W9-BIT-108

ENCYCLOPEDIA OF AMERICAN INDUSTRIES

3RD EDITION

VOLUME 2: SERVICE & NON-MANUFACTURING INDUSTRIES

ENCYCLOPEDIA OF AMERICAN INDUSTRIES

3RD EDITION

VOLUME 2: SERVICE & NON-MANUFACTURING INDUSTRIES

REBECCA MARLOW-FERGUSON, EDITOR

Detroit
New York
San Francisco
London
Boston
Woodbridge, CT

Encyclopedia of American Industries

Third Edition

Copyright Notice

Library of Congress Card Number: 00-106822

ISBN 0-7876-4273-8 (Set)
ISBN 0-7876-4274-6 (Volume One)
ISBN 0-7876-4275-4 (Volume Two)

Printed in the United States of America

CONTENTS

VOLUME 1

Tobacco Products

Textile Mill Products

Apparel & Other Finished Products Made from Fabrics & Similar Materials

Lumber & Wood Products, Except Furniture

Furniture and Fixtures

Paper & Allied Products

Printing, Publishing & Allied Industries

Chemicals & Allied Products

Petroleum Refining & Related Industries

Rubber & Miscellaneous Plastics Products

Leather & Leather Products

Stone, Clay, Glass & Concrete Products

Primary Metals Industries

Fabricated Metal Products, Except Machinery/ Transportation Equipment

Industrial & Commercial Machinery & Computer Equipment

Electronic & Other Electrical Equipment & Components, Except Computer Equipment

Transportation Equipment

Measuring, Analyzing & Controlling Instruments

Miscellaneous Manufacturing Industries

VOLUME 2

Agriculture, Forestry, & Fishing

Mining Industries

Construction Industries

Transportation, Communications, Electric, Gas, & Sanitary Services

Wholesale Trade

Retail Trade

Finance, Insurance, & Real Estate

Service Industries

PUBLIC ADMINISTRATION

Introduction

The *Encyclopedia of American Industries (EAI)* is a major business reference tool that provides detailed, comprehensive information on a wide range of industries in every realm of American business. Volume one provides separate coverage of 459 manufacturing industries. Volume two presents 545 essays covering the vast array of service and other non-manufacturing industries in the United States. Combined, these two volumes provide individual essays on every industry recognized by the U.S. Standard Industrial Classification (SIC) system. Both volumes of *EAI* are arranged numerically by SIC code for easy use. Additionally, each entry in the third edition includes the corresponding North American Industry Classification System (NAICS) code(s).

Content and Arrangement

Industry Essays. The *Encyclopedia*'s business coverage includes information on historical events of consequence, as well as relevant trends and statistics entering the twenty-first century. Sections of coverage in an essay may include the following:

- Industry Snapshot: Provides an overview of the industry and identifies key trends, issues, and statistics.
- Organization and Structure: Discusses the configuration and functional aspects of the industry, including government regulation, sub-industry divisions, and interaction with other industries.
- Background and Development: Relates the industry's genesis and historical development, including major technological advances, scandals, pioneering companies, major products, important legislation, and other factors that shaped the industry.
- Current Conditions: Provides information on the status of the industry in the late 1990s to early 2000s, with an eye to industry challenges on the horizon.
- Industry Leaders: Profiles major companies within the industry and includes discussion of financial performance.
- Workforce: Contains information on the size, diversity, and characteristics of the industry's workforce.
- America and the World: Discusses the global marketplace for the U.S. industry, as well as international participation in U.S. markets.
- Research and Technology: Furnishes information on major technological advances, areas of research, and their potential impact on the industry.
- Further Reading: Provides users with suggested further reading on the industry. These sources, many of which were also used to compile the essays, are publicly accessible materials such as magazines, general and academic periodicals, books, annual reports, and government sources, as well as material supplied by industry associations. This edition also includes references to numerous Internet sources. When available, the URL address and updated or visited date of these resources is included, although such addresses are apt to change frequently.

Graphs. The *Encyclopedia of American Industries* includes more than 350 informative, easy-to-read graphs detailing a wide range of key economic and business information. Graphs without source information have been compiled from the research material used to write the essay or from original research.

Conversion Tables. Two industry classification tables allow cross-referencing of SIC categories with the NAICS industry codes. (Please see below for additional information.)

Indexes. The *Encyclopedia of American Industries'* index contains alphabetic references from both volumes to companies, trade associations, significant business trends, government agencies, historical figures, and key legislation. It also includes cross-references for acronyms and variant names.

About Industry Classification

Encyclopedia of American Industries offers tools to analyze industries using two industry classification systems. The primary system, the Standard Industrial Classification (SIC) system, was established by the U.S. government to provide a uniform means for collecting, presenting, and analyzing economic data. SIC codes are still widely used by federal, state, and local government agencies; trade associations; private research organizations; and business professionals to promote comparability in the presentation of statistical data. In addition, *EAI* includes reference tables for the 1997 North American Industry Classification System (NAICS), which has been adopted by the U.S. government as its new standard for economic data. Each essay includes the corresponding NAICS code(s) as well.

1987 Standard Industrial Classification (SIC). Each SIC code classifies business and nonprofit establishments by the types of activities in which they are engaged; in other words, it is "industry-oriented." An establishment is an economic unit where a service is performed or a product is manufactured or sold (generally at a single physical location). To be recognized as a separate industry within the SIC system, a set of establishments must be statistically significant according to criteria such as the number of persons employed and the volume of business conducted. Each establishment is placed in an SIC category according to its primary activity, which is determined by the industry from which it derives the most revenue. Many large companies, however, operate multiple establishments and may participate in several industries, thus it is possible for a company to be a leading force in SIC categories outside of its primary industry.

The SIC system comprises four levels of classification, as described below:

- Divisions: The broadest SIC categories are divisions that define an activity in very general terms: Agriculture, Forestry, and Fishing; Mining; Construction; Manufacturing; Transportation, Communications, Electric, Gas, and Sanitary Services; Wholesale Trade; Retail Trade; Finance, Insurance, and Real Estate; and Public Administration, for example.
- Major Groups: Within these broad categories are major groups. Each begins with a unique two-digit code that makes up the first two numbers of the complete four-digit SIC code. In the case of Manufacturing, the major group codes range between 20 and 39. Examples of two-digit groups in Manufacturing are: Food & Kindred Products (20); Tobacco Products (21); Furniture & Fixtures (25); Printing, Publishing, & Allied Industries (27); and Industrial & Commercial Machinery & Computer Equipment (35).
- Industry Groups: Major groups are further subdivided into three-digit industry groups. Each is assigned a three-digit code based on the two-digit code for its major group. For example, Printing, Publishing & Allied Industries is broken down into 271 for Newspapers, 272 for Periodicals, and 273 for Books.
- Industries: Industry Groups are divided still further into specific classifications that are assigned complete, four-digit codes based on the Industry Group. These four-digit classifications are the basis for the industries detailed in *EAI*.

1997 North American Industry Classification System (NAICS). Although NAICS has officially replaced the SIC system, industry information is still maintained in SIC categories for this edition. The *Encyclopedia of American Industries* provides conversion tables to compare SIC data with NAICS data, which the governments of Canada, Mexico, and the United States jointly adopted. It includes broad classifications that are common among the three nations as well as unique national-level classifications. Industries are specified within NAICS by up to six digits, however in some cases the most specific category is only five digits. The conversion tables provided in this book reflect the U.S. version of NAICS, which contains six digits.

NAICS is similar in principle to the SIC system but differs in industry specificity and grouping; NAICS is "production-oriented," or dependent on the activity of the industry. Also, although the U.S. Census Bureau calls NAICS a hierarchical numbering system, it does not have broad terms broken down into narrower terms, broken down into sub-classifications, then sub-sub-classifications—as with the SIC system.

Unfortunately, total reliance on NAICS data means the loss of historical information for some industries. To help combat this, in 2001 the Census Bureau is slated to release its information in both SIC and NAICS formats.

Comments and Suggestions

Questions, comments, and suggestions regarding the *Encyclopedia of American Industries* are welcomed. Please contact:

The Editor
Encyclopedia of American Industries
Gale Group
27500 Drake Rd.
Farmington Hills, MI 48331-3535
Telephone: 248-699-4253
Toll-Free: 800-347-GALE
URL: http://www.galegroup.com

Foreword

Expansion Sustained: A Macro View of U.S. Economic Activity and Industry Trends

A multitude of events, most perhaps coincidental, converged to produce the thriving U.S. economy of the 1990s and early 2000s. By most measures, the period of expansion has been the longest in U.S. history, as well as one marked by a particularly elusive mix of favorable conditions. Vigorous macroeconomic growth, low price inflation, high labor participation rates, rising personal incomes and wealth, and a sharply rising stock market are only some of the auspicious hallmarks of the vibrant, world-leading economy.

To keep everything in perspective, though, it's useful to consider the unlikely convergence of events that intensified and prolonged the expansion. To take only a few examples, such diverse influences as very inexpensive oil prices (until late 1998); economic troubles in Asia, Russia, and Latin America; and the commercialization of a communications network known as the Internet all worked to the U.S. economic benefit. Cheap oil, for instance, helped keep price inflation down and, in doing so, probably helped forestall the Federal Reserve's raising of interest rates. Meanwhile, currency slumps and economic problems elsewhere in the world helped funnel capital into U.S. markets, fueling price growth in the stock markets and, at least temporarily, providing capital to U.S. businesses. And for its part, the Internet's mainstream emergence triggered a deluge of spending on computer hardware, software, and services extending to nearly every sector of the economy. Had the timing been different, and had there not been such a convergence, the economy might have puttered out years earlier.

But far from puttering out, the U.S. economy bareled forward, breaking records with surprising ease and causing some economists to rethink their theories about sustainable growth. In 1999 the U.S. gross domestic product approached $9.26 trillion in current dollars, marking a robust 4.2 percent gain after inflation is factored out. That came on the heels of two previous years of 4-plus percent growth in real terms. All the while, inflation remained largely at bay, and the U.S. unemployment rate hovered at 30-year lows.

Both companies and individuals benefited from the 1990s expansion. Corporate earnings at U.S. firms advanced decisively throughout the decade, with before-tax profits more than doubling between 1990 and 1999. In the meantime, real disposable personal income grew by about 26 percent in total over the period, or by about 15 percent on a per capita basis.

Internet and E-commerce Increasingly Pervasive

Moving on to events that have contributed to economic growth, an obvious question is, what is the impact of the Internet on traditional industries and the economy as a whole? Clearly, any attempt at a comprehensive answer could fill an entire book, and on just one industry at that. With that in mind, there are several broad implications to consider.

Online Marketplaces. Whereas in the mid- and late 1990s most Internet activity was confined to individual companies and trade organizations establishing a presence, since the late 1990s a new crop of sites has been recreating industries and vertical supply chains online. A few examples of these electronic marketplaces:

- The metals industries have multiple sites devoted to trading metals online.
- Three top paper companies in 2000 announced a global online marketplace that allows businesses to buy and sell forest products in a multi-vendor environment and do so seamlessly by integrating their purchasing and logistics systems with the site.

Changes on the Horizon

The following industries are expected to experience the greatest change in net output—positive or negative—through 2008

Biggest Gainers	**Annual growth**
1. Computer and office equipment	14.5%
2. Electronic components	10.9%
3. Computer and data services	10.3%
4. Car rental services	9.3%
5. Communications equipment	8.1%

Biggest Decliners	**Annual decline**
1. Watch and clock manufacturing	-11.7%
2. Luggage/handbag manufacturing	-2.2%
3. Bowling centers	-2.2%
4. Bookbinding	-1.9%
5. Newspapers	-1.4%

Source: *Monthly Labor Review*, Bureau of Labor Statistics, November 1999

- A large truck-parts manufacturer has launched a site to enable online purchases of parts and trucking-related services from a variety of providers.

These sites and a multitude of others aim to offer a competitive, usually neutral exchange that lets companies and consumers quickly determine a range of prices and options available and complete a transaction on the spot. The emphasis in the future, moreover, will be on providing value-added information and services via the online marketplace beyond simply quoting prices and entering transactions.

The trend toward industry marketplaces online, most pronounced in the lucrative business-to-business e-commerce category, is likely to get much bigger. Forrester Research, a market research firm, predicted that by 2003 the business-to-business online market would be worth $2.7 trillion—and more than half of those sales would be conducted through online marketplaces. In perhaps a less rigorous survey of business-to-business conference attendees, Forrester found that fully 71 percent of corporate leaders expected their companies to participate in such marketplaces by 2001.

Competitive Impact. Aside from shifting business and consumer transactions to an electronic medium, e-commerce promises to upset the competitive status quo in some industries. One reason is rising cost transparency associated with the Internet. As buyers gain access to fuller information about how much competing products cost and how much components of those products sell for, they'll enjoy a stronger negotiating position with suppliers. This means many suppliers will increasingly compete on price—potentially cutting into profits—and find it necessary to justify their mark-ups if they're not the low-cost producer.

Ultimately, as well, winners and losers will emerge in the e-commerce field. Developing and maintaining sophisticated e-commerce sites requires considerable skill and resources, and for some companies the investment will exceed the revenue potential. This is already apparent in several of the online retail categories, where competition for consumer mind share and market share is intense and even the leaders have had a tough time turning a profit, let alone the lower-tier players. This dynamic is widely expected to result in retail consolidation as the less able competitors are bought out, refocused, or simply go out of business, all this while online sales continue to grow in the aggregate at phenomenal rates. Observers see this weeding out as a necessary stage in the evolution of e-commerce.

Robust Capital Flows and Investment

Investment is a means of generating new growth opportunities by funding promising economic endeavors. By most measures, the U.S. economic investment climate was markedly robust in the 1990s. This includes not only the celebrated gains in the stock markets, which were awash with capital from both domestic and international sources, but also strong advances in corporate fixed investment and research and development (R&D). Expansion in these areas is usually seen as a platform for future economic growth.

Overall, Federal Reserve statistics pinpointed growth in gross private domestic investment at nearly 47 percent between 1995 and 1999. Private investment in equipment and software, a major component of corporate fixed investment, grew in the late 1990s at a torrid 8 to 12 percent a year, two to three times the rate of growth in the broader U.S. economy. Spending on information technology hardware and software contributed heavily to the increase.

Meanwhile, R&D spending trailed somewhat because of cutbacks in federal grants for research. R&D is responsible for, among other things, breakthrough technologies that can greatly impact entire industries and, potentially, the economy as a whole. Spending in this area grew at a more modest average of 6.6 percent annually from 1995 to 1999, according to a report compiled by the National Science Foundation (NSF), yet that rate still outpaced GDP growth. While federal support has diminished since the early 1990s, corporate R&D funding has more than picked up the slack, and now accounts for almost three-quarters of R&D spending in the United States. The NSF estimated total R&D outlays in 1999 at $247 billion.

Venture Capital. Venture capital has also become a key source of financing for new, innovative companies. The use of venture capital, privately placed equity (and sometimes debt) funding for start-up companies, burgeoned in the 1990s with the influx of new Internet-related companies, and more importantly, the boom in Internet stocks. Venture capital firms take massive stakes in risky albeit promising companies in hopes of cashing out handsomely months or years later when the companies go public. In 1999 venture capital in the United States soared to $36.5 billion, almost three times the 1998 level and a sixfold increase from 1995.

Despite its dramatic rise, venture capital directly impacts only a narrow portion of the economy—primarily Internet and health-care technology concerns. In the late 1990s between 1,000 and 2,000 companies a year, only a fraction all new start-ups, received venture backing. Total funding through venture capital also pales in comparison to other modes of investment, which measure in the hundreds of billions of dollars and even trillions.

Soaring Stocks. The buoyant stock markets represent a different kind of investment—that of capital—and often a more speculative kind. Nonetheless, they have been an increasingly important source of operations funding for start-ups and acquisitive companies. Increasing reliance on market equity has fed into so-called New Economy theories, which hold that, among other things, new technology companies—especially Internet firms—aren't as burdened by higher interest rates as traditional companies because they hold less debt. However, this assertion has been hotly contested and the evidence for it is spotty.

Still, the price growth of technology shares, in particular, has been staggering. From mid-1990 to mid-2000, the NASDAQ Composite Index, a broadly based stock gauge with heavy technology weighting, skyrocketed 600 percent. And that's even after a precipitous decline in early 2000, when the index peaked above the 5,000 mark, but soon tumbled back to the 3,500 range. A handful of computer and Internet firm shares grew by even greater multiples, although there was also no shortage of also-rans that failed to deliver exponential investment growth.

Other leading indexes such as the New York Stock Exchange Composite Index and the Standard & Poor's 500 also recorded sharp gains in the 1990s, although not nearly as big as the NASDAQ's. All told, the NYSE Composite, a broad measure of established, large-capitalization stocks, rose 220 percent from mid-1990 to mid-2000, while the narrower S&P 500, another large-cap metric, climbed 282 percent.

Reasons Behind the Rally. A few trends have contributed to the prolonged stock rally. For one, an ongoing trend toward self-managed 401(k) retirement plans has funneled vast sums of cash into the market, particularly into mutual funds. U.S. assets held in mutual funds more than doubled from $1.9 trillion in 1995 to more than $4.5 trillion by the end of 1999, based on statistics published by the Federal Reserve. Estimates by industry groups placed the 1999 value at closer to a whopping $6 trillion. While either figure includes asset appreciation in the general stock market and other sources, to give an indication of how much new money has been flowing into funds, one estimate valued new inflows into mutual funds at $165 billion in 1999 alone.

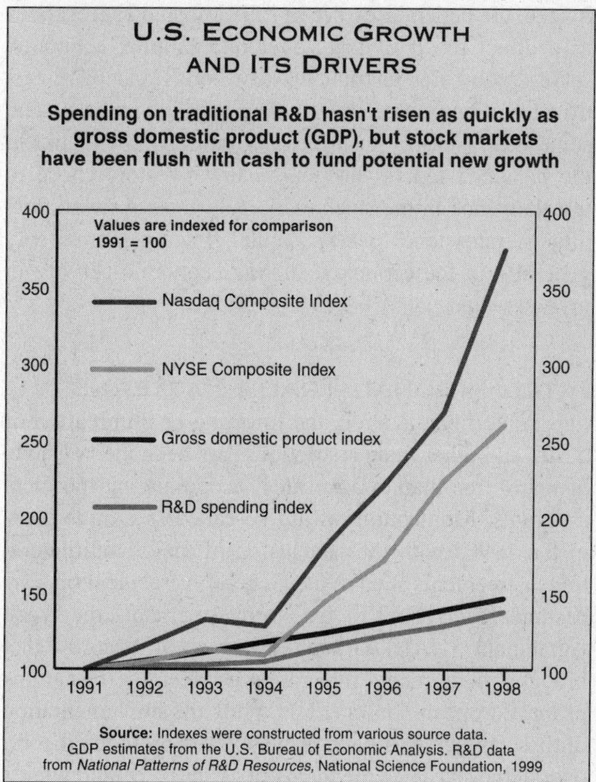

Source: Indexes were constructed from various source data. GDP estimates from the U.S. Bureau of Economic Analysis. R&D data from *National Patterns of R&D Resources*, National Science Foundation, 1999

Another event that helped ignite the U.S. stock markets was, oddly enough, economic crisis elsewhere in the world. In the wake of the Asian currency crisis of the late 1990s, when fiscal vagaries in up-and-coming Southeast Asian countries triggered a debilitating withdrawal of international capital from several of the region's emerging markets. Global investors effected a so-called flight to quality by pumping their money into U.S.-based assets. A similar story unfolded in Russia in 1998, when the country's currency collapsed amid foreign investors' jitters over ineffective reforms and political corruption in that beleaguered country.

Back at home, continued low interest rates helped stimulate demand for stocks over bonds and other more rate-sensitive investment vehicles in the United States.

Indeed, the Federal Reserve in 1998 lowered interest rates as a direct result of fears over international economic strife. With safer instruments like bonds and bank certificates of deposit offering underwhelming returns—and some U.S. Treasury securities in shorter supply thanks to the balanced federal budget—many investors chose to test their luck in the stock markets instead. As well, low interest rates tend to keep capital flowing more freely generally in the economy, fueling economic activity in myriad ways.

International Trade Patterns

Trade liberalization, the lowering or elimination of tariffs and other trade restrictions, has been the keystone of many free-market advocates' economic and political programs. Momentum toward so-called free trade grew in the 1990s with the conclusion of major multilateral trade agreements such as the General Agreement on Tariffs and Trade (GATT), the North American Free Trade Agreement (NAFTA), and a series of accords that brought about greater integration between the 15 nations of the European Union (EU). While the implementation of these agreements hasn't always lived up to the theory, overall they've been the main policy thrust behind what's known to many as globalization, or the expansion of corporate enterprises and their supply chains across international boundaries.

According to World Trade Organization (WTO) figures, in 1999 countries exported a collective $5.6 trillion in merchandise (including some double counting from re-exports) and $1.3 trillion in commercial services. Western Europe, including both EU and non-EU countries, is the world's largest exporting region, supplying about 42 percent of global exports in 1999. Asia and North America followed, with 27 percent and 17 percent, respectively. The regional rank order was the same for imports, although North America occupied a larger share.

U.S. Trade Performance. Despite perennial worries about the trade deficit, the United States remains the world's largest single-nation exporter of merchandise, shipping nearly $700 billion worth in 1999. It leads the next-largest exporter, Germany, by a comfortable margin, and for the most part, U.S. exports have been growing faster than either Germany's or those of Japan, the third-largest exporter. Top U.S. export sectors in terms of dollar value include aerospace, electronic and mechanical components (especially semiconductors), motor vehicle parts, computer equipment, and telecommunications equipment. Those five industry groups accounted for 20 to 25 percent of all U.S. exports in the late 1990s. Canada, Mexico, and Japan were the largest destination countries, and the EU ranked number two (behind Canada) when treated as a single market.

Meanwhile, the sectors most dependent on foreign-made goods include some of the same: motor vehicles, computer equipment, oil, electronic and mechanical components, and parts and accessories for office equipment. Altogether, the United States imported $1.059 trillion worth of products in 1999, leaving a yawning merchandise trade gap of $364 billion. In descending order, the largest suppliers of imports into the United States include Canada, Japan, Mexico, China, and Germany. Thus, the United States maintains trade deficits with most of its biggest trading partners, but it does have country-level surpluses with a number of smaller partners, including the Netherlands, Australia, Belgium, Egypt, Argentina, and Hong Kong.

Trade in services remains a bright spot for observers who lament the merchandise trade deficit, although there are some indications that the services trade has been losing a bit of its luster. In 1999 the United States exported $252 billion worth of services, including foreign tourism, royalties, and professional services rendered abroad. That compares with $182 billion in imports. However, the trade surplus in services has been narrowing since its 1997 peak at $82 billion; it fell to $74 billion in 1998 and to just below $70 billion in 1999. Economic softness in parts of Asia and Latin America contributed to the declines. But some economists believe services are an inherently shallow base on which to build an export program, and thus weren't swayed even when the surplus was mounting.

Interpreting the Trade Deficit. The U.S. trade deficit widened significantly throughout the 1990s in the face of a strong U.S. dollar, substantial wealth creation domestically, and economic troubles in some parts of the world. These and other circumstances conspired to create heightened demand for foreign-made goods, and only moderate demand for U.S. goods abroad. The problem isn't that U.S. exports haven't been growing, but that imports have climbed consistently at a faster pace.

All of this feeds into the continuing debate over whether a massive trade deficit is really a problem when most of the other economic ducks are in a row, so to speak. Mainstream economic theory holds that trade deficits are harmful over the long term because they usually lead to current account deficits for a country, where the current account is an economic concept encompassing the net national income from international transactions. The current account deficit, in turn, demonstrates that foreign entities are getting an increasing share of U.S. dollars and assets.

And here's where the damage might be done: as emerging economies regain their steam after the late-1990s setbacks, foreign holders of U.S. currency could begin to rid themselves of dollars and dollar-denominated assets in favor of assets based elsewhere. The resulting

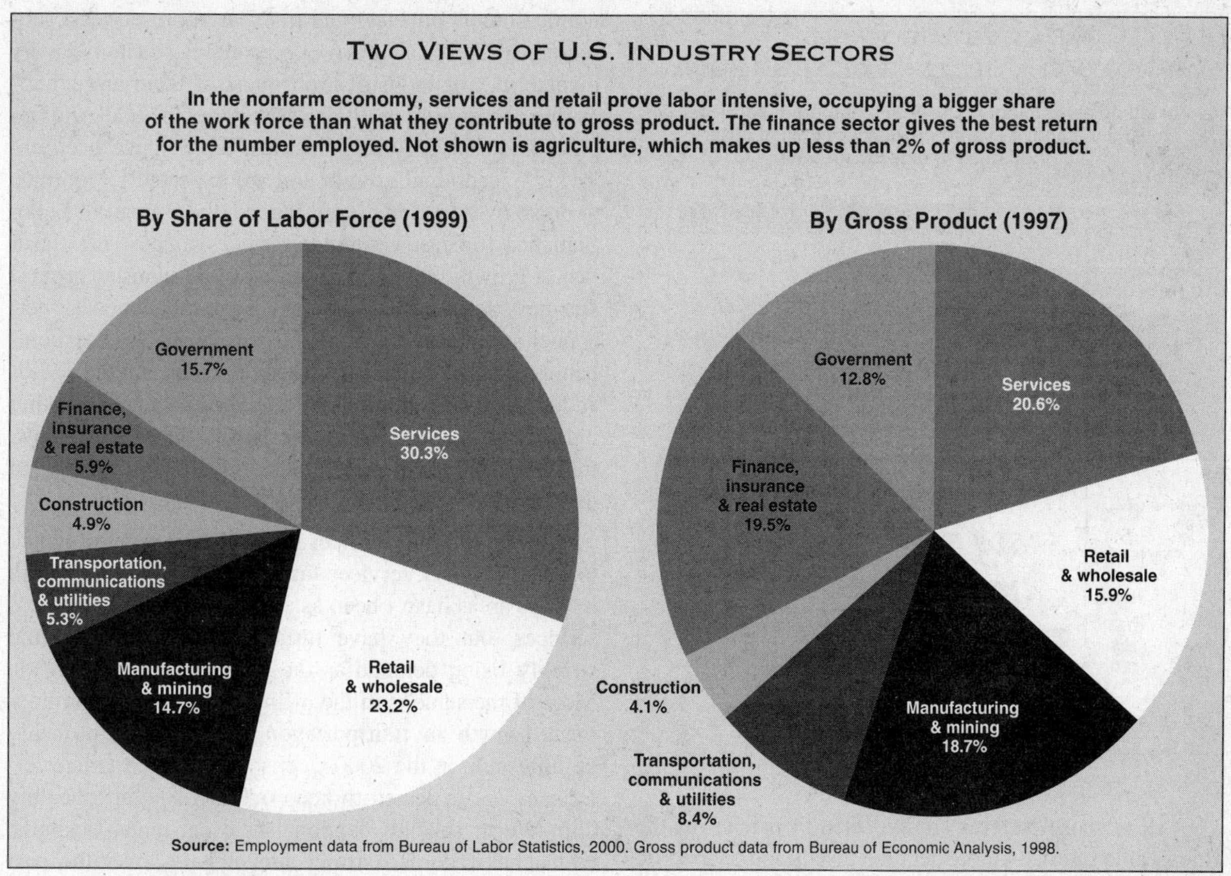

influx of dollars in the foreign exchange markets would likely drive the dollar's value down, particularly if the transition is sudden. A weak dollar would, over time, tend to improve the trade balance by making imports into the United States less attractive on price and exports out of the United States more attractive on price. But correcting the balance that way, according to many economists, would probably be an unpleasant process to say the least. A declining dollar would tend to cause price inflation, and as a result, interest rates would creep upward. Further into the vicious cycle, tighter control on capital flows would tend to slow purchases, and ultimately, economic growth. The dismal outcomes could include rising unemployment, stagnant or bearish financial markets, and in the worst case, recession.

Each step in the pernicious cycle has been observed in recent times. Indeed, the late-1990s Asian financial crisis stemmed in large part from capital flight and currency sell-offs in otherwise economically dynamic countries. However, the question is, at what point is a current account shortfall bad enough to cause such an adverse chain of events? Clearly that threshold is harder to reach with an economy as large and as stable as that of the United States. Even clearer is the plain fact that the United States has been running current account deficits for the better of two decades, through bad economic times and good.

Sector Trends

Macroeconomic forces aside, a host of industry- and sector-specific trends add texture to the U.S. economic mosaic. The most important of these trends are already rooted firmly in the economy:

- Widespread investment in information technology and communications infrastructure continues to stimulate brisk demand for products and services in those areas.
- Electronic transactions increasingly alter and supplant physical transactions in sectors as diverse as entertainment, consumer retailing, wholesaling, and banking, to name a few.
- Manufacturers cope with declining profitability on sales of physical products by bundling them with value-adding services.
- Commoditized, low-value-added manufactures and services are being sought more and more from foreign providers with lower overhead costs.
- Seemingly contradictory binges of outsourcing and mergers/acquisitions continue at large corporations as they try to optimize their economies of scope and scale.

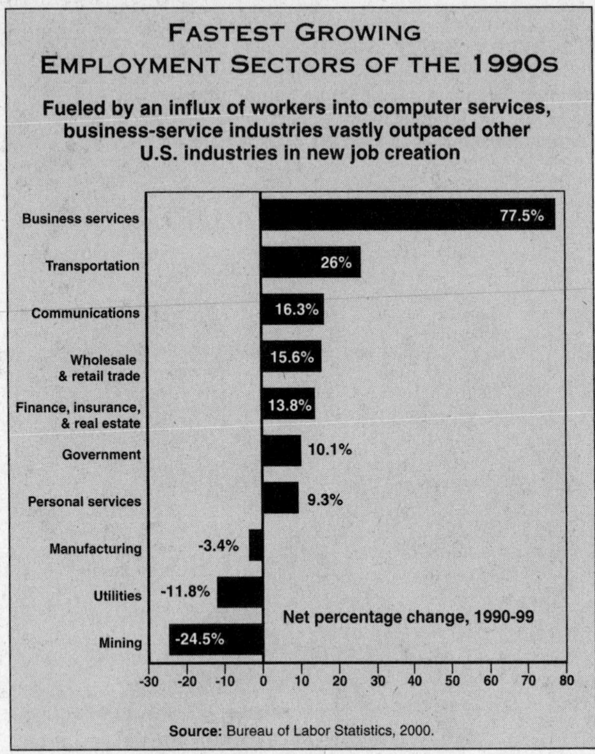

All of those patterns are expected to persist for the foreseeable future. A more detailed discussion of specific sectors follows.

Manufacturing. It's well documented that manufacturing industries as a whole are in the midst of a long-term decline as a proportion of the U.S. economy. A few manufacturing industries have suffered real setbacks because of changing technology and market forces, foreign competition, and other factors, but in general the decline is the result of simply a slower rate of growth than other sectors of the economy, notably service industries.

U.S. employment in manufacturing has diminished slightly since the 1980s, and a forecast by the Bureau of Labor Statistics anticipates a very minor further decrease in the early 2000s. Manufacturers of nondurable goods like apparel, food, and chemicals are expected to deliver the weakest performance within the sector, both in terms of employment declines and the value of industry sales.

By contrast, makers of durable goods such as industrial machinery, computers and communications devices, semiconductors and electronic components, and medical goods are predicted to fare better. Some will actually boost their employment levels modestly, and overall they're likely to continue increasing productivity and output at vibrant rates throughout the first decade of the twenty-first century.

Business and Transportation Services. Services of all sorts are expected to occupy a growing share of U.S. economic output. Business and transportation services, subsectors of the broader service economy, contain a very diverse mix of industries, but most of them are experiencing robust growth. Business services include the computer and data service industries, which have been enjoying exceptional growth and are expected to continue to do so over the long term. Indeed, the Bureau of Labor Statistics forecast computer services to post the third-fastest growth rate in gross output of all industry groups. Business services also contain such specialties as personnel and recruiting firms and equipment leasing companies. All combined, business services in the 1990s added more new employees to their ranks than any other industry sector, and while the rate is expected to slow, the sector's growth is apt to continue outpacing that of the broader economy well into the 2000s.

Transportation services range from passenger transit to cargo delivery services via air, land, and sea. Growth in these areas hasn't been as swift as in general business services, but they have turned in solid results amid steadily rising demand as the broader economy grows. More of the same is in the offing. Although net employment growth in transportation services will probably be miniscule in the 2000s, consolidation and greater efficiency are expected to keep output rising at a healthy clip. Worth special mention is the car-rental business, which has recorded strong annual gains over the past decade and is projected to continue that trend in coming years.

Communications Services. The communications sector is one of the pillars of the information economy, and indeed, the world economy. The sector's prominence has risen considerably as its infrastructure has grown ever more vital to modern lifestyles and economic activities. Whether it's traditional wireline phone service, wireless communications, high-speed data networks, or entertainment and rich-content electronic media, demand for communications services has swelled in recent years as technological change and deregulation have helped usher in new forms of service at increasingly affordable rates.

The communications industries are undergoing tremendous consolidation, as witnessed by an array of once unthinkable mergers in the late 1990s and early 2000s among local-service carriers, long-distance providers, wireless services, Internet access providers, cable TV system operators, and content providers. Many expect the momentum toward consolidation to continue. As a result, job growth in most communications businesses will be subdued. But industry revenues on the whole will remain on a steady upward track, even as service prices continue to drop.

Retail and Wholesale Trade. With a few exceptions, the retail and wholesale sectors aren't known for dramatic growth. Rather, they tend to eke out a modest existence by sheer volume of transactions, benefiting from the fact most personal consumption spending is channeled through retail firms. In essence, retailers are logistics and marketing specialists who take a vast, disorganized universe of products and render them accessible and possibly more attractive to potential buyers. Meanwhile, wholesalers work behind the scenes, supplying retailers and other businesses with a preordained assortment of goods.

Thus, because their main function is in aggregating merchandise for sale, retailing and wholesaling face more than most sectors a potentially drastic paradigm shift with the onset of electronic commerce. Some prognosticators have gone so far as to say the customary wholesale business could be eliminated entirely by a combination of e-commerce and powerful chain retailers that can negotiate directly with manufacturers. Retailers, too, must contend with unfavorable economics versus virtual storefronts—the infrastructure of a retail chain is costly and inefficient compared to a high-tech inventory and outsourced logistics system. It's precisely with such a system that some electronic challengers hope to wrest market share from traditional retailers.

Still, retailers have several things going for them. In some cases, such as with food purchases, many observers believe that consumers will be reluctant to give up the tactile and visual experiences of shopping in a store, and they'll hesitate to give up the spontaneity of deciding what to buy just minutes before they consume it. Retailers' existing physical infrastructure and market share also provide a powerful platform from which to launch integrated e-commerce/traditional retail ventures. As for conventional wholesalers, they have some infrastructure and market advantages as well, but are probably more vulnerable in the long run.

Whatever the impact of e-commerce, traditional wholesalers and retailers aren't likely to be extinct anytime soon. But their tepid growth rates are expected to slow further in the early 2000s, including both the rate of new job creation and the rate of sales growth. Restaurants, especially, are predicted to lag. Retail and wholesale saw substantial consolidation during the 1990s, and more of the same is anticipated in the 2000s.

AGRICULTURE, FORESTRY, & FISHING

SIC 0111

WHEAT

This industry consists of establishments primarily engaged in the production of wheat, or whose sales of wheat account for more than 50 percent of total value of sales for their agricultural production.

NAICS CODE(S)

111140 (Wheat Farming)

INDUSTRY SNAPSHOT

Wheat farms in the United States produced more than 2.5 billion bushels of grain in 1998, harvesting approximately 59 million acres with yields of individual classes of wheat ranging from 33-67 bushels per acre. Wheat is the third largest crop in the United States in terms of acres harvested, with Kansas, North Dakota, Montana, Washington, and Oklahoma harvesting the most. Average prices for the six classes of American wheat was $2.45 to $2.75 per bushel and depended on an enormous range of environmental, political, economic, and technological factors. Although used as livestock feed, wheat is largely used to make flour and more than 50 percent of total consumption in 1998 was accounted for in exports.

Due to the importance of U.S. wheat in international trade and the integral role the U.S. Department of Agriculture (USDA) played in every sector of the agricultural economy, wheat farmers were in many ways more affected by shifts in the political climate than by actual weather conditions.

The United States wheat industry was also a world leader in research and development, a point underscored by the unparalleled variety of wheat grown by American farmers. While the Hard Red Winter Wheat (HRW) crop is much larger than other wheat crops (accounting for about 69 percent of the total wheat crop value), there were five other commercial classes of U.S. wheat: Hard Red Spring (HRS), Soft Red Winter (SRW), White, Durum, and Red Durum.

Distribution, Production Conditions, and Use. Although wheat is grown in virtually every state, the focal point of the industry is in the central and southern Great Plains Region where Hard Red Winter Wheat is produced. There, in states like Kansas, Oklahoma, Nebraska, Texas, and Colorado, the winters are cold and dry, and the summers hot. Precipitation, which varies over the region (between 13 and 30 inches annually), can fluctuate drastically and droughts periodically afflict wide areas for a succession of years. Farms are generally large, and employ extensive, as opposed to intensive, methods of crop production. Wheat farmers employ various systems of crop rotation depending on a specific field's soil moisture. Most often, farmers alternate a year of wheat with a year of fallow to conserve soil moisture, and HRW wheat is sown in late autumn and harvested in the spring. Wheat production is highly mechanized in the region. A farm worker can typically sow 100 acres or combine-harvest 50 acres in a workday. When milled, HRW wheats produce strong baking and high-quality breadmaking flours.

The main region for Hard Red Spring wheat is the northern Great Plains region, where winters are too harsh for HRW production. The soils are deep, rich, black or brown grassland soils. HRS wheat is usually sown in late April and harvested in August. On average, 80 percent of the annual 15 to 25 inches of rainfall comes during this short growing season. A great variety of crops are used in rotation with wheat and summer fallowing becoming rare except in the driest areas. The climatic and soil conditions give HRS wheat a high protein content, strong gluten, and high baking strength. Its flour is excellent for breadmaking, and can support weaker flours when combined with them in breads.

The Pacific Northwest is the third significant American wheat-producing region. There, on the Columbia Plateau in the valley of the Columbia River, large areas of rolling farmland are protected by mountains and the climate is moderated by the Japanese Current. Most of the wheat grown in this region is white-grained, or ''White wheat.'' It is produced in semi-arid zones (10-20 inches of rainfall/year), sown in autumn, and harvested in the spring. Because of the varying altitudes, however, almost all other kinds of wheat (including various wheats falling under the ''White'' designation) are also cultivated. The region's wheat production, crop rotation, and mechanization methods are similar to those used by farmers in the Great Plains. Because of the different topography of the Columbia Plateau, however, combines are often specially designed with self-leveling mechanisms to operate on hillsides. Most White wheat flour is suited only for pastry and crackers.

The Eastern part of the country produces wheat on a much smaller scale than the rest of the country and also generally produces inferior wheats of a softer texture and lower protein content. The majority of the wheat in this region, including Soft Red Winter in the central and southeastern states and White in New York and Michigan, is grown as part of a complex crop rotation system on farms that specialize in other agricultural products. However, the farming methods used on these smaller farms have often resulted in higher wheat yields than those recorded in the major wheat regions.

ORGANIZATION AND STRUCTURE

Wheat farmers are part of a large and increasingly complex agribusiness commodity system. The multileveled structure of the wheat industry as a whole includes farm suppliers, storage operators, processors, wholesalers, and retailers, as well as government institutions, futures markets, and trade associations. Despite the continuing movement toward expansion and consolidation, however, the wheat farmer is still, by and large, an independent operator. Farmers generally till and harvest their own land and sell goods to the highest bidder at the next level of the wheat system, usually a grain elevator operator or a miller-agent.

Certain support and control structures are necessary to ensure an adequate wheat supply for the consumer market while controlling production levels to secure price levels. With one harvest a year for each class of wheat, combined with year-round consumption, imbalances between supply and demand are sometimes immense. Moreover, forecasting supplies can be difficult, since such forecasts must rely on weather conditions, which affect both the quality and quantity of wheat from year to year. In addition, technological advances have resulted in higher yields, which makes projections even more indeterminate. Consequently, without price supports, wheat farmers can fall prey to severe price, and thus, income, swings. The economic, social, and political repercussions of such fluctuations demand that the government assume some control of the wheat growing industry.

Government Programs. The USDA submits a new wheat program every year as an amendment to a larger legislative act (like the Food, Agriculture, Conservation, and Trade Act), under which all agricultural activity is regulated. In these programs, the USDA makes adjustments to various price and income support strategies. First, the wheat program (as any other commodity program) bases support payments on a certain fixed ''eligible production,'' which is defined as a farm's wheat acreage multiplied by its yield (both averaged over five years). Exceeding the set acreage makes a farmer ineligible for payments, while exceeding the yield means that only the excess production is excluded from program benefits. To give wheat farmers some flexibility in planting decisions, there are ''flex acreage'' provisions that allow farmers to set aside some program acreage to lie fallow or to plant with other crops. Other provisions affecting a farmer's acreage are Acreage Reduction Programs (ARPs), which are designed to control production, raise market prices, and lower government outlays. The USDA usually requires program participants to idle some percentage of their base acreage, a number that is set annually by the Secretary of Agriculture.

Perhaps the most important annual figures released in wheat programs are the target prices for each class of wheat. For each bushel of eligible production, the wheat farmer is assured of receiving the target price, and he also receives deficiency payments equal to the difference between the target price and either the current market price or the loan rate, whichever is highest. If the target price is $4 per bushel and farmers can only get $3.50 for a bushel (either as a loan or as an actual price), then they receive a deficiency payment of $.50 per bushel. Additionally, loan rates are set by the government and also act as price supports, because they are nonrecourse loans in which the government's right to recovery is limited to the crop used as collateral. If the market price is close to, or below, the loan rate, then the wheat farmer simply defaults on it and transfers title of his crop to the government. Excess units of production, while not eligible for deficiency payments, are included in the loan program; consequently, loan rates are important to consider when making planting decisions.

Although these price and income support provisions directly influence wheat farmers, there are many other programs under existing agricultural legislation that also profoundly affect a farmer's business. Other types of government assistance include wheat stock control mechanisms, credit programs, and crop insurance and disaster payment provisions.

In order to give the farmer some control over the point at which his wheat enters the market, the government established the Farmer-Owned Reserve (FOR). Under the direction of the Secretary of Agriculture, the FOR makes multiyear loans to wheat producers to maintain reserve stocks. Whenever less than 300 million bushels of wheat are maintained in the FOR and the market price is less than 140 percent of the nonrecourse loan rate, participation in the FOR is encouraged through incentives like raising storage payments. By the same token, if participation exceeds 30 percent of the estimated use of wheat, the Secretary of Agriculture closes the reserve. Once the market price exceeds the target price or 140 percent of the loan rate for the year in which the crop is harvested, a farmer enrolled in the FOR no longer receives storage payments and can market his wheat.

The other stock control mechanism is the Commodity Credit Corporation (CCC), which acquires surplus wheat through loan forfeitures and direct purchases; it then releases its stocks only under certain domestic and foreign programs. In early 1999, the USDA's CCC purchased more than 1 million metric tons of hard red winter wheat. Valued at approximately $133.5 million at the time, it was the largest purchase of wheat on a single day by the CCC.

Programs that provide either direct credit or credit guarantees are essential to wheat producers. The Farmer Credit System (FCS), not formally a government agency even though it is sponsored by the USDA, provides credit and related services to wheat farmers. However, since 1987, the FCS has operated in conjunction with a new entity, the Federal Agricultural Mortgage Corporation (''Farmer Mac''), which establishes underwriting standards for agricultural mortgages, and, to a degree, covers defaults. Finally, the Farmer's Home Administration (FmHA) is a guarantor of loans made by agricultural lenders, and also acts as a lender of last resort for family farmers who are unable to obtain credit under reasonable terms.

A variety of crop insurances are available to farmers to insure some portion of their established yields, with premiums subsidized by the government. Historically, farmers have not purchased insurance, which cannot cover all of their losses. Disaster payment legislation has, thus, regularly been passed to cover major droughts or flooding.

The last two major areas of government intervention in the wheat growing industry—trade and environmental conservation—serves to illustrate the larger context in which the industry operates. Primarily as a way of protecting American farmland from erosion (but also to control soil salinity and off-farm environmental threats), the USDA solicits bids from year to year for enrollment in its Conservation Reserve Program (CRP). If a farmer's bid is accepted, the farmer enters into a 10- to15-year contract with the government, under which he/she agrees not to plant on a certain acreage without the Secretary of Agriculture's approval; in return, the farmer receives an annual payment.

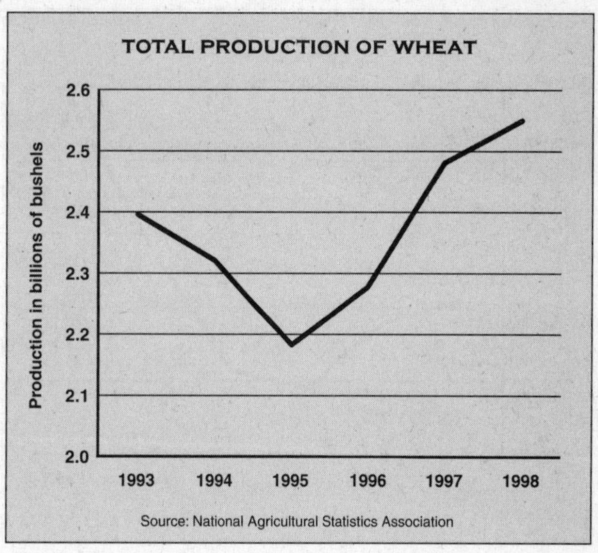

Associations and Commissions. The government plays a significant role in the wheat growing industry largely because farmers asked for assistance, and there are several organizations through which farmers can voice their concerns. The National Wheat Council (NWC) was formed in 1965 to coordinate the activities and interests of the wheat complex as a whole. The National Association of Wheat Growers was organized 15 years prior to the NWC as a nonprofit organization designed to promote the specific interests of wheat farmers. It acts primarily as a lobbying organization, focusing on legislative matters. The group also funds research on improving the quality and yields of American wheat and works in coordination with other wheat industry associations in market promotion. In addition to this national institution, there are many wheat associations and commissions at the state level as well. State associations are involved in state policy, while commissions are nonpolitical bodies that are supported by a fee automatically charged against each bushel of wheat sold in a state—the county elevator operator usually acts as a collection agency. Commissions also administer research, education, and promotion programs. Because of the success of wheat price support programs, the National Farmers Organization (NFO)—which is a prominent bargainer for other commodities—

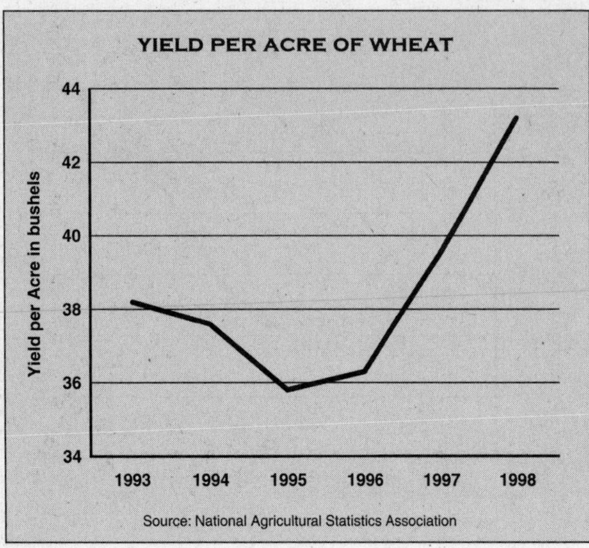

has not become a major player in the wheat growing industry.

Farmer Cooperatives. Although the majority of farms are nonintegrated, and the need for farmer cooperatives has diminished with the steady support of the government, such joint venture groups still make up a substantial portion of American wheat farming. In this type of common-ownership organization, farmer members pool their crops and store them in their own cooperative-owned elevators. Farmer-cooperative commission agents then sell the wheat, in many cases, to farmer-cooperative terminal elevators. The attempts by farmer cooperatives' to control the marketing and processing channels have also brought about a few farmer-cooperative exporters and flour millers.

Background and Development

Wheat was introduced to North America by explorers, traders, settlers, and soldiers in the sixteenth and seventeenth centuries. Spanish wheats were cultivated in the southeast and British and French wheats were produced in the northeast. The first permanent American wheat cultures were developed at the Jamestown colony in Virginia and at Plymouth, Massachusetts in the early 1600s. New York was the largest wheat-producing state until the late nineteenth century. The center of the wheat industry shifted to new territories as progress was made in railway construction and farming mechanization. In the midwestern wheat belt, the wheat economy developed into its present form, with railroad and commissions agents and, eventually, farmer cooperatives, overseeing it from production to consumption.

In the first part of the twentieth century the technological revolution affected every phase of wheat operations, and economies of scale and specialization strategies began to develop. Together with increases in domestic and foreign demand, the industry developed rapidly. It was not until after World War II, however, that the government began to intervene and established itself as an important ''market'' for wheat.

The American wheat farming industry has followed the general agricultural movement of consolidation and reduction. In recent decades, both the number and size of U.S. wheat farms has been decreasing. Most importantly, the proportion of tenant operators was increasing, and that of owner-operators was decreasing. Still, even with yields rising almost annually, production leveled off and supplies have generally been down.

There has been a trend toward less government involvement in the agricultural sector as a whole, and wheat farmers generally viewed this optimistically. 1996 ushered in a new era of market-dependent farm after Congress passed the ''Freedom to Farm'' bill, which curtailed government involvement by gradually reducing farm subsidies over a seven-year period set to end in 2002. This bill allows farmers to sow as many acres as the market dictates, without having to rely on government planting stipulations. Still, the government has planned to maintain some control to avoid surplus or shortage crises. Wheat growers have been encouraged by the increasing domestic demand for wheat since 1970. In 1993, the per capita level of consumption increased to its record high of 143 pounds. Furthermore, 1995-96 brought the industry some of its highest prices ever, averaging $4.55 per bushel from almost 70 million acres with a yield of 35.9 bushels per acre.

Current Conditions

High wheat production in the United States and globally since 1995, along with a weak demand, is driving down prices. As a result of the high yields in 1998, wheat prices failed to break $3.00 per bushel for the first time since 1990. U.S. wheat supplies are at their highest level since 1987. In the fall of 1998, the USDA announced wheat donation programs to needy countries in an effort to curb the excess stock; however, the USDA has predicted high wheat supplies again for the 1999-2000 season.

The estimated cash value of wheat supplies in 1998 wass $6.9 billion, down from $8.6 billion in 1997. The lower value of wheat was primarily due to the Federal Agriculture Improvement and Reform Act of 1996 (commonly called the Farm Bill). Since the bill allowed greater flexibility for farmers to respond to market price and demand changes, the USDA estimated that farmers planted the lowest wheat acreage in more than 10 years in 1998. Wheat farmers stocks from previous crops are high, thus demanding a lower planting. Despite a lower value, wheat is still the third largest cash crop in the United States.

Lower acreage and yields were projected by the USDA to reduce the U.S. wheat output in 1999 to the lowest level since 1973. Producers were encouraged to switch to other crops or leave more land fallow, due to lower returns on their crops. Globally, wheat production was expected to be down, as major wheat exporters' supplies were large.

WORKFORCE

A noteworthy development in the American wheat farm work force was the growing numbers of tenant operators, farmers who cultivated their wheat on rented land. Approximately 15 percent of all wheat was produced through tenantries, while only 35 percent was produced by full ownership farmers. Another significant development is the aging of the wheat industry's work force. The largest numbers of wheat producers are between the ages of 55 and 64. Moreover, while the number of farmers over 64 years of age is increasing, the number under 35 is decreasing. As the industry has grown more and more mechanized, young people in wheat farming communities have had to find other types of employment.

AMERICA AND THE WORLD

U.S. wheat growers produce much more wheat than the domestic market can consume; consequently, they market their wheat aggressively to other countries in order to sustain themselves. Although the United States is still the number one exporter of wheat, its market share has been reduced dramatically since the 1970s. Both China and the former Soviet Union, for example, were expected to reduce their purchases of U.S. wheat by between 25 percent and 40 percent in the 1990s. This development has forced the United States to seek out other major markets.

The passage of the North American Free Trade Agreement (NAFTA) was expected to create a major market for U.S. wheat in Mexico. Because global wheat reserves in 1998 were at their lowest level since the mid-1970s, the United States and other international wheat producers have taken advantage of the renewed and increasing demand for wheat. The demand for wheat has continued to exceed production in part because of the increased demand for meat such as beef, pork, and poultry. As meat played a greater role in the world's diet, the demand for wheat indirectly went up. A *Business Week* report noted that for every one pound of pork, for example, a hog required the sustenance of four pounds of wheat.

Two major developments in U.S. wheat exportation occurred at the end of the twentieth century. In late 1998, Brazil agreed to re-open its market to U.S. wheat. Closed to U.S. wheat importation since 1996, Brazil lifted the embargo after a series of negotiations with the USDA. In mid-1999, President Clinton lifted U.S. sanctions on food and medicine for Libya, Sudan, and Iran. As a result, Libya bought 16,000 tons of wheat in late 1999.

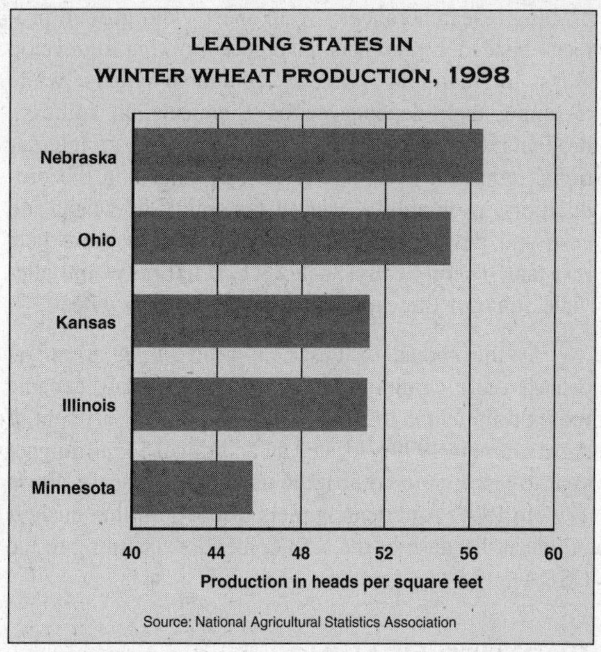

Trade Expanding Provisions. An important program geared toward international trade in wheat was the Export Enhancement Program (EEP), under which the government offered subsidies to domestic exporters. Although these subsidies were available (under certain guidelines) to exporters of any commodity, they have been used primarily to counteract European Community (EC) competition in wheat and wheat flour. The United States also offered loan guarantees to foreign purchasers of U.S. wheat, and under Public Law 480 (or the 1954 Food for Peace Program) provided some surplus wheat to low- and middle-income countries through subsidized sales or as donations. In return, the revenue the country generated went toward specific developmental projects. Public Law 480 funds were also regularly used to support wheat farmers' associations and commissions. There was a smaller Food for Progress program (Section 416 of the Agricultural Act of 1949) geared toward the implementation of market-oriented agricultural reform in less wealthy countries as well. These programs were all under constant scrutiny of American wheat farmers to ensure that they continued to generate business for them.

RESEARCH AND TECHNOLOGY

Land grant universities like Texas A&M and Kansas State University perform a great deal of research that has been very successful in developing stronger strains of wheat and more effective chemical fertilizers. Yields are expected to continue to rise as a result of this work. Increasingly, however, concerns for the environment are pushing researchers away from sheer yield growth projects. Instead, researchers have been working to develop ways to maintain farmers' profitable yields while lessening their dependence on chemicals. In addition, droughts and sun-scorched farms have led to international nonprofit research efforts for enhancing the productivity, profitability, and sustainability of wheat and corn and developing a wheat hybrid that is more heat resistant. Theoretically, such a wheat hybrid would alleviate some of the capriciousness of growing wheat.

As the spread of Fusariam head blight, a fungal disease more commonly known as wheat scab, became more prominent in the late 1990s, the U.S. Department of Agriculture in 1999 allocated an additional $3 million per year to research to combat the devastating disease. From 1991 to 1997, American farmers lost 470 million bushels of wheat, because of the scab epidemic, according to the USDA.

FURTHER READING

Burns, Greg, and Dave Lindorff et al. ''The New Economics of Food.'' *Business Week,* 20 May 1996.

Carini, Maureen. ''Outlook Tempered by Weak Worldwide Demand.'' *S&P's Industry Survey Vol. 1,* 29 July 1999/Agribusiness Industry Survey.

Economic Research Service. ''U.S. Wheat Supplies Remain Large in 1999/2000.'' *Agricultural Outlook,* August 1999. Available from http://www.econ.ag/gov/epubs/pdf/agout/aug99/ao263d.pdf

Economic Research Service. ''Record U.S. Wheat Yield, Large Stocks Pressure Prices.'' *Agricultural Outlook,* August 1998. Available from http://www.econ.ag/gov/epubs/pdf/agout/aug98/ao253d.pdf

Frey, David E. ''Major Breakthrough in Libya.'' 17 November 1999. Available from http://www.smallgrains.org

United States Department of Agriculture. ''Glickman Announces Largest Wheat Purchase Ever by CCC.'' 26 March 1999. Available from http://www.usda.gov/ews/releases/1999/03/0135

SIC 0112

RICE

This industry consists of establishments primarily engaged in the production of rice, or whose sales of rice account for 50 percent or more of the total value of sales for their agricultural production.

NAICS CODE(S)

111160 (Rice Farming)

INDUSTRY SNAPSHOT

Rice farms in the United States grew to almost 9,300 in the 1990's. With more than three million acres harvested annually, rice production remains stable. Peaking at $1.75 billion in 1997, the value of rice production is among the top 20 crops in the United States. Valued at $1.62 billion, rice farms harvested 3.31 million acres in 1998.

BACKGROUND AND DEVELOPMENT

Although rice is not considered a major American crop, the American rice industry is more than 300 years old. Rice was introduced in America around 1685, when a British sea captain, John Thurber, brought a load of the grain to the colonies from Madagascar. Rice first appeared as a commercial crop in the Carolinas in the seventeenth century. After peaking in the mid-nineteenth century, rice production in South Carolina and Georgia began to decline as a result of the Civil War, bad weather, and increasing competition from Louisiana. The industry began to shift toward plantations along the Mississippi River where steam-powered river pumps provided a more efficient irrigation system than the Carolina tidal gates. Soon thereafter, the industry developed in the milling and shipping center of New Orleans, and grew rapidly and independently amid the explosive transformations of the American industrial economy in the early twentieth century.

Depending largely on government acreage allotment, conservation, marketing, and loan and deficiency payment programs, which adjust incentives annually to control production, between 2.5 and 3.5 million acres of U.S. farmland have been used for rice cultivation annually. Most of this land was in the Mississippi River Delta in Louisiana, Arkansas, Mississippi, and Missouri. Texas and California provided the two other major rice farming centers, with Florida adding marginally to the total.

Because of its capital intensive nature and its extensive use of irrigation and canal systems, the rice industry naturally aligned itself to the technological progress of the industrial revolution and modernized much faster than the cotton and sugar industries. In addition, the industry's development of a coordinated network among its various milling interests, distributors, and broker/agents, was a useful organizational model for other southern agricultural industries. The modern rice industry has concentrated far more on distribution and marketing channels than on production.

With a growing year spanning from August to July, modern rice production has been aided by the use of land plans that till and level the soil, creating fields that slope slightly for uniform flooding and controlled draining. Rice farmers also have relied on lasers to determine where to place water control levees. Sowing has been facilitated by the use of seed drills and airplanes in the early spring. During the growing season, rice must be kept constantly in a water depth of two to three inches. Rice producers also apply fertilizer from airplanes to yield consistent and healthy crops. After the rice matures, the fields are drained. At harvest time, farmers use combines to cut rice, separate the grain from the stalk, and convey the grain into trucks. The trucks then transport the grain to dryers where warm air removes moisture until it is ready for shipment to rice mills.

Domestic consumption of rice subsumes three primary uses: direct food use, processed food use, and beer production use. Direct food use has constituted the largest segment of rice consumption at 58 percent of overall use. Growing over the years, processed food use has accounted for 25 percent of total domestic rice consumption. In this market, use in cereal has long been the highest, making up 44 percent of the processed food division. Other noteworthy processed foods containing rice include candy bars, soups, and crackers. Finally, beer production constitutes 17 percent of total domestic consumption.

In the mid- to late 1990s, U.S. rice production accounted for approximately two percent of the world total with annual sales consistently over $1 billion. The United States has ranked tenth as a producer of rice and second, behind Thailand, as an exporter of rice, averaging around 20 percent of the annual world export market share for many years, until India's emergence as a major rice exporter in 1995. After India's foray into the export market, the United States became the third leading exporter. With a small but expanding domestic consumption base, the industry has, from its inception, relied heavily on foreign markets in selling its high quality rice varieties. During the 1980s, Latin America became the largest customer for American rice; however, lower prices and proximity began to favor Thailand and other exporting countries in the competitive European, North African, and Asian markets. As Americans became increasingly health conscious in the 1980s, domestic consumption of rice began to rise. Use of rice in processed foods such as cereals and candy also contributed to the increased consumption of rice. Breweries have also used rice consistently as a cereal adjunct for making beer. By 1991, domestic use had actually overtaken exports as a proportion of total annual rice production. In 1995, domestic per capita rice consumption climbed to its all time high: nearly 25 pounds per capita—up almost 10 pounds from its 1985 level. With stiff competition worldwide from less expensive rices, American rice producers have begun concentrating increasingly on national demand as domestic prices often exceed international prices, forcing competitors to characterize the United States as a residual rice exporter.

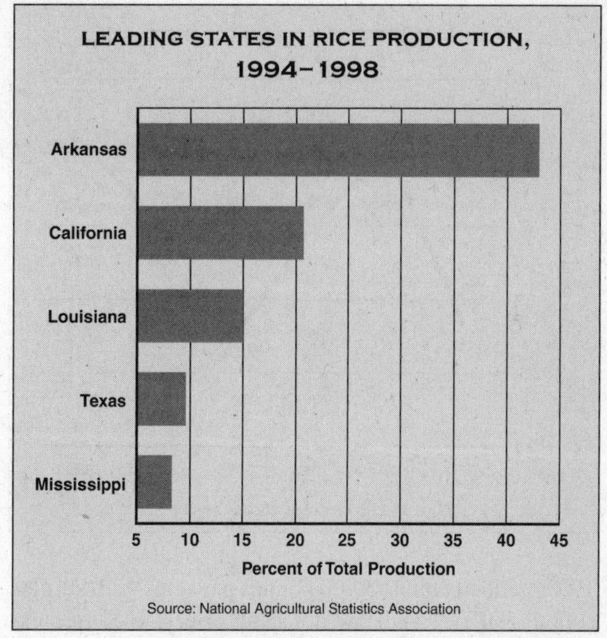

CURRENT CONDITIONS

The trend of market dependence, which began in the early 1990s, has persisted and will likely constitute the rice production situation in the future. Government assistance to rice farmers has gradually decreased in an effort to wean rice farmers off of government subsidies and safety nets, and to make them more market dependent. As rice related legislation became increasingly crucial, the USA Rice Federation formed in 1994 to represent the industry and to lead policy making, research, education, and efficiency initiatives and endeavors to benefit all segments of the industry. President Clinton, in 1996, signed the long-anticipated landmark Federal Agriculture Improvement and Reform Act, the so-called ''freedom to farm'' bill, that called for the incremental reduction of farm subsidies over a seven-year period, after which government income support would cease altogether. Before, the government had issued subsidies to producers who agreed to not plant an overabundance of rice and other grains. With this piece of legislation, the government paid subsidies to farmer whether or not they planted anything for the seven year transition period. Rice producers have confronted this significant transition from government income support to becoming independent by devoting increased attention and effort to advancing rice production technology and efficiency, i.e., to developing methods for yielding larger crops with less effort, using less acreage. These moves, rice producers hoped, would stabilize the volatility of the coming farming age and counteract losses incurred from the loss and diminution of farm subsidies.

Rice production efficiency has continued to increase. The 1998 growing year, although not as productive as

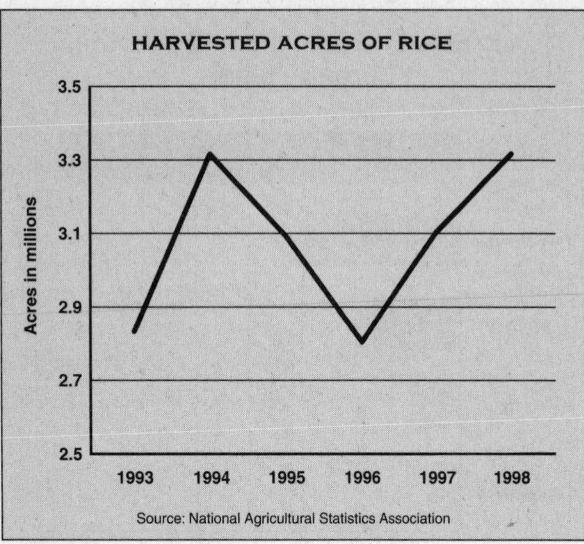

1997, yielded almost 5,900 pounds per acre. With surplus supplies of rice and low domestic prices, U.S. rice exports increased to 85.2 million hundredweight (cwt) in 1998.

Further Reading

"Clinton Signs Farm-Subsidy Overhaul." *Facts On File World News Digest,* 4 April 1996.

Coats, Robert C., and Gail L. Cramer. "Rice Policy." Available from http://ianrwww.unl.edu/farmbill/rice.htm.

Food and Agriculture Policy Research Institute. "Rice." Columbia, MO: 23 May 1996. Available from http://ssu.agri.missouri.edu.ssu/fapri/title.htm.

Meyers, Richard. "USA Rice VP Column" Arlington, VA: USA Rice Federation, March 1996. Available from http://www.usarice.com/COMMUNIC/vprm396.htm.

USA Rice Federation. "Facts about USA Rice." Arlington, VA, 1996. Available from http://www.usarice.com/rice.htm.

U.S. Department of Agriculture. Economic Research Service. *Rice Situation & Outlook Yearbook* Washington, 1996. Available from http://usda.mannlib.cornell.edu/reports/erssor/field/rcs-bb/1996/rice_outlook_report_12.13.96.

U.S. Department of Agriculture. Economic Research Service. *Rice Outlook* Washington, DC: 12 November 1998. Available from http://usda.mannlib.cornell.edu/reports/erssor/field/rcs-bb/1998/RCS0698.ASC

SIC 0115

CORN

This entry includes establishments primarily engaged in the production of field corn for grain or seed. Establishments primarily engaged in the production of sweet corn are classified under **SIC 0161: Vegetables and Melons,** and those producing popcorn are classified under **SIC 0119: Cash Crops Not Elsewhere Classified.**

NAICS Code(s)

111150 (Corn Farming)

Industry Snapshot

The United States is the world's leading producer and exporter of corn, growing about two-thirds of the world's supply. Argentina, the second largest exporter, is a distant second. Although corn is grown in all 50 states, approximately 75 percent of it corn comes from the section of the Midwest known as the Corn Belt, which consists of parts of Illinois, Indiana, Iowa, Michigan, Minnesota, Missouri, Nebraska, Ohio, South Dakota, and Wisconsin. The leading corn-producing states are Iowa and Illinois. In 1998/99 the U.S. corn crop was estimated at 9.73 billion bushels with a total estimated weight of 247.5 million tons.

Throughout the 1990s corn was the number one U.S. crop in terms of acreage, with more than 70 million acres devoted to it. Throughout the decade, planted acreage of corn has accounted for approximately 24 percent of all major field crops, the highest in the United States. Corn is the leading U.S. feed grain. The record 5.9 billion bushel usage estimated for 1998/1999 would top the previous high of 5.7 billion for 1997/1998. Corn was a major source of livestock feed, and approximately 50 percent of the annual harvest of corn was fed to chickens, hogs, and cattle.

In 1999 total corn supplies showed a sharp increase. Corn had a large variety of industrial and food applications. Although sweet corn was classified elsewhere (as a vegetable rather than a grain), field corn was an ingredient in many processed foods including breakfast cereals, salad dressings, margarine, syrup, soft drinks, and snack items. Corn had also been adapted for use in the manufacturing of ceramics, construction materials, disposable diapers, paper goods, textiles, and health and medical products such as penicillin, antibiotics, and vitamins. It had also been converted into fuel (ethanol) and biodegradable plastic.

Organization and Structure

Harvesting. In terms of harvesting, corn is the largest U.S. crop. Corn is planted in the spring and harvested in the summer and fall. The marketing season for the crop runs from September 1 to August 31.

Most corn is harvested with a combine, which picks the corn from the stalk, removes the husks, and shells and cleans the corn. The shelled corn is dried for storage. Corn can also be harvested with a machine that picks the corn and strips the husk but leaves the kernels on the ear. The ears are then stored in bins that allowed the corn to dry.

Harvesting of corn for grain begins when the moisture content is about 28 percent, and harvesting for silage corn begins when the moisture is about 50 percent. A forage harvester chops the corn stalks close to ground level and grinds it into small pieces. The silage is blown into a wagon following behind and is then stored in a silo where fermentation preserves it.

Federal Price Supports. Government price supports for corn began with the Agricultural Adjustment Act of 1933. The legislation granted federal payments to farmers who reduced production of surplus crops. In 1938 Congress enacted a law to set up nonrecourse loans that gave farmers money for their crop so they could hold onto it and sell it when prices went up. The loans also guaranteed the farmers a minimum price for their corn. If the farmers could not sell their crop at a higher price than the government had lent them against the crop, they could simply forfeit the crop to the government. However, the 1996 ''Freedom to Farm'' legislation promised to end this method of agricultural support. The law called for the gradual reduction of loans over a seven year period, ending with the termination of government subsidies altogether after 2002. This move, the government hoped, would make farmers more dependent on the market and less on the government.

Acreage Reduction Programs (ARP) paid farmers to set aside an amount of land on which they would not grow corn; the amount of land set aside depended upon the corn reserves already available. However, the optimal amount of set-aside land depended upon one's perspective. For example, the agriculture secretary announced a five percent set-aside for 1992, ordering all farmers who received government corn subsidies to set aside five percent of their corn acreage. Farmers wanted to see higher set-asides to limit production and keep prices up. Grain companies, however, wanted to see no land set aside in order to increase production and lower prices to make corn more competitive on the world market.

A government program for conservation reserves paid farmers not to plant corn or other crops on highly erodible cropland for ten years. They instead were required to plant grass or another ground cover and could not use that land for hay or grazing their livestock. According to James Bovard, a policy analyst and author of *The Farm Fiasco,* the conservation program was idling land that was equivalent to the entire state of Ohio and would cost the United States more than $20 billion by the time it expired in 1999. Bovard claimed that this program paid three times the going price for renting land.

Corn and other feed-grain supports raised costs for livestock producers, and those expenses were passed on to consumers. However, farmers and others who supported the government agricultural programs claimed

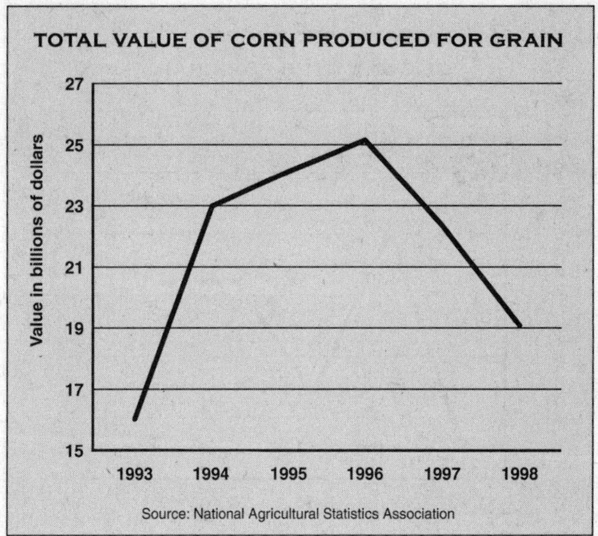

that U.S. consumers had stable food supplies and prices because of the programs.

Critics contended that these programs, which were initially adopted in 1933 to confront an emergency situation, had become a burden to U.S. consumers and taxpayers and were hurting the United States in world trade. While U.S. farmers were being paid not to plant, thus reducing the amount of grain available for export, farmers in some nations were planting as much as they could to take over world markets, the critics said. Among the critics were grain dealers who urged that the United States and other countries end price supports and exercise free trade policies instead.

BACKGROUND AND DEVELOPMENT

Corn has figured strongly in the history of people in America. Native Americans cultivated it long before the Europeans arrived. Corn became a staple in the diet of the Europeans, and each wave of settlers moving farther and farther west across the continent carried corn to plant.

In 1837 John Deere introduced a steel plow, which made turning the heavy Midwestern soil easier because soil did not stick to it as it did to wood or cast-iron plows. Mechanical corn planters were also developed during the 1800s. Mechanical corn pickers became common in the 1930s and 1940s.

During the 1920s corn pushed wheat aside as the country's main grain crop. This was due in part to the changing eating habits of Americans, who began eating more poultry, red meat, and dairy—and less bread and other wheat products. Poultry, cattle, and dairy livestock thrived on corn, which was cheap and abundant.

Since 1920 the total number of farms has declined from 6.5 million to less than 2.2 million. During that same time, the average farm size has grown from less than 150 acres to 450 acres. Much of this consolidation

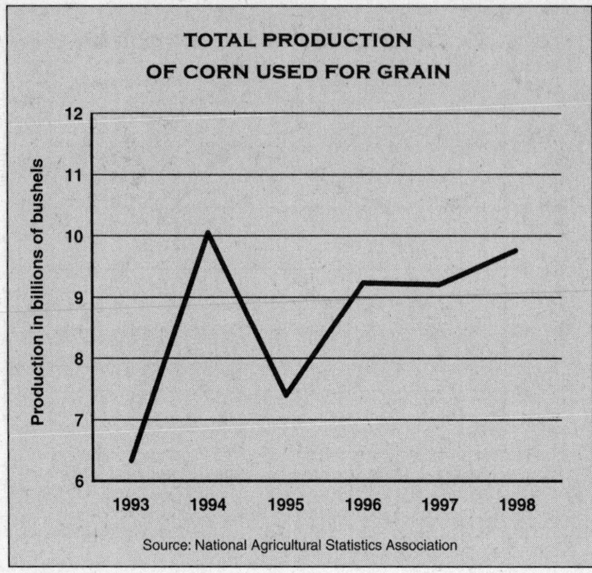

was due to technology, as improvements in seeds, fertilizer, and machinery allowed fewer people to farm more acreage.

During the 1970s easy credit prompted many farmers to purchase expensive machinery and more land. The value of farmland tripled and, in some cases, quadrupled. In the early 1980s, however, the value of farmland in the Corn Belt dropped 52 percent, according to Hugh Ulrich in *Losing Ground.* Interest rates shot up and grain exports dropped, resulting in low prices and a surplus of grains. Farmers were unable to repay their loans; in order to maintain their income, they bought and planted more acreage and went deeper into debt. Droughts in 1986 and 1988 decreased production, and farmers needed federal aid. The mid-1980s saw thousands of family-owned farms fail. However, in the 1990s corn became a precious commodity domestically and internationally with its multifarious food and industrial applications.

Current Conditions

With the development of better hybrids and improved production methods, farmers could grow more grain even though they were planting less acreage. In 1932 almost 2.9 billion bushels of corn were grown on almost 110.5 million acres, resulting in an average production of about 28.4 bushels per acre. Twenty years later, three billion bushels were grown on only 81.8 million acres, for an average of 37.6 bushels per acre. Although weather, soil, disease, and pests played a big part in the size of the crop each year, production and production efficiency has continued to increase, culminating in 1994's record harvest of 10 billion bushels, with a yield of 138.6 bushels per acre. However, in 1995, production declined when 71 million acres yielded 7.4 billion bushels, an average yield per acre of 113.5 bushels. In 1997 acreage was up to 73.7 million with the average yield of 127 bushels per acre. In 1998 both harvested acreage and average yield increased; acreage went up to 73.8 million and yield went up to 132 bushels per acre.

A large portion of the corn grown in the United States was still used by the farmers who grew it or by their neighbors. About 60 percent of the crop was consumed by livestock on the farm on which the corn was grown or by animals on nearby farms.

Corn that went on the market for export, industrial use, or trade passed through the hands of agribusinesses, such as Cargill or Continental Grain. These privately-held grain trading companies bought corn, stored it in their huge grain elevators, processed it into cornstarch or corn syrup, or sold the corn and milled corn products in the United States and around the world.

The rest of the crop was exported or sold for processing to other companies. Wet millers prepared the crop for use, with starch being the leading product. Corn oil is produced by pressing the germs of the corn and is used in making margarine, mayonnaise, and other foods. Further processing turns corn starch into corn syrup or high fructose corn syrup. High fructose corn syrup has emerged as the leading sweetener in the United States, with more consumed per capita than cane sugar and beet sugar combined. It is produced by converting some of the glucose in cornstarch into fructose and is now used in place of other sugars in soft drinks and processed foods. It became popular with food and beverage processors because it was cheaper than cane and beet sugar, which were supported by federal price levels and quotas on foreign sugar. In the late 1990s, industrial demand for corn as high fructose corn syrup was expected to increase.

The North American Free Trade Agreement (NAFTA) of 1993 has brought the U.S. corn industry increased access to the Mexican market. Corn exports to Mexico have risen, because the trade accord has reduced support for Mexican corn growers, forcing the country to rely on imported corn. In its first year of implementation, Mexico imported 2.5 million metric tons (98.5 bushels) of corn. Another emerging key importer of U.S. corn was the Pacific Rim in Asia. The U.S. Department of Agriculture (USDA) has predicted that exports would rise to 2.9 billion bushels by 2004. While smaller field crop growers viewed the 1996 Farm Bill with trepidation, corn growers remained unfazed as demand for corn has continued to increase.

Pollution and Erosion. The increase of crop yield has been taking its toll on the nation's water supplies. Pesticides and fertilizers have contaminated ground water in major agricultural areas and have invaded the drinking water of people who depend on wells for their water. The nation's fertile topsoil has continued to erode and, as farms have expanded, erosion has become more of a problem because larger fields are more vulnerable to topsoil erosion. Use of heavier equipment has also contributed to the problem.

As the United States and other nations began to deal with environmental issues more intensely, erosion and pollution caused by farming received more attention, especially from farmers growing corn.

RESEARCH AND TECHNOLOGY

Improved Seeds and Techniques. Farmers have always tried to find the best ways to increase crop yield and quality. They knew that the size of their crop depended on the seed they used, so they saved the best and largest ears of corn for seed. They carefully observed the results of their seed selection and learned to develop strains adapted for their locations and conditions. Farmers could increase the quality of their crop and the bushels per acreage yield by selecting the right seed. Scientists and farmers began to apply knowledge of hybrid corn-seed breeding, which involved fertilizing one strain of corn with another to produce corn with particular characteristics.

Some industry observers expected that, in the beginning of the next century, biotechnologists would be able to genetically engineer seeds to produce corn with specific traits such as modified proteins, oils, or starches—as well as resistance to disease and insects. To this end, the National Corn Growers Association (NCGA) implemented the National Corn Genome Initiative (NCGI) and has endeavored to create a comprehensive gene map of corn in order to realize the corn industry's goals of creating corn hybrids for different environments, thus reducing the reliance on pesticides and fertilizers. The NCGA has been seeking federal funding to fuel this costly project.

As of early 1999, it was estimated that hundreds of transgenic varieties of seeds were commercially available. These included mostly corn, soybean, cotton, and canola. Between 1997 and 1998, global acreage planted to commercial transgenic crops, excluding China, increased 250 percent, according to the International Service for the Acquisition of Agri-Biotech Applications (ISAAA). Corn and soybean together made up 82 percent of the 1998 acreage.

In 1998 only two genetic traits were devoted to almost all of the crop acreage in the country—herbicide and insect resistance. At the same time, less than 1 percent of acreage was devoted to "quality traits" like improved nutritional features. Genetically altered crops available at the end of the century had a negligible impact on prices received by farmers because the products were indistinguishable from conventional crops. More enhanced traits are expected in the future and will most likely increase the value of crops.

Corn-Based Products. In 1975 a team of USDA scientists developed a starch substance that could absorb 2,000 times its weight in moisture. This discovery was widely applied by manufacturers of disposable diapers.

Ethanol, a corn-based fuel, increased corn demand on an even larger scale. Sales of ethanol have skyrocketed. Only a few million gallons of the fuel were produced in the early 1980s. By the late 1980s, more than 850 million gallons were produced, and 86 percent of it was distilled from corn. Although some analysts predicted that ethanol use would rise steadily in the 1990s, ethanol use increased only slightly: about 7 percent of the U.S. corn crop or 600 million bushels of corn generally have been used to generate 1.5 billion gallons of ethanol.

When the Environmental Protection Agency (EPA) mandated that lead be removed from gasoline, ethanol became an octane booster, for ethanol added to gasoline created an oxygenated fuel that cut carbon monoxide exhaust emissions. Sixty major metropolitan areas in the United States failed to meet EPA carbon monoxide levels and were mandated to oxygenate gasoline during the winter months. The ethanol industry grew rapidly from 1980 to 1986, but when crude oil prices dropped, the ethanol market dried up. Moreover, ethanol, also known as gasohol, was an expensive product.

Corn was also becoming an environmentally-friendly product in the plastics industry. New technology was able to process starch into methylglucoside, a biodegradable plastic. This corn plastic breaks down after being buried in landfills for only seven months, while oil-based plastic never breaks down completely. Corn has also been used to create calcium magnesium acetate (CMA), a deicing substitute for rock salt. Since CMA contains neither sodium nor chloride, this deicer was safe for watersheds and agricultural areas, and it would not damage roads, bridges, and automobiles.

FURTHER READING

"Corn." *CRB Commodity 1999 Yearbook,* 1999.

National Corn Genome Initiative. "The National Corn Genome Initiative." St. Louis, MO: National Corn Growers Association, May 1995. Available from http://www.inverizon.com/ncgi/early/NCI_NCI.html.

National Corn Growers Association. "World of Corn On-line." St. Louis, MO: National Corn Growers Association, 1996. Available from http://www.ncga.com/02world/page02.html.

Ohio Corn Marketing Program. "Corn and the Environment," 3 December 1995. Available from http://www.ohiocorn.org/env/ethanol.htm.

"Tortilla Wars: NAFTA Opens Floodgates to Cheap Corn from USA." *The Progressive,* June 1999.

United States Feed Grains Council. "The Impact of NAFTA," 3 June 1996. Available from http://www.grains.org/policy/nafta.htm.

"U.S. Corn Prices to Remain Weak Despite Record Domestic Use." *Agricultural Outlook,* October 1999. Available from http://www.econ.ag.gov/cpub/pdf/agout/oct99/ao265d.pdf.

SIC 0116

SOYBEANS

This industry consists of establishments primarily engaged in the production of soybeans.

NAICS CODE(S)

111110 (Soybean Farming)

INDUSTRY SNAPSHOT

Soybeans are the second largest cultivated crop in the United States, behind corn, with almost 70 million acres harvested annually. In 1998, the United States produced more soybeans than any other country in the world, producing nearly 48 percent of the world's total. According to American Soybean Association, soybeans provided 82 percent of the edible consumption of fats and oils in the United States in 1998.

Soybeans, which possess high quantities of protein, and soybean products are used in a wide range of food and industrial products. Soy products have three major divisions: soy oil products, whole bean products, and soy protein products. Food products include baby food, cereal, diet foods, imitation meats, processed meats, soy sauce, tofu and miso, salad dressings and margarine, cooking oil, candy, and baked goods. Soybeans are used in pet foods and as the leading source of protein meal for U.S. livestock. Industrial uses for soybeans include wallboard and plywood, medicines, soaps and disinfectants, pesticides, fertilizers, candles, linoleum, and varnish, fire extinguisher fluid, and paint.

ORGANIZATION AND STRUCTURE

Federal policies have affected the output and price of U.S. soybeans. The government has supported soybean prices by setting the bottom price for both soybeans and other competing crops. Under the U.S. Department of Agriculture's (USDA) Commodity Credit Corporation, farmers could borrow money against their crops when they harvested them, with the harvest serving as collateral, and could sell their harvest at any time. At the end of nine months, the farmer had to repay the loan or forfeit the harvest to the government. This program has allowed farmers to sell when prices were high and thus more easily pay back the loan, and it has guaranteed them a minimum price set by the USDA even if market prices dipped below the loan rate. Soybean prices for the most part have been at or above the government loan rate since 1950.

Although there were no restrictions or production quotas for soybeans, programs controlling the production of other crops, such as wheat, feed grains, cotton, and rice, have often cut down on the number of acres available for soybean cultivation, since supply control programs for other commodities prohibited the planting of other crops on that acreage. Reduction of potential soybean acreage, however, has reduced supply and maintains higher soybean prices.

BACKGROUND AND DEVELOPMENT

Soybeans, legumes related to clover and peas, were cultivated in Eastern Asia 5,000 years ago, but they were not grown in the United States until the beginning of the nineteenth century, when they were grown experimentally for use as livestock feed. When soybeans were processed into oil and meal, the primary use was for fertilizers. Their use as fodder grew also, but the events of World War II created an increased demand for soybeans for human and animal consumption, causing its industrial applications to expand as well. Because soybeans were an inexpensive protein source, their use has been credited with aiding in the expansion of the poultry industry in the 1970s and 1980s.

Controversy and drops in exports ensued in 1996 when U.S. producers tried to sell a mixture of regular and genetically engineered soybeans to the European market. Though U.S. policy did not require labeling of genetically engineered products, European customers demanded to receive only soybeans that were not tampered with genetically. This controversy cost producers $150 million, almost 10 percent of their European exports.

Although soybean producers have viewed with consternation agricultural bills such as the 1990 five-year act that preserved price controls for soybeans and other crops, they were pleased with the Federal Agriculture Improvement and Reform Act of 1996, which alleviated the fears generated by the preceding agricultural legislation. The American Soybean Association (ASA) welcomed the bill, with its more equitable rate of marketing loans that allows soybean growers similar funds as other major cash-grain growers are eligible to receive. Indeed, soybean production was expected to benefit dramatically from the FAIR legislation because of high domestic and international demand for soybeans. The increasing success of soybeans began in 1994/95, when soybean oil consumption, for example, increased to 13 billion pounds. Moreover, soybean yields, which started to increase prior to the bill, have continued this trend. 1994 brought the soybean industry its record yield at 41.4

bushels per acre, up substantially from 1993's 32.6 bushels per acre yield, with the total soybean yield a record 2.5 billion bushels. Since 1994, soybean yields have consistently been high as a result of the FAIR Act's provision to allow farmers the flexibility to plant more acres of soybeans.

CURRENT CONDITIONS

According to the American Soybean Association, soybeans were planted on a record 72.4 million acres in 1998, producing the largest soybean crop ever grown. Prices paid to farmers per bushel were the lowest average since 1985, making the 1998 crop value of $13.9 billion lower than previous years.

Soybeans are grown in more than 30 states, making soybeans the second largest crop in cash sales in the United States, and the largest value crop export. Soybeans and products are now promoted by the ASA in more than 100 countries.

The United States has continued to dominate the export market, in part because of production efficiency, which has created an abundance of soybeans and soy products for exportation, giving U.S. producers the advantage of offering their product at a lower price than producers from competing countries. According to the ASA, U.S. soybean and soybean products exports totaled $7.4 billion in 1998.

FURTHER READING

American Soybean Association. ''ASA Positive on New Farm Bill.'' St. Louis: ASA, 4 April 1996. Available from http://www.oilseeds.org/asa/fb_signd.htm.

American Soybean Association. ''1999 Soy Stats.'' St. Louis: ASA, 1999. Available from http://www.unitedsoybean.org/99soystats/

Food and Agriculture Policy Research Institute. ''Soybeans.'' Columbia, MO: 1996. Available from http://ssu.agri.missouri.edu.ssu/fapri/report/195/execsum/text/beans.htm.

Ibrahim, Youssef M. ''Genetic Soybeans from U.S. Alarm Europeans.'' *New York Times,* 7 November 1996.

United Soybean Board. ''U.S. Soybean Market Opportunities Emerging in Vietnam.'' Urbana, IL, 26 October 1996. Available from http://spectre.ag.uiuc.edu/~usb/usbnews10_2696.html.

U.S. Department of Agriculture. Economic Research Service. ''Oil Crops Yearbook.'' Washington, DC: 29 October 1996. Available from http://usda.mannlib.cornell.edu/reports/erssor/field/ocs-bby/oil_crops_yearbook_10.29.96.

U.S. Department of Agriculture. Economic Research Service. ''Oil Crops Outlook.'' Washington, DC: 12 November 1999. Available from http://usda.mannlib.cornell.edu/reports/erssor/field/ocs-bb/1999/ocs1199.pdf

SIC 0119

CASH GRAINS, NOT ELSEWHERE CLASSIFIED

This industry includes establishments primarily engaged in the production of cash grains, not elsewhere classified. Primary cash grains in this classification include dry field and seed peas and beans, safflowers, sunflowers, and popcorn. The industry also includes farms growing barley, buckwheat, lentils, oats, sorghum, rye, mustard seeds, cowpea and flaxseed.

NAICS CODE(S)

111130 (Dry Pea and Bean Farming)
111120 (Oilseed (except Soybean) Farming)
111150 (Corn Farming)
111191 (Oilseed and Grain Combination Farming)
111199 (All Other Grain Farming)

Major members of this industry, such as barley, oats, sunflower seeds, sorghum, and dry beans combined for more than $4.2 billion in sales in 1997, according to the U.S. Department of Agriculture (USDA). This group of cash grains accounted for more than 42 million acres of farmland in the mid-1990s, which yielded more than 1 billion bushels per year. Cash grains, like most U.S. crops, had depended on government price supports since the Great Depression. In 1996, however, Congress passed the Federal Agriculture Improvement and Reform Act, or ''freedom to farm'' legislation, to gradually decrease subsidies over a seven-year period and to eliminate them by 2002, ushering in a new era of market-dependent farming. The United States had more than 175,000 farms producing in this industry in 1997.

Barley. About 60 percent of the barley grown in the United States was used for livestock feed, especially dairy and beef cattle. Another third of the crop was used for malt by the food and brewing industries. Barley has been affected by acreage reduction programs through which the U.S. government has paid farmers to suspend the planting of barley on portions of their land. In some years, USDA payments accounted for one-fourth of barley farmers' income. In 1998, barley production was estimated at 352 million bushels, yielding 60.1 bushels per acre nationally. North Dakota was the top barley producing state, followed by Idaho, Montana, Washington, and Minnesota. These five states produced more than 75 percent of the 1998 U.S. barley crop.

Genetic research may enhance barley's future by developing breeds of barley that can yield leavening flour for breads—conventional barley flour alone cannot yield raised loaves of bread—and that are resistant to disease. If biotechnology produces such a barley hybrid, then the

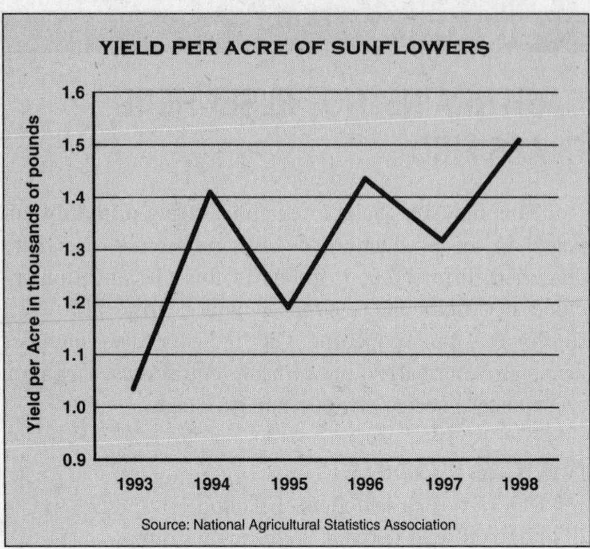

Source: National Agricultural Statistics Association

demand for barley would likely increase because of its growing efficiency: barley yields about 35 more bushels per acre than wheat.

Sorghum. Valued at $1.45 billion in 1997, sorghum (cereal grasses, also called milo) was used primarily for livestock feed. Close to two-thirds of the sorghum grown in the United States was used as livestock feed. About one-third of the U.S. sorghum production was exported, primarily to Japan, Mexico, and Argentina. Applications of sorghum in food, seed, and industrial processing account for about two percent of the U.S. crop. The use of sorghum in liquors has been its most common food application. Sorghum was also processed into starch, oil, and dextrose. Production has suffered a modest decline since the early 1990s. Sorghum, which has competed with corn as a primary livestock feed, was expected to gradually increase to occupy more than 10 million acres and yield 68 bushels per acre in the coming decade, stabilizing after that. In the 1997 production year, growers planted 10.1 million acres, and yielded 69.5 bushels per acre.

Oats. Oats, the smallest agricultural contracts traded on the Chicago Board of Trade, were used as a cash grain as well as for on-farm uses as straw, pasture, forage, or as a companion crop to help establish an alfalfa crop or other legume crop. Leading states in oat production included Iowa, Minnesota, South Dakota, and Wisconsin. Total domestic oat sales experienced a 33 percent decline between 1992 and 1995, plummeting from roughly $400 million in 1992 to $265 million in 1995. In 1996, oat production dropped to its lowest level on record with only 155 million bushels harvested, a 5 percent decrease from the previous record low. These trends reflected that oats had become less profitable than other grains and that U.S. crops were viewed as inferior to foreign oats. In 1997, oat production increased to more than 2.9 million bushels harvested. Oat consumption in general gained ground as food in the early 1990s because of their health benefits; medical research suggested that oats could lower cholesterol-but an increasing proportion of this consumption was of foreign oats.

Rye. A minor crop in the United States, rye was used primarily as livestock feed and is often mixed with other grains. Rye, especially rye flour, is also used for food. Less than three million acres were planted annually during the 1980s. Approximately one-third of the acreage was harvested, and the rest was grown for grazing, ground cover in the winter, or was plowed under to enrich the soil. Leading rye-producing states were South Dakota, Georgia, North Dakota, and Minnesota. In 1997, 341 thousand bushels of rye were harvested, valued at $31.9 million.

Dry Beans. The United States has consistently been a major dry bean exporter, ranking second behind China in exports and fifth in the world in production. Leading states producing dry beans comprised North Dakota, Michigan, and Nebraska. Dry edible beans, including pintos, garbanzos, navy beans, limas, black, and black eye, have constituted this industry's third largest segment with annual sales of $640 million in 1995. With mild fluctuations, dry bean production has risen and has been predicted to continue this trend, regularly yielding more than 20 million hundred weight (cwt.) since the record yield in 1980. In 1997, the average yield of dry beans was 1,695 hundredweight (cwt) per acre from 1.9 million total acres. The largest dry bean crops were pinto, navy, black, and great northern beans. Pinto bean crops totaled more than 41 percent of the all dry bean production.

Sunflower/Safflower. Sunflower and safflower seeds produced nearly 4.2 billion pounds from just over 3.1 million acres of farmland in 1997. Sunflower production has maintained this level of production with 2.85 million harvested acres in 1997. These seeds were primarily used in cooking oil, as the oil content of sunflower seeds is typically 40 percent or higher. Safflower oil had a peripheral industrial application, because it resembles linseed oil, and safflower cakes were used as high-protein livestock supplement. Sunflower seeds became more acceptable in international markets, and demand was expected to increase. In the mid-1990s, the United States was the third leading supplier of sunflower oil, producing more than 1.5 million metric tons annually.

Popcorn. Popcorn is native to the Americas and has been cultivated and eaten by Native Americans for centuries. In the early 1990s, the United States grew nearly all the popcorn used in the world. Nebraska, Indiana, and other Corn Belt states have consistently been the leading popcorn producers in the United States. By 1996, with higher profit margins for growing regular dent corn, popcorn production had begun to decline.

FURTHER READING

Fitzgerald, Anna. "Crop Decline: The U.S. Isn't Feeling Its Oats." Gannett News, 1 August 1996.

Food and Agriculture Policy Research Institute. Columbia, MO, 1996. Available from http://www.ssu.agri.missouri.edu/ssu/fapri/title.htm.

U.S. Department of Agriculture. Economic Research Service. "Dry Edible Beans." Washington, DC: 1996.

U.S. Department of Agriculture. *United States Crop Rankings—1997.* Washington, DC:1997. Available from http://usda2.mannlib.cornell.edu/data-sets/crops/9X180/98180/crprnkus.txt

SIC 0131

COTTON

This industry classification includes establishments primarily engaged in the production of cotton and cottonseed.

NAICS CODE(S)

111920 (Cotton Farming)

INDUSTRY SNAPSHOT

Farmers harvest approximately 15 million bales of cotton every year from an average of more than 12 million acres planted annually. Cotton's many uses make it a major U.S. textile export, increasing in 1997 to 3.7 million bale equivalents shipped. Often overlooked as significant, the cottonseed produces more than 9 billion pounds of feed for livestock on average and more than 154 million gallons of cottonseed oil (used for a variety of food products ranging from margarine to salad dressing) annually. According to the National Cotton Council, cotton stimulates an estimated $120 billion in business revenue on the nation's economy, the largest of any U.S. crop.

BACKGROUND AND DEVELOPMENT

Earliest records of domesticated cotton or Gossypium date back to 5000 B.C. and traces of cotton processed into cloth have been found in Peru with the estimated date of 2500 B.C. Since the eighteenth century, the United States has reigned a leading producer of cotton, usually the second largest. Virginian colonists grew and exported small amounts of cotton since the founding of the colony in 1607 using imported seed from the West Indies, but it was the invention of Eli Whitney's cotton gin in 1793 that allowed cotton to become a major component of the American economy. According to Harold Woodman, author of *King Cotton and His Retainers,* exports of cotton increased from 500,000 pounds in 1793 to more than 90 million pounds in 1810. In the three decades preceding the American Civil War, cotton production accounted for more than half of the nation's exports. Spurred by continuing worldwide demand, U.S. cotton production and acres planted grew steadily until reaching its peak in 1925, when 45 million acres of American soil were planted with cotton. By the early 1990s, U.S. mills annually consumed some four billion pounds of cotton.

The mechanization of cultivation and harvesting led to dramatic changes in the U.S. cotton industry. In the early 1950s, only 18 percent of U.S. cotton was harvested mechanically; by 1967 that figure had jumped to 95 percent, and productivity increased with mechanization. As a result, total acreage devoted to cotton production dropped 75 percent between the 1920s and the 1990s, while annual production stabilized at approximately 16 million bales. U.S. cotton growers produced close to 20 percent of the world's cotton supply throughout the 1980s, and approximately half of their annual production during that time was exported.

Because cotton requires warm conditions for germination and growth, it has always been grown in the southern regions of America, from Virginia to California. For three centuries, U.S. cotton production was centered in the area stretching from the Atlantic coast westward to central Texas. However, the increasing availability of irrigation facilities has allowed western growers to produce cotton that is more consistent in color and weight. By 1995, the largest producers of cotton were Texas and California, with annual harvests of about 4.5 million and 2.5 million bales respectively. Although California growers plant approximately one-quarter the number of acres as Texas growers, their yield per acre has often been triple that of Texas growers.

Two kinds of cotton are grown in the United States: American upland cotton, which accounts for 95 to 98 percent of production, and Amer-Pima, which accounts for two to five percent of production. Cotton seed is planted mechanically between February and June and is harvested in the fall, usually before the first frost. The cotton plant grows three to six feet tall, has broad bushy leaves and a stalk that measures up to an inch in diameter. After flowering, the cotton plant produces a boll which contains the seeds and fiber that are eventually harvested. Cotton bolls are harvested mechanically after the plants have been defoliated, either by frost or by application of chemicals. The harvested bolls are cleaned, ginned (a process that strips the fibers from the seeds), packed into bales weighing approximately 500 pounds, classified according to staple (fiber) length, grade, and character, and then brought to market. The longest cotton fibers are processed into yarns for making fabrics, the shorter fibers, called linters, are used as a source of cellulose for industrial applications. The seeds are processed into cot-

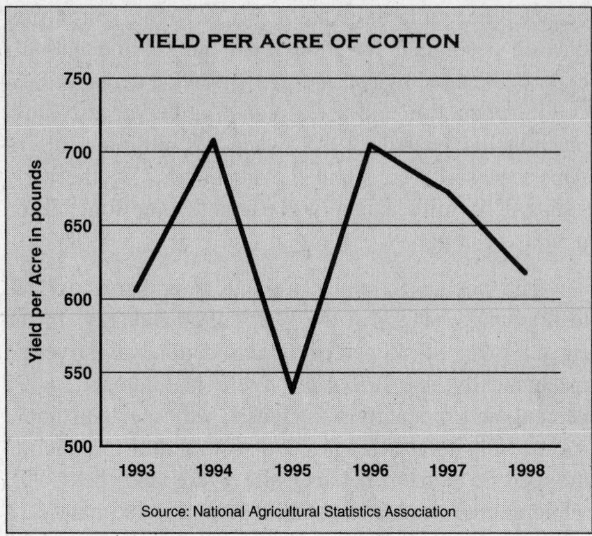

tonseed oil, while the seed husks are used as a feed for livestock.

The emergence of the man-made fiber market in the mid-1970s represented the greatest challenge to cotton's dominance of the world fiber market. With the introduction of fibers such as polyester, cotton's share of the clothing market fell from 50 percent in 1970 to 34 percent in 1975, according to *The Economist.* The cotton industry responded to this challenge by forming Cotton Incorporated, a promotional organization funded by voluntary levies paid by cotton growers. During the 1980s and 1990s, cotton began to reclaim the fiber and lint market: recapturing a 50 percent share of the U.S. retail clothing market, indicative of its success worldwide.

CURRENT CONDITIONS

Cotton is produced on more than 35,000 farms in the United States, with 98 percent grown in fourteen states. Texas is the largest grower, producing more than 5.15 million bales of cotton in 1999, while California, the second largest, produced only 2.15 million.

Though the cotton industry had been stabilized by U.S. government subsidies and price supports that have eased the pressures of a volatile world cotton market since 1933, Congress passed the 1996 Freedom to Farm Bill, bringing about a new era of market-dependent farming. The bill called for the freezing and incremental reduction of farm subsidies over a seven-year period ending altogether in 2002. According to *Journal of Commerce and Commercial,* analysts predicted that the legislation would benefit cotton production and exportation. The forecast asserted that growers would shift acreage from less profitable and marketable crops to ones like cotton with strong national and international demand.

As with other agricultural products, cotton producers have faced pressure to implement more environmentally-friendly production techniques. Retailers and manufactures such as Esprit, O Wear, Eco Sport, and GAP have called for an increased supply of organic cotton and have begun to market organic cotton products. In the 1980s, the United States accounted for only 3 percent of the world's farmland but almost 25 percent of the world's pesticide use.

As organic cotton can cost up to three times as much to produce as traditional cotton, customers buying the clothes manufactured with pure organic cotton were not pleased with the prices. After spiking to more than 25,000 acres in 1995, organic cotton farming dropped to 10,000 acres in 1996. Since the rise and fall, retailers and manufacturers have introduced new blended cotton clothing which allow customers the benefit of organic cotton, while keeping the prices down. According to the Organic Trade Association's 1997-1998 survey, more than 4 million pounds of organic cotton was grown in Arizona, California, Missouri, New Mexico, and Texas. According to Ecomall.com, in 1997, more than 1 million pounds of organic cotton was purchased by Levi's, the largest apparel user of cotton in the world.

FURTHER READING

Apodaca, Julia Kveton. ''Potential of Organically Grown Cotton.'' Available from http://www.ecomall.com/greenshopping/panna3.htm.

McConnell, Jane. ''Organic Cotton Clothing Industry Booming.'' Available from http://www.ecomall.com/greenshopping/mothero.htm.

Montgomery, Delia. ''Organic Cotton: A Better Alternative.'' Available from http://www.ecomall.com/greenshopping/chiceco5.htm

National Agricultural Statistics Service. ''Cotton and Wool Outlook.'' December 1999. Available from http://www.usda.gov/nass/

National Cotton Council of America. ''Cotton: Profile of a Resourcesful Industry.'' 1999. Available from http://www.cotton.org/ncc/education.

National Cotton Council of America. ''Frequently Asked Questions About Cotton.'' 1999. Available from http://www.cotton.org/ncc/education/cotton_faq.htm.

Sparrow, David. ''The Benefits of Organic vs. Chemically-Treated Cotton.'' Available from http://www.ecomall.com/greeenshopping/ahappy.htm.

SIC 0132

TOBACCO

This classification covers establishments primarily engaged in the production of tobacco.

NAICS CODE(S)

111910 (Tobacco Farming)

INDUSTRY SNAPSHOT

This industry, which is composed of approximately 65,755 small farms in the United States, grows and sells tobacco to cigarette companies and other tobacco product retailers. The links between tobacco and several serious diseases such as cancer and emphysema, however, first suggested in the 1960s and confirmed in the 1990s, have posed serious threats to the industry. Through the 1990s, criminal and civil lawsuits against cigarette manufacturers focused public attention on the role of the tobacco industry in promoting health-threatening products and contributed to diminished demand for tobacco. Increased exports of foreign-grown tobacco also affected American growers. However, changes in federal regulations and in harvesting and processing techniques have somewhat mitigated the uncertain future of tobacco farming.

ORGANIZATION AND STRUCTURE

Small farms, particularly in the southeastern regions of the United States, grow most of the nation's tobacco. The total number of farms producing tobacco in the United States dropped from 512,000 in 1954 to only 89,706 in 1997, and the number classified as tobacco farms—organizations deriving at least 50 percent of sales from tobacco—dropped to 65,755. Though tobacco farms have increased in size since the 1950s, by 1997 their average size was only 150 total acres, with 44 acres of cropland and only 9.9 acres devoted to tobacco production. In 1997, 60 percent of tobacco farms were owner-operated and 29 percent were operated by part-owners. Only eight percent were run by tenant farmers. Total revenues for tobacco farms in 1997 averaged $32,700. Approximately 56 percent of tobacco farmers report off-farm earnings.

The major tobacco growing states are North Carolina, Kentucky, and Tennessee. With South Carolina, Virginia, and Georgia, they produce about 94 percent of the tobacco grown in the United States. In all, 17 states grow appreciable acreage of tobacco. Establishments from North Carolina and other states compete with each other at tobacco auctions, where major tobacco companies purchase their crops.

Flue-cured tobacco is produced in the southeastern Coastal Plain and the Piedmont region from Virginia to Florida. This variety of tobacco is by far the greatest component (about 95 percent) used in American cigarettes. Flue-cured is also the kind of tobacco most used in exported products. Fire-cured, or Class 2, tobacco is produced in central and western Virginia, Tennessee, and Kentucky. This tobacco has broad, dark green leaves, which are heavily drooping and gummy to the touch.

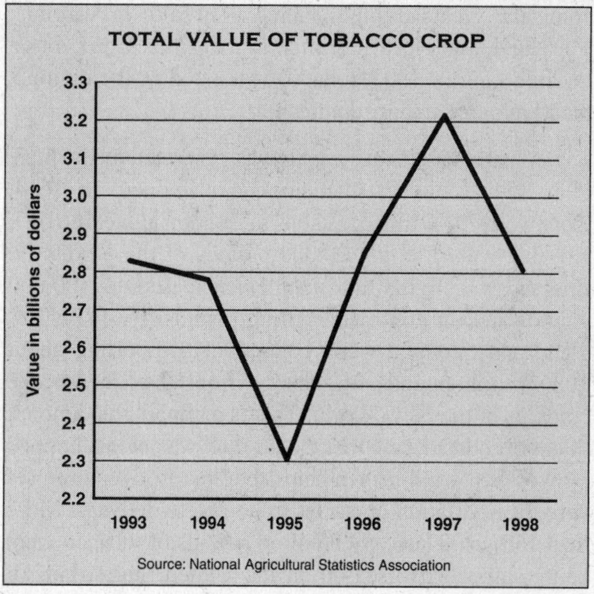

After curing they are light to dark brown and strong in flavor. Class 2 tobacco is principally used in snuff in the United States, but it is also used for cigar manufacture and chewing tobacco in other countries. All other American tobacco is air-cured and is principally used in cigars, except for the light air-cured and Maryland types. Burley is currently grown in Kentucky and Tennessee, and to a lesser extent in Ohio, Indiana, Virginia, West Virginia, and North Carolina. Major cigar tobacco districts include New England, Pennsylvania, Ohio, Wisconsin, Georgia, and Florida.

Priming and stalk cutting are the two methods of harvesting used in tobacco production. Three methods of curing—flue-curing, fire-curing, and air-curing—are used. Curing barns are typically 18 to 20 feet tall. Ventilators permit the flow of ambient air around suspended stalks of stalk-cut tobacco or around suspended leaves of flue-cured and cigar wrapper tobacco. Supplemental heat is used on air-cured tobacco during inclement weather. Before tobacco is suitable for consumption, it must be fermented and aged, which brings the tobacco leaves to their peak color and aroma and eliminates harsh or bitter taste. Finally, most tobacco products in the United States have various amounts of sweeteners, flavorings, or humectants added to increase or modify their natural flavor and aroma.

BACKGROUND AND DEVELOPMENT

As one of the first native crops to be commercially grown and marketed, tobacco has long reigned as a key crop in the American South. Historical records indicate that commercial cultivation of the crop began as early as 1612. In the eighteenth century, tobacco became such a coveted item that it was being used as legal tender for payment of wages, taxes, and debts. In fact, it had become the greatest single source of wealth in Virginia, Maryland, and North Carolina at that time. Until cotton became king in 1803, tobacco was rated as the nation's most valuable export commodity.

A large part of this wealth was generated by the huge international market that quickly developed. In 1614, there were 7,000 tobacco shops in London alone. In 1617, Virginia was shipping 20,000 pounds of the product to England; by 1628, this number increased to 500,000 pounds and, in 1638, 1.4 million pounds. By 1771, England and Scotland were, collectively, importing about 102 million pounds of tobacco from the Chesapeake colonies in the New World. This is a remarkable amount of export considering that the product was being shipped by wooden, wind-driven ships that had to overcome severe transportation obstacles to complete delivery. More than 150 years later, 590 million pounds of tobacco were being shipped overseas from the United States, half of this still passing through the Virginia ports.

In the early part of the nineteenth century, tobacco began to lose its place as the premier export to the Old World. More of it began to be consumed at home. Farmers and other consumers took to the pipe along with their chewing habits. As snuff became more and more associated with British dandyism, pipe smoking took first place as the desired mode of tobacco consumption.

The quality of most tobacco during antebellum years was poor compared to today's standards. In New England, a harsh, narrow leaf called ''shoe-string'' was produced. The South grew a dark, heavy ''shipping leaf'' that was quite different from the light, sweet Bright tobacco raised today. This all changed in 1864 with White Burley, a strain of tobacco that was remarkable for its capacity to absorb sugar and flavoring, which was first produced at this time. Burley was first grown prodigiously in Ohio; today it is predominantly a product of Kentucky and Tennessee. The effect of Burley on the industry cannot be overestimated. It revolutionized smoking and the chewing industry after the Civil War and had an equally strong impact on the cigarette industry during World War I.

A significant part of the industry's history has to do with the search for superior tobacco products abroad. This search was primarily focused on Cuba and Mexico. A large part of this was due to the popularity of Cuban cigars in America. Cigar imports from the Antilles reached the 4 million mark by 1811. A booming cigar industry sprang up in Havana during this time and has not abated since.

Cigars achieved their prominence as a symbol of aristocracy during the ''Brown Decades,'' after the Civil War. It was also during this era that modern cigarettes began to appear on the scene. All cigarettes were initially ''roll-your own.'' It was not until 1866 that tailored cigarettes were produced in America and England. These also were hand-rolled, since the modern machine-produced methodology for cigarette manufacture had not yet been invented. These cigarettes were also larger than the cigarettes we are familiar with and were often made from Turkish tobacco grown in Greece, Bulgaria, and Turkey. New York, with its preponderance of immigrants and large pool of inexpensive labor, served as a central site of cigarette production and mass consumption.

Though tobacco has historically been a labor-intensive crop, averaging as much as 300 hours of labor per acre, new techniques for producing, harvesting, and curing have reduced labor and permitted increased acreage per farm. Flue-cured tobacco, once tied by hand, is now marketed as loose leaf. The introduction of mechanical harvesters also reduced labor, as did the shift from sheets to bales. Successful growth of tobacco also requires a good supply of well-developed seedlings for transplanting. On American farms, these are usually produced in a cold frame covered with cheesecloth, plastic, or glass. The tobacco seeds are sprinkled on top of the soil and then tamped firmly into the ground. A high state of fertility and adequate soil moisture must be maintained throughout the growing season to ensure vigorous production. Tobacco crops are also regularly attacked by fungi, bacteria, viruses, and a number of other harmful parasites that must be combated by raising disease-resistant crops. Without such varieties of tobacco, the industry would not be viable in certain areas of the United States.

Despite these difficulties, tobacco remains relatively lucrative for small farmers. It is the most profitable crop in the southeastern region of the United States, generating relatively high prices per acre. In Kentucky, for example, tobacco comprised only 1 percent of farmland in 1992 but generated 40 percent of net farm returns and, in 1994, each acre of tobacco grown in the United States for domestic use generated more than $43,000 in state and Federal excise taxes at the retail level. Estimates suggest that, for farmers, one acre of tobacco can net between $1,200 and $1,500 compared to about $75 per acre for corn or soybeans. For this reason, many tobacco farmers continue to resist pressure to shift from tobacco to other crops, though demand for tobacco has declined significantly and continued price supports are far from certain. From 1981 to 1997, U.S. tobacco production declined about 20 percent and cigarette consumption fell about 24 percent. During the past two decades, America's share of the world tobacco market has also declined. Because of a Clinton Administration tariff proclamation in 1995, imports into the country increased about 27 percent. The import of less-expensive cigarettes composed of foreign-grown tobacco also had a negative impact on domestic industry sales.

Government Legislation. The U.S. government became involved in the tobacco industry in the 1930s, when its main purpose was to stabilize tobacco prices. Designating tobacco as a basic, storable commodity, the Agricultural Adjustment Act of 1933 resulted in cash payments to tobacco farmers who restricted production. Although the legislation was found unconstitutional just several years later, substitute legislation authorized payments to farmers who followed soil conservation guidelines. Because of the need of buyers and producers for uniform standards on which to base marketing decisions, Congress enacted the Tobacco Inspection Act of 1935, thereby setting the framework for the development of tobacco grade standards. The Act also enabled the distribution of daily price reports for each grade and authorized the Secretary of Agriculture to designate tobacco auction markets, where growers would receive mandatory inspection of their tobacco. The Agricultural Act of 1938 called for marketing quotas for specific types of tobacco.

Legislation had become extremely tight in the late 1990s. When plans were made in 1996 to authorize the Food and Drug Administration (FDA) to classify nicotine as a drug, leading tobacco-growing states argued that ensuing new regulations would severely impact Virginia's $5 billion tobacco industry (of which $175 million went to farmers), and result in a loss of jobs, loss of tax base, reduced ability to finance schools and other government services, as well as jeopardizing sporting and cultural events sponsored by brand name tobacco products. On the other hand, studies by anti-smoking groups predicted exactly the opposite, suggesting that lost jobs and revenues would be more than compensated for by new jobs and industry. The FDA, for one, argued that its restrictions would have a relatively minor effect on U.S. tobacco sales and cost just 2,500 agricultural jobs. Though tobacco companies first resisted FDA regulation of tobacco, in 1998 they agreed to cooperate with the Clinton Administration's efforts and accept FDA regulation. Later that year, however, a federal court ruled that the FDA did not have the legal authority to regulate tobacco, reserving this power for Congress.

CURRENT CONDITIONS

Changing attitudes toward smoking have forced the cigarette industry to change the way it sells cigarettes. Though the link between the inhalation of tobacco smoke and such diseases as heart disease, cancer, and emphysema was first publicized in 1964 in a report to the U.S. Surgeon General, tobacco companies successfully evaded any legal responsibility for producing and marketing a dangerous product for decades. But this changed in the 1990s. By 1998, the leading U.S. tobacco companies agreed to pay $206 billion to 46 states to settle a plethora of suits filed to recover Medicaid money states spent to treat smoking-related diseases. Individual and class action suits also resulted in massive damage payments and, in October 1999, the nation's largest cigarette maker, Philip Morris, admitted that scientific evidence shows that smoking causes lung cancer.

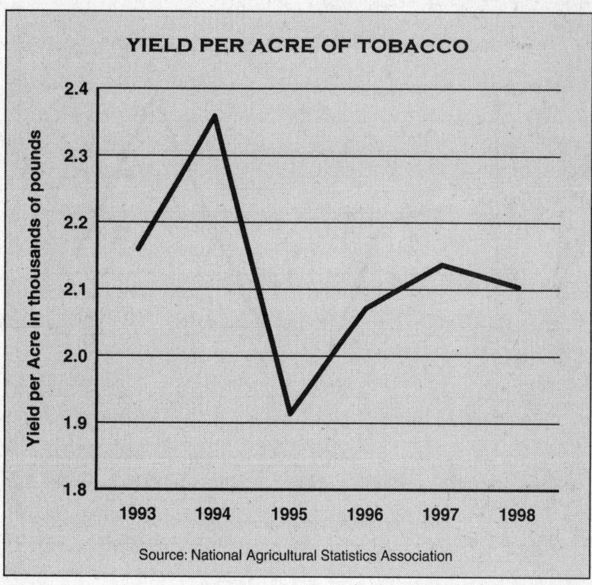

The impact of this admission, and judgments of liability in smoking-related deaths, have weakened tobacco companies' financial performance and contributed to reduced demand for American tobacco. In 1998, U.S. cigarette consumption dropped seven percent from the previous year, and production declined six percent during the same period. Exports also fell, declining seven percent in 1999. Though cigar consumption rose by a staggering 50 percent from 1993 to 1997, price increases on cigarettes and a tax hike of 10 cents per pack, effective January 2000, are expected to further reduce demand for tobacco.

Quotas for 1999 were reduced by 29 percent for Burley tobacco and 17 percent for flue-cured, with the effective quote for 1999 nearly 20 percent lower than the previous year. Tobacco farmers expected to harvest about 650,000 acres of tobacco in 1999—about 11 percent less than in 1998. The U.S. Department of Agriculture expects that production will continue to decline by about a third from 1997 to 2007. At the same time, price increases and impending tax hikes will further decrease consumption. Price supports for the 1999 crop, however, were up slightly.

Tobacco growers and legislators have disagreed on how to respond to declining demand for U.S. tobacco. While a provision of the 1998 legal settlement requires cigarette makers to pay $5.1 billion to compensate grow-

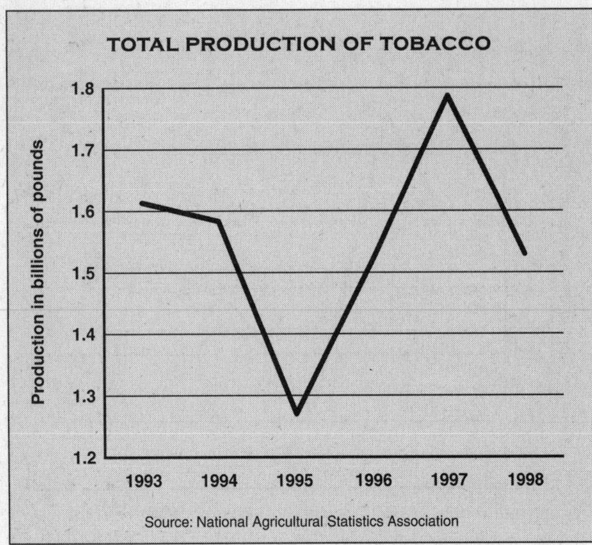

ers for decreased demand, farmers in many states complain that this is only a fraction of what they need. Kentucky Senator Wendell Ford introduced a bill to compensate tobacco farmers $4 a year for every pound of quota lost, while keeping the present quota and price support system intact. Senate Agriculture Committee chair Richard Lugar, in contrast, argued that federal regulation makes tobacco growing less competitive. His proposal, costing about $15 billion, would buy out existing quotas and phase out federal price supports. The Lugar bill would also provide tobacco-producing regions with $300 million in aid.

In 1999, tobacco farmers pushed for receipt of $328 million from a proposed $7.4 billion farm aid package. Though legislators from tobacco states argued that tobacco growers had a right to be compensated, like other farmers, for lost income, others argued that the government should not be involved in helping tobacco farmers produce a crop associated with major health risks. Frustrated with continued quota cuts, growers of flue-cured tobacco in five states planned to file a suit in November 1999 against state and federal officials and cigarette makers, seeking up to $18 billion in damages.

Eliminating federal controls, analysts believe, will almost certainly lead to fewer but larger tobacco farms, which will be able to produce their crop more profitably than smaller operations. This trend could eliminate as many as half the small tobacco farms in some areas. Yet 56 percent of tobacco farmers in the United States report income from off-farm work, which could compensate for lower profits from tobacco crops. Demographic patterns also suggest that a significant number of American tobacco farmers, whose average age is 53.5 years, may be nearing retirement and be willing to accept a government buyout.

AMERICA AND THE WORLD

Although global tobacco leaf production increased in the mid-1990s, reaching 14 billion pounds and accounting for 40 percent of the tobacco used in the United States, the effects of new legislation and decreasing demand have become felt by tobacco growers world wide. Reacting to lower market prices and predictions of increased stocks, Zimbabwe reduced its 1998 tobacco plantings by eight percent. Brazil and Malawi also reported reductions. U.S. Department of Agriculture (USDA) forecasts for 2000 indicate that world tobacco production will total 6.3 million kilograms, about 0.2 million kilograms above expected consumption. In 1998, Tobacco producers were led by China (2,525 million kilograms), the United States (746 million kilograms), India (635 kilograms), Brazil (468 kilograms), the European Union (349 kilograms), and Zimbabwe (220 kilograms).

International tobacco advertising regulations greatly affected the major countries around the world, as well as in the United States, in the mid- to late 1990s. Canada, for example, banned cigarette vending machines and tobacco brands' sponsoring of sporting events. In Norway, an existing law banning tobacco advertisements became stricter by including indirect advertisements. Tobacco advertising in Poland was banned on private and state radio and television media, and the European Union dealt a severe blow to the European tobacco industry when it banned advertising and sponsorship, to begin in 2002. The World Health Organization (WHO) and the World Bank have also instituted tobacco control initiatives. Tobacco growers, representing about 33 million workers worldwide, are making plans to develop a global alliance to advocate for their interests.

FURTHER READING

"Court Rules FDC Lacks Authority to Limit Tobacco." *New York Times,* 15 August 1998.

Economic Research Service, U.S. Department of Agriculture. "Cigarette Consumption Continues to Slide." *Tobacco-Summary,* 21 April 1999.

Economic Research Service, U.S. Department of Agriculture. *U.S. Tobacco Farming Trends,* 1999. Available from http://www.econ.ag.gov/briefing/tobacco/Agcensus.htm.

Edgecliffe-Johnson, Andrew. "Tobacco Stocks Hit by Ruling." *The Financial Times,* 21 October 1999.

Estrada, Richard. "Tobacco Growers Posed to Get Freedom to Farm." *Modesto Bee,* 26 April 1998.

Glantz, Stanton A., Brion J. Fox, and James M. Lightwood. "Tobacco Litigation: Issues for Public Health and Public Policy." *Journal of the American Medical Association,* 5 March 1997.

"Growers' Association Meets WHO." *World Tobacco,* March 1999.

L'Heureux, Dave. "Quota Losses May Bring Lawsuit from South Carolina Tobacco Growers." *Knight-Ridder/Tribune Business News,* 21 October 1999.

Meier, Barry. "Philip Morris Admits Evidence Shows Smoking Causes Cancer." *New York Times,* 13 October 1999.

———. "Remaining States Approve the Pact on Tobacco Suits." *New York Times,* 21 November 1998.

"Senate Seeks to Aid Tobacco Growers." *USA Today,* 6 August 1999.

Solman, Paul. "Tobacco Crop Falls as Cigarette Sales Drop." *The Financial Times,* 22 October 1999.

Thompson, Christian. "Tobacco Industry Braces for Major Changes." New York: Reuters Limited, 22 June 1997.

"Tobacco Country Fights Back." *The Economist,* 21 March 1998.

"Tobacco Growers Link Arms." *The European,* 9 November 1998.

U.S. Department of Agriculture. *Tobacco.* Washington: Economic Research Service, 1997.

U.S. Department of Agriculture. *Tobacco Division History,* 1997. Available from http://www.usda.gov/ams.

U.S. Department of Agriculture. *Tobacco Yearbook.* Washington: Economic Research Service, 6 May 1997.

SIC 0133

SUGARCANE AND SUGAR BEETS

This industry classification includes establishments primarily engaged in the production of sugarcane and sugar beets.

NAICS CODE(S)

111991 (Sugar Beet Farming)
111930 (Sugarcane Farming)

BACKGROUND AND DEVELOPMENT

The story of the sugar industry in the United States is in fact the story of two industries, one devoted to producing sugarcane and the other to producing sugar beets. Before the twentieth century, sugarcane accounted for 95 percent of world consumption of sugar. However, modern planting and refining techniques helped make sugar beet production profitable. By the 1980s, sugar beets and sugarcane shared equally in the U.S. sugar market. Sugarcane was introduced to the United States from the Caribbean region by Jesuit priests traveling to Louisiana in 1751, and the first U.S. sugar refinery was built in the same state in 1795. Sugarcane is produced only in Florida, Hawaii, Louisiana, and Texas. Western pioneers desiring their own source of sugar began sugar beet production in the United States around 1870, but their efforts proved unprofitable until the development of irrigation systems in the 1890s. Beet production provided 25 percent of the nation's sugar needs by 1920. The Red River Valley area of Minnesota and eastern North Dakota are the largest U.S. beet producing regions.

Sugarcanes and sugar beets are grown mainly to produce table sugar and sucrose. Sugarcane is also produced to manufacture alcohol as fuel for vehicles. Although refining processes for sugar sources are similar, cultivation and harvesting techniques are quite different. Sugarcane is planted using stalk cuttings, and matures between eight and sixteen months, depending on the region. A crop of sugarcane may produce acceptable yields for two to three years before being replanted and, in the case of Hawaii, where there is no danger of frost, can be harvested year round. Sugarcane is most often harvested mechanically, with specially-designed harvesters that cut the stalk at the bottom, strip the unneeded leaves and top, and transfer the cane to a wagon. Prior to mechanical harvesting, sugarcane production required vast numbers of laborers who, in many cases, worked under conditions of slavery or near-slavery.

Grown primarily in twelve states, sugar beets, on the other hand, are harvested annually, and have benefited greatly from the attention of agricultural specialists who devised seed types and planting methods that encourage maximum yields. Still, great care must be taken to ensure adequate distance between plants, weed control, planting depth, and proper fertilization. One study showed that 50 percent of sugar beet production costs were expended in cultivation. However, mechanical cultivation and harvesting equipment makes labor costs in sugar beet production negligible. Both sugar industries have attained yields that are among the highest in the world: the average yield for sugarcane was 38.2 tons per acre in 1998-99, while it was 22.5 tons per acre for sugar beets.

CURRENT CONDITIONS

The U.S. sugar industry has long been bolstered by government programs designed to elevate the prices that sugar producers receive for their product. According to Robert Barry, a government agricultural economist, "Sugar is the most price-volatile among internationally traded commodities." Prices for sugar have traditionally gone through dramatic swings, none more so than during the 1980s, when prices reached a high of 29 cents a pound in 1980 only to fall to an average of 6.5 cents a pound between 1982 and 1987. During that same time, world production costs ranged from 12.6 to 15.4 cents a pound. The situation reversed itself from 1996 through 1998, when U.S. raw sugar prices averaged 22.2 cents per pound and world sugar prices averaged 11.6 cents per pound; in 1999, the world price dropped to 6.0 cents per pound.

In 1996, the U.S. government sought to alleviate farm subsidies and loans altogether. The 1996 Farm Bill called for the freezing and gradual reduction of agricultural loans and subsidies over a six-year period, resulting in termination of the program in 2002. Government assistance had been especially important to sugar producers because of the market's volatility. Though the bill met stiff resistance from sugar producers and lobbyists, it eventually passed, leading to some closures. In 1999, the U.S. General Accounting Office estimated that raw sugar prices cost domestic sugar users about $400 million annually and recommended that USDA should operate the sugar program in a manner that minimizes costs to sugar users.

The sugar industry went through a number of changes beginning in the 1970s. Per capita consumption of sugar (both beet and cane) plummeted from 1970, when it stood at roughly 102 pounds, to 1980, when it stood at about 60 pounds. However, the consumption rate has increased mildly since then: in 1995, per capita consumption was 65 pounds. The corn sweetener market, which claimed per capita consumption in 1993 of 79 pounds, has claimed much of sugar's old market share. This led to a reduction in cane sugar refineries, from 22 in 1981 to 12 in 1998.

Sugar farmers, especially in Florida, have also been faced with environmental concerns. In 1991, the state was sued by the federal government to clean up the discharge from sugar farms. Parts of Florida's Everglades are choked with cattails, a weed that grows from run-off from sugar fields. In 1999, the federal government revealed the Restudy, a major plan to clean up the Everglades.

Since the U.S. Department of Agriculture (USDA) and other agricultural agencies have predicted that domestic and world sugar consumption would continue to gradually increase, both sugarcane and sugar beet production has continued to increase: in 1998, U. S. sugar production was about 8.0 million tons, up from 7.3 million tons in 1996. In 1998, U.S. consumers used 9.9 million tons of sugar, about 16 percent of which was imported. Sugar beets accounted for 4.2 million tons, or 52 percent of the total sugar crop in 1998-99 (from a harvest of 1.45 million acres); this was 9.3 percent above 1997-98, and a 25 percent share of the $6 billion white sugar market. Sugarcane production was estimated at 3.9 million tons, with increases in Florida and Texas compared to the previous year. Beet sugar production was forecast to increase by more than 7 percent in 1999-2000, requiring 50,000 more acres and a crop of about 32.0 million tons. Cane sugar production is forecast to reach 3.9 million tons, slightly above the previous year.

The USDA reported that the sugarcane value in 1994 was $896 million for both sugar and seed, while sugar beets reached the value of $1.2 billion. In 1995 Minnesota, Idaho, North Dakota, California, and Michigan led in sugar beet production, while Hawaii led in sugarcane production. Also, in commemoration of Louisiana's 200th anniversary for growing sugarcane, Pepsi Cola announced that it would develop a version of its soft drink called ''Louisiana Pepsi'' using sugarcane sugar from this state, instead of the traditional corn sweetener.

Industry Leaders

According to Ward's Business Directory 2000, the leading sugar farmers include A and B Hawaii Inc. at over $200 million in sales and 1,500 employees; its subsidiary Hawaiian Commercial and Sugar Co. at $110 million and 1,000 employees; and Sterling Sugars Inc. with $34 million in sales and 200 employees. U.S. Sugar and Flo-Sun are leaders in Florida; each controls 40 percent of the state's sugar industry. The 1996 Farm Bill is forcing these companies to diversify to survive. U.S. Sugar has a joint marketing venture with sugar beet producers and has moved into citrus production.

America and the World

Low world sugar prices threatened U.S. import protections in 1999 and was predicted to increase Mexico's access to the U.S. sugar market. USDA forecast above-quota imports from Mexico at 260,000 tons in 1999/2000, compared to 155,000 tons the previous year. Mexico already has duty free access to the United States for around 28,000 tons as guaranteed by NAFTA. In 2000/01 this access increases tenfold. Duty-free access allows Mexico to sell at the U.S. domestic price and keep the difference.

Further Reading

''America's Sugar Industry: Bittersweet.'' *The Economist,* 5 June 1999.

ASCS Commodity Fact Sheet: Sugar. Washington, DC: U.S. Agricultural Stabilization and Conservation Service.

Palmer, Doug.''World Prices, NAFTA Reshape N. American Sugar Market.'' *Reuters Business Report,* 20 July 1999.

''Sugar Program, Changing the Method for Setting Import Quotas Could Reduce Cost to Users.'' *Government Accounting Office Report.,* Federal Document Clearing House, Inc., 26 July 1999.

U.S. Department of Agriculture. ''Agricultural Statistics 1995-6.'' Washington, DC: June 1996. Available from http://www.usda.gov/nass/pubs/agr95_96/acro9596.htm.

U.S. Department of Agriculture. ''Sugar and Sweeteners.'' Washington, DC: 19 December 1996. Available from http://usda.mannlib.cornell.edu/reports/erssor/specialty/sss-bb/1996/sugar_and_sweeteners_summ ary_12.19.96.

Ward's Business Directory of U.S. Public and Private Companies 2000. Detroit: Gale Group, 2000.

SIC 0134

IRISH POTATOES

This industry classification includes establishments primarily engaged in the production of potatatoes, except sweet potatoes, which are part of **SIC 0139: Field Crops Except Cash Grains, Not Elsewhere Classified.**

NAICS CODE(S)

111211 (Potato Farming)

The potato, a member of the nightshade family that produces thick, fleshy tubers from underground stems, was introduced into the United States around 1719, but it was not mentioned in crop production data until the 1840 census, which listed 160.4 million pounds of potatoes grown. American per capita potato consumption peaked in the early twentieth century at 198 pounds, dropped to about 103 pounds by 1956, and rose again to its 1998 level of 141 pounds per person as people consumed more processed potatoes. Of the potatoes reaching the consumer market in 1998, 31 percent were distributed fresh, while 69 percent were processed, either frozen as chips or shoestrings, dehydrated, or canned. In addition, a portion of each year's 30 million hundredweight crop (hundredweight is a unit of measure equaling 100 pounds, abbreviated cwt.) is used for seed and for feeding livestock. Although there are more than 80 varieties of potatoes planted in the United States, 6 varieties dominate production: Russet Burbank, Russet Norkotah, Atlantic, Ranger Russet, Frito-Lay, and Shepody.

American potato farmers plant relatively few acres, just 1.377 million in 1999, yet the high yield of Irish potatoes allows them to supply domestic potato production of almost 500 million cwt of potatoes per year, according to U.S. Department of Agriculture (USDA) statistics. In fact, the Irish potato yields more food per unit area of land planted than any other major crop. Potatoes are grown commercially in 35 American states, from Alaska to Maine to Florida, but more than 72 percent of the 1999 potato crop was produced by just eight states: Colorado, Idaho, Maine, Minnesota, North Dakota, Oregon, Washington, and Wisconsin. Idaho, the most renowned potato-producing state, led the United States in 1999 with 133.3 million cwt of potatoes from 395,000 acres planted, representing approximately 28 percent of the total U.S. potato crop. Altogether, U.S. growers tend to produce about 7 percent of the world's potatoes.

Mechanization revitalized potato farming by reducing the amount of manual labor involved. Seed potatoes (precut sections of potato) are planted using an automatic planter pulled behind a tractor. Such planters can plant

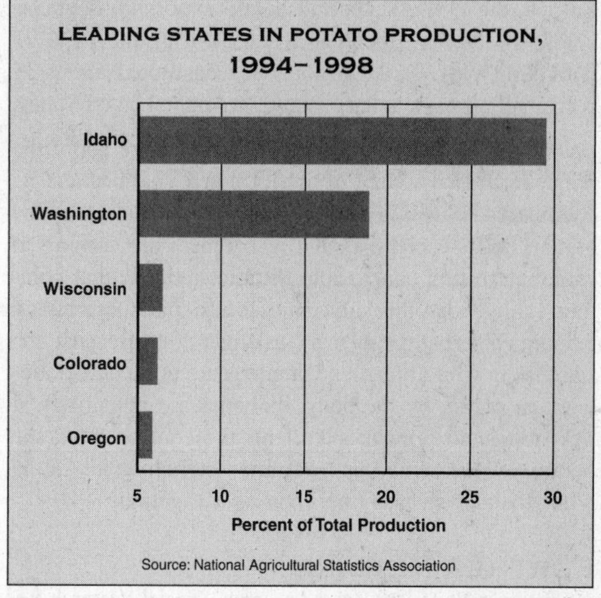

four or more rows at a time and require only a tractor driver and a tender. Potatoes are harvested mechanically as well, with machines that dig out the entire potato plant, shake free excess dirt and rocks, and deposit the potatoes in an adjacent truck. In the southern United States, potato farmers are able to reap four harvests per year, while in the northwestern states, where most of the U.S. crop is grown, potatoes are harvested primarily in the fall. After they are harvested, potatoes are placed in cool (45-60 degrees Fahrenheit), humid storage areas to allow for healing of surface damage, a process called curing. Because potatoes are distributed throughout the year, roughly 63 percent of each year's potato crop is placed in storage, where the potatoes are maintained in carefully controlled conditions to prevent rot, dehydration, and a wide range of diseases.

In recent years researchers have attempted to counter various diseases that can affect potato crops. One promising experiment undertaken by Purdue University researchers was to take a gene from tobacco plants and insert it into potato plants. "This gene codes for a protein, called osmotin, that brings death to the fungi by chemically drilling holes in their cell membranes," noted *Business Week* in 1994. "For humans, the protein is probably safe . . . since it's produced by many food plants." Testing continues on the potato, as well as other crops such as soybeans, corn, and tomatoes.

The potato crop's value reached $3.0 billion in 1996. Major potato producers include Sunny Farms and Anthony Farms, Inc., which averaged about $8 million and $7 million in sales from potatoes per year, respectively. The 1996 growing season also brought U.S. farmers their record crop of 449 million cwt. from some 1.4 million acres. With increased potato production in Canada and

Europe, the USDA expected potato exports to decrease below the crop's 5 percent average during the 1996-97 marketing year. In 1998 potatoes constituted about 37 percent of all vegetable consumption in the United States.

In recent years, as research reveals more about the potato both as a source of nutrition and vitamins and its chemistry—how it is metabolized and synthesized by the human body—scientists and researchers are coming to some interesting conclusions. Studies indicate that potatoes rank with other glycemic foods: potatoes raise a person's blood sugar as much as sugar does. Because the starches in white bread and potatoes are quickly metabolized as sugars by the body, diabetics are potentially at risk; some nutritionists and scientists recommend that the potato be reclassified as a complex carbohydrate, along with rice and pasta, rather then as a vegetable.

Further Reading

American Institute for Cancer Research, Special Research Report, 22 January 2000. Available from http://airweb@aircr.org.

Collins, Karen, R.D., "Potatoes: Friend or Foe?" *Nutrition Notes, MSNBC,* 22 January 2000. Available from http://MSNBC.com/Healthpage/NutritionNotes/.

Port, Otis. "Bioengineering Comes to the Potato Patch." *Business Week,* 16 May 1994.

U.S. Department of Agriculture. National Agricultural Statistics Service. "Agricultural Statistics 1998." Washington, D.C., 1999. Available from http://www.usda.gov/nass/pubs/agr 97_98/agr97_pdf.

U.S. Department of Agriculture. "Vegetables and Specialties." Washington, DC: 22 November 1999. Available from http://usda.mannlib.cornell.edu.

SIC 0139

FIELD CROPS EXCEPT CASH GRAINS, NOT ELSEWHERE CLASSIFIED

This entry includes establishments primarily engaged in the production of field crops, except cash grains, not classified elsewhere. This category includes a range of crops for human or livestock consumption, encompassing farms that produce alfalfa, broomcorn, clover, grass seed, hay, hops, mint, peanuts, sweet potatoes, timothy, and yams. This category also includes establishments deriving 50 percent or more of their total value of sales of agricultural products from field crops, except cash grains, but less than 50 percent from products of any single industry.

NAICS Code(s)

111940 (Hay Farming)
111992 (Peanut Farming)
111219 (Other Vegetable (except Potato) and Melon Farming)
111998 (All Other Miscellaneous Crop Farming)

Sweet Potatoes and Yams. Yams grown in the United States are actually a variety of sweet potato, but with a moister, golden red flesh. Sweet potatoes are light yellow or pale orange in color. Yams are grown primarily in North Carolina, account for about half of all sweet potato consumption in the United States, and are consumed mainly in the northeast and mid-Atlantic states. California is the leading producer of sweet potatoes, with Louisiana, Georgia, and Alabama following as major producers. With increasing production and sales of sweet potatoes, 1995 brought the industry production level of 12.9 million hundredweight (cwt.), averaging 154 cwt. per acre from 83 thousand acres harvested. In 1997, 83,300 acres were harvested, producing 13.5 million cwt. In the mid-1990s, per capita consumption of sweet potatoes was 4.7 pounds in contrast to the consumption of more than 50 pounds of Irish potato products.

Hay. Grass, alfalfa, clover, and timothy are all used for livestock fodder. Farmers grow hay for their own livestock or for commercial sale. Some dairy farmers buy grain and use their fields for quality forage crops since well-managed alfalfa, for example, can provide more net income per acre than grain crops such as corn or soybeans, according to farmers and researchers in the trade journal *Implement & Tractor.* In 1997, harvested hay continued the trend of decreased production with 60.8 million acres harvested with a total of about 150 million tons of hay. However, harvesting efficiency has increased as growers gleaned a record 2.50 tons of hay per acre in 1996. Yet the reduced levels of overall production have driven hay prices up.

According *Implement & Tractor,* Wisconsin researchers have found that the nutritional value of alfalfa and other hays depends on when it is cut and have noted that milk production of dairy cattle rose dramatically when cows were fed alfalfa that was harvested at first flower. In some areas, hay marketing cooperatives hold regular hay auctions with hay-testing services, since demand is up for high quality hay for dairy cattle.

Peanuts. Peanuts have ranked as the eighth leading field crop with an annual value of about $1.2 billion. In 1990, the United States was the third largest producer of peanuts in the world, according to the *National Food Review.* The United States produced about 3.9 billion pounds of peanuts in 1998, with the southeast producing 75 percent of the crop and the southwest and northeast producing the rest. Georgia is the leading producer averaging about 50 percent of the country's total peanut crop per year. Of the 2 billion to 2.5 billion pounds annually consumed by humans, 50 percent is used in peanut butter and the other 50 percent is used in candy products and snack nuts.

The peanut industry has been regulated by government price support and quota programs since the 1930s. Though support prices guarantee peanut farmers a minimum price for their crops, the Federal Agriculture Improvement and Reform Act of 1996, or Farm Bill, reduced and froze the loan rate at 10 percent. The government also imposes production quotas on regions and even on individual farms within the regions, according to the unit's historical share of production; the nation's total production quota is based on expected food and seed use for the coming year. However, the 1996 Farm Bill called for the elimination of the floor quota, because, in recent years, production had fallen below the 1.35 million tons stipulated in the 1990 bill. The legislation allows for the annual determination of the year's quota to avoid the previous situation of being manacled to a quota from years before. The government has set up a two-tiered pricing system that distinguishes between "quota peanuts" and "additional peanuts." Quota peanuts are used for domestic food products or for seed and receive higher price supports than additional peanuts. Additional peanuts can be sold only for export or for processing into peanut oil or peanut meal. Farmers may produce both quota and additional peanuts.

Mint. Oregon is the leading producer of peppermint, followed by Washington and Idaho. Production costs can be high for growers. Spearmint is primarily grown in Washington, Wisconsin, and Indiana. Mint varieties, as herbs and oils, have a host of applications, including being a spice, a cosmetic agent, an ingredient in tea, and a flavoring for toothpaste.

FURTHER READING

"Crop Production." Washington, D.C.: U.S. Department of Agriculture, 10 November 1999. Available from http://www.usda.mannlib.cornell.edu.

National Agricultural Statistics Service. "Vegetables and Melons" Washington, D.C.: U.S. Department of Agriculture, 1996. Available from http://www.usda.gov/nass/pubs.

SIC 0161

VEGETABLES AND MELONS

This entry includes establishments primarily engaged in the production of vegetables and melons in the open, including asparagus, beans, broccoli, cabbage, cantaloupe, cauliflower, celery, sweet corn, cucumber, green peas, lettuce, onions, peppers, squash, and tomatoes.

NAICS CODE(S)

111219 (Other Vegetable (except Potato) and Melon Farming)

Of the produce included in this category, tomatoes, onions, and iceberg lettuce led per capita consumption in the late 1980s and throughout the 1990s. Vegetables and fruits (truck farm products) are the second largest food group in the United States by volume and consumption, behind milk and dairy products. California, Florida, Texas, Arizona, and New York are the largest truck farming states. Produce is sold directly to processors, wholesalers, retailers, or consumers by truck farmers. Large truck farms usually specialize in one or two crops for shipment to the rest of the country, while smaller farms may grow a large variety for sale at local farmers' markets, stands, and stores. Smaller farms may also market their produce together through a cooperative in order to negotiate better prices.

Truck farms developed as people moved to cities and could no longer grow their own produce. With the building of railroads and highways, and the development of refrigerated transportation, truck farmers were able to ship their produce farther. Trucks and trains could carry out-of-season produce to the north from truck farms in the south.

Truck farmers in the United States have had to contend with periodic scares regarding the safety of fruits and vegetables. Various consumer and environmental groups claimed that too many pesticides, fungicides, and other chemicals were used on crops. Government agencies and industry groups, however, have insisted the food supply is safe and any chemical residue is well within government limits. Domestic growers have also defended their produce from fears about contaminated imports. Because produce is integrated into stores, usually without differentiation between foreign and domestic products, domestic growers have been concerned their produce would be affected by any suspicion about the quality of the imported goods.

In 1992 the Environmental Protection Agency (EPA) issued new rules requiring employers to protect farm workers from pesticide poisoning, although these national rules were still not as strict as those in place in California. The new rules barred employees from going back into freshly sprayed fields, with the quarantine periods ranging from 12 hours to three days, depending upon the chemical used. After pesticide concern continued to escalate, President Clinton signed a bill in 1996 that required the EPA to establish safe levels of tolerance for pesticide residue on both fresh and processed fruits and vegetables. The bill also mandates that the EPA register all new and old pesticides. Chemicals that cause "unreasonable adverse effects" will not be registered, according to this piece of legislation. The bill also covers

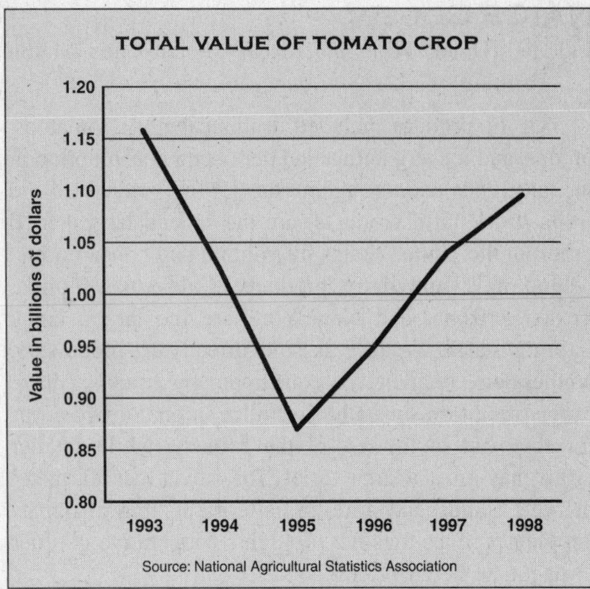

imported produce, calling for the rejection of any imports with unregistered pesticide residue or tolerance-excessive residue of any sort.

Tomatoes. Florida tomato growers compete with Mexico for winter tomato sales. In 1992, Mexican farmers were able to deliver tomatoes to the U.S. border at about half the $9 production cost of a Florida-grown 25-pound box of tomatoes. However, in 1996, after receiving petitions from concerned growers, the United States and Mexico reached an agreement that would place a lower limit on the cost of a 25-pound box. The pact does not restrict the amount of tomatoes the United States imports; instead it ensures price equity. The tomato processing business had been very profitable and the industry expanded quickly, resulting in over production and excess capacity. Even though processing tomato farmers reduced acreage by 25 percent in 1992, the California yield was about 7.4 million tons of processing tomatoes.

In 1997, the United States imported almost 1.8 billion pounds of fresh tomatoes, exporting only 332 million. In 1998, total U. S. harvest was 114,800 acres. Of that total, Florida harvested 40,600 and California harvested 32,000.

California, Mexico and Florida also produced the first genetically-altered tomato. After five years of testing, the United States Food and Drug Administration(USDA) approved for public consumption the first genetically altered food in 1994. Tomatoes grown by Calgene Inc. were cleared for distribution to the public under the Flavr-Savr brand name. The tomatoes, which are more expensive than tomatoes grown through more traditional means, were created when scientists isolated the gene that causes tomatoes to soften. They then manipulated its genetic make-up to slow down the softening process, allowing more time on the vine for it to ripen. Public interest groups however, allege that the altered tomatoes carry a gene that causes the plant to become resistant to antibiotics and charge that the presence of the gene may cause humans to build up the same resistance. Supporters of the process however, argue that health concerns are unfounded and point to the superior taste that results from the procedure.

Tomatoes have also received some positive media attention as a Harvard medical researcher, Edward Giovannucci, MD, announced a preliminary link between tomato consumption and the reduced risk of developing prostate cancer. Tomatoes contain lycopene, a red carotenoid related to beta-carotene, to which Giovannucci has attributed this salubrious effect.

Current Conditions

In 1998, producers devoted almost 3.3 million acres to growing vegetables and melons, producing nearly 37 million tons. The USDA estimated the value of the 1998 crop to be about $9.4 billion. Fresh vegetable and melon use is expected to increase, rising to a level of 147 pounds per person fueled in part by growing demand for tomatoes, watermelons, and romaine lettuce. In 1996, tomato production reached one of its highest levels ever. Processed vegetable and melon consumption had increased as well, averaging 133 pounds per person, according to the USDA. The United States remained one of the largest producers and exporters of canned vegetables throughout the 1990s, although, the United States has also increased its imports of fruits and vegetables, especially from the Caribbean and Latin America.

In 1998, top growers in terms of acreage were R.D. Offut Company, Grimmway Farms, and Tanimura and Antle. Ranked by revenue, the top growers in 1999 were Tanimura and Antle of Salinas, California, with $378 million, and Dole Fresh Vegetables, also of Salinas, with $250 million.

The 1996 Farm Bill introduced a new era of market-oriented production that had ramifications on all agricultural sectors. Analysts received the bill favorably because the legislation offered farmers more flexibility and yet protected specialty crop growers from market fluctuations by stabilizing the commodity market. The bill was also expected to promote more sound business practices through the alleviation of surplus production, making U.S. producers more competitive.

Further Reading

Lazich, Robert S., ed. *Market Share Reporter,* Detroit: Gale Group, 1999.

Schierow, Linda-Jo. ''Pesticide Policy Issues.'' Congressional Research Service. Washington, DC: 4 December 1996. Available from http://www.cnie.org/nle/pest-2.html#summ.

U.S. Department of Agriculture and National Agricultural Statistics Service. "Statistics of Vegetables and Melons." Washington, DC: 2000. Available from http://www.usda.gov/nass/pubs.

Ward's Business Directory of U.S. Private and Public Companies, Detroit: Gale Group, 1999.

SIC 0171

BERRY CROPS

This industry covers establishments primarily engaged in the production of cranberries, strawberries, and bush berries. Agricultural products in this last category include blackberries, blueberries, currants, dewberries, loganberries, boysenberries, and raspberries.

NAICS CODE(S)

111333 (Strawberry Farming)
111334 (Berry (except Strawberry) Farming)

INDUSTRY SNAPSHOT

The berry industry in the United States has a history as old as the continent. Native American peoples relied heavily on certain berries as a staple in their diet and passed on their knowledge of the fruit to the first European colonists. The production of cranberries, strawberries, blueberries, and raspberries is a profitable agricultural enterprise that began in the early nineteenth century. In more recent decades, the industry has been dominated by large commercial farms, particularly in states like California, Oregon, and Washington. Research and development factors have become an influential element in the industry, as increasingly larger berry-growing companies employ scientists who work to genetically improve the fruit. Researchers also strive to combat the possible side effects of one uncontrollable factor—the weather. A late spring frost can seriously damage a farm's entire harvest.

Fluctuations in consumer preferences also play a significant role in the industry. For instance, cranberries—fruit indigenous to North America—enjoyed a surge in popularity in the late 1980s and throughout the 1990s. Wisconsin is the leader in cranberry production, followed by Massachusetts, New Jersey, Oregon, and Washington. In 1998, farmers harvested 36,600 acres, which yielded 5.46 million barrels. This total was down 1 percent from the previous year, but acreage increased 3 percent from 1997, which set a new record. The average yield per acre was 149.1 barrels. Production of strawberries, the largest segment of this classification, is led by the state of California, which produces nearly 80 percent of the nation's entire berry crop and nearly 10 percent of the world's annual supply. An estimated 759,000 tons of strawberries went to market in 1995.

Production of cultivated blueberries, cultivated blackberries, boysenberries, loganberries, and raspberries rose 5 percent, while the value of production declined mildly to $201.5 million in 1995. Cultivated blueberries have undergone a popularity increase over the last decade. New Jersey, Michigan, and North Carolina have been the leading producers of blueberries, while small commercial farms operating in California, Indiana, Maine, and Massachusetts also account for a percentage of the total blueberry output.

ORGANIZATION AND STRUCTURE

The berry industry in the United States is increasingly dominated by large agricultural enterprises. These farms employ a staff of horticulturists to develop and perfect new varieties of berries. Production and processing work on both commercial and smaller farms is carried out by large numbers of seasonal workers at harvest time. The berries are shipped out to a distribution center, where each farm receives the market price for its crop. Fresh berries destined for supermarkets are then shipped as quickly as possible, while the rest of the fruit is sent to processing centers to be frozen or used in other products such as juices. Larger commercial enterprises may have an in-house marketing staff that works with grocers to place their product in large eye-catching displays. However, much of the advertising end of the berry business is taken care of by umbrella groups. For instance, Ocean Spray Cranberries, Inc., a Lakeville, Massachusetts-based cooperative of growers, has launched national print, television, and radio advertising campaigns to increase consumer awareness of the fruit. In the strawberry industry, growers belong to the California Strawberry Advisory Board, a collective organization responsible for marketing the fruit at both the height of strawberry season as well as in leaner months. The last type of group relies heavily on cooperative advertising efforts with grocery chains and produce retail outlets, but this is sometimes a difficult task. The campaign must be coordinated based on predictions of the likely date of the crop's ripeness, coupled with incorporation of other factors such as weather conditions and shipping problems.

CURRENT CONDITIONS

The production and sale of all types of berries have benefited from increased consumer health consciousness. Beginning in the 1980s, people began to incorporate more fresh fruits and vegetables into their diets as a way to reduce fat and increase vitamin and nutrient intake. Research in the 1990s revealed that berries are high in vitamin C and fiber, are low in calories, and contain high levels of antioxidants. The demand for berries of all types has dramatically increased over the years and in some cases has even doubled.

Cranberry harvests have also enjoyed a boom in recent years. In 1977 total output was 2.1 million barrels, valued at $38.1 million. By 1995 production had doubled to over 4 million barrels, valued at $230 million. The forecast for the 1999 crop was estimated at a record high 5.81 million barrels, which would be up 6 percent from both 1997 and 1998. Of all the major cranberry producing states, only Washington expected a decrease. Production in Wisconsin was estimated to be 2.6 million barrels. This record high figure is up 2 percent from the 1998 production and 13 percent from 1997. The Massachusetts crop was expected to produce 2.1 million barrels, an increase of 12 percent from the previous year. New Jersey was forecasting production of 580,000 barrels, up 11 percent from 1998, while Oregon was forecasting production of 370,000 barrels, an increase of 4 percent from 1998. The Washington crop was forecast at 160,000 barrels, down 5 percent from 1998 and 3 percent from 1997. Factors contributing to the state's decrease included a cool spring that hampered pollination and set, as well as insect and weed problems.

Much of the increases in these harvests are due to improvements in crop management that allow growers to harvest more berries per acre and at the same time better control over some effects of inclement weather. Sales of fresh cranberries are tied to a short season in the fall, when they are harvested. This segment accounts for only 5 percent of the fruit's sales, but the product's use in traditional holiday dishes generates a strong demand during those few weeks. Dried cranberries or ''craisins,'' on the other hand, have helped expand the cranberry market beyond seasonal demand due to their use in cereals and fruit mixes.

Strawberry production is the most viable of all subindustries classified in the category. In recent years both its production and value has escalated substantially. In 1977 total production was 6.6 million hundredweight (domestic strawberry production is gauged by the hundredweight, a standard of measure equivalent to 100 pounds), and the value of that year's crop was $219 million. By 1995, production had doubled to 15 million hundredweight, and its value had more than tripled to $753.5 million. The majority of the strawberry proceeds, $633.6 million, came from fresh-market sales, while about $120 million came from processing sales. The U.S. Department of Agriculture (USDA) reported that the United States exported about 60.6 million pounds of fresh strawberries and about 20.5 million pounds of frozen strawberries in 1995. Per capita consumption of fresh strawberries leveled off a bit in 1995 to 3.76 pounds after the record level of 4.09 pounds in 1994. Frozen strawberry consumption, however, increased to 1.14 pounds, just slightly below 1971's record of 1.27 per capita level.

Research and Technology

Combatting insect population and the ravages of horticultural diseases is a major preoccupation of berry growers across the United States. In states where a certain fruit is a vital component of the area's agricultural economy, government-financed research stations exist to study growing methods and problems. In the Massachusetts Cranberry Experiment Station, for instance, horticulturists and entomologists discovered in 1929 that the blunt-nosed leafhopper was responsible for the scourge of the ''false-blossom'' disease, which had devastated cranberry harvests for decades. They researched ways to eradicate it through pesticides and fertilizers. Cranberry producers have also experimented with increasing the yield from each crop in processing the berry. Since 1955, they have managed to triple the amount of product from each acre.

In the strawberry industry, research has played a vital role in the development of the business since World War II. Working with the California Department of Agriculture, growers were able to create new varieties of the fruit that could better withstand insects and the vagaries of rain and wind. Research into improved growing and harvesting methods, in conjunction with university agricultural labs, also made a great impact on the state's strawberry industry. By the early 1990s, one acre of land could produce twenty-five tons of the fruit, a tenfold increase over a decade. Other research has looked at increasing the amount of nutrients in fruits. In the 1980s government researchers detected traces of ellagic acid in strawberries, a compound thought to have cancer-inhibiting qualities. Since then, experiments have been conducted to increase the amount of the acid in the fruit as well as in other berries. Research reports made public in 1993 asserted that raspberries and strawberries were found to have their own natural mold-inhibiting compounds. Termed 2-nonanone, this compound occurs naturally in the fruit; when used to chemically treat the berry, it further prolongs the shelf life of the fruit with no adverse effects.

Research has also played a role in creating new product segments in this industry. The boysenberry is a recent type of fruit developed from loganberry, blackberry, and raspberry strains, yielding a seedless berry ideal for jams.

In 1998, five new cultivars of blackberries, blueberries, and strawberries were developed and released that had the advantage of ripening before or after the typical growing season, which made the berries available longer throughout the summer. The new berry cultivars were also developed to produce much larger fruit than existing commercial counterparts. One of the cultivars, the Black Butte berry, is almost twice the size of most fresh blackberries. The Siskiyou cultivar, which ripens a couple weeks ahead of the main berry season, has already developed a niche market. The Chandler cultivar, a highbush blueberry, is a large midseason berry that provides ripe fruit for 4 to 5 weeks. Most blueberries only ripen over a three-week period. Two new strawberry cultivars, named Firecracker and Independence, will produce berries longer, thus extending the strawberry season up to 3 weeks.

FURTHER READING

Agricultural Research Service. *Bigger, Better Berries Available Soon,* 11 November 1999. Available from http://www/.ars.usda .gov/is/AR/archive/Jan98/berro198.htm.

ICFTU Online. *Strawberry's Bitter Taste,* 28 November 1999. Available from http://www.icftu.org/english/pr/1998/ epr01109-980506-nd.htm.

National Agricultural Service. *Cranberries,* 17 August 1999. Available from http://usda.mannlib.cornell.edu/reports/nassr/ fruit/zcr-bb/cran0899.txt.

U.S. Department of Agriculture and National Agricultural Statistics Service. ''Agricultural Statistics 1995-1996.'' Washington, DC: GPO, 1996. Available from http://www.usda.gov/ nass/pubs/agr95_96/agr95_5.pdf.

U.S. Department of Agriculture. ''Fruit and Tree Nuts.'' Washington, DC: GPO, 23 September 1996. Available from http:// usda.mannlib.cornell.edu/reports/erssor/specialty/fts-bb/1996/ fruit_and_tree_nuts_09.23.96.

SIC 0172

GRAPES

Establishments in this industry are primarily engaged in the production of grapes.

NAICS CODE(S)

111332 (Grape Vineyards)

INDUSTRY SNAPSHOT

Grape production has consistently constituted one of the largest U.S. non-citrus fruit crops, usually competing with apples for the greatest amount of total fruit produced. In the general fruit category, however, grapes have always trailed oranges. The farm value of the grape crop has totaled approximately $1.5 billion to $2 billion each year since the mid-1980s. The two types of establishments engaged in the production of grapes in the United States are grape farms and vineyards. Grapes are grown for table use, processed into wine or juice, canned or frozen, and dried for raisins. California, Washington, and New York lead the country in grape production, although California alone produces about 90 percent of the country's grapes. California also leads in wine consumption. California had more than 100 wine grape farms in 1999.

While European grape varieties account for 90 percent of cultivated grapes in the world, early attempts to grow them in the United States were unsuccessful because of native pests and diseases. As a result, U.S. grape growers began domesticating native species. The Concord grape, an American variety, is a favorite of eastern growers and accounts for 80 percent of the eastern crop. Most eastern grapes are processed into grape juice and wine, while California is the major table grape growing region of the country.

Grape growing is labor intensive. The vines are trained to grow on a system of stakes and wire and are pruned to develop the desired shape for maximum production and quality. Hand pruning continues throughout the year. Other practices used by growers to increase production or quality include thinning of the berries, and clusters and girdling.

The many diseases and pests that attack grape vines are a continuing threat to the industry. Throughout the late 1980s and early 1990s, the Napa Valley of California was infested with a new strain of root pest. Industry losses as a result of the infestation were estimated to be $600 million.

Harvesting is also an arduous task, especially for table grapes, because they require special care to avoid bruising. Because of the higher cost for field labor, mechanical picking is used for grapes intended for wine or raisins.

The California Table Grape Commission has identified several important trends that benefit the grape industry. First, the large number of two-income households in the United States have increased the demand for convenience food items, and health-conscious consumers find that grapes meet all the criteria in convenience and nutrition. Second, children are playing a growing role in the marketplace with grapes being their number one snack food choice.

Exports of California table grapes to other countries have increased at record levels each year since 1985 and by the early 1990s represented 14 percent of the total crop. A saturated domestic market, a willingness of American farmers to grow varieties favored by foreign buyers, adoption of international packaging, and improvements in handling and shipping are credited with the dramatic rise in exports. California also hosts a thriving vineyard economy, producing many world-famous red and white wines. About 680 wineries in California produce over 90 percent of the country's wine. For red wine, the grape varieties zinfandel, cabernet sauvignon, and merlot made up 59 percent of California's red wine variety grape acreage in 1995 and 30 percent of the state's total wine variety grape acreage. For white wine, the grape varieties chardonnay, colombard, and chenin blanc made up 80 percent of the state's white variety grape acreage and 40 percent of California's total wine variety grape acreage.

Current Conditions

Research and innovation, coupled with encouragement from state governments, have transformed grape growing in the United States. Laws encourage research and promotional activities; new pest controls have reduced the amount of chemical control; and new cultivation techniques have increased quality. One of the most dreaded grape enemies is phylloxera, an aphid-like insect that attacks susceptible grape rootstock. Private industry and universities have developed varieties of grapes that offer greater diversity and that have superior pest tolerance and extended growing seasons.

In 1997, the major fresh fruit consumed by Americans were bananas, apples, oranges, and grapes. Combined, they accounted for 66 percent of fruit eaten. Per capita consumption rose for grapes alone, due to increased grape production and imports. Raisin consumption increased slightly after three years of decline. Grape juice consumption increased 5 percent in 1997, when Washington's grape production increased 122 percent, 81 percent of which was processed into juice. Wine consumption continues to increase, from 1.79 gallons per person in 1994 to 2.65 gallons in 1997. Prices for fresh-market grapes were about 30 cents per pound ($600 per ton), down 25 percent from the previous year. Processing grape prices increased by 3 percent.

California's grape crop was estimated at 11.3 billion pounds in 1998, down 15 percent from 1997's bumper crop. Thirteen percent of this production went to table varieties, 46 percent to wine varieties, and 41 percent to raisin varieties. All three types decreased, from 9 percent to 20 percent. Bearing acreage increased by 3 percent. Total U.S. grape production was forecast to reach 12.5 billion pounds, 14 percent below the previous year. This reduction in grape production led to an increase in fresh grape prices.

U.S. fresh grape imports increased by 15 percent during the 1997-98 marketing season. Imports from Chile accounted for more than 75 percent of the total. Other leading importers are Mexico and South Africa, increasing by 12 percent and 37 percent, respectively. Exports increased by 33 percent to more than 600 million pounds. Major markets including Canada, Hong Kong, and Mexico, all increased. Taiwan, the fourth largest market, declined 25 percent.

U.S. wine exports increased by 25 percent in 1997 compared to the previous year, with the European Union, Canada, and Japan making up a combined 74 percent of the total. This trend continued in 1998. Imports of grape juice rose 7 percent in 1997, with the European Union, Mexico, and Brazil shipments increasing. Imports declined in 1998 due to the record crop the previous year. Export of grape juice increased by 10 percent, but declined in 1998 due to the Asian economic crisis. Exports of raisins declined 9 percent in 1997, while imports increased by 2 percent.

U.S. grape production was forecast to reach 6.56 million tons, up 11 percent from 1998 and down 10 percent from 1997. California's grape production increased 10 percent from 1998 to 5.9 million tons. California, along with New York, Pennsylvania and Washington, accounted for 99 percent of the 1999 production. A cool summer in California, however, led to one of the state's latest wine grape harvests in history. Although the California Department of Food and Agriculture estimated the harvest would reach 2.9 million tons, producers expected only 2.8 million tons, 20 percent to 40 percent below historical averages. Alfred G. Scheid, CEO of Scheid Vineyards Inc., estimated the grape crop would be 20 to 25 percent below normal.

Industry Leaders

Some of the leading grape producers are the National Grape Cooperative Association Inc. of Westfield, New York, with annual sales of $550 million; Guimarra Vineyards Corp. of Bakersfield, California, with estimated sales of $100 million; and Delicato Vineyards with estimated sales of $79 million.

The majority of fresh grape imports during the winter come from Chile. Chilean production of table grapes was expected to decline in 1998/1999 due to lower vineyard yields. More than half of this country's table grape production goes to the export market, which was expected to decline only slightly. Imports of Chilean grapes to the United States increased by 64 percent and 12 percent in January 1999 and February 1999, respectively, compared to the previous year. Total U.S. fresh grape imports were up 12 percent from the same period the previous year.

Further Reading

"California Winemaker Predicts Grape Crop to Be Down 25 Percent." *The Monterey County Herald.* Knight-Ridder/Tribune Business News, 5 August 1999.

"Economic Research Service: Fruit and Tree Nuts, Part I." M2 PressWIRE, 3 September 1998.

"Economic Research Service: Fruit and Tree Nuts Yearbook Summary" M2 PressWIRE, 15 October 1998.

Estrada, Richard. ''Late Bloom, Cool Summer Force One of Latest-Known Wine-Grape Harvests.'' *The Fresno Bee.*Knight-Ridder/Tribune Business News, 1 December 1999.

Hurley, Sue. ''Growers Increasingly Tap into Wine Market.'' *St. Louis Post-Dispatch.* 2 September 1999, 1.

National Agricultural Statistics Service. ''Crop Production.'' M2 PressWIRE, 12 August 1999.

U.S. Department of Agriculture. National Agricultural Statistics Service. ''Agricultural Statistics 1995-1996.'' Washington, D.C.: 1996. Available from http://www.usda.gov/nass/pubs/agr95_96/agr95_5.pdf.

U.S. Department of Agriculture. ''Fruit and Tree Nuts.'' Washington, D.C., 23 September 1996. Available from http://usda.mannlib.cornell.edu/reports/erssor/specialty/.

U.S. Department of Agriculture. '' Fruit and Tree Nuts.'' M2 PressWIRE, 1 April 1999.

Ward's Business Directory of U.S. Private and Public Companies, 2000. The Gale Group, Detroit, 2000.

SIC 0173

TREE NUTS

This classification covers establishments primarily engaged in the production of tree nuts, including almonds, filberts, macadamia nuts, pecans, pistachios, and walnuts.

NAICS CODE(S)

111335 (Tree Nut Farming)

INDUSTRY SNAPSHOT

Nuts are high in unsaturated fat and low in saturated fat, and they are considered to be a high energy food containing dietary fiber and essential vitamins and minerals. Most varieties are used throughout the year as nutritious snacks. Products containing nuts include ice cream, candy, assorted baked goods, and even, in the case of almonds, cosmetics.

The United States is a dominant world player in the commercial production of tree nuts with 875 companies claiming tree nut production as their primary operation. The total crop value of tree nuts produced in the United States was reported by the U.S. Department of Agriculture (USDA) to be approximately $1.4 billion in 1998. By contrast, the value of the 1971 crop was only $194 million. In addition, the per capita consumption rate was 2.2 pounds in 1998.

California alone grows 70 percent of the world's almond crop. Almonds generate $1 billion in sales annually, making them California's number-one export. California is also the second largest producer of pistachios in the world. U.S. production values of pistachios were $194 million in 1998.

Filberts or hazelnuts are grown in Oregon and Washington State, and production has more than tripled in 20 years, according to the USDA. The value of the 1998 crop was estimated at more than $42 million.

Macadamia nuts are native to Australia but have become an important crop in Hawaii in less than 50 years. The outlook for macadamia nut producers is especially bright, as demand continues to exceed the available supplies. The value of the 1998 crop was $37 million.

The pecan, the black walnut, and the butternut (white walnut) are native to the United States. Pecans grow in the central and southern United States, which hosts Georgia as the leading pecan producer. Native walnuts grow throughout the central Mississippi Valley and the Appalachian regions. Only the imported English or Persian walnut, grown in northern and central California and Oregon, is considered to be of commercial importance. Production values for 1998 were $177 million for pecans and $229 million for walnuts.

Almonds, the sixth largest U.S. food export, are shipped to more than 90 foreign countries. Europe and Japan are the largest markets. Exports to Europe received a boost with the passage of the General Agreement on Tariffs and Trade (GATT). Before its passage, almond shipments over 100,000 pounds incurred a 7 percent tax. A 2 percent tariff was imposed on shipments under 100,000. GATT doubled the allowable tonnage under the 2 percent limit and provided for a gradual decrease of the 7 percent tariff to 5.5 percent.

Tree Nut Production in America. These nuts are grown in orchards using modern cultivation methods that include supplemental irrigation, fertilizers, and insect and disease control for maximum productivity. Harvesting is mechanized, with the exception of macadamia nut gathering, in which the nuts are shaken from the trees and transported to processing factories. Here the hulls or shells are mechanically removed, and then they are electronically sorted and graded.

BACKGROUND AND DEVELOPMENT

Government agencies have been instrumental in establishing the importance of tree nuts in the United States. Several important pieces of legislation have been implemented over the years, such as the almond marketing order that established the Almond Board of California in 1950 to stabilize the volatile almond market, and the creation of the California Pistachio Commission in 1981 to aid the development of the industry. In addition, the USDA has been instrumental in developing more productive varieties of pecans that have expanded the industry.

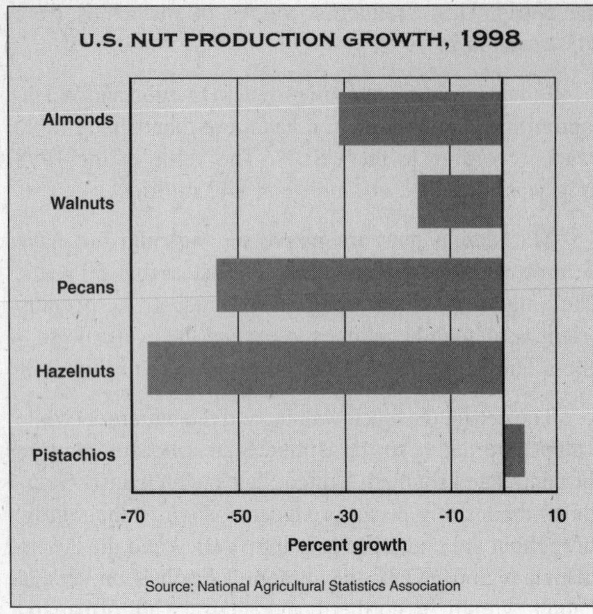

Though the consumption level dropped to a mere .5 pounds per capita, the 1995 almond crop still brought in a USDA-estimated $1 billion. That same year California yielded 148 million pounds of pistachios from about 60,000 acres, a crop valued at about $141.6 million.

Although well below 1993's record crop of 365 million pounds, 1995's 268-million-pound crop was much stronger than the previous year's 199-million pound yield. The USDA estimated that the 1995 crop had a value of almost $250 million. The 1994 walnut crop weighed in at more than 235,000 tons with a value by the USDA at nearly $239 million. In 1995, the United States exported 38,396 metric tons of shelled walnuts.

CURRENT CONDITIONS

After jumping to an all-time high of $2 billion in 1997, the production value of tree nuts dropped back to $1.4 billion the following year. Much of this was due to the on-year, off-year nature of almond farming. In 1997, an on-year, almonds accounted for 61 percent of the U.S. tree nut production with a record value of $1.1 billion.

At the close of the twentieth century, tree acreage continued to increase. Domestic consumption climbed to 611 million pounds, or 2.2 pounds per person. This measurement reflected a rise in the consumption of almonds, pecans, and pistachios, as well as a 14 percent increase in the sale of imported nuts.

INDUSTRY LEADERS

Founded in 1910 as the California Almond Growers Exchange, Sacramento-based Blue Diamond Growers is the largest almond grower-owned cooperative with 4,000 members. Blue Diamond's members produce one-third of California's almond crop with average annual sales of $500 million.

Diamond Walnut Growers, Inc., of Stockton, California, produces 50 percent of the country's walnut crop. Based in Hawaii, C. Brewer & Company and its subsidiary, the Mauna Loa Macadamia Nut Corporation, posted 1997 sales of $231 million.

FURTHER READING

Blue Diamond Growers Home Page, 1998-2000. Available from www.bluediamondgrowers.com.

Graebner, Lynn. ''Small Crop, Big Return for Almond Growers.'' *The Business Journal Serving Greater Sacramento,* 16 December 1996.

U.S. Department of Agriculture. ''Agricultural Statistics 1977-1999.'' *National Agricultural Statistics Service.* Washington, D.C., 1999. Available from http://www.usda.gov/nass/pubs/agr.

Ward's Business Directory of U.S. Private & Public Companies 1999. Detroit: Gale Research, 1998.

SIC 0174

CITRUS FRUITS

This industry consists of establishments primarily engaged in the production of citrus fruits.

NAICS CODE(S)

111310 (Orange Groves)
111320 (Citrus (except Orange) Groves)

INDUSTRY SNAPSHOT

Citrus fruits include oranges, tangelos, temples, tangerines, lemons, limes, and grapefruits. Oranges make up about 65 percent of total worldwide citrus production; tangelos, temples, and tangerines make up 15 percent; lemons and limes 10 percent and grapefruits, 10 percent. Oranges and grapefruit account for approximately 90 percent of U. S. citrus production.

With more than 20,000 U. S. producers of all sizes, no one grower is dominant in the production phase. The industry governs its own marketing orders. Growers heed marketing factors as they specify grade and standard of crop leaving the region. They control the amount of product leaving the region during marketing season, and designate periods when no new product can be shipped. Growers also provide market support such as research and price information, and provide market development programs.

ORGANIZATION AND STRUCTURE

Florida, California, Texas, and Arizona, all subtropical regions, produce the bulk of citrus fruits in the United States. Tropical cultivation is not as productive since seasonal changes are necessary for proper fruit growth. Citrus trees can withstand short periods of light frost, but hard frosts of long duration can be devastating.

The modern citrus industry depends on regular and frequent irrigation, fungicides, herbicides, pesticides, and other fertilizers. Harvesting is still often accomplished through manual means, although mechanical techniques are increasingly being used.

In the fresh fruit market, there is a great deal of competition, especially considering that, since around 1970, the per capita consumption of fresh oranges has declined, and since 1976, the consumption of fresh grapefruit has also decreased. With some fluctuations in between, per capita consumption of oranges has dropped from 16.2 pounds in 1970 to 13.1 pounds in 1994, while grapefruit consumption tapered off from 8.2 pounds in 1970 to 6.1 pounds in 1994. Of the total orange harvest in 1995, only 20 percent was consumed as fresh fruit, while 47 percent of grapefruits were consumed fresh. In the United States, almost all fresh citrus was garnered from domestic sources.

Processed fruit takes two forms: ready-to-serve juice (also known as single-strength equivalent, or SSE) and concentrate. Both forms have become very popular among consumers, mostly for their convenience. The variety of canned, frozen, and ready-to-serve juices in supermarkets is clear evidence of how the public responds to the processed product.

Citrus growers in the United States generally operate under one of three production philosophies. The first of these is to physically hand the fruit over to a packinghouse, processor, or middleman. A second option involves contracting with the packinghouse, processor, or middleman before the fruit is ready for harvest. In both cases, the seller and buyer agree to a satisfactory price before the fruit goes to market. The third option is an arrangement wherein the grower places his fruit along with a number of individual growers into a ''pool'' for sale on the open market. Profit is then determined by the selling price of the pooled fruit.

Citrus processing is a lucrative business. In addition to the primary products of frozen concentrate, chilled juice, and canned juice, processing also yields a number of by-products such as food additives, pectin, marmalades, cattle feeds (from the peel), cosmetics, essential oils, chemicals, and medicines. The processor can sell all these products to the appropriate industry for a profit.

BACKGROUND AND DEVELOPMENT

Until the 1950s, citrus fruits were cultivated and traded on a local basis almost exclusively. Speed and care in shipping the perishable fruits were of great concern. However, the development of citrus concentrate in the late 1940s had a lasting impact on the citrus industry worldwide. Concentrating the fruit permitted the storage, transportation, and transformation of product far from the groves. In contrast to fresh fruit consumption, processed citrus consumption has remained fairly stable since 1972. According to the Florida Department of Citrus, Economic and Marketing Research Department, per capita orange consumption in processed form (frozen concentrated juice, chilled juice, and canned single-strength) has fluctuated little since the early 1970s. Since the 1970-71 growing season, retail prices have risen steadily, in large part because of the healthy market for frozen concentrated orange juice.

By the 1995-96 growing year, Florida processed about 85 percent of the oranges and grapefruits grown in the United States, including 64 percent of its own orange production and 57 percent of its grapefruit crop. This process effort yielded 94 percent of the nation's frozen concentrated orange and canned orange juice, as well as 76 percent of canned grapefruit juice. In 1996, the USDA projected that U.S. orange juice production would rise to its record level of 1.3 billion SSE gallons. However, not all of the fruit processed was domestically grown. Nearly half of all processed juices available in America come from imported juice concentrate. Under the North American Free Trade Agreement (NAFTA), for example, the United States must import 44.1 million (SSE) gallons.

In recent years, cooperatives have been created in all four citrus producing states; in Florida they account for 22 percent of that state's processing volume. Conglomerate integration—firms that are subsidiaries of national food conglomerates—is also a significant presence in the industry, processing 35 to 45 percent of all the citrus that Florida processes.

CURRENT CONDITIONS

According to the U.S. Department of Agriculture (USDA), the citrus industry, which is based primarily in Arizona, California, Florida, and Texas, produced 13.7 million tons of citrus fruit during the 1998-99 growing season, as opposed to the record-high 17.8 million tons produced the previous season. The drop in production was attributed to poor weather in Florida and California. Oranges constitute the country's largest fruit crop with nearly 10 million tons produced in 1999, having a value estimated at $2.57 billion by the USDA.

The total orange-bearing acreage has been relatively stable since the 1957-58 growing season, and reached its peak during the early 1970s. However, after receding for

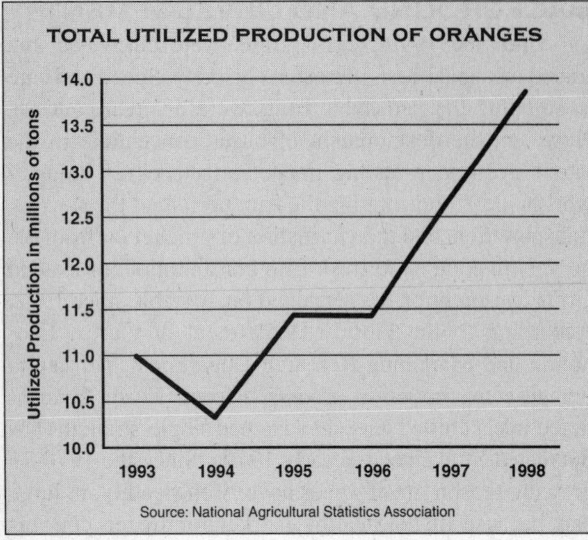

a period following the 1979-80 season, the total acreage devoted to citrus production began to rise in 1996-97, but has fallen off slightly since then. According to the National Agricultural Statistics Service (NASS), a division of the USDA, in the 1998-99 growing season, approximately 1.1 million acres were devoted to citrus production. Among the four major producing states, the orange-bearing acreage and production were as follows: Florida had 70 percent of the acreage and 79 percent of the production; California, with 28 percent of the acreage, produced 17 percent of the production. Texas and Arizona together claimed approximately 5 percent of total orange-bearing acreage.

Florida, as the major supplier of grapefruit, held around 74 percent of the acreage of the crop and produced 77 percent of the fruit. Accounting for nearly 23 percent of the acreage, Texas and California together provided around 22 percent of the domestic grapefruit total to the marketplace. In 1998, California produced 12 percent of the crop, while Texas produced 10 percent.

The citrus industry has also been enmeshed in controversy in recent years. Citrus growers have long enjoyed the benefits of Depression-era laws that established quotas governing citrus sales. As *Business Week* notes, these ''industry panels set total weekly sales ceilings'' and divided sales allotments among the growers, ''a practice economists criticize because it inflates consumer prices.'' Deepening concern about reputed abuse of the quotas by Sunkist and a number of its leading cooperative members prompted the government to eliminate 1993 marketing orders for navel oranges. With the quotas effectively blunted, wholesale prices plunged. Sunkist has been particularly wounded, both by the allegations and the financial difficulties brought on by the removal of the quotas. Despite their ongoing tribulations, however, Sunkist, with a total income of $1.1 billion, remains the world citrus industry's wholesale giant.

Industry Leaders

Leading establishments in the citrus fruit production industry are located in Florida and California. Companies such as Duda and Sons Inc., Lykes Bros., Inc., Orange-Co Inc., and Ben Hill Griffin Inc. are among the leaders in Florida, while leading companies in California include Royal Citrus Co., Limoneira Co., ET Wall Co., and Pandol Brothers.

The best known distributor of citrus fruits in the United States is Sunkist Growers, Inc. For the past 104 years it has been the dominant force for citrus growers in California and Arizona, and is a formidable presence in Florida as well. It operates a cooperative of some 6,000 members and accounts for 65 percent of the growers in the states of California and Arizona.

America and the World

The largest citrus producing countries, accounting for more than 70 percent of the world's supply, include the United States, Brazil, Japan, Spain, Italy, Egypt, South Africa, and Morocco, with Brazil leading the world in citrus production. With oranges and grapefruit accounting for approximately 90 percent of all U.S. citrus production, Florida has become a world player; it, along with Brazil, produces most of the world's concentrate.

While the U.S. fresh and processed orange industry is domestically oriented, imports are expected to grow largely due to two factors: the heightened demand for chilled orange juice and improved port facilities. At the same time, these improved facilities allow for more exports, a facet of the industry that growers are trying to enhance. The United States exports orange concentrate to both Canada and Mexico. These exports account for less than 10 percent of the total American domestic supply. Demographically and in price structure, the Canadian market differs little from the United States, and before 1986, Canada was the major purchaser of U.S. exports of orange concentrate. Since January 1994 when the NAFTA guidelines were implemented, frozen concentrated orange juice (FCOJ) exported to Mexico has quintupled, whereas the importing of SSE orange juice has gradually decreased about 20 percent of what it was in 1990. Also on account of NAFTA, which gives products from the United States preferential treatment, all citrus juices made from only one fruit must come only from NAFTA-grown fruit.

In contrast, the European market is very different demographically from the United States. European imports from other suppliers, such as Spain, are priced substantially lower than the American product. To alleviate the disparity, the industry has proposed a two-price system, in order to maintain the price of concentrate sold domestically (already higher relative to the rest of the world), and export the concentrate at a lower price to successfully compete.

To further interest in concentrate produced in the United States, which has been steadily declining in popularity for ten to fifteen years, growers have advanced programs in quality control, packaging innovations, and cross-merchandising, where, for example, FCOJ is paired and successfully marketed with another breakfast food such as waffles. The Duty Drawback Program is another program designed to encourage processors to develop foreign markets. It states that if, within a three-year period, a processor or importer exports a specific quantity of concentrate, duties paid on imports of ''like concentrate'' will be refunded, or ''drawn back.''

The export of fresh grapefruit is also of concern to U.S. growers, especially when dealing with Japan. Trade restrictions, import quotas, embargoes, and tariffs have resulted in substantially higher prices for American grapefruit in the Japanese market, yet, even with home-grown grapefruit available, the demand in Japan for fresh grapefruit allows U.S. growers to capitalize on the market.

FURTHER READING

Florida Department of Citrus. Economic and Market Research Department. ''Citrus Reference Book, 1999.'' Florida. April 1999. Available from http://www.fred.ifas.ufl.edu/citrus/

Lubove, Seth. ''Rebellion in the Orange Groves.'' *Forbes,* 5 Oct. 1998, 76-77.

Merli, Richard. ''There's a Silver Lining in Frozen Orange Juice.'' *Frozen Food Age,* July 1999, 16.

U.S. Department of Agriculture. ''Foreign Agricultural Service.'' Washington, DC: 1999. Available from: http://www.fas.usda.gov/info/factsheets/nafta.html and http://www.fas.usda.gov/itp/policy/nafta/orange.html

U.S. Department of Agriculture. National Agricultural Statistics Service. ''Agricultural Statistics 1999.'' Washington, DC: 1999. Available from: http://usda.mannlib.cornell.edu/usda/ess_entry.html

Ward, Ronald W., and Richard L. Kilmer. *The Citrus Industry: A Domestic and International Economic Perspective.* Ames, IA: Iowa State University Press, 1989.

SIC 0175

DECIDUOUS TREE FRUITS

This classification includes establishments primarily engaged in the production of deciduous tree fruits. Establishments primarily growing citrus fruits are classified in **SIC 0174: Citrus Fruits** and those growing tropical fruits are classified in **SIC 0179: Fruits and Tree Nuts, Not Elsewhere Classified.**

NAICS CODE(S)

111331 (Apple Orchards)
111339 (Other Noncitrus Fruit Farming)

The deciduous fruit industry consists of farms and orchards that maintain and harvest a variety of fruits, specifically apples, apricots, cherries, nectarines, peaches, pears, persimmons, plums, pomegranates, prunes, and quinces. According to the U.S. Department of Agriculture, apples led 1998 crop production with 5.5 million tons, followed by 1.2 million tons of peaches, 926,000 tons of pears, and 542,000 tons of prunes and plums. The value of the apple crop alone in 1995 was in excess of $1.8 billion. The apple crop also constitutes the country's third largest fruit crop, trailing grapes and oranges.

In 1998, more than 1.8 million acres of farmland were devoted to the growth of major deciduous fruits in the United States. This is indicative of the steady market for deciduous fruits, as the acreage devoted to deciduous fruits 15 years earlier was about 1.7 million acres and harvesting techniques have allowed growers to glean more fruit from fewer trees.

Deciduous fruits are divided into two groups according to climate requirements: warm-temperate fruits, and cool-temperate fruits. Warm-temperate fruits include apricots, peaches, and plums. Cool-temperate fruits include apples, pears, and cherries. Both categories need a certain, short-period of low temperatures during winter dormancy, called a chilling period, in order to flower and produce fruit.

Chilling periods vary greatly not only among disparate fruits, but among different varieties of the same fruit as well. For example, some varieties of peaches require 250 hours of chilling while others demand as many as 1,000 hours. Apples and cherries generally need more than that. An inadequate chilling period can result in a number of problems. Flower buds may die or blossoms may drop before they open. Those flowers that do develop may not set fruit, or the fruit may be undersized. Growers consider the chilling period of primary importance in the success or failure of their crops. These temperature conditions therefore preclude commercial production of deciduous fruits in colder or warmer climates.

In 1999, top producers by revenue were CM Holtzinger Fruit Company, with $35 million, and Wells and Wade Fruit Company, with $25 million. Both companies were located in Washington. The previous year, top apple and pear companies by acreage were Stemilt Management and Naumes. Top stone fruit companies were Gerawan Farming and Lane Packing.

Apples. More land was devoted to the growing of apples than any other fruit in this category. Leading apple-producing states were Washington, New York, Michigan, and California. Out of nearly 11 million pounds of apples produced in 1998, more than 56 percent was fresh-market sales, while about 12 percent was canned. U. S. producers faced consistent worldwide demand for apples, though competition from France and New Zealand remained strong. In the 1997-98 marketing year, Taiwan, Canada, and Mexico were the major importers of U.S. apples, accounting for more than 60 percent of all U.S. apple export, according to the USDA.

Apricots. Apricot production in the United States has been fickle in the last decade. Although the production level climbed to 153,200 tons in 1994, it plummeted to a mere 58,500 in 1995. In 1998 production was back up to 118,000. California, Washington, and Utah were the leading apricot producing states in 1998. California, however, produced nearly 96 percent of the crop. The domestic usage distribution for 1998 was as follows: 22,278 tons were fresh market, 40,700 tons were canned, 9,000 tons were dried, and 10,400 tons were frozen.

Cherries. Cherries, classified as two types, (sweet and tart), have met increasing demand over the last decade. Whereas in 1986, cherry production yielded under 2,500 tons, in 1998 production yielded more than 384,000 tons. The value of the 1997 crop was estimated at about $323 million. Sweet cherries accounted for more than half of the total cherry production. Leading sweet cherry producing states include Washington, Oregon, Michigan, and California. Leading tart cherry producing states included Michigan, Utah, and Wisconsin. In 1998, 113,600 tons, sweet and tart combined, were frozen, while about 52,350 tons were canned or otherwise processed. There were 110,310 tons of fresh cherries.

Peaches. In 1998 for example, growers harvested more than 2.4 million tons of peaches. Inclement weather damaged the crops of Georgia and South Carolina in 1996, causing overall production to drop to its lowest level since 1983 at under 2 billion pounds. The value of peaches however, rose within this same period from 14 cents per pound in 1986, or a $311 million total value, to more than 18 cents per pound, or $413 million total value. California, South Carolina, Georgia, and New Jersey ranked as the leading producers of peaches in the United States. Of 1998's total crop, more than 1 million pounds were sold as fresh-market fruit, while about 985,000 pounds were processed as canned peaches and 185,800 pounds were frozen. Canada, Japan, and Latin American countries have been major importers of U. S. canned peaches.

Pears. The United States was the leading producer of pears with a total of 947,000 tons in 1998. Italy, Spain, and Japan were distant followers. Consequently the United States could export a large portion of its pear crop. Approximately one third of U.S. pears were exported in 1995: 137,000 tons of fresh pears and 153,000 tons of processed pears, of which 12,000 tons were canned. In 1998 fresh market sales of pears accounted for 519,895 tons while about 404,000 tons were processed. Washington, California, and Oregon consistently led the country in pear production. The Pacific Bartlett variety accounted for more than 50 percent of the U. S. pear crop, according to the USDA.

Plums and Prunes. From 1986 to 1995, plum and prune production fluctuated. Whereas producers yielded 247,000 tons in 1994, only about 124,000 tons were produced in 1995 and 25,500 tons in 1998. The value of the crops also vacillated, with 1994's crop worth $79.3 million, while 1995's soared to $1.1 billion and 1998's fell to a mere $7.7 million. Exportation of plums and prunes amounted to about 70,000 tons of fresh and about 70,575 tons of dried in 1998. Oregon and Idaho were the leading producers of plums and prunes. Washington had cut production in half since 1986.

FURTHER READING

Lazich, Robert S. ed. *Market Share Reporter.* Detroit: Gale Group, 1999.

U.S. Department of Agriculture and National Agricultural Statistics Service. ''Agricultural Statistics 1995-1996.'' Washington, DC: 1996. Available from http://www.usda.gov/nass/pubs/agr95_96/agr95_5.pdf.

U.S. Department of Agriculture. ''Statistics of Fruits, Tree Nuts, and Horticultural Specialties.'' 2000. Available from http://usda.mannlib.cornell.edu/reports.

Ward's Business Directory of U.S. Private and Public Companies. Detroit: Gale Group, 1999.

SIC 0179

FRUITS AND TREE NUTS, NOT ELSEWHERE CLASSIFIED

This category covers establishments primarily engaged in the production of fruits and nuts, not elsewhere classified. This classification also includes establishments deriving 50 percent or more of their total value of sales of agricultural products from fruits and tree nuts (Industry Group 017) but less than 50 percent from products of any single industry.

NAICS CODE(S)

111336 (Fruit and Tree Nut Combination Farming)
111339 (Other Noncitrus Fruit Farming)

This relatively small American industry produces fruits that are normally grown in more tropical regions of the hemisphere. Members of this category are avocado orchards, banana farms, coconut groves, coffee farms, date and fig orchards, kiwi fruit farms, olive groves, and pineapple and plantain farms. Avocado, olive, and date production comprises the bulk of crops in this category. Most producers are small commercial enterprises situated in warmer states such as Hawaii, California, and Florida. The number of such farms engaged in producing fruits and tree nuts in this industry has been in steady decline since the 1980s. The production value for tree nuts was $1.66 billion in 1995, while the value of U.S. fruit production was $9.06 billion. Figures from 1996 showed an estimated 346 establishments in this industry classification, employing roughly 7,700. Sales were $8.163 billion, with the average amount per establishment at $24.8 million.

In 1999 the two top companies were Dole Food Company of Westlake Village, California, with over $4.3 billion in revenue; and Chiquita Brands International, of Cincinnati, Ohio, with over $2.4 billion.

Looking at the individual components of this industry classification is necessary due to great fluctuations in various crop yields from year to year. The apparent lack of any one statistical pattern over a span of a decade may be due to the fragile nature of such perishables as avocados and olives. These smaller, exotic crops are extremely dependent on favorable weather conditions for the success of the year's harvest. The import market also plays some role in the fluctuation within the industry.

California avocados continue to yield steady profits for growers, who produce about 90 percent of the American avocado crop; Florida produces almost all of the rest. During the 1990s, production continued to rise steadily, as did overall crop value—$277.5 million for the 1997-98 season in the combined two states, for 178,000 tons. Many U.S.-grown avocados are exported to Canada, Japan, the Netherlands, and France. In 1995 the U.S. Department of Agriculture (USDA) considered rescinding a rule dating from 1914 that banned the import of some Mexican-grown avocados. California growers, however, showed vociferous opposition, since the Mexican product fails pest-contamination standards and could spread crop-damaging organisms to American avocado crops.

California is also the center of olive production in the United States. Black olives are the most commonly grown variety. The output from the state's olive groves varies greatly from year to year; crop value reached $40 million in 1998. In this sector approximately 2 to 5 percent of the year's crop is crushed for oil. Much of the rest is canned or used in other products.

Date production in the United States is centered primarily in Coachella Valley, an arid region about 130 miles east of Los Angeles. In the early years of the twentieth century, ranchers received date plantings from the USDA as an incentive to settle the region. The industry did not begin to thrive until 1913, when a collective organization was formed to purchase imported date plants from North Africa. In 1998 production was 22,200 tons.

The center of the U.S. fig-growing industry is likewise located in California. Per capita consumption in the United States, however, has declined steadily since the 1960s and in 1995 reached .0124 pounds per person. Though they are grown year-round, fig harvest is at its heaviest during the fall months. In 1993 production reached the highest levels since 1966—59,000 tons—but sunk to 40,000 by 1998. Imported figs from Turkey and Spain provide the greatest competition to American fig growers.

Hawaii is the center of the coffee-growing industry in the United States; it is also the locus of American banana production. This state's annual banana yield has seen steady increases since the 1980s—with some declines from year to year. In 1998, 20,000 tons were produced. As a further boon, U.S. banana consumption rose 26 percent from 1989 to 1995, but the largest American grower—Cincinnati-headquartered Chiquita Brands International—performed poorly as a result of a corporate takeover; in 1995 the value of one of its shares rose only one cent. Chiquita's main rival, the Dole Food Company, assumed Chiquita's former number-one spot in the market.

In this industry, growers of fruits and tree nuts face stiff competition from foreign competitors. This sector of agriculture in the United States is relatively small compared to its status in other countries. For instance, countries in North Africa produce a sizable portion of figs and dates for export abroad, while olive tree acreage figures for areas in the Middle East, Greece, and Italy are staggering. In such countries these industries have been vital components of the local economy for literally thousands of years. Coffee growers in the United States face heavy competition from foreign countries—most notably Brazil, Mexico, and Ecuador. However, American growers are finding some success in the cultivation of exotic fruits such as mangoes and passion fruit.

FURTHER READING

Agricultural Statistics 1998. Department of Agriculture, 2000. Available from http://www.usda.gov.

National Agricultural Statistics Service. *Statistics of Fruits, Tree Nuts, and Horticultural Specialties.* 2000. Available from http://usda.mannlib.cornell.edu.

Ward's Business Directory of U.S. Private and Public Companies. Detroit: Gale Research, 1999.

SIC 0181

ORNAMENTAL FLORICULTURE AND NURSERY PRODUCTS

This category includes establishments primarily engaged in the production of ornamental plants and other nursery products, such as bedding plants, bulbs, florists' greens, flowers, shrubbery, potted plants, flower and vegetable seeds and plants, and sod. These products may be grown outdoors, or under cover of a greenhouse, frame, cloth house, or lath house.

NAICS CODE(S)

111422 (Floriculture Production)
111421 (Nursery and Tree Production)

Nursery and greenhouse marketings accounted for nearly 5 percent of all farm income. In 1997, nursery and greenhouse products accounted for more than $7.63 billion in sales after showing slow growth in the previous seven years. The wholesale value of floriculture crops was estimated at $3.93 billion in 1998.

Nursery crops, turfgrass, bulbs, and groundcovers accounted for 63 percent of retail sales in 1996. Cut flowers and greens were 7.8 percent of sales, while bedding plants were 16 percent. Potted flowering plants were 8 percent of the market, slightly higher than foliage plants' 6.9 percent.

California, Florida, Texas, Michigan, and Ohio were the top producers of bedding plants. They accounted for 51 percent, or $1.81 billion, of the 1998 value of floriculture crops. Bedding plants included impatiens, petunias, geraniums (the 1998 top-seller), marigolds, pansies, and more. Begonias, zinnias, salvia, gerbera, dusty miller, snapdragons, alyssum, and coleus also had a healthy share of the market.

The floriculture market increased by 1 percent in 1998, after having slowly but steadily climbed throughout the decade from $2.5 billion in 1990 to $3.9 billion in 1998. Bedding and garden plants accounted for the majority of the growth, while the cut-flower industry suffered in part due to increased foreign competition. Potted flowering plants were also down, while foliage gained a mere 1 percent. California was the highest producer in the U.S. market, and in 1998 the state's crop was valued by the U.S. Department of Agriculture (USDA) at $769 million. In 1998 the United States had 14,308 operations in the field of floriculture with the majority having sales in the $100,000-$499,999 range.

The more than 1,900 poinsettia growers in the United States sold more than 63,000 potted poinsettias in 1998, with an average wholesale value of $4.15 a plant and a total market value of more than $211 million. California provided 21 percent of that value. This was down 7 percent from 1997, and the potted flowering plant value was down 3 percent, at $701 million.

The U.S. wholesale flower market was a $419 million concern in 1998, down 11 percent. The total number of growers dropped by 135 in 1998, leaving 694 in production. More than 70 percent of all roses are now imported, making for steep foreign competition for local growers of all varieties of cut flowers.

Also in 1997, according to the USDA, the amount of covered area in floriculture crop production was 1.07 billion square feet, up 15 percent. Greenhouse space was 654 million square feet of this covered area, while film plastic structures were 463 million square feet. Shade and temporary cover accounted for 420 million square feet of covered area, the remaining area being rigid plastic or glass greenhouse area.

Operations increased the use of hired workers in 1998. Overall, 86 percent used hired workers in 1998, compared with 80 percent in 1997.

The cut-flower industry continued to suffer from foreign competition, particularly from warmer climates where growers do not need to heat greenhouses and labor is less expensive. The cut-flower industry was down 11 percent in 1998, and there were only 132 businesses growing roses, down from 273 in 1987. According to an article in the *Detroit Free Press,* domestic flowers were on average one-third more expensive than imports and domestic growers were touting freshness as the main advantage of their product. Imports accounted for approximately 60 percent of cut flowers sold in the United States, with the top import countries being Colombia, Ecuador, and the Netherlands.

The month of May, which includes Mother's Day, accounts for approximately 11 percent of florists' annual sales. According to industry statistics, the personal consumer breakdown of floriculture was as follows: outdoor bedding/garden plants, 49 percent; cut flowers, 28 percent; flowering/green houseplants, 23 percent.

Industry leaders included Hines Horticulture, Inc., with 1998 sales of $235 million; The Scotts Company, with 1999 sales of $1.65 billion; and Color Spot Nurseries, with 1999 sales of $206 million. The mega-company Monsanto, with 1998 sales topping $8.6 billion was also a major player, as well as being in a variety of other related feed and seed agricultural businesses. Other industry leaders included Ohio-based Yoder Brothers Inc., Idaho-based Rogers Seed Company, and California-based Monrovia Nursery Company.

FURTHER READING

National Agricultural Statistics Service. *Floriculture Crops, 1998 Summary.* Washington, DC: NASS, June 1998.

Parker, Jocelyn. ''South American Rose Imports Crowd U.S. Growers.'' *Detroit Free Press,* 14 July 1999.

Society of American Florists. *About Flowers.* Available from http://www.aboutflowers.com.

U.S. Department of Agriculture. *Ornamental Crops Market Reports.* Available from http://www.ams.usda.gov/fv/mncs/orntren2.htm.

SIC 0182

FOOD CROPS GROWN UNDER COVER

This industry consists of establishments primarily engaged in the production of mushrooms or fruits and/or vegetables grown under cover.

NAICS CODE(S)

111411 (Mushroom Production)
111419 (Other Food Crops Grown Under Cover)

In 1987, 21,055 farms were growing saleable greenhouse crops, mushrooms, and sod under glass or other types of protective covering in the United States. Those crops covered approximately 762 million square feet of greenhouse or shelter space. Combined with their counterparts grown in the open, those crops had sales value of $5.77 billion for that year.

Mushrooms are by far the largest segment of crops grown under cover. According to the U.S. Department of Agriculture (USDA), there were 357 mushroom growers in the United States in the 1995-96 season. That figure has been declining steadily since the end of 1989, when the number peaked at 502. With a growing year extending from July 1 to June 30, the 1994-95 season brought the mushroom industry its highest level of production at 789 million pounds—a value of nearly $760 million. Production tapered off slightly in the 1995-96 season, with yields of 787 million pounds valued at $758 million, an average of 96.3 cents a pound. The USDA estimated that the 1996 per capita consumption rate was 3.9 pounds per person, of which fresh mushrooms accounted for slightly over half the total. Approximately 99 percent of these mushrooms were of the *Agaricus* variety. Agaricus mushrooms—which include Brown, Portabella, and Crimini mushrooms—generated $773.5 million in sales for 1998, and the crop weighed in at 808.6 million pounds. Nearly half the Agaricus mushrooms grown in the United States come from Pennsylvania, which produced 353 million pounds in the 1995-96 season. California ranks second with 131 million pounds.

Production of specialty mushrooms for the 1997-98 season totaled 9.5 million pounds, and had a value of about $26.8 million. The two most common types of specialty mushrooms are shiitake and oyster mushrooms. The sale of 5.5 million pounds of shiitake mushrooms totaled slightly over $20 million during 1994-95. Almost 2 million pounds of oyster mushrooms, valued at $4.5 million, were sold that same year.

The top two companies in the industry as of 1999 were Monterey Mushrooms, Inc. of Santa Cruz, California, with $160 million in sales; and Vlasic Farms, Inc. of Blandon, Pennsylvania, with $150 million in sales.

In the 1990s, the trend in the mushroom industry has moved toward lower prices, due to an increased supply of fresh mushrooms. Production efficiency allows growers to harvest about 5.75 pounds per square foot. This trend was temporarily reversed in 1993 because of production problems, accompanied by minor labor disputes in Pennsylvania and the closure of one major producer. For the last few years, exports of fresh mushrooms have amounted to between 15 and 18 million pounds annually. In 1997, China, Indonesia, and India imported the most U.S. canned mushrooms, respectively.

Early in 1993, the National Mushroom Research and Promotion Act was passed. Under the act, producers and importers of fresh mushrooms with sales of at least 500,000 pounds can be assessed up to one cent per pound by the Mushroom Council to be used in generic promotion and research.

FURTHER READING

U.S. Department of Agriculture. National Agricultural Statistics Service. ''Statistics of Fruits, Tree Nuts, and Horticultural Specialties.'' Washington, D.C.: 2000. Available from http://www.usda.gov/nass/pubs.

U.S. Department of Agriculture. ''Vegetables and Specialties.'' Washington, D.C.: 22 November 1996. Available from http://usda.mannlib.cornell.edu/reports.

SIC 0191

GENERAL FARMS, PRIMARILY CROP

This industry classification is comprised of establishments deriving at least half the value of their total agricultural sales from crops, but less than 50 percent of the sales are from the products of any single, three-digit industry group. Crop farms deriving 50 percent or more of their total agricultural sales from products classified within a single three-digit grouping are classified according to that grouping.

Specified three-digit classifications are: 011 cash grains (wheat, rice, corn, and soybeans); 013 field crops (cotton, tobacco, sugarcane, sugar beets, and potatoes); 016 vegetables and melons; 017 fruits and tree nuts (berries, grapes, citrus and tree fruits such as apples, cherries, peaches, and pears); and 018 horticultural specialties (ornamental and nursery products and food crops grown under cover such as mushrooms and bean sprouts).

NAICS Code(s)

111998 (All Other Miscellaneous Crop Farming)

Industry Snapshot

Farming has long been one of the staple industries in the U.S. economy, and by the end of the twentieth century, the United States was the world leader in crop harvesting. Like many industries, crop farming was in the midst of rapid consolidation in the late 1990s, in which large agribusiness firms increasingly took the place of smaller family farms, resulting in reduced employment levels as farms try to boost efficiency to remain competitive.

The total land in farms in the United States has fallen about 6 percent since the early 1990s, with the largest portion of this decline in cropland, indicative of the trend toward fewer smaller and medium-sized farms and an increase in those farms with more than 5,000 acres. About 1.66 million farms contained harvested cropland, according to the *1997 Census of Agriculture*, amounting to more than 431 million acres, or 46 percent of all farmland in the United States. About half of all these farms derived less than $10,000 in market value from their farm commodities, while only 8 percent garnered more than $250,000. The total market value of agricultural crops sold in 1997 reached $98 billion. Nearly half of this total was derived from various grains, of which the largest portion came from corn for grain, which brought sales of $46.6 billion. Other major crops included soybeans, with $15.62 billion in revenues; fruits, nuts, and berries, with $12.7 billion; vegetables, with $8.82 billion; wheat, with $7.17 billion; cotton and cottonseed, with $5.98 billion; other grains, with $2.97 billion; and tobacco, with $2.924 billion.

Despite dismal commodity prices through the late 1990s, overall farming business has managed to remain fairly stable. In 1999 net income for the U.S. farm industry was $44.6 billion, just below 1990's average of $45.5 billion. One of the major causes of the slight decline was the severe drought that ravaged the northeast region's farming in 1999. Meanwhile, U.S. wheat consumption declined by about 5 million bushels in 1999, when consumption totaled 910 million bushels. However, much of the overall stability was maintained by the higher margins enjoyed by the larger agribusiness firms; thus the farming industry's steady income was small consolation for the average small farmer.

General crop farms accounted for 44,597 of the nation's 1.9 million farms in 1997 and harvested a total 27.2 million acres. The average size of a general crop farm was 609 acres, higher than the average for all U.S. farms (487 acres) and for all crop farms (259 acres). The market value of all commodities produced by general crop farmers was approximately $7 billion, for an average of $156,737 per farm. The vast majority of this total was derived from crops, although general crop farmers also received $924 million from livestock and related products.

In addition to battling chronically low agricultural-commodity prices in the late 1990s, farmers faced a host of challenges relating to environmental and health concerns. As consumers and regulators placed heightened emphasis on water and land conservation and the minimization of pollutants, many farmers have rapidly attempted to reorganize their production to become more environmentally sound. Moreover, concern was on the rise over the presence of chemicals in foods, forcing farmers to rethink their pest- and quality-control practices. Finally, the practice of genetically modifying seeds and foods has generated national and international controversy relating to environmental, economic, health, and ethical concerns.

Organization and Structure

In 1997 86 percent of farms classified in the industry were owned by sole proprietors. Nine percent were organized as partnerships. Two percent were family corporations, and about two percent were held by non-family corporations. The remainder were operated by other entities such as cooperatives, institutions, and estates. These statistics were comparable to the ownership structure for all U.S. farms.

Farm operators were classified by their ownership interest in the land. Full owners owned the land they operated; part owners operated part of their own land and rented the remaining land; tenants rented the land they worked. Sixty percent of all general crop farms were predominantly operated by full owners, while partners operated 30 percent and tenants ten percent.

Background and Development

European colonists learned about cultivating plants indigenous to the United States, developed an agricultural industry, and modified it to suit their own needs. European settlers brought horses and oxen to the continent and put them to work as draft animals. They imported seeds and introduced wheat, rice, barley, oats, rye, and buckwheat. In areas with rich soil, abundant production soon surpassed local demand, and, during the seventeenth century, exports were used to finance imports of manufactured goods. Crop production varied by area; in New York, Pennsylvania, New Jersey, and Delaware, farmers were primarily grain producers. In addition to grains, farmers in Maryland, Virginia, and North Carolina grew tobacco and vegetables. Rice and indigo were the main crops in South Carolina and Georgia. Commercial production of indigo, which had prospered under British rule because of preferential trade treatment, ceased following the Revolutionary War. Cotton was not fully developed as a commercial crop until later.

Colonies were generally forbidden to trade with countries other than their ''mother'' country. English colonies traded only with England; Dutch colonies traded only with Holland; Spanish colonies traded only with Spain; and French colonies traded only with France. This type of trade restriction was one of the contributing factors leading to the Revolutionary War.

Events surrounding the war's conclusion set the stage for the development of farming practices within the United States. Under the terms of the peace treaty signed in 1783, England surrendered its claim to the colonies and its claim to an additional 237 million acres located west of the Ohio River. The original 13 states agreed that the western territory would be held in public domain by the federal government for the purpose of distributing it equitably to settlers.

The process of selling units of western land to farmers began in 1785, two years before the Constitution was adopted. Under the terms of the Land Survey Ordinance, lands were portioned off into townships containing 36 sections of 640 acres (one square mile per section). These were further subdivided into 16 units. Farmers could purchase up to four units, equaling one-quarter section (a total of 160 acres), at one dollar per acre. Within 10 years of the end of the Revolutionary War, an estimated 100,000 settlers had begun farming in the Ohio River valley and the Cumberland River valley.

Farmers who moved west often left depleted soils in the east. Overproduction of single crops such as cotton or tobacco drained the land of the nutrients needed to maintain soil fertility. Thomas Jefferson was a leader against the practice of single-crop agriculture. He believed that farms should be diversified and self-sufficient. His experiments with crop rotation and botanical research made significant contributions to the nation's agricultural industry. Jefferson also developed an improved ''moldboard'' to improve plowing efficiency. (A moldboard was the part of a plow that turned the soil.) To help farmers share agricultural knowledge, agricultural societies were formed.

A major innovation occurred at the end of the eighteenth century when Eli Whitney invented the cotton gin, a mechanical device able to separate cotton fibers from cotton seeds. The combination of the cotton gin and slave labor made cotton a profitable crop for plantation-style agriculture. Another crop grown on plantations was tobacco. As the South increased its reliance on single-crop, nonfood agriculture, it became dependent on imports from other regions for food.

The nineteenth century opened with new opportunities for farming in America. The United States purchased the Louisiana Territory in 1803, opening up possibilities for new settlers from the Mississippi Delta to the Dakotas. The century also brought a mechanical revolution to farming. John Lane introduced the all-steel plow. Cyrus McCormick invented the horse-drawn reaper, a device able to harvest more than ten acres per day—a four-fold increase over what a skilled worker could harvest. McCormick's reaper was first built in 1831 and patented in 1834. Other nineteenth century farm machinery developments included two-row corn planters, combines, threshing machines, and hay balers.

As the nation's infrastructure developed, the ability to transport western farm products to eastern markets improved. The number of settlers moving west increased and demand for western land intensified. The Preemption Act of 1841 allowed squatters the right to purchase up to 160 acres at $1.25 per acre. The Swampland Act of 1849 was designed to create more cultivatable land by draining swamps.

Cotton and tobacco continued to make major contributions to the country's economy. In 1850 almost half of all U.S. exports were cotton shipments headed for English textile mills. In 1859 U.S. tobacco growers harvested 430 million pounds, a 106 percent increase over a ten-year period. In 1860 approximately 60 percent of the nation's working population was involved in the farming industry. Their efforts brought a steady increase of U.S. agricultural products to the world marketplace.

The Civil War disrupted farming, particularly in the South where plantations were devastated and the region's economy ground to a halt. According to J. J. McCoy in *To Feed a Nation,* the cash value of southern plantations fell by 48 percent between 1860 and 1870. The post-Civil War years in the South saw an increase in the numbers of tenant farmers and an increase in the number of diversified farms as the region made an attempt to improve its production of food.

During the Civil War, several major agricultural initiatives were undertaken. On May 15, 1862, President Abraham Lincoln signed legislation creating the U.S. Department of Agriculture (USDA). Also in 1862, the Homestead Act was implemented. Under its provisions, heads of households could receive up to 160 acres of publicly held property, for a filing fee of $10, if they farmed it for five years.

In 1877 the Desert Land Act provided another means by which settlers could receive land. The act required that lands received be irrigated. It also recognized that arid land was less productive than other types of land and, as a result, permitted people to acquire up to 640 acres. In 1887 the Hatch Experiment Station Act was passed to fund agriculture experiments and investigations in all states and territories. In 1889 the USDA was promoted to the level of a cabinet office and began publishing its *Yearbook of Agriculture.* In 1898 the USDA established an office for the systematic introduction of foreign plants. The long-standing governmental policy of converting publicly held lands to private hands was challenged in the 1890s by a Conservation Movement. Under the influence of conservationists, the government started setting aside public lands to preserve forests and watersheds.

During the first decades of the twentieth century, U.S. farmers prepared for war in Europe. Government pronouncements encouraged the production of excess food in anticipation of heavy export possibilities. Farmers expanded operations and put more land under cultivation. When the United States entered the war, labor shortages intensified the development of costly labor-saving machinery. High commodity prices during the war years led to high profits for farmers. Following the war, however, European nations had no money with which to buy American products. The export market failed to meet expectations, and U.S. farmers were forced to sell surplus crops at low prices.

During the 1920s, the U.S. farming industry endured a time of crisis. In 1922, for an average farmer, the estimated cost of growing a bushel of oats was more than the sale price. Between 1922 and 1927, an estimated one million people left farms in search of other work. Small farmers could not afford to purchase the labor-saving machinery necessary to reduce their costs or buy expensive improved seeds to improve per acre yields. In addition, share croppers and tenant farmers, unable to make use of modern farming methods, relied on traditional methods, which caused damage to the soil and further reduced crop yields. As a result, poor farmers became poorer, and soil depletion problems worsened, particularly in the South and the Southwest. Soil erosion led to dust storms that were exacerbated by drought conditions. In Kansas, Missouri, and Oklahoma, the topsoil blew away, resulting in the Great Dust Bowl. Throughout the 1930s, federal efforts were aimed at improving the farmers' economic plight and preserving the nation's soil.

With war again brewing in Europe, farmers once more were encouraged to expand production in anticipation of increased demand for U.S. products abroad. In a series of events paralleling those of the World War I era, heavy demand existed during the war years and exports plummeted following the war. Farm surpluses once more led to declining crop prices and difficult economic conditions for farmers. In 1948 Congress passed the Agricultural Adjustment Act, which included price supports for farm products.

Despite the economic turmoil, technological advances for the farming industry continued. The 1950s and 1960s brought expanded reliance on machinery. By 1955, sprinkler irrigation systems were being used on two million acres. A mechanical tomato harvester was developed in 1959. Tractor sales increased, and the development of a tractor-mounted electric generator enabled farmers to use electricity in remote areas.

Traditional plowing methods were blamed for fostering soil erosion. During the late 1980s, researchers estimated that four billion tons of soil were lost every year to erosion. Although crop management practices aimed at reducing soil losses by reducing or eliminating plowing had been under investigation since the 1930s, they did not become feasible until the development of chemical weed control methods during the 1960s. During the fuel crises of the 1970s, farmers began to look more favorably on the possibility of eliminating plowing.

The advent of giant machinery transformed the farming industry. Large machines required large areas to operate efficiently. In addition, they needed uniform conditions. As a result, small and mid-sized diversified commercial farms became less profitable. Owners found it necessary to supplement their incomes with non-farm work. Some sold family farms to larger entities. According to a USDA estimate, five to eight percent of all farmers left farming in 1985. By 1997 the farm population totaled 5.02 million, representing only 1.9 percent of the total U.S. population.

As the number of farms in the United States fell, the average number of acres per farm increased. Between 1970 and 1980, average farm size grew from 374 acres to 426 acres. By 1997 it stood at 487 acres. Total acreage in farms overall, however, decreased. In 1970 the nation's farms totaled 1.1 billion acres; in 1980, only one billion acres were classified as farmland and, in 1990, the total had dropped further to 960 million acres. By 1997 U.S. farmland totaled 931.79 million acres.

Current Conditions

The farming industry in the late 1990s was plagued by the lowest commodity prices in decades. This trend was especially harmful to small farmers, who require a greater percentage of their budget to move products to market. By 1999, however, the entire industry was growing desperate. Corn output that year totaled 1.47 billion bushels, marking the third-largest single-year drop (about 3 percent) in U.S. history. The drought that hit the American northeast that summer exacerbated the problem. Profits, meanwhile, continued their decade-long decline. According to USDA reports, only 23 cents of every dollar spent on food represented farm value. The largest component cost of food was labor (38 cents), a figure that rose 4 cents during the 1990s. Other costs included packaging (8.5 cents), transportation, machinery, depreciation, advertising, fuels, taxes, and interest.

One reason for low farm profits was the existence of a surplus for many farm commodities. The Federal Agriculture Improvement and Reform Act of 1996 (FAIR), also known as the Freedom to Farm Act, was designed to help alleviate surpluses in traditional crops—such as corn and soybeans—by encouraging farmers to diversify into new crops. Congress drafted the bill to encourage U.S. producers to become more market-oriented in operations and not rely as heavily on government supports, subsidies, and planning. This new legislation marked the beginning of the gradual departure of government from farming and planting decisions. FAIR called for the elimination of price supports after 2002, with price support payments decreasing over the years leading up to 2002.

While this law was always a thorn in the side of small farmers and populist farming organizations for reducing government programs to aid farmers, generally to the advantage of large agribusiness firms, the Freedom to Farm Act has met with increasing calls for reexamination from the latter groups as the slumping commodities prices began to eat into profit margins. The American Farm Bureau Federation in 1999 voted to reexamine Freedom to Farm, seeking greater crop and revenue insurance and assistance programs. The House of Representatives Agriculture Committee was expected to hold hearings in 2000 regarding changes to the act. It was widely expected that the Freedom to Farm Act would be overhauled before its provisions were to expire in 2002.

Despite Freedom to Farm, the U.S. farming industry still relies heavily on governmental subsidies. In 1999 the U.S. government made $38 billion in farm subsidy payments. Intense lobbying also brought $7.4 billion in relief aid in the fall to help farmers recover from the drought.

In addition to facing economic challenges, the agricultural industry found itself under increasing criticism regarding environmental concerns. One issue regarded water conservation, as environmentalists spearheaded efforts to reduce consumption levels. A total of 279,442 farms, covering 55.06 million acres, utilized irrigated land in 1997. This represented 15 percent of all farmland. More than 50 million acres of this total was on harvested cropland. The average crop farm irrigated 197 acres in 1997, up from 159 acres a decade earlier. Although innovations in irrigation systems helped lessen water requirements, some people claimed that irrigating crops was depleting the nation's fresh water supply. Greater empha-

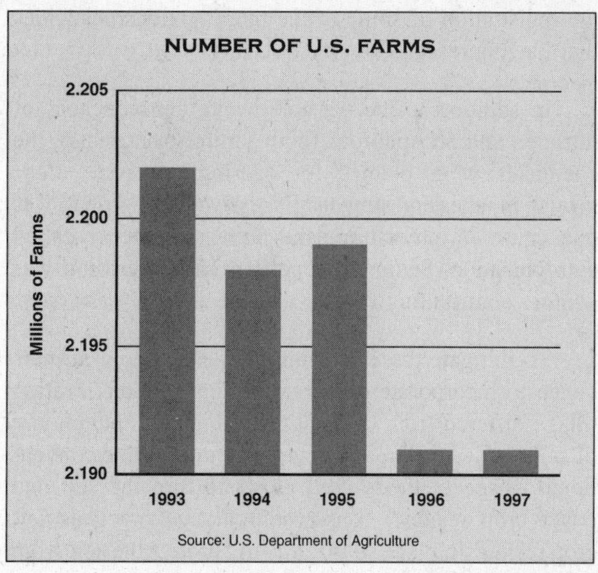

sis on efficiency led to positive developments; however; between 1982 and 1997, the rate of erosion by water on U.S. croplands was reduced by 24 percent.

Farms were also blamed for polluting water supplies. Contamination resulted from discharges of chemicals used in pesticides and fertilizers and sediment from soil erosion. Some critics estimated that as much as 80 percent of the nitrogen and phosphorous in the nation's fresh water supplies came from agricultural run-off. An estimated 55 percent of impaired river miles and 58 percent of impaired lake acres were attributed to agricultural run-off. In addition to surface water, ground water supplies were impacted. One study estimated that half of the nation's drinking water wells contained detectable levels of nitrate. Nitrate levels higher than those recommended by the Environmental Protection Agency (EPA) were found in 2.4 percent of rural private domestic wells and 1.2 percent of community water systems.

In an effort to alleviate the problem, some farms installed grass waterways to catch sediments and to filter phosphorous and pesticides out of run-off. Catch basins were sometimes used to help control the flow of water from irrigation systems. Researchers also investigated ways to reduce nitrate contamination of ground water supplies by improving plants' ability to use nitrogen. Fertilizer application methods were also under review. In addition to FAIR, President Clinton also signed the Federal Insecticide, Fungicide, and Rodenticide Act (FIFRA) and the Federal Food, Drug, and Cosmetic Act (FFDCA) into law in 1996. These acts require the EPA to set tolerance levels for pesticide residue on fresh and processed foods. The former act regulates the manufacturing, sale, and use of pesticides, while the latter governs pesticide residues. The EPA must also register all new farm chemicals and re-register all old pesticides, denying the registration of some of the more noxious pesticides that have unreasonable effects.

In addition to the possible health consequences of nitrogen and phosphorous (both fertilizer nutrients), the chemicals were blamed for causing excessive algae growth in lakes and streams. Excessive algae growth was one cause of premature lake aging, a process called eutrophication. Sediment deposit from soil erosion was another contributing factor.

To mitigate these growing problems, many farmers began to incorporate conservation tillage. Conservation tillage differed from conventional tillage by the amount of soil surface covered with crop residue. While conventional tillage methods used plows to turn the soil and cover crop residue, conservation tillage practices left crop residue in place so that it could protect the soil from excessive wind and water erosion. Crop residue also helped retain moisture and reduce the need for irrigation. Although conservation tillage methods were effective in helping reduce soil erosion, they typically required specialized equipment and relied on chemical herbicides to control weeds. The principal methods of conservation tillage used during the early 1990s were called no-till, ridge-till, strip-till, and mulch-till (also called reduced-till). No-till leaves the soil undisturbed from harvest to planting, with the exception of periodic nutrient injections; weed control is accomplished primarily with herbicides. Ridge-till conservation tillage likewise leaves the soil undisturbed save for nutrient injections, while weed control is handled either by herbicides or cultivation; ridges are rebuilt during conservation. Finally, mulch-till disturbs the soil just prior to planting. No-till practices left the most plant residue on the soil and reduced soil losses by more than 75 percent. Other conservation tillage methods varied in effectiveness but generally reduced soil losses by 50 to 75 percent. Some type of conservation tillage was utilized on 109.8 million acres in 1997, while an additional 40 million acres were farmed in narrow strips to help prevent erosion.

Another area of conflict between farmers and environmentalists concerned the use of wetlands. During the early years of the twentieth century, the USDA promoted a policy of transferring wetlands to private ownership. USDA-endorsed programs were aimed at draining swamps and ''reclaiming'' land for cultivation purposes. During the mid 1970s, the USDA revised its policies concerning wetlands. In 1985 the Food Security Act defined wetlands based on soil and vegetation types and stopped price support payments to farmers who continued converting wetlands to crop lands. The American Farm Bureau Federation, lobbying on behalf of its member farmers, successfully opposed more restrictive federal wetlands regulations in 1989. By 1997 255,410 farms totaling 29.49 million acres were protected under Conservation Reserve or Wetland Reserve Programs.

Not all farmers, however, were opposed to the efforts of the environmental movement. Some favored alternative agricultural methods relying on crop rotations to disrupt the reproductive cycles of weeds, insects, and crop diseases. Alternative agriculture, also called organic or natural, was a labor-intensive practice, and such crops were typically more expensive than those produced on farms employing traditional forms of cultivation.

Many general crop farmers have been successful in finding their niche in the growing organic-foods industry. Targeting customers concerned with the health and environmental risks associated with chemicals, pesticides, and genetically modified foods, the organics sector has emerged from specialty health stores and a fringe customer base to assume a significant position in the mainstream consumer market. Organic agricultural products constituted the fastest-growing sector of the farming industry during the 1990s, with annual sales of $5 billion in the United States by 1999. Organic farmers eschew the synthetic chemicals and gene-tampering technologies many farmers use to boost yields and create more productive livestock. To qualify as organic, crops must be completely free of such chemicals, a fact that demands organic farmers to plan carefully far in advance to ensure appropriate planting patterns. Organic crops must be maintained on land that is free from any chemical infiltration, including soil and water supplies. Because of the greater risk and investment required, organic farming is a more costly undertaking than non-organic farming, and thus organic commodities fetch a higher price at the market.

One of the hottest issues relating to agriculture in the late 1990s was the use of biotechnology to genetically alter seeds in order to boost yields or enhance food quality. More than 40 genetically engineered crops were developed between 1995 and 1999, while the amount of farmland devoted to such crops continued increased tenfold, reaching 76 million acres. About 37 percent of corn and nearly half of all soybeans incorporated biotech engineering. For many years, such crops were used primarily in livestock feeds, though that was changing by the end of the 1990s, when such products were increasingly being sold directly to consumers.

One reason for the turn toward biotechnology in crop production is the realities of demographics and geography. While the world population is expected to surpass the 10 billion mark by 2030, analysts project that farmers could face a severe shortage of adequate farmland. As a result, the ability to boost yields and limit pest infestation has increasingly become a priority. However, biotech alteration is also emblematic of the trend toward consolidation within the farming industry, as bigger farms attempt to produce more for less input in order to remain competitive.

While proponents of genetically modified food technology contend that its use will lead to benefits for producers and consumers alike in the form of greater yield, lower costs, and higher-quality products, criticism has been widespread, emanating from environmental activists decrying the polluting effects of soil and water; health monitors concerned about the safety to humans of genetically modified food consumption; and consumer advocates and small farmers worried about the potential monopoly power wielded by large agribusiness concerns working with biotechnology firms.

Environmentalists and industry analysts further warn that the continued use of such powerful pest-control mechanisms will effectively result in the breeding of more powerful, and more resistant, ''super pests.'' These fears were acknowledged by the technology's leading industry proponents, who insisted that, for that reason, the technology must be more rapidly developed and implemented in order to stay a few steps ahead of the pest evolution.

Small farmers were most particularly concerned with the rising use of technology designed to manufacture seeds that are sterile. Farmers have always saved seeds at the end of the year's crop harvest for use in the following year's planting. By introducing destructive toxins that render the seeds sterile, companies' genetically modified seeds are often engineered to be usable only once, thus forcing farmers to repurchase seeds from the manufacturers every year. In addition to the potential health hazards posed by these toxins, the degree of control this practice could afford seed suppliers has many farmers concerned. Moreover, biotechnology firms increasingly insist on legal agreements with farmers that those seeds that are fertile be used only once, a move that has hardly been popular among farmers.

Concerns about genetically modified food were for many years far more widespread in Europe and Japan than in the United States. By the end of the 1990s, that was still true, but the margin was diminishing rapidly. Many large U.S. firms have noticed this trend and fear the potential economic damage they could sustain by over-investing in a product line that consumers come to avoid. As a result, some farmers have announced that they were placing restrictions on the genetic modification of crops while they wait to see how negative public opinions eat into the market for such foods.

Farmers have begun, especially in 1999, to take advantage of electronic commerce on the World Wide Web to market their products. Web sites acting as bulletin boards as well as online auction sites took off in the late 1990s, affording farmers a relatively cost-effective way to take their products to market and purchase necessities such as agricultural chemicals. By the end of 1999, however, Internet access was mainly concentrated among the largest farm operations; only 29 percent of all U.S. farms were online, but more than half of that figure was derived from farms with annual sales of more than $250,000. At any rate, the Internet is viewed by analysts as an indispensable aspect of farming's future, likely to spur an increased trend toward specialty niche crops with significant value-added properties.

INDUSTRY LEADERS

One of California's largest agricultural companies, Sun World International, a division of the water and agricultural resources firm Cadiz, Inc., was one of the leading general crop farm operations in the late 1990s. Established in 1976 and headquartered in Coachella, California, the firm quickly became one of the leading producers of a range of commodities, including carrots, green onions, cantaloupes, and seedless watermelons. Sun World was an innovator in growing and marketing unique crop varieties, relying on selective breeding programs to develop branded produce; by the late 1990s, the company operated the world's largest fruit-breeding programs. Sun World farmed about 14,000 acres of agricultural crops.

Sun World provided 75 different products to markets in all 50 states and more than 30 countries. It was noted for its many alliances with academic and research organizations aimed at the enhancement and modification of its breeding programs.

WORKFORCE

Employment in the U.S. farming industry has been declining rapidly for many years. About 2.2 million people worked in farming in 1997, down from 2.8 million in 1994. Over the longer term, the drop is even more dramatic; in 1950, the farming industry employed 9.9 million. Moreover, increasing numbers of farm operators supplement their income with other employment. In 1997 only 50.3 percent of all farmers claimed farming as their principle occupation; more than 60 percent of farm operators supplemented their income with other employment.

Career opportunities included jobs in production, processing, and marketing. Wages varied widely according to the size and structure of the farm, the nature of the job held, and the education level of the employee.

The most common job in the farming industry was hired farm labor, the majority of whom were field laborers. A total of 1.29 million individuals were hired farm laborers in 1999, of whom about 1 million were hired directly by farm operators. Eighty-five percent of hired laborers were men, while 52.0 percent were white, 42.0 percent were Hispanic, and 5.5 percent were African-American. The average hired worker earned $7.77 per hour in 1999, though among field laborers, the average dropped to $7.31. The average workweek totaled 42.5 hours of labor. Part-time workers accounted for 17 percent of hired farm labor.

Farm operators contracted to hire an average of about 300,000 workers per month in 1998. Farm labor contractors met with a great deal of criticism in the 1990s by those claiming that they allow farmers to sidestep labor laws and depress wages.

America and the World

Although the United States contains less than seven percent of the land in the world, the country produced 13 percent of the world's farm commodities. The U.S. Department of Agriculture estimated that the United States controls 47 percent of the world market for soybeans, 19 percent of the world's cotton, 12 percent of all wheat, and 36 percent of the world's corn.

The leading crop exports for U.S. farmers include coarse grains, with exports of $9.3 billion in 1997; soybeans, with $6.3 billion; wheat, with $6.9 billion; and cotton, with $3 billion in exports. Significant trading partners included Japan ($11.7 billion), Canada ($6.1 billion), and Mexico ($5.4 billion). The North American Free Trade Agreement (NAFTA) has been responsible for increasing trade among the United States, Canada, and Mexico. Other major export markets were in western Europe ($8.2 billion), Asia ($14.8 billion), and Latin America ($10.5 billion).

The United States also imported about $2.6 billion in grain and feeds, while other leading import commodities included those that were not grown or could not be grown domestically, such as fruits and nuts, coffee, cocoa, vegetables, and grain.

In addition to regular sales of agricultural production, the U.S. government funded exports of food under its Food for Peace program. The Food for Peace program began in 1959 and provided food items from U.S. surplus production to developing nations.

According to some industry forecasters, the demand for U.S. products on the global market would decline as other nations developed their own farming industries. Low labor costs in some countries were expected to enable them to produce crops more cheaply than could be accomplished in the United States. In addition, improved technology, such as the availability of advanced irrigation systems, was improving the ability of some countries to grow crops. For example, Saudi Arabia achieved self-sufficiency in wheat production using a center-pivot irrigation system. Thus, U.S. producers expected to face increased competition as more countries entered the trade market and improved their agricultural conditions at home. However, as consolidation of farming grows, highly leveraged agribusiness firms are likely to wield greater influence on the world market. Moreover, as land availability diminishes and genetically modified crops take on heightened priority, the globalization of farming will likely help major U.S. players. One of the central tasks of U.S. officials is the strengthening of accords relating to intellectual property rights to be enforced by the World Trade Organization. Such provisions would grant patent control to developers and owners of GM technology, thereby allowing them to charge other businesses for the use of such technology.

Research and Technology

Historically, technological advances in the agricultural industry focused on increasing land productivity and reducing labor costs. The mechanical revolution in farming, which began during the nineteenth century, accelerated through the middle of the twentieth century. For example, to produce one acre of corn in 1850, it took approximately 30 to 35 hours using draft animals, a walking plow, and hand planting procedures. In 1930 it took approximately six to eight hours using horses and early tractors. In 1995 the same task took two and a half hours using a tractor, a 5-bottom plow, a 25-foot tandem disk, a planter, an herbicide applicator, and a combine. Increasing crop yields also reduced the amount of land necessary to meet the nation's per capita food and fiber needs from about four acres in 1900 to less than two by 1995.

During the latter part of the twentieth century, however, the focus of agricultural research shifted to environmental issues. Pesticides (such as DDT) and herbicides (such as 2,4,5-T) were criticized for their potential negative human health consequences. Researchers intensified their efforts to produce less toxic alternatives.

Computer technology was also being used to bring about agricultural advancements. Geographic information systems (GIS), computer modeling and simulation, and fertilizer- and irrigation-monitoring systems were among the many computer-based systems that were popular with farmers in the late 1990s. One of the primary functions of such technology was to help increase farm profitability through the reduction of resource use. GIS, which combines farm-positioning sensors, aerial photography, and farm-equipment sensors, was particularly poised as a primary tool by which farmers can analyze the myriad factors and data necessary for farmers to most efficiently utilize their land, boost yields, and cut down on resource consumption. The accumulated information affords farmers the ability to analyze specific factors, such as soil nutrients, in particular plots of land on their farms, thus enabling them to make effective decisions about water allocation, fertilizer application, crop selection, pest control, and so on. Moreover, computer-based precision irrigation systems monitor crops to ensure that they receive the appropriate amount of water, which can be applied automatically when the system deems it necessary.

The 1996 Freedom to Farm Act put an end to the long-standing farm subsidy through which the farming industry benefited from the government-developed satellite mapping systems. Farmers used these systems to aid in the selection of farmland for qualities such as richness of soil and the availability of resources such as water. Because farmers, under Freedom to Farm, are no longer required to report acreage and planting patterns to the Department of Agriculture, the government's aerial photo-mapping system was rendered obsolete. The larger agribusiness farms were expected to take over this role, providing this much-needed service to the farming industry for a fee.

FURTHER READING

"Are Bio-Foods Safe?" *Business Week,* 20 December 1999.

Farm Facts. Park Ridge, IL: American Farm Bureau, 1997. Available from http://www.fb.org/today/farmfacts.

"Forage Production Continues to Dominate Ag Land Use." *Feedstuffs,* 11 October 1999.

Holmberg, Mike. "Confronting the Backlash: The Push for Segregation is Leading to New Efforts to Promote GMOs." *Successful Farming,* January 2000.

"Is the Sun Setting on Farmers? Many Can't Survive the 'New Agriculture'." *New York Times,* 28 November 1999.

Mirasol, Feliza. "Bioengineered Foods Gain Wider Acceptance in the U.S." *Chemical Market Reporter,* 6 September 1999.

McCoy, J.J. *To Feed a Nation.* Camden, NJ: Thomas Nelson, 1971.

Philips, Jim. "Changes Coming for Freedom to Farm?" *Progressive Farmer,* 18 January 1999.

Philips, Jim. "'Reexamining' Freedom to Farm." *Progressive Farmer,* 18 January 1999.

Philips, Jim. "To Rewrite the Farm Bill." *Progressive Farmer,* 4 January 2000.

"Price Pressure on Major Field Crops to Continue in 1999/2000." *Frozen Food Digest,* October 1999.

Schulman, Richard D. "Modern Technology Meets Traditional Farm Practices." *Geo Info Systems,* February 1997.

Tai, Nikki. "U.S. Proves Fertile for GM Crops: Use of the Technology is Spreading Rapidly." *Financial Times,* 18 March 1999.

U.S. Department of Agriculture. National Agricultural Statistics Service. *1997 Census of Agriculture.* Washington, D.C.: 1999.

U.S. Department of Agriculture. National Agricultural Statistics Service. *Farm Labor.* Washington, D.C.: 19 November 1999.

"Wheat Export Forecast Lowered." *Milling & Baking News,* 14 December 1999.

SIC 0211

BEEF CATTLE FEEDLOTS

This classification covers establishments primarily engaged in the fattening of beef cattle in a confined area for a period of at least 30 days, on their own account or on a contract or fee basis. Feedlot operations that are an integral part of the breeding, raising, or grazing of beef cattle are classified in **SIC 0212: Beef Cattle, Except Feedlots.** Establishments that feed beef cattle for less than 30 days, generally in connection with their transport, are classified in **SIC 4789: Transportation Services, Not Elsewhere Classified.**

NAICS CODE(S)

112112 (Cattle Feedlots)

INDUSTRY SNAPSHOT

The grain-growing region of the Midwest dominated the U.S. cattle feeding industry in the 1970s. Huge American grain surpluses caused by government price supports provided cheap food for livestock and made cattle feeding a standard practice in the nation's beef industry. Iowa was the nation's leading cattle feeder during this period, feeding over 4 million head per year, or approximately 20 percent of nation's cattle. Nebraska and Illinois were the other top cattle feeding states in the Midwest. These three states combined with California to account for 62 percent of all fed cattle in the United States.

Across the country a majority of American cattle were fed by small, farmer-owned operations. These farmers used cattle to market their grain. If grain was drawing a satisfactory price, farmers would sell it outright. But if farmers were unsatisfied with the price of corn, barley, or oats, they might market their grain indirectly by feeding it to cattle or hogs. Midwestern feed farmers typically acquired their cattle by attending livestock auctions themselves or by having commission buyers purchase steers or heifers that had been raised and bred by ranchers. The cattle would then be placed in pen lots on the feeders' farms. Small mills on the farms processed the grain used to feed the cattle. For decades this was how the majority of U.S. cattle were "finished." (The "finishing" period was once referred to as "fattening." But as Americans began to limit their fat intake, feeders decided to refer to this stage of the cattle's growth as finishing.)

The geographic center of the cattle feeding industry began to shift from the Midwest to the Southern plains states in 1972. By the 1980s the biggest cattle feeders were located primarily in Texas, Nebraska, Kansas, and Colorado. During the 1990s these four states accounted for over 60 percent of the total beef production annually. Iowa had fallen to fifth place among cattle feeding states by 1999, marketing only about 1 million finished cattle a year, or about 5 percent of the nation's total. This represented a drop for the Iowa cattle feeding business of more than 3 million head since 1970. California and Montana also experienced severe declines in their cattle feeding business, both down more than 25 percent since the 1970s.

Several reasons explain why the nation's cattle feeders moved. First, the Southern plains states provided tax incentives for cattle feeders to leave the Midwest. Second, it was much cheaper to feed and slaughter beef in modern facilities that were located far from large population centers, where wages and land values were high and environmental restrictions were often prohibitive. Third, low transportation costs made shipping boxed beef across the country cheaper than shipping grain to feedlots. Fourth, many cattle feeders in the plains states transformed the grazing land surrounding their feedlots into farmland that grew grain to feed the cattle, increasing the efficiency of their operations and decreasing the need to buy grain from the Midwest. Fifth, several Midwest cattle feeders began focusing their operations on growing corn and soybeans to capitalize on the grain market boom of the 1970s.

Cattle feeding operations also grew larger as they migrated to the plains states. In 1980 small farm feedlots with fewer than 1,000 head accounted for 25 percent of fed cattle sold in the country. By 1997 these feedlots made up only 15 percent of the fed cattle sold. At the same time, the share of cattle in medium (capacity for 16,000 to 31,999 head) and large (capacity for at least 32,000 head) commercial feedlots increased from 43 percent in 1980 to nearly 60 percent in 1997. Large commercial feedlots experienced the largest increase in share, accounting for 35 percent of cattle on feed in 1999 as compared with only 22 percent in 1980. In Kansas the percentage of cattle fed in large feedlots rose to 87 percent in the 1990s, while in Texas it rose to 97 percent. In these and other large cattle feeding states it was not uncommon to see feedlots capable of holding over 100,000 head of cattle at any one time.

Organization and Structure

The feeding of grain to cattle is unique to the United States. Americans and an increasing number of international consumers have developed a taste for American grain-fed beef, as opposed to beef cattle fattened on grass only. The cattle that are fed in U.S. feedlots are young steers and heifers that have been weaned from their mothers, perhaps run on grass for another season or two, and then placed in the feedlot for further finishing. Typically this finishing period lasts between 110 and 150 days, during which the cattle may grow from 800 pounds to 1,250 pounds by eating a ration containing grain, by-products, and hay that gives American beef its unique taste known throughout the world.

Prior to the 1970s farmer feeders would send their "fat" cattle to an auction or terminal market and packers would have representatives there to buy them. But by 1993 less than 7.6 percent of fed cattle were purchased by packers through public auctions. Instead, packers staffed their own buyers, who visited the huge feedlots and perused the "show lists," which are pens containing cattle being sold that week. After settling on a price for particular cattle, buyers then purchased the cattle directly from the feeder.

Because ranchers have been increasing their investment in genetic technology, a growing number of them have been retaining ownership of their cattle from the time they are born until the time they are processed by packers. Owning cattle through the finishing stage allows ranchers to be rewarded directly when their cattle are sold to satisfy packer and consumer demands. Ranchers, however, are more vulnerable than other farmers during market drops. Under retained ownership agreements ranchers can buy feed outright and pay only a yardage charge, pay a set price per pound gain, or pay only for the amount of feed used.

Cattle are pen lotted in a feedlot after being vaccinated. They are lotted by owner, and pen riders check the cattle daily and pull any sick or nonperforming cattle. Some feeders keep feed in front of the cattle at all times, while others feed them twice a day with huge feed trucks that place the feed in bunkers. The feed is mixed either in a large mill or by trucks that mix it while carrying it to the cattle. The ration contains grain, hay, and by-products such as cottonseed and almond hulls. Computers keep track of the amount of grain consumed, the cost of grain, the cattle's daily weight, and the number of days on feed. When the cattle are eventually processed the owner receives a computer report with all of this information.

Cattle are fed by investors, ranchers, or packers, who want to guarantee a steady supply of cattle for their packing plants. Such cattle are referred to as "captive supply." The captive supply generally represents about 20 percent of the cattle on feed at any one time, and the government watches this number as an indicator of packer concentration. When cattle are considered good enough to be graded "Choice," they can be sold in a variety of ways. They might be sold by the pound while the cattle are still alive or they might be sold "in the meat," based on what they weigh when hanging on a packer's rail. The cattle business is currently attempting to achieve "value-based marketing," whereby cattle are priced according to the quality and amount of meat in the carcass rather than by their weight alone. Thus, there is a growing trend toward selling cattle on "grade and yield.'' This strategy helps prevent packers from buying overly fat animals.

BACKGROUND AND DEVELOPMENT

The Corn Belt states have suffered the largest loss of market share. Just as many industrialists left the Rust Belt for the Sun Belt, cattle feeders in 1990s fled the Corn Belt for Texas and the plains states and have been thriving there since. More than half of all beef slaughtered in this country is processed in plants west of the Mississippi River. Most cattle feeding takes place between the western bank of the Mississippi and the eastern slope of the Rocky Mountains in large feedlots that commonly contain more than 50,000 head of cattle.

According to industry analyst Topper Thorpe, beef production continued to concentrate within a 400-mile radius of Grand Island, Nebraska. Where Iowa, Minnesota, and Missouri once fed 17 percent of America's cattle, they accounted for barely 10 percent in the 1990s. The eastern Corn Belt also suffered in the 1990s, as states in that region accounted for just 7 percent of total U.S. fed cattle. Lack of financing hurt farmers throughout the Corn Belt, causing many to go out of business or shift their resources to other endeavors. The Corn Belt also became less environmentally suited to feedlots as population density increased. Additionally, increased federal regulation made the feedlot business more costly and burdensome. Regulations governing water quality, runoff, erosion, and drainage forced many small operators out of business.

Changes in the meat packing industry also helped transform the feedlot business. More than 405 packing plants shut their doors since the mid-1980s. In the 1990s three large corporations controlled nearly 80 percent of U.S. boxed beef production. To be competitive a packing house should process over 500,000 head per year, and most of these superplants relocated to the plains states. If the location of American feedlots were plotted on a map and then dovetailed with an overlay of a map identifying the packing houses, they would form a heart shape covering the nation's midsection. Nebraska, Kansas, Texas, and Colorado have the largest number of processing facilities. They are also the four largest packer states.

CURRENT CONDITIONS

The business aspect of the feedlot industry has become increasingly sophisticated. Most feedlot managers have computers on their desks to check current prices, futures, and the amount of grain consumed on their farms. Advanced communication devices allow managers to track the performance of individual animals from ranch to feedlot to packing plant. Ten years ago tracking individual animals involved a blizzard of paper and a bevy of manpower. Today the job is made easier by computers, electronic identification tags, high-speed data transmission networks, and specialized software. Computers sort the data. Electronic tags track the animals. Software makes the system work. But it is communications devices and data transmission networks that tie the system together by allowing managers to easily access, collect, and share data. Ranchers use the beef quality data from packers to improve herd genetics, while feedlots use the data to decide which ranches best suit their needs.

Cattle feeders hope that this technology increases their profit margins. The feedlot industry returned to profitability in the late 1990s after sagging earlier in the decade. Cheap feed prices in 1999 made it more profitable to fatten cattle than to slaughter them. In August 1999 cattle prices rose 3.4 per cent, while the cost of corn, the main ingredient in livestock feed, rose only 2.2 per cent. Feedlots had faced negative margins since late 1997, with losses accelerating in February 1998 due to the sharp break in fed cattle prices as the domestic market adjusted to larger supplies of higher quality beef than normally would have entered the export market.

Downsizing. Nearly all segments of the beef cattle industry were in a downsizing mode during the 1990s. The consolidation was especially pronounced in the feedlot sector. In the mid-1960s there were 200,000 feedlots scattered around the country. In 1997 that figure had fallen to 110,000 lots. But the largest 2 percent were marketing 95 percent of the nation's fed cattle. Those numbers are not expected to change much in the first few years of the twenty-first century.

The feedlot industry requires individual farmers to invest a great deal of capital in their cattle. A typical steer going on feed costs a cattle feeder over $600, and at least another $200 in costs are incurred during the feeding phase. Consequently, many small cattle feeders teetered on insolvency or went out of business in the 1990s. As the packing industry became concentrated, packers started looking to build fiscally sound strategic alliances with their suppliers. Packers were not inclined to build such alliances with financially unstable smaller feeders. Marketing alternatives for smaller feeders dwindled as fewer fed cattle were marketed at auction. Large feeders were better able to hedge their cattle using futures contracts. The practice of hedging saved many feeders from the wild price swings common to the cattle business. Large diversified companies were also more resilient during lean years than their unvariegated smaller competitors.

Mad Cow Disease. Bovine spongiform encephalopathy (BSE), commonly called ''Mad Cow Disease,'' shocked the beef-eating world in 1986 and culminated in a frenzy in 1995 as producers in the United Kingdom found escalating numbers of afflicted cattle throughout the country. BSE is a fatal disease that affects the central nervous system of cattle. The U.S. Department of Agriculture promptly attempted to allay consumers' concerns by releasing studies showing that no cases of BSE existed in the United States. As a precautionary measure, the United States does not import cattle from countries with reported cases of BSE. Moreover, many scientists contend that the disease is not transmissible through an infected cow's meat or through physical contact.

Nonetheless Texas cattle ranchers sued talk-show host Oprah Winfrey for defamation in 1996, after one of her guests told a national television audience that the cattle industry had potentially exposed Americans to Mad Cow Disease by feeding cows the remains of live animals. Winfrey then exclaimed that her guest had ''just stopped [her] cold from eating another burger!'' The cattle ranchers blamed Winfrey for sagging beef prices, and requested money damages totaling $11 million. Winfrey argued that the dip in cattle prices was caused by high feed costs, oversupply, and low prices of competing meats. In 1998 a federal jury in Amarillo, Texas, sided with the talk-show host.

INDUSTRY LEADERS

In an industry dominated by large corporations, the largest at the end of the twentieth century was Continental Grain. Its home office was located in Chicago, Illinois, but the company owned feedlots in six different states. Continental Grain was capable of feeding 405,000 cattle at one time, and marketing nearly 1 million fed cattle during the course of a year. Like the small farmer feeders, Continental Grain used cattle to market its grain, but on a much larger scale.

Cactus Feeders of Amarillo, Texas, ranked second among U.S. cattle feeders, owning six lots with a capacity for 350,000 head of cattle. ConAgra Cattle Feeding of Greeley, Colorado ranked third, owning four lots with a capacity for feeding 320,000 head. National Farms Inc., of Kansas City, Missouri, ranked fourth, owning seven lots with a capacity for 274,000 head. Caprock Industries (a division of Cargill) of Amarillo, Texas, ranked fifth nationally among cattle feeding businesses, owning four lots with a capacity for feeding 263,000 head of cattle.

J.R. Simplot of Idaho, who had been included on *Forbes* list of the 400 richest men in America, was another leader in the cattle feeding industry. Simplot gained his fortune through potato farming and became one of the largest cattle feeders in the United States. He developed a system of feeding the potato waste from his french fry plants to cattle in his feedlots. Simplot was also one of the largest ranchers in the country.

Some industry leaders such as ConAgra ran both meat packing and feedlot operations. ConAgra fed its cattle in Colorado and Idaho, and was also a major meat packer. ConAgra entered the cattle feeding business to assure a ready supply of cattle for its processing plants. The company's biggest acquisition was the purchase of Monfort of Greeley, Colorado, which had once been among the largest cattle feeders in the country. Monfort was also one of the country's largest lamb packers.

As the feedlot business entered a new millennium, industry experts warned that even some of the leading cattle feeders might be forced to downsize or go out of business. According to industry analyst Topper Thorpe, efficiency would separate the successful cattle feeding operations from those that fell by the wayside. Several recent studies have been released concerning efficiency in the beef industry. In 1997 Idaho researchers released two studies showing that rainbow trout that had been given the cattle hormone bovine somatotropin (BST) grew nearly 70 percent faster and 50 percent more efficiently than untreated fish. Prior to these studies BST had been used to boost milk production in dairy cattle. But the growth hormone is now being studied for its stimulation in beef cattle. In 1998 scientists at the Agricultural Research Service Grazinglands Research Laboratory in El Reno, Oklahoma, released a three-year study showing that beef cattle finish as efficiently on grass pastures with a low grain supplement as they would on a mostly grain diet.

The beef industry as a whole closed the twentieth century on a mixed note. Annual per capita beef consumption declined to about 66 pounds in 1999, after peaking at 87 pounds in 1976. Public perceptions that red meat is less healthy than chicken, turkey, or pork were largely to blame for the fall. Beef has lost much of its market share to pork and poultry, going from 59 percent in 1980 to about 46 percent in 1999. Industry reports predict that by 2004 beef's market share will further drop to 26 percent, pork will advance to 26 percent, and poultry will rise to 47 percent. But beef is still America's favorite source of protein. The United States produced a record amount of beef in 1999. At the same time, consumers were spending $5 per capita more on beef in 1999 than the year before. The beef industry also began a $25 million marketing campaign in 1999. Advertisements reprised the catchy ''Beef: It's what's for dinner'' tag line, and beef companies introduced a host of new products.

FURTHER READING

Bigness, John. ''Beef Industry Tries New Products to Cut into Chicken Sales.'' *Knight-Ridder/Tribune Business News,* 18 June 1999.

National Cattlemen's Association. *Cattle and Beef Handbook.* Englewood, CO: National Cattlemen's Association, 1996.

———. *Facts Machine.* Englewood, CO: National Cattlemen's Association, 1996.

Nicholson, Nancy. ''Plenty of Beef Behind U.S. Drive on Hormones in Meat.'' *Scotsman,* 26 April 1999.

''Questions and Answers about Bovine Spongiform Encephalopathy.'' College Station, TX: Texas A & M University, 1996.

U.S. Bureau of the Census. ''U.S. Bureau of the Census.'' 1999. Available from http://www.census.gov.

U.S. Department of Agriculture. *Ag Statistics, 1995.* Washington, DC: GPO, 1996.

———. ''U.S. Department of Agriculture.'' 1999. Available from http://www.usda.gov.

U.S. Department of Commerce. ''U.S. Department of Commerce.'' 1999. Available from http://www.doc.gov.

SIC 0212

BEEF CATTLE EXCEPT FEEDLOTS

This classification covers establishments primarily engaged in the production or feeding of beef cattle, except feedlots. Establishments primarily engaged in raising dairy cattle are classified in **SIC 0241: Dairy Farms.**

NAICS CODE(S)

112111 (Beef Cattle Ranching and Farming)

INDUSTRY SNAPSHOT

There are 1.06 million independently owned farms and ranches producing beef cattle for breeding and for feeding in the United States. Although dairy farmers produce 20 percent of the beef in this country, that beef is largely a by-product of the milk business and is not included in this industry classification. This category includes all activities of ranchers or beef farmers up to the time their cattle are sent to the feedlot. Issues regarding the operation and management of feedlots are discussed in **SIC 0211: Beef Cattle Feedlots.**

The sale of cattle and calves is the largest segment of the American agricultural economy, which in turn comprises 16 percent of the gross national product. Moreover, sales of cattle and calves account for almost one fifth of the country's farm and ranch cash receipts. Beef cattle are one of the few agricultural commodities produced in all 50 states and the industry comprises more than 1 million businesses.

In some regions of the country, mostly the West, cattle producers are referred to as ranchers and their operations are known as ranches. In parts of the Midwest and the East beef cattle producers are more apt to be called farmers. In 1998, cattle sales totaled almost $36 billion. This represents 18.4 percent of all farm sales that year. By the time the cattle were processed and the beef placed in coolers in retail stores, they generated an additional $5 or $6 for every dollar of beef produced on the farm or ranch. The National Cattlemen's Association estimates that beef cattle contribute slightly less than 1 percent to the total gross domestic product.

Beef has been central to America's dining habits for a long time. Recently, however, poultry has made great strides in eroding that primacy. Much of poultry's popularity has been attributed to lower prices and low fat content. The beef industry has worked hard to produce and promote a leaner product, and cites that one-third of all Americans have eaten some type of ground beef in the past 24 hours. Despite the many advances of the poultry industry, beef surpasses its competitors in both production and sales.

The United States is the largest producer of beef products in the world, although it ranks fourth in total number of beef animals. This high production rate is made possible by the high efficiency of U.S. producers. The United States is the third largest exporter of beef in the world. It is also the largest importer of beef, particularly of ground beef in frozen form. Despite a recent drop in annual beef consumption, U.S. per capita beef consumption ranks third in the world.

Texas has the largest number of beef cows, followed by Kansas, Nebraska, Oklahoma, and Missouri. In 1998, the USDA estimated that there were close to 100 million beef animals in the United States, which produced about 25.6 billion pounds of beef at the retail level. Production methods have changed dramatically since the trail driving days; yet many of the traditions have been preserved.

ORGANIZATION AND STRUCTURE

Because a vast amount of acreage is needed to support beef cows, cattlemen own or manage more land than any other single industry. In the meadows of Montana or the irrigated pastures of California, one acre of land supports a cow and her calf for an entire year. In the deserts of the Southwest, however, an entire section of land, or 640 acres, can support only a handful of cows.

More than 1.2 billion acres of this country are considered agricultural lands by the USDA; this comprises approximately 50 percent of the United States and two-thirds of the contiguous states. Though two-thirds of this land is considered to be grazing land, 90 percent of it is unsuitable for growing commercial crops because of limited rainfall, steep slopes, rocky terrain, or poor soil. Thus, the land can only be used for pasturing beef cattle, sheep, goats, bison, horses, and wild animals.

These grazing lands are ideal for cattle, because the cattle can convert grass and other forages into high-protein food sources. The typical beef cow does not spend a single day in a cattle fattening feedlot, but instead lives on grass and hay her entire life, being retained for breeding and nursing. Her offspring may be fattened in a feedlot for 20 percent of their lives or her female offspring may be kept as replacement females. A typical range cow loses her productivity between the ages of 8 and 10 and must be replaced.

The cow is like a factory for the beef industry: she generates more cattle. Beef cows have a nine-month gestation period and usually give birth to a single calf either in the fall or the spring. These calves are called ''commercial'' cattle as opposed to ''purebreds,'' which are born from both a sire and dame of purebred ancestry. The majority of calves in this country are born in the spring and sold in the fall. The average calf weighs between 80 and 85 pounds at birth and lives on a diet of grass and its mother's milk. The calves run beside their mothers until they are weaned, which usually occurs when the calves are between 6 and 8 months old. At this age, the calves usually weigh between 500 and 550 pounds, though there are significant variations due to management and feed conditions.

While they are still running alongside their mothers, the calves are gathered or rounded up much like they were in the early days of ranching. The calves are then branded by their owners and vaccinated for a variety of diseases. Bull calves are altered or castrated, at which time they are called steers. Steering a bull prevents fighting, accidental breeding with cows and heifer calves, and allows for easier management.

Before the calves are weaned, bulls are turned in with the cows to breed them. Normally, between 80 and 90 percent of the cowherd will be bred successfully. Those cows that don't conceive are referred to as ''open'' and are sold for beef. The bulls that are used are usually purebred cattle in which multigeneration pedigrees have been maintained by a breed association. These bulls are produced by purebred breeders whose sole intent is to provide seedstock for the commercial beef cattle producer. These purebred producers test their cattle for weight gain and meat quality and keep extensive records on their pedigreed livestock. When commercial producers subsequently purchase bulls in the spring or fall of the year, they are aided by a pedigree and by computerized records that indicate how a particular sire's offspring might perform. The price of these commercial bulls usually ranges from $1,500 to $4,000, while the purebred sire that was used to produce them might cost upwards of $20,000. It is not uncommon for a particularly good purebred bull to be syndicated for several hundred thousand dollars or to be purchased by a bull stud. The use of artificial insemination and embryo transfer has become commonplace in the beef cattle industry and has made it possible to use genetics from the best cows to produce several offspring per year instead of a single calf.

When the calves are ready for weaning they can be sold through an auction market or over a satellite video hookup known as a satellite auction. They may also be traded in-country by an order buyer, or the cattlemen may prefer to retain ownership. The calves are then run as ''stockers.'' Stockers go back to feeding on grass until the time they weigh approximately 800 pounds. Other weaned calves may go straight into the feedlot for the final finishing stage and skip the stocker stage completely. As cattlemen continue to improve the genetics in their herds, many calves are weaning in excess of 650 pounds and reaching a finished weight of 1,250 pounds in the feedlot when they're just over one year old.

Many ranchers consider themselves nothing more than grass farmers. Their job is to convert grass to beef as efficiently as possible. Cattle spend between 80 and 100 percent of their lives on grazing lands and have played a role in sustainable agricultural systems for centuries. Their manure and urine naturally fertilize the grasslands and their hoofing action breaks up the crust of the soil. When they are run in the proper manner without overgrazing, cattle play a key role in maintaining soil productivity and keeping forages in a healthy condition. These forages in turn protect soil from wind and water erosion, and leguminous forages, such as alfalfa, add nitrogen to the soil.

Current Conditions

While per capita consumption decreased during the 1980s and 1990s and beef lost market share to poultry, the industry experienced one of the most prolonged profitable periods in its history. This is probably due to the fact that hundreds of thousands of beef producers left the industry during the last downturn in the cattle market. Several factors have been responsible for the decline in beef consumption since 1986.

Competing Meats. Per capita annual boneless beef consumption in the United States stood at 64.7 pounds in 1998. This was down considerably from 1975 when per capita consumption peaked at 95 pounds, yet per capita consumption has stabilized in the 1990s. With ebbs and flows, consumption levels have remained at 62 to 65 pounds, signaling that major declines may be over.

A combination of factors contributed to beef's decline in the late 1980s. Competition from competing meats got the attention of beef producers as poultry challenged beef's position as ''The King of Meats.''In the early 1990s, the poultry industry proudly announced that more chicken was consumed per person in this country than beef. This was the first time in the industry's history that beef was displaced as the most consumed meat in the country, in terms of poundage. Cattlemen like to point out, however, that beef at the retail level is a 94 percent boneless product, while chicken is only 69 percent boneless. On an edible meat basis, therefore, Americans still eat more beef, 64.7 pounds versus 49.2 pounds of chicken in 1998. On a dollar basis the difference is more dramatic. Americans spent $187.91 per person on beef in 1998 compared with $125.16 on pork and $112.50 on chicken. As the largest dollar volume item sold in grocery stores, beef represents more than 6 percent of all grocery store sales. It is estimated that in 1999, Americans consumed 36.5 pounds of beef cuts compared to 27.7 pounds of ground beef.

However, beef producers are still concerned about beef's declining market share. In the late 1980s, for example, cattlemen began to voluntarily assess themselves one dollar per head every time a beef animal was sold and pooled these proceeds toward advertising, research, and education. Much of that money was spent on finding better ways to compete with poultry and seafood.

The War on Fat. After experiencing decades of adulation from the public, the beef industry faced a host of new problems and new adversaries beginning in the early 1980s. The cattle industry was unaccustomed and unprepared for this avalanche of negative publicity. First there was the ''war on fat.'' A Gallup poll in the early 1990s determined that the top dietary concern among consumers was the amount of fat in their food. This caught the beef cattle industry off guard.

American cattle differ from most beef animals produced in the world because they are grain fed. This grain finishing period, which usually lasts around 100 days, is unique to this country. It makes for a better tasting piece of beef, but it also increases the amount of fat in the beef carcass. In surveys of American beef consumers, taste remains the number one reason why they select beef over competing meats. This taste is achieved by intermuscular marbling, the tiny flecks of fat visible to the eye in steaks and roasts. This marbling is what gives beef its flavor and is one of the main criteria used in determining the grade and the price of beef.

Because of the manner in which beef animals distribute fat, intermuscular marbling is the last place where fat is deposited. Before the fat is distributed as intermuscular marbling, it is first deposited on the outside of the animal, visible to the consumer as the outer rind of fat on a piece of steak. Studies sponsored by the Meat Board estimated that the beef industry was producing 2,825 truckloads of fat at 40,000 pounds per load annually. This inefficient production of fat was costing all segments of the industry $4 billion annually. This figure, however, still does not represent the loss of per capita consumption that may have been attributable to fatty beef.

Faced with this dilemma the beef industry declared its own war on fat. Due largely to a program sponsored by commercial beef producers, retailers have reduced the amount of external fat on meat cuts by 27 percent. The fat rind on most cuts is trimmed to one-quarter and even one-eighth of an inch. In some cuts, the fat trim is completely removed.

Commercial cattle producers have also responded by using new genetic enhancements on their cattle. Throughout its history, the U.S. beef industry has relied largely on three breeds of cattle—Angus, Hereford, and Shorthorn. These breeds were of English descent and were introduced to this country when pioneer cattlemen wanted to improve the degree of muscling found in Longhorn cattle.

In their quest to find faster growing and leaner breeds cattlemen looked to Europe for new genetics, and since the 1960s there has been a constant parade of new breeds of beef cattle into the United States. Beginning with the Charolais from France, it is estimated that there have been over 76 different breeds of beef cattle introduced into the United States. Some of these breeds, such as the Charolais, Simmental, and Limousin have made major contributions to the beef industry, while many others were quickly discarded. These breeds from Europe became known as the ''Continental Breeds'' or ''Exotics.'' Although they have not displaced Angus and Hereford as the most popular beef breeds, they are quite commonplace in crossbreeding programs.

It has become the norm in the beef industry to blend the genetics from two or three breeds for maximum heterosis or hybrid vigor. This results in faster growth, increased disease tolerance, and leaner beef. A cattleman, for example, might breed a Hereford bull with an Angus cow and then cross the resulting crossbred female with an exotic breed. Such crosses have become extremely popular and have helped reduce fat.

As fat content has decreased some critics argue that the flavor of beef has suffered. Consequently, beef producers are faced with the challenge of producing animals whose meat has the taste Americans prefer without the fat.

Value Added Products. Beef is still largely sold as a generic product in retail grocery stores, whereas chicken and pork are often sold as ''branded'' products with fancy packaging and attractive labels. The beef industry has struggled with the concept, launching many private label brands with little success. However, the meat packing industry is concentrated in the hands of three major packers who have shown a reluctance to enter the branded meat business. This factor has also contributed to the decrease in the per capita consumption of beef.

Several breed associations have attempted to market a branded product with their breed name on the package. In many cases they have backed up the labels with extensive advertising programs. Many exotic breeds attempted to market ''lite'' beef with fewer calories and less fat. Other companies have introduced organic and ''natural'' beef products. Of the more than 200 companies that have tried to discover and exploit such niche markets, less than a dozen remained in business in the 1990s. The industry continues to search for ways to successfully brand beef, seeing it as a way to increase sales.

The most successful branded product has been Certified Angus Beef. This brand features highly marbled Angus beef. A great deal of effort goes into selling Angus beef carcasses to restaurants and high-end retail stores.

Beef Safety. Throughout the 1990s, beef producers faced a challenge from outbreaks of a strain of E. coli. Ground beef is the product most affected by the bacteria, as E. coli do not penetrate the inner muscling of steaks and roast and are easily destroyed when the outside meat is heated, seared, or barbecued. The safety hazard occurs when the E. coli are ground up with the hamburger, and the meat is not cooked at temperatures high enough to destroy the bacteria. The E. coli incidents were thought to be a problem with culled beef and dairy cows that are ground for hamburger. These outbreaks caused new labeling laws on meat products that urged consumers to follow proper cooking instructions and not to eat rare hamburger. New studies on irradiation and acid rinses of beef carcasses were also implemented. The USDA insists that despite the E. coli incidents beef remains a very safe food. In 1996, President Clinton announced a new, expanded meat inspection program that requires the participation of the private sector as well as the USDA. The USDA implemented the Hazard Analysis and Critical Control Points (HACCP) system to replace the look-touch-smell system that began in 1907. The new system also requires companies to use antimicrobial chemical sprays and irradiation to combat meat contamination hazards; to determine where in the production process contamination takes place and prevent it from occurring; and to submit samples to the USDA.

Concern for bovine spongiform encephalopathy (BSE), popularized as "Mad Cow Disease," came to a head in the 1990s as producers in the United Kingdom continuously found escalating numbers of afflicted cattle throughout the country. BSE is a fatal disease that affects the central nervous system of cattle. The USDA estimated that 171,000 head of cattle were diagnosed with BSE in Great Britain between 1986 to 1998. Several other European countries reported indigenous cases of BSE. During the past 10 years, the USDA BSE Working Group has taken aggressive measures to prevent BSE from entering the United States. Additionally, the U.S. government and the USDA have conducted studies showing that no cases of BSE exist in the United States. As a precautionary measure, the United States does not import cattle from countries with reported cases of BSE. Moreover, many scientists contend that the disease is not transmissible through an infected cow's meat or through physical contact.

The industry has long been haunted by critics, consumers as well as researchers, who object to the use of hormones in modern day beef production. Although the hormones occur naturally and are administered in small doses, the critics say that they pose health risks. The debate will likely intensify as new biotech products, such as BST, are introduced. These hormones produce meat and milk more efficiently and with less fat. Companies that have attempted to market such hormone-free products have not fared well economically.

Challenges to the Industry. Beef cattle producers have been facing an increasing number of challenges from environmentalists. Although cattle ranchers consider themselves "the original environmentalists," they are facing increasing federal environmental regulations involving endangered species and wetlands protection. As the largest private land owners in the country, ranchers are most affected by laws that restrict the rights of private property owners. Such issues have begun to overshadow diet and health concerns. Because the cattle business provides the primary livelihood for thousands of small communities, the resolution of such environmental issues as endangered species and wetlands protection is of vital importance.

Some environmental groups have questioned the amount of grazing land devoted to the cattle industry. Buffalo grazing developed our nation's grasslands. Beef cattle replaced the buffalo, and in the early years of the industry some abuses existed when rangeland was free for the taking and there were no fences. Cattle barons ran as many cattle as they could and during years with inadequate rainfall some rangelands deteriorated. However, according to the U.S. Bureau of Land Management, the overall condition of the national rangelands, both public and private, has improved during the past 50 years. Eighty-seven percent of this land is considered "stable or improving." However, the National Resources Conservation Service of the USDA considers only 39 percent of rangelands to have no serious resource problems. They hope to increase this to 45 percent by the year 2002.

Although there is no government price support program for beef cattle, the government does operate a Conservation Reserve Program (CRP), whereby cattle producers and farmers are paid to keep previously farmed or marginal lands out of production for ten years. Since 1980, 45 percent of cattle producers have participated in some form of government conservation program. During the same period 64 percent have participated in private conservation programs, such as rotational grazing and range management systems. Range science concepts are relatively new and have only been put into practice since the 1960s. New ideas are emerging almost daily as to how beef cattle can best be integrated into an environment that also accommodates wildlife and growing numbers of people.

The beef cattle industry faced many other challenges during the 1990s. Although vegetarianism has remained relatively stable at about 3 percent of the population, an increasing number of people are occasionally eating vegetarian dinners. Although beef is a nutrient-dense food with a caloric content similar to that of chicken, it is generally not perceived as such by a large part of the general population. Health care and nutritional experts recognize, however, that beef can be part of a well-balanced diet because it is a good source of iron, zinc, and vitamin B-12.

Exports. Although there were difficulties in marketing beef during the 1980s and 1990s, there have also been some stunning success stories. The most economically significant success for the industry has been the increased demand for American beef internationally. The United States produced 24.9 percent of the world's beef supply in the 1990s, with exports representing 9 percent of the value of all U.S. beef production. From 1981 to 1998, export values increased from $1.9 billion to $4.4 billion. It is estimated that between 10 and 12 percent of the value of every steer produced domestically comes from the added demand created by the export market. Consequently, the National Cattlemen's Association was very much in favor of the North American Free Trade Agreement (NAFTA), because Mexico is a growing market for American beef. Exports to Mexico increased nearly 47 percent during 1994, the first year of NAFTA. This was followed by a brief downturn with the devaluation of the Mexican Peso, but rebounded by the end of the decade. NAFTA has been criticized for contributing to lower domestic cattle prices in the face of foreign imports, in spite of the fact that NAFTA did not change the regulations on cattle imports. Beef exports also suffered somewhat due to the slowdown in the Asian economy, and are down from a high of $5.3 billion in 1995. In 1999, 82.7 percent of exports went to Japan, Mexico, Canada, and the Republic of South Korea. European markets are less receptive to U.S. beef which has been treated with hormones. Despite these slowdowns exports significantly exceed imports, and there continues to be a strong export market for U.S. beef and by-products.

WORKFORCE

The largest cattle ranch in the United States is the family-owned King Ranch in Texas. While much of the West was settled by large ranchers with investor money from England, today the American cattle industry is largely made up of small, family producers. In 1996 79.8 percent of U.S. beef operations had less than 50 head of cattle. The King Ranch's herd of 35,000 reveals the extremes in the modern day beef industry.

Approximately 98 percent of all American cattle producers are considered small or midsize (less than 500 cattle) by the National Cattlemen's Association. These ranchers raise the majority of the nation's beef cattle, accounting for 86 percent in 1996. While the cattle feeding and meat packing industries continue to become more concentrated in the hands of fewer and larger corporations, the beef cow herds remain in the hands of small or midsize producers. Cattle are also raised as a sideline, a hobby, or in conjunction with a farming operation. In addition, they are often used to consume what is left after crops have been harvested.

The work on a typical ranch varies with the season. In winter, when grass is dormant or covered with snow, the cattle must be fed hay. Ranchers usually grow and store this hay in the summer, but some ranchers purchase their hay. In the spring and summer, cattle are branded and worked; this requires hiring more hands. Several ranches share cowboys during these roundups. One of the more difficult chores comes at calving time, when cowboys routinely check the cows and heifers. Heifers are females that have not yet had a calf and usually have much more difficulty calving than an aged cow. A cowboy must often assist heifers in the birthing process.

In Nevada, male and female ranch workers are referred to as buckaroos, in Texas they may be called cowpunchers, and in Montana they are cowboys. Though they are referred to by a variety of names, these workers generally perform the same duties and receive a fairly low wage for their work. Typically they are given a house, a ration of beef per year, a pickup truck, and a monthly salary that ranges from $650 to $2,000. The National Cattlemen's Association estimates that the industry produces about 186,000 full-time jobs.

The beef cattle industry is steeped in tradition. For example, 42 percent of U.S. beef cattle operations with more than 100 head of cattle have been in the same family for over 50 years, and 21 percent have been in the same family for 75 years. Many of these firms are known by the brand they give their cattle, such as the Pitchfork or the Four Sixes. The latter brand is simply 6666, which is said to be the poker hand the founder of the ranch was holding when he won the ranch.

While being a cowboy used to be a romantic notion, far fewer young men and women had aspirations of becoming cowboys in the 1990s. It is projected that the need for cowboys will continue to decline through 2006. The production of beef remains high, but this is due more to the increased weight of animals than to larger herds.

There are several barriers to entry into this industry. It is difficult to find a ranch in America today that will be profitable. Ranches are often priced according to cow/calf unit, which is the amount of land necessary to run a cow and her calf for one year. This calculation is used to figure the carrying capacity of the land. Typically a ranch today sells for $1,500 to as high as $3,000 per cow/calf unit.

Many ranches were up for sale in the 1990s and a lot of them had federal land grazing permits. Most eastern cattle ranches are composed entirely of ''deeded land.'' In the West, however, the government owns sizable amounts of land in each state. For example, the federal government owns 86 percent of Nevada, 52 percent of Oregon, 49 percent of California, 64 percent of Idaho, 67 percent of Utah, 49 percent of Wyoming, and 41 percent of Arizona. This land has traditionally been rented to public lands ranchers who run their cattle part of the year on these marginal lands. These ranchers own small deeded ranches and use much of the farming land for hay production. The deeded acreage is usually surrounded by large blocks of federal land. Ranchers often lease this ground from the federal government as a means of supplying cattle with water. The rancher is responsible for maintaining fences and overseeing the property. These lands are governed under a multiple-use concept, which means that other citizens can use the lands as well. However, Congress has attempted to increase the land rent and put constraints on the public lands ranchers.

Research and Technology

There were about 100 million cattle in the United States during the 1990s, and the industry was producing as much beef as it did in the 1970s when its cattle inventory numbered 120 million. Such efficiency has been made possible by the use of technology—new breeds, computerization, and increased mechanization. Output per man hour in agriculture has increased twice as fast as that in manufacturing industries. American beef cattle producers are producing nearly 25 percent of the world's beef supply with just 10 percent of the world's cattle population. Other countries have been unable to match U.S. efficiency standards. For example, prior to the breakup of the Soviet Union, they had nearly 20 percent more cattle than the United States but produced 20 percent less beef.

The use of production testing and artificial insemination has made it possible to use the best genetics the industry has to offer. Fertilized eggs from superior producing cows are being flushed and then implanted in lower quality recipient cows so that their offspring will have highly predictable traits for growth and meat quality. In effect, the recipient cow acts as a surrogate mother for a calf that carries none of her genes.

Breed associations keep extensive computer records and the use of ''Expected Progeny Differences'' has made it possible for a rancher to select his cattle using statistical analysis.

Money from ranchers' voluntary dollar per head assessment is being pooled and used to map the genes of beef cattle. It is expected that such research will allow future ranchers to implant genes for tenderness, marbling, or any number of economically important beef cattle traits.

Quality control became the watchword of the industry in the 1990s. The beef cattle industry initiated its own Beef Quality Assurance program to assure consumers that beef is a wholesome food. Beef Quality Assurance programs have been sponsored by 41 states, which account for 98 percent of all cattle marketed. Additionally, the Pathogen Reduction Act of 1996 required the industry to update its inspection methods, which had changed little in the previous 50 years. During 1996-1999 the new inspection methods were put into effect. As of January 20, 2000 all raw meat and poultry products were being inspected using methods capable of detecting invisible pathogens.

Microchips and scanners are being tested as means to maintain cattle identification. For instance, a calf could be implanted with an identification chip at birth and when that animal's carcass is hung on the rail the chip could be scanned and the individual could be traced back to its original owner. The chip could also reveal vaccination records, pedigree information, and feedlot data. Such information would allow the industry to identify superior producing animals and weed out those of poorer quality.

Further Reading

Beef Today Magazine. Available from http://www.farmjournal.com/magazines/articles.cfm?id=4.

BeefNutrition Web Site. Available from http://www.beefnutrition.org.

Cattle-Fax. *Cattle Industry Data, Analysis, Research and Education.* Available from: http://www.cattle-fax.com/.

Meat and Poultry Online Web Site. Available from http://news.meatandpoultryonline.com/.

National Cattlemen's Beef Association. *Beef Demand Shows Improvement after 20-Year Slide,* November 1999. Available from http://www.beef.org/newsrels/rel_ncba/ncba99_1102a.htm.

National Cattlemen's Beef Association. *Industry Factsheets.* Available from http://www.beef.org/librfacts/factsheets_industry.htm.

National Resource Conservation Service. *Healthy, Productive Grazing Land.* Available from http://www.nhq.nrcs.usda.gov/land/strat/graz.html.

National Resource Conservation Service. *National Resources Inventory.* Available from http://www.nhq.nrcs.usda.gov/NRI/intro.html.

National Resource Conservation Service. *Private Grazing Land.* Available from http://www.nhq.nrcs.usda.gov/land/env/use4.html.

Occupational Outlook Handbook. Available from http://stats.bls.gov/ocohome.htm.

Texas Agricultural Extension Service. *Cattle Grazing on Land Formerly Enrolled in the CRP Program.* Available from http://agecoext.tamu.edu/commodity/crp/four/cattle.htm.

Texas Agricultural Extension Service. *Conservation Reserve Program Publications.* Available from http://agecoext.tamu.edu/commodity/crp/list.htm.

U.S. Department of Agriculture. *Census of Agriculture.* Available from http://www.nass.usda.gov/census/.

U.S. Department of Agriculture. *Food Safety and Inspection Service.* Available from http://www.fsis.usda.gov/.

U.S. Department of Agriculture. *Foreign Agricultural Service.* Available from http://www.fas.usda.gov/.

U.S. Department of Agriculture. Marketing and Regulatory Programs. *Animal and Plant Health Inspection Service.* Available from http://www.aphis.usda.gov/.

U.S. Department of Agriculture. National Agricultural Statistics Service : Cattle. Available from http://www.usda.gov:80/nass/pubs/stathigh/1996/cattle.htm.

U.S. Department of the Interior. Bureau of Land Management. *National Commercial Use Activity.* Available from http://www.blm.gov/nhp/pubs/rewards/1999/2natcomm.htm.

SIC 0213

HOGS

This category covers establishments primarily engaged in the production or feeding of hogs on their own account or on a contract or fee basis. A general trend toward vertical integration in the industry has resulted in larger, more integrated hog operations that often play diverse roles—including breeding, raising, feeding, feed production, butchering and processing, distribution and marketing—in the process of getting hogs from the weaning pen to the market place.

NAICS CODE(S)

112210 (Hog and Pig Farming)

INDUSTRY SNAPSHOT

In September 1998, the United States pork herd reached its highest level in over a decade, with the U.S. Department of Agriculture estimating that American producers maintained about 62 million hogs on farms and feedlots. That was up from 61.2 million the previous year. By January 1999, it was estimated that 99.2 million were slaughtered throughout the year. The U.S. hog inventory is only about 8 percent of the world total, but slaughter is up to 10-12 percent. In 1998, per capita pork in the country reached 51.9 pounds. Besides meat, pork products provide a broad range of needs, serving as a source for over 40 drug and pharmaceutical products as well as varied industrial and consumer products, from chemicals to leather goods. Such widespread demand fueled increasingly fierce competition, with a general trend toward larger farms and vertically integrated operations that controlled every step of the production process, from birth to grocery store sales. With escalating competition, industry leaders in the 1990s strove to increase pork's market share by appealing to consumers. Lower prices resulting from supply surfeits of the early 1990s were a start. But the pork industry was faced with the task of reversing years of market decline largely brought on by consumers' growing health concerns, which had resulted in a general shift in consumption from pork, beef, and red meats to less fatty fish and poultry. In 1986 the National Pork Producers Council (NPPC) launched its ''Pork—the Other White Meat'' promotional campaign to emphasize a new health-awareness in the industry and to lend fresh pork a brand name type identity. In 1996, NPPC began a new phase of its campaign, emphasizing the versatility of pork, epitomized by its ''Taste What's Next'' slogan.

In December 1991 the University of Wisconsin, working with the U.S. Department of Agriculture and the hog-raising industry, published findings that indicated that pork examined in 1990 contained 31 percent less fat, 17 percent fewer calories, and 10 percent less cholesterol than its equivalent in the *1983 USDA Nutrient Handbook.* The NPPC estimated that in contrast to the hog of the 1950s, the hog of the 1990s contains 50 percent less fat. Whereas before the average hog had 2.86 inches of backfat, now the average hog only has 1.1 inches. According to the NPPC, by the turn of the century corporate farms selling more than 50,000 hogs a year could produce up to 30 percent of the nation's pork. In 1995, 80 percent of the nation's hogs came from farms that produced over 1,000 hogs a year. Furthermore, a 1993 survey by Brock Associates of Milwaukee and Elanco Animal Health division of Eli Lilly & Co., suggested that the country could have as few as 100 producers by the year 2050. The majority of survey participants—250 leading hog producers, veterinarians, meatpackers, and scientists—believed that the pork industry would move along the same lines that the poultry industry had in previous years, with a massive shakedown in the number of small or independent producers. Industry observers noted that hog production was rapidly becoming less labor-intensive and more capital-intensive, a condition that had not been problematic for corporate outfits able to bring significant resources to bear. Independent farmers, however, have to compensate for their lack of capital through extra work and by securing the latest technology through public universities, cooperative deals, and other sources.

Competition for such resources to acquire the necessary funding for the buildings, equipment, and technology needed to produce the most competitive hogs has grown increasingly fierce. Producers have to seek increasingly tight financing through combinations of credit institutions, investor groups, insurance companies, and allied industries such as feed producers and packers. Financing is contingent on overall efficiency, management ability, complete and accurate records, and a sound business plan. In order to best meet such demands, producers have to rely increasingly on genetics, nutrition, and advanced record-keeping systems.

The Typical Hog Farm. Whether corporate or independent, typical hog farms have operated along roughly similar lines, consisting of designated buildings or areas for breeding, farrowing, nursing, growing, and finishing the animals. Depending on various factors—available capital, amount and type of labor, future plans, existing facilities, and management style—a producer could provide a comfortable and efficient environment in many ways. To conserve land for harvesting purposes and to better control animal environments, producers increasingly turned to enclosed buildings for the different stages of production. In the past, fully controlled environments were almost exclusively reserved for nurseries, where baby pigs had to be carefully protected against weather, insects, and disease.

From Gestation to Market. The gestation period for a sow or gilt (young female that has not yet had its first litter) lasts 114 days, during which a careful diet is provided to ensure a healthy litter. Farrowings averaged 8.8 pigs per litter in feeder pig production and 8.52 pigs saved in farrow-to-finish operations, with average pigs weaned increasing to 8.4 in 1995 up from 7.1 in 1980. Facilities for farrowing (giving birth to baby pigs) ranged from pasture systems with A-frames or other types of shelter to confined quarters that could be totally or partially confined. Though significantly more expensive, total confinement facilitated handling of hogs, disease control, feeding control, and reduced labor expenditure for the farmer.

After three to five weeks, pigs are weaned (removed from their mother) and moved to a nursery—dry, warm, and draft-free facility that generally features slotted floors to keep the young animals free of their own waste. After reaching an age of eight or nine weeks, by which time the pigs weigh an average of 50 pounds, the pigs are moved to another area for growing until they reach roughly 120 pounds; finally, they are finished (fattened or fed in preparation for slaughter) until they've reached the marketable weight of 220 to 250 pounds.

Feed and Supplements. From farrow to finish, food intake is carefully monitored to assure proper growth and development and, above all, marketable fat-to-muscle ratio. They are usually fed a ration of 20 percent protein in the nursing stage, changed in an incremental fashion to 13 to 15 percent for finishing. U.S. producers tended to prefer corn as the staple diet, supplemented by high-protein soybean meal and other feeder concentrates usually acquired from specialized feed producers.

Breeding. Generally, eight major breeds remained prominent in the United States throughout the 1990s: Yorkshire, Landrace, Chester White, Berkshire, Hampshire, Duroc, Poland China, and Spot. Purebred hogs are generally raised to be sold to commercial producers as seed stock for crossbreeding purposes. The objective of crossbreeding programs is to combine the most desirable traits of select breeds in order to arrive at the desired characteristics of leanness, meatiness, feed efficiency, growth rate, and durability. In the 1990s, farmers have increasingly depended on the research and expertise of independent breeders to provide them with stock designed to yield a more competitive hog herd. In addition, a growing proportion of breeding stock consists of hybrid (crossbred) hogs. Hybrid hogs have become a significant part of breeding stock replaced annually in the U.S. herd.

Whether a producer secures breeding stock from a breeder or from the resident herd, choice of breeders can make or break a herd. Considerations in boar selection include such traits as temperament, birth rate, feed efficiency, carcass merit, feet and leg soundness, and past performance records with litter mates. Sow herd replacements are often gilts from large litters that exhibited fast growth and leanness.

Three basic breeding systems have been commonly employed: the simplest lets one boar run with a group of sows and gilts. Although such a method requires little labor, it complicates the detailed record keeping of breeding dates. Another option is a hand breeding system that puts one boar with one female at a time; this puts less stress on the boar and is easier for record keeping. A third breeding method involves artificial insemination. This route requires the greatest level of management for the producer, but minimizes the spread of disease organisms or uncontrolled genetic material.

The Market. Once a hog has reached an average of 230 pounds and 4.5 to 6.5 months of age, it is considered ready to market. The producer has several options at this juncture, including livestock exchanges, cooperative marketing agreements, terminal markets, auctions, and direct sales to packers. Terminal markets are typically located near major metropolitan areas, where commission firms represent the producer before the product is brought to nearby slaughtering plants. Auctions, on the other hand, were developed to provide a point of sale for small lots of livestock in rural communities. Direct sales to packers became increasingly popular with advances in animal transportation vehicles, which facilitated both delivery of livestock to packers and shipment of dressed carcasses to consumption centers.

Playing off the ever-shifting forces of supply and demand, producers can also sell their product at livestock exchanges, hedging their hogs on futures markets like the Chicago Mercantile Exchange (CME). Market prices for hogs and pork products can be extremely volatile, influenced by a wide range of factors, including seasonal and cyclical supply fluctuations; shifting consumer demand patterns due to seasonal influences like holidays and temperature patterns; the impact of the fortunes of competing products like beef and poultry; and the price of grains, such as corn and soybeans, that serve as hog feed.

Industry Cooperation. In order to best address changes in production, marketing, technology, and consumer preferences, pork producers have organized at local, state, and national levels. In addition to countless cooperatives and local clubs and councils, the pork industry was represented by four main organizations in the 1990s: the National Pork Bureau (NPB), the National Pork Producers Council (NPPC), the Pork Industry Group (PIG) of the National Live Stock & Meat Board, and the U.S. Meat Export Federation (MEF).

The National Pork Bureau was established by Congress under provisions of the Pork Promotion Research and Consumer Information Act of 1985. Its purpose was to organize and manage funds raised by a legislative check-off on all hogs and pork products sold domestically and imported, at the rate of 35 cents per $100 of value. The NPB contracted different organizations to coordinate specific checkoff-funded programs. The NPPC, for example, coordinated national product promotion and marketing efforts. That group was also responsible for a wide range of programs in producer research and education. The MEF assisted NPPC in cultivating foreign markets of U.S. pork. PIG coordinated informational programs aimed at health care professionals and schools, including nutrition and product research related to pork.

BACKGROUND AND DEVELOPMENT

Dating back 40 million years according to fossil records, hogs were domesticated in China by 4900 B.C. and in Europe by 1500 B.C.. The animal was reputedly brought to the New World from Europe by Columbus and then, more notably, by Hernando de Soto, who was dubbed ''the Father of the American Pork Industry'' for landing hogs at Tampa Bay, Florida, in 1539. By the time of de Soto's death in 1542, his herd of 13 had grown to 700 strong. Pork colonization continued with other explorers: Hernando Cortez introduced hogs to New Mexico in 1600 and Sir Walter Raleigh brought them to the Jamestown Colony in 1607.

Hog population grew alongside, and sometimes in conflict with, humans—a long solid wall was constructed on the northern edge of Manhattan Island to control roaming hogs, eventually becoming the Wall Street area of the country's largest city. By the end of the seventeenth century, the typical farmer owned between four and five hogs, which were raised largely on Indian corn. Pioneers carried a growing hog population westward in the nineteenth century.

By the mid-1800s, pork was being commercially slaughtered in Cincinnati, which acquired the moniker Porkopolis as a result. During this period, 40,000 to 70,000 hogs per year were driven along trails to eastern markets. The development of railroad lines and eventually the refrigerated railroad car ushered in the modern era of the hog industry. The midwestern states led the nation in hog production after 1920.

CURRENT CONDITIONS

Despite high industry numbers, 1998 proved to be a hard year for the small, independent hog producer in the United States. Live hog prices fell to an inflation adjusted 50 year low. This situation for the small farmer continued a trend that saw the industry concentrating itself into corporate based finishing and marketing operations. In 1998 more than 50 percent of the inventory share of the U.S. hog marketings came from the large contract hog operations. In this contractual situation, the contractor agrees to provide the hogs, feed, medication and supplies. The contractee supplies the housing, utilities and labor.

Animal Rights. The pork industry's efforts to produce an efficient, lean pig, as well as the consumption of its product have aroused animal rights groups. Common ground between these two groups is perhaps impossible to achieve, since the industry's livelihood is predicated on continued consumption of pork and other hog byproducts. But numerous, if not effective, measures had been taken over the years. As early as 1873 legislation—the Humane Treatment of Livestock Act—was enacted to prevent cruelty to livestock while in transit on railroads. It was repealed and replaced in 1906 by the 28-hour law controlling feed and water availability and handling procedures of livestock. The Humane Slaughter Act of 1958 also contained humanitarian guidelines, though no noncompliance penalties were enforced. These and numerous other rules continued to spark controversy over such issues as animal confinement, feed supplements, and slaughtering methods. Groups such as the People for the Ethical Treatment of Animals (PETA), a Washington, D.C.-based nonprofit animal protection organization, continue their opposition to the pork and beef industries.

Drugs and Pork. Concerns were also voiced by consumers, veterinarians, hog buyers, and the NPPC over the use of drugs by hog farmers. Efforts have been mounted in recent years to develop better methods of detecting drug residues in table-ready pork in an effort to alert producers and curtail the practice. Industry interest also revolved around the possible uses and abuses of porcine somatotropin (PST), a growth hormone that would greatly reduce fat while increasing lean meat and diminishing the amount of feed needed for a pound of weight.

Meat Inspection Policy. In 1996 President Clinton announced a new, expanded meat inspection program that would require the participation of the private sector as well as the USDA. The USDA implemented the Hazard Analysis and Critical Control Points (HACCP) system to replace the look-touch-smell system that began in 1907. The new system requires companies to use new technology, anti-microbial chemical sprays, and irradiation, to combat meat contamination hazards, to determine where in the production process contamination takes place and prevent it from occurring, and to submit samples to the USDA. Besides these measures, the NPPC has taken steps to ensure pork does not become contaminated. Calling for participation at the producer level as well as at the processing level, the NPPC strove to reassure consumers of pork's safety.

Industry Leaders

In 1999 the leading pork producers in the United States were the Smithfield Foods/Murphy/Tyson, of Smithfield, Virginia, followed by ContiGroup Companies, of Kansas City, Missouri; Seaboard Corporation, of Shawnee Mission, Kansas; Prestage Farms, of Clinton, North Carolina; and Cargill, Incorporated, of Minneapolis, Minnesota. According to the U.S. Department of Agriculture, the leading hog-producing states during the 1990s included Iowa (24.1 million annually); North Carolina (11.4 million); Minnesota (9.7 million); Illinois (9.6 million); Indiana (7.8 million); and Nebraska (7.3 million). Other leading states included Missouri, Ohio, South Dakota, and Kansas.

America and the World

The United States imported and exported substantial quantities of hog products in the 1990s and is among the world's largest pork exporters in the world, exporting 449,000 metric tons in 1998 compared to 474,000 in 1997. The world's leading exporter of pork in 1998 was Denmark with 4.8 million metric tons. The top customers for U.S. pork exports in 1998 were Japan, Russia, Canada and Mexico. In 1996 U.S. exports of pork reached the $1 billion mark, and the NPPC attributed this in part to the implementation of the General Tariffs and Trade Agreement (GATT) and to the North American Free Trade Agreement (NAFTA).

Various socioeconomic forces in Europe complicated import/export relations with the United States in the 1990s. Continued restructuring of agriculture, among other things, in Eastern Europe, coupled with civil war in the former Yugoslavia resulted in substantial declines of imports from those areas. The European Community (EC) continued to out-price Danish and Dutch products in the United States, while the NPPC accused the EC of aggressive export subsidies to unfairly capture markets at the expense of American and other exporters. The NPPC also claimed that the EC had a long record of manipulating meat inspection standards to limit meat entry into the European market.

Research and Technology

Checkoff-funded programs organized by the pork industry forged ahead in research and development toward efficient and safe pork production that would better attract domestic consumers and compete in world markets. Of the many advances sure to affect the hog industry of the future, several could be especially notable, including the use of repartitioning agents as feed additives to encourage less fat, leaner meat, and faster growth; and biotechnology that would advance gene mapping to a point where growth, fat-to-lean ratio, and prolificacy could be better controlled from the laboratory.

Further Reading

Freese, Betsy. ''Pork Powerhouses.'' *Agriculture Online,* 1996. Available from http://www.agriculture.com/contents/sf/porkpwr/pp.html.

Looker, D. ''Riding Out Low Hog Prices with Contracts.'' *Successful Farming,* May/June 1998.

Pork Facts, 1996-1997. Des Moines, IA: National Pork Producers Council (NPPC), 1996. ''Pork Powerhouses,'' *Successful Farming,* October 1999.

Steever, Tom. ''Hard Times for Pork Producers.'' *Focus on Agriculture.* Jan. 1999. Available from: http://www/fb.com/views/focus

''USDA Modernizes 90-Year Old System of Meat Inspection Final Rule.'' National Technical Information Service. Springfield: November 1996.

United States Department of Agriculture and National Agricultural Statistics Service. ''Statistics of Cattle, Hogs, and Sheep.'' Washington, DC: 1996. Available from: http://www.usda.gov/nass/pubs/agr95_96/agr95_7.pdf.

SIC 0214

SHEEP AND GOATS

This classification covers establishments primarily engaged in the production of sheep, lambs, goats, goats' milk, wool, and mohair, including the operation of lamb feedlots, on their own account or on a contract or fee basis.

NAICS CODE(S)

112410 (Sheep Farming)
112420 (Goat Farming)

In 1999 there were 68,810 sheep operators in the United States. The number of operations has continued to drop each year since 1992 when the U.S. Department of Agriculture (USDA) reported about 100,000 sheep operations. Although sheep and goats are produced in every state, the 17 western states produce 80 percent of the total U.S. flock. Sheep and goats are among the most versatile animals in the world. They can live in many climates from the desert Southwest to the colder climates of Wyoming, and they can efficiently turn barely edible browse into food and fiber. Many farmers use sheep to clean up crop residues. In the West, sheep are often run on alfalfa fields under temporary fence. Goats, however, are even more hearty than sheep, and, therefore, can make do on land that even sheep cannot.

Sheep. In eastern states the farm flocks are generally small, while in the West the flocks are much larger, often numbering in the thousands. The top five sheep-producing states are Texas, California, Wyoming, Colorado, and South Dakota.

Along with the decline of operations is the decline in gross sheep and lamb production. According to *USDA-NASS Agricultural Statistics,* in 1999 the total number of sheep and lambs was 7.2 million, valuing $640 million. The number slaughtered in 1998 was 3.8 million, yielding about 249 million pounds. In 1999, preliminary cash receipts from sales of sheep and lambs was $500 million, according to the *USDA Economic Research Service.*

Sheep production in the United States is unique among all sheep-producing countries, because the U.S. market emphasis is on meat, rather than wool production. Three-fourths of the American sheep producer's income is derived from the sale of meat, whereas, in the rest of the world, wool is the primary commodity. Sheep that are processed before the joints in their legs ossify produce meat referred to as "lamb," while older sheep produce mutton. There is a very distinct difference between the two types of meat, and lamb is priced significantly higher.

The female sheep is called a ewe and she may give birth to one or more lambs. The national average is 1.1 lambs per ewe per year. Sheep producers are weaning 20 percent more lambs per ewe in this country than 10 years ago. The lambs are raised in the spring and are processed for meat when they reach approximately 125 pounds at 5 to 6 months old. Most lambs go straight to processing right off grass, but some lighter lambs may spend the final finishing stage in a feedlot eating a high-concentrate grain ration. Many sheep flocks are still herded by Basque shepherds and their well-trained dogs.

Consumer demand for the taste of fresh American lamb is growing, especially at restaurants, where usage is up dramatically. Consumers are eating 16 percent more lamb than ever before and retailers are allocating 38 percent more shelf space to selling American lamb. Lamb prices commanded by producers, however, have fallen in recent years, while the retail price of lamb has risen.

The sheep industry has experienced some wild price swings. In just one year the price of lamb per head fell from $100 to $45. Prices rose in 1996 to $86.50 per head, yet they have fluctuated greatly in the past decade. American lamb producers blamed the lamb packing industry, which has become concentrated into a few hands, and imports from Australia and New Zealand for their losses. To differentiate their fresh product from frozen imported products, the American Lamb Council launched a program in 1990 to label and market selected fresh American lamb that is leaner than the imported product. The program has been successful and that product now accounts for 22 percent of the American lambs being marketed.

In recent years increased imports of lamb meat from Australia and New Zealand has endangered the survival of U.S. sheep producers, according to the American Sheep Industry Association. In September 1998, the American Sheep Industry Association and industry supporters filed a Section 201 trade action petition with the U.S. International Trade Commission. The Trade Commission investigated the effects of increased lamb imports on the U.S. sheep industry and reported recommendations to the White House. On July 7, 1999, President Clinton imposed a three-year tariff-rate quota program and $100 million in assistance to the sheep industry. The program began in July 1999, and imposed a tariff on all lamb imported from Australia and New Zealand.

Although the United States is not a major player in the world wool market, U.S. wool is known for its bright color and strength. Domestic wool production fell to 53.8 million pounds in 1997 after climbing to 89.2 million pounds in 1989. Because of the fluctuations in payments, however, farmers have continued to shy away from wool production. World output of wool is 6 percent higher than demand, and it could take 10 years just to eliminate the wool stockpiled in Australian warehouses. The sheep industry remains a vital contributor to the U.S. economy. Sheep contribute $7 billion to the gross national product when domestic lamb and wool production is sold at the retail level. The production of lamb and wool in this country accounts for 350,000 jobs.

Sheep killed by animal predators is a serious issue for livestock operators. In the mid-1990s, predators ac-

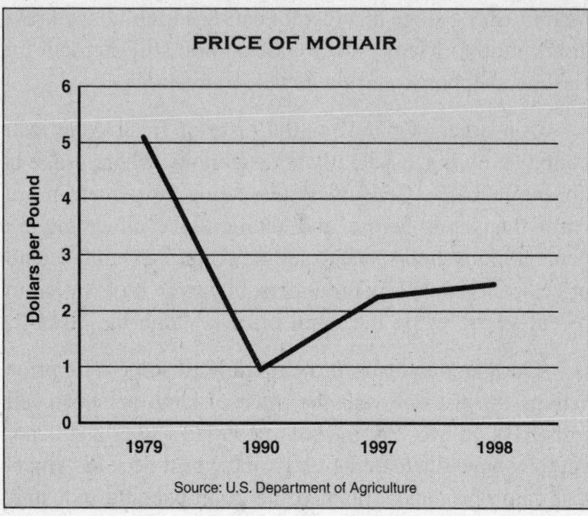

counted for approximately 42 percent of sheep and lamb losses, resulting in lost income of an estimated $35 million, according to the American Sheep Industry Association. Coyotes are the major predator of sheep and lambs.

Goats. The American goat industry is made up of milk goats that are run in small farm flocks and back yard operations as well as large mohair operations primarily in the dry and arid southwestern states. Mohair, like wool, creates a versatile fabric for warm and cold weather and can be found in apparel and furniture. Goat meat has increased in popularity in the United States, as well.

Texas is the leading mohair producing state, while New Mexico, Oklahoma, and Arizona produce nearly all of the rest of the country's mohair. The four-state total for goats clipped in 1998 was 705,000 head, down from 936,000 head in 1997, according to *USDA-NASS Reports*. In 1998, each goat averaged a clip of 7.2 pounds, down slightly from 7.3 pounds in 1997. The goat producer received approximately $2.48 a pound for the mohair in 1998, up from $2.25 per pound in 1997. The USDA estimated that the value of the 1998 yield was $12.6 million.

According to the United States Department of Agriculture, during World War II and the Korean conflict the United States imported half the wool required for military uniforms and blankets. The National Wool Act of 1954 was enacted to reduce dependency on foreign wool imports and increase domestic production by providing a subsidy for wool and mohair producers in the United States. The subsidy provided direct payment to farmers based on their production: the more wool they produced the more federal funding they received. A portion of the import tax levied on wool provided the money for the subsidy program. In 1955 the amount of wool sheared was 283 million pounds compared to 89 million pounds in 1988. The price of mohair dropped from $5.10 per pound in 1979 to just $0.95 per pound in 1990. In 1993, Congress voted to eliminate the subsidy at the end of the 1995 fiscal year, saying the program had failed to increase domestic wool production, disproportionately benefited the few largest producers, and wool was no longer a strategic material. The Federal Agriculture Improvement and Reform Act of 1996 upheld the earlier elimination of wool and mohair subsidies, in an effort for the government to reduce spending.

FURTHER READING

American Sheep Industry Association. *An Outline of the President's Decision On the Section 201 lamb imports case*, 8 July 1999. Available from http://www.sheepusa.org/news/cfapps/articleView.

American Sheep Industry Association. *Sheep and Predator Management*. 12 January 2000. Available from http://www.sheepusa.org/environment/predator.html.

American Sheep Industry Association. *U.S. Sheep Industry Files Petition for Import Relief*, 1 February 1999. Available from http://www.sheepusa.org/news/cfapps/articleView.

United States Department of Agriculture, Economics and Statistics System. *Agricultural and Finance (AIS,)* December 1999. Available from http://usda.mannlib.cornell.edu/reports/erssor/economics/ais-bb/199/ais73.pdf.

United States Department of Agriculture, National Agricultural Statistics Service, Agricultural Statistics 1999. ''Cattle, Hogs, and Sheep.'' Washington, D.C.: 1999. Available from http://www.usda.gov/nass/pubs/agr99/99_ch7.pdf.

United States Department of Agriculture, National Agricultural Statistics Service, Agricultural Statistics Board. *Wool and Mohair,* March 1999. Available from http://usda.mannlib.cornell.edu/reports/nassr/livestock/.

United States Department of Agriculture. *USDA01: End the Wool and Mohair Subsidy*, 15 January 2000. Available from http://www.npr.gov/library/reports/.

SIC 0219

GENERAL LIVESTOCK, EXCEPT DAIRY AND POULTRY

This classification covers establishments deriving 50 percent or more of their total value of sales or agricultural products from livestock such as cattle, hogs, sheep, and goats, but with less than 50 percent deriving from any single one of those livestock categories.

NAICS CODE(S)

112990 (All Other Animal Production)

The multi-faceted, diversified livestock farm has faded from the American landscape in the late 1990s because of industry emphasis on specialization. Large farms focused on raising a single animal were poised to all but replace diversified farms and ranches by the end of the twentieth century. Cattle production, for example, grew into an enormous industry. In 1997 the industry reported sales of $40.5 billion. Additionally, there were fewer than 1,000 farms with cattle numbering greater than 5,000, but these farms accounted for 33 percent of the country's cattle production and more than 42 percent of cattle value. Cattle farms with less than 100 head of cattle continued to decline in both number of farms and in dollar value production.

Farmers grazed herds on harvested crop land, which made cattle raising a lucrative side-business. Many smaller farms were able to support small- to moderate-sized herds this way.

Like the cattle industry, many hog producers became increasingly larger operations as well. In this $13.8 billion industry, liberal production laws in states such as North Carolina have attacked large corporate hog farms, but the trend in hog production favors the growth of large scale organizations. The number of farms that sold more than 7,500 hogs and pigs in 1997 reached 3,314, up from 1,431 only five years prior. This does not mean that ranchers and farmers have given up on diversifying their operations. The species of livestock and the character of the business has changed, though, over the years, and those establishments that fit in this classification are apt to be small family-run outfits.

Nevertheless, several of the larger beef cattle operations have made some moves toward diversification. Some are also involved in the raising of horses. With the growing popularity of team penning, cutting, roping, and other equine recreational sports, the sale of working ranch horses has become an important source of income for a number of smaller ranches.

Historically, cattle and sheep bred in America did not graze the same land; indeed, cattlemen and sheepherders often viewed each other as rivals. This has changed, however, as studies have indicated that running cattle and sheep together helps keep predators at bay. Sheepherders now believe that coyotes are intimidated when cattle are present, thus drastically cutting sheep losses. Running the two species together is also becoming popular for another reason. Overgrazing of plant species is decreased because the cattle eat the grasses while the sheep eat broad-leafed weeds, forbes, and shrubs. Running the two species together is thus a growing phenomenon in parts of the country to both protect the livestock and the land.

FURTHER READING

''Meat and Poultry Facts.'' American Meat Institute, 1992.

United States Department of Agriculture and National Agricultural Statistics Service. ''Statistics of Cattle, Hogs, and Sheep.'' Washington, DC: 1995-1996. Available from http://www.usda.gov/nass/pubs/agr95_96/agr95_7.pdf.

United States Department of Agriculture and National Agricultural Statistics Service. *1997 Census of Agriculture—United States Data.* Available from http://www.usda.gov/nass/pubs/agr97/agr97_7.pdf.

SIC 0241

DAIRY FARMS

This classification includes establishments primarily engaged in the production of cows' milk and other dairy products and in raising dairy heifer replacements. Such farms may process and bottle milk on the farm and sell at wholesale or retail. However, the processing and/or distribution of milk from a separate establishment not on the farm is classified in manufacturing or trade. Establishments primarily producing goats' milk are classified in **SIC 0214: Sheep and Goats.**

NAICS CODE(S)

112111 (Beef Cattle Ranching and Farming)
112120 (Dairy Cattle and Milk Production)

INDUSTRY SNAPSHOT

Dairy farming is one of the leading agricultural activities in the United States with dairy cash receipts totaling over $20 billion a year. Cash receipts in 1998 totaled $24.3 billion, which was 16 percent above the 1997 figure. Because of scientific advances increasing milk production, the total number of dairy cows in the United States has been declining steadily since 1970, while the total output and the output per cow have increased significantly. Milk sales constitute about 12 percent of all money made from agricultural activities. Of the roughly 2 million farms in the country, less than 10 percent were dairy farms by the close of the century. In 1955, however, there were as many as 2.8 million dairy farms. (The U.S. Census defined a farm as any place with $1,000 or more of annual gross sales from agricultural goods.) A milk policy administered by the U.S. Department of Agriculture (USDA) has supported milk prices for dairy farmers and also bought back surplus milk, though the government is in the process of weaning farmers of such programs. Such policies have helped dairy farmers but raised the retail price of milk and other dairy products, making U.S. dairy products unattractive in the world market.

ORGANIZATION AND STRUCTURE

Number and Size of Farms. Every state in the country has dairy farms; however, warmer climates are not generally suited to efficient year-round milk production. Basically, about 88 percent of milk produced in the United States is produced in the 22 states considered to be the nation's Dairy Belt. The Dairy Belt is in the northern region, extending from New York to Minnesota, though California is the largest milk-producing state in the country. Wisconsin, a Dairy Belt state, is the second largest dairy-producing state. Wisconsin led in dairy production for many years, earning the state the title ''The Dairy State,'' but California surpassed it in total dairy production in 1994 and has held the lead ever since. For 1997 and 1998, California produced 7.1 billion pounds of milk during the April-June quarter (the season of highest milk production), while Wisconsin produced 5.8 billion. Other leading dairy states are New York, Pennsylvania, and Minnesota.

Since the 1950s, the number of farms has decreased 50 percent and the number of farms with dairy cows has decreased almost 90 percent. This is due to the shift toward larger scale, industrial dairy farms. A farm with 100 milking cows was considered big in 1950, while farms with 5,000 milking cows were becoming the norm toward the end of the twentieth century.

As recently as 1987, more than 70 percent of the American dairy farms had fewer than 72 cows, but this large segment of the dairy farmer population produced only about 37 percent of milk sold. However, in the mid- to late 1990s the USDA reported that larger farms of 100 or more head accounted for 68.4 percent of the country's total dairy herd. In the south and the west, dairy farms of 500 head or more are increasing. Dairy farming in the nation's Dairy Belt in the north is also headed toward larger, mass-production enterprises, although at present smaller herds still predominate this area. Yet larger dairy farms are able to take advantage of the advances in technology, including fully automated milking parlors, computerized feeding systems, and genetically engineered drugs and hormones, allowing these farms to produce even more milk per head and weakening the ability of small- and medium-sized farms to compete. Many small- and medium-sized farms sell their milk to member-owned dairy cooperatives that process and distribute the milk and other dairy products.

Marketing Orders. For purposes of administration of the government milk subsidy program, dairy farmers in much of the country are part of marketing orders, which are geographic zones set up by the government during the Depression to regulate milk pricing. Farmers voted to form these orders, and the government set the minimum prices for each order that bottlers and other milk processors had to pay. Not all areas chose to be part of this system, but as of 1994, 38 orders regulated about 70 percent of U.S. milk production.

Dairy Farming Regulations. State and local laws regulate conditions under which milk is produced, collected, and processed because it is so easily contaminated. Most milk is sold as Grade A when dairy farms meet strict sanitation standards. Milking machine equipment must be washed and sanitized, and the milk house and milking parlor floors must be kept clean. Farmers must also test their cattle for disease periodically, vaccinate all calves against the disease brucellosis, which affects humans, and remove sick cows from the herd. On the other hand, milk that fails to meet these standards is sold as Grade B.

Background and Development

Dairy cows have been an important part of life in America since the first English settlers arrived in Jamestown in the early 1600s. Cattle continued to move west with the settlers. Each family kept two or more cows with their ''dry'' times staggered so that they would have milk year round.

As towns grew, farmers kept more animals and sold any surplus milk they had. Because milk was highly perishable, farmers could not live very far away from consumers. In the mid-1800s, as the big cities expanded, farms became further removed from consumers, and transportation of milk before it spoiled became a problem. But as more and more railroad lines were built, milk could be transported by train as far as 50 miles. Sanitation and refrigeration were a problem though, and it wasn't until they were dealt with that dairy farming could become a major industry.

Pasteurization, developed by Louis Pasteur in France in the 1860s, kept milk safe longer and enabled milk to be shipped farther. However, this process was not widely used in the United States until the early 1900s. Further development of refrigerated transportation and methods to retard spoilage also contributed to the growth of dairy farming.

The five most important dairy breeds in the United States in the late 1990s were Holstein, Jersey, Ayrshire, Brown Swiss, and Milking Shorthorn. Each breed has a different strength, either in quantity of production, composition of its milk, or suitability to a region's conditions. Eighty-five percent of dairy cattle in the United States are Holsteins, which produce large quantities of milk. Jerseys produce the milk richest in butterfat and protein, and they also tolerate heat better than other breeds.

Current Conditions

During the period of 1996-1998, United States Dairy farmers had an annual production rate of almost 72 million metric tons of milk. Throughout the 1990s the U.S. milk cow inventory steadily shrank but milk production per cow increased. The number of dairy cows in 1998 was estimated to be 9.2 million head. In 1997, the number

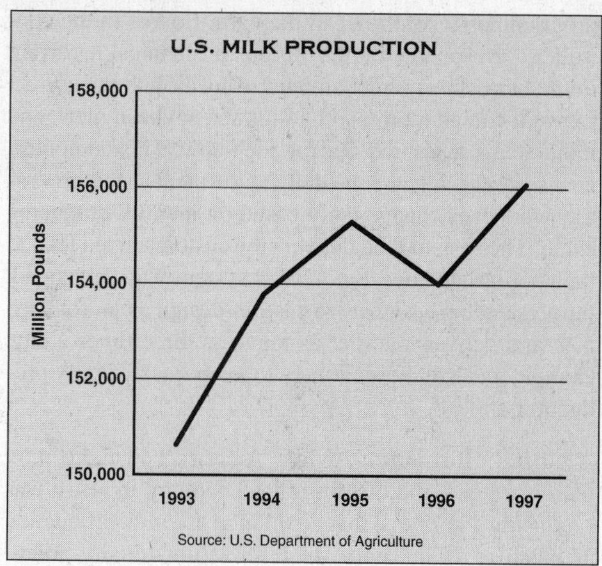

was about 9.3 million. In the period between 1993 and 1997 the average was about 9.5 million. Dairy products that come from milk include butter, cheese, ice cream, sherbet, frozen yogurt, and dry milk

The United States remains the largest producer of milk with 72.6 million metric tons in 1999. India, with 36 million metric tons was a distant second, yet it produced its volume with more cows than the United States. This disparity in milk per cow stems from the ability of U.S. cows to yield 7.3 kilograms of milk per cow, while India's cows only averaged 1.9 kilograms per cow. Industry analysts predicted that the trend of larger dairy farms with fewer cows would persist, followed by a concentration of dairy processing as well.

The 1996 Federal Agriculture Reform and Improvement Act (FAIR) addressed a lot concerns that had been brewing over the decades about milk price regulation, price supports, and market orders. For years, critics had demanded changes in these dairy-management policies. FAIR called for the elimination of the milk price support program that will take effect in 2000. The price support amount was scheduled to decrease from $10.35 to $9.90 over the period leading up to 2000. After that, the subsidy will become a recourse loan—an inventory loan from the government—for processors who have butter or cheese in storage. The government hoped this move would get rid of the floor on dairy products.

The 1996 Farm Act also nixed the fee assessed for maintaining the price-support program. Dairy farmers welcomed this change, because, under the 1990 Farm Bill, they had to pay $.11 per hundredweight. Though not fully articulated within FAIR, the milk marketing order system will undergo modification as well. FAIR mandated the reduction of the current 33 orders to just 10 to 14. In addition, the Agricultural Marketing Service (AMS) and the USDA have three years to develop and put into action reformed milk marketing order system, which among other things, will include a replacement formula for the old Minnesota-Wisconsin Price Series where the standard for milk prices was based on the cost for producing Grade B milk in these two states. With the elimination of the price support program, analysts believe exports could rise, because the support program kept U.S. prices well above competitors' prices. Furthermore, the 1996 Farm Act allowed The National Dairy Promotion and Research Board to use check-off revenue for international marketing. FAIR also strengthened The Dairy Export Incentive Program (DEIP) and called for the establishment of a dairy export trading company. Making the United States a more viable contender in the world dairy market, legislators hope, will lubricate the transition from price support to market dependence.

However, the government continued to set minimum prices for milk, based on the farm's distance from Eau Claire, Wisconsin, which is in the heart of dairy country. Theoretically, the price was based on how much shipping milk from Eau Claire would cost if supplies were not available locally. Milk for drinking was worth between one and two cents more per gallon for every 100 miles from Eau Claire. Under this policy, farmers in Texas were paid more for milk than Wisconsin dairy farmers. And processors had to pay at minimum a regional price set by government guidelines. Milk has been the only commodity for which the agriculture secretary can dictate the minimum price to be paid a farmer.

The complicated system, which requires 500 Department of Agriculture employees to administer and takes up three volumes of the *Code of Federal Regulations,* was instituted in the 1930s before refrigerated transportation was widely available. The south had often faced milk shortages because milk was perishable in the heat and raising cows in that climate was very expensive. Southern farmers were paid a bonus as incentive to expand. However, technology today reduces the cost of shipping milk from surplus states, such as Wisconsin, to distant destinations. Technology has also developed new options for shipping milk. For example, in the 1970s, scientists devised a way to remove water from milk to make it less expensive to ship. But the federal rules made reconstituted milk more expensive than local milk, so this technology has not been pursued.

The Eau Claire rule led to an increase of dairy farming in warm regions even though they were not efficient places to run dairy farms. While many Midwestern farmers claim they are hurt by the regulations, farmers from many other regions support the Eau Claire rule, since they fear that revocation of that rule would result in the shipment of Wisconsin milk across the country, driving thousands of dairy farmers out of business. Southern farmers especially oppose deregulation, claiming they could not afford to remain in business without price supports.

Industry Leaders

In 1996, Aurora Dairy Corp. of Westminster, Colorado, came in first with an inventory of 20,000 cows. Joseph Gallo Farms of Atwater, California was second with 15,100 cows. Another California dairy came in third, Hettinga Dairies of Corona, with 13,600 cows. Braum's Dairy Farms, located in Tuttle, Oklahoma, claimed fourth place, followed in fifth place by Larson Dairy of Okeechobee, Florida. Las Uvas Dairy of Hatch, New Mexico came in sixth. MacArthur Farms also in Okeechobee, Florida was ranked seventh, followed by eighth ranked Case Van der Eyk, Jr. of Ontario and Tipton, California. Closing out the top ten dairy producers were Knevelbaard Dairies of Corona, California, ranking ninth, and, finally, Shamrock Farms of Chandler, Arizona was ranked the tenth largest dairy in the United States.

Workforce

Dairy farmers and workers put in long hours with few days off since the cows must be milked twice a day every day. Farmers must also keep the barns and pens cleared out, clean milking equipment, and keep track of each cow's food consumption and milk production. Most dairy farmers also plant crops to provide feed for their cattle in the winter. Many smaller dairy farms have been in the same family for a few generations, but very few new family farms have been started in recent years because the costs of land, equipment, and a dairy herd are prohibitive. But the increase in larger dairies is changing the landscape of dairy-related employment. On a large dairy farm in Oklahoma, Braum's Dairy Farm, employees earn $8 to 9 per hour, working in six-day intervals punctuated by two days off. The dairy also provides benefits and a savings plan. However, such wages and amenities are not feasible for smaller farms.

Because of their increasing size, the larger dairy farms don't depend as heavily on human labor as they once did. A large portion of the tasks associated with dairy farming are automated, even the milking of cows.

Research and Technology

Computers. Many farms have joined the computer age, enabling farmers to keep track of food consumption and milk production to better manage their herds and their finances. Computerized systems also allowed farmers to design better feeding programs for their herds. Computer controlled trolley systems allowed some dairy farmers to deliver just the right food mix to each individual cow, based on the cow's current milk production, age, weight, overall health and its stage in the lactation cycle. A personal computer in the farmer's home is linked with a programmable controller in the barn. Boards in the controller correspond with the various mechanical hardware in the barn. The correct amount of feed, with the correct ratios of forage (corn and hay), grain, soybean meal, and minerals, is measured out for each cow. This computerized system can make the daily adjustments necessary, as a cow's needs change daily based on its milk-producing cycle. The system then delivers the custom-mixed feed to the appropriate cow. Before this system was developed, farmers had no easy way to custom-design a diet for each cow and deliver that diet as much as three times a day. Computers also allow farmers to keep track of milk production as well.

Artificial Hormones. While America had more milk than it needed, the budding biotechnology industry was producing a hormone that could increase milk production as much as 25 percent, which drove down dairy prices. Bovine somatotropin (BST), a natural protein found in cattle, has been artificially produced in pharmaceutical labs. Farmers remained skeptical about its use: Would it drive down prices by producing a glut of milk? Would consumers believe milk was tainted if it had artificial BST? Companies producing the artificial protein said BST was present in all milk, and milk from cows treated with laboratory BST did not have any higher BST content than milk from untreated cows.

Dairy farmers were in a difficult position: they had already learned to increase milk production through better feed and breeding methods, but BST promised to further increase milk production with even smaller herds. Farmers feared that use of the hormone would produce a vast surplus of milk that would bring prices down. Still, the USDA predicted that 60 percent of dairy cows would be given the hormone by the year 2000. Farmers were not as enthusiastic about the hormone as the pharmaceutical companies, but farmers who wanted to stay competitive would have to give BST to their herds.

Further Reading

Knunston, Ron. et al. ''Economic Status of the Dairy Industry.'' June 1996.

Looker, Dan. ''The Milk Meisters.'' *Agriculture Online.* June 1996. Available from: http://www.agriculture.com/.

———. ''The Milk Meisters II.'' *Agriculture Online.* November 1996. Available from: http://www.agriculture.com/.

United States Department of Agriculture and National Agricultural Statistics Service. ''Dairy, Poultry, and Eggs.'' Washington, DC: 1995-1996. Available from: http://www.usda.gov/nass/pubs/agr95_96/agr95_8.pdf.

United States Department of Agriculture and National Agricultural Statistics Service. ''Milk Production, Disposition, and Income 1998.'' Washington, DC: May 1999. Available from: http://usda.mannlib.cornell.edu/reports/nassr/dairy/pmp-bbm/milk0599.txt.

SIC 0251

BROILER, FRYER, AND ROASTER CHICKENS

This category includes establishments primarily engaged in the production of chickens for slaughter, including those grown under contract.

NAICS CODE(S)

112320 (Broilers and Other Meat-Type Chicken Production)

INDUSTRY SNAPSHOT

Although the number of chicken farms decreased by half over the last 50 years, output rose dramatically, from about 1.5 billion birds in 1959 to almost 8.0 billion in 1999. Farms raising 10,000 or more chickens increased from 2,254 in 1959 to 14,473 in 1987, and supplied 93 percent of all chickens produced.

The industry survived the late twentieth century recession reasonably unscathed. In the early 1990s, it benefitted from unprecedented consumer demand for poultry. In 1992 sales of chicken outstripped those of red meat for the first time. By 1999, chicken gained a 41 percent share of the meat market.

Chicken was also being marketed more widely, particularly in fast food restaurants. Between 1970 and 1990, about 25,000 outlets introduced chicken in the form of sandwiches or nuggets. There was also steady growth in the number of specialist fast food chicken chains, such as KFC and Church's Fried Chicken. The broiler, fryer, and roaster industry and the fast food industry have worked closely together to develop products especially for these markets.

ORGANIZATION AND STRUCTURE

In the 1990s, 7 to 10 companies controlled about 50 to 60 percent of the chicken market. These were vertically integrated concerns—companies with control over every stage of poultry growth and production from egg production to broiler slaughter.

By the end of the twentieth century, independent farmers under contract to large poultry companies grew 89 percent of the chickens, a 10 percent decrease from the mid-1990s. The remainder were farmed directly by the companies themselves. Under the contract system, the company provided the chicks, feed, medication, and transportation to market. The farmer furnished the housing, equipment, labor, and miscellaneous supplies, and agreed to raise the birds until slaughter. Farmers were generally paid according to how much feed was needed for the birds to achieve market weight. The less they needed, the cheaper the chickens were to produce and the more farmers earned.

BACKGROUND AND DEVELOPMENT

Broiler production increased from 34 million in 1934 to approximately 6 billion in 1990. Output has increased in all but five of the last 50 years. Better breeding, feeding, and disease Control—combined with more sophisticated housing—reduced broiler production time by two weeks between 1980 and 1990. In 1935, it took a farmer 16 weeks to produce a 2.9-pound broiler, with 4.5 pounds of feed needed per live weight. By 1988, a farmer could produce a four pounder in just six weeks, on less than two pounds of feed per live weight. This increase was realized by the use of intensive farming methods; new systems of temperature, feed, and water control; careful breeding; and the use of antibiotics to speed the birds' growth.

Increased national and international demand for chicken and chicken products fueled steady industry growth, about 5 percent per year since the early 1960s. In 1995, chicken producers raised about 7.33 billion birds with sales of over $11.4 billion. Total broiler production continued to increase, surpassing 1995's approximately 34 billion pound level of production. About 50 percent of chickens were sold directly to consumers, another 40 percent were sold to restaurants, and 10 percent went for export or pet food.

Despite a sustained drop in the price of chickens in 1994 and 1995, in 1996 wholesale prices for broilers climbed to about 60 cents per pound, while broiler parts held at roughly $1.92 per pound for boneless breasts and about 96 cents for breasts with ribs on. Retail prices ranged from 98 cents per pound for fresh whole broilers to about $2.05 for bone-in breasts.

In 1996, per capita consumption of chicken stood at 72.9 pounds. The type of chicken consumed changed in the latter part of the twentieth century. Chicken was marketed as ''whole,'' ''cut-up and parts,'' or ''further processed.'' Sales in the latter two categories rose steadily, partly due to the fact that consumers considered them time-saving. The market share of cut-up and parts grew from 15 percent in 1962 to 56 percent in 1990. Sales of further processed chicken also increased, from 2 percent market share in 1962 to 26 percent in 1990, of which boneless chicken comprised 80 percent. Also included in this category were value-added products such as nuggets, which became very popular in the 1990s; chicken strips; patties; and versions of buffalo wings.

However, sales of whole chickens plummeted to about 20 percent of all chicken sales in 1994. This trend continued throughout the 1990s and was predicted to continue into the next century. On the other hand, the popularity of rotisserie chicken, as marketed by restaurants such as Boston Market, somewhat stabilized whole chicken sales.

In 1996, the U.S. Department of Agriculture (USDA) revamped its meat inspection system to ensure a high standard of safety. Under the new system, scientific tests and modern technology supplanted the former system, which relied on the inspectors' abilities to perceive contamination themselves. The new method, the Hazard Analysis and Critical Control Points (HACCP), required poultry companies and the USDA to participate in an effort to reduce and prevent contamination.

CURRENT CONDITIONS

By the close of the twentieth century, there were 175 poultry-processing plants in the United States. The industry employed approximately 240,000 workers. In 1999, 8 billion chickens were slaughtered. Per capita consumption was 75 pounds, with consumers spending $40 billion on chicken products annually. Boneless chicken breasts continued to be the most popular cut.

Controlling the spread of disease and ensuring worker safety will most likely continue to be two of the major challenges facing the poultry industry in the next century. For example, chicken feed contained large amounts of the strengthening nutrient phosphorus, which was difficult for chickens to digest. Therefore, the chickens' waste material, much of which was used as manure, also contained high levels of phosphorus. When the manure ran off into ponds and streams, human water supplies were endangered.

Industry researchers and scientists from the University of Delaware were developing a corn hybrid with a more easily digestible phosphorus. However, processors still faced public perception of the negative effects of genetically altered foodstuffs. At the close of the century, Perdue Farms was considering a ban on genetically altered corn for its chickens.

Worker safety was also a concern, since increased product demand and faster machinery had significantly increased the USDA-maximum production line speed from 70 birds per minute in 1979 to 91 birds per minute in 1999. The rate of worker injuries had also increased so that cumulative-trauma disorders, such as carpal tunnel syndrome and tendinitis, were 16 times the national average among poultry workers. The National Institute for Occupational Safety and Health determined that 49 percent of the workers in one plant's deboning line sustained injuries to their upper bodies. Additionally, a study of 51 plants conducted by the Occupational Safety and Health Administration (OSHA) in 1997 concluded that 40 percent of worker injuries resulted from falls on slippery factory floors.

INDUSTRY LEADERS

The industry was dominated by Tyson Foods, Inc. in the 1990s producing over 25 million head of chicken. Second in sales and production was ConAgra, Inc., producing about 13 million head. Other industry leaders included Gold Kist, Perdue Farms, and Pilgrim's Pride.

Tyson Foods, Inc., based in Springdale, Arkansas, was the world's largest producer, processor, and marketer of poultry-based foodstuffs. The bulk of its business (71 percent) was concerned with value-enhanced poultry products, such as chicken patties, precooked and prepackaged chicken, and Rock Cornish hens. Tyson controlled all aspects of its poultry production, from genetic research and breeding, to hatching, rearing, and feed milling. It was also concerned with veterinary and technical services, transportation, and delivery. With 66,000 employees, Tyson posted sales of $7.4 billion in 1998.

John Tyson, the father of the current chairman, Don Tyson, entered the poultry business in the 1930s, although it was not until 1947 that the company was incorporated under the Tyson name. After starting out as a dealer in chicken, John Tyson began raising them. During the 1950s, the company significantly expanded, and in 1958 it opened its first processing plant in Springdale, Arkansas. In 1960, Don Tyson became manager. Three years later, he renamed the company Tyson's Foods, Inc. and introduced Tyson Country Fresh Chicken, packaged birds that have become the company's mainstay. In 1971, the name was changed yet again to Tyson Foods, Inc.

Although the company has grown steadily over the years, a veritable explosion in its trade occurred in the 1980s, as health conscious consumers switched from red meat to chicken. By 1985, it had achieved $1 billion in annual sales. Between 1984 and 1989, Tyson's profits more than quadrupled, while its revenues tripled. Tyson Foods had consolidated its dominance of the market by purchasing key poultry operations, including Prospect Farms, Consolidated Food's (now Sara Lee) Ocoma Foods Division, Heritage Valley, Lane Processing, and the Tasty Bird division of Valmac. In 1989, it beat out rival ConAgra, Inc. for control of Holly Farms, the nation's leading brand name broiler producer. Tyson was also involved in the Mexican food business, produced by-products for pet food, and acquired a stake in a fishery.

Headquartered in Springdale, Arkansas, the chicken capital of the nation, Tyson Foods also had processing plants in 13 states. By the twenty-first century, it was run by CEO and president, Wayne Britt. In addition to being number one in the U.S. market, Tyson exported to Canada, Mexico, Central America, the Caribbean, the Commonwealth of Independent States, the Middle East, the Far East, Sweden, and the United Kingdom. Japan had also become an important customer of Tyson chicken:

Tyson supplied Japan with over 50 percent of all its U.S. chicken imports.

Tyson Foods' chief competitor was ConAgra, Inc., a diversified food company that was number two in the U.S. food business in the 1990s, placing after Philip Morris' Kraft General Foods. The company as a whole earned $23.8 billion in fiscal 1998 for all of its divisions and employed a total of 82,629 people. It also had stakes in the agriculture industry. ConAgra has been involved in the broiler industry since 1982 when it brought Country Pride, a leading producer of broilers. It continued to market chickens under this label and also under its Country Skillet and Frozen Banquet brands. Based in Omaha, Nebraska, the company has trading offices in 26 countries and was run by CEO and president Bruce Rohde.

ConAgra, Inc. came into existence in 1919 as the Nebraska Consolidated Mills Company. Its founder, Alva Kinney, concentrated on the grain milling business, and it was not until the late 1940s that the company entered the prepared foods industry. The company continued to diversify through the 1960s, when it first gained an interest in the chicken market, developing poultry growing and processing sites in Georgia, Louisiana, and Alabama. In 1965, it expanded into the European market, eventually forming a partnership with BioterBiona, SA, a Spanish breeder of chickens, other livestock, and animal feed. In 1971, the company changed its name to ConAgra, meaning ''in partnership with the land.'' It was first listed on the New York Stock Exchange in 1973.

During the early 1970s, the company languished as many of its acquisitions failed to thrive. In 1975, former Pillsbury executive Charles Harper was brought in as president to turn ConAgra around. He purchased Banquet Foods Corporation in 1980 as a way to increase ConAgra's share of the chicken market. In 1982, ConAgra moved into first place in the chicken industry when it formed Country Poultry, Inc. By the following year, the division was the nation's biggest poultry producer, with more than a billion pounds of brand-name broilers. In 1987, it tightened its grip on the broiler industry when it bought Longmont Foods, another poultry producer. It has since been pushed into the number two spot by Tyson Foods. Competition between the two companies intensified in 1999 when Tyson filed suit against ConAgra, charging ConAgra with luring away four top-ranking Tyson employees and stealing company secrets.

Atlanta-based Gold Kist Poultry Group, a farmers' cooperative formed in 1933, reported sales of $1.65 billion in 1998 and employed 16,500 people. Perdue Chickens, a privately-run company headed by James Perdue and based in Salisbury, Maryland, reported sales of between $1.5 and $2 billion in the 1990s and employed 19,000 people. Pilgrim's Pride, reported $1.3 billion in sales and 13,000 employees in 1998. Lonnie ''Bo'' Pilgrim, CEO, heads Pilgrim's Pride, which is based in Pittsburg, Texas. Leading chicken-producing states included Arkansas, Georgia, Alabama, North Carolina, and Mississippi.

WORKFORCE

U.S. chicken processors employ a total of about 240,000 workers. Approximately 73 percent of chicken farms employed under four workers in the 1990s, and over 9 percent employed between five and nine workers. About 4.5 percent of operations employed over 100 people, while 2 percent employed between 10 and 14, and 3 percent, between 20 and 49. Approximately 1 percent employed between 15 and 19 and 1 percent between 50 and 99 workers.

Although most poultry farmers worked as independent contractors for the large poultry companies, their relationship was usually one of dependence. Fewer poultry producers meant that farmers often had no choice but to take what they could get. Although they may have depended on a company for their livelihood, they did not enjoy the benefits of employment, such as workers' compensation, health insurance, or paid vacation time. In order to be eligible for a contract, growers had to invest heavily in plants and equipment, thus tying themselves up with debt for long periods of time. Their contracts with poultry companies did not last the length of their mortgages, but were automatically renewable unless either party wished to cancel. In practice, this meant that farmers were guaranteed no more than the next flock of chickens.

Although there was some talk of setting up a growers' organization to lobby for legislative change in the industry, growers were fearful of being boycotted or blacklisted by the producers if they tried to organize. The poultry industry's political clout was legendary. Its political action committee contributed hundreds of thousands of dollars to politicians, particularly those from the South. John Tyson, head of the largest poultry company, was a personal friend of former-president Bill Clinton and contributed generously to his election campaign. The poultry companies defended the contract system by pointing out that they provided employment, and that they offered farmers a steady income. About 58 percent of the chicken farmers earned between $50 and $250 thousand in 1996. Some earned far less and others considerably more. Top growers often received bonuses from the poultry companies.

Some steps to protect the growers have been taken, although growers said they did not go far enough. They wanted to see laws that would require poultry companies to: pay them within a specified time; provide for mediation in the case of disputes; allow growers to recoup their investment if the contractor backed out of the deal; adjust prices for growers whose income was affected by weight; and prevent unfair trade practices.

America and the World

Most of the market leaders had a stake in the poultry market abroad. For example, Tyson Foods, Inc. had important markets in western Europe, the Caribbean, Mexico, and the Pacific Rim. The latter alone accounted for almost 50 percent of all exports in this category. Demand for U.S. chicken had also increased in Russia and former Soviet Union countries. The USDA estimated that Russia imported more than 990,000 tons of chicken in 1997, generating $793 million in revenue for the American poultry industry.

Because of Hong Kong's reversion to Chinese rule, its imports of U.S. chicken have been somewhat uncertain yet remained strong. China drastically increased its imports of U.S. chicken, making it one of the largest customers in the late 1990s. South Africa also imported 50 percent more U.S. chicken in 1996 than in 1995. Exports to Mexico, Canada, and Japan also rose significantly and were expected to remain high. Soaring to record highs in all sectors, total poultry exports amounted to 5.4 million pounds with a value of $2.5 billion.

Research and Technology

Research remained focused on ways to help farmers improve their yields in order to satisfy the ever growing demand for chicken. Technological leaps in the late twentieth century allowed farmers in the 1990s to produce more birds in a day than farmers in the 1930s did in an entire year. The aim of much of these efforts was to produce a stress-free environment for the birds. One company even came up with red-tinted contact lenses for chickens which, it claimed, "lowers the chicken's social stress" level.

Further Reading

Cook, Christopher D. "Fowl Trouble." *Harper's*, August 1999.

Dun's Census of American Business. New Jersey: Dun and Bradstreet, 1996.

Hoover's Handbook of American Business. Austin, TX: Reference Press, 1996.

National Technical Information Service. "USDA Modernizes 90-Year-Old System of Meat Inspection Final Rule." Springfield: November 1996.

Roston, Eric. "Will the U.S. Chicken Out on Russia?" *Fortune,* 23 November 1998.

U.S. Department of Agriculture and National Agricultural Statistics Service. "Dairy, Poultry, and Eggs." Washington, DC: 1995-1996. Available from: http://www.usda.gov/nass/pubs/agr95_96/agr95_8.pdf.

U.S. Department of Agriculture. *Poultry Outlook.* Washington, DC: 18 November 1996. Available from: http://usda.mannlib.cornell.edu/reports/erssor/livestock/ldppbb/1996/poultry_outlook_11.18.96.

U.S. Poultry and Egg Export Council. Available from http://www.usapeec.org.

SIC 0252

CHICKEN EGGS

This category includes establishments primarily engaged in the production of chicken eggs, including table eggs and hatching eggs, and in the sale of cull hens.

NAICS Code(s)

112310 (Chicken Egg Production)

Industry Snapshot

According to *Dun's Census of American Business,* there were 1,026 chicken egg farms in the late 1990s, a decline of several hundred farms from the early 1990s. However, another 160 farms claimed this industry as a secondary SIC. Four hundred and seventeen of the chicken egg farms were fairly small, employing under five people, while the remainder ranged in size from 10 employees to more than 100. Overall production was heavily consolidated by a few companies who ran massive operations; upwards of one million birds was not uncommon at these farms.

Background and Development

The chicken egg farm industry has been strong since the beginning of the 1990s, although it is subject to fluctuations. The size of the nation's laying flock has varied in the past few decades, with a noticeable effect on price. Although the national laying flock has steadily decreased from 317 million in 1967 to 290 million in 1983 to 258 million in 1998, the production level has increased over the years from 170.5 billion cases in 1984 to an estimated 192.5 billion in 1999.

In 1993, large eggs sold for 76 cents per dozen, but in 1996, prices increased dramatically to a record average high around 90 cents per dozen. By 1998, the price was back down to 78 cents. Egg farmers tried to affect future pricing by slowing the rate of increase of the broiler hatching egg flock, thus reducing production. The flock grew by only a fraction of a percent in 1995 and only 1 percent in 1996, compared with a 6 percent growth rate in 1991. Therefore, prices rose in late 1995 and remained strong throughout 1996.

The production rate on some egg farms is impressive in comparison with other livestock farms. Some farms have 1.5 to 2 million laying hens, producing about 400 million eggs a year. The number of farms with 1 million or more hens, or layers, has increased in the 1990s. ''Large complexes of a million or more layers are one result of increases in layer productivity and feed conversion rates, and developments in egg handling and processing technology,'' according to the U.S. Department of Agriculture (USDA). Sources in the business claim that the number of large egg farms (more than 75,000 layers) has grown by 20 percent since 1980, whereas the overall number of farms has declined. This move toward larger facilities, to take advantage of economies of scale, is expected to continue.

However, the factory-style facilities designed to accommodate large flocks frequently attract criticism for the manner in which the birds are treated. Space is at a minimum, and the layers are often literally ''henpecked'' by frustrated fellow birds; they also are given antibiotics to reduce the diseases that spread easily in this environment. It is this type of farming, though, that allows for high levels of production and low prices. The alternative is ''free-range'' eggs produced by hens that are allowed to roam freely and are not confined to a cage. However, because production is limited, ''free-range'' eggs are more expensive than factory-produced ones.

In larger ''corporate'' chicken farms, eggs are collected via machinery and conveyor belts that transport the eggs directly from the layers to cleaning stations where they are washed, ridding them of bacteria, dirt, and blood spots. Even though the USDA has not established a storage time limit, eggs are generally stored for one to seven days prior to being shipped to stores. Throughout the storage and transportation period (pre-market), eggs are refrigerated to ensure freshness and safety. Due to the grand scale of production, modern egg farms require extensive capital investments in the form of environmentally-controlled shelters, computerized egg flow controllers, and packaging machinery.

CURRENT CONDITIONS

Although annual per capita egg consumption fell substantially throughout the 1980s and early 1990s (from 275 in 1980 to 225 in 1992), it rose to 245 eggs in 1998. Analysts have attributed egg consumption growth to the fact that more people were using more egg products than in previous years. Broken shell egg production and consumption also has continued to increase. For example, 1.5 billion eggs, or 257 million pounds, were used in the manufacture of liquid, frozen, or dried egg products in January 1997, which is 9 percent more than during the same period in 1996.

Egg products are regarded as more versatile and safer than shell eggs since they are pasteurized to eliminate bacteria. According to the USDA, ''Eggs are increasingly being broken and used in liquid, dried, and frozen form by food manufacturers, as well as by hotels and restaurants. Part of this increase reflects restaurants buying liquid pasteurized eggs instead of shell eggs. It also reflects growth in supermarket sales of convenient, value-added products in forms other than shell eggs.'' Increased demand for egg products has led many egg farmers to build egg breaking and processing plants on their properties. Several farmers have also introduced a production process dedicated to egg products, where eggs are automatically transported by conveyor belt from the hens to breaking and processing stations.

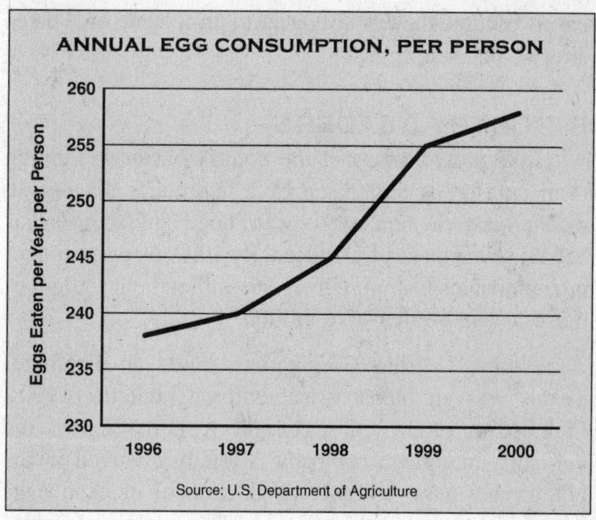

Source: U.S. Department of Agriculture

Of 1997's 77.5 billion eggs, table eggs accounted for 65.4 billion eggs, while hatching eggs amounted to 12.0 billion.

Most chicken egg farms earned less than $250,000 in the late 1990s. Just 41 farms were reported by *Dun's* as earning more than $5 million. While 102 farms earned less than $50,000, 248 posted revenues of $50,000-$100,000, and 316 earned $100,000-$250,000. Additionally, 88 chicken egg farms reported a gross income of $250,000-$500,000, while 60 earned $500,000-$1 million. Finally, 54 egg farms earned $1-5 million.

At the end of the twentieth century, the five top egg-producing states represented one-half of all U.S. layers. In 1998, Ohio surpassed California as the nation's top egg-producing state with 28 million laying flocks to California's 25 million. They were followed by Iowa (23.7 million), Pennsylvania (21.4 million), and Indiana (21.3 million.)

Prevention of salmonella poisoning from eggs was a major concern of the industry. Of the 67 billion eggs consumed by Americans each year, the Federal Drug Administration (FDA) estimates that one in 20,000 carries salmonella bacteria. Date-stamping on egg cartons and better consumer education were two recommendations from the government. In August 1999, Rose Acre

Farms became the first producer to print "laid on" dates directly on their eggs.

Industry Leaders

Like most aspects of the poultry business, the egg farm industry is dominated by a few major players. In recent years, the tendency toward huge egg factories has become even more pronounced. By 1999, 60 egg-producing companies had more than one million layers; eight of those had more than five million.

Pilgrim's Pride Corporation, based in Pittsburg, Texas, was an industry leader throughout the 1990s. Founded in 1963 by CEO Lonnie A. (Bo) Pilgrim, the vertically-integrated company is totally involved in the poultry business, with the production of chicken eggs being just one of its concerns. The company's chief markets are the western United States and Mexico; it also exports to Eastern Europe and the Pacific Rim. In 1998, the company reported total revenues of $1.3 billion and employed 13,000 people.

Although an industry leader, Pilgrim's Pride has had financial problems. Until the mid-1980s, the company's sales grew by about 20 percent annually. However, this growth was financed by massive debt, equivalent to four times the value of the company's equity. In the mid-1980s, the company started reducing its debt, but suffered badly from falling prices for its products. To protect itself, Pilgrim's Pride entered the prepared chicken market in 1986.

After reaching an all-time financial low in 1988, the company rebounded in 1989. Its decision to surrender the ailing retail market and concentrate on the food service industry had proven savvy. It also benefited from entry into the Mexican market. As a result, its net sales increased by 30 percent to give the company a profit-to-sales ratio of more than 3 percent. Sales continued to rise through 1991 due to Pilgrim's Pride's expansion within the Mexican market, increased export sales, and steady demand for its further processed and prepared chicken products. Pilgrim's Pride's profits, however, did not keep pace, but instead fell by 21 percent.

In 1992 Bo Pilgrim sold off 18 percent of his stock to the Archer-Daniels-Midland (ADM) Co. as part of a deal that enabled Pilgrim's Pride to extend its loan maturities. Pilgrim controlled approximately 65 percent of the company. As part of the agreement, Pilgrim's Pride agreed to indemnify ADM against losses for an unspecified period of time. The deal also stipulated that ADM cannot control more than 20 percent of the firm.

In addition to rescheduling loans in 1992, Pilgrim's Pride attempted to deal with its financial woes by appointing a new president, Monty Henderson, to replace William Voss. Henderson sought to postpone the company's loan repayments, consolidate its indebtedness, and improve Pilgrim's Pride's operating and financial flexibility.

Another major chicken egg producer in the 1990s was Cal-Maine Foods Inc., based in Jackson, Mississippi. Its primary classification is as a producer of chicken eggs. It is also involved in raising hogs and beef cattle. The company employed 1,650 people in 1998. Cal-Maine earned about $2.8 billion in 1996.

The Albertville, Alabama, division of Hudson Foods Inc. was also a prominent egg producer in the 1990s; the division was also involved in poultry production. The entire Hudson empire earned $13 billion in 1998 and employed 11,470 people.

Another leader of the 1990s was Sun City Industries, based in Fort Lauderdale, Florida. Its primary business was egg production, although it also maintained a food-service division. It employed 300 people and posted revenues of $91.1 million in 1998, half of which came from egg production. Finally, Hillandale Farms of Florida Inc. has been a key egg producer. In 1998, the company reported revenues of $45 million and employed 20 people.

Workforce

Egg farms are generally highly automated operations that can function with a minimal staff. In 1996, 484 farms employed 0-4 workers, 208 employed 5-9, 83 farms had 10-14, and 41 had 15-19 workers. Additionally, 111 egg farms had a staff of 20-49 workers, while 49 had 50-99, and 32 farms had more than 100 workers.

America and the World

The United States has been one of the world's largest egg-producing countries. Only China, with an annual production of 284 billion eggs, ranks higher. U.S. egg exports in 1998 equaled 1.5 million cases.

The most important markets for U.S. eggs are Japan, Hong Kong, Canada, Mexico, Germany, and the Netherlands. Japan, Canada, and Mexico were responsible for 80 percent of U.S. egg exports in the 1990s. Many other countries also rely on the United States for their eggs. Sales of egg products to the United Arab Emirates increased by 71 percent in the first quarter of 1996, constituting 10 percent of all exports, although they tapered off later in the year. However, during the same period, Hong Kong and Mexico increased their importation of U.S. eggs. In addition, the European Union has created a new market for U.S. eggs. Analysts predicted egg exports to continue increasing through the end of the decade due to escalating production and lower domestic prices.

FURTHER READING

American Egg Board. "Egg Industry Facts Sheet," 1999. Available from http://www.aeb.org/eii/facts/industry-facts.html.

American Egg Board. "U.S. Egg Production, Population and Distribution," 1999. Available from http://www.aeb.org/eii/facts/us-prod.html.

Cohen, Andy. "What You Didn't Learn in Marketing 101." *Sales & Marketing Management,* August 1999.

Dun's Census of American Business 1996. Bethlehem, PA: Dun and Bradstreet, 1996.

Turcsik, Richard. "Good Egg." *Progressive Grocer,* October 1999.

U.S. Department of Agriculture. "Layers and Egg Production," 31 January 1997. Available from http://usda.mannlib.cornell.edu/reports/nassr/poultry/pec-bbl/layers_and_egg_production_annual_01.31.97.

SIC 0253

TURKEYS AND TURKEY EGGS

This category includes establishments primarily engaged in the production of turkeys and turkey eggs.

NAICS CODE(S)

112330 (Turkey Production)

Turkey production in the United States has been on the decline in the late 1990s after peaking with a record 310 million birds produced in 1996, according to the U.S. Department of Agriculture (USDA). In 1999, U.S. turkey production dipped to 273 million birds, down from 285 million in 1998 and 301 million in 1997.

Over these years, North Carolina has remained the turkey capital, producing 46.5 million birds in 1999, down from 50 million birds in 1998. In the same period, the second-largest producer, Minnesota, produced 43.5 million birds, a slight decrease from the 44.5 million turkeys produced in 1998. Arkansas was a distant third, producing 27 million turkeys in 1999, while fourth-ranked Virginia produced 24 million. Missouri, producing 22 million birds in both 1998 and 1999, moved up to the fifth-place spot, nudging out California, which had been the third-leading producer in the 1980s and early 1990s. During 1999, these states accounted for 71 percent of all turkeys produced in the United States.

Turkey production in 1998 totaled 7 billion pounds live weight, down from 7.23 billion the previous year. Producers received an average price of 38 cents per pound in 1998, down from 39.9 cents in 1997. Also in 1998, the value of turkeys produced dropped to $2.66 billion, down 8 percent from $2.88 billion in 1997.

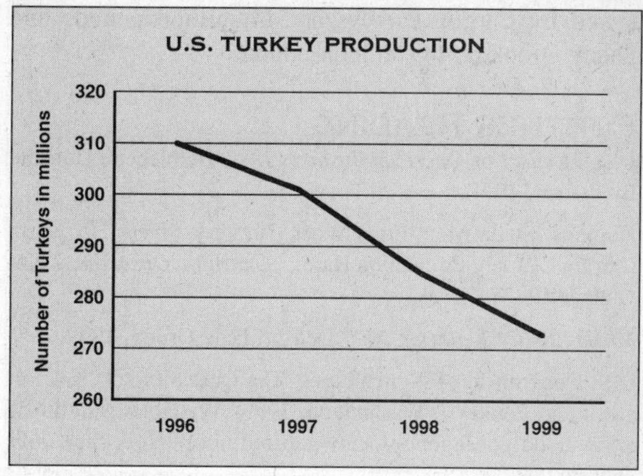

While the numbers have been on the decline in the late 1990s, turkey growers in the 20 states that produced 96 percent of all turkeys in 1999 planned to increase by 1 percent the number of birds raised in 2000. The USDA predicts moderate expansion through 2002, as feed prices decline and producers see an increase in returns. Beyond that, the USDA expects production after 2003 to increase by less than 1 percent each year as feed costs increase at a faster rate than turkey prices. Growth in exports during this time is also expected to be slow as turkeys face competition from low-priced pork trimmings.

In the late 1990s, the turkey industry grappled with many problems, including flattened consumption, weak selling prices, increasing problems with turkey disease, high feed costs, excess inventories, and low selling prices. Technology also hurt the industry. Genetic engineering has produced turkeys with larger breasts, leading to excess inventories. According to the USDA, turkeys slaughtered in December 1999 were 4 percent heavier than they were the year before, averaging 25.7 pounds per bird. Also, more and more processors are using less meat and supplementing with fillers—like basting solutions—in place of meat. This has led to a glut of turkey. In 1997, the amounts in cold storage were running 30 million to 50 million pounds above normal. Breast meat sold at $1.45 a pound in 1997, 30 percent lower than the $2.07 offered in 1995.

While the number of turkeys produced has declined, so has the number of establishments engaged in the industry. In 1997, according to *Dun's Census of American Business,* there were 574 such establishments, compared with 614 in 1996 and 805 in 1992.

According to the *Market Share Reporter 2000,* the industry is led by Jennie-O Turkeys, a wholly owned subsidiary of Hormel Foods Corporation; it produces about 891 million pounds (live weight). Butterball Turkey, a ConAgra subsidiary, produces 846 million pounds to finish just behind Jennie-O. Wampler Turkeys is the third-leading producer, with 650 million pounds, followed by Cargill Turkeys at 514 million pounds and Shady Brook at 489 million pounds.

FURTHER READING

Dun's Census of American Business 1997. Bethlehem: Dun and Bradstreet, 1997.

Hopkins, Stella M., "Price Woes, Mystery Illness Hit North Carolina Turkey Production Hard." *Charlotte Observer,* 7 November 1997.

Market Share Reporter 2000 Detroit: Gale Group, 1999.

U.S. Department of Agriculture. "The Outlook for U.S. Livestock and Poultry." Washington: 1999. Available from http://www.usda.gov/agency/oce/waob/outlook99/speeches/069/shagam.txt.

U.S. Department of Agriculture. National Agricultural Statistics Service. "Dairy, Poultry, and Eggs." Washington, 1995-1996. Available from http://www.usda.gov/nass/pubs/agr95_96/agr95_8.pdf.

———. "Livestock, Dairy, and Poultry Monthly." Washington: 20 March 1997. Available from http://usda.mannlib.cornell.edu/reports/erssor/livestock/ldp-mbb/1997/livestock_dairy_and_poultry_03.20.97.

———. "Poultry—Production and Value 1998 Summary." Washington: April 1999. Available from http://usda.mannlib.cornell.edu/reports/nassr/poultry/pbh-bbp/plva0499.txt.

———. "Turkeys." Washington: 12 January 2000. Available from http://usda.mannlib.cornell.edu/reports/nassr/poultry/pth-bbt/tuky0100.txt.

SIC 0254

POULTRY HATCHERIES

This category includes establishments primarily engaged in operating poultry hatcheries on their own account or on a contract or fee basis.

NAICS CODE(S)

112340 (Poultry Hatcheries)

This is a small industry, with only 746 businesses operating primarily as poultry hatcheries in 1997, according to *Dun's Census of American Business,* down from 783 the previous year. The number has been falling in the late 1990s due in part to massive vertically integrated operations that produce chickens in great quantities and raise them from hatchery to slaughterhouse. Another 158 businesses, however, claimed **SIC 0254: Poultry Hatcheries** as a secondary SIC in 1997.

As this industry is highly automated, most operations have a small staff. In 1997, over half of the poultry hatcheries (415 operations) employed fewer than five workers. The remainder of the establishments maintained staffs of various sizes; 72 businesses had 5 to 9 employees, 40 had 10 to 14, 28 employed 15 to 19 people, 93 had 20 to 49, 34 had 50 to 99 workers, and only 45 had more than 100 employees.

A few companies controlled the majority of the hatchery market in the late 1990s. These were mainly giant, vertically integrated operations that had multiple interests in the poultry business. The remaining hatcheries were mostly family-run operations, with a majority, 231, making between $100,000 to $250,000 in annual revenues. Many of these smaller businesses produced chicks on a contract basis for the large poultry companies. Thirty-nine hatcheries earned less than $50,000 in 1997, while 89 earned $50,000 to $100,000. Another 231 operations earned $100,000 to $250,000, and 59 had $250,000 to $499,000 in revenues. Continuing up the scale, 44 companies earned from $500,000 to $999,000, while 60 earned $1,000,000 to $5,000,000. Finally, 53 poultry hatcheries earned more than $5 million. A number of poultry hatcheries were not accounted for in regard to profits.

In November 1999, hatcheries produced 674 million broiler-type chicks, down 1 percent from November 1998. However, egg-type chicks hatched during this period increased to 33.1 million, up 6 percent from 1998. Georgia, Arkansas, and Alabama, respectively, produced the most broiler-type chicks in November 1999; Indiana, Iowa, and Pennsylvania led with the most egg-type chicks hatched in November 1999.

As of December 1, 1999, there were 614 million broiler-type chicks in incubators in the United States, down 1 percent from 618 million a year before. There were also 29 million egg-type chicks in incubators, down 7 percent from 32 million a year before.

The value of broilers produced during 1998 hit $15.1 billion, up 7 percent from $14.2 billion in 1997. The United States produced 7.93 billion broilers in 1998, up 2 percent from 1997. Revenues at hatcheries may be on the rise because poultry production is expected to increase by about 5 percent in 2000 due to low feed costs and an increasing domestic demand for poultry—up 5 to 7 percent annually.

The nation's number one chicken producer, Tyson Foods Incorporated, is a vertically integrated operation with $7.36 billion in sales in fiscal 1999, down .7 percent from $7.41 billion the previous year. Tyson, based in Springdale, Arkansas, employs more than 60,000 people across the United States and Mexico and operates 54 hatcheries. Although it is the industry leader, it is primarily classified as a poultry slaughterer and processor, producing 6.4 billion pounds of chicken per week in 1998.

Agri International Inc., an Atlanta-based poultry hatchery, is the second largest company in this industry.

It's primarily classified as a hatchery and secondarily as a broiler, fryer, and roaster farm. Agri International is owned by Gold Kist Inc. and, according to *Agriculture, Mining, and Construction USA,* employs 13,000 people and has estimated sales of $1.2 billion.

The third largest chicken hatchery operation is Purdue Inc., based in Showell, Maryland, with $530 million in sales and 3,200 employees. Fourth place is held by Wampler-Longacre Chicken Inc., based in Broadway, Virginia, earning an estimated $370 million and employing 4,000 people. The fifth largest company in this industry is McCarty Farms Inc., based in Magee, Mississippi, which operates primarily as a hatchery. It employed 3,000 workers and earned approximately $250,000.

FURTHER READING

Agriculture, Mining, and Construction USA. Detroit: Gale Research, 1998.

Dun's Census of American Business 1997. Bethlehem, PA: Dun and Bradstreet, 1997.

Tyson Foods Inc. ''About Tyson.'' Available from http://www.tyson.com/corporate/About/today.asp.

U. S. Department of Agriculture. National Agricultural Statistics Service. ''Broiler Hatchery.'' Washington, 19 March 1997. Available from http://usda.mannlib.cornell.edu/reports/nassr/poultry/pbh-bb/1997/broiler_hatchery_03.19.97.

U. S. Department of Agriculture. National Agricultural Statistics Service. ''Chickens and Eggs.'' Washington, 21 March 1997. Available from http://usda.mannlib.cornell.edu/reports/nassr/poultry/pec-bb/1997/chickens_and_eggs_03.21.97.

U. S. Department of Agriculture. National Agricultural Statistics Service. ''Poultry Highlights.'' Washington, 30 December 1999. Available from http://www.nass.usda.gov/ca/rev/poultry/912poltb.htm and http://www.nass.usda.gov/ca/rev/poultry/912polna.htm.

SIC 0259

POULTRY AND EGGS, NOT ELSEWHERE CLASSIFIED

This category includes establishments primarily engaged in the production of poultry and eggs, not elsewhere classified. This industry also includes establishments deriving 50 percent or more of their total value of sales of agricultural products from poultry and eggs (Industry Group 025), but less than 50 percent from products of any single industry.

NAICS CODE(S)

112390 (Other Poultry Production)

This industry had just 272 businesses operating under this primary SIC in 1997, according to *Dun's Census of American Business.* Another 38 establishments claimed **SIC 0259: Poultry and Eggs, Not Elsewhere Classified** as a secondary SIC. Included in this industry were businesses engaged in operating duck farms, geese farms, pheasant and pigeon farms, quail and squab farms, and poultry egg farms, except chicken and turkey eggs.

Although accounting for only a small percentage of overall poultry and poultry egg sales, the geese, pheasant, pigeon, and other birds farmed in this industry benefitted from brisk sales throughout the mid-1990s, as consumers' taste shifted from red to white meat. Consumption, however, flattened toward the end of the decade. According to the U.S. Department of Agriculture (USDA), the amount of poultry in this category (other than duck) slaughtered under federal inspection decreased from 14.5 million pounds (live weight) in 1998 to 14 million pounds in 1999. During this same period, the number of ducks slaughtered under federal inspection increased from 2.0 million birds, or 13.6 million pounds (live weight), in December 1998 to 2.1 million, or 14.5 million pounds (live weight), in December 1999.

In 1997, the majority of poultry farms in this category were small-scale operations employing less than five people and earning less than $250,000 per annum. Of the operations surveyed by *Dun's,* 127 farms earned between $100,000 and $250,000, and 30 establishments earned less than $50,000. Another 40 operations made between $50,000 and $100,000, while 24 operations reaped from $250,000 to $500,000 in revenues. An additional 12 farms had between $500,000 and $1 million in sales, and another 14 of them earned from $1 million to $5 million. Finally, just five companies reported more than $5 million in revenues. A total of nine companies were unaccounted for as far as earnings were concerned.

More than 75 percent of the businesses in this group, (a total 205 establishments), employed zero to four workers in 1997, according to *Dun's.* Almost 11 percent (30 businesses), had between five and nine employees. Another 17 farms had 10 to 14 people on staff, while two had between 15 and 19. Finally, six farms had between 20 and 49 employees; another six, from 50 to 99; and an additional six had more than 100 workers.

FURTHER READING

Dun's Census of American Business, 1997. Bethlehem, PA: Dun and Bradstreet, 1997.

U.S. Department of Agriculture. National Agricultural Statistics Service. ''Poultry Slaughter.'' Washington, DC: 4 March 1997. Available from http://usda.mannlib.cornell.edu/reports/nassr/poultry/ppy-bb/1997/poultry_slaughter_03.04.97

U. S. Department of Agriculture. National Agricultural Statistics Service. ''Poultry Slaughter.'' Washington, DC: 4 February

2000. Available from http://usda.mannlib.cornell.edu/reports/nassr/poultry/ppy-bb/2000/psla0200.txt.

SIC 0271

FUR-BEARING ANIMALS AND RABBITS

This classification covers establishments primarily engaged in the production of fur and fur-bearing animals and rabbits. These include chinchilla farms, fox farms, fur farms, mink farms, and rabbit farms.

NAICS CODE(S)

112930 (Fur Bearing Animal and Rabbit Production)

In 1998 there were 439 establishments that raised mink for pelts. Utah had the largest percentage of farms, with more than 26 percent, followed by Wisconsin and Minnesota. Of these, 31 establishments also raised fox. Value of the 2.94 million pelts produced that year was $99.1 million.

The majority of fur-bearing animal farms were small-scale operations that earned less than $250,000 in 1996. Approximately 115 farms reported 1996 revenues of less than $100,000. The largest grouping, about 250 farms, made between $100,000 and $500,000, while 21 garnered more than $500,000 during the year, and 10 producers earned between $1 and $4 million. However, no operation reported revenues of over $5 million. Most of the establishments in this industry employ fewer than five people.

In recent years, the fur-bearing animal raising industry has suffered the ill effects of fur's increasingly negative image. Many stores have closed down their fur departments under pressure from animal rights activists and in response to decreasing sales. As a result, sales of fur-bearing animals to the retail fur industry have steadily declined over the past few years. Although sales increased during the boom years of the 1980s, they plunged again as resistance became more pronounced. High-profile protest groups such as People for the Ethical Treatment of Animals (PETA) have proven adept at casting the industry in an unflattering light. PETA has launched many rescue missions where members target fur farms and release the animals. In the 1990s the industry made a comeback, as fur came to be regarded as a versatile fabric, and the American economy improved.

Mink has generally accounted for 50 to 60 percent of all fur production and sales. Only 659,900 females were bred in 1999, compared to 733,000 in 1998. Most pelts produced that year were of the standard color class, followed by mahogany, gunmetal, ranch wild, and demibuff. Despite increased production and sales, the fur industry faces an uncertain future.

FURTHER READING

Dun's Census of American Business, 1996. Bethlehem, PA: Dun & Bradstreet Corporation, 1996.

U.S. Department of Agriculture. ''Mink.'' *National Agricultural Statistics Service.* Washington, D.C., 2000. Available from http://usda.mannlib.cornell.edu/reports/nassr/other/zmi-bb/mink0799.txt.

SIC 0272

HORSES AND OTHER EQUINES

This classification covers establishments primarily engaged in the production of horses and other equines such as burros, donkeys, and mules.

NAICS CODE(S)

112920 (Horse and Other Equine Production)

INDUSTRY SNAPSHOT

In 1908, when Henry Ford rolled out his first car, there were more than 21 million horses in the United States. That number eventually shrank to three million, as horses were no longer needed to pull military cannons, plow fields, or haul freight. The horse raising industry has been a resilient one, however. By 1996 the number of horses in the United States had risen back to 7 million head.

Horses have long done America's hard work. Horses are still used on ranches and feedlots. Occasionally helicopters or motorcycles are used to gather and check cattle, but the horse is still the preferred method of transportation for the modern-day cowboy. Horses and mules are also still used as pack animals and carriage animals. Primarily, however, most horses in the United States in the late 1990s were used for pleasure. While rodeo, recreational riding, and horse shows increased in popularity, horse racing was in decline—although exports of horses used for racing did increase. As a result, although yearling thoroughbred sales took by far the most money, the most growth was seen in other breeds, including unfamiliar breeds such as miniature horses.

ORGANIZATION AND STRUCTURE

Horse breeding establishments usually specialize in one breed of horse for a particular usage. For example, a quarter horse breeder may produce horses to be used solely for herding, cutting cattle, or quarter horse racing, whereas a paint breeder may raise horses to show at halter in a show ring, or vice versa. Whatever the purpose, the breeder depends on the reproductive capacity of the stallion and the brood mare band.

Successfully breeding domesticated horses is one of the more difficult tasks in raising livestock. A stallion that is capable of achieving a conception rate of 75 percent is regarded as acceptable, compared with a conception rate of 90 percent for a stallion in the wild, who would run with 30 to 40 mares.

Well-grown fillies (young female horses) can be bred when they are two years old so they will first foal when they are three years of age. Many breeders think it best to wait until the filly is three before breeding her for the first time. If she is properly cared for, a mare will reproduce up to 15 years of age, and even longer in many cases. Mares can be pasture bred, hand bred (a method where the stallion is brought to the mare), or artificially inseminated, a growing practice. Some breed associations, though, do not allow a foal to be registered if it was conceived through the use of artificial insemination. The Jockey Club, the main registrar of thoroughbred horses, is one of the last breed organizations that will not allow this method.

Stud farm establishments provide standing exceptional stallions, enabling horse owners to bring their mares to get bred to an animal they could not otherwise afford. The owner of an exceptional stud horse may own his/her own band of mares or only breed outside mares belonging to other people for a stud fee. Most horse farms and ranches have a combination of the two.

Foals that have just been weaned from their mother's milk in auction sales or through what is called "private treaty" can be sold as weanlings or retained on the farm and broken (the practice of training a horse to accept a saddle, a bit, and a rider) for riding. This training usually begins when the foal is about 18 months old.

Horses that show promise can be campaigned at horse shows, endurance races, ropings, rodeos, polo matches, or numerous other activities. A firm that is in the business of breeding horses may sell the offspring once a year at a production sale or consign them to an auction. There are literally hundreds of auctions around the country where such animals are consigned and sold to prospective buyers. These auctions usually feature one breed of horse.

BACKGROUND AND DEVELOPMENT

The horse, humankind's primary method of transportation until relatively recent times, was of vital importance to America's development. Horses pulled the heavy Conestoga wagons between the Ohio and Mississippi Rivers and were the main tools of working farmers. In eighteenth- and nineteenth-century America, the horse was held in such high esteem that theft of such an animal was commonly held to be a hanging offense. In addition to its important role in commerce and transportation, the horse was an important military supply.

When horses became unnecessary as central vehicles for transportation, their numbers dwindled. Dozens of breed associations, however, launched attempts to preserve many breeds of horses and the traits for which those horses were best known. These breed registries maintained studbooks, kept track of pedigrees, published their own magazines, and sponsored shows for their breed. In 1997 there were more than 150 breed organizations in the United States.

The revenue generated by the horse industry does not lie in breeding alone. The American Horse Council, the national legislative board for the horse industry, claimed that in 1992 horse shows generated $223 million annually, rodeos generated 104 million annually, and racetrack wagering by 71 million people totaled $14 billion.

Even the federal government is in the horse business. On vast acreage owned by the Bureau of Land Management (BLM) wild horses and burros still run free. Due to the overpopulation of such equines the government regularly gathers up the horses and maintains them in a horse feedlot, or offers them for adoption to the general public for a small fee. Between 1981 and 1984, more than 11,000 of these animals were rounded up and removed from the Naval Air Weapons Station, which works with the BLM in managing these wild herds.

Tax law changes in 1986 dealt a devastating blow to the horse industry. Prior to that time horses could be depreciated rapidly and their owners received a 10 percent investment tax credit just for the pleasure of owning a horse. The sudden excess of horses triggered a dramatic increase in the number of animals slaughtered for human consumption abroad. Despite half-hearted attempts to market horse meat in the United States, consuming the flesh of an equine is still considered taboo in this country, even though it is legal.

Residents of France, Belgium, Japan and many other parts of the world include horse meat in their diet. The United States is the largest producer and exporter of horse meat, with 15 horse slaughter plants. As of 1996, 90 percent of the processed horse meat was exported to other countries, with the remaining ten percent going into fertilizer and dog food. Seventy-two percent of U.S. overseas horse meat sales went to France, Belgium, and the Netherlands. Mexico and Canada took 11 percent, and Japan buys 3 percent; some of the horse meat also finds its way to Southeast Asia and South America. A growing contingent of animal rights groups have targeted the practice, hoping to see it outlawed entirely or regulated out of business.

Types of Horses Bred. The American quarter horse is the most popular and the largest equine breed registry membership, with more than 288,000 horse breeding members in 77 countries around the world. The quarter horse was developed in this country and derives its name from the fact that it is the fastest horse in the world in running the quarter mile.

The Thoroughbred is the most popular horse used for racing in this country and is quite commonly bred to horses of other breeds to add speed and versatility. The number of Thoroughbred breeding operations is the highest in Kentucky, with Florida second and California third.

A rapidly growing breed is the American paint horse. These are beautifully colored horses with much the same athletic ability as the quarter horse. Pinto horses are colored like the paints but have their own breed registry.

Arabian horses have been the breed of choice for entertainers and celebrities seeking tax write-offs. Historically, the Arabian is the oldest major pure breed of horse. They are unexcelled in endurance races and because of their beauty are popular with people who show horses at halter. Their popularity has grown rapidly among amateur competitors in all fields and Arabian interest by young competitors has grown by 88 percent since 1988, due partly to the fact that in 1992 there was more than $300,000 in prize money awarded in Arabian horse shows.

One of the most distinctly marked breeds of horse is the Appaloosa, the breed with spots on its rump. The Appaloosa Horse Club is responsible for maintaining the purity of this breed, which first achieved fame as the horse ridden by the Nez Perce Indians of Idaho. As the history of the Wild West continues to be of interest in Europe, so too has the popularity of the Appaloosa grown abroad. International registrations recently surged 65 percent in just one year, and in 1992 there were 526,000 registered Appaloosas in existence throughout the world. Very few of these horses, however, were actually purebred Appaloosas—less than 3,000.

The American Morgan was the first and the oldest recognized American breed, and was developed entirely in this country. In the 200 years of its existence in America, 125,000 purebred Morgans have been registered.

There are dozens of other breeds of horses, including the Missouri fox trotter, Peruvian Paso, American Indian horse, Palomino, American mustang, Paso Fino, Icelandic, the Standardbred, Tennessee Walking Horse, and several breeds of draft horses, including Percheron, Belgian, and Clydesdale. The sport of draft horse pulling experienced significant growth in the early 1990s, with contests and demonstrations held at numerous county and state fairs.

Current Conditions

The market in horses increased throughout the 1990s, after peaking and then declining in 1986. In 1996, estimates maintained a count of more than 7 million horses in America, representing a growth rate of 20 percent over the past decade. Another common standard for measuring the growth of the industry is the thoroughbred foal count, which had increased sizably every decade since 1910, until beginning to fall in the late '80s. By this standard, the industry was still in a slump at the end of the century, but showing some signs of modest gains. The foal count was 51,296 in 1986, and 40,333 in 1990, before reaching a low of 31,874 in 1995. Estimates for 1998, 1999, and 2000 show small but steady increases: 32,800; 33,265; and 33,360, respectively. The different standards for growth reflect the decreasing popularity of horse racing in America—gate numbers decreased by half between 1980 and 1997—and increasing interest in horses for other purposes.

According to a 1998 article in *The Economist,* part of this growth reflects a late 1990s fad for the horse as a status symbol: ''What the new owners will do with their purchases varies, but not many will work them or even ride them. The horse trade has become a metaphor for what is happening to the West. Horses, like the ranch land from which they spring, are being bought for their looks, not their usefulness.'' A 1998 study from the U.S. Department of Agriculture also suggested that most horses were maintained for personal use. Over two thirds of horse owners kept them primarily for pleasure; only 15 percent used them primarily for farm or ranch work. In the states surveyed, more than 45 percent of horse owners owned only one or two horses.

For many horse owners, the animals were also considered an investment. This has long been true with thoroughbred racehorses, but a less obvious choice that became more common in the late 1990s was miniature horses. Linda Brown, a Texas breeder of miniature horses, told the *Dallas Business Journal* in 1999 that ''A miniature horse has a possibility of making your initial investment back for you almost every year.'' In 1999, a high quality miniature horse could sell for as high as $42,000, and even more for a show champion—over $100,000. More commonly, the horses sell for $1,500 to $10,000. While the most common way for breeders to profit was through selling offspring, some owners of miniature horses made money by using the ponies for children's parties, school programs, and private lessons. Of the nearly 78,000 miniature horses registered worldwide, more than 13 percent were in Texas. Over half of these horses sold were exported.

The use of horses for logging has also increased. According to the North American Horse and Mule Loggers Association, membership went up by a sizeable 440 percent between 1991 and 1997. Horse logging, using breeds including Percherons and Belgians, has the advantage of being much kinder to the environment, although it is also more expensive than mechanized alternatives. The method is best suited to thinning existing stands of trees or clearing small lots or home sites, making large-scale growth for horse sales in this market unlikely.

The popularity of Arabian horses led to problems with determining the purity or integrity of a horse's breeding, particularly with South American breeders. In 1997, the Arabian Horse Registry of America was expelled from the World Arabian Horse Organization for refusing to register horses it considered impure. In 1998, Arabian Horse America was founded to support the industry of Arabian horse breeding in America, another sign of the breed's growing popularity. Arabian racing was also a growing sport: between 1996 and 1997, the number of horses racing went up nearly 8 percent, with purses totaling $4.5 million. The Arabian Horse Registry of America reported 391,414 Arabians registered in 1998.

The purity of Appaloosas also became an issue as the breed became more popular in the 1990s. In 1997, a movement was started to find and breed "Foundation Appaloosas," in order to help the pure breed survive.

In the racehorse market, as thoroughbred prices edged higher in the late 1990s, other groups of horses became popular with less wealthy consumers. A quarter horse yearling cost up to $10,000 less than a thoroughbred, and because it could begin racing sooner, an owner could begin making money from the horse more quickly. Quarter horses made up 39.5 percent of horses by breed. Sales of two-year-old horses also increased as more horses from that age group began to win big-money races. Some industry observers suggest that an excess of top-quality yearlings helped to create the market, which was popular with buyers looking to start racing sooner than they could with yearlings. The growth of this market created new opportunities for investors, who purchased yearlings and trained them for resale, sometimes reaping returns of more than 2000 percent from their initial investment.

In 1999, horse sellers took advantage of a new tool for boosting sales: the Internet. Industry leader Keeneland held auctions using live audio and video, and the results were unprecedented. *Computerworld* reported record-breaking sales: "A one-day record was set on November 8 when sales totaled $99.3 million. The 1999 September yearling sale was the largest in Keeneland's history. It sold nearly 3,500 horses—about 10percent of the 1998 U.S. foal crop. It ended the 11-day auction with gross sales of $233 million, a 38percent increase from last year."

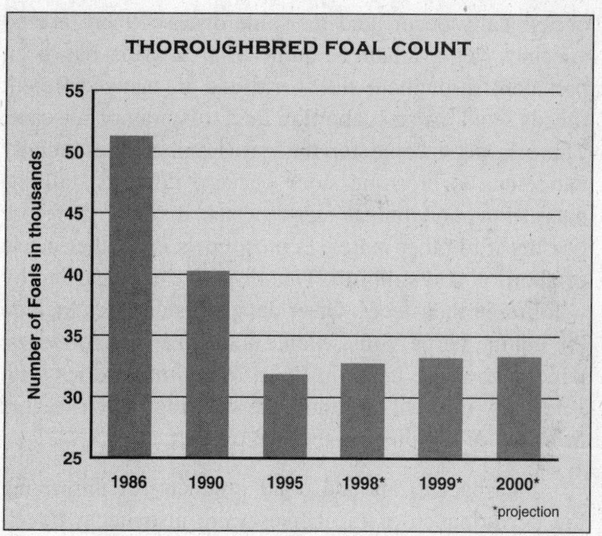

INDUSTRY LEADERS

Most operations in this industry are small and privately owned. Of the largest organizations with the highest revenues, most are breeders and sellers of thoroughbred racehorses. By revenue, the largest operation in 1998 was Keeneland Association of Lexington, Kentucky, with operating revenues of $19 million. Others included Whitewood Stable Inc., from The Plains, Virginia, and Jonabell Farm Inc. and Calumet Farm Inc., both of Lexington, Kentucky.

AMERICA AND THE WORLD

Exports in horses increased steadily from the mid-1980s. Main importers of U.S. horses in 1996 included Japan, the United Kingdom, Canada, Ireland, and France. In 1997, John Dunn reported in *Florida Trend* that "Some breeders even worry the U.S. [breeding] industry is in danger of losing its top bloodstock to the Japanese, who have paid top dollar for American thoroughbreds." In 1998, more than 18 percent of registered American Quarter Horses—the most popular exported breed—were in foreign countries. Other popular breeds for export included thoroughbreds, used for racing, and Tennessee Walking Horses, which are used for English riding. The foreign popularity of the Tennessee Walking Horse (TWH) created a 72 percent increase in TWH Association membership between 1993 and 1998; most exported TWHs went to Western European countries. A growing market for thoroughbreds in 1998 was South Korea, which made an arrangement with breeders in Maryland worth more than $3 million.

RESEARCH AND TECHNOLOGY

The main threat against horse breeders in this country were various diseases that can affect the breeding stock, as well as the general horse population. Vaccinations are the main prevention against disease, as well as cleanliness in the breeding facility, however, outbreaks occasionally occur, and for some diseases there are no vaccines yet available. Equine viral arteritis has been prevalent throughout the world and in many different breeds, and causes abortion and respiratory disease. There is no vaccine for this virus and it is especially dangerous to breeding stock because infected stallions may show no clinical signs of the disease, therefore passing it to other mares. Leptospirosis is another cause of abortion and stillbirth. This disease can be carried by wildlife, in their feces. Other dangerous diseases include the equine herpesvirus, equine influenza, and rotavirus, which can cause death in foals. Many universities with veterinary medical programs are studying these diseases in hopes of eliminating them altogether.

Pharmaceuticals and other products for improving the performance of racehorses were also being developed. In 1997, Aphton Corp. announced that it was ready to market its ulcer medication designed for stressed-out thoroughbreds, whose ulcers cost owners upwards of $75 million per year. In 1998, Special Devices Inc. announced that it was researching the possibility of developing its bone fasteners, already tested on humans, for large animals. These too could be used for racehorses, among which leg fractures are very common.

FURTHER READING

The Arabian Horse Registry of America. ''AHRA Expelled From International Group Over Refusal to Register Impure Horses.'' 12 November 1997. Available from http://www.theregistry.org/press.

———. ''Arabian Horse America Founded to Promote the Arabian Breed.'' 16 March 1998. Available from http://www.theregistry.org/press.

Borstein, Larry. ''Quarter Horses Beat Thoroughbreds for the Less Well-Heeled.'' *Orange County Register,* 7 June 1997.

Brennan, Fran. ''Miniature Horse Breeders Combine Love of Animals and Business.'' *Miami Herald,*28 April 1997.

Carfagno, Jacalyn. ''Market for Two-Year-Old Horses Increases as More Win Big.'' *Lexington Herald-Leader,* 11 April 1997.

Curry, Kerry. ''Miniature Horses Can Be Lucrative for Owners.'' *Dallas Business Journal,* 14 May 1999.

Dunn, John. ''Back on its feet.'' *Florida Trend,* September 1997.

The Jockey Club. *The Jockey Club 2000 Fact Book.* Available from http://home.jockeyclub.com/factbook/index.html.

Joseph, Priscilla. ''Wranglers Round Up Equine Exports.'' *AgExporter,* January 1998.

''The Lawn-Ornament Trade: Horses in the West.'' *The Economist,* 23 May 1998.

McGeever, Christine. ''Keeneland Races to the Web Block; Auctions Broadcast Via Streaming.'' *Computerworld,* 22 November 1999.

Robertson, Kathy. ''New Aphton Deal Bets on Racehorses Getting Ulcers.'' *Sacramento Business Journal,* 8 August 1997.

———. ''Firm that Helps Bones Mend Sizes Up New Market: Horses.'' *Sacramento Business Journal,* 17 July 1998.

Sather, Jeanne. ''Horses, Mules Bring in the Log Harvest.'' *Puget Sound Business Journal,* 14 March 1997.

''A Thousand Guineas, and More: Yearling Sales.'' *The Economist,* 26 September 1998.

U.S. Department of Agriculture. *Equine '98.* Available from http://www.aphis.usda.gov/vs/ceah/cahm.

SIC 0273

ANIMAL AQUACULTURE

This industry classification includes establishments engaged in the production of finfish and shellfish within a confined space and under controlled growing and harvesting procedures. It includes farmed aquatic animals intended as human food (catfish, trout, and oysters), bait (minnows), and pets (goldfish and tropical aquarium fish). Establishments primarily engaged in hatching fish and in operating fishing preserves are classified in **SIC 0921: Fish Hatcheries and Preserves.**

NAICS CODE(S)

112511 (Finfish Farming and Fish Hatcheries)
112512 (Shellfish Farming)
112519 (Other Animal Aquaculture)

The aquaculture industry entered the 1990s with significant economic promise. Production was small but growing, and aquaculture crops had doubled between 1975 and 1983. In the late 1990s, however, the U.S. aquaculture industry met with relatively flat growth in the per capita consumption of seafood. What little growth occurred was attributed to the increase in population in the Unites States of 1 to 2 million annually. Of total seafood consumed, shrimp, salmon, tuna, and catfish accounted for 50 to 60 percent in 1998, according to the National Marine Fisheries Service. The U.S. Department of Agriculture predicted that competition from the growing pork and poultry industries would pose greater challenges in the twenty-first century.

Despite somewhat slow growth, consumption of farm-raised seafood was on the rise. According to the United Nations's Food and Agriculture Organization, aquaculture production more than doubled in the decade ending 1999, producing aquatic animals and plants worth more than $42 billion. Sales of catfish from growers to processors were predicted to reach between $420 and $430 million in 1999. These figures represent substantial growth over 1985 statistics, when aquaculture posted U.S. farm receipts valued at only $205 million. Seafood industry analysts expect aquaculture to play an ever-increasing role in providing fisheries products to the marketplace.

The aquaculture industry is not, however, limited to seafood production. Ornamental fish exports increased in the late 1990s, particularly to Asia, where economies began to recover from recessions and financial crises. During the first half of 1999, U.S. ornamental fish exports rose 11 percent over the previous year, and exports to Hong Kong, which had been virtually nil in the first half of 1998, increased more than 400 percent. Exports to European nations, including the United Kingdom and Belgium, also rose. Canada remained the primary market for U.S. ornamental fish exports, though Canadian shipments declined 5 percent in the first half of 1999.

Although aquaculture is a relative newcomer to U.S. economic importance, the industry itself is not new and has applications in many parts of the world. The Japanese have raised oysters for centuries; the ancient Romans also raised oysters. Many Pacific island nations have turned swampy seaside areas into simple fish farms.

During the 1860s, the United States developed techniques for raising salmon and trout in captivity. By 1990, nearly all catfish, rainbow trout, and hybrid striped bass consumed in U.S. restaurants were harvested from fish farms.

Catfish. Sales of catfish remained strong in the late 1990s, with 1998 sales from growers to processors reaching 564.4 million pounds. This marked an 8 percent increase over 1997 sales. Catfish sales were to continue rising in 1999, and sales were expected to total between 585.0 and 595.0 million pounds for estimated sales of $420 to $430 million. Production remained strong due to stable prices and lower feed costs. The leading catfish producing states include Alabama, Arkansas, Mississippi, and Louisiana, which together account for more than 90 percent of total catfish production. Mississippi experienced the largest pond acreage growth in the late 1990s with a 5,000 acre expansion. Catfish farmers used 172,200 acres of ponds in the first half of 1999. Of these acres, 138,700 acres were devoted to foodsize catfish production, while 24,600 were used for fingerlings (feeding), and 5,530 for broodfish (breeding) production.

Shrimp. Shrimp is one of the most highly regarded crops. It is the most popular seafood product in the United States and boasts the highest consumption. In 1998, shrimp accounted for about 19 percent of per capita seafood consumption, a record high. Shrimp are especially suitable for farming because of their high market value, rapid growth, and low position on the food chain. Successful shrimp culturing operations are already underway in Ecuador, Thailand, and China, and aquaculturists predict their growth in the United States. Furthermore, the importance of U.S. shrimp farms increased in the late 1990s as shrimp imports began to decline, due to greater domestic demand by some key shrimp-exporting countries. Domestic shrimp production was down in 1998. The wild harvest of shrimp produced 278 million pounds that year, the lowest harvest since 1983. Despite the declines in imports and domestic production, demand was expected to remain strong through 2000.

Tilapia. Production of tilapia in the United States continued to increase in the late 1990s, with the north central region dominating tilapia production. Production was expected to expand in the north central and southern regions as well. If live product continued to generate greater demand than processed product, long-term prospects were not exceedingly optimistic for domestic growers. The U.S. Department of Agriculture, however, expected the larger long-term market demand to be for processed products. In 1998, tilapia imports totaled 94 million pounds, liveweight, compared to domestic production of about 18 million pounds, liveweight.

Mussels, Clams, and Oysters. Exports of clams and oysters declined slightly in the late 1990s but were expected to grow over the following several years as Asian economies recovered. Imports of clams, oysters, and mussels all increased, and mussels represented the fastest-growing mollusk import. Production of mussels fell throughout the 1990s, though Washington State continued to produce quality mussels. Mussels farmed in Washington State were generally larger and meatier than wild mussels and commanded a higher price.

FURTHER READING

U.S. Department of Agriculture. National Agricultural Statistics Service. "Aquaculture." Washington, DC, 4 March 1997. Available from http://usda.mannlib.cornell.edu/reports.

U. S. Department of Agriculture. National Agricultural Statistics Service. "Catfish Production." Washington, DC, 3 February 1997. Available from http://usda.mannlib.cornell.edu/reports.

U.S. Department of Agriculture. "Aquaculture Outlook." Washington, DC: Economic Research Service, 3 March 1999. Available from http://usda.mannlib.cornell.edu/reports.

U.S. Department of Agriculture. "Aquaculture Outlook." Washington, DC: Economic Research Service, 4 October 1999. Available from http://usda.mannlib.cornell.edu/reports.

SIC 0279

ANIMAL SPECIALTIES, NOT ELSEWHERE CLASSIFIED

This category includes establishments primarily engaged in the production of animal specialties, not elsewhere classified, such as pets, bees, worms, and laboratory animals. This industry also includes establishments

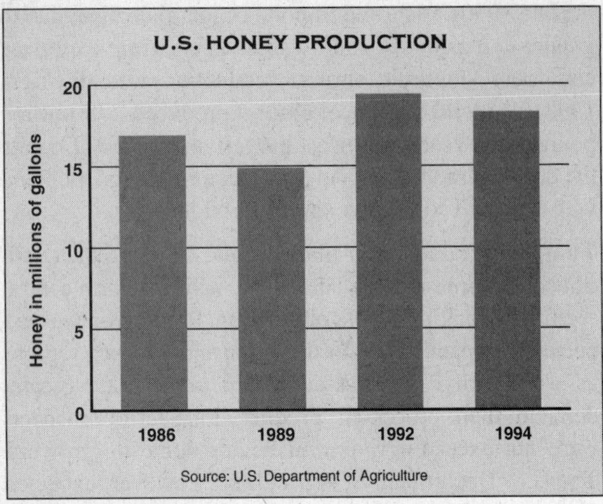

deriving 50 percent or more of their total value of sales of agricultural products from animal specialties, but less than 50 percent from products of any single industry. Establishments included in this group are alligator farms, apiaries, aviaries, cat farms, dog farms, frog farms, honey production farms, kennels that breed and raise their own stock, laboratory animal farms (rats, mice, guinea pigs), rattlesnake farms, and silk and silkworm farms.

NAICS Code(s)

112910 (Apiculture)
112990 (All Other Animal Production)

Developments in this industry in the late 1990s included rising sales of exotic birds, which pet owners increasingly preferred over cats and dogs, as well as the expansion of the market for reptiles and their prey, crickets. Informed consumers who saw the poor breeding conditions of exotic birds began to demand better breeding practices. The growth of the exotic bird market spurred growth in the entire pet industry. Fluker Farms Inc. of Baton Rouge, Louisiana, which led the industry in breeding and supplying reptiles and crickets, sought to strengthen its market by expanding into iguana breeding; they also added novelties to its feed supplies like chocolate-covered crickets, which it sold in the United States as well as in Japan.

Industry leader Charles River Laboratories of Wilmington, Massachusetts, with sales of $221 million in 1998, was sold by parent company Bausch and Lomb Inc. to Global Health Care Partners in July 1999. Charles River dominated the industry by supplying laboratory animals to research facilities. Though renounced conspicuously by animal rights groups and activists, laboratory animal production was a successful facet of this industry, due to the constant demand for medical research. The industry's second leading company was Denver-based Covance Research Products Inc., with sales of $25 million in 1997. The remainder of the list of industry leaders is dominated by overseas operations.

As of 1996, approximately 2,043 U.S. business establishments were engaged in animal breeding specialties, according to *Dun's Census of American Business.* This amount marked a steady decrease from 1993's 2,500 operations. The majority of these businesses reported sales of under $1 million in 1996, with only six establishments reporting more than $5 million in revenues. The majority of these establishments were small-scale operations, employing fewer than five people. Less than 5 percent of the businesses operating in this industry had payrolls exceeding 10 workers.

Honey. Honey production in the United States has fluctuated since 1986, when beekeepers garnered about 16.9 million gallons of honey. In 1989 production fell to only 14.9 million gallons, then rose in 1992 to 19.4 million gallons. In 1994 production dropped slightly to 18.3 million gallons. The United States exports a small portion of its honey each year. Some 705 thousand gallons were exported in 1994. Since domestic consumption outweighed production by about 28 million gallons, however, the United States imported about 10.4 million gallons in 1994.

Llamas. As competition in many show animal industries has escalated, many farmers have turned to llama production. In 1996 the International Llama Registry reported 13,409 llama farms in the United States. Producers—both professional and amateur—gravitated towards llamas because of their relatively low cost and their low-maintenance dispositions. Llamas do not require expensive feed; they can thrive on hay. The average llama sold for $750 in 1996, although high quality show animals cost upwards to $15,000.

Further Reading

''Bausch & Lomb finds buyer for animal research unit.'' *The New York Times,* 27 July 1999.

Crispell, Diane. ''Lleapin' Llamas.'' *American Demographics* 18, no. 12 (1996): 25.

Dun's Census of American Business, 1996. Bethlehem, PA: Dun and Bradstreet, 1996.

Infotrac Company Profiles, 20 January 2000. Available from http://web5.infotrac.galegroup.com.

Michele Picozzi. ''Fluker Farms celebrates Ruby Jubilee: the cricket business develops into an international success.'' *Pet Product News,* August 1997.

Samuelson, Kathleen. ''Bird business.'' *Pet Product News,* February 1999.

U. S. Department of Agriculture. *Agricultural Statistics.* Washington, 1995-96. Available from http://www.usda.gov/nass/pubs/agr95_96/agr95_2.pdf.

SIC 0291

GENERAL FARMS, PRIMARILY LIVESTOCK AND ANIMAL SPECIALTIES

This classification includes establishments deriving 50 percent or more of their total value of sales of agricultural products from livestock and animal specialties and their products, but less than 50 percent from products of any single three-digit industry group.

NAICS CODE(S)

112990 (All Other Animal Production)

INDUSTRY SNAPSHOT

Livestock, poultry, and their products generated sales of $98.8 billion in 1997, up from $87.4 billion in 1992. Of that total, general livestock farms accounted for only a very limited number, as most sales in this category come from farms specializing in a specific animal. General livestock farms tend to be small, with fewer than 50 employees and modest sales, though some, such as Euribrid BV, a subsidiary of The British Petroleum Company PLC, and Nevada Nile Ranch Inc. registered multimillion-dollar sales volumes. Farmers in this category mostly maintained traditional livestock, such as sheep, cattle, hogs, turkeys, and chickens, though many diversified into more specialty animals, such as elk, bison, and llamas. In addition, most general livestock farmers harvested traditional crops as well, either for feed or for retail.

The roots of general farming in the United States go back many years. A period of specialization occurred in the nineteenth century; general farming, however, remained ubiquitous but was concentrated particularly in the Appalachians. Farm wisdom advises against ''putting all your eggs in one basket,'' and there are many beneficial combinations of different types of livestock and crops.

CURRENT CONDITIONS

Perhaps the most severe challenge facing general livestock farmers at the beginning of the twenty-first century was the severe lull in agricultural-commodity prices, due in large part to the massive production levels generated by large-scale factory farming; factory farms, generating an increasing share of national agricultural output, are further able to produce their goods at lower costs, further exacerbating the pricing crisis. The net result has been to squeeze small and mid-sized farmers, which constitute the bulk of the general livestock farms in the United States, out of the market place if they are unable to find an appropriate niche allowing them to create economies of scale.

Many livestock farmers have been successful in finding their niche in the growing organic-foods industry. Targeting customers concerned with the health and environmental risks associated with chemicals, pesticides, and genetically modified foods, the organic sector has emerged from specialty health stores and a fringe customer base to assume a significant position in the mainstream consumer market. Organic agricultural products constituted the fastest-growing sector of the farming industry during the 1990s, with sales of $5 billion in the United States by 1999. A typical use of livestock in conjunction with raising organic crops involved grazing cattle through rotations of oat and soybean fields, thereby improving soil conditions and helping to control weeds.

Organic farmers eschew the synthetic chemicals and gene-tampering technologies many farmers use to boost yields and create more productive livestock. Both the animals themselves and all the feed they consume must be completely free of such chemicals in order to be labeled organic, a fact that demands organic farmers plan carefully far in advance to ensure appropriate feed supplies and access. Organic livestock must be maintained on land that is free from any chemical infiltration, including soil and water supplies. Moreover, animals themselves must be carefully monitored for illnesses, to which they are more susceptible that their non-organic cousins since organic animals cannot be administered antibiotics used to stave off disease; thus, an animal discovered with a communicable disease must immediately be removed from the herd lest it affect the remaining supply. Because of the greater risk and investment required, organic farming is a more costly undertaking than non-organic farming, and its consequent products fetch a higher price at the market.

The health and safety concerns related to livestock farming have assumed increasing prominence on the national scene. The Environmental Protection Agency (EPA), in conjunction with the National Pork Producers Council, addressed environmentalists' protests over on-farm odors and waste disposal, particularly on pork farms, with the development in 1997 of the On-Farm Odor/Environmental Assistance Program (OFO/EAP), whereby risk factors are identified and assessed. This environmental-management program was designed to reduce odors and prevent contamination of surface or ground water. It calls for periodic governmental inspection (with the cooperation of farmers) of farming sites, buildings, manure-handling systems, deceased-animal disposal methods, and land application. The OFO/EAP's checklist includes questions about seepage in the building's foundation, cleanliness of animal-storage facilities, pipe conditions, and drainage facilities and equipment. As a cooperative program rather than a mandate, farmers are encouraged to consider the financial benefits afforded by implementing sanitary environmentally sound waste-management systems.

Chickens, longtime barnyard fixtures, have been used as scavengers, feeding on spilled feed and insects around barns and rabbitries, resulting in savings in feed costs and improved sanitation of the animals' living areas. However, the type of environment has had to be carefully matched with the right type of chicken. For example, only non-flying chickens typically are used near rabbit cages; otherwise, they fly on top of the cages and contaminate them with their droppings. Other types of scavengers have filled similar roles. Earthworms, for example, have been kept under rabbit cages with success, for they can process the rabbit droppings and can themselves be sold as bait.

Other symbiotic relationships have been successfully fostered in livestock farming. Hogs have been kept with cattle to feed on waste grain. Goats have a rather hardy digestive system, but they are usually kept alone due to their differences from cattle in size and temperament. Horses seem to act as catalysts to tetanus in goats; these two species, therefore, are not usually kept together, or tetanus shots are used as a precaution. Goats, meanwhile, are not usually stored with sheep, due to the high susceptibility of both to parasites. Cattle, sheep, and goats, though, have grazed open pastures together successfully, because each feeds on different levels of vegetation.

Food-born illnesses, such as E. coli, salmonella, listeria, and others, garnered a great deal of attention in the late 1990s; there were an estimated 60 million cases of such illnesses in the United States in that period. In California, 1.5 million pounds of low-heat processed milk was withheld from the market in 1999 when it was learned that 140 cows on a California ranch had died from exposure to botulism; this was only thirteen months after some 400 cows had met a similar fate at another California dairy farm. The disease was tracked to large bales of hay, suggesting that the attempts by some farmers to cut costs by packaging hay in larger bales was creating compromised feed allotments.

U.S. Department of Agriculture USDA regulations prohibit fowl from dairy barns, due to the birds' susceptibility to tuberculosis. Waterfowl tend to be more resistant to tuberculosis than chicken and pheasants. Unlike most emerging focus on food-borne illness in the farming industry, concern over tuberculosis infection is targeted more at small farms and ''homesteads'' than at factory farms, since the former's birds tend to be free-ranging and are kept longer than. Chickens more than two years old are more likely to spread the disease, which can be transmitted to humans either directly from the birds or through cattle or swine. Soil contamination is also a threat that can persist even after the affected birds are destroyed.

A study conducted by the University of California Agricultural Issues Center concluded that an outbreak of bovine spongiform encephalopathy (BSE), also known as ''mad cow'' disease, like those that have plagued the United Kingdom's beef industry since the mid-1980s, could cost the U.S. agriculture industry more than $14 billion—$8 billion from farm income. The key to preventing such damage, the researchers said, was to detect the disease before it diffused throughout the food industry. While no evidence has yet been discovered that the disease has entered the U.S. market, heightened international trade, the trend toward factory farming, and a surge in cases of food-born illnesses have stirred fears that an outbreak could potentially infiltrate the U.S. food supply. BSE causes a fatal, degenerate brain disease in cattle. It has been caused by sheep material, infected with transmittable spongiform encephalopathies (TSEs), used in cattle feed.

To accommodate public outcry against these increasing tendencies, the federal government has sprung into action. The Food and Drug Administration (FDA) has placed limits on the amount of aflatoxin, which results from mold growth on livestock feed, that can appear in human or livestock items for consumption. Meanwhile, the EPA has taken regulatory steps aimed at imposing pollution-discharge permits on the nation's larger farms by 2005, affecting everything from feed supplies to equipment. These and similar developments are expected to increase costs to farmers in the form of testing and prevention systems and other expenses relating to staving off food-born illnesses and livestock contamination.

More broadly, however, factory farms themselves have come under fire, even from the Department of Agriculture, for the perception that they inherently lend themselves to pollution and food contamination. While the trend in all agricultural sectors has been toward larger, more centralized farming, such farms have been found to be fertile ground for manure spills that contaminate water and kill fish, as well as for high levels of nitrogen- and phosphorous-based water contamination. This has focused attention on the comparative benefits of small-scale farming, which has been gradually displaced by factory farms. After years of protests from small farmers and environmentalists, the prominence of food-born illnesses and contamination have lead the Department of Agriculture to investigate the possibilities of reversing the long shift toward factory farming. While most industries have experienced a tightening concentration of ownership and production, the immediate negative consequences of this pattern in the agricultural industry have forced regulatory bodies to reconsider traditional policies. Federal tax programs, for instance, have long been tilted in favor of large agribusiness, offering incentives for capital-intensive expansion of operations, as well as exemptions from federal labor laws for large farms dependent on hired labor. For general livestock farmers, the majority of whom are relatively small, these developments could be a welcome form of relief.

FURTHER READING

"BSE Could Cost the United States $14 Billion Over Five Years, Researchers Estimate." *World Food Chemical News,* 9 June 1999.

"Canada Agrees to Reduce Barriers Against U.S. Farm Products." *New York Times,* 5 December 1998.

Cochrane, Willard Wesley. *The Development of American Agriculture.* Minneapolis: University of Minnesota Press, 1979.

"Is the Sun Setting On Farmers? Many Can't Survive the 'New Agriculture'." *New York Times,* 28 November 1999.

Knight, Danielle. "Environment-Food: Quit Hogging the Environment." *Interpress Service,* 7 April 1998.

"Milk Products Scrutinized After California Dairy Cows Die from Botulism." *Food Chemical News,* 7 June 1999.

National Agricultural Statistics Service. *1997 Census of Agriculture.* Washington, D.C. : U.S. Department of Agriculture, 1999.

Petrak, Lynn. "Environmental Commitment." *National Provisioner,* September 1999.

"Sweet Harvest." *Food & Beverage Marketing.* February 1998.

SIC 0711

SOIL PREPARATION SERVICES

This category covers establishments primarily engaged in land breaking, plowing, application of fertilizer, seed bed preparation, and other services for improving the soil for crop planting. Establishments primarily engaged in land clearing and earth moving for terracing and pond and irrigation construction are classified in **SIC 1629: Heavy Construction, Not Elsewhere Classified.**

NAICS CODE(S)

115112 (Soil Preparation, Planting and Cultivating)

The soil and topography of the land, along with the climate of an area, determines the type of farming that can be done. For example, wheat, corn, and other grains are most efficiently grown on level land where large, complex machinery can be used. These crops are commonly grown on the prairies and plains of Iowa, Illinois, Indiana, Nebraska, Ohio, Kansas, and southern Minnesota and Wisconsin. Cotton, tobacco, and peanuts—all crops that require longer growing seasons—are primarily grown in the South. Most of the country's fruits and vegetables are grown in California, Texas, and Florida.

To promote growth and germination, soil must provide water, heat, oxygen, and essential nutrients. The soil must also be compressible enough to allow root penetration and plant growth. Among the most important operations in the crop preparation industry are tilling, liming, and fertilizing soils in preparation for crop planting.

Tilling is commonly done for several reasons: to eradicate crop residuals from previous plantings, such as corn stalks or wheat stubble; to destroy weeds; and to modify the structure of the soil to accommodate planting. Traditional tilling, which typically involves plowing, leaves less than 15 percent of plant residue on the soil surface. It temporarily aerates the soil and controls weeds, but over the long term, decomposing plants and compaction destroy the structure of the soil and actually reduces aeration.

To combat the problems resulting from conventional tilling, soil preparers increasingly turned to conservation tillage in the late 1990s. Conservation tillage systems leave at least 30 percent crop residue after planting and minimize water runoff and soil. The practices can stave soil erosion by as much as 90 percent. The most common types of conservation tillage are no-till, ridge-till, and mulch-till. The no-till system involves leaving the soil undisturbed from harvest to planting except for nutrient injection and controlling weeds primarily with herbicides. The ridge-till system also leaves the soil undisturbed from harvest to planting except for nutrient injection, but weeds may be controlled with herbicides and/or cultivation and the ridges are rebuilt during cultivation. The mulch-till system disturbs the soil prior to planting and accomplishes weed control with herbicides and/or cultivation. Many U.S. farmers also utilized reduced tillage methods, which leave 15 to 30 percent crop residue after planting. According to the Conservation Technology Information Center, 37 percent of the 294.6 million acres of farmland in the Unites States used conservation tillage methods in 1997, and 77 million utilized reduced tillage systems. Mulch-till was the most commonly used conservation tillage method, used on 60 million acres.

Liming involves spreading agricultural lime, containing calcium carbonate and magnesium carbonate, to soils with undesirably high levels of acidity, thereby increasing their pH levels. Optimal lime requirements depend on both the condition of the soil and the crop to be planted.

A fertilizer is any natural or synthetic origin that is spread in soils to supply one or more essential nutrients. Fertilizer carriers or materials that are mixed together and processed to produce fertilizer are mixed fertilizers. Fertilizers come in several forms: solid, liquid, or gas. The most commonly used fertilizers contain various concentrations of nitrogen, potassium, and phosphorus. The National Agricultural Statistics Service (NASS) Prices Paid Index

(PPI) indicated that nitrogen fertilizer costs rose in October 1999. The increased costs were offset by lower prices for mixed fertilizers and potash and phosphate materials. The NASS also reported that U.S. farm expenditures on fertilizer, lime, and soil conditioners declined between 1997 to 1998, from $10.9 million to $10.6 million.

Environmental concerns over fertilizer use became increasingly publicized in the 1990s, particularly regarding the contamination of ground water from nitrogen supplies. Farmers began turning to crop preparation services for custom application of fertilizers, as Federal and State laws required licensed applicators for many more chemicals. Domestic farmers also started using different fertilizer management methods, including foliar fertilization application—direct application of fertilizer to plant leaves—and fertilizing several times during the growing season rather than applying fertilizer once. It was thought that several smaller applications of fertilizer lessened the amount of nitrates seeping into the ground. Farmers also began to test and analyze soil and plants to better assess the need for fertilizing. Because of the low cost of nitrogen, however, farmers were hard-pressed to drastically cut their usage.

One important operation for the soil preparation services industry is the decontamination of soils. Volatile organic compounds (VOCs) are among the most problematic soil contaminants. A number of methods for VOC decontamination were tested in the 1990s, and the vapor extraction system was among the most effective of these, with 85 to 100 percent removal rates. The problems involved in accommodating environmental regulations passed in the late 1990s, particularly regarding site remediation and containment, suggest that soil decontamination will remain an important activity for the industry.

There are few firms whose primary activity is soil preparation services. The largest of these is Waste Stream Technology Inc. of Buffalo, New York. Waste Stream was founded in 1986 and generated sales between $1 and $2 million during 1999. The firm is involved in the bioremediation of contaminated soils and provides environmental laboratory services for soil, water, and waste. Waste Stream is a subsidiary of the publicly held Sevenson Environmental Services of Niagara Falls, New York. Another key player in the industry is Soil Solutions in Winston-Salem, North Carolina.

FURTHER READING

American Farm Bureau. *Farm Facts,* 1996. Available from http://www.fb.com/newvoa/ffindex.htm.

Kelly, Dave. ''Environment-Friendly Conservation Tillage a Growing Practice on America's Farms.'' American Farm Bureau Federation. 24 October 1997. Available from http://www.fb.com/issues/analysis/tillage.html.

Stroud, Jenni. ''Techno-Farmers Get Precise Results.'' *St. Louis Post-Dispatch,* 10 February 1997.

U.S. Department of Agriculture Economic Research Service. ''Agricultural Chemical Expenses Continued to Rise Despite Fall in Crop Production.'' 1997. Available from http://www.econ.ag.gov.

U.S. Department of Agriculture Economic Research Service. ''Conservation Tillage Usage Reaches 35 Percent of U.S. Planted Area.'' 1997. Available from http://www.econ.ag.gov.

U.S. Department of Agriculture Economic Research Service. ''Fertilizer Expenses Pushed Up by Higher Nutrient Prices.'' 1997. Available from http://www.econ.ag.gov.

U.S. Department of Agriculture National Agricultural Statistics Service. ''Agricultural Prices.'' 29 October 1999. Available from http://usda.mannlib.cornell.edu/reports/nassr/price/pap-bb/1999/agpr1099.txt.

U.S. Department of Agriculture National Agricultural Statistics Service. ''Farm Production Expenditures Summary.'' July 1999. Available from http://usda.mannlib.cornell.edu/reports/nassr/price/zpe-bb/fpex0799.txt.

Ward's Business Directory of U.S. Private and Public Companies, Detroit: Gale Research, 1997.

SIC 0721

CROP PLANTING, CULTIVATING, AND PROTECTING

This group covers establishments primarily engaged in performing crop planting, cultivating, and protecting services. Establishments engaged in complete maintenance of citrus groves, orchards, and vineyards are classified in **SIC 0762: Farm Management Services.**

NAICS CODE(S)

481219 (Other Nonscheduled Air Transportation)
115112 (Soil Preparation, Planting and Cultivating)

The crop planting, cultivating, and protecting industry encompasses a variety of services, including: aerial dusting and spraying; bracing of orchard trees and vines; citrus grove cultivation; corn detasseling; hoeing; insect control for crops, with or without fertilizing; irrigation system operation; planting crops; pruning orchard trees and vines; weed control; and other miscellaneous activities. The highly fragmented industry is dominated by small, private, local companies. As a result, statistical data on this group is scant.

Most industry activities, such as corn detasseling and hoeing, are relatively self-explanatory. One of the larger and more complex services is aerial application, or crop dusting, which usually entails dusting or spraying crops of large acreage with pesticides and weed control chemicals from an airplane. By 1999, aerial application was used for more than 65 percent of crop chemical applications in the United States, according to the National Agricultural Aviation Association (NAAA). Besides increasing the speed and efficiency of the dusting process, aerial crop dusting eliminates the need to apply chemicals with wheeled vehicles that could damage crops.

The need for crop services is an indicator of the trend toward advanced, large-scale farming practices that accelerated during the post-World War II U.S. economic expansion. During the 1950s, 1960s, and 1970s, U.S. farms became increasingly mechanized to take advantage of economies of scale. Importantly, the development of advanced pesticides, herbicides, fertilizers, and other chemical treatments resulted in an entire chemical application services industry. Likewise, new machinery significantly increased the amount of cultivated land which a single land owner could efficiently manage. Aerial crop dusting, performed as early as the 1920s using World War I surplus aircraft, for example, gave way to advanced higher-altitude craft by the early 1950s.

Indeed, while farmers during the early 1900s usually performed most crop management activities, many farm owners in the 1990s are more business owners and managers than conventional farmers. Farm owners commonly contract planting and seeding, irrigation, pest control, and other duties to specialized outside service providers.

The trend toward greater farm automation continued into the late 1990s. Aerial crop dusting, for example, became a complex, high-tech endeavor, with advanced crop dusting systems employing global positioning systems (GPS) to indicate precise location and to show which rows of crops need dusting. The modern systems are more efficient than the previously used flagging system, which required on flagmen on the ground to communicate where spraying or dusting was needed. Modern aerial dusters, which cost anywhere between $100,000 and $500,000, also benefit from on-board computers that automatically control spray width and coverage density. Computer systems are also capable of plotting fields and provide information about the best path for dusting a certain area, taking into consideration applicable weather conditions. Crop dusters also use computers to keep track of the types and amounts of chemicals used, as well as when and where they were sprayed.

Environmental safety of crop protection products (chemicals used to control insects, diseases, and/or weeds) became an increasingly important focus in the 1990s. Pesticide sales in the United States reached $7.9 billion in 1995, the latest year for which data is available, making this industry, and its impact on the environment, a significant public concern. The Food Quality Protection Act, signed into law in August 1996, provided some significant changes in food safety and pesticide laws, including major revisions in pesticide registration and use provisions of chemicals.

In the late 1990s, state representatives continued to promote legislation regulating pesticide use, and despite a 1997 report by the Environmental Protection Agency (EPA) that indicated pesticide usage among U.S. farms had dropped significantly since the all-time high in 1979, activist groups contended that pesticide use was on the rise, and controversy over the safety of pesticides grew stronger. The American Crop Protection Association (ACPA), to which most major pesticide manufacturers and distributors belong, has been instrumental in providing information on regulatory changes as well as promoting the environmentally sound use of crop protection products. The ACPA notes that pesticides used on U.S. farm fields are rigorously tested, and only about one out of 20,000 pesticides is approved for usage on crops. Still, such groups as the Environmental Working Group and Pesticide Action Network North America lobby for more stringent controls on pesticide use and advocate less toxic pest control methods, such as crop rotation, introduction of beneficial insects, mulching, and use of low-toxicity pesticides such as sulfur, soaps, and biopesticides.

One of the largest providers of crop services in the United States during the 1990s was Lykes Bros. Inc., of Florida. Established in 1875, Lykes is a major player in Florida agribusiness. It generated sales of about $450 million in 1999 in its diversified operations.

FURTHER READING

American Crop Protection Association. "Representing the Crop Protection Industry." Available from http://www.acpa.org/public/info/indexaboutacpa.html#represent.

———. "A Look at Provisions of The Food Quality Protection Act of 1996." Available from http://www.acpa.org/public/issues/fqpa/indexfqpa.html.

Bell, R. W. "Crop Dusters: Those Daring Young Men in Their Flying Machines." *The Pamlico News,* 26 May 1999.

SIC 0722

CROP HARVESTING, PRIMARILY BY MACHINE

This industry encompasses establishments primarily engaged in mechanical harvesting, picking and combining of crops, and related activities, using machinery provided by the service firm. Crops undergoing mechanical harvesting include berries, fruit, cotton, grain, nuts, sugar beets, sugarcane, and vegetables. Companies that provide threshing, combining, silo filling, and hay mowing and baling services are also included in this classification. Farm labor contractors providing personnel for manual harvesting are classified in **SIC 0761: Farm Labor Contractors and Crew Leaders.**

NAICS Code(s)

115113 (Crop Harvesting, Primarily by Machine)

Industry Snapshot

This industry is comparatively small—sales of the top five companies in this segment were about $204.5 million annually in the 1990s, and a portion of this amount was contributed from other divisions of the companies. The industry is dominated by family-owned companies. Crop harvesters, both manual and mechanical, are directly reliant on the economic fortunes of the American farming community, the sole client of the harvesters.

Organization and Structure

American agribusiness is a huge, diversified industry and encompasses several specialized sectors. Besides the farmer (also called the grower), who manages the land and cultivates the crops, there are industries based around companies that harvest, process, distribute, and transport farm products and farm supplies. There are also industries based around companies that supply materials and services to the farmer. Contract or custom harvesters are part of the former group.

It is increasingly common for farmers to enter into contracts to sell their produce before it has matured. Contract farming is an arrangement with a buyer, such as a food processor or marketer, to sell and ship the produce to the buyer upon harvesting. The custom harvesting company may be an intermediary part of this arrangement. If the company has been contracted to do the harvesting, it may also make the arrangements for selling and shipping the product to the buyer on the grower's behalf.

The farmer agrees to a price at the time of the contract. This arrangement can benefit either the grower or the harvester/buyer, depending upon supply and demand of the particular type of crop at harvest time. If there is a nationwide bumper crop of green beans, and the farmer is selling green beans, the farmer may get a higher price for the crops with a contract than if he or she waited for the harvest and bid with many other farmers waiting to sell their beans. If crop production is low, creating high demand, the buyer comes out ahead because the farmer could have sold for a higher price, had he or she known there would be a smaller supply. The custom harvester, having agreed to buy a crop at a certain price before it has matured, is subject to similar losses or gains.

The custom harvester contracts production with the food processor. The contract will specify the delivery of tons of produce per day, which will fluctuate according to weather conditions or other variables. The custom harvester also contracts with the grower to produce the crop. The harvester begins working with the grower when it is time to plant the crop. The harvester's field representative works with the grower to coordinate various facets of the planting process. For the harvester, this is to set standards for the crop and ensure quality control. The field representative delivers the seed and develops the timing for planting, fertilizing, and harvesting the crop. The grower pays for the seed, because it is held against his or her account when the grower is paid for the harvested crop.

Large harvesters generally have a variety of equipment that enables them to harvest the crop of their choice. They harvest with their own machinery, load the produce onto their own semi- tractor-trailers, and ship it to the processor. Large contract harvesters also have trucking and communications systems in place. These systems are crucial because, in order to fulfill the contract with the processor, the harvesting company may have to send trucks, equipment, and harvesting crews to different states for harvesting jobs. They go wherever they need to fill the packing window. Weather can determine the order in which the harvester chooses the farms. Timing is crucial, because each crop matures at a different rate and must be harvested at its peak. Increasingly, harvesting companies use computers to track the planting dates, varieties, and pesticides (herbicides, fungicides, insecticides) used by different growers. The time frame for a harvesting job can range from a few days to two weeks, depending upon crop, terrain, and size of acreage.

Mechanically-Harvested Crops. In deciding whether to harvest mechanically or manually, farmers must consider what type of crop and plant is being harvested. Grain crops are harvested mechanically. In the case of vegetable crops, however, they may be harvested mechanically if a hardy variety or if not intended for the fresh market. Many fruits and vegetables, especially citrus fruits, are harvested almost exclusively by hand because they must arrive on the fresh market in perfect condition, and mechanical harvesting can scratch or bruise produce. Damage is a major concern of reap harvesting. Damage is usually minimal if the harvesting equipment is kept clean and adjusted correctly for the crop. Even with hand harvesting, however, machinery, such as conveyor belts, will likely be used to transport the fruit from the field, to cool it and perhaps wrap it. Farmers may also choose to harvest by hand if they have secured a high price for their crop and can afford manual labor. They may combine their options within the same crop, picking large, mature vegetables first by hand for the fresh market and then bringing in machinery to harvest smaller vegetables for sale to a processor.

Time is also a major consideration. If farmers need to harvest quickly, they will need to harvest mechanically. In deciding whether to harvest by themselves or to contract with a custom harvester, farmers have another set of factors to consider. If the farmers have a lot of acreage, they may own a combine harvester. Often, they will make arrangements to harvest the crops of their neighbors as well. If the farmers grow grain and do not have enough acreage to justify making the capital investment in a combine harvester (about $120,000), they will need the services of a contract harvester.

Convenience and assistance may be a factor as well. Farmers may find it easier to have the input of the custom harvester in determining crop planting, timing, harvesting, and sale issues. Even if the farmers do own a combine harvester, they may still contract a custom harvester. One reason is that the window of opportunity for harvesting is small. Farmers may need to get grain out of the field immediately or risk losses because of bad weather, for example. If they don't have the capacity to do the job themselves, they may seek help from a custom harvester.

Equipment. The combine harvester used for grains tends to be different from the one used for vegetables, although the manufacturers strive to make the machines more interchangeable through modifications. Harvesting machinery is generally classified by crop. A harvester must be adjusted to harvest a specific crop and to keep trash out of the load. A grain harvester is called a combine harvester because it cuts, threshes, and cleans grain in one operation. Corn is harvested by mechanical pickers that snap the ears from the stalk so that only the cobs are harvested. Stripper-type cotton harvesters strip the entire plant of both open and unopened bolls. Hay and forage machines include mowers, crushers, windrowers, field choppers, balers, and grinders.

Root crops such as potatoes are harvested with diggers, which often pull up rocks and unwanted vegetation with the potatoes. Some machines can sort this trash out, while other machines carry people who sort it by hand. Sugar-beet harvesters lift the whole root from the ground, clean it, and deliver it to a bin. Vegetable crops such as broccoli, asparagus, celery, lettuce, and cabbage are still harvested largely by hand.

For the fresh market, some vegetables and nearly all fruits are still harvested by hand. For processing, drying, and occasionally for fresh market, mechanical tree and bush shakers with catching belts, bins, pallets, and electric lifts reduce harvesting and handling labor.

Background and Development

Some custom harvesters are family-run outfits that started as growers, purchased expensive harvesting equipment, and entered into agreements with other local farmers to harvest their crops. They are likely to grow crops and maintain livestock in addition to their harvesting operations. Others are large and sophisticated operations that coordinate production with the grower from planting to sale and delivery.

The history of mechanical harvesting itself dates back to Cyrus McCormick's marketing of the mechanical reaper in the early 1840s. The reaper could harvest grains only; mechanical harvesters for root and vegetable crops weren't invented until the 1930s. McCormick's invention was an important part of the agricultural revolution that began in the eighteenth century.

The agricultural revolution dramatically increased a farmer's ability to produce crops. The technique of crop rotation allowed farm land to be used continually. Machinery allowed ever larger areas to be worked, and farmers increased their acreage. When mechanical harvesters and other devices were created to do formerly manual labor, production increased to a level that surpassed national consumption. The McCormick reaper permitted the cultivation of the vast Midwestern plains states.

The proportion of human labor used in the production of farm goods dropped by measurable degrees as a result of farming advances, while capital spending on feed, machinery, fertilizer, and other farming staples increased dramatically.

Farmers now rely heavily on specialized technology to sustain and increase production. Farmers are also highly dependent on outside sources for their equipment and services, such as custom harvesting. Because of these specialized interrelationships, farmers and the businesses that support them have also necessarily become increasingly sophisticated in their cash management techniques.

Current Conditions

Because this industry sustains itself by providing services to farmers, it is affected by many of the same economic, climactic, and industrial conditions that affect farmers. The 1990s saw a slight improvement in the American farm economy. Net farm cash income was more consistent and higher than in previous years. Farmers who stored grain were able to take extra advantage of relatively high commodity prices. After grain reserves reached historically low levels in 1993-94, producers expanded their crops to keep up with increased national and international demand.

In 1998 about 9.76 billion bushels of corn were produced, the second highest on record and a 6 percent increase over the 1997 crop. Soybean production also fared well in 1998 with a record high harvest. Despite excessive heat in the Southeastern and Mid-Atlantic states, which caused some damage and lower yields, total production reached 2.76 billion bushels, a 3 percent increase over 1997 figures. Wheat production also experienced a banner year, and the approximately 2.55 billion bushels produced represented the largest crop since 1990. Wheat production was up 3 percent from 1997.

In the late 1990s efforts to develop new machines to facilitate the labor-intensive harvesting of crops intensified. In Florida, for example, providers of citrus for the production of juice faced labor shortages, and exploration of mechanical harvesting options became necessary. The most promising type of mechanical harvesting system appeared to be the "continuous canopy shake and catch," which resulted in as much as a 75 percent decrease in harvesting costs. These systems were appropriate only for fruit destined for juice production, as fruit for fresh consumption would suffer from too much damage from the machinery.

In 1997 farmers spent a total of $24.21 billion on farm services, up from $23.50 billion in 1996. This figure covered all farm services, not only expenditures for the mechanical harvesting of crops. Also in 1997, according to the U.S. Department of Commerce, factory shipments of farm machinery and equipment rose 16 percent from 1996 to total $13.99 billion. Harvesting machinery shipments rose 10 percent, from $2.96 billion to $3.24 billion, and haying machinery increased 18 percent to reach $792.5 billion in 1997. These figures suggested continued and increasing use of mechanical harvesting equipment on U.S. farms.

Industry Leaders

Among the leaders in the mechanical harvesting services industry in the 1990s were Noblesse Oblige Inc. of Seeley, California; Apio of Guadalupe, California; and Fresh Western Marketing of Salinas, California. Other companies engaged in providing mechanical harvesting services were geographically clustered in agricultural regions in such states as Texas, Kansas, Oklahoma, Indiana, Wisconsin, Florida, and California.

Further Reading

Jackson, Jerry. "Harvesting Machines Shake Up Tradition." *Orlando Sentinel,* 12 March 1999.

U.S. Department of Agriculture. National Agricultural Statistics Service. "Statistical Highlights, 1998-99: Farm Economics." Washington, DC: U.S. Department of Agriculture, 1999. Available from http://www.usda.gov/nass/pubs/stathigh/1999.

U.S. Department of Commerce. "Farm Machinery and Lawn and Garden Equipment, 1997." Washington, DC: Economics and Statistics Administration Bureau of the Census, 1998.

SIC 0723

CROP PREPARATION SERVICES FOR MARKET, EXCEPT COTTON GINNING

This classification covers establishments primarily engaged in performing services on crops, subsequent to their harvest, with the intent of preparing them for market or further processing. Establishments primarily engaged in buying farm products for resale to other than the general public for household consumption and which also prepare them for market or further processing are regarded as wholesale trade establishments. Establishments primarily engaged in stemming and redrying tobacco are classified in **SIC 2141: Tobacco Stemming and Redrying.** Establishments engaged in ginning cotton are classified in **SIC 0724: Cotton Ginning.**

NAICS Code(s)

115114 (Postharvest Crop Activities (except Cotton Ginning))

The scope of operations included under the crop preparation services for market industry is large. It includes bean, grain, and seed cleaning; corn, peanut, and nut shelling; fruit and vegetable sorting, grading, and cooling; grain, hay, fruit, and vegetable drying; packaging of fresh or farm-dried fruits and vegetables; potato and yam curing; grain fumigation; custom grinding; and tobacco grading.

The leading firm in the crop preparation services for market industry was Deli Universal Inc. of Richmond, Virginia, with just under $2 billion in sales for its fiscal year ended June 30, 1998. The second-leading company was Golden Peanut Co. of Alpharetta, Georgia, with sales of $310 million for its fiscal year ended June 30, 1995, according to the most recent information available on Infotrac databases. Golden Peanut specialized in peanut flours, which it roasted to achieve the color and flavor of roasted peanuts. Used in peanut butter flavored confections, these flours controlled fat migration and extended shelf life.

Next in the industry was Dole Fresh Vegetables of Salinas, California, with $250 million in 1997 sales. Diamond Walnut Growers Inc. of Stockton, California, followed close on its heels with sales of $223 million for its fiscal year ended July 31, 1998. Rounding out the top five was Jimbo's Jumbos Inc. of Edenton, North Carolina, with sales of $190 million for its fiscal year ended July 31, 1995, according to the most recent information available on Infotrac databases.

The *Occupation Outlook Quarterly* reported in 1996 that between 1983 and 1994, employment in agricultural services grew from 22 percent to 32 percent of total agricultural employment. The agricultural services industry had over 837,000 wage and salary jobs, coupled with more than 300,000 self-employed workers. Most managed crop production activities while others managed livestock and dairy production. Earnings in crop preparation can vary greatly, depending on the season. Many workers find work only in the growing or harvesting seasons and are unemployed or work in other jobs during the rest of the year.

There were 61 firms in the industry with $1 million or more in sales in 1997. These firms employed over 9.7 million. Of the top ten firms in the industry, five were headquartered in California.

FURTHER READING

American Farm Bureau. *Farm Facts,* 1996. Available from http://www.fb.com/newvoa/ffindex.htm.

Bluford, Verada. ''Agricultural Services.'' *Occupational Outlook Quarterly,* Fall 1996.

Infotrac Company Profiles. Available from http://web5.infotrac.galegroup.com.

''Nuts.'' *Candy Industry,* May 1999.

Ward's Business Directory of U.S. Private and Public Companies, Detroit: Gale Research, 1997.

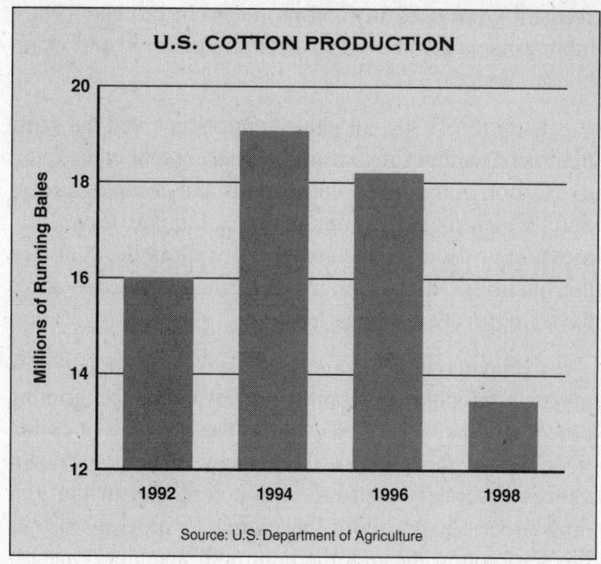

SIC 0724

COTTON GINNING

This category includes establishments engaged in cotton ginning.

NAICS CODE(S)

115111 (Cotton Ginning)

Cotton gins are machines used to separate cotton fibers from cotton seeds, a process that must be done before cotton fibers can be used for textiles. High quality cotton is the combined result of the original characteristics of the fiber and the degree of cleaning and drying it receives. The amount of trash and moisture in the cotton helps to determine the efficiency of the overall ginning process.

In 1999, cotton gins in the United States produced approximately 15.9 million bales of cotton. Some establishments operated a single gin, while larger companies operated as many as two dozen gins each. Texas and California are the leading cotton-producing states; nearly one third of all cotton grown in the United States was ginned in Texas. California was second in the nation in cotton ginning production, representing 13 percent of total U.S. production, followed by Mississippi with a little less than 11 percent.

In 1999 the two industry leaders were Anderson Clayton Corporation of Fresno, California, with $35 million in sales; and Lyford Gin Association of Lyford, Texas, with $19 million in sales.

Eli Whitney, a schoolteacher from Massachusetts, is generally given credit for inventing the first cotton gin in 1773. Whitney's gin, which he patented in 1774, was actually an improvement on an earlier invention known as the Churka gin. The Churka gin used rollers to loosen the cotton fibers, but it was almost useless on the tight, fuzzy variety of cotton that was grown in the Southern states. Whitney replaced the rollers with revolving wooden spikes that pulled the fibers down narrow slots, through which the seeds could not fall. A brush would then clean the cotton from the spikes. The hand-cranked Whitney gin drastically improved the pace of cotton cleaning and made cotton a profitable crop for Southern farmers.

Hodgen Holmes, a mechanic who had worked for Whitney, further improved the cotton gin by replacing the spikes with saw-toothed metal cylinders, which were more effective in grabbing hold of the cotton fibers. Holmes, who received a patent on his gin in 1776, also opened up the bottom of his gin so cotton could be fed into the top of the machine in a continuous process. Mechanical cleaners were added to the basic cotton gin in the 1840s to remove the leaves and stems left by harvesting. The first drier to reduce the moisture content of the cotton before ginning was patented in 1929.

Although the basic technology developed by Whitney and Holmes has remained in use, modern gins have become much more complex. In the early 1960s, cotton ginners developed an improved version of the Churka roller gin for use on long-fiber Pima cotton grown in the Southwest. These roller gins used two knife blades, one revolving and one stationary, to separate the cotton from the seeds. Pima cotton accounted for about 5 percent of the cotton grown in the United States.

Many ginners also sold or processed cottonseed for additional revenue. According to the National Cotton Council of America, more than five billion pounds of cottonseed and cottonseed meal were used annually for feeding livestock. Another 100 million gallons of cottonseed oil were used in food products. In the late 1980s, more ginners also began to offer compressing and warehouse services.

Until the 1990s, all ginned cotton received the same treatment, without regard to its trash content or its quality. Cotton ginning is a voluminous and complex procedure, which makes it impossible for humans to visually measure or decipher the amount of trash in the cotton or the quality of it; however, new technological advances have improved this situation.

Computerized advancements, for example, now make it possible to monitor and evaluate the ginning process online, as well as evaluate the response of cotton fiber during the process. These new technological advances accurately measure each component of the ginning process, and allow the ginner to process various types of cotton through the minimum machinery necessary to obtain maximum returns while keeping the fiber quality in tact.

In 1929 the Department of Agriculture established the U.S. Cotton Ginning Research Laboratory in Stoneville, Mississippi. The research laboratory has received several public service patents for developments that have improved cotton ginning. In 1938, the National Cotton Ginners Association, located in Memphis, Tennessee, was chartered to provide a national voice for several state and regional associations. In the 1990s, the association conducted a gin safety program, disseminated information on technology, and acted as a liaison between the ginning industry and machinery manufacturers. It also tracked federal legislation that affected the industry, including proposals affecting occupational health and safety, migrant workers, and clean-air regulations.

Since then, the effects of cotton processing on human health have been well documented by the National Cotton Ginners Association and the U. S. Department of Labor. The evidence indicates that the dust from cotton processing may be hazardous to a person's health. Many contaminants have been identified that could cause serious respiratory diseases. Because of these dangers, employers are required to limit the level of breathable cotton dust in the air and take other safety measures, such as supplying employees with respirators, periodic medical examinations, and training programs.

FURTHER READING

Anthony, Stanley. "Ginning Control Can Optimize Fiber Quality." *TextileWorld,* September, 1996.

Introduction to a Cotton Gin, Memphis, TN: National Cotton Ginners Association & the U.S. Department of Agriculture, n.d.

Johnson, Fred, "A Short History of the National Cotton Ginners Association." Memphis, TN: unpublished manuscript, 1992.

National Agricultural Statistics Service. "Cotton Ginnings," 2000. Available from http://usda.mannlib.cornell.edu.

U. S. Department of Labor. *Cotton Dust.* http://www.osha-slc.gov/Oshdoc/Fact_95_23.html, 1995.

Ward's Business Directory of U.S. Private and Public Companies Detroit: Gale Group, 1999.

SIC 0741

VETERINARY SERVICES FOR LIVESTOCK

This industry consists of establishments of licensed practitioners primarily engaged in the practice of veterinary medicine, dentistry, or surgery for cattle, hogs, sheep, goats, and poultry. Similar establishments primarily engaged in veterinary medicine for all other animals are classified in **SIC 0742: Veterinary Services for Animal Specialties.**

NAICS CODE(S)

541940 (Veterinary Services)

Roughly half of the food Americans eat is derived from animals (in the form of meat and dairy products). Thus, the focus of this industry is largely aimed at maintaining adequate and safe food supplies for humans through the treatment of injuries and diseases of livestock. Because disease accounts for billions of dollars in lost revenue for the livestock industry—around $3 billion in the 1980s and 1990s—veterinary establishments specializing in preventive medicine for larger animals (cattle, sheep, and swine) are integral to increasing livestock productivity and profitability.

Approximately 4,000 private veterinary practices were solely "country vet" practices or large animal clinics, providing treatment and preventive services, including the advising of private and commercial ranchers and farmers on the care and management of livestock and poultry in the 1990s. Although some practitioners specialize in dairy or beef cattle exclusively, most establishments also provide services for sheep, goats, and pigs; a small percentage also treat poultry.

In contrast to the rest of the veterinary industry, where services are most often rendered in a clinic or hospital setting, most veterinary services for livestock are performed on site—that is, in a barn, out in the field, or on a ranch. An experienced livestock practitioner treating predominantly large animals grossed about $61,000 in the late 1990s for services rendered, and veterinarians treating large animals exclusively earned about $76,000. Neophyte veterinarians just entering the profession earned just over $37,000. On the other hand, federally employed veterinarians of various capacities (nonsupervisory, supervisory, and managerial) averaged about $68,000 in the late 1990s.

The U.S. Department of Agriculture (USDA) provides veterinary services for researching livestock regulatory medicine. About 2,000 veterinarians were federally employed and engaged in the control and/or elimination of livestock disease and the protection of the public from animal diseases in the 1990s. These services were conducted through the Veterinary Services (VS) division of the Animal and Plant Health Inspection Service, a branch of the USDA. In the late 1990s the VS group worked to eradicate such diseases as cattle brucellosis, swine brucellosis, bovine tuberculosis, and swine pseudorabies. The division was also responsible for compiling information on the state of animal health in the United States—particularly livestock and poultry—through its National Animal Health Monitoring System, a program established in 1983. The USDA also used recently trained veterinarians as meat inspectors.

Another branch of the USDA, the Livestock and Poultry Sciences Institute, conducted research with the aim of increasing profitability, production efficiency, and the quality and value of livestock products. Among the Institute's laboratories were the Animal Improvement Programs Laboratory, the Meat Science Research Laboratory, and the Growth Biology Laboratory, which conducted research pertaining to the improvement of the growth and development of cattle, poultry, and swine.

Although the practice of caring for and treating animals dates back to ancient Egypt, veterinary services in the United States did not develop until the late 1880s, in response to the growth of the livestock industry. During the late nineteenth century and the first half of the twentieth century, almost all veterinary activities in the United States were associated with livestock, especially cattle, hogs, and sheep. A growing concern for public health in relation to the meat supply gave rise to a need for trained individuals capable of curing and preventing livestock diseases.

The first veterinary practitioners for livestock were generally farmers and ranchers who tended their own animals but otherwise had no formal training. In the late 1800s, however, veterinary schools in the United States began cropping up to provide a more specialized education in this field. At about the same time, state agencies became involved in the regulation of livestock health standards and the licensing of veterinary practitioners, moving livestock health care from the local farm or ranch to a more institutional setting.

The increasing population of the United States has created the need for additional food-producing animals. The current emphasis on scientific methods of breeding and raising livestock and poultry is expected to become even more prevalent, requiring additional specialization in the area of veterinary services for these animals. Advances in livestock production have also created a need for veterinary services related to contamination of the food chain by toxic chemicals. Thus, the demand for veterinary services related to the livestock industry is expected to increase, especially in the area of nutrition and disease control, as the continued integration of veterinary services with the livestock industry will be essential in order to address issues of food safety, quality of environment, and animal welfare.

FURTHER READING

American Veterinary Medical Association. ''General Position on Food Animals.'' 1999. Available from http://www.avma.org/care4pets/polfood.htm.

U.S. Department of Agriculture. Animal and Plant Health Inspection Service. ''Veterinary Services: Protection Animal Health and Promoting Trade.'' Washington, DC: October 1998. Available from http://www.aphis.usda.gov/oa/pubs/Vsbro.pdf.

U.S. Department of Labor. *Occupational Outlook Handbook, 1998-99 Edition.* Washington, DC: Bureau of Labor Statistics, September 1998. Available from http://www.bls.gov/ocohome.htm.

SIC 0742

VETERINARY SERVICES FOR ANIMAL SPECIALTIES

This industry consists of establishments of licensed practitioners primarily engaged in the practice of veterinary medicine, dentistry, or surgery for animal specialties, including horses, bees, fish, fur-bearing animals, rabbits, dogs, cats, and other pets and birds, except poultry. Establishments primarily engaged in the practice of veterinary medicine for cattle, hogs, sheep, goats, and poultry are classified in **SIC 0741: Veterinary Services for Livestock.**

NAICS CODE(S)

541940 (Veterinary Services)

INDUSTRY SNAPSHOT

The veterinary services industry is responsible for the care and treatment of companion animals (pets), sport animals (e.g., racehorses), and some livestock, as well as the protection of the public from exposure to animal diseases such as rabies. These services are generally performed by more than 73,000 licensed veterinarians and animal health technicians in the United States, often within the confines of one of the 22,400 animal hospitals and clinics in existence during the late 1990s.

According to the American Animal Hospital Association (AAHA), it is estimated that Americans spent about $20 billion in 1997 on veterinary services for their pets. It is expected that this amount will continue to increase by as much as 10 percent per year.

Organization and Structure

The term veterinary clinic is used to describe any veterinary establishment where animals are seen, usually as outpatients needing such services as physical exams, vaccinations, and treatment of minor illnesses and injuries. A veterinary hospital is an establishment that has facilities to treat animals needing to be hospitalized for more than a day. Treatments requiring overnight stays include surgery (most commonly spaying and neutering), tooth extraction, bone repair, and the suturing of wounds.

Because of the substantial investment needed for drugs, instruments, and other start-up costs, most veterinary establishments are group practices, either partnerships or larger facilities that hire individual veterinarians and technicians as employees. Smaller establishments may consist of one to three veterinarians and a technician, who may also serve as receptionist and bookkeeper. Larger establishments may employ several veterinary specialists, additional technicians, an animal dietician, a dental hygienist, and an office manager.

Veterinary Centers of America, Inc. (VCA), based in Santa Monica, California, is the country's largest provider of comprehensive health care services for animals. By 1999, the company owned about 190 animal hospitals in 27 states. VCA's twelve diagnostic laboratories provided services for more than 13,000 animal hospitals throughout America. The company owned 50.5 percent of Vet's Choice pet food and had investments in Veterinary Pet Insurance. Veterinary Centers of America, Inc. reported 1998 sales at $281 million, a 17.4 percent growth over 1997. VCA had 3,036 employees at the end of 1999. Hill's Pet Nutrition, Petco, and PETsMART were it's closest competitors at the close of the century.

About 75 percent of the industry is comprised of veterinarians in private practice. Of these, approximately 40 percent treat small animals, which may be either dogs and cats exclusively, or may include birds, rabbits, hamsters, monkeys, snakes, turtles, and other companion animals. Small-animal services involve pharmacy, surgery, dentistry, ophthalmology, cardiology, orthopedics, oncology, nutrition counseling, obstetrics, radiology, anesthesiology, and internal medicine. Mobile and house-call facilities often have established relationships with local veterinary hospitals so that surgical facilities are available when needed.

Geographical region seems to influence the type of veterinary practice. In metropolitan areas, for example, services are generally aimed at treating small companion animals; in rural areas, establishments are more likely to treat livestock and horses.

Large-animal practices comprise about 13 percent of the industry. Except for horses, these establishments are covered under **SIC 0741: Veterinary Services for Livestock.** Those veterinary services specializing in horses often care for racing horses; such establishments are better compensated financially than most others. Roughly 40 percent of establishments are mixed practices, involving both clinic and house-call facilities. Some of these facilities are affiliated with zoos and primarily provide preventive treatment and health upkeep, including vaccinations, dental care, worming, and grooming.

The cost of routine veterinary services is paid for directly by the individual. However, since the early 1980s, health insurance covering accidents, major injuries, and certain chronic illnesses for dogs and cats has been available in most states. For an annual premium of about $50 to $220, with a deductible ranging from $20 to $300, animal owners can purchase major medical benefits for their pets that like those available for humans. As a result, there is a growing trend to continue care for many animals that would have previously undergone euthanasia.

All personnel engaged in the private sector of the industry must be licensed. Veterinarians are required to have a Doctor of Veterinary Medicine (D.V.M. or V.M.D) degree from one of the 27 accredited colleges of veterinary medicine, and must pass state board proficiency examinations. Those engaged in specialty services must complete an approved residency program, as well as pass board exams and other board requirements. Some states require licensing of animal health technicians based on minimum educational requirements, an examination, and a fee. In addition, some larger companies, such as VCA, require their vets to have a minimum number of hours of continuing education on a yearly basis. Veterinarians employed by the government need not be licensed.

Background and Development

Because most of the procedures and medicines developed for the treatment of human diseases were first tested on animals, the advancement of veterinary medicine, and therefore the development of the veterinary services industry, is closely related to the advancement of human medicine. Although people have kept animals for companionship for thousands of years, the need for practitioners of veterinary medicine did not arise in the United States until 1883, when bans on interstate transportation and exportation of diseased animals to Europe began to hurt this country's growing livestock industry.

The establishment of the Veterinary Division of the U.S. Department of Agriculture (USDA) in 1883 was the first step toward recognition that treatment and preventive care of animals was a necessity. In May 1884 Congress passed an act that established The Bureau of Animal Industry (BAI). Among its aims was "to provide means for the suppression and extirpation of . . . contagious diseases among domestic animals."

With the industrialization of the United States came shorter work hours, more leisure time, earlier retirement, and longer life expectancies. Animals' status as pets began to receive greater attention and a corresponding demand for better veterinary services resulted. According to a 1990 survey, approximately 43 percent of all households had pets, whereas only 38 percent had children. Many of these pet owners treat their animals as family members, which includes ensuring that they receive competent medical care.

Current Conditions

By 1999, 75 percent of all licensed veterinarians worked in private practice and 58 percent of those specialized exclusively to small animals. These veterinarians were responsible for the care of 53 million dogs and 59 million cats along with other pets such as rabbits, ferrets, guinea pigs, hamsters, rodents, turtles, and other reptiles.

Veterinary services and specialties exist for nearly all human equivalents, including chemotherapy, CAT scans, ultrasound, prosthetic hip surgery, pacemaker implants, electrocardiograms, kidney transplants, arthroscopic surgery, dental care, and acupuncture. As a result, the industry is expected to become more and more specialized in the coming years. The rising popularity of medical insurance for pets is already allowing more pet owners to afford these technologically-advanced treatments that otherwise would have been too expensive, and some believe that the small, one- to three-person practice will eventually be replaced by large, centralized veterinary hospitals with staffs of 30-50 specialized veterinarians and technicians.

A trend toward more unconventional methods of private practice, such as mobile clinics, low-cost spay clinics, vaccination clinics, and tax-exempt government-subsidized animal welfare groups, has already been noted. Some veterinary facilities also are taking a more holistic approach, considering environmental factors, nutrition, and the psychological needs of animals.

In an effort to increase revenues, veterinary establishments now include the sale of over-the-counter drugs and pet supplies such as food and parasite-control products. This practice allows for competition with feed stores, pet health centers, and pet supply stores, which also tend to offer free advice on the use of drugs and other animal health products.

The industry is expected to grow faster than the average of all occupations through the year 2006 with a higher demand for specialized facilities in metropolitan areas. An increasing need for additional small-animal clinics is predicted as the pet population increases, although small animal practices might become more competitive because most graduates preferred to live in more populated areas rather than rural ones caring for larger animals. Large, multi-hospital corporations (such as Veterinary Centers of America) and clinics that incorporate pet stores and grooming all in one facility may be one way to counteract competition and increase revenues. Advertising, including television, direct mail, newspapers, Yellow Pages advertisements, and advertisements in professional publications, once shunned, will also play a greater role as this industry develops.

Workforce

The veterinary services industry employs approximately 73,000 people, about 90 percent of whom are doctors of veterinary medicine. Veterinary assistants, technicians, and office workers make up the remainder of the work force. By 1997, women accounted for nearly 40 percent of all practicing veterinarians in the United States. The 1998-1999 college enrollment for veterinarians showed 9,055 students, of that total 6,296 were female and 2,759 male.

In 1998, licensed practitioners first starting out in the industry earned an average salary of about $31,000 annually. Those with six or more years experience averaged between $60,000-$75,000, less than half the average gross of a doctor of human medicine and about two-thirds as much as a human dentist with comparable experience.

Entry level animal-health technicians, many of whom are trained in laboratory procedures, assisting and monitoring patients, preparation for surgery, administering medication, and feeding, are paid an average of $16,000 a year. Salaries increase gradually with experience, ranging from about $23,390 to $28,390 after seven years. The low starting salaries, coupled with the lack of financial growth, has led to a shortage of qualified technicians at a time when the industry itself has become more and more technically-oriented.

America and the World

The World Veterinary Association (WVA) met for the third time in March 1999 to discuss animal welfare throughout the world. The association scheduled meetings at three year intervals. One of the association's objectives was to develop a policy statement to help set worldwide standards. Another major concern was the potential of diseases being spread across country borders. The organization prides itself on keeping politics out of the discussions and maintaining animal welfare their priority.

FURTHER READING

American Veterinary Medical Association. *News.* 1999. Available from http://www.avma.org.

American Veterinary Medical Association. ''World Veterinary Association stresses science, not politics.'' 15 May 1999. Available from http://www.avma.org/onlnews/javma/.

Bess, Jack. ''Animal Medical Care Now Rivaling Treatment Level Delivered to Humans.'' *American Medical News,* 33, 12 January 1990: 3-4.

Hoover's Company Capsules. 1999. Available from http://www.hoovers.com/co/.

Hyten, Todd. ''Chain Takes Big Bite out of Veterinary Clinics.'' *Boston Business Journal,* 7 June 1996: 1.

Occupational Employment Statistics, 1998. U.S. Department of Labor, Bureau of Statistics, 1998. Available from http://www.stats.bls.gov.

SIC 0751

LIVESTOCK SERVICES, EXCEPT VETERINARY

This classification covers establishments primarily engaged in performing services, except veterinary, for cattle, hogs, sheep, goats, and poultry. Dairy herd improvement associations are also included in this industry. Establishments primarily engaged in the fattening of cattle are classified in **SIC 0211: Beef Cattle Feedlots.** Establishments engaged in incidental feeding of livestock, often during periods of transportation, as a part of holding them in stockyards for periods of less than 30 days are classified in **SIC 4789: Transportation Services, Not Elsewhere Classified.** Establishments that perform services, except those in the realm of veterinary services, for animals not classified as livestock are classified in **SIC 0752: Animal Specialty Services, Except Veterinary.**

NAICS CODE(S)

311611 (Animal (except Poultry) Slaughtering)
115210 (Support Activities for Animal Production)

INDUSTRY SNAPSHOT

The raising of cattle, sheep, hogs, goats, and poultry requires several specialized husbandry skills, many of which are performed by members of the livestock service industry. These services range from artificial insemination to pedigree record keeping to sheep dipping and shearing.

Labor use on American farms and ranches has changed dramatically since World War II. In 1950 nearly 10.0 million workers were employed on farms and ranches, but by 1969 this figure had been reduced to 3.1 million. In the subsequent decades, this number continued to drop and held at a little more than 2.0 million in the 1990s. This decrease was the result of the trend towards fewer and larger agricultural enterprises and the increasing use of technological innovation. One result of increasing concentration and the development of very large poultry and livestock feeding enterprises has been the switch from family labor to the increased use of temporary workers. In the 1990s, 239,724 operations or 12 percent of all farms relied on contract labor, a sizable increase from 1980 when only about 2 percent did. These establishments provide a range of livestock maintenance services.

In 1999, the four top companies ranked by revenue were Kane-Miller Corp. with $96 million, ABS Global, Inc., with $91 million, Pig Improvement Company, Inc., with $85 million, and 21st Century Genetics Cooperative, with $24 million.

ORGANIZATION AND STRUCTURE

Breed Associations. These organizations perform many services, including tracking of pedigree information and performance records. Typically, a breeder of purebred livestock registers the offspring of his herd or flock shortly after they are born. To be registered in the national herd book these animals must be of purebred parentage, meaning that both sire and dam were previously recorded with the breed registry. Breed associations keep these records and in so doing maintain the purity of the breed. Most breed associations have a paid field staff whose job it is to assist the purebred breeders in filling out the paper work, designing breeding programs, and even aiding in the selection and procurement of seedstock.

Increasingly it has fallen to the breed associations to also keep performance data on livestock animals. Breeders send in such data as birth weights, weaning weight information, or—in the case of dairy cows—milk production figures. The breed association then gathers up all the data from the participating breeders and publishes this information in the form of sire summaries and ''expected progeny differences.'' This computer-generated data aids purebred and commercial breeders in selecting those animals with the highest production traits. The role of the various breed associations is rapidly expanding, primarily because of their large databases of performance information. This data has become increasingly valuable as the animal industries turn to what is known as ''value-based marketing.'' Purchasers of livestock—feedlots, dairies, piggeries, and processors—demand to know the performance ability and meat quality of the animals before they purchase them.

Examples of breed associations in the beef industry include The American Hereford Association and the American Angus Association. The Holstein Association keeps pedigrees and production information for Breeders of registered Holstein dairy animals. There are more than a dozen sheep registries, including the American Hampshire Sheep Association, the American Suffolk Sheep Society, and the National Suffolk Sheep Association.

Artificial Breeding Services. Another service industry common to most domesticated livestock establishments is the artificial insemination stud and breeding service. Artificial insemination is widely used in dairy cattle and poultry and to a lesser extent with beef cattle and hogs. Those employed in the breeding industry purchase or lease superior animals, house them at their facilities, collect their semen regularly, merchandise the semen, and ship it in frozen nitrogen to their livestock-raising customers. Recent technological innovation is making it possible to sex the semen so that a producer can determine the gender of the resulting offspring.

The concept behind artificial insemination is the same for all species; however, the procedures vary from animal to animal. When superior producing male animals are identified their semen is drawn and extended. Extension is the process whereby 10 cubic centimeters of semen is extended to provide 100 or even 200 doses. For cattle, the semen is frozen and then sold by the straw or ampule to other breeders who in this manner can use the best genetics available. In the case of dairy animals, it might be possible for a superior dairy bull to produce a million offspring through insemination techniques. Without the use of this technology, the bull's number of offspring and his contribution to the breed would be significantly reduced. But for hogs, the semen must be fresh in order to work. Hence, artificial insemination is more difficult for pigs and has not been as successful. Operations offering this service try to accommodate hog farmers within a 50 mile radius of the operation's headquarters. Computers and refrigerated trucks play a crucial role in the tracking and expeditious delivery of the hog semen.

In the case of artificial insemination for poultry, the inseminator collects semen from roosters and, using a microscope, records the motility and morphology of the semen. A specified amount is then placed into a syringe-like inseminating gun and the semen is injected into the oviduct of the hen or through a tiny hole in the egg shell. The use of artificial insemination in poultry has expanded such that it accounts for nearly 99 percent of all new birds in the turkey production industry. This production route has resulted in turkeys with much more meat than the average bird of a few years ago. Typical turkeys now have so much meat on their breasts that they are unable to mate in the usual manner.

Technological innovation and research has led to another breakthrough in reproductive physiology—embryo transfer. Just as it is desirable to increase the offspring from a superior male, so too is it advantageous to increase the number of offspring from a superior female. By taking the eggs from an animal's ovary, implanting them in a petri dish with genetically superior semen, and then implanting them back into a recipient female, the breeding potential of superior females is being expanded. The recipient female actually gives birth to an animal that has none of her genes. These tasks are performed by a growing number of businesses located throughout the country.

Central Test Stations. Testing stations are also common to several species of livestock. Sometimes associated with a university, these test stations can also be individually owned. It is the purpose of a test station to feed, weigh, measure, and record the performance of bulls, rams, and boars. The data is used to compare consignments from several breeders and in many cases the animals are then sold at auction to go into other seedstock operations. Through the use of centralized testing stations the universities and land grant colleges have played a vital role in identifying animals with superior genetics.

Fitting Services. The showing of hogs, sheep, goats, and cattle at livestock fairs and expositions is often left to professional fitters. Animals entered in these contests are groomed, fed, and hauled from one fair to another, often by fitting services that perform these services either for a flat fee or a percentage of the prize money. In many instances one fitter's string of show animals might include animals from several different breeders.

Custom Slaughtering. The people who perform these services are few and far between. It is illegal to raise an animal, have it custom slaughtered, and then sell that animal's carcass or meat to another individual without having it inspected by a government inspector. Therefore, most custom slaughtering is done for ranchers or raisers of livestock on animals they have raised for their own family's consumption.

Specialized Species Services. In many instances the services required by one animal species are unique to that animal. Specialized services regarding sheep include sheep herders, sheep shearers (usually contract labor, with payment either by the head or for a flat fee. This is difficult, highly-skilled work), fleece tiers, lambers (individuals hired during birthing season to aid the ewes in delivery), and trappers. The trapper hunts, kills and traps predatory animals that are killing lambs and sheep.

The Animal Damage Control program of the USDA provides direct assistance to private individuals to help protect their animals from injury and damage caused by wild animals. Under the Animal Damage Control Act of 1931 there are state and federal funds available to help pay for the services of a trapper. In the past trappers used to work for a bounty, but most are now independent contractors since most bounties have been discontinued. The trapper's practices and methods are much more regulated and controlled than in the past.

Specialist positions in the poultry service area include caponizers, who castrate cockerels (very young male chickens) to prevent the development of secondary sex characteristics; debeakers; poultry vaccinators; and chick graders and sexers. In the area of dairy cattle, while most work on the modern day dairy is performed by the facility's employees, milk testing is one task that is ''farmed'' out. The milk tester or sampler can either work for a dairy herd improvement association, a breed association, or an independent service. It is the tester's job to collect milk samples from dairies, processing plants or tank trucks for lab analysis.

Further Reading

Tevlin, Jon. ''Making Bacon.'' *Corporate Report—Minnesota,* 26 October 1995.

U.S. Department of Agriculture. *Agricultural Statistics,* Washington, DC: GPO, 1995-1996.

Ward's Business Directory of U.S. Private and Public Companies. Detroit: Gale Group, 1999.

SIC 0752

ANIMAL SPECIALTY SERVICES, EXCEPT VETERINARY

This classification covers establishments primarily engaged in performing services for pets, equines, and other animal specialties. These establishments include kennels, animal shelters, stables, breeders of animals other than livestock, pet registries, and a host of other animal care services. Establishments primarily engaged in performing services other than veterinary for cattle, hogs, sheep, goats, and poultry are classified in **SIC 0751: Livestock Services, Except Veterinary.** Establishments primarily engaged in training racehorses are classified in **SIC 7948: Racing, Including Track Operation.**

NAICS Code(s)

115210 (Support Activities for Animal Production)
612910 (Pet Care (except Veterinary) Services)

Industry Snapshot

About 60 percent of all U.S. homes sheltered a pet of some sort in the late 1990s. Dogs, cats, birds, and fish were the most popular types, with about 59 million cats and 52.9 million dogs existing in the United States. Though cats outnumbered dogs, dogs were found in 4.2 million more U.S. households than cats, according to a study conducted by the American Veterinary Medical Association's Center for Information Management. There was a rise in the number of household with no pets, but there was also an increase in the number of households with more than one pet. An estimated 58.9 percent of U.S. households owned one or more pets in 1996, and 45.7 percent of these homes owned dogs, cats, or both. Because of the nation's affinity for pets, a growing number of animal specialty services have emerged to provide a wide range of general breeding, grooming, care, and training services.

Though dogs and cats were the most popular of companion animals, bird ownership increased from 11.0 million in 1991 to 12.6 million in 1996, a rise of 14.5 percent. Other household pets that enjoyed increased popularity in the 1990s included rabbits, hamsters, guinea pigs, ferrets, gerbils, snakes, lizards, and turtles.

Animal caretakers outside the farm held about 125,000 jobs in the mid- to late 1990s. Most of these workers were employed in boarding kennels and veterinary facilities. Other employers included animal shelters; horse stables; and local, state and federal agencies. According to the U.S. Census Bureau, one out of every six animal caretakers was self-employed and more than a third worked only part-time. Of these 125,000, about 16,000 people held positions as trainers or breeders.

Pedigree Record Services. The American Kennel Club of New York keeps a list of the number of dogs registered to purebred parents. The Kennel Club's list of the top 50 dog breeds includes such standbys as Labrador Retrievers to breeds growing in popularity such as the Rottweiler (which jumped from the fourth most registered breed in 1991 to second in 1992). In contrast to the widespread interest in purebred dog breeds, only a small percentage of cats are registered with one of the official registering bodies. The largest such body is the Cat Fancier's Association, which sponsors 650 member clubs scattered across the country. The Cat Fancier's Association recognized 36 breeds as of 1997, and in February 1998 the Sphynx was accepted as a new breed. Popular cat breeds included the Persian, the Maine Coon, the Siamese, and the Abyssinian.

Boarding Kennels. Kennels care for small companion animals when their owners cannot. Kennels are used primarily as temporary homes while the pet owner is gone on business or vacation. There is much more to managing a kennel than feeding the animals, cleaning cages, and maintaining dog runs: attendants are often called upon to perform basic acts of first aid, bathe and groom animals, and clean their ears and teeth. At the better kennels, the attendants also play with the animals, provide companionship, and observe behavioral changes that could indicate illness or injury. Often, kennels also sell pet food and supplies, teach obedience classes, help with breeding, and arrange transportation.

Groomers. People who specialize in the maintenance of the appearance of pets are called groomers. Some operate out of kennels while others maintain their own independent businesses. Most groomers learn their trade by working for an established groomer but a few schools do exist that teach the basic skills. The groomer combs, clips, and shapes the animal's coat according to a set of established breed guidelines.

Animal Breeding. The small animal breeder raises animals for a variety of purposes. A breeder of dogs may produce the very best bird dog for hunting or fancy poodles for exhibiting in the show ring. Whatever the animal's purpose, the breeder's task is to produce the animal that is both phenotypically and genotypically demanded by the customer. In the case of dogs, these styles are constantly changing and the breeder must be on a constant look-out for outstanding genetic stock to improve the breed and his profitability. There are numerous pet publications dealing with specific breeds that carry advertising for stud dogs and litters. Numerous shows, trials, and exhibitions allow breeders to display their excellence in direct competition. Through such endeavors the better dogs become well known and can command impressive fees.

Animal Shelter. More commonly known as "the pound," the animal shelter provides for the basic maintenance of pets that are lost or abandoned. The shelter screens applicants for adoption, vaccinates newly admitted animals, provides spay and neuter clinics and, as a last resort, euthanizes severely injured or unwanted pets. A survey sponsored by the National Council on Pet Population Study and Policy polled more than 1,000 U.S. animal shelters for the years 1994, 1995, and 1996. The total number of dogs entering these shelters rose from 2.11 million in 1994 to 2.15 million in 1996. The number of cats entering these shelters increased as well, from 1.67 million in 1994 to 1.71 million in 1996.

A major problem facing the small animal care industry is the frequency with which euthanasia is used—more than 15 million dogs and cats had to be euthanized in 1996. According to the National Council on Pet Population Study and Policy survey, about 1.98 million of the dogs that entered shelters in 1996 exited, either through adoption, reclamation by owner, or euthanasia. Of the 1.98 million dogs, 55.5 percent were euthanized. Of the 1.58 million cats that left shelters, 71.2 percent were euthanized in 1996. Overpopulation and unwanted pets were the biggest reasons for these statistics and have prompted shelters to initiate concerted education efforts aimed at lowering those numbers. Recent budget cuts have also forced some shelters to support their populations with food processed from the remains of euthanized animals.

Shelters can be maintained by county, state, and local governments or may be sponsored by charitable institutions and foundations. They are almost always non-profit organizations. One of the most important functions performed by shelters are the vaccination clinics they sponsor on a community-wide basis. They also maintain and operate pet ambulances or trucks in order to respond to emergency calls. It also falls within their jurisdiction to investigate complaints of animal cruelty. Most animal shelters will also aid the urban resident when he is faced with a pest or a livestock rancher who is experiencing losses due to roving packs of wild dogs. In ridding communities of rabid or vicious animals, the shelters work closely with county law enforcement officials.

Large Animal Specialty Services. The use of horses for recreation and competition has increased dramatically in recent years and produced a corresponding increase in demand for training and boarding services. Among these equine services are horse stables, which provide boarding accommodations for horses whose owners do not possess the facilities to house their animals. Fees, which can be tallied on a monthly or daily basis, are broken down for food and board and additional expenses such as veterinary care. Horse training is another key element of this industry. Horses used for pleasure riding, endurance racing, cutting, team penning, showing at halter, or any of the other number of activities must be properly trained.

Some operations also offer horse mating services, which have proven to be quite lucrative. Top breed stud fees continued to rise through the late 1990s, but the rate of increase slowed slightly between 1999 and 2000. For example, according to figures compiled by publishing company The Blood-Horse Inc., the average stud fee for 138 stallions that had two or more crops racing was an estimated $23,134 in 2000, a 9.1 percent rise from the 1999 average of $21,207. The 1998 average was $19,735. The most expensive stallions commanded the highest stud fees and represented the fastest growing portion of the stud fee market in the late 1990s. The average fee for this small group of stallions was $175,000 for 2000, a 25 percent increase over the 1999 average of $140,000.

FURTHER READING

American Veterinary Medical Association. Center for Information Management. "U.S. Pet Ownership and Demographic Sourcebook." 1997.

Biles, Deirdre B. "Demand for the Suppliers." *The Blood-Horse,* 29 November 1999. Available from http://www.bloodhorse.com/features/stud_fees1129.html.

Fossell, Eric. "Warm Companions." *The Herald-Dispatch,* 9 June 1997. Available from http://www.4yi.com/060997kittens/060997kittens.html.

Munk, Nina. "Nice Work if You Can Get It." *Forbes,* 3 June 1996.

U.S. Department of Labor. *Occupational Outlook Handbook, 1998-99 Edition.* Washington, DC: Bureau of Labor Statistics, September 1998. Available from http://www.bls.gov/ocohome.htm.

"U.S. Pet Market Continues to Grow." *Pet Product News,* August 1996.

U.S. Department of Commerce. *Statistical Abstract of the United States, 1996-1997.* Washington, DC: GPO, 1996.

SIC 0761

FARM LABOR CONTRACTORS AND CREW LEADERS

This category describes establishments primarily engaged in supplying labor for agriculture production of harvesting. Establishments primarily engaged in machine harvesting are classified in Industry 0722 (see **SIC 0722: Crop Harvesting, Primarily by Machine**).

NAICS CODE(S)

115115 (Farm Labor Contractors and Crew Leaders)

More than 500 farm labor contractors were in operation in the United States in 1998, directly employing more than 6,700 individuals. This industry is heavily concentrated in the western United States, particularly in California. Farm labor contractors and crew leaders overcome language barriers and handle paperwork as they recruit, hire, fire, supply, pay, and transport workers for the U.S. agriculture labor market. Contractors are required by law to ensure that all employees performing under their administration are certified in accordance with federal regulations, and are legally responsible for all violations.

Observers have long levied a variety of criticisms at farm labor contractors, most of them stemming from contractors' heavily reliance on migrant labor, including illegal immigrants. The percentage of farm laborers who were migrant workers, a classification that includes all agricultural workers who must travel such a distance as to make it impractical to return to their residence the same day, fluctuates from about 6 percent in the winter months to about 12 percent in the summer.

One of the most frequent criticisms aimed at farm labor contractors (FLCs) and crew leaders is the allegation that they allow growers to sidestep labor laws. Critics say many FLCs short workers on pay, or extract profits from workers for such things as tool rent, transportation, and lodging. Further, critics say, FLCs contribute to worker poverty, income inequality, poor conditions, a regular influx of new undocumented immigrants, and decline of the farm labor movement.

Criticism may be merited. In 1995 the U.S. Department of Labor fined growers and contractors $2.1 million for underpayment of 2,700 farm workers on 800 farms nationwide. Particularly in the FLC-heavy California, the dependence on illegal farm labor, most notably from previously untapped regions in Mexico, has skyrocketed to an estimated 43 percent of hired farm workers. The increasing use of illegal immigrants have not abated despite a number of federal actions aimed at reducing the number of such immigrants entering the United States. In all, about 91 percent of such workers in 1999 were from Mexico, 80 percent were men, and 75 percent earned less than $10,000 per year, although 61 percent were married and 56 percent had children.

To stem the tide of illegal farm labor, state and federal legislatures have made moves to implement "Alien Agriculture Worker Programs," which compel farm labor contractors to become officially sanctioned by their state government to hire "guest" workers for a given period each year.

Meanwhile, farm laborers were exposed to alarmingly dangerous work conditions. Fatal injuries claimed about 700 farm workers in the mid 1990s, while 64,813 suffered nonfatal injuries. The majority of these incidences involved hired laborers.

Contractors insist they've been unfairly criticized. Child labor and workplace safety violations are declining. An advocacy group, the National Farm Labor Contractors Association, established in 1967 and based in Fresno, California, lobbies lawmakers on behalf of FLCs, gives legal advice, and provides training, a newsletter, phone numbers, and reference materials.

Nationally, FLCs hired an average of 300,000 workers per month in 1999, averaging about $8.00 per hour in wages. About one-third were based in California. Crew sizes vary from 20 to 60 workers, depending on the crop and locale. Western FLCs tend to be large. The average number of workers employed by California FLCs in the 1990s was 800. FLCs were the fastest-growing employer in California agriculture, accounting for 90 percent of the seasonal worker employment since the mid-1980s.

California is home to most of the largest FLCs in the nation. The largest was Valley Pride, Inc. of Castroville, California, with $22 million in annual sales and 400 employees. Also based in California was Tara Packing in Salinas, with $21 million in annual income and 600 employees. Other major FLCs include Vegpacker, Inc. of Yuma, Arizona, with sales of $7 million and 250 employees; Emco Harvesting of Yuma Arizona with $18 million in revenues; and 5A Harvesting Co. of Labelle Florida.

FURTHER READING

''13 Needless Deaths.'' *The New York Times,* 11 August 1999.

Greenhouse, Steven. ''U.S. Expands Protection for Contract Farm Labor.'' *The New York Times,* 12 March 1997.

''Number of Illegal Farm Workers in California Increases.'' *Fresno Bee,* 17 December 1998.

Sevilla, Graciela. ''U.S. Harvest-Time Sweeps Reveal Abuses.'' *The Arizona Republic,* 25 June 1999.

SIC 0762

FARM MANAGEMENT SERVICES

This category describes establishments primarily engaged in providing farm management and maintenance services for farms, citrus groves, orchards, and vineyards. Such activities may include supplying contract labor for agricultural production and harvesting, inspecting crops and fields to estimate yield, determining crop transportation and storage requirements, and hiring and assigning workers to tasks involved in the harvesting and cultivating of crops; but establishments primarily engaged in performing such services without farm management services are classified in the appropriate specific industry within Industry Group 072. Workers with similar functions include agricultural engineers, animal breeders, animal scientists, county agricultural agents, dairy scientists, extension service specialists, feed and farm management advisors, horticulturists, plant breeders, and poultry scientists.

NAICS CODE(S)

115116 (Farm Management Services)

The overall trends in the farming industry portends good news for farm managers. With an increasing consolidation and centralization of farming activities and a more market-oriented approach to the business, farmers are likely to find farm managers ever-more attractive. In 1997, over 60 percent of all U.S. farmland was operated by someone other than its owner. There were about 500 farm management firms operating in the United States in 1998, employing about 4,700 workers. The industry is served by the American Society of Farm Managers and Rural Appraisers.

Professional farm managers have a variety of duties and responsibilities. For instance, the owner of a large livestock farm may employ a farm manager to supervise a single activity such as feeding the animals. At the other end of the spectrum, a farm manager working for an absentee farm owner may have the responsibility for all functions, from planning the crop to participating in the planting and harvesting activities. Professional farm managers must be able to establish output goals, determine financial constraints, and monitor production and marketing. Farm management firms often handle the financial business of client farms, including the buying and selling of products and even the farmland itself. In addition, a number of firms provide consulting services to farmers and farming companies.

Many types of farming are seasonal. Although farm managers on crop farms tend to work all day during the planting and harvesting seasons, they often work on the farm less than 7 months a year. They spend the rest of the year planning the next season's crops, marketing their output, and repairing machinery. Farm managers can achieve Accredited Farm Manager (AFM) certification by the American Society of Farm Managers and Rural Appraisers, after sufficient academic training and job experience.

As more people without agricultural backgrounds come to regard farmland as a good investment rather than a vocation, and as family farms give way to corporate farms, farm managers are growing in number and influence. A 1999 survey conducted by the American Society of Farm Managers and Rural Appraisers revealed that about half the farm management firms in the United States expected to be managing more agriculture products than banks in within a few years.

Among the leading farm management services firms are: Orange-co, Inc. of Bartow Florida, with 500 employees and sales of $119 million; Farmers National Company, with 130 employees, $18.5 billion in sales and 3,700 clients throughout the Midwest; Indian River Exchange Packers of Vero Beach, Florida, employing 350 workers; Alliance Argonomics, Inc. of Mechanicsville, Florida, with $24 million in sales; and Sun-Ag, Inc. of Fellsmere, Florida, with a payroll of 550 employees.

The late 1990s was a difficult time for many farmers. The industry's vigorous competition, exacerbated by the lowest agricultural commodity prices in decades heightened the demand for shrewd management practices. Proper crop, soil, and feed management systems could make or break a farming enterprise in this environment.

Of growing importance was the handling of efficiency measures to cut down on costs and pollution, especially in the socially and economically sensitive areas of water and fertilizer management. Farms were falling under heavy scrutiny by environmentalists, consumers, and the U.S. Department of Agriculture to diminish waste production and eliminate pollution.

One avenue by which farm managers were beginning to recognize financial and efficiency gains was in the trading of emissions between agricultural and industrial operations. Farmers were increasingly called on to overhaul animal-waste-management and fertilizer-application systems and in general gear agricultural processes toward the limiting of greenhouse-gas emissions in accordance with the U.S. standards adopted by President Clinton at the Kyoto Conference in 1997. While the practice of pollution trading has existed for years, it traditionally involved the transfer of pollution credits from one party to another. Greenhouse-gas emissions, on the other hand, involve the actual purchase of the reductions in agriculturally based emissions by industrial firms who can then allocate the emissions allotment in accordance with their industry's regulations. It thus creates a financial incentive for farm managers to streamline farming operations for greater efficiency.

Farm managers need to keep abreast of continuing advances in farming technologies. In the late 1990s, more and more farm managers were using precision agriculture or site-specific farming methods to customize the placement of seed, fertilizer, and chemicals to get more bushels of grain from their land, reduce waste, and prevent pollution of streams. For instance, in 1997, Ag Technology Inc. estimated that 8,000 yield monitors were in use across the United States. Yield monitors attached to combines measure the harvest as the combine gathers it. Over one-third of the farm managers using yield monitors also used a global positioning satellite, paired with a receiver that correlates the satellite reading with a fixed point on the ground. Some farm managers are supplementing these technology tools with Geographic Information System, a mapping software.

The passage of the Federal Agriculture Improvement and Reform (FAIR) Act, popularly called Freedom to Farm, was a significant event in this industry in 1996. This new legislation marked the beginning of the gradual departure of government from farming and planting decisions. Once this law was passed, farms began moving toward a market-oriented approach to operations. While this law was always a thorn in the side of small farmers and populist farming organizations for reducing government programs to aid farmers, generally to the advantage of large agribusiness firms, the Freedom to Farm Act has met with increasing calls for reexamination from the latter groups as the slumping commodities prices began to eat into profit margins. It was widely expected that the Freedom to Farm Act would be overhauled before its provisions were to expire in 2002.

Further Reading

Bureau of Labor Statistics. U.S. Department of Labor. *Occupational Outlook Handbook, 1998-99 Edition.* Washington, D.C.: GPO, 1998.

"Is the Sun Setting on Farmers? Many Can't Survive the 'New Agriculture'." *New York Times,* 6 December 1999.

Philips, Jim. "Reexamining Freedom to Farm." *Progressive Farmer,* 18 January 1999.

Schulman, Richard D. "Modern Technology Meets Traditional Farm Practices." *Geo Info Systems,* February 1997.

"Unique Emissions Trading May Open Door for Others." *Pollution Engineering,* December 1999.

SIC 0781

LANDSCAPE COUNSELING AND PLANNING

This classification includes establishments engaged in landscape planning and landscape architectural and counseling services.

NAICS Code(s)

541320 (Landscape Architectural Services)

541690 (Other Scientific and Technical Consulting Services)

The service industry of landscape counseling and planning is primarily composed of private landscape architecture firms and self-employed landscape architects, although the federal government also hires landscape architects for projects similar to those done by private firms. The American Society of Landscape Architects reported in 1999 that approximately 80 percent of its 12,000 members were engaged in private practice, with another 15 percent working in local, state, or federal government and 5 percent in academic practice. Major architectural and engineering firms have also started offering in-house landscape architectural services.

Landscape architects working in this industry are responsible for the design and implementation of land use for areas such as parkways, golf courses, parks, shopping malls, and the areas surrounding private homes and businesses. They plan the location of buildings, roads, and walkways; arrange flowers, shrubs, and trees; and design streets to maximize pedestrian access and safety. Landscape architects are hired by a wide variety of groups including real estate developers, municipalities, private citizens, and private businesses.

Often working in conjunction with architects and engineers, landscape architects combine engineering, horticultural, and design skills to create satisfying and efficient environments. They also work to prevent or solve environmental problems due to construction. Once given a particular assignment, a landscape planner conducts detailed analyses of the existing soil composition, vegetation, water drainage, and slope of the land. Next, initial drawings outlining plans for the site are submitted to the client. If the plans are accepted, the landscape architect makes a formal proposal that may include written reports, sketches, models, photographs, land use studies, and cost analyses. Most landscape architecture firms also supervise contractors during the installation of their plan. Commonly, the landscape architecture firm is present at the opening of the site and available for assistance or consultation through the first six months of existence.

As an art form, landscape architecture can be traced back to the ancient world. The Renaissance enthusiasm for open space, including ornate villas and outdoor piazzas, influenced the chateaux and urban garden movement in seventeenth century France, which produced such masterpieces as Andre le Notre's gardens at Versailles. In eighteenth century England, landscape planners such as Lancelot ''Capability'' Brown emphasized naturalistic rather than geometric forms, notably in Brown's remodeling of the grounds of Blenheim Palace. Sir Humphrey Repton, however, reintroduced formal motifs in such public spaces as Victoria Park in London in 1845 and Birkenhead Park in Liverpool in 1847. These projects greatly influenced the development of landscape planning in the United States and Canada. In the 1850s the title ''landscape architect'' was first used by Frederick Law Olmsted who worked with Calvert Vaux to design New York's Central Park, one of the first urban renewal projects in the country. An advocate of public space as a means of making cities more livable, Olmsted also designed the grounds of the U.S. Capitol in the 1879s and was instrumental in developing numerous public parks around the country.

In 1899 the American Society of Landscape Architects (ASLA) was formed by Olmsted's followers. By 1999, the ASLA had approximately 12,000 members. Though the profession grew slowly during the first half of the twentieth century, with landscape architects earning modest salaries, the profession experienced significant growth during the 1980s and 1990s. By 1999, almost 60 universities and colleges in the United States offered accredited baccalaureate and post-graduate programs in landscape architecture, and commissions for landscaping outnumbered the professionals available to execute them.

For many years the design work involved in landscape planning was done by hand at drawing boards but, in the late 1990s, an increasing number of landscape architects were using computer aided design (CAD) systems to assist them in creating designs. Advances in global positioning systems and computerized Geographic Information Systems (GIS) have benefited landscape architects who work on large-scale projects such as land planning, recreation, campuses, and greenways. Video simulation, a technological tool that helps clients visualize a proposed site plan, is also increasingly used.

The demand for landscape counseling services has a direct correlation to economic conditions relative to private construction rates, building costs, interest rates, growth of business and industry, and government funding of parks and other outdoor facilities. Although only about a quarter of their work is residential, landscape architects have experienced increased opportunities in the residential market due to its robust growth through the 1990s. Prices for private residential commissions have increased from a high of about a quarter of a million dollars to commissions of $500,000 or more. In 1999, a private residential landscape commission in California was reported to cost $17 million. Remodeling is also a strong factor in landscape commissions as more homeowners and businesses are becoming aware that landscaping can provide a 100 to 200 percent return, with property value increases between 14 and 25 percent.

The most significant opportunities for landscape architects during the early 2000s, however, will be in environmental design and public projects. Water quality issues in particular will demand the profession's specialized skills. *Landscape Architect and Specifier News* predicts that landscape architects will become major players across the nation in compliance with waste disposal procedures, water quality protection, and land preservation. In addition, landscape architects will displace engineers as leaders on such projects as planned communities, transportation corridors, and urban planning. Federal initiatives—such as the Environmental Protection Agency's (EPA) Sustainable Development Challenge Grant (SDCG) Program, which provides seed money to encourage local projects that use sustainable development strategies to address serious environmental problems—will also greatly expand opportunities for landscape architects. In addition, passage of TEA-21, which authorizes federal funding for transportation projects, will offer significant possibilities for landscape architects through the early 2000s. Some landscape architects have even started using their skills to improve indoor environments, which further expands the industry's already broad scope.

Industry leaders in this field in 1999 included Environmental Industries, Inc. and its Valley Crest Landscape

Inc. subsidiary, both of which are based in Calabasas, California; SWA Group, headquartered in Sausalito, California; Environmental Earthscapes Inc. of Tucson, Arizona; and Green Thumb Enterprises Inc., based in Chantilly, Virginia. Environmental Industries, Inc., which has designed such major projects as the Las Vegas Strip beautification project and the grounds for the Getty Center in Los Angeles, posted 1998 sales of $350 million, a 2.9 percent increase from the prior year. The company is the nation's largest commercial landscaping business and specializes in landscape construction and maintenance, lawn care, and nursery work in addition to landscape consulting and planning. Environmental Industries' major competitors lagged with sales between $10 and $15 million.

Landscape architects must study engineering and graduate from an accredited program in their field. They must then complete a two-year apprenticeship program and pass a rigorous three-day examination to obtain state licensing. Apprentice landscape architects can earn between $45 and $75 an hour, with licensed principals earning from $90 to $200 per hour and annual salaries of between $50,000 and $150,000. By 1999, earnings for licensed landscape architects surpassed those for building architects. Landscape designers, who do not have to graduate from any program or pass any licensing tests, perform many of the same tasks as landscape architects, such as the design of hardscaping with walls and walkways, but average about $50 per hour. Though the majority of landscape architects remain in private firms, an increasing number are migrating to large-scale design firms that offer landscape planning as one of a range of diversified services.

Further Reading

American Society of Landscape Architects. ''Landscape Architecture: Defining the Profession,'' 1995. Available from http://www.asla.org.

''Architects, Designers, and Contractors.'' *Boston Globe,* 21 October 1999.

Hoover's Company Capsules. ''Environmental Industries, Inc.,'' 1999. Available from http://www.hoovers.com.

''In Olmsted's Footsteps.'' *Boston Globe,* 21 October 1999.

''Landscape Architect's Diverse Lot.'' *Puget Sound Business Journal,* 21 February 1997.

''LASN Predicts. . . .'' *Landscape Architect and Specifier News,* 1999. Available from http://www.landscapeonline.com.

''Local Communities Build Sustainable Future with EPA Awards.'' *Landscape Architecture News Digest,* 7 October 1999.

''Outlook 1999.'' *Landscape Architect and Specifier News,* 1999. Available from http://www.landscapeonline.com.

''The Profession of Landscape Architecture.'' American Society of Landscape Architects, 1998. Available from http://www.asla.org.

SIC 0782

LAWN AND GARDEN SERVICES

The lawn and garden services industry is comprised of establishments primarily engaged in performing a variety of landscape maintenance services. Companies that install artificial turf are included in **SIC 1799: Special Trade Contractors, Not Elsewhere Classified.**

NAICS Code(s)

561730 (Landscaping Services)

The industry encompasses an abundance of firms that provide a wide range of services, including sod laying, lawn mowing, and seeding. Firms can also serve niche markets such as lawn mulching, cemetery maintenance, garden planting, fertilizing, lawn spraying and treating, highway center-strip maintenance, and athletic field and golf course turf installation.

Typically, companies in this industry fertilize four to six times and apply herbicides two or three times a year. Some may offer a soil test or a lawn analysis. One kind of lawn management offered by some companies is called Integrated Pest Management, which operates on the idea that all pests cannot be killed, but need to be reduced to acceptable levels through monitoring and total yard management.

The lawn and landscape industry established itself as an important component of the service sector of the economy in the late 1990s. A 1997 Gallup poll revealed that homeowners spent over $14 billion a year on professional landscape, lawn care, and tree care services, and an estimated $4 billion a year on lawn care products. Between 1994 and 1997, 22 percent of the 100 million households in the United States utilized professional lawn care services. The Professional Lawn Care Association of American projected these numbers to continue increasing.

An identifiable lawn and garden service industry did not emerge until the post-World War II U.S. economic expansion. Housing developments ballooned from just 139,000 in 1944 to 1.9 million per year in 1950, and thousands of tract subdivisions were built on the perimeter of urban America. As an entire suburban culture emerged, replete with private lawns and gardens, the demand for landscape services flourished.

More recently, strong housing starts throughout most of the 1980s, as well as favorable demographic trends, boosted sales in many traditional segments of the landscape services industry. Relatively new services, such as chemical lawn treatments and hydroseeding, also offered growth opportunities. A general trend toward more elaborate landscaping bolstered industry profits as well. Although stalled housing developments and a virtual depression in commercial construction markets soured demand for new landscape installations in the late 1980s and early 1990s, many landscape maintenance firms enjoyed steady growth.

The continued rise in two-income families throughout the 1990s left homeowners with less available time for lawn care. People also became more aware of the positive environmental effects of lawns such as oxygen production, temperature modification, and pollutant absorbent. In 1994, consumers spent $13.4 billion on professional services, an increase of $900 million over 1993. Do-it-yourself lawn and garden activities contributed an additional $25.9 billion. In 1995, more than 20 million households used landscape, lawn care, and tree care professionals, spending an average of $710 per household; homeowners in the South accounted for 39 percent of the total. In 1999, American lawns covered over 25 million acres in the United States.

The lawn and garden services industry is mostly comprised of thousands of small, privately owned firms. An example of a successful local lawn and garden maintenance firm in the mid-1990s was Arrowhead Landscaping of Arizona. Despite the U.S. economic recession, Arrowhead's landscaping business flourished during the early 1990s. Its owners launched the company in 1982, after they shut down their homebuilding business, Arrowhead Construction, when construction markets stalled. By 1993, Arrowhead had grown into one of Phoenix's largest landscape contractors. In the mid-1990s, the company cultivated growth by stressing environmentally friendly, "green" landscape installation and maintenance services.

Like Arrowhead, many other industry participants were hopping on the environmental bandwagon of the mid-1990s. At the annual Turf Foundation Conference in Ohio, for example, the number of exhibitors specializing in natural landscape products for lawn care professionals jumped from 0 in 1987 to 12 in 1993. New high-tech natural products included slow-growing golf course turf and insect resistant grass seed.

Other technological advances that affected the industry included Magic Circle Corporation's new Dixie Chopper, a hydrostatical driven mower. The mower incorporated a turbine-powered military helicopter power unit and boasted a maximum mowing speed of 18 miles-per-hour. Such technological advances and environmental concerns have brought the industry greater expansion and success.

A series of mergers throughout the 1990s resulted in the domination of the industry by one firm. TruGreen merged with ChemLawn in 1992, creating the nation's largest professional lawn care provider, which specialized in chemical landscape treatments. TruGreen ChemLawn generated mid-1990s sales of $350 million with about 8,000 employees. In the mid-1990s the second largest and fastest-growing company was Barefoot, Inc. of Ohio. Following rapid expansion through mergers and acquisitions, Barefoot garnered mid-1990s sales of $95 million and was active in 75 metropolitan markets. But in 1997, TruGreen ChemLawn purchased Barefoot as well as Orkin Lawn Care, and in March 1999 the company further added LandCare USA, Inc., to its list of acquisitions, thereby solidifying its control of the commercial landscaping market.

The Professional Lawn Care Association of America (PLCAA), organized in 1979, promotes education, legislation, and public awareness of the environmental and aesthetic benefits of turf. The PLCAA represents more than 1,200 lawn and landscape companies, industry suppliers, and grounds managers in the United States, Canada, and other countries. They have also established a training program for lawn and garden professionals.

FURTHER READING

Lawn and Lawn Care Services, "Consumer Information Sponsored by Member Businesses." Council of Better Business Bureaus, Inc., 1995. Available from http://www.bosbbb.org/lit/0118.htm.

Professional Lawn Care Association of America. "The Importance of Turf." Available from http://www.plcaa.org/prof.html.

———. "U.S. Households Invest $14.2 Billion in 'Green Home Improvement'." 10 April 1996. Available from http://www.plcaa.org/news.html.

TruGreen-ChemLawn, Available from http://www.trugreen.com.

Ward's Business Directory of U.S. Private and Public Companies, Detroit: Gale Research, 1997.

SIC 0783

ORNAMENTAL SHRUB AND TREE SERVICES

Companies primarily engaged in performing a variety of shrub and tree services make up the ornamental shrub and tree services industry. Activities common to this industry include ornamental bush and tree planting, pruning, bracing, spraying, removal, and surgery. Tree trimming around utility lines also constitutes a significant share of industry revenues. Companies that perform lawn and garden installation and maintenance are described in **SIC 0782: Lawn and Garden Services,** and companies offering shrub and tree services for farm crops are included in **SIC 0721: Crop Planting, Cultivating, and Protecting.**

NAICS Code(s)

561730 (Landscaping Services)

Industry Snapshot

The ornamental shrub and tree industry consists mainly of small, family-owned businesses; most companies offer the service in addition to lawn care and maintenance. Working with shrubs and trees requires more education than merely working on lawns, since there are more plants and pests to know. Nearly a $39-billion industry, ornamental shrub and tree services attracts many firms to the field. The failure rate is high, though, and many companies don't survive the first few years.

Weather plays a big role in the industry, and the drought along the mid-Atlantic caused a dramatic decrease in business for firms in this area. Hurricanes can actually be beneficial for shrub and tree firms, as the destruction opens an opportunity for re-landscaping. Strong housing starts are also advantageous for business.

With the booming U.S. economy of the late 1990s, landscaping services of all kinds have been in high demand. Labor shortages plagued the industry, with a better-educated younger generation looking for white-collar opportunities.

Organization and Structure

The biggest difference between lawn care and maintenance and ornamental shrub and tree services is education of employees. A company adding shrub and tree care to its business must invest at least six months into education. There are hundreds of shrub and tree types, not to mention pests and pest control. The commitment is costly in terms of time, and companies adding shrub and tree specialists need to be assured their investments will be worth the effort.

This extremely fragmented industry is dominated by thousands of small, privately held companies. Of the 70,000 companies responding to a 1999 *Lawn & Landscape Magazine* survey, more than 3700 said they offered ornamental shrub and tree services.

Background and Development

The popularization of the gasoline-powered truck during the early 1900s made it possible for growers to easily transport trees and shrubs, prompting the development of a recognizable industry for ornamental plants. However, it was the rapid proliferation of suburbia during post-World War II economic and population growth that spawned a widespread demand for shrub and tree services. Growth in the number of installation and maintenance contracts for corporate campuses, residences, institutions, and other landscape markets bolstered industry growth throughout the mid-1900s.

Strong housing starts, increased spending on homes by baby boomers, and a general trend toward more elaborate landscapes in both commercial and residential sectors aided many industry participants during the 1980s.When housing developments stalled and commercial construction markets collapsed in the late 1980s and early 1990s, however, many ornamental tree and shrub service companies suffered. Steady utility tree trimming markets and a revival in housing starts in 1992 and 1993 helped to buoy diminished earnings for some competitors. In addition, a string of natural disasters, including Hurricane Andrew in 1992 and the 1993 floods in the Midwest, hiked demand in some regions.

Housing starts were increasing through the mid-1990s, and by March 1997, the rate of starts was approximately 1.4 million. This increase was encouraging news for the industry.

In the mid-1990s, ornamental shrub and tree service companies tried to take advantage of a trend toward naturalized landscapes. Another growing segment of the industry was the relocation of mature trees from development sites to zoos, housing communities, or commercial properties. Companies also strived to invent advanced strains of shrubs and trees that would deliver improved performance and aesthetics. Utility line tree trimming companies grappled with increased community environmental sensitivity, which forced some companies to adopt low-impact trimming techniques. Many power companies simply suggest carefully planning the planting of trees and shrubs to avoid future problems with power lines—large trees should be at least 30 feet away from utility lines.

From 1995 to 1996, landscaping tree shipments increased—an indication that the industry was doing well. In 1995, evergreen trees were most popular with 51.8 million units shipped; this increased to 60.2 million in 1996. Shade trees accounted for 37.5 million units in 1995 and increased to 46.6 million in 1996. Flowering trees accounted for approximately 27 million units in 1995, increasing to about 33 million in 1996. About 11 million fruit/nut trees were shipped in 1995; in 1996 about 13 million units were shipped.

As the industry was evolving, more companies, such as Asplundh, were becoming concerned with regulations in order to comply with safety standards. Work crews and customers were often supplied with information on new regulations—including OSHA changes, ANSI standards, and state wage guidelines.

CURRENT CONDITIONS

With the economy booming in the late 1990s, both corporations and private homeowners were spending more on landscaping. The Christmas holiday was a busy time, with malls and office buildings often erecting large, living, Christmas tree displays. Some of these displays could cost up to $100,000.

In 1998 ornamental shrub and tree services accounted for 5.3 percent of the lawn and landscaping industry's companies. In an annual survey of members by *Lawn & Landscape Magazine,* almost three-quarters said they would have higher sales in 1999 compared to 1998. Tree and ornamental pruning accounted for 10.1 percent of lawn and landscapers sales volume (behind lawn mowing and landscape construction/installation). Profitability was up too, with 83.2 percent of members saying their profits would go up an average of 22.9 percent. The industry as a whole had double digit growth in 1999.

The U.S. Department of Agriculture (USDA) defines environmental horticulture as trees, outdoor plants, bulb, turfgrass, and groundcovers, excluding bedding and garden plants. In 1998 the USDA reported that the environmental horticulture industry took in $7.7 billion—up 33 percent since 1991. At the retail level, which includes delivery and landscaping services, environmental horticulture accounted for $38.8 billion in sales or $120 per person.

INDUSTRY LEADERS

Most of the companies in the ornamental tree and shrub industry are small, privately held firms. One leader is Asplundh Tree Expert Co. The company mainly trims trees for public utilities to clear lines. Asplundh reported 1998 sales of $1 billion and employed 21,000 people in the United States, Canada, New Zealand, and Australia.

Environmental Industries is a landscaping company that provides shrub and tree services; the company projected sales of $425 million in fiscal 1999. The company grows more than 3 million trees and has contracts for more than 6,000 gardens—both indoor and outdoor. The company has 37 locations in seven states and 1,500 nursery acres in California.

WORKFORCE

The labor shortage has been felt across the lawn and landscaping industry. Younger people, who typically fill the labor-intensive positions in the industry, are better educated than ever before and tend to have higher career aspirations. Government restrictions on the hiring of immigrants have hurt the pool of labor also.

RESEARCH AND TECHNOLOGY

The biggest technological advance in the shrub and tree industry is microinjection. Microinjection allows for application of a pesticide in small, concentrated amounts under the bark of a tree. Contractors no longer need to worry about poisoning themselves or other people in the area. The technique saves time because the contractors don't need to notify neighbors, barricade the area, and don special equipment. The only drawback to microinjection is tree wounding, so contractors must take care how they inject the tree.

FURTHER READING

Asplundh Homepage, 1999. Available from http://www.asplundh.com/index.html.

''Asplundh Tree Expert Co.'' *Infotrac,* 17 November 1999.

Clancy, Dave. ''Getting Started in Tree & Shrub Care.'' *Lawn & Landscape Magazine,* October 1999.

''Environmental Industries.'' *Infotrac,* 17 November 1999.

''Floriculture and Environmental Horticulture-Summary.'' *Economic Research Service, U.S. Department of Agriculture,* 1 October 1999. Available from http://www.usda.mannlib.cornell.edu/reports/erssor/specialty/flo-bb/flo-1999.asc.

''Housing Starts Fall in March.'' Washington, D.C.: National Association of Homebuilders, 16 April 1997. Available from http://www.nahb.com/bakbeg2.html.

''The Labor Crisis.'' *Lawn & Landscape Magazine,* 1999. Available from http://www.lawnandlandscape.com/soi/99soi/99soi_labor.htm.

Lincoln Electric System. ''Planting Trees and Shrubs Information,'' June 1996. Available from http://www.les.lincoln.ne.us/cust/plant.htm.

Lubove, Seth. ''Green Begets Green.'' *Forbes,* 14 December 1998.

''Market Overview.'' *Lawn & Landscape Magazine,* 1999. Available from http://www.lawnandlandscape.com/soi/99soi/99soi_market.htm.

West, Bob. ''Money Can Grow on Trees.'' *Lawn & Landscape Magazine,* August 1999.

West, Bob, and Nicole Wisniewski. ''State of the Industry Report.'' *Lawn & Landscape Magazine,* 1999. Available from http://www.lawnandlandscape.com/soi/99soi/99soi_report.htm.

SIC 0811

TIMBER TRACTS

This category includes establishments primarily engaged in the operations of timber tracts or tree farms for the purpose of selling standing timber. Establishments not holding timber tracts as real property (not for sale of timber) are classified in **SIC 6519: Lessors of Real Property, Not Elsewhere Classified** and logging establishments are classified in **SIC 2411: Logging.**

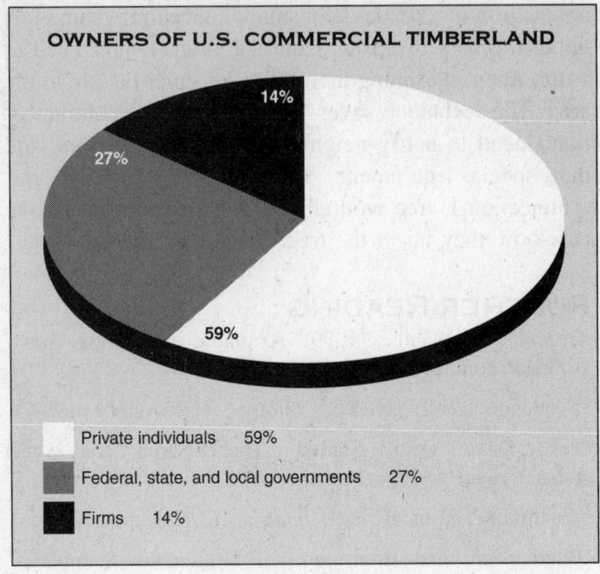

NAICS CODE(S)

111421 (Nursery and Tree Production)
113110 (Timber Tract Operation)

In the United States 737 million acres, or about one-half of the country, is wooded. This amounts to about two-thirds of the nation's presettlement forested land. About 490 million acres of this forested land is classified as timberland, or land capable of growing 20 cubic feet of wood per acre per year. About 131 million acres are owned by the federal government and other state and local governments. The remaining 288 million acres are in relatively small tracts owned by individuals, with 70 million acres being owned by commercial firms. In 1995, 1.6 billion tree seedlings were planted in the United States. Annually about 4 million seedlings are planted every day. Washington, Oregon, and California are the country's largest timber producing states and timber is the South's largest agricultural product.

Live Christmas trees are grown in all 50 states. According to the National Christmas Tree Association, 33 million live Christmas trees were sold in 1997, up from 31 million sold in 1996 but down from the 37.1 million sold in 1995. For every Christmas tree cut and sold, the industry plants 2 to 3 seedlings. The industry employs about 100,000 full and part time workers and there are approximately 5,000 cut-and-choose farms. Depending on the species, it takes between 7 and 15 years for a tree to grow to an average cuttable height of 6 feet. The retail cost per foot for Christmas trees generally ranges from $3.10 to $5.65. The biggest expense for farmers is pruning each tree every year so that they maintain the classic, conical shape demanded by consumers. The leading states for Christmas tree production are Oregon, Michigan, Pennsylvania, California, and North Carolina. The most popular trees are the balsam fir, Douglas fir, Fraser fir, noble fir, Scotch pine, Virginia pine, and white pine. The Scotch pine is usually the largest selling tree, capturing between 30 and 40 percent of the market. According to the U.S. Department of Agriculture, the annual value of the U.S. Christmas tree harvest is around $440 million, with about 17,000 farms working nearly 137,000 acres.

Tree farms cover a wide range of businesses. After they have cut the original stumpage, giant corporations like Weyerhaeuser plant second- and third-growth on vast timber holdings, which they may keep for their own use or sell. Small tree farmers manage woodlands that range from a few acres to several hundred acres. Some may keep the timber for a small sawmill they own, but most sell the stumpage, either for use in mills or as Christmas trees. Several of the giant timber producers run programs that assist small landowners in exchange for first rights on the timber.

The industry continues to face competition from artificial tree makers, who captured half the market in the early 1990s. Most artificial trees are manufactured in Korea, Taiwan, and Hong Kong. These producers promote their trees as fire-resistant and perfectly designed, with no needles to be swept up. In addition, some argue that artificial trees are more ecologically responsible because they can be used more than once. The tree growers, in turn, say that real trees are a renewable, recyclable resource, while artificial trees contain nonbiodegradable plastics and metals.

According to the Western Wood Products Association, demand for lumber in 1998 and 1999 was at an all time high. Demand is expected to slip slightly in 2000 but nonetheless remain high. It is estimated that 53.3 billion board feet of lumber was sold in 1999. This is an increase of 2.2 percent over 1998 and higher than the prediction of 52.3 billion board feet for 2000. In 1999, 17 billion board feet came from the western United States with a regional prediction of 16.6 billion board feet for 2000. The U.S. Department of Commerce estimates that 81 percent of softwood lumber and 65 percent of structural wood panels are used for residential and light commercial construction. The 1999 value of shipments for sawmills and planning mills also was estimated to be worth nearly $28.3 billion. Steve Lawser of the Wood Component Manufacturers Association told *Wood & Wood Products* that lumber and materials account for 53 percent of the total cost of producing wood components. This figure is up from 43 percent in 1985.

It is estimated that the United States imported 18.96 billion board feet of lumber in 1999, mostly from Canadian lumbering operations. Exports were an estimated 1.35 billion board feet in 1999. In 1998, exports were down due to the Asian financial crisis. Exports are expected to climb 4.3 percent in 2000. The pulp and paper industry, a major consumer of forest products, is cautiously optimistic about market demand in 2000 and hopes that 2001 could be a strong year. *Pulp & Paper* forecasts industry operating rates to rise from 91 percent in 1999, to 91.9 percent in 2000, and 93 percent in 2001.

Industry leaders and their total 1997 sales are: International Paper ($20 billion); Weyerhauser ($11.2 billion); Champion International ($5.7 billion); Boise-Cascade ($5.5 billion); and Georgia-Pacific's Timber Co. ($551 million), Kimberly-Clark ($12.5 billion) is a major manufacturer of personal paper products, but in 1999 it began divesting itself of its timberland operations. In June of that year, for instance, the company sold 460,000 acres of timberland in Alabama, Mississippi, and Tennessee to Joshua Management LLC for approximately $400 million. Also in 1999, the Timber Co. sold 194,000 acres of California timberland to the Hawthorne Timber Co. for $397 million. The Timber Co. manages about 5 million acres of timberland across the country.

FURTHER READING

Darnay, Arsen J., Ed. *Agriculture, Mining, and Construction USA.* Detroit: Gale, 1998.

Hoover's Masterlist of Major U.S. Companies 1998-1999. Austin, Texas: Hoover's Business Press, 1998.

Iwanski, John. "Where Will The Wood Industry Be In 2005?" *Wood & Wood Products.* December 1999, 174-181.

"Kimberly-Clark Is Selling 460,000 Acres of Timberland." *New York Times.* 11 June 1999, C4.

National Christmas Tree Association. *National Christmas Tree Association.* St. Louis: National Christmas Tree Association, 1999. Available from http://www.christree.org.

Routson, Joyce. "North American Industry Outlook Bright Over Next Two Years." *Pulp & Paper.* January 2000, 36-48.

Standard & Poor's Corp. *Industry Surveys: Paper & Forest Products.* New York: Industry Surveys, 1999.

Starkman, Dean. "Most U.S. Paper, Forest-Products Firms Are Expected to Post Strong Results." *Wall Street Journal.* 6 July 1999, 22A.

Tardiff, Joseph C., Ed.*U.S. Industry Profiles: The Leading 100.* 2nd Edition Detroit: Gale, 1998.

"Timber Company To Sell California Woodlands." *New York Times.* 2 November 1999, C4.

U.S. Dept. of Agriculture. National Agricultural Statistical Service. *1999 Census of Agriculture.* Washington D.C.: GPO, 1999. Available from http://www.nass.usda.gov/census.

U.S. Industry & Trade Outlook '99. New York: DRI/McGraw-Hill: Standard & Poor's; Washington D.C.: U.S. Dept. of Commerce/International Trade Association.

Western Wood Products Association. *WWP: Western Wood Products Association.* Portland, Oregon: Western Wood Products Association, 1999. Available from http://www/wpa.org.

SIC 0831

FOREST NURSERIES AND GATHERING OF FOREST PRODUCTS

This category covers establishments primarily engaged in growing trees for purposes of reforestation or in gathering forest products. The concentration or distillation of these products, when carried on in the forest, is included in this industry. Forest products typically gathered are: balsam needles, ginseng, huckleberry greens, maple sap, moss (including Spanish and sphagnum varieties), teaberries, and tree gums and barks. The industry also includes forest nurseries; rubber plantations; gathering, extracting, and selling of tree seeds; lac production; and distillation of gums, turpentine and rosin, if carried on at the gum farm.

NAICS CODE(S)

111998 (All Other Miscellaneous Crop Farming)

113210 (Forest Nurseries and Gathering of Forest Products)

The term "forest products industry" (FPI) is used to describe all industries dependent upon forest products including the lumber, wood pulp, and paper industries and those activities covered by SIC 0831. However, those activities covered by SIC 0831 are a relatively small part of total FPI activities.

Since the mid-1950s, the forest products industry shifted from a proliferation of companies operating in specialized areas toward a consolidation of operations within large, diversified conglomerates with national and international interests. Reflecting these patterns, most forest nurseries and operations involved in the gathering of forest products became affiliated with larger operations in the parent industries of **SIC: 6519 Timber Tract Real Estate** or **SIC 2411: Logging.** Furthermore, in 1986 the standard industrial classification (SIC) system itself was altered to reflect industry trends toward less specific groups. That year, **SIC 0831: Forest Nurseries and Gathering of Forest Products** was created by merging three formerly independent forestry-industry categories: **SIC 0821: Forest Nurseries and Seed Gathering, SIC 0842: Extraction of Pine Gum,** and **SIC 0849: Gathering of Forest Products, Not Elsewhere Classified.**

The American FPI produces about $230 billion worth of goods annually according to the American Wood Preservers Institute. The industry employs approximately 1.6 million in the planting, growing, managing, and harvesting of trees and in the production of wood and paper products. The FPI ranks among the top 10 manufacturing employers in 46 of the 50 states, with an annual payroll of around $46 billion. Washington, Oregon, and California are the largest timber producing states. Timber is the South's largest agricultural product, employing one of every nine southern manufacturing workers.

About one-half of the United States (737 million acres) is covered with trees. This represents about two-thirds of the presettlement forested land in the country. Two-thirds of America's forest land, or about 490 million acres, is classified as timberland, or forest capable of growing 20 cubic feet of wood per acre per year. Of this, 131 million acres (27 percent) are owned by the federal government and by state and local governments, 288 million acres (59 percent) are in relatively small tracts owned by individuals, and 70 million acres (14 percent) are owned by the FPI. About 4 million tree seedlings are planted in the United States daily. In 1995, 1.6 billion such seedlings were planted.

In the United States, the largest timber holding companies also are the largest forest nursery and forest product gatherers. In 1997, some of the largest forest product companies were International Paper, Georgia-Pacific, Kimberly-Clark, Weyerhaeuser, Boise-Cascade and Champion International. Despite the preeminence of these giant companies, many of which are major paper manufacturers, the FPI also is populated with small nurseries, maple syrup producers, owners of small timbered tracts who have them logged for personal income, and even individual ginseng gatherers. Other small companies focus on unique products, such as, sphagnum peat moss, bark nuggets, and mulches. Because of the diverse nature of SIC 0831 classification and the fact that much of the economic activity represented by it comes from individuals and small cottage industries, comprehensive economic statistics are difficult to come by.

It is estimated that in 1998 the FPI as a whole was made up of 2,713 establishments that employed 20.4, million people and had a total payroll of approximately $488 million. The average payroll per employee was $21,409. In 1995, Oregon had the largest number of establishments with 344. Other important states were Washington (218), California (183), Alabama (152), Georgia (150), and Florida (108).

One niche of the FPI that does get reported is maple syrup production. In 1998, U.S. forests produced 1.6 million gallons of maple syrup worth $31.5 million. New England states produced nearly $18.4 million worth of maple syrup, with Vermont leading with 360,000 gallons. In 1998, production was down 11 percent from 1997 and down 26 percent from 1996. This drop in production is blamed on warm weather and ice storms. In 1997, there were 4,850 farms producing maple syrup on 120,863 acres. Sap was gathered from 6.7 million taps.

Ginseng is a medicinal root that traditionally has been gathered in the wild and exported to China and other Asian countries. Most gathering is done by individuals under permits issued by states. Although wild ginseng commands the highest prices, the herb also is cultivated on farms. In 1992, 824 farms produced 1.7 million pounds of ginseng on 1,505 acres. Wisconsin led the United States in cultivated ginseng with 785 farms responsible for 97 percent of U.S. production and 95 percent of cultivated acreage. In 1992, 1.9 million pounds of ginseng worth $104.5 million were exported, 1.7 million of which were cultivated.

The overall paper and forest products industry was on the upswing between spring 1997 and fall 1998. However, this recovery over previous years was set back by the Asian economic crisis. The driving force behind this improvement was largely due to increased activity in paper and packaging. But as this economic sector retreated markedly in late 1998, the wood products sector, which had been slow earlier, began picking up. This revival continued especially through the second quarter of 1999. ''Wood, wood, wood is good,'' according to industry analyst Mark Wilde in a *Wall Street Journal* interview. ''Anything related to building products, it's going to be a blow out.'' Standard & Poor's, however, was less optimistic for the year 2000 and expected the wood products sector to show a decent performance but one that would not match the boom seen in the second quarter of 1999. A solid domestic demand for wood products is expected to be matched by high supplies.

Exports have played an increasingly important role in the FPI. In fact, according to Standard & Poor's, 65 percent of the industry's shipment growth between 1988 and 1998 came from export sales. In 1998, exports by U.S. paper manufacturers totaled $13.7 billion. Although this was down 5.5 percent from 1997, that year tallied the second highest total on record. These exports represented 8 percent of the industry's 1998 shipments. Total industry exports of paper, pulp, and various forest products totaled 12 million tons in 1998, down from 13 million tons in 1997.

In 1995, approximately five new trees were planted for every American. Approximately 43 percent of these 1.6 billion seedlings were planted by the FPI. Naturally regenerated trees totaled in the millions. In the 1980s and early 1990s, forest nurseries were affected by increased efforts at global reforestation. Fighting on behalf of cleaner air, endangered species such as the northern spotted owl, and the ecological preservation of old-growth and tropical forests, environmental groups gained tremendous clout. Regarding the spotted owl, only 200 pairs were known in the 1970s, but by early 1992, approximately 3,510 owl pairs were known. In 1995, estimates in California alone were as high as 8,000 pairs. In addition, numerous studies tied the effects of deforestation to depletion of the earth's protective ozone layer and the subsequent warming of atmospheric temperatures. Tree nurseries kept up with increased reforestation efforts. During fiscal 1990, public and private forest owners in the United States regenerated 2.86 million acres by tree planting and artificial seeding. Most forest products companies developed third-generation seedlings to genetically maximize growth, height, shape, and resistance to drought and disease on their tree farms. Such seedlings often yielded increases of 50 to 60 percent per acre of timber. From 1985 to 1995, forest product companies spent more than $100 million on wildlife and environmental research, employing more than 90 wildlife biologists. During this time, approximately $400 million of land (about 1 million acres) were donated by the FPI for conservation, recreation, and social causes. In 1994, the industry aligned itself with the U.S. Department of Energy to create Agenda 2020, which is an effort to address environmental and productivity improvements during the next century.

Many of these efforts were aimed at reversing a decline in U.S. forest acreage that began in the early 1970s and continued well into the 1980s. It is estimated that the United States lost nearly 1.5 million acres of forest land each year during this period. However, reforestation efforts began to take hold in the 1990s and U.S. forest depletion dropped to about 500,000 acres annually. Despite these efforts government sources still predict a 4 percent decline in U.S. forest land by 2040. Also continuing into the twenty-first century is the ongoing conflict between those forces that want to use public and private forest land for environmentally conscious purposes and those forces that are market driven. Activists are also beginning to rally against genetically modified trees, fearing that wind-borne pollen, which can travel up to 600 kilometers, will trigger unanticipated hazards.

Forest products are both biodegradable and recyclable. Trees also are a renewable resource, and approximately 95 percent of the bark and wood residues from producing lumber and plywood are used for energy and other products. It is estimated that more than 90 million short tons of paper and paperboard are used every year in the United States. Americans now recover about 45 percent of all paper used in the United States, and the paper industry had set a goal to recover more than half of all paper in use by the year 2000. By 1999 Americans were using, on a per capita basis, 749 pounds of paper annually, or the equivalent of a tree 100 feet high and 16 inches in diameter.

It is estimated that in 1998 the FPI employed about 20.4 million workers. Many of these workers classify as forest products technicians and forestry technicians. The former perform supervisory and technical jobs, mostly for private companies that operate lumber mills or manufacture wood products. Salaries for this classification range from $18,000 to a little more than $21,000, and employment outlook is fair. Forestry technicians aid professional foresters in the management of forest resources and work for government agencies as well as private companies. The pay scale for this job classification varies greatly, from $12,500 to $28,000 a year, depending on education and experience. Employment outlook is poor.

Another job classification in the FPI is that of Forester. Foresters work for private industry and government agencies and perform a wide variety of tasks. Foresters must have a bachelors degree and many have masters and doctorate degrees. The average starting salary for foresters ranges from $19,500 to nearly $43,000 depending on education. In 1997, the average salary for federal foresters, including those in supervisory positions, was $47,600. Employment growth is expected to be as fast as the average.

Like many other sectors of the U.S. economy the FPI has been going through an ongoing process of acquisitions and mergers. Major transactions in the last few years include a $6.5 billion merger between Jefferson Smurfit and Stone Container in 1998. The resultant Smurfit-Stone Container Corp. is the world's leading paper based packaging company. In 1999, International Paper Co. acquired Union Camp in a stock deal valued at $7.9 billion, and Weyerhauser reached an agreement to purchase Canada's MacMillan Bloedel for $2.45 billion. According to economist Richard Diamond these industry mergers and acquisitions are driven by a number of motives including economic efficiency, diversification, self-defense, and market power.

Prior to the 1998 merger, the Stone Container Corp. had 1997 sales of $4.85 billion and 24,600 employees, while Jefferson Smurfit had sales of $3.23 billion and 15,800 employees. By late 1998 Smurfit-Stone began exiting the market pulp business by closing two mills that had been part of Stone Container's operations. The mills were closed for market reasons.

Other industry leaders include: the International Paper Co. ($20 billion, 82,000); Georgia-Pacific ($13 billion, 46,500); Champion International ($5.7 billion, 24,000); Boise Cascade ($5.5 billion, 22,514); and Georgia-Pacific's Timber Co. ($551 million, 500).

FURTHER READING

American Forest & Paper Association. *American Forest & Paper Association: Improving Tomorrow's Environment Today.* Washington D.C.: American Forest & Paper Association, 1999. Available from http://www.afandpa.org.

American Wood Preservers Institute. *American Wood Preservers Institute.* Fairfax, Virginia: American Wood Preservers Institute, 1999. Available from http://www.awpi.org/forestry.html.

Career Information Center. 7th Edition. New York: Macmillan Reference USA, 1999.

Darnay, Arsen J. ed. *Agriculture, Mining, and Construction USA.* Detroit: Gale, 1998.

Diamond, Joseph, Daniel Chappelle, and Jon Edwards. ''Mergers and Acquisitions in the Forest Products Industry.'' *Forest Products Journal.* April 1999, 24-35.

Hoover's Masterlist of Major U.S. Companies. Austin, Texas: Hoover's Business Press, 1998.

''No GM Tree Hugging.'' *Chemical Week.* 24 November 1999, 52.

''Outlook 2000 Looks Promising.'' *Pulp & Paper.* January 2000, 39-59.

Routson, Joyce K. ''More Forest Industry Mergers . . .'' *Pulp & Paper.* March 1999, 79.

''Smurfit-Stone Closing Two Pulp Mills.'' *Pulp & Paper.* February 1999, 19-20.

Society of American Foresters. *Society of American Foresters.* Bethesda, Maryland: Society of American Foresters, 1999. Available from http://www.safnet.org.

Standard & Poor's Corp. *Industry Surveys: Paper & Forest Products.* New York: Industry Surveys, 1999.

Starkman, Dean. ''Most U.S. Paper, Forest-Product Firms Are Expected to Post Strong Results.'' *Wall Street Journal.* 6 July 1999, 22A.

Tardiff, Joseph C. *U.S. Industry Profiles: The Leading 100.* 2nd. Ed. Detroit: Gale, 1998.

''U.S. Capacity Growth Lowest in 40 Years.'' *Pulp & Paper.* February 1999, 17-19.

U.S. Dept. of Agriculture. *1999 Census of Agriculture.* Washington, D.C.: GPO, 1999. Available from http://www.nass.usda .gov/census.

U.S. Dept. of Agriculture. *New England Agricultural Statistics Service: Maple Syrup.* Concord, NH: New England Agricultural Statistics Service, 1999. Available from http://www.nass.usda .gov/nh/maple.htm.

U.S. Department of Labor. *Occupational Outlook Handbook, 1998-99 Edition.* Washington: GPO, 1999.

SIC 0851

FORESTRY SERVICES

This industry classification includes establishments primarily engaged in performing, on a contract or fee basis, services related to timber production, wood technology, forestry economics and marketing, and other forestry services, not elsewhere classified, such as cruising timber, fire fighting, and reforestation.

NAICS CODE(S)

115310 (Support Activities for Forestry)

INDUSTRY SNAPSHOT

One-third of the United States is forest land. The challenge for federal government, activists groups, and private companies is how best to put the resources to work, yet preserve old growth trees and animal habitats. Forestry products account for $230 billion in sales and the industry employs 1.5 million people. Products manufactured by the industry include paper and lumber.

Federal regulations regarding the industry are numerous. They encompass everything from road construction to reforestation mandates. Many in the industry see these regulations as excessively burdensome and a barrier to trade. However, for many years private companies harvested trees on public lands, paying nothing to the public coffers and having little regard to the impact of wholesale tree clearing. The U.S. Forest Service stepped in, and with the help of public pressure due to awareness to the need for the forests, set up regulations.

Foreign countries continue to place high barriers to trade for the forestry industry. The United States had a 1998 deficit of more than $9 billion in this sector, and while the industry continues to grow around the world, the U.S. forestry industry saw a drop in production—about 2 percent in lumber and 6 percent in paper products.

ORGANIZATION AND STRUCTURE

During the start of the twentieth century, the economic future of the United States was heavily dependent on the ''perpetual supply of timber,'' as noted in a 1923 editorial in *The Timberman,* a leading forest products journal. The forestry services industry took hold from a philosophy that the nation's forest land was a resource that had to be serviced, protected, and renewed, rather than just harvested and diminished. Protection from wildfires and pest infestation of the nation's forests were essential for survival.

As the timber industry grew and became more competitive, so did related services: timber cruisers hiked though forests to assess logging conditions and estimate the volume of marketable timber; and estimators, log graders, and scalers inspected logs for defects, measured them to determine volume, and estimated marketable content or value for pulpwood and other uses. Timber and related industries grew at a fast pace along with the demand for skilled loggers.

Vast Forest Resources. As the growth of forest land that required servicing increased, so did the growth for the demand of the forestry services industry. In 1996, over 737 million acres—or approximately one-third of the total U.S. land area—was forested. In Oregon, Washington, and California, more than 10 million acres of old-growth forest can be found. Nonfederal public agencies, the forest industry, farmers and ranchers, and other private individuals owned the majority of this forest land.

Fire fighting and prevention, pest control, and forest management plans took hold in the 1980s and 1990s due to the new philosophy of managing the U.S. forests as complex ecosystems containing interdependent communities of plants, animals, and microbes. This new way of looking at forests was greatly influenced by the declining number of U.S. forest lands during the early 1970s. Reforestation and new forestry management efforts started, in part to prevent the decline of 1.5 million acres each year between 1970 and 1987. The efforts paid off, for by the early 1990s, the rate of U.S. forest depletion had decreased to approximately half a million acres per year. However, government sources still project a decline of 4 percent of forest land to about 703 million acres by the year 2040.

International Forest Servicing. The issues of deforestation, acid deposition, climate change, and endangered species were problems that crossed national boundaries. During the 1980s and 1990s, natural resource issues helped create an international forestry emphasis. Many U.S. companies and organizations specializing in forestry services increasingly contributed to reforestation efforts in forests from the Amazon to Malaysia. The authorization of the 1990 Farm Bill communicated to the world that the U.S. Forest Service supported forestry services work on an international basis. It coordinated efforts with the U.S. Department of State and other organizations. The Foreign Operations Appropriations Act of 1990 authorized increased funds for international forestry services performed by various agencies including the U.S. Agency for International Development (AID). By 1991 international operations had gained such clout that the Forest Service elevated the International Forestry Staff to division status. In addition to internationalization on the federal level, private industry leaders were performing forestry services around the world.

Public vs. Private Services. Historically, the forestry services industry has been divided between federal and private control, with the two sectors often overlapping in cooperative efforts as well as disputes. With the rise of industrial forestry in the late 1900s, budding forestry products companies developed individual management plans, fire and pest control systems, and business priorities. As early as 1904, the Weyerhaeuser Company reforested 1.3 million acres of timberland in Washington state, and following the 1903 and 1908 fires in the Northeast and the 1902 and 1910 fires in Idaho and the Northwest, private companies drafted the first fire protection organizations.

The scene changed dramatically, however, with the 1905 establishment of the U.S. Forest Service. After the 1920s, the Forest Service began a campaign advocating the federal regulation of private timber harvesting. Even though federal forests accounted for less than one-fifth of total U.S. forest land, government regulations influenced private industry in such areas as logging, road construction, reforestation mandates, taxation of private forests, and use of herbicides and pesticides. Entering the 1990s, private forest land owners and forest industry leaders took issue with many federal regulations, arguing that forest management plans for public forest lands were incompatible with market-driven interests of private foresters.

BACKGROUND AND DEVELOPMENT

Since its creation, the U.S. Forest Service, the largest bureau in the U.S. Department of Agriculture, served as an innovator and driving force in forestry services. The Forest Service managed the National Forest System (made up of 191 million acres) and worked with state land management organizations to help private landowners apply sound natural resource management practices on their lands. The service's research division strived to develop the means and understanding to enhance and protect productivity of forest lands, with special emphasis on natural resource issues of national and international scope. Finally, the international forestry arm of the U.S. Forest Service facilitated the exchange of technical expertise and managerial skills with other nations.

At the turn of the twentieth century, public forests had become an immense timber commons with no established property rights and no incentives for responsible harvesting or reforestation. By the 1860s and 1870s, exploitation of vast timber tracts began to stir national attention. A new awareness emerged; in his famous study, ''Man and Nature'', George Marsh described the central role of forests in overall environmental health, from erosion control to water flow. In addition, the Timber Culture Act of 1873 granted settlers 160-acre tracts provided they planted and sustained trees on a quarter of the land, and in 1875 the American Forestry Association was founded.

Over the next two decades, a series of measures were taken to control the occupancy and use of forest lands. After legislation to set aside national forest reserves was introduced in 1876, 15 years elapsed until the Reform Act of 1891 finally provided for the creation of forest reserves. By 1892, U.S. President Benjamin Harrison had contained 13 million acres in forest reserves, and by 1893 President Grover Cleveland oversaw an addition of 4.5 million acres.

When the National Academy of Sciences appointed a study commission to consider the future of the forest reserves in 1896, Gifford Pinchot, the future head of the U.S. Forest Service, rose to prominence. His advocacy of forest management aimed at productive use emphasizing timber harvesting spurred the 1897 passage of the Forest Reserve Act, which established regulations for the use of forest reserves. Prompted by Pinchot, President Theodore Roosevelt provided the final impetus for the Transfer Act of 1905, whereby forestry management was consolidated in the Bureau of Forestry within the U.S. Department of Agriculture. The Forest Service had been created.

A drive for public regulation of private timber harvest gained considerable impetus with the 1919 meeting of the Society of American Foresters, chaired by Pinchot. The committee forecast that the nation would face a veritable "timber famine" within 50 years if forestry management were not reformed. Under the guidance of Pinchot, the U.S. Forest Service embraced ideals of scientific forestry management, with many critics claiming that it proceeded to employ the gusto of scientific methodology without any of the benefits of scientific problem solving.

With the passage of time came the implementation of numerous programs granting the U.S. Forest Service greater importance and scope in the forestry services industry. The Clarke-McNary Act of 1924 facilitated the transfer of federal funds and programs to state and local programs. With the New Deal came the 1933 National Plan for American Forestry (also called the Copeland Report), calling for greater federal forest lands and national forest management.

Starting in the late 1950s, the Forest Service forged a general plan of national forestry management that continued to carry substantial influence well into the 1990s. The Multiple-Use Sustained-Yield Act of 1960 mandated that production of timber supplies in national forests be continuous and that a variety of goods and services—including timber, hunting, fishing, and recreation—be produced. The 1974 Forest and Rangeland Renewable Resources Planning Act (RPA) concluded that major shortages of timber were likely to develop and encouraged long-range planning processes. The National Forest Management Act of 1976 provided additional guidance on planning and management of the National Forest System. These acts served as the building blocks for the Forest Service's application of multiple-use forestry management into the 1990s.

American Tree Farm System. In order to foster the sound management of privately owned woodlands, the forest products industry organized the American Tree Farm System, a nationwide conservation program dating back to the 1920s. The program demonstrated that privately owned forest lands could be managed in the public interest without the supervision of the Forest Service.

The Tree Farm program began in 1941, when Weyerhaeuser Timber Co. called on the public and local foresters to help protect one of its major tracts in western Washington. The resulting Clemons Tree Farm, named after the pioneer logger Charles H. Clemons, set the precedent for a wide line of similar organizations. Later that year, the West Coast Lumberman's Association and the Pacific Northwest Loggers Association (later the Industrial Forestry Association) established the West Coast Tree Farm Program for the Douglas fir region of western Oregon and Washington. Other tree farms opened throughout the United States, including the Western Pine Association, with a 450,000-acre tract in eastern Oregon and the Arkansas Forestry Commission. Before long, the program went national.

In November of 1941, the American Forest Products Industries (AFPI), then a subsidiary of the National Lumber Manufacturers Association (NLMA), assumed major sponsorship and national promotional role. The organization's dictates were systematically set forth in the *Principles of the American Tree Farm System* of 1954. The AFPI assumed administrative control on a national level, but also divvied out responsibilities to key local forest industry committees around the country. When the AFPI was reorganized as the American Forest Institute (AFI) in the mid-1960s, the tree farm program lost central support and cohesiveness until the mid-1970s. By 1980, however, the American Tree Farm System registered 38,926 certified tree farms occupying 79.6 million acres of industry-owned and nonindustrial forest land. A green and white diamond-shaped tree farm sign became the symbol for sound private forest management.

Fire Control. The rise of industrial forestry called for new perspective on fire management. Private timber owners were instrumental in forming the first fire protection agencies. In the early 1900s, fire protection associations emerged in California, the Lake States, Georgia, Kentucky, West Virginia, Pennsylvania, and New Hampshire. One of the most renowned and longest lasting organizations was the Western Forestry and Conservation Association (WFCA), founded in 1909 and boasting members in 11 states and Canada by the early 1980s.

After the General Land Office (GLO) transferred management and fire control of the national forest reserves to the U.S. Forest Service in 1905, the federal role in fire control moved to the foreground. The Forest Service controlled the national forest system, promoted cooperative fire control programs with states and private industry, and led research and planning initiatives toward development of modern forest fire control.

In early 1993, the focus of aerial fire fighting focused on improvements in safety and efficiency for this type of forestry service. NASA-Ames, the Bureau of Land Management, and the USDA-Forest Service signed an agreement to look at air traffic control issues around a fire area to improve communication and safety, work on a standard phraseology for working to extinguish the fire area, and introduce advanced navigation systems with electronic chart displays that reduce disorientation and improve safety and efficiency.

Affiliated government agencies worked separately, but in harmony with the Forest Service. The Forest Service made ties with the National Weather Service in forecasting and monitoring fires. It also chaired the Forest Protection Board from 1927 to 1933, serving as a central hub for cooperative action. Around 1934, the technique known as smoke jumping was introduced, incorporating military paratrooper training strategies to combat fires. During the New Deal, federal involvement assumed the cloak of the Civilian Conservation Corps (CCC). When the Grazing Service and General Land Office reorganized as the Bureau of Land Management (BLM) in 1946, it became the largest federal fire service beside the Forest Service.

Following World War II, CCC ranks had been gravely depleted. Sparked in part by fears of ''mass fires'' used as offensive weapons by wartime enemies, the Forest Service carried fire-control efforts into the general public. The Cooperative Forest Fire Prevention Campaign featured Smokey the Bear, a character who spread fire safety messages to a broader audience. By the mid-1950s, the Forest Service assumed responsibility for coordinating wildland and rural fire protection the entire United States, providing material support and planning assistance to state and rural fire agencies. In the 1960s, the Forest Service increased its emphasis on the control of wilderness fires. Over the next decades, fire protection services continued to grow and evolve along with changing technology and new forest conditions.

Social Changes. What started in the early 1990s as a small voice of reform in the U.S. Forest Service has turned out to exemplify the debate over the role of the forest industry and the move to protect forests. The Association of Forest Service Employees for Environmental Ethics (AFSEEE) was created for government employees who feared their livelihoods in the U.S. Forest Service could be in jeopardy when environmental assessments might harm the prospects for timber sales. A U.S. Forest Service biologist, Marynell Oechsner, was asked to study how a proposed timber sale would affect wildlife in the Kootenai National Forest in northwestern Montana. She stated it would endanger a species of bear in the forest. The forest was also home to a large number of employed timber workers. She claimed during a Congressional hearing that her U.S. Forest Service supervisor pressured her into deleting the report's findings, which unfavorably affected the bear's habitat, because it would adversely impact the timber companies in the area. Jeff Debonis, a former Forest Service employee who founded AFSEEE, stated, ''There's a civil war going on in the Forest Service.'' Career foresters who believe the agency balances environmental and logging policies are pitted against younger employees who worry that the agency is too beholden to the logging industry. In the mid-1990s, AFSEEE had 8,000 members, 2,000 of whom were U.S. Forest Service employees. Its purpose is to fight for Forest Service employees' rights to express professional opinions without the threat of job termination.

The forest industry, as well as its professionals, has been forced to change due to social, economic, and political pressures in the last decade that have reduced the number of acres that can be harvested for timber. Many in the industry looked first to public agencies and forest product corporations for employment, but even at the largest single employer, the Forest Service in the U.S. Department of Agriculture, the word ''downsizing'' is frequently spoken. However, many owners of small forest tracts are hiring forestry consultants to help manage land. The reductions in timber cutting on national forests have caused lumber and timber prices to rise. As profits from timber growing increase, forest product companies, especially the ones with large land holdings, are using more of the services that this industry sector can offer.

Deforestaion. Starting in the mid-1980s, world attention veered toward the interrelated problems of global deforestation—especially in tropical forests—and its possible contributions to such environmental problems as global warming. At the 1990 Economic Summit in Houston, Texas, President Bush proposed a global forest convention to address problems of deforestation, biodiversity, and forest management. At the 1991 Economic Summit in London, these concerns were reiterated in anticipation of the Earth Summit meeting scheduled for June of 1992 in Brazil. Capitalizing on many of the issues raised in these conferences, U.S. President Bill Clinton and his running mate, Al Gore, attracted considerable support of environmentalist groups in the 1993 presidential elections.

By 1993 more than 100 acres of rain forest were being destroyed every hour. The worst victims were the particularly fragile and ecologically rich rain forests in Brazil, Indonesia, and other locations. In the 1990s, attention was also focused on the former Soviet Union, where huge tracts of untapped timber were in danger of uncontrolled exploitation. International pressure to curb deforestation in such areas assumed many forms: diplomacy and negotiations around committee tables; export bans and taxes on tropical wood products in Indonesia, Malaysia, and the Philippines; and such creative alternatives as debt-for-nature swaps. Illustrating this last strategy, in 1987 Conservation International acquired $650,000 of Bolivia's debt in exchange for that government's establishment of a 1.5-million hectares forest reserve to be managed for sustainable development. These and other measures required substantial funding: the World Resources Institute (WRI) estimated a cost of approximately $8 billion to tackle deforestation between 1985 and 1990 alone.

Public vs. Private. Another condition affecting the forestry services industry was the ongoing battle between the use of public and private forest land for market-driven purposes or for more environmentally conscious purposes, whether or not they made money. At the center of this contentious issue stood the fate of old-growth forests in the Pacific Northwest. Actions to protect diverse ecosystems of the ancient forests raised concern over the impact on small, timber-dependent communities. The northern spotted owl, a regional inhabitant protected under the Endangered Species Act of 1990, became a focal point for the spotty differences between environment and industry, and between public and private forest lands. Many critics of the established system proposed complete privatization of timberlands, arguing that the federally managed system of multiple use and sustained yield also lost tremendous amounts of public money. Additionally, a new challenge to the spotted-owl logging protection arose in March 1997 when a federal appeals court allowed for new timber industry challenges to Northwest logging reductions that were ordered by President Clinton in 1993. Clinton's Northwest Forest Plan dropped logging levels on national forests in Oregon, Washington, and Northern California to approximately one-fourth the annual averages of the 1980s. The plan intended to protect the old growth forests that were inhabited by the owl, which was declared an endangered species in 1990. The logging industry alleged the administration violated many procedural requirements that prevented government officials who drafted the plan from obtaining critical information that formulated the logging strategy. The Northwest Forestry Association believed if the information from the industry was permitted, much more logging would have been made available to timber harvests.

New Forestry Initiatives. Moving into the 1990s, the forestry services industry saw the enactment of numerous forest-related initiatives. 1991 marked the first year of the America the Beautiful program by which the Forest Service worked with state foresters to plant a goal of 970 million trees in rural areas and 30 million trees in urban areas. In March of 1991, the National Tree Trust, a private nonprofit group designed to raise funds for tree planting, opened offices in Washington, D.C. In October of 1993, President Clinton announced the recognition of National Forest Products Week, a period during which Americans were invited to participate in ceremonies and activities calling attention to the need for healthy and productive forests. And following a program calling for ''New Perspectives,'' or ''New Forestry,'' from the 1990s on, the Forest Service tried new ways of incorporating the concept of biodiversity into national forestry management. The course of the forestry services industry was bound for change into the twenty-first century.

In 1995, a new study was underway using a $1-million 260-foot construction crane to study the Columbia Gorge forests. Cranes have been in use since 1990 to study the rain forest canopies of Venezuela and Panama, but this is the first time the higher canopies of the temperate forest was studied. The product is a joint effort of the U.S. Forest Service and the University of Washington. Temperate woodlands are estimated to be 40 percent of the world's forests, containing tree species that are the most commercially viable. The study seeks to understand the workings of mature forests, so that new ways of harvesting the timber can be found while also preserving its ability to regrow logged sections.

Current Conditions

Realizing that the Forestry Service needs to work with local citizens and companies, the Camino Real Ranger District of New Mexico's Carson National Forest developed the Northern New Mexico Collaborative Stewardship (NNMCS). The fighting between all groups around the forest had reach a bitter pitch—companies and workers wanted fewer restrictions on using wood and environmentalists wanted more. The Forestry Service was in the middle and came up with an innovative way to manage all concerns. They literally went door-to-door surveying the surrounding community about concerns for management of the forest.

The NNMCS brings together people, organizations, and/or companies with conflicts and works with them for solutions. The Forest Service feels they are not just responding to one crisis after another, but preventing problems from getting out of control. In one case, the problem of Camino Real's overgrowth was explored, as the practice of control fires has been eliminated. To thin tree by hand was expensive, but the solution brought forth was to raise money to train Native Americans how to thin the forest. Local Hispanic communities used the wood for cooking and building.

Camino Real won an Innovations in Government Award in 1998, along with $100,000. Recipients of the award have to use 80 percent of the money to set up the prize-winning program in other areas. The toughest challenge is not only convincing local communities to work with the Forest Service, but also convincing government employees to work with the communities.

Industry Leaders

Looming over even the biggest private wood products companies, the U.S. Forest Service remained the largest player in the forestry services industry. In the 1990s, the organization reported $3.42 billion in expenditures.

Still, the combined ownership of the forest industry, farmers, and other private concerns accounted for roughly 70 percent of timberland in the United States by the mid-1990s. Much of that land depended on forestry services provided by private companies. After the 1950s, however, the forest products industry saw a consolidation of specialized companies into large and diversified organizations. Forestry services were increasingly performed by subsidiaries or divisions of larger forestry products and related companies. Therefore, the industry leaders in forestry services tended to overlap with leaders in the forest products industry.

International Paper (IP) was the leader in forest products in 1999. The company has $24.0 billion in annual sales and operates around the world. IP reported $6.3 billion in sales for the third quarter of 1999, a gain of 5 percent from the previous year. Other leaders include Georgia-Pacific, with reported sales of $5.5 billion in the third quarter of 1999, up from $3.4 billion in 1998; and Boise Cascade, with reported 1999 third quarter sales of $1.8 billion.

WORKFORCE

The industry of forestry products employs 1.5 million people in the United States. The U.S. Forestry Service has 29,500 permanent employees and anywhere from 3,000 to 15,000 contract, summer, and seasonal workers.

In the U.S. Forestry Service the top positions are chief, deputy chiefs, regional foresters, and stations directors. The positions command a salary of $90,000 to $120,000 per year. Many other positions are paid according to market conditions.

There are 17,150 logging tractor operators with a mean annual wage of $23,810. Log-handling equipment operators make a mean yearly wage of $24,430 and there are 18,120 employed. There are 11,480 fallers and buckers and they make a mean yearly wage of $27,200. Choke setters receive $27,040 annually and comprise 2,960 workers. There are 20,330 forest and conservation workers receiving a mean yearly wage of $24,670. Log graders and scalers make up 3,790 of the industry's employees and have a mean annual wage of $23,250.

Due to high trade barriers in other countries, the United States imports more forestry products than it exports. As a result, the number of jobs in this industry declined by 2.6 percent in 1998—a total of 17,800 jobs.

AMERICA AND THE WORLD

By the 1990s, the forestry services industry had become international in scope, with most important issues and projects crossing national borders. One example of such internationalism was the decision of the U.S company Applied Energy Services (AES) to reforest 52 million trees in Guatemala in order to offset carbon dioxide emissions from its coal-fired power plant in Connecticut. AES's planting project began in June of 1989, with a projected time frame of 10 years and a cost of $15.7 million.

The Forest Service also stressed international operations. Among them, it worked with over 100 organizations and numerous countries on its Tropical Forestry Program. Latin America, the Caribbean, and South Pacific gained the most attention in that area. The Forest Service also cooperated with foreign countries—including Spain, Israel, and Brazil—in managing fires and forest insect and disease problems. In the early 1990s, the home front, too, was in the process of change. Congressional debates on the North American Free Trade Agreement (NAFTA) bore strongly on the dynamics of the North American wood products industry and, by extension, on the role of forestry services in Mexico, the United States, and Canada.

International concern about deforestation stemmed from links between rates of forest destruction and global warming. Increased carbon dioxide in the earth's atmosphere was shown to trap the sun's heat. Since trees replace the carbon dioxide with oxygen, researchers maintained that fewer trees contributed to more carbon dioxide and faster global warming, with potentially devastating consequences to world ecosystems. In 1991 the Global Change Research Program was initiated by the Forest Service to increase understanding of climate changes.

A project that was born out of the concern for the growing buildup of atmospheric carbon dioxide and the increased threat of global warming uses aircraft for reforestation. A former aeronautical engineer and Israeli immigrant, Moshe Alamaro, was working on a project to drop tree seedlings in open-topped cones from aircraft in order to reach previously inaccessible areas. These ''aerial bombs'' as they are referred to, bear one-year old tree seedlings. Areas that are being sought to plant this way are war-torn battlefields, empty deserts, and steep slopes. This wasn't the first time aerial seeding has been tried however. Shortly after WWII, the mountain states in the United States were the site of similar efforts, but rodent predation often got to the edible seeds before they had a chance to grow. Today's technology incorporates the use of rodenticides to increase the tree seed's chances of survival. Honolulu was also a site back in 1925 for aerial seeding after a fire ravaged several acres of forest land.

The forestry industry continued to fight high trade barriers in other countries in the late 1990s. In contrast, other countries face little regulation when exporting forestry products to the United States. During the Uruguay Round of world trade talks, Japan declined to open its wood market to foreign competition and the European Community decided not to phase out tariffs on paper products for 10 years. As a result, by 1998 the United States had a deficient in this industry of $9.4 billion, up from $3.0 billion in 1994.

Research and Technology

In the early 1990s, the advent of the technology called global positioning systems (GPS) revolutionized the way foresters work. It is comprised of high tech software, computers, and satellites that can locate a point anywhere in the world. Hand-held GPS receiver systems are now available at affordable prices that give an instantaneous readout of the receiver's longitude, latitude, and elevation. Forestry applications are: improved mapping of roads and walking trails; exact acreages for harvesting, planting, or burn sites; better night walking; increased accuracy finding archaeological sites or specific wildlife habitats; and exceptional tracking of every vehicle in a forest fleet.

Further Reading

Baker, Beth. ''U.S. Forest Service Program Builds Bridges Between Government and Public.'' *BioScience,* January 1999.

Boise Cascade & American Forest and Paper Association. ''Quick Facts About Our Industry.'' April 1997. Available from http://www.bc.com/indust.html.

''Financial Highlights.'' *Boise Cascade,* 24 November 1999. Available at http://www.bc.com/boise99_3qtr/1fin_high.htm.

''Georgia-Pacific Group Reports Strong Third Quarter Earnings.'' *Georgia-Pacific,* 21 October 1999. Available at http://www.gp.com/center/gpnews/c-1555.html.

''International paper Reports Strong Improvement in Operating Earnings for Third Quarter.'' *International Paper,* 12 October 1999. Available at http://www.internationalpaper.com/ca/page/pr101299.html.

''John Dillion Testifies Before Congress to Urge Global Free Trade in the Forest Products Sector.'' *International Paper,* 5 August 1999. Available at http://www.internaitonalpaper.com/ca/page/pr0805099.html.

''1997 National Ocupational Employment and Wage Estimates.'' *Occupational Employment Statisitics,* 24 November 1999. Available at http://www.stats.bls.gov/oes_stru.htm#70000.

Raloff, Janet. ''Bombs Away! Reforesting Inaccessible Regions from on High.'' *Science News,* January 1997.

SIC 0912

FINFISH

This industry classification includes establishments primarily engaged in the commercial catching or taking of finfish, including cod, menhaden, pollack, salmon, and tuna.

Industry Snapshot

The United States has three major shorelines, situated along the Atlantic Ocean, the Gulf of Mexico, and the Pacific Ocean. Together these shores, including those of Alaska and Hawaii, span more than 12,000 miles. As do many other nations, the United States holds economic jurisdiction over waters out to a distance of 200 nautical miles. This area is called the nation's exclusive economic zone (EEZ). The U.S. EEZ contains more than 2.2 million square miles. These waters are estimated to contain about 20 percent of the harvestable seafood in the world.

In 1998 the U.S. commercial fishing industry landed 7.8 billion pounds of finfish, down from 8.3 billion pounds in 1997. The finfish landed in 1998 comprised 85 percent of all edible and industrial fish products landed. Finfish made up 82 percent (5.9 billion pounds) of all edible fishery products landed and 96 percent (1.9 billion pounds) of all industrial fishery products landed.

Annual per capita consumption of fishery products rose from 12.7 pounds in 1981 to a high of 16.2 pounds in 1987. From 1987 to the mid-1990s, consumption fell and stabilized at approximately 15.0 pounds per person per year. Although the National Fisheries Institute set a goal of increasing annual per capita consumption to 20.0 pounds by the year 2000, it was more likely that growth in the industry would come from increases in exports and from the expansion of nonedible markets, such as the production of livestock feed. In 1998 per capita consumption of fish and seafood stood at 14.9 pounds. Finfish, fresh and frozen, made up 5.8 of the 14.9 total pounds, with tuna leading the pack at 3.4 pounds per capita consumption.

Organization and Structure

Historically, independent fishermen caught fish and sold them to local packers or processors who resold them to retail markets. Although the U.S. fishing fleet still contains independent fishermen, large corporations are becoming increasingly involved in all aspects of seafood distribution.

The U.S. fisheries industry is managed by the National Marine Fisheries Service (NMFS). The NMFS is responsible for regulating commercial fishing, finding ways to control overfishing of exploited species, collecting data, and publishing reports about commercial landings. The fishing industry, however, remains a lightly regulated one. Critics of the NMFS have at times accused the agency of concentrating efforts on helping fishermen maximize profits at the expense of protecting fish populations.

The NMFS, however, has instituted a number of measures designed with the fish population in mind. One way in which the NMFS has regulated fishing is through the use of limited seasons for selected species. Because of intense pressure on selected populations, some seasons are short. Pacific halibut, for example, was once fished during a six-month season. By 1991 the season was limited to two 24-hour periods. In September 1991 approximately 6,000 boats landed 23.7 million pounds of halibut in one day.

The NMFS has also tested the use of quotas and limited entry into established fisheries as a means of regulating stressed fish populations. Such programs have included a moratorium on new entrants into the fishery, quotas based on catch histories of the vessel or fisherman, quotas based on a percentage of the total allowable catch, quotas on specific poundage, quotas based on vessel size or gear, and quotas that can be purchased or traded.

BACKGROUND AND DEVELOPMENT

Commercial fishing is one of America's oldest industries. The bountiful waters off the continent's East Coast attracted fishermen from Scandinavian countries possibly as early as 1,000 years ago. The ocean also provided employment for many European settlers during the seventeenth and eighteenth centuries. Technological innovations and the institution of regulatory agencies during the 1800s prepared the industry for the modern era.

The techniques of netting, harpooning, and pole-and-line fishing used by early fishermen were eventually replaced by more efficient methods of catching fish. Trawling—pulling a funnel-shaped bag to scoop fish from the ocean floor—was introduced in the middle of the nineteenth century. Purse seines, nets that trap fish by closing in a manner similar to a drawstring purse, were introduced early in the twentieth century. Together, purse seines and trawlers catch more fish worldwide than all other types of fishing gear.

Legislation. In addition to technological innovations, the middle of the nineteenth century also saw some fishery resources dwindle. To protect the resources, the government assumed responsibility for fisheries management. In 1871 Congress created the U.S. Commission on Fish and Fisheries. The commission was charged with the responsibility of investigating food-fish populations and making recommendations. In 1956 Congress passed the Fish and Wildlife Act, which established the Bureau of Commercial Fisheries under the auspices of the Fish and Wildlife Service. The National Environmental Policy Act of 1969 included the requirement that an environmental impact statement be prepared for fishery regulations. Both the Endangered Species Act of 1969 and the Marine Mammal Protection Act of 1972 placed restrictions on allowable catches of threatened species and species that interact with threatened species.

One of the most significant pieces of legislation to affect U.S. commercial fishing was the Magnuson Fishery Conservation and Management Act of 1976 (Magnuson Act). The Magnuson Act extended the U.S. coastal jurisdiction from 12 miles to 200 miles from shore and gave the federal government exclusive authority over domestic and foreign fishing operations within the exclusive economic zone.

Depletion of Fish Populations. The U.S. commercial fisheries industry entered the 1990s with promise and problems. Consumer demand was expected to remain stable, total catches were on an upward trend, and increases in sales were expected to be limited only by the availability of preferred species. The problems centered on charges that fish populations were being seriously depleted because of the combined impacts of overharvesting and environmental degradation. Amos Eno, spokesman for the non-profit National Fish and Wildlife Foundation, told *U.S. News & World Report,* ''Marine fisheries are the nation's single most threatened resource.''

At the beginning of the 1990s catches of many important species were significantly down across the lower 48 states from their level in the 1980s. In addition to habitat impairment, conservationists and environmentalists blamed the drops on overfishing. Critics of the fishing industry claimed that nearly half of the U.S. coastal finfish populations were being depleted because the size of harvests outweighed the ability of the populations to reproduce themselves. Some scientists estimated that as many as 14 species faced commercial extinction, a state wherein too few fish of that species would remain to harvest them economically. The New England, Middle Atlantic, South Atlantic, and Gulf regions all saw total catches drop below their 1980 levels, although rising prices helped stabilize the value of the harvest.

One important species of fish cited as an example was menhaden, an oily, bony fish that is related to herring and harvested in the Atlantic and Gulf of Mexico. Large-scale harvesting of menhaden began in the nineteenth century following the discovery that its oil could be used as a substitute for whale oil. Twentieth century uses for menhaden included the production of fish oil, the production of fish meal, and as a bait fish.

Although the Gulf population remained stable, the Atlantic menhaden population saw wide fluctuations. The largest Atlantic landings took place in the mid-1950s.

During the middle of the following decade, the larger, older fish disappeared and landings tumbled. During the 1970s the population appeared to make a tentative comeback, but in 1982 the Atlantic States Marine Fisheries Commission found it necessary to recommend protective regulations. In 1985 U.S. fishermen landed 2.7 billion pounds of menhaden, but Atlantic takings declined steadily. As a result, the last meal plant in Maine was shut down in September 1988. By 1995 total landings of menhaden had fallen to 2.0 billion pounds. In 1998 menhaden landings stood at 1.7 billion pounds, down from 2.0 billion in 1997. Atlantic takings stood at 608 million pounds.

Bycatch. ''Bycatch'' was another problem plaguing the fishing industry during the early 1990s. Bycatch refers to unintentionally caught fish, birds, marine mammals, and turtles that are seriously injured or killed. In 1990 Alaskan trawlers fishing primarily for pollack reported throwing away 550 million pounds of other edible groundfish such as cod and halibut. In the late 1990s, 3.5 million fishing boats around the world were catching about 84 million metric tons of fish, plus 27 million tons of bycatch that was discarded. The practice was condemned by critics as wasteful, and fishermen realized that public concern over real or even perceived threats to nontarget species could have negative consequences. Indeed, concern about the number of dolphins killed as a result of bycatching prompted several well-publicized boycotts of leading tuna producers in the 1980s.

In an effort to avoid further legislative involvement, fishermen organized the National Industry Bycatch Coalition in 1992 to discuss possible solutions. The coalition's goals included the development of new technologies for cleaner fishing, promotion of education in how to use bycatch-reduction gear; support of management style changes to reduce throw-away rates; reduction of bycatch of threatened, endangered, and overfished species to the absolute minimum; reduction of the rate of bycatch mortality; and the development of valuable uses for dead bycatch. The coalition also expressed a determination to work with conservation groups rather than adopt an adversarial stance.

Current Conditions

In 1996 Congress passed a bill aimed at fish conservation that required the NMFS, along with eight regional fishing councils from across the nation, to formulate plans to eradicate overfishing, minimize bycatch, and reduce the loss of marine habitats—especially on the sea bottom, which is damaged by trawling. But as the 1990s came to an end, many were questioning the outcome of the law and if steps being taken were enough. Fisheries biologist Joshua Sladek-Nowlis of the Center for Marine Conservation told *Business Week* the reductions were ''too little too late.'' Fishermen called the tougher regulations on fishing overkill.

Fishermen are often in agreement with conservationists and environmentalists in discussing ominous environmental trends in the areas of breeding-ground pollution, shoreline development, and loss of wetlands. Approximately 75 percent of U.S.-produced seafood need bays and estuaries for breeding grounds; both types of marine environments have suffered from pollution. Several states have been particularly hard-hit in this regard. The state of Louisiana loses about 50 square miles of breeding ground every year. California has lost more than 90 percent of its original coastal wetlands.

According to a 1998 report by the National Academy of Sciences, overexploitation was responsible for a 30 percent decline of fish stocks worldwide. Also, 44 percent were nearing exploitation, the report said. It was also noted that in U.S. waters, 80 percent of commercial fish stocks were disappearing.

In 1997 Alaska led the nation with the most fishing vessels and boats, with 16,442. Louisiana was second with 13,637, and Florida a distant third with 9,085.

Industry Leaders

In the late 1990s, leading companies in the industry included Zapata Corporation, Omega Protein (a 60 percent-owned public subsidiary of Zapata), and Talmadge Brothers Inc. Zapata, of Houston, Texas, had 1998 sales of $133.6 million, an increase of 13.6 percent from 1997, and employed 1,322. The company operated a fleet of more than 65 fishing vessels and about 35 spotter aircraft for use in fishing operations.

America and the World

Prior to World War II, Japan, which has a long history of relying on sea resources, had the largest fishing operations in the world. By the 1930s the Japanese fleet fished many areas of the Pacific, including Bristol Bay, Alaska. World War II interrupted commercial fishing, but the following years saw an explosion of fishing fleets. In 1948 Japan maintained its position as the world's leading fishing nation in terms of number of pounds caught. The U.S. fishing fleet landed the second-largest catch, followed by Norway, the Soviet Union, the United Kingdom, and Canada. Competition increased during the late 1950s and early 1960s as Soviet factory vessels began operating off the eastern coast of the United States and in Alaskan waters. During 1966 the combined Soviet and Japanese fleets took approximately 3 billion pounds of fish from the Bering Sea and the Gulf of Alaska. U.S. harvests, however, entered a state of decline and by the mid-1960s the United States ranked only sixth in the world. Japan had fallen to second, and Peru, with massive catches of Peruvian anchovies, had assumed the top position.

In 1974 a new international law of the sea was agreed upon, although it was not officially ratified until 1982. Under its terms, many countries declared exclusive economic zones (EEZs) that extended 200 miles from their shores. In a similar move, the United States adopted the Magnuson Act in 1976, legislation that created a 200-mile U.S. EEZ. Under the Magnuson Act the only foreign fishing allowable within the EEZ was that portion of the allowable catch not taken by U.S. vessels. The Magnuson Act, however, did permit joint ventures in which foreign vessels were permitted to receive fish from U.S. vessels. The fish were considered part of the U.S. harvest in such instances.

Overfishing remains a severe problem internationally, with stocks of food fish dropping severely in Southeastern Asian waters, the North Sea, and the Mediterranean Sea. The reduced fish stocks threaten not only American and European industries, but also the economies of some developing countries. Part of the problem lies in the fact that western-style management techniques out-compete traditional Third World country industries. Between 1989 and the mid-1990s, fishing catches worldwide increased from approximately 100-million metric tons to 109-million metric tons. According to a report in *International Agricultural Development,* 7.5 million people in India relied directly on commercial or personal fishing for their livelihoods, while in the Philippines 38,000 fishermen were put out of work because of overfishing and competition each year. Exports of fish made up a significant proportion of the gross national product of Thailand. Western countries have taken some steps to address these concerns. The European Union, for example, adopted a strategy that called for a 20 percent cut in its fishing fleet between 1993 and 1996, but most fisheries management experts believed that this might not be enough.

The quality of fish taken by both western and other fleets also declined precipitously in the late twentieth century. Takes of many of the most profitable species—sea shrimp, Atlantic Ocean cod, herring and mackerel, Pacific Ocean perch, tuna, and halibut—were cut in half in the 20 years between 1970 and 1989. Most of the increase since 1989, according to *International Agricultural Development,* was in less lucrative species, especially Alaskan pollack, jack mackerel from Chile, Japanese and South American pilchards, anchoveta, and shark. These species were also considered less nutritious than the more profitable kinds.

Overall, the United States was successful in the finfish industry during the 1990s. In 1998 U.S. imports totaled 5.6 billion pounds, while exports totaled 4.5 billion pounds. Imports in 1997 stood at 5.4 billion pounds, while exports stood at 5.0 billion pounds.

RESEARCH AND TECHNOLOGY

The two essential ingredients in the fishing industry are detecting fish (hunting) and catching fish (gathering). Until the modern era, fish detection was done primarily by the eye. The twentieth century introduced new methods of looking for fish. Aircraft scouting, satellite data, echo sounders, and other electronic equipment enabled fishermen to search more efficiently. Innovations were also made in catching fish. Nets made of new materials were rot resistant, less susceptible to abrasion, and more elastic. Larger purse seines became possible when better methods of hauling them were developed. Trawling became more efficient and diverse when faster and lighter trawls were made.

The Redmond, Washington, Marine Conservation Biology Institute estimated that in 1998, there were 89,000 trawling vessels in operation across the globe and they fished an area larger than the lower 48 states. Many equate trawling with clearcutting forests. But the fishing industry declared that the analogy was nothing more than a public relations spiel and said that they were striving to make changes to minimize impact on fish habitats in order to protect the resources that provided their livelihood.

Research continued during the 1990s on ways to improve on the various aspects of finfish harvesting. Areas under exploration included the introduction of electrical devices to herd fish into nets, the use of acoustical devices to hear noises characteristic of particular species, the development of more sophisticated methods of determining detailed water conditions, and determination of the applicability of luring fish with light, sound, chemicals, and electricity.

In addition to the technical aspects of finding and catching fish, researchers continued looking into ways to ameliorate the social, political, and economic problems of the industry. Promoters researched fish species not previously used commercially and worked on finding processing methods to make underexploited stocks more acceptable to American consumers. New versions of bycatch-reduction gear were being developed and tested. Scientists continued in their endeavors to understand interspecies relationships in an effort to make fisheries management more successful.

Also, the advent of global positioning systems and depth sounders made it easier for fishermen to find stocks. Likewise, the development of ''rockhoppers,'' which rolled along the bottom, allowed sea bottoms, including coral reefs, to be fished. At one time this was impossible to do.

Despite modern innovations, commercial fishing at the dawn of the twenty-first century was still basically a hunting and gathering operation. As research efforts continued, modern technological advances aimed at improving the livelihood of fishermen often seemed to run at cross purposes with regulatory efforts to preserve fish stocks.

FURTHER READING

"Fisheries: Overfishing Nets Disaster." *International Agricultural Development,* May/June 1995.

"Hook, Line, and Extinction." *Business Week,* 14 December 1998, 166.

Knickerbocker, Brad. "Trawling Blamed for Loss of Marine Habitat." *Christian Science Monitor,* 17 December 1998.

National Marine Fisheries Service. *Fishery Market News.* Available from http://remora.ssp.nmfs.gov.

———. "U.S. Commercial Landings" and "Per Capita U.S. Consumption." Available from http://www.nmfs.gov/trade/default.html.

U.S. Bureau of Labor Statistics and U.S. Bureau of the Census. *Trade & Employment.* Washington, DC: GPO, 1996.

U.S. Bureau of the Census. *Statistical Abstract of the United States, 1996.* 116th ed. Washington, DC: GPO, 1996.

SIC 0913

SHELLFISH

This industry classification includes establishments primarily engaged in the commercial taking of shellfish. The shellfish designation includes mollusks (such as clams, mussels, oysters, and squid) and crustaceans (such as crabs, crayfish, lobsters, and shrimp). Establishments primarily engaged in shellfish farming are classified in **SIC 0273: Animal Aquaculture.**

NAICS CODE(S)

114112 (Shellfish Fishing)

In the mid-1990s the U.S. commercial fishing industry landed 1.26 billion pounds of shellfish. The National Marine Fisheries Service (NMFS) 1998 annual report on fisheries in the United States indicates declines in 1998 and 1997. The NMFS reports 1.24 billion pounds U.S. domestic landings of shellfish in 1997, worth $1.68 billion. Preliminary results for 1998 indicate further declines—1.22 billion pounds of shellfish were landed for a value of $1.65 billion. In 1998, shellfish landings accounted for approximately 13 percent of all U.S. domestic commercial fish landings.

The market for seafood was growing slowly in the late 1990s, and shellfish imports decreased throughout the decade, especially for shrimp, which decreased to 299 million pounds in 1999, a two percent drop from the previous year. In addition, prices dropped to a value of $1.2 billion. Crawfish imports and exports had dropped even more severely in 1999. Imports of clams, mussels, and oysters rose, while exports for clams and oysters fell slightly over previous numbers. Mussels were the fastest growing mollusk import, with 1999 totals estimated at 19.1 million pounds.

In 1999 the United States imported more than 53,750 metric tons of shellfish, down from $3.73 billion in 1994. U.S. exports followed a similar trend. The 1999 value of exported shellfish was 18,321 metric tons. More competition was expected to come from other meat producers, but higher imports were expected from Asian countries, notably Japan, into 2000.

The largest potential for growth in consumer shellfish demand in 2000 and beyond was expected to be shrimp. Industry analysts, however, question whether fishermen can harvest increased amounts of shrimp without damaging the ability of populations to sustain themselves.

The shellfish industry entered the 1990s with a myriad of regulatory and management challenges. Many East Coast shellfisheries were recovering from sharp declines during the middle years of the 1980s when algae blooms ravaged fertile scallop grounds and decimated clam populations. Oyster stocks from Long Island to the Chesapeake Bay were threatened by viral oyster diseases. Catches of Alaskan crab, which had dropped from 347 million pounds in 1980 to 129 million pounds in 1985, totaled 281 million pounds in 1990.

As past methods of managing shellfish populations through the use of quotas and limited seasons have not proven entirely successful, government agencies are analyzing new approaches. For example, in 1990 an innovative management plan for surf clams replaced a policy under which vessels could work a total of only 144 hours annually. The new system, designed to be more flexible, permitted the sale and transfer of allocations.

Regulators are also looking for ways to control bycatch problems. "Bycatch" refers to unintentionally caught fish, birds, marine mammals, and turtles that are killed in the harvesting process. Because shrimp are traditionally caught in trawls (net devices pulled behind the boat) they catch significant quantities of other marine animals. Shrimp bycatch was blamed for reductions in red snapper populations and for thousands of turtle deaths. Some reports estimated that as many as 50 to 75 percent of juvenile red snapper were being caught and discarded annually by shrimpers. In addition, a study done by the National Academy of Sciences estimated that trawls killed up to 50,000 turtles per year.

One apparatus under consideration to reduce trawl bycatch is called a Turtle Excluder Device (TED). TEDs operate by holding the net open so turtles can escape rather than asphyxiate. Florida began requiring shrimpers within state waters to use TEDs during the middle of

1990. Shrimpers expected TED regulations to become more widely enforced and anticipated Finfish Excluder regulations as well.

One major threat endangering shellfishing today is the algal blooms known popularly as "red tides." Shellfish, which are mostly filter feeders, siphon the algae out of the water and feed on it, retaining any toxins in their own bodies. These toxins can then be transferred to people who eat the shellfish, resulting in a syndrome known as paralytic shellfish poison (PSP). Since 1972, "red tides" have increased in frequency worldwide and resulted in the closing of many clamming beds. George's Bank off Cape Cod, Massachusetts, for instance, was closed in 1989 after an algal bloom close by. Many of its shellfish species remain unsafe for consumption today. In the United States, however, PSP poses a very small threat to human life, thanks to efficient monitoring of algal events. The year 1999 saw major institutes conducting research into water contaminations.

Leaders in the industry as of 1999 included Salt Creek Inc. and Shafmaster Fishing Company.

FURTHER READING

National Marine Fisheries Service. *Fisheries of the United States, 1998.* Silver Spring, MD: NMFS Fisheries Statistics and Economics Division, 1999. Available from http://www.st.nmfs.gov/st1/fus/fus98/index.html.

National Marine Fisheries Service. *Imports and Exports of Fishery Products Annual Summary, 1998.* Silver Spring, MD: NMFS Fisheries Statistics and Economics Division, 1999. Available from http://www.st.nmfs.gov/trade/index.html.

Parker, Henry S. and Robert J. Wright. "Agriculture and Marine Environments." *Agricultural Research,* January 1999. Available from http://www.ars.usda.gov.

U.S. Bureau of Labor Statistics and U.S. Census Bureau. *Trade & Employment.* Washington, DC: GPO, 1996.

U.S. Census Bureau. *Statistical Abstract of the United States: 1996.* 116th ed. Washington, DC: GPO, 1996.

U.S. Department of Agriculture, Economic Research Service. "Aquaculture Outlook." Washington, D.C.: U.S. Department of Agriculture, 4 October 1999. Available from http://usda.mannlib.cornell.edu.

Ward's Business Directory of U.S. Private and Public Companies. Farmington Hills, MI: Gale Group, 1999.

SIC 0919

MISCELLANEOUS MARINE PRODUCTS

This industry classification covers establishments primarily engaged in miscellaneous fishing activities, such as catching or taking of miscellaneous marine plants and animals. Plants and animals covered under this code include seaweed, sponges, sea urchins, terrapins, turtles, and frogs. Cultured pearl production also falls under this classification.

NAICS CODE(S)

114119 (Other Marine Fishing)
111998 (All Other Miscellaneous Crop Farming)

The primary marine animal featured under this heading is the turtle. Turtles became popular for meat and soup shortly after Columbus discovered the New World. By 1878 an estimated 15,000 green turtles were shipped annually from the Caribbean to European markets. The market for the turtle remained undiminished in the 1990s.

The turtle's popularity as a meal item has created a serious threat to its ability to sustain its population. In addition to risks associated with over-harvesting and habitat loss, thousands of turtles have been injured or drowned as a result of commercial fishing operations.

Many species of sea turtles, such as the hawksbill turtle, Olive ridley, Kemp's ridley, and the green turtle, have been listed as endangered or threatened. In 1973 the Convention on International Trade in Endangered Species of Wild Fauna and Flora drafted a resolution to prohibit the trade of endangered or threatened species including the imperiled sea turtles. The agreement was signed by 95 nations.

The diamondback terrapin population has also dwindled, a victim of over-harvesting and diminished habitat. The diamondback terrapin, which lives in estuaries and salt marshes along the eastern seaboard and through the Gulf of Mexico region, is regarded by many culinary experts as the best tasting species of turtle.

In 1920 the population of diamondback terrapins plummeted, spurring the institution of regulatory measures designed to protect it. Governmental agencies undertook breeding efforts to reestablish it in some areas. During the 1960s the diamondback population started to show signs of recovery; however, market demand also increased. In 1989 New York established more stringent regulations defining the size and season for taking turtles. Some environmentalists charge that the rules are inadequate, and they predict another population crash.

Another well-known miscellaneous marine product is seaweed. The two centers of seaweed production in the United States are located in New England and California. Although seaweed is used as a food in Asia, its primary uses in the United States are industrial. Seaweed is used to make agar, which is a jelly-like substance used in laboratories as a culture media and also used as a thickener in food processing; alginates, which are thickeners and stabilizers used in food processing; and algin, a substance used in food processing, pharmaceuticals, the rubber industry, the dairy industry, and the textile industry. A process developed in Scotland in 1950 to make liquid fertilizer from seaweed has also increased its popularity over the years.

Another, lesser-known, commercially taken marine product is the sea urchin. In December 1991 urchins from Maine were bringing fishermen about 40 cents per pound. Urchins are typically caught by divers and exported for uses like urchin roe—a traditional food in Japan. Urchins' popularity as an export item, however, has caused concern about the possibility of over-fishing domestic stocks. Because of falling California landings in 1990, regulators have re-issued seasonal, geographic, and size requirements on red sea urchin catches.

However, with the recovery of the economy in 1993, the miscellaneous marine products industry had started recovering as well. In 1995, the total value of imports in this industry was placed at $118.9 million. The value of imports the previous year was only $90.1 million, representing a 32 percent increase.

Imports of sea urchins were valued at over $8 million in 1998, for a total of 3,130 metric tons. Exports that same year were valued at over $9 million, for a total of 1,856 metric tons. For frog legs and meat, the totals were $10 million imports and $3 million exports, for 1,706 and 662 metric tons, respectively.

Seaweeds and algae imports were valued at $77 million in 1998, and exports were valued at $58 million. Sponges were valued at $1 million for imports and $8 million for exports.

Imports of cultured pearls was valued at over $280 million in 1998, and exports were valued at over $9 million. Of the top five importers of cultured pearls—Mikimoto USA, Frank Masteloni & Sons, Imperial Pearl Syndicate, Honora Ltd, and Assael International—only one was not U.S. owned.

Further Reading

National Marine Fisheries Service. *Imports and Exports of Fishery Products.* 2000. Available from http://www.nmfs.gov.

U.S. Department of Labor. Bureau of Labor Statistics. *Trade & Employment: Absolute Change and Percent Change, 1995 and 1994.* Washington, DC: GPO, 1996.

SIC 0921

FISH HATCHERIES AND PRESERVES

This category covers establishments primarily engaged in operating fish hatcheries or preserves. Establishments primarily engaged in raising and harvesting aquatic animals are classified in **SIC 0273: Animal Aquaculture.**

NAICS Code(s)

112511 (Finfish Farming and Fish Hatcheries)
112512 (Shellfish Farming)

Fish hatcheries were developed during the latter part of the nineteenth century in an effort to supplement dwindling fish stocks. In nature, fish lay thousands of eggs, but most juveniles die in massive numbers because of insufficient food, predators, and diseases. In hatcheries, eggs hatch under controlled conditions and juveniles are able to grow in a protected environment. These conditions result in diminished losses and young fish can be returned to their natural environment in sufficient quantities to replenish populations.

In 1871, The National Fish Hatchery System (NFHS) was established by Congress through the creation of a U.S. Commissioner of Fish and Fisheries. In 1885, the first hatchery programs were undertaken by the NFHS in an effort to replenish shad and lobster populations. By 1916 the federal government operated more than 100 hatcheries, and many states also had opened their own hatcheries. Fish populations being augmented with hatchery stock included cod, pollack, haddock, flounder, salmon, and lobster.

Hatcheries were also involved in the intentional transplanting of species. Although most programs failed and new stocks did not take hold, there were notable successes. Shad and striped bass (rockfish), two of Atlantic species, were introduced to Pacific waters. Both flourished and briefly sustained commercial fishing. Overfishing, however, led to government action to protect remaining stocks. Although commercial harvesting was prohibited, striped bass and shad continued to be abundant, popular game fish.

Hatchery development began to slow during the 1930s because programs were unable to demonstrate increases in commercial harvests. Hatchery-raised fish were often less able to survive in a natural environment because they were conditioned to being fed, fell prey more readily than wild stock, and were susceptible to stunting, diseases, and parasites as a result of overcrowded conditions in hatchery ponds. Additionally, although millions of fish were released, they represented only a tiny fraction of the ocean's natural population and, as a result, did not make a significant difference.

Because of these problems, fish hatcheries began evolving in different ways. Private, commercial hatcheries redirected themselves toward raising harvestable crops of fish under controlled conditions (see **SIC 0273: Animal Aquaculture**). One remaining type of private, commercial hatchery was the fish preserve. Fish preserves provided a controlled environment for people—usually from urban areas—to visit and experience the thrill of catching a fish. Public hatcheries backed away from commercial species, instead focusing their efforts on replenishing game stock. Even the NFHS shifted its focus and diversified many of its programs to ensure a future for the aquatic ecosystems of the United States. In the late 1990s, U.S. Fish & Wildlife Service hatcheries delivered fish to area bodies of water, while fishermen followed or waited.

As the fish hatchery industry entered the 1990s, most were publicly owned. In 1990 Alaska's fishery enhancement division transferred the last of its commercially oriented hatcheries to private aquaculture associations. Remaining government-owned hatcheries refocused their efforts toward producing fish for sportsmen and enhancing fish populations in rural areas in which they are depended on for subsistence. But the late 1990s saw increased hatchery activity and success. The NFHS integrated the work of fish hatcheries and fisheries management to procure more efficient national restoration programs such as those for Great Lakes lake trout, Atlantic Coast striped bass, Atlantic salmon, and Pacific salmon. In 1997, the NFHS included 72 fish hatcheries, 5 fish technology centers, and 9 fish health centers. The NFHS focused their resources on restoring, maintaining, and recovering native and endangered fish populations, maintaining the National Broodstock Program, (which ensures the availability of disease-free eggs and larvae for various programs), evaluation of hatchery stocking programs and recreational fisheries, and developing and encouraging partnerships between governments and the private sector to provide greater opportunities for conserving and enhancing aquatic ecosystems. In addition, new vaccines were being developed to help fight fish diseases.

According to a Washington Office Fish Hatchery Species report, more than 168 million fish were distributed from hatcheries in the United States and more than 137 million eggs produced. Most of the fish distributed, or 60.4 percent, were cold-water species with Fall Chinook Salmon accounting for nearly half of the total cold-water distribution. Cool-water species made up 24.5 percent. Walleye distribution accounted for 78.3 percent, Northern Pike made up 18.9 percent, and the remaining 2.8 percent of the fish was split among 13 other species. Although warm-water species accounted for the least number of total fish, the group consists of 30 different species, twice as many as cold- and cool-water species. Striped bass accounted for 41.1 percent of the warm-water distribution and together, bluegill, largemouth bass, channel catfish, and American shad made up 45.7 percent of distribution.

In the late 1990s, 45 states were involved in the distribution of fish and fish eggs from hatcheries. The state of Washington led the nation, responsible for 24.8 percent of all distributed fish. California had 10.8 percent and Wisconsin accounted for 7.0 percent. Illinois was the leading fish-egg producing state with Washington and Wisconsin following, respectively.

FURTHER READING

Aquaculture Outlook. *U.S. Department of Agriculture.* 2000. Available from http://usda.mannlib.cornell.edu.

''Doctoring Fish—New Vaccines for Aquaculturists.'' *Agricultural Research,* October 1999.

McCoy, John.''A Truck Runs to It.'' *Field and Stream,* April 1998.

U.S. Fish and Wildlife Service. Division of Fisheries Internet Information Center. Available from http://www.fws.gov/~r9af/index.html.

U.S. Imports and Exports of Fishery Products. *National Marine Fisheries Services.* 2000. Available from http://www.st.nmfs.gov.

Ward's Business Directory of U.S. Private and Public Companies, Detroit: Gale Research, 1999.

SIC 0971

HUNTING AND TRAPPING AND GAME PROPAGATION

This category includes establishments primarily engaged in commercial hunting and trapping, or in the operation of game preserves.

NAICS CODE(S)

114210 (Hunting and Trapping)

Hunting and trapping are among the oldest industries in the United States. Trading in beaver pelts played a role in the western expansion of the United States. As areas became overexploited, the commercial trade moved further and further west. During the nineteenth century, there were few ordinances governing the taking of fur-bearing animals. As a result some species were threatened. One of the first animal management regulations regarded fur seals. Under the terms of the Alaska Convention of 1911, Japan, Russia, Canada, and the United States agreed to limit catches according to governmental rules. The resulting regulations enabled seal populations to recover and sustain themselves.

The twentieth century brought other regulations to the industry. Seasons for taking animals were open or closed based on the management needs of specific populations. Many jurisdictions instituted laws requiring trappers to check their traps at frequent intervals, usually every 24 hours. The Endangered Species Confiscation Act of 1969 listed animals ''threatened with world-wide extinction'' and prohibited trading in them.

During the 1960s and 1970s, the United States saw growing antagonism between members of the animal rights movement and trappers and hunters. Animal rights activists aimed their efforts at reducing demand for fur products, which resulted in price declines. Trappers and hunters responded by developing programs in conjunction with governmental regulators to manage populations of wild animal stocks at sustainable levels and to seek more humane trapping techniques.

There are 23 fur-bearing species in the United States spread among all the states, except Hawaii. Of those 23, 8 make up about 92 percent of the annual fur harvest. The species are, in descending order: muskrat, raccoon, opossum, nutria, beaver, coyote, mink, and gray and red fox (gray fox and red fox are often counted together).

Today, the U.S. fur industry is divided into two segments: ''wild caught'' and ''ranch farmed''. Wild-caught pelts account for the majority of U.S. fur production, but ranch-farmed pelts are worth much more and account for a larger percentage of annual sales. In 1997, there were 200,000 registered trappers in the United States. Mink pelt production in the United States in 1998 totaled 2.94 million pelts, down 2 percent from 1997. Wisconsin, the major mink producing state, produced 800,500 pelts in 1998. Total mink pelts produced in 1998 were valued at $72.9 million dollars, down 26 percent from $99.1 million in 1997. The two major American fur markets are in New York and Chicago, and there are more than 1,500 retail stores in the United States specializing in fur garments.

Most of the ranch farming in the United States involves mink, but a significant number of fox farms exist as well. Less than $100 million in mink, or 95 percent of mink produced in the United States, is exported annually, which accounts for 10 percent of the world's mink supply.

Although hunting and trapping have traditionally involved taking animals for their pelts and skins, the 1990s saw increases in other occupations within this classification. Experienced hunters and trappers turned to work as guides for hunting parties. Some trappers focused their efforts on catching animals for research or wildlife management programs. A growing specialty was the practice of capturing wild animals in urban areas so that they could be removed to other environments. Another component of this category is the game preserve, where game populations are controlled to provide a hunting experience for visitors.

FURTHER READING

Ballard, Camela Kai. ''Fur Farming: From Cages to Coats.'' *The Planet Magazine,* 1996.

Bureau of Labor Statistics. ''Fishers, Hunters, and Trappers,'' 1999. Available from http://www.fedstats.gov/index20.html.

Fur Industry in America, 1999. Available from http://www.fur.org.

U.S. Department of Agriculture. *1999 National Agricultural Statistics Service,* 1999. Available from http://www.usda.mannlib.cornell.edu/reports.

MINING INDUSTRIES

SIC 1011

IRON ORES

This classification covers establishments primarily engaged in mining, beneficiating, or otherwise preparing iron ores and manganiferous ores valued chiefly for their iron content. This industry includes production of sinter and other agglomerates except those associated with blast furnace operations. Blast furnaces primarily engaged in producing pig iron from iron ore are classified in **SIC 3312: Steel Works, Blast Furnaces (Including Coke Ovens), and Rolling Mills.**

NAICS CODE(S)

212210 (Iron Ore Mining)

INDUSTRY SNAPSHOT

Virtually all of the iron ore mined in the world is used in steelmaking. In the United States, the largest producers are concentrated in a few states that account for the country's national output of usable iron ore. According to the U.S. Geological Survey, mines in Minnesota, Michigan, and six other states shipped about $1.9 billion worth of usable iron ore in 1998, slightly up from the $1.7 billion shipped in 1996.

The U.S. iron ore industry is dependent on the domestic steel industry, most notably the large integrated steelworks along the Great Lakes. These integrated manufacturers use blast furnaces to turn iron ore, coke, and limestone into pig iron and then into steel.

High labor and fuel costs, declining ore grades, and the inland location of the country's mines make it difficult for the United States to compete in the world iron ore market. U.S. iron ore producers are meeting these demands by making higher-quality fluxed iron ore pellets that can meet the tight chemical and physical specifications that are needed to make higher quality steels.

U.S. iron ore production decreased in the late 1990s in response to the Asian financial crisis that began in 1997 when Thailand devalued its currency and set off a chain reaction of devaluations in the region. Foreign producers, unable to find buyers for their steel products in their depressed regions, supplied low-cost exports to the United States, thereby decreasing the need for domestic iron ore.

In September 1999 U.S. mine production of iron ore dropped 14 percent from where it was in August 1999, according to the U.S. Geological Survey. Production, at 3.3 million metric tons (mmt), was the lowest it had been since August 1993 when it sank to 2.8 million metric tons. Shipments dropped 3 percent and mine stocks were down 20 percent as compared to August 1999.

ORGANIZATION AND STRUCTURE

The United States maintained a close relationship with Canada in regard to iron ore trade. Over the course of the 1990s, the United States was a net importer to meet demands for iron ore. Since 1990, about 54 percent of U.S. imports have come from Canada, while 99 percent of U.S. exports went there. The reasons for the tight relationship included ownership and proximity. In 1998 Canadian steel mills owned part of three of the nine iron ore producers that accounted for 99.5 percent of the U.S. ore produced. Likewise, one U.S. iron ore company and one U.S. steelmaker had partial ownership of one of three iron ore producers in Canada. Also, the proximity of the countries and the location of the Great Lakes, which were used for transportation, meant lower shipping costs for each country.

The high-grade direct shipping ore of Michigan and Minnesota has all been mined in the United States. Lower-grade taconite, which requires the more expensive processes of beneficiation and pelletizing, makes up the bulk of U.S. mining today. Many of the pelletizing and taconite mining facilities are in the interior of the country forcing higher transportation rail costs to ship to the Mid-Atlantic and Alabama steelworks. Since these mines are far away from saltwater harbors, imported iron ore from Canada, Brazil, and Venezuela makes up a large portion of iron ore consumed on the East Coast.

For the inland steelmaking region, those same high rail costs that keep U.S. iron ore from being competitive for use at coastal steelworks also act to keep foreign ores from being used in their region. The St. Lawrence Seaway is an inexpensive transportation route to the Great Lakes, but it can also become a bottleneck for iron ore carriers trying to supply the steelworks in this region. Some oceangoing iron ore carriers cannot enter the Great Lakes because of the short gate-to-gate river locks.

Similarly, U.S. iron ore bound for foreign shores on 1,000-foot ships cannot leave the locks. Ore often has to be off-loaded onto smaller gulf vessels or transferred to rail cars at Philadelphia or Baltimore. Sometimes, to reach the many steelworks in the Pennsylvania and Ohio River Valley, iron ore is barged up the Mississippi River through the Port of New Orleans.

A handful of states account for the country's national output of usable iron ore. Minnesota and Michigan are by far the largest providers of iron ore in the country. In 1998 Minnesota produced 4.1 million metric tons of ore, excluding by-product ore, out of the 62,591 total U.S. production, while Michigan produced 1.3 million metric tons. In 1999 Minnesota continued its dominance with 3.3 million metric tons in production.

Background and Development

Making up 5 percent of Earth's crust, iron is the fourth-most abundant rock-forming element. Iron ore is the primary source of iron for the world's iron and steel industries, and is the cheapest and most widely used metal.

The first known use of iron ore from the United States was when several barrels of ore were shipped from Virginia and Maryland to England for testing in 1608. The ore was found to be of good quality, and an attempt was made to build an ironworks near Falling Creek, Virginia. An Indian raid in 1622 ended that early undertaking.

In 1645 Massachusetts became the first regular production site for iron ore in the colonies with the building of the Hammersmith ironworks just north of Boston. Other furnaces built in Rhode Island, New Jersey, and Connecticut soon followed. During the next 100 years, iron making spread southward and westward, with many new mines opening to meet the surging demand. By the beginning of the Revolutionary War, iron ore was mined and smelted in 12 of the 13 colonies. Pennsylvania became the center of iron making.

By the 1840s, the northeastern furnaces began to close because of a scarcity of charcoal and ore, but smelting in Tennessee, Missouri, Alabama, and Texas easily met the demand. In 1844 the discovery of the reserves contained in the Marquette Range in Michigan supplied new hard ores. Before the completion of the Sault Ste. Marie shipping canal in 1855, development of the industry in this region was slow, but with this new transportation route came further development of the Lake Superior region. By 1885 the Gogebic and Menominee Ranges of Michigan and Wisconsin began producing more than two million metric tons of ore, more than 20 times the volume produced in 1860. Smaller mines in New York, Tennessee, and the Mid-Atlantic states couldn't compete with the high grades and low water transportation costs of ore coming out of this region. Production from the Vermilion Range in the 1880s and the discovery of the Mesabi ores in the 1890s helped to close most of the Eastern mines in the United States by the turn of the century. Birmingham, Alabama, became a major iron ore center at this time.

Iron ore properties in the Lake Superior district were bought by steel companies, and small mines were consolidated into larger ones by the mergers of large mining companies. The structure of the iron ore industry today is a direct result of the consolidations that took place between 1893 and 1905.

In the 1950s hundreds of U.S. mines closed because of greater imports, the rising costs of underground mining in America, and depleted ores of higher grades. By 1981, 15 mines accounted for 90 percent of America's iron ore production. Only five years later, increasing steel imports and two severe recessions reduced the number of iron ore mines from 15 to 10. The numbers were slightly up in 1991, when iron ore was produced by 20 companies operating 24 mines (21 open, 1 underground), 16 concentration plants, and 10 pelletizing plants. But by 1998, iron ore was being produced by only 12 complexes with 12 mines (11 open pit, 1 underground), 10 concentration plants, and 10 pelletizing plants. In 1998, 5 companies operating 9 mines produced 99.5 percent of the ore.

The U.S. steel industry accounts for 98 percent of domestic iron ore consumption. While steel consumption remained strong in the United States in 1998, a large portion of that consumption was of steel imports, which were cheaper for U.S. consumers because of the combination of the strong dollar and depressed foreign markets where producers could not sell their products.

Electric arc furnace steelmaking in the United States, which accounted for 43 percent of total steelmaking in 1993 and does not use iron ore, is the technology most often used by minimills, the chief competition of integrated outfits. Minimills substitute metal and iron scrap for iron ore to melt in their furnaces and have made great inroads into integrated steel's market share over the past decade. The minimills, however, during the 1990s, were faced with 50 percent increases in scrap prices, and as a result they were forced to vertically integrate, sometimes taking on the cost structures of their larger integrated competitors. But minimills remained strong competitors. Their share of the steel market, which stood at 15 percent in 1970, increased to more than 43 percent by 1997. By the end of the decade, flat-rolled minimills were expected to add to the flat-rolled market 10-15 million tons of capacity.

CURRENT CONDITIONS

The U.S. steel industry accounts for 98 percent of iron ore consumption. In 1998 the reported U.S. consumption of ore and total agglomerate was 79.0 million metric tons of iron ore, slightly down from the 79.5 million metric tons consumed in 1997.

In the late 1990s, imports of low-priced steel plagued U.S. producers, especially following the Asian financial crisis that began in 1997. While the market seemed to be picking up in 1998, which had been looking like a good year with domestic iron ore production and consumption rates into the third quarter exceeding those of 1997, the rates dropped off at year-end because of record imports of low-priced steel. As a result, two of the seven iron ore producers in Minnesota's Mesabi iron range reduced production. Though U.S. steel consumption remained strong that year, a majority of that consumption was met by steel imports. The strength of the U.S. dollar against foreign currencies made imports cheaper. The Asian financial crisis also made imports more enticing. As Asian economies weakened, steel consumption in that region declined and the area's producers looked to the U.S. market to sell their products. Throughout 1998, the United States imported vast amounts of inexpensive semifinished steel. These falling world export prices also hurt domestic steel producers. Diminished steel demand in the Asian region, coupled with a strong dollar, and declining world export prices were expected to cause the United States to continue this trend of importing mass amounts of low-priced steel into the next century.

In 1998 domestic iron ore mine production dropped from 1997's 63.0 million metric tons to 62.0 million metric tons, or 6 percent, of the 1,020 million metric tons produced worldwide. Through September 1999, domestic iron ore production stood at 42.4 million metric tons, down 9.5 percent from the 46.9 million metric tons produced from January through September 1998. Domestic iron ore shipments stood at 61.3 million metric tons in 1998, down 2 percent from the 62.8 shipped in 1997, but a 31 percent improvement from the low of 42.0 million metric tons in 1986.

INDUSTRY LEADERS

At the close of the twentieth century, leading companies included Cleveland-Cliffs Inc., with $503 million in sales, and Oglebay Norton Co., with $161 million, both based in Cleveland, Ohio. Other leaders included Rouge Steel Co., based in Eveleth, Minnesota, with $150 million in sales; Northshore Mining Corp., of Silver Bay, Minnesota, with an estimated $110 million; and Tilden Mining Co., based in Ishpeming, Michigan, with an estimated $45 million.

WORKFORCE

In 1996 most iron ore mine workers were union members of the United Steelworkers of America. For decades, up until 1983, union contracts often included generous increases in wages and benefits. But the 1982 recession, subsequent large layoffs, and the need to reduce operating costs brought about new working relationships between the unions and company management. Reductions in real wages, more flexible work rules, and management/labor cooperation were more the norm in the late 1990s.

Mines also began offering incentive bonus plans. In 1997, 55 metal mines had incentive bonus plans, and in the past decade, the number of mines offering bonuses rose 37 percent. Bonuses were awarded generally for productivity, safety, profit, attendance, commodity price, and/or meeting sales goals. According to a 1998 study by Western Mine Engineering Inc., the most common bonuses were fixed bonuses awarded for having a specific period accident-free, according to a report in *American Metal Market.*

Total employment in 1998 increased to 11,103, up 7.8 percent from the 10,236 in 1996, and up substantially from the approximately 7,000 total employment in the late 1980s, but down 72 percent from the industry peak of 40,100 back in 1953. Average hourly wages were up to $23.89 in 1998, according to *Agriculture, Mining, and Construction USA.* This was an increase of 4 percent over the previous year.

AMERICA AND THE WORLD

In 1998 world iron ore production was at 1,020 million metric tons, slightly down from the 1,040 million metric tons produced in 1997, which was a new record for world production. China was the world's largest producer of iron ore with an estimated output of 240 million metric tons in 1998. The next closest country was Brazil with 180. The United States came in with 62 million metric tons.

World iron ore production was expected to increase to 1,240 million metric tons by 2006, according to Sydney, Australia-based AME Mineral Economics. Australia's production was predicted to rise from 140 million metric tons in 1995 to more than 167.5 million metric tons in 2005. Since China's steel production doubled since 1986, it was expected to become the largest steel producer in the world by the year 2000. Korea and India also experienced dramatically increased output from 1985 to 1995 and were expected to continue their growth into the twenty-first century.

From 2000 onward, world iron ore demand was expected to grow steadily and reach 1.1 billion metric ton in 2004, according to *American Metal Market.* According to AME Mineral Economics, it was expected that after the massive drop in 1999, iron ore prices would level out with the possibility for a recovery of about 2 percent in 2000. In the long range, however, real prices were expected to decline.

The United States produced 6 percent of the world's iron ore in 1998, continuing a steady downward trend from its 11.9 percent world market share in 1970. Imports for consumption in 1998 increased to an estimated 18.5 million metric tons from 1994's level of 17.5. Imports of iron ore reached its peak of 48.8 million metric tons in 1974. Exports for 1998 stood at an estimated 6.4 million metric tons, up a bit from the 6.3 million metric tons exported in both 1996 and 1997.

World resources were estimated to exceed 800 billion tons of crude ore containing more than 230 billion tons of iron, with U.S. resources estimated at about 110 billion tons of ore containing 27 billion tons of iron. U.S. resources, however, were mainly low-grade taconite-type ores that required beneficiation and agglomeration for commercial use.

Research and Technology

Technological advances during the 1990s affected the structure of the iron ore industry in the United States. Many of the integrated steelworks began using fluxed pellets, which were created by adding fluxstone, limestone, and/or dolomite to the iron ore during the balling stage. A more reducible type of iron ore pellet was thus created. In 1990 U.S. production of fluxed pellets made up 39 percent of total iron ore pellet production. In many cases, integrated steelworks were trying to meet the growing fluxed pellet demand.

In the late 1990s, stricter environmental regulations restricting coke oven gas emissions closed some older integrated facilities. But in the end, the closures forced the development of new technologies for those firms providing alternatives to scrap. With the closures, companies became concerned about the availability of low-reside scrap and invested in alternative iron-making technologies. Direct-reduced iron, or DRI, is an alternative to scrap. At the turn of the century, there were five proposed projects that would boost the U.S. DRI capacity from .5 million metric tons annually to more than 4 million metric tons if the projects were completed.

Further Reading

Cleveland-Cliffs Inc. *Productions and Sales Information,* February 1997. Available from http://www.sec.gov/edgar/data/764065/0000950152-97-002212.txt.

Darnay, Arsen J., ed. *Agriculture, Mining, and Construction USA.* Detroit: Gale Research, 1998.

Hagopian, Arthur. "Australian Iron Ore Projects Stalled." *American Metal Market,* 31 May 1999, 3.

Kertes, Noella. "Mine Wages on Rise: Survey." *American Metal Market,* 14 July 1998, 2.

Kirk, William S. "Iron Ore." *U.S. Geological Survey, Mineral Commodity Summaries,* February 1997.

———. "Iron Ore." *U.S. Geological Survey, Mineral Commodity Summaries,* 1998. Available from http://minerals.usgs.gov/minerals/pubs/commodity/iron_ore/340399.pdf. Accessed 14 December 1999.

———. "Iron Ore in January 1997." *U.S. Geological Survey, Mineral Industry Surveys,* 18 March 1997.

———. "Iron Ore in September 1999." *U.S. Geological Survey, Mineral Industry Surveys.* Available from http://minerals.usgs.gov/minerals/pubs/commodity/iron_ore/34000999.pdf. Accessed 14 December 1999.

———. "Minerals Yearbook: Iron Ore 1995." *U.S. Geological Survey, Mineral Industry Surveys,* Washington, DC: Bureau of Mines, 1996.

U.S. Bureau of the Census. *Census of Mineral Industries.* Washington, DC: GPO.

Value Line Investment Survey. New York: Value Line Publishing.

SIC 1021

COPPER ORES

This category includes establishments primarily engaged in mining, milling, or otherwise preparing copper ores. This industry also includes establishments primarily engaged in the recovery of copper concentrates by precipitation and leaching of copper ore.

NAICS Code(s)

212234 (Copper Ore and Nickel Ore Mining)

INDUSTRY SNAPSHOT

A global commodity business, copper mining and milling is subject to swings in both prices and production levels, depending on world markets and individual companies' operating strategies. World demand for copper has grown steadily over the past two decades, but in the late 1990s ambitious copper producers, including many located in Chile, the world's largest copper-producing country, ramped up new mining capacity faster than the market could absorb their production. In addition, economic weakness in Asia and Latin America in the late 1990s left global demand growth at a slower pace than some producers anticipated. As a result, copper prices slumped by as much as 50 percent in the latter half of the 1990s, especially during 1998 and 1999, reaching Great Depression-era levels adjusted for inflation. Soft prices decimated copper companies' profits and triggered a frantic round of consolidation among major producers. Prices were expected to recover in 2000 and 2001, as the industry curbed excess production and economic growth resumed in Asia and Latin America.

The United States is the world's second-largest copper producer and a net importer of copper, obtaining about 16 percent of its copper from abroad as of 1998. That year, U.S. mines turned out 1.85 million metric tons of copper, or 15 percent of world production, and employed 13,000 people. Based on the 1998 average world price of $0.76 a pound, U.S. copper production was worth approximately $3.3 billion. The U.S. Geological Survey estimated net U.S. consumption of unmanufactured copper materials in 1998 at more than 3 million metric tons.

ORGANIZATION AND STRUCTURE

Stages of Production. Copper extraction and processing involves several stages, which vary with the kind of ore and technology being used. Integrated producers are involved in all of the stages, including ones that are considered outside the scope of this industry classification. Also, because copper ores are recovered along with a variety of other useful minerals, most copper-mining companies also have side businesses to handle other metals, such as gold, silver, and molybdenum.

Copper ore, which may be mined underground or, more commonly, at the surface in an open pit, is unearthed with digging equipment or explosive devices. The material is then transported by conveyor or by truck to a mill or plant, often on site, that crushes and grinds the ore into a powder.

In the next step, called concentrating, the powder is mixed with water and chemicals, which cause copper sulfide ores to float to the top, where they may be separated from some of the other minerals. Once the copper is skimmed, the copper mix, or concentrate, may be piped as slurry to another site for additional processing, or it may be dried and transported via truck or ship.

Meanwhile, the leftover liquid, known as tailings, can be processed further for copper oxide ores and other useful minerals. This material can be broken down further by treating with acid, known as leaching, and applying one of several methods to separate the copper from other substances.

Concentrate must be purified and refined before it yields copper that is ready for manufacturing applications. While for classification purposes this advanced processing is the domain of **SIC 3331: Primary Smelting and Refining of Copper,** in practice many of the major copper-mining firms are involved to some degree in these activities. Many mines have smelters or refineries on site.

Copper Sales and Markets. Large copper producers typically sell their products in two ways: by contract and on the spot markets. Contracts are usually for one to three years and may involve selling copper ores or concentrates at various points in the production process, depending on the client's needs and capabilities. While many manufacturers require copper in a state that's ready to go directly into their products, and thus purchase it as refined cathode, rod, or wire, others buy concentrate and do their own smelting, refining, shaping, and so forth.

Copper is also sold on the open market. Major world markets such as the London Metal Exchange provide a large and efficient medium for financial transactions relating to the copper trade. Transactions may take the form of spot contracts, in which the parties arrange for the physical transfer of copper, or futures/options contracts, which are market instruments that enable financial hedging against adverse price movements, but no physical exchange occurs. A variety of copper trading firms and brokerages also act as intermediaries for bringing together buyers and sellers.

Copper Use By Sector. According to annual figures from the Copper Development Association, a leading trade group, building construction consumes the largest share of copper in the United States, representing 41.8 percent of all consumption as of 1997. Copper products are used in a variety of building construction materials including insulated wire and piping. Single family homes in the United States, for example, use an average of 422 pounds of copper in their construction.

Electrical and electronic products account for another 25 percent of the U.S. copper market. Copper's electrical conductivity properties enable it to be widely used for telephone and power lines. In addition, copper is used in underground lines and small gauge wire. However, fiber optics, which uses thin strands of glass to transmit light signals, has made significant inroads into the telecommunications market.

Other notable sectors that consume copper include the transportation equipment, industrial machinery, and consumer goods industries. Transportation equipment makes up 12.8 percent of U.S. copper consumption. Cars, trucks, and vans use copper in their electrical systems and have been increasing their use of copper—about 56 pounds were used per car in 1998, as opposed to 30 pounds in 1981. The popularity of larger models, like sport-utility vehicles, and the growth of electronic features in cars have contributed to copper's success in the transportation sector. Industrial machinery and equipment manufacturing represents an additional 11.5 percent of the copper market. Industrial machinery, air conditioners, and farm machinery all use copper products in their construction. Consumer products, like hair dryers, knives, and coffee makers, constitute 9 percent of the U.S. copper market.

Copper Production. The United States has two major copper-producing regions: the Butte district of Montana and the region composed of Arizona, New Mexico, Utah, and Nevada. In 1998, just 15 U.S. mines supplied 97 percent of national copper output. Arizona is the largest copper-producing state, generating 65 percent of the total U.S. output as of 1996.

Copper is a relatively homogeneous product. Copper mined and processed in Arizona is in essence the same as copper mined and processed in Chile. Therefore, success in the copper industry depends on keeping production costs low compared to market prices. Major production costs for U.S. producers include labor costs, environmental regulations, and energy costs. New technical processes have also been central to keeping costs down.

Background and Development

Copper has been mined since ancient times. The Egyptians, for example, mined copper 5,000 years ago. In the United States, significant copper mining began in 1845 when the Pittsburgh and Boston Company started a mine in Michigan's Upper Peninsula. According to Hildebrand and Mangum, there were 25 mining companies located in the Upper Peninsula by 1850. The Calumet and Hecla Mining Company, founded in 1870, quickly became a dominant copper producer. Michigan's Upper Peninsula was the only significant copper-producing region during this period. In the late 1870s, Butte, Montana, experienced a mining bonanza. The copper mines in Butte were the largest underground copper source ever found. The vast Western copper deposits eventually eclipsed the original Michigan mining operations.

Technological innovations changed the nature of copper mining. The early mines were underground operations. Innovations like nitroglycerin, power drills, electric power, and steam shovels increased the productivity of copper mining. Eventually massive open-pit operations replaced underground mines. Milling and smelting technology also improved.

The industry eventually recognized that economies of scale were the key to efficient and profitable copper mining. Hildebrand and Mangum point out that this major innovation resulted from a combination of smaller technological breakthroughs like gravity separation, the Chilean mill (for grinding separated ore), and the steam shovel. In addition, copper mining companies eventually recognized that large initial fixed costs became insignificant when a copper mine produced a huge output. Following World War II, massive open-pit mining and the consolidation of large integrated companies became the norm in the industry. By the 1990s, the U.S. copper industry, dominated by a handful of industry leaders, was the world's second-largest copper producer.

Current Conditions

With copper prices at historic lows in the late 1990s, a wave of consolidation swept through the U.S. industry, highlighted by several prominent shutdowns and mergers. Australia-based Broken Hill Proprietary, operating as BHP Copper Co. in the United States, had closed all of its U.S. copper operations by 1999, after acquiring them in its ill-timed purchase of Magma Copper Co. just four years earlier. BHP's mines had produced around 10 percent of U.S. copper output, but the company was not one of the low-cost producers and was hit especially hard when copper prices plummeted. Other companies closed individual mines in an effort to cut their losses and ease the glut of copper on the market.

Mergers have been another legacy of rock-bottom copper prices. In 1999, Asarco Inc. and Cyprus Amax Minerals Company began merger talks to form what would have been the world's second-largest copper company. The parties estimated that a merger would save some $200 million a year in operating costs between the two. Then, in a surprise move, the largest U.S. copper firm, Phelps Dodge, made bids for both Asarco and Cyprus, proposing a three-way merger that would have created the world's largest copper concern. The targeted firms, however, balked at Phelps Dodge's offer on grounds that it was too little and shortchanged their shareholders. While executives at Asarco and Cyprus were determined to fend off Phelps' overtures, some shareholders of the respective companies opposed the Asarco-Cyprus deal. Meanwhile, Phelps continued to make its case aggressively, threatening a lawsuit and a proxy battle and, eventually, increasing its offering price.

As relations between Asarco and Cyprus began to cool, a fourth company, Grupo Mexico S.A. de C.V., entered the fray. Grupo Mexico, a diversified mining company, offered to merge with Asarco at more attractive terms than either of the earlier offers. Phelps chose not to match the new offer. In the end, two mergers were inked: Phelps with Cyprus, and Asarco with Grupo Mexico.

The production cuts during this period of consolidation were expected to help shed the oversupply of copper, although certain producers outside the United States have proven more reluctant to curtail their output. Still, as demand revived in depressed areas like Asia, copper consumption was forecast to catch up with supply. After a devastating first six months of 1999, when copper averaged $0.65 a pound, prices rebounded modestly in the latter part of the year, to the mid-70 cent range, after several of the closures had been announced. Some analysts expected this trend to continue throughout 2000 and into 2001, with prices expected to average 80 cents during 2000.

INDUSTRY LEADERS

Phelps Dodge. Now with Cyprus Amax Minerals under its umbrella, Phelps Dodge Corporation is by far the largest copper producer in the United States and second largest in the world. In 1998, Phelps' U.S. operations produced an estimated 610,000 metric tons of copper. The Phoenix-based company was founded in 1834 as a partnership between Anson Greene Phelps, William Dodge, and Daniel James. The company purchased two copper mines in the 1880s. By 1906, the company's copper mining and smelting operations had become so successful that it moved exclusively into the copper industry. Today, Phelps' Morenci mine, at Greenlee, Arizona, is the largest in the United States. Revenues from all Phelps operations, including its non-copper business lines, totaled $3.1 billion in 1998.

Cyprus Amax Minerals Company was the third-largest U.S. based copper producer before the 1999 acquisition. Cyprus Amax itself was the result of a 1993 merger between Cyprus Minerals Company and Amax Inc. In 1998, the company reported production of 274,000 metric tons of copper from its U.S. mines. Cyprus Minerals was founded in 1916 by Charles Gunther and Philip Wiseman. Its first mining operations were located on the island of Cyprus during the 1920s and 1930s. As of 1998, Cyprus Amax reported total revenue of $2.6 billion from all operations.

Asarco/Grupo Mexico. Asarco Inc. was founded in 1899 by Henry Rogers and Adolph Lewisohn. Originally named the American Smelting and Refining Company, Asarco concerned itself primarily with copper, lead, and silver smelting and refining. By the 1990s, Asarco had become a fully integrated copper mining and processing organization, producing an estimated 294,000 metric tons of copper in the United States during 1998. The company's consolidated revenues that year were approximately $2.3 billion.

Grupo Mexico actually had historical ties to Asarco, originating as Asarco's Mexican operations and later taking the name Asarco Mexicana. The company gradually gained majority control by Mexican business concerns and grew through a series of mergers and acquisitions. In addition to its mining activities, Grupo Mexico operates two railroads by agreement with the Mexican government. Some observers speculated that Asarco's stake in a Peruvian mining company was a major reason for Grupo Mexico's bid for Asarco.

Rio Tinto plc. Though not a U.S. based company, London-based Rio Tinto plc is noteworthy within the U.S. copper industry both as the parent company to several U.S. copper concerns and as a major world copper producer. Its biggest U.S. holding is Kennecott Utah Copper Corp., which operates Bingham Canyon, near Salt Lake City, one of the largest copper mines in the United States. The site also includes a major smelting and refining operation that can accommodate all of the mine's output. Among its other global interests, Rio Tinto has a 30 percent stake in Chile's Escondido mine, the world's largest copper mine. Rio Tinto likewise has a minority stake in Freeport-McMoRan Copper & Gold, Inc., a U.S. based holding company with large copper operations in Indonesia.

WORKFORCE

The U.S. copper industry employed an average of 13,000 people in 1998. The United Steelworkers Union represents most employees. Major occupations in the U.S. copper industry include mining managers, mining geologists, valuation engineers, mining engineers, design engineers, shift bosses, blasters, miners, and construction equipment operators.

AMERICA AND THE WORLD

Chile is the world's largest producer of copper, twice as big as the United States, with 3.66 million metric tons of copper output in 1998. The United States was second with 1.85 million metric tons. Based on U.S. Geological Survey statistics, other major producers in 1998 included Indonesia (750,000 metric tons), Canada (710,000), Australia (600,000), Peru (450,000), and Russia (450,000). In Chile and in other nations, government ownership of mines is commonplace.

RESEARCH AND TECHNOLOGY

A notable advance in copper mining technology is the solvent extraction-electrowinning (SX-EW) method of production. The SX-EW process involves saturating copper bearing ores with sulfuric acid solutions. After the sulfuric acid dissolves the copper, it is recovered by the electrowinning process, where the dissolved copper is deposited onto charged cathodes. The process is significantly less expensive than traditional methods because it involves fewer steps. It also reduces air pollution control costs because it avoids the smelting process. Currently, only oxide and secondary sulfide ores can be processed with the SX-EW process. These ores are located close to the surface where they have been exposed to oxygen. It is estimated that only 15 percent of world copper reserves and 13 percent of U.S. copper reserves can be processed via the SX-EW method. However, coupled with other new lower-cost processing methods, use of the SX-EW process can significantly reduce production costs, and thus large U.S. producers have been quick to adopt it.

FURTHER READING

Copper Development Association. *The Copper Page.* New York, 1999. Available from www.copper.org.

Edelstein, Daniel L. "Copper." *Mineral Commodity Summaries.* Washington, D.C.: U.S. Geological Survey, January 1999. Available from minerals.usgs.gov.

———. "Copper." *Mineral Industry Surveys.* Washington: U.S. Geological Survey, July 1999.

International Copper Study Group. "The Numbers." *Copper Bulletin.* Lisbon, Portugal, 1999. Available from www.icsg.org.

SIC 1031

LEAD AND ZINC ORES

This category covers establishments primarily engaged in mining, milling, or otherwise preparing lead ores, zinc ores, or lead-zinc ores.

NAICS CODE(S)

212231 (Lead Ore and Zinc Ore Mining)

INDUSTRY SNAPSHOT

According to the U.S. Department of the Interior, U.S. Geological Survey, lead and zinc account for 2 and 3 percent of U.S. nonferrous metals production, respectively. In 1997 approximately 29 establishments were engaged in the production of lead and zinc ores. Overall, U.S. reliance on importation of these metals was limited, with 35 percent of U.S. zinc consumption derived from imported product and 14 percent of lead consumption obtained from imports. A lack of capacity in zinc refinery production in the late 1990s resulted in increased export of zinc concentrates coupled with imports of zinc metal, a situation projected to continue in the United States through 2005. The special properties of lead, especially its resistance to corrosion, make it extremely useful for nuclear insulation and applications such as X-ray protection. Zinc is also used in the production of nonferrous alloys and is useful as a corrosion inhibitor, especially as a protective coating on steel.

In keeping with a rebound of the industry, and despite a surplus of lead, revenues from the two ores increased by $0.33 billion between 1996 and 1997—from $1.20 billion to $1.53 billion. Zinc production rose modestly, from 620,000 metric tons in 1996 to 630,000 in 1997; likewise, lead production increased from 430,000 to 440,000 during that time. Yet the price of lead, which traditionally averaged 30 cents per pound, hovered at 24 cents per pound in 1998, as a result of oversupply. Despite stable long-term growth from 1986 to 1997, by the end of the twentieth century lead and zinc production in the United States failed to recapture the high levels attained earlier in 1970. As a result, domestic zinc output failed to meet demand.

ORGANIZATION AND STRUCTURE

Lead mining is located primarily in Missouri, Alaska, Colorado, Idaho, and Montana. Ninety-two percent of U.S. lead product is extracted from nine mines in Alaska and Missouri; Alaska accounts for about one-half of total U.S. lead production. Zinc output is concentrated in Alaska, Missouri, New York, and Tennessee. The lead and zinc industry consolidated operations gradually after production peaked in 1970: where 88 establishments existed in 1977, the number fell to 36 firms in 1996, and only 29 remained in 1997.

Manufacturers of lead and zinc intermediate products for industrial use are the principal purchasers of lead and zinc.

BACKGROUND AND DEVELOPMENT

The mining of lead and zinc ores originated in Colorado in the early 1800s. The production of these base metals became closely intertwined because both were extracted from the same ores—although in different proportions. After recovery, lead and zinc are separated in the smelting process, whereby the ore is processed and reduced to a metal. Until the beginning of the twentieth century, lead and zinc production was strictly a U.S. affair, and before World War II, the United States was generally not dependent of foreign zinc suppliers. During most of that time, exports exceeded imports by a small margin. After World War II, the United States became a small net importer.

Zinc imports increased from 39,000 tons per year in 1939 to an average of 375,000 tons from 1946 to 1950 and 534,000 for the period from 1951 to 1953. The industry became heavily concentrated during this period, and by 1952 there were 912 lead and zinc mines in the

United States, but only 193 of them accounted for 95 percent of the market. A few corporations dominated the industry, with ten companies controlling 65 percent of total U.S. lead output and ten companies controlling 62 percent of the zinc market. Of those corporations, seven dominated in both groups. Control of the smelting market for zinc and lead ores was even more concentrated.

U.S. firms soon lost their competitive position internationally as the demand for lead and zinc expanded far faster than domestic production. Foreign producers expanded production and sent large quantities of their surpluses to the United States. The market shift coincided with the termination of price controls in the United States in 1946 and the suspension of import duties for several years following World War II. These tactics were needed because the war had depleted the country's stocks, yet demand from the U.S. government increased with the onset of the Korean War.

By the late 1960s imports of zinc exceeded domestic production by more than 50 percent, and domestic production of lead just barely exceeded imports in 1969. Secondary production of lead (essentially from scrap) overtook primary production, reaching more than one-half of total production in the late 1970s.

An overall downturn in lead and zinc mining began in 1970. By 1980 U.S. production of zinc fell to less than 10 percent of total world production, and Soviet and Japanese companies accounted for much of the world market. Total production indexes for the industry as a whole reveal a decline of nearly one-half from 1970 to 1986. During the 1980s lead production declined by more than 10 percent, but zinc production increased by more than 50 percent. The loss of several key markets for lead, including the abandonment of lead as an anti-knocking additive to gasoline and the discontinued use of lead as an insulator in water pipes, contributed to lower demand beginning in the 1970s. The use of lead in products that might come into contact with humans (such as paints and pipes) was gradually curtailed because of the risk of lead poisoning, and studies suggested that exposure to lead impaired brain development in children. The U.S. Bureau of Mines projected that annual lead demand to fall at a rate of 0.5 percent to 1.5 percent per year in the 1990s.

Tariffs on zinc were phased out gradually as part of the U.S.-Canada Free Trade Agreement of 1989. That situation, combined with the rollback of world trade barriers, encouraged competition on the part Mexican and Peruvian zinc products to seek duty-free markets in the United States. Finally, after the fall of the Soviet Union in 1989, lead and zinc from its former member states flooded the world market, putting downward pressure on prices. The Bureau of Mines estimated world reserve base of zinc at 400 million tons and reserves at 150 million tons, with the United States having the largest reserves. The world reserve base was approximately 120 million tons at the end of 1995.

A series of circumstances caused lead and zinc prices to fluctuate in the early 1990s. Initially, a strike at Doe Run Company, one of the country's primary producers, created a decline in production; but a subsequent strike at the Trail smelter in Canada led to price increases. Later, in 1996, Doe Run experienced a loss of an estimated 5,400 metric tons of lead production as the result of a shutdown for a furnace repair at a secondary lead smelter in Boss, Missouri. Around that same time ASARCO, Incorporated announced the indefinite closing of its Leadville, Colorado zinc-lead-silver mine but reversed that decision in early 1997 and resumed full production. Zinc prices, which had dropped during 1996, turned steadily upward in early 1997 as the U.S. economy began to recover from an earlier recession, and consumption rose by 8 percent.

CURRENT CONDITIONS

Lead. The primary demand for lead in 1999 resulted from growing demand for rechargeable automobile batteries. Additionally, lead-acid storage batteries served as the primary component in uninterruptible power supplies (UPS) for computer backup systems, a market projected to increase by 5-7 percent at the turn of the century. Use of lead shielding for protection from X-ray exposure and lead glass for computer displays and television tubes also contributed to increased demand. The expansion of the secondary (recycled) lead supply—70 percent of total production—combined with improved methods for primary production contributed to a market surplus in the late 1990s. Even as the demand for lead grew toward the turn of the twenty-first century, prices dropped to 24 cents per pound in 1998 from a peak of 35 cents in 1996.

Zinc. The properties of zinc as a corrosion inhibitor make it valuable for the galvanizing process, and the rubber industry uses zinc oxide in making white paint and pigments. In 1996 a rise in U.S. zinc consumption reflected an economic rebound by industries such as construction that use galvanized steel extensively. Worldwide zinc consumption increased by 5.7 percent, and subsequent price reductions forced mine closures and caused a deficit in zinc concentrate. A slight, sudden surge in refined zinc production (up 1.6 percent), pushed the level up to 5.7 million metric tons in 1998, from an earlier pattern of 5.4 to 5.5 million metric tons of annual output that emerged from 1991 to 1997. Cominco Red Dog (zinc) Mine in Alaska expanded production by 50 percent to meet the demand, yet the deficit lingered due to sluggish smelter production. Domestic production remained flat against strong competition from imports, largely from Canada and Mexico. Unlike lead, only 30 percent of zinc came from recycled materials, and the shortage endured throughout final years of the century.

INDUSTRY LEADERS

Nearly all of the leading companies in the industry engage also in other types of metals mining. ASARCO Incorporated of New York is a conglomerate with a major interest in copper as well as lead and zinc and the manufacturing of specialty chemicals. ASARCO appeared at number 500 on the *Fortune* 500 in April of 1998.

Doe Run Company of St. Louis, owned by New York's Renco Group, was also a major player in the industry. The company, which led the world in the production of primary lead, was ranked second worldwide in led production in 1999. Also prominent is Cominco, Limited, parent company to Cominco Alaska, operators of Alaska's Red Dog Mine. Red Dog was the largest known zinc ore body worldwide at the close of the 1990s. The total zinc reserves at Red Dog were estimated at 138 million tons at end of 1995, with new deposits discovered in 1999. Total zinc and lead production at Red Dog was reported at 600,000 metric tons annually in 1999.

AMERICA AND THE WORLD

World prices for lead and zinc fell during the third and fourth quarters of 1997 as a result of Asian monetary crises and resultant slowdowns and outright stoppages of production in southeast Asia. The crisis, manifested most severely in Thailand, Malaysia, Korea, and Japan, caused significant reductions in the demand for metals. The countries affected by the crisis accounted collectively for 25 percent of world lead consumption and 30 percent of zinc. Earlier, in 1995, Japan and South Korea alone accounted for 22 percent and 21 percent respectively of U.S. lead and zinc ore exports. The emergence of China into the lead/zinc market just prior to the crisis contributed to an international product deficit in that market as a result of work stoppage associated with the crisis. The situation was further aggravated when Canada, a major supplier to the United States, experienced a 3 percent reduction in zinc mine output in 1998.

Zinc Expansion. In 1999 the Asturiana del Zinc in Spain, prepared to increase operations by 37 percent, to become the second largest producer of zinc worldwide.

New production startups in 1998 included the Western Metals' Pillara mine in Australia; overall Australian zinc output remained stable. Also significant were refinery expansions in Korea and Finland: 27 percent production increase at Korea Zinc's Onsan refinery, and 32 percent expansion at Outokumpu's Kokkola refinery. Cominco's Red Dog Mine in Alaska expanded to boost production by 50 percent in the second half of 1998.

FURTHER READING

"About Doe Run." *Doe Run.* Available from http://www.doerun.com/ENGLISH/html/about_doe_run.html.

Barry, Susan (ed.) *U.S. Industry and Trade Outlook.* New York: McGraw Hill, 1999.

Deelo, Michael L. "1999 Annual Commodities: Lead." *Engineering & Mining Journal,* 1 March 1999.

Fortune, 27 April 1998.

Plachy, Jozef. "Zinc." *Mineral Commodity Summaries.* Washington, DC: U.S. Geological Survey, 1996.

———. "Zinc." *Minerals Yearbook.* Washington, DC: U.S. Geological Survey, 1996.

Smith, Gerald R. "Lead." *Mineral Commodity Summaries.* Washington, DC: U.S. Geological Survey, February 1997.

———. "Lead." *Minerals Yearbook.* Washington, DC: U.S. Geological Survey, February 1997. Yates, E. M. "1999 Annual Commodities: Zinc." *Engineering & Mining Journal,* 1 March 1999.

SIC 1041

GOLD ORES

This category covers establishments primarily engaged in mining gold ores from lode deposits or in the recovery of gold from placer deposits by any method. In addition to ore dressing methods such as crushing, grinding, gravity concentration, and froth flotation, this industry includes amalgamation, cyanidation, and the production of bullion at the mine, mill, or dredge site.

NAICS CODE(S)

212221 (Gold Ore Mining)

INDUSTRY SNAPSHOT

Mined on every continent except Antarctica, gold is used for a wide variety of applications ranging from jewelry and the arts to dentistry, electronics, and diverse industrial applications. In 1998, U.S. gold mine production was valued at approximately $4 billion. Of that, jewelry and other art-related pursuits accounted for 55 percent of U.S. gold consumption, industrial uses for 38 percent, electronics for 4 percent, and dental use for 3 percent, according to statistics from the U.S. Bureau of Mines. As a precious metal, gold is traditionally used as a backing for paper currency systems and as a hedge against inflation. Of all the gold produced by the United States, 90 percent came from 30 mines.

An estimated 89,000 tons of gold make up the world's resources, according to the United States Geological Survey. The United States has 12 percent of these resources. World leaders include South Africa, the

United States, and Australia. Other major producers include Brazil, Canada, Russia, and China. World bullion reserves for 1994 were estimated by the Bureau of Mines at 34,500 tons.

ORGANIZATION AND STRUCTURE

Price. After gold peaked in 1987 at $500 an ounce, the industry was characterized as being on a downtrend that continued into the late 1990s. Worldwide deflationary forces—including stagnant economic growth, tepid money supply growth, and weak commodity prices—threatened to continue dampening new gold prices. Gold prices in 1998 were $295.24 per troy ounce, well below the $370 per ounce of 1996.

Declining prices curtailed worldwide exploration spending, which in turn diminished the prospects of new mine supply. In addition, the combination of lower prices and rising production costs precipitated cutbacks at many mines and the closure of numerous others. Production costs in the mid-1990s were estimated at somewhere around $200 per troy ounce. With many companies implementing cost-saving measures, in 1992, average Western world cash and total costs were reduced by 5 percent to $247 per ounce, and 4 percent to $300 per ounce, respectively.

Speculative Demand and World Events. The key swing factor for gold prices has traditionally been speculative demand, arising from the role of gold as a hedge against inflation and backing for currency. Adverse conditions in developed countries intensified deflationary forces in the early 1990s, placing significant downward pressure on gold prices as recession extended from U.S. to German and Japanese economies by 1992.

World events apart from economics, particularly war and political turmoil, also traditionally spur gold price fluctuations, even events in countries thought not to impact industrialized nations; however, as early as 1994, the Commodity Research Bureau predicted "gold's pivotal role in the world's financial structure is dissipating."

Money Supply and Gold Speculation. Another key factor in the early 1990s was the indirect effect of money supply growth on gold speculation. Riding on the heels of runaway debt built up in the 1980s, the monetary climate of the early 1990s was characterized by general bank resistance to lending and by wariness or inability of companies and consumers to borrow. By 1992, growth of the M-2 money supply hovered at 1.6 percent, the lowest in over 30 years. According to Standard & Poor's, such a slow rate of money supply growth tended to favor deflation, which in turn, dampened speculation in gold.

Among industrialized nations, a notable exception to stagnant money growth was Germany, which took measures to counteract excessive money supply growth and inflation in 1992 and ended up sending shock waves through European currency markets. After the Bundesbank raised its discount rate in mid-July 1992 to 8.75 percent, the highest since 1931, other countries in the European Monetary System (EMS) were forced to raise their rates to maintain the value of their currencies vis-a-vis the deutsche mark. Artificially high interest rates spurred deflationary measures throughout Europe. Nevertheless, European currency did not stabilize, and the European Monetary System's exchange rate mechanism (ERM) was rocked by turmoil (the Spanish peseta was devalued by 5 percent, and the pound and lira were suspended from ERM to find their own levels in the market). Given the depth of the European currency crisis, the dollar gold price underwent little change, partly because investors' "flight" funds were largely channeled into the U.S. dollar itself, not its gold equivalent, and partly because foreign exporters kept their dollar-denominated prices steady, at the expense of profit margins, in an attempt to maintain market share in the United States.

Both China and Brazil asserted intentions to gain better control over their national gold industries. The Chinese government, in mid-1994, announced intentions to shut down unauthorized markets and give the nation's central bank control of all aspects of gold production and trading; by 1999, China had increased its gold production and mining efficiency. Brazil similarly gained a better grasp of production in the Amazon.

The Official Sector. Constituted by central banks and government agencies, the official sector drew much discussion over the role and influence of its gold holdings. For the better part of the 1980s, official sector institutions were net buyers of gold, becoming marginally net buyers by 1990. Turmoil of the ERM played an additional role in highlighting the importance of reserve liquidity insured by the sales. Influxes of gold to the market by European bank sales in 1992 and again in 1999 and 2000 were not as damaging as many analysts anticipated. Unexpectedly high demand for jewelry fabrication absorbed a good deal, and a significant portion of the Dutch sale circumvented the market to land in several Asian central banks.

Forward Selling. Adapting to the pressure of low prices, many producers received prices much higher than the spot price "fixed" in London by forward selling their gold. By agreeing to deliver gold at a specified future date and price, producers not only obtained a premium to the spot market price, but also hedged against market decline. In late April 1992, North America's leading gold producer, Newmont Mining, prepaid at $336 an ounce all remaining 375,000 ounces of a 5-year, 1-million-ounce gold loan for a gain of roughly $40 million. While many analysts hailed the transaction as establishing a new bottom for the gold market, Standard & Poor's projected that most producers, forbidden by higher production costs to gamble on future gold prices, would continue to sell at available rallies, contributing to declining prices. In the 1990s, fewer companies would make profits by forward selling their production.

Supply. Even with lower price trends, Western world gold mine production reached a record 1,782 tons in 1991 and mining companies still spent more on gold exploration than for any other metal or mineral, according to the *Financial Times Mining International Year Book 1993.* Although Canada, western Europe, the Philippines, and several Latin American countries saw declines in production for 1992, overall world mine production was sustained by increased output from the three largest producers (South Africa, the United States, and Australia) and such key developing countries as Indonesia, Papua New Guinea, Ghana, and Chile; consequently Western world gold production rose by almost 4 percent to 1,841 tons in 1992. Throughout the early 1990s the average world mine production had been about 66 million troy ounces.

Starting in 1991, the dramatic upheavals in the former Soviet Union also contributed to surges in market supplies of gold, as stocks were sold for desperately needed foreign currency. The ability of Russian mines to sustain increased levels of production remained a topic of debate into the mid-1990s. The former Soviet Union produced 12 percent of the world's gold in 1993. Despite record production levels in 1992, the rate of production growth declined as compared to Western world production increases of 128 metric tons and 51 metric tons in 1989 and 1990 respectively. Many analysts cited diminished increases in production as a sign that mine supply was reaching its peak. The Gold Institute, a trade organization based in Washington, D.C., projected that world gold mine output would eventually taper off.

Background and Development

A Shining Past. Its sparkling character, beautiful hue, and unique metallurgical properties—including resistance to tarnishing and corrosion and virtual indestructibility—have set gold on the throne of coveted precious metals since early history. Ancient Egyptian, Minoan, Assyrian, and Etruscan artists produced elaborate gold artifacts as early as 3,000 B.C. As increasingly complex economic systems evolved, gold was used as a high-denomination currency and, eventually, as a backing for paper-currency systems.

The Source. Naturally occurring gold is dispersed throughout the earth's crust and is usually combined with other elements such as silver, copper, platinum, and palladium. In addition, small amounts of gold are usually recovered as a by-product in the refining of such base metals as copper and lead. Gold ores, large and rare masses of rock that are very rich in the metal, are usually quartz lodes (also called veins) or deposits that fed off of river bed gravel or quartz conglomerate beds (termed blankets or reefs). One of the best known reefs is the South African Witwatersrand system in the Transvaal and Orange Free States. Though gold occasionally appears in rock formations as visible flakes, grains or nuggets, it remains for the most part invisible until separated from ore and refined. The principal ores are calaverite, a telluride (containing tellurium) containing 40 percent gold; and sylvanite, a mixture containing 28 percent gold and variable amounts of silver.

Mining History. Ancient Near Eastern civilizations made profitable use of gold culled from alluvial deposits in and along streams. Egyptian monuments dating back to the first dynasty (c. 3100 to c. 2890 B.C.) depicted the washing of gold ores. Gold deposits were also exploited throughout regions including the Aegean, Libya, Persia (later Iran), India, and China. By the Middle Ages in Europe, gold was mined in Saxony and Austria and, to a lesser extent, Spain.

With the European colonization of the Americas in the sixteenth century, gold production reached unprecedented levels, as output from mines worked by slaves was supplemented by hoards taken from native palaces, temples, and burial sites. Well into the seventeenth and eighteenth centuries, South American mines accounted for the majority of world gold production. In the early nineteenth century, massive deposits were uncovered in Russia, making it a world leader in gold mining from the 1820s to the late 1830s.

The discovery of gold in California and Australia in the mid-nineteenth century brought a veritable explosion of gold production. Prospectors flocked to California to participate in the gold rush of 1849, earning themselves the name ''49ers.'' From 1890 to 1915, world production of gold jumped again, with major developments in Alaska, Yukon Territory, and South Africa, as well as Canada in the 1920s. Moving into the twenty-first century, primary production of gold was carried out in South Africa, Australia, Brazil, Canada, the United States, and several republics of the former Soviet Union, now the Commonwealth of Independent States (C.I.S.). Although gold markets became increasingly convoluted, steady advances in mining and refining technology—such as the development of the heap-leach process in the mid-1980s—continued to increase efficiency and permit mining of less accessible and lower-grade ores.

Mining. Gold is recovered by three basic mining methods: placer mining of alluvial deposits, lode or vein mining, and recovery as a by-product of base-metal mining. In placer mining, the oldest method, the high-density gold is separated from the lighter, siliceous material (called the matrix or gangue) in which it is found.

Though the basic principles of placer mining are essentially the same, methods of varying sophistication were developed according to the scale of particular mining operations and the types of terrain exploited. The simplest method of placer mining, practiced by the individual miners in the great American gold strikes of the nineteenth century, was panning—a technique by which several handfuls of siliceous material were placed in a pan or batea (a wooden bowl for washing gold that was commonly used in Mexico) and repeatedly washed with large amounts of water until the denser materials, including gold, were left at the center of the pan. To ''sift'' greater amounts of material, cradles (also called rockers) were developed in which material was ''rocked'' with the aid of water, and dense materials collected in riffle. Pieces of wood or iron were perpendicularly attached to the bottom and sides of the cradle.

Several other large-scale placer methods are used as well. In hydraulic mining, powerful jets of water are directed at thick beds of gravel to break them down and wash the residue through lines of sluices designed to separate gold particles. The subsequent discarding of large amounts of residue into adjacent rivers and farmlands, however, resulted in injunctions that limited the practice in America after 1880. Large-scale placer mining continued to develop, however, with the late nineteenth century invention of the gold-mining dredge in New Zealand. Originally used in the rivers of New Zealand, California, and Russia, the dredge technique later evolved into the paddock dredge, developed in the western United States, which replaced the need for riverbeds by starting with a dredging pond and continuously shifting the pond by redistributing mining wastes and tailings as the dredge moved across a designated terrain.

In addition to placer techniques, methods for underground mining of gold lode or vein deposits closely resemble the pit- and shaft-mining methods used for other metals and minerals. In general, a vertical shaft was sunk to gain access to lodes, often at great depths, by designing stopes—underground excavations wherein ore-bearing materials are produced—suitable to specific sites. The basic sequence of activities constituting the mining cycle is comprised of: rock breaking (drilling and blasting); mucking (loading); and transporting (hauling and hoisting).

Recovery. After ore is mined, its gold content must be recovered by one or several techniques that vary according to the type and amount of ore. The process of amalgamation, in use since the mid-nineteenth century, applies the principle that gold particles wetted by mercury adhere to each other and to copper plates coated with mercury. Amalgamation remained a commonly used technique for bulk recovery of gold, even as other, more efficient methods evolved.

One such method, the cyanide process, was introduced in South Africa in 1890 and became the industry norm. The process depends on a series of chemical reactions to flux off (remove by heating) base metals contained in the gold ore. Finely ground ore is first treated with dilute solution of sodium cyanide (or calcium cyanide with lime and natural oxygen), yielding a water solution of gold cyanide and sodium cyanoaurite. After being deoxygenated, the mixture was mixed with zinc dust to precipitate the gold and other metals dissolved by the cyanide. The precipitate is then treated with sulfuric acid to remove residual zinc and copper before it is again washed, dried, and melted with fluxes to dissolve any remaining copper and to fuse gold and silver. The end result, a mixture of gold and silver called doreé, is then cast in preparation for assaying (a complex process for determining purity).

The 1980s saw the development of heap leaching, a low-cost technique for recovering gold from low-grade ores, mining waste, or milling tailings, which has resulted in large new supplies of gold. The ore is crushed and ''heaped'' on large pads, where a process of sprinkling cyanide acid solution leaches the gold in bulk.

Refining. After doreé is recovered from ore, various refining processes are then applied to produce gold metal ready for the market. Two common methods are the Wohlwill process and the Miller process. The Wohlwill process uses direct and alternating currents to electrolyze doreé gold in a chloride solution. Gold on the doreé anode dissolves and accrues to the cathode, yielding gold of at least 99.95 percent purity. The silver is converted into chloride, while platinum or palladium in the anode dissolves and has to be recovered by further treating the electrolyte. The alternative Miller process is often preferred because of its faster rate of production. Chlorine is bubbled through molten doreé, converting the metals into chlorides. Although the purity of gold refined by this method—at least 99.5 percent pure—falls slightly below that of the Wohlwill process, a faster rate of production makes it the preference for most refiners.

CURRENT CONDITIONS

In 1997, 301 establishments in the industry had sales of $3.95 billion. The United States imported 257,000 kilograms of bullion and 2,540 kilograms of gold ores and concentrates for consumption in 1998. Conversely, the United States exported 430,000 kilograms of bullion and 401 kilograms of ores and concentrates.

Environmental Issues. The gold ore industry responded on numerous fronts to the environmental concerns of the 1980s and 1990s. Such issues as waste water, waste disposal, and land reclamation placed additional planning and economic pressures on mining companies, prompting many to seek development in other countries with less stringent regulations. Three environmental acts carried particular weight: The Resource Conservation and Recovery Act (RCRA) required mine owners to comply with terms of the National Pollutant Discharge Elimination System (NPDES), which called for the monitoring and testing of water runoff. The American Mining Congress challenged the rule but was overridden in a 1992 court decision.

Tensions between mining and environmental interests were epitomized in *Colorado v. Idarado Mining Co.,* decided in February of 1989 by a U.S. District Court in Colorado. Pursuant to the Comprehensive Environmental Response, Compensation, and Liability Act (CERCLA), a proposal calling for a 50-cent-per-pound tax on sodium cyanide used in gold mining was considered. These and other environmental issues put the gold ore industry on guard as it moved into the twenty-first century.

Amending the 1872 Mining Law. From the late 1980s onward, both Houses of Congress focused considerable attention on measures aimed at reforming the 1872 Mining Law governing use of federal lands by mining companies, with emphasis on increasing revenues for leasing or sales of mineral-rich government lands and on environmental protection standards for mining of such lands. Specific controversy revolved around the fee required to patent a claim on federal land; still at $5 per acre in 1993, critics argued that the country was consequently losing out on the exploitation of precious natural resources. Many experts and mining executives on the other hand, feared proposed royalty payments of 8.0 to 12.5 percent would adversely effect the gold mining industry. An economic impact study by Evans Economics indicated that an 8 percent royalty on hard-rock mining would cut into U.S. gold and silver mining by 26 and 7 percent, respectively, over a 10-year period.

In the mid-1990s, both the House and the Senate passed bills that would eliminate the ability of mining companies to take title to valuable federal lands containing gold, silver, and other ''hard rock'' minerals for only a few dollars an acre.

INDUSTRY LEADERS

In the late 1980s, the gold mining industry was hit by a merger rush, with many so-called ''brie-and-chablis'' miners—those running small and cost-effective operations supported by innovative financing—joining forces to form big and viciously competitive units. ''One plus one may equal three,'' in terms of investor interest, explained Jeffrey A. Nichols, president of American Precious Metals Advisors, in a 1991 article for *Agence France Presse.* In June 1988, for example, five Canadian companies merged to form Corona Corp., which produced about 458,000 ounces of gold that year. The 1987 merger of Placer Development, Dome Mines, and Campbell Red Lake Mines resulted in the formation of Placer Dome Inc., North America's second largest gold mining operation at the time.

Consolidation in the metals industry continued in 1996. Acquisition of Santa Fe Pacific Gold Corp. was the object of a bidding war between Newmont Mining and Homestake Mining Company in 1996.*Forbes* attributes the contraction to the relative ease of purchasing a company compared to the expenses associated with finding and mining new gold reserves.

South Africa. The world's largest producer of gold, South Africa also moved into the 1990s as the world's highest-cost producer. Due to deepening mines, an ongoing diminution of ore grades, and labor-intensive practices, South African miners resorted to self-preserving measures including high-grading (i.e., focusing first on those portions of a mine containing high-grade ore) and reductions in operating expenses across the board. The government eased restrictions on some operations to allow work on Sunday, despite continued adherence to the politically sensitive blanket ban on Sunday mining. And allying market demand with production, many houses increased forward positions on the hedging market in attempts to secure upward prices for future output. Some of the country's biggest mines included Freegold, Vaal Reefs, Driefontein, Randfontein, and Elandsrand.

An ongoing research program of the Chamber of Mines of South Africa focused on highly integrated mining systems, incorporating several options to conventional drilling and blasting cycles. The effort, initiated in the mid-1970s, yielded numerous advances, including light, hand-held hydraulic drills with performance characteristics surpassing those of their heavier, immobile counterparts; a portable gold analyzer, developed in cooperation with EG&G Oretec, which scanned faces and blasted muck piles with X-ray fluorescence to measure gold concentrations; and others. Further, as South African mines exhausted easily accessible ores and tended toward deeper levels, new technology was designed to encounter the high stresses of such environments and to maintain acceptable working conditions far underground. Most South African advances would eventually benefit the industry worldwide.

North America. Canada's Barrick Gold Corp. was the largest North American gold producer, according to*Forbes,* with an average sales growth of 38.3 percent in a five-year period, ending in 1996.

As the world's second largest gold producer, the United States shipped about $3.6 billion in gold mill bullion and placer gold and $164 million in gold concentrates in 1997; this represented an increase in value of about $400 million in bullion and placer gold and an approximate doubling of the amount of gold concentrates that had been shipped in 1992. Mine production facilities in the U.S. consisted of 252 operations with various combinations of underground, open-pit, or combination mines, most with processing plants. About 25 mines contributed 80 percent of all gold produced in the United States. Nevada, Alaska, Arizona, Colorado, and California are the leading gold mining states.

Alaska's ten largest placer mines accounted for 58 percent of the 1994 gold production. It was also in that state in 1994 that the tenth largest nugget of placer gold in Alaskan mining history was discovered. The Silverado Mines Ltd. unearthed a 41.3 ounce nugget from its Nolan Mine. Alaska produced 18,300 kilograms of gold in 1998.

Leading mines in the nation include Goldstrike, Carlin Mines Complex, Twin Creeks, Bingham Canyon, Homestake, and Nye, Nevada's Smokey Valley Common Operation. Newmont Gold Company is among the country's largest producers. Nevada produced 273,000 kilograms of gold in 1998—74 percent of the nation's total.

The industry significantly changed in July 1992 when Homestake Mining Co. acquired International Corona, making Homestake the largest gold miner outside of South Africa. Further corporate change occurred in January 1993, when Santa Fe Pacific Minerals Corp.'s "coal-for-gold" swap with Hanson's Gold Fields Mining Co. enabled Santa Fe to acquire several new mines.

The first day of commodities trading in 2000 saw gold decline in price by $6 per ounce to $283.70 per ounce. This drop was attributed to traders' dumping of gold purchased in December 1999 as a precaution in preparation for Y2K.

Europe. Although they produces little gold, European countries influenced the 1999 gold market. European banks, notably those in England, have been selling off gold reserves, a practice the United States Treasury claims it will avoid. During the last three weeks of 1999, the Dutch central bank sold three metric tons of gold, and announced plans to release a total of 100 metric tons of the metal by September 2000. The introduction of the Euro, the so-called "single currency" of Europe, makes the future of gold's role in the world's financial balance unknown and so makes gold prices, mining, and all related activities volatile.

Australia. With production of 256 tons in 1994, Australia was the third largest world gold supplier. Its leading mines include Super Pit, Boddington, Telfer, and Tick Hill; the territory of western Australia produces about 76 percent of that nation's gold. Traditionally characterized by shallow open pit mining—primarily of oxide ores—with relatively short life spans, Australian operations increasingly moved into underground mining of sulfide ores in the mid-1990s and began more extensive use of heap-leach recovery methods (the process contributed to a 13.8 percent rise in production at the Telfer mine in 1992). The Australian mine industry found itself embroiled in land tenure disputes linked to court rulings protecting traditional aboriginal lands from mining exploration and development.

Other traditional gold producing nations include the Commonwealth of Independent States (C.I.S.), China, Brazil, Papua New Guinea, Indonesia, Chile, Ghana, and Columbia. C.I.S. production was difficult to precisely assess in the mid-1990s due to a combination of factors, including new payment systems in most C.I.S. mines, delays in payments, and the impact of inflation and currency depreciation. China also increased the size and productivity of its mines and the modernity of its equipment.

WORKFORCE

With trends in the early 1990s toward price decline and austerity measures to increase efficiency while lowering cost, the gold industry expected bleak new employment prospects. In South Africa alone, over 36,000 gold-mine positions were eliminated in 1991, with another 15,000 following in June 1992. In a June 1991 *Agence France Presse* article, outgoing South African Chamber of Mines President, Clive Knobbs, warned that "the implication of additional gold mine closures presents a depressing picture," with possible loss of 136,000 additional jobs if 10 ailing mines were to close down.

Employment in this sector in the United States was at approximately the same level in 1992 and 1997 with 17,500 employees in 1997 (18,200 persons in 1992); payrolls were comparable with $778 million in 1997 ($784 million in 1992, which represented a doubling from 1984 figures), according to U.S. Census Bureau statistics. The 15,500 production workers in the industry made an average hourly wage of $21.07 in 1997.

To recover ore from complex deposits that cannot be mined or leached by conventional methods, pressure oxidation and bio-oxidation processes have been developed and patented to extract refractory gold by environmentally friendly methods. A $3-million investment and five years of study at the Twin Creeks deposit operated by Newmont Gold Co. near Golconda, Nevada, yielded a patented process requiring careful design of the milling process to blend the several types of ore present in the deposit. These oxidation methods are also expected to be adopted by other mining ventures.

FURTHER READING

Brierley, Corale L. "Bacterial oxidation: master key to unlock refractory gold ores?" *Engineering & Mining Journal* May 1995.

Brimelow, Peter. ''What is gold worth?'' *Forbes Magazine*4 October 1999. Available from http://www.forbes.com/forbes/99/1004/6408073a.htm.

Cope, Louis W. ''Sage mill patent turns waste to ore.'' *Engineering & Mining Journal* January 1998.

Knight-Ridder Financial/Commodity Research Bureau. *The CRB Commodity Yearbook 1995.* John Wiley & Sons, Inc., 1995.

''Metals.'' *Forbes.* 13 January 1997.

Reuters Limited. ''Gold Drops in First Trading Day of 2000.''4 January 2000. Available from http://dailynews.yahoo.com/h/nm/20000104/bs/markets_commodities_1.html.

Reuters Limited. ''Summers: US Not Selling Any Gold Reserves.''8 January 2000. Available from http://dailynews.yahoo.com/h/nm/20000108/bs/economy_gold_2.html.

Reuters Limited. ''Supply deficits to support gold and silver CRU.''12 January 2000. Available from http://biz.yahoo.com/rf/000112/12.html.

U.S. Census Bureau. ''Gold Ore Mining.'' *1997 Economic Census: Mining Industry Series.* December 1999.

U.S. Department of the Interior. *Minerals Yearbook: Metals and Minerals,* Washington, DC: GPO, nd.

U.S. Geological Survey. ''Mineral Industry Surveys.'' Washington, DC: GPO, 1999.

SIC 1044

SILVER ORES

This category covers establishments primarily engaged in mining, milling, or otherwise preparing silver ores, including the production of bullion at the mine or mill site.

NAICS CODE(S)

212222 (Silver Ore Mining)

INDUSTRY SNAPSHOT

Most world silver is produced as a byproduct or coproduct in the mining of other metals—such as copper and gold, and to a lesser degree, lead and zincem. The outlook for silver production tends to overlap with the outlooks for other metals. Primary producers, which account for roughly one-third of world silver supply, are more vulnerable than diversified metal producers to swings in the historically volatile silver market.

Silver entered the 1990s with a downward trend in price, suggesting a dreary outlook for many primary producers. The average Comex silver price of $5.32 for 1996 represented a fall of 24 percent from $7.01 in 1987. The sustained effects of a worldwide recession fueled a continuing stream of deflationary news that precipitated lower silver prices by reducing investors' interest in silver's traditional role as a hedge against inflation. With market prices often dipping below bare-minimum production costs, many primary producers were forced to close or cut back operations. Though prices declined through the early 1990s, silver's market fundamentals continued to improve, with constrained supply and increasing demand. In addition, fabrication demand remained solid in spite of the weak worldwide economy. Recognizing the seeming disparity between investor disinterest and silver's market potential, many analysts projected new rallies for the metal with the onset of economic recovery.

By 1993, the downward trend in silver prices steadied after bottoming out at $3.51 per ounce on February 22, 1991, the lowest price in 18 years. Greater interest on the part of investors prompted a partial return to the disproportionate rallies and collapses that have traditionally characterized speculative interest in the metal. While prices fell below $3.60 per ounce in February 1993, the rest of the year showed new promise. By March, prices had topped the $4 per ounce threshold, riding largely on the back of a rising gold price. From mid-March to mid-May, silver prices rose to $4.75 an ounce and then jumped again to over $5 an ounce in July, to hover just above the much-watched $5 level for the rest of 1993 and into 1994. This was welcome news to silver mining operations across the country and worldwide. In May 1995, the price broke the $6 barrier for one day for the first time since 1989. Throughout 1995 and 1996, the prices remained comparatively stable between $4.86 and $5.79 per troy ounce. Most analysts attributed the boost in performance to optimism about the U.S. and European economies and to buying activity among fund investors in the Middle East and United States. Some analysts expected continued upward price patterns with inflationary economic growth, while others regarded such precious metals rallies as temporary developments. The average silver price for 1998 was $5.10 per troy ounce. The industry shipped $121.5 million worth of silver in 1997.

ORGANIZATION AND STRUCTURE

Most silver is produced from argentiferous ores—the sulfides of lead, copper, and zinc—which may contain varying amounts of silver, depending on their location. Silver is also found as deposits of native silver (usually in alloy form), as sylvanite (gold and silver telluride) ores, and in many naturally occurring minerals, including galena (lead sulfide), argentite (silver sulfide), cerargyrite (silver chloride) and others.

Extraction and Refining. Various methods are employed to extract silver or a combination of silver and gold from ores, scrap, alloys, and used photographic materials. As most silver is a by-product of copper, lead, and zinc ore treatment, the precise process differs with each ore. In every case, however, the silver is finally collected in the form of crude silver or silver-gold bullion. The former is refined by a process involving smelting in a furnace with lead oxide, fluxes, and a reducing agent to produce a purer alloy of silver and gold called doreé. An oxidized lead residue melts away in the process.

Two primary methods—electrolysis and parting—are used to separate silver and gold in silver-gold bullion. In electrolysis, electric current is passed through a silver nitrate water solution, with silver, gold bullion, doreé serving as the anode. In the parting method, the doreé is dissolved in a bath of hot concentrated sulfuric or nitric acid. Gold is recovered from the residue, while the clear solution is treated with ferrous sulfate to precipitate the silver, which is filtered off and melted into bars. In 1996, approximately 2,000 tons of silver were recovered from recycled materials according to the U.S. Geological Survey, Mineral Commodity Summaries.

BACKGROUND AND DEVELOPMENT

Silver's aesthetic and practical value, as well as its relative rarity, have earned it a position among precious metals for thousands of years. As a noble metal, it resists oxidation and demonstrates excellent properties of conductivity, making it particularly useful in both ornamentation and as a practical conductor of electricity and heat for numerous applications. Although it tarnishes easily in the presence of certain sulfur compounds and scratches easily in its pure form, it is the whitest of all metals and an excellent reflector of light—capable of reflecting up to 95 percent of incident light rays in the visible spectrum. Silver's chemical symbol, Ag, was obtained from the Latin name for silver, *Argentum*, which means bright and shining.

Early History. Silver was one of the first metals after gold and copper to be humanly molded, and silver artifacts have been found in Near Eastern tombs dating back to 4,000 B.C. The Romans developed a method of separating silver from ore by a heating process, which was used into the Middle Ages, when silver-copper mines were exploited in central Europe. By the sixteenth century, the Spaniards had discovered enormous silver and gold deposits in Central and South America. Mexico largely supported Spanish colonial wealth until its independence in the early nineteenth century. Into the 1990s however, much of the silver remained, leaving Mexico the world leader in silver production. Minas de las Rayas, a mine that began operating in 1558, as well as other mines and general sites, still produced silver into the 1990s. Until the discovery of the Comstock Lode strike in the Sierra Nevada area of the United States, Central and South America almost exclusively supplied world silver. Moving into the twentieth century, Western world silver leaders were Mexico, the United States, Canada, Peru, and Bolivia.

CURRENT CONDITIONS

U.S. silver mine production was valued at $338 million from about 76 mines in 1998, an increase of more than $200 million from the previous year. The Silver Institute, a Washington D.C.-based industry research group, projected that world silver production would reach 14,347 metric tons in 1994, followed by 14,622 metric tons in 1995 and 14,912 metric tons in 1996. (One metric ton is equivalent to 1,000 kilograms and to 32,151 troy ounces.) The actual production, according to the Silver Institute, was 14,266 tons for 1994, and 15,073 for 1995. According to the U.S. Geological Survey, world silver production was estimated at 16,200 metric tons in 1998, a slight decrease from 1997's 16,400 tons. Given the magnitude of price declines however, silver output remained relatively resilient due to the large portion—up to 70 percent—typically produced as a byproduct of copper, lead, zinc, and gold mining activity.

Silver Supply and Stocks. The early 1990s also saw dramatic reductions in secondary silver supply. Compared with the early 1980s, silver supply from scrap during the 1990s fell to approximately half its former level and hovered around the 100-million-ounce (3,215-metric-ton) mark. Reasons for the decline included lower prices, the prevalence of lower-content scrap, and restrictive sales policies on official reserves. Most secondary recovery came from photographic scrap materials, which remained economically recoverable even at $3.50 an ounce, while recovery of the lower silver content in electronic scrap became less desirable.

Other secondary sources also declined. Most notably, the U.S. Defense Department's National Stockpile inventory of surplus silver was reduced from nearly 4,300 tons in 1982 to nearly 1,100 tons in 1998. Several regulations were enacted in the early 1990s to control the rate and nature of the National Defense Stockpile: a 1992 law restricted the disposal of silver from the stockpile to coinage programs or government contractors for use in government projects. Between 1981 and 1992, 65 million ounces of stockpile silver were used for coinage programs and roughly 3.5 million ounces were delegated to contractors, according to the Silver Institute. In 1992 Dennis E. Wheeler of the Idaho-based Coeur D'Alene Mines Corp. predicted that the national defense stockpile's supply of silver would be gone by 1997, at which time the U.S. Mint—a unit of the U.S. Department of the Treasury, which since 1985, has consumed roughly 45 percent of stockpile silver—would buy the metal from domestic producers. The Silver Institute forecasts depletion of silver stocks in the first quarter of the twenty-first

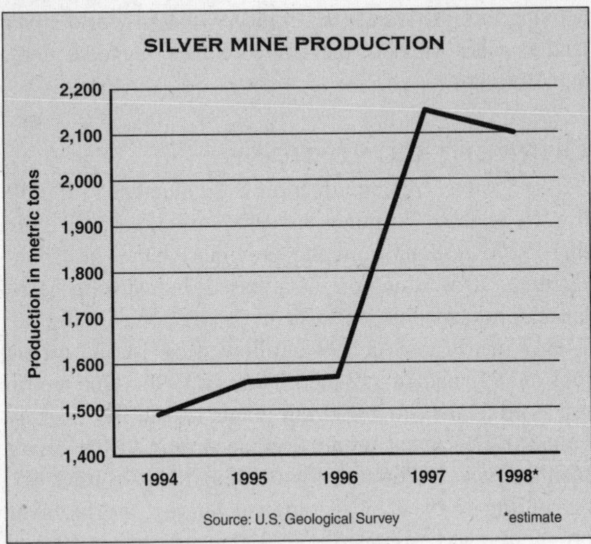

century if the yearly average reduction continues as previously illustrated.

Even while diminishing supplies and fairly stable production cast a positive light on supply/demand ratios for silver, many wary investors pointed to massive visible supplies that they feared would virtually flood the market. A 1993 study conducted by Charles River Associates and published by the Silver Institute, however, indicated that only a small proportion of the worldwide silver stocks were not readily available to the market. Total aboveground stocks were estimated at 19.1 billion ounces: 1.4 billion ounces of bullion, 1.2 billion ounces of coins and medallions, and a majority 16.5 billion ounces in silverware and art forms. Of that total, the study estimated that the only ''truly available stocks,'' under realistic market conditions, were minute.

Consumption. Through the early 1990s, silver consumption continued to grow at a moderate pace, slowed by domestic recession and sluggish European economies while sustained by the low cost of raw materials and by the emerging economies of Southeast Asia. World consumption of silver was 588.4 million ounces in 1991, up 0.5 percent from 585.4 million ounces the preceding year, according to Handy & Harman. The United States and Germany accounted for substantial increases in coinage and were joined by India in significantly increasing silver use for industrial purposes.

In the fabrication of silverware and jewelry, 1998 worldwide demand amounted to 244.4 million ounces, an 11 percent drop from 1997. Demand in this sector dropped 17 percent in 1998 in India alone, where jewelry, silver gift items, and silverware make up two-third's of that nation's demand for the metal; this was significant enough to affect worldwide assessments of demand. In 1996, demand in the jewelry and silverware area had increased 15.6 percent with another increase of 5.3 percent in 1997. The 1998 decline was attributed to silver prices and poor economic conditions in India and East Asia. In the United States, demand for the fabrication sector rose to 214.4 million ounces, a rise of 13 percent. For the tenth year in a row, 1998 fabrication demand was greater than the supply from mine production and recycling. The gap was bridged by supply hedging on the part of suppliers and probably some disinvestment. Sales of designer jewelry and white metals including sterling silver were strong in 1998, and these fashion trends and the supply of disposable income are expected to continue well past 2000.

Industrial consumption in the United States also continued to grow but at a rate that was not expected to materially affect prices. Worldwide, the industrial sector continued to be the largest consumer of silver in 1998. The photography market retained its leading position as a silver end-user (28 percent of industrial demand in 1998, for example). This was expected to drop, however, as digital imaging becomes more widespread. Other significant markets included: electrical and electronic products—20 percent in 1996; sterling ware, electroplated ware, and jewelry—10 percent; and brazing alloys and solders—5 percent. The metal is also used for hundreds of other applications. Its excellent and long-lasting conductivity, even in high temperatures, makes it the material of choice in batteries requiring little space, long life and high voltage, as in hearing aids, space technology, submarines, and portable television sets. Silver's germicidal properties make it particularly suitable for medical applications such as bone-replacement plates and sutures, antiseptic drainage tubes, and water purifiers. Its reflectivity also makes silver a perfect coating for high-quality mirrors. Among other uses, it serves as a freeze-resistant alloy in diesel locomotives and airplanes and is used as a colloidal catalyst in various vapor-phase organic chemical reactions.

The particularly volatile nature of silver prices has been partly attributed to the metal's dual role as both a precious metal and an industrial material. As a precious metal, silver benefits from the same interests that influence gold prices (and other precious metals) as hedges against inflation. Thus, upturns in gold prices starting in 1993 were accompanied by similar patterns in silver prices; yet silver enjoyed a bigger boost relative to gold because of the notion that, as an industrial metal, it could benefit the most in the event of an economic recovery, according to Bette Raptopoulos, from Prudential Securities Inc. in *American Metal Market.*

Silver-Free Photography. Silver-halide salts (including silver chloride, silver iodide, and silver bromide) darken when they are exposed to light. As a result of this property, silver halide is coated on photographic film, paper, and plates, which makes the photographic industry the largest end-user by far for industrial silver. New developments in photography have some members of the silver industry uneasy. Some analysts fear that new technologies in electronic imaging that do not depend on silver-based chemistry will phase out traditional photographic practices, causing significant losses to the silver industry. Other industry observers, however, feel that such new technologies may actually offer new and related growth opportunities to silver-based imaging.

The silver industry showed signs of a possible upswing in 1994, after more than six years of price decline, but the price of silver has remained between $4.86 and $5.79 per troy ounce. The unpredictable metal's standing is predicated on a combination of complex factors, including inflationary trends, continued fundamentals favoring constrained supply and increased demand, prices of base metals from which it was produced, and investor interest.

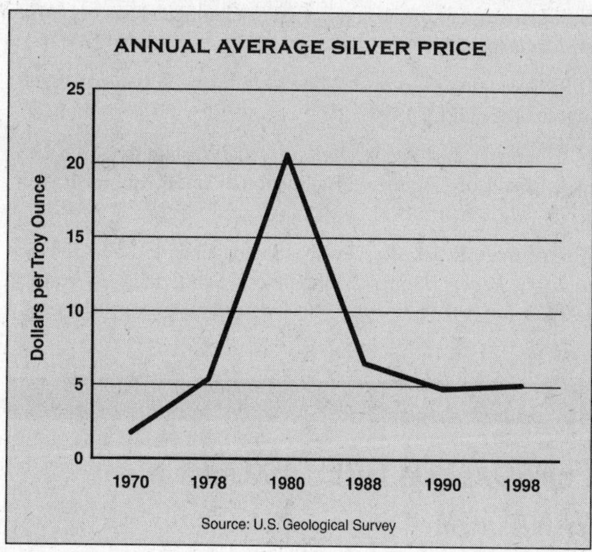

INDUSTRY LEADERS

Nevada was the largest of the 16 silver-producing states in 1998, with Alaska second, Arizona third, and Idaho fourth. According to the United States Geological Survey, 30 fabricators were responsible for 90 percent of the silver used in art and industry.

According to the U.S. Geological Survey, 1995's leaders in silver production were:

- Idaho: Black Pine Mine (nearly 2 tons of silver) and Lucky Friday mine (52 tons of silver)
- Montana: Montana Tunnels Mine (33 tons of silver) and Zortman-Landusky Mine (16 tons of silver)
- Nevada: Battle Mountain complex (6 tons of silver), McCoy and Cove Mine (27 tons of silver), and Rochester Mine (202 tons of silver)

WORKFORCE

In 1997, the 16 American operations producing crude silver ore, silver concentrate, mill bullion, and placer silver employed about 800 employees with a total annual payroll of $32 million. Only five of the 16 operations employed more than 20 people. The 700 production workers in this industry earned an average hourly wage of $19.19.

AMERICA AND THE WORLD

International supply in 1998 was led by Mexico, Peru, and the United States. Australia (900 metric tons) and Canada (1,200 metric tons) were also major producers according to 1996 figures. Mexico had produced 2,400 metric tons in 1995 and 1996. Even so, Mexican mines suffered dramatically from lower silver prices, particularly because they produced silver primarily as a byproduct or coproduct of lead and zinc, two base metals that also suffered price declines in the 1990s. United States mines, on the other hand, were less affected because they generally extracted silver as a byproduct of copper, which remained relatively profitable.

With the significant political changes in Eastern Europe of the early 1990s, silver production data were available from those regions for the first time. The Silver Institute estimated production in those so-called transitional economies as follows: the Commonwealth of Independent States (C.I.S.—the republics that were formerly the Soviet Union) at 39 million troy ounces from 1992 to 1996; Poland at 28.9 million troy ounces for the same period; China at 6.4 million troy ounces; Bulgaria at 3.1 million troy ounces; and North Korea at 1.6 million troy ounces.

Between 1994 and 1997, Canada accounted for 26 percent of American imports, Mexico accounted for 24 percent, Germany for 9 percent, and Peru for 8 percent. The United States imported 3,140 metric tons of silver and exported 2,490 tons in 1998.

FURTHER READING

Dun & Bradstreet Marketplace, *Industry: Silver Ores,* Marketplace Information Holdings, Inc., 1995. Available from http://www.mktplace.com/members/anal/reports/rpt1044.htm.

Kahaner, Larry, ed. ''World Mine Production of Silver, 1994-1998.'' *The Silver Institute,* Washington, DC: 1996.

Reese, Robert G. *Mineral Commodity Summaries, U.S. Department of the Interior, U.S. Geological Survey,* February 1997.

———. *Minerals Yearbook, U.S. Department of the Interior, U.S. Geological Survey,* 1996.

The Silver Institute. *World Silver Survey.* Washington, DC: 1996.

U.S. Census Bureau. ''Silver Ore Mining.'' *1997 Economic Census: Manufacturing Industry Series.* December 1999.

U.S. Department of the Interior. U.S. Geological Survey. *Mineral Industry Surveys.* 14 March 1997.

U.S. Geological Survey. ''Mineral Industry Surveys.'' Washington, DC: GPO, 1999.

*U.S. Industry and Trade Outlook, 1998*Washington, DC: U.S. Department of Commerce/International Trade Administration, 1998.

Zimmerman, R., *et al.* ''Jewelry Sector Update.'' *The Jewelry Industry Report* Janney Montgomery Scott, Inc., 25 August 1999.

SIC 1061

FERROALLOY ORES, EXCEPT VANADIUM

This category covers establishments primarily engaged in mining, milling, or otherwise preparing ferroalloy ores, except vanadium. The mining of manganiferous ores valued chiefly for their iron content is classified in **SIC 1011: Iron Ores.** Establishments primarily engaged in mining vanadium ore are classified in **SIC 1094: Uranium-Radium-Vanadium Ores,** and those mining titanium ore are classified in **SIC 1099: Miscellaneous Metal Ores, Not Elsewhere Classified.** The ferroalloy classification includes the following ores: chromite, chromium, cobalt, columbite, ferberite, huebnerite, manganese, manganite, molybdenite, molybdenum, molybdite, nickel, psilomelane, pyrolusite, rhodochrosite, scheelite, tantalite, tantalum, tungsten, wolframite, and wulfenite. While production and consumption of particular ores can vary as much as their names, industry-wide trends tend to influence ferroalloys as an overall group of ores serving related applications responding to similar market forces.

NAICS Code(s)

212234 (Copper Ore and Nickel Ore Mining)
212299 (Other Metal Ore Mining)

Industry Snapshot

The ferroalloy industry is serviced by dozens of international mining companies, often with special subsidiaries responsible for specific alloys. As ferroalloys are primarily used in the production of steel, the state of worldwide steel production impacts that of the ferroalloy industry. Ferroalloys serve three main functions in steel: they help eliminate undesired elements such as oxygen and sulfur; they impart special characteristics, such as heat- and corrosion-resistance and strength; and they neutralize undesirable elements in the steel.

Starting in 1995, steel production began a decline that has affected prices and demand for many ferroalloys. By 1997 the steel market appeared to have settled down and prices were on the verge of rising, which in turn could have a domino effect on the ferroalloys industries. After experiencing a steady decline in the first half of the 1990s, the ferroalloys markets appear to be leveling off but with few signs of future growth.

From 1989 onward, ferroalloys underwent substantial market decline, largely spurred by a decline in steel production in the United States and other Western nations. Several economic factors placed continued strain on steel—repercussions from the oversupply and price boom of the late 1980s, a flood of exports from Commonwealth of Independent States (CIS) and China, and the lingering effects of worldwide economic recession in the early 1990s. A glut of low-priced imports forced many ferroalloy companies, including world giants, to drastically reduce production and contend with losses and severely reduced profits. Moving into 1993, established market economy countries (EMEC) did not compensate for these factors with sufficient reduction of output, resulting in growing inventories and uncomfortably low commodity prices. From 1993 onward, stainless steel producers in the Western World experienced an annual growth of about 10 percent per year, forcing many to operate at full capacity. However, ferroalloy production forged ahead in anticipation of future demand a little too soon, causing a market flooded by ferroalloys.

By the mid-1990s, industry analysts anticipated a turnaround in the nonfuels minerals industry, particularly in metals. With modernized plants, lower operating costs, and more efficient workforces, producers were poised to capitalize on moderate economic expansion. Forecasts for the late 1990s indicated increases in commercial building construction, infrastructure projects, and the motor vehicle industry, spurring demand for many types of steel and, consequently, for ferroalloys.

Organization and Structure

The Market. Like mining in general, the ferroalloy industry is organized along the complex lines of worldwide consumption and supply, with different countries consuming different metals—in varying quantities—according to the demands of their industrial bases and capital goods markets. The London Metal Exchange (LME) served as the general barometer of price fluctuation in metals trading, reflecting the ever-shifting balance between world demand and supply of those commodities.

Ferroalloys and the Former Soviet Union. Due to the complexity of international forces governing consumption and supply, however, the industry's organization seemed anything but organized, as evidenced by the turmoil following the collapse of the Soviet Union in the early 1990s. Before that event, the metal mining industry was still coping with the adverse effects of a recession taxing the Anglo-Saxon economies and eventually Japan and Germany as well. For the most part, metal mining companies weathered the storm by repairing their balance sheets with high metals prices in the late 1980s. Industry stocks were cautiously maintained at low levels, while the rapid growth of newly-developing countries translated into new demand for most metals minerals and ferroalloys.

The collapse of the Soviet Union, however, placed tremendous strain on the supply side of the metals industry with no apparent let-up in sight. Seeking hard currency to prop up its staggering economy, the Commonwealth of Independent States (CIS) began aggressively exporting any commodities of immediate value, with LME-traded metals and precious metals at the top of the list. The old Soviet Union had been a leading customer for ores as well as the world's leading producer of iron ore, lead, manganese, nickel, and potash. The crisis prompted convulsions in the economies of Russia and other republics and caused severe industrial production problems, effecting a virtual halt to imports of minerals and metals. Consequently, Western stocks soared and prices plummeted, forcing Western mining companies to slash capital spending and exploration expenditure to a minimum and absorb serious short-term losses.

While the CIS may lessen supply of metals exports, Chinese producers fill in the holes, resulting in an abundance of metal on the market. Many analysts predicted that the CIS would not only develop substantial new markets for metals, but that it would become net importers as well. China's ore grades are lower than in Western countries, and mine output is falling, while production costs rise. For example, the worldwide market continues to rely on China and the CIS for most of its tungsten. Still, unknown stockpile levels have left questions in the minds of analysts as to how much and how long an oversupply situation will last for ferroalloys. In mid-1996, it became apparent that production of at least tungsten, and quite possibly other metals, in the CIS, which had declined between 1990 and 1994, was experiencing an increase in global demand. That higher demand is expected to spur additional production. Tungsten production in the CIS totaled 9,500 metric tons in 1995, a 9 percent increase from the 8,800 metric tons of 1994. Any shortfall in Chinese production was expected to be taken care of by CIS producers.

BACKGROUND AND DEVELOPMENT

The mid-nineteenth century saw an explosion in U.S. mining, with the discovery of great mineral deposits, the development of transcontinental railroads, and a rapidly growing population. Responding to such growth, the American Institute of Mining and Metallurgical Engineers (AIME) was founded in 1871 (it was eventually renamed the American Institute of Mining, Metallurgical and Petroleum Engineers in 1956). Since that time, the ferroalloy industry became fundamentally international in scope, depending on worldwide producers to stabilize the delicate balance between consumption and supply and thereby stabilize prices.

From the mid-1980s onward, several new factors further influenced the industry. Roughly 100 years after the beginning of the industrial revolution that proved so bountiful for ferroalloys, many western countries, particularly the United States, began a trend of deindustrialization, with employment in industrial areas shifting toward service-oriented sectors. In 1986, the U.S. Department of Labor included ferroalloy ores mining on a list of industries that were expected to experience more than a 20 percent decline in output over a 15-year period.

With diminished threat of war with the former Soviet Union, attention shifted to management of the so-called ''peace dividend,'' which included some funds that would have been formerly allotted to ferroalloys in the defense industry. In 1992, the U.S. Department of Defense announced an ambitious plan to sell many of its stockpiles of ferroalloys, including cobalt, nickel, manganese metal and ore, ferromanganese, derrochrome, chrome ore, and silicon carbide. Debate continued over the wisdom of the sales, however, spurring mixed reactions from legislators and ferroalloy industry groups. The government stockpiles have been severely depleted since that 1992 decision, and sales now have little effect on the market.

Environmental Issues. As world attention shifted increasingly toward environmental issues, the ferroalloy industry responded on numerous fronts. Issues such as waste water, waste disposal, and land reclamation placed additional planning and economic pressures on mining companies, prompting many to seek development in other countries with less stringent regulations. The minerals industry was primarily controlled by three environmental acts: The Resource Conservation and Recovery Act of 1976 (RCRA), regulating both hazardous and nonhazardous solid waste; The Clean Water Act (CWA), regulating surface water discharges; and The Clean Air Act (CAA), regulating air emissions. Many clauses included in these and other environmental acts met with industry resistance due to increased costs of doing business or even prohibition of some practices deemed standard in the past. In 1990, for example, the EPA required mine owners to comply with terms of the National Pollutant Discharge Elimination System, which called for the monitoring and testing of storm water runoff. The American Mining Congress challenged the rule but was overridden in a 1992 court decision. The result of such proposed legislation has been to force companies to take extra environmental precautions, incurring an added expense over the cost of producing the same metals in other countries. The effect has been to put American companies at a slight disadvantage, at least.

Federal Lands. Another factor affecting the development of the ferroalloy mining industry—and, indeed, mining in general—was the availability of federal lands, which traditionally accounted for about 75 percent of U.S. metals mining. As minerals exploration and mining were dependent on access to these lands, growing efforts to limit or restrict access to federal lands for mining have understandably captured the industry's attention. Natural resource development prescriptions stipulated by the U.S. Forest Service and the Bureau of Land Management grew in scope. From the mid-1960s to mid-1990s, more than 96 million acres of federal lands were withdrawn from mineral entry and placed in the National Wilderness Preservation System. Compounding these debates about mining on federal land were ongoing reinterpretations of key elements in the 1872 Mining Law that determined issues of self-initiation, free access, and security of tenure for mining operations on federal lands.

CURRENT CONDITIONS

The early 1990s saw a deterioration of the domestic ferroalloy industry performance, reflecting a fall in Western world steel production, a sustained flood of exports from the CIS and China, and a backlash from oversupply dating back to the late 1980s. World crude steel output for the first 10 months of 1996 was down by 1.4 percent. Prices, and the purchase of, ferroalloys should reflect that trend. Specifically, specialty steel production saw a decline in 1996, forcing Western molybdenum production to fall. Surveying the specific performances of key metals—nickel, chromium, molybdenum, cobalt, manganese, niobium, and tungsten—yields a clearer picture of the ferroalloy industry in general.

Nickel. A highly ductile and heat- and corrosion-resistant metal, nickel is used primarily in stainless and specialty steel production, plating, and high-temperature superalloys. Overall nickel production was expected to rise in 1997 by 30,000 tons to 730,000 tons, according to *American Metal Market.* But this amount is unlikely to satisfy the rise in consumption. Global production in the early 1990s was headed by Russia and Canada, followed by Australia, New Caledonia, and Indonesia. The only U.S. producer, Cominco Resources International Ltd.'s Glenbrook Nickel in Riddle, Oregon, was forced to temporarily curtail operations to cope with low metal prices.

Chromium. Resistant to tarnish and corrosion, Chromium—which derives its name from chrome, the Greek word for color, due to the lustrous nature of its compounds—is primarily used to produce stainless steel and to harden steel alloys. It is also used as corrosion-resistant decorative plating and as a pigment in glass. It is found primarily in chromite, a combination of iron, chromium, and oxygen. Prices for chromium products slowly rose in 1996 after a long sea-saw (1989-1993), only to come crashing down. A 15 percent increase in production capacity worldwide did not help the situation, especially when faced with a tight steel situation. In the early 1990s, South Africa led the world in mining of chromite and high-carbon ferrochrome, the chief ferrochromium product, followed by Yugoslavia and Turkey. South African producers expanded their production capacity between 1995 and 1997, with four existing ferrochrome producers bringing out almost 800,000 metric tons per year on-stream. Additionally, a joint venture between China's Eastern Asia Metal Investment and Corp. and Northern Province Development Corp. in South Africa should produce new ferrochrome capacity. In addition, near St. Petersburg, Russia, TDR International was in the process of building 16.5-MW furnaces, capable of producing as much as 150,000 tons per year.

Molybdenum. First used widely in World War I to toughen armor plating, molybdenum is commonly used as an alloy to strengthen steel and inhibit rust and corrosion. Accounting for approximately 90 percent of world output, the United States, Chile, Canada, and the CIS were the world's leading producers in the 1990s. In the United States, the major producers were Climax Molybdenum Co., a subsidiary of Amax Inc.; Cyprus Amax Minerals Company; Kennecott Corporation; Magma Copper Co.; and Montana Resources Inc. The world's three largest producers were Cyprus, Climax, and Corporacion Nacional del Cobre de Chile (Codelco), Chile's state-owned giant. Western demand for molybdenum fell from a record 235 million pounds in 1995 to about 220 million pounds in 1996.

Cobalt. In use since at least 2250 B.C. as a colorant in Persian glass, cobalt is mainly used in high-temperature alloys, magnetic alloys, and hard-facing alloys resistant to abrasion. The largest producers of cobalt were Zaire (with an output of 6,625 tons), Zambia, and Canada, which sold primarily to the United States because of economic shipping arrangements. Cuba was also a large cobalt producer—one market research firm estimated its holdings at 29 percent of world reserves—but remained unable to sell its materials in the United States. Although a major consumer of cobalt, the United States stopped producing the metal in 1971. The early 1990s market was characterized by several salient factors: a significant reduction of cobalt consumption for military and aerospace applications; the growing importance of Russian cobalt, which was typically of a lower grade but drew business away from African suppliers by virtue of its lower price; and new chemical applications for the metal as regulations on desulfuration of diesel fuels increasingly took effect and drove use of cobalt as a petroleum catalyst.

Manganese. In addition to its critical role in steel production, manganese is used in dry-cell batteries, pig iron, animal feed, fertilizers, and other chemicals. South Africa and the CIS held more than 80 percent of world resources in the early 1990s. In the late 1990s, the United States, which had no significant manganese mine production of its own, imported supplies primarily from Gabon, Brazil, Australia, and Mexico.

Niobium. Commonly known as columbium, niobium is one of the refractory metals primarily used as a microalloying element in high-strength and stainless steels. It is also a common ingredient in superalloys, popular in the aerospace industry, and carbide cutting tools. Three mines were almost exclusively responsible for world niobium production: the Araxa mine and smelter of Companhia Brasileira de Metalurgia e Mineralcao (CBMM) and the Catalao mine operated by a subsidiary of the Anglo American Group, both in Brazil; and the Niobec, Quebec, mine in Quebec, Canada.

Tungsten. Also called wolfram, tungsten is found in wolframite and scheelite ores and is primarily used as a carbide to harden metal-cutting tools and as a alloying agent in steel making. Its good thermal and electric conductivity also make it very suitable for electric contact points and lamp filaments. In the 1990s, China led in world tungsten production, followed by Australia, Austria, Bolivia, Brazil, Burma, Canada, North and South Korea, Peru, Portugal, Spain, and Thailand. The United States played a relatively small role in the tungsten industry, with two plants for the production of tungsten concentrated in California and a handful of processors elsewhere. In late 1996, exports of tungsten from Russia and China fell. China is the world's largest tungsten exporting country, with a current mine output at almost 80 percent of the world's supply. The U.S. tungsten market was expected to bounce back in 1997, according to *American Metal Market,* to strong levels last seen in 1995. U.S. demand for primary tungsten was forecast at 8,400 tons for 1997, up from 8,200 tons in 1996.

RESEARCH AND TECHNOLOGY

Many employment opportunities in the ferroalloy industry involve implementation or operation of new tools and technologies designed for greater efficiency, safety, and environmental benefit. In addition to innovative mine environments to maximize safety, transportation, communication, and yield of large mine operations, companies and specialty metal mining services drew on new computer technology to assist in all phases of industry activity. In 1990, for example, Australia's Mount Isa mine used an Integrated Mine Planning system (IMPS)—a computer-aided drafting (CAD) system for geological interpretation and modeling. The system enabled engineers to integrate information from various departments (geology, mine design, and survey) and evaluate complex criteria—such as test clearances, drivers' lines of sight, and mobile equipment specs and compatibility all at once. Other mining companies began using a new system designed to rapidly determine ore contacts and grades in underground metal mining. By measuring differences in the physical characteristics of relatively small mineral samples culled from drill holes, the system vastly reduced the amount of expensive core drilling sampling and assaying required for mine planning. Sandvik Rock Tools made further developments in drilling systems, developing a computer program to simulate drilling conditions through all types of percussive drilling conditions. Graphically displayed results and data are then used to develop optimum rock drilling tools and to maximize drilling energy efficiency in a wide range of tools.

FURTHER READING

Fineberg, Seth. "Elkem Keeps Eye Open for Manganese Ore Deal." *American Metal Market,* 29 August 1996.

———. "Cuba's Nickel, Cobalt Attract Gencor." *American Metal Market,* 19 November 1996.

Larkin, Kay, ed. *Financial Times International Yearbooks: Mining.* United Kingdom: Longman, 1992.

Ozols, Victor. "Cobalt Alloy Makers Mull Capacity Boost." *American Metal Market,* 28 January 1997.

U.S. Census Bureau. *1997 Economic Census.* "Mining-Industry Series." Washington, D.C.: GPO, November 1999. Available from http://www.census.gov.

SIC 1081

METAL MINING SERVICES

This classification covers establishments primarily engaged in performing metal mining services for others on a contract or fee basis, such as the removal of overburden, strip mining for metallic ores, prospect and test drilling, and mine exploration and development. Establishments that have complete responsibility for operating mines for others on a contract or fee basis are classified according to the product mined rather than as metal mining services. Establishments primarily performing hauling services are classified under transportation.

NAICS CODE(S)

213114 (Support Activities for Metal Mining)
541360 (Geophysical Surveying and Mapping Services)

INDUSTRY SNAPSHOT

While most large national and international mining companies retain private divisions specially outfitted for mining services, even the largest companies continue to contract specialty mining services companies for jobs requiring particular expertise, extra speed, or outside consultation. Total sales for the industry topped $11 million in 1997.

In 1999 one of the leading U.S. companies for metal mining services was Battle Mountain Gold Co., of Houston, Texas, a public, stand-alone company specializing in gold mine exploration and mining of gold and silver and metal mining services, with 1999 sales of $228.2 million. The company produces more than 890,000 ounces of gold per year. Other leaders were Anglo American plc, with 1998 sales of $1.0 million, and Newmont Mining Corporation, with 1999 sales of $1.4 billion. Newmont's subsidiary, Newmont Gold, is the largest U.S. gold producer.

Organization and Structure

The metal mining services industry, composed of 362 companies nationwide, offers a wide range of services. Geographically speaking, the state of Nevada has the most companies engaged in mining services. Most of these companies are small operations engaged in the physical tasks involved in mining, as well as in planning, development, and exploration. Some companies specialize in preparing mine shafts and tunnels, while others offered test boring services. In this age of outsourcing, the metal mining services industry should be growing, but the decline in overall mining is limiting its growth.

Current Conditions

The overriding trend in modern metal mining has been toward the development of improved equipment to ensure better working conditions, the potential exploitation of lower-grade ores, and the design and construction of bigger and deeper mines. Where companies involved in metal mining services did not themselves develop new technologies toward such ends, they made use of a plethora of advances made by other mining companies and associations.

MINExpo International, an annual event held in Las Vegas, is a dynamic forum displaying many of the latest mining technologies, including: Integrated Mine Planning System (IMPS), a system for geological interpretation and modeling featuring computer-aided drafting (CAD) technology that allows engineers to manipulate plans, design options, and even insert equipment within specific parameters; hydraulic drills that replace pneumatic models; computer-controlled underground drilling jumbos; computer programs to help evaluate and plan ventilation systems and other mine conditions; a variety of communication systems; and other advances that are intended to benefit the metals mining services and their workers.

Workforce

Occupational opportunities in the mining services industry range from those involved in the physical tasks related to mining to those responsible for the planning and development of mining, testing, and prospecting. In the mining, quarrying, and tunneling domain, the industry employs workers as varied as rock splitters—who separate rough dimensions of rock and ore using jackhammers, wedges, and feathers—and mining machine operators, responsible for the operation of equipment including truck-mounted or portable drills, continuous mining machines, channeling machines, and cutting machines for underground excavation.

In the planning and development domain, the metal mining services industry employs a wide variety of mining engineers trained in locating, extracting, and preparing metals for industry use. In addition to designing and supervising most functional aspects of metal mines, such engineers conceived new plans and equipment to improve safety and health conditions, environmental compatibility, and efficiency of mines.

Workers filled approximately 3,827 jobs in 1995, reflecting a declining trend in job opportunities by the year 2000. More than 44 percent of the mining services companies employed two to four workers.

While more than half of the 4,200 jobs held by mining engineers in the mid-1990s were in the mining industry, a large percentage transferred each year to other occupations, such as engineering consulting, government agencies, and manufacturing. Nevertheless, increasingly stringent environmental standards, as well as moves to increase production capacity and productivity while reducing operating costs, promised new challenges and some new opportunities for mining engineers in the metal mining services industry.

Further Reading

Metal Statistics 1999: The Statistical Guide to the Metals Industries. Chilton Publications, 1999.

"Mining Annual Review." *The Mining Journal, Ltd.*, July 1995.

Occupational Outlook Handbook, 1995-96. Washington, D.C.: U.S. Department of Labor, 1995.

SIC 1094

URANIUM-RADIUM-VANADIUM ORES

This category covers establishments primarily engaged in mining, milling, or otherwise preparing uranium, radium, or vanadium ores.

NAICS Code(s)

212291 (Uranium-Radium-Vanadium Ore Mining)

INDUSTRY SNAPSHOT

Domestic uranium mining is essentially a dying industry, no longer kept afloat by the military demand that launched mining in the 1940s, nor the commercial nuclear power industry that provided the major source of more recent demand. In 1992, production of uranium ore from underground mines fell near zero, with any production of uranium coming from by-products. As an indication of the collapse of uranium mining, total mine production peaked in 1980 at 21,850 tons of ore before declining to 1,550 tons in 1995; 1992 marked the first year since in 1948—when uranium mining was initiated in the United States—that no new ore was mined from underground mines. Current U.S. demand for uranium is about 22,550 tons per year, of which only seven percent is met by new domestic production. According to the U.S. Energy Information Administration, an estimated 500,000 tons of uranium was in inventory in 1995. At the end of 1995, only six mines were active; of these six mines, two were by-product recovery plants.

In 1987, approximately 101 establishments were engaged in the extraction of uranium, radium, and vanadium ores from mines in the United States. These establishments employed about 2,300 workers, who produced about $268 million worth of ores. The number of employees had dropped to 1,200 by 1992 (48 percent below the 1987 total) and then to about 700 (70 percent below the 1987 total) by 1997. Value added through mining increased in 1997 to $90 million, as compared with $69.4 million in 1992; the 1997 figure was a substantial decline, however, from the 1987 value of $174.7 million. Furthermore, these figures were down sharply from the 1982 census, when output value was $223.9 million, value added was $578.8 million, and the industry employed 10,500 workers. Industry shipments totaled $103.2 million in 1997.

Uranium. The collapse of uranium production in the early to mid-1990s was an intensification of the steady decline of U.S. uranium mining since the late 1970s. Import pressure remained strong. In fact, 83 percent of U.S. demand for uranium was satisfied through imports in 1998—imports as a share of domestic consumption rose from a low of 26 percent in 1983 to 51 percent in 1988, 45 percent in 1989, and 80 percent in 1990—mostly from low-cost producers such as Canada and Australia. Net imports fluctuated around zero in the 1960s and 1970s as the government tried to maintain self-sufficiency, but the U.S. market was swamped by imports in the 1980s. In 1998, Canada supplied 34 percent of the United States' foreign-origin uranium, while Russia supplied 14 percent, Australia supplied 13 percent, and South Africa and Uzbekistan both supplied 6 percent. The United States sold 15.1 million pounds of uranium to foreign suppliers and utilities in 1998, 11 percent less than 1997.

In addition to the relatively high cost of mining uranium in the United States, which has hurt the industry's competitive position worldwide, the U.S. uranium industry has always relied heavily on federal government subsidies and protection to keep its markets afloat. Thus, as federal support for the industry was gradually removed, the industry's viability quickly came into question. Because uranium is a one-market commodity, the fall in nuclear-powered electricity generation negatively affected the uranium market. Even uranium inventories held by U.S. utilities continued to fall in the early 1990s. This growing supply-demand gap has sent prices plummeting, creating, from the industry's perspective if not a social perspective, unwanted additions to inventories from nuclear disarmament.

The federal government remains a primary producer and purchaser of uranium ores. To counteract the import dependency, the United States instituted restrictions on imports from former Eastern Bloc countries—mainly Russia, Kazakhstan, Kyrgyzstan, Tajikistan, Ukraine, and Uzbekistan.

Radium. Radium is a white metal that does not occur in a free state; it must be refined from pitchblende and occurs naturally only as a disintegration product in the radioactive decay of thorium, uranium, or actinium. Radium itself continues to decay into radon, bismuth, polonium, lead, or thallium. Radium was important for radiation treatment of cancer, but it has been replaced by other isotopes that can be produced at a lower cost and have greater effectiveness in treatment. It was also used for petroleum prospecting but has also been replaced in this application. Radium coating of instrument dials and clock faces to make them glow in the dark ceased in the 1930s when the toxicity of the paint was found to cause cancer and anemia in workers.

Vanadium. Vanadium, a mineral which is found in the same ores as uranium, is primarily a one-market commodity used as an alloy in iron and steel. Small amounts of vanadium can produce high-strength steel for bridges, buildings, pipelines, and automobiles due to the weight savings it brings to these applications. Steel production, which typical accounts for about 90 percent of vanadium demand, began its recovery in the first half of 1992. Vanadium consumption in the United States for the first half of 1995 increased about 10 percent over that in the same period of 1994. Though consumption in the tool steel sector fell 16 percent, consumption in the full alloy sector was up 9 percent. With the cost and mining of vanadium so intertwined with uranium, both industries are strongly affected by U.S. government policy. Vanadium is also seen as a strategic and critical mineral for

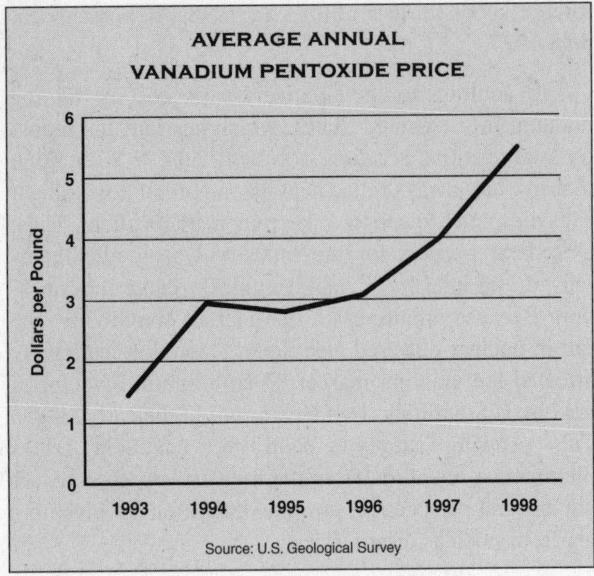

defense, energy, and transportation industries and thus import dependence is a perennial concern. According to the U.S. Geological Survey, in 1998 carbon steel accounted for 38 percent of domestic vanadium consumption (an estimated 4,700 metric tons), high-strength low-alloy steel accounted for 20 percent, full alloy steel comprised 19 percent, and tool steel accounted for 10 percent.

Vanadium and uranium are mined together, then separated by liquid extraction techniques. Columbrium, manganese, molybdenum, titanium, and tungsten can be substituted for vanadium to some degree and in some applications. While it is difficult to establish specific reserves, the largest reserves of vanadium are found in South Africa, China, the former Soviet Union, Australia, and the United States. Vanadium resources in the United States are sufficient to satisfy domestic needs. Nevertheless, foreign suppliers met a substantial portion of vanadium demand. In 1998, South Africa controled 89 percent of the vanadium pentoxide market, China held a 6 percent market share, and Russia had 4 percent of the market.

Eight U.S. companies mined or milled vanadium in 1998. Raw materials used in milling vanadium included Idaho ferrophosphorus slag, petroleum residues, spent catalysts, utility ash, and vanadium-bearing iron slab. End-use distribution of vanadium from U.S. plants goes to transportation, which used 30 percent, the machinery and tools industry bought 27 percent of output, and building and heavy construction, 22 percent, among others. Vanadium averaged $4.00 per pound in 1998.

Organization and Structure

In 1997, 29 operations employed about 700 people who were engaged in the production of uranium, radium, and vanadium ores. Per production worker, the average value added in 1997 was $175,700. By comparison, in 1992, approximately 102 establishments employed 1,011 workers. For the same year, the average value added per production worker was $57,800. When ranked by the number of establishments per state, the top three were Colorado, Wyoming, and Texas.

In the mid-1990s, it was estimated that the largest two companies accounted for $5.3 million worth of uranium-vanadium industry ore sales, and ten companies were responsible for nearly all of the output of the industry. Only 3 of the largest 14 companies were publicly traded, and the remainder were subsidiaries or divisions of other corporations. Of the 29 establishments reporting to the U.S. Census Bureau in 1997, only five employed 50 or more persons. Of the total of 29 establishments, 23 were producing establishments; six operated mines only; nine operated mines with preparation plants; two were separately operated preparation plants; and six were non-producing establishments. From 1972 through 1997, the primary materials consumed in the extraction of uranium compound ores, when ranked by cost, came in the form of other minerals and the use of installed machinery, followed by purchased electric energy.

The product output shipments for the entire industry can be broken down into crude ores and uranium-vanadium concentrates. The largest component of the $103.2 million of 1997 shipments was uranium concentrates with $73.9 million; uranium-vanadium ores made up the balance with $29.3 million. The precise amounts of uranium and vanadium concentrates and ores were not separately reported to the Census Bureau. The decline of these annual shipment figures from 1982 to 1997 is startling—from $763.2 million to $103.2 million.

For the industry as a whole, uranium-vanadium-radium miners and milling companies turned a profit in the early 1990s for the first time since 1983. Though net income in those years was still quite small, translating into a rate of profit of less than 5 percent, peak losses in the mid-1980s ranged from over $400 million (nominal dollars) to around $100 million.

Exploration expenditures for new mines peaked at $626 million in 1978 and continued on a downward slide to $50.8 million in 1983, to $14.5 million in 1992, and to a slight increase of $15.1 million in 1997. In the early 1990s, foreign-controlled companies accounted for 55 percent of exploration in the United States.

Background and Development

The exploration and mining of radioactive ores began around the turn of the century when sources of radium were sought for use in luminous paints for instruments such as watch dials and for medical purposes. In 1910, Marie and Pierre Curie refined pitchblende to isolate the metal after Madame Curie had discovered polonium, also in pitchblende. In fact, radium is a radioactive decay product of uranium that was initially perceived to have more uses than uranium and to be more valuable. Uranium was used only as a pigment for coloring glass and painting china until the dawn of the age of atomic weapons and energy.

Radium's chemistry was first understood by the Curies and Andre-Louis Debierne in 1910. Initially, it had more commercial applications than uranium or vanadium, but it has essentially lost its commercial value because it has been replaced in most applications by safer, cheaper, and more effective materials and because it is difficult to isolate.

Because vanadium is often found in the same ores as uranium, its history closely parallels the history of the uranium industry. Originally isolated and discovered in lead ores by Mexican mineralogist Andres Manuel Del Rio in 1801, successful commercial applications wouldn't follow until the beginning of the next century. The basic chemistry was worked out by German chemist F. Wohler.

By 1941, the United States became the largest producer of vanadium. During World War II, stable demand for war output and stable pricing structure from the Office of Production Management helped bolster the industry. Later, production was increased to meet the demand for the Korean War. By 1958, however, the U.S. stockpile reached its limit so the government reduced its vanadium purchases, focusing more attention on uranium. With its primary market saturated, production declined, and the AEC stopped purchasing vanadium concentrate—leaving the industry subject to the vagaries of the steel market.

Throughout its history, the uranium industry has been regulated by the federal government. More specifically, the origin of the uranium industry is intimately connected with the heightened U.S. national security following World War II. Originally spawned, nurtured, and subsidized by government programs to develop the atomic bomb, uranium prospecting was encouraged solely for military needs. Later, when the guaranteed military market dried up in the 1960s, the government's industrial policy toward uranium shifted towards helping to foster a new source of demand—commercial nuclear power. Then, when import competition threatened the viability of the industry, the government would impose limits on imports to protect domestic industry.

The U.S. military's explosion of the Trinity device in New Mexico on July 16, 1945, introduced the world to the atomic age. At that time, the United States purchased uranium for military purposes only. In fact, only the U.S. government could legally own uranium ore. (It gradually reduced its purchases until 1970, when it cut its purchases

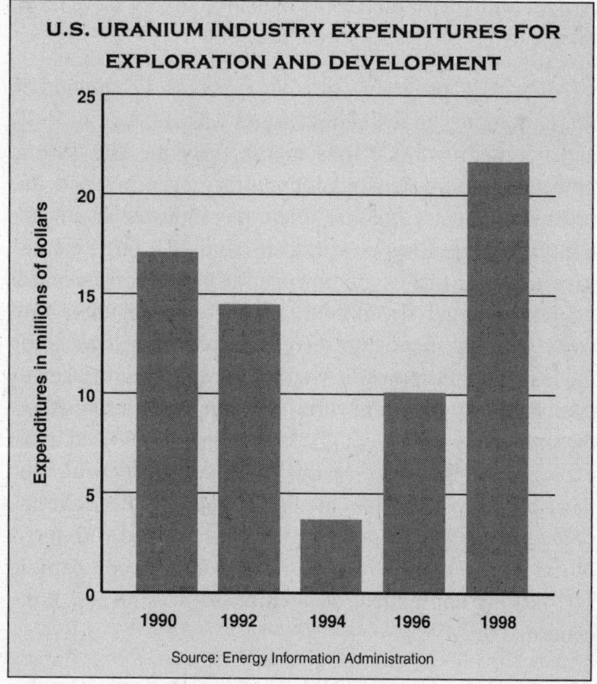

entirely.) Until that time, much of the uranium for the Manhattan Project was purchased overseas. In 1943, however, the Union Mines Development Corporation, assisted by the government, operated mills to process additional uranium for the war effort.

On August 1, 1946, the Atomic Energy Commission (AEC), a civilian agency, was created for the purpose of procuring uranium for military needs. The AEC launched a domestic program to stimulate war production from U.S. deposits. In pursuit of its stated goal to push ''nuclear security,'' the AEC offered bonuses for discoveries of ''yellowcake'' (as uranium was often called), established prices for ores, offered development and transportation allowances, built miles of access roads and pushed mill construction by subsidizing mill costs. More importantly, the AEC provided a guaranteed market for the ore. The AEC encouraged exploration in the Colorado Plateau region and many new discoveries led to a number of mining and milling facilities and new ore mining and processing methods were developed.

The federal government owned 90 percent of the western lands where uranium was sought. Navajo Indians and Mormons did much of the early prospecting of the region during the ''uranium rush'' unleashed by the AEC. Over 5,500 people took to the plains in pursuit of profits and what was considered patriotic service. At first, large corporations were unconvinced that they could profit over the capital investment required and the Geiger counter evened out the competition. By the early 1950s, with many small companies generating profits at guaranteed prices, and a guaranteed market with demonstrated large reserves, the industry became less speculative and larger companies entered the industry, among them large oil interests.

The AEC program was a huge success. Production of uranium oxides in the United States was 100 tons in 1948 and boomed to 8,000 tons in 1965. By the late 1950s, however, falling demand for military purposes and the resultant industry shakeout left the industry in uncertainty. Waiting for a new market required a large capital investment. Smaller companies went out of business while the larger diversified companies, with their low costs and high-quality reserves, simply shut down their nuclear operations while waiting for the new market to take root. At this time, the oil companies established themselves as the ''energy companies,'' and led new exploration. Reserves at this time were plentiful, but more costly to mine than in other countries. The shakeout of capacity left the industry more concentrated with most of the reserves held by large oil and mining companies. The milling component of the industry was far less concentrated.

The Shift to Commercial Nuclear Power. By the 1960s, military demand was declining and a new source of profitable demand for uranium had to be found, namely commercial nuclear power. The AEC would be involved in a reactor development program for demonstrating the potential use of nuclear power to generate electricity in commercial power plants. It would also provide research and development and technical assistance, encourage property development, and secure stockpiles to meet military needs. Further encouragement of uranium production was provided by the 1964 passage of the Private Ownership of Special Nuclear Materials Act, which privatized many of the government's roles in the industry. Despite relative privatization, the AEC nonetheless sought to protect the industry to maintain a viable domestic uranium industry.

The program was very successful for industry growth for several decades. U.S. utilities ordered 249 commercial nuclear power plants between 1953 and 1978; more than half of them were built, and 109 were operable by the early 1990s. The decline in demand for nuclear-generated electricity was due primarily to the OPEC oil embargo; the Three Mile Island nuclear power plant disaster; and the increasing costs of building and operating nuclear power plants.

The industry, seduced by prices that increased by over 700 percent from 1972 to 1979, stepped up exploration and production during this period; however, high utility rates and energy conservation efforts slowed utility demand and deterred construction of nuclear plants. These utilities had stockpiled uranium inventories—averaging two-year supplies. Consequently, utilities cut back on uranium orders. Still, many mine producers expanded their activities, knowing that with utilities bleeding off their inventories, the situation could not last.

The boom of this period led to serious oversupply problems. With its high unit labor costs and safety requirements, the U.S. industry was at a competitive disadvantage on the world market and the U.S. government stepped in to protect the industry, placing an embargo on foreign uranium. Following the sevenfold increase in prices from 1972 to 1976, it was alleged that an international cartel—which included Canada, Australia, South Africa, and England—conspired to fix prices.

By the late 1970s, production was up, demand for nuclear fuel was down, and inventories were high. Prices fell to around $40 a pound. Even deeper problems led many to question the viability of the industry at the time. One of the contributing factors to declining demand for uranium was the strong antinuclear campaign following the accident at the Three Mile Island plant in the spring of 1979. Because uranium is essentially a one-market metal, any wholesale shift to other energy sources such as coal would be disastrous for the industry. Fortunately for the uranium producers, coal had problems of its own, notably its environmental costs.

During this period, declining interest in and direct opposition to the nuclear industry led to more stringent environmental regulations. This increased the cost of nuclear power and reduced the demand for uranium ore. Uranium mill dumping into rivers and wind erosion of exposed tailing piles meant an increased public pressure for additional control measures and cleanup activities. The Uranium Mill Tailings Radiation Control Act (UMTRCA) of 1978 was designed to deal with these problems. The Nuclear Regulatory Commission (NRC) was established, and many mines were shut down or dismantled altogether.

Although the industry as a whole faced severe decline through most of the 1980s and early 1990s, some surviving companies showed signs of strength. One leading mining and milling company, Uranium Resources, Incorporated, posted a 41 percent decline in 1992 net income, but in 1997 the Dallas-based company had revenues of $12.9 million for 1992, and had contracts in place with utilities through 1998—worth around $60 million. Mergers and acquisitions in general increased the profitability of remaining firms by reducing capital stock value.

By the early 1990s, the uranium industry as a whole showed positive rates of profit for the first time since 1982. Following losses as high as 67 percent (net income on total equity in 1988 and 1989) and 21.6 percent (net income on total assets in 1985), the industry scored profit rates of around 3 to 4 percent on total equity and 1 to 2 percent on total assets in the early 1990s. The eight active uranium mines in 1996 were: the Crow Butte mine in

Nebraska (operated by Fernet Exploration of Nebraska); the Canon City, Colorado, mine (run by the Cotter Corporation); Nevada's Apex Deposit (owned by Strathmore Resources Limited; the Ambrosia Lake, New Mexico, site (operated by the Rio Algom Mining Corporation); the Churchrock, New Mexico, Mine (run by Uranium Resources, Incorporated); the Holiday-El Mesquite mines in Texas (owned by Malapai Resources); and the Sunshine Bridge and Uncle Sam mines located in Louisiana (operated by Freeport Uranium Recovery). Of these facilities, the Freeport Uranium Recovery operation was the sole producer of uranium by-products. The remaining plants used ''in situ'' leaching (ISL) methods which involved recovery by chemical leaching of the valuable components of uranium deposits without physical extraction of the mineralized rock. In 1998, Rio Algom Mining Corporation started up an ISL project at Smith Ranch, Wyoming.

Maintaining the industry's viability entailed massive consolidation and concentration of assets, at rock bottom prices, into the hands of fewer companies. Plateau Resources, which operated the Shootaring Canyon uranium mining facility in southern Utah, was acquired by U.S. Energy Corporation, thereby raising its stake in the uranium market. The U.S. Energy Corporation (USEC) was a creation of the U.S. government in the 1960s when the federal government began to provide uranium enrichment services. Through the Energy Policy Act of 1992, USEC was privatized. In another major deal, Pikes Peak Mining was sold in its entirety by Nerco Minerals to Independence Mining for $21 million. In another deal, Exxon Corporation sold its Bullfrog uranium deposit in Garfield County, Utah, to Energy Fuels Exploration—with total reserves of 20 million plus pounds of uranium oxide.

Government action in the 1990s hurt the uranium industry, while at the same time protecting it from foreign competition. First, Russia was given most-favored-nation trading status in 1992. The U.S. government agreed to buy bomb-grade uranium from Russia's dismantled nuclear warheads and convert it into fuel for commercial nuclear power plants, an action that further depressed demand for domestic uranium. As a result of the glut of uranium, imports from Russia rose from near zero to over 2,700 tons. Second, the remaining companies sought protection from international competition. This issue focused primarily on the independent republics of the Commonwealth of Independent States.

In July 1992, the U.S. Department of Commerce imposed duties of 115.82 percent against six former Soviet republics—Russia, Kazakhstan, Uzbekistan, Ukraine, Kyrgyzstan, and Tajikistan, all of which posed substantial competitive threats to U.S. uranium. In August 1993, the U.S. International Trade Commission set a

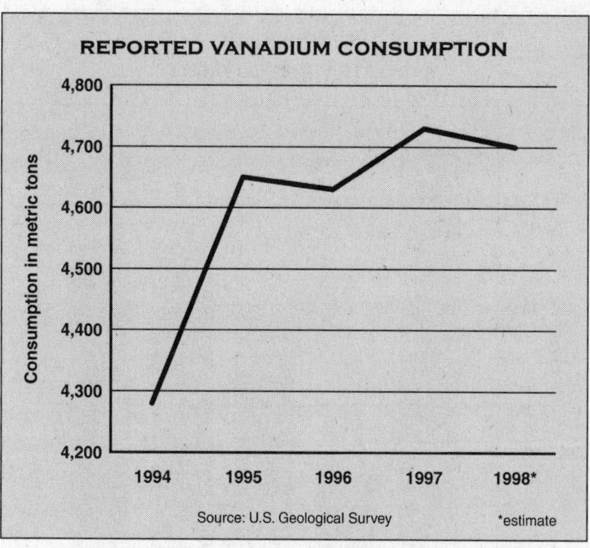

129 percent anti-dumping duty on uranium imports from Ukraine, excluding highly enriched uranium. Then in October, the U.S. Department of Commerce banned imports from four of the above countries. A two-tier pricing system resulted with U.S. importers paying nearly one-third more—about $8.75 a pound (in 1998) for uranium concentrates; this compares with $8.10 per pound (1998 average) of uranium from the former Soviet Union republics. All of these actions, along with an anti-dumping case brought against the former Soviet bloc nations have been credited with a 25 percent increase in the spot market price for U.S. uranium.

In the 1990s, uranium supplied about 6 percent of the world's energy. According to the U.S. Energy Information Administration, 43 percent of Western Europe's electricity came from nuclear facilities. Though world nuclear power has grown since 1973 from 191 billion kilowatt hours to just over 2 trillion, the nuclear energy industry—which is the prime user of uranium—is essentially flat.

The viability of the industry has been uncertain for quite some time. In the early 1980s, the issue was examined by congressional inquiry. Congress passed the U.S. Nuclear Regulatory Commission Authorization Act of 1983 to assess the industry's viability on a periodic basis. World uranium production expanded, while consumption remained steady. Most of this demand was projected to be met by Canadian producers, which accounted for 26 percent of world uranium production the early 1990s, while U.S. production was projected to fall to around 3.1 million pounds by 1996. Even the once prolific producers fell by the wayside; production in the former East Germany ceased while elsewhere, such as Czechoslovakia and Bulgaria, production reorganized, and the former Soviet republics jockeyed for some sort of potential cooperative production agreement.

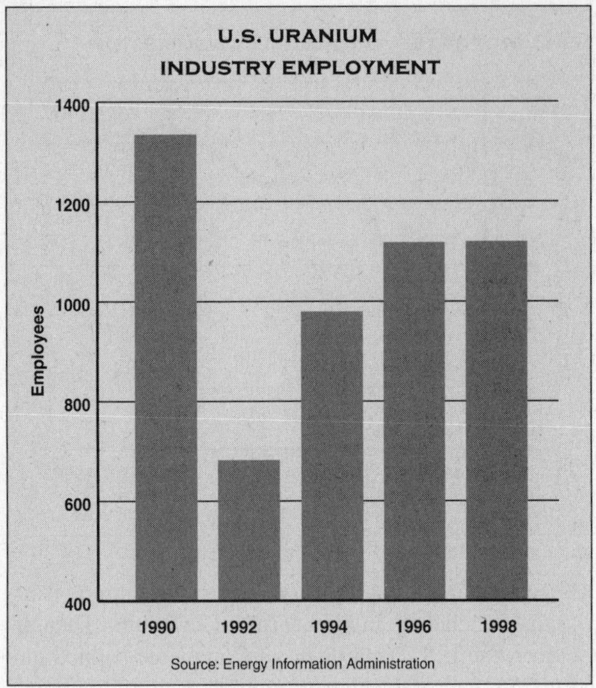

Source: Energy Information Administration

Current Conditions

As of 1999, Cameco (based in Saskatchewan, Canada) is the largest producer of uranium in the world with 27.6 million pounds in 1998, and the firm is most likely (according to industry forecasters) to claim the highest share of the world market. Cameco acquired Uranerz in 1998 as part of the ongoing consolidations and closures claiming many members of the industry. Uranerz had been Cameco's partner in the Key Lake, Rabbit Lake, Crow Butte and McArthur River projects. The McArthur River site, located about 620 km north of Saskatoon, Saskathchewan, is the largest known deposit of high-grade uranium ore in the world . When fully developed by 2002, McArthur River will produce about 18 million pounds per year of commercial-grade uranium. Cameco Corporation operates the mine and owns about 70 percent of the deposit with Cogema Resources, as the owner of the remaining 30 percent.

As of 1998, Russia's stockpile of commercial grade uranium continued to control secondary sources of uranium and therefore, to limit worldwide production. The size of the stockpile was not easily assessed primarily because of questions about Russia's ability to reprocess spent fuel; it is estimated that the stockpile will reach a minimum between 2003 and 2007. Russia has claimed that its Krasnokamensk, Siberia, mine will increase production four times over by 2010, but experts consider this statement inflated. Kazakhstan and Uzbekistan are better positioned for growth despite that fact that their huge, low-grade sources require in-situ leaching; profits from gold mines have generated much-need capital for the uranium operations.

U.S. government inventories are to be sold off through the U.S. Enrichment Corporation at 20 million pounds per year from 1999 through 2004. Worldwide projections by the U.S. Energy Information Agency suggest that requirements for uranium production will remain flat until 2010.

Meanwhile, environmental cleanup continued with the Environmental Protection Agency (EPA) and the U.S. Department of Energy announcing a cleanup of radioactive, uranium-mine waste on land controlled by the Energy Department at the Bluewater Mine near Prewitt, New Mexico. Other cleanups in the early 1990s included two sites on Navajo Nation land—an adjacent mine on privately owned land was also cleaned up by private companies in accordance with an EPA order. Radiation levels in these areas posed a serious health threat to people living in the vicinity. The cleanup included sealing mine openings and moving and covering mine waste, with bulldozed areas replanted with grass and sloped to resist erosion. The economic effects of environmental reclamation claimed corporate victims, however. In December 1999, Atlas Corporation of Colorado filed for reorganization which included the responsibility for remediating its Moab, Utah, uranium tailings piles. International effects of environmental activism include pressure to close nuclear power reactors in Switzerland, Sweden, and Germany despite studies showing that nuclear power is needed to reduce greenhouse gases, global warming, and acid rain.

From the vanadium side of the industry, suppliers continued to be in a situation of oversupply, despite reduced production by the largest producer, Highveld Steel & Vanadium Corporation of the Republic of South Africa. The pattern of vanadium consumption in the United States was not expected to change much in late 1990s to early 2000, but will remain subject to cycles in domestic and global steel production.

Shipments of concentrated uranium totaled 49.9 million pounds in 1998, and U.S. uranium exploration companies held 825,000 acres. Their expenditures that year totaled $21.7 million, 29 percent less than 1997 expenditures. Three states (Texas, New Mexico, and Wyoming) had 74 percent of the U.S. $30 per pound uranium reserves in 1998, according to the Energy Information Administration (EIA).

Workforce

Employment figures for 1998 were relatively unchanged from 1997, but significant changes occurred within the industry. Mining employment and processing both had major increases in their workforces (25 percent and 16 percent, respectively), while reclamation and milling employment both had serious decreases (31 percent and 9 percent respectively). Exploration employment was unchanged. Colorado, Texas, and Wyoming accounted for 72 percent of the total U.S. workforce in 1998, according to the EIA.

At the height of uranium mining (1961 and 1962), there were 925 mines with 5,500 miners in 1961 and 1962. From a peak of 12,000 employees in 1977, employment has declined to 2,300 in 1987 and 682 workers in 1992; but it rebounded to 1,120 employees in 1997. Value added per employee did increase from 1992 to 1997 to $175,700 per production employee; the value added was $57,800 in 1992 and $76,000 in 1987.

With the mining of ores at a virtual standstill, and output coming mainly from by-product operations, employment for all occupations including mining, exploration, milling, and processing are all projected by the U.S. Energy Information Administration to decline, alongside the decline of the industry in general. Mining employment in 1998 was 518 people.

Health Hazards. It is now well-known that even low levels of radiation cause serious health risks; however, it wasn't until the late 1960s that major health and safety regulations were enacted for uranium mining. In 1967, the Walsh-Healy Act imposed health standards in the mines. From 1979 to 1981, congressional hearings were held to investigate the link between mining in unventilated mines and lung cancer. The EPA instituted regulations dealing specifically with the mining of uranium ores in 1982. Some of the new rules dealt specifically with worker exposure. Mill operators were required to install protective barriers to minimize radioactive exposure and earthen covers to minimize emissions.

In addition, strict cleaning and work rules were established, which meant lower thresholds for the work week in order to minimize exposure. In 1990, after many defeats in the legislative and judiciary branches, the U.S. Congress passed compensatory legislation, called the Radiation Exposure Compensation Act, which called for compensation of uranium miners who were exposed to radioactivity during the peak years of uranium mining. By 1995, the small number of uranium miners who worked in mining or milling were much more closely monitored for health risks.

FURTHER READING

''Atlas Corporation Receives Approval for Its Plan of Reorganization,'' *PR Newswire,* 20 December 1999.

''Cameco Corporation: Mining Begins at McArthur River Uranium Operation,'' *BusinessWire,* 7 December 1999.

Hobbs, G. Warfield. ''Resources Trends on the Rise.'' *Oil and Gas Journal,* 4 September 1995.

Martin, R. *Energy Minerals,* Lafferty, Harwood & Partners, Ltd., 16 January 1999.

''Mellow Yellow.'' *The Economist,* 10 August 1996.

Pool, Thomas C. ''Uranium: low prices bring closures, cutbacks, and consolidation''*Engineering & Mining Journal,* March 1999.

Taylor, Theodore B. ''A Ban on Nuclear Technologies.''*Technology Review,* August/September 1995.

U.S. Census Bureau. *Uranium-Radium-Vanadium Ore Mining: 1997 Economic Census, Mining Industry Series.* August 1999.

U.S. Department of Energy. Energy Information Administration, Office of Coal, Nuclear, Electric and Alternate Fuels. *Domestic Uranium Mining and Milling Industry 1995: Viability Assessment.*Washington, DC: GPO, 1995.

U.S. Department of Energy. Energy Information Administration. Office of Coal, Nuclear, Electric and Alternate Fuels. *Uranium Industry Annual 1998* Washington, DC: GPO, 1999.

SIC 1099

MISCELLANEOUS METAL ORES, NOT ELSEWHERE CLASSIFIED

This category covers establishments that are primarily engaged in mining, milling, and preparing miscellaneous metal ores. Production of metallic mercury by furnacing or retorting at the mine site is also included.

NAICS CODE(S)

212299 (Other Metal Ore Mining)

INDUSTRY SNAPSHOT

Metal ores included in this category include: aluminum, antimony, bastnasite, bauxite, beryl, beryllium, cerium, cinnabar, ilmenite, iridium, mercury, microlite, monazite, osmium, palladium, platinum, quicksilver, the rare-earth metals, rhodium, ruthenium, rutile, thorium, tin, titaniferous-magnetite (chiefly for titanium content), titanium, and zirconium. The actual mining of these ores declined for two decades beginning in the 1970s. Production fell by 10.7 percent through the mid-1990s. In addition, environmental pressure for stricter regulation on mining and recycling strained the mining of ores. In the late 1990s metals mining increased slightly, although the value of the mined ore failed to register an increase when adjusted for inflation. Likewise wages for mining employees increased, but failed to match inflation.

United States consumption of the miscellaneous metals overall exceeds production, especially for the platinum-group metals and tin. U.S. industry in turn relies on imported product to satisfy its needs, and a trade deficit exists in these areas. Additionally the U.S. government maintains a strategic stockpile of product, especially of import-dependent metals, that is crucial to the military and to the national security. The stockpile serves to sustain military reserves at adequate levels and creates a small, insulated metals market with limited fluctuation for certain producers. Specific metals in the U.S. government stockpiles include bauxite, titanium, platinum, and tin.

ORGANIZATION AND STRUCTURE

The production of miscellaneous metals is segregated into mining and metal refining according to respective metal product. Individual metal production is subdivided further into primary and secondary production. In the 1990s approximately 14 percent of mining firms in the industry additionally operated preparation plants. Virtually all of the total product output (99 percent) was from primary products. The industry's market structure grew more concentrated during the final decades of the twentieth century, and the number of mining establishments fell to under 50 by the late 1990s after achieving a dramatic peak of 236 in 1982.

In terms of geographic concentration, the largest number of firms mining miscellaneous metal ores is located in the Pacific region of the United States (California, Washington, and Oregon). The second greatest concentration was in the mountainous western region (Montana, Nevada, and Utah). California ranked first among the United States, with ten sites, followed by Montana with five, Arkansas with four, and Florida and Utah with two each.

The principal economic sectors or industries responsible for the purchase of miscellaneous metal ores are manufacturers of intermediate products for industrial use.

BACKGROUND AND DEVELOPMENT

The mining of the miscellaneous metals is very much intertwined because multiple products are frequently extracted from the same ores; separation of the individual metal products occurs in the smelting process whereby reduction of the ores takes place.

Aluminum. Aluminum is the second most abundant metallic element in the earth's crust after silicon. The use of aluminum exceeds that of any other metal except iron, and it is important in nearly all segments of the world economy. The United States is the leading producer of primary aluminum. Aluminum's prime use is in packaging, aerospace, and increasingly in construction. In addition, aluminum competes with other metals and plastics for an increased share of the automobile market. Aluminum experienced a boom in world demand in the early 1980s, then dropped suddenly on the world market until 1986. The industry rebounded after 1986, buoyed by increased applications of aluminum products, and grew by more than 32 percent from 1986 to 1992.

Antimony. Most production of antimony in the United States is the result of a byproduct or is a co-product of mining, smelting, and refining other metals and ores that contain small quantities of antimony. Foreign deposits far outweigh domestic deposits, and U.S. users of antimony depend on suppliers in Bolivia, China, Mexico, and South Africa. Antimony has a variety of manufacturing applications, but is mainly used in batteries.

Beryllium. Beryllium is important in industrial and defense applications and is known for its high strength, light weight, and high thermal conductivity. It is used in components for aircraft, satellites, electronics, oil drilling equipment, and consumer goods. The U. S. beryllium industry is the largest in the western world.

Bismuth. Bismuth has been replacing lead (which is highly toxic) in many applications. For example, a bismuth and brass alloy was developed to replace leaded brass in some plumbing applications. In the United States, only ASARCO, Incorporated produces primary bismuth, while a number of smaller firms produce secondary bismuth product mainly from scrap.

Mercury. U.S. production of this key metal was a very small percentage of a declining world market. Manufacturers sought substitutes for mercury, especially for its primary use in batteries. New technology enabled reduction of the mercury content of some batteries by as much as 98 percent. A temporary suspension of mercury sales from the National Defense Stockpile in 1994 resulted in dramatically increased quantities of imported mercury in 1995. Sales were prohibited, not to resume until the U.S. Environmental Protection Agency and the Defense Logistics Agency might determine a safe method of selling the mercury to ensure against environmental damage. Consumption as a percentage of supply remained largely unchanged because of the ongoing elimination of mercury from many products and processes, and because of accelerated efforts to recycle product.

Platinum-Group Metals. Six closely related metals comprise the platinum-group metals: platinum, palladium, rhodium, ruthenium, iridium, and osmium. These are among the scarcest of all metal elements and are used in mostly commercial applications. Platinum and palladium (a platinum substitute) dominate this product grouping. These metals are used as emission catalysts for automobiles and in electronics and glass applications. Platinum is highly valued for its corrosion resistance and catalytic activity.

South Africa is the world's largest producer of platinum, furnishing 75 percent of the metal. Russia is also a critical producer in the world market for this metal group. Production of the platinum ores—platinum and palladium—increased in the early 1990s. Platinum production rose from 1,430 kilograms in 1989 to 2,000 kilograms in

1991, while palladium rose from 4,850 kilograms to a high of 6,780 kilograms in 1992, but fell again to 6,000 kilograms by 1994. In terms of revenue, U.S. mine production of platinum and palladium topped $60 million in 1994, and remained essentially unchanged in 1995.

Rare-Earth Ores: Lanthanides, Yttrium, and Scandium. This group of metals includes 17 elements. In 1995 more than 50 percent of the world total (28,700 metric tons) came from one company in California. The United States was a leading producer and processor of rare-earth ores and continued to be a major exporter and consumer of these products. Domestic ore production was valued at $82 million in 1995. Three companies refined these ores with plants in Arizona, California, and Tennessee, reaching an estimated value of more than $500 million. The uses of these metals range from catalysts in petroleum, chemical, and pollution control to metallurgical uses as iron and steel additives, and as alloys to ceramics and glass additives.

Thorium. Thorium is a naturally radioactive element and is extremely expensive to mine—environmental regulations and waste disposal mandate costly extraction and transport procedures. Domestic production of monazite ceased in 1994 as a result of decreased demand for thorium-bearing minerals. Only a small portion of the mined thorium is for consumption, while most is disposed of as waste. Its uses include refractory applications, lamp mantles and lighting, and welding electrodes.

Tin. One of the earliest metals known to humankind, tin is used in a variety of applications. Most known for tin cans, tin is also a component of solder used to weld electronic circuitry. Tin is highly valued for national security purposes by the U.S. military, and is the most collected of all metals in the National Defense Stockpile. Tin production occurs in many countries throughout the world, but U.S. production supplies only a very small percentage of the world market. Domestic consumption of tin exceeds production, and the deficit justifies the high level of defense stockpile.

Titanium. Two firms in Nevada and Oregon produce titanium, most known as a metal alloy used to lighten aircraft and spacecraft. Two titanium sponge producers and nine other firms in seven states produced the total U.S. output in 1995. About 30 companies also produce titanium forgings, mill products, and castings. In 1995 an estimated 65 percent of the titanium metal produced in the United States was used in aerospace applications. The remaining 35 percent was used in the chemical processing industry, mostly as a white pigment in paints, paper, and plastics. It is also used in ceramics, chemicals, welding rod coatings, heavy aggregate, and steel furnace flux. E.I. du Pont de Nemours & Co., Inc. (Du Pont) is the largest integrated producer of titanium products. According to the U.S. Bureau of Mines, U.S. companies own or control almost one-half of the world's productive capacity for titanium pigments. In 1995 titanium dioxide pigment was valued at $2.6 billion and was produced by five companies in 11 plants in nine states.

Zirconium. U.S. mining interests produced about one-seventh of the total tonnage of zirconium in 1992. Its ore, zircon, is generally recovered from operations in Florida and New Jersey. Zircon is used in refractories, foundry sands, and ceramic opacities. Its ore contains both zirconium and hafnium, two of the mainstay nuclear metals used in reactor cores.

CURRENT CONDITIONS

The actual mining of many of these ores has been in decline since the 1980s, falling by 11 percent through the mid-1990s. Indeed, U.S. consumption became almost entirely import-dependent in some of these metals categories. Foreign producers supply approximately 90 percent of U.S. platinum, along with 98 percent of U.S. bauxite, and 77 percent of U.S. tin.

Aluminum Surplus. Aluminum production is a major industry among the miscellaneous metals. Untypical of this industry, the United States is the largest producer of aluminum worldwide. Two of the top three U.S. producers of aluminum together produce one-sixth of the world's aluminum, earning combined revenues of $20.5 billion annually. Production of this metal rebounded to 3.6 metric tons in 1997, of which 33 percent was secondary (recycled) product. Despite high aluminum consumption in the United States, there resulted an aluminum surplus that left prices in a slump in 1998. A recovery occurred in 1999 as the surplus abated; prices rose by $1.25 per pound over the course of the calendar year. At the beginning of the new century, world prices soared past $75 per pound. In the United States, where demand was strong, merchant prices approached $80 per pound.

Rare Ores. Demand for platinum jewelry consumed approximately one-half of the world market for this precious metal at the end of the 20th century, while the car industry—historically a key consumer of platinum—turned increasingly to palladium catalysts as a substitute. Nevertheless a chronic slump in the production of platinum persisted throughout the 1990s. Russian shipments declined by more than one-third in 1999, thus aggravating the shortage and curtailing supplies of platinum everywhere. Record deficits persisted throughout the year despite unusually high levels of production in South Africa, which is the main supplier worldwide. With a global deficit of 530,000 ounces, prices rose by 30 percent—to $456 per ounce—during the final months of the century.

Other Metals. In 1999, analysts projected a demand for more than one million metric tons of zirconium by the year 2000, up from 900,000 in 1996; the United States was among the three largest producers of zirconium, after Australia and South Africa. U.S. bauxite production, in contrast, makes up less than one percent of world production totals. Most of the domestic ore is used in the production of abrasives, chemicals, propellants, and refractories. Processing plants convert more than 95 percent of U.S. bauxite into alumina, thus the world output of bauxite increased with the upswing in aluminum production.

Titanium was described as a roller coaster industry by Myra Pinkham in *Amerian Metal Market.* Volatile fluctuations in demand for the metal are attributed to fashion whims brought about by ''designer'' sports equipment made from titanium. Emerging industrial markets in gas and oil exploration, combined with traditional aerospace applications maintain the stability of the industry. In 1999 more than one-half of product distribution, or 23 million pounds went to the commercial airline industry. An additional 8 million pounds went to the military, with 19 percent for industrial applications, and consumer markets using 8 percent of the total tonnage. A strong market in 1998 led analysts to project U.S. shipments of 50 million pounds for 1999 plus 27 million pounds of imports, in a stable but sluggish world market for titanium.

Environmental Considerations. The momentum toward greater environmental consciousness continued to exert downward pressure on metals demand, especially toxic metals such as mercury. Increasing regulatory controls on mining activities resulted in escalated costs for producers. Incentives abounded for scientists to develop synthetic substitutes for many of the toxic primary metals. Additionally, use of these products was discouraged.

Mercury mining interests, long under scrutiny because of the toxicity of the metal, remained under strict operational guidelines from most governments. The mercury industry not only began to embrace recycling, but also introduced new technology in 1994 to replace mercury battery cells with a new type of membrane cell. U.S. mine production of mercury declined dramatically, by one-third from 1980 to the mid-1990s. Production of the metal virtually collapsed from a level of 1,057 metric tons in 1980 to just 58 metric tons in 1991. Production rose slightly to 64 metric tons in 1994, but political pressure to eliminate the metal from the environment altogether continued through the end of the century.

Most of the mercury produced in the United States in the year 2000 was from secondary (recovered) product, from such items as obsolete batteries and electrical appliances, and from used fluorescent tubes. The combination of all sources, including the mercury obtained as a by-product of gold mining, brought the total value of U.S. mercury to under $4 million. The Universal Waste Law of 1995 was amended on July 9, 1999, to become effective on January 6, 2000. The amendment specified proper disposal procedures for fluorescent light bulbs to prevent the mercury-coated tubes from ending up in landfills, and to recycle more product in the process.

Industry Leaders

It is difficult to identify precise market shares for individual companies, since nearly all of the leading companies engage in activities classified within other industries. These include **SIC 1041, Gold Ores; SIC 1455, Kaolin and Ball Clay; SIC 1459, Clay, Ceramic, and Refractory Minerals, Not Elsewhere Classified; SIC 3312, Steel Works, Blast Furnaces (Including Coke Ovens), and Rolling Mills;** and **SIC 3339, Primary Smelting and Refining of Nonferrous Metals, Except Copper and Aluminum.** Among the leading companies with interests in the miscellaneous metal ores was the U.S. Steel Group of Pittsburgh, Pennsylvania with nearly $5 billion total sales in all arenas including production of the miscellaneous metals. The leading company devoted primarily to production of miscellaneous metals ores was Cominco American, Inc., of Spokane, Washington. Cominco had total sales of $400 million in the mid-1990s. Other leading firms in the industry included Magnesium Corporation of America, of Salt Lake City, Utah with sales of $100 million; and Stillwater Mining Company of Nye, Montana, with sales of $54 million. Placer Dome U.S., Incorporated of San Francisco, California, showed sales of $93 million; and RGC(USA) Mineral Sales, Incorporated of Green Grove Springs, Florida, with sales of $30 million.

Workforce

The mining of primary metals is considered to be the most dangerous type of mining. The average occupational injury incident rate per 100 full-time employees for total primary metal production was 16.5 incidents. Overall employment in the industry followed a cyclical pattern of rise and fall, beginning with 1,800 workers in the entire industry in 1972. In 1982 the numbers rose to 2,100, then fell to 1,500 by 1992. Of the 1,500 employed in 1992, approximately 1,100 were classified as production workers. The employment of production workers followed a similar curve, bottoming out at approximately 75 percent of total employment. Total industry employment remained essentially flat from 1972 to 1987, with numbers rising from 1,800 in 1972 to a peak of 2,100 in 1982 and then falling to lower levels throughout the 1990s. The companies involved in miscellaneous ore production employed an average of 31 workers.

AMERICA AND THE WORLD

While virtually all of these metals have vital industrial applications in the world economy, the largest reserves, in most cases, are found outside the United States. According to the U.S. Bureau of Mines, the United States only serves as a net exporter of aluminum, beryllium, and rare-earth ores.

The small share and relative descent in U.S. production in this industry has been attributed to several economic pressures. First in most cases, the most productive mines for many of these metals are not located in the United States. Second, an explosion of supply coming from Russia, which is rich in mineral reserves, has led to an oversupply on the world market in the mid-1990s. Also, the downward pressure on prices and a great degree of uncertainty among producers has led to a U. S. decline in production. Aluminum, platinum, and titanium, for example, experienced severe losses in the face of worldwide competition and a major imbalance in supply and demand. Finally, the demand for many of these metals is directly connected to the world's industrial activity, thus the worldwide increase in demand for the industry's products in 1996. In many cases, U.S. companies curtailed production, giving them even less of a market share.

In 1999 Russia announced the discovery of a major titanium/zirconium deposit, anticipated to be the largest in the world and totaling seven billion tons of ore. The deposit is anticipated to produce 106 million tons of titanium and 26 million tons of zirconium. Prior to the discovery Russia produced no titanium and a maximum of 5,000 tons of zirconium concentrate annually.

FURTHER READING

Barry, Susan (ed.) *U.S. Industry and Trade Outlook.* New York: McGraw-Hill, 1999.

''Buying Is Weaker than Forecast Earlier.'' *Purchasing,* 4 November 1999.

Carlin, James F. ''Tin.'' *U.S. Department of the Interior, Bureau of Mines Minerals Yearbook 1995, Volume 1: Metals and Minerals,* Washington, DC: GPO, 1995.

''Commodity Price Index.'' *Economist,* 20 November 1999.

Gambogi, Joseph M. ''Titianium and Titanium Dioxide.'' *U.S. Department of the Interior, Bureau of Mines, Minerals Yearbook 1995, Volume 1: Metals and Minerals,* Washington, DC: GPO, 1995.

Guzzo, Maria. ''Mercury Falling.'' *Pittsburgh Business Times,* 10 December 1999.

Hedrick, James B. ''Rare Earths.'' *U.S. Department of the Interior, Bureau of Mines, Minerals Yearbook 1995, Volume 1: Metals and Minerals,* Washington, DC: GPO, 1995.

Hedrick, James B. ''Thorium.'' *U.S. Department of the Interior, Bureau of Mines, Minerals Yearbook 1995, Volume 1: Metals and Minerals,* Washington, DC: GPO, 1995.

Jasinski, Stephen M. ''Bismuth.'' *U.S. Department of the Interior, Bureau of Mines, Minerals Yearbook 1995, Volume 1: Metals and Minerals,* Washington, DC: GPO, 1995.

Kramer, Deborah A. ''Beryllium.'' *U.S. Department of the Interior, Bureau of Mines, Minerals Yearbook 1995, Volume 1: Metals and Minerals,* Washington, DC: GPO, 1995.

Llewellyn, Thomas O. ''Antimony.'' *U.S. Department of the Interior, Bureau of Mines, Minerals Yearbook 1995, Volume 1: Metals and Minerals,* Washington, DC: GPO, 1995.

Pinkham, Myra. ''Titanium Industry Looks for New Applications.'' *American Metal Market,* 16 December 1999.

Plunkert, Patricia A. ''Bauxite and Alumina.'' *U.S. Department of the Interior, Bureau of Mines, Minerals Yearbook 1991, Volume 1: Metals and Minerals,* Washington, DC: GPO, 1995.

Reese, Robert G. ''Mercury.'' *U.S. Department of the Interior, Bureau of Mines, Minerals Yearbook 1995, Volume 1: Metals and Minerals,* Washington, DC: GPO, 1995.

Reese, Jr., Robert G. ''Platinum Group Metals.'' *U.S. Department of the Interior, Bureau of Mines, Minerals Yearbook 1995, Volume 1: Metals and Minerals,* Washington, DC: GPO, 1995.

Regan, Bob. ''Aluminum at 28-Month High.'' *American Metal Market,* 10 January 2000.

''Reynolds Agrees to Bid from Alcoa Inc.,'' *Washington Times,* 20 August 1999.

Templeton, David A. ''Zirconium and Hafnium.'' *U.S. Department of the Interior, Bureau of Mines, Minerals Yearbook 1995, Volume 1: Metals and Minerals,* Washington, DC: GPO, 1995.

SIC 1221

BITUMINOUS COAL AND LIGNITE SURFACE MINING

This classification covers establishments primarily engaged in producing bituminous coal or lignite at surface mines or in developing bituminous coal or lignite surface mines. This industry includes auger mining, strip mining, culm bank mining, and other surface mining, by owners or lessees or by establishments that have complete responsibility for operating bituminous coal and lignite surface mines for others on a contract or fee basis. Bituminous coal and lignite preparation plants performing such activities as cleaning, crushing, screening, or sizing are included if operated in conjunction with a mine site, or if operated independently of any type of mine.

NAICS CODE(S)

212111 (Bituminous Coal and Lignite Surface Mining)

INDUSTRY SNAPSHOT

The U.S. bituminous coal industry is the second largest in the world, accounting for about 27 percent of global production in the mid-1990s. In addition, approximately 25 percent of total world coal reserves are located on U.S. lands, providing enough coal to meet an estimated 450 years of domestic demand. Bituminous and lignite surface mining represents about 60 percent of total industry output.

Coal generates more than 50 percent of U.S. electric power and accounts for about 25 percent of total U.S. energy consumption. It also represents a major export product. In 1998, American producers exported approximately 76 million tons of coal (not including lignite or anthracite). The coal industry shipped about $20 billion worth of coal per year in the early 1990s, while employing more than 100,000 workers. An additional 100,000 to 150,000 U.S. workers held jobs that were dependent on the industry's output, such as coal transportation.

The coal industry in the mid-1990s was characterized by price erosion, strict environmental controls, labor unrest, increasing foreign competition, stagnant growth in demand, and increasing energy taxes. To combat these negative influences, producers were striving to raise productivity, increase surface mining, consolidate, and take advantage of new environmental technologies. Industry participants already had experienced significant achievements in these areas by 1997 and expect to continue in the same positive direction into the beginning of new century.

Organization and Structure

According to the Energy Information Administration, 1,750 mines operated in 25 states in 1998. Surface mining was the exclusive mining technique used in 9 of those states. Mines range in size from small facilities that generate several thousand tons of coal per year to mammoth surface operations that extract 10 to 20 million tons per year. The surface and underground mining industry produced more than 1.1 billion tons of coal in 1998.

The Mining Process. Surface mining usually is practiced on relatively flat ground; the coal is recovered from a depth of less than 200 feet. At mines where the coal is located on steep inclines, though, material may be excavated from open pits that can reach depths of several hundred feet.

To reach coal deposits, miners must first remove the overburden, or strata, that covers the coal bed. Between 1 and 30 cubic yards of strata must be excavated for each ton of coal recovered. Dragline excavators, power shovels, bulldozers, front-end loaders, scrapers, and other heavy pieces of equipment are used to move the strata and extract the coal.

The two common methods of surface mining are strip and auger. At strip mines, large drills bore holes in the strata. Explosives are placed in these cavities and detonated. Power shovels or draglines operating at surface level then move the broken strata, while power shovels below dig up the coal and load it into trucks. The strata and coal are removed in long strips. This is done so that the debris from the newest strip can be dumped into an adjacent strip, from which the coal already has been recovered.

Auger mining consists of boring a series of holes that are 2 to 5 feet in diameter and 300 or more feet deep. This parallel and horizontal pattern is carved into a seam of coal that already has been exposed by an outcropping or by strip mining methods. No blasting takes place and the overburden is left intact. The coal simply is removed and loaded into waiting trucks. Auger mining frequently is used in open-pit mines where the strata is too thick to economically remove using strip methods.

Because surface mining is less expensive and more productive than traditional underground mining, new surface extraction technology has allowed this method to dominate U.S. coal production. Moreover, producers are able to remove an estimated 90 percent of the coal at surface mines, while underground mines permit only a 50 to 80 percent extraction rate, depending on the mining method used.

After it is processed, different types of coal are often blended to produce uniform grades of commercial material. Blending also may occur at the point of use. Coal preparation plants can produce anywhere from 200 to 20,000 tons of coal per day. From the preparation plant, 70 percent of the coal is delivered to users by rail. Barges and ships deliver an additional 20 percent of industry output. Some coal also is stored for future use.

Coal Products. Four grades of coal mined in the coal industry include lignite, subbituminous, bituminous, and anthracite. Each grade differs in moisture content, volatile matter, and fixed carbon content. Anthracite, the highest grade material, accounts for less than one half of one percent of total output, and is classified in its own industry (see **SIC 1231: Anthracite Mining**).

Bituminous coal, or soft coal, is the most common type of coal produced in the United States. It represents more than 70 percent of total industry output and accounts for approximately 50 percent of total U.S. reserves. The mineral is composed of 80 to 90 percent carbon and about 10 to 20 percent moisture. A ton of bituminous coal typically generates 19 to 30 million BTUs and ignites at between 700 and 900 degrees fahrenheit. Bituminous coal possesses a relatively low sulfur content, which causes it to burn more cleanly than some lower grades. Because of its properties, bituminous coal is the principal steam coal used for generating electricity.

It also is the primary coking coal used in the steel-making process.

Bituminous coal can be further categorized as low-, medium-, and high-volatile coal, according to its moisture content and heating capacity. Low- and medium-volatility grade bituminous coal typically generates between 26 and 30 million BTUs per ton. High-volatile coal, in contrast, usually produces anywhere from 18 to 29 million BTUs per ton. For comparison, a ton of bituminous coal, assuming an average 22 million BTUs, produces about the same amount of energy as one cord of hardwood, 22,000 cubic feet of natural gas, or 160 gallons of fuel oil.

Subbituminous coal has a 75 to 85 percent carbon content. It produces 16 to 24 million BTUs per ton and is used primarily to generate electricity. In 1995, subbituminous coal represented 31.7 percent of industry output. Although its sulfur content is low relative to lignite, a high moisture content, along with other negative properties, makes it less desirable than higher coal grades for most applications.

Lignite, the lowest ranked coal, is a brownish-black mineral containing a moisture content of 30 to 40 percent. It produces about 9 to 17 million BTUs per ton and ignites at roughly 600 degrees Fahrenheit. Because it deteriorates rapidly in air, has a high sulfur content, and is liable to combust spontaneously, lignite mainly is used to generate electricity in power plants that are close to mines. In 1995, lignite accounted for 8.3 percent of industry production. Lignite also is subject to high royalties charged by the federal government.

Coal Consumers. In 1998, 83 percent of the coal produced in the United States, 912.1 million short tons, was consumed by utilities. Percentage-wise, this was down from 88 percent in 1995. Coal-fired facilities produced approximately 55 percent of the total electricity generated domestically.

The second largest coal customer was the general industry sector, which accounted for 76.5 short tons of coal in 1998. Industry uses for coal include production of materials such as calcium carbide, silicon carbide, refractory bricks, carbon and graphite electrodes, and various food and paper products. Coal also is used to produce gall and stone, primary metals, textiles, and plastics. One of the largest industrial uses of coal is cement production. In fact, 90 percent of U.S. cement plants use coal—at a rate of about 1 ton for each 3.5 tons of cement produced.

Iron and steel manufacturers are the third largest coal consumers. These industries use coal to produce coke—a primary ingredient in the smelting of iron. In 1995, approximately 27.6 million short tons of coal was used in the processing of iron and steel.

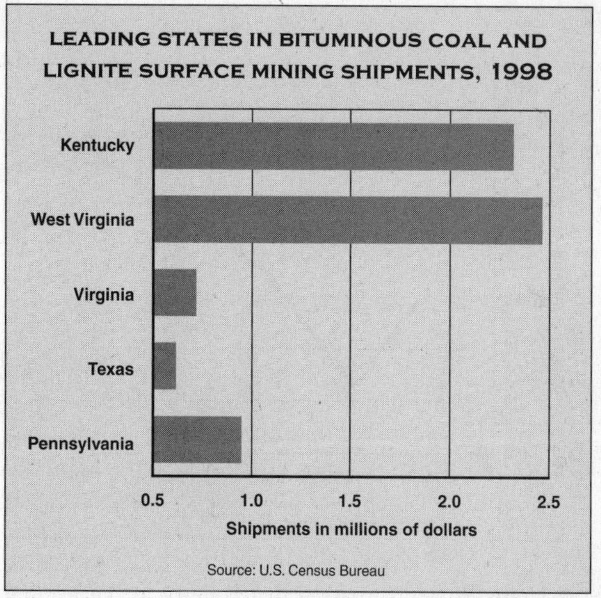

BACKGROUND AND DEVELOPMENT

Coal is not a true mineral, but rather an organic compound formed from the remains of living organic material that flourished 250 to 400 million years ago. The Chinese are believed to be the first to have used coal, in about 1000 B.C. The Romans also are believed to have burned the material. The first written history of coal dates back to 1200 A.D., when metalworkers in Europe were observed using it.

Widespread use of coal did not occur in Europe until the fifteenth and sixteenth centuries. Advances that significantly promoted the use of coal during the eighteenth century included Abraham Darby's methods of using coal instead of charcoal in blast furnaces and forges, as well as the coal-burning steam engine developed by James Watt.

Although coal mining was taking place in North America as early as 1701 in Virginia, it was not until 1745 that coal was mined in the colonies on a commercial scale. During the American Revolution, when European sources of coal became inaccessible, the fledgling industry's importance increased. By the early 1830s, many small coal mining operations had sprung up along rivers in Appalachian regions. In the 1840s, the industry mined its first 1 million tons.

The advent of the steam locomotive in the middle and late 1800s prompted a huge expansion of the coal industry, as producers took advantage of that important new channel of distribution. This development, in conjunction with the start of the Industrial Revolution, resulted in huge industry growth. Between 1865 and 1905, for instance, production ballooned from 182 million tons to 928 million tons. Although the United Kingdom led world coal production throughout the nineteenth century,

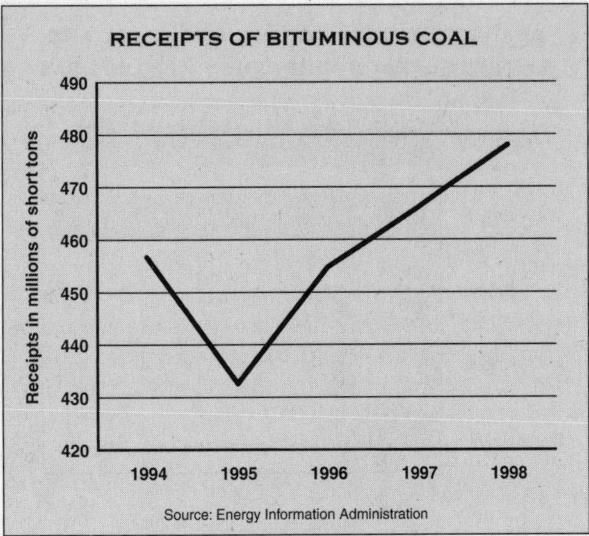

the United States surpassed that country as the leading producer in 1900. In that year, U.S. companies mined 250 million tons of coal. By 1935 world output stood at 1.18 billion tons.

Growth in the use of coal, mostly to generate energy and to create iron and steel, continued at a moderate pace until the middle 1900s in most industrialized countries. By 1958 annual demand for coal in the United States stood at about 400 million tons. However, massive growth in demand in previously undeveloped regions such as the former U.S.S.R. and China had pushed global consumption past 2.5 billion tons by the 1950s.

In the 1950s and 1960s demand for coal realized solid growth in the United States, despite the increasing popularity of alternative energy sources such as petroleum and hydro-power. During those decades, a booming post-war economy spurred demand for coal by utilities and iron and steel makers, as well as other commercial industrial sectors.

Growth of Strip and Auger Mining. Coal was first taken directly from exposed ledges and outcroppings. When this meager supply was consumed, however, miners began to scratch beneath the earth's crust using surface, or open-cut, mining equipment. After easily accessible surface coal had been extracted and the strata became too thick to remove, companies were forced to mine for coal using costly underground operations. Underground mines, though, could not safely access coal that was close to the earth's surface because the risk of the mine collapsing was too great. For this reason, much of the coal that lay just beneath the earth's surface, but also under thick strata, remained inaccessible.

In the 1960s and 1970s, improved earth-moving equipment catapulted the surface, or strip mining, industry to center stage. New tools allowed miners to remove overburden more than 200 feet thick. Massive power shovels, many taller than a 12-story building, were developed that could remove up to 115 cubic yards of debris in a single bite. New earth hauling trucks had equivalent capacities. Similar advancements propelled auger-mining technology, which originated in the 1940s. Indeed, massive drills, conveyors, and haulers made auger mining, like strip mining, preferable to many forms of underground mining.

Coal companies were finding that, in most cases, they could extract coal using new surface mining techniques more cheaply and efficiently than they could using even the latest underground mining technology. Surface mining accounted for only 35 percent of total U.S. coal production in 1965. By the late 1970s, however, auger and strip mining operations accounted for a full 60 percent of industry output. Because surface mining is not always applicable in mountainous regions, such as Appalachia, coal extracted from underground mines accounted for 38 percent by 1995.

Labor Influence. The early mining industry in the United States and Europe was characterized by a history of worker exploitation and dismal and dangerous working conditions. For these reasons, the impetus to form and maintain strong labor unions has played an integral role in the development of the industry.

The first U.S. coal labor union appeared in Illinois in the 1890s. By 1900 unions were present in 5 other states. Eventually, the United Mine Workers of America (UMW), a national organization, became the dominant labor influence in the industry; by 1940 the UMW represented more than 800,000 mine workers. Federal and state governments also became active in the protection of mine workers in the first half of the century. Following a succession of mine explosions in 1907 that killed thousands of miners, the Bureau of Mines (BOM) was created. Several states also began requiring mine safety inspections.

The industry death toll continued to rise, however, prompting the federal government to establish mine safety standards in 1941, although these regulations were not enforced until 1946. In 1969 Congress passed the important Coal Mine Health & Safety Act (CMHSA). Adding to federal and state efforts were international organizations, such as the Coal Mining Industrial Committee, which was formed in 1945 to improve mine workers' conditions on a global scale. Between 1968 and 1991, mine fatalities decreased from .27 fatalities per 200,000 man-hours to .05—a reduction of 81 percent. Injures declined as well, by about 29 percent.

By the 1960s, labor organizations had become so strong in the mining industry that about 75 percent of all coal was produced by UMW members. Furthermore, several other unions appeared, including the Progressive Mine Workers of America, the International Brotherhood of Electrical Workers, and the International Union of Operating Engineers. These combined labor forces vastly improved wages and working conditions for miners in the 1960s, 1970s, and 1980s. Critics, however, argued that labor unions had become too strong and were sapping coal industry productivity and health.

The 1970s and 1980s. Many coal producers fell on hard times during the 1970s—a result of several factors. A principal reason for the industry's decline was a marked decrease in productivity and an increase in salaries and benefits. Federal safety regulations, for instance, were blamed for slashing productivity by almost 50 percent between 1969 and 1978—from 1.95 miner hours per ton to 1.04. CMHSA regulations forced companies to hire more personnel and alter existing labor practices that were deemed unsafe or unfair.

Of critical importance to the coal mining industry in the 1970s, as well as in the 1980s and 1990s, were federal environmental regulations that cut into the profits of industry players. A series of state and federal bills dealing with land reclamation, for instance, were blamed for decreased productivity at surface mines—down to 3.03 tons produced per man hour in 1977 from 4.74 tons in 1974. The Surface Mining Control and Reclamation Act (SMCRA) of 1977 also set up a provision for cleaning up old mining sites. That provision, which among other things instituted a tax of 35 cents per ton on all surface-mined bituminous coal, generated $256 million in 1996.

Another factor that hurt producers in both the 1970s and 1980s was a decrease in the growth of coal demand. Hydro, nuclear, natural gas, and oil sources continued to reduce coal's total contribution to domestic energy consumption. Although coal production grew at a rate of 5.7 percent in the 1970s and 3.8 percent in the 1980s, this was down from a 7.3 percent annual growth rate in the 1950s and 6.6 percent average annual growth during the 1960s.

During the 1980s, however, many coal producers succeeded in overcoming the profit barriers that arose during the 1970s. Although total growth in demand for coal declined in the 1980s, the industry was able to increase its contribution to total U.S. energy consumption from a low of 17.6 percent in 1973 to more than 25 percent in the late 1980s. Even a significant reduction in the use of coal by iron and steel producers was not enough to offset increased consumption by utilities, which were seeking less expensive alternatives to oil.

Coal companies also enjoyed increased success in increasing productivity and extracting labor concessions in the 1980s. Technological advancements in automation and mining techniques allowed producers to realize massive productivity gains between 1980 and 1990. Productivity at surface mines shot up from about 3 tons per man-hour in the late 1970s to more than 6 tons per hour by 1990, and continued to rise. As a result, total industry employment declined from about 240,000 workers in 1978, when 665 million tons of coal was shipped, to 81,000 workers in 1995, when 1.12 billion tons of coal were produced.

As industry employment diminished and new surface mining plants opened in western states, labor's influence on the industry declined. Indeed, the portion of coal produced at UMW mines had declined to about 30 percent of the total by 1990, while the percentage of U.S. coal mined by members of all labor unions had fallen to only 55 percent. By 1995, about 27 percent of miners at surface mines belonged to the UMWA, and another 11 percent belonged to other unions.

Industry participants also insisted that they had made strides in meeting environmental challenges, pointing to new mining, processing, and coal burning technologies. Environmental groups, however, remained opposed to many aspects of the coal mining industry.

Despite successes in the 1980s, industry profit growth was held in check by relatively stagnant demand growth and declining prices. Production outpaced demand, forcing prices down. Between 1992 and 1995, for instance, the price of coal dropped from $21.03 per ton to $17.52 per ton, using constant 1992 dollars.

CURRENT CONDITIONS

Overall coal production realized very modest gains from 1991 to 1998, averaging less than 1 percent annual growth. There was a slight decrease from 1994 to 1995, but figures for 1996 indicated growth of more than 2 percent. Surface mining, however, grew steadily. While coal production east of the Mississippi, where most underground mines were located, fell 3.9 percent from 1994 to 1995 to 544 million short tons, coal production in the western states, where surface mines predominate, increased by 4.6 percent to a record 489 million short tons. In 1998 surface production stood at 686.6 million short tons. Prices continued to decline, though, at the same time that production costs were rising.

Mines continued to close and employment continued to decline across the whole coal mining industry, with a net loss in 1995 of 250 mines and about 7,000 miners. Employment at surface mines declined by 9.9 percent from 1994 to 1995, to about 32,000 miners. However, productivity continued to increase. Miner productivity east of the Mississippi grew to 3.45 short tons per miner per hour, while in the west productivity rose 7 percent to 14.18 short tons.

Phase one of the Clean Air Amendment Act of 1990, which set a goal of cutting sulfur dioxide emissions nationwide by 10 million tons by the year 2000, went into effect on January 1, 1995. The law required electrical generating plants to lower smokestack emissions of sulfur compounds, but gave utilities wide latitude in how this might be accomplished. Plants that exceeded requirements received allowances that could be sold or exchanged on the open market. Because of this market-based approach, the legislation had not, by the time phase one went into effect, had the calamitous effect that some analysts had feared. Most utilities had not found it necessary to install expensive scrubbers, but had found switching to low-sulfur coals and purchasing allowances adequate to meet the law's requirements. Midwestern mines that produced coal with a higher sulfur content felt the impact of the legislation most severely, while western low-sulfur coal producers experienced some relative benefit. The threat of increased environmental controls related to carbon-dioxide emissions and land reclamation was, however, a source of concern for many producers.

The Future of Coal. Electric utilities continued to consume the vast majority of surface-mined coal and lignite. In 1998, electric utilities used 912 million short tons. A study by Resource Data International Inc., reported in July 1996, projected continued domination of electricity generation by coal through the year 2015. Annual increases of 1.3 to 2.1 percent were forecast.

Another segment in the energy market that held promise for coal producers was non-utility power producers. Since passage of the Public Utility Regulatory Policies Act (PURPA) of 1978, several new types of non-regulated power facilities had developed. These entities usually sold their output to public utilities. Non-regulated facilities included non-utility generators, independent power producers, and cogenerators.

The domestic demand for coking coal was expected to continue to decline. Accounting for 25 percent of industry output in 1950, the demand for coking coal to produce iron and steel in the United States commanded only 3.4 percent of production in 1991. In 1993 consumption of coking coal hit a low of 31 million short tons, but had risen to 33 million tons in 1995. By 1998, that figure had declined to 27.6 million.

INDUSTRY LEADERS

The coal industry has undergone a period of consolidation that began in the mid-1970s. Since that time, the number of coal producers declined from 2,300 to about 1,500 by 1993. The number of mines those companies operated fell during the same period from 6,200 to 3,200. In the 1970s, a number of energy companies such as Exxon, Shell, and Sun Oil had acquired coal properties in an attempt to diversify, but soft prices for both coal and oil encouraged many of these companies to sell off some or all of these acquisitions. Large coal operators such as Peabody Holding, Zeigler Coal, and Cyprus AMAX Minerals purchased many of these existing mines.

In an effort to increase their capital strength and benefit from economies of scale, larger mining companies also were acquiring or merging with competitors. In 1995, the 10 largest coal producing companies accounted for 51 percent of the total production for the year. In 1984 this percentage was only 29 percent. The surface mining industry, compared to the overall mining industry, was even more concentrated, as a few massive surface mines dominated the industry. Of the 20 highest producing mines in 1995, 19 were surface mines located west of the Mississippi, and together accounted for 28.9 percent of total U.S. coal production. The top 9 mines were all surface mines in Wyoming and accounted for 18.8 percent of production.

In 1998 the largest U.S. producer of coal was Peabody Holding Co., part of the British-owned Hanson PLC. Peabody's output from both underground and surface mines in 1998 was 160.1 million tons. The next largest producers were Cyprus AMAX, Consol Coal Group, Kennecott Energy Co., and Atlantic Richfield Co.'s ARCO Coal. However, in April 1997, Atlantic Richfield reported that it was likely to divest itself of its coal mining operations in both the United States and Australia. Arch Coal Inc. was the sixth largest U.S. coal company, with annual production of 48.4 million tons.

WORKFORCE

The number of workers employed by U.S. coal producers continued declining in 1998 to about 81,000 (excluding management and office workers). Although surface mining operations are less susceptible to labor cutbacks than underground mining facilities, surface mines are considerably less labor intensive and provide fewer job opportunities per ton of coal produced than do underground mines. Labor positions in the surface mining industry are concentrated in the maintenance and operation of heavy machinery. In addition, surface mining companies have a higher proportion of management and clerical workers than the overall coal industry.

Employment opportunities in the surface mining industry have been limited. Labor unions have pushed hard to get companies that have opened new surface mining operations to employ workers that were displaced from underground mining jobs. This factor, in addition to constantly rising automation and productivity, make coal industry employment highly competitive. Even new positions in management remained limited in the early 1990s—a result of generally tepid industry growth.

AMERICA AND THE WORLD

Of the estimated 490 billion tons of coal reserves in the United States, only about 150 billion tons are accessible through surface mining. Nevertheless, this reserve ensures a dominant U.S. position in the future global coal mining industry. In addition to healthy reserves, U.S. coal companies have achieved the highest productivity of any coal-producing nation. While the United States places second to Australia as the largest coal exporter, America remained the largest total coal producer until the early 1990s when China assumed the lead.

The amount of coal exported from the U.S. has increased. In 1998, exports stood at 76.2 million tons. The primary reason for the increase was the substantial growth in the demand for U.S. steam coal. Exports to Europe more than doubled between 1994 and 1995. At the same time, the United States imported less than one percent of its coal needs. Canada overtook Japan as the single largest consumer of U.S. coal in 1998, absorbing 19.2 million tons to Japan's 7.7 tons. Other countries importing U.S. coal include Brazil (6.5 million tons in 1998), the UK (5.9 million tons), and Italy (5.3 million tons).

Despite its strong export position, the 1998 figure represents only 7 percent of total U.S. production for the year. The price per exported ton fell from $44.36 in 1996 to $34.30 in 1998. In fact, U.S. share of the world coal market has fallen dramatically since the 1950s. From 1960 to 1990 the country's global market share fell from 50 percent to approximately 25 percent. This decline was a result of increased production by several other countries, many of which are not subject to environmental regulations and labor controls that constrain U.S. producers. South Africa and Australia, particularly, have proven themselves effective competitors for global market share. Other countries with a small but growing output of coal include Indonesia, Colombia, and Venezuela.

Producers also have kept a close eye on China, which produced 1.2 billion tons in 1998—and which boasts massive coal reserves in excess of 800 billion tons. China's export potential clearly is formidable. The country has continued to strive to upgrade its production and distribution infrastructure with the help of Japanese investment capital and has embarked on an ambitious nuclear energy program. China hoped that increased domestic use of nuclear energy would allow it to divert more of its coal production to the export market. Other countries that were striving to garner global coal market share in the early 1990s included Columbia, Venezuela, and Indonesia. These three, along with Canada, make up the major exporters to the United States.

RESEARCH AND TECHNOLOGY

To maintain economic viability and their position in the global export market, U.S. surface mining firms have continued to rely on technological advances to overcome imposing barriers that face them. Of great importance were projects to improve the cleanliness and efficiency of coal-fired electric power plants. The U.S. Department of Energy was developing five categories of research. Low-emission boiler systems incorporated advanced combustion and innovative flue gas cleaning systems in the initial design for new power plants. Pressurized fluidized bed combustion captured sulfur pollutants inside the boiler instead of in the stack, and allowed combustion at temperatures below the point at which most nitrogen pollutants form. The integrated gasification combined cycle (IGCC) employed coal gasification rather than traditional combustion and combined a steam turbine driven by exhaust heat with the gas turbine driven by the coal gas. Indirectly fired cycles employed a design that heated a working fluid such as air to turn the turbine rather than the hot gases of combustion. Finally, integrated gasification-fuel cell combinations would link a coal gasifier with a fuel cell. By 1995, pressurized fluidized bed combustion systems and IGCC systems were in commercial use. The primary goals of the industry at present are to produce coal more efficiently and more safely, as well as to encourage scientists to find cleaner ways in which it can be used.

FURTHER READING

''Arco Says Considers Disposal of Coal Assets.'' *Reuters Business Report,* 1 April 1997.

Bonskowski, Richard. ''The U.S.Coal Industry in the 1990s: Low Prices and Record Production.'' September 1999. Energy Information Administration, Office of Coal, Nuclear, Electric and Alternate Fuels, U.S. Department of Energy. Available from http://www.eia.doe.gov.

Brogan, Pamela. ''Coal Health Care Bill: Will It Be Surplus or Deficit?'' *Gannett News Service,* 22 June 1995.

Byrne, Harlan S. ''Power Play.'' *Barron's,* 16 September 1996.

Chambers, Ann. ''Coal to Dominate Generation to 2015.'' *Power Engineering,* July 1996.

Massey, David. ''Coal: An Industry in Transition.'' *Electric Perspectives,* 1 January 1995.

National Mining Association. ''Salient Statistics of the Mining Industry.'' Available from http://www.nma.org/salient.html.

U.S. Department of Commerce, Bureau of the Census. *1997 Economic Census.* Available from http://www.census.gov.

U. S. Department of Energy. ''The Department of Energy's Clean Coal Power Program.'' Availble from http://www.fe.doe.gov/coal_power/advpwr.html#cleanpower.

U.S. Department of Labor. Mining Safety and Health Administration. ''Mine Accident, Injury, Illness, Employment, and Coal Production Statistics, 1996.'' Available from http://www.msha.gov/ALLCOAL.HTM.

SIC 1222

BITUMINOUS COAL UNDERGROUND MINING

This classification includes establishments primarily engaged in producing bituminous coal in underground mines or in developing bituminous coal underground mines. This industry includes underground mining by owners or lessees or by establishments that have complete responsibility for operating bituminous coal underground mines for others on a contract or fee basis. Bituminous coal preparation plants performing such activities as cleaning, crushing, screening, or sizing are included if operated in conjunction with a mine. Independent bituminous coal preparation plants are classified in **SIC 1221: Bituminous Coal and Lignite Surface Mining.**

NAICS Code(s)

212112 (Bituminous Coal Underground Mining)

Industry Snapshot

Underground coal mining has been practiced in the United States since the 1800s and was the dominant mining technique for most of the twentieth century. By the late 1990s, underground U.S. mines were producing more than 430 million tons of coal per year. In addition, bituminous coal mining operations were responsible for exporting more than 76 million tons of product in 1998.

Despite its large size and its importance to energy and industrial markets, the U.S. underground coal mining industry is in some fundamental ways a troubled one. These difficulties first manifested themselves in the late 1960s and have continued unabated throughout the 1990s. A primary threat to industry participants has been the rapid proliferation of relatively efficient surface mines. Other detriments though, include increasing environmental constraints, labor problems, stagnant growth, and foreign competition.

Organization and Structure

In 1998 there were about 860 underground coal mines in operation. Underground mines were more prevalent in the East, accounting for 64 percent of production. The majority of these mines were located in the Appalachian region. Surface coal mines were located primarily in the West, with the largest surface mines in the world found in the Powder River Basin. (see **SIC 1221: Bituminous Coal Surface Mining**).

Steam coal, which represents the large majority of industry output, is most often used to power electric utilities. General industry, such as glass making and cement production, accounts for the next large portion of coal consumption. Metallurgical coal, or coking coal, is used for iron and steel production. Although they are classified as part of the same industry, these three segments differ in their reserve base, production facilities, distribution channels, and marketing requirements.

Besides regional distinctions and differences in mining techniques, underground mines differ in the quality and type of bituminous coal they produce. Eastern underground coal, for instance, is more likely to exhibit coking properties. Coal mined from underground operations in the northeast typically has a high energy content and contains a widely varying amount of sulfur, a pollutant that is believed to be a major source of acid rain. Eastern Appalachian coal is most likely to have a very high sulfur content, while central Appalachian coal is comparatively low in sulfur. Much of the underground coal mined in the Midwest, such as Illinois Basin coal, is also high in sulfur.

Because it has a higher energy content and costs much more to produce, coal extracted from underground mines is more expensive than surface-mined coal. Appalachian coal, for instance, was priced at $28.24 per ton in 1995. In contrast, western surface mined coal was selling at $9.63 per ton. High transportation costs associated with western-mined coal tends to reduce this great disparity, though.

Underground Mining Methods. Companies engaged in this industry extract coal that lies 200 to 1,000 feet below the earth's surface, though some mines are as deep as 2,000 feet. Underground mines consist of a series of parallel and interconnecting tunnels from which the coal is cut and removed with special machinery. The process is complex and sometimes dangerous. The mine must be adequately ventilated to protect miners from dust and explosive methane gas that is released by the coal. In addition, careful ground control must be practiced to prevent the roof of the mine from collapsing on workers and equipment.

Three types of underground operations are distinguished by the method used to access the coal mine. Drift mines are characterized by the use of a level tunnel leading into the mine, while slope mines have an inclined tunnel and shaft mines utilize a vertical tunnel. The primary methods of extracting coal from all of these mines are room-and-pillar, long-wall, and shortwall.

Room-and-pillar mining is often the least efficient method. It often allows recovery of only about 50 percent of the coal, although there are occasions when this methodology can achieve a much greater recovery percentage. Long-wall and shortwall mining, in comparison, extracts up to 80 percent of the usable coal. In a room-and-pillar operation, coal is mined in a series of rooms cut into the coalbed. Pillars of unmined coal are left intact, and serve to support the mine roof as miners advance through the coal seam. Sometimes the coal in the pillars can be extracted later in the ''retreat'' phase.

The two basic types of room-and-pillar mining are conventional and continuous. Conventional mining consists of a series of operations that involve cutting and breaking up the coalbed, blasting the bed, and then removing the shattered coal. Continuous mining, on the other hand, uses a machine that digs and loads coal in one operation, without blasting. The majority of room-and-pillar coal was extracted using continuous mining in the 1990s.

Long-wall mines use huge machines with cutting heads. The heads are pulled back and forth across a block of coal up to about 600 feet long. Coal is sheared and plowed into slices that are removed by a conveyor. Movable roof supports allow mined-out areas to cave in behind the advancing machine. In the mid-1990s, long-wall systems accounted for about half of all coal mined underground. Shortwall mining is similar to long-wall operations, but the continuous mining machine shears smaller blocks of coal, generally less than 150 feet long.

BACKGROUND AND DEVELOPMENT

Bituminous underground coal was created during a 250- to 400-million-year process in which the ocean covered and compressed organic deposits. Low grade coal material that eventually developed below the ocean floor was further compacted into higher grade bituminous coal. More extreme pressure, resulting from the folding of the earth's surface into great mountain ranges, such as the Appalachians, produced the highest grade coal. This high-grade coal is most likely to be found in the United States in underground mines along the eastern seaboard.

The first coal mined from the famous Appalachian bituminous coal field, which is more than 90 miles long and covers 63,000 square miles, occurred in the mid-1700s. Most of this coal, though, was simply dug from exposed coal seams on the earth's surface. During the 1800s, after the easily removable surface coal had diminished, underground mining became the industry standard. By the early 1830s in fact, underground mines were operating in many parts of Appalachia as well as in several areas along the Mississippi River. In 1840, the U.S. coal industry mined its first one million tons.

As the coal industry gained strength in the 1850s and 1860s, the federal government began to play an increasingly important role in its development. Concerned about the loss of valuable federal coal reserves, Congress enacted the first legislation dealing specifically with federal coal resources in 1864. The legislation provided for the sale of coal lands at public auction for a minimum of $20 per acre, compared to $1.25 per acre for other types of land. The law was modified in 1865 to require that purchasers be miners, and that one buyer could acquire no more than 160 acres.

The Coal Lands Act of 1873 added further regulations to the sale of lands with coal reserves by stipulating new prices for federal lands that were located near railroads. This Act remained the dominant law regulating federal coal reserves until the 1920s, when The Mineral Leasing Act was passed. The Mineral Leasing Act of 1920 essentially ended an era of federal coal disposal. By requiring mining companies to lease, rather than purchase, coal reserves, the Act instituted an ideology of close government planning and supervision of federal coal production.

The Industrial Revolution. By the late 1800s, U.S. coal production had reached a staggering 250 million tons per year. As the industry expanded, huge numbers of miners were employed to work underground. Besides suffering dismal working conditions for relatively low pay, miners were also exposed to serious hazards. Unsafe mining practices often resulted in cave-ins or explosions that killed hundreds of workers at a time, and poor ventilation gave many miners ''black lung,'' an ailment caused by inhaling large amounts of coal dust.

To relieve the plight of underground miners, federal and state government bodies began regulating and mandating safety standards in the early 1900s. In addition, workers succeeded in forming powerful labor unions that forced improvements in working conditions and higher salary scales. Although workers began forming state unions as early as the 1890s, the United Mine Workers of America (UMW) had become the dominant force for change in the industry by the 1930s. By 1960, UMW members were responsible for 75 percent of industry output.

At the same time that industry workers were making gains, underground coal mining companies were also realizing successes. Industrial growth in the early 1900s pushed U.S. coal production to more than 500 million tons per year in the early 1920s, the large majority of which was extracted from underground mines. International demand for U.S. coal following World War II further aided the companies; exports reached a record 80 million tons per year in the mid-1950s. Furthermore, the introduction of long-wall systems in the 1950s rapidly increased industry productivity. These factors combined to enable many coal companies to reap huge profits between 1900 and 1950.

Total demand for U.S. coal subsided after World War II—a result of the proliferation of alternative fuels such as natural gas and oil. Nevertheless, coal producers benefitted from the huge productivity gains achieved in the 1950s and 1960s because of the introduction of new mining techniques and advances in machinery. Although coal production fell to about 400 million tons per year by the late 1950s, worker productivity increased 50 percent and payroll costs declined between 1940 and 1960. In addition, an increase in the demand for underground-mined metallurgical coal helped offset decreasing demand in other areas. The United States became a major supplier to Japan and Europe, who were trying to rebuild their countries. Until the late 1970s in fact, the United States supplied 30 to 50 percent of those regions' import demand. Many underground coal mining companies were thus able to maintain profit growth throughout the 1960s.

Industry Downturn. In the late 1960s and early 1970s, the underground bituminous coal industry suffered serious setbacks. Most importantly, coal production in the United States rapidly shifted from underground mines in the East to surface mines in the West. New surface mining technology and machinery, which allowed companies to surface-mine coal at drastically reduced costs, accelerated this trend in the 1970s and 1980s. Furthermore, western mine operators were able to employ mostly non-union labor—a factor that eventually weakened organized labor's influence on underground mining companies across the country.

Also during the 1970s and 1980s, domestic demand for metallurgical coal, which is primarily supplied by eastern underground mines, dropped from about 10 percent of total industry production to 4 percent. Because metallurgical coal is usually of a higher grade than steam coal, the loss of this high-income domestic segment constituted a serious blow to many Appalachian mine companies. The drop reflected the overall decline in the late 1960s and 1970s of the U.S. iron and steel industry, which was battered by foreign competition and productivity losses, among other problems.

Adding to industry turmoil in the 1970s and 1980s were stringent new environmental regulations and an increase in foreign competition in the export market. The loss of world export market share hit underground mining companies particularly hard, as they produced a proportionately larger share of export coal than do surface mining firms. Because of new safety and environmental requirements, moreover, underground mine productivity fell from 1.95 tons per miner hour in 1969 to just 1.04 tons by 1978.

As producers battled on several fronts, total demand for underground coal rose only 2 percent between 1980 and 1990. New legislation, much of it intended to protect the environment from both surface and underground mining operations, further pressured the industry. The Surface Mining Control and Reclamation Act (SMCRA) of 1977, the 1988 National Bituminous Coal Wage Agreement (NBCWA), the Ford-Wallop Agreement, parts of the Comprehensive National Energy Policy Act, and several other legislative efforts increased downward pressure on coal industry profits, although environmental groups continued to protest that the measures were insufficient.

The net effect of western mining growth, diminished demand in some high-margin markets, and new regulations contributed to the decline of underground mining. Despite an overall rise in coal consumption to more than 950 million tons by 1990, the share of U.S. coal produced by underground miners plummeted from 65 percent in 1965 to about 40 percent by 1985. Even massive gains in productivity during the 1980s, to 2.54 tons per miner hour, were unable to restore profits for many ailing companies.

Current Conditions

Though the number of underground mines dropped in the 1990s—in 1993 there were more than 1,100 U. S. mines but in 1998 there were only about 860—underground mining production increased through the 1990s, rising from about 351 million tons in 1993 to 430 million tons in 1998. The increase in production was due primarily to the trend toward larger and more efficient mines. The increasing use of long-wall and continuous mining methods also helped boost productivity.

The year 1998 was extraordinary for overall coal production, which reached a record 1.12 billion tons, according to an estimate from the Energy Information Administration. This amount, which was the fifth straight year U.S. coal production output was more than a billion tons, reflected an increase of 2.6 percent over 1997 numbers and 18.3 percent over 1993 figures. Output in the East accounted for 51 percent, or 570.6 million tons of the total, while production in the West reached a record 547.6 million tons, 49 percent of the total. Though coal production continued to migrate to the West, underground operations continued to dominate production in the East. Data from the Energy Information Administration revealed that productivity levels, when calculated in terms of tons per miner, had more than doubled since 1985. The number of miners employed as underground miners however, had declined. While more than 64,000 underground miners had been employed in 1993, this figure dropped to 51,000 in 1998.

According to a 1998 survey by the National Mining Association, the four top-producing underground mines included the Enlow Fork Mine in Pennsylvania, the Twentymile Mine in Colorado, the Bailey Mine in Pennsylvania, and the Mountaineer Mine located in West Virginia. Wyoming and West Virginia were the top coal producing states in the nation, producing about 314 million and 171 million tons, respectively, in 1998. West Virginia was the leader, however, in 1997 in terms of shipments of processed bituminous coal from underground mining operations, followed by Kentucky, then Pennsylvania.

The federal government owned about a third of the U. S. coal resources in 1998, according to estimates by the Bureau of Land Management. The governments reserves consisted of about 92 billion short tons of recoverable coal reserves, considerably more than the 20 billion tons held by the next largest holder of reserves, the Great Northern Limited Partnership. The Peabody Group came in third with an estimated 10.3 billion tons, followed by CONSOL Energy Inc., and Arch Coal, Inc. Each had less than 4 billion tons of coal reserves.

Phase One of the Clean Air Amendment Act of 1990, which set a goal of cutting sulfur dioxide emissions nationwide by 10 million tons by the year 2000, went into effect on January 1, 1995. The law required electrical generating plants to lower smokestack emissions of sulfur compounds, but gave utilities wide latitude in how this might be accomplished. Plants that exceeded requirements received allowances that could be sold or exchanged on the open market. Because of this market-based approach, the legislation had not, by the time Phase One went into effect, had the calamitous effect that some analysts had feared. Most utilities had not found it necessary to install expensive scrubbers, but had found switching to low-sulfur coals and purchasing allowances adequate to meet the law's requirements. Midwestern mines that produce coal with a higher sulfur content felt the impact of the legislation most severely, while western low-sulfur coal producers experienced some relative benefit. The threat of increased environmental controls related to carbon-dioxide emissions and land reclamation was however, a source of concern for many producers.

The Clean Coal Technology Program, a partnership between the U.S. government and private industry, began in 1986 with the goal of developing options for controlling hazardous emissions. With an investment of more than $6 billion, by the late 1990s the program had about 40 projects either completed or in development. These projects included advanced power generation systems designed to increase coal-to-electricity efficiencies, environmental control devices to reduce pollution in a cost-effective manner, and efficient coal processing and cleaning processes.

Future Expectations. The underground mining industry will continue to struggle against regulatory, as well as natural market pressures. The threat of further federal involvement in the coal industry creates an unpredictable business environment and should reduce future investment in the coal industry. Coal production continued to move toward the western portion of the United States, and surface mining, as well as long-wall and continuous mining methods, made gains.

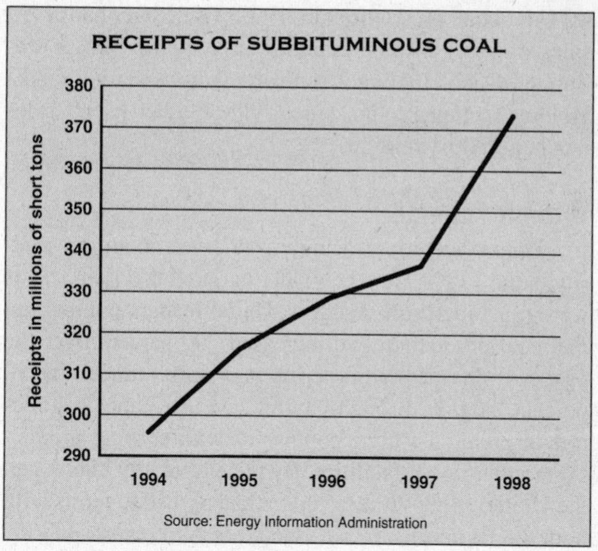

INDUSTRY LEADERS

The coal industry has undergone a period of consolidation that began in the mid-1970s. Since that time the number of coal producers declined from 2,300 to about 1,500 by 1993. The number of mines those companies operated fell during the same period from 6,200 to 3,200, and to 2,104 in 1995. In the 1970s, a number of energy companies such as Exxon, Shell, and Sun Oil had acquired coal properties in an attempt to diversify, but soft prices for both coal and oil encouraged many of these companies to sell off some or all of these acquisitions.

Consolidation among coal companies was extensive in 1998. Arch Coal purchased the U.S. coal interests of ARCO, and AEI Holding Company, Inc., acquired the coal interests of both Zeigler Coal Holding Company and Kindill Mining, as well as the Martiki Coal Company, a subsidiary of MAPCO Coal Inc. In addition, AEI secured a portion of the coal properties of Cyprus-Amax Coal Company. Other acquisitions included the Kennecott Energy Company purchase of Kerr-McGee's Jacobs Ranch Mine, the American Coal Corporation's buyout of Kerr-McGee's Galatia Mine, and MAPCO Coal Inc.'s purchase of the Cimarron Division of Andalex Resources.

The largest U.S. producer of coal in 1998 was Peabody Group, which had 25 U.S. mines and 4 in Australia. The company produced 168.5 million short tons, which accounted for 15.1 percent of total U. S. coal production. Peabody had sales in fiscal 1999 of $2.39 billion. The second largest producer of coal in the United States was Arch Coal, Inc., which produced more than 110 million tons of coal per year in the late 1990s. In 1998 Arch's output made up 9.4 percent of total U.S. coal production. The company had 1998 sales of $1.5 billion. The third biggest producer was Kennecott Energy Company, with an output of 102.6 million tons, and the fourth biggest was CONSOL Energy Inc., which produced 6.6 percent of U.S. coal production in 1998. CONSOL had 1999 sales of $1.11 billion. Another large coal producer was Zeigler Coal Holding Company, a subsidiary of AEI Holding Company, Inc., since 1998. Zeigler's 1997 sales reached $800.8 million.

WORKFORCE

Unions were increasingly concerned about job security in the 1990s. Coal companies argued that rising costs were pinching profit margins. Union leaders pointed out that coal production had increased 200 percent over the past two decades, while costs had been reduced by 50 percent, largely through payroll savings. Labor negotiators also charged mine companies with shifting production to non-union facilities. By the end of 1993 however, the United Mine Workers union had agreed to terms with both the Bituminous Coal Operators Association and the Independent Coal Bargaining Alliance, the multi-employer bargaining groups of the industry, and had signed five-year contracts. This was only accomplished however, after bitter strike actions and negotiations with the association.

Job opportunities are expected to continue to degenerate in the underground coal mining industry. According to the Bureau of Labor Statistics, employment in the coal mining industry was expected to decline about 35 percent from 1998 to 2008. In 1998 about 91,600 people worked in the coal mining industry. Of these about 16,240 worked in mining, quarrying, and tunneling occupations. By 2008 the number employed in the coal mining industry was expected to drop to about 59,400 overall, with 12,078 in mining, quarrying, and tunneling occupations.

AMERICA AND THE WORLD

The United States was the second largest coal exporting nation in the world in the mid-1990s, accounting for approximately 24 percent of the global export market. In 1998, U.S. companies exported about 76 million tons. More than 59 percent of U.S. coal exports were metallurgical grade in the mid-1990s, which was primarily produced in eastern underground mines. Much of the high-grade steam coal exported was also produced in that region. West Virginia alone distributed 49 percent of U.S. coal exports in 1995. The leading customers for U.S. bituminous coal in the late 1990s were Canada, Japan, Brazil, and the United Kingdom, in that order.

Foreign Investment. A weak foreign dollar, the exit of traditional steel, oil, and utility interests, and the decline of European coal industries combined to generate an influx of capital into the U.S. coal industry in the early 1990s. The most significant move was made in 1990 when U.K.-based Hanson PLC acquired Peabody Holding (for which it paid $1.25 billion), America's largest coal producer. Similarly, Rheinbraun A.G., of Germany, paid $890 million for a stake in CONSOL Energy, the nation's second largest producer. Kennecott Energy was also acquired by the British conglomerate RTZ. At the same time, U.S. companies such as Cyprus AMAX, ARCO, and Peabody, were involved in coal mining ventures in Australia and South America.

RESEARCH AND TECHNOLOGY

To combat regulatory entanglement, stagnant prices, and increased competition, underground coal companies were increasingly looking to advanced mining and coal burning technologies for help. In addition, the industry was seeking new uses for its products that could open new markets.

Of critical and immediate importance to the underground coal mining industry was clean-burning coal technology that could reduce sulfur emissions and allow utilities to comply with new CAAA standards. Failure to achieve success in this area will likely result in many power plants converting to alternative fuels, a development that would devastate high-sulfur underground mining regions. The U.S. Department of Energy, working with researchers in coal companies and utilities, was developing five categories of research. Low-emission boiler systems incorporated advanced combustion and innovative flue gas cleaning systems in the initial design for new power plants. Pressurized fluidized bed combustion captured sulfur pollutants inside the boiler instead of in the stack, and allowed combustion at temperatures below the point at which most nitrogen pollutants form. The integrated gasification combined cycle (IGCC) employed coal gasification rather than traditional combustion and combined a steam turbine driven by exhaust heat with the gas turbine driven by the coal gas. Indirectly fired cycles employed a design that heated a working fluid such as air to turn the turbine rather than the hot gases of combustion. Finally, integrated gasification-fuel cell combinations would link a coal gasifier with a fuel cell.

The Wabash River coal gasification repowering project in Terre Haute, Indiana, demonstrated on a commercial scale and in a commercial utility environment that IGCC technology can effectively meet both energy and environmental needs. Wabash River, a joint venture of Destec Energy Inc. and PSI Energy Inc., was selected as a Department of Energy demonstration project in September 1991, and went on line in August 1995. The plant was built in the 1950s, but the project replaced 1 of 6 original coal fired units with a new gasification process and combined cycle power block.

Several more unusual approaches to meeting government regulations were being explored. Microterra Inc., of Florida, was trying to patent a system that utilized genetically engineered bacteria that lived on a diet of sulfur. A prototype system was already being used by Freeport

McMoran Inc. Porter's system differed from past efforts by other researchers in that it consumed sulfur in 36 to 48 hours, compared to 10 to 48 days for similar systems.

Another approach reported in the mid-1990s used pellets of zinc titanate to absorb the sulfur. The advantage being tested was that the hot coal gas produced in the coal gasification process has to be cooled only to about 1,000 degrees Farenheit to remove the sulfur instead of to room temperature as in other processes. The zinc pellets are dropped through the column of hot gas, absorbing sulfur as they fall, and then returned to the top of the column in an elevator. In another project, researchers were striving to replace coke used in processing iron and steel with ''formcoke,'' made from less expensive and more abundant non-metallurgical grade coals.

FURTHER READING

Brogan, Pamela. ''Coal Health Care Bill: Will It Be Surplus or Deficit?'' *Gannett News Service,* 22 June 1995.

Byrne, Harlan S. ''Power Play.'' *Barron's,* 16 September 1996.

Chambers, Ann. ''Coal to Dominate Generation to 2015.''*Power Engineering,* July 1996.

Massey, David. ''Coal: An Industry in Transition.'' *Electric Perspectives,* 1 January 1995.

National Mining Association. ''1998 Coal Producer Survey Special Report.'' July 1999. Available from http://www.nma.org/CPS%20Map%2098.html.

''Salient Statistics of the Coal Mining Industry: 1993-1998.'' Available from http://www.nma.org/coalstats.html.

Prince, Cathryn. ''Eastern Fights to Shed $100M Coal Act Liability.'' *Boston Business Journal,* 10 February 1995.

''Scientist Believes His Zinc Pellets Can Aid Gasification Plants.'' *Power Engineering,* October 1996.

U.S. Department of Commerce. ''Bituminous Coal Underground Mining 1997.'' Economic Census, October 1999. Available from http://www.census.gov/prod/ec97/97n2121b.pdf.

U.S. Department of Energy. Office of Fossil Energy. ''Clean Coal Technology Demonstration Program.'' Available from http://www.fe.doe.gov/.

U.S. Department of Energy. Energy Information Administration.*Coal Annual 1995.* Washington: GPO, 1996.

U.S. Department of Labor. *Occupational Outlook Handbook, 1998-99 Edition.* Washington: Bureau of Labor Statistics, September 1998. Available from http://www.bls.gov/ocohome.htm.

U.S. Department of Labor. Mining Safety and Health Administration. ''Mine Accident, Injury, Illness, Employment, and Coal Production Statistics, 1996.'' Available from http://www.msha.gov/ALLCOAL.htm.

Wollensky, Jug. ''Wabash River Successfully Demonstrates Commercial IGCC.'' *Modern Power Systems,* 1 July 1996.

SIC 1231

ANTHRACITE MINING

This category covers establishments primarily engaged in producing anthracite or in developing anthracite mines. All establishments in the United States that are classified in this industry are located in Pennsylvania. This industry includes mining by owners or lessees, or by establishments that have complete responsibility for operating anthracite mines for others on a contract or fee basis. Also included are anthracite preparation plants, whether or not operated in conjunction with a mine.

NAICS CODE(S)

212113 (Anthracite Mining)

INDUSTRY SNAPSHOT

Anthracite is a hard coal containing a high percentage of fixed carbon and a low percentage of volatile matter, such as sulfur and ash, containing more than 90 percent of fixed carbon, less than 5 percent of volatile matter (gases), and a very small percentage of moisture (usually less than 5 percent). With these desirable qualities, anthracite coal is ranked higher than other, more commonly used coals like bituminous and lignite because it has more than twice the energy content of these other coals. Thus, it provides a longer burning potential and is, accordingly, a higher energy fuel.

In 1997, 131 mines were engaged in the extraction of Pennsylvania anthracite, employing 1,094 miners. Production for the year was 4.6 million short tons, less than 0.5 percent of total U.S. coal production. Most of the original markets for anthracite were relinquished long ago to natural gas, fuel oil, and other coals such as bituminous and lignite coal. In the mid-1990s, anthracite maintained a small share of a niche market, consisting primarily of coal-fired home-heating units. In fact, anthracite mining has been declining steadily for many years, from peak production in 1918 when anthracite mines produced 99.6 million short tons.

ORGANIZATION AND STRUCTURE

Both surface and underground methods were used in the extraction of anthracite. In 1995, 270,000 short tons were produced by underground mines and 4.1 million tons by surface mines. Surface mining is usually practiced on relatively flat ground; the coal is recovered from a depth of less than 200 feet. To reach coal deposits, miners must first remove the overburden, or strata, that covers the coal bed. Between 1 and 30 cubic yards of strata must be excavated for each ton of coal recovered. Dragline excavators, power shovels, bulldozers, front-end loaders, scrapers, and other heavy pieces of equipment are used to move the strata and extract the coal.

The two common methods of surface mining are strip and auger. At strip mines, large drills bore holes in the strata. Explosives are placed in these cavities and detonated. Power shovels or draglines operating at surface level then move the broken strata, while power shovels below dig up the coal and load it into trucks. The strata and coal are removed in long strips. This is done so that the debris from the newest strip can be dumped into an adjacent strip, from which the coal has already been recovered.

Auger mining consists of boring a series of holes that are 2 feet to 5 feet in diameter and 300 or more feet deep. This parallel and horizontal pattern is carved into a seam of coal that has already been exposed by an outcropping or by strip mining methods. No blasting takes place and the overburden is left intact. The coal is simply removed and loaded into waiting trucks. Auger mining is frequently used in open-pit mines where the strata is too thick to economically remove using strip methods.

Underground mines consist of a series of parallel and interconnecting tunnels from which the coal is cut and removed with special machinery. The process is complex and sometimes dangerous. The mine must be adequately ventilated to protect miners from dust and explosive methane gas that is released by the coal. In addition, careful ground control must be practiced to prevent the roof of the mine from collapsing on workers and equipment.

Three types of underground operations are distinguished by the method used to access the coal mine. Drift mines are characterized by the use of a level tunnel leading into the mine, while slope mines have an inclined tunnel and shaft mines utilize a vertical tunnel. The primary methods of extracting coal from all of these mines are room-and-pillar, longwall, and shortwall, but no anthracite mines used longwall systems.

Room-and-pillar mining is often the least efficient method. It allows recovery of only about 50 percent of the coal, although there are occasions when this methodology can achieve a much greater recovery percentage. Longwall and shortwall mining, in comparison, extracts up to 80 percent of the usable coal. In a room-and-pillar operation, coal is mined in a series of rooms cut into the coalbed. Pillars of unmined coal are left intact, and serve to support the mine roof as miners advance through the coal seam. Sometimes the coal in the pillars can be extracted later in the ''retreat'' phase.

The two basic types of room-and-pillar mining are conventional and continuous. Conventional mining consists of a series of operations that involve cutting and breaking up the coalbed, blasting the bed, and then removing the shattered coal. Continuous mining, on the other hand, uses a machine that digs and loads coal in one operation, without blasting.

Longwall and shortwall mines use huge machines with cutting heads. The heads are pulled back and forth across a block of coal up to about 150 feet long in shortwall mining, though much longer in longwall. Coal is sheared and plowed into slices that are removed by a conveyor. Movable roof supports allow mined-out areas to cave in behind the advancing machine.

Anthracite reserves totaled more than 7 billion short tons in Pennsylvania in 1990, with smaller amounts (less than 300 short tons) existing in Colorado, Virginia, Arkansas, and New Mexico. By far the greatest concentration of anthracite reserves were in several counties in northeastern Pennsylvania, specifically Lackawanna, Luzerne, Carbon, Columbia, Northumberland, Dauphin, Schuylkill, and Lebanon, with more than one-third of the reserves lying in Schuylkill county.

Background and Development

The history of anthracite mining in the United States dates back to before the industrialization of the country, when material needs were largely met through subsistence agriculture, and craft-type production methods dominated the economy. The shift to an economy dominated by factory production methods was accompanied by growth in anthracite mining, providing a striking case study of the origins of industry in the United States. Historian Alfred Chandler argued that anthracite was a primary factor in facilitating factory production methods in the northeastern United States, suggesting that anthracite mining played a key role in the timing and pattern of economic development in the United States during the mid- to late 1800s.

Well before it was mined for profit, anthracite was discovered by Native Americans near Nazareth, Pennsylvania, around 1750. By the 1790s, settlers began exploring the possibility of using anthracite for commercial and industrial purposes.

During the Revolutionary War, anthracite was burned in forges for the production of weapons. When the war ended, the population of the country was less than four million and most of the output of the country was agricultural. A profitable market for anthracite would emerge as merchants sought higher levels of profitability, bringing forth factory production methods and a rise in demand for mineral production.

One impediment to coal production was the lack of transportation infrastructure, which made the cost of getting coal to market prohibitive. Part of the rise of anthracite production can thus be tied to the construction of canal and railway systems, which lowered the cost of transportation. By the War of 1812, demand for coal by the government led to shortages in Baltimore, Philadelphia, and New York, which hastened the decision to develop additional anthracite sources.

Much of the early mining was undertaken by small scale entrepreneurs. Development would be intertwined with the development of extensive canal systems constructed in the 1820s and 1830s, and later the railroad, eventually leading to the union of the most successful anthracite firms with railroad companies.

The development of canal systems between 1815 and 1834 enabled coal to reach expanding textile markets on the East Coast. In fact, between 1815 and 1834, $10 million was spent by the government and private interests to construct canals to bring anthracite deposits of northeast Pennsylvania to the Atlantic seaboard, thereby providing a way for a cheap fuel to reach expanding markets. The Erie Canal, the Delaware Canal, and the Hudson Canal were all developed specifically for the purpose of allowing growing anthracite companies like the Lehigh Coal and Navigation Company and the Schuylkill Navigation Company to haul anthracite.

The Industrial Revolution. As the industry advanced, early mining methods were rapidly replaced by more machine-intensive methods of production, which raised productivity and reduced labor time. Mines became much more productive, but along with this trend, mining accidents increased, leading to many worker casualties from explosions, fires, floods, and collapsing ceilings and walls. Consequently, workers began organizing to fight against increasingly intolerable work conditions.

From the 1830s to the 1870s, Pennsylvania produced more anthracite than bituminous coal. Anthracite had specific applications in steel production and was the most used of all types of coal at the time. By the early 1860s, anthracite fueled booming iron production in Pennsylvania and became a primary fuel for the textile industry in New England. The boom years of 1863 and 1864 in the northeastern United States were driven by the need for blankets, firearms, and other goods needed for the prosecution of the Civil War. Other contributing factors during this period were tariffs placed on imported manufactured goods and the creation of a national currency and a national banking system.

With the increasing growth of the railroad industry, the demand for pig iron and iron production rose as well, which meant more anthracite coal was needed. Total coal production leaped from just under 17 million tons in 1861 to nearly 72 million tons in 1880. At this time, competition in the highly profitable anthracite industry was fierce. Not only were many capitalists entering the industry to take advantage of the higher than average profit rates and low wages, but firms were also guaranteed a relatively controlled work force.

Labor Disputes. At this time, the federal government was fostering manufacturing activity, but was hardly a friend of labor in the Pennsylvania anthracite mines. With the industry expanding vigorously in the post-Civil War boom era, miners were being pushed to their physical limits for very low wages. Paid low piece-wages while working long hours under extremely hazardous conditions, miners also had to pay exorbitant prices at company-owned stores. In addition, 600 workers had died in mining accidents in the Pennsylvania mines from 1863-1870. As labor organized, the government called in the army to crush strikes in 1864. Strike leaders were arrested and martial law was declared in the Pennsylvania coal towns. The miners responded by organizing under the Workingmen's Benevolent Association (WBA). Due partly to fierce competition in the coal industry, which prevented coal owners from uniting against the miners, the WBA was able to forge a unified force of all miners, skilled and unskilled, throughout the industry, as opposed to separate "craft" unions that were the dominant form of labor organization at the time. As a result of this collective action, the WBA, after a bitter six-month strike, won better working conditions, a "sliding scale" wage system by which wages rose or fell according to the market price of coal, and a mining inspection law from the Pennsylvania legislature.

As the country slipped into a prolonged depression in the 1870s, anthracite prices and profits collapsed and workers struggled to maintain their living standards. A wave of strikes swept the nation in the mid-1870s, with the Long Strike in eastern Pennsylvania standing as one of the most dramatic and important. The conflict plagued eastern Pennsylvania, with many firms using private police forces to infiltrate and suppress unions. The conflict was often violent.

Despite intense competition among mining companies, management's response to the labor movement was much more organized and aggressive this time around. The anthracite mining industry was changing, becoming more concentrated as a result of competition, which engendered far more failing companies than profitable companies. A leading company was Reading Railroad, an anthracite and railroad concern headed by Franklin Gowen, which became the largest coal operator in eastern Pennsylvania. Gowen circled the wagons of other coal operators and took on the WBA.

Responding to a five-month strike in 1874, Gowen stockpiled coal, then, in the winter of 1874-1875, shut down his mines, inflicting tremendous hardship on the miners and their families. Following a long, violent struggle—with Gowen's private police firing indiscriminately into crowds of workers, and strikers often attacking scab workers and strike breakers with clubs and stones—workers eventually succumbed, conceding a 20 percent wage cut, and returned to work in nonunion mines. Several miners were tried for alleged violent attack and convicted, despite questions about testimony of security agents for the companies. The union was decimated and would not emerge again until the end of the century, when the United Mine Workers of America (UMWA) came into existence.

The depression dragged on for many years. The UMWA was involved in strikes across the country, including a key strike in Pennsylvania in 1894, but with the union severely weakened from the impact of the prolonged depression, the coal miners lost a battle of attrition.

Many more strikes would rock the industry around the turn of the century. One major 1901 in the anthracite fields of Pennsylvania drew the attention of President Theodore Roosevelt, who, after threatening to order U.S. troops to seize the mines, convinced the mine owners to settle with the UMWA. Roosevelt had taken on the owners, who were being particularly strident in the struggle, and won support as a populist.

By the end of the nineteenth century, Pennsylvania anthracite was shipped by boat and rail to almost every major city in the country, becoming the most important domestic fuel for industrializing America. By the turn of the century, Luzerne county ranked as the third most populous county in the state, while Lackawanna County ranked as the fourth largest. These counties were growing up on coal, a resource that made the region a major commercial center.

Entering the twentieth century, use of anthracite was clearly on the rise, when production reached 57.3 million tons and grew to more than 100 million tons by World War I. Output increased every year in the late nineteenth and early twentieth century, reaching its peak in 1917, when the industry employed more than 150,000 anthracite miners. From 1870 to 1920, more than 50 percent of all hard coal produced came from the northern Pennsylvania fields. Profitability was very high, with mining costs at the point of extraction only 75 cents while the selling price ranged from $15 to $18. At this time, anthracite was used as a bunker fuel during World War I, but this was less than 20 percent of all end uses. Most anthracite was used as space heating fuel for industrial, commercial and residential purposes. In addition, a small portion of anthracite was used for electrical power generation and by the steel industry. Most anthracite was used domestically with little being exported.

The value of anthracite properties was estimated by the U.S. Coal Commission to be almost $1 billion. However, coal costs began to rise while prices remained constant. Other troubles arose because of changes in steel production. Coke, which has many of the advantages of anthracite, but is derived from soft coal, increasingly came into competition with anthracite. The harder anthracite could not compete, primarily because production costs were too high.

To exacerbate the situation, the highly centralized industry also was accused of operating as a monopoly, with a small number of firms regulating pricing and controlling 90 percent of the market. There had been a close connection between the mining and distribution of anthracite and the control of these companies by ''anthracite railroads.'' Suits were brought against the Lehigh Valley and Reading companies.

In 1923, seven large companies owned and controlled an estimated 75 to 80 percent of the mining, transportation, and hauling of anthracite, each of which was controlled by the railroads. The remaining anthracite producers were considered small independent miners who leased coal mines. The large interests were accused of price collusion. The debate raged over whether these large interests should be allowed to operate as railroads, or coal miners, or both. Some of the large companies were: The Reading Company, Philadelphia and Reading Railroad Company, Philadelphia and Reading Coal and Iron Company, Lehigh Valley Railroad Company, Lehigh Valley Coal Company, and Coxe Brothers Co.

In a ruling similar to the Supreme Court decision that broke-up Standard Oil in 1911, the seven large companies were forced to dissolve in accordance with the Sherman Anti-Trust Act. By 1922, profit rates for the industry fell to around 12.1 percent, while the debate on price fixing and regulation continued. Meanwhile, the costs to the smaller independent companies rose as rents charged by land owners increased. With the tendency of coal prices to reflect the cost of the largest company, the price of anthracite rose.

In addition, strike and labor resistance continued to plague the mining industry. Several long and costly strikes occurring after World War I that involved the complete cessation of anthracite production lent support, from the mine owners' perspective, to promoting substitute fuels. Major strikes were carried out during the 1920s and 1930s.

Anthracite production began to decline before the Great Depression. Following the expansion of mining, which came with the high profitability enjoyed during World War I, demand for coal fell, and more cost-efficient oil and natural gas were used. Supply for all types of coal was outrunning demand by two to one and prices were plummeting, eroding profits, and consequently production was cut back. Companies were going under, closing some union mines, and labor was severely hurt, with working conditions becoming harsher, wages falling, and the intensity of labor increasing. The UMWA was completely demoralized following an important strike in 1927.

Market demand continued to shift away from anthracite and oil, while natural gas became more attractive and more widely distributed. Space heating applications, which had been a major portion of anthracite consumption at the turn of the century also declined. Production fell precipitously, from 69.4 million tons in 1930 to 9.7 million tons in 1970. A slight resurgence in the demand for anthracite occurred in the late 1970s because of an increase in home heating units in New England and from a switch to coal as a consequence of rising oil and natural gas prices.

Though it did not lead to a major rejuvenation of the industry, one of the salvation's for anthracite producers in the 1970s was the use of anthracite for space-heating purposes in U.S. military installations overseas. The Defense Department's space heating equipment, originally designed to burn coke, accommodated only anthracite rather than bituminous coal.

The 1980s saw a brief surge in the demand for anthracite primarily because of a rise in the purchase of coal stoves, as homeowners sought alternatives to rising oil and natural gas prices. But the industry had trouble meeting the demand because of its inflexibility, leading to huge price increases. The industry tried to remedy this by increasing mining capacity to ensure protection of its key market, the residential space-heating market. By this time anthracite composed less than one percent of the coal market. In 1977, the federal government gave brief attention to the industry, forming the Anthracite Task Force in 1977 and the Office of Anthracite within the U.S. Department of Energy. This was more appearance than action, however as very little federal assistance was forthcoming.

CURRENT CONDITIONS

The anthracite coal mining industry remained in a basically stagnant condition in 1995. Since 1991 the number of operating mines had fallen by 24 percent and the number of miners by about 8 percent. Productivity per miner increased during this same period, but was still well below that of bituminous miners. Expressed in 1997 dollars, the price for anthracite averaged $31.24 per ton, while the average price for all U.S. coal was $16.142.

The outlook for real growth in the industry was grim. With the market for anthracite flat, there was little incentive for mining companies to open new mines or install production enhancing technology such as longwall systems. In 1997 there were only 68 establishments with 1,094 employees.

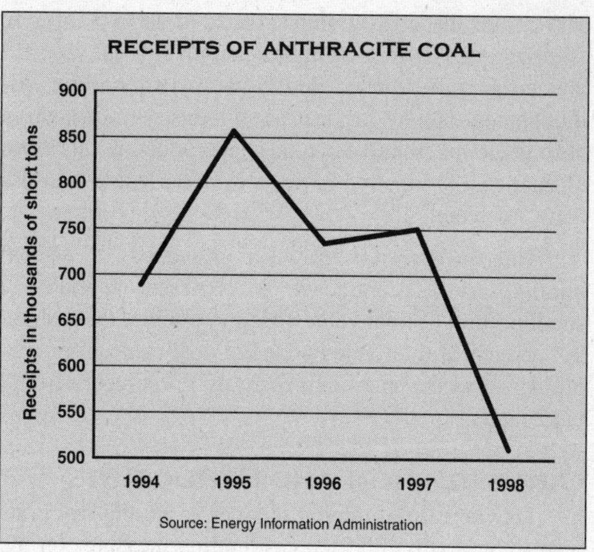

FURTHER READING

Massey, David. "Coal: An Industry in Transition." *Electric Perspectives,* 1 January 1995.

National Mining Association. "Salient Statistics of the Mining Industry," 1999. Available from http://www.nma.org/salient.html.

U.S. Department of Energy, Energy Information Administration. *Coal Annual 1998.* Washington, D.C.: GPO, 1997. Available from http://www. eia.doe.gov.

U.S. Census Bureau *1997 Economic Census.* "Mining-Industry Series." Washington, D.C.: GPO, July 1999. Available from http://www.census.gov.

SIC 1241

COAL MINING SERVICES

This category covers establishments primarily engaged in performing coal mining services for others on a contract or fee basis. Establishments that have complete responsibility for operating mines for others on a contract or fee basis are classified according to the product mined, rather than as mining services.

NAICS CODE(S)

213113 (Support Activities for Coal Mining)

INDUSTRY SNAPSHOT

The companies classified in this category are a small but growing part of the overall coal industry. According to the most recent data from the Census of Mineral Industries, the industry employed a workforce of 4,990 production workers in 1997, 7 percent above the figure for 1992. Total value of shipments and receipts was $578.1 million. These workers added value through their services to the coal mining process of $536.5 million. Although this figure was higher than in 1987, it was still above the peak reached in 1982 at $418.1 million. Although coal mining services as an industry has grown in absolute terms (relative to total coal production), its share of total coal production in terms of dollar value was less than 2 percent.

Thus, in spite of its growth as an industry, those coal mining services contracted out represent a relatively small portion of total value added in mining. Only about 2.2 percent of total value added in coal came from coal mining services, up from a share of 1.7 percent of total value added in 1972.

Organization and Structure

The increase of mining services as an industry in its own right largely reflected cost-cutting measures on the part of the coal mining industry. They often cut costs by increasing use of nonunion workers to perform many of the tasks previously performed by union workers. Contract mining services also grew due to the fact that many larger coal interests simply diversified their operations or got out of certain aspects of coal mining.

With specific services contracted out, firms can avoid a large commitment of capital investment and small entrepreneurs have seen a profitable opening. Thus, faced with erratic demand conditions, the industry has seen an increase in flexible conditions of production, including just-in-time production methods, which create smooth production, reduce turnover times, and thereby reduce downtime. Flexible work rules involving eradication of union work rules—or at the very least, union cooperation—have contributed to mine efficiency. In any case, with various degrees of contract services, the number of large independent operators continues to decline according to some industry observers, with efficiency forcing the competition process.

In 1997, approximately 306 establishments (and 280 companies) provided services to the coal industry on a contract basis. These companies provided services ranging from removal of overburden, stripping the mine face, auguring or culm bank mining, drilling services, mine tunneling, and shaft sinking. Most of these establishments and multi-establishment firms were small; only 50 had more than 19 employees and, of these, only fourteen had 100 or more.

The most significant revenue source in the coal mining services industry was strip mining, which totaled $6.7 billion in industry shipments in 1997. Stripping overburden followed with $81.2 million. Sinking mine shafts and driving mine tunnels generated revenue of $34.6 million, and drilling and blasting generated $36.3 million. Other coal mining services not specifically classified produced $199.2 million in industry revenue, and another $198.9 million was estimated from incomplete data, including data for smaller enterprises.

In terms of major area of geographic concentration, the larger companies engaged in coal mining services (with 20 or more employees) were concentrated in West Virginia, Kentucky, Pennsylvania, and Ohio, in that order. These firms accounted for approximately 71.0 percent of the workforce and 66.8 percent of the value of shipments and receipts.

Background and Development

Coal mining services are defined more according to company organization rather than by type of activity. In other words, for a given technique of extracting coal, a number of activities are undertaken including sinking shafts, stripping, tunneling, drilling, coal recovery, transportation, and others. For any particular mine, these activities may take place under the auspices of one establishment, or some of the services may be outsourced to a contracting company for a fee. In the case where one particular establishment has complete responsibility for the operation of the mine, the activities are classified according to the product mined, whereas specific activities performed by contracting companies on a fee basis are counted as part of the coal mining services industry.

The specific types of services that may fall under coal mining services, for all types of coal—anthracite, bituminous, and lignite—include anthracite mining, auger mining services, bituminous coal mining, draining or pumping of coal, drilling, lignite mining, overburden removal of coal, sinking shafts, stripping services, and tunneling.

The Commerce Department, at one point, classified coal mining services according to the product mined. Thus, anthracite mining services and bituminous coal and lignite mining services were classified separately. When the number of anthracite mining service companies went to 57, however, the Commerce Department created a SIC classification for coal mining services in general.

Historical Precedents. With its small but integral connection to the coal industry in general, the coal services industry rises and falls with coal mining. Mining services have been an integral part of the rise of coal in the United States, whether they were part of the mining companies operations or provided through companies that contracted with the mine owners and operators. In general, the evolution of mining services connected with coal mining and the rise of separate companies providing these services relates to the changes in production techniques in the extraction of coals and the efficiency of production methods. Thus, the separation of the industry called mining services is somewhat artificial, or at the very least, a changing one.

In fact, the early techniques of coal mining were exceedingly simple—simply carrying coal from the exposed vein. Of course, these primitive methods were rapidly replaced by a more refined division of labor, and eventually, by machinery, which rationalized the production processes and reduced the total labor time required per unit of coal mined.

In the early years of coal mining, primitive production methods meant individual workers owned and operated their own tools and were paid piece-wages, according to the amount of coal mined. This involved the simple act of shoveling coal into a pile, then throwing it into an empty mine car—human muscle. According to Keith Dix, as late as 1948, one-third of the nation's underground coal was still loaded by hand. The early miners used their own tools, paid the company blacksmith to keep them sharp, and worked the mines and railroad track owned by the company. The miner also bought his own blasting powder, lamp oil, and other supplies, and even purchased his means of subsistence from the company stores. Thus, the early miner was an independent craftsperson combining a high level of knowledge and skill.

While increases in productivity came fast and furious in coal mining, the labor process in mining coal, during any period, involved essentially five tasks: sinking a shaft for an underground mine, penetrating a slope, or uncovering a surface vein; undercutting the coal vein face; drilling the face; blasting the coal; and shoveling the broken coal into cars.

Mechanization to reduce costs, and to overcome the resistance of an increasingly militant mine workers union, proceeded quickly. First, undercutting machines developed, and eventually, the mechanization of hauling, drilling, and cleaning followed. The result was higher capital equipment requirement per worker, vast improvements in labor productivity, and a decline in labor requirements. Impediments in transportation to markets were overcome by agreements with the developing railroad industry near the turn of the century.

The Ups and Downs of the Coal Industry. While precise records of coal mining services as an industry were not kept by the government until the late 1960s, coal mining services has undoubtedly been a part of coal mining from the time of its inception. The railroads provided the impetus for the coal boom during the first two decades of this century, but when the railroads switched to the oil burning diesel engine, coal lost a major customer. This, accompanied by the switch of home heating to oil and gas, deflated the coal industry in the post-World War II period. Following the protracted boom immediately following World War II, by 1961 coal output declined to 1939 levels.

In the early 1960s, mechanization (which reduced unit costs), the decline in general transportation costs, and the surge in demand for electricity brought the industry to life. The rise in electricity demand between 1962 and 1966 produced a boom in the coal industry of over 26 percent. Smaller, more efficient, continuous mining companies also increased the intensity of labor, further reducing costs. The surge in demand from electrical utilities, which comprised over 50 percent of coal industry sales, led to two of the most dynamic decades in U.S. coal history in the 1960s and 1970s. This dynamic led to concentration and consolidation of industry capital and to the rise of small contracting companies.

The number of mining service establishments more than doubled from 191 in 1972 to 422 in 1982. The massive rise in productivity allowed for relatively high wages in the industry and exports boomed, with foreign customers seeking low-cost, high-quality U.S. coal. The markets for steel (coal's second largest customer) also came to life in the postwar boom. Nuclear power was a small, but growing, government-subsidized industry at this time.

Though the 1970s witnessed a slowdown in coal productivity, this trend reversed in the 1980s. After an austerity campaign, the introduction of continuous mining techniques, and further advances in mechanization in cutting, drilling, and loading, the 1980s witnessed a resurgence in productivity growth and a reduction in necessary workers. This shakeout in the industry also led to a decline in the proportion of union mines. In the non-union shop, mine operators implemented work rule changes—allowing flexible work teams, cross-training, and fewer and longer shifts. In addition to the relative hardship of laborers, industry leaders faced a highly uncertain and sluggish demand in an industry where many firms struggled to finance the large scale capital investment that was required to compete.

CURRENT CONDITIONS

The U.S. coal industry was still strong in the mid-1990s, second only to China in terms of coal production, but growth was sluggish and prices continued to fall. Electric utilities remained by far the largest consumers of coal, and demand from this sector was expected to remain steady well into the future. The industry was marked by consolidation as smaller, less efficient mines closed and some large non-mining corporations who had acquired coal mines during the seventies sold withdrew. Large mining companies expanded by acquiring these existing operations more often than by opening new mines. Production shifted west where economies of scale could be brought to bear on operating costs, and where large deposits of the low-sulfur coals desired by the utilities were located. Surface mines in the western states accounted for 49 percent of production;

in fact, the nine largest mines in the United States were in low-sulfur beds in Wyoming and represented 25 percent of coal production.

Given these conditions, in which narrow profit margins forced coal operators to seek every possible means of lowering operating costs, expanding opportunities existed for mining service companies, which were able to accomplish some aspects of the mining process at a lower cost. Companies in this industry segment provided much needed flexibility to mine operators.

INDUSTRY LEADERS

Although there were a fairly large number of firms classified in this industry in the late 1990s, the consolidation and influx of foreign companies that marked the coal industry at large were evident in coal mining services also. The largest companies in the field in the late 1990s were subsidiaries of major corporations, such as Texas Utilities Mining Co., a subsidiary of Texas Utilities Company, which reported 1999 sales of $17.1 billion. The North American Coal Corporation, a subsidiary of NACCO, a diversified conglomerate, reported revenues of $2.66 billion. Other large operators included several subsidiaries of Tenneco Inc., First Mississippi Corporation, and Flour Corporation. Logan and Kanawha Coal Company, classified in both bituminous coal mining and coal mining services industries and headquartered in West Virginia, reported revenues of more than $100 million.

FURTHER READING

Chambers, Ann. ''Coal to Dominate Generation to 2015.'' *Power Engineering,* July 1996.

Dix, Keith. *What's A Coal Miner To Do? The Mechanization of Coal Mining.* Pittsburgh: University of Pittsburgh Press, 1988.

Massey, David. ''Coal: An Industry in Transition.'' *Electric Perspectives,* 1 January 1995.

U.S. Bureau of the Census. *1997 Economic Census.* Washington, D.C.: GPO, 1999. Available from http://www.census.gov.

U.S. Department of Energy. Energy Information Administration. *Coal Annual 1995.* Washington, D.C.: GPO, 1997.

U.S. Department of Labor. Mining Safety and Health Administration. ''Mine Accident, Injury, Illness, Employment, And Coal Production Statistics, 1999.'' Available from http://www.msha.gov/ALLCOAL.HTM.

SIC 1311

CRUDE PETROLEUM AND NATURAL GAS

This industry consists of companies that are primarily engaged in the operation of properties for the recovery of hydrocarbon liquids and natural gas. These companies may perform any or all of a broad range of activities. They may explore tracts onshore and offshore for crude petroleum and natural gas; drill and complete wells; equip wells for production; supply services to increase or maintain the recovery of oil and gas; or provide any of the other services necessary to prepare the product for shipment from the production site. This industry includes companies that produce oil and gas from oil shale and oil sands, or that recover hydrocarbon liquids and natural gas through the gasification and liquefaction of coal. The industry also encompasses firms that are responsible for operating oil and gas wells for others on a contract basis. Oil field service companies that perform services for operators are classified in **SIC 1382: Oil & Gas Exploration Services.**

NAICS CODE(S)

211111 (Crude Petroleum and Natural Gas Extraction)

INDUSTRY SNAPSHOT

The early 1990s were a time of struggle for U.S. crude petroleum and natural gas companies. Low oil and gas prices combined with slow economic growth, drilling bans, and lawsuits, all limiting exploration. Oil production continued its long decline. The mid-1990s, however, showed a large increase in revenues, and while domestic production stagnated, production overseas was growing. By the late 1990s, crude oil production in the United States fell, even in Alaska, while natural gas production rose slightly.

Exxon Corporation continued to be the leader in the United States, with annual sales reported at $117.5 billion. Other leaders were the Royal Dutch/Shell Group, Mobil Corporation, and BP Amoco. In 1998 Exxon and Mobil announced they would merge, creating a supersized oil giant, and bringing together again descendants of the old Standard Oil machine. The companies received regulatory clearance for the merger by the end of 1999.

After Russia, the United States was the world's second-largest producer of natural gas. Production gains in the Gulf of Mexico, Arkansas, and Colorado were credited with the increase in total gas production in 1998.

ORGANIZATION AND STRUCTURE

Two types of companies are involved in the crude petroleum and natural gas business: the independents and the majors. The majors are large, vertically integrated companies that explore, produce, refine, and sell oil and gas to end consumers. These companies benefit most from the economies of scale. In contrast, the independent operators produce oil and gas to sell to others who then refine and distribute it.

While major oil companies usually funded drilling programs out of their own resources, independents relied heavily on outside investors. Favorable tax treatment for investors in oil and gas limited partnerships helped fuel an unprecedented boom of exploration and drilling in the late 1970s and early 1980s. In a limited partnership there are two kinds of partners, limited and general. General partners, like limited partners, invest money and share the risk of drilling programs. Unlike limited partners, general partners handle the day-to-day management of the business. Usually, there are several limited partners, but only one general partner.

Company Size and Distribution. The companies in the crude petroleum and natural gas industry range from enormous conglomerates that employ 100,000 people and generate revenue of more than $100 billion, to companies reporting less than $1 million in revenue with few employees. Despite the fact that some firms are very large, 53 percent have fewer than five employees and report revenues of $50 million or less. The industry reported 325,900 employees in 1998.

Regulatory Climate. Historically, the federal government has both helped and hindered the industry. The 1990 Omnibus Budget Reconciliation Act encouraged production by granting a tax credit for projects using enhanced recovery. It expanded the use of deductions for intangible drilling costs and the percentage depletion allowances, and provided a special deduction for independent oil and gas producers to apply against the alternative minimum tax. The decision to cancel the 1990 sale of leases for exploration on the outer continental shelf off California, the Gulf Coast of Florida, and the Northeast, however, hindered the discovery of new oil. The Oil Pollution and Liability Act of 1990 prohibited oil and gas exploration off the coast of North Carolina. That same law also hampered production by imposing federal liabilities on vessels and facilities for oil spills. In addition, the act allowed states to impose their own forms of liability independently. As a result, drillers paid higher insurance rates for their offshore activities.

BACKGROUND AND DEVELOPMENT

Crude petroleum has been used since ancient times. It has caulked boats, cured ailments and aches, and lighted the lamps of home and the fires of war. But it was the demand for lamp oil that triggered the creation of the oil and gas industry. Overfishing had decimated the whale population, the primary source of lamp oil. Experts speculated that the supply of kerosene, made from petroleum collected at ground seepages, could be increased and solve the problem. A group of investors, led by George Bissell, a New York attorney, and James Townsend, a banker from New Haven, Connecticut, decided to finance the drilling of the first petroleum well.

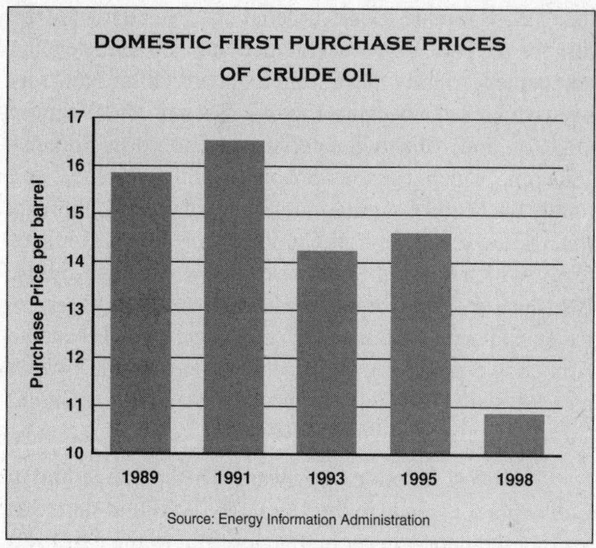

Boom and Bust. On August 27, 1859, the well was completed in Titusville, Pennsylvania, by Edwin L. Drake. Drake's success triggered a frantic search for oil in the area, and boomtowns sprang up quickly. While the first wells required that petroleum be pumped from the ground like water, it wasn't long until the first flowing well, producing 3,000 barrels per day, was discovered several miles from Drake's well. New refineries were built closer to the wells, and existing refineries increased capacity. Soon, hundreds of small companies were involved in drilling for oil.

Seven years later, however, the once-bustling streets of Titusville were nearly deserted. A legal loophole, "the rule of capture," led the fledgling oil companies to take as much oil as possible from the ground as quickly as possible. This practice promptly ruined the oil-producing capabilities of the underground field and the wells ceased to produce. The industry had completed its first boom/bust cycle.

The cycle was a phenomenon that the industry has been unable to shake for more than 100 years. After the Civil War, the United States began a period of massive economic expansion and development. The need for petroleum and its products greatly increased.

Standard Oil Trust. In 1871 the industry was in a panic; too many wells were producing too much oil. The price of kerosene fell by more than half, and many refineries were losing money. This alarmed a commodities trader-turned-refiner named John D. Rockefeller. He decided that the best way to save the industry was to limit the intense competition by combining most of the refineries into one company. Eventually, Rockefeller's Standard Oil Trust controlled 90 percent of the refining capacity in the United States. But the company's questionable business practices came to light and, in 1890, the Sherman Antitrust Act was passed by Congress. In 1911 the U.S. Supreme Court ordered that Standard Oil be dissolved. The trust was divided into 33 independent companies. Among these were Standard Oil of New Jersey (which later became Exxon); Socony and Vacuum Oil Co., Inc. (the two later merged to form Socony-Vacuum, which became Socony-Mobil Co., Inc., and finally the Mobil Corporation); Standard Oil of California (later known as Chevron Corporation); Standard Oil of Ohio (which became Sohio and later was bought by the British Petroleum Company p.l.c. as part of its BP America subsidiary); Standard Oil of Indiana (which became Amoco Corporation); and Atlantic Petroleum (which merged with Richfield to become Atlantic Richfield Company, also known as ARCO).

The quest for oil led westward. The first large find in California was made in the 1890s. By 1903 that state was leading the nation in oil production. But to the east lay a larger discovery. In the Texas town of Corsicana, south of Dallas, civic leaders were upset when they discovered oil while drilling for water in 1893. The new well marked the beginning of the Texas oil industry.

It was south of Corsicana, however, that the Texas oil industry had one of its grandest openings. On January 10, 1901, Lucas No. 1 on Spindletop Hill near Beaumont blew in at 75,000 barrels per day, a real Texas gusher. Spindletop was followed by other major discoveries in Texas, Oklahoma, and Louisiana. The result was a surplus of U.S. oil that would last for nearly 70 years.

New Market. Originally, the quest for petroleum was driven by the need for kerosene, a cheap lamp fuel. Yet when Thomas A. Edison invented the electric light, the need for kerosene decreased. The budding auto industry, however, needed gasoline. By 1910 gasoline sales exceeded kerosene sales. William Burton, a Standard Oil scientist, was working on a new process—thermal cracking—that more than doubled the yield of gasoline from a barrel of oil. When Standard Oil was dissolved, Burton's new employer, Standard Oil of Indiana, began using his discovery. Soon the process was licensed at refineries across the country, and petroleum production soared.

Natural Gas. After World War II, the nation implemented the lessons it had learned: petroleum had figured mightily in the success of the Allies. It was clear that measures to conserve the resource had to be taken, and exploring the possibilities of natural gas seemed a logical avenue. In the Southwest where it was produced, natural gas was used to heat communities near the gas fields. Most of it, however, was burned in bright flares on the high plains. Transporting natural gas to the major markets in the industrial Northeast required a 1,300-mile pipeline.

In 1947 the government sold the ''Big Inch'' and the ''Little Inch,'' two petroleum pipelines that had carried crude oil and gasoline from the Southwest to the Northeast during World War II. Texas Eastern Transmission Co. immediately converted them to gas pipelines. El Paso Natural Gas brought gas to Los Angeles, California, through another pipeline called the ''Biggest Inch.'' In 1950 gas consumption rose to 2.5 trillion cubic feet (tcf), more than doubling the consumption of four years earlier.

Offshore Exploration. While most oil men were busy drilling on land, some saw the potential off the coast of the United States—especially Louisiana. Because of their state's abundance of marshes, Louisiana oil men had been drilling over water since the early 1900s. The first over-water rigs were land derricks built on wooden platforms supported by creosoted pilings. It was a costly method, but the rewards from the rich Louisiana reservoirs could be worth the expense.

In 1945 a controversy arose over whether the southern states or the federal government owned the rich oil fields on the continental shelf in the Gulf of Mexico. At stake were billions of dollars in potential revenue. If the land belonged to the states, as they claimed, the taxes, royalties, and other revenue would make them among the wealthiest in the nation. On November 14, 1947, the first deep offshore oil well was completed in the Gulf of Mexico, 45 miles south of Morgan City, Louisiana. Three years later, the value of the area was confirmed as five more major oil fields were discovered.

In 1950 the U.S. Supreme Court declared the offshore waters the province of the federal government. The question of how the lands would be managed was settled by Congress. It passed two acts, the Submerged Lands Act and the Outer Continental Shelf Lands Act, firmly establishing the federal government as the owner, yet allowing leasing of the land for exploration. The Court decision created a major revenue source for the federal government. Between 1970 and 1989, the federal government received a total of $55 trillion from its offshore oil and gas leases. In 1983 alone, the offshore oil industry turned over more than $6 trillion to the U.S. Treasury.

Although oil had been discovered and produced off the shores of other states, Louisiana remained the undisputed U.S. leader in offshore oil wells. In 1990 there were 3,612 oil and gas platforms in federal waters off Louisiana. Marathon Oil and Texaco announced in December 1996 that they made a new oil discovery 130 miles south of New Orleans in the Gulf, and this single well field was expected to recover about 10 million barrels of oil equivalent. The Vermilion 279 property was producing 979 barrels of oil and 4.2 million cubic feet of gas per day from two wells. The Gulf of Mexico was the only place where production was slated to increase in the United States.

Using the Oil Weapon. On October 6, 1973, the high holy day of Yom Kippur, Egypt and Syria launched surprise attacks against Israel. When the Soviet Union resupplied Egypt and Syria with weapons, it was clear that Israel was in danger. When the United States sent supplies, the Organization of Petroleum Exporting Countries (OPEC) retaliated with an oil embargo. Other countries were granted varying amounts of oil, depending on their relations with OPEC. For those who could buy OPEC oil, the price jumped from $2.90 per barrel in September to $11.65 in December. Non-OPEC nations also raised their prices. The nations of the world faced a global recession that rivaled the Great Depression.

New Era. By mid-1974, the Yom Kippur War was over. The effects of the embargo lingered for a long time, however. Besides forcing a settlement in the war, the embargo signaled that the OPEC nations controlled their own oil. Soon after the fighting ended, the OPEC countries nationalized their petroleum industries. The OPEC member countries would pay the oil companies for operating the oil fields and refineries, but those companies no longer had an equity interest in the oil.

This shift in control forced the companies to rethink where and how they would obtain their oil. What they decided shifted the balance of petroleum power again. By the late 1970s, the U.S. demand for oil began to drop for the first time since the 1930s. Stringent conservation measures, especially a mandatory increase in automobile fuel efficiency, had made the nation less dependent on OPEC oil. Moreover, new non-OPEC fields in Alaska, Mexico, and the North Sea were coming on stream. The surge in prices brought in a great deal of money for the oil companies, creating an exploration boom. At the peak of the boom, more than 4,000 rigs drilled for oil both onshore and offshore the United States.

High energy prices intensified the search for more secure sources of petroleum in oil shale and tar sands. Oil shale contains kerogen, an organic material that forms oil when the shale is heated to high temperatures. An estimated 550 billion barrels of recoverable oil existed in the oil shale deposits of the western United States. Researchers realized that if the cost of recovering it compared favorably with the price of crude oil, it would ensure the energy security of the nation. Experiments were initiated in the 1960s, but were shelved when energy prices dropped in the 1980s. Nonetheless, the federal government continued low-level research in the area. Another area of exploration was tar sands, deposits of very thick crude petroleum. Three experimental projects in tar sand production were successful, but additional research was funded at a very low level.

Coal gasification was used to make almost all the fuel gas sold for residential and commercial use from the late 1800s to the 1940s. As natural gas became more available, the market for coal gas diminished to near zero. Yet, interest in gasification was revived after the 1973 oil embargo. The high crude oil prices made the cost of gas made from coal competitive again. Out of all the projects, only one actively produced synthetic natural gas for pipeline distribution in the early 1990s—the Great Plains Synfuels Plant in North Dakota. In another project of the early 1990s, the federal government funded an experimental coal liquefaction plant in Wyoming to produce synthetic fuel gas and formcoke—made from coal char and much like ordinary coke.

After nationalization, OPEC's announced strategy was to stabilize prices by persuading its members to reduce production. But decreased production meant less income, and the OPEC countries had become accustomed to large profits. One by one, the members of OPEC broke ranks, selling more oil than the agreed upon amount. As a result, prices began to tumble. When the price of oil hit bottom, it was less than $10 per barrel, a far cry from the $30 per barrel OPEC had commanded at the peak of its power. In the United States, the number of rigs drilling for oil plummeted, until they were counted by the hundreds instead of the thousands.

Even in their disagreement, the OPEC oil ministers controlled prices. If they lowered their income, they also seriously slowed the discovery of new sources of oil outside OPEC. Steadily rising consumption would eventually increase the world's dependence on their oil.

Shifting Sites. The U.S. crude petroleum and natural gas industry moved into a period of decline after 1986 when production hit 8.35 million barrels per day. Three major factors figured in the decline: a shift away from petroleum as an energy source, low crude oil prices, and increasingly stringent environmental regulations—including drilling bans in some of the most promising areas of development. The number of rotary rigs drilling in the United States in 1995 was 723, a decrease of 52 rigs from 1994. This was the second-lowest count since World War II, and a drastic decrease from the nearly 4,000 that were in operation in 1981. But in the first nine months of 1996, the number rose to 761, with 39 percent drilling for oil, 60 percent for gas, and 1 percent miscellaneous. As a result, the major thrust of drilling and exploration moved outside of the United States. Low crude oil prices also curbed the development of other sources of hydrocarbon liquids, such as oil shale, tar sands, and coal liquefaction.

Despite the fact that oil supplied a smaller percentage of the total U.S. energy demand, that demand increased significantly. As a result, the absolute amount of oil used by the United States continued growing (at a time when worldwide use remained stable). By 1992 nearly 2 million miles of gas pipelines linked wells with consumers. Dependence on foreign oil imports reached a

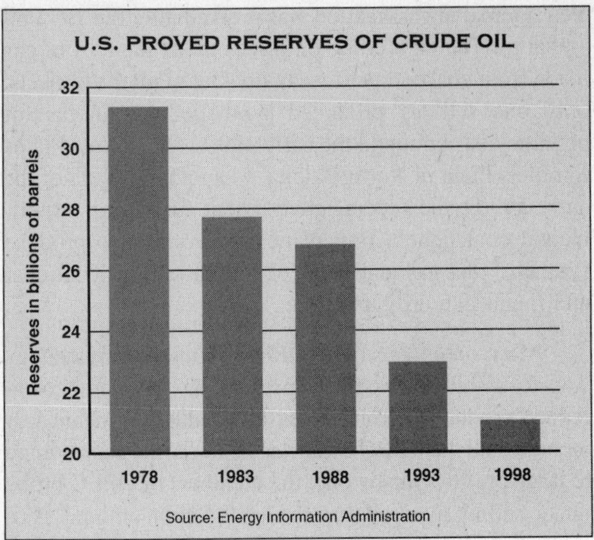

record-high 48.2 percent of domestic demand in 1993, up from 31.5 percent in 1985. In 1992 the amount of natural gas consumed rose 4.1 percent to 19.83 trillion cubic feet (tcf). The figure rose to 21.99 tcf in 1996, and consumption for 1998 was estimated at 23.25 tcf.

CURRENT CONDITIONS

Americans increased their dependence on foreign oil, from 45 percent in 1993 to 53 percent in 1998. In 1998 the United States imported an average of 8.55 million barrels of crude petroleum per day. After remaining flat for a few years, in 1998 crude oil production in the United States began to fall, from 6.45 million barrels per day in 1997 to 6.24 million barrels per day in 1998. By February 1999 the production levels were the lowest in 50 years, dropping from 6.38 million barrels per day in February 1998 to 5.94 million barrels per day. While production declined, the reserves of crude oil rose, to 222.5 billion barrels in 1997, an increase of 2.4 percent.

Through the year 2002 the forecast was for increased production of petroleum around the world, but with a continuing decline in the United States, down 5 percent. As the United States was forecasted to continue its increase in oil consumption—to 21.5 million barrels a day by 2005—the country's dependence on imported oil was also expected to rise, to 10.14 million barrels per day.

The industry in the United States also changed where it got its petroleum. In 1974 the United States produced 8.8 billion barrels per day, with 81 percent from the lower 48 states, 2.2 percent from Alaska, and 17 percent from offshore. In 1998 the output was 6.4 billion barrels per day and the percentages were: lower 48 with 57 percent, Alaska with 19 percent, and offshore with 24 percent. The forecast for the year 2005 was 5.8 million barrels per day, with 54 percent from the lower 48, 16 percent from Alaska, and 30 percent coming from offshore drilling. The Gulf of Mexico was the area where nearly all offshore drilling occurred in the United States. The increase in offshore drilling was attributed to advances in deepwater production and drilling and legislation aimed at providing royalty relief to the crude oil companies.

In the first six months of 1999 the large integrated oil companies of the United States cut back spending on exploration and production by 10 percent, compared to the same time in 1998. Companies had cut back their upstream spending in the United States by a quarter, while maintaining or increasing the spending in foreign countries. Some analysts, noting total upstream budgets, expected the spending to rise dramatically in the second half of 1999. Some smaller firms were being more aggressive in upstream investment, with some spending more than 75 percent of their yearly upstream budget in the first six months of 1999, with the implication that they would go over budget by the end of the year.

While natural gas production rose in the United States—averaging 18.97 trillion cubic feet (tcf) in 1998, up from 18.90 tcf in 1997—imports rose 4 percent during that period, due to increased demand. Production was expected to increase in the United States over the next few years, with improved technologies for recovery and storage. The forecasts for natural gas production were 20.27 tcf in 2000 and 22.25 tcf by the year 2005.

Consumers are demanding ever more efficient energy sources and this will push demand for natural gas to about 2 percent per year. With more Americans choosing products based on environmental considerations, natural gas wins over petroleum products. The combination of deregulation and plans for more electricity generation plants to be powered by gas will lead to increased demand.

For the industry as a whole, the rotary rig count declined to 502 as of March 1999, the lowest ever. Of those 502 rigs, 78 percent drilled for natural gas and 22 percent for oil. In 1998 there was a drop of 13 percent in well completions—10,711 for gas, 8,720 for oil, and 5,453 dry wells.

INDUSTRY LEADERS

In 1998 the top production companies were Exxon, with sales of $117.5 billion; Royal Dutch/Shell, with $107.8 billion; BP Amoco, with $68.3 billion; and Mobil, with $46.3 billion. Exxon was the flagship of the Standard Oil Trust and was incorporated in 1882. It was the world's largest publicly owned integrated oil company. Mobil Oil, the second largest in the United States and third largest worldwide, started in 1866 in Rochester, New York, as Vacuum Oil Co., and was also part of the Standard Oil Trust. It merged with Socony in 1931, became Socony-Mobil in 1955, and Mobil Oil in 1966. In

1998 Exxon and Mobil agreed to merge into a new company called Exxon Mobil.

BP Amoco was a result of a merger in 1998, the world's largest between industrial companies. William Knox D'Arcy founded BP in the early 1900s. D'Arcy was convinced (and eventually proven right) that there were large oil deposits in Iran (then Persia). BP remained a heavy presence in the Middle East for 60 years, before concentrating in the United Kingdom and the United States. Amoco was founded by John D. Rockefeller in 1889 and folded into his giant Standard Oil. In 1911 Amoco became an independent company. Scientists at Amoco developed the process that increased octane levels in gasoline in 1912.

Shell had humble beginnings as a bric-a-brac shop in 1833, with part of its enterprise the sale of exotic sea shells. When owner Marcus Samuel died, the thriving business was continued by his sons, and had its first foray into the oil industry in 1878, handling consignments of cased kerosene, and eventually became Shell Transport. Standard Oil made several unsuccessful attempts to buy or control Shell, and in 1907, Shell and Royal Dutch merged, with Royal Dutch holding 60 percent ownership and Shell Transport 40 percent ownership—exactly as it stands today. The Royal Dutch/Shell Group is the second-largest petroleum company in the world.

The industry was being held to an increasingly higher environmental standard, especially offshore. Drilling and production wastes once held acceptable were declared toxic. For example, a machine shop that removed scale from the inside of drilling pipes found out the scale was radioactive. The oil companies that sent the pipe to the shop agreed to a multimillion-dollar settlement out of court. Early estimates were that thousands of workers and their families might have been exposed to harmful radiation and clean-up costs might reach several hundred million dollars.

Environmentally related situations continue to plague petroleum companies. In 1989 the largest oil spill in United States history took place in Prince William Sound, Alaska. Seven years later, a U.S. District Court judge ordered Exxon to pay compensatory damages of more than $5 billion. Exxon filed an appeal. In January 1997, Ecuador's attorney general stated that Texaco Oil was responsible for unprecedented and continuing damage to the health and well-being of Ecuadorian Indians. They joined a $1 billion class-action lawsuit against Texaco. Shell Petroleum in Nigeria was accused of environmental devastation and exploitation in Ogoni, a small, highly populated area of the Niger Delta. There have been several well-publicized incidents and community disruption to Shell Nigeria's operations.

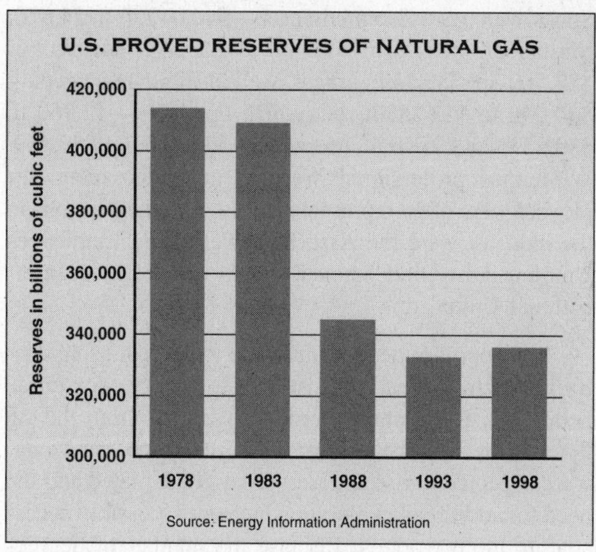

The bad publicity from environmental disasters continues to afflict the oil industry. Russell Mokhiber of *Corporate Crime Reporter* and Robert Weissman of *Multinational Monitor* complied a list called the ''Top 100 Corporate Criminals.'' The list appeared in an article written by Michelle Bier in the *Oil Daily* and oil companies were featured prominently. Exxon, in making the list twice at numbers 5 and 96, was called a ''criminal recidivist corporation.'' The two incidents involving Exxon were the spill in Prince William Sound and a spill of 567,000 gallons of home heating oil. The latter spill occurred in Arthur Kill, a waterway between New York and New Jersey, and resulted in Exxon pleading guilty to federal charges in 1991 and paying a $200,000 fine.

But Exxon had company on the list. Chevron Corporation was placed at number 41 when it pleaded guilty to discharging oil and grease off a drilling platform in Santa Barbara, California. The company was fined $8 million. At number 77 was Unocal Corporation, which leaked oil at its field in Guadalupe, California. It was estimated that the company leaked as much as 8.5 million gallons. Five other oil or petroleum related companies made the list.

WORKFORCE

In 1998 the crude petroleum and natural gas industry employed more than 325,900 people. Among the job titles were administrators, accountants, civil engineers, insurance specialists, human resource specialists, public relations practitioners, and marketing and sales managers. Peculiar to the industry are gas engineers, geologists, geophysicists, seismic surveyors, derrick men, drillers, floormen, mud engineers, mud loggers, mud men, petroleum engineers, roughnecks, roustabouts, swampers, tank strappers, and wildcatters.

Wages in the industry ranked above average. Annual salaries in 1997 for those who worked in the United

States were: petroleum engineer—$40,040 to $124,820; roustabout—less than $11,960 to $23,399; surveyor—$27,560 to $89,959, oil/gas well drilling managers—$40,040 to $124,820; rotary drill operators—11,960 to $89,959; and derrick operators—$11,960 to $50,439. While most professionals were not unionized, other employees were often represented. Two prominent unions in the industry were the Associated Petroleum Employees Union and the Oil, Chemical and Atomic Workers International Union.

Job opportunities remained fair to poor, due to industry restructuring and consistently low prices for crude petroleum. Restructuring produced layoffs from the rig floor to the boardroom. Long-term oil prices, however, were expected to rise as reservoirs were depleted and the need for additional exploration increased, possibly necessitating more workers. Because the number of degrees granted in the field has traditionally been low, the number of job seekers was not likely to exceed the number of positions available in the near future. Recent setbacks were offset by the increased demand for these professionals in environmental protection, reclamation, cleaning up contaminated sites, and in assisting private companies and government comply with more numerous and complex regulations. Job prospects for geoscientists were expected to grow 10-20 percent through 2005. In addition, overseas opportunities existed for many of the skilled and technical professions.

America and the World

The United States has been a leader in international oil exploration and production. U.S. companies have played roles in the discovery and production of oil in major fields in Mexico, Venezuela, Saudi Arabia, Kuwait, and Libya. While exploration and oil drilling have decreased in the continental United States and Alaska, all of the major American oil companies have increased their presence overseas. It is important to note that more than 75 percent of proven oil reserves are controlled by OPEC, although the vast majority of oil is consumed by non-OPEC nations—therefore giving OPEC a tremendous influence on the world oil and gas market.

American oil exploration, and that of other non-OPEC countries, slowed in contrast to OPEC exploration. Meanwhile, the major U.S.-based petroleum companies became increasingly involved in foreign exploration. In the early 1990s, money allocated to foreign exploration and development topped 50 percent of all exploration spending, as compared to 27 percent in the mid-1980s. In 1998, for example, Exxon spent about 45 percent on production in the United States and about 55 percent in the rest of the world. World political and economic developments of the 1990s made it more feasible and profitable to increase American investment in foreign exploration. U.S. companies increased their investment in many areas of the world, particularly in Latin America. The natural gas industry in Central and South America presented great potential. With the exception of Argentina and Venezuela, the industry was underdeveloped, with reserves equivalent to those found in North America.

The dissolution of the Soviet Union provided increased opportunities for investment in that area's oil reserves. The CIS (Commonwealth of Independent States) saw the rise of joint exploration and drilling ventures, especially in Russia, between U.S. and Russian companies. While instability in the former Soviet Union slowed the natural gas industry, this was seen as a short-term problem.

Another area of increasing American investment was Southeast Asia, where U.S. exploration spending grew the most from the mid-1980s to the mid-1990s. The economies of Asian countries became increasingly industrialized in recent years, and many governments in Asia, including China and Vietnam, actively courted foreign investment and participation in local drilling by outside companies. Deepwater fields offshore in the Philippines showed great promise as well.

After decades of being a net exporter of petroleum, the United States crossed the line into international interdependency sometime in 1970, when production hit its peak and the last of the oil surplus that had guaranteed energy independence had been pumped into the pipeline. Other countries, particularly South Africa and Canada, were leaders in developing technology for the use of coal as a source of petroleum and gas. South Africa had the largest commercial coal gasification plant and the only commercial coal liquefaction plant in the world. But while oil production decreased, natural gas production in America was increasing and was expected to remain on an upward swing until 2015. As the largest supplier of natural gas after Russia, American companies were putting more effort into drilling for gas domestically rather than petroleum.

Research and Technology

In the crude petroleum and natural gas industry, research and development occurs in both the laboratory and on the drilling rig. Directional drilling and enhanced oil recovery have been two of the latest areas of research and development. Directional drilling rapidly gained importance by allowing several wells to be drilled into different areas from a single derrick. The technique proved especially valuable offshore, where the cost of establishing a platform ran into the hundreds of millions of dollars. Onshore, directional drilling also limited environmental damage by reducing the number of rig locations needed.

Another advantage to directional drilling was the ability to drill a well horizontally across the top of a formation to maximize oil or gas recovery. Directional drilling is done with steerable drill bits that allow drillers to change the direction of the hole from the surface at any depth specified. A turbine motor, powered by the pressurized drilling mud circulating through the well, provides a high-speed twist to the drill bit.

Enhanced oil recovery—the third phase of oil recovery—became increasingly important as oil fields matured. In primary recovery, natural gas or water pressure drives the oil through the rock formation into the well. Sometimes the pressure is high enough to raise the crude to the surface, but often it must be pumped out. Production reduces the pressure until the driving force can no longer push the oil through the formation fast enough for economical recovery.

In secondary recovery, gas or water pressure is added to push the oil to the well. Enhanced, or tertiary, recovery begins when secondary recovery methods no longer produce enough oil to make the well profitable. Tertiary recovery uses a variety of techniques to wring the last bit of recoverable oil from the rock formation. The techniques fall into four categories: thermal—combustion, steam soak, steam drive, steam flood, hot water drive and electromagnetic; gas—hydrocarbon gas, carbon dioxide, nitrogen or flue gas; chemical—alkaline, foam and polymer; other—microbial.

Oil Shale, Tar Sands. In the early 1990s the attempt to produce liquids from oil shale involved several steps. The shale was mined, crushed, and heated in a retort to produce shale oil. Major problems with the technique included how to dispose of spent shale. In an oddity of nature, when oil is recovered from shale, the shale expands. Research in oil shale technology, like that for tar sands technology, had been all but completely shelved because of low oil prices.

Coal Gasification, Liquefaction. In the early 1990s, the $2.1 billion Great Plains Synfuels Plant in North Dakota produced more than 171 million cubic feet of synthetic natural gas per day using lignite (soft) coal mined in the state. The gas was then sold to a pipeline company for distribution in the eastern United States. Design of the plant began in 1973 as an effort to reduce the nation's dependence on foreign energy.

The success of the plant was costly. The federal government guaranteed $2.02 billion in loans to build the plant, and private sector partners agreed to provide up to $740 million of their own funds. Four years after construction began, the private sector sponsors withdrew and defaulted on the loans, despite the fact that the plant was earning revenue in excess of operating costs. The plant was sold in 1988 with $84 million and a share of future profits going to the federal government.

Coproducts had become important sources of revenue for the Great Plains Synfuels Plant. The plant produced 35 million pounds of phenol annually for plywood and chipboard resins. From the facility's oxygen plant, commercial quantities of xenon and krypton gases were being recovered and sold to lighting manufacturers. Other products included anhydrous ammonia, sulfur, and liquid nitrogen.

Coal liquefaction, also called mild gasification, began to emerge from the purely experimental stage in the early 1990s. While promising technologies had been discovered, they required crude oil prices in the $38-per-barrel range to be feasible. The price of crude ranged between $12.50 per barrel (1986) to about $20 per barrel in the early 1990s. Commercialization may depend on making commercial quantities of high-value chemical coproducts. The solid product of mild gasification can be made into formcoke and used in blast furnaces. Because the product would come from new plants meeting the most stringent environmental standards, instead of traditional coke ovens, the environment would benefit as well.

Also in the early 1990s, a Wyoming project that received federal funding under the U.S. Department of Energy Clean Coal Technology Program was to produce two products, one solid, the other liquid. The solid product was a low-sulfur, high-energy, coal-like fuel able to be burned in power plants and meet strict emissions standards. The liquid fuel could be used directly as a boiler fuel or as a refinery feedstock to produce gasoline and diesel. When fully operational, the plant was expected to produce 180,000 tons of high-energy solid fuel and 150,000 barrels of liquid each year using 1,000 tons of sub-bituminous coal per day. In all, 32 coal gasification and liquefaction projects were in various stages of development across the United States. But as crude oil prices increased, the economic benefits of coal liquefaction were beginning to attract attention. The Sierra Pacific Power Company's Pinon Pine Project was a showcase demonstration plant showing how clean affordable electricity could be generated from coal, one of America's most abundant resources. In its gaseous form, coal can be cleaned of more than 95 percent of its sulfur pollutants and virtually all of its ash impurities. The project began in 1992 and was scheduled to run until 2000. By 2010, technology improvements will be able to lower the cost to 75 percent of what it is today.

FURTHER READING

Brier, Michelle. "8 Industry Firms Qualify for Ranking among Top Corporate Criminals." *Oil Daily,* 4 October 1999.

"Crude Petroleum." *WEFA Industrial Monitor 1999-2000.* New York: John Wiley and Sons, 1999.

"Crude Petroleum and Natural Gas." *U.S. Industry & Trade Outlook '99.* New York: McGraw-Hill, 1999.

Exxon Corp. "1998 Financial and Operating Review." *Exxon Annual Report,* 1998. Available from http://www.exxon.com/exxoncorp/news/publications/98_fo/upstream2.html, 17 November 1999.

Galarza, Pablo. "Investing/Stocks/The Deal: Exxon and Mobil Cheap Oil Isn't the Only Reason that the Biggest Merger Ever Makes Sense." *Money,* 1 February 1999.

Independent Petroleum Association of America. "State of the U.S. Oil and Natural Gas Industry." Available from http://www.ipaa.org/departments/information_services/state_of_the_industry.htm.

Merolli, Paul. "Majors' Spending Declines 10 Percent from Last Year." *Oil Daily,* 30 July 1999.

"Natural Gas." *WEFA Industrial Monitor, 1999-2000.* New York: John Wiley and Sons, 1999.

"Petroleum and Natural Gas." *U.S. Industry Profiles: The Leading 100,* 2nd ed. Detroit: Gale Research, 1998.

Royal Dutch/Shell Group. "Income/Adjusted CCS Earnings." *Royal Dutch/Shell Annual Report,* 1998. Available from http://www.shell.com/reports98/items/shell_172.html, 17 November 1999.

"Sierra Pacific Power Company's Pinon Pine Project - A Preview of the Future." Project Facts, Department of Energy, Office of Fossil Energy. Available from http://www.metc.doe.gov/projfact/power/igcc/siercct.html.

U.S. Department of Energy. Energy Information Administration. "Outlook Assumptions." Available from http://www.eia.doe.gov/emeu/steo/pub/otlkasum.html.

SIC 1321

NATURAL GAS LIQUIDS

This category includes establishments primarily engaged in the production of liquid hydrocarbons from oil and gas field gases. Establishments recovering helium from natural gas and establishments recovering liquefied petroleum gases incidental to petroleum refining or to the manufacturing of chemicals are classified in a range of chemical and allied product manufacturing industries.

NAICS CODE(S)

211112 (Natural Gas Liquid Extraction)

Natural gas liquids (NGL) are found in natural gas, often in association with crude oil production. NGL is a reservoir portion of natural gas that is stripped out as a liquid at the surface by special processing facilities. NGL typically contains 35 percent ethane, 30 percent propane, 17 percent natural gasoline, 12 percent butane, and 6 percent isobutane. NGL should not be confused with natural gas, which is composed primarily of methane. NGL is denser than natural gas and becomes combustible at different concentrations than methane, according to the American Gas Association. Also, NGL is not liquefied natural gas, which is condensed natural gas that is compact and therefore convenient for overseas shipping.

NGL appears in a gaseous state at normal temperatures and pressures. NGL is removed from the gas stream at an extraction plant when the gas is processed. Using the most modern extraction technique, up to 90 percent of the NGL can be recovered from the gas stream. After the NGL is extracted, it is mixed together and transported to a fractionation center, where it is divided into individual gas products. The two largest centers are located in Texas and Kansas. Furthermore, Texas, Louisiana, Oklahoma, Wyoming, Kansas, and New Mexico together accounted for 87 percent of all NGL production throughout the 1990s. In addition, the 20 largest gas processing companies controlled 75 percent of NGL production, according to the *Oil and Gas Journal.*

The chemical industry accounted for 53 percent of the total demand for NGL products ethane and propane in the mid-1990s—up about 3 percent from earlier in the decade. NGL is used as feedstock to produce chemicals and plastics. One common product called ethylene is composed of 75 percent NGL. According to the *Oil & Gas Journal,* worldwide demand for NGL should rise significantly through the year 2010 because of feedstock usage, especially in the manufacturing of ethylene.

The Clean Air Act goaded butane demand by requiring gasoline composition to include a 12 to 15 percent greater oxygen content. Methyl tertiary butyl ether (MTBE), which has a high oxygenate content, has been the most highly regarded oxygenate to be used. MTBE is composed of 75 percent butane. The retail industry accounts for 30 percent of NGL demand. Propane is used for home heating, cooking, and transportation purposes.

The U.S. Department of Energy reported that 690 million barrels of NGL were produced in 1998. Most of the domestic supply of more than 70 percent of NGL was derived from natural gas processing plants. Refiners accounted for about 20 percent, and the rest of the supply came from imports, according to the *Oil and Gas Journal.*

In 1995, the United States increased its NGL reserves by 3 percent or 229 million barrels—the first increase since 1988; this increase pushed reserve levels up to 7.4 billion barrels. Total discoveries of NGL reserves also rose in 1995 by 10 percent with the largest share of the discoveries (33 percent) in Texas. In addition to the increasing reserves and discoveries, the NGL future looks promising as the Gas Processors Association predicted strong demand for NGL in the future as industrial and developing countries increase their use of cleaner burning fuels.

A leading producer of NGL throughout the 1990s in the United States has been GPM Gas Corporation (formerly Phillips 66 Natural Gas), located in Bartlesville, Oklahoma. Founded in 1985, and restructured and renamed in 1992, its parent company is Phillips Petroleum Company. GPM Gas Corp. produced 169,000 barrels of NGL per day in 1998, a 2 percent increase over 1997. The company owns or has interest in 16 gas liquid plants and approximately 28,000 miles of gathering lines. Philips Petroleum Company reported 1999 sales of $14 billion with sizable contributions from GPM. Another NGL industry leader has been Warren Petroleum Company, a private division of Chevron Corporation. After a merger with another leading producer, NGC Corp., Warren increased its plants to 57 and increased its production level to a potential yield of 120,000 barrels per day of gas liquids.

FURTHER READING

Phillips Petroleum Company. ''Gas Gathering, Processing and Marketing,'' 1999. Available from http://www.phillips66.com/keybusb.html.

U.S. Department of Energy. ''Natural Gas Liquids.'' Washington, D.C.: 1997. Available from http://www.eia.doe.gov.

SIC 1381

DRILLING OIL AND GAS WELLS

The category includes establishments primarily engaged in drilling wells for oil and gas field operations for others on a contract or fee basis. This industry includes contractors that specialize in spudding in, drilling in, redrilling, and directional drilling.

NAICS CODE(S)

213111 (Drilling Oil and Gas Wells)

INDUSTRY SNAPSHOT

According to estimates by the United States Census Bureau, there were 1,638 oil and gas well companies in operation in 1997. They Employed 53,865 people with an annual payroll of $1.9 billion and sales of $7.3 billion.

The states with the highest number of businesses in this industry in 1997 were: Texas, with 448 companies employing 14,322 people; Oklahoma, 164 companies with 3,680 employees; Ohio, 71 companies with 549 employees; Kansas with 66 companies employing 784 employees, and California with 60 companies employing 2,298 people.

Statistics from the Independent Petroleum Association of America (IPAA) indicate the industry's peak year was 1982, with nearly 13,000 drillers in operation.

The number of domestic rigs has continued to decline, despite the fact that demand for oil and gas continues to grow. Drilling contractors moved their rigs from the Gulf of Mexico to the North Sea. Much of the oil and gas used in the United States was imported in the 1990s. Because of consumer demand, the United States imported up to 47 percent of the total domestic petroleum consumed. Nearly eight million barrels of crude oil and related products per day were imported in 1992. Natural gas imports reached two trillion cubic feet, which accounted for 10 percent of total gas consumption. Oil consumption was up 3 percent in 1999, but domestic oil production declined 4 percent, resulting in a greater need to import oil. In 1999 the U.S. Department of Energy (DOE) estimated that 56 percent of oil was imported; the DOE also forecast that the figure would rise to 70 percent by 2020.

In the mid-1980s when Saudi Arabian crude oil flooded the market, the price of crude oil fell to $10 a barrel. American crude oil producers were hurt, but the rest of the domestic industry remained profitable, primarily due to strong consumption rates for refined petroleum products and chemical sales. The operators and producers of crude oil who survived the 1980s confronted an industry-wide collapse in 1991 and 1992.

In the early 1990s, the entire industry was afflicted with an array of problems, according to *Standard & Poor's Industry Surveys.* The fall of natural gas prices sent the rig count plummeting to the lowest number in 50 years; drillers were most affected. Intense gasoline price competition led to the collapse of refining and marketing margins. An economic slump in the United States and a surplus of gas also contributed to weak prices.

Industry analysts continued to offer conflicting views regarding the future of the oil and gas industry through the mid-1990s—eventual recovery, little or no recovery, growth in the natural gas sector only. For the drilling sector of the industry, economic recovery was contingent on many factors, all related to the supply and demand for oil and its related products. Various indicators included economic growth in the United States, consumption rates, oil and gas prices, Organization of Petroleum Exporting Countries (OPEC) production and export rates, and the development of new markets for exploration.

Earlier in the 1990s, Standard & Poor's (S&P) anticipated U.S. oil consumption to approximate one-half of real growth in Gross Domestic Product (GDP). With long-term real GDP growth forecast at 2.5 percent annually, S&P predicted oil consumption to increase approximately 1.0 percent annually during the 1990s. Oil consumption did, in fact, rise from 17.979 million barrels a day in 1992 to 19.653 million barrels a day in 1999.

Gasoline consumption remained the largest component of total domestic petroleum use, with home heating oil in second place. Market analysts asserted that as Americans purchased more sports vehicles, which consume more gasoline than conventional automobiles, U.S. consumption of gasoline increased. Increased consumption was also attributable to industrial and utility users who had dual burning capacity and switched from heavy fuel to natural gas. Natural gas consumption increased 4 percent over 1992 to capture approximately 25 percent of the U.S. energy market in 1993.

Natural gas can be found by itself or in association with crude oil. Natural gas is one of the cleanest burning fuels, producing primarily carbon dioxide, water vapor, and small amounts of nitrogen oxides. Prices of natural gas averaged $1.86 per thousand cubic feet in 1992, up 13 percent from the 1991 average of $1.59. According to the IPAA, 1991 prices were abnormally low due to the warmer weather and the early release of gas from storage. By 1997, however, prices had risen to $2.42. Preference for natural gas continued to grow throughout the decade. The IPAA projected an annual growth rate of 1.7 percent through 2010.

According to an industry report by Hanifen Imhoff, Inc. Investment Bankers, U.S. demand for natural gas had exceeded supply in 1996. By late 1995 the natural gas industry faced numerous challenges attributable to increased demand for natural gas, limited sources of new gas supplies domestically and in Canada, and record low levels of gas storage. The industry also faced low average natural gas prices in 1995, which discouraged exploration drilling activity. As a result, producers cut capital expenditures; productive capacity, subsequently, was reduced during the 1995-96 heating season. Although market analysts projected continued low capacity through 1997 and projected natural gas prices in major regional hubs to nearly double from 1995 prices, prices only rose to $2.42 per thousand cubic feet.

From 1989 through 1991, oil consumption fell. According to the *Oil and Gas Journal*, this continued decline was a result of a depressed level of drilling activity, the natural production decline rate of mature reservoirs, and a lack of access to prospective onshore and offshore areas. According to IPAA, crude oil production averaged 7.2 million barrels per day in 1992, which was the lowest level in 30 years. The trend continued and fell to 6.3 million barrels per day by 1998.

Oil prices averaged $12.12 per barrel in 1998, rose to $17.21 in 1999, and the DOE projected that they would continue to rise to an average of $21.86 per barrel in 2000. Natural gas prices also rose from $2.38 per million BTU in 1998, to $2.64. in 1999, and were expected to rise to an average of $2.89 in 2000.

Perhaps reflecting the price increase in crude oil, the U.S. rig count rose to 763 in November, 1999, compared to 696 in 1998. The Canadian rig count was 336 in 1999, almost double the 183 operating in 1998. Only international drilling activity showed a decrease from 724 rigs in September 1998, compared to 557 in September 1999.

Saudi Arabia has been the dominant member of OPEC and maintained the highest share of OPEC oil export revenues. Other top OPEC oil exporters included Iran, Venezuela, Iraq, and Nigeria.

In the first half of the 1990s, U.S. exploration was centered in the Gulf of Mexico. According to Hanifen Imhoff Inc., this drilling activity was primarily caused by natural gas prices and deliverability. As consumption of natural gas increased at the end of the twentieth century, companies continued to search for new sources of crude oil. Opportunities for international petroleum companies to explore, develop, and produce crude oil and natural gas in many areas of the world increased rapidly, particularly in the Asia-Pacific region.

Organization and Structure

Contract drilling firms work with the well operators. Operators are the companies that decide what kind of well to drill and determine its specifications. Operators hold the lease rights and operate the lease as well. According to the *Fundamentals of Petroleum,* almost 98 percent of all gas and oil wells in the United States have been drilled by contract drilling firms. The drilling contractor usually is assisted by other companies, or subcontractors, that furnish specialized well services such as casing and cementing **(see SIC 1389: Oil and Gas Field Services, Not Elsewhere Classified)**.

To remain financially viable, drilling contractors began to diversify their businesses to include other oil-related services. Rowan Companies Inc., for example, diversified into an international aviation organization operating helicopters and fixed-wing aircraft. Between 1983 and 1995, while the drilling industry was in a state of turmoil and a period in which Rowan lost $342 million, its aviation division contributed more than $178 million in earnings. To diversify, Rowan Companies also operated another division, LeTourneau, Inc., a mini-steel mill and manufacturing facility that produces heavy equipment for the mining, timber and transportation industries, an international aviation service business operating helicopters and fixed-wing aircraft, and a marine division that has built more than one-third of all mobile offshore jack-up drilling rigs.

Drilling contractors are primarily responsibile for drilling wells, redrilling, reworking wells, and spudding (or startup) services. During 1995, Rowan Companies conducted offshore drilling operations in the Gulf of Mexico, the North Sea, offshore eastern Canada, and offshore Trinidad. The overall activity rate of its 21 offshore rigs in 1995 was 90 percent, up from 85 percent in 1994. Its drilling operations yielded an operating profit of $2.3 million, down $2.7 million from 1995.

Varco International, Inc., a manufacturer of products used in the oil and gas well drilling industry worldwide, reported that sales for 1999 totaled $80 million, down from $96.1 million in 1998. The reduced level of incoming orders in 1999 as compared to 1998 reflected the continued low level of worldwide drilling activity and the absence of new rig construction.

Drilling contracts specify a drilling contractor's obligations to the operating company. The drilling contract is important to both the drilling contractor and the operating company because it details responsibilities and expectations, such as the depth of the well, start date, and sizes of the hole and casing. Operating companies rely primarily on two kinds of drilling contracts: turn-key and footage or daywork. Using a turn-key contract, the operating company is required to pay a set fee to the drilling contractor upon completion of the well. The contractor furnishes all the materials and labor, controlling the entire drilling process independently. Under a footage contract, a rate per-foot-drilled is established. This contract usually includes a daywork payment to compensate the drilling contractor for days when drilling has been suspended. This payment covers situations when the drilling rig is on site but has to perform nondrilling duties that are vital to well completion.

Drilling Rigs. All drilling rigs are designed to extract a significant amount of petroleum which is trapped underground in a porous or permeable rock formation. The most common form of drilling rig has been the rotary rig. With rotary drilling, the rock formation is penetrated by a rotating bit connected to a hollow drill pipe. Fluid is pumped through the pipe so that the rock cuttings can be brought to the surface. Two or more diesel or gas engines provide the required 1,000 to 3,000 horsepower, depending upon well depth and rig design. Rotary rigs are usually portable, so the contractor can be relatively mobile.

The operating equipment of a rotary rig can be divided into three systems: hoisting, rotating, and circulation. Wells are drilled using tremendous amounts of pipe and drill collars, sometimes weighing as much as 500,000 pounds. In order to move these items, the rig must have a hoisting system. The rotating system provides the power to the bit by turning it in the wellbore. The rotary method

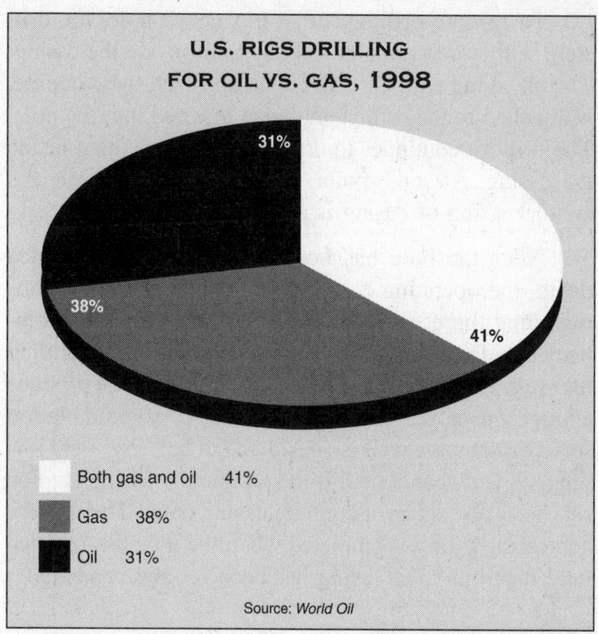

spins the bit further and further into the ground, while the drill is lubricated to keep it cool and to flush out excess matter. The drill collar is heavier than the drill pipe and is used on the bottom of the string to put weight on the bit. The bit chews up the rock formation and dislodges it. The hardness of the formations determines the type of bit to be used. The circulating system is used to remove rock cutting and to cool the bit. Drilling fluid, often called mud, is a mixture of clays, chemicals, and water or oil, and is circulated in the drill hole.

Preparing a drill site requires many steps. The contractor must first clear and level the land, build access roads, make water available, and dig a pit to serve as a waste protector. At the site of the borehole, the contractor moves in the rig and other necessary equipment. Once the rig is in position over the conductor hole, the drilling begins to create the surface hole. The first drilling is accomplished by using a large bit attached to a drill collar, which is lowered into the conductor hole, with sections of the drill pipe added until the bit is on the bottom. Additional joints of drill pipe are added to the drill stem every 30-40 feet. At some depth, when the hole has been created beyond the gravel beds and other near-surface materials, the drilling subsides and the drill stem is lifted out of the hole.

Pulling out the entire drill stem and bit is known as tripping out. Once the pipe is out, a casing crew moves in and runs the surface casing. Casing is a steel or iron pipe lowered into the well to prevent the walls from caving during drilling and to keep gas and water from entering the well. Casing services are usually provided by an oil and gas field services subcontractor. Once in place, the casing is cemented by a subcontractor.

To resume drilling, or to trip into a hole, the drill stem with a new, smaller bit has to fit inside the casing. The bit, along with the drill collar, and each stand of pipe, is attached to the drill stem and is lowered into the hole. The drill bit continues to drill through the cement inside the casing. At some point, the drilling stops again and another string of casing is set into the hole.

After the hole has been drilled to its determined depth, the operating company completes all evaluations regarding the economic viability of the hole. The company decides whether to set the production casing or plug the well. If it is determined that the well can not produce enough oil or gas to compensate the costly completion services, then the well is considered to be ''dry'' and it is plugged and abandoned. If the production casing is to be set, it will be set by a contract casing crew. The drilling contractor's job is completed when the hole has reached final depth and the casing has been set and cemented.

BACKGROUND AND DEVELOPMENT

The petroleum pioneers based their drilling methods on the process of drilling for water: digging by hand. In 1857, operator Edward L. Drake and driller Billy Smith in Titusville, Pennsylvania, decided to try drilling for oil by hammering a pipe into the ground. The citizens of Titusville thought the project was foolishness and called the contraption ''Drake's Folly.'' Even the financial backers of the venture gave up on the scheme and wanted Drake to abandon the project. But the driller, Billy Smith, did not give up, and soon enough the drill pipe struck oil. By the start of the 1860s, Titusville was covered with derricks and the first oil boom had begun.

Early drilling methods relied on the cable-tool method, which was a rope or chain that suspended drilling tools into the well bore. Various methods were used to actually pound the drill bit into the ground. The tool's strings were relatively light and the bit ''looked something like a funnel.'' The process allowed the drill to penetrate one to two feet before the bit became dull. The drilling tools had to be removed from the well, the bit sharpened, and attached to a larger reaming instrument. If necessary the hole was pumped out, and the entire process began again. Versions of cable-tool drilling have been modernized and used in shallow wells. The cable-tool drilling system does not use injecting fluid or mud. Thus, the hole still has to be bailed out in order to remove cuttings produced during the drilling process.

Unlike the impact action of the cable system, in rotary drilling, the power of the bit comes from a rotating motion that turns the bit in the wellbore. The circulation of fluid was an innovation by the Baker brothers in the 1880s. Fluid circulation allows particles of soft rock to float up the shaft and out of the way of the drill bit. The Bakers used their rig for drilling water wells in the Great Plains. The technique was also successful in the soft soil of Texas, where the great Corsicana oil field was discovered.

The petroleum industry's offshore operations began in the 1930s. Drilling in the shallow bays of the Louisiana and Texas Gulf coasts was conducted on wooden platforms mounted on timber piles. Most of the early activities in water-covered areas were designed to recover oil from reservoirs already defined on shore.

The offshore industry grew with the development of submersible and semi- submersible rigs, drill ships, and barges. Each year, independents dramatically increased their presence offshore, in both traditional production areas and in frontier deepwater leases. In 1999 more than 400 independents were active in the Gulf of Mexico, with at least 60 independents participating in the development of deepwater leases.

As the rig counts in American waters have declined, offshore drilling in other parts of the world has steadily increased. According to *Oil & Gas Journal,* a report by Infield Systems Ltd. noted that more than 1,400 new oil and gas fields will be developed before the end of the decade. According to the *New York Times,* rig operators pulled their equipment out of the Gulf and hauled it to areas with more oil, including Venezuela, West Africa, and the North Sea.

According to IPAA, there were 835 U.S. rigs in operation in 1992. IPAA attributed the decrease in the number of operating rigs to the expiration of Section 29 tax credits and warm weather patterns. Some analysts predicted that the industry would pick up by 1993, estimating an average of 1,200 wells. Yet, the rig count stood at an average of 827 during the first half of 1998.

Environmental Issues. Industry leaders, such as those present at the 1992 Offshore Technology Conference, complained that the rapid decline in rig count has been due to rising costs, and also to excessive environmental regulations. As these and other drilling experts have commented, the petroleum industry has been increasingly subjected to environmental considerations, a trend that continued throughout the decade.

The industry was mainly concerned with U.S. national energy policies. The Clean Air Act promoted the development and use of natural gas, which burns cleaner than other fuels. Although this legislation seemed to boost the natural gas market, it also included more stringent emission standards for offshore drilling, which directly affected well completion costs for drilling contractors. As new environmental laws and regulations were introduced, drilling contractors had to spend capital to meet standards set by these laws.

CURRENT CONDITIONS

To meet demand, crude oil and petroleum products were imported at the all-time high rate of 10.4 million barrels per day in 1998, while exports measured 0.9 million barrels per day. Between 1985 and 1998, the rate of net importation of crude oil and products more than doubled from 4.3 million barrels per day to 9.5 million barrels per day. The share of U.S net imports that came from OPEC nations reached 72 percent in 1977, subsided to 42 percent in 1985, and climbed back to 51 percent in 1998. Total net imports as a share of petroleum consumption reached a record high of 51 percent in 1998. The five leading suppliers of petroleum to the United States in 1998 were Venezuela, Canada, Saudi Arabia, Mexico, and Nigeria.

The price paid by refiners for crude oil in 1998 averaged $12.57 per barrel. When adjusted for inflation, the price was $11.15, fully 35 percent below the previous year's price and 79 percent lower than 1981's record inflation- adjusted price of $53.39 per barrel.

Up from less than $15 in early June of 1999, a jump in September of world oil prices put crude back to above $21 a barrel, the highest since 1997. The jump came on top of hefty fuel duty increases. The signs of a strengthening recovery in Japan and South East Asia drove the upward twist in oil prices.

The United States produced 19.0 trillion cubic feet of natural gas in 1998, well below the record-high 21.7 trillion cubic feet in 1973. Gas well productivity peaked at 435 thousand cubic feet per well per day in 1971, then fell steeply through the mid-1980s before stabilizing. Productivity in 1998 was 146 thousand cubic feet per well per day.

Annual petroleum consumption rose in the United States until 1973, when the Arab OPEC embargo stalled the annual increases for two years. Consumption peaked in 1978 at 18.9 million barrels per day. Rising prices over the next few years lowered consumption, which fell to 15.2 million barrels per day in 1983. Consumption began to rebound the following year and was boosted by plummeting crude oil prices in 1986. By 1998 it had reached 18.7 million barrels per day, close to the all-time high.

The resurgent U.S. natural gas market and new opportunities for work abroad should provide growth in the industry. Operators are expected to use more turnkey operations, risk sharing, partnerships, and to seek outside sources for certain services rather than developing them in-house, explained Sam Albright, of Howard, Weil, Labouisse, Friedrich, Inc., at the International Association of Drilling Contractors (IADC) Annual Meeting. Albright added in *Drilling Contractor* that the oil industry is restructuring and consolidation will continue for the next few years. "This is an industry in transition, he said. It is responding to contraction in the market. It's our view that even if a recovery is out there, there are stray secular forces that are driving this industry toward change."

Outlook. *Annual Energy Outlook 1999* (AEO99) projected rising demand and prices for natural gas. Increased demand will provide additional economic incentives for the investments in infrastructure, rigs, drilling, and manpower development needed to meet the necessary increases in gas production. As a result, industry experts suggest that the natural gas industry will be in a position to meet the challenge of satisfying projected demand.

The AEO99 also predicts that onshore and offshore production will increase by 57 and 14 percent, respectively, and pipeline capacity will increase by 32 percent over 1997 levels. This prediction seemed validated at the close of the 1990s; according to Baker Hughes (October, 1999), 761 U.S. rigs were in operation as well as 557 international rigs.

With higher utilization, day rates increased and contract terms lengthened. These factors, coupled with a continuing trend of consolidation among the remaining drilling contractors, place this segment of the industry in its strongest position since 1982. Still, except for some very specialized rigs, day rates are far below the level which would justify new rig construction.

INDUSTRY LEADERS

On July 13,1999 Schlumberger Ltd. announced that it had agreed to merge the offshore drilling operation, Sedco Forex, with Transocean Offshore, to create the world's largest offshore drilling company. The merged company would be called Transocean Sedco Forex. Both companies said the spinoff was in response to the increasing costs and technological demands of offshore drilling, which is taking place in deeper waters than in previous years.

BP Amoco PLC, which formed in 1998 from the merger of British Petroleum and Amoco, produces oil in 24 countries and has proven reserves of 14.8 billion barrels of oil. Headquartered in London, its 1998 revenues were more than $100 billion and it employs 96,000 people. The daily production of BP Amoco is 1.9 million barrels of crude oil and 5.7 billion cubic feet of natural gas. It is the largest U.S. oil and gas producer and one of the top two gas producers in Canada. BP Amoco also manufactures petrochemicals and specialty chemicals.

Texaco, Inc., headquartered in White Plains, N.Y. has operations in approximately 30 countries throughout the world. Texaco is the third largest oil producer with more than 24,000 employees and revenues of more than $3 billion. Texaco claims total reserves of 4.7 billion barrels of oil. It is involved in two extensive U.S. joint ventures, Equilon (Shell) with a 44 percent stake, and a 33 percent stake in Motiva (Shell and Saudi Aramco). Texaco also owns half of Caltex Petroleum, an international refining and marketing joint venture with Chevron.

Ultramar Diamond Shamrock Corp. with headquarters in Greenwich, Connecticut, was originally formed in April 1992, via a merger with the United States and Canadian refining and marketing operations of Ultramar PLC from LASMO PLC, a British oil and gas exploration and production company. The company employs 24,000 people, and revenues in 1998 were almost $12 billion. Ultramar Diamond Shamrock Corporation is a leading independent refiner and marketer of high-quality petroleum products in the central and southwest United States, and the northeast United States, and eastern Canada. This independent oil refining and marketing company owns seven refineries with a total capacity of 685,000 barrels per day.

DRECO, a National Oilwell Technology, designs and supplies drilling, workover, and coiled tubing rigs and associated equipment worldwide for land and offshore use. In 1997, National Oilwell and DRECO merged to form a worldwide comprehensive oil well drilling, equipment servicing, production, design, manufacturing, and supply organization with 125 distribution centers, 11 manufacturing facilities, five engineering offices, and worldwide sales offices.

Workforce

According to the IPAA, employment in the exploration and production sector of the oil and natural gas industry in 1997 averaged 320,000, compared to 310,700 in 1996. Ten years ago, 557,600 people earned their living in this sector. This loss of experienced personnel constrains the industry's current rebound.

The 1997 U.S. census reported that 1,371 companies employed 53,865 people in the oil and gas industry. Annual payroll was $1.9 billion. Employment was highest in Texas, Oklahoma, and Ohio.

America and the World

The Department of Energy (DOE) has forecast strong opportunities for the export of U.S. energy services and technology through 2010. The international market for oil and gas exploration, excluding former Eastern bloc nations and China, has been predicted to increase to $1.3 trillion per year from 1991 through 2010, as reported in *Oil & Gas Journal.* The DOE has estimated that U.S. vendors can capture $955 billion or 74 percent of that market.

According to the International Trade Administration, Department of Commerce, the Middle East and North Africa region is of vital strategic interest to the United States and is of economic importance as a major source of the world's energy supplies. Export figures from the region support that assesment—Persian Gulf countries (Bahrain, Iran, Iraq, Kuwait, Qatar, Saudi Arabia, and the United Arab Emirates), as of February, 1998, produced 26 percent of the world's oil, and held 65 percent of the world's oil reserves. Saudi Arabia and Kuwait alone accounted for about 12 percent of total U.S. crude oil imports.

Canada was the world's fifth largest energy producer, after the United States, Russia, China, and Saudi Arabia. The United States is Canada's major trade market for energy products, accounting for 91 percent of all Canadian energy exports (including nearly all of Canada's oil, natural gas, and electricity exports). Despite low oil prices in 1998, Canada's overall energy outlook was good. The country possessed abundant quantities of gas, coal, uranium, and oil, and was a major net energy exporter.

Latin America is also a promising market, especially Venezuela and Columbia. Although both have political risks, a joint venture has already begun between Benton Oil & Gas Co. and Vinccler CA producing 2,100 barrels a day in Venezuela. According to the *Wall Street Journal,* this has been the first Venezuelan oil field operated by a U.S. company since the industry was nationalized in the mid-1970s. Southeast Asia has become a lead target for development by U.S. firms. As the 1993 *U.S. Industrial Outlook* reported, ''governments in the subcontinent are actively seeking foreign investment through the production stage, and U.S. development spending has grown at a more rapid rate in Southeast Asia than in any other foreign area.''

Although overseas work can prove to be lucrative, it is not without its problems, most of which are not related to the task of drilling. Instead, contractors will have to learn about customs, work habits, and social behaviors for each country. Also, each market is decisively different, so what is known about one market will not be easily transferred to the next. Moreover, some overseas markets, have grown to expect contract drillers to provide integrated services, ''where the driller's participation in the planning and the management of the drilling programs are the norm rather than the exception,'' reported Luigs in *Oil & Gas Journal.*

Research and Technology

Advances in research and technology in the contract drilling industry will continue to be the most critical factor to keep companies competitive. Continual improvements in technology and procedures have resulted in lower drilling costs and improved safety. At an IADC annual meeting, both Suzanne Cook, industry analyst and first vice president of Merrill Lynch and Co., and Matt Simmons, president of Simmons and Co., International, agreed that ''savvy exploitation of technology is one of the keys to repositioning for the future.'' Technological issues boil down to how to drill a well more efficiently and cost effectively. ''The reality for operators is more and more marginal fields and more and more pressure on regulatory and environmental fronts, all at a flat crude price,'' noted Bob Agnew, Drilling Manager for Exxon International, in *Drilling Contractor.*

Other technological advancements already in use are rig computerization and automation for daily drilling operations, such as Microsoft's Project Manager software. As reported in *Drilling Contractor,* Global Marine has developed a Rig Efficiency Program and has used the Microsoft program to monitor and analyze the performance of all its operations on every company rig around the world. Simmons added that while technology has profoundly changed the drilling industry, few advances have threatened to replace the rig itself. ''For most of the important new technical advances to work, it is important that a modern, well-operated drilling rig is present,'' Simmons said in *Drilling Contractor.* ''While the use of coiled tubing or slim-hole drilling could take a few wells away from the traditional contractor, these can easily be offset by a wider number of holes drilled through the application of 3D seismic drilling or the use of horizontal drilling.''

Horizontal drilling uses drill bits driven by motors actually in the bits, instead of above ground motors, and can be directed with the help of computers and detailed mapping. Drillers use horizontal drilling in aging fields where earlier attempts might have missed oil trapped in narrow, vertical rock formations. Texas has remained the dominant region for horizontal drilling, with 81 percent of all horizontal wells. Some companies have begun to use the technique to search for new discoveries in North Dakota, Wyoming, and Colorado, where rock layers are similar to the ones in Texas fields, according to *The New York Times.*

According to the 1997 Swift Energy Annual Report, while horizontal drilling was still a small segment of the total drilling activity in the United States, its percentage of the total drilling activity increased sharply during the 1990s. Between 1991 and 1996, the number of horizontal wells drilled rose by 28 percent, while the total number of drilled wells fell by 23 percent.

In the field of exploration and production, technology revolutionized the way oil was found and gas was produced. Mobile Oil developed a new software that mimicked the way the human brain's neural network processes information. Using supercomputers, this tool integrated signs of gas, oil, or water from well measurements into a ''big picture,'' provided by high-definition seismic readings taken over hundreds of square miles. Predictions could then be made regarding a reservoir's hydrocarbon locations. With this detailed reservoir picture as a guide, zones could be tested using flexible drilling technologies.

FURTHER READING

Annual Energy Outlook 1999. Available from http://www.eia.doe.gov/oiaf/aeo99/issues.html.

Baker Hughes 1999. Available from http://www.bakerhughes.com/.

Davis, Neal C. *National Energy Information Center,* 18 June 1998. Available from http://www.eia.doe.gov/emeu/finance/usi&to/up_98.html.

Mobile Oil Company. Available from http://www.mobil.com/cgibin/bld_frameset.cgi?CONTENT=/clim_opeds/980820_oped.html.

''Natural Gas and Offshore Drilling Stocks.'' Hanifen Imhoff Inc. Investment Bankers, 26 June 1996.

Palmeri, Christopher. ''Annual Report on American Industry: Energy.'' *Forbes,* 13 January 1997.

Swift Energy 1997 Annual Report. Available from http://www.swiftenergy.com/SFY/Ann_rpts/97rpt/HTML/Ar97ab05.htm.

''Varco Announces Third Quarter Results.'' *Corporate Press Release,* 14 October 1996.

SIC 1382

OIL AND GAS FIELD EXPLORATION SERVICES

This category covers establishments engaged primarily in performing geophysical, geological, and other exploration services for oil and gas on a contract or fee basis.

NAICS CODE(S)

541360 (Geophysical Surveying and Map Services)
213112 (Support Activities for Oil and Gas Field Exploration)

INDUSTRY SNAPSHOT

Companies performing oil and gas exploration services are most often divisions or subsidiaries of major oil companies, although the industry also boasts several significant independent contractors. Many of the industry's leaders are known as integrated companies, which cover the entire oil and gas industry, from exploration to refining to distribution. As such, the exploration branch of the industry is affected by trends in the field as a whole. For example, in 1998 a drop in world oil prices led to a collapse in exploration and drilling activity. Drilling activity in the United States fell 12 percent, to an annual average of 831 active rotary rigs. The American Petroleum Institute reported that completion of U.S. oil wells, natural gas wells and dry holes declined by 21 percent in the third quarter of 1999 compared with the same period of 1998. In 1998, crude oil reserves decreased 7 percent, from 22,546 million barrels (MMbbls) in 1997 to 21,034 MMbbls in 1998. This level reflects an historic low not seen since 1935, during the depression. Natural gas liquid reserves fell 5.6 percent to 7,524 MMbbls in 1998. And dry natural gas reserves declined 2 percent to 164,041 billion cubic feet (Bcf) in 1998, breaking a four-year run of annual increases.

In 1998 there were a total of 24,884 wells in the United States, an increase of 2,703 from 1995; of these 8,720 were completed for oil; 10,711 for gas; and 5,453 were dry holes. Baker Hughes, Inc., an oil field service company, reported a dramatic drop in domestic drilling since late 1997. The September 1997 U.S. rig count topped 1,000; by December 1998, it dropped to 647, reaching the lowest level since 1950. Partly because the United States is considered a mature oil region, the major American companies—Exxon/Mobil, Texaco and Chevron (which, along with the European giants British Petroleum/Amoco/Arco and Royal Dutch/Shell, control the American market)—focused their exploration efforts elsewhere. The Energy Information Administration reported that the increases in the U.S. majors' exploration and development expenditures have mostly been directed toward the North Sea and Southeast Asia.

Organization and Structure

Much of the exploration process is done before wells are actually drilled. Once a company obtains the mineral rights to the land it wishes to drill, three-dimensional (3-D) seismography, above ground sonic sampling, and other methodologies are utilized to determine where oil is most likely to be found. Once seismographic data about either underground or sea floor rock is collected, it is analyzed for signs of oil or gas deposits, a process that takes several months. A likely area is then selected, and exploratory or ''wildcat'' wells are drilled to confirm suspicions. If the area is known to have oil, ''development'' wells are drilled. There are legal regulations on the number of wells that can be drilled in a given area by ''infill drilling.'' Drilling to test the possibilities for expanding an oil field is done with ''stepout'' wells. Finally, wells that turn up no product, or too little to make continued drilling feasible, are called ''dry holes.''

While drilling, a rig (made up of a derrick and surface equipment) is set up over the target area, and a bit attached to a drill stem is lowered into the earth. In the most common setup—rotary drilling—a rotating bit connected to a hollow pipe breaks up the earth. Fluids (''mud'') made up of clay, water, and other ingredients are injected through the pipe to cool the rotating bit and carry broken rock back to the surface. Often a hollow casing is placed in the well to keep the walls from caving in and to protect the contents of the well from outside influences of water or gas. Both oil and gas are removed through narrow tubing implements that bring the substances to the surface.

The crude oil that wells up without pumping is culled using primary recovery methods, during which time most of the available oil is recovered. In secondary recovery, additional effort must be expended to remove the oil. Most often, the well is flooded with water to flush out the oil. Finally, in some wells, tertiary recovery methods such as injecting steam or gases into the well help flush out the heaviest, most viscous oil. Wells may be ''shut in,'' their valves closed, during the wait for a pipeline connection or even when the oil and gas market is depressed and further drilling becomes financially difficult. Once a well is dry, it is plugged—filled with cement or mud—and abandoned.

Drilling for natural gas is similar to drilling for oil, but gas must be liquefied before it can be shipped. Apart from the natural gas liquids (NGL) that occur naturally at a well, all gas obtained must be cooled and pressurized into liquid natural gas (LNG) for transportation. NGL is mainly ethane, propane, butane, and natural gasoline; the gas from LNG is mainly composed of propane, propylene, butanes, and butylenes.

The amount of oil obtained is measured in barrels (bbls.), one of which is equal to 42 U.S. gallons. Natural gas is measured in thousand cubic feet (mcf), one of which equals 1 million BTUs of energy at one atmosphere of pressure. One barrel of oil is equal to six mcf.

Background and Development

Field exploration in the petroleum industry began in earnest in 1859, when Edwin Drake drilled the first successful oil well in Titusville, Pennsylvania. Previously, oil was obtained only where it seeped from the ground. Drake's discovery went to feed the burgeoning need for kerosene for lamps; soon, lamp oil made from oil replaced that made from coal.

Among the rash of speculators who entered the exploration business was John D. Rockefeller, who soon turned away from exploration (which he considered too much of a financial risk) and moved toward refining and transporting the fuel already obtained. For the next 50 years, Rockefeller's Standard Oil Company expanded by any means necessary, engaging competitors in price wars or buying them out when they became a threat. Standard Oil remained unchallenged until exploration in Texas, Louisiana, and Oklahoma led to the rise of companies such as Gulf and Texaco. While Standard's oil fields were in the United States, it began exporting its products to the European and Far Eastern markets, competing with both Shell (then the Shell Transport and Trading Company) and the Royal Dutch Petroleum Company. Standard Oil made several unsuccessful attempts to buy or control Shell. Royal Dutch and Shell began cooperating with each other, partly in an attempt to compete with Standard Oil, and eventually united into one company, today the second largest worldwide. In 1909 the Standard Oil Trust was deemed illegal under antitrust charges and the U.S. Supreme Court ordered it to be dissolved. Broken up into over 30 companies, the offshoots of Standard Oil still retained immense industry influence, eventually spawning Jersey Standard (later Exxon), Socony and Vacuum (later Mobil), Standard of California (later Chevron), Atlantic (later ARCO), and Standard of Indiana (Amoco), among others.

U.S. exploration on the part of the major American oil companies (known as the Seven Sisters) produced what for a while seemed to be a never-ending stream of resources. It was not until the 1920s that they began foreign exploration, and then mostly to check the power of British companies drilling in the Middle East. But foreign exploration came with a price; in the 1940s Venezuela demanded half of the income generated from drilling within its borders; other countries followed suit, stemming in part from the huge profits flowing into U.S. companies from overseas. Challenges also came from smaller independent oil companies such as Marathon and Getty. At the same time, exploration efforts uncovered new sources of revenues in natural gas, often found with oil deposits. Once it was discovered how to trap and transport the gas, it became another focus of exploration.

Another challenge to American oil companies came with the 1960 formation of the Organization of Petroleum Exporting Countries (OPEC), consisting of eight Middle Eastern countries that were heavy producers of oil. This cartel used its power to push up the price of oil from $1.80 a barrel in the 1960s to more than $3.00 a barrel in 1973. Prices rose further when a 1973 OPEC embargo aimed at punishing U.S. support of Israel led to a national energy crisis in which America was made aware of its dependence on foreign oil. Meanwhile, American oil companies came under attack for profiting unfairly from the embargo. The state of the oil and gas exploration industry was further impacted by increased emphasis on alternative energy sources such as hydroelectric, nuclear, and solar energy.

In the late twentieth century, the oil industry made significant cutbacks in exploration, production, and corporate staffs. Slim profits, surplus inventories, and low prices cooled the fever to explore for new oil and gas fields. In some cases, such as with the 1984 purchase of Gulf Oil by Chevron, companies were bought out or restructured. By the early 1990s, the industry had still not re-attained boom status; it entered 1994 with several years of cutbacks, employee layoffs, and flat earnings behind it. By the mid-1990s, though, the downhill slump did an extraordinary turn around. U.S. oil companies experienced strong profits during the second quarter of 1996. Compared to the same period only one year earlier, Mobil's profits were up 337 percent, Texaco's 154 percent, Chevron's 44 percent, Amoco's 13 percent, and ARCO's 11 percent. Exxon experienced a 4 percent decrease in profits, but showed a strong net income in the fourth quarter, which was 49 percent higher than the same period in 1995. For the year in total, all showed strong profits, including Exxon, whose 1996 income was up 16 percent from that reported in 1995. ARCO announced that 1996 was one of the most successful years in the company's 130-year history. The increase in profits has been credited to high crude oil and natural gas prices, and also to strong margins in refining and marketing operations. Mergers and acquisitions reached $14.5 billion in the first half of 1996, up from $11.5 billion for all of 1995. Among the largest of these moves was Tenneco's $4.0 billion sale of its pipeline to El Paso Natural Gas Co.; Mobil's planned merger of its European refining and marketing operations with British Petroleum; and Mobil's $1.4 billion takeover of Australia's Ampolex Ltd.

According to *Industry Surveys,* the dawn of the 1990s was "the worst of times for domestic contract drillers." Natural gas prices fell to record lows in the early part of the decade and oil companies spent approximately 10 percent less in 1992 on new well exploration than they had the previous year. U.S. production fell to 9.0 million barrels per day (b/d) in 1992, down from 10.0 million b/d in 1987, continuing its slow slide as more companies pursued international drilling at the expense of U.S.-based exploration. Despite the gains in the industry, U.S. production had fallen below 7.0 million b/d, a low not seen since the 1950s.

In 1996, production was 6.7 million b/d, with 1.4 million b/d from Alaska and the remainder from the lower 48. Alaska was seen as the only U.S. state with the possibility of harboring large untapped oil and gas reserves, but new exploration on federally owned lands has been forbidden by Congress, spurred on by a growing environmental movement. The only real growth sector was offshore, primarily in the Gulf of Mexico. For example, the Federal Energy Regulatory Commission (FERC) had approved the Gulf of Mexico Discovery Project for Discovery partners MAPCO and Texaco, a 150-mile offshore Gulf pipeline accessing deepwater production from existing a and planned locations. Ashland Oil began production on Vermillion Block 410 offshore Louisiana, and a second platform with four wells was scheduled for production in 1997. At the beginning of 1997, Amoco announced that it would develop the deep water Gulf of

Mexico Marlin prospect with Shell Deepwater Development, Inc. It was expected to cost $500 million to develop and ultimately would produce 250 cubic feet of gas and 40,000 barrels of oil per day.

Environmental concerns had also increased the cost of local drilling, further spurring American exploration firms to turn their attention to drilling outside of the United States, where regulation was sometimes slack and the possibility of untapped reserves significant. While exploration services underwent shifts in fortune prior to the 1990s, those changes were most often due to economic or political factors (such as the OPEC oil embargo of the mid-1970s) rather than environmental ones. However, The Oil Pollution Liability and Compensation Act of 1990 and the Clean Air Act of 1990 had some direct effect on exploration practices (the latter, among other things, tightened emission standards for offshore drilling activity). But most effects on exploration remained indirect—most new regulation and fines applied to vehicles, oil refineries, ships, and pipeline operations, the costs of which would reach oil and gas companies in general and then trickle down to exploration expenditures. With government rewarding the use of diesel fuel alternatives, more energy was being put into natural gas exploration and production than into crude oil.

Current Conditions

In the late 1990s, U.S. drilling activity took a major dive, due to plummeting world oil prices, but made a remarkable recovery by the end of 1999. Oil drilling in the United States hit an historic low in 1999, with one of the smallest number of total well completions in the modern petroleum era. Operators drilled 18,600 in 1999, off from an estimated 23,900 drilled in 1998, the lowest number in 6 decades. Slack profits in oil and gas production operations accounted for the decline in investment in U.S. exploration and development. Oil prices bottomed out at $11.26 a barrel in February of 1998, but rebounded to $25.70 a barrel in December of 1999.

After peaking in 1970, domestic crude oil production has fallen by an average of 1.5 percent per year. In 1997, crude oil production in the United States declined by 56,000 barrels a day to an average of 6.4 million barrels per day (MMb/d), down from 6.5 MMb/d during the same period in 1996. Alaska, which produced 1.3 MMb/d, accounted for 20 percent of total U.S. production in 1997. The lower 48 states averaged 5.1 MMb/d. Total natural gas production in 1997 was estimated at 19.0 trillion cubic feet (Tcf) compared to 18.7 Tcf in 1996. Domestic crude oil production was expected to increase by only 0.1 percent in 1998 and decline by 2 percent in 1999.

Since 1986, the U.S. petroleum industry has shrunk: higher-cost companies have left the industry and big-budget projects have been scrapped. Despite the slow growth, U.S. companies have made significant efficiency gains, as the cost of adding reserves (finding costs) has declined. A general reduction in activity combined with more selective drilling (often called ''prospect high grading'') account for this drop. Moreover, technological advances in exploration and drilling have made many projects more profitable. Finally, corporate downsizing and industry mergers have reduced operating costs by streamlining resources and eliminating redundancies.

The Gulf of Mexico and California were two areas in the United States where experts forecasted an increase in crude oil production. Offshore production, mostly concentrated in the Gulf of Mexico, accounted for 21 percent of total U.S. production in 1997, up from 15 percent in 1989. The Energy Information Administration predicted that offshore Gulf of Mexico production would show a sustained increase well into the future, while onshore production in the lower 48 states would decline steadily over the next two decades. Major U.S. operators continued to evaluate and develop large prospects in the Gulf of Mexico using the latest in deepwater technology. California's San Joaquin Basin saw the largest reserve increases in 1997. New methods, such as the application of the continuous-injection steam flood process, were expected to increase production and lower per-barrel production costs in the Basin's Kern River Field.

Industry Leaders

The *Financial Times* reported that the petroleum industry has been transformed by what it called a new order of mega-majors. Impelled by low oil prices and a desire to cut costs, petroleum corporations stepped up their merger activity in the late 1990s. The largest industry marriages occurred between BP and Amoco, Exxon and Mobil, and Total and PetroFina. In addition, on April 1, 1999, BP Amoco agreed to purchase Arco.

Exxon's merger with Mobil, completed in the third quarter of 1999, created the world's largest company, with revenues estimated at $164 billion and the equivalent of 21 billion barrels of oil in proven reserves, according to the *Financial Times*. The consolidation also gave the company key access to some of the world's most lucrative oil basins, including offshore West Africa and the Caspian Sea, as well as a strong position in natural gas markets in North America, Europe, and Asia-Pacific. Based on oil reserves, the new company would rank second after BP Amoco/Arco. In gas, it would be second to Royal Dutch/Shell.

Smaller companies had also been gaining ground in the development of U.S. oil and gas resources. The share of oil and gas production from nonmajors (also known as ''independents'') increased from 40 percent of total U.S. production in the late 1980s to nearly 50 percent in

1996. Nonmajors' accounted for 60 percent of total U.S. production of natural gas from U.S. offshore areas in 1996. Nonmajor companies tended to drill smaller fields that had faster depletion rates than those of the majors. But like the majors, the smaller companies were able to reduce their finding costs to levels equivalent to the majors'.

WORKFORCE

Corporate mergers have not boded well for the job market in oil and gas exploration. The *New York Times* reported on Exxon Mobil Corporation's plan to cut its payroll by 16,000 jobs, approximately 13 percent of its workforce by 2002. This streamlining, however, did not affect skilled exploration workers. With prospects beckoning overseas, the demand for technical experts was expected to rise.

Oil and gas exploration teams require a variety of subject expertise. Geophysicists, who apply the principles of physics to the science of geology, and geologists, who study the formation of the earth, evaluate incoming data from seismic vessels and onshore data collection. Then, they use sophisticated computer systems to interpret the data and make recommendations for when and where to drill. Engineers are needed to design oil and gas rigs and to oversee their use on site. Oil rig workers, who may live for weeks at a time on offshore rigs, are needed to operate the equipment. The oil companies themselves employ executive and clerical staff on the corporate level, but in the wake of increased cutbacks in the 1990s, these jobs were increasingly difficult to obtain. Companies were relying more and more on contract or freelance work instead of large, permanent staffs.

AMERICA AND THE WORLD

The American oil and gas industry is inextricably linked to the world industry. In 1997-98, financial crises spread throughout the world—from Southeast Asia to Brazil to Russia—causing a huge drop in worldwide petroleum demand; hence the collapse of oil prices.

Because decisions about exploration are linked to the proven reserves of oil and gas available, it is important to note that more than 75 percent of proven oil reserves are controlled by OPEC, although the vast majority of oil is consumed by non-OPEC nations, giving OPEC a tremendous influence on the world oil and gas market. In 1998, OPEC countries decided to raise their production quotas, flooding the market with excess supplies and driving prices downward. However, in April of 1999 the OPEC consortium agreed to cut their production to drive up world demand, and oil prices soon rebounded.

American oil exploration, and that of other non-OPEC countries, has slowed in contrast to OPEC exploration. With the end of the Gulf War, members of OPEC followed the lead of relatively moderate Saudi Arabia and stabilized their pricing while increasing both exploration and production.

Meanwhile, the major U.S.-based petroleum companies were becoming increasingly involved in foreign exploration. In the early 1990s, money allocated to foreign exploration and development topped 50 percent of all exploration spending, as compared to 27 percent in the mid-1980s. In 1996, Exxon spent twice as much on foreign exploration as for domestic. Mobil Co. spent $830 million on domestic exploration and $1.8 billion on overseas. In addition to the many reasons for decreasing domestic exploration mentioned earlier, world political and economic developments of the 1990s made it more feasible and profitable to increase American investment in foreign exploration. Along with maintaining an already strong presence in the Mexican and Latin American markets, U.S. companies have increased investments in other areas of the world.

The dissolution of the Soviet Union provided increased opportunities for investment in that area's oil reserves. The Commonwealth of Independent States (CIS) has seen the rise of joint exploration and drilling ventures, especially between U.S. and Russian companies. The Caspian Sea, which borders Russia, Azerbaijan, Iran, Turkmenistan, and Kazakhstan, is one of the world's hottest new investment zones, with estimates of oil reserves ranging from 30 billion barrels to 200 billion barrels according to Steve LeVine of the *New York Times*. Another area of increasing American investment is Southeast Asia, where U.S. exploration spending grew the most from the mid-1980s to the mid-1990s. The economies of Asian countries have become increasingly industrialized in recent years, and many governments in Asia, including China and Vietnam, have actively courted foreign investment and participation in local drilling by outside companies.

However, U.S. companies do not have a free rein to invest anywhere they choose. Politics trumps economics in petroleum-rich countries whose governments have offended the United States. Sanctions continue to Iran, Iraq, and Libya, putting U.S. companies at a disadvantage to their foreign competitors. U.S. companies must also adhere to relatively stringent environmental and labor codes compared to their competitors.

RESEARCH AND TECHNOLOGY

Fortune magazine reported on the dramatic strides in oil exploration technology. In 1965, drillers could only operate in water up to 300 feet deep. By the late 1990s, Chevron was leasing blocks of land in the Gulf of Mexico 9,000 feet underwater. Some experts said that drilling in 10,000 feet was imminent. Chevron and other companies were developing a technique called subsea mud-lift drilling, which enabled drillers to leave residue on the ocean floor instead of sucking it up through a pipe. This method could save drillers $5 million to $10 million per well.

New tools like three-dimensional seismic analysis allow oil companies to bounce sound waves off oil-bearing deposits and translate the patterns into 3-D models. Drilling rigs using the technique find productive wells more than 70 percent of the time, compared to a 40 percent success rate with conventional seismic analysis, according to *Fortune*. In addition, producers could extract more oil from existing wells. *Oil and Gas Journal* reported on a new fracturing technique that allowed gas drillers to stimulate existing wells rather than drilling new wells. Major U.S. producers could pump as much as 50 percent of the oil from a given pool, compared to a worldwide average of less than 35 percent.

As the large oil companies cut back on domestic exploration through the 1990s, it became even more important to make as certain as possible the profitability of those explorations that were undertaken. Technology for assessing the shape of underground earth formations and oil and gas deposits was introduced as early as 1927 by Schlumberger Ltd., which maintained a hold on the industry through 1996, with nearly $9 billion in annual revenues. Schlumberger's Maxis service, which assesses the characteristics of earth around a well, was introduced in the early 1990s. At a time when profits were flat and downsizing common, Schlumberger doubled its jobs in 1992, testament to the industry's ever-increasing reliance on high technology.

But Maxis was only one of many high-technology innovations that reduced oil exploration costs and more than halved finding costs for natural gas in the late 1980s and early 1990s. Other innovations included horizontal drilling, three-dimensional (3-D) seismography, and improvements in drilling in light sands. The majority of innovation was in offshore drilling, which required much technological innovation in both the exploration and drilling stages. The Machar project in the North Sea used both advanced technology and an innovative system to tap a difficult oil well. Discovered in 1972 and estimated to hold 55 million barrels of recoverable oil, the reservoir was too complex to confidently evaluate with the technology of the day, and considered too marginal economically. In 1994, British Petroleum enlisted what became the Turnkey Additional Production (TAP) alliance, which drew together contractors to supply the best possible solutions, one of them being Schlumberger Integrated Project Management (IPM), managing well engineering and well construction. All parties participated in risk and reward, so all focused on reducing risk, maximizing efficiency, and maximizing return. Decisions were made rapidly by those nearest the action, instead of relying on a chain of management. The results were quick and impressive; instead of the usual one to two years typical when using the conventional approach, appraisal oil flowed in just 19 weeks. At the end of the 25-month project, there had been no work loss due to accidents, no leaks or spills, and an overall efficiency 7 percent above plan.

Although invented in the 1960s, three-dimensional (3-D) seismography only became viable in the 1980s with advances in the computer and acoustical industries. Ships equipped with two cables each carrying two source arrays (or "seismic streamers") cruise areas of suspected undersea oil and gas deposits. The streamers give off electric or air detonations whose waves are reflected off underwater rock formations below the level of the sea floor. Data is then processed onshore and the undersea floor mapped. Although ships covered much terrain, it could take as much as a year and a half to interpret the data gained from 100 square miles. Because of the presence of above ground structures, 3-D seismography was impractical on land. Instead, trucks called "thumpers" sent sonic waves through the ground by hammering the earth at specific sites; the wave data was then collected and interpreted.

Data interpretation is highly technical and involved; it uses excessive amounts of computer storage space, plus specialized computer software that sorts and analyzes the streams of incoming data. However, advances in proprietary hardware and software were speeding up the process.

FURTHER READING

Durgin, Hillary. "Merger of Giants Rewrites Rules for the Oil Business." *Financial Times,* 23 November 1999.

"Frequently Asked Questions." Washington, DC: Independent Petroleum Association of America. Available from http://www.ipaa.org/FAQs.htm.

LeVine, Steve. "A Cocktail of Oil and Politics; U.S. Seeks to End Russian Domination of the Caspian." *New York Times,* 20 November 1999.

"Machar and Beyond: A New Path to Profitable Growth." New York: Schlumberger, Ltd. Available from http://www.slb.com/ir/ar/ar96/feature/machar1.htm.

"Oil & Gas News." *Aral Energy News.* Available from http://www.aral.com/newog.htm.

Petzet, G. Alan. "U.S. Drilling at Historic Low, Canada's Drop Not So Severe." *Oil & Gas Journal,* 26 July 1999.

Reeves, Scott R., Lawrence J. Pekot, James R. Ammer and George J. Koperna, Jr. "Novel Fracturing Enhances Deliverability." *Oil & Gas Journal,* 15 November 1999.

"State of the U.S. Oil and Natural Gas Industry." Washington, DC: Independent Petroleum Association of America. Available from http://www.ipaa.org/departments/information_services/state_of_the_industry.htm.

Taylor, Alex, III. "Oil Forever." *Fortune,* 22 November 1999.

U.S. Department of Energy. "Energy Information Administration." Available from http://www.eia.doe.gov.

U.S. Department of Labor. *Occupational Outlook Handbook.* Washington, DC: GPO, 1996.

SIC 1389

OIL AND GAS FIELD SERVICES, NOT ELSEWHERE CLASSIFIED

This industry includes establishments primarily engaged in performing oil and gas field services, not elsewhere classified, for others on a contract or fee basis. Services included are excavating slush pits and cellars; grading and building of foundations at well locations; well surveying; running, cutting, and pulling casings, tubes, and rods; cementing wells; shooting wells, perforating well casings; chemically treating wells; and cleaning out, bailing and swabbing wells.

Establishments that have complete responsibility for operating oil and gas wells for others on a contract or fee basis are classified according to the product extracted rather than as oil and gas field services. Establishments primarily engaged in hauling oil and gas field supplies and equipment are classified in a range of Transportation and Public Utilities Standard Industrial Classifications. Establishments primarily engaged in oil and gas machine shop work are classified in **SIC 3599: Industrial and Commercial Machinery and Equipment, Not Elsewhere Classified.**

NAICS CODE(S)

213112 (Support Activities for Oil and Gas Field Exploration)

INDUSTRY SNAPSHOT

Companies categorized in this industry provide specialized services to assist in the excavation of oil and gas. These companies are used by drilling contractors to provide services in producing new wells and maintaining existing wells.

When the price of natural gas fell in the United States during the early 1990s, operators reduced most of their drilling plans, which adversely affected the oil field service companies already suffering due to the decline in the overall U.S. market. Many service companies have begun to diversify into other oil field services not directly related to production or well completion. Halliburton Company, a leader in the oil field services industry, purchased both 60 percent of Texas Instruments' Geophysical Services (GSI) and Geosource, another geophysical service company. The company also bought Gearhart Industries, a wireline service company, and merged it with Welex to form Halliburton Logging Services. In the second quarter of 1996, they announced plans to acquire Landmark Graphics Corporations, the leading supplier of integrated exploration and production information systems and professional consulting services for the petroleum industry. Schlumberger Ltd., another industry leader, also has been investing in artificial intelligence technology. The company bought GECO to provide marine seismic analysis and acquired Prakla Seismos for onshore seismic operations. They have also entered a joint venture in a smart card and pay phone plant in China. At the end of January 1997, barely two months after beginning production, their factory in Hunan shipped its one millionth smart card. Pay phone production has also reached volume status with an output of 1,000 units per month. Schlumberger Electronic Transactions, a unit of Schlumberger Ltd., supplies cards, terminals, and management systems across the entire range of magnetic and chip card applications and is considered the industry's leading single source supplier.

With nearly all of the world's major energy fields already found, according to *The Value Line Investment Survey* in 1993, the future of oil and gas excavation will be dependent on the search for smaller pools. This effort, in addition to the extension of production from existing wells, should increase the demand for oil field service companies. Therefore, those companies providing high tech services, such as three-dimensional seismography, extensive data gathering methods, seismic exploration services, and enhanced oil recovery skills should find a competitive but productive market in the 1990s.

ORGANIZATION AND STRUCTURE

Companies classified in this industry provide services intended to increase or improve well production. Services are provided throughout the life of the well, including the initial drilling, the completion phase that sets production, and the maintenance or stimulation of existing wells.

Casing and Cementing. Casing and cementing services are provided when the well is drilled. Casing is a large steel pipe, inserted into the wellhole and cemented into place. Oil well cementing is a mixture of water and cement that is pumped into the space between the casing and the wellbore, known as the annular space. The cement bonds the casing to the formation, providing structural support and directing fluid movement. Cementing also limits pipe corrosion, prevents natural gas blowouts, and aids in maximizing production circulation.

Testing Services. After the well has been drilled to its determined depth, evaluations are made to determine if the hole will produce a sufficient amount of oil and gas. Downhole formations can be analyzed by five different methods: well logging, drill stem testing, potential testing, bottomhole pressure testing, and productivity testing.

Completion Services. If it is determined that the well should be completed, the service company will lay production casing and complete the well, bringing the flow of liquid to the surface. Specific types of completion services depend upon the formation of the hole. The open-hole and liner methods are available, although the perforated casing technique has become the most commonly used completion method.

Using perforated casing, the casing wall is pierced to provide holes through which formation fluids may enter the wellbore. These holes are created either by bullet or jet perforating. Bullet perforators are lowered into the hole and fired electronically from the surface. However, jet perforating, using shape-charge explosives, has become more widely used because it produces maximum penetration, especially in hard rock.

Well Stimulation Services. Additional treatment to increase fluid flow rates may be needed to make existing and producing wells commercially viable. These treatments include hydraulic fracturing, acidizing the reservoir, and explosives. The rock type and the existing formation structure determine the selected approach.

Hydraulic fracturing is the use of specialized fracturing fluids blended with water to form a gel that is pumped downhole. This gel forces the petroleum reservoir to split open along the bedding surfaces and fracture zones extending beyond the wellbore. A greater reservoir drainage area is exposed to the wellbore, enhancing the flow of liquid. Reservoir rocks with poor permeability can be treated with acids in order to increase the wellbore's drainage area. Depending upon the structure of the reservoir, acidizing and hydraulic fracturing can be used together.

Originally used in the 1880s, explosives have reappeared as a modern well service method. Explosives are used with certain kinds of tight formations that do not respond to the other treatments. Explosive fracturing enlarges the wellbore by detonation either in the borehole or away from the wellbore.

Establishments engaged in this industry also often provide routine maintenance work on wells already in production. One of the most common well servicing operations is the artificial lift installation. When a well is first drilled, the fluid is expected to flow to the surface. In order to maintain maximum recovery from the well, however, most need some form of artificial lift to help raise the fluid to the surface. Types of artificial lifts include gas lifts, sucker rod pumps, hydraulic pumps, and submersible pumps. Maintenance service also includes replacing parts, repairing tubing leaks, working on malfunctioning downhole equipment, and providing well clean-out services.

CURRENT CONDITIONS

The economic condition of oil field service companies is predicated on that of the oil and gas industry in general. Service-related work has been contingent on the number of rigs in operation, the price of oil and gas, and the demand for energy.

Rig Count. In the early 1980s, the number of operating rigs in the United States rose to more than 4,500. By 1995, the rotary rig count for the United States was 723, a decrease of 52 rigs from 1994. Forty-five percent of the rigs were drilling for oil, 53 percent for gas, and 2 percent miscellaneous. The rotary rig count has improved for the first nine months of 1996, with 39 percent drilling for oil, 60 percent for gas, and 1 percent miscellaneous. According to the Independent Petroleum Association of America (IPAA), crude oil production averaged 7.2 million barrels per day in 1992, the lowest level in 30 years. It continued to decline; it averaged 6.6 million barrels per day in 1995 and less than 6.5 in 1996. However, the natural gas industry has been growing, with production at 19.01 trillion cubic feet (tcf), an increase from 18.8 tcf in 1995. Continued growth was projected through the end of the century. In 1998 the rotary rig count averaged 827 rigs for the United States—a decrease of 116 over one year ago. The rotary rig count dropped to an all time low of 502 through March 26, 1999. Twenty-two percent of the rigs were drilling oil, while seventy-eight percent were drilling for gas.

Price for Oil and Gas. Natural gas prices fell to $1.00 Mcf ($6 per barrel of oil), the lowest level since the mid-1970s. As of June 1992, natural gas prices had rebounded to $1.50 per Mcf ($9 per barrel of oil equivalent), and continued to rise, fluctuating between $2.00 and $2.55 per Mcf. The prices remained about $2.00 per Mcf through 1998.

The well head price for crude oil has shown a sharp increase from the early 1990s. It averaged $16.54 in 1991, and hit a high of $23.02 in the fourth quarter of 1996. Crude prices fell slightly, averaging between $21 and $21.50 per barrel. The average decline of about $1 per barrel was seen in the first quarter of 1997, partially due to the influx of Iraqi oil. Iraq has been permitted to sell oil on the world market, about 600,000 barrels a day, for humanitarian reasons (supplying its people with food and medicine). Gasoline prices, as well, continued to rise into the 2000s.

During recent years, when both oil and gas prices were low, service companies had been in demand to aid in workovers of existing wells, rather than assist in the costly process of new well generation. Service companies with technologically advanced products and services have fared the best, offering well production service that is both affordable, yet profitable.

Demand for Oil and Gas. Faster economic growth in the United States boosted the demand for energy, including oil and natural gas. With long-term real gross domestic product (GDP) growth forecast at 2.2 percent annually, *Industry Surveys* has predicted oil consumption to increase approximately 1 percent annually during the 1990s.

Consumption of natural gas has also increased, gaining 3.8 percent over 1992's rate to capture approximately 25 percent of the U.S. energy market in 1993. In 1996, 21.99 tcf of natural gas was consumed, and usage was expected to rise to 22.38 tcf in 1997 and 24.5 tcf in 1998. Natural gas maintained its popularity throughout the decade; this preference was beneficial to service companies, since it should translate into an increase in drilling sites and, subsequently, site maintenance opportunities.

In addition to the domestic market, service companies based in the United States should find a variety of overseas market opportunities. High-potential countries include the Commonwealth of Independent States (CIS) and the Asia-Pacific region, a growing energy market.

INDUSTRY LEADERS

Halliburton Co. Dallas-based Halliburton Company provides oil field services, construction services, and insurance as an underwriter of property and casualty insurance. Its oil field service and products group provides start-to-finish service in the drilling and production of oil and gas wells. One of the many companies within this group is Halliburton Services, the world's largest supplier of cementing, stimulation, water and sand-control services and related downhole tools.

Erle Halliburton founded his company in 1919, then called the Better Method Oil Well Cementing Company. He provided a service using cement to hold a steel pipe in a well, which assisted in the drilling and production process. Although this technique was not initially accepted, it has become a common practice throughout the industry. In 1921 Erle Halliburton moved to Duncan, Oklahoma, and in 1924 he incorporated the company as Halliburton Oil Well Cementing Company.

With the purchase of other companies experienced in the oil and gas markets, Halliburton built up its oilfield service business from the 1950s to 1970s. Two particularly important acquisitions were the addition of Welex, a well-logging company, in 1957, and Brown & Root, experts in the construction of offshore and drilling platforms, in 1966.

Halliburton has operations in 120 countries providing construction, drilling, and well maintenance services. It reported 1999 sales of $14.9 billion and 103,000 employees.

Schlumberger Ltd. New York-based Schlumberger Ltd. provides oilfield services, exploration services, well site and contract drilling, and computer-aided engineering services in more than 100 countries. In January 1993, Schlumberger purchased Dow Chemical's 50-percent interest in the Dowell Schlumberger group of companies. This group provides various oil and gas field services and is divided into the following entities: coil tubing, drilling fluids services, cementing, design and evaluation, and industrial cleaning.

Schlumberger was created by two brothers, Conrad and Marcel Schlumberger, who believed that the earth's surface could be measured by electrical resistance. The company began in 1927, when the Schlumberger brothers lowered an instrument down a well to assess the surrounding rock formation.

The company's oilfield services unit provides 75 percent of the company's revenues. Schlumberger reported 1999 sales of $8.9 billion and 64,000 employees.

AMERICA AND THE WORLD

Companies from the United States have played roles in the discovery and production of oil in major fields in Mexico, Venezuela, Saudi Arabia, Kuwait, and Libya. While exploration and oil drilling have decreased in the continental United States and Alaska, all of the major American oil companies have increased their presence overseas. The American oil and gas industry is inextricably linked to the world industry. Overseas operations have been particularly interested in service companies because of their ability to provide well workover and stimulation services to existing wells. Many countries have numerous wells in existence, but due to a lack of technology, have not been able to maximize production. The situation in the Commonwealth of Independent States is a particularly intriguing one.

The CIS holds an estimated 6 percent of the world's proven oil reserves and 37 percent of the natural gas reserves. According to *Oil & Gas Journal,* the older fields should offer tremendous opportunities for Western service firms to achieve considerable production improvements through the use of relatively straightforward procedures such as well workovers, equipment repairs, and regular preventive maintenance programs. Estimates of the number of wells in need of workover have been as high as 20,000. Area instability since the early 1990s has slowed progress somewhat, both in renovating old wells and in new drilling and pipelines. But it is predicted that the region will experience enormous growth in the long term, and in the next 10 to 20 years, the former Soviet Union will be the largest supplier of natural gas. The Yamal pipeline project, if successful, will run 4,000 km connecting Siberia with Western Europe. It's scheduled completion is 2010.

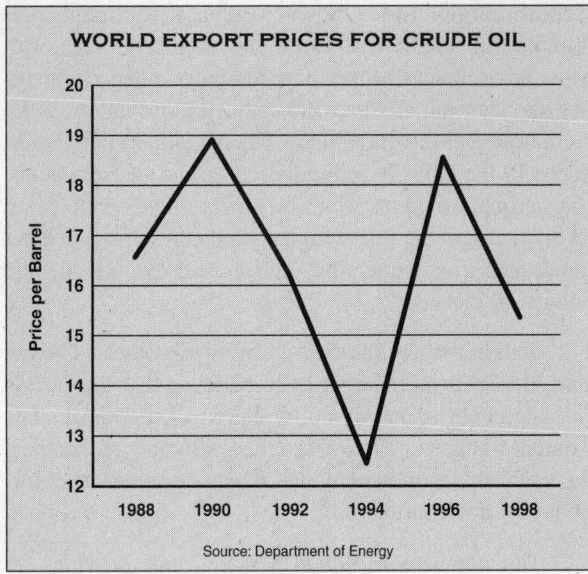

Source: Department of Energy

Furthermore, *Oil & Gas Journal* notes that the Department of Energy (DOE) regards China as an enormous growth market for oilfield service companies. The DOE has stated that the worldwide market for oil and gas exploration services, excluding China and the CIS, was $38.2 billion in 1990 and will grow to $1.3 trillion per year to 2010. Moreover, the DOE has calculated that American vendors can capture $995 billion, or 74 percent of that market. This will likely translate into substantial opportunities for companies providing support services to oil and gas exploration services.

Other areas of Asia show great potential as well for the service companies. Spending by American oil companies was highest in Southeast Asia during the past decade, indicating a vested interest in the region. Vietnam and the Philippines also show great promise for oil exploration offshore, which in turn will be a profitable opportunity for service companies.

Latin America and Africa also are growing markets. The natural gas resources in South America are largely underdeveloped but the industry is expected to undergo increased development, incurring a need for skilled personnel to build and maintain rigs and pipelines. The oil wells of Columbia and Peru are expected to double their production by the end of the century. Several natural gas pipeline projects are also planned in South America, the two most ambitious being the Bolivia-Brazil pipeline and the Argentina-Chile pipeline. After the year 2000, the African nations of Chad, the Ivory Coast, and Somalia, among others, are expected to join the market as oil producers.

FURTHER READING

''State of the U.S. Oil and Natural Gas Industry.'' Washington: Independent Petroleum Association of America, 1999. Available from http://www.ipaa.org/departments.

U.S. Department of Energy. Energy Information Administration. *Outlook Assumptions.* Washington, D.C.: GPO, 1997. Available from http://www.eia.doe.gov.

SIC 1411

DIMENSION STONE

This category covers establishments primarily engaged in mining or quarrying dimension stone. Also included are establishments engaged in producing rough blocks and slabs. Establishments primarily engaged in mining dimension soapstone or in mining or quarrying and shaping grindstones, pulpstones, millstones, burrstones, and sharpening stones are classified in **SIC 1499: Miscellaneous Nonmetallic Minerals, Except Fuels.** Establishments primarily engaged in dressing (shaping, polishing, or otherwise finishing) blocks and slabs are classified in **SIC 3281: Cut Stone and Stone Products.** Nepheline syenite mining operations are classified in **SIC 1459: Clay, Ceramic, and Refractory Minerals, Not Elsewhere Classified.**

NAICS CODE(S)

212311 (Dimension Stone Mining and Quarry)

INDUSTRY SNAPSHOT

In 1996, 145 U.S. companies produced 1.33 million tons of dimension stone for use in building, monuments, and curbing with a total value of $231 million., Roughly 234 quarries operated in 1996 in 36 states, with those in Indiana, Georgia, Vermont, and Wisconsin accounting for 45 percent of the national output. Of the total industry tonnage, 42 percent was granite dimension stone, 31 percent limestone, 13 percent sandstone, 3 percent slate, 3 percent marble, and 8 percent other types of dimension stone. By 1998, a total of 189 establishments produced $117.3 million in shipments of dimension stone.

New construction of hotels, stores, and office buildings led to a 14 percent increase in nonresidential construction sector that boosted dimension stone industry sales in 1995. Although the use of dimension stone in the high-end single-family housing sector was hampered by a decrease in residential construction in 1995, a growing trend toward the use of granite and marble dimension stone in residential kitchens and bathrooms, limestone dimension stone in landscaping stone and ledges, and ''worked'' or hand-carved dimension stone and roofing slate in residential homes indicated that the residential segment would continue to be an expanding market for U.S. dimension stone producers.

In the mid-1990s, the U.S. dimension stone industry continued to cope with fluctuating prices, trade deficits, high production costs, and competition from substitute materials such as steel, aluminum, reinforced concrete, lightweight and low-cost facing materials, plastics, glass, aluminum, and porcelain-enameled steel. As a result, industry firms looked to the development of niche markets in granite and marble dimension stone for kitchens and bathrooms; limestone for landscaping, ledges, and tiles; and worked or hand-carved stone for custom-built houses. A trend toward the use of so-called natural stone, including acid-washed and hard-to-polish stones, continued to be fueled by its ability to lend a rough, bucolic feel to home designs. The major segments of the U.S. dimension stone industry were expected to grow at the following rates to the turn of the century: 2.6 percent for granite; 3.7 percent for limestone; 3.8 to 5 percent for slate, and 2.0 to 4.5 percent for marble.

ORGANIZATION AND STRUCTURE

The U.S. quarrying industry as a whole encompasses two major sectors: crushed stone and dimension stone. Dimension stone accounted for 56 percent of all rock produced by U.S. firms in 1995. One-quarter was used in rough blocks in building, 12 percent was used in ashlar (a squared cut of stone used as facing material), another 12 percent for rough blocks for monuments, 4 percent for dressed (or trimmed and smoothed) stone for monuments, and almost 50 percent for other uses. Within the dimension stone segment, companies mine, cut, and in some instances prepare stone blocks for such uses as building stone, monument stone, paving stone, and curbing. The dimension stone industry traditionally has accounted for only 0.5 to 1.0 percent of the 1 billion total tons of stone produced annually.

Among the many minerals mined for use as dimension stone by U.S. producers are basalt and diabase. Although these minerals, known collectively as trap rock or ''trap,'' are primarily used in crushed stone, small amounts are quarried, cut, and polished as ''black granite'' for dimension stone. Because trap rock dimension products are low-cost commodities in the stone market, they become less profitable as they are transported farther from mining locations. As a result, proximity to end-use markets or inexpensive modes of transportation are considered more important than their properties as minerals.

Another material commonly used as dimension stone is granite. The granite category includes ''true'' granite, granite gneiss, syenite and diorite, and some forms of granite-gabbro. Dimension granite is used in monuments and memorials; in heavy construction as large blocks; in residential and other buildings as foundation blocks, steps, and columns known as ashlar (when cut to regular shapes and sizes); and as paving stones and curbstones. Factors influencing the value of dimension granite deposits include color, uniformity of texture, and hardness. Besides final appearance, these factors also affect the cost of quarrying, cutting, and ''dressing'' or processing the rock.

The production of dimension granite historically has occurred in three regions: New England, the Southeast, and the midwestern states of Minnesota, Wisconsin, and South Dakota. Smaller amounts of dimension granite were produced in 14 other states. In 1995, 42 companies in 19 states produced 495,000 tons of dimension granite valued at $104 million.

Limestone is another material with numerous applications as dimension stone. Mines in Indiana traditionally have accounted for 60 percent of the dimension limestone produced in the United States. Dimension limestone is used nationally for the exteriors of commercial and institutional buildings as ''Indiana'' or ''Bedford stone.'' Valuable properties of dimension limestone include uniformity of color and texture as well as the absence of elements such as stain-forming iron sulfide and quartz or chert, which impeded extraction of the stone. In 1995, 29 companies in 13 states produced 363,000 tons of dimension limestone, with a value of $61 million.

Dolomite is a geologically recrystallized form of limestone used for dimension stone, and polished crystalline limestone is sold as ''orthomarble.'' When first quarried, orthomarble is soft and easily worked and can be readily planed and carved into desired shapes. Orthomarble mines in eastern Tennessee produce a limestone known as ''Tennessee marble'' that ranges in color from light gray to pink, red, and brown, and is used in interior floors, panels, wainscoting, windowsills, and to a lesser extent in exterior construction.

Another popular material used as dimension stone is marble. The term marble applies commercially to any stone, other than granite, that had an attractive appearance and takes a polish. Most rock marketed as marble is not true marble but metamorphic marble, crystallized limestone, cave onyx, travertine, or verde antique (or serpentine). The most common element in true marbles is calcite, although the highest grades of statuary stone are more than 99 percent calcium carbonate. Pure marble is white, but common color variations include light gray, green, red, cream, and black.

Major uses for cut and polished marble are as architectural and statuary stone. In the mid-1990s, more than 50 percent of marble production was utilized in constructing building exteriors as well as interior floors, steps, sills, wainscoting, columns, and trim. Most of the remainder became memorial or statuary stone. Important properties affecting the value of dimension marble include color, texture, hardness, porosity, solubility, and strength. Marble can be worked profitably only on a large scale, and new quarries cannot be economically opened or old ones extended without positive indications that a large bed of stone is present.

In 1995, seven companies in six states and Puerto Rico produced 39,600 tons of marble with a value of $21.1 million. The states of Vermont and Georgia produced the bulk of building and monument marble, but other producing states included Alabama, Colorado, Maryland, and North Carolina. Vermont marble quarries were often as deep as 400 feet, and single blocks of Vermont marble weighing as much as 65 tons were used for such purposes as fountain base stones. Georgia marble was used in buildings, monuments, and memorials. Well-known marble structures include the Buckingham Fountain in Chicago and the face of the New York Stock Exchange.

Sandstone provides another material appropriate for use as dimension stone. Dimension sandstone is used for exterior facing and trim on large buildings, for "ashlar" in residential construction, as flagstones and curbstones, and in retaining walls and bridge abutments. Dimension sandstone ranges in texture from very fine to coarse and in deposit depth from a few inches to 200 feet. Some of the most desired colors in sandstones include shades of gray and tan. Uniformity of color in dimension stone is typically favored, but some producers market dimension stones that oxidized during weathering to produce aesthetically appealing spotted and streaked patterns. In 1995, 29 companies in 15 states produced 145,000 tons of dimension sandstone with a value of $17.2 million.

Dimension slate is widely used for roofing purposes because it is easily prepared and fixed, weatherproof and durable, and often cheaper than and superior to other roofing materials. An average roofing tile of the highest grade of rock is only about five millimeters thick, which reduces strain on walls and roof supports. In addition to its use in roofing and flagstones, much dimension slate historically was produced as "mill stock" for switchboards and electrical panels, blackboards, mantels, baseboards, steps, sills, and grave vaults. Colored slate, which included red, purple, green, black, and gray, was favored for flagstone. In 1995, 17 companies in eight states produced 35,600 metric tons of dimension slate with a value of $21.6 million.

Background and Development

Techniques for quarrying dimension stone varied according to the type of rock, the depth of the deposit, and the end-use of the mined stone. Unlike some other minerals, which were processed into their marketable form at processing plants and simply extracted from the ground in the most economical fashion possible, the specific end-use of a dimension stone product determined the procedure used to quarry it. Ideal end-products—large, solid, relatively flawless blocks of stone of attractive texture and color—were carefully cut from quarries one by one.

The exact type of quarry excavated by industry firms depended on the nature of the terrain in which the deposit was located. A deposit extending into a hill, for example, could be entered from the side by digging a "bench" quarry. Such quarries provided long, high faces from which the granite could be blasted, as well as direct approaches to the quarry for removal of the mined rock. When granite deposits were located under flat ground, a pit quarry had to be excavated—either wide and shallow quarries for deposits of uniform quality extending over large areas, or deep quarries extending from 20 to 300 feet for narrow deposits of great depth.

Most dimension stone was cut from the quarry face into large blocks, undercut at quarry "floor" level, and pried free by wedging. The stone was then cut into "mill blocks" of the desired size (typically from 10 to 60 feet long, 4 feet wide, and 4 to 12 feet thick) by drilling and wedging, and then hoisted from the quarry by derricks. Although light blasting was sometimes used to loosen deposits, explosives were usually avoided because they could damage the rock.

Granite and sandstone quarrying usually involved "broaching," wire sawing, or jet piercing mining methods after the covering rock and silt were removed by scrapers or steam shovels. Broaching consisted of drilling a row of closely aligned holes in the rock face with tungsten carbide drill bits, then removing the blocks between the holes with broaching tools. Wire sawing involved the application of tensioned single- or triple-strand wire cables up to 16,000 feet long, which were drawn through pulleys. The cables formed a "saw" that was held against the rock and fed with a mixture of water and sand, cutting the stone by abrasion at a rate of about two inches per hour (in hard granite). When cutting was completed, channels of about a quarter of an inch wide and 50 to 70 feet deep remained from which the mill blocks could be extracted.

In sandstone and granite deposits with inherent strains or internal pressure, the drilled holes sometimes closed around the drill bit, rendering it ineffective. In such cases, a jet-piercing drill—in which a combustible mixture of oxygen and fuel from the drill's nozzle was used to blast the rock into fragments—could be employed to cut an eight-inch channel through the deposit face. Blocks could then be cut into the desired dimensions and lifted from the quarry by derricks into rail cars for transport to the dressing or preparation mill.

Another method traditionally used by dimension granite miners in shallow quarries involved drilling six- to eight-foot holes (depending on the desired size of the block) and placing small explosive charges into them to create a ''parting'' in the rock. Compressed air then was forced into pipes cemented in the holes, separating the desired sheet from the rock below. Using this method, granite miners could peel off segments of stone in desired sizes as they were needed.

In marble, limestone, and soft sandstone quarries, electrically powered channeling machines with steel chisels—which moved in a chopping motion back and forth on a track—could be used to cut through the stone. Such machines usually left channels about 2 inches wide, 10 to 12 feet deep, and 4 feet apart. After these initial cuts, drill holes were made into the rock and blocks were loosened from the quarry floor by wedges inserted in the holes. These loosened blocks could then be fashioned into smaller blocks using the ''plug and feather'' method. Feathers were elongated strips of iron, which were inserted in rows of drill holes. Plugs, or steel wedges, were driven between the ''feathers'' and alternately struck until a fracture appeared, forcing the feathers and loosening the stone.

Marble quarrying was typically affected by such factors as the ''dip'' or shape of the marble beds, the quality of the deposit, the expected price of the mined rock, the thickness of the overburden, and the uniformity of the marble. The chief goal of marble quarrying was to produce sound blocks of uniform quality, and quarrying procedures were tailored to each deposit. Marble beds of high value could be worked laterally or vertically through deep cuts made in the marble, while gently dipping layers of marble between solid walls of earth could be worked in deep open quarries.

In a typical marble mining operation, channel cuts were made six feet apart and eight feet deep across the quarry floor. The ends of the resulting strips were cut away from the walls, leaving blocks free to be drilled, wedged, and lifted out. Using this technique, the quarry floor was gradually lowered by successive eight-foot ''benches.''

Since most dimension stone was mined and dressed through contracts for specific jobs, preparation plants or mills operated by industry firms kept extensive drafting and pattern-making departments to anticipate required stone sizes. Drawings were prepared that detailed the exact dimensions of the requested stone, which were then referred to regularly during the stone finishing or dressing stage. Sawing, planing, rubbing, and polishing with stoneworking machines were among the processes employed in the finishing stage. Finished stones were then carefully marked and packed for shipment.

Between 1987 and 1992, employment in the U.S. dimension stone industry increased 8 percent to 1,400. Companies with five or fewer employees comprised more than one-third of the industry's total shipments in dollar terms, and the number of industry establishments employing twenty or more employees fell from 13 percent in 1987 to only 10 percent in 1992. In 1992, nearly 79 percent of the industry's work force was involved in production, development, and exploration activities at an average income of $19,455. Nonproduction workers averaged annual wages of $30,333.

Major dimension stone industry events in the mid-1990s included major new industry projects, expanding reliance on foreign sources, and new technologies. In 1995, after many delays, the Denver International Airport opened a massive construction project that featured 20,000 square feet of two-centimeter thick marble slabs from the Colorado quarry that had supplied marble for the Lincoln Memorial and the Tomb of the Unknown Soldier. In July 1995, the Korean War Veterans Memorial was also unveiled, in which 41 panels of granite formed a 164-foot-long reflective wall on which were etched photographic images of the conflict. Although exports of U.S. dimension stone (primarily to Italy) decreased slightly in 1995, imports (mostly of dimension granite) rose to $476 million, primarily from Italy, Spain, India, and Canada. Indian green marble found growing use for kitchen countertops, and low-priced Chinese marble emerged as a new product in the U.S. market.

New technologies included ''thermally stable'' waterjet stone-cutting drill bits for increased penetration rates and extended bit life and computerized wire saws that could cut complex images on monument faces. The images etched on the surface of the Korean War Veterans Memorial, for example, were made by high-precision etching and contour-cutting laser technology made possible by advances in computerized design. Fueled by the growing demand for ''natural stone'' finishes, new quarry and processing technologies emerged that permitted the fabrication of very thin stone products. Computers also aided the marketing efforts of industry firms. The explosion of the World Wide Web as a marketing tool in the mid-1990s enabled some dimension stone producers to display their wares through digitized images of their stone products on their own web pages.

CURRENT CONDITIONS

A 1997 industry periodical described a new extraction method that used diamond wire sawing machinery (as opposed to traditional hydraulic and mechanized drilling, smooth blasting, and wheel loading). The new technique, manufactured by Blue Pearl, reportedly resulted in smoother surfaces and reduced waste. Such new ways of extracting granite were tested in the United States, as well as Japan, Finland, Italy, and South Africa.

The National Mining Association (NMA) was formed in 1995 from the union of the National Coal

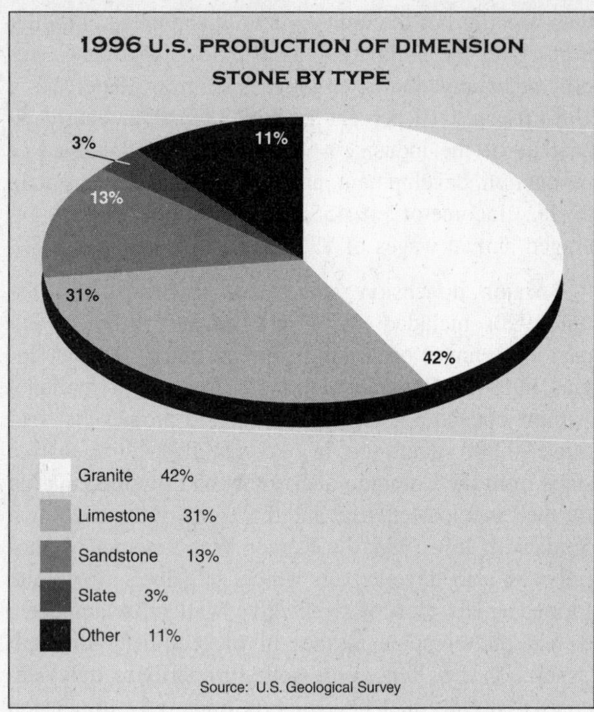

Association and the American Mining Congress. The group, which represented the entire mining industry, said its initiatives would include advocating for policy and legislation that will promote the health of the industry. Specifically the group was concerned with, in the words of 1995 association president Richard Lawson, the perception of the ''environmental lobby [that] argues that 'public' land must be forever held virtually as wilderness in the public interest.'' The NMA expressed concern that such environmental initiatives could make resources, including lands which were home to mineral resources, available only to select ''special interests.''

The mining industry and the NMA seemed to be heading toward victory with a mid-1999 legislative initiative regarding mineral dumping. The United States Senate overturned a Department of Interior law that had required that mining companies use only five acres per mining claim for waster rock piles and runoff from the mining process. The bill was scheduled for conference committee hearings in 1999 to determine an outcome.

Industry Leaders

Cold Spring Granite Company, Rock of Ages Corporation, Fletcher Granite, Indiana Limestone, Georgia Marble, and Halquist Stone were among the industry's leading companies in the mid-1990s. In 1997, Rock of Ages, which maintained 46 granite quarries, billed itself as the ''world's leading supplier of granite products'' for memorials, mausoleums, and estate pieces. Primarily a supplier of granite blocks to other manufacturers, Rock of Ages was capable of producing 63,000 cubic meters of granite every year from its quarries. By the end of 1998, Rock of Ages had 100 retail outlets in 15 states and sold products wholesale to more than 2,100 United States independent retailers. Company sales during 1998 were $82.7 million, representing an annual sales growth of 52.6 percent. The company employed 985 people.

Georgia Marble was founded in 1835 by an Irish immigrant stone cutter. By 1997, the company was a subsidiary of IMETAL and the largest producer of marble products in the world, with more than 300 marble products produced by its industrial, consumer, and dimension stone divisions. Its dimension stone operations produced structural (panels, columns, and floor tiles) and memorial dimension stone, and its marble stones have been used in the memorials of such prominent Americans as Warren Harding, Thomas Jefferson, and Martin Luther King Jr. In the late 1990s the company had a sales range of $50 to $100 million.

Further Reading

''Annual Review 1995.'' *Mining Engineering,* May 1996.

Casteel, Kyran. ''Stepping Stone.'' *World Mining Equipment,* June 1997.

''Georgia Marble Co.'' *Hoover's Online.* Woburn, MA: Corporate Technology Information Services Inc., 2000. Available from http://www.hoovers.com/co/corptech/5/0,2282,13145,00.html.

''Industrial Minerals 1995.'' *Mining Engineering,* June 1996, 21.

Lawson, Richard L. ''The New National Mining Association.'' *Vital Speeches,* 1 August 1995.

''Rock of Ages Corporation.'' *Hoover's Online.* Hoover's Inc., 2000. Available from http://www.hoovers.com/co/capsule/5/0,2163,54315,00.html.

U.S. Geological Survey. *Mineral Commodity Summaries,* February 1997.

SIC 1422

CRUSHED AND BROKEN LIMESTONE

This industry consists of establishments primarily engaged in mining or quarrying crushed and broken limestone, including related rocks, such as dolomite, cement rock, marl, travertine and calcareous tufa. Also included are establishments primarily engaged in the grinding or pulverizing of limestone, but establishments primarily engaged in producing lime are classified in **SIC 3274: Lime.**

NAICS CODE(S)

212312 (Crushed and Broken Limestone Mining and Quarrying)

Crushed limestone production is the largest of three related industries that extract and process nonfuel, nonmetallic minerals. Primarily employed as aggregate, which refers to a wide number of sand, gravel, and stone mixtures, crushed stone is an essential component of the U.S. infrastructure because of its use in the construction of highways, airports, river locks and dams, railroad ballast, and breakwaters. It is, however, considered a ''high-volume, low-value commodity'' with relatively stable prices since the 1970s, according to the U.S. Geological Survey.

The crushed stone industry is the largest nonfuel mining industry in the United States, with 3,400 quarries in 48 states. Limestone and related rocks account for the vast majority—71 percent in 1998—of crushed stone production and sales in the United States. The essential make-up of limestone is calcium carbonate (CaCo3). If 10 percent or more of magnesium carbonate is present it is called ''magnesian'' or ''dolomitic'' limestone. Usually the term ''limestone'' acknowledges the presence of dolomite.

The industry has posted modest gains in the 1990s. In 1998 the United States produced 1.1 billion metric tons of crushed stone, including approximately 920 million metric tons of limestone. Production grew by an average of 3 percent in the mid-1990s, and a 3 percent increase in production was expected for 1997. Total crushed stone output in 1998 was valued at $8.8 billion. There were 27,565 workers employed in the broader crushed stone industry in 1997, according to the U.S. Census Bureau.

In the past most crushed and broken stone has been mined from open quarries. Today, the trend has been more toward underground mining. Underground room-and-pillar mines are operated on a year round basis and do not require as much material removal. Additionally, underground mining requires less surface space and consequently avoids the ever-increasing cost of land. Another benefit for the underground mine operator is the availability of valuable storage space.

The high cost of transporting crushed stone has dictated that stone be mined and quarried as near as possible to the market centers or manufacturing plants that use it. However, increasing land values and environmental concerns have made it necessary to move crushed stone quarries further away from customers and have driven up the cost of the delivered material for some producers. Overall, however, prices have remained stable since the 1970s, growing just over the rate of inflation due in part to productivity gains and competition.

The average unit value of crushed stone is also expected to increase as a result of rising costs of labor, energy, and the rising costs of processing equipment. In the area of environmental concern, most states are now requiring crushed stone operations to submit environmental impact reports, and soon a reclamation plan and a use permit application will be required.

In the mid-1990s, eleven states accounted for 50 percent of the total U.S. output of crushed limestone and dolomite: Florida, Texas, Pennsylvania, Georgia, North Carolina, Kentucky, Illinois, Ohio, Missouri, Virginia, and Tennessee. The central and eastern regions of the United States contain its largest reserves of limestone. Three companies were the leading U.S. producers in 1999. They were Redland Stone Products Company, Florida Crushed Stone Company, and ECC Calcium Products Inc.

Among market economy countries, the United States is far and away the largest producer of crushed and broken stone. Major international producers include Australia, Canada, Germany, France, Japan, and the United Kingdom. Because of high transportation costs, the international crushed stone trade remains quite minor. Nearly 80 percent of the tiny U.S. crushed stone import market is held by Canada and Mexico.

The outlook for limestone, and crushed stone in general, is generally favorable entering the twenty-first century. The industry was expected to continue to achieve modest growth fueled by several national and state highway repair initiatives as well as the relatively strong U.S. construction market.

FURTHER READING

Tepordei, Valentin V. ''Crushed Stone.'' *Minerals Yearbook.* Washington: U.S. Geological Survey, 1996.

U.S. Bureau of the Census. *1997 Economic Census,* Washington, DC: 2000. Available from http://www.census.gov.

U.S. Geological Survey. *Mineral Commodity Summaries.* Washington, DC: 1999.

Ward's Business Directory of U. S. Public and Private Companies. Detroit: Gale Group, 1999.

SIC 1423

CRUSHED AND BROKEN GRANITE

This classification covers establishments primarily engaged in mining or quarrying crushed and broken granite, including related rocks, such as gneiss, syenite, and diorite.

NAICS Code(s)

212313 (Crushed and Broken Limestone Mining and Quarrying)

The top crushed and broken granite producer in the late 1990s was the family-owned Luck Stone Corp. of Richmond, Virginia, with $95 million in sales for its fiscal year ended October 31, 1998. The company, founded in 1923 and now run by the third generation of the Luck family, was the twelfth largest producer of crushed stone in the United States, operating 14 crushed stone plants, one sand-and-gravel plant, and five retail stores in Virginia and North Carolina. Its automated, noise-controlled crushers had the capacity to produce and ship over 600,000 tons of stone daily, as compared to its 1923 capacity of 100 tons produced manually by men with sledgehammers, loading mule-drawn carts by hand. Retail stores, part of the Architectural Stone division, offered crushed stone to construction professionals as well as the general public for diverse uses such as in fireplaces and garden pathways. The second-place company in the late 1990s was W.W. Boxley of Roanoke, Virginia, with $40 million in sales for its fiscal year ended February 28, 1998. North Carolina Granite Corp. of Mount Airy, North Carolina, generated $24 million in 1998 sales.

The industry is composed primarily of small independent operators, with a few large companies producing a significant percent of total granite output. In 1995 approximately 150 companies operated 365 granite quarries in 34 states. On a state-by-state basis, Georgia led U.S. production in 1995, followed by North Carolina, Virginia, South Carolina, and Arkansas. Together, these states made up more than 73 percent of total production.

A small but healthy segment of the U.S. crushed stone industry, crushed granite accounted for approximately 15 percent of U.S. production in the mid-1990s. In 1996, the United States produced nearly 200 million metric tons estimated at $1.3 billion. In general, granite production growth and prices have exceeded the average for crushed stone in the 1990s. As with most types of crushed stone, the majority of crushed granite—roughly 56 percent—is used as construction aggregate.

Civil engineers found granite as early as 1871 along the main coastal line of the Southern Pacific railroad. As track was laid throughout California, engineers discovered that granite was the perfect ballast material for railroad beds. With the inception of automated, steam-powered crushers, the mining and production of granite improved significantly.

When crushed to powder, tiny fragments of separate substances can be picked out of granite. These secondary or compositional particles include quartz, feldspar, and mica. As the most common igneous rock in the earth's crust, granite has been mined voluminously for decades.

The introduction of giant, mobile primary crushers in mining operations at granite quarries unleashed enormous production and profit potential. Other recent technological innovations used in granite mining include conveyors that move rock from the primary crusher to wash plants and secondary crushers; state-of-the-art, computer-controlled automated trucks and rail car loading systems; and the complete control and monitoring of all quarry operations by large computer systems.

Further Reading

Barksdale, Richard D., ed. *The Aggregate Handbook.* Washington: National Stone Association.

Constantino, Darren. ''More than luck.'' *Pit & Quarry,* November 1998.

Infotrac Company Profiles, 20 January 2000. Available from http://web5.infotrac.galegroup.com.

U.S. Geological Survey. *Mineral Industry Surveys.* Washington, 1997.

SIC 1429

CRUSHED AND BROKEN STONE, NOT ELSEWHERE CLASSIFIED

This classification covers establishments primarily engaged in mining or quarrying crushed and broken stone, not elsewhere classified. Types of stone processed by this industry include basalt, diabase, dolomitic marble, gabbro, marble, mica schist, onyx marble, quartzite, sandstone, and volcanic rock.

NAICS Code(s)

212319 (Other Crushed and Broken Stone Mining and Quarrying)

In 1998, about 71 percent of the crushed stone produced in the United States was limestone and dolomite (see **SIC 1422: Crushed and Broken Limestone**), followed by granite at 16 percent (see **SIC 1423: Crushed and Broken Granite**), traprock at 7 percent, as well as sandstone, quartzite, shell, marble, calcareous marl, volcanic cinder and scoria, and slate, which combined to account for the remaining 6 percent of stone production. Only the latter 13 percent of crushed stone production is included in this industry.

In 1999, the United States produced roughly 450 million metric tons of crushed stone valued at $900 million. The industry has enjoyed modest growth in the 1990s, fueled in part by increased federal spending on highway construction and maintenance. Although the recessions of the 1980s and 1990s affected the stone crushing industry, it recovered in the mid-1990s to produce consecutive years of record output. A large part of this resiliency has been attributed to aggregate's vital role as an ingredient in cement, concrete, and asphalt products.

The mining of aggregate was relatively unorganized and undocumented in the nineteenth century. It was not until 1882, when the U.S. Geological Survey began compiling an annual *Mineral Resources of the United States* publication, that the classification, method, and organization of the aggregate industry began to take shape. The *Mineral Resources of the United States* added its first chapter on stone in 1889. Aggregate production was originally reported in dollar amounts of product sold but has since been assessed in terms of both tons and dollar value of product sold or used. Production volume of crushed stone has escalated dramatically throughout the twentieth century. The dollar value of crushed stone in 1900 was $24 million. In 1950, this increased to $422 million, representing 325 million tons of crushed stone. The crushed stone industry in 1998 was valued at more than $8 billion, representing over 1.5 billion metric tons produced.

The crushed stone industry has been labor intensive since its inception in the late 1800s. Early production advancements came in the first decade of the twentieth century when company-owned steam locomotives and quarry cars replaced steam tractors and mule-powered carts in quarry operations. Characterized by innovation and inventiveness, the stone crushing industry also improved the quantity and quality of production when it began incorporating sophisticated processing equipment and quarry machines in the 1940s. Product quality and quality control have increased steadily throughout the twentieth century as technology has continued to keep pace with the production demands of the stone crushing industry. The largest association concerned with the health of this and other nonmetallic mineral mining and quarrying industries is the National Stone Association, which was founded in Columbus, Ohio in 1918 by a group of concerned quarry operators.

Production of traprock is concentrated in Oregon, Virginia, Washington, New Jersey, and Idaho. Sandstone and quartzite operations are centered in Arkansas, Pennsylvania, and South Dakota. California, North Carolina, and Georgia also produce significant shares of other miscellaneous stone.

The industry is comprised of many small companies and a few large corporations. In 1997, 462 establishments employed 8,036 workers. Vulcan Materials Co. of Birmingham, Alabama was the leading crushed stone producer by output in 1999, with 136 active crushed stone operations and $1.6 billion in total sales (including non-stone sales). Other leaders included Martin Marietta Materials Inc., Trap Rock Industries Inc., and Georgia Marble Company.

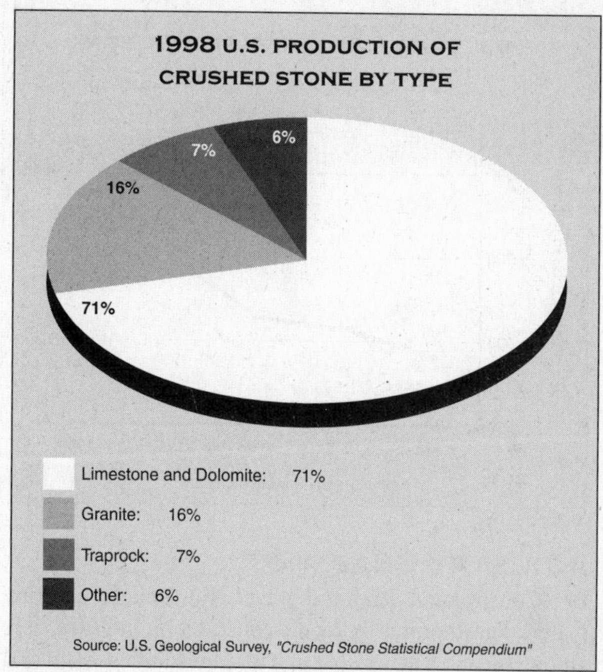

FURTHER READING

Barksdale, Richard D., ed. *The Aggregate Handbook.* Washington: National Stone Association.

U.S. Census Bureau. *1997 Economic Census.* 20 March 2000. Available from http://www.census.gov.

U.S. Geological Survey. *Crushed Stone Statistical Compendium.* Washington, 1999.

U.S. Geological Survey. *Mineral Commodity Summaries.* Washington, 1999.

U.S. Geological Survey. *Mineral Industry Surveys.* Washington, 1999.

SIC 1442

CONSTRUCTION SAND AND GRAVEL

This category covers establishments primarily engaged in operating sand and gravel pits and dredges and in washing, screening, or otherwise preparing sand and gravel for construction uses.

NAICS CODE(S)

212321 (Construction Sand and Gravel Mining)

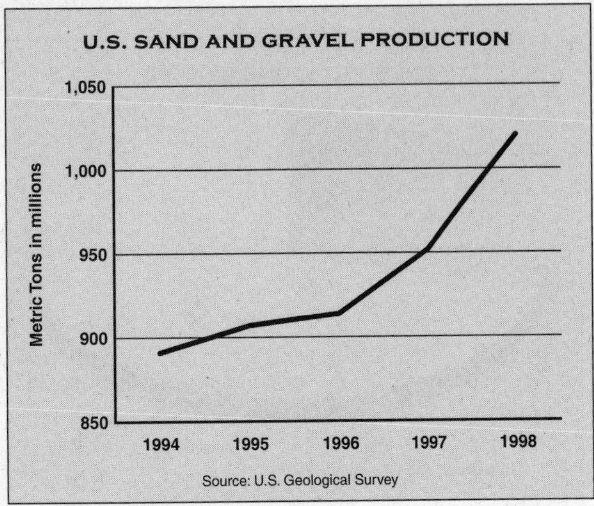

INDUSTRY SNAPSHOT

Construction sand and gravel is a fundamental raw material used primarily by the construction industry. It is among the most accessible of natural resources. Sand and gravel production benefitted from the increasing growth in the construction industry in the mid- to late 1990s. As a result, construction sand and gravel production in 1997 increased 4.2 percent over 1996 production to reach a total of 952 million metric tons. In 1998 more than 3,600 companies in 50 states produced more than 1 billion metric tons of construction sand and gravel worth an estimated $4.7 billion. Ten states accounted for about 47 percent of U.S. output of construction sand and gravel. In order of volume, the leading states were California, Texas, Michigan, Ohio, Arizona, Washington, Utah, and Colorado. More than 40 percent of the total output was used for unspecified purposes. Of the remainder, 43 percent was used as aggregate in concrete, 23 percent for road stabilization and road base and coverings, 13 percent as aggregate in asphaltic and other bituminous mixtures, and 13 percent as construction fill.

ORGANIZATION AND STRUCTURE

Sand is composed of particles of feldspar, limestone, slag, gypsum, coral, or quartz formed by such natural processes as erosion and weathering. Gravel consists of pebbles, stones, and rock fragments broken from larger deposits of such minerals as shale, quartz, granite, or sandstone by water or ice erosion. Gravel occurs geologically in riverbeds and seas but is more commonly found in dried-up streambeds formed by glaciers during the Ice Age. Sand is graded for commercial use by passing the grains through standardized sieves, which yield such classifications as very fine, fine, medium, coarse, and very coarse. The five standard gravel sizes are also classified according to the sieves through which they pass. Acceptable sizes for commercial sand and gravel vary with the engineering organization, highway department, or government agency setting the standard and are occasionally revised.

Sand and gravel is primarily used by private construction firms and government agencies in the construction and paving industries. It takes the form of ''aggregate'' in concrete, portland cement, asphalt, mortar, and plaster, or can be used alone as ''fill'' in the construction of building foundations, runways, highways, dams, and a wide range of other applications. The commercial use of sand and gravel is so extensive that the growth or decline of production by industry firms is considered a reliable indicator of the country's economic activity.

Roughly 80 to 85 percent of the weight of concrete is typically contained in its sand and gravel aggregate content. In other words, one ton of concrete usually contains about 1,700 pounds of sand and gravel. An estimated 54,000 pounds of sand and gravel is used in the construction of a typical new American home. Traditionally, roughly twice as much gravel is used as sand in the United States. The term *fine aggregate* is often used to describe commercial sand, and *coarse aggregate* to describe gravel. (In addition to sand and gravel, aggregate might also contain crushed stone.)

In the 1990s firms in the sand and gravel mining industry shared a number of characteristics with other U.S. mining industries, including equivalent production methods for blasting, drilling, loading, transporting, crushing, screening, and ''beneficiation'' (removal of impurities) of the mineral. Firms in sand and gravel and other mining industries also placed great emphasis on geological, management, and fundamental technical expertise and shared the same environmental, safety, and land rehabilitation concerns.

The sand and gravel mining industry is distinguished from other mining industries, however, by the number and size of its mining operations. Mining firms outside the industry generally operate fewer mines, which are on average much larger than sand and gravel operations. While the market for sand and gravel and other aggregates is highly localized (generally within 40 miles of the quarry), the market for metals and their derivative minerals is much wider (approximately 300 miles for some industrial minerals) and in many cases international in scope. Finally, the amount of capital investment, time, and financial risk required to develop a metal mine is substantially larger than is common in the sand and gravel industry.

In the 1990s the aggregates industry as a whole was a mature industry tied closely to general economic cycles. The range of firms in the sand and gravel industry extended from small, temporary roadside pits working deposits of 20,000 cubic yards with portable equipment to major facilities extracting thousands of tons per day and maintaining stockpiles of processed sand and gravel in excess of 100,000 cubic yards. In the late 1990s the trend in the industry was a continued shift from the small, ''family-run'' mining operations toward consolidation of industry activities among a few large companies. One factor fueling this trend was the requirement by government environmental agencies that firms entering the industry file environmental impact statements beforehand, which eliminated many prospective small firms with limited start-up capital. Although the majority of industry firms were private establishments, by the mid-1990s more than 50 percent of aggregates consumed went to public construction projects.

Background and Development

Before sand and gravel deposits can be mined, they first have to be located, thoroughly analyzed, and mapped. Geologists, engineers, or other exploratory personnel first consult geologic maps and reports on topography, hydrology, and geology for the potential site, then visually inspect places where the deposits protrude to the surface or are exposed in streambeds and highway ''cuts.'' Samples of the subsurface deposit can be extracted using soil augurs or test borings, and electrical resistivity tests or other geophysical test might also be conducted from the surface to analyze the deposits.

''Petrographic'' analyses of deposits supply information about the average shape, hardness, and size of the sand and gravel particles; the amount of sand relative to the amount of gravel; the presence of ''coatings'' on the rock particles; and the existence of any chemically reactive properties or impurities in the particles. After these analyses are completed, a thorough three-dimensional map of the deposit is prepared indicating the extent, depth, and variation of the deposit.

The optimal sand and gravel deposit contains a wide range of particle sizes, from fine to coarse. It consists of particles that are round, hard, solid, resistant to temperature and moisture changes, chemically inert, and ''clean'' (free of organic matter, mica, and soil), in sufficient quantities to justify extraction. The ideal deposit is also located near transportation routes to a permanent source of demand for the processed product. Factors such as compressibility, elasticity, thermal conductivity, chemical alkali reactivity, or specific gravity also might be important for sand and gravel intended for special-purpose concretes. In large or laterally extensive deposits, ''exploration'' by geologists or engineers often continues after mining of the deposit begins. These experts constantly update the levels of overburden (overlaying soil) and grades and supplies of remaining sand and gravel as the deposit is worked.

Because sand and gravel is a readily available commodity of low unit value, the economic viability and final market price of a deposit is determined by such factors as the costs of labor, extraction, and shipment to end-use markets. Transportation costs in the aggregates industry as a whole traditionally average about 50 percent of the price paid by customers, so a deposit located far from transportation or sizable markets might be economically worthless regardless of its extent and quality.

Transportation of the mined sand and gravel to the processing or preparation plant is usually accomplished by conveyor belt, truck, or railcar. The processes employed at the preparation plant to ready the sand and gravel for shipment depend on the nature of the specific deposit and the intended end use. In general, it is washed to remove soil and other impurities, screened or otherwise ''classified'' to divide it into its various grades, crushed to remove oversized particles, and subjected to various separation techniques to remove remaining impurities and undesirable minerals.

If the sand and gravel mined from a deposit are not of a grade adequate for a market's needs, they can be upgraded artificially at the processing plant by washing, screening, and combining particles until they become the required size. Separation techniques include ''sink-float'' solutions, in which unwanted impurities sink to the bottom of a receptacle or settling pond while the sand and gravel float, or ''heavy-heavy-media'' methods, in which gravitational or other forces are used to differentiate the sand and gravel from the impurities. In other methods, separation of sand and gravel from impurities is accomplished using inertial, aerodynamic, or centrifugal principles.

Current Conditions

Between 1945 and 1966 the sand and gravel industry experienced an uninterrupted period of growth, with combined tonnage of aggregates increasing from 266,000 tons to 1.5 billion tons. Following the completion of the federal government's massive highway construction project begun in the 1950s, industry growth leveled off at roughly 7 percent annually between 1973 and 1988. By 1990, however, the industry was growing at only about 2.5 to 4 percent annually and fell off even further during the recessionary years of the early 1990s.

In the mid-1990s the sand and gravel mining industry continued to be affected by fluctuations in demand by the home-building industry; federal construction-oriented legislation such as the Intermodal Surface Transportation and Infrastructure Act; continuing expenses for compliance with environmental regulations (such as the Clean Water Act and Federal Water Pollution Control Act); and cost increases stemming from the longer distances industry firms were forced to cover to bring sand and gravel from their quarries to the end market.

In 1993, however, the sand and gravel industry began to show signs of a recovery from the recession of the early 1990s, its worst period since the Great Depression. Although construction of apartments and office buildings, which traditionally required much larger amounts of sand and gravel than single-family homes, had been stagnant in the early 1990s, construction of highways, power plants, and electrical utility structures rose markedly in 1993. Together with the rise in residential housing starts, this construction spurt contributed to a boom period for the industry that continued through the late 1990s.

In the 1990s trends in the U.S. construction sand and gravel industry centered on three basic factors: consolidation, transportation, and automation and new operating methods. The wave of consolidation that struck the industry in the 1980s continued into the late 1990s as the larger producers gobbled up smaller operations at the rate of about 130 acquisitions a year. As the number of unexhausted quarries near major markets continued to decline, industry firms were also faced with higher costs of hauling their products from their increasingly remote quarries. Rail transportation, which had traditionally been reserved for hauls of 300 miles or more, began to edge into the trucking industry's historical hold over the aggregates transport business, and experts predicted that by the year 2046 most sand and gravel would be shipped by railcars.

The industry also began to rely increasingly on automation and innovative methods to streamline the rock extraction and preparation process and cut costs. Underground mining, for example, enabled some industry firms to sidestep the controversial issue of the environmental impact of surface strip mining on unspoiled land. More fuel-efficient equipment, electric rather than gas-powered machinery, and the operation of sand and gravel mines at night promised to reduce the industry's energy costs. Enhanced rock blasting technology offered improved efficiency and better rock fragmentation and driverless rock-hauling trucks guided remotely by Global Positioning Satellites promised to reduce employee accidents and personnel costs. Industry leaders increasingly envisioned a future in which highly automated sand and gravel ''industrial centers'' would incorporate asphalt, ready mix, and pipe production facilities within the traditional quarry. A new emphasis on quality management techniques, customer-driven ''value-added'' business approaches, and the introduction of new, specifically sized and hybrid aggregate products also hinted at the future shape of the industry.

The passage of the Transportation Equity Act for the 21st Century in 1998 led to an increase in funding for highway construction and maintenance, which in turn assured continued demand for aggregates. In addition, the Balanced Budget Act of 1997 included a provision to increase appropriations to the Highway Trust Fund. This additional yearly amount of $6 to $7 billion was expected to fuel road construction and thereby provide steady demand for construction sand and gravel.

Construction sand and gravel production continued to increase in 1999, and the total outlay for the first nine months of 1999 reached 816 million metric tons, a 2.8 percent increase over the comparable period in 1998. The top five producing states in the third quarter of 1999 were California, Michigan, Ohio, Texas, and Minnesota. Together, the states produced 36.4 percent of the total U.S. output of construction sand and gravel. Among geographic regions, the leading area was East North Central, producing 21.7 percent of the U.S. total. Ranking second among sand and gravel producing regions was the Pacific, which contributed 18.8 percent, followed by the Mountain area, which produced 17.2 percent.

Though the late 1990s were a positive period for the construction sand and gravel segment, construction spending was expected to decline in the early part of the twenty-first century, resulting in lower demand for aggregates, according to the CIT Group, Inc. Public works projects such as road and highway construction were expected to remain steady, while residential and nonresidential construction were expected to decrease somewhat in 2000. The CIT Group expected that production of sand and gravel would reach record levels in 1999 but fall by 5 million short tons in 2000.

Industry Leaders

The leading U.S. aggregate producing firms (including crushed stone) in 1998 were Vulcan Materials Company, with 222 active operations; Martin Marietta Materials, Inc., 304 operations; Hanson Building Materials America/Hanson Aggregates, 144 operations; Oldcastle, Inc./Materials Group, 183 operations; Lafarge Corporation, 79 operations; and Calmat Company, with 30 operations. Among construction sand and gravel producers, the leading companies in order of output in 1997 were Calmat Company; Cornerstone Construction & Materials, Inc./Hanson Industries; Martin Marietta Materials, Inc.; Lafarge Corporation; and Granite Construction Company.

Consolidation and acquisitions continued to be the trend in the late 1990s. In 1997 Martin Marietta Materials acquired several operations of American Aggregates Corp. from CSR America. This purchase included more than 25 production facilities. The company also bought Nuckolls Aggregates, with operations primarily in north central Iowa. Lafarge's acquisition of Redland Plc transformed Lafarge into one of the largest aggregates producers in the world. It also made Lafarge the fourth largest producer of aggregates in the United States, up considerably from 36th place in 1996. In early 1999 Vulcan acquired Calmat, the leading producer of aggregates in California.

AMERICA AND THE WORLD

Beginning in the late 1970s foreign acquisitions of U.S. sand and gravel mining firms began an upward spiral that would see thirty major purchases of U.S. aggregate producers concluded between 1979 and 1990 alone. Firms from the United Kingdom, France, Belgium, Ireland, and Australia were among the many foreign owners of U.S. construction sand and gravel producers in the early 1990s. Led by the United States, the North American sand and gravel market was the world's largest in the 1990s, but import-export activity was relatively low. In 1997, for example, U.S. imports and exports accounted for less than 1 percent of domestic consumption. The U.S. exported about 1.43 million tons of construction sand in 1997, primarily to Mexico and Canada. Exports of construction gravel in 1997 dropped 15 percent from 1996 amounts. About 81 percent of total exports of gravel were to Canada. Imports in 1997 reached 1.61 million tons, an increase of about 28 percent from 1996 imports. About 73.9 percent of imported construction sand and gravel was from Canada, and 15.1 percent came from the Bahamas.

FURTHER READING

''Aggregates Industry Will Level Off, According to CIT Outlook.'' The CIT Group, Inc. Available from http://www.citgroup.com/newswire/outlooks/aggregates.asp.

''Annual Review 1995.'' *Mining Engineering,* May 1996.

Bolen, Wallace P. ''Sand and Gravel, Construction.'' *Minerals Information 1997.* Reston, VA: U.S. Department of the Interior. U.S. Geological Survey. Available from http://www.minerals.er.usgs.gov/minerals.

Copple, Brandon. ''Smashing Success.'' *Forbes,* 26 July 1999.

''Industrial Minerals 1995.'' *Mining Engineering,* June 1996.

Meyer, Drew. ''Trends in the North American Aggregates Industry.'' *Aggregates Manager,* December 1996. Available from http://www.aggman.com/.

Mineral Industry Surveys. U.S. Department of the Interior. U.S. Geological Survey, 1999. Available from http://minerals.er.usgs.gov/minerals.

Pit & Quarry. Advanstar Communication.

Rock Products. Intertec Publishing Corp.

Tepordei, Valentin V. ''Crushed Stone: Statistical Compendium.'' U.S. Department of the Interior. U.S. Geological Survey. Available from http://minerals.er.usgs.gov/minerals.

SIC 1446

INDUSTRIAL SAND

This category covers establishments primarily engaged in operating sand pits and dredges, and in washing, screening, and otherwise preparing sand for uses other than construction, such as glass making, molding, and abrasives.

NAICS CODE(S)

212322 (Industrial Sand Mining)

INDUSTRY SNAPSHOT

In 1998, 80 U.S. companies in 36 states produced an estimated 29,000 metric tons of industrial sand with a total value of $532 million. A total of 140 individual operations employing 2,739 quarry and mill employees were active in 1997, and Illinois, Michigan, Texas, California, and Wisconsin produced 45 percent of the national industrial sand total for 1998.

ORGANIZATION AND STRUCTURE

Glass Sand. The single most common use of industrial sand (37 percent of total tonnage in 1998) is in glass making, where glass or quartz sand constitutes 52 to 65 percent of the weight of finished glass. Glass sand requires a high percentage of silica—the principal ingredient of sand—because the presence of other elements such as iron oxide and clay introduces visible impurities that mar the glass's transparency. Few sandstones or natural sands (such as beach or dune sand) are pure enough to yield glass without ''beneficiation,'' or the removal of impurities through processing. Glass sands are graded according to average grain size, which can be determined by passing them through sieves of varying calibers.

The container glass industry was one of the largest consumers of silica-based glass sand in the United States in the mid-1990s, but the trend toward glass recycling, as well as increased plastic bottle and aluminum can packaging, weakened demand for silica sand. Some states require that 35 percent of container glass be comprised of recycled glass, with the potential for increases of as high as 65 percent recycled glass content by 2005. This trend was partly offset in the mid-1990s, however, by heightened demand for flat glass, special-purpose glass, glass microwave packages, and glass containers for sparkling and flavored waters.

Molding Sand. Molding or foundry sand is traditionally the second most common use (23 percent in 1998) of industrial sand. Sand is used in these applications to make molds into which molten metal is poured in metal casting and as the ''core'' sand used in such molds to produce hollow areas in the final casted product. Sand needs to

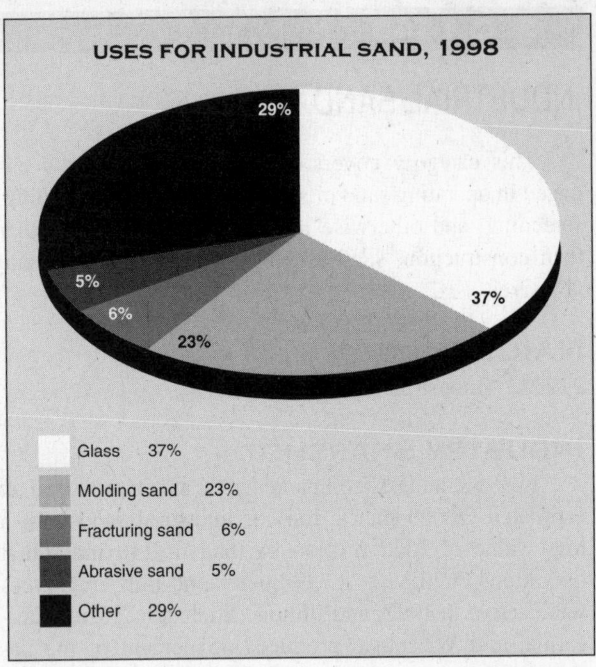

contain several properties to be used in foundry or molding applications. Internal cohesiveness and heat resistance—or refractoriness—enable the mold to withstand the high temperatures of the metal casting process (in steel applications, temperatures of 1340 to 1500 degrees Fahrenheit). Second, the sand's moisture content, and the type and amount of bonding agent (such as clay) within it, govern its ability to withstand the pressure exerted by the casted metal during heating. A third requirement is the sand's permeability, or its ability to allow water vapor and gases from the molten metal to escape during the casting process for cooling. Finally, the sand's composition and texture determine whether it will react chemically with the casted metal and whether it will create a smooth surface on the metal when it cooled.

While so-called naturally bonded molding sand contains enough clay and other bonding material to be used in metal casting without the addition of other bonding ingredients, synthetic molding sand consists of silica sand to which a specific amount (about 5 to 10 percent) of fire clay, bentonite, or other bonding material is added artificially. In the mid-1990s the trend toward greater use of these synthetic molding sands continued, and spurred by government regulations governing the disposal of used industrial sand, the use of recycled or reclaimed foundry sand increased. Both these trends affect future demand for industrial sand.

Fracturing Sand. Fracturing or hydraulic ''frac'' sand, also known as ''proppant'' sand, accounted for 6 percent of U.S. industrial sand production. It is comprised of washed and graded high silica-content quartz sand with a grain size of between 0.84 and 0.42 millimeters and is used in high-pressure fluids pumped into oil and gas wells to enlarge or scour out openings in oil- or gas-bearing rock or to create new fractures from which oil or gas can be recovered. Traditionally, the ''fracture treatment'' at an average well uses 26,000 pounds of fracture sand, and annual demand for fracture sand increases or decreases with the level of activity in the oil and gas industry.

Abrasive Sand. Abrasive sand and blast sand, which accounted for 5 percent of total industrial sand tonnage in 1998, include quartz-based silica sand used in sandpaper, glass grinding, stone sawing (as in dimension stone manufacturing), metal polishing and metal casting cleaning, and in sandblasting to remove paint, stain, and rust. While sands with angular-shaped grains are often used because they cut faster, sands with rounded grains last longer and yield a smoother finish.

Other Uses. Other traditional applications of industrial sand include engine sand, fire or furnace sand, and filtration sand, which together comprised 29 percent of the industry's total tonnage in 1998. Engine sand is laid on railroad tracks to provide traction for train engines in wet or slippery conditions. Fire or furnace sand is generally coarser than the sand used in metal molding. It is used in building floors for acid open-hearth furnaces and in lining the cupolas and ladles that contain molten metal in the foundry industries.

Filtration sand is used by municipal water departments to remove bacteria and sediment from water supplies. Although filtration sand is generally mined from the same quarries as molding and glass sands, it has to be free of clay, lime, and organic matter as well as insoluble in hydrochloric acid. Other industrial uses include enamel manufacture, various metallurgical applications, and the production of phosphoric acid for the fertilizer industry.

Producing Regions. The sand used in industrial applications is mined from silica sand and sandstone deposits in 35 states. Approximately 75 percent of the sand derived from dunes and glacial lake beds is sandstone. Silica sand is composed almost exclusively of grains of quartz and includes between 95 and 99 percent (or more) silicate.

Industry firms in New Jersey traditionally supply special-purpose industrial sand (abrasives, fire sand, etc.), while silica miners in Pennsylvania provide sand for refractory bricks. Deposits in eastern Ohio are a source of sandstone sand that, when finished and sized, is used for clay-free molding sand and high-purity glass sand. Sandstone pebbles from the same region are often crushed and used in the production of ferrosilicon and silica brick. Industry mines in northwestern Ohio and southeastern Michigan historically produce very pure quartz sandstone for high-quality glass sand, and industrial sand mines in California have provided materials for superduty silica brick and glass-making applications since the mid-1950s.

BACKGROUND AND DEVELOPMENT

Mining Methods. The method by which industrial sand deposits are mined depends on the solidity or degree of ''cementation'' of the mineral. Natural sand deposits such as dunes and coastal beaches can be worked simply by using loading and hauling equipment. However, in deposits where the ''overburden'' or covering deposits are unusually deep—as in some locations in Missouri—underground mining uses the traditional ''room-and-pillar'' method, in which sections of the deposit are mined around supporting ''pillars'' of the mineral.

By far the most common means of extraction, however, is the mining of open pits or quarries. The term *quarry* is traditionally assigned to hard mineral deposits—such as the harder varieties of sandstone—requiring blasting or crushing, while *pit* technically refers to softer mineral deposits that can be mined using digging techniques.

Firms involved in quarrying operations use drills to make ''shotholes'' spaced at calculated intervals parallel to the rock face and with a diameter, depth, and angle sufficient to dislodge a specific volume of rock when explosive charges are detonated in them. The explosives are of a quantity and type needed to shatter the rock face and break the sand deposit into sizes convenient for loading.

Firms mine deep sand deposits in dry pits in progressive steps or terraces connected by ramps. They use light blasting, mechanical excavators, or high-pressure jets of water to dislodge the lighter earthy material and expose the heavy sand rock for mining. In some low-lying sand deposits, water naturally seeps into the pit as material is removed, so sand can be extracted as in riverbeds using ''drag lines,'' chain buckets, ''grab dredgers,'' or suction pumps. In pits with sufficiently deep water levels, floating grab dredgers and drag lines can be used to haul the sand to the surface.

Processing. While molding or foundry sand may be marketed without preparation other than crushing, glass sand is washed, dried, and screened, and may also be treated by electromagnetic, electrostatic, flotation, or other techniques to remove heavy mineral impurities like clay. Blast sand may be processed by breaking large sand grains into marketable grades using a high-speed rotary impact mill. Quartzite sandstone used to make silica bricks is crushed and screened into particle sizes of about 0.132 inches.

Recent Developments. In 1995 the U.S. industrial sand industry experienced several facility closures as well as a few major mergers and acquisitions, including Fairmount Minerals' purchase of two Ohio companies to fortify its third-place position in the industry. The biggest corporate news, however, is the announcement by U.S. Borax, the parent company of the industry's largest producer, U.S. Silica, that it planned to divest its subsidiary from its corporate stable.

Major changes in the end uses for industrial sand continued to affect the demand for the industrial sand mining industry's products. The greatest new product advances in 1995 occurred in the silica chemicals and glass and advanced materials industries. Rhône-Poulenc Basic Chemicals and PPG Industries announced new precipitated silica plants in Illinois and Louisiana, respectively; Dow Corning launched a new line of ''resin modifiers'' based on silicone powder for use in flame-retardant thermoplastics; and Ford Motor Company announced the development of an all-fiber, glass-reinforced composite car body design that if adopted by the auto industry would increase the demand for the industrial sand industry's glass sand products. By using silica as an ingredient in the ceramic portion of such aluminum-and-ceramic composites, manufacturers could produce industrial materials with the strength of steel but with a fraction of its weight and cost. The growing importance of the semiconductor industry also promised to expand the silica sand industry's sales, and Samsung Electronics and Intel Corporation announced major new plants in Texas and Arizona, respectively.

CURRENT CONDITIONS

In 1998 the United States remained the world's largest producer and consumer of industrial sand and gravel due to the wide range and high quality of its deposits and the advanced processing techniques used to mine them. The United States exported 2 million metric tons of industrial sand, primarily to Canada (roughly three-quarters of all exports) followed by Mexico, Asia, and Europe.

From 1997 to 1998 exports nearly doubled due to increased demand from Mexico. U.S. industrial sand imports were much smaller, totaling 65,000 metric tons in 1995 and traditionally came from pits in Australia and Belgium. Besides the United States, the leading industrial sand producers worldwide in 1998 were the Netherlands, Germany, Austria, and France.

Health and environmental issues continue to have a major impact on the industrial sand mining industry in 1998. In 1992 the International Agency for Research on Cancer identified crystalline silica as a probable human carcinogen, and the U.S. Occupational Safety and Health Administration (OSHA) therefore required that industrial sites using or receiving more than 0.1 percent of crystalline silica notify workers of its potential health dangers.

Industry firms began labeling bags and filing Material Safety Data Sheets to comply with federal, state, and local regulations regarding crystalline silica content, and garnet and granular slag were investigated as alternative sources of blasting and filtration sand. Establishments were expected to move into lower-population zones at the end of the twentieth century.

Recycling regulations also affected the industrial sand industry's sales, as manufacturers sought ways to reuse foundry sand and the recycling of glass bottles and other products threatened to reduce the overall demand for new sand-based glass. The use of polyethylene terephthalate (PET) in the manufacture of beverage bottles and of plastic optical fiber products in fiberoptic communication applications—an area traditionally dominated by silica-based glass—also represented new threats to the industrial sand industry's future sales.

Industry Leaders

The largest producer of industrial sand in the United States in 1999 was JM Huber Corporation of Edison, New Jersey. Second was Unimin Corporation of Connecticut, which produced the broadest range of ceramic grade silica, nepheline syenite **(SIC 1459: Clay, Ceramic, and Refractory Minerals, Not Elsewhere Classified)**, feldspar **(SIC 1459: Clay, Ceramic, and Refractory Minerals, Not Elsewhere Classified)**, and micron-sized silica. Its trademarked ''QIP'' quality assurance program enabled it to offer minerals of the highest grades of chemical purity and uniformity. In 1995, the nation's third-largest industrial sand producer by 1999, U.S. Silica of West Virginia, was put up for sale by its corporate parent U.S. Borax and Chemical Corporation of California (in turn owned by RTZ Corporation Plc of Great Britain). In late 1995 D. George Harris and Associates, a New York industrial management and advisory firm, purchased U.S. Silica. Fourth in the industry was Morie Company Inc., of New Jersey.

Further Reading

Bolen, Wallace P. ''Minerals Information, 1997.'' *Industrial Sand and Gravel.* U.S. Geological Survey. Available from http://minerals.er.usgs.gov/minerals.

———. ''Minerals Information, 1999.'' *Industrial Sand and Gravel: Statistical Compendium.* U.S. Geological Survey. Available from http://minerals.er.usgs.gov/minerals/pubs/commodity/sand_&_gravel_industria l/stat/.

Economic Census, 1997. Bureau of the Census, 2000. Available from http://www.census.gov.

''Fairmount Minerals Sells Majority Stake.'' *Pit & Quarry.* 88, no. 10 (April 1996), 10.

Mineral Commodity Summaries. United States Geological Survey, 1999. Available from http://minerals.er.usgs.gov/minerals.

''U.S. Silica on the Block.'' *Pit & Quarry,* 87, no. 11 (May 1995).

SIC 1455

KAOLIN AND BALL CLAY

This category covers establishments primarily engaged in mining, milling, or otherwise preparing kaolin or ball clay, including china clay, paper clay, and slip clay. Establishments primarily engaged in grinding, pulverizing, or otherwise treating clay, ceramic, and refractory minerals not in conjunction with mining or quarrying operations are classified in **SIC 3295: Minerals and Earths, Ground or Otherwise Treated.**

NAICS Code(s)

212324 (Kaolin and Ball Clay Mining)

Industry Snapshot

In the late 1990s, roughly 30 U.S. firms operating 110 mines produced 10.6 million metric tons of kaolin and ball clay. Of the total U.S. production of clay and shale in 1998, which reached 41.6 million metric tons with a value of $1.66 billion, kaolin accounted for about 64 percent of the value. Eleven states, led by Georgia, produced kaolin in the late 1990s. Kaolin's primary uses are for paper coating and filling (56 percent), refractories (14 percent), fiberglass (7 percent), paint (5 percent), and other uses (18 percent).

The ball clay segment of the industry was rather small and consisted of five companies in five states in 1998. Tennessee was the leading supplier of ball clay, producing 63 percent of the total U.S. output. Following Tennessee were Texas, Kentucky, Mississippi, and Indiana. U.S. production of ball clay in 1998 reached 1.13 million metric tons with an approximate value of $51.1 million. The major ball clay markets in the United States were floor and wall tile (30 percent), sanitary ware (21 percent), pottery (10 percent), and other uses (39 percent).

Organization and Structure

Clays are classified according to their relative plasticity or malleability, their strength when moist (green strength), their strength after drying (dry strength), their air shrinkage properties, and their vitrification range. Vitrification refers to the process by which clay molecules begin to fuse when exposed to heat. A clay's vitrification range therefore describes the temperature levels between which the clay begins to fuse and when it achieves its final fusion or hardness.

Clays are often mixed or blended to achieve the desired properties dictated by their end use. Thus, whiteware ceramic consists of kaolin, ball clay, feldspar, and ground silica. Kaolin, or china clay, derived its name from the hill where it was first extracted in Kao-Ling, China. Historically, more than half the annual U.S. production of kaolin was used as filler and coating material in high-quality paper. Along with wood pulp, kaolin traditionally constituted a large percentage of the paper's content. The properties that recommend kaolin as a paper clay include natural brightness, ink absorption characteristics, chemical inertness, and superior dispersability when introduced into the water solutions from which the final paper mixture is derived.

There are no commercial substitutes for kaolin as an ingredient in coated paper. The increasing scarcity of wood pulp and the high costs of transporting kaolin outside the southeastern United States however, spurred the papermaking industry to develop alternatives to kaolin as a paper filler in the 1980s. The invention of lime- and calcium carbonate-based alkaline paper manufacturing techniques meant that papermakers would require less wood pulp for paper production. It also meant that they could avoid the high transportation costs associated with kaolin paper fillers—resulting in a potentially long-term loss of demand for the industry's kaolin mining firms.

However, in addition to its uses in papermaking, kaolin is also favored as a filler in rubber production for its low cost and stiffening or reinforcing characteristics, as well as for the properties that recommended it in papermaking. Comparatively smaller amounts of kaolin have been used as extenders and fillers in the manufacture of paint, linoleum, leather, wallpaper, textiles, and fertilizers. Other uses of kaolin include the production of fungicides and insecticides and the manufacturing of porcelain, chinaware, and other ceramic products. Highly refined kaolin has also been used in cosmetics and pharmaceutical products.

Although kaolin as a commodity is relatively inexpensive, it is less common than other clays and therefore has a higher unit price compared to them. Because kaolin has a low per ton price compared to other nonclay commodities, it yields its producers only slim profit margins—unless it could be extracted and processed in greater bulk without added cost or offered to the market in a refined, higher-priced form. For example, in the late 1980s, Georgia-based Nord Kaolin Company introduced a line of customized kaolin-based pigments to act as "opacifiers" to reduce the transparency of paper and to augment the printing quality and whiteness of premium or "glossy" magazine paper, lightweight periodicals paper, and uncoated copier paper. The firm sold more than 12,000 tons of such kaolin-based pigment paper products in 1992.

Historically, about 90 percent of U.S. kaolin production came from mines in Georgia and South Carolina, but North Carolina provided another source of workable deposits. The United States and Great Britain historically led world production of kaolin. In the late 1960s, the kaolin production by Germany, India, and France combined amounted to less than one-third the kaolin production of Great Britain alone.

Ball clay, a light-burning, high-grade ceramic clay, derived its name from the shape it took when it was removed from open pit mines in the early days of the clay mining industry in Great Britain. More than 89 percent of U.S. ball clay originated in western Tennessee and Kentucky, but other mined deposits existed in California, Maryland, Mississippi, and New Jersey. Ball clays differ in color, plasticity, strength, and firing properties, but almost all their uses are ceramic. High-grade ball clay is used in the manufacture of dinnerware, porcelain, and ceramic-based bathroom fixtures. Ball clay is also used to produce "wad" and "sagger" clays used in ceramic kilns to protect and support the clay being baked. Ball clay is shipped in bags and bulk carload lots—in ground, "air floated," lump, or shredded form. Like kaolin, ball clays are produced in relatively small quantities compared to other clays and thus have a generally higher unit price.

BACKGROUND AND DEVELOPMENT

Kaolin and ball clays were most often mined by directing hydraulic high-pressure jets of water on the clay faces of open pits, loosening the soft clay from the deposit. The liquefied clay mixture or "slip" was then raised by bucket elevator to a flume or chute that transported it to the preparation plant. In other methods, the clay was mined by removing the overburden (or overlay of soil or rock) by power shovel or dredging "dragline" machine. The exposed clay was then mined by a power shovel and delivered to the preparation plant by conveyer belt, truck, or rail.

At the preparation plant, the clay mixture was refined and "de-watered" by mechanical drying equipment and filter presses. The undesired grit minerals (such as sand, rutile, or mica) were separated from the clay by such processes as grinding, washing, screening, settling, and/or flotation (in which the extracted mixture was immersed in a solution that caused the undesired elements to sink to the bottom while the clay rose to the surface).

The mining industry as a whole has traditionally faced very high capital costs associated with its exposure to weather-related work interruptions, the cost of exploration activities and preparation of feasibility studies, the expense of acquiring and holding rights to mineral properties, the cost of purchasing and maintaining equipment, and the expense of developing and operating the mines and preparation plants. The mining operations of kaolin and ball clay producers were also governed by environmental regulations that required them to control dust emissions, reclaim strip-mined sites, and purify production waste materials.

CURRENT CONDITIONS

Kaolin. The United States remained the world leader in kaolin production in the late 1990s. In 1998, 80 quarries in 11 states produced 9.45 million metric tons of kaolin, up from 9.28 million metric tons produced the previous year. About half of the kaolin produced was water washed. U.S. exports of kaolin in 1998, according to the U.S. Bureau of the Census, were estimated at about 3.55 million metric tons, and imports from foreign sources totaled approximately 52,900 tons. The primary supplier of kaolin imports was Brazil, which supplied 70 percent of the total. Brazil became a major supplier of kaolin only in the late 1990s. In 1998, total world production of kaolin was estimated at 39.8 million metric tons, with Uzbekistan ranking as the leading producer worldwide after the United States.

The leading U.S. producers of specialty clays in the late 1990s included Engelhard Corporation, which produced both kaolin and fuller's earth; ECC International LTD; Thiele Kaolin Co.; Dry Branch Kaolin Co.; and J.M. Huber Corp. The major companies were active in consolidation attempts, and in 1999 IMETAL SA finalized its purchase of ECC International LTD. As a result, IMETAL formed a Pigments and Additives Group that consisted of ECC International's kaolin operations, previously acquired Dry Branch Kaolin Co., Georgia Marble Co., and Dry Branch Kaolin's portion of the Rio Capim Caulim kaolin facilities in Brazil. Engelhard continued to expand its kaolin operations, and in 1997 the company allotted $45 million to update its calcining operations. Other major activities in the clay segment included the acquisition of A.P. Green Industries Inc. by Global Industrial Technologies Inc., the parent company of Harbison-Walker Refractories Co., and the purchase of Evans Clay Co. by United Catalysts Inc., the parent company of Albion Kaolin Co.

Ball Clay. In 1998, the U.S. ball clay mining industry produced an estimated 1.13 million metric tons, up from 1.06 million metric tons in 1997. The largest increase in demand and consumption was for sanitaryware. Positive sales for ball clay were attributed largely to the steady growth in construction, both commercial and residential, and home renovations. The construction segment provided consistent demand for sanitaryware, tile, and whiteware. Ball clay exports in 1998 were 140,000 tons, according to the U.S. Bureau of the Census. The U.S. imported about 2,670 tons of ball clay in 1998.

FURTHER READING

U.S. Department of the Interior. U.S. Geological Survey. *Mineral Industry Surveys.* June 1999. Available from http://minerals.er.usgs.gov.

U.S. Department of the Interior. U.S. Geological Survey. *Mineral Commodity Summaries.* January 1999. Available from http://minerals.er.usgs.gov.

Virta, Robert L. ''Clay and Shale.'' U.S. Department of the Interior. U.S. Geological Survey. 1998. Available from http://minerals.er.usgs.gov.

SIC 1459

CLAY, CERAMIC, AND REFRACTORY MINERALS, NOT ELSEWHERE CLASSIFIED

This category covers establishments primarily engaged in mining, milling, or otherwise preparing clay, ceramic, or refractory (heat-resistant) minerals, not elsewhere classified. Establishments producing clay in conjunction with the manufacture of refractory or structural clay and pottery products are classified in manufacturing in the major group for stone, clay, glass, and concrete products.

NAICS CODE(S)

212325 (Clay and Ceramic and Refractory Minerals Mining)

INDUSTRY SNAPSHOT

Firms in this industry extract raw minerals used in a wide variety of industrial and consumer applications with the most common end use being refractory materials for the manufacture of glass, ceramics, and industrial uses.

ORGANIZATION AND STRUCTURE

Common Clay and Shale. Industry firms produced 24.5 million metric tons of common clay and shale in 1998. About 44 percent of all common clay and shale was used to make bricks for the construction industry. In 1998, common clay and shale accounted for 70 percent of the total output of all clay minerals (including those produced by firms not classified in this industry) sold or used in the United States.

Common clay alone was used to manufacture bricks (50 percent of output), cement (25 percent), and in lightweight aggregate (16 percent). Other uses for common clay alone include such heavy clay products as building brick, flue linings, sewer pipe, drain tile, structural tile, terra cotta, and portland cement clinker (slag). In descending order of output, Alabama (2.40 million metric tons), North Carolina (2.38 million metric tons), Texas (2.12 million metric tons), and Georgia (1.65 million metric tons) were the largest producers of common clay in 1998.

Shale is one of the most common sedimentary rocks and thus usually has a lower unit price than rarer clays such as kaolin and ball clay. Shale's industrial applications include heavy ceramic ware, portland cement manufacture, and lightweight construction aggregate. The choice of shale as an ingredient in these applications is governed by such factors as its suitability compared with other industrial minerals, the presence of other useful minerals in the market for which it is to be produced (i.e., pumice, sand and gravel, slag, or crushed stone in the lightweight aggregate industry), and its economic viability with respect to other competing minerals such as clay.

Bentonite. The United States was the world leader in the production of bentonite throughout the 1990s, and the 19 industry companies produced an estimated 3.82 million metric tons in 1998 from mines in 11 states. In 1998, bentonite's specific end uses were as a foundry sand-bonding agent (25.5 percent), in iron ore pelletizing (15.6 percent), as a drilling mud (19.6 percent), and as a clumping agent in pet waste litter (22.8 percent). Bentonite's other uses included the manufacture of decolorizing oils; catalysts for the production of polymers, plastics, and resins in the petrochemical industry; absorbent materials for industrial plants; cattle feeds; and a thickening agent for the production of paints, hand lotions, and pencil lead.

As ingredients in the drilling mud used in the oil-well drilling industry, bentonite-based products aid in the removal of drill cuttings, thicken drilling fluids, stabilize well walls, and reduce friction. Bentonite is also used as an ingredient and preblend in the production of metal casting products for automobiles, kitchen appliances, and other products; as a binding agent in iron ore pelletizing processes in the steel industry; and as a water-absorbing sealant or liner in underground or waterproofed structures.

Fuller's Earth. The United States was the world leader in fuller's earth production throughout the 1990s. Fuller's earth derived its name from the ancient practice of using earth to clean wool—a process known as "fulling." Fuller's earth became a generic name for clay- and earth-based minerals that had the property of chemically colorizing vegetable oils and minerals. The product is used to decolorize soy oils, petroleum products, tallow, and cottonseed oil, as well as in such applications as insecticide production, oil well drilling, mud, manufacture, and as a filler. Fuller's earth is also used in the manufacture of traditional or nonclumping cat litter products. In 1998, 72 percent of all fuller's earth mined in the United State was for use as an absorbent, and another 6 percent of total output served as a dispersant in insecticide.

Feldspar. Feldspar is the most common igneous rock mineral and the most plentiful mineral in the earth's crust. In 1998, 70 percent of all feldspar (including aplite) sold or consumed in the United States is in the glass-making industry, including the manufacture of glass fibers and glass containers in which it enhances glass's durability, hardness, and resistance to erosion. Feldspar is also commonly used as a flux in the manufacture of ceramics and its other end uses include the manufacture of pottery, plumbing fixtures, electrical porcelain, ceramic wall and floor tiles, glass, dinnerware, television picture tubes, and glass fiber insulation. In 1999, industry firms in seven states (primarily North Carolina) produced an estimated 900,000 metric tons of feldspar with a value of $45 million.

Nepheline syenite is a feldspathic mineral that provides alumina and alkali used in glass making and serves as a flux in ceramic product manufacturing to lower melting temperature. Pegmatites are the minerals from which feldspar is mined; feldspar is the most plentiful mineral present in pegmatites.

Fire Clay. In 1995, 69 percent of the 583,000 tons of fire clay produced in the United States was used in refractory products such as calcines (metal oxides produced by roasting or calcination), firebrick, grogs (crushed material used to make refractory products, such as crucibles, to limit shrinkage), high-alumina brick, saggers (fireclay boxes for firing more delicate ceramics), refractory mortars and mixes, and ramming and gunning mixes. Other uses include lightweight aggregates, portland cement, and pottery. Roughly 12 percent of fire clay production is used as a dispersant in insecticides. In 1998, Missouri produced the most fire clay for the United States, followed by Ohio, South Carolina, California, Kentucky, Alabama, and New Mexico.

Magnesite. The United States has been the world's biggest producer of metallic magnesium since World War II. Magnesium is the third most abundant element in seawater and the eighth most abundant element in the Earth's crust. Magnesium and its compounds are recovered from seawater (74 percent in 1998) and from mineral deposits of magnesite, dolomite, and olivine. Magnesium is employed primarily as an alloy in the aluminum used to make everything from beverage cans, aircraft, automobiles, and machinery. It has also found uses in the desulfurization of iron and steel and in the chemical, agricultural, and construction industries. In 1998, 62 percent of U.S. magnesium compounds were used in refractories, as for example, in the linings of iron and steel furnaces;

thus, the magnesite mining segment of the industry is strongly affected by economic trends in the iron and steel industry. Magnesium compounds are also used in agricultural, chemical, environmental, and industrial capacities.

Kyanite. Kyanite and its two related minerals, andalusite and sillimanite, are used primarily in the glass-making, metallurgy, refractory, and ceramic industries. With most mines located in Georgia, Virginia, and North and South Carolina, the American kyanite mining segment is the world's second largest producer in 1999, with an estimated 90,000 metric tons. South Africa ranked first with 250 metric tons, or 61 percent of the world total. Andalusite is mined from deposits in California and used in the manufacture of spark plugs and other porcelain requiring high heat-resistant properties in electrical and chemical applications.

Kaolin. Kaolin is a clay mineral that is used as a pigment in the production of paint, paper, plastic, ink, polish, ceramics, cement, fiberglass, adhesives, and rubber. Kaolin is distinguished from other clay minerals like illite, montmorillonite, vermiculite, and several other groups by chemistry, particle shape and structure, and properties like conductivity and light refraction. All clays are very fine in structure, and their differences require techniques like electron microscopy or X-ray diffraction to measure. These same differences, however, greatly affect the behavior of kaolin (or any of the other clays) in product applications. Kaolin is also used as a paper coating (100,000 tons) and in refractories (210,000 tons).

In 1998, 25 firms in 11 states produced 9.28 million metric tons valued at $1.05 billion. This was a slight increase from th 9.28 million metric tons produced the previous year. Georgia is the leading state in kaolin production, followed by South Carolina, Alabama, and Arkansas.

CURRENT CONDITIONS

Common Clay and Shale. In 1995, more than two hundred of the firms in the common clay and shale segment of the industry mined these minerals for use in the manufacture of their own products, and only about 10 percent of the estimated 25.6 million metric tons of common clay and shale produced in 1995 was sold to other firms. A significant trend in this portion of the industry was the consolidation of industry firms in reaction to the prohibitive costs of transporting mined clay and shale. Thus, many smaller industry firms operated through local ownership companies, while larger firms contained transportation costs by owning and operating a number of strategically located pits and fabricating facilities.

In 1998, 24.5 million metric tons of common clay and shale was sold by the United States. More than 50 percent is used as brick, with 21 percent being used as cement, and 10 percent being used as concrete blocks.

Bentonite. Bentonite Baroid Drilling Fluids and Amcol International announced that they would construct a bentonite blending plant for foundry compounds in Texas in the 1990s.

Fuller's Earth. Seventeen companies operating 37 quarries in 11 states produced 2.4 million metric tons of fuller's earth in 1998. World production of fuller's earth, 3.3 million tons in 1998, was led by the United States and Germany.

Feldspar. In 1998, 9 U.S. firms produced an estimated 900,000 metric tons of feldspar and aplite with a value of $45 million. The three largest producers supplied over 60 percent of this total. In the mid-1990s industry leader Feldspar Corporation expanded its North Carolina production capacity by 120,000 tons and opened a new mine in Georgia. In 1999, the United States only imported 6,000 metric tons for consumption, 96 percent of which was supplied by Mexico. A booming housing market helped the U.S. ceramic tile market value increase 8.7 percent in 1998, to $1.7 billion. Import penetration in this market was 67 percent, however.

Fire Clay. In 1998, 16 U.S. firms operating 49 quarries in 7 states produced 410,000 metric tons valued at $7.52 million, down from 583,000 metric tons in 1995. Most producers were refractory manufacturers that used the clay in the fabrication of firebrick and other refractory materials.

Magnesite. In 1998, four companies in California, Delaware, Florida, and Texas extracted magnesium compounds from seawater; three companies in Michigan extracter magnesium compounds from brine wells; and two companies in Utah recovered magnesium compounds from lake brine. U.S. production of magnesium compounds reached an estimated 440,000 metric tons in 1998, up 28 percent from 1994. Domestic production wasn't enough to satisfy demand though, as 220,000 metric tons were imported, 69 percent of which came from China. In the mid-1990s, a worldwide shortage of magnesium supplies led to the highest magnesium prices since it was first manufactured commercially in 1915. As a result, the increased use of magnesium in diecasting applications in the auto industry was dealt a significant setback, as both Ford Motor Company and General Motors Corporation decided against switching from steel and aluminum, respectively, to magnesium in their assembly plants. Nevertheless, in 1995 two major industry producers, PQ Corporation and Great Salt Lake Minerals Corporation, announced significant capacity expansion programs.

Kyanite. In the mid-1990s the kyanite industry was positively affected by new developments in the refractory market. So-called monolithic refractories, that is, refractories that are made of a single piece, found expanded uses in new high-temperature manufacturing processes being adopted in the iron and steel, cement, glass, and other refractories industries. In particular, industry firms like Kyanite Mining Corporation of Virginia, C-E Minerals of Georgia, and North American Refractories were expected to benefit from the emergence of new refractory materials that help the steel industry in its quest to produce ever purer grades of steel. In 1999, U.S. consumption of kyanite reached 104,000 metric tons. Refractories accounted for 90 percent of use. The U.S. exported 35,000 metric tons of kyanite and imported 10,000 metric tons, all from South Africa.

INDUSTRY LEADERS

Leading firms in the clay, ceramic, and refractory minerals industry in the late 1990s included Amcol International (formerly American Colloid) of Illinois, Stancorp Inc. of Ohio, Oil-Dri Corporation of America of Illinois, Martin Marietta Magnesia of Michigan, Harbison-Walker Refractories & Minerals of California, and American Premier of Nevada. In 1998, 49 percent of Amcol's $552.1 million in sales derived from its bentonite minerals division; Amcol is the leader in the manufacture of such clay-based products as scoopable cat litter.

In 1999 Utah Clay Technology (UCT), a firm that makes high-quality kaolin, leased 7,000 acres of land in southern Utah from Utah Kaolin Corporation. UCT's kaolin reserves are estimated to have increased by over 200 million tons through this mining lease. Hecla Mining Company of Coeur d'Alene, Idaho, is also a key supplier of kaolin and other clay mineral from mines in Mexico, Venezuela, and the United States as of 1999. Creative uses of mining properties around the world characterize forward-looking leaders in the clay minerals industry.

FURTHER READING

"AMCOL International Corporate Report," 18 April 2000. Available from http://www.amcol.com.

"Hecla Mining Preferred Stock Dividend Scheduled for January Payment." *BusinessWire,* 16 December 1999. Available from http://finance.individual.com/.

Hoover's Online Company Profiles. "AMCOL International Corporation," 18 April 2000. Available from http://www.hoovers.com.

"Industrial Minerals 1995." *Mining Engineering,* June 1996.

U.S. Bureau of the Census. *The Census of Mineral Industries: General Summary, 1992,* 1995. Available from http://www.census.gov.

U.S. Bureau of the Census. *1992 Census of Mineral Industries, Industry Series,* 1995. Available from http://www.census.gov.

U.S. Geological Survey. *Mineral Commodity Summaries,* April 2000. Available from http://minerals.usgs.gov/minerals/pubs/commodity/.

U.S. Geological Survey. *Mineral Industry Surveys.* Available from http://minerals.er.usgs.gov.

U.S. Geological Survey. *Mineral Yearbook 1995,* 1996. Available from http://minerals.er.usgs.gov.

"Utah Clay Technology Acquires Strategic Mining Lease." *PR Newswire,* 15 December 1999. Available from http://finance.individual.com/.

Vita, Robert L. "Clay and Shale—1998." Washington, DC: GPO 1999. Available from http://www.usgs.gov.

SIC 1474

POTASH, SODA, AND BORATE MINERALS

This category covers establishments primarily engaged in mining, milling, or otherwise preparing natural potassium, sodium, or boron compounds. Establishments primarily engaged in mining common salt are classified in **SIC 1479: Chemical and Fertilizer Mineral Mining, Not Elsewhere Classified.**

NAICS CODE(S)

212391 (Potash, Soda, and Borate Mineral Mining)

In 1999 the majority of potash production took place in New Mexico, where five mines were in operation. Michigan and Utah also had potash production facilities. In the crop year which ended June 1999, about 1.3 million metric tons of potash were produced in the United States. The fertilizer industry accounted for about 90 percent of U.S. potash sales, and the chemical industry used about 10 percent. Roughly 50 percent of the potash extracted in 1998 was produced as potassium chloride, with potassium sulfate and potassium magnesium sulfate—both for fertilizing certain crops and soils—representing the remainder of potash production. Of the world's potash reserves, the largest percentage was located in Canada and Russia.

As a fertilizer, potash was used for such crops as soybeans, tobacco, potatoes, sugar beets, and corn, and the potash mining industry was thus subject to the seasonal fluctuations of the agricultural market. Before the Civil War, U.S. production of potash involved removing it from wood ashes through a leaching process. In 1916 potash began to be extracted through crystallization from saltwater lake brines in southern California, and later

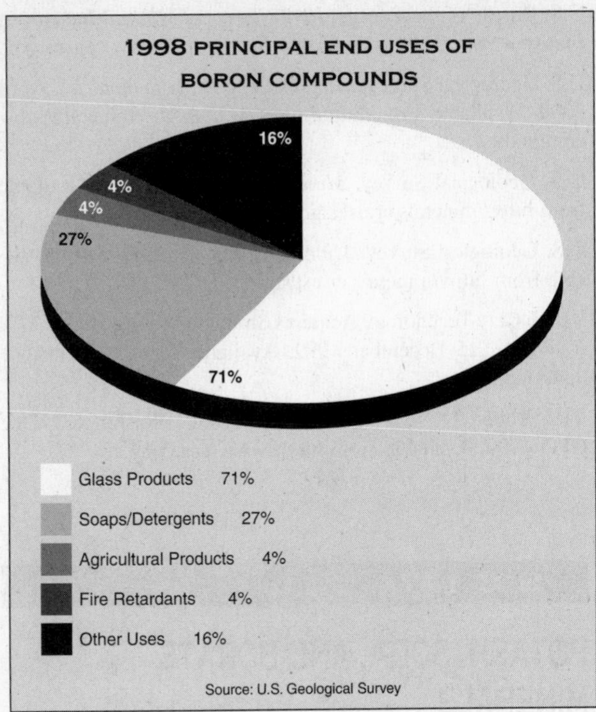

potash was mined from deposits discovered in New Mexico, which became the primary source of domestic potash in the United States. Following the oil crisis of 1979, demand for potash in developed nations declined, but in 1986 began a steady climb of 140,000 short tons a year.

By the 1990s the world's potash markets were in oversupply, and in the late 1990s potash producers were forced to operate at reduced capacity. In addition, potash production was affected by economic crises afflicting Asia, as demand from Asia for imported grains declined. In 1998 U.S. farmers began to curb usage of fertilizers, and sales of potash began to fall. Based on data from the U.S. Bureau of the Census and the U.S. Geological Survey, it was estimated that consumption of potash fell about 12 percent in 1998 from 1997 figures. Exports in 1999 rose 7 percent over 1998 exports, with approximately 70 percent of total exports going to Latin America. Imports in 1998 declined by about 10 percent compared to 1997 imports.

By 1999 there were only four potash-producing companies in operation in the United States, down from ten companies in 1996. The four companies worked a total of seven production facilities. In 1997 Mississippi Chemical Corp. closed down its Eddy Potash Mine located in New Mexico. Also that year IMC Global Inc. acquired Western Ag-Mineral, and in 1998 IMC purchased Harris Chemical Group, Inc., which included the Great Salt Lake Minerals Corp. Other consolidations led to Canadian-based Potash Corporation's ownership of the Moab Salt Company in Utah and Reilly Industries, Inc.'s ownership of the Reilly-Wendover potash site.

The soda ash mining segment of the industry, the world's largest, consisted of six U.S. companies in Wyoming and California, which in 1998 produced 10.1 million metric tons of soda ash. Soda ash, a form of sodium carbonate, is used in the production of such chemicals as sodium bicarbonate, sodium sulfate, sodium chromate, sodium phosphate, sodium silicate, potassium chloride, potassium sulfate, sodium sulfite, sodium tripolyphosphate, and chemical caustic soda. In 1998 the most common end uses of these soda ash products were glass (49 percent); chemicals (26 percent); soap and detergents (12 percent); distributors (5 percent); flue gas desulfurization (3 percent), pulp and paper and miscellaneous (2 percent each); and water treatment (1 percent). Other applications of this ''non-table salt'' group of sodium or saline minerals were the production of photographic darkroom materials and wood fibers for the manufacture of wrapping paper and carton board, and the processing of textile fibers, dye manufacture, and leather tanning. Alum, Glauber's salt, and trona were other forms of sodium salts mined by industry firms. Sodium sulfate in particular was used as a substitute for salt in the dyeing processes of the textiles industry and in the glass, powdered laundry detergent, and pulp and paper industries.

Though natural soda ash production declined 6 percent in 1998 compared to 1997, it was expected that global demand for soda ash would grow about 1.5 to 2 percent a year in the early part of the twenty-first century. U.S. soda ash exports fell by about 13 percent in 1998. Economic problems in Asia affected overseas demand for U.S. soda ash, and exports to Indonesia, the Republic of Korea, and Thailand fell from 26 percent of total exports in 1996 to 16 percent in 1998. Exports to Brazil, Chile, Japan, Mexico, and Taiwan, however, grew to 38 percent of total exports in 1998, up from 32 percent in 1996.

Foreign investment in the U.S. soda ash industry increased throughout the 1990s. In 1981 foreign investment accounted for only 10 percent of soda ash production, but by 1998 foreign investment was 46 percent of capacity. European companies owned about 22 percent of soda ash production operations in Wyoming in 1998. The percentage had been higher—35 percent—in 1995, before Rhône Poulenc SA of France sold its Wyoming plant to Korea's Oriental Chemical Industries.

Significant activities of soda ash-producing companies in the late 1990s included OCI Chemical Corp.'s expansion project, which increased annual capacity from 2.09 million tons to 2.81 million tons. In 1998 IMC Global bought several soda ash operations, including North American Chemical Co.'s Searles Lake, California, plant; the White River Nahcolite facility in Colorado; the Harris Chemical Group's Matthes & Weber synthetic soda ash plant in Germany; and the Penrice Soda Products synthetic soda ash facility in Australia. Also, American Soda LLP, Inc., proposed a $400 million soda ash project in western Colorado.

The term *borate minerals* encompasses such boron-producing minerals as borax and kernite and includes colemanite, ulexite, and probertite. Boron was used in gasoline, jet and rocket fuel, and as an ingredient in industrial plasticizing and dehydrating processes. Borax was used in the production of enamel for bathtubs, stoves, refrigerators, and metal signs, and as an agent for ensuring brilliance and clarity in the manufacture of glass. Other uses for borax included disinfectants, preservatives, starches, lumber treatment, detergents, fertilizers, weed killers, and metallurgical applications. Borax and other borate compounds were also used as intermediate chemicals in a wide variety of industrial processes. Colemanite and ulexite were used in glass manufacturing and in the production of glass wool used for insulation.

U.S. production of boron minerals was centered in California and handled by four companies. The three regions responsible for much of the production were Kern County, San Bernardino, and Inyo County. The four borate mineral producers were American Borate Co., Fort Cady Minerals Corp., North American Chemical Co., which was owned by IMC Global, and U.S. Borax, Inc. The United States was the largest producer of boron compounds globally in 1998 and exported roughly 50 percent of its output. The largest producer of boron ore globally was Turkey. The United States continued to import borates, primarily from northern Chile. The principal end uses of boron compounds in 1998 were glass products (71 percent), soaps and detergents (5 percent), agriculture (4 percent), fire retardants (4 percent), and other uses (16 percent).

FURTHER READING

''Industrial Minerals 1995.'' *Mining Engineering,* June 1996.

Kostick, Dennis S. ''Soda Ash.'' U.S. Department of the Interior. U.S. Geological Survey, 1998. Available from http://minerals.er.usgs.gov.

Lyday, Phillis A. ''Boron.'' U.S. Department of the Interior. U.S. Geological Survey, 1997. Available from http://minerals.er.usgs.gov.

Potash & Phosphate Institute, Norcross, Ga., 770/447-0335. Available from http://www.agriculture.com/contents/ppi/.

U.S. Department of the Interior. U.S. Geological Survey. *Mineral Commodity Summaries.* January 1999. Available from http://minerals.er.usgs.gov.

U.S. Department of the Interior. U.S. Geological Survey. *Mineral Industry Surveys.* November 1999. Available from http://minerals.er.usgs.gov.

Searls, James P. ''Potash.'' U.S. Department of the Interior. U.S. Geological Survey, 1998. Available from http://minerals.er.usgs.gov.

SIC 1475

PHOSPHATE ROCK

This category covers establishments primarily engaged in mining, milling, drying, calcining, sintering (heating without melting), or otherwise preparing phosphate rock, including apatite.

NAICS CODE(S)

212392 (Phosphate Rock Mining)

In 1997, 20 U.S. firms employed 3,858 workers. In 1998 mines produced an estimated 44.6 million metric tons of phosphate rock, with a value of $1.14 billion f.o.b. mine. The United States is the world's leading producer and consumer of phosphate rock, over 90 percent of which is used to produce chemical fertilizers. In 1998 it accounted for about one-third of total global production. The states of Florida and North Carolina produced 83 percent of the total U.S. phosphate rock output, with Idaho and Utah contributing the rest. In 1998 U.S. phosphate production grew for the sixth consecutive year.

The mineral phosphate took over 150 natural forms and was required by all plant and animal life for existence. All of the U.S. production of phosphate minerals—and 90 percent of worldwide production—was the sedimentary phosphate rock known as phosphorite, which was largely comprised of carbonite apatite. The phosphate rock mining and preparation industry produced the phosphorus that comprised one of three primary ingredients of agricultural fertilizers.

A substantial percentage of mined low-grade phosphate was used in an untreated state as soil fertilizer. This natural phosphate released its phosphorus content into soils relatively slowly, however, so greater volumes had to be extracted to achieve the same effects as more concentrated processed phosphate fertilizers. Common forms of treated or processed phosphate compounds include phosphoric acid, triple superphosphate, ammonium phosphate, and superphosphate. The harvesting of one ton of wheat required the application of about 18 pounds of phosphoric acid fertilizer, which was usually applied to the soil through irrigation water.

In addition to its use as a fertilizer, phosphate rock provided orthophosphoric acid and elemental phosphorus, which were used in applications such as leavening agents, photographic chemicals, water softeners, oil refining, beverages, insecticides, ceramics, detergents, plasticizing chemicals, and scouring powders. Phosphate rock was also widely used as a source of fluorine for making plastics and resins, laboratory dies, refrigerants, solvents, lubricants, and aerosol propellants. Phosphorus also played a role in the production of explosives and fireworks and in steel production. Phosphate rock found in Idaho contained vanadium, which was used as a bonding agent in the manufacture of titanium steel, as a stabilizing agent in steel production, and as a rust-resistant element in high-speed tools.

The extremely high costs of acquiring and holding mineral properties, conducting feasibility studies and exploration operations, purchasing and maintaining mining equipment, and developing and operating the mines themselves, made the mining industry one of the most capital-intensive in the United States. Historically, the majority of phosphate rock mined in the United States was extracted from open pits, but the number of underground mining operations gradually increased. Open pit mining was performed by large excavating machines, which stripped the ''overburden'' (nonproductive overlay) and removed it from the site. A typical operation involved washing the mined phosphate with a hydraulic jet and then pumping it in liquefied ''slurry'' form to a washing plant. The phosphate was then mechanically graded by size, concentrated, and dried.

Phosphate mining began in Idaho in 1906 and in Montana in 1920. The use of phosphate fertilizers in sugar beet fields first occurred in the western United States in the mid-1930s. The production of phosphate rock grew rapidly during World War II and reached 10.7 million metric tons by 1950. And by 1964, 23.3 million metric tons were produced in the United States alone. Although worldwide consumption of phosphate fertilizers increased from the 1970s to the 1990s, its rate of growth steadily fell off, from 5 percent a year to 2 percent or lower by the mid-1990s.

The most important trend in the U.S. phosphate mining industry in 1998 was industry consolidation. Grain surpluses, an excess supply of phosphate fertilizer worldwide, and depressed prices between 1981 and 1986 forced North American phosphate producers to seek greater efficiencies, and in 1996 Potash Corporation of Saskatchewan (PCS) bought two phosphate mines and chemical plants in Florida to complement its existing phosphate complex in North Carolina. The purchase gave it control of approximately 39 percent of U.S. phosphate reserves, the largest in the industry, and made PCS the third largest phosphate producer in the world. Similar consolidation activities by U.S. phosphate mining firms—such as the merger of IMC Global and Vigoro—created significant economies of scale within the industry by 1995. Several idle mines had been purchased and were expected to reopen in 1999. That year, the industry was dominated by IMC-Agrico Company, of Uncle Sam, Louisiana, which reported revenues of $184 million.

Industry firms also turned to advanced mineral processing technologies such as the WPPA manufacturing process. As a result, coupled with increased global demand for phosphate-based agricultural fertilizer, the outlook for the U.S. phosphate mining industry in the late 1990s was favorable. U.S. phosphate rock mines were operating at 90 percent of capacity in 1995 and wet-process phosphoric acid and elemental phosphorus facilities at close to 100 percent capacity. In the long term, however, U.S. producers faced the eventual depletion of domestic phosphate reserves, particularly in Florida, and because of the high cost of developing new U.S. phosphate deposits at least one industry expert predicted that by the early years of the twenty-first century the United States would have to import more phosphate than it produces.

In 1998 U.S. phosphate exports continued a decline that began in 1992, with roughly half of all exports going to Asian countries. In 1996 the United States imported 1 million tons of phosphate rock, virtually all of it from Morocco. International production of phosphate rock centered in the former Soviet Union, Norway, South America, Egypt, Israel, Jordan, and Africa. As of 1999, analysts expected that demand and consumption would both continue to increase.

Further Reading

Bureau of the Census.*1997 Economic Census,* 2000. Available from http://www.census.gov.

''Industrial Minerals 1995.'' *Mining Engineering,* June 1996.

Rabchevsky, George A. ''Phosphate Rock.'' *U.S. Geological Survey—Minerals Information,* 1998. Available from http://minerals.er.usgs.gov.

U.S. Geological Survey. ''Marketable Phosphate Rock in February 1999.'' *Mineral Industry Surveys.* Available from http://minerals.er.usgs.gov.

U.S. Geological Survey. *Mineral Commodity Summaries,* February 1999. Available from http://minerals.er.usgs.gov.

Ward's Business Directory of U.S. Public and Private Companies, Detroit: Gale Research, 1999.

SIC 1479

CHEMICAL AND FERTILIZER MINERAL MINING, NOT ELSEWHERE CLASSIFIED

This category covers establishments primarily engaged in mining, milling, or otherwise preparing chemical or fertilizer mineral raw materials, not elsewhere classified. Establishments primarily engaged in milling, grinding, or otherwise preparing barite not in conjunction with mining or quarry operations are classified in **SIC 3295: Minerals and Earths, Ground or Otherwise Treated;** similar establishments preparing other minerals of this industry are included here. Establishments primarily engaged in producing salt by evaporation of sea water or brine are classified in **SIC 2899: Chemicals and Chemical Preparations, Not Elsewhere Classified.**

NAICS CODE(S)

212393 (Other Chemical and Fertilizer Mineral Mining)

INDUSTRY SNAPSHOT

The 66 companies participating in the chemical and fertilizer minerals industry in 1998 generated more than $270.5 million in shipments. Industry employment in the mid 1990s totaled 4,100 workers, almost 54 percent of whom were involved in production, development, and exploration activities. Of the industry's 99 producing establishments, 45 percent operated only mines, while 20 percent operated mines in conjunction with preparation plants. Only 27 percent of the industry's establishments had more than 20 workers in 1998. In 1992 the majority of industry establishments were in Texas (16), followed by Louisiana, with 13 establishments.

ORGANIZATION AND STRUCTURE

The major products mined by the chemical and fertilizer minerals industry included salt, sulfur, barite, fluorspar, lithium, and strontium. The largest single product category was salt, which represented 48 percent of the value of all industry shipments and was primarily produced in Louisiana, Texas, and New York. The United States was the world's largest producer of salt in the 1990s. Twenty-eight U.S. companies operated 64 salt-producing plants in 14 states in 1995, producing salt in four basic forms: salt in brine (50 percent of all salt sold or used), rock salt (32 percent), vacuum pan salt (10 percent), and solar salt (8 percent). Eight of the companies produced more than 1 million tons of salt each in 1995, accounting for 89 percent and 93 percent of the industry's total production and total dollar value, respectively.

There were roughly 14,000 end uses for salts, with the largest being chemicals (45 percent), road de-icing/ice control salt (28 percent), salt sold to distributors (9 percent), food and agricultural salt (including table salt, 7 percent), industrial uses (8 percent), primary water treatment applications (1 percent), and exports/other uses (2 percent). Along with limestone, coal, and sulfur, salt was one of the four most important minerals used by the chemicals industry. As early as 1939, salt was being used in the production of 74 industrial chemicals in the form of sodium and chlorine, and the largest U.S. salt mining or producing firms historically were operated by chemical companies that processed the extracted salt into commercial products. Salt was used by the chemical industries as a feedstock in the manufacture of chlorine and caustic soda, which was used to make everything from soap, dyes, and dairy products to glass, pulp, and paper. Other uses included water conditioning and treatment processes, textiles and rayon manufacturing, metallurgical applications, leather treatment, agriculture, refrigeration, meat packing, and fish curing.

U.S. salt producers accounted for about 22 percent of the world's total production in 1995, and six industry firms exported 93 percent of all salt sold overseas: Akzo Nobel Salt Inc., Cargill Salt Co. and its affiliate Leslie Salt Co., North American Salt Co., Morton Salt Co., Western Salt Co., and United Salt Co.

In 1995, 46.5 million metric tons of domestic and imported salt was used in the United States. In 1970 50 salt-producing companies had operated 95 plants in the United States. By 1995, several factors had reduced this industry segment to 28 companies and 64 plants. Among these factors were cheaper salt imports, intensified market competition, surplus production capacity, and high energy and labor costs. Among the major salt industry events of the mid-1990s were the announcement of a joint venture between Continental Salt, Eastern Cargill Inc., and Petroquaimica de Venezuela, S.A. to produce solar salt, and the decision by Akzo Nobel Salt Inc. not to replace its collapsed and flooded rock salt mine in Retsof, New York—the largest underground room-and-pillar salt mine in the hemisphere—with a new mine. Instead Akzo decided to sell virtually all its North American and Caribbean salt operations (valued at $450 million) to agricultural giant Cargill Inc., strengthening Cargill in its struggle with Morton Salt for industry dominance.

The second largest segment of the miscellaneous chemicals and fertilizer minerals mining industry was sulfur, which comprised 36 percent of the value of all industry products. In the mid-1990s, the United States remained the world's largest producer and consumer of sulfur, one of the four most widely used industrial minerals in the chemical industry. Unlike most other major mineral commodities, sulfur is primarily used not as part of a finished product but as a chemical reagent, namely, sulfuric acid, the most widely produced chemical in the United States. In 1995, 90 percent of all sulfur output was consumed in the form of sulfuric acid **SIC 2819: Industrial Inorganic Chemical Manufacturing,**) and it was used to make everything from insecticides, soaps, leather, and textiles to artificial fertilizers, paints, dyes, and paper. Two-thirds of all sulfur consumed in the United States in 1995 was used in agricultural chemicals, mainly fertilizers, but also in the manufacture of a myriad of industrial products.

The world sulfur industry was divided into two categories: producers who extracted sulfur or pyrites as their primary mining objective, and those who extracted it solely as a byproduct of the mining of other minerals. In 1995, this indirect or ''involuntary'' production of sulfur accounted for almost three-quarters of the world's sulfur production. In 1996, $450 million of elemental or unrefined sulfur was produced by more than 160 operations in 32 U.S. states and territories. Three-quarters of the world's output of elemental sulfur was ''involuntary,'' that is, it was recovered from natural gas processing, petroleum refining, and coking plants. Fifty-nine U.S. companies in 28 U.S. states and territories produced recovered sulfur in 1995, led by Exxon Co. U.S.A., Standard Oil Co., Mobil Oil Corp., Shell Oil Co., and Star Enterprises. Elemental sulfur was also produced using the Frasch hot-water method, in which native sulfur found in salt domes and sediment was melted underground and brought to the surface with compressed air. In 1995, two U.S. Frasch-method sulfur mines operated in Louisiana and Texas.

In the early 1990s, global demand for sulfur declined due to decreased demand for the phosphate fertilizer that represented a major market for sulfur producers. Between 1991 and 1994, for example, cheap Canadian and Polish imports had caused prices to plummet from $147.50 per long ton to $85. Conditions had improved somewhat by 1995, but the combination of improved production and falling consumption produced excessive inventories and still deflated prices. Prices for Canadian sulfur imports dropped so low that some Canadian producers held back sulfur sales to the United States in fear of antidumping penalties, but several Canadian sulfur firms were nevertheless found guilty of price gouging and were slapped with import duties by the U.S. government. Industry leader Freeport-McMoran's expansion of its sulfur operations in the early 1990s continued in 1995 when it acquired the sulfur operations of competitor Pennzoil Sulphur Co., making Freeport the last Frasch-method sulfur producer in North America.

The third largest product in the miscellaneous chemical and fertilizer mineral mining industry was barite, which represented 3 percent of the value of all industry shipments. Roughly 34 U.S. companies—14 mines and 20 mills—produced 540,000 tons of barite, with a value of $30 million, in 1996, primarily from sites in Nevada. Almost 90 percent of the barite sold in the United States in the mid-1990s was used as a weighing agent in oil- and gas-well-drilling fluids to maintain pressure and prevent blowouts. It was also used as a weighing additive in cement, rubber, and urethane foam and for metal protection and gloss in automobile paint primer and leaded glass, as well as a raw material in barium chemicals. It has found uses in everything from automobile brake and clutch pads, concrete vessels for holding radioactive materials, cathode-ray tube faceplates and funnelglass, as a filler in linoleum, paper, and rubber, as an ingredient in the manufacture of white pigment, inks, oil cloth, and leather, and in the production of glaze, enamels, detonators, and signal flares.

An oversupply of barite for the oil industry—the end user of 90 percent of all barium produced—in the mid-1990s caused the consumption of ground barite to grow only slightly to 1.3 million tons in 1996. Despite a trend toward the use of more efficient wells—resulting in lower demand for new barium—the number of U.S. rotary oil rigs grew from 762 to 790 between December 1995 and July 1996, fueling a need for fresh barium. However, most exploratory and development oil drilling occurred outside the United States in the mid-1990s, and because it was not cost-effective to ship a low-unit-value commodity like barium overseas, the barium mining industry's future growth depended on the unlikely discovery of new gas reserves in the United States.

Other minerals mined by industry firms in the 1990s included pyrites, fluorspar, lithium carbonate, strontium, wollastonite, natural wollastonite, and natural iron oxide pigments. Major end uses for fluorspar included lead, silver, copper and gold smelting, aluminum manufacturing, high-octane gasoline production, enamel manufacturing, refrigerant, plastics, and insecticide production, the manufacture of opaque glass and colored cathedral glass, and steel production (a single ton of steel requires approximately seven pounds of fluorspar). Lithium compounds have historically been used in roughly 20 industrial applications, including the production of synthetic vitamins, the manufacture of special-purpose alloys, use in aluminum lithium composite alloys for commercial and military aircraft, and in nuclear energy applications, among other uses. Spodumene, lepidolite, and amblygonite were mined by industry firms primarily for their lithium content. Almost 70 percent of strontium consumed in the United States was used in the manufacture of X-ray-blocking faceplate glass for television picture tubes. Celestite and strontiate were strontium-based minerals also mined by this segment of the industry. Other minerals mined in comparatively small quantities by industry firms included arsenic, brimstone, alunite, guano, marcasite, mineral pigment, ocher, pyrrhotite, and umber.

Current Conditions

According to a report by IMC Global, a leading company in the industry, world events toward the end of the twentieth century seemed to indicate that a demand for mineral and chemical fertilizers would continue. The report cited in particular increased gross domestic product (GDP) rates in the United States (3.9 percent) and China (8 percent) that exceeded the worldwide GDP (2.5 percent) in 1998. IMC Global also cited predicted GDP increases in the United States, China, Japan, and India; speculating that increased economic growth, coupled with rising population pressures, would increase the demand for grains and meats. World population, which stood at 6 billion people in 1999, was predicted to reach

6.5 billion people by 2005. The report also noted strong farm financial conditions, as average annual growth of farms had increased almost 5 percent during the second half of the 1990s. But another IMC Global report, which focused on world grain production, stated that grain production at the end of the twentieth century was at its lowest amount in three years. While Congress helped farmers with supplemental farm income (government payments to American farmers were doubled during 1998), farm policy at the end of the 1990s allowed farmers flexibility to align planting decisions with market conditions. During 1998 and 1999, United States crop acreage was expected to decrease and crop nutrient consumption would remain the same or decrease slightly from the previous year.

World phosphate production rose 3 percent between 1997 to 1998, at 28 million tons. The United States accounted for 41 percent of the production. The United States remained a world leader in the export of concentrated phosphate export products; and 1998 exports showed an annual increase of 7 percent (at 12 million tons).

Global potash production increased 2 percent annually in 1998 at almost 26 million tons. North America remained the leader in producing and exporting potash products. North American offshore potash-related export dropped 8 percent between 1997 to 1998, and this trend was expected to continue. The consumption of potash was predicted to grow 12 percent up to the year 2002.

Salt production in North America increased 1 percent between 1997 to 1998, at 55.1 million tons. North America produced 28 percent of the world's salt. The United States exported 0.8 million tons and imported 9.3 million tons of salt in 1998.

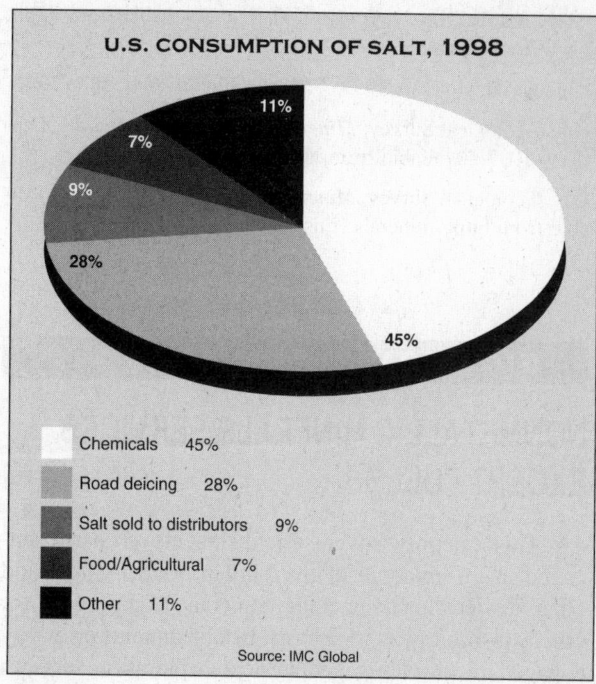

INDUSTRY LEADERS

The leader in the chemical and fertilizer minerals industry in the 1990s was Freeport-McMoran Inc., of Louisiana, with close to 8,000 employees and $957.5 million in 1996 sales. In addition to producing, distributing, and selling phosphate fertilizers—in which it was the leading U.S. firm—the company also explored for, mined, developed, produced, processed, transported, and marketed sulfur and other minerals, owned and operated laboratory and pilot plant facilities for analyzing minerals, performed metallurgical work, and conducted testing and research activities. Freeport-McMoran was founded in 1981 through the merger of Freeport Minerals Co. and McMoran Oil & Gas. To strengthen its mineral assets while lessening its dependence on the fertilizer market, in the 1980s CEO James Moffet had begun diversifying and expanding, investing more than $1 billion in new sulfur reserves, adding geothermal properties and oil and gas assets, and opening phosphate mines in Florida. In 1988, however, two major mineral discoveries—a gold, silver, and copper mine in New Guinea and the world's second-largest sulfur discovery in history in the Gulf of Mexico—compelled Moffet to change course. To pay for the development of these sites, it sold its geothermal properties and part of its oil and gas, fertilizer, and gold properties, betting that the two discoveries were worth the risk in company capital. Moffet's bold move depended for its success on a resurgence in mineral prices, however, that, by 1996, had not yet arrived, and a lawsuit filed by New Guinea tribesmen claiming Freeport-McMoran had violated their land and culture put a crimp in Moffet's strategy. One investment firm had downgraded Freeport-McMoran to a "neutral" rating over the company's "high-risk" strategy, and Rene L. Latiolais had replaced Moffet as the company's CEO. In 1997 Freeport-McMoran was acquired by IMC Global Inc. at a value of $748 million. The companies had collaborated in a prior partnership (IMC-Agrico) which made phosphate fertilizers. By the late 1990s IMC Global was the third largest world producer of salt (behind Rohm and Haas' Morgan Salt and Cargill, respectively). IMC Global had 1999 sales of $2.3 billion (a 12.1 percent annual sales growth) and employed 11,244 people in 1998.

FURTHER READING

"Agricultural Outlook," 1999. Available from http://www.imcglobal.com/generalinformation/agoutlookframe.html.

"Cargill Buys Akzo's Salt Business." *Chemical Week,* 21 August 1996.

"Crop Nutrients and Salt Situation." Available from http://www.imcglobal.com/generalinformation/cnss/word/Doc4overview.doc.

''IMC Global, Inc.'' *Hoover's Online.* Available from http://www.hoovers.com.

''Industrial Minerals 1995.'' *Mining Engineering,* June 1996.

U.S. Geological Survey. *Mineral Commodity Summaries,* February 1997. Available from http://minerals.er.usgs.gov.

U.S. Geological Survey. *Mineral Yearbook 1995,* 1996. Available from http://minerals.er.usgs.gov.

SIC 1481

NONMETALLIC MINERALS SERVICES, EXCEPT FUELS

This category covers establishments primarily engaged in the removal of overburden, strip mining, and other services for nonmetallic minerals, except fuels, for others on a contract or fee basis. Establishments primarily engaged in providing geophysical exploration services for metal mines are covered in **SIC 1081: Metal Mining Services.** Establishments primarily engaged in performing oil and gas field geological exploration services are covered in **SIC 1382: Oil and Gas Field Exploration Services.**

NAICS Code(s)

213115 (Support Activities for Non-metallic Minerals, (except Fuels))

541360 (Geophysical Surveying and Mapping Services)

In addition to performing contracted strip mining (19.0 percent of total industry receipts) and overburden removal (8.0 percent), industry firms performed general non-testing drilling and blasting (7.0 percent), miscellaneous mining services (3.5 percent), and prospect and test drilling (3.0 percent). Industry firms also offered geophysical exploration services, sank mine shafts, and drained and pumped mines—all on a contract basis and all within the nonmetallic minerals mining industry. However, almost 60 percent of the industry's total receipts derived from for-contract mineral services performed by firms classified as mining rather than mining services companies and from industry firms too small to be canvassed by the Bureau of the Census.

The U.S. nonmetallic minerals mining industry was traditionally considered highly capital intensive. Before a mining firm could begin to consider establishing a mine at a site suggested as potentially viable by geological literature and maps, a complex range of activities had to be undertaken to ensure that a workable deposit of economically viable mineral existed at the location. Extensive exploratory and assessment activities were conducted; highly detailed maps were made of the prospective deposit; and costly and sophisticated equipment was brought in to test, dig, develop, work, and maintain the mining operation. Because most costs at a mine are fixed, the more ore that can be processed lowers the producer's total cost per ton. High-volume, highly efficient mineral extraction is thus crucial, and contractors in the mineral services industry play a key role in this process. Because smaller mining firms either did not have the capital resources to perform exploration and extraction activities or wished to restrict themselves to the operational side of mining, they turned to independent contractors who specialized in the techniques and technologies of mineral geophysics and mine engineering to perform a broad range of mining support activities.

Projects performed by these nonmetallic minerals service contractors prior to the actual working of a mine included analyzing the surface geology for outcroppings or other indications of the underlying mineral, as well as conducting geophysical surveying or mapping operations using aerial photography, satellite imagery, or seismic, gravitational, magnetic, electric, or other methods of geological analysis. Drilling or boring test shafts (usually with an electrical, gas-powered, or pneumatic diamond drill) helped determine if a ''showing'' of a desired mineral was actually and extensively located at the site. The extracted cores or ''cuttings'' from these tests were used to gauge the quality, subsurface shape and variation, depth of overburden (unwanted mineral, soil, or rock covering the deposit), geographical extent, and potential processability of the mineral at a deposit.

When the precise range and nature of the deposit was documented, nonmetallic minerals service firms might also be contracted to develop the mine by sinking shafts, boring mine tunnels, stripping and removing overburden, or blasting the deposit face with explosives to dislodge the mineral from underground, an open pit, or a shallow strip mine. Industry firms might also be retained to perform the actual mining of the mineral or to develop or maintain the mine.

For example, many mines suffered from accumulation of subsurface water, surface runoff, or water associated with the mining operation itself. Industry contractors were often hired to install the draining or pumping infrastructure to prevent water from entering the operation and clear the mine of existing water levels. This facet of the industry activity alone could necessitate the installation and operation of a drainage system so complex that computer planning software would be required to assess the viability of networks containing as many as 20 drainage pumps, 50 regulators, and numerous line segments, valves, and fittings.

In the mid-1990s, the nonmetallic minerals services industry continued to benefit from advances in sensing, automation, and computer technology. New unmanned "walking machines" loaded with cameras, sensors, and measuring equipment have enabled researchers to explore inhospitable terrain remotely and may prove to have applications in the field of mineral exploration. An automatic mining machine was successfully tested in an underground coal mine in West Virginia in the mid-1990s, offering industry firms the potential to remotely investigate and then mine underground deposits without endangering their work force. Space-age sensing and mapping technology also enabled scientists to search for mineral deposits with much greater sensitivity and speed. The staggering growth in the power of computer microprocessors has also allowed scientists to collate and analyze enormous volumes of data about mineral structures, hazards, and resources that previously would have taken years to gather. By the mid-1990s, computer-controlled X-ray diffractometers could also determine a mineral's structure within a matter of minutes. The rapid advances in laser range-finding technology, three-dimensional digital mapping software, computer-aided design programs, and data acquisition and processing systems promised to give the mineral services industry new opportunities to provide the mining industry with precise data about the volume of material extracted, scrap volumes, topographical features of a deposit, and a host of other factors.

Among the largest firms in the industry in 1999 were Soil Sampling Service Inc. of Puyallup, Washington, and GZA Drilling Inc. of Brockton, Massachusetts. The nonmetallic minerals industry employed approximately 106,000 people in the late 1990s, indicating a steady increase since 1993, when employment reached the decade low of 101,500 people. Approximately 81,000 employees in 1996 worked in production areas, earning an average of $13.42 per hour, an increase of about 14 percent from 1990. By the mid-1990s, imports increased slightly to $540 million. Exports increased just 4 percent from 1994 to 1995, reaching $214 million.

FURTHER READING

Bemis, Bruce. "Laser Imaging, Software, Will Be Tool for Land Developers." *Birmingham Business Journal,* 3 June 1996.

"Bureau of the Census." *1997 Economic Census* 2000. Available from http://www.census.gov.

Matty, Jane M. "Technological Innovations." *Rocks & Minerals* January/February 1995.

Soil Sampling Service Inc. Company Profile. Puyullap, Washington: Soil Sampling Service, Inc.

Ward's Business Directory of U.S. Private and Public Companies. Detroit: Gale Research, 1999.

SIC 1499

MISCELLANEOUS NONMETALLIC MINERALS, EXCEPT FUELS

This category covers establishments that primarily mine, quarry, mill, or otherwise prepare nonmetallic minerals, except fuels. This industry includes shaping natural abrasive stones at the quarry. Establishments that primarily produce blast, grinding, or polishing sand are classified in **SIC 1446: Industrial Sand,** and those calcining gypsum are classified in **SIC 3275: Gypsum Products.**

NAICS CODE(S)

212319 (Other Crushed and Broken Stone Mining and Quarrying)

212399 (All Other Non-Metallic Mineral Mining)

Some of the most economically significant minerals mined by industry firms included garnet, gemstones, graphite, gypsum, industrial diamonds, perlite, and quartz. Other minerals produced include asbestos, asphalt, burrstone, calcite, catlinite, corundum, cryolite, diatomite, emery, fill dirt, gilsonite, greensand, Iceland spar, meerschaum, mica, millstone, oilstone, ozokerite, peat, pipestone, pozzolana, pumice, pyrophyllite, rubbing stone, scoria, scythestone, vermiculite, whetstone, wollastonite, and wurtzilite.

Garnet was used primarily for industrial applications, particularly as an abrasive or as a filtration medium. Of the world's industrial garnet output, just under a third was from the United States. Five U.S. companies—Barton Mines Corp., NYCO Minerals, Inc., Patterson Materials Corp., Emerald Creek Garnet Co., and Cominco American Inc.—produced a record high amount of about 74,000 metric tons of garnet in 1998 worth about $7.1 million. The United States was the largest consumer of industrial garnet in the world, and garnet was used for air/water blasting media (45 percent), water filtration (15 percent), abrasive powders (15 percent), and water jet cutting (7 percent), which used concentrated, high-pressure water jets for precision cutting of metals, composite materials, fabrics, and fiberglass. Demand for industrial garnet was expected to remain strong through the early part of the twenty-first century, and new facilities, expected to produce at least 120,000 tons, were planned or under construction in the late 1990s.

Minerals were defined as gemstones less by geological properties than by end use—any mineral or other material whose aesthetic qualities recommended it for decorative or ornamental uses could be called a gem stone. The terms precious and semiprecious described the relative economic value of gemstones and other minerals,

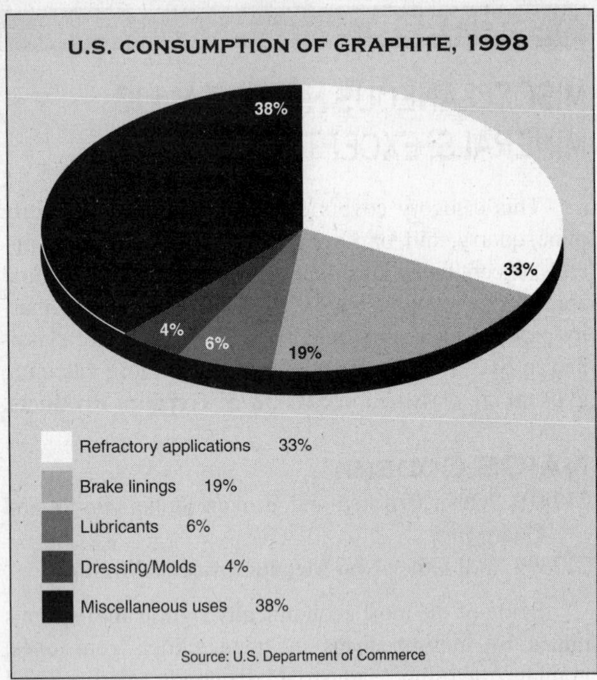

and most gemstones fell into the precious stone category, including: jade, corundum (rubies and sapphires), diamond, quartz (including amethyst and agate), garnet, turquoise, and several stones not mined by industry firms.

U.S. production of natural gemstones was valued to be at least $14.3 million in 1998. Though production of natural gem materials took place in every U.S. state, four states produced the majority of the total output in 1998: Tennessee, Arizona, California, and Oregon. The United States produced less than 1 percent of total global output. The United States, however, was the largest market for gemstones in the world, accounting for about 35 percent of world demand. Gem stone diamond production in the United States was virtually nil in 1998, as the nation's only commercial diamond mine, Kelsey Lake in Colorado, stopped production and was put up for sale.

Graphite is a soft, carbon-based mineral that is classified into two general types: natural and synthetic. Natural graphite is further subdivided into three types: flake, high-crystalline, and amorphous. In the late 1990s, natural graphite was used for refractory applications (33 percent), brake linings (19 percent), lubricants (6 percent), dressings and molds in foundry operations (4 percent), and miscellaneous uses (38 percent). Graphite consumption in the United States fell by 16 percent between 1997 and 1998, and about 200 manufacturing companies used natural graphite. The United States relied on imports from China, Mexico, Canada and Brazil for its natural graphite supply, since it was not mined domestically in 1998. The majority of amorphous graphite came from Mexico.

The United States was the largest producer and consumer of gypsum in the world, contributing 18 percent of world output in 1998. Of the estimated 31 million tons produced domestically, the majority was used for the manufacture of wallboard and plaster products. Gypsum was also used for cement production, agricultural applications, smelting, and glassmaking. Growth in the construction industry led to increased demand for wallboard in the late 1990s. The majority of crude gypsum was mined by three companies—U.S. Gypsum Co., Georgia-Pacific Corp., and National Gypsum Co.—though a total of 32 companies participated in crude gypsum mining.

Industrial diamonds were crystallized carbon of a quality and color unsuitable for decorative gem stone use. Industrial diamonds generally ranged from yellow-brown to black in color and because of their hardness, diamonds found applications in virtually every major manufacturing industry. The United States produced about 140 million carats in 1998 and was a leading producer of synthetic industrial diamonds. Du Pont Industrial Diamond Division and GE Superabrasives were the only two U.S. companies that produced synthetic industrial diamonds in 1998. The United States was also the leading consumer of industrial diamonds, and in 1998 consumption increased to a record high of 270 million carats. Industrial diamonds were used by such U.S. industries as construction, computer chip production, mining services, transportation systems, and machinery production.

In 1998, domestic processed perlite production was 688,000 tons with a value of $24.8 million. Eight companies operating 10 mines in six states in the West produced crude ore, with the majority of domestic production coming from New Mexico. The primary uses of perlite in the late 1990s included building construction (71 percent), horticultural aggregate (10 percent), filter aids (9 percent), and fillers (7 percent). Imports and exports of processed (sized and dried) and expanded perlite increased in 1998. The majority of exports were to Canada, and imports of processed perlite came primarily from Greece.

Quartz was one of the most common minerals that found many industrial and decorative applications. Large flawless quartz crystals were used to make radio circuits, radar, television, telephone circuits, ultrasonic equipment, and quartz oscillator plates in electronic products; as prisms, wedges, and lenses in optical spectrographs, microscopes, and other optical instruments; and as an abrasive in glass and refractory brick production. Crystalline quartz, including clear quartz, rose quartz, and yellow quartz, was used for decorative carvings and semiprecious stones. Amethyst and agate were quartzes used as gemstones.

Most of the quartz crystal used in the manufacture of electronics goods were cultured quartz crystals as opposed to natural crystals. The United States stopped mining lascas, which was used to produce cultured quartz crystals, in late 1997; however, four domestic companies continued to produce cultured quartz crystals using imported, mostly from Brazil, and reserved lascas. The continued growth of the U.S. consumer electronics market was expected to keep demand for quartz crystal strong.

FURTHER READING

Balazik, Ronald F. ''Diamond, Industrial.'' U.S. Department of the Interior. U.S. Geological Survey. 1998. Available from http://minerals.er.usgs.gov.

''Garnet, Industrial.'' U.S. Department of the Interior. U.S. Geological Survey. 1998. Available from http://minerals.er.usgs.gov.

''Gemstones.'' U.S. Department of the Interior. U.S. Geological Survey. 1998. Available from http://minerals.er.usgs.gov.

''Gypsum.'' U.S. Department of the Interior. U.S. Geological Survey. 1998. Available from http://minerals.er.usgs.gov.

Bolen, Wallace P. ''Perlite.'' U.S. Department of the Interior. U.S. Geological Survey. 1998. Available from http://minerals.er.usgs.gov.

Kalyoncu, Rustu S. ''Graphite.'' U.S. Department of the Interior. U.S. Geological Survey. 1998. Available from http://minerals.er.usgs.gov.

U.S. Department of the Interior. U.S. Geological Survey. *Mineral Commodity Summaries.* January 1999. Available from http://minerals.er.usgs.gov.

CONSTRUCTION INDUSTRIES

SIC 1521

GENERAL CONTRACTORS—SINGLE-FAMILY HOUSES

The category covers general contractors primarily engaged in construction activities (including new work, additions, alterations, remodeling, and repair) of single-family houses.

NAICS CODE(S)

233210 (Single-Family Housing Construction)

INDUSTRY SNAPSHOT

Traditionally quite fragmented, the single-family home-contracting industry consolidated rapidly throughout the mid- and late 1990s. However, by 1998 the industry leader, Pulte Corporation, still accounted for only 2.3 percent of new housing starts, while the top 100 firms accounted for just 28 percent. According to the 1997 census, the industry consisted of 116,537 establishments that employed 570,990 workers whose work was valued at $78.5 billion.

The single-family home construction industry comprises general contractors that are primarily engaged in building, remodeling, and repairing houses. Included in this industry classification are prefabricated housing assembled on-site and town-house construction. The single-family home construction industry is vital to the U.S. economy; in addition to supplying jobs, tax revenue, and housing for Americans, the single-family construction industry also serves as an important indicator of the nation's economic health and general standard of living.

That feature was exceptionally welcome to contractors in the late 1990s as the raging stock market and strong economy created strong demand for new homes. The sustained surge in housing starts, which began in 1992 and continued through 1999, was made possible by an improved national economic picture and low interest rates. However, at the turn of turn of the twenty-first century, a rise in interest rates cut into single-family home starts, where growth rates had already begun to slow, especially among low-end housing. Wealthier home buyers were less affected by interest rate increases, further emphasizing a trend toward more expensive homes. Fixed mortgage interest rates had declined for most of the 1990s before rebounding in 1999.

The rate of home ownership reached a record 67 percent of U.S. households in 1999, a figure that was expected to reach 70 percent by 2010. However, declining numbers of people will be entering the prime home-buying ages of 25 to 45 following the aging of the baby boomers during that period. Moreover, a decreasing proportion of this age bracket was purchasing homes; despite rising income levels among those 25 to 45, more people than ever opted to live in apartments. This shift was attributed mostly to lifestyle changes among younger people entering the housing market, who tended to prefer living in proximity to entertainment venues and shopping.

Furthermore, the rising costs of land, labor, and materials were among the primary challenges to single-family homebuilders at the close of the 1990s. Drywall and lumber prices, which tend to be somewhat unstable, were particularly inflated, while increases in land costs have been less pronounced, though some strong markets, especially in southern cities, have experienced significant escalation. The shortage of skilled labor, meanwhile, was viewed by some analysts as the most pressing concern facing the industry as it entered the twenty-first century.

ORGANIZATION AND STRUCTURE

The single-family housing construction industry is unique for an industry of its size because it is highly fragmented and dispersed. The typical home is built by a contractor that produces fewer than 25 houses each year, while about half of all industry employees work at firms with less than 20 workers. While some larger contractors maintain building operations in a number of sectors, about 75 percent of establishments engage only in single-family housing construction. These firms also account for 55 percent of industry employees.

Nonetheless, in alignment with most industries in the 1990s, single-family construction was rapidly consolidating. The top construction firms on *Builder* magazine's ''Builder 100'' list have continued to expand their market share throughout the decade, particularly toward the late 1990s. The top five single-family contractors have accelerated their market share the fastest, achieving 30 percent of the top 100's share in 1997, compared with 21 percent two years earlier. Altogether, the five largest contractors generated revenues of $14.9 billion in 1998, up from $11.3 billion in 1997.

The relative, though diminishing, lack of concentration in the industry reflects the labor intensity and logistical complexity characteristic of on-site homebuilding. Regional and state building codes, trade unions, demographics, and environmental regulations combine to make the competitive structure of each local market unique. Many workers from various trades must be coordinated to complete a home. Moreover, many construction materials are less expensive when purchased regionally. Finally, the localized nature of housing markets prohibits many national economies of scale.

Over the last two decades, the south and west have proved the most fertile ground for new housing construction. The leading states for single-family construction in 1997 were California, with 13,000 establishments generating sales of $18.1 billion; and Florida, with 6,740 establishments engaging in work valued at $12.1 billion. Other leading states included Michigan, New York, and Texas.

Large contracting companies that do compete nationally are often relatively decentralized—consisting of generally autonomous regional operating companies. The various units of the corporation benefit from financial strength, as well as geographic and market diversification. The few contractors that compete overseas usually do so through foreign-owned subsidiaries. Although U.S. manufacturers sell and ship significant amounts of manufactured housing to countries such as Mexico, the homes themselves are usually assembled and finished by foreign contractors.

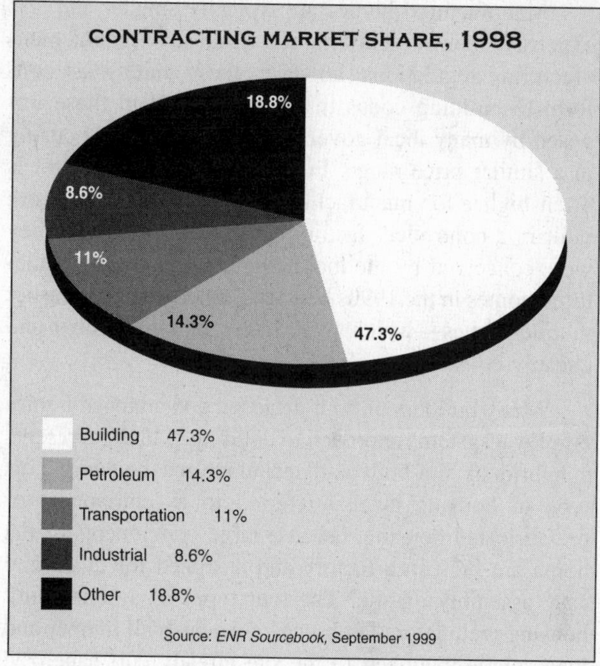

General contractors in the industry operate in a variety of ways. Some contractors actually purchase property and perform all construction work themselves. In other cases, a general contractor may be hired by a developer or landowner to provide construction services. General contractors commonly subcontract some, or a majority of, building activities to other firms. In any case, the general contractor is ultimately responsible for the finished product.

Products and Services. Two broad categories of homes are constructed or assembled on-site by the industry—attached and detached. Attached homes, commonly called town houses, can be owned by their occupants rather than rented. They are similar in construction to some apartment rental complexes, but town houses are separated from adjoining units by a ground-to-roof wall. In contrast to rental facilities, attached homes also have completely separate utilities and do not share infrastructure.

Detached homes are usually built on a lot that is owned by the same party that possesses the house. They typically have front, back, and side yards and are more expensive that attached homes. In 1998, 1.03 million detached homes were constructed, accounting for more than 90 percent of the single-family market. Approximately 8 percent of these homes were manufactured houses, which means that they were almost completely manufactured off-site, shipped to a lot, and assembled by a general contractor. Only the on-site assemblage of the home is classified as a single-family home construction activity.

Manufactured homes are typically smaller and less expensive than site-built homes. Because of federal manufacturing regulations, however, these units must conform to building codes that are stricter than those imposed by many local governments for site-built housing in a similar price range. Furthermore, quality control is often higher for manufactured homes because they are built in a controlled, factory environment. Though they were conceived by the mobile home industry, manufactured homes in the 1990s bear little resemblance to earlier mobile homes—which were often temporary-sited and cheaply constructed.

Many builders of both detached and attached homes employ a systems approach to building, which represents a hybrid of site-built and manufactured housing. This type of housing is also referred to as component or prefabricated housing, because large components of the home are built in a factory and designed for quick and easy assembly on-site. The four types of systems-built housing include pre-cut homes, for which all lumber and materials are shipped to the site already cut; panelized homes, for which the main wall panels are shipped to the site—often with plumbing and wiring already installed; sectional homes, which are more than 90 percent complete when they leave the factory and have cabinets and flooring already installed; and log homes, which are essentially factory made kit homes. Furthermore, half of the new, larger manufactured homes currently built are placed on privately owned, scattered building sites and into housing subdivisions.

In addition to new home construction, single-family home contractors also are engaged in maintenance-and-repair and home improvement work. Maintenance and repair included painting, mudjacking, replacement of appliances, and similar work. Improvements consisted of additions and alterations to existing structures involving major interior and exterior changes. Replacement of major items such as furnaces and water heaters are also considered home improvements. Americans spent a record $121 billion on home improvements in 1998. As baby boomers reach middle age, Americans are staying in their homes longer than they did previously. The median number of years Americans remain in one home is now 13 versus 10 a decade ago. Nearly two-thirds of the dollars Americans spend on home improvements are targeted for optional upgrades, such as kitchens, bathrooms, and family rooms, rather than for repair work. In 1989, the split was approximately 50-50.

Financial Market Influence. The single-family home construction industry is extremely susceptible to changes in economic factors and financial markets. There is a significant and direct negative correlation, for example, between federally controlled interest rates and the volume of new homes under construction. When the interest rate attainable on mortgage loans is low, housing starts are relatively high because of increased affordability. For example, a $100,000, 15-year home loan requires a buyer to make monthly payments of $899 per month when the interest rate is fixed at seven percent. When the interest rate rises to 12 percent, however, that monthly payment jumps to $1,200. In such an environment, builders will have to offer incentives to increase sales. As a result, the housing industry, like mortgage rates, is highly cyclical.

In addition to interest rates, contractors are also affected by consumers' access to capital. For this reason, several government sponsored enterprises, as well as private companies, make up the secondary mortgage market. This market consists of investors who buy mortgages from primary lenders, such as banks and thrifts, so that the lenders can use that money to make new loans. By backing mortgage loans, as well as mortgage securities created from pools of loans, the government helps to insure a steady supply of capital to build, maintain, and improve housing.

Background and Development

During the nineteenth and early twentieth centuries, when a large majority of Americans lived in rural areas, people who could afford to build a home often acted as the general contractor in the construction of their own home. They hired local builders and tradesmen with money that they had saved or borrowed from family members. Few regulations existed to insure structural soundness or safety of new homes, and little long-term financing existed for prospective homeowners. Indeed, by the time the Great Depression hit, less than half of all U.S. families owned a home.

In an effort to increase home ownership, the Federal Housing Administration (FHA) was created in 1934. By insuring home mortgages, the FHA made it possible for banks to make relatively low interest loans to home buyers. By the early 1940s, Americans were building about 100,000 new homes each year. Outdated and often lacking basics such as indoor plumbing and electricity, however, nearly half of the homes in the nation were considered substandard. Furthermore, most families still could not afford to buy a home, choosing instead to rent housing or live with family members. In 1942 the United States home ownership rate stood at approximately 46 percent.

The housing environment began a radical transformation in the mid-1940s for several reasons. Most important, much of the demand that had existed for new housing during World War II had gone unmet as the country poured its resources into fighting a war. When soldiers returned home and started families, housing demand ballooned even further. The number of U.S. births leapt from less than 3 million in 1945 to about 3.75 million in 1947.

Coinciding with the jump in demand was the development of the Veterans Administration Home Loan Guaranty Program in 1944. Using a Veterans Administration (VA) loan, war veterans were able to obtain mortgage loans with little or no down payment. Besides insuring VA and FHA loans, the federal government also set a maximum interest rate that lenders could charge. Credit and tax policies, such as tax-deductible mortgage interest payments, were also used by the government to spur home ownership. Furthermore, the National Housing Act of 1949 set a national goal of providing ''a decent home and suitable living environment for every U.S. family.'' As a result of government incentives and strong demand, both single and multi-family housing starts boomed—skyrocketing from 139,000 in 1944 to 1.9 million by 1950.

Throughout the 1950s and 1960s as the postwar economy flourished, families flocked to the housing market in a buying frenzy. Thousands of tract subdivisions were built on the perimeter of urban America—typically offering quality detached homes for less than $10,000 in the 1950s, with mortgage payments of less than $100 per month. Indeed, during the 1950s and 1960s an entire suburban culture emerged. Enormous street grids with identical homes in the early 1950s soon gave way to more elaborate and attractive neighborhood layouts that offered a variety of cape cod and ranch style home designs. Split-level homes and garages also became dominant features in many communities.

In addition to the rise in the number of U.S. homes in the 1950s and 1960s, housing quality improved. Besides new federal and state regulations that mandated structural integrity and uniform infrastructure, new construction techniques increased home quality and affordability. Component construction, for instance, let builders efficiently erect large numbers of units. Plywood replaced expensive boards and drywall was introduced as an improvement to lath and plaster construction. Portable generators, power trowels, backhoes, and other heavy equipment allowed contractors to realize massive productivity gains. Although less than 2 percent of homes in 1960 had air-conditioning, almost all new homes sported indoor plumbing, central heat, electricity, and gas. Furthermore, most newer homes in the 1960s had more than one bathroom.

Despite cyclical downturns caused by interest rates and energy prices, the housing industry remained healthy throughout the 1960s and 1970s. For instance, although single-family housing starts dropped by 50 percent in 1966 to about 800,000, they peaked in 1972 at about 1.3 million. After falling to approximately 850,000 in 1975, housing starts rose to more than 1.4 million in 1977. Despite increasing land and construction costs, housing starts in general surged in the 1970s as baby boomers matured and began buying homes. In the 1970s, housing prices outran inflation by an average of 3 percent per year. By 1980 the U.S. home ownership rate had risen to more than 65 percent.

While the number of Americans owning their own home had steadily risen during the 1970s, housing quality and construction productivity also advanced. Fiberglass and plastic products—used for everything from bathroom fixtures and plumbing to siding—helped to allay the impact of rising material and energy costs. Furthermore, by 1979 the share of new homes that offered central air-conditioning had risen to more than 60 percent. Most important, rising energy costs had caused builders to increase the efficiency of their products with better windows and doors, insulation, and heating and cooling equipment.

The 1980s and 1990s. Although contractors began construction on nearly 1.2 million new homes in 1979, the industry was devastated in the early 1980s by soaring interest rates. As mortgage rates skyrocketed past 16 percent, housing starts collapsed to 705,000 in 1981 and then to only 663,000 during 1982. Many builders filed for bankruptcy in the severely depressed market. Contractors that survived the shakeout, however, were greeted by falling interest rates in 1983 that continued through 1987. Single-family housing starts lurched 62 percent in 1983, to about 1.1 million. Throughout the mid-1980s, in fact, new home construction inched upward to nearly 1.2 million starts by 1986.

Despite apparently healthy construction activity in the 1980s, single-family home contractors were failing to achieve growth rates attained in the three previous decades. Several factors indicated that the industry was declining. Of immense importance, the affordability of housing for younger buyers began slipping—after peaking in 1980. Although the total home ownership rate only declined from 65.6 percent in 1980 to 63.9 percent in 1990, the rate for the population in the 30 to 34 age bracket plummeted from 61.1 percent to 51.8 percent. Furthermore, the ownership rate for 35- to 39-year-olds fell from 70.9 percent to 69.8 percent during the 1980s. The ownership rate for the 25- to 29-year-old age bracket recessed even more.

To make matters worse, housing starts began slowly declining in 1987 as interest rates edged upward and the U.S. economy began to fall into a recession. Despite the government's lowering of mortgage rates in 1990, housing starts quickly plummeted to 895,000 in 1990 and to only 840,000 in 1991. In addition, contractors were also battling rising expenses associated with burdensome regulations and material costs. Although the generally distressed industry forced many builders across the nation into bankruptcy, contractors in some regions of the country fared much worse than others.

After a five-year decline in housing starts—one of the longest in U.S. history—the single-family home construction industry experienced a relatively weak recovery in 1992. The early 1990s housing slump differed from past slowdowns, since the recession in the early 1990s hit upper and middle-income white-collar wage earners—the bulk of the housing market—the hardest. Earlier recessions had a greater impact on blue-collar workers (who are more likely to rent). In addition to job losses, construction loans for builders remained suppressed throughout the early 1990s. Total construction lending by commercial banks, for instance, declined more than 40 percent between 1989 and 1992. Small construction companies that supply the large majority of U.S. homes were especially crunched by tight credit.

Contractors were especially disappointed by weak growth in 1991 and 1992 in remodeling and repair expenditures, which are traditionally relatively impervious to cyclical downturns. Although new home construction generally drives the industry, remodeling and repair contracts had grown during the 1980s to account for more than 45 percent of the value of all single-family home construction.

CURRENT CONDITIONS

One impetus for the rapid consolidation of the single-family home-contracting industry was the parallel consolidation that has characterized lumber and building material (LBM) dealers. Builders recognized that by pooling resources they were more easily able to demand better pricing deals, thus maintaining leverage over suppliers. LBM dealers followed suit following the same logic, thus producing a self-replicating trend. While small, localized contractors tend to enjoy relative stability in their immediate markets, mid-sized contractors found it increasingly difficult to establish economies of scale. Thus the mid- and late 1990s witnessed these firms' increasing absorption into their larger competitors, who were more capable of hedging against increases in material and labor costs, the prime factors holding the single-family home construction market in check in the late 1990s. Analysts agree that the wave of consolidation is not likely to break in the near future. Smaller and niche custom builders can remain healthy, however, especially as long as the vigorous economy continues.

The industry's previous stabs at consolidation were less than spectacular, with firms quickly realizing diminishing returns after 10,000 homes built. Leading firms in the late 1990s combated this tendency by decentralizing managerial structures to allow for greater autonomy at the local levels within the organization.

The market for professional remodeling continued its strong showing for the 1990s, worth $40 billion in 1998 and expected to reach $45 billion by 2003. A good portion of this success owed to demographic trends. Whereas the home building market of the early 1990s was driven by the tendency for consumers to "downsize" to smaller homes, particularly as baby boomers' "empty nests" led them to abandon their larger homes, the strong economy of the late 1990s produced many more customers for building additions and remodeling.

Factory-built homes also registered strong growth. These buildings, alternately called systems-built or modular homes, incorporate building methods that are virtually identical to those of standard detached homes, but that occur in a factory, thus avoiding weather-related delays. Modular homes are shipped to the site in fewer than ten pieces before construction is finished on-site. Modular homes often weigh as much as 30 percent more than conventional homes. Most modular homes can be completed in 30 to 60 days; however, they are still a small market sector, totaling only 8 percent of all homes built in 1997.

In 1998, the average interest rates on 30-year fixed-rate mortgages fell to 6.94 percent, down from 8.36 percent in 1994 to reach the lowest level since the early 1960s. Mortgage originations reached a record $1.5 trillion. As a result, more households could claim the income necessary to purchase their own home. The housing market has thus responded in kind. Meanwhile, houses themselves continued to grow. The average new home in 1999 covered 2,190 square feet, compared to 1,645 square feet in 1975 and 2,095 in 1995. An estimated 31 million homes exceeded 2,400 square feet or larger by 1998. The average size of a single-family home lot was 13,795 square feet. The median home price in 2000 was $135,000.

Finally, the growing numbers of new homes also included a greater range of features. In 1997, about 82 percent of new homes had central air-conditioning and 78 percent had at least a two-car garage; 50 percent of the homes had at least 2.5 bathrooms and about 69 percent had fewer than four bedrooms; about 80 percent of all new homes were built in metropolitan areas. Thirteen percent lacked garages or car ports; but 61 percent were equipped with a fireplace, 37 percent with a basement, and half had two or more floors. Nearly two-thirds were fueled by gas, 32.2 percent by electricity, and only 2.7 percent by oil.

Regional Differences. Despite strong overall business in the single-family housing industry, some regions experienced stronger growth rates in housing starts in the late 1990s. In 1999, sales increased in all regions except the northeast. Midwest housing sales increased by 5 percent, while those in the south and west experienced a 2 percent growth. Total housing starts in 1997 were broken down by region as follows: the south started 630,000 new home projects, the west 335,000, the Midwest 292,000, and the northeast 127,000. The generally more built northeastern market faced higher taxes relating to land development and building. Seventy-five percent of households in the rural United States are homeowners.

Rising Costs. Escalating construction costs, attributable to a variety of factors, were a primary cause of declining home ownership among younger Americans in the mid- and late 1990s. One reason that costs were rising was a jump in the price of land, materials, and labor necessary to build homes. The cost of materials for single-family home contractors totaled $42 billion in 1997. In addition, more restrictive land regulations increased land costs, largely a result of emerging anti-growth initiatives to combat urban sprawl and environmental degradation that have reached U.S. legislatures. In general, land prices have increased less dramatically than those for building materials, though stronger markets have achieved double-digit growth. Meanwhile, indeed, costs associated with new impact fees, building codes, environmental rules, safety laws, and other regulations were increasingly squeezing contractors, especially mid-sized firms.

Builders also suffered from bloated costs associated with the tight labor market and the scramble to find a shrinking number of skilled laborers, including managerial workers. In addition to wages, the cost of complying with federal worker safety regulations in the late 1990s often exceeded $1,000 for a 2,200 square foot home.

After the deregulation of the thrifts, the traditional source of financing for home builders, culminated in the Savings & Loan crisis of the 1980s and 1990s, home builders were forced to seek alternative financial sources. In recent years, they have tended to settle on the stock and bond mortgages, where the lucrative business in the 1990s is expected to cool but remain stable in the early 2000s. This development has been particularly beneficial to large firms with greater capital pools and the geographic reach to concentrate business in regions with strong local economies.

Future Expectations. Along with the overall economy, the U.S. single-family home-construction market was expected to cool from its robust growth in the early 2000s. Total housing starts were at 1.47 million units for 2000, a decline from 1999's 1.65 million. Single-family starts are expected to be 1.145 million, down from 1.245 million in 1999.

While an aging population was expected to prove a boon to housing construction well into the 2000s, fewer younger people were entering the single-family housing market. Moreover, younger professionals were increasingly opting to live in apartment complexes. The homeownership rate among those aged 25 to 34 was expected to remain fixed at about 45.6 percent until 2010. For those between the ages of 35 to 44, the rate was likely to increase only marginally, from 66.1 percent in 2000 to 67.9 percent in 2010. The expected rate improves among older demographics. Meanwhile, minority groups watched their homeownership rate increase; about 45 percent of all African-American households were homeowners in 1998, up from 43 percent in 1994; while Hispanics' homeownership rate increased from 42 percent to 45 percent in that period. Contractors were expected to rely heavily on minorities and immigrants to fuel the single-family homebuilding market in the early 2000s.

With fewer households forming, it would seem likely that housing starts would, in turn, be affected negatively. While the new household projections from the Census Bureau seem to justify a lower level of housing starts, the housing market is more complicated than a simple one-to-one relationship with household formations. For example, regional shifts in the population require that homes be constructed where the population is moving. In the 1990s, there was a dramatic population shift toward the South and West, a trend expected to accelerate in the 2000s. This movement will justify a larger number of starts in these areas than the national household statistics might suggest.

INDUSTRY LEADERS

The largest builder of single-family detached homes in the United States in 1995 was Pulte Corporation, headquartered in Arlington, Virginia. Pulte employed 4,600 employees. The firm broke new ground in 1998 by constructing more than 20,000 homes, closing a total of 20,359, in 1998 on its way to revenues of $3.6 billion. The company's 43 years of unbroken profitability was an extraordinary accomplishment in such a cyclical industry.

Centex Corporation achieved revenues of $4.75 billion in 1998, though not all of this derived from the single-family homebuilding sector. Established in 1950, Centex employs 11,000 workers and also engages in financial services related to construction.

Kaufman & Broad Home Corporation, founded in 1957, acquired seven homebuilders between 1996 and 1999, positioning itself as one of the leading single-family housing contractors with a payroll of 3,500 employees. Like Pulte, Kaufman & Broad topped the 20,000 mark for new home starts in 1998, while bringing in revenues of $3.7 billion.

Other leading single-family home contractors included D.R. Horton, with 1998 revenues of $2.4 billion and 2,750 employees; Lennar Corp., with $2.41 billion in sales and 4,100 workers; Ryland Group, with sales of $1.77 billion; and U.S. Home Corporation, with $1.5 billion in revenues in 1998.

Workforce

About 571,000 workers were involved in single-family construction in 1998, including 368,000 construction workers, who earned an average of $16.50 an hour. In the overall construction industry, there were about 250,000 construction managers, approximately one-fifth of which were self-employed and earned an average of $28,000 per year, though experienced managers sometimes earned up to $100,000.

Research and Technology

Housing contractors have been quick to incorporate the latest technology into their operations. In the late 1990s, the use of computer-aided design (CAD) and "virtual models" to optimize design and construction greatly streamlined the building process.

Steel producers were aggressively positioning themselves to establish inroads in the construction market. While only 50,000 steel-framed homes were built in 1997, the steel industry is aiming for a 25 percent market share by 2003. Steel costs are generally higher than those for wood (about $3,000 more for a 2,000 square-foot home). However, while wood prices were rising quickly in the late 1990s and generally tend to fluctuate, steel prices remain fairly stable.

Industry advances in productivity and technology since World War II created vast improvements in the quality, integrity, and comfort of housing. The percentage of new homes with more than 2,400 square feet, for example, increased from 11 percent in 1977 to 31 percent by 1997. During the same period, the percentage of new houses with a garage for two or more cars jumped from 60 percent to 78 percent. Likewise, 50 percent of all new homes had two-and-a-half or more bathrooms in 1995, compared to 23 percent in 1977, while central air conditioning was featured in 82 percent of new homes, up from 54 percent in 1977.

Builders have also been able to improve housing through the use of cheaper and stronger materials, such as plastics and alloys. Bathtubs and sinks made of cultured marble generated huge savings for buyers. Integrated energy and communications systems have allowed significant gains in energy efficiency. Between 1980 and 1987, new systems and insulation helped to decrease average household energy consumption from about 140 million BTUs to less than 120. Other amenities, such as electric garage openers and security systems, have added to home quality as well.

Further Reading

Demaster, Sarah. "Report Says Americans Spending More on Homes." *National Home Center News,* 8 March 1999.

Goch, Lynna. "Home Improvement." *Best's Review Property/Casualty Edition,* September 1999.

"Homeward Bound." *Forecast,* July 1999.

Maynard, Roberta, and Rebecca DePietropaolo. "Big Builders Break Away." *Builder,* May 1999.

"NAR: Study Show Need for Continued Home Ownership Efforts." *National Mortgage News,* 16 August 1999.

Rebane, Kirk A. "Determining Worth in the Consolidation Era." *National Home Center News,* 9 August 1999.

"Residential Builders Cater to Baby-Boomers Eager to 'Do Your Own Thing'." *Philadelphia Inquirer,* 28 February 1999.

Thomas, Karen. "Johnson: Homeownership Will Grow Over Next Decade to New High of 70 percent." *National Mortgage News,* 22 November 1999.

U.S. Department of Commerce. Bureau of the Census. *1997 Economic Census-Construction Series.* Washington, D.C.: GPO, 29 November 1999.

U.S. Department of Commerce. International Trade Administration. *United States Industry & Trade Outlook 1999.* New York: The McGraw Hill Companies, 1999.

"Virginia-Based Nationwide Homes Builds on Success in Modular Homes." *Roanoke Times,* 7 June 1999.

SIC 1522

GENERAL CONTRACTORS—RESIDENTIAL BUILDINGS, OTHER THAN SINGLE-FAMILY

This industry consists of general contractors primarily engaged in the construction of residential buildings other than single family homes. This type of construction includes new work, additions, alterations, remodeling, and repair of such establishments as apartment buildings, dormitories, and hotels and motels.

NAICS Code(s)

233320 (Commercial and Institutional Building Construction)

233220 (Multi-Family Housing Construction)

Industry Snapshot

Multifamily residential construction enjoyed strong sales and a promising market for new projects in the late 1990s as the U.S. economy maintained its voracious expansion. The industry was composed of 7,544 establishments that employed nearly 60,000 workers, including 40,100 construction workers, and produced annual shipment values of $20 billion. Demand for multifamily housing was expected to increase by one percent annually until 2010.

After apartment construction outpaced demand through the early and mid-1990s, resulting in increased vacancy rates, contractors were forced to scale back new starts and derive greater shares of revenue from remodeling and repairs, a market that was expected to maintain its strong growth for years to come. By the end of the decade, however, demand had resurfaced, leading a resurgence of new building activity. Revenues for new apartment buildings totaled $11.5 billion in 1998, while additions, alterations, and reconstruction garnered $2.5 billion. Maintenance and repair brought builders an additional $739 million. The total value of work for other residential buildings was $338 million.

Hotel construction, meanwhile, continued its recovery from the economic recession of the early 1990s. A notoriously volatile sector, construction spending reeled from the recession, dropping 35 percent in 1991 and another 47 percent in 1992. By 1995 the sector had dusted itself off and regained its healthy position in the construction industry, reaching $6.4 billion. Total spending for hotel construction reached $17.0 billion in 1999, up from $14.9 billion in 1998, and was particularly strong in the luxury hotel market. Analysts familiar with gluts in this market sector expected that building would cool along with the U.S. economic expansion in 2000, when total spending was estimated to reach $15.4 billion. Costs for luxury-hotel development rose more quickly than for mid-scale and economy lodging facilities, increasing 5 percent in 1998, while occupancy rates declined. However, the luxury sector was not expected to be overbuilt until the mid-2000s.

Leading multifamily construction markets in 1999 were located mostly in the South or West: Dallas, Texas; Orlando, Florida; Houston, Texas; Atlanta, Georgia; and Seattle, Washington. Hotel construction, meanwhile, has been strongest in the Pacific and mid-Atlantic regions, while trailing off in the south, central, and mountain regions. The states with the greatest concentration of multifamily construction companies included New York, with 1,017 establishments employing 4,700 workers and receiving revenues of $1.23 billion; California, with 736 establishments enjoying sales of $1.10 billion and employing 3,900; Florida, with 4,728 workers in 485 establishments generating revenues of $2.35 billion; and Texas, where $1.02 billion in sales were raked in by 2,300 employees working for 325 establishments.

The rising costs of land, labor, and materials were among the primary challenges to multifamily contractors at the close of the 1990s. Drywall and lumber prices were particularly alarming, while increases in land costs have been less pronounced, though some strong markets, especially in southern cities, have experienced significant escalation.

Organization and Structure

General contractors are licensed professionals who agree to arrange a project in agreement with certain plans, specifications, and other related documents. A written contract usually documents the specific terms. The responsibility of a general contractor extends to every aspect of construction, except those items so designated within the contract documents. General contractors are frequently referred to as builders; however, a developer or owner is also commonly referred to as a builder. Therefore, for purposes of understanding, a general contractor is one who contracts with owners to construct the owners' projects.

Multi-unit housing consists of two or more unit structures and includes apartment buildings, dormitories, condominiums, and some townhouses. Apartments constitute approximately 90 percent of all multi-unit construction. Multi-unit construction experienced unexpectedly strong sales in the late 1990s relative to single-family detached homes, despite a strong economy that would normally favor single-family home purchases.

This industry also includes companies that provide maintenance and repairs, as well as new construction improvements to existing buildings. In general, improvement refers to additions and alterations involving major interior and exterior changes to existing residential structures, and the replacement of major individual items such as furnaces and water heaters.

Establishments engaged in the erection of residential prefabricated buildings (except single-family structures) are also included in this industry. Prefabricated buildings are those that are built with various forms of factory-made items, ranging from simple components (for example, roof trusses, wall panels, and prehung doors and windows) to three-dimensional, 95-percent complete modular units. These buildings are constructed from wood **SIC 2452: Prefabricated Wood Buildings and Components** or metal **SIC 3448: Prefabricated Metal Buildings and Components.** Such structures were gaining popularity in the mid- and late 1990s as improved technology, materials, and building processes eliminated much of the negative public perception formerly associated with pre-fabricated housing.

A knowledge of the legal aspect of the construction business is a critical component in understanding this complex industry. Construction contractors operate under a significant amount of federal, state, and local regulation, and thus often utilize members of the legal profession. The attorney a contractor selects must be experienced and have complete knowledge of contract law with particular reference to laws that affect contracts between general contractors, owners, and subcontractors. In fact, due to the complex and diversified components inherent in the general contracting business, one attorney often cannot handle all legal requirements of a general contractor. The various arenas of law that impact general contractors that may require legal representation include negotiations, preparing and reviewing contracts, labor law, lien laws, bankruptcy laws, litigation, corporate structure, and general counsel. The extent of the contractor's general business operations and the legal issues regarding individual projects should be the determining factors when a contractor elects to use more than one legal firm or attorney. Attorney services are needed for almost every step of the construction process. Therefore, the choice of a competent general contracting attorney is often one of the most crucial decisions a general contractor can make.

Another aspect of the legal portion of general contracting is the vast array of government laws. These laws include both local and area laws. Examples of such laws include laws relating to the inspection and approval of works, the acceptance of plans, the use of certain materials, the conditions under which labor may be employed, and health and safety regulations. Moreover, equipment that comes on site has to be certified safe for use under the conditions of use.

Many large contractors have organized their own legal department, usually employing lawyers that are experts in construction law. These legal departments will often perform many of the functions described above that are necessary for a general contractor to operate their business.

Current Conditions

Demographic and lifestyle trends favored the multifamily residential construction industry in the late 1990s. Despite rising income levels among the prime home-buying age group (25 to 45), more people than ever opted to live in apartments; in fact, the fastest-growing financial-demographic group for apartments was made up of individuals who earn more than $50,000 per year. This shift is attributed mostly to lifestyle changes among younger people entering the housing market, who tended to prefer living in proximity to entertainment venues and shopping. Moreover, the faster pace of living among young professionals helped spark a preference to avoid the continuous upkeep associated with detached homes. To accommodate these developments, multifamily housing facilities increasingly feature such amenities as swimming pools, fitness centers, and gardens. Apartment starts totaled 261,000 units in 1998. For contractors, high-rise apartments experienced the highest expense increase in 1998, at 6.1 percent; in contrast, low-rise expenses increased by only 1.7 percent. For all building types in 1998, rental-unit starts totaled 286,000, achieving sound levels after the unsustainable highs of the late 1980s.

Older customers also wielded tremendous influence on construction activity, as assisted-living housing facilities exploded in the late 1990s. In 1998, construction reached 32,600 units, up 46 percent from 1997; an additional 31,300 units were produced in 1999. However, most analysts expected that the boom was at an end by 2000. Prices per unit skyrocketed as well, from a median of $39,755 in 1993 to $86,667 in 1995. Florida, California, and Texas were the leading markets for assisted-living housing, accounting for 28 percent of the national total in 1999.

Another market fueling multifamily residential housing construction was low-income housing, spurred by tax-exempt municipal bonds and housing tax credits, which finance multifamily building. Private-activity multifamily housing bond issues skyrocketed from $322.0 million in 1992 to $2.3 billion in 1998. Meanwhile, helping to hedge against some of the more dramatic market swings, particularly those relating to land costs and occupancy rates, was the growing popularity of real estate investment trusts (REITs), which were expected to help stave off a financial windfall in the case of a market glut.

Industry Leaders

While contractors in this industry tend to be rather small with limited market reach, a few firms stood out as clear market leaders. A.G. Spanos Construction of California, one of the largest apartment builders with nearly 12,000 in annual starts, boosted its revenues 62 percent to $1.2 billion in 1999, while maintaining a payroll of 600 employees. JPI of Irving, Texas, achieved revenues of $504.0 million in 1998 while starting 9,935 building projects. Trammell Crow Residential of Atlanta, Georgia, garnered $767.0 million from residential starts in 1998. Colson & Colson Construction of Salem, Oregon, had 5,125 rental starts in 1998 that brought in revenues of $675 million.

Workforce

The construction industry has always been labor intensive. This fact has not cheered contractors in the late 1990s, as an extremely tight labor market has led to wage pressures, causing many industry players to fear further inflation of construction prices. Some analysts suggest that the shortage of skilled labor was the most serious problem facing the industry at the end of the 1990s.

Nearly 60,000 employees were engaged in multifamily construction in the late 1990s. Construction workers in 1998 earned an average of $16.50 per hour. Craftsmen generally acquire skills during an apprenticeship, usually over a period of four years.

To help alleviate the industry's shortage of skilled laborers, the University of Florida established the Florida Academy of Construction Trades through its School of Building Construction, designed to speed prospective construction workers through a training program in half the time it would take them through the standard apprenticeship route. The school, with training programs based on the standards set by the National Center for Construction Education and Research, was set to open its doors in the fall of 2000.

FURTHER READING

"Assisted Living Facilities Prosper in Tampa, Fla., Area." *Tampa Tribune,* 14 August 1999.

Avidon, Eric. "Census Bureau Finds Potential Homeowners Prefer Renting Apartments." *National Mortgage News,* 13 December 1999.

Avidon, Eric. "Rise in Apartment Rents Generates More Income for Multifamily Sector." *National Mortgage News,* 30 August 1999.

"Building Construction Academy to Address Nationwide Labor Shortage." *ENR,* 6 January 2000.

Millan, Mert. *General Contracting.* New York: McGraw-Hill, 1990.

"Multifamily Spending Remains Strong." *Building Design & Construction,* November 1999.

Saphir, Ann. "Report: Assisted-Living Prices Are At Premium." *Modern Healthcare,* 21 June 1999.

Sichelman, Lew. "Apartment Market Value Very Strong Nationally, with L.A. at Top." *Mortgage Servicing News,* August 1999.

U.S. Department of Commerce. International Trade Administration. *U.S. Industry and Trade Outlook 1999.* New York: The McGraw Hill Companies, 1999.

Vadum, Matthew. "Housing: Housing-Credit Competition Kick-Starts Multifamily Market." *The Bond Buyer,* 12 October 1999.

Yetzer, Elaine. "Development Costs Begin to Stabilize." *Hotel & Motel Management,* 4 October 1999.

SIC 1531

OPERATIVE BUILDERS

This category covers builders primarily engaged in the construction of single-family houses and other buildings for sale on their own account rather than as contractors. Establishments primarily engaged in the construction (including renovation) of buildings for lease or rental on their own account are classified in the Real Estate Operators (Except Developers) and Lessors industries.

NAICS CODE(S)

233210 (Single-Family Housing Construction)
233220 (Multi-Family Housing Construction)
233310 (Manufacturing and Light Industrial Building Construction)
233320 (Commercial and Industrial Building Construction)

INDUSTRY SNAPSHOT

According to the most recent statistics from the U.S. Census Bureau, the operative building industry (including single-family, multi-family, industrial, and office buildings) included 21,000 firms of all sizes employing 140,000 people, with construction work valued at $72 billion.

ORGANIZATION AND STRUCTURE

Unlike general contractors who perform construction work on a for-hire basis for the owner or owners of a development, operative builders are the owners of the structures they erect and act as their own general contractor. In addition to construction, operative builders also engage in land acquisition, sales, and a host of other non-construction activities associated with developing and selling properties. Historically, operative building has traditionally accounted for a comparatively small percentage of construction. Typically during the 1990s, operative builders employed fewer construction workers than general contractors and employed a higher proportion of non-construction employees such as executives, salespeople, administrative staff, and other professional categories, reflective of their wider involvement in site development, property sales, and other activities not performed by general contractors.

Although operative builders were primarily involved in construction, their principal industry activities also included subdivider and site development work, real estate management activities, land sales, construction-related activities, and miscellaneous operations. The vast majority (95 percent) of the construction performed by industry firms involved the erection of new buildings and service facilities and the installation of equipment such as elevators, heating and air conditioning, and plumbing. A small proportion of construction activities involved renovation work, such as additions, alterations, or reconstruction, and maintenance and repair.

An important component of the industry's non-construction-related activities was the acquisition of land for development of its own properties or for resale in developed, undeveloped, or partially developed form to purchasers such as other builders. Industry firms considering the purchase of a tract of land evaluated it on its cost, or based on marketing and demographic studies conducted by the operative builder or by consultants.

Other criteria included financial and legal considerations, governmental approvals and entitlements, environmental factors, the firm's experience in a particular market, real estate market trends and the health of the economy in general. Engle Homes of Florida, for example, primarily purchased land already "improved" for building construction, land requiring site improvements, and "options" on improved land permitting the company to buy the site when market demand warranted construction. Firms that can afford to carry the costs of a large undeveloped "land inventory" may ultimately benefit from having purchased large tracts rather than several smaller, more expensive parcels when it comes time to construct a large master-planned community on the site. It generally takes five years to develop purchased land into master-planned communities or subdivisions, while smaller, more conventional residential projects take two to three years to complete. The purchase of land tracts involves a "contingency period" while zoning, environmental, and other governmental and infrastructure requirements are met.

In the 1980s and early 1990s, several factors compelled the building industry to seek new means for acquiring financing for land purchases: the federal Tax Reform Act of 1986, the revision of commercial banks' loan underwriting standards, and the decline of the U.S. savings and loan industry. One such approach was the formation of "land bank partnerships" in which investors pooled their resources to purchase land and used provisions in the tax code to avoid the costs associated with carrying the debt from the purchase of land on their balance sheets.

After purchasing land for a master-planned community, industry firms must determine the layout, size, and style of each of the site's lots, as well as the design of the overall community. A product line is then developed, based on such factors as existing housing, the expenditure for the lots, and the projected needs of the specific market. Once these general guidelines are established, the firm seeks the necessary governmental approvals, performs specific site planning, constructs or contracts for the construction of roads, sewers, water and drainage facilities, and, if necessary, conducts other engineering operations.

The development of the "balloon frame" building technique in the 1830s, with which homes could be constructed by laborers rather than skilled carpenters, represented the birth of modern, industrialized home construction methods in the United States. Contemporary two-story homes are generally constructed using a "platform frame" method in which the studs that support the roof rest on the second story rather than extending all the way to the ground floor as in traditional balloon frames. Single-family homes—both detached and attached—were the most common structures erected by operative builders during the late 1980s. The modern home is much more than a frame, floor, roof, and walls, however; home builders must install pipes for plumbing, fiberglass for insulation, ductwork for heating and air conditioning, special flooring for bathrooms and kitchens, and conduits for electrical wiring, as well as a wide range of building components.

Office buildings, industrial buildings and warehouses, and commercial buildings such as stores, restaurants, and service stations represent a not insubstantial amount of construction activity. Industry firms also developed and constructed condominiums, defined as townhouses, apartments, or any other structures in which the purchaser owns title to the three-dimensional space occupied by the unit as well as an undivided interest in the building's common property. Industry firms also developed cooperative apartments, which have the same physical form as condominiums but in which purchasers hold stock in the company that owns the apartment rather than owning a unit of space. Industry firms also engage in speculative building—structures built in the expectation of future demand without prearranged purchasers.

The operative building market, like other construction markets, is "counter cyclical." Operative builders are significantly dependent on the freeing up of credit from lending institutions that occurs when depressed economic conditions limit the number of industrial or manufacturing borrowers seeking loans for expansion. Because money loaned by banks and other financial institutions is more readily available to home-buyers and construction firms when the economy is in the trough of an economic cycle, the home building industry generally begins to improve when economic conditions are at their worst, thus earning the designation "counter cyclical." Home builders also are strongly affected by interest rate levels and general consumer confidence. Other economic factors affecting the home building industry include demographic trends, such as the number of adults in the prime home-buying years (ages 25-44), changes in the mortgage financing industry, increases in energy costs and property taxes, labor and building materials costs, and changes in consumer preferences.

The residential building industry during the 1990s, was highly competitive, with only a few firms competing at the national level. Builders compete on the basis of location, reputation, quality of construction, price, design quality, and amenities, among other factors. Builders with strong administrative and paperwork processing operations, superior on-site management, and sound construction systems were generally the most competitive.

Most residential building firms (including operative builders) were small, with the number of units constructed by a single establishment averaging 25 or less per year. Such firms often started out by building a small number of homes, acquiring additional land, and then gradually expanding their market geographically and perhaps demographically as well, offering, for example, ''first home'' residential construction, then moving up to expensive high-end home construction. Among the preliminary activities that may be conducted by start-up builders before beginning their first construction project were: market research of the communities in which they intend to sell, prearrangement of financing for their initial construction activities, analysis of competition, exploration of business relationships with construction suppliers, installation of computer-aided design computer systems for floor plan design and modification, or consultations with area realtors and investors. Using specialized formulas, builders conducting market research were able to determine with some accuracy how many homes of a certain type would be purchased in a particular subdivision or development.

Builders may finance their construction activities through revolving lines of credit offered by commercial banks using the firm's inventory of homes as collateral. The actual amount of credit extended to the builder may be based on the value of the homes the builder has sold and may be about 50 percent of the home's intended sale price. Builders can expect profits of perhaps 15 percent of the sale price of a home. Larger home builders tend to have the financial resources to survive housing downturns and exploit emerging housing trends.

An important initial decision for the operative builder during the 1990s was the choice between constructing and marketing individually designed homes or offering so-called ''market units,'' a choice between unique home specifications and floor plans or more generic housing specifications keyed to a specific demographic market, master-planned development, or architectural style. Some firms offer a ''personal builder'' program in which home buyers can modify the builder's design plans to arrive at a ''semi-customized'' home. Other builders may purchase pre-designed house plans from ''plan service'' firms, thus eliminating design and architectural costs from their budgets. In fact, many builders use the elevations provided in catalogs of home plans such as *Sweet's Catalogue Files* rather than incur the expense of retaining an architect.

The types of homes built by industry firms during the 1990s were as diverse as the U.S. housing market itself, ranging from government subsidized lower-income developments to customized, high-end estate homes. Housing markets can be classified according to taste, race, family status, location (neighborhood as well as region), employment patterns, income, or age. Across all housing levels several trends have merged since the late 1970s. Mean home size has continued to increase and the percentage of new homes with 2,400 square feet of space or more has risen notably. Between 1978 and 1995 the percentage of homes with central air conditioning grew from 58 percent to 80 percent, those with two-car garages or larger increased from 52 percent to 76 percent, and homes with two-and-half baths or more nearly doubled, growing from 25 percent to 48 percent.

One of the largest hurdles faced by prospective operative builders was arranging financing through banks, which are much more inclined to lend money to established builders. In some markets construction financing was provided to builders by their suppliers (such as lumber companies) which could monitor the builder's financing needs and construction progress by observing how much materials they had ordered or used. Other sources of residential building loans include pension funds and insurance companies. Because construction costs can vary significantly over a two-month period, some builders planned to construct only the number of homes projected by their monthly research, then concentrated on selling the homes before beginning actual construction.

Industry firms generally sell their homes through independent brokers or by employing salespeople retained on commission. These salespeople operated out of model homes and conducted tours, providing floor-plans and describing prices and design options. Available homes were advertised in newspapers, magazines, billboards, brochures, on radio, through out-of-state home shows, direct mail, video tapes, or special promotional events. Major sources of sales include referrals from customers or members of a region's home-building, real estate, architectural, or financial community, from traffic through model homes, and through bidding on planned residential development projects in competition with other builders.

Operative building firms may also maintain customer service departments that conduct home orientation tours for buyers before the final sale as well as resolving problems occurring after the sale is final. In the mid-1990s, the largest costs incurred by operative builders were: construction on work subcontracted to other builders (35-40 percent of industry outlays); materials, components, and supplies (20-22 percent); and payroll (about 8 percent). Industry firms took advantage of a number of strategies to control their costs including using subcontractors to perform home construction and site improvement on a fixed-price basis, obtaining volume discounts on construction materials and other special pricing arrangements from subcontractors, obtaining zoning entitlements before making land purchases, and minimizing their inventories of unsold homes by building a limited number of speculative homes in order to meet short-term demand. Some larger home-builders elected to lessen the financial risk inherent in residential construction by having a range of projects under development in several communities in each market at one time, thus minimizing their dependence on the success of any single project.

In 1993, *Builder* magazine listed the following factors as the problems most often cited by home builders as ''critical'' to the success of their operations: worker's compensation claims; increasing lumber prices; Occupational Health and Safety Administration inspections; storm water management and permit regulations; environmental regulations concerning protection of wetlands; government environmental impact fees; endangered species regulations; economic confidence levels; government procedures for development approval; and mandated health insurance legislation. Other problems affecting some home-builders include poor design and shoddy workmanship, such as the use of moist lumber, poor soil testing, or inadequate concrete mixes.

Among the range of secondary activities engaged in by industry firms in the 1990s were the sale of improved lots, mortgage origination and title insurance services, cement aggregate and gypsum wallboard manufacture, and the purchasing and selling of undeveloped land. Other activities included the sale and asset management of commercial properties and sites, residential and commercial property rental, real estate investment trust (REIT) management, development and marketing of vacation ownership resort communities, savings and loan operation, and aluminum and wood building component manufacturing.

CURRENT CONDITIONS

The states with the largest number of operative builders (single-family construction) in the late 1990s were California and Florida, followed by New York, Pennsylvania, and Michigan. North Dakota, Alaska, South Dakota, Hawaii, and Wyoming have the lowest number of firms operating in this industry.

As of the mid-1990s, most operative building industry establishments specialized in detached single-family housing construction, about 10 percent specialized in attached single-family housing construction, about 3 percent specialized in apartment building construction, and only 1 percent specialized in office building construction and other commercial building construction.

Trends in the operative building industry in the 1990s included the continuing increase in the use of prefabricated and component parts, such as pre-finished walls, partitions, and stairs. Also, operative builders used a greater amount of non-wood construction materials in response to rising lumber costs and increased their reliance on computer-aided design and other software for home design and business tracking activities. Other characteristics of the industry in the 1990s included: a continuation of the trend toward larger homes (between 1950 and 1995 average home size rose from 983 square feet to 2,095 square feet); improved construction tools and equipment; decreasing union representation among construction workers; a continuation of the rise in average home prices and land costs; an increase in the number of mergers and acquisitions among the largest national home-builders; increases in the amount of remodeling activities performed by industry firms; and gradual increases in the percentage of U.S. households owning homes.

As the economy continued its healthy growth through the end of the 20th century, more people bought new homes, and the new homes they bought became increasingly lavish. By the late 1990s many people believed the market was ready to peak, but the attractiveness of home ownership, coupled with low mortgage rates, continued to keep it active.

INDUSTRY LEADERS

Dallas-based Centex Corporation was the largest operative builder in 1999, with sales of $5.2 billion and 13,161 employees. Centex builds homes in 20 states and also in the United Kingdom. It also owns 80 percent of manufactured-housing producer Cavco Industries. Other companies with a strong presence include Pulte Corporation, based in Bloomfield Hills, Michigan. Pulte, which builds single-family homes across several price ranges, had 1999 sales of $3.7 billion and 4,300 employees. The Ryland Group, based in Columbia, Maryland, focuses on the ''typical'' middle-class home; it had 1999 sales of $2.0 billion and employed 2,119 people. Toll Brothers, which focuses on luxury housing, operates in 18 states. The Huntington Valley, PA company had 1999 sales of $1.5 billion and 2,208 employees.

The Rouse Company, based in Columbia, Maryland, is a real estate investment trust (REIT) that specializes in retail properties such as shopping centers; its 1998 sales were $768 million and the company had 4,126 employees.

Other companies include Engle Homes, Inc., based in Boca Raton, Florida (sales in 1999 were $742 million and the company has 870 employees); Atlanta-based Beazer Homes ($1.4 billion in 1999 sales, 1,468 employees); and Hovanian Enterprises, Inc. of Red Bank, New Jersey (1999 sales of $948 million; 1,356 employees).

FURTHER READING

Hoover's Company Capsules. Austin, Texas: Hoover's Inc., 1999. Available from http://www.hoovers.com.

U.S. Census Bureau. *1997 Economic Census.* Washington, DC: GPO, 1999. Available from http://www.census.gov.

SIC 1541

GENERAL CONTRACTORS—INDUSTRIAL BUILDINGS AND WAREHOUSES

This category covers general contractors primarily engaged in the construction, alteration, remodeling, repair, and renovation of industrial buildings and warehouses, including aluminum plants, automobile assembly plants, food processing plants, pharmaceutical manufacturing plants, and commercial warehouses. General contractors working on nonresidential buildings other than industrial buildings and warehouses are classified in **SIC 1542: General Contractors—Nonresidential Buildings, Other Than Industrial Buildings and Warehouses.**

NAICS CODE(S)

233320 (Commercial and Institutional Building Construction)

233310 (Manufacturing and Light Industrial Building Construction)

INDUSTRY SNAPSHOT

Like all construction activity, this category of nonresidential construction is crucially dependent on overall U.S. and regional economic health. Specifically, construction of industrial building and warehouses is intimately tied to trends and conditions in the U.S. manufacturing sector; individual projects were, moreover, bound to the economic health of whichever industries were sponsoring those projects.

Contractors of industrial buildings and warehouses experienced dramatic growth through the mid-1990s, from $18.4 billion in 1994 to $32.2 billion in 1997, as the U.S. manufacturing sector picked itself up from its early 1990s recession. In addition to general U.S. economic strength, the explosive wave of modernization programs among U.S. industrial firms was largely responsible for this upswing, as technological innovation flourished as the focus of the consolidating industrial industries' competitive strategies. More than half of total spending in 1997 went toward the construction of manufacturing and light industrial buildings, which accounted for $17.6 billion. Of that figure, $10.9 billion was for the construction of new buildings, while additions, maintenance, and repair accounted for the remainder. Manufacturing and light industrial warehouses constituted the second largest sector in this industry, totaling $7.06 billion, while commercial warehouses brought in an additional $1.04 billion.

With the surging U.S. economy expected to slow somewhat, spending on all construction of industrial buildings and warehouses was projected to decline to $30.1 billion in 2000. While three-fourths of industrial modernization spending is for new equipment, analysts expect that the residual amount for new construction would largely sustain contractors during a potential downturn. Offsetting these positive developments, however, is the increasing tendency among the U.S. manufacturing industries to close down production facilities in the United States in order to take advantage of lower production costs overseas.

ORGANIZATION AND STRUCTURE

In this sector of the construction industry general contractors generally bid for a project, assuming responsibility for the project's planning and overall development. Often, however, the general contractor delegates performance of many specific tasks to specialty subcontractors.

Once a contractor is chosen to undertake a given project, he or she often remains in close communication with its owner over many aspects of construction detail while at the same time coordinating the work of various subcontractors and teams of employees. Given the inherent complexity of this arrangement, successful management proved one of the industry's greatest challenges. Project often fail due to miscalculation of budgets and missed deadlines, often attributed to the lack of an efficient communication process between contractors and owners.

CURRENT CONDITIONS

Contractors benefited from the booming U.S economy in the late 1990s, in particular the raging stock market, which encouraged investment in new buildings and modernization schemes as manufacturing industries attempted to increase efficiency through technological innovation. Contractors were called in for building and remodeling projects to accommodate the new production methods and equipment.

Manufacturers that expanded or relocated in the mid- and late 1990s at the greatest rate were those involved in semiconductor manufacturing, pharmaceuticals, food and kindred products, and paper and allied products. Companies within the pharmaceutical industry as well as semiconductor manufacturers are particularly in constant need of new research, development, and production facilities since their products face ever-shortening product life cycles. In order to be competitive, many manufacturers also need to upgrade into facilities fully equipped to provide advanced telecommunications and computer systems. Moreover, the importance increasingly attached by companies around the world to reducing hazards to the environment is seen as likely to create further remodeling and new construction opportunities.

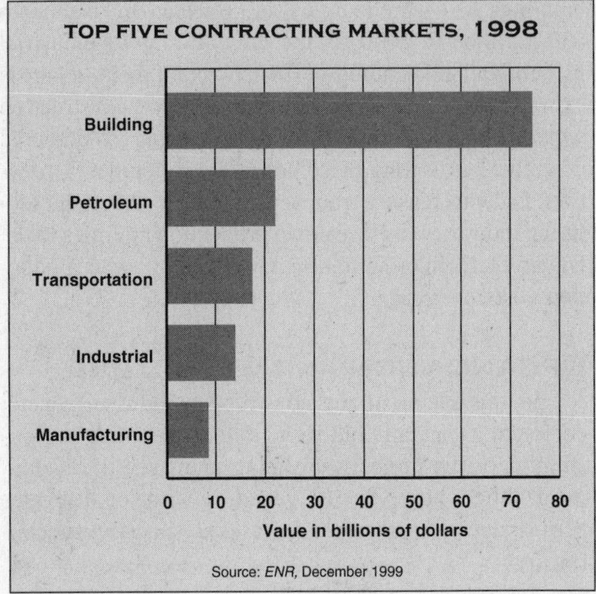

The food industry, for instance, demanded the construction, expansion, or renovation of a record 867 plants in 1998, an increase of 14.7 percent from the year before. Analysts attributed the bulk of this growth to increasing automation in production. Companies such as Coca-Cola, ConAgra, and Frito-Lay all had a number of projects underway in 1999, with Kraft leading the sector with 24 projects. The food industry in general was leaning toward larger facilities in which automation could be most economically applied.

Also impacting the industry in the 1990s was the increasingly stringent loan requirements set up by banks in the wake of the savings and loan crisis. To counter banks taking a risk position in these projects, developers and their subsequent construction firms were often asked to take an equity position or become a part owner in projects they design or build. Meanwhile, however, the growing strength and popularity of real estate investment trusts (REITs) will help maintain healthy funding for construction in this sector, even in the face of concerns over oversupply or pending interest-rate increases.

The nonresidential repair and renovation market, in general, was seen as having a more secure future than that of new construction. The commercial building boom of the 1980s produced, among other results, record vacancy rates for warehouses, and this over-supply was expected to diminish the market for new warehouse construction for some time. Instead, manufacturers were generally trying to reflect their industries' tightening concentration by expanding their capacities—in short, fewer but larger facilities.

Contractors in this construction sector remained somewhat wary, however, over the increased international presence of the U.S. manufacturing industries. With relaxed trade and investment restrictions, a strong dollar relative to foreign currencies, and the lure of cheaper labor and materials costs overseas, larger firms with capacity to move production facilities to foreign markets are seeing increasing reasons to do so. However, such practices will likely also lead to a rise in warehouse construction, as goods produced abroad are shipped to the U.S. and readied for domestic distribution.

Industry Leaders

The top contractors in this category in the late 1990s were generally engaged in other construction sectors as well. Fluor Corporation of Irvine, California, posted sales of $12.4 billion in 1998 for all its operations and employed 53,560 people. Bechtel Corporation of San Francisco, a private company founded in 1898 and still run by its founding family, employed 40,000 people and generated worldwide sales of $12.6 billion in 1998, of which 38 percent derived from North American work. Kellogg Brown & Root, based in Houston, Texas, was the construction unit of Haliburton Company, with sales of $5 billion and 35,000 employees. JA Jones Construction Co. of Charlotte, North Carolina, maintained a payroll of 10,000 workers and generated about $1.5 billion in revenues.

There were large numbers of generally small firms tackling a wide variety of projects within a frequently confined geographical area. Nearly half of all establishments in this category employed fewer than 5 workers, while 85 percent employed fewer than 20. With the exception of the giants undertaking business not only nationally but also internationally, even those contractors doing business in more than one state typically relied overwhelmingly on contracts in the state in which they were headquartered for the bulk of their profits.

Workforce

About 5 percent of the U.S. labor force is employed by one branch or another of the construction industry. The industrial building and warehouse sector employed about 139,000 individuals at the end of the 1990s. Construction workers in this category earned an average of $16.50 per hour. The states employing the greatest number of construction worker were Texas, with 10,000; Alabama, with 7,200; and California, with 6,300.

Despite its size, this workforce was by no means monolithic. Employment in construction was seasonal, leading to pronounced swings in the number of workers employed over the course of a year. Moreover, the skilled members of the work force engaged in a wide variety of different crafts or specialties. As a result, no single voice could adequately represent the various needs and interests of all of these workers, which somehow had to be accommodated to general concerns. Such considerations were particularly important because labor and management are more intimately tied than in many other industries. That is, in addition to wages and working conditions, unions must negotiate with contractors on issues such as training procedures and hiring practices. Especially in the late 1990s, when skilled labor was in exceptionally short supply, employers and unions were increasingly forced to negotiate to preserve job opportunities. Skilled labor in this category earned about $29 per hour.

Further adding to the lack of uniformity in the workforce were the tendencies for skilled workers to identify with their specialties rather than with a particular employer, as well as for all employees to change employers often, to switch frequently from site to site, to work beside teams hired by other employers, and to engage to an unusual extent in self-supervision.

Supervising contractors typically worked their way into that position from a beginning in some particular craft or specialty. Traditionally, academic training has played a minor role in preparing contractors for their career, though the inherent complexity of managing construction projects—especially the larger ones—seemed likely to make higher levels of education increasingly desirable.

FURTHER READING

Delano, Daryl, ''Nonresidential Spurt Mostly Commercial.'' *Contractor,* November 1999.

Ferrante, Maria A. ''1999 Construction Survey: New Technology Ignites Plant Expansions.'' *Food Engineering,* April 1999.

U.S. Census Bureau. *1997 Economic Census.* Washington, D.C.: GPO, 1 September 1999.

U.S. Department of Commerce. International Trade Administration. *U.S. Industry and Trade Outlook 1999.* Washington, D.C.: GPO, 1999.

SIC 1542

GENERAL CONTRACTORS—NONRESIDENTIAL BUILDINGS, OTHER THAN INDUSTRIAL BUILDINGS AND WAREHOUSES

This category covers general contractors primarily engaged in the construction, alteration, remodeling, repair, and renovation of nonresidential buildings, other than industrial buildings and warehouses. Included are nonresidential buildings of commercial, institutional, religious, or recreational nature, such as office buildings, churches and synagogues, hospitals, museums and schools, restaurants and shopping centers, and stadiums. General contractors primarily engaged in the construction of industrial buildings and warehouses are classified in **SIC 1541: General Contractors—Industrial Buildings and Warehouses.**

NAICS CODE(S)

233320 (Commercial and Institutional Building Construction)

Nearly 31,000 establishments were engaged in this industry in the late 1990s, employing about 472,000 people. As with the construction industry in general, nonresidential construction benefited from a surging U.S. economy. The demand and spending for all types of construction in this sector was commensurate with general economic strength, measured by gross domestic product and interest rates. The specific construction categories of this sector are further affected by a range of variables, such as demographic trends, legislation regarding public expenditures and business developments, and social trends.

Private nonresidential construction in the United States has fluctuated according to the success of key sectors such as office buildings and institutions. An industry high mark of nearly $200 billion in 1990 was the last good turn for several years. In 1992, nonresidential construction spending dropped to approximately $155 billion. Increases followed in the mid-1990s, before cooling somewhat by 1997, when industry sales totaled $175.2 billion.

The states that experienced the greatest levels of construction activity in this sector included California, with 3,722 establishments employing 31,200 workers and generating sales of $17.97 billion; and Texas, whose 2,857 firms enjoyed sales of $12.47 billion and employed 24,050.

Office Construction. The 1980s saw tremendous growth in new office construction, but the overproduction and subsequent economic recession resulted in such a glut that vacancy rates became a nationwide problem. In 1983, the national metropolitan office vacancy rate stood at approximately 12 percent; by 1990, that rate had risen to 17 percent and peaked at 19 percent two years later. In 1998 the rate was at its lowest mark since the early 1980s, at 8.9 percent.

Office construction spending experienced a long-awaited resurgence in the late 1990s, from $36.2 billion in 1997 to $47.5 billion in 1999. While this was excellent news for contractors, the 1999 revenues were still 35 percent below their record 1985 level. As the economy as a whole was expected to cool off from its late 1990s surge, the rate of office building construction growth was likely to slow somewhat, with sales projected at $49.1 billion in 2000. Meanwhile, lending institutions have eased some of their restrictions on commercial real estate loans. Still, history-conscious contractors remained cautious. Eyeing the slower growth rate for white collar employment and the economic trend toward downsizing, builders wary of a repeat of the late 1980s disaster were likely to try and rein in runaway construction, which was expected to result in a moderately increased office vacancy rate, reaching 13.5 percent by 2004.

Retail Construction. In contrast to office construction, the retail construction market has remained strong since the 1980s. Spending on retail construction rose steadily during the late 1990s, from $42 billion in 1996 to $55.4 billion in 1999. About half the value in this category is related to the construction of shopping centers. Especially in recent years, such construction was geared toward big box stores—large non-mall discount stores specializing in focused product categories.

While many analysts feared that this market sector was currently overbuilt, the strength and popularity of real estate investment trusts (REITs) was likely to help maintain strong commercial spending and stave off a severe financial windfall in the face of a market glut.

Institutional Construction. This sector includes a wide range of building types, including hospitals, schools, prisons, government buildings, and others. This type of construction has generally been more stable than all other sectors of nonresidential construction. As a result, it commands an increasing share of the total industry spending. In 1995, institutional building construction accounted for half of all spending in this industry; in 1998, that had risen to 61 percent, at $105.5 billion. Furthermore, institutional spending was expected to increase more rapidly than other sectors, reaching $114.1 billion in 2000.

Educational building construction was very healthy in the late 1990s, with optimistic forecasts into the following decade. Sales in 1998 reached $39.5 billion and were expected to increase to $44.0 billion by 2000. Seventy percent of this construction was of primary and secondary schooling facilities, while colleges, universities, and other educational institutions accounted for the remainder. The vast majority of this construction (80 percent) was for public institutions, though that figure was likely to diminish as state and local budgets continued to be strained while calls for voucher programs and other shifts toward private schooling increased. Furthermore, as more schools place a priority on full Internet service and technological facilities, the construction of new buildings and remodeling of existing ones will follow.

The construction of healthcare facilities was largely dependent on legislative activity, which was in an uncertain state of limbo in the late 1990s. As a result, spending was down slightly in this sector, though much less for private hospitals than for public care facilities. Seventy percent of spending in this sector went toward hospitals and clinics, though nursing homes and outpatient centers claimed an increasing proportion of the market. Healthcare building construction generated sales of $17.1 billion in 1999, down from $17.6 billion in 1998. More optimistically, however, analysts expected healthcare facilities to be among the fastest-growing sectors in the entire construction industry in the early 2000s. An aging population is a prime factor for this projected growth, especially as nursing homes and similar facilities flourish.

Other types of institutional facilities maintained steady, if modest growth, with the exception of prisons, which experienced a tremendous boom in the 1990s as the U.S. prison population skyrocketed past the 2 million mark. Public safety buildings generated $6 billion in construction sales in 1998.

Other Construction. Construction of religious institutions, nonresidential farm buildings, and recreational facilities have experienced little growth in the mid- and late 1990s. Spending in all these areas totaled less than $13 billion in 1997.

Industry Leaders

While the majority of companies engaged in nonresidential construction other than industrial buildings and warehouses employed fewer than 8 workers, a handful of firms commanded a substantial market share, though most of those firms' operations included construction activity that extended beyond what fits into this industry.

HBE Corporation was established in 1960 and employed 7,000 workers in the late 1990s. Its flagship operation is HBE Hospital Building and Equipment Company, which designs, plans, and builds healthcare facilities. HBE also performs construction activity for the financial services industry, building banks and credit unions. Sales totaled $1.3 billion in 1998.

Hellmuth, Obeta, and Kassabaum engaged in a wide range of construction activities, including commercial, recreational, and institutional facilities, including U.S. government buildings. The firm maintains a payroll of more than 2,000 workers.

Other leading firms include: Clark Construction Group of Bethesda, Maryland, with 1,500 employees and sales of $1.2 billion; Perini Corporation of Farmingham, Massachusetts, with 2,700 employees and sales of $1.3 billion; and Turner Corporation of New York, New York, with 2,800 employees and $2.8 billion in sales.

Further Reading

Saphir, Ann. ''Erector Set.'' *Modern Health Care,* 6 December 1999.

Delano, Daryl. ''Nonresidential Spurt Mostly Commercial.'' *Contractor,* November 1999.

"Real Estate." *Business Week,* 11 January 1999.

U.S. Department of Commerce. International Trade Administration. *U.S. Industry and Trade Outlook 1999.* Washington, D.C.: GPO, 1999.

SIC 1611

HIGHWAY AND STREET CONSTRUCTION

This industry covers general and special trade contractors primarily engaged in the construction of roads, streets, alleys, public sidewalks, guardrails, parkways, and airports. Special trade contractors primarily engaged in the construction of private driveways and sidewalks are classified in **SIC 1771: Concrete Work.**

NAICS Code(s)

234110 (Highway and Street Construction)

Industry Snapshot

Three quarters of highway construction is for roads, called flatwork. In 1998, the Transportation Equity Act for the 21st Century (TEA-21) was signed into law, allowing for nearly $200 billion for highway construction and maintenance from 1998-2003. Most of the money for federally-subsidized highway and airport projects comes from excise taxes on fuel, airplane fares, trucks, and related products. Americans also spend more than $1 billion annually on tolls.

These numbers reflect the significant impact the industry has on the nation's economy. For instance, the U.S. Department of Commerce estimates that every $1 spent on construction results in $2.23 generated in the economy on a short-term basis. In terms of the specific contribution to the economy from investment in road construction, each $1 million generates 63 jobs (13 at job sites, 13 by suppliers, and 37 through related service industry jobs created). In 1986, 272,000 workers were engaged in highway and street construction projects, according to the U.S. Department of Labor. In 1997, the number was up to 302,000. The industry's impact has been felt for years. In 1982, 504,878 people were employed by state, county, and local highway departments. This represented a total payroll of $9.3 billion. Directly related to the highway and street construction industry is the manufacture of construction equipment. Approximately 61,200 Americans are employed in this industry, which generates $2.95 billion according to 1986 statistics compiled by the Construction Industry Manufacturers Association. The total impact of the highway and street construction industry ranks it as one of the major industries in the country. It is estimated that total spending related to public and private spending on highway construction and maintenance equals $700 billion, or 18 percent of the GNP. More than 1.5 million jobs are created by federal, state, and local government spending on road construction.

Organization and Structure

There are a number of different categories of independent contractors that make up the highway and street construction industry. Each of these specializes in a different facet of the industry. The employment change for highway maintenance workers was expected to decline into 2006, but employment prospects were expected to grow rapidly. The total number of highway and street construction employees is estimated at more than 302,100. There are more than 100,000 firms in the construction industry, a figure that far outnumbers the total aggregate of firms in all other manufacturing sectors.

Despite the vast number of firms, the average size of most firms is relatively small. Many of these, in fact, are comprised of only one individual performing a specialized task in the construction project. Although there are a number of exceptions to this, the overwhelming majority of contract construction firms have no employees at all, except for the self-employed owner and operator of the firm. Despite this, small firms in the industry account for only 6 percent of the industry's total volume, according to available statistics. Most of the construction activity in the industry, about two-thirds, is carried out by small to medium-size contracting firms having less than 100 employees.

Construction contractors typically limit their activity to a specific, local jurisdiction. These are, more often than not, the states in which they are located. In fact, only one out of eight contractors performs out-of-state work.

The construction contracting business can be a precarious one. Contractors hire employees on an ad hoc basis after securing contracts; very rarely are two contracting jobs the same, and contractors have to meet the labor and material requirements of each job and its particular specifications. Also, contractors have very little control over the development of new business or increased demand for their services. The industry and nature of the work also demand that contractors adhere to strict completion schedules. The nature of the industry mandates that contractors and the heavy construction machinery they need to do the job must be mobile. Each contracting firm must be able to restructure and equip his organization according to the requirements of the contract and transport crew and materials to the construction site. Inevitably, this leads to increased management problems and expense, and requires specific organizational skills on the part of the contractor.

Of the contracting businesses that fail, the most common reason is that individual contractors have to cover the cost of labor and machinery rentals—usually within 10-30 days. This leaves most contractors operating with a minimum of working capital. As a result, most contractors show a lower profit margin than other major industries. Because of the risk involved in underwriting the construction project, most general contractors subcontract different aspects of the project to specialty contractors. This minimizes their investment and risk and increases the likelihood they will earn a reasonable profit from each job. Street and highway construction contractors, however, use their own equipment and underwrite the job when they can, thus maximizing the profit margin, although this increases the financial risk of the project.

The highway and road construction industry is labor sensitive and intensive. Most of the costs in other construction fields incur increased material expenses. Because highway and road construction is more labor sensitive, it tends not to be as affected by increased material costs. For instance, where material costs account for 42.9 percent of residential construction, they consume only 32.6 percent of highway and street construction. Overall, 37 cents of every construction dollar is spent on materials, 40 cents on labor, and 23 cents for miscellaneous expenses, such as equipment, services and supplies, rentals, and overhead. Whatever is left after these expenses constitutes profit.

Contractors have had limited success in passing rising labor and material costs on to customers because demand for their product has not kept pace with inflationary trends of labor and material required to manufacture the product. This is especially the case with highway and street construction.

The primary federal agency concerned with this industry is the Department of Transportation's Federal Highway Administration. The FHWA administers an annual, multi-billion dollar program of financial assistance to the states. The estimated budget for the FHWA in 1999 was $28.7 billion.

The agency is also responsible for the development and distribution of the latest technology to meet the need of federally financed road programs. It serves as the highway design and construction agent for the U.S. federal government, and regulates and enforces federal requirements relating to the safety of operation and equipment of commercial motor carriers engaged in interstate or foreign commerce.

Through cooperation with major financial and developmental institutions such as the International Bank for Reconstruction and Development, the Inter-American Development Bank, the Export-Import Bank, the United Nations, the Organization of American States, and the Agency for International Development, FHWA provides technical help in highway technology nationally and internationally.

Background and Development

The history of the road and highway construction industry can be traced back to the invention of the automobile in 1892. The number of cars, buses, and trucks escalated quickly, and today there are more than 200 million vehicles. But it became apparent, even in 1900, that the nation's road system would soon see a period of major expansion.

Road and highway builders organized an association in 1902 that represented them as an industry. It evolved from a bicycle group founded 22 years earlier called the League of American Wheelmen. The history and growth of the American Road and Transportation Builders Association (ARTBA) parallels that of the construction of roads and highways that exploded in the early twentieth century and has continued ever since.

ARTBA, based in Washington, D.C., is a federation of private firms, public agencies and associations. It is the only national association to represent all sectors of the transportation construction industry to the Executive and Legislative branches of government as well as federal agencies. Its primary goal is to advocate strong federal investment in transportation infrastructure. Its more than 5,000 members as of 2000 include the chief executive officers of large transportation construction firms in the United States, owners and partners of planning, engineering and design firms, and heavy equipment purchasing directors with all 50 state Departments of Transportation, major public works departments, and county transportation departments.

The Office of Road Inquiry, which became the Office of Public Roads, was formed in 1905. With the inception of highway departments in 16 states by 1906, road construction escalated dramatically.

The Federal-Aid Road Act of 1916 was the harbinger of voluminous road construction across America. It has fueled transportation construction, from single-lane roads in rural America to the super interstate highways that traverse the nation. The act was officially signed into law by President Woodrow Wilson on July 11, 1916. This made substantial money available for heavy construction of roads and ratified several principals and objectives that have remained in place to the present. The legislation established the federal-state relationship that determined that federal help would be channeled through the states, which were responsible for implementation of heavy construction projects. The act also provided for the institution of a state matching requirement that would operate in tandem with federal contributions to highway and road construction. Finally, the Act put forth financial distribution formulas that would determine the distribution of money, based on demographics such as population, area, and road mileage.

Although this program was supposed to promote and support the federal-aid highway program for three years, it was extended for two more years because of the onset of World War I. In 1921, Congress once again set out to create an ambitious highway development program, using the 1916 law as a paradigm that would set the pace and structure for completion of the basic structure of the federal highway program. The pace at which the industry has subsequently developed has been largely determined by the categories of funding established by the 1921 legislation, which established the principle of contract authority; this allowed highway money to be obligated to the states even if they had not been appropriated. Basically, this meant that construction could begin with the apportionment of money becoming a financial obligation of the federal government. Soon, numerous contractors began major construction projects before the money was in hand, knowing that the federal government would eventually pay for it.

It was only a few years after this revolution in highway legislation, 1925, that the U.S. Numbered Highway System became a reality. The entire street and highway development program leaped forward when Col. H. L. Bowlby, Chief of the War Materials Division of the U.S. Bureau of Public Roads, was elected ARTBA president. This led to further organization of the heavy construction industry, coordinated with the federal government's ambition to build an arterial transportation infrastructure throughout the nation. The creation of the Highway Research Board of the National Academy of Sciences was another watershed event that escalated quality road construction in America.

In the meantime, ARTBA elected J.H. Cranford as president in 1924. This was the first time a contractor had been elected to head the organization and increased the association's efficacy in promoting and lobbying for work and money from the federal government. ARTBA also established a Manufacturers Division. This was created as the result of affiliation with the Highway Industries Association, today's Construction Industry Manufacturers Association. This and other divisions created by ARTBA served to increase the specialized focus of the group and organized street and highway contractors in a way that increased their credibility and productivity as an industry.

Road construction, similar to most other industrial initiatives, slowed during the Depression era. States began leveraging gas taxes and vehicle registration charges as a way to underwrite the cost of highway construction. Prodded by the industry to use creative means to stimulate the economy and increase and improve the nation's streets and highways, Congress initiated huge public works programs that included substantial highway construction projects. The industry continued to lobby on Capitol Hill, urging continued highway development projects, even as the Depression abated and the Second World War drained the nation's manpower and financial and material resources. As the industry argued, a well-constructed and maintained road and highway system was needed to facilitate the nation's war effort.

Highway construction that was needed to move men and material during World War II took precedence over all other heavy construction during the war. It was during this period, however, that more emphasis was placed on road and highway safety, and engineers and designers threw themselves into these efforts with a vengeance.

It became evident by the mid-1950s that an expanded highway construction program was urgently needed. Increased motor traffic and reliance on the automobile as the primary mode of conveyance throughout the United States, civil defense plans during the Cold War, and the deferral of highway construction during the World War II years placed the industry at the center of the nation's economic stage. The industry surged forward after Congress authorized a 40,000-mile national highway network in 1944, named the "Interstate" system three years later. Appropriation of money proved difficult, however, and financing of the bill had to compete with other federal-aid highways at a 50-50 matching ration.

The situation changed drastically, however, in favor of the industry in 1956. This is when the government enacted the federal-aid Highway Act of 1956, which represented a redesign of the interstate system. The Highway Trust Fund was set up to pay for this initiative and it was decreed that the federal government would pay 90 percent of the cost. This put the industry at the forefront of major government initiatives aimed at mobilizing America. The "Golden Years of Road Building" were at hand.

Building the interstate system took precedence over all other heavy road construction activities and was the primary focus of the highway construction industry for the next 10 years. As the project neared completion, the industry began to focus more on other modes of transportation. Counsels were established throughout the country to advise governments and industry on construction of airports, public transit, rail, and highway maintenance and improvement.

Federally-funded highway construction and improvement projects and mass transit programs all felt the impact of the Surface Transportation Assistance Act as the result of a congressional decision made in 1978. Shortly after this, the industry met one of its biggest challenges to date: support of the re-authorization of the federal-aid highway program in 1982. The Reagan Administration announced it would support increased highway user fees to back funding for highway construction and maintenance programs and the jobs they would create. After much congressional debate and negotiations, the bill was finally passed in January 1983. This led to a five cents per-gallon increase on the gas tax. One cent of this tax was set aside for funding mass transit programs.

Another battle ensued in 1986 when re-authorization of highway and mass transit programs was addressed by Congress. After an adjournment late in the year, Congress declared the legislation a high priority in January 1987. The industry lobbied heavily as money for highway and mass transit programs began to dry up. Although Reagan vetoed the measure, he was overridden by Congress and road building moved into high gear once again.

The federal surface transportation program would be overhauled in 1991 and this consumed the industry's attention in the late 1980s. Completion of the interstate system, coupled with fiscal restraints and tight budgets in government, did not bode well for the road and highway construction industry.

Congress developed the Intermodal Surface Transportation Efficiency Act (ISTEA), and The House Public Works & Transportation Committee recommended a five cents per-gallon fuel tax. Debate and lobbying continued, much of which was focused on the prevention of using federal fuel taxes to decrease the federal deficit. In 1991, Congress enacted the massive and complex ISTEA which changed and rewrote the federal highway law for the first time since 1916. Authorizations of funding equal to $155 billion was provided over the next six years for federal highway and mass transit programs. President George Bush signed ISTEA into law on December 18, 1991. In 1997, President Bill Clinton offered the National Economic Crossroads Transportation Efficiency Act (NEXTEA) as a guideline for highway construction spending over the following six years.

Public investment in the nation's network of roads and bridges has been declining steadily, according to an analysis by Apogee Research, Inc., of Bethesda, Maryland. Investment that was 1.4 percent of the gross national product in 1958 had declined to 0.7 percent in 1988.

The fiscal health of the Highway Trust Fund could meet the need of an immediate requirement for highway improvement expenditures. The balance in the federal Highway Trust Fund at the end of fiscal year 1987 was $9.4 billion. Revenue accruing to the Highway Trust Fund during fiscal year 1987 totaled $12.7 billion, and expenditures equaled $12.8 billion. Federally-aided highway program obligations totaled $12.9 billion during fiscal year 1987.

Several states have committed themselves to substantial road building programs, despite the fact that total state government spending on road construction has increased only slightly faster than the inflation rate. Voters in California approved a relatively large gasoline tax to pay for billions of dollars in road improvements. The California legislature, in the meantime, approved the implementation of four toll roads. The state suffered a tremendous blow in January 1994, however, when a massive earthquake crippled the highway system of Los Angeles, its most populous city. Repairs to the area's highways and bridges cost billions of dollars and took years to complete.

The Highway Bill, passed in December 1992, provided more money for highway maintenance. Industry skeptics were discouraged by the fact that the allotment was to be spent over a five-year period. Moreover, the bill had no incremental spending built into it. Nevertheless, industry was encouraged by the aspect of the bill that allows states and municipalities to own stretches of road and bridges they build and to collect tolls for their use. It was hoped that this may inspire the issuance of tax-free bonds to initially finance construction of local roads and highways, given that revenue would be generated from their construction and use.

About 25 percent of highway construction in 1992 was in the areas of bridge construction, overpasses, and tunnels. Flatwork (primarily roads) accounted for the remaining 75 percent of the work. Analysts believe bridge work will grow faster than road work in the coming years, mainly because of the need to replace aging, unsafe bridges. Federal Highway Administration reports indicate that 23 percent of the highway bridges in the United States were structurally deficient, and an additional 21 percent were functionally or structurally obsolete in 1990. This will naturally require that the industry put a great deal of work into repairing and rebuilding these structures.

Due to the limited lifespan of most highways and roads, maintenance and repair expenditures have continued to grow since the 1970s. This reflects the increase in the number of these structures as well as their age. According to the *U.S. Industrial Outlook,* the current-dollar cost of highway maintenance and repair, in 1992, was about $21 billion, compared with $32 billion in highway construction put in place. ''While some of the work was routine maintenance such as mowing grass,'' the report said, ''much of it was typical construction activity such as repaving roads and painting bridges. Highway maintenance and repair expenditures will probably grow more rapidly than new construction over the next decade.''

CURRENT CONDITIONS

According to President Bill Clinton's statement of March 12, 1997, concerning NEXTEA, there were approximately 12 million people employed in transportation and transportation-related industries. One million of those jobs had been created since 1994. This represented just over 10 percent of the total civilian work force. The NEXTEA program proposed about $175 billion be spent between 1998 and 2003 for the improvement of bridges, highways and transit systems. NEXTEA authorized an 11 percent increase over the Intermodal Surface Transportation Efficiency Act (ISTEA) of 1991. It concentrated on improving border crossings and developing major trade corridors within the United States. According to President Clinton, this bill would create tens of thousands of jobs. From another angle, an analysis by the American Road and Transportation Builders Association (ARTBA) found that Clinton's 1998-2002 transportation budget would "throw 106,000 transportation construction industry employees out of work over the next five years."

On June 9, 1998, the Transportation Act for the 21st Century (TEA-21) was signed into law. Nearly $200 billion was allocated for highway construction and maintenance from 1998-2003, picking up where ISTEA left off.

For financial year 2001 under TEA-21, federal investment in highways should exceed $30 billion for the first time, reaching $30.4 billion. This marks a 5.7 percent increase from 2000's $28.8 billion. A large part of this increase is the result of higher-than-expected gas tax revenues that contribute money to the Highway Trust Fund (HTF). Core highways pending in this plan is expected to be $872 million for 2001, an increase of 3.2 percent over the previous year.

The highway program under TEA-21 has seen exceptional growth—more than most other programs under the government budget. Between 1997 and 2001, federal highway investment will have grown 65 percent. Of the entire construction expenditures in the federal budget, transportation composes 70 percent. The highway program is 60 percent of this total.

Although spending on operations and maintenance has remained relatively stable since completion of the interstate system, there has been a steady trend toward disinvestment on the part of the federal government. Although capital investment has been declining, highway use in this country has increased dramatically, according to the report. In 1962, the United States spent $42 for every 1,000 vehicle miles traveled (VMT) on highway infrastructure. Expenditures leveled off at around $16 per 1,000 VMT in the mid-1990s.

From 1970-90, VMT averaged a growth of 3.3 percent compounded annually. But for the first five years of the 1990s, growth slowed to 2.3 percent. A statement issued by the U.S. Department of Transportation in May 1996 found lower growth rates consistent with Highway Performance Monitoring System forecasts which showed nationally 2.37 percent compound annual growth over the next 20 years. The report reasoned that vehicle ownership rates may have reached a saturation point with ownership at one vehicle for personal use per household driver in 1990.

Driver licensing rates have approached saturation as men are at 93 percent and women at 83 percent of the driving age population. Women have closed this gap since the 1970s and are near men's licensing rates in the high driving age groups. Also, the age structure of the population had a great effect on travel with the baby boom generation entering the high driving age groups during the late 1970s and 1980s. A decline in the number of new drivers is evident now that the baby boom phenomena has passed.

The highway and street construction industry was also hurt by the recession at the beginning of the 1990s. Federal and local governments, burdened with tightened budgets and swelling deficits, had difficulty maintaining existing highway, airport, and street construction projects; new street construction initiatives were sparse as well.

Despite this, road and bridge construction increased slightly during 1992. The demand for improvement of essential arterial transportation systems necessitated work on major roads and highways and this helped to keep contractors working. New construction suffered as money was directed toward highway maintenance and repair.

Many analysts feel that growing concern about the state of the nation's infrastructure, including its highway system, could result in a period of robust growth for members of the highway construction industry during the 1990s. At the very least, highway construction expenditures will need to keep pace with the demands for road maintenance and repair throughout the nation. This is needed to insure the transportation infrastructure—an essential component of the American economy—retains its structural integrity and efficiency.

INDUSTRY LEADERS

In 1999, the highway and street construction industry leaders were: Kiewit Construction Group, Inc., of Omaha, Nebraska, with $2 billion in revenue and 11,000 employees; APAC Inc., of Atlanta, Georgia, with $1.3 billion in revenue and 7,500 employees; and Granite Construction Inc., of Watsonville, California, with $1.2 billion in revenue and 3,900 employees.

WORKFORCE

The U.S. Department of Commerce estimates that road building generates more than 1.5 million American jobs. The federal-aid highway construction program alone generated nearly 750,000 jobs.

In 1999, this industry employed 302,100 workers, of which 253,600 were in production. An average workweek was 46.1 hours at a rate of $17.87 per hour.

AMERICA AND THE WORLD

The U.S. highway and road system has not kept pace with those of competitors throughout the world. Highway capital investment relative to the economies in Japan, Korea, and Germany, for instance, has been significantly higher over recent years than similar investment in America. In 1988, for example, Japan spent more than 1.8 percent of its Gross National Product (GNP) on highway infrastructure. That's almost triple the amount that the United States invested in highways, 0.7 percent of its GNP.

Comparing capital spending per vehicle miles traveled (VMT), it is obvious Japan is substantially outspending other nations in highway development and maintenance. In 1988, Japan invested $150 for every 1,000 VMT—nine times the U.S. investment. In the same year, Korea spent $95 per 1,000 VMT and Germany expended $30 per 1,000 VMT. The U.S. spent only $16 per 1,000 VMT.

Despite lagging investment, America's road building technology remains strong. In fact, although the United States comes up short in terms of highway infrastructure investment, it continues to export highway technology to other nations through the Department of Transportation's FHWA.

RESEARCH AND TECHNOLOGY

New technology in highway construction and maintenance offers significant opportunities to the industry in terms of the ability to meet safety concerns, energy concerns, and other transportation challenges. Computerization has already changed the automobile and promises to revolutionize the mechanical and physical aspects of the car as we know it. Computerization and telecommunications, industry visionaries say, may result in completely automated vehicles traveling automated highways. This would result in improved travel-time, energy conservation, lower operating costs, reduced environmental pollution, and improved highway safety.

Addressing the subject of technology and highway construction and administration, Thomas D. Larson, U.S. Federal Highway Administrator, said ". . . the research and technology component of a potential future highway program will provide the expanded level of funding necessary to support a long-term aggressive commitment to improving highway productivity through the development, demonstration, and deployment of available and evolving technology for both operations and construction."

Proposed legislation envisions a program with the following components:

- Attention to long-range fundamental and applied research and development activities for pavement and structure materials and construction methods, safety and traffic research, and improved techniques and technologies for environmental management.
- A focus on intelligent vehicle/highway systems programs in four key areas—advanced traffic management systems, advanced driver information systems, automated vehicle control systems, and advanced commercial vehicle operations.
- A program for motor carrier research activities, including vehicle characteristics, human factors studies, regulatory and program analysis, and other motor carrier-related research.

The highway construction industry has already instituted high-tech methods of dealing with traffic management and safety throughout the United States.

One example of this approach is the INFORM system on Long Island, New York. Conceived as an FHWA research and development project, the system features variable message signs that inform motorists of unusual congestion, and also implements ramp metering and signal control on affected freeways and arterials.

The Smart Corridor in California is a 12.3 mile stretch of the Santa Monica Freeway that features coordinated traffic data and management strategies with the California Department of Transportation, the California Highway Patrol, the City of Los Angeles Department of Transportation and the City of Los Angeles Police Department. By linking traffic control centers, and developing a common database of information, the coordination of strategies such as ramp metering policies, parking enforcement, signal timing, and detours around congested areas will be possible.

In Philadelphia, I-95 is being transformed into a high-tech, traffic management super highway. An elaborate traffic management plan with advanced technologies, such as integrated ramp metering and signal control, will be used to alleviate traffic congestion, integrate public transit and automobile traffic, and mitigate air and noise pollution.

A new technology to highway construction in 1996 was the use of rubberized asphalt. Roads made with recycled tire chips showed less frost heave than conventional roads. Tire chips also proved much better than soil as an insulator, limiting the depth of frost and therefore the damage of winter. Using rubber in retaining walls reduced the pressure on those walls, allowing them to be lighter, thinner and less expensive.

Studies by FHWA and university research programs in 1995 aimed to use robotics in highway construction. These included the development of an Automatic Pavement Crack-Sealing Machine and a Pothole-Repairing Machine. Another area of research was directed at improving work zone safety and minimizing traffic congestion with the use of robotic aids.

One of the most environmentally sound research strategies in the highway construction industry was for the use of waste materials and byproducts in place of conventional asphalt. In 1994, research was done to help implement materials such as blast furnace and steel slags, carpet fibers, coal ash byproducts, including fly ash, and bottom ash, glass, municipal solid waste combustion ash, recycled plastic, roofing shingle wastes and rubber tires into roads and highways.

Further Reading

''Analysis of the President's Proposed Transportation Budget FY 2001-2005.'' American Road & Transportation Builders Association, 10 March 2000. Available from http://www.artba.org.

''Construction Trades Occupations.'' *1998-99 Occupational Outlook Handbook,* 2000. Available from http://stats.bls.gov.

Dah-Cheng Woo. ''Robotics in Highway Construction and Maintenance.'' *Public Roads,* Winter 1995, 26-30.

Economic Census 1997. *Bureau of the Census.*2000. Available from http://www.census.gov.

Employment Statistics*Bureau of Labor Statistics.*2000. Available from http://www.bls.gov.

''Highway Information Update.'' 22 May 1996. Available from http://cti1.volpe.dot.gov/ohim/vol1no1.html.

''President Clinton's Remarks on Rollout of NEXTEA.'' 12 March 1997. Available from http://www.fhwa.dot.gov/reauthorization/31297pc.htm.

''President Clinton Unveils Reauthorization Proposal for Transportation for the Twenty-First Century.'' U.S. Department of Transportation, 12 March 1997. Available from http://www.dot.gov/affairs/dot3097.htm.

''Proposed Clinton Budget Plan Would Slash Highway and Airport Programs.'' American Road and Transportation Builders Association, 7 February 1997. Available from http://www.artba-hq.org/docs/newsrel/1997/97-02-07.htm.

''TEA-21.'' *Federal Highway Association,* 2000. Available from http://www.fhwa.dot.gov.

''Tire Chips in Road Construction.'' *Biocycle,* September 1996.

U.S. Industry and Trade Outlook '99. The McGraw-Hill Companies, 1999.

U.S. Transportation Construction Industry Profile. Washington: American Road & Transportation Builders Association.

Ward's Business Directory of U.S. Private and Public Companies. Detroit: Gale Research, 1999.

SIC 1622

BRIDGE, TUNNEL, AND ELEVATED HIGHWAY CONSTRUCTION

This category covers general contractors primarily engaged in the construction of bridges; viaducts; elevated highways; and highway, pedestrian, and railway tunnels. General contractors engaged in subway construction are classified in **SIC 1629: Heavy Construction, Not Elsewhere Classified.** Special trade contractors primarily engaged in guardrail construction or installation of highway signs are classified in **SIC 1611: Highway and Street Construction, Except Elevated Highways.**

NAICS Code(s)

234120 (Bridge and Tunnel Construction)

Industry Snapshot

According to the 1997 U.S. Census there were approximately 1,171 bridge, tunnel and elevated highway construction contractors. These firms employed more than 47,000 people and generated more than $7 billion in construction projects. The average salary per industry employee was $38,000. Establishments employing 20 or more employees represented 42 percent of all industry firms but accounted for almost 92 percent of the work done.

Organization and Structure

Roughly 25 percent of the money spent on highway construction in the United States is used for bridge, tunnel, and elevated highway construction, with the remainder spent on ''flatwork'' such as highways and interstates. The vast majority of the construction work performed by industry firms in 1992 (72 percent) was for bridge and elevated highway construction, while tunnel construction composed only about 12 percent of industry construction. The remaining 17 percent of the industry's construction work encompassed highway, street, and related facilities construction; sewage treatment and water treatment plant construction; and sewer, water main, and related facilities construction. In 1992, 884 industry establishments specialized in bridge and elevated highway construction, while only 122 firms specialized in tunnel construction.

Like general contractors in residential and building construction, general contractors in the bridge, tunnel, and elevated highway construction industry generally assume responsibility for managing an entire construction project, but they may subcontract all or part of a project to various subcontractors. The design and construction of some construction projects may be awarded to a prime contractor and several subcontractors or to a single prime contractor, or the project may be awarded to two or more firms operating in a joint venture. Contractors bid on jobs based on estimates, and the difference between the lowest and highest bids depends on the accuracy of the estimates made of the job's cost. For example, the six bids received by the Florida Department of Transportation in 1994 for the construction of a bridge—a $7 million project; emdiffered by only several hundred thousand dollars. Boston's mammoth Central Artery/Tunnel Project (known as ''the Big Dig'') involved more than 200 design and construction contracts encompassing tens of thousands of intercontract and intracontract dependencies. Typically, bid prices for highway construction projects tend to go up as the number of bidders declines on any given project.

In cost-reimbursement contracts, builders were paid for justifiable costs incurred during the project, while fixed-price contracts required builders to absorb any cost overruns themselves. Incentive and performance-based construction contracts rewarded contractors who completed projects by prescribed deadlines or ahead of schedule.

Any construction projects using federal funds were required by law to be awarded on the basis of competitive bids, except in the case of emergencies or if the highway agency could demonstrate a more cost-effective way of assigning contracts. Government agencies also considered service, contractor guarantees, past experience with particular contractors, and options offered by individual bidders when evaluating bids. In order to avoid the appearance of relying on ''sole sourcing'' for public construction projects, some government agencies wrote project specifications in language general enough to attract several potential bidders. Some government public works agencies held ''pre-bid'' conferences with prospective contractors to make possible the dissemination of information on a project. Such conferences enabled local contractors or experts with specialized knowledge to add input that could help either the agency formulate specifications on the job or assist contractors in modifying their bids.

In the 1990s, federal highway and public works' agencies increasingly involved themselves in the execution of construction projects. Known as ''partnering,'' this trend changed the way bridge, tunnel, and elevated highway construction projects were conducted. In the early 1990s, the distinction between private and public construction—at one time determined by which sector paid for the construction work—was determined by which sector owned the project. Industry projects were funded by a combination of federal and state funds. In a typical example from the early 1990s, the Federal Highway Administration(FHWA) paid 80 percent for a cable-stayed bridge across the Mississippi River, while the Illinois Department of Transportation paid the remaining 20 percent.

Driven by their need to find alternative funding sources, a growing number of public agencies developed new financing strategies such as public-private joint ventures that allowed state agencies to take advantage of bond market investment funds. The 1991 federal transportation bill also enabled private construction firms for the first time to operate toll collection facilities while they repaired bridges, tunnels, or highways in order to finance their work without having to invest as much of their own capital up front.

By the early 1990s, 89 percent of state highway agencies were using some form of ''team building'' or partnering process and 85 percent incorporated partnering directly into their construction projects. Private and public partnering took several forms, including committing to a joint mission statement or project charter, reaching agreements on quantifiable objectives of performance, creating an issue-resolution ''ladder'' to streamline decision making, and jointly developing team-building and problem-solving skills to enhance ''team'' productivity. An advantage of public-private partnering is that it allows private contractors to review a construction project with a state administrator and, if necessary, adjust a project's specifications so that contractor capabilities and project requirements meshed.

Almost 67 percent of the value of all industry construction work in 1997 was new construction, with the remainder divided between additions, alterations, and reconstruction—which accounted for 26 percent of the value of the industry's construction work—and maintenance and repair, which represented almost 7 percent.

The public-private partnership funding mechanism flourished in the late 1990s as construction costs continued to spiral upward and resistance increased to full public funding of transportation projects. In 1999, Bechtel Group and Kiewit Pacific entered into a contract with the state of Washington, forming a non-profit corporation to finance and build a companion bridge to the existing Tacoma Narrows bridge. This new bridge is the first major suspension bridge to be constructed in the United State since the 1970s.

The public-private agreement is also an excellent way for a community to acquire a much larger dollar value of improvements for a given amount of public money. This improves the transportation infrastructure and provides many more jobs than a project built solely with public money. In addition to the $350 million used

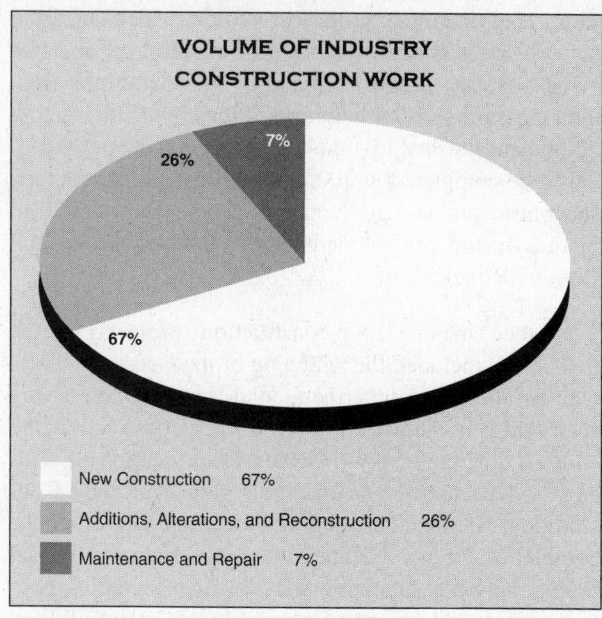

to build the bridge, the state of Washington will invest another $350 million for approaches to the new bridge and to Interstate 5.

Although public-private partnerships have been successful in smoothing the resistance to new bridge and highway projects, it is usually necessary for these new facilities to charge tolls. This presents another avenue of resistance to highway improvements. In addition to the new Tacoma Narrows suspension bridge, Washington state had five other projects on its wish list; these projects failed to go forward because of resistance from anti-toll activists.

BACKGROUND AND DEVELOPMENT

Although ancient Roman techniques for constructing stone bridges were sophisticated, it was not until the principles of physics were applied to bridge construction in the nineteenth century that bridge building made the transition from craft to a technical and scientific profession. In 1816 the first suspension bridge in the world was constructed over the Schuykill River near Philadelphia by U.S. builders. American bridge construction firms erected the country's first iron arch bridge in Pennsylvania between 1836 and 1839, the first all-metal truss bridge in 1840, the first iron girder railroad bridge in 1845, and the first U.S. bridge with concrete piers or foundations in 1848. In the mid-1850s wrought iron began to replace stone in some bridges, increasing their length and durability, and private U.S. firms began to manufacture ''proprietary'' bridges to be marketed to railroads and government agencies, a practice that continued until the turn of the century. After 1856, the invention of the Bessemer process for producing steel by reducing the carbon content of iron made possible the incorporation of steel into bridge construction. In 1855, John Roebling designed the first stiffened suspension bridge in Niagara Falls, New York, and 28 years later introduced the use of high-strength steel wire in the supporting cables of the famous Brooklyn Bridge. Civil engineering bridge science came into its own in the 1880s when poor bridge design and cheap building materials led to rail bridge collapses that called attention to the need for systematic analysis of bridge design and construction methods. In the United States, a premium was placed on inexpensive design, which led to the predominance of the simple triangulated truss design (first used with for wood bridges and later for iron bridges).

Although systematic tunneling for military and other purposes dates back at least to the Roman Empire, the first tunnel in the United States was the Erie Canal, constructed between 1817 and 1825. Because early locomotives did not have the power to climb steep slopes, blasting tunnels through mountains was a necessity. The first such railroad tunnel, constructed for the Allegheny Portage Railroad in Pennsylvania, was completed in 1832 and extended the distance record for rail tunnels from 850 feet to four miles. By 1850, 29 railway tunnels had been built in the United States using only picks, shovels, and explosives. The first steam-operated percussion rock drill was patented in 1849. Compressed air percussion drills came into use in 1851.

Nitroglycerin first was used for blasting purposes in the construction of the Hoosac Tunnel in Massachusetts in the mid-1850s, but by 1865 the excavation of a single cubic yard of rock still required almost four man-hours of labor. The invention of a stable form of nitroglycerin, dynamite, in 1869 made the construction of tunnels for such historic rail lines as the Union-Pacific transcontinental route more practicable. The first underwater railroad tunnel was constructed in 1890, connecting Michigan and Ontario, Canada, and in the same year the first underwater tunnel for horse-drawn carriages was built in Chicago. Although few early tunnels had any linings at all, when used linings consisted of cast iron rings. This lining method was gradually replaced by such early tunnel-lining materials as timber, brick, and mortar. Tunneling technology was greatly advanced with the development of the Greathead ''shield'' excavator around the turn of the century, which used air pressure to hold back walls of water so workers could tunnel underwater.

In 1956 President Dwight Eisenhower initiated a mammoth federally funded program to create a national interstate highway system, later named the Dwight D. Eisenhower System of Interstate and Defense Highways. The system offered industry firms enormous new revenue sources in the construction of bridges, tunnels, and elevated highways. By the mid-1990s, the system, renamed the National Highway System (NHS), encompassed more than 225,000 miles of roads nationwide.

The longest railroad tunnel in North America, measuring 7.7 miles, was constructed in the state of Washington in 1929. As the century progressed, new tunneling techniques began to see wider application. For example, the immersed tube tunnel, also known as the build-and-sink method, enabled underwater tunnels to be built from the surface by lowering prefabricated sections into trenches excavated from the river floor. The first such tunnel was built under the Detroit River between 1906 and 1910 and a second on the west coast in 1925. In the second half of the twentieth century, tunneling methods, materials, and excavating tools continued to evolve in sophistication and versatility, culminating in the construction of the Channel Tunnel (Chunnel) between Great Britain and France in the 1980s and 1990s. Although the construction of the Chunnel required no radical new departures in tunneling science, its sheer scale, expense, and technical success made it perhaps the single most important tunneling project in history. The engineering success of the tunnel (though marred by its great expense and a major tunnel fire in 1996) led some engineers in the mid-1990s to explore the idea of tunnels connecting Russia and Alaska across the Bering Straits and Morocco and Spain across the Straits of Gibralter.

About 25 percent of the value of highway construction consisted of bridges, overpasses, and tunnels in 1993, while flatwork (primarily roads) accounted for the remaining 75 percent. According to a U.S. Department of Transportation report on the status of the nation's highways, bridges, and transit systems, $49.9 billion was required to maintain the condition and performance of the nation's highways and bridges in 1994. In 1991 it was estimated that approximately 72 percent of existing U.S. bridges were built before 1935 and estimates of the nation's roughly 575,000 bridges that were structurally or functionally deficient in the early 1990s ranged from 14 to 40 percent, with those in New York in most need of repair. In addition, the Federal Highway Administration estimated that another 21 percent of U.S. bridges were not only deficient but obsolete, leaving a grand total of 225,000 to 231,000 below-par bridges nationwide. Roughly 42 percent of the backlog for bridge rehabilitation in the early 1990s involved pavement costs, and the remaining 58 percent was for constructing additional capacity. By 1996 the estimated cost of upgrading the backlog of deficient U.S. bridges had risen to about $72 billion. By 1998 the value of new construction for highways, including elevated highways and bridges, was expected to increase to almost $39 billion.

Perhaps the largest single bridge, tunnel, and elevated highway construction project in the United States in the mid-1990s was the $7.7 billion Central Artery/Third Harbor Tunnel project in Boston, which consisted of an immersed three-quarter mile tube tunnel and elevated highway system designed to connect several Boston neighborhoods with the rest of the city. With roughly 22 percent finished by mid-1996, the project was expected to be completed in 2004. A total of 100 contractors, subcontractors, and government agencies were involved in the Boston project, led by the Bechtel Group and Parsons Brinckerhoff.

Other major U.S. construction projects in the mid-1990s included the widening of the George P. Coleman Bridge in Virginia (the second-largest double-swing span bridge in the world) by Tidewater Construction; the construction of the Des Plaines River section of Chicago's deep tunnel and reservoir plan by Kenny Construction, Kiewit Construction Group, and J.F. Shea; the completion of the Cumberland Gap Highway Tunnel project between Kentucky and Virginia (including two-lane tunnels and seven roadway bridges); and a $3 billion deep tunnel wastewater collection, treatment, and disposal system in Singapore by CH2M Hill and Parsons Brinckerhoff. In the mid-1990s New York City mayor Rudolf Guiliani began pushing the construction of a multibillion dollar water tunnel to supplement New York's water supply.

CURRENT CONDITIONS

In November 1995, President Clinton signed the National Highway System Designation Act of 1995, which injected an additional $5.4 billion into the federal contribution set aside for the NHS. By one estimate each $1 billion of federal highway aid created roughly 7,900 full-time, on-site construction jobs in the United States. One provision of the act also raised the maximum federal share for toll project funding to 80 percent, up from a variable 50 to 80 percent previously.

The Intermodal Surface Transportation Efficiency Act (ISTEA)—an annually budgeted omnibus transportation legislation package—and FHWA funds accounted for a large percentage of the revenues of industry firms. In 1991, ISTEA provided $130 billion in transportation funding. In mid-1998 President Clinton signed a funding bill that was a follow-up to the 1991 ISTEA legislation. Called the "Transportation Equity Act for the 21st Century" (TEA-21), it provides $217 billion through the year 2003 for all types of surface transportation. It is the largest public works legislation in US history. Since it was signed into law, implementation of the act was passed to each state's transportation agency along with the state's share of the funding. The state is responsible for parceling out its share of the funds for use in highway, bridge and tunnel projects. The transportation industry is watching carefully how the money is distributed and how well transportation contractors and government are prepared to fill the transportation needs of the next century.

States have received this funding with mixed blessings. For instance, California's share of the TEA-21 funding is more than $14 billion; this money will fill a large void in funding caused by the voters' rejection of $4 billion in transportation bond issues in the late 1990s. Although Illinois's allocation is expected to be $5.3 billion, the state ranks first in truck traffic, yet it only has the sixth highest level of funding in the TEA-21 package. New York's $8 billion allocation is music to the state's ears;—with this money New York will be able to complete even the smaller projects that usually get pushed aside when transportation priorities are assigned.

INDUSTRY LEADERS

The five leading bridge-building firms in 1999 were Peter Kiewit Sons, Inc (with $258 million in sales), Traylor Brothers ($139 million), MCM Construction ($132 million), Skanska USA ($129 million) and Balbour Beatty Construction ($97 million). Peter Kiewit Sons also led the list of transportation construction firms with $1.61 billion in sales. Rounding out the top five were Bechtel Group ($1.29 billion), Granite Construction ($700 million), Tutor-Saliba ($610 million) and Skanska USA ($492 million).

Peter Kiewit Sons was formed in the 1880s by a Dutch immigrant brick maker and under the founder's son the firm built dams, power plants, and canals during the New Deal and highways after World War II. In the mid-1990s, Kiewit formed a joint venture with the Bechtel Group called United Infrastructure Co. to design, build, finance, and operate private toll roads, bridges, water pipelines, and treatment facilities.

The states with the greatest number of industry establishments in the 1990s were New York (96 establishments), Pennsylvania (66), Ohio (57), and Texas (56). The state highway departments with the largest budgets for new bridge construction contracts in 1994 were estimated to be New York with $394 million, Illinois with $224 million, and Ohio with $150 million.

WORKFORCE

The bridge, tunnel, and elevated highway industry encompassed a wide diversity of engineering specializations in the mid-1990s. A typical advertisement placed in the jobs section of the World Wide Web site of *Road and Bridges* (a leading industry trade magazine), for example, called for an ''engineering project analyst'' to join up with a state's department of transportation and ''assist in contracting for engineering consultant services for highway design projects.'' His or her responsibilities included determining fees and statistical measures and assisting in the development of agreements with consulting engineers. In addition to requiring state licensure as an engineer, the job required ''experience in planning and design of highway improvement projects and knowledge of state government procurement practices.'' The pay range was $41,800 to $54,725. For a salary of between $45,470 and $64,230 a year, an engineering design manager for a municipal construction agency might be required to review private construction development projects, resolve right-of-way issues (i.e., legal arrangements allowing highway projects to be built on specified lands), and oversee municipal permit work.

Structural engineers might be called on to design multispan concrete bridges; to have expertise in designing drilled piers, analyzing soil reports, and driving piles, caissons, abutments, and mats for bridge foundations; and to have experience drafting plans and sections with computer-aided design (CAD) software. With a B.S. degree and two years of specific experience, an entry-level engineer who qualified for this position might expect to be paid at least $35,000 per year. The majority of the states in the country did not require engineers to possess a degree to practice the profession in the mid-1990s.

Project managers for a freeway construction firm could be expected to prepare design reports, environmental assessments, traffic management analyses, or bridge condition reports and be able to assume overall control of a project involving professionals from several firms. Geotechnical engineers conducted soil analyses to determine the suitability of a site for heavy construction foundations. Other engineers were required to have experience in traffic-flow theory and related modeling software as well as have thorough knowledge of such industry manuals as the *Highway Capacity Manual.* A senior bridge and highway engineer acted as a technical reviewer for quality assurance of bridge and highway designs, plans and construction documents, and condition inspection procedures and reports.

Project schedulers are generally required to utilize such project scheduling software systems as Primavera System Inc.'s P3 as well as have experience analyzing the impact of change orders, tracking delays, and scheduling large complicated heavy construction projects. So-called special trade contractors perform such tasks as painting and electrical work, and general superintendents directed all functions of large construction operations according to established schedules and procedures. Estimators gather basic data on proposed construction projects from engineering or architectural plans and site inspection and computed the cost of construction, factoring in profit and overhead. Other integral industry positions included expediters, materials purchasing agents, marketing managers, drafters, construction inspectors, job site safety directors, office managers, and foremen.

Construction occupations in the bridge, tunnel, and elevated highway industry were similar to positions in the construction industry as a whole but also included mining industry-related positions such as mining or tunneling machine operators and drainage constructors. The most important construction occupations included electricians, cement masons, painters, reinforcing ironworkers, structural ironworkers, heavy construction and highway laborers, crane operating engineers, operating engineers of light equipment, operating engineers of heavy equipment, sheet metal workers, and carpenters.

Union efforts in the 1990s to increase membership levels in the heavy construction and highway industries included strategies carried out by the AFL-CIO and its building and construction trades department to challenge contractors on their compliance with environmental regulations, membership campaigns targeting specific corporations, political pressure, and agreements for union-only representation in major government and private projects. Highway and heavy construction work such as bridge, tunnel, and elevated highway construction has historically been one of the most dangerous occupations in the United States. In the early 1990s, the National Transportation Safety Board (NTSB) issued reports calling for safeguards in highway construction sites, such as separating traffic lanes in detoured highway construction areas and redesigning highway work zones. Another area of concern stemmed from the unique hazards associated with working in confined spaces such as sewer and tunnel construction projects. Historically, about 50 workers per year died in confined space construction accidents and another five thousand suffered serious injuries. In 1993, the Occupational Health and Safety Administration (OSHA) issued new rules governing the safety of workers in confined spaces, requiring employers to warn employees about potential hazards, provide them with protective and emergency equipment, and ensure they follow specific procedures before entering confined work spaces.

America and the World

Beginning in the early 1970s, the world's construction industry became increasingly international in scope, and early on U.S. contractors dominated the global scene. In 1992, U.S. firms were awarded about 49 percent of all international construction contracts, including contracts awarded to foreign subsidiaries of U.S. firms. Beginning at least in the 1980s, however, U.S. construction firms began to fall behind Japanese and European contractors in the development of new construction technologies and building methods and by 1992 were losing market share in international contracts at a rapid clip. By one estimate, U.S. firms were 10 years behind the pace in construction technology and took twice as long on average as the Japanese to erect a structure. And according to a study by the U.S. Department of Commerce, American construction firms could no longer bring either ''strong technological or management advantage'' to the bidding process for international infrastructure contracts.

Construction firms in Japan—the world's largest market at $700 billion in 1995—were the world leaders in the use of high-performance steel, automated equipment, and intelligent buildings and systems, and European firms were the leaders in high-performance asphalt, tunneling, high-speed rail work, and marine construction. The leading U.S. construction firm with more than 50 percent of its revenues from transportation construction work (including bridges, tunnels, and elevated highways) was Kiewit Construction Group of Omaha, Nebraska (52 percent), which, however, only ranked 59th worldwide in 1995 revenues.

In the mid-1990s, the largest foreign construction firms with more than 50 percent of their revenues deriving from transportation construction work were Bouygues SA of France, Toa Corporation of Japan, China Railway Construction Corporation, China Harbor Engineering Co., and Ret-Ser Engineering Agency of Taiwan. Although lagging in the global bridge, tunnel, and elevated highway market, U.S. construction firms in general continued to be the leaders in the Middle East, Latin America, and Canada.

The most promising international markets for industry firms during the early 1990s were located in developing countries where anticipated transportation infrastructure needs were estimated to cost as much as $100 billion a year. Nations in the Far East and Pacific Rim, particularly Vietnam, Cambodia, and China, were expected to be the site of much of the international bridge and tunnel industry's most significant projects in the 1990s and beyond. In the mid-1990s, an increasing number of major international infrastructure projects were being developed on a ''build-own-operate-transfer'' (BOOT) basis. In BOOT contracts, which were invented by the Turkish government in the 1980s, the construction firm not only performed the construction work but also operated the finished facility until it became profitable, at which point it transferred ownership to the local government. Another international trend that had just begun to have an affect on the bridge, tunnel, and elevated highway industry was the privatization of international infrastructure work, especially in developing countries with little capital to spend on huge projects. In these arrangements, the builder itself offered to supply the project funding—for a power plant or toll road, for example—and expected to recoup its investment from the income generated by the project when it was operational.

Of the 50 largest U.S construction contractors in the mid-1990s, the vast majority earned significant portions of their business from international work. Although U.S.

construction firms did not have a strong presence in international transportation construction work in the mid-1990s, several major U.S. construction firms did a substantial amount of transportation construction work overseas (which in addition to bridges, roads, and tunnels included airports, canals, locks, marine facilities, dredging work, and railroad construction). Kiewit Construction Group, for example, derived 36 percent of its revenues—its largest segment—from transportation-related construction projects. Morrison Knudson of Boise, Idaho, derived 35 percent of its total market from such construction work, and the Parsons Corporation and Ellis-Don Construction Inc. derived 12 and 22 percent, respectively, of their revenues from international transportation projects.

RESEARCH AND TECHNOLOGY

Innovations in bridge, tunnel, and elevated highway construction technology in the 1990s occurred in three broad areas: improvements in construction materials, improvements in construction tools and equipment, and wider use of sophisticated engineering and management computer software and automation technologies.

Materials. Although steel has been a highly popular material for bridge and tunnel construction and continued to prove its usefulness in new weathered and improved grades, industry researchers in the 1990s continued to look for other suitable materials. One such alternative was aluminum, which the American Association of State Highway and Transportation (AASHT) officials began recommending as a practical substitute for steel girders and subfloors in bridges. Because of its light weight, anticorrosive properties, and favorable weight-to-strength ratio, aluminum was also used for bridge decks in place of other construction materials.

Although steel has been used almost exclusively as the material for liner plates along the walls of tunnels, plastic polymers offered cost savings in construction time, labor, and equipment in certain tunneling operations. Similarly, the search for alternatives to the traditional welded wire highway concrete reinforcement led to the development of fiber-reinforced concrete using acrylic, nylon, carbon, and polyethylene materials among others to create stronger, more sound, and cheaper concrete reinforcing materials. Another reinforcement alternative, glass-fiber-reinforced concrete, was also comparatively inexpensive and offered versatility and light weight. Concrete reinforcement using steel fiber has been in use since the late 1950s and was also gaining wider use as an alternative to traditional reinforcing materials in the early 1990s. Plates made of carbon steel were also introduced as a reinforcing element in highway and bridge construction. Other innovations in bridge, tunnel, and elevated highway construction materials included the use of electrical current, called cathodic protection, to counter corrosion of concrete by road salts as well as new technology for making and installing buried segmental precast arch structures for use in road and rail bridges and tunnels.

Between 1988 and mid-1993, the FHWA's Strategic Highway Research Program developed 130 products aimed at improving highway construction and operation methods, including new pavement engineering techniques and concrete and asphalt with enhanced performance characteristics. By 1996, more than 100 case studies reporting the program's development of successfully implemented technologies had been documented. These included a new road-surfacing material known as Superpave, spray-injection technologies for filling potholes, bridge management software, and concrete anticorrosion technologies. Similarly, the FHWA's Geotechnical Research program developed improvements for bridge foundations, retaining walls, and embankments and maintained experimentation sites for assessing new methods for quantifying the properties and behavior of soils to predict their suitability for highway and bridge construction.

According to a July 1999 article in *ENR*, a leading industry journal, cable-stays and composites represent the future of bridge building materials. Bridges will last longer and will require less maintenance. In the traditional suspension bridge, thick cables are strung from the support towers and the bridge deck hangs from smaller cables attached to the thicker cable. Cable-stayed bridges are similar except that the cables that hold the bridge deck are attached directly to the support towers. Along with new technology in the manufacture and composition of the towers and cables, it is believed that bridges of the future will also have traffic monitoring and de-icing systems to help with operation and maintenence.

Equipment. Among the many advances in bridge, tunnel, and elevated highway construction equipment in the 1980s and 1990s was the increased use of highway and bridge surface groovers and grinders using diamond-tipped saw blades to cut grooves into pavement for vehicle traction and water drainage. Also utilized more frequently was an underground excavating machine for cutting two-lane road arch tunnels through hard granite. The machine formerly had been used only in underground mining, offering an alternative to drilling and breaking rock by hydraulic wedge or nonexplosive demolition.

Software and Automation. The introduction of engineering/design and project management software had a profound effect on the way bridge, tunnel, and elevated highway construction firms conducted their business. Among the advantages such packages offered was the capability to produce clean and accurate technical drawings by users without drafting skills, correct and replot drawings in a fraction of the time required by manual methods, quickly optimize designs to explore alternative approaches to a project, and better understand a project's total design features through three-dimensional visualization and imaging features.

On the project management and administrative side of construction operations, software programs like "AutoProject" or Primavera's P3 facilitated easy scheduling and project monitoring, time/cost trade-off analyses, and customized reports. Packages like "WinEst" provided building construction estimating features for the Windows operating system and allowed construction managers to create detailed project estimates. Quick scheduling also was completed with Critical Path Method software programs to monitor the progress of individual contracts and an entire construction project.

In the 1990s Japanese firms began dominating the global construction market by integrating automated construction systems and robotics into their construction projects. Systems like Obayashi Corporation's Automated Building Construction System enabled structures to rise up in twice the time as traditional methods. Automated machines delivered the building materials, from columns and beams to floor panels and interior fittings, to the floor under construction, which was enclosed in a climate-controlled "factorylike" environment. Robots then precisely positioned the materials at their appropriate points on the construction floor, and automatic welding machines welded the columns and beams. When the floor was finished, an integrated hydraulic system lifted the entire "shop" up one level to start the process anew. Such systems not only shortened construction schedules by allowing around-the-clock construction, they ensured that the structure was of uniform quality and reduced labor costs and construction site injuries. Using such technologies, by the mid-1990s the Japanese construction firms had become the world's most competitive.

As in many other U.S. industries, the emergence of the Internet and the World Wide Web in the mid-1990s gave industry firms new opportunities to market themselves inexpensively through company web sites and links to construction industry organizations, journals, and databases. By mid-decade the construction industry was also experimenting with processing federal construction grants remotely through the Web.

Further Reading

Bennett, Nancy. "The National Highway System Designation Act of 1995." *Public Roads,* Spring 1996.

"Bond Measures Win Big With Voters: $8.3 Billion OK'd." *The Bond Buyer,* 4 November 1999.

"Cable-Stays and Composites among Bridges of the Future." *ENR,* 26 July 1999.

"Chicago Tunnel on Track." *ENR,* 18 September 1995.

Daniels, Stephen. "Bechtel Signs Contracts for Suspension Span and Light Rail." *ENR,* 5 July 1999.

"ENR Sourcebook." *ENR,* September 1999.

Flynn, Larry. "Bridge Trends Buoy Industry." *Roads and Bridges,* 1 November 1996.

Ichniowski, Tom. "A Solid Market Shapes Up for 1996." *ENR,* 29 January 1996.

"Is Harbor Tunnel Worth the Billions?" *New York Times,* 25 February 1997.

Robertson, Scott. "High Steel Benefits from Bridge Replacement Bill." *American Metal Market,* 1 September 1999.

Sheriff, Margie. "Innovations in Technology." *Roads and Bridges,* 1 March 1996.

"TEA-21: Action Shifts to States." *ENR,* 19 October 1998.

"Tighter Squeeze on Road Jobs." *ENR,* 21 June 1999.

SIC 1623

WATER, SEWER, AND UTILITY LINES

This industry covers general and special trade contractors primarily engaged in the construction of water and sewer mains, pipelines, and communications and power lines.

NAICS Code(s)

234910 (Water, Sewer and Pipeline Construction)
234920 (Power and Communication Transmission Line Construction)

According to the U.S. Census Bureau, there were 8,042 companies involved in water, sewer, and pipeline construction in 1997. Their 162,566 employees earned $5.5 million. Work completed by this industry was valued at $22.2 million. The cost of materials, components, supplies, and fuels was $7 million, and capital expenditures were $945,000.

The three segments of the water, sewer, and utility lines construction industry share a common trait: project-based organizational structure. To facilitate project completion, various general contractors and subcontractors form transitory networks that sometimes last for several years. Nevertheless, the three segments of the industry are distinguished from each other by their key stakeholders, market segments, and projected growth rates.

The utility construction industry is exceptionally sensitive to fluctuations in tax legislation and the investment community, and it experienced a decline during the mid-1990s. The pipeline construction industry, however, benefitted from declining spot market prices and increased consumer demand for natural gas. As a result, there was a dramatic increase in building for that sector. The water and sewer construction segments respond to legislative actions and government spending. Decreased federal outlays and financially strapped state and local governments slowed growth for this segment of the industry. Legislative mandates that foster modernization and replacement of older aqueduct systems were expected to create long-term growth, however.

Private Electrical Utility Construction. This segment of the heavy construction industry includes the building of new power plants, transmission lines, pollution control facilities, conversion of existing power plants from oil/gas to coal, and modernization of existing power plants. Spending on utility construction slowed considerably after the passage of the 1986 Tax Reform Act. According to a U.S. Industry and Trade Commission report, the inflation-adjusted value of electrical utility construction dropped by 47 percent during the 1980s. Other factors that contributed to the slowdown included excess capacity, changing regulatory policies, dissatisfaction in the investment community, and overseas nuclear-generation disasters.

By the early to mid-1990s, however, demand for electrical energy was increasing rapidly, which encouraged the industry to consider building more electrical generation facilities. DRI/McGraw-Hill estimated in *Electrical World* that one-third of the nation's growth in electrical generation capacity through 2001 would come from retooling and reconfiguring existing power plants rather than new construction, which tends to be far riskier and requires more regulatory permits. In addition, pollution control spending was expected to increase because of environmental restrictions and a federal government program aimed at subsidizing "clean coal" technology.

Oil and Natural Gas Pipeline Construction. The oil/natural gas industry uses pipelines primarily to acquire and transport natural gas. Long-distance, high-pressure "trunk lines" are the most efficient and economical method of transporting gas from areas of production to areas of consumption. Due to seasonal fluctuations in gas demand, transmission companies and large distributors maintain storage facilities near final markets and production markets. At "city-gate" facilities (located as the pipelines near consumer markets) pressure in the pipeline is reduced and an odorant is added to the gas to make any leaks more noticeable. Finally, end-use pipelines distribute gas to homes and businesses.

During the mid-1990s recently completed construction projects and system expansions were consolidated into the interstate pipeline grid. The construction of new long-line pipeline systems slowed as the industry moved toward projects such as mainline extensions and lateral facilities to reach specific customers.

Gas pipeline companies reported an industry gas-plant investment of more than $59.8 billion in 1995, up from $55.5 billion in 1992. Despite nearly stagnant operating revenues, natural gas and petroleum liquids pipeline companies increased their net incomes slightly in 1995 by improving their efficiency.

New natural gas pipelines from Canada and the Gulf of Mexico began coming online in the late 1990s. The increased supply caused some dips in the price of natural gas, but these fluctuations were generally offset by increased demand for energy. In contrast to the utility construction segment of the industry, world pipeline construction is a rapidly expanding industry. Developing regions of South America and Asia have large capacity, international gas pipeline projects underway that will continue past the year 2000.

Water and Sewer System Construction. Water and sewer construction is heavily influenced by growth or decline in the construction industry, since new homes require a water supply and sewage treatment facilities. Developers and local utilities usually pay for water and sewer systems for new subdivisions. During the early and mid-1990s the industry grew moderately, but some projects were postponed because of problems with financing by local governments. This was particularly true of sewer projects. The industry did benefit, however, from federal legislation. The Safe Drinking Water Act Amendments of 1996 required system upgrades, and the Water Resources Act of 1991 increased federal funding for water supply construction.

In 1998 *Forbes* magazine reported that there were almost 60,000 U.S. water companies owned by cities or private enterprises, and many cities were placing their water supply services up for bid. Some U.S. waterworks projects were being taken over by foreign companies.

Leading companies in the water, sewer, and utility line construction industry in 1999 included Qwest Communications International Inc., of Denver, Colorado; Morrison Knudsen Corp., of Boise, Idaho; MasTec Inc., of Miami, Florida; and Perini Corp., of Framingham, Massachusetts. One of the largest companies operating in this segment was EMCOR Group Inc., of Norwalk, Connecticut. Previously known as Jamaica Water Power, EMCOR had declared bankruptcy in 1993, was restructured, sold some of its businesses, and acquired others, including Marelich Mechanical Company in 1998 and Poole & Kent in 1999. Poole & Kent had nearly $400 million in annual revenues, largely from the construction of water and wastewater treatment plants.

Another huge company in the industry, Suez Lyonnaise des Eaux, was based in France but expanded its global operations in 1998 by bidding successfully for the contract to supply water to Atlanta, Georgia. In 1997 the company reported U.S. revenues of $500 million. Another French company, Vivendi, had U.S. revenues of $490 million in 1997.

Further Reading

Hendricks, Colin. ''Natural Gas Industry Experts Differ over Future Gas Prices, Supply and Demand.'' *Houston Business Journal,* 15 August 1997.

Jones, Terril Yue. ''Water, Water Everywhere.'' *Forbes,* 30 November 1998.

True, Warren R. ''U.S. Pipelines Continue Gains into 1996.'' *Oil & Gas Journal,* 25 November 1996.

U.S. Bureau of the Census. *1997 Economic Census.* Washington, DC: GPO, 1999. Available from http://www.census.gov/prod/ec97/97c2349a.pdf.

U.S. Department of Labor. Bureau of Labor Statistics. *Career Guide to Industries.* Washington, DC: GPO, 1998.

———. *Occupational Outlook Handbook,* 1998-99 ed. Washington, DC: GPO, 1998. Available from http://stats.bls.gov/ocohome.htm.

White, Brian. ''New Pipeline Construction—Status Report 1994-1995.'' *Gas Energy Review,* 2 June 1995.

''World Pipeline Construction Plans Show Increase into Next Century.'' *Oil & Gas Journal,* 6 February 1995.

SIC 1629

HEAVY CONSTRUCTION, NOT ELSEWHERE CLASSIFIED

This classification covers general and special trade contractors primarily engaged in the construction of heavy projects, not elsewhere classified.

NAICS Code(s)

234930 (Industrial Nonbuilding Structure Construction)
234990 (All Other Heavy Construction)

Industry Snapshot

The heavy construction business is divided into several specific categories that represent separate building and development industries. There remain, however, multiple specialty construction activities that cannot be easily classified. Consequently, this miscellaneous heavy construction industry was named to encompass and represent these specialties. This industry is composed of companies primarily engaged in the construction of heavy projects not classified elsewhere. The array of categories in this group include athletic field and golf course construction, clearing of brush and land, land drainage, canal and channel construction, chemical complex or facilities construction, dam and dike construction, hydroelectric plant and petrochemical plant construction, missile facilities construction, pier, wharf and waterway construction, pond construction, power plant construction, and railroad construction.

The structure, history, and current status of this industry is closely related to, and often overlaps, the major divisions of the overall construction industry. Therefore, this entry stresses many of the unique specialties that are considered miscellaneous, and serves to tie-up loose ends of the heavy construction market that are not addressed in other standard industrial classifications. For more information on the structure and history of this industry, see related entries in the heavy construction industry.

The U.S. construction industry overall continued to grow throughout the late 1990s, largely as a result of a strong economy, which drove building in both residential and nonresidential markets. Based on a 1999 *ENR* survey of the top 400 contractors, revenues increased 12.9 percent from 1997 to 1998—13.1 percent domestically and 11.8 percent in foreign markets. Of the specialties that make up this classification, transportation was the largest domestic market, up 12.8 percent in 1998. Estimated 1998 revenues for all establishments in this classification were $44.7 billion, reflecting total growth of almost 31 percent since 1992.

Apart from a strong economy, factors influencing the growth of this industry were government initiatives and regulation, a trend toward privatization both domestically and internationally, and increased concern for the environment. The international construction market was very important to the larger firms in this industry; despite soft markets in Asia—the result of weak currency and the collapse of many Asian economies—contracts for power plants, water treatment facilities, and dam projects overseas were a major source of revenues for American firms.

Prospects for the near future in this industry were generally considered bright by industry analysts and insiders. The opening of foreign markets to American construction companies created great potential for further international growth, while domestic government-funded initiatives were slated to carry over several years. Transportation was expected to remain especially strong.

Organization and Structure

Because the miscellaneous heavy construction industry is actually a conglomeration of many distinct activities performed by diverse companies, there is not a formal structure by which it is characterized. Likewise, few statistics exist that provide a representative picture of the companies within the industry or the markets that they serve. Many of the firms in this industry are active in several areas, while others are highly specialized. Furthermore, it is difficult to distinguish this classification from other sectors of the overall construction industry because many of the miscellaneous activities are closely related to other markets. For instance, aqueduct construction is not part of this industry, but both canal building and waterway development are included. Similarly, subway tunnel construction is part of the industry, but highway tunnel work is not encompassed by this classification.

Most companies in this industry usually act as general contractors for specific construction projects. This means that they sign a contract with the entity for whom the job is being done and are responsible for seeing that all work pertaining to the job is accomplished. Responsibilities of general contractors include hiring and managing sub-contractors. In some cases, however, companies in this industry act merely as sub-contractors, serving as part of a team of companies working to construct a project rather than orchestrating and managing the entire job.

Although huge multinationals dominate the top 10 lists of industry leaders, most companies in this industry are quite small. According to the *1997 Economic Census,* there were 15,475 establishments classified as Heavy Construction, n.e.c., with a total of 192,974 employees—an average of 12.5 employees per establishment, which marks a decline from the average of 19.2 in 1992. The vast majority of establishments indicated that at least 51 percent of their business was specialized; taking into consideration both the number of establishments and the size of those establishments, the most common areas of specialization included conservation and development, sewage and water treatment plants, and mass transit construction. Larger corporations may achieve specialization through divisions and subsidiaries, or through joint ventures with more specialized firms.

Industry Divisions. Many of the miscellaneous projects in the heavy construction industry are so irregular that they cannot be comfortably categorized with a significant number of other activities. For instance, removing underwater timber and extinguishing oil well fires are both relatively distinctive enterprises. On the other hand, a few broad categories exist that encompass many of the miscellaneous activities, and thus bring some order to this industry classification.

A 1999 survey of the top 400 contractors broke down as follows: Forty-seven percent of 1998 revenues in the construction industry came under the general category of building, most of which does not fit into this classification. The remaining 53 percent was split among various specialties, including several in this classification.

Transportation took 11 percent of the market, with $17.2 billion in revenues. This sector grew steadily from 1995, with a substantial jump in 1998. Some of the projects included in this miscellaneous heavy construction field are subways, railroads, and canal construction, including repair work on existing projects. Three hundred and ninety-three companies specialized to some degree in mass transit construction alone.

Power-related construction had 4.2 percent of revenues, with $6.6 billion dollars. Spending on power-related construction had been declining since a high of over $7 billion in 1995, but also posted a substantial increase in revenues between 1997 and 1998. Construction projects that fall under this category include new power plants, conversion of existing power plants from oil and gas to coal, modernization of power plant buildings, and myriad modern, unconventional power plant projects, which are spurred by technological advances. With the inclusion of power and telephone lines, 511 establishments specialized to some degree in this sector of the industry.

Sewage and wastewater treatment, and related projects, took 1.7 percent of the market, with $2.6 billion in revenues. Figures from 1998 held steady from 1997, which marked a steady drop from a peak of near $3.3 billion in 1996. Work in this category primarily entails contracts related to water and sewage treatment plant construction and renovation, including filtration and desalinization plants. Sewer and water line development is not considered part of the miscellaneous heavy construction industry. Six hundred and sixty-nine establishments considered this one of their specialties.

Other water projects, such as reservoirs and dams, represented 1.3 percent of the market, with $2.0 billion in revenues. Spending on water construction showed a significant increase between 1995 and 1996, and remained relatively steady through 1998.

The ''Other'' category took had 3.1 percent of the total market, with $4.8 billion dollars. A few of these activities include furnace construction for industrial plants, kiln construction, missile facilities development, pile driving, underwater rock removal, construction of industrial baking ovens, and development of chemical complexes and facilities. Sports and recreation facilities, such as golf courses, racing speedways, tennis courts, or ice rinks, also fall under this classification.

A category of construction that split among these and other categories was conservation. Some of the jobs included in this heavy construction industry include breakwater construction, brush clearing and cutting, land clearing, drainage project construction, dredging, earth moving (not related to building construction), flood control project development, land and sea reclamation, pond construction, and water power plant development. Over 3,000 establishments considered this their specialty to some degree; 2,146 specialized completely in this area.

Background and Development

Although the success of individual specialties within the industry varied widely in the 1980s and early 1990s, the industry followed the same economic pattern as the general construction market. Most commercial construction sectors boomed during the mid-1980s but became recessed in the late 1980s and early 1990s. In contrast, industrial and public construction remained comparatively stable.

The health of the miscellaneous heavy construction industry was similar to that of the overall construction industry in the mid-1990s. However, a greater proportion of these miscellaneous projects were related to public works (except military installations) and industrial activity, rather than commercial construction. Because the commercial sector was the most depressed segment of the construction industry, the market for miscellaneous projects was not as adversely affected as other construction markets by the economic downturn of the late 1980s and early 1990s.

For example, total expenditures for commercial construction plummeted about 40 percent between 1985 and 1992, falling from approximately $87 billion to $54 billion. During the same period, however, the value of all work done in the construction industry fell about 13 percent, to an annual rate of just under $410 billion by the end of 1991. Furthermore, spending in several sectors that represented disproportionately large amounts of miscellaneous construction actually increased. Spending on water supplies increased from $3.5 billion in 1989 to about $4.8 billion in 1992. Similarly, spending on all miscellaneous private structures increased from about $2.3 billion in 1989 to about $2.9 billion during 1992.

Despite the industry's resilience, most contractors that offered miscellaneous heavy construction services were still striving to recover from unfavorable market conditions which began in the late 1980s and lingered into the mid-1990s. Several factors contributed to these conditions: increased competition from global competitors, as well as from domestic contractors that were fleeing from depressed market segments; lower profit margins caused by increased competition; a weak economy, which was resulting in a general reduction in the demand for new construction and was generating fewer tax dollars for public improvement projects, and; a lack of capital available to finance new projects.

Conservation. In 1992 the value of new conservation construction amounted to approximately $4.5 billion, reflecting a growth of 5 percent. This figure excluded repair work on existing facilities, but included some work classified in other construction industries.

In 1993, federal expenditures accounted for more than 80 percent of the activity in the conservation category and were administered by three federal agencies: The Army Corps of Engineers, the Bureau of Reclamation, and the Tennessee Valley Authority (TVA). The Army Corps of Engineers' hydropower facilities accounted for 30 percent of the U.S. power generating capacity in 1993.

Although the last of the Bureau of Land Reclamation's ''mega-dams'' were put into place in Arizona and Utah in 1993, several new smaller projects were planned. The Army Corps of Engineers was planning significant rehabilitation expenditures for major repairs of its dams, many of which were built in the 1940s and 1950s. Other conservation construction spending was slated by the TVA, which launched a $100-million redevelopment program in 1991 for dam repairs. Furthermore, more than $1 billion of spending was earmarked for flood control projects in such states as California and New Jersey.

One of the more ambitious conservation projects proposed in 1993 was an effluent diversion plan in the San Francisco Bay area. This $3-billion proposal, developed by the city's Department of Public Works, called for treating, storing, and delivering municipal wastewater to farmers nearly 50 miles away. Part of the plan proposed spending an additional $200 million to construct a seven-mile tunnel across the city that would transport effluence to the ocean.

Utilities. Although the inflation-adjusted value of electric utility construction (excluding water power) dipped by 47 percent during the 1980s, the decline appeared to have leveled off in the early 1990s. The market for power plant retrofits, which increase plant efficiency or convert plants to run on different fuels, was especially promising. In fact, expenditures for the maintenance and repair of electric utilities were almost as great as new utility construction spending in the mid-1990s. This phenomenon was due in part to increased regulatory requirements and financial risks associated with building new utility facilities.

Transportation. Growth in mass transit construction activity, much of which falls into the miscellaneous heavy construction industry, received a significant boost by the Intermodal Surface Transportation Efficiency Act (ISTEA) of 1991. ISTEA was created to generate as much as $90 billion in additional funds for new mass transit projects between 1992 and 1997. ISTEA was also responsible for much of the projected 21 percent growth in the Department of Transportation's mass transit spending for 1994. The Federal Highway Administration recognized that economic and environmental constraints of the 1990s would make it impossible to build the 34,000 lane miles needed to meet U.S. traffic demand, and consequently focused on boosting rail industry prospects.

Although traditional railroad construction, which is also part of the industry, was relatively stagnant in the early 1990s, there was growth in the rehabilitation of commuter and intercity tracks. For instance, Amtrak was electrifying a line between New Haven and Boston under a $300-million construction contract. At least $500 million of additional spending would improve other areas of Amtrak's Northeast corridor. Additionally, Los Angeles was continuing construction of a multi-billion dollar, 400-mile regional rail system in 1993.

Water and Sewage. Spending on new water and sewage projects in 1992 was approximately $13.4 billion, up from $11.7 billion in 1989. Much of that amount, however, was spent on activities such as pipeline and manhole construction, which are classified in other industries.

Most of the growth in this division of the industry was dependent on increased federal spending on municipal water supply construction allocated by The Safe Water Drinking Act and The Water Resources Act. For instance, in 1993 the Environmental Protection Agency (EPA) estimated that it would take $110.6 billion over 20 years to deal with U.S. water pollution.

Aside from wastewater treatment and water supply facilities, filtration was a growing market, as the federal government forced localities to improve their water supplies. In 1992, San Francisco was ordered to initiate a $500-million surface water filtration program. The city of New York was facing a potential $5 billion investment in filtration systems. Other domestic opportunities for water and sewage facilities contractors existed in the West and Southwest, where disappearing or contaminated water supplies were forcing many cities to resort to desalinization to supplement drinking water supplies.

CURRENT CONDITIONS

While most indicators project growth in this industry, the cost of construction materials and labor was also expected to rise, as supply struggled to keep up with demand. In 1999, the price of gypsum wallboard went up 36 percent, plywood 22 percent, wall insulation 18 percent, and lumber 17 percent. On the other hand, the price of steel decreased as much as 13 percent, although prices were expected to rise through 2000 as demand increased and imports of lower-priced foreign steel decreased. Loss of productivity due to labor shortages was blamed for up to 15 percent increases in building costs; large amounts of overtime—with 60-hour weeks not uncommon—also cut into contractors' margins.

Conservation and Water. The Water Resources Development Act of 1999 (WRDA) was expected to make

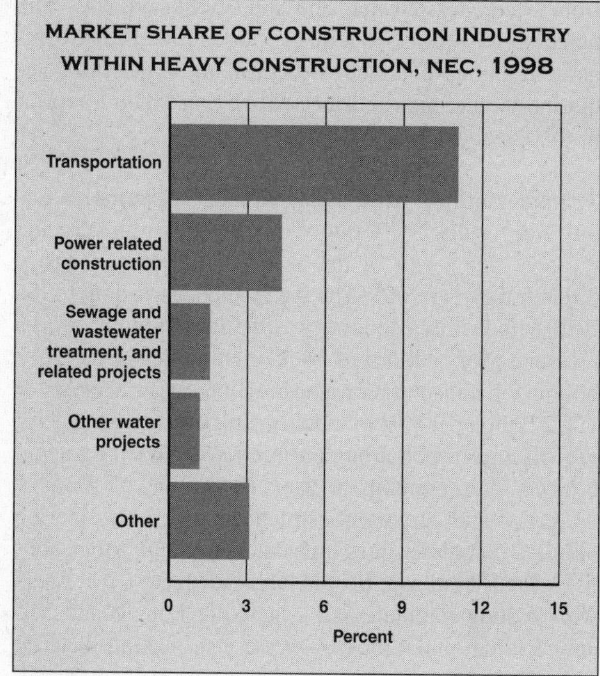

available over $4.3 billion dollars for 45 major conservation projects, including flood control and dredging. That federal money was expected to be matched by local money, bringing the total to $6.3 billion. One goal of the bill was to develop nonstructural methods of flood control, including the restoration of wetlands and floodplains. "Challenge 21," as the project was called, was slated to receive $200 million of the federal WRDA money. Major dredging projects included Oakland Harbor (receiving $128.1 in federal money) and Savannah Harbor ($145.2 million); beach-rebuilding projects were planned for mid-Atlantic states including Delaware and New Jersey. Congressional members also mentioned the possibility of a similar act in the year 2000, which might include significant funding for the restoration of the Florida Everglades.

In late 1999, the House considered reauthorizing the Clean Water Sate Revolving Load Fund program, which expired in 1994. A bill co-sponsored by Rep. Sue Kelly (R-N.Y.) and Rep. Ellen Tauscher (D-Calif.) would fund the program at $3 billion per year for five years. Part of that money would be earmarked for smaller projects in less populated areas.

Increasing concerns about the environment were also a boon for firms specializing in these areas of the industry. According to a 1999 report in *ENR,* "municipalities face the twin challenges of expanding populations and ever-stricter state and federal standards for water and wastewater treatment." The top 200 firms focusing on environmental engineering earned $26.7 billion in revenue in 1998, marking an 11 percent increase from the year before. Forty-seven percent of that revenue came from water, wastewater, and solid waste projects. The potential for profits from this sector spurred heavy competition among contractors, with many larger firms acquiring smaller niche businesses to expand their footprint in this area.

Transportation. The passage of the Transportation Equity Act for the 21st Century in year 1998 was expected to boost this sector of the heavy construction industry through the year 2005. The Act, which, according to the WEFA Industrial Monitor, was the largest public works measure ever authorized by Congress, set aside $217 billion for transportation construction, at an average of $26.2 billion per year over five years. Important areas for growth in transportation construction included light rail projects—representing at least 10 percent of TEA-21 projects—and airport construction. Cities considering building commuter lines included Cleveland, Minneapolis-St.Paul, Madison, Seattle, and Salt Lake City. Areas with existing commuter rail—including Long Island, Miami, Boston, and Chicago—were also making plans to extend services.

High-speed rail was another beneficiary of TEA-21 funding, with $121.5 million in earmarked funds from 1998 to 2004—plus another $1 billion to study magnetic levitation technology. High-speed rail, which travels at speeds from 150 to 300 mph, was primarily considered for areas with high population density and heavily touristed areas, including lines from Anaheim, California, to Las Vegas, Nevada; from Orlando International Airport to Disney World; between Dallas, Houston, and San Antonio; and between San Francisco, Los Angeles, and San Diego.

Using trains for airport transportation was another growing trend: as of 1998, 166 cities worldwide either had or were planning or building such systems. An expansion project underway for San Francisco International Airport carried a price tag of $1.1 billion; a new system for JFK in New York was projected to cost $1.5 billion. Parsons Brinckerhoff was the general engineering consultant for the San Francisco project, while the JFK project was a joint venture of Bombardier Transportation, Skanska USA, STV, Inc., Alcatel Canada, and Perini Corp.

Traditional rail was on the rise in the late 1990s as well, for both passengers and freight, as infrastructure investments reached record highs. Capital spending by ''Class I'' railroads was over $6.26 billion in 1997, as railroads increased capacity to compete directly with the trucking industry. Several railroad companies announced plans in 1998 to spend even more: Union Pacific planned to spend $1.4 billion, CSX Corp. announced nearly $320 million in construction projects, and Dakota, Minnesota & Eastern Railroad was seeking federal approval for a $1.2 billion expansion.

Utilities. ''Utilities and independents are building power plants again,'' according to a year 2000 report in *Forbes.* Deregulation was one of the main factors in the increase in power plant construction, especially renovating existing facilities. According to a 1998 article in *ENR,* ''Deregulation has set the stage for massive restructuring and is expected to force companies to reuse and to retrofit existing facilities for cost reasons. Utilities are auctioning off assets and buyers are finding that repowering plants are more cost-effective than constructing new ones.''

Industry Leaders

Because miscellaneous heavy construction markets are so fragmented, no companies that are engaged primarily in this industry dominate it. Although some of the largest construction companies in the world complete numerous projects within the industry, these companies are not dedicated to projects included in the miscellaneous heavy construction market. Rather, the industry is mainly composed of thousands of unique small and mid-size companies. Many of these companies specialize in a single activity, such as brush-clearing or pier construction. According to Katherine Grieder of Insurance Marketing Research, ''Approximately $4.1 billion in premium, or 75 percent of the total, is in small and medium sized accounts. The average premium per account of $12,300 for small firms and $124,000 for medium sized firms makes this a much sought after area for independent agents.''

Ranked by total sales (which may include projects not included in this classification), the top five companies in this industry in 1998 were Foster Wheeler Corp. ($4 billion), Peter Kiewit Sons Inc. ($3.4 billion), Bechtel Petroleum Chemical and Industrial ($1.4 billion), Washington Corporations ($1.2 billion), and MW Kellog Co. ($1.2 billion).

Rankings within particular classifications give a clearer picture of who leads the industry in each sector. For light rail, the top three in 1998, based on contracting revenue, were Skanska (USA) Inc., Peter Kiewit Sons, and Raytheon Engineers and Constructors. In power plants, the top three were Bechtel Group Inc., Black & Veatch, and Raytheon Engineers and Constructors. Leading the list for wastewater treatment plants were Skanska (USA) Inc., TIC-The Industrial Company, and Danis Environmental Industries Inc.—this was the only area in water treatment, including desalinization, dams and reservoirs, and sewers, in which Peter Kiewit Sons was not one of the top three.

WORKFORCE

Although employment in the entire construction industry dropped from over 5 million to less than 4.5 million during the recession of the late 1980s and early 1990s, the miscellaneous heavy construction industry fared better than most other segments of the construction market. In fact, certain areas of this industry were realizing significant employment growth in the 1990s. Most growth was expected to occur in sectors that benefited from increased federal spending or from federal mandates requiring businesses and localities to invest in construction.

Significant growth was expected to occur in miscellaneous activities related to environmental construction such as wastewater treatment, retrofits of energy producing facilities that were polluting the atmosphere, and land reclamation. Greatest growth, however, was likely to occur in international markets, which were seven times larger than the U.S. market and were growing at a relatively rapid pace.

Job positions in the miscellaneous heavy construction industry were similar to those available in related heavy construction industries. Jobs in construction management, skilled trade work, physical labor, equipment operation, and sales were representative of the overall construction industry. Growth was most likely to occur in positions that required technical knowledge, as more firms were relying on advanced technology to reduce costs and become more competitive in the crowded market.

A multitude of niche opportunities existed in miscellaneous projects, as well. For instance, high-paying jobs in weapons disarmament and battlefield reclamation were on the rise as foreign governments increasingly sought U.S. expertise in removing and detonating live explosives that remained after armed conflicts. Another growing field was removal of underground storage tanks, many of which were leaking hazardous residues and were contaminating surrounding soil and water tables.

AMERICA AND THE WORLD

At the close of 1999, the United States was the world's largest construction market, with $725.5 billion in total construction spending—surpassing economically depressed Japan, which was the largest market in the mid-1990s. Japan was second, with $677.1 billion in spending, and a 2.3 percent growth rate expected between 1999 and 2003. China was a distant third, with $340.8 billion in spending, but an anticipated growth rate of 10 percent for the period 1999-2003. Other markets expected to see growth rates of 8 percent or higher included Italy, Spain, Australia, Mexico, India, and Switzerland. The market with the highest predicted growth was Korea, with 12.3 percent. Overall, in the world's 58 largest construction markets—from countries representing 97 percent of the total world economy—$3.52 trillion was spent in 1999, and the 1999-2003 growth rate was projected at 5.1 percent. Only Brazil was expected to show a slight decline in growth.

Based on growth in the early 1990s, industry watchers had anticipated an even larger Asian market, but the collapse of several Asian economies in the late 1990s changed the forecast. Particularly for U.S. construction firms on the West Coast, soft spending in former growth leaders Japan and Korea affected all areas of the construction industry. Bart Eberwien, vice president of Hoffman Construction Co., told *ENR* "Even for a bunch of concrete pourers like us, it's a worldwide economy. Once the world's second-largest economy [Japan] went into a nosedive, it affected all of our customers." Temporary instability caused by the introduction of the Euro (the European Union's common currency) slowed the growth of markets in Europe as well.

Of markets in this industry classification, the largest share of international revenues went to transportation construction—20.9 percent, or $24.3 billion (based on surveys of the top 225 international contractors). Water, power, and sewer/waste construction took a combined total of 12.2 percent of the international market, with $14.2 billion in revenues.

Decreased restrictions on foreign involvement and increased privatization in public works projects created opportunities for U.S. construction firms. In February 2000, India announced plans to build the world's largest hydroelectric power plant, at an estimated cost of $23 billion (U.S.). The plant was planned to have a capacity of 21,000 megawatts, and to be built on the river Brahmaputra, in northeast India. The National Hydroelectric Power Corporation encouraged U.S. construction companies to pursue contract opportunities on the project through the U.S.-Asia Environmental Partnership.

Contracts in light rail increased overseas as well as domestically. In late 1999, China announced plans to start an extensive light rail development in 2001, including a subway line in the Northeastern city of Shenyang, and above-ground commuter rail in Changchun and Harbin. Competition for the projects was expected to be intense; only 30 percent of total project value was open to foreign participation. U.S. companies with investments in Chinese concerns, however, would be considered domestic, giving heavily globalized companies a significant advantage.

Environmental and Utility Opportunities. As in U.S. markets, the greatest area of growth for miscellaneous contractors overseas was in the area of environmental construction. American specialty contractors have dominated this industry segment. For example, U.S. firms took the lead in extinguishing more than 900 oil well blazes in Kuwait following the Gulf War of 1991. Growing markets in waste cleanup and water treatment abroad were likely to lure more U.S. companies overseas. Another potential area for international growth was in flood control, as several Asian nations announced plans for major flood control efforts in the second half of 1999.

A characteristic of many foreign environmental projects in the industry is immensity. The average overseas utility project in the 1990s was 4.5 times larger than the typical U.S. project. An example of one of these massive projects was in progress in Pakistan in the mid-1990s. This multi-billion-dollar plan would eventually create an entirely new river system that would allow more efficient and environmentally safe irrigation. The master plan called for the construction of over 2,500 miles of channels, drains, and irrigation canals. In addition to irrigating soil, the system would carry 2,700 cubic feet of refuse water per second to the Arabian Sea. More Western firms were expected to receive contracts for the project as the amount of work exceeded the capacity of Pakistan's construction industry.

The construction of the Katse Dam and two massive accompanying diversion tunnels in Africa was another example of projects that were increasing the foreign market for U.S. firms in the industry. The project, which started in the tiny mountain country of Lesotho in 1991, will carry water and generate power for the Republic of South Africa. The $5-billion effort, which will provide 29 years worth of construction activity, will result in the continent's tallest dam.

In 1999, Bechtel, already a leader in international construction, announced expansion of its relationship with Royal Dutch/Shell Group, an alliance expected to enhance their competitiveness in seeking contracts to build power plants abroad. The joint venture is known as Intergen, based in Houston. One of its biggest projects as of 1999 was China's largest private coal-fired power plant, built to provide power for most of southern China. The global trend toward the privatization of power plants previously run by national governments—particularly in Latin America and Asia—drove the market for power plant construction up; strategic alliances with key players in foreign markets became essential for U.S. companies like Bechtel to compete.

Research and Technology

An area of growth that has been of particular interest to specialty contractors is alternative energy production facilities. For instance, the first compressed air energy storage unit was completed in 1991. In addition, Hawaii's National Energy Laboratory launched construction of an ocean thermal energy conversion unit in 1992, which was designed to generate electricity by exploiting temperature variations of seawater at different depths.

Other advances in technology offered the potential for growth in wind power plant construction, development of large-scale solar-thermal facilities, and construction of onsite "fuel cell" generation facilities. Fuel cell power plants employ clean electrochemical reactions that generate the useful by-products of steam and heat. New waste-to-energy projects were also beginning to increase, following a lull in the early 1990s. Delaware, for example, unveiled a plan for a $275 million, 2,400-ton-a-day plant that would burn virtually all the state's combustible, non-recyclable waste.

U.S. dollars began moving from defense to private industry, particularly environmental industries, in the early 1990s. Nevertheless, U.S. construction companies lagged behind many other industrialized nations in the percentage of revenues invested in research and technology in the mid-1990s. In sharp contrast, Japan's construction contractors spent about $100 million on research in 1992, almost twice as much as their U.S. counterparts. Japanese firms also were forming more joint research ventures between government agencies and other industries. As a result, Japanese miscellaneous heavy construction contractors were setting the pace in three critical growth areas: mass transit, automation, and tunneling. For instance, Japan had already developed an automated rail setter by the mid-1990s, which could lay rail for subway systems. Furthermore, it was nearing completion of an automated tunneling system.

Despite Japanese advances, U.S. firms were breaking new ground and innovating at a record pace, particularly in wastewater and water treatment. For instance, the National Environmental Technology Applications Corp. (NETAC) in Pittsburgh was working with contractors to use X-ray fluorescence technology to analyze soils and sludge for heavy metals. In another breakthrough, the company designed a portable system for screening soil and water samples for volatile organic compounds. NETAC also had developed a biotreatment system that used proprietary microbes and enzymes to cleanse wastewater.

American construction firms were also leading the global industry in development of new software that served miscellaneous heavy construction firms. One of the newest software breakthroughs was 3-D computer modeling. This process allowed construction managers and job site engineers to construct projects on their computers, piece by piece, before implementing the construction on the ground, thereby reducing completion time and costs. This 3-D modeling technology had already been used in the construction of cogeneration plants, where animated diagrams showed exactly how the projects would come together and how they would later function.

In addition to increasing research expenditures, the U.S. government was trying to increase industry awareness of new research and technology being developed. Northwestern University, with an $18-million grant made possible by ISTEA, was striving toward this goal through development of the Infrastructure Technology Institute. The purpose of the Institute was to transfer knowledge from research to practical applications in the field.

FURTHER READING

Armistead, Thomas F. "Rebound Anticipated as Deregulation Kicks In: Engineers Look for Release of Pent-up Demand." *ENR,* 14 September 1998.

"China: Light Rail Transportation Projects." *International Market Insight Trade Inquiries,* 20 January 2000.

Cho, Aileen. "Keeping on Track: Heavy Rail Work Speed Up, Boosted By New TEA-21 Bill." *ENR,* 27 July 1998.

"Construction Industry Forecast." *Real Estate Finance Journal,* Fall 1996.

Daniels, Stephen H., and Tim Grogan. "Prices Mask Inflation." *ENR,* 20 December 1999.

"Engineering Report Delivers New Planning Tool." *American City & County,* February 1996.

Fisher, Daniel. "Industry Buzz." *Forbes,* 10 January 2000.

Ginsberg, Steve. "Power Play: Bechtel Group Ditches Go-It-Alone Strategy." *The Business Journal,* 23 July 1999.

"Hunan to Use Overseas Loans to Improve Flood-Control Works." *Xinhua News Agency,* 10 August 1999.

Ichniowski, Tom. "Congress Clears $4.3-billion Bill." *ENR,* 6 August 1999.

Ichniowski, Tom and Tim Grogan. "Key Markets Will Rebound in '97." *ENR,* November 1996.

"India: World's Largest Hydroelectric Power Plant to Be Built." *International Market Insight Reports,* 4 February 2000.

Kim, S.C. "Challenges, But Another Chance." *Business Korea,* July 1996.

Krizan, William G., and Richard Korman. "Light Funding Burdens Heavy Market." *ENR,* 20 May 1996.

Reina, Peter. "Reports Measure World Market." *ENR,* 6 December 1999.

Reina, Peter, et al. "The Top 225 International Contractors." *ENR,* 16 August 1999.

Rogers, Magdalene. "Borneo: Osu Briefed on Flood Control Project." *Borneo Bulletin,* 16 November 1999.

"Trends in U.S. Construction, 1996 to 2000." *Construction Review,* Winter 1995.

Tulacz, Gary J. "Reports Measure World Market." *ENR,* 6 December 1999.

———. "Good Times are Shared By All." *ENR Sourcebook,* September 1999.

U.S. Census Bureau. *1997 Economic Census.* Washington: GPO, 1999. Available from www.census.gov.

Vantuono, William C. "You can get there from here." *Railway Age,* June 1998.

"Vietnam Speeds Up Construction of Flood Control Projects." *Xinhua News Agency,* 18 August 1999.

WEFA Industrial Monitor. New York: John Wiley, 1999.

Winston, Sherie and Tom Ichniowski. "Clean Water Bill to Reform State Loan Funds Introduced." *ENR,* 30 August 1999.

Wright, Andrew G., et al. "The 'Other' E-biz Continues to Grow." *ENR,* 5 July 1999.

SIC 1711

PLUMBING, HEATING, AND AIR CONDITIONING

This industry classification covers special trade contractors primarily engaged in plumbing, heating, air conditioning, and similar work. Sheet metal work performed by plumbing, heating, and air conditioning contractors in conjunction with the installation of plumbing, heating, and air conditioning equipment is included here, but roofing and sheet metal work contractors are classified in **SIC 1761: Roofing, Siding, and Sheet Metal Work.** Special trade contractors primarily engaged in electrical work are classified in **SIC 1731: Electrical Work.**

NAICS CODE(S)

235110 (Plumbing, Heating and Air-Conditioning)

The U.S. plumbing, heating, and air conditioning industry included 84,876 establishments in 1997. According to the 1997 Economic Census published by the U.S. Department of Commerce, these establishments had combined employment of 788,930, with the average firm employing between 8 and 9 people. Larger establishments, with 20 employees or more, accounted for 10 percent of the total number of establishments while bringing in 62 percent of all business done by this industry in 1997. Average hourly earnings for HVAC Mechanics and Installers was $14.02 in 1996 with a yearly wage of $28,040. Plumbers earned an average of $530 per week in 1998. Apprentices earned half the wage paid to their more experienced counterparts.

The U.S. plumbing, heating, and air conditioning industry produced $87.3 billion in total dollar value of business in 1997. The cost of materials, components, and supplies for this industry was $33.0 billion, and $8.8 billion was spent on subcontracted construction work. The cost of power, fuels, and lubricants for the industry was $1.1 billion. Total industry payroll costs in 1997 were $25.7 billion.

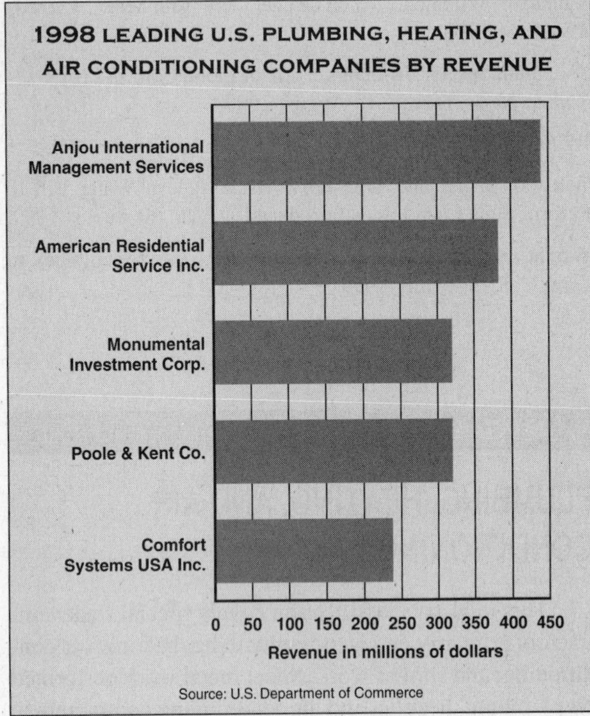

The plumbing, heating, and air conditioning industry is the largest of the more than 20 special trade contractor groups as classified by the U.S. Department of Commerce. In the mid-1990s, it was benefiting from the growing U.S. housing market. Housing construction continued its record growth in response to a strong economy and low interest rates. There were approximately 1.18 million building permits issued for single family housing in 1998 and 424 thousand building permits issued for multi-family units. This was vital for the plumbing, heating, and air conditioning industry, since 28 percent of its construction work was done on detached single-family houses in 1997. Industrial buildings accounted for another 15 percent of its work, followed by office buildings at 11 percent, and other commercial buildings at 9 percent. Other categories made up the remainder of the total.

Severe winter weather in some areas of the country in 1995 and 1996 proved to be a good business opportunity for this industry. Water damage from frozen pipes and frozen water mains required expensive repairs. Also, the nation's aging housing stock meant that many homes built during the building boom that followed World War II needed replacement heating and air conditioning systems as well as plumbing repairs, which helped to boost industry sales.

One trend affecting the plumbing, heating, and air conditioning industry in the mid-1990s was the continuing shortage of skilled tradespeople. Jobs in the construction image continued to suffer an image problem with high school students. A survey conducted by National Business Employment Weekly, reported that jobs in construction ranked 248 out of a possible 250. Dancers and lumberjacks were the bottom two career choices after construction. The labor shortage was causing firms involved in construction to increase wages, stretch schedules, and, in some cases, reduce the quality of construction.

While there are thousands of small, independent contractors in this industry, there are also very sizable major companies leading the industry. Ranked according to revenues, the top five companies in 1998 in the plumbing, heating and air conditioning industry were: Anjou International Management Services ($440 million), American Residential Service Incorporated ($383 million), Monumental Investment Corporation ($320 million), Poole & Kent Company ($320 million)—a subsidiary of Monumental Investment Corporation—and Comfort Systems USA Incorporated ($238 million).

Further Reading

"Build YOUR Future; Careers in Construction."*Craft Information.* Available from http://careers.nccer.org/craft_info/earning_potential.asp.

Donohue, Gerry. "Labor Drought." *Builder,* July 1996, 168.

Emerson, Jim."Plumbers."*Direct,*November 1998, 91.

Patrick, Stephanie."Building Boom, Labor Bust."*Dallas Business Journal,*April 1999, 31.

"Residential Construction Forecast: Slower in 2000."*Air Conditioning, Heating & Refrigeration News,* November 1999, 18.

Seiders, David. "1997 Housing Forecast." *Builder,* January 1997, 316.

U.S. Department of Commerce. *1997 Census of Construction Industries.* Washington: GPO, 2000.

SIC 1721

PAINTING AND PAPER HANGING

This classification includes special trade contractors primarily engaged in painting and paper hanging. Special trade contractors primarily engaged in roof painting are classified in **SIC 1761: Roofing, Siding, and Sheet Metal Work.**

NAICS Code(s)

235210 (Painting and Wall Covering Contractors)

Painting and paper hanging is a diverse, highly fragmented industry. In 1997, there were 37,480 industry establishments in the United States, with total employment of 195,331, according to the U.S. Census Bureau.

The painting and paper hanging industry produced $13 billion in income in 1997. Of this amount all but

$51,000 was for construction work. The establishments in this industry paid $3 billion for materials, components, and supplies and $966 million for construction work subcontracted out to others. The cost of power, fuels, and lubricants for the industry was $217 million.

While most of the establishments in this industry are small, independent contracting companies, there are several large corporations. In 1999, the top three companies (by annual revenue) were Brock Enterprises, of Beaumont, Texas ($203 million); Cannon Sline Inc., of Philadelphia and Houston ($90 million); and Long Painting Company, of Seattle ($30 million). In most regions of the United States, individual contractors and contracting companies are available and handle most industrial and residential contracts. Contractors involved in painting and paper hanging are often represented by one of several industry groups or associations, such as the Painting and Decorating Contractors of America.

The painting and paper hanging industry is closely linked with overall trends in the construction industry, since the painting of new and remodeled buildings account for most of the industry's business. For that reason, the painting and paper hanging industry saw sustained growth in the early to mid-1990s. A long economic expansion, which began in 1992 and continued into 1997, combined with relatively low interest rates, kept housing starts growing steadily from 1992 through 1996. The number of single family housing starts in 1999 were at their highest since 1978. Though expected to decline in 2000, starts still were expected to be at a high enough level to sustain growth in many construction industries, including painting and paper hanging. Consequently, employment outlook in this industry was expected to grow fairly steadily into 2006.

The type of work done by painting and paper hanging firms varies by the type of construction being done. For example, new detached single family houses accounted for 25.6 percent of all work done by this industry in 1992, up sharply from 20.1 percent in 1987. New office buildings were the next largest category of work done, at 12 percent, down from 13.9 percent in 1987. Industrial buildings and warehouses accounted for 11.8 percent of all work in 1992, while other commercial buildings accounted for 9.9 percent. Other buildings and construction projects accounted for the remaining 39.7 percent of the work in 1992.

The painting and paper hanging industry benefited from the relatively high level of housing starts from 1992 to 1999. For example, in 1999, starts were estimated at a rate of more than 1.7 million units, the highest in more than two decades. Workers earned an average of $15.89 per hour for a 38.2 hour workweek in 1999. One negative trend in the 1990s was the shortage of skilled laborers. The construction boom of the early to mid-1990s meant that painting and paper hanging firms had to compete more intensively for skilled labor and increase compensation for their employees. The shortage produced quality problems, increased prices, and stretched schedules for many firms.

FURTHER READING

Bureau of Labor Statistics. *1998-99 Occupational Outlook Handbook,* 20 March 2000. Available from http://stats.bls.gov.

1997 Census of Construction Industries. Washington, D.C.: U.S. Department of Census, 2000.

Donohue, Gerry. ''Labor Drought.'' *Builder,* July 1996, 168.

Employment Statistics. Washington, D.C.: Bureau of Labor Statistics, 20 March 2000. Available from http://www.bls.gov.

Housing Starts Increase in December. National Association of Home Builders, 20 March 2000. Available from http://www.nahb.com.

Seiders, David. ''1997 Housing Forecast.'' *Builder,* January 1997.

''Volatile Homebuilding Market Reignites.'' *Standard & Poor's Industry Surveys,* 22 February 1996.

SIC 1731

ELECTRICAL WORK

This category covers special trade contractors primarily engaged in electrical work at the site. The construction of transmission lines is classified in **SIC 1623: Water, Sewer, Pipeline, and Communications and Power Line Construction,** and electrical work carried on in repair shops is classified in **SIC 7622: Radio and Television Repair Shops; SIC 7623: Refrigeration and Air-Conditioning Service and Repair Shops;** or **SIC 7629: Electrical and Electronic Repair Shops, Not Elsewhere Classified.** Establishments primarily engaged in monitoring of burglar and fire alarms with incidental installation are classified in **SIC 7382: Security Systems Services.**

NAICS CODE(S)

561621 (Security Systems Services (except Locksmiths))

235310 (Electrical Contractors)

INDUSTRY SNAPSHOT

The electrical contracting industry in the United States is made up of a few large firms doing business in many regions, and a large number of small companies that generally serve customers in their local vicinities. Many of these smaller firms are family owned. Most work in this industry depends on intense competitive bidding, and the obtaining and completing of contracts makes for fluctuating needs for skilled electricians. Most electrical contract work companies are nonunion, but there is a strong union that is influential in some parts of the industry.

In the late 1990s, the industry had 65,031 establishments with 646,719 employees. The dollar value of business done in 1999 by these establishments was $76.5 billion, of which $43 billion was for electrical work. Ten percent of the establishments had 20 or more employees and did business amounting to 60 percent of the electrical contract revenues that year.

In the early 1990s the specialty contracting business generally had lower revenues and profit margins than in prior years. The industry experienced growth in the mid-1990s, however, due to nationwide economic improvement and a boom in housing construction. By the late 1990s the industry was booming, growing faster than any other type of construction contracting. Both the amount and nature of work continues to expand as electrical contractors move into the data and voice line communication installation businesses.

Organization and Structure

While the wide range of company sizes and large number of firms in electrical contracting make for diversity of operations, there are certain patterns relating to the types of customers and jobs, internal functions, costs, union and nonunion conditions, trade associations, training, and governmental regulations and standards.

Customers and Jobs. Electrical contracting firms as well as other trade contractors generally do their work at the construction or facility site, though some specialty work may be done in their own shops. When a new building is constructed, these trade contractors are retained by a general contractor who is responsible for the entire building's construction. The specialty contractors, however, are sometimes subcontractors of other subcontractors and, at other times, especially with repair and maintenance jobs, may deal directly with the facility's owners. The ultimate customers are individual homeowners, businesses, institutions, and governmental agencies, each of which has its own manner of dealing with contractors and subcontractors.

Size of Operating Units. About 10 percent of electrical contracting establishments in 1997 had 20 or more employees, and these establishments controlled 60 percent of all business. Only 9 establishments had 1,000 or more employees. Establishments are considered to be generally permanent places where estimating, procurement, and management of work is done for one or more sites. Larger firms may have a number of such establishments.

Internal Functions. Whether an electrical contracting firm is an individual or a company with 500 employees, it performs the necessary business functions of marketing, estimating, planning, scheduling, purchasing, accounting, and training. The estimating function is especially important in the electrical contracting industry because many jobs are obtained on the basis of competitive bids. Jobs bid too low result in losses, and bids that are too high result in business lost to lower bidding competitors.

Costs. Principal costs are materials and labor. In 1997 the cost of materials and supplies amounted to 36.6 percent of the total value of electrical contractors' work, and their payrolls came to 33.5 percent of that total. Other costs included subcontracted work, rentals for machinery and facilities, fuel, and other overhead and administrative costs.

Unions. The International Brotherhood of Electrical Workers (IBEW) is an AFL-CIO affiliate that dates back to the 1890s. Generally the electrical contractors in larger cities have had larger numbers of union employees. The number of nonunion shops increased during the 1980s and the IBEW launched a campaign to strengthen its membership. Membership is still down from its high of more than 1 million. In the late 1990s the IBEW counted 750,000 members in more than 1,100 local unions in both the United States and Canada.

Standards and Regulations. The National Electrical Code (NEC) was established to provide electrical work guidelines to assure avoidance of hazards. The code was fostered by the American National Standards Institute and by the National Fire Protection Association. The code is revised and updated every three years to meet changing technology and improve safety features. In 1996 the National Electrical Contractors Association introduced the National Electrical Installation Standards (NEIS) for electrical products and systems. Not intended for regulatory use, they are voluntary standards intended to create a more specific definition for what is meant by the ''neat and workmanlike'' standards that the NEC refers to, creating a baseline level for quality and workmanship in electrical construction. Other specifications under development by NEIS at the end of the 1990s included standards for electrical symbols, industrial lighting systems, motor control systems, raceways, cables, hazardous locations, industrial heat tracing systems, and telecommunications.

Regulation. Local and state authorities generally require adherence to code and most have set up their own supplementary procedures and regulations to monitor its enforcement. Most localities require that electricians performing commercial and industrial work be licensed as journeymen, and some localities provide a ''residential wireman's'' license for residential work only. Work permits and inspections are required for new construction, and most cities require yearly code inspections for commercial buildings. In addition, the Underwriters Laboratory has provided a service to manufacturers of electrical and other products to analyze and certify approval to those products that the laboratory has determined meet its minimum safety standards.

BACKGROUND AND DEVELOPMENT

Commercial use of electrical products and services developed rapidly in the late 1880s after Thomas Edison's invention of the incandescent lamp and other applications. Electrical products and service businesses grew along with related organizations, associations of electrical contractors, and electricians' unions. Although growth has been quite continuous, there have been cycles with downswings, as in the early 1990s.

One measure of the continuing growth in the electric industries is the fact that the amount of electricity used in American homes tripled in the four decades after 1950. Other data showed growth and change in the structure of the electrical contracting industry in the years between 1972 and 1999. The number of employees reached an all-time high in 1999, and the number of establishments continually increased.

Electrical contracting firms, however, like all construction businesses, have always been subject to significant up and down cycles according to economic conditions. The late 1980s and early 1990s were a period of decline in new construction, and electrical contractors were affected accordingly, as the specialty contracting business in general had lower revenues than in prior years. Most recently the addition of "limited energy systems," such as voice-data lines and fiber optics, has expanded the work of electrical contractors.

Unions and Associations. The National Electrical Contractors Association was founded in 1901 and by 1999 boasted 118 local groups and 4,000 contractor members. It has traditionally worked with union leaders in developing training programs and negotiating relationships. Independent Electrical Contractors, Inc. (IEC), formed in 1958, represents primarily open-shop electrical contractors and also administers apprentice training activities. By the year 2000 the IEC grew to a 76-chapter association representing more than 3,500 electrical contractors and nearly 70,000 electrical workers. The International Brotherhood of Electrical Workers (IBEW), founded in 1891, is an affiliate of the AFL-CIO.

CURRENT CONDITIONS

During the second half of the 1990s an ever increasing number of electrical contractors branched into the quickly expanding systems work, which included low voltage applications such as building alarm systems, automatic building controls, and voice-data communications lines. An increasing number of customers hired electrical contractors solely for their installations of telecommunications wiring and infrastructure. By 1999 standard electrical work accounted for only 60 percent of industry sales, with systems work accounting for 33.5 percent and the remaining 6.5 percent classed as other.

To stay competitive, many firms sought business in the adaptation of old facilities to meet current and future computer needs, such as installation of systems for new technologies. More and more firms also offered design services to customers. Moreover, a large percentage of homes built before 1970 had electrical systems that were inadequate for their current and future needs, indicating continuing business potential for electrical contracting firms in that area. Maintenance and building modernization accounted for nearly 25 percent of industry sales by the end of the 1990s.

INDUSTRY LEADERS

Most electrical contracting firms were quite small and were limited to a specific geographical area. Also, most such firms provided electrical contracting services only, whereas other outfits engaged in additional contracting work, such as carpentry or masonry. Quite a few construction companies specializing in other fields performed electrical work as well. In the late 1990s, the top three electrical contracting firms in terms of revenue, according to *Electrical Contractor Magazine,* were EMCOR Group Inc., Integrated Electrical Services Inc., and Building One Services Corp.

EMCOR Group. Based in Norwalk, Connecticut, EMCOR Group was the largest electrical and mechanical construction firm, and ranked first among electrical contractors, with $123 billion in revenue in 1998. The EMCOR Group acquired several large industry leader firms, such as Dynalectric. EMCOR boasted 90 offices worldwide and more than 18,000 employees, with more than a third of its business outside the United States. EMCOR worked with a wide variety of industries and offered complete project design and construction in all phases of mechanical and electrical construction.

Integrated Electrical Services. Based in Houston, Texas, Integrated Electrical Services grew rapidly since going public in January 1997. With 1999 sales of more than $103 billion dollars and an astounding one year growth figure of 167 percent, it was ranked second in the industry. Integrated Electrical managed this rapid growth by acquiring a large number of smaller companies, and offered services in every aspect of electrical contracting, including commercial, industrial, residential, service, power line and information technology.

Building One Services. Based in Minnetonka, Minnesota, Building One's home page touted that it was ''consolidating the fragmented facilities services industry to become a national single-source provider of facilities services for commercial, retail and industrial facilities.'' Services provided by the company included electrical, mechanical, janitorial, and maintenance management. With $91 billion in revenue in 1998, Building One ranked third in the nation, covering all aspects of electrical contracting, from electrical wiring to building automation.

Workforce

The principal technicians in the electrical contracting industry were journeyman electricians, who had the skills, training, and experience to perform the demanding work. The union status of a contractor had a significant effect on the relationships between management and the electricians as well as the individual firms' apprentice training approach. Wages varied with job requirements and were influenced significantly by the wage levels in the locality. Jobs for electricians were found in all areas of the country, and at all times of the day.

Approximately 50 percent of electricians were employed in the construction industry and 10 percent were self-employed. The remaining 40 percent worked in a wide variety of other industries and provided a broad rage of business functions, including estimating, engineering, planning and scheduling, purchasing, material control, and accounting.

Unions. The share of construction work undertaken by union shops has decreased. In 1997 approximately 18.6 percent of construction workers were represented by unions, according to the U.S. Bureau of Labor Statistics. The International Brotherhood of Electrical Workers (IBEW) began a campaign to increase union membership among electrical contracting firms that had been open-shop firms. This campaign was part of an AFL-CIO construction-worker crusade called COMET (Construction Organizing Membership Educational Training). It was expected that the members of Independent Electrical Contractors (IEC), which are open-shop firms, would carry on various efforts to maintain their open-shop status. Union membership was heaviest among larger firms and in the major urban areas.

In the union apprentice training program, contractors and the union collaborated in organizing and administering training courses. IBEW and the National Electric Contractors Association had a joint committee that established training standards for the local groups' guidance and promoted journeyman and apprenticeship training. In open-shop localities, training programs were run by the IEC.

Pay. The rates of pay for electricians varied considerably, affected by supply and demand, union presence, and historical wage levels in particular geographic regions. In 1996 the average income for full-time electricians was approximately $32,000, with the lowest 2 percent earning less than $18,000 and the highest 10 percent earning more than $52,000, according the U.S. Bureau of Labor Statistics.

America and the World

The various elements of the American construction industry increasingly looked to international opportunities since around 1980. Despite difficulties gaining entry into foreign markets, demand grew most strongly in the Pacific Rim. The largest market for U.S. contractors was Europe. American-based design firms received $7 billion in international billings in 1997, and American general contractors received $25 billion in foreign contracts that same year, according to the U.S. Department of Commerce. In 1997 the United States held the largest percentage, slightly less than 25 percent, of the international contractors market share. U.S. construction exports were predicted to continue to grow by 2 to 5 percent in the coming years, despite the downturn in the Asian economy.

Research and Technology

Electrical contractors, as well as construction firms in general, continued to rely on computer programs, such as computer-aided design (CAD), for a variety of functions. According to a survey conducted by the Electrical Contracting Foundation, from 1995 to 1996 the use of CAD for design and development in the electrical contracting industry rose 8 percent and continued to rise. Through the use of CAD 3-D modeling, construction companies could now detect design interferences and problems earlier in the development of a project. Also the rapid development of the Internet dramatically increased the need for systems work involving upgraded building wiring and fiber-optic cable work.

Deregulation. Since the passage of the Energy Policy Act of 1992, the door opened to deregulation of the electric utility industry. Various states passed legislation that required deregulation in the late 1990s and early twenty-first century. Industry analysts predicted nationwide deregulation of the utility industry, and it began in several states. While the majority of the impact of this regulation would be felt by utility providers, it remains to be seen how this would effect the status of electrical contractors.

Further Reading

''The 50th Annual Report on American Industry.'' *Forbes,* 12 January 1998. Available from http://www.forbes.com.

"50 Largest Electrical Contractors." *Electrical Contractor Magazine.* Available from http://www.ecmag.com/feature/50largest.htm.

"Guide to the Electrical Contracting Market." *Electrical Contractor Magazine,* 1999. Available from http://www.ecmag.com/research/guide.

NECA-NEIS Codes and Standards. Available from http://www.neca-neis.org.

U.S. Bureau of the Census. "County Business Patterns." *Census of Construction Industries.* Washington: GPO, 1997. Available from http://www.census.gov.

———. *Economic Census. Industry Series. Construction.* 1997. Available from http://www.census.gov.

U.S. Department of Commerce. International Trade Administration. *U.S. Industry & Trade Outlook '99.* Washington, DC: GPO, 1999.

U.S. Department of Labor. Bureau of Labor Statistics. *Labor Force Statistics from the Current Population Survey.* Washington: GPO, 1999. Available from http://www.bls.gov.

———. *Occupational Outlook Handbook,* 1998-99 ed. Washington, DC: GPO, 1998. Available from http://stats.bls.gov/ocohome.htm.

SIC 1741

MASONRY, STONE SETTING, AND OTHER STONE WORK

This category covers special trade contractors primarily engaged in masonry work, stone setting, and other stone work. Special trade contractors primarily engaged in concrete work are classified in **SIC 1771: Concrete Work;** those engaged in digging foundations are classified in **SIC 1794: Excavation Work;** and those engaged in the construction of streets, highways, and alleys are classified in **SIC 1611: Highway and Street Construction, Except Elevated Highways.**

NAICS Code(s)

235410 (Masonry and Stone Contractors)

Industry Snapshot

The masonry, stone setting, and other stone work industry includes the laying of cement blocks and bricks, chimney construction, and stone and marble work, both utilitarian and decorative. While some contractors use techniques in existence for centuries, others rely on the latest advances in method and machinery. For example, buildings of rough stone or brick remain dependent on construction techniques developed thousands of years ago, while the cutting and polishing of stone was accomplished in the 1990s with highly accurate and sometimes electronically controlled machinery.

As a business, masonry remained a relatively small part of the construction specialty trades group, accounting for only 1.6 percent of total construction revenues in 1992. Masonry contractors often worked as subcontractors to general contractors on construction projects, but some also worked for the facility owners on repair and maintenance jobs, or on projects such as the installation of a new marble floor in an old building.

Organization and Structure

Masonry contracting establishments are considered offices managing work at one or more constructions sites. While some of the larger masonry contractors serve customers from several offices over a wide territory, most firms are relatively small, privately or family-owned businesses serving local customers. Most masonry work is performed by specialists, with only about 6 percent contracted to firms primarily engaged in other construction specialties. Furthermore, some masonry specialists limit the scope of their business to specific materials such as brick, cement blocks, or stone. One of the largest masonry firms, The Western Group, works primarily in restoration and renovation projects.

Masonry contract work is done on a variety of structures. According to the U.S. Census Bureau, the industry is broken down by revenue as follows: single-family houses (26.0 percent), office buildings (12.5 percent), stores, restaurants, and gas stations (12.5 percent), industrial buildings (8.7 percent), schools (6.2 percent), apartment buildings (5.7 percent), houses (5.4 percent), hospitals (3.9 percent), other institutions (3.6 percent), warehouses (3.5 percent), heavy industrial facilities (2.2 percent); churches (2.0 percent), and other construction (7.8 percent). Of the total construction amounts, about 76 percent represented new construction, 24 percent additional alterations or reconstruction, and 10 percent maintenance and repair.

Masonry contracting companies all performed the necessary business functions of marketing, estimating, planning, scheduling, purchasing, accounting, and training. Since most contracts were secured on the basis of competitive bids, the estimation function was regarded as one of the most important in the business, requiring special skills and experience. Bids that were too high resulted in losing contracts to competitors, whereas jobs bid too low could result in losses for the contractor. Masonry was also subject to national, state, and city building codes, which required the full understanding and compliance of the masonry firm management and technicians.

In 1997, payroll represented the main cost of operating masonry contractor businesses, representing an average of 33 percent of total revenues. The cost of building materials represented about 30 percent of revenues, and work subcontracted to other firms represented an average of 6 percent of revenues. The balance went toward overhead and administrative costs, plus profit.

Background and Development

Masonry had its origins in Mesopotamia around 4000 B.C., when mud or clay bricks were used in construction. In Egypt, around 2600 B.C., cut stone was introduced in the construction of religious facilities and monuments. These early stone works exhibited remarkable engineering skills as they included stone pieces of several tons in size which were fitted with exacting tolerances. In the Americas, dry stone construction was also used, primarily for religious edifices, by the early Aztec, Mayan, and Inca civilizations.

The Romans brought several innovations to stone construction techniques. They used mortar extensively and developed vaults and domes in large structures with buttresses to reinforce large scale buildings. These features were later incorporated into Gothic cathedrals, which represented an unsurpassed artistic achievement in masonry workmanship.

The development of steel and reinforced concrete in the nineteenth century rendered stone arches and vaulting obsolete and led to the development of the modern skyscraper. In the twentieth century, the most common masonry application involved the use of concrete blocks, which proved both economical and durable. Moreover, concrete blocks provided excellent insulation against extreme temperatures and noise, were fire-resistant, stood up well in earthquakes, and needed little maintenance. In the United States, an industry standard developed in which concrete blocks, with mortar, measured 8 inches by 8 inches by 20 inches.

Much of the stone used in American masonry projects—granite, limestone, marble, sandstone, and slate—was purchased from foreign sources, and a lesser amount of stone quarried in the United States was sold overseas. In 1991, domestic stone production was valued at $197 million, with the following six states as the highest producers: Georgia, Vermont, Minnesota, North Carolina, Texas, and Indiana. Stone imports for domestic use that year were valued at $475 million, with Italy serving as the source of about half the worldwide stone production.

Current Conditions

Industry revenues have stagnated or declined since the 1980s. In 1997, the industry generated $12.3 billion in revenues. Projects were handled by 22,614 establishments with 164,236 employees. Employment projections remain low into 2006. Although construction will increase, demand for masonry will not increase at a similar rate. Average wages were $17.29 per hour in 1999.

The early 1990s were a relatively slow period for masonry contractors, as well as for other construction specialties, because several years of high vacancy rates caused office construction in 1992 to drop to 35 percent below its peak in 1985. Keeping skilled masons on the payroll during this slack time became problematic, and some masonry contractors cross-trained their masons in other skills in order to retain them.

Industry Leaders

The industry leaders as of 1999 were Cajun Constructors Inc. of Baton Rouge, with sales of $110 million; Masonry Technology Inc., of Garland, Texas, with $65 million in sales; and Seedorff Masonry Inc., of Strawberry Point, Iowa, with sales of $58 million.

Workforce

Steeped in centuries of tradition, masonry work required specialized skills and often, artistry. The homes, cathedrals, and other buildings masons helped produce prompted a high esteem for the profession and many masons derived considerable personal satisfaction from their creative efforts.

Formal apprenticeship and training programs for the industry were administered by the International Masonry Institute, an organization formed jointly by contractors in the masonry industry and the International Union of Bricklayers and Allied Craftsmen. Less formal training was also available through on-the-job guidance by senior, experienced masonry craftspersons.

In 1992, construction workers comprised 87 percent of the industry's work force, while about 13 percent performed a broader rage of business functions including estimating, engineering, planning and scheduling, purchasing, material control, and accounting. Although some seasoned masons had a broad range of skills and experience, from laying cement blocks to carving or repairing stone ornamentation, most specialized in one skill. Considerable physical strength was required for laying cement blocks, while stone work was more precise and therefore, required more patience and an eye for detail.

Most masonry contractors' employees are members of the International Union of Bricklayers and Allied Craftsmen. Others belong to the Laborers International Union. Both unions are affiliated with the AFL-CIO and membership remains particularly strong in urban areas.

America and the World

While some of the larger masonry companies had branch operations throughout the United States, few were engaged in business on a global scale. American general contractors that performed construction overseas generally subcontracted work to established local masonry firms or acquired foreign operations near the job site. Foreign general contracting companies performing construction work in the United States were more common.

RESEARCH AND TECHNOLOGY

Several masonry methods and techniques led to changes in the industry. The development of modular stone wall panels for high-rise buildings, which consisted of steel frames, anchoring devices, and stone, glass, and other exterior materials, made construction of walls more speedy and economical. The modular process also enabled the use of thinner stone panels, leading to lighter and less costly materials.

An injection system for applying epoxy—used to secure threaded rods to reinforced brick masonry walls—helped make the walls better equipped to withstand the effects of an earthquake. Moreover, aqueous silicon solutions were introduced to new water repellents to help prevent damage to walls from the freezing and thawing of absorbed moisture. Improved durability in concrete was achieved by adding supplementary materials made from industrial by-products, thereby conserving natural resources. Technological developments also resulted in using robots in the industry for excavating, pipe mapping, and building masonry walls and wall partitions.

FURTHER READING

U.S. Bureau of the Census. *1997 Economic Census.* Washington, DC: GPO, 2000. Available from http://www.census.gov.

U.S. Bureau of Labor Statistics. *Employment Statistics.* Washington, DC: GPO, 2000. Available from http://www.bls.gov.

U.S. Bureau of Labor Statistics. *1998-99 Occupational Outlook Handbook.* Washington, DC: GPO, 2000. Available from http://stats.bls.gov.

———. *County Business Patterns—1994.* Washington, DC: GPO, 1996.

Ward's Business Directory of U.S. Public and Private Industries. Detroit: Gale Group, 1999.

SIC 1742

PLASTERING, DRYWALL, ACOUSTICAL, AND INSULATION

This category is comprised of special trade contractors primarily engaged in applying plain or ornamental plaster, or in the installation of drywall and insulation. Activities include taping and finishing drywall, applying solar-reflecting insulation film, installing lathing, and constructing ceilings.

NAICS CODE(S)

235420 (Drywall, Plastering, Acoustical and Insulation Contractors)

The U.S. plastering, drywall, acoustical, and insulation industry included 20,457 establishments in 1997. These establishments had total employment of 266,710, with the average firm employing 13 people, according to the *1997 Economic Census* published by the U.S. Census Bureau. Larger establishments (defined as those with 20 employees or more) accounted for just 16 percent of the total number of establishments while taking in 62 percent of all business done by this industry in 1997.

The U.S. plastering, drywall, acoustical, and insulation industry produced $22.6 billion in total dollar value of business in 1997. The cost of materials, components, and supplies for this industry was $7.3 billion and $2.3 billion for construction work subcontracted out to others. The cost of power, fuels, and lubricants for the industry was $220 million.

This industry changed markedly in the twentieth century. In the early 1900s most walls and ceilings were constructed with wood laths and plaster. Homeowners commonly performed much of the work themselves. Thermal and acoustical insulation, if any, generally consisted of natural materials. After World War II, gypsum wallboard began to displace the lath and plaster, and various synthetic insulation products were introduced. New construction materials, along with a massive demand for plaster and insulation during the post-war building boom, created a specialized industry.

Because of its heavy dependence on new construction, the industry is cyclical. Commercial and residential construction growth during the mid-1980s generated a steady demand for specialty plaster contractors as gypsum wallboard sales surged past $2.6 billion. Conversely, a depression in commercial development and a recession in housing starts quashed industry growth from the late 1980s through the early 1990s. As the demand for gypsum products slipped to about $2 billion in 1992, many wallboard contractors suffered major setbacks, but sustained growth in housing starts gave the industry a strong boost in the mid-1990s. After dropping to 1.01 million in 1991, housing starts rose to 1.45 million in 1996.

In the midst of a nationwide construction boom during early 1999, builders faced a labor shortage followed by a widespread shortage of drywall that was expected to continue for at least six months, including the busy summer building season. Prices increased substantially, construction projects fell behind schedule, and some retail outlets limited drywall purchases to 20 sheets per customer. Drywall manufacturers responded by building new factories, re-opening facilities that had been closed, and increasing production at existing plants. Some companies hoped to import drywall from Canada, Mexico, and other foreign sources; this was a difficult proposition, though, since drywall cannot survive accidental contact with rain or other dampness and it is so brittle that it tends to break in transit.

The plastering and insulation contracting business was comprised mainly of thousands of small, privately owned firms. Some of the industry leaders, however, were large contracting companies with additional operations in other segments of the construction industry. The top five firms in the plastering and insulation contracting business by revenue, as of 1998, were Rust Industrial Services Inc. of Westchester, Illinois ($750 million); APi Group Inc. of St. Paul, Minnesota ($535 million); Performance Contracting Inc. of Shawnee Mission, Kansas ($481 million); Pacific Coast Building Products Inc. of Sacramento, California ($360 million); Irex Corp. of Lancaster, Pennsylvania ($315 million); and Performance Contracting Group Inc. of Lenexa, Kansas ($269 million).

Further Reading

Fanjoy, Rob. ''Drywall Well Drying Up.'' *Professional Builder,* April 1999.

Scott, Jonathan. ''Builders Kept Hopping in Quest to Discover Supply of Drywall.'' *Memphis Business Journal,* May 14, 1999.

Seiders, David. ''1997 Housing Forecast.'' *Builder,* January 1997.

U.S. Census Bureau. *1997 Economic Census.* Washington, D.C.: GPO, 1999.

U.S. Department of Labor. Bureau of Labor Statistics. *1998-99 Occupational Outlook Handbook.* Washington, D.C.: GPO, 1998.

U.S. Department of Labor. Bureau of Labor Statistics. *Career Guide to Industries, 1998-99 Edition. Bulletin 2503.* Washington, D.C.: GPO, 1998.

SIC 1743

TERRAZZO, TILE, MARBLE, AND MOSAIC WORK

This category covers special trade contractors that primarily set and install ceramic tile, marble, and mosaic, and those that mix marble particles and cement to make terrazzo at construction sites. Companies that primarily make pre-cast terrazzo steps, benches, and other terrazzo objects are in **SIC 3272: Concrete Products, Except Block and Brick.**

NAICS Code(s)

235420 (Drywall, Plastering, Acoustical and Insulation Contractors)

235430 (Tile, Marble, Terrazzo and Mosaic Contractors)

Terrazzo, tiles, marble, and mosaic have been used in construction for centuries, lending charm and elegance to houses, churches, and public buildings. This respected craft requires skill but offers the opportunity for artistic expression, particularly in the use of terrazzo and mosaic materials.

The U.S. Department of Labor reported that approximately 29,000 tilesetters were employed in 1996. Those who were employed by contractors tended to be assigned to nonresidential construction projects. Almost half were self-employed and worked primarily on residential projects. During the late 1990s, the industry included many companies that served customers locally, although some firms covered broader areas.

Much of the marble and other material used in this industry is imported from countries such as Italy. Terrazzo originated hundreds of years ago when Venetian craftsmen discovered a new use for discarded marble chips. Terrazzo is made by mixing pebbles or chips of stone or glass in cement, then polishing the surface to make it smooth. Terrazzo is one of the most durable flooring surfaces, and it can also have aesthetic qualities.

Tiles traditionally are square pieces of fired clay used to cover exterior or interior surfaces such as floors, walls, or roofs. Craftsmen in this trade also use thin slabs of vinyl, wood, cork, and other materials in a similar way. Most civilizations since 3000 B.C. have used ceramic tiles, often for decorative purposes. Because they are durable and easy to clean, tiles are commonly used in areas such as bathrooms, swimming pools, and medical operating rooms.

Marble is a metamorphic rock often with irregular markings from impurities, which add to its appeal and beauty. It has been used in many architectural landmarks including the Parthenon and the Taj Mahal.

Mosaic is a decorative surface made by setting small colored pieces, such as tile, in mortar or other adhesive. Employed in architecture since 3000 B.C., mosaic is still used in places where a waterproof, hygienic surface is required, especially if decoration is also desired.

Although this industry is based on a craft that is centuries old, some new methods have been developed to make the work easier or less expensive. In contrast to the traditional methods of setting and polishing terrazzo or laying out tile and mosaic at the construction site, some manufacturers began selling prefabricated materials. Other innovations included vinyl tile designed to look like natural formations, as well as new lightweight panels and bonding materials that made tile more suitable for exterior surfaces, even on high-rise buildings.

In 1997 the U.S. industry employed 39,755 workers in 6,847 businesses, compared to 31,300 workers in 5,800 firms in 1994. The total industry payroll for 1997 was $1.064 billion. Businesses with fewer than 20 employees made up 93 percent of all firms in the industry. Those small companies accounted for 58 percent of the $3.53 billion terrazzo, tile, marble, and mosaic work completed that year.

For a typical contractor in this field in 1997, materials, components, and supplies constituted the principal expenses, amounting to $1.29 billion. Payroll was next with $1.06 billion, while work subcontracted to other firms amounted to $201 million. Other expenses included fuels, overhead, and administration.

In 1998 the largest companies in this industry included Catello Tile and Marble of Las Vegas, Nevada, with 350 employees and annual sales of $25 million. K-Lath Div. of Monrovia, California, had 50 employees and estimated sales of $25 million. Tomlinson Engineering Co. of Charlotte, North Carolina, had 160 employees and sales of $16 million. R.S. Andrews Services Inc. of Atlanta, Georgia, had 160 employees and sales of $15 million. Twin City Tile and Marble Co. of St. Paul, Minnesota, had 135 employees and estimated sales of $12 million.

Several trade associations serve contractors and manufacturers in this industry. They include the National Terrazzo and Mosaic Association, the Ceramic Tile Institute of America, the Marble Institute of America, the National Tile Contractors Association, the International Brotherhood of Painters and Allied Trades, and the International Union of Bricklayers and Allied Craftsmen.

FURTHER READING

U.S. Census Bureau. *1997 Economic Census.* Washington, D.C.: GPO, 1999.

U.S. Department of Labor. Bureau of Labor Statistics. *1998-99 Occupational Outlook Handbook.* Washington, D.C.: GPO, 1998.

U.S. Department of Labor. Bureau of Labor Statistics. *Career Guide to Industries, 1998-99 Edition. Bulletin 2503.* Washington, D.C.: GPO, 1998.

SIC 1751

CARPENTRY WORK

This category includes special trade contractors primarily engaged in carpentry work. Establishments primarily engaged in building and installing cabinets at the job site are classified in this industry. Establishments primarily engaged in building custom cabinets for individuals in a shop are classified in **SIC 5712: Furniture Stores.** Carpentry work performed by general contractors engaged in building construction is classified in **SIC 1500: General Building Contractors.**

NAICS CODE(S)

235510 (Carpentry Contractors)

INDUSTRY SNAPSHOT

Carpentry is the work of cutting and joining timber to create frames for housing and items such as doors, windows, cabinets, and staircases. Work in this industry includes cabinet work performed at the construction site, carpentry work, folding door installation, framing, garage door installation, ship joinery, store fixture installation, trim and finish, and prefabricated window and door installation. It is a very strenuous occupation due to long periods of standing, climbing, bending, and kneeling.

Carpenters rely heavily on the health of the economy and especially the success of the housing industry since their work consists mainly of building or renovating residential structures. The housing industry can be positively or negatively affected by factors such as interest rates fluctuations and availability of mortgage funds. Throughout the recession of the early 1990s, carpenters suffered as the number of housing starts declined. As the economy improved in the mid-1990s, so did the availability of carpentry work.

The price of lumber fluctuated wildly throughout the 1990s, and in April 1996, the Clinton administration imposed tariff sanctions on Canadian lumber beyond a certain amount. This good intention backfired and caused lumber prices in the United States to skyrocket, and soon building and construction costs went up. Construction growth for new housing was expected to reach 1.54 million units in 2000. Overall prospects in the industry are positive through the year 2006, as the remodeling industry shows promise of becoming stronger, and replacement carpentry needs escalate.

ORGANIZATION AND STRUCTURE

Nearly 500,000 carpenters belong to the United Brotherhood of Carpenters and Joiners, a labor organization located in Washington, D.C., which is actively involved in the construction industry. The union supports building contractors who work with union carpenters. The union also studies health and safety aspects of carpentry work, which has the highest serious injuries rate in the United States. The union has been studying the ergonomics of carpentry in hopes of reducing workplace accidents by developing preventive on-the-job techniques.

The union, in conjunction with contractor trade associations, also provides training and apprenticeship programs, which are greatly needed in this industry. As carpentry work becomes more specialized and involves potentially dangerous materials such as asbestos removal, formal training will become increasingly necessary.

Other groups primarily interested in carpentry are the Associated Builders and Contractors, of Rosslyn, Virginia; the Associated General Contractors of America, Inc., of Washington, D.C.; and the National Association of Home Builders, also located in Washington, D.C.

The construction industry can be divided into three major contract divisions: general building contractors, heavy construction contractors, and special trade contractors (including carpenters). General building contractors build residential, industrial, and commercial buildings, while heavy construction contractors build structures like roads, highways, and bridges.

Special trade contractors usually focus on one trade and work under the direction of general contractors, architects, or property owners. Beyond completing their work to specification, special trade contractors have no responsibility for building the structure in its entirety.

According to *Occupational Outlook,* "Carpenters are involved in many different kinds of construction activities. They cut, fit, and assemble wood and other materials in the construction of buildings, highways and bridges, docks, industrial plants, and many other structures. The duties of carpenters vary by type of employer. A carpenter employed by a special trade contractor, for example, may specialize in setting forms for concrete construction or in erecting scaffolding, while one who is employed by a general building contractor may perform many tasks, such as framing walls and partitions, putting in doors and windows, hanging kitchen cabinets, and installing paneling and tile ceilings."

Background and Development

When both commercial and residential buildings were made primarily from timber, the carpenter was the critical element needed for construction. Over time, the scope of the carpenter's work has changed. As the materials for commercial buildings switched to primarily concrete and steel, the demand for carpenters has shifted to the framework for houses and commercial structures and residential remodeling. A carpenter's work also may extend to interior jobs, requiring some of the skills of a joiner. These skills include making door frames, cabinets, countertops, and assorted molding and trim.

The standard tools used by a carpenter have been hammers, pliers, screwdrivers, awls, planes (hand-held blades), crosscut saws, rip saws, tenon and dovetail saws, and levels, in addition to an assortment of power tools. Lightweight cordless pneumatic and combustion tools like nailers and drills, and sanders with electric speed controls are being used increasingly more. These help carpenters to be more efficient and work faster; they also reduce fatigue. Carpenters have used wood as a building material for centuries; however, as the world's supply of wood continues to shrink, alternative building materials, such as partial-wood products, have begun to be developed and used in residential construction.

For carpenters who work predominately in residential construction, the state of the housing industry is critical. The recession of the early 1990s hit the housing market particularly hard. With weak employment trends, potential buyers postponed purchasing new homes. The housing market's recovery was stalled by a lingering and severe credit crunch, an unanticipated rise in lumber costs, and low consumer confidence levels. Fueled by lower interest rates, the housing industry began a slow but steady rebound in 1994. Although the pace of economic growth stalled during the first quarter of 1994, a surge in housing sales at the end of 1993 forecasted a strong performance for 1994. In 1993 the construction of 100,000 new single-family homes generated over 200,000 construction jobs and $4.4 billion in wages, according to the National Association of Home Builders (NAHB). The NAHB predicted a 4 percent rise in single-family housing starts for 1994.

Carpenters work closely with, and are greatly affected by, the remodeling industry. Once thought to be recession-proof, the residential repair and remodeling (R&R) market declined by 8.7 percent during 1991. Spending for additions and alterations dropped the most, by 17 percent. Despite this fall, the remodeling sector should continue to provide carpenters with steady work. Remodeling totalled approximately $113.5 billion in 1993. NAHB predicted that remodeling activity would climb to $124.9 billion in 1994.

Carpenters who work in the remodeling sector should benefit from two major demographic factors. First, as baby boomers enter their high income-producing years, they will be purchasing new or existing homes. Also, the aging U.S. housing stock will need to be updated or replaced. Out of the 100 million homes in the United States, nearly 60 percent are at least 22 years old.

Impact of the High Cost of Lumber. Despite the increased number of jobs available for carpenters in the mid-1990s, the construction and housing industry continued to be burdened by the high cost of lumber. When logging stopped in the national forests of the Pacific Northwest, a lumber shortage ensued. Home builders and remodelers have been the primary users of lumber, accounting for nearly 65 percent of all framing timber. After hovering at just over $200 per 1,000-board-feet throughout the 1980s, the price of framing lumber rose and dropped sporadically during 1992 and 1993, according to NAHB. The price increase was blamed on the cessation of virtually all logging in the national forests of the Pacific Northwest. Logging was halted by court order as environmental organizations fought to protect the habitat of the Northern Spotted Owl, a threatened species in Washington, Oregon, and Northern California.

A near-instantaneous shortage of lumber from national forest land, one of three major sources of timber, caused a 74 percent price increase between October 1992 and 1994. This price increase added between $4,000 and $5,000 to the cost of building a typical 2,000-square-foot home, according to NAHB. Although lumber prices fell somewhat from a high of $510 per 1,000-board-feet, the Northern Spotted Owl issue has yet to be resolved.

Impact of Labor Union Activity. In an effort to get contractors to use union workers, labor groups have been subsidizing organized labor by using a tactic called ''job targeting.'' Although some contractors have aggressively opposed job targeting, smaller operators have welcomed the arrangement because it allows them to gain market share by underbidding their nonunion contractor. By late 1992, more than 500 local unions nationwide had begun to implement this practice, according to the *Wall Street Journal.*

When a construction job comes up for bid, a local union will ''target'' a contractor and offer to make a payment. This allows the union contractor to come in with a lower bid than a nonunion competitor. Although originally intended to stem the flow of jobs to nonunion workers, *Wall Street Journal* staff reporter Barbara Marsh noted that ''some local unions apparently use targeting to persuade nonunion contractors to go union.'' In fact, Marsh continued, ''target programs can pose such a competitive threat that nonunion contractors are trying to stop them in court.''

Health and Safety Issues. With the highest serious injury rate in the United States, health and safety concerns continue to be a major issue both to carpenters and the contractors who employ them. Because over half of all workers' compensation dollars have been used for the treatment of musculoskeletal injuries, the United Brotherhood of Carpenters launched a pilot program to address the ergonomics of carpentry by exploring how job-related tasks impact the worker and provide preventive training at the apprenticeship level, according to *Engineering News Record.* An ergonomist and a health and safety team will study carpenters at job sites to better understand the contributing factors to the most prevalent injuries. The team will compare workers' compensation data from state and area health and welfare funds, according to *Engineering News Record.*

The union also has begun to study carpentry in relation to health implications for its workers. Carpenters have been dying an average of six years younger than other Americans, reported Hazel Bradford in *Engineering News Record.* Carpenters have a 150 times greater chance of dying from mesothelioma, an asbestos-related disease. Cancer deaths for carpenters have been 50 percent higher than the general population, while deaths from emphysema, bronchitis, and asthma have been three times higher. From its findings, the union hopes to establish medical screenings and early warning programs for its members. The union also plans an educational campaign aimed at reaching both apprentices and journeymen (trained union workers) through educational programs. Special attention will be given to work regarding asbestos, lead, and hazardous wastes.

Current Conditions

Due to replacement needs, more than 100,000 job openings are thought to become available every year from 1997 to 2005, according to the Bureau of Labor Statistics. The number of job openings in the carpentry field is relatively higher than in other fields because of the high turnover rate and the difficulty in finding steady work. Those entering the field should expect to experience periods of unemployment. Many construction projects are short-term, and the industry itself tends to be cyclical.

The rate of employment may be adversely affected by the use of prefabricated components. These new materials require minimal installation time, allowing carpenters to finish jobs faster and as a result, fewer carpenters are needed. For example: prehung doors and windows and prefabricated wall panels, stairs, and partitions are easily installed; entire roof assemblies can be lifted into place by cranes; and better adhesives reduce the time waiting for pieces to join. But overall, employment was expected to grow at a high rate of increase into 2006, due to renovation and replacement demands.

Industry Leaders

It is difficult to determine exactly how many carpentry contractors exist in the United States because carpentry contractors generally are small establishments, and many self-employed carpenters serve as their own contractors. Plus, the housing industry is highly fragmented, lacking national general contractors or specialty trade contractors. A typical American home builder is a local contractor who constructs fewer than 25 houses each year and works with local subcontractors, labor, and suppliers. The largest companies involved in carpentry, according to *Ward's Business Directory of U.S. Private and Public Companies* (1999) were BT Mancini Company Inc., Center Brothers Inc., Door Systems Inc., and J Mar and Sons Inc.

WORKFORCE

In 1997, 230,409 people were employed in the carpentry industry. Eighty percent of those worked for contractors; they built, remodeled, and repaired buildings and other structures. The others worked for manufacturing firms, government agencies, wholesale and retail establishments, and schools. About 40 percent were self-employed. According to the Bureau of Labor Statistics, $17.39 per hour was the median pay for carpenters who were not self-employed in 1999.

Carpenters learn their trade through both on-the-job training and formal education. Most employers recommend an apprenticeship, but the number of available programs, usually administered by local chapters of Associated Builders and Contractors, Associated General Contractors, and the United Brotherhood of Carpenters, has been limited.

As skilled workers become scarce, and jobs become more demanding, the need for more training programs will increase. The industry will demand more knowledgeable workers. ''There's more complex instrumentation, new materials,'' Cliff Mumm, president of Houston-based Becon Construction, told the *Wall Street Journal.* Computer and math skills in addition to special new skills, such as hazardous waste cleanup, will be in demand.

Some organizations have begun to provide additional training programs, starting in high school and offering apprenticeships upon graduation. Associated Builders and Contractors has begun four-year training courses in five construction specialties. The group works with both employers and high school students in 19 school districts in Texas. The Laborers International Union and Associated General Contractors trained about 33,000 U.S. and Canadian workers in construction skills in 1992. The group also planned to train another 29,000 workers in hazardous-waste cleanup.

RESEARCH AND TECHNOLOGY

With rising timber costs, the construction industry continues to look for alternative building materials to use instead of lumber and plywood in residential construction. Some viable options have been engineered wood products, concrete, structural foam sandwich panels, and laminated fiberboard structural sheathing. Engineered wood products (EWPs) have been on the market for years. These products are a combination of wood fibers with adhesives and have been used to form beams, headers, joints, and other structural framing products. EWPs do not use raw materials from the U.S. timber supply. Instead these products have been made from smaller trees and inferior species once thought to be unsuitable for building materials. ''Engineered lumber is structurally superior to ordinary lumber,'' Tom Denig, president of Trus Joist MacMillan told *Nation's Building News.* ''It's stronger and can span greater distances than ordinary lumber. And it has most of the moisture removed during the manufacturing process, so it won't change shape before or after it's installed.''

Laminated fiberboard and foam core structural sandwich panels are two other alternative building products. Fiberglass sheathing is a lightweight panel made from wood and agricultural by-products. The panel consists of fibrous plies laminated under pressure and covered with aluminum foil or polyethylene. Foam sandwich panels are made of two strong, stiff skins, usually strand board or plywood, and separated by a light-weight, but thick, core of polystyrene. The fiberboard can be used in place of plywood sheathing on exterior walls, and the foam core panels can be used instead of wooden wall and roof systems.

FURTHER READING

Grogan, Tim. ''Forecast: Getting Back on Track.''*Engineering News Record,* 23 December 1996, 30.

———. ''Summary: Lumber Prices Zap Indexes.'' *Engineering News Record,* 23 December 1996, 27-9.

''Housing Starts Increase in December.''*National Association of Home Builders,* 2000. Available from http://www.nahb.com.

''Manufacturing Climbs Value-Added Ladder.'' *Global Economic Outlook.* October 1996, 10-11.

U.S. Department of Labor. Bureau of Labor Statistics. ''Carpenters.'' *1998-99 Occupational Outlook Handbook.* Available from http://stats.bls.gov.

U.S. Department of Labor. Bureau of Labor Statistics. *Employment Statistics,* 2000. Available from http://www.bls.gov.

Ward's Business Directory of U.S. Public and Private Companies. Detroit: Gale Research, 1999.

Winston, Sherie. ''Carpenters Get Crash Course on Becoming More Business-Like.'' *Engineering News Record,* 23 December 1996, 10.

SIC 1752

FLOOR LAYING AND OTHER FLOOR WORK, NOT ELSEWHERE CLASSIFIED

This category includes special trade contractors primarily engaged in the installation of asphalt tile, carpeting, linoleum, and resilient flooring. The industry also includes special trade contractors engaged in laying, scraping, and finishing parquet and other hardwood flooring. Establishments primarily engaged in installing stone and ceramic floor tile are classified in the Masonry, Stonework, Tile Setting, and Plastering industries; those installing or finishing concrete floors are classified in **SIC 1771: Concrete Work;** and those installing artificial turf are classified in **SIC 1799: Special Trade Contractors, Not Elsewhere Classified.**

NAICS CODE(S)

235520 (Floor Laying and Other Floor Contractors)

The U.S. floor-laying industry is characterized by a large number of special trade contractors who perform work for a general contractor or an architect. In 1997, 12,078 of these establishments operated in the United States. Carpet installers may also install other types of flooring, such as tile and/or vinyl and linoleum.

The health of the floor-laying industry is closely tied to that of the housing and construction industry; when housing starts slow, as they did in the early 1990s, floor layers lose work. The rate of employment for carpet layers, however, generally remains stable, since so much of their work involves the replacement of carpet. Although there was a small decline in the housing market early in 1995 following a three-year upswing, the market recovered by 1996, providing a steady supply of work for flooring contractors.

Much of the floor-laying industry works in the residential repair and remodeling (R&R) market. Renovation and repair increased dramatically in the mid-1990s, reaching an all-time high in 1995 of $69.5 billion in total revenue. Fueled by lower interest rates, the housing industry continued the slow but steady rebound begun in 1993. According to the National Association of Home Builders (NAHB) in 1995, ''Manufactured housing placements exceeded the 300,000 unit mark for the first time in over two decades.'' The NAHB predicted a 7 percent rise in housing starts for 1996, and reported a two decade high of more than 1.7 million units for 1999.

Approximately 50,000 workers were employed in carpet installation in the mid-1990s, according to the U.S. Census Bureau, and 60,533 workers were reported industry-wide in 1997. While some carpet installers worked for flooring contractors or floor covering retailers, two out of every three were self-employed. Typically, carpet installers have been concentrated in urban areas that have high levels of construction activity. Because carpet installation often provides entry-level jobs, more than 30 percent of the industry's workers were between the ages of 16 and 29 in 1990. Women represent a growing but still small proportion—9 percent of total employment in 1990—of workers in the industry. Employment in the flooring industry was expected to grow at an average rate through 2006 due to the continued need to renovate and refurbish existing structures and a growing demand for carpet in new industrial plants, schools, hospitals, and other commercial buildings.

Carpet and other flooring installers may belong to either the United Brotherhood of Carpenters and Joiners of America or the International Brotherhood of Painters and Allied Trades.

Of all floor coverings, carpet continues to be the most popular product for both residential and commercial buildings. In the 1990s, carpet accounted for 76 percent of the total flooring market (both residential and commercial). For houses built with plywood rather than hardwood floors, wall-to-wall carpet is a necessity. Commercial properties, such as offices and shopping centers, also use carpet to cover concrete floors. And, as previously stated, carpet continues to be used largely in renovation work. As new fibers are developed, particularly those that are stain and crush resistant, more durable, and in a wider range of colors, the demand for carpet will continue to grow. Over the past decade, however, hardwood floors have experienced a resurgence in popularity and usage. Vinyl and linoleum manufacturers are also improving their products: the newer vinyls come with a glossed finish, requiring less maintenance to retain original appearance. Most are available without patterns (they may have a fleck or pebble-grain design), but more are becoming available with stylish patterns, in order to compete with the commercial carpet market.

The four industry leaders in 1999 were Continental Flooring Company; Hagopian and Sons, Inc.; Kalman Floor Company; and Wilson Floors Inc.

FURTHER READING

The Carpet and Rug Institute. ''Carpet and Rug Institute.'' Dalton, GA: 1997. Available from http://www.carpet-rug.com.

National Association of Home Builders. ''Housing Forecast.'' Washington, DC: 1996. Available from http://www.nahb.com.

———. ''Housing Starts Increase in December.'' 2000. Available from http://www.nahb.com.

Seiders, David F. ''Key Points in the Housing Outlook.'' Washington, DC:National Association of Home Builders, 1996. Available from http://www.nahb.com/bakbeg2.html.

U.S. Bureau of the Census. ''Economic Census 1997.'' Available from http://www.census.gov.

U.S. Department of Labor. Bureau of Labor Statistics. *Occupational Outlook Handbook, 1998-99 ed.* Washington, DC: GPO, 2000.

SIC 1761

ROOFING, SIDING, AND SHEET METAL WORK

Special trade contractors primarily engaged in the installation of roofing, siding, and sheet metal work. Sheet metal work performed by plumbing, heating, and air-conditioning contractors in conjunction with the installation of plumbing, heating, and air-conditioning equipment are classified in **SIC 1711: Plumbing, Heating, and Air-Conditioning.**

NAICS Code(s)

235610 (Roofing, Siding, and Sheet Metal Contractors)

Industry Snapshot

Construction services offered by the roofing, siding, and sheet metal industry include architectural sheet metal work; erection and repair of metal ceilings; copper smithing in connection with construction work; metal downspout installation; sheet metal duct work; metal gutter installation; roof spraying, painting, or coating; all roofing work, including repairs; siding installation; skylight installation; and tinsmithing in connection with construction work.

Organization and Structure

The construction industry can be divided into three major divisions: general building contractors, heavy construction contractors, and special trade contractors, which include those who install roofing. General building contractors build residential, industrial, and commercial buildings, while heavy construction contractors build structures such as roads, highways, and bridges.

Special trade contractors usually focus on one trade and work under the direction of general contractors, architects, or property owners. Beyond completing their work to specification, special trade contractors have no responsibility for building the structure in its entirety.

Besides new installations or re-roofing, the market can be divided by type of roof, either low-slope or steep-slope. The low-slope market includes commercial and industrial buildings and some apartment houses. The steep-slope market is primarily residential.

Sometimes working in conjunction with architects, roofing contractors choose from a selection of materials that include thermoset single plies (e.g., EPDM, CSPE/Hypalon, PVC), built-up roofing (BUR), and fiberglass, and organic asphalt shingles. In the re-roofing industry the contractor decides what type of roofing system to use and which manufacturer's product to install. With new installations the architect usually decides which roof system to use, and, most of the time, the contractor still chooses the manufacturer.

Background and Development

For roofers who work predominantly on newly built homes, the state of the housing industry is crucial. The recession of the early 1990s hit the housing market and roofing contractors particularly hard. Renovation and repair increased slowly but steadily during the mid-1990s, reaching $69.5 billion by 1995. The recovery of the housing market led to significant increases in both re-roofing and new construction in the West (86.4 percent), with moderate increases in the Northeast (36.0 percent) and Midwest (16.8 percent). In the South, however, there was a 17.4 percent decline.

The state of the home remodeling industry also greatly affected roofing contractors, since a large percentage of their business derives from re-roofing projects. The residential repair and remodeling (R&R) market was once thought to be recession-proof. The recession of the early 1990s proved that theory wrong, but the market recovered and increased to about $113.5 billion by 1993.

Roofing contractors who worked in the remodeling sector stood to benefit from two major demographic factors. First, as baby boomers entered their high income-producing years, they would be purchasing new or existing homes. Also, the U.S. housing stock became fairly old. Of the 100 million homes in the United States, nearly 60 percent were at least 22 years old.

Some roofing contractors rebounded from the recession with a booming roofing business. These contractors were re-roofing faulty plywood that was widely used in the eastern and southern United States in the 1980s. The chemically treated, fire-resistant roofing substance known as FRT deteriorated and lost strength when subjected to high heat and humidity, causing roofs to sag and leak. It was estimated that between 250,000 and 1 million roofs would need to be replaced.

Current Conditions

According to the *1997 Economic Census* published by the U.S. Census Bureau, the U.S. roofing, siding, and sheet metal contracting industry comprised 30,557 companies. These businesses employed a total of 253,315 people. The average firm employed 8 people. The 27,645 companies with fewer than 20 employees accounted for $10.78 billion (45 percent) of total revenues generated by the industry. The cost of materials, components, supplies, and fuels amounted to $8.9 billion, while the cost of construction work subcontracted out to others totaled $2.0 billion.

Of the industry's $24.15 billion in total revenues, $2.09 billion was generated by architectural sheet metal contractors; $509 million by carpentry contractors; $343 million by heating, ventilation, and air-conditioning contractors; $14.40 billion by roofing contractors; $2.80 billion by sheet metal contractors (except those involved in heating, ventilation, air-conditioning, and plumbing); $2.40 billion by siding contractors; $610 million by specialty sheet metal contractors (including those who worked on decking and metal ceilings); $694 million by other construction activities; and $177.90 million by other business activities.

INDUSTRY LEADERS

The roofing industry typically consists of numerous small roofing firms and a few larger companies, which often operate additional construction and manufacturing businesses. Among the largest companies involved in the roofing, siding, and sheet metal industry, Bradco Supply Corp. of Avenel, New Jersey, employed 1,100 people in 1998 and had estimated annual sales of $475 million. Pacific Coast Building Products Inc. of Sacramento, California, had 2,500 employees and sales of $360 million. Young Sales Corp. of St. Louis, Missouri, had 700 employees and sales of $129 million. Astrotech International Corp. of Pittsburgh, Pennsylvania, had 1,051 employees and sales of $122 million. Bryant Universal Roofing Inc. of Phoenix, Arizona, had 1,200 employees and sales of $110 million.

WORKFORCE

Workers in the sheet metal industry typically learn their trade through apprenticeship, including four or five years of hands-on training at job sites and at least 144 hours per year of classroom education. Others start as helpers, learning informally from experienced workers on the job and progressing gradually to more skilled tasks. They often study at vocational schools to supplement their practical experience.

On-the-job training is the most common way of entering the roofing industry, but some people learn the trade through a three-year apprenticeship that typically includes 144 hours of classroom education and at least 2,000 hours of hands-on training at job sites. Labor unions usually offer roofing and sheet metal work apprenticeship programs, often under the auspices of local union- management joint training committees.

According to the *U.S. Occupational Outlook Handbook,* roofers held approximately 138,000 jobs in 1996. Self-employed roofers represented 3 out of every 10 jobs and mainly specialized in residential work. Some roofers were members of the United Union of Roofers, Waterproofers & Allied Workers. According to the *ENR,* average hourly earnings for union roofers in 1997 were $25.75.

Sheet metal workers held approximately 110,000 jobs in 1996. Seven out of every ten worked for plumbing, heating, and air-conditioning contractors. Most of the others worked for roofing and sheet metal contractors, and a few worked for other general or special trade contractors. Relatively few sheet metal workers were self-employed. Most were members of the Sheet Metal Workers' International Association. Average hourly earnings in 1997, according to *ENR,* were $31.87.

Employment for roofers is expected to increase more slowly than the average for all occupations through the year 2006, and for sheet metal workers, it is expected to increase about as fast as the average.

FURTHER READING

"Housing Forecast." Washington, DC: National Association of Home Builders, 1996. Available from http://www.nahb.com/.

Kane, Karen. "How Was 1995?" *Professional Roofing,* March 1996.

National Roofing Contractors Association 1995-1996 Annual Market Survey. Rosemont, IL: National Roofing Contractors Association, April 1996.

Seiders, David F. "Key Points in the Housing Outlook." Washington, DC: National Association of Home Builders, October 1996. Available from http://www.nahb.com/bakbeg2.html.

U.S. Census Bureau. *Economic Census 1997.* Washington, DC: GPO, 1999.

U.S. Department of Labor. Bureau of Labor Statistics. *Occupational Outlook Handbook, 1998-99.* Washington, DC: GPO, 1998.

U.S. Department of Labor. Bureau of Labor Statistics. *Career Guide to Industries, 1998-99 ed. Bulletin 2503.* Washington, DC: GPO, 1998.

SIC 1771

CONCRETE WORK

Special trade contractors primarily engaged in concrete work, including portland cement and asphalt. This industry includes the construction of private driveways and walks of all materials. Concrete work incidental to the construction of foundations and concrete work included in an excavation contract are classified in **SIC 1794: Excavation Work;** and those engaged in construction or paving of streets, highways, and public sidewalks are classified in **SIC 1611: Highway and Street Construction, Except Elevated Highways.**

NAICS CODE(S)

235420 (Drywall, Plastering, Acoustical and Insulation Contractors)

235710 (Concrete Contractors)

INDUSTRY SNAPSHOT

Concrete—a mixture of portland cement, sand, gravel, and water—is used for the construction of everything from patios and floors to dams and highways. Special trade contractors involved in concrete work provide the following products and services: private asphalt parking areas; blacktop work; concrete work for private driveways, sidewalks, and parking lots; culvert construction; curb construction; pouring concrete to build foundations; grouting work; gunite work; parking lot construction; patio construction; sidewalk construction, except public; and stucco construction.

The U.S. Census Bureau reported that 30,417 establishments were involved in concrete contracting in 1997. These companies employed 262,256 workers and had a combined payroll of $6.9 billion. The industry's work was valued at $25.8 billion. The cost of materials, components, supplies, and fuels was $9.8 billion.

ORGANIZATION AND STRUCTURE

The construction industry can be divided into three segments: general building contractors, heavy construction contractors, and special trade contractors, which includes those engaged in concrete work. General building contractors build residential, industrial, commercial, and other buildings, while heavy construction contractors build structures such as roads, highways, and bridges. Special trade contractors usually focus on one trade and work under the direction of general contractors, architects, or property owners. Beyond completing their work to specification, special trade contractors have no responsibility for building the structure in its entirety.

Concrete can be classified by the type of aggregate or cement used, by specific characteristics, or by production methods. Ordinary structural concrete is characterized by its water-to-cement ratio. The lower the water content, all else being equal, the stronger the concrete. For concrete to set properly, however, the mixture needs to have enough water to ensure that the aggregate particles are encompassed by the cement paste, that the space surrounding the aggregate is filled, and that the concrete is liquid enough to be poured and spread effectively. The composition of concrete varies because different aggregates are used from market to market, depending upon what kind of sand and rock is available and least expensive.

Concrete's range of durability is determined by the amount of cement in relation to the aggregate, with relatively less aggregate present in strong cement. The strength of concrete is measured in pounds per square inch (psi) of force needed to crush a concrete sample of a given age or hardness. Concrete's strength can be affected by environmental factors, especially temperature and moisture.

Cement, through its use in concrete, is used in all types of construction. The Portland Cement Association estimated that in the mid-1990s about 55 percent of cement shipments in the United States was consumed in building construction, with 22 percent used for residential and 19 percent for commercial construction. Public works construction consumed about 42 percent of cement shipments, with most going to the building of streets and highways.

By far the largest customer for portland cement at that time was the ready-mix concrete industry, which purchased about 71 percent of the total shipments. Another 13 percent went to concrete producers of blocks, pipes, precasts, and prestressed products; 5 percent to highway contractors; 4 percent to building materials dealers; 3 percent to other contractors; and 4 percent to all others, including the government.

BACKGROUND AND DEVELOPMENT

Long before the discovery of cement, ancient civilizations used clay as a bonding substance. The Egyptians used a material made from lime and gypsum that resembled modern-day cement. Derived from limestone, chalk, or oyster shells, lime continued to be the primary cementing agent until the early 1800s.

In 1824 English inventor Joseph Aspdin burned and ground together a mixture of limestone and clay. This concoction, called portland cement, became the cementing agent used in concrete from that time on.

In 1867 Joseph Monier, a Parisian gardener who made pots of concrete reinforced with iron mesh, received a patent for reinforced concrete. This product, sometimes called ferroconcrete, consisted of concrete hardened onto imbedded metal, usually steel. The reinforcing steel contributed tensile strength.

A later innovation in masonry construction was the use of prestressed concrete, which neutralized the stretching forces that would rupture ordinary concrete. Because it achieved its strength without heavy reinforcements, prestressed concrete could be used to build light, shallow structures such as bridges and roofs.

During the 1980s cement imports became a significant part of the domestic supply, peaking in 1987 at more than 17 million short tons. The reason for this rise in imports was weak worldwide demand combined with strong U.S. demand, which made the United States a target for excess supplies produced by foreign cement manufacturers. Low water transportation costs during the 1980s also was a key. Canada was the largest supplier of cement to the United States through 1985. Mexico became the primary source from 1986 through 1989, supplying 28 percent of total U.S. imports in 1989.

U.S. consumption of cement (the major component of concrete) was 84 million short tons in 1993. Cement was used to build highways and other public works and to rebuild structures damaged by natural disasters, such as the hurricane in southern Florida, the earthquake in Los Angeles, and the flood in Midwest river basins. During the mid-1990s the concrete industry benefitted from a slow but steady recovery in the housing industry. New home building traditionally used about one-third of the cement consumed annually in the United States.

Prices for concrete varied widely and depended on the proximity of the nearest mill. Transportation costs continued to be a major factor in determining costs, because concrete was so heavy and had to be delivered on a timely basis. In 1994 the U.S. Justice Department began investigating possible price fixing, since the average cost of cement had jumped from $5 to about $50 a ton within one year.

CURRENT CONDITIONS

In 1997 the work done by concrete contractors was valued at $25.8 billion. New construction amounted to $18.7 billion. Additions, alterations, and reconstruction amounted to $3.6 billion. Maintenance and repair amounted to $3.2 billion. Of the $17.2 billion derived from building construction, $6.8 billion was from single-family houses. Of the $8.3 billion derived from non-building construction, $5.3 billion was from work done on private driveways and parking areas, and $1.5 billion was from work done on projects such as highways and streets.

About 9 percent of the 30,417 establishments in this industry had at least 20 employees. These larger firms accounted for 53 percent of the total value of work done in this field, 55 percent of the total payroll, and 62 percent of the $2.2 billion in work subcontracted out to other companies. There were 2,471 concrete contractors in California; 1,873 in Texas; and 1,773 in Florida. Other states with a high concentration of firms in this industry included Illinois, Michigan, Missouri, New York, Ohio, and Pennsylvania.

From 1997 into 1999 the construction industry grew rapidly as the nation experienced a surge in housing starts. The construction boom was due to a robust economy, generally mild weather, and the need to repair and rebuild after natural disasters such as ice storms in the Northeast and devastating rainstorms in the West. For the building industry, 1998 was one of the best years on record.

INDUSTRY LEADERS

During the late 1990s the residential and commercial concrete industry was a mixture of large public companies, such as cement manufacturers, and small independent concrete contractors and laborers. Among the largest companies involved in the industry was Weatherford US Inc. of Bel Air, Texas, with 2,960 employees and sales of $380 million in 1998. The firm was a division of Weatherford Enterra Inc., an international energy service and manufacturing company based in Houston. Other industry leaders included A. Teichert and Son Inc. (Sacramento, California) with 2,100 employees and $280 million in sales; Walsh Group Ltd. (Chicago, Illinois) with 3,500 employees and $1,170 million in sales; Washington Construction Group Inc. (Highland, California) with 1,000 employees and $229 million in sales; Kasler Corp. (Highland, California) with 512 employees and $210 million in sales; and Ray Wilson Co. (Pasadena, California) with 350 employees and $200 million in sales.

WORKFORCE

Most concrete masons worked for concrete contractors or for general contractors on projects such as highways, bridges, shopping malls or large buildings such as factories, schools, and hospitals. A small number were employed by firms that manufactured concrete products. Fewer than 1 out of 10 concrete masons were self-employed, a smaller percentage than in other building trades. Most self-employed masons specialized in small jobs, such as driveways, sidewalks, and patios.

Concrete masons who worked full time and belonged to a union reported average hourly earnings of between $15 and $45 in 1996. Concrete masons often work overtime, because a job must be completed once the concrete has been placed. Overtime tends to be paid at premium rates.

As the construction industry boomed, contractors had trouble finding enough workers and building supplies. The widespread labor shortage ran from 1997 into 1999. To attract workers, companies increased wages and overtime pay, but many were nevertheless forced to settle for laborers who were inexperienced or insufficiently trained. The shortage of workers stemmed from a trend among young people to attend college instead of entering the skilled trades. In addition, many construction workers had left the industry during the slump of the early 1990s.

Concrete masons generally learned their trade through on-the-job training or apprenticeship programs. Many concrete workers belonged either to the Operative Plasterers' and Cement Masons' International Association of the United States and Canada or to the International Union of Bricklayers and Allied Craftsmen.

RESEARCH AND TECHNOLOGY

The future of the concrete industry lay in continued development of high-performance concrete products. Since the start of the 1980s, concrete formulations changed to create an entirely new generation of high-strength products. What was once considered strong was 7,000 to 9,000 psi, but new products reached 15,000 to 20,000 psi. These concrete products became popular for use in tall buildings, bridges, offshore structures, and pavements.

FURTHER READING

Gallun, Alby. "Construction Labor Market: Tighter in '97." *Business Journal-Milwaukee,* 28 March 1997.

McCarthy, Mike. "Construction Boom Spurs Worries of Labor Shortage." *Sacramento Business Journal,* 26 September 1997.

Marcelonis, Judi. "Construction Employment and Earnings Make Solid Gains." *Industrial Distribution,* June 1998, S6.

"Newsline: Construction Rate Rises." *Pit & Quarry,* February 1999, 6.

Seiders, David F. "Labor Noose Tightens." *Builder,* February 1999, 52.

Thompson, Boyce. "A Year to Remember." *Builder,* May 1999, 17.

U.S. Department of Commerce. Census Bureau. *Economic Census 1997.* Washington, DC: GPO, 1999. Available from http://www.census.gov/prod/ec97/97c2357a.pdf.

U.S. Department of Labor. Bureau of Labor Statistics. *Career Guide to Industries.* Washington, DC: GPO, 1998.

———. *Occupational Outlook Handbook,* 1998-99 ed. Washington, DC: GPO, 1998. Available from http://stats.bls.gov/ocohome.htm.

SIC 1781

WATER WELL DRILLING

This category covers special trade contractors primarily engaged in water well drilling. Establishments primarily engaged in drilling oil or gas field water intake wells on a contract or fee basis are classified in **SIC 1381: Drilling Oil and Gas Wells.**

NAICS CODE(S)

235810 (Water Well Drilling Contractors)

The U.S. water well drilling industry included 3,862 establishments in 1997. These establishments had total employment of 21,214, with the average firm employing between 5 and 6 people, according to the *1997 Economic Census* published by the U.S. Department of Commerce. (The total number of establishments was up from 3,638 in the early 1990s.) Larger establishments (defined as those with 20 or more employees), accounted for 4 percent of the total number of establishments while taking in 21 percent of all business done by this industry in 1997.

Establishments engaged in water well drilling in the United States tend to be small, independent contractors. Even the industry leaders tend to be small, seldom generating more than $20 million in annual revenues. Some of the largest companies have diversified into other areas of construction or other types of drilling projects, such as oil, natural gas, and geothermal wells.

The nation's water supply comes from surface sources such as lakes, rivers, and streams, in addition to vast underground aquifers. Groundwater has often been preferred over surface water for use in homes and industry because it is relatively inexpensive to develop and treat, it contains no sediment, its chemical quality remains constant, and facilities to develop it can be situated on small plots of ground.

Contractors who drill wells to tap into underground water are largely dependent on new construction. In fact, community water mains and wells for single-family houses account for the vast majority of all business done by this industry. In 1997 water mains and related facilities accounted for 60 percent of the industry's work, while wells for single-family houses accounted for 25 percent.

In the early to mid-1990s the number of water wells drilled ranged between 260,000 and 290,000. Housing starts at that time remained fairly strong, rising to 1.45 million in 1996 after dropping to 1.01 million in 1991. The water well drilling industry was mature and somewhat overserved from both a manufacturing and distribution standpoint. Manufacturers had excess capacity, and distributors were readily available to serve contractors. The environmental business had been the source of most growth for some years. Drillers who offered new and differentiated products were seeing success in their marketing efforts. Increasing emphasis on service and quick responses to customer needs was separating the firms that were growing from those that were merely retaining their market share.

The U.S. water well drilling industry produced $2.2 billion in total dollar value of business in 1997. The cost of materials, components, and supplies for this industry was $743 million, and $59.4 million for construction work was subcontracted out to others. The cost of power, fuels, and lubricants for the industry was $88.6 million. Total payroll for this industry in 1997 was $576 million.

In 1997 there were 311 water well drilling firms based in Texas, 268 in Michigan, 251 in Florida, 229 in California, 167 in North Carolina, 152 in Wisconsin, 139 in Pennsylvania, 130 in New York, and 120 in Georgia. The dollar value of construction work completed was highest in California, Florida, and Michigan.

In 1998 the U.S. Department of Labor predicted that industries engaged in the supply of water would be among the fastest-growing public utilities because of factors such as the nation's expanding population and the increasing number of new housing projects connected to community water sources. The construction industry, however, was expected to grow at an annual rate of about 9 percent through the year 2006. This growth rate was slower than the average for all the nation's industries.

As of 1998 the industry leaders in well drilling (by revenue) were: Marley Company, Mission Woods, Kansas ($580.0 million); Beylik Drilling Inc., La Habra, California ($53.0 million); Barnwell Industries Inc., Honolulu ($11.9 million); Water Resources International Inc., Kamuela, Hawaii ($11.0 million); and Charles Sargent Irrigation Inc., Broken Bow, Nebraska ($7.7 million). Other industry leaders included True Geothermal Energy Company, Raba-Kistner Consultants Inc., R. E. Chapman Company, Weeks Drilling and Pump Company Inc., and Grabow Well Drilling Company.

FURTHER READING

Seiders, David. ''1997 Housing Forecast.'' *Builder,* January 1997, 316.

U.S. Bureau of the Census. *Economic Census 1997.* Washington, DC: GPO, 1999. Available from http://www.census.gov/prod/ec97/97c2358a.pdf.

U.S. Department of Labor. Bureau of Labor Statistics. *Career Guide to Industries.* Washington, DC: GPO, 1998.

''Volatile Homebuilding Market Reignites.'' *Standard & Poor's Industry Surveys,* 22 February 1996, B92.

SIC 1791

STRUCTURAL STEEL ERECTION

This category covers special trade contractors primarily engaged in the erection of structural steel and of similar products of prestressed or precast concrete.

NAICS CODE(S)

235910 (Structural Steel Erection Contractors)

INDUSTRY SNAPSHOT

According to the U.S. Census Bureau, there were 4,238 establishments engaged in structural steel erection in 1997. These establishments generated an estimated $8.1 billion worth of business. Major uses of structural steel included office and industrial buildings; commercial buildings, including retail stores, restaurants, and service stations; apartment buildings, hotels, and motels; warehouses; and highways, bridges, tunnels, and other transportation facilities. Single-family homes accounted for a very small percentage of the structural steel used in the United States.

The structural steel erection industry had a payroll of $2.3 billion in 1997 and employed more than 72,300 workers. There are many construction trades represented by the industry, but those workers directly responsible for raising the steel-beamed frames that support most high-rise buildings, bridges, and industrial plants are known as ironworkers and are often celebrated for their daring feats hundreds of feet above the ground. The industry also employed approximately 12,378 workers who were not involved in construction. Larger establishments, employing 20 or more workers, accounted for 71 percent of all business.

BACKGROUND AND DEVELOPMENT

French architects began using iron to form the framework of their roofs about 1780. By the 1830s they also were using a form of masonry reinforced with imbedded iron bars that is regarded as the precursor of reinforced concrete. English builders began relying on iron in the construction of factories about 1850, primarily in an effort to make the buildings fireproof. Columns, beams, and window frames were made of cast iron, while exterior walls were made of brick or stone. Many commercial buildings also used iron, with elaborate facades often constructed entirely of cast iron and glass.

Builders in the mid-1800s also used wrought iron, which could be hammered into a sheet and laid between wooden beams, or vice versa, for added strength. Iron plates also were sometimes riveted to the ends of these beams to create an early I-beam. The first I-beams made entirely of wrought iron were produced in Paris about 1847. The Trenton Iron Works in Trenton, New Jersey, began rolling wrought-iron I-beams in 1854. The first wrought iron I-beams produced in Trenton were shipped to New York where they were used to rebuild the six-story Harper Building, which had burned in 1853. The building also had a cast-iron front.

Bridge builders also began using iron to replace wood and stone in the late eighteenth century. Abraham Darby, an Englishman credited with originating the coke blast furnace, designed and built the famous Coalbrookdale Bridge over the Severn River in 1779, using wedged-shaped sections of cast iron to form the arch. The 100-foot bridge was still standing more than 200 years later. The first bridge in the United States made entirely of cast iron was built in 1840 and spanned the Erie Canal at Frankfurt, New York. The first railroad bridge made entirely of cast iron was built in 1845 at Manayunk, Pennsylvania.

In 1886, a bridge being built across the St. Lawrence River near Montreal needed to pass through part of the Caughnawaga Indian reservation. To obtain permission, the bridge builder agreed to hire local Indians. The Indians proved adept at the work, and several tribes, especially the Iroquois, later earned reputations for high-steel construction work.

However, bridges made of cast iron often shattered and collapsed under the tremendous weight of the steam locomotives, so bridge builders turned to wrought iron, which has greater elasticity under stress. Later, bridge builders turned to steel for even greater strength. The first bridge to use arches made of steel was built at Kuelenberg, Holland, in 1868, and spanned the Rhine River. The Eads Bridge, which was built in 1874 and spanned the Mississippi River at St. Louis, was the first bridge to use steel arches in the United States. The rest of the bridge was made of wrought iron. The first all-steel bridge was built over the Missouri River at Glasgow, Montana, in 1879.

Besides being used in bridges, steel was crucial to the erection of the world's first tall buildings. In the early 1850s, Elisha Graves Otis, an American inventor, developed an improved elevator with safety devices to keep it from falling. About the same time, Henry Bessemer in England and William Kelly in the United States developed a process that made it possible to produce large quantities of inexpensive steel. Together, the Bessemer process and the Otis elevator gave rise to the modern structural steel erection industry. Safe elevators made it practical to build taller structures, and cheap steel provided architects with a way to support taller buildings without relying on thick, windowless walls of masonry.

William Le Baron Jenney, a Chicago architect, built the first metal-frame skyscraper, the 12-story Home Insurance Building, in the mid-1880s. Jenney used an iron framework for the first six floors to carry the weight of the building into the foundation. He used steel beams for the top six floors. According to Douglas Alan Fisher in *The Epic of Steel,* the first building with a frame made entirely of steel probably was the Rand McNally Building completed in Chicago in 1890. By 1900, buildings had reached 30 stories. The Empire State Building, built in 1931, was originally 86 stories. It was later raised to 102 and remained the United States' tallest building until the Sears Tower in Chicago was built in 1972.

Current Conditions

The structural steel erection industry reflected general economic trends in the United States. With an economic downturn in the late 1980s and early 1990s, there was less construction of new factories and office buildings, which depressed the industry. However, structural steel and prestressed or precast concrete remained the primary construction materials for large-scale projects, and the industry was expected to rebound with another spurt in new construction. In 1998, the United States also was becoming increasingly concerned with the deteriorating transportation infrastructure. With thousands of railroad and highway bridges needing repair, the outlook for the structural steel erection industry was strong. Employment outlook was uncertain though, due to the slow rate of growth for new construction.

Industry Leaders

The leading company in this industry in 1999 was Pitt-Des Moines Inc. Engineered Construction Division, of Clive, Iowa. Pitt-Des Moines reported revenue of $177 million. Second was Schuff Steel Company, of Phoenix, Arizona, which reported $138 million in revenue.

Workforce

Structural steel erection workers held approximately 70,000 jobs in 1997. Nearly 6 of every 10 worked for structural steel erection contractors. Very few were self-employed. Many were members of the International Association of Bridge, Structural and Ornamental Ironworkers. According to the *Engineering News Record* (*ENR*), union wages for structural steel erection workers in the 1990s averaged about $27 an hour. Earnings of these workers can be reduced due to poor weather and the short-term nature of the work in the construction industry.

Further Reading

U.S. Bureau of the Census. *Economic Census 1997.* Available from http://www.census.gov.

U.S. Department of Labor. Bureau of Labor Statistics. *Occupational Outlook Handbook.* 19998-99 ed. Available from http://stats.bls.gov.

*Ward's Business Directory of U.S. Public and Private Companies.*Detroit: Gale Group, 1999.

SIC 1793

GLASS AND GLAZING WORK

This category is comprised of establishments primarily engaged in cutting, coating, tinting, and installing glass. Companies that install automotive glass are described in **SIC 7536: Automotive Glass Replacement Shops.**

NAICS Code(s)

235920 (Glass and Glazing Contractors)

This industry consists of a few companies offering a range of services. Common industry activities include installing plate glass in storefronts and other commercial buildings, cutting and installing windowpanes for homes, and tinting windows. Other niche markets exist for firms that install revolving glass doors; cut and install mirrors and safety glass; create custom glass doors, signs, shelves, and glass tabletops; or cut and install architectural and ornamental custom glass work.

The U.S. glass and glazing work industry included 4,714 establishments in 1997. These establishments had total employment of 35,823, with the average firm employing seven people, according to the 1997 Economic Census.

The industry totaled $4 billion in business in 1997. The cost of materials, components, and supplies was $1.7 billion with $95 million for work subcontracted to others. The cost of power, fuels, and lubricants for the industry was $50.5 million. Total industry payroll costs in 1997 were $1 billion.

Although glass was invented in about 4000 B.C., it wasn't until the early twentieth century that advancements in manufacturing technology made it inexpensive and widely available. In 1900, the use of glass was primarily limited to windows, mirrors, optical lenses, and containers. During the early and mid-1900s, however, glass applications proliferated. As the U.S. economy boomed after World War II, the demand for glass by commercial, institutional, and residential sectors ballooned, spurring growth in the glass installation and glazing industry.

By the mid-1980s, the United States was consuming about $2 billion worth of non-automotive flat glass, much of which was installed by contractors in the glass and glazing industry. Approximately 80 percent of that glass was construction industries, with the remainder used to make signs, mirrors, solar panels, and other specialty products.

A recession in commercial and residential building markets in the early 1990s curtailed glass shipments and cut the need for glass installation contractors. U.S. glass demand plummeted 8 percent per year between 1990 and 1992, to less than $1.5 billion, as building contractors faced a major economic setback. Glass contractors also suffered as trends in architectural design moved away from the expensive glass office enclosures and stoic glass buildings so popular the decade before.

However, the sustained economic recovery in residential housing that began in 1992 continued past the middle part of the decade, spurring renewed demand for glass contractors. Single-family houses accounted for 16.3 percent of the value of construction work done by this industry in 1992, up sharply from 10.6 percent in 1987, according to the U.S. Economic Census. However, the leading category of construction work done by the glass and glazing work industry in 1992 was ''other commercial buildings,'' such as stores and restaurants, with 28 percent of the total (up from 21.7 percent in 1987). Office buildings accounted for another 21.5 percent of the industry's work in 1992, but this was down sharply from 28.8 percent in 1987.

Industry trends that began in the 1980s included greater use of riot- and bulletproof glass, more skylights and windows in residences, and greater use of metal frames and finishes. By the mid-1990s many successful glass and glazing contractors were concentrating on developing niche markets, including the installation of energy-saving glass and safety glass. Some also expanded their services to include such activities related to glass installation as designing and building window frames. Technological advances in the mid-1990s that affected the glass and glazing work industry included a new ''two-phase'' adhesive glazing technique that lowered costs and enhanced aesthetics.

This industry has supported several thousand small contractors, but there are several large firms that lead the industry. In 1999, the top two companies (by total annual revenue) in the industry were Harmon Contract, of Bloomington, Minnesota, ($170 million), and Benson Industries, Inc., of Portland, Oregon, ($106 million).

FURTHER READING

Seiders, David. ''1997 Housing Forecast.'' *Builder,* January 1997, 316.

U.S. Department of the Census. *1997 Economic Census,* 20 March 2000. Available from http://www.census.gov.

''Volatile Homebuilding Market Reignites.'' *Standard & Poor's Industry Surveys,* 22 February 1996, B92.

Ward's Business Directory of U.S. Private and Public Companies. Detroit: Gale Research, 1999.

SIC 1794

EXCAVATION WORK

This category covers special trade contractors primarily engaged in excavation work and digging foundations, including digging and loading. Contractors in this industry may also perform incidental concrete work. Contractors primarily engaged in concrete work are classified in **SIC 1771: Concrete Work.** Those primarily engaged in trenching or in earth moving and land clearing not related to building construction are classified in the major group for heavy construction other than building construction, contractors.

NAICS CODE(S)

235930 (Excavation Contractors)

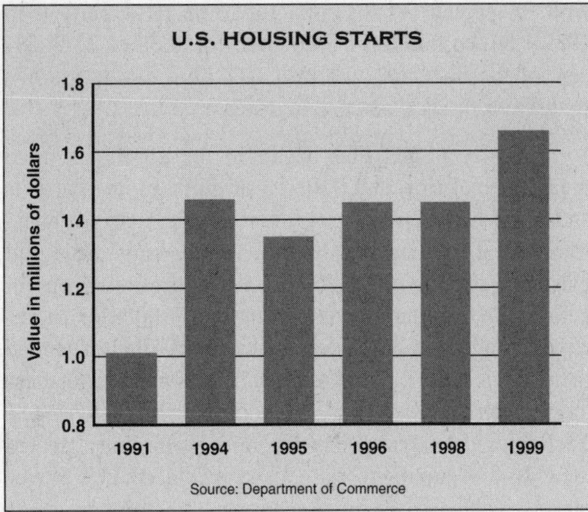

The U.S. excavation work industry included 18,229 establishments in 1997. These establishments had total employment of 116,237, with the average firm employing between five and six people, according to the *1997 Economic Census* published by the U.S. Department of Commerce. Larger establishments (defined as those with 20 or more employees), accounted for 4 percent of the total number of establishments while taking in 21 percent of all business done by this industry in 1997.

In 1997 this industry produced $14 billion in total dollar value of business. The cost of materials, components, and supplies for this industry was $3 billion and $1 billion for construction work subcontracted out to others. The cost of power fuels and lubricants for the industry was approximately $580 million. Total payroll for the industry in 1997 was $3.35 billion.

The status of the U.S. excavation industry generally mirrors the country's economic climate, in particular the demand for construction of detached single-family homes. In 1997 single-family homes accounted for 36 percent of the value of all excavation work in the United States, while other commercial buildings represented 17.3 percent and educational buildings 3.6 percent.

The U.S. excavation work industry benefited from the sustained demand for single- and multi-family housing in the mid-1990s. The recession of the early 1990s dropped housing starts to just 1.01 million in 1991, but the economic recovery that began in 1992 helped housing starts rise each year to a peak of 1.46 million in 1994. While starts dropped back to 1.35 million in 1995, they rose again to 1.45 million in 1996. In 1998 housing starts matched the 1996 number of 1.45 million, down slightly from the previous year. New construction is expected to experience a steady increase over the next three years, according to the U.S. Department of Commerce.

While construction trends were slightly up throughout the United States in the mid-1990s, some areas were growing faster that others, and excavation work in these areas was booming. Not surprisingly, most growth occurred in southern and southwestern states, which have experienced the strongest population growth in the United States during the 1980s and 1990s. Each of the top 50 markets experienced growth of 20 percent or better in 1997, with Dallas, Houston, Phoenix, Atlanta, and Las Vegas among the top areas. Florida leads the way in growth, attracting aging baby boomers who are looking for retirement homes or communities in warmer climates.

Small, independent operators remain the backbone of the excavation work industry. They generally work as subcontractors to home building companies, commercial construction firms, and others. Still, several large companies hold dominant market positions in this industry, though they tend to be regional and not national in scope. In 1999 the top five companies in the excavation work industry (by revenue) were: Freesen Inc., Illinois ($80 million); Ryan Incorporated Central, Wisconsin ($78 million); Glasgow Inc., Pennsylvania ($75 million); George J. Igel and Company, Inc., Ohio ($50 million); and Beaver Excavating Company, Ohio ($40 million).

The two dominant costs of doing business in the excavation work industry are materials components and supplies, costing the industry approximately $2 billion in 1997 and payroll which cost $3.3 billion. Other costs include: electricity ($34 million); rental cost for machinery, equipment, and buildings ($7.7 million); and cost of repairs to machinery and equipment ($6.4 million).

Further Reading

Kennedy, Kim. ''Top Markets for Apartment Construction in 1998.'' *Building Design & Construction,* March 1998.

National Association of Home Builders. *Facts & Figures.* Available from http://www.nahb.com.

U.S. Department of Commerce. *1997 Economic Census: Construction Industry Series.* Washington, D.C.: U.S. Department of Commerce, 2000.

U.S. Industry & Trade Outlook '99. Washington, D.C.: The McGraw-Hill Companies and U.S. Department of Commerce, 1999.

SIC 1795

WRECKING AND DEMOLITION WORK

This category covers special contractors that primarily wreck and demolish buildings and other structures, except marine property. They may or may not sell material salvaged from demolition sites. Businesses that do marine wrecking are in **SIC 4499: Water Transportation Services, Not Elsewhere Classified.**

NAICS CODE(S)

235940 (Wrecking and Demolition Contractors)

Despite opposite objectives, wrecking firms are grouped in the larger trade construction industry. This is due to the similar physical and economic nature of demolition and construction work; they use many of the same tools, and the former activity often precedes the latter.

The wrecking and demolition industry is grouped into two sections: building and non-building demolition. The first category destroys houses, commercial establishments, and office buildings; the second removes highways, streets, and other non-inhabitable construction projects. Companies in the wrecking and demolition industry may specialize in one type of task—for example, demolishing small single-family homes.

According to U.S. Census Bureau statistics, there were 1,542 firms in this industry in 1997. These companies employed 18,820 workers and reported $2.3 billion in sales for 1997, compared to 14,109 workers, and $959 million in sales for 1987. Payroll costs for 1997 were $592 million, up from $261 million in 1987. Many of these firms were small, family-owned companies already in business for a generation or two.

Before the 1930s, buildings were usually demolished by hand tools, which could take many months for an average-sized building. Newer building techniques developed in the early twentieth century gave rise to larger, sturdier buildings. This development, coupled with methods developed in post-World War II Britain to clear building debris, brought new demolition techniques. Because the German air force bombed so much of London, civilian and army units mobilized to help clear the destroyed buildings. These first methods were primitive, but the need to clear large sections of rubble and debris eventually led to quicker and more large-scale building removal techniques.

Another effect of World War II on the wrecking industry was a U.S. construction boom in the prosperous years afterward. The returning troops, a population shift away from urban and industrial areas, and a baby boom led to severe housing shortages in many parts of the country. It also was necessary to clear older sections of cities to make room for new apartments and houses. The push toward urban renewal also played a role in the development of the industry. This idea began in the 1930s, when Roosevelt's administration tried to improve living conditions in poor urban areas where old tenements housed people in crowded, unsanitary conditions. The U.S. Housing Authority, the forerunner of the Department of Housing and Urban Development (HUD), began in 1937 to clear large tracts of slums and erect federally-subsidized housing. More wrecking and demolition firms set up shop to meet the higher demand. Urban renewal continued to effect the demographics of American cities well into the 1970s.

The decline of American manufacturing since the 1970s showed in the number of related edifices torn down in 1987—15 percent were former industrial buildings. The next largest group was commercial structures, such as stores and restaurants, which made up 12.4 percent of the buildings demolished. Office buildings were next, with 10.1 percent of the total, followed by single-family homes at 5.8 percent. The rest of the structures torn down by the industry in 1987 were, in descending order, highways and streets, blast furnaces, petroleum refineries or other heavy industrial complexes, hospitals and other institutional buildings, apartment buildings, and warehouses.

Various demolition methods, ranging from the traditional wrecking ball to explosives, were often used in conjunction. The largest expense for industry firms was often payroll costs. Generally these costs took one-third of the wrecking or demolition company's operating budget. Supplies and materials were the next biggest expense, while other pre- or post-demolition work, if contracted out to other companies, was an additional cost. Many smaller firms could not afford to own their own heavy equipment because the purchase price and maintenance costs were prohibitive. A thriving sister industry in equipment rental was another segment of the wrecking and demolition business. Insurance costs were also high, due to the relative danger of demolition work.

In 1999, the industry leader was Walsh Group Limited, of Chicago, with $11 billion in revenue. Following behind were Cleveland Wrecking Company, of Los Angeles, with $64 million, and Brandenburg Industrial Service Company, of Chicago, with $60 million.

FURTHER READING

U.S. Census Bureau. "Wrecking and Demolition Contractors." *1997 Economic Census—Manufacturing.* Washington, DC: U.S. Department of Commerce, 1999. Available from http://www.census.gov/prod/ec97/97c2359d.pdf.

Ward's Business Directory of U.S. Private and Public Companies. Farmington Hills, MI: Gale Group, 1999.

SIC 1796

INSTALLATION OR ERECTION OF BUILDING EQUIPMENT, NOT ELSEWHERE CLASSIFIED

Special trade contractors primarily engaged in the installation, erection, or dismantling of miscellaneous building equipment make up this industry, which encompasses numerous firms that offer a wide range of services. Common activities include the installation, repair, and dismantling of conveyor systems, dumbwaiters, dust collecting equipment, elevators, incinerators, industrial machinery, power generation devices, revolving doors, and vacuum cleaning systems.

NAICS Code(s)

235950 (Building Equipment and other Machinery Installation Contracts)

In 1997, the businesses classified in this industry included 4,489 establishments, employing 75,510 total workers with a payroll of $3.1 billion.

The installation or erection of building equipment industry produced $9.3 billion in total revenue in 1997. The cost of materials, components, and supplies for this industry was $2.0 billion, while $609 million worth of construction work was subcontracted out to others. The cost of power, fuels, and lubricants for the industry was $96 million.

Most contractors in this industry rely heavily on new commercial, industrial, and institutional construction. In 1992, for example, industrial buildings accounted for 31.6 percent of the value of construction work done by this industry, followed by office buildings at 16.9 percent, and other commercial buildings at 13.3 percent.

When building markets boomed during the mid-1980s, most specialty contractors realized healthy growth in billings and profits, and demand for items such as industrial machinery, elevators, and revolving doors increased. Contractors in this business, however, have to cope with the extremely cyclical nature of the nonresidential construction market, and this fluctuating cycle was most clearly evident during the late 1980s and early to mid-1990s. For example, industrial building construction expenditures in the United States advanced from $15 billion in 1987 to $23.8 billion in 1990. In 1991, for instance, construction in this category fell to $22.3 billion and continued falling to $20.7 billion in 1992 and to $19.5 billion in 1993. Nonetheless, the industrial building market bounced back in 1994, to $21.1 billion and $24.1 billion in 1995.

The cycle in office building construction, the second largest market for contractors in SIC 1796, has been even more pronounced. Construction in this category peaked in 1989 at $31.5 billion. By 1993, however, construction expenditures in this category had dropped by half, to just $15.4 billion, before recovering slightly to $17.0 billion in 1994 and $19.4 billion in 1995.

This cycle has a profound impact on contractors in this industry category. During good times, specialty contractors enjoy healthy profit margins, expanding business, and steady demand for their services. In bad times, many contractors manage to stay afloat only by taking on installation and repair jobs at very low profit margins. In the early to mid-1990s, for example, elevator contractors were emphasizing elevator retrofits that integrated advanced technology. They were also striving to increase their share of the airport and health care elevator markets.

The long-term outlook for this industry appears to be mixed. While commercial construction benefited from the extended economic expansion of the mid-1990s, overbuilding in many regions somewhat dampened the industry's recovery. Some commercial construction companies are looking overseas for growth, and the best-equipped contractors in this industry may be able to follow that business.

Privately owned companies dominate this diverse industry. The largest companies in the industry tend to be diversified contractors that have interests in many different areas. As a result, their activities in this industry category are just a small part of their overall business. Industry leaders by revenue, as of 1999, were Millar Elevator Service Company, of Holland, Ohio ($176 Million); Harco Technologies Division, of Medina, Ohio ($93 million); and General Elevator Company, Inc., of Baltimore, Maryland ($66 million).

Further Reading

U.S. Bureau of the Census.*1997 Economic Census,* 20 March 2000. Available from http://www.census.gov.

"Volatile Homebuilding Market Reignites." Standard & Poor's Industry Surveys, 22 February 1996, p. B92.

Ward's Business Directory of U.S. Private and Public Companies. Detroit: Gale Research, 1999.

SIC 1799

SPECIAL TRADE CONTRACTORS, NOT ELSEWHERE CLASSIFIED

The special trade contractors, not elsewhere classified industry is comprised of a plethora of firms that provide a broad range of miscellaneous construction services. Examples of industry activities include bathtub refinishing, gasoline pump installation, grave excavation, swimming pool construction, post hole digging, wallpaper stripping, mobile home setup, house moving, fire escape installation, bowling alley construction, artificial turf installation, and sandblasting.

NAICS Code(s)

235210 (Painting and Wall Covering Contractors)
235920 (Glass and Glazing Contractors)

562910 (Remediation Services)
235990 (All Other Special Trade Contractors)

The special trade contractors industry included 25,932 establishments as of 1997. These establishments had total employment of 198,141 with the average firm employing 8 people, according to the 1997 Economic Census published by the U.S. Department of Commerce.

The U.S. special trade contractors industry produced $17.9 billion in total dollar value of business in 1997. The cost of materials, components, and supplies for this industry was $5.4 billion; $1.6 billion was spent for construction work subcontracted to others. The cost of power, fuels, and lubricants for the industry was $329 million. Total industry payroll costs were $5.1 billion.

While this diverse industry is hard to classify, the Department of Commerce survey noted that the industry's leading business category (based on value of construction work) was other commercial buildings, such as stores, restaurants, and auto service stations. This category accounted for 14.1 percent of construction work done by this industry in 1992, followed by outdoor swimming pools at 13.9 percent, industrial buildings and warehouses at 10.5 percent, fencing at 10.2 percent, single-family houses at 8.3 percent, and office buildings at 8.2 percent. A variety of other construction work accounted for the remainder of the total.

Although each sector of the industry is impacted by different factors, most specialty contractors are heavily dependent upon housing starts or new commercial and institutional construction. During the mid-1980s most contractors enjoyed steady expansion as commercial and residential building flourished. Likewise, when housing starts and commercial development stalled in the late 1980s and early 1990s, many contractors suffered immense setbacks. Total U.S. construction expenditures, in fact, actually declined 10 percent in inflation adjusted dollars between 1986 and 1992.

However, the construction industry saw strong growth between 1992 and 1999, as the general economy recovered, interest rates stayed relatively low, and housing starts boomed. For example, after dropping to just 1.01 million in 1991, single family and multi-family housing starts in the United States rose every year to 1.46 million in 1994. While starts dropped back to 1.35 million in 1995, they rose again to 1.45 million in 1996 and were about 1.7 billion in 1999, a two-decade high.

These stable housing starts and a rise in nonresidential construction were expected to keep this industry growing through the late 1990s. Total new construction expenditures were expected to rise from $405.9 billion in 1994 to $435.6 in 1998 in inflation adjusted dollars. That would mean average annual real growth of 1.8 percent. Spending on other commercial buildings, the special trade contractors industry's leading category of work, was expected to rise from $20.4 billion in 1994 to $22.6 billion in 1998.

Most companies in this industry were small, privately held, local enterprises. There were several industry leaders, though many of them also had interests in other industries. As of 1999, leaders in the specialty contractors industry were, by revenue: REXX Environmental Corporation, of New York, New York, with $1.3 billion; Anco Industries Inc., of Baton Rouge, with $125 million; and Western Group/Western Waterproofing Company Inc., of St. Louis, with $120 million each.

FURTHER READING

National Association of Home Builders. ''Housing Forecast.'' Washington, DC: 1996. Available from http://www.nahb.com.

Seiders, David. ''1997 Housing Forecast.'' *Builder,* January 1997, 316.

U.S. Department of Commerce. *1997 Economic Census.* Washington, DC: GPO, 2000. Available from http://www.census.gov.

''Volatile Homebuilding Market Reignites.'' *Standard & Poor's Industry Surveys,* 22 February 1996, B92.

Ward's Business Directory of U.S. Public and Private Companies. Detroit: Gale Group, 1999.

Transportation, Communications, Electric, Gas, & Sanitary Services

SIC 4011

RAILROADS, LINE-HAUL OPERATING

This category covers establishments engaged primarily in line-haul railroad passenger and freight operations. Railways primarily engaged in furnishing passenger transportation confined principally to a single municipality, contiguous municipalities, or a municipality and its suburban areas are classified in **SIC 4111: Local and Suburban Transit** and **SIC 4119: Local Passenger Transportation, Not Elsewhere Classified.**

NAICS Code(s)

482111 (Line-Haul Railroads)

Industry Snapshot

Line-haul is defined as ''the movement of freight between terminals.'' More generally, line-haul railroads are those that transport passengers or freight long distances on a network of tracks that disperse goods and passengers across the United States. In 1997 line-haul railroads carried 40 percent of the nation's intercity freight as measured by ton-miles, compared to 28 percent by trucks, 14 percent by water, and 18 percent by pipelines.

In 1998 there were more than 500 railroad companies operating in the United States, generating $36 billion in operating revenues. Most of that business was handled by Class 1 railroads, defined as those railroads with revenues of more than $95 million. The top five Class 1 railroads (Union Pacific, Burlington Northern Santa Fe, CSX Transportation, Norfolk Southern, and Conrail) accounted for a combined $31 billion in revenues.

Rail freight volume increased by more than 30 percent between 1990 and 1997, with Class 1 rail freight volume reaching 1.3 trillion ton-miles in 1997. Railroads carried 70 percent of all motor vehicles shipped from manufacturing sites, 65 percent of the nation's coal, and 40 percent of all U.S. grain and farm products. Major freight railroads operated more than 19,000 locomotives in 1996, and the industry had a total fleet of more than 1.24 million freight cars with an aggregate capacity of 118.6 million tons, an increase of nearly 10 percent since 1990.

The 30 regional lines, by contrast, operated over 18,800 miles of track and brought in $1.55 billion in operating revenues. Smaller railroads that operate less than 350 miles of track are called shortline railroads; there were 500 of these nationwide operating a total 26,546 miles of track. Amtrak, the government-supported passenger rail system also known as the National Railroad Passenger Corporation, was the only passenger carrier with national impact, carrying more than 20 million intercity passengers yearly. It operated over 23,750 route miles owned by freight railroads and 750 miles of its own track.

Organization and Structure

In the years from 1987 to 1992, the railroad industry began to pull out of the slump it had seen in the 1970s and 1980s. In 1995 railroads realized significant productivity gains with freight revenue ton-miles per employee rising to 7 million, up 11.1 percent over 1994 figures, and a dramatic 233 percent increase over the 1980 totals. In 1995 the industry's fleet expanded for the third year in a row to 69.4 million, up 7 percent from 1994 and twice the comparable 1980 level. Meanwhile, rail freight rates fell sharply and steadily, lagging behind the overall inflation rate every year since 1983, with the exception of 1998, when rates rose 1.2 percent. Costs, however, also declined since the early 1980s, resulting in widening margins for the railroads.

Rail traffic increased steadily in the 1990s, growing by 30 percent between 1990 and 1997. In 1998 rail traffic increased 2.1 percent to 1.377 trillion ton-miles, due in part to a 3.7 percent increase in U.S. industrial output. Demand for rail service was influenced by several factors, including retail sales, general manufacturing levels, export and import trade, and housing and commercial construction. Coal was the industry's largest source of traffic, accounting for 44 percent of volume and 22 percent of revenues in 1997. Grain, another major source of traffic, accounted for 8 percent of the industry's volume and revenues.

Nearly 70 percent of all rail freight was transported under contract relationships between railroads and shippers. Meanwhile, railroads would operate almost exclusively on privately owned rights-of-way, and would spend large sums of money on restoration of these rights-of-way, maintenance, and equipment investment.

One of the most notable investments in new equipment came in 1984 with the advent of double-stack containers—boxcar containers that fit on a lowered platform and could be stacked one on top of the other, doubling the amount a single train could carry—immediately improved the feasibility and profitability of rail transport.

Another important innovation was the increase in intermodal transport, a system in which freight containers are attached to truck beds for shipments to rail yards, then transported by rail to a distribution ''hub,'' where they were again picked up by trucks for the final leg of their journey. These containers could also be transported by ship to port locations where they were transferred to rail for the journey inland. Intermodal transport allowed for both speed and low cost when transporting goods; due to decreased wind resistance of the lower-stacked cars, it cut fuel consumption by 20 percent. More importantly, the system changed the relationship between rail and trucking companies—once intense rivals for the same business—by encouraging cooperation and new business collaboration for the benefit of both industries. Between 1980 and 1997, intermodal traffic grew from 3 million containers to 8.7 million. By 1997, intermodal transport accounted for more than 17 percent of rail revenues, second only to coal, which accounted for 22 percent.

A side effect of intermodal shipping was the adoption of a hub-and-spoke network for shipping, in which fewer cities (hubs) served as drop-off points for goods initially shipped by truck. This system reduced the number of stops that had to be made by a single train, speeding up travel time for many routes and reducing overall customer costs.

BACKGROUND AND DEVELOPMENT

Railroads, defined as vehicles that move along a track on flanged wheels, have been in use since the sixteenth century, when human- or horse-pulled carts on tracks were used in Europe to haul ore out of mines. The first mechanically self-propelled railroad system was created in 1681 by Ferdinand Verbeist, a French Jesuit missionary in Peking, China. It was not until 1804, however, when the steam locomotive was invented in Wales, that the railroad's potential as a system of mass transportation was realized. In the westward expansion of the United States, the railroad industry became significant both as a key factor in national growth, and as a formidable economic force in its own right.

In 1825 John Stephens of Hoboken, New Jersey, built the first American steam locomotive, ushering in an era of development that would make the railroad industry an integral part of the expansion of America. Only two years later, the Baltimore and Ohio Railroad Company (B&O) was created to carry passengers and goods from Baltimore to Ellicott City, Maryland, 13 miles away. As B&O expanded in the following years (its tracks reached West Virginia by 1834), railway companies sprang up in other areas of the country during the 1830s, many of which were to become the Class 1 railways of the present.

Railroad building continued at an amazing pace between 1830 and 1860. With their ability to connect places previously separated by prohibitive distance, the railroads made possible the settlement of the western half of the continent. Railroads also liberated the country from its reliance on water transportation and made it possible for cities to grow away from rivers and canals, as the new lines could deliver goods and building materials to new homesteaders and carry raw materials to other cities. It became physically and economically possible to tap the continent's huge reserves of raw materials such as lumber. New cities and towns were formed due to their proximity to railroad lines; in some ways the industry determined the political and social geography of westward expansion. In 1869 the first transcontinental railroad was created when the tracks of the Union Pacific from the East met those of the Central Pacific from the West at Promontory, Utah. America had entered the Railway Age.

By the beginning of the Civil War, 30,000 miles of track had been laid across the country. Railroads played an important strategic role in that conflict, as they were a means of delivering crucial supplies and troops. The Union army's control of railroads—the owners of which were located mainly in the industry-rich North—was a significant factor in its eventual victory.

Big Business. From the end of the war in 1865 until the turn of the twentieth century, the industry grew at a fantastic rate, becoming America's first "big business." Although the railroad expanded the possibilities for agricultural sales, it did so at a price. Future conflicts between industry and agriculture were foreshadowed when, during the economic depression of the 1870s, a farmers' group called the Grange protested the high rates charged by railroad "middlemen" to ship their goods. The case went to the Supreme Court. Its decision of 1877, *Munn v. Illinois,* gave states the power to regulate business with a strong public aspect like that of the railroads. National (long haul) rates remained unregulated, however, leaving the industry open for control by businesses of national stature.

The development of the railroads was inextricably linked to that of other industries. Andrew Carnegie's innovations in steel allowed the creation of rails that were much more durable than the previous ones made of more malleable iron. The increase in anthracite coal mining in the late nineteenth century reduced the price of coal and made coal-fueled steam engines cheaper and more feasible; the railroads, in turn, made it possible to transport and distribute coal and steel to new towns and cities, many of which were centered around mills and factories needing these goods. The railroad thus became an essential link in the cycle of industrialization of the 1870s and 1880s that made mass production and mass marketing a way of life for a growing nation.

It took a new organization of business on a greater scale to support all this growth; in the last quarter of the century, the rise of big business was seen nowhere more clearly than in the railroads. Initially the competing companies fought rate wars to lure customers, but bankruptcy followed for many. In the late 1870s, railroad executives set up "pools," informal rate-setting agreements that fixed rates in a market. They also cut wages, which eventually led to the formation of unions to protect worker rights.

The railroads' profit margins, coupled with their workers' unstable and often dangerous working conditions, created an increasingly explosive atmosphere in the industry. In 1877 railroad workers staged what was to become the first nationwide strike, a conflict that required military and police intervention. In the years between 1881 and 1905, the country witnessed 36,757 strikes, a situation that resulted in the creation of unions such as the Knights of Labor and the American Federation of Labor. These unions forced the railroads, among other businesses, to improve working conditions, reduce hours, and pay wages negotiated by the unions and company management.

The growth of the rail industry continued unchecked through the beginning of the next century. Despite the Sherman Antitrust Act of 1890, industry saw the formation of several huge trusts, made up of formerly competing companies, that controlled certain industries almost exclusively and made competition by smaller rivals nearly impossible. In 1902 President Theodore Roosevelt directed that a suit be filed against the railroad monopoly established by James J. Hill and J. P. Morgan. When that succeeded, he gave the Interstate Commerce Commission (ICC), which had been established in 1887, the authority to regulate monopolies and enforce rates. Although it did not end the tendency in the industry towards establishing trusts, the ICC did serve as a regulatory eye until it was abolished in 1995 and replaced with the Surface Transportation Board.

Profits Level Off. Railroads continued to expand their business and their track miles until well into the 1920s, at which point the industry reached a level of maturity that was reflected in a leveling off of profits and growth that continued for the next few decades. As passenger air travel, and later air shipping, became more common and less expensive in the 1950s and 1960s, the railroads entered a period of decline that would not change until the 1980s. As it was still used to ship raw materials such as coal, grain, and lumber, the industry did little to reflect the nation's shift from a service and industrial economy to an information economy in the 1970s and 1980s.

The railroad industry suffered in the 1980s as increased reliance on trucking and other modes of transportation and the perception of railroads as antiquated, contributed to slow growth. The advent of innovations, however, such as double-stack containers, intermodal shipping, and computer-controlled dispatching, changed both perceptions and profits.

Deregulation. Another boon to the freight rail industry was industry deregulation. The Staggers Rail Act of 1980 reduced the ICC's regulation of rates and service, and in the following year the ICC exempted all intermodal traffic from rate controls. In addition, the ICC exempted boxcar and trailer-on-flatcar traffic and the transport of some agricultural products, lumber, and transportation equipment. Industry analysts credited this loosening of regulations with rail companies' increased investment in equipment, especially intermodal containers.

Deregulation also spurred Class 1 railroads' sales of branch lines to smaller companies. In contrast to the mergers of the 1980s, which analysts said left the largest railroads weighted down by debt and property, the sales of the early 1990s helped the industry as a whole. Smaller lines were able to offer improved local service, while still maintaining connection to the larger lines' nationwide network of tracks. In addition, smaller railroads often hired nonunion employees, who generally were unable to bargain for higher wages. Without union regulations, lines were also able to staff trains more lightly; they could rely on improved computer tracking and monitoring that could be handled by a two-person crew. Shorter lines also had the advantage of being able to offer more personal service to smaller customers.

In 1994 the ICC approved the merger of Burlington Northern (BN) with the Atchison, Topeka and Santa Fe Railway Company. This created the country's biggest railroad, with $7 billion in combined revenues and 33,000 miles of track. BN already operated the longest rail system in North America, with 24,500 miles of track spanning 25 states and 2 Canadian provinces.

In late 1996 CSX Corp. attempted to take over Conrail with an $8.4 billion offer. Norfolk Southern immediately countered with a $9.1 billion hostile takeover bid. After several months of wrangling and opposition from several sources over the proposed takeover, the two railroad giants agreed to divide Conrail's assets between themselves. After two years of planning, CSX and Norfolk Southern finally divided Conrail in 1999. CSX acquired 4,000 miles of track for $4.2 billion, while Norfolk Southern took 7,200 miles of track for $5.8 billion. The deal left most of the railroad traffic in the eastern half of the United States under the control of the two companies.

Another major consolidation in the railroad industry took place late in 1996, when Union Pacific acquired Southern Pacific. Following the acquisition, Union Pacific experienced two years of service interruptions as it tried to integrate the two rail systems. It was estimated that the interruptions cost shippers $2 billion and Union Pacific $1 billion.

CURRENT CONDITIONS

While the merger of Union Pacific and Southern Pacific resulted in two years of service interruptions, it was hoped that the acquisition of Conrail by CSX and Norfolk Southern would go more smoothly. Service delays and misdirected freight cars, however, were reported in the months following the Conrail breakup in mid-1999. Because of these delays, United Parcel Service of America Inc.—one of the nation's largest rail shippers—diverted part of its Conrail business to trucks.

By 1999 Union Pacific appeared to have successfully integrated the Southern Pacific system into its operations. Through mid-1999 the company reported a 7 percent gain in rail traffic, the most of any major rail line.

The railroad industry enjoyed growing margins, as costs fell faster than rail rates during the 1990s. In addition, favorable economic conditions and a robust economy have contributed to steady increases in rail traffic. Following a 0.5 percent decline in rail traffic in 1997—due to factors such as the Asian financial crisis, traffic problems at Union Pacific, and soft demand from the coal and grain industries—rail traffic rebounded in 1998, rising 2.7 percent as the overall economy increased industrial output by 3.7 percent.

The future of the rail industry is affected heavily by industries that produce the goods being shipped. Those industries relying most heavily on rail transportation for shipping their products included steel, coal, chemicals, pulp and paper, automobiles, construction, and agriculture. Coal alone made up approximately 40 percent of rail shipments, so the coal industry's economic status had a strong effect on the fortunes of the railroads.

INDUSTRY LEADERS

The top Class 1 freight railroads of 1998, generally considered to be the industry giants, included Union Pacific, with $9.2 billion in revenues; Burlington Northern Santa Fe, $8.9 billion; CSX, $5.0 billion; Norfolk Southern, $4.2 billion; and Conrail, $3.7 billion. In 1999 Conrail's assets were split between CSX and Norfolk Southern in a $10.3 billion deal. After the split, CSX owned 23,100 miles of track, third behind Union Pacific and Burlington Northern Santa Fe, while Norfolk Southern ranked fourth with 21,400 miles of track.

Illinois Central, the nation's sixth-largest railroad in 1998, with revenues of $700 million, was acquired by Canadian National Railway Co. for $2.4 billion in a deal that was approved by the Surface Transportation Board in March 1999. The acquisition added 2,600 miles of U.S. track, ranging from Chicago to the Gulf of Mexico, to Canadian National's 13,750-mile system in Canada and six northern U.S. states. Following the acquisition, Canadian National expected revenues of C$5.2 billion (US$3.5 billion).

Through a series of acquisitions, RailAmerica, Inc. emerged as the largest regional and short- line operator. Toward the end of 1999 the company acquired RailTex of San Antonio for $325 million. The deal gave RailAmerica ownership or an interest in 51 railroads with 12,500 miles of track in the United States, Canada, Mexico, Chile, and Australia. RailAmerica expected 2000 revenues to reach $450 million.

Amtrak was established by Congress in 1971. Operating with the benefit of government subsidies and federal grants for equipment, Amtrak had yet to show a profit by 1999. In 1997 Congress passed the Amtrak Reauthorization Act, which among other things created the Amtrak Reform Council (ARC). The ARC was responsible for monitoring how Amtrak would use the $2.2 billion it received as a result of the Taxpayer Relief Act of 1997. With Wisconsin Governor Tommy G. Thompson appointed the new board chairman in 1998, Amtrak was attempting to become self-sufficient by 2002, when Congress would end its operating subsidies. For 1999 Amtrak projected an operating loss of $930 million, followed by a loss of $908 million for 2000. Congress set aside $609 million for Amtrak's use in fiscal 1999 and $571 million for fiscal 2000.

In the 1990s Amtrak's challenge was to become profitable while improving travel time by incorporating high-speed passenger trains that would create competition with commuter air flights, especially in the congested Northeast. This goal is helped by rail travel's role in reducing traffic congestion and pollution when used as an alternative to automobile travel—trains emit 10 to 30 percent less pollution than do autos and trucks. Amtrak's first high-speed train, called Acela, was scheduled to debut in spring 2000. The 150-mile-an-hour train was expected to add $180 million in annual profits and help Amtrak compete against airline shuttles in the northeast corridor.

WORKFORCE

Rail workers have long been unionized, and the unions have made rail employees as a group one of the highest-paid segments of the working population. Labor costs, including wages, accounted for 37 percent of all railroad operating costs in 1995 (as compared with 48 percent in 1982). But the increasing automation of trains, centralized dispatching, and company mergers, combined with companies' desire to cut operating costs as much as possible, have endangered several key employment positions. In addition, faster trains mean that crews, who are paid bonuses for miles traveled over a set limit, often earn bonuses of up to 70 percent of a day's wages for an eight- or ten-hour day. Companies are eager to cut these bonuses, but the power of the unions is strong.

The 11 largest Class 1 railroad companies, plus Amtrak, employed nearly 210,000 workers in 1995. Regional railroads employed 10,647 employees and short lines, 13,269 employees. Although the early 1990s saw rail profits rise, corporate mergers and increased mechanization led to a decline in the number of rail employees during the same period.

By 1992 most carriers employed only two-person crews, with an engineer and a conductor controlling each train, the brake operator having become superfluous on most runs. A 1993 agreement between Burlington Northern Railroad and the United Transportation Union negotiated a crew reduction agreement that would phase out the position of brake operator on express trains. This agreement cost the railroad a great deal of money in early retirement packages (estimated to be $80,000 each for 1,500 employees) but would likely reduce a high percentage of Burlington's business costs. The industry as a whole was expected to save $600 million per year as a result of that job title's elimination.

Other negotiations proved more difficult. Collective bargaining occurred throughout 1991 between the freight railroads, Amtrak, and the railroad employees' unions (most notably the International Association of Machinists, or IAM), with most disputes being settled that year. Yet by June 1992, IAM and the freight rail companies had still not reached an agreement. This situation, combined with Amtrak's stalled negotiations with two of its unions, led to a strike and a national rail shutdown on June 24, 1992. After Congressional intervention forced binding arbitration, all disputes were resolved by August 2, 1992. It is likely that labor disputes will continue to mark the rail industry, as technical advances shift emphasis from physical labor such as brake operation to more technical and managerial jobs such as engineering.

Each train is run by an engineer, who holds the highest rank on a train and is in charge of the train and its crew. The engineer checks the train for mechanical and safety problems before each run, starts and stops the train, and monitors its progress throughout a trip. Trained as ''firers'' (a term surviving from the days of steam locomotives) or assistant engineers, engineers must learn how to run and monitor all trains owned by their employer and must be familiar with tracks, signals, and hazards of each route. In 1993 starting engineers earned an average of $35,000 to $45,000 per year, reflecting the job's status as the highest-paid railroad worker.

All trains also employ a conductor who is responsible for the train crew and the passengers or freight. On freight trains, the conductor logs the contents of each freight car and ensures that the contents are deposited at their destinations along the route. On passenger trains, the conductor collects passenger fares, helps passengers with any needs or requests, and alerts the engineer when all passengers at a given stop have left the train. Conductors also act as an information conduit between the dispatchers, station managers, etc., and the engineer. In 1993 the average annual starting salary for a conductor was $32,000 to $35,000.

Some trains employ an assistant engineer (''fireman'' or ''firer''), who aids the engineer in running and monitoring the trains—this position is being phased out due to the increasing computerization and the mechanization of trains, terminals, and freight yards. Firers perform engine maintenance and repair and serve as emergency replacements for engineers. Brake operators (previously called ''brakemen'') maintain braking equipment and lights and add and remove cars at station stops. Brake operators also are disappearing from trains due to railroad-union negotiations; they are being eliminated mainly through attrition and early-retirement incentives. In 1993 firers earned an average yearly starting salary of $16,000 to $25,000, and brake operators had a starting salary of $30,000.

AMERICA AND THE WORLD

Regional trade agreements, railroad cooperation, railroad mergers, and transportation innovations have all had an impact on the growth and development of rail transportation. The U.S.-Canadian Free Trade Agreement, signed in 1988, resulted in Class 1 railroads on both sides of the border accelerating their connections into each other's territory. The North American Free Trade Agreement (NAFTA), which diminished most trade barriers, and a wave of rail mergers in the United States in 1994 and 1995 further hastened this trend.

With trade between the United States and Canada forcing a north-south orientation, railroads shifted their east-west systems accordingly. Both shared track, railbeds, and operations on both sides of the border. U.S. railroads gained entry to Canada through interline agreements with Canadian railroads. The Atchison, Topeka and Santa Fe Railway Company, for example, entered into an interline connection with the Canadian National Railway Company's Grand Trunk line at Chicago. This enabled the railroad to provide service between Mexico and Canada.

NAFTA resulted in U.S., Canadian, and Mexican rail carriers capitalizing on increased transborder trade. Rail traffic to Mexico began growing when the country first began easing trade barriers in 1988, and reached new highs in 1993 with NAFTA. In 1994 cargo volumes for Canadian railroads accounted for about one-quarter of the southbound export tonnage moving across the U.S. border. The pact particularly benefitted U.S. producers of grain, automobiles, lumber, and other goods suited for transport by rail.

American companies worked especially hard with the Mexican national rail system, FNM (Ferrocarriles Nacionales de Mexico), to simplify border regulations and increase rail traffic between the two countries. For example, FNM adopted Union Pacific's computerized monitoring and tracking system, while Concarril, a Mexican company, began building cars for the Atchison, Topeka, and Santa Fe Railway. Shipments of goods between the two countries had already increased in the early 1990s, even before the implementation of NAFTA, with more American-made automobiles and Pacific Rim imports being shipped by train to Mexico.

In 1994 Union Pacific derived $348 million in revenues from Mexico traffic, up 20 percent from the previous year, and handled 55 percent of cross-border rail traffic. Southern Pacific, the largest double-stack carrier to Mexico, handled the second-largest amount of cargo. Southern Pacific invested directly in Mexico's infrastructure and developed a network of distribution centers at Mexican rail ports that enabled timely unloading. In 1993 it completed construction on an intermodal facility at Monterrey, operated by Mexican firms. Union Pacific expanded its presence in Mexico in 1997 by entering into a joint venture to operate the Pacific-North Railway. In 1999 it increased its ownership to 26 percent of Grupo Ferroviario Mexicana, parent company of Ferrocarril Mexicano, the operator of the privatized former Pacific-North region of the Mexican National Railway.

RESEARCH AND TECHNOLOGY

Among the newest innovations in the railroad industry was EDI, or electronic data interchange, which allowed the railways to track goods and trains more closely and quickly than in the past. The primary EDI system, ATCS (advanced train control systems), controlled trains using telecommunications technology and computer tracking. With ATCS, train crews could stay informed of all train operations, a development that could improve safety and reliability and reduce costs.

Norfolk Southern established an EDI system called Thoroughbred, which allowed the carrier to closely track cargo, gave customers up-to-the-minute status reports on their shipments, and provided delivery schedules. Likewise, the Atchison, Topeka and Santa Fe Railway launched Santa Fe Direct, a real-time EDI system to track shipments that went beyond its rail service. Union Pacific's computerized car locator system, on which all U.S. and Canadian locator systems were based, installed its system at 10 railyards in Mexico. In 1994 data was integrated into the U.S. and Canadian systems making it possible for a Canadian shipper to send freight out on a Canadian National or Canadian Pacific car all the way to Mexico City without the car being opened, and know where the goods were anytime and anywhere.

Technology refinements in the use of intermodal containerized freight, the means by which containers could be interchanged between rail, seagoing, and trucking modes, resulted in railroads moving freight faster and more efficiently. Statistics from the Association of American Railroads indicated that the use of intermodal peaked in 1994 with 8.13 million trailers and containers in use, then slacked off in 1995 to 8.07 million, only to rebound to 8.7 million in 1997. The engineering of double-stack trains, a means by which one container is literally stacked on top of another, also made it possible for a train to carry the equivalent of 200 trucks, thereby saving fuel and labor costs while improving efficiencies. Platforms on which the containers were secured provided a smoother ride for materials and products.

Once industry standards became hammered out, some industry observers felt that ATCS would provide near-instantaneous data on car location, switching records, car scheduling, and other factors that affected the smooth synchronization of a vast network of trains. Of course, the up-front costs were great, but ATCS was one step toward further computerizing a large and complex industry.

Other innovations included ISS (Interline Settlement System) and REN (Rate EDI Network), industry-wide standards of computerized data management that would manage revenue sharing among railroads when goods were shipped on more than one line, as was often the case, and speed billing and dispute resolution within the industry. An information system called Railinc, used widely in the industry, already sped customer service and tracking. Finally, it was predicted that the rail industry would take advantage of handheld ''slate'' computers that would allow crews to forward information to central schedulers ''on the fly,'' or as it was taken down. All of this automation, based on smaller networked computer systems rather than large central mainframe machines, could lead to a continuing decentralization of control and information that would allow greater flexibility and improved response on the part of each company and the industry as a whole.

A major development affecting passenger rail service, and especially Amtrak, was high-speed rail passenger systems, which ran at 125 miles or more per hour and brought train travel to a speed where it could compete with air travel over shorter distances, both in regard to cost and convenience.

High-speed rail systems fell into two categories, steel-wheel-on-steel-rail and magnetic levitation systems. Among the more traditional wheel-on-rail trains, the fastest of which could reach 187 miles per hour, France's TGV train was the most successful. As of 1993, a privately financed TGV system was planned by the Texas High-Speed Rail Authority to link Dallas/Fort Worth, Houston, San Antonio, and Austin by 1999. Privately financed for $7 billion, the system would be the first of its kind in the United States.

Magnetic levitation (maglev) technology, which used magnetic forces to propel, brake, and control trains traveling up to 300 miles per hour, was tested in Germany and Japan. The trains, which were separated from the tracks by a magnetic field, were not yet in commercial use. A planned maglev system, however, that would connect the Orlando, Florida, airport and the Disney World complex, was planned, with backing from American, German, and Japanese investors.

Among other developments in the industry were new fuels for locomotives. In 1991 Burlington Northern, in conjunction with Air Products & Chemicals, Inc., developed a locomotive that could be run on refrigerated liquid methane, a natural gas derivative. The use of such fuels could reduce fuel costs for rail companies, as well as cut down on polluting emissions.

Railroads invest heavily in technologies that would improve safety and efficiency. By July 1997 railroads had two-way end-of-train braking devices installed on all trains that routinely traveled at speeds greater than 30 miles per hour. Railroads replaced older wheels with heat-treated curved plate wheels, which were developed following research in the late 1980s. Positive train separation systems were being tested to reduce the chance of mainline collisions. The latest rail transport and safety improvements were tested at the Transportation Technology Center, a 52-square-mile facility operated by the Association of American Railroads.

FURTHER READING

Association of American Railroads. ''Economic Linchpin: The American Rail Industry.'' Available from http://www.aar.org/comm/statfact.nsf.

———. ''Intermodal Transport: Fastest Growing Segment of the Railroad Industry.'' Available from http://www.aar.org/comm/statfact.nsf.

———. ''National Railroad Passenger Corporation (Amtrak).'' Available from http://www.aar.org/comm/statfact.nsf.

———. ''New Technologies Improve Safety & Efficiency.'' Available from http://www.aar.org/comm/statfact.nsf.

———. ''An Overview: Railroads—The Engine That Drives America.'' Available from http://www.aar.org/comm/statfact.nsf.

———. *Railroad Facts.* 1999 ed.

———. *Railroads Rip Bottleneck Scheme as Reregulation,* 16 October 1996.

Burke, Jack. ''Rail Attacks Bottlenecks.'' *Traffic World,* 21 October 1996.

''CN-IC Gets STB Final Approval.'' *Chemical Week,* 9 June 1999.

''Conrail Breakup Creates Congestion.'' *Chemical Week,* 7 July 1999.

Dinsmore, Christopher. ''Norfolk Southern Chief's Ultimatum Draws Results in Conrail Bid.'' *Knight-Ridder/Tribune Business News,* 5 March 1997.

''$8.4-Billion Rail Merger Would Be Largest.'' *Pulp & Paper,* December 1996.

''Fast Train to Nowhere?'' *Business Week,* 27 September 1999.

''Freight Delays Follow Conrail Carve Up.'' *Pulp & Paper,* August 1999.

''Grows to 12,000 Miles.'' *Railway Age,* September 1999.

Hassler, Darrell. ''Canadian National, Illinois Central Railways Merge.'' *American Metal Markets,* 16 July 1999.

''RailAmerica to Fold in RailTex.'' *Railway Age,* November 1999.

Rasmussen, Jim. ''Conrail Split Avoids Depths of Union Pacific's Woes.'' *Knight-Ridder/Tribune Business News,* 14 September 1999.

Reinke, Jeff. "A New Direction for Amtrak?" *Mass Transit,* July/August 1999.

"Shippers Wary of Conrail Breakup." *Purchasing,* 15 July 1999.

"Shortline Consolidation." *Chemical Week,* 27 October 1999.

"Tracking Mergers." *American Shipper,* January 1999.

"UP Doubles Stake in Mexico." *Railway Age,* March 1999.

SIC 4013

RAILROAD SWITCHING AND TERMINAL ESTABLISHMENTS

This category covers establishments engaged primarily in the furnishing of terminal facilities for rail passenger or freight traffic for line-haul service and in the movement of railroad cars between terminal yards, industrial sidings, and other local sites. Terminal companies do not necessarily operate any vehicles themselves, but they may operate the stations and terminals. Lessors of railway property are classified in **SIC 6517: Lessors of Railroad Property.**

NAICS Code(s)

482112 (Short Line Railroads)
488210 (Support Activities for Rail Transportation)

Industry Snapshot

Between 2,500 and 3,000 rail transit stations were in the United States in the late 1990s. About 600 were operated by Amtrak alone. These stations and track terminals served about 15 large freight railroads and more than 600 small, regional railroads. As mass transit systems continued to spread across America, rail tracks and terminals shared by more than one railroad company became an increasing concern. A train going just 30 mph needs two-thirds of a mile to stop; a train going 50 mph needs 1.5 miles warning time to stop. High speed trains traveling in excess of 125 mph were also being placed into the rail system. The July 1999 crash of two trains near Calcutta, India, killed several hundred people and was caused by the error of a railroad switching employee.

The human error factor however, which accounted for the majority of train switching accidents, was being eliminated from the industry. As trains became more electronically controlled, safety for passenger and freight cargo rose dramatically. Approximately 80 percent of railroad tracks in the United States used a technology employing electromechanical relay signal systems. However, wireless microprocessors, using computer signals, were rapidly replacing the relay systems. The result was a less expensive and more safety-oriented rail system that was expected to grow through 2006.

Background and Development

Railroad switching and terminal establishments for line-haul railroads are the connection points that facilitate the movement of tons of goods on and off trains, as well as the assembly and tracking of those trains. Closely tied to the railroads' increased profitability in the 1990s was tighter scheduling and dispatching made possible by high-technology tracking systems that aided crews in train turnover, which can reach hundreds of trains a day.

In order to cut costs and attract new truck-to-rail business, railroad companies have begun to upgrade their transfer terminals. At the heart of this activity was a desire to facilitate the movement of intermodal traffic. In 1997 Illinois Central upgraded its transfer terminal at Harvey outside of Chicago to increase its intermodal business. Norfolk International Terminals constructed a new intermodal transfer container facility to increase the facility's intermodal rail handling capacity.

With the merger of major railroad companies in the United States, railroad executives anticipate a potential bottleneck at terminals with some railroads not having easy access to switching. In 1997 the issue became heated with the potential of some form of re-regulation coming to the industry.

The biggest technological advance affecting railroad terminals was the use of computer networking and scheduling to speed jobs that were once handled by paperwork and tracked by human operators. These advances, which in the long run save money for railroads and make them able to compete with other forms of transportation, have shaken up the industry and reduced the number of workers necessary for a task. Automatic Train Control System (ATCS) networks, used by most Class 1 (large railroad) lines, are based on transponders attached to tracks at certain intervals and triggered by passing trains.

With ATCS, information gained from the transponders is sent via fiber-optic cable or telephone line to a regional data center or directly to the switching yard to which a passing train is headed. This information, once gathered, allows switching establishments to react more quickly to changes on the line, as well as to assign incoming trains to certain tracks in the yard. Switching establishments, which may or may not be run by the railroads that use them, can use up to 100 track segments on which cars and locomotives are coupled and uncoupled, loaded and unloaded.

ATCS was being implemented in four areas—work order reporting, locomotive performance monitoring, track force equipment management, and positive train separation and control. The U.S. Department of Transportation's (DOT) Federal Railroad Administration (FRA), in cooperation with the industry, conducted a safety inquiry into this new technology and reported to Congress the feasibility of implementing ATCS in a way that would enhance the safety, efficiency, productivity, and customer service capabilities in the railroad industry.

Union Pacific's rail complex in North Platte, Nebraska, the world's largest, can deal with up to 700 trains in a day by way of its computerized command center. Outside Albany, New York, Conrail's Selkirk Yard sorts 3,200 freight cars per day, thanks to computer scheduling and track assignment. Finally, a move by the railroads to a hub-and-spoke system of organization reduces local stops and focuses time and money on larger, more centralized switching establishments (see **SIC 4011: Railroads, Line-Haul Operating**).

CURRENT CONDITIONS

The Surface Transportation Board Reauthorization Act of 1999, introduced to Congress by the DOT in October 1999, was intended to extend the Surface Transportation Board (which replaced the Interstate Commerce Commission) for another two years. A key provision of the act was the mandate calling for reciprocal switching in railroad terminal areas. It is anticipated that the act will enhance competition among terminal providers, which is something that rail shippers have been demanding for some time.

Interest in passenger rail continues to grow, with both intercity and rapid transit applications. The Congressional fiscal year 2000 budget for the federal transit program was $5.8 billion, with the passenger railcar-building industry being a key beneficiary. It is expected that after completing the 3,000-unit backlog (of January 1999), the industry will receive another 6,200 rail car orders through 2004.

To meet the new demand, corollary industries were also experiencing commensurate growth. For example, Harmon Industries, manufacturer of signaling and safety systems, posted a record $265 million in sales for 1998. The company offers a six-week training program to train switch operators in crisis situations, which are simulated in its 3,500-square-foot lab, complete with two full-size switching machines and three railroad crossing gates.

Another corollary industry is that of renovating and refurbishing train stations that service switching terminals. The nonprofit Great American Train Foundation published its first ''Guidebook on Train Station Revitalization'' in 1999 to assist local governments and communities in transforming railroad stations into multimodal centers of transportation, commerce, and economic development.

WORKFORCE

Railroad terminals use a hierarchical employment structure much like that found in the larger railroad industry, in which engineers, conductors, and brake operators work together on operations. In the terminals, however, job descriptions are slightly different. Railyard engineers oversee the movement of cars within the freight yard or terminal and the assembly of trains. Yard conductors oversee all yard employees, instructing them in assembling and disassembling trains and switching cars between tracks. Yard brakers (or ''yard helpers'') assist the conductor and do much of the physical labor of coupling and uncoupling cars. In addition to the yard crew, railroad terminals employ clerks, maintenance workers, and signalers and signal maintainers. Passenger terminals also employ station agents and ticket agents, who deal directly with the public.

Because of continued automation, the industry is expected to lose employees,—declining to 143,000 by 2006, which represents about a 24 percent drop from 1995.

FURTHER READING

Burke, Jack. ''UP Ready to Take Over SP.'' *Traffic World,* 9 September 1996.

''DOT Proposes STB Reauthorization Bill.'' *Logistics Management & Distribution Report,* November 1999.

''IC to Double Size of Chicago Bulk Terminal.'' *Rail Business Week,* 3 February 1997.

Johnson, Gregory S. ''Widespread Delays in Railroad Service Worry Shippers.'' *Journal of Commerce,* 1 May 1996.

''Preserving Railroad Stations.'' *Public Management,* October 1999.

''Rail Intermodal Yard Greatly Increases NIT's Handling Facility.'' *The Virginia Maritimer,* June/July 1996.

Roth, Stephen. ''Training Showpiece.'' *Kansas City Business Journal,* 19 March 1999.

Vantuono, William. ''Passenger Trains for the 21st Century.'' *Railway Age,* May 1999.

SIC 4111

LOCAL AND SUBURBAN TRANSIT

This industry consists of establishments primarily engaged in furnishing local and suburban mass passenger transportation over regular routes and on regular schedules, with operations confined principally to a municipality, contiguous municipalities, or a municipality and its suburban areas. Also included in this industry are establishments primarily engaged in furnishing passenger transportation by automobile, bus, or rail to, from, or between airports or rail terminals, over regular routes, and those providing bus and rail commuter services.

NAICS CODE(S)

485111 (Mixed Mode Transit Systems)
485112 (Commuter Rail Systems)
485113 (Bus and Motor Vehicle Transit Systems)
485119 (Other Urban Transit Systems)
485999 (All Other Transit and Ground Passenger Transportation)

INDUSTRY SNAPSHOT

Despite America's complaints of traffic congestion, pollution, gasoline prices, and lack of available parking, the truth is, and remains, that Americans love their automobiles. ''Public transit'' and ''mass transit'' systems, once buzz words of futurists, have become terms that hardly cause interest among those who would best be served by such systems. Two studies released in September 1998 by the Reason Public Policy Institute (RPPI) indicate that, despite $180 billion in federal funds from 1988 to 1998, public transit systems have failed to relieve the very problems used to justify their fiscal costs: traffic congestion, transportation for the poor, and local maintenance of fiscal responsibility for transit.

The sheer convenience of a personal automobile appears to be one of the biggest obstacles to the appeal of public transit. While most transit systems are intended to alleviate ''rush hour'' traffic associated with commutes to and from work, the truth is that almost 40 percent of morning traffic, and a clear 60 percent of afternoon rush hour traffic, is not even work related. Moreover, most transit systems were designed to serve urban metropolises and their suburbs, but only 19 percent of all commuters live in suburbs while working in the central cities. In fact, in 1995, public transit systems served only about one percent of total surface miles nationwide. Added to this is the fact that Americans do not often go straight home from work: they pick up the kids, drop off their dry cleaning, or go out to eat—still another reason why car pools have not worked. Public transit, as we know it, simply cannot compete with private transportation when considering such realities.

For years, the mass transit industry had carried the stigma of the ''one percent argument,'' the system would service only one percent of all trips made by persons. The argument has been close to reality: light-rail systems are used by only 5 percent of commuters, once the multibillion dollar systems have been completed. Public transit in general has historically served a captive clientele: persons without drivers licenses or without vehicles, comprising about 70 percent of all riders, according to the National Urban Transit Institute at the Center for Urban Transportation Research. Ultimately, government subsidies to maintain the failed systems were averaging almost $10 dollars per one-way passenger and, in cities like Los Angeles, ran as high as $40 dollars per commuter rail trip.

But all is not for naught. As the 1990s ended, the statistical wake-up calls urged cities and policy-makers to shift focus. Instead of trying to increase ridership with billion-dollar subsidies, they needed to develop other innovative transportation solutions. As a result, the industry has been paving its way toward an effective and appealing solution to ease public transportation concerns.

ORGANIZATION AND STRUCTURE

Passenger transit is considered an essential public service in the United States. As such, large sums of government financial assistance are pumped into transit systems throughout the country every year. Since World War II, private transit companies have been converted into public enterprises on a huge scale. This trend was facilitated by the passage of the Urban Mass Transit Act of 1964. This act was created largely as a measure to save mass transit from disappearing, since the postwar rise in automobile use had pushed many transit companies into insolvency. By 1990, public transit systems accounted for 86 percent of the industry's vehicles, 94 percent of its vehicle miles operated, and 94 percent of its unlinked passenger trips.

Transit Modes. Local and suburban passenger transit includes several different transportation modes. The most common mode found in the United States is the motorbus, which sees heavy use throughout the country. In large cities, heavy rail systems, which generally means subways and elevated rails, are also common. Commuter trains, light rails, and trolleys are also part of the local transit network. This industry also includes vanpools, airport shuttles, and other transportation to transit terminals, provided they run over regular routes on fixed schedules.

Distribution. Obviously, the need for transit grows with population size. In general, smaller urban areas use more buses and vanpools, while rail systems are found primarily in only the largest cities and their metropolitan areas. More than half of the nation's road transit systems are located in urbanized areas with populations under 50,000. Of the 20 all-rail transit systems in the United States, 15 are in cities with populations in excess of two million. California and New York have the most transit systems in operation, each state containing 362 systems. Texas, with 238, is the only other state with more than 200 transit operations.

Organizations. The American Public Transit Association (APTA) is an organization of mass transit operators in the United States and Canada. Based in Washington, the APTA has more than 1,000 members. The APTA is generally considered the definitive source of transit information in the United States. Its members include organizations involved in every facet of mass transit, including construction, design, financing, planning, and supplying. The APTA was created in 1974 upon the merger of the American Transit Association (ATA), founded in 1882 as the American Electric Railway Association, and the Institute for Rapid Transit (IRT). The federal agency that oversees the industry is the Urban Mass Transit Administration (UMTA), an arm of the U.S. Department of Transportation.

BACKGROUND AND DEVELOPMENT

Urban mass transit in the United States began to appear in the early part of the nineteenth century. In 1827, a horse-drawn stagecoach line began operating in Manhattan. Designed and planned by Abraham Brower, the line started out as a single 12-passenger vehicle, built by the coach-making company Wade & Leverich, running up and down Broadway. Two years later, Ephraim Dodge followed suit in Boston. Meanwhile, a more comfortable vehicle called an omnibus was gaining popularity on the streets of London and Paris. Brower took notice of the omnibus' success in Europe and, within four years of their New York introduction, over 100 omnibuses were rolling on New York's grid of streets. By 1844, omnibus service was also available in Philadelphia, Boston, and Baltimore.

Beginnings of Rail Service. At the same time that road transit was developing in the United States, street railway lines were making their debut. In 1832 John Mason, president of the Chemical Bank, founded the New York and Harlem Railroad, which initially ran along the Bowery from Prince Street to 14th Street, and eventually stretched all the way to Harlem. New Orleans launched a similar streetcar line in 1835, but this mode of transit did not really catch on until the 1850s, when Brooklyn, Cambridge, Philadelphia, Baltimore, Pittsburgh, Cincinnati, and Chicago all had horsedrawn rail lines built.

By 1882, more than 400 street railway companies were in business in the United States, with a total capital investment of $150 million. Those companies operated 18,000 streetcars and owned 100,000 horses or mules. Approximately 1.2 billion passengers were riding in railcars annually. That year, the American Street Railway Association was formed in Boston as a nationwide trade organization.

The first successful cable-powered transit line began operating in San Francisco in 1873. Cable cars spread across the country more quickly than horsecars had, and by 1883, cable lines were operating in Chicago, Philadelphia, and New York. The New York line included a route across the newly built Brooklyn Bridge. Over nine million passengers rode cable cars across the bridge in the cable line's first year of operation. In 1888, the first successful electric-powered street railway line was launched in Richmond, Virginia. Powered by a small, stationary copper wire, this line quickly made cable cars—with their cumbersome systems of pulleys, wheels, and underground vaults—obsolete.

The next major development in urban transit was the elevated rail. Although elevated lines had popped up in New York throughout the second half of the nineteenth century, it was not until financier Jay Gould took them over and combined them into a single entity, the Manhattan Railway, that the "els" became an important transit system. By 1893, the New York els carried 500,000 passengers a day. Steam powered elevated lines also appeared before the turn of the century in Kansas City, Missouri and Sioux City, Iowa, but these ventures were short lived. The Chicago "L" opened in 1892, and it was there that the first electric powered elevated rail was unveiled in 1895.

Ground was broken in 1900 for the nation's first subway system, New York's Interborough Rapid Transit (IRT). On the system's first day of operation in October of 1904, 150,000 passengers paid five cents each to ride the new trains. The IRT quickly grew to resemble the sprawling system it is today.

The period between World War I and World War II was the golden age of the trolley. Trolleys were operating in virtually every city in the United States by 1917, covering 45,000 miles of track. By the mid-1920s, however, ridership had already begun to decline, largely due to competition from gasoline powered buses and the emerging automobile. The trolley industry was saved by the development of the PCC car, named for the Electric Railway Presidents' Conference Committee that had spawned its design. The PCC car—lighter, more comfortable, and better performing than previous streetcars—was a major success, and revived streetcar business through the 1930s and early 1940s. After World War II, however, trolley ridership tailed off permanently.

Shift to Public Sector. The huge surge in the use of automobiles in the postwar era made it extremely difficult for transit companies to operate at a profit. In order for urban transit to survive, a shift from private to public ownership of many major systems became necessary. Under public control, transit systems were expected only to cover operating expenses, such as salaries and routine maintenance, through passenger fares. Capital expenses, such as facility construction, could be met through bond issues or taxation. New York's subway companies and Cleveland's transit were taken over by government agencies as early as 1940 and 1942. Chicago and Boston followed in 1947.

Rise of Buses. Another postwar trend was the shift from streetcars to buses as the main form of surface transit. By 1960, buses had an annual ridership of 6.5 billion, compared to 463 million streetcar passengers. This transition was assisted by the actions of companies like National City Lines, a transit holding company whose standard procedure was to absorb smaller street rail companies and quickly convert them into motorized bus operations. In 1964, Congress passed the Urban Mass Transit Act, creating a role for the federal government in ensuring the survival of local transit.

Ridership Decline. The decline in transit ridership eased a bit in the early 1970s, as concerns about energy consumption and environmental issues arose. One result of this modest resurgence was the development of light rail transit (LRT), which first appeared in the form of rehabilitation projects on old trolley lines. After successful LRT systems were launched in Canada in the late 1970s, LRT lines began operating in San Diego in 1981, Buffalo in 1984, and Portland, Oregon in 1986. Several other cities have built LRT systems since then.

In the United States in the mid-1990s, there were about 6,000 transit systems in operation. Those systems had active fleets containing 118,000 vehicles. Motorbuses made up the largest portion of transit vehicles, numbering 67,000. Ten thousand heavy rail cars and 4,500 commuter rail cars comprised another sizeable share. In 1995, the transit industry had operating funds of $17.6 billion. Nearly half of this revenue was in the form of government assistance from local, state, or federal sources. Passenger fares accounted for about 40 percent of total revenue, just more than $6 billion in 1995. Of the 8.4 billion trips taken on transit in 1994, 5.4 billion were made on buses and 2.7 were made by rail.

Despite the small rebound in the popularity of mass transit that took place in the 1970s, Americans were using it at a lower rate than ever before in the mid-1990s. Only about 5 percent of commuting was done via public transit systems, down from 9 percent in 1970. The exception to this trend was the increased use of vanpools, airport shuttles, and other smaller, nonpublic transit designed for special use.

Government Funding. Since 1974, nearly $70 billion in federal funds have been pumped into the nation's public transit systems. Although federal spending on local transit tailed off somewhat during the Reagan and Bush presidencies, this was offset by increases in local and state funding. In addition, the Intermodal Surface Transportation Efficiency Act of 1991 authorized $31 billion in federal spending from 1993 through 1997.

Despite this huge outlay of money, there is little evidence to suggest that riders are choosing transit systems over their cars. In some cases, newly built rail systems are merely drawing passengers from existing bus routes. Several new systems, such as Miami's $1.2 billion, 21-mile rail system, are attracting fewer passengers than were projected at higher than predicted costs. In 1989, Miami's system drew only 15 percent of its projected ridership and cost triple the forecast amount per car to run. A trolley system in Los Angeles cost $700 million more to construct than was projected and ran slower than the bus routes it was designed to replace.

CURRENT CONDITIONS

In 1998, almost 8.7 billion persons used public transit at least once, an increase of 4.6 percent from 1997. Buses carried the largest number, approximately 5.2 billion in 1998. Heavy rail carried 2.6 billion riders, light rail had 278.8 million riders, and commuter rails carried 378.6 million. The trollybuses reported a loss, although they still carried 117.4 million passengers in 1998. All in all, 1998 was the third consecutive year that public transit ridership was increased (by almost the same percent in 1997).

Light rail use increased in Portland, San Diego, Baltimore, Dallas, Denver, Boston, Los Angeles, St. Louis, and Sacramento in 1998. Philadelphia and Pittsburgh reported decreases, as did Buffalo, New York. During the same year, commuter rail systems increased their passenger numbers in Boston, Los Angeles, and North San Diego County in California. Tri-Rail suffered a 6.8 percent loss.

With an eye toward the future, public-private partnerships in the public transportation industry are increasingly common. For example, California's Route 91 express lanes in busy Orange County were converted to a fully automated toll road, complete with a toll-free "three +" lane for car-poolers. The project represented a partnership between the California Department of Transportation (CALTRANS) and a consortium of private companies, including one French firm. CALTRANS saved the $130 million construction cost, in return for a 30-year lease to the companies, to build and operate the toll road. The 10-mile, four lane toll road opened in December 1995, but as of January 1998, was losing money. Even with $3.20 tolls at peak hours, traffic congestion continued during rush hour, and the revenue loss was attributed to the car pool lanes.

The Future. The end result is that fewer and fewer people are commuting to work. Even in New York, where the subway is still king, only 53 percent of the population take transit to work, down from 62 percent in 1970 and 56 percent in 1980. Still, industry officials are committed to the survival of mass transit. Money from the government is likely to continue flowing, as solutions are sought to the problems associated with large-scale automobile use, which include highway congestion, pollution, and excessive use of energy.

INDUSTRY LEADERS

The largest public transit system in the United States by far is New York's Metropolitan Transportation Authority (MTA), which accounts for about one-fourth of the nation's total trips. MTA reported a 7.71 percent increase in ridership for 1998. Its subway system makes 61 percent of the nation's heavy rail trips. Other large public transit systems include Chicago's Regional Transportation Authority, the Los Angeles-based Southern California Rapid Transit District, and the Washington Metropolitan Area Transit Authority.

In the private sector, the clear industry leader is New Jersey Transit Bus Operations Inc., a subsidiary of the huge New Jersey Transit Corporation. In addition to local buses, New Jersey Transit also operates intercity bus and commuter rail services. The Bus Operations subsidiary has annual revenue of $194 million. Another large local bus line operator in the private sector is Liberty Lines Transit Inc., based in Yonkers, New York. Liberty Lines, founded in 1955, generates $32 million in annual revenue.

WORKFORCE

There are more than 300,000 employees in the transit industry. About 179,000 of these are employee in the motorbus sector; 52,000 in heavy rail; 37,000 in demand response; 22,500 in commuter rail; and the remainder in other areas. Of all personnel, 49 percent are vehicle operators or conductors, 27 percent are maintenance workers, and 24 percent work in other fields.

RESEARCH AND TECHNOLOGY

The technology of mass transit changes constantly. Many of the industry's developments have been in the area of communications. The Intelligent Mobile Data Network (IMDN) is a network of base stations and antennas scattered over a metropolitan area that can efficiently function as both a communications system and a vehicle locator. Wireless transmission systems, in conjunction with new camera technology, are also being developed for security use on rail platforms. Fare collection is another area that sees constant technological change. Many larger systems are incorporating fare cards, which allow passengers to prepay for a variable number of trips. Some industry observers see fare cards as the first step toward the use of debit cards or a system similar to those used with automatic teller machines. In 1999, Motorola announced its contract with Nanjing, China, to provide public transit riders with custom smart cards for payments of ferry, subway and bus fares. Motorola also services the Washington and San Francisco markets with smart cards. By 2002, Motorola will service 26 transit agencies.

As environmental concerns continue to trouble the transit industry, the search for efficient alternate fuels for buses remains an ongoing task. Sacramento has experimented with bus engines that run on natural gas, while Los Angeles is testing methanol and electric power. In Peoria, Illinois, ethanol made from corn, an abundant local resource, is being examined as a possible engine fuel for buses.

FURTHER READING

DeLong, James V. "Running Around." *Reason,* May 1999.

Dunn Jr., James. "Transportation." *American Behavioral Scientist,* September 1999.

Ford, Tom. "RTA's Berea Plan Stopped in Tracks." *Crain's Cleveland Business,* 11 October 1999.

"Global Briefs." *Wireless Week,* 27 September 1999.

"Public Transit is Largely Ineffective." *Society,* January/February 1999.

"Transit Update." *Railway Age,* July 1999.

"Transportation Survey Sheds Light On Urban Transit." *American City & County,* May 1999.

Vantuono, William C. "Why *Transit* Works: Real-World Conservatives Take Another Look." *Railway Age,* July 1999.

SIC 4119

LOCAL PASSENGER TRANSPORTATION, NOT ELSEWHERE CLASSIFIED

This industry classification includes establishments primarily engaged in furnishing miscellaneous passenger transportation, where such operations are principally within a municipality, contiguous municipalities, or a municipality and its suburban areas. Establishments primarily engaged in renting passenger automobiles without drivers are classified in services, Industry Group 751: Automobile Rental and Leasing, without Drivers. Establishments primarily operating ski lifts, tows, and other recreational lifts are classified as **SIC 7999: Amusement and Recreation Services, Not Elsewhere Classified.**

NAICS CODE(S)

621910 (Ambulance Service)
485410 (School and Employee Bus Industry)
487110 (Scenic and Sightseeing Transportation, Land)
485991 (Special Needs Transportation)
485999 (All Other Transit and Ground Passenger Transportation)
485320 (Limousine Service)

A diverse range of transportation modes makes up this industry classification. Among the types of companies in this group were ambulance services, limousine services (with drivers), and aerial tramways and cables cars that were not for amusement or scenic use. Sightseeing buses (noncharter), vanpool operations, and hearse rentals with drivers were also classified in this industry. There were 7,915 establishments classified in this industry in the 1990s, according to *County Business Patterns.* Almost 3,500 of them were very small operations, with fewer than five employees. The industry employed 130,677 people, with a total annual payroll of $2.2 billion.

Ambulance Services. The top companies in this catch-all industry were ambulance services. Collectively, ambulance services in the United States generated about $7 billion a year in revenue. Following a wave of consolidation in the early and mid-1990s, two clear industry leaders emerged: American Medical Response (AMR), whose parent company, Laidlaw Inc. of Ontario, Canada, also merged in San Diego-based Med Trans; and Rural/Metro Corp. of Scottsdale, Arizona. Prior to the merger, the Colorado-based AMR had annual revenue of $725 million and 17,000 ambulances operating in 38 states. Med Trans had $500 million in revenue and 12,000 employees. In late 1999, however, Laidlaw announced its intention to sell AMR, which reported flat profit margins during late 1998 and 1999. Its competitor remained Rural/Metro Corp. of Dallas/Fort Worth, Texas, the second-largest ambulance service, with $250 million in revenue. By late 1999 Rural/Metro had taken over two of AMR's most lucrative 911 contracts, one alone worth $53 million.

The outlook for growth in the ambulance business in the 1990s was favorable, due to an aging population and health care reform measures, which resulted in patients being shifted between facilities more frequently. The industry faced increasing competition, however, for hospital and health maintenance organization contracts from public fire departments, whose personnel were also trained to respond to medical emergencies. Nearly 60 percent of all calls to fire departments in 1995 were medical aid requests.

The Balanced Budget Act of 1997 had significant effects on the ambulance industry, tightening the criteria for Medicare reimbursement of emergency ambulance claims. By 1998, the Health Care Financing Administration had published its Medicare ambulance fee schedule and final rules for determining ''medical necessity.'' The new rules required physician certification for nonemergency ambulance services. Most ambulance companies relied heavily on Medicare claims for business; in some states having large Medicare beneficiary populations, Medicare ambulance services could constitute as much as 60 percent of all transport revenues.

Limousine Services. Limousine services made up another significant share of the miscellaneous local passenger transportation industry. By 1999 there were more than 9,000 limousine companies in the United States, controlling a $4.4 billion industry. Carey International, Inc., an industry leader, was expected to triple in size by 2002, with 1998 revenues near $124 million. In June 1999 Carey acquired Classic Limousine Airport Service Inc., with revenues of $12 million and 100 chauffeur employees. In the late 1990s Carey was publicly traded and operated in 420 cities and 65 countries. Another leader, International Limousine Service Inc., covered only the Washington, D.C., area, but maintained a fleet of 75 vehicles, and had shuttled the likes of Congresspersons, Bob Hope, and even Mother Teresa around town. The company anticipated 1999 earnings of $5 million. New York and New Jersey also led in the number of limousine companies operating in the New England area.

As the industry grew in size, limousine services sought to widen their customer base by appealing to businesspeople in addition to their usual wedding and prom ridership. In particular, gains were made in the limousine industry's battle against taxicabs and shuttles for airport runs, for which the cost of limousine service was not much higher than for a cab in some places. In New York and elsewhere, however, proposals to allow liveries and limousines to make on-street pickups (strongly opposed by taxicab associations) continued to be a controversial issue in the area of local passenger transportation.

In the 1990s vanpools also sprang up to fill the gaps left by ordinary forms of local transit. VPSI (formerly Van Pool Services Inc.) was founded in 1973 as an in-house ride-sharing program for Chrysler employees during the energy crunch of that year. It subsequently blossomed into a profitable company subsidiary. National Themes, Ltd. also created a niche in major cities such as New York and Chicago, transporting patrons between bars, restaurants, sports arenas, and other nightspots. Kids Kab, founded in 1991 in the Detroit area to take children to their various activities, was an immediate hit among suburban working mothers. By the mid-1990s there were more than 250 similar companies nationwide.

FURTHER READING

Austin, Marsha. ''Laidlaw Slides AMR Division off Its Books.'' *Denver Business Journal,* 22 October 1999.

Austin, Marsha, and Aldo Svaldi. ''Ambulance Giant Races for Revamp.'' *Denver Business Journal,* 5 March 1999.

Bhambhani, Dipka. ''Retiree Steers Washington, D.C., Limousine Firm Back to Profitability.'' *Washington Times,* 22 November 1999.

DeSantis, Solange. "Laidlaw Agrees to Buy Ambulance Firm and Plans with Rollins to Merge Units." *Wall Street Journal,* 7 January 1997.

Feldman, Amy. "Driving Billy." *Forbes,* 11 March 1996.

Jeter, Lynne Wilbanks. "Ambulance Services Struggling with BBA Cuts." *Mississippi Business Journal,* 15 November 1999.

"Medicare Announces New Ambulance Coverage Regulation." *Health Care Financing Review,* Winter 1998.

Spiegel, Peter. "At Your Service." *Forbes,* 5 October 1998.

Strempel, Dan. "Classic Limousine Founders Drive a Multimillion-Dollar Deal." *Fairfield County Business Journal,* 2 August 1999.

U.S. Census Bureau. *County Business Patterns 1997.* Washington, DC: U.S. Census Bureau, 1999.

Woodbury, Richard. "Ambulance Chasing." *Time,* 9 December 1996.

SIC 4121

TAXICABS

This category covers establishments engaged primarily in furnishing passenger transportation by automobiles not operated on regular schedules or between fixed terminals. Taxicab fleet owners and organizations are included, regardless of whether drivers are hired or rent their cabs or are otherwise compensated. Establishments primarily engaged in furnishing passenger transportation by automobile or bus—to, from, or between airports or rail terminals—over regular routes, are classified under **SIC 4111: Local and Suburban Transit.** Taxicab associations and similar organizations that supply maintenance and repair services to their members are classified under **SIC 4173: Bus Terminal and Service Facilities.**

NAICS CODE(S)

485310 (Taxi Service)

INDUSTRY SNAPSHOT

In the latter 1990s, U.S. consumers spent an estimated $10.5 billion annually on taxis. Approximately 355,000 people were employed in the industry as owners, managers, drivers, dispatchers, or mechanics. About three out of every four drivers were either independent contractors licensed through and renting their vehicles from the taxi companies, or owner-operators affiliated with a taxi company or association. Overall, the U.S. taxi industry consisted of 130,000 fleets of 25 or more vehicles in 1996. Of these, 175,000 vehicles were licensed taxis and 30,000 were hired cars, also referred to as executive sedans or liveries. The remainder were minibuses or vans, many of which were wheelchair-accessible for transporting the elderly and disabled. In 1998, at least 29 cities had accessible taxis for physically impaired passengers. The industry continues to face competition from limousine services, executive sedans, and airport/hotel shuttle services.

ORGANIZATION AND STRUCTURE

Most taxi companies followed a similar organizational pattern. Managers—sometimes the company owners—ran the business, hired drivers, and performed other administrative duties. Dispatchers took calls and assigned cabs to passenger locations. In large companies, some dispatchers worked in two-person teams, one taking incoming calls and the other dispatching them. The position of dispatcher once represented a promotion awarded to experienced cab drivers, whose familiarity with the city best qualified them for the job. However, the increase in computer-based dispatching in the early 1990s prompted cab companies to favor computer skills over specialized knowledge of local geography when filling the dispatcher position.

Regulation of the U.S. taxi industry varied from city to city. While almost all cities had some form of licensing requirements, larger urban areas had the strictest regulations. In New York, for example, the number of licenses or "medallions" allotted the industry remained at 11,787 from 1937 until 1996. In 1996, 133 additional medallions were auctioned at prices between $172,000 to $221,000. Applicants for a taxi driver's license in New York were required to complete a 40 to 80 hour training course and pass an English exam as well as a final exam. About 30 percent of applicants failed the English exam, and 33 percent failed the final exam. Boston's regulations were similar to those of New York, with the number of available medallions frozen at 1,525 and selling for approximately $90,000 in the 1990s.

In most cities, regulations focused on fares charged to customers, with rates assigned to designated zones of the city. Seattle and Phoenix experimented with deregulating their cab industry in 1979 and 1982, respectively. Fare limits were imposed only on trips to and from airports, to protect tourists from unscrupulous drivers. After some initial price wars, cab fares eventually stabilized in Phoenix, but Seattle reregulated its industry in 1996, following years of declining service quality. The new regulations called for dress codes, standard per-mile fees, mandatory geography and language testing for drivers and age limits on vehicles.

CURRENT CONDITIONS

Government incentives for alternative fuels in the latter 1990s provided ample opportunity for city and county governments to convert their vehicles to energy-efficient fleets. In 1998, Ford Motor Company began offering $5,000 incentives to taxi operators who buy Ford's compressed-natural-gas Crown Victoria taxi vehicles. The biggest market so far has been New York City, where more than 105 vehicles have been sold. A joint venture between British, Belgian, and an American company built electric-powered taxis starting in 2000 for use in New York City. London's Zevco (Zero Emissions Vehicle Company) was the world's first company to launch the first fuel-cell powered taxi.

INDUSTRY LEADERS

Due to increasing decentralization in the industry, large taxi operations with operations beyond the local level were essentially non-existent in the mid-1990s. While some industry analysts felt that the cab business was too fragmented to support a national company, the acquisition of Yellow Cab Services Corp., of Houston, Texas, by Coach USA in 1996 gave an indication of how the taxi industry might be consolidated in the future. Founded in 1995, Coach USA quickly became the nation's leading provider of motor coach charter and tour services by acquiring a dozen independent bus companies. The acquisition of Yellow Cab Services, which had operations in Texas and Colorado, played into Coach's plan to provide full-service passenger ground transportation within its operating areas. In 1998, Coach owned nine taxi companies. It reported $625 million in revenues for 1997.

WORKFORCE

Until the mid-1970s, drivers were usually employees of cab companies, with salaried jobs and standard benefits. However, in the late 1970s most companies began hiring drivers as independent contractors. Under this arrangement, drivers paid a flat per-day fee to the company and paid for all expenses out of their take from fares but did not receive employee benefits such as insurance. In another, similar arrangement, some drivers earned a percentage of total fares, plus tips, which averaged 15 percent of a fare. Work hours varied, with full-time drivers often working as many as twelve hours a day, six days a week. Cab drivers' average salary was reported at $20,000 to $40,000 a year in 1997.

Studies performed by the National Institute for Occupational Safety and Health in the 1990s indicated that in the U.S. workforce, cab drivers were at the greatest risk of being killed on the job. These studies reported that from 1990 to 1992, 22.7 out of every 100,000 cabbies were murdered while performing work-related duties. The national average rate of death at the workplace during this time was 0.70 per 100,000 workers. In 1998, 82 taxi drivers lost their lives on the job, roughly 60 percent from assault and violence, and the other 40 percent from transportation accidents.

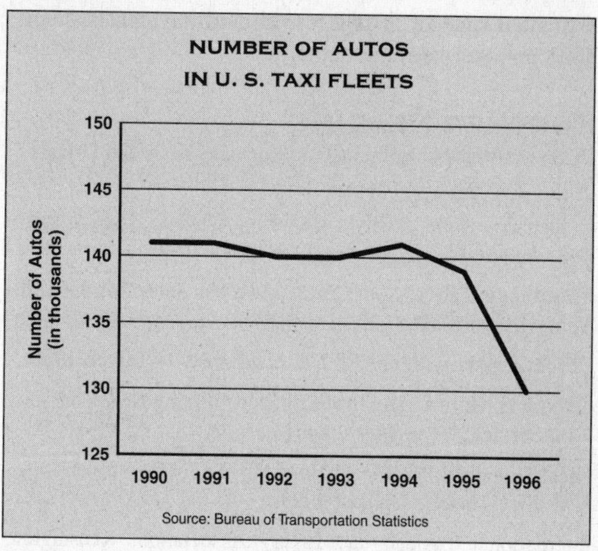

AMERICA AND THE WORLD

A self-drive taxi system, jointly developed by the French government and the car maker Renault, began testing in Paris in 1996. Under this system, drivers who registered for ''smart cards'' could access and drive 50 electric cars scattered around the city, then abandon the car when they reached their destination. French officials hoped this hybrid public-private form of transportation would ease traffic congestion by encouraging drivers to leave their own cars at home. New York City's 12,000-car taxicab fleet was poised for a makeover following the decision by General Motors to discontinue production of the Chevrolet Caprice, which, along with Ford Motor Company's Crown Victoria, made up the majority of the city's cabs. The mix of cars in the next generation fleet promised to strike a decidedly contemporary note with the addition of Ford Explorers and Honda Odyssey mini vans, approved for use by the Taxi and Limousine Commission (TLC) after withstanding six months of testing. The TLC also approved a number of sedans for experimental use, including the Lincoln Town Car and the Mercury Grand Marquis. In keeping with tradition, the new cabs were to be yellow.

RESEARCH AND TECHNOLOGY

In addition to the efforts to incorporate more alternative-fuel vehicles into taxi fleets, several other innovations were changing the way businesses operated in the 1990s. Early experiments with satellite dispatching systems—in which a satellite identified a cab's position to within 10 feet computerized and dispatch instructions appeared on a terminal on the cab's dashboard—reportedly doubled ridership for some taxi companies. Satellite dispatching systems allowed more efficient assignment of cabs to passengers and offered customer service features such as a customer ''call out'' system, in which a computer called the customer and gives an estimated time of arrival, credit card payment systems, and computerized rate quotation.

FURTHER READING

"Council Votes Unanimously to Regulate Taxis and Drivers." *Seattle Post-Intelligencer,* 22 October 1996.

Culbertson, Katie. "City's Cab King Sold to Texas Firm." *Indianapolis Business Journal,* 16 March 1998, 1.

"Ford Calls Cabs to Spur CNG Crown Vic Sales." *Automotive News,* 13 April 1998, 22.

"From Russia with Guv." *The Economist,* 11 March 1996.

Gilbert, G. Gorman and Bruce Shaller. "Fixing New York City Taxi Service." *Transportation Quarterly,* Spring 1996.

Hicks, Jonathan P. "Illegal Vans Move Closer to Licensing." *New York Times,* 8 August 1995.

International Taxicab and Livery Association, Kensington, Maryland.

Jabez, Alan. "Taxis You Can Drive and Dump." *The Times,* 12 January 1997.

Jacobs, Andrew. "The Airy Fare: 3 Wheels, 4 Bits, a Pedal a Minute." *New York Times,* 19 November 1995.

Milbank, Dana. "The London Taxi May Go the Way of the London Bridge." *Wall Street Journal,* 7 April 1995.

"New Taxis." *Crain's New York Business,* 8 February 1999, 42.

Perez-Pena, Richard. "For 53, the Promise of America Fits on a Taxicab." *New York Times,* 11 May 1996.

Reuland, Fred. "Hail Accessible Taxis!" *Inside MS,* Fall 1998, 42.

"A Spoke in their Wheels." *The Economist,* 29 July 1995.

Snow, John. "Taxi Company Goes High-Tech." *Financial News and Daily Record,* 1 January 1997.

"Space-Age Cabs." *The Economist,* 1 August 1998, 68.

Suzuki, Peter T. "Unregulated Taxicabs." *Transportation Quarterly,* Winter 1995.

Thompson, Norm. "'Bye Caprice, Hello Minivan: N.Y. Cabs Get New Makeover." *Christian Science Monitor,* 11 December 1996.

U.S. Department of Labor. Bureau of Labor Statistics. *Occupational Outlook Handbook 1998-99.* Washington, D.C.: 1999. Available from http://stats.bls.gov/cfoi/cftb0115 and http://stats.bls.gov/oco/ocos138.htm.U.S. Department of Health and Human Services.

U.S. National Institute of Occupational Safety and Health. *Violence in the Workplace: Risk Factors and Prevention Strategies.* Washington, D.C.: 1998.

Ward's Business Directory of U.S. Private and Public Companies. Detroit: Gale Research, 1997.

Wildgoose, P. "London Taxicabs Fight the Minicab Menace." *Wall Street Journal,* 17 May 1995.

Wilgoren, Jodi. "The Last New York *Checker* Turns Off Its Meter For Good." *New York Times,* 27 July 1999, A1.

Windeler, Robert. *Back Stage,* 12 November 1999, 55.

Zeiger, Dinah. "Satellites to Track Taxi Cabs." *Denver Post,* 23 May 1996.

SIC 4131

INTERCITY AND RURAL BUS TRANSPORTATION

This category includes establishments primarily engaged in furnishing bus transportation, over regular routes and on regular schedules. The transportation is principally outside a single municipality, outside one group of contiguous municipalities, and outside a single municipality and its suburban areas. Charter bus transportation services are classified in **SIC 4141: Local Bus Charter Service** and **SIC 4142: Bus Charter Service, Except Local.**

NAICS CODE(S)

485210 (Interurban and Rural Bus Lines)

INDUSTRY SNAPSHOT

Intercity and rural bus transportation appears to be a declining industry. In 1990, there were roughly 43 million intercity regular route bus passengers in the United States, half as many as in 1983. According to the Department of Transportation, only 28 companies were providing regular route intercity bus service, and only one carrier, Greyhound, maintained a national network in 1999. The decrease in passenger miles was largely due to competition from private automobiles, Amtrak, and the airlines, which offered greater speed and convenience at a comparable price. The number of locations served by intercity bus lines also declined in the 1990s, totaling about 4,275 in 1996, fewer than half the number served in the early 1980s.

In a 1998 American Travel survey conducted for the Bureau of Transportation Statistics, two-thirds of intercity bus trips are less than 300 miles one-way. Nearly the same percentage applies to the number of passengers traveling alone, and having annual household incomes of less than $25,000. Thirty-six percent have full-time jobs; another 21 percent are retired. Surprisingly, bus passengers are more likely to be young adults than middle- or senior-aged people. Single women make up 41 percent of intercity travelers.

ORGANIZATION AND STRUCTURE

For years, Greyhound has dominated the intercity and rural bus transportation industry. The carrier's position was secured in 1987 when Greyhound acquired

Trailways, the nation's second largest bus line. That purchase left Greyhound the only bus line in the United States with routes covering the entire country. In the 1990s, 27 Class I bus companies (companies that earned more than $10 million annually) competed with Greyhound to provide regular route intercity bus service regionally. Greyhound accommodated about 58 percent of the industry's passengers in 1995, as compared to the next three largest carriers, which together carried only about 28 percent of intercity bus passengers.

Trade Associations. A number of trade associations served a variety of functions in the bus industry. The American Bus Association, in Washington, D.C., was founded in 1926. Of its 500 bus operator members, 75 provided intercity service on regularly scheduled routes. Another Washington, D.C. group, the National Bus Traffic Association, founded in 1933, served as a publisher of bus tariffs. The National Trailways Bus System was what remained of the Trailways system after the Greyhound merger. The system was an association of 32 independent, intercity bus companies, which coordinated schedules and promoted a unified approach to marketing and operating procedures.

BACKGROUND AND DEVELOPMENT

Intercity bus services sprang up independently in different regions across the United States in the early part of the twentieth century. Some of the earliest intercity bus lines began as extensions of urban jitney operations. Minnesota is often named as the birthplace of intercity bus transportation. The Mesaba Transportation Company, of Hibbing, Minnesota, transported miners between mining villages over regularly scheduled routes as early as 1913. Around the same time, the Pickwick Transportation Lines initiated intercity bus service in Southern California. By 1918, this company had expanded its service area to include Northern California and Oregon.

As road conditions improved, bus companies began to appear by the hundreds across the country. Over 4,000 intercity bus companies were in operation by 1926. Soon, the number of companies began to decrease as the industry consolidated. Mergers, acquisitions, and bankruptcies became commonplace, a trend that continued until the 1970s.

In December 1926, the Motor Transit Corporation, a $10 million holding company, was organized by Eric Wickman, the founder of the early Hibbing bus operation. A few years later, the Motor Transit Corporation was restructured as the Greyhound Corporation. Greyhound acquired smaller bus companies and had routes covering most of the United States by the mid-1930s. In 1936, the National Trailways System was formed by an association of railroad-owned bus lines, including Missouri Pacific Trailways, Burlington Trailways, and Santa Fe Trailways. As the system grew through acquisitions, it evolved into the Continental Trailways System, a nationwide bus service. In 1943, the Continental Coach Company was launched. Continental, after changing its name to Transcontinental Bus System, was a nationwide line by 1953.

World War II brought about a dramatic increase in intercity bus ridership. Between 1940 and 1945, traffic grew from 10 billion to 27 billion passenger miles. After the war, the share of the intercity travel done by bus began to decline, although the number of bus travelers remained fairly steady. By 1960, only about 2.5 percent of intercity trips were made by bus, compared to a wartime peak of 10 percent.

As competition from air travel and improvements in automobiles increased, the industry's share of passengers eroded further. In the 1970s, the bus lines came under pressure from low fares offered by Amtrak. The deregulation of airlines also brought about the emergence of low-cost air operations. These events cut into the profitability of the bus lines significantly. Between 1975 and 1982, intercity bus service (measured by number of weekly bus departures) declined by nearly 5 percent a year. Greyhound lost about 30 million passengers, roughly half of its ridership, between the mid-1960s and the mid-1980s.

Greyhound spent the late 1980s and early 1990s in the throes of a drivers' strike and its consequences. The strike resulted in a number of violent confrontations and quite a bit of negative publicity for the company. Four months after the strike began, Greyhound declared bankruptcy. The company emerged from bankruptcy in 1992 under new ownership and management.

Role of Government. Federal agencies had no jurisdiction over bus companies that operated within one state. Bus lines whose routes crossed state borders fell under the regulatory jurisdiction of the Surface Transportation Board (STB), formerly the Interstate Commerce Commission (ICC). Regulation was cut sharply, however, by the Bus Regulatory Reform Act of 1982. Following the 1982 Bus Act, entry into the industry was open, and applications for authority to operate rarely were challenged. Minimum insurance coverage and knowledge of safety regulations were the only requirements to prove a carrier's fitness to operate. Passenger carriers were required to file rate information with the STB, but these filings seldom were rejected since 1982. Only Class I companies were required to report financial statistics to the STB. Federal regulations pertaining to intercity bus drivers were somewhat stricter. Drivers had to be at least 21 years old and were required to pass a physical examination. Drivers operating vehicles designed to carry 16 or more passengers were also required to obtain a commer-

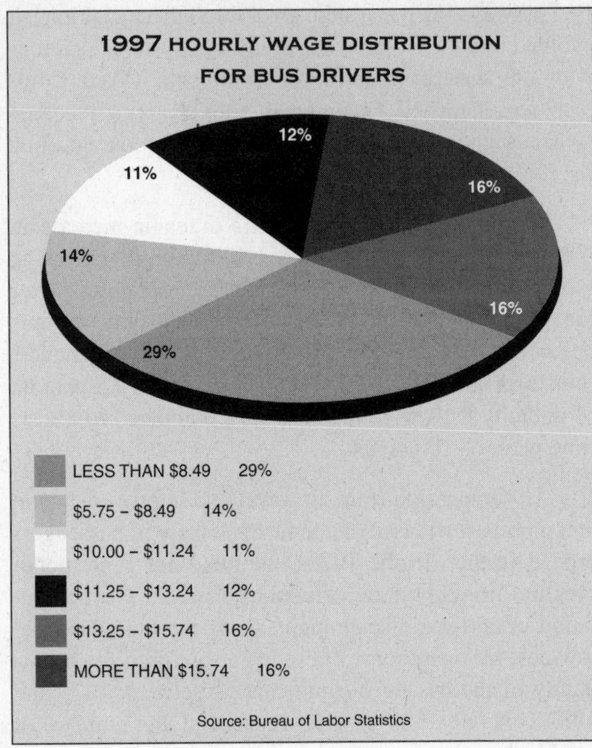

cial driver's license from the state in which they lived. Additionally, most intercity bus companies required drivers to complete two to eight hours of classroom and behind-the-wheel training that included instruction in federal and state driving regulations and safe-driving practices.

Government Regulation. Regulation of intercity bus transportation arose during the industry's infancy. Pennsylvania became the first state to regulate the operation of passenger buses in 1914. By 1925, a majority of states had followed suit. That year, the industry's first national organization, the National Motor Bus Association, was formed. The U.S. Supreme Court determined, however, that state regulatory agencies had no jurisdiction over interstate bus lines. It was not until 10 years later, with the passage of the Motor Carrier Act of 1935, that the ICC was authorized to regulate fares, safety, routes, entry, exit, mergers, transfers of operating rights, and other service and financial matters of the interstate bus lines.

In the 1970s, Greyhound began to push for deregulation of the intercity bus industry in hopes of competing more effectively with the heavily subsidized Amtrak rail service. The ICC made entry regulations more liberal in 1977 and 1978. In 1980, the Motor Carrier Act was amended by Congress. The new version of the Act made the process of applying for operating authority easier and required quicker decisions on the applications.

The Bus Regulatory Reform Act of 1982 brought about major changes in the industry. Entry was liberalized to the point where any prospective carrier that was "fit, willing, and able" was granted authority, barring evidence that this authority was contrary to the public interest. The Act also empowered the ICC for the first time to overrule state regulatory authorities on matters of intrastate rates if their rulings were harmful to interstate commerce. A 1992 report by the General Accounting Office (GAO) suggested that the deregulation that took place in 1982 did not address the causes of the industry's decline, and a major result of the deregulation was the elimination of service to areas where there are fewer transportation alternatives, particularly rural areas and small towns.

Since deregulation in 1982, hundreds of routes in rural areas have been discontinued. Many of the areas that are no longer served are not accessible by air or rail systems, leaving residents without automobiles completely isolated. A 1992 study by the GAO recommended that the best way to address this problem was through more widespread use of a set-aside provision in the Intermodal Surface Transportation Efficiency Act of 1991. Section 18(i) of the Act requires each state to set aside money to support intercity bus transportation. By 1992, 20 states had instituted such programs, which included subsidies to firms for continuing service on endangered routes, price breaks on vehicles, and financing for building and repairing terminals.

INDUSTRY LEADERS

In March 1999, Greyhound merged with Laidlaw, Inc., boasting 22.6 million passenger boardings for 1998. Passenger revenues for Greyhound Lines were $727.8 million for 1998. The company had a fleet of 2,677 buses that year, and had 13,400 employees nationwide.

Although Greyhound was the only bus line with a nationwide scope in 1999, several other companies had achieved solid positions in specific regions. With projected 1999 revenues of $73 million from its intercity, charter and other bus services, the 800-employee Peter Pan Bus Lines, Inc., of Springfield, Massachusetts, more than doubled its earnings from the early 1990s to become the second largest player in the intercity bus travel market. The company's growth came out of aggressive marketing efforts to increase ridership, including the addition of express services between major cities and advertisement on rock music radio stations to attract college students. In 1998, Peter Pan Bus Lines was voted the safest bus company in America by the National Safety Council.

Other prominent companies—all of which operated in the New York metropolitan area—included Connecticut Limousine, with $20 million in revenue from its intercity bus service in 1995; Hudson Transit Lines Inc., with $19 million; and New Jersey Transit Bus Operation, Inc., also with $19 million.

WORKFORCE

The 1997 National Occupational Employment and Wage Estimates report published by the Bureau of Labor Statistics listed 187,630 "transit and intercity" bus drivers for 1996. Although the mean hourly wage was $13.21 an hour in 1998, 32 percent were earning between $32,000 and $40,000 annually. Full-time drivers could earn more than $48,000 a year. Local transit companies in metropolitan areas with more than 2 million people were paying an average hourly rate of $15.43 and $17.06 in 1997. School bus drivers earned an average $11.50 per hour. Employment opportunities through the year 2006 was expected to remain good, increasing at about the same rate as all occupations.

RESEARCH AND TECHNOLOGY

Advances in technology historically played a part in the rise and fall of the intercity bus industry. It was improvements in road conditions and the development of the interstate highway system that made a nationwide network of bus routes possible. Later, the increased availability of private automobiles and affordable air travel contributed to the bus lines' loss in ridership share.

Since fuel was a major cost in running a bus company, companies were always on the lookout for equipment that would improve fuel efficiency. Diesel engines were in regular use in buses since the 1950s, and steady advances were made in their engineering, leading to developments such as the turbocharged diesel engines introduced around 1980. In 1992, a new bus called the Neoplan Cityliner was unveiled in Colorado. Used mostly for organized tours in the early 1990s, the Cityliner featured a smoke-free diesel engine that polluted significantly less than traditional models. Bus manufacturers were also experimenting with fueling buses by way of pollution-free battery cells.

In the mid-1990s, technological innovations in intercity buses focused largely on reducing trouble-shooting and repair time. The newest motor coaches featured sophisticated systems monitoring and recording devices that allowed drivers and maintenance personnel to diagnose malfunctions in a fraction of the time previously required. Buses were likely also to sport electronic brake and steer-by-wire systems, similar to the fly-by-wire systems used in airplanes, which would offer drivers better feedback and control of the vehicle as well as increased ease of maintenance.

FURTHER READING

Bernier, Brad and Tom Seekins. "Rural Transportation Voucher Program for People with Disabilities: Three Case Studies." *Journal of Transportation and Statistics,* May 1999, 61.

"Company Notebook." *Business West,* December 1998, 60.

"Fact Sheet." Greyhound Lines Company Information, 1999. Available from http://www.greyhound.com/company/factsheet.shtml.

"Greyhound Drives Deeper Into Mexico, Seeks Hispanic Riders." *Wall Street Journal,* 10 January 1997.

Mogelonsky, Marcia. "Busing It." *American Demographics,* May 1998, 42.

"Motorcoach Industry Facts," December 1996. Washington, DC: American Bus Association.

O'Brien. "The *Peter* Principal." *Business West,* November 1999, 22.

Schneggenburger, Martin. "Gentlemen, Start Your Computers." *Metro Magazine,* March/April 1996.

"Greyhound, Amtrak to Join Some Terminals." *Wall Street Journal,* 27 October 1995.

"Greyhound Sees Growth During Next Few Years." *Wall Street Journal,* 24 May 1996.

U.S. Department of Labor. Bureau of Labor Statistics. *Occupational Outlook Handbook 1998-99.* Washington, DC: 1999. Available from http://stats.bls.gov/news.release.ocwage.t01.htm.

U.S. Department of Labor. Bureau of Labor Statistics. *Employment, Hours and Earnings, United States, 1988-98.* Washington, DC: 1998.

U.S. Department of Transportation. Bureau of Transportation Statistics. "BTS Issues Report Showing Fourth Quarter 1995 Operating Results of Ten of the Nation's Largest Bus Companies." 7 November 1996.

SIC 4141

LOCAL BUS CHARTER SERVICE

This category includes establishments primarily engaged in furnishing local bus charter service where such operations are located principally within a single municipality, contiguous municipalities, or a municipality and its suburban areas.

NAICS CODE(S)

485510 (Charter Bus Industry)

The local bus charter service industry—whose primary business is in local sightseeing tours and airport shuttle service—grew rapidly after 1982. The number of employees increased from 3,781 in 1982 to 8,782 in 1997, and the number of establishments in the industry grew from 163 to 503 during those years. More than 40 percent of these establishments employed fewer than five people; fewer than nine establishments employed more than 100 people. The average salary for all employees in 1997 was $16,094.

All of the top eight firms in the local bus charter service industry in 1997 were private independents, many of which were located in the southern and western parts of the United States. In order of descending operating revenue, these companies were the industry leaders: Gray Line Tours of Southern Nevada, with $8 million in revenue and 330 employees; Eyre Bus Service Inc. of Glenelg, Maryland, with $7 million in revenue and 100 employees; Peerless Stages Inc. of Oakland, California, with $4 million in revenue and 100 employees; Capital Motor Lines Inc. of Montgomery, Alabama, with $3 million in revenue and 200 employees; Gulf Coast Motor Line Inc. of Largo, Florida, with $2 million in revenue and 100 employees; Huntleigh Transportation Services Inc. of Hazelwood, Missouri, with $2 million in revenue; Browder Tours Inc. of Memphis, Tennessee, with $1 million in revenue; and Gwen Tours Inc. of New Orleans, Louisiana, with under $1 million in revenue.

Affiliates of the Dallas-based Gray Line Worldwide, a sightseeing and tour operator association with a global membership of 150 companies, provided charter services and airport transfers across the country to accommodate local niches. Gray Line of San Francisco offered sightseeing expeditions around the city as well as tours to nearby attractions such as the Napa Valley wine country. They also offered their tours in a number of foreign languages to accommodate the international tourist. Gray Line of Alaska maintained a fleet of more than 150 motorcoaches and offered over a dozen different land tours of the state, some lasting as long as ten days. In addition to its 21 daily sightseeing tours, Gray Line of Las Vegas did a high volume of business in airport shuttle service. With 65 coaches and 68 minibuses, its Airport Express service carried 2.4 million passengers to and from more than 70 hotels in the Las Vegas area in the mid-1990s. In 1996, Gray Line Worldwide announced plans to expand its membership and increase its electronic booking capacity.

FURTHER READING

Del Rousso, Laura. ''Gray Line Begins Offering Tours of Wine Country Year—Round.'' *Travel Weekly,* 18 July 1994.

''Gray Line Traffic Surging Into 1995.'' *Travel Weekly,* 21 November 1994.

Long, Felicity. ''Gray Line to 'Review and Refine' Standards of Member Firms.'' *Travel Weekly,* 23 September 1996.

1997 Gray Line Travel Guide. Dallas, TX: Gray Line Worldwide, 1997.

U.S. Bureau of the Census. *County Business Patterns 1997, United States.* Washington, DC: U.S. GPO, 1997.

Ward's Business Directory of U.S. Private and Public Companies, Detroit: Gale Research, 1997.

SIC 4142

BUS CHARTER SERVICE, EXCEPT LOCAL

This category covers establishments engaged primarily in furnishing bus charter service, except local, where such operations are principally outside a single municipality, outside one group of contiguous municipalities, and outside a single municipality and its suburban areas.

NAICS CODE(S)

485510 (Charter Bus Industry)

INDUSTRY SNAPSHOT

In the 1990s, there were less than 1,000 nonlocal charter bus companies in the United States, employing less than 20,000 people. The 50 largest charter bus companies maintained an average fleet size of 255 coaches, with each coach traveling an average of 65,000 miles a year. In the early 1990s, the industry had revenues of about $894,000 annually.

The cost of a 40-foot motor coach started at $270,000 for a basic model, and ranged upwards of $300,000 for coaches outfitted with video equipment and luxury interiors. To maintain a 40-foot charter bus, charter companies spent an average of $12,000 per year in the early 1990s; the average operating cost for a 40-foot coach in 1996 was $1.46 per mile, including driver's wages, fuel, and normal equipment usage. Most charter bus companies charged customers—largely private groups paying for one-time trips—either by the mile or by the hour. The average per-mile rate in 1996 was $2.09. The average hourly charge was $46.

Although many private motor coach companies used their buses for multiple modes of transport, the majority of time (66.6 percent) was spent on charter services, with coaches doubling as tour buses 22.5 percent of the time. Although the linehaul and passenger bus businesses were separate industries, a minority of private passenger bus companies also reported performing regular route intercity service and hauling services.

CURRENT CONDITIONS

According to American Bus Association (ABA) surveys, the top three events/activities used by groups for bus charters in 1998-1999 were theater shows, gaming/casinos, and sightseeing. On the down side, growth in the number of casino charter traffic nationally has increased the number of accidents and fatalities involving interstate bus travel.

Future growth in the charter bus industry was favorable in the latter 1990s, based on the growing p opulation of affluent and active senior citizens. To accommodate a more comfort-conscious ridership, charter buses were increasingly incorporating ergonomic seat designs, user-friendly lavatories, and kitchen galleys for refreshments.

INDUSTRY LEADERS

In the late 1990s, the largest provider of charter bus service in the United States was Coach USA, of Houston, Texas, with revenues of over $625 million in 1997 from all its operations. Formed as a company in 1995 with the intention of consolidating independent charter bus operators under a single corporation, Coach became an industry sensation after buying a dozen companies that operated more than 1,700 coaches in nine states. By 1998, Coach had spent $500 million in acquisitions. Under a decentralized management strategy, the acquired companies maintained their individual operating practices and identity while turning finance and marketing functions over to Coach. Coach's chief executive, Richard Kristinik, said that lower financing costs, insurance premiums, and equipment costs were among the benefits of consolidation. Of Coach's 52 subsidiaries in 1998, 43 were motor coach operations.

Another prominent charter company is Greyhound Lines, which primarily offers scheduled bus services but also engages in charter bus services, shipping services, and food services. Greyhound merged with Laidlaw, Inc. in 1999. Total revenues for the Greyhound Lines in 1998 was $728 million. Also prominent in the industry are Westours Inc., of Seattle, Washington, with $28.5 million in revenue and 299 coaches; Blue Bird Coach Lines Inc., of Olean, New York, with $14 million in revenue and 138 coaches; and Kerrville Bus Company Inc., of Kerrville, Texas, with $8 million in revenue and 98 coaches.

WORKFORCE

The charter bus industry work force consisted primarily of owners or managers (in smaller companies, often the same person), dispatchers, maintenance workers, and drivers. The largest number of employees in the industry were drivers. Of drivers employed by charter companies which were surveyed in the mid-1990s, 8 percent were members of a union, while the rest were independent contractors earning an average of $8.14 an hour. Drivers transporting more than 16 passengers were required to have a commercial driver's license issued by their home state, and drivers conducting interstate travel were required to be at least 21 years of age. Many employers offered training for the requisite written and behind-the-wheel testing.

In most cases, charter bus drivers were assigned to a trip with the group chartering a bus, and remained with that group for the duration of the trip; in the case of intercity charters or tours, drivers remained with the group for several days. Drivers often were assigned on a per-trip basis and available work hours varied greatly, with more work available in the summer months and around the winter holidays. Senior drivers were guaranteed more work than new hires, who might be ''furloughed'' when no work was available.

FURTHER READING

Bayles, Fred and Jayne O'Donnell. *USA Today,* 26 May 1999, 15.

Card, Andrew H., Jr., Secretary of Transportation. *National Transportation Statistics Annual Report.* Washington, DC: U.S. Department of Transportation, 1997.

Culbertson, Katie. ''City Cabs King Sold to Texas Firm.'' *Indianapolis Business Journal,* 16 March 1998, 1.

''Fact Sheet.'' Greyhound Bus Lines. Available from http://www.greyhound.com, 1999.

Furgo, Frank. ''The Phenomenal Rise of Coach USA.'' *Bus Ride,* February 1997.

Magenheim, Henry. ''Holiday Displays Helping Expand the Appeal of Coaches: ABA.'' *Travel Weekly,* September 30, 1999, M1.

''METRO's 1997 Top 50 Motorcoach Fleet Survey.'' *Metro Magazine,* January/February 1997.

''Motorcoach Industry Facts.'' American Bus Association, Washington: December 1996.

''1996 Industry Survey.'' *Destinations,* August 1996.

U.S. Bureau of the Census, *County Business Patterns 1994, United States* Washington, D.C.: U.S. Government Printing Office, 1996.

U.S. Department of Labor. Bureau of Labor Statistics. *Occupational Outlook Handbook 1996-97.* Washington, D.C.: 1996. Available from http://stats.bls.gov/oco/ocos242.htm.

U.S. Department of Transportation. Bureau of Transportation Statistics. ''BTS Issues Report Showing Second Quarter 1998 Operating Results of 18 of the Nation's Largest Motor Carriers of Passengers Companies.'' 1998.

Ward's Business Directory of U.S. Private and Public Companies. Detroit: Gale Research, 1997.

SIC 4151

SCHOOL BUSES

This category covers establishments engaged primarily in operating buses to transport pupils to and from school. School bus establishments operated by educational institutions are considered auxiliaries. This category does not include companies offering only bus manufacturing or maintenance.

NAICS CODE(S)

485410 (School and Employee Bus Industry)

In 1999, the school busing industry consisted of 418,000 school buses covering 4.5 million miles at a cost of nearly $10 billion. Nearly half of the nation's children—24 million—rode buses to and from school. In 1997, 60 percent of all school buses were owned and operated by individual school districts, many maintaining as few as one or two buses; the remaining 40 percent of vehicles belonged to private companies that contracted their services with school districts. According to County Business Patterns, there were 4,332 school bus service establishments in 1997 employing 147,704 people. About a third of these establishments were small organizations with four or fewer employees. The annual total payroll of these companies was $1.8 billion.

Largely unregulated until the latter part of the twentieth century, the school bus industry began with the manufacture of vehicles owned by individual schools and districts and developed concurrently with the automobile industry. In the late 1960s, bus companies were exposed, peripherally, to the struggle for racial integration of American schools and, more directly in the early 1970s, to the automobile safety movement led by activist Ralph Nader. In the 1990s, bus companies continued to be subject to national and state safety legislation; during this time, a debate over the need for school bus seat belts was tabled, as advocates on either side of the issue failed to turn up conclusive information. In August 1998, the National Highway Traffic Safety Administration announced an extensive two-year research program to consider alternative methods for potentially improving federal school bus passenger crash protection requirements. Nevertheless, fatalities in school bus-related accidents continued to decline, with a 19 percent reduction in deaths from 1980 to 1990. In the 1990s, there was an average of 32 school-age children fatalities each year.

Safety issues largely impelled innovations in the school bus industry in the mid-1990s. Since many fatalities occurred when buses hit riders passing through the bus driver's blind spot, some buses were being equipped with automatic ''crossing gates'' that swung out when the bus stopped, forcing children to walk 10 feet in front of the bus when crossing the street. Other school districts were equipping school buses with on—board video cameras as a deterrent to unruly or dangerous behavior among riders. In a more controversial development, some school districts were choosing to raise money by allowing advertisements to be painted on the sides of their school buses. New York City hoped to bring in $53 million over nine years from contracts signed with commercial advertisers in 1996.

Because most school bus providers were school districts, management was often handled from within the district. Although there were jobs in management and maintenance, by far the largest number of employees working in school busing were drivers. In fact, in 1998, nearly 75 percent of bus drivers in the United States operated school buses. In general, drivers worked an average of 20 hours or less per week during the school year. Wages for drivers employed by public school systems ranged from $9.93 to $13.06 an hour during the 1996-97 school year. School bus drivers were required to get a commercial driver's license from their state of residence and in some cases were subject to a background investigation for criminal misconduct or a history of mental illness. Drivers generally received one to four weeks of driving instruction in addition to classroom training on state and local laws, safe driving practices, and first aid and emergency evacuation procedures. Aside from driving, they were responsible for checking their vehicles for safety and reliable operation as well as issuing reports on fuel consumption, number of students and trips, and hours worked.

In 1999, the largest provider of school bus service in the United States, by far, was Laidlaw, Inc. of Canada. A diversified company in Burlington, Ontario, Laidlaw operated 39,000 school buses in 44 states and Canada, carrying a total of 2 million children each day. After acquiring a number of the leading private school bus operators in the 1990s—including Mayflower Contract Services Inc. of Shawnee Mission, Kansas; National School Bus Service of Barrington, Illinois; and Vancom Inc. of Oakland Terrace, Illinois—Laidlaw claimed a 34 percent share of the U.S. market in 1999. Laidlaw's closest competitors included Ryder Student Transportation of St. Louis, Missouri, with 10,000 buses; Atlantic Express of Staten Island, New York, with 5,230 buses; and Durham Transportation Inc. of Austin, Texas, with 3,500 buses.

FURTHER READING

Card, Andrew H., Jr. *National Transportation Statistics Annual Report.* Washington, D.C.: U.S. Department of Transportation, 1998.

Stead, Deborah. ''Corporations, Classrooms and Commercialism.'' *New York Times,* 5 January 1997.

Stone Lombardi, Kate. ''Peril Rides the School Bus.'' *New York Times,* 10 March 1996.

U.S. Department of Labor, Bureau of Labor Statistics. *Occupational Outlook Handbook 1998-99.* Washington, D.C.: U.S. GPO, 1996. Available from http://stats.bls.gov/oco/ocos242.htm.

Ward's Business Directory of U.S. Private and Public Companies. Detroit: Gale Research, 1997.

The ABCs of School Busing, National School Transportation Association, 2000. Available from http://www.schooltrans.com/abcs.htm.

1997 County Business Patterns. Tech Talk, U.S. Census Bureau, 2000. Available from http://tier2.census.gov/techtalk.htm#SOFTWARE/.

Top 50 Contractor Fleets "Top 50 Contractors—1999." Schoolbusfleet.com, 2000. Available from http://www.schoolbusfleet.com/Resource/.

SIC 4173

TERMINAL AND SERVICE FACILITIES FOR MOTOR VEHICLE PASSENGER TRANSPORTATION

This industry includes establishments primarily engaged in the operation of motor vehicle passenger terminals and of maintenance and service facilities, not operated by companies that also furnish motor vehicle passenger transportation. Establishments that are owned by motor vehicle passenger transportation companies and are primarily engaged in operating terminals for use of such vehicles are classified in the same industry as establishments providing motor vehicle transportation. Separate maintenance and service facilities operated by companies furnishing motor vehicle passenger transportation are treated as auxiliaries. Establishments that provide motor vehicle maintenance or service for the general public are classified in various automotive repair industries, such as **SIC 7533: Automotive Exhaust System Repair Shops** and **SIC 7538: General Automotive Repair Shops.**

NAICS Code(s)

488490 (Other Support Activities for Road Transportation)

In 1997, there were 30 establishments in the industry employing a total of 215 people. Combined, their annual payroll totaled $5 million.

The majority of motor vehicle passenger terminals and maintenance facilities in the United States, whether their mode of transportation was bus, train, or some other method, were owned and operated by companies that were also directly involved in the transport of passengers. As a result, the terminal and service facility operations of those companies—from Greyhound to Amtrak—were treated as part of their overall transportation services and were classified with those services, rather than in this industrial classification. In 1999 Greyhound operated 150 terminals and employed a total of 4,500 employees in its terminals alone. In larger urban areas, a government-run, regional transportation authority usually maintained terminals.

The independent facilities in this industry suffered as a result of waning intercity bus ridership during the final decades of the century. In the 1920s, more than 4,000 intercity bus companies operated in the United States, and, by the mid-1940s, the bus transport industry registered 27 billion passenger miles annually. The popularity of this mode of transportation in turn spurred the success of terminal and service facilities of the time. Due to the increasing availability of personal-use vehicles, however, more and more Americans traveled between cities in their own vehicles. By 1998, nearly 80 percent of long distance trips were made by personal vehicle. According to the U.S. Department of Transportation's *Transportation Statistics 1998 Annual Report* the total intercity bus ridership accounted for only 2.1 percent of total highway miles traveled.

The trend among publicly run regional transportation facilities moved toward intermodal transportation terminals that accommodated inter-city bus lines, passenger railroads, transit rail and buses, commuter rail, and subways all under one roof. In the mid-1990s, Boston, Newark, New Jersey, San Francisco, and Atlanta were all in various stages of designing intermodal facilities that made passenger travel more convenient. Acting as landlords, the transportation authorities leased space to their terminal tenants. In Boston's newly intermodal South Station, for example, prime bus bays were leasing for about $35,000 a year in 1995. Another trend in ground transportation terminals focused on establishing a more customer-friendly ambiance and providing both passengers and city residents with a greater diversity of services. By the late 1990s, the Port Authority of New York and New Jersey had transformed the Port Authority Bus Terminal in New York City, long associated with grime and criminal activity, into a shopping and entertainment center. Through aggressive marketing, the Port Authority attracted a host of upscale retailers, including drug stores, coffee and pastry vendors, and florists. It also installed a new 30-lane bowling alley, patronized primarily by corporate leagues and local families. In 1999, the George Washington Bridge Bus Station followed suit, upgrading its facilities with the same type of retailers and services.

Further Reading

"Bus Terminals Are Big Business." *Metro Magazine,* September/October 1995.

Deutsch, Claudia H. "A Former Haven of Sleaze Is Now a Refuge of Retail."*New York Times,* 17 March 1996.

1998 Transportation Statistics Annual Report, U.S. Department of Transportation, 2000. Available from http://www.bts.gov/programs/ats/.

Greyhound Lines Company Profile. Greyhound, 2000. Available from http://www.greyhound.com.

1997 County Business Patterns. U.S. Census Bureau. Available from http:tier2.census.gov/cgi-win/cbp/Detail.exe.

SIC 4212

LOCAL TRUCKING WITHOUT STORAGE

This category covers establishments primarily engaged in furnishing trucking or transfer services without storage for freight generally weighing more than 100 pounds, in a single municipality, contiguous municipalities, or a municipality and its suburban areas. Establishments primarily engaged in furnishing local courier services for letters, parcels, and packages generally weighing less than 100 pounds are classified in **SIC 4215: Courier Services Except Air;** those engaged in collecting and disposing of refuse by processing and destruction of materials are classified in **SIC 4953: Refuse Systems.** Those establishments involved in removing overburden from mines or quarries are classified in various mining industries, while establishments such as construction contractors engaged in hauling dirt and rock as part of their construction activity are classified in various construction industries.

NAICS CODE(S)

562111 (Solid Waste Collection)
562112 (Hazardous Waste Collection)
562119 (Other Waste Collection)
484110 (General Freight Trucking, Local)
484210 (Used Household and Office Goods Moving)
484220 (Specialized Freight (except Used Goods) Trucking, Local)

Trucks represent virtually the sole means of transporting freight in intracity and local markets—operating zones of 50 miles or less. Such diverse products as bakery goods, dry cleaning, auto products, fuel for service station pumps, and vending machine supplies are only a few of the enormous variety of goods delivered by local trucking firms.

Although over-the-road intercity truckers are the most visible segment of the industry as a whole, the trucking industry itself grew out of local, short-haul trucking in the early years of the twentieth century, when automobiles began to be converted into trucks to haul the freight traditionally transported by horse-drawn wagons.

The industry is divided into two types of establishments: private carriers who own or lease trucks to transport their products to customers, and for-hire carriers who contract with shippers to transport their goods for them. All companies in this industry are divided roughly in half between corporations and individual proprietorships or partnerships. In 1998, some of the larger firms in this segment of the trucking industry were Schneider National Inc., based in Green Bay, Wisconsin, which had sales of $2.7 billion and 17,000 employees. Lowell, Arizona-based J.B. Hunt Transportation Services Inc. held the number two spot with sales of $1.8 billion and more than 14,000 employees. Other industry leaders included Landstar System, Inc. and American Freightways Corporation.

The industry's largest segment, in terms of number of establishments, is comprised of local delivery firms transporting packages weighing more than 100 pounds. Almost one-third of all of these firms reported annual revenues of less than $1 million. Although major intercity ground transport firms and air cargo companies also operated local large-package delivery establishments, by far the most common local large-package delivery establishments were smaller firms with names like Susie's Speedy Service or Lickety Split Couriers. The package delivery segment also included messenger services, grocery and food product transporters, newspaper distribution truckers, legal and medical delivery services, and the large-package delivery departments of taxicab companies.

Another important segment of the local non-storage trucking industry is comprised of light haulage and cartage truckers including warehouse goods transporters, freight forwarders (see **SIC 4731: Arrangement of Transportation of Freight and Cargo**), and distributors and goods transfer services. The industry also includes significant numbers of dump truck hauling firms, local log and timber transporters, bulk mail contract carriers, and ''star route'' carriers, which transport goods between transportation modes, such as from a port to a railhead.

In the late 1990s, a smaller segment of the local non-storage trucking industry consisted of highly specialized carriers such as hazardous materials transporters, like Enviroguard Technologies and Omega Environmental Control; local animal, livestock, and horse transporters, such as Ft. Worth Cattle Express and Hickory Hill Horse Transport; and local pet transporters, such as Pet'in on the Ritz and Happy Tails to You. The industry also included a variety of local household goods movers who did not offer storage services, ranging from the local divisions of large intercity movers, like Bekins, to smaller firms, like Starving Scholars Movers, Shleppers Movers, and Load, Lock, and Roll Moving.

By the late 1990s, many local non-storage-trucking firms were unionized. Overall, trucking and courier services employed about 1.7 million people in 1996. The average hourly wage for non-supervisory workers was $13.21, up from $12.94 in 1995.

FURTHER READING

U.S. Department of Commerce. *Census of Transportation 1987.* Washington, DC: GPO, 1991.

U.S. Department of Labor. Bureau of Labor Statistics. *Employment, Hours, and Earnings, United States, 1988-96.* Washington, DC: GPO, 1996.

U.S. Department of Labor. Bureau of Labor Statistics. *1998—1999 Occupational Outlook Handbook.* Washington, DC: GPO, 1999.

SIC 4213

TRUCKING EXCEPT LOCAL

This category covers establishments primarily engaged in furnishing ''over-the-road'' trucking services or storage services, including household goods either as common carriers or under special or individual contracts or agreements, for freight generally weighing more than 100 pounds. Such operations are principally outside a single municipality, outside one group of contiguous municipalities, or outside a single municipality and its suburban areas. Establishments primarily engaged in furnishing air courier services for individually addressed letters, parcels, and packages generally weighing less than 100 pounds are classified in **SIC 4513: Air Courier Services** and other courier services for individually addressed letters, parcels, and packages generally weighing less than 100 pounds are classified in **SIC 4215: Courier Services Except Air.**

NAICS CODE(S)

484121 (General Freight Trucking, Long-Distance, Truckload)

484122 (General Freight Trucking, Long-Distance, Less than Truckload)

484210 (Used Household and Office Goods Moving)

484230 (Specialized Freight (except Used Goods) Trucking, Long-Distance)

INDUSTRY SNAPSHOT

Approximately 433,435 interstate motor carriers were on file with the federal Department of Transportation's Office of Motor Carriers in 1997. Of these, approximately 70 percent operate six or fewer trucks and 79 percent operate 28 or fewer trucks.

According to Insurance Market Research (IMR) Corporation, in 1998 there were approximately 122,934 trucking and warehousing companies in the United States, employing about 1.8 million people. The American Trucking Association notes that the 5.5 billion tons of freight transported by intercity and local trucks each year represents about 55 percent of the total domestic tonnage shipped. Some 37 percent of the total tons shipped are general freight; 63 percent are bulk goods.

Increased internal competition for a static trucking services market, growing competition for freight dollars as a result of intermodal and ''double stack'' rail technologies, and increased rail industry efficiency continued to restrict industry profits, weed out leveraged and marginal firms, and increase consolidation among industry leaders and surviving firms. The industry looked to new truck tracking and information technologies, nontraditional markets such as express delivery of light freight, increased entree to intrastate markets, and general improvements in the U.S. economy to enhance industry revenues. The industry's ability to integrate new technologies and exploit global trends in freight transport conditioned its future strength.

ORGANIZATION AND STRUCTURE

The nonlocal trucking industry is divided into several segments that are based on the size of freight shipments (truckload, less-than-truckload), the type of goods hauled (household goods, general freight), the size of the trucker's market (regional, national), and the nature of the availability of the trucker's services to shippers (common, contract, or private carriage). Thus, an industry firm can be categorized as a regional contract carrier who hauls less-than-truckload shipments of general freight or as a national common carrier who hauls truckload shipments of bulk goods, and so on. National carriers have the equipment, facilities, and operating authority to transport freight cross-country while regional carriers primarily serve smaller multistate geographical areas such as the southern states or the West Coast. Long-haul transport is defined as shipments of 200 to 1,000 miles or more, and short-haul transport refers to shipments of 50 to 700 miles, depending on the carrier and other variables. ''Off-the-road'' transport refers to primarily agricultural- and construction-related trucking involving minimal use of public roads.

Less-than-Truckload. Less-than-truckload (LTL) carriers haul shipments of 10,000 pounds or less in combined lots from more than one shipper. Although modern trucks can carry loads of 40,000 pounds or more, a ''truck load'' has traditionally been defined as 10,000 pounds. LTL carriers, then, are distinguished from truckload (TL) carriers not by the weight of individual trucks but by the number of individual shipments that comprise the truck's load. Unlike TL shipments, which typically involve the direct hauling of one shipper's freight from origin to destination, LTL shipments usually involve five phases: pick-up, sorting at a distribution terminal or transfer hub, line haul (the main, and longest, leg of the shipment), sorting at a destination facility, and final delivery. The

LTL market is divided evenly between general freight carriers and carriers of small packages (shipments weighing less than 500 pounds). The deregulation of the trucking industry in 1980 resulted in a flood of new TL firms, but the prohibitive costs of entry limited the number of new carriers in the LTL segment. A national LTL carrier must be able to finance a large sales force, expensive technology, and approximately 500 distribution terminals.

Shorter routes and increased use of information technology had the greatest impact on the for-hire trucking segment of the industry. Shippers continued to streamline product manufacturing cycles and required just-in-time delivery schedules. This, in turn, placed greater demand for shorter, more reliable truck supply routes. For-hire trucking firms were also faced with growing competition from doublestack rail. It forced many of them to surrender a number of long-haul routes to the railroads. Acknowledging the trend, a growing number of trucker-railroad alliances were formed. Under these partnerships, truckers handled pick-up and delivery.

Truckload. TL carriers haul shipments of 10,000 pounds or more from origin to destination. In 1992, roughly one-quarter of the nonlocal trucking industry's general freight tonnage was hauled by about 40,000 direct origin-to-destination TL carriers. With an onslaught of mergers, in 1995 there were some 20,000 truckload providers in the country. The TL segment hauls about 80 percent of all intercity freight and includes for-hire and private carriers. Because TL firms do not need to maintain intermediate freight consolidation facilities, the TL segment has historically been characterized by comparatively low start-up costs. When deregulation removed restrictions on new businesses entering the trucking industry, the TL segment experienced fierce competition among a large number of new, poorly capitalized firms. About two-thirds of the trucking industry consisted of such new often high-debt, low-income firms. The largest TL carriers had low profit margins, market shares of only 1 percent to 3 percent, and revenues that ranged between $30 million and $40 million (compared with the several billion dollar revenues of the largest LTL carriers).

Common Carriers. Common carriers are ''for-hire'' public truckers whose operating authority is conditioned on the availability of their services to any shipper who buys them. Historically, common carriers have been categorized according to the cargo they carry and the routes they cover: ''regular'' (or specific, limited routes) and ''irregular'' (unrestricted routes).

Contract Carriers. Contract carriers provide trucks, equipment, and services (such as fleet maintenance or customer billing) on an exclusive, guaranteed basis for shipping customers who prefer the convenience of leasing trucks to owning them. As dedicated contract carriers, truck leasing firms (such as Ryder Systems) may lease drivers in addition to trucks. Such firms may also provide fuel, safety training, insurance, maintenance and other services to their customers. Contract carriers are often common carriers with an additional operating authority that allows them to contract out their services and have historically transported TL shipments. The growth of just-in-time inventory management techniques, however, has created a niche for contract carriers to haul lighter LTL ''time-sensitive'' parts or materials from warehouse to plant for primarily large industrial firms.

For-hire. There were approximately 48,000 for-hire carriers in the 1990s. These carriers offer their services either impartially to all shippers (common carrier authority) or exclusively for specific shippers (contract carrier authority). In 1993, distribution of goods by the nonlocal for-hire trucking segment represented nearly 40 percent of the total industry. By 1994, that percentage had increased to 42.5 percent. Additionally, 60 percent of the freight hauled by for-hire truckers was categorized as general freight, and 25 percent of that freight tonnage was hauled by for-hire truckers and consisted of direct origin-to-destination TL shipments.

Private Carriers. The private carriage market consists primarily of manufacturers, builders, retailers, or other firms (such as Sears Roebuck and Wal-Mart Services) who own, lease, or control truck fleets for the exclusive transport of their own goods or products. Many older private trucking fleets were created as alternatives to the inflated shipping costs charged by truckers in the industry's preregulated, heavily unionized years. Private fleets were maintained by 33 percent of manufacturing firms, 55 percent of food processing companies, 65 percent of the wood and lumber industry, and 75 percent of the construction materials industry. Private carriage allows shippers to maintain greater control over scheduling and freight handling and to customize service for specialized equipment or products.

Types of Freight. Although the trucking industry hauled 55 percent of total U.S. freight tonnage in 1994, that tonnage represented nearly 75 percent of the total dollar value of U.S. freight, reflecting the dominance of the trucking industry in the transportation of high-value goods and commodities.

Traditionally, the types of freight truckers are authorized to transport have been classified in three ways: ''specific'' commodities (in which a trucker is authorized to carry only certain, specified goods); ''specialized'' commodities (in which the commodities truckers are authorized to carry are classified in broader but still limited terms, for example, ''iron or steel articles''); and ''general'' commodities (which includes all goods except ''household goods, heavy and bulky articles, new automobiles, dangerous or explosive articles, livestock, articles of unusual value and articles injurious or contaminating to other commodities''). More narrowly classified, nonlocal trucking freight can be further divided into general freight or packaged merchandise; agricultural goods; hazardous materials; and miscellaneous goods. In the early 1990s, 70 percent of all steel, sheet metal, wire pipes, rods, semifinished metal products, and lumber and wood products were shipped by truck as well as nearly 85 percent of all food, furniture, rubber products, fixtures, appliances, and plastics goods. The nonlocal trucking industry also hauls bulk commodities, automobiles, glass products, industrial water, heavy machinery, refrigerated liquids and solids, liquid petroleum products, building materials, synthetic fuels, and cargo requiring flatbed or specialized trailer transport.

Household Moving. The trucking industry includes 115,000 (local and nonlocal) household goods movers such as North American Van Lines, Mayflower Group, and Allied Van Lines. In the 1980s and 1990s, many household goods movers began to break out of the static, seasonal residential moving market by providing warehousing, logistics, LTL and even intermodal service. In 1994 the household goods industry accounted for 4.6 percent of the industry's distribution and 7.8 percent of its revenues.

Competitiveness. Industry firms distinguish themselves from their competitors through financial strength, quality of sales force, shipment tracking technology, breadth of route coverage, efficient claim settlement, delivery performance, proper billing, size and quality of fleet, insurance coverage, and superior safety records. Larger national carriers can also provide the benefits of economies of scale including lower equipment, advertising, and insurance costs as well as sophisticated management techniques, more efficient administrative procedures, and extensive financial resources. Many of the large national carriers have also entered into logistics services, whereby they offer customers the ability to track their shipments as they travel from point of departure to destination.

Rate Bureaus. Trucker's rates are determined by nine regional rate bureaus that meet on a regular basis to determine rate increases for the carriers in their region based on those firms' revenue needs. Rate bureaus also provide legal services, disseminate financial reports and market information, categorize shipments, and provide smaller carriers with rating software. Deregulation permitted carriers to publish rates independently of the Interstate Commerce Commission (ICC) and as a result the majority of large carriers withdrew from the rate bureaus between 1991 and 1992.

Rate bureaus continued to play a role in the nonlocal trucking industry, however, because international and intrastate rates could not be published independently and smaller carriers' budgets prevented them from performing the kinds of services provided by the bureaus. In the early 1990s, 25-30 percent of all general freight was transported under rates published by rate bureaus. Historically, two or more general rate hikes (of between 3.5 percent and 4.8 percent in 1992, for example) are implemented per year, but truckers' discounts (often ranging between 30 and 50 percent) reduce the de facto rates charged to shippers. Before industry deregulation in 1980, the ICC monitored rates more closely. However, because deregulation brought free market forces into play, new rates that did not reflect economic realities tended to regulate themselves down to natural levels by way of rollbacks and discounts.

Intermodal. From a manufacturers' perspective, the biggest advancement in trucking industry came when truckers began entering into alliances with railroads in 1990. Among them were J.B. Hunt Transport Services Inc. and Schneider National which formed alliances with Conrail, Norfolk Southern, Southern Pacific, Union Pacific and Burlington Northern. Such alliances offered manufacturers the speed and flexibility of trucks and the low cost of rail service. As a result, trucking companies began to use equipment that accommodated intermodal containers rather than tractor trailers so that containerized cargo could be easily moved between both transportation modes. In intermodal arrangements, truckers team with rail or maritime freight carriers to haul goods in generic dual-use containers.

The trucker supplies the shorter origin-to-railhead and railhead-to-destination portions of the transport and splits the revenue from the haul with the railroad according to an agreed-upon formula. The percentage of general freight truckers' vehicle-miles transported using intermodal rose from 1 percent in 1970 to as high as 15 percent for some TL carriers in 1991.

The advantages of container freighting—decreased theft, lower transport and handling damages, better driver retention through assignment of long hauls to railroads, and new markets for trucking companies—were virtually doubled with the introduction of ''double stack'' intermodal transport in 1984. In double stack arrangements, containers are ''piggybacked'' on top of each other on a rail car to increase hauling capacity.

BACKGROUND AND DEVELOPMENT

The invention of the combustion engine and the automobile in the nineteenth century and the development of the first public highways mark the origins of the modern trucking industry. The first transcontinental transport of freight by truck took place in 1912, and within five years the U.S. Army's request for a vehicle capable of hauling troops and war materials led to the creation of a fleet of trucks and specially trained drivers that formed the core of a new civilian trucking industry after World War I. While the industry began to establish itself as a serious competitor to the railroads, the Federal Highway Act of 1921 laid the groundwork for a national highway system that by the early 1990s stretched 45,000 miles.

Several factors contributed to the rise of the trucking industry in the following half century: a shift of population and industry away from cities and railheads to suburban locations accessible only by truck; a continuing federal mandate for a network of national highways; the inherently superior cost efficiencies of trucks relative to railroads with respect to loading facilities and shipment packing and handling; and the greater flexibility of trucks in providing specialized routes and delivery schedules.

Regulation. Faced with increasing competition from the trucking industry, the rail industry pushed for legislation that resulted in The Motor Carrier Act (MCA) of 1935, which gave the Interstate Commerce Commission broad powers to approve acquisitions and mergers; classify commodities that are covered by and exempt from regulation; and govern the routes, services, and rates charged by the trucking industry. The 17,000 truckers in the industry during that period were granted perpetual ''grandfather'' operating authority, while potential new entrants had to meet restrictive requirements regarding the ''public convenience and necessity'' of proposed services. The MCA also guaranteed all communities route service regardless of the cost of such service to the trucking industry.

Over the years, federal regulation emerged as an artificial structure for maintaining wages and profits above natural market levels. Under ICC protection the trucking industry's share of total national intercity freight ton-miles (a measure of freight traffic expressed as one ton multiplied by one mile) grew from 9.7 percent to 22 percent between 1939 and 1974, and its share of the dollar value of U.S. freight began to surpass the railroads for the first time.

Deregulation. Although deregulation of the trucking industry had been contemplated as early as the Truman Administration, it wasn't until the late 1970s that significant reform of the industry began to appear possible. When it passed, the Motor Carrier Act of 1980 radically altered the nonlocal trucking industry by eliminating ICC control over companies' abilities to enter the industry, determine their rates and routes, and enlarge their operations through acquisition, merger, or route extension.

The most immediate impact of the MCA of 1980 was seen in the number of failures of poorly capitalized new firms and noncompetitive existing firms, and the influx of new carriers in the TL segment where start-up costs were less prohibitive. The number of trucking business failures jumped from about 400 in 1980 to over 1,561 in 1986; a total of 11,000 failures were recorded between 1980 and 1989. However, 19,000 new firms entered the industry between 1980 and 1982 alone, and the number of for-hire carriers with ICC-granted operating authority grew from less than 20,000 in 1980 to almost 50,000 in 1992.

Rate Undercharging. Since deregulation, industry firms began resorting to broad discounting programs to provide customers with rates more attractive than published tariffs. In the early 1990s, bankrupt truckers began suing brokers and their shipping customers for the difference (estimated at more than $2 billion) between these unfiled discount rates and official published rates. In 1990, the U.S. Supreme Court ruled that shippers were obliged to pay the difference between filed tariff rates and rates negotiated with defunct truckers. Two years later, the ICC eliminated all regulations covering motor carrier contracts, making binding agreements between shippers and truckers easier to enforce and thus reducing the future likelihood of undercharge disputes.

Intermodal. Although some rail hauling of empty and loaded truck trailers existed in the 1950s and truckers subsequently began buying ''piggyback'' services from railroads, it wasn't until 1989 that the trucking and rail industries formally recognized the importance of intermodal transport with the signing of the first major intermodal agreement between a trucking firm (J.B. Hunt Transport) and a competing rail carrier (Atchison, Topeka and Santa Fe Railway). Between 1970 and 1991 alone, the percentage of vehicle-miles transported using intermodal by some TL carriers rose from 1 percent to 15 percent. In 1991, the Intermodal Surface Transportation Efficiency Act (ISTEA) was adopted, with the goal of reducing the amount of paperwork required by forcing states to adopt uniform measures, such as making fuel tax payments to a single state.

CURRENT CONDITIONS

While the long-distance LTL segment experienced decreased revenues, regional LTL carriers experienced double digit growth by encroaching on the overnight delivery market once monopolized by small-package ground couriers, which are covered in **SIC 4215: Courier Services Except Air.** This trend was fueled by the widespread adoption of so-called ''zero-inventory'' production techniques by U.S. manufacturers, which entailed the creation of distribution centers or parts storage facilities within a delivery zone of two days or less in traveling distance from manufacturers' sites. The growing emphasis on regional markets was also enhanced by the industry's need to retain drivers by offering them shorter hauls, the rail industry's increasing competitiveness in long-distance freight, and growing emphasis by shippers on on-time delivery guarantees.

Legislation. Congress passed the International Registration Plan and International Fuel Tax Agreement, taking effect in 1996 and 1998 respectively, to allow truckers to avoid repetitive state-by-state vehicle registration requirements and fuel tax payments. The Clinton administration's gasoline and diesel fuel tax ratified in 1993 added 4.3 cents to per-gallon fuel costs, raising industry operating expenses by an estimated $3 billion annually.

Additionally, several federal programs continued to affect the trucking industry's response to safety concerns. The Motor Carrier Safety Assistance Program, for example, gave the Federal Office of Motor Carrier Safety and relevant state agencies greater latitude in carrying out annual vehicle safety inspections. The resulting $6,000 to $9,000 per truck spent annually by the industry on maintenance and repair was expected to be offset by lower insurance premiums and cost savings derived from fleets maintained in optimal operating condition.

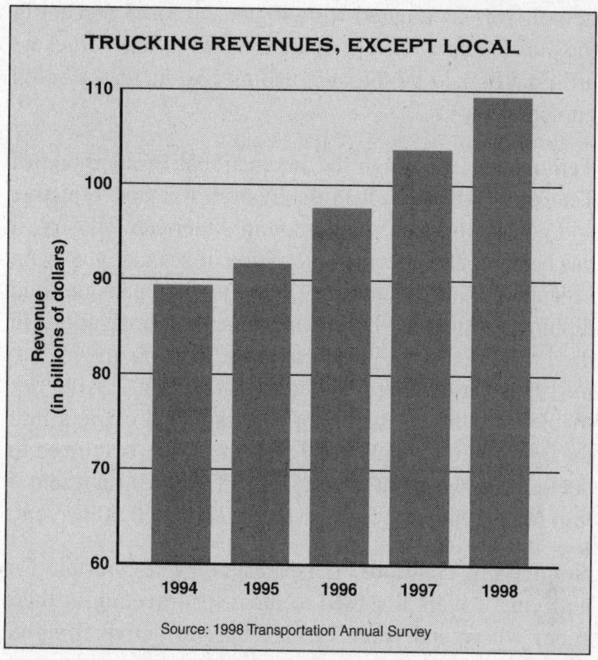

INDUSTRY LEADERS

Three firms dominate the national LTL general freight market. Together, Consolidated Freightways, Yellow Freight, and Roadway Express, Inc. command more than one-third of LTL revenues. Although no national TL carrier claimed a monopoly of the TL market, several firms, including Schneider National, J.B. Hunt Transport, and Werner Enterprises, Inc. have historically led that industry segment. The contract carrier/truck leasing sector is dominated by Ryder Systems, Inc. Penske Truck Leasing, and Rollins Truck Leasing Corp. Historical leaders in the nonlocal household goods moving segment include North American Van Lines, Mayflower Group, and United Van Lines.

Consolidated Freightways (CF), which had operating revenues of $2.2 billion in 1997, maintains 714 terminals and 30 freight consolidation hubs throughout North America and operates a fleet of 63 freight aircraft and 54,000 trucks, vans, trailers, and tractors. Its 96 percent on-time record was among the industry's best performance records. CF was founded in 1929 as Consolidated Truck Lines of Portland, Oregon. When it formed Freightways Manufacturing in 1939, it became the first trucking company to make its own vehicles. The company was also a pioneer in the use of aluminum as a truck fabrication material and diesel fuel as a standard fuel source.

WORKFORCE

The trucking industry as a whole employed more than 9.3 million people in 1995. That year there were 2.9 million truck drivers. Nearly 59 percent were employed in wholesale/retail sector and 20 percent in the manufacturing sector. Only 23 percent employed were minorities and 4.5 percent were women. In total, $275.2 billion in annual wages were paid to employees throughout the trucking industry. Drivers operating heavy specialized trucks earned the highest annual salary in 1995 ($35,400). Tank drivers followed with an annual average wage of $35,300; refrigerated truck drivers, $35,100; LTL truck drivers, $33,600; TL truck drivers, $33,000; general cargo truck drivers, $32,200; and private fleet truck drivers earning the lowest average annual salary at $32,100. Trucking jobs are expected to grow through 2005, keeping this industry in the top 25 occupational groups identified with projected employment growth. An estimated 879 truck drivers lost their lives during 1998, 82 percent as a result of transportation accidents.

Fewer than 60 percent of new truck drivers lasted longer than four weeks on the job, and driver turnover rates (which rose as high as 100 percent for some firms) were considered to be among the most critical issues facing the industry. The president of American Trucking Association, Walter McCormick, Jr., in a 1998 interview for *Traffic World,* indicated that the lack of trained drivers was of top concern for the industry. Besides bonuses, benefits, and higher pay, methods used to retain drivers included expanded use of husband and wife teams, ''relay'' driving in which routes normally handled by one driver are divided up, increased scheduling of short hauls, and equipment amenities designed to make the driver's job less taxing.

Large LTL freight carriers with unionized employees often pay out 60 percent to 65 percent of their revenues in wages and benefits (including wages to independent drivers) compared with 40 percent to 45 percent in the mostly nonunion TL segment. Long-distance truckers are usually paid by the mile and receive increases based on seniority.

Teamsters. Although the International Brotherhood of Teamsters (IBT) has historically been the most effective and politically influential union in American industry, it has been plagued by a long tradition of scandal involving organized crime connections, racketeering, pension fund dipping, insurance abuses, and federal investigation. In the 1970s, the IBT represented about 500,000 drivers, but by 1980 that number had declined to 300,000. After deregulation allowed scores of nonunionized carriers into the industry, the number of Teamster drivers continued to decline. Between 1981 and 1991, Teamster representation in the regulated for-hire sector alone fell 50 percent.

Nondriving Positions. Dispatchers are responsible for notifying drivers assigned to them (or traveling in their zone) where and when to pick up and deliver freight. They routinely juggle a continuously changing roster of drivers, destinations, routes, schedules, and freight categories to determine the most efficient distribution of the company's fleet resources.

Raters determine the minimum amounts a company can quote its customers for shipping freight based on such variables as the type of commodity to be shipped, current shipping rates and discounts, competitors' rates, and the relative profitability of the shipment.

While dispatchers focus on specific shipping zones and individual drivers, planners are responsible for the efficient distribution of drivers throughout whole regions and must take into consideration such factors as fluctuating seasonal shipping levels or mistaken sales of company services to unserviced areas.

AMERICA AND THE WORLD

U.S. involvement in foreign trucking has historically centered primarily on the Canadian market. The degree of internationalization in the industry was expected to grow, however, as a result of the ratification of the North American Free Trade Agreement (NAFTA) in late 1993, the implementation of new phases of the General Agreement on Tariffs and Trade, the emergence of a formally unified European economy, and the openings to trade offered by the democratization of the former Soviet Union and Eastern Europe.

Canada. The United States and Canada trade more goods with each other than with any other economies, resulting in transportation costs—including trucking—of $4 billion to $7 billion a year. In 1989, Canada and the United States signed a trade agreement to promote cross-border commerce, which was expected to be further bolstered by the gradual implementation of NAFTA throughout the 1990s.

The NAFTA agreement called for opening cross-border traffic in the U.S. and Mexican border states by 1996. Other geographic and ownership access would be expanded by 2000, and virtually all access and investment restrictions on trucking companies would be lifted by 2003.

Before NAFTA, Mexican cross-border trucking was highly restricted. Mexico required foreign shippers to use Mexican drivers and Mexican equipment to handle shipments there. This forced U.S. shippers and carriers to form alliances with Mexican carriers. In response to the restrictions, the United States established an embargo in 1982 that limited Mexican access to U.S. markets. U.S. certificates of registration restricted Mexican carriers' access to a border zone generally ranging 10 to 25 miles north of the U.S. border. But just before NAFTA's passage some 4,354 Mexican carriers held registration certificates. Only three Mexican motor freight carriers, however, held broader authority and none held 48-state authority.

U.S. trucking companies sending freight to Mexico were especially subjected to lengthy delays at border crossings since their trailers had to be unloaded from their tractors and re-loaded onto Mexican tractors. With NAFTA's passage, American truckers won access to all of Mexico in 1999, and Mexican truckers were granted full access to the United States.

NAFTA was regarded as bad news for U.S. trucking companies that faced difficulties retaining drivers for long hauls. Mexico lacked good roads, hotels, communications, and gas and repair stations—four requirements of most truckers. Meanwhile, the Mexican government began efforts to build a 7,240-mile network of superhighways that would crisscross the nation and connect most of Mexico's major ports with its principal commercial and industrial centers. As more American and Asian manufacturers began using Mexico for assembly of products, and trade increased with all of Latin America, many executives began seeing the traditional East-West, West-East trade routes replaced with an emphasis on North-South, South-North routes. The devaluation of the peso in 1995, however, had devastating effects on U.S. truckers operating there, causing many to rethink their involvement in Mexico.

Amendments to Mexico's federal weights and measures law in 1994 were met with enthusiasm by U.S. truckers. The new law lowered Mexico's weight limit for trucks to just under 90,000 pounds for an 18-wheel tractor-trailer, only 10,000 pounds shy of U.S. limits. Trucks from Mexico had been weighing in excess of 140,000 to 160,000 pounds, an amount considered unsafe in the United States. Prior to the amendment, many Mexican vehicles weighing high amounts came across the border into the United States since resources to monitor all vehicles at border crossings were lacking.

With the advent of the European Union in 1992, U.S. carriers quickly established a presence to control the European leg of their shipments. European operators like steamship line Nedlloyd began offering land-based transportation in Europe and employed the services of U.S. trucking companies to provide the U.S. leg of the shipment. Nedlloyd Road Cargo signed a contract with Consolidated Freightways's subsidiary Con-Way in 1992 to provide door-to-door LTL service between the United States and Europe, with Nedlloyd handling the European part of the venture. Carolina Freight opened an office in Rotterdam, the Netherlands, to provide faster service for its customers' European needs. Dutch motor carrier Bleckmann B.V. handled sales and marketing for Carolina's transportation services within the Dutch market, served as its general agent within the United Kingdom, and provided international trucking services within Europe. In 1993, Yellow Freight and The Royal Fran Maas group in Europe entered into an agreement to provide transatlantic LTL shipments.

The trend in the European trucking industry was toward increased concentration of business activities within the industry, decreased border restrictions, harmonization of excise duties and value-added taxes, and increased grants of operating authority for trucking firms.

New Markets. The number of trucking companies with international operations has grown, and American nonlocal truckers have been among the most active global firms. Expanding and potential markets included South America (arrangements by Consolidated Freightways and Carolina Freight, for example, with Argentina/Chile and Colombia, respectively), the Pacific Rim (direct service by Roadway Express to Australia, New Zealand, and 10 Asian countries), Russia (joint marketing agreement by Mayflower Transit with SovTransavto in 1990), and China (U.S.-China shipping accord signed in 1992).

RESEARCH AND TECHNOLOGY

The nonlocal trucking industry has not historically been associated with advanced technologies. Reliable braking and cab heating systems didn't come into use until the 1940s, the diesel engine wasn't common until the 1950s, and as late as 1971 few trucking companies used computers for even basic office-related administrative applications. By the early 1990s, however, a typical heavy truck featured three to 20 forward gears, electronically controlled fuel-injection systems, aerodynamic airfoils, and roof-mounted satellite antennae linked to computers inside the cab and remote data storage centers.

The areas of technology with the greatest potential impact on the nonlocal trucking industry were vehicle and freight tracking systems and information storage and interchange systems. Because these technologies enabled industry firms to increase productivity, enhance responsiveness to customers, and distinguish themselves from competitors, they played increasingly critical roles in the industry's profitability in the early 1990s.

Tracking technologies use sophisticated computer systems to record the progress of freight from origin to destination and satellite technologies to provide precise locations of fleet trucks. Bar code labels on freight packages and portable bar code scanners permitted industry firms to process extensive data on individual loads and monitor the movement of those loads during transport. Such electronic data interchange (EDI) systems allowed truckers to "capture" data automatically and permitted shippers to link up with a carrier's computer to access data on proof of delivery, invoices, shipment routing, and freight consolidation in "real time," with greater accuracy, and with reduced administrative paperwork and storage.

Handheld, laptop, and dashboard-mounted computers let truckers communicate with company computers, keep track of information on fuel taxes and fuel management performance, store navigational maps and information on truck stops and repair facilities, record departures and arrivals, send and receive messages, monitor vehicle speed and engine conditions, and register mileage or the results of trailer inspections.

Although satellite technology for vehicle tracking and navigation has been available since the early 1980s, active industry interest began only in 1987 when the first LT carriers began installing satellite tracking equipment. These systems enabled trucking firms to locate trucks to accuracies of 300 yards by linking on-board computers with company dispatchers via specialized satellites. Less expensive "meteor burst" systems bounced VHF radio waves off meteor trails to obtain the same positioning coordinates offered by satellite signals.

Using satellite tracking equipment, C.R. England and Sons achieved 98 percent on-time performance in the early 1990s. Although satellite tracking systems can add as much as 2 percent to operating costs, 2,000 U.S. trucking fleets had two-way satellite data links in 1992, and 30,000 trucks were equipped with position location systems. The number of trucks equipped with vehicle tracking equipment was expected to continue to grow.

Legislation. Several industry innovations have been direct responses to government regulations in the areas of vehicle emissions, radar evasion devices, and highway safety. Environmental Protection Agency pollution mandates and related clean air laws drove industry firms in the 1980s and 1990s to explore alternatives to diesel and gasoline fuels. In 1993, for example, all trucks were required to begin using low sulfur fuels. Although the practicality of other fuel sources such as compressed natural gas and liquid petroleum was unclear in the early 1990s, research breakthroughs in fuel modification, exhaust after-treatment, and engine redesign resulted in reductions in diesel engine emissions of 40 percent over preregulatory levels.

So-called ''double-bottoms''—trucks hauling two trailers—were estimated to increase truckers' load capacity by 35 percent, offering the industry improved ability to compete with rail carriers' stacked container methods. In the early 1990s, industry firms continued to push for legislative reforms permitting them to use double- and triple-trailers and other ''longer combination vehicle'' arrangements more widely.

Other Technologies. A wide range of technology applications were introduced or were under development, ranging from ''early warning systems'' that use radar technology to inform drivers when they are approaching a vehicle too quickly; cab-mounted computers that reduce accidents by enabling dispatchers to remotely monitor the status of the driver and vehicle; electronic systems for registering automatic payment of tolls without requiring trucks to stop; systems for automatically monitoring freight and engine temperatures and setting temperature levels in refrigerated vehicles; and diagnostic and prognostic software packages that allow engine computers to predict component failure based on engine performance trends.

Trucks themselves have been subject to technological research and advancement. German truck manufacturers Freightliner and Mercedes Benz tested a second generation of truck design that uses an interactive video computer system. Called Vector, the system video tapes the highway as the truck drives along, interprets data such as speed and traffic, and directs the truck as to what speed it should operate. Application of this technology was not expected to reach the marketplace until well into 2000.

Potentially important technologies outside of the truck cab included laser image-processing and optical character recognition devices for speeding up paperwork using electronic scanning techniques; driver training simulators based on aerospace industry designs; shipment planner software to allow truckers to reduce ''deadhead'' (or empty trailer) miles; and fax and voice response systems that provide shippers with constantly updated rate quotes, transit times, and locations of in-transit shipments.

FURTHER READING

American Trucking Association, Regulated Motor Carriers statistics, 1998.

Bowman, Robert J. ''Battling for Turf.'' *Distribution,* July 1996.

Buxbaum, Peter A. ''Shippers Benefit from Truckload Consolidation.'' *Transportation & Distribution,* July 1995.

Engel, Cynthia. ''Competition Drives the Trucking Industry.'' *Monthly Labor Review,* April 1998. Available from http://stats.bls.gov/opub/mlr/1998/04/art3exc.htm

Flanagan, William G. ''Travel & Transport.'' *Forbes,* January 1, 1996.

Global Industry Profiles Detroit: Gale Research, 1995.

''Standard Trucking and Transportation Statistics, January/February 1997.'' ATA Statistics Department, American Trucking Association, Alexandria, Va.

''Trucking and Warehousing.'' *Rough Notes,* October 1999, 119.

U.S. Department of Commerce. *U.S. Industrial Outlook 1998-1999.* Washington: 1999.

U.S. Department of Labor. *Occupational Outlook Handbook.* Washington, D.C.: 1998.

SIC 4214

LOCAL TRUCKING WITH STORAGE

NAICS CODE(S)

484110 (Local General Freight Trucking, Local)
484210 (Used Household and Office Goods Moving)
484220 (Specialized Freight (except Used Goods) Trucking, Local)

This category covers establishments primarily engaged in furnishing both trucking and storage services, including household goods, within a single municipality, contiguous municipalities, or a municipality and its suburban areas. Establishments primarily engaged in furnishing warehousing and storage of household goods when not combined with trucking are classified in **SIC 4226: Special Warehousing and Storage, Not Elsewhere Classified.** Establishments primarily engaged in furnishing local courier services for letters, parcels, and packages weighing less than 100 pounds are classified in **SIC 4215: Courier Services Except Air.**

The local trucking and storage industry consists of firms that provide storage, warehousing, and other services in addition to transport within an operating radius of 50 miles, which usually includes an urban area and its suburbs. The industry is divided between firms that transport and store furniture and household goods locally (58 percent of all industry establishments in 1992) and firms that transport and store other goods locally (41 percent). In 1992, over 4,500 firms in the industry employed over 64,000 workers and generated almost $4.2 billion in total revenues. By 1998 total revenues reached $6.1 billion, an increase from the $5.8 billion of 1997. Although revenues were on the increase during the 1990s, there were expected to be less than 2,500 establishments employing just over 51,500 workers by the year 2000.

In 1994, three-quarters of the industry's revenues derived from motor carrier work (including the leasing of trucks with drivers). A total of 63 percent of these revenues came from local trucking and the remainder from long-distance trucking. The industry's nonmotor carrier derived revenues from such activities as parking and storing vehicles, snow plowing, repair work and truck terminal leasing for other carriers, and the lease and rental of vehicles without drivers. Industry firms are generally classified as ''specialty freight'' carriers because the materials they transport—typically household goods—require special equipment for loading, unloading, or transport.

Local firms that both moved and stored household goods comprised roughly 20 percent of the total U.S. household goods moving industry in 1987, with the remainder divided between non-local household goods movers and local truckers that did not offer storage. Typically, most residential moves occur in the summer, and industry revenues often drop by as much as 50 percent during the winter months. As a result of such revenue fluctuations, many local moving and storage firms have supplemented their core moving business with other services, including off-season commercial and business office relocation, less-than-truckload (i.e., under 10,000 pounds of goods per truckload) freight transport, and third-party logistics, and warehousing.

A growing trend in American industry in the 1980s and 1990s was the ''just-in-time'' production management system in which manufacturers lowered their inventory costs by maintaining only a short-term stock of manufacturing materials. Shippers of manufacturing materials responded to this trend by warehousing goods in the same locality as their customers, enabling them to respond more quickly to continual changes in their customer's orders while also lowering shipping expenses. Local trucking and storage companies participated in this trend by providing transport, warehousing, and logistics services to shippers and their customers. In third-party logistics arrangements, local trucking and storage firms provided storage, inventory control services, packing or crating of goods, or pickup and delivery of shipments. Goods were stored in the customer's warehouse, the trucking firm's warehouse, or in ''dedicated'' warehouses owned by the trucking firm but maintained exclusively for the customer. Inventory management could be

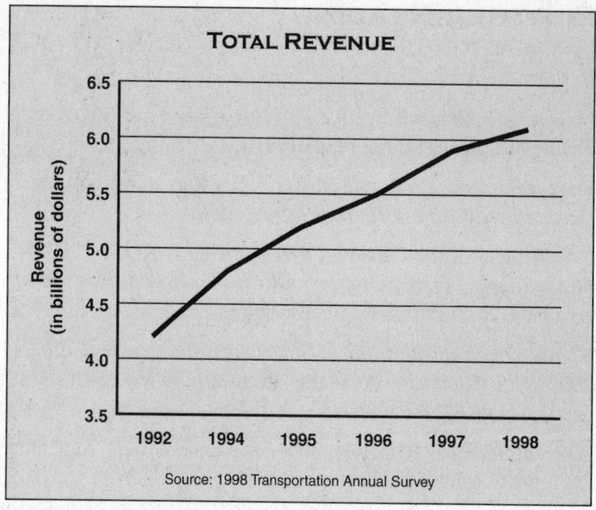

handled by the customer in the trucker's storage facility or by the local trucking firm itself. Some firms maintained small warehouses called ''parts banks'' where important components were kept ready for immediate (one to four hour) delivery to customers.

Many of the same firms that dominated the national intercity moving industry in the late 1990s—Bekins, Mayflower, Allied, North American, and U-Haul, for example—also operated in the local trucking and storage industry and were among the leaders in developing the nontraditional less-than-truckload and logistics services markets. Far more common, however, were smaller firms such as Kane Is Able Inc., Nice Jewish Boy Moving and Storage, Frozen Food Express, and Beverly Hills Transfer and Storage Inc.

In addition to national moving companies and smaller trucking and storage firms, the local trucking and storage industry includes a variety of specialized carriers, such as merchants' goods delivery services, refrigerated meat transporters, data transport and storage firms, liquid tank truckers, container and intermodal companies, cement hauling firms, bus companies, farm goods transporters, crane and excavation companies, as well as the local trucking and storage divisions of such national rail carriers as CSX and Norfolk Southern.

In the mid-1990s important trends in the local-trucking-with-storage industry included continued diversification into new areas of business: some companies, for example, would offer to pack up a company's computers, move them to its new office, and reinstall them so employees could begin work immediately. As intense competition in the industry drove down truckers' wages, industry firms also concentrated on developing ways to retain drivers, such as only hiring drivers from within the company or offering generous benefits and profit-sharing plans.

FURTHER READING

Byrd, Alan. "Good Service Moves Joiner to Success." *Orlando Business Journal,* 21 October 1996.

MacDonald, Mitchell E. "It's Not Just a Van Line Anymore." *Traffic Management,* February 1991.

Starzynski, Bob. "Virginia Mover Takes Care of Employees." *Washington Business Journal,* 8 July 1996.

U.S. Bureau of the Census. *Current Business Reports, BT/94, Motor Freight Transportation and Warehousing Survey: 1994,* Available from http://www.census.gov.

Census of Transportation, Communications, and Utilities, 1992: U.S. Summary, Available from http://www.census.gov/epcd/www/uc92h42.html.

General Statistics. GaleNet, 2000. The Gale Group. Available from www.galenet.com.

U.S. Census Bureau. *1998 Transportation Survey Tables,* 1999. Available from http://www.census.gov/ftp/pub/svsd/www/tas.html/.

SIC 4215

COURIER SERVICES EXCEPT AIR

This category covers establishments primarily engaged in the delivery of individually addressed letters, parcels, and packages (generally under 100 pounds), except by means of air transportation or by the United States Postal Service. Delivery is usually made by street or highway within a local area or between cities. Establishments primarily engaged in furnishing air delivery of individually addressed letters, parcels, and packages, except by the United States Postal Service, are classified in **SIC 4513: Air Courier Services,** and establishments of the United States Postal Service are classified in **SIC 4311: United States Postal Service.**

NAICS CODE(S)

492110 (Couriers)
492210 (Local Messengers and Local Delivery)

INDUSTRY SNAPSHOT

In 1998, 5,966 industry establishments employed more than 350,000 workers and generated more than $40 billion in revenues. About three-quarters of the firms in this industry were local surface or ground-based couriers (those with an operating radius of 50 miles or less), and the remainder were nonlocal couriers. Despite the name recognition owned by industry leader United Parcel Service (UPS) and its smaller competitors, local-market establishments with five or fewer employees and annual revenues between $100,000 and $250,000 were the most common business type in the industry.

ORGANIZATION AND STRUCTURE

The diversity of business activities performed by industry firms was reflected in the number of establishments for whom courier service was not their sole business. For example, industry firms included bus lines (Greyhound Lines), messenger services (Dial-A-Messenger), armored car services (Hudson Armored Car & Courier Service), temporary employment firms (Speedy Temporary Employment & Courier Service), business-only couriers (Business Mail Express), food product delivery companies (Culinary Shuttle), bicycle courier companies (Boulder Bicycle Couriers), newspaper publishers (Fairbanks Daily News-Miner), specialized bank document couriers, couriers who provided "in-house" service for business clients within a single office building, and a wide variety of smaller firms.

The vast majority of industry firms serviced local markets, for example, a single urban market and its environs, and offered no air delivery service. A national local-based ground courier company like U.S. Delivery Systems, for example, used acquisitions of these smaller local courier companies to become a national presence in the same-day non-air express courier market by 1997, with operations in roughly 115 U.S. cities. In addition to its traditional "point-to-point" local messenger services, U.S. Delivery offered such services as grocery delivery, home catalogue merchandise delivery, and local just-in-time warehousing for manufacturers in other markets.

The U.S. ground courier industry delivers packages and parcels generally weighing from 70 to 100 pounds for business and residential customers. (In 1994, however, UPS raised its weight limit to 150 pounds.) The types of delivery available ranged from overnight (or "next-day") service to two-day and three-to-five-day service with a range of additional services such as international delivery, same-day intercity air delivery (packages picked up in the morning and delivered before 5 p.m. that day), and even express overnight service to Europe by 8:30 a.m. the next day. While overnight air service was increasingly the most dominant delivery service provided by air couriers in the mid-1990s, same-day, two-day, and three-day ground service remained the staple of industry firms.

The industry continued to offer a wider range of services and rates to capture the many specialized niches of the package shipping market. For example, UPS introduced five new rate tiers based on commodity density, also later adding another tier for light and bulky parcels. One such service, accepting packages weighing 100 pounds or more, helped UPS and other carriers compete with the small-package niche of the less-than-truckload (LTL) segment of the trucking industry, which transported consolidated loads from different shippers that consisted of individual packages of 500 pounds or less.

These traditionally general freight carriers began reacting to the ground couriers' co-optation of their small package business by adopting the same operating strategies that helped the leading couriers dominate their industry: local pick-up and delivery of small packages and parcels, the creation of geographical distribution networks or hubs, and the use of tracking software and high-tech sorting facilities.

The leaders of the air and ground courier industries maintained extensive networks of drop boxes and staffed drop-off centers in addition to providing on-site package pick up. UPS, for example, had roughly 35,000 unstaffed drop-boxes and other drop-off facilities in operation, Airborne Express maintained roughly 8,000 such facilities, and Federal Express maintained about 370 company storefronts and 165 staffed drive-through pick-up and drop-off facilities for its customers. In 1997, UPS' delivery network consisted of over 500 aircraft, 147,000 vehicles, and 2,400 facilities. The company serviced 200 countries and delivered 1.6 million parcels and documents (air business only). By comparison, in 1999 Federal Express had 600 planes, 33,000 package drop-off locations, and 5,000 retail service outlets; it serviced 210 countries and had a daily volume of about 2.4 million air express parcels and documents.

BACKGROUND AND DEVELOPMENT

UPS was formed in 1907 as American Messenger Company, a telephone message service in Seattle, Washington. In 1913, the company changed its name to Merchants Parcel Delivery when it began delivering small parcels for local department stores. When the company changed its name again to United Parcel Service in 1930, it had expanded its service areas to northern California, New York, New Jersey, and Connecticut. UPS began operating in Los Angeles in 1952 and in the years that followed gradually expanded its services throughout the nation.

As late as 1970, Federal Express was the only package courier in the United States specializing in express delivery, when the USPS began to offer business customers priority mail delivery on an experimental basis. Within five years, the USPS was publicly acknowledging UPS as its principal competitor while Federal Express, aided by a 1974 UPS strike and its memorable slogan "When it absolutely, positively has to be there overnight," began to emerge as the major force in the air segment of the courier market. UPS responded by offering air delivery services, though initially through the use of charter air services. In 1982 it offered guaranteed next-day air delivery to anywhere in the United States and began buying its own air fleet.

In 1986, UPS began automating its operational systems with a five-year $2 billion technology upgrade program that was bolstered by an additional $500 million technology investment each year thereafter. It also countered FedEx's catchy corporate slogan with one of its own: "We run the tightest ship in the shipping business." By 1987 UPS owned 90 planes, by 1988, it offered international service to 41 countries, and between 1987 and 1992 it acquired 16 firms. In 1990, UPS bought a 9.5 percent stake in Mail Boxes, Etc., a franchise neighborhood-oriented mailing and business service company that began offering UPS to its customers for the shipping needs. Between 1991 and 1992, UPS acquired three European courier firms and by 1993, UPS was delivering 11.5 million packages and documents a day, and boasted over 1 million regular customers. In 1996 it paid $110 million in sponsorship and marketing/advertising fees to be the official sponsor of the summer Olympic games in the company's hometown of Atlanta.

The major competitors in the ground courier industry continued to wage a fierce price war with each other and with the air courier industry. This battle resulted in lower rates for small package shippers but reduced earnings for firms in an industry already characterized by narrow profit margins.

The rapid spread of fax and e-mail technology in the 1980s and 1990s represented a significant source of competition for ground couriers (primarily in the same-day delivery niche) and was estimated to have cost the courier industry $75 million in lost business in 1990 alone. At the same time, the adoption of cost-saving "just-in-time" or zero-inventory management policies by many American businesses in the same period created a demand for truckers capable of providing same-day warehouse-to-customer transport of time-sensitive parts and manufacturing materials. Because of the quick-delivery, short-haul nature of many courier firms, this growing market represented a natural niche for the ground courier industry.

Major industry events of the mid-1990s included the 1996 merger of U.S. Delivery Systems and Corporate Express in the same-day courier segment of the industry; the purchase of three smaller services by Consolidated Delivery and Logistics the same year; United TransNet Inc.'s acquisition of Eddy Messenger Service; and the merger of Quick International Courier and Specialty Mailing Inc. U.S. Delivery Systems, of Houston, Texas, continued its bid to become the leader of the U.S. same-day, point-to-point local courier industry by buying more than 33 smaller delivery services in 85 U.S. cities between 1994 and 1995. In 1996, UPS announced a joint venture with China's Sinotrans-Pekair transportation company to share its express delivery technology in the Chinese market, and established a major new Asian-Pacific air express hub in Taiwan. In 1997, UPS also began selling passenger seats on its weekend air freight flights to exploit the revenue potential of its fleet on Saturdays and Sundays.

Despite UPS' seemingly unassailable dominance of the U.S. ground courier industry, it was never very far away from bad press. In the early 1990s, for example, the carrier was accused of practicing anti-union employment policies, failing to ensure worker safety at package-sorting facilities, raising package weight limits without appropriately retraining employees, and refusing to pay workers overtime for extra hours and missed lunches (resulting in a class-action lawsuit settled out of court for $14 million). Between 1993 and 1995 UPS spent about $1 billion on safety equipment and worker-training programs. However, UPS still had problems. It struggled with charges that it used predatory pricing tactics, and in 1996 the International Transport Workers' Federation launched a campaign to unionize UPS's non-U.S. work force.

In the 1980s and 1990s, UPS, one of only three U.S. companies that competed nationally for small package delivery (Roadway Package system, Inc., and the USPS being the other two), and Federal Express—the air courier leader—increasingly encroached on each other's traditional markets, so much so that the differences between the two firms in services offered and size of fleet were almost negligible. Although UPS did not enter the air courier business until the 1980s, by 1995 double-digit growth in its air express operations allowed a UPS spokesperson to admit that air freight delivery had "changed the way we do everything. It is absolutely core to our business now." By late 1995 UPS' air express business was accounting for 25 percent of its annual revenues.

CURRENT CONDITIONS

Despite the growth in electronic transmission of data and information, courier services maintained healthy markets into the millennium. For the 1999 Christmas holiday season, UPS expected to deliver 18 million expedited packages on Christmas Eve alone. Normal daily averages for UPS were about 12.5 million per day for 1999.

One of the biggest contributors to the continued success of courier services was the 1998-99 rapid growth of e-commerce, including on-line shopping wherein on-line retailers delivered their parcels—as consumers often requested—by courier shippers. The convenience of the entire transaction outweighed hefty delivery charges for a generation of Web-users accustomed to near-instant gratification. In 1998, UPS shipped approximately 55 percent of all items bought on the Internet during the holiday season; the U.S. Postal Service delivered another 32 percent, followed by FedEx at 10 percent.

As competitors' prices remained parallel, the only real room for growth was overseas, and all three companies sought to secure these lucrative markets. However, higher fuel costs cut deeply into profits in 1998 and 1999, and UPS and FedEx announced increases in their charges of about 3 percent, starting in early 2000.

INDUSTRY LEADERS

The most successful couriers remain the large national companies such as UPS, Federal Express, DHL Worldwide Express, Roadway Package System Inc., Purolator Courier, Emery Air Express, and Airborne Express, which offered air courier and ground operations and competed directly with the ground-only couriers for business. In fact, the largest air couriers maintained sophisticated and extended surface operations that dwarfed the scope of services offered by the majority of companies in the ground courier industry. Another important provider of services closely related to the ground courier industry was USPS, which began to market itself as a direct competitor to UPS and Federal Express in the delivery of two- to three-day parcels and documents.

As 1999 came to an end, UPS announced a public offering of about 10 percent of its shares. In 1998, the company earned $1.7 billion on revenues of $24.8 billion. It also had a 24 percent return on equity in 1998. This was true despite brewing labor problems from the Teamsters, who filed a grievance in late 1999, claiming that the company failed to meet its obligation under a settlement from the 1997 strike.

Conversely, FedEx earned $503 million on revenues of $15.9 billion in 1998. Despite a revenue increase in 1999, earnings were down sharply, attributable to rising fuel costs. With a fleet of 600 aircraft, FedEx was paying 82 cents per gallon for fuel, compared to 51 cents the previous year. Fuel costs alone dropped quarterly operating income by $55 million. Notwithstanding, FedEx carried into 2000 its status as the world's largest express-delivery company, with 145,000 employees.

Among closest competitors was RPS, an offshoot of trucking firm leader Roadway Express ($2.3 billion in sales in 1996). Established in 1985, RPS was closely modeled on UPS and matched its mentor in everything from delivery times to pricing structures. Though its areas of delivery were less inclusive than UPS', in the 1980s it began coaxing customers away by offering the volume discounts UPS initially hesitated to offer. It also distinguished itself from its larger role model by offering cheaper rates for packages under 70 pounds and by waiving weekly account fees in weeks during which its customers had not shipped anything.

Other leading industry firms included Central Freight Lines, J. B. Hunt Transport, Mayflower Group, TNT Red Star Express, Viking Freight Inc., and Pony

Express Courier. A host of smaller industry firms included Courier Dispatch Group, Lanter Company, and Choice Courier Systems.

AMERICA AND THE WORLD

The 1993 North American Free Trade Agreement (NAFTA) continued to expand Canadian and Mexican markets for American couriers, and Mexican businesses continued to integrate courier delivery services into their business operations at a rapid pace. UPS promptly announced plans to open terminals or otherwise enlarge their Mexican operations, but in 1995, it terminated a large portion of its Mexican operations over frustrations with Mexican regulations and customs delays.

UPS Canada Ltd. and Purolator Courier Ltd. remained the two largest Canadian ground couriers. Roughly 60 larger Canadian firms offered local, regional, provincial, national, and international ground and air courier service in the $5 billion Canadian courier industry, among them such firms as Associated National Couriers, Priority Courier, Challenger Courier, Hotline Express, and Sameday Right-O-Way. Checker Courier, a division of Checker Cabs Ltd., began to violate Canada Post's legislated monopoly on letter delivery by offering next-day business mail delivery for 35 cents, nearly a dollar lower than Canada Post's required $1.29 charge. Canada Post refused to prosecute, however, on the grounds that the violations were not yet a ''major'' problem. Canada's private courier companies formed a Coalition for Canada Post Accountability to seek reform of Canada Post's monopoly over mail delivery, arguing that its purchase of Purolator represented an unfair interference in the free trade of commercial courier services.

Due to Europe's small population and size relative to the United States, its courier services market is better suited to ground-based companies than to air carriers. The emergence of a unified European economic market in the 1990s, and the elimination of national border restrictions were expected to substantially increase business opportunities for ground couriers operating in Europe. A European Court ruling in the early 1990s, which declared that European postal authorities could not prevent private firms from competing for package delivery business, reflected the increasingly liberalized inter-European courier services market. In August 1996, the British government suspended the Royal Mail's monopoly over British letter delivery for one month, allowing private courier services to enter the letter courier market. America's UPS expected the liberalized European courier market to result in annual growth of $2 billion in its European courier business revenues through 2000.

Before the recession of the early 1990s, the British courier industry had experienced annual growth rates of 10 to 20 percent. The recession affected the same-day light van and motorcycle courier segment most severely, but two- to three-day and next-day delivery services also experienced average declines of 15 percent. The British courier industry includes such firms as Instone Air Services, Datapost, Speedbird Courier, Securicor, and Lynx Express Delivery, which is a subsidiary of Britain's largest road transport company, NFC Plc. Other couriers serving Britain and Europe include UPS and the Netherlands-based TNT Express, Europe's oldest courier.

While nonlocal general freight truckers expanded their European markets through partnerships with European carriers, UPS used a strategy of outright acquisition. For example, UPS bought French, Austrian, and Dutch firms to increase its European business. In the same period, UPS also announced courier service to Hungary, Yugoslavia, Poland, Romania, Russia, and Czechoslovakia. Rather than develop its own European air fleet, UPS contracted with local European firms to handle the forwarding of packages flown into European terminals by UPS planes.

RESEARCH AND TECHNOLOGY

In its operations centers, shipping points, and package pickup and delivery trucks, the U.S. ground courier industry was transformed by mobile communications technology and electronic scanning, tracking, and billing technology. Faced with increasing competition from Federal Express in the late 1970s and early 1980s, industry leader UPS inaugurated a technology modernization program in the mid-1980s that transformed it into a technology-driven enterprise with a management information systems (MIS) staff of 4,000. In 1990, UPS began installing a cellular phone system in 50,000 of its fleet trucks that enabled customers to determine the exact status of their packages in real time for a cost of 75 cents. The $150 million system, called DIAD (Delivery Information Acquisition Device), used an electronic pen and clipboard device carried by the driver and was based on ''image capture'' software that recorded the customer's signature and the package's bar code data. When the driver attached the clipboard to an adapter in the truck, the data was sent via UPS's ''UPSNet'' system to the company's main data center for customer access. Among other advantages, the system largely eliminated the problem of verifying illegible signatures, thereby tripling the number of next-day air deliveries made without errors, and enabling UPS to include an electronic ''replica'' of the recipient's signature when providing the shipper with a proof of delivery. In 1992, UPS introduced GroundTrac for electronically tracking packages passing through the UPS system. It also began investing in coded package labels capable of containing more data than existing bar code labels.

UPS also established a toll-free hot line that shippers could call to get a faxed sheet displaying the time and location of their package's delivery and the name of the person who signed for it. By 1996 this simple fax system had evolved into UPS's interactive home page on the World Wide Web through which customers could check the status of their shipments. Customers also could schedule pickups, get price estimates for shipping their packages, and make billing inquiries. By 1997, Federal Express's online system claimed more than 400,000 customers who generated more than 60 percent of the company's two million-plus daily transactions. In January 1997 alone, more than 800,000 packages were tracked via the Web, and its Internet transactions were growing at the rate 10 to 12 percent a month.

Other advanced technology applications in the ground courier industry in the 1990s included parcel processing systems capable of sorting 20,000 packages per hour, and satellite computer systems that could locate courier fleet trucks as closely as 300 yards or better.

FURTHER READING

''Competition Fierce in Complex Business of Delivering Packages.'' *Marketing News* 29, no. 11, 5.

''Deliverance for UPS?'' *Atlanta Business Chronicle* 18, no. 36, 6A.

''Delivering Growth.'' *Fortune,* September 4, 1995, 137.

''Follow the Flag of Convenience.'' *Economist,* 22 February 1997, 75.

Gillam, Carey. ''Delivering the Dream.'' *Sales & Marketing Management* 148, no. 6, 74.

''Hauling UPS's Freight.'' *Time,* January 29, 1996, 59.

Hawcroft, Sam. ''United Parcel Service Joint Venture in Beijing.'' *Asian Business Review,* August 1996, 21.

Lee, Mie-Yun. ''Are You Sure It's as Easy as Signed, Sealed and Delivered?'' *Business First—Western New York,* April 1, 1996, 17.

Pols, Mary F. ''Postal Service, UPS Face Busiest Days.'' *Contra Costa Times,* December 18, 1999.

Smith, Marjie. ''Canada Post Irks Couriers.'' *Northern Ontario Business,* July 1995, 27.

''Thirty-five Cents per Letter.'' *Alberta Report/Western Report,* June 26, 1995, 15.

Thompson, Richard. ''Federal Express' Memphis, Tenn.-Based Parent Reports Low Earnings.'' *The Commercial Appeal,* December 17, 1999.

Thurmond, Jeffery. ''Shipping into the Next Century.'' *National Public Accountant,* June 96, 13.

''UPS: Will This IPO Deliver?'' *Business Week,* November 15, 1999.

''UPS Hubs in Taiwan.'' *Asian Business Review,* May 1996, 23.

''UPS Pins Its Future Growth on the Skies.'' *Atlanta Business Chronicle,* December 8, 1995, 3A.

''U.S. Delivery, Corporate Express Agree to Merger in Same-day Arena.'' *Traffic World,* January 29, 1996, 33.

U.S. Bureau of Transportation Statistics, ''Selected Earnings Data, Class 1 Motor Carriers of Property, 1997 (UPS, Inc. statistics),'' August 3, 1998.

SIC 4221

FARM PRODUCT WAREHOUSING AND STORAGE

This category includes establishments primarily engaged in the warehousing and storage of farm products. Farm product warehouses provide temporary storage for non-perishable agricultural products such as grain. Establishments primarily engaged in refrigerated warehousing are classified in **SIC 4222: Refrigerated Warehousing and Storage.**

NAICS CODE(S)

493130 (Farm Product Storage Facilities)

INDUSTRY SNAPSHOT

Consumer demand is one of the most important factors that stimulates consolidation and vertical integration of the farm product warehousing industry. This development mirrors what has already occurred in other agriculture sectors such as pork, poultry, and vegetable processing. In the 1990s, per capita consumption of cereal and flour products was up 25 percent since 1968, while consumption of animal products expanded 1 percent. After four consecutive years of abundant harvests worldwide, the 1999 international demand for farm produce was weak, forcing farm prices to drop, domestically and on exports. Conversely, as demand waned, storage warehousing and insurance on agricultural products increased. Commercial storage of grain alone in 1999 was estimated at 8 billion bushels, with another 11 billion stored on farms. This was notwithstanding $53 billion in U.S. farm exports in 1998.

BACKGROUND AND DEVELOPMENT

Warehousing was established as a significant link between producers and consumers by 1783, particularly at port cities. Before elevator mechanization, grain was stored and shipped in sacks or barrels. A chain-bucket system to move grain from bins into elevators was invented in 1785 and improved in 1843, achieving widespread use by the 1860s. Before modern roads and rail transportation, country storekeepers doubled as warehousers who traded commodities and offered credit. Transportation and storage improvements made it profitable to grow grains at greater distances from major markets, spurring the development of commodity exchanges.

The warehousing industry refined its basic function from simple storage and handling of bulk materials toward supplying the market with custom products; the baking industry launches 1,000 new products a year to satisfy demand for variety, quality, safety, convenience, price, and environmental compatibility. The shift demanded skillful management and specialized knowledge as warehousing evolves from high-volume processing to a transitional role in value-added product innovation.

Communication skills became more important as grain handlers link producers and manufacturers. Computer-literate elevator personnel—fluent in crop varieties, fertilizers, finance, marketing, and sales—offer a wider range of services to high-tech farmers and end-users. Growers delivered a variety of grains as raw materials for developing niche markets. In addition to cash crops such as corn, wheat, and soybeans, farmers produced barley, durum, rice, sunflowers, flax, edible beans, and other specialty crops. Advances in genetics and grain monitoring spurred demand for specialized end products. Crops were manipulated for food quality, protein yield, and mold resistance. Insects were detected by acoustic monitors. Nucleic acid probes discovered microbes, pesticides, and antibiotics.

Over 9,000 elevators were in operation in the United States in 1982, dropping to fewer than 8,000 by the mid-1990s. The top 44 U.S. firms primarily in the farm product warehousing and storage business posted total earnings between $1 and $3 billion in the 1990s. Some of the larger companies were Federal Compress and Warehouse Company Inc., of Memphis, Tennessee; Prairie Central Cooperative Company Inc., of Chenoa, Illinois; and international food products giant Archer-Daniels-Midland Company (ADM) of Decatur, Illinois. Archer-Daniels, whose 1999 sales were $14.3 billion, owned 800 trucks, 2,000 river barges, and 13,000 rail cars. Another giant, Continental Grain Inc., was acquired in 1999 by Cargill, Inc., a commodities trading and processing company. Continental had owned 54 grain storage and transport facilities in the United States, which were transferred in the deal.

As 1999 came to a close, agricultural commodities stocks were large,—not only from 1998 surplus, but also from record crop harvests. Storage and warehousing was bulging at the seams, but farmers tried to offset storage costs by self-storing as much as possible. Total crop receipts for 2000 were expected to be approximately $1.7 billion below 1999, and the lowest since 1994. To offset this decline, governmental assistance was enhanced, including emergency assistance legislation in the form of loan deficiency payments in October 1998 and October 1999.

FURTHER READING

Archer Daniels Midland Company Annual Report 1996. Decatur, Ill.: Archer Daniels Midland Company, 1996.

Beurskens, Frank. *Change in the Grain Warehousing Industry.* Bloomington, Ill.: 1994. Available from http://www.agribiz.com/fbFiles/readings/MEGA.html.

Burns, Greg. ''Archer Daniels Midland Tells Unhappy Shareholders of Plans to Cut Costs.'' *Chicago Tribune,* October 22, 1999.

Burns, Greg. ''Exporters Such As Archer Daniels Midland Accept Slow Progress on Trade.'' *Chicago Tribune,* December 3, 1999.

Cook, Michael. *Food and Agricultural Markets: The Quiet Revolution.* National Planning As sociation, 1994. Available from http://www.agribiz.com/fbFiles/tNews/cook.html.

''Emergency Assistance Legislation Boosts 1999 Farm Income to above the 1990-1999 average.'' USDA, available at http://www.econ.ag.gov/briefing/farmincome/fore/fore.htm

Keith, Kendall. ''Competitiveness In Agriculture and Food Marketing.'' FDCH Congressional Testimony, October 20, 1999.

National Agricultural Statistics Service, USDA. Available from http://usda.mannlib.cornell.edu/reports/nassr/

Pedraza, Juan Miguel. ''North Dakota Elevators Tower Over the Economic Landscape.'' *Grand Forks Herald Tribune,* August 4, 1996.

Shean, Tom. ''Government Restricts Commodities Trader From Buying Rival's Grain.'' *The Virginian-Pilot,* July 15, 1999.

SIC 4222

REFRIGERATED WAREHOUSING AND STORAGE

NAICS CODE(S)

493120 (Refrigerated Storage Facilities)

This category includes establishments primarily engaged in the warehousing and storage of perishable goods under refrigeration. The establishments may also rent locker space for the storage of food products for individual households and provide incidental services for processing, preparing, or packaging such food for storage. Establishments primarily selling frozen foods for home freezers (freezer and locker meat provisioners) are classified in **SIC 5421: Meat and Fish (Seafood) Markets, Including Freezer Provisioners.**

In 1999 roughly 240 companies provided public refrigerated warehousing and storage services in more than 625 facilities. According to the International Association of Refrigerated Warehouses (IARW), there was a record total of 2.1 billion cubic feet of refrigerated/frozen storage in North America in 1999. The USDA estimated 2.73 billion cubic feet, but this figure included private as well as public storage space. The five states containing the largest gross general warehouse capacity were California, Florida, Washington, Texas, and Wisconsin. According to the USDA, there has been a 59 percent increase in capacity in the past 10 years. While refrigerated storage is generally used for food products, it also serves the pharmaceutical, chemical, medical and scientific industries as well.

Cold storage operators have historically acted as middlemen between the manufacturers and the grocery or convenience store retailers. They provide storage and distribution services for domestic and international clients. These operators have been able to meet the needs of their clients by offering, through the latest technology, an efficient and inexpensive way to store their goods.

Many cold storage warehouses are at seaports where volumes of perishables are imported and exported. Berkshire Foods Inc. operates the cold storage facility at the Port of Savannah, Georgia, which is owned by the Georgia Ports Authority. Berkshire also operates four warehouse facilities, which include more than 4 million cubic feet of freezer space at −5 to −30 degrees Fahrenheit.

Companies, including seaports, that would otherwise have to operate large warehouses and spend considerable resources on computerized tracking systems are able to avail themselves of services from the cold storage operators. Throughout the second half of the twentieth century, cold storage operators developed expertise through experimentation and the application of new technology that food manufacturers were anxious to use. With the passage of time, the reproduction of this expertise became costly and time-consuming for food manufacturers. Therefore, food manufacturers elected to outsource their food storage needs to a refrigerated storage expert.

Since the 1970s, moreover, the use of artificial preservatives as a means of keeping food fresh has come under increasing scrutiny from health-conscious consumers. As a result, the demand for frozen foods, which do not contain as many preservatives, has increased. Cold storage providers were indirect beneficiaries of this evolving market trend.

IARW listed the top refrigerated warehouse companies in 1999 as: Americold Logistics, with 519.5 million cubic feet in 99 facilities; Millard Refrigerated Services, with 164.8 million cubic feet in 24 facilities; CS Integrated, with 140.6 million cubic feet in 29 facilities; United States Cold Storage, with 102.0 million cubic feet in 31 facilities; and Associated Freezers, with 61.8 million cubic feet in 20 facilities. Other industry leaders include Versacold Group, Nordic Refrigerated Services, Atlas Cold Storage, and Interstate Warehousing. Americold was sold to a real estate trust partnership in 1997 for $1 billion.

In addition to the IARW, the industry is also promoted by an organization known as the World Group, which celebrated its twentieth anniversary in 1998. World Group is a consortium of eight public refrigerator warehouse companies in the United States and Canada. Their common interests are to promote state-of-the-art technology and to simplify manufacturers' distribution processes.

Further Reading

"Capacity of Refrigerated Warehouses, 1997." USDA National Agricultural Statistics Service, January 1998. Available from http://usda.mannlib.cornell.edu/reports/nassr.

Merli, Joseph. "IARW Census Lists Top 20 PRW Firms." *Frozen Food Age,* October 1999.

Walker, Susanne. "Crescent Reportedly Looking to Sell Americold Stake to Vornado." *Real Estate Finance & Investment,* January 1999.

"The World Group, at 20, Looks to Upcoming New Initiatives." *Frozen Food Age,* March 1998.

SIC 4225

GENERAL WAREHOUSING AND STORAGE

This category includes establishments primarily engaged in the warehousing and storage of a general line of goods. The warehousing of goods at foreign trade zones is discussed under **SIC 4226: Special Warehousing and Storage, Not Elsewhere Classified.** Field warehousing is found under **SIC 7389: Business Services, Not Elsewhere Classified.**

NAICS Code(s)

493110 (General Warehousing and Storage Facilities)
531130 (Miniwarehouses and Self Storage Units)

Industry Snapshot

Operating between shippers and carriers, companies engaged in the general warehousing business were third parties in the transportation industry. These businesses provided a variety of transportation and distribution services in addition to storage. As the industry entered the new millennium, large general warehousing companies offered value-added services ranging from customer billing to salvage and scrap disposal, and were marketing themselves as logistics services providers rather than as storage companies.

Logistics, a term the transportation industry borrowed from the military, refers to all phases of the distribution process. Logistics-related services were provided by various industries including public warehouses, parcel express, and freight transport. In the 1990s, boundaries between these industries were blurring, and an integrated logistics industry was emerging.

The general warehouse industry enjoyed strong growth in the early 1990s, but began to slack toward the end of the decade. According to Insurance Market Research (IMR) Corp., there were 123,384 trucking and warehousing firms in the United States, in all categories. Between 40 and 50 percent of all public warehousing revenue was from the subcategory of general warehousing and storage. The growth of the industry was a result of the trend by manufacturers and distributors toward "outsourcing," or using third-party support for operations outside the core business. During this time, an increasing number of manufacturers and distributors contracted with general warehouses instead of operating in-house warehouses. However, by the end of the 1990s, warehousing costs had risen so high that the Warehousing Education & Research Council (WERC) confirmed a 1999 *decrease* in the number of operating warehouses.

Organization and Structure

General warehousing companies received and shipped goods on behalf of their customers, serving as middlemen in the transportation process and a vital part of the logistics business. Although some of the large general warehousing companies, such as GATX Logistics, Inc. and DMSI, Inc., of Charlotte, North Carolina, operated their own trucking fleets, normally an independent carrier was used to transport the goods. The carrier was chosen either by the customer or by the warehouse operator who then acted as the customer's agent.

Like most transportation-related businesses, the general warehouse industry was well-organized on a national level. Four trade associations, Affiliated Warehouse Companies, Allied Distribution, American Chain of Warehouses, and American Warehouse Association, founded in 1953, 1933, 1911, and 1891, respectively, maintained national networks for marketing, sales, and industry lobbying. Because this industry operated between the vast manufacturing industry and the powerful transport industry, national organization was critical to the preservation of its own interests.

Competitive Structure. Although eight multi-regional companies dominated the general warehousing business, dozens of medium and small companies operated throughout the country. Entry into this industry was relatively easy for businesses proposing to operate locally; expanding demand and low start up costs encouraged new entrants. In fact, from 1988 to 1993 the number of firms in the industry nearly tripled. Entering the mid-1990s warehouse expenditures were declining due to lowered costs of data processing equipment, furniture, and overhead labor. Self-storage companies found the conditions particularly inviting. Public and contract warehouse operators involved in logistics, however, faced an increasingly competitive environment in which service and technology were critical to success.

Although expanding demand and relatively low barriers to entry encouraged new entrants, competition for national market share was strong. Once a shipper chose a warehouse operator, especially one that offered logistics support, a strong relationship developed, and the cost of switching to another warehouse operator was high. Expanding market share, therefore, was difficult. The largest firms faced competition from national trucking companies and specialized distribution services in the logistics sector. In the warehouse sector, these companies competed with manufacturers' in-house storage operations. To gain market share, the national operators invested heavily in technology to differentiate their services.

Background and Development

General warehouses have operated in the United States since colonial days. Located in major ports such as Boston, these early warehouses were used as repositories for goods being shipped to and from England. These warehouses served as temporary housing for the exports of raw materials, such as cotton, and imports such as finished goods like textiles.

It was not until the completion of the railroad trunk lines around 1860 that warehouses began to move from the port cities into the nation's interior. During this time, industry was developing in the northeastern states, and the western farm lands were producing corn and wheat for consumption in the east and for export.

General warehouses grew with the nation's economy. As production techniques became more efficient, finished goods were produced faster, allowing manufacturers to develop inventories that required storage. Manufacturers that could not afford to maintain a warehouse paid a public warehouse operator to store finished products and raw materials. Often, manufacturers would ship their products to and from warehouses at major railroad terminals.

From its inception, the primary function of the general warehouse industry was storage. During the twentieth century, however, the transportation industry became more complex. Manufacturers faced several regulations regarding interstate shipping and had to choose between hundreds of transport companies in the truck, rail, and air freight transport business. Moreover, the deregulation of trucking in the early 1980s caused an explosion in the number of companies providing truck services. As the transportation landscape became more difficult to navigate, shippers turned to warehouse operators for more services including the arrangement of freight distribution.

The increased reliance on warehouse operators for services other than storage prompted some warehouses to diversify into different transportation areas. After deregulation of the truck business, for example, some warehouses operated private trucking fleets used for distribution. Others became involved in combining small shipments of freight from various shippers into truckload shipments. These types of services were more typical of freight forwarders or transport companies than of general warehouse operators. At the same time, however, freight forwarders and truckers were offering storage services in addition to their primary functions.

Such overlap in services resulted in the emergence of the logistics industry. In fact, the various industries already providing logistics-related services were involved in a cooperative marketing campaign called "Think Logistics." The marketing effort was developed in the wake of research indicating that, according to Michael Jenkins, president of the American Warehouse Association, the "traditional lines between freight transportation and warehousing, or brokerage and warehousing, or even manufacturing and warehousing were beginning to blur." By the mid-1990s, many warehouse operators had developed from temporary caretakers of raw materials and finished goods into logistics experts.

The precarious position of the general warehouse operator, between shippers and carriers, was illustrated in the legislative battle over "carrier undercharge." Carrier undercharge occurred when truck companies quoted shippers lower freight rates than were prescribed by the various rate bureaus throughout the country and then failed to file the discounted tariffs with the rate bureaus. An undercharge crisis occurred in the early 1990s when many truck companies went bankrupt. During the reorganization or failure of these truck companies, it became clear that some carriers had charged rates that did not match those on file at the Interstate Commerce Commission (ICC). In the wake of these discoveries, shippers were receiving bills for "carrier undercharge" from the trustees of the bankrupt truck companies. Often the undercharge bill arrived months or years after the freight was shipped.

By 1992, undercharge claims exceeded $30 billion. In cases in which warehouse operators arranged the transportation of a manufacturer's goods, the warehouse operator received the undercharge bill. At this point, the warehouse operator had to either risk sabotaging a business relationship by trying to recover the undercharge costs from the true shipper, his client, or pay the bill himself.

The undercharge debate raged in Congress for years. In 1993, Congress passed the Negotiated Rates Act, legislation that set procedures for resolving claims involving unfiled, negotiated transportation rates. The legislation favored shipper interests and included a subsection allowing the public warehouse to settle for 5 percent of the claim, with any disputes settled by the ICC.

The fact that the public warehouse industry was mentioned specifically in this legislation attested to its lobbying skills and highlighted the industry's ability to defend its interests. Had this legislation not been passed, warehouses were in a position to lose millions of dollars in undercharge payments and court battles related to the payments.

In the mid-1990s, co-ops become the latest trend among suppliers and distributors, as companies combined their resources into one network to take advantage of economies in transportation and warehousing. Most of their arrangements were made by suppliers or shippers through third parties. These types of arrangements benefited companies by reducing inventories, extending buying power, saving costs, improving service, and producing less paperwork.

The general warehousing industry was the beneficiary of corporate America's strategic responses to the 1989-90 recession. Corporate downsizing, inventory management, and increased customer service all became important competitive priorities as manufacturers struggled to turn a profit in a weak economy. General warehouse operators provided the services necessary for companies to employ these strategies.

Corporate Downsizing. Faced with an increasingly competitive business environment and a weak economy, many large corporations underwent major downsizing during the early 1990s. As a result, operations not related to the core business of the corporation were eliminated. Often, these operations were connected with in-house storage and distribution. Many large manufacturing companies such as Eveready Battery Corp. considered public warehousing to be a cheaper and more efficient alternative to operating company-owned warehouses. Eveready switched to 100 percent public warehousing in the early 1990s; as a result, in 1992, Eveready estimated that it saved $2.1 million, at a cost of $1.4 million.

Mothercare, a 200 store maternity retailer, also switched from private to public warehousing during the early 1990s. Mothercare hired DMSI to handle its logistics, from arranging transportation into DMSI warehouses to distributing merchandise by means of the DMSI fleet. In New Jersey, general warehouse storage was booming in 1999, with more than 60,000 people employed in the industry in that state. Volkswagen, Barnes & Noble, Tommy Hilfiger, and Howmedica all had built distribution centers in New Jersey in the latter 1990s.

Also affecting the evolution: increased competition from alternative formats, such as mass merchandisers and warehouse clubs caused food distributors to rethink and reengineer their distribution strategies. For Fleming Companies, of Oklahoma City, Oklahoma, the nation's largest supermarket distributor, this meant fundamentally reinventing its business. For years, Fleming had served as the ''middle man'' between product manufacturers and grocery store retailers. By 1996, it operated as a major distributor and supplier of virtually every national brand and high-volume private label, as well as a variety of general merchandise and full lines of perishables, including meats, dairy and delicatessen products, frozen foods and fresh produce. By incorporating ''Efficient Consumer Response'' (ECR), Fleming repositioned itself as a value-added marketing and distribution company providing goods and services. ECR made it possible for customers to pick and choose which services they wanted and pay for only those used. In 1996, Fleming's sales topped $17 billion. That same year, Fleming had 41 supply centers nationwide, and 44,000 employees servicing more than 3,500 supermarkets in 42 states, the District of Columbia and several foreign countries. It operated approximately 370 company-owned stores.

Inventory Management. In addition to corporate downsizing, American businesses were eager to increase inventory turnover as a means of streamlining operations. As a result, Just-in-Time (JIT) inventory management was being used by more companies than ever before. In fact, logistics expert Robert V. Delaney of Cass Logistics estimated that by 2000 close to 40 percent of U.S. products would be shipped on a time-based standard, and that most deliveries from warehouses would be completed in 37 hours or less.

However, the successful execution of JIT required constant monitoring of inventory levels and flexibility on the part of shippers. JIT generally required more frequent, but smaller shipments of goods to and from warehouses. Public and contract warehouses were often better equipped than in-house warehouses to execute time-based inventory management. A critical advantage held by public warehouses was their ability to create economies of scale in distribution. In 1992, public contract warehouses shipped nearly 2 trillion pounds of product from their warehouses. With this volume, the warehouses often had more leverage than a small manufacturer with suppliers and carriers. The warehouse operator, therefore, could dictate the size and frequency of the shipment to meet JIT inventory requirements.

Furthermore, public warehouses could dedicate more resources to inventory management than would be efficient for some manufacturers. Expensive technology such as Electronic Data Interchange (EDI), bar coding, radio-frequency technology, scanners and specialized logistics software was critical to the successful implementation of JIT and prohibitively costly to some companies. Public warehouses, however, were able to spread the cost of this technology over many customers. By 1996, transport and logistics industries had become the world leaders in the use of advanced technologies such as EDI. USCO Distribution Services, of Naugatuck, Connecticut, for example, repaired personal computers, printers, and monitors for IBM. Some companies stated that they used public warehouses for service rather than storage.

Current Conditions

The 1999 Annual Report published by *Logistics Management & Distribution* confirmed the shift to fewer but larger warehouse facilities. Warehousing costs, as a percentage of sales, rose 3.72 percent between 1997 and 1998. To compensate, warehouses began adding assembly, prepackaging and special labeling ''value-added services'' for their customers.

Respondents to a 1998 WERC member survey indicated that companies had decreased the number of warehouses in their networks by more than 2.5 percent for 1998 and expected to do the same in 1999. Manufacturing companies led the greatest decline, projecting a 23 percent decrease in the number of warehouses used (wholesalers predicted a slight increase).

New facilities in 1999 were estimated at 40 to 80 percent larger than existing warehouses. While this was expected to contain some of the rising costs, other factors could not be controlled. According to the 600-member International Warehouse Logistics Association (IWLA), labor, information technology, and ISO 9000 certification compliance remained key budget expenses at the end of the 1990s.

Industry Leaders

The top 1998 general warehouse contractors (by square foot of warehouse space) were: Exel Logistics Americas (25.0 million square feet); GATX Logistics (23.0 million); Tibbet & Britten (15.1 million); DSC Logistics (11.8 million); and the Kenco Group (11.2 million).

Jacksonville, Florida's GATX Logistics, a subsidiary of GATX Corporation, continued to expand in global logistics warehousing, revenues having been so high from its Mexico City facility in 1997 that it opened a similar facility in Santiago, Chile, in 1998, and expanded another 250,000 square feet in the Grand Prairie, Texas, Great Southwest Industrial District. In 1999, it also announced plans to open a 300,000 square foot building in Hebron, Kentucky. The company's net income for the third quarter of 1999 increased 11 percent to $42 million, with third quarter net earnings of $1.1 million.

RESEARCH AND TECHNOLOGY

Employing the latest standards in shipping and warehouse technology was an industry standard for general warehouse operators. Because so many of the companies marketed themselves as logistics experts and as purveyors of value-added services, having the latest technological innovations was necessary to meet customer expectations. Within the warehouse industry itself, moreover, flexibility and efficiency were necessary to the survival of a firm. Technology enabled businesses to maintain levels of productivity.

One type of technology that saw rapid acceptance throughout the transportation industry was electronic data interchange (EDI). Allowing shipper and receivers to transmit invoices electronically, this mainframe computer system greatly reduced the routine paperwork associated with distribution. EDI was used by many large companies throughout the nation, putting pressure on general warehouse operators to install the system if they wanted to do business with these large companies.

In addition to EDI, general warehouses used electronic devices such as bar coding and radio frequency monitoring. These innovations enhanced the productivity and efficiency of warehouse operations and simplified inventory tracking. As customer expectations became more stringent and competition in the general warehouse industry increased, more warehouses were forced to invest in technology to remain contenders.

Improved technology appeared to contribute to the growth of the general warehousing industry. As traditional in-house storage and management facilities became obsolete, and the cost of upgrading outweighed the benefits of maintaining the facility, manufacturers looked to general warehouses to provide the high tech warehousing facilities necessary for survival.

FURTHER READING

Andel, Tom. "Cost Cutting Adds to Your Value." *Transportation & Distribution,* April 1996.

———. "There's Power in Numbers." *Transportation & Distribution,* August 1995.

———. "Forge a New Role in the Supply Chain." *Transportation & Distribution,* February 1996.

Andel, Tom, and Sarah Bergin. "Does Your Warehouse Have More Service in Store?" *Transportation & Distribution,* April 1996.

"Avante Garde: GATX Distributes Mexico." *Export Today,* August 1999.

Bronstad. " GATX Adding 250,000 SF to GSWID Space." *Business Press,* 24 September 1999.

"GATX Opens Facility." *The Business Journal of Jacksonville, Florida,* 19 November 1999.

"Public Warehousing Service." *Motor Freight and Warehousing Survey: 1995.* U.S. Bureau of the Census, 1997.

"Services to the Industry." *Chemical Week,* 27 October 1999.

Thuermer, Karen. "Fleming Cos. Flexes Its Logistics to Meet Retailer Demands." *Traffic World,* 12 August 1996.

"Trucking & Warehousing." *Rough Notes,* August 1998.

"Warehousing: Costs Are Rising." *Logistics Management & Distribution,* July 1999.

"Warehousing is Location, Location, Location." *Logistics Management & Distribution,* July 1999.

Zuckerman, Amy. "Sizzling Pace of Technology, But Brutal Competition Propel Revolution in Warehousing and Distribution." *Traffic World,* 22 April 1996.

SIC 4226

SPECIAL WAREHOUSING AND STORAGE, NOT ELSEWHERE CLASSIFIED

This category includes establishments primarily engaged in the warehousing and storage of special products, not elsewhere classified, such as household goods, automobiles (dead storage only), furs (for the trade), textiles, oil, chemicals, lumber, whiskey, and goods at foreign trade zones. Warehouses primarily engaged in blending wines are classified in **SIC 5182: Wine and Distilled Alcoholic Beverages.**

NAICS CODE(S)

493120 (Refrigertated Storage Facilities)
493110 (General Warehousing and Storage Facilities)
493190 (All Other Warehousing and Storage Facilities)

The special warehousing and storage industry is a heterogeneous group of companies serving a variety of niche-oriented markets. Businesses in this industry serve clients with both specific and unique storage needs. Because of this diversity, changes in the types of firms in operation occur frequently. In 1995, approximately 1,400 firms engaged in special storage and warehousing, and, when combined, generated roughly $2.8 billion in operating revenues. Revenue growth in the 1990s for this industry has averaged more than 10 percent annually. Employment in this industry was estimated at 20,000 workers.

The majority of special warehousing and storage businesses in the 1990s were involved in petroleum bulk storage and oil and gasoline storage. Most of these warehouses were located in the vicinity of oil refineries in Texas and Oklahoma.

A growing trend in the industry, however, is indicated by the steadily rising number of firms offering storage services at foreign trade zones. These facilities have expanded their services in response to increasing international trade. Frequently, these foreign trade zone warehouses are operated by companies whose primary business is custom house brokerage, classified in **SIC 4731: Arrangement of Transportation of Freight and Cargo.**

Companies engaged in petroleum-related storage benefited from the passage of the Clean Air Act and other environmental regulation requirements. Because states like California adopted stringent pollution control requirements in the mid-1990s, petroleum companies were forced to deliver the cleanest burning fuel available to certain markets. This clean burning fuel is shipped and stored separately from conventional gasoline and is often blended with special additives, such as oxygenates, before final delivery to gas stations.

These storage and handling requirements were taxing for gasoline manufacturers with large, inflexible operations. The petroleum storage operators, however, were positioned to capitalize on the increased storage and processing demands. These specialty warehouse operators provided customers with safe, efficient, and reliable alternatives to storing and processing the fuel in-house.

While many companies provided petroleum storage, GATX Terminals, Inc., the largest independent bulk terminal operation in the world, controlled the domestic industry. The company boasted 73 million barrels of storage worldwide, employed 6,000 workers in all operations, and generated approximately $298 million in gross income for fiscal 1996. In 1996 GATX reported that 54 percent of its storage revenues came from petroleum, 25 percent from chemical storage, 20 percent from pipelines, and 1 percent from other products. GATX's bulk-liquid storage, distribution, and pipeline business rose sharply in 1999, with third quarter 1999 net earnings at $6 million.

As with petroleum storage, demand for foreign trade zone storage increased in the 1990s. As companies expanded internationally, their traditional storage and distribution operations have, in some cases, fell behind the competition. Rather than building large international transportation departments, some companies chose to hire outside companies to manage international storage and distribution. In an effort to better serve customers, some foreign trade zone warehouse operators introduced customs brokerage services and freight forwarding, in addition to warehousing. These comprehensive packages provide customers with one-stop shopping in the international logistics market.

FURTHER READING

GATX Corporation. *GATX Corporation 1996 Annual Report.* Chicago, 1997.

''Service to the Industry: GATX Profits Up.'' *Chemical Week,* 27 October, 1999,

U.S. Bureau of the Census. *Motor Freight Transportation and Warehousing Survey: 1995.* Washington, DC: GPO, 1997.

———. *Statistical Abstract of the United States 1996.* Washington, DC: GPO, 1996.

SIC 4231

TERMINAL AND JOINT TERMINAL MAINTENANCE FACILITIES FOR MOTOR FREIGHT TRANSPORTATION

This category includes establishments primarily engaged in the operation of terminal facilities used by highway-type property carrying vehicles. Also included are terminals that provide maintenance and service for motor vehicles. Terminals operated by motor freight transportation companies for their own use are classified in **SIC 4212: Local Trucking Without Storage; SIC 4213: Trucking, Except Local; SIC 4214: Local Trucking With Storage;** or **SIC 4215: Courier Services, Except by Air.** Separate maintenance and service facilities operated by motor freight transportation companies are classified as auxiliary.

NAICS CODE(S)

488490 (Other Support Activities for Road Transportation)

Only a handful of companies—52, according to the U.S. Department of Commerce's *County Business Patterns 1994*—provided trucking terminal facilities in 1994 (the last report available). While there are thousands of trucking terminals in the United States, most of these facilities are operated by trucking companies themselves and therefore are not included in this category. The 52 establishments employed 533 employees. The majority of the establishments (35) employed one to four workers, while only one company employed more than 100. The annual payroll for the entire industry stood at $15.78 million in 1994.

Although trucking terminals provide a number of services, including showers for truckers and truck maintenance and repair, these establishments are primarily used for their storage and consolidation facilities. Freight is combined and redistributed at these terminals in an effort to reduce the distances and costs of transportation. Terminals, therefore, are located in areas where the demand for transportation is high, and terminals are continually relocated according to shifting traffic patterns.

The truck terminal industry boomed after the deregulation of the industry as a whole in 1980. Deregulation resulted in a 160 percent increase in the number of registered truckers between 1980 and 1991. These new truck companies were often small operations that could not afford to operate their own terminals. As the industry moved into the 1990s, however, shifts in both the economy and in distribution patterns reversed the truck terminal expansion. Although an increase in traffic in the southeastern United States fostered terminal growth in the south, many existing terminals were closed in the early 1990s.

A number of factors precipitated the terminal closings, such as the waning health of the trucking industry. By the late 1980s, many of the smaller operators who emerged after deregulation had been forced out of business. The post-deregulation boom was ended by the recession and an increase in competition from parcel carriers such as United Parcel Services. The remaining companies were large and generally operated their own terminal facilities. Even these large trucking companies were forced to streamline their terminal networks in the 1990s.

The focus on efficiency and quality in the 1990s further encouraged terminal closings. Shippers and truckers were committed to reducing cargo damage and handling costs. These reductions were often achieved by minimizing the number of times freight was handled. As such, truck terminals were eliminated from the transportation equation if their use proved unnecessary according to freight handling standards, which emphasized efficiency over short-term cost savings.

One bright spot in the trucking terminal facility industry was the growth of the intermodal industry in the 1990s. Intermodalism, or piggybacking, is the use of two or more modes of transportation for freight movement. Often, railroads were unable to obtain right-of-way into ports because of the unavailability of land, creating an opportunity for intermodal truck terminals to be built in major ports. According to the 1997 *Transportation Statistics Annual Report* of the U.S. Department of Transportation's Bureau of Statistics, intermodal truck-rail shipments for 1993 (the latest statistic available) accounted for 41 million tons of cargo, with a gross value of $83 billion dollars. Employment statistics for 1998 indicated that the transportation services industry as a whole employed 417,000 people in 1996.

The truck terminal industry appeared to be in transition in the 1990s. Although the decline of the trucking industry had a negative impact on terminals, the growth in intermodal service presented opportunities for truck terminal facility expansion. Truck terminal owners continue to reevaluate location and access in search of new opportunities in a shrinking market.

Further Reading

U.S. Department of Commerce. *County Business Patterns 1994.* Washington, DC: GPO, 1996.

U.S. Department of Transportation. *Transportation Statistics Annual Report 1997.* Table 9-5. Washington, DC: GPO 1997

SIC 4311

UNITED STATES POSTAL SERVICE

This industry includes all establishments of the United States Postal Service.

NAICS Code(s)

491110 (Postal Service)

Industry Snapshot

The U.S. Postal Service is one of the largest organizations in the world. In fiscal 1998 it had more than 775,000 employees and handled about 198 billion pieces of mail through an extremely complicated system of carefully coordinated activities. In addition to the national headquarters in Washington, D.C., the U.S. Postal Service consisted of regional and field division offices that together supervised 38,000 post offices, branches, stations, and community post offices throughout the United States. The U.S. Postal Service had a fleet of more than 200,000 vehicles and shipped 10.5 million pounds of mail daily on commercial airlines, making it the nation's biggest shipper. It was the largest civilian employer in the United States.

The U.S. Postal Service was created as an independent establishment out of the old Post Office Department by the Postal Reorganization Act of 1970, and commenced operations on July 1, 1971. The industry was highly labor intensive, with employee wages and benefits accounting for 85 percent of the system's total costs. To cope with its soaring costs, the organization increased postal rates consistently, from 6 cents at the onset of the Postal Reorganization Act to 33 cents in 1999 for first-class letters. It also faced increasing competition from private mail and package delivery services and new technologies such as facsimile services and electronic mail and bill paying that reduced the need for postal services.

ORGANIZATION AND STRUCTURE

The purpose of the U.S. Postal Service was to process and deliver mail to individuals and businesses within the United States. This mission also entailed handling mail efficiently and protecting it from loss or theft. The Postal Service handled about 198 billion pieces of mail in 1998 through its interrelated system of 38,000 post office branches.

Organizational Hierarchy. At the top of the Postal Service's organizational hierarchy is a team of 39 officers. In charge of these officers is the postmaster general (PMG) and the deputy postmaster general, whose authority derived from the Postal Reorganization Act. The PMG is appointed by the 9 governors of the Postal Service, who are, in turn, appointed by the president with the advice and permission of the Senate for overlapping 9-year terms. The governors and the PMG together appoint the deputy PMG, and these 11 people together form the board of governors. The remaining officers are appointed by the PMG, and the board of governors determines the nature and scope of activities of these officers. These officers consist of 2 associate postmasters general, 5 senior assistant postmasters general, 19 assistant postmasters general, 6 other headquarters functional heads, and 5 regional postmasters general. In addition to these officers, there are approximately 800 other persons in senior management positions in the country.

Geographical Distribution. The activities of the Postal Service are divided over five postal regions: central, eastern, northeastern, southern, and western. The reason for such field division is to reduce administrative layers and incorporate operating management expertise as near as possible to the locations where postal services are offered to the public. Each of the five regions has a number of "field divisions" that are regarded as the Postal Service's key organizational units, with all other local offices reporting to a division. Moreover, there are 74 field divisions located in key cities throughout the country, and there is a regional chief inspector at each of the five regions of the Postal Service. Any information or complaint with regard to postal violations is required to be presented to the closest postal inspector in authority. The five regional postmasters general are in charge of all the postal activities in a geographical region.

Economic Structure. The Postal Service is not considered a business, but rather a governmental institution designed to serve the U.S. public. When Congress created the Postal Service as an "independent establishment" of the federal government, however, one of the main objectives was to assure financial stability and self-sufficiency for the organization. In the 1970s this seemed a highly ambitious goal. At that time not only did the Postal Service suffer from long-standing operating problems and deficit-producing services, but it also faced a high inflation rate and rising cost of fuel. To cover its costs, the Postal Service received operating subsidies from the government, but these were discontinued in 1982, and the Postal Service has been self-supporting since that time.

The Postal Service is not supported by taxes or government appropriations. As a self-supporting organization, it must obtain its funds from its operating activities or through borrowing. Under this policy its debt reached nearly $10 billion. From 1971 to 1994, prior years' losses accumulated to nearly $9 billion. The Postal Service began to achieve positive net income in 1995, then reported four consecutive years of positive net income through 1998, when it had an operating surplus of $550 million. From 1995 through 1998 the Postal Service had cumulative earnings of $5.1 billion. Its debt was reduced from $9.9 billion in 1992 to $6.4 billion in 1998.

As postage rates were held steady from 1995 until the January 1999 increase, the Postal Service's costs rose over 19 percent for such things as fuel, rent, utilities, salaries, and benefits, causing net income to decline during that period. New postage rates are reviewed and recommended by an independent body, the Postal Rate Commission, and then approved by the board of governors, a process that typically takes a year and a half.

Revenues come from different classes of mail. In 1998, 86 percent of all Postal Service revenue came from three classes of mail: first-class mail (56.6 percent), standard mail (22.9 percent), and priority mail (6.9 percent). Standard mail includes advertising mail, formerly known as third-class or bulk-rate mail.

BACKGROUND AND DEVELOPMENT

The U.S. Postal Service has a long and rich history that began in the early days of the colonial period. This historical period gave birth to the first American post office. Following repeated failures to develop a postal system in colonial America in the seventeenth century, the British government delegated this critical responsibility to Thomas Neal in 1692. Neal's mail service was a dismal failure, and by 1707 the British government acquired the rights to the mail system. Although this new system was more successful than Neal's and broke even in the 1720s, it did not produce a profit until 1761. This newfound profitability was partly due to the management skills of Benjamin Franklin, who became co-deputy postmaster general in 1753, and partly due to a reciprocal agreement between the colonies and England.

Ironically, the successful postal service improved England's control over the American colonies at a time when the relationship between the two was deteriorating. The high postal rates were considered a prime example of ''taxation without representation,'' and some Americans started to send mail via ''alternative'' mail distribution sources, such as postmen not associated with the British mail system who delivered mail for far less than what the colonial post office charged.

In 1774 Maryland newspaper publisher William Goddard initiated an independent postal system called the ''Constitutional Post,'' which eliminated the need for alternative postmen. In 1775 the Second Continental Congress acquired the Constitutional Post and successfully ran the system throughout the Revolutionary War. In 1782 the Confederate Congress wrote an innovative, first-ever postal law allowing the Post Office a monopoly in the carrying and delivering of mail, establishing the office of postmaster general, setting postal rates, and carefully detailing the operating regulations of the postal service.

In 1792 the new Constitution gave Congress the right to establish post offices and roads. Therefore, Congress created a new postal law that established a new U.S. Post Office. This new law was more an addendum to the law of 1782 than a radical new legislation. The primary contribution was the establishment of the principles of the nation's postal policy, which stipulated that the Post Office was to be self-supporting (using any profits to expand the postal service), and that Congress (not the PMG) was to approve post offices and post roads. Therefore, Congress would completely control the post office and its growth. Moreover, the PMG was given the responsibility of managing the postal service, which included providing an annual budget to Congress that estimated the needs of the department.

In response to complaints by both rural and urban customers concerning high postal rates in 1851, Congress reduced the rates and stated that this would in no way reduce the postal service, even if postal deficits resulted from this action. Therefore, a customer-service policy, as opposed to a ''self-supporting'' policy drove the Post Office. This new policy eliminated distance as a factor in determining the price of a letter and led to greater use of the mail service through the modernization of the postal system, although it also produced annual postal deficits.

The next phase of the history of the U.S. Postal Service consisted of a series of significant events, including: initiation of mandatory prepayment of postage and the use of stamps in the 1850s; institution of a registered letter service in 1855 and a city free-delivery system in 1863; development of the first railroad post office in 1864, which revolutionized postal service by allowing employees to sort mail as they traveled on trains; introduction of mail delivery to farm homes in 1896 and parcel service to rural areas in 1913; use of automobiles to deliver the mail, replacing horses, in the early 1900s; and initiation of the first regular airmail service between Washington and New York in 1918. In 1964 zip codes were introduced to identify each postal delivery area in the United States. ''Zip'' is an acronym for ''zone improvement plan.''

Postal Reorganization Act of 1970. The Postal Reorganization Act of 1970, which created the current structure of the U.S. Postal Service, was the most detailed and radical reorganization in two centuries. The postal department was removed from the president's cabinet, and Congress was no longer able to set both postal employee wages and postal rates. The ''new'' Postal Service was able to run more like a business enterprise—for example, it could hire its own personnel.

Other specific changes resulting from the act included: establishment of the board of governors to oversee operations; creation of the independent Postal Rate Commission to provide advice to the board of governors on postal rates and classifications; establishment of provisions for an independent personnel system and direct collective bargaining between postal management and unions; authorization of a general ''public service'' subsidy in an amount equal to 10 percent ($920 million) of the fiscal 1971 appropriations to the Post Office Department through the year 1979, and declining by 1 percent per year through 1984—by which time the Postal Service was expected to be self-sufficient; provision of a plan for gradually phasing out the preferential rates for various categories of mail, and assuring that rates covered only those costs directly applicable to the class plus some ''reasonably assignable'' portion of the system's institutional costs; and authorization to modernize the postal system through borrowing money and issuing public bonds up to $10 billion.

Current Conditions

The Postal Service played a significant role in the development of the United States. Not only did it foster unity among the diverse individuals scattered over the nation, but it also contributed largely to the development of U.S. business. Over the years the U.S. Postal Service has received criticism about frequent rate increases, slow service, and lost mail. Proponents countered that the U.S. Postal Service actually improved the performance of the U.S. mail system in many dimensions, including finances, productivity, and service delivery.

The 1990s, and most notably the years under Postmaster General Marvin Runyon (1992-98), marked a turning point for the Postal Service. From 1995 through 1998 the Postal Service had cumulative earnings of $5.1 billion, compared to cumulative losses from 1971 to 1994 of $9.9 billion. Under Runyon's leadership, the Postal Service successfully set and communicated clear objectives and improved automation, service, and customer satisfaction. It began using private sector tools, such as accepting credit cards and adopting longer hours, to better meet its customers' needs.

Independent surveys confirmed that the Postal Service was achieving higher customer satisfaction. In 1998 the Pew Research Center for the People and the Press reported that 89 percent of Americans rated the Postal Service the most favorably of any federal agency. According to a 1998 Roper Survey, 78 percent of all Americans had a highly or moderately favorable opinion of the Postal Service, the highest ranking of 15 federal agencies.

The Postal Service has an extraordinary tradition of public service. It evolved with the transportation, communications, and technology infrastructure of the United States. It changed the way it operated, found new ways to serve customers, and became more efficient. At the end of the twentieth century the U.S. Congress was seeking ways to clarify the Postal Service's role. As Postmaster General William J. Henderson noted in the 1998 Annual Report, "The potential exists for a redefinition or perhaps even a reregulation of our services."

WORKFORCE

More than 775,000 people were career employees of the Postal Service in 1998, making it the number one civilian employer in the United States. These individuals worked in facilities with contingents varying in size from 1 to more than 40,000 employees. The largest category of postal employees consisted of clerks and mail handlers, which constituted 44 percent of the workforce, or about 350,000 individuals. The next largest category included delivery carriers and vehicle drivers, constituting 237,000 employees, or 30 percent of the total workforce. Nearly 8 percent of this figure, or 65,000 individuals, were full- and part-time rural delivery carriers who performed a variety of tasks. More than 50,000 people held supervisory and managerial positions, and more than 29,000 attended to building and vehicle maintenance. There were 28,000 postmasters in total, and the rest of the workforce filled a number of specialized jobs that ranged from security officer to the postmaster general.

The postal employees in the United States are unionized. The four major organizations that represent the postal workforce in collective bargaining with management over wages and other terms and conditions of employment are: the National Association of Letter Carriers (NALC); the American Postal Workers Union (APWU); the National Rural Letter Carriers' Association; and the National Post Office Mail Handlers, Watchmen, Messengers, and Group Leaders Division of Laborers' International Union of North America. The APWU and the NALC, representing clerks and carriers respectively, were the two largest of these organizations.

During the early 1990s the U.S. Postal Service suffered a series of highly publicized, unfortunate incidents involving disgruntled or former employees. At post offices in several cities, such an employee brought a gun to work and shot fellow workers and managers. These incidents occurred far more frequently at post offices than in other businesses, raising concerns about the working environment. Some observers attributed the violence to the fact that relations between post office workers and management had grown increasingly tense, and claimed that some disturbed individuals were unable to handle the everyday stress of the job. Others blamed the strong employee unions for making it difficult for managers to discipline or terminate workers with behavioral or emotional problems. The Postal Service tried to address these concerns through reorganizations, offers of counseling, and training programs.

AMERICA AND THE WORLD

Despite growing concern, the U.S. Postal Service maintained the lowest postal rate among many industrialized nations. For example, U.S. first-class postage, which was increased to 33 cents in 1999, still compared favorably to the 1998 rates (converted to U.S. currency) charged in Great Britain, at 44 cents; Italy, at 48 cents; France, at 53 cents; Japan, at 59 cents; Switzerland, at 65 cents; and Germany, at 66 cents.

RESEARCH AND TECHNOLOGY

Advances in electronic technologies changed the way that people communicate with each other and represent a long-term threat to the Postal Service. The improved capabilities of electronic communication technologies, such as microcomputers, facsimile systems, high-speed printers, broadband satellite connections, and video display instruments, made communication quicker and mail delivery less necessary. Two technological advances that presented alternative channels to mail delivery were of particular concern to the Postal Service: electronic funds transfer and electronic mail.

Electronic Funds Transfer. Financial institutions in the early 1990s increasingly substituted paperless, computer-based systems of transferring funds for conventional payment systems such as mail delivery. Electronic systems for funds transfer had two primary applications that directly affected the Postal Service's activities: direct electronic deposit of payments, often called direct deposit, allowed people to bypass the mail system and electronically deposit their paychecks, retirement benefits, dividends, or Social Security benefits; and payment of bills through preauthorized debits allowed people to pay bills electronically at any convenient automated teller machine, without ever using the Postal Service. Moreover, with a personal computer and a modem, people could contact their financial institution electronically from home or work, and pay bills on the spot without ever using the mail system. As of 1998 the Postal Service recognized electronic bill paying as a potential long-term threat to its profitability.

Electronic Mail. The use of fax machines and electronic mail (e-mail) became more prevalent in the 1990s. With the rise of the Internet, many individuals began to have e-mail capabilities at home as well as at the office. Again, these developments were not perceived as a current threat to the Postal Service, but something to be watched.

In the early 1990s the U.S. Postal Service also made strides toward automating some of its operations, including mail sorting. For instance, businesses that sent many pieces of mail daily could obtain lower rates by adding bar codes to envelopes for easy sorting. Industry analysts claimed that the Postal Service stood to gain $40 to $80 million in annual cost savings for each 1 percent of the mail it processed automatically. By the end of the decade the Postal Service was using sophisticated sorting equipment and handwriting recognition technology to process mail more efficiently and accurately. It put two bar codes on all uncoded letter mail, one of which was a fluorescent ID tag that could in the future be used to provide real-time information about the mail stream.

In 1999 the Postal Service introduced PC Postage, which enabled customers to purchase and print postage using their computers and the Internet. The PC Postage products were developed by private companies and approved by the Postal Service after successful testing and evaluation. To purchase postage, a customer had to establish a connection with a PC Postage vendor's Internet site. The prepaid postage could be either stored in a small security device attached to the customer's personal computer, or stored on the vendor's Internet site. Vendors established their own license and service fees, and the Postal Service received full payment for the amount of postage printed. The markings produced by PC Postage products to represent postage were called Information Based Indicia.

FURTHER READING

Kellner, Mark A. "Printing Postage by Computer." *Nation's Business,* March 1999.

U.S. Postal Service. "Information Based Indicia Program Press Kit." August 1999. Available from http://www.usps.gov/news/press/ibip_presskit/background.htm.

———. "1997 Annual Report," and "1998 Annual Report." Available from http://www.usps.gov/history/annual.htm.

SIC 4412

DEEP SEA FOREIGN TRANSPORTATION OF FREIGHT

This category includes companies primarily engaged in operating vessels for the transportation of freight on the deep seas between the United States and foreign ports. Establishments operating vessels for the transportation of freight which travel to foreign ports and also to noncontiguous territories are classified in this industry. A related industry group is **SIC 4424: Deep Sea Domestic Transportation of Freight.**

NAICS CODE(S)

483111 (Deep Sea Freight Transportation)

INDUSTRY SNAPSHOT

Deep sea foreign transportation of freight was greatly affected by the global economy and international competition. U.S. companies in this industry competed with each other and with foreign carriers. Competition in the industry is heightened in part because of U.S. regulations that tended to make costs for U.S. shipowners higher than for ships bearing the flags of other nations. Many American-owned ships carried flags of nations with lower levels of expenses in order to stay competitive in the cargo transport business. By operating under the authority of other countries, shipping operations in America estimated they could cut labor costs by as much as 80 percent.

In 1999, U.S. merchant ships operating in the deep sea foreign transportation of freight carried a total of one billion tons of cargo, according to the U.S. Transportation Institute. The United States remained the world's largest trading nation, with export and import trade equaling one-fourth, or $500 billion of total world merchandise trade. By far, the majority of this trade cargo was transported by water. Notwithstanding, as of 1999, the U.S. ranked fifteenth in number of oceangoing vessels, and the U.S. flag merchant fleet ranked eleventh on a deadweight tonnage basis. The U.S. fleet's share of oceanborne commercial foreign trade, by weight, was less than five percent.

Although tonnage of foreign merchandise trade had increased over previous years, rising costs and price competition still meant declining profits for U.S. shipowners. Some shipping firms received subsidies from the U.S. government to compensate for high U.S. flag operating costs. These subsidies fell under the Maritime Security Program in which steamships were made available to the U.S. Defense Department should the need arise.

By 1997, there were 495 active, privately owned U.S. vessels of 1,000 gross tons or more engaged in oceangoing transportation of freight, according to the U.S. Bureau of Transportation Statistics. As of April of 1999, the U.S. flag merchant marine's active oceangoing fleet consisted of one passenger ship, 15 dry bulk ships, 81 container ships, 26 roll-on/roll-off vessels, 120 tankers, and 24 ''other'' ships, including breakbulks, partial container ships, refrigerated cargo ships, barge carriers, and specialized cargo ships. The 1999 U.S. flag vessel manpower pool was about 6,000 (not including passenger/combination ships).

The outlook for the U.S. flag fleet is predicated on several factors: foreign competitors; costs of labor, fuel, insurance, and other operating expenses; and volume of trade in relation to available cargo space. Overcapacity has been a problem for U.S. and foreign merchant fleets for many years, resulting in lower freight rates.

In the latter 1990s, the top foreign-trade water gateways for freight cargo (ranked in descending order, based upon trade dollars) were: the Port of Long Beach, California; the Port of Detroit, Michigan; the Port of Los Angeles, California; the Port of New York, New York; and the Port of Buffalo-Niagara Falls, New York.

Organization and Structure

The U.S. merchant deep sea fleet is made up of three categories of service: liner, non-liner (or tramp), and tanker.

Liner service includes regular, scheduled stops at ports along a route. Vessels operating as liners may be owned or chartered by an operator. Operators must accept any legal cargo they are equipped to carry, unless it does not meet the minimum freight requirements of the operator. Liner service usually carries manufactured goods. Often, two or more carriers along a route form ''conferences'' in order to regulate rates and competition. All conference members must charge the same freight rates, although rates may fluctuate according to supply and demand for cargo space. Liner service vessels are designed to handle the cargo most often shipped along their routes. Trip frequency depends upon the demands for shipping along that route. As of 1998, there were 108 private container ship and roll-on/roll-off (Ro-Ros) vessels in the active oceangoing U.S. flag fleet.

Non-liner, or tramp, shipping is scheduled individually by a customer who charters the ship to carry its cargo. Tramps usually carry only one type of bulk cargo, such as coal, ores, grain, lumber, or sugar. On occasion, two shippers of the same commodity may charter the ship jointly. Freight rates vary depending on the negotiations of the shipowner and shipper and the supply of and demand for cargo space. The tramp freight market peaked in 1995, and continued to decline except for a few peak rate periods.

Tanker service carries liquid cargoes, especially crude oil and petroleum products. Tankers may be operated by privately-owned companies for charter or by the oil company or other company as part of its entire industrial organization. Exxon Corporation has one of the largest tanker fleets in the world with a special department to oversee its operation of its fleet. Oil companies also charter extra ships as needed.

However, oil companies are not the only companies to employ their own ships exclusively for their own trade. Other companies may have specialized ships for transport of their goods. United Brands, for instance, a banana-growing and distributing concern with headquarters in the United States, operated a fleet of refrigerated vessels for transport of its produce.

Some companies chartered ships on a long-term basis. This provided many of the same advantages of owning a fleet without the enormous investment. By owning a fleet or contracting for long-term charter, the shipper was able to maintain complete control over shipping schedules. It could divert its ships to ports where demand for the product was high, and it could engage for service a fleet of ships with crews that had experience in handling a particular commodity.

Ships became increasingly more specialized during the twentieth century, and specialized ships were built to carry such diverse products as bulk cement, liquid chemicals, coal, iron ore, liquefied natural gas, newsprint and other paper products, petroleum and petroleum products, wood chips and wood pulp, refrigerated foods, and heavy equipment such as railroad locomotives or electric generator parts. Because many specialized ships were so expensive to build, a shipowner could agree to have a ship built for a company with the stipulation that the company lease the ship for most of its active life.

There were several federal agencies that administered laws and policies concerning the U.S. merchant fleet. The main agency was the Maritime Administration (MARAD), which was charged with coordinating the requirements of shipowners, ship builders, shippers, and labor unions for both domestic and foreign trade. In the late twentieth century, MARAD initiated and administered construction and operating subsidies, capital construction funds, and market development and maritime training.

BACKGROUND AND DEVELOPMENT

Since the earliest days in the United States, the federal government has considered the maintenance of a viable merchant fleet to be a priority for national security and the health of its foreign trade. During wars and other emergencies, the U.S. military chartered private ships to transport supplies.

Congressional legislation throughout U.S. history has helped to protect and promote the U.S. merchant fleet. Legislation in 1845 required the U.S. Post Office to transport mail abroad on U.S. merchant ships. Mail contracts were offered as incentives to shipping companies to establish shipping lines with Cuba, Panama, and major European ports. The law also stipulated that merchant ships could be converted to warships if necessary. The Military Transportation Act, passed in 1904, directed the U.S. Army and Navy to give preference to U.S. flagships for the transportation of supplies for direct support of military operations abroad.

The Merchant Marine Act of 1928 offered incentives to the shipbuilding industry to build new ships so that U.S. fleets could compete more effectively in the world market. This legislation, however, failed to spur the construction of many new ships and U.S. foreign shipping continued to decline as it had for many years.

The Merchant Marine Act of 1936 has been called the Magna Carta for U.S. shipping. It called for the first direct aid to merchant fleets for construction and operation. It also authorized the government to build ships and charter them to private companies for operation on foreign routes if private citizens did not provide that service. It required subsidized fleets to set up special funds to replace aging ships, provided loans and mortgage insurance, and authorized a training program for American crew members. That landmark piece of legislation was followed in 1954 by the ''Fifty-Fifty Law,'' which required that at least half of the country's foreign aid or humanitarian aid cargoes be carried abroad by U.S. merchant ships.

A weak merchant marine was regarded as unacceptable to the U.S. Department of Defense, as the military has historically relied on private ships to carry military cargo during emergencies. Although all U.S. presidents since George Washington have recognized the importance of a strong merchant marine for the nation's security, the industry has not always received the support it needed to remain viable and to compete successfully with foreign ship operators. Presidents George Bush and Bill Clinton promised reform in order to maintain the shrinking U.S. merchant fleet, which carried only about 15 percent of U.S. exports in the early 1990s, according to *The Wall Street Journal.* The National Performance Review headed by former Vice President Al Gore made several reform recommendations regarding the maritime industry, including striking down legislation that forced U.S. flag ships to carry military and aid cargoes; curtailing subsidies; repealing antitrust protection for carrier conferences established under the 1984 Shipping Act; and extending the U.S. flag to carrier lines that had foreign investors.

The Merchant Marine Act of 1970 was an attempt to counter several growing problems in the shipping industry. The U.S. fleet at that time carried only a small portion of the nation's foreign trade and a large portion of its ships were due to be scrapped because of age within the next few years. The 1970 legislation called for the construction of 300 merchant ships, deferred taxes for U.S. shipping companies if the money was put into funds to replace aging vessels, and operating and construction subsidies.

Despite the best intentions and stated policies of the U.S. government, American companies engaged in foreign deep sea transportation have been in trouble for many years. Operation Desert Shield and Operation Desert Storm, the 1990-91 confrontation with Iraq over its invasion of Kuwait, called for a gigantic shipping effort to bring American supplies and equipment to the Middle East. The military enlisted the services of the merchant marine for this task. It also used several dozen chartered transport ships it kept fully loaded and ready. However, even these privately owned ships could not handle the demand of military shipments, and the U.S. was forced to turn to foreign transport to carry equipment and supplies. During the build-up of forces, almost half of the 200 ships carrying equipment to Saudi Arabia were foreign-owned. This dependence on foreign vessels was, in part, a consequence of the U.S. fleet's incompatibility with military needs. The U.S. military needed Ro/Ro (roll on/roll off) ships for ease of transport, but according to a *Fortune* magazine article, half the U.S. fleet was comprised of oil tankers, and the rest were container ships or bulk carriers. *Fortune* also noted that although ships were much larger than in 1950, the U.S. shipping capacity had slipped by a third during that time.

Like the rest of the world's fleets, U.S. bulk carriers and supertankers were aged and worn. But replacing them was expensive ,and the industry could be unable to afford replacements because of its perennially shaky financial standing. After years of debate, the U.S. Congress finally passed the Maritime Security Act in 1996 by an overwhelming margin. This act reformed outdated maritime regulations and ensured that privately owned merchant ships would be available to meet national security sealift requirements. It also established a program to provide participating carriers with $1 billion in operating assistance over 10 years.

Prior to passage of the act, the two largest U.S. shipping companies, American President Companies and

CSX Corporation's Sea-Land Service, Inc., considered registering their fleets overseas and flying the flag of another nation unless the United States relaxed its rules and regulations, which shipowners regarded as prohibitively expensive. One of those restrictive rules stated that shipping lines must buy ships built in the United States in order to receive operating subsidies. John Lillie, president of the American President Lines Ltd. (APL), said that ship lines needed to have more freedom to buy vessels overseas because of the lower costs of those products.

Despite threats that even surpassed the passage of the Maritime Security Act, in January 1997, APL chose to remain a U.S. flag carrier, retaining at least a 51 percent U.S. ownership, by enrolling 9 of its largest ships in the Maritime Security Program in return for $2.1 million per ship in annual subsidies for a total $18.9 million. Its other 38 vessels were enrolled in December of 1996. Nevertheless, APL Limited announced in April of 1997 that it was merging with Neptune Orient Lines LTD, a Singapore-owned and operated steamship line.

''The future of the shipping industry belongs to those who have a global vision, and the strategy and critical mass to realize that vision,'' said Timothy Rhein, president and CEO of APL. ''Moreover, this merger in no way lessens APL's commitment to the U.S. flag and American seafaring labor as part of our commitment to the Maritime Security Program.''

Sea-Land Services, Inc. also applied to the Maritime Security Program. The U.S. government accepted 15 of its ships. For this, Sea-Land received $2.1 million per year for each ship participating in the program.

Legislation to deregulate the ocean shipping industry continued to be debated within the halls of Congress after the National Industrial Transportation League proposed the issue in January 1995. Such reform would enable shippers to operate in a more certain regulatory environment, and according to steamship lines, would improve shipper-carrier relations and the efficiency of American exporters, plus reduce the federal government's involvement in unnecessary regulation.

In March of 1997, legislation to allow confidential contracting between individual ocean common carriers and shippers, and other measures such as the making public of tariffs and the reduction of time required to post such a tariff rate increase, was proposed to change the Shipping Act of 1984. Called the Ocean Shipping Reform Act, the bill, in essence, would eliminate the Federal Maritime Commission (FMC) and transfer remaining functions to an expanded and renamed Surface Transportation Board. If passed, the regulatory changes would take place in 1998 with the FMC eliminated in 1999.

Tankers and Oil Spill Legislation. Transport of oil in bulk began in the late 1880s. Tankers in the more than 100 years since then have changed dramatically, with ship work handled more by computers, thus cutting back on the size of the crew. The enormous size of the tankers of the modern era has also increased the risk of oil spills and the impact such spills can have on the environment. The Alaskan oil spill in Prince William Sound by the *Exxon Valdez* in 1989, which caused significant ecological damage to the area, thus served as a catalyst in the institution of stricter environmental regulations for tankers and other vessels.

A U.S. law passed in 1990 that required all tankers sailing in U.S. waters to be equipped with double hulls to prevent spills if the outer hull was damaged. The shipping industry claimed that another rule included in the act could shut down the shipping industry in U.S. waters. The rule required carriers to provide environmental-liability guarantees in the form of insurance, letters of credit, surety bonds, or Protection and Indemnity (P&I) clubs that insured more than 95 percent of the ships traveling in U.S. waters. However, the liability allowed was open-ended, making it impossible to find guarantors. This rule was not implemented pending resolution of the problem.

CURRENT CONDITIONS

Although the number of oceangoing vessels had dramatically decreased, fleet productivity, in terms of cargo-carrying capacity, improved by 42 percent since 1972. The last ODS contract (operating differential subsidy) expires in 2001. As of January 1999, three companies still held ODS contracts that covered seven vessels in the bulk trades: Ocean Chemical Carriers, Ocean Chemical Transport, and Liberty Maritime. Under 1996's Maritime Security Program (replacing ODS), 47 U.S. flag vessels remained as participants. Companies which were awarded MSP agreements included: American Roll-On Roll-Off Carrier, American Ship Management, Central Gulf Lines, Farrell Lines, First American Bulk Carriers, and Waterman Steamship Lines.

The annual inflation rate for water transportation as of November 1999 was approximately 6.1 percent, a dramatic increase from 1997's 0.5 percent. Another 4 percent increase was expected for 2000. The biggest hike was for inbound deep-sea foreign transportation of freight.

The economic boom of the mid-1990s caused many shipowners to replace their aging vessels, the new vessels being delivered 18 to 24 months later, just when the bottom fell out of the market. The Baltic Freight index struck bottom and Japanese steel production dropped 13 million tons between 1998 and 1999. Seaborne trade in chemical products dropped one percent in 1998, and U.S.

petrochemical shipments to the Far East dropped 18 percent. Although domestic business was booming, the Far East crisis left many owners of new vessels ''all dressed up with nowhere to go.'' Consequently, in 1998, demolition of older vessels increased as owners attempted to avoid continued financial losses. The biggest demolition efforts in 1998 were in the Handy size (20/49,999 deadweight) of vessels in the 20 to 25 year age range.

RESEARCH AND TECHNOLOGY

Foreign shipping benefited from a revolutionary improvement first introduced in domestic transport in 1956—containerization of freight as part of an integrated transportation system. Prior to this new design, cargo was lifted aboard either in separate packing crates or bundled on pallets. However, container shipping involved large containers that fit the chassis of a tractor trailer and that could be packed and sealed by the manufacturer, transported via truck to the ship terminal, removed from the truck chassis, and placed in the cargo hold of the ship with a large crane that was actually part of the ship. At its destination port, the container was lifted off the ship, placed on the truck chassis, and driven to its ultimate destination. The containers could also be hauled by train if necessary. This innovation eliminated much of the handling that cargo once required. With this integrated system, it was handled once to pack it and once to unpack it, neither time by ship personnel, thus reducing the risk of damage and liability on the part of the shipowners.

Containerization also led the way to Ro/Ro (roll-on/roll-off) ships with their gigantic cargo doors on the sides and stern that allowed large vehicles or other large cargo to be driven or rolled on and off. Conversion to containerships was an expensive investment for shipowners, terminal operators, and port agencies. The adoption of containerships also led to the establishment of new companies that bought containers and leased them to the shipowners, thus removing from the shipowners the complex problem of keeping track of the whereabouts of empty containers.

In recent years, American President, Sea-Land, and smaller independent shipping lines have installed sophisticated computers and information technology to provide shippers with access to information about their cargo, keep track of rates, and allow customs officers to screen cargo while the ship is still at sea.

The next decade may well be marked by the introduction of significantly faster shipping vessels. David L. Giles, an aeronautical engineer, has invented a new craft dubbed FastShip. The new breed of freighter would be 863 feet in length and marry jet-ski technology to a novel hull design 100 feet shorter than the conventional superfreighter. FastShip is estimated to cross the North Atlantic at speeds up to 40 knots in 3.5 days as compared to existing ocean service requiring seven to eight days. If successful, its biggest benefit will be delivering high-value time-sensitive (HVTS) cargo, such as automobiles and automotive parts, pharmaceuticals, apparel and other consumer goods, on a door-to-door basis in 5 to 7 days as opposed to the current 14 to 35 days that existing services require. Japanese researchers are experimenting with ships driven by superconducting electromagnets and ships propelled by water jets and powered by gas turbine engines. Further in the future, a Techno-Superliner may be capable of traveling between Japan and the United States in three days.

FURTHER READING

Barnes, David. ''Maritime Deregulation.'' *Traffic World,* 10 March 1997.

Bergin, Sarah. ''How Ocean Carriers Are Staying Afloat.'' *Transportation & Distribution,* February 1997.

CSX Corporation, 1995 Annual Report & Form 10-K.

Logistics Management & Distribution Report, November 1999.

''Lykes in Critical Talks to Restructure Debt.'' *Traffic World,* 12 February 1996.

''Sea-Land Breezing Along.'' *Distribution,* March 1997.

The Transportation Institute. ''Industry Profile.'' 1999. Available from http://www.trans-inst.org/1am.html.

Thuermer, Karen E. ''Ocean Carriers Turn to Bigger Ships, New Technology to Meet Customer Demands.'' *Traffic World,* 5 February 1996.

''Top Foreign Trade Freight Gateways: 1996. (Table 13)'' U.S. Dept. of Commerce, Bureau of the Census, Foreign Trade Division, 1997.

''Table 2: Number of Vehicles (Oceangoing ships).'' U.S. Department of Transportation, National Transportation Statistics, 1998. Available from http://www.bts.gov/ntda/nts.

Ventham, D.J. ''Deep-Sea Shipping: Hope Seen for Long-Haul Market Stability in 2000.'' *American Metal Market,* 23 November 1999.

Young, Ian. ''Chemical Shipowners Grapple With Overcapacity.'' *Chemical Week,* 16 June 1999.

SIC 4424

DEEP SEA DOMESTIC TRANSPORTATION OF FREIGHT

This industry consists of establishments primarily engaged in operating vessels for the transportation of freight on the deep seas between ports of the United States, the Panama Canal Zone, Puerto Rico, and U.S. island possessions or protectorates. Also included are operations limited to the coasts of Alaska, Hawaii, or Puerto Rico. Establishments engaged in operation of vessels for transportation on the deep seas between the United States and foreign ports are included in the entry for **SIC 4412: Deep Sea Foreign Transportation of Freight.** Establishments primarily engaged in transportation of freight on the Great Lakes and St. Lawrence Seaway are included in **SIC 4432: Freight Transportation on the Great Lakes—St. Lawrence Seaway.** Establishments performing transportation of freight on the intracoastal waterways paralleling the Atlantic and Gulf coasts are classified in **SIC 4449: Water Transportation of Freight, Not Elsewhere Classified.**

NAICS Code(s)

483113 (Coastal and Great Lakes Freight Transportation)

Industry Snapshot

Deep sea domestic transportation of freight is part of a massive interrelated system of transport of manufactured and raw materials. Tank ships, which include tanker barges and liquefied natural gas vessels, and bulk carriers, which include tug barges, comprised 122 of the 149 privately owned U.S. flag merchant vessels operating in the domestic trade in 1999. Of these, 58 tankers and 4 bulk carriers operated on the coastal waters, and 37 tankers and 1 bulk carrier operated on noncontiguous waters. Additional vessels in active deep-sea domestic trade during 1999 included 19 containerships and nine roll-on/roll-off (Ro-Ro) ships.

Although the health of the industry depends in large part on the health of the U.S. economy, domestic deep sea transportation plays an important role in the nation's private and public interests. Ocean-going domestic vessels facilitate business between various areas of the country by providing relatively low-priced shipping service and are part of the vast network of trains, trucks, and inland water carriers that keeps the nation's commerce moving. The industry also supports millions of other jobs at shipbuilding yards, seaports, and terminals. In addition, the domestic waterborne shipping industry is vital to national defense interests, as it has relieved rail congestion and provided transport of military equipment and supplies during periods of national emergency.

In 1995, the deep sea sector of the U.S. domestic transport industry carried approximately 1.1 billion short tons (2,000-pound tons), according to the U.S. Army Corps of Engineers. Total coastal waterborne commerce for that year (by type of traffic) was 266.6 million tons. Nearly 440 billion ton-miles were spent in coastal/deep sea commerce in 1995.

Much of the success of the U.S. deep sea domestic industry over the years has been reliant upon oil drilling in Alaska. Since the 1989 oil spill disaster involving the *Exxon Valdez* in Alaska's Prince William Sound, new laws aimed to prevent oil spills in U.S. waters have become a serious concern for U.S. shipping companies. The Oil Pollution Act of 1990 required that all oil products be conveyed in double-hulled ships in order to prevent a repeat of the *Exxon Valdez* spill. The law also required each carrier to provide a guarantee of financial responsibility in the event of a spill. Shipowners claimed that the law, as written, threatened the survival of domestic shipping.

Organization and Structure

The U.S. deep sea fleet consists of three categories of service: liner, nonliner (or tramp), and tanker service.

Liner service includes regular, scheduled stops at ports along a designated route. The operators either own or charter the ships and must accept any legal cargo they are equipped to carry, unless it does not meet the minimum freight requirements. Liner service usually carries manufactured goods. Often, two or more carriers form "conferences" in order to regulate rates and competition along a route. All conference members must charge the same freight rates, although the laws of supply and demand may affect rates from one sailing to the next. Frequency of trips depends upon the demands for shipping along the route.

Nonliner, or tramp, service is scheduled individually by a customer who, in essence, is chartering the ship to carry its cargo. Tramps generally carry only one type of bulk cargo, usually a raw material such as coal, ores, grain, lumber, or sugar. On occasion, two shippers of the same commodity charter a ship jointly.

Merchant ships have become increasingly more specialized, especially during the last half of the twentieth century. Special ships were designed to carry bulk cement, coal, iron ore, liquefied natural gas, wood chips and pulp, refrigerated foods, and heavy equipment. These ships, operating as nonliner service, were often on long-term lease by one company. Because the ships were so expensive to build, the shipowner could require the company to sign a long-term lease for most of the life of the vessel before beginning construction.

Tankers carry shipments of liquid cargoes, especially crude oil and petroleum products. Oil companies could own and operate their own tanker fleets and charter privately owned ships as needed. At the end of the 1990s, the Exxon Corporation owned one of the largest tanker fleets in the world and had a special department to oversee its operation.

The transport of oil in bulk began in the late 1880s. Tankers in the 100 years since then have changed dramatically, with ship work handled more by computers, thus cutting back on the size of the crew. The enormous size of the tankers of the modern era has also increased the risk of oil spills and the impact such spills can have on the environment. The infamous Alaskan oil spill in Prince William Sound by the *Exxon Valdez* in 1989, which caused significant ecological damage to the area, thus served as a catalyst in the institution of strict environmental regulations for tankers and other vessels.

One innovation in oil product shipment was the tug-barge. The bow of the tug fits into a notch in a barge weighing up to 20,000 tons and pushes the barge. This vessel was devised as a way to cut shipping costs on tanker routes from the Gulf of Mexico north along the eastern seaboard of the United States. The tug-barge requires only a fraction of the crew needed aboard a tanker.

Domestic shipping includes coastwise, intercoastal, and noncontiguous services. Coastwise shipping refers to movement of cargo along the coastlines of the 48 contiguous states. This includes shipment of goods between the Atlantic and Gulf coasts. For the most part, tankers and ocean tug-barge systems carry petroleum and tramps carry dry bulk cargoes along this route.

Intercoastal shipping includes movement of cargo between Gulf and Pacific ports and between Atlantic and Pacific ports. Most traffic of this type consists of oil tankers carrying their cargo from Alaska to Gulf ports. Noncontiguous shipping includes service to Alaska, Hawaii, and U.S. territories and possessions. Outbound Alaskan shipping consists largely of petroleum products and crude oil; inbound service carries consumer goods for state residents. Hawaii and Puerto Rico rely on deep sea freight to transport goods in and out of their islands.

Several federal agencies promoted and regulated the U.S. merchant ships before the Maritime Administration (MARAD), part of the Department of Commerce, was given jurisdiction in 1950. The Merchant Marine Act of 1970 strengthened and expanded the MARAD's function. It brought the many facets of the merchant marine together in order to ensure the strength of the industries involved, including shippers, shipbuilders, and shipowners, as well as the various unions in each of those industries. MARAD guarantees loans for shipbuilding as well as providing other subsidies and tax benefits for construction of new ships by fleet owners.

BACKGROUND AND DEVELOPMENT

Cargo ships showed little design improvement between 1850 and the late 1950s. Cargo of various shapes and sizes was stored in five different cargo holds. But in the late 1950s and the 1960s, ship design and the shipping industry were revolutionized.

In 1956, when the T-2 tanker *Ideal X* left Houston, Texas, a new era of deep sea shipping was launched. Shipowner Malcolm P. McLean had initiated a new approach to shipping cargo by which the functions of both truck and ship were combined in an integrated transportation system. McLean had modified a 35-foot long tractor-trailer, so that the ''container'' holding the cargo could be lifted off the tractor-trailer chassis. These containers could then be loaded onto the ship by crane and stacked in rows. When the cargo reached its destination, each container was lifted off the ship and put back on a truck chassis. The cargo no longer had to be loaded and unloaded onto trucks at the ship terminal. The containers were packed and sealed by the shipper, then unpacked by the recipient of the goods at its ultimate destination rather than at the terminal. The containers could also be transported aboard freight trains. Not only did this new integrated transportation system save time, it drastically reduced the number of times a crate or pallet of packages was handled, thus eliminating instances when damage could occur.

Further development brought the addition of a shipboard crane so that the ships could unload at any port as long as there was a dockside apron large enough to accommodate a truck-tractor. The use of the container shipment method also cut down on the number of hours a ship had to be in port loading and unloading, thus resulting in less ''down time.'' This reduced the number of ships needed to maintain a specified frequency of service on a scheduled route. This revolutionary method of shipping quickly caught on among domestic and foreign carriers.

Roll-on/Roll-off (Ro-Ro) ships were a variation of the container ship; containers were placed on wheeled conveyors that are driven aboard the ship through huge cargo hold doors in the sides and stern of the ship. The containers were moved by ramps and elevators to their places in the cargo hold. The driver's cab was detached from the conveyor and driven back on shore. The container and conveyor remained on board to be unloaded at their destination. Roll-on/Roll-off ships were used to convey vehicles or other large cargo.

A speedier version of the container ship is the LASH vessel. LASH ships (standing for Lighter Aboard Ship) are about 800 feet long. Barges (lighters) loaded with cargo are hoisted on board the LASH vessel by a crane on board the ship and stored in cargo holds.

The federal government has long held that a strong merchant marine was in the best interest of the country, both militarily and economically. Various laws and acts have been passed by Congress to protect and promote the merchant fleet operating in foreign and domestic trade. The Merchant Marine Act of 1920 called for a merchant marine of ''the best equipped and most suitable types of vessels sufficient to carry the greater portion of its commerce and serve as a naval or military auxiliary in time of war or national emergency.'' According to this 1920 law, ships carrying cargo between domestic ports must be U.S. flag ships, owned by U.S. citizens and built in U.S. shipyards, thus protecting domestic trade from foreign competition.

In March of 1997, legislation to allow confidential contracting between individual ocean common carriers and shippers was proposed by Congress to reform the Shipping Act of 1984. Called the Ocean Shipping Reform Act of 1998, the bill, in essence, eliminated the Federal Maritime Commission (FMC) and transferred remaining functions to an expanded and renamed Surface Transportation Board.

The domestic fleet was a relatively old one, but shipowners were reluctant to replace their aging ships very quickly because of low profit margins. In 1994, for example, one merchant vessel capable of carrying seven gross tons and one tanker capable of hauling 17 gross tons were constructed, according to figures available from the U.S. Maritime Administration. No new ships were constructed in 1993, and in 1992, three merchant vessels with a total of 44 gross tons hauling capability, one cargo vessel capable of carrying 32 gross tons, and two tankers with a hauling capability of 12 gross tons were constructed. According to the *U.S. Industrial Outlook,* published by the U.S. Department of Commerce, the shipowners were facing stricter laws governing hazardous materials, waste disposal, vapor recovery, crewing requirements, and inspections. Any new regulations would affect profits and expenses of fleet owners.

Presidential administrations have also supported proposals to help boost the U.S. shipping lines and make them more competitive. President Bill Clinton indicated support to revitalize U.S. shipping and a number of potential remedies were under consideration, including regulatory relief, tax credits, and bankruptcy law revisions. In the wake of the *Exxon Valdez* oil spill in Alaska, however, the Oil Pollution Act of 1990 called for stronger regulation of oil transport. A rule from that same act, designed to strengthen pollution controls and clean-up laws, was intended to insure that oil shipping firms would be able to pay for damages from oil spills. The rule required ship operators to obtain a Certificate of Financial Security from the Coast Guard for each ship over 300 gross tons. This stipulation included not only oil tankers and barges but other ships as well because they carry oil as fuel.

The regulation called for operators to show proof of financial responsibility in the form of insurance, letters of credit, surety bonds, or other backing. However, the agency that provided the guarantee would also be liable for damages. Protection and Indemnity (P&I) clubs insured more than 95 percent of the ships traveling in U.S. waters or between U.S. and foreign ports. In this case, however, they refused to act as guarantors for environmental accidents because the regulation left the amount of liability open-ended and allowed any person, state, or local government to sue for the cost of cleanup, loss of natural resources, destruction of personal or real property, and loss of revenue or earning capacity. Insurance did not provide sufficient levels of coverage, so the law made shipowners responsible for paying the difference. Oil shipping firms insisted that this rule would shut them down. The rule was not implemented, pending further discussions on its potential ramifications for the industry.

Current Conditions

Overall, the 1999 domestic deep sea industry appreciated about a 1.5 percent increase in rates over 1998. There was no expected increase for 2000. The flat market was attributable to many factors, including a weak foreign market, high fuel costs, and excess cargo tonnage. In June of 1999, Peter Finnerty, Vice President of Public Affairs for Sea-Land Service, Inc. and of Maritime Affairs for CSX Corporation, testified before the U.S. Congress on behalf of the proposed United States Flag Merchant Marine Act of 1999. The House Bill proposed several tax rule changes which would hopefully generate private investment capital for new U.S. flag ships. In 1999, Sea-Land Service, Inc., operated a fleet of 100 container ships under both foreign and domestic flags. However, declining revenues forced its sale by CSX Corporation, its parent, to A.P. Moller-Maersk Line for $800 million. CSX retained Sea Land's domestic shipping business, worth $700 million. Despite the one-time charge-off of $315 million in profits as a result of the sale, CSX nonetheless reported third-quarter 1999 earnings of $123 million.

To help finance a cargo terminal to be used by the new Maersk-Sea-Land merger interests, the Port of Los Angeles announced in November of 1999 that it would sell $300 million in bonds in 2000. The merger of the two shipping interests will create the largest shipping company in the world. Upon completion of the terminal, the new Maersk Sealand will move from the Port of Long Beach to the Port of Los Angeles, bringing with it an estimated $2.2 billion in revenues over the next several years.

Industry Leaders

In addition to the Maersk-Sea Land leaders, Atlantic Richfield Co.'s ARCO Transportation Co. was one of the largest domestic deep sea carriers. However, in 1999, a pending merger with BP Amoco for $26 billion was conditioned upon the divestiture of certain gas interests in the North Sea, which could greatly affect the future of its deep-sea domestic freight operations. Other leaders in the industry included Alexander and Baldwin Inc., operating primarily as a deep sea domestic with some manufacturing and other concerns; Midland Enterprises, engaged primarily in inland and ocean-bound transportation and towing; and Crowley American Transport, which offers triple-deck barges and container ships (roll-on/roll-off and lift-on/lift-off) service to and from U.S. ports to Puerto Rico.

RESEARCH AND TECHNOLOGY

Shipping lines have invested in more sophisticated computer equipment to help track cargo and display information about the size, weight, origin, or destination of specific containers. Computers were increasingly used to perform many of the tasks that crew members once performed on board. Technology has also allowed shippers to access information about the progress of their own cargo.

FURTHER READING

Barker-Benefield, Simon. ''Transport Firm CSX Earnings Beat Analysts' Estimates.'' *The Florida Times,* 29 October 1999.

Figler, Andrea. ''Port of Los Angeles Plans Issue to Help Shipping Giant.'' *Bond Buyer,* 12 November 1999.

''Industry Profile: Domestic Deep Sea Trades.'' The Transportation Institute, 1999. Available from http://www.trans-inst.org/ind_profile.html.

''International Tax Rules.'' FDCH Congressional Testimony by Peter J. Finnerty, July 1999.

Jones, Chip. ''Richmond, Va.-Based Transportation Company Changes Name.'' *Richmond Times,* 18 November 1999.

''Maersk/Sea Land Takeover Cleared by EC.'' *American Shipper,* November 1999.

''Market Watch.'' *Logistics Management & Distribution Report,* November 1999.

''Newsbriefs.'' *Chemical Week,* 6 October 1999.

''Sea-Land Reports Loss Despite Pacific Rebound.'' *American Shipper,* December 1999.

Skerret, P.J. ''Designing Better Tankers.'' *Technology Review,* August/September 1992.

U.S. Department of Commerce. *Statistical Abstract of the United States, 1996* Washington: GPO, 1996.

Warner, David. ''Oil Shippers on Troubled Waters.'' *Nation's Business,* October 1992.

''Waterborne Commerce of the United States: 1995.'' U.S. Army Corps of Engineers, 1995.

SIC 4432

FREIGHT TRANSPORTATION ON THE GREAT LAKES-ST. LAWRENCE SEAWAY

This category covers establishments primarily engaged in the transportation of freight on the Great Lakes and the St. Lawrence Seaway, either between U.S. ports or between U.S. and Canadian ports.

NAICS CODE(S)

483113 (Coastal and Great Lakes Freight Transportation)

INDUSTRY SNAPSHOT

In 1999, there were 37 active bulk carriers, 7 active ITB (Integrated Tug/Barge) carriers, 2 active tankers, and 2 active ITB tankers engaged in the transportation of domestic freight on the Great Lakes and upper St. Lawrence River. Additionally, 20 bulk carriers were temporarily inactive or laid-up inactive, as was one ITB carrier. The total 1999 U.S. Great Lakes fleet (in excess of 1,000 gross registered tonnage) was 69 vessels. These ships also carried freight between U.S. and Canadian ports. Federal cabotage laws required that cargo shipped between U.S. ports be carried in ships built and registered in the United States, and owned and crewed by U.S. citizens. Ships of other maritime nations also sailed the Great Lakes-St. Lawrence Seaway. Any U.S. flagged ships involved in international trade other than to Canadian ports would be classified elsewhere. According to the U.S. Coast Guard, an estimated 500,000 private sector jobs were dependent upon Great Lakes commercial shipping in 1999. Actual shipboard jobs in the Great Lakes during 1999 were approximately 1,344 (432 licensed, 912 unlicensed), according to the Maritime Association.

The principal cargoes shipped on the Great Lakes-St. Lawrence Seaway were iron ore and coal. Freighters carried iron ore mined in Minnesota and Michigan to steel mills in Illinois, Indiana, Michigan, and Ohio. A single Great Lakes freighter could carry enough iron ore to produce the steel needed to build 87,000 automobiles. The second-largest cargo was coal, mined primarily in West Virginia, Kentucky, Pennsylvania, Ohio, and Illinois, and was shipped to utilities and factories in the upper Great Lakes states and Canada. Great Lakes freighters also carry low-sulfur Western coal shipped initially by rail to Superior, Wisconsin. The U.S. fleet typically hauled millions of tons of cargo annually during a nine-month navigation season. The principal cargoes of foreign transporters were wheat, barley, corn, and other grains from the Midwest and Canada that are destined primarily for European markets. In 1997, internal waterways, including the Great Lakes, hauled 1,016 million tons of cargo, up slightly from 1996. Specifically, the Great Lakes saw 123 million metric tons of cargo move through its waters, despite inactivity during freeze-over months. In 1998, 97 percent of U.S. flag Great Lakes cargoes moved by self-propelled vessels rather than barges.

Nearly all of the U.S. flag ships engaged in freight transportation on the Great Lakes were members of the Lake Carriers' Association, founded in 1880 and one of the oldest active trade organizations in the United States. The Cleveland-based organization listed 14 members who owned 63 vessels. This included two steel companies that operated ore carriers. The fleet included 60 dry-bulk carriers and three double-hulled tankers. Their collective cargo capacity was more than 1.8 million tons.

Background and Development

The Great Lakes constitute the single largest body of fresh water in the world, covering more than 95,000 square miles. Lake Superior alone covers 31,700 square miles, making it the world's largest freshwater lake. With their connecting waterways, the five Great Lakes—Superior, Michigan, Huron, Erie, and Ontario—also constitute the world's largest inland water transportation system. Eleven hundred miles separate Duluth, Minnesota, the western-most point of Lake Superior, from the St. Lawrence River, which stretches another 800 miles to Quebec, where it empties into the long, narrow Gulf of St. Lawrence. This waterway provides access for the transport of goods from the heart of the Midwest directly to the Atlantic Ocean.

This massive, interconnected waterway has been an important trade route for more than three centuries. As early as 1660, French explorers were transporting furs by canoe from the upper reaches of Lake Superior to Quebec on the St. Lawrence River. In 1679, the explorer Sieur de La Salle built the *Griffin,* the first commercial vessel on the Great Lakes. Built and launched above the falls on the Niagara River, which connects Lake Ontario and Lake Erie, the *Griffin* was also the first ship to sail on the upper Great Lakes.

La Salle sailed the *Griffin* to Green Bay, then a French outpost on the western shores of Lake Michigan, where it was loaded with furs. The five-man crew of the *Griffin* then set out on the return trip, while La Salle headed south to explore the Illinois River. The *Griffin* never survived its maiden voyage, however, as it was apparently lost during a violent storm. Father Louis Hennepin, who sailed with La Salle, later wrote an account that suggested the *Griffin* foundered on Lake Dauphin, the French name for Lake Michigan. In 1890, a lighthouse keeper discovered seventeenth-century artifacts and four skeletons in a cave on Manitoulin Island in Lake Huron, but the *Griffin* and the chest of gold coins it reportedly carried were never found.

Struggle for Control. The next ships to sail the Great Lakes after the ill-fated *Griffin* were warships built on Lake Ontario in the years leading up to the French and Indian War, in which France and England struggled for control of the profitable North American fur trade. The first naval battle fought on the Great Lakes took place in 1756, and the English commander fled without firing a shot. However, British forces eventually captured Quebec and Montreal, the two most important French settlements. In 1763, France ceded Canada and most of its possessions east of the Mississippi River to Great Britain. The English established a shipyard at Navy Island on the Niagara River and built the first commercial ships to sail the upper Great Lakes since the *Griffin.*

In 1783, following the Revolutionary War, the Treaty of Paris established the Great Lakes as the boundary between the United States and Canada, with the exception of Lake Michigan, which was entirely in U.S. territory. However, the Great Lakes remained the ''English Seas'' until Oliver Hazard Perry defeated the British fleet in the Battle of Lake Erie during the War of 1812. The Battle of Lake Erie was the last naval engagement fought on the Great Lakes. Neither the United States nor Canada now maintain warships or fortifications on the lakes. Although the international boundary runs down the middle of the lakes, the two countries have granted admiralty and criminal jurisdiction to each other covering the entirety of the Great Lakes.

Canals Expand Great Lakes Trade. The Great Lakes and the St. Lawrence River were always connected by natural waterways, but not all of those waterways were navigable. Fur traders were able to portage around the spectacular falls on the Niagara River or the much smaller falls on the Saint Mary's River, which linked Lake Superior with Lake Huron. But larger ships of commerce were unable to sail the entire stretch of the Great Lakes or navigate the Lachine Rapids on the upper St. Lawrence River.

The Erie Canal, completed in 1825, was the first navigable waterway to link the Great Lakes with the Atlantic Ocean. It connected the city of Buffalo, at the eastern edge of Lake Erie, to Albany, 363 miles away. From there, ships were able to reach the harbor at New York by sailing down the Hudson River. The *St. Clair* became the first ship to travel all the way from Detroit to the Atlantic, lowering its masts at Buffalo so it would fit under the bridges as it was towed down the canal by mules.

With the opening of the Erie Canal, the cost of transporting freight from Lake Erie to New York fell from $120 a ton to $4 a ton. Several other canals were also dug in the early nineteenth century, linking other inland waterways with the Great Lakes. The Ohio-Erie Canal, also opened in 1825, ran from Cleveland to Akron, Ohio, and then followed the Scioto River to the Ohio River. The Miami-Erie Canal linked the Great Toledo with the bustling Ohio River port at Cincinnati. The Illinois and Michigan Canal, completed in 1848, is often called the single most important factor in the development of the state of Illinois. It linked the growing port at Chicago with the Mississippi River.

In 1829, a Canadian company opened the Welland Ship Canal, which further encouraged trade on the Great Lakes by making it possible to sail between Lake Erie and Lake Ontario. The original canal linked Lake Ontario with the Welland River, which flowed into the Niagara River above the falls. A laborious system of 40 locks lifted and lowered the ships. In 1833, the canal was extended from Port Robinson on the Welland River to Port Colborne on Lake Erie, entirely bypassing the 25-mile-long Niagara River. Canal reconstruction conducted between 1873 and 1887 reduced the number of locks to 25; a new canal completed in 1932 further reduced the number of locks to eight.

The opening of the Welland Canal left only Lake Superior cut off from the rest of the Great Lakes, since the 42-mile-long Saint Mary's River contained several stretches of rapids and a 19-foot waterfall. In 1668, French trappers established a portage and trading post on the river at the city of Sault Sainte Marie. Then in 1797, the Northwest Fur Company, an English enterprise, built a single-lock canal around the falls, which allowed canoes and flat-bottomed boats to navigate the river. However, the canal was destroyed by American troops during the War of 1812. In 1850, John Jacob Aster's American Fur Company built a tramway to carry cargo between Lake Huron and Lake Superior, but the need remained for a navigable waterway. With the growing importance of Lake Superior trade, entire ships were sometimes dragged between the lakes on wooden rollers.

Soon after Michigan became a state in 1837, Governor Stevens T. Mason announced plans to build a canal on the American side of the Saint Mary's Falls. However, the proposed canal would have crossed the Fort Brady military reservation, and a detachment of U.S. soldiers stopped the project less than a week after it was started. Michigan then began lobbying Congress for permission and a federal grant to build the canal. For years the request went nowhere, reportedly blocked by Henry Clay, the powerful senator from Kentucky, who declared Lake Superior ''beyond the farthest bounds of civilization, if not the moon.''

Sentiment changed dramatically after 1844, when William Burt, a deputy U.S. government surveyor, accidentally discovered vast amounts of iron ore along the shores of Lake Superior. Jacob Houghton, a member of the surveying team, later wrote, ''As we looked at the [compass], to our astonishment, the north end of the needle was traversing a few degrees to the south of west. Mr. Burt called out, 'Boys, look around and see what you can find.' We all left the line, some going to the east, some going to the west, and all of us returned with specimens of iron ore, mostly garnered from outcrops.''

In his first State of the Union Address in 1851, President Millard Fillmore told Congress that a canal bypassing the Saint Mary's Falls ''would be national in its purpose and benefits.'' In 1852, Congress granted Michigan a 400-foot right-of-way across the Fort Brady reservation. It also donated 750,000 acres of federally-owned land in Michigan to pay for the project. In 1853, the Saint Mary's Falls Ship Canal Company broke ground on what would become the first of the Soo Locks.

The Saint Mary's Canal was completed in July of 1855. The brig *Columbia,* with six barrels of ore from the iron range at Marquette, became the first vessel to pass through the locks and sail down the river onto Lake Huron. More than 14,000 tons of ore were carried through the canal in 1856, the first full year of operation. That figure had risen to more than 153,000 tons by 1861, in time to play a major role in providing munitions for the North during the Civil War. In 1876, more than a million tons of iron ore, copper, grain, and other cargo passed through the canal, which by then had been expanded with a second lock to handle larger ships. In 1881, Michigan relinquished control of the canal to the federal government. The Canadian government opened the Sault Sainte Marie Canal on its side of the river in 1895. In 1900, 19 million tons of iron ore were shipped from the Great Lakes. By 1905, the tonnage had nearly doubled to 37 million tons. In 1855, the cost of hauling iron ore was $3 a ton; by 1900, it was 60 cents.

A second canal was built on the U.S. side of the Saint Mary's River in the early 1900s, and the twin Davis and Sabin locks were opened. The original South canal was expanded in 1943 with the MacArthur Lock. The largest of the Soo Locks, the 1,200-foot Poe, was opened on the South canal in 1969. The Soo Locks have been called the single most important development in the Great Lakes shipping industry. Each new lock was bigger than the last, and gave rise to bigger and wider freighters.

Great Lakes Freighters. Although steamships made their appearance on the Great Lakes in 1816, they were primarily engaged in passenger service or package delivery. A few masted steamers were used as cargo carriers in the mid-1800s, but nearly all freight was carried in wooden sailing ships. The most common freighters were known as Great Lakes schooners and were characterized by long, narrow beams. By one account, there were more than 1,700 schooners plying the Great Lakes in the 1870s, carrying grain, lumber, coal, and iron ore. The last full-rigged schooner ever built on the Great Lakes was the *Cora A,* launched in 1889 at Manitowoc, Wisconsin.

In the 1880s, however, shipbuilders began turning to steam and steel. The first Great Lakes freighter to be built of iron was the *Onoko,* launched in 1882. The *Onoko* was 300-feet in length, had a vast unobstructed cargo space, and could carry up to 3,000 tons. The *Onoko,* which operated for 33 years before being lost on Lake Superior, became the prototype for hundreds of Great Lakes freighters that would follow. Most freighters mimicked the *Onoko's* long, low-riding cargo hold with a forecastle for crew and bridge and a housing at the stern for the engines.

The earlier Poe lock, which opened on the Saint Mary's River in 1896, could handle ships with twice the cargo capacity of the *Onoko,* and the Great Lakes shipping industry was quick to take advantage. The 412-foot *Sir Henry Bessemer,* with a capacity of 6,700 tons, was launched the same year the lock opened. The 454-foot *Malietoa,* launched in 1889, could carry 7,500 tons, a record which lasted until the 540-foot *Augustus B. Wolvin* took on 10,500 tons in 1904. More than 100 freighters the size of the *Wolvin* were launched in the first decade of the twentieth century, but even those giant ships were outclassed by 600-foot freighters with 15,000-ton capacities when the Davis and Sabin locks opened in 1914 and 1919, respectively.

The first freighter to carry 20,000 tons was the *Wilfred S. Sykes,* launched in 1949, following completion of the MacArthur lock. The *Sykes,* owned by the Inland Steel Corporation and still in operation in 1993, was nearly 700-feet long and 70-feet wide, and had a draft of 37 feet. The largest of the U.S. locks, also named Poe for the one it replaced, was dedicated in 1969, and opened the way for the latest generation of Great Lakes freighters—1,000-foot supercarriers capable of taking on loads of 60,000 tons or more.

St. Lawrence Seaway. The St. Lawrence River is the second longest river in Canada. It flows northeast from its headwaters at the eastern end of Lake Ontario to the Bay of St. Lawrence, 800 miles away. Part of the river forms the boundary between the province of Quebec and New York State. Navigating the lower St. Lawrence, from Montreal to Quebec, was always relatively easy. However, between Lake Ontario and Montreal, the upper St. Lawrence drops from 245 feet above sea level to 20 feet in a series of rapids, making access difficult.

In 1895, Canada and the United States began discussing the possibility of deepening the upper St. Lawrence and constructing a series of locks to open the river to international trade. In 1929, the International Joint Commission, established 20 years earlier to administer the boundary waters, recommended a combined navigation and power-generation project. In 1932, Canada and the United States signed the St. Lawrence Deep Waterway Treaty, which called for building a 27-foot-deep waterway between Lake Erie and Montreal, plus the construction of four hydroelectric plants. Several commercial interests opposed the project, including the railroads and coal companies, and the U.S. Senate rejected the treaty in 1934.

In 1941, the war in Europe revived interest in the proposed seaway, and the two countries signed the Great Lakes-St. Lawrence Basin Agreement, which added a power plant at Niagara Falls to the original proposal. The proposal still needed Congressional approval, but when the United States entered World War II a few months later, the issue was set aside. In 1942, power shortages in Ontario and New York delayed production of war materials, and President Franklin D. Roosevelt considered an executive order to begin the St. Lawrence project. He dropped the idea because it would take at least three years to bring the first power plant on line. The proposal languished in Congress until 1951, when Canada announced plans to proceed on its own. Congress then began serious discussions and approved U.S. participation in the project in 1954.

The St. Lawrence Seaway opened officially on June 26, 1959. Parts of the seaway lie entirely within Canada, while other sections lie within the United States. Although the St. Lawrence Seaway opened the Great Lakes to international trade, Great Lakes freighters and most ocean-going vessels built after 1970 were too large to use the locks.

The Dangers of Great Lakes Shipping. Hundreds of ships and thousands of lives have been lost during violent storms on the Great Lakes. As Jacques Marquette, one of the first white men to explore the region, wrote in the seventeenth century, ''The winds from the Lake of the Illinois no sooner subside than they are hurled back by the Lake of the Hurons, and those from Lake Superior are the fiercest of all. In the winter months there is a succession of storms; and with these mighty waters all about us, we seem to be living in the heart of a hurricane.'' In one terrible storm alone, in November 1913, more than 235 sailors were killed and 10 Great Lakes freighters lost. But the most famous shipwreck in Great Lakes history was the *Edmund Fitzgerald.*

In November 1975, the *Edmund Fitzgerald,* a freighter loaded with 26,000 tons of taconite iron pellets, was nearing the safety of Whitefish Bay, north of the Soo Locks. A brutal storm with hurricane-force winds and 30-foot waves had been battering the *Edmund Fitzgerald* for hours. The captain, a 44-year veteran of the Great Lakes, radioed a ship not far behind that the *Edmund Fitzgerald* was taking on water, but that there was no immediate danger. Suddenly, the *Edmund Fitzgerald* disappeared from the other ship's radar. The next day, searchers found some debris, but no sign of the ship nor any of its 29 crew members.

Initial reports suggested the *Edmund Fitzgerald* was lifted by two waves, one at the stern and one at the bow, causing the unsupported weight of its cargo to snap the 729-foot ship in two, sending it instantly to the bottom of the lake. However, after locating and photographing the ship several months later, a Coast Guard investigation determined the most likely cause of the disaster was flooding of the cargo holds, which caused the *Edmund Fitzgerald* to suddenly dive bow first below the water, much like a submarine. The Great Lakes Association presented a third possibility. The industry position was that the ship hit a shoal when it came too close to an island, which tore open the hull. Whatever the cause, the ship broke in two, coming to rest in 525 feet of water with the stern half upside down.

As the size of ships operating on the Great Lakes grew, their numbers decreased. In the early 1950s, there were more than 300 U.S. flagged ships operating on the Great Lakes, but that number fell to about 120 by the end of the 1970s. A nationwide recession took a further toll on shipping in the 1980s, reducing the number of vessels to just 45 by 1986. By 1995, the number had increased to 59 ships in operation on the Great Lakes. It must be noted however that modern Great Lakes freighters carry substantially larger cargoes then their smaller predecessors. In 1995, for instance, the fleet boasted 13 self-unloaders that were 1,000 feet long. These 13 ships had the same carrying capacity as 65 of the older 600-foot vessels.

Iron ore for the steel industry has long been the primary cargo for U.S. flagged ships on the Great Lakes. Therefore, the Great Lakes shipping industry was seriously affected by economic conditions that crippled midwestern steelmakers in the 1980s, especially the influx of cheap foreign steel and a general economic recession. In bullish economies, United States and Canadian Lakes freighters carried as much as 100 million tons of ore in a single season, generally from late March to early January, before ice closed the Soo Locks. However, from 1983 until the early 1990s, the Great Lakes fleet averaged about 60 million tons per year. In 1995 the Great Lakes vessels carried 70.6 million net tons of iron ore as compared to 64.3 million net tons in 1991.

Coal was the second largest cargo for Great Lakes shippers. Most of the coal was mined in the Appalachian regions of West Virginia, Kentucky, Pennsylvania, and Ohio, and shipped by rail to ports on Lake Erie. From there, it was distributed by freighters to utilities and industries throughout the Great Lakes region. Midwest coal also was loaded at Chicago and Thunder Bay, Ontario. Low-sulfur coal from the Powder River Basin in Wyoming and Montana was loaded at Superior, Wisconsin, which shared a harbor with Duluth, Minnesota. Low-sulfur coal was used by utilities on the Lower Great Lakes because burning it produced less sulfur dioxide, a major cause of air pollution. In 1995, coal shipments totaled 32.9 million net tons, down from 35.3 million in 1991.

Other Great Lakes cargoes included limestone and gypsum for the steel industry, cement, and liquid bulk products such as asphalt, gasoline, and light heating oil. In 1995 Great Lakes freighters carried 34.6 million net tons of limestone and gypsum, 4.6 million tons of cement, and 4.7 million tons of liquid bulk products. In the same year, 18.8 million net tons of grain was carried on the Great Lakes. This represented the most U.S. grain shipped on the Great Lakes since 1984 and was fueled by strong overseas markets and ample stocks from a good growing season. Dry and liquid-bulk commerce on the Great Lakes totaled 173.6 million net tons in 1995.

The 1995 navigation season on the Great Lakes was blessed by favorable weather and a favorable economic climate. The season opened on March 25 and by May 1 all 59 U.S. flag self-unloaders available for service were in operation. The season closed on January 15, 1996 for a total of 297 days. The 1996 season was expected to be a repeat of the 1995 season. This optimistic prediction was based on select sectors of a strong U.S. economy. Especially important was a growing foreign market for steel, which was expected to boost iron ore shipments, long a mainstay of Great Lakes commerce. By early 1996, industry insiders were hopeful about the year's grain shipments, but by mid-year optimism had turned to pessimism. A quick drop in grain shipments forced shipping concerns to tie up some of their vessels. Winnipeg based Seaway Bulk Carriers was forced to sideline 12 of their 24 grain carriers. Canadian movement of grain through the end of June was down by 1.4 million metric tons as compared to 1995, while U.S. shipments were down 1.7 million metric tons compared to a year earlier. The drop was blamed on low grain supplies not low demand or low prices. The low supply of grain was due to a late winter and wet spring which delayed the planting of wheat in many regions.

The Jones Act. Passed in 1920, the Jones Act required that cargo shipped between U.S. ports be carried in vessels that were owned, crewed, and built by U.S. citizens. Other cabotage laws set similar standards for passenger service, towing in U.S. harbors, and salvage operation in territorial waters. Initially, the Jones Act was passed to ensure the safety of U.S. ports and guarantee that the United States would maintain a strong merchant marine. In lobbying for continued enforcement, the Lake Carriers' Association also pointed out that by protecting the Great Lakes fleet from foreign competition, the Jones Act provided the assurance that shippers needed to invest in safe, modern vessels that are manned by seaman who are certified by the U.S. Coast Guard.

In 1996, however, the Coastal Shipping Competition Act (H.R. 4006) was introduced in the U.S. House of Representatives. This bill was similar to legislation introduced in the U.S. Senate earlier in the year. These bills, if passed, would allow foreign-flag, foreign-built vessels to carry U.S. products between U.S. ports. Adherents of the legislation claim that the lack of adequate waterborne transportation vessels had a negative effect on the movement of American products between American ports. In other words existing American flag vessels were inadequate to meet the demand. This forces businesses and consumers to purchase foreign goods that could be moved between U.S. ports on foreign vessels. Opponents of the legislation, which included the Lake Carrier's Association, believed that repealing the Jones Act would result in the loss of 125,000 American jobs on the Great lakes and decimate the domestic shipbuilding industry.

Winter Navigation. When the Soo Canal was opened in 1855, the weather controlled the navigation season. Fierce gales would begin whipping across Lake Superior in November, sending most Great Lakes schooners scurrying for port. By mid-December, ice closed the canal completely, and shipping did not resume until the spring thaw. The steel-hulled steamers that began replacing the schooners in the 1880s were better suited to challenge the weather. As bigger and more powerful ships were able to break through the ice, the closing date was pushed back steadily to as late as mid-January. From 1974 to 1979, the locks were open year-round.

Environmentalists raised concerns in the 1980s that year-round operation might have adverse affects on water levels in Lake Superior and the lower Great Lakes and that ships forcing their way through ice-covered channels might cause damage to the shoreline. Such concerns prompted the Soo Canal to revert to a navigation season based on the formation of ice. In 1990, the Army Corps of Engineers said it found no evidence of environmental damage and set January 15 as the official closing date. In 1993, although environmental groups still objected, the Corps recommended March 21 as the official date to open the locks. The Lake Carriers' Association supported establishment of a fixed navigational season. In early 1996, however, the U.S. Army Corps of Engineers published a notice in the Federal Register proposing that the Soo Locks open on March 25, fixing the Great lakes navigation season from that date until January 15. The Lake Carrier's Association saw this set season as a compromise they could live with.

Another issue on the Lake Carriers' Association agenda was the status of the Coast Guard's icebreaker, the *U.S.S. Mackinaw.* As the navigational season above the Soo Locks lengthened, freighters occasionally needed the *Mackinaw* to free them from unusually heavy ice build-up and to keep the shipping lanes open. For example, gale force winter winds on Lake Superior have been known to create six-foot-high windrows of ice at the Duluth/Superior harbor in a matter of hours. The *Mackinaw* was also needed to break up ice in the St. Clair River north of Detroit twice in the 1980s. In the late 1980s, the Coast Guard announced that it would decommission the *Mackinaw* because of budget problems, but the Lake Carriers' Association convinced Congress to save the icebreaker. A modernization program that the association said would cut the *Mackinaw's* $3 million operating expense in half was scheduled to begin in 1993. In its annual report for 1992, the Lake Carriers' Association said, "The March 21-January 15 navigation season so necessary to the continued health of the Great Lakes economy can be attained with certainty only if the *Mackinaw* is primed and ready for the ice seasons that accompany the opening and closing of navigation."

By 1996, however, the Lake Carrier's Association was beginning to modify its stand on the *Mackinaw.* Christened in 1944 the *Mackinaw* was the most powerful of the nine Coast guard icebreakers operating on the Great Lakes. Capable of generating 10,000 shaft horsepower and displacing 5,000 tons, no windrow of ridged ice on the Lakes proved too much for the *Mackinaw.* While recognizing that the 51-year-old cutter was structurally sound and internal modernization could be cost-effective, they questioned the economic viability of year-round maintenance on a vessel used only during the winter shipping season. The Association noted that an off-season use for the vessel could not be found and that the *Mackinaw* was "underutilized" during the summer months. They noted that it was perhaps time to "plan for a post-*Mackinaw* world." One option was the possible leasing of an ice-breaker. In the interim the Association planned to continue to support the operation of the *Mackinaw* and if a replacement was ever planned, the Association felt it should be a multi-purpose vessel adaptable to a variety of year round tasks. In late 1999 the Coast Guard officially announced that the *Mackinaw* would be decommissioned following the 2005-2006 season. Renovating it would have cost $147 million, but a new vessel would only cost an estimated $128 million. As of 1999, the *Mackinaw* averaged 134 days out of port per year, it was hoped that her replacement would sail 185 days per year.

Industry Concerns. Twenty-two of the U.S. flagged ships operating on the Great Lakes in 1993, representing almost 70 percent of the American fleet's total cargo capacity, were called Poe-class vessels. This meant they were too large to use any of the locks at Sault Sainte Marie except the Poe Lock, which was opened in 1969. In 1986, Congress authorized the construction of a second Poe-sized lock as part of the Water Resources Development Act. However, the law required that local funding pay 35 percent of the cost, and the lock was never built.

In 1992 the Lake Carriers' Association estimated a new Poe-sized lock would cost $400 million, with local costs of $140 million. In lobbying for full federal funding, the association warned that any lengthy closure of the Poe Lock would bring much of the U.S. flag shipping on the Great Lakes to a standstill. Canadian ships and other foreign-flagged vessels small enough for the locks on the St. Lawrence Seaway would not be affected.

Another environmental concern for Great Lakes carriers was the disposal of materials dredged from ports and navigation channels. Each inch of reduced draft in waterways reduced the amount of cargo that could be carried by a 1,000-foot freighter by roughly 270 tons. With shoreline erosion, storm runoff, and airborne dirt, dredging was an ongoing requirement. Until 1970, sediment was disposed of by dumping it in deep water areas. But sediment, especially from industrial ports, was often contaminated with petroleum products and other chemicals. In the 1970s, the federal government began requiring that material dredged from harbors be stored in government-built confined disposal facilities. As a result, in the early 1990s, some harbors had not been dredged in nearly 20 years. According to the Lake Carriers' Association, disposal facilities at Duluth and Cleveland would be full by the end of the century, and all but two of the remaining 24 disposal facilities would be full by 2006.

The association urged the federal government to allow non-polluted sediment to be dumped in deep water or used constructively for projects such as beach replenishment. Under the association's plan, disposal facilities would be reserved for contaminated sediment. The association also urged the federal government to pay part of the cost of dredging and for the construction of new disposal facilities where containment was necessary.

Current Conditions

In 1999, the estimated capacity of the U.S. flag Great Lakes fleet (in excess of 1,000 gross registered tonnage) was 732,403 deadweight tons (dwt.) for dry bulk active carriers (plus another 222,968 dwt. for inactive laid-up carriers; 78,465 dwt. for active (plus 3,413 dwt. for inactive) ITB bulk carriers; and 9,758 dwt. for the active tanker (and 8,150 dwt. for the inactive tanker). Total 1999 dwt. capacity was 1,060,157. As of September 1999, rate hikes for cargo shipments on the Great Lakes had varied less than 0.4 percent overall from those of 1998. (This statistic was controlled by supply and demand.) However, 1998 business had been significantly better than 1997, with a 4 to 6 percent increase overall.

Industry Leaders

American Steamship Company. The American Steamship Company was founded in 1907 by Adam E. Cornelius, Sr. and John J. Borland, Sr. The Oswego Shipping Company purchased American Steamship in the 1960s, and sold the company in the 1970s to the GATX Corporation. The company's headquarters are in Buffalo, New York. American Steamship's 770-foot *St. Clair* set a record in 1997 by delivering the largest coal cargo (45,411 tons) to a Canadian Great Lakes port west of the Welland Canal (Nanticoke).

In 1998, American Steamship operated 10 self-unloading freighters with a total gross registered tonnage of more than 190,000 tons and a mid-summer capacity of more than 345,000 gross tons. In cargo capacity, American Steamship was the largest of the U.S. flagged Great Lakes shipping companies. Seven of the company's lakers were Poe-class vessels, including the 1000-foot *Indiana Harbor,* which carried a U.S. flag record 64,390 tons of iron ore in one trip through the Soo Canal in 1986. In the 1990s, American Steamship carried about 50 percent of the coal shipped on the Great Lakes. It also carried iron ore and stone.

Interlake Steamship Company. The Interlake Steamship Company, headquartered in Cleveland, Ohio, was the second largest Great Lakes freight company in terms of cargo capacity. In 1998, the company operated nine vessels with a total capacity of just over 390,000 tons. It was one of two companies operating 1,000-foot self-unloading bulk carriers on the Great Lakes in 1998. In May, 1998, its *Elton Hoyt 2nd,* at 698 feet, was the longest vessel to ever navigate the Federal Channel in Cleveland's Cuyahoga River, known for its twisting path. In 1999, Interlake moved it Great Lakes office from Cleveland to a new $5.2 million building in Richfield.

Oglebay Norton Company. The Oglebay Norton Company was founded in 1890 by Earl W. Oglebay and David Z. Norton. Oglebay was an experienced shipping agent and Norton was a former bank head cashier acting on behalf of oil magnate John D. Rockefeller, who had purchased iron-bearing land in the Mesabi range of Minnesota. Both Oglebay and Rockefeller were associated with the Tuttle family, pioneers in iron-ore shipping on the Great Lakes. As a teenager in the 1850s, Rockefeller worked for shipping agents Isaac Hewitt and Henry Tuttle. The firm of Hewitt & Tuttle later became H.B. Tuttle & Company. In the 1880s, Oglebay became acquainted with Horace Tuttle, who was then running the company founded by his father. In 1884, Tuttle & Company became Tuttle, Oglebay and Company. Horace Tuttle died in an accident in 1889 and in the following year Tuttle,

Oglebay and Company was dissolved and succeeded by Oglebay Norton.

Oglebay Norton managed sales and shipping for Rockefeller's Lake Superior Consolidated Iron Mines until 1901, when Rockefeller sold his ships and mining interests to the U.S. Steel Corporation. Oglebay Norton continued as shipping agents for other mining interests, eventually acquiring a fleet of ships and forming the Columbia Steamship Company in 1920. The *Edmund Fitzgerald* was the flagship for the Columbia fleet from 1958 until it sank in 1975. More recently, the company's 1,000 foot *Columbia Star* set a coal cargo long-haul record of 70,903 net tons on July 6, 1997.

In 1928, the company also began manufacturing equipment for the steel-making industry. The company began shipping coal in 1936. In 1939, Oglebay Norton formed the Reserve Mining Company and began mining taconite, a low-grade iron ore previously considered useless. As high-quality iron-ore reserves dwindled, taconite grew in importance. From the 1970s on, almost all iron ore mined in Michigan and Minnesota was taconite.

In 1997, Oglebay Norton operated the largest fleet among Great Lakes shipping companies. Among its 12 vessels were two 1,000-foot freighters, the *Columbia Star* and *Oglebay Norton,* each of which could carry more than 60,000 tons. The fleet's cargo capacity was about 340,000 tons. The *Oglebay Norton* set a record in 1992 by hauling 59,078 tons of limestone from Cedarville, Michigan to Ludington, Michigan. In 1986, the same ship, then known as the *Lewis Wilson Foy,* carried a record 72,351 tons of iron ore. In 1996 Oglebay Norton did $189 million in business.

Other members of the Lake Carriers' Association operating vessels on the Great Lakes in 1997 included the Bethlehem Steel Corporation of Chesterton, Indiana, which operated two 1000-foot freighters to provide iron ore to its steel mills. The Inland Steel Company of East Chicago, Indiana also operated its own fleet of three smaller iron-ore freighters.

FURTHER READING

"Another Strong Season." *Seaway Review,* January-March, 1996.

Barker, James R. "FDCH Congressional Testimony," presented September 15, 1998. Senate Commerce, Science and Transportation Economics Reports/Data, 1998.

Bullard, Sam and Jennifer Beauprez. "Interlake Steamship Cruising to New Richfield Home." *Crain's Cleveland Business,* 1 June 1998.

The Detroit Marine Historian, March 1998.

"The Forecast for 1996: Most Likely a Repeat." *Seaway Review,* April-June 1996.

Hatcher, Harlan. *The Great Lakes.* New York: Oxford University Press, 1944.

———, and Erich A. Walter. *A Pictorial History of the Great Lakes.* New York: Crown Publishers, 1963.

Havighurst, Walter. *The Great Lakes Reader.* New York: The Macmillan Company, 1967.

"The Jones Act Debate Continues." *Seaway Review,* October-December 1996.

Katz-Stone, Adam. "The Party's About Over: MAC Will No Longer Break The Ice." *Navy Times,* 22 November 1999.

Lake Carrier's Association. *1995 Annual Report, 1996 Objectives.* Cleveland: Lake Carrier's Association, 1996.

"Market Watch." *Logistics Management & Distribution Report,* November 1999.

Stonehouse, Frederick. *The Wreck of the Edmund Fitzgerald.* AuTrain, Michigan: Avery Color Studios, 1977.

The Transportation Institute."Industry Profile: 1999." Available at http://www.trans-inst.org/ind_profile.html.

SIC 4449

WATER TRANSPORTATION OF FREIGHT, NOT ELSEWHERE CLASSIFIED

This category includes establishments primarily engaged in transportation of freight on all inland waterways, including the intracoastal waterways on the Atlantic and Gulf Coasts. Transportation of freight on the Great Lakes and the St. Lawrence Seaway is classified in **SIC 4432: Freight Transportation on the Great Lakes–St. Lawrence Seaway.** Establishments primarily engaged in providing lighterage and towing or tugboat services are classified in Industry Group No. 449: Services Incidental to Water Transportation.

NAICS CODE(S)

483211 (Inland Water Freight Transportation)

INDUSTRY SNAPSHOT

There are approximately 12,000 miles of navigable inland waterways used by the domestic shipping trades in the United States. This statistic does not include the Great Lakes merchant marine trade, which if included, would almost double the statistic. In 1997, the industry was served by 3,284 towboats, 25,648 dry cargo barges, and 3,286 tanker barges. Excluding Great Lakes shipping, the inland trade industry moved 631 million metric tons of freight in 1997. In 1999, freight moved along the inland and coastal waterways constituted 15 percent of all U.S. freight.

The inland and intracoastal navigation system is operable in water from 6 to 9 feet in depth, but several thousand miles are considerably deeper. The most important inland waterways for commerce are the Mississippi River System, the Gulf Intracoastal Waterway, the Columbia River System, the McClellan-Kerr Arkansas River Navigation System, the Tennessee-Tombigbee-Mobile River System, and the Hudson River-New York State Barge Canal System. About one-third of all inland traffic is on the Mississippi River, followed by the Ohio River, the Gulf Intracoastal Waterway, the Illinois Waterway, and the Tennessee River, in that order.

Most freight consists of dry bulk cargo and is carried aboard barges known as hoppers. This includes grain, coal, and chemicals. Petroleum products, which account for about 40 percent of the inland waterways cargo, are carried in tank barges. Ocean-going tank barges used on the Gulf and Atlantic Intracoastal Waterways may carry as much as 225,000 barrels of oil. Tonnage is high during the crop harvest months, but the Upper Mississippi and Missouri Rivers are closed to barge traffic in winter.

Inland waterway transportation of freight is considered the safest, least polluting, and most cost efficient of all freight transportation in the United States. Waterway transportation of freight is more than twice as energy efficient as rail transportation and eight times as efficient as truck transportation. The U.S. Coast Guard enforces regulations regarding design, construction, and operation of towboats and river barges. In addition, the Coast Guard is responsible for licensing crews aboard the vessels. Cabotage laws require that vessels involved in inland water transportation of freight be built, owned, and crewed by American citizens or U.S. owned companies.

BACKGROUND AND DEVELOPMENT

Mississippi River System. The Mississippi River system consists of the Mississippi and Ohio Rivers and their tributaries. It was the busiest and most important inland waterway in the United States in the early 1990s, accounting for about 40 percent of all freight shipped on the nation's inland and intracoastal waterways. More than 700 million tons of both international and domestic freight were carried annually on the Mississippi River in the 1990s, with an additional 480 million tons each year via internal traffic. Of the international and domestic freight, nearly 70 percent was internal Mississippi River freight.

More than 100,000 barges and half the 7,000 ocean-going vessels traveling the Mississippi call at the Port of South Louisiana at the mouth of the river. The port, extending 54 miles along the Mississippi, was the largest tonnage port in the United States, and the third biggest in the world, handling 216 million tons of cargo in 1998.

The Mississippi River is the longest river in the United States, flowing more than 2,300 miles from northwestern Minnesota to the Gulf of Mexico. More than 1,800 miles are considered navigable. A series of 29 dams and locks constructed by the Army Corps of Engineers after World War I ensured a minimum depth of nine feet on the upper Mississippi as far north as Minneapolis. Below St. Louis, the Mississippi reaches depths of 100 feet or more. The Mississippi River-Gulf Outlet, a 76-mile canal between New Orleans and the Gulf of Mexico, was completed in 1963. It opened the port of New Orleans to ocean-going vessels and cut more than 40 miles off the river's winding course through the treacherous Mississippi Delta.

The Ohio River is more than 980 miles long, beginning at Pittsburgh, where it is formed by the confluence of the Allegheny and Monongahela Rivers, and flowing to Cairo, Illinois, where it joins the Mississippi. It is the second largest barge line in the inland waterways system. The only serious impediment to navigation on the Ohio was removed in 1830 with the construction of the Louisville and Portland Canal around the Falls of the Ohio at Louisville, Kentucky. A system of 41 moveable dams completed in 1929 eliminated the problem of low water and permitted year-round navigation. Major tributaries to the Mississippi and Ohio Rivers include the Tennessee, Arkansas, Cumberland, Missouri, and Illinois Rivers.

The Mississippi and Ohio Rivers were opened to exploration by the French in the 1600s, but did not become important rivers of commerce until the beginning of the nineteenth century. Settlers began moving into the Ohio Valley about the time of the American Revolution, and records indicate shipments of flour from Louisville to New Orleans as early as 1782. In 1783 a Louisville merchant advertised goods from Philadelphia that had been shipped up the Mississippi. Commerce was occasionally interrupted as Spain, which had obtained the Louisiana Territory from France in 1762, strictly controlled trade on the Mississippi and periodically closed the river to foreign navigation. In 1801, Spain ceded the territory back to France, which sold it to the United States in 1803 in the Louisiana Purchase.

With access to the Gulf of Mexico guaranteed by the Louisiana Purchase, southbound commerce on the Mississippi grew rapidly with pork, corn, whisky, hides, and other agricultural products from the Ohio Valley shipped aboard flatboats or the more colorful keel boats, which could haul up to 10 tons. Strong river currents kept trade moving in one direction until the introduction of the steamboat in about 1817. Within just a few years, 60 steamboats plied the waters of the Mississippi and Ohio Rivers. By the mid-1830s, there were more than 230 such boats. By the 1840s, steamboats regularly carried grain and lead from the upper Mississippi, coal from the Ohio

Valley, and cotton, sugar, and molasses from the South. Stern-wheelers, introduced in the late 1850s, could carry up to 350 tons of cargo while still maintaining less than three feet of draft. Rates for freight shipped from New Orleans to Louisville fell from $5 per hundred weight in 1815 to only 25 cents in 1860. Rates for the return trip fell from $1 to 32 cents.

The commercial importance of the Mississippi River System, especially for east-west trade, began to decline in the 1850s with the construction of railroads, which could deliver goods faster and more directly. This became especially apparent during the Civil War, when the Confederacy mistakenly believed it could cripple the Union by controlling the Mississippi. After the war, shipments of coal increased dramatically, but railroads captured most of the grain and cotton trade. Between 1870 and 1891, the number of steamboats on the Mississippi and Ohio Rivers dropped from almost 500 to about 150. Barges, pushed ahead by steamboats, began to carry much of the remaining river trade. In 1904, the steamboat *Sprague* set a record by guiding a "tow" of 56 barges loaded with 53,000 tons of coal from Cairo to New Orleans. Steamboats continued to operate on the Mississippi and Ohio Rivers until the early 1900s, when they were replaced by diesel powered towboats. Although called towboats, the vessels actually pushed their "tows."

The United States recognized the importance of river freight during World War I when the railroads were unable to meet the increased demands for shipping, and the government was forced to build an emergency fleet of barges and towboats. This led to a revival of trade on the Mississippi River System in the 1920s, when the upper Mississippi channel was dredged to a depth of nine feet and a series of moveable dams made it possible to navigate the Ohio during low-water months. Shipments on the Ohio increased from 7 million tons in 1915 to 22 million tons in 1929. The Inland Waterways Corporation, created by Congress in 1924 to regulate freight transport on the rivers, also developed a radically new towboat design with increased power which further revitalized the industry. In 1938, Congress authorized the construction of floodwalls along the Ohio and reservoirs on its tributaries to control flooding. In 1944, Congress also passed the Flood Control Act, which included provisions for a 12-foot channel and a series of dams on the upper Mississippi, and modernization of locks and dams on the Ohio. Work on the improvements did not begin until 1954.

Nearly 35 percent of the freight carried on the Mississippi River System in the early 1990s was petroleum products. Coal accounted for about 25 percent. Tows on the lower Mississippi often included as many as 40 barges—the equivalent of 600 railroad cars of freight—and were the size of four football fields.

Intracoastal Waterways. The Gulf Intracoastal Waterway is a natural, sheltered waterway completed in 1949 that follows the coastline of the Gulf of Mexico for 1,065 miles from Brownsville, Texas, to Carrabelle, Florida. The Atlantic Intracoastal Waterway is also a system of rivers, bays, estuaries, and inlets that stretches 1,200 miles from Miami, Florida, to Trenton, New Jersey. There are three major canals along the Atlantic Intracoastal Waterway: the Chesapeake and Delaware Canal across northern Delaware, which connects Chesapeake Bay with the Delaware River just south of Philadelphia; the Dismal Swamp Canal, south of Norfolk, Virginia; and the Caloosahatchee River-St. Lucie Canal across southern Florida. Vessels traveling the Atlantic Intracoastal Waterway are exposed to the ocean for less than 100 miles during the entire route.

Columbia Snake River System. The Columbia Snake River System is the longest river in the United States to flow into the Pacific Ocean. It is the nation's second largest waterway. From its headwaters in the Canadian province of British Columbia, the Columbia flows southwest through Washington state before turning westward to form much of the northern border of Oregon and joining the Snake River at Lewiston, Idaho. Along its course is 465 miles of navigable waterways and 36 large and small ports. Eleven dams on the American portion of the Columbia, including the Grand Coulee Dam, account for nearly one-third of the hydroelectric power produced in the United States. Ocean-going vessels can travel inland on the Columbia as far east as Pasco, Washington, while barges can navigate further up the Columbia and onto the Snake River as far as Lewiston, Idaho. Freight hauled on the Columbia consists primarily of grain and other agricultural products. One-third of all U.S. wheat exports move out of the Columbia River to world markets. Potatoes are another major export commodity moving downriver from Lewiston, Idaho; Pasco, Washington; and Umatilla, Oregon.

Steamboats first appeared on the Columbia in 1851, running between Astoria, Oregon, on the Pacific Coast and Portland, Oregon, 113 miles inland, and on to the Cascade mountain range. A mule-powered portage railroad, built in 1853, allowed steamboats to go as far as The Dalles, Oregon. The Oregon Steam Navigation Company, a monopoly controlling steam transportation on the Columbia and Willamette Rivers, was formed in 1861. During the 1860s, the Columbia and Snake Rivers were important routes for miners flocking to Idaho and Montana, and some steamboats managed to traverse the rivers nearly to the gold fields. However, the commercial importance of the Columbia and its tributaries did not begin to grow until after 1873, when construction of the Oregon City locks on the Willamette allowed grain from the fertile upper Willamette Valley to be shipped directly to Portland.

Other improvements followed. Locks were built on the Columbia at the Cascades between 1878 and 1898, and the Celilo Canal at The Dalles opened in 1915. The Bonneville Dam, just west of The Dalles, was completed in 1937. A towboat demonstrated the feasibility of shipping grain by barge all the way from Lewiston in 1945, but large shipments did not begin until the Lower Granite Dam was opened in 1975.

McClellan-Kerr Arkansas River Navigation System. The Arkansas River is the longest tributary of the Mississippi, flowing more than 1,450 miles from central Colorado to the eastern edge of Arkansas, where it enters the Mississippi. The first steamboat reached Little Rock, Arkansas in 1822, and Fort Gibson, Oklahoma, in 1827. The 436-mile-long McClellan-Kerr Navigation System was completed in 1971, and opened the Arkansas to barge traffic as far west as Tulsa, Oklahoma. The four largest cities in Arkansas, including Little Rock, are all located along the river.

Tennessee-Tombigbee Waterway. The Tennessee River is the largest tributary of the Ohio River and is part of the Mississippi River System. From its headwaters in Knoxville, Kentucky, the river flows southwest through Tennessee and into Alabama before turning north and eventually emptying into the Ohio at Paducah, Kentucky. The Tennessee-Tombigbee Waterway, a $2 billion inland waterway, opened in 1985 by connecting the Tennessee with the Black Warrior and Tombigbee Rivers in Alabama. Nicknamed the Tenn-Tom, the 234-mile long waterway connects 16,000 miles of 14 major navigable inland waterway systems in middle America with deepwater ports on the Gulf of Mexico. The Tombigbee flowed into the Mobile River, providing shorter access to the Gulf of Mexico. While estimates projected 20 million tons would be shipped on the Tenn-Tom per year, that figure had only reached 8 million tons by 1995. With the construction of the Trico Steel and British Steel mini mills in Decatur and Mobile, Alabama, in 1996, tonnage from these two mills alone were projected to represent an additional 2.5 million tons of cargo annually. Companies shipping via the waterway claimed large savings over conventional modes of transportation.

Hudson River-New York State Barge Canal System. At one time, the New York State Barge Canal System was the most important inland waterway in the United States. The famed Erie Canal from Lake Erie to the Hudson River was completed in 1825, and provided the United States with a navigable waterway from the Atlantic Ocean to the upper Great Lakes. The canal, enlarged several times between 1825 and 1862, was one reason that New York City developed into the nation's financial center.

Like the Mississippi River System, however, the Erie Canal declined in importance after the Civil War because of competition with the railroads. In 1903, New York State passed a $100 million bond issue to upgrade the Erie Canal and to connect it with three smaller canals to create the toll-free New York State Barge Canal System, which opened in 1918. The smaller canals linked the Erie Canal with Lake Ontario, Lake Champlain, Seneca Lake, and Cayuga Lake. More than 90 percent of the state's population now lives within 20 miles of the Hudson River or the canal system.

In 1993 and several years following, unusually heavy rains in the upper Midwest caused the Mississippi and its tributaries above St. Louis to swell to record flood levels, inundating towns along the rivers and destroying billions of dollars worth of farm crops and personal property. The Great Flood of 1993 and floods that followed also had a devastating effect on the inland waterways shipping industry. In 1997, the U.S. Army Corps of Engineers informed the port of New Orleans that it would take all summer to restore a 45-foot draft in the Southwest Pass, the channel used by ocean-going vessels to enter Louisiana's five deepwater ports, because of the millions of tons of sand and silt from devastating Ohio River Valley floodwaters.

Ironically, in 1993 the inland waterways shipping industry was only beginning to recover from a drought in 1988, when water levels on the Mississippi and Ohio Rivers fell to their lowest point since 1871. More than 100 towboats ran aground on the upper Mississippi during the summer, periodically closing the river to traffic. Those towboats that did manage to navigate the low water were forced to reduce the load and number of barges in their ''tows'' by two-thirds, from an average of 50 to 16 barges, which reduced profitability and forced companies to increase rates.

CURRENT CONDITIONS

Overall demand for inland waterway shipping grew only slightly during the 1998-1999 trade season. With an aging barge fleet, capacity was expected to decrease, to keep rates up, while volume was expected to expand less than 0.5 percent through 2010. One exception was the Mississippi River, which had a good season in 1999. Its rates were generally higher than the 6.1 percent average rate increase appreciated by the water transportation industry overall.

On the Tennessee-Tombigbee Waterway, 1998 steel hauling traffic increased by 140,000 tons from 1997, and as of June 1999, was up an additional 50,000 tons from 1998. Overall tonnage in all categories on the ''Tenn-Tom'' during 1998 was up about 2 percent, with a total 1998 tonnage trade of 9.3 million tons. Traffic on the Tenn-Tom was expected to increase again in 2000, due to the new Boeing plant in Decatur, Alabama, which would begin building Delta Five Rockets.

As of January 1, 1999, all members of the American Waterways Operators (AWO) must participate in its Responsible Carrier Program (RCP) as a condition of membership. The requirement was precipitated by the 1994 accident involving a barge which struck an unlit railroad bridge in fog, causing the railroad track alarm to malfunction. As a result, Amtrak's Sunset Limited derailment killed 42 people. The new RCP requirements exceed federal safety standards and regulations, incorporating only the best industry practices available, in an effort the increase industry safety.

On the federal front, the Army Corps of Engineers' Water Resources Development Act (WRDA) of 1999, with another scheduled for 2000, has provisions which address not only safe water supplies, but increased funding for development of domestic water transportation systems.

Industry Leaders

Until 1998, three main carriers had controlled 50 percent of the covered hopper barge fleet. But in 1998, two barge lines joined under the American Commercial Lines name, giving American control of 447 inland tank barges. However, in 1999 CSX, parent company of American Commercial Lines, sold 60 percent of American's shares for $695 million cash and $155 million in securities, as part of a partnership deal with the Vectura Group. Later in 1999, CSX was looking to divest its interest in the remaining 40 percent. American and Kirby Lines of Houston, Texas, accounted for 40 percent of the U.S. liquid barge fleet. Other leaders included Hollywood Marine, Marathon Oil, Ingram Barge, and Coastal Towing companies.

As of October 1999, another major merger took place. Top-ranked Kirby acquired Hollywood Marine for $322.2 million. Kirby then controlled 767 inland tank barges, giving Kirby 26 percent of total U.S. tank barge capacity.

Research and Technology

A significant development in the inland waterways trade fleet has been the conversion digitized Army Corps of Engineer maps of the entire inland river system, hooking them to Global Positioning Systems (GPS) installed on each boat. Such information, as applied to this industry, assists captains in pinpointing their exact locations on the river, their relative positions as to oncoming traffic, and their expected itineraries based upon speed and direction.

Another key issue carrying over into 2000 was the upgrading and replacement of an aging fleet in general. Barge construction has been accelerated to meet the expected demands of the first decade, with state of the art jumbo open and covered hopper barges costing approximately $235,000 to $275,000 each to build. A total of $1.4 billion dollars of capital would be required by the industry by the year 2005.

Further Reading

"Barge Fleet Rebounding Slowly, Study Says." *Journal of Commerce,* 28 February 1996.

Boehlert, Sherwood L. "Fiscal 2000 Water and Environment Budget." FDCH Congressional Testimony, 10 February 1999.

Gillette, Becky. "Tenn-Tom Shipping Up Slightly Despite Commodities Downturn." *Mississippi Business Journal,* 5 April 1999.

"Market Watch." *Logistics Management & Distribution Report,* November 1999.

Morton, Roger. "Keeping Up With The Flow." *Transportation & Distribution,* August 1999.

"N.O. Channel Clogged." *Traffic World,* 21 April 1997.

Sauer, Pamela. "M&A Hits Inland Liquid Bargers." *Chemical Market Reporter,* 22 November 1999.

Snadowsky, Leslie Tamar. "Bulking Up." *New Orleans City Business,* 3 May 1999.

"The Great Waterway: A Guide to Marine Facilities and Industrial Properties on the Columbia River System." *Merchants Exchange and the Columbia Snake River Marketing Group,* 1997.

"The Port of South Louisiana." *Handbook and Directory,* 1996.

The Transportation Institute. *Industry Profile: 1999.* Available from http://www.trans-inst.org/ind_profile.html.

U.S. Department of Commerce. *Statistical Abstract of the United States, 1996.* Washington: GPO, 1996.

"Water Transportation Industry Yearbook." WEFA, 14 December 1998.

SIC 4481

DEEP SEA TRANSPORTATION OF PASSENGERS

This category includes establishments primarily engaged in operating vessels for the transportation of passengers on the deep seas.

NAICS Code(s)

483112 (Deep Sea Passenger Transportation)

483114 (Coastal and Great Lakes Passenger Transportation)

Industry Snapshot

The passenger cruise industry, as we know it today, was formed around 1970 when approximately 500,000 people took overnight cruises. Since that time, the number of passengers has increased dramatically, reaching an estimated 6.45 million people in 1998. According to Cruise Lines International Association (CLIA), this number was expected to reach nearly 7 million by the year 2000. To encourage this activity, cruise line companies have continued to work with airlines to offer built-in fares. According to CLIA, the cumulative market potential for the cruise industry had been projected to hit between $50 and $90 billion between 1995 and 2000.

The North American cruise industry, which included the United States and Canada, was a $7.5 billion industry representing approximately 90 percent of the worldwide cruise market. By January 1998, approximately 135 ships were serving the North American market, with an aggregate capacity of 124,000 berths. Total berth capacity was expected to increase 50 percent by 2000. A fast-rising segment of the North American cruise industry is the short ''getaway'' cruise market. CLIA reported that in 1998, 1.7 million Americans took a cruise of five days or less, with 1999 estimates at 2 million passengers.

More than half of all cruises leaving from North American ports traveled to the Caribbean, about 13 percent traveled to Europe, and 9.5 percent traveled to Alaska. The most popular U.S. port for embarkation was Miami, followed by San Juan, Port Canaveral, Port Everglades, and Los Angeles. Delaware, the District of Columbia, Florida, Georgia, Maryland, North Carolina, South Carolina, Virginia, and West Virginia contributed the most to the cruising business with more than 38 percent taking two- to five-day cruises and 22 percent taking six- to eight-day cruises.

Since the mid-1980s, the cruise industry has conducted extensive market and consumer research. As a result, the industry has added new destinations, new ship design concepts, new on-board/on-shore activities, new themes, and new cruise lengths to reflect the changing vacation patterns of the public.

The cruise industry continues to have a very close working relationship with the travel agency community. An estimated 95 to 97 percent of all passengers were projected by the Cruise Lines International Association to have been booked through travel agents. Travel agencies found that cruises were profitable to sell and many people who take a cruise want to repeat the experience.

ORGANIZATION AND STRUCTURE

Cruise lines generally offered either luxury, mass market, or specialty cruises, although some analysts believed two more distinct categories have emerged: super-luxury cruises catering to the very rich and shorter, budget-priced cruises targeting middle-income vacationers.

Luxury cruise lines included companies such as Seabourn Cruise Lines and the Royal Viking Line, which emphasized personal service aboard relatively small cruise ships. The *Song of Flower,* a luxury ship owned by Seven Seas Cruise Line, Ltd., was typical of the luxury segment, carrying 172 passengers and 144 crew members.

The mass-market category included such highly advertised companies as Carnival Cruise Lines, Princess Cruise Lines, and Royal Caribbean Cruise Lines. These companies offered resort-style cruises aboard mammoth ships. In 1996 Carnival launched the world's first 100,000-ton *Destiny.* Carnival operated 13 ''Fun Ships'' in 1999, carrying more than 1 million guests annually.

The specialty cruise segment included companies such as Clipper Cruises and Windstar Cruises that offered adventure cruises to exotic ports of call aboard small ships that often carried as few as 100 passengers. Destinations included Africa, the Amazon, Antarctica, and seldom-visited islands in the Caribbean and South Pacific. Specialty companies also offered theme cruises with lecturers or celebrity hosts from the world of science, entertainment, or sports. The Cunard Steamship Co. offered murder mysteries aboard the famous *Queen Elizabeth 2 (QE2)* and opera and classical music experiences in which amateurs were invited to study and play alongside professionals aboard the *Sagafjord.*

At least five companies offered around-the-world cruises, including Cunard's cruises aboard the *QE2,* which had accommodations that included ''penthouse'' apartments that cost $400,000 for the entire 100-day cruise—and the apartments were always booked. The *QE2,* built in 1967 and refurbished at a cost of $160 million in the 1980s, also offered the only shipboard Harrod's department store. The *QE2* ran aground off the coast of Massachusetts in 1992 and tore a 300-foot gash in its hull, but was back in service in 1993.

Registry. U.S. cruise industry vessels were primarily of Panamanian, Liberian, or Bahamian registry, which provided cruise line operators with significant tax breaks over U.S. registration. Foreign registration, known as ''flags of convenience,'' also allowed U.S. ships to hire foreign crews and escape strict U.S. safety inspections. The only U.S. flagged ships in the North American deep-water cruise industry were those operated by American Hawaii Cruises and Clipper Cruise Lines.

Likewise, major cruise companies, although they operated from U.S. ports and their headquarters were in the United States, were often incorporated elsewhere to avoid U.S. taxes. For example, the corporate headquarters for Carnival Corporation, the largest North American cruise operator, were in Miami, but the company and its cruise subsidiaries were incorporated in Panama, the Netherlands Antilles, the British Virgin Islands, the Bahamas, and Liberia.

National Organizations. Cruise Lines International Association (CLIA), headquartered in New York, was formed in 1975 to promote the cruise industry and provide training to affiliated travel agencies. In 1996, 26 cruise lines belonged to CLIA, as did 22,000 affiliated travel agencies. Travel agents began actively suggesting cruises as a vacation alternative in the 1980s. Cruise-only travel agencies have since been formed and large agencies have created cruise divisions. CLIA also sponsors National Cruise Vacation Month in February. The International Council of Cruise Lines, headquartered in Washington, D.C., lobbied on behalf of foreign-flag cruise ships operating out of U.S. ports.

BACKGROUND AND DEVELOPMENT

Until the early 1800s, most ocean-going vessels sailed only when they had a full load of cargo and the weather was favorable. Passengers were secondary. However, in January of 1818, the Black Ball Line in New York began regularly scheduled service between the United States and England. The first ship, the *James Monroe,* left New York Harbor on time, despite a blizzard, and arrived in Liverpool three weeks later. The Black Ball Line proved so successful that other ships began regular service. ''Packet ships,'' as they were known, were the first ships to concern themselves with the comfort of their passengers.

In the 1830s, steamships began to replace packet ships for carrying mail and passengers. The Pacific Mail Steamship Company, an American line founded in 1848, eventually came to dominate passenger service across the Pacific, but English companies dominated transatlantic service. One of these companies was the Cunard Steamship Co., Ltd., founded in 1840 by Samuel Cunard. Cunard was a Canadian who won the contract to deliver mail between England and Halifax, Nova Scotia. He and English partners formed the British and North American Royal Mail Steam Packet Co., which was renamed the Cunard Line in 1878. The first Cunard ship was the *Britannia,* which set sail from Liverpool on July 4, 1840. The ship carried a cow on board to provide passengers with fresh milk during the 14-day crossing. By 1880, the Cunard Line operated 19 ships that provided regular transatlantic passenger service.

Notable Firsts. In 1852, the *City of Glasgow,* owned by the British Inman Line, became the first ship to provide regular transatlantic passenger service without also having a contract to deliver mail. The *Glasgow* was also the first ship to be fitted with a spar deck covering part of the main deck. The spar deck provided passengers with a sunny recreation area in good weather and protection on the main deck during bad weather.

In 1879 another Inman ship, the *City of Berlin,* became the first passenger ship outfitted with electric lights. The Inman Line was also the first to carry immigrants to the United States on a regular basis in ''steerage class.'' Throughout most of the nineteenth century, passengers traveling in steerage slept wherever there was space in the hold and provided their own food or ate out of communal kettles. Signs aboard Cunard Line ships cautioned that ''passengers of the First and Second Class are requested not to throw money or eatables to the steerage passengers, thereby creating disturbance and annoyance.'' By the end of the nineteenth century, carrying immigrants was profitable for most passenger ships. The International Navigation Company of Philadelphia, later to be known as the American Line, purchased the Inman Line in the late 1890s.

The first organized recreational activities aboard an oceangoing passenger ship may have been aboard the *Great Eastern* in 1858. A commercial failure, the *Great Eastern,* owned by the Eastern Navigation Company, was the largest ship of its day. It was also the first ship with enough space for passengers to congregate on deck. On its maiden voyage, passengers organized a marathon and played ninepins. Most on-board recreation would be organized by passengers until after World War I, when deck tennis, shuffleboard, quoits, dancing, and bingo became popular ship-sponsored activities.

In 1870 the *Oceanic,* owned by the Oceanic Steam Navigation Company, became the first ship with multiple passenger decks. The *Oceanic* also offered passengers an on-board saloon and oversized cabins equipped with electric bells to summon stewards. In the 1880s, the *Umbria* and the *Etruria,* owned by the Cunard Line, became the first ships with refrigeration for food storage.

Superliners. By the early 1900s, Germany had begun to dominate transatlantic passenger service with luxury liners that rivaled the most posh European hotels. The *Amerika,* owned by the Hamburg-Amerika Line, was the first ship equipped with an elevator. It also boasted of an on-board restaurant operated by the Ritz-Carlton Hotel in London. Even the famed Cunard Line was losing money to the German competition, and American financier J. P. Morgan, who had purchased the White Star Line, was ready to buy the Cunard Line. However, the English government saved Cunard by subsidizing the construction of two new ships, the *RMS Mauretania* and *Lusitania.*

The *Mauretania* and *Lusitania,* launched in 1907, were the first ''superliners,'' the largest and most luxurious passenger ships yet built. Aboard these English superliners two cruise traditions arose: dressing for dinner and the ship-board romance. Cunard's advertising promised, ''Passengers will remember how romantically the glowing phosphorescent waves curled back in the ship's wake falling forever in flakes of diamond and pearl. They will remember how readily the damsel of their choice could be persuaded to a secluded spot in order to observe this poetic phenomenon.''

In 1911 the White Star Line surpassed even Cunard for luxury when it launched the *Olympic.* In addition to the amenities that had become standard, the *Olympic* was outfitted with a swimming pool, Turkish baths, and a tennis court. The ill-fated *Titanic,* which sank on its maiden voyage in 1912, was a sister ship to the *Olympic.* White Star never fully recovered financially from the sinking of the *Titanic.* In 1934, the Cunard Line purchased White Star and became Cunard White Star Ltd.

The *Lusitania* also earned a place in history when it was sunk by a German U-boat in 1915. Although kept secret by the U.S. and British governments for nearly 50 years after the sinking, the *Lusitania* was carrying tons of munitions for the English war effort, in violation of U.S. neutrality laws. Considered unsinkable by many, the *Lusitania* sank in only 21 minutes after being hit by a single torpedo, which detonated the contraband cargo. Nearly 1,200 people were killed, including 128 Americans, hastening U.S. entry into World War I.

After World War I, the largest of the German ocean liners were divided among the Allies. The United States Line got the *Vaterland,* which it renamed the *Leviathan.* The *Leviathan* became the first ship to launch a mail plane from its decks in 1927. Cunard, which lost 22 ships during the war, was given the *Imperator.* It was rechristened the *Berengaria* and became the line's flagship. White Star got the *Bismarck,* which it renamed the *Majestic.* The *Majestic* was the largest ocean liner afloat until 1935, when the French launched the 80,000-ton *Normandie.* The *Normandie,* described as a floating luxury hotel, included 28 six-room suites, 30 two-room suites, and 24 verandah suites along with the usual array of staterooms, each of which had a private bath. The ship also had an air-conditioned dining saloon, a movie theater, and a glass-enclosed garden complete with fountains and caged song birds.

The years between 1920 and 1940 were considered the glamour days for transatlantic passenger ships. The rich and famous from Europe and the United States often took long, slow, luxurious, pampered trips at sea, which were captured by the newsreels to be shown to common folks in movie theaters. However, the Depression of the 1930s almost destroyed the Cunard Line. Again the British government came to the rescue by subsidizing the construction of two more ships, the *Queen Mary* and *Queen Elizabeth.* The *Queen Mary,* launched in 1936, became the new symbol of luxury, surpassing even the *Normandie,* which was destroyed by fire in New York Harbor in 1942. Only 350 of the *Queen Mary* 's 1,100 crew members were needed to operate the ship; the other 750 catered to the needs of 2,100 passengers. The *Queen Elizabeth* was launched in 1940, but was soon converted into a troop carrier during World War II.

After World War II, the glamour of cruises faded. Jet planes replaced ships for those who could afford to fly, crossing the Atlantic in hours instead of days. By the 1960s, most passenger ships had become drab and dingy. In 1952, the American Line launched the *United States,* which was the largest passenger ship ever built in the United States and the fastest oceangoing passenger ship in service. However, a lack of passengers forced the ship to be mothballed in 1969. Cunard also sold the *Queen Mary* in 1967, symbolizing the end of an era. The ship became a tourist attraction in Long Beach, California. The *Queen Elizabeth* was sold in 1968, leaving Cunard with only one ship, the *Queen Elizabeth 2.* The original *Queen Elizabeth* caught fire and sank in Hong Kong Harbor before it could be turned into what was planned to be a floating university. Cunard repositioned itself as a cruise line in the 1970s.

The modern cruise industry began to take shape in the late 1960s. Faced with declining demand for transatlantic passenger service, especially during the winter when the North Atlantic was stormy and cold, passenger lines began offering vacation cruises to warm-weather locations. Instead of the transportation business, they were becoming part of the tourist and vacation industry. Princess Cruise Lines, founded in 1965, was one of the pioneers in this emerging industry, leasing a converted ferry from the Canadian Pacific Railway during the winter months to offer cruises from Los Angeles to Mexico. However, several business historians considered Carnival Cruise Lines and its co-founder Ted Arison to have actually invented the modern cruise industry in the mid-1970s.

Miami-based Carnival Cruise Lines was founded in 1972 as a subsidiary of the American International Travel Service. The company purchased the former *Empress of Canada* passenger liner, renamed it the *Mardi Gras,* and invited 300 travel agents to sail on its maiden voyage, which almost proved disastrous. The *Mardi Gras* ran aground before it cleared the Port of Miami. By 1974, Carnival was near bankruptcy. Arison assumed more than 5 million dollars in debt and bought American International Travel's interest in the cruise line for one dollar.

What followed was a remarkable, serendipitous turnaround. Even with a complete remodeling, the *Mardi Gras* remained an aging, inefficient passenger ship. During the energy crisis of the 1970s, it was forced to sail slowly to save on fuel. To fill the additional time at sea between ports of call, Arison added a disco, comedians, singers, and other live entertainment. He also encouraged less formality, more casual dress, and a festive atmosphere. The crew began to call the *Mardi Gras* the ''fun ship,'' and Carnival began advertising that time aboard ship was as fun and exciting for the passengers as the exotic destinations they were sailing to.

The ''Fun Ship'' marketing strategy, adopted as a registered trademark of the Carnival Cruise Lines, was an enormous success. Based on two people per cabin, the *Mardi Gras* sailed at more than 95 percent capacity in 1974 and 100 percent capacity in 1975. At the end of the year, Carnival purchased a second ship, the former *Queen Anna Maria,* which it renamed the *Carnivale.* A third refurbished ship, renamed the *Festivale,* was added in 1978. It was then the largest and fastest cruise ship sailing between Miami and the Caribbean. Over the next four years, Carnival built four new superliners and quickly became the largest cruise line in the world, capturing a quarter of the North American market and carrying twice as many passengers as its nearest competitor.

The cruise industry also received an invaluable boost from ''The Love Boat,'' a popular TV series that aired on network television for nine seasons beginning in 1977. ''The Love Boat,'' which featured a ship owned by Los Angeles-based Princess Cruise Lines, revived the Golden Era link between ocean liners and romance, and made the point that cruises were not only for the rich. ''The Love Boat'' was a staple among syndicated reruns into the 1990s.

A 1997 Cruise Lines International Association (CLIA) study identified some interesting—and favorable—trends in the passenger cruise industry. The study reported that by 1997, approximately 11 percent of the U.S. population had taken a cruise, compared to just 4 percent a decade earlier. The fastest growing segment of those taking cruises was passengers between the ages of 25 and 39 years old, and the average household income was about $50,000 per year.

An issue brought to the forefront by the International Council of Cruise Lines was the need for industry-wide international and national regulations governing the care of sick or injured passengers on cruise ships. For example, Holland America Lines, a passenger line with an excellent reputation for safety and sanitation, reported 325 to 375 emergency disembarkments in an average year. Council statistics indicated that if Holland America's figures were the industry norm, annual evacuations from ships would total roughly 3,760 to 4,350.

Only Norway, Britain, and Italy had any rules regarding cruise line medical care. The majority of deep water vessels calling on U.S. ports, however, were registered in the Bahamas, Liberia, Panama, Norway, and Italy. The U.S. Coast Guard does conduct sanitation inspections of these foreign ships.

Attendees of an International Council of Cruise Lines meeting on the topic in early 1996 recommended guidelines outlining the basic, advanced life support and cardiac life support that should be available on board by medical staff; medical staff should be certified in competencies, including emergency medicine, family practice and internal medicine, emergency and critical care, advanced care for injured patients, and minor surgical skills. Approval of such recommendations, however, was expected to be a long process.

CURRENT CONDITIONS

A sign of the times in the 1998-99 booming economy was the proliferation of mergers and acquisitions in corporate America, and the cruise industry was no exception. American Classic Voyages Company (AMCV, Nasdaq) announced an agreement to purchase the *New Amsterdam* from Holland America Lines for $114.5 million, with contingencies. The 1,200-passenger ship was expected to cruise the Hawaiian Islands beginning in the fall of 2000. AMCV reported a $2.2 million earnings loss for the first six months of 1999; however, its second-quarter 1999 earnings were $2.3 million.

Carnival Cruise Line had attempted to buy out Norwegian Cruise Lines, but in December 1999 dropped its bid when Norwegian sold two of its ships in order to meet loan payments. Norwegian officials projected a $92 million profit for 2000. Its 1999 earnings were approximately $40 million.

Royal Caribbean Cruise Lines received negative press in 1999 for its plea-bargained agreement to pay $18 million in fines for illegal dumping of waste oil and sewage in Alaskan waters. It had previously conceded similar dumping near Puerto Rico, only after being caught falsifying log records and proffering false testimony during Congressional inquiry. Notwithstanding, the company's annual revenues were more than $1.9 billion by September 1999, with gross profits of $686 million.

A 1998 newcomer to the cruise industry was Disney, spending $130 million to launch its *Disney Magic,* followed by the launch of a sister ship, *Disney Wonder,* in August 1999. Both ships boasted 2,400 berths and three on-board restaurants.

INDUSTRY LEADERS

Founded in 1972 as Carnival Cruise Lines, Inc., and renamed in 1993, the Carnival Corporation was the largest cruise operator in the world, with 13 vessels. In addition to Carnival Cruise Lines, which remained an operating division, the company owned and operated the Holland America Line and Windstar Cruises. It also owned a 25 percent interest in the Seabourn Cruise Line. The company employed approximately 1,400 full-time and 300 part-time employees engaged in shoreside operations. Carnival also employed approximately 360 officers and 8,900 crew and staff on the Carnival ships. Carnival's 1999 earnings were $1 billion.

The Carnival Cruise Lines division of Carnival operated ten ships offering mass-market cruises, including the *Sensation,* a 2,600-passenger superliner launched in 1993. That same year, Carnival signed a contract to build the largest cruise ship in the world capable of accommodating 3,000 passengers. Called the *Destiny,* it became the world's first 100,000-ton cruise ship upon its delivery in late 1996. In 1995, two other superliners, the *Fascination* and *Imagination,* were launched into service. Two more Fantasy-class ships were scheduled for 1998 and a sister ship to *Destiny* in 1999.

Royal Caribbean Cruise Lines, founded in 1969, became one of the world's largest cruise band by passenger capacity in the mid-1990s by offering more than 50 different itineraries ranging in length from 3- to 15-night cruises. In 1995, it had a nine-ship fleet that called at more than 130 destinations on four continents. Among its fleet were the 2,354-passenger *Majesty of the Seas*; 2,354-passenger *Monarch of the Seas*; 2,276-passenger *Sovereign of the Seas*; 1,600-passenger *Nordic Empress*; 1,512-passenger *Viking Serenade*; 1,402-passenger *Song of America*; 1,004-passenger *Song of Norway*; 714-passenger *Sun Viking*; and 1,804-passenger *Legend of the Seas.* Between 1996 and 1998, five additional megaships were planned to be launched for Royal Caribbean: *Splendor of the Seas, Grandeur of the Seas, Rhapsody of the Seas, Enchantment of the Seas,* and *Vision of the Seas.*

The Holland America Line, which Carnival purchased in 1988, was one of the oldest names in passenger ship history, dating back to 1873 and the Netherlands America Steamship Company. More than 1 million immigrants came to the United States aboard Holland America ships between 1873 and World War I. Holland America provided regular transatlantic passenger service until the late 1960s, when it retired the *Nieuw Amsterdam* and devoted attention to the cruise industry. Under Carnival's ownership, the Holland America Line added two new ships in 1993 and in 1994. Holland America offered premium-priced cruises to Alaska, Europe, and the Caribbean. In 1993 Holland America also resumed around-the-world cruising.

Windstar Cruises, founded by Circle Line Cruises in 1986, offered luxury adventure cruises aboard four-masted schooners with computer-controlled sails. Each of Windstar's 440-foot windjammers, the largest sailing ships ever built, carried about 150 passengers in a yacht-like environment. Windstar's North American cruises were primarily to small warm-weather ports in the Caribbean and focused on water-sports such as scuba diving and windsurfing. The line also offered cruises in the Mediterranean, South Pacific, and Southeast Asia. Circle Line sold Windstar to Holland America in 1988. Carnival acquired Windstar when it purchased Holland America.

Seabourn Cruise Lines, founded in 1987 by Atle Brynestad, a Norwegian entrepreneur, offered luxury cruises aboard two 200-passenger, all-suite ships, the *Seabourn Pride* and the *Seabourn Spirit.* Along with luxury accommodations, the Seabourn ships offered underwater observation rooms and sea-level platforms for water activities. Carnival purchased a 25 percent interest in Seabourn in 1992, with an option to acquire another 25 percent. Carnival also owned minority interests in Admiral Cruises and the Royal Caribbean Cruise Line, which had more passenger capacity than any other single cruise line. In 1993, Royal Caribbean operated nine ships with a combined passenger capacity of nearly 15,000, and had scheduled three more 1,750-passenger ships by 1997.

The Cunard Line, one of the oldest passenger ship companies in the world, is a wholly owned subsidiary of the multinational Trafalgar House PLC, based in London. Founded in 1840 by Samuel Cunard to deliver mail between England and Halifax, Nova Scotia, the Cunard Line included such famous ships as the *Lusitania,* sunk by a German U-Boat at the beginning of World War I, and the *Queen Mary.* Cunard headquarters were moved to New York in 1977. In the 1990s, Cunard offered cruises to more than 300 ports of call. It also was the only ship line providing scheduled passenger service between the United States and Europe. Kloster Cruise, Ltd., founded in 1906, is the parent company of the Norwegian Cruise Line, the Royal Cruise Line, Ltd., and the Royal Viking Line. Norwegian Cruise Line was founded in 1966 and offered one class of service aboard smaller ships in the Caribbean. The Royal Cruise Line, founded in 1971, offered luxury air/sea packaged cruises around the world. The Royal Viking Line, founded in 1972, offered luxury specialty cruises, including world affairs cruises in conjunction with Georgetown University, celebrity chef cruises in conjunction with the James Beard Foundation, and environmental programs. In 1988, Royal Viking launched the 758-passenger *Royal Viking Sun,* one of the most spacious ships in the cruise industry at the time.

Princess Cruise Lines was the third largest cruise line in the North American market with a fleet of ten ships. Princess was founded in 1965 by Seattle entrepreneur Stanley MacDonald, who leased the 318-passenger *Princess Patricia,* a converted ferryboat, from the Canadian Pacific Railway during the winter months and offered cruises between Los Angeles and Mexico. Princess continued to operate ships under charter until 1971, when it purchased the *Island Venture,* which was renamed the *Island Princess.* In 1974, Princess was purchased by the P&O Lines, a venerable British firm which added the *Sun Princess* to the Princess fleet. In 1977, Princess became the model for the hit television show ''The Love Boat,'' which provided market exposure to Princess and the cruise industry. To be launched in 1998, the line planned to add two new ships: the *Dawn Princess,* the sister ship to *Sun Princess,* and the 104,000-ton *Grand Princess,* reportedly the largest cruise ship ever built.

The Miami-based Celebrity Cruises, founded in 1972, was one of the largest companies in the luxury segment of the cruise industry. In 1995, the company had $39 million in revenues and 350 employees. The company operated two divisions, Celebrity Cruises and Fantasy Cruises. Celebrity Cruises offered Caribbean cruises sailing from Fort Lauderdale year-round. In the winter, it also offered Caribbean cruises departing from San Juan and Bahamas cruises departing from New York. Fantasy Cruises offered trips to the Caribbean, Europe, Scandinavia, the Mediterranean, and South America. Celebrity Cruises introduced combined fly/cruise packages to the cruise industry.

The New York-based Club Med, founded in 1984, was best known as a resort operator. However, in 1990 the company entered the luxury cruise industry with the launching of *Club Med 1,* which was the world's largest sailing ship. The five-masted *Club Med 1* carried 386 passengers and provided sports-oriented cruise adventures in the Caribbean from its home port in Martinique. With a shallow, 16-foot draft, the ship was able to enter harbors inaccessible to most cruise ships. The ship also featured a sports platform that unfolded from the stern, allowing passengers to windsail, water-ski, or scuba dive. In 1992, the company launched *Club Med 2,* also a sailing ship, which was based half the year in New Caledonia and half the year in Guam.

WORKFORCE

The majority of jobs aboard cruise ships generally fall into three categories: crew, food service, and accommodations. Crew was comprised of deck hands, engineers, and maintenance. Food service was comprised of all the jobs associated with running restaurants, including managers, waiters, cooks, and kitchen staff. Accommodations was comprised of all the jobs associated with running a hotel, including reservations, laundry service, and housekeeping. The ships also employed numerous clerical personnel, activities directors, and managers of the on-board retail shops and passenger services. Cruise ships were also among the largest employers of entertainment, including singers, comedians, dancers, and stage actors for musicals produced at sea.

Although many on-board cruise line employees were not from the United States, CLIA estimated that the North American cruise industry generated 475,000 jobs for U.S. workers in 1998. Average salaries for cruise jobs ranged from about $12,000 a year plus tips for assistant waiters to $50,000 for top ranking ship's officers. Employees also received room and board.

RESEARCH AND TECHNOLOGY

In 1992, Diamond Cruise, Ltd., a joint venture based in Helsinki, Finland, that included Japanese, Finnish, and American investors, launched the *Radisson Diamond,* the largest twin-hulled cruise ship in the world. The 354-passenger ship, which flew the Finnish flag, was managed by Minneapolis-based Radisson Hotels International, and catered to an upscale business clientele. The cost of sailing on the *Radisson Diamond* was about $600 per day, among the highest in the industry.

In addition to luxury accommodations, including 123 of 127 staterooms with outdoor balconies, the *Radisson Diamond* offered complete conference facilities, including an eight-channel satellite communications systems for voice, data, and fax transmission. But the most innovative feature about the $125 million ship was its hull. The catamaran-like hull was designed to increase the ship's stability and reduce the rolling and pitching that caused seasickness. The *Radisson Diamond* was about the same width as other modern cruise ships but only about half the length at 410 feet. The ship was also slower and had a deeper draft than single-hulled ships, which made it impossible to dock at some ports.

Other groups were considering even larger cruise ships, including the 5,600-passenger *Phoenix World City,* designed by a consortium of German shipbuilders. The *Phoenix World City* would include three eight-story hotels atop a 1,243-foot split-stern hull. There would be room between the semi-catamaran hull to dock four 400-passenger ships for day excursions. Another design by the leading French shipbuilder was a circular ship that would look like an island resort from above, complete with an amusement park, lagoon, and sandy beaches.

Royal Caribbean's *Splendour of the Seas,* launched in March 1996, offered an ultra high-tech interior design. Its atrium/lobby area soared seven decks in height to the base of the ship's Viking Crown Lounge, accessible by two panoramic glass elevators. Radiating light throughout the enormous atrium was a sculpture made out of brilliant glass to symbolize the sun, sky, and earth. The circular Viking Crown Lounge served as an observatory by day and a disco by night. Its dining rooms were designed to take advantage of 20-foot windows that offered views of the sea. Its Solarium and Spa offered a Greek theme with bubbling fountains, whirlpools, lounge chairs, and a caf. A 4,500-square-foot canopy, the largest on board any ship, was used to shade an 18-hole, 6,000-square-foot miniature golf course. This golf course, designed to recreate famous courses around the world, was the second placed aboard a cruise ship. It included trees, sand traps, water hazards, bridges, and foliage. An 802-seat theater contained an orchestra pit that could be raised and lowered, as well as a computerized set rigging system that moved sets on and off stage. Royal Caribbean's megaship, *Grandeur of the Seas,* launched in December 1996, introduced an innovated procedure for ship stabilization while docked or moored out in harbor. Computers and satellites enabled the placement of the ship and held it stationary without the use of an anchor, anchor chains, and potential damage to the ocean floor. The procedure made it possible for the ship to make more port calls and sped up the arrival and departure of the vessel.

Celebrity Cruise Line's ships, *Galaxy* and *Century* offered an interactive entertainment system from which passengers could make reservations for shore excursions and learn about special events, or use as an information system for business. Another feature was ship-to-shore video conferencing.

Crystal Cruises introduced a Computer University at Sea program in January 1997, which enabled passengers to become more computer literate. Norwegian Cruise Line's ship, the *Dreamworld,* was the world's first ship to offer SeaVision, a fully-digital interactive television system, on 10 cruise ships. By touching the television remote control, passengers could preview shore excursions, purchase tours, order room service, shop, or engage in a host of other services. The ship's captain could also use SeaVision to notify and instruct passengers in the event of an emergency.

Some industry analysts questioned the wisdom of building megaships so big that passengers would not know they were at sea. However, they also agreed that with the industry growing so rapidly, someone would test the market.

FURTHER READING

Beirne, Mike. "Carnival Augments Six Lines' Image." *Brandweek,* 12 April 1999.

Chater, Amanda. "1998: Food Spending Tops $527 Mil., Ship-Counts Up." *Food Service Director,* 15 April 1999.

Corzo, Cynthia. "Cruise Line Offers Two-Night Florida-to-Nassau Getaways." *The Miami Herald,* 25 June 1999.

"The Cruise Industry—an Overview." New York: Cruise Lines International Association, January 1996.

"In Brief." *Waste News,* 13 December 1999.

"Cruise Industry Expects to Set New Marks for 1997, CLIA Study Shows." New York: Cruise Lines International Association, 1997. Available from http://www.ten-io/clia/news/expect97.html.

Grimm, Matthew. "Bells and Whistles To Go." *Brandweek,* 15 June 1998.

Havre, Randy. "American Classic Voyages In For Smooth Sailing." *Pacific Business News,* 15 October 1999.

Kremer, Gloria Hayes. "HiTech on the High Seas." *Montgomery Newspapers,* 19-20 March 1997.

McDowell, Edwin. "Law Firms in Four States File Suits Challenging the Port Charges Assessed by Cruise Lines." *New York Times,* 28 April 1996.

Royal Caribbean Cruise Lines Financial Report for 1999. Available from http://www.hoovers.com.

Stieghorst, Tom. "Carnival Drops Bid for Cruise Line." *Sun-Sentinel* South Florida, 16 December 1999.

Verrier, Richard. "New Cruise Ship Arrives at Port Canaveral, Fla." *The Orlando Sentinel,* 15 November 1999.

Wade, Betsy. "Assessing Ships.' Medical Care." *New York Times* 4 February 1996.

SIC 4482

FERRIES

This category includes establishments primarily engaged in operating ferries for the transportation of passengers or vehicles. Establishments primarily engaged in providing lighterage services are classified in **SIC 4499: Water Transportation Services, Not Elsewhere Classified.**

NAICS CODE(S)

483114 (Coastal and Great Lakes Passenger Transportation)

483212 (Inland Water Passenger Transportation)

INDUSTRY SNAPSHOT

As of early 1999, there were 138 ferry establishments operating in 35 states in the United States, including both private and government-run ferries. After falling to historic lows in the 1970s, U.S. ferry services began enjoying a revival in popularity as commuters sought alternatives to overcrowded highways.

ORGANIZATION AND STRUCTURE

Ferries in the United States run the gamut from small floating parking lots capable of carrying a few dozen cars a short distance to huge ferryliners, such as those servicing the Alaska Marine Highway, that are capable of carrying hundreds of automobiles. Some even provide passengers with conveniences ranging from lounges and cafeterias to overnight accommodations on trips that could last up to a week. Some old-fashioned rope or steam-operated paddle-wheel ferries still run as tourist attractions and as a living monument to the long history of ferries in the United States.

Multi-route ferry systems, such as the Alaskan system or the Washington State Ferry System, are often operated by state departments of transportation. However, many commuter routes in urban areas such as New York and San Francisco are privately operated. Highway river crossings are characterized by a mix of government and privately run services. Federal law requires that all passenger ferries be inspected by the U.S. Coast Guard. There was no national organization of ferry operators, though many of them belonged to the American Waterways Operators.

BACKGROUND AND DEVELOPMENT

Ferries are commonly defined as boats that carry passengers or vehicles across narrow bodies of water in return for payment. They have a long history. Even Charon, ferryman for the dead in ancient Greek mythology, demanded payment before transporting souls across the river Styx into Hades, prompting Greeks to place coins in the mouths of the dead before burying them.

The earliest accounts of European exploration in North America record instances of Native Americans charging to carry passengers across rivers in birch bark canoes. There are, in fact, written accounts of wagons being loaded into two canoes paddled side-by-side. Many early government treaties conferred the right of ferriage to the Indians, but the Indians were shunted aside as soon as a ferry route became profitable, as John Perry points out in *American Ferryboats.*

As late as 1828, 10 years after Illinois became a state, the Winnebago Indians controlled the important commercial ferry route across the Rock River at modern day Dixon. When the Winnebago monopoly was challenged in 1827, the Indians destroyed both the offending ferryboat and ferry house. Eventually, ferriage rights were negotiated as part of the Treaty of Green Bay. French trapper Joe Ogee established the first non-Indian ferry in 1829. In 1832, Ogee sold the ferry to John Dixon, and the community became known as Dixon's Ferry.

Piecing together a history of the early American ferryboat industry is difficult because few official records were kept. What is known was usually gleaned from the diaries of travelers, or as was often the case, when squabbles over who had the legal right to provide ferriage ended up in court. However, by the 1640s, there were several established ferry routes in the American colonies. In 1630, the Massachusetts Bay Colony issued a request for someone to begin ferry service between Boston and Charlestown. The first regular ferry service between New Amsterdam on Manhattan Island and Brooklyn on Long Island is known to have been in operation by 1643, and probably for several years before that.

In 1654, New Amsterdam also passed what may have been the first ferry ordinance in the New World. The ordinance declared that no one could provide ferriage without a license, that ferry service must adhere to a regular schedule, and that ferry operators must provide shelters for passengers on both shores. Despite the ordinance, however, ferry service between Manhattan and Brooklyn was a contentious free-for-all for more than 100 years as the two communities argued over which had the right to carry passengers across the East River. The dispute often turned ugly, as when Brooklyn radicals burned the ferry house belonging to the officially chartered and licensed New York Corporation. Brooklyn finally won the legal right to provide its own ferry service in 1775. Although the colony of New York appealed to the Court of King George III, the appeal was never heard because the American colonies declared their independence in 1776.

Current-Driven Ferries. Initially, Indian canoes were replaced on ferry routes by flat-bottomed boats that were either rowed, poled, or paddled across the stream or river. On open water, ferryboats were often fitted with sails. The first technological improvement was simply to string a rope across the river. The rope allowed the ferry to be pulled across. But more importantly, it acted as a restraint so that the ferry would end up at the right point on the opposite shore instead of being pushed downstream by the current. This made it feasible to build permanent docks, rather than allowing the ferries to run aground along the riverbank somewhere close to their destination. In some places, horses or windlasses were used to pull the ferries.

The use of ropes led to the development of ''current ferries.'' Ferry operators discovered they could use water power to drive the boats by turning them at a slight angle to the river current, much like tacking in a sailboat, except the rope also kept the ferry from moving downstream. The return trip could be made by reversing the angle of the ferry. The current ferry established the pattern of double-ended ferryboats, which removed the need to turn the boat around. Eventually, wire cables replaced ropes, but current ferries remained the most common short-haul ferries in the United States into the nineteenth century. Another innovation was the pendulum ferry. Apparently fairly popular in Europe, although rare in the United States, pendulum ferries took advantage of a mid-river island to anchor a rope or cable strung along a line of floating platforms. Such ferries would then swing across the river at the end of the rope pendulums.

Team Boats. Current ferries were fine for narrow rivers that could be spanned by ropes or cables, but broad rivers or coastal bays required a different source of power. The "team boat," which appeared in America in the early nineteenth century, used mules or horses carried aboard the ferry to power a capstan or treadmill that drove a paddle wheel. The Romans apparently used oxen in a similar manner to propel war boats, but team boats were considered an ingenious new invention by early Americans. The first team boat in the United States is believed to have been put in service in 1814 on a run between Brooklyn and Manhattan. The *Long Island Star* reported that the boat took 8 to 18 minutes to cross the East River and carried an average of 200 passengers, plus horses and vehicles. The team boat was the principal type of ferry for open water for almost two decades, until the steamboat replaced it. However, many team boats operated well into the twentieth century.

Steam Ferries. Steamboats, including ferries, were operating in the United States as early as 1786. However, credit for creating the first practical, commercial steamboat is usually given to Robert Fulton in 1807. Fulton was a successful jeweler and painter of miniatures before he turned his attention to science and engineering in the late eighteenth century. He invented a number of labor saving machines and designed several experimental submarines between 1797 and 1806. The following year, Fulton directed the construction of a steamboat originally known as the *North River Steamboat* and later renamed the *Clermont.* For many years, the *Clermont* carried passengers and cargo up and down the Hudson River, but it was never used as a ferry.

In 1808, Fulton formed New York and Brooklyn Ferry Associates and established a watershed business relationship with Robert R. Livingston, former United States Ambassador to France who had signed the Declaration of Independence and negotiated the Louisiana Purchase. Several years before, around 1790, the governments of Pennsylvania, New Jersey, and New York each granted exclusive license to American inventor John Fitch to operate steam-driven vessels on the waters bordering their states. Fitch later transferred the license to operate in New York waters to Livingston, a former business partner who was also presiding judge of the New York court of chancery when the monopoly was granted. Since obtaining the franchise, Livingston had also received permission to double ferry tolls once steam ferries were put in operation.

When Livingston joined up with Fulton, team-boat ferry operators were told they should be prepared to go out of business. The New York Legislature even agreed to extend Livingston's monopoly an additional five years for every steamboat that he and Fulton put in service. However, before they were able to launch their first steam ferry, another entrepreneur beat them to it.

John Stevens, a former business associate of both Fitch and Livingston, had launched his first steam ferry in 1809. He wanted to run between Hoboken, New Jersey, and New York, but because of Livingston's monopoly, he decided to operate between Philadelphia and Trenton, New Jersey, across the Delaware River. In 1810, Stevens obtained a ferry license from New York City, in conflict with the state license. Stevens tried to reach an amicable agreement with Fulton and Livingston, but when negotiations failed, Stevens went ahead and launched the *Juliana,* the first steam ferry in New York waters, in 1811. The *Juliana,* however, challenged the Fulton-Livingston monopoly for only one season. Soon after the ferry was launched, the New York Legislature enacted a law that allowed the seizure of any steamboat not authorized under the state monopoly. The next summer, the *Juliana* was literally chased out of New York waters. Stevens returned to using team boats on his Hoboken to New York run.

Fulton and Livingston launched their first steam ferry, the *Nassau,* in 1814. It ran between Manhattan and Brooklyn. The *Long Island Star* reported of the *Nassau,* "The captain, lordly as old Neptune, drives his splendid car regardless of wind or tide, and is able to tell with certainty the hour of his return."

Gibbons v. Ogden. The New York seizure law, and a similar law passed by New Jersey in retaliation, seriously retarded development of the ferry industry and perpetuated the use of team boats. The laws also led to the first case ever decided by the U.S. Supreme Court under Article I, Section Eight of the U.S. Constitution, known as the commerce clause.

In 1824, the Court agreed to hear the now-famous case of *Thomas Gibbons v. Aaron Ogden.* The ferry, heavily loaded with 27 boxcars, sank in Lake Michigan, about seven miles from Milwaukee, during a fierce storm in 1929. Fifty-nine crew and passengers died.

Between 1920 and the early 1960s, ferries on Lake Michigan were also an important conveyance for passengers heading to vacation resorts in Michigan and Wisconsin. However, interstate highways built in the 1960s cut into this passenger service. When the railroads were deregulated in the late 1970s, many of the ferry routes were abandoned. The last railroad to operate ferry service on the Great Lakes was the Chesapeake and Ohio, then known as the Chessie System. In 1983, the railroad's ferry service between Ludington, Michigan and Kewaunee, Wisconsin, was purchased by the private Michigan-Wisconsin Transportation Company for $3—$1 for each of the ferries then in operation.

The Michigan-Wisconsin Transportation Company went out of business in 1990, temporarily ending more than 140 years of continuous ferry service on the Great

Lakes. In 1991, the *Badger,* the last Great Lakes car ferry, was purchased by a former chief engineer for the Pere Marquette Railway. Lake Michigan Carferry Services, Inc. began operation in 1992, between Manitowoc, Wisconsin, and Ludington. The four-hour trip was at least six hours faster than driving by car around the southern end of the Lake and through Chicago.

Puget Sound Navigation Company. Small steamboats, known as the Mosquito Fleet, were operating on Puget Sound, in what is now the state of Washington, as early as 1836. The first ferryboat was the *City of Seattle,* launched on New Year's Eve in 1888. It operated between Seattle and West Seattle for more than 25 years. By the early 1900s, there were at least 70 ferryboats crisscrossing Puget Sound on 70 different routes.

Puget Sound Navigation Company, a subsidiary of the Alaskan Steam Ship Company, began operating ferryboats in 1898. Also known as the Black Ball Line because of its flag, Puget Sound Navigation became the largest licensed ferry operator in the United States in the 1930s with a fleet of more than 30 boats, many of them purchased from San Francisco ferry operators after the Golden Gate Bridge opened in 1937. Puget Sound Navigation controlled most major ferry routes on Puget Sound as a state-regulated monopoly from 1935 until 1951 when it became part of the Washington State Ferry System. It was also responsible for all passenger vessels operating on Puget Sound being called ferryboats. In the early 1900s, only steamboats operating on the shortest routes were commonly called ferries. But in 1909, Canada passed a law limiting the number of passengers that ocean steamships could carry based on gross tonnage. The law was to benefit the Canadian Pacific Railway, which operated steamships between Seattle and Vancouver, in the province of British Columbia. Canadian Pacific's luxury steamships were larger but carried fewer passengers than the vessels operated by Puget Sound Navigation. But Charles Peabody, chairman of Puget Sound Navigation, declared publicly that his vessels were ferryboats, not ocean steamships. Puget Sound Navigation continued carrying boatloads of passengers between Seattle and Vancouver, and the Canadian government never challenged the definition. Passenger boats on Puget Sound have been considered ferryboats ever since.

Puget Sound Navigation is also known for operating the *Kalakala.* Originally built as a passenger ship in San Francisco and converted to carry automobiles on Puget Sound in 1935, the futuristic-looking *Kalakala* was the world's first streamlined ship. It could carry 110 cars and 2,000 passengers, and was probably the most photographed ferry in the world. More than 6 million passengers rode the *Kalakala* between 1935 and 1941 alone. It was in service on Puget Sound for 32 years.

In the late 1940s, a series of labor strikes and declining ridership forced Puget Sound Navigation to seek a 30 percent rate increase from the State of Washington. The state refused, and Alex Peabody, who had succeeded his father as president, threatened to suspend service, which he did on February 29, 1948. Peabody and Washington State reached an agreement and service was restored a few weeks later. However, Washington state also began to explore the possibility of buying Puget Sound Navigation and operating the ferry service as a public transportation system. Peabody resisted at first, but in 1951 his financial backers forced him to sell, leading to the creation of the Washington State Ferry System.

Ferries began making a comeback in the 1980s as traffic congestion, air pollution, and urban stress became critical problems. In New York, five private ferry operators began service on nine routes between 1986 and 1992. In 1992, New York City offered free use of terminal facilities for ferry operators who agreed to undertake routes specified by the city. Other cities to experience a renaissance in ferry service included Boston, Detroit, and Fort Lauderdale, Florida. Ferry service across San Francisco Bay resumed in 1989 when an earthquake damaged the Bay Bridge. The ferry was so popular that a rival ferry began service in 1990. Both ferry systems planned to add routes, and city transit officials expected 6 to 8 percent of all San Francisco Bay area commuters to be riding ferries by 2000. Many of these new ferries were high-speed, high technology catamarans.

Current Conditions

In early 1999, *Fast Ferry* magazine reported that there were approximately 1,250 fast ferries operating in the world. Traveling 25 to 35 knots, they are capable of carrying at least 50 passengers, or a combination of freight and passengers, making them ideal, alternative transportation in congested areas near waterways. Some of the new market areas include service from Boston to Martha's Vineyard and Nantucket, and a $1 billion Water Transit System planned for San Francisco's Bay Area. Smog-sensitive Californians were pleased to learn that the proposed system, covering 440 miles of water routes, would produce only one-sixtieth (1/60) of the amount of nonmethane hydrocarbons as would vehicular traffic moving the same number of persons.

The Great Lakes ferry system had 20 ferry services going into the 1998 season, serving both upper and lower Michigan. For fiscal year 1997, Great Lakes ferries carried 722,420 passengers, 448,221 vehicles, and completed 64,860 ferry crossings.

One of the most successful ferry shuttle services in the country is operated by the Massachusetts Bay Transportation Authority (MBTA). Ridership has doubled between 1997 and 1999. Its biggest passenger commuter ferry service carried 380,000 passengers a year in the Boston Harbor area. Another service from Lovejoy Wharf to the World Trade Center, with a stop at the new Federal Courthouse, was carrying 2,240 one-way passengers per month by mid-1999.

INDUSTRY LEADERS

Washington State Ferries. In the early 1990s, the state of Washington operated 25 ferries on 11 routes, making it the largest ferry operator in the United States. In 1992, more than 23 million passengers rode Washington State ferries, more than the number of passengers who rode Amtrak trains or used the Seattle-Tacoma International Airport. In 1992, Washington State ferries also carried nearly 10 million cars and other vehicles on routes crossing Puget Sound. The year 1992 marked the tenth straight annual increase in passengers and vehicles for the ferry system,

The largest of the Washington State ferries were the *Spokane* and the *Walla Walla,* jumbo ferries that could each carry more than 2,000 passengers and 200 automobiles. When they were built in 1972, the *Spokane* and the *Walla Walla* were the largest ferryboats in the world. The smallest of the Washington State fleet was the 86-foot *Tyee,* a passenger-only ferry that could carry 200. The longest of the ferry system's routes is the 40-mile international trip between Anacortes, Washington, and Sidney on Vancouver Island in British Columbia, Canada. The route winds its way through the San Juan Islands and takes approximately three hours. The shortest route is less than two miles between Tacoma and Vashon Island. Fares ranged from $5.50 for a driver and automobile on most routes to $26 on the Anacortes-to-Sidney route.

Ferry operators in Washington advertised the scenic beauty of the Puget Sound as early as 1890, and nearly 60 percent of the passengers in 1992 were recreational riders, making the ferry system one of the state's biggest tourist attractions. The Washington State Ferry System officially began operation in 1951, when the state purchased the Puget Sound Navigation Company, which had operated as a regulated monopoly since 1935. In addition to the state system, there were 13 other ferries in Washington operated by county or private enterprises.

Alaska Marine Highway. The Alaska Marine Highway was created in 1960, a year after Alaska became the 49th state. In 1992, the system operated eight ferryliners that served three different regions of Alaska. More than 415,000 passengers rode the ferries, which also transported more than 110,000 automobiles. The state Department of Transportation and Public Facilities operates the Alaska Marine Highway.

The Alaska Marine Highway was designed to serve the communities of southeast Alaska, most of which could not be reached by highways. The ferries travel the Inside Passage, a natural seaway protected from the open ocean by the Alexander Archipelago. The first ferries ran between Haines and Juneau. Service was extended north to Skagway and south to Prince Rupert in 1961, and further south to Seattle in 1967. In 1989, Bellingham, Washington, replaced Seattle as the southern terminus of the line.

The trip between Bellingham and Skagway takes three-and-a-half days and covers more than 1,100 miles. Most of the Alaska ferryliners provide staterooms, showers, and food service. Passengers are also allowed to spread sleeping bags on the floor of the passenger lounges at night. Many passengers pitched tents on the open rear deck of the ferryliner.

In 1964, the Alaska Marine Highway created a second ferry system to serve communities in south-central and southwest Alaska, eventually extending from Whittier on Prince William Sound as far west as Dutch Harbor in the Aleutian Islands. All of the routes combined served 32 ports in Alaska, British Columbia, and Washington state, and covered more than 3,500 miles.

In addition to providing transportation for residents of Alaska, the state ferry system also carried thousands of tourists annually. In 1992, the state Department of Transportation estimated that one of every 12 tourists reached Alaska via the Alaska Marine Highway. Tourists riding the ferryliners spent an estimated $26 million annually. In 1992, the Alaska Marine Highway employed more than 1,000 workers.

In 1991, the Alaska Marine Highway began a six-year program to refurbish its ferryliners, which ranged in age from the *Taku,* built in 1963, to the *Aurora,* built in 1977. The program also included replacing the *Malaspina,* also built in 1963, with a new ferryliner to be launched in 1996. Like the *Malaspina,* the new ferryliner would carry 500 passengers and would take over the Bellingham to Skagway route. The system's largest ferryliner was the 418-foot *Columbia,* built in 1974, which could carry 625 passengers and 158 automobiles.

New York City Area Ferries. Among the best-known ferries in the United States are the blue and orange Staten Island Ferries. The ferries provide the only direct link between the New York City boroughs of Manhattan and Staten Island. More than 370,000 people lived on Staten Island in the early 1990s. The ferries also provide tourists with a waterborne view of the Statue of Liberty in New York Bay. In recent years, the ferries averaged more than 20 million passengers annually.

The first official ferry service between Manhattan and Staten Island was chartered in 1712. Cornelius Vanderbilt operated one of three Staten Island ferry companies during the early 1800s. In 1853, Vanderbilt merged his service with the rival services. The Staten Island Railroad operated the ferry service from the late 1850s until 1905, when New York City purchased the route, making the Staten Island Ferries the first publicly owned mass-transit system in the United States. The cost of riding the Staten Island ferry remained five cents from 1897 until 1975.

As highways in the New York City area became increasingly more congested with commuters bound to and from work, a number of other ferry services were established. These new ferry routes link points wholly within the city, as well as points in New Jersey, Long Island, and Connecticut with the city. Unlike the publicly operated Staten Island Ferries, these newcomers to ferry service in the city are mostly privately run.

North Carolina Ferry Division. The North Carolina Department of Transportation operated the second largest ferry operation with 21 vessels on seven routes in 1993. The ferries carried about 700,000 cars a year. North Carolina, with its many inlets and offshore islands, entered the ferry business in 1934 when it began subsidizing a private ferry at Oregon Inlet. The state took over the Oregon Inlet ferry in 1950. The first state-owned ferry service, however, was on Croatan Sound. The state purchased the ferry operation in 1947 from the widow of a private operator.

Between 1947 and the early 1960s, the state inaugurated or acquired several more ferry routes using surplus World War II-type Landing Craft Tank (LCT) and Landing Craft Utility (LCU) vessels purchased from the U.S. government. Many of those ferry crossings were later eliminated by bridge construction. The first modern doubled-ended ferries were put in service in 1957. All of North Carolina's ferries were operated toll-free until 1961, when the state assumed operation of the Pamlico Sound ferry between Atlantic and Ocracoke Island. In 1962, the state began ferry service between Knotts Island and Currituck to cut in half a 90-minute school bus ride for children living on the island.

The North Carolina Department of Transportation Ferry Division was created in 1977, combining an early ferry operations department and a maintenance facility at Manns Harbor. In 1993, the newest ferry route was another Pamlico Sound crossing between Ocracoke and Swan Quarter on the mainland. It was also the longest route at 26 miles. The newest ferry in operation was the *Governor Russell,* completed in 1992, which could carry 34 vehicles and 225 passengers. The oldest ferry in operation was the *Hattaras,* an LCU built in 1953.

Of the private ferry service operations around the country, the largest in the mid-1990s was run by Catalina Channel Express, Inc., based in San Pedro, California. Catalina Channel Express operates passenger-auto ferries from the greater Los Angeles area to Catalina Island. The second largest private ferry operation, Cross Sound Ferry Services, Inc., runs boats across Long Island Sound between Connecticut and the north shore of New York's Long Island. It is based in New London, Connecticut. Based in Alameda, California, Harbor Bay Maritime is the third largest private ferry operation in the United States. It operates ferry routes in the San Francisco Bay Area. Based in Boston, Bay State Cruise Co., Inc., was the fourth largest private ferry operation in 1996, followed by Harbor Boating, Inc., in Baltimore.

FURTHER READING

"History of the North Carolina Ferry Division." Raleigh, N.C.: North Carolina Department of Transportation.

U.S. Census Bureau. "1992 Census of Transportation, Communications, and Utilities." Available from http://www.census.gov/epcd/ec92/uc92tabl.txt.

Ward's Business Directory of U.S. Private and Public Companies. Detroit: Gale Research, 1996.

SIC 4489

WATER TRANSPORTATION OF PASSENGERS, NOT ELSEWHERE CLASSIFIED

This category covers establishments primarily engaged in furnishing water transportation of passengers, not elsewhere classified.

NAICS CODE(S)

483212 (Inland Water Passenger Transportation)
487210 (Scenic and Sightseeing Transportation, Water)

This industry is comprised of a number of different operations. Airboats, or swamp buggies, provide transportation primarily for sightseers in swamps and marshy areas; excursion and sightseeing boats offer passenger tours and non-deep water cruises; canal boats give passengers the opportunity to explore historic canals. In the mid-1990s, 751 establishments offered services in this industry, employing 8,687 yearly, with an annual payroll of $188 million. More than half of these establishments employed fewer than five individuals, and only 17 employed more than 100.

Not only because of their unspoiled beauty and diversity of wildlife, but also because of their inaccessibility without the aid of a knowledgeable guide, swamps represented an ideal setting for services offering sightseeing tours on such watercraft as airboats (swamp buggies).

The airboat tour industry experienced two events that have had and will continue to have polar impacts on the viability of the industry. First, since the vast majority of the airboat tour business in the United States is centered in Florida, the crash of ValuJet Flight 592 on May 15, 1996 brought to the nation's attention the potential importance of airboats in search-and-rescue scenarios where a large-scale disaster occurs in an area such as a swamp, virtually inaccessible by other more traditional means. Commercial airboats were among the first vehicles used to access the crash site for the rescue and evacuation of potential survivors, and eventually were used to transport various personnel to and from the site, including relatives of victims.

Conversely, the battle between environmentalists and airboat operators in Florida has been heating up. According to the environmentalists, airboats have contributed greatly to increased ecological pressure placed on swamps—most notably, the Everglades. The intrusion of these vehicles and the sightseers they bring is causing a loss of habitat for endangered and threatened species. Environmental groups were looking to enact legislation to curtail airboat use.

Other such businesses, however, based their tourist appeal not on remoteness from civilization, but rather on the historical connections between industry and natural or man-made waterways. Disused canals held great natural beauty, but also served as a reminder of a key moment in the nation's past (the brief and yet crucial role of canals in opening up the West and fostering the growth of the U.S. economy) and of a time when the forces of industrialization and the natural world co-existed on a more equal footing. One example was the Chesapeake and Ohio canal, connecting Cumberland, Maryland, and Washington, D.C. The canal became a historic park, thanks in part to the efforts of Supreme Court Justice William O. Douglas, who successfully opposed plans to turn the route into a scenic autoway.

The nation's excursion boat business continued to expand, offering the public activities ranging from dinner yacht cruises to steamboat rides to canal cruises to charter canal boats to rides on official U.S. Mail boats. Riverboat rides continued to be popular on river ports, especially throughout the Mississippi/Missouri/Ohio River systems and in the Tennessee River Valley.

Additionally, many individuals were seeking to explore shipwrecks, initially protected on account of their historical significance. These wreck sites have become "bottomland preserves" providing additional sources of tourist revenue for local businesses offering water transportation services shuttling tourist, marine biologists, and scuba enthusiasts to and from sites.

According to the U.S. Transportation Institute's *Industry Profile,* as of January 1999, riverboat gambling operations were state-authorized in Illinois, Indiana, Iowa, Louisiana, Mississippi, and Missouri, cumulatively operating approximately 50 self-propelled vehicles. There were an additional 26 U.S. flag "cruise-to-nowhere" gaming vessels operating from U.S. ports, primarily in Florida. There were three traditional steamboats offering cruises on the Mississippi and Ohio Rivers. The Delta Queen Steamship Company will be operating five coastal steamers in the next decade, construction of the first to begin in 2000.

FURTHER READING

"Cattails Crowding Native Sawgrass Out of Everglades." *The Palm Beach Post,* 15 July 1996.

"Florida to Limit Frog Hunts." *The Associated Press News Service,* 5 August 1996.

"In the Line of Fire." *The Palm Beach Post,* 16 July 1996.

"Industry Profile." The U.S. Transportation Institute, 1999.

"Rejuvenated Lake Kissamee Opened." *The Tampa Tribune,* 8 June 1996.

Standard & Poor's Register of Corporations, Directors, and Executives. Volume 3. New York: McGraw-Hill Companies, 1996.

U.S. Bureau of the Census. *1994 County Business Patterns.* Washington: GPO, 1996.

SIC 4491

MARINE CARGO HANDLING

Establishments primarily engaged in activities directly related to marine cargo handling from the time cargo, for or from a vessel, arrives at shipside, dock, pier, terminal, staging area, or in-transit area until cargo loading or unloading operations are completed. Included in this industry are establishments primarily engaged in the transfer of cargo between ships and barges, trucks, trains, pipelines, and wharfs. Cargo handling operations carried on by transportation companies and separately reported are classified here. This industry includes the operation and maintenance of piers, docks, and associated buildings and facilities; but lessors of such facilities are classified in **SIC 6512: Operators of Nonresidential Buildings.**

NAICS CODE(S)

488310 (Port and Harbor Operations)
488320 (Marine Cargo Handling)

INDUSTRY SNAPSHOT

According to 1999 statistics, more than 2 billion tons of foreign and domestic commerce move through U.S. ports each year. Port and harbor facilities provide employment for companies that load and unload ships, transfer cargo from one mode of transport to another, or provide storage facilities. In the United States, approximately 800 firms participated in marine cargo handling operation in the 1990s. More than 21,000 people were employed in the industry, generating an annual payroll of nearly $1.8 billion.

Ports on the U.S. West, East, and Gulf coasts include both public facilities governed by port authorities and privately held terminals. Companies employ stevedores or longshoremen to load and unload breakbulk, bulk, or container ships. Most of these workers belong to a longshoremen's union. The goals of these unions are to preserve longshore employment and to raise the wages of its members. In 1999 the West Coast trade represented about 50 percent of the total containerized waterborne trade in the United States, moving $266 billion in cargo in 1998.

Containerization, or the use of standardized containers to ship bulk cargo, was one of the most important innovations in the marine cargo handling industry. This standardization of cargo handling produced both increased productivity and reduced labor needs. Another fundamental change in the industry was the growing usage of computerization in nearly every aspect of work, both in the office and on the wharf. The development of automation and containerization, including the growing use of robotics, could eventually make marine cargo handling completely automated.

ORGANIZATION AND STRUCTURE

America's busiest ports, by tons of cargo, were the ports in South Louisiana, Houston, New York, New Orleans, Baton Rouge, Corpus Christi, and Valdez, Arkansas. Port authorities were created from the 1920s to the 1950s, when port cities realized the economic impact shipping had on not only their city, but also the general public. During that 30-year period, large amounts of public funds were spent to repair and replace cargo and port facilities. But by the start of the 1990s, many were found to be in poor financial shape. Only 33 percent of the ports on the North Atlantic coastline showed a profit before tax support—and only the Pacific ports, especially those in Southern California, consistently reported profits prior to subsidy. Privatization of the industry has been contemplated by several port authorities, particularly in Washington, but most of the industry remained in the hands of private sector interests.

Companies that handle cargo at the ports, generally referred to as terminal operators, provide a variety of services to incoming and outgoing shippers. Usually these include loading and unloading ships, transferring cargo from one mode of transport to another, and storing cargo. Employees of marine cargo handling companies that actually perform the loading and unloading are called stevedores or longshoremen. Many employees belong to one of two unions, the International Longshoremen's Association (ILA) or the International Longshoremen and Warehousemen's Union (ILWU).

On the shipping end of the industry, as of 1999, the Pacific Maritime Association represented approximately 100 stevedore companies, terminal operators, and shipping lines on the West Coast. About 14,500 dock workers were employed by its member concerns. The American Shippers Association reported 700 members in 1999. These associations provide a unified front for negotiating in obtaining favorable rates and services, promoting fair competition, and bargaining with the longshoremens' unions.

BACKGROUND AND DEVELOPMENT

Since the 1960s, the cargo handling industry experienced tremendous changes. As early as the 1940s, mechanized cargo handling began in North America. However, its growth during the 1960s and the containerization movement during the 1970s resulted in great changes in worker activities, costs, and productivity levels. "The new mechanical equipment for container handling introduced into many ports in the 1960s and 1970s was designed to lift large heavy units and move them rapidly to land transport. This equipment replaced manual effort and greatly speeded the whole process of loading and discharging ships," A. D. Couper explained in *New Cargo Handling Techniques: Implications for Port Employment and Skills.* "Later, the more repetitive and simple tasks in these systems began to be taken over from human operators by the application of automation. This allowed faster movements, stacking, and retrieval, which in turn helped speed the handling of containers on and off vessels."

The three kinds of cargo handled by stevedores included breakbulk, bulk, and containerized. Breakbulk general cargo vessels totaled 21 percent of the world's shipping by gross registered tonnage (grt). Breakbulk general cargo ships were self-sustaining in cargo handling, meaning that they did not need on-shore handling equipment. Many ships even carried their own containers in order to operate at ports lacking adequate handling facilities. These kinds of ships included coasters, tramps (cargo vessels lacking a regular schedule), and cargo liners.

Handling breakbulk cargo was normally labor intensive and time consuming, requiring the movement of sheds close to the berth and the availability of equipment for lifting and moving cargo. On the ship, moving cargo usually involved making slings or trays and carrying or hauling heavy cargo into the center of the hatch to remove it from the ship. Movement of breakbulk cargo required extra caution when pipes, plates, and other awkward loads or dangerous materials had to be transported. Work on the wharf included making up slings and landing loads onto vehicles. Use of fork-lift trucks and mobile cranes, both introduced to most ports during the 1960s, was fundamental in removing much of the hard labor from onshore cargo handling.

Bulk cargo vessels ranged from 50,000 to 150,000 deadweight tons (dwt), and most of the larger modern vessels were without cargo-lifting equipment. These kinds of vessels included bulk carriers, ore carriers, timber carriers, and combination carriers for ore and oil, and for ore, dry bulk, or oil. Bulk cargoes such as ore, coal, coke, bauxite, sand, and salt once were handled using buckets, scoops, and baskets. However, the loading and unloading of bulk cargo was mechanized long ago. Bulk terminals handled a combination of commodities such as grain, wood chips, and scrap metal, while others housed a single commodity such as iron ore, copper ore, or minerals. Liquid bulk cargo such as crude oil and petroleum products accounted for more than 40 percent of the cargo engaged in seaborne trade. Handling of liquid bulk was almost entirely automated, thus requiring limited manpower.

The development of standardized modular containers for transporting bulk goods became known as containerized cargo. Standardization included the maximum weight of individual containers, specific lifting points, and uniform shapes. Due to containerization, much of the handling equipment in ports around the world also became highly standardized. Most manufactured goods and primary products were carried by containers. Only very large items were excluded, but even logs and timber could be carried in specially designed containers. Although standard in size, containers were built using a variety of materials, and could be refrigerated, heated, ventilated, or specially equipped to handle virtually any kind of cargo. The use of standardized containers reduced the time it took to load or unload a vessel, thereby increasing productivity and reducing port labor needs. The speed and volume of cargo handling continued to increase during the 1990s, as container systems become more widely accepted.

Due to these technological advancements in cargo movement, the job of stevedoring has changed over the past 70 years. What used to be laborious, physically demanding manual labor was replaced with handling diverse materials and operating highly technological equipment. The expansion of containerization also modified cargo handling operations, since ports had to be equipped with special cranes capable of lifting these containers.

Having the most profound impact on containerization and cargo handling operations were the number of huge containerships that came on line in the mid-1990s. To replace inefficient ships, meet shippers' demands, and maximize loads, larger, faster and more efficient containerships began to be introduced on certain trade lanes. The largest, dubbed supercontainers or post-Panamax vessels, were engineered to carry 4,000 to 5,000 20-foot equivalent units (TEUs), rather than the most prevalent generation capacity of 3,000 to 3,400 TEUs. Such huge vessels impact land operations such as on-dock rail facilities and intermodal connections. In addition, cranes must have a broad enough reach to stretch across six containers.

Ports, such as the major U.S. West Coast gateways of Los Angeles and Long Beach, California, positioned their operations to accommodate these huge supercontainerships. In 1995, the Port of Los Angeles embarked on a $600 million expansion plan. At the close of 1996, the Port of Long Beach and Chinese steamship line China Ocean Shipping Co. (COSCO) finalized plans for a $200 million marine terminal to accommodate post-Panamax ships. Six cranes with the capability to reach across 18 to 20 rows of containers were ordered for the terminal. Since 1994, the port had undergone more than $1.35 billion in property purchases and capital projects to expand and upgrade its cargo handling capabilities. It would become the largest container terminal in the United States.

Other port volumes reflected not the importance of containerized cargo but the difficulty they had in sustaining its business. On the West Coast, the Port of Long Beach accounted for 31.4 percent of all West Coast containerized volumes. On the East Coast, the Port of New York and New Jersey remained the busiest container port with some 40 percent of the North Atlantic business.

A more current problem facing all U.S. ports was the ongoing controversy about how to dispose of the muddy silt dredged to keep the harbors navigable. Much of the silt contained environmentally hazardous pollutants, which created dredging permitting delays. Through the lobbying efforts of the American Association of Port Authorities, amendments to the Water Resources Development Act (WRDA) were proposed to Congress. They called for a national dredging policy that would enable the U.S. Army Corps of Engineers to dredge more efficiently. Provisions in the act called for authorizing equitable federal cost sharing and dredged material disposal facilities, the prompt removal of obstruction to navigation, and capping of local cost sharing during the feasibility stage of project development. Until a solution could be agreed upon by all concerned parties, the heightened environmental issues about pollution in dredged materials was expected to create additional delays, increased costs, and lost business for American ports. The ports began looking for ways to share the costs of dredging, claiming they were the cause of the problem, but a solution had yet to be finalized.

Facing their own financial constraints, terminal operators explored the idea of forming partnerships among themselves, a process dubbed by the shipping industry as ''rationalization.'' By forming regional port authorities, terminal operators working with a shipping line in one port could form a partnership with operators in other ports that served the same shipper. The operators would divide the revenue generated for the work done in all the ports under an agreed-upon formula. Using this arrangement, the shipping line would benefit by receiving a volume discount, while the terminal operators would gain additional business without investing in equipment, office space, and labor. Several examples of regional port authority alliances included the Virginia Port Authority, the Port Authority of New York and New Jersey, and the Delaware River Port Authority. Prior to forming the Virginia Port Authority, competition between Norfolk, Portsmouth, and Newport News was so intense, steamship lines decided to call on other East Coast ports.

Many of the major container shipping lines began taking their stevedoring and terminal work in-house, virtually squeezing independent stevedoring operations out of the market. Edward DeNike, senior vice president of Stevedoring Services of America in Seattle, Washington, suggested in the *Journal of Commerce and Commercial* that independent operators should expand their services and embrace intermodal operations—the combination of different modes of transport. Working with 25 steamship operators, Stevedoring Services has become an intermodal operator with its 22 rail ramps, nine chassis pools, and a computer services division. Direct Container Line, Inc., also launched an intermodal container service between Japan and Mexico. The company offered Japanese shippers and Mexican importers door-to-door service that took 14 to 16 days, nearly 20 days faster than all-water cargo transportation.

Often companies that offered intermodal services were classified as non-vessel operators (NVOs). These companies did not own any vessels; instead, they either coordinated the transportation of several shipments in one container and were called ''consolidators,'' or they handled the complete transportation of full boxloads, and were called ''multimodal operators.'' Combined transport, such as the marriage of rail and trucking, generally was most developed within the North American market, followed by the European Community. Intermodalism had yet to pick up in Asia.

CURRENT CONDITIONS

On May 1, 1999, the ocean and inland container transportation industry became deregulated under provisions of the Ocean Shipping Reform Act of 1998 (OSRA). The Act's provisions intended to open competition in the industry. One of the key changes under the new law was the elimination of filing requirements with the Federal Maritime Commission of all contracts between container ship operators, importers, and exporters. Under OSRA, such contracts may remain confidential and unavailable to competitors' inquiries. Although intended to challenge price-fixing and favoritism, smaller shippers feared that it would promote unequal bargaining power among shippers. Small to medium-sized companies began to form alliances in order to leverage their negotiating power and keep them competitive in the market. In September of 1998, three California consolidators—Direct Container Line, Brennan International, and Conterm Consolidation Services—formed the New American Consolidators Association (NACA) to combine their buying and negotiating power. In early 1999, the National Customs Brokers & Forwarders Association of American Shippers Association (NCBFAASA) was formed, already up to 90 members by July of 1999.

Contract negotiations between the Pacific Maritime Association and the International Longshoremen and Warehousemen's Union during the summer of 1999 caused slowdowns and backups at the Ports of Long Beach and Los Angeles, creating a ripple effect along the entire coast. At one point, crane drivers shut down the Port of Oakland, California on July 7, further exacerbating the tense bargaining. A three-year contract was finally agreed upon in November of 1999, with voting approval by more than 80 percent of the union's members, with only 60 percent required. In 1998, average earnings for West Coast union workers were between $99,000 and $125,000 annually, including overtime and shift differential. Average hours worked per week were 54 hours.

In other industry news, the Port of Galveston (Texas) reported a 172 percent increase in net income for the first half of 1999, compared to the same period in 1998. The Port of Tacoma (Washington) and Hyundai Merchant Marine announced the opening of Hyundai's 60-acre container terminal, which features on-dock ship-to-rail transfer capability for auto shipments.

In December of 1999, workers at the Long Beach port rejected a proposed automated computer system intended to facilitate job dispatching to allow longshoremen to start work on time. The union has generally been wary of automation, fearing job elimination and general cutbacks. However, the Port of Savannah (Georgia) announced in 1999 that it would install integrated computer software for its container-management operations, ranging from gate operations to bookings, billings, and work-order tracking.

INDUSTRY LEADERS

Ryan-Walsh, Inc., became well known throughout the maritime industry as a bulk cargo and container handling company. It was a subsidiary of Pittsburgh-based Vectura Group, Inc., a holding company that also owned National Marine, Inc., a barge transportation company based in New Orleans. In 1992, Ryan-Walsh acquired the cargo handling operations of Palmetto Shipping and Stevedoring Co. in the ports of Charleston, South Carolina, and Savannah and Brunswick, Georgia. Ryan-Walsh already operated in 24 ports along the South Atlantic and Gulf coasts, including the three ports previously served by Palmetto. That same year, the company also became the stevedoring contractor at a new warehouse at the Alabama State Docks, where the company invested $2 million for pulp and paper handling systems.

Direct Container Line (DCL), based in Carson, California, became the leading U.S. export non-vessel operating common carrier (NVOCC), specializing in the movement of less than container load (LCL) freight. Although focused on service to the Pacific Rim, Direct Container Line worked with export shippers and freight forwarders to ship and consolidate freight from virtually any U.S. port to most major markets. Company chairman Owen G. Glenn founded Pacific Forwarding Group in Australia in 1975 and formed Direct Container Line in 1978. In 1998, DCL operated 13 offices and 25 receiving terminals in the United States.

International Terminal Operating Company, Inc. (ITO) was founded in 1921 by Captain Franz Jarka. Originally called The Jarka Corporation, the company specialized in handling freight and passengers in the Port of New York. Soon, The Jarka Corporation expanded its services to encompass the ports of Boston, Philadelphia, Baltimore, and Hampton Roads, Virginia. In 1962 ITO was acquired by Ogden Corporation. In 1983, the company merged with John W. McGrath Corporation, which included Atlantic and Gulf Stevedores, Inc., and integrated their North Atlantic and Gulf Coast operations. Ogden and McGrath continued to share ownership of ITO.

ITO opened its first public container handling facility in 1967, and it was among the first to utilize computers in its terminal operations. The company used the latest technology to coordinate all its port activities, including receiving and delivery functions, cargo documentation, and terminal security. ITO worked with many of the largest container, breakbulk, and specialized cargo carriers in the world and became one of the largest stevedores and marine terminal operators in the United States. Headquartered in Jersey City, New Jersey, ITO operated in 25 ports on the Gulf and Atlantic coasts. *Ward's 1997* reported that the company generated $32 million in revenues.

Van Ommeren offered logistical services for tank storage, shipping, and other transport services. With a total of 31 terminals in Europe, America, and Asia, the company had more than 11 million cubic meters of storage capacity, and became of one of the three largest independent storage companies in the world. Van Ommeren also operated a fleet of 28 ships transporting mineral oil products, chemicals, gases, and animal and vegetable oils and fats. Van Ommeren had 4,800 employees in 25 countries.

WORKFORCE

Crews of stevedores or longshoremen typically loaded and unloaded ships and moved cargo in and out of warehouses. Longshoremen employment began to decline in the 1950s, and most workers depended upon the International Longshoremen's Association (ILA) or the International Longshoremen and Ware-housemen's Union (ILWU) to preserve existing longshoring jobs. The ILWU represented more than 8,000 longshoremen working in California, Oregon, and Washington ports. The ILA had about 30,000 members from Maine to Texas, although the number working at any given time was much smaller.

Longshoremen labor disputes dominated the maritime industry. In the past, tremendous pressure was placed on shippers by the unions due to their competitive rivalry. Faced with declining memberships, each tried to obtain higher settlements, an accomplishment that could be used to attract new union members. These continual attempts to raise wages and protect a declining number of jobs resulted in several major strikes during the 1960s, 1970s, and 1990s.

Earnings for longshoremen remained relatively high compared to the average earnings in American industry. For example, full-time workers of International Longshoremen's and Warehousemen's Union at the ports of Long Beach and Los Angeles earned an annual salary of $99,000 in 1998, including shift differential and overtime. Wages also varied according to the kind of cargo handled. Moving distress cargo and explosives brought in double the hourly rate of general cargo. Cargo that was 32 degrees Fahrenheit or below also received a slightly higher hourly rate than general cargo.

AMERICA AND THE WORLD

Many ports throughout the world have prepared for the anticipated growth in container traffic, which was projected to increase for all of the world's major trades. According to the Drewry report, world container trade was forecasted to grow at an average of 4.6 percent annually through the 1990s, but with noted regional variations.

Trade with Asia and Latin America was projected to grow the fastest. Container traffic between Europe and Asia should expand at a faster rate than the U.S./Asian route. Forecasts called for 6 to 8 percent expansion from

Asia to Europe and roughly a 6 percent increase from Europe to Asia. Europe/Far East trade growth should remain at or near double-digit growth, mainly due to imports.

A more uncertain region was South America. Many ports located there lacked planning, financing, or room for expansion. These factors, coupled with a recent trade boom, caused a shipping ''bottleneck.'' However, North American/South American volumes were expected to continue to grow at a respectable rate, but at a slower pace than the previous two-year boom. In particular, American shippers saw an end to the double-digit growth in cargo traffic to South America, due to the anticipated entry of global carriers, accompanied by fears of overcapacity and falling freight rates. Unlike the South American ports, those in the United States and Europe were well equipped to handle increased container traffic and should not require large investments. However, some observers foresaw increased competition among the European ports.

In the meantime, the labor unions also began gearing up for the ''internationalization'' of shipping lines and increased containerized cargo traffic. Since both of these factors posed a formidable threat to future longshoremen employment, ILWU officials met with labor delegates from 15 Pacific Rim nations in San Francisco in April 1993 to explore the possibility of international solidarity among shipping employees. One suggested way of showing international labor support was that when one union came under attack by a particular company, other unions—through their operations with that company—would send a message of protest. ''Sympathy strikes'' and boycotts are generally prohibited in the United States, but other forms of protest are generally permitted.

Research and Technology

Widespread introduction of computers affected all forms of port activities and extended into every sector of cargo handling. A number of ports in North America and Europe introduced computers for office administration tasks, such as payroll and accounting. Several ports applied computers to the actual work of container control and cargo clearance, and they also developed their own information retrieval systems. Computers eventually were used for all aspects of port operation, and in the not-too-distant future, containerized cargo might be electronically inspected for damage, logged in by some type of electronic or laser-sensing device, coded, and recorded by computer.

One example of advanced computer technology was the development of Automated Guided Vehicles (AGVs). These unmanned, computer-guided, chassis-like carriers were introduced by Europe Combined Terminals BV and Sea-Land Service, Inc. in the Port of Rotterdam in 1993. They are capable of performing much of the work comm only done by a driver pulling a chassis by positioning itself under the quayside gantry crane while being loaded or unloaded. When fully loaded, it proceeded to the stacking crane where the box was removed. The AGV received directions from the terminal's Process Control System (PCS), which controlled all the computerized operations at Delta/Sea-Land. The ECT-Delta/Sea-Land facility in the Port of Rotterdam cost $275 million and took 10 years to complete. However, the system would be able to accommodate an increase in the terminal's capacity over the next 10 to 15 years.

An even more recent invention is the Robotic Machine, created by Paul Dunstan, president of Robotic Container Handling Co., of Bellevue, Washington. This dockside machine consists of a rack system with a computer-controlled container handler similar to a straddle carrier that stores and unloads containers. Its biggest advantage is its design to load and unload 1 million cargo containers a year in a terminal area covering only 50 acres. Each custom-built machine is 2,000 feet in length and capable of processing more than 50,000 cargo containers a month. Its biggest benefit is being able to reduce ship time in port by more than 50 percent. North American ports had often been criticized for lagging far behind international ports for container utilization per terminal acre. Singapore, for example, averages some 20,000 container moves an acre each year. (In the United States, that figure is 5,000 moves).

In the face of continued automation and computerization throughout the marine cargo handling industry, labor unions began trying to prevent the elimination of jobs. Now the unions faced ''a new, more sophisticated menace'' with the industry's push toward further computerization and the introduction of robotics. Yet, employers claimed that to match their competitors, they must invest in the new equipment and advanced technology. Recognizing that reality, the ILA took the position of not blocking progress in its entirety, but instead claiming jurisdiction over the automated jobs.

Further Reading

Bechard, Theresa. ''Ocean Shipping Deregulation to Start.'' *Pacific Business News,* 30 April 1999.

Burnson. ''Terminal Operators Stand United in Contract Talks.'' *Logistics Management & Distribution Report,* November 1999.

DiBenedetto, William. ''Inventor Hopes to Put Robots on the Docks Unloading Boxes.'' *Journal of Commerce,* 2 December 1996.

Direct Container Line, Inc. (DCL), 1999. Available from http://www.dclusa.com.

Gibbs, Al. ''Crane Drivers Shut Down Oakland, Calif. Port.'' *The News Tribune,* 7 July 1999.

———. "Romance Has Little to Do with Regional Port Alliances." *Journal of Commerce,* 16 September 1996.

"International News Notes." *Logistics Management & Distribution Report,* September 1999.

Kamhix, Jacob. "Matson Boosts Cargo Capacity in Case of Strike." *Pacific Business News,* 11 June 1999.

Machalaba, Daniel. "U.S. Ports Are Embarking on a Shake-out." *Wall Street Journal,* 18 October 1996.

Mongelluzzo, Bill. "Longshoremen Reject System to Automate Job Dispatching." *Journal of Commerce,* 14 December 1999.

Murchinson, George M. "Let's Build for the Future." *The Port of Long Beach Report,* fall 1996.

"One Step Back." *Distribution,* October 1996.

"Strength in Numbers." *Logistics Management & Distribution,* July 1999.

SIC 4492

TOWING AND TUGBOAT SERVICES

This classification covers establishments primarily engaged in furnishing marine towing and tugboat services in the performance of auxiliary or terminal services in harbor areas. The vessels used in performing these services do not carry cargo or passengers.

NAICS CODE(S)

483113 (Coastal and Great Lakes Freight Transportation)
483211 (Inland Water Freight Transportation)
488330 (Navigational Services to Shipping)

INDUSTRY SNAPSHOT

Approximately 15 percent of the total amount of transportation in the United States travels through inland waters, while 4 percent of this traffic takes place on the Great Lakes, and 5 percent along coastal ocean routes. Operators of tows and tugboats work these inland waterways, providing services such as docking ocean vessels, shifting floating equipment with harbors, marine towing services, tugboat services, and undocking ocean vessels.

Cargo transported along the U.S. inland waterways can be moved by barge or towboat. Barges range from 100 to 300 feet in length, carry a wide variety of cargo, and serve as a floating work station for offshore construction. Some barges certified for coastal and ocean service are capable of transporting liquid cargoes, such as oil. Companies that operate tugs and towboats usually have barges in their fleets. However, barge operations have been classified separately under **SIC 4449: Water Transportation of Freight, Not Elsewhere Classified.**

Many different types of tugs and towboats work the various inland waterways. Towing-supply vessels are from 150 to 222 feet in length and are used for towing drilling rigs, service and supply rigs, and offshore structures from shore. Supply vessels are 160 to 252 feet in length and handle supplies, equipment, and materials. They are usually outfitted with special pneumatic tanks for bulk cargoes and can be adapted to perform research. Utility, production, and line handling vessels are much smaller than the other two types, ranging from 65 to 130 feet long. They can transport crews and light equipment, carry supplies, and are often utilized as a general utility vessel. Offshore tugs are for any kind of ocean towing. They tow mobile drilling rigs and service the construction and pipe laying industry. They are also used for commercial ocean towing. Inland towing vessels range in horsepower from 400 to 2,000 and are used for any kind of coastal and river towing. They can tow drilling rigs and barges within various coastal area inland waterway systems, such as lakes and bays. They are also commercial tows providing service to industrial clients. Crew boats are much smaller than the other types of vessels, from 76 to 125 feet in length; they can transport light cargo and passengers at high speeds.

BACKGROUND AND DEVELOPMENT

Establishments that provide marine towing and tugboat services primarily work the inland waterways of the Atlantic, Gulf, and Pacific coasts; the Mississippi River; the Great Lakes; and the domestic ocean. These North American waterways comprise more than 26,000 miles of navigable rivers, canals, lakes, and coastal regions. The largest is the Mississippi River system, which runs more than 8,950 miles through the middle of the United States and intersects with the Missouri and Ohio rivers.

One of the earliest functions of the tugboat was to tow sailing ships into and out of the harbor and to assist in berthing (docking and undocking). The tug was also used to assist steamships. Although these vessels were able to enter and leave the harbor on their own, they were unmanageable to dock. Even though ships continue to be built with increased power and maneuverability, the tug remained necessary due to the ships' corresponding increase in size and tonnage.

Currently, the auxiliary propulsion force of tugs and towboats can serve many purposes. Large ships need tugs to assist in docking operations, to maneuver in confined waters and narrow channels, and to escort to clear waters. Items such as barges, cranes, "A" frames, derricks, lighters, tank barges, and railroad floats are towed by tugs. Towing also may be necessary to move a non-self-propelled piece of floating equipment. Such items might include mining equipment, drill rigs, dredges, barges, floating towers, ''dead'' ships, scrap hulls, and damaged marine equipment.

Tows have been ideal for river trade due to their shallow draft and ability to navigate the upper reaches of the Mississippi, Missouri, Ohio, and Columbia Rivers. Unlike ships, tugs are adaptable to changing needs with a minimum of delay because tugs do not have to wait until cargo is discharged before moving on to another job. The use of tows and barges has historically been one of the least expensive ways to transport coal, lumber, ore, oil, and bulk cargoes in the river and coastal trades.

Canal tugs operate on the canals of inland waterway and intracoastal systems and are designed to pass under low bridges covering most waterways. Railroad tugs haul car floats that transport railroad freight cars. The railroad tug must maintain a tight schedule and therefore has been specially designed for maneuverability, power, and visibility.

Coastal tugs are heavier than harbor tugs, and consequently have greater horsepower, larger all-around dimensions, and increased fuel capacity. American ocean tugs have been among the largest towing vessels utilized worldwide, second only to the enormous river towboats. Actually, the ocean tug is similar to a small ship. It has a large fuel capacity, quarters for a crew, and stores provisions for extended operations. Rescue and salvage tugs are at least as large as ocean tugs and contain extensive equipment for diving and salvage work. These vessels usually operate on short notice.

In the 1980s, inland waterway commerce rose slowly. However, the towing and tugboat services industry, especially the inland towing sector, was slowed by ''the effects of overcapacity and slower-than-expected growth in markets for grain and other bulk materials,'' according to *American Shipper.* The Midwest flooding of 1993 further hindered the industry; tugboat and towing operations came to a complete halt on the Mississippi River at the height of the shipping season. Widespread economic growth in 1993, however, gave industry operators reason to believe that tugboat and towing services would be in high demand for the next several years.

Environmental concerns, especially relating to the prevention of oil spills, led to increased competition among tug service operators on the West Coast. As the state laws regarding tanker movement in the San Francisco bay have tightened, some tug operators already have begun to purchase specially equipped vessels to use as escorts in the area. More specifically, California's Office of Oil Spill Prevention and Response established new rules that require tankers to have a tug escort when moving in and out of the San Francisco bay. The ruling mandated that tankers carrying a minimum of 5,000 tons of oil must have enough tugs on hand to provide one horsepower of pulling power for every deadweight ton. The bay area has been home to several major oil terminals and bulk ports, and has at least 1,000 tankers travel into the area annually.

Tanker operators were hoping that double-hulled vessels would be exempt from the escort requirements; that has yet to occur. The average tug escort costs between $8,000 and $10,000, depending upon the size of the vessel and the distance traveled. Tanker operators estimated that using tug escorts could add more than $1 million a year to the cost of their shipping operations. The California ruling also mandates that the ''best achievable technology'' must be used to avoid accidents. Tug operators are hopeful that the use of tractor tugs will become mandatory.

Hoping to take advantage of the new oil-spill prevention laws, Crowley Maritime Corp. planned to spend nearly $100 million on a fleet of these specialized tugs. ''This is the Swiss Army knife of tug boats,'' Crowley's engineering manager, Ed Schluter, told interviewers in *Popular Science.* The article featured the two 153-foot, 10,200 horsepower tractor tugs built by Crowley and delivered to Alaska's Alyeska Pipeline Company in early 1999.

The U.S. inland towing industry spent the 1980s recovering from the boom in shipbuilding during the 1960s and 1970s. However, many vessels in the tug and towing industry have reached the end of their economic life span—approximately 20 years—and some operators actually have begun to update their fleets. National Marine, for instance, spent more than $10 million annually from 1988 to 1992 on new vessels. National's efforts to improve their fleet included a purchase of three 6,800-horsepower linehaul towboats. Such new models incorporate the latest technology and have been built to operate in an increasingly restrictive regulatory environment.

The National Transportation Safety Board (NTSB), the Coast Guard, and the tugboat industry have been exploring increased requirements for towboat pilot licensing, mainly resulting from major incidents occurring in the past few years. A 47-death accident occurred in 1993 when barges being pushed by a tug in heavy fog conditions hit and damaged a bridge. The result was an Amtrak train plunged into an Alabama river. The NTSB's recommendations were drafted into new rules by the U.S. Department of Transportation, and included increased proficiency requirements for towboat pilots as well as regular performance evaluations, plus mandates that towboats be equipped with current radar systems and appropriate charts and compasses. In January 1996 near Rhode Island, a Scandia tugboat was pulling a barge, which carried 4 million gallons of fuel oil. The Scandia became disabled by fire resulting in the barge leaking 800,000 gallons of oil. A representative of Soundwaters

Environmental Group, Stephen Tarrant said, ''This incident is just a reminder that something like that can happen at any point.'' In fact, between 1986 and 1994 tugboats and barges were accountable for 23 percent of all oil spills, compared with tankers, which comprised 60 percent, and 8 percent were attributable to oil drilling rigs, according to Coast Guard statistics.

The American Bureau of Shipping is an industry regulatory organization that conducts annual inspections of larger tugs, such as the Scandia. However, coastal tugs are usually small enough to be prohibited from requiring inspection by the Coast Guard. Oil companies, which charter tugs, frequently have their own inspections. Jack Morgan of American Waterways Operators claims Coast Guard and industry studies indicate that ''two-thirds of the accidents are human error rather than equipment failure.'' Fires and electrical failures account for 1.7 percent of towing vessel accidents, according to Coast Guard statistics. After the Amtrak derailment, the Coast Guard increased requirements for licensure of tugboat skippers, including formal training in the use of radar. Federal regulations already mandate that the captain and pilot have firefighting training and equipment. In addition, towing firms and the industry association have agreed to improve training and equipment by 1998. According to Capt. Richard Stewart, head of the U.S. Merchant Marine Academy's Marine Transportation Department, ''The Coast Guard and the tug industry have taken some real strong steps to improve operations.''

Current Conditions

According to industry statistics, the domestic deep-sea trade was supported in 1999 by 1,879 registered tugboats. The inland industry at that time was served by 3,284 registered tugs, and the Great Lakes were serviced by 210 tug boats. These statistics did not include barges. The National Shipyard Association reported that 24 tugboats were under construction in the U.S. shipbuilding industry for 1998.

A few maritime events during 1998 and 1999 were illustrative of the versatile applications of tow and tug boat services. When two Carnival cruise ships caught fire in two separate incidents (July of 1998 and September of 1999), tow boats pulled the damaged ships safely back into harbor. Elsewhere, on an historic December 31, 1999, the government of Panama assumed control of the massive Panama Canal. In the late 1990s, tug boats were often called upon to assist super-sized Panamax vessels into the lock chambers by maneuvering the vessels into position and pushing on the stem of the vessels. Even though this assistance facilitated the passage of such wide-berthed ships (with less than 12 inches separating the ships' sides and the Canal walls) through the Canal, the vibratory damage to the concrete lock walls has become increasingly alarming to the U.S. government. The ability of the Panamanian government to assume maintenance and upkeep on the Canal was of heightened international significance for the twenty-first century.

Industry Leaders

Crowley Maritime Corporation. Headquartered in Oakland, California, Crowley has more than 100 offices in major ports and cities. A family-owned operation, the company had about 5,000 employees and generated an estimated $1.1 billion in annual revenues in 1998. Crowley Maritime Corporation was founded more than 100 years ago when Thomas Crowley, Sr., began a ferry service with an 18-foot Whitehall rowboat. Working in the San Francisco bay, Crowley hauled transport crews, merchants, supplies, and equipment from the docks to cargo ships anchored in the bay. In latter 1999, the company decided to divest its interest in South American operations, which produced two-thirds of its revenues.

Crowley Maritime has been an industry leader in instituting computer technologies. Crowley utilizes automated tariff retrieval systems, electronic data exchange, data communications, and electronic imaging. More than 150 users work with Crowley's automated tariff retrieval system to produce rate quotations, billings, audits, and other tariff-related functions. Customers can access the data through a mainframe computer located at company headquarters in Oakland, California. Crowley also joined in the Information System Agreement (ISA), a group created in 1991 by American President Line Ltd., Maersk Inc., P&O Containers, and Sea-Land Service to exchange information in the maritime industry. The group has been working with ports and government agencies to ''streamline'' electronic data exchange (EDI) standards on a global basis, and published a 600-page EDI implementation guide. In early 1999, Dakota Creek Shipyard signed a $26 million contract to build three new tugboats for Crowley in Valdez Harbor and Prince William Sound.

Tidewater, Inc. A New Orleans-based public company, Tidewater owns and operates marine vessels used by the international offshore energy market. Founded in 1956, the company had 6,400 employees and generated $546.5 million in annual revenue in the early 1990s. In 1992, Tidewater merged with Zapata Gulf Marine Corporation, its marine service joint venture. Tidewater's Marine Division provides a full range of marine services including the transportation of supplies, materials, and personnel; towing of mobile drilling rigs and construction barges; positioning and anchor handling of drilling rigs and construction and pipe laying barges; standby services; and diving and marine maintenance support. Tidewater reported net income of $18.9 million for its second quarter in 1999, on total revenues of $138.9 million, down substantially from the previous year. However, its stocks were up going into the third quarter.

National Marine, Inc. A New Orleans-based company that was a private subsidiary of Vectura Group, Inc., National Marine operated tugboats and barge lines. The company was founded in 1973, had about 225 employees, 55 tow boats, 700 barges, and $135 million in 1997 revenue. National Marine had one of the most varied fleets operated by any company on the inland waterway system. However, in 1998 Vectura merged National Marine with CSX's American Commercial Lines in a joint venture, paying more than $800 million for a 34 percent ownership interest. The new company, retaining the American Commercial Lines name, had 4,500 barges and 195 tow boats.

Other notable companies in the industry include Moran Towing Corporation of Greenwich, Connecticut; McAllister Towing and Transportation Company, Inc., headquartered in New York; Foss Maritime Co. of Seattle, Washington; Sause Brothers Ocean Towing Company, Inc. of Portland, Oregon; Hvide Shipping, Inc. of Fort Lauderdale, Florida; Cenac Towing Company of Houma, Louisiana; and Brix Maritime Co. of Portland, Oregon.

RESEARCH AND TECHNOLOGY

In May of 1998, Halter Marine company of Gulfport, Texas, announced the development of a new class of harbor tug boats, called ship docking modules (SDMs). These 90-foot-by-50-foot tugs are especially designed to assist in maneuvering ships into tight dock spaces. They are equipped with 4000 hp. twin Caterpillar diesel engines and can provide 100 percent power in any direction.

FURTHER READING

Bleyer, Bill. ''On the Water: New Wave of Rules for Barging.'' *Newsday,* 4 February 1996. Available from http://www.elibrary.com/id/2525/.

Carlsen, Clifford. ''Crowley Unloads Big Cargo: S. American Business.'' *San Francisco Times,* 13 August 1999.

''Crowley Maritime Corporation.'' Oakland, CA: Crowley Maritime Corporation, 1996. Available from http://pwr.com/crowley/marinfo.html.

''Industry Profile: 1999.'' The Transportation Institute. Available from http://www.trans-inst.org/ind_profile.html

''McAllister Towing and Transportation Company, Inc.'' New York: McAllister Towing and Transportation Company, Inc., 1997. Available from http://www.ships-service.com/mcallister/about.html.

Puckett, Kenneth P., Capt. ''Impact of Transfer of Panama Canal.'' FDCH Congressional Testimony, Panama Canal Hearings. 8 December 1999.

Salvail, Andre and Thomas Caywood. *New Orleans City Business,* 3 July 1998.

Stewart, Stephen. ''Oil Price Rise Slow to Affect Service-Company Earnings.'' *New Orleans City Business,* 22 November 1999.

Stover, Dawn. ''Newsfronts: Science & Technology.'' *Popular Science,* May 1999.

Wilson, Jim and Stefano Coledan. ''The Shape of Tugs To Come.'' *Popular Mechanics,* May 1998.

Wojcik Kochaniec, Joanne. ''Fire, Storm Disrupt Cruise.'' *Business Insurance,* 27 September 1999.

SIC 4493

MARINAS

This category covers establishments primarily engaged in operating marinas. These establishments rent boat slips and store boats, and generally perform a range of other services including cleaning and incidental boat repair. They frequently sell food, fuel, and fishing supplies, and may sell boats. Establishments primarily engaged in building or repairing boats and ships are classified in **SIC 3731: Ship Building and Repairing** or **SIC 3732: Boat Building and Repairing.** Establishments primarily engaged in the operation of charter or party fishing boats or rental of small recreational boats are classified in **SIC 7999: Amusement and Recreation Services, Not Elsewhere Classified.**

NAICS CODE(S)

713930 (Marinas)

INDUSTRY SNAPSHOT

According to 1998 statistics, 13 million families owned boats in the United States, and 570,000 new boats (all types) were sold that year. The National Marine Manufacturers Association reported that another 8 million persons were interested in buying a boat some time in the future. In 1997, 9,967 marina facilities provided storage space and sold marine-related services and products to recreational power and sail and commercial water craft owners. No standardized format for determining marina industry assets exists, because a ''marina'' may refer to a facility with only four docks or one with thousands of slips as part of a larger facility. The marina industry experienced rapid growth and increased annual sales in all climate zones from 1982 through 1987, the year retail sales topped $8 billion. This was the longest period of uninterrupted growth in the industry's history. From the late 1980s through the early 1990s, the industry suffered increasing financial difficulties. In 1992, boat slip vacancies averaged from 20 to 30 percent, although this figure was less in the Sunbelt states. By 1996, even marinas in southern California were experiencing increasing vacancy rates, some exceeding 40 percent—and generally, vacancies signify additional marina retail losses. A slip customer purchases more products and equipment from the marina than the boating public based elsewhere. Marina expansion and development slowed in the early 1990s, a reflection of a stagnant national economy and poor weather conditions. By the latter 1990s, the number of marinas in operation had stabilized, with a prediction for increased growth due to the positive economic outlook. *Boating Industry's* 1998 random survey of marinas around the country indicated stable occupancy rates, with a slight increase, and a 90-plus percent occupancy rate during peak seasons.

In the 1990s, marina owners and operators began to address several challenges to the industry, including periods of economic instability, increased marina insolvencies, stringently enforced environmental regulations, a lack of natural waterfront with adjacent land, and the loss of traditional lending sources. Conversely, market forces created more demand for marina facilities, especially in the Southeast and the West.

Organization and Structure

Marinas, always on or adjacent to the water, have varied physical shapes and sizes, offer a diverse range of services, and lend themselves to different ownership arrangements. Each marina has limitations and options to serve the boating public.

A marina rents, leases, or sells slips, usually in a boat basin with piers and stationary or floating docks. More than 8,000 marinas, with about 400,000 slips, sell marine services. There are moorings and anchorages for about 33,000 boats. More than 200 dry slip or land-based, often stacked, boat facilities store up to 150,000 boats on racks in buildings or on open land. Approximately 1,100 boat yards provide wet slips. More than 100 dockominiums berth boats in clusters of individually owned docks. More than 80 percent of the marinas provide yard services to maintain, repair, or build boats.

Financial Structure. Marinas are located on gravel pits, reservoirs, lakes, rivers, coastal waterways, and oceans. All marina ownership is held by the owner of the associated upland. Water rights are leased from the government. In many states, a government body holds coastal water rights for the public interest.

About 70 percent of marinas are privately owned, profit-making businesses that sell services to the public. About 1 to 2 percent of the marinas are cooperative, condominium, housing development and yacht club marinas, which serve their members and offer reciprocity privileges to other associations. The remaining 30 percent are municipal, state, and federal government marinas, which are open to the public at minimal or no cost—although some federally owned marinas are exclusively used by the military.

More than 70 percent of the marinas are owner-operated, stand-alone facilities. Corporations, families, and retired business owners provide slips and sell fuel and minimal ship stores. Investment sources are often friends, family, local banks, and savings and loans establishments. Larger marinas are often expanded owner-operated facilities.

The full-service marinas are owned by private or publicly traded real estate corporations. Some offer extensive boat yard services. Others are development complexes. They showcase marinas in two architecturally consistent mixed-use categories that maximize land-bound sales. Urban revitalization complexes integrate commercial space with residences. Resorts emphasize water- and land-based recreation and sports. Investment sources are banks, savings and loans establishments, venture capitalists, private and public industrial and recreational development bonds, investment banking, pension funds, and life insurance companies.

Full-service marinas have broad profit centers. Product sales are derived from slip and building fees, diesel, gasoline, propane and alcohol fuels, engine oil, vending machine products, marine and grocery goods, electronics, custom-built equipment, and boats. Services available include boat washing and cleaning; wood, fiberglass, rigging, engine, and propeller painting, maintenance, and repair; haul outs; and diving.

Marinas rent or lease wet or dry storage by the boat's or slip's length or slip's square footage. Marinas charge transient boats a daily or weekly rate. Permanent customers pay a monthly, seasonal, off-season, or annual rate based on competitive, comparable local prices. Therefore, other sales usually account for a significant amount of marina profits.

The full-service marina draws the demanding boating public with amenities, including but not limited to, deep water for boating; safe tie-ups; launching ramps; dock hand and concierge service; water, electricity, television, and telephone service to the boat; sewage pumping; storage facilities; and various other benefits.

Background and Development

The early concept of the marina, including public access and common ownership of waterfront property for commerce and transportation, dates to Roman Law of 2,000 years ago. The concept was lost during the Dark Ages. The Magna Carta restored public rights to coastal tidelands in 1215 A.D.

In the United States, marinas developed slowly. The U.S. Congress passed The River and Harbor Act of 1899, which authorized the Secretary of the Army, through the

Army Corps of Engineers, to approve the building of any structure on or over navigable waters. Recreational boating increased. The wealthy built private harbors in the early 1900s. By the 1930s, the term marina—Italian for small craft harbor—described the recreational boat facility.

After World War II, the middle class bought recreational boats with discretionary income. The marine industry used lighter-weight aluminum and fiberglass developed during World War II to mass-produce durable, low-maintenance marina docks and other products. Simpler welding techniques refined steel construction for hoists. Inexpensive concrete was also available for piers, docks, and pilings.

Until the 1960s, most marinas were owner-operated. Then, developers showcased the marina as the first stage in long-term, mixed-use plans for urban revitalization and resort complexes. As a result of the increased recreational boating across the country, Congress broadened The River and Harbor Act in 1968 to require approval for building recreational structures, further protecting U.S. waterways.

In the 1970s, a series of devastating events rocked the marine industry. Double-digit inflation, 20 percent interest rates, fuel pump lines, the Arab oil embargo, a federally proposed weekend energy conservation motor boating ban, and environmental regulations all adversely affected the marina economy.

Legislation. The federal Water Pollution Control Act amendments of 1972 required permits to regularly discharge waste water. The Coastal Management Act controlled development to protect water quality and coastal and inland wetlands. The Clean Water Act of 1977 further protected natural resources. The Environmental Protection Agency and the National Oceanic and Atmospheric Administration released guideline documents to control non-point source pollution.

The early 1980s provided the marina industry with a friendlier business atmosphere. Increased discretionary spending, tax changes, declining interest rates, and laxly enforced regulations all spirited growth. Amendments to The Federal Tax Reform Act of 1986 allowed private marinas on port district property to continue tax exempt financing for equipment, docks, and marina-related buildings.

The marina industry has remained non-standardized. According to Neil Ross, past president and co-director of the International Marina Institute, the marina industry, in its evolution, is like the roadside service industry when motels were replacing family-owned cabins. However, it is changing rapidly in response to management, environmental, and real estate demands and opportunities.

Approximately 80 percent of tidal flow and inland coastline is private commercial and residential space. Marinas only allow their customers and service workers access due to security and insurance regulations. Actual public access to waterfront is limited to the 20 percent of municipal, state, and federal marinas. This limited shoreline is proving insufficient to meet the needs of the expanding boating public.

The marina industry coordinates with government, banks, and insurance companies to maximize cost-effective, creative business procedures. Financiers consolidate foreclosed marinas into $100 to $150 million portfolios for publicly traded real estate investment trusts, freeing banks from the responsibility of disposal. Developers submit long-term plans to accelerate the three- to five-year complicated government permitting process for dredging and filling. Brokers sell dockominiums and other large facilities so developers immediately recoup some investment costs. Investors replace owner-operated businesses with retail chains and franchises to cut costs. In addition, cash-strapped municipalities increasingly investigate the sale of public marinas to private owners. Dry stack marinas, which require less waterfront volume, are an increasing presence as well.

Industry Leaders

Marinas vary widely in terms of size, services, and dockage capacity. However, the largest marina businesses provide full services. In the late 1990s, four top industry leaders were American Commercial Lines, Inc., of Jeffersonville, Indiana (In 1998 American merged with the Vectura Group's National Marine); ATC Leasing of Kenosha, Wisconsin, a subsidiary of Jupiter Industries, Inc.; Richard Betram & Co., Inc., of Miami, Florida; and Skipper Marine Corp. of Milwaukee, Wisconsin. Skipper bought four boat dealerships in Michigan during 1999, bringing its total sales outlets to eleven. In addition, it operated 20 marinas in four states.

These corporations own and/or operate marinas as part of larger hotel resort complexes that include other sports and recreational facilities. The largest marina in the United States is Marina del Rey (California), which boasts more than 8,000 slips—the majority occupied by large yachts. Westrec, a management company, controls chains that include over three dozen marinas.

Workforce

The marina industry's lack of standardization is reflected in its employment practices. Marinas generally employ staff and bring in independent contractors or concessionaires to whom the marina may lease space and/or charge to work in the facility.

The stand-alone marina labor force includes the self-employed owner/operators and additional staff as needed, who serve as dock masters, retailers, maintenance managers, and bookkeepers. For 1996, the average number of employees for each marina was between 2.5 and 4 per 100 berths; these were often part-time employees. During slow times of the year, the staff repaired facilities or worked at other marinas, often in a warmer climate zone. Full-service marinas often employed highly specialized employees as well. Various general managers, service managers, operations managers, and controllers were often part of the payroll of larger establishments.

The industry as a whole was standardizing employment and training. The International Marina Institute began a certified marina manager program in 1992, which emphasized standardizing accounting and other financial procedures, environmental processes, and education of customers. The Marina Operators Association of America had more than 300 members, primarily owners and managers representing large marinas, who participated in ongoing information programs. The International Marina Institute had 350 dues-paying members in the mid-1990s, and promoted growth and professional development among members and their staffs.

RESEARCH AND TECHNOLOGY

New technologies boost marina profits and management efficiency, provide weather protection, meet environmental regulations, and expand space. Marina franchises and management companies are fledgling innovations. Management retraining and computer software lead in office and on-the-dock changes.

In the realm of structural changes, docks and other structures are increasingly made of refined composite structures designed to withstand the elements more effectively than wood. Marinas have increasingly turned to new products with environmental and fire-resistant attributes. Engineers in the 1990s have also redesigned boat yard and dockside disposal systems to meet environmental regulations. Space limitations are resolved with offshore islands for docking, refueling, and mixed-use facilities such as floating hotels. Another area of enhanced development in the latter 1990s was the increased space for dry-dock storage created by new technology and equipment facilitating dry-*stack* storage. Older marinas continued to utilized large vacant parcels of real property to store boats off-season. However, new technology, including the development of powerful forklift-type vehicles, permit the lifting and stacking of boats into shelf-like racks for off-season storage.

FURTHER READING

Gay, Lance. ''Golf Courses, Marinas Benefit from Disaster Relief Funds.'' Scripps Howard News Service, 6 September 1996.

''Just the Stats.'' *Salt Water Sportsman,* September 1999.

Kirton, Darrell. ''Prospective Boat Owners.'' *Motor Boating & Sailing,* June 1998.

Manning, Joe. ''Milwaukee-Based Boat Retailer Buys Four Dealerships in Michigan.'' *The Milwaukee Journal Sentinel,* 20 October 1999.

Marina Inventory 1997. Washington: National Marine Manufacturers Association, Boat Facilities Development Division, 1997.

Marinas 1996. Washington, DC: National Marine Manufacturers Association, Boat Facilities Development Division, 1996.

Rogers-Harrington, Joan. ''Marina Survey 1999.'' *Boating Industry,* November 1999.

Ross, Emma. ''Sabal Bay Battle Draws to a Close.'' *Naples Daily News,* 20 July 1996.

Simpson, John. ''Appraising Proposed Marina Dry Stack Storage.'' *Appraisal Journal,* July 1998.

SIC 4499

WATER TRANSPORTATION SERVICES, NOT ELSEWHERE CLASSIFIED

This classification covers establishments primarily engaged in furnishing miscellaneous services incidental to water transportation, not elsewhere classified, such as lighterage, boat hiring, except for pleasure; chartering of vessels; canal operation; ship cleaning, except hold cleaning; and steamship leasing. Establishments primarily engaged in ship hold cleaning are classified in **SIC 4491: Marine Cargo Handling;** and those primarily engaged in the operation of charter or party fishing boats or rental of small recreational boats are classified in **SIC 7999: Amusement and Recreation Services, Not Elsewhere Classified.**

NAICS CODE(S)

532411 (Commerical Air, Rail, and Water Transportation Equipment Rental and Leasing)
488310 (Port and Harbor Operations)
488330 (Navigational Services to Shipping)
488390 (Other Support Activities for Water Transportation)

The miscellaneous water transportation services industry covers a variety of services related to water transportation. These include boat livery, except pleasure; commercial boat rental; canal operation; cargo salvaging from distressed vessels; chartering of commercial boats; dismantling ships; lighterage; operation of marine railways for dry-docking; marine salvaging; marine surveying, except cargo; marine wrecking; piloting vessels in and out of harbors; ship cleaning, except hold cleaning; ship registering, including surveying and classifying ships and marine equipment; and steamship leasing. These duties usually are performed dockside and include loading and unloading of railroad cars, trucks, barges and containers; building grain feeders; lashing and strapping cargo; and repairing shipping pallets. Cleaning crews wash and paint surfaces, clean oil tanks, take inventory, clean and wash decks, clean and check lifeboats, clean the quarters, and sort and check laundry. Additional services can be provided by towing and barge operators. Such work includes lighterage or the transfer of goods from ship to barge.

This industry also includes companies that repair, salvage, or scrap ships, and organizations that conduct safety inspections, called classifications societies. The leading societies are Lloyd's Register of Shipping (U.K.), Nippon Kaiji Kyokai (Japan), and the American Bureau of Shipping (U.S.). By the end of the 1980s, members of the maritime industry had become highly critical of classification societies for their reduction in standards, charging that the changes had led to increased passenger and vessel loss and the decline of maintenance standards throughout the world. In an attempt to prevent additional losses, the International Association of Classification Societies has begun to implement ''enhanced surveys'' for tankers and bulk carriers, vessels with the greatest potential for loss.

In the 1990s there were approximately 1,000 establishments employing about 8,600 workers in miscellaneous water transportation services. These figures represent a slight decline from the early 1990s and reflect ongoing consolidation within the industry. Total payroll was valued at roughly $300 million and the industry was worth an estimated $1 billion in annual revenues.

In recent years, many ship repair companies have been hesitant to work on some vessels, fearing they will be held liable for any subsequent malfunction. Moreover, underwriting agencies have become more cautious of paying claims that have been the result of poor maintenance rather than damage caused by an accident. This wariness has created an environment wherein ships needing repairs are more likely to be relegated to the scrapheap. However, this market has been saturated and rates for scrap metal have remained low. The shipping industry estimates that some 200 million deadweight tons of ships probably need to be eliminated by the end of the century.

The uncertainty of the ship-repairing sector kept many companies from expanding. San Diego, California's private ship-repair industry received $238 million from the U.S. Navy in 1998. Although the 1999 budget was $260 million, the locals are still recouping from the slag following 1997's $282 million. The private ship-repair industry takes in about 40 percent of U.S. Department of Defense work, the other 60 percent going to public shipyards. In 1998, it was 34 and 66 percent. The same was not true in the Norfolk, Virginia area, where the Navy paid private companies $942 million for ship maintenance work in fiscal year 1998, as opposed to only $417 million going to the Navy shipyard. At Puget Sound, Todd Pacific Shipyards of Seattle entered a $100 million multi-year contract with the Navy in 1999 for alteration and repairs on aircraft carriers, representing the first such contract award to private industry.

Most companies in the industry are privately held and generally provide only one or two of the services included under this classification. No companies primary to this industry earned more than $100 million annually. Entering the late 1990s, some of the largest firms included Marmac Corporation of Parkersburg, West Virginia; Gulf Star Holdings of Metairie, Louisiana; and American Overseas Marine Corporation of Quincy, Massachusetts.

A collateral but important component of the water transportation industry is the servicing and dredging of ports, channels, and marina ingress/egress waterways throughout the United States. According to the Transportation Institute, the U.S. flag dredging fleet in 1999 was comprised of approximately 365 pipeline dredges, 180 mechanical dredges, and 23 hopper dredges. The largest purchaser of marine dredging services was the federal government, through the Army Corps of Engineers. The maintenance-dredging budget runs from $220 to $260 million annually. New dredging work each year will add another $50 to $180 million. Shore protection services, environmental clean-up, and wetlands restoration are slow-growing corollary dredging trades, with the exception of shore protection, which jumped from $25 million to about $90 million in 1999.

FURTHER READING

Cahlink, George. ''Partnerships Dock at Shipyards.'' *Federal Times,* 29 March 1999.

Holcomb, Henry J. ''Philadelphia Area Loses Navy Ship Repair Jobs to Norfolk, VA.'' *The Philadelphia Inquirer,* 8 October 1999.

''Industry Profile 1999.'' The Transportation Institute. Available from http://www.trans-inst.org/ind_profile.html.

Siedsma, Andrea. ''Local Shipyards Are Dealing With Yo-Yo Funding.'' *San Diego Business Journal,* 13 April 1998.

SIC 4512

AIR TRANSPORTATION, SCHEDULED

The scheduled air transportation industry primarily has been engaged in furnishing passenger air transportation over regular routes and on regular schedules. This industry includes Alaskan carriers operating over regular or irregular routes.

NAICS Code(s)

481111 (Scheduled Passenger Air Transportation)
481112 (Scheduled Freight Air Transportation)

Industry Snapshot

The passenger air transportation industry provides air travel to both domestic and international destinations. What once began as a mode of transport for the U.S. mail has become a multi-billion dollar industry. For 1998 the industry had estimated revenues of $90.5 billion. Passenger air travel has continued to dominate all other modes of transportation in the commercial inter-city market, accounting for $82 billion or 91 percent of the airline industry's revenues in 1998. Air travel has become so commonplace that, according to an Air Transport Association (ATA) Gallup poll, nearly 75 percent of all Americans have flown on a commercial airliner at least once.

The airline industry enjoyed a remarkable turnaround between 1992, when a $2.6 billion operating loss occurred, to 1998 when the top ten airlines earned $8.0 billion before special charges. Airline profitability can be affected by several factors, most of which were favorable during the 1990s. Labor willingly made concessions and gave up billions of dollars worth of wages to help the major airlines achieve profitability. New airline management shifted the industry's strategic focus from market share, which was very costly, to cutting costs and improving profits. As the industry faced overcapacity, orders for new airplanes were cut drastically, contributing to a healthier bottom line. Finally, the industry enjoyed a steep decline in fuel prices through 1998.

The leading airport entering the twenty-first century in terms of volume was Chicago O'Hare Airport, with more than 70 million passengers transported in 1997. Atlanta Hartsfield International transported more than 68 million passengers. Dallas/Fort Worth International edged past Los Angeles International Airport for the third spot with 60.5 million passengers compared to 60.1 million passengers for Los Angeles.

Three carriers have historically dominated the industry. United Airlines, American Airlines, and Delta Air Lines have become the best-known domestic carriers and, in total, captured 54 percent of the market share in 1998. With number four airline Northwest Airlines capturing an 11.9 market share, the top four airlines accounted for nearly two-thirds of the industry's revenue passenger miles. These carriers and others have experienced significant financial improvements since the early 1990s, because economic conditions in the United States and operating costs in the industry have improved. Of the ten leading U. S. airlines, only one—Southwest—posted a profit in 1992. American, United, and Delta combined lost approximately $2.5 billion that year, despite revenues of more than $37 billion. However, the industry in three year's time turned around to the point that American, United, and Delta made approximately $46.6 billion in revenues and $1.6 billion in net profits in 1996. The trend continued in 1998, with United reporting $17.6 billion in revenues, American $17.4 billion, and Delta $14.4 billion.

Organization and Structure

The U.S. Department of Transportation (DOT) has categorized airlines based on their annual revenues into three groups: major, national, and regional/commuter.

Major airlines are carriers with more than $1 billion in annual revenues. This category once included Eastern, Pan Am, Northwest Airlines, Continental, Republic, America West, and Trans World Airlines (TWA). By the early 1990s, many of these companies were in some form of bankruptcy or had shut down operations completely. The result of these and other closings was the consolidation of assets among the three strongest majors: American Airlines, Delta, and United. Also new to this category was Southwest Airlines, formerly a national airline, which offers short-haul, point-to-point service with minimal amenities.

Airlines with annual revenues of $100 million to $1 billion are generally categorized as national airlines. Although this category has been called ''national,'' the name is not based on geographic boundaries, as only a small number of carriers actually have nationwide routes.

A carrier with less than $100 million in annual revenue has been classified as a regional/commuter airline, according to the DOT. By the start of the 1990s, approximately 140 carriers were in operation, but the top 50 regional/commuter carriers accounted for approximately 97 percent of the group's revenue passenger miles.

Hub-and-Spoke System. The major airlines operate under the hub-and-spoke system set up after passage of the Airline Deregulation Act of 1978. This system created central hubs across the United States where feeder flights were directed. Passengers from the feeder flights transferred to numerous other flights provided at the hub to their final destinations. The hub-and-spoke system has been advantageous to the major airlines in creating additional service to more destinations and allowing more efficient use of planes, terminals, ground equipment, and employees.

Unlike many other countries, the U.S. government has not owned or operated an airline in any form. Instead, all U.S. airlines have been either public or privately held companies. Government involvement in the industry has been in the form of regulatory agencies, congressional acts, and appointed commissions.

BACKGROUND AND DEVELOPMENT

The creation of the passenger airline industry was contingent on the development of the aviation industry. With the first successful flight by the Wright brothers in Kitty Hawk, North Carolina, in 1903 the aviation industry began. However, the general public did not eagerly embrace air travel, thinking that it was a dangerous mode of transportation. Thus, the development of an aircraft for passengers, which in those days was called a ''heavier-than-air craft,'' moved slowly.

The country's preparation and eventual entry into World War I provided the necessary stimulus for developing the aircraft industry, if only for wartime usage. But as quickly as the U.S government supported aviation during the war, it pulled all support and funding after the war, which virtually halted the industry.

The popularity of air travel exploded, though, with the successful overseas flight of Charles Lindbergh in 1927. Various air transport holding companies were created, such as Aviation Corporation, launched by financiers W. Averill Harriman and Robert Lehman. The air transport division of this company was called American Airways. In 1928, another holding company was created by Boeing and its air transport division—United Aircraft and Transportation Corporation. By 1931, United Air Lines was created as the management company for United Aircraft's four transport companies.

Mail Service Spurred Industry Development. The airline industry developed in large measure because of efforts to improve the U.S. mail service. Congress appropriated monies for a trial mail run and flights were originally made by Army planes and pilots. Soon after, the U.S. Post Office put together its own fleet of planes for mail delivery service. By 1920, flights were being made from New York to San Francisco during daytime hours.

Since the post office planes were allowed to carry only mail, political pressure mounted to turn this service over to private airline operators that could expand their cargo. In 1925, the Kelly Airmail Act gave private airlines, via a system of competitive bidding and subsidies, the opportunity to serve as mail carriers. The first national aviation policy, the Air Commerce Act of 1926, established provisions for the regulation of air traffic, the registration of aircraft, and the production of pilot licenses. Passenger volume per year grew from 6,000 to 400,000, and carriers proliferated. Air traffic across the nation grew increasingly disorganized, however. The McNary-Waters Act of 1930 gave the nation's postmaster general the authority to manage the industry. While the bidding system nominally remained in place, Postmaster General Walter Brown, who had lobbied for his expanded powers, arranged a meeting wherein the airlines negotiated territories among themselves. As a result, three primary routes were established—north, middle, and south—across the United States, with United, American, and TWA controlling one route each.

Brown's dictatorial power over the airline industry, however, came under increasing criticism. With the entrance of the Roosevelt Administration in 1933, congressional hearings were held that included the investigation into the awarding of mail contracts. Under pressure from Senator Hugo Black, President Roosevelt cancelled all of the mail contracts, deeming them illegal, and turned over the mail delivery service to the Army Air Corps. This decision turned out to be a disastrous mistake because the Corps pilots were unfamiliar with the territory and had to fight treacherous winter weather. By the third week, five pilots had been killed in various crashes and public outcry persuaded President Roosevelt to return the mail service to contractors.

Under the 1934 Air mail Act, the postmaster general's power over the industry was diluted, and measures to ensure truly competitive bidding were established. New airlines as well as established ones made low bids in an effort to snare market share and, as a result of the fierce competition, no carrier was able to make a profit.

Civil Aeronautics Act. The desperately competitive industry seemed in danger of destroying itself. The government reacted by passing the Civil Aeronautics Act in 1938. The legislation created the Civil Aeronautics Authority (CAA), an independent regulatory bureau. This organization later was named the Civil Aeronautics Board (CAB). The CAB regulated passenger fares and airmail routes, monitored acquisitions and mergers, and distributed routes to airlines. The policies implemented by the Board in the 1930s remained intact for nearly 40 years, resulting in a sort of stagnation in the industry. No new major carriers established themselves during that time, a period in which the number of major airlines dwindled to nine.

America's entry into World War II required the country's commercial fleet of planes to be sent overseas, along with flight personnel. The war increased the development of aircraft, not only for wartime use, but also for post-war commercial aviation. The 1950s brought both the introduction of the electronic reservations system and cross-country jet service. Advances in passenger comfort and plane capacity further aided the industry. During the 1950s and 1960s, companies continued to buy modernized planes, while expanding service to both domestic and international destinations.

The Federal Aviation Act was passed in 1958 after a midair collision of two planes over the Grand Canyon. The Act created the Federal Aviation Agency, which was responsible for developing an air traffic control system. In 1967 the Agency was renamed the Federal Aviation Administration (FAA) and was put under the control of the U.S. Department of Transportation (DOT), which was also created that year.

Industry Deregulation. In the 1970s, the industry underwent a tremendous transformation. Industry players were rocked by expensive new aircraft purchases and fuel costs that, because of oil supply concerns, reached as much as 30 percent of operating expenses. Labor costs soared as well, while service demand remained tepid. The airline industry was in serious trouble.

During this same period, cries calling for repeal of the 1938 legislation that froze the industry for so long grew louder. Critics contended that the airline industry had become a sluggish, ineffective entity in the regulatory environment in which it functioned. Events of the mid-1970s seemed to support this viewpoint. Thus, the Airline Deregulation Act of 1978, which removed governmental control of routes and fare pricing, was passed and signed by President Carter.

The airline industry felt the effects of deregulation almost immediately. New players in the industry proliferated, both at the national and regional level. Established regional airlines, meanwhile, viewed deregulation as an opening to expand their influence. Competition quickly grew fierce across the industry, and established giants scrambled to keep pace with new, more nimble companies armed with modern aircraft that fit their needs and strategies that jelled with the hub network concept.

In the mid-1980s, the industry was swept by a wave of mergers, acquisitions, and bankruptcies. These mergers were approved by the Department of Transportation rather than the Justice Department (the Justice Department assumed power over airline mergers in 1988). This consolidation of the industry left eight airlines controlling more than 90 percent of U.S. air traffic. The industry boomed with increased traffic and first-time air travelers because of drastic reductions in fares and the addition of cities serviced by air transportation. The industry encountered significant problems as well, however. Demand for new aircraft exceeded manufacturers' supplies, creating a situation wherein, by the late 1980s, 20 percent of U.S. planes in operation were older than the 20-year standard life. Safety concerns mounted as well after several major airplane crash disasters resulted in the loss of hundreds of lives. Critics contended that the airlines were not paying sufficient attention to maintenance needs because of cost concerns.

Perhaps the biggest threat to the domestic airline industry, however, was the most basic one: the inability to make a profit. Operating costs, especially in the realm of labor, coupled with incessant fare wars in which ticket prices were often slashed as much as 50 percent, battered the industry's major companies.

The benefits of deregulation to the customer have been proven, according to James Landry, president of the Air Transport Association of America (ATA), in a 1993 editorial in *Dallas Morning News.* Since 1979, passenger enplanements had increased by more than 70 percent, revenue had tripled from $27 billion to more than $77 billion, and nearly 90 percent of all passengers during the 1980s traveled on discounted fares.

Daunting financial difficulties for the carriers persisted into the early 1990s. In 1993, due to financial problems that challenged the airline industry, the Clinton administration created the National Commission to Ensure Strong Competitive Airline Industry. This group produced a 90-day study of public-policy changes to be enacted in order to maintain profitability.

Staged Strong Recovery After 1992. The passenger air transportation industry made an unprecedented turnaround in profitability, traffic, and price stability in the 1990s. The industry had flourished from the late 1950s through the early 1970s, as U.S. airline passenger traffic grew at 13 percent a year. By the early 1990s, however, the industry had been hit hard by the Gulf War, rising fuel prices and other operating costs, fare wars, rising debt service costs, and the slowdown of the American economy. On average, the industry's annual growth in traffic was less than one percent from 1987 through 1992, and even this dismal rate was achieved by selling seats below cost. ''In short, there has been little or no true growth in revenue passenger miles since 1986,'' reported *Forbes* in 1993.

Consolidation in the industry was forecast to pick up as the major airlines became profitable once again. In late 1996, American and British Airways, Continental and Delta, and USAir and United toyed with the idea of joining forces. However, none of these happened in 1996, and pilots, unions, and government anti-trust sentiments tended to hamper merger prospects.

Successful nationals provided service to a niche market, did not interfere with the majors, and operated from airports with minimal competition. Examples included Southwest Airlines at Dallas Love Field, Midway Airlines at Midway Airport in Chicago, and America West in Phoenix. Alaska Airlines has remained the only large, successful national airline in operation, with more than 50 percent market share of the Pacific Northwest/Alaska market.

Regional airlines have continued to flourish for two reasons. First, in an effort to cut costs, the majors have ''handed over'' to affiliated regional airline routes that were not profitable for them. Customers were attracted to fly on the regional line with the enticement of gaining frequent flyer miles. With this arrangement, the major airline maintained its name recognition without having to run an unprofitable route.

The majors' withdrawal of jet service to certain markets also presented opportunities for non-affiliated regional airlines. Defying negative trends, several small airlines such as Reno Air Inc., Skybus Corp., and Kiwi International Air Lines Inc. started operations during the early 1990s. Tapping into the glut of planes and unemployed workers created by the industry shake-out of the late 1980s, 17 airlines had applied to become certified for chartered service by the end of 1991.

During the early 1990s, carriers put forth a serious effort to control operating costs by cutting personnel, reducing salaries, trimming flight schedules, and retiring older aircraft. The industry benefited from 1994 through 1996 as the capacity glut diminished.

At the beginning of 1996, profits and traffic in the airline industry were affected by the expiration and reinstatement of a 10 percent federal excise tax on domestic airline tickets. Congress let the tax expire at the end of 1995, but reinstated it on August 17, 1996. The airlines lowered prices during this time and traffic increased—as did profits. However, the tax expired again at the end of 1996, and was reinstated in March 1997. This time, most airlines (except Southwest) raised prices after the reinstatement. Wall Street analysts predicted that strong airline traffic and lower fuel costs would have a more positive effect on the industry, despite the reinstatement of the federal excise tax and any threat of future price wars.

CURRENT CONDITIONS

Fuel prices were at 30-year lows by the end of 1998, helping to support profits in the airline industry, even as the industry was hit by several one-time events that served to drive down profits compared to 1997. These included a lengthy pilot strike against Northwest Airlines, which drove the company into the red for 1998. While the industry reported an increase in overall revenues from $88 billion in 1997 to $90.5 billion in 1998, the top nine airlines reported a 15 percent decline in earnings for the year. Cost-cutting measures, including lowering commissions paid to travel agents, helped improve profits in some cases.

While America West, the ninth-ranked airline in terms of passengers and revenue passenger miles in 1997, was courted by United Airlines and Delta Air Lines in early 1999, nothing came of it by the end of the year. In fact, following about a dozen airline mergers in 1986 and 1987, there has not been a major airline merger in the 1990s, although Northwest took a majority stake in Continental Airlines in 1998. However, negotiations continue among the major airlines. American Airlines was courting US Airways in 1999, a combination that would result in the nation's largest airline.

Rather, airlines have joined forces through alliances with other domestic and international carriers. Code-sharing, whereby one carrier's flight schedules are coded under an affiliated carrier's symbol on airline reservation systems, have become popular ways of forming alliances. The top five airlines have formed clusters of code-sharing alliances with international carriers, making it easier for customers to book connecting flights. United Airlines leads the Star Alliance with Lufthansa, Scandinavian Air System, All Nippon Airways, and Air Canada. American's One World Alliance includes British Airways, Quantas, TACT, and other Latin American carriers. Delta is seeking to join Air France's Atlantic Excellence partners, which includes Swissair and Sabena.

INDUSTRY LEADERS

The U.S. air transportation industry has been dominated by the strength and size of three domestic carriers: American, United, and Delta. The industry also has been greatly affected by the emergence of national airlines that provide service to niche markets. One company that has served as a model for this type of operation has been Southwest Airlines.

United Airlines. With corporate headquarters near Chicago O'Hare International Airport, United Airlines Inc. claims to be the largest air carrier in the world and the largest majority employee-owned company. It offers nearly 2,300 flights a day to 135 destinations in 28 countries and one U.S. territory. In addition to its main Chicago hub, the airline has four other U.S. hubs in Denver, Los Angeles, San Francisco, and Washington, D.C. In 1997 it was the industry leader in terms of revenue passenger miles (121,350 million) and operating revenues ($17.3 billion). It held a 20 percent market share based on revenue passenger miles in 1998.

The company began with Varney Airlines, which later became a part of Pacific Air Transport and National Air Transport. This company merged into Boeing Air Transport, part of Boeing Airplane Company and Pratt & Whitney. In 1931, United Airlines was organized as a management company for the airline division and became a separate business entity three years later. In 1961, United Airlines acquired Capital Airlines, added 7,000 employees, increased the route system, and gave United claim to the title of the world's largest privately owned airline.

Following tough negotiations with its unions in the mid-1990s, the pilot and machinist unions and the non-union ground support groups along with management agreed to an employee stock ownership plan that placed 55 percent of the company stock in employee hands. United became the largest employee-owned company in the United States. All parties participated in the ESOP except United's flight attendants. According to *Valueline,* labor relations have been a strong point for United. Settlements with its pilots and mechanics have been signed to restore the wage levels that preceded the buyout by the year 2000. To reach this agreement, some profit-sharing rights were given up by the workers.

American Airlines. American Airlines, Inc. has long been the main subsidiary of AMR Corporation, with headquarters in Fort Worth, Texas. American Airlines was once the largest carrier in the world, serving more than 200 cities worldwide. With more than 110,000 employees, American completes more than 2,000 departures daily and operates from seven hubs. In 1997 it ranked second in the industry in terms of revenue passenger miles (106,936 million) and operating revenues ($15.9 billion). It held a 17.6 percent market share in 1998 in revenue passenger miles.

In 1999 American's parent company spun off its 83 percent interest in Sabre Holdings Corp. by distributing its Sabre shares to AMR shareholders, subject to a favorable ruling from the U.S. Internal Revenue Service. Sabre had been reorganized in 1996 from being a part of American Airlines into a separate subsidiary through an initial public offering. Sabre provides American with substantially all of its information technology, including reservations, flight operations, and other real-time services.

American Airlines, previously named American Airways, started as the air transport division of the holding company Aviation Corporation. In 1934, the company was renamed and C.R. Smith was appointed president. Smith continued to serve in this position until 1968 when he was named Secretary of Commerce by President Lyndon B. Johnson.

Delta Air Lines. Delta Air Lines, with headquarters at the Hartsfield Atlanta International Airport in Atlanta, Georgia, once offered the most extensive transatlantic service of any carrier in the world. The company operates 2,800 flights daily to more than 220 cities in 34 countries. Delta has more than 60,000 employees and a fleet of 543 jet aircraft. In 1997 Delta ranked third in the industry in terms of revenue passenger miles (99,624 million) and operating revenues ($14.2 billion). It held a 16.4 percent market share in 1998 in terms of revenue passenger miles.

Delta was founded in 1925 in Monroe, Louisiana, as Delta Air Service, a crop dusting company. Passenger service began in 1925 with flights to Dallas, Texas, and Jackson, Mississippi. The company merged with Northeast Airlines in 1972. Delta announced 1992 revenues of $10.84 billion but was unable to post a profit for the year. Instead, the company lost more than $500 million. However, revenues and profits increased substantially during the 1995 and 1996 time period. Revenues reached $12.5 billion and profits reached $156 million in 1996.

Southwest Airlines. Once a regional airline, Southwest Airlines is a short-haul, low-fare, high-frequency, point-to-point carrier. By avoiding hub-and-spoke service, it is able to provide more direct nonstop routings, thus minimizing connections, delays, and flight times. Based in Dallas, Southwest Airlines initiated service in 1971 with flights to Houston, Dallas, and San Antonio. In 1991, the company moved into the major category due to its increased revenue. By 1999, the company was serving 52 cities in 26 states. The airline has been noted for its consistent profitability, and it was the only major carrier from 1990 through 1997 to make a profit. In 1998 it reported net income of $433.4 million on operating revenues of $4.2 billion. In 1998 it ranked seventh in revenue passenger miles (28,359 million) and eighth in operating revenues. In 1998 it held a 4.7 percent market share and was eighth among all U.S. airlines.

Other top ten airlines included Northwest Airlines, US Airways, Continental Airlines, Trans World Airlines, and America West. Of these companies, Continental, Trans World, and America West went through and survived bankruptcy proceedings in the early 1990s.

WORKFORCE

Following deregulation in 1978, employment in the airline industry increased from 340,000 jobs to more than 530,000 jobs in the early 1990s. In 1997, total employment by the 10 major carriers was 450,753 workers. James Landry, president of ATA, stated in a 1993 editorial in the *Dallas Morning News* that "Despite . . . layoffs and salary cuts, airline employees remain one of the best paid workforces in the United States, with the average wage and compensation package exceeding $51,000 per year, nearly twice the national average." A popular way to reduce wages in 1995 and 1996 was the use of employee stock payments. TWA, United, Northwest, and Southwest all reached agreements with their labor unions to exchange equity for wage increases.

Deregulation, though, also created differences between the airlines and various unions, which at the end of the 1970s filled 90 percent of all industry jobs. New airlines were able to operate with much lower labor costs than established outfits, and the industry giants soon decided that they had to reduce their labor costs in order to compete. While at some airlines, unions and management were able to reach agreements (equity for wage concessions, etc.), other companies resorted to measures that brought turmoil across the industry. Braniff Airlines and Continental Airlines both utilized Chapter 11 bankruptcy regulations in the early 1980s to nullify existing labor contracts. Chapter 11 regulations enabled the companies to return to business without union employees if they so desired. In Continental's case, they fired their employees after filing for bankruptcy, then re-hired them as non-union employees at wages that were in some cases more than 50 percent lower than prior to Chapter 11. This maneuvering galvanized unions across the industry, spurring them to protect themselves legally.

With the exception of American Airlines, company relationships with labor unions significantly improved in 1995 and 1996 from earlier years. Management of major carriers such as United Airlines and American Airlines demanded concessions from unions to cut costs, while unions dug in their heels; but both airlines resolved the issues, United with an employee buyout and American with the flight attendants—but only after a costly strike. Northwest Airlines was able to reach an agreement with labor in July 1993 with wage reductions and other concessions in exchange for 30 percent of the airline's preferred stock and an increased voice in operations. United's successful ESOP was touted as a model of employer-employee relationships by the Clinton administration, and other carriers with higher labor costs may try similar employee buy outs to solve the problem of high labor costs.

Differences between labor unions and the airlines are sometimes exacerbated by the airlines practice of taking two to three years to negotiate a labor contract. Labor costs as a percentage of the airlines' operating expenses increased steadily during the 1990s, from 31.6 percent in 1990 to 35.5 percent in 1998. As the airlines dragged their feet in contract negotiations, groups of employees were often left working without a contract. Short of striking, unions have resorted to tactics such as informational pickets at airports, presenting their cases to the general public. Northwest Airlines was hit by a costly airline pilots strike in 1998, and pilots at American Airlines staged a sick-out in early 1999. Although the airlines profitability in the late 1990s was in part the result of earlier wage and benefits concessions on the part of unionized workers, the airlines appeared reluctant to make suitable offers to unions representing their pilots, flight attendants, and machinists.

Future trends in hiring airline industry employees will always be contingent on the strength and pace of the industry's economic outlook. While airlines are making good money, job security will probably always be tenuous, especially at the less-profitable carriers. The prospect of future airline mergers may also have a negative effect on industry employment. The emergence of new regional airlines has provided some opportunity for employment, but wages have been lower than the industry standard due to the large number of experienced unemployed airline workers. Computer-related jobs, such as systems analysts and reservations and keyboard operators will continue to be in demand as companies become increasingly automated.

AMERICA AND THE WORLD

The U.S. Department of Transportation's Office of International Aviation reported that 48.7 million passengers traveled by air between the United States and the rest of the world during the first half of 1995. This was a 6 percent increase in passenger traffic compared to the first half of 1994. In June 1995, approximately 9.3 million passengers traveled by air in U.S. international markets, which was about 7 percent greater than the same period in 1994. In the first half of 1995, New York, Miami, Los Angeles, Chicago, and Honolulu were the top five U.S. international gateways. Miami recorded an 11 percent increase, with 674,000 passengers. The greatest passenger loss was felt in Boston, where a drop of 6 percent, or 88,000 passengers, occurred in the first half of 1995. The top five country markets for U.S. international travel were Canada, Japan, the United Kingdom, Mexico, and Germany.

More than 1.25 billion passengers per year rely on the world's airlines for business and vacation travel. The world's airline industry transports approximately a quarter of the manufactured exports by value. In the early 1900s, approximately 22 million jobs were in the world airline industry, producing approximately $1 trillion in annual gross output.

Between 1994 and 2010, passenger and freight traffic were expected to increase at an average annual rate of 5 to 6 percent, which is significantly greater than the growth in global GDP. Estimates are that by the year 2005, there could be in excess of 2 .5 billion air travelers per year. By the year 2010, the world airline industry could exceed $1.7 trillion with more than 30 million jobs provided.

Growth in international travel will be contingent on the successful application of Open Skies legislation and other agreements with foreign governments and carriers. Open Skies agreements have offered airlines from foreign countries almost unlimited access to the U.S. market and freedom to set prices. The first-ever Open Skies aviation agreement was signed on September 4, 1992, between the United States and the Netherlands. The agreement allowed the integration of the operations of KLM Royal Dutch Airlines, the Netherlands flag carrier, and Northwest Airlines, in which KLM would own a major interest.

The European Community (EC) has been working on its own version of Open Skies deregulation. The initial resolution, effective January 1993, abolished the web of government-to-government agreements, which allocated routes within the EC and fixed fares. The 12 EC community nations and their seven partners in the European Free Trade Area (EFTA) have been trying to create a common market within Europe and to develop a cohesive group in order to gain access in the U.S. market.

The impact that the EC liberation policy will have on U.S. carriers has yet to be determined. But as *Air Transport World* noted, ''Whether they view competition from U.S. carriers as threat or potential opportunity, all are adamant that Washington open up the U.S. market before Europe makes a move. And none appear to feel particularly hampered by having to continue bilateral negotiations with the United States, for lack of a united position.''

International markets in 1999 appeared to be on the eve of deregulation. The United States continued to push for open international aviation markets. International carriers were preparing for deregulation by building international hub systems and forming strategic alliances. Two leading international alliances involving U.S. carriers were the Star Alliance, led by United Airlines and including Lufthansa, Scandinavian Air System, All Nippon Airways, and Air Canada. American's One World Alliance included British Airways, Quantas, TACT, and other Latin American carriers. Air France was the lead airline in the European alliance, Atlantic Excellence, which included Swissair and Sabena.

RESEARCH AND TECHNOLOGY

From improved reservations computer systems to high-tech amenities for business travelers to advances in aircraft design, computer software technology is expected to have a tremendous impact on the future of the airline industry. Most airlines have had home pages on the World Wide Web since 1995. Those sites began by simply displaying flight information, but soon the airlines were using the Internet to book flights and offer special discounts. By registering at an airline's Web site, consumers could benefit from unannounced specials and receive weekly briefings on discounts via e-mail. Booking flights via the Internet has the potential of saving airlines a percentage of the $5.6 billion they paid in commissions to travel agents in 1998, an expense that accounted for nearly seven percent of total airline costs. Online booking and ticket less travel enable the airlines to realize additional savings in the cost of processing tickets by being able to reduce the number of customer service operators and reservation clerks they employ. It was estimated that Internet purchases of airline tickets amounted to $2 billion in 1998, up sharply from $827 million in 1997 but still only 2.5 percent of passenger revenues.

High-tech amenities for the business traveler may be the next battleground for customer service among the major domestic carriers. Satellite-based telephone systems capable of handling calls to and from anywhere in the world have been placed on board planes, and in-flight faxes, computer, and data transmission services are commonplace.

The most significant advances in communications technology continue to be in the design, development, and operation of the airplane itself. ''Satellite-guided landings have marked more addition to the panoply of technologies that allow airplanes virtually to fly themselves. Hands-off piloting, navigation, and landing of aircraft have become a routine part of civil aviation,'' reported *Scientific American* in 1991.

Computer technology will continue to refine the cockpit. By 1980, instrumentation and control systems had created the autopilot and ''blind flying'' instruments, which allowed a plane to fly straight and level even if the pilots removed their hands from the controls. By 1988, aircraft automation took a further step with the introduction of the Airbus A320. The flight control computers on board actually told the pilot how to fly the plane and could prevent the pilot from exceeding the aircraft's structural limitations.

Modern aircraft have become so automated that some pilots and even some aircraft manufacturers have grown concerned about excessive reliance on the automated systems. New training programs have been established to combat this fear of over-reliance. Although advances in technology will continue to assist in the creation of safer and more fuel-efficient planes, the captain of a plane cannot be eliminated or automated out of the cockpit.

Additionally, according to an Airports Council International survey, ''The new generation of large aircraft currently on the drawing boards of aircraft manufacturers could reduce airport capacity and have considerable cost implications for the world's airports.'' Approximately $105 million in infrastructure modifications may be needed to accommodate these new planes. The 600-plus passenger aircraft lower the unit operating costs and increase capacity for the airlines, but the modifications to runways, taxiways, and aprons could cost an average of $62 million per airport. Changes to passenger terminals and operational facilities could add another $43 million in costs.

FURTHER READING

Air Transport Association. ''Industry Information: 1998 Annual Report, Highlights.'' Available at http://www.air-transport.org/public/industry/37.asp.

———. ''Industry Information: Leading U.S. Airports.'' Available at http://www.air-transport.org/public/industry/47.asp.

———. ''Industry Information: Top 25 Airlines in 1997.'' Available at http://www.air-transport.org/public/industry/47.asp.

———. ''Welcome to the Air Transport Association: Airline Customer Service Commitment.'' Available at http://www.air-transport.org/.

''Air Transport Industry.'' *Valueline,* March 1997.

Airports Council International. ''The Economic Benefits of Air Transport.'' May 1997.

AMR Corporation. ''AMR Corp. Announces Plan to Spin Off Sabre into Fully Independent Technology Company.'' Company news release, 14 December 1999. Available at http://www.amrcorp.com/news/dec1499.htm

Feldman, Joan M. ''To Phase or Not to Phase.'' *Air Transport World,* April 1999.

Flint, Perry. ''A Tough End to a Good Year.'' *Air Transport World,* March 1999.

Hall, Thomas C. ''AA, US Airways to Merge?'' *Dallas Business Journal,* 2 April 1999.

''Nosedive.'' *Business Week,* 8 March 1999.

Schmeltzer, John. ''American Airlines' Parent to Spin Off Shares in Reservations Firm.'' *Knight-Ridder/Tribune Business News,* 14 December 1999.

Southwest Airlines. ''Southwest Airlines Fact Sheet - November 1999.'' Available at http://www.southwest.com/about_swa/press/factsheet.html.

Standard & Poor's Industry Surveys: Airlines. New York: Standard & Poor's, 4 November 1999.

United Airlines. ''United Airlines Overview.'' Available at http://www.corporate-ir.net/ireye/ir_site.zhtml?ticker=UAL&script=2100.

U.S. Department of Transportation. *Federal Aviation Administration Forecasts, Fiscal Years 1991-2002.* Washington, DC: GPO.

Yahoo! ''Delta Air Lines.'' Available at http://dir.yahoo.com/Business_and_Economy/Companies/Travel/Airlines/Delta Air Lines.

Yahoo! ''Southwest Airlines.'' Available at http://dir.yahoo.com/Business_and_Economy/Companies/Travel/Airlines/Southwest Airlines.

Yahoo! ''United Airlines,'' at http://dir.yahoo.com/Business_and_Economy/Companies/Travel/Airlines/United_Airlines.

SIC 4513

AIR COURIER SERVICES

The air courier services industry includes establishments primarily engaged in furnishing air delivery of individually addressed letters, parcels, and packages (generally under 100 pounds), except by the U.S. Postal Service. While these establishments deliver letters, parcels, and packages by air, the initial pick-up and the final delivery are often made by other modes of transportation, such as by truck, bicycle, or motorcycle. Separate establishments of air courier companies engaged in providing pick-up and delivery only; ''drop-off points;'' or distribution centers are all classified in this industry.

Establishments of the U.S. Postal Service are classified in **SIC 4311: United States Postal Service;** and establishments furnishing delivery of individually addressed letters, parcels, or packages (generally under 100 pounds) other than by air are classified in **SIC 4215: Courier Services, Except by Air.**

Establishments primarily engaged in undertaking the transportation of goods from shippers to receivers for charges covering the entire transportation but making use of other transportation establishments for delivery, are classified in **SIC 4731: Arrangement of Transportation of Freight and Cargo.**

NAICS CODE(S)

492110 (Couriers)

INDUSTRY SNAPSHOT

Definition of Service. The air courier industry is a division of the air cargo industry. As defined by the Air Transport Association (ATA), cargo is the total volume of freight, mail, and express traffic. The air courier division includes both freight (generally under 100 pounds) and express mail. As defined by the ATA, freight and express mail are commodities of all kinds including small packages, counter service, express service, and priority reserved freight. Air courier service does not include the delivery of U.S. mail.

Major Integrators. In general, two kinds of companies have provided air courier service in the United States. First have been the integrators or all-cargo companies such as Federal Express and DHL. These companies have a fleet of planes, carry cargo only, usually fly at night, and have ground transportation and personnel for door-to-door pick up and delivery.

According to *Distribution* magazine's Annual Report, integrators have controlled 90 percent of the domestic market for envelopes, packages, and freight. These companies have been Federal Express, Airborne, Burlington, Air Express, DHL, Emery Worldwide, and United Parcel Service (UPS).

Combination Carriers. Air courier service also has been provided by passenger airlines, such as American Airlines. These companies transport cargo (freight, express, and mail) in the holds of their passenger aircraft. They fly during the day since passenger traffic is their first priority. Passenger airlines have provided service similar to integrators, except most airlines have to subcontract ground transportation. Airlines also provide airport-to-airport deliveries.

Eleven passenger airlines once included all-cargo aircraft in their fleets. As of 1999, Northwest Airlines, with ten 747-200s, was the only U.S. passenger airline operating all-cargo equipment. The other ten retired the all-cargo aircraft from their fleets by the end of 1984.

Air Forwarders. Both major integrators and combination carriers have worked with air forwarders to provide shipping services. Air forwarders are companies that arrange the complete shipping process and receive charges for the entire transportation. These companies do not own or operate aircraft and have to purchase space on the planes of airlines or integrators for their packages. Although air forwarders were the precursor to the air courier industry, these companies are not represented in this industry, but are classified in **SIC 4731: Arrangement of Transportation of Freight and Cargo.**

Revenue Generated by the Industry. According to Federal Aviation Administration (FAA) forecasts, freight and express mail (air courier) services have reached over 14 billion revenue ton miles (RTMs) annually. A revenue ton mile (RTM) equals one ton of revenue traffic transported one mile. Both domestic and international RTMs for freight/express have been approximately 7 billion RTMs annually.

Most Used Airports. The airport that has received the most air cargo (freight, express, and mail) has been New York's John F. Kennedy Airport (JFK) with 1.2 million tons of cargo enplaned and deplaned annually. Los Angeles International and Chicago O'Hare came in second, each with approximately 1.1 million tons annually.

Kinds of Service. Companies within the freight/express mail division of the air cargo industry have offered various services related to time-sensitive delivery conditions. Customers can request next-morning or afternoon delivery, same-day service, or second-day delivery. Most international express service required a few days for delivery, depending upon the country's customs procedures and regulations.

BACKGROUND AND DEVELOPMENT

The U.S. airmail system was the forerunner to the air courier industry (or express mail industry). The U.S. airmail system also spurred the growth of the air passenger industry and the creation of the modern airlines. Yet, the air courier industry and the time-sensitive delivery of letters and parcels remained dormant until the late 1970s.

Prior to deregulation of the air cargo industry in 1977, air transport of packages was made by the U.S. Postal Service or air forwarders. Time-sensitive shipments were not possible because air forwarders did not operate their own planes and had to depend upon the scheduled service of the airlines.

Deregulation in 1977. Following deregulation, the air cargo industry underwent dramatic changes, as air forwarders and ground transportation operators acquired their own aircraft and became integrators. Some passenger airlines also began to pick up some market share, but it was the all-cargo carriers (or integrators) that created the express delivery service that has been most commonly known as air courier service.

Creation of the Hub System. Development of the hub system made possible the large-scale, overnight deliveries, and essentially the very existence of the modern air courier industry. Federal Express initiated the hub system, and it has remained the standard operating method in use.

Using this system, all freight is originally shipped to the company's central hub, where it is sorted and rerouted to its final destination. As the air courier industry has grown, some regional hubs have been formed to serve particular areas of the country. Only integrators use the hub system. Passenger airlines, instead, provide point-to-point service.

Air Express Service. The rapid growth of the air courier industry during the 1980s was primarily due to the success of express delivery service. This particular service has been dominated by the integrators. From 1982 to 1990, the domestic air express market grew at an annual rate of nearly 19 percent. In 1999 the air express industry continued to grow, along with air cargo. Air express deliveries accounted for 60 percent of air shipments in 1998, with overnight letters and envelopes alone accounting for 27 percent of the industry (in both shipments and revenues).

Standard & Poor's Industry Surveys suggested that the factors that contributed to the growth of air express service included: the need for the rapid delivery of documents and small packages in an information- and service-based economy; the development of centralized distribution systems; the adoption of just-in-time inventory and production systems; and the willingness of shippers to pay premium fees for such services.

Competition. A flurry of overnight express companies appeared on the scene during the 1980s. By 1992 only seven significant air carriers remained in the express service business. Five companies continued to dominate the category in 1999: the U.S. Postal Service (USPS), the world's largest air-and-ground package delivery company, which offers express mail along with other options; Federal Express, the world leader in the overnight package delivery market; DHL, the world's largest and most experienced international air express network; and Airborne Express, the third largest air express carrier.

Many analysts have considered the status of the air freight industry as a vanguard of the direction of the overall economy. During tight economic times, people cut costs by using the more economical two-day delivery service. As conditions improve, traffic in the more expensive, priority overnight service increases.

A Mature Market. Compared to the growth rates of the 1980s, the cargo industry (freight, express, and mail) slowed by the early 1990s. For example, annual growth in 1990 was 2.2 percent, compared to the 7 percent annual rate during the 1980s. Part of the slower growth rate was not only due to the recession, but also to the use of long-range cargo aircraft in the Persian Gulf War.

By 1993 a general upturn in air cargo was reported in both domestic and international markets. Moreover, steady growth in express service (or courier service) has been predicted for the next decade, especially in the international arena. In 1996 air cargo traffic was at a 10-year high; total air cargo was up 30.5 percent from September 1995 to September 1996. All of the major air express carriers experienced growth in the late 1990s.

Service-Oriented Competition. As the express service industry has continued to mature, integrators have turned to service refinements as a competitive tool. Services such as guaranteed early morning or afternoon deliveries have become commonplace. Second-day service has been expanded, and weight limits have been raised. Extensive tracking processes and communications networks have been established to automate billing and accounting services for customers.

Status of Combination Carriers. The integrators have continued to dominate market share of the express service industry, as most U.S. combination carriers still treat cargo as a secondary service. Although most airlines could compete with integrators in head-to-head competition, they haven't yet done so. However, *Standard & Poor's Industry Surveys* reported that the larger airlines have begun to focus more on this area, aided by expanded fleets and larger aircraft. Airlines have emphasized improved customer service and have attempted to gain a strong foothold in the small shipment sector.

CURRENT CONDITIONS

According to the Colography Group, an Atlanta-based research firm specializing in the air-freight and air-express industries, there were 2.8 billion domestic air shipments made in 1998. The U.S. Postal Service (USPS) moved 1.3 billion Express and Priority Mail parcels and represented 45 percent of the domestic market. In late 1999 USPS announced an affiliation with DHL Worldwide Inc. for expedited global service to 65 countries.

Overall, the 1998 industry realized a modest 7.6 percent increase from 1997. Federal Express captured 25.6 percent of the public market, followed by UPS at 15.6 percent, and Airborne Express at 11.3 percent, but the lion's share of the market remained with USPS. As of 1999, there were 18 listed companies operating in the air courier industry, only 3 of which were publicly held. 216,000 employees worked in the $22.8 billion industry.

INDUSTRY LEADERS

Federal Express. Federal Express had 26 percent of the private market share in 1998, and 45 to 50 percent market share in the air express service division. Each day, Federal Express delivers approximately 2.8 million items.

The company began operations in 1973, and is known as the creator of the hub system of distribution. By 1999 Federal Express had 145,000 employees worldwide and served 185 countries. It operated 600 aircraft and 38,000 vehicles and had 550,000 Powership and FedEx automated systems in its integrated network. Frederick Smith was chairman, president, and chief executive officer of the company. Federal Express's headquarters are located in Memphis, Tennessee.

Federal Express has also been the industry leader in various technological advancements. The company was the first to develop a computerized tracking system that could tell where any package was at any time from pick-up to delivery. Federal Express created the customer service system with 32 call centers worldwide that handled 300,000 calls daily. The company also developed the digitally assisted dispatch system (DADS), which communicates to couriers through computers in their vans. In 1998 they had revenues of $15.9 billion, with profits at $503 million. Federal Express became a publicly held company in 1978 and is listed on the New York Stock Exchange.

United Parcel Service. United Parcel Service (UPS), headquartered in Atlanta, Georgia, was the second largest private express courier in the United States and the world's largest package delivery company, as well as the leader for domestic air shipments in 1998.

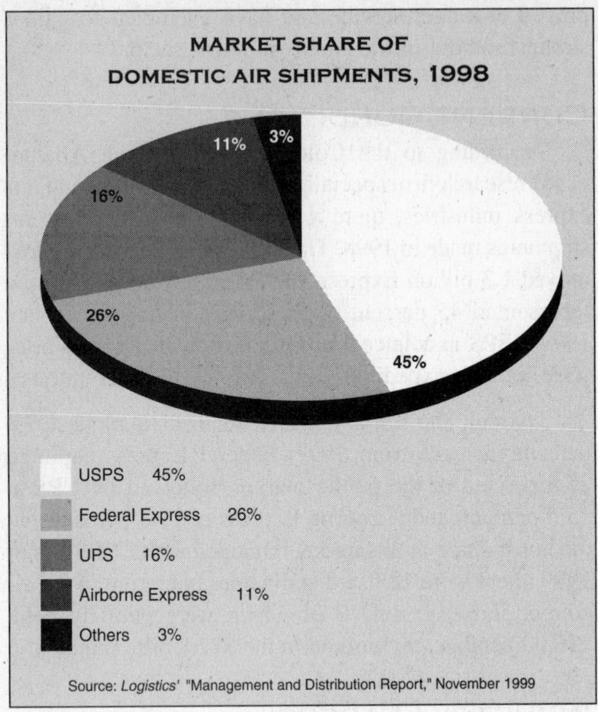

Source: *Logistics'* "Management and Distribution Report," November 1999

The company was founded in Seattle, Washington, in 1907, furnishing messengers for errand service. The company merged with a competitor in 1913 and took its name, Merchants Parcel Delivery, reflecting the company's concentration on retail packages. In 1919 the company changed its name to United Parcel Service (UPS) in the process of expanding its business into California and eventually to all of the West Coast.

In 1929 UPS began air delivery along the West Coast, but its airline, called United Air Express, ended operations in 1931 due to the depressed economy. During the 1930s and 1940s, the company concentrated on retail delivery service and opened major urban areas in the Midwest and eastern United States. UPS renewed its air service in 1953, and major cities on the East and West Coasts became connected with two-day service. By 1975 UPS had become the first company to service every address in the 48 contiguous states.

UPS entered the overnight delivery business in 1982, offering UPS Next Day Air to 24 major metropolitan areas. UPS was already the largest carrier of packages in the United States, but the packages were primarily transported by ground service. On a daily basis, UPS delivers by air more than 1.78 million express mail packages, with UPS Next Day Air and 2nd Day Air Services combined. The company services more than 200 countries and territories and every address in the United States. With 336,000 employees in the U.S. daily automatic pick-up, service is provided to more than 1.7 million shipping customers, to 6 million ultimate receivers. UPS operates 149,000 vehicles, including package cars, vans, tractors, and trailers; and 500 aircraft. By 1999 it had affiliated itself with more than 100 e-commerce entities to provide Web-based services. In 1998 the company had sales of $24.8 billion on a volume of 3.15 billion packages, with a net income of $1.7 billion. Near the end of 1999, UPS announced that it would offer more than 100 million shares on the public market at $36 to $42 per share.

Airborne Express. Airborne Express was the third largest air express carrier in the United States in the mid-1990s, second only to Federal Express and United Parcel Service. Airborne operated its own airline, ABX Air, Inc., with 82 planes in its fleet and its own ground transportation vehicles. It is the only U.S. air cargo company to own an airport. The Airborne corporate office is in Seattle, Washington; and as of 1997, Robert S. Cline was chairman and chief executive officer of the company.

Airborne Express operated as a freight forwarder until 1980 when it expanded into an overnight air express company. The company, initially Pacific Air Freight, merged with Airborne Freight Corporation of California in 1968, taking the Airborne name. The company first began operations by leasing the services of Midwest Air Charter in Wilmington, Ohio. With deregulation in 1977, Airborne began to purchase its own fleet of aircraft, which reduced the company's dependence on chartered space on other airlines. In 1980 Airborne acquired Midwest Air Charter and the Wilmington Airport and turned the property into the company's hub airport. In 1995 the company expanded their fleet with the acquisition of Boeing 767-200 aircraft and opened a second runway. They also formed Airborne Alliance Group, a consortium of transportation, logistics, third-party customer service operations, and high-tech companies providing value-added services.

Airborne has been moving freight internationally for more than 40 years. The company has operated overseas with a combination of its own facilities and foreign service partners. Airborne has entered into joint operating agreements with other large, well-established transportation companies worldwide. Overall net earnings were $120 million in 1997 on revenues of $2.9 billion.

DHL Worldwide Express. DHL is the carrier with the most worldwide coverage, operating 1,600 offices around the globe. DHL employs 50,000 people with 9,000 of them in the United States, and serves nearly 80,000 destinations in 224 countries and territories. Handling more than 65 million shipments each year, the company works out of 13 hubs, beginning operations out of a brand new Miami facility in 1997. They had 275 gateways, owned 33 aircraft, and chartered 48 other planes. DHL's domestic hub is located at the Greater Cincinnati/Northern Kentucky Airport.

DHL Airways Inc. was founded in 1969 by Adrian Dalsey, Larry Hillblom, and Robert Lynn (hence DHL) as a shuttling service between Hawaii and San Francisco. In 1971 the company was the first international air express company to provide service to the Pacific Rim, starting with the Philippines. Service was extended to Japan, Hong Kong, Singapore, and Australia in 1972. DHL moved into Europe in 1974, Latin America in 1976, the Middle East in 1977, and to Africa in 1978. It was the first company to bring air express service to the Eastern Bloc countries in 1983 and to the People's Republic of China in 1988. The DHL Worldwide Express network is part of both DHL Airways Inc., based in Redwood City, California, which provides service to the United States and its territories; and DHL International, Ltd. in Brussels, which operates in all other areas of the world. Japan Airlines and German airline Lufthansa each own 25 percent of DHL International, and Japanese securities firm Nissho Iwai owns an additional 7.5 percent. The estate of the company's late cofounder, Larry Lee Hillblom, owns 60 percent of DHL Airways and 24 percent of DHL International. In 1999 DHL announced a deal with the Boeing Company for the long-term lease of 44 Boeing 757 special freighters to assist with the expanding global express delivery market. DHL also announced that it would be selling 23 percent of the company in 2001. Finally, in November 1999, DHL announced an agreement with Mail Boxes, Etc. to use their 3,300 franchise locations for the marketing and servicing of DHL international services.

Another carrier is Emery Worldwide, which was a $2 million global, multi-modal transportation and logistics company. They had 580 service agencies in 95 countries, owned 98 aircraft, and had a ground fleet of 2,000 trucks. In 1997 the U.S. Postal Service awarded Emery with a $1.7 billion 58-month contract to create and operate a new network for the exclusive handling of priority mail.

Burlington Air Express had 185 offices in North America and 325 internationally for a worldwide total of more than 500 offices in 18 countries. They specialized in transportation and logistics services for industrial shippers and primarily handled large package shipments (from over 10 lbs. up to 1,000 lbs.) They did not, however, offer residential delivery. The company operated out of its hub in Toledo, Ohio.

WORKFORCE

In spite of the recession during the early 1990s, the express service of the air cargo industry had continued to grow along with career opportunities. Employment opportunities in the industry have been greatest in major metropolitan areas. In 1997 Federal Express had to advertise nationally for employment in Indianapolis because there weren't enough qualified applicants to fill the job openings locally. At the end of the 1990s, job outlook was favorable because of the expected growth in the global market serviced by the same carriers.

Employees with experience in industry-specific software and knowledge of Electronic Data Interchange (EDI) will be needed, as companies head toward greater interconnectivity with client companies. To provide service to their customers, these companies will need Information Systems (IS) professionals with experience in developing various programming languages, such as C and C++, under the Unix operating system. Computer networking skills also have become critical because companies have been adding new client sites to their network. With industry trends suggesting that the overnight express service will continue to lead in the growth figures for the industry, IS employment opportunities remain strong throughout the 1990s.

AMERICA AND THE WORLD

By far the most important factor in the global expansion of this industry was the 1999 World Trade Organization (WTO) meeting in Seattle, Washington. At stake was China's anticipated contribution to a global air cargo value which in 1998 surpassed the $2 trillion mark (including ground services). In December 1999, Federal Express, UPS, and Polar Air Cargo companies were all filing documents with the U.S. Department of Transportation in an attempt to secure rights to provide service for ten new authorized round-trip flights to China, the newest member of the WTO. Currently, the market is held by United and Northwest Airlines, and Federal Express. Those three entities would like to keep it that way. The Department of Transportation was expected to announce its decision in 2000, with service flights to begin in 2001.

The Northwest Airlines pilot strike in 1998 greatly impacted both domestic and global air courier markets. Notwithstanding, the industry expects a 7 to 10 percent annual growth rate for the next several years. The 1998 global air-cargo market (including air and ground services) brought in revenues of $8 billion. DHL was providing about 40 percent of the global express courier market.

RESEARCH AND TECHNOLOGY

Advances in computer technology, software development, and the communications industry have provided the air courier industry with the necessary tools for efficient and timely functions related to all aspects of operations. Everything from hand-held computers, to online, real-time data systems has allowed air courier companies to communicate more effectively with ground personnel and their customers. Continued advances will bring additional automation and provide improved accuracy in delivery and billing and improved service to the customer.

EDI. Electronic Data Interchange (EDI) is a computer-to-computer exchange of information between businesses. This information, such as inventories and purchase orders, travels over phone lines. Many overnight delivery companies have developed their own PC-based EDI systems to use at their client sites. For example, UPS' Maxi-Ship system consists of a PC, UPS-developed EDI software, and a printer. The system enables their clients to produce all shipping documentation and manage all cost accounting within their own offices.

Federal Express' system is called PowerShip. It too is an internally developed computer system that allows their customers to generate their own billing labels and invoices and track their own packages through the Fed Ex delivery system. The Federal Express EDI system resolved their paperwork problem identified by their salespeople as a burdensome task, by performing four customer functions. First, it generates the shipping label. Second, it prints a manifest of what was shipped at the end of each day. An invoice is automatically generated, and shipping charges are accrued and sent to the home office system for billing procedures. The third function is an array of shipping management and reporting. And finally, PowerShip allows customers to access the Federal Express' computerized package-tracking system. More than 25,000 Federal Express customers began to use this system in the mid-1990s. Customers who do as little as $75 worth of shipping per day with Federal Express can receive this system. For those with access to the Internet, it was possible to track your own package online, using the Federal Express Web site.

Cellular Technology/UPSnet. UPS entered the cellular market with the development of one of the first cellular data networks in the country. The system, called UPSnet, transmits air and ground package delivery information in real-time that can be accessed by any ground transportation vehicle anywhere in the country.

To process delivery data for transmission on UPSnet, a driver first obtains a customer signature on a Delivery Information Acquisition Device (DIAD), a hand-held computer that captures signatures electronically. Next, the driver attaches the DIAD to UPS' DIAD Vehicle Adapter, which is inserted in a cellular telephone modem in the truck. The modem then transmits the information from an external transceiver on board to cellular switches provided by four different cellular carriers and to a UPSnet packet switch. The information is transmitted to a mainframe system at the UPS worldwide data center in Mahwah, New Jersey. UPSnet was expected to be installed in more than 50,000 vehicles in the UPS fleet.

Teller Machines Drop-Off Boxes. Federal Express had been test marketing its own new product, a self-service center based on Automated Teller Machine (ATM) technology. Anyone with a credit card or a prearranged Federal Express account number would be able to drop off an overnight letter or small package at this self-service center at any time. All labeling and billing would be executed on a touch-screen terminal similar to a bank ATM. The system, known as Federal Express Online, has a touch screen video display terminal that offers computer menus for making an address label or choosing either next-day or two-day delivery service. Payment is made by running a credit card through a magnetic slot.

The self-serve center processes the information, sends it over telephone lines to a local or regional database computer that authorizes the credit card transactions, stamps a time on the bar-coded address label, and confirms the delivery address for the customer. These centers were planned to be used around-the-clock, and were intended to complement and possibly replace some of the 29,000 Federal Express drop-off boxes. The company hoped that increased automation would reduce costs and improve service.

FURTHER READING

''Air Cargo Tells New Story.'' *Transportation & Distribution,* December 1999.

Aurentz, Tim. ''Air Cargo Carriers.'' *Des Moines Business Record,* 17 December 1996.

''Boeing, DHL Sign Freighter Conversion Deal.'' *Business Times,* 26 November 1999.

''Business This Week.'' *Economist,* 18 December 1999.

Corder, David R. ''USPS Delivers New Low-Cost Mail Option.'' *Business Journal Serving Jacksonville & Northeast Florida,* 12 November 1999.

Dinell, David. ''Cargo Traffic at 10-Year High.'' *Wichita Business Journal,* 8 November 1996.

Henterly, Meghan. ''DHL Bracing for Competition on Its Overseas Turf.'' *Gannett News Service,* 11 June 1996.

''Mail Boxes, Etc., DHL Sign Deal.'' *Business Journal Serving San Jose & Silicon Valley,* 26 November 1999.

Nelms, Douglas W. ''Airborne - All The Way.'' *Air Transport World,*August 1998.

Orr, Deborah. ''The Post Office With a Ticker.'' *Forbes,* 29 November 1999.

''Pipeline.'' *IPO Reporter,* 8 November 1999.

''Tenth Freighter for Northwest.'' *Transportation & Distribution,* December 1999.

Thompson, Richard. ''Federal Express' Memphis, Tenn.-Based Parent Reports Low Earnings.'' *The Commercial Appeal,* 17 December 1999.

''U.S. Postal Service Dominates Domestic Air Cargo.'' *Logistics Management & Distribution Report,* November 1999.

Yung, Katherine. ''Airlines, Cargo Carriers Fight to Add New Flights to China.'' *The Dallas Morning News,* 7 December 1999.

SIC 4522

AIR TRANSPORTATION, NONSCHEDULED

This category includes establishments primarily engaged in furnishing nonscheduled air transportation. Also included in this industry are establishments primarily engaged in furnishing airplane sightseeing services, air taxi services, and helicopter passenger transportation services to, from, or between local airports, whether or not scheduled.

NAICS CODE(S)

621910 (Ambulance Services)

481212 (Nonscheduled Chartered Freight Air Transportation)

481211 (Nonscheduled Chartered Passenger Air Transportation)

487990 (Scenic and Sightseeing Transportation, Other)

INDUSTRY SNAPSHOT

According to *Ward's Business Directory of U.S. Private and Public Companies 2000,* the U.S. nonscheduled air transportation industry was made up of at least 33 companies that generated $4 billion in revenue in 1999, employing 27,000 workers. This nonscheduled segment of the air transportation industry included all companies that provided charter service, airlines carrying passengers and/or cargo, and helicopter services. One major characteristic of the nonscheduled industry was that companies operated on the basis of full-plane sales. Using this procedure, the total aircraft capacity was sold to an organization, such as a ticket wholesaler. In general, these wholesalers were tour operators, military and governmental agencies, specialty charter customers, and sponsors of incentive travel packages. Most charter carriers, either passenger or cargo, were small operations working within a niche market.

ORGANIZATION AND STRUCTURE

According to *The Air Charter Journal,* there were 20,000 aircraft, from jets to turboprops, as well as 3,000 operators available for charter throughout the world as of March 1999. The nonscheduled airline industry included charter passenger airlines and air taxi services. Charter passenger airlines provided service to vacation or leisure destinations and marketed their services through the use of tour operators, travel agencies, or destination resort operators, which included cruise ship operators. With medium- to large-size planes in their fleet, charter carriers also provided service to the U.S. military and other groups. Air taxi services companies provided short-haul, on-demand transportation—in which case they were called ''Part 135'' operators—and helicopter service. Part 135 operators fly planes with less than 30 seats and have relied largely on corporate-oriented clientele. Most carriers also utilized their fleets for sightseeing trips, commutes between airports, emergency medical transportation, and the delivery of workers and equipment to offshore oil well sites. Helicopter services provided similar on-demand corporate transportation.

Scheduled Traffic and Capacity. Charter carriers typically board between 1.0 and 1.5 million passengers annually, and log more than 18 billion revenue passenger miles (RPMs), a measurement based on one fare-paying passenger transported one mile. Charter airlines logged 9.1 billion of their RPMs in domestic service and 8.7 billion RPMs in international service. In comparison, annual enplanements for the scheduled airline sector average 554.2 million per 12-month period, producing 547 billion RPMs. While charter airlines fly fewer people, they tend to fill more seats on their planes. Nonscheduled carriers average 70-75 percent load factors (a measure of seats filled), while scheduled airlines typically realize much lower load factors.

With regard to charter service in the United States, it is estimated that 17 percent of charter certificates were held on a single pilot basis. More than 14 percent of all piston charter operators stopped their operations, according to *The Air Charter Journal.* Regulations and insurance costs were cited as the reason in 40 percent of these cases, and 15 percent cited lack of business opportunities.

Load factors for specific charter airlines usually have been higher than the overall industry average, running anywhere from 80 to 100 percent. For example, Trans National Travel (TNT), with its twice-weekly charter flights from Providence, Rhode Island, to Bermuda, achieved a 95 percent load factor, according to *Travel Weekly.* Load factor directly affects fare structure. With fares based on a load factor of 80 percent or more, each seat can be sold at a deeper discount. However, unlike scheduled carriers, if a charter cannot meet these numbers, the flight is canceled. Therefore, charter operators work in high-demand markets and will pull out of the market when demand falls.

Nonscheduled airlines, like charter services, can access approximately 5,000 different airports in the United States. In comparison, scheduled airlines can use only 500 airports around the United States. Charter airlines rarely engage in direct competition with scheduled airlines. Instead, charters usually work in markets not directly served by the scheduled carriers. For example, Passport Travel, a Kansas City-based planner of Las Vegas trips, could not secure transportation through a scheduled carrier once the major hub in their market closed. ''We had been contracting blocked space on America West, but they decided to run their own tour packages in direct competition with us,'' said Sharon Lewis, director of marketing for Passport Travel, in *Travel Weekly.* As a result, PTI Tours, the wholesale division of Passport Travel, chartered a 166-seat plane for the summer and was responsible for filling those seats.

In the 1990s, depending on aircraft type, country, and personnel, the hourly and overnight waiting charges varied widely. Rates in the United States were around $50 to $100 per hour for standby, and $75 to $300 for overnight. Rates in Europe for hourly waiting charges were between 3 to 7 percent of hourly flight charges, as reported in *The Air Charter Guide.* Taxes can often be charged as a percentage of the entire cost of the trip. In the United States, an 8 percent levy was typical for aircraft over 6,000 lbs. According to *The Air Charter Journal,* chartering an aircraft ranged in price from $1,379 per hour in the Southeast to $1,608 per hour in the North Central region. The number of planes also varied from four in the Northwest and South Central regions to 27 in Northeast and Southwest.

Some charter airlines work directly with cruise lines and operators of other vacation sites. Miami Air International, created in October 1991, was formed to serve the cruise industry, according to *Travel Weekly.* The carrier's first contract, with Seawind Cruises, had them offering transportation between Miami and the island of Aruba, where Seawind was based. The carrier also had a long-term contract with Club Med to bring vacationers from Miami to the club's villages in St. Lucia, Martinique, the Dominican Republic, and Guadeloupe.

Generally, a charter airline will enter into a contract with a tour operator 4 to 6 months in advance of the service to be provided. At the time the contract is executed, tour operators are required to pay the charter a deposit. The balance must be paid to the charter carrier at least two weeks prior to the flight date. If the tour operator fails to make the necessary payment, the carrier must either cancel the flight within ten days prior to the flight date, or, pursuant to the U.S. Department of Transportation (DOT) regulations, perform under the contract in spite of the breach by the operator.

All charter carriers are subject to the jurisdiction of and regulation by the DOT and the Federal Aviation Administration (FAA) under the Federal Aviation Act. The DOT is responsible for regulating economic issues affecting air service, including air carrier certification and fitness, insurance, leasing arrangements, allocation of route rights, authorization of proposed charter operations, and consumer protection. In 1993 the DOT enacted a major overhaul of charter airline regulations, simplifying the arrangement and sales of charter services while providing adequate consumer protection.

BACKGROUND AND DEVELOPMENT

Charter airlines have existed in the United States since the onset of commercial aviation, offering supplemental service to that provided by scheduled operators. Charter airline companies, generally small operations flying a few older aircraft, have never been well known among air travel consumers. The deregulation of the airline industry in the early 1980s offered severe challenges to charter airlines, primarily because it encouraged commercial airlines to offer low fares and plentiful flights to leisure travelers. Many charter carriers, seeking to protect their traditional business, could not compete with the larger commercial carriers and left the business.

While deregulation hampered the charter airline industry in one area, it helped in another. Due to the creation of the hub-and-spoke system, also a product of deregulation, many smaller cities have lacked direct or nonstop service, especially to leisure destinations. Successful charter operations have found niche markets in these cities and have avoided direct conflict with scheduled carriers.

Charter airlines have struggled to improve their image with the flying public. When the largest charter carrier, American Trans Air (ATA), began operations in 1973, the industry had a reputation for ''rusty planes, lousy in-flight service and long delays,'' said George Mikelsons, chairman of Amtran, the parent company of ATA, in *Travel Weekly.* ''It has been a very slow process to get people comfortable with the fact that you can buy a charter flight that is at least the equal of coach class on a good scheduled carrier.''

Forecast for Charter Airlines. Charters usually cost 20 percent less than a scheduled carrier's ticket prices. However, if the major scheduled carriers are undergoing a price war among themselves, the price differential between the scheduled airlines and charters can sometimes significantly narrow. The charter business has succeeded because it is efficient; maintaining that efficiency through finding and effectively serving niche markets will be critical to the industry's success throughout the 1990s. ATA officials believe that the consolidation of the scheduled industry actually will help the charter market. Their reasoning has been that as markets become more consolidated, airlines will be less willing to price seats for tour packages. Also, as the scheduled carriers bring their tour operations in-house, they will be less willing to deal with operators outside their airlines. In turn, independent tour operators will have to depend on charters.

As reported in *Travel Weekly,* The National Parks Overflights Act of 1997, introduced by Senator John McCain of Arizona, has the potential to significantly reduce the amount of air touring travel in the Grand Canyon National Park. The U.S. Air Tour Operators Association from Las Vegas represents 50 air tour operators, and the association didn't favor the effort to reduce national park noise. The bill would give the U.S. Department of the Interior the ability to establish flight restrictions, curfews, and flight-free zones over certain national parks, and it requires the Interior and Transportation Departments to study and create a plan that would implement quieter air technology for flying over national parks.

Part 135 Operations. Some carriers have begun to operate under the umbrella of a larger charter, such as AMRCombs. Others have ventured into additional markets, such as providing contingency service. United Parcel Service (UPS) developed a contingency program dubbed the ''Lear Operation,'' according to *Business & Commercial Aviation.* Under this program, if a UPS shipment will miss the primary package sort at the hub, the company will call on Part 135 on-demand charter companies to deliver the stranded packages. Some operators have kept their planes at UPS's Louisville, Kentucky, hub to increase their availability.

Executive Jet Aviation, Inc. has created a ''timeshare'' program called NetJet. Instead of owning an entire jet, Net-Jet ''Lets executives use planes anywhere in the continental U.S. within four hours—for the expense of owning just a piece of the plane,'' reported Andrea Rothman in *Business Week.* Corporations purchasing shares in the program are guaranteed that NetJets arrive prepared to fly, and they eliminate maintenance needs, leasing fees for hangars, and a pilot's salary.

Helicopter Service. Helicopter companies supporting the oil industry, police and public service operations, and the medical profession were all expected to see continued growth through the end of the 1990s. Those companies offering diversified service have been best equipped to produce consistent earnings. For example, Petroleum Helicopters has worked primarily with the oil and gas industry in the Gulf of Mexico, but also has become involved in the emergency medical service (EMS) business, reported Nicholas Kernstock in *Aviation Week & Space Technology.* Keystone Helicopters, a subsidiary of Keystone Flight Services, has split its contracts between EMS (approximately 80 percent) and on-demand charter and corporate management flying (20 percent). Keystone president Peter Wright predicted that thé public sector will be the fastest growing market in the helicopter industry.

Another successful approach for helicopter service has been ''to fully develop and dominate a niche market,'' reported *Aviation Week & Space Technology.* For example, Portland-based Columbia Helicopters has been one of the few commercial operators of heavy-lift aircraft worldwide. The company has specialized in heli-logging, which does less damage to the land than conventional logging methods.

CURRENT CONDITIONS

Industry analysts reported an 8.3 percent price rise in 1998 for the charter services sector of the nonscheduled air transportation industry. The overall industry rose at a somewhat lesser pace for 1998. The robust economy was identified as the key market influence, but the 1998 Northwest pilot strike also contributed greatly to the enhanced charter airline market.

In 1999, however, all the new airplanes that were ordered in anticipation of a continued growth market were being delivered, and a glut of available seat space began to cut into profits. By August 1999, there were 500 domestic planes still sitting, available for purchase or lease—about 100 more than in August 1998. To balance this, 268 aging aircraft were removed from the fleet in 1998, followed by 241 in 1999, and an anticipated 286 in 2000.

In addition to retiring older planes, another key development in the latter 1990s was the rise in ''fractional ownership'' contracts. Under such plans, companies may purchase, for example, 50 flight hours annually on a standard business jet by purchasing one-sixteenth ownership interest for approximately $500,000 to $600,000. In comparison, the company would spend $6.6 million to purchase the plane outright, in addition to another $1.2 million annually for maintenance and crew.

INDUSTRY LEADERS

American Trans Air has been the largest U.S. charter airline, holding more than 40 percent of the charter market. At the end of 1996, revenues were estimated at $550 million. A privately held subsidiary of Indianapolis-based Amtran, Inc., the airline has 26 medium- to long-range aircraft in its fleet. The leisure travel market has comprised the largest part of Amtran's business, accounting for nearly 62 percent of total revenues and nearly 71 percent of available seat miles (ASMs) in 1992. The airline also has flown military charters, with a peak year in 1991 transporting U.S. troops to the Persian Gulf conflict. Amtran operates other travel-related subsidiaries, including a travel agency; a training school for pilots, mechanics, and flight attendants; an executive air charter service; and a freight forwarder. Amtran employs approximately 3,500 people.

World Airways provides worldwide, nonscheduled air transportation of passengers and cargo for commercial and government customers. World Airways has twelve

McDonnell Douglas aircraft in the long-range international market. The airline's business has been seasonal, with the highest travel figures from May through July and in December. According to *Insiders' Chronicle,* the company's largest customer has been the U.S. Military Airlift Command, which accounts for nearly half of its consolidated revenues. Malaysian pilgrims traveling to Mecca also generated 15 percent of annual revenues under a contract with Malaysian Air. World Airways, which recently became independent of WorldCorp, its previous holding company, had 844 employees in 1998, with negative sales and net income for that year. WorldCorp continues in bankruptcy proceedings.

A relatively new entrant into the U.S. charter industry is United Parcel Service. In March 1997, the company intended to fly weekend travelers who book flights through cruise lines or tour operators, the typical charter vacationer. The company's Boeing 727 planes usually remain idle on weekends, but the firm will move 113 seats and carpeting into some of its aircraft to obtain a slice of the charter market.

The industry remained ripe for entrepreneurial interests through 1999. Aero Jet Services of Scottsdale, Arizona, began in 1997 with less than $20,000. Its revenues for that year were $1 million, followed by $2 million in 1998, and the company expected to close out 1999 with more than $6 million. The company's employees grew from three in 1997 to 14 in 1999, managing seven planes for its air-charter business.

AMERICA AND THE WORLD

Charter airline service in Europe, as opposed to that in the United States, offers significant competition to the scheduled airline industry for passenger traffic to leisure destinations. In fact, charter airlines have traditionally carried slightly more than half of all European travelers. The charter industry's success has been due in part to the fact that charter carriers have been subject to fewer regulations than the scheduled airlines. Thus the European market has been of interest to American charter companies like ATA simply because charter services are well known and well liked throughout Europe.

In January 1993, the European version of open skies legislation was enacted, removing government restrictions on air fares and on cabotage throughout the European Community member countries. This program has allowed airlines to set fares at any level. In 1997, carriers were also able to offer services on domestic routes in other member states. Such legislation was expected to have the same effect on the European charter industry that deregulation had on the U.S. charter industry. Industry leaders predicted that the charter carriers will lose market share as the scheduled airlines become free of capacity and price restraints, thus reducing possibilities for American firms to expand into European markets.

RESEARCH AND TECHNOLOGY

The charter industry's ability to compete on a price basis will be contingent on the efficiency of its aircraft operations. Therefore, some U.S. companies have begun to update their fleets. Amtran has added a sixth extended-range Boeing 757 to its fleet, according to *Travel Weekly.* Lauded for its fuel efficiency and endurance, the 757 can amass up to 300 flight hours a month, and will be used by ATA for transatlantic charters and military transportation. Another aircraft that may aid in competitive pricing is the new Airbus A320 aircraft, Europe's high-tech twinjet. Dubbed by its manufacturer as "the most advanced airliner in the world," the A320 "burns 40 percent less fuel than the 727-200, and is more efficient than the latest aircraft in the 737 and MD-80 families as well," reported Bill Poling in *Travel Weekly.*

The helicopter section of the unscheduled industry should also profit from technological advancements. Of particular importance will be the military tiltrotor. The aircraft can function as a helicopter on takeoffs and landings, but is capable of flying at a cruising speed of 300 knots per hour at an altitude of 20,000 to 25,000 feet as a conventional fixed-wing aircraft. While it remains uncertain whether this aircraft will be ordered by the military, the helicopter may be introduced into the civilian market by the turn of the twenty-first century.

FURTHER READING

The Air Charter Guide Web Site, 1995-2000. Available from http://www.guides.com/acg/guide/datasources.asp.

Brackey, Harriet Johnson. "If They Aren't Buying Jets, Executives Lease, Buy an Interest in Them." *The Miami Herald,* 4 November 1999.

Cohen, Warren. "That 'P' in UPS Stands for People." *U.S. News & World Report,* 17 March 1997.

Federal Aviation Administration. *FAA Aviation Forecasts, Fiscal Years 1991-2002.* Washington, D.C.: Department of Transportation.

Flint, Perry. "A Slight Imbalance." *Air Transport World,* December 1999, 34.

Graham, Philip. E-mail response to question about charter terminology. *The Air Charter Guide,* 27 February 2000.

Kosdrowsky, Terry. "Charter Airlines Cash In On Northwest's Pending Strike." *Crain's Detroit Business,* 24 August 1998, 30.

Pina, Michael. "Air Tour Group Criticizes Bill Limiting Flights Over Parks." *Travel Weekly,* 24 February 1997.

Sioc, Cindy Vargo. "Air Charters Reach New Heights." *South Florida Business Journal,* 17 April 1998, 1B.

Thomas, William D., and Joseph Kowal. "Producer Price Highlights, 1998." *Monthly Labor Review,* July 1999, 3-15.

U.S. Bureau of Transportation. ''Bureau of Transportation Statistics May 1997.'' Available from http//www.bts.gov/oai/indicators/top.html.

Ward's Business Directory of U.S. Public and Private Companies 2000. Detroit: Gale Research, 1999.

Winograd, Jeanne. ''Catering to High-Flying Clients.'' *Business Journal of Phoenix,* 18 June 1999, 23.

Woods, Lynn. ''Pay Now, Fly Later: Just Make Sure You're Not Left High and Dry.'' *Kiplinger's Personal Finance Magazine,* March 1997.

World Airways financial information provided by *Hoover's Online,* 1999. Available at http://www.hoovers.com.

WorldCorp, Inc. ''WorldCorp, Inc. Form 10-K.'' Herdon, Va.: WorldCorp, Inc., December 1992.

SIC 4581

AIRPORTS, FLYING FIELDS, AND AIRPORT TERMINAL SERVICES

This category includes establishments primarily engaged in operating and maintaining airports and flying fields; in servicing, repairing (except on a factory basis), maintaining, and storing aircraft; and in furnishing coordinated handling services for airfreight or passengers at airports. This industry also includes private establishments primarily engaged in air traffic control operations. Government air traffic control operations are classified in **SIC 9621: Regulation and Administration of Transportation Programs.** Aircraft modification centers and establishments primarily engaged in factory type overhaul of aircraft are classified in transportation equipment industries, and flying fields maintained by aviation clubs are classified in **SIC 7997: Membership Sports and Recreation Clubs.**

NAICS Code(s)

488111 (Air Traffic Control)
488119 (Other Airport Operations)
561720 (Janitorial Services)
488190 (Other Support Activities for Air Transportation)

Industry Snapshot

According to Ward's 2000 Business Directory of U.S. Private and Public Companies, in 1999, there were approximately 48 public and private companies in the airports, flying fields, and services industry, which generated $20.6 billion in sales and employed 133,300 workers. The firm Mergeglobal Inc. estimates that the direct economic impact of U.S. airports was estimated at $200 billion, and total economic impact at $575 billion. The North American Airports Council International (NAACI) reported that there were 416 U.S. airports that had scheduled airline service and another 149 with nonscheduled airline service. The NAACI also reported, ''Approximately half a billion passengers travel through U.S. airports annually, approximately nine million metric tons of air cargo are handled by U.S. airports annually.'' 1999 U.S. airline fleets totaled 4,133 planes.

The airport, flying field, and airport terminal services industry can be divided into two distinct parts. One segment of the industry offers airport terminal services, covering everything from baggage handling to food service. Typically these companies work with commercial airlines, both domestic and international, and airport management. The other segment of the industry offers aircraft services, including maintenance, repair, aircraft conversion, and sales of equipment and parts. These companies work with commercial passenger airlines, but have also provided service to the U.S. military, to makers and end users of general aviation aircraft, and to air cargo carriers.

Airports that can increase the number of runways and thus increase capacity stand to benefit more than those airports that do not have more room for additional runways. Airplane passenger mind-sets have changed significantly since the early days of flight, and many airports across the country are finding that they need to update their facilities to reflect this change. The five largest airports in the United States by passenger traffic in 1997 were: Chicago O'Hare (70.4 million), Atlanta Hartsfield (68.2 million), Dallas/Ft. Worth International (60.5 million), Los Angeles International (60.1 million), and San Francisco International (40.5 million). The NAACI estimates that airport costs represent approximately 5 percent of total airline costs.

The aircraft and airport services industry has always included a broad range of companies, from small private firms, to divisions of large conglomerates that offer transportation-related services, to divisions within an airline operation. A long recession in the passenger airline industry from 1988 to 1992 hurt the industry, and many airlines ceased operations, merged with other airlines, or cut back in service. All service companies, especially those dependent on the large air passenger carriers, struggled to survive. Smaller maintenance companies merged operations, while the larger conglomerates sold off unprofitable services. Surviving companies diversified both their services and their markets, and many moved into the international arena. However, during the latter 1990s, (but for the Northwest pilot strike in 1998) the industry reported steady profits and earnings were expected to continue to grow through the third millennium A.D.

ORGANIZATION AND STRUCTURE

Airports in the United States typically contract with outside vendors for the services they provide to their customers, both airlines and passengers. Those vendors, which make up the companies listed in this industry, provide a number of services to people and to planes. Providers of airport terminal services operate food and beverage concessions, gift shops, and newsstands in airport terminals, while providers of airport passenger services offer bus and limousine operations, consulting and training services, passenger screening, airport security, interline baggage service, and skycaps. Aircraft in-flight service companies provide catering operations for commercial passenger airlines.

Other companies provide aircraft terminal services, including ground handling services for commercial carriers, aircraft fueling and cleaning, and baggage handling. Maintenance, repair, and overhaul (MRO) companies provide heavy maintenance, usually working on aging-aircraft programs or on conversions for commercial carriers and military aircraft. Fixed-base operation (FBO) vendors work as a ''service station'' for aircraft, providing refueling and ground handling services for corporate jets and general aviation aircraft. FBOs sometimes have a terminal lounge for flight crews. Aviation aftermarket companies sell parts and equipment for new or used aircraft, usually as a division of an aerospace company.

Depending upon the type of service provided, aircraft and airport service companies operate on airport grounds, within the airport terminal, or at nearby hangers or production facilities. Most companies have corporate headquarters physically removed from these working sites.

The combination of the Gulf War, skyrocketing fuel prices, airline fare wars, rising debt service costs, and the slowdown of the American economy had a devastating effect on the financial condition of several domestic airlines in the late 1980s and early 1990s—and left no airline untouched. By 1993 the air transportation industry had lost a record $10.5 billion, three large carriers had ceased operations, two were operating in bankruptcy, and one had just emerged from bankruptcy protection. Companies providing service to the air transportation industry shared in the recession; however, the unprecedented recovery of the airline industry in 1995 through 1996 helped rebuild many of the service companies that survived the downturn.

Passenger Services. During the slowdown of the early 1990s, companies providing terminal services were hard hit by price-conscious travelers who limited their out-of-pocket spending in the airports. One company, Dobbs Subsidiaries, a division of the Dial Corporation, was sold to Host International in 1992 due to rising costs. In turn Host, a division of the Marriott Corporation, not only lowered its prices and offered promotions, but also redesigned its concession stands and brought in well-known, fast food chains to entice passengers to use their services.

Unlike most of the other companies in this industry, those offering in-flight catering have been directly dependent upon the operations of the major commercial passenger airlines. Companies capable of accommodating the ever-changing demands of these carriers during the turbulent years of 1988 to 1993 were the ones who survived. Dobbs International was one such company. According to a company report prepared by Donald, Lufkin, Jenrette Securities, despite the difficulties posed by the price wars in the airline industry, Dobbs continued to earn more in revenues and profits because of its success in winning new contracts. Consequently, Dobbs has maintained approximately a 19 percent market share. Other catering companies included CaterAire (formerly Marriott), with 26 percent, Onyx (formerly Sky Chefs), with 19 percent, and UAL Services, with a 15 percent market share.

Aircraft Services. Maintenance operations were also affected by the recession, but this segment of the service industry stabilized by the end of 1993, due in part to diversification. For example, Pemco Aeroplex, a large third-party maintenance operator, maintained a 50-50 mix of military and civilian work to level off the peaks and valleys of the market.

Many providers of fixed-base operations responded to the recession by consolidating operations. The best-known merger took place between Page Avjet Airport Services and Butler Aviation International, creating the world's largest multisite FBO company. Some industry analysts have predicted that merged operations such as these may be the model for FBOs of the future.

Future Growth. The industry was expected to grow significantly into the twenty-first century. Projected future growth in airline fleet size was predicted to be a positive factor for those companies that provide maintenance and repair services.

Many airport and aircraft service companies have looked to strategic alliances or partnerships to create further market growth. For example, UNC, Inc. has developed long-term contracts with major aviation firms and has formed trading company partnerships to add leasing and parts distribution services.

Air transport service companies will continue to improve their services with a reliance on computerization. For example, UNC, Inc. has been using cutting-edge information technology to provide its customers with computerized online parts status. Commodore Aviation also has become completely computerized, allowing instant tracking of work-hours required and materials expended.

CURRENT CONDITIONS

While 1998 data was affected by the September 1998 Northwest Airlines pilot strike, domestic air traffic nonetheless reported a 4.9 percent increase. However, the net effect of this was lost in the fact that *capacity* rose 9.5 percent during the same period. This resulted in the overall load factor dropping 2.9 points to 65.9 percent. The excess domestic capacity resulted in a 2 percent decline in average ticket price.

Customer satisfaction with airport services also plummeted in 1999 following the January 1999 snowstorm that closed down Detroit's Metropolitan Airport, also a hub for Northwest Airlines. Ostensibly because of poor airport services planning, dozens of airplanes were stuck on ramps, while others sat parked at the gates, filled with passengers. Several immobilized planes kept their passengers on board without food, air, or working toilets for nine hours. Less than one month later, American Airlines pilots staged a sickout, again leaving passengers stranded or without comparable flight substitutions. These and other events resulted in Congressional hearings intended to mandate industry-wide changes. However, during the first six months of 1999, the airlines industry made more than $1.3 million in direct political contributions, $3 million in lobbying, and another $1 billion in ''soft money'' for political action committees. In the end, Congress backed off, and the airlines were permitted to submit their own voluntary plans for service improvements to the Department of Transportation by early 2000. Several airlines began implementing their voluntary plans in December 1999, according to the Air Transport Association (ATA). As of December 1999, the ATA represented 28 major U.S. carriers, which accounts for 98 percent of all domestic air travel. In June 2000 the Department of Transportation is expected to present an interim report on the efficacy of the voluntary plans to Congress and a final report in December 2000.

In 1999 airports and airlines spent $2.3 billion on Year 2000 (Y2K) readiness plans.

INDUSTRY LEADERS

A leader in airport and aircraft services has been DynCorp's Commercial Aviation Services Group, better known as DynAir. With approximately 4,000 employees and $1.2 billion in revenue, DynAir has provided total ground support services to both domestic and international carriers at more than 80 airports in the United States. DynAir has delivered services to over 100 airlines on more than 150,000 flights, and has processed more than 15 million passengers annually. With facilities in Arizona, Florida, and Texas, DynAir has offered a complete range of aviation-related technical services to the operations of commercial aircraft, including periodic checks, nonroutine maintenance, structural inspections, repair and overhaul, and stripping and painting. Other specialized services have included the repair, modification, and installation of transport aircraft avionics and navigation systems, including windshear alerts, weather radar and radio altimeter systems, complete cargo handling, and fueling services for commercial and general aviation customers. DynAir Technical Services has also provided the professional expertise of contract engineers, mechanics, and technicians.

Ogden Aviation Services, the world's largest independent provider of airport services, worked with more than 80 airports in the United States and abroad and with more than 180 commercial airlines. The company has provided fueling facilities, baggage loading and offloading, aircraft cleaning and maintenance, and passenger checking. A private subsidiary of the Ogden Corporation, Ogden Aviation Services is headquartered in New York. As of December 1998, Ogden had 21,970 employees and reported 1998 net income of $87 million on sales of $1.69 billion.

Dobbs International has been one of the world's largest airline caterers, providing in-flight food service for domestic and international airlines at 52 kitchens in 44 airports in the United States and Great Britain. Dobbs International has served 11 major U.S. airlines, 19 national carriers, and 36 international carriers. The company employed 180 workers in the mid-1990s, and the corporate office is located in Memphis, Tennessee.

The Dial Corp. terminal service subsidiary, Aircraft Service International, Inc., is a key player in this industry. Since 1958, the company has provided aircraft ground handling services such as fueling, aircraft cleaning, and baggage handling for all major domestic airlines and for 27 foreign airlines at 26 airports throughout the United States and in the Bahamas and London. The company employed 2,300 people in the 1990s, and corporate headquarters were located in Miami, Florida. The company reported 1998 earnings of $737 million on revenues of $1.52 billion.

One of the premier suppliers of aircraft maintenance, repair, and overhaul services has been Tramco Inc., a subsidiary of BF Goodrich Aerospace. With the completion of its 625,000 square-foot hanger, Tramco Inc. increased its facility to more than one million square feet, allowing the company to overhaul four wide-body aircraft at one time. Tramco Inc. has performed maintenance for the fleets of Federal Express, Southwest Airlines, and United Parcel Service (UPS). Tramco Inc. employed approximately 2,000 workers in the 1990s. Company headquarters are located in Everett, Washington.

UNC, Inc., once a builder of nuclear reactors, has become a profitable supplier of equipment to the aviation industry. The company had 35 facilities in 17 states and employed 3,800 people in the mid-1990s. Approximately 80 percent of its 1992 revenue came from overhauling aircraft engines and accessories, providing pilot training services, refurbishing and overhauling helicopters, and providing trading, leasing, and other parts distribution services. The other 20 percent came from making aircraft parts and engines. UNC, Inc. is a private company with corporate headquarters in Annapolis, Maryland.

E-Systems Inc., a premiere defense electronics company, has worked repeatedly with the U.S. Department of Defense, maintaining and equipping RC-135 reconnaissance aircraft. Serv-Air, Inc., a wholly owned subsidiary of E-Systems, has been a leader in aircraft and logistics programs, operations and maintenance services, special operations support, and communications systems integration, test, and repair. Serv-Air was awarded a two-year, $25-million contract in June 1993 to perform aircraft and flight simulator maintenance and technical services at the NASA Ames Research Center in Mountain View, California. With general offices in Greenville, Texas, Serv-Air had nearly 3,000 employees.

Created in 1981 as a subsidiary of AMR Corporation, AMR Services Corporation has provided flight operations services, including passenger services, cargo handling and warehousing, cabin services and facility cleaning, fuel services, and aircraft handling services. The company also has operated flight service centers, marketed used aircraft, provided ground transportation services, and offered security services. By late 1988 AMR Services owned 10 FBO locations and offered its services to 55 airlines at 51 airports in the United States and Canada. AMR Services employed approximately 5,500 workers in the 1990s, and was headquartered at Dallas/Fort Worth International Airport.

Lockheed Space Operations, a private subsidiary of the Lockheed Corporation, has provided launch pad preparation, operation and maintenance of facilities, flight hardware processing, and flight technology services. With headquarters in Titusville, Florida, the Space Operations division employed approximately 6,500 workers in the 1990s.

WORKFORCE

According to the North American Airports Council International, U.S. airports provide nearly 8 million jobs and $575 billion of economic impact to the communities they serve. Most of the employment in the airport, flying field, and airport terminal services industry has been concentrated in the maintenance, repair, and aircraft service segment. Additional employment in this industry can be found in companies that are not considered primary providers, but have been secondary providers of services categorized in this industry. These companies generally have included the food, beverage, and other airport terminal services companies.

Some companies, such as Commodore Aviation, have a large part-time contingency employment base, which has offered flexibility in an industry that has been highly seasonal. For example, Commodore Aviation has full-time employment of about 150 people, but has operated with a total of 180 to 500 employees, based on workload needs.

According to the U.S. Department of Labor, jobs in the air transportation industry have been projected to increase 37 percent over the period from 1990 to 2005—much faster than the overall average. An increase in passenger and air cargo traffic—and related employment—has been anticipated in response to increases in population, income, and business activity. New technology was not expected to have any significant effect on air transportation in the long-term future, as most labor saving technology has already been introduced.

It was estimated that 1 in every 15 people employed in the United States owed his or her job to civil aviation, and jobs directly attributable to U.S. airports were estimated at 2.3 million, with total jobs attributable to U.S. airports estimated at 7.6 million. Job opportunities in this industry varied by occupation. Sources estimated that for every $1 billion invested in airport development, 50,000 jobs were created and sustained. Due to an expected shortage in qualified applicants, the job market for aircraft mechanics has been expected to be very favorable in the long-term future. Job opportunities have also been predicted to be good in entry-level positions where job turnover has been high, such as baggage handlers, aircraft and interior cleaners, and food service workers.

FURTHER READING

"Airlines Begin Service Plans." *Travel Weekly,* 20 December 1999, 2.

"Airports: The Facts." North American Airports Council International. May 1997. Available from http://www.aci-na.org/facts.html.

"Air Transport Industry." *Valueline,* 21 March 1997.

Belden, Tom. "One Year After Detroit Debacle, Customers Filing More Complaints About Airlines." *The Philadelphia Inquirer,* December 1999.

Hoover's Online. 1999. Available at http://www.hoovers.com. for financial information on The Dial Corporation, DynCop, and Ogden Aviation.

Kaye, Ken. "ValuJet Crash Spurred Tightening of Aviation Safety Rules." *Sun-Sentinel, Florida,* 6 December 1999.

"North America Report." *Air Transport World,* December 1999, 15.

"Top 30 ACI Airports by Passenger Traffic." North American Airports Council International. May 1997. Available from http:/ /www.aci-na.org/facts.html.

U.S. Department of Labor. *Career Guide to Industries.* Washington, D.C.: GPO.

Ward's Business Directory of U.S. Private and Public Companies, 2000. Detroit: Gale Group, 1999.

SIC 4612

PIPELINES, CRUDE PETROLEUM

This category covers establishments primarily engaged in the pipeline transportation of crude petroleum. Field gathering lines are classified in oil and gas extraction industry sections. This major group includes establishments primarily engaged in the pipeline transportation of petroleum and other commodities, except natural gas. Pipelines operated by petroleum producing or refining companies and separately reported are included. Establishments primarily engaged in natural gas transmission are classified under **SIC 4922: Natural Gas Transmission.**

NAICS CODE(S)

486110 (Pipeline Transportation of Crude Oil)

INDUSTRY SNAPSHOT

According to U.S. Department of Transportation statistics, in 1997 there were 114,000 miles of pipelines transporting crude oil throughout the country. Notwithstanding the dependence of the world's economy on crude oil as a fundamental source of energy, the crude petroleum pipelines industry has experienced stagnant growth, stemming from profound structural changes in both the global market for crude oil and the world economic order. Changes in factors affecting the consumption and production of crude oil impact crude petroleum pipeline establishments since the demand for pipelines to transport crude oil is a derived demand. The change in the global supply of oil from a shortage situation in the early 1970s to a surplus situation in the latter 1990s characterizes the general economic environment that crude petroleum pipeline establishments face. In addition to the uncertain economic climate, the crude petroleum pipeline industry is confronted by several challenges at the start of the twenty-first century. These challenges include increasingly stricter environmental protection regulations, the development of natural gas as a substitute for crude oil-based energy products, and the depletion of crude oil reserves. Because companies have explored and produced more crude petroleum, they have also increased capital spending on pipelines. Company profits have also increased—spurred on by lower operating costs and moderate expanses in deliveries.

ORGANIZATION AND STRUCTURE

The crude petroleum pipeline industry consists of companies that are capital-intensive. As start-up costs for capital intensive organizations are high, entry into the industry is restrictive, as is indicated by the relatively small number of firms operating with headquarters in the United States. On the other hand, the day-to-day maintenance of capital intensive industries tends to be relatively moderate, enabling successful companies within the industry to take advantage of economies of scale.

The overwhelming majority of crude petroleum pipeline companies with corporate offices in the United States operated as subsidiaries of other corporate entities. Of the companies headquartered in the United States, only a few were independently listed on any stock exchange. Many of the subsidiary companies were affiliated with the major oil company giants. Examples include Exxon Pipeline Company, Mobil Pipeline Company, and Chevron Pipe Line Company. The maintenance of a vertically integrated relationship between the oil industry and the crude petroleum pipeline industry indicates a desire on the part of the giant oil companies to control the entire process of production and the natural economies that emerge from capital-intensive industries.

In addition, the Federal Energy Regulatory Commission (FERC) oversees the liquids pipeline industries, legislating and monitoring them. The FERC does not regulate the construction of pipelines and crude petroleum prices; rather it strives to make pipeline transportation an equitable means of shipping petroleum products. Through the FERC, shippers can gain fair access to pipeline transportation, just service conditions on a pipeline, and reasonable rates for transporting petroleum products via pipelines.

BACKGROUND AND DEVELOPMENT

The concept of using pipelines to transport liquids can be traced to both the ancient Romans and Chinese, who developed systems of pipelines and viaducts, utilizing gravity as the mechanism for transporting water. Such early pipeline transportation systems were limited by the terrain of the surrounding countryside due to the lack of an effective lift mechanism.

The discovery and subsequent drilling of crude oil in Pennsylvania by Col. E. L. Drake in 1859 created the need for a cost-effective method to transport the crude to market. Drake laid a two-inch, cast-iron pipeline, roughly 6.2 miles long, and the crude petroleum pipeline industry was born. However, the operation of the pipeline was short-lived. A group of local teamsters, fearing the elimination of their jobs, destroyed the pipeline soon after its operation began. Even so, pipeline transportation of crude petroleum proved to be both viable and cost-effective, and the industry grew concurrent with the nation's expanding oil industry.

Until World War I, crude pipelines were made almost exclusively from wrought or cast iron. After the war, improvements in steel quality led to its utilization as the primary material used in the construction of pipeline. Pipe diameter could be increased from 8 to 26 inches using steel. Also, the introduction of electric arc welding in the 1930s eliminated the ''weak link'' of screwed couplings.

During the 1930s and through World War II, significant developments took place in the crude oil pipeline industry. The utilization of the ''spread'' method of pipeline construction lowered construction costs and made the use of pipelines as a method of transporting crude oil more competitive. Furthermore, the size of pipeline projects grew, both in the United States and internationally. In 1934, a 12-inch pipeline over 620 miles long in length was constructed from Kirkuk, Iraq, to the Mediterranean Sea. During World War II, a 24-inch crude petroleum pipeline 1,240 miles long was laid from Texas to New York. Advances in both the materials used in the construction of pipeline and in the construction techniques allowed for the development of pipeline that could withstand greater pressure per square inch and that could transport more crude in less time.

The post-World War II era witnessed the peak of crude petroleum pipeline construction. Driven by a demand for oil that doubled roughly every ten years, ''Big-Inch'' pipelining became prevalent on a worldwide scale. Pipe size increased from 24 inches to 56 inches in diameter, expanding the capacity to transport crude oil. A better understanding of corrosion led to the development of pipe coatings of bitumen or coal tar enamel over glass-fiber wrappings. With the development of X-ray scanning technology, pipeline could be examined for weaknesses that would have gone undetected in the past. During the 1960s, construction of crude petroleum pipelines moved offshore with discoveries of oil in the Gulf of Mexico, the Arabian Gulf, and the North Sea.

From 1970 through the 1990s, the crude petroleum pipeline industry experienced a period of stagnant growth, both domestically and internationally. While interstate liquid pipeline mileage totaled 173,532 miles in 1972, the total mileage had dropped to 168,364 by 1990. New construction of domestic crude oil pipelines dropped from 1,966 miles in 1980 to 240 miles in 1990. In the United States, retirement of old pipeline had outpaced the construction of new pipeline, and this trend was also evident on a worldwide scale. World totals of new construction in 1980 equaled 8,129 miles. New constructions totaled 652 miles in 1990.

This trend of stagnant growth in the crude petroleum pipeline industry has been attributed to several events. Low oil prices, caused by a surplus or glut in the market for crude oil, had a significant influence on the market for crude oil pipelines. Also, stagnation in the domestic and world economies caused uncertainty and increased risk, especially for industries in which the time between project development and project completion is measured over a period of years. Furthermore, political instability led to a period of restructuring, as markets adjusted to such events as the end of the Cold War, the aftermath of the Gulf War, and the amalgamation of European countries in the European Community. Finally, preservation of the environment has become a global concern, and the world's industrialized nations have adopted a more active role in regulating the environmental impact of most industrial activities.

The primary players in the crude petroleum pipeline industry continue to be the giant, multinational or state-owned oil companies. Given the commitment of the multinational companies to maintaining control over the entire process of production, capital maintenance and development of crude pipeline are likely to continue at a pace calculated to maximize return on investment. Similarly, state-owned oil companies possess the capability to take advantage of large-scale operations and are able to utilize their unique position to expand operations. Furthermore, multinational and state-owned oil entities are able to absorb short-term market irregularities and to capitalize on their tremendous market power. Of the crude petroleum pipeline companies operating with corporate headquarters in the United States, about 80 percent operated as subsidiaries of other corporate entities. The majority of these were in some manner affiliated with the large oil companies.

With the impact of industry on the environment becoming a global issue, both domestic and international organizations have become politically active in attempting to protect the environment from the excesses of industrialization. In the United States the Environmental Protection Agency (EPA) has been given broad powers to oversee and regulate industrial activities in order to control environmental pollution. Legislation affecting the crude petroleum pipeline industry includes the Oil Pollution Liability Act of 1990. The crude petroleum pipeline industry may continue to feel the effects of this trend toward increased regulation in the form of increased risk of litigation and higher operation costs.

Projections for domestic and world crude oil consumption reflect modest increases of 5 to 10 percent. Though the industry has shown signs of recovery, given the maturity of the crude petroleum pipeline industry and the relative longevity of pipeline once constructed, increases in sales revenue, profits, and new construction may become stagnant again after a few years. Consequently, intriguing new uses for old pipeline systems are being explored, including the use of existing pipeline to encase fiber-optic lines used in the telecommunications industry. Williams Telecommunication, the sister company of Williams Pipe Line Company of Tulsa, Oklahoma, is regarded as an innovator in this field. As new technologies are developed, the crude petroleum pipeline industry has the opportunity to respond in unique and innovative ways.

CURRENT CONDITIONS

In 1998, crude oil prices dropped to the lowest they had been since 1973. However, in the latter months of 1999, OPEC gained control of its production quotas again, and prices increased more than $10 per barrel. The volatile market again caused global uneasiness and heightened interest in alternative markets and sources.

To that end, of key import was the November 1999 agreement between Turkey, Georgia, and Azerbaijan to build a 1,080-mile pipeline from the Caspian Sea to the Mediterranean. Several multinational corporations and U.S. companies, including the new BP-Amoco, Exxon, Chevron, and Texaco, contributed $50 billion to the project. The new pipeline would bypass Iran and Russia, and secure U.S. access to the Caspian basin. It would also have the secondary effect of enhancing the presence of American political and commercial interests in Central Asia. The Caspian basin deposits were believed to be second in size only to the Persian Gulf, but more recent seismic results indicate that they are substantially smaller, about the size of those in the North Sea.

On the domestic scene, Pacific & Texas Pipeline and Transport Company entered into a joint venture agreement in November 1999 to build and operate a 1,075-mile, 42-inch crude oil pipeline and fiber-optic system which would run from the Port of Los Angeles to Midland, Texas. (The fiber-optic system will be entrenched alongside the pipeline, thus contributing to cost-sharing and environmental conservation. The other party to the joint venture is Pan Kai Development USA, Inc. Bethlehem Steel, Ingersoll Rand, and Westinghouse are involved in the actual construction of the pipeline.

INDUSTRY LEADERS

According to the *Pipeline & Gas Journal*'s 1999 Annual 500 Report, the top 5 liquid pipeline companies (ranked by 1998 crude oil deliveries) were: Equilon Pipeline Company LLC, (1.023 billion barrels); Lakehead Pipe Line Company (570 million barrels); Alyeska Pipeline Service Company (440.5 million barrels); LOOP Inc. (335 million barrels); and Marathon Ashland Pipe Line LLC (331.5 million barrels). Exxon and Chevron ranked sixth and seventh, respectively, with Mobil Pipe Line Company ranking tenth (258.8 million barrels).

With respect to ranking by *miles of pipelines,* the 1999 Annual Report ranked the top 5 companies as: Equilon (10,090 miles); Williams Pipe Line (7,070 miles); Marathon Ashland (6,273 miles); Mobil Pipe Line (6,169 miles); and Exxon Pipeline (5,609 miles).

WORKFORCE

Throughout the 1990s, control of the domestic pipeline industry was in the hands of between 25 and 40 companies, employing approximately 15,000 persons. The relatively small number of persons employed in the industry reflects the capital-intensive nature of crude petroleum pipeline companies, where the emphasis is on capital rather than labor. Employment trends in industries wherein establishments are primarily engaged in the pipeline transportation of petroleum and other commodities (except natural gas), of which the crude petroleum pipeline industry constitutes the major segment, reflect a trend toward downsizing in regard to the labor force.

RESEARCH AND TECHNOLOGY

The basis for technological advances in the crude petroleum pipeline industry centers on the search for improved materials, the development of improved methods of welding or ''jointing'' the pipe, the refinement of specialty pipe for use under extreme environmental conditions, and the investigation of new applications and alternative uses for the pipeline.

Refined steel pipe remains the industry mainstay, allowing for pipe sizes up to 56 inches in diameter. The utilization of new industrial processes permitting refinement of the alloying process remains the most promising area of technological advance in this area. The fatigue life of "Big-Inch" pipe is also affected by conventional arc welding and jointing techniques. Arc welding makes steel pipe susceptible to hairline cracks and hardening in the areas of the pipe close to the welds. Alternative methods indicating the most promise include flash butt welding, friction welding, electron beam welding, screwed and bonded coupling, and cold forging.

The materials used to construct the pipe and the jointing technique used to bond pipe together will be determined in large part by the environmental conditions at the site of the pipeline. Thus, innovation in creating pipe resilient to temperature extremes and able to withstand the pressures of off-shore and underwater operations will continue to drive research and development.

Alternative applications of crude petroleum pipelines include using the lines to transport other materials as well as use of retired pipeline to encapsule fiber-optic communication lines. Coal slurry is regarded as a primary alternative for transport using the lines, as both domestic and international analysts maintain that coal reserves may constitute as much as four times the amount of oil available. Research continues on finding ways to modify existing pipeline for such use, and such innovations may provide extensive changes in the crude petroleum pipeline industry.

FURTHER READING

Hundley, Tom. "New Caspian Pipeline Will Keep Oil Flowing in Friendly Territory." *Chicago Tribune,* 24 November 1999.

"Newsline." *Underground Construction,* November 1999, 5.

Piller, Dan. "Crude Oil, Natural Gas Prices Switch Directions Over Past Six Months." *Fort Worth Star-Telegram,* 30 November 1999.

Standard & Poor's Industry Surveys. New York: Standard & Poor's Corporation, 1996.

True, Warren. "U.S. Pipelines Continue Gains into 1996." *Oil and Gas Journal,* 25 November 1996, 39.

Tubb, Jeff, et al. "P&GJ's 19th Annual 500 Report." *Pipeline and Gas Journal,* November 1999, 42.

U.S. Department of Energy. "The U.S. Petroleum and Natural Gas Industry," 20 March 2000. Available from http://www.eia.doe.gov/emeu/finance/.

U.S. Department of Transportation. *Transportation Statistics Annual Report 1999.* Washington, D.C.: 1999.

Ward's Business Directory of Private and Public Companies 2000. Detroit: Gale Research Group, 1999.

SIC 4613

PETROLEUM PIPELINES, REFINED

This category covers establishments primarily engaged in the pipeline transportation of refined petroleum products of petroleum, such as gasoline and fuel oil. Linking all petroleum pipeline industries together is Industry Group 461: Pipelines, Except Natural Gas, which includes the other major subcategories of the petroleum pipeline industry, **SIC 4612: Crude Petroleum Pipelines** and **SIC 4619: Pipelines, Not Elsewhere Classified.**

NAICS CODE(S)

486910 (Pipeline Transportation of Refined Petroleum Products)

INDUSTRY SNAPSHOT

Pipelines are the leading method of transporting refined petroleum, and they are an especially important mode of transportation in the United States where large volumes of oil must be moved over land. Manufacture of refined petroleum is classified in **SIC 2911: Petroleum Refining;** fuels classified as refined petroleum products include gasoline, kerosene, distillate fuel oils, residual fuel oils, and lubricants—essentially any product made from the distillation of crude oil or redistillation of unfinished petroleum derivative.

The United States has an extensive network of pipelines for the transport of refined petroleum owned and managed, for the most part, by the large, vertically integrated operations of the major oil companies. In total, firms in the industry operated a network moving petroleum products through 86,500 miles of pipeline as of 1997, or approximately 46 percent of the total petroleum pipelines (crude and refined). Though pipeline grew at a crawling pace from the mid-1980s through the mid-1990s, the late 1990s ushered in a more successful period for the industry, and demand for refined petroleum products was predicted to increase modestly in the United States and abroad.

In 1997, there were approximately 200,000 total miles of liquid pipeline in the United States (crude and refined). The pipeline network contains gathering systems of pipelines, which are used to bring crude petroleum from the oil fields and pump it to storage. Then, oil fields have a network of small-diameter "gathering lines" collecting crude oil from individual wells and transporting the output to a large-diameter "trunk line" for shipment to a refinery. Next, pipelines move refined products to markets.

The ups and downs of the industry have been attributed to several economic forces. The growth of pipelines in general is linked, and ultimately limited by, oil production. Thus, industries like petroleum pipelines in general, and refined products pipelines in particular, are subject to competition from other transport industries such as water carriers, motor carriers, and railroads. As a method of transportation, pipelines transport about 50 percent of refined petroleum, compared to water carriers, which transport about 40 percent. Railroads and trucks transported the remaining percentage of total petroleum (total crude and refined products).

On the negative side, however, three major spills in the 1990s put a dent in the pipeline industry's relatively clean safety and environmental track record. More stringent environmental regulations are being put in place as the twenty-first century approaches and, as might be expected, the larger, vertically integrated producers are in the best position to manage the transition.

Organization and Structure

Between 40 and 50 companies were estimated to be in some way involved in the operation of refined petroleum pipelines in 1998, with 32 officially reporting to the Department of Energy. Market concentration was also relatively high in the refined petroleum pipeline industry, which has been under allegations of antitrust violations. Because of the heavy involvement of the large oil interests, it is difficult to differentiate the pipeline components of their operations from the other components. Nonetheless, of those firms whose principal business was identified to be refined petroleum pipelines, the top 6 firms controlled only 11 percent of the market.

The petroleum industry consists of four distinct, but connected, vertical levels as outlined by author and analyst Stephen Martin. These are: production, refining, marketing, and transportation. The refined products segment manufactures finished products ranging from petroleum coke to motor gasoline to fuel oil, heating oil, and jet fuel. Connecting the mines to the refinery and the refinery to the market are specialized transportation networks including pipelines, trucks, railroads, and, most notably, water carriers (tankers and barges).

Pipelines have historically been the most cost-effective means of transportation of petroleum products. Having the advantage of economies of scale, pipelines have construction costs that are proportional to pipeline radius, but pipeline capacity is roughly proportional to the square of the radius. Thus, for example, if pipeline radius is doubled, pipeline capacity will increase by a factor of about four.

While the share of railroads and truck methods has remained virtually unchanged, pipeline's share rose to around 60 percent in the mid-1970s (through 1977) then declined to 45.5 percent in 1983 but bounced back to a 54 percent share in the 1990s. Water carriers surpassed pipelines for a short period in the early 1980s but have largely played second fiddle to pipeline market share; water carriers' share of the market declined from 50 percent in 1985 to about 40 percent in 1995. Aside from their economies of scale, pipelines are viewed (with the exception of recent history when two accidents have marred their record) as a safer and more environmentally sound method of transporting petroleum. Historically, spills from pipelines have been dwarfed by tanker spills.

Pipeline operations are large, capital-intensive facilities, and are often part of larger companies operating pipelines for their own use. By law, however, no company can deny access to independent shippers in order to gain market share. Throughout the twentieth century, however, oil companies have been accused of using exclusive control over pipelines to gain expanded control of markets. Because pipelines are such a critical link in the petroleum production process, much regulation exists at the federal level, primarily from the Interstate Commerce Commission (ICC), in order to ensure access of all producers to pipelines and to set rates. In addition to monitoring competitive practices, the ICC sets rates and collects reports that are required to be filed by the companies.

Background and Development

According to analyst Stephen Martin, the first attempt to transport petroleum by pipe was made by James Hutchings in 1862. Although he failed, his efforts drew attention to other possible means of transporting oil, specifically: to the low cost of pipelines; and, to avoid the market power of the railroads. By the turn of the twentieth century there were 6,800 miles of crude oil pipeline in the United States. The market for pipelines at the time was dominated (90 percent) by the Standard Oil Company. By 1906, the Interstate Commerce Act made interstate pipelines subject to federal regulation, a move directed largely at abuses by Standard Oil.

Refined petroleum pipelines began being used in 1930, as firms discovered that many different products could be shipped through the same pipeline. The emerging cities in the Midwest and West, moreover, created new markets for refined petroleum, and pipelines won out as the least expensive method of transporting the growing number of refined petroleum products. More than 3,800 miles of refined petroleum pipelines were placed in operation from 1930 to 1931 and another 2,300 miles through 1941.

During World War II much transportation of the oil products was diverted from tankers to pipelines. Tankers were needed for the war effort, and it was becoming increasingly difficult for the U.S. Navy to devote resources to protect ships transporting oil from the Gulf

Coast to the eastern seaboard. As an added boost to the industry, the federal government helped build the War Emergency Pipeline (WEP), which spanned 1,475 miles and was used for the transport of refined petroleum. The availability of water carriers after World War II is cited as the only impediment to the complete monopolization of the oil transport industry by the pipeline. Other modes of transportation—rail and trucking—held only small niches of the oil transportation market. Figures on intermodal competition showed that, by the early 1970s, pipeline costs were 1/5 as high as rail rates and 1/28 as high as truck rates. Water transport costs were the only serious competitive threat.

Despite the success of the pipeline industry, a major concern of federal regulators has been that the oil companies exert substantial market control over production and distribution. In 1976, 90 percent of crude pipeline shipments reported to the ICC originated in pipelines that were owned or controlled by the 16 major U.S. oil companies. Nearly 75 percent of refined petroleum shipped that came from refineries went into pipelines owned by the major companies. Only 13 percent of refined petroleum was moved by pipeline firms not involved in other segments of the oil industry.

The expansion of the refined petroleum pipeline industry and its profitability are ultimately limited by two key forces. The first is the force of competition, here in the form of other modes of transporting oil, most notably water carriers such as oil tankers. This includes cost competitiveness, environmental safety, and the industry's ability to absorb the costs of increased environmental regulations. The health of this industry is also limited ultimately by the production of the refined petroleum products that it transports.

In 1992, as part of the revised Clean Air Act, it was mandated that the nation's cities burn cleaner gasoline to cut carbon monoxide levels. The law led to greater reduction of carbon monoxide by 1995, and forced cities with severe air pollution to use even cleaner gasoline. However, the National Petroleum Refiners Association estimated that the Clean Air Act cost the industry between $10 to $30 million.

The law created problems for pipeline companies, who were now required to sell different gasolines in different cities at the same time. Gas sold in one city might have tighter restrictions than those of a gas sold in another city serviced by the same pipeline. This forced firms to separate different batches of gasoline along pipelines, which was more expensive for pipeline companies. Nonetheless, overall refinery throughputs have increased over the years, even if only marginally at times.

Despite the industry's renewed economic success, pipe fractures and spills have besmirched its reputation as the safest method of transport. A 1993 spill occurred in the Potomac River near Washington, D.C., and in 1994 a more virulent pipeline disaster dumped about 1.2 million gallons into the San Jacinto River, outside Houston, and caught on fire. In 1996, the U.S. Transportation Department's Office of Pipeline Safety issued a report that revealed the serious condition of the country's largest pipeline, which extends from Texas to New Jersey, owned by Colonial Pipeline Co. The report indicated that the pipeline contained frail, corroded, and cracked portions as well as profound pressure control problems. The report also stated that without repair, operation of the pipeline could prove hazardous to the environment and to life, according to the *Wall Street Journal.* The pipeline, which delivered over 75 million gallons of fuel per day, ran only 20 feet away from homes and businesses in areas. A few months prior to the report, a pipe segment ruptured in Greenville, South Carolina, spewing about a million gallons of fuel into the Reedy River—the fifth largest pipeline spill in the United States. After mending this fracture, Colonial agreed to test and repair the whole pipeline. Colonial estimated that the repairs would run almost $21 million.

CURRENT CONDITIONS

The U.S. Department of Transportation reported in 1999 that there were 86,500 miles of products, or refined oil, pipeline in the country, as of 1997. When added to the 114,000 miles of crude oil pipeline, the total miles of pipeline were over 200,000, approximately 65 times the entire width of the country.

Two major refined pipeline projects in the latter 1990s were the cross-border pipeline connecting Brownsville, Texas, to Matamoros, Mexico, scheduled for completion near the end of 1999; and a joint pipeline project between Williams Company and Texaco Pipeline Inc., connecting Texas, Oklahoma, and some Kansas lines to provide a new route for Gulf Coast refined products and liquid petroleum gas. The Texas-Mexico pipeline was being constructed for the Penn Octane Corporation to sell directly to Pemex, the state-owned Mexican oil company, as well as independent distributors.

With respect to the refined products industry, several major changes occurred in 1998 and 1999. Mergers, consolidations, divestitures, and frank exits within the industry brought many smaller companies into the fold. By 1999, small refining companies constituted 36 percent of the total U.S. refining capacity. On the other end of the spectrum, one of the biggest mergers was the December 1998 $53 billion transaction joining BP America with Amoco (the new company known as BP-Amoco). Not far behind was the December 1999 merger of Mobil Corporation with Exxon Corporation, an $87 billion transaction considered the largest industrial merger ever. As a condition precedent to the final merger, Mobil agreed to sell off its 300 retail gas stations in New Jersey in order to satisfy the Federal Trade Commission's and 29 states' antitrust claims.

INDUSTRY LEADERS

According to *Pipeline & Gas Journal*'s 19th Annual 500 Report, in 1999, the leading company for throughputs was Equilon Pipeline Company LLC, the newly formed company resulting from the combined Shell Pipe Line Corp. and Texaco Pipeline Inc., with a daily throughput of 1.33 million barrels.

When ranked by products deliveries, the top 5 companies in 1999 were: Colonial Pipeline Co. (708 million barrels); SFPP Kinder Morgan, LP (382 million barrels); Buckeye Pipe Line Co., LP (313 million barrels); Equilon (301 million barrels); and Marathon Ashland Pipe Line LLC (289 million barrels).

With respect to revenues, the leading 5 companies for 1999 (reporting 1997 operating revenues) were: Exxon Pipeline ($588 million); Colonial Pipeline ($562 million); BP Pipelines (Alaska), Inc. ($550 million); Equilon ($378 million); and Lakehead Pipe Line Co., LP ($288 million).

RESEARCH AND TECHNOLOGY

The companies themselves have adopted new technology to enhance supervisory control and data acquisition (SCADA) systems, such as 32-bit computers and distributed processing to increase efficiency. Colonial Pipeline and Amoco Gas are two companies that are installing new SCADA and software systems. These new systems are projected to increase efficiency and ease of use in the management of data traffic. For example, using these systems, pipeline systems can easily be drawn and monitored or scanned with graphics software.

Finally, deterioration in pipeline safety has plagued certain companies in the industry. Despite the relatively good safety record of oil pipelines, the National Transportation Safety Board (NTSB) began studying pipeline safety in the wake of two spills of diesel fuel caused by the ruptures of Colonial Pipeline Company pipelines near Simpsonville, South Carolina, and Reston, Virginia, in 1991 and 1993, respectively. As a result, the NTSB is studying 400 pipelines to develop techniques for identifying damaged pipelines.

FURTHER READING

Binkley, Christina. ''U.S. Agency Says Pipeline is 'Hazardous'.'' *Wall Street Journal,* 25 September 1996, 1.

''Cross-Border Pipeline Nears Completion.'' *Pipeline & Gas Journal,* November 1999, 10.

Perone, Joseph R. ''Mobil Agrees to Sell New Jersey Gas Stations for Merger with Exxon.'' *The (Newark) Star-Ledger,* 1 December 1999.

Thompson, Jim. ''New Route for Gulf Coast Products.'' *Pipe Line & Gas Industry,* May 1998, 19.

Tubb, Jeff, et al. ''P &GJ's 19th Annual 500 Report.'' *Pipeline & Gas Journal,* November 1999, 42.

U.S. Department of Commerce. *Statistical Abstract of the United States.* Washington, D.C.: GPO, 1996.

U.S. Department of Energy. *The U.S. Petroleum and Gas Industry (Performance Profile: Executive Summary).* Available from http://www.eia.doe.gov/emeu/perfpro/execsum.html.

SIC 4619

PIPELINES, NOT ELSEWHERE CLASSIFIED

This category covers establishments primarily engaged in the pipeline transportation of commodities, except crude petroleum, refined products of petroleum, and natural gas. Establishments primarily engaged in the pipeline transportation of refined petroleum are classified in **SIC 4613: Crude Petroleum Pipelines,** and those engaged in natural gas transmission are classified in **SIC 4922: Natural Gas Transmission and Distribution.** Most notably, the industry includes coal slurry pipeline operations and metal ore concentrates.

NAICS CODE(S)

486990 (All Other Pipeline Transportation)

According to data collected by the U.S. Bureau of the Census in the 1990s, approximately 59 establishments were primarily engaged in the operation of pipelines for the transportation of coal slurry, metal ore slurry, phosphate slurry, etc., and other types of pipelines, not elsewhere classified. These establishments employed more than 640,000 workers for a total industry payroll of about $40 million. This industry's employment comprised only a scant 8 percent of the total employment for the broader pipeline industry, which is mainly comprised of petroleum and natural gas pipelines.

Firms in the industry are typically either small companies focused exclusively on pipeline transportation or larger firms primarily involved in other lines of business. Industry participants include Black Mesa Holdings of Tulsa, Oklahoma; Sabine Pipe Line Company of Houston, Texas; American Pipeline Company of Houston, Texas; Arco Pipe Line Co., an Atlantic Richfield Company subsidiary; Enron Liquids Pipeline L.P. of Houston, Texas, and the J.R. Simplot Company.

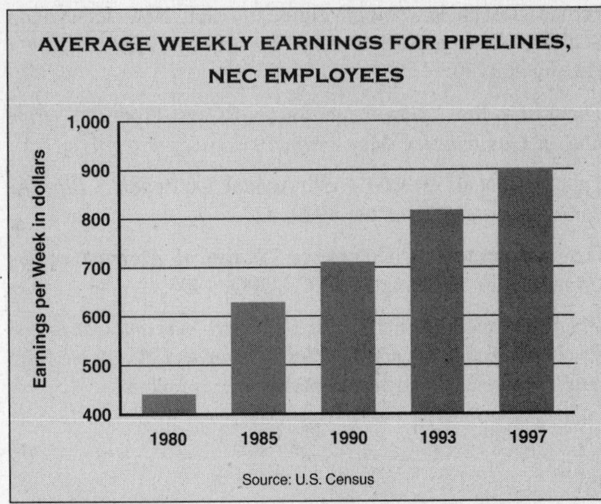

Most of the U.S. pipelines operated by this industry transport coal suspended in water (crushed/mashed coal mixed with water to create slurry). The United States operates an extensive slurry pipeline system, and pipelines are operated throughout the world, transporting not only coal but other metal ore concentrates. Coal, however, was the first slurry system to be developed, and in 1995 total U.S. coal-slurry output totaled 100 million short tons, including transport by tramway and conveyor. The key developmental factor in coal-slurry technology was its cost competitiveness when compared to other methods of transporting coal. The expense associated with building roads and railroads to the mouth of the mines was prohibitive, and the slurry alternative required a much smaller capital investment. As such, the Black Mesa Company began operating a coal slurry line in 1970 that transported coal 273 miles from a mine in northeast Arizona to a power plant in southern Nevada. This became the prototype for most slurry pipelines, and, in the late 1990s, pipelines stretch as long as 1,500 miles.

The coal slurry technology involves transporting pulverized coal suspended in water and pumped through pipelines. From the mine, the coal is crushed, formed into slurry, suspended in water, and pumped through the pipe to the power plant. At the end of its journey, the slurry is placed in storage tanks, where various processes remove the water from it. The final result is coal that can be used for burning.

Modern slurry systems were initially developed after World War II and, although coal is the most common commodity transported via slurry, other concentrates—iron-ore concentrate, copper ore, phosphate-rock concentrate, limestone, and the mineral gilsonite—are transported as well. The South American Alumbrera pipeline, completed in early 1998, is the world's longest copper ore concentrate slurry pipeline, traversing 312 kilometers through the Andean desert, vast grazing lands, rain forests, and flat pampas in Tucumn.

In recent years, pipelines have been built for the transport of carbon dioxide, hydrogen, ethylene, and other liquids. In 1997, pipelines transported about $18 billion dollars worth of hazardous materials (excluding petroleum and its byproducts, kerosene, etc.) that consisted primarily of flammable liquids such as refrigerated liquid ethylene, butane, sodium hydroxide solutions, propylene, benzene, and butadiene.

FURTHER READING

''Controlling the Flow.'' *Mechanical Engineering,* December 1998, 74.

''The Slurry Pipeline & Filter Plant.'' *Engineering & Mining Journal,* May 1998, 52.

Stockfisch, Jerome. ''Florida Phosphate Mining Industry Faces Environmental, Foreign Challenges.''*Tampa Tribune,* August 16, 1999.

U.S. Bureau of the Census. *Census of Transportation, Communications, and Utilities.* Washington, DC: GPO, 1995.

U.S. Bureau of the Census. ''The Official Statistics.'' *Statistical Abstract of the United States: 1998.*Washington, DC: GPO, October 2, 1998.

SIC 4724

TRAVEL AGENCIES

This industry comprises establishments primarily engaged in furnishing travel information and arranging tours, transportation, rental cars, and lodging for travelers. Establishments primarily engaged in arranging and assembling tours directly to travelers or through travel agents are discussed in **SIC 4725: Tour Operators.**

NAICS CODE(S)

561510 (Travel Agencies)

INDUSTRY SNAPSHOT

As retail outlets for the travel and tourism industry, travel agencies have benefited from the explosive worldwide growth of this industry during the late twentieth century. While travel and tourism may not account for as high a percentage of the diversified U.S. economy as it does of other nation's economies, it is estimated that more than $400 billion is spent on travel and tourism annually in the United States, with almost 30 percent passing through more than 30,000 travel agency locations across the country.

According to the U.S. Census Bureau's *Statistical Abstract of the United States: 1999,* about one in four travelers now uses a travel agent to make business reservations; approximately one in nine (or 11 percent) uses a travel agent for pleasure/vacation trips. Travel agency sales, which recently increased to 40 percent utilization, are generally broken down by destination, purpose, and, most importantly, by ''product'' or supplier. In terms of travel destinations, the ratio of revenue from domestic travel to that of foreign travel has been fairly constant at 70 percent to 30 percent. The type and purpose of travel, on the other hand, has shown a marked change over the years and has altered the entire structure of the travel agency industry in the United States. Business travel, which expanded enormously through the 1980s, has narrowly surpassed personal and pleasure travel in total annual sales.

Ultimately, the two most significant factors affecting the future of the industry are mergers and acquisitions and Internet competition. Many travel agencies have risen above or met the competition by opening their own Web sites on the Internet for the convenience of travelers. Forrester Research Group estimated that $12 billion dollars was spent in 1999 for online travel bookings. This segment of the industry is expected to grow from 3 percent to 10 percent of the total travel business by 2003.

ORGANIZATION AND STRUCTURE

The travel agency industry is young, dynamic, and in a relatively constant state of transformation and growth. While no longer expanding at the explosive rate (almost 20 percent annually) of the early 1980s, the industry continues to grow—in terms of the number of locations]—by nearly 6 percent every year.

Regional Distribution. Travel agencies can be found in virtually every community in the United States. The greatest share of travel agency locations has been in the eastern United States (30 percent), with the western United States close behind (28 percent); the South has a 22 percent share; and the Midwest has 19 percent. Central city locations account for more than 50 percent of the total, and the uneven growth of the 1980s—with the suburbs and small towns gaining disproportionate numbers of locations—not only subsided, but reversed itself. The share of rural and town locations dropped quite significantly to 9 percent, from nearly 12 percent in the late 1980s. With the emergence of Satellite Ticket Printers (STPs), automated ticket distribution machines began to replace branch offices altogether, a trend which may well continue.

Consolidation. In examining location revenue trends in the travel agency marketplace, the pattern seems somewhat obscure. Not only is the proportion of larger agencies (those with more than $5 million in revenue) growing rapidly, but the proportion of smaller ones (grossing under $1 million) is increasing at an equally conspicuous rate. The percentage of the industry's large locations has risen steadily to 11 percent, and their share of total industry revenue has risen to more than 33 percent. At the same time, small locations make up almost 30 percent of the industry. While seemingly contradictory, these trends are, in fact, results of the same overall movement of the industry towards consolidation into a number of ''mega-agencies,'' or regional and national branch and franchise networks. Such firms have the resources to set up large offices in prime locations and to establish small branch agencies that are run in coordination with the main offices. Whether or not these smaller branches are profitable, they do augment name recognition, which is of utmost importance to any agency in this increasingly competitive market.

The steady expansion of the industry in the 1990s had a completely different character than the boom period advances of the 1980s. The segment of the industry that expanded most in the 1980s—comprising the majority of the independent, single-location agencies with between $1 million and $5 million in revenue—came under pressure. The majority of agency locations still fell into this category in the 1990s, but it was a dwindling majority. Especially significant was the decrease in agency locations at the lower end of this group—those grossing between $1 million and $2 million—which were not as eagerly pursued by the acquisition-minded mega-agencies as were those locations with greater revenues.

The high level of consolidation activity in the travel agency industry is best assessed through the steep upturn in acquisitions. Almost a third of all agencies have acquired another agency already, and there are no signs of the buying spree slackening. In 1991 American Express Company purchased Lifeco of Houston, a firm whose airline ticket sales exceeded $1 billion annually. This acquisition provided a new scale for the already highly charged marketplace environment. Many smaller agencies also felt they had much to gain in terms of access to the latest technological innovations and overall support than they had to lose in giving up their autonomy. For this reason, they pursued buyers. Typically, the cost of purchasing an agency location is set at between 3 percent and 7 percent of its latest annual sales.

Smaller Agencies. Despite the industry's consolidation, it remains first and foremost an industry of small businesses. Even in the face of intensifying competition, single-location firms still make up the vast majority of agencies, and in addition, they have successfully developed alternative business strategies to stay afloat. One common tactic is to seek out corporate clients—89 percent of all agencies handle at least one corporate account. While only large agencies can manage the travel accounts of most medium-sized and large corporations, these accounts make up about only 28 percent of all the corporations that use travel agencies. The rest (those with fewer than 100 employees) compose a huge market for the

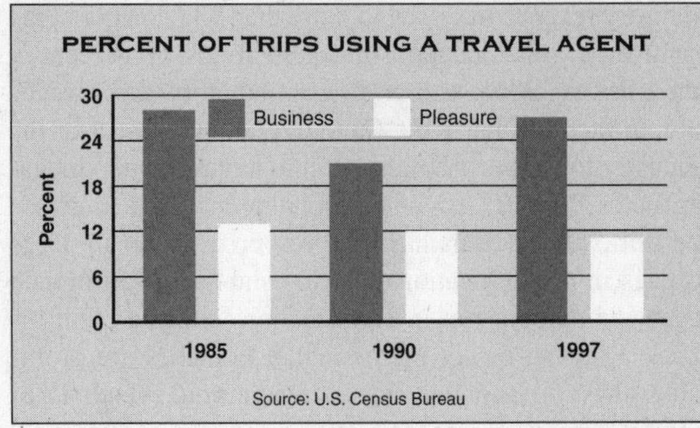

services of smaller agencies. The average number of corporate accounts an agency manages dropped to 38 from a high of 43 in 1989, proof that small agencies have made inroads into the realm of business travel. Quite simply, more agencies are attracting fewer business clients: certain companies may feel better served by an agency without too many other commitments. The particularized service that a small agency can provide has proven to be an effective selling point in building an agency's business travel base.

Promoting themselves in terms of the unique, personal service that they offer, small agencies have also secured a place in the leisure travel market, a market in which the travel agent is often solicited as an advisor to the traveler. Although not widespread, there has been some noteworthy fragmentation of the leisure market into agencies specializing in travel niches (e.g., student travel, or travel to a certain part of the world).

Consortiums. Membership in travel consortiums is seen as a way of benefiting from consolidation without ceding direct control of the business. Through consortium membership, an agency develops close working relationships with other member agencies. An increase in purchasing power results in significantly higher override commissions from preferred suppliers and in cheaper access to expensive services that foster office efficiency. These immediate paybacks, however, are not the only focus. Many agencies feel consortiums, through annual meetings and newsletters, ensure that they remain up to date on broad developments in the industry. Consortiums also give travel agents a unified voice that increases their ability to influence supplier developments that affect them. In the 1990s nearly half of all U.S. travel agencies became affiliated with a consortium of some sort, and there are few signs of this trend slowing, since business travel consortiums have begun to catch up to leisure travel consortiums in membership numbers.

Of course, consortiums are not only set up for small agencies, and the growing number of business travel associations are welcoming more and more mega-agencies. Access to consortium arrangements will ultimately serve to protect the travel agency industry from complete consolidation by ensuring that it retains some degree of its small-business character while still adjusting to the increasingly complex demands of the American traveler.

Trade Associations. In seeking greater efficiency and better returns in the 1990s, an industry proliferated with independent operators, consortiums, and mega-agencies still sought a kind of uniformity. Market-driven joint ventures were not, however, the only coordinating mechanisms that served to integrate the industry. For example, several large trade associations act to influence government policy decisions on behalf of the travel complex as a whole. These associations also provide educational services for their members and promote the benefits of using travel agents. The largest of these trade associations, the American Society of Travel Agents (ASTA), boasted 29,000 travel agents in 170 countries in 1999. Seventy to 75 percent of this nonprofit organization's funding comes from its member dues, the rest from an annual conference. The second largest trade association, the Association of Retail Travel Agents (ARTA), has a much smaller membership—3,000 travel agents—and a more specific agenda of promoting their interests. Other important travel agent associations include the Travel and Tourism Research Association and the Alliance of Independent Travel agents. Related associations include the American Bus Association, American Hotel & Motel Association, and Cruise Line International Association.

While providing services for travel agents, such associations also legitimize the trade itself. Because only Rhode Island requires its travel agents to be licensed, an ASTA or ARTA membership offers assurance to both suppliers and consumers that an agent has some qualification beyond the easily obtainable agency accreditation, which is granted by the Airlines Reporting Corp. (ARC). In what has become a very technical field, there has been an increasing need for further standards of expertise, and educational bodies such as the Institute of Certified Travel Agents (ICTA) have begun to serve a crucial role. The ICTA, a 16,000-member association that seeks to improve the level of competence within the industry, offers a course through which agents can become Certified Travel Counselors (CTC), a title which already carries significant weight within the industry. Another certification which has come into demand with the growth of corporate travel is that of Certified Meeting Professional (CMP), which allows an individual to oversee every aspect of a business meeting.

Nine states currently require some regulation, certification or registration of retail sellers of travel services: California, Hawaii, Illinois, Ohio, Rhode Island, Washington, Iowa, Florida, and Oregon.

Suppliers. Travel agencies rely entirely on commissions from their suppliers. Commissions, as a rule, are set at 10 percent of a booking, but slightly different arrangements can be made with each supplier. Travel agents may contact several suppliers to set up an appointment with each or use one of two coordinating bodies accepted by various suppliers as a kind of clearinghouse establishing the validity of agents. ARC agents are allowed to use standard ticket stock for more than 100 domestic and international carriers. ARC also provides weekly reconciliation of sales, refunds, exchanges and commission payments to travel agents via a third party. While ARC appointment is not required of agents, it would be difficult to provide full services without it. A minimum of $20,000 is required to be appointed or retained by ARC. This acts as both a financial screen and a protection against default.

Airlines are the only suppliers who give significant commission overrides (marginally higher commissions) to agencies with which they have a preferred supplier relationship, whether negotiated through a consortium or through the agency itself. These overrides appear to be relatively effective in influencing agents' booking habits. More than two-thirds of all agencies book particular carriers in order to receive overrides, and these locations obtain overrides on about a third of all the air tickets they book. It is more common for overrides to be passed on to a business client than to a leisure client, mainly because the market for corporate accounts is highly competitive and, because of the higher prices a corporate traveler generally pays for last-minute scheduling, the commission will already be substantial. The use of overrides for leisure travel is on the rise, however, as it becomes an increasingly competitive sector.

The industry's dependence on air travel resulted in a marked consistency of products offered by travel agencies. Airline tickets make up nearly 60 percent of a travel agency's business on average, more than all other ''travel products'' combined. This attachment to the airline industry poses problems for some travel agencies, and so has prompted an effort within the industry to decrease dependence on airline ticket sales. With air travel continuing to increase, however, this dependency may be unavoidable. The remainder of a travel agency's business comes from cruise bookings (which make up 16 percent of total industry sales), hotel bookings (12 percent), car rentals (8 percent), and rail travel and other bookings (4 percent).

Tour and vacation packages, organized through tour operators with minimum arrangements, have increased in popularity. Packages allow for better control of costs in advance, and assure the customer that they will be taken care of in case of an emergency. For agents, they are easily put together and provide higher, more dependable commissions. Specialized tours (often called Foreign Individual Tours or FITs) are becoming confined to the luxury market, a welcome trend for agents because FITs are often time-consuming to organize.

Car rental companies use a variety of strategies to lure travel agency business, including commission incentives, free client upgrades, low familiarization trip rates, and frequent contests. Regardless of what kind of inducement is offered, however, car rental bookings are still generally viewed by agents as an added service for their clients. More often than not, an agent will make car reservations based on the efficiency and dependability of the car rental company's system rather than on what rewards are being offered. Payment of commissions has become less of a problem as car rental companies have begun to centralize their payment systems and have designated full-time agent assistants to deal with travel agent inquiries or commission payment concerns. In 1997 a New York State Court of Appeals ruled that rental companies cannot refuse to rent automobiles to drivers on the basis of age. Drivers under 25 or 21 were routinely denied rental because of higher accident rates. Since other states are considering similar legislation, this could, according to a Hertz Corporation spokesman quoted in *ASTA Travel Industry Headlines,* give car rentals ''virtually unlimited exposure'' to insurance liabilities.

As more hotels acknowledge their dependence on travel agents for reservation bookings, the relationship between the two industries is greatly improving. Evidence of this is seen in the effort by many hotels to simplify and speed up the payment of travel agency commissions. In the past, commission payments could take anywhere from a few days to a couple of months and come with confusing statements from branch hotels. Now, a large hotel company, with a centralized commission payment system, issues payments and statements regularly from one office that deals with individual branch problems internally. Such centralization safeguards travel agents from having to spend valuable time chasing down commissions and makes agents far more comfortable in booking hotel reservations.

STPs and On-Site Agents. In order to meet corporate demand for efficiency and specialized service, two strategies were adopted to better manage the travel accounts of large companies. Some agencies are offering to install satellite ticket printers in corporate offices so that a ticket and/or boarding pass can be distributed directly and immediately to the client. Some 13 percent of all agencies use such delivery systems, with the average number for an agency location being three. A smaller but growing number of agencies have gone so far as to set up on-site departments for their major clients (those who contribute more than $41 million in sales, for instance). Such departments, which are run and paid for by the agency but work

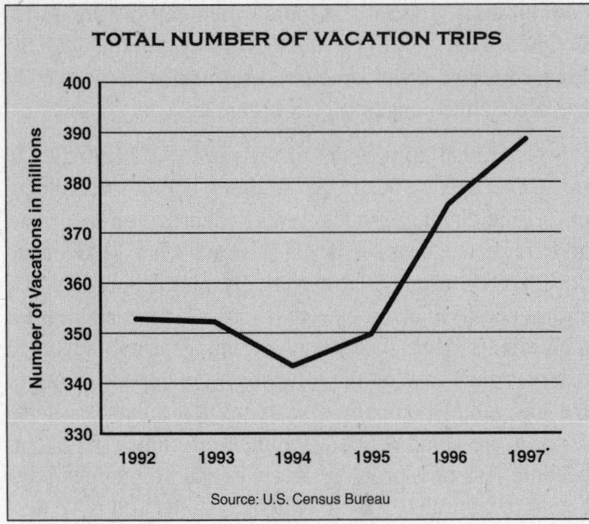

in client-supplied office space, give the company more direct control over its travel arrangements and thus create savings and enforce travel policy. On-site agents also work in conjunction with in-house travel departments to set budgets, negotiate with vendors, and create travel expense reports.

Background and Development

The Early Years. Because travel agency surveys have only been taken since the early 1970s, it is difficult to speak with much certainty about the state of the industry prior to this time, except to note that it bore little resemblance to the industry of the 1990s. ASTA was founded in 1931 as a society for steamship agents, at a time when steamships and trains were the predominant means of travel. A small group of agents booked tour packages and cruises in these early days. Later, with the spread of air travel, particularly with the introduction of larger passenger jets in the 1960s, travel agencies became much more prominent. Despite their prominence, travel agencies still remained a select group. For a long period of time, an agent actually had to be appointed by an airline commission in order to book airline tickets. In many ways this obstacle spurred the industry's expansion into car rentals and hotel bookings. For many years, however, travel agencies remained essentially unsustainable without inside connections to the airline industry.

The Deregulation Watershed. In 1978 the Carter administration's airline deregulation legislation, designed by Alfred E. Kahn, chairman of the Civil Aviation Board, transformed the industry completely. In just three years the number of agency locations rose by 30 percent, from 14,804 in 1978 to 19,203 in 1981, and the average revenue per agency was up 23 percent, from $1.3 million to $1.6 million. Such broad-based, steep increases were, and remain, unparalleled and clearly point to deregulation as a watershed in the history of the travel agency industry. By eliminating fixed pricing and opening up air travel to competition, deregulation allowed more people to travel more cheaply. The benefits of travel agency services also suddenly became much clearer. With a floating market, and new airlines either popping up or going under with shocking speed, travel agencies were in a better position than anyone else to find the best ticket at the best price. Companies suddenly forced to trim budgets also came to be recognize travel agencies as the most cost-effective mode of ticket distribution.

Since the early post-deregulation years, travel agents' enthusiasm for airline competition has cooled somewhat. In particular, the frequent price wars create havoc for travel agencies. When special fare offers are made, for instance, not only are agents unprepared, but their reservation systems are rarely loaded with new fares fast enough to avoid problems. Despite the fact that agencies continue to handle nearly 80 percent of airline ticket sales, no true partnership has evolved between the two industries. As a percentage of all travel agency revenue, revenue generated by the airlines has, in fact, fallen moderately from 63 percent in the early 1980s to around 56 percent. Both sides have tried to reduce their co-dependence; the airlines have developed frequent flier programs as alternatives to preferred supplier relationships, and travel agencies have built closer ties to other suppliers.

A number of travel agents and tour operators were upset when the U.S. Travel and Tourism Agency was eliminated in 1996 along with its $16.3 million budget. This made the United States the only major country without a national tourist agency. Private industry stepped in, and the new United States National Tourism Organization Act was passed by the United States Senate in September 1996. It is estimated to have an $80 million budget to promote the United States to foreign tourists. Patterned after the U.S. Olympic Committee, the National Tourism Organization is funded by business sponsors who pay an annual fee to use its logo in advertising and promotion. The organization's avowed goal is to put the United States back on top of the international tourism market.

Despite a leveling off in overall growth, the U.S. travel agency industry remains vibrant and is well-placed to benefit from the promise of future increases in both leisure and business travel. Even in a prolonged recessionary period, cumulative agency revenues have remained up, and it appears that there is still some room for agencies to grow within the travel complex. While they have no real competition in airline ticket sales, tours, and cruises, their proportion of the car rental and hotel reservation markets show room for growth. Even without any marked improvement in their relationship with these two suppliers, however, the industry is so closely aligned to the airline and cruise industries that the years ahead, while they may show further consolidation and cost containment, will surely be prosperous. In addition, the recent focus on airline industry upheaval and the Clinton administration's commitment to airline industry reform is welcome news to agencies who continue to depend on that sector of the travel economy. With the outgrowth of consortiums and mega-agencies, travel agencies have more leverage than ever before, which will enable them to play a significant role in airline industry reforms. Finally, and perhaps most importantly, travel agencies have proven themselves flexible enough to adapt to the ever-changing habits of American travelers.

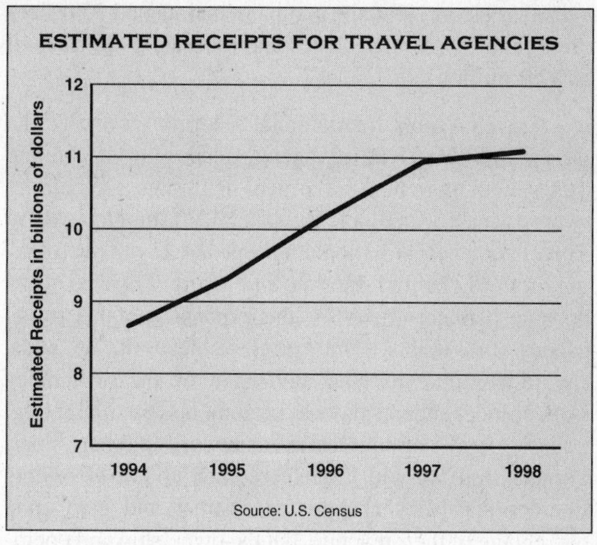

CURRENT CONDITIONS

Travel is currently the leading services export in the United States, bringing in $93 billion (including water transportation) from 46.4 million international visitors in 1998, which was $18.7 billion more than U.S. travelers spent abroad that year. Travel and tourism is also the third largest retail industry, next to automobile dealers and food stores. Total 1998 output from both domestic and international travel was $1.15 trillion dollars, which was 13.6 percent of the Gross National Product (GNP). The entire industry employed 7.58 million people in 1998, up from 6.6 million in 1995. Travel within the United States continues to represent a large segment of the industry: in 1998, Americans spent $424 *billion* on travel away from home without leaving the country. According the the U.S. Census Bureau, travel agencies brought in approximately $11.1 billion in receipts for 1998.

Post-deregulation commissions continued to drop through the latter 1990s as commission caps, ticketless travel, and cost cutting all began to take their toll. In October 1999 airlines cut their commissions to travel agencies down to 5 percent, the third reduction since 1995. In effect were a $50 commission cap on round-trip domestic flights and a cap of $100 on international flights. Electronic ticketing and Internet booking remained the biggest threats to travel agency income. According to ASTA, however, travel agents were still booking about 80 percent of all flights in 1999 despite the continued threat of direct online purchasing. Some of the most frequented Internet travel sites in 1999 included BizTravel.Com, GetThere.com, Priceline.com, and Travelocity.

Travel Weekly's "1999 U.S. Consumer Travel Survey" reported that travel agents ranked higher than doctors, lawyers, and stockbrokers with respect to the value provided for the work (they were out-ranked by teachers, pharmacists, and accountants). Notwithstanding, the Federal Trade Commission (FTC) reported that Americans lose $12 billion yearly in travel fraud, mostly from non-registered agencies.

INDUSTRY LEADERS

In 1997 Carlson Companies Inc. and Accor SA of Paris merged to create a new company, Carlson Wagonlit Travel Inc., the first true global travel company, with international management and total sales of $9 billion. Travel Group, a subsidiary of Carlson Companies, Inc. based in Minneapolis, is the world's largest travel agency chain. Formed in 1887, Carlson's most extraordinary period of expansion began some 100 years later in the late 1980s. From 851 locations in 1988, Carlson has grown to include about 3,000 offices. Carlson Companies, the parent organization, now comprises more than 100 companies and a worldwide workforce of more than 100,000 people who speak about two dozen languages and represent 125 countries. In 1998 Carlson Wagonlit Travel reported sales of $11 billion (a 3.8 percent growth from the previous year), with 20,100 employees.

A.T. Mays Ltd., Carlson Wagonlit Travel's U.K. leisure company, and ARTAC World Choice (formerly Association of Retail Travel Agents Consortia and the Alliance of Independent Travel Agents) announced a proposal in January of 1997 that would create the largest travel agency network in the United Kingdom, with more than 1,000 offices and 12 percent of the leisure travel market share.

GetThere.Com (the former Internet Travel Network) went public on November 23, 1999 with an IPO (intitial public offering) of 5 million shares. American Express and United Airlines own 15 percent and 28 percent of the company, respectively. The company reported $6.4 million in sales for 1999.

After Travel Services International, Inc. went public in 1997, it acquired 20 smaller companies and made them subsidiaries. In 1999, the company maintained 35 offices throughout the United States and reported 1998 sales of $129.9 million.

Travel Agents International (Florida) is one of the largest franchised travel agency chains in the United States, with more than 360 offices in 38 states. According to president Roger Block, the state of Washington, where Travel Agents International has opened 22 offices (ranking it third, behind Florida and North Carolina), has become a major focus for the expansion of his travel agency and others. The franchise network, he adds, should continue to take advantage of the difficulties smaller independents have in keeping up with marketing, training, and communications networks. When small agencies link up with franchises such as Travel Agents International, they change their names and give up a percentage of their revenue, but the ownership and operation of the agency remain independent.

Apex Travel of San Jose, California, epitomizes the aggressive regional travel agency. Bought in 1992 by Roger Hunt, the company already has seven branch offices and air ticket sales volume of around $35 million. Having bought one of the area's largest independents, Travel Systems Inc. (with sales of more than $5 million), Apex has targeted San Francisco and the East Bay area as its next market. They project revenues to soon top $45 million. Mr. Hunt feels confident that his regional agency, which specializes in corporate travel, will have no trouble competing with the largest agency presence in northern California, American Express Travel Related Services Co. Inc., which is owned by the credit card company. American Express, with total sales of almost $300 million, has also been expanding in the region and now has 34 offices. However, Mr. Hunt believes Apex, as a purely regional entity, can be more responsive to the needs of its clients than a national agency.

Travelfest, whose owner sold his chain of bookstores to Barnes & Noble, is a travel agency superstore of thousands of square feet, open from 9:00 a.m. to 11:00 p.m. seven days a week, and featuring videos, globes, and other travel-related items in addition to ticket sales. Capitol Prestige Travel Incorporated, a franchise of Carlson Wagonlit Travel, relies on independent home-based agents, with minimum training and computer hookups to cut costs. PCTravel, a Web site claiming 70,000 registered users, has minimal marketing costs and relies on the traveler to do much of the work. Aspen Travel provides personalized service for large corporations in Los Angeles, New York, and Miami, catering to the personal whims of traveling executives. Travelogue Company makes effective use of Docunet Incorporated, which prints tickets for a flat $4 each, which allows their clients to pick up phone-generated ticket requests at any of 50 sites. Premier Travel Partners completely eliminates commissions by providing on-site full-time contract travel service. The client pays for the cost of the agent and/or a flat monthly fee. The American Wilderness Experience, which specializes in exotic travel, has grown into a $2.4 million enterprise.

Air Travel Card is a business payment center with cards issued globally by more than 25 airlines, accepted by 200 airlines worldwide, and established accounts with more than 100,000 corporations. It is the only corporate charge card with no annual fees, no deposits, no per-card charges, and no fees for management reports. Corporations may choose to establish cardless accounts for their employees. American Express and Microsoft signed an agreement to develop an online corporate booking service that will list discounts and monitor corporate limitations.

WORKFORCE

According to the *U.S. Occupational Outlook Handbook,* there were 142,000 travel agents in 1996, about 10 percent of which were self-employed. The American Society of Travel Agents (ASTA) and the Institute of Certified Travel Agents (ICTA) both offer self-study and group courses. There are no federal licensing requirements, but nine states require some form of registration or certification. Employment of travel agents is expected to grow through 2005 primarily by the establishment of new agencies. The full impact of changes in the industry has yet to be determined. The industry is sensitive to the economy, the perception of air safety, and political crises.

On average, travel agencies employ 6.5 employees in an office: 1 manager agent and 5.5 agents, the majority of whom are women. For those who are full-time employees receiving a straight salary (73 percent of all agents), 1996 median salaries ranged from $16,000 to $38,000 annually, depending on experience. ASTA noted that some suppliers pay a commission, usually 10 percent, but the majority of inside agents are salaried.

With greater economic pressures, though, agencies have been slowly turning away from straight salary compensation and moving toward compensation packages that combine salary and commissions. Such plans are viewed as ways to ease the strain of flat revenues and rising salaries while bringing employee earnings in line with productivity. Agents paid in this manner (21 percent of all agents) tend to earn 6 to 11 percent more than their straight salary counterparts. Compensation packages have increased competition among agents, however and concern for a friendly office environment has kept most agencies from resorting to paying commissions, which generally range from 25 to 30 percent of an agent's total earnings.

Benefits packages have also been an area of debate in the industry, with rising health insurance rates the primary focus. Only 31 percent of agencies cover the full cost of their employees' health insurance, and the numbers are decreasing. To help small independents, ASTA has a nationwide health plan that covers more than 1,000 agencies, but the costs are still regarded as far too high by many employers. Still, health insurance ranks second behind familiarization trips as the benefit most commonly provided for by the employer. Agencies that are willing to share some of the costs of such packages can offer substantially lower wage contracts. With skyrocketing health care costs, agents are focusing more and more on benefits packages when choosing an agency.

Research and Technology

Travel agencies have provided fertile ground for the application of cutting edge computer technology. Computer reservation systems (CRSs) are used by all but 4 percent of the industry. Of the five CRS vendors, Sabre has the largest market share of the industry at 35 percent; the other vendors include Apollo (23 percent), System One (20 percent), Pars (17 percent), and Data II (9 percent). Agents have become very comfortable with using CRSs and have started to employ them in uses beyond airline bookings. More car rental companies and hotels can be accessed through CRSs than tour companies and cruises, and agents have responded by making the majority of both their car and hotel reservations (68 percent and 53 percent, respectively) by computer. The most important specialized software to appear in conjunction with CRSs is the fare-auditing scan, which checks a system for better fares and/or routing. Such software has already given many large corporate agencies an invaluable marketing tool. Other quality-control software, such as automated accounting systems (used by 51 percent of all agencies), should continue to proliferate within the industry. The U.S. Department of Transportation, in fact, expected to issue new CRS rules that will make it easier for agencies to buy third-party software and hardware for accessing their CRSs.

The emergence of Satellite Ticket Printer Networks (STPNs) and Electronic Ticket Delivery Networks (ETDNs) promises to have a major impact on travel agency ticket delivery. Starting in 1986, STPNs allowed agencies to set up ticket machines on client premises. The advent of third-party ticketing networks, used by agencies who can't afford to establish networks themselves, has given agents the ability to issue tickets through their STPNs at a number of different locations. New networks are being developed that are essentially the same manner as STPNs but are not agency accredited by the Airlines Reporting Corp. (ARC). The ARC is expected to approve them, however, and many envision ticketing locations popping up in much the same as automated bank tellers machines. Without agency accreditation, though, ETDN vendors will neither sell tickets nor offer any kind of travel counseling.

Electronic ticketing and bookings via the Internet are revolutionizing the industry. Because of reduced personal interaction, electronic tickets promise to slash transaction costs. Several airlines are promoting direct self-ticketing. USAir Group Incorporated has provided its Priority Travelworks disks, which allow online reservations to 70,000 of the 19 million people in its frequent flyer program. United Airlines Incorporated sells its online connection for $24.95 a year but also provides for free drinks coupons and headsets. It also charges $2.50 per hour of connect time which is waived with the online purchase of a ticket. Northwest Airlines Incorporated's online registration is available through Compuserve. Delta, TransWorld Airlines Incorporated, and others plan to introduce their versions. The airlines are well positioned to capture online traffic because of their share in reservation systems such as Sabre, Apollo. and Worldspan, which are used by travel agents.

Hotels, travel agents. and quasi-travel agents have also taken to the Internet to allow do-it-yourself bookings to save costs, frequently providing access to databases previously reserved for travel agents and posting significant sales. For example, the Marriott hotel chain allows reservations over the Internet. The travel industry has embraced the Internet at a pace second only to the computer industry, but there are mixed reactions as to the impact of the Internet on travel agencies. Some feel that the ability to make one's own reservations and bookings will eliminate the need for a travel agent, but there is also the speculation that the fundamental role of the travel agent will remain unchanged; that is, they will continue to act as travel consultants because of their knowledge of the industry, although they may work in-house for larger corporations.

Further Reading

''1999 U.S. Consumer Travel Survey.'' *Travel Weekly,* 25 October 1999.

American Society of Travel Agents (ASTA). ''ASTA Travel Industry Headlines: Last Update: 28 March 1998.'' Available from http://www.astanet.com/www.astanet/news/headlines.html.

Corzo, Cynthia. ''Airlines Commission Cuts Puts Pressure on Travel Agents.'' *Miami Herald,* 14 October 1999.

Dunfee, Thomas W. ''Ethical Issues Confronting Travel Agents.'' *Journal of Business Ethics,* February 1996.

Epstein, Gene. ''Economic Beat: A Glance at a Nation's Travel Market Offers a Glimpse of the State of Its Economy.'' *Barron's,* 3 June 1996.

Feiertag, Howard. ''Industry Segments Must Unite to Battle Bogus Travel Agents.'' *Hotel & Motel Management,* 17 June 1996.

Fenn, Donna. "Can the Boss Make the Upgrade?" *Inc.*, May 1996.

Green, Judson. "The Travel Agency Business." *Vital Speeches of the Day,* 1 February 1996.

Gunther, Marc. "Travel Planning in Cyberspace." *Fortune,* 9 September 1996.

Jarrett, Ian. "Travel Agents Have Doubts About the Net." *Asian Business,* September 1996.

"Opening Address Eyes Upside, Downside of Growth." *Travel Weekly,* 20 December 1999.

Reamy, Lois Madison. "Making the Most of Electronic Travel." *Institutional Investor,* April 1996.

Rothman, Howard. "Tapping the Great Outdoors." *Nation's Business,* April 1996.

Rowe, Megan. "The Smart Business Hotel." *Lodging Hospitality,* October 1996.

Rutledge, K. "Travel Industry Dealing with Business of Busy People." *Nashville Business Journal,* 9 September 1996.

Thuermer, Karen E. "A Tour of an Overlooked Export Sector." *World Trade,* November 1996.

"Travel Agents' Value Ranks Higher Than Doctors."' *Travel Weekly,* 25 October 1999, 91.

———Travel Industry Association of America (TIA). "Fast Facts" and "Industry Profile." 1999. Available from http://www.ita.org.

"Travel Safety Survey." *Security Management,* December 1996.

Underwood, Elaine. "Delta Sales Staff Claims New Baggage." *Sales & Marketing Management,* May 1997

U.S. Department of Commerce. Economics and Statistics Administration. Bureau of the Census. *Statistical Abstract of the United States 1999.* Washington, DC: GPO, 1999.

"Vacations from Hell." *Consumer Reports,* January 1999.

Willens, Michele. "How to Avoid the Vacation from Hell." *Money,* June 1996.

Wintrob, Suzanne. "Red Arrow Charts Cautious Path Through IT." *Computing Canada,* 20 June 1996.

———. "Travel Agents Told to Prepare Themselves for Change." *Computing Canada,* 11 April 1996.

Wolff, Carlo. "Tapping into the Travel Bazaar." *Lodging Hospitality,* March 1996.

SIC 4725

TOUR OPERATORS

This classification comprises establishments primarily engaged in arranging and assembling tours for sale through travel agents. Tour operators primarily engaged in selling their own tours directly to travelers are also included in this industry.

NAICS CODE(S)

561520 (Tour Operators)

INDUSTRY SNAPSHOT

Within the entire U.S. travel and tourism industry, the packaged tours industry constitutes the second largest revenue-producing sector of the travel services group, bringing in about half the revenues of air carriers alone. As of 1998, the entire travel and tourism industry was the nation's leading services export, and the third-largest retail industry, next to automotive dealers and food stores. To provide some perspective to the enormity of the economic impact of travel and tourism on the U.S. economy, in 1998, domestic and international travelers contributed $1,155 trillion dollars, or 13.6 percent, to the nation's gross domestic product.

From this enormous market, tour operators earn their revenue by providing a host of travel services to a travel agent, who then sells these services to tourists. The types of tours provided vary widely according to the type of tour operating business concerned, ranging from arranging transportation, lodging, meals, and a guide for a week-long, gorilla tracking expedition in Africa, to the simple service of providing newly arrived guests to Hawaii with ceremonial leis. Tour operators frequently offer the following advantages: cheaper price, grouped travel with others with similar interests or same socio-economic level, predetermined costs, and pre-planned activities.

Historically, tourists who have chosen to arrange their vacations through a tour operator rather than through a travel agency have done so for several different reasons, which, over the course of the modern travel industry's existence, have fluctuated in their relative importance to the tour operator industry. Initially, tourists were attracted by the cheaper total price of their vacations when purchased from a tour operator; they also preferred to travel with a group, have the trip's budget determined beforehand, and not having to worry about what to do, where to go, and how to get there. These benefits, economy, and ease of travel that motivate a consumer to consider a tour package essentially predicate the industry's existence. Throughout the tour operator industry's development, these advantages attracted a certain portion of those contemplating travel, although the number of tourists motivated by economy and ease of travel has varied during different phases of the industry's history.

As time progressed and more people found the time and the extra finances to travel, the tour operator industry also began to attract a new type of customer not necessarily interested in traveling with a group or particularly interested in saving money. These tourists had traveled to numerous destinations numerous times, becoming somewhat inured to the attraction of a particular destination. Instead of traveling, for example, to France for the seventh time, a tourist might consult with a tour organizer to arrange a trip to France specifically tailored to the tourist's interests. As the tour operator industry entered the 1990s, these types of tourists represented a growing part of the industry's customer base and led to the creation of fantastic, sometimes eccentric, tours.

ORGANIZATION AND STRUCTURE

On a broad level there are two types of businesses that generate revenue from arranging transportation and entertainment for tourists: wholesale travel businesses and retail travel businesses. Tour operators generally function as wholesalers, although like travel agencies, they may operate as retailers or both. Wholesalers in the travel industry secure large blocks of hotel rooms, or sections of seats on an airplane, or large volumes of any other travel-related commodity by paying a deposit for such reservations. By reserving, for example, 200 rooms in a particular hotel, the wholesaler receives a discounted price from the hotel operator, primarily because the wholesaler has assumed the risk of having the 200 hotel rooms remain vacant, a risk the hotel operator would otherwise assume. To generate revenue and mitigate its newly assumed risk, the wholesale concern then attempts to occupy these 200 hotel rooms with tourists by selling the rooms through a retail concern. The distinction between the wholesaler selling through the retailer rather than to the retailer is an important one, since the retailer, usually a travel agency, does not pay for the block of rooms (thereby assuming the inherent risk), but only attempts to occupy the rooms for the wholesaler, for which the retailer receives a commission from the wholesaler.

Frequently, as a result of the vertical integration by the travel industry, a travel wholesaler also may own a travel retail business and, if so, functions as a wholesaler and a retailer, reserving large blocks of transportation or lodging space, then selling these reservations directly to tourists through its retail travel agency. Some tour operators operate as such, selling tour packages directly to tourists, while others sell tour packages through retail travel agencies, in both cases assuming the risk that the tours offered may not attract any customers. Multi-mode tours are increasingly included in travel packages, for example cruise-tours using planes, boats, and buses offered by Carnival, Holland-America, et al.

The many types of tours offered by tour operators generally fall under four different tour categories, although a particular tour may incorporate characteristics from more than one category. Tours may be designed and organized to suit the desires of a specific group of tourists, such as a tour of Rome organized exclusively for lawyers, or a tour of the museums in Rome for art lovers. Tours of this type are known as Special-Interest Tours, which may or may not be led by a tour guide. In early 2000, the Yahoo Web site listed 36 specialized tour categories with a combined total of 946 listings under all categories. Adventure tours lead the group with 601 sublistings, followed by bus tours (42), EcoTours (36), educational and sports tours (33 each), and spiritual/self-discovery tours, which had 27 listings. Other tour operator categories of interest included spring break, whale watching, fishing, gambling, and bird watching.

Tours that are led by a tour guide and are comprised of a group of tourists not necessarily familiar with each other are classified as Escorted Tours. During these tours, a tour director travels with the group and assumes responsibility for confirming hotel reservations, scheduling transportation, overseeing the handling of baggage, leading the group on sight-seeing excursions, and providing language translation when necessary. Generally, during escorted tours, travelers follow a scheduled itinerary created by the tour operator, and travel as a group to appointed destinations at predetermined times.

Foreign Independent Tours (FIT) or Domestic Independent Tours (DIT) allow travelers more freedom to vacation on their own without following a scheduled itinerary or traveling with a group, yet these tours still offer the traveler the convenience of paying for all facets of a trip prior to departure, including transportation, transfers, lodging, sight-seeing excursions, and often some meals. This type of tour is divided into two varieties: those tourists traveling on an independent tour outside their home country are on a FIT, while those traveling inside their home country are on a DIT. Thirty-six percent of the National Tour Operators Association offered packaged FITs in 1996.

Group Inclusive Tours (GIT) are the fourth category of tours offered by tour operators and comprise groups of travelers that share a particular mutual affiliation, such as belonging to the same club or business organization. This type of tour differs from an Escorted Tour in that the travelers in a GIT share a commonality among them, while the members of an Escorted Tour share no common bond, other than perhaps living in the same region. GITs are also distinct from Special-Interest Tours, not because of the composition of the tour members, but because of differences in the tours themselves. Tourists on Special Interest Tours travel to a particular destination for an experience that somehow is reflective of their mutual interests, while travelers in GITs form a group merely to pool their purchasing power and realize savings.

Some tour operators offer travel services only after the tourist or group of tourists arrive at their destination. These tour operators, known as ground operators, often specialize on a particular destination and consequently are located in proximity to the particular destination. As a result, many tour operators are located in regions of the

United States that are typically thought of as popular tourist destination points, such as California, Florida, and Hawaii.

Although the tour operator industry is densely populated, the capital required to enter the business is relatively high, making entry into the industry more difficult than the number suggests. Since tour operators generate revenue by paying large deposits for travel commodities that, with hope, will be paid for by future customers, the fledgling tour operator must have enough capital to secure the necessary reservations without first having the opportunity to generate any revenue. Moreover, the tour operator is required to pay in-full for reserved travel commodities, whether or not the tour attracted any tourists, putting the large deposits at risk. Consequently, the number of tour operators is constantly in flux because some companies fail, particularly smaller ones with limited cash reserves, and new companies are established.

Professional Associations. There are two principal associations concerned with tour operators with a combined membership of more than 4,000 in 1999. The United States Tour Operators (USTOA) was one of the largest, with a 1999 budget of $930,000 and a membership of 524. Members must be in business at least three years, carry a minimum of $1 million liability insurance and are required to have 18 industry and financial references. The million dollar security is in the form of a bond and is used solely to reimburse consumers for tour payments or deposits lost in the event of bankruptcy, insolvency, or cessation of operations involving an active USTOA member. The National Tour Association contains 3,800 members and has a staff of 20. Its monthly magazine has a circulation of 5,200.

BACKGROUND AND DEVELOPMENT

The concept of traveling for pleasure is a relatively recent phenomenon that emerged in the latter half of the twentieth century, when society as a whole became more affluent, achievements in aviation made inexpensive air travel available to the masses, and the basic desire to spend vacations away from home combined to make travel, and particularly long-distance travel, a popular and widespread activity. Whether this transformation of the human mindset was merely the product of a people suddenly and inexplicably desirous for travel, or the result of effective marketing by both national governments and commercial interests is not clear, but whatever the root of the new desire to travel, it did not surface until the dawn of the jet age.

For Americans, travel by plane first became available in the 1930s, when airline service was first established, but many could not afford to fly, and perhaps even more felt no desire to fly, preferring instead to remain close to home. It was not until after World War II that Americans began traveling by plane to any appreciable extent, an activity facilitated by a dramatic increase in their discretionary income and the affordability of travel. But even then, not many traveled, at least not by plane, for it would be another twenty years until more than one in two Americans had ever flown in an airplane. Nevertheless, once Americans began to travel in the 1950s, tour packages designed and arranged by tour organizers appeared immediately, signaling the genesis of the modern tour operator industry at roughly the same time the overall travel industry began to mature into a formidable economic force.

Of course, the tour operator industry did not wholly depend upon air travel to generate revenue. Bus loads of high school and college students traveling together during spring vacations during the 1920s most likely constituted the formal beginnings of the industry. But the business created from those traveling to foreign countries or across the United States by airplane, had a significant effect on the development of the industry. During the 1950s, the tour operator industry benefited from several key attributes peculiar to the experience tour organizers offered. First and perhaps most important, tour packages were generally more affordable than traveling independently. Packages usually offered inclusive fares, leaving the tourist with little to pay for after departure and virtually no travel details to arrange either before departure or once traveling. Group travel also companionship in unfamiliar places and unfamiliar cultures. Many tourists traveling during the 1950s were experiencing their first journey of any distance from home. Travel for some represented a somewhat frightening—albeit exciting—endeavor. The tour operator industry was well-equipped to assuage this sentiment with comparatively cheap prices, the convenience of pre-arranged travel plans, and the security and camaraderie provided by group travel. Poised as such, the tour operator industry secured a viable foothold in the then burgeoning travel industry, establishing for itself a particular type of clientele that consistently fueled its growth.

By the beginning of the 1960s, tourism was big business, amounting to roughly $30 billion a year in the United States. Nearly 124 million Americans traveled each year during the first years of the decade. An appreciable portion traveled internationally, spending more than $2 billion annually in foreign countries. During the 1950s, international travel had become enough of an economic force to attract the attention of government officials. In fact, the Eisenhower administration's attempts to incorporate travel as a focus of foreign economic policy led to the formation of the U.S. Office of International Travel in 1958. Although no branches were established overseas, the Office of International Travel acted as promoter and served as a liaison between the travel industry and government agencies affecting the industry's operation abroad.

Despite federal promotion, several years after the creation of the Office of International Travel the number of U.S. tourists traveling overseas still outnumbered the number of foreign tourists traveling in the United States. By the beginning of the 1960s, this disparity had widened,—creating an industry trade deficit of nearly $1 billion annually. In 1961 the John F. Kennedy administration created the United States Travel Service (USTS) as part of the International Travel Act. With more power than the Office of International Travel and with branches overseas, the USTS, operating within the Commerce Department, promoted travel to the United States and facilitated that travel wherever possible.

The promulgation of the International Travel Act and the consequent creation of the USTS provided a tremendous boost to the tour operator industry, primarily because the USTS, focused on persuading large groups of tourists to visit America. Large groups of people translated into tours for tour organizers, who now found themselves infused with business created by the government. With an initial $2.5 million annual budget earmarked for travel promotion, the USTS, through its Visit U.S.A. program, enabled tour operators to reach a much wider audience than their individual marketing budgets would have allowed. In one of the first successes of the Visit U.S.A. program, 400 Swiss tourists came to, America paving the way for additional groups numbering as high as 700, to come from Britain, France, and Germany.

While foreign travel to the United States began to pick up in the 1960s, another tour type began to grow in popularity. At this time exotic tours such as safaris, gave hunters an opportunity to shoot wild game in such distant venues as Mongolia, Serbia, and Africa. Despite being considerably expensive—priced between $3,000 and $9,000 in the mid-1960s excluding airfare—safari tours attracted up to 200,000 tourists each year by the end of the decade.

A larger niche within the tour operator industry was experiencing an increase in popularity, further bolstering the industry's record growth during the 1960s. This niche would later be known as the Special-Interest Tour, which included a group of people with mutual interests traveling together to a particular destination. Some of these tours offered virtually no savings to the group traveler when compared to traveling alone. This development, along with the growing number of people paying for expensive safari tours, signified a subtle but crucial change in the reasons tourists selected tour organizers to arrange their vacations. Previously, lower vacation costs were the primary advantage tour operators offered tourists, and in the 1960s that continued to support the industry's existence. Now, however, tourists also were opting for tour operators solely due to their talents at organizing vacations. This evolution occurred slowly, but would prove to be one of the industry's primary selling points.

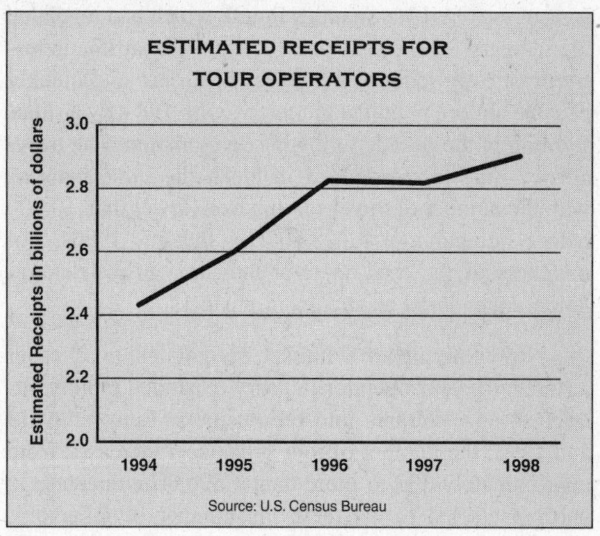

As the tour operator industry broadened its scope, the U.S. tourism deficit also continued to broaden. Despite the efforts of Kennedy's Visit U.S.A. promotional program, the tourism deficit had increased from $1 billion at the beginning of the 1960s to $1.6 billion by 1965, prompting the country's next administration to design a new international tourist program to somehow keep the gap from increasing.

Shortly after assuming office, the Lyndon Johnson administration created the See the U.S.A. program, similar to Kennedy's program in name, but decidedly different in its objective. Instead of solely promoting travel to the United States from overseas, See the U.S.A. also attempted to curb the number of U.S. citizens traveling abroad. For several years the idea of levying a ''travel-tax'' of $50 to $100 was contemplated. Although the threat of an international travel-tax initially produced the opposite of its intended effect—spurring travel abroad before the tax was implemented—other components of See the U.S.A. essentially promoted U.S. destinations for U.S. citizens, which had a positive affect on tour organizers' business. Cities with warm climates and popular tourist attractions in such states as California, Florida, and Hawaii, benefited enormously from the promotional efforts of See the U.S.A., which induced travelers to vacation within U.S. borders.

The next significant federal involvement in the travel industry came in 1978, when the Airline Deregulation Act ended the regulation of domestic air transportation. Regulation had in effect made the industry a consortium of closely allied companies forming what resembled a cartel. Once deregulated, the airline industry assumed its own course of development, unfettered by the strict controls of the Civil Aeronautics Board, which had regulated the industry for the previous 40 years. The airline industry drastically reduced the prices of airfare and quickly became a more populated industry, with 198 new airlines forming in the decade following deregulation. The travel agency industry responded in much the same manner, with the number of travel soaring from fewer than 10,000 before deregulation to 28,000 by the mid-1980s. For members of the tour operator industry, airline deregulation engendered an upturn in business.

Now catering to a market invigorated by cheaper airfares, the tour operator industry expanded rapidly, attracting new entrants into the business. Between 1973 and 1993, the number of tour organizers increased from approximately 350 to more than 1,500. This increase in participants led to a rise in the number of fallacious, which hurt the industry for the next 20 years and enticed the government to consider regulation of the industry.

Aside from this undesirable manifestation of the industry's growth, the Airline Deregulation Act of 1978 also led to an increase in the industry's sales volume, as travel agents increasingly turned to tour operators to realize larger profits. The precipitous decline in airfare prices proved to be a boon for airline companies, but travel agents dependent on commissions suffered from the drop in ticket prices. To ameliorate their position, travel agencies turned to tour operators and began selling more tours, which offered a much higher commission than cheaper airline tickets.

Buoyed by these beneficial developments as it entered the 1980s, the tour operator industry faced an additional regulatory change. In 1982 the Civil Aeronautics Board, still in the process of dismantling itself after the 1978 Airline Deregulation Act, decided as one of its final acts to deregulate the sale of airline tickets in 1985. This decision put to rest a system that had allowed only airlines and travel agents accredited by an airline industry group to issue tickets. This practice had forced many tour operators to sell tours through retail travel agencies. With greater freedom to enter the retail market, tour operators continued to attract additional business and competition for the second consecutive decade.

As tourists seek more adventuresome and exotic tours in wilderness and other uninhabited areas, concerns about the ecological impact on these environments will continue. In 1995 the National Parks Airspace Management Act sought to allow the National Park Service to control airspace above national parks in addition to directing the Federal Aviation Administration (FAA) to develop more stringent federal regulations for air tour operators. The act was aggressively fought by the United States Air Tour Association as well as the Aircraft Owners and Pilots Association because it would shift control over air space from the FAA to the Park Service, which both groups felt would be unacceptable.

The air tour operator industry noted that aircraft flying over the Grand Canyon, the central focus of the contested airspace, flew well-defined corridors away from popular areas over only 14 percent of the entire Grand Canyon National Park. It was also noted that complaints had decreased by 92 percent from 100 to 8 complaints per million visitors. The National Park Service reported that 92 percent of respondents to a survey reported no adverse sound impact from overflights.

The strength of the national air tour industry was also noted. The estimated impact of the air tour industry was $625 million. The 275 air tour operators conducted 285,714 flights in 962 aircraft during 428,571 flying hours and carried 2 million passengers annually; 1.2 million of which were foreign passengers. A total of 240,000 handicapped passengers flew on air tours. The accident rate was 1.9 per 100,000 hours flown. The environmental impact of air tours on the ground was none according to USATA.

CURRENT CONDITIONS

According to U.S. Census Bureau reports, tour operators brought in revenues of $2.9 billion dollars in 1998. Going into the millennium, two key issues dominated the industry: the trend toward mergers and the competition from Internet providers. Forrester Research reported that more than $12 billion in revenues was generated from on-line bookings in 1999. Although this constitutes less than three percent of the total travel business, it is expected to grow beyond 10 percent by 2003. Employment in the travel industry as a whole was expected to continue to grow through 2006, with faster than average earnings increases.

In late 1999, the U.S. Department of Commerce announced its second round of competition to encourage the development of new tourism itineraries across the nation. The Department announced five themes that highlight the diverse culture and heritage of the country, and competing tour operators would develop new, never-yet-sold itineraries. The five theme choices were: From Sea to Shining Sea, I Have a Dream, Food for the Soul, Lady Liberty, and America's Cultural Mosaic. The winning tour operators would become official ''American Pathways 2000'' partners in conjunction with the Department's Office of Tourism. American Pathways 2000 includes the NTA, the American Bus Association, the USTOA, the Receptive Services Association, and the International Association of Convention and Visitor Bureaus (IACVB).

INDUSTRY LEADERS

Aside from large travel, passenger transportation, and entertainment concerns that also sell tour packages, most independent tour operators are small and privately held. Leading operators included Mark Travel Corporation of Milwaukee, Wisconsin, which had 1998 revenues of approximately $1 billion and 2,400 employees worldwide; Certified Tours Inc. of Fort Lauderdale, Florida, with 800 employees; and Group Voyagers of Littleton, Colorado, with 500 employees.

The industry's Tour Operator (TOP) program under the umbrella of the American Society of Travel Agents has developed several safeguards to protect consumers from fraud or misrepresentation. Tour operators must have been in business for the past three years, must participate in one of four approved consumer protection plans, subscribe to a $1 Million Errors & Omissions policy naming travel agents as additional insurers, accept travel agent bookings and pay commissions, comply with federal and state travel regulations, respond to Better Business Bureaus and other complaints within 30 days, and subscribe to a prescribed Code of Ethics. The four protection plans with a brief description of their coverages are outlined below.

The U.S. Tour Operators Association requires that a $1 million security deposit in the form of a bond, letter of credit, or certificate of deposit be used solely for reimbursing consumers who have lost tour payments or deposits because of the bankruptcy, insolvency, or cessation of operations of one of its active members. The funds are also available to consumers whose company failed to refund monies within 120 days of cancelation of a tour or package.

The National Tour Association's Consumer Protection Plan applies to qualifying deposits or prepayment for packaged travel placed by a travel agent on behalf of the consumer. Losses are limited to $250,000 per bankrupt member with maximum liabilities limited to the total assets of the fund at the time.

The Travel Funds Protection Plan is an escrow account for individual deposits by agreement with tour operators and the bank. The deposit account is controlled by the First Bank of America, automatically debits air fare, and releases payment to the tour operator for land and lodging related cost five days after the tour is complete. None of the consumer's money is available to the tour operator in the interim.

The Federal Maritime Commission Program requires owners, operators, and charters of vessels with accommodations for 50 or more passengers embarking from U.S. ports (including territories and possessions) to demonstrate fiscal responsibility in the form of a surety bond, financial guaranty, self-insurance, or an escrow account to protect passengers against loss in the event of nonperformance of water transportation.

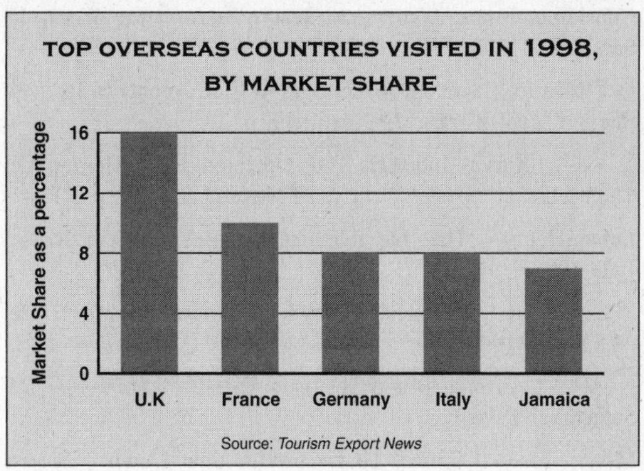

AMERICA AND THE WORLD

Since the late 1980s, the United States has held a trade surplus in travel expenditures, i.e., international tourists spent more in the United States than U.S. travelers spent abroad. In 1998 this surplus totaled an estimated $18.7 billion. International visitors generated an estimated $91.3 billion in U.S. travel revenues for 1998. Florida, California, New York, Hawaii, and Nevada, were leading U.S. destinations for foreign travelers. Nationals of Canada, Mexico, Japan, the United Kingdom, and Germany made up more than half of the international visitors to the United States.

International travel by residents of the United States has also grown steadily. In 1998, 23.1 million U.S. residents traveled overseas. Top international destinations for U.S. travelers in 1998 were the United Kingdom (16 percent); France (10 percent); Germany (eight percent); Italy (eight percent); and Jamaica (seven percent). Most travelers left the country from (in descending order) New York City, Washington, DC, Los Angeles, Miami, and Chicago.

FURTHER READING

Agency Group 04. "U.S. Department of Commerce and American Pathway Partners Announce Second Round of the American Pathways 2000 Program." FDCH Regulatory Intelligence Database, October 8, 1999. Available from http://ita.doc.gov.

Amercian Society of Travel Agents. "Tour Operator Program (TOP) Approved Consumer Protection Plans." Available from http://www.astanet.com/astanet/news/CPPS.html.

Bartlett, Tony. "NTA Panelists: Operators Require Flexibility, Creativity." *Travel Weekly,* 2 December 1999, p. 8.

"Bids for Balkantourist." *East European Markets,* 17 February 1995.

"Carnival Offers Stock and Cash for Airtours." *New York Times,* 23 February 1996.

Considine, Pippa. ''The Last Resort.'' *Marketing Week,* 15 September 1995.

Del Rosario, Laura. ''NTA Strives to Lure Agents to Its Web Site.'' *Travel Weekly,* 19 July 1999, p. 24.

———. ''Survey Indicates Tour Operators Have Mergers On Their Minds.'' *Travel Weekly,* 29 November 1999, p. 22.

Lefer, Henry. ''The 'Flexible Flier'.'' *Air Transport World,* June 1995.

Marsh, Harriet. '''Honest' Policy Fails Thomson.'' *Marketing,* 23 January 1997.

———. ''Airtours Brand Set for a Facelift.'' *Marketing,* 19 September 1996.

Morris, Jerry. ''Cruise, Tour Operator Shut Down.'' *Boston Globe,* 5 November 1995.

National Tour Association, Inc. ''Tour Operator Data.'' Memorandum dated April 17, 1996.

Tharpe, Gene. ''How to Seek Funds from Tour Operator.'' *Atlanta Journal Constitution,* 1 April 1995.

''Tourism Export News—1998 Annual Data on U.S. Resident Travel to Overseas Destinations.''

The International Trade Administration, U.S. Department of Commerce, 1998. Available from http://tinet.ita.doc.gov.

Travel Industry Association of America. Available from http://www.tia.org/press/fastfacts13.stm

U.S. Bureau of the Census. *Statistical Abstract of the United States 1998.* Washington, DC: GPO, 1998.

Wilkening, David. ''Business Briefs.'' *Travel Weekly,* 2 August 1999, 48.

Yenkel, James T. ''When a Tour Operator Goes Belly Up.'' *Washington Post,* 14 May 1995.

SIC 4729

ARRANGEMENT OF PASSENGER TRANSPORTATION, NOT ELSEWHERE CLASSIFIED

This category covers establishments primarily engaged in arranging passenger transportation, not elsewhere classified, such as ticket offices, not operated by transportation companies, for railroads, buses, ships, and airlines.

NAICS CODE(S)

488999 (All Other Support Activities for Transportation)
561599 (All Other Travel Arrangement and Reservation Services)

According to *Ward's Business Directory of Private and Public Companies 2000,* the industry reported 1999 revenues of $903 million, with an employee work force of 4000. This diverse industry is just one part of the much larger travel industry. The independent establishments in this category engage in businesses ranging from the sale of cruiseline tickets to the organization of vanpools or carpools. These establishments, however, are not affiliated with the passenger carriers or transportation companies to whose services they provide access. They only sell the tickets for passage via various means of transportation. Another sector of business activity for the industry involves the organization of car or van transportation for certain groups. Clients for these types of establishments may include individuals with disabilities who need transportation and are not able to use public or personal transportation; elderly individuals; or those for whom other forms of transportation are not available or feasible.

The industry is influenced by trends and demographics within the United States and foreign travel markets. By the mid-1990s, U.S. travelers took nearly 1.1 billion personal trips annually. In addition to U.S. travelers, the industry benefits from international tourism in America. Expanding international tourism—one of the largest sources of foreign dollars flowing into the U.S. economy—will continue to benefit this industry. Overall, continued growth was expected for the broader travel industry.

The industry is predominantly serviced by either smaller, more specialized firms or larger companies engaged primarily in other lines of business. Leading firms specializing in this industry include Worldspan LP of Atlanta, Georgia; Boston Coach of Chelsea, Massachusetts; and Commuter Transportation Services of Los Angeles, California.

Worldspan is jointly owned by Delta Air Lines Inc., Trans World Airlines Inc., and Northwest Airlines Inc., for which it provides customer reservation systems. It works through a network of 18,000 affiliated travel agencies in 60 countries. Worldspan also offers specialized services for business travel. The company reported 1998 sales of $637 million. It had 3,100 employees in 1998, representing a 3.3 percent growth from 1997.

On a related front, e-commerce and the Internet has produced ''priceline.com,'' which gives Internet-users the ability to bid on prices on non-committed travel accommodations for airline tickets, hotels, car rentals, and other travel-related services, free of charge. As of 1999, the corporation (Priceline.com Incorporated) had two shareholders controlling 55 percent of the company.

FURTHER READING

Priceline.com. Hoover's Online. Available at http://www.hoovers.com.

U.S. Census Bureau. *1992 Census of Transportation.* Washington, DC: GPO, 1995.

U.S. Census Bureau. *Service Annual Survey: 1995.* Washington, DC: GPO, 1997.

Ward's Business Directory of Private and Public Companies, 2000. Detroit: Gale Group, 1999.

Worldspan. Hoover's Online. Available at http://www.hoovers.com.

SIC 4731

ARRANGEMENT OF TRANSPORTATION OF FREIGHT AND CARGO

This category includes establishments primarily engaged in furnishing shipping information and acting as agents in arranging transportation for freight and cargo. Also included in this industry are freight forwarders, which undertake the transportation of goods from the shippers to receivers for a charge covering the entire transportation, and, in turn, make use of the services of other transportation establishments as instrumentalities in effecting delivery.

NAICS Code(s)

541618 (Other Management Consulting Services)
488510 (Freight Transportation Arrangement)

Industry Snapshot

Companies engaged in the freight transportation arrangement business offer numerous services ranging from import advice to shrink-wrapping freight crates. These firms are transportation middlemen that support the movement of cargo through the services they offer. Although relationships between forwarders and carriers may develop, the companies involved in arranging freight transportation are not affiliated with any particular carrier.

State-of-the-art automation and a strong customer orientation were the hallmarks of the industry as it entered the millennium. The high cost of automation, and a growing demand for large companies with extensive international networks, created an environment in which smaller firms found it difficult to operate. These small firms competed on their ability to provide tailored customer service; however, the industry appeared to be in a consolidation phase, as were many other industries. Although customer service continued to be a priority, the larger firms were better suited to compete in the increasingly international and automated environment.

Organization and Structure

Freight transportation arrangements are rendered by two major types of establishments: freight forwarders and customs brokers. Although many large companies offer both types of services, the businesses are distinct.

Freight Forwarders. Freight forwarders operate under many names and licensing requirements. All freight forwarders, however, are transportation intermediaries that arrange the movement of cargo according to customers' needs. Supplementary services such as shipment tracing, warehousing and storage, and the preparation of letters of credit also are offered by forwarders. Freight forwarders often are referred to as ''transportation architects.''

Through working with numerous air, road, rail, and water transportation companies, these establishments endeavor to find the least expensive and most efficient freight routings possible. Their services are popular with shippers because freight forwarders are not affiliated with one carrier and therefore are not biased or restricted. Also, forwarders are known for their expertise in the ever-changing regulations that affect cargo movements such as hazardous goods handling, documentation, and insurance. The carriers, in turn, welcome the business from forwarders. In fact, smaller carriers, who cannot afford to maintain sales staffs, depend on the business tendered by forwarders.

All forwarders that are involved in ocean, truck, or rail forwarding must be licensed by either the Federal Maritime Commission (FMC) or the Interstate Commerce Commission (ICC). However, the majority of freight forwarders are licensed by the Federal Maritime Commission as Ocean Freight Forwarders. Some Ocean Freight Forwarders, known as Non-Vessel Operating Common Carriers, operate as third party carriers and issue their own bill of lading. Since deregulation of the United States air transportation industry, air freight forwarders have not been subject to formal licensing requirements; however, most air cargo agents that are involved in international forwarding are endorsed by the International Air Transportation Authority (IATA).

Customs Brokers. Customs brokers provide services to importers and exporters and facilitate the clearance of shipments through customs. One particularly important service offered by a licensed customs broker is advice on regulations and laws pertaining to customs clearance and the power to argue on behalf of a client during the clearing process. In this regard, a customs broker is similar to a lawyer. Brokers may also provide advice and information on quotas for controlled commodities, trademark restrictions, and dumping duties, among other topics.

The customs brokerage industry is highly regulated by the U.S. Department of the Treasury. According to Section 641 of the Tariff Act, customs brokers must be individually and personally licensed by the Treasury, and brokerage firms must obtain a separate license. In the

1990s there were approximately 3,500 individually licensed customs brokers in the United States. In order to be licensed, an individual must pass a comprehensive test, which often is passed by fewer than 40 percent of the test-takers.

Financial Structure. The rate structure for both freight forwarders and customs brokers is extremely competitive. These establishments operate on very thin profit margins. Freight forwarders generate revenue through transportation charges, fees for additional services such as warehousing or shrink-wrapping freight, and commissions from carriers. Customs brokers' revenue sources include document preparation fees, charges for customs clearance, and charges for post clearance services.

BACKGROUND AND DEVELOPMENT

The primary means of transporting freight over land through the seventeenth century was pack horses. In the mid- to late eighteenth century, the first freight transportation establishments sprang into existence as services via pack horses. Ironically, supplying pack horse freight transportation frequently cost more than current airline freight rates. Even though traveling over land entailed a much shorter distance east to west than using water routes, the latter was much more practical and cost effective, so the majority of freight was moved over the Mississippi River, the Gulf of Mexico, and the Atlantic Ocean.

In the first half of the twentieth century, the United States mainly relied on truckers, oil pipelines, and inland-waterway carriers for freight and cargo transport. In the 40-year period from 1915 to 1955, railroad freight traffic decreased by 29 percent (as measured in ton-miles). Airlines accounted for less than 1 percent of freight transportation. Yet, the total freight traffic increased approximately 350 percent as a result of the boom in commerce and manufacturing.

Transportation middlemen, performing services similar to modern freight forwarders, operated in Europe in the 1600s. In the United States, these intermediaries arranged transportation by means of stagecoach, river boat, horse, and rail in the eighteenth and nineteenth centuries. However, the birth of the modern freight forwarding industry in the United States did not occur until after World War II, when the IATA allowed air freight forwarders and air cargo agents to solicit freight independently of the air carriers.

The deregulation of the trucking industry in 1980 contributed to a tremendous proliferation of forwarders. Deregulation resulted in a staggering increase in the number of registered truckers, causing confusion in the shipping community. Freight forwarders were needed to help shippers choose from the many newly established trucking companies. As a result, the number of forwarders swelled from 70 in 1980 to 6,000 in 1991. Many of these forwarders were small and barely solvent.

The growth of intermodal traffic during the 1980s and early 1990s also contributed to a rise in the number of forwarders. Intermodal transportation, the movement of freight via two or more modes of transportation, grew faster than the economy in 1992. Freight forwarders were particularly well-received in the intermodal industry because of their willingness to take responsibility for the cargo as it moved over different modes of transportation. In this way, one bill of lading was issued for the shipment. In 1992, between 400 and 500 forwarders handled approximately 35 percent of all rail intermodal traffic.

Although customs brokers operated as far back as Phoenician times, they have only operated since the early 1900s in the United States. The existence of customs brokers in the modern world can be attributed to myriad tariff laws that the United States and other countries enforce. In 1989, every shipment imported into the United States was subject to 500 pages of customs regulations and 14,000 tariff items. Moreover, importers must comply with regulations put forth by approximately 40 U.S. regulatory agencies, such as the Food and Drug Administration and the Federal Communications Commission.

The demand for freight forwarders has remained stable. However, forwarders and customs brokers have found it difficult to maintain their profit margins, which are estimated to range between 5 and 10 percent. Lower freight rates reduced the commissions forwarders earned from the carriers. Additionally, the costs of automation and improved customer service eroded profit margins. Overall, forwarders and customs brokers significantly improved their service level without a corresponding increase in their rates.

The safeness of cargo and the adequacy of inspections has been an issue in recent years. Freight is only subject to inspection when the shipper is unknown to the freight forwarder; shippers familiar to freight forwarders comprise 80 percent. However, most cargo shipments are not X-rayed or inspected as a matter of routine, and hazardous materials inspectors lack proper training.

In 1989 the presidential commission on aviation security issued the recommendation that airlines rather than freight forwarders be responsible for screening cargo. Until that time, the Federal Aviation Administration (FAA) stipulated that freight forwarders comply with a security program. However, that stipulation went largely unenforced because the Civil Aeronautics Board became defunct in 1984, and it was their responsibility to monitor freight forwarding firms. In 1992, the FAA suggested ways to make freight forwarders accountable for security.

Then, in 1994, the FAA began requiring that airlines only conduct business with air forwarders who submit safety plans that adhere to a set of established federal guidelines.

The globalization of the market created challenges for forwarders and brokers. Logistics appeared to be the smallest hurdle, while increased competition from large integrated carriers who took full responsibility for cargo and promised shippers door-to-door service over great distances was more difficult for forwarders and brokers to overcome. To mitigate this threat, forwarders and brokers continued to emphasize their ability to provide the customized service not offered by mega-carriers. Freight transportation arrangers, however, were establishing more overseas networks in response to this globalization.

Current Conditions

In 1997, there were 9,152 establishments directly involved in the arrangement of freight and cargo transportation. This smaller subgroup generated $7.9 billion in revenues and reported a workforce of 72,358. The entire industry, including 6,630 freight forwarders, reported 15,782 establishments and revenues of $16.2 billion.

In early 1999, the National Customs Brokers and Forwarders Association of America (NCBFAA), representing 700 members, petitioned the FMC to declare forwarders as shippers, thereby making them eligible to joins shippers' associations. Memberships in such associations would help to streamline the end-to-end transportation package, as well as to enhance their bargaining powers in securing competitive rates.

Freight forwarders with global skills and connections will continue to be in demand the most. Worldwide e-commerce sales are expected to reach $3.2 trillion by 2003, according to Forrester Research Inc. Moreover, international shipments—13 million per day in 1999—are growing at 18 percent annually. International transportation logistics experts who are knowledgeable in import duties, shipping charges, taxes, and returns processing will be worth their weight in gold. However, to avoid potential delays in the end-to-end transport of goods, companies are turning more and more to overnight air shipments. In 1999, 80 percent of overnight shipments took place in the United States, but the market for overseas shipments was growing twice as fast. By shipping overnight through companies such as DHL and Federal Express, manufacturers could eliminate or reduce their contracts with intermediaries such as freight forwarders and have the shipments go straight through to their destinations.

America and the World

The arrangement of freight transportation continued to develop into a global industry. Shippers found the international market to be particularly demanding because of high costs and complicated tariff schedules, rendering the services of freight forwarders and customs brokers especially valuable. Although international forwarding problems have arisen, such as an FMC sanction against Korean forwarders in 1992, most international forwarding has been negotiated without incident. Shippers in the Far East are unusually receptive to the use of transportation intermediaries.

The freight forwarding community itself attained an international perspective. An excellent example of its global character is United Shipping Associates, a band of 30 small companies from around the world that joined together in an effort to compete with the larger forwarding companies. Although the group was headquartered in Boulder, Colorado, approximately one-third of its members were non-U.S. companies. Through the association, the members developed an international network comparable to that of a large international firm.

Globalization continued to challenge transportation intermediaries as the industry entered the new millennium. Continued effects of the North American Free Trade Agreement (NAFTA) were positive, as U.S.-Canada trade has grown by more than 80 percent in the last 10 years. In 1999, trade between these two countries had reached $1 billion in goods and services crossing the border every day. Ties with Mexico were more controlled: in 1999, Mexican trucks were officially allowed limited access to four border states only. This followed a 1997 audit which found that more than 3.5 million trucks had crossed the border into the United States, with only 17,000 of them being inspected for safety. Half of those inspected failed the inspection.

Smaller carriers were forced to develop innovative marketing schemes to compete with large firms, while the large firms focused on improving global networks and customer service. Although globalization, together with automation, appeared to favor the larger firms, smaller firms continued to court shippers with their strong service orientation.

Research and Technology

The freight transportation arrangement industry was swept by automation in the late 1980s and early 1990s. Contributing to the growth of automation was the desire of U.S. Customs to create a paperless environment and the growth of just-in-time inventory management.

The U.S. Customs Department's automation initiative forced forwarders and brokers to embrace technology. All customs brokers licensed after September 1988 were required to be proficient in the Automated Broker Interface (ABI), a component of the Automated Commercial System, which is Customs' system for reducing paperwork. Although this system increased the efficiency and speed of customs transactions, some firms objected to its use on the grounds that it was costly and difficult to implement. Smaller firms claimed the costs were prohibitive. Nevertheless, the Customs Department continued to promote ABI and other automated systems designed to revolutionize the customs clearing process. Another automated filing system was implemented in 1999 to assist Mexican exports across the U.S. border. A joint effort between the Bureau of the Census, the Department of Commerce, and the Laredo (Mexico) Freight Forwarding Association resulted in the automated filing of shipper export declarations (SEDs). By electronically transmitting them in advance of the shipment, forwarders can track shipments more readily and learn when they have cleared the border.

In addition to Customs' officially sanctioned automation directive, customers themselves demanded up-to-the-minute information which could only be provided by computer. As more businesses adopted time-based inventory management systems, the demand for flexible and responsive distribution services, as well as accurate and timely information on shipments, increased. Forwarders were forced to install computers to meet these demands.

In an effort to provide this information, many companies replaced their own computer programs with Electronic Data Interchange (EDI), a mainframe system which provided customers with on-line access to information on shipments. EDI was originally heralded for its ability to reduce administrative costs; however, its power to enhance customer service propelled its use in the 1990s.

EDI allowed the freight transportation industry to meet many of the demands of shippers. One of EDI's more popular features is electronic document transmission, including electronic invoicing and remittance. Moreover, the system is well-equipped to meet the demands of just-in-time delivery by minimizing errors and reducing order cycles. The information available through EDI is, however, second hand. Freight forwarders and customs brokers must obtain the status of shipments from carriers before the information is available to customers. Many EDI users are trying to gain direct access to carrier systems in order to better serve their customers.

Further Reading

Fitzpatrick, Michele. ''Logistics of Transport May Be E-Commerce's Greatest Obstacle.'' *Chicago Tribune,* 29 December 1999.

Grossman, William L. ''History of Transportation.'' *Colliers Encyclopedia.* 28 February 1996, v22. Available from http://www.elibrary.com/id/2525/.

National Customs Brokers & Forwarders Association of America, Inc. *Customs Brokers: Import Specialists.* New York, 1999. Available from http://www.ncbfaa.org/.

Sowinski, Lara L. ''Moving Goods In and Out of Emerging Markets.'' *World Trade,* December 1999, 60.

Standard and Poor's Industry Surveys. New York: Standard & Poor's Corporation, 1999.

Tanzer, Andrew. ''Warehouses That Fly.'' *Forbes,* 18 October 1999, 120.

Terrazzano, Lauren. ''Airlines lack real information on cargo they carry.'' *Newsday,* 18 December 1996.

U.S. Census Bureau. *1997 Economic Census* 5 January 2000. Available from http://www.census.gov/econ/www/servmenu.html.

White, Michael D. ''NAFTA Shipping Still Negotiating The Curves.'' *World Trade,* September 1999, 54.

SIC 4741

RENTAL OF RAILROAD CARS

This category includes establishments primarily engaged in renting railroad cars, whether or not also performing services connected with the use thereof, or in performing services connected with the rental of railroad cars. Establishments, such as banks and insurance companies, which purchase and lease railroad cars as investments are classified based on their primary activity.

NAICS Code(s)

532411 (Commercial Air, Rail, and Water Transportation Equipment Rental and Leasing)
488210 (Support Activities for Rail Transportation)

Industry Snapshot

Railcar leasing companies are intermediaries in the transportation industry—they do not solicit or transport freight. Rather, they support the movement of products through the services they offer. Shippers and railroads are the primary customers of railcar leasing companies. Because the anticipated usage time of railcars is relatively short, shippers and railroads tend to lease equipment in order to preserve capital and avoid the prohibitive costs of purchasing and maintaining the specialized equipment.

In the 1990s, most of the firms were small to medium-sized, with fleet sizes averaging around 5,000 cars. A few companies, however, eclipse these average-sized operators in size and market share. These large firms own tens of thousands of railcars.

Railcar leasing companies benefitted from a railroad renaissance in the 1990s. Rail transportation's reputation improved during this period in the wake of service and quality enhancements by the major railroads. Rail popularity also was augmented by an increase in intermodalism—the transportation of cargo via two or more modes of transportation, such as truck and rail.

ORGANIZATION AND STRUCTURE

Leasing companies offer two basic leasing options: capital leases and operating leases. A capital lease bestows all the economic benefits and risks of the leased property on the lessee. These contracts usually cannot be canceled and the lessee is responsible for the upkeep of the equipment. Capital leases usually amortize the value of the equipment over the life of the lease. An operating lease, also called a service lease, is written for less than the life of the equipment and the lessor handles all the maintenance and service. The operating lease usually can be canceled if the equipment becomes obsolete or unnecessary. Most railcar leasing companies are either operating or capital leasing companies, though some of the larger companies have separate operations offering both types of leases.

Railcar leasing companies are further categorized by their areas of specialization. The largest lessors have the resources to offer diversified fleets, although more often than not they are best known for their expertise in a few railcar markets. The average-sized leasing company is decidedly niche-oriented. There are many types of railcars including boxcars, tank cars, and covered hoppers. These cars are designed to carry specific cargos and have different maintenance needs. Leasing companies with average-sized fleets tend to specialize in one or two specific railcar types.

Financial Structure. Several elements affect the earnings of railcar leasing companies: new car purchases; the number of cars leased (called the utilization rate and expressed as a percentage of the total fleet); and leasing rates. New cars are purchased during, or in anticipation of, strong economic periods and when tax laws favor investment. Utilization rates usually reflect the overall health of the economy. Though long term leases sustain utilization rates during recessionary periods, it is difficult to maintain utilization rates above 90 percent during a weak economy. From 1920 through 1994, leasing rates were regulated by the Interstate Commerce Commission (ICC); freight car rates were subsequently determined by free-market forces.

BACKGROUND AND DEVELOPMENT

The railcar renting industry emerged in the late nineteenth century in response to a growing demand for specialty freight cars. By the late 1800s, rail tracks had stretched across the nation; shippers of perishables, such as fruit, and liquids, such as oil, were anxious to take advantage of distant yet rail-accessible markets. Without refrigerator cars or liquid carrying (tank) cars, these shippers were restricted to local markets. Since the railroads were unwilling to provide these cars because of their high cost and seasonal or otherwise uneven demand, the shippers built and maintained private car fleets themselves. The larger shippers rented their cars to smaller shippers who could not afford to maintain their own fleets.

Although the early private freight car companies often were regarded as negative additions to the railroad family, these companies were essential to the development of a number of American industries. For example, midwestern meat packers that were forced to ship only during the cold winter months could operate 12 months a year when refrigerated cars were introduced. Similarly, fruit growers in California could ship perishables all the way to the east coast in refrigerated cars.

Moreover, the mobility of the private railcar fleet suited the shorter seasons of other fruit growing regions. These fleets could follow harvests around the country; peach growers in Georgia, whose crops were harvested in June, had access to refrigerated cars until the end of their summer season, at which point the growers from Michigan could rent the cars for their fall harvest. Since the railroads operated in a specific region, these short demand cycles discouraged railroads from purchasing the refrigerated cars. The private railcar fleets were more flexible than individual railroad fleets.

Although the private car industry originally focused on the short-term needs of shippers and railroads, the advent of the long-term lease enhanced the industry's strength and size. Throughout railroad history, leases were negotiated between shippers or railroads and banks; however, these leases were financing instruments. The notion of long-term leasing specialty cars was not introduced until 1902, when Max Epstein, the founder of the large lessor GATC began leasing tank cars. The long-term lease has provided a buffer against economic slumps, allowing some companies to coast through difficult periods on the income from old leases.

The financial arrangements between private car companies and railroads were numerous and varied during the railroad boom; however, the Transportation Act of 1920 empowered the ICC to set maximum and minimum car-hiring rates. Since the availability of specialty cars was vital to the health of both the shippers and the growing industrial economy, particularly because oil was transported in specialty cars, every effort was made to eliminate discriminatory pricing even before the Transportation Act was passed. Nevertheless, despite the efforts of the ICC and other regulatory agencies, discriminatory practices did exist. In fact, Standard Oil Co., which controlled the Union Tank Car Co., was repeatedly accused of manipulating the supply of tank cars to its advantage.

One particularly unpopular practice, used often by Armour Car Lines, a refrigerated car specialist, was the exclusive contract. In this arrangement, the railroads agreed to use only one private car company for all of a particular type of traffic. The car line was obligated to provide enough equipment to handle all the shipments, and to bear the icing costs associated with refrigeration. These contracts were considered discriminatory and monopolistic.

As a result of these types of practices, the industry was highly regulated for more than 70 years. In 1992, however, the ICC voted to eliminate the rate prescription policy in an effort to promote competition and efficiency. Under this deprescription plan freight cars ordered or put into service on or after January 1, 1991, became subject to free-market rates. Car hire rates for equipment ordered or in service prior to that date were frozen at 1990 levels. The ICC voted to implement the deprescription plan gradually, beginning on January 1, 1994, with complete free market rates prevailing after December 31, 2000. This legislation represented a significant break from traditional railroad-related policy.

More than anything, the costs associated with specialty cars continued to motivate shippers and railroads to lease. In fact, in the interest of streamlining, some shippers who owned small specialty fleets chose to enter sale-leaseback agreements. By selling their cars to an operating lessor and leasing them back under an operating lease, the shipper transferred all maintenance responsibility to the lessor and shed a business that was usually cumbersome to manage and unrelated to the principal revenue-generating operation. This type of arrangement was typical of the emphasis on cost cutting and efficiency.

The 1990s brought competition from banks searching for financing activities, and weakness in the airline industry created a financial lease vacuum. The relative health of the railroad industry provided an attractive alternative for bankers looking for finance leasing opportunities. This available financing, coupled with low rates made buying railcars an attractive alternative to leasing.

Current Conditions

The industry employed slightly more than 2,000 workers in 1997 (the latest U.S. Census Department statistics available), with an annual payroll of $123 million. The 1998 domestic market was slightly depressed because of international economic slumps, particularly in the steel and grains markets. Because of the uncertainty of the market's future, railcar lessors were offering longer-term leases at low rates to accommodate the shippers and keep their business.

However, 1998 and 1999 were good years to become more competitive and upgrade the fleets. New construction of railcars was close to 70,000 units in 1998. Larger (5000+ cubic feet) grain cars and aluminum coal cars were two of the upgrades most in demand. By 1999, lessors owned more than 50 percent of the North American railcar fleet.

One novel way for securing business was for the lessors to lease railcars themselves. For example, industry leader GATX Corp. added 6,100 new railcars to its fleet between 1997 and 1999. But it did not purchase the railcars; it leased them from investors who put up the purchase money in return for a stake in the rent when GATX re-leases them to customers.

Industry Leaders

For the most part, the railcar leasing industry is a niche-oriented business comprising small to medium firms, specializing in one or two specific types of railcars. However, a few giant and diversified leasing companies have dominated the industry.

By far the largest lessor is General Electric Capital Railcar Services, a wholly owned subsidiary of GE Capital. A merger with Itel in 1992 left GE Railcar with a fleet of 140,000 freight cars, the largest and most diversified fleet in the industry. The company also had the most extensive repair network with 11 railcar repair facilities, 9 mobile repair facilities and 6 wheel shops in the United States and Canada. Despite the size and diversification of its fleet, GE is best known for its boxcars. GE Capital's overall 1998 sales were $41.4 billion.

The disproportionate size of GE Railcar is evident from the fact that the runner up in diversified leasing, U.S. Rail, owned 20,000 cars in 1996. U.S. Rail is a division of Ford Financial Service's U.S. Leasing Co. Like GE, U.S. Rail acquired a substantial number of cars in the early 1990s, of which 4,800 were obtained from the auction of Chrysler Rail. These large car acquisitions, resulting from mergers and bankruptcies, contributed to the concentration of the industry into the hands of a few major players.

Although no other non-bank diversified freight car lessors approached the size of U.S. Leasing, some of the niche-market companies were quite large. In the tank car industry two companies surpassed the diversified freight car runner-up: Union Tank Car and GATX. GATX's General American Transportation, which constitutes 29 percent of overall sales, remains a U.S. leader with 100,000 cars in 1999. This number represented 26 percent of the national tank car fleet. Another major niche player was TTX Co., which specialized in intermodal cars. TTX generated approximately $937 million in sales in 1998, and continued to prosper with the intermodal freight transportation industry, which grew faster than the economy in 1998.

RESEARCH AND TECHNOLOGY

Since its inception, the railcar leasing industry has capitalized on the fact that specialized cars are expensive to purchase and maintain. These specialized cars were developed in response to the specific needs of shippers and railroads. As cargo became more specialized, so did the cars in which the cargo was transported. Going into the mid-1990s, technology and innovation continued to enhance the industry. Railcars evolved from refrigerated cars to ultra-modern designs such as GATC's Arcticar, a cryogenically cooled railcar for frozen food transport.

Oftentimes, a new railcar design created a niche market. This type of opportunity occurred when Greenbrier/Gunderson introduced the Autostack car in 1992. The development of this car addressed the surge in intermodal traffic. The railroads and the transportation industry overall saw an increase in intermodalism in the 1990s. Intermodal transportation is the use of two or more modes of transportation to move cargo. Greenbrier/Gunderson's Autostack car is a technologically advanced design used to transport automobiles via sea and land. The Autostack was such a successful innovation that a separate leasing company called Autostack began operations in 1992. This new car virtually created its own market.

The 1990s, however, added a twist to the specialization effort. The search for streamlining and cost savings encouraged the development of designs that made operations more efficient. General Electric Railcar, for example, redesigned the boxcars used by paper shippers to reduce cargo damage. These changes, such as watertight seals and the elimination of protrusions inside the boxcar that could damage the cargo, reflected the emphasis on quality and efficiency in the 1990s.

Advances in railcar designs and increased confidence in rail transportation continued to bolster the industry. Despite economic factors such as low interest rates that promote buying over leasing, railcar leasing companies were optimistic. Technology and specialization continued to be the critical factors contributing to the success of the railcar leasing industry. One area of design development at the end of the decade was in grain and plastic pellet cars, now ranging in size from 5,100 cubic feet to the giant 5,300-cubic-foot covered hopper. The 286-cubic-foot rapid-discharge aluminum coal car also was considered a good investment.

FURTHER READING

GATX Annual Report,1996. Chicago: GATX, 1997.

GE Capital Annual Report, 1996. GE Capital, 1997.

Hoover's Company Capsules for GATX, GE Capital and TTX. *Hoover's Online,* 1999. Available from http://www.hoovers .com.

Knapp, Kevin. ''GATX is Trying to Switch Wall St. to Different Track.'' *Crain's Chicago Business,* 3 May 1999, 4.

Kruglinski, Anthony D. ''How International Trade Is Impacting The Lease Fleet.'' *Railway Age,* October 1998, 12.

———. ''Leasing Helps Drive a Market in Cars.'' *Railway Age,* June, 1998, 37.

McConnell, Sheila. ''Employment Benchmarks for Industries Not Published Monthly, March 1991-98.'' *Employment & Earnings,* June 1999, 1.

Standard and Poor's Industry Surveys. New York: Standard & Poor's Corporation, 1997.

U.S. Census Bureau. *County Business Patterns 1995.* Washington: GPO, 1997.

Welty, Gus. ''Freight Cars: The Market is Healthy, The Innovators are Busy.'' *Railway Age,* September 1996.

''Zero Mileage Contracts.'' *Traffic World,* 23 December 1996.

SIC 4783

PACKING AND CRATING

This industry includes establishments that derive more than 50 percent of their revenues from packing, crating, and otherwise preparing goods for shipping. Establishments primarily engaged in packaging and labeling merchandise for purposes other than shipping, such as retail packaging, are classified in **SIC 7389: Business Services, Not Elsewhere Classified.**

NAICS CODE(S)

488991 (Packing and Crating)

Approximately 800 establishments comprised this small industry in the 1990s, generating estimated combined revenues of $530 million. The industry employed approximately 8,000 workers in the 1990s; wages in the industry were considerably lower than the average for transportation and utility workers.

Most large manufacturers in the United States pack or crate their own goods for shipment rather than relying on the specialty firms in this industry; this industry's services are also offered by many firms primarily engaged in other activities, such as shipping of freight. Firms in the industry typically offer a line of shipping-related services, such as supplying packing materials, physically packaging goods to the sender's specification, and transporting goods to and from the packaging plant. Some businesses also arrange for the final shipment of goods, either through third-party services or through their own shipping networks, and may offer clients insurance policies on goods shipped and computer tracking of goods. Firms specializing in the shipping aspects, however, are not included in this industry.

Characteristic of the 1990s was the rise in small business start-ups. With them came the reality that many otherwise-successful entrepreneurships could not afford the packaging and crating of their own goods. A niche market was born: the ''co-packing'' industry. The term was first used in France in 1998, but quickly spread to the United States. Its concept was simple: by out-sourcing the packing end of the business, many small companies could now direct their resources to sales and marketing. By 1999, co-packing was common jargon in smaller businesses, and had been employed in several larger ones, including Land O'Lakes Dairy Foods and Quaker Oats.

The vast majority of companies in this industry are small, regional concerns, none of which generate more than $100 million in annual sales. Some of the successful firms by sales volume were Venchurs Packaging of Adrian, Michigan; Paco Packaging Inc. of Lakewood, New Jersey; Howard Ternes Packaging Co. of Redford, Michigan; and Export Packaging Co. of Moline, Illinois.

FURTHER READING

Clark, Gerry. ''Land O'Opportunity.'' *Dairy Foods,* September 1999, 17.

Connolly. ''Co-Packing is Big for Small Businesses.'' *Boston Business Journal,* November 26, 1999, 13.

''Co-Packing Links Packaging and Logistics.'' *Paperboard Packaging,* September 1998, 19.

Holleran, Joan. ''All That is ABC.'' *Beverage Industry,* April 1999, 24.

U.S. Census Bureau. *Census of Transportation, Communication, and Utilities Industries.* Washington: GPO, 1995.

U.S. Census Bureau. *County Business Patterns 1995.* Washington: GPO, 1997.

SIC 4785

FIXED FACILITIES AND INSPECTION AND WEIGHING SERVICES FOR MOTOR VEHICLE TRANSPORTATION

This category covers establishments primarily engaged in the inspection and weighing of goods in connection with transportation or in the operation of fixed facilities for motor vehicle transportation, such as toll roads, highway bridges, and other fixed facilities, except terminals. Included in this industry category are companies that check boat cargo before it is transported on trucks; operate highway bridges, tunnels, and toll bridges; operate truck weighing stations; and conduct various inspections. It encompasses firms that serve private facilities as well as companies that contract to perform services for state and federal regulatory agencies. Because the industry is dominated by private, localized firms, statistical data is sparse. Notwithstanding, government statistics indicate that in 1998, tolls at bridges, tunnels, road stations, and ferry facilities brought in $9.1 billion in total receipts. By far, the lion's share of receipts came from toll road facilities ($6.7 billion).

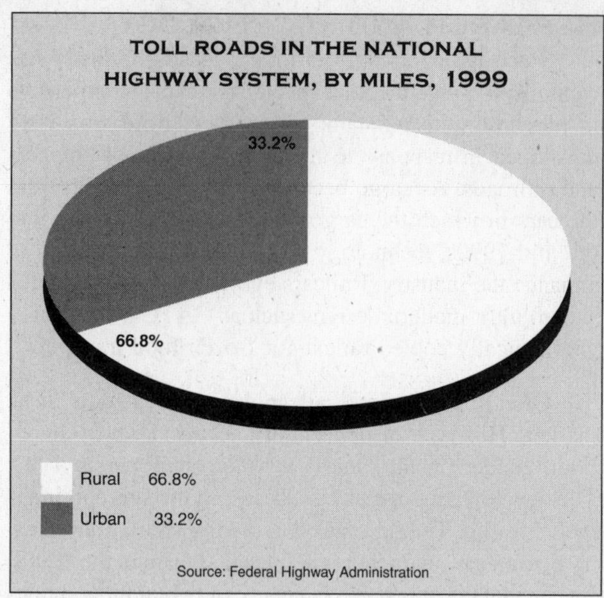

NAICS CODE(S)

488390 (Other Support Activities for Water Transportation)

488490 (Other Support Activities for Road Transportation)

The industry is largely driven by the need to monitor, for both trade and regulatory purposes, the $300 billion U.S. trucking industry. More than 50,000 trucking companies existed in the 1990s. They had access to 3.9 million miles of roads, including 45,000 miles of interstate highways. As a result, numerous enterprises have emerged to operate infrastructure, such as toll bridges, and to help enforce a glut of government restrictions. As of 1999, there were 4,715 miles of rural/urban toll roads and 4,533 miles of the national highway system under toll.

On the federal level, the U.S. Department of Transportation (DOT) and the Interstate Commerce Commission (ICC) are the primary sources of industry regulations and often employ contractors to enforce their codes. Among other duties, the DOT is responsible for maintaining the highway system and developing and enforcing safety measures. The DOT's Motor Carrier Safety Assistance Program (MC-SAP) of 1982, for example, conducts annual safety inspections of many of the nation's 250,000 large trucks. The ICC regulates carrier rates and services and enforces weight and size restrictions on trucks that use interstate highways. During the latter part of the 1990s, several states were implementing the Commercial Vehicle Information Systems and Networks (CVISN), an automated electronic system for screening trucks in lieu of having them stop for weight and safety inspections. The nationally-standardized system is expected to decrease congestion at weigh stations and more efficiently target high-risk operators.

Commercial trucking has been an important mode of commercial transportation in the United States since the 1930s. The ICC, which was formed in 1887, began regulating the industry in 1935 under the Motor Carrier Act. It was not until the 1950s and 1960s, however, that a large inspection and weighing industry emerged to monitor the trucking industry, which was booming. When the DOT was established in 1966, a profusion of new rules were developed that created a need for commercial motor vehicle inspection and weighing services.

Although the use of motor vehicles for the transport of commercial goods increased significantly during the 1980s and early 1990s, the trend since the early 1980s had been toward federal deregulation. The Intermodal Surface Transportation Efficiency Act (ISTEA) of 1991 mandated uniform state standards that substantially reduced the need for many types of interstate inspection services by the late 1990s. On the other hand, new opportunities for government contractors will likely arise from expanding DOT commercial transport safety programs.

Companies that operate toll roads, bridges, and tunnels benefitted from growing trucking activity throughout the 1990s. Although railroad and plane commercial shipping industries were becoming more competitive, the trucking industry was benefitting from reduced regulations and the integration of new information systems that were boosting efficiency. Advanced satellite systems, for example, had been launched early in the decade to track and coordinate truck transportation networks.

Commercial truckers were expected to boost their 80 percent share of the U.S. freight industry. However, job growth in the weighing and inspection industry was expected to diminish because of labor-saving automation, such as bar-code scanners and vehicle tracking information systems. Automation will reduce toll road and bridge operation jobs as well. In 1999, there were 118 toll facilities that operated with electronic technology, up from 49 in 1995.

Other technologies expected to be implemented on a wide scale early in the new millennium include infrared inspections, which use infrared "guns" aimed at passing trucks to check for faulty brakes, exhaust leaks, overinflated tires, and other hazardous conditions. Collision-warning devices—radar-activated flashing lights which signal when a truck is advancing too quickly on a car or when a truck is about to veer into a car hidden in its blind spot—also are expected to enhance the safety of transportation on the nation's roads.

FURTHER READING

"The Killer Trucks." *U.S. News & World Report,* 13 September 1999.

U.S. Census Bureau. *County Business Patterns 1997.* Washington: GPO, 1999.

U.S. Census Bureau. *Census of Transportation, Communication, and Utilities Industries 1992.* Washington: GPO, 1995.

U.S. Department of Labor. *Occupational Outlook Handbook, 1996-1997 Edition.* Washington: GPO, 1996.

U.S. Department of Transportation. "A CVISN Fact Sheet," 1999. Available from http://www.dot.gov/.

———. "Toll Facilities in the United States." Available from http://www.fhwa.dot.gov/ohim, 1999.

SIC 4789

TRANSPORTATION SERVICES, NOT ELSEWHERE CLASSIFIED

This category covers establishments primarily engaged in furnishing transportation or services incidental to transportation that are not classified elsewhere. Included in this industry are stockyards that do not buy, sell, or auction livestock; and pipeline terminals.

NAICS CODE(S)

488999 (All Other Activities for Transportation)
487110 (Scenic and Sightseeing Transportation, Land)
488210 (Support Activities for Rail Transportation)

This composite industry was worth less than $1 billion in 1997. Its 100 establishments employed less than 2,000 people in the United States. Largely made up of small and mid-sized companies, the industry included such companies as Rescar, Inc. of Downers Grove, Illinois, a railcar service company which offers technical compliance consulting and fleet management services; Trancisco Industries, Inc. of San Francisco, California, another railcar maintenance firm; and St. Louis Refrigerator Car Co. of St. Louis, Missouri, a subsidiary of Anheuser-Busch Companies Inc. that likewise services railroad cars.

The U.S. Department of Agriculture generally controls the rail stockyards industry. The USDA administers the Packers and Stockyards Act of 1921. The Act contains various financial protections for the industry, and serves as the policing law to control unfair, deceptive or anti-competitive practices. The 1999 budget for the Packers and Stockyards Administration Association was $13.5 million, with 178 employees.

One of the largest pipeline terminals is the Alyeska Valdez Marine Terminal, which services the Trans Alaska Pipeline system. Alyeska, which delivers 20 percent of the nation's domestic crude oil supply, loads an average of 42 tankers per month at the Valdez terminal.

FURTHER READING

''Rescar Supports Customers.'' *Transportation & Distribution,* January 1999, 16.

Lugar, Richard, U.S. Senator. FDCH Political Transcripts, Senate Agriculture Committee, July 27,1999.

Malone, Bob, President, Alyeska Pipeline Service Company. ''Y2K and Oil Production and Shipping.'' FDCH Congressional Testimony, April 22, 1999.

U.S. Census Bureau. *County Business Patterns 1995.* Washington: GPO, 1997.

U.S. Census Bureau. *Summary Statistics for the United States: 1997.* Washington: GPO, 1999.

SIC 4812

RADIOTELEPHONE COMMUNICATIONS

Establishments included in this category are primarily engaged in providing two-way radiotelephone communications services, such as cellular telephone services. This industry also includes establishments primarily engaged in providing telephone paging and beeper services and those engaged in leasing telephone lines or other methods of telephone transmission, such as optical fiber lines and microwave or satellite facilities, and reselling the use of such methods to others. Establishments primarily engaged in furnishing telephone answering services are classified in **SIC 7389: Business Services, Not Elsewhere Classified.**

NAICS CODE(S)

513321 (Paging)

513322 (Cellular and Other Wireless Telecommunications)

513330 (Telecommunications Resellers)

INDUSTRY SNAPSHOT

The first wireless telecommunication services, apart from radio, were developed in the 1960s, and the first experimental cellular systems were installed in 1979. Even by 1985, only a few hundred thousand Americans were using cellular telephones. Rapid growth during the 1980s and 1990s, however, catapulted the wireless telecommunication industry to prominence.

The wireless telecommunication services industry in the late 1990s was comprised primarily of cellular telephones, paging services, and personal communications service (PCS) networks. These various services allow customers with mobile telephones to send (and receive) calls to (and from) people with landline phones, pagers, or hand-held wireless phones. Increasingly, data of various types including short messages, news reports, and Internet content were also transmitted over digital wireless systems. Cellular service subscribers typically pay a monthly subscription fee plus an additional per-minute usage charge. According to the Cellular Telephone Industry Association (CTIA), in June 1999 there were an estimated 76 million mobile wireless subscribers, generating about $37 billion per year.

Like the rest of the telecommunications industry, the wireless industry was marked by significant turbulence as the 1990s drew to a close. The sweeping changes in the regulatory landscape brought about by the Telecommunications Reform Act of 1996, and the emergence of PCS systems as viable competition to cellular networks, promised lower costs and improved services to consumers. It also increased the stakes tremendously for industry players. A Yankee Group report predicted that the eventual value of the market would mushroom to more than $313.2 billion worldwide by 2002, up from $87.2 billion in 1996.

ORGANIZATION AND STRUCTURE

At the end of the 1990s the general consolidation of the telecommunications industry had blurred the distinction between the traditional landline telephone companies and wireless. Companies that aspired to be dominant players in the industry moved to establish themselves in all types of communication delivery. Moreover, success in the fiercely competitive mobile market was seen to hinge to a great extent on national coverage. However, the huge capital investment required to build the networks necessary to be a big winner created the need for mergers, joint ventures, and other forms of strategic alliances.

How a Cellular System Functions. A cellular telephone system consists of three main components: the cellular site or station, the mobile telephone switching office (MTSO), and the mobile telephone unit or pager. The mobile telephone unit is simply a low-powered portable transceiver. A pager is a wireless receiving device.

The term ''cellular'' refers to the network of cells or transceivers that support a company's service area. Each service area is broken down into several communication cells that have a radius of 2 to 20 miles. Each cell is equipped with a low-power transceiver and antenna, known as a base station, which sends and receives wireless telephone transmissions. Ideally, the cells should be arranged so that they efficiently canvass an entire service area, but cells often overlap or miss certain areas.

When a mobile phone user makes a telephone call, the transceiver in his cell receives the call and immediately routes it to the regional MTSO that oversees all the cells in its service area. The MTSO, which acts as a central nervous system, is connected to each cell by a landline or a microwave link. The MTSO analyzes the telephone call to determine whether the caller is a ''roamer'' (someone operating outside of their home service area) or a subscriber. Once it determines how to bill the call, the MTSO connects the call to a landline, or ''trunk.'' Depending on the number dialed, the call will be routed to a long-distance or local carrier. Among other tasks, the MTSO monitors the caller's signal strength within other cells. If the caller passes from one cell to another, the MTSO will ''hand-off'' the call to the next cell without interruption.

When a caller on a landline telephone calls a cellular phone user, the call is received by the MTSO, which sends an individualized ''page'' message to its cell sites to locate the mobile phone. The cellular phone responds to the page by sending a signal to the cell, after which the MTSO causes the mobile phone to ring. If the user elects to answer the call, the MTSO establishes contact between the communicators. The entire process requires only milliseconds. The MTSO works similarly for cellular callers that are contacting other mobile phones, and for callers that are trying to reach a person's paging device.

Advantages. The advantage of using a cellular system is ''frequency reuse.'' Because the Federal Communications Commission (FCC) grants a limited number of channels, or frequencies, to the cellular telephone service industry, it would be impossible to have only one or a few transceivers in each service area. Multiple cells allow the same channel, or frequency, to be used by many callers in the same service area. Furthermore, each cell can be subdivided into sectors, usually three, using directional antennas. As a result, a single service area can have thousands of callers communicating on several hundred designated channels.

PCS. PCS systems operate similarly to cellular services. However, PCS systems use comparatively low-powered phones that operate at a higher radio frequency. As a result, the systems use smaller cells that allow a greater concentration of users. In addition, PCS systems utilize digital technology that transmits a caller's voice as a numerical code. Most standard cellular systems, in contrast, use analog technology that mimics sound waves, though many systems were being converted to digital in the second half of the 1990s. Digital transmission delivers greater sound quality and makes more efficient use of limited frequencies.

The net result of PCS differences is a cellular network with as much as 20 times the capacity of a standard cellular service area. This increased capacity will allow PCS to spread costs over a potentially larger subscriber base. In addition, PCS phones require less power, weigh less, and are cheaper to manufacture. In 1996, PCS calling rates were running 15-20 percent lower than cellular in the same markets. PCS has the potential to allow a cellular user to utilize the same phone number for his landline and wireless communication devices, so that other callers would not have to know his location before they called.

Besides increasing the efficiency and sound quality of wireless telecommunication systems, advancing digital technology also promised to open an entirely new market to the cellular service industry—data transmission. Many analysts expected data transmissions to rise rapidly in the next decade, as users of new electronic devices begin transferring digitized data over telephone lines and wireless systems. Although existing cellular systems allowed users to transmit data over analog systems, such transmissions were typically troublesome and expensive. Signal fading and interference often hampered the process, though new Cellular Digital Packet Data (CDPD) standards and digital packet-switched networks offered potential solutions to analog transmission problems.

Regulation. Under regulations enacted in 1981, two operating licenses were granted for each Cellular Graphic Service Area (CSGA): One license was given to the local landline carrier or phone company, and the other was awarded to a wireless carrier through a lottery. Each carrier received half of the available frequencies. In addition, each of 428 designated Rural Service Areas (RSAs) were served by one or two carriers. In September of 1993, the FCC initiated a set of rules aimed at governing PCS. The commission allocated significant bandwidth for PCS licenses and divided the United States into 51 major trading areas (MTAs). The MTAs contained 492 basic trading areas (BTAs), each of which corresponds to a metropolitan area. The FCC auctioned off the licenses for these markets in six blocks between December 1994 and January 1997. Some blocks, called the ''entrepreneur blocks,'' were set aside for bidding by businesses with gross revenues of less than $125 million and total assets under $500 million. Provisions were also made for companies owned by women and minorities.

The Telecommunications Act of 1996, signed into law February 8, 1996, swept away 62 years of regulation of the telecommunications industry. The legislation was intended to promote competition across the industry, resulting in the development of new technology, the creation of new businesses and new jobs, and ultimately lower prices. Local telephone companies (telcos), long-distance providers, wireless companies, and cable television operators would be free to offer any and all telecommunications services. Since all the major landline entities were already cellular providers, this did not have an immediate effect on the wireless industry, but the long-range goal of the major industry players was to provide ''one stop shopping'' for consumer's telecommunications needs, leading to a general consolidation of the industry.

Background and Development

The Detroit Police Department used the first mobile radio system on April 7, 1928. The spectrum for radio transmission was broadened seven years later to include FM, or frequency modulation, signals. FM transmission technology paved the way for the mobile radio systems, which were widely used during World War II. After the war, American Telephone and Telegraph (AT&T)—which at the time held a virtual monopoly over phone service in America—introduced the Improved Mobile Telephone Service (IMTS), which made possible extremely limited cellular communication systems. The service was so restrictive that even by 1970, the Bell system in New York City could simultaneously sustain a total of only 12 mobile-phone conversations. Bell Laboratories developed the cellular telecommunication concept during the 1960s. In the early 1970s, using a relatively small amount of bandwidth allocated by the FCC for mobile telephone communication, several crude wireless phone services began. A total of 44 channels were available. Only a few channels were allocated to each major metropolitan area because of the risk of interference from high-powered mobile transmitters.

As technology improved during the 1970s, the federal government began to reconsider cellular potential. Around 1980, under the guidance of AT&T, the first practical framework for mobile service in the United States, advanced mobile phone service (AMPS), was born. The FCC allocated space for AMPS in the Washington, D.C. test market, but it was not until 1983, in the Chicago and Baltimore markets, that companies provided relatively inexpensive, efficient consumer cellular service in the United States. In 1982, the FCC allocated the equivalent of 622 additional channels to the cellular mobile phone industry, resulting in a flurry of activity and capital investment in high-tech cellular networks. An additional 166 channels were assigned in 1986, bringing the total to 832. In addition, frequency reuse strategies exponentially expanded the capacity of pre-1980s systems.

Foreseeing a bright cellular future, phone companies and well-heeled private start-ups began investing heavily in the development of cellular networks. Besides the local telephone operating companies, major players included communication giants such as AT&T and McCaw Cellular Communications. Industry investment grew from $354 million in 1984 to $1.43 billion in 1986. A still insignificant subscriber base resulted in a capital investment per subscriber of nearly $4,000 in 1984 and about $2,300 in 1986.

As cellular systems gained public acceptance and service and phone prices began to fall during the mid-1980s, the industry started to gain momentum. Cellular service revenues climbed from around $1 billion per year in 1985 and 1986 to about $4 billion in 1989. During the same period, the aggregate U.S. subscriber base rocketed from several hundred thousand to nearly 4 million. Encouraged by booming sales, cellular service providers continued to sacrifice short-term profits as they fueled massive capital investment programs. As cumulative industry outlays ballooned from $1.74 billion in 1987 to a staggering $5.21 billion by 1990, increased usage reduced the total investment per subscriber to $1,189.

Lower prices and new high-tech phones and accessories contributed to increased cellular service during the early 1990s, despite a lingering U.S. and global recession. The number of cellular users soared to about 10 million in 1992, reflecting an annual growth rate of about 20 percent. Only a few years earlier, analysts had predicted that the industry would achieve the 10 million mark around the turn of the century. Likewise, industry revenues almost doubled 1989 levels when they rose to more than $7 billion. The industry passed a major milestone in June of 1992, when service was established in the last of the 305 MSAs, paving the way for a seamless national cellular network.

The most significant trend in the wireless communications industry in the later 1990s was the shift toward PCS. Some industry participants viewed it as an expansion of local telephone networks, while others saw it as a way to bypass landline communications. Many companies saw PCS as an extension of the existing cellular network and others thought of it as a replacement. The FCC envisioned PCS as including a wide variety of services including mobile telephone, paging, cordless telephones, and other related wireless communication technologies. The FCC granted some experimental licenses in 1990, and the first commercially available network began in the Washington-Baltimore area in late 1995.

The first PCS licenses, for the 51 major trading areas (MTAs) in the United States, were auctioned off between December 1994 and March 1995. Eighteen bidders won 99 licenses, earning $7.7 billion for the U.S. Treasury. The number of licenses purchased for each market put tremendous competitive pressure on everyone. Financial pressure was also great because of the cost of building the networks along with the cost of the licenses. Moreover, many communities opposed the construction of the many transmitting towers necessary for the low-power networks. The FCC, however, along with most industry observers, expected the investment to pay off bountifully within 10 years.

In the face of PCS expansion, cellular companies tended to reduce investment in new cells and turned to other strategies to head off new competition. Some directed funds into stronger marketing efforts while others, like AT&T Wireless, switched more networks over to digital systems, advertising the first nationwide digital wireless service.

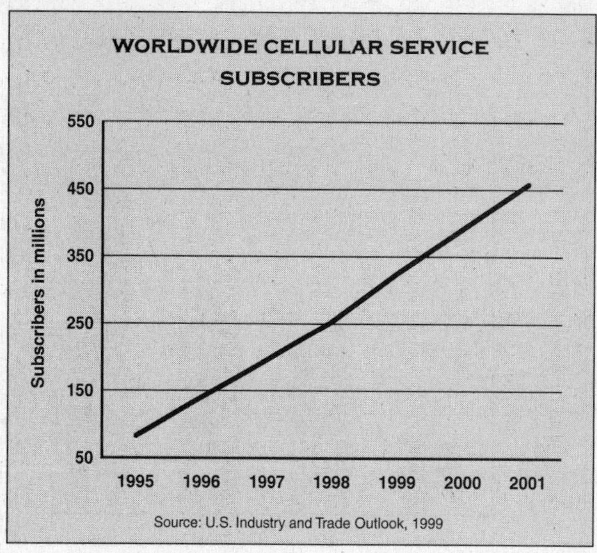

CURRENT CONDITIONS

As the 1990s drew to a close, the wireless communications industry continued its explosive growth. Between June 1998 and June 1999, the industry experienced its greatest one-year increase in subscribers—25.5 percent, to more than 76 million, according to the CTIA. Total annualized revenue for service in June 1999 was estimated at $37 billion, an increase of 26 percent. Capital investment also surged 33.1 percent, reaching a total cumulative investment of more than $66 billion. The first half of 1999 exhibited a new phenomenon in this industry—the average monthly local wireless phone bill increased, by a little less than one dollar. At $40.24 it was still much less than half the figure in 1987 when it was $98.83. A report by J. D. Powers and Associates said that in 1998 wireless customers used the phones an average of 199 minutes per month, whereas usage in the first ten months of 1999 was up to 242 minutes. The growth in usage was expected to continue.

Service continued to improve as well, as more systems were converted to digital transmission and as carriers extended geographic reach. AT&T Wireless announced a new rate plan called Digital One that eliminated roaming and long distance charges. Other companies that served wide geographic areas followed with similar plans.

Satellite-Based PCS. Piggy-backing off the PCS concept were several proposals for massive global satellite communication networks that would vastly expand the reach of terrestrial PCS. Ideally, the systems would allow phone users to communicate with anyone in the world through their mobile phone, while bypassing long-distance landline carriers. Although the service would not initially compete with land-based cellular services because of price differences, economies of scale and decreasing fees could eventually allow satellite systems to dominate global telecommunications.

The first such network to go into service was the Motorola-inspired Iridium, Inc. Iridium established a global satellite network that allowed customers to call or be called anywhere on earth, any time, using hand-held wireless telephones. According to the plan, 66 low-orbit satellites were interconnected with earth stations and public telephone networks. Iridium, with the financial backing of investors on almost every continent, launched its first satellite in 1996 and began offering commercial service in 1998. Marketing efforts were not as successful as expected, however, and in August 1999 the company filed for bankruptcy protection. ICO Global Communications, a similar satellite venture, followed suit later that month. A third enterprise, called Globalstar, began rolling out its service to selected customers and partners around the world in October 1999.

High-tech entrepreneurs Craig O. McCaw and Bill Gates proposed the most ambitious satellite plan in 1994. McCaw sold his McCaw Cellular Communications to AT&T Wireless in 1994 for $11.5 billion, and subsequently launched Teledesic Corporation. Gates, the founder of Microsoft, invested $4 billion of his own money in the venture largely on the basis of McCaw's track record in growing McCaw Cellular. Dismissed by critics, the Gates/McCaw venture called for a $9-billion network of 840 low-orbiting satellites. McCaw's vision differed from others in that, instead of creating a globe-girdling telephone network, his aim was to span the world with a satellite based Internet. Teledesic was scheduled to begin offering service by 2001. In the meantime, McCaw and others involved with Teledesic announced plans to invest in ICO Global, thus hoping to salvage that effort and protect the satellite communication vision.

The Future. New products and services that will complement existing wireless and PCS systems are expected to emerge. New digital systems and services, for exam-

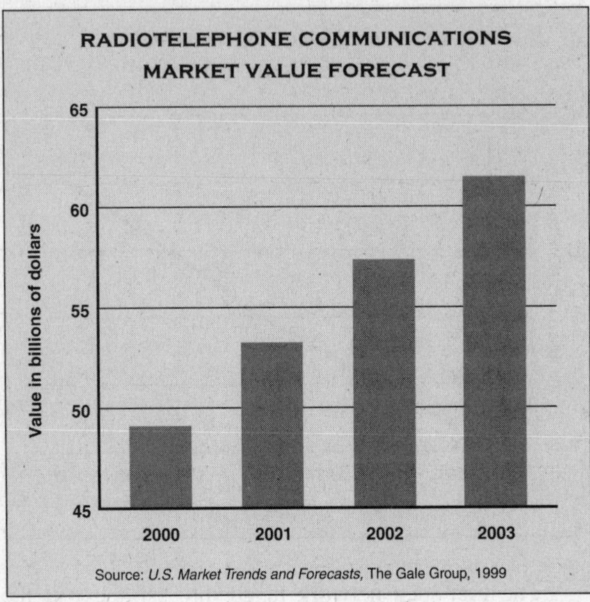

ple, will allow people to integrate computers, personal digital assistants, and other information devices into wireless communications. At the end of 1999 early adopters could already purchase hand-held wireless devices to send and receive e-mail, browse the Internet, and even trade in the stock market. According to the WDF Primer from the Wireless Data Forum, estimates of the potential market for the wireless data industry range as high as $37.5 billion for the year 2002 for wireless Internet applications alone.

One technological issue that remains is competing standards for digital transmission. Some major carriers have rolled out systems using code division multiple access (CDMA) technology, while others were based on time division multiple access (TDMA). The European industry has adopted Global System for Mobile (GSM). Various industry groups and regulatory bodies such as The International Telecommunication Union (ITU) were working on the thorny issue of the next generation of wireless technology, loosely referred to as 3G. ITU-200 is a standard that specifies a minimum set of capabilities for 3G services, including high-bandwidth communication anywhere in the world, global roaming, and a single system for residential, office, and mobile use. The primary decision yet to be made was the choice of a CDMA or TDMA air interface. At the end of the 1990s it seemed unlikely that a single technology would be agreed upon, but standards were set that would most likely ensure compatibility in user equipment.

INDUSTRY LEADERS

The numerous mergers involving wireless carriers made it difficult to identify exactly who was the absolute leader in the industry, but *Global Wireless* said in May 1999 that when all the deals were completed SBC Wireless would have the most subscribers in the United States with approximately 11.3 million, Bell Atlantic Mobile next with 11 million, AT&T Wireless with 9.5 million, AirTouch with 7.9, and Bell South with 4.6 million. However, in September Vodafone, AirTouch, and Bell Atlantic announced a deal to merge their wireless businesses, and in October MCI Worldcom made a bid to buy Sprint. Consolidation of the industry was not yet complete, but it was evident that in the end a very small number of companies would dominate not just wireless but the entire telecommunications industry. The Vodafone-Air Touch-Bell Atlantic entity would most likely have the largest wireless subscriber base in the United States and in the global market, for at least a while. AT&T Wireless, with its national footprint, would also remain a dominant force, but the MCI Worldcom-GTE-Sprint entity would also have a huge subscriber base in wireless as well as landline service.

The largest independent wireless carrier was Nextel Communications, which enjoyed the financial backing of Craig McCaw and, more recently, Microsoft. It also walked away from a merger deal with MCI Worldcom in May 1999. In July it was estimated that Nextel had 3.6 million wireless subscribers in the United States, in 92 of the top 100 markets encompassing about 70 percent of the country's population. Nextel began life as a Special Mobile Radio provider, serving customers such as trucking firms, but in recent years has moved into the cellular market. Nextel's phones often have a special two-way radio feature in addition to regular cell phone features. It also provides Internet-ready phones, and boasts of the largest guaranteed all-digital wireless network in the United States.

AMERICA AND THE WORLD

U.S. telecommunication service providers were the most competitive in the world, and maintained a substantial lead in most technologies at the end of the 1990s. Technological experience, marketing know-how, and one of the least regulated communications environments in the industrialized world contributed to global dominance. However, as global competitors raced to capture a share of the burgeoning wireless market, overseas competitors were giving U.S. cellular companies a run for their money. The United Kingdom launched the first PCS network in the early 1990s, for example, and Mannesman Mobilfunk, a German consortium, began service through the first digital GSM network. By the second half of the 1990s every country in Europe had adopted the GSM standard.

As global wireless telecommunication markets heated up, growing at twice the rate of the domestic market, U.S. service providers were aggressively chasing foreign dollars. AT&T, MCI Worldcom, and almost all other major communications firms were actively pursuing partnerships and acquisitions throughout the world. Overseas investment in the U.S. wireless industry was allowing many foreign competitors to participate in North American markets and to form global partnerships with technological leaders. Despite extensive worldwide interaction between wireless services, major impediments to the creation of a seamless global network remained at the end of the 1990s. Most notable was the lack of uniform technological and regulatory standards.

Wireless in the Third World. As many of the major wireless service providers set their sights on expanding into the leading industrialized nations, some of the savviest visionaries were eyeing third world markets. Recognizing that half of the world's population lives more than 200 miles from the nearest telephone, many companies were striving to devise a blanket service that could deliver inexpensive wireless telephone service to every person on the globe. Even if a company could capture just 1-2 percent of the global marketplace, it would enjoy a subscriber base of 50-100 million people.

To many observers the concept seemed logical. Although the United States boasted 58 telephones per 100 people, the telephone saturation rate in truly populous countries, such as China and Indonesia, was in the area of 1 percent. Furthermore, to achieve its high telecommunication rate, the United States had invested the equivalent of $320 billion dollars in equipment by 1992 to serve a population of only 250 million. For a fraction of that amount, some companies reasoned, a comprehensive global satellite network could be established that would put wireless telephone capabilities in the hands of every person in the world.

Such a system could potentially render comparatively expensive landline systems obsolete. Even phone users in the United States would be tempted to eliminate local phone service in favor of a less-expensive, easier-to-use mobile phone system. Users could carry a phone in their pocket or on the wrist and either make calls or be reached at any destination. Similar thought processes had evoked visionary schemes like Iridium and Teledesic, which were scheduled to become fully operational shortly after the turn of the century.

FURTHER READING

Barker-Benfield, Simon. ''Competition Drives Costs Down for Cellular-Telephone Users.'' *The Florida Times-Union (Jacksonville, FL),* 31 October 1999.

''Boards Study Bell Atlantic-Vodafone Deal.'' *The New York Times,* 14 September 1999.

Blumenthal, Robin Goldwyn. ''Follow Up: One Record Down.'' *Barron's,* 11 October 1999.

Cellular Telecommunications Industry Association. ''Semi-Annual Wireless Industry Survey.'' November 1999. Available at http://www.wow-com.com.

Emmett, Arielle, Peter Meade, and David Kopf. ''By Leaps and Bounds: Cellular CDMA Surges.'' *America's Network,* 1 September 1996.

Federal Communications Commission. Wireless Telecommunications Bureau. ''Auctions Fact Sheet.'' Washington, DC: GPO, January 1996. Available from http://www.fcc.gov/wtb/aucfct.html.

———. ''Broadband PCS Fact Sheet.'' Washington, DC: GPO, February 1997. Available from http://www.fcc.gov/wtb/bbfctsh.html.

———. ''FCC Auction Events.'' Washington, DC: GPO, February 1997. Available from http://www.fcc.gov/wtb/auctions/summary/aucevent.gif.

———. ''FCC Auction Revenues; Completed Auctions.'' Washington, DC: GPO, February 1997. Available from http://www.fcc.gov/wtb/auctions/summary/revenue.gif.

———. ''Narrowband PCS Fact Sheet.'' Washington, DC: GPO, January 1997. Available from http://www.fcc.gov/wtb/nbfctsh.html.

———. ''Personal Communications Services.'' Washington, DC: GPO, March 1996. Available from http://www.fcc.gov/wtb/pcssrv.html.

Fernandez, Bob. ''Iridium Casting a Shadow Over Satellite Industry.'' *The Arizona Republic,* 19 October 1999.

Forward Concepts. ''3G Cellular Market Opportunities.'' 1998. Available at http://www.wirelessdata.org.

''Gates Buys into Wireless Internet.'' *Sydney Morning Herald,* 12 May 1999.

''Globalstar Introduces Satellite Telephone Service.'' *Canada NewsWire,* 19 October 1999.

Hamblen, Matt. ''Wireless Merger a Boon for National Coverage.'' *Computerworld,* 27 September 1999.

Healey, Jon. ''Telecommunications Highlights.'' *Congressional Quarterly,* 17 February 1996.

Herschel Shosteck Associates. ''Mobility, Portability, Ubiquity: What Will Be the Model for Wireless Data Access?.'' 1998. Available at http://www.wirelessdata.org.

Kupfer, Andrew. ''Craig McCaw Sees an Internet in the Sky.'' *Fortune,* 27 May 1996.

Ledahl, John. ''Only the Strong Survive.'' *Telephony,* 4 November 1996.

''Nextel Changes Chairman, Reports Growth in Subscribers.'' *Associated Press Newswires,* 15 July 1999.

''PCS Takes on Cellular.'' *Telephony,* 4 November 1996.

''Top 20 U.S. Cellular Carriers.'' *Global Wireless,* May 1999.

Wireless Data Forum. ''WDF Primer.'' November 1999. Available at http://www.wirelessdata.org.

Young, Shawn. ''AT&T Wireless CEO Eyes Market Share Gains with New Rate.'' *Dow Jones News Service,* 3 November 1999.

SIC 4813

TELEPHONE COMMUNICATIONS, EXCEPT RADIOTELEPHONE

This category covers establishments primarily engaged in furnishing telephone voice and data communications, except radiotelephone and telephone answering services. This industry also includes establishments primarily engaged in leasing telephone lines or other methods of telephone transmission, such as optical fiber lines and microwave or satellite facilities, and reselling the use of such methods to others. Establishments primarily engaged in furnishing radiotelephone communications are classified in **SIC 4812: Radiotelephone Communications,** and those furnishing telephone answering services are classified in **SIC 7389: Business Services, Not Elsewhere Classified.**

NAICS CODE(S)

513310 (Wired Telecommunications Carriers)
513330 (Telecommunications Resellers)

INDUSTRY SNAPSHOT

Since the invention of the telephone in 1877, the demand for telecommunication services has steadily expanded. Even when competition from wireless systems increased during the 1980s, wireline service sales grew at a rate of more than 5 percent annually, and long distance calling volume expanded by 12 percent. In 1998, total local service revenue exceeded $101 billion, and toll service revenues topped $105 billion, according to figures from the Federal Communications Commission (FCC).

The Telecommunications Reform Act of 1996 made the most sweeping changes in the industry in 62 years. Aimed at reducing segmentation between local phone service, long distance service, wireless service, and cable television, the act sought to lower prices, improve services, drive greater technological innovation, and create new business and jobs for the United States. At the end of the 1990s one of the most obvious results of the reform was the rapid pace of mergers and acquisitions in the industry. For example, if all the mergers announced in 1998 and 1999 went through, the only regional Bell holding company created by the break up of AT&T in 1984 remaining in the year 2000 would be Bell South.

ORGANIZATION AND STRUCTURE

The wireline telecommunication services industry includes firms that provide electronic communications using wire networks or fiber-optic lines. The massive U.S. wireline infrastructure incorporates 750,000 miles of aerial wire, 3.5 million miles of cable, and more than 4.5 million miles of optical fiber. The Federal Communications Commission (FCC) reported that in July 1996 all the telephone companies together served 93.9 percent of U.S. households.

Although the Telecommunications Act of 1996 removed legal barriers in general, the industry was still largely divided into long distance carriers and local telephone companies (telcos). Local telcos provide basic telephone services. They bring telephone access lines into homes, hook up new customers, and service local lines and equipment. Telcos also connect customers to long distance carriers, and sometimes handle intrastate toll calls that are considered long distance.

In addition to basic services, many local telcos also publish phone directories, offer operator assistance, and provide numerous add-on services. Examples of such services are: voice mail; caller identification; call-waiting; touch-tone dialing; wide area telephone service (WATS); separate digital lines; 1-900 billing services; and video conferencing.

By far the majority of local telephone lines are serviced by the Bell Operating Companies (BOCs)—called''Baby Bells,'' because they are the offspring of the 1984 American Telephone and Telegraph Company (AT&T) divestiture. At the time of the breakup there were already a few established independent local phone companies, notably GTE. Together these companies and the BOCs are referred to as Incumbent Local Exchange Carriers (ILECs), as opposed to new local carriers, called Competitive Local Exchange Carriers (CLECs).

In addition to the BOCs and independents, competitive access providers (CAPs) offer local telephone services. Started in 1992, CAPs typically furnish dedicated fiber-optic telephone lines that connect corporations and long distance carriers. Because CAPs are not subject to the same pricing regulations with which the BOCs must comply, they can often deliver service to high-volume corporate customers at reduced rates. Early on some observers feared that these companies would siphon off debilitating amounts of high margin business, but the telcos have not suffered greatly from their presence. The terms CAP and CLEC are now often used interchangeably.

Long distance carriers, the other division of the wireline telecommunication services industry, provide national and international services via wire and fiber-optic lines. Their services often utilize satellite and microwave systems as well. Long distance carriers typically pay a hefty fee to have local carriers route long distance calls to their lines, although the rates have steadily declined since 1997.

Since 1984, when its virtual monopoly of the telephone industry was ended by the Federal courts, AT&T

has steadily lost market share in the long distance segment. The FCC reported that in 1998, AT&T held a 43 percent share of long distance revenue, although its revenue increased by 16 percent over the previous year. MCI Worldcom held about a 25.6 percent share, while Sprint had about 10.5 percent.

AT&T, MCI Worldcom, Sprint, and some other large services are referred to as"facilities-based" carriers, because they maintain the infrastructure necessary to connect calls. In addition to facilities-based carriers are"resellers," companies that complete customer calls using a transmission facility leased from a large carrier. The largest of these in 1998 was Teleglobe (formerly Excel), which enjoyed a 3.3 percent share of residential long distance revenue.

Digital Communications. Most telephone networks transmit voice and data communications using analog technology, which sends a type of sound wave over the phone line. A digital system sends bits of numeric data, making it much faster, cheaper, and more reliable than analog transmission. In addition to the data communication options offered by the standard carriers and the CAPs, a new breed of wireline service companies are providing data communication services. Value-added network (VAN) providers furnish contract services such as electronic mail, credit card verification, and electronic data interchange. These companies typically lease lines—which they use to set up data communications networks for their customers—from carriers at bulk rates. Many VANs are able to efficiently link a company's global computer networks, and by contracting with a VAN, a company can avoid incompatible national regulatory and technical communications standards, and receive consolidated billing.

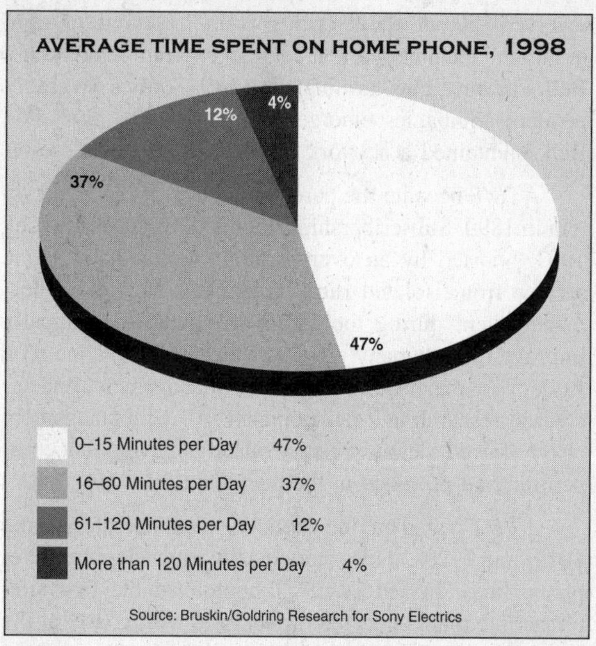

BACKGROUND AND DEVELOPMENT

The first attempts at an electrical telegraphing system occurred in the mid-1700s in Europe. One experimental system used 26 wires—one for each letter of the alphabet. Numerous telegraph models were developed with limited success during the late 1700s and early 1800s. American Samuel F.B. Morse introduced the first commercially successful telegraph in 1844."What hath God wrought?" were the first words to be transmitted on the 37-mile pole line between Baltimore, Maryland, and Washington, D.C. Under Morse licenses, open-wire pole lines were soon erected all over the United States and Canada.

Alexander Graham Bell is credited with inventing the telephone in 1876, although fellow American Elisha Gray's work closely paralleled Bell's efforts up to that time. The technology was immediately put to use in sophisticated telephone systems by the National Bell Telephone Company (originally the Bell Telephone Company). Western Union Telegraph Company also began offering phone service, using technology developed partly by Gray and Thomas Edison. But as a result of an out-of-court settlement regarding a patent dispute, Western Union sold its phone operations to Bell in 1879.

The public embraced Bell's phone service immediately. By March of 1880, there were more than 30,000 U.S. telephone subscribers and 138 telephone exchanges. By 1887, just ten years after the commercial introduction of the telephone, there were more than 150,000 subscribers and about 146,000 miles of wire. In addition, nearly 100,000 people had phone service in Europe and Russia.

As telephone services proliferated, a demand for long distance services arose. Bell established the American Telephone and Telegraph Company in 1885 as its long distance subsidiary. Important equipment and wire advances allowed commercial service to be implemented between Boston, Massachusetts, and Providence, Rhode Island by the 1890s. Distances gradually increased with the introduction of new equipment, such as relays, loading coils, amplifiers, and repeaters. Although microwave systems allowed limited telephone communications with overseas telephone users in the 1940s, large-scale wireline telecommunication was not available until the 1950s.

Bell Telephone and AT&T. Broad patent rights enabled the National Bell Telephone Company, which became the American Bell Telephone Company in 1878, to completely dominate the telephone service and equipment industry throughout the late 1880s and early 1900s. Bell built a nationwide network by licensing local operating companies to deliver service for 5 to 10 years. Bell received $20 per phone each year and reserved the right to buy the local network at contract expiration. Although Bell's patent rights terminated in 1894, only a few independent companies emerged as competitors. By 1899, Bell maintained a network of 800,000 lines.

AT&T became the parent company of the Bell system in 1899. Subscribership ballooned to 3.12 million by 1907, boosted by an overwhelming demand for phone service from isolated rural Americans. Moreover, new management during the 1910s was able to drastically improve the company's performance. AT&T adopted a strategy of expansion, centralized management, and increased research and development. AT&T management also followed a monopolistic course, believing that competition had no place in the telephone industry.

AT&T began buying up independent operators in the 1910s and 1920s. It also started delivering telegrams over phone lines. In 1915, AT&T completed the first telephone line that connected the east and west coasts of the United States. By 1921, AT&T served 64 percent of the 21 million phones installed in the United States and owned many of the networks used by almost all of its independent competitors. By 1929, the company was generating annual revenues of more than $1 billion. Despite setbacks during the Great Depression, AT&T service continued to expand at a rate of more than 1 million new customers every year during the late 1930s and 1940s. In 1955, it laid the first transatlantic cable, linking its customers to Europe.

AT&T grew quickly during the 1950s and 1960s, meeting surging demand with an influx of new products, services, and technological breakthroughs. By 1966, the company had over one million employees and served about 85 percent of the households in the areas in which it operated. Despite pressure by antitrust regulators to cede its market dominance, AT&T continued to grow during the 1960s and 1970s, becoming the largest company in the world. By the early 1970s, AT&T was serving roughly 80 percent of the phone users in the United States and providing 90 percent of all long distance service. Antitrust suits filed separately by MCI and the Justice Department in 1974 signaled an end to the company's unfettered reign.

The Communications Act of 1934 established telecommunications as a regulated industry under the jurisdiction of the FCC. The act directed the FCC to regulate the industry based on "public interest" rather than free market competition. For most of the twentieth century, the FCC believed that a regulated monopoly that could establish a standard nationwide telephone network was in the best interest of the public. The FCC and state regulatory bodies set the rates that AT&T could charge for their services, allowing the company to cover its costs but not generate excess profits. In addition, the Justice Department kept an eye on AT&T to make sure that it did not illegally compete in other industries.

In the 1970s, antitrust pressures began to change regulator's attitudes toward AT&T. Many people felt that AT&T and its Bell companies did not have enough of an incentive to install new technology and improve efficiency. Furthermore, potential industry competitors were pressing for permission to compete with AT&T using proprietary technologies. MCI, for example, wanted to compete using its microwave long distance technology. Although MCI received permission to offer limited service during the early 1970s, its 1974 suit was the regulatory turning point.

In 1982, after a lengthy court battle, AT&T agreed to divest its operations. The monopoly was broken in 1984, when AT&T was divided into eight pieces. Under the Modification of Final Judgement (MFJ), AT&T became a regulated long distance carrier, and its 22 BOCs were organized into seven regional holding companies. Among other results of industry deregulation, competitors were allowed to enter the long distance service industry. Federal and state regulators planned to slowly remove restrictions on AT&T as competitors became established. When AT&T was divided in 1984, it had sales of $36 billion from long distance toll services. This represented 88 percent of U.S. wireline long distance services sales. In 1995 its toll service revenues were $47 billion, but this represented only 55.6 percent. By 1998 its share was down to 43.1 percent.

Regulators began to loosen restrictions on AT&T and the Baby Bells in the late 1980s. In 1989 they removed profits caps on AT&T, and in 1991 they reduced pricing constraints. In 1995 the FCC ended its classification of AT&T as a "dominant carrier." The Baby Bells, though still hampered by state price and profit regulations, were enjoying greater flexibility and competing in some new markets in the mid-1990s. For example, U.S. West formed partnerships with several CAPs outside of its local service region to offer data-transport services.

The Telecommunications Act of 1996, signed into law February 8, 1996, swept away 62 years of regulation of the telecommunications industry. The legislation was intended to promote competition across the industry, resulting in the development of new technology, the creation of new business and new jobs, and ultimately lower prices. Local telcos, long distance providers, wireless companies, and cable television operators would be free to offer any and all telecommunications services.

A major provision held that the Baby Bells—and any new local telephone network developers—must allow competition for local service using their local networks. They are also required to allow the resale of their services, much like long distance service is resold by a great number of small long distance companies. Finally, they must provide the customers of these resellers the same type and quality of service that they provide their own customers.

The major benefit of the new regulations for the Baby Bells is freedom to enter the long distance market upon demonstrating that they have opened local networks to viable competition. Having done so, they will also be able to join with other companies, local or long distance, to form subsidiaries to offer long distance service jointly. The goal is to provide"one stop shopping" for all telephone services.

One of the goals of Federal regulation continues to be universal service. Companies that provide service in a region must make it available to everyone at an affordable price, even in areas where the costs of providing the service are much higher. Companies that offer such service receive subsidies from a fund that, under the new legislation, will be supported by all interstate telecommunications providers.

Other provisions of the Act allow BOCs to manufacture telecommunications equipment. It further allows telephone companies to offer video programming, and other utility companies to offer telecommunications services through subsidiaries set up for that purpose.

CURRENT CONDITIONS

A defining characteristic of the telecommunications industry throughout the 1990's was the large number of mergers, acquisitions, and joint ventures. In anticipation of deregulation, many companies joined with companies in other segments of the industry. In 1994, for example, AT&T acquired McCaw Cellular Communications, the largest cellular provider in the United States. at the time. Altogether, 746 such transactions were announced in the industry between January 1994 and June 1996, with a value estimated at $110.7 billion. Nearly 73 percent were mergers of service providers, i.e., wireline, wireless, and cable TV operators. The rest involved equipment and software providers.

In 1998 mergers and acquisitions in the U.S. telecommunications industry were valued at $234.8 billion, four times the figure for 1997. Among these were the merger of MCI and WorldCom, Ameritech and SBC Communications, AT&T and TCI, and Bell Atlantic and GTE. Early in 1999 the trend continued as AT&T made a deal for MediaOne Group, a major cable company, MCI Worldcom made a bid for Sprint and Sprint PCS, and Vodafone AirTouch announced a merger with Bell Atlantic, the largest U.S. local phone company. A relative newcomer, Qwest Communications International, primarily a long distance provider to business, closed a deal for U.S West, the Denver-based BOC. Industry analysts expected the trend toward consolidation to continue into the new century, including more international ventures as the European market moved toward deregulation beginning in January 1998.

The industry as a whole continued its steady growth. Total local service revenues in 1998 were reported by the FCC at $101.9 billion, an increase of 5.6 percent. Competition, however, had not developed to any great extent, as the ILECs accounted for more than 96 percent of the revenue. Even so, there was some improvement, since in 1993 they accounted for 99.7 percent. The long distance segment of the market showed similar growth, with an increase of 6.1 percent in long distance conversation minutes. Long distance showed somewhat more competition than local service, with AT&T holding only 43.1 percent of the market. MCI Worldcom garnered 25.6 percent, and Sprint captured 10.5 percent. All other long distance carriers together held the remaining 20.8 percent.

The growth in popularity of the Internet, as a business tool as well as a medium for nonbusiness consumers, was having an impact on the strategy of industry players. AT&T's bid for MediaOne, the leading cable company, as well as other cable carriers, had in view cable's potential for carrying large amounts of digital data, as well as local telephone traffic. Other wireline industry powers were acquiring wireless cable companies and other new companies developing Local Multipoint Distribution Systems (LMDS) and Multichannel Multipoint Distribution Systems (MMDS), both for their potential to provide a way to bypass the local telephone company and for their potential to provide the broadband delivery of data necessary for the Internet.

INDUSTRY LEADERS

Though steadily losing market share in the highly competitive long distance market after 1984, AT&T remained the largest company in the industry, with 1998 revenues of $40.6 billion. Since 1984 its toll revenues rarely declined from quarter to quarter, and dipped only twice from one year to the next. Besides being the largest long distance carrier, AT&T's wireless subsidiary was one of the country's largest cellular providers. At the end of the 1990s it was still the standard against which the others were measured.

MCI Worldcom had 1998 long distance revenues of $24.1 billion. Worldcom had been a rather small reseller of long distance in the early 1990's, but followed the path of mergers and acguisitions to become the second largest U.S. long distance carrier. If its acquisition of Sprint is completed it will have the highest capitalization of any company in the industry, though its share of the long distance market will still be slightly smaller than AT&T's.

Sprint Corporation also continued to grow, from toll revenues of $8.5 billion in 1997 to $9.9 in 1998, reflecting a market share of 10.5 percent. Sprint's wireless subsidiary, Sprint PCS, was the fastest growing wireless system in 1999, which contributed greatly to its appeal for MCI Worldcom.

Qwest Communications, before the acquistion of U.S. West, was the fourth largest long distance carrier, with revenues in 1998 of about $2.3 billion. Telelglobe Companies' Excel Telecommunications, a reseller of long distance service, ranked fifth in 1998 with revenues of $1.2 billion.

In the local service market, the Baby Bells continued to dominate, although their number was diminishing. Prior to 1998, Bell Atlantic had merged with NYNEX, and SBC Communications had emerged out of the union of Southwestern Bell and Pacific Telesis. During 1999, SBC acquired Ameritech, the midwestern Baby Bell, leaving only U.S. West and Bell South. Bell Atlantic also completed a merger with GTE, the largest non-Bell company, and Qwest made a deal for U.S. West, leaving Bell South as the sole remaining BOC.

The new broadband wireless technologies LMDS and MMDS posed a threat, at least potentially, to the ILECs. Teligent, Inc., a CLEC operating in 34 markets, used such fixed wireless technolgy along with broadband wireline facilities to provide high bandwidth communications services to businesses in cities such as New York, San Francisco, Chicago, and Baltimore. Led by former AT&T chief operating officer Alex Mandl, the company has attracted attention and funding beyond its size. Their aim, according to Teligent President Kirby Pickle, is to offer their clients savings of up to 30 percent over current communication expenses.

AMERICA AND THE WORLD

In the late 1990s, U.S. telecommunications service providers remained the most competitive in the world. Technological experience, marketing know-how, and one of the least regulated communications environments in the industrialized world contribute to their global dominance. But many nations were catching up to the United States, and some analysts believed that U.S. providers were missing the boat on some important new technologies. During the 1980s, for instance, Germany invested an average of $305 annually per telephone in its telecommunications infrastructure. Japan invested about $244 dollars per phone. The United States spent an average of only $218 per year. Likewise, U.S. investment in ISDN (Integrated Services Digital Network), the potentially vital global digital standard, lagged behind its major trading partners. On the other hand, U.S. wireline service providers were far ahead of most of their foreign counterparts in the transition to wireless telecommunications, which could eventually dominate landline services.

As the new, post-Telecommunications Act environment took shape, the industry leaders in the United States were clearly determined to maintain American leadership in the global market.

RESEARCH AND TECHNOLOGY

Besides capital spending on labor-saving automation, U.S. wireline telecommunication service industry investments were targeted at several emerging technologies in the mid-1990s. The most important area of research and development was digital transmission. Both long distance and local carriers were racing to develop and integrate new digital technology that would increase line capacity and speed, and allow the efficient transmission of data, voice, and video. ISDN deployment was being retarded by the lack of agreed standards in the U.S. Telcos were also investing in other data transmission technologies, such as Switched Multimegabit Data Service (SMDS), frame relay, and asymmetric digital subscriber line (ASDL). These technologies, combined with advancing fiber-optic and ISDN efforts, resulted in vast data transmission improvements. Technologies not traditionally associated with wireline networks were also attracting attention from the industry, including fixed wireless systems and cable modems.

An important element of the move to digital transmission was the development of a fiber-optic network, the basis of the much-touted''information superhighway.'' Fiber-optic networks can carry a lot more traffic than copper, making them much more suitable for the transport of large volumes of data and video. In 1998, local carriers increased their deployment of fiber by 21.5 percent, with ILECs deploying 2.1 million miles of fiber and CLECs deploying 1.3 million. The effort by the CLECs represented an increase of 73 percent over the previous year.

FURTHER READING

Chen, Kathy, and Leslie Cauley. ''AT&T Expects to Complete MediaOne Purchase.'' *Wall Street Journal,* 11 October 1999.

Federal Communications Commission. Common Carrier Bureau Industry Analysis Division.*Second 1999 Trends in Telephone Service Report.* Washington, DC: September 1999. Available from http://www.fcc.gov/Bureaus/Common_Carriers/FCC-State_Link/

Gibson, Stan.''RBOC Network Thrust Invades Rivals' Turf.'' *PCWeek,* 10 April 1995.

Girard, Kim.''Baby Bells Call in New Data Pipe Technology.'' *Computerworld,* 26 August 1996.

Healey, Jon.''Telecommnications Highlights.'' *Congressional Quarterly,* 17 February 1996.

"Leaders: A High-Wired Act." *The Economist,* 9 October 1999.

McElroy, Coleen, and Andrew Brooks. "Qwest and Global Crossing Compromise: Both Get What They Want." *National Post,* 19 July 1999.

Pappalardo, Denise. "IXCs Turn to Wireless for Local Service Options." *Network World,* 10 May 1999.

Ribbing, Mark. "Va. Firm Vies with Bell for Business; Telegent Offers Phone, Internet Services in 23 Markets Now." *The Baltimore Sun,* 9 February 1999.

"SBC Communications Purchase." *Wall Street Journal,* 11 October 1999.

"Teligent Levels the Playing Field for Small and Mid-Sized Businesses in Charlotte, Nashville, and Portland." *PR Newswire,* 13 October 1999.

Todd, Karissa. "The Heat Is On." *Wireless Review,* 15 July 1999.

U. S. Department of Commerce. *U.S. Industrial Outlook 1994.* Washington, DC: GOP: January 1995.

Verity, John W. "Calling All Net Surfers." *Business Week,* 5 August 1996.

SIC 4822

TELEGRAPH AND OTHER MESSAGE COMMUNICATIONS

This industry covers establishments primarily providing telegraph and other nonvocal message communications services including cablegram, electronic mail, and facsimile services. Also within this industry are establishments providing one or more of the following services: mailgram, photograph transmission, telegram, telex, and various telegraph services. Online and Internet services, many of which provide electronic mail services, are classified under **SIC 7375: Information Retrieval Services.**

NAICS Code(s)

513310 (Wired Telecommunications Carriers)

Industry Snapshot

The telegraph and other message services industry was an industry in decline at the end of the 1990s. The telegraph was the oldest form of telecommunications but was steadily being replaced by newer forms of data transmission such as e-mail over the Internet. Western Union, long the U.S. leader in this industry, was still a vibrant company, and still offered telegraph and telex service, but had turned to various forms of money transfer as its bread-and-butter. Newer methods of non-vocal message transfer, such as broadcast facsimile and fax-on-demand services, were still viable businesses, but served rather specialized markets.

Background and Development

The word "telegraph" has been in use since 1792 when Frenchman Claude Chappe of France used it to describe a visual signaling system he invented. However, it was Samuel F.B. Morse—sending a message using his new system of dots and dashes between Baltimore and Washington, D.C., on May 24, 1844—who set a communications revolution in motion. On October 24, 1861, America's two coasts were linked by a single telegraph wire. This event put the legendary Pony Express out of business. In 1866 the Western Union Telegraph Company introduced stock tickers, enabling stockbrokers to receive minute by minute information from the New York Stock Exchange.

Even after the invention of the telephone by Alexander Graham Bell in 1876, the telegraph continued to be a vital communications medium. In 1930, the telegraph began to increase in popularity following a 40-year decline, a result of the use of teletypewriters, which did not require a skilled operator to use Morse Code and had the added benefit of providing a printed record of a communication. In 1933 Western Union introduced the singing telegram. In the 1960s the telegraph lines and poles that blanketed the nation were replaced by a microwave radio system.

Until the 1970s, telegrams and telexes were the most frequently used ways of transmitting written messages within the same day. The development of communications satellites and related technological improvements further enhanced the flexibility of the telegraph. But with the increasing use of personal computers and modems, and the advent of the "Information Superhighway" for person-to-person communications (either from one computer to another or through electronic bulletin boards and online service providers), the telegraph no longer had the same prominence it enjoyed for most of the twentieth century.

Western Union, the largest telegram and mailgram service in America, saw a dramatic drop in its service levels over the years—from an all-time high of 200 million telegrams at its height in 1929 to less than 1 million at the start of the 1990s. In 1980, there were 8 telegraph carriers, according to the U.S. Federal Communications Commission's *Statistics of Communications Common Carriers.* By 1994, there were 2. Operating revenues showed a similar downward trend, decreasing from $1.008 billion in 1980 to $579 million in 1994. U.S. revenue from international telegraph service declined from $63 million in 1980 to $4 million in 1997. International telex service revenues declined from $325 million to $110 million over the same period.

CURRENT CONDITIONS

Although still available at the end of the 1990s, the telegram and the telex were relics of a bygone age. Specialized forms of message delivery services, however, continued to fill certain market needs. Western Union listed at least 20 different services on its Web site. Many of these were ways to pay bills, transfer money, or collect money owed, but others were various forms of message delivery, including the famous singing telegram. Among its services for businesses and organizations were the Hotline, a method organizations could use to enable their members and supporters to send a message to government officials or other decision-makers.

Another form of message delivery service that had a ready market at the end of the century was facsimile. Many small businesses such as packaging stores, print shops, and even convenience stores sold facsimile services for the many consumers that did not own a fax machine. On a bigger scale, a number of businesses provided a range of facsimile services for business. Broadcast fax enabled an organization to send a message to a list of fax telephone numbers very similar to a mass mailing. Fax-on-demand services provided businesses an automated system to supply documents of many kinds to interested parties by fax. The company providing the service would store the client's documents electronically, and anyone who wanted a document, such as a sales brochure or product information sheet, could simply call a toll-free number, identify the document wanted, and receive it by fax in just a few minutes.

INDUSTRY LEADERS

Western Union, perhaps the oldest company in the telecommunications industry, now is a subsidiary of First Data Corporation, the leading bank card transaction processing company in the United States. Although it still offers telegraph and other message services, Western Union's 26,000 agents, many of which are located in supermarkets, primarily transfer money, sell money orders, and collect debt payments. The company provides many such financial services for consumers who don't use banks. A new service developed with Electronic Data Services Corp. enables money transfer via ATM machines. The sender uses a debit card to initiate the transfer but the recipient doesn't have to own a card. Instead, the recipient uses codes received from the sender to access the money from another ATM.

Premiere Technologies Inc., formerly Xpedite Systems Inc., is a leader in document distribution services. It offers broadcast facsimile and fax-on-demand services, as well as telex, cablegram, and mailgram services both domestically and internationally.

FURTHER READING

Blake, Linda and Jim Lande. ''Trends in the U.S. International Telecommunications Industry.'' Washington: Federal Communications Commission, September 1999.

''Cardless Transfer Is Ready for Bankless Customers.'' *Bank Network News,* 9 June 1998.

''EDS, Western Union Offer Cardless ATMs.'' *Virtual Finance Report,* 1 June 1998.

Lewis, Len. ''Money Matters.'' *Progressice Grocer,* June 1997.

''Premiere Technologies, Inc.'' Available from http://www.xpedite.com.

''Western Union: Company History.'' Available from http://www.westernunion.com/english/about/history.html.

''Western Union: List of Services.'' Available from http://www.westernunion.com/english/product/menu.html.

''Western Union: Message Services.'' Available from http://www.westernunion.com/english/telegrams/tam.html.

SIC 4832

RADIO BROADCASTING STATIONS

This industry consists of establishments engaged in broadcasting radio programs to the public. This includes commercial, religious, and educational stations and establishments primarily engaged in broadcasting and broadcasters that produce radio program materials used by other stations.

NAICS CODE(S)

513111 (Radio Networks)
513112 (Radio Stations)

INDUSTRY SNAPSHOT

In 1999 this industry consisted of approximately 12,200 radio stations in the United States, including more than 4,900 commercial AM stations, more than 5,300 commercial FM stations, and more than 1,800 noncommercial FM stations. The industry enjoyed increasing advertising revenues during the 1990s, from $10.7 billion in 1994 to an estimated $15.2 billion in 1998. Advertising revenues grew at about 12 percent a year. Although the success of radio might seem paradoxical in the age of computers, 99 of every 100 households had a radio, with the average number of radios per household at 5.6. The typical listener tuned in for three hours and 20 minutes on average each day.

Regulatory changes following the passage of the Telecommunications Act of 1996 increased the limit on the number of radio stations one company could own. As a result, there was a sharp increase in the level of merger and acquisition activity resulting in industry consolidation. That trend had not abated by the end of 1999. Indeed, the largest merger in the history of radio was announced in November 1999, when Clear Channel Communications, which owned the largest number of radio stations in the United States, acquired AMFM Inc. (formerly Chancellor Media Corporation) for $23.5 billion. The growing consolidation of radio station ownership was expected to not only affect programming, but to also shrink the number of people employed in the industry.

ORGANIZATION AND STRUCTURE

The radio station industry is divided into two basic groups, commercial and noncommercial stations. Commercial stations earn their revenues from advertisers who pay for radio advertising time based on listener ratings. Noncommercial stations (also called ''educational'' or ''public'' stations) earn revenues from public subscriptions or, in the cases of colleges and religious stations, from the institutions they represent.

Network programs, mainly news, are transmitted to many more radio stations than are owned by the network. Similarly, outside programming, such as pop music's Top 40 countdowns, are produced within the entertainment industry and sold on tape to stations throughout the country.

Many of the large radio stations hire media research firms. The differences between large and small stations are also revealed by their internal organization. Large stations have additional station management and employ promotion and public a to better understand listener tastes. Small radio stations conduct these services exclusively in-house ffairs directors.

BACKGROUND AND DEVELOPMENT

The first radio station in the United States was KDKA in Pittsburgh, which began operating in 1919. The concept of using radio waves to broadcast information and entertainment spread quickly, and by 1922, 570 licensed stations operated in America. With this emerged the idea of networking, where stations form chains to broadcast programs simultaneously. In 1926 National Broadcasting Company (NBC) was established with two networks of 24 radio stations under its parent company RCA. By 1928 Columbia Broadcasting Systems (CBS) had established a network of 16 stations.

During the 1920s this industry saw many innovations as stations experimented with power, looking for ways to increase frequency distance and strength, and with acoustics, learning which environments blocked out unwanted background sounds. The 1930s witnessed a large increase in radio listeners. This was due in large part to the Great Depression. ''As businesses failed, radio flourished,'' observed Michael C. Keith and Joseph M. Krause in *The Radio Station.* ''The abundance of escapist fare that the medium offered, along with the important fact that it was provided free to the listeners, enhanced radio's hold on the public.'' As the depression came to a close, World War II would continue to keep the public tuned in, and by 1939, 1,465 stations were licensed in America, with network stations having 90 percent of the audiences.

The early 1940s continued with a slow and steady increase in the number of radio stations operating, and by 1945, 95 percent of all homes in America had radio. The end of the 1940s saw an emerging interest in television, which took away from radio's audiences. As noted later, however, by Keith and Krause, ''although television usurped radio's position as the number one entertainment medium . . . radio's total reach handily exceeds that of the video medium. More people tune into radio for its multifaceted offerings than to any other medium—print or electronic.''

Television's presence had a negative impact on the radio industry's expectations for growth and the formats of radio programs. Across America many radio stations owners sold their stations; others kept their stations, but sold their large studios intended for staged performances. Radio stations changed their format during the 1950s from presenting story and news programs, which were more graphically presented on television, to mostly music. The fifties also saw a development that helped radio retain some level of popularity; the transistor radio—created at Bell Laboratories—allowed radio manufacturers to produce small portable radios, bringing this medium outdoors and into cars.

During the 1950s and into the 1960s, FM radio stations, which were created in the 1940s, appeared with a better, static-free sound quality than existing AM bands. By 1961 FM offered stereo sound as well. These features appealed to audiences of special interest groups, such as classical music fans. By the end of the 1970s there were 2,000 FM radio stations in the United States, but with many of them operating for limited hours and regarded as providing only background music.

During the 1960s the growth in rock and roll recordings and the widespread acceptance of portable radios helped AM stations to continue to flourish. By the end of the sixties, there were 4,300 AM stations in the United States; of those, roughly half transmitted only during the daytime.

The 1970s and 1980s saw a change from AM to FM stations, as FM stations started to offer programming similar to AM, mainly popular and rock and roll music, and had better sound quality. By the mid-1980s, FM radio had taken over much of AM's audiences, and held 70 percent of the nation's radio listeners. AM radio stations reacted to their loss of popularity by offering more news and talk radio and some converted their equipment for stereo broadcasting. AM radio, however, was predicted to experience further losses, and eventual closure of the band. Michael C. Keith suggested in *Broadcasting* that sound quality had not had as strong an impact on AM radio's difficulties as had their lack of "imaginative, stimulating programming."

Radio Stations and the Government. Throughout the history of this industry, government legislation played a major role. In 1927 the newly formed Federal Radio Commission ordered electronic requirements on equipment, the costs of which caused nearly 150 stations to close, including 100 educational stations. In 1934 the Federal Communications Commission (FCC) was established. This governing body issued licenses for television and radio stations and enforced regulations dealing with ownership practices, radio frequencies, and broadcast programming (the most notable being restrictions on offensive language).

During World War II the FCC placed a wartime freeze on the establishment of new radio stations. At this time, the FCC also ordered this industry to conserve its power use by 10 percent, allowing energy use for other industries contributing to the war effort.

Throughout its history, the FCC influenced programming by legislation related to issues such as rebuttal practices for editorial statements and political remarks and restrictions against offensive language. The Communications Act of 1934 prohibited the FCC from censorship, but they could enforce criminal fines and probations of license for "obscene or indecent language." In 1978 the Supreme Court affirmed that the FCC had the authority to act against radio (and television) stations that broadcast indecency during times that children were likely to be listening. The FCC, however, did not enforce fines until 1987.

In 1940 the FCC set up a duopoly policy limiting station owners to only 1 AM station and 1 FM station in a given locality and up to 4 stations nationally. In the 1970s the laws on this were changed to 7 AM and 7 FM stations. In the 1980s the FCC eased regulations further to 12 AM stations and 12 FM stations nationally. By 1992 the FCC allowed owners 2 AM stations and 2 FM stations in a single locality and 18 AM stations and 18 FM stations nationwide. When the Telecommunications Act of 1996 was passed, these rules were changed yet again; the act lifted all national restrictions and increased single market ownership to 8 stations, with a maximum of 5 FM stations.

Controversy over Arbitron. Arbitron, a national research firm, provided the ratings used by radio stations and their advertisers to determine advertising prices and other marketing terms. Arbitron used a combination of statistics based on government census reports and data collected from diaries filled in by sample groups of listeners. Radio stations paid for this service by purchasing periodic reports and surveys. Over the years there was tension between station owners and Arbitron for the most part about the accuracy of ratings, but also in the 1990s about Arbitron's pricing policies. Listener diaries relied on the accuracy of listeners and on the size of the sample group. Arbitron's pricing policies drew criticism from the Radio Advertising Bureau and the National Association of Broadcasters because Arbitron changed their policy from charging stations based on their revenues to charging them based on the size of their listenerships.

CURRENT CONDITIONS

The Telecommunications Act of 1996 had a dramatic impact on the radio industry. The largest radio corporations, which had grown in profit and size during the 1980s by acquiring additional stations, were given the opportunity to expand even further, thanks to the looser ownership guidelines. The resulting consolidation of station ownership among a relative handful of large companies was characterized as "the modern version of the Oklahoma land rush," by the *Pittsburgh Post Gazette.* Broadcast companies quickly sought to achieve a concentration of stations in single major markets. This boon to large companies meant the prospect of hard times for small owners and for radio station employees. The *Minneapolis Star and Tribune* reported an estimated 30 percent employment cut in the industry, on a national basis. Listeners, however, were expected to benefit, as "the remaining fewer owners will be freer to try new niches . . . an owner of multiple stations will not want his or her own stations to compete with each other."

During the year following deregulation, the size of the growing companies was tested at the urging of advertising executives. As a result, the U.S. Department of Justice ruled that broadcasting companies would be limited to a 40 percent share of any given market. Radio advertising revenues increased by 12 percent in 1998 to $15.2 billion. Ad revenues were conservatively forecast to increase by another 9 or 10 percent in 1999, based on a 9 percent increase for local advertising, 12 percent for national spot advertising, and 11 percent for network advertising. Strong advertising growth was supported by a robust economy, continuing industry consolidation, new advertisers, and cross-media marketing.

Major industry consolidations included the $4.1 billion merger of Chancellor Media and Capstar Broadcasting in 1998, which created the nation's largest radio station owner in terms of 1998 revenue. As of March 1, 1998, Chancellor owned 97 stations (69 FM and 28 AM).

Through the Capstar merger and other acquisitions, Chancellor owned 465 stations by the end of 1998 and had estimated 1998 revenues of $1.9 billion. A year later, in November 1999, Chancellor—which had changed its name to AMFM Inc. earlier in the year—was acquired by Clear Channel Communications, which owned 459 stations at the end of 1998, for $23.5 billion, in the largest merger in radio history.

Another major acquisition affecting the radio industry was the merger of CBS Corp. and Viacom, valued at $36 billion, in 1999. In 1998 CBS had acquired 98 radio stations from American Radio Systems Corp., vaulting it into the second spot among radio station owners in terms of 1998 revenues, estimated at $1.7 billion. Viacom's acquisition of CBS, though, was expected to force the new company to divest up to ten radio stations. In the Washington, D.C.-Baltimore, Maryland, market, for example, Viacom and CBS together owned 11 radio stations, exceeding FCC limits.

Industry Leaders

Companies owning radio stations grew dramatically since the passage of the Telecommunications Act of 1996. Pending mergers between AMFM Inc. and Clear Channel Communications, and between Viacom and CBS, needed to pass regulatory approval, which might require the new entities to divest some of their radio holdings. Clear Channel put up 103 stations for sale in November 1999 as part of its acquisition of AMFM. As of the end of 1998, the top five radio station owners in terms of revenues were Chancellor Media (465 radio stations, $1.9 billion estimated 1998 revenue), CBS Radio (163 stations, $1.7 billion), Clear Channel (459 stations, $1.2 billion), ABC Radio (43 stations, $355 million), and Cox Radio (56 stations, $284 million).

Following its acquisition of AMFM, Clear Channel was clearly the industry leader. It would own 830 radio stations in 187 U.S. markets—including 47 of the top 50 markets—as well as two radio networks (Premiere and AMFM Radio Networks), interests in more than 240 international stations in 32 countries, more than 425,000 outdoor advertising displays in 35 domestic and 29 international markets, 19 television stations, and equity interests in other radio industry-related properties. Overall annual revenues were projected to reach $5 billion in 2000 and $5.5 billion in 2001.

Citadel Communications was ranked eighth among radio station owners in terms of revenues at the end of 1998, with 116 stations and $164 million in revenues. Before the end of 1999 it acquired 35 radio stations for $190 million from Broadcast Partners Holdings LP, giving Citadel ownership of 161 radio stations in 34 markets and projected 1999 revenues of more than $200 million. Following the acquisition, Citadel was ranked the sixth-largest radio group.

Hertel Broadcasting, which changed its name to Hispanic Broadcasting Corporation in 1999, was radio's largest Hispanic broadcaster. At the end of 1998 it was ranked seventh among all radio station owners in terms of revenue, with 42 stations and $182 million in 1998 revenue. In 1999 it created the HBC Radio Network, took a 4.1 percent interest in Z-Spanish Media, and acquired a second Spanish-language radio station in Las Vegas, Nevada.

America and the World

Since radio frequencies operate at low and medium levels, there has not been an international market for radio stations in the strict sense. High-frequency (shortwave) bands, however, were allocated for broadcast between nations through the U.S. Information Agency. Most of these stations were managed by Voice of America (VOA), Radio Free Europe, and Radio Liberty, which broadcast mostly in foreign languages and were not regulated by the FCC.

For more than 40 years, these services were government owned, but in the early 1990s a presidential task force suggested privatization on the premise that pro-Western ideals were not needed in the newly democratized Eastern Europe. The VOA Europe responded by airing English-language popular music and selling advertising time. Such formats were expected to be successful, especially in Eastern Europe, where there was a strong interest in American culture and in learning English; moreover, at this time many new radio stations in Eastern Europe were run on small budgets, where the use of prerecorded popular programs had a market. In 1996 Voice of America broadcasts expanded to Tuzla, Bosnia-Herzegovina, while U.S. troops participated in peacekeeping efforts in that country. That same year, the Asia Pacific Network was also created, having been mandated by the U.S. International Broadcasting Act of 1994. The act prescribed a ''new broadcasting service to the people of the People's Republic of China and other countries of Asia, which lack adequate sources of free information and ideas, which would enhance the promotion of information and ideas, while advancing the goals of U.S. foreign policy.''

Research and Technology

Satellite transmission and Internet broadcasting—known as ''netcasting''—promised to radically change the radio industry at the start of the twenty-first century.

Satellite Radio. During much of the 1990s radio broadcasters awaited the formulation of FCC guidelines that would give them the ability to market national services akin to that of cable television. In 1997 the FCC auctioned two satellite radio licenses to CD Radio for $83.3 million and its rival, XM Satellite Radio, for $89.8 million. Using a technology called the unified S-band, these satellite services sought to offer a range of programming choices to a national audience. It was estimated that these services would cost consumers about $10 a month, plus about $200 for the receiver. After spending 1999 signing up content providers, CD Radio and XM Satellite Radio were set to launch satellites in early 2000.

Internet Radio. A less pressing but inevitable source of competition was developing on the Internet. Netcasting of radio programming was hampered by technological obstacles that reduced the quality of its sound, but showed a potential to provide listeners with unprecedented options. As computer technology became more mainstream, with more than one-third of American households equipped with computer modems in 1999, competition for the ''desktop'' audience increased. Most radio stations had their own web sites by 1999, and about half of those in the top 100 markets supplied streaming audio via the Internet. According to an Arbitron survey released in February 1999, nearly 13 percent of people in the United States had listened to radio on the Internet, up from 6 percent in July 1999.

Low-Power Radio Stations. A low-power FM (LPFM) radio station initiative introduced by the FCC in 1999 might result in competition for local listeners with established FM stations. Since 1978, when noncommercial educational radio licenses were discontinued because of interference concerns, only college radio stations and specialized programming such as traveler's advisories had operated legally at low power. Between 1997 and 1999, the FCC shut down 480 LPFM stations that were operating without a license. Most of them specialized in alternative music, commentary, and news stories targeted to local communities. During 1999 the FCC commissioned studies of the interference issue and invited comments on the LPFM initiative. While its proposal to license LPFM stations attracted the opposition of the radio establishment, it was supported by religious broadcasters and a coalition called the Media Access Project.

Digital Radio. In November 1999 the FCC formally began the process of creating a terrestrial digital radio service. It began evaluating competing technologies, with ''in-band, on-channel'' appearing to be the favored technology. Companies such as USA Digital Radio, Lucent Technologies, and Digital Radio Express, however, were pursuing competing technologies. The FCC has studied digital radio since 1990. In 1995 the FCC approved a satellite-delivered digital radio system, with two such systems expected to go online in 2000. By 1999 the agency felt that digital technology offered promise for a land-based service.

FURTHER READING

Bachman, Katy. ''Heftel Doubles Its Bets.'' *Mediaweek,* 15 March 1999.

———. ''New Acquisitions Make Citadel a Bigger Fortress.'' *Mediaweek,* 1 November 1999.

———. ''New Name, New Strategy in Store for Chancellor.'' *Mediaweek,* 24 May 1999.

———. ''The Next Wave.'' *Mediaweek,* 12 April 1999.

Bomann, Mieke H. ''Microradio Stations Pitch for Local Air Time.'' *Nation's Cities Weekly,* 6 September 1999.

''By Any Other Name, Heftel's Clout Grows.'' *Mediaweek,* 19 April 1999.

''Chancellor Puts Itself on the Block.'' *Billboard,* 6 February 1999.

Crotty, Cameron. ''The Revolution Will Be Netcast.'' *Macworld,* October 1996.

Ditingo, Vincent M. ''Radio.'' *Broadcasting & Cable,* 4 January 1999.

Freeman, Michael. ''CBS Projects Radio Station Sales after Viacom Deal.'' *Mediaweek,* 22 November 1999.

''Hammock Year Stints TV; Radio, Cable Warm Up.'' *Advertising Age,* 19 August 1996.

Herndon, John. ''Radio May Be the Next Domain for 'Superstation' Concept.'' *Austin American-Statesman,* 16 May 1996.

''Hot Properties.'' *Broadcasting & Cable,* 8 November 1999.

''Internet Audio Growing.'' *Television Digest,* 6 September 1999.

''It Was a Busy Week for Chancellor Media Corp.'' *Broadcasting & Cable,* 29 March 1999.

''LPFM Bill Introduced.'' *Television Digest,* 22 November 1999.

McConnell, Bill. ''First Step for Digital Radio.'' *Broadcasting & Cable,* 8 November 1999.

McCord, Julia. ''Religion on the Radio.'' *Omaha World Herald,* 20 May 1995.

''McDonald's of the Airwaves.'' *Economist (U.S.),* 9 October 1999.

''Online Radio Listening Doubles in 6 Months.'' *Content Factory,* 8 February 1999.

''Radio Deals, Revenue Booming.'' *Billboard,* 17 July 1999.

Rathbun, Elizabeth A. ''Citadel Builds 153-Station Radio Group.'' *Broadcasting & Cable,* 1 November 1999.

———. ''Clear Channel, Jacor Spin-Offs.'' *Broadcasting & Cable,* 15 February 1999.

———. ''A Radio Record.'' *Broadcasting & Cable,* 25 October 1999.

Taylor, Chuck. ''Federal Communications Commission.'' *Billboard,* 1 May 1999.

Taylor, Chuck, et al. ''Big Deal Rocks Radio Biz.'' *Billboard,* 16 October 1999.

———. "Radio Eyes Potential of New Media." *Billboard,* 18 September 1999.

Teinowitz, Ira. "Huge Merger Deals Inked in Radio, Telco." *Advertising Age,* 11 October 1999.

Teinowitz, Ira, and Michael Wilke. "Justice Dept. Sets 40 Percent as Guide on Radio Mergers." *Advertising Age,* 18 November 1996.

Weiskind, Ron. "Land Rush in the Radio Business." *Pittsburgh Post Gazette,* 25 May 1996.

SIC 4833

TELEVISION BROADCASTING STATIONS

This category covers establishments primarily broadcasting visual programs by television to the public, except cable and other pay television services (discussed in **SIC 4841: Cable and Other Pay Television Services**. Included in this industry are commercial, religious, educational, and other television stations. Also included are establishments primarily engaged in television broadcasting and that produce taped television program materials. Separate establishments primarily engaged in producing taped television program materials are classified in **SIC 7812: Motion Picture and Video Tape Production.**

NAICS CODE(S)

513120 (Television Broadcasting)

INDUSTRY SNAPSHOT

As the television broadcasting industry prepared to enter the twenty-first century, it faced a staggering number of challenges brought on by new competition, regulatory changes, and technological developments. Among the long-established networks—ABC, CBS, and NBC—the struggle for the top ratings position was intensified as two of the three acquired new owners. In 1995 ABC was purchased by Disney and CBS was purchased by Westinghouse. CBS subsequently merged with Viacom Inc. in 1999. The established networks also had to contend with Fox Broadcasting, which established itself in the 1990s as the fourth major broadcast network. Smaller "netlets," not yet meeting the Federal Communications Commission's definition of a network, were established by Paramount and Warner Brothers in 1995, and in 1997 Pax Communications launched a seventh network, PAX TV. Audiences for network broadcasters were being eroded by the increased reach of cable television, direct broadcast satellite operators, and even the rise of the Internet. New federal rules regarding ownership, programming content, and digital transmission continue to reshape the competitive landscape.

In this frenetic atmosphere, the once-bleak outlook of the networks in the early 1990s improved considerably. Although they continued to see a drop in audience share from the previous decade, the networks still held a strong position in prime-time ratings and saw increased advertising revenues. Beginning in 1995, the major networks gained new syndication revenues resulting from a relaxation of federal regulations. They also began creating their own cable networks, such as ESPN2 and MSNBC, using their considerable production resources. Furthermore, viewing audiences had made it clear that they did not want cable television service that did not include local broadcast network affiliates. Thus, the networks became increasingly concerned with production and programming, as they created a strong role for themselves in the growing system of television delivery and services. Writing for *Time,* Richard Zoglin commented, "If the network business is thriving, it is as a radically different sort of business. The line between distributors (the networks) and suppliers (outside producers) is being blurred. The networks, given the chance to produce and own their own shows, are acting more like studios, while the studios, afraid of being squeezed out, are trying to become networks."

ORGANIZATION AND STRUCTURE

The networks include in their stables both network-owned stations, which are often flagship stations in major media markets, and affiliated stations, independently owned stations that have contractual agreements with a network to broadcast its line of programming. *Variety* noted in December 1996 that the merger of Westinghouse with CBS "had no greater impact than on the station side, where both companies had established strong station businesses long before their teaming." At the same time, the acquisition of New World Communications by Fox Televisions Stations Group contributed to the radical changes that took place among station holdings. Fox vaulted from being a medium-sized group to being the largest operation by the end of 1998, with 23 stations (including channels in New York, Los Angeles, Chicago, and Philadelphia) and 35 percent penetration of U.S. television households. Paxson Communications ranked second with 55 stations reaching 31 percent of U.S. television homes. CBS followed with 14 network-owned stations (including stations in New York, Los Angeles, Chicago, and Philadelphia), reaching 31 percent of all American homes. NBC ranked fourth with 12 stations (including channels in New York, Chicago, Los Angeles, and Washington, DC) and 27 percent penetration. ABC, which had led the industry in 1992, ranked sixth with 10 network-owned stations (including stations in New York, Los Angeles, Chicago, and Philadelphia) and 24 percent penetration. Tribune Broadcasting was ranked fifth with 19 stations and 26.5 percent penetration.

The shake-up in station ownership started in May 1994, when Fox lured 12 stations affiliated with the other networks, including several in major markets, to its side. This affiliation switch, the biggest in television history, signaled a significant change in the balance of power between the networks and individual television stations. Dennis FitzSimons, president of Tribune Television, noted in *Business Week* that the deal highlighted "the importance of the distribution of programming—something that has been ignored recently. Furthermore, it gives the control back to the stations." Fox's success in these matters subsequently inspired the creation of additional netlets, the United Paramount Network (UPN) and the Warner Brothers (WB) Television Network, which launched in January 1995 with more than 80 percent national coverage.

Background and Development

The first television networks in America—NBC, ABC, CBS, and DuMont—were actually at first divisions of major radio networks or subsidiaries of television and radio manufacturers. Recognizing that centralized sales and distribution companies could be more profitable than scattered businesses, networks offered programs to individual stations that the affiliates could not afford to underwrite individually. Advertisers were fond of the network arrangement as well, for it enabled them to reach the entire nation with one commercial contract rather than dozens.

In the early years of television, the networks competed for programs, viewers, and advertisers in much the same manner as they do today. CBS was the recognized leader of the networks by any measure, while a number of other fledgling networks failed to crack the wall separating the leading triumvirate from the rest of the pack. The DuMont Network was the hardiest of the challengers; at one point DuMont had 80 stations under its banner and twice that many part-time affiliate subscribers. The company's financial fortunes fell, however, and ABC plucked a number of the network's chief attractions. By 1955 the company folded; the affiliates it owned became the Metromedia chain of independent stations.

With the outbreak of World War II, England and Germany, America's chief competitors in television technology, halted their research programs. By remaining at peace for two additional years before entering that conflict, by continuing government-sponsored television research even during the war, and by realizing the benefits of advances in electronics that resulted from the war effort, the United States took a major lead in this technology.

The Federal Communications Commission (FCC) then sought nationwide standards guaranteeing that all Americans could enjoy equal access to television and that no single television company, beginning with industry pioneer NBC, could achieve a monopoly. From this point on, much of the government's regulation of the limited available airwave space reflected the dichotomy described by Andrew F. Inglis in *Behind the Tube*: television "is regarded as an essential public service . . . to which every citizen is entitled. On the other hand, it has been regarded as a business that is regulated by the risks and rewards of the free market . . . to meet the needs and desires of the public."

Initially, the high costs of establishing a television station and the paucity of television sets meant that losses far outweighed profits. The popularity of the television increased dramatically in a very short time, however, and profits in the industry grew every year between 1951 and 1986, at which point growth was stalled, "partly as a result of competition from cable and VCRs and partly as a result of rapidly escalating program costs," Inglis noted. Network growth was also radically affected by the growing pay television industry that, by the early 1990s, established itself as a major rival. The big three broadcast networks had a 91 percent share of the prime-time television audience during the 1978-79 season, which dropped to 75 percent in 1986-87, and further to 61 percent in 1993-94. Part of an overall loss in audience share, however, was credited to the success of Fox Broadcasting, which drew viewers with its coverage of National Football League (NFL) games and strong children's shows.

Competition. In 1995 cable systems actually experienced a drop in subscribers and reached about 65 percent of television homes. Subscribers balked at price hikes that followed rate deregulation and some opted for satellite television services. In order to give broadcasters the chance to compete against pay television services and the netlets, the FCC agreed to gradually lift a ban on the syndication of network programming. Previously, networks were wholly dependent on advertisers for their revenue and had access to the airwaves only by permission of the government, while cable companies could charge subscribers as well as advertisers. In 1993 the networks gained rights to profit from reruns of their prime-time shows. This triumph for the networks affected the outside producers that made and financed much of the prime-time programming. Permitted to undertake a greater proportion of in-house production of prime-time programming, the networks could now negotiate for more financially rewarding deals with outside producers. By 1995 all such restrictions on network ownership of programming and on their right to syndicate programs were lifted.

Networks War with Nielsen. With an eye on advertising revenues, the networks found fault with Nielsen Media Research, the company that had long provided the broadcasters and advertisers with viewership ratings.

Changes in Nielsen methodology coincided with a reported decline in NFL football ratings, which caused both NBC and Fox to question their validity. CBS also complained about the accuracy of ratings for the *CBS Evening News.* The networks were concerned that Nielsen's new methods of selecting participants and an increased sample size were skewing the resulting ratings. In December 1996, Fox, CBS, NBC, and ABC joined ranks to criticize the research company by placing ads in media and advertising trade publications that denounced Nielsen's claims of reliability. As *Broadcasting and Cable* reported, the ads read ''Our confidence in Nielsen is DOWN'' and ''There is a growing disparity between local overnight ratings and national ratings.'' At the same time, the FCC was asked to investigate Nielsen's services.

Programming Content Debate. Another issue that the networks and the cable television industries faced was that of violent programming content. Under pressure from the federal government, CBS, ABC, NBC, and Fox all agreed to place parental advisory labels on violent programming—in order to avoid having a system imposed upon them. The group unveiled its age-based ratings system that was similar to that of the movie industry in December 1996, which labeled programs (with the exception of news) with one of six categories ranging from children's programming to shows for mature audiences: TV-Y, TV-Y7, TV-G, TV-PG, TV-14, and TVM. Viewers saw the appropriate icon in the upper left corner of the television screen at the beginning of the program and, if the program exceeded one hour in length, at the beginning of subsequent hours. On June 4, 1997, television executives met with representatives of the American Medical Association and the National PTA to review the ratings system. Several networks agreed to add V (for violence), S (for sexual content), and L (for language) to the age-based system.

At the same time, the federal government was proceeding with plans to give parents the ability to black out violent programming with a device called the V-chip. Mandated by the White House and Congress in 1996, television manufacturers were waiting for FCC specifications before adding the chip to new television models and designing V-chip converter boxes. By 1999 V-chips were being installed in new television sets, and the broadcast networks were implementing a system that would help parents select programs based on their content. Many of the major cable networks were also committed to designing their own rating system, although some refused to comply based on First Amendment issues.

CURRENT CONDITIONS

Myriad issues continued to unfold across the broad range of communications and information industries, including increased competition resulting in audience erosion, industry consolidation, changing rules and regulations, and new technologies. While cable companies were once the competitive focus of television broadcasters, in 1999 they were facing competitive challenges from the growing popularity of the Internet as well as from film studios, cable companies, telephone companies, computer companies, consumer-electronics companies, and publishers.

Industry Consolidation. ABC, CBS, and NBC took in more than 40 percent of the advertising revenue for the television broadcast industry, and they were expected to continue to dominate television advertising and viewership. In addition to providing programming, the networks also owned television stations. At the end of 1998 the top 25 owners controlled 36 percent of the nation's estimated 1,200 commercial stations. During 1999 several major deals were announced that would further concentrate the industry. Viacom announced a $35.9 billion buyout of CBS. NBC announced it would acquire a 32 percent interest in Paxson Communications, which owned or had a significant financial stake in 72 television stations, for $415 million. Following its announced merger with Viacom, CBS offered $2.15 billion to acquire Chris-Craft Industries, which operated 10 television stations (including stations in New York City and Los Angeles) and owned 50 percent of UPN.

In late 1999 current FCC regulations limited companies from owning stations that reached more than 35 percent of the national television audience. The industry, however, expected the ownership limit to be raised, sooner if not later. NBC, for example, could not acquire more than a one-third interest in Paxson under FCC ownership limits, because Paxson-owned stations were already reaching more than 34 percent of television viewers. NBC, however, had an option to acquire up to 49 percent of Paxson after February 1, 2002, if the FCC raised its current ownership limit.

Audience Erosion. The top four networks experienced declining viewerships from 1997 to 1999 and, for the future, faced the possibility of an explosion of competitors. The advent of digital television will boost channel capacity, making cable networks even more formidable competitors. For the 1999-2000 season, fewer than half of the new network shows were expected to achieve a double-digit share of audience, compared to 1997-98 when 76 per cent of the new network shows achieved a 10 or better audience share.

Among the major networks the battle for prime-time ratings continued to be very intense and very close. In the 1998-99 season CBS barely edged NBC for the top spot with a 9.0 household rating and 14.3 audience share, compared to NBC's 8.9 household rating and 15 percent audience share. ABC ranked third, followed by Fox, WB, and UPN.

Digital Television. At the close of 1996 the industry moved one step closer to digital transmission of television signals, as the FCC selected a DTV standard. The ''Grand Alliance Standard'' was adopted minus specifications regarding picture formats on which the broadcast, computer, and film industries could not agree. Video compression, sound delivery, and transmission of signals were part of the specifications. The commission still needed to determine how long broadcasters could use existing analog channels, how digital channels would be assigned, and if high-definition programming would be required. The FCC also mandated that all television stations be capable of transmitting high-definition television by the year 2006.

INDUSTRY LEADERS

The three leading broadcast networks—ABC, CBS, and NBC—were also the longest established. In terms of prime-time ratings, ABC was the leading network at the beginning of the 1990s, but by the 1998-99 season had been overtaken by both NBC and CBS, with CBS edging out NBC for the top spot in ratings for the season. In terms of station ownership, ABC owned 10 stations with a market penetration of 23.9 percent at the end of 1998, CBS owned 14 stations with 30.8 percent market penetration, and NBC owned 12 stations with 26.9 percent penetration. ABC was owned by the Walt Disney Co., NBC by General Electric, and CBS was acquired by Viacom in 1999. The combination of Viacom and CBS was expected to result in an $80 billion media giant, second in size only to Time Warner, Inc. among media companies. All three broadcast networks and their parent companies had ownership interests in cable television networks and other media properties.

The Fox Broadcasting Company was launched in 1986 and aggressively pursued young viewers, especially teenagers and adults aged 18-34. By the 1998-99 season Fox was established as the fourth broadcast network; it finished second to NBC in the key demographic of adults aged 18-49 and first among teenagers. Fox Broadcasting was part of the Fox Entertainment Group, which also included Twentieth Century Fox Film, Twentieth Century Fox Television (production), Twentieth Century Television Stations (station ownership), Fox News Channel, Fox Sports Networks, and the FX cable channel. Through Fox Television Stations, the company owned 22 television stations. Fox's parent company was Rupert Murdoch's News Corporation, which owned 81.4 percent of Fox Entertainment following an initial public offering that made 18.6 percent of the company's stock available to the public.

With an interest in 72 television stations, Paxson Communications owned the largest broadcast television station group. In 1999 NBC invested $415 million in Paxson and took a 32 percent ownership interest in the company. In 1997 Paxson launched a new network, PAX TV, which contributed to a net loss of $137.9 million in 1998 on revenues of $134.2 million in fiscal 1998. PAX TV reached approximately 74 percent of U.S. households in 1999 through 72 company-owned stations and 51 network affiliates.

In addition to its pending acquisition of CBS and ownership of several cable channels, Viacom was the parent company of the Paramount Stations Group. It owned 19 stations and was the sixth-largest television broadcasting group in the United States by reach, covering 25.6 percent of all U.S. viewing households. Viacom was also a co-owner of UPN, and all of the Paramount stations were UPN affiliates.

Other major television station owners included Tribune Broadcasting, a subsidiary of the Tribune Co., which owned and operated 18 major market television stations reaching more than 75 percent of U.S. television households. Toward the end of 1999 Tribune Broadcasting was in the process of acquiring Qwest Broadcasting, a minority-owned corporation that owned two WB affiliates in New Orleans and Atlanta.

At the end of 1999 Dallas-based A.H. Belo Corporation owned 26 television stations with a 14 percent market penetration. Chris-Craft Industries, which owned 10 stations, including one in New York City and one in Los Angeles, was being sought by CBS, which offered $2.15 billion to acquire the company in November 1999. Rounding out the top 10 station owners were Gannett Broadcasting, with 19 stations at the end of 1998, and USA Broadcasting with 13 stations.

FURTHER READING

Accas, Gene. ''Divining Prime Time 1999-2000.'' *Broadcasting & Cable,* 16 August 1999.

Auletta, Ken. ''Marriage, No Honeymoon.'' *New Yorker,* 29 July 1996.

Boliek, Brooks. ''Paxson-NBC Heats Up Ownership Debate.'' *Back Stage,* 24 September 1999.

Broadcasting & Cable Yearbook 1999. New Providence, NJ: R.R. Bowker, 1999.

Flint, Joe. ''Fox Clan Grows.'' *Variety,* 16-22 December 1996.

Fox Entertainment Group. ''Overview and Chairman's Review.'' Available from http://www.corporate-ir.net/ireye/ir_site.zhtml?ticker=fox&script=2100&layout=6.

Freeman, Michael. ''Tribune Agrees to Buyout of the Rest of Qwest.'' *Mediaweek,* 15 November 1999.

Gunther, Marc, and Henry Goldblatt. ''Turnaround Time for CBS.'' *Fortune,* 19 August 1996.

Hofmeister, Sallie. "Westinghouse/CBS to Launch First Cable Channel." *Los Angeles Times,* 21 August 1996.

Knestout, Brian P. "Viacom and CBS Make it a Blockbuster Night." *Kiplinger's Personal Finance Magazine,* November 1999.

Lesly, Elizabeth. "Six Months after Westinghouse Took Over, the Network May Be Waking Up." *Business Week,* 3 June 1996.

Levin, Gary. "Eye Web Marriage Survives First Year." *Variety,* 16-22 December 1996.

McClellan, Steve. "CBS Bids $2 Billion for Chris-Craft." *Broadcasting & Cable,* 8 November 1999.

———. "Combined Nets Take Aim at Nielsen." *Broadcasting & Cable,* 30 December 1996.

———. "War at NBC, ABC at Peace." *Broadcasting & Cable,* 5 July 1999.

McConnell, Chris. "Broadcasters Arm for ATV Fight." *Broadcasting & Cable,* 21 October 1996.

———. "DTV Standard: It's Official." *Broadcasting & Cable,* 30 December 1996.

"NBC-Paxson $415-Million Deal Designed to Avoid FCC." *Television Digest,* 20 September 1999.

Paxson Communications. "NBC Makes Strategic Investment in Paxson Communications," 16 September 1999. Available from http://www.paxson.com/press/default2.htm.

———. "Paxson Reports Fourth Quarter and Year End 1998 Results." Available from http://www.paxson.com/financenews/Q4_1998_operating_results.htm.

Rice, Lynette, and Rich Brown. "Networks Rolling out TV Ratings." *Broadcasting & Cable,* 30 December 1996.

Schlosser, Joe. "Disney Closes TV Ranks." *Broadcasting & Cable,* 12 July 1999.

———. "Reinventing ABC." *Broadcasting & Cable,* 30 August 1999.

Schmuckler, Eric. "Slow Start for UPN, WB." *Mediaweek,* 27 February 1995.

Schneider, Michael. "Nielsen, Networks Ratings War Mounts." *Electronic Media,* 16 December 1996.

Silver, Marc. "Would You Care for a V or an S with Your PG?" *U.S. News & World Report,* 16 June 1997, 59.

Standard & Poor's Industry Surveys: Broadcasting & Cable, New York: Standard & Poor's, 1999.

Torpey-Kemph, Anne. "Belo Wraps Phoenix Buys." *Mediaweek,* 8 November 1999.

———. "Cable Nets OK V-Chip Ratings System." *Mediaweek,* 26 July 1999.

Tribune Company. "Company Overview." Available from http://www.tribune.com/about/index.htm.

Viacom Inc. "Television." Available from http://www.viacom.com/unitbyseg.tin?sBusSegmentNickname=tv.

Zoglin, Richard. "Network Crazy." *Time,* 16 January 1995.

SIC 4841

CABLE AND OTHER PAY TELEVISION SERVICES

This industry covers establishments primarily engaged in the dissemination of visual and textual television programs, on a subscription or fee basis. Included in this industry are establishments which are primarily engaged in cable casting and which also produce taped program materials. Separate establishments primarily engaged in producing taped television or motion picture program materials are classified in **SIC 7812: Motion Picture and Video Tape Production.**

NAICS Code(s)

513210 (Cable Networks)

513220 (Cable and Other Program Distribution)

Industry Snapshot

The cable television industry was developed in the United States in the late 1940s to serve small communities unable to receive conventional television signals due to difficult terrain or physical distance from television stations. Cable also provided improved television reception to remote areas. The original systems were centered around a collective antenna for regions with poor or nonexistent reception. Cable systems located their antennas in areas where reception was good, picked up broadcast signals and then relayed them by cable to subscribers for a fee. In 1950 cable systems operated in only 70 communities and served 14,000 subscribers.

By 1995 there were approximately 11,800 cable systems with 62 million subscribers (65.3 percent of all television households) in the United States. The average cable system provided 30 or more channels as well as other services such as custom programming and pay-per-view options. The average monthly fee for a cable subscription was $23.00.

By 1999 the number of cable subscribers had risen modestly to 67 or 68 million. However, through digital compression cable operators were able to offer more than 100 channels. Between 1995 and 1999 cable fees had risen faster than the rate of inflation. Even though there are thousands of cable operators, the industry has been dominated by the top 25 companies, which in 1999 accounted for more than 90 percent of U.S. subscribers. Following passage of the Telecommunications Act of 1996, which removed several regulations regarding ownership, the industry experienced increased merger and acquisition activity that is likely to continue. This activity resulted in further consolidation within the cable industry.

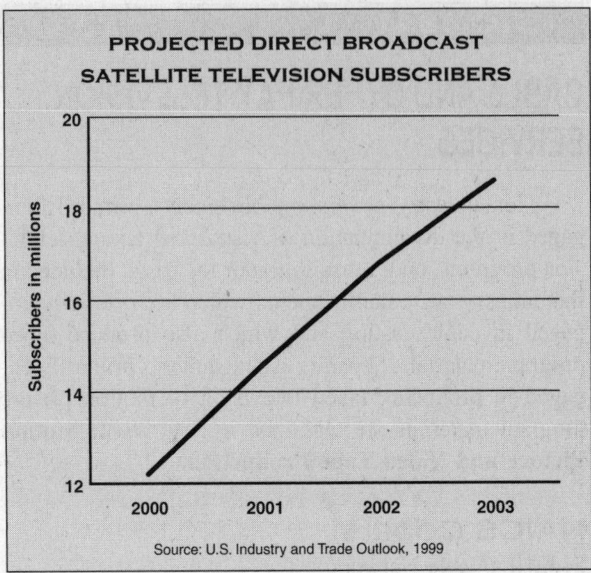

During the late 1990s, however, satellite television services made their presence felt in the pay television industry by providing an alternative to increasingly expensive cable service. Providers dramatically reduced set-up costs by cutting satellite dish prices to $200 and, after this purchase and installation fees, gave viewers many more channels for a monthly fee that rivaled cable rates. The biggest drawback to satellite television was its inability to carry local broadcast channels, but this limitation was removed by federal legislation toward the end of 1999. Satellite services claimed only 4 percent of the market in 1996. The fastest growing segment of the satellite service industry was direct broadcast satellite (DBS), which grew from 2.3 million subscribers in 1995 to 8.2 million subscribers in 1998. The number of DBS subscribers was projected to double by 2002.

ORGANIZATION AND STRUCTURE

Traditional underground cable lines are just one of several methods used to transmit video signals from the broadcaster to the home. Pay television companies must decide which transmission method or combination of methods is the most effective in serving their customers. Overall, there are four basic ways to broadcast a video signal:

- Terrestrial, a transmission tower on the ground sends a picture directly to a television aerial. This is easy to install but reception is often poor and only a few channels can be carried. This is the method traditionally used to broadcast network channels.
- Coaxial or Fiber-Optic Cable, are TV signals that travel through an underground cable. Installation is time-consuming and expensive. Cable is used primarily in densely populated urban areas.
- Microwave, multichannel, a multi point distribution system (MMDS) carries signals from a television studio to a microwave transmitter, which then relays them to rooftop receivers on apartment blocks. These receivers are relatively small dishes that are easy to install and maintain. Microwave transmission is a low cost alternative to cabling and is feasible in areas where there are large distances between transmitting stations and subscribers (e.g. South America).
- Satellite, a broadcaster uplinks a signal to a transponder on a satellite, which re-transmits either to home dishes or to a satellite master dish (SMATV) located on the roof of a high-rise block. Satellite transmission is common in remote rural areas. Subscribers pay hook-up and access fees to the satellite owners.

Cable television operators rely primarily on four revenue streams; advertising, installation services, basic cable subscriptions, and premium channel subscriptions. The industry posted revenues of $37 billion in 1997, of which $18.4 billion were basic subscription revenues and $7.5 million were advertising revenues. Cable operators were expected to enjoy a trend of increasing subscription and advertising revenues for the foreseeable future.

Cable Regulation. The domestic cable industry is highly regulated by the U.S. government. Regulations affect cable system ownership, rate structures, channel limits, types of programming, and permission to access programming. This involvement is due to the high fixed investment in installation; the industry lends itself to being a natural monopoly with limited competition; and the sensitive nature and importance to national security of communications technology.

Ownership in the cable television industry is fragmented because of the regulatory environment in which companies compete. The Federal Communications Commission (FCC), the government agency empowered to regulate cable TV companies, has given municipalities the authority to grant cable licensing contracts on a geographic basis. Municipalities generally bid out these contracts and then grant exclusive franchise rights to provide service in a given area in return for a commission of three to five percent of revenues.

In 1986 the FCC decided to allow cable companies to freely set monthly service rates and rate increases in any market that already provided at least three over-the-air broadcast signals to nonsubscribers. Prior to 1986, cable companies were limited to a mandated five percent cap on annual rate increases. Re-regulation was proposed in 1992 because various groups claimed that the cable industry abused its privilege to set monthly rates by gouging consumers. Congress, under pressure from consumer groups, haggled with President George Bush, who was against re-regulation. After a failed attempt by the FCC to control the situation by redefining some rules, Congress overrode the president's veto and passed the controversial Cable Television Consumer Protection and Competition Act of 1992. This bill reversed cable companies' freedom to set rates. However, local governments were given the power to regulate rates for basic cable programming in their areas.

The act also contained programming regulations. Programming could no longer be denied to competitors and it must be offered at "fair terms." The bill required cable companies to pay royalties to over-the-air broadcasters. Networks have complained for years that cable companies were in essence charging subscribers for network developed programming that was free to them and pocketing a subscriber fee. One other provision of this bill limited the size of multiple system operators and the number of channels a system could devote to programming in which it had an interest.

New technologies have also prompted cable companies to team with telecommunication companies in order to provide interactive services to subscribers. In August 1992 the FCC permitted Tele-Communications Inc. (TCI) and Cox Enterprises to buy Teleport Communications Group, a company that connects long distance carriers and provides large corporations with private fiber-optic communications networks. This ruling opened the door by allowing cable companies to enter the telecommunications business and vice versa.

Telephone companies were slow to react to this decision, primarily due to regulatory concerns. Not until February 1993, when Southwestern Bell Corp. announced that it agreed to purchase two cable TV systems in the Washington, D.C. area, did a telephone company move into traditional cable markets. This action led other telephone companies to search for cable acquisitions.

A regulation implemented in June 1992 allowed the television networks to buy local cable TV systems. However, a TV network's cable holdings could not exceed 10 percent of the nation's homes that are passed by cable wire or 50 percent of the households in a single market. In addition, a 1984 ruling stated that a company cannot own a TV station and a cable system in the same market. The intended effect of these rulings was to speed up the unraveling of traditional network and affiliate relationships. The resulting alliances between cable and over-the-air industries would impact the competitive environment among entertainment providers.

The Telecommunications Act of 1996 also did much to deregulate cable television, with the hope of further stimulating competition in the television industry. The act served to revise 62 years of telecommunications law and eliminated some of features of the 1992 Cable Act that were seen as punitive by the industry. Most notably, fees for upper service tiers would be deregulated on March 31, 1999 in large cable systems, while such services were deregulated immediately in smaller franchises. The bill also eliminated the 1984 restriction that prevented individual companies from zoffering cable and phone services to the same market.

Government regulations have a significant impact on the ways in which cable companies compete. In the mature cable TV market, revenue growth comes primarily from rate increases. Government regulations will impact existing companies by limiting revenue growth from this source. In the long run, the industry is expected to benefit from being pushed to develop other revenue resources, such as cable modems and telecommunication services. The regulatory environment is constantly changing—and there are gains that will accrue to the companies best able to influence and adjust to new regulatory initiatives.

CURRENT CONDITIONS

The cable television industry has proved to be very resilient. The industry has successfully responded to recession, regulation and deregulation, and the entry of meaningful video service competitors such as telephone companies, direct broadcast satellite systems (DBS), and computer firms. The future appears to hold more of the same. The introduction of new technologies and system upgrades will continue to make it possible for cable firms to vastly expand channel capacity and services. The cable companies that are leading the way in these developments are expected to reap the lion's share of success. The keys to competitive advantage in the cable industry today are investment in fiber-optics, digital compression, and research and development into new services; ability to influence and/or respond quickly to changing regulatory elements; programming capabilities; visionary management; and economies of scale. At the same time, however, satellite television providers made impressive progress in building their subscriber base, and several new players began providing satellite services.

Investment in Fiber-Optics and Digital Compression. Investment in fiber-optic technology and digital compression is allowing cable providers to expand channel capacity, offer interactive services, and carry voice, data, and video signals simultaneously on a single line. Each of these areas represents a significant opportunity to increase revenue. Both technologies, however, require an enormous investment for cable companies. Installation of fiber-optic cable and the introduction of digital boxes in cable homes will be a gradual process.

Fiber-optic cabling improves signal quality and range. Companies that invest in fiber-optics to improve transmission quality should have an advantage in the bidding process used to award franchise rights for geographic areas. The greater the number of franchise rights, the greater the number of subscribers, and the greater the amount of total revenue accruing to a company. Four of the largest players in the industry, TCI, Time Warner, Continental Cablevision Inc., and Cablevision Systems Corp.) have invested heavily in this strategy. TCI invested $2 billion in the mid-1990s, a clear indication that the industry views investment in fiber-optics as a critical component in ensuring long-term financial success.

Expanded channel capacity allows cable providers to increase revenue by offering additional programming and pay-per-view channels. The creation of new cable networks was straining the existing cable carriage space in 1997, as CBS, A&E (Arts and Entertainment), Rainbow Programming, and BET (Black Entertainment Television) all prepared to start major cable networks. The need to expand channel capacity was underscored by the fact that many new networks were finding their first home on satellite television, where a greater number of channels are offered.

Expanded channel capacity also allows cable companies to offer advertisers more options. Traditionally the broadcast networks have demanded the highest advertising dollars and yet devoted less on-air time to commercials than cable networks. During the mid-1990s, however, cable advertising revenues increased, and the cable networks began increasing the minutes per hour devoted to advertising. Between 1990 and 1998 advertisers increased their spending on cable television from $1.1 billion to $6.7 billion.

Studies have shown that the total time Americans spend viewing television is rising, while the audience share of the three major networks continues to decline. *Advertising Outlook in Industry Surveys* noted that, ''For the most part, FOX and advertiser-supported cable networks gained the viewers that the networks lost.'' This statement suggests that viewers are spending a larger proportion of their viewing time watching cable channels as opposed to network programming. This increased viewership should also serve to position cable companies to gain a large percentage of increasing advertising dollars.

Ability to Influence and Respond to Regulation. Because regulations change so frequently, the ability to influence and leverage new regulations becomes a crucial success factor. If a company can dictate how a regulation is written or interpreted in order to exploit an internal core competency, then they will be best positioned to profit from the change. Conversely, cable companies can be negatively impacted by regulations that restrict their ability to expand service areas, affect rate structures, and introduce new products.

During the late 1990s, cable operators and telephone companies entering the television business were not only adjusting to the new FCC guidelines set by the Telecommunications Act of 1996, they also faced the demands of local governments—who were trying to maintain local control of rates and public rights-of-way. An April 1996 ruling eliminated rate regulation in areas where a cable company had non-DBS competition. Local governments complained that better proof of the new competition's effectiveness was needed in each case before rate deregulation was allowed. Squabbles of use of public rights-of-way also cropped up, as in the case where the city of Troy, Michigan required TCI to obtain a telecommunications franchise when it wanted to create a new system. Such arguments prompted cable and telephone companies to join in asking the FCC to rein in local regulators.

Programming Capabilities. A *MediaWeek* poll revealed that 65 percent of cable TV subscribers would cancel their subscriptions if broadcast signals were dropped. The poll suggests that network-affiliated TV stations have considerable leverage in their retransmission consent fee negotiations with cable providers. But, ironically, the networks are waiving retransmission consent fees in exchange for getting the cable operators to air network-owned cable programs. The potential for revenue growth in the current cable industry is primarily through controlling programming. Offering more options to the customer results in increased advertising income and subscription revenue. This increased cash flow assists in the development of new and improved services, further driving the company's revenue growth.

Economies of Scale. Size is necessary to achieve economies of scale and to provide cash flow for investments into research and development, development of new programming and markets, and acquisitions. Large companies can gain economies of scale in purchasing equipment, satellite time, and programming. In addition, by being large enough to be able to purchase its own satellite, a cable company gains significant control over costs and programming. Through ownership of large libraries of information (music, video, etc.), the cable company not only controls costs, but also drives other competitors through access to that programming. Finally, programming consists mainly of large fixed costs; with a large cable company, this fixed cost is spread over a larger base, resulting in increased profits. This is particularly important for development of fiber-optics.

Satellite and Telephone Company Competition. Customer dissatisfaction and rising cable costs have served to feed the growing satellite television industry with new viewers. At the beginning of 1999 direct broadcast satellite (DBS) had about 10.5 million subscribers compared to cable's 67 million, but it was growing by 26 percent a year in spite of not being able to provide local broadcast channels. However, at the end of 1999 that roadblock was removed when the U.S. Congress passed legislation that would allow DBS to offer local channels, thus giving satellite subscribers access to broadcast network programming.

Satellite television also underwent major changes among its key players in the late 1990s. Primestar, the second largest DBS provider with 2.3 million subscribers, was sold in January 1999 by its cable company owners to DirectTV, the industry leader. However, the sale did not guarantee DirectTV would pick up all of Primestar subscribers, thus leaving the door open to EchoStar, which moved up from third to second in the industry and was regarded as the fastest growing DBS company. EchoStar had recently picked up the assets from Rupert Murdoch's failed satellite venture. DirectTV was owned by Hughes Electronics, which in turn was owned by General Motors. In December 1998 DirectTV acquired United States Satellite Broadcasting, which provided top-of-the-line premium services that customers could order on top of the 185 channels offered by DirectTv. As of 1999 neither DirectTV nor EchoStar were profitable, and EchoStar was carrying nearly $2 billion in debt.

Phone companies have been investing in and upgrading phone lines to fiber optics for sometime—with the intention of transmitting video signals. Companies such as Tele-Communications, Inc., U.S. West, Bell South, Time Warner, Microsoft, IBM, Sony Corp., Intel, and Silicon Graphics are trying to position themselves as major providers of service and support in this emerging playing field. Even utilities are laying fiber-optic cable when they install new lines in order to position themselves as water, gas, electric, voice, data, and video providers.

By 1996, however, it was clear that the movement into television programming and delivery services had slowed. One telephone group, made up of Bell Atlantic Corp., NYNEX Corp., and Pacific Telesis Group, made news when it decided to sell Tele-TV, a television programming business. The companies had committed to pooling $300 million dollars in the joint venture. At the time, opportunities in long distance telephone service and Internet access appeared to have greater potential rewards. One area where potential for telephone company participation looked more promising was in markets with under 50,000 people. These markets were deregulated in 1996 to allow cable and telephone companies to enter each other's service area.

Industry Consolidation. The entry of AT&T into the cable industry, as well as major mergers and acquisitions following passage of the Telecommunications Act of 1996 have resulted in more subscribers for the top cable operators. Size and clout were becoming more significant factors, with new technologies such as wireless, fiber-optics, and digital compression requiring large investments. By 1999 the top 10 cable operators accounted for 71 percent of all U.S. cable subscribers, compared to 45 percent in 1994. In mid-1999 the top five cable operators (AT&T, Time Warner, Comcast, Charter, and Cox) controlled nearly 68 percent of all U.S. cable subscribers. However, the industry leader board was likely to continue to change, with merger and acquisition activity continuing to show strength.

INDUSTRY LEADERS

The names of the industry leaders changed dramatically in 1998 and 1999, and industry rankings are likely to change frequently as competitors seek to add more subscribers through mergers and acquisitions. Two new top 10 cable operators emerged in 1998-99: AT&T, ranked number one with 16.2 million cable homes, and Charter Communications, owned by Microsoft cofounder Paul Allen. AT&T acquired the largest cable operator, Tele-communications Inc. (TCI), in mid-1998 for approximately $50 billion in stock. Then AT&T outbid Comcast Corporation to purchase fifth-ranked cable giant, MediaOne Group Inc. for $62 billion. The purchase would add MediaOne's 4.9 million subscribers as well as an interest in Time Warner's 11.2 million subscribers (because of MediaOne's 25.6 percent ownership interest in Time Warner Entertainment). With an interest in 32.1 million subscribers, though, AT&T was running up against the FCC's rule limiting cable operators to owning systems that served 30 percent of cable subscribers. In October 1999 the FCC revised its ownership limit, allowing cable operators to serve 30 percent of all video subscribers, including satellite subscribers as well as cable subscribers. According to *Broadcasting & Cable,* that would raise the effective limit to about 24.6 million of all 67 million cable homes in the United States.

Charter Communications is a relative newcomer to the cable industry. Founded in 1993 in St. Louis by Harold Wood, Barry Babcock, and Jerry Kent—all former executives of Cencom Cable Associates—Charter Communications was the tenth-ranked cable operator in 1998 when it was acquired by Microsoft cofounder Paul Allen for $4.5 billion. Earlier in the year Allen had acquired Marcus Cable for $2.8 billion. Marcus and Charter each had about 1.2 million subscribers at the time, giving Allen control of 2.4 million subscribers and the seventh-largest MSO. Additional acquisitions gave Charter a customer base of 6.2 million in 40 states, making it the fourth-largest cable operator in 1999.

In 1999 Gannett Co. exited the cable industry by selling its cable subsidiary, Cablevision, for $2.7 billion to Cox Communications. Cablevision served about 522,000 subscribers in Kansas, Oklahoma, and North

Carolina. Following a string of acquisitions for Cox, the addition of Cablevision's subscribers gave Cox a base of 6 million subscribers, putting it at the number five position behind industry leaders AT&T and Time Warner, number three Comcast, and number four Charter Communications.

Time-Warner Cable. Time Warner is the world's largest media and entertainment company. Time Warner Cable (TWC) is one of the many media/entertainment subsidiaries that deal with businesses ranging from Time, Inc. (publishing) to Warner Bros. Records (music) to HBO (programming). The parent company was made even bigger—worth some $20 billion by its acquisition of Turner Broadcasting System Inc. In 1999 TWC was the second largest cable operator in the United States, with more than 13 million subscribers. TWC has aggressively sought multiple cable systems within the same geographic locations. Known as "clustering." this process achieves superb operating efficiencies and economies of scale. The strategy has resulted in TWC becoming the best clustered cable operator, with 86 percent of its customers clustered in systems of 100,000 subscribers or more.

Known as the industry leader in fiber-optic cable installation and interactivity, TWC delivered the world's first interactive cable TV service to New York in 1991. The 150-channel system, called Quantum, provides locally targeted programming as well as 57 pay-per-view channels. As the industry leader in the percentage of subscribers in fiber-optic addressable systems (81 percent), Time Warner is well-poised to progressively bring its customers into the mainstream of advancing cable technologies. In 1999 the company began an aggressive national roll out of the first phase of its new digital cable service, and by the end of the year expected to have upgraded 85 percent of its cable plant.

Comcast Corporation. With 4.5 million customers in 21 states, Comcast Cable held on to its third place among cable operators in 1999. Like Time Warner Cable, Comcast Cable clustered its subscribers, with 80 percent of its customers located in 10 large geographic clusters and each cluster serving more than 100,000 customers. In November 1999 Comcast acquired Philadelphia-based cable operator Lenfest Communications for $5.3 billion. The acquisition increased Comcast's subscriber base by 20 percent to 7.2 million subscribers.

Direct Broadcast Satellite Companies. The two leading DBS companies at the end of 1999 were DirectTV Inc. and EchoStar Communications Corporation. After acquiring Primestar, DirectTV had 7.8 million customers at the end of 1999. DirectTV was a unit of Hughes Electronics Corporation, which provided digital television entertainment and satellite and wireless systems and services. Hughes Electronics in turn was a unit of General Motors Corporation.

Headquartered in Littleton, Colorado, EchoStar Communications Corp. was founded in 1980 and filed for a DBS license in 1987. It established EchoStar Satellite Corporation to build, launch, and operate DBS satellites, and in 1992 was given a DBS orbital slot. In 1995 the company established the DISH (Digital Sky Highway) Network and launched its first DBS satellite. By 1999 EchoStar was considered the fastest growing DBS company, and in October 1999 it added its three millionth customer.

AMERICA AND THE WORLD

The cable industry is highly regulated, not only in the United States, but also overseas. As a result, high entry barriers exist causing companies to compete on a national basis. U.S. companies serve U.S. subscribers, European companies serve European subscribers, etc. Because the U.S. market is saturated, American companies are looking to expand overseas in an effort to sustain growth. Asia, Latin America, and Europe have been identified as areas with high potential. The strategies companies are pursuing to break into overseas markets include joint ventures and alliances.

The major obstacles companies must overcome to become global are government regulation and lack of infrastructure. In Asia, for example, most governments still maintain tight control over the industry, which limits a foreign national company's ability to compete. Often, they restrict the screen time allotted to foreign programs and limit transponder hours. Cultural and industrial issues influence government regulation. Japan and Malaysia worry that foreign programming could upset the country's social harmony, while local monopolies exert their influence to prevent competition.

However, market demands are forcing Asian governments to either loosen the grip of state broadcasting monopolies or set up new channels to meet the demands of viewers for higher quality programs. Hong Kong is leading the change in Asia, with Singapore, South Korea, and Taiwan following.

Regulations in Europe are easing slightly. The presence of the European Union has allowed for the development of some unified standards. However, European countries are reluctant to allow U.S. companies to expand into their markets due to cultural differences.

Lack of capacity is also a major factor limiting U.S. companies' entrance into foreign markets. There is a need to develop a cable infrastructure in growth regions. For example, there are simply not enough satellite transponders servicing overseas locations. In the United States, there is one transponder for every 300,000 people.

In Europe, the ratio is one per one million people, while in Asia it is one per six million people. Using the existing system can be costly to a broadcaster. The broadcaster can expect to spend $1 to 1.5 million American dollars per year to rent a transponder. In addition, there are usually local government license fees, plus fees to landlords for the use of high-rise apartments.

In addition, Latin America suffers not only from a severely lacking cable infrastructure, but also a lack of financial resources. This has led regional cable companies to rely on MMDS as the transmitting method. MMDS, while still regarded as a start-up technology, has proven to be a low-cost, reliable method of delivering pay television, relative to cable and satellite broadcasting.

The cable industry will never be more than a multi domestic industry so long as regulation denies ownership of all or a majority share of a local cable company by a foreign organization. The opportunities for growth in the emerging markets will be enjoyed by local companies, but the opportunities for cross-border operations still exist. A lack of technology and programming expertise provides opportunities for U.S. companies to partner with the regional operators to gain footholds in overseas markets, preempting European and Asian providers. However, as these new markets grow, they will develop the programming to cater to local preferences and culture. To stay competitive, U.S. companies will have to adapt and develop programs for these new markets, instead of just offering dubbed-over U.S. programming.

RESEARCH AND TECHNOLOGY

Cable television companies are most anxious to implement system upgrades using digital compression and fiber-optic cable. They also hope to answer consumer demands for fast access to the Internet by providing high-speed cable modems.

Although there have been a number of advances in cable technology, the most promising is digital compression. Compression technologies enable broadcasters to squeeze several channels of video programming onto a single existing channel in much the same way as compression software conserves storage space on a computer. Compression converts the analog signals, currently used in broadcasting, to digital signals. This allows 10 channels to be transmitted along the same bandwidth of coaxial cable that would normally be capable of handling a single uncompressed signal. Compression would allow cable companies to offer more than 500 channels, 10 times the number available today.

Even with the advent of compression technology, coaxial cable does have its limitations. Coaxial cable uses radio waves to transmit video images. Its drawbacks include a limitation on the number of signals that can be transmitted simultaneously and the distance that such signals can travel before they begin to degrade. Its advantage is that it is already installed in millions of homes across the country. Fiber-optic cable, on the other hand, uses light to transmit video images. It is superior to coaxial cable in terms of bandwidth or signal capacity, transmission speed, signal distance, and clarity. However, fiber-optic cable has a daunting limitation—it is prohibitively expensive.

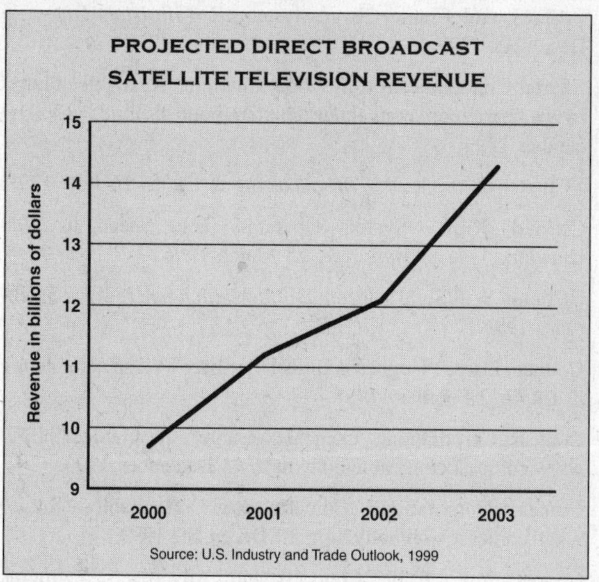

Fiber-optics technology has allowed companies to develop "video-on-demand." an interactive service that may be the wave of the future. It allows customers to order the transmission of movies and special events by using a hybrid television/computer terminal and enables them to view these programs at their leisure. These systems are expected to be able to handle high-definition television and provide links to computers, facsimile machines, and personal communications networks. The one drawback to the video-on-demand concept is that the subscriber cannot pause, rewind, or otherwise fiddle with the program, capabilities taken for granted when using a VCR.

The development of cable modems has allowed cable companies to enter the Internet access business. At a time when established providers such as CompuServe and America Online are struggling to deal with quickly expanding numbers of Internet users, cable operators hope to use the superior speed of cable modems to lure away their customers. Cable modems take advantage of the industry's use of coaxial cable, which can provide transmission speeds up to 400 times faster than traditional phone lines.

FURTHER READING

"Allen Buys More Cable Systems." *Television Digest,* 3 August 1998.

''AT&T and Charter Swap Systems.'' *Television Digest,* 6 December 1999.

Charter Communications. ''About Charter.'' Available at http://www.chartercom.com/about_charter/about_us.html, 13 December 1999.

''Charter on the Rise.'' *Broadcasting & Cable,* 16 June 1997.

Cleland, Kim. ''System Operators Tout Speed to Web Crawlers.'' *Advertising Age,* 25 March 1996.

''Clinton Will Sign Telecom Bill.'' *Multichannel News,* 5 February 1996.

Colman, Price. ''Hughes is Bullish on DirecTV.'' *Broadcasting & Cable,* 2 February 1998.

Comcast Corporation. ''Comcast—Cable.'' Available at http://www.comcast.com/cable/body.htm, 13 December 1999.

Comcast Corporation. ''Comcast Corp.'' Available at http://www.comcast.com/body.htm, 13 December 1999.

Cooper, Jim. ''Cable Connects with Advertisers.'' *Adweek Eastern Edition,* 20 September 1999.

Cooper, Jim. ''Comcast.'' *Mediaweek,* 22 November 1999.

''Cox Buys Multimedia.'' *Television Digest,* 2 August 1999.

DirectTV. ''DirectTV Applauds Passage of Satellite Home Viewer Act.'' company press release, 19 November 1999, at http://www.directv.com/press/pressdel/o,1112,244,00.html

EchoStar Communications Corp. ''A History and Profile of DISH Network and Echostar Communications Corporation.'' Available at http://www.dishnetwork.com/profile/history.htm

Grone, Jack. ''Cencom Chiefs Form New Firm.'' *St. Louis Business Journal,* 7 December 1992.

Haddad, Charles. ''Assembling a $20 Billion Company.'' *Atlanta Constitution,* 13 September 1996.

Halonen, Doug. ''Baby Bells' Video Fever Cools Down.'' *Electronic Media,* 16 December 1996.

Healey, Jon. ''Lawmakers Clear Way for Digital Satellite Television Service to Expand.'' *Knight-Ridder/Tribune Business News,* 2 December 1999.

Hendrickson, Paula. ''Telco Reform Liberates Small-Market Cable Biz.'' *Advertising Age,* 25 March 1996.

Higgins, John M. ''Allen's Big Buy Not His Last.'' *Broadcasting & Cable,* 3 August 1998.

Hofmeister, Sallie. ''Satellites Face Woes as They Tug at Cable.'' *Los Angeles Times,* 12 November 1996.

Jessell, Harry A. ''Cable's Performance Gap.'' *Broadcasting & Cable,* 15 July 1996.

Lieberman, David. ''Comcast, Cox Join TCI Online.'' *USA Today,* 6 June 1996.

———. ''Upgrade Costs Frighten Some Firms Off Fast Track.'' *USA Today,* 5 February 1997.

McConnell, Bill. ''AT&T Getting Its Way.'' *Broadcasting & Cable,* 11 October 1999.

McConnell, Chris. ''Tug-of-War Over Cable Plans.'' *Broadcasting & Cable,* 10 June 1996.

———. ''Cable and Phone Companies Take on Local Regulators.'' *Broadcasting & Cable,* 30 December 1996.

McConville, Jim. ''DBS Competition Takes Off.'' *Broadcasting & Cable,* 16 September 1996.

———. ''New Cable Networks Scramble for Space.'' *Broadcasting & Cable,* 30 December 1996.

Oslund, John J., and Ann Merrill. ''US West Deal a Defining Point in Digital Age.'' *Minneapolis Star Tribune,* 28 February 1996.

''Satellite Broadcasting Galloping.'' *The Economist (US),* 30 January 1999.

Standard & Poor's Industry Surveys: Broadcasting & Cable. New York: Standard & Poor's Corporation, 8 July 1999.

Stern, Christopher. ''Birds to Sing Local Songs in 14 Cities.'' *Variety,* 29 November 1999.

Time Warner Inc. ''Broadband Wagon.'' New York, 1997.

———. ''Time Warner Cable.'' Available at http://www.pathfinder.com/corp/about/cablesys/twcable/index.html, 13 December 1999.

SIC 4899

COMMUNICATIONS SERVICES, NOT ELSEWHERE CLASSIFIED

This category covers establishments primarily engaged in furnishing communications services, not elsewhere classified. Examples of such services include radar station operation, radio broadcasting operated by taxicab companies, satellite earth stations, satellite or missile tracking stations operated on a contract basis, and tracking missiles by telemetry and photography on a contract basis. Establishments primarily engaged in providing online information services on a contract or fee basis are classified in **SIC 7375: Information Retrieval Services.**

NAICS Code(s)

513322 (Cellular and Other Wireless Telecommunications)

513340 (Satellite Telecommunications)

513390 (Other Telecommunications)

Industry Snapshot

Because of an increased interest in communications technologies and information transmission, satellite systems have been driving growth and commanding high visibility in **SIC 4899: Communications Services, Not Elsewhere Classified.** Continued expansion of this industry was anticipated, in response to increased demand for services to small mobile satellite terminals and telephones, the need for more television relay services, expansion of the Internet, and the growth of direct television broadcasting via high-powered satellites. In addition to many established weather, communications, and remote-sensing satellites, a few multiple-satellite systems were in operation in 1999, and many more were planned.

ORGANIZATION AND STRUCTURE

Commercial space launches, satellite communications goods and services, and satellite remote sensing are the major segments of this industry and provide the bulk of industry's revenue. Voice and data communications, mobile services, vehicle tracking and navigation, and broadband data transmission for the Internet are emerging segments. Beginning with its inception in the 1960s, this industry has been the realm of government agencies, the military, and international consortia. In the last decade, however, new technologies and increased privatization have resulted in new applications for satellite services and earth stations.

Communications Satellites. Communications satellites allow the exchange of live television programs and news and sports events—such as the Olympics—between nations and continents. Linking earth stations located in more than 50 countries carry international telephone services. Communications satellites transmit signals via microwaves, which are very short radio waves sent from or received by bowl-shaped reflectors or from antennas. Earth-based (terrestrial) systems send out extremely high frequency signals from transmitters to repeater stations and back to receivers. The waves form narrow beams, which travel in straight lines. For this reason, receivers must be located within line of sight of one another and usually are placed on towers. Transoceanic microwave systems became feasible with the advent of satellite technology.

Satellite systems work in much the same way as terrestrial systems, except that the signals are relayed from an earth station to an orbiting satellite. The equipment aboard the satellite receives these signals, amplifies them, and rebroadcasts them to another earth station. Satellites are better suited for long-haul, single-to-multipoint transmissions than are terrestrial systems, because they are not susceptible to being blocked by geographical obstructions. Satellites also are preferable for reaching regions where the cost of laying cable would be prohibitive. Their large bandwidth accommodates a variety of video and data transmissions. Compared to terrestrial systems, satellite systems have the disadvantages of echo, less signal security, and a slight transmission delay which varies according to the altitude of the satellite.

As a transmission technology, communications satellites also compete with fiber-optic cables because both systems transmit data. Over time, the cost of transmitting information via satellite has become almost as low as the cost of transmitting via land. It is unlikely that one technology will win out over the other, because each has its advantages. A study done by COMSAT Corp. showed that "satellites and cable will play complementary roles in voice, data, and video communications. Complementary technologies will become increasingly important because of growth in international broadcasting, advances in computer technology, and increases in demand for worldwide, instant voice and data communications."

The satellites considered to be the most competitive alternatives to cable are Ku-band, beam-hopping, multibeam satellites. These conserve energy by allowing simultaneous switching among beams. Other cable competitors are C-band, fixed multibeam satellites that use a series of beams but do not permit rapid switching between them. The beam-hopping, multibeam system costs an estimated 27 percent less than cable, while the fixed multibeam was estimated to cost nearly half as much as cable. Ka-band is being proposed for higher speed transmission for broadband Internet access.

The part of a communications satellite that is "for sale" is the transponder, which broadcasts signals. Transponders are transmitter/receiver devices. Early satellites had single transponders, but in the 1990s some satellites had as many as a dozen or more (which are leased full-time or occasionally). The cost of leasing varies, depending upon variables such as the time of day, frequency, power, duration of lease contract, orbital position, and type of satellite. The rate for domestic analog C-band channels can range from $200 to $600 per hour, or $55,000 to $230,000 per month. Leasing a higher-frequency, Ku-band transponder can range between $250 to $800 per hour, or $150,000 to $210,000 per month.

Fixed and Mobile Services. Fixed satellite services (FSS), which include fixed broadcasting, data transmission and telephone service, accounted for about 85 percent of all U.S. satellite service revenues. An estimated 65 percent of these revenues were generated by video transmissions for news feed services, cable TV networks, and national broadcast networks. The advantages of communications satellites have made their services attractive for "narrowcasting" applications for educational or corporate programming. Private business television (BTV) is a rapidly growing area of information transmitted via private networks with very small aperture terminals (VSATs). Users have grown to rely on these systems for intracorporate data, video, and telephone communications. Retail companies use VSATs for credit card authorization and remote inventory control, and the travel industry relies on VSAT services for its reservation systems.

Mobile satellite services (MSS) are a more recently developed services market. Whether mobile satellite services will continue to expand will depend on the allocation of enough of the radio frequency spectrum to accommodate multiple communications systems. Market growth will depend in part on the success of newer technologies based on clusters of microsatellites in low orbits, as opposed to traditional technologies based on very large, high-cost satellites in geostationary orbits. Satellites in lower orbits are less expensive to build and launch, but more of them are required to cover the same areas as a larger satellite in geosynchronous orbit. Satellites in low earth orbit are referred to as LEO systems.

Both domestically and abroad, land mobile satellite services (LMSS), which include applications such as navigational services, cellular telephone services, and digital radio, are expected to be the fastest-growing MSS application. About 80 percent of mobile satellite service revenues come from LMSS applications, such as location and messaging services for trucks; aviation and shipping make up the balance of the mobile market.

Remote Sensing. Remote sensing is the gathering and storage of information around the earth's surface—such as weather patterns—via optical and infrared cameras, radar, or other sensing equipment in an orbiting spacecraft. Uses for remote sensing satellite data include agricultural forecasts, shipping, fishing, oil and mineral prospecting, cartography, forestry, and pollution surveys. In the mid-1900s, about 200 domestic companies offered remote sensing software, systems hardware, and consulting.

BACKGROUND AND DEVELOPMENT

Between 1958 and 1963, the United States launched several experimental communications satellites, including Score, Echo, Telstar, Relay, and Syncom. Built by American Telephone and Telegraph Co. (AT&T), Telstar was launched on July 10, 1962. Telstar was powered by solar cells and chargeable batteries, and it demonstrated international satellite communications capabilities by transmitting American speech and television transmissions to Europe. In December of the same year, NASA launched its communications satellite, Relay, for communication experiments. On July 26, 1963, Hughes Aircraft Co.'s Syncom II, the first synchronous communication satellite, was launched by NASA. Hughes' Syncom III, launched the following August, relayed the first sustained trans-Pacific television broadcast during the 1964 Olympics.

Many satellites have been launched for military use. The largest satellite ever built (1,600 pounds, versus less than 200 for most satellites) was launched in 1969 and was designed for use by the U.S. Army, Navy, and Air Force in communicating with mobile field units, aircraft, and ships. The first commercial satellite, Early Bird, was launched in April of 1965. Commercial activity in this sector heated up in the 1980s following new federal policies to privatize space activities. The technology used in commercial satellites, such as satellite launch vehicles and guidance systems, was originally developed for military purposes.

In 1962, the U.S. Communications Satellite Act provided that the sole right of U.S. ownership of satellites for international communications would rest with a single private corporation, the Communications Satellite Corp. (Comsat), that was incorporated in 1963. This move prompted European common carriers to band together into a consortium. In August of 1964, the International Telecommunications Satellite Consortium (Intelsat), an international corporation for the construction, launching, ownership, and operation of communication satellites, was established. Intelsat was an international not-for-profit consortium of 143 countries whose members contribute capital in proportion to their use of the system and receive a return on their investment. All users paid Intelsat utilization charges, which vary depending on the type, amount, and duration of the service used. The Intelsat system provided four major services to users in more than 180 nations: public switched telephone services; private line network (business) services; broadcasting (video and audio) services; and domestic and regional services. The Intelsat system was accessed by thousands of earth stations, ranging in size from 50 centimeters to 30 meters. COMSAT was the U.S. government's representative to Intelsat, and was the sole source of access to Intelsat for U.S. companies.

A new generation of satellites was launched in the early 1990s to replace aging satellites with higher-powered, higher-capacity models, many with combinations of both C-band and Ku-band capacity. The life of a satellite is determined by its altitude and how much fuel it has to power the onboard rockets that keep it in its orbital pattern. This fuel usually runs out after about a decade of operation. The new satellites contain twice as many transponders as their predecessors and have the digital compression technology to expand their capacity by squeezing several channels of video per transponder. One example of the new breed of high-capacity satellites is AT&T's Telstar 401, which began operation in January of 1994. Telstar 401 has 24 C-band transponders and 24 Ku-band transponders.

Demand was expected to remain high for small, low-cost satellites, called lightsats and microsats. Lightsats weigh less than 1,000 pounds and microsats less than 250 pounds. These smaller models are increasingly the models of choice for new communications systems. In 1994, Hughes Communications Inc. began its direct-to-home satellite service, DirecTV, which incorporates the United States' first high-powered direct broadcast satellite. DirecTV delivered more than 150 channels of programming to homes using 18-inch dishes and receivers. Similar services were launched by RCA Corp. and other companies.

An offshoot of direct-to-home satellite communications was the use of DSS technology to facilitate computer communications. Competing directly with the telephone companies and the new cable modems announced by the cable industry, the satellite industry—led by DirecTV—began offering high-speed satellite links to the Internet. According to DirecTV, its direct broadcast satellite (DBS) system, when combined with a personal computer, would allow consumers to receive digital video programming and a variety of new entertainment, multimedia, and interactive data services on their PCs. The key advantage of the system was its speed. At up to 30 megabytes per second (mbps), the new DirectPC system allowed users to download information and files more than a thousand times faster than standard modem connections.

CURRENT CONDITIONS

At the end of the 1990s satellite based communication was poised for great expansion. In 1996 there were 54 commercial satellites in orbit around the earth, but by 1999 the number had more than tripled (to 175) and more than 500 were scheduled to be launched in the next 3 to 5 years. Most of these were elements of systems or constellations of multiple satellites, ranging from a few GEO satellites to hundreds in low earth orbit (LEO). Although the number of such systems changed as the sponsoring companies consolidated their efforts and new proposals were put on the table, there were about 29 constellations launched or planned in 1999. These systems targeted 4 different applications: voice, broadband data transmission, messaging, and geodesy and navigation.

The first of these new systems to actually get into service was Iridium, a 66-satellite network for mobile telephone service. It began voice and pager service in 1998, but filed for bankruptcy protection in August 1999. It had problems with supplying its handsets, which also were very expensive compared to a regular mobile phone, and its per minute charges were high. These factors, combined with other marketing and support failures, resulted in much slower growth in the number of subscribers than was expected, and the company was unable to meet some of its debt payments.

ICO Global Communications, another voice-oriented satellite venture, also filed for bankruptcy protection in August 1999, in part because the problems with Iridium made it difficult to attract the investors it needed to proceed. ICO stands for Intermediate Circular Orbit, which is another name for medium earth orbit (MEO). Service was expected to start in summer of 2000, using a system of 9 or 10 MEO satellites. ICO began as a spin-off from Inmarsat, which offered an expensive mobile voice service previously, and uses technology already proven in service. Globalstar, the second voice-oriented system to begin service, suffered a major setback when it lost 12 satellites in a failed launch in September 1998. Nevertheless, it began limited "friendly user" service in October 1999. The full system was designed to use 48 satellites and cover the world between 68 degrees north and south latitudes. Its initial service coverage was much smaller.

Satellites were expected to provide 10 to 15 percent of the global broadband Internet and data transmission service early in the next century. This market was projected to grow from $200 million in 1999 to $37 billion by 2008, according to Pioneer Consulting. The most ambitious and well publicized broadband scheme was Teledesic, which dubbed itself "the Internet in the Sky." Its initial backers were Bill Gates, CEO of Microsoft, and Craig McCaw, highly successful pioneer of cellular telephone service. It was planned to use 288 LEO satellites to provide Internet access anywhere in the world, beginning service in 2004. Systems planned to compete in this market included SkyBridge, an 80-satellite LEO constellation backed by Alcatel, the Paris-based telecommunications equipment manufacturer, and Spaceway, a constellation of GEO satellites backed by Hughes Electronics, the leading U.S. satellite builder and operator. Hughes also has filed with the Federal Communications Commission (FCC) for a MEO constellation of 20 satellites and another GEO system of 14 satellites.

A number of satellite ventures designed to forward messages—short non-voice transmissions—were planned or underway. Although much less glamorous than global mobile telephone or broadband Internet access, these systems have immediate real-world applications. Orbcomm had 35 of its satellites in orbit by 1999, out of a proposed 48. The Orbcomm system was designed to enable businesses to track remote assets such as trailers, heavy equipment, gas storage tanks, and wells and pipelines, and maintain communications with remote workers anywhere on the globe. Leo One, a 48-satellite constellation, planned to offer store-and-forward messaging. E-Sat planned a six-satellite system focused on meter reading applications.

Satellite-based navigation systems were well established by the end of the 1990s, but additional constellations were planned. The Global Positioning System (GPS), funded and operated by the U.S Department of Defense, was a system of 24 active satellites that enabled users to determine their position using satellite radio signals. Civilian users could use the Standard Positioning Service (SPS) without charge or restriction. Glonass was a similar Russian system in use. GNSS-2 was planned by the European Community to create a navigation system independent of foreign military control.

In September 1999 the first commercial remote imaging satellite was launched. It was designed to take black-and-white and full color photographs of any place on earth. Journalists were looking forward to using its images, which were to be of much higher resolution than what was previously available. Frost & Sullivan, a technical marketing research firm, expected the market for satellite imaging to grow at an annual rate of 17.1 percent through 2005. New remote sensing satellite systems were planned, including Skymed-Cosmos, focused on the Mediterranean basin, and Tsinghua, designed for disaster monitoring. Remote sensing using single satellites already was well developed by the end of the 1990s.

INDUSTRY LEADERS

According to the Satellite Industry Association, U.S. satellite manufacturing revenues reached $17.6 billion in 1998, up 10 percent from 1997, while satellite services revenue was $26.2 billion, an increase of 23 percent. A measure of future growth potential in the industry was the amount of investment in satellite projects, which had reached $5 billion in the first 9 months of 1999, as opposed to $4.2 billion in all of 1998. The previous record was $5.7 billion in 1997, according to investment bank Bear Sterns & Co. This was public debt and equity money, and did not include the large amounts of investment by strategic partners in the many joint projects in this industry.

The leading satellite company, as opposed to generic space company, was Hughes Electronics, a subsidiary of General Motors. Now almost entirely a builder and operator of satellites, its revenues in 1998 totaled $5.6 billion. One of Hughes' subsidiaries, DirecTV, had 7.74 million subscribers to its satellite TV service in October 1999. This gave it 71 percent of the satellite TV market, but its main competitor, EchoStar, was recording very rapid growth.

Boeing was the world's largest space company, but was not a major player in the satellite business. Lockheed Martin, the second largest space company, also was not a major factor in the commercial satellite industry, although that would change if its proposed acquisition of Comsat Corp. received congressional approval. Loral Space and Communications, the ninth leading space company in the world, earned most of its revenue in 1998 through its satellite manufacturing arm. Loral also had significant assets in satellite operation services. Satellite manufacturing revenues were $1.4 billion in 1998.

A relative newcomer to the industry was Orbital Sciences Corp. (OSC). Through various subsidiaries it operated the Orbcomm network of messaging satellites, the Orbview-1 atmosphere monitoring satellite, and the Orbview-2 multispectral imaging satellite. Two additional Orbview satellites were to be launched soon. Total revenues for OCS in 1998 were $734.28 million, which yielded a net loss of $6.37 million, mostly due to startup expenses.

AMERICA AND THE WORLD

The U.S. space industry supplied about 60 percent of the world's satellite requirements in 1998, according to Euroconsult. Conversely, all segments of U.S. space commerce have some foreign direct investment. Because most satellites move over many countries and because satellites lend themselves most of all to international services, and because satellite systems are very expensive, the industry is marked by a great deal of international collaboration. Nearly all the commercial satellite constellations in operation or planned were joint ventures that involved non-U.S. companies and in some cases foreign governments.

FURTHER READING

Anderson, Karen.''Eagle Eye in the Sky.'' *Broadcasting & Cable,* 25 October 1999.

Foley, Theresa.''Star Attractions.'' *Communications Week International,* 16 August 1999.

Golden, Paul''Analysts Say Consolidation Likely for Satellite Industry.'' *Global Wireless,* October 1999.

''An Industry's Brightest Days: Growing Its Subscriber Pie to Awesome Numbers.'' *Satellite News,* 22 November 1999.

Mooney, Elizabeth V. ''SkyBridge to Compete with LMDS Carriers.'' *RCR Radio Communications Report,* 13 September 1999.

Nairn, Geoff. ''Sector Is Reinventing Itself for the Next Millennium.'' *Financial Times Survey Edition,* 18 November 1998.

''New Focus for U.S. Satellite Industry.'' *Interavia Business & Technology,* September 1999.

Price, Christopher. ''SkyBridge to Lift Capacity of System Satellites Cost Increased to $4.2 BN.'' *Financial Times London Edition,* 1 June 1999.

''Satellites: The New Direct-to-Consumer Model.'' *America's Network,* 15 September 1998.

Shiver, Jube, Jr. ''The Cutting Edge/Focus on Personal Technology Satellites at Risk in Crowded Skies.'' *Los Angeles Times,* 11 November 1999.

Smith, Bruce A. ''Remote Sensing.'' *Aviation Week & Space Technology,* 11 October 1999.

Thyfault, Mary E. ''Satellites Reposition for Broadband - A Batch of Service Providers Shift to Internet and Data.'' *tele.com,* 8 November 1999.

Wood, Lloyd. ''Lloyd's Satellite Constellations.'' Available at http://www.ee.surrey.ac.uk/Personal/L.Wood/constellations/overview.htm.

SIC 4911

ELECTRIC SERVICES

This industry classification includes establishments engaged in generating, transmitting, and distributing electricity. Establishments providing electric services in combination with other services, where the electric services account for less than 95 percent of revenues, are classified in **SIC 4931: Electric and Other Services Combined; SIC 4932: Gas and Other Services Combined;** or **SIC 4939: Combination Utilities, Not Elsewhere Classified** according to the major service supplied.

NAICS CODE(S)

221111 (Hydroelectric Power Generation)
221112 (Fossil Fuel Electric Power Generation)
221113 (Nuclear Electric Power Generation)
221119 (Other Electric Power Generation)
221121 (Electric Bulk Power Transmission and Control)
221122 (Electric Power Distribution)

INDUSTRY SNAPSHOT

The electric service industry is less than 150 years old, but it runs America. In the span of a century, electricity replaced gas as a preferred means of lighting and succeeded steam engines in many growing industries. Electric service utilities are the nation's largest business, gauged according to capital investment and market value. Electricity is so widely available in modern American society that service disruptions are newsworthy. Throughout the twentieth century, its use consistently increased. Although industry forecasters disagree about how rapidly demand will continue to grow, they generally agree that demand for electricity will continue to increase into the foreseeable future.

Electricity is measured in watts. A watt is a basic unit of electrical power equal to about 1/746th of one horsepower. A kilowatt is equal to 1,000 watts; a megawatt is equal to one million watts; a gigawatt is equal to one billion watts. Electricity is sold in kilowatt-hours (kWh). One kWh equals the amount of electrical energy needed to keep ten 100-watt bulbs burning for one hour. Not all the electricity generated is available to be sold. Some is used by the power plant and some is dissipated during transmission and distribution. Furthermore, because electricity cannot be stored, it must be used or lost.

The Energy Policy Act of 1992 was the beginning of the deregulation of the electric services industry. By 1999, almost half of the states had passed, or had pending, new legislation which provided for restructuring of the industry, open access to transmission lines, and wholesale/retail competition among producers, transmitters and distributors of electricity.

ORGANIZATION AND STRUCTURE

There are several kinds of electric service establishments in the United States. Investor-owned companies are owned by shareholders; cooperative utilities are owned by their members and are operated to meet members' needs. Public utilities are nonprofit government agencies such as municipalities, public power districts, and irrigation districts. The federal government also produces electricity under the direction of agencies such as the U.S. Army Corps of Engineers and the U.S. Bureau of Indian Affairs. The largest federal producer is the Tennessee Valley Authority, which provides electricity to both wholesale and retail markets.

Although public utilities and rural cooperatives account for about 90 percent of the nation's more than 3,200 electricity utilities providers, they are generally small. Cooperative electric utilities provide service to their members, who are usually in rural areas where investor-owned electric utilities would find it uneconomical to operate because of low population densities. In 1999, there were 932 cooperatively-owned utilities, 2,010 non-profit publicly-owned and 10 federally-owned utilities, and 267 for-profit, investor-owned utilities.

Electricity providers differ not only by class of ownership but also vary greatly in size, services, profitability, and organization. An integrated utility may operate its own generation plants as well as maintain its own transmission and distribution lines. Other companies may distribute electricity to customers but buy it from other producers rather than generate it. Some rural cooperatives operate with less than 100 employees and own under $1 million in total assets. Some corporations supply electricity to customers through subsidiary companies in several states. These giant organizations may employ tens of thousands.

The North American Electric Reliability Council (NERC) was established in 1968 by the electric utility industry and consists of ten regional reliability councils. The councils are responsible for setting and maintaining standards to foster reliable service within the three power grids that supply electricity to the contiguous United States: the Eastern Power Grid (also known as the Seven Interconnected Regions Power Grid), the Western Power Grid, and the Electric Reliability Council of Texas Power Grid. As of 1998, there were more than 200,000 circuit miles of high-voltage transmission lines in the three power grids.

Electric service producers operate several types of generating stations in order to meet customers' constantly changing energy demands. Three classes of power plants are base-load, intermediate-load, and peak-load stations. Base-load plants serve to meet the normal minimum demand of a company's customers. They are usually the largest and most efficient of a company's generating

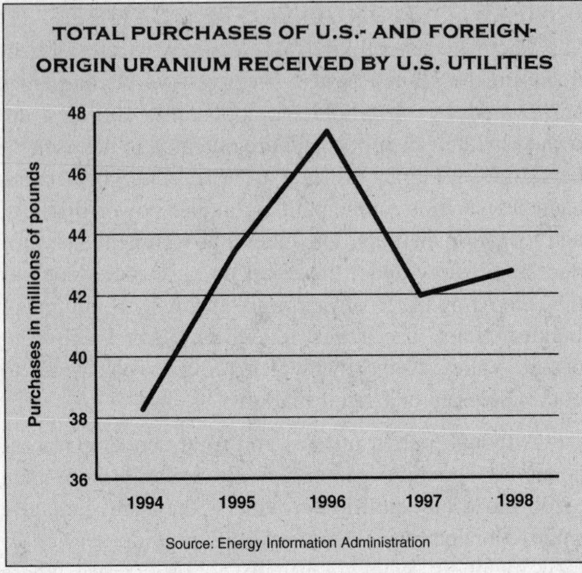

units. Intermediate-load plants handle increases in demand that are less than the highest, or peak, demands. They perform as transitional power providers and can function as standby units when unexpected problems arise. Peak-load generating stations are used to meet short-term, high demand. Peaking units are usually quick starting but the least efficient.

Electricity is created by electric generators that convert mechanical energy into electric power by rotating a magnet within coiled wires. The mechanism that causes the magnet to rotate is called a ''prime mover.'' Different kinds of prime movers are used to generate electricity in different circumstances. Most generators are turbines that are spun when a liquid or gas is forced against their blades. Steam, hot air or combustion gases, and water are the most common prime movers.

Steam turbines produce most of the electricity generated in the United States. The steam required to operate the turbines is created through burning fossil fuels, such as coal, petroleum, and gas, or through nuclear fission. Steam turbines generally operate in base-load power stations. Gas turbines and internal-combustion engines are most frequently used as peaking units. A type of gas turbine that operates in conjunction with a steam turbine is called a combined-cycle generating unit and is typically used for intermediate-level generation. Hydroelectric-generated power is created when flowing or falling water is used to spin a turbine. Hydroelectric units can serve as base-load or peaking stations.

Background and Development

America's demand for electricity began during the last two decades of the nineteenth century. In October 1879, Thomas Edison created the first long-lasting incandescent light bulb. In December of the following year, he founded the Edison Electric Illuminating Company in New York for the purpose of building the nation's first centralized generating plant. The company's Pearl Street station took two years to build, and on September 4, 1892, its generator was turned on. It supplied electricity for 158 lamps, 52 at the editorial office of the *New York Times* and 106 in financier J. P. Morgan's office. A year later, the company was serving 513 customers. By the end of the decade, Edison's companies had constructed 500 isolated-generating units and 58 centralized-power stations.

Edison faced competition from George Westinghouse, a proponent of alternating current, who purchased the United States Electric Light Company. Alternating current, shunned by Edison who preferred direct current (DC), gradually emerged as the preferred form of electricity because it could be transmitted at lower costs. The industry expanded as new companies began producing the products innovators created, including longer-lasting light bulbs, different kinds of generators, and motors.

By the turn of the century, one out of every 13 factories utilized electric motors. Cities replaced gas street lamps with electric lights. Electric trolleys became a preferred mode of transportation. Generators became larger and more efficient. Technologies to transmit power over longer distances was developed. Increased production created economies of scale and lower prices. In 1892 the cost per kilowatt-hour from a centralized station was 22 cents; thirty years later the cost was seven cents.

In 1907, Wisconsin and New York became the first two states to establish independent regulatory commissions. By the end of World War I, 26 other states had established similar commissions. Under the direction of state regulators, electric service companies became public utilities instead of competitors. Regulators established service territories and granted specific companies monopolies within the territory. One motivating factor that led to the establishment of monopolies was the goal of eliminating the expense of duplicate transmission systems.

During the 1920s, holding companies acquired the largest portion of America's generating capacity. By the middle of the decade, 16 companies controlled about 75 percent of the nation's electricity. Many companies continued to operate independently, while others cooperated with neighboring utilities to form power pools, agreements under which companies shared resources to achieve greater efficiency and reliability.

In 1920, Congress enacted the Federal Power Act to regulate licensing of nonfederal hydroelectric ventures; the Federal Power Commission was created to enforce its provisions. The act was amended in 1935 to include regulations for interstate transmission, and monitoring rates for wholesale transactions of electric power.

By the mid-1930s, electric services were commonplace in urban but not rural areas. An estimated 85 percent of farms still had no electricity. On May 11, 1935, President Franklin Roosevelt created the Rural Electrification Administration to fund projects undertaken by rural cooperatives.

In 1935, Congress passed the Public Utility Holding Company Act (PUHCA). PUHCA outlawed pyramiding and limited holding companies to single-integrated operating systems. The act was opposed by the nation's large holding companies, who had to reorganize in accordance with its provisions.

World War II brought increased demands for electric power. Following the war, further improvements in generators and transmission technologies increased the availability of low-priced electricity. Between 1945 and 1965, the average generating plant size multiplied sevenfold and demand increased at a rate of approximately 7.8 percent per year. The 1940s also ushered in the nuclear era. On December 3, 1942, Enrico Fermi created the first self-sustaining nuclear chain reaction. The first usable electricity generated by atomic power occurred at the Argonne National Laboratory in Idaho on December 20, 1951. In 1957, the Shippingport Nuclear Station in Pennsylvania became the country's first nuclear plant to supply electricity to a utility's power grid.

During the 1960s nuclear power gained prominence. Seven new reactors were ordered in 1965, 20 in 1966, and 30 in 1967. Despite growing anti-nuclear sentiments among segments of the U.S. population, nuclear power continued to contribute a growing amount of electricity to the nation. In 1979, an accident at the Three Mile Island station in Pennsylvania led to increased scrutiny of the nuclear power industry and new regulations exacerbated the financial difficulties many nuclear projects faced.

No new domestic orders for nuclear power plants have been placed since 1978, but electric utilities have continued to complete plants that were under various stages of construction. From 1980 to 1990 the number of operating nuclear plants in the United States increased from 70 to 111.

Other transformations also challenged the electric service industry during the 1970s. The Arab oil embargoes of 1973 and 1979 disrupted fuel oil supplies and increased prices. Inflation and high interest rates caused base-load plant construction costs to soar. Measures necessary to protect the environment brought increased regulatory requirements. As prices increased and the economy slowed, demand dropped to under three percent per year.

In 1977, Congress created the Department of Energy. The Federal Power Commission was abolished and its responsibilities were split between the Department of Energy and the Federal Energy Regulatory Commission (FERC). In 1978, Congress passed the Public Utility Regulatory Policies Act (PURPA). One of PURPA's goals was to encourage conservation and efficiency in power generation. PURPA injected competition into the electric service industry by requiring utilities to purchase electricity from certain producers defined as ''qualifying facilities'' (QFs). As a result, cogeneration facilities (plants that produced electricity along with other forms of energy) and small producers relying on renewable resources such as water, wind, solar, and geothermal power began supplying power to the nation's power grids.

By 1988 nontraditional producers of electricity produced six percent of the total generation in the United States. Forecasters expected independent producers to play an increasing role and to provide as much as 15 percent of the nation's power by the end of the twentieth century.

As the electric services industry entered the 1990s analysts debated whether new generating capacity was necessary. Many older base-load plants were reaching the end of their licensed operating span. An estimated 25 percent of the country's fossil-fueled generating plants were scheduled to reach the end of their planned life span by the year 2000.

The approach of the twenty-first century left many problems unsolved and questions unanswered: the growth of nonutility generating companies led to questions about accessing transmission lines, a comprehensive national nuclear waste management program remained elusive, forecasters disagreed about whether the nation possessed sufficient generation capability to meet demands in the new century, and provisions of the Clean Air Act Amendments of 1990 required changes in generation technologies.

In addition to regulations on gaseous emissions, the Clean Air Act of 1990 listed 189 elements and compounds to be studied to determine regulatory requirements for their emission. One element was mercury. During normal operations in coal-burning generating units, mercury turns into a gas that can escape regular emissions collection systems. Because of the environmental problems inherent in fossil-fueled generation, some utilities expressed a renewed interest in nuclear generation. Nuclear fission creates heat without producing combustion by-products. Consequently, its proponents offered it as a clean alternative to fossil fuel.

Also in 1990, the Nuclear Power Oversight Committee identified 14 issues that needed to be addressed before substantial expansion of America's nuclear generating capacity would be practical. The areas included improving operations at existing plants, resolving waste storage issues, establishing consistent regulations and standardized reactor designs, political support, and available financing.

Nonutility generating companies represented a likely source of additional power production in the early 1990s. In 1992, Congress passed a comprehensive Energy Act which removed restrictions on independent power producers and opened wholesale markets to competition. Under the terms of the legislation, independent power producers were granted access to utility transmission lines. In addition, the act enabled large holding companies to operate in multiple states more freely.

The North American Electric Reliability Council estimated that national reserve capacities, a measure of unused generating ability, would drop below 20 percent by the end of the century and that in some areas reserve capacity would fall more. Some industry analysts calculated that high demand increases would accompany a recovering economy. They predicted reserves would be insufficient to meet the nation's needs in the twenty-first century. The Energy Information Association, an agency of the Department of Energy, projected demand increases between 1990 and 2010 in the range of 1.3 to 1.9 percent per year.

By the mid-1990s, the electric services industry had entered a period of radical change. Technological advances and an increasing demand for customer choice had prompted public utilities commissions in over 20 states, as well as the FERC, to propose deregulation of electricity generation, slowly exposing existing monopolies to competition, and giving consumers the opportunity to buy power from any broker or supplier, not just their local monopoly.

On April 24th 1996, the FERC officially opened the electric services business to competition with two separate rulings, Order Nos. 888 and 889. The first, Order No. 888, required that public utilities offer to sell electric power to other providers or utilities at the same rates they charged themselves. At the same time, the utility providing transmission service (the ''wheeling utility'') would be compensated for the use of its lines. Order No. 889 required electric utilities to establish electronic systems to share information about available transmission capacity.

By 1997, competition in the industry had accelerated dramatically, spurred by the rise of a growing number of independent power producers, brokers, and energy marketers. In the third quarter of 1996 alone, these tough new competitors sold enough electricity to power 31 million homes—this from an industry that had not even existed a few years earlier. Independent producers and marketers came in all sizes, from small brokers such as California-based New Energy Ventures to Houston-based giant, Enron.

CURRENT CONDITIONS

During 1998, California, Massachusetts, and Rhode Island added to the ranks of states that opened their retail electricity markets. As of April, 1999, there were 19 states with legislation allowing retail competition.

The deregulation of the industry also created spin-off markets in wholesale auctions of electricity and the trading of electricity futures and options contracts on the New York Mercantile Exchange (NYMEX). Moreover, a new type of monopoly entered the market. In 1998, almost two-thirds of electric utilities did not have their own generating capacity; about 55 percent of domestic consumed electricity had been sold to the utilities by other utilities or nonutilities. When power producers began to increasingly use natural gas, a new utilities super-power appeared on the horizon. Instead of natural gas companies buying out their smaller natural gas competitors, they began buying out electric utilities companies to provide multiple services to end-users. Thus, by the millennium, some of the largest utilities providers were in fact ''hybrid'' entities offering both electricity and natural gas services to their customers. Consequently, by 1999, the new monopolies were power companies which generated, transmitted and distributed electricity, plus offered consumers their natural gas and sometimes their water, all on one monthly bill.

A newcomer to industry jargon in 1998 was the ''ISO,'' or Independent System Operator, which the industry set up to operate power transmission systems as the competition in the wholesale market intensified. Five ISOs were operating across the nation in 1999, to ensure non-discriminatory access to transmission grids.

Sales of electricity to ultimate consumers increased by 3.2 percent in 1998, for a total of 3.24 trillion kWh. The industry generated $218 billion in sales for 1998, although the national average revenue per kWh decreased for the fifth year in a row. Coal remained the leading source for power generation, holding about 51.7 percent of the 1998 market, followed by nuclear power (18.6 percent) and natural gas (15 percent). Nuclear powered generation had actually dropped between 1995 and 1998, but the nation experienced sustained above-normal temperatures during the summer of 1998, resulting in high demands for electricity; seven nuclear units that had been out of service were restarted during 1998. Residential end-users captured the largest share of the market, at 35 percent, followed by industrial users at 33 percent and commercial users at 29 percent.

With respect to environmental concerns, air emissions from electric utility fossil-fueled plants were estimated to have increased in 1998. The largest noxious agent, carbon dioxide, increased by an estimated three percent in just one year.

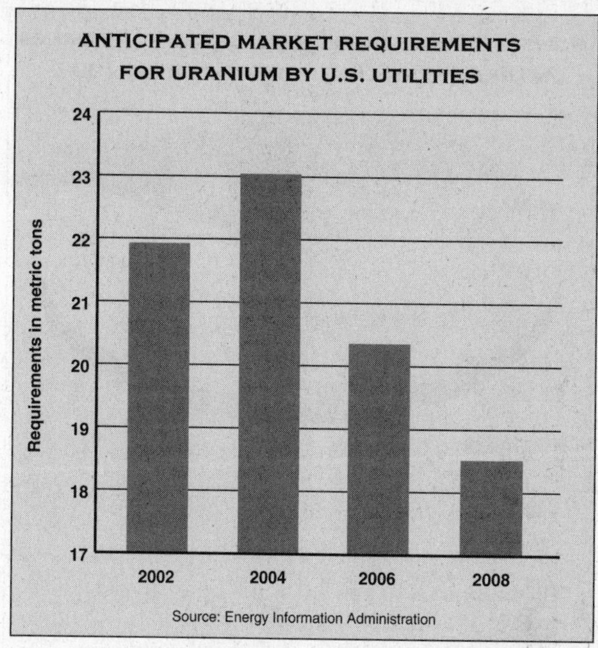

INDUSTRY LEADERS

Reliant Energy, Inc. (formerly Houston Industries) provides energy to more than 13 states, South America, and India. The company serves 1.6 million electricity customers and 2.8 million natural gas customers in the United States alone. It reported 1999 sales of $15.5 billion.

Another giant is Dominion Resources, Inc., which, through its subsidiaries, distributes electricity to two million people, and also serves another two million gas customers. The company reported 1998 sales of $6.08 billion.

Other leaders include AES Corporation of Virginia, with more than 100 facilities in 20 countries, considered the leading power plant company in the United States; Philadelphia-based PECO Energy, which planned to merge with Chicago's Unicom (parent of Commonwealth Edison) in 2000; and Edison International, which serves not only 11 million Southern California residents, but also owns power plants in Africa, Asia, Europe and the Middle East.

WORKFORCE

Despite reductions in numbers of workers, the electric services industry continues to be a major employer, providing jobs for more than 400,000 people in the United States. The utility industry employs people in four major areas: generation, transmission, distribution, and administration. Because the industry relied on emerging technology, it needed engineers and scientists as well as clerks and technicians.

AMERICA AND THE WORLD

In 1998, the United States led the world in net generation of electricity, with 3.6 trillion kWh produced; Japan was second. Other leaders included China, Russia, Canada, Germany, and France. The United States imported 39.5 billion kWh from Canada and exported 12 billion kWh back to Canada.

Although the United States led the world in fossil and nuclear generation, it was second in hydroelectric production. Canada was the world's top hydroelectric producer, with 319 billion kilowatt-hours of hydroelectric power generated. Canada was followed by the United States (304 billion kWh), Brazil (225 billion kWh), Russia (173 billion kWh), Norway (118 billion kWh), and China (143 billion kWh).

Nuclear power was also a method through which some countries were addressing pollution concerns. Lithuania produced a greater percentage of its domestic electricity (85 percent) through nuclear generation than any other nation. The United States produced the world's largest amount of electricity from nuclear power (673 billion kWh), yet nuclear generation accounted for only about 22 percent of its total production. Behind the United States, other top nuclear countries included France (358 billion kWh), Japan (286 billion kWh), and Germany (154 billion kWh).

RESEARCH AND TECHNOLOGY

As the electric service industry prepared for the twenty-first century, researchers were studying many potential technological innovations. Advanced light-water reactors (ALR) were being developed by General Electric and Westinghouse. Another improvement over older, conventional reactors was the use of passive safety systems, which depended on natural physical laws (such as gravity) rather than human intervention to respond to problems.

Electric utilities implemented a number of methods to reduce sulfur emissions from burning coal. Some began using a process in which the coal was crushed and treated to reduce its sulfur content. Others switched from high-sulfur content coal to low-sulfur coal. Still other utilities invested in a process called ''flue gas desulfurization'' (commonly referred to as ''scrubbing'') to remove sulfur from the gases created by combustion. One promising innovation was the development of an integrated gasification combined-cycle (IGCC) power plant. The IGCC generator was designed to use partially oxidized coal as a fuel, a process that virtually eliminated air pollutants.

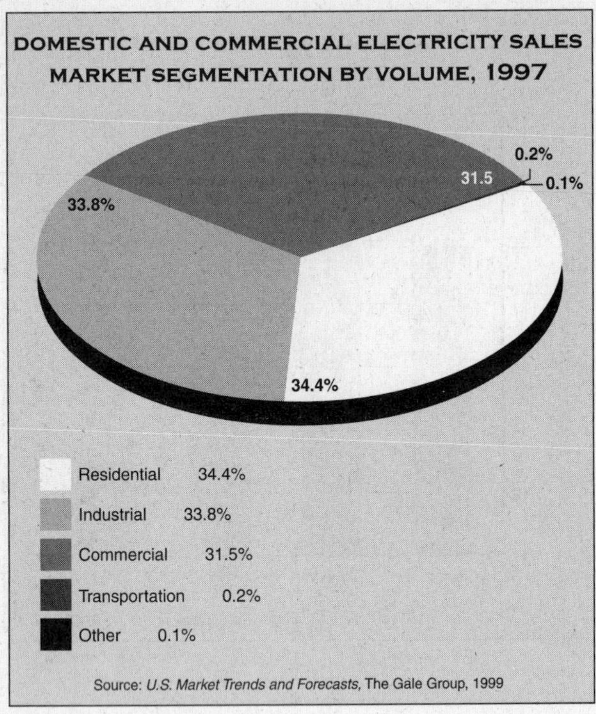

In the 1990s, the combined output from all other renewable sources, such as hydroelectric, wind, geothermal, and biofuels (which included wood, waste, and alcohol fuels) totaled only about one percent of the electricity generated in the United States. One hopeful experiment with solar generation was conducted in a California desert. Approximately 900 mirrors were set to focus light from the sun and generate 10 megawatts of power. If the project met expectations, Southern California Edison planned to consider building 200 megawatt plants using the technology. In another solar project, Southern California Edison and Texas Instruments were testing a new type of solar cell using tiny silicon balls. The material, called ''Spheral Solar'' held promise for application in remote sunny areas, especially in Third World nations.

Developments in wind generation technology also looked encouraging. During the early 1980s wind generators produced power at an average cost of 30 cents per kilowatt-hour. By the early 1990s costs had dropped to 11 cents per kWh. Researchers hoped that improved technology would produce wind-generated power at a cost of six cents per kWh by 2010. Site selection for wind generation was critical because even small differences in average wind speed had substantial effects on the amount of electricity generated.

Another source of renewable energy under exploration was geothermal power. Most of the geothermal production in the United States was from a single plant operated by the Pacific Gas and Electric Company in California. Investigators were researching methods to extract heat from hot dry rock, which is found everywhere on earth at sufficient depths. One study underway in New Mexico during 1992 offered promising results. Scientists drilled a hole 12,000 feet deep and pumped water into it. They were able to extract 100 gallons of water per minute at temperatures high enough to generate electricity.

Not all the research underway during the decade involved power generation. Many utilities were investigating robot technology for use in operations, maintenance, transmission, and distribution. Interest in robotics intensified when utilities realized that robots could be used in potentially hazardous situations. The use of robots helped reduce human exposure to radiation following the Three Mile Island accident. Robots could also work on lines carrying live current or inside vessels with toxic substances. A robot able to perform maintenance tasks on live wires was commercially introduced and another, able to inspect high-voltage lines and towers, was under development. A pipe-crawling robot, developed by Public Service Electric & Gas's Energy Technology Development Center, was able to inspect pipes where human access was impossible and perform some types of repairs.

In 1996, the world's first utility-scale molten carbonate fuel cell (MCFC) power plant began operation in Santa Clara, California. Generating two MW of power from natural gas without combustion and with very low emissions, the plant was part of a demonstration program closely monitored by more than 30 utilities who had signed tentative commitments to purchase commercial MCFC units.

Further Reading

''Competition in the Electric Power Industry.'' *The Electric Power Industry Today.* Edison Electric Institute, February 1997.

''Electric Utilities.'' *Standard and Poor's Industry Surveys.* New York: MacGraw Hill, September 1997.

''Energy Secretary O'Leary to Dedicate Tampa Electric's Polk Power Plant.'' TECO Energy, 1997. Available from http://www.teco.net.

''Generation.'' Electric Power Research Institute, 1997.

Lazich, Robert S., ed. *Market Share Reporter.* Detroit: Gale Research, 1997.

Mack, Toni. ''Electric Utilities.'' *Forbes,* 13 January 1997.

Navarro, Pete. *Power Unleashed.* Hemisphere, Inc., 1997.

U.S. Department of Energy. ''Electric Power Annual,'' 1998. Available from http://www.eia.doe.gov/cneaf/electricity.

U.S. Department of Energy. *Changing Structure of the Electric Power Industry: Selected Issues,* 1998. Available from http://www.eia.doe.gov/cneaf/electricity.

SIC 4922

NATURAL GAS TRANSMISSION

This industry classification includes establishments engaged in the gathering, transmission, and storage of natural gas. Establishments involved in natural gas exploration and drilling are classified under oil and gas exploration industries. Establishments involved in both the transmission and distribution of natural gas are classified in **SIC 4923: Natural Gas Transmission and Distribution.** Establishments involved in natural gas distribution to end users are classified in **SIC 4924: Natural Gas Distribution.**

NAICS CODE(S)

486210 (Pipeline Transportation of Natural Gas)

INDUSTRY SNAPSHOT

Natural gas, as it exists in the ground, is not a single kind of gas, but rather a mixture of hydrocarbons, molecules made up of hydrogen and carbon, existing naturally in a gaseous state. The hydrocarbon gases include methane, ethane, propane, butane, and, frequently, impurities such as water, hydrogen sulfide, nitrogen, and helium. Methane, the lightest of the gases, is the most important gas for the energy industry. The heavier gases (ethane, propane, and butane) are sometimes included in the natural gas mixture transported by a pipeline, but usually they are removed for use in other industries, such as in the manufacture of industrial chemicals.

Traditionally, the natural gas industry has consisted of three primary activities: exploring for and producing natural gas; transporting the gas from production centers to market regions; and distributing gas to end users. Throughout the development of the industry, some companies have been involved in all three areas, while others have focused their efforts on only one or two.

The natural gas transmission segment of the industry includes gathering lines, storage facilities, and pipeline systems. Gathering lines transport gas from producing wells to facilities, where impurities are removed, and to processing plants that separate methane from other types of natural gas. Methane can then be injected into storage or sent through transmission pipelines.

ORGANIZATION AND STRUCTURE

Within the United States, gas flows primarily in a northeasterly direction toward the eastern states and the Midwest from four major producing areas centered in Texas, Oklahoma, Louisiana, and the Gulf of Mexico. A smaller, but increasing, amount of gas is transported from Texas and Canada into California. Most of the natural gas is transported through interconnected webs of underground pipelines. Individual pipes vary in size from about five feet in diameter to less than an inch. The largest pipes collect gas in producing areas; the smallest pipes deliver gas to individual households. By the latter 1990s, more than 256,000 miles of pipeline transported the gas to 47 of the contiguous states (Vermont imported its gas from Canada).

Long-distance pipelines transport gas under pressure, usually about 1,000 pounds per square inch. The gas travels through the pipeline at a rate of about 15 miles per hour. As it moves through the system, local gas utilities and large individual users, such as industrial customers or electricity-generating power plants, make withdrawals. To keep the gas moving, compressor stations along the pipeline restore gas pressures, which otherwise would drop because of withdrawals and friction.

One advantage to natural gas as an energy source is that it can be stored. Natural gas usage fluctuates seasonally, typically showing slack demand during the summer months and dramatic increases during the winter when it is used for space heating. During times of low use, inexpensive gas can be purchased and injected into storage for use during times of high demand when the price usually is higher. Some companies meet more than half of their winter deliveries with gas from storage.

Not all gas in storage is available for use, however. In order to maintain adequate pressure in a storage reservoir, a quantity of gas, referred to as ''base gas,'' must be maintained. The gas available to be withdrawn is called ''working gas.''

BACKGROUND AND DEVELOPMENT

The natural gas supplied in the United States comes from two basic kinds of sources, referred to as conventional and unconventional. Conventional gas is recovered from gas fields, both onshore and offshore. According to a traditionally held belief, conventional natural gas deposits were formed through long geological processes in combination with the decay of biological material. Under appropriate conditions, the gas became trapped in permeable rock and was covered by an impermeable cap.

Gas reservoirs consist of areas where the gas is contained within porous rocks and between the pieces that make up rocks. The amount of gas a rock formation can hold is based on how many of these tiny holes exist within the structure. Natural gas within a porous rock formation is prevented from migrating to the surface and into the atmosphere when a nonporous cap covers it.

Unconventional gas reservoirs have different geological characteristics. Some types of unconventional gas resources include: ''tight gas'' or ''tight sands gas,'' which is found in low-permeability rock; ''Devonian shale gas,'' which is found in shale deposits from the

Devonian geological period, approximately 350 million years ago; ''coal-bed methane,'' which is natural gas that has been formed along with the geological processes that formed coal; ''natural gas from geopressurized aquifers,'' which refers to gas dissolved under high pressure and at high temperatures in brines located deep beneath the earth's surface; ''gas hydrates,'' which are ice-like structures of water and gas located under the permafrost; and ''deep gas,'' which is found at levels much deeper than conventional gas. Although there is no scientific consensus, some believe deep gas originated from inorganic sources and that it exists everywhere as a result of the geological processes that formed the earth. Of the unconventional gas sources, the one most important to the gas transportation industry was coal-bed methane.

Recorded use of natural gas dates back thousands of years. The ancient Chinese used natural gas, piped through bamboo poles, to boil water to make salt. In the seventh century, natural gas transported through secret pipes fueled ''eternal fires'' in temples near the Caspian Sea, where people came to see the mystery and to worship.

In the United States, natural gas discoveries date back to 1775. George Washington reportedly saw flames rising from water near the location of present-day Charleston, West Virginia. That same year, other gas discoveries were made by French missionaries in the Ohio Valley.

In 1821 the discovery of natural gas in a well in Fredonia, New York, led to the nation's first pipeline. William Aaron Hart piped gas from a 27-foot-deep well to provide lighting for nearby buildings. Two other major developments occurred in 1872. The nation's first long pipeline (25 miles) was completed and provided natural gas to Rochester, New York. Also, the first iron pipeline transported natural gas, carrying it 5.5 miles to serve about 250 customers.

Toward the end of the nineteenth century, natural gas fields in Ohio, Pennsylvania, and West Virginia yielded nearly 80 percent of the natural gas produced in the United States. The National Transit Co., a subsidiary of John D. Rockefeller's Standard Oil Co., transported the largest share of the nation's gas. In 1898, Standard founded the Hope Natural Gas Co. to serve the West Virginia area, and the East Ohio Gas Co. to serve residential and industrial users in Ohio.

At the turn of the century, large gas fields were discovered in Texas, Louisiana, and Oklahoma. As a result of their discovery, national production doubled between 1906 and 1920. By 1925, approximately 3.5 million customers used natural gas, most of them living within a few hundred miles of the producing sites. Lack of pipelines and other means of transportation thwarted efforts to fully utilize the resource.

Seamless, electrically welded pipe developed in the late 1920s enabled pipeline companies to carry gas at higher pressures. This meant that large quantities could be transported over longer distances. The world's first high-pressure, thin-wall, large-diameter gas transmission line was constructed in 1930 by the Natural Gas Pipeline Co. It transported gas produced in Texas, Oklahoma, and Kansas to the Chicago area. The nation's first all-welded, high-pressure natural gas pipeline was constructed by the Hope Natural Gas Co. in 1936.

The development of pipeline technologies made long-distance gas transmission feasible, and the 1930s brought an increased awareness of the product's potential as an important energy resource. Until that time, gas was discovered almost incidentally as the nation searched for oil reserves. If a company drilled for oil and found nothing, it could simply walk away from the dry well. Gas wells, on the other hand, were considered a nuisance, because if a company struck gas, the well had to be capped. If gas was discovered along with oil, the gas was routinely burned off, a procedure called ''flaring.''

The mid-1930s marked a time of changes in governmental regulation of the gas industry. In 1935, the Public Utility Holding Company Act required holding companies to divest themselves of public utility subsidiaries. As a result, ownership of many local distributing companies changed.

In 1938, in response to Federal Trade Commission reports that pipeline companies were employing monopolistic price setting practices, Congress passed the Natural Gas Act, under which natural gas became a regulated commodity. The Federal Power Commission, given the responsibility of administering the Natural Gas Act's provisions, assumed control over pipeline rates. Actual price controls on gas were not instituted until after World War II.

World War II played an important role in the development of the U.S. natural gas pipeline industry. During the war years, the Axis powers sank tankers transporting fuel oil from Texas to the eastern seaboard. To help transport oil for the war effort, the government built two large-diameter oil pipelines between 1942 and 1944. Following the war, these pipelines were sold and became part of the nation's transcontinental natural gas pipeline grid. The result was that by 1947 gas from Texas could be piped to both U.S. coasts.

Offshore drilling technologies also were developed during the late 1940s. The first offshore lease sales were held by the state of Louisiana on August 14, 1945. The first successful offshore Gulf of Mexico production began in 1947.

Technological advances proceeded as methods for underground storage were created. In 1951, Consolidated Natural Gas and Texas Eastern Transmission Corp. opened one of the world's largest underground gas storage facilities at Oakford Field in southwestern Pennsylvania. At the facility, natural gas was stored in an existing, but depleted, gas field.

In 1954, the U.S. supreme court's Phillips decision expanded the federal government's jurisdiction by granting the Federal Power Commission the authority to regulate the interstate gas market and control gas prices. This decision created a division between interstate and intrastate sales. The division between interstate and intrastate markets, which had begun to affect the availability of natural gas as early as the mid-1960s, became more profound. Because pipeline companies could get higher prices in intrastate markets, nationwide supplies began to dwindle. In 1975, the Federal Power Commission issued Order 533, which permitted pipeline companies to transport gas on behalf of end users who purchased it directly from producers. The order was intended to help large users avoid supply cuts because of declining gas supplies on the interstate market.

Low price ceilings also affected the rates at which new gas fields were discovered. Exploration began declining during the late 1960s, and as the discovery rate dropped, some industry watchers concluded that the nation was running out of natural gas reserves.

In 1973, however, production of natural gas in the United States was at its highest at 21.7 trillion cubic feet. Increases in natural gas production helped offset reductions in oil imports due to the OPEC oil embargo. U.S. natural gas consumption also peaked in the early 1970s. During 1972, the nation consumed 22.1 trillion cubic feet and set record usage levels in the residential, industrial, and electric utility sectors.

A cold winter during the 1976-77 heating season highlighted supply problems within the natural gas industry. Some large companies, like Consolidated Natural Gas, were forced to cut deliveries to industrial customers holding ''interruptible'' contracts. Typically, gas had been sold under ''interruptible'' or ''noninterruptible'' agreements. Interruptible contracts, primarily sold to industrial users with the ability to switch to other types of fuel when necessary, called for the delivery of gas when supplies were available. Noninterruptible contracts, which were more expensive, called for a guaranteed amount of gas to be delivered.

Localized gas shortages during the late 1970s caused concerns about its availability and led to increased interest in expanding storage capacities. The gas shortages also led to the Powerplant and Industrial Fuel Use Act of 1978, which placed restrictions on the use of natural gas for generating electricity and for industrial uses. Congress also passed the Natural Gas Policy Act of 1978, which called for price deregulation and increased exploration and development, especially of potential nonconventional gas supplies. The act attempted to correct the price distinctions between interstate and intrastate markets by setting different prices on different categories of gas for both types of markets. It also made provisions to phase out wellhead price controls and to make pipelines more accessible to gas users wishing to purchase transportation services only.

Until the creation of the U.S. Department of Energy (DOE) in 1977, statistical information regarding the natural gas industry was compiled by the Bureau of Mines under the auspices of the U.S. Department of the Interior. Thereafter, the Energy Information Administration, an agency within the DOE, assumed responsibility for collecting information regarding the natural gas industry. Also during this time, the duty of regulating interstate natural gas markets was transferred from the Federal Power Commission to the Federal Energy Regulatory Commission (FERC), an independent office of the DOE.

FERC launched its restructuring efforts in the mid-1980s, and the process was completed with the issuance of Orders 636 and 636A in 1992. The new regulations were intended to promote competition within the industry and to restructure interstate pipelines by requiring them to offer their services separately rather than bundled together. Formerly, pipelines bought and sold gas at unit prices that included associated charges for transportation and storage. Without the ability to access pipeline delivery services separately from gas purchases, customers were unable to buy gas from other suppliers.

The new regulations required pipeline companies to ''unbundle'' services. This meant that they could not exclusively sell packages combining sales, transportation, and storage services. The restructuring orders dictated that all services be offered and priced separately. As a result, customers were allowed to buy gas from sources other than the pipeline. Consequently, many pipeline companies abandoned their customary merchant function, turning their attention toward selling gas transportation services and leasing storage capacity.

The unbundling of pipeline services brought open access to gas transportation service. Large end users and local distribution companies increasingly made separate agreements under which gas purchases were arranged with producers or brokers, and transportation services were purchased from pipeline companies.

Also, as part of its Order 636, FERC identified four types of costs pipeline companies could recover from their customers, including gas utilities, as they sought to comply with the new regulations. The costs pipeline companies were permitted to pass on were: the cost of purchased gas that would have been recaptured under previously existing bundled contracts; the cost associated with reforming or canceling remaining contracts to buy gas; the cost of abandoning facilities or contracts rendered unnecessary; and the cost of installing new facilities required to comply with the regulations.

The gas transportation industry began responding to these legislative initiatives in the 1980s. Additional FERC orders issued during 1983 and 1984 addressed questions surrounding access to natural gas transportation systems. In January 1985, under the deadline set by previous regulations, most price controls on gas expired.

The environmental advantages of natural gas remain significant, especially when compared to coal, which still fuels the bulk of the electricity generated in the United States. Used as a fuel in a power plant, natural gas produces 100 percent less sulfur pollution than a coal plant; 100 percent less ash, sludge or solid waste; 95 percent less particulate emissions; and 81 percent less nitrogen oxide emissions. According to one natural gas company, substitution of natural gas for coal globally on a 50/50 basis by the year 2010 would result in a 35 percent decrease in the volume of global carbon emissions.

CURRENT CONDITIONS

In 1999, natural gas was the leading source for heating energy in the United States, holding more than 50 percent of the market. Heating oil still controlled 30 percent of the market, and electricity controlled 10 percent. The remaining 10 percent was divided among miscellaneous heat energy sources such as coal, wood, and propane. By 2010, government analysts predict annual consumption of natural gas to be near 30 trillion cubic feet. To satisfy that anticipated market, as much as $32 billion will be needed for new pipelines, and more than $2 billion for storage facilities.

Notwithstanding, in December 1999, FERC voted 3-2 to refuse certification of the proposed $678 million, 401-mile Independence Pipeline intended to carry natural gas from the western United States and Canada to the East Coast. FERC also issued a hold on the $528 million Transco Market Link project connecting Pennsylvania and New Jersey, as well as the $125 million ANR SupplyLink Project between Chicago and Ohio. FERC's hold was intended to address not only environmental concerns for the high-pressure pipelines, but also to address objections to the ostensible need. Meanwhile, American Natural Resources Corp. (ANR) proposed in December 1999 to build a 130-mile pipeline under Lake Michigan to connect Milwaukee, Wisconsin, with northern Indiana. Its competitor, Wicor, Inc., concurrently proposed a 150-mile Guardian Pipeline from Joliet, Illinois, to Ixonia, Wisconsin. ANR remained the top company nationally in 1999, when ranked by total gas throughput (4,511,426 Mmcf).

INDUSTRY LEADERS

According to *Pipeline & Gas Journal's* 1999 Annual 500 Report, El Paso Energy Corp. was the newest leading gas transmission company (by pipeline miles) in the United States, controlling an acquired 32,000 miles of pipeline, which spread coast to coast and border to border. Other leaders were GPM Cas Corp. (28,000 miles of gathering pipeline); Northern Natural Gas Co. (16,613 miles); and Columbia Natural Gas Co. (13,459 miles).

One of the largest overall companies in this industry is Enron Corp., headquartered in Houston, Texas. With more than $40 billion in 1999 revenues and a 27 percent net income growth for that year, Enron and its four major business units are well positioned to take advantage of the global trend toward increased consumption of natural gas. Through its subsidiaries, Enron is the largest buyer and seller of natural gas in North America, the largest supplier of natural gas to America's electric generation industry, and operator of one of the largest transmission systems in the western hemisphere (the second largest in the world).

Interstate gas pipeline companies operated by Enron include Northern Natural Gas, Transwestern Pipeline, Florida Gas Transmission, Northern Border Pipeline, and Transportadora de Gas del Sur in Argentina. Northern Natural Gas transports gas from western Texas to the upper Midwest. States served include Iowa, Wisconsin, and Minnesota. Total 1999 pipeline miles for the company were 32,000.

Enron's system also reaches beyond U.S. borders. The Northern Border Pipeline, operated by Enron and 35 percent owned by the company, receives Canadian gas at Monchy, Saskatchewan, and delivers it to the upper Midwest market. In South America, Enron and three partners acquired a 3,800 mile portion of Argentina's natural gas pipeline system.

Enron also operates natural gas processing plants which provide ethane, propane, butane, and other natural gas liquids to the marketplace. In November 1992, the company completed a new plant to produce methyl tertiary butyl ether (MTBE). MTBE is a component used to produce reformulated gasoline, mandated for use in several urban areas under the terms of the 1990 Clean Air Act.

Another leading gas transmission enterprise, The Williams Companies Inc., operated 27,000 miles of coast-to-coast pipeline in 1999, as well as its own reserve containing 708 billion cubic feet of natural gas. The company not only is involved in gathering, processing, and transporting natural gas, it also operates a 20,000-

mile communications field made by installing fiber-optic cable inside unused pipelines.

In addition to providing natural gas transmission services, The Williams Companies offer field services, petroleum services, and exploration and production services under the umbrella of the Williams Energy Group. The merging of these units, according to company spokespersons, is meant to ''leverage existing assets to compete in virtually every segment of the huge and evolving unregulated energy market.'' The Williams Communications Group includes: WilTel, which provides a full range of telecommunications services including data, voice, video, and Internet transmission; Vyvx, which provides terrestrial fiber-optic and satellite multimedia transmission services; Global Access; and Williams Learning Network.

The Williams Cos., with 21,000 employees, reported 1998 sales of $7.26 billion and a one-year sales growth of 73 percent. Its 1998 net income was $128 million.

America and the World

Imports and exports both played an important role in U.S. natural gas markets. During the 1990s imports from Canada and exports to Mexico were at their highest levels in history. Net imports of natural gas from Canada were 3.0 trillion cubic feet in 1998, constituting 14 percent of overall 1998 U.S. gas consumption. The United States also imported liquefied natural gas from Algeria (69 billion cubic feet in 1998). The liquefied natural gas, transported by special tanker ships and kept in liquid form through refrigeration and pressure, entered U.S. pipeline systems after being re-gasified at special facilities in Louisiana.

Canadian gas, however, accounted for the bulk of U.S. imports. The North American energy giant TransCanada controls 13,888 miles of pipeline in their Alberta System, 9,176 miles of the Canadian mainline, and 110 miles of ANG Pipeline. In 1999, TransCanada also had partnership interests in 7,100 miles of North American pipelines.

In terms of natural gas production, the United States ranked second in the world, averaging about 17 trillion cubic feet per year. The world's top producer, the former Soviet Union, produced about 26 trillion cubic feet per year. Canada ranked third, producing about 3.5 trillion cubic feet annually. The world's fourth largest producer, the Netherlands, supplied about 3 trillion cubic feet per year. The Netherlands obtained gas from both onshore and offshore facilities, exporting it through pipelines to Germany, Belgium, France, and Italy.

One of the longest international gas pipeline systems, the Trans-Mediterranean Pipeline, stretched more than 1,500 miles from the Sahara Desert in Algeria (on the north African coast) to northern Italy. The Trans-Mediterranean was designed to transport gas under the Mediterranean sea, deliver it to markets in Italy, and eventually link to a European pipeline grid.

In the latter 1990s, worldwide demand for natural gas stood at approximately 77 trillion cubic feet. By 2015, demand was expected to more than double, reaching 135 trillion cubic feet. In North America, natural gas usage for industry and electric power generation was expected to lead growth in gas demand with U.S. energy consumption expected to increase by 30 percent over the 1995 to 2015 time frame. On a worldwide basis, consumption of natural gas was growing at a rate of nearly 3 percent annually, compared to 1 percent for other fossil fuels, and another 355,000 miles of natural gas pipelines were to be added to the world gas grid by 2015—mostly in Asia, Europe, the Middle East and Africa. This growing demand coupled with the trend toward privatization brought on by the FERC's deregulatory measures, as well as easier access to foreign markets, boded well for U.S. gas transmission companies. Companies like Enron and Williams moved quickly to establish themselves in international markets and to consolidate their positions at home.

Further Reading

Cook, Linda, Sheila M. Darnell, and Ann M. Ducca. ''U.S. Natural Gas Imports and Exports-1998.'' U.S. Dept. of Energy, Energy Information Administration, Natural Gas Monthly Report, August 1999.

———. *Corporate Profile.* Houston: Enron, 1997.

Griffin, Jeff. ''Pipeline Growth Potential Viewed With Cautious Optimism.'' *Underground Construction,* November, 1999, 34.

Haferd, Laura. ''Federal Regulators Delay Plans for Pipeline Through Ohio.'' *Akron Beacon Journal,* 16 December 1999.

Hoover's Online: Company capsules for Enron Corp. and The Williams Companies. Available from http://www.hoovers.com, 1999.

Ives, George Jr., ed. ''A Step Forward.'' *Pipe Line & Gas Industry,* September 1998, 5.

''Let Guardian Proposal Sink or Swim on its Own.'' Editorial, *Business Journal Serving Greater Milwaukee,* 17 December 1999, 46.

Tubb, Jeff. ''P&GJ's 19th Annual 500 Report.'' *Pipeline & Gas Journal,* November 1999, 42.

U.S. Dept. of Transportation, *Transportation Statistics Annual Report 1999.* Washington, D.C.: 1999.

The Williams Companies, Inc. *Annual Report 1996.* Tulsa: Williams Companies, 1997.

SIC 4923

NATURAL GAS TRANSMISSION AND DISTRIBUTION

This industry classification includes establishments engaged in both the transmission and distribution of natural gas. Establishments involved in natural gas transmission, but not its distribution to end users, are classified in **SIC 4922: Natural Gas Transmission.** Establishments involved in natural gas distribution, but not its transmission from supply regions to market areas, are classified in **SIC 4924: Natural Gas Distribution.**

NAICS CODE(S)

221210 (Natural Gas Distribution)
486210 (Pipeline Transportation of Natural Gas)

INDUSTRY SNAPSHOT

Composed almost entirely of methane, natural gas is a combustible gaseous fuel used in residential and commercial applications. It is produced, transported, and consumed in measures associated with cubic feet. One cubic foot is equal to the volume of gas that could be contained in a cubic area measuring one foot in all three dimensions under a pressure of 14.73 pounds per square inch at 60 degrees Fahrenheit. Although the energy content of natural gas can vary depending on its precise chemical composition, 1,000 cubic feet of natural gas has the energy equivalent of approximately one million British thermal units (Btu). A Btu is a standard unit used to measure the amount of heat produced by an energy source.

By the end of the 1990s, natural gas supplied about one-half of the nation's energy needs. Industry watchers noted several trends indicating increased reliance on natural gas. For example, in 1990, natural gas was used in 59 percent of new single-family home construction, up from 43 percent in 1985. By 1999, it was up to 70 percent. According to the American Gas Association (AGA), there were more than 1.3 million miles of natural gas transmission and distribution pipelines traversing the nation, delivering supplies to 60 million commercial and residential customers. The U.S. imported about 14 percent of its natural gas in 1998, primarily from Canada. Conversely, the U.S. exported natural gas to Japan (66 billion cubic feet) and Mexico (53 billion cubic feet) in 1998.

In the late 1990s, natural gas usage was also becoming increasingly important in generating electricity. Much safer than nuclear energy and significantly cleaner for the environment than coal-burning, natural gas took over as the energy source of choice in power generation plants and many industrial complexes. The effects of the Clean Air Act were expected to expand its role even farther. In addition, natural gas played a significant role in industrial cogeneration (retaining and distributing the heat energy produced by generating electricity).

ORGANIZATION AND STRUCTURE

Natural gas is transported and distributed under a myriad of federal and state regulations. Interstate pipelines fall under the jurisdiction of the Federal Energy Regulatory Commission (FERC). Local distribution companies (called LDCs or gas utilities) fall under the domain of their state's public utility commission.

The complete natural gas distribution chain, from the point of its production to the point of its use, was historically comprised of controlled monopolies. During the 1980s and early 1990s, deregulation brought increased competition and fragmented the industry. Before deregulation, producers supplied gas to transporters. Transporters provided gas, primarily under wholesale agreements, to distributors. Distributors delivered gas, primarily under retail agreements, to end users. Following deregulation, the natural gas industry saw the expansion and extension of traditional roles as well as the introduction of new participants such as brokers, independent marketers, marketing affiliates, and consultants.

Various segments of the natural gas industry are represented through trade associations. The American Gas Association represents the interests of local distributing companies. The Natural Gas Supply Association represents major gas producers. The Interstate Natural Gas Association of America represents pipelines. Some other related organizations include: the Independent Petroleum Association of America, representing small independent gas producers; the Domestic Petroleum Council, representing some large independent gas producers; and the Process Gas Consumers, which is comprised of industrial gas users. The Natural Gas Council represents producers, pipelines, and local distributors. It works to increase gas availability and the reliability of natural gas supplies as well as to promote increased consumption.

BACKGROUND AND DEVELOPMENT

The origin of the natural gas industry can be traced back to Titusville, Pennsylvania, in 1859. Former railroad conductor Colonel Edwin Drake struck oil 69 feet below the surface of the ground in the small town. The spot marked the first transportation pipeline in the United States, running just more than 5 miles.

Because there was no easy way to transport natural gas into homes, it was used primarily to light city streets in the nineteenth century. The 1885 invention of the Bunsen burner, which mixed air with natural gas, allowed the use of the fuel's thermal properties. Gas producers responded to the discovery by promoting natural gas as a heating fuel for use in warming water or cooking food.

Natural gas was not, however, widely used until after World War II, after which metallurgy advances, welding techniques, and pipe rolling greatly improved the methods of transporting the fuel. Thousands of miles of pipeline were laid from the post-War period through the 1960s, when natural gas began to be widely used in American industry as well.

Congress passed the Natural Gas Act of 1938, marking the first governmental regulation of the industry. This act sought to protect consumers from the monopolies that were forming in the industry by regulating the price of natural gas. The gas shortages in the 1970s and 1980s caused the eventual move away from price regulation, which resulted in increased demand for gas supply and decreased prices. Marketplace competition led to innovation and technological improvements. The deregulation of segments of the industry has, overall, had positive results with regard to pricing and demand. Because natural gas is often thought of as the cleanest source of energy, the Clean Air Act Amendments of 1990, which called for cleaner fuel sources, also boosted the demand for natural gas.

Domestic demand for natural gas hit its peak in 1972 when consumption was 22 trillion cubic feet. In succeeding years, questions about gas availability and climbing prices led to shrinking demand. Consumption fell to 16 trillion cubic feet in 1986 before beginning to grow again. By the early 1990s, natural gas was making a sustained comeback which continued into the millennium. Natural gas gained popularity as a favored fuel because of its environmental advantages and its availability as a domestic resource.

CURRENT CONDITIONS

Gas service is provided in all 50 states by 1,200 gas distribution companies, pulling from about 288,000 natural gas wells. In 1999, American users consumed approximately 20 trillion cubic feet of natural gas. By 2010, that figure is expected to reach 30 trillion cubic feet. The largest percentage of consumption goes to residential users, who account for about 50 percent. U.S. industry uses about 40 percent. A small amount, equal to approximately 0.0004 trillion cubic feet, has been used to fuel natural gas vehicles. As the industry continues to deregulate, prices to end-users continue downward. In the ten years between 1987 and 1997, prices dropped an average of 14 percent, while the industry grew annually by approximately two percent.

Between 1999 and 2000, 84 new pipeline projects were proposed, which would increase delivery capability by 23.2 billion cubic feet per day. Year 2000 expenditures for pipeline development and expansion were estimated at $6 billion. There were 410 underground natural storage sites in the U.S. as of the end of 1998, with the largest number of them located in the Midwest (128).

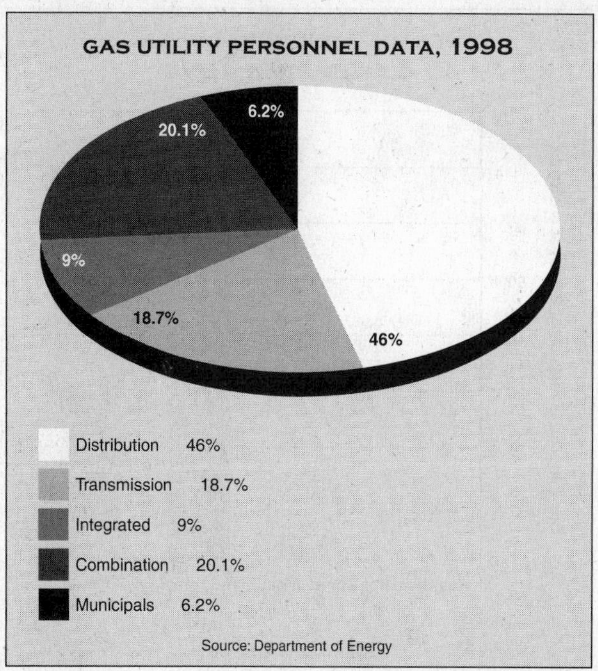

The latter 1990s saw many nuclear power plants and coal-burning power facilities shut down or convert to natural gas facilities. This was particularly true in the eastern half of the nation, in highly-industrialized areas.

INDUSTRY LEADERS

Amidst a rapidly-changing industry characterized by continuous mergers, trades, and acquisitions, *Pipeline & Gas Journal*'s 1999 Annual 500 Report listed some of the then-current leaders. Southern California Gas Co, a subsidiary of Pacific Enterprises (one of the largest natural gas transmission and distribution holding companies) was the leading LDC, with 4.9 million customers, up another 76,000 meters from just the previous year. Southern reported 1997 operating revenues of $2.4 billion. Next was Pacific Gas & Electric Co. (PG&E), which in 1999 reported 3.8 million gas customers. In 1999, PG&E was considered the largest utility holding company in the U.S., with 4.6 million electric customers in addition to its gas customers. Although it controlled 9,000 miles of pipeline, in early 2000, the company was expected to sell its gas lines to El Paso Natural Gas Company, a major transmission pipeline leader. PG&E's 1998 revenues were just under $20 billion. Net income was $719 million.

Another multifaceted natural gas enterprise was Consolidated Natural Gas Company (CNG). CNG, with headquarters in Pittsburgh and New York operated one of the nation's largest natural gas systems and marketed natural gas and electricity throughout North America.

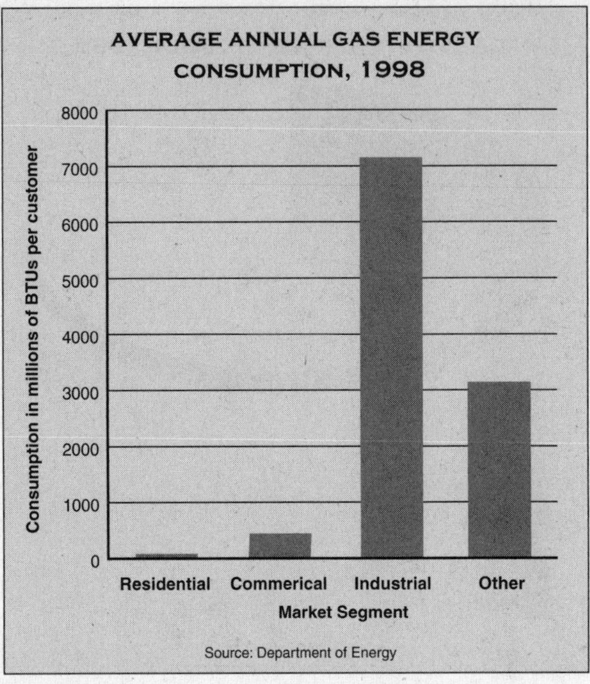

The company had more than $5 billion in assets and nearly $3 billion in 1998 sales. Its subsidiaries operate in all segments of the gas industry, including exploration, production, transportation, storage, purchasing, reselling, and distribution. The company controlled 10,000 miles of pipeline and a network of 27 underground storage facilities with a capacity totaling more than 885 billion cubic feet, making it the largest gas storage network in the United States. The gas storage fields receive injections of gas during low demand periods to help meet high demand during the winter heating season. In December 1999, CNG and Dominion Resources announced their merger plans for 2000 which would create the largest integrated natural gas and electric power company in the U.S.

While traditional transmission and distribution gas companies like CNG and Pacific Enterprises have been reorganizing to adapt to industry-wide changes, non-traditional entities called GTMs (gatherers, transporters, and marketers) have been emerging. GTMs operate in a more flexible environment because they are not tied to pre-existing, long-term contracts. Two of the nation's leading GTMs are Associated Natural Gas Corporation and Western Gas Resources, Inc. Both are headquartered in Denver.

But nothing was to compare with the biggest collaboration in the industry which occurred in the final hours of 1999: the joint natural gas venture between Phillips Petroleum's GPM Gas Corp. and Duke Energy. The spin-off company was to be called Duke Energy Field Services, and would be the nation's largest natural gas gatherer and processor. Duke will own 70 percent of the new venture. The company will control 57,000 miles of pipeline, with a daily production of 5 billion cubic feet of natural gas, and 400,000 barrels of natural gas liquids, in 67 plants across the country.

RESEARCH AND TECHNOLOGY

In 1999, Congress appropriated $246 million for natural gas Research, Design, & Development programs at the Department of Energy (DOE). Priority projects included natural gas turbines and microturbines, natural gas cooling technologies, and natural gas vehicles and fuel cells. The Gas Research Institute also announced its 1999 Pacesetter Awards to member companies who help promote adoption of new natural gas technologies. 1999 winners included Enron Gas Pipeline Company for surveying 160 compressor stations for fugitive emissions, using the Hi-Flow Sampler for leak detection and measurement, and the City of Richmond, Virginia, for helping to secure a gas industry consortium and co-funding for testing Methane de-NOX reburn technology at a 240-MW coal-fired plant.

Overall, research efforts undertaken by transmission and distribution companies focused primarily in two areas: expanding natural gas markets and improving natural gas conveyance. One of the most popular technologies under investigation was the evolution of natural gas fueled vehicles (NGVs). In 1999, about 60,000 NGVs were in operation in the United States, increasing in number by about 10,000 annually. Although the amount used for NGVs accounted for only a small fraction of U.S. natural gas consumption, it represented a 26 percent increase over 1990. Four states—Arizona, Indiana, Ohio, and Washington—made up approximately 60 percent of the nation's demand for natural gas for vehicle use. Advanced NGVs have been proven to reduce carbon monoxide and nitrogen oxide emissions by as much as 90 percent. As of 1999, the AGA announced that 13 states had 30 or more compressed natural gas (CNG) vehicle fueling stations, and usage is expected to increase.

Another emerging technology involved gas-powered cooling for refrigeration and air conditioning. Although large air conditioning systems have already been developed for use in industrial and commercial applications, air conditioning units small enough for private home use have been typically electric. That trend began to reverse in the 1990s, and the industry expected to introduce its first residential model natural gas dehumidifier in 2000. In 1999, gas-powered appliances were typically about ten percent more expensive to purchase than their electric counterparts, but were less expensive to operate. In addition to expanding markets for natural gas, gas cooling technologies were expected to help reduce summer peaks in demand for electricity.

During the 1990s, several gas distribution companies were experimenting with first generation natural gas fuel cells, manufactured by United Technologies Corporation (Connecticut) and by Westinghouse. Natural gas fuel cells produce electricity and heat by combining hydrogen in the gas with oxygen in the air. Brooklyn Union Gas Company, for example, installed a 200-kilowatt fuel cell at a health care facility in New York, and Southern California Gas Company installed fuel cells for diverse customers including hospitals, food-processing facilities, and a mass transit agency. Because natural gas fuel cells yield low emissions at their point of use, the technology looked promising for densely populated areas and for use inside buildings. Under early gas fuel cell agreements, fuel cells were installed and maintained by local utilities who charged for the electricity and heat used.

In the arena of natural gas conveyance, one area under investigation was pipeline maintenance. According to estimates of the U.S. Department of Transportation, approximately 800,000 to 900,000 leaks in gas mains and service lines occur every year. In addition to presenting a potential disaster, lost gas represents lost earnings. In order to make gas line repairs, utilities must find the precise location of defective pipe segments, remove soil or pavement at the site, repair or replace the pipe, and then restore the site. However, in 1999, the Gas Research Institute announced a joint venture with Germany's Karl Weiss GmbH & Company to bring to North America the new ''trenchless'' technologies for pipeline maintenance (requiring only two digging holes) and installation of the cured-in-place (CIP) liners to service lines and mains. New technology has increased the development of polyethylene piping, which can withstand higher pressures, from 100 to 125 psig. Other developments include new devices for detection of natural gas leaks. Overall, the industry spent $4 billion in 1999 for safety, with reportable incidents dropping from 290 in 1988 to 206 in 1998.

A pipe repair technique being jointly developed by Consolidated Natural Gas Company, East Ohio Gas Company, and PLS International (a company specializing in robotics technology) was called the PLS 3000. The PLS 3000 system used a sealed probe to examine low-pressure gas lines while they were still in use. The probe was expected to help identify specific problems such as water infiltration, pipeline distortions, cracks, or other problems in the pipes and pinpoint their locations. Although early models proved expensive, initial users judged the PLS 3000 cost effective in urban areas where excavation costs were substantial.

FURTHER READING

''Association News.'' *Pipeline & Gas Journal,* October 1999.

Cook, Linda, Sheila M. Darnell, and Ann M. Ducca. ''U.S. Natural Gas Imports and Exports-1998.'' U.S. Dept. of Energy, Energy Information Administration, Natural Gas Monthly Report, August 1999.

Consolidated Natural Gas Company. *Corporate Profile.* Pittsburgh: Consolidated Natural Gas Company, 1997.

''Deal of the Century.'' *Philips Business Information Highlights,* 27 December 1999.

Donovan, Dan. ''Dominion Resources, CNG Set Anticipated Merger Closing Date of January 28, 2000.'' CNG Press Release, December 17, 1999. Available from http://www.shareholder.com/cng/news/19991217-12639.htm.

''Enova Corporation and Pacific Enterprises Announce Strategic Combination of Equals.'' Enova Corp. Pacific Enterprises, 14 October 1996.

''Gas Industry Online.'' American Gas Association. 1997. Available from http://www.aga.com.

Griffin, Jeff. ''Pipeline Growth Potential Viewed With Cautious Optimism.'' *Underground Construction,* November 1999.

''Interview With American Gas Association Chairman Dick Terry.'' *Pipe Line & Gas Industry,* April 1999.

McDowell, Bruce. ''Natural Gas Utilities Deliver Natural Gas-And Broader Choices-To Residential Customers.'' *Pipline & Gas Journal,* November 1999.

''Natural Gas Week.'' National Gas Supply Association, 1997. Available from http://www.gri.org.

Pacific Enterprises. *1996 Annual Report,* 1997 Los Angeles: Pacific Enterprises.

Reed, Ted. ''Energy, Phillips Petroleum Plan Natural-Gas Venture.'' *The Charlotte Observer, N.C.,* 18 December 1999.

''Resources: Keeping Natural Gas Vehicles on the Go?'' *Government Procurement,* December 1999.

''Six Gas Companies Receive '99 GRI Pace Setter Awards.'' *Pipe Line & Gas Industry,* June 1999.

Tubb, Jeff, et al. ''PG&J's 19th Annual 500 Report.'' *Pipeline & Gas Journal,* November 1999.

U.S. Department of Energy, Natural Gas Statistics available from http://www.eia.doe.gov/pub/oil_gas/natural_gas/presentations/1999.

Vanderwater, Bob. ''Phillips Petroleum, Duke Energy Enter Natural Gas Venture.'' *The Daily Oklahoman,* 21 December 1999.

SIC 4924

NATURAL GAS DISTRIBUTION

This industry classification is comprised of establishments engaged in the distribution of natural gas to end users. Establishments involved in both the transmission and distribution of natural gas are classified in **SIC 4923: Natural Gas Transmission and Distribution.**

NAICS CODE(S)

221210 (Natural Gas Distribution)

INDUSTRY SNAPSHOT

From the years 2000 to 2015, natural gas consumption in the U.S. is expected to increase 25-30 percent (or about 2 percent annually, according to the U.S. Department of Energy). As of 1999, 70 percent of new homes being built were piped to receive natural gas. The biggest gain in usage, however, is expected to come from electric utility companies, which continue to shut down their nuclear energy or coal-burning facilities and convert to natural gas energy.

The natural gas distribution system continues to ''unbundle'' in a deregulated industry, giving end-users more choices than ever as to who delivers their gas supplies. Growing numbers of private entities have taken over the distribution of natural gas from traditional ''utilities'' companies, such that by 2000, more than 77 percent of natural gas consumed in the U.S. could be purchased from sources other than a local natural gas utility. Many local distribution companies (often referred to as LDCs or gas utilities companies) saw their largest and most profitable customers switching to alternate gas sources. In some cases, industrial users and electric utilities contracted with pipeline companies to construct direct access to transmission systems and bypass the LDC altogether. In other instances, the customer purchased the actual gas from independent suppliers but continued to buy transmission services from the LDC.

To cope with the changing industry environment, LDCs have begun far-reaching marketing efforts. They have offered services to large industrial users, such as natural gas storage, in attempts to keep profitable customers within the system. They have obtained new industrial customers by promoting fuel switching away from electricity and oil. LDCs have also expanded efforts aimed at increasing demand through the development of new technologies, including vehicular natural gas and natural gas fuel cells.

ORGANIZATION AND STRUCTURE

Gas utility companies receive their supplies of gas from a transmission system at a transfer point called the ''City Gate.'' The utility then delivers the gas through mains and distribution lines to end users in a particular geographic area. There are four traditional classes of gas utility customers: individual residences, commercial establishments, industrial facilities, and electric utilities. There are two types of customers within these classes. ''Core'' customers require stable amounts of gas on demand because gas is their only source of fuel. ''Noncore'' gas customers can switch to other types of fuel when gas is unavailable or too expensive. Residential and commercial customers are typical core customers; industrial and electric-generating companies are examples of non-core customers.

Local distribution companies are subject to regulation by state public utility commissions (PUCs). PUCs establish rates for different classes of customers. Prices per unit are typically lower for larger users. In setting rates, PUCs attempt to find an appropriate balance between the differing interests of consumers, who want low rates, and company investors, who seek adequate returns on their investments.

In addition to state PUCs, federal regulations also influence the gas distribution industry. In 1992, the Federal Energy Regulatory Commission (FERC) issued its Order 636. Although Order 636 had its most direct impact on the gas transmission industry, it also affected local distribution companies. Its provisions necessitated changes in the way distribution companies arranged for gas purchases, transportation, and storage. FERC's order also permitted pipelines to pass transition costs on to distribution companies.

BACKGROUND AND DEVELOPMENT

The nation's earliest gas distribution companies delivered synthetic gas, manufactured from coal, to cities for use in lighting. In the late 1800s, naphtha gas (derived from crude petroleum) replaced coal gas. By the time the first company to distribute natural gas, the Fredonia Gas Light and Water Works Company, was formed in New York, approximately 300 companies were already delivering manufactured gas. Other local distribution companies were formed in the closing years of the nineteenth century. Two examples are Brooklyn Union Gas Company, which was incorporated in 1895, and East Ohio Gas Company, founded in 1898 by the Standard Oil Company. Many early gas distribution companies were owned by holding companies involved in other segments of the natural gas industry. The Public Utility Holding Act of 1935 required large holding companies to divest themselves of their public utility companies.

In 1937, Texas became the first state to require the addition of an odorant in distributed natural gas. Ethyl mercaptan, originally introduced in Germany in 1880, aided in detecting natural gas leaks and provided an early warning system to help prevent disasters. The use of mercaptans and mercaptan blends gave natural gas, a compound that has no inherent smell, a distinctive odor.

During World War II, fuel oil and gasoline rationing led to an expansion of natural gas markets. Production during the war years increased by 55 percent. Natural gas was a key ingredient in more than 5,000 industrial processes, and was used as an industrial fuel and in the manufacture of explosives. Natural gas usage continued to increase following the war and from 1945 to 1954 consumption doubled.

To meet demand, local distribution companies purchased gas from an available pipeline that reached their area. The pipeline typically sold the gas at a single price that represented an average of all the categories of gas handled by the pipeline and included charges for transportation and storage. Changes in federal regulations during the 1980s and 1990s required pipelines to ''unbundle'' their services and offer gas utilities access to gas transmission services separately from gas purchases. As a result, local distribution companies were permitted to buy gas from a variety of sources.

As the gas distribution industry entered the 1990s, residential use accounted for about one-fourth of the nation's natural gas consumption. Because residential use fluctuated according to weather patterns, weather was an important issue. The industry judged ''normal weather'' as the mean of temperatures experienced over a 30-year period, and adjusted its norms every ten years. A ''degree day'' was defined as a measurement comparing the daily mean temperature to a guide of 65 degrees Fahrenheit. Although the decade began amid a series of years with warmer than average temperatures and a slowed economy, demand for natural gas was growing.

Environmental and conservation efforts contributed to increased demand for natural gas. In some instances, state regulatory agencies required electric utilities to use more natural gas and to encourage their customers to switch away from using electricity during peak demand periods. Often the preferred replacement fuel was natural gas.

The states of Wisconsin and Vermont required electric utilities to help retail customers shift away from electricity as their primary source of energy in instances where switching to fuels would be cost effective. Under the ruling, residential customers with electric heat were offered assistance in converting to other fuels.

Maximizing use of their system's capacity by providing gas to a variety of users is a vital concern to local distribution companies. Gas utilities hoped that improvements in natural gas cooling technologies for uses such as refrigeration and air conditioning would help balance winter and summer demand.

Another concern facing local distribution companies was ''bypass.'' Bypass referred to a process under which natural gas suppliers provided direct sales and service to large users, circumventing the local gas utility. According to bypass proponents, the practice provided an opportunity for customers to shop around for the best gas prices. According to critics, bypass provisions unfairly impacted small users, such as residential customers, because the distribution companies lost substantial loads resulting in higher fixed costs being passed on to the remaining customers.

For the nation as a whole, deregulation meant that industries that used a lot of natural gas became more competitive internationally, while consumers paid more of the real cost of the gas they used. Analysts saw the trend towards ''unbundling,'' as it came to be known, as being in the consumer's best interest; an increasing number of companies began to offer ''unbundled'' delivery at the residential level, as well as to larger customers. In spite of deregulation and other changes, profits among natural gas distributors continued to soar.

CURRENT CONDITIONS

As of August 1999, residential end-users in 23 states and the District of Columbia were able to purchase natural gas from one of several suppliers, but have their local utility company deliver it. These options accommodated roughly 22 million (or 40 percent) of the 55 million households with natural gas service. Between 1996 and 1999, four million residential customers actually switched to a non-utility supplier. According to a December 1998 report published by the U.S. General Accounting Office (GAO), residential customer choice programs resulted in individual savings of 1 to 15 percent on the total gas bill. The state of New York was a leader in offering customer choice to residential customers, and Ohio made customer choice a state policy. As of 1999, Georgia had the largest number of residents exercising purchase options. The state's largest natural gas utility, Atlanta Gas Light, continued to offer delivery services of natural gas, irrespective of the residential user's purchase source. In 1997, 88 percent of all gas consumed by electric utilities companies was purchased under this option, as was 33 percent in commercial/industrial facilities.

The American Gas Association (AGA) has estimated that overall natural gas consumption will increase 40 percent by the year 2015. By 2010, the U.S. will use 30 trillion cubic feet (tcf) annually. In order to accommodate these needs, industry analysts have estimated new pipeline costs to be as much as $32 billion, plus another few billion to provide for storage. States in New England are anticipated to be the first to require more pipeline construction, as nuclear and coal energy facilities continued to shut down and/or convert to natural gas. The Southeast is also a priority.

According to *Pipe Line & Gas Industry*'s 1999 interview with Dick Terry, chairman of AGA, residential natural gas customers paid 14 percent less for natural gas in 1997 than they did in 1987. Much of this savings was attributable to ''unbundling'' and gas utilities' reduction in operating and maintenance costs, down by nearly 2 percent annually between 1990 and 1995. The price drop

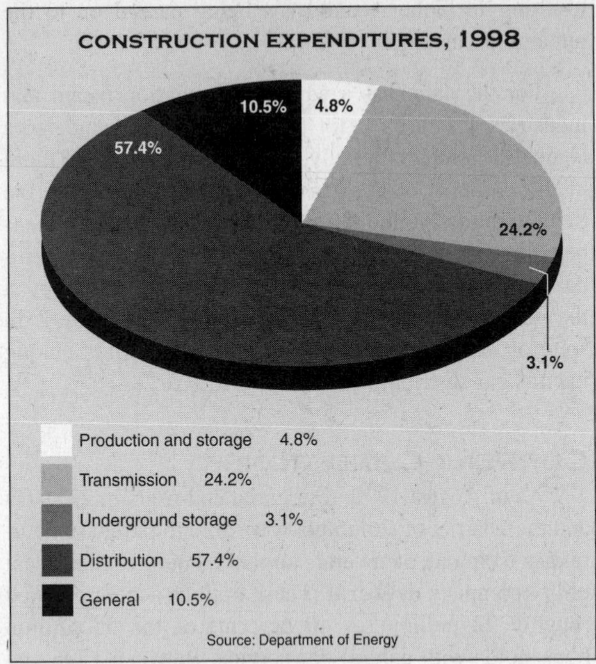

was more dramatic for the larger users, electric utilities and industrial customers, who paid 17 to 18 percent less.

Other factors have contributed to the steady but consistent growth of the industry. New technology has increased the development of polyethylene piping that can withstand higher pressures, from 100 to 125 psi. Other developments include new devices for detection of natural gas leaks. Overall, the industry spent $4 billion in 1999 for safety, with reportable incidents dropping from 290 in 1988 to 206 in 1998. Finally, in 1999, the Gas Research Institute announced a joint venture with Germany's Karl Weiss GmbH & Company to bring to North America the new ''trenchless'' technologies for pipeline maintenance (requiring only two digging holes) and to install the cured-in-place (CIP) liners to service lines and mains.

INDUSTRY LEADERS

In a rapidly-changing industry characterized by continual mergers, trades, and acquisitions, *Pipeline & Gas Journal*'s 1999 Annual 500 Report listed some of the leaders. Southern California Gas Co, a subsidiary of Pacific Enterprises (one of the largest natural gas transmission and distribution holding companies) was the leading LDC, with 4.9 million customers. Southern reported 1997 operating revenues of $2.4 billion. Next was Pacific Gas & Electric Co. (PG&E), which in 1999 reported 3.8 million gas customers. In 1999, PG&E was considered the largest utility holding company in the U.S., with 4.6 million electric customers in addition to its gas customers. Although it controlled 9,000 miles of pipeline, in early 2000, the company was expected to sell its gas lines to El Paso Natural Gas Company, a major transmission pipeline leader. PG&E's 1998 revenues were just under $20 billion. Net income was $719 million.

One of the fastest-growing LDCs was Southwest Gas Corporation, exemplary of the unbundled industry's opportunities. In 1999, Southwest obtained its gas from approximately 70 suppliers, then forwarded it to end-users through its 22,000 miles of transmission and distribution pipeline. Southwest reported 1998 sales of $917 million, a 25 percent increase from the previous year.

Other industry leaders were Public Service Electric & Gas, with 3.7 million customers and 1997 revenues of $1.5 billion, Consolidated Natural Gas Co. (CNG), with 1.88 million customers and 1997 revenues of $1.5 billion, and Nicor, with 1.9 million customers and 1997 revenues of $1.22 billion.

FURTHER READING

''Association News.'' *Pipeline & Gas Journal,* October 1999.

Griffin, Jeff. ''Pipeline Growth Potential Viewed With Cautious Optimism.'' *Underground Construction,* November 1999.

''Interview With American Gas Association Chairman Dick Terry.'' *Pipe Line & Gas Industry,*April 1999.

McDowell, Bruce. ''Natural Gas Utilities Deliver Natural Gas—And Broader Choices—To Residential Customers.''*Pipline & Gas Journal,* November 1999.

Standard & Poor's Industry Surveys. New York: McGraw Hill. October 1996.

Tubb, Jeff, et al. ''PG&J's 19th Annual 500 Report.'' *Pipeline & Gas Journal,* November 1999.

U.S. Department of Transportation, BTS. *Transportation Statistics Annual Report 1999.*Washington, DC: 1999.

SIC 4925

MIXED, MANUFACTURED, OR LIQUEFIED PETROLEUM GAS PRODUCTION AND/OR DISTRIBUTION

This industry classification includes establishments involved in manufacturing and/or distributing manufactured gas, liquefied petroleum gas (LPG), or mixtures of manufactured gas with natural gas. Examples include blue gas, coke oven gas, manufactured gas, synthetic natural gas from naphtha, and liquefied petroleum gas distributed through mains. Establishments involved in the sale of liquefied petroleum gas in steel containers are classified as **SIC 5984: Liquefied Petroleum Gas (Bottled Gas) Dealers.**

NAICS CODE(S)

221210 (Natural Gas Distribution)

Manufactured gas, liquefied petroleum products, and gas mixtures play an important role in specific industrial applications and in places beyond the reach of natural gas pipelines. Some of the most widely used manufactured or liquefied petroleum gases include coke oven gas, water gas, naphtha gas, acetylene, propane, and butane. Coke oven gas and water gas are both derived from coal. To make coke oven gas, vapors are collected from heated coal and then purified. Water gas is produced by forcing steam through hot coal or coke. Naphtha gas is made from crude petroleum. Acetylene can be made from water and calcium carbide or by breaking apart methane molecules. Propane and butane are both natural gas liquids. They are typically separated from methane during natural gas processing.

Although the ability to produce manufactured gas from coal dates back to the early years of the 1600s, the technology to use it commercially did not develop until the closing years of the eighteenth century. In Great Britain, William Murdock was the first to make large-scale application of gas lighting. Murdock installed outside factory lighting and 900 gas lamps in British cotton mills. In subsequent years, coal gas increased in popularity for municipal lighting. In 1817, Baltimore became the first U.S. city to contract for gas street lighting.

The gas industry grew during the 1800s, until the introduction of electric lamps drew lighting customers away from coal gas. The manufactured gas industry lost more customers during the early 1900s as natural gas became more widely available. By the early 1960s, the volume of natural gas sold was about 50 times greater than the volume of manufactured gas. By 1990, manufactured gas accounted for only about 1 percent of the gas consumed in the United States.

The decline of the manufactured gas industry continued in the 1990s as the popularity of natural gas increased. Notwithstanding, there remained a market for manufactured gas. For example, in 1997, Indianapolis Power & Light (IP&L) converted some of its coal-burning boiler units to steam boilers using coke oven gas. The utility signed a 20-year agreement to purchase the coke-oven manufactured gas from Citizen's Gas & Coke Company in Indianapolis. The conversion from raw coal-burning was expected to reduce air pollution of sulfur dioxide emissions by 2,200 tons per year. IP&L provided electric service to about 410,000 customers and 270 commercial customers.

The increased presence of liquefied natural gas (LNG) in the market facilitated distribution to areas previously out of reach, and led to numerous closings of manufactured gas plants. Nationally, these closed plant sites were considered potential environmental hazards due to the presence of numerous toxic substances that may have been manufactured or buried there. In December, 1999, the town of Mount Belvieu, Texas was host to an environmental battle over the renewal of permits for operators of LPG storage wells. Most of these underground wells were in salt caverns located under the town itself. But in recent years, many salt caverns in the Southwest have had problems with salt dissolves coming from the caverns and polluting the indigenous soil and water. Also in 1999, the U.S. Department of Transportation settled its two-year legal battle over its interim rules for excess flow valves on cargo tanks, following an incident in North Carolina which resulted in the release of 50,000 gallons of propane.

INDUSTRY LEADERS

One of the largest distributors of manufactured gas in the United States was Gasco. Gasco, originally named Honolulu Gas Company, was established in 1904 to provide gas service to Hawaii's largest city. Hawaii, being separated from the contiguous United States, was never linked to the mainland's transcontinental natural gas pipeline grids. Gasco was purchased from BHP Hawaii Inc. in 1997 by Citizens Electric for $100 million. However, in latter 1999, parent company Citizens Utilities decided to sell off its interest in Gasco and focus instead on telecommunications.

Another leading company involved in the production of manufactured gas was Indianapolis Coke, the manufacturing division of Indiana-based Citizen's Gas and Coke Utility, the only gas distribution utility in the United States that still mixed coke oven gas in its send-out product. Serving approximately 250,000 customers, the company produced a variety of coke mixtures for industrial use by pouring a raw coal mixture into ovens 50 feet wide and 15 feet tall, heating it to over 1800 degrees Fahrenheit, and baking it in the absence of air for 26 to 30 hours. Once produced, the coke was cooled and sized according to whether it was to be used in the steel, mineral wool, sugar beet, or secondary smelting industry.

Overall demand for LPG was up in 1999 by over 2 percent from 1998. As of August 1999, propane suppliers were showing good profits for that year, with an average net income of 16 cents per gallon. Some of the leading companies included AmeriGas, Cornerstone, Ferrellgas, Heritage, Star Gas, and Suburban Gas Company.

FURTHER READING

''Citizens Gas & Coke Utility Profile.'' Citizens Gas & Coke Utility, Indiana, 1997.

''Deliveries Drop Despite Strong Economy.'' *LP/Gas,* September 1999.

''History of Indianapolis Coke.'' Indianapolis Coke, 1997.

"IP&L Converts Perry K Boilers to Coke Oven Gas." *Coal Age,* February 1997.

Hoover's Company Profiles. Austin, TX: Hoover's Inc., 1997. Available from http://www.hoovers.com/.

"LP/Gas Stock Index." *LP/Gas,* August 1999.

Richards, Don. "Mount Belvieu Fights Permit Renewals." *Chemical Market Reporter,* 27 December 1999.

Schupphaus, Klaus. *Steel Times,* May 1997.

"Settlement Finally Reached On DOT Cargo Tank Requirements." *LP/Gas,* June 1999.

"Two Hawaii Utilities On the Block." *Pacific Business News,* 25 June 1999.

SIC 4931

ELECTRIC AND OTHER SERVICES COMBINED

This industry classification consists of companies primarily providing electricity, but also furnishing other utility services. Companies in which the electricity sales account for 95 percent or more of the revenues are listed in **SIC 4911: Electric Services.**

NAICS CODE(S)

221111 (Hydroelectric Power Generation)
221112 (Fossil Fuel Electric Power Generation)
221113 (Nuclear Electric Power Generation)
221119 (Other Electric Power Generation)
221121 (Electric Bulk Power Transmission and Control)
221122 (Electric Power Distribution)
221210 (Natural Gas Distribution)

BACKGROUND AND DEVELOPMENT

The roots of the U.S. electric utility industry can be traced back to 1878, when the first private electric company, Edison Electric, began operating in New York City. The first city-owned electric system began operating in Butler, Missouri, in 1881. By 1900, utilities of both types had proliferated; there were more than 800 publicly owned systems and about 2,000 private power companies. Most electric utilities were vertically integrated, controlling generation plants as well as the transmission and distribution lines to customers in multiple states.

Modern state utility regulation was born in Wisconsin in 1907. The Wisconsin Public Utilities Commission charter served as a model for other state efforts. It was the first to require operating permits for all utilities to initiate service, and it was the first to regulate rates of service and to control the issuance of securities by regulated public utilities.

From 1910 through the 1920s, the number of electric utilities declined. Many were controlled by a small number of holding companies, which were, in turn, owned by other holding companies. By 1932, three holding companies controlled 45 percent of all U.S. electricity generation. They charged excessive rates, had high debt-to-equity ratios, engaged in self-dealing, and provided unreliable service. Most highly leveraged holding companies that stayed solvent in the 1920s collapsed after the stock market crash, unable to service their debt.

The 1930s saw federal government involvement in power production in rural areas through the Tennessee Valley Authority, the Rural Electrification Administration and five federal Power Marketing Administrations formed to sell cheap power to municipal and cooperative systems.

In 1935, Congress passed the Federal Power Act and the Public Utility Holding Company Act. The Federal Power Act created a Federal Power Commission (now the Federal Energy Regulatory Commission) to regulate interstate and wholesale electric power transactions. The Public Utility Holding Company Act required holding companies that own or control more than 10 percent of another utility to provide the Securities and Exchange Commission with detailed financial information.

Between 1935 and 1978, little changed. In 1978, primarily in response to the oil crisis, Congress passed The Public Utility Regulatory Policy Act (PURPA), designed to lessen domestic dependence on foreign oil and encourage alternate energy sources. PURPA required utilities to purchase electricity generated by small independent producers using wind or geothermal energy, or by cogenerators, which simultaneously produce electricity and thermal energy. Congress also passed the Fuel Use Act, which prohibited burning natural gas in new power plants to conserve what was then thought to be a dwindling supply.

The next major change was the Energy Policy Act of 1992, which increased competition in wholesale energy markets, allowing utilities to operate independent generating plants outside service territories and enter into wholesale power agreements. However, authority over retail electric sales—sales of electricity directly to homeowners and businesses—was left to regulatory commissions in each of the 50 states.

In 1996, the Federal Energy Regulatory Commission issued Order 888 and Order 889, two final rules governing access to utility power lines. Order 888 required utilities to offer nondiscriminatory access to their power grid, even to direct competitors. Order 889 required utilities to share information about available transmission capacity through electronic information systems. FERC also announced a new policy to review proposed mergers in 12 to 15 months.

The industry has been in the process of transitioning to a competitive market since the early 1990s, and the final outcome of that ongoing national debate has been uncertain. Part of the uncertainty stemmed from a bifurcation in regulatory responsibilities between federal and state governments. Federal law regulated the wholesale power market, that is, sales or bulk power between power suppliers or across state lines. State regulators, however, regulated sales of power to retail end-users, such as homes and businesses.

About 30 to 40 percent of a burned fuel's energy is converted to usable electricity. The remaining thermal energy (the heat produced by the burning fuel) is dissipated into the atmosphere without recapture. Because of the low energy efficiency of electricity-producing plants, research focused on recapturing some of the lost thermal energy. This process, known as ''cogeneration,'' allows plants to produce and market both electricity and the heat that is produced in the process (usually in the form of piped steam heat).

CURRENT CONDITIONS

A new wave of large ''cogeneration'' projects emerged toward the latter decade and into the millennium, representing viable power sources. Most cogenerated power remains in the manufacturing sector, with the paper and chemical industries as leading users. The potential savings in energy remains tremendous. For example, in 1998, more than 2.66 trillion cubic feet of natural gas, almost 60 million barrels of petroleum and 56.80 million short tons of coal were all burned off in order to produce electricity.

With the continued deregulation of electricity and rising environmental concerns, the appeal of on-site electric generation continues to grow. One California study has predicted that on-site (distributed) generation will double by 2004. Power shortages and price hikes during the summer of 1998 stimulated further interests in the advantages of on-site generation.

The Federal government has also taken a renewed interest in cogenerated power because of the decrease in global carbon emissions. On December 10, 1998, the Department of Energy announced its goal to double the capacity of cogenerated power by 2010. Partially in anticipation of this expected growth, the Comprehensive Electricity Competition Act of 1999 contained provisions addressing required interconnections between cogenerative power producers and distribution utilities.

INDUSTRY LEADERS

Trigen Energy Corporation, with 46 cogeneration and district energy facilities, supplies steam hot water, electricity, and chilled water to its 1,500 industrial and commercial customers in Canada, Mexico and the U.S. It is also a leader in converting biomass to energy. Trigen reported a 77.8 percent increase in net income for 1999, with overall sales of $280.4 million. Trigen, which produces and sells electricity as a by-product of its heat and power generation, is considered the leading thermal science company in North America.

Another industry leader is Cogeneration Corporation of America (CoGenAmerica), which owns five facilities that produce both electric and thermal energy for commercial and industrial users and utilities companies. It has plants in Illinois, New Jersey, Oklahoma and Pennsylvania. Sales for this company in 1998 were $74 million, with a one-year net income growth of 65.8 percent.

Primary Energy, Inc., a subsidiary of NiSource Inc., announced in November 1999 its plans to enter a joint agreement with LTV Steel Co. to build a cogeneration facility for LTV at its East Chicago plant. The designed gas-fired blast furnace for the plant will convert waste gas into clean, usable electricity. Completion was scheduled for late 2001. NiSource (formerly NIPSCO Industries) was another leader in combination-energy offerings to its customers. In 1999, it served 416,000 electricity customers,700,000 gas customers in Indiana and another 300,000 in New England, plus water utilities and natural gas marketing. The company employs over 6,000 and reported 1999 sales of $3.14 billion.

FURTHER READING

Battles, Stephanie J. ''Generation in the Manufacturing Sector: A Historical Perspective.'' Presentation to the 20th Annual North American Conference of the U.S. Association for Energy Economics, Affiliated with the International Association for Energy Economics, August 1999.

FERC Approves Colorado Merger, Process Speeding Up. Energy Online, LCG Consulting. 13 March 1997. Available from http://www.energyonline.com/Restructuring/news_reports/fr_mergs.html.

FERC Finalizes Electric Industry Restructuring Rule. Public Utility Topics: Electric & Gas Industries. Coopers & Lybrand L.L.P. June/July 1996. Available from http://www.colybrand.com/industry/utility/util696a.html.

FERC's New Merger Policy. Public Utility Topics: Electric & Gas Industries. Coopers & Lybrand L.L.P. February 1997. Available from http://www.colybrand.com/industry/utility/util971a.html

Hoover's Company Capsules used for NiSource, Trigen, and Cogeneration Corporation of America. Austin, Texas: Hoover's Inc., 1999. Available from http://www.hoovers.com.

''Investor-owned utilities expected to dwindle down to 80 by year 2000.'' *Electric Light & Power,* September 1996.

Kamat, Dilip, Ostrowski, Ken and Stuebi, Richard, ''Winning in the Emerging Energy Services Business,'' *The Electricity Journal,* August/September 1996.

Mack, Toni. ''Annual Report on American Industry: Electric Utilities.'' *Forbes,* 13 January 1997.

''NiSource Subsidiary, LTV Sign Cogeneration Project Agreement Primary Energy to Build Plant at LTV's Indiana Harbor Plant.'' PR Newswire, 20 November 1999. Available at http://www.prnewswire.com

Penn, David W. *Public Power's Vital, Procompetitive Role in the U.S. Electricity Industry's Future.* Remarks delivered at the Annual Conference of Michigan State University's Institute of Public Utilities, 11 December 1995.

Pospisil, Ray. ''Cogeneration Reflux.'' *Chemical Week,* October 28, 1998, 29.

Saunders, Barbara. ''U.S. gas/electric megamergers may slow as new policies tested.'' *The Oil and Gas Journal,* 3 February 1997.

Santa, Donald F. *Energy Restructuring Issues.* Remarks delivered at Arthur Andersen's 17th Annual Energy Symposium, 10 December 1996.

Studness, Charles M. ''Converging Markets: The First Real Electric/Gas Merger.'' *Public Utilities Fortnightly,* 1 October 1996.

Thierer, Adam D. *Energizing America: A Blueprint for Deregulating the Electricity Market.* The Heritage Foundation. Washington, 23 January 1997. Available from http://www.heritage.org/heritage/library/categories/regulation/bg1100.html.

''Trigen Declares Quarterly Dividend.'' PR Newswire, 12 December 1999. Available from http://www.prnewswire.com.

U.S. Department of Energy. Energy Information Administration. *Annual Energy Outlook 1998 With Projections to 2015.* Available from http://www.eia.doe.gov/oiaf/aeo97/elefut.html.

———. *Electric Power Annual 1999,* Vol. I and II. Available from http://www.eia.doe.gov/cneaf.

U.S. Department of State. United States Information Agency. *Energy Restructuring in the United States.* Available from http://www.usia.gov/abtusia/posts/GE1/wwwh0000.html.

Warkentin, Denise. ''FERC Adopts new utility industry merger standards.'' *Electric Light & Power.* February 1997.

Wright, John W., gen. ed. *The Universal Almanac 1996.* Kansas City: Andrews and McMeel, 1995.

SIC 4932

GAS AND OTHER SERVICES COMBINED

This industry classification consists of companies primarily providing gas distribution services, but also supplying other utility services. Companies in which natural gas distribution accounts for 95 percent or more of revenues are classified in **SIC 4924: Natural Gas Distribution.**

NAICS Code(s)

221210 (Natural Gas Distribution)

Organization and Structure

Gas utilities, called local distribution companies (LDCs), provide customers with two services: gas transportation, or moving the gas from the pipeline to the customer, and supply, whereby the LDC buys the gas and resells it to the customer. The LDC transports gas for all its customers and supplies gas to other suppliers. The utility earns a rate of return for transporting gas but receives nothing for supplying it to those other than end-use customers. The LDC earns the same fee for transporting gas, regardless of who supplies the gas.

Gas utilities have several competitive advantages over electric utilities. While electric utilities were just beginning to experiment during the mid-1990s with allowing customers to choose among energy suppliers, large gas customers were extending the freedom to choose their gas supplier to the smallest of customers, including homeowners. Both industries were deregulated.

By the end of the 1990s, natural gas supplied about half of the nation's energy needs. When electric utilities providers began to use natural gas for electric power generation, a new utilities superpower appeared on the horizon. Instead of natural gas companies buying out their smaller natural gas competitors, they began aligning with electric utilities companies to provide multiple services to end-users. Thus, by the millennium, some of the largest utilities providers were in fact ''hybrid'' entities offering electricity and natural gas services to their customers. These ''cogeneration'' facilities appeared to be on the rise nationally and internationally. Another spin-off industry from these consolidations was the combination of gas pipelines and fiber-optic networks, thus servicing the energy and communications businesses.

Background and Development

While state governments began to regulate the venting of natural gas in the late 1920s, federal government regulation of interstate sales of natural gas was a product of already existing federal regulations governing interstate sales of electricity. The same public outcry that led to passage of the Federal Power Act and the Public Utilities Holding Company Act in 1935 led Congress to create regulations for natural gas. (See **SIC 4931: Electric and Other Services Combined.**)

The Natural Gas Act, passed in 1938, was even more stringent than its electricity counterpart, giving the Federal Power Commission (now the Federal Energy Regulatory Commission) explicit authorization to fix ''just and reasonable'' pipeline rates, ban discriminatory tariff practices, and determine legitimate costs. In 1942, the

Act was amended to require interstate sales of gas for resale elsewhere to be at the lowest possible rate.

Historically, the same type of regulation used for electric utilities has been applied to interstate natural gas pipelines. Tariffs were set to recover the costs of operation and gas purchases, depreciation of investments in facilities, and to provide a regulated rate of return on business assets.

In 1954, the Supreme Court of the United States decided the Federal Power Commission had authority to regulate prices all the way back to the well. After delaying its response to the court's mandate for several years, the commission began regulating wellhead gas prices on a case-by-case basis, then experimented with setting ''area rates'' based on broad geographic regions. There were higher rates for ''new gas,'' or newer discoveries, and lower rates for ''old gas,'' or existing production.

During the late 1960s, regulated prices for interstate pipelines were relatively cheap compared with prices in intrastate markets. Within higher intrastate market prices, interstate pipelines, who could pay only the low regulated prices, were unable to meet growing demand for gas supplies.

Burgeoning demand for natural gas forced pipelines and LDCs, to allocate demand. The imbalance between demand and supply brought increasing pressure on Congress to deregulate wellhead prices.

In 1978, Congress passed the Natural Gas Policy Act, an extremely complex law with more than 20 different categories of gas and prices ranging from $0.30 per thousand cubic feet (mcf) to $10.00/mcf. But by the early 1980s, gas demand dropped due to a recession, and improved production technologies made gas available in almost unprecedented volumes. The supply and demand equilibrium was again out of sync. In 1989, Congress passed legislation phasing out price controls on most types of natural gas.

In 1992, the Federal Energy Regulatory Commission issued Order 636, which forced gas transmission companies to become common carriers of natural gas and ordered them to redesign their rate structures, essentially changing the way local gas distribution utilities obtain their natural gas. That same year, Congress passed the Energy Policy Act, which increased competition within the electricity industry. In 1996, FERC issued Orders 888 and 889, final rules governing access to utility power lines. FERC also announced a policy to consider mergers within a 15-month period.

Current Conditions

According to the 1997 Economic Census, 119 establishments reported combined services, with their primary service being gas distribution. The industry was worth $2.85 billion. These figures did not include another 145 establishments of combined service (electricity-gas) where the primary service was electricity. That industry was worth $28 billion in 1997 in comparison.

However, by 1999, the gap had significantly decreased, due in large part to advanced technology for shared trenches between natural gas distribution and fiber-optic networking. Using thousands of miles of pipeline routes, pipeline companies have coupled with communications companies to create dual-service routes, making pipeline assets much more profitable and cutting costs for laying communications cable lines. As of 1999, about 200,000 miles of fiber-optic line existed in the United States. Because of increased need for Internet and telecommunication lines, that figure was expected to double by 2002.

Only 14 states had enacted laws permitting utilities to enter the telecommunications business as of 1999, but many states were expecting to do so soon. Traditional utilities were experiencing slow annual revenue growth rates, while the telecommunications business continued to experience double digit growth rates.

Industry Leaders

Houston pipeline giant Enron Corp. merged with Portland General Electric in 1999. Shortly thereafter, its Enron Communications subsidiary began plans for a 17,000-mile line system for telecommunications using its lines along with other systems. As of 1999, Enron was projecting a 15 percent annual growth for the foreseeable future.

Notwithstanding, El Paso Energy Corporation, the biggest pipeline company in the United States, also began partnerships in 1999 with communications companies needing more fiber-optic miles.

Another giant in 1999 was Pacific Gas & Electric Co. (PG&E), which reported 3.8 million gas customers. In 1999, PG&E was considered the largest utility holding company in the United States, with 4.6 million electric customers in addition to its gas customers. Although it controlled 9,000 miles of pipeline, in early 2000, the company was expected to sell its gas lines to El Paso Natural Gas Company, a major transmission pipeline leader. PG&E's 1998 revenues were just under $20 billion. Net income was $719 million.

Another multifaceted natural gas enterprise was Consolidated Natural Gas Company (CNG). CNG, with headquarters in Pittsburgh and New York, operated one of the nation's largest natural gas systems and marketed natural gas and electricity throughout North America. The company had more than $5 billion in assets and nearly $3 billion in 1998 sales. Its subsidiaries operate in all segments of the gas industry, including exploration, production, transportation, storage, purchasing, reselling, and distribution. The company controlled 10,000 miles of pipeline and a network of 27 underground storage facilities with a capacity totaling more than 885 billion cubic feet, making it the largest gas storage network in the United States. In December 1999, CNG and Dominion Resources announced their merger plans for 2000, which would create the largest integrated natural gas and electric power company in the United States.

Other types of deals are emerging as well. In January 1997, PacifiCorp announced a joint venture with a Lakewood, Colorado, natural gas company, KN Energy Inc., to provide utilities with two-way interactive metering services that could also provide satellite television, Internet services, and long distance telephone services, among others.

Research and Technology

The deregulation of the utilities industries in the 1990s opened the door for significant cross-mergers between gas and electric companies. By the end of the decade, shared technologies enhanced the profitability of both industries: pipeline companies, which traditionally held rights-of-way over miles of lines, could now have a financial stake in sharing those routes and passageways with other industries. Moreover, the growing technology created a form of commodity trading: fiber-optic bandwidth futures, which Enron hoped to begin selling.

Within the natural gas supply market, progress in technologies associated with exploration and development of gas reduced costs and expanded the amount of gas that can be economically recovered from a well. Some examples are the use of advanced computer-imaging technologies to explore underground reserves, offshore drilling deep in the Gulf of Mexico, and unconventional recovery techniques for getting more gas from reserve wells.

Technological advances in generation technologies were also important. For example, 60 percent of all additions to electric generating capacity since 1990 have been natural gas, and state-of-the-art gas turbines were increasingly being used in electricity production. Also, a significant opportunity existed in distributed power generation—modular electrical generators ranging in size up to 50 megawatts. These new turbines were easy to site and build, allowing them to serve one large customer or several large customers in one area. They also made maximum use of the gas distribution network already built to accommodate the customer's needs.

Further Reading

A.G.A. Publishes 50th Edition of Gas Facts. American Gas Association. Washington, 21 January 1997. Available from http://www.aga.com/pr15.html.

Ban, Stephen D. ''Challenges for Gas Technology in a Restructured Electric Industry.'' *The Electricity Journal,* May 1996.

Bergstrom, Stephen W., and Callender, Terry. ''Gas and power industries linking as regulation fades.'' *The Oil and Gas Journal,* 12 August 1996.

Can Electricity and Natural Gas Produce 'Infotainment? Energy Online, LCG Consulting. 24 January 1997. Available from http://www.energyonline.com/Restructuring/news_reports/news/or_pc-kn.html.

Cissna, Tami. ''Strategic Benefits Emerge in Electric-Gas Alliance.'' *Electric Light & Power,* July 1, 1999, 1.

Consolidated Natural Gas Company. *Corporate Profile.* Pittsburgh: Consolidated Natural Gas Company, 1997.

''Deal of the Century.'' *Philips Business Information Highlights,* December 27, 1999.

Donovan, Dan. ''Dominion Resources, CNG Set Anticipated Merger Closing Date of January 28, 2000.'' CNG Press Release, December 17, 1999. Available at http://www.shareholder.com/cng/news/19991217-12639.htm.

''Enova Corporation and Pacific Enterprises Announce Strategic Combination of Equals.'' Enova Corp. Pacific Enterprises, 14 October 1996.

Freedenthal, Carol. ''Industry Convergence: Where is It Really Headed?'' (Editorial) *Pipeline & Gas Journal,* December 1996.

Freedenthal, Carol. ''Marketing Takes Center Stage as Gas and Electric Companies Compete.'' (Editorial) *Pipeline & Gas Journal,* November 1999, 4.

Hoover's Company Capsules used for Reliant Energy, CNG, Dominion Resources, Southwest Gas Corp. and PG&E. Austin, Texas: Hoover's Inc., 1999. Available from http://www.hoovers.com.

''Newsline.'' *Underground Construction,* 3 July 1999.

''PG&E Buys Valero Energy for $1.5 Billion.'' *The Electricity Daily,* 4 February 1997.

Saunders, Barbara. ''U.S. Gas/Electric Megamergers May Slow as New Policies Tested.'' *The Oil and Gas Journal,* 3 February 1997.

Studness, Charles M. ''Converging Markets: The First Real Electric/Gas Merger.'' *Public Utilities Fortnightly,* 1 October 1996.

Vanderwater, Bob. ''Phillips Petroleum, Duke Energy Enter Natural Gas Venture.'' *The Daily Oklahoman,* 21 December 1999.

Walsh, Jennifer. ''Houston-Area Pipeline Firm Sees the Light in Fiber Optics.'' *Houston Chronicle,* 22 June 1999.

U.S. Census Bureau, *The Official Statistics,* 1997 Economic Census. Available from http://ww.census.gov/prod/ec97/97t22-us.pdf.

SIC 4939

COMBINATION UTILITIES, NOT ELSEWHERE CLASSIFIED

This industry classification includes combination electric and natural gas utilities not categorized elsewhere.

NAICS CODE(S)

221111 (Hydroelectric Power Generation)
221112 (Fossil Fuel Electric Power Generation)
221113 (Nuclear Electric Power Generation)
221119 (Other Electric Power Generation)
221122 (Electric Power Distribution)
221210 (Natural Gas Distribution)

INDUSTRY SNAPSHOT

The governmental deregulation of the utilities industries in the 1990s was intended in part to break up monopolies and create market competition. The privatization of the industry forced more cost-effectiveness, and ultimately consumers were paying between 7 and 15 percent less for natural gas in 1997 than they were ten years previously. However, the utilities companies used the profits to buy out smaller competitors on the open market—something not possible when the utilities were under governmental rather than Wall Street's control.

BACKGROUND AND DEVELOPMENT

By the turn of the twentieth century, there were more than 2,000 private utilities and more than 800 publicly owned utilities in the United States. About three dozen of these early companies were combined electric and gas distribution companies. This occurred at a time when municipal lighting and heating were largely produced through the generation of synthetic coal gas. When street lighting was developed, the gas producers became electric suppliers. When natural gas became available in the 1900s, the utilities continued to serve as gas suppliers as well.

In the early 1900s, state governments began regulating electric utilities; state regulation of the venting of natural gas used in electricity production began in the late 1920s. Complaints of excessive rates charged by utilities for electric service led Congress to pass two pivotal laws in 1935: The Federal Power Act and the Public Utility Holding Company Act. The first law created a Federal Power Commission (now the Federal Energy Regulatory Commission, or FERC) to oversee interstate power transactions and transactions between wholesale bulk energy suppliers. The second law reined in previous abuses linked to pyramiding holding companies in the United States. A third influential law was the Natural Gas Act of 1938, which gave FERC authority to fix pipeline rates. In 1942, the act was amended to regulate interstate sales of gas.

Historically, the same type of regulation used for electric utilities has been applied to natural gas utilities. In 1954, the Supreme Court of the United States gave FERC the authority to regulate prices all the way back to the well. The commission experimented with "area rates" that set higher rates for new gas discoveries and lower prices for "old gas," or existing production. During the late 1960s, burgeoning demand for natural gas forced gas utilities to allocate demand. In 1978, Congress stepped in again by enacting the Natural Gas Policy Act, an extremely complex law with more than 20 different categories of gas prices. By 1989, Congress gave up trying to regulate supply and demand, passing legislation to phase out price controls on most types of gas.

In 1992, FERC issued Order 636, which forced gas transmission companies to redesign rate structures, essentially changing the way local gas distribution companies obtained natural gas. That same year, Congress passed the Energy Policy Act, which increased competition within the electricity industry. In 1996, FERC issued Orders 888 and 889, final rules governing access to utility power lines. FERC also announced a new policy to consider mergers within a 15-month period.

Natural gas companies that have strong marketing capabilities have even stronger impetus to acquire or merge with electric companies in order to increase the gas companies' share of the power marketing pie. Gas marketers with the ability to also market power will buy a foothold in the electricity market through acquisitions or strategic alliances.

In the past, when gas-to-gas company mergers were proposed, they were reviewed by the Federal Trade Commission and other agencies. Electric utility mergers, however, are overseen by FERC, but even FERC doesn't know how to handle overlap between an electric company and a gas company. The agency did address electric and gas mergers in its new merger policy, issued in late 1996; these mergers were to be considered on a case-by-case basis. FERC was being cautious because a large number of mergers in an industry will reduce the number of active players in the market, raising questions of market power. Combination utilities in retail markets that were once the province of two distinct, unaffiliated gas and electric companies raised similar issues of market power and customer choice.

CURRENT CONDITIONS

In the latter half of the 1990s, natural gas took over 50 percent of the energy market. As older nuclear power facilities and coal-burning electric utilities companies shut down, they were replaced by or converted to natural gas energy facilities. When electric utilities providers began to use natural gas for electric power generation, a new utilities super-power appeared on the horizon: instead of natural gas companies buying out their smaller natural gas competitors, they began aligning with electric utilities companies to provide multiple services to end-users. Thus, by the millennium, some of the largest utilities providers were in fact hybrid entities offering both electricity and natural gas services to their customers.

INDUSTRY LEADERS

Notwithstanding FERC's caution, between 1997 and 1999 mergers and acquisitions among the natural gas and electric power industries became the rule rather than exception among larger powers. In 1997, Reliant Energy bought out NorAm Energy Corp. During the same year, the natural gas company Entex, an affiliate of NorAm, merged with Houston Industries, which controlled Houston Light & Power. In February 1999, all were subsumed into the surviving Reliant Energy, Inc. Reliant now covers 13 states, parts of South America, and India. It services 1.6 million electricity customers and 2.8 million natural gas customers. Reliant also serves 9.5 million Latin American customers, and has a 52 percent stake in a Dutch company slated to develop in Europe. The company reported 1999 sales of $15.3 billion dollars.

Another major pact was the merger in early 2000 of Dominion Resources and Consolidated Natural Gas Company (CNG), pending only a final approval from the Virginia State Corporation Commission. The Securities and Exchange Commission (SEC) had already approved the merger on December 15, 1999. The surviving entity (Dominion Resources, Inc.) would become the largest fully integrated natural gas and electric company in the U.S. With $25 billion in combined assets, the new company will serve almost four million retail customers in five states. Just prior to the final merger agreement, CNG had rejected Columbia Energy's offer to buy it out. Columbia remains one of the largest U.S. gas companies. At the same time, Dominion was securing an agreement with General Electric Company to purchase ten of its gas-fired electric generation turbines. Dominion's 1998 sales were $6.0 billion. CNG had reported $2.7 billion for 1998.

Duke Power's merger with PanEnergy created a third giant. The survivor, Duke Energy, again merged with Phillips Petroleum in 1999, creating Duke Energy Field Services, the largest natural gas gatherer and processor in the country. Duke's stock is expected to earn $4.00 per share in 2000.

FURTHER READING

Bergstrom, Stephen W., and Callender, Terry. ''Gas and Power Industries Linking as Regulation Fades.'' *The Oil and Gas Journal,* 12 August 1996.

Cissna, Tami. ''Strategic Benefits Emerge in Electric-Gas Alliance.'' *Electric Light & Power,* 1 July 1999, 1.

''Citizens Utilities Acquires Conference-Call USA.'' *Citizens Utilities,* 4 December 1996.

Freedenthal, Carol. ''Industry Convergence: Where is It Really Headed?'' (Editorial). *Pipeline & Gas Journal,* December 1996.

———. ''Marketing Takes Center Stage as Gas and Electric Companies Compete'' (Editorial). *Pipeline & Gas Journal,* November 1999, 4.

Hoover's Company Capsules. Austin, Texas: Hoover's Inc., 1999. Available from http://www.hoovers.com.

''PG&E Buys Valero Energy for $1.5 Billion.'' *The Electricity Daily,* 4 February 1997.

Penn, David W. *Public Power's Vital, Procompetitive Role in the U.S. Electricity Industry's Future.* Remarks delivered at the Annual Conference of Michigan State University's Institute of Public Utilities, 11 December 1995.

Reed, Ted. ''Energy, Phillips Petroleum Plan Natural Gas Venture.'' *The Charlotte [NC] Observer,* 18 December 1999.

Saunders, Barbara. ''U.S. Gas/Electric Megamergers May Slow as New Policies Tested.'' *The Oil and Gas Journal,* 3 February 1997.

Studness, Charles M. ''Converging Markets: The First Real Electric/Gas Merger.'' *Public Utilities Fortnightly,* 1 October 1996.

Thierer, Adam D. *Energizing America: A Blueprint for Deregulating the Electricity Market.* Washington, DC: The Heritage Foundation, 1997. Available from http://www.heritage.org.

U.S. Department of State. United States Information Agency. *Energy Restructuring in the United States.* Available from http://www.usia.gov/abtusia/GE1/wwwh8003.html.

SIC 4941

WATER SUPPLY

This category includes establishments primarily engaged in distributing water for sale for residential, commercial, and industrial uses. The industry is dominated by government controlled establishments such as municipal service districts and public utilities. However, private companies are active in the construction and improvement of water supply facilities and infrastructure. Water distributed for irrigation purposes is classified in **SIC 4971: Irrigation Systems.**

NAICS CODE(S)

221310 (Water Supply and Irrigation Systems)

INDUSTRY SNAPSHOT

There were a minimum of 55,000 water systems supplying water to more than 225 million Americans in 1999. To help ensure the safety of the nation's drinking water, the government is providing more than $9.6 billion through the year 2003 to help these systems to comply with safe drinking water regulations. Total compliance with amendments to the Safe Drinking Water Act (SDWA) of 1996, as well as agency coordination under the 1998 Clean Water Action Plan, will cost more than $1 trillion dollars by 2030. Of greatest concern was the nation's groundwater, which by 1999 was being withdrawn at a rate of approximately 77.5 billion gallons per day. Of sobering reality is the fact that every gallon of water withdrawn from the ground takes an estimated 280 years to replace. Although surface water from streams and lakes is replaced rapidly, it was ground water that supplied 95 percent of rural America's drinking water and half of the nation'drinking water in 1999. Furthermore, groundwater provided more than 40 percent of all crop irrigation and livestock watering. Thus, the alarming potential for human consumption of contaminants became an increasing concern.

By the millennium, more than 80 percent of U.S. water companies were controlled by governmental entities. However, an increasing number of smaller utilities were being acquired by larger systems, a trend that industry experts called consolidation. There also was an increase in privatization—private companies that contract to operate or to purchase the public utilities. Moreover, many larger systems were investing in new testing and treatment methods. They also were improving their systems' infrastructure by replacing miles of 70- to 100-year-old municipal water pipes. The entire industry had been bolstered in the 1990s by federal amendments to the 1996 SDWA and the 1998 Clean Water Action Plan.

ORGANIZATION AND STRUCTURE

The water supply industry is highly fragmented and consists mainly of municipal utilities or regional entities. In 1997, the United States Environmental Protection Agency (EPA) divided the nation's 55,000 water systems into three categories: 694 large systems served more than 50,000 people, 6,800 medium systems served between 3,301 and 50,000 people, and 46,500 small systems served fewer than 3,300 people. The largest system serves 16 million; the smallest serves 25 people.

A water utility or company is responsible for providing its community with water that is free of objectionable tastes and odors and does not contain significant color or turbidity. The water also must meet strict federal, state, and local health and safety regulations. It is the utility's job to build and maintain a distribution system that is capable of providing an adequate and uninterrupted supply of water for residential, commercial, industrial, and institutional customers. In addition, the water supplier must maintain adequate water pressure for the community's firefighting needs.

Although most water supply entities are owned or controlled by local or regional governing bodies, a variety of organizational structures are represented in the industry. In addition, water and wastewater management systems are often integrated, resulting in an organization that also operates a sewerage system and waste treatment facilities. The two primary categories of water suppliers are local and regional.

Local organizations include utilities arranged under various management structures. A utility commission, for example, is governed by a policy-making body such as an appointed or elected commission or board of directors. This utility structure offers the advantage of removing the policy-making body from direct political influence. Furthermore, the revenues required by the utility are generated by the commission specifically for water supply purposes with no competition from general city funds. A utility controlled by elected council, in contrast, often is subject to political forces from other city departments and divisions with which the council members also are associated. Planning decisions can become complex and are sometimes bogged down by political infighting. The advantage of a utility that is controlled by a common governing body, as opposed to a separate utility commission, is that the goals of the water utility can be more easily coordinated with the aims of other city departments and agencies.

Regional water authorities provide service directly to customers or through smaller government entities, such as cities and townships. Regional authorities provide many economies of scale that increase water quality and reduce costs. They also offer the advantage of a coordinated large-scale water system that would be impossible to achieve with scattered independent local utilities. However, regional systems must transport water over greater distances, which can reduce efficiency.

An increasing number of for-profit entities were supplying water needs in the late 1990s. These companies either operate and maintain some portion or all of the water utility's operation. Also, there are a few instances of outright sale of a utility to a private company. In 1999, an estimated 20 percent of all water suppliers were managed or owned by private companies.

Source and Price. Water companies extract water mainly from natural and man-made reservoirs, underground aquifers, and waterways. In addition, some water is reclaimed through wastewater treatment, and a small amount of water is derived through desalinization. The water typically is pumped to a treatment center where

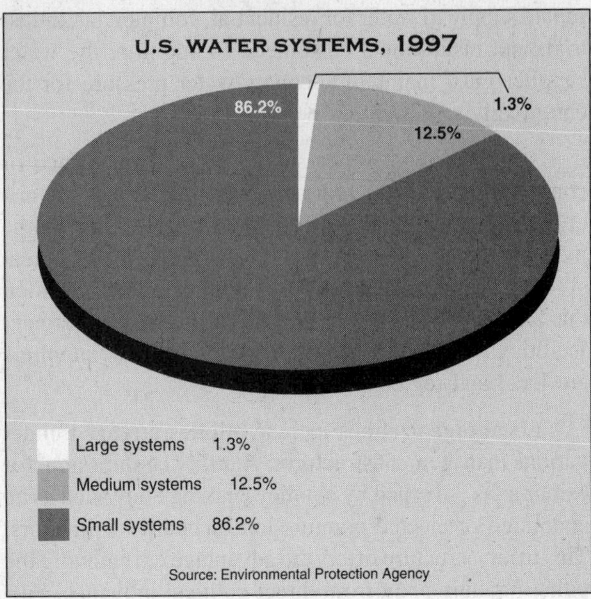

impurities are filtered out. Before distribution, the water is purified with chemicals such as chlorine and aluminum sulfate.

Besides natural impurities and sediment, a variety of manmade contaminants and sources must be countered by water treatment managers. Sources of pollutants include septic tanks, landfills, surface impoundments, pesticides and fertilizer used on millions of acres of farmland, highway salt, and thousands of industrial chemicals that enter the environment every day.

Revenues for water companies and utilities are generated through taxes and securities issues. Much of their income, however, is derived from water usage fees. A common traditional rate structure is the declining block rate. Under this system, customers pay a fee for each unit of water they use—the fee declines for each subsequent block of water consumed. Two other rate structures are the flat rate and the increasing block rate, which are greater incentives for consumers to conserve water.

BACKGROUND AND DEVELOPMENT

Although water supply systems have been in existence since the beginning of history, community water treatment and delivery systems similar to those existing today did not appear in the United States until the late 1800s. Demand for water treatment proliferated during the industrial era when the urban population grew and more people had access to indoor plumbing and municipal water supplies. During the economic expansion that followed World War II, demand for water increased as industrial, residential, and agricultural needs increased.

New federal regulations that mandated cleaner water also were important to industry growth. The Water Facilities Act of 1937, the Water Pollution Control Act of 1948, and the Water Supply Act of 1958 were three of the first federal initiatives that helped to expand the industry. In addition to setting water quality standards for communities, these laws also arranged to channel vast federal resources into the development of water supply and treatment systems. Other significant legislative efforts included the Water Resources Research Act of 1964, the Water Resources Planning Act of 1965, and the National Environmental Policy Act of 1969.

Some of the most sweeping and consequential laws propelling industry growth were enacted in the 1970s, when environmental concerns became paramount. The Water Bank Act of 1970, the SDWA of 1974, and the Clean Water Act of 1977 were three important laws that increased the importance of both water and wastewater treatment facilities. These laws resulted in billions of dollars worth of public water treatment projects. New legislation and government expenditures continued in the 1980s, with the passage of laws such as the Water Resources Research Act of 1984, amendments to the SDWA in 1986, and the Water Supply Act of 1988.

During the 1960s, 1970s, and 1980s, water standards were tightened, regulations increased, and communities continued to spend billions of dollars on water systems. By the mid-1990s, the cost of complying with the SDWA was estimated to cost water companies from 15 to 50 percent of their annual capital budgets.

Competition for Water Sources. Globally, 12,500 cubic kilometers of fresh water is available per person each year (the figure includes water stored by dams and reservoirs). However, the supply is unevenly distributed, and a large percentage is lost to flooding. Global demand for water has risen sharply since World War II. Between 1920 and 1940, for example, global water demand rose from about 400 to 600 cubic kilometers per year. By 1960, the figure had grown to 2,000 cubic kilometers. By 1980 and 1990, world demand increased to about 3,000 and 3,500 cubic kilometers per year, respectively. By 2000, this number was expected to be approximately 3,800 cubic kilometers per year. Water supplies in various regions of the globe are under increasing stress in the face of increasing population and scarcity of natural supplies. In other areas, water supplies are adequate, but poor irrigation practices consume supplies. An average of 87 percent of accessible fresh water resources in the world are consumed by irrigation and agriculture, leaving a limited supply for industrial and residential demands.

In North America, fresh water available per person each year is 10,500 cubic kilometers (the figure includes water stored by dams and reservoirs). This supply also is unevenly distributed; the western United States is classified as an arid and semi-arid region. The U.S. Geological Survey breaks down the consumption of fresh water this way: irrigation, 40 percent; thermoelectric power, 39 percent; public supply, 11 percent; industry, 6 percent; livestock, 1 percent; domestic, 1 percent; mining, 1 percent; commercial, 1 percent.

Water supply scarcity is a critical problem in arid and semi-arid western states, where irrigation consumes 90 percent of accessible fresh water supplies. In a number of western states, water is being drawn out of aquifers faster than nature replenishes it. Most notable is the depletion of the Ogallala Aquifer, which sits beneath 115 million acres between Texas and Nebraska. Recognizing the problem, governors of the western states issued a policy statement calling for increasing efficiency in water use management. Agencies of the federal government also were beginning to implement water use efficiency measures, and set new standards for water-conserving plumbing fixtures. Water conservation measures were becoming a way of life in the 1990s.

These measures are needed, according to the U.S. Geological Survey report, because the era of using big water projects such as dams and reservoirs to control water supply is over. Instead, existing water resources will have to be managed effectively.

Amendments to the SDWA in 1996 had a positive reception from the nation's water suppliers and companies that supply water equipment, services, and materials. The amendment introduced flexibility into the requirements for testing of contaminants—testing could be limited to those that were most likely to be found in their supplies and those most likely to harm certain members of the community, such as pregnant women, the elderly, and the young. Water systems that already were in compliance with the 1986 SDWA would need to make minor investments to comply with the 1996 amendments. In addition, the SDWA created a revolving loan fund to help water systems to come into compliance with the legislation.

The EPA surveyed a sampling of the nation's 55,000 water systems to determine what infrastructure changes would be necessary through the year 2014 to meet the revised safe drinking water standards. The EPA reported that $12.1 billion would be needed immediately to comply with the current SDWA. The survey showed that 84 percent of that amount is needed to test and treat water supplies for microbiological contaminants. However, through the year 2014, infrastructure needs were large, totaling $138.4 billion. This figure included the replacement or refurbishment of distribution piping and water storage tanks, and adding or improving sources of water. Medium and smaller sized water systems needed the most funding to comply with the SDWA. The revolving loan fund for upgrading community drinking water systems allots $9.6 billion or $1.2 billion annually through the year 2003.

Since most of the country's water systems are small (90 percent of them provide for 10 percent of the people), they had smaller budgets for the costly upgrading or replacement of infrastructure. Consolidation with larger, usually investor-owned utilities was becoming more commonplace. Large investor-owned companies such as American Water Works and United Water Resources, two utilities which were actively acquiring in the late 1990s, had resources and economies of scale that small water suppliers didn't have.

In addition, cities with larger waterworks utilities have switched or were considering bids for privatization, either by way of outright sale, lease, or management contract. An analyst quoted in *Civil Engineering* suggested that the proportion of public utilities to private may reach 50/50 by the year 2020. Cities that have some form of privatized water systems included Phoenix, Indianapolis, New Orleans, Houston, and Colorado Springs. The 1997 changes to Internal Revenue Service regulations regarding fees, length of contracts, and the sale of facilities were considered a positive sign to an estimated 30 U.S. cities considering this type of public-private "partnership" in the last years of the decade.

Public concern about the safety of drinking water increased since the 1993 cryptosporidium outbreak in Milwaukee, which resulted in more than 400,000 illnesses and 100 deaths. One quality control expert called cryptosporidium the biggest challenge faced by the water supply industry in 40 years. In 1997, the EPA asked water systems serving more than 100,000 users to conduct pilot tests for treatment of cryptosporidium. Not only is this micro-organism highly resistant to treatment, it also is difficult to detect. In 1999, four people died and dozens were hospitalized following ground water contamination from manure runoff into a local well feeding the county fairgrounds. In September 1999, New Jersey residents had to boil their tap water for almost a week following flood-related sewage contamination.

The EPA reported that in the 1990s alone, there were more than 370,000 confirmed releases of oil contaminants from leaking underground storage tanks. A contaminant "buzz word" at the end of the century was MTBE (methyl tertiary butyl ether), a common gasoline additive that has caused fairly widespread contamination of the country's drinking water—about 9 percent of all samples taken. A known carcinogen, MTBE is not removed by conventional treatment or filtration processes. For this reason, a growing number of states, including California, have banned the use of MTBE in gasoline. Under the 1998 Clean Water Action Plan, states had identified more than 20,000 lakes and stream segments that had contaminants exceeding one or more of the quality standards.

CURRENT CONDITIONS

A 1999 survey conducted for the Water Quality Association found that 60 percent of adults believe that their health is affected by the quality of drinking water, and nearly 50 percent reported that if purchasing a home, they would more likely purchase one with a home water treatment device. Approximately 75 percent of all Americans expressed concerns about the quality and safety of drinking water. By 1999, Americans were spending $3 billion annually on bottled water and home water treatment units.

In October 1999, under provisions of the amended SDWA, most Americans received their their first annual drinking water quality report from their local water supplier. Starting in 2001, the EPA will require suppliers that serve more than 10,000 people to begin monitoring for 12 unregulated contaminants. The purpose of the new requirement is to help determine whether these contaminants are present at a level or frequency that would warrant regulation at a later date. On October 19, 1999, the EPA also signed a proposed version of a radon monitoring rule for eventual implementation. It requested $41.5 million for its fiscal year 2000 budget, although it was authorized $54.6 million.

In 1999, the EPA began publishing survey results of approximately 935 public beaches that regularly monitor water quality. The agency's own review of 1,062 coastal beaches and the Great Lakes the previous year indicated that 350 had an advisory or closing, mostly as a result of fecal coliform contamination.

Also signed into law in 1999 were the Water Resources Development Act, authorizing $6.3 billion for flood control and shore protection by the U.S. Army Corps of Engineers, and the long-winded Chippewa Cree Tribe of the Rocky Boy's Reservation Indian Reserved Water Rights Settlement and Water Supply Enhancement Act of 1999. Under the latter Act, the United States became a party to the eight-year negotiations between the tribe and the state of Montana over water supplies on the reservations, as well as future rights to water stored in the Tiber Reservoir.

One of the most important pieces of legislation to appear in 1999 was the EPA's new rule regarding Class V injection wells, which numbered from 700,000 to one million that year. These wells are used primarily for the inground disposal of antifreeze, motor oil, gasoline, human waste, and other waste materials associated with light industries such as commercial printers. Eventually, these toxic materials are leached into ground water and end up being consumed by humans in diluted amounts. Under the new rule, large capacity wells and cesspools will be prohibited from use by April 2000, and all such wells will be phased out by 2005.

INDUSTRY LEADERS

American Water Works is the largest investor-owned water utility in the United States, with operations in 22 states and an estimated 4,000 employees serving 19 million consumers. With $1.26 billion in 1999 revenues, analysts expected American Water Works to invest approximately $250 million in 2000 to upgrade treatment facilities. A few of its competitors, although considerably smaller, included United Water Resources, Vivendi, and Philadelphia Suburban.

The Metropolitan Water District of Southern California (MWD) is the largest provider of drinking water in the United States, serving about 16 million people through 27 public agency members. The Water District is part of a project involving private firms to make seawater drinkable. The district also was involved in making $7 billion in capital improvements in the final years of the decade.

RESEARCH AND TECHNOLOGY

In 1999, a research team from the New Jersey Institute of Technology announced the development of a new technique designed to rid water of organic microbes without the carcinogenic after-effect of heavy chlorination. The Spectral Fluorescent Signatures targets carbon-based pollutants that are the most likely to become carcinogenic following disinfection. If eventually implemented after further testing, the proposed treatment technique would reduce byproduct formation, thereby reducing the amount of additives needed to disinfect water.

The University of Cincinnati has been working on the use of glowing zebrafish to identify pollutants in drinking water. Firefly genes were inserted into the DNA of the inch-long zebrafish, causing them to light up when exposed to PCBs. University staff have stressed that the fish are not harmed and eventually lose their glow when removed from polluted areas.

Another non-chemical way to disinfect water is through the use of ultraviolet (UV) light rays. Although the technology has been known for several years, it has not been used widely for drinking water application in the United States. Conversely, it is commonly used in Europe, and especially in Finland. Because of concerns about the carcinogenic properties of chlorine, there has been renewed interest in the development of UV treatment facilities in the United States.

Plans for a desalinization plant that would convert seawater into a portable or drinkable source were launched by the West Coast Regional Water Supply Authority in Florida. Another desalinization venture was undertaken by MWD, the largest provider of water in the country, which also faced a severe water deficit. Four private companies with interest and expertise joined

MWD in the venture. In the late 1990s, there only were two desalinization plants in the United States, one in Key West, Florida, and the other in Santa Barbara, California.

FURTHER READING

Agency Group 5. ''Most Americans Receive Their First Local Drinking Water Reports.'' FDCH Regulatory Intelligence Database, 21 October 21 1999.

Agency Group 5. ''President Clinton Signs Into Law Amdinistration's First Indian Water Rights Settlement.'' FDCH Regulatory Intelligence Database, 10 December 1999.

''Agency Releases Monitoring Schedule.'' *Pollution Engineering,* 3 November 1999.

Bogo, Jennifer. ''Oil and Water Don't Mix.'' *E Magazine,* September/October 1999, 44.

Carpenter, Denise L. ''World Outlook: The Water and Wastewater Business Sector.'' *Water Online.* 1997. Available from http://www.wateronline.com.

''ENR Forecast '97.'' *Engineering News Record,* 27 January 1997.

''EPA Puts Beach Survey Results on Web.'' CNN on-line news. Available from http://cnn.com/NATURE/9906/14/beach.enn/index.html.

Gullick, Richard W. and Mark W. LeChavallier. ''Occurrence of MTBE.'' *Journal AWWA,* January 2000, 100.

Heavens, Alan J. ''New Faucet Aims to Improve Water.'' *The Philadelphia Inquirer,* 23 December 1999.

''Joint Venture to Develop Promising Sea Water-Drinking Water.'' *Water Online,* 1996. Available from http://www.wateronline.com.

Kolch, J. ''Disinfecting Drinking Water With UV Light.''

Kucera, Daniel J. ''Gleanings on Water and Wastewater.'' *Water Online,* 1997. Available from http://www.wateronline.com.

———. ''New IRS Rules Enable Longer Term Privatization Management Contracts.'' *Water Online,* 1997. Available from http://www.wateronline.com.

''Northern New Jersey Utilities Again Compete in Unregulated Market.'' *The Record,* Hackensack, N.J., 20 December 1999.

Maldonado, Monica. ''Public Water in Private Hands.'' *Civil Engineering,* January 1997.

Milner, John W. ''Water Utility Industry.'' *The Value Line Investment Survey (Part 3—Ratings & Reports),* 7 February 1997.

O'Connor, Marjie. ''Treat Your Water Better.'' *Contractor,* December 1999.

''Perceptions of Tap Water.'' *Environment,* 8 November 1999.

Powers, Mary Buckner. ''Tax Changes To Ease Long-Term Management by Private Sector.'' *Engineering News Record,* 3 February 1997.

''Reading Your Water Report.'' *Consumer Reports,* October 1999, 52.

Rubin, Debra K., and William J. Angelo. ''New York's Green Garb.'' *Engineering News Record,* 17 February 1997.

Soast, Allen. ''As Federal Programs Slow, Locally Funded Work Grows.'' *Engineering News Record,* 27 January 1997.

United Nations Commission on Sustainable Development. ''Comprehensive Assessment of the Freshwater Resources of the World.'' *United Nations,* April 1997. Available from http://www.un.org./dpcsd/dsd/freshwat.htm.

United States Environmental Protection Agency. ''The Drinking Water Infrastructure Needs Survey.'' *Environmental Protection Agency,* January 1997. Available from http://www.epa.gov/OGWDW/docs/needs. src]United States Environmental Protection Agency. ''SDWA Section 1429 Ground Water Report to Congress.'' *Environmental Protection Agency,* January 1999. Available from http://www.epa.gov/OGWDW/docs/needs.

Van Cranebrock, Allen. ''Teams Vie To Build and Run Seattle Water Plant.'' *Puget Sound Business Journal,* 6 December 1996.

''Water/Wastewater Market Poised for More Growth.'' *Water Online,* 1997. Available from http://www.wateronline.com.

''Water/Wastewater Utilities Win Own Competitions To Operate Their Facilities.'' *Water Online,* 1997. Available from http://www.wateronline.com.

''Zebrafish May be Toxin Detectors.'' Associated Press Online, 26 December 1999.

Zimoch, Rebecca. ''Organic Contaminant Screening Process For Drinking Water Developed.'' *Water Engineering & Management,* 10 November 1999.

SIC 4952

SEWERAGE SYSTEMS

This category includes establishments primarily engaged in the collection and disposal of wastes transported through a sewer system. These private and public organizations usually treat the wastewater they collect before discharging it back into the environment.

NAICS CODE(S)

221320 (Sewage Treatment Facilities)

INDUSTRY SNAPSHOT

Conventional sewerage treatment in the U.S. today releases nearly 27 million tons of carbon dioxide into the air each year. Wastewater management has become big business now that federal amendments to the Safe Drinking Water Act (SDWA) of 1996 and the Clean Water Action Plan of 1998 have put new life, and new money, into environmental protection. Concurrently, the increasing deregulation of public utilities and the privatization and/or public-private partnership development in wastewater treatment has caused the industry to grow at a faster pace than other industries in the United States. The Environmental Protection Agency (EPA) has put teeth into its legislation by imposing criminal and civil penalties on violators of the wastewater cleanup mandates. From Royal Caribbean Cruise Line's 1999 multi-million-dollar fine for dumping waste into the intracoastal waters, to the $1.3 million fine and prison sentence for a Richmond, Virginia wastewater treatment executive, EPA continued to show that it meant business when it said ''clean up.''

ORGANIZATION AND STRUCTURE

Organizations in the wastewater industry are responsible for collecting wastewater from homes, businesses, and institutions, for treating wastewater to acceptable standards before discharging it into a waterway, and for disposing of residues called sludge. These activities entail building, operating, and maintaining a transport system, and constructing and operating primary treatment facilities that remove or dilute toxins, synthetic debris, human waste, and other refuse.

Wastewater managers are expected to devise a system that transports wastewater as much as possible by gravity and that offers almost no threat of disruption of flow or service. The manager must also ensure that wastes do not seep into water supplies and that plant effluents are treated in a manner that does not significantly harm the environment. In accomplishing their duties, managers must comply with numerous state and federal regulations, financial restrictions, and political pressures. In addition, wastewater managers are often charged with developing resource recovery programs.

The majority of wastewater treatment plants consist of holding reservoirs that contain, chemically treat, and aerate wastewater until pollutants have settled out and the water can be safely jettisoned into a natural waterway. A few treatment plants use other systems. Approximately 300 municipal and industrial artificial marshland wastewater treatment systems were in operation across the country in the late 1990s. These marshes use plants and microorganisms to absorb and biodegrade the organics.

The two main sources of wastewater are residential and industrial. The large majority of residential wastewater is discharged into local sewer systems and treated by local utilities or publicly owned treatment works (POTWs). In 1999, there were approximately 16,000 POTWs across the nation. However, it was estimated that millions of homes still maintained on-site disposal systems, including septic tanks, cesspools, and outhouses—septic tanks alone numbered over 23 million in 1999.

Industrial waste is often pretreated at its source to remove hazardous wastes that require special handling. After being treated in surface impoundments or on-site treatment plants, the water is either discharged directly into the environment or released into local POTWs. About 80 percent of all industrial wastewater is eventually processed by POTWs. Industries that discharge waste into POTWs become subject to many of the same state and federal standards that regulate municipal wastewater facilities.

Types of Organizations. Most organizations that provide wastewater treatment services are publicly owned, and operated as nonprofit entities. They may be established under a variety of organizational structures. A regional wastewater authority, for example, provides service either directly or through governmental entities such as cities, townships, water and sanitation districts, and counties. The regional authority may provide direct service and billing to individual customers, or it might offer wholesale service to several governmental entities that would in turn provide service and billing to local customers.

Large centralized treatment facilities, such as regional authorities, benefit from economies of scale. The drawback of this type of arrangement, however, is that centralized facilities often require pumping of wastewater over long distances. As a result, they tend to be less energy efficient and produce greater amounts of residue in a concentrated area than satellite (or local) treatment plants. Municipal special service districts, which represent a more localized wastewater organizational structure, avoid these drawbacks. Localized utilities though, often have higher costs and lack capital for investment in new technology.

In addition to POTWs, some wastewater treatment facilities are operated by private companies that have a profit motive. These companies bid to either own or manage the wastewater plants or a portion of the operation for a set period of time. The private company's incentives for providing quality service are not only profit but also winning the bid again when the contract ends. The private companies also inject private capital into the operation, which frees the community's capital for other uses.

BACKGROUND AND DEVELOPMENT

The first sanitary sewer system was built in 1843 in Hamburg, Germany. Twelve years later, construction began in Chicago on the first U.S. sewer system. In the 1870s, the first U.S. wastewater treatment plants were built. By the end of World War II, wastewater treatment plants served nearly 30 percent of the 145 million Americans. As the population and housing boomed across the United States after the war, so did wastewater treatment plants and sewer systems.

The proliferation of professional wastewater treatment was stimulated by federal government efforts to control pollution caused by residential and industrial discharge. The Federal Water Pollution Control Act

(WPCA) of 1956, for instance, established a grant program to help communities construct state-of-the-art facilities. Amendments to the WPCA in 1972, as well as the Clean Water Act of 1977, boosted development of wastewater infrastructure by mandating clean water standards. For example, the National Pollutant Discharge Elimination System (NPDES), created by the Clean Water Act, set limits on the amount and quality of effluent and required all municipal and industrial dischargers to obtain permits.

A few of the other laws and regulations that impacted the wastewater industry, either directly or indirectly, included the Water Facilities Act of 1937, the Water Resources Research Act of 1964, the National Environmental Policy Act of 1969, and the Safe Drinking Water Act of 1974. In the 1980s, important legislation included the Comprehensive Environmental Response, Compensation, and Liability Act (CERCLA) of 1980, amendments to the Safe Water Drinking Act in 1986 and 1996, the Resource and Conservation Recovery Act (RCRA), and the Water Quality Act of 1987. The Safe Water Drinking Act was amended in 1996. The Clean Air Act and the Clean Water Act of 1998 were essentially reauthorizations of the earlier acts.

When the number of contaminants, particularly chemicals, began increasing at a rapid pace, Americans began to demand a cleaner environment, and federal regulations became more stringent during this time. As a result, the number and capacity of wastewater treatment plants ballooned. Privatization was one technique used to control the rising cost of POTWs. Private wastewater companies typically existed only in areas that were too small or remote to support a municipal treatment system. New legislation encouraged many communities to privatize utilities to achieve cost savings. Initial results of privatization efforts were mixed, and some analysts suggested that private companies often operated at a higher cost than municipally owned systems.

The federal government however, continued to encourage municipalities to take on waste water treatment responsibilities. An EPA grant program was announced in 1997 for rural communities with fewer than 3,000 residents. These communities were eligible to receive grants from a $50 million fund established by the EPA and authorized by congressional appropriations in 1996 as part of the Clean Water State Revolving Fund loan program. This loan fund offered loans at low interest for wastewater treatment and projects.

Because this loan source was shrinking just at the time equipment from the 1970s and 1980s needed improvements, more plants were looking at the feasibility of privatization. In addition, changes in 1997 to Internal Revenue Service (IRS) regulations regarding fees, length of contracts, and the sale of facilities were considered a positive sign to an estimated 30 U.S. cities considering this type of public-private ''partnership.'' The percentage of public to private wastewater plants could reach 50/50 by the year 2020.

Because in some locales water and wastewater are under the same roof, there are many variations of private involvement in public wastewater plants. Some companies may operate just one phase of the operation, and in another city, one company may operate and maintain the entire water and wastewater process. An industry consultant estimated that in 1997 there were more than 500 contracts for facilities with capacities greater than 1 million gallons per day (mgd). Some cities had successful arrangements while others found private involvement problematic. Some of the cities that have some form of privatized wastewater systems are Indianapolis, Indiana; Cranston, Rhode Island; New Orleans, Louisiana; Fulton County, Georgia; and Schenectady, New York.

CURRENT CONDITIONS

In 1999, the Association of Metropolitan Sewerage Agencies (AMSA) represented more than 210 wastewater treatment facilities nationwide, up from 160 members just a few years previously. AMSA members now serve the majority of the country's sewered population. Collectively, AMSA facilities treated and reclaimed approximately 18 billion gallons of wastewater each day in 1999. AMSA reported that sewer service rates rose a modest 2.3 percent in 1998, about 0.7 percent above the level of inflation as measured by the Consumer Price Index.

AMSA is a member of a coalition of 60 public and private groups known as the Rebuild America Coalition. The group focuses attention on strengthening the nation's infrastructure at the federal, state and local government level. The 1999 Rebuild America Infrastructure Survey, released in January, 1999, indicated that 70 percent of Americans surveyed stated that quality infrastructure was ''very important'' to their quality of life. According to the survey, an easy majority of the American public would support an one percent increase in taxes for the guaranty of safe and efficient sewage and water treatment and the return of fishes to local waterways. Only 13 percent of those surveyed believed that the quality of their tap water had improved in the previous five years. Conversely, 30 percent believed that water quality of local rivers, lakes and coastal areas had actually deteriorated. As of 1999, local governments shouldered 90 percent of the funding burden for clean water programs. Americans were split in their opinions as to whether this burden should shift to federal government or remain with the state and local communities.

During the latter years of the decade, global warming and *El Niño* seasons created numerous floods and heavy rains. Sewer overflows (SSOs) became a national nightmare. The EPA attempted to form a committee to draft national policies for the prevention of SSOs during heavy storm events, at a proposed cost of more than $80 to 90 billion to the American public. In July 1999, five national organizations, including the AMSA, the National League of Cities, and the National Association of Counties, walked out of committee talks in protest of the proposed EPA regulations. As one participant noted, ''Leaving communities vulnerable to lawsuits and enforcement actions is no way to deal with this issue. The realities of operating a sewage collection system have somehow been lost in these talks.''

INDUSTRY LEADERS

On the stock market, wastewater is grouped among the environmental industries, which has been called a ''mature'' market. Analysts at Value Line Investments saw some bright spots among wastewater's publicly traded companies. Ionics Inc. of Watertown, Massachusetts had well-defined, longer-term earning prospects because of its technology and sales in chemical and electronic filtration systems that purify water to extremely high levels. Ionics reported $351 million in sales for 1998.

Another company mentioned by Value Line experts for potential growth in the late 1990s was U.S. Filter of Palm Desert, California. U.S. Filter acquired Wheelabrator, one of the pioneers in operating and maintaining public wastewater utilities, in 1997 from WMX Technologies of Oak Brook, Illinois. This acquisition established U.S. Filter as North America's largest private water and wastewater service organization, operating more than 200 municipal and industrial water and wastewater treatment plants with $1 billion in annual revenue.

An example of one of the largest publicly owned and operated wastewater utilities in the United States is the Hyperion treatment facility, the largest of Los Angeles, California's four wastewater plants. Hyperion serves 4 million people in a 600 square mile area. The plant can handle 450 million gallons of wastewater per day and is unique in that it burns its sludge residue to help produce the energy that operates the plant.

WORKFORCE

Workers in the wastewater treatment industry are typically employed by POTWs, engineering and construction companies that build and improve facilities, or consulting firms. The industry hires a disproportionate share of engineers and chemists. Consultants typically provide services such as hydraulic analysis and modeling, feasibility and financial studies, design and specifications for construction, lab services, resource recovery, hazardous waste management, and environmental litigation.

According to the U.S Bureau of Labor Statistics (BLS), the industry employed approximately 98,000 persons in 1996, and predicted good job opportunities through 2006.

RESEARCH AND TECHNOLOGY

Several companies continued to offer marsh wastewater treatment, called constructed wetlands for smaller communities. This treatment method is estimated to cost 50 percent less than traditional mechanical treatment systems and operates without chemicals. The ''living machine'' is an artificial marsh, using tanks rather than a pond, where organisms and plants do the same work of biodegrading and absorbing. This is an alternative in locations where soil conditions prevent the use of a pond. Living Earth Technology Co. installed its system in one municipality and found it about 15 percent less expensive in terms of capital costs than competing technology, and approximately the same in terms of operating costs. There was 66 percent less sludge than conventional methods, and no chemicals were used to treat the wastewater. Therefore none of the remaining waste was considered an environmental hazard.

An article published in the Winter 1998/Spring 1999 issue of *Earth Island Journal* proposed the adoption of ''sewage forests,'' trees specifically planted and grown near sewage treatment plants. According to the article's author, Daniel Wickham, not only do the trees seem to thrive in the fertilized soil, but they provide a tremendous service by absorbing phenomenal amounts of carbon dioxide from the atmosphere. He cited one such experimental forest in Martinez, California, where redwoods have grown 40 feet tall in as little as nine years.

A new process for wastewater treatment systems in cold climates uses modified snowmaking equipment to treat wastewater without the use of chemicals. The process, similar to freeze drying, flash freezes the wastewater after solids have been removed. The quick freezing explodes bacteria and separates gases as the water is sprayed into the air. Harmless nutrients remain, which are released into the soil during the spring thaw.

Of course, making lemonade from bad lemons is the American Way. In September, 1999, the ThermoEnergy Corporation announced its creation of a thermochemical process which makes combustible fuel oil out of wastewater sludge. The Sludge-To-Oil Reactor System (STORS) boasted a nonbiological technology which eliminates the anaerobic sludge digestion unit from wastewater treatment. The company alleged that the resulting fuel product has 90 percent of the heating value of diesel fuel.

On-site sewerage treatment plants are used by companies such as Anheuser-Busch, Inc. The company reduced its wastewater treatment costs by installing anaerobic/aerobic bio-energy recovery systems. The new technology required about 75 percent less energy than traditional aerobic treatments, and cost about half as much to install. Methane gas produced by the new system replaced about 15 percent of the natural gas used as fuel at the breweries. On-site treatments are not limited to factory settings—a Santa Monica office park has on-site sewage treatment plant, which uses the treated water for its lake and landscaping.

FURTHER READING

"$50 million EPA Grants Program for Rural Community Wastewater Projects." *Water Online,* 1996. Available from http://www.wateronline.com.

American Water Works Association. *Journal of the AWWA,* Vol. 91, No. 1, 1999.

Association of Metropolitan Sewerage Agencies. News Releases Online from http://www.amsa-cleanwater.org.

Angelo, William J. "Snowfluent Spices Up Snowmaking Equipment." *Engineering News Record,* 17 February 1997.

Carpenter, Denise L. "World Outlook: The Water and Wastewater Business Sector." *Water Online,* 1997. Available from http://www.wateronline.com.

"Case Study #2: Advanced Wastewater Treatment Plants." *The Indianapolis Experience,* 1997. Available from http://www.ci.indianapolis.in.us.

"Clean Water Needs Survey." *Environmental Protection Agency,* 1997. Available from http://www.epa.gov/own/wm049000.htm.

"A Commitment to Quality Control." *Water Environment WEB,* 1997. Available from http://www.wef.org/docs/commitment.html.

"Congress Urged to Act on Risk Assessment." *Chemical Market Reporter,* 3 February 1997.

"Creating Fuel Oil From Wastewater Sludge." *Civil Engineering,* September 1999.

Dutton, Gail. "Managing Water Resources." *Management Review,* May 1995.

"ENR Forecast '97." *Engineering News Record,* 27 January 1997.

"Former Executive of Richmond Wastewater Treatment Business Sentenced to Three Years in Jail and Ordered to Pay $1.3 Million Fine." FDCH Regulatory Intelligence Database, EPA, 2 September 1999.

"Global Competitiveness of U.S. Environmental Technology Industries." *U.S. International Trade Commission,* 1997. Available from http://www.usitc.gov/332s/water.htm.

Hoover's Online Company Capsules, 1999. Available from http://www.hoovers.com.

"How Common Are Septic Tanks?" *Colorado Water Resource Research Institute,* 1997. Available from http://www.colostate.edu/Depts/CWRRI/onsite/howcom.html.

"Industry Doings." *Water Online,* 1997. Available from http://www.wateronline.com.

Laughlin, James. "Job Outlook Good for Plant Operators." *WaterWorld,* October 1999.

Lewis, Mark. "Plants Do the Dirty Work: Cleaning Wastewater, Saving the Environment." *Nation's Cities Weekly,* 23 September 1996.

Maldonado, Monica. "Public Water in Private Hands." *Civil Engineering,* January 1997.

Mays, Susan and Paul Roy. *Pollution Engineering,* June 1999.

Shaw, Susan E. and Stig Regli. "US Regulations on Residual Disinfection." *Journal of the AWWA,* Vol. 91, No. 1, 1999.

"Study Building Guidelines for Plant Performance Evaluation." *Engineering News Record,* 26 December 1996.

Wickham, Daniel. "Sewage Forests: Cleaning Water and Cooling the Planet." *Earth Island Journal,* Winter 98/Spring 99.

———. "New England Cities Queue Up with Privatization Proposals." *Engineering News Record,* 25 November 1996.

SIC 4953

REFUSE SYSTEMS

This category includes establishments that are primarily engaged in the collection and disposal of solid waste. Firms in the industry operate incinerators, solid waste treatment plants, hazardous waste facilities, landfills, and other disposal sites and services. Companies that only collect and transport waste without such disposal are classified in **SIC 4212: Local Trucking Without Storage.**

NAICS CODE(S)

562111 (Solid Waste Collection)
562112 (Hazardous Waste Collection)
562920 (Materials Recovery Facilities)
562119 (Other Waste Collection)
562211 (Hazardous Waste Treatment and Disposal)
562212 (Solid Waste Landfills)
562213 (Solid Waste Combustors and Incinerators)
562219 (Other Nonhazardous Waste Treatment and Disposal)

INDUSTRY SNAPSHOT

In the late 1980s and early 1990s, the refuse industry was struggling to overcome the effects of a recession, which included reduced waste and a more competitive business environment. Many refuse companies were also buckling under stringent new environmental regulations. As it entered the millennium, the industry was continuing to seek new ways to safely handle growing amounts of waste at the same time that landfill space was rapidly declining. The industry placed a greater emphasis on recycling efforts, and by 1998, there were 9000 curbside recycling programs in the U.S. There also was a strong move toward privatization of former municipal operations, consolidation of firms, and increased flexibility of government regulation of the industry. About 2,400 landfills were still functional in 1997 and these, along with hundreds of incinerators, consumed the bulk of America's trash (not including hazardous waste).

However, by 1999, new problems loomed on the horizon. Of major concern was that the ''clean-up'' of America was causing new toxic byproducts. MTBE additives to gasoline fuel, ostensibly to reduce air emissions, ended up contaminating ground water. Methane gas fumes released from landfills had reached toxic levels in many states, and dioxin, a byproduct of incinerated waste, was brought under EPA monitoring. Moreover, chloroform, a byproduct carcinogen created during the disinfection phase of water treatment, was detected in high levels in approximately one to three percent of drinking water samples reported in 1999 by the U.S. Geological Survey.

Organization and Structure

The refuse industry traditionally has been fragmented in comparison to other businesses. Organizations range from local firms and government bodies that manage consumer garbage to companies that handle hazardous and specialty waste. However, from the mid-1990s on there has been a trend toward acquisition of smaller firms and privatization of former municipal efforts, which often are absorbed by large private companies. Municipal and government entities, which owned 85 percent of landfills in the early 1990s, owned less than 70 percent by 1997. Several large U.S. corporations also have become active in all aspects of waste management on a global scale.

The two largest segments of the refuse management market are municipal solid waste (MSW) and hazardous waste. MSW includes non-hazardous garbage discarded by homes, businesses, and governments. In 1997, 217 million tons of MSW was generated across the nation, constituting eight million tons more than in 1996. The lion's share of trash was paper and yard trimmings, which accounted for 51 percent of all MSW. By 1999, nearly 30 percent of MSW was recycled. Recycled solid waste prevents the release of more than 33 million tons of carbon into the atmosphere each year.

Hazardous waste includes liquid and solid materials that are toxic or radioactive. Liquid waste commonly emanates from nuclear energy facilities and U.S. Department of Defense activities. Solid waste often comes from mining and milling operations (especially from extracting uranium ore), sludge in abandoned storage tanks, and contaminated equipment and structures. Large amounts of both solid and liquid hazardous materials also emanate from chemical, medical, and petroleum industry activities, as well as from mishandling of those wastes by businesses, governments, and consumers.

Disposal Methods. By 1998, landfills were managing about 55 percent of MSW, 30 percent was being recycled, and 15 percent combusted. In raw figures, this meant that approximately 60 million tons of material was recycled rather than dumped into landfills or incinerated. The highest recycle recovery rates are batteries (93.3 percent) and paper/paperboard products (41.7 percent). About 41 percent of yard trimmings is also recycled.

Like MSW, most hazardous waste is landfilled. Various types of toxic waste are also incinerated and even recycled. Solid waste landfills differ from MSW fills in that they are usually built to contain the waste for a long period of time, and a greater effort is made to break down or neutralize the refuse, thus making hazardous waste fills more expensive to build and operate. Highly radioactive waste may be sealed in special drums or tanks where it can be held indefinitely.

Background and Development

Municipal Solid Waste. Prior to the industrialization of the United States, most people managed their own waste. Garden and organic waste was composted and used as fertilizer and soil conditioner. Scrap wood, glass, metal, and other debris were often taken to a local dump or burned on one's property. A garbage collection and landfill industry emerged however, as industrialization occurred and large urban areas began to develop in the 1800s. In fact, WMX Technologies, Inc., one of the largest refuse companies in the world, originated in 1894 as a collector of Chicago's waste.

The waste disposal industry flourished after World War II. As the U.S. economy and population expanded, so did the amount of garbage produced per capita. By 1960, in fact, Americans were discarding a combined total of over 100 million tons of garbage per year, prompting some people to call ours the ''disposable society.'' In order to handle mass quantities of garbage created by the new suburban consumer society that evolved in the 1950s and 1960s, municipalities began building large numbers of landfills and incinerators. By the early 1970s, 300 to 400 municipal landfills were opening each year.

During the 1970s, the MSW environment began to change. In addition to the fact that many landfills were becoming saturated, environmental problems began to plague landfill operators. Some landfills were emitting hazardous gases and fluids that were seeping into the air and water. Americans became more conscious of the need for safer and more attractive waste management. Federal initiatives that impacted the refuse industry included the Clean Air Act, the Clean Water Act, and the Safe Drinking Water Act. Recycling programs, such as the ''one-bag'' and ''blue-bag'' programs, emerged in several states. Consumers also became less receptive to landfill development, thus coining the acronym NIMBY (not in my backyard).

It was not until the 1980s that North American landfill capacity began to shrink. Public opposition to new landfills posed major barriers to refuse organizations. Furthermore, new federal and state environmental regulations made it increasingly difficult and expensive to operate existing landfills. During the 1980s, the number of landfills opened each year declined between 50 and 200 while existing landfills closed at a high rate. The total number of dump sites dropped from 14,000 in 1980 to 6,000 by 1990, and then to only 3,000 by 1996.

Despite society's apparent concern over MSW and the environment in the 1970s and 1980s, both personal and commercial waste volumes continued to grow at a record pace. By 1992, the average American was producing four pounds of trash per day. Landfills were further stressed by curbside collection of yard waste, which was not commonly practiced until the mid-1980s. The total amount of U.S. trash had ballooned to over 280 million tons per year.

Waste companies responded to refuse growth and market demands for safer, less conspicuous disposal by stepping up recycling operations and by developing other disposal options, such as WTE. By the late 1980s, recycling programs processed 15 percent of all MSW, and about 125 WTE plants consumed nearly 15 percent of all refuse. The future importance of innovative waste management companies seemed clear to investors. Many refuse companies enjoyed skyrocketing stock prices and healthy profit growth.

Hazardous Waste. At the same time that the MSW industry was rapidly growing, government and industry began producing large amounts of toxic and radioactive waste that would eventually result in the proliferation of an entire hazardous waste industry. New synthetic chemical products that were developed during the war, for instance, were offered to the public on a broad scale in the 1950s and 1960s. Industrial wastes that resulted from production of these chemicals were often carelessly dumped in waterways, landfills, and wells. Furthermore, the Department of Defense, which was busy creating a nuclear defense system, jettisoned mass amounts of highly radioactive materials.

By the 1970s, the refuse industry began to respond to societal concerns about the environment. Toxic substances, including some that had seeped into aquifers or had been used to produce children's clothing, resulted in a new category of refuse called ''hazardous waste.'' Prompting the formation of the hazardous waste industry were federal mandates regarding toxic refuse. The Resource Conservation and Recovery Act (RCRA) of 1976, for instance, was implemented to control the creation and disposal of hazardous materials.

Laws that followed RCRA in the 1980s included the 1984 Hazardous and Solid Wastes Amendments (HSWA); the Comprehensive Environmental Response, Compensation, and Liability Act (CERCLA or Superfund), which designated billions of federal dollars for clean up; the Toxic Substances Control Act; and the 1986 Superfund Amendments and Reauthorizations Act (SARA). CERCLA earmarked over $9.6 billion for hazardous waste cleanup in the 1980s, much of which went to contractors in the refuse industry. In addition, the federal government required companies to spend additional billions to recover toxic waste sites.

Like MSW, the creation of hazardous waste continued to grow during the 1980s and early 1990s. By 1985 ten times more chemicals were in use than in 1970. In the early 1990s, synthetic chemical manufacturers were producing 220 million tons per year of about 58,000 different chemicals. In addition to growing amounts of hazardous waste produced in the United States in the early 1990s, refuse companies also benefitted from ongoing CERCLA cleanups. By 1990, the Environmental Protection Agency had identified 1,224 priority cleanup sites, as well as over 31,000 sites that needed attention. In addition, the General Accounting Office estimated that 130,000 to 425,000 potentially hazardous sites existed. The average bill for a Superfund site cleanup in the early 1990s exceeded $26 million.

Stock prices of refuse companies during the late 1980s and early 1990s reflected the surging demand for both MSW and hazardous waste services. The average earnings per share for the ten largest companies, for instance, jumped from 59 cents to over 70 cents in 1990 alone. Stock prices of those firms peaked in 1990 as well, rising from about $22 to an average of almost $30. In the early 1990s however, most refuse firms were stalled by an industry recession.

Several factors contributed to the slowdown in the early 1990s. MSW tonnage dropped to around 280 million tons per year by 1993. The amount of money spent on hazardous waste cleanup also declined in the weak economy. In addition, larger amounts of garbage were being collected for recycling. Because recycling is labor-intensive and there is relatively little demand for recycled products, it offers low profit margins. A weak economy also played a role in keeping prices down, as stagnant waste growth created a more competitive business environment.

Adding to the plight of the refuse industry in the early 1990s was a proliferation of the NIMBY attitude and increasingly stringent environmental regulations. These two factors were reducing the number of new landfills that were opening and were forcing many operators to close their fills or comply with expensive new regulations. In 1991 for example, an average of 63 landfills per state were shut down, while an average of only ten new dump permits and six landfill expansion permits were allowed.

Regulations and public opposition also squelched the WTE market for waste in the early 1990s. Although the number of plants in operation grew from 30 in 1991 to 61 by 1993, the number of plants planned for future construction fell from 220 in 1988 to only 48 in 1993. Furthermore, by 1993 a full 50 plants had been shut down for environmental reasons, up from 37 in 1991, and 27 in 1988. More WTE closings were expected as the cost of retrofitting existing plants for cleaner operation spiraled.

Privatization became more prevalent, with municipal ownership of solid waste landfills falling to 70 percent by 1996 and private firms picking up the formerly public operations. This shift was largely due to municipal budget cuts and increased regulatory compliance costs.

CURRENT CONDITIONS

Overall, the waste management and disposal industry experienced less than five percent growth annually for the latter years of the decade. In early 1999, the industry reported an annual revenue of $40 billion, with private industry controlling approximately 67 percent. The industry also reported a 20 percent annual decline in disposal volume. However in 1997, the EPA increased the goal for recycling to 35 percent of total volume, and by 1999, several communities had reached or surpassed that goal. (The national average in 1999 was 28 percent.) Some states were taking more drastic measures. California had hoped to cut its overall refuse by 50 percent, but missed that goal even though it did accomplish an impressive 33 percent. Minnesota was considering a law to ban *all* dumping in landfills.

But no state caught the attention of the industry more than New York, which plans to close its half-century-old Staten Island landfill by the end of 2001. The landfill has been home to New York City's 13,000-ton daily trash load for fifty years. Of concern to citizens of neighboring states, as well as to legislators, is the absence of laws preventing interstate dumping, and many Americans living in the East are wary of their states taking on New York's trash, even if they have the room and can use the money. For example in 1997, Pennsylvania imported 6.3 million tons of trash from other states and buried it in its landfills for a fee. Virginia had also been a high-volume trash importer. However, in 1998, barges of trash traveling the historic James River on their way to landfills began spilling and leaking their loads into the river. At about the same time, New York papers featured Governor James Gilmore wearing latex gloves and showing the press items of medical and human waste that had been mixed with Brooklyn garbage. A shocked citizenry began to mobilize their political support, and as of early 2000, several state legislators had bills pending which address the potential ban of imported trash. Continuing negotiation of a proposed international hazardous waste treaty may result in bans on shipments of certain wastes to developing nations, which could otherwise become dumping grounds for other nations' unwanted and dangerous refuse.

On November 8, 1999, the EPA published its plan to implement emission guidelines for MSW landfills, focusing on the recovery of methane gases released into the atmosphere. Emissions from MSWs and industrial landfills had increased almost 20 percent between 1990 and 1997. EPA's stated goal was to reduce landfill methane emissions by 50 percent by 2000.

INDUSTRY LEADERS

The multinational waste management and environmental services firm Waste Management Inc. remains the largest in the industry. With $13 billion in annual revenues in 1999, it owned 319 landfills and 650 hauling operations across the country. However, it reported losses of $770 million in 1998, which followed a $1.2 billion loss in 1997.

In early 1999, Allied Waste Industries Inc. bought out Browning-Ferris Industries, Inc. which had been the second largest private company. By December 1999, Allied was selling off some of its operations to reduce its debt. Browning-Ferris had been the most profitable company in 1998 before being bought; it reported just under $339 million in profits for 1998.

The nation's fastest-growing private hauler in 1999 was Independent Environmental Service Inc, which purchased 25 other companies in 1999. IESI expected to bring in $140 million for 1999.

Firms were also beginning to venture into central and eastern Europe, which was projected to have a solid and hazardous waste and soil remediation market of $6.35 billion in 1997, perhaps rising to about $13 billion by 2010.

RESEARCH AND TECHNOLOGY

The industry would increasingly be affected by new technologies related to packaging, waste transportation, and hazardous waste disposal. Recycling services were becoming a more important part of waste management services, even though residential recyclables recouped only a fraction of the cost necessary to collect and process them. Therefore, new recycling technologies, such as papers and inks that are easier to process, would play a critical role in MSW profitability.

Additionally, great strides were made in the development and promotion of refuse derived fuel under what has been referred to as waste-to-energy (WTE) technology. In 1999, the U.S. had 103 WTE facilities, which operated mostly as joint ownerships/partnerships with local governments.

National Environmental Technology Applications Corp. represented one firm on the technological edge. This firm devised a mile-deep tube that could pressurize hazardous sludge for use as bricks, road base material, and structural fill. Importantly, advances in scrubber technology could revive the ailing WTE sector, allowing cleaner emissions from energy plants at reasonable costs. WMX had already developed new fabric filters and dust collectors that allowed it to convert trash to energy more efficiently and cleanly.

FURTHER READING

"1999 Timeline." *Waste News,* 20 December 1999.

"A Year Best Forgotten." *Waste News,* 20 December 1999.

Brown, Bob. "IESI Buys 14 Firms." *Waste News,* 23 August 1999.

———. "Stericycle Moves to Front of Line." *Waste News,* 19 April 1999.

"Browning-Ferris Industries - Company Report." *Investext,* 7 August 1996.

Defendis, Megan. "Recycler's Revenues Increase." *Waste News,* 28 September 1998.

"Environmental Industry Hits $180 Billion in Revenues." *Waste Age,* October 1996.

"Environmental Services Industry—Industry Report." *Investext,* 15 May 1996.

"European Solid Waste Management—Where Is It Heading?" *Waste Age,* June 1996.

Ewel, Dexter. "Garbage: Can'Keep it Out, Can't Keep It In." *Bio Cycler,* March 1999.

"Forces of Change in the Solid Waste Industry." *Waste Age,* May 1996.

Hickman, Lanier. "Garbage: Bin There, Done That." *American City & County,* November 1999.

"High Growth Potential in CEE Markets." *Haznews,* 1 March 1997.

Hill, Michael. "A Trend Toward Smart Regulations." *Environmental Solutions,* January 1997.

Kertes, Noella. "Superfund Resolution Sought." *American Metal Market,* 28 January 1997.

"Medical Waste Steps to the Future." *Waste Age,* July 1996.

"Municipal Solid Waste Disposal Trends 1996 Update." *Waste Age,* May 1996.

"Philip Environmental Inc. and Allwaste Inc. To Merge." *Business Wire,* 6 March 1997.

Sanders. "Trash Haulers' Prices Going Up With More Hauler Consolidation." *New Hampshire Business Review,* 5 November 1999.

"Solid Waste Industry Report." *Investext,* 16 September 1996.

"Solid Waste Management Services Are on the Rise as Municipalities Privatize." *PR Newswire,* 10 February 1997.

"SPI, Greenpeace Tussling Over Waste Treaty." *Plastics News,* 10 March 1997.

"The Cleanup of Contaminated Federal Facilities." *Industrial Health & Hazards Update,* 1 January 1997.

"The Third Annual Waste Age 100." *Waste Age,* September 1996.

"Transamerican Waste Industries, Inc. Completes Acquisition Adding Approximately $15 Million in Annual Revenue." *Business Wire,* 31 January 1997.

Truini, Joe. "Trash Bags Lots of Cash." *Waste News,* 12 July 1999.

"Trash Timeline: 1000 Years of Waste." *Waste News,* 3 May 1999.

"United Waste Developing Into an Industry Leader." *Fairfield County (CT) Business Journal,* 27 January 1997.

"U.S. Environment Industry Generates $180b in 95 Revenues." *Eco-Log Week,* 16 August 1996.

"US Environmental Market Growing." *Haznews,* 1 September 1996.

U.S. Environmental Protection Agency's *MSW Report 1998* Executive Summary, Available from http://www.epa.gov/epaoswer/non-hw/muncpl/mswrpt98/execsumm.txt. Other EPA information from http://www.epa.gov/outreach.

"Valuation of the Waste Management Industry." *Weekly Corporate Growth Report,* 1 February 1999.

"Waste News Stock Market." *Waste News,* 20 December 1999.

"WMX Reverses Global Ambitions." *Haznews,* 1 March 1997.

"WMX to Idle 3,000, Refocus on Roots in Trash Hauling." *St. Louis Post-Dispatch,* 5 February 1997.

Wolpin, Bill. "A Strong Current of Change." *World Wastes,* April 1998.

Wood, Daniel B. "Recycling Revolution Loses Its Fervor." *Christian Science Monitor,* 9 November 1999.

SIC 4959

SANITARY SERVICES, NOT ELSEWHERE CLASSIFIED

This category includes establishments primarily engaged in cleanup and maintenance activities that are not classified in other sanitary industries. Activities covered by this industry classification include beach maintenance and cleaning, malaria control, mosquito eradication, oil spill cleanup, snowplowing, street sweeping, and vacuuming airport runways.

NAICS Code(s)

488119 (Other Airport Operations)
562910 (Remediation Services)
561710 (Exterminating and Pest Control Services)
562998 (All Other Miscellaneous Waste Management)

Most establishments in the industry are small, local companies that operate on a contract basis, typically for business and municipal clients. For instance, many firms that offer commercial snowplowing, street cleaning, and runway clearing services are small, family-operated businesses. These companies typically act as subcontractors and bid on service contracts for property managers, government agencies, or institutions. The combination of the labor and capital intensive nature of sanitation services and the competitive bidding process results in characteristically low profit margins for industry participants. Furthermore, low barriers to entry create an extremely competitive pricing environment.

An example of an entrepreneurial company in this industry is the Greater Philadelphia Commercial Residential Services Co. (CORS). Started in 1996 as a graffiti-removal company, CORS could not turn a profit because business owners were unwilling to pay for services that they believed should be paid for by local government or the graffiti wrongdoers. Since CORS company assets already included vehicles with mounted pressure washers, the company broadened its market by offering industrial cleaning and environmental services. In 1999, services included pressurized surface cleaning, street cleaning and interiors cleaning. Corporate revenues went from an $11,000 loss in 1997 to nearly $1.2 million in 1999.

Some 1,200 establishments performed miscellaneous sanitation services in the United States in the 1990s. They employed approximately 8,000 laborers and generated receipts of more than $700 million. Such firms benefited from an emphasis by commercial property managers on increased maintenance to retain tenants. This, combined with moderate growth in government spending, was partially offsetting increased competition and stagnant prices among sanitary industry participants.

Environmental awareness of unhealthy conditions has helped the industry. In 1999, the U.S. Environmental Protection Agency (EPA) began publishing survey results of approximately 935 public beaches which regularly monitor water quality. The EPA's own review of 1,062 coastal beaches and the Great Lakes the previous year indicated that 350 had an advisory or closing. Beach maintenance often was contracted out to private companies, but remained a local responsibility. In Hollywood, Florida, for example, the public works division purchased a sanitizer that cleans the beach sand and redistributes it along its 5 miles of beaches. Each year, crews collect more than 500,000 pounds of litter, and 440 cubic yards of shoreline debris.

A bright spot in the industry has been oil spill cleanup services. This segment was benefiting from stringent new federal regulations enacted during the cleanup of the 11-million gallon Exxon Valdez spill in 1989. Notwithstanding, in that incident, less than 50 percent of the rescued wildlife had survived. Ten years and $45 million later, 1999 populations for the bald eagle and river otter appeared to have recovered. Sea otters, harbor seals, harlequin ducks, herring, salmon, and one pod of killer whales were reported as ''not recovering.'' With respect to salmon in 1999, patches of residual oil could still be found adjacent to some intertidal spawning habitats, having continued negative impact on salmon embryos, according to the National Marine Fisheries Service (NMFS).

Many companies and city governments established oil spill readiness plans that provided for quick mobilization of spill cleanup contractors in the event of an emergency. Companies most likely to benefit in this sector are those that have access to the latest technology related to disaster cleanup equipment and chemicals. Major companies in the industry included Waste Management Inc. (formerly WMX Technologies) of Oak Brook, Illinois; and Handex Environmental Recovery Inc. of Morganville, New Jersey.

By the millennium, increasing numbers of Americans were washing with antibacterial soaps, drinking bottled water, employing the latest electronic pest deterrents, and contributing to environmental charities in record amounts. According to a 1999 study released by the American Enterprise Institute, this was with good reason—it found that basic public health measures, including ''drinkable water and sanitation services,'' have the greatest effect on life expectancy.

Further Reading

Batin, Chris. ''A Decade After Disaster.'' *Outdoor Life,* 13 October 1999.

Bennett. ''Sweeping In Profits.'' *Philadelphia Business,* 29 October 1999, 21.

''Drugs and Life Expectancy.'' *Futurist,* 15 November 1999.

''Public Works Department Leads City's Environmental Efforts.'' *American City & County,* March 1998, 78.

U.S. Census Bureau. *County Business Patterns 1997.* Washington: GPO, 1999.

U.S. Census Bureau. *Census of Transportation, Communication, and Utilities Industries.* Washington: GPO, 1995.

SIC 4961

STEAM AND AIR CONDITIONING SUPPLY

This industry comprises companies that produce and/or distribute steam and heated or cooled air for sale.

NAICS CODE(S)

221330 (Steam and Air-Conditioning Supply)

The steam and air conditioning supply industry consists mainly of a few big competitors that produce and sell steam and hot air. The industry also encompasses some miscellaneous activities, including production of geothermal steam and trailer-mounted air conditioning units used as back-up cooling systems.

One growing segment of this industry is cogeneration. Cogeneration is a process that conserves fuel by improving energy efficiency in power plants. When power plants create energy using thermal processes, excess heat is produced. However, only 30 to 40 percent of that thermal energy is converted to usable electricity. Many power plants try to capture this excess heat and deliver it directly to a nearby consumer in the form of hot air or steam. These plants, by capturing the heat, are able to produce and sell both heat and power.

An electric utility plant, for example, might capture heat dissipated during steam production. It could then channel the heat through an underground pipe or vent to, for example, a nearby automobile factory for the factory's heating needs. This is like a car's heating system, which vents residual heat dissipated by the engine back to the car's interior.

Plants using cogeneration typically operate at about 80 percent efficiency, meaning 80 percent of the energy source converts to usable power. Traditional power plants, by comparison, operate at closer to 40 percent efficiency. Although cogeneration has been understood for decades, it was not until the 1980s and 1990s that energy plants started cogeneration programs.

One of the largest cogeneration projects of the 1990s was done by Virginia Electric & Power Co. In 1993, this utility asked state regulators to approve a company plan to build and own ten ''dispersed energy facilities'' in its territory, to help industrial customers save money. Other utilities observed Virginia Power's efforts, and some analysts predicted similar cogeneration efforts may end the construction of traditional centralized power plants.

A new wave of large cogeneration projects emerged toward the latter half of the decade and into the millennium, representing viable power sources. Most cogenerated power remains in the manufacturing sector, with the paper and chemical industries as leading users. The potential savings in energy remains tremendous. For example, in 1998, more than 2.66 trillion cubic feet of natural gas, almost 60 million barrels of petroleum and 56.8 million short tons of coal were all burned off in order to produce electricity.

With the continued deregulation of electricity and rising environmental concerns, the appeal of on-site electric generation continues to grow. One California study has predicted that on-site (distributed) generation will double by 2004. Power shortages and price hikes during the summer of 1998 stimulated further interests in the advantages of on-site generation.

The Federal government has also taken a renewed interest in cogenerated power because of the decrease in global carbon emissions. On December 10, 1998, the Department of Energy announced its goal to double the capacity of cogenerated power by 2010. Partially in anticipation of this expected growth, the Comprehensive Electricity Competition Act of 1999 contained provisions addressing required interconnections between cogenerative power producers and distribution utilities.

Trigen Energy Corporation, with 46 cogeneration and district energy facilities, produces steam hot water, electricity, and chilled water to its1,500 industrial and commercial customers in Canada, Mexico and the U.S. It is also a leader in converting biomass to energy. Trigen reported a 77.8 percent increase in net income for 1999, with overall sales of $280.4 million. Trigen, which produces and sells electricity as a by-product of its heat and power generation, is considered the leading thermal science company in North America.

Another industry leader is Cogeneration Corporation of America (CoGenAmerica), which owns five facilities that produce both electric and thermal energy for commercial and industrial users and utilities companies. It has plants in Illinois, New Jersey, Oklahoma, and Pennsylvania. Sales for this company were $74 million in 1998, with a one-year net income growth of 65.8 percent.

In November 1999, Primary Energy, Inc., a subsidiary of NiSource Inc., announced its plans to enter a joint agreement with LTV Steel Co. to build a cogeneration facility for LTV at its East Chicago plant. The designed gas-fired blast furnace for the plant will convert waste gas into clean, usable electricity. Completion was scheduled for late 2001. NiSource (formerly NIPSCO Industries) was another leader in combination-energy offerings to its customers. In 1999, it served 416,000 electricity customers, 700,000 gas customers in Indiana and another 300,000 in New England, plus water utilities and natural gas marketing. The company employs over 6,000 and reported 1999 sales of $3.14 billion.

FURTHER READING

Battles, Stephanie J. ''Generation in the Manufacturing Sector: A Historical Perspective.'' Presentation to the 20th Annual North American Conference of the U.S. Association for Energy Economics, affiliated with the International Association for Energy Economics, August 1999.

Hoover's Company Capsules used for NiSource, Trigen, and Cogeneration Corporation of America. Austin, Texas: Hoover's Inc., 1999. Available from http://www.hoovers.com.

Kamat, Dilip, Ken Ostrowski and Richard Stuebi. ''Winning in the Emerging Energy Services Business,'' *The Electricity Journal,* August/September 1996.

''NiSource Subsidiary, LTV Sign Cogeneration Project Agreement Primary Energy to Build Plant at LTV's Indiana Harbor Plant.'' PR Newswire, November 20, 1999. Available at http://www.prnewswire.com.

Pospisil, Ray. ''Cogeneration Reflux.'' *Chemical Week,* October 28, 1998, 29.

Saunders, Barbara. ''U.S. gas/electric megamergers may slow as new policies tested.'' *The Oil and Gas Journal,* 3 February 1997.

Studness, Charles M. ''Converging Markets: The First Real Electric/Gas Merger.'' *Public Utilities Fortnightly,* 1 October 1996.

''Trigen Declares Quarterly Dividend.'' PR Newswire, 12 December 1999. Available at http://www.prnewswire.com.

U.S. Department of Energy. Energy Information Administration. *Annual Energy Outlook 1998 With Projections to 2015.* 20 March 2000. Available from http://www.eia.doe.gov/oiaf/aeo97/elefut.html.

U.S. Department of Energy. Energy Information Administration. *Electric Power Annual 1999,* Vol. I and II, 20 March 2000. Available from http://www.eia.doe.gov/cneaf.

U.S. Department of State. United States Information Agency. *Energy Restructuring in the United States,* 20 March 2000 Available from http://www.usia.gov/abtusia/posts/GE1/wwwh0000.html.

SIC 4971

IRRIGATION SYSTEMS

This industry consists of establishments primarily engaged in operating water supply systems for the purpose of irrigation. Establishments primarily engaged in operating irrigation systems for others, but do not themselves provide water, are classified in **SIC 0721: Crop Planting, Cultivating, and Protecting.**

NAICS CODE(S)

221310 (Water Supply and Irrigation Systms)

The Center for Irrigation Technology at the California State University describes irrigation as the artificial application of water to crops to ensure adequate moisture for growth. Irrigation systems ship water from its source to where it is needed. The U.S. Environmental Protection Agency (EPA) reported that in 1999, approximately 64.1 percent of withdrawn ground water was used for irrigation.

Water supply systems primarily utilized for irrigation purposes are in operation all over the world. Generally, water for irrigation falls under the responsibility of a water management district. These entities can be state, local, or federally operated public agencies or mutual associations, private agencies, or co-ops. Some are for-profit organizations, but most fall in the category of nonprofit.

One of the earliest water supply system co-ops in America, according to Robert Morgan, author of ''Water and the Land—A History of Irrigation in America,'' was organized in Salt Lake City, Utah, around 1847 by Mormons who built an irrigation system for their community.

Irrigation water supply systems are structured differently in different parts of the United States. Large irrigation systems are prevalent mainly in the western United States, while other areas of the country generally experience enough rainfall to satisfy agricultural requirements. However, irrigation projects of some kind dot the whole country. According to *Irrigation Journal,* water supply systems in the western United States fell off in total surface irrigated acreage in recent years, while the eastern areas of the country have shown an increasing usage of irrigation systems, despite the rainfall advantages they enjoy. Notwithstanding, approximately 75 percent or more of harvested cropland in several Western states is irrigated, and the greatest volume of irrigated water use remains in the western and southeastern states.

There are four basic irrigation systems now in use. Those systems are: surface systems that employ wild flood, border, basin, and furrow methods; sprinkler systems that use hand-moved and mechanically-moved aluminum pipe, plastic hose, and solid set arrangements; drip systems that are placed above or below the ground; and sub-surface systems that encourage a high water table to rise in the root zone of the plant.

Attaining irrigation efficiency for the user is a top goal of the districts and water resource departments that monitor the water supply systems. Every effort is made to schedule the release of water to most effectively meet the crop's water needs. Water is expensive, so it is for the benefit of the supplier as well as the user to make optimum use of the water. As *Landscape and Irrigation* magazine noted, ''With today's expensive water, it takes good design, proper installation, rigorous maintenance and careful irrigation scheduling to achieve good irrigation efficiency.''

Water pricing systems for irrigation vary throughout the country. Water from surface storage facilities is less expensive than water from State Water Projects (SWP). In California alone, there are approximately 385 water districts. These include commercial water service agencies and mutual associations that sell water at cost for agriculture within the district service area. Some of the organizations are nonprofit. Each water supplier provides the water within a structure that allows them to set the cost and objectives according to their own policies. The result is that there are many water pricing systems in use. The water price range for agricultural water can vary from $1 to $300 per acre-foot, which often dictates the type of crops that can afford to be irrigated.

Many technological advances during the last century have resulted in the expansion of irrigated agriculture and of the construction of dams and reservoirs to regulate the distribution of water resources. There are actually four sources of water available for irrigation purposes: ground water, surface water, atmospheric water, and ocean water. The most widely used of these is surface water, which comes in the form of rivers, streams, lakes, and oceans. Ocean water is the least utilized of these for irrigation purposes, except in arid areas such as the Middle East where desalination projects are bringing new technology to agricultural development.

A steady growth of agricultural crops is necessary in order to keep up with the world's population growth. To make water supplies available for irrigation, there are hundreds of water districts throughout the world. However, water scarcity remains the single greatest threat to global food production. According to a 1999 Worldwatch Institute Report, the world's human population derives about 40 percent of its food from irrigated land. Irrigation, in turn, consumes or depletes over 70 percent of the world's water supplies. It has been estimated that each gallon of water withdrawn from the ground takes 280 years to replace. Worldwatch is calling for a ''blue revolution,'' to radically reduce water depletion. One of the most promising efforts is in developing ''drip irrigation'' systems which could decrease water use by as much as 70 percent. Its technology is premised upon a slow drip of water directly to plant roots through a system of perforated plastic tubing. Not only does it conserve water, it also prevents run-off of nutrients from overly-flushed soil, and uses less energy than traditional irrigation techniques.

FURTHER READING

Barker, Randolph; David Seckler; Upali Amarasinghe. ''The World's Water.'' *Choices: The Magazine of Food, Farm & Resource Issues,* 1999 Fourth Quarter, 28.

Johnson, Dan. ''Solving Water Scarcity.'' *Futurist,* December 1999, 9.

''The Evaporation of Hope.'' *Earth Island Journal,* Winter 1999/2000, 14.

U.S. Environmental Protection Agency. ''SDWA Section 1429 Ground Water Report to Congress.'' January 1999, available from http://www.epa.gov/safewater/annual.

Wholesale Trade

SIC 5012

AUTOMOBILES AND OTHER MOTOR VEHICLES

This classification covers establishments primarily engaged in the wholesale distribution of new and used passenger automobiles, trucks, trailers, and other motor vehicles, including motorcycles, motor homes, and snowmobiles. Automotive distributors primarily engaged in selling at retail to individual consumers for personal use, and also selling a limited amount of new and used passenger automobiles and trucks at wholesale, are classified in **SIC 5511: Motor Vehicle Dealers (New and Used).**

NAICS Code(s)

421110 (Automobile and Other Motor Vehicle Wholesalers)

Industry Snapshot

In 1997, the United States had a total of 495,457 wholesale establishments. They employed almost 5.8 million people with a total payroll of $173 billion. In general, the wholesale industry remained fragmented, composed of some large firms and many small ones, but growing industry concentration threatened that pattern throughout the late 1980s and early 1990s. Motor vehicles and parts accounted for about 25 percent of all wholesale trade, with motor vehicles claiming about 75 percent of that category by sales volume. In 1997 the U.S. *Census of Wholsesale Trade* reported $278.9 billion in sales of automobiles and other motor vehicles.

The auto industry plays an integral part in the American economy and everyday life. In 1998, it employed 998,000 workers; an increase of 99,000 from 1995 and the highest level since 1979. Nearly 2 million are employed indirectly as dealers and suppliers at 4,000 facilities and 22,000 dealerships. The U.S. automobile industry is the number one U.S. manufacturing industry and contributes $300 billion to the U.S. economy or 3.5 percent of the nation's gross domestic product. Indirectly, one in every seven jobs in America relates to the manufacture, sale, operation, or maintenance of motor vehicles.

The automotive industry also forms the core of America's industrial strength. In a typical year, it generates one-sixth of all U.S. manufacturers' shipments of durable goods and consumes 30 percent of all the iron, 15 percent of all the steel, 25 percent of all the aluminum, and 75 percent of all the natural rubber bought by all industries in the nation. In 1998 personal consumption expenditures for new and used automobiles and trucks were $229.5 billion. This was an increase of $16.8 billion over 1997 spending.

Organization and Structure

The *Census of Wholesale Trade* breaks down typical wholesaling activity into three categories based on business ownership, ownership of goods sold, and the character of typical transactions. Merchant wholesalers are independent or chain operations which take title to the goods they sell from a manufacturer and sell to a variety of clients. Approximately 60 percent of all wholesale sales are made by these firms. Manufacturers' sales branches and offices are owned by the product manufacturer or producer and sell to retail outlets and franchised dealers. The majority of motor vehicle wholesale sales fall into this category. Finally, agents, brokers, and commission merchants are independent merchants who buy or sell products for others. Sales for this category usually relate to commissions and fees. In the automotive sector, the auto auction, classified under this category, was growing in importance in the early 1990s. Wholesale motor vehicle auctions have become the primary means of used motor vehicle distribution in the United States. In 1995 the 252 National Auto Auction Association (NAAA) member auctions resulted in more than 15 million wholesale transactions with total sales prices exceeding $60 billion.

Generally, automobile manufacturers maintain a network of franchised retail dealers who sell to the public and provide customer support and service. To maintain a unified corporate presence, the manufacturers also establish separate wholesale sales offices which set and monitor dealer sales practices, advertising and marketing campaigns, and retail pricing ranges. Because these transactions are internal to the corporate entities and regarded as proprietary in nature, little specific information is available.

Many sales are made to franchised dealers, but the manufacturers' sales offices also sell to fleet purchasers and rental agencies with guaranteed buy-backs after three to six months. In 1991, rental companies bought one-fifth of all new cars sold that year. In many cases, those rental firms were owned by the car manufacturer.

Auctions. With dealers swamped with the growing volume of quality used cars, the manufacturers have increasingly shipped bought-back vehicles, known as program cars, to national auction chains, which have gained in size and popularity in recent years. Traditionally, the auto auction had been a small mom-and-pop operation designed mainly to redistribute used cars between differently branded dealerships or between regions of varying consumer market preference. Dealers of one type of car who took a competing make as a trade-in could wholesale the used car at an auction rather than display it on their own lots. In the late 1980s, however, some large players entered the auction arena and began consolidating many of the smaller operations into regional and national chains, transforming the industry into a high-tech ''stock'' market for motor vehicles.

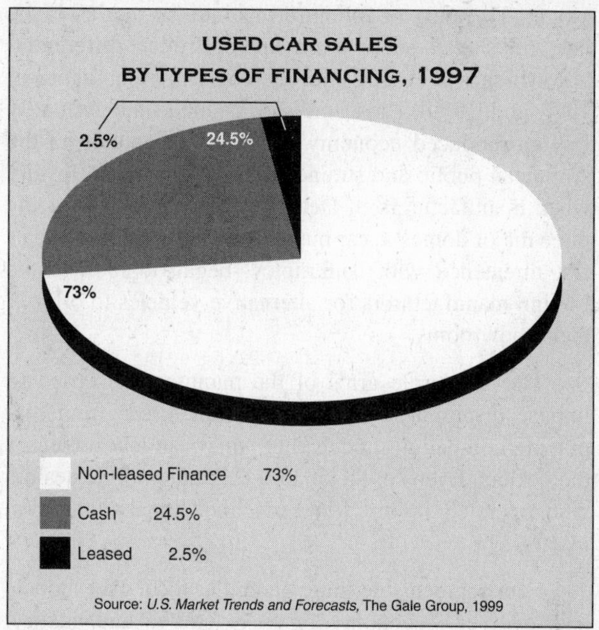

Source: *U.S. Market Trends and Forecasts*, The Gale Group, 1999

BACKGROUND AND DEVELOPMENT

Henry Ford's concept of mass manufacturing on the assembly line meant that his fledgling auto industry needed a means of mass marketing its product. Ford intended to build as many copies as possible of a universal automobile which everyone would buy. To do so, he and his competitors set up a network of small dealers who would buy the product and promote it locally, freeing up the manufacturer to concentrate on the technical development of the product and the evolution of the manufacturing process. This was particularly important in those early days of the industry, when communications were slow and unreliable. Making local managers and independent entrepreneurs responsible for everyday business decisions created a flexible and responsive marketing system.

As the American consumer's appetite for various models of automobiles increased, other manufacturers entered the arena. To maintain market share, Ford dropped the price of his Model T to almost one-half its initial offering, but still erosion continued. Innovation and product improvement picked up speed in the 1920s, prompting Ford to close his plant in 1926 for nine months to design and retool for his Model A. When he reopened, he found he had a new competitor, Chrysler, which produced few of its own components but responded quickly to market demand by sourcing parts and systems from supplier firms.

During this heady period of product innovation, the dealer network played a less important role in gaining and maintaining corporate profits than did the actual product. Those early years saw the complete domination of the world automotive market by American manufacturers, but the rapid acceleration of car production after World War II attracted global players. America's world share peaked at 82 percent in 1947, but declined since that time until the early 1990s, when domestic manufacturers once again increased their global market share. The American auto industry regained some of its market share between 1993 and 1996—particularly with pick-up trucks, minivans, and sport utility vehicles—but auto sales continued to fluctuate.

After 1948 the majority of technical development came to an end, and product lines within manufacturers became less differentiated. At that point, product loyalty and customer service at the dealer level became paramount. The entry of foreign firms into the market in the late 1950s again set up a measure of product differentiation which was eroded after the OPEC oil embargoes of 1973 and 1979. Those oil shocks made the primarily foreign-produced economy car more acceptable to the American public and strained the ties of product loyalty when manufacturers in Detroit, the headquarters of the three major domestic car makers, failed to respond. Dealers, threatened with bankruptcy, began to look to the foreign manufacturers for alternative vehicles to offer in their showrooms.

The wholesale arms of the manufacturers tried to impose discipline by forbidding franchisees from displaying competing models, but American law protected the dealers. Even so, the 50,000 U.S. automobile dealers who operated in the 1940s declined to about 18,000 in 1997.

Four segments defining particular niches for models had evolved—economy, sports, family, and luxury. Within those categories, the product became increasingly undifferentiated as technological advances slowed. By the early 1990s, all the manufacturers were selling products with many similarities, which made the wholesale aspect of the business an especially important factor. As noted by the National Association of Wholesaler-Distributors, competition in the distribution of cars and trucks became particularly heated.

The 1980s saw a decline in the fortunes of the American automotive industry. Sales of all cars, motorcycles, and heavy trucks plummeted in the face of increasing competition from abroad. Only recreational vehicles and light trucks maintained their sales strength. This general downturn in the retail arena had a corresponding effect on the wholesale industry.

According to Federal Reserve Chairman Alan Greenspan, the seeds of that downturn could be seen in the drop in the number of vehicles per household, which occurred between 1979 and 1983, and the rise in the relative age of vehicles on the road. That resulted in a pent-up demand somewhere in the neighborhood of 10 million units which produced a selling boom between 1983 and 1987. However, those gains evaporated in the slow economic growth of the late 1980s and early 1990s. In 1990, total sales of all new cars in the United States dropped close to their 1982 level of 7.9 million units. From 1991 to 1994 auto sales climbed. Sales of U.S. produced cars increased while sales of imports decreased. In 1995, total import sales declined—from about 9 million sold in 1994 to 8.6 million sold in 1995—but total sales of U.S. produced cars continued to climb.

Moreover, competition in the industry from manufacturers abroad had increased in strength. Sales of imported cars rose from 21.9 percent of all new sales in 1979 to 26.4 percent in 1990 according to *Monthly Labor Review,* and the output of transplants—foreign car manufacturing plants built in the United States—rose from nothing in 1982 to 14.4 percent of sales in 1990. At the same time the wholesale price of the vehicles was dropping. In *Applied Economics,* Edward Millner compared the average wholesale price of domestic cars in the period 1954-74, before the OPEC oil shocks, to the period 1975-86. He found prices in the later period to be lower than those of the earlier period despite the fact that the costs of doing business had increased.

The sales of imports dropped steadily between 1991 and 1995, but foreign car manufacturers continued to build plants in the United States. Over the past decade Japanese companies have invested $12 billion in U.S. facilities and employ about 40,000 American workers. Toyota opened a $700 million light truck plant in Indiana in 1998, creating 1,300 jobs. BMW opened a plant in 1994 in South Carolina, and by the end of 1995, production totaled 12,000 units. Mercedes Benz opened a $300 million plant in Alabama in 1997, employing 1,500.

With foreign automobiles being manufactured in the United States by American workers and American cars being built overseas by foreign workers, the distinction between domestic and import has become blurred. According to a 1996 poll by the Japan Automobile Manufacturers Association (JAMA), a majority of Americans believe that a car by any name is American if it was built in this country. Nearly three-quarters believe that a car made abroad is foreign, even if it's sold by Ford Motor Co., Chrysler Corp., or General Motors Corp.

Entering the mid-1990s, however, it appears that General Motors, Ford, and Chrysler—the ''Big Three'' of American car making—had arrested their long decline. In 1997 Ford's trucks set all-time high sales records. According to their 1996 Annual Report, Chrysler Corporation increased their vehicle shipments by almost 300,000 from 1995 to 1996, and total revenues were $8 billion higher in 1996 than in 1995. Indeed, the economic fortunes of all three automakers improved dramatically in the early and mid-1990s, a welcome sight for the wholesaling divisions of those companies.

The Development of the Auto Auction. In 1995, approximately 20 percent of all U.S. new car sales were to rental companies. Often these vehicles return to the hands of the manufacturer. Handling such volumes of essentially used vehicles proved a headache for the wholesale divisions, even after they established factory-direct operations to move thousands of vehicles every week from rental agencies to dealer lots. In response, the wholesalers looked to another, more traditional used-car wholesaler already established in the industry. The auto auction provided an ideal distribution tool.

The traditional auto auction was a small operation that essentially exchanged vehicles between dealers, but the 1980s saw a revolution in the marketing device. Anglo American Auto Auctions Inc. and its British Car Auction Group (BCA) targeted the American lease and fleet operations, drawing on its extensive European experience to transform the American industry. Between 1979 and 1988 the number of vehicles sold by about 300 wholesale-dealer auctions doubled to 4.5 million units per year.

Growth slowed toward the end of the decade. The NAAA expected sales of 10 million units by its 215 auction operators in 1990, but sales for the year only reached 7.7 million units. By 1996 the number of NAAA auction operators had increased to 252, and 14 million vehicles would be offered for sale in member auctions in the United States, Canada, Australia, Denmark, and Japan.

Like other wholesaling segments, this part of the industry has become increasingly concentrated. The three largest players competed with each other throughout the late 1980s by buying up smaller auctions across the nation. In 1987 the largest player, Manheim Auctions, Inc., moved 600,000 cars through 21 sites for a 13 percent market share. A new challenger, General Electric Capital Corp. (GECARS), responded with 450,000 vehicles at 17 locations. BCA followed with 415,000 through 20 facilities. In 1991, Manheim and GECARS merged under the Manheim name to form an auction giant with 46 locations and expectations to sell as many as 2 million cars annually. In 1995 Manheim was the world's leading auto auction operation and sold 4 million cars that year. In 1996 the Manheim, of Atlanta, Georgia, bought the Greater Auction Group, which has operations in five states. With its acquisition, Manheim operated 62 auctions in the United States and Canada and employed 18,000 people. Dealers were their biggest customers.

Current Conditions

According to the National Automobile Dealers Association (NADA), in 1998, 31 percent of the used cars that dealers retailed were bought at auto auctions. Dealers had increased their use of the auto auctions as a source for their inventory of used cars. The record 31 percent share reported in 1998 was a substantial increase from the 10 percent of dealer used car inventory reported in the early 1980s.

The growth in automotive leasing had a direct effect on the growth of auctions. Automakers used the auctions to dispose of their off-lease vehicles. The off-lease activity began at a time when fleet incentives and rental returns began to wane. As a result, auto auctions experienced more growth through the end of the twentieth century.

Dealers became more comfortable using the auction as a source when program cars, rental fleets bought by the manufacturers, were offered in the 1980s. In 1998, new car dealers retailed 12 million used vehicles and wholesaled another 7.3 million, according to NADA. They also reported the average price of a used vehicle sold by a new car dealer was $12,500, up from $12,100 the previous year.

NAAA's data, gathered from its members, showed more than 8.6 million used cars and trucks were sold through their auctions in 1998. The value of the vehicles was reported to be $66.7 billion. There was a total of 14.5 million vehicles handled. In 1999, the association had 204 member in the United States.

Industry Leaders

Manheim, founded in 1945, was the world's largest operator of wholesale automobile auctions. Manheim had 83 locations in 1999. The company operated facilities in North America and the United Kingdom in 1998, and made its first move into continental Europe in 1999 with the acquisition of a French group, Societe d'Expertise Agenaise (SEA). In 1998, Manheim offered more than 6.5 million vehicles for sale, with a sale value of $35 billion. ''Manheim Online'', a division of Manheim Auctions, Inc., enabled dealers to buy pre-owned vehicles from manufacturers and captive finance companies via the Internet. In 1998, $275 million worth of auctioned vehicles were sold through the site, up from $58 million in 1997. Manheim is a subsidiary of Cox Enterprises, Inc.

Insurance Auto Auctions, Inc., a leading U.S. auto salvage company, was founded in 1982. The auction provided insurance companies with a cost-effective means to process and sell total loss and recovered-theft vehicles. The salvage industry was a $3 billion industry at the turn of the century. Insurance Auto Auction reported 1998 sales of 287.1 million with net income of $7.2 million—an increase over 1997 sales of 259.3 million. In October 1999, the company had 50 auction sites across the United States.

America and the World

Professional Auto Remarketing, a subsidiary of Adesa Corporation, offered import services for used cars from Canada to the United States. Wholesaling of the Canadian used vehicles to the United States increased from 24,000 units in 1997 to 78,000 units in 1998. The weak Canadian dollar made the Canadian vehicles a great value for U.S. dealers. With the Canadian dollar having a value of 65 cents, American dealers could buy wholesale a vehicle such as a 1998 Explorer 4x4 at a savings of more than $3,200 U.S. dollars. Professional Auto Remarketing, changed its name to PAR North America in July 1999. The company was based in Indianapolis, Indiana.

Research and Technology

The United Recyclers Group were developing a modern operating system and data base in 1999. The new Recycler's Management Information System (RMIS), when developed, would assist members in the recycling of more than 200,000 vehicles annually. This technology will make the salvage inventory information easier to access for customers and more manageable for the recyclers. The group has more than 200 recyclers with revenues of more than $400 million.

Workforce

The labor force in the wholesale trade segment of industry had been decreasing as many small firms had been forced out of business or were consolidated into larger entities. However, in the automotive wholesale industry, employment experienced a slow but steady growth. As the volume of off-lease and dealer consignment vehicles grew, so did the need for personnel to handle the increased activity. The need to physically move large volumes of automobiles and trucks spurred growth in the employment of personnel to shuttle these vehicles. Many of these positions were filled by retirees on a part-time basis.

Further Reading

American Automobile Manufacturers Association. Available from http//www.aama.com.

Auto Connect. ''Manheim Auctions Makes First Move into Continental Europe.'' 1999. Available from http://wwwautoconnect.com

———. ''Manheim Auctions Adds Post-Sale Vehicle Inspections.'' 8 February 1999. Available from http://www.autoconnect.com

Automotive Recyclers Association. ''What is the ARA?'' 1999. Available from http://www.autorecyc.org/docs

Automotive News. ''Manheim Online.'' 25 January 1999.

Cox Enterprises, Inc. ''Corporate.'' 1999. Available from http://www.cnnfntech.newsreal.com/c_info/1/3/ov

Darney, Arsen J., and Mary Alampi, eds. *Wholsesale and Retail Trade 1995.* Detroit: Gale Research, 1995.

Haddad, Charles. ''Cox Names 2 Executives to Lead Manheim Auctions Division.'' *The Atlanta Journal and Constitution,* 28 October 1995.

Hoover's Company Capsules. Available from http://www.hoovers.com.

Insurance Auto Auction, Inc. ''Annual Report.'' 1999. Available from http://www.cnnfntech.newsreal.com/c_info/0/2/afn

Insurance Auto Auction, Inc. ''Insurance Auto Auction Acquires Auto Disposal Company (ADC).'' 17 February 1999. Available from http://www.autoconnect.com

Insurance Auto Auction, Inc. ''Insurance Auto Auctions Introduces FastTrack Appraisal Services.'' 10 May 1999. Available from http://www.autoconnect.com

Manheim. ''Manheim Auctions Invests More Than $50 in Technology.'' 8 Februrary 1999. Available from http://www.manheim.com

''Manheim Auctions Makes Acquisition.'' *Atlanta Journal and Constitution,* 18 July 1996.

National Auto Auction Association Web Site. Available from http//www.naaa.com.

Sawyers, Arlena. ''ADESA Unit Offers Import Assistance from Canada.'' *Automotive News.* 12 July 1999.

———. ''Used Cars—Auction Uniformity Urged.'' *Automotive News,* 20 September 1999.

———. ''Used Cars—Survey: Auctions Sold $66.7 Billion in Vehicles in '98.'' *Automotive News,* 4 October 1999.

———. ''Title-Branding Law Is Hot Issue with Auction Group.'' *Automotive News.* 30 August 1999.

U.S. Department of the Census. *Wholesale Trade.* 1997. Available from http://www.census.gov.

U.S. Department of Commerce. *1994 County Business Patterns.* Washington, DC: GPO, 1995.

SIC 5013

MOTOR VEHICLE SUPPLIES AND NEW PARTS

This industry classification is comprised of establishments primarily engaged in the wholesale distribution of motor vehicle parts and supplies such as accessories, tools, and equipment. Establishments primarily engaged in the distribution of used motor vehicle parts are classified in **SIC 5015: Motor Vehicle Parts, Used.**

NAICS Code(s)

441310 (Automotive Parts and Accessories Stores)
421120 (Motor Vehicle Supplies and New Part Wholesalers)

Industry Snapshot

According to the U.S. Bureau of Census, there were 28,002 establishments classified in **SIC 5013: Motor Vehicle Supplies and New Parts** in 1997. Overall, the industry provided jobs for 271,270 people with a payroll of $6.5 million, which represented a slight decrease in employment and payroll compared to 1994. Combined sales were reported at more than $91 billion in 1997.

Background and Development

Traditionally, the distribution process for delivering motor vehicle supplies and parts to the marketplace took place in three steps. Manufacturers sold products to warehouse distributors who then sold them to ''jobbers'' who, in turn, sold them to customers such as service stations. Jobbers offered benefits such as the extension of credit and wholesale discounts and often sold items at retail price to the "do-it-yourself" market segment. Warehouse distributors provided other advantages, such as accessible inventory and a process for returning defective parts and stock that did not sell.

A variation of this process, termed "programmed distribution", emerged as jobbers united to make purchasing decisions. The largest and one of the oldest organizations of this type was the North American Parts Association (NAPA), which provided services such as volume buying, private labeling, and advertising.

During the 1980s and early 1990s, the distribution process evolved: jobbers began to make purchases directly from manufacturers, bypassing the warehouse distributors. Some claimed it would reduce costs by streamlining the industry; others claimed it merely shifted the costs of maintaining an inventory and handling returns to the manufacturer.

CURRENT CONDITIONS

According to *Automotive Marketing Online*, the major trends in the motor vehicle supplies and new parts industry are consolidation, specialization, and assimilation. Through consolidation, the number of establishments increases while the number of owners decreases. In 1987, for example, the top 100 chains owned 2,771 stores; by contrast, in 1999, the top four chains owned more than 6,000 stores. Another growing trend is specialization: in the 1990s, establishments that specialized in specific types of products fared better than those who stocked a more general inventory. Finally, through assimilation, the lines between the traditional and retail channels have been blurred, and the use of the three-step distribution process has declined. All three of these trends will affect the way the automotive aftermarket industry does business in the future.

Although *Chilton's Automotive Marketing* reported an overall slowing trend in the growth rate in the automotive aftermarket as a whole, it indicated positive signs for the future, based on the aging of the car population and the rise in miles driven. The U.S. International Trade Administration predicted excellent opportunities for U.S. suppliers in the Mexican automotive parts market.

INDUSTRY LEADERS

In 1999, the top industry leader in motor vehicle supplies and new parts was newcomer Delphi Automotive Systems, based in Troy, Michigan. With $28 billion in sales and 216,000 employees, Delphi was by far the biggest company in this industry. Next on the list was Genuine Parts Co., based in Atlanta, Georgia, with $6 billion in sales and 24,500 employees, followed by GM Service Parts Operations, based in Flint, Michigan, with $5 billion in sales and 15,000 employees. These three companies accounted for over half the total sales and nearly half the employees in the U.S. automotive aftermarket industry in 1999.

FURTHER READING

"After Show Review." *Chilton's Automotive Marketing,* December 1995.

The Big Emerging Markets: 1996 Outlook and Sourcebook. Lanham, MD: Bernan Press, 1995.

"Big Three Now Serve Half the Jobbers, What Will They Do in 1997?" *Market Line,* January 1997. Available from http://am.chilton.net/197ml.htm.

"The Evolution of the Aftermarket: Traditional, Retail, Today." *Automotive Marketing,* April 1997. Available from http://am.chilton.net/evtrd.htm.

"Market Statistics: Top 25 Parts Jobbers and Auto Retail Chains." *Automotive Week,* April 1997. Available from http://www.auto-week.com/stats.htm.

"The Merging Aftermarket." *Automotive Marketing Online.* Available from http://www.automotivemarketing.com/mgmkt.html.

U.S. Census Bureau. *1992 Census of Wholesale Trade—U.S. Summary. Motor Vehicles and Motor Vehicle Parts and Supplies.* Washington: GPO, Updated 1997. Available from http://www.census.gov/epcd/ec92/wc92h501.html.

Ward's Business Directory of U.S. Private and Public Companies. Volume 5. Detroit: Gale Group, 1999.

Wholesale and Retail Trade USA. Detroit: Gale Research, 1995.

SIC 5014

TIRES AND TUBES

This industry category includes companies that primarily wholesale new and used tires and tubes for passenger and commercial vehicles. It also includes companies that wholesale tire and tube repair materials.

NAICS CODE(S)

441320 (Tire Dealers)
421130 (Tire and Tube Wholesalers)

In 1997, according to U.S. government statistics, there were 4,146 businesses grouped in this industry. The majority operated as merchant wholesalers, or companies who take title to the goods they sell. Other companies were grouped as either manufacturers' sales branches and offices or as agents, brokers, and commission merchants.

Total industry sales for 1997 were $20.09 billion, with an annual payroll of $1.02 billion. In 1997 approximately 46,341 employees were in the industry. *Modern*

Tire Dealer estimated that 279 million replacement tires to be sold in 1998. The industry is predicting a bright outlook for the 2000s based on the high volume of car sales in the late 1990s. By 1999 major brand tires accounted for less than 50 percent of the market. At the same time, sales by establishments more likely to buy directly from manufacturers (such as chain stores, department and discount stores, and warehouse clubs) continued to increase through the end of the century.

One of the largest establishments classified in this industry was TBC Corporation, with net income for the first nine months of 1999 at $560.3 million, up 17 percent from same period 1998. TBC began in 1956 as a tire wholesaler. By the late 1990s, TBC's products included several private label tires under such brand names as Sigma, Cordovan, and Multi-Mile. They also sold aftermarket automotive supplies such as tubes, batteries, custom wheels, ride-control products, filters, brakes, chassis parts, and automotive service equipment.

TBC tires were made under contract by U.S. and non-U.S. corporations and received at the company's 1.3 million-square-foot distribution complex in Memphis, Tennessee. Through its network of more than 185 regional distribution centers, the company sold products through 20,000 independent tire dealers in North America.

In 1996 TBC acquired Big O Tires, a franchise founded in 1962. Big O is headquartered in Englewood, Colorado, and was one of the fastest growing retail dealers in America by 1999.

Other leaders in this category include companies selling new and re-treaded tires, such as Bandag, Inc. of Muscatine, Indiana. Bandag serves independent dealers throughout America as well as dealers in Africa, Asia, Europe, and South America. The ''Bandag Method'' retread tire lasts approximately 15 percent longer than other retread tires. Brad Ragan, Inc. of Charlotte, North Carolina, operates 28 retail tire and appliance stores in 28 states and is majority-owned by Goodyear.

Further Reading

Bandag, Inc. *Company History,* November 1999. Available from http://www.bandag.com.

Big O. ''Overview,'' November 1999. Available from http://www.bigotires.com.

''Hoover's Company Capsules.'' Austin, Texas: Hoover's, Inc., 1999. Available from http://www.hoovers.com.

TBC Corp. ''TBC Corporation.'' Memphis: TBC Corp., 1999. Available from http://www.isysit.com/tbc/new.html.

U.S. Department of Commerce. Bureau of the Census. *1992 Census of Wholesale Trade.* Washington, D.C.: GPO, 1997.

SIC 5015

MOTOR VEHICLE PARTS, USED

This industry classification is comprised of establishments primarily engaged in the distribution of used motor vehicle parts at both the wholesale and retail level. It also includes establishments primarily engaged in dismantling motor vehicles for the purpose of selling parts. Establishments engaged in dismantling motor vehicles for the purpose of selling scrap are classified in **SIC 5093: Scrap and Waste Materials.**

NAICS Code(s)

421140 (Motor Vehicle Part (Used) Wholesalers)

The Automotive Recyclers Association (ARA) reported 1997 gross annual revenues of $7.05 billion in the U.S. The same year 4.7 million vehicles were acquired for the purpose of recycling. There are more than 6,000 automotive recycling businesses in the United States employing more than 46,000 people. An estimated 86 percent of these establishments are full-service and employ 10 or fewer people.

During the early years of the automotive industry, the need for replacement parts became apparent. Although manufacturers typically provided parts for their vehicles through franchised distributors, many car makers did not survive the early decades of the twentieth century, thus leaving ''orphan'' vehicles behind. These vehicles had a need for replacement parts that no manufacturer was producing.

Replacement parts became available through two channels. Some companies purchased tracings, drawings, and blueprints for parts from bankrupt manufacturers in order to fabricate replacement parts. Others obtained parts from broken-down vehicles and reconditioned them for resale. As the automotive industry matured and cars became an ubiquitous part of the American landscape, the need for replacement parts continued to grow.

The National Automotive Parts Association (NAPA) was founded in 1925 to meet America's growing need for an auto parts distribution system. This distribution system accommodated 200,000 part numbers in 1999. NAPA members supplied new and reconditioned products to repair shops, service stations, fleet operators, automobile dealers, and individual consumers.

The leader in this market in 1998 was Genuine Parts Company (GPC), which operates the NAPA outlets. Genuine Parts Company was founded in 1928. It was a service organization that engaged in the distribution of automotive replacement parts. In 1998, its NAPA Auto Parts Group increased sales by 6 percent. In 1998, total sales for Genuine Parts Company were $6.6 billion, an increase of 10 percent over 1997 levels.

Blonders of Hartford, Lubacks and Co., Recycled Auto Parts of Brattleboro Inc., and Road Tested Recycled Auto Parts Inc. were also well known in the industry.

In 1998, a reported 205 million vehicles were in use in the United States with an average age of eight years. As the total number of motor vehicles increased, so did the market for used auto parts. A major channel for obtaining these was through recyclers of scrapped or wrecked vehicles. Used parts often cost substantially less than new parts and could be located quickly through communications systems that linked auto recycling businesses, according to Brad Rose of the Automotive Recyclers of Michigan.

Ford Motor Company entered the recycling business in 1999. Ford purchased ''Kwik-Fit,'' Europe's largest independent ''Fast-fit'' repair chain, and a facility in Tampa, Florida, to disassemble cars and trucks. Customers included insurers and body shops and retail customers.

Ford opened a Web site where customers could order parts online and the recycling unit would deliver it by express mail. Eventual plans were to distribute recycled parts from its factories.

FURTHER READING

Automotive News. ''U.S. Vehicle Population 1999,'' 1999.

Automotive Recyclers Association. ''ARA to Seek Meeting with Ford as Auto Maker Announces Entry into Auto Recycling Industry,'' 27 April 1999. Available from http://www.autorecyc .org/docs.

———. ''Automotive Recyclers Association Voices Support of English-Tanner Tax Credit Legislation for Recycling Equipment,'' 22 October 1999. Available from http://www .autorecyel.org/docs.

''Auto Parts (Replacement) Industry.'' *Value Line Investment Survey,* 14 March 1997.

''Cars, Light Trucks Reach Record Age of 8.8 Years.'' *Aftermarket Business,* January 1996.

Czurak, David. ''Auto Recycling: Old Idea Gets Global Boost.'' *Grand Rapids Business Journal,* 8 April 1996.

Daily Auto Insider. ''Ford Sees Junk Cars as $1 Billion Business,'' 27 April 1999. Available from http://www.autorecycl .org/docs.

Dun's Census of American Business 1996. Bethlehem, PA: Dun & Bradstreet, Inc., 1996.

Genuine Auto Parts. ''1998 Annual Report Highlights,'' 1999. Available from http://www.genpt.com.

SIC 5021

FURNITURE

This classification comprises establishments primarily engaged in the wholesale distribution of furniture, including bedsprings, mattresses, and other household furniture; office furniture; and furniture for public parks and buildings. Establishments primarily involved in the wholesale distribution of partitions, shelving, lockers, and other store fixtures are classified in **SIC 5046: Commercial Equipment, Not Elsewhere Classified.**

NAICS CODE(S)

442110 (Furniture Stores)
421210 (Furniture Wholesalers)

INDUSTRY SNAPSHOT

The wholesale distribution of furniture industry is subdivided into two categories: establishments engaged primarily in the sale of household and lawn furniture, and establishments primarily engaged in the sale of office and business furniture. According to statistics compiled by the U.S. Department of Commerce, 6,819 establishments were listed in this classification in 1987. Combined sales totaled $18.63 billion. In 1998, the number of establishments was predicted to increase to 7,663 with about 81,000 employees, generating roughly $31 billion in sales.

CURRENT CONDITIONS

Barrons reported that the furniture industry experienced a slump from 1988 until mid-1992 when a ''stop-and-start'' recovery process began. Conditions within the furniture industry reflected the nation's general economy as consumers postponed purchases. As a result, when the economy began to improve, there was a pent-up demand for industry products, and the American Furniture Manufacturers Association (AFMA) predicted an increase in furniture shipments. AFMA also predicted an increase in the value of shipments of 7.6 percent in 1999, and a smaller increase of 2.1 percent for 2000. Consumer demand was expected to increase by 5.5 percent and 4.5 percent for 1999 and 2000, respectively.

This industry is affected by interest rates and the housing market. When these economic indicators are stable and strong, the furniture industry generally has higher retail sales. Following a slump in the early 1990s, the International Wholesale Furniture Association found more than 90 percent of survey respondents reported sales increases in 1993. Sales continued to climb in 1994 and 1995. Throughout 1995, monthly sales for furniture and home furnishings were between $3.1 and $3.4 million. Housing starts were forecast to increase by 2.9

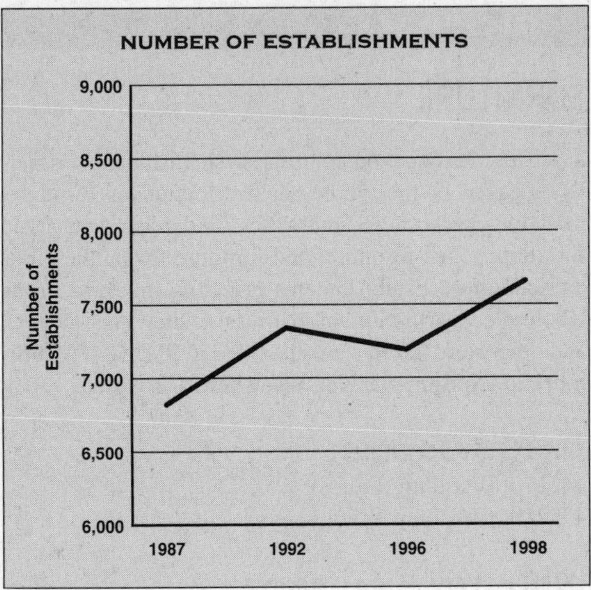

percent in 1999, followed by only 0.3 percent in 2000. In the late 1990s, much of this industry's strength has come from the industrial (offices, hotels, restaurants) side of the market. The office furniture market is estimated at $12 billion. Another forecast predicts 50 million U.S. households will feature some sort of home office by 2002.

The largest type of customer, furniture stores, represented 69.4 percent of sales. Other types of customers included rental dealers (19.2 percent of sales), manufactured homes (4.9 percent), specialty stores (2.5 percent), interior designers (1.4 percent) and institutional buyers (0.5 percent). The two largest product categories, living room/upholstered and bedroom, accounted for half of the sales.

Customary distribution channels within the industry, however, have changed. To reduce costs and improve efficiency, many manufacturers have increased their direct sales to retailers and rental dealers. As a result, wholesalers faced a shrinking number of traditional customers, and innovative wholesale concepts, such as warehouse clubs and electronic shopping networks, emerged. Wholesalers are also being threatened by large discount department stores such as Wal-Mart. In 1999, Kmart launched its Solutions electronic shopping program, which offers a mix of bedding, recliners, home office and home entertainment furniture. Consolidation of furniture manufacturers is another trend in the industry.

Industry Leaders

California had the most establishments in the United States, with 1,017 or 14.1 percent of the U.S. total. The state employed more than 10,000 and generated 13.2 percent of U.S. sales. The other states having 7 to 8 percent of U.S. establishments were New York, Florida, and Texas. Together these states accounted for 18.9 percent of U.S. sales.

In the late 1990s, industry leaders included Value City Furniture Division of Ohio, Office Depot Incorporated Business Services Division of California, and TAB Products Company, also of California.

Workforce

The wholesale trade workforce is expected to show an overall increase by 2005. Jobs with the highest increases are expected to be traffic, shipping, and receiving clerks (41 percent), general managers and top executives (36 percent), blue collar worker supervisors (28 percent), and truck drivers (28 percent).

Further Reading

Craver, Richard. ''Technology Growth Sparks New Demand for Home-Office Furnishings.'' *High Point Enterprise,* 22 October 1999

Darnay, Arsen J. and Gary Alampi, eds. *Wholesale and Retail Trade USA.* Detroit: Gale Research, 1995.

''Monthly Wholesale Trade: Sales and Inventories.'' *Current Business Reports,* U.S. Department of Commerce, October 1999.

''Office Furniture Firms Face Challenges, As Market Changes, Competition Grows'' *Wall Street Journal,* 13 July 1999

Quarterly Economic Forecast American Furniture Manufacturers Association, July 1999.

''Ratings and Reports.'' *Value Line Investment Survey.* New York: Value Line Publishing, 17 January 1997.

Sloan, Carole. ''Kmart to Boost Furniture.'' *Furniture Today,* December 1999. Available from http://www.furnituretoday.com/news/index.html.

U.S. Department of Commerce. *Combined Annual and Revised Monthly Wholesale Trade.* Washington, DC: GPO, April 1996.

U.S. Industry and Trade Outlook. U.S. Dept. of Commerce/International Trade Administration and McGraw-Hill, 1999.

Ward's Business Directory of U.S. Private and Public Companies. Detroit: Gale Group, 2000.

Wholesale and Retail Trade USA Detroit: Gale Group, 1999.

SIC 5023

HOMEFURNISHINGS

This industry classification contains establishments primarily engaged in the wholesale distribution of home furnishings and housewares. Products of the industry include antiques, china, glassware and earthenware, lamps (including electric), curtains and draperies, linens and towels, and carpets, linoleum, and all other types of hard and soft surface floor coverings.

NAICS CODE(S)

442210 (Floor Covering Stores)
421220 (Home Furnishing Wholesalers)

Establishments primarily engaged in the wholesale distribution of electrical household goods are classified in **SIC 5064: Electrical Appliances, Television and Radio Sets.** Establishments primarily engaged in the wholesale distribution of precious metal flatware are classified in **SIC 5094: Jewelry, Watches, Precious Stones, and Precious Metals.**

The homefurnishing wholesale industry is divided into four categories: establishments primarily engaged in selling china, glassware, and crockery; sellers of linens, domestics, draperies, and curtains; sellers of floor coverings; and sellers of other types of home furnishings. Industry sales were $18.8 billion in 1998. The number of establishments was estimated at approximately 44,000 in 1997 with an estimated payroll of $1.4 billion, according to the *1997 Economic Census.*

Industry watchers predicted industry expansion during the 1990s. *HFD* reported that demographic projections favored growth. The number of U.S. residents in the 35 to 55 age bracket was increasing, and that group typically included a higher percentage of home owners than older or younger segments of the population. The Furniture Buying Index showed a one point increase in January 2000 to 85—the first rise in five years. The index was at its highest point in aJanuary since 1993, when it reached 102.

Single-digit unemployment and a record-setting stock market as the new century began boded well for sales. But a high level of consumer debt or falling consumer confidence could moderate any gains.

Home fashions analysts identified three major design trends: casual and traditional; pure and simple; and crafted and contemporary. Casual and traditional combined classic and eclectic pieces with easy-care fabrics. Pure and simple styles were comparable to uncluttered country. Crafted and contemporary featured bright colors and patterns.

Flooring distributors noted a shift in traditional distribution channels as more carpeting retailers turned to direct mill purchases. The number of retailers purchasing carpeting from distributors fell in the early 1990s. However at the beginning of 2000, Don Whitfield, division vice president for Shaw Rugs, said that''continued economic growth will spur double-digit rug industry growth for the next 5-6 years.''

The market influence of wholesale warehouse stores also was growing. There also were more distribution warehouses, conceived to cater to interior designers, builders, and decorators rather than retailers or the general public, and they were growing more popular.

The two states with the industry's highest number of establishments and dollar value of sales were New York and California. In 1997 New York's 1,059 establishments posted sales of $5.4 billion, and California's 1,288 recorded $5.9 billion in sales.

FURTHER READING

Craver, Richard. ''Furniture-Sales Index Indicates Consumer Confidence Remains Strong.'' *High Point Enterprise,* 31 December 1999.

Herlihy, Janet. ''Rug Industry Recommends Sunglasses for Future.'' *HFN,* 30 August 1999.

''Outlook for the Whitewares Industry.'' *Ceramic Industry,* March 1999.

''Ratings and Reports.'' *Value Line Investment Survey.* New York: Value Line Publishing, 15 October 1999.

U.S. Bureau of the Census. *1997 Economic Census.* Available from http://factfinder.census.gov.

Valero, Greg.''Distribution Evolution.'' *Flooring,* September 1998.

SIC 5031

LUMBER, PLYWOOD, MILLWORK, AND WOOD PANELS

This classification is comprised of wholesale distributors of rough, dressed, and finished lumber (other than timber). Establishments operate with or without yards. Principal products include plywood, reconstituted wood fiber products, doors and doorframes, windows and window frames (all materials), wood fencing, and other wood or metal millwork.

NAICS CODE(S)

444190 (Other Building Material Dealers)
421310 (Lumber, Plywood, Millwork, and Wood Panel Wholesalers)

During the early 1990s, establishments involved in the wholesale distribution of lumber and other wood products faced a number of challenges stemming from depressed economic conditions and an uncertain political climate. As the nation's economy stagnated, many large retail outlets began bypassing wholesalers in favor of direct purchasing channels. Some smaller retail outlets were forced to close, leaving a diminished number of traditional customers for wholesalers. In addition, uncertainty about the nation's timber policy led to fluctuating prices and concerns about product availability. In the late 1990s, however, the booming U.S. housing market led to an increase in new construction, reducing inventories and increasing the price of lumber.

According to figures compiled by the U.S. Department of Commerce, 8,364 establishments participated in this industry in 1992, having combined sales of more $56 billion. Sales of plywood, millwork, and wood panels represented $28.9 billion of that amount. Lumber sales, totaling $27 billion, were divided between establishments with yards ($14.6 billion) and without yards ($12.4 billion). By 1995, 8,584 firms were in operation, having 122,769 employees, a payroll of $3,794,600 and estimated sales of almost $70 billion. Of the firms reporting, 78 percent had less than 20 employees. Employment was expected to remain relatively flat through the close of the century, with total sales reaching almost $76 billion.

The do-it-yourself (DIY) market represented approximately $117 million in retail sales in 1993. Sales made by DIY retailers rose 12 percent between 1988 and 1993, and industry watchers anticipated that 150 new warehouse-style stores would begin operating in 1994. By 1995, however, the DIY market had flattened considerably and, in 1997, it was declining. In contrast, the professional builders' market continued to increase, beefing up sales for building supply giants such as Home Depot—which controlled 42.8 percent of retail building supply sales in 1996—and the North Carolina-based Lowe's Companies.

According to Business Trend Analysts, manufacturers' sales of millwork were forecast to increase 3.2 percent in 1999 from a 1998 market that totaled $12 billion,. Market segments that showed significant increases included flush-type, solid-core doors with hardboard faces (up 7.8 percent), hardwood stairwork (up 7.7 percent), and wood patio doors (up 6.7 percent). In 1999, the U.S. paneling market was dominated by furniture and molding/millwork at 44 and 21 percent, respectively. Doors and wall paneling each had 9 percent.

According to *Wholesale and Retail Trade USA,* the top five companies in this industry by total annual sales are Nissho Iwai America Corp ($12.0 billion), HomeBase Inc. ($4.4 billion), Universal Corp. ($4.1 billion), Crane Co. ($1.8 billion) and 84 Lumber Co. ($1.6 billion). In 1998, Crane Co. acquired the Consolidated Lumber company, a one-step wholesale distributor of lumber and millwork products based in the greater Kansas City area, for $41 million.

Other significant companies in the industry include Carter Lumber Co., North Pacific Group Inc., Hardware Wholesalers Inc., and Boise Cascade Corporation's Building Materials Distribution Division.

Further Reading

Benderoff, Eric. ''Giants March Tall Despite Slow Year.'' *Building Supply Business,* Des Plains, IL: Cahners Publishing, April 1996.

''Crane Co. Acquires Consolidated Lumber.'' *PR Newswire,* 1 July 1998.

Ewubdm Terzah. ''Lumber's Strength Defies Bearish Trend.'' *Wall Street Journal, Eastern Edition,* 26 January 1999.

Business Trend Analysts. ''News Release,'' 9 July 1999. Available from: http://www.businesstrendanalysts.com/PRMWK.shtml.

''U.S. Paneling Market, 1999.'' *Wood Digest* March 1999.

Darnay, Arsen J., and Joyce Piwowarski, eds. *Wholesale and Retail Trade USA, 2nd Edition* The Gale Group, 1998.

SIC 5032

BRICK, STONE, AND RELATED CONSTRUCTION MATERIALS

This classification comprises establishments primarily engaged in the wholesale distribution of stone, cement, lime, construction sand, and gravel; brick (except refractory); asphalt and concrete mixtures; and concrete, stone, and structural clay products (other than refractories). Distributors of industrial sand and of refractory materials are classified in **SIC 5085: Industrial Supplies.** Establishments primarily engaged in producing ready-mixed concrete are classified in **SIC 3273: Ready-Mixed Concrete.**

NAICS Code(s)

444190 (Other Building Material Dealers)

421320 (Brick, Stone and Related Construction Material Wholesalers)

Typically, firms in the industry supply mineral-based building materials to building contractors and developers. Strong housing and commercial building markets in the mid- to late 1990s continued to provide slow but steady growth for industry sales. According to the CIT Group/Equipment Financing, residential construction increased by 5.6 percent in 1999, but was projected to decrease by 3.5 percent in 2000. Nonresidential construction was expected to flatten in 1999 and decrease slightly in 2000. According to the U.S. Census Bureau, new construction increased by 6 percent during the first 10 months of 1999, compared to the same period in 1998.

The U.S. industry was worth an estimated $11.9 billion in 1995, a growth of approximately 18 percent since 1992. Sales were projected to be slightly lower at $11.3 billion in 1998.

Merchant wholesalers—those who take title to the goods they sell—account for 79 percent of the industry's establishments; 17 percent are manufacturers' sales branches and offices; and the remaining 4 percent are agents, brokers, and commission merchants. Combined, there were approximately 4,200 establishments in the industry in the mid-1990s, employing a labor force of roughly 32,000. The number of establishments were projected to increase to about 4,800 in 1998, with a total workforce of roughly 35,000.

By products sold, the segment consisting of brick, block, tile, and sewer pipe commanded approximately 54 percent of industry sales in the 1990s. These were followed by cement, lime, and related products at 25 percent; and sand, gravel, and stone at 21 percent of industry product share. Sand and gravel production was expected to increase by 6.3 percent in 1999, but decrease slightly in 2000, according to the CIT Group. Although crushed stone production increased by 5.5 percent in 1999, it was projected to remain flat in 2000.

The industry is geographically distributed throughout the United States, with the Midwest, Southeast, and West having a slightly higher share than elsewhere of the industry's establishments. California, Texas, and Florida lead in the number of establishments and employees.

Industry leaders include Granite Rock Company of Watsonville, California; Walker and Zanger Inc. of Mount Vernon, New York; Livingston-Graham, Inc. of Irwindale, California; and Hudson Companies of Providence, Rhode Island.

FURTHER READING

"Financial Group Says Aggregate Industry Will Level in 2000." *Rock Products,* August 1999.

"October 1999 Construction at $699.3 Billion Annual Rate." Press release, U.S. Bureau of the Census, 1 December 1999. Available from http://www.census.gov/const/c30_curr.html.

U.S. Bureau of the Census. *1992 Census of Wholesale Trade.* Washington, DC: GPO, 1995.

U.S. Bureau of the Census. "Current Business Reports." *Combined Annual and Revised Monthly Wholesale Trade.* Washington, DC: GPO, 1996.

Ward's Business Directory of U.S. Private and Public Companies. Detroit: Gale Group, 2000.

Wholesale and Retail Trade USA Detroit: Gale Group, 1999.

SIC 5033

ROOFING, SIDING, AND INSULATION MATERIALS

This industry consists of establishments engaged in the wholesale distribution of roofing and siding (except wood) and insulation materials. Such establishments include those engaged in wholesale distribution of asphalt felts and coatings; fiberglass insulation materials; roofing, asphalt, and sheet metal; shingles (except wood); and siding (except wood).

NAICS CODE(S)

421330 (Roofing, Siding, and Insulation Material Wholesalers)

The wholesale roofing, siding, and insulation industry grew steadily in the early to mid-1990s, with sales rising from $14.43 billion in 1992 to $15.65 billion in 1996. At the same time, companies in the industry were consolidating—the number of establishments dropped from 2,848 in 1992 to 2,659 in 1996. Despite the decrease in establishments, employment remained relatively stable, dropping only slightly from 30,060 in 1992 to 29,523 in 1996. The industry's payroll grew from $921.9 million in 1992 to $1.02 billion in 1996. While many of these establishments were solely concerned with the wholesale distribution of roofing, siding, and insulation materials, publicly held corporations such as Boise Cascade Corporation and Owens-Corning Fiberglass Corporation also have established their presence in the industry via subsidiary divisions.

The wholesale roofing, siding, and insulation industry is dominated by large firms. The top five companies in the industry had revenues of $500 million or more. The revenue leaders in this industry, according to Wholesale and Retail Trade USA and Ward's Business Directory 2000, were T.J.T. Inc. of Emmett, Idaho ($2.5 billion); American Builders and Contractors Supply Company Inc. Beloit, Wisconsin ($960 million); Boise Cascade Corp. of Boise, Idaho (estimated $956 million); Cameron Ashley Building Products Inc. of Dallas ($762 million); and Rugby USA Inc. of Deerfield, Ill. ($500 million). Other leaders included Patrick Industries Inc., Elkhart, Indiana ($404 million); Irex Corp., Lancaster, Pennsylvania ($244 million); Shook and Fletcher Insulation Co. ($250 million); Roofing Wholesale Co. Inc. of Phoenix, Arizona; and Harvey Industries of Waltham, Massachusetts ($160 million).

Inextricably tied to the larger construction industry, companies involved in wholesale distribution of roofing, siding, and insulation materials keep a close eye on such key economic indicators as housing starts, which provide a particularly accurate barometer of trends in this support industry. In the mid-1990s, housing starts were very strong. After dropping to just 1.014 million in 1991, single family and multi-family housing starts in the United States rose every year to a peak of 1.457 million in 1994. While starts dropped back to 1.354 million in 1995, they rose again to 1.451 million in 1996. Though housing starts jumped to 1.66 million in 1999, the economy is expected to slow, resulting in housing starts to drop by an estimated 3.6 percent to 1.61 million in 2000.

U.S. demand for residential/commercial/light industrial siding material is expected to reach 9 billion square feet per year, valued at more than $7 billion. The market for specialty roofing is more than $1 billion.

Further Reading

Darnay, Arsen J. and Gary Alampi. *Wholesale and Retail Trade USA.* Detroit: Gale Research, 1995.

"Despite Slower Economic Growth, Housing Forecast is Promising." *PR Newswire,* 21 December 1999.

Kurpiel, Fred. "Fiber-Cement Siding is Tomorrow's Growth Product." *Wood Technology,* January/February 1998.

Seiders, David. "1997 Housing Forecast." *Builder,* January 1997.

"Volatile Homebuilding Market Reignites." *Standard & Poor's Industry Surveys,* 22 February 1996.

Ward's Business Directory of Public and Private U.S. Companies 2000. Detroit: Gale Group, 2000.

Wholesale and Retail Trade USA, 2nd Edition. Detroit: Gale Group, 1998.

SIC 5039

CONSTRUCTION MATERIALS, NOT ELSEWHERE CLASSIFIED

This industry comprises establishments engaged in the wholesale distribution of mobile homes and of construction materials that are not classified elsewhere. Some industry products are awnings, grain storage bins, and septic tanks. The industry also includes establishments primarily engaged in the wholesale distribution of mobile homes, prefabricated buildings, and glass. Establishments primarily engaged in selling construction materials to the general public are classified in **SIC 5211: Lumber and Other Building Materials Dealers.** Establishments primarily engaged in marketing heavy structural metal products are included in **SIC 5051: Metals Service Centers and Offices.**

NAICS Code(s)

444190 (Other Building Material Dealers)
421390 (Other Construction Material Wholesalers)

Sales of the wholesale construction materials industry were dropping in early to mid-1990s, from $9.22 billion in 1992 to $6.9 billion in 1996. During the same period, the number of establishments in the industry dropped, from 4,049 in 1992 to 3,870 in 1996. Employment in the industry also declined from 36,978 in 1992 to 34,114 in 1996. The industry's payroll, however, grew slightly, from $970.9 million in 1992 to $1.02 billion in 1996.

As wholesalers of construction materials entered the 1990s, they faced economic challenges and changing industry conditions. Major retailers were growing in size and turning increasingly to direct purchasing and retail buying groups. Small building supply retailers were closing. This led to a diminished number of traditional wholesale customers, a situation reflected in the industry's dismal sales numbers in the mid-1990s.

A large portion of construction materials wholesalers' sales are generated by building supply retailers who operate a small number of stores. However, these are precisely the type of retailers who were being put out of business in the mid-1990s by building supply superstores such as Home Depot. Larger retailers—those with an annual sales volume of at least $50 million—were more likely to purchase directly from manufacturers.

Surviving wholesalers in this industry grew larger and were able to operate on lower profit margins. Industry analysts predicted that only those wholesalers able to offer value-added services would survive. Typical value-added services included inventory management, financing, training, ad development, and merchandising assistance.

Manufactured housing represented one portion of the industry experiencing growth in the mid-1990s, a dramatic reversal of fortune from the 1980s. Manufactured housing units are shipped from plants, either single wide or as single sections of multiwide housing units. Some manufactured housing is not used for dwellings, but for light commercial use, classrooms, or clinics.

Manufactured home sales declined each year between 1983 and 1991 and were down to about 170,000 units in 1991. However, sales rose dramatically to 210,800 in 1992 and about 265,000 in 1993, increases of 23 and 26 percent, respectively. In 1994 the industry grew another 9 percent, to 290,000 units and jumped to over 375,000 in 1998, according to the Manufactured Housing Institute. In 1999, one out of every three presold single-family homes was manufactured, and there were about 10 publicly traded manufactured housing companies. In the first 11 months of 1999, production was up 5.2 percent (around 346,000 homes), compared to the previous year's 329,000. Because of zoning restrictions in major cities, manufactured homeowners and developers have focused on moving to rural areas.

Builders of traditional homes began diversifying into creating developments of manufactured homes in the mid-1990s. For example, Centex Corp., the largest-volume U.S. home builder, agreed to acquire Cavco Industries, Phoenix, a major manufactured housing company, in December 1996. Also, Pulte Home Corporation, an-

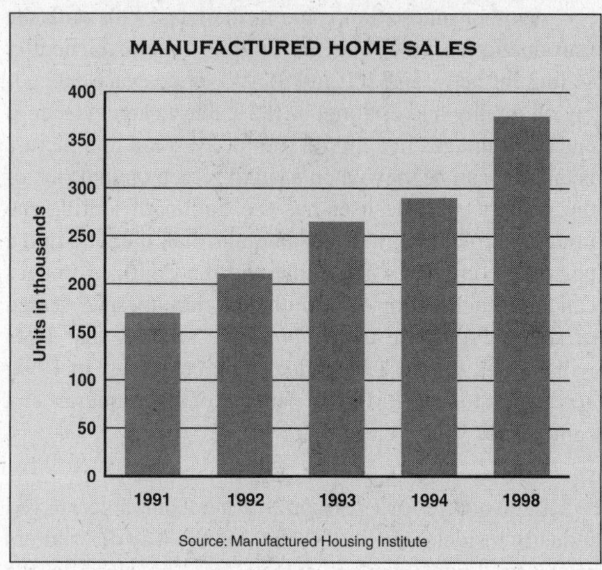

other high-volume home builder in the United States, developed six manufactured housing communities in 1995 and 1996 and had plans to build more. American Homestar ranked ninth among manufacturers nationally in 1997, out of about 100 companies, up from 18th the previous year.

The popularity of manufactured housing was spurred by the rising cost of traditional ''stick'' built homes and a dramatic improvement in manufactured housing quality, according to *Builder* magazine. A shortage of skilled tradespeople has made manufactured housing an attractive and cost effective means of developing lower-income communities, the magazine said. Today's manufactured houses are also larger and come with more features, resembling site-built houses but at a lower cost: 50 to 60 percent less.

While sales in the wholesale building material industry were declining, the largest players in the industry remained very large. All of these companies, however, have extensive interests outside of the industry. According to *Wholesale and Retail Trade USA, 2nd Edition,* the five largest companies in this industry by revenue were: HomeBase Inc. of Irvine, California ($4.4 billion); 84 Lumber Company of Eight Four, Pennsylvania ($1.6 billion); Boise Cascade Corp. of Boise, Idaho (about $1.0 billion); Cameron Ashley of Dallas, Texas ($762 million); and Sun Distributors L.P. of Philadelphia, Pennsylvania ($652 million). Other significant companies in the industry included, VVP America Inc., L and W Supply Corporation, and Wolohan Lumber Company.

FURTHER READING

Buchta, Jim. ''The Chaning Face of the Mobile Home.'' *Minneapolis Star Tribune,* 31 July 1999.

''Builders Place Bets on Manufactured Housing.'' *Builder,* March 1997.

1992 Census of Construction Industries. Washington: U.S. Department of Commerce, 1995.

Chuang, Tamara. ''Manufactured Homes Have Rich History, Profitable Future.'' *Arlington Morning News,* 12 January 1999.

Darnay, Arsen J., and Gary Alampi. *Wholesale and Retail Trade USA.* Detroit: Gale Research, 1995.

Reagor, Catherine. ''Prefab Homes Go Upscale/Grab Bigger Piece of Housing Market.'' *Arizona Republic,* 29 May 1999.

Wholesale and Retail Trade USA, 2nd Edition. The Gale Group, 1998.

SIC 5043

PHOTOGRAPHIC EQUIPMENT AND SUPPLIES

This industry classification comprises establishments primarily engaged in the wholesale distribution of photographic equipment and supplies, including cameras, darkroom apparatus, and photographic film. Establishments primarily engaged in the wholesale distribution of items such as photocopy, microfilm, and similar equipment are classified in **SIC 5044: Office Equipment.**

NAICS CODE(S)

421410 (Photographic Equipment and Supplies Wholesalers)

INDUSTRY SNAPSHOT

In 1997, there were an estimated 1,207 establishments in this industry, down from 1,424 the previous year. The number of establishments had been steadily dropping since a high of 1,556 in 1987, but had remained rather steady from 1993-96 with an estimated 0.3 percent change. States with the largest number of establishments in 1996 were California (with 238) and New York (with 190)—combined, these states together accounted for just under a third of all establishments. The industry generated $8.3 billion in sales for 1997.

CURRENT CONDITIONS

Overall demand for photographic equipment and supplies was generally flat throughout the early 1990s. The 1999 value of shipments was expected to be $24.7 billion. Photographic industry shipments through 2003 are expected to show modest growth reaching $26.7 billion. The United States ranks as the world's second largest exporter of photographic equipment and supplies after Japan. In 1997, U.S. exports were worth $4.7 billion, 4 percent more than 1996.

In 1997, 32.4 percent of American households had film processed. Of these households, 28.3 percent processed 35mm film, 1.2 percent processed advanced photo system (APS) film, 5.8 percent processed disposable-camera film, and 2.9 percent processed other types of films. Of all rolls processed that year, 80 percent were 35mm print film, excluding disposable cameras. Also in 1997, 12.8 percent of American households obtained at least one camera or camcorder, and 11.5 percent bought at least one camera or camcorder.

Unit share was lost by the popular 35mm format in 1997 because of the growing popularity of APS and digital cameras. In 1998, the unit share by camera type purchases, according to Photo Marketing Association International (PMA), was: 35mm lens shutter with 46.5 percent; camcorder with 22.4 percent; APS with 8 percent; 110 with 7.6 percent; instant with 5.5 percent; 35mm SLR with 4.1 percent; digital still camera with 3 percent; and professional medium and large format with 2.9 percent. The 1997 unit shares by outlet type for camera and camcorder purchases were: discount stores with 39.8 percent; electronic/video stores with 15.1 percent; camera stores with 11.1 percent; unclassified types of stores with 8 percent; department stores (not discount) with 7.4 percent; mail order with 6 percent; catalog showroom with 5.4 percent; warehouse clubs with 3.8 percent; and drugstores with 3.3 percent.

Background and Development

The 1990s saw the introduction of two products that continue to have a profound effect on the photographic equipment and supplies industry. APS, a new kind of camera and film and photofinishing option, first appeared in 1996. Using a 24mm format the APS film cassettes and cameras were developed by five major camera and imaging companies—Kodak, Fuji, Canon, Minolta, and Nikon.

One advantage of the APS format is its simple film loading procedure. Loading a standard 35mm film canister can be tedious since it has to be manually wound around a spool, the leader cannot be used for photographic images, and once in the camera it is not practical to remove the film unless it is rewound into its canister. APS cassettes are dropped into the camera. The ''smart'' cassette then tells the camera to move the film to the first unused frame. The cassette can be removed at any time and reloaded. In this sequence the APS cassette will instruct the camera to advance the film to the next available frame. APS systems and their cameras also allow the user to choose from three formats for every frame shot. The ''classic'' format is similar to the standard 35mm format, the ''HDTV'' format is slightly wider, and the ''panoramic'' format approximates 3:10 ratio framing. In 1997, 11.2 percent of cameras bought in the United States were APS format, up from 6.4 percent in 1995.

Another innovation came in the late 1990s with the introduction of the filmless digital camera. Generally selling for between $200 and $1,000 (prices vary depending on quality and options) in 1999, these cameras record and store images in a digital format. As soon as a picture is taken it can be viewed on a small screen on the back of the camera and the user has the option of storing the imaging or deleting it. The camera is then plugged into a personal computer via a cable and the digitized images can be brought up on the computer's monitor and printed or stored for future use. *Kiplinger's* predicts that 1999 will see the sale of 1.6 million digital cameras. In 1998, according to the PMA, 3 percent of all cameras and camcorders sold were digital.

In an article for *PTN* Lorraine DarConte interviewed industry insiders who saw changes in the way distributors relate to digital cameras which are ''as close to the computer/electronic industry as to the photo industry,'' according to Michael Hess, vice president of marketing for Tiffen/Saunders. Martin Lipton, national sales manager for Argraph Corp., also saw changes ahead for distributors of photo equipment and supplies. ''Distributors that involve themselves in digital photography have to make themselves aware of a vast new body of information. They have to be the teachers and fonts-of-knowledge for many of their dealers.'' Josh Blank of Mardel Photo Supply agreed. ''Digital photography brings with it a new set of challenges for the traditional photographic distributor. Digital imaging and printing require product knowledge, new inventory stocking requirements for the showroom and constant updates on competitive products.'' Bob Rose, vice president of Bogen saw electronic induced changes in the way dealers and distributors interact. ''Probably one of the biggest changes for distributors,'' Rose said, ''is dealing with more computer-literate dealers. People are constantly asking us for more information via e-mail and fax machines.'' Bogen's sales representatives also access the Internet to check inventory and expedite orders while in the field. Liz Kleider, president of Kleider Inc. expected profound changes in consumers because of electronic innovations. Kleider said, ''I see two distinct camps emerging in our industry: those who believe in 'pictures' and those who call them 'images,''' Kleider said. ''The traditional photographic picture is to hold in your hand, to mail, to exhibit, and store. Besides, it can be produced cheaply. The electronic image is exciting in its versatility and mobility. But it is more fleeting, and capture into a more stable medium is still quite expensive.'' Writing for *Photo Marketing* Alfred DeBrat suggested that retailers align themselves with photo equipment distributors who grew into digital imaging from the photographic rather than the electronic side of the business. Digital imaging products can thus be discussed using a 'common language' as opposed to distributors of electronic products "who may speak an unfamiliar language of bits, bytes, and megapixels."

INDUSTRY LEADERS

One of the largest wholesale distributors of photographic equipment and supplies in the United States is Minolta Corporation, of Ramsey, New Jersey. Minolta was incorporated in 1959 to market products created by the Minolta Camera Co., Ltd., a Japanese manufacturer of cameras and accessories. Minolta offers products including cameras, and computer-based digital information and imaging systems. Minolta employs nearly 4,000 people in the United States and had 1998 sales of about $1.1 billion.

Another major wholesale distributor is Olympus America, Inc., a subsidiary of Japan's Olympus Optical Co. Ltd. Olympus America was established in 1968 in Melville, New York, as a division of the Olympus Corporation. The company employs 1,500 people and had 1998 sales of about $223 million. It distributes photographic supplies not only to retailers, but to hospitals and government organizations as well, and markets Olympus scientific products.

Like many other industries, distributors of photographic equipment and supplies were expected to go through a period of buy-outs, mergers, and acquisitions. "Buy-outs and mergers will continue a while longer among dealers as well as distributors because many feel it's the only way to survive," according to Kleider. Hess saw major retailers altering the way distributors do business. "Through direct sourcing or private labeling, major retailers can either eliminate the distributor's share in the price of a product, or keep it for themselves in the form of increased profit margins," he said. Hess believed that major retailers often have more buying power than the distributors.

The Tiffen Manufacturing Corp. of Hauppauge, New York, is a major manufacturer of photographic equipment and supplies, especially glass filters for still, video, and motion picture/television photography. In 1998, Tiffen acquired the Saunders Group making Tiffen "the world's largest maker and distributor of filters and accessories for the consumer imaging and motion picture industry." Tiffen also offers filters and accessories for the digital camera market. In 1998, Tiffen had sales of $27 million and employed 270 people. Tiffen has also entered into an agreement with photo giant Eastman Kodak, of Rochester, New York, to market, sell, and distribute Kodak filters, step tablets, control devices, and darkroom accessories. Tiffen will also introduce consumer and professional photographic accessories to be sold as Kodak Gear and Kodak ProGear.

WORKFORCE

In 1996, the photgraphic equipment and supply industry employed 32,615 workers and had an annual payroll of $1.336 billion. Photographic equipment wholesalers averaged 19 employees per establishment, while all of wholesaling averaged only 12. Payroll per employee was also higher in the photographic equipment wholesale trade when compared to the wholesale industry average. Photographic wholesalers' average payroll per employee was $36,519, whereas the entire wholesale industry averaged $29,919.

FURTHER READING

DarConte, Lorraine A. "Digital Imaging, the Internet and the Millennium." *PTN.* June 1998, 12+.

Darnay, Arsen J., and Alampi, Gary, eds. *Wholesale and Retail Trade USA.* Detroit: Gale Research, 1995.

D & B Million Dollar Directory: America's Leading Public & Private Companies. Bethlehem, PA: Dun & Bradstreet, 1999.

DeBat, Alfred. "What Digital Distributors Can Do For Retailers." *Photo Marketing.* January 1999, 25-29.

Henry, Ed. "Digital Cameras: Fun Without Film." *Kiplinger's Personal Finance Magazine.* November 1999, 128-131.

Minolta USA. *Minolta USA.* Ramsey, NJ: Minolta USA, 1999. Available from: http://www.minoltausa.com.

Olympus Corp. *Olympus: Focus On Life.* Melville, NY: Olympus Corp., 1999. Available from: http://www.olympusamerica.com.

Photo Marketing Association International. *1998 PMA U.S.A. Consumer Photo Buying Guide.* Jackson, MI: Photo Marketing Association International, 1998.

Schaub, George. "Film Star: A New Film Promises To make Cameras Smaller and Picture-Taking Easier." *Popular Mechanics.* May 1996, 68+.

Tardiff, Joseph C. ed. *U.S. Industry Profiles: The Leading 100.* 2nd ed. Detroit: Gale, 1998.

Tiffen Manufacturing Corp. *Tiffen: Helping Create The World's Greatest Images.* Hauppauge, NY: Tiffen Manufacturing Corp., 1999. Available from: http://www.tiffen.com.

"Tiffen To Acquire Saunders Group." *Photo Marketing Newsline.* May 6, 1998, 1.

U.S. Census Bureau. "1997 Economic Census—Wholesaling." Washington: GPO 1999.

U.S. Industry & Trade Outlook '99. New York: DRI/McGraw-Hill: Standard & Poor's; Washington, DC; U.S. Dept. of Commerce/International Trade Association, 1998.

SIC 5044

OFFICE EQUIPMENT

This entry includes establishments primarily engaged in the wholesale distribution of office machines and related equipment, including photocopy and microfilm equipment; safes and vaults; accounting and adding machines; calculating machines; cash registers; duplicating machines; mailing machines; mimeograph equipment; typewriters; and addressing machines. These establishments also frequently sell office supplies, but establishments primarily engaged in wholesale distribution of office supplies are classified in **SIC 5111: Printing and Writing Paper, SIC 5112: Stationary and Office Supplies,** or **SIC 5113: Industrial and Personal Service Paper.** Establishments primarily engaged in wholesale distribution of office furniture are classified in **SIC 5021: Furniture,** and those involved primarily in wholesale distribution of computers and peripheral equipment are classified in **SIC 5045: Computers and Computer Peripheral Equipment and Software.**

NAICS Code(s)

421420 (Office Equipment Wholesalers)

Fueled by the strong U.S. economy and by the advent of digital copiers, the office equipment industry experienced bounding growth throughout the 1990s. Industry Analysts Inc., of Rochester, New York, conducted a 1999 survey of 135 office equipment dealerships, which were experiencing increased sales of 8 to 10 percent that year. Another market research firm, Dataquest, of San Jose, California, had projected U.S. placements of 180,000 digital copiers in 1998; actual placements more than doubled this projection, with 377,710 digital copier placements that year. Combined 1998 placements of analog and digital copiers numbered 1,927,600 units, an increase of 9.9 percent compared to 1997 placements. Dataquest projections called for continued expansion of the total copier market over the three years after 1998 before decreasing to 2.1 million units by 2003. This would represent sales increases from $425.8 million in 1998 to a projected $36.1 billion in 2003.

Industry Analysts attributed the hot digital copier market to organizations replacing analog copiers with digital technology, which suggested finite growth once full digitalization was achieved. However, the trend toward digital networking encouraged the purchase of multiple copiers that could be interlinked, which could buoy sales once analog copiers are phased-out. Industry Analysts also projected a shift in income for companies from hardware sales to technical support, as office equipment such as copiers were integrated into more complex systems requiring more sophisticated and knowledgeable users, and hence more support.

Industry Snapshot

The number of office equipment wholesalers decreased in the 1990s due to consolidation, forcing dealers to accept tighter profit margins. Like distributors in other industries, office equipment dealers found that the way to maintain or increase their market share was to emphasize the service they provided that customers would not find in the superstores and other discount outlets. To broaden their appeal, many distributors also developed online catalogs for easy customer use.

The office machinery wholesale industry has become intensely competitive as profit margins have tightened. Many buyers of office equipment order through wholesale distributors rather than through retail outlets or direct from the manufacturer. Dealers selling low-end copiers and other equipment encounter tough competition from superstores and discounters, whose prices appeal to small and medium-sized businesses that do not qualify for the volume discounts given to large companies.

Background and Development

Xerox Corporation, the inventor of the copier in 1949, led the office equipment industry until the 1970s when Japanese rivals entered the market. Xerox sales representatives found themselves competing against local distributors of Minolta Camera Co. Ltd., Toshiba Corporation, and other companies. At the premium-priced end, Eastman Kodak Co. had become a powerful competitor as well. Xerox's quality-improvement strategy, however, helped the company regain much of its market share (about 38 percent in 1991). Xerox sells and rents machines and provides special financing to its largest accounts. Because Xerox machines are usually high-end products and small or new businesses do not qualify for Xerox's low interest financing, entrepreneurs often turn to the distributors of the lower-priced Japanese machines to buy or rent.

Wholesale distributors of office equipment have traditionally been part of a two-tier distribution system in which they bought merchandise from the manufacturers and sold it for profit to other retailers or industrial and commercial clients. They maintained deep inventories, often by taking loans against those inventories. To remain competitive, they needed to continually expand their services, expand geographically, and diversify their product markets.

Current Conditions

Distributors of office equipment, although not so vulnerable to the spending habits of individual consumers, had to contend with downsizing and layoffs at businesses across the country. Superstores have vied for the small to midsized business market and have been very successful in part because they offered smaller businesses discounts for which they had never qualified before. Smaller distributors, who could not profitably compete with the superstores for their customer base, had thus been endangered.

Dealers, however, stressed the value-added service that they could provide to business customers of the retail outlets they supplied. Value-added service was one advantage that wholesalers stressed in their competition with superstores. Value-added services included on-call technical expertise; special financing arrangements; assistance in customer materials management costs; product lines tailored to specific customers; specially designed, labeled, or customized products or catalogs; next-day delivery; aftermarket products and service; just-in-time inventory controls; online reporting; and usage reports. Intense competition, though, often prevented dealers from charging fees for these services, which adversely affected their already tight profit margins.

Long-standing dealers of office equipment were angered by the generous discounting some manufacturers extended to office supply superstores. According to the National Office Machine Dealers Association (NOMDA), manufacturers were selling to the discounters at a better price than they sold to dealers. They noted that the superstores did not have to bear the expense of supporting repair, training, and technical service networks that the dealers maintained.

Although manufacturers, through the large retailers, realized the benefits of reaching out to the small business and home-office market they might not have reached through traditional distributor channels, superstores were a mixed blessing to them. The superstores offered minimal service, and the manufacturers assumed increased responsibility for handling repair and warranty problems. Dealers, on the other hand, carried a large inventory of parts, provided training with the equipment they sold, and provided same-day, on-site repair of the equipment.

The remaining larger distributors competed for the corporate dollars of national companies. To be competitive, however, they offered a wide range of products and services since customers often look to deal with one supplier rather than many.

INDUSTRY LEADERS

In January 1997, Alco Standard Corp. completed a long-contemplated consolidation by adopting IKON Office Solutions as its name for its office products division. IKON, which stands for I Know One Name, was previously one of the world's leading office machine companies. Alco spun off its paper distribution arm, Unisource Worldwide, the largest paper distributor in North America, to Alco's shareholders. In 1997, IKON had 87 companies under its umbrella, with more than 800 offices worldwide.

In February 1999 IKON announced a partnership with Canon U.S.A. Inc. to market Canon's imageRUNNER digital products. However, an increased backlog of Canon digital products later in the year (among other issues) hampered the company's fiscal-year results. Fiscal-year 1999 revenues amounted to $5.5 billion, a drop of 1.9 percent from 1998. Additionally, IKON shareholders sued the company for misleading financial projections, winning a $111 million settlement in December 1999. IKON's settlement did not admit guilt.

Another leading wholesale distributor was Lanier Worldwide Inc., a billion-dollar subsidiary of Harris Corporation. Lanier markets copiers, fax machines and dictation equipment, telephones, integrated computer software and networking systems, and other office equipment. In 1996, they were given the Business Technology Association Award of Excellence in the category of office machine sales revenue of $10 million or more. Lanier had more than 1,600 sales and service offices in 100 countries. Estimated results for the second quarter ending Dec. 31, 1999, indicated net income to be softer than in previous years, due to decreasing prices in the industry, the strength of the Japanese yen, and uncertainties surrounding the effects of the so-called Y2K bug. In November 1999 Lanier announced an alliance with Hewlett-Packard Co. to market HP copier multifunction peripherals.

Danka Business Systems, PLC, of the United Kingdom, was another major wholesaler, employing 22,000 people in more than 700 offices in 35 countries. Danka is a major independent supplier of automated office equipment such as photocopiers, facsimile machines, and the related parts and service. Danka was the main distributor of Kodak printers and copiers.

RESEARCH AND TECHNOLOGY

Wholesale distributors have applied computer technology to improve profit margins. This has improved the productivity of many functions, including purchasing, delivery, storage, and shipping. It also improved inventory, credit, and information management.

FURTHER READING

Business Technology Association. ''An Overview: The Thriving U.S. Economy, Information Technology and the Business Equipment Market,'' and ''IKON Agrees to Pay $111 Million to Settle Shareholder Lawsuit.'' Available from http://btanet.org.

Cohan, Robin. ''Corporate Profile for Danka Business Systems PLC.'' *Business Wire,* 17 May 1996.

Dinell, David. ''Office Automation Plans Changes.'' *Wichita Business Journal,* 18 October 1996, 6.

Farrell, Michael. ''Brunswick Copier Firm Hopes to Duplicate Parent's Success.'' *Capital District Business Review,* 24 June 1996. Available from http://www.amcity.com/albany/stories/062496/story3.html.

IKON Office Solutions. Available from http://www.ikon.com.

Lanier Worldwide, Inc. Available from http://www.lanier.com.

Larson, Mark. ''Enlarged Image: DISC Sale Brings Expansion Cash.'' *The Business Journal of Sacramento,* 9 December 1996. Available from http://www.amcity.com/sacramento/stories/120996/story3.html.

Lummus, Laurey. ''Harris Garners Large Contract.'' *Colorado Springs Business Journal,* 11 October 1996.

''Office Buyers Take on Industry Challenges.'' *Purchasing,* 20 April 20, 1995.

''Systems, Inc. Acquired by Alco Standard.'' *Middlesex Magazine & Business Review,* February 1996.

''The Week in Business.'' *Tampa Bay Business Journal,* 13 January 1997. Available from http://www.amcity.com/tampabay/stories/011397/weekinbiz.html.

SIC 5045

COMPUTERS AND COMPUTER PERIPHERAL EQUIPMENT AND SOFTWARE

This industry consists of establishments primarily engaged in the wholesale distribution of computers, computer peripheral equipment, and computer software. These establishments also sell related supplies, but establishments primarily engaged in wholesaling supplies are classified according to the individual product for example, computer paper in **SIC 5112: Stationery and Office Supplies.** Establishments primarily engaged in the wholesale distribution of modems and other electronic communications equipment are classified in **SIC 5065: Electronic Parts and Equipment, Not Elsewhere Classified.** Establishments primarily engaged in selling computers and computer peripheral equipment and software for other than business or professional use are classified in **SIC 5734: Computer and Computer Software Stores.**

NAICS Code(s)

421430 (Computer and Computer Peripheral Equipment and Software Wholesalers)
443120 (Computer and Software Stores)

Organization and Structure

Five distinct segments exist within the traditional electronics wholesale distribution arena: full-line distributors, technical and professional distributorships, regional and local distributorships, hardware distributors, and software distributors. The limited focus of the respective wholesaler segments distinguishes each from the mixed-sales distributor segments.

Full-line Distributors. Full-line distributors predominate the computer wholesale industry with the broadest product and customer base. Sales in this segment represent 35 percent of the total traditional distribution market and 23 percent of U.S. wholesale computer-distribution network revenue.

Hardware Distribution. Hardware distributors accounted for 22 percent of the non-systems products. Regional and local distributors within the wholesale category account for 28 percent of the traditional distribution total and 18 percent of the U.S. wholesale computer distribution revenue. These distributors emphasize sales to independent dealers and fulfillment services.

Technical Distributors. Most of the wholesalers in this industry segment supply goods to corporations. Typical product lines include disk drivers, terminals, computers, keyboards, printers, and other computer equipment. Up to 20 percent of sales in the industry are commonly filtered to corporations via systems integrators and value-added reseller (VAR) channels. In the early 1990s technical distributors accounted for approximately 10 percent of the traditional distribution total and 7 percent of the U.S. wholesale computer distribution revenue. This segment is characterized by an overriding value-added focus consisting of integration and networking services. High-end product mixes involving complex hardware and software configurations predominate in this market.

Software-only distributors accounted for a scant 4 percent of traditional distribution sales. Their primary focus was on the sale of educational and entertainment software to the mass market. They also played an important role in bringing new software products to the market.

The wholesale computer distribution market generated $17 billion in sales in 1992 and rose to $21.5 billion in 1993, continuing a precedent of growth in the industry. The market reached $36.5 billion by 1996, and by 1999 sales among the leading four distributors alone topped $46.5 billion, with original equipment manufacturers (OEMs) excluded from the tally.

Background and Development

A vital transformation occurred in the computers and computer peripheral equipment and software industry during the late 20th century. Industry standards evolved, markets solidified, and customer sophistication matured to new levels. Most significant among the changes was a dramatic shift toward complex network configurations, as a dramatic proliferation of new hardware technology emerged and expanded the functionality of desktop computers. The result was an expansion in the retail computer industry that spurred wholesale and manufacturing markets. Any doubt that the wholesale distribution segment of the industry was a powerhouse was erased in 1992 when IBM, Apple, and Compaq entered the industry. Concurrent with these developments, the larger national wholesalers formed new divisions to pursue such areas as retail sales, direct fulfillment, and emerging technologies.

Following the peak years between 1991 and 1993, there were 38,000 jobs lost in the wholesale sector. The business computer market segment became saturated at 90 percent by 1996, according to a report in *Monthly Labor Review.* In the face of a waning business market, distributors turned their attention to the new mass market of home consumers who were captivated by the power of the Internet. The market for home computers expanded dramatically at that time with the innovation of easy-to-use Internet software interfaces called browsers. The industry rebounded, employment increased by 4 percent, and the industry recovered 32 percent of the lost jobs. Additionally, the expansion of the home computer industry fueled a new market for pre-packaged software. Advances in CD-ROM technology resulted in lower equipment prices for associated peripherals such as optical drives and spurred sales of both hardware and software in the process.

CURRENT CONDITIONS

In 1995, computer manufacturers began to encourage competition among wholesale distribution channels by opening the market to unhindered competition. The practice, called "open sourcing," absolved dealers from the requirement to contract exclusively with a specified wholesaler. "Second sourcing," a modified version of open sourcing, limits competition by permitting no more than two wholesalers to enter the channel. As a result of open sourcing policies, competition increased within the industry. Wholesalers were forced to compete and flourish or else to withdraw from the marketplace. Between 1992 and 1995 the number of wholesale distributors dropped nearly in half, from 300 to less than 180.

Likewise, software distributors encountered new challenges in the mid-1990s. In response to the burgeoning popularity of the Internet, some software manufacturers established on-line outlets and sold products directly to consumers over the World Wide Web. The new on-line method of distribution enabled the $30 billion software industry to distribute their product directly to a rapidly expanding Internet consumer market and bypass the wholesale industry entirely.

INDUSTRY LEADERS

In 1999 more than 50 wholesale firms continued in existence, with the most prosperous reporting double-digit growth patterns. At the top of the wholesale industry that year, Ingram Micro, Incorporated of Santa Ana, California, a public company, ranked at number 55 on *Fortune's* list of 500 leading public corporations. Ingram reported annual sales of $22 billion in 1998 for close to 33 percent growth. The corporation was the world's largest computer wholesaler, with one-third of its business from international markets. The second largest company, Tech Data Corporation of Clearwater, Florida, reported $11.5 billion in sales for a growth of more than 63 percent. Tech Data appeared at number 145 among the *Fortune* 500—up from 305 and 224 in 1997 and 1998 respectively. CHS Electronics Incorporated followed closely at number 189 in 1999. CHS, also based in Florida, dealt exclusively at the international level. The firm reported sales growth of nearly 80 percent. Other significant businesses included Intelligent Electronics, and MicroAge. Computer manufacturer Packard Bell NEC Incorporated eliminated its wholesale distributorship program in 1997. They experienced a significant decline in market share as a result and moved to realign with its former distribution partners, MicroAge and Tech Data, less than one year later.

FURTHER READING

"CHS Electronics, Inc.," *Hoover's Online,* 5 January 2000. Available from http://www.hoovers.com/.

"Computer Products Distribution & Support," *Hoover's Online,* 5 January 2000. Available from http://www.hoovers.com/.

Freeman, Laura, "Job creation and the emerging home computer market," *Monthly Labor Review,* 1 August 1996.

"Ingram Micro Inc.," *Hoover's Online,* 5 January 2000. Available from http://www.hoovers.com/.

Judge, Paul C. "Surviving the Age of the Internet." *Business Week,* 3 June 1996.

Lazich, Robert S., ed. *Market Share Reporter.* Detroit: Gale Research, 1999.

Snyder, Bill. "Middle of It All." *PC Week,* 13 February 1995.

Studt, Tim. "Downloading Software from Web Sites." *R & D,* November 1996.

"Tech Data Corporation," *Hoover's Online,* 5 January 2000. Available from http://www.hoovers.com/.

SIC 5046

COMMERCIAL EQUIPMENT, NOT ELSEWHERE CLASSIFIED

This industry classification is comprised of establishments primarily engaged in the wholesale distribution of commercial machines and equipment, not elsewhere classified. Products of the industry include commercial cooking and food service equipment, partitions, shelving, lockers, store fixtures, electrical signs, balances and scales (except laboratory), mannequins, and vending machines.

NAICS CODE(S)

421440 (Other Commercial Equipment Wholesalers)

Commercial wholesaling, not elsewhere classified was valued at an estimated $15 billion in 1995. Slightly less than 5,000 establishments in the industry employed approximately 45,000 people in the mid-1990s. This segment is part of the professional and commercial equipment and supplies market, which made up 19 percent of the entire wholesale distribution of durables in 1997, totaling $256 billion. Wholesale durable goods sales was forecast to grow 4.4 percent in 1999 and 5.2 percent in 2000.

Two key lines of business characterize the industry: restaurant and hotel equipment, and store machines and equipment. Restaurant and hotel suppliers produced about 60 percent of the industry's sales versus store machine wholesalers' 40 percent share. Sales in the hospitality side of the industry have generally grown faster than those of the store equipment segment.

In the late 1990s, domestic restaurant chains and their suppliers increased their presence overseas. Unit openings in Europe and elsewhere by restaurant chains were expected to be twice that as in the United States. Since these restaurants prefer American equipment, this growth offered opportunities for both manufacturers and distributors. Distributors supporting overseas markets must be able to handle post-sales service requirements, local order fulfillment, and language barriers.

Sales of store fixtures increased dramatically during the 1970s and the 1980s, but stalled during the first years of the 1990s. Growth was attributed to the number of shopping malls under construction during the period. According to the report, the number of shopping malls in the United States had increased from 3,500 in the mid-1970s to about 35,000 in the early 1990s. As a result, the combined value of wood and nonwood store fixture shipments went from $1.75 billion in 1975 to $6.19 billion in 1990. As the construction of retail outlets slowed and overall economic growth lost momentum, demand for industry products leveled off.

During the mid-1990s, suppliers of store fixtures expected growth to come from three areas: renovations necessitated under the provisions of the Americans with Disabilities Act; government requirements; and vendor shops—distinctive spaces within retail establishments devoted to specific products. These three areas, however, were not expected to provide growth as dramatic as had been experienced during the previous two decades. In the late 1990s, wholesalers faced competition from manufacturers as they began selling via the Internet. For instance, St. Louis-based NU-ERA Group now has an online catalogue and Newark, New Jersey-based Handy Store Fixtures offers 2,000 store fixtures for sale on their Web site.

The majority of firms that distribute miscellaneous commercial equipment in the United States are typically quite small. Leading firms by revenues in the late 1990s, most of which were restaurant and hotel suppliers, included Gordon Food Service Inc. of Grand Rapids, Michigan; Performance Food Group Co. of Richmond, Virginia; SYSCO Food Services of Walnut, California; International Dairy Queen Inc. of Minneapolis, Minnesota; and Nobel (subsidiary of Sysco Food Services) of Denver, Colorado.

FURTHER READING

McDonald, Jack. ''Learning to Serve the Global Market.'' *Foodservice Equipment & Supplies,* July 1999.

''Surfing for Fixtures.'' *Discount Merchandiser,* August 1999.

U.S. Bureau of the Census. *1992 Census of Wholesale Trade.* Washington, DC: GPO, 1995.

———. ''Current Business Reports.''. *Combined Annual and Revised Monthly Wholesale Trade.* Washington, DC: GPO, 1996.

Wholesale and Retail Trade U.S.A. 1998. Detroit: Gale Group, 1998.

''Wholesaling: Economic and Trade Trends.'' *U.S. Industry & Trade Outlook '99.* U.S. Department of Commerce/International Trade Administration and McGraw-Hill, 1999.

SIC 5047

MEDICAL, DENTAL, AND HOSPITAL EQUIPMENT AND SUPPLIES

This industry classification is comprised of establishments primarily engaged in the wholesale distribution of instruments, apparatus, and equipment to medical and dental practitioners, clinics, and hospitals. Products of the industry include surgical instruments, artificial limbs, operating room equipment, X-ray machines, hospital beds, medical and dental laboratory equipment, and professional supplies. The industry also includes wholesale distributors of industrial safety devices such as first-aid kits and face and eye masks.

NAICS CODE(S)

421450 (Medical, Dental and Hospital Equipment and Supplies Wholesalers)

446199 (All Other Health and Personal Care Stores)

The U.S. Bureau of the Census, in its *1992 Economic Census,* reported a total of 9,521 establishments operating within this industry. Their combined sales totaled $51.7 billion. The establishments were subdivided into two categories: wholesalers engaged primarily in the distribution of medical and hospital equipment and supplies, and wholesalers engaged primarily in the distribution of dental equipment and supplies. Medical and hospital wholesalers formed the largest segment of the industry, accounting for 8,598 establishments and sales of $48.5 billion. Dental wholesalers accounted for 923 establishments and sales of $3.2 billion.

During the early 1990s, rising health care costs led many hospitals to form alliances and make group purchasing decisions. Critics of the policy claimed that the situation created an adversarial relationship between the medical community and its suppliers because the purchasing groups left distributors with unprofitable margins.

In addition to concern over cost containment, the medical community faced increasing pressure to reduce its impact on the environment. Costs related to the disposal of medical waste, including toxic and hazardous materials, were mounting. Medical administrators called upon manufacturers and distributors to help provide products able to serve patients' needs and also reduce waste.

As the 1990s continued, suppliers engaged in cutthroat competition and managed care placed additional pressure on the industry. Hospitals began to complain about declining standards of service, even from the major national suppliers. As a result, suppliers found themselves competing to provide improved service at lowered prices. ''Activity-based costing,'' in which prices are based on actual costs rather than a negotiated price plus a set shipping cost, became popular. Some hospitals turned to regional distributors and even took back some functions formerly performed for them by distributors.

Not surprisingly, many smaller companies folded or were acquired by larger companies. For instance, in 1994 Owens & Minor Inc. acquired third-ranking distributor Stuart Medical. Even the largest companies suffered a decline in profits. The average pretax profit margin for hospital distributors fell to 1.8 percent in 1994 and was expected to drop still more.

In the latter part of the 1990s, the remaining national medical-surgical distribution companies were struggling to maintain their standing, with regional distributors and drug distributors providing additional competition. In 1999 the industry leaders were Allegiance Corporation of McGaw Park, Illinois (a spinoff from Baxter International, which had broken up); Owens & Minor Inc. of Richmond, Virginia; and Fisher Scientific Co., of Hampton, New Hampshire.

A majority of companies in this business were small: 12,900 had fewer than 5 staff members. An additional 3,919 firms employed 5 to 9, and 1,437 employed 10-14 people. When ranking by sales, firms were more in the mid-size range, with 6,808 with sales between $250,000 and $499,000. Of the remaining establishments, 2,882 firms had sales between $100,000 and $249,000, while there were almost an equal number above that mid-size range, with 2,443 companies with sales of $500,000 to $999,000.

One tool available to help medical supplies distributors locate specialized products was a CD-ROM database provided by MDI (Medical Data Institute) called EPIC Plus. The EPIC Plus system provided suppliers with an up-to-date database of more than 500,000 products produced by more than 2,000 manufacturers and wholesalers. The system was used by the Health Industry Distributors Association (HIDA) and recommended by the Independent Medical Distributors Association (IMDA), an organization formed to facilitate the exchange of ideas among medical suppliers and to meet the needs of firms involved in the distribution of specialized medical products.

FURTHER READING

Dun's Census of American Business 1997. Parsippany, NJ: Dun & Bradstreet, 1997.

Hensley, Scott. ''Healthcare Supply King: McKesson-General Medical Pact to Create Largest Supply Center.'' *Modern Healthcare,* 3 February 1997.

———. ''Outlook 1997: Seeking Synergies: Purchasing Industry to Focus on Digesting Consolidation.'' *Modern Healthcare,* 6 January 1997.

Independent Medical Distributors Association. ''A Specialist Needs Specialized Service.'' Mission, KS: IMDA, nd.

Scott, Lisa. ''Materials Management; Squeezed Distributors Try New Methods.'' *Modern Healthcare,* 27 May 1996.

———. ''Outlook 1996: Consolidation Likely in Hospital Supply Industry.'' *Modern Healthcare,* 1 January 1996.

———. ''Suppliers Endure Large Doses of Change.'' *Modern Healthcare,* 21 October 1996.

U.S. Census Bureau. *1992 Economic Census.* Washington, D.C.: GPO, 1995.

Ward's Business Directory of U.S. Private and Public Companies, 1999. Detroit: Gale Research, 1999.

SIC 5048

OPHTHALMIC GOODS

This category covers establishments primarily engaged in the wholesale distribution of professional equipment and goods used, prescribed, or sold by ophthalmologists, optometrists, and opticians, including ophthalmic frames, lenses, sunglass lenses, contact lenses, and optometric equipment and supplies.

NAICS Code(s)

421460 (Ophthalmic Goods Wholesalers)

Background and Development

Some historians believe eyeglasses originated in Europe during the thirteenth and fourteenth centuries. Others attribute them to China, claiming Marco Polo introduced them to Europeans. Following the invention of Gutenberg's press and the ensuing availability of printed material, demand soared.

The now common frame form—with side arms fitting over the ears—was introduced in 1746. Benjamin Franklin invented bifocals in 1752. Contact lenses were first offered in 1888. Other major innovations include the 1959 development of variable strength corrective lenses, and the 1971 availability of ''soft'' contact lenses.

Current Conditions

In 1994, according to *American Demographics,* about 25 percent of Americans under 35 wore prescription eyeglasses, 15 percent wore contact lenses, and less than 2 percent wore bifocals. Among those aged 35 to 54, the respective percentages were 38, 12, and 14. Of those 55 and over, 42 percent had glasses, 3 percent wore contacts, and 39 percent used bifocals.

Questions about the appropriate distribution of contact lenses surfaced when the U.S. Food & Drug Administration termed them ''medical devices'' which could only be dispensed by professionals or by prescription. Improving technology simultaneously increased the number of people who could wear them.

Because of their large, low-wage labor forces, overseas manufacturers captured the market for frames and low-end sunglasses by the mid-1990s, but the United States remained a leader in lens technology, high-end sunglasses, and contact lenses. In 1995, the *Monthly Labor Review* projected employment in ophthalmic goods would remain flat for the next 10 years, while output would grow 3.9 percent annually.

Furthermore, in the late 1990s, an aging U.S. population increasingly desired improved types of both reading and computer glasses.

In 1997, according to *Dun's Census of American Business, 1997,* there were 1274 establishments in this category; and by far the largest number, 599, employed four or less people. There were 281 units with between five and nine employees; 123 with ten to 14 employees; and 52 with 15 to 19 employees. There were 108 stores with 20 to 49 employees, 47 with 50 to 99, and only 33 with 100 or more employees.

The breakdown by sales was somewhat balanced, with 259 units reporting gross sales of $100,000 to $249,000, 243 garnering sales between $250,000 to $499,000, 159 selling between $500,000 to $999,000, and 207 with gross sales between $1 million and $5 million. There were only 96 units selling less than $100,000 and 89 at more than $5 million.

Industry Leaders

Industry leaders include Bonneau Co of Dallas TX, Charmant Incorporated USA, Bolle America, Inc., and Moonlight Products.

Further Reading

Cowie, Denise. ''Thinner, Lighter Lenses Get Consumer's Attention.'' *Knight-Ridder News Service,* 13 April 1995.

Crispell, Diane. ''Contact Lenses or Glasses?'' *American Demographics,* June 1995, 38.

Franklin, James C. ''Industry Output and Employment Projections to 2005.'' *Monthly Labor Review,* November 1995, 45.

U.S. Bureau of the Census. *1992 Census of Wholesale Trade.* Washington, DC: GPO.

''Vision Correction and Contact Lenses.'' *Contact Lens Council.* Available from http://www.iglobal.com/CLC/clc-01.htm.

SIC 5049

PROFESSIONAL EQUIPMENT AND SUPPLIES, NOT ELSEWHERE CLASSIFIED

This industry classification covers establishments primarily engaged in the wholesale distribution of professional equipment and supplies that are not categorized elsewhere. It includes wholesale distributors of drafting instruments, laboratory equipment (other than medical and dental), and scientific instruments.

NAICS CODE(S)

421490 (Other Professional Equipment and Supplies Wholesalers)
453210 (Office Supplies and Stationery Stores)

Wholesale distributors of medical and dental laboratory equipment are classified in **SIC 5047: Medical, Dental, and Hospital Equipment and Supplies.**

INDUSTRY SNAPSHOT

According to the U.S. Census Bureau, some 2,700 establishments composed this industry in the mid-1990s, and employed an estimated 34,000 people in the United States. Their combined sales were estimated at $11 billion in 1995. The industry accounts for roughly 6 percent of the broader professional and commercial equipment category, which sold an estimated $190 billion in products in 1995.

The industry is divided into two general categories: wholesalers primarily engaged in the distribution of religious and school supplies, and wholesalers primarily engaged in the distribution of other professional equipment and supplies. Sellers of religious and school supplies represented 27 percent of industry establishments and accounted for 24 percent of its sales.

In the 1990s, one of the most promising product segments was laboratory equipment. Some industry analysts predicted that provisions of the Clean Air Act of 1990 would bring steady growth in U.S. sales of instruments and apparatus used to measure and control pollutants. Pollution abatement programs undertaken in other countries around the world were expected to create similar increases in other markets.

Sales of school equipment, however, were uncertain. One industry participant stated that the school market was ''characterized by tight funding and restricted budgets.''; typically, such conditions tend to stifle market growth.

CURRENT CONDITIONS

This industry consisted of just over 7,000 establishments in 1997 according to *Dun's Census of American Business.* The largest group, comprising 2,076 units, reported sales between $250,000 and $499,000 in 1997. The next biggest category included slightly smaller operations with gross revenues between $100,000 and $249,000 in 1997: 1,143 wholesalers fell into this group. Interestingly, the next largest group was at the higher end of the scale, with gross revenues of $1 million to $5 million, with 1,104 establishments. More than 842 units had sales between $500,000 and $1 million; about 319 distributors had annual sales volume between $50,000 and $99,000. Only 82 sold between $1,000 and $50,000 worth of stock in 1997, while 339 units reported more than $5 million in annual sales.

Almost half of the distributors in this category (4,399) employed less than five workers in 1997. 1,311 businesses had between five and nine employees; 517 staffed between 10 and 14 workers; and 214 employed from 15 to 19. A slightly larger number of establishments (412) employed between 20 and 49 workers. There were 127 with between 50 and 99 employees, and just 82 with over 100.

INDUSTRY LEADERS

One of the nation's leading distributors of professional equipment and supplies in the late 1990s was the VWR Scientific Products Corporation. Founded in 1852, VWR provides laboratory equipment, chemicals, and supplies to customers around the world. VWR also offers value-added services such as warehouse management systems, electronic order entry, electronic data interchange, and bar coding for more efficient inventory control. The company posted sales of $1.3 billion in 1998, nearly tripling its revenues within five years. Other leaders were Carl Zeiss, Inc. of Thornwood, New York, Mitutoyo/MTI Corp. of Aurora, Illinois, and Crocker Fels Co. of Cincinnati, Ohio.

FURTHER READING

U.S. Bureau of the Census. *1992 Census of Wholesale Trade.* Washington, DC: GPO, 1995.

———. ''Current Business Reports.'' *Combined Annual and Revised Monthly Wholesale Trade.* Washington, DC: GPO, 1996.

VWR Corporation. *1998 Annual Report* West Chester, PA, 1999.

SIC 5051

METALS SERVICE CENTERS AND OFFICES

This industry comprises establishments primarily engaged in marketing semifinished metal products (except precious metals). Products of the industry include aluminum and copper (sold in bars, rods, sheets, pipes, plates, etc.), iron and steel products (such as rough castings, bearing piles, flat products, and semifinished products), lead, mercury, tin and tin base metals, and zinc. The industry also includes establishments engaged in the wholesale distribution of wire products (such as screening and bale ties), metal bars, nails, and metal tubing. Establishments primarily involved in the wholesale distribution of metallic ores (including precious metal ores) are classified in this industry. Establishments primarily involved in distributing semifinished precious metals are classified in **SIC 5094: Jewelry, Watches, Precious Stones.**

NAICS Code(s)

421510 (Metals Service Centers and Offices)

The U.S. Department of Commerce reported a total of 10,281 establishments within this industry in 1987. They were subdivided into three classifications: ferrous metals service centers (those operating with a warehouse), ferrous metals sales offices (those operating without a warehouse), and nonferrous metals service centers and offices. Ferrous metals contain iron; nonferrous metals do not contain iron. Economic census reports forecast the total number of establishments would dip slightly in the beginning of the decade and stand at 10,261 by 1996.

In 1987 the U.S. Department of Commerce reported that this industry employed 137,009 workers. Establishments within the industry posted a combined annual payroll of $3.85 billion for that year. In 1996 approximately 144,048 individuals were employed by metals service centers and offices, while total industry sales were in excess of $5.4 billion.

Ferrous metals service centers represented the largest segment of the industry. They numbered 5,840 establishments, and their combined sales totaled $47.8 billion. Ferrous metals sales offices numbered 2,388, with $28.5 billion in sales. The 2,053 nonferrous metals service centers and offices had combined sales of $24.8 billion.

According to *Purchasing magazine,* service centers supply a third of all the metal fabricated by manufacturing. These service centers shipped an estimated 32.8 million tons in 1998 (an increase of 4.1 percent compared to the previous year), out of the 128 million tons of ferrous and nonferrous metals consumed in North America. Since total metals demand was expected to drop by 2 to 3 percent in 1999, metals service center shipments were expected to decline by about the same amount. *Purchasing*'s Metals Distribution Index was thus expected to drop from 148.8 to 142.6. Other industry analysts predict that market share of service centers will grow, reaching 40 to 45 percent within a decade or so.

Metals service centers received shipments from mills and prepared products for manufacturers and other end users. Both aluminum and steel service centers suffered from a nationwide economic downturn during the early years of the 1990s. As the economy recovered, so did shipments. Steel service shipments increased from about 27 million tons in 1994 to around 30 million tons in 1998, according to *Purchasing magazine*. However, shipments were expected to drop to about 30 million tons in 1999. Aluminum center shipments increased from a little more than 2 billion pounds in 1994 to nearly 2.4 billion pounds in 1998. These shipments were expected to increase slightly in 1999. Copper center shipments peaked in 1994 at more than 500 million pounds, then declined in 1998 to around 460 million pounds, with another drop expected in 1999.

According to statistics offered by the Steel Service Center Institute (SSCI), almost 45 percent of domestically produced stainless steel and 30 percent of carbon industrial steel was purchased and distributed through steel service centers. SSCI also said that shipments reached a record of 28.8 million tons in 1997, compared to 27.1 million tons in 1995. Average daily shipments increased by 8 percent in 1997 compared to the previous year.

Following the general trend in the wholesale industry, there was significant consolidation through mergers of metals service centers in the late 1990s, with 1997 and 1998 being peak years. This trend was expected to continue in 1999 though at a slower rate. One of the biggest during 1997 was the merger of Tubesales and Williams & Co. to form TW Metals of Exton, Pennsylvania. In the first quarter of 1999 there were seven acquisitions involving steel and aluminum centers.

Customers also began putting more challenging demands on metals service centers during the same period. These included meeting promised delivery dates and consistently providing high-quality goods at competitive prices, according to *Purchasing magazine.* New areas of customer service were also being added, including supply of finished parts and management of logistics. These developments are blurring the lines between service centers and independent processors.

Based on *Purchasing*'s annual survey, the top 100 service centers reported an 8 percent increase in sales (to $32.7 billion) in 1998, compared to the previous year. The top 11 each have sales of $1 billion or more, and their combined 1998 sales grew by 9.5 percent to more than $16 billion, nearly half of what the entire top 100 did as a group., The majority of service center companies are much smaller, however—nearly 90 percent of 975 North American centers listed by *Purchasing* magazine have annual sales under $100 million. Thirty-nine percent have their corporate offices headquartered in the Midwest, while 72 percent operate service centers where most manufacturing is located. Construction is the largest market.

Purchasing's Top 11 companies, according to 1998 annual sales, are Ryerson Tull Inc. of Chicago, Illinois ($2.8 billion); Thyssen Inc. of Detroit, Michigan ($2.5 billion); Metals USA Inc. of Houston, Texas ($1.5 billion); Reliance Steel & Aluminum Co. of Los Angeles, California ($1.35 billion); MacSteel Service Centers USA of Torrance, California, Russel Mettals Inc. of Ontario, Canada, and Samuel, Son & Co. (each at $1.2 billion); Carpenter Steel Service Centers of Reading, Pennsylvania ($1.18 billion); North American Metals Distribution Group of Coon Rapids, Minnesota ($1.16 billion); Preussag North America Inc. of Atlanta, Georgia ($1.12 billion); and Earle M. Jorgenson Co. of Brea, California ($1 billion). Ward's Business Directory 2000 also listed two Japanese subsidiaries: Marubeni America Corp. and Mitsui and Company, both of New York City, among the top leaders.

FURTHER READING

Darnay, Arsen, and Gary Alampi, eds. *Wholesale and Retail Trade USA.* Detroit: Gale Research, 1995.

Petry, Corinna C. ''Service Center Daily Shipping Rate Climbs.'' *American Metal Market,* 26 February 1997.

Robertson, Scott. ''Another Strong Year for Service Centers.'' *American Metal Market,* 27 January 1997.

''Service Center Forecast.'' *AMM Online,* 20 January 2000. Available from: http://www.amm.com/inside/2000/jan/0120si.htm.

''Service Centers.'' *AMM Online.* 23 September 1999. Available from: http://www.ammm.com/inside/1999/092399si.htm.

''Service Centers Set Shipping Record in 1997'' *New Steel,* March 1998. Available from: http://www.newsteel.com/news/NW980311.htm.

Stundza, Tom. ''Buyers Ask Service Centers: What Happened to JIT? And A Few Other Things.'' *Purchasing,* 6 May 1999. Available from: http://www.manufacturing.net/magazine/purchasing/archives/1999/pur0506.99/051dist.htm.

———. ''Top 100 Metal Service Centers: The Big Keep Getting Bigger.'' *Purchasing,* 6 May 1999. Available from: http://www.manufacturing.net/magazine/purchasing/archives/1999/pur0506.99/051mtop.htm.

Ward's Business Directory of U.S. Private and Public Companies 2000. Detroit: Gale Group, 2000.

SIC 5052

COAL AND OTHER MINERALS AND ORES

This industry comprises establishments primarily engaged in the wholesale distribution of coal and coke, metallic ores (such as copper, iron, and lead), and nonmetallic minerals (except crude petroleum). It also includes establishments engaged in the wholesale distribution of precious metal ores (such as gold ore and silver ore).

Establishments primarily engaged in the wholesale distribution of semifinished precious metals are classified under **SIC 5094: Jewelry, Watches, Precious Stones, and Precious Metals.** Establishments primarily engaged in the wholesale distribution of nonmetallic minerals used as construction materials are classified under **SIC 5032: Brick, Stone, and Related Construction Materials.** Establishments primarily engaged in the wholesale distribution of crude petroleum and petroleum products are classified under **SIC 5171: Petroleum Bulk Stations and Terminals.**

NAICS CODE(S)

421520 (Coal and Other Mineral and Ore Wholesalers)

According to the U.S. Census Bureau, 756 establishments were classified in 1997; this figure has declined consistently since the 1980s. They were subdivided into establishments primarily engaged in wholesaling coal, accounting for approximately 75 percent of establishments; and those primarily engaged in wholesaling other minerals and ores, which made up the remaining 25 percent. Coal sales were around $12 billion, and sales of other minerals and ores topped $2 billion. Total sales for this industry reached $14.8 billion.

The majority of industry establishments are merchant wholesalers. Sales by merchant wholesalers, however, typically represent only a third of industry sales. The establishments classified as manufacturer sales branches and offices represent approximately 48 percent of industry sales. Agents, brokers, and commission merchants make up the remainder of industry sales. The states with the most establishments were Pennsylvania and Kentucky.

Some of the leading companies in this industry, according to Ward's Business Directory 2000, include Arch Coal Sales Company Inc. of St. Louis, Missouri, with annual sales around $1 billion; Electric Fuels Corp. of St. Petersburg, Florida, with estimated sales over $600 million; and Hickman Williams and Co. of Livonia, Michigan, with annual sales around $290 million. The top ten coal distributors in 1997 were Atlantic Richfield Co.; Arch Mineral Corp.; A.T. Massey Coal. Co. Inc.; Consol Energy Inc.; Cyprus AMAX Minerals Co.; Kennecott Energy Co.; Kerr-McGee Coal Co.; Peabody Holding Co.; Texas Utilities Co.; and Zeigler Coal Holding Co. According to the Energy Information Administration, these top 10 companies accounted for 53 percent of the total market.

FURTHER READING

Coal Distribution Report. Energy Information Administration. Available from: http://www.eia.doe.gov/cneaf/coal/cia/t60p01.txt.

U.S. Census Bureau. *1992 Census of Wholesale Trade.* Washington: GPO, 1995.

U.S. Census Bureau. *1997 Census of Wholesale Trade.* Washington: GPO, 1999.

Ward's Business Directory of U.S. Private and Public Companies 2000. Gale Group, 2000.

Wholesale and Retail Trade USA '98. Gale Group, 1998.

SIC 5063

ELECTRICAL APPARATUS AND EQUIPMENT, WIRING SUPPLIES, AND CONSTRUCTION MATERIALS

This category covers establishments primarily engaged in the wholesale distribution of electrical power equipment for the generation, transmission, distribution, or control of electric energy; electrical construction materials for outside power transmission lines and for electrical systems; and electric light fixtures and bulbs. Construction contractors primarily engaged in installing electrical systems and equipment from their own stock are classified in **SIC 1731: Electrical Work.**

NAICS Code(s)

444190 (Other Building Material Dealers)

421610 (Electrical Apparatus and Equipment, Wiring Supplies and Construction Material Wholesalers)

Industry Snapshot

Following a relatively stagnant period in the early 1990s, sales of electrical equipment picked up significantly. By 1997, sales had grown by 5.2 percent over the previous year. However, 1998 marked a slow down in sales, a trend that was expected to continue in subsequent years. Wholesalers of electrical equipment had already responded to the industry's slump of the late 1980s and early 1990s by consolidating with competitors and improving customer service, trends that continued even after the market for these goods began to improve. These steps were made necessary by increased competition from non-traditional outlets for electrical equipment. Still, wholesalers remained the largest category of distributors for these items, sales of which reached $91 billion dollars in 1997. Like other wholesalers, those who deal in electrical apparatus and equipment benefited from the sustained growth of the U. S. economy in the second half of the 1990s.

Organization and Structure

Electrical equipment wholesale companies, or merchant wholesalers, purchase or take title to goods produced by manufacturers and resell the goods to retailers, or other wholesalers, at a profit. They help to lubricate the U.S. economy by providing retailers with goods to sell, and by finding and cultivating markets for manufacturers' products. Historically, this industry has been fragmented, with establishments focusing on local markets and specializing in particular items. For instance, California alone had more than 1,600 electrical equipment wholesale establishments in 1997. Still, throughout the 1990s, a few large wholesalers acquired smaller, regional outlets in order to gain efficiency of scale for their operations.

Transactions by merchant wholesalers account for a majority of equipment sales. In addition to merchant wholesaling, some transactions involve agents and brokers. Although the agents and brokers work as middlemen between producers and retailers, they are usually compensated directly by the manufacturer in the form of fees and commissions. The third type of wholesale establishments are manufacturers' sales offices and branches, which sell their equipment directly to retailers.

In addition to buying, selling, and shipping products between producers and retailers, wholesale companies have recently begun to provide more value-added services to their customers. In the case of industrial electrical equipment, wholesalers often provide engineering and technical consulting. They might also arrange to have products customized or repaired. Wholesalers of contractor and consumer electrical supplies might arrange special financing plans, help retailers develop just-in-time inventory systems, or provide overnight delivery services for specialty items. Many wholesalers also incorporate a shifting price scale that favors customers who purchase the most.

Products. The wholesale market for electrical supplies is divided into industrial and consumer products. Wholesalers deliver industrial electrical equipment primarily to utility companies and to firms engaged in heavy industries. The four primary types of equipment are transformers, switchgears, motors and generators, and relays and controls. Transformers are used by utilities to regulate and deliver power to their customers and by industries to change voltage for varying equipment needs. Smaller transformers are used in a variety of products from doorbells to low-voltage lighting and security systems. Switchgear products include panelboards, circuit breakers, fuses, and other devices used to generate, transmit, and distribute electricity. Motors and generators are used by utilities, industry, and residential consumers alike. Industrial relays and controls are used to start, regulate, stop, and protect electric motors. With the expansion of the Internet and company intranets, an increasing amount of electrical wholesale companies are expanding into the data and communications market, offering a wide range of structured cables and systems.

The total market for industrial electrical equipment in 1998, a large part of which was served by wholesalers, was almost $37 billion. Transformers accounted for 15 percent of the market, while switchgear and complementary apparatus represented about 21 percent. Motors and generators made up about 32 percent of sales, as did relay and control devices. While the market for these items increased by 5 percent between 1996 and 1997, the next two years saw slower growth of only about 1 percent annually.

Products offered by wholesalers for residential, commercial, and construction markets were numerous. Major retailers of such equipment included hardware stores, home centers, discount stores, and construction supply centers. Major product categories were: lighting fixtures, current-carrying wiring devices for residential homes, and non-current-carrying devices for commercial applications. These categories encompassed such items as light bulbs, lugs and connectors, insulators, hangers and fasteners, flashlights, conduits, circuit breakers and panels, coaxial cable, capacitors, alarm systems, batteries, wire, and other related supplies.

The market for electric lighting and wiring equipment, most of which was served by wholesalers, rose significantly in the mid-1990s, and in 1996, the total value of shipments exceeded $24.5 billion. This figure represented an increase of 24 percent over four years. Wiring devices and lighting fixtures represented nearly equal shares of that figure. In 1997 sales of lighting fixtures for commercial and industrial uses reached $4 billion, almost double the $2.3 billion in sales for residential use. In addition, sales of miscellaneous items, like batteries and flashlights, added significantly to non-industrial wholesale revenues.

BACKGROUND AND DEVELOPMENT

Although Benjamin Franklin conducted some of the first experiments related to electricity in the mid-1700s, public supplies of electricity were not a reality in most advanced countries until the late 1800s. Not until after the turn of the century, moreover, did identifiable industries arise to meet the demand for industrial and residential electrical equipment. Indeed, rapid U.S. industrialization between 1900 and 1929 spurred demand growth for all types of electrical equipment, as well as for wholesale and retail distributors that could bring products to the market.

The U.S. economic expansion after World War II proved to be a boon for electrical equipment wholesalers. As the population expanded, particularly in the 1960s, sales of industrial equipment to utilities and factories ballooned. Sales of electrical supplies and lighting fixtures to residential markets also accelerated, as housing starts soared past 1 million per year in the 1960s, and fluctuated as high as 1.4 million annually during the 1970s.

Wholesalers became an integral factor in the distribution of electrical equipment and supplies to all markets. Hardware stores sprang up across the United States from the 1950s through the 1970s to serve burgeoning suburbia. These outlets looked to wholesalers for help in finding and supplying products, managing inventory, and marketing their goods to consumers. Likewise, agents and brokers, as well as manufacturers' branches, helped to supply and advise industrial and utility customers that sought heavy-duty electrical equipment. Wholesalers also devised catalogs and distribution facilities to help them efficiently supply contractors, property managers, and other commercial customers.

Although sales growth began to slow in the late 1970s, partially as a result of the energy crunch, wholesalers continued to realize steady growth in demand throughout the early 1980s. The reduction in sales growth for new industrial and utility installations was partially offset by an increase in sales of replacement equipment and retrofits. Furthermore, strong commercial and residential construction markets were boosted by a rise in sales of electrical supplies for home remodeling and repair.

By the mid-1980s, wholesalers supplied the lion's share of a $23 billion market for industrial and utility equipment, and a $12 billion market for lighting and wiring supplies. Total merchant wholesale sales of electrical goods, which included many products sold by other industries, approached $90 billion. Revenue and profit growth remained relatively steady through 1988, as sales of all electrical wholesale goods climbed to $110 billion and lighting and wiring sales jumped to about $14 billion.

The electrical apparatus and equipment wholesale industry began to experience difficulty in the late 1980s and early 1990s. A U.S. economic recession compounded problems that had begun in the early 1980s. Demand for electric energy equipment, for instance, stagnated at about $21 billion (in constant 1987 dollars), and sales of electric wiring and lighting devices fell more than 1 percent per year between 1989 and 1992. Plummeting housing starts contributed substantially to declines in both market segments. The subsequent economic recovery boosted both residential and commercial construction, which in turn brought growth in the sales of electrical apparatus. The total $91 billion market for these goods in 1996 marked an increase of nearly 22 percent from 1992.

Competition. Even as their market grew, wholesalers had to deal with new sources of competition. Giant hardware supply warehouses, such as The Home Depot, Inc., and Lowe's Companies, Inc., continued to expand, encroaching on markets traditionally dominated by hardware and lighting stores. These organizations often sidestepped the traditional wholesale industry by going straight to the manufacturer for their products, often ordering products in bulk at a lower price. Many wholesalers feared that their markets could wane while profit margins withered. Do-it-yourself homeowners, as well as construction and maintenance contractors, discovered that they could obtain lighting, wiring, and other electrical supplies at significant discounts at the larger supply warehouses, compared to electrical wholesalers and specialty distributors. Supply warehouses were not able to compete as easily in the commercial and industrial product markets. Since opening their first stores in the early 1980s, some warehouse chains realized stunning growth rates. By 1999, Home Depot alone had more than 900 stores. In the late 1990s a new form of competition emerged both for traditional wholesalers and large superstores. Manufacturers began offering their wares directly to their customers on the Internet. Direct Internet sales offered manufacturers the opportunity to sell their products directly to the end customer, eliminating the middle man and increasing their profits. This development created agreement among competitors on the same side of the issue, as some traditional wholesalers expressed support for Home Depot's threat not to deal with manufacturers who competed with their stores.

Current Conditions

With the growth in the market for electrical apparatus and wiring throughout the middle and end of the 1990s, major wholesalers became able to use their resources to acquire smaller regional distributors. Besides increasing the larger wholesalers' market share, these acquisitions also created more locations for them throughout the United States. Some large companies also increased their market share by landing exclusive contracts as suppliers for government agencies.

Electrical apparatus and wiring wholesalers also sought ways to improve customer service as a means of improving sales. Like wholesalers of other kinds of goods, electrical supply distributors turned to the Internet as a potentially powerful and convenient tool. However, by the late 1990s the percentage of their business done on the Internet remained insignificant. W.W. Grainger, Inc., for instance, received less than 1 percent of its revenue from Internet sales. Explanations for why the customers for these products were slow to make use of the new technology ranged from their lack of computers with Internet capability to their insistence on negotiating prices instead of ordering online.

Another method by which wholesalers attempted to increase customer convenience was through cooperation with non-competing wholesalers. In these arrangements, a wholesaler of electrical equipment would agree to pool their catalogs with distributors of other kinds of items that might be of interest to their customers. Such arrangements offered customers one-stop shopping.

Industry Leaders

While some *Fortune* 500 firms participated in the electrical apparatus and equipment, wiring supplies, and construction materials wholesale industry, many local and regional firms did business around the country. None of the largest companies exclusively sold items that fall into this category.

Graybar Electric Company, Inc., an employee-owned company based in St. Louis, Missouri, generated $3.7 billion in sales in 1998, most of that amount coming from electrical apparatus and equipment. About 40 percent of its sales went to electrical contractors. Forced to downsize and reorganize during the construction slump of the late 1980s and early 1990s, the company diversified once the economy improved. After buying a minority interest in a Canadian computer networking firm in 1994, Graybar divided its operations between its electrical products and its data and communications line of goods. Graybar continued to expand internationally in 1998, opening a subsidiary in Chile.

WESCO International, Inc., was the second largest wholesaler of electrical apparatus and equipment behind Graybar, earning more than $3 billion in sales in 1998. Originally a part of Westinghouse, WESCO became an entity unto itself in 1994. The company embarked on a series of a acquisitions, including Industrial Electric Supply Company and Statewide Electrical Supply in 1999. WESCO expanded from 250 branches in 1994 to more than 330 in 1998, with locations in Europe and Asia as well as North America.

Besides selling electrical equipment, W.W. Grainger, Inc., of Lincolnshire, Illinois. provided a wide variety of industrial supplies and equipment to its customers. Its total sales for 1998 reached $4.3 billion, a significant portion of which came from electric motors and lighting equipment. Grainger was one of the first electrical wholesalers to use the Internet as a sales tool. Its catalog went online in 1995, and in 1999 Grainger opened the online store OrderZone.com.

Workforce

Employment in the overall wholesaling industry grew slightly along with the U.S. economy in the middle and late 1990s, even though the economic slump in the preceding years had led to workforce reduction, accompanied by increased automation. In 1997 6.6 million people were employed in wholesaling, up from 6 million in 1992. In the field of durable goods wholesaling, which includes electrical apparatus and equipment, nearly 4 million people were employed in 1997, 500,000 more than five years earlier. The Bureau of Labor Statistics projected small growth in the wholesale workforce into the twenty-first century.

AMERICA AND THE WORLD

The market for electrical apparatus and equipment is an international one, and major wholesalers in the field have operations around the world. Besides having distribution centers in other countries, the 1990s saw American wholesale firms creating alliances with, and buying interests in, companies in other countries. Graybar, for example, invested in Canadian companies. WESCO likewise expanded its global operations. Besides its outlets in the Middle East and the Pacific Rim, the company also joined forces with an Australian mining and steel company in 1997.

RESEARCH AND TECHNOLOGY

Technological advances in the electrical supplies wholesale industry were limited primarily due to automation and information systems, namely incorporating the Internet into their business operations. Major distributors put their catalogs online to allow customers to place orders conveniently. Some wholesalers joined with other companies that distributed different kinds of goods that their customers were likely to need, providing one-stop online shopping by making multiple catalogs available at one website.

These arrangements were expected to appeal to large customers who negotiated prices for bulk purchase in advance. Such firms could use secured Internet connections to conduct their dealings with the wholesalers with whom they had contracts. Some occasional buyers would also find the Internet convenient for quickly filling one-time orders. Many purchasers from wholesalers, though, might still prefer in-person negotiation for their orders. Hardware stores, for instance, need to keep just the right amount of inventory in stock. WESCO developed a way to help such customers in remote areas by sending out trucks stocked with supplies, which the customer could then purchase as needed when the truck arrived. This method cut out the delay between order and delivery that even the Internet couldn't remove.

FURTHER READING

Avery, Susan. "To Manage Content, Distributors Form Partnerships." *Purchasing,* 10 December 1998.

Cremeans, John E., ed. *Handbook of North American Industry.* Washington, DC: Bernan Press, 1999.

Daniels, Steve. "High-Tech Turmoil Hits Firms: Computer Snafus Bruise Grainger." *Crain's Chicago Business,* 26 July 1999.

Darnay, Arsen J., ed. *Manufacturing USA.* Detroit: Gale Research, 1996.

Darnay, Arsen J., and Gary Alampi, eds. *Wholesale and Retail Trade USA.* Detroit: Gale Research, 1995.

"Distributor Alliances Continue to Form, Strengthen." *Purchasing,* 15 February 1996.

Elliott, Heidi. "E-Commerce Coming, But What Is It? Distributors Counting on the Internet, But Not Yet Certain Exactly What Services Will Be There." *Electronic News,* 8 February 1999.

Frook, John Evan. "Grainger Retools Strategy to Sell Web Marketing: Finds Its Customers Ill-Equipped, Salesforce Reluctant." *Crain's Chicago Business,* 16 November 1998.

"Graybar Electric Company, Inc." *Hoover's Online.* Austin, TX: Hoover's, 1999. Available from http://www.hoovers.com.

"Home Depot Tells Vendors to Stay off the Net." *Industrial Distribution,* September 1999.

National Electrical Manufacturers Association. "NEMA: Setting Standards for Excellence." Rosslyn, VA: 1996. Available from http://www.nema.org.

U.S. Bureau of the Census. *1995 Annual Survey of Manufactures, Value of Product Shipments.* Washington, DC: U.S. Bureau of the Census, January 1996. Available from http://www.census.gov.

U.S. Bureau of the Census. *1997 Economic Census.* Washington, DC: U.S. Bureau of the Census, 1999. Available from http://factfinder.census.gov.

U. S. Bureau of the Census. *Statistical Abstract of the United States.* Washington, DC: GPO, 1998.

U. S. Industry & Trade Outlook '99. New York: McGraw-Hill, 1999.

"WESCO International, Inc." *Hoover's Online.* Austin, TX: Hoover's, 1999. Available from http://www.hoovers.com.

"WESCO Managers Execute $1.1 Billion Buyout." *Industrial Distribution,* June 1998.

"WESCO on Wheels Improves Service to Remote Locations." *Purchasing,* 16 September 1999.

"W.W. Grainger, Inc." *Hoover's Online.* Austin, TX: Hoover's, 1999. Available from http://www.hoovers.com.

SIC 5064

ELECTRICAL APPLIANCES, TELEVISION AND RADIO SETS

This industry is comprised of establishments engaged in the wholesale distribution of household electrical appliances (such as refrigerators, freezers, dishwashers, and laundry equipment), household and motor vehicle electronic sound or video equipment, and radio and television sets. The industry also includes establishments primarily engaged in the wholesale distribution of household nonelectric appliances (such as gas clothes dryers and gas refrigerators).

NAICS Code(s)

421620 (Electrical Appliance, Television and Radio Set Wholesalers)

According to Gary Shapiro, president of the Consumer Electronics Manufacturers Association (CEMA), 1998 was one of the most important years for his industry with its transition to predominantly digital technology. This transformation posed many challenges; for example, the industry already enjoyed high household product penetration, so convincing consumers to replace analog technology products with similar products carrying digital technology would be difficult. MP3 technology, which allows Internet surfers to download digital music from World Wide Web sites, poses another challenge, because ease of access makes it more difficult for the music copyright holders to receive compensation for their work. CEMA worked with Congress to protect the interests of the consumer electronics industry (which manufactures MP3s and similar technologies) while bringing the United States into compliance with the World Intellectual Property Organization's copyright treaty. Despite these challenges, the consumer electronics industry enjoyed a record sales volume increase of 5 percent, to $76 billion in factory sales for 1998.

Industry insiders worry that the advent of digital technology will adversely affect sales in categories that have not fully transformed from analog technology. However, combination television/video cassette recorder sales increased to 3,147,000 units in 1998, totaling $832 million. Sales of projection televisions increased 16 percent to top one million units for the first time, representing a $1.6 billion value. The color television category as a whole reached its second-highest sales mark in history with 27 million sets, and a factory value of $8.7 billion. Video cassette recorder sales of 18 million units, worth $2.4 billion, broke the previous year's record peak. Portable audio products' factory sales amounted to $2.5 billion, an increase of 9 percent.

Sales increases in most categories of electrical appliances were similar to the sales increases experienced in the consumer electronics industry. Gas range shipments increased by 6.2 percent, from 186,000 in January 1996 to 197,500 in January 1997, and freezer shipments increased 6.8 percent from 90,000 in January 1996 to 96,100 in January 1997. However, electric range shipments declined by 1.7 percent, from 303,100 in January 1996 to 297,800 in January 1997, and refrigerator shipments fell 3.3 percent, from 564,500 in January 1996 to 554,800 in January 1997. Dryers, both gas and electric, had a 1.9 percent increase, offset by a 2.7 percent drop in automatic washer sales, resulting in an 0.5 percent drop in total home laundry equipment shipments.

According to the 1992 Census of Wholesale Trade, a total of 3,785 electrical appliance, television, and radio wholesalers posted sales in excess of $46.9 billion. Statistics from CEMA suggested a steady increase in sales for consumer electronics wholesalers over the subsequent four years. For 1993, CEMA reported wholesalers posted $51.0 billion in sales. Sales rose to $56 billion in 1994, $62 billion in 1995, and an estimated $68.0 billion for 1996. Between January 1996 and January 1997, shipments increased in all categories tracked by CEMA except laser disc players, which declined 41.5 percent from 13,018 shipments to 7,613. But in all other categories of televisions and related equipment (color televisions, color television/VCR combinations, projection televisions, home VCRs, and camcorders), the increase in shipments averaged from 0.6 percent (color televisions) to 20.8 percent (camcorders).

One of the trends that will help the continued increase in television and related product sales is the growing interest in direct-to-home satellite systems. As of March 1997, more than 1 million subscribers a year were being drawn away from cable, bringing the total who have this equipment to more than 4.4 million subscribers. This 1 million subscriber shift enabled an additional 322,000 households to downgrade cable options to ''basic'' service, according to estimates from a national survey conducted by CEMA. CEMA estimated that the switch resulted in a $1.4 billion annual revenue loss for the cable industry.

The survey, based on 1,000 randomly selected direct-to-home satellite owners, found that 87 percent purchased their equipment to improve picture quality. Given that 96 percent of those surveyed said they would recommend this technology to their friends, this trend is likely to impact wholesale sales of televisions and related appliances. Similarly, the advent of digital television broadcasts on November 1, 1998, is good for the consumer electronics industry. CEMA estimates that 30 percent of American households will have digital television sets by 2006, a prediction that will fuel sales in the consumer electronics industry.

Further Reading

Kitchen, Steve. ''Annual Report on American Industry: Consumer Durables.'' *Forbes,* 13 January 1997.

Shapiro, Gary. ''1998 and Beyond.'' Available from http://204.245.190.25/market_overview/uceit_99/1998.cfm

U.S. Department of Commerce. *Statistical Abstract of the United States 1996: The National Data Book.* Washington DC: Bureau of the Census, 1996.

SIC 5065

ELECTRONIC PARTS AND EQUIPMENT, NOT ELSEWHERE CLASSIFIED

This industry consists of companies that wholesale electronic parts and electronic communications equipment not classified elsewhere. Industry products include semiconductors, modems, telephone equipment, amateur radio communications equipment, recording, cassettes, diskettes, and public address equipment.

NAICS CODE(S)

421690 (Other Electronic Parts and Equipment Wholesalers)

The electronic parts and equipment industry began in the late nineteenth century, when it primarily served the telegraph industry. After Alexander Graham Bell invented the telephone (1875), and Thomas Edison invented the light bulb (1879), the United States used more electricity. And, as manufacturers offered new electric inventions, wholesale distribution systems were developed to deliver these products to market.

The industry fell into a recession during the 1980s but rebounded by 1987, only to experience a second setback in industry growth—to less than 2 percent—in 1991. Conditions improved slightly in late 1992, as delivery lead times increased; the number of electronic parts distribution companies totaled 15,329 by the end of that year, and combined industry sales totaled $106 billion. Yet, just as industry forecasters predicted that U.S. exporters would sell more to developing markets in Asia, Western Europe, Canada, and Mexico, the industry suffered a recurrence of depressed conditions. A renewed slump in the distribution industry began in 1995 and lasted for three years. During the remainder of the 1990s, industry players moved toward consolidation; and, due in part to instability in Latin America and an economic crisis in the Far East, U.S. exports slowed dramatically. Distributors rushed to synchronize supply with demand during this decline, which, unfortunately, lasted into the third quarter of 1998. Finally, near the end of the fiscal year, stock prices in the industry hit bottom—a four-year low that was broken by a subtle climb in prices at the beginning of 1999. Distribution margins, however, remained low, as key consumers such as computer manufacturers continued to drive prices down with bulk purchases. Observers reiterated that success in the distribution channels hinged on the ability to sustain growth in the existing high-volume transaction environment.

In early 1999, guardedly optimistic forecasters predicted a turnaround for the electronic component distribution industry, and analysts pressed firms to merge and consolidate in apprehension of a continually temperamental economic climate. Analysts further concluded that the continued growth of distribution channels necessitated the conscientious implementation of dynamic efficiency controls to coordinate supply with demand within a fluctuating marketplace.

During the early 1990s, the nation's largest independent electrical and telecommunications distributor was Graybar Electric Company, Incorporated. The diversified Graybar, headquartered in St. Louis, Missouri, operated at 275 U.S. locations throughout North and Central America, and the Pacific Rim.

Dominance of the industry shifted to Arrow Electronics, Incorporated of Melville, New York in the mid-1990s, although Graybar continued its activity. Arrow, primarily a supplier of passive components, interconnect products, and computer peripherals, boasted key clients including Intel and Texas Instruments. Arrow moved to acquire a number of smaller distributors throughout the remainder of the decade, and by 1998 the distributor employed 9,700 workers. Arrow reported $8.345 billion in annual sales that year, of which an estimated 65 percent were from semiconductors.

Second to Arrow in the distribution industry, Avnet, Incorporated of Phoenix, Arizona derived approximately 50 percent of its business from the distribution of semiconductors to major producers including National Semiconductor, Intel, and Advanced Micro Devices. Avnet reported $6.35 billion annual sales during fiscal 1999 and increased its employee count by 5.7 percent to achieve a workforce of 8,200. In January of 1999, when Arrow announced a merger with Bell Industries' Electronics Distribution Group, Avnet rebounded with the acquisition of Marshall Industries in mid-year. Arrow Electronics and Avnet thereby commanded over 45 percent of the market, according to a report in *Electronic Buyer News.* Forecasters predicted continued single-digit growth as the industry moved into the third millennium.

FURTHER READING

Damron, Rob, ''Business & Finance: Is this upturn cyclical or seasonal? . . .'' *Electronic Buyer News,* 9 November 1998.

Jorgensen, Barbara, ''Distribution: More globalization in '99?,'' *Electronic Buyer News,* 4 January 1999.

Matsumoto, Craig, ''News: Avnet-Marshall deal opens gate for Asian IC makers.'' *Electronic Engineering Times,* 5 July 1999.

Sheerin, Matthew, ''Viewpoints: Distribution and the urge to merge.'' *Electronic Buyer News,* 12 July 1999.

Walser, Clarke L., ''Quarterly Financial Review: Distribution: Distribs mulling murky 1999.'' *Electronic Buyer News,* 8 February 1999.

U.S. Bureau of the Census. *1987 Census of Wholesale Trade: Geographic Area Series.* Washington, DC: GPO, 1989.

SIC 5072

HARDWARE

This industry comprises establishments primarily engaged in the wholesale distribution of general hardware items and cutlery. Products include bolts, nuts, washers, rivets, screws, brads, locks (and related materials), and hand tools (including power handtools). Establishments primarily engaged in the wholesale distribution of nails, non-insulated wire, and screening, however, are included in **SIC 5051: Metals Service Centers and Offices.**

NAICS Code(s)

421710 (Hardware Wholesalers)

In 1996, there were an estimated 8,000 establishments engaged in the wholesale distribution of hardware, a dramatic increase from 1991's total of 7,083. In 1994, hardware wholesalers employed more than 100,000 people and posted an annual payroll in excess of $3 billion. Wholesale sales reached more than $8.7 billion, with the top four co-op companies claiming 95 percent of that total. Cotter & Company (True Value) had $2.6 billion in sales, ACE Hardware generated $2.3 billion, ServiStar claimed $1.7 billion, and Hardware Wholesalers Inc. (HWI) had $1.6 billion. All remaining co-op members shared nearly $4.1 million in sales. By 1996, the industry as a whole was expected to generate more than $35 billion in sales.

During the 1990s, the hardware industry began to change. The combined effects of consolidation and the growth of the ''Do-It-Yourself'' (DIY) industry squashed the small, independent hardware stores, the industry's traditional customers, and simultaneously expanded the dominance of the large, warehouse-style retailers, such as Home Depot, which made purchases directly from manufacturers. In 1999, Home Depot expected to at least double its chain of 800 stores by 2003. Lowe's followed the lead of Home Depot and, after it acquired Eagle Hardware's 36-store chain in 1999, the company planned to add between 80 and 85 stores to its base of 484. Home Depot and Lowe's were expected to generate sales of more than $50 billion the same year, which is 25 percent of the DIY market.

In early 1997, the DIY industry had a value of $140 billion. The top 100 retailers held about one-half of the market share. One response to this challenge was the 1997 merger of Cotter & Company with ServiStar Coast to Coast Corporation. This venture helped its members by reducing costs and improving efficiency, and it was expected to benefit customers in terms of lower prices. The new company, TruServ Corporation, has annual sales of more than $3 billion and employs almost 6,000.

Cotter & Company is the largest full-line hardware distributor in the United States, as measured by sales volume. Cotter, a privately held dealer cooperative with headquarters in Chicago, Illinois, operates 15 distribution centers and employs more than 4,000 people. The company supplies nearly 6,000 True Value members across the United States and in 50 countries. In 1995, Cotter generated revenues of $2.4 billion.

Another merger involved Do it Best Corp.'s (formerly Hardware Wholesalers Inc.) acquisition of Our Own Hardware. Hardware Wholesalers had 1997 sales around $1 billion and employed more than 1,000. In 1999, Do It Best Corporation beat both Home Depot and Lowe's to Web prominence and became the largest hardware store on the Internet, with more than 70,000 items for sale. Other dealer-owned wholesale companies have commitments to e-commerce, unlike the big three retailers.

ACE Hardware Corporation, based in Oak Brook, Illinois is second in sales volume. ACE, another dealer-owned cooperative, supplied products to more than 5,000 stores through its 18 distribution centers. In 1998, the company reported sales of $3.1 billion, and employed more than 4,700 people.

Further Reading

Darnay, Arsen J., and Gary Alampi, eds. *Wholesale and Retail Trade USA.* Detroit: Gale Research, 1995.

Dobie, Maureen.''Do-It Best Learns Internet a Good Place to Market Hardware.'' *Indianapolois Business Journal,* 30 August 1999.

''Home Center Industry Tailors Itself to Consumers.'' *Chain Store Age,* August 1999.

Lazich, Robert S., ed. *Market Share Reporter.* Detroit: Gale Research, 1997.

Ward's Business Directory of U.S. Private and Public Companies 2000. Detroit: Gale Group, 2000.

elcome to Home Improvement Market.'' Radnor, PA: Chilton Company, 1997. Available from http://www.homemkt.com/.

''Welcome to Hoover's Online.'' Austin, TX: Hoover's, Inc., 1997. Available from http://www.hoovers.com.

Wholesale and Retail Trade USA, 2nd Edition. Detroit: Gale Group, 1998.

SIC 5074

PLUMBING AND HEATING EQUIPMENT AND SUPPLIES (HYDRONICS)

This industry consists of companies that primarily wholesale hydronic plumbing and heating equipment and supplies. Industry products include: steam and hot water boilers, prefabricated fireplaces, oil burners, plumbing fixtures, solar heating panels, and water softeners. Companies that primarily install plumbing and heating equipment from their own stock are in **SIC 1711: Plumbing, Heating and Air Conditioning.**

NAICS CODE(S)

444190 (Other Building Material Dealers)

421720 (Plumbing and Heating Equipment and Supplies (Hydronics) Wholesalers)

The British conglomerate Wolseley plc, the largest distributor of heating and plumbing products worldwide, owned two of the top three industry leaders in this category: Ferguson Enterprises, Inc. (purchased in 1982 and based in Newport News, Virginia) and Familian Corp. (purchased in 1987 and based in Los Angeles, California). On June 18, 1998, Wolseley announced its integration of Familian into Ferguson with the new, single entity headed by Ferguson president Charles A. Banks. The companies generated approximately $2.3 billion in combined sales for 1997. The merger brought the employee count of the combined company to almost 7,000 and the number of locations to 391 in 41 states, the District of Columbia, and Puerto Rico.

According to trade publications, Ferguson ranked as the largest distributor of plumbing supplies in the United States; the third largest for pipe, valves, and fittings (PVF); and the fifth largest for heating and cooling (HVAC) equipment. Ferguson achieved its market dominance through integrated inventory strategies: first, local market needs determined branch inventory; second, Ferguson located its distribution centers strategically to maximize accessibility; and third, Ferguson offered just-in-time inventory delivery for products not in stock. Primus, Inc., of Dayton, Ohio, represented the other of the top three industry leaders before the consolidation of Ferguson and Familian. Primus garnered sales of $829 million with 2,962 employees in 1998, $780 million in 1997 sales with 2,175 employees, and $700 million in 1996 sales with 2,150 employees.

In 1994, according to the U.S. Department of Commerce, 9,341 establishments did business in this industry, compared to 8,931 in 1987. Of this total, 7,930 were merchant wholesalers (wholesalers who take title to the goods they sell); 1,118 were agents, brokers, and commission merchants. The remaining 278 were manufacturers' sales branches and offices. Combined sales for all establishments topped $27.8 billion in 1992, compared to $23.2 billion in 1987.

According to the *Annual Benchmark Report for Wholesale Trade,* wholesalers of hardware, plumbing and heating equipment, and supplies saw April 1999 sales (seasonally adjusted) of $68.7 billion. This amount was projected to increase through 2000.

FURTHER READING

''Ferguson Enterprises, Inc.,'' 21 November 1999. Available from http://www.ferguson.com.

Hoover's Company Capsules. Austin, TX: Hoover's, Inc., 1999. Available from http://www.hoovers.com.

''Primus, Inc.,'' 21 November 1999. Available from www.activedayton.com/business/localbusiness/mv100/primus.html.

U.S. Bureau of the Census. *1992 Census of Wholesale Trade.* Washington, D.C.: GPO, 1995.

''Wolseley, plc,'' 21 November 1999. Available from http://www.wolseley.com.

SIC 5075

WARM AIR HEATING AND AIR CONDITIONING EQUIPMENT AND SUPPLIES

This industry includes companies that wholesale warm air heating and air conditioning equipment and supplies. Industry products include air conditioning equipment (except room units), air pollution control equipment, electric heating furnaces, humidifiers and dehumidifiers (except portable units), and ventilating equipment.

NAICS CODE(S)

421730 (Warm Air Heating and Air-Conditioning Equipment and Supplies Wholesalers)

In 1997 the U.S. Census Bureau reported that there were 799 establishments manufacturing equipment for air conditioning, warm air heating, and commercial and industrial refrigeration. These operations shipped $22.9 billion worth of merchandise, spent $12.5 billion on materials, and invested $569 million in buildings and other structures, machinery, and equipment. About 63 percent of these establishments employed at least 20 people, and 33 percent employed at least 100 people. The largest concentrations of facilities in this classification were in Texas, California, New York, Illinois, and Florida.

Some growth was predicted for this industry from selling through nontraditional channels such as the Internet. Changing Environmental Protection Agency (EPA) regulations were also expected to increase sales, since the phasing out of older refrigerants would create a demand for replacement units. Supermarkets, restaurants, and high-rise buildings were among those converting to new refrigeration and air conditioning systems through the year 2000.

The U.S. Census Bureau estimated that the main product of 133 of these establishments was mechanically refrigerated, self-contained heat transfer equipment. These operations shipped $5.4 billion worth of merchandise and employed 29,110 people. Products in this category accounted for about 19 percent of total industry shipments in 1997. The largest value of shipments in this segment originated in New York, Georgia, Tennessee, Texas, and Kentucky. This industry employed 120,002 people, including 91,566 production workers who earned an average hourly wage of $12.65. Total payroll was $3.7 billion.

Unitary air-conditioners, not including air source heat pumps, were the main product at 55 facilities. These operations shipped $6.0 billion worth of merchandise and employed 24,194 people. Products in this category accounted for 20 percent of total industry shipments. The largest value of shipments in this segment originated in Pennsylvania, Texas, and Ohio. Room air conditioners and dehumidifiers, except portable units, accounted for 4 percent.

Warm air furnaces (including duct furnaces and humidifiers) and electric comfort heating equipment were the main products at 33 establishments. These operations shipped $1.7 billion worth of merchandise and employed 7,234 people. Products in this category accounted for 9 percent of total industry shipments. The largest value of shipments in this segment originated in Tennessee and Ohio.

Air source heat pumps, not including room air-conditioners, accounted for 4 percent of the industry's shipments; and ground and ground water source heat pumps accounted for less than 1 percent. Parts and accessories for air-conditioning and heat transfer equipment accounted for 9 percent. The largest value of shipments in this segment originated in Tennessee, New York, Missouri, and Ohio.

Among companies whose primary products fell into this classification, ACR Group Inc. (Philadelphia, Pennsylvania) had 330 employees and sales of $117.9 million in 1998. Previously known as Time Energy Systems Inc., this firm manufactured various climate control products. Another company, Gensco Inc. of Houston, Texas, had 500 employees and estimated sales of $117 million. Gensco manufactured furnace duct pipe, elbows and fittings, and custom-cut flexible ducting.

Of other diversified companies that made products in this category, W.W. Grainger Inc. (Lake Forest, Illinois) was one of the largest with 15,250 employees and sales of $4.34 billion in 1998, up from $3.2 billion in 1995, and $2.6 billion in 1993. The company's Grainger Division, a nationwide distributor of air compressors, air conditioning and refrigeration equipment and components, and other tools and equipment, served more than one million customers and had several hundred branches located nationwide. During the 1990s the company put its 67,000-item product catalogue on the World Wide Web and on CD-ROM to reach still more customers.

Other industry leaders included Primus Inc. (Dayton, Ohio), with 2,175 employees and sales of $780 million in 1998; and United Refrigeration Inc. (Philadelphia, Pennsylvania), with 1,175 employees and estimated sales of $384 million.

FURTHER READING

ACR Group Inc., company website. Available from http://www.acrgroup.com.

Allen, Margaret. ''United Refrigeration Eyes Expansion: Company Plans Move to Warehouse.'' *Dallas Business Journal,* 6 August 1999.

Avery, Susan. ''Grainger Develops New Web Site for 'One-Stop' MRO Purchases.'' *Purchasing,* 25 March 1999.

''Cooling Showcase: Flexibility by Design.'' *Air Conditioning, Heating & Refrigeration News,* 12 April 1999.

Darnay, Arsen J., and Gary Alampi, eds. *Wholesale and Retail Trade USA.* Detroit: Gale Research, 1995.

Gensco Inc. company website. Available from http://www.gensco.com.

Hoover's Company Capsules. Austin, TX: Hoover's, Inc., 1997. Available from http://www.hoovers.com.

Primus Inc. company website. Available from http://www.primus.au.

United Refrigeration Inc. company website. Available from http://www.uri.com.

U.S. Department of Commerce. Census Bureau. *1992 Census of Wholesale Trade.* Washington, DC: GPO, 1995.

U.S. Department of Commerce. Census Bureau. *1997 Economic Census.* Washington, DC: GPO, 1999. Available from http://www.census.gov/prod/ec97/97m3334d.pdf.

W.W. Grainger, Inc. company website. Available from http://www.grainger.com.

SIC 5078

REFRIGERATION EQUIPMENT AND SUPPLIES

This industry consists of companies that primarily wholesale refrigeration equipment and supplies. Industry products include beverage coolers, refrigerated display cases, drinking water coolers, ice cream cabinets, ice-making machines, walk-in and reach-in commercial refrigerators, and refrigerated soda fountain fixtures. Companies that primarily install refrigeration equipment from their own stock are in **SIC 1711: Plumbing, Heating and Air-Conditioning.**

NAICS CODE(S)

421740 (Refrigeration Equipment and Supplies Wholesalers)

In 1999, the industry experienced an acute shortage of R-134a, a key refrigerant for production, due to increased demand for use in flat-tire inflators, increased exports to fill the European demand, a scarcity raw materials to manufacture R-134a, and the shutdown of three Japanese producers of the refrigerant. R-134a prices rose more than 70 percent in February and March 1999. Refron, Inc. of Long Island City, New York, one of the market leaders, took advantage of this shortage to advertise its inventory of rare CFC refrigerants. The company's sales grew in 1998 by 2,389 new customers.

August 1999 shipments of unitary air-conditioners and heat pumps as tracked by the Air-Conditioning and Refrigeration Institute fell compared to 1998 shipments. In January 1998 sales dropped to about 350,000 from almost 400,000 in January 1997. However, shipments rose by 10.4 percent in September 1999 over the previous year, making the August drop seem like an anomaly.

Also in 1999, the Environmental Protection Agency flexed its muscle by enforcing its 1992 Refrigerants Recycling regulations. First, the EPA fined the City of New York $50 million for venting refrigerants into the atmosphere by not removing them before crushing refrigerators and air conditioners for disposal. The EPA also enforced its anti-leakage regulations by fining GTE in California $85,000 for insufficient repair work on its refrigeration system. The agency simultaneously proposed lower allowable leakage rates, dropping the acceptable level from 35 percent to as low as 5 percent, depending on the type of system.

In September 1995, the Environmental Protection Agency' enacted its Clean Air Act Amendment, tightening leak repairs for owners and operators. Still, as the economy improved and interest rates went down, refrigeration equipment and supplies sales rose during the mid-1990s.

A poor economy during the early 1990s lowered refrigeration equipment sales. Large refrigeration equipment buyers, such as supermarkets, had trouble obtaining credit, and slim profit margins effected industry expansion. Mobile vehicle refrigeration systems sales fell from 60,070 units in 1989 to 50,800 in 1990. Sales of drinking water coolers also dropped from 984,061 units in 1989 to 886,175 in 1990.

Ice-making machines sales rose, from 195,959 units in 1989 to 200,818 in 1990, but stayed below the 243,771 units sold in 1988. Among other factors, lower sales were blamed on slow growth in the fast food restaurant industry. According to one account, about 70 percent of ice machine shipments during the early 1990s were replacements rather than new purchases. In addition to the fast food industry, who use ice machines for soft drinks, other ice machine buyers include hospital emergency rooms, food processors, and pre-cast concrete pourers.

According to government statistics, there were 1,421 establishments in this industry in 1994, down from 1,513 in 1987. Combined sales totaled approximately $3.7 billion in 1996, up from $2.68 billion in 1987. Merchant wholesalers—wholesalers who take title to goods they sell—made up the largest number of these companies, with 1,252 establishments. The industry employed 10,373 people, with an annual payroll of $303 million in 1992, compared to 12,281 people paid a total of $303 million in 1987. The employment rate was also expected to fall to 11,561. California had the most establishments, with 191, and generated 12.4 percent of U.S. sales. Texas had 108 establishments and generated 7.9 percent of U.S. sales.

FURTHER READING

The Air Conditioning and Refrigeration Institute. Available at: http://www.ari.org.

Darnay, Arsen, J. and Gary Alampi, eds. *Wholesale and Retail Trade USA.* Detroit: Gale Research, 1995.

"Environmental Protection Agency." *Federal Register,* 8 August 1995. Available from http://www.epa.gov/ozone/title6/608/leakfrm.txt.

"R-134a Shortage Takes Industry by Surprise, Prices Rise," and "EPA Enforces Venting Regulations and Proposes Tougher Leak Repair Rules," *The Refron Reporter.* Available at: http://www.refron.com.

U.S. Department of Commerce, *1992 Census of Wholesale Trade.* Washington, DC: Bureau of the Census, 1995.

SIC 5082

CONSTRUCTION AND MINING (EXCEPT PETROLEUM) MACHINERY AND EQUIPMENT

This industry is comprised of establishments involved primarily in the wholesale distribution of construction, mining, and logging machinery and equipment. Industry products include cranes, dredges, and draglines (except ships), excavating machinery, front-end loaders, quarrying machinery and equipment, road construction and maintenance machinery, scaffolding, power shovels, and drilling equipment. Establishments engaged in marketing machinery and equipment for oil wells, however, are included in **SIC 5084: Industrial Machinery and Equipment.**

NAICS Code(s)

421810 (Construction and Mining (except Petroleum) Machinery and Equipment Wholesalers)

As a whole, this industry consisted of an estimated 5,300 establishments that employed more than 87,500 workers in the late 1990s. Industry sales were valued at more than $44.7 billion in 1997, representing a preinflation growth of nearly 50 percent from sales of roughly $30 billion in 1995. In the 1990s, the U.S. states with the highest sales volume included Illinois, Pennsylvania, Texas, California, Colorado, and Florida, which together accounted for more than 40 percent of the industry's output in that decade.

Demand for construction equipment fluctuated in accordance with spending in the construction industry. The industry managed to weather the global recession of the early 1990s with little more than a slowdown in sales' growth. Fairly dramatic growth characterized the industry during the mid- to late 1990s, despite a nationwide trend toward business consolidation in most other sectors. Within this industry, sharp increases were seen in both the number of establishments and the size of their workforces.

As the industry entered the new millennium, it faced increased competition from such nontraditional participants as equipment rental services and large-format warehouse retailing. Industry analysts advised distributors dealing with contractors to focus on niche products and full-service offerings in order to keep their customers from turning to do-it-yourself retail outlets. Moreover, information technologies like the Internet provided new marketing challenges to the industry by allowing potential customers to easily reach outside of their local area to obtain equipment. As a result, numerous participants in the industry, as well as their trade associations, established Internet sites to reach the newly widened market.

Two major players in the wholesaling of construction and mining machinery in the late 1990s were Caterpillar Inc. of Peoria, Illinois, and CNH Global N.V., which is headquartered in the Netherlands but operates in more than 15 countries, including the United States. Both companies manufacture this equipment and market it through their own networks of distributors. Furthermore, both companies loom large in the production of agricultural equipment, which is not covered by this industry. Caterpillar's 1999 sales totaled $19.7 billion, off 6.1 percent from 1998, while CNH Global reported 1998 sales of about $5.47 billion, down 5.6 percent from the previous year.

Further Reading

Associated Equipment Dealers, Inc. *Construction Equipment Distribution.* Oak Brook, IL: 1997. Available from http://www.aednet.org/ced/cedhmpg.htm.

Darnay, Arsen J., and Joyce Piwowarski, eds. *Wholesale and Retail Trade USA,* 2nd ed. Detroit: Gale Group, 1998.

U.S. Bureau of the Census. *1997 Economic Census.* Washington: GPO, 1999.

SIC 5083

FARM AND GARDEN MACHINERY AND EQUIPMENT

This industry is primarily engaged in the wholesale distribution of agricultural machinery and equipment, including devices used to prepare and maintain soil and to plant, protect, irrigate, and harvest crops. The industry also supplies equipment and machinery to dairy and livestock operations.

NAICS Code(s)

421820 (Farm and Garden Machinery and Equipment Wholesalers)

444210 (Outdoor Power Equipment Stores)

Industry Snapshot

In 1996, there were an estimated 7,980 establishments within this industry. Combined sales totaled almost $28.3 billion. Subcategories were farm dealers (7,238 establishments with sales of $14.72 billion); wholesale distributors to nonfarm accounts, including exports (2,150 establishments with sales of $9.6 billion); and lawn and garden machinery and equipment (1,354 establishments with sales of $5.17 billion). Total sales in 1998 were projected to increase slightly to about $28.7 billion.

Current Conditions

The trade journal *Appliance Manufacturer* projected growth in the market for consumer lawn and garden products in 1998 of 2.9 percent to almost 8 million units. The Outdoor Power Equipment Institute (OPEI) predicted increases in shipments of walk-behind power mowers in 1998 of 2.5 percent; decreases in riding mowers of 10 percent; growth for lawn and garden tractors of 6.3 percent; and increases in tiller shipments of 3.6 percent. Overall, shipments rose 5 percent to 7.7 million units for 1998.

According to the Freedonia Group, sales of U.S. power lawn and garden equipment are expected to rise 4.2 percent per year through 2002, when the market will reach nearly $9 billion. This market includes lawn mowers, turf and grounds equipment, garden tractors and tillers, trimmers and edgers, and show throwers. U.S. exports of lawn and garden equipment are two-thirds the value of imports, according to the U.S. Department of Commerce. The biggest markets for exports are Canada, France, Germany, the United Kingdom, and Australia.

Sales of tractors and combines were up significantly in 1996, according to the Equipment Manufacturers Institute. The strength of the farm economy, rising net farm income and a decline in the ratio of debt to assets, contributed to farmers' willingness to buy agricultural equipment. However, depressed grain and livestock prices led to a decrease in North American retail demand for farm equipment in 1999. Hans Becherer, chairman and CEO of Deere & Co. expected a reduction of 25 percent or more. Since the early 1970s, the number of U.S. farms has decreased by one-third, from 3 million to 2 million.

Industry Leaders

AGCO Corp., Deere & Co., and Case Corp. were important agricultural machinery manufacturers with extensive distribution networks. Consolidation continues as companies acquire other equipment makers. In 1998, Case Corp. bought Tyler Industries, a manufacturer of agricultural sprayers. Major wholesalers include RDO Equipment Co., IIC Industries Inc., and Richton International Corp.

Workforce

The industry employed approximately 84,659 people in 1996. Its annual payroll approached $2.4 billion. States with the highest number of establishments were Texas (754), California (684), Iowa (574), and Illinois (519).

Further Reading

Becherer, Hans. ''From Deere & Co.: Farming's Promising Future.'' *Des Moines Register,* 6 June 1999.

Darnay, Arsen J., and Gary Alampi, eds. *Wholesale and Retail Trade U.S.A.* Detroit: Gale Group, 1999.

''EMI Industry Outlook.'' *Implement & Tractor,* January/February 1996.

''Farm Equipment Maker Case Corp. Plans to Buy Tyler Industries of Benson'' *Minneapolis Star Tribune,* 27 March 1998.

''Lawn & Garden Equipment to Near $9 Billion in 2002'' *Appliance Manufacturer,* February 1999.

Milligan, Valerie. ''Farmers Gearing Up, Businesses Reap the Benefits.'' *Times-Republican* (Marshalltown, Iowa), 21 January 1996.

''On Solid Ground.'' *Appliance,* October 1996.

Shepherd, Mary. ''A Different Set of Tracks.'' *Implement & Tractor,* September/October 1996.

Shepherd, Mary. ''Focus Groups, Field Tests and Feedback Result in New Products.'' *Implement & Tractor,* September/October 1996.

U.S. Department of Commerce. *1992 Census of Wholesale Trade—U.S. Summary.* Washington, DC: Bureau of the Census, 1997. Available from http://www.census.gov/epcd/ec92/wc92tabl.txt.

U.S. Industry & Trade Outlook '99. U.S. Dept. of Commerce/International Trade Administration and McGraw-Hill, 1999.

Ward's Business Directory of U.S. Private and Public Companies, 2000: Companies Ranked by Sales within 4-Digit SIC. Detroit: Gale Group, 2000.

SIC 5084

INDUSTRIAL MACHINERY AND EQUIPMENT

This industry is comprised of establishments involved in the wholesale distribution of industrial machinery and equipment, not elsewhere classified. Products of the industry include chainsaws, citrus processing machinery, conveyor systems, industrial cranes, derricks, industrial diesel engines, elevators, ladders, lift trucks, machine and machinists' tools, oil refining machines, packing machinery, industrial paint spray equipment, wood pulp manufacturing machinery, industrial pumps and pumping equipment, industrial sewing machines, shoe manufacturing and repairing machinery, smelting machinery, welding machinery, and winches. The wholesale distribution of all machinery, equipment and supplies—which includes this category—makes up 15 percent the durable goods market for 1997, which totaled $193 billion.

NAICS Code(s)

421830 (Industrial Machinery and Equipment Wholesalers)

According to the U.S. Census Bureau, there were nearly 30,000 establishments employing approximately 268,000 people in the industrial machinery and equipment industry in the mid-1990s. These were subdivided into six groupings: food-processing machinery, equipment, and parts made up approximately 5 percent of sales; general-purpose industrial machinery, equipment, and parts accounted for about 36 percent; metalworking machinery, equipment, and parts accounted for 12 percent; materials handling equipment and parts accounted for 13 percent; oil well, oil refinery, and pipeline machinery, equipment, and supplies garnered 9 percent; and other industrial machinery and equipment made up the remaining 25 percent. Industry payroll in 1994 exceeded

$10 billion, and estimated 1995 combined sales totaled $105 billion. Sales were expected to only increase slightly during the late 1990s, while employment was expected to remain relatively flat.

The top states, based on number of establishments and sales volume, largely mirrored the concentration of the U.S. population. These were Texas, California, Illinois, New York, Ohio, New Jersey, North Carolina, and Michigan. Together, these eight states generated more than half of all industry sales. Pennsylvania and Florida were also leaders in number of establishments.

Industrial equipment sales suffered downturns during the early 1990s as lean fiscal performances stalled new plant investment in many sectors served by this industry. Recovery began in 1993, and the industry posted healthy sales' growth and modest profits in the mid-1990s. Trying to post higher returns, many in the industry reconfigured the way their companies distributed industrial machinery. Other industry strategies aimed at further increasing market strength included reducing costs, outsourcing distribution-related services, and seeking out new business, especially through the exploration of foreign markets. Strong prospects for export growth included Canada, Mexico, South America, the United Kingdom, France, Germany, Australia, Japan, China, and Africa.

One of the leading industrial distribution firms in the United States is Dresser Industries Inc. of Dallas, Texas, with annual sales of more than $7.4 billion and 31,000 employees. Other top companies include Unisource Worldwide Inc. of Berwyn, Pennsylvania ($7.1 billion, 14,000 employees); BET Plant Services USA Inc. of Atlanta, Georgia ($4.8 billion and 12,5000 employees); LTV Corp. of Cleveland, Ohio ($4.4 billion and 15,5000 employees); and W.W. Grainger Inc. of Lincolnshire, Illinois ($4.1 billion and 14,600 employees). Following the integrated supply trend in the wholesaling industry, W.W. Grainger established an alliance with VWR Scientific Products in 1997 to service consolidated customer orders.

Other leading companies include WESCO Distribution Inc. of Pittsburgh, Pennyslvania; Duferco Energy Group, Inc. of Houston, Texas; Stewart and Stevenson Services of Houston, Texas; Airgas Inc. of Radnor, Pennyslvania; and National-Oilwell Inc. of Houston, Texas.

FURTHER READING

Cort, Stanton. ''Industrial Distribution: How Goods Will Go to Market in the Electronic Marketplace.'' *Business Economics,* Washington, DC: January 1999.

U.S. Bureau of the Census. *1992 Census of Wholesale Trade.* Washington, DC: GPO, 1995.

———. *County Business Patterns 1994.* Washington, DC: GPO, 1996.

U.S. Industry & Trade Outlook '99. U.S. Department of Commerce/Industrial Trade Administration and McGraw-Hill, 1999.

Wholesale and Retail Trade U.S.A. 1998. Detroit: Gale Group, 1998.

Workman, Michael. ''Industrial Distribution 50th Annual Survey.'' *Industrial Distribution,* 1996. Available from http://www.manufacturing.net/magazine/id/spot/exec.htm.

SIC 5085

INDUSTRIAL SUPPLIES

This industry comprises establishments engaged in the wholesale distribution of industrial supplies that are not included in another classification. Products of the industry include abrasives, bearings, industrial diamonds, printers' ink, refractory materials, rope (except wire), valves and fittings (except plumbers' valves and fittings) and non-paper containers such as bottles, crates, drums, and metal pails.

NAICS CODE(S)

421830 (Industrial Machinery and Equipment Wholesalers)

421840 (Industrial Supplies Wholesalers)

Plumbers' valves and fittings are included in **SIC 5074: Plumbing and Heating Equipment and Supplies (Hydronics).** Wire rope is included in **SIC 5051: Metals Service Centers and Offices.**

The 15,900 establishments in this industry employed some 161,000 workers in 1995, according to the U.S. Census Bureau. These establishments were subdivided into six specialties: general-line industrial supplies (approximately 15 percent of establishments); mechanical power transmission supplies (18 percent); hydraulic and pneumatic supplies (10 percent); industrial valves and fittings (9 percent); welding supplies 13 percent); industrial containers and supplies (9 percent); and other industrial supplies such as abrasives, mechanical rubber tools, ropes, cordage, and industrial diamonds (26 percent). Estimated industry-wide sales totaled more than $60 billion in 1996.

During the early 1990s, the Industrial Distribution Association (IDA) reported that conditions within the industry were changing. The institutional market for industrial supplies, including governments, schools, and hospitals, had fallen considerably from its mid-1980s high. The IDA ranked metals fabrication supply as the leading national market for industrial suppliers. Other industries representing major clients included chemical, automotive, aircraft, and construction establishments.

The abrasives market also suffered from the general economic downturn. Noting variations by geographic region, however, abrasives sales were expected to rebound in the more robust mid- and late 1990s global economy. Abrasive distributors had strong sales in 1997 and many companies expected their 1998 sales to top 1997 levels. Certain niche markets were forecast to increase significantly.

The role of bearing distributors began changing in the late 1990s. Manufacturers began demanding that distributors form partnerships with customers, to both deliver product and to participate in the design and selection processes. This demand was in response to increasing overseas competition. The distributor is expected to bring extra value to the customer, including an integrated supply contract, just-in-time delivery and 24-hour product availability.

The integrated supply trend is expected to continue, as are acquisitions, making companies become even larger. Companies like FedEx and UPS are entering the industrial distribution market and therefore conventional distributors will have to focus on providing technical services and customer support to increase revenue. Industry experts estimate that approximately 25 percent of all large company purchases were linked to an integrated supply program in 1999.

Industry leaders include Applied Industrial Technologies of Cleveland, Ohio with annual sales of more than $1.1 billion; Motion Industries Inc. of Birmingham, Alabama with sales of $1 billion; McJunkin Corp. of Charleston, West Virginia with sales of more than $727 million; PrimeSource Corp. of Pennsauken, New Jersey with sales of more than $450 million; and Kaman Industrial Technologies of Windsor, Connecticut with sales of $400 million. Other leaders include Lawson Products Inc. of Des Plaines, Illinois; Fairmont Supply Co. of Washington, Pennsylvania; and Industrial Distributors Group Inc. of Tucker, Georgia. Some companies were acquired by others, including Dixie Bearings Inc. (a subsidiary of Applied Industrial Technologies) and Berry Bearing Co. (a subsidiary of Motion Industries Inc.).

FURTHER READING

''Abrasives Industry Braces for Growth.'' *Industrial Distribution,* February 1998.

Burke, Mel. ''Distributors Must Rethink Selling Methods.'' *Industrial Distribution,* July 1998.

Darnay, Arsen J., and Gary Alampi, eds. *Wholesale and Retail Trade USA.* Detroit: Gale Group, 1998.

Johnson, John R. ''Millennium of Change.'' *Industrial Distribution,* December 1999.

U.S. Bureau of the Census. *1992 Census of Wholesale Trade.* Washington, DC: GPO, 1995.

Ward's Business Directory of U.S. Private and Public Companies 2000. Detroit: Gale Group, 2000.

SIC 5087

SERVICE ESTABLISHMENT EQUIPMENT AND SUPPLIES

This industry comprises establishments primarily engaged in the wholesale distribution of equipment and supplies for barber shops, beauty parlors, power laundries, dry cleaning plants, upholsterers, undertakers, and related personal service establishments. Other products of the industry include carnival and amusement park equipment, firefighting equipment, janitors' supplies, and voting machines.

Service establishment equipment and supplies wholesalers specialize in one of four areas: beauty and barber equipment and supplies, custodial equipment and supplies, laundry and dry cleaning equipment and supplies, and other service establishment equipment and supplies.

NAICS CODE(S)

421850 (Service Establishment Equipment and Supplies Wholesaler)

446120 (Cosmetics, Beauty Supplies, and Perfume Stores)

Unisource Worldwide Inc. of Berwyn, Pennsylvania led the industry with sales of more than $7.4 billion for its fiscal year ended September 30, 1998. Sally Beauty Company Inc., headquartered in Denton, Texas, followed with sales of almost $1.3 billion for the same fiscal year. Fastenal Co. of Winona, Minnesota placed third in the industry with 1999 sales of $609.2 million. Reinhart Institutional Foods Inc. of La Crosse, Wisconsin generated $415 million in 1997, the most recent year available. Clark Foodservice Inc. of Elk Grove Village, Illinois rounded out the top five industry leaders with 1998 sales of $310 million.

Unisource employed 13,400 workers who together generated total revenues of $553,530. Reinhart, although it placed fourth in total sales, was second in sales-to-worker ratio, with 750 employees producing $553,333 in revenue—just under $200 per employee less than the leader Unisource. Of the top five sales leaders, Clark placed third in this category with $413,333 sales for its 750 employees, exactly $140,000 less than Reinhart. Fastenal placed fourth with $201,388 sales for its 3,025 employees, and Sally Beauty placed fifth with $161,375 in sales for its 8,000 employees.

The National Association of Wholesalers (NAW) issued a report in 1992 titled *Facing the Forces of Change 2000: The New Realities in Wholesale Distribution.* The report, based on the findings of a commissioned study undertaken by Arthur Andersen Company, included equipment and supply distributors among the examples of types of companies encountering competition from innovative market channels. Traditional merchant wholesalers, who represented 93.5 percent of industry establishments in the government's census, were expected to face the stiffest competition. Alternate channels included manufacturer direct sales, retail formats such as buying clubs and warehouse clubs, and inventory service providers such as subcontractors offering product assembly or transportation coordination. Merchant wholesalers were not expected to increase their market share in the overall national economy, however.

The industry employed 65,300 workers in 1994 with a payroll of $1.74 billion. Combined, industry sales amounted to an estimated $13 billion in 1996.

Further Reading

Arthur Andersen & Co. *Facing the Forces of Change 2000: The New Realities in Wholesale Distribution.* Washington: Distribution Research & Education Foundation, 1992.

Darnay, Arsen J., and Gary Alampi, eds. *Wholesale and Retail Trade USA.* Detroit: Gale Research, 1995.

Infotrac Company Profiles, 18 February 2000. Available from http://web4.infotrac.galegroup.com.

U.S. Bureau of the Census. *1992 Census of Wholesale Trade.* Washington: GPO, 1995.

SIC 5088

TRANSPORTATION EQUIPMENT AND SUPPLIES, EXCEPT MOTOR VEHICLES

This industry is comprised of establishments engaged in the wholesale distribution of transportation equipment and related supplies, excluding motor vehicles. Ships (except pleasure craft), combat vehicles, guided missiles, and space vehicles are included in the industry. Self-propelled golf carts, railroad equipment, and aircraft parts and supplies are also included. Establishments primarily engaged in the wholesale distribution of motor vehicles are included in Industry Group 501 (motor vehicles and motor vehicle parts and supplies). Establishments primarily engaged in the wholesale distribution of pleasure boats are included in **SIC 5091: Sporting and Recreational Goods and Supplies.**

NAICS Code(s)

421860 (Transportation Equipment and Supplies (Except Motor Vehicles) Wholesalers)

Three separate specialties constitute this fragmented category. By number of establishments, the largest classification is aircraft and aeronautical equipment and supplies; followed by marine machinery, equipment, and supplies wholesalers; and other transportation equipment and supplies wholesalers—including sellers of equipment and supplies used by railroads, streetcars, buses, tramways, aerial hoists, and horsedrawn vehicles.

U.S. Airways Group Inc. of Arlington, Virginia, led the industry with 1999 sales of almost $8.6 billion. Two New York City-based firms—Mitsubishi International Corp. and Sea Containers America Inc.—followed with 1998 sales of more than $7.1 billion and almost $1.3 billion respectively. Houston-based Stewart and Stevenson Services Inc. generated sales of more than $1.2 billion for its fiscal year ended January 31, 1999. AAR Corp., headquartered in Elk Grove Village, Illinois, rounded out the top five industry leaders with sales of $918 million for its fiscal year ended May 31, 1999.

Stewart and Stevenson Services Inc. (SSSS) was awarded a $5 million Systems Technical Support (STS) service contract in early 2000 from the United States Army for support of its Family of Medium Tactical Vehicles (FMTV). The contract, administered by the Army's Tank, Automotive, and Armaments Command (TACOM), added up to $47 million in total revenue over four years. The company was extremely familiar with the equipment it would maintain, as SSSS manufactured 11,400 FMTVs from 1992 through 1998 for the Army.

During the early 1990s, the aerospace industry experienced declines in both the defense and civil segments. Although industry analysts anticipated recovery in the commercial segment of the industry during the second half of the decade, continuing stagnation in the defense market was expected because of continued U.S. government downsizing. The best growth opportunities were for niche segments such as business and commuter jets, spare parts, and maintenance and overhaul in the commercial sector. Small commercial aircraft running regional services were a growing trend in the late 1990s. Industry performance as a whole continued to be mixed as the industry supplanted its defense-based revenues with commercial and industrial sales. The industry grossed an estimated $23 billion in 1996 and employed approximately 37,000 workers.

Further Reading

Darnay, Arsen J., and Gary Alampi, eds. *Wholesale and Retail Trade USA.* Detroit: Gale Research, 1995.

Infotrac Company Profiles 18 February 2000. Available from http://web4.infotrac.galegroup.com.

U.S. Bureau of the Census. *1992 Census of Wholesale Trade.* Washington: GPO, 1995.

SIC 5091

SPORTING AND RECREATIONAL GOODS AND SUPPLIES

Establishments in this entry are primarily engaged in the wholesale distribution of sporting goods and accessories; billiard and pool supplies; sporting firearms and ammunition; and marine pleasure craft, equipment, and supplies. Establishments primarily engaged in the wholesale distribution of motor vehicles and trailers are classified in **SIC 5012: Automobiles & Other Motor Vehicles.** Those distributing self-propelled golf carts are classified in **SIC 5088: Transportation Equipment & Supplies,** and those distributing athletic apparel and footwear are classified in Industry Group 513: Apparel, Piece Goods, and Notions.

NAICS CODE(S)

421910 (Sporting and Recreational Goods and Suppliers Wholesalers)

INDUSTRY SNAPSHOT

As with other wholesale industries, sporting and recreational goods wholesale distributors were undergoing a period of consolidation early in the 1990s. Rather than competing with the manufacturer's prices, wholesale distributors opted to emphasize value-added services not offered by manufacturers, in an effort to regain a larger portion of the market.

In the early 1990s, many small and medium-sized distributors, as well as several smaller retailers, went out of business. According to an industry study released by a Chicago stock brokerage firm, however, some smaller distribution firms maintained an important place in the industry, handling markets and products too small for the large firms. Nevertheless, the study found that consolidation has led to fewer but stronger competitors offering an array of advantages, including volume discounts, better financing options, value-added services, and larger warehouses to accommodate a variety of product lines. Consolidation and growth also enabled distributors to take advantage of the most up-to-date computer technology in warehouse and inventory operations.

The late 1990s in the sporting goods industry were characterized by mergers, acquisitions, and cut backs among both manufacturers and retailers. The Sporting Goods Manufacturers Association (SGMA) ''1999 State of the Industry Report'' noted the major mergers in 1998: The Sunbeam Corporation acquired the Coleman Company in a $2.1 billion deal. In the fitness sector, Cybex acquired Tectrix; Schwinn bought Hebb Industries and GT Bikes; Precor procured Pacific Fitness; and Icon acquired the trademark rights to Nordic Track. SLM acquired Sports Holdings Corporation and became the largest hockey company in the world.

In reaction to sales declines in the U.S. market for licensed products, a shift away from athletic footwear to ''brown shoes,'' and slower international sales growth due to the Asian and Brazilian financial crises, both Nike and Reebok announced employee layoffs and the Russell Corporation closed 25 of its 90 production facilities, cutting 22 percent of its workforce. As the number of vendors and manufacturers consolidated, a ''consolidation of retailers also occurred, resulting in fewer, but larger, operators of sporting goods stores.'' The largest sporting goods retail merger in 1998 was Gart Sports and SportMart. The Venator Group closed 467 Kinney and 103 Footquarters stores in 1998, converting many of the storefronts to Lady Foot Locker. The Sports Authority reduced its store count to 196 by closing 18 stores in 1998.

ORGANIZATION AND STRUCTURE

The sporting and recreational goods market is largely seasonal, requiring manufacturers to deliver product lines in a timely fashion in order to take advantage of the limited period of demand for many products. According to a 1997 survey of sporting goods buyers by *Sporting Goods Business* magazine, almost 75 percent of the buyers surveyed were buying closer to the selling season, rather than overstock products during the off-season.

Because of the wide range of sports and other activities serviced by this industry, many retailers specialized in providing equipment for certain activities, such as fishing, firearms, boating, and so on. Other distributors specialized by market, dealing primarily with team equipment for schools and other institutions. Still others directed their business toward equipment popular in specific regions of the country, for example, providing fishing and hunting gear in rural areas. The latter strategy, in particular, gave smaller dealers or distributors an advantage over the superstores and chains, in that such operations could specialize in providing specific regional information, advice, and products.

CURRENT CONDITIONS

The sale of wholesale sporting goods, including footwear and sports apparel, totaled more than $45.62 billion in 1998, reflecting a one percent growth over 1997. Sports apparel sales ($19.55 billion) grew by 5 percent over 1997, outpacing sports equipment and athletic footwear. According to the SGMA ''1999 State of the Industry Report,'' total sporting goods manufacturers' sales—inclusive of sporting goods equipment, sports apparel and athletic footwear—were expected to increase by only 2.4 percent in 1999. The SGMA also noted that slow growth during the late 1990s could be attributed to the ''over-saturation of the metal golf club market, weakness in the in-line skating market, a lack of innovative, new products, and relatively flat participation in team sports.'' Women's products and the fitness equipment market are two areas that offered the most promise for growth for the industry.

In the early 1990s, sales of golf equipment, accessories and apparel soared due to the participants desire to have the latest and greatest equipment on the course. Sales of over-sized drivers, titanium clubs and graphite shafts largely contributed to the growth of the entire category. In 1998, the market for golf equipment reached its saturation point and golf product sales reflected only a 2 percent growth rate. The SGMA projected that the 1999 golf market would be flat.

Skiing, also a high-priced sport, was hurt by recession and by several bad winters. At least 30 percent of ski shops went out of business between 1983 and 1993. Sales dropped consistently throughout the 1990s, and retailers were carrying less inventory in their stores. Because of the decline in sales, for several recessionary years in the late 1980s and early 1990s manufacturers did not have the resources to develop and produce dramatically innovative equipment, so skiers were less likely to invest in new skis, poles, or boots. The ski market also had more competition from other outdoor sports such as snowboarding.

Women's participation and interest in sports reached an all-time high during the mid-to-late 1990s. According to American Sports Data, Inc., ''37 million females participated on a frequent basis in some sport, fitness or outdoor activity in 1997—a 16 percent increase since 1987.'' Three U.S. women's teams captured gold medals in the 1996 Olympic games in soccer, hockey and softball; women's professional sports leagues such as the Ladies Professional Golf Association (LPGA) and the Women's National Basketball Association (WNBA) were able to bring in major corporate sponsors and land cable and network television coverage; and U.S. Women's Soccer Team won the 1999 World Cup. The national and international media coverage helped women's sports capture significant marketing dollars. Since 1990, the unit sales of women's sports apparel has increased by 38 percent. A study by the Sporting Goods Manufacturing Association noted that women's in-line skating grew in popularity by more than 300 percent between 1992 and 1995. Other sports reflecting significant growth due to women's participation include tennis, working out with free weights, stair-climbing, treadmills, step aerobics, camping with tents and stationary bikes. The SGMA projected that both manufacturers and retailers would need to ''become more aggressive in courting the female consumer,'' noting that products for women would be a ''growth category in an otherwise saturated market.''

The SGMA also points to the exercise and fitness equipment category as another key driver for sales in 1999. Sales for exercise and fitness equipment reached $2.7 billion in 1997. From 1987 to 1997, sales of cardiovascular exercise machines increased 63 percent and strength training equipment increased by 44 percent. A 1997 study by Target Management found that nearly one-third of U.S. households own and use exercise equipment such as treadmills, stationary bikes and free weights in their homes. Health club memberships have also dramatically increased, from 13.8 million in 1987 to 22.5 million in 1998, which resulted in increased sales of exercise and fitness equipment.

The SGMA addressed what growth rates retailers and manufacturers could expect in other areas of the sporting goods industry noting that, ''Camping, water sports, and soccer are expected to post sales increases in the mid single digits, while sales of tennis and bowling/billiards should grow minimally (about 2 percent). The in-line skate market will continue to contract . . . and archery will experience a modest decline in sales.''

Industry Leaders

One of the industry leaders in the wholesale sporting and recreational goods and supplies industry was SCP Pool Corp., based in Covington, Louisiana with $335 million in sales in 1998. Gander Mountain Inc., in Wilmot, Wisconsin came in with $292 million in sales in 1998, Ellett Brothers, Inc. of Chapin, South Carolina ($153 million), and Salomon North America Inc. of Georgetown, Massachusetts ($130 million), were the only other companies to boast 1998 sales of more than $100 million. Outdoor Sports Headquarters Incorporated (OSHI), a subsidiary of Centuri Incorporated, a distributor of a general line of sporting goods, had sales of $110 million in 1991, but only $90 million in 1998. Nine other companies in this industry reflected total yearly sales of $50 million or more in 1998.

Research and Technology

In the mid-1980s, OSHI and other distributors introduced the opportunity for customers to purchase powerful new computer systems that could track, report, and forecast inventory needs and quickly compute sales and profits. The systems offered customers several unique advantages. Programs could update inventory, track sales taxes, and create mailing lists. Given a certain amount of information regarding individual sales, the system might recommend additional products for the retailer to promote. The OSHI system provided firearms records required by the Bureau of Alcohol, Tobacco, and Firearms, as well as fishing and hunting license records. Furthermore, some programs allowed dealers to access the wholesaler's mainframe to obtain information on the status of the wholesaler's inventory. Other options included allowing the retailer to place an order directly to the wholesaler's computer, quickly learning whether the order qualified for any incentive programs. Some computer programs could also update prices in the dealers' computers, forecast seasonal sales based on the sales in previous years, track special orders, and generate daily sales reports.

Distributors were also increasingly relying on computerized distribution centers to improve service and profits. Easton Aluminum, the official supplier of equipment to the U.S. Olympic Archery Team, built a 100,000 square foot, state-of-the-art distribution center that has served as a model for distributors and manufacturers. Located in Salt Lake City, this distribution center replaced four warehouses, one for each division of the company, providing a more stable distribution of merchandise in an industry that experienced severe peaks and valleys due to the seasonal nature of sporting goods. The system also allowed Easton to maintain extremely accurate inventory records.

Recognizing that the market is consumer-driven, both manufacturers and retailers used computer technology to gather market and consumer information. Retailers can track customer preferences from point-of-sale (POS) information and use it to manage inventory accurately. Manufacturers can use this same information to react to top-selling products or discontinue shipments of slow-sellers. Both the retailer and manufacturer benefit by reducing the need for inventory build up and markdowns.

The Internet became an integral part of business in the late 1990s, changing how and where consumers shop. The number of retailers in all categories selling on-line to consumers increased from 12 percent in 1997 to 39 percent in 1998. The Internet allows retailers to store data regarding customer purchases, birthdays, and demographics. Retailers can use the information to suggest gifts, cross-promote products and refer users to partner sites. On-line retailers such as Sports Superstore Online (www.shopsports.com) and Fogdog Sports (www.fogdog.com) challenge the current model of "brick and mortar" retail establishments. In addition to offering products to consumers, many companies used the Internet to facilitate business-to-business e-commerce such as automating their inventory, offering customer service, distributing products, and utilizing order fulfillment functions. Forrester Research in Cambridge, Massachusetts, projected that business-to-business e-commerce revenues would reach an estimated $186 billion, compared to consumer revenues reaching $18.4 billion by 2001.

FURTHER READING

"1999 State of the Industry Report." Sporting Goods Manufacturers Association (SGMA), 1999. Available from http://www.sportlink.com/research/1999_research/99soti.

Brooklyn Public Library. *Business Rankings Annual 1999.* Farmington Hills, MI: The Gale Group.

"Buying Cycles." *Sporting Goods Business,* 7 July 1997.

Carr, Robert E. "Consolidation Is Not Over." *Sporting Goods Business,* 27 January 1989.

"Don't Sideline Women's Sports." *Discount Store News,* 2 June 1997.

Feitelberg, Rosemary. "Why Wall Street Likes Nike." *Women's Wear Daily,* 21 March 1996.

Gallagher, Julia. "Women's Teams Deliver Sales Bounce." *Footwear News,* 3 February 1997.

Lloyd, Brenda. "SGMA See 7 percent Gain in Activewear Sales." *Daily News Record,* 17 February 1997.

Standard & Poor's Register of Corporations, Directors and Executives. New York: McGraw-Hill Companies, Inc., 1997.

U.S. Department of Commerce. *U.S. Industry and Trade Outlook, 1999.* New York: McGraw Hill Companies, Inc., 1999.

SIC 5092

TOYS AND HOBBY GOODS AND SUPPLIES

This category includes establishments primarily engaged in the wholesale distribution of games, toys, hobby goods and supplies, dolls, craft kits, model kits, children's vehicles, fireworks, and playing cards.

NAICS CODE(S)

421920 (Toy and Hobby Goods and Supplies)

INDUSTRY SNAPSHOT

In April, 1999, the International Council of Toy Conferences announced that toy sales worldwide in 1998 reached $67.8 billion. In 1997, the American toys and hobby goods wholesaling industry was composed of 3,229 establishments and 36,337 employees. Sales for that year amounted to $20.2 billion.

Wholesale distributors of toys experienced a shrinking customer base in the early 1990s, as national toy store chains and discount stores began to buy directly from manufacturers. Sales in the mid-1990s continued to grow, up by 20 percent from 1992 to $20 billion. However, since 1992 expenses have been rising faster than sales. While toy distributors were once the most important customers at toy fairs, Toys 'R' Us became the leading toy retailer in the mid-1990s and had the most purchasing clout with toy manufacturers, accounting for 20 percent of U.S. toy sales in 1996. Sydney Ladensohn Stern and Ted Schoenhaus, authors of *Toyland: The High Stakes Game of the Toy Industry,* wrote that toy manufacturers referred to the wholesale distributors as "dinosaurs because they used to be the toy company's most powerful customers, and today they are almost extinct." However, wholesale distributors of toys continue to supply smaller, independent toy stores and department stores, and still regarded their industry as playing a pivotal role in the toy marketplace.

Even toy specialty retailers were not immune to a shifting market, however. By 1998, Toys 'R' Us had been surpassed by Wal-Mart as leading toy retailer. Wal-Mart commanded 17.4 percent of the market, while Toys 'R' Us dropped to 16.8 percent of the market.

Acknowledging changes in the marketplace, the Toy Wholesalers Association changed its name to the Toy and Hobby Wholesalers Association in 1989. Like wholesalers in other industries, toy and hobby wholesalers refocused their business to provide value-added services generally not offered by manufacturers.

Current Conditions

Value-added Services and the Role of the Distributor. Consolidation of toy manufacturers and retailers meant massive changes for the distribution network of the toy industry. Eliminating the added expense of distributorships, major toymakers were able to offer volume discounts to toy stores and other retailers of toys. Furthermore, toy store chains such as Toys 'R' Us established their own distribution centers from which to supply their stores. In 1995, the pressure on distributors increased as more manufacturers went to direct distribution of their products, an effort led by Marvel comic books and Citadel Miniatures. This second wave in the direct distributorship drive proved even more vexing for the wholesalers because the manufacturers involved introduced the licensing of retail outlets. These licensed dealers received delivery of new product releases before non-licensed dealers and wholesalers, which further tightened the market for distributors.

Consequently, toy and hobby wholesale distributors targeted smaller retail stores and chains, offering merchandise from the smaller manufacturers. They also expanded their industry to include the distribution of hobby and craft items. Distributors recognized that service was vital to their survival in a tough market.

William L. MacMillan, executive director of the Toy and Hobby Wholesalers Association in 1991, noted in a 1991 article in *Playthings* magazine that the distributor could still offer many unique services to both retailers and manufacturers. For instance, the distributor, having associations with thousands of products and retailers, was able to provide valuable information to toymakers and toy sellers. MacMillan suggested that the wholesaler could act as a consultant to new retailers, advising them about such issues as the proper quantities to keep in stock and the benefits of certain promotional techniques. Furthermore, MacMillan observed, the distributor could provide valuable services to manufacturers by offering information on how various products were selling in specific markets, providing advertising aid through distributor-sponsored promotions and in-store displays, and providing sales training to store personnel.

The distributors' volume buying power meant they could offer retailers lower prices than the manufacturer, and by maintaining fully stocked warehouses, distributors also helped save retailers and manufacturers inventory space. In addition, a computer network for ordering, sales, and inventory became perhaps the most important value-added service. Through such a network, distributors provided an efficient means of sharing information with both manufacturers and retail clients.

According to a survey of the entire wholesale distribution industry, consolidation of the distribution industry led to fewer but stronger competitors able to offer a wide range of services including volume discounts, improved financing options, and adoption of state-of-the-art warehouse technology.

Although consolidation of the retail toy industry forced many distributors out of business, those that remained were more efficient and were able to explore smaller manufacturers and retail accounts, including independent drug and specialty stores.

Craft and Hobby Boom. The crafts and hobby industry experienced a renewed popularity in the early 1990s, probably due to a return to homemade gifts and decorations prompted by economic recession. A 1994 survey by the trade group Hobby Industries of America found that participation in crafts or hobbies had increased, with 81 percent of U.S. households participating in a particular craft or hobby, compared to 77 percent four years earlier.

New Technology's Impact. Probably the most intriguing change in the toy industry was the birth of the Internet. Companies such as eToys, founded in 1996, gained considerably publicity during the 1999 Christmas season. eToys offered buyers the opportunity to shop at home for hard-to-find toys rather than braving crowded stores and frenzied shoppers. The company's sales in 1999 were $30 million, but that represented a 4,267 percent jump from the previous year. There are numerous concerns and challenges surrounding the concept of e-trade, but there is no question that as the technology improves, online toy shopping will become an important element of the sales structure.

INDUSTRY LEADERS

Among the leaders in this field at the end of the 1990s were Ben Franklin Crafts Inc., with more than $350 million in annual sales and more than 200 workers, and Applause Enterprises Inc.—with $300 million in sales and more than 1,700 employees in 1999.

Ben Franklin Retail Stores Inc. had franchised variety and crafts stores throughout the U.S. by the end of the 1990s. The company also owned and operated a chain of Ben Franklin superstores. The parent company was the wholesale distributor for both the variety and craft franchises.

Ben Franklin managers from all over the nation entered orders into electronic data collection terminals for the information to be transmitted to the main computer in Wichita, Kansas. Orders were sorted and transmitted to the appropriate regional distribution center.

Applause Enterprises is best known for its plush toys, including characters from Sesame Street and Disney. It was created in 1995 when Dakin, a plush toy manufacturer, merged with a company founded by Wallace Berrie (brother of rival novelty manufacturer Russ Berrie), and in addition to plush toys it produces items such as magnets, keychains, and tableware decorated with its licensed characters (such as Looney Tunes and the Muppets).

AMERICA AND THE WORLD

By the mid-1990s, wholesale toy distributors were not a significant presence in foreign markets, and during this time, toy manufacturers themselves were investing in distributorships in foreign nations. Mattel Inc. acquired a majority stake in Auritel S.A., a Mexican toy marketer and distributor with sales of more than $65 million a year. Auritel manufactured and distributed Mattel toys as well as marketing and distributing other toy brands in Mexico. Tyco Toys Inc. also acquired a majority share in a Mexican distributorship of Tyco toys. Tyco maintained that the company, Munecas y Juguetas Ensueno S.A., was the second largest toy company in Mexico.

FURTHER READING

Hartnett, Michael. ''Kmart lures Shoppers with New Convenience Format.'' *Stores,* February 1996, 18.

Hoover's Company Capsules. Austin, TX: Hoover's Inc., 1999. Available from http://www.hoovers.com.

''Infant and Pre-School Toys.'' *EIU,* January 1996, 53-64.

International Council of Toy Industries. ''ICTI Announces Worldwide Toy Sales at $67.8 Billion in 1998,'' 19 April 1999. Available from http://www.toys-icti.org.

MacMillan, William L. ''The Economy Is Right for Toy Wholesalers.'' *Playthings,* November 1991, 38.

Reynolds, Simon. ''Discovery Channel Explores Wild World of Retailing.'' *Stores,* May 1996, 40-43.

Toy Manufacturers of America, 10 February 2000. Available from http://www.toy-tma.com.

U.S. Census Bureau. *1997 Economic Census—Wholesale Trade.* Washington: GPO, 2000.

SIC 5093

SCRAP AND WASTE MATERIALS

This industry category includes establishments primarily engaged in assembling, breaking up, sorting and distributing scrap and waste materials. The industry also includes auto wreckers engaged in dismantling automobiles for scrap. Those establishments engaged in dismantling cars for the purpose of selling secondhand parts are classified under **SIC 5015: Motor Vehicle Parts—Used.**

NAICS CODE(S)

421930 (Recyclable Material Wholesalers)

INDUSTRY SNAPSHOT

The United States generates more than 200 billion pounds of municipal waste annually, distributed as follows: paper, 38 percent; yard trimmings, 18 percent; metals and plastics, 16 percent; other waste, 28 percent. In addition to collection, the scrap and waste materials industry operates the sorting and recycling services that help to reduce the amount of waste sent to landfills. To that end, it also processes for wholesale distribution a wide variety of materials including bags and bottles, fur cuttings and scraps, nonferrous metal wastes and scraps, and rubber scraps. The industry's primary output, however, has been wastepaper and ferrous scrap metals such as iron and steel.

ORGANIZATION AND STRUCTURE

Scrap Wastepaper. Wastepaper processors use large balers to bundle compressed wastepaper—such as newsprint, cardboard, or office paper—for shipment to paper mills for recycling. Recycling efforts by the scrap industry increased substantially during the final decades of the twentieth century, recovering 45 percent—45 million tons—of all paper and paperboard used nationally in 1997; recycled office paper alone increased to 48 percent, up from just 15 percent in 1990. The industry set a goal to recycle 50 percent of all paper, and 65 percent of office paper by the year 2000.

Export markets increased by 285 percent from the mid-1980s and the mid-1990s, and prices for recycled paper products soared in 1995, but fell again in 1996. A subsequent no-growth forecast for the entire paper industry late in 1998 led producers to forestall plans to increase plant capacity for recycling of paper products as the 1990s drew to a close. At that time the American Forest & Paper Association projected a continued 2.1 percent annual growth for recovered fiber, which reflected a 75 percent decline from previous growth. Revised projections called for recycled paper to flatten and stabilize at 36 percent of total product, with printing and writing paper down at 10 percent. The lower projections stemmed from an ongoing pattern of lack of demand. Meanwhile, paper recovery in Japan and Europe remained above 50 percent.

To help bolster the market, companies developed chemicals and techniques for improving the marketability of recycled paper products. Ponderosa Fibers of Baltimore, Maryland, developed a method for removing fluorescence from office wastepaper, and Cytec Industries Inc. of West Paterson, New Jersey, introduced a chemical that reduced bleeding of ink in recycled paper products. A growing trend among producers in 1998 was to move aggressively toward lowering the chlorine content through substitution, with a goal of achieving elemental chlorine-free (ECF) pulp.

Scrap Iron and Steel. Scrap iron and steel companies collect junked cars, steel from buildings, and scrap from metalworking industries, then process it for use by steel mills. Processors are required to remove and properly dispose of many hazardous wastes before shredding any metal scraps. Of particular concern is the disposal of shredder fluff—the waste left after processing metals—which often contains high levels of oils, PCBs, lead, and cadmium. At least 75 percent of shredder waste is recoverable. Ways to recycle this waste are being studied by government and industry researchers alike.

In the mid-1990s. U.S. steelmakers were using more than 70 million tons of scrap metal annually to produce new steel. Globally, the use of scrap metals reached 400 million tons. Some analysts predicted that this demand on a global scale would keep prices high throughout the 1990s. However, demand leveled off by 1996, and prices for ferrous scrap metals dropped. A 1997 rebound in prices, offset by a monetary crisis in Asia, led to an industry slump at the close of the decade. The industry recycled 1.9 million tons of steel in 1998, or 72.1 percent of eligible steel—a decline of 8.9 percent from the 1997 recycling level of 81 percent. The decrease resulted from excessively low steel prices brought about by the economic crisis in Asia and by "steel dumping" (excessive cheap exports) by foreign nations. Analysts detected some improvement early in 2000 as Asian recovery progressed, and secondary producers fought to maintain an effective price differential between primary and secondary product.

Scrap Plastic. The United States used more than 30 billion pounds of plastics annually in the 1990s, of which the recycling rate was nearly 20 percent. By the late 1990s, more than 15,500 U.S. communities—representing nearly 50 percent of the U.S. population—had access to some form of plastics recycling.

In response to the growth in plastics recycling, research and development departments sought ways to use various types of recycled plastics. One industry association listed more than 1,300 uses for recycled plastics, including products such as PCV pipes, lawn furniture, and auto dashboards. A technique called pyrolysis can convert plastics from shredder fluff into fuel oil. This process is being tested by the Illinois-based Argonne National Laboratory.

Industry Leaders

The largest company in the solid waste handling industry in 1999 was Waste Management Inc. of Houston, Texas—formerly USA Waste Services. Waste Management took its new name following a 1998 acquisition of the former Waste Management Corp. A *Fortune* 500 company, Waste Management reported $12.703 billion in sales, for 386-percent growth in 1998. Waste Management maintains operations worldwide through Waste Management International. Allied Waste Industries Inc., with $1.7 billion in holdings, assumed the rank of second largest waste handler, following its acquisition of BFI. Allied Waste reported $1.575 billion in sales for 1998.

Among recycling firms, IMCO Recycling Inc. of Irving, Texas, is the world's largest recycler of aluminum, with 20 plants in the United States, and overseas operations in Wales and Germany. IMCO sells to General Motors, Alcoa, and Kaiser Aluminum among others. IMCO's 1999 sales totaled $765 million.

Junk Conglomerates. In 1999 two major corporations entered the salvage arena. Prior to that time, according to the Automotive Recyclers Association in 1997, that industry involved 5,500 independent firms engaged primarily in parts recycling, for estimated collective revenues of $7.05 billion annually. A survey conducted by the association and reported in *Automotive News* revealed that 86 percent of U.S. junkyards maintained a staff of 10 or fewer employees in 1997. The scenario shifted course between April of 1999 and January of 2000, as the giant automaker, Ford Motor Co., entered the marketplace through a wholly owned subsidiary called Greenleaf Acquisitions. The incorporation of Greenleaf was a critical move in a new diversification strategy underway at Ford, and by January of 2000 Greenleaf had expanded into 6 of the United States and had acquired a total of 20 previously independent junkyards. At that time the company indicated plans for international expansion into Canada, Mexico, and Europe. Management projections held that Greenleaf's annual sales might surpass $1 billion at an undetermined time in the future, primarily through the salvage car parts market. Ford's entry into the salvage market followed an earlier move by LKQ Corp. to diversify into junkyards in 1999.

RESEARCH AND TECHNOLOGY

Power of Plastic. A $20 million plant for gasification of recycled plastic—the world's first facility of its kind—was under construction at Varkaus, Finland, in 1999. The plant, designed to recycle aluminum and plastic packaging, promised to convert the waste into gas energy. Common types of refuse included in this category include paper cartons designed to contain liquid, as such cartons typically contain 30 percent plastic and aluminum foil. The new plant, designed to support recovery of aluminum, can operate at 95 percent energy savings over aluminum ore processing. Prior to the Varkaus plant, aluminum recovery from cartons was considered unfeasible. Corenso United Oy, Foster Wheeler, and VTT Energy undertook the construction of the plant as a joint venture. VTT Energy is a research organization that pioneered the gasification technology in the early 1980s. The plant, according to projections, will produce more than 2 million kilograms of aluminum every year, for export to Sweden. Also in Europe, in 1999 German researchers reported initial success with near-infrared spectroscopy (NIR) as a method for determining the paper content of plastic for recycling. NIR can be implemented more cheaply and faster than current chemical processes in use.

Automation. A process that automated the sorting of waste was designed by National Recovery Technologies Inc. of Nashville, Tennessee, in conjunction with the U.S. Department of Energy's Office of Industrial Technologies. Not only did this new technology allow for sorting according to material, but also according to more specific characteristics such as color, or particular type of plastic. With these new advances, up to 1,500 tons of municipal solid waste can be processed in one day. The EddySort system, manufactured by Wendt Corp. of New York, can recover virtually all nonferrous metal from automobile shredder fluff. Overall, automating the recycling process improves both the speed and efficiency of the recovery of hazardous wastes. Technologies also are being introduced to improve or provide additional applications for recycled paper and plastics, which ultimately will strengthen the market for industry products.

FURTHER READING

"Allied Waste Industries, Inc." *Hoover's Online,* 18 February 2000. Available from wysiwyg://13/http://www.hoovers.com/co/capsule/6/0,2163,15676,00.html.

Amerman, Don. "U.S. Recycling Rockets." *Journal of Commerce and Commercial,* 3 June 1996.

"BFI's Affiliate, Otto Waste Services, Aquires P&R Waste Services." *Research: Shareholder News for Browning-Ferris Industries, Inc.* 1997. Available from http://www.researchmag.com/news/bfi_1.htm.

Ducey, Michael J. "Softness slows enviro-paper shipments." *Graphic Arts,* October 1998.

"Entrepreneurs Surf the Waste Stream." *Biocycle,* November 1996.

Finchen, Kirk. "Recycled Capacity Floods Market Despite Potential Fiber Storage." *Pulp & Paper,* April 1997.

Giltenan, Ed. "Ups and Downs of Recycling." *Chemical Marketing Reporter,* 26 August 1996.

Goodwin, Morgan. "Fluff Attracts Further Pyrolysis Research." *American Metal Market,* 10 October 1995.

———."Auto Shredder Fluff Recycling Research Nears Payoff." *American Metal Market,* 11 March 1996.

Harkki, Pekka. "Producing electricity from plastic packaging." *Modern Power Systems,* September 1999.

Hoffman, Bryce. "Fod finding treasure in trash." *Automotive News,* 3 January 2000.

Holman, Hugh F. "Waste Firms Must Rethink Strategy." *Waste News,* May 1997. Available from http://www.wastenews.com/subscriber/opinion/2384.html.

"IMCO Recycling Inc." *Hoover's Online,* 18 February 2000. Available from wysiwyg://17/http://www.hoovers.com/co/capsule/2/0,2163,13732,00.html.

Marley, Michael. "Auto Bundle Price Rise Tops $8/T.." *American Metal Market,* 28 April 1997.

"New Megadeal Holds Promise." *Waste News,* April 1997. Available from http://www.wastenews.com/subscriber/opinion/2382.html.

Null, David. "Risks of Recycled Fiber Projects Make Virgin Fiber More Attractive." *Pulp & Paper,* July 1996.

Oline, Mark. "DCR Downgrades Browning-Ferris Industries, Inc." *Envirobiz,* 19 November 1996. Available from http://www.envirobiz.com/newsdaily/pr11201.htm.

"Plastics Recycling Backgrounder." *The Plastics Resource,* 1997. Available from http://www.plasticsresource.com/Docs/apc/bk_rcycl.htm.

Prindiville, Sheila. "Bonds in Good Shape." *Waste News,* April 1997. Available from http://www.wastenews.com/subscriber/opinion/2385.html.

"Steel's Status." *Appliance Manufacturer,* November 1999.

"Recycling." *U.S. Environmental Protection Agency,* 1997. Available from http://www.epa.gov/epaoswer/non-hw/recycle.htm.

''Recycling Plastics and Other Materials from Scrapped Automobiles.'' *Argonne National Laboratory Programs and Capabilities,* 1997. Available from http://www.anl.gov/LabDB/Current/Ext/H201-text.007.html.

''1995 Recycling Rate Study Backgrounder.'' *The Plastics Resource,* 1997. Available from http://www2.plasticsresource.com/Docs/apc/bk_95rts.htm.

''Success Story.'' *Industry Week,* 15 April 1996.

United Waste Systems, Inc. Web Site. *United Waste Systems, Inc.* 1996. Available from http://www.uwst.com.

''Paper or plastic? New test has the answer.'' *Science News,* 20 March 1999.

''Waste Management, Inc.'' *Hoover's Online,* 18 February 2000. Available from wysiwyg://10/http://www.hoovers.com/co/capsule/4/0,2163,15374,00.html.

Worden, Edward. ''Scrap Tags Stalled, Auto Wreckers Told.'' *American Metal Market,* 28 October 1996.

Worden, Edward. ''Scrap dealers welcome higher 2000 price tags.'' *American Metal Market,* 6 January 2000.

Zulpo, Margaret. ''High Newsprint Prices Cause Recycling to Grow in Tulsa, Okla.'' *Knight-Ridder/Tribune Business News,* 13 April 1996.

SIC 5094

JEWELRY, WATCHES, PRECIOUS STONES, AND PRECIOUS METALS

This industry classification comprises establishments involved in the wholesale distribution of jewelry, watches, precious stones, and precious metals. Products of the industry include clocks, coins, gem stones, pearls, precious metals bullion, silverware, and trophies. Establishments primarily engaged in the wholesale distribution of precious metal ores are included in **SIC 5052: Coal and Other Minerals and Ores.**

NAICS Code(s)

421940 (Jewelry, Watch, Precious Stone, and Precious Metal Wholesalers)

Organization and Structure

The industry employed more than 50,000 and generated sales of about $44 billion in 1998. Sales in jewelry stores increased about 8.5 percent from 1997 to 1998 to $22 billion, and about 40 percent of sales occurred in the fourth quarter of 1998, in keeping with traditional holiday sales trends. Other than jewelry stores, gemstones, jewelry, precious metals, and watches are sold by department stores, warehouse stores, home shopping television, catalogs and showrooms, and over the Internet.

Over 28,000 jewelry stores across America accounted for approximately half of the nation's jewelry sales in 1998. Consolidation occurred as large chains purchased others, and growth took place as these same chains expanded their number of outlets in shopping malls. Zale Corporation acquired Peoples Jewelers of Canada in June 1999, but Service Merchandise (a major catalog showroom) filed for bankruptcy, also in 1999; these events show that this industry is both highly competitive and risky. Retailers have sought new ways of improving product value. As a result, jewelry imports have increased from 26 percent in 1983 to 52 percent in 1997. With economic declines in Asia, Asian wholesalers have turned to the United States and Europe with increased volumes of exports.

Background and Development

Jewelry is as universal and ancient a form of adornment as clothing. It has been made of a variety of materials from human hair to precious metals and gems, and has been used to signify social status, wealth, official or political rank, holidays and celebrations, and fad and fashion. Its forms have included items for the head (hairpins, headbands, crowns, earrings, and lip and nose rings); neck (pendants and necklaces); chest (brooches, cloak clasps, buttons); waist (belts and girdles); and arms and legs (bracelets, anklets, and rings). As an industry, jewelry has been represented in all the major civilizations by goldsmiths, metalworkers, gem cutters, and many others. The Byzantine Empire (approximately the 6th to 13th centuries) with its profusion of gold and enamel and the European Renaissance (the 15th to 17th centuries) characterized by the use of gemstone-emblazoned fabrics and chains, ropes, pendants, and girdles were perhaps the greatest moments in the history of jewelry.

Watches were developed around 1450-1500 when the coiled spring made the invention of the pocket watch possible. By the 17th century, crystal faces to protect the workings, bearings, hairsprings, and balance wheels were standard. Watches were handcrafted by skilled artisans until about 1800 when machine-made parts led to mass production. Electric and electronic watches were introduced in the 1950s and 1960s.

During the first few years of the 1990s, conditions within the jewelry, watches, precious stones, and precious metals industry were unstable. In 1993, the number of establishments was about 6,800 and sales were about $45 billion, which was up from a 1990-91 low of about 6,000 establishments and $40 billion in sales. High numbers of retailer bankruptcies, fluctuations in international currency exchange rates, and the recession in the United States and abroad led to reduced profitability for wholesale dealers.

In January 1994, however, *Jewelers' Circular-Keystone* reported that conditions appeared to be improving. Some diamond dealers attributed the turn-around to the repeal of the federal luxury tax in 1993. During 1994, the heaviest projected demand was for diamond jewelry, loose diamonds, and karat gold jewelry.

Gem stones were also experiencing an upswing. Industry forecasters expected growth in ruby, sapphire, emerald, tourmaline, and tanzanite sales. The highest projected demand was for stones in earth tones, such as orange and peach.

Pearl dealers also anticipated improving conditions. Although high-quality Japanese pearls remained expensive and in short supply, forecasters predicted that increased supplies of Chinese freshwater pearls and South Sea pearls would help bring prices down in the lower-quality sector of the pearl market. This, coupled with increased demand, was expected to yield higher net profits.

Watch suppliers also expected sales to increase slightly during 1994. Annual U.S. watch sales were pegged at 65 million units with women's and jewelry watches, sport watches, upscale watches, two-tone watches, stainless steel watches, and watches with lighted dials remaining popular.

In the mid-1990s, jewelers were trying to lower their business costs, increase productivity, and tighten their customer base to increase profitability. The diamond trade was having especially low confidence due to foreign competition.

The states with the highest number of establishments were New York (2,339) and California (1,203). Together, they generated about 34.0 percent of U.S. sales. Connecticut had only 58 establishments but generated 44.7 percent of U.S. sales or $18.4 billion. Some of the most successful companies in this industry were Bulova Corporation, of New York; Citizen Watch Company of America Incorporated, of New Jersey; Bijoux Terner L.P., of Florida; and Swiss Army Brands, Inc. of Connecticut.

CURRENT CONDITIONS

Jewelers improved their prospects substantially in the late 1990s by better marketing and improved tracking of supplies, demand, and sales; they also were able to capitalize on simple demographics as the United States emerged from the recession earlier in the decade with baby boomers reaching their maximum earnings years and investing their income in jewelry. The large jewelry chains are continuing to consolidate into the 2000s, and retailers are optimistic about trends and fashions in jewelry and watches and growth of markets at a range of income levels.

Jewelers credit the bridal business with 30 to 50 percent of their revenue. Holidays and gift-giving opportunities, including a substantial promotion related to the Millennium, are also major factors in sales of watches and jewelry. Year-round spending and the growth of purchases among women of jewelry for themselves have made jewelers less dependent on December holiday sales, despite cyclic sales related to the economy and, to a lesser degree, the seasons.

Jewelry sales also depend heavily on fashion trends. In 2000 and beyond, colored gemstones, designs from natures, diamonds in virtually any form, yellow gold, white metals, princess-cut gemstones, Tahitian pearls, and invisible necklaces are expected to be among the most popular.

In precious metals, gold commodity prices have continued to drop to the year 2000, but jewelry manufacturers and retailers have yet to pass savings along in lower prices because, given the metal's volatile price, they are protecting their ability to pay higher prices for gold over the coming years. Sales of silver jewelry and other white metals were strong from 1996 through 1998, and forecasters expect this trend to continue. Platinum is the strongest of the precious metals in sales and totaled 7 percent of total jewelry sales in 1997 (compared to 3 percent in 1993). China and Japan lead the world in consumption of platinum jewelry.

Hong Kong and China produced 80 percent of the 500 million watches made in 1997. Quartz analog and digital watches are 93 percent of the total number of imported units.

INDUSTRY LEADERS

The top 20 firms in jewelry sales consisted of about 50 percent jewelers only. Tiffany & Co., Whitehall Jewelers, and the Piercing Pagoda were the only three companies with both unit growth and sales that exceeded 20 percent. For the industry as a whole, 1998 sales growth was 7 percent (compared to 8.7 percent in 1997) and unit growth was 2.3 percent (3.8 percent in 1997). The two major television shopping networks generated about 3 percent of industry-wide sales in 1996 through 1998. Of the three corporate leaders, Tiffany & Co. epitomized quality and name recognition worldwide; in the second quarter of 1999, Tiffany's earnings increased 63 percent.Whitehall Jewellers, Inc., has 276 stores in 31 states and has projected earnings growth rates of 30 percent and 22 percent for fiscal 1999 and 2000, respectively. Following a massive reorganization in the late 1980s, Zale Corporation is the largest specialty retailer (per 1999 statistics) with 1,300 stores in the United States, Canada, and Puerto Rico under several firm names; they also have considerable direct mail and online sales.

Internet sales of jewelry and watches are anticipated to rise to $56 million in 2000 and $140 million by 2001. Polygon Network, Inc., maintains Web sites for approximately 3,000 retailers and suppliers on six continents as well as providing online information resources. The Network experiences daily transactions of about $3 million and, as of 2000, holds a loose diamond inventory valued at about $100 million.

Research and Technology

Sellers of diamonds are increasingly threatened by sales of cubic zirconium and other, less expensive ''diamond look-alikes''. The largest diamond marketer worldwide, De Beers, is experimenting with ''diamond branding'' to mark the firm's name and identification numbers on diamonds. Development of this technique includes reader machines to detect the tiny, laser-cut inscriptions. Production of synthetic gemstones continues to be a strong research field.

Further Reading

Darnay, Arsen J, and Gary Alampi, eds. *Wholesale and Retail Trade USA.* Detroit: Gale Research, 1995.

U.S. Bureau of the Census. *Combined Annual and Revised Monthly Wholesale and Retail Trade.* Washington, DC: GPO, April 1996.

Ward's Business Directory of U.S. Private and Public Companies. Detroit: Gale Research, 1997.

Zimmerman, R., et al. ''Jewelry Sector Update.'' *The Jewelry Industry Report,* Janney Montgomery Scott, Inc., 25 August 1999.

SIC 5099

DURABLE GOODS, NOT ELSEWHERE CLASSIFIED

This industry classification includes wholesale distributors of durable goods that are not categorized elsewhere. It includes distributors of prerecorded audio cassettes, compact discs, and phonograph records; fire extinguishers; firearms and ammunition, except sporting; coin-operated game machines; luggage; monuments and grave markers; musical instruments; nonelectric signs; and forest products, except lumber, such as cordwood, hewn logs, and wood chips.

NAICS Code(s)

421990 (Other Miscellaneous Durable Goods Wholesalers)

Industry Snapshot

In 1997 Dun and Bradstreet listed 26,841 establishments in the durable goods industry, which generated $659 billion in sales, up from $617 billion in 1996. The industry also generated profits of approximately $107 billion dollars, up $15 billion from the previous year. In 1998 profits dropped to roughly $100 billion, due in large part to struggling overseas economies, especially in Asia. Orders for durable goods rose again in 1999, to a record $186 billion dollars in August. But over the next two months the U.S. Department of Commerce reported that orders for durable goods had fallen 1.3 percent.

Current Conditions

General merchandise such as luggage, nonsporting firearms, and non-electronic signs accounted for approximately 32 percent of sales in the durable goods industry during the 1990s; musical recordings made up 26 percent; forest products excluding lumber were 24 percent; musical instruments and supplies accounted for 4 percent; fire extinguishers and safety equipment totaled 2 percent; and other durable goods filled out the remaining 12 percent.

Industry Leaders

Samsonite was the world's largest manufacturer of luggage in the 1990s. The maker of American Tourister, Lark, and Samsonite brand names reported more than $175 million in U.S. sales during 1997 and employed 7,300 workers.

There were more than 1,100 U.S. nonelectronic sign makers in 1997, but only a fraction reported annual sales in excess of $1 million. Display Technologies, Inc. was one of the leading sign makers in the country during the late 1990s. Display Technologies, of Orlando, Florida, posted sales of approximately $66 million in 1997 and employed 525 workers. In 1999 Display Technologies bought Lockwood Group Inc., a commercial sign manufacturer in Atlanta, Georgia. Revenue for Lockwood totaled more than $10 million in 1998.

Dun and Bradstreet listed 158 U.S. dealers of nonsporting firearms in 1999. Most such dealers had less than 10 employees and reported sales between $50,000 and $500,000, with more successful dealers commonly being located in higher crime areas like Los Angeles, California.

Warner-Elektra-Atlantic Corp., a subsidiary of multimedia conglomerate Time Warner Entertainment Co., L.P., was one of the nation's leading distributors of prerecorded music over the past 10 years. It had sales of more than $222 million in 1997 and employed approximately 1,200 people. Yamaha Corporation of America (a subsidiary of Yamaha Corporation headquartered in Japan) was one of the leading U.S. distributors of musical instruments. It posted $185 million in sales during 1997 and employed approximately 1.000 workers.

WORKFORCE

The durable goods industry employed 72,000 workers in the mid-1990s, and had an annual payroll exceeding $2 billion. The average industry worker brought home approximately $588 dollars per week in pay in 1997. A 1999 survey of leading U.S. employers indicated that the biggest demand for workers in 2000 would come from durable goods manufacturers, 30 percent of which reported plans to hire employees, while 9 percent had plans to lay off workers. Nonetheless, payrolls in the durable goods industry fell by 6,000 workers during a nineteen-month period ending in November 1999. But the workers who remained worked less on average than they did in previous years. One study showed that employees in durable goods manufacturing worked 45.2 hours per week in January 1999, 3.1 hours per week less than in January 1998.

FURTHER READING

Darnay, Arsen J., and Gary Alampi, eds. *Wholesale and Retail Trade USA*. Detroit: Gale Research, 1995.

Time Warner Entertainment Company, L.P. *Annual Report*. New York, 1996.

U.S. Bureau of the Census. Available from http://www.census.gov.

U.S. Department of Commerce. Available from http://www.doc.gov.

U.S. Department of Labor. Available from http://www.dol.gov.

SIC 5111

PRINTING AND WRITING PAPER

This industry classification includes wholesale distributors of printing and writing paper. Products of the industry include fine paper, envelope paper, and groundwood paper. Wholesale distributors of computer paper and stationery are classified in **SIC 5112: Stationery and Office Supplies.**

NAICS CODE(S)

422110 (Printing and Writing Paper Wholesalers)

INDUSTRY SNAPSHOT

Judging from paper production capacity in the United States, the late 1990s represented a time of ''ultra slow'' capacity growth, according to the 40th annual Capacity Survey conducted in 1999 by American Forest & Paper Association (AF&PA). The 1998 Capacity Survey was the first to identify a leveling of growth in aggregate paper production capacity in the United States, with an expansion rate of 0.6 percent. Capacity Survey results for 1999 confirmed this slowdown, with aggregate production capacity falling 0.5 percent, to 101.3 million tons. Projections for aggregate production capacity remained very slow, predicting increases of 1.1 percent in 2000, 0.7 percent in 2001, and 0.4 percent in 2002.

Whereas printing and writing paper experienced capacity growth at an average annual rate of 2.2 percent throughout the 1990s, in 1999 this trend nosedived, with 1999 capacity of 29.1 million falling 1 percent under 1998 projections. Producers expected the capacity growth rate to flatten to an average rate of 0.7 percent throughout the projection period, lasting until 2002. The survey cited at least three factors contributing to such slow growth: increased competition, the migration of industry capital to meet external demands, and mill shutdowns.

Printing and writing paper is grouped in four large categories: uncoated groundwood, coated groundwood, uncoated freesheet, and coated freesheet. ''Groundwood'' refers to paper made from mechanical pulp, and ''freesheet'' refers to paper made from chemical pulp (see **SIC 2611: Pulp Mills**). ''Coated'' refers to paper that has been treated to improve printability and/or appearance. Printing and writing papers range from the lower-quality paper used to print advertising circulars to the high-quality coated paper used to print upscale magazines. These categories do not include newsprint, considered to be a low-quality paper.

The projected growth rate for uncoated groundwood capacity called for an average annual increase of 1.9 percent from 2000 to 2002. Even with this growth, however, total uncoated groundwood capacity in 2002 would be 4 percent lower than the 1996 total of 2.3 million tons, the category's peak capacity. Projections for coated groundwood peg capacity at 4.6 million tons in 2002, representing the same capacity as a decade earlier. Whereas coated free sheet capacity rose at an annual rate of 4.6 percent in the 1990s, producers expected this growth rate to flatten to 1.9 percent per year, with most of this growth concentrated in a few companies. Projections for uncoated free sheet production call for a capacity increase of 0.6 percent in 2000, and then remain flat through 2002.

CURRENT CONDITIONS

The growing popularity of electronic modes of communication such as the Internet, electronic mail, and voice mail certainly contributed to the slowdown in demand for printing and writing paper in the late 1990s. These means of communication were still in their infantile phases in the early and mid-1990s, and did not impact

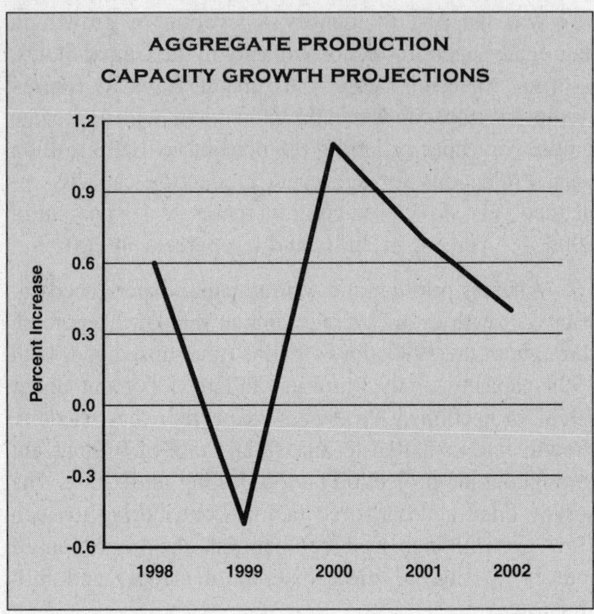

the industry. In fact, wholesalers of printing and writing paper showed consistent sales growth in the early to mid-1990s, moving from $32.3 billion in 1990 to $37.9 billion in 1993 and $43.2 billion in 1996, sustaining average growth of 5.6 percent, well ahead of inflation.

In 1996, there were more than 2,300 establishments in the wholesale distribution of printing and writing paper. In that year, the industry employed just over 39,700 workers, and its annual payroll was $1.68 billion. Total shipments of printing and writing paper by U.S. paper mills to distributors and wholesalers amounted to 25.2 million tons in 1995, about 28 percent of total U.S. paper production.

Over the past few decades, printing and writing paper distributors have had to deal with wide price swings brought about by the volatile market for paper products. For example, after several years of below average pricing in the early to mid-1990s, the average price for all pulp, paper, and paperboard products rose 34 percent in 1995, with some printing and writing grades rising as much as 75 percent. However, in 1996, prices dropped as much as 30 percent in some grades. This volatility is brought about by a complex cycle of mill capacity additions, changes in inventory, and paper usage. For example, as the cost of printing and writing paper soared in 1995, publishers and printers increased their inventories dramatically in anticipation of future price increases. When publishers and printers began using this inventory, they stopped buying new supplies and prices for printing and writing paper tumbled.

For distributors and wholesalers, this makes business planning difficult. When demand and prices are high, they can make incremental profits, but down cycles are difficult since they are carrying the double burden of excess inventory and low unit prices.

In the mid-1990s, distributors and wholesalers of printing and writing paper focused on forming st rategic alliances with major commercial printers and with other high-volume end users. In some cases, distributors became sole suppliers to certain printers. On the ''imaging'' side of the business, the growth of desktop computers, software graphics programs, and new output devices challenged paper distributors to more closely match paper requirements to their customers' imaging needs. To do this, distributors have had to provide more technical assistance to customers.

Industry Leaders

As in other industries, diversification, acquisitions and mergers dominated the business plans of the leading companies. Unisource Worldwide, Inc. of Berwyn, Pennsylvania, was the largest independent marketer and distributor of printing and imaging paper in North America, with 13,400 employees and revenues in fiscal 1998 of $7.4 billion. However, for the six months ending March 31, 1999, Unisource experienced sales of $3.29 billion, a decrease of 12 percent due to price deflation. On May 25, 1999, Georgia-Pacific Corp., of Atlanta, Georgia, merged with Unisource.

International Paper Co., of Purchase, New York, the other major player in this industry, relied on diversification to balance its business. Revenue losses due to Hurricane Floyd in September 1999 were offset by an increase of more than 400 percent in earnings in the U.S. papers segment of the company, which it ascribed to favorable pricing, internal cost-cutting, and other streamlining as a result of International Paper's merger with Union Camp earlier in 1999.

Further Reading

American Forest & Paper Association. ''Slow Capacity Growth to Continue, Paper Industry Survey Indicates.'' Available from http://www.afandpa.org/news/PressReleases/capacity99_rel.html.

''Coated Free-Sheet: Robust Year Ends on Down Note.'' *Pulp & Paper,* March 1996.

Darnay, Arsen J. and Gary Alampi, eds. *Wholesale and Retail Trade USA.* Detroit: Gale Research, 1995.

''Georgia-Pacific and Unisource Worldwide to Merge.'' Available from http://www.newswire.ca/releases/May1999/25/c6928.html.

International Paper Co. Available from http://www.marketguide.com.

Paper, Paperboard, Pulp Capacity and Fiber Consumption. Washington, DC: American Forest & Paper Association, 1996.

U.S. Trade and Industrial Outlook, 1997-1998. New York: McGraw-Hill, 1997.

SIC 5112

STATIONERY AND OFFICE SUPPLIES

This entry includes establishments primarily engaged in the wholesale distribution of stationery and office supplies, including computer and photocopy supplies, envelopes, typewriter paper, file cards and folders, pens, pencils, social stationery, greeting cards, carbon paper, business forms, looseleaf binders, and inked ribbons.

NAICS CODE(S)

453210 (Office Supplies and Stationery Stores)
422120 (Stationery and Office Supplies Wholesalers)

INDUSTRY SNAPSHOT

In October 1999 the Business Products Industry Association (BPIA) reported on a new study conducted by the National School Supply and Equipment Association (NSSEA) suggesting that the education segment represented a growing outlet for the industry. The 1999 State of the School Market Report noted the increase in annual expenditure per pupil—to $7,000 from $5,000 a decade earlier—as well as record enrollment increases three years in a row, with projected record-breaking enrollment every year through the early 2000s. National spending on K-12 education increased by 51 percent in inflation-adjusted dollars since the 1970s. This growth in education ensured business for the industry, as most of its products catered to students or school administrators.

The 1997 BPIA Leadership Council Meeting identified four major trends affecting the industry: vendor consolidation, globalization, internal competition within the industry, and liquidizations of family-owned businesses. Whereas the office supply and stationery wholesale industry had a large number of establishments operating in the mid-1990s (just over 11,450, though most were small, employing an average of 12 people), this number diminished in the late 1990s.

As part of the consolidation trend within the industry, larger national distributors established networks of distribution centers to serve targeted regions. National distributors also turned to technology to help make them competitive with the many regional distributors. To enhance service to customers and ensure quick delivery, many distributors converted their ordering, billing, and warehouse operations to sophisticated computer hardware and software systems so inventory could be tracked easily and orders filled within 24 hours.

Meanwhile, large retailers and warehouse clubs such as OfficeMax, Staples and Office Depot were usurping the role of distributors and buying directly from the manufacturer, their large size and vast networks facilitating the volume buying power of wholesalers. These retailers grew quickly by targeting corporate purchasers and expanding their service capabilities.

Smaller distributors were operating on increasingly narrower margins and serving a shrinking market of retail stores, and many went out of business due to a poor economy and fierce competition. Those that did survive did so by reevaluating their pricing and service policies, finding that while they often could not beat the discounters' prices, they could provide value-added services as part of the traditional two-tier distribution system. Wholesale distributors then focused on ways to better serve retail clients and to help those clients provide better customer service.

As for globalization, Paine Webber analyst Aram Rubinson pointed out at the BPIA Leadership Council Meeting that international expansion did not succeed as well for Staples as it had for Viking, a contract stationer, because Viking didn't have to invest in brick-and-mortar infrastructure as Staples did. United efforts within the industry also promoted globalization. For example, in February 1997 the National Purchasing Association (NPA) formed a marketing alliance with Basic Office Products Canada and Integra of the U.K. These three groups represent a total of 600 individual dealer locations with combined sales volume of about $2 billion in office product consumables.

ORGANIZATION AND STRUCTURE

Traditionally, wholesalers buy merchandise from a manufacturer and resell it at a profit to other wholesalers, retailers, or industrial and commercial customers. To compete with wholesalers, superstores such as OfficeMax, Staples and Office Depot provide small businesses, and the distributors who supply those dealers, with similar merchandise for lower prices. As competition for smaller businesses intensified, larger distributors began focusing more on commercial accounts. For example, United Stationers targets commercial accounts with $5 million or more in annual revenue, servicing industry office complexes of 50 or more employees. Unisource Worldwide also reports success in attracting and retaining regional and national accounts. In fiscal 1995, these key customers contributed more than $600 million to Unisource revenues.

Wholesale distributors have also tried coordinating their efforts with the superstores rather than trying to compete with them. United Stationers began testing a distribution system with the largest office supplies superstore, Office Depot. United received products from 10 different manufacturers at its Atlanta distribution center, and then within 24 to 36 hours shipped the merchandise to 31 Office Depot stores in the southern United States.

United also performed this service for smaller dealers and for some manufacturers by delivering products to the manufacturers' key accounts.

Many retailers and their commercial customers have begun operating on "just-in-time" delivery, requiring their distributors or manufacturers to ship supplies as quickly as possible. With just-in-time buying, dealers or their customers place smaller orders more often, saving them space and inventory time and avoiding tying up their money in supplies that might sit on the shelves for months. For commercial and industrial accounts, just-in-time also reduced the theft that often occurs in business.

Just-in-time ordering prompted retailers to more fully computerize their sales and inventory information, making it readily available to their distributors, or manufacturers if they dealt directly. With state-of-the-art computer equipment, suppliers could perform some of the inventory management tasks and determine what items needed to be restocked. Because dealers were keeping less inventory on hand, however, they had to ensure that the distributor could get merchandise to them quickly, often for next-day delivery.

The office supply wholesale industry also had to compete with the convenience of catalog and direct mail marketers with whom customers could place orders by calling a toll-free number or using a fax machine. These suppliers also operated on slim profit margins and dealt directly with the manufacturers.

Distributors of stationery and office supplies saw steadily growing sales in the 1990s. Total sales for this industry grew from $27.8 billion in 1990 to $33.5 billion in 1993 and $39.3 billion in 1996. Average annual growth for that six-year period was 6.9 percent, well ahead of inflation. In 1994 and 1995, larger distributors posted strong earnings growth. One particularly strong growth area was contract business forms management.

Industry Leaders

United Stationers Inc., of Des Plaines, Illinois, was the nation's largest wholesale distributor of business products in North America, with a distribution network of 66 Regional Distribution Centers serving more than 20,000 resellers. United Stationers had record net sales of $878 million in the third quarter of 1999, up 10.4 percent from its net sales in the third quarter of 1998 at $795 million. Third quarter 1999 net income similarly rose to $22.3 million, up from $19.9 million in the third quarter of 1998. Net sales over the first nine months of 1999 amounted to $2.5 billion, up 10.7 percent compared to the same nine-month period in 1998, when net sales reached $2.3 billion.

In 1992, United Stationers acquired Stationers Distributing, the fourth largest distributor in the industry at half the size of United. The acquisition strengthened United's position in Texas and the western United States, since United was dominant in the Midwest and Northeast.

U.S. Office Products claimed to be "one of North America's leading providers of office supplies" and other professional needs. The company performed poorly in the second quarter of 1999, with revenues falling 1.6 percent from the same quarter of 1998 because of diminished North American sales, particularly in the Office Supplies Division. Overall revenues for the company for the third quarter 1999 were $642.5 million as compared to $677.2 million during the same period of 1998. Half-year results showed a more dramatic decline: $1.27 billion for 1999, compared to $1.33 billion, a difference of $60 million.

Other major competitors in the industry include Unisource Worldwide, of Wayne, Pennsylvania; ResourceNet, of International Paper, in Purchase, New York; Genuine Parts Co., of Atlanta, Georgia; Boise Cascade Office Products, of Itasca, Illinois; S.P. Richards Co., of Smyrna, Georgia; and Corporate Express Inc., of Broomfield, Colorado. In May 1999, Georgia-Pacific Corp., of Atlanta, Georgia, merged with Unisource.

Research and Technology

Wholesalers have applied advanced computer technology to improve their slim profit margins. This technology improved productivity of all functions, including purchasing, delivery, storage, picking, and shipping. It also improved inventory as well as credit and information management. Using electronic document interface (EDI) technology wholesale distributors, superstores, warehouse clubs, mail order houses and dealers can input an order and trigger the shipping and billing, resulting in faster turnaround, less paperwork, and savings on handling.

Further Reading

Alco Standard Corporation Annual Report 1995. Wayne, PA: Alco Standard Corporation, 1996.

Business Products Industry Association. "Industry Trends Debated at Leadership Council Meeting." and "School Market is New 'Growth Business.'" Available from http://www.bpia.org.

Cohen, David, et al. *The Value Line Investment Survey (Part 3-Ratings & Reports),* 27 January 1995.

Darnay, Arsen J. and Gary Alampi, eds. *Wholesale and Retail Trade USA.* Detroit: Gale Research, 1995.

International Paper Company Annual Report 1995. Purchase, NY: International Paper Company, 1996.

"More International Alliances Seen from Dealer Groups." *Business Product Industry Association Industry Report,* 15 March 1997.

"United Stationers Reports Third-Quarter Sales up 10 Percent and Earnings Up 25 Percent." Available from http://www.corporate-ir.net.

"US Office Products Reports Results for Second Quarter of FY 2000." Available from http://www.corporate-ir.net.

SIC 5113

INDUSTRIAL AND PERSONAL SERVICE PAPER

This category includes establishments primarily engaged in the wholesale distribution of wrapping and other coarse paper and paperboard, as well as converted paper and related disposable plastics products, such as bags, boxes, dishes, eating utensils, napkins, and shipping supplies. It includes wholesale distribution of corrugated and solid fiber boxes, fiber cans and drums, pressed and molded pulp goods, pressure sensitive tape, sanitary food containers, and paper towels.

NAICS CODE(S)

422130 (Industrial and Personal Service Paper Wholesalers)

INDUSTRY SNAPSHOT

Judging from paper production capacity in the United States, the late 1990s represented a time of "ultra slow" capacity growth, according to the 40th annual Capacity Survey conducted in 1999 by the American Forest & Paper Association (AF&PA). The 1998 Capacity Survey was the first to identify a leveling of growth in aggregate paper production capacity in the United States, with an expansion rate of 0.6 percent. Capacity Survey results for 1999 confirmed this slowdown, with aggregate production capacity falling 0.5 percent, to 101.3 million tons. Projections for aggregate production capacity remained very slow, predicting increases of 1.1 percent in 2000, 0.7 percent in 2001, and 0.4 percent in 2002.

Whereas the production capacity for most grades of industrial and personal service paper ran flat or grew slightly, one component of the industry represented sustainable growth. The annual rate of using recovered paper to make industrial papers was projected to rise 1.8 percent from 2000 to 2002, bringing recovered paper's share of total consumption from 36.1 percent in 1998 to 37.1 percent in 2002. The production capacity for tissue paper grew to 7.1 million tons in 1999, an increase of 3.4 percent. However, projections called for slower capacity growth through the next three years, with rates descending from 2.8 percent in 2000 to 1.7 percent in 2001 and 0.2 percent in 2002.

Containerboard and boxboard capacities were slated to run fairly flat, with the former only growing 0.5 percent annually from 2000 to 2002 and growth of the latter falling from 1.2 percent in 2000 to 0.6 percent in 2001 before bottoming out at 0.3 percent in 2002. Milk carton and food service board capacity grew by 2.5 percent in 1999, but was expected to level off during the first three years of the millennium. The production capacity of kraft paper, used to line corrugation, fell to 2.1 million tons in 1999, a dramatic decrease of 3.8 percent. However, its capacity levels were expected to level as well, dropping only 1.1 percent in 2000 and then leveling off by 2002.

Wholesale distributors of industrial and personal service paper saw a steadily increasing market in the 1990s, with sales growing from $37.0 billion in 1990 to $46.7 billion in 1996. This represented average annual growth of 4.4 percent, keeping the industry growing moderately in real (inflation adjusted) dollars. The industry was also growing in terms of employment in the 1990s, with 69,700 employees in 1990 increasing to 75,300 in 1996. There were 5,668 establishments involved in wholesale distribution of industrial and service paper in 1996, up from 4,667 in 1990, according to U.S. Department of Commerce figures. Most of these were small operations, however, averaging 12 employees per establishment.

CURRENT CONDITIONS

Establishments in this industry are concentrated in the most densely populated areas to be close to their customers. About half of all industrial and personal service paper is distributed by paper merchants and the other half is marketed and distributed by the paper manufacturers' own sales representatives and distribution services. Many of the largest manufacturers of industrial and personal service paper distribute their goods from distribution centers near their plants and mills.

Given the small size and large number of distributors in this industry, the market is considered to be highly fragmented. Market share is spread among the thousands of local and regional U.S. distributors, with only a few operations being considered national in scope. However, larger firms such as International Paper and Unisource Worldwide have been consolidating the distribution system in recent years by buying up smaller competitors to provide single-source purchasing for a range of industry products. These distributors are taking advantage of a trend in which their major customers establish company-wide supply contracts, eliminating some of the buying autonomy of their local units.

In addition to single-sourcing, a major strategy for paper distributors has been to offer several services to clients, including: on-call technical expertise; overnight delivery; just-in-time inventory controls; and electronic data interchange (EDI), which allows suppliers, distributors, and customers to write electronic purchase orders, track inventory and sales, and collect other information as part of the distribution process.

INDUSTRY LEADERS

Leading companies included International Paper Co., of Purchase, New York, and Unisource Worldwide, of Berwyn, Pennsylvania. International Paper employed 80,000 workers as of the beginning of 1999, and its revenues totaled $18.28 billion over the first 9 months of 1999, representing a rise of 2 percent. Revenue losses due to Hurricane Floyd in September 1999 were offset by an increase of more than 400 percent in earnings in the U.S. papers segment of the company, which it ascribed to favorable pricing, internal cost-cutting, and other streamlining as a result of International Paper's merger with Union Camp earlier in 1999.

Unisource Worldwide, employed 13,400 workers and generated revenues of $7.4 billion in fiscal 1998. However, for the six months ending March 31, 1999, Unisource experienced sales of $3.29 billion, a decrease of 12 percent due to price deflation. On May 25, 1999, Unisource and Georgia-Pacific Corp., of Atlanta, Georgia, announced a merger.

Other major players in the industrial and personal service paper distribution industry included units of the following paper manufacturing firms: Champion International Corp., of Stamford, Connecticut (through its Nationwide Papers Division); Mead Corp., of Dayton, Ohio; and Georgia-Pacific. Leading independent operations include McCarty-Holman Co., of Jackson, Mississippi; Martin-Brower Co., of Downers Grove, Illinois; Central National-Gottesman, of Purchase, New York; and Bunzl Distribution, of St. Louis, Missouri.

FURTHER READING

American Forest & Paper Association. ''Slow Capacity Growth to Continue, Paper Industry Survey Indicates.'' Available from http://www.afandpa.org/news/PressReleases/capacity99_rel.html.

Darnay, Arsen J. and Gary Alampi, eds. *Wholesale and Retail Trade USA.* Detroit: Gale Research, 1995.

''Georgia-Pacific and Unisource Worldwide to Merge.'' Available from http://www.newswire.ca/releases/May1999/25/c6928.html.

International Paper Co. Available from http://www.marketguide.com.

International Paper Co. Available from http://www.internationalpaper.com.

''Kraft Paper: Lower Operating Rates and Price Levels for Kraft Paper Mills.'' *Pulp & Paper,* November 1996.

Paper, Paperboard, Pulp Capacity and Fiber Consumption. Washington, DC: American Forest & Paper Association, 1996.

SIC 5122

DRUGS, DRUG PROPRIETARIES, AND DRUGGISTS' SUNDRIES

This industry classification includes establishments engaged in the wholesale distribution of items such as prescription drugs, proprietary drugs, druggists' sundries, and toiletries. Products handled by industry participants include antiseptics, bandages, blood plasma, cosmetics, hair preparations, perfumes, pharmaceuticals, nonelectric razors and razor blades, toothbrushes, and vitamins. Establishments primarily involved in the wholesale distribution of surgical, dental, and hospital equipment are included in **SIC 5047: Medical, Dental, and Hospital Equipment and Supplies.**

NAICS CODE(S)

422210 (Drugs, Drug Proprietaries, and Druggists' Sundries Wholesalers)

The number of establishments in the drugs, proprietaries, and sundries industry steadily increased throughout the decade, from approximately 5,200 in 1990 to more than 6,000 by 1996. In 1997 the number had reached 8,053. Combined, these companies posted combined sales of approximately $203 billion in 1999. The industry employed approximately 190,000 workers in 1997, with an annual payroll totaling slightly more than $8 billion.

Establishments within the industry were subdivided into two categories. The largest—specialty-line pharmaceuticals, cosmetics, and toiletries—was comprised of 69.8 percent of the industry's total number. Their sales, totaling $42.17 billion in the mid-1990s, accounted for 65.6 percent of the industry's sales. The other category—general-line drugs—was comprised of wholesalers who were distinguished from specialty-line sellers on the basis of their commodity-line mix.

According to U.S. government predictions, demand for pharmaceuticals was ''insensitive'' to the national economy, meaning that fluctuations in the country's overall business climate had little impact on demand for the industry's products. National concern over rapidly rising costs, however, was mounting and bringing change to traditional distribution patterns. Price increases, which marked the early to mid-1990s, were beginning to slow during the final years of the decade.

One industry leader is McKesson HBOC, based in San Francisco and formed when McKesson (distributor of pharmaceuticals) bought HBO and Company (healthcare information systems and technology). The company posted 1999 sales of $30.4 billion and 24,600 employees.

Other leaders were Cardinal Health of Dublin, Ohio, with 1999 sales of $25.0 billion; Bergen Brunswig Corporation of Orange, California, with 1999 sales of $21.2 billion; and AmeriSource of Malvern, Pennsylvania, with 1999 sales of $9.8 billion.

FURTHER READING

Hoover's Online. *Hoover's Company Profiles.* Austin, TX: April 2000.

U.S. Department of Commerce. Economics and Statistics Administration. *1997 Economic Census-Wholesale Trade.* Washington, D.C.: GPO, March 2000. Available from http://www.census.gov.

SIC 5131

PIECE GOODS, NOTIONS, AND OTHER DRY GOODS

This industry comprises wholesale distributors of piece goods, yarn goods (made from natural or manmade fibers), notions (including sewing accessories and hair accessories), and other dry goods. Products of the industry include belt and buckle assembly kits, buttons, shoulder pads, textiles, thread, apparel trimmings, and zippers. The industry also includes converters who buy fabric goods (except knit goods) in the grey market, contract to have them finished, and sell the finished product at wholesale. Converters of knit goods, however, are included in Industry Group 225. Establishments engaged primarily in the wholesale distribution of items considered home furnishings are classified under **SIC 5023: Homefurnishings.**

NAICS CODE(S)

313311 (Broadwoven Fabric Finishing Mills)
313312 (Textile and Fabric Finishing (except Broadwoven Fabric) Mills)
422310 (Piece Goods, Notions, and Other Dry Goods Wholesalers)

In 1996, there were approximately 4,800 establishments in the piece goods and notions industry, an increase of 2 percent over 1990. Sales for the industry totaled about $32 billion in 1996, up about 16 percent over 1990's total of $27 billion. The states with the largest number of establishments in the industry were New York (34 percent) and California (16 percent). In 1997 the industry had 5,666 establishments with 45,435 employees. Sales fell somewhat to approximately $26 billion.

Sellers of fabric goods and craft items to retailers experienced an upswing during the early to mid-1990s. According to a report in *Adweek's Marketing Week,* as Americans began spending more time at home, sales for sewing and craft shops increased. Fabric wholesalers supplying the apparel industry, however, saw their customers dwindle in size and numbers. Industry employment decreased in the apparel industry during the first half of the 1990s. Thread sellers were expected to be unaffected because apparel cut in the United States and shipped abroad for assembly was ordinarily sewn with American-produced threads. Additionally, non-apparel uses for industry goods were steadily increasing into the 2000s.

One of the largest organizations involved in this industry was Marubeni America Corporation. Marubeni America, a wholly owned subsidiary of Marubeni Corporation (a Japanese general trading company), was incorporated in 1951. Its headquarters were located in New York City, and the company operated 14 other branches and offices throughout the United States.

Marubeni America's Textile Division offered an assortment of products in the international marketplace. According to a published company statement, although fabrics represented the ''backbone of the division's success,'' the company was expanding its interest in natural and synthetic fibers, yarns, and raw American cotton.

Marubeni America operated other product divisions in addition to its Textile Division. These included metal and mineral, machinery, chemical, plastics and inorganic chemicals, agri-commodity, and general merchandise. Total sales for the company in 1999 were more than $100 billion.

Other industry leaders include ITOCHU International Inc. (ITOCHU Cotton Inc.) and China Industrial Group, both located in New York City.

FURTHER READING

Hoover's Online. *Hoover's Company Profiles.* Austin, TX: April 2000.

U.S. Department of Commerce. Economics and Statistics Administration. *1997 Economic Census-Wholesale Trade.* Washington, D.C.: GPO, March 2000. Available from http://www.census.gov.

SIC 5136

MEN'S AND BOYS' CLOTHING AND FURNISHINGS

This industry classification is comprised of wholesale distributors of men's and boys' apparel and furnishings. Products of the industry include shirts, trousers, sportswear, suits, ties, work clothing, hosiery, underwear, nightwear, outerwear and overcoats, gloves, hats, scarves, and umbrellas. Wholesale distributors of men's and boys' shoes, however, are included in **SIC 5139: Footwear.**

NAICS Code(s)

422320 (Men's and Boys' Clothing and Furnishings Wholesalers)

Approximately 5,000 establishments were primarily engaged in the wholesale distribution of men's and boys' apparel and furnishings in 1997. The industry's sales were estimated to total in excess of $33.3 billion, an increase from the $28.1 billion reported by the *1992 Census of Wholesale Trade.*

In the late 1990s, New York led the nation with both the highest number of establishments (1,024) and the highest dollar amount of sales ($7.8 billion). California was second with 817 establishments and sales of $4.5 billion.

In fall 1996, *Occupational Outlook Quarterly* provided a solemn forecast for employees in the apparel industry. During the later part of the twentieth century, increasing globalization and new technological developments played a role in the continuous decline in the industry. From 1970 to 1996, employment in the overall apparel industry declined by about 33 percent to around 915,000 workers by the mid-1990s. This industry in particular reported 62,253 employees in 1997.

One industry leader was Polo/Ralph Lauren L.P. Ralph Lauren began his career in 1967 when he designed wide ties and started the Polo label. The following year, he established the Polo by Ralph Lauren menswear company. Throughout the following decades he also established successful womenswear, fragrance, accessories, and home furnishing lines.

The *Daily News Record* reported in late 1996 that Polo/Ralph Lauren generated more than $500 million in retail sales of men's furnishings in the United States and internationally; this number remained virtually unchanged in 1999. In 1996, the company had 2,700 employees; this number increased to 6,800 in 1999. Polo/Ralph Lauren had licenses throughout the United States and in more than 30 countries. It sold the resulting products through independently licensed and company-owned Polo stores and through upscale department stores.

Other important companies were Tommy Hilfiger Corporation; L.L. Bean, Inc.; and J. Crew Group Inc.

Further Reading

Curan, Catherine. ''Purple Reign.'' *Daily News Record,* 6 December 1996.

Hoover's Online. *Hoover's Company Profiles.* Austin, TX: April 2000.

Mittelhauser, Mark. ''Job Loss and Survival Strategies in the Textile and Apparel Industries.'' *Occupational Outlook Quarterly,* fall 1996.

U.S. Department of Commerce. Economics and Statistics Administration. *1997 Economic Census-Wholesale Trade.* Washington, D.C.: GPO, March 2000. Available from http://www.census.gov.

SIC 5137

WOMEN'S, CHILDREN'S, AND INFANTS' CLOTHING AND ACCESSORIES

This industry comprises wholesale distributors of women's, children's, and infants' clothing and accessories. Products of the industry include blouses, dresses, skirts, sportswear, unisex clothing, underwear, lingerie, hosiery, outerwear, hats, handbags, ladies' handkerchiefs, gloves, and mittens. Wholesale distributors of baby goods and diapers and distributors of hospital gowns are also included. Wholesalers engaged in the distribution of women's, children's, and infants' footwear, however, are classified under **SIC 5139: Footwear.**

NAICS Code(s)

422330 (Women's, Children's and Infants' Clothing and Accessories Wholesalers)

Approximately 8,200 establishments were engaged in this industry in 1997. Their estimated combined sales totaled $40.6 billion, up by nearly $10 billion from *1992 U.S. Census of Wholesale Trade* data. Additionally, this industry employed more than 76,000 workers in the late 1990s.

Much of the industry's activity was centered in New York and California. Combined, these two states accounted for 54.2 percent of the number of industry establishments and 61.0 percent of its sales.

According to several U.S. business publications including *Forbes,* the North American Free Trade Agreement (NAFTA) was the impetus behind a massive shift of U.S. garment production from Asia to Mexico. Half of the apparel sold in the United States was imported from other countries and, after the 1994 NAFTA agreement, apparel exports from Mexico grew to $3.3 billion. In early 1997, Mexico was the highest U.S. source of imported apparel. Sent to Mexico mainly in the form of cut pieces to be sewn, U.S. apparel exports almost doubled to about $2.5 billion a year after NAFTA. The change in production from Asia to Mexico helped lower U.S. clothing costs between 1994 and 1997.

One of the largest industry establishments was Nitches, Inc., formerly known as Beeba's, Inc. The company began operation as a women's sportswear wholesaler in 1973 and imported finished garments, primarily all-cotton and cotton-blend items, from approximately 20 countries and resold them to retailers such as Wal-Mart Stores, Inc.; Mervyn's; The Limited Stores, Inc.; J.C. Penney Company, Inc.; and Target Stores, Inc. In 1996, Nitches reported that it competed "on a basis of price, quality, reliability of service and fashion focus," with experience in handling a variety of women's, children's, maternity, and plus-size apparel.

In 1996, the California-based Nitches imported finished garments from 15 foreign countries and continued a policy of seeking national diversity in its arrangements with manufacturers. Nitches reported sales of $31.5 million in 1999. The company had 40 full-time employees during 1999, which was down approximately 50 percent from the mid-1990s. This decline in the number of employees followed a trend that *Occupational Outlook Quarterly* predicted would continue in the apparel industry beyond the year 2000.

FURTHER READING

Hoover's Online. *Hoover's Company Profiles.* Austin, TX: April 2000.

Mittelhauser, Mark. "Job Loss and Survival Strategies in the Textile and Apparel Industries." *Occupational Outlook Quarterly,* fall 1996.

Ramey, Joanna. "Wholesale Prices on Women's Up a Bit in December From November." *Women's Wear Daily,* 1 February 1996.

U.S. Department of Commerce. Economics and Statistics Administration. *1997 Economic Census-Wholesale Trade.* Washington, D.C.: GPO, March 2000. Available from http://www.census.gov.

SIC 5139

FOOTWEAR WHOLESALERS

This industry consists of establishments that engage in the wholesale distribution of athletic and other footwear of leather, rubber, and other materials.

NAICS CODE(S)

422340 (Footwear Wholesalers)

INDUSTRY SNAPSHOT

Footwear wholesalers benefited greatly during the 1980s and 1990s from the booming popularity of athletic and other sport-oriented casual shoes. Nearly 180,000 employees at domestic manufacturers lost their jobs between 1968 and 1995, according to the Footwear Industries of America (FIA) trade group, but footwear wholesalers flourished by importing inexpensive models. Nike, Inc. and Reebok International Ltd. fueled the industry by making casual footwear a fashion staple.

ORGANIZATION AND STRUCTURE

The Commerce Department divides footwear wholesalers into three categories: merchant wholesalers (who take title to the goods they sell); manufacturers' sales branches and offices (which are kept apart from manufacturing plants for marketing purposes); and agents, brokers, and commission merchants (who buy and sell products owned by others on a commission or agency basis). Additionally, the footwear market is divided into several sections: women's and misses' footwear; men's, youth's and boys' nonrubber footwear; children's, infants', and babies' nonrubber footwear; leather athletic footwear; sneakers, rubber and plastic protective footwear; and house slippers. By way of imports, wholesalers play a major role in each of these markets and dominate several.

According to the *1992 Census of Wholesale Trade,* almost 80 percent of the total establishments in the industry were merchant wholesalers, and they accounted for nearly 75 percent of all sales. Manufacturers' sales branches and offices comprised 1.5 percent of the total establishments and tallied less than 9 percent of sales. Over 19 percent of the establishments and 16 percent of the sales were attributed to agents, brokers and commission merchants.

The payrolls of footwear wholesalers have grown substantially in recent years, largely mirroring their increased activity as domestic production declined and imports rose. Annual payrolls at all footwear wholesaling establishments jumped 13.7 percent between 1992 and 1996, and the sales per establishment increased 43.9 percent. By 1995, average annual pay for agents, brokers and commission merchants was $61,015; employees in manufacturers' sales branches and offices received $50,557; and merchant wholesalers were paid $37,825.

BACKGROUND AND DEVELOPMENT

The distinction between domestic manufacturers, wholesalers, and retailers had grown fuzzier due to the domination of imports in the U.S. footwear market. Traditionally, footwear wholesalers served as the middlemen between footwear manufacturers and footwear retailers. In the 1990s, however, more and more of these manufacturers were based outside the U.S. In addition, with many domestic manufacturers seeking to replace lost sales by boosting their own foreign production, and powerful domestic retailers sourcing directly from factories abroad in an attempt to reduce costs, smaller wholesalers began facing stiff competition from firms that were once their partners.

Nike and Reebok, along with other U.S. firms that produce footwear in the factories of foreign shoe firms, can take advantage of the extremely low wages paid abroad and solidify their positions. South Korean manufacturers, who dominated the high-quality U.S. import market in the early 1990s, fell from favor in recent years as wages increased. Major U.S. companies like Nike and Reebok gradually moved their higher-level production to other countries in Southeast Asia causing employment in South Korea's footwear industry to drop 40 percent between 1990 and 1993. Chinese manufacturers, on the other hand, continued to dominate the low-priced footwear market because their wages remained extremely low. Footwear continues to represent over 15 percent of China's entire light industry sector's exports.

Industry sales for footwear wholesalers was $19.9 billion in 1996, more than 22 percent higher than 1990 and almost 52 percent greater than 1987. More than 21,800 people were employed by 1,534 footwear wholesalers in 1996, drawing an annual payroll of $1 billion. Millions of other workers around the world also found employment as a result of the American demand for footwear and imports from their production—mostly from China, Brazil and Indonesia—now account for almost 89 percent of all U.S. shoe sales.

Current Conditions

The primary function of independent footwear wholesalers operating in the United States is to stock the shelves of shoe retailers with a wide variety of brands and products. The operations of these companies, however, were dwarfed by those of the wholesale divisions of America's two leading athletic footwear manufacturers, Nike and Reebok (Reebok generated $3.2 billion in sales for fiscal 1998.) These two firms have established themselves as major consumer brands of footwear and other related athletic apparel products with the power to act as their own wholesale importers.

1999 predictions called for continuing flat sales for footwear wholesalers, remaining at about $35 billion per year with a mere 1 percent rate of annual growth. Industry insiders attributed this stagnancy to oversupplied inventories, especially in athletic footwear (which makes up about 40 percent of the overall market) and to poor sales for women's nonathletic shoes (which account for over 35 percent of market).

Industry Leaders

Besides Reebok and Nike, the big names in the Footwear wholesale industry were the St. Louis-based Brown Shoe Co., with $1.8 billion in fiscal 1998 sales, Spalding Holdings Corp., with $800 million in 1998 sales, and Items International Airwalk Inc., with $236 million in fiscal 1997. Brown's sales increased 4.2 percent to $429.1 million in the third quarter of 1999, with wholesale sales slipping from $119.2 million to $116.7 million. Airwalk took advantage of the cash infusion resulting from the 1998 buyout by Sunrise Capital Partners to diversify into apparel, buying into the brand's appeal internationally, where it was not as well known as a shoe company as in the United States.

Workforce

The changes in the industry all but eliminated the role of so-called jobbers, or middlemen who resold closeout, seconds and overrun shoes to retailers, as manufacturers sold directly to merchants and computerized their inventories. Estimates pegged the number of jobbers in 1997 at half the number there were a decade earlier.

In 1992, according to the Commerce Department, there were 21,826 employees in the footwear wholesaling industry. Of them, 18,710 worked for merchant wholesalers; 1,689 for manufacturers' sales branches and offices; and 1,427 for agents, brokers and commission merchants.

Sales per employee for all footwear wholesalers that year were quite high, and growing. With relatively few employees, the industry generated more than $16.2 billion in total sales and sales per employee averaged $744,635—up nearly 20 percent from 1987. This compared favorably to the 1992 sales-per-employee average of $539,753 for all wholesalers.

America and the World

By the mid-1990s, once successful foreign producers in regions like Taiwan and South Korea were suffering losses similar to those experienced by domestic manufacturers during the 1970s and 1980s. An increased standard of living in these countries led to rapidly rising wages, which made it increasingly difficult for them to compete with other lower wage countries such as China, Indonesia, and Mexico. As a result, Taiwan and South Korea dropped from being the fourth- and fifth-largest importers of shoes to America in 1992 to the seventh- and eighth-largest in 1995. The heated foreign competition, though, is good news for American footwear wholesalers and, ultimately, the U.S. consumer.

FURTHER READING

"Current Highlights of the Nonrubber Footwear Industry," Washington D.C.: Footwear Industries of America, 25 July 1996. Available from http://www.fia.org.

McAlister, Robert. "Jobbers need true grit to survive." *Footwear News,* 28 July 1997.

Plotkin, Amanda. "Airwalk Team Push to Bolster Brand." *Footwear News,* 15 November 1999.

Solnik, Claude. "Airwalk Searching for U.S. Companies to Fill Out its Licensing Portfolio." *Footwear News,* 6 September 1999.

SIC 5141

GROCERIES, GENERAL LINE

This category covers establishments primarily engaged in the wholesale distribution of general lines of groceries. Specialty establishments—those involved in such activities as roasting coffee, blending tea, or grinding and packaging spices—are not included in this classification. Wholesalers responsible for the distribution of specific grocery classes are classified under specific wholesale distribution areas such as **SIC 5142: Packaged Frozen Foods; SIC 5143: Dairy Products, Except Dried or Canned;** and **SIC 5145: Confectionery.**

NAICS CODE(S)

422410 (General Line Grocery Wholesalers)

INDUSTRY SNAPSHOT

Wholesale food distributors provide food and related products (health and beauty aids, cleaning products, and other general grocery items) to retail grocery stores, convenience stores, and other retailers that sell food products. Food distributors can provide other services to their retail customers as well—advertising, merchandising, accounting, real estate site location, and financing. Their infrastructure usually includes warehouse facilities, truck fleets, and related information technology systems.

The U.S. wholesale food distribution industry reflects the ups and downs of the retail food industry, which has been subject to slow, or even negative growth during the late 1980s and 1990s. Historic low levels of food inflation, weak consumer spending, and the rapidly changing face of the retail grocery industry (including the growth of so-called "wholesale club" stores and the decreasing influence of the independent grocer) have all taken their toll on the retail and wholesale food industries in the 1990s.

Retail grocers—and the wholesalers that depend upon them—have also seen a growing portion of their sales being taken away by restaurants. In the 1990s, restaurants have emphasized value and convenience to lure new customers, and an increasingly time-stressed public has responded by eating out or buying takeout food in increasing numbers. To counter this, a number of retail grocers began offering prepared food as early as the mid-1980s. They began with salad bars and soon were offering sandwiches, microwaveable dinners, pizza, and soups. In 1998, 83.6 percent of supermarkets offered some sort of prepared foods. This figure was actually down by 10 percentage points from the previous year, but retailers claim they are still committed to offering prepared meals.

Another factor contributing to the decline of the food wholesaler is the trend toward self-distribution. Grocery chains are increasingly moving in this direction, causing wholesalers to expand their client base to take on more (and often smaller) independent grocers. With the number of independents shrinking annually, this pool is becoming limited, forcing some wholesalers to look to mergers as their only way of surviving.

ORGANIZATION AND STRUCTURE

To be profitable, wholesale distribution must operate on a local or regional level. The most successful distributors, therefore, have either located their warehouse near a targeted metropolitan area or have set up a system of branch warehouses to limit the distance their truck fleets must travel to deliver goods to retailers.

There are a variety of wholesale distributors in the United States today. The specialty wholesaler provides a limited range of products—gourmet foods, spices, candy, or greeting cards. These wholesalers usually provide a range of services that include point-of-sale merchandising material, display suggestions, and product servicing such as stock rotation and monitoring of product displays. Rack jobbers provide a limited line of products—usually health and beauty aids, housewares, toys, and other types of non-food merchandise with distinctive marketing requirements different from those needed for food items—for which they assume complete responsibility on the in-store level.

Full-service wholesalers offer complete lines of grocery and non-grocery products; they also often provide lines of general merchandise, dairy, bakery, frozen foods, fresh meat, and fresh produce. Besides the food products themselves, full-service wholesalers provide help to the retailer in advertising, merchandising, and procuring products they may not warehouse. For example, a wholesaler may not actually stock fresh meat in its own warehouse, yet it may help retailers in obtaining and marketing fresh meat products. Among the range of merchandising services a full-service wholesaler may provide its retail customers are retail accounting, site selection, store design and interior layout, personnel training, display, promotion, advertising, suggested retail selling prices, and advisory help in projecting and controlling sales, gross margin, expenses, and net profit. In some instances, a full-service wholesaler may make private or controlled brands available to its retail customers.

The retailer-owned wholesaler represents the efforts of a number of retailers to join forces (sometimes under a common name) to operate their own warehouses and shipping lines. The cooperative effort makes it possible for retailers to obtain merchandise at the lowest feasible cost. In addition to providing lines of food products, the retailer-owned wholesaler also supplies group advertising, merchandising, and other services. Among the largest retailer-owned wholesalers are the Wakefern Food Corporation of New Jersey and Certified Grocers of California, Ltd.

Background and Development

In the early history of American food merchandising, retailing, wholesaling, and importing were often carried out by the same organization. It was not until the 1850s that the three activities began to distinguish themselves. Between 1850 and 1900 specialized wholesaling became common as service wholesalers provided a complete line of grocery products, including non-food items and perishables, to independent retail food stores.

During the early twentieth century, the number of service wholesalers grew rapidly. As chain stores developed and flourished, beginning with the founding of the Great Atlantic & Pacific Tea Company in 1912, wholesalers and retailers formed voluntary and retailer-owned groups. As supermarkets flourished between 1930 and 1965, marketing strategies on the retail and the wholesale level began to evolve, and major changes in food distribution took place. Retailer-owned and voluntary group wholesalers grew in number; at the same time, food wholesalers began to streamline and automate their distribution processes to cut costs and boost efficiency.

Among the earliest wholesaling leaders were the Independent Grocers Alliance (IGA Stores), founded in 1926, and Nation-Wide Stores, founded in 1928. These early wholesalers saw their role not only as stocking retailers' shelves, but also serving as merchandising experts to help increase profits.

Intense competition marked the 1970s and 1980s. The high inflation rates of the 1970s, coupled with the energy crisis, contributed to a general downturn in the industry. The industry profile was also in flux during this period because of changes in the retail food industry. Small retailers began expansion into multiple stores, sometimes also increasing their geographical dispersion. As chains spread out, the costs of moving goods to them from warehouses increased; some of the multiple-store owners turned to new distributors closer to their branch stores, while others began their own warehouse operations. The 1980s saw the consolidation of many food chains and the subsequent closing of warehouses that proved to be redundant.

Current Conditions

The trend toward self-distribution which began in the 1980s is one of the most serious threats facing the wholesale grocery industry. Wholesalers have historically made their biggest profits from servicing small regional independents, many of which were non-unionized and therefore able to save in labor costs. As the small independents consolidated into regional chains, the few independents left lost their labor cost advantage, since the chains gained labor concessions from their unions.

The strength of regional chains allowed them to negotiate price concessions from wholesalers and reduce their use of the supplementary services for which the wholesalers previously charged. Many of the remaining small independents have been unable to compete against new formats such as combination stores and wholesale clubs. Consequently, competition for the wholesalers has increased as has margin pressure, and they have had to deal with the growing clout of surviving customers and the threat of self-distribution.

With the move to self-distribution, wholesalers must either acquire new accounts or take over other wholesalers to maintain sales volume. Today, the bulk of wholesaler business is derived from small-volume independents and relatively small chains. Regional chains and such nontraditional food retailers as "deep discount" drug stores and "club" stores have forced wholesalers to invest more heavily in the weaker companies they supply to maintain their volume.

The largest wholesalers—most notably Supervalu and Fleming Companies, Inc.—have responded to these pressures not only by acquiring other wholesalers but also by significantly increasing their presence on the retail side of the grocery industry. By 1998, Fleming derived 31 percent of its revenue from retail operations. Supervalu, meanwhile, had reached as high as 16th place among U.S. food retailers in 1998. Essentially, these wholesalers were creating their own self-distributing chains through their acquisitions of retail chains and encroaching on retail territory, just as retailers have been encroaching on wholesaler turf.

Another major source of competition for the industry is the proliferation of alternative format stores, including warehouse clubs, deep discount drugstores, mass merchandisers, and supercenters. Analysts expected these new alternatives to capture a greater market share from traditional retail outlets as alternative outlets offer more food and food-related products.

A new wrinkle in the grocery industry is the on-line grocer business, which allows people to shop for groceries on the Internet. An estimated 90,000 households bought groceries on-line in 1998, and according to *eMarketer,* a newsletter that tracks on-line business, that number will grow to 6.9 million by the end of 2002, accounting for some $33.6 billion in sales. The market leader, Peapod, Inc., launched its site in 1989 and within 10 years had filled more than 1 million orders. Although it posted sales of $69.3 million in 1998, it lost $21.6 million the same year. When it began, it served only the Chicago area; today it serves San Francisco, Boston, Houston, Dallas, Austin, Columbus, and Long Island.

Webvan, which started up in the summer of 1999, plans to have warehouses in 10 major U.S. markets by the end of 2000. It is owned by Louis Borders (of Borders Books and Music fame). Netgrocer, with 1998 sales of $5 million, is the only on-line grocer that delivers nationwide, but charges more for deliveries than other companies. There are drawbacks to on-line grocery shopping; for example, most services do not deliver perishable goods. As the industry grows, however, it is likely that these issues will work themselves out.

The wholesale food industry has been forced to consolidate to remain profitable. In the past, voluntary wholesalers—firms that derive the majority of their revenues from independent stores operating under voluntary group banners—were the primary source of acquisition and growth for wholesalers. A growing number of other types of small wholesalers are also being acquired by their larger counterparts.

Wholesalers will need to know that the price of services they provide for their independent customers will not be affected by costs related to distribution inefficiencies. They will also need to secure favorable terms from manufacturers and pass along these savings to their customers, thus leveling out price differences among all types of retailers. Cutting down on excess inventory is also seen as a key to future grocery wholesalers' success.

A shrinking client base is one of the major reasons for the high consolidation rate in the wholesale food industry. The fate of the independent supermarket is a good illustration: According to *Progressive Grocer,* independents accounted for 65 percent of supermarket sales in 1952, 42 percent in 1972, 29 percent in 1992, and 16 percent in 1998. Large chains, convenience stores, and alternative-format stores have all taken market share away from independents. Another contributing factor is the capital-intensive nature of the wholesale grocery industry, which requires constant investment in systems, technology, and warehouse enhancements. Smaller wholesalers may have difficulty financing these commitments.

INDUSTRY LEADERS

The largest food wholesaler in the United States at the end of the 1990s was also a food retailer and manufacturer of food products. Supervalu Inc. (formerly known as Super Valu Stores Inc.), with headquarters in Eden Prairie, Minnesota, reported 1998 revenues of $11.84 billion. A wholesaler of groceries, drugs, sundries, and toiletries, Supervalu supplied 4,600 stores in 48 states. It also operated several chains of retail grocery stores and made peanut butter, nuts, and candies. Supervalu has grown rapidly in recent years through acquisitions, most recently signing an acquisition agreement with Richfood, Inc. of Richmond, Virginia, in June 1999 (Richfood, the ninth largest wholesaler, had 1998 sales of $3.01 billion.)

The second largest food wholesaler was Fleming Companies Inc., of Oklahoma City, Oklahoma, which had sales of $11.47 billion in 1998. A publicly held company founded in 1916, Fleming supplied more than 3,100 stores in 46 states and exports food products as well. In the 1990s, Fleming solidified its wholesaling and retailing operations through several acquisitions.

FURTHER READING

eMarketer Special Issue on Online Grocers. 7 January 2000. Available from http://www.emarketer.com/eservices/000099_grocers.html.

Food Marketing Institute. *The Food Marketing Industry Speaks, Fiftieth Anniversary,* 1999.

Food Marketing Institute web site. Available from http://www.fmi.org.

''66th Annual Report of the Grocery Industry.'' *Progressive Grocer,* April 1999.

Weinstein, Steve. ''Are Wholesale Changes Necessary?'' *Progressive Grocer,* March 1996, 47.

SIC 5142

WHOLESALE PACKAGED FROZEN FOODS

Included in this category are establishments primarily engaged in the wholesale distribution of packaged quick-frozen vegetables, juices, meats, fish, poultry, pastries, and other ''deep freeze'' products. Establishments primarily engaged in the wholesale distribution of frozen dairy products are classified in **SIC 5143: Dairy Products, Except Dried or Canned,** and those distributing frozen poultry, fish, and meat that are not packaged are classified in **SIC 5144: Poultry and Poultry Products, SIC 5146: Fish and Seafoods,** and **SIC 5147: Meats and Meat Products,** respectively.

NAICS CODE(S)

422420 (Packaged Frozen Food Wholesalers)

Like the wholesale grocery industry in general, the wholesale packaged frozen food industry is sensitive to the ups and downs of the retail food industry. Supermarkets anticipate continued growth in interest by consumers of frozen foods. The modern consumer with a busy schedule liked the convenience of quick meals, and 80 percent preferred eating at home. Data for 1997 showed frozen foods sales exceeded $24 billion. The dinner and entrée category was the best selling in the market, showing $4.5 billion in sales in 1997. As the 1990s drew to a close, wholesale packaged frozen food companies faced increasing competition and were turning to technology to help stay competitive.

Some packaged frozen food wholesalers are specialty wholesalers offering just a few products—premium frozen novelties or frozen diet foods, for example. Besides selling frozen food, these wholesalers generally provide point-of-sale merchandising material, display suggestions, and product servicing such as stock rotation and product display monitoring.

For the most part, however, frozen foods were provided to retailers by full-service wholesalers, businesses that offer complete lines of grocery and non-grocery products and help the retailers with advertising, merchandising, and getting products they did not warehouse. Competition increased in this sector during the 1990s, and many large companies introduced sophisticated computer programs to track orders and deliveries.

Some frozen foods are distributed through the wholesale/retail chain by retailer-owned wholesalers, retailers who operate their own warehouses and shipping lines. The cooperative effort makes it possible for retailers to obtain merchandise at the lowest possible cost. The retailer-owned wholesaler also supplies group advertising, merchandising, and other services.

History. The father of the frozen food industry, Clarence Birdseye, began experimenting with frozen food products in 1915; by 1930, General Foods Corp. began marketing a line of frozen poultry, meat, fish, fruit, and vegetables in retail grocery stores under the Birdseye name.

In the industry's infancy, frozen food processors marketed their wares through company-owned branches or regional wholesale distributors. This distribution pattern was expanded in 1945 when the Snow Crop Marketers Co. (New York City) introduced a direct sales program to chain stores, voluntary groups, and retail cooperatives. Frozen food products are now distributed through public warehouses or private distribution centers.

Frozen foods were profitable for both manufacturers and wholesalers. They became the primary players in a category supermarket industry analysts call "meal replacement"—that is, food for people too busy to cook. From 1996 to 1997, frozen food sales increased 3.2 percent. According to a 1997 survey conducted by *Frozen Food Age*, a family with teenagers spent an average $58 a week on frozen foods. The Great Lakes and the Plains had the greatest growth in frozen food sales for the time period covered by the survey.

The fastest growing segment in frozen foods was in natural or organic foods. In 1996 and 1997 natural brands increased 63.5 percent in dollar volume, against mainstream brands' 2.4 percent. Consumers were becoming health conscious and eager to buy products for healthy lifestyles.

The leader in the wholesale frozen food industry is the Houston, Tex.-based SYSCO Corp., which reported $17 billion in sales in 1999, a 13.7 percent increase from 1998. Chiefly a supplier to the food service industry, SYSCO specializes in the wholesale distribution of more than 275,000 types of prepared frozen meals, condiments, and deli meats. Distributing their products to approximately 300,000 foodservice customers, including restaurants, hospitals, and schools, SYSCO employed about 35,100 workers in 1999 in almost 100 facilities throughout North America. Top competitors are: Alliant Foodservice, Ameriserve, and U.S. Foodservice.

FURTHER READING

"Big 3 Duke It Out in Frozen Entrees." *Advertising Age,* 30 January 1995.

"Frozen Dinners Attack Appetite for Carryout." *Advertising Age,* 2 September 1996.

"Good Times Roll for Public Cold Storage Operators in United States and Canada." *Quick Frozen Foods International,* October 1999.

Harrison, Dan. "Natural Frozens Surge: No Matter How You Slice It, Natural Frozen Foods are Coming on Strong." *Frozen Food Age,* September 1998.

"Industry Trends." Available from http://www.affi.com, 2000.

Hoover's Company Capsules. Hoover's Inc., 1999. Available from http://hoovers.com.

Litwak, David. "Frozen Natural Foods: Thawing Mainstream Retail Resistance." *Supermarket Business,* 15 October 1999.

Saulnier, John M. "Covering the World of Frozen Foods Since 1959: A Look Back and Forward." *Quick Frozen Foods International,* July 1999.

Sturman, Chris. "The Outlook For Cold Storage." *Frozen and Chilled Foods,* December 1998.

Thayer, Warren. "Retailers Eye Share Gains by Frozen, Private Label." *Frozen Food Age,* May 1998.

Ward's Business Directory of U.S. Private and Public Companies. Detroit: Gale Group, 1999.

Wellman, David. "New Life in the Freezer Case." *Supermarket Business,* February 1999.

SIC 5143

DAIRY PRODUCTS, EXCEPT DRIED OR CANNED

This classification covers establishments primarily engaged in the wholesale distribution of dairy products such as butter, cheese, ice cream and ices, and fluid milk and cream. This industry does not include establishments primarily engaged in pasteurizing and bottling milk. Establishments primarily engaged in the wholesale distribution of dried or canned dairy products are classified in **SIC 5149: Groceries and Related Products, Not Elsewhere Classified.**

NAICS CODE(S)

422430 (Dairy Products (except Dried or Canned) Wholesalers)

Farm milk prices began plummeting in November 1996, causing many dairy farmers to lose up to a third of their income. The industry was quick to react: within a half year, four of the industry-leading cooperatives entered merger discussions, and within a year the co-ops had inked an agreement pending approval by the Department of Justice antitrust division. Even as the justice department approved it, industry insiders questioned whether it sacrificed competition for the sake of increased efficiencies. Merger proponents pointed out that dairy cooperatives have been consolidating since long before economic techno-globalization ushered in the late 1990s consolidation craze.

One of the industry leaders, San Antonio-based Associated Milk Producers Inc. (AMPI), was the product of the merging of 100 smaller cooperatives. The parent company opted out of the 1997 merger discussions, but its subsidiary AMPI Southern Region of Arlington, Texas joined the "super cooperative," Dairy Farmers of America, which also included Mid-America Dairymen of Springfield, Missouri, Milk Marketing of Strongville, Ohio, and Western Dairymen Cooperative of Thornton, Colorado.

Mid-America was the country's biggest cooperative at the time of this merger, with 12,000 members, while AMPI was the second-biggest, with 8,000 members. Besides price stabilization, the goal of the consolidation was to take advantage of government deregulation, which left the industry to regulate itself; in the absence of government oversight, control of the industry would revert to the strongest coalition.

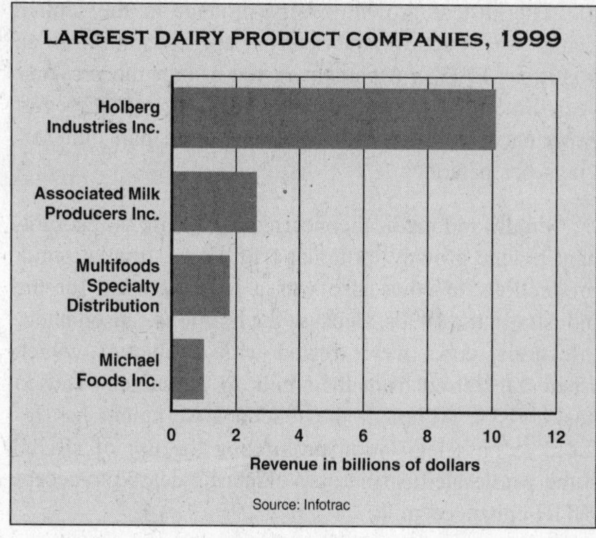

Holberg Industries Inc. of Greenwich, Connecticut, led this industry with 1998 sales of over $10 billion on the work of 19,800 employees. AMPI followed, with Multifoods Specialty Distribution of Englewood, Colorado, bringing up third place with sales of $1.8 billion for its fiscal year ended February 28, 1999. Minneapolis-based Michael Foods Inc. generated 1998 sales of more than $1 billion. AMPI North Central Region, which also chose to forego merger talks, garnered 1997 sales of $928 million to round out the top 5 industry leaders.

Milk consumption in the United States began to lag behind other beverages in the 1960s; by the late 1990s, it was fourth behind soft drinks, coffee, and beer. Part of the decrease can be tied to health concerns as a cholesterol- and calorie-conscious public became aware of whole milk's high fat content. Many consumers tended to cut milk from their diet completely, believing, erroneously, that lower fat milks were also lower in nutrients. Further research proved otherwise and consumption of lower fat milks increased. In the period between 1970 and 1974, 78 percent of all beverage milk consumption was of whole milk. By the mid-1990s, reduced-fat milk accounted for 50 percent of all beverage milk consumed. Skim milk consumption increased from 5 percent in the early 1970s to 13 percent in 1994. In addition, promoting the health benefits of lowfat milk, the industry embarked on a $52 million ad campaign in the mid-1990s featuring popular celebrities.

Consumption of fluid cream products such as half-and-half, light cream, heavy cream, and sour cream increased in the 20 years from 1974 to 1994 with per capita consumption rising from 10 half-pints in 1974 to 15 half-pints in 1994. The average consumption of cheese for the same period more than doubled: from 12.9 pounds per person in 1974 to 26.8 pounds per person in 1994. Much of the cheese was consumed on pizzas and in convenience foods.

The fastest growing dairy product in the United States was yogurt. Americans spent $3.6 million on yogurt in 1995, a 6 percent increase over the previous year. Since 1974, the per capita consumption of yogurt experienced a threefold increase to nine half-pint servings per person.

Public and medical concern over the use of recombinant bovine growth hormones (rBGH) to stimulate milk productions in cows also was a primary issue for the industry in the 1990s. Because the hormone caused udder infections, cows were treated with antibiotics, which when transferred from their milk to consumers, caused health risks. Although the federal government has refused to pass legislation prohibiting the use of rBGH, some wholesale distributors voluntarily ceased to accept rBGH-enhanced milk.

Prices for wholesale dairy products remained relatively stable through the mid-1990s, according to *Standard & Poor's Industry Surveys.* The nutritional value of dairy products and the controls placed on the pricing of these products have protected the industry from the "shoppers' mood swings" that have caused dramatic rises and falls in other areas of the wholesale and retail food industries.

The structure of the wholesale milk industry is somewhat different from that of other wholesale food product operations. In most metropolitan areas, local milk producers make it unnecessary for wholesalers, either chain store or affiliate, to operate their own fluid milk facilities. Instead, distributors arrange with one of the local milk companies for their fluid milk sales. These local producers are responsible for supply and delivery to stores. They also are in charge of producing private-label milk and milk products, which they distribute directly to the retailer.

In rural areas, when local sources are not available, wholesalers usually handle fluid milk through their own distribution centers. These wholesalers may be full-service wholesalers, providing not only dairy products but also complete lines of grocery and nongrocery products. Besides the food products themselves, full-service wholesalers provide assistance to the retailer in advertising, merchandising, and procuring products they may not warehouse.

The retailer-owned wholesaler may also provide fluid milk to a number of outlets. This type of wholesaler represents the efforts of a number of retailers to join forces (sometimes under a common name) to operate their own warehouses and shipping lines. The cooperative effort makes it possible for retailers to obtain merchandise at the lowest possible cost. In addition to providing lines of food products, the retailer-owned wholesaler also supplies group advertising, merchandising, and other services.

Ice cream, butter, and cheese may be handled by retailer-wholesalers, full-service wholesalers, or, in the case of some premium products, by specialty wholesalers. This type of wholesaler provides a limited range of products and a variety of services, including point of sale merchandising material, display suggestions, and product servicing such as stock rotation and monitoring.

Further Reading

Barrett, Rick. "Dairy Cooperatives Plan Merger to Boost Depressed Prices." *Knight-Ridder/Tribune Business News,* 22 May 1997.

"Dairy Co-Op Closing Local Headquarters." *San Antonio Business Journal,* 12 January 1996.

"Dairy Co-Op May Relieve TCBY's Bottom-Line Pressure." *Nation's Restaurant News,* 3 April 1995.

Infotrac Company Profiles, 12 December 1999. Available from http://web6.infotrac.galegroup.com.

Kurtzweil, Paula. "Companies, Employees Answer to Corrupt Milk Practices." *FDA Consumer,* October 1996.

Perman, Stacy. "Milk Shakes It Up." *Time,* 25 November 1996.

"U.S. Food Consumption." *Food Review,* May 1996.

Wren, Worth Jr. "Dairy Farmers of America Represents the Merger of Four Cooperatives." *Knight-Ridder/Tribune Business News,* 10 December 1997.

SIC 5144

POULTRY AND POULTRY PRODUCTS

This category encompasses establishments primarily engaged in the wholesale distribution of poultry and poultry products, except canned and packaged frozen foods. Not included are establishments primarily engaged in the killing and dressing of poultry, which are classified in **SIC 2015: Poultry Slaughtering and Processing.** Establishments primarily engaged in the wholesale distribution of packaged frozen poultry are classified in **SIC 5142: Packaged Frozen Goods,** and those distributing canned poultry are classified in **SIC 5149: Groceries and Related Products, Not Elsewhere Classified.**

NAICS Code(s)

422440 (Poultry and Poultry Product Wholesalers)

In the late 1990s, the poultry industry contended with ongoing consumer concern over salmonella contamination. According to a poultry consumption survey presented at the 1997 Poultry Science Association meeting,

80 percent of the 50 respondents expressed concern over microbial contamination, and 40 percent considered poultry ''unsafe.'' However, Agriculture Secretary Dan Glickman announced September 28, 1998 that over a six-month period earlier that year, salmonella prevalence in broiler chickens was cut in half, from 20 percent before January 1998, to 10.4 percent in 1998. This decrease continued the trend of lowering salmonella rates in broilers, which were as high as 50 percent in the 1980s. Although this news should have alleviated concerns over salmonella contamination, it came on the heels of a report from the Centers for Disease Control and Prevention announcing that salmonella DT-104 was developing resistance to antibiotics.

The U.S. government, in 1997, challenged food industries, including poultry wholesalers, to develop methods of detecting salmonella and other food-borne pathogens, some of which have developed resistance to antibiotics. Industries are asked to design controls for all production phases—including transportation, shipping, tracking, and shelving—focusing on temperature, prior cargoes, and sanitation.

Methods either in use or under study include sturdier machine-assembled reusable shipping containers doubling as retail shelves, computerized order placement, and tracking and bar coding. Pathogen eradication and tracking technology includes food irradiation and genetic ''fingerprinting.'' Control points could monitor temperatures and times with package sensors both en route and during loading and storage. Pathogen source control may involve such ideas as coating chicken feed with red pepper to repel rodents.

In 1996, the top 48 companies accounted for 99 percent of the U.S. broiler output, carrying out all phases of production including wholesale distribution. The top 10 firms processed and shipped 66 percent of the U.S. ready-to-cook broiler product. The top 34 producers posted sales of $18.7 billion in 1996.

The U.S. broiler industry grew from 5 to 8 percent each year from 1992 to 1996. The U.S. Department of Agriculture reported broiler production at 34 million birds in 1934, rising to more than 5 billion birds by 1989, and more than 8 billion in 1996. The top 27 turkey processors slaughtered 6.87 billion pounds of live birds in 1996. Egg producers reported a total of 174.4 million layers in 1995.

In 1997, Tyson Foods Incorporated of Springdale, Arkansas, the nation's largest broiler company, merged with Hudson Foods Inc. A massive recall of 25 million pounds of ground beef produced at Hudson's Columbus, Nebraska plant in August 1997 due to suspected E. coli contamination debilitated business and the company lost $21.2 million that year. Meanwhile, Tyson's fiscal 1997 sales (excluding beef and pork and other non-poultry sales) increased 4.5 percent over the previous year's sales.

Independent companies specializing in wholesale distribution of fresh and frozen poultry handled 22.2 percent of all U.S. broiler production in 1995, most of which is sold to retail grocers, restaurants, and institutions, according to the National Broiler Council of Washington, D.C.

Ward's Business Directory lists Zacky Foods of South El Monte, California, as the nation's top wholesale distributor of poultry and poultry products. However, Zacky operates hatcheries, feed mills, and processing plants as well as distribution centers, ranking 28th in sales among vertically integrated U.S. broiler firms. Subtracting Zacky's $600 million in sales, the top 33 wholesale distributors posted revenues of $1.1 billion for 1996. This figure includes the sale of wholesale distributors of eggs and egg products.

Behind Zacky in sales was Norbest Incorporated of Midvale, Utah, at $200 million in sales for 1996, followed by Troyer Foods of Goshen, Indiana, at $190 million. Howlett-Olson Egg Company of Las Vegas, Nevada, posted $120 million in revenue; followed by Crystal Farms Refrigerated Distribution of Minneapolis, Minnesota, at $110 million. The next 16 firms posted annual sales ranging from $76 million to $10 million.

The U.S. poultry industry started on small farms, where chickens and eggs provided family income. Hatcheries, feed stores, and poultry processing facilities sprang up in grain-producing regions of the Midwest, connected to markets by collection and distribution centers. Integration developed as feed dealers and manufacturers merged with hatcheries and processors. Large wholesalers began to dominate the market in the mid-1940s in response to consumer demand and the ability to preserve and ship fresh products.

FURTHER READING

''Assorted News Briefs.'' *Poultry,* October, 1998. Available at http://www.mtgplace.com.

Bowers, Pam. ''Companies Grapple with Earnings Outlook.'' *Poultry Marketing and Technology: The Meating Place,* December 1995. Available at http://www.mtgplace.com.

Christensen, Heidi. ''A Look at the Key Element in Product Marketing, Product Integrity and Consumer Satisfaction—Packaging.'' *Poultry Marketing and Technology: The Meating Place,* June 1996. Available at http://www.mtgplace.com.

Dunn, Dr. Joseph A. ''Domestic Poultry Food Containing Capsaicin.'' Amherst, NY: Snyder Seed Corporation. Available at http://www.reeusda.gov/new/sbir/phase1.htm.

Food Safety from Farm to Table: A New Strategy for the 21st Century. Washington, DC: U.S. Department of Agriculture,

U.S. Environmental Protection Agency Centers for Disease Control and Prevention. February 1997.

Gardner, F.A. and Dale Hyatt. *Poultry Industry Characteristics.* Texas A&M University Department of Poultry Science, October 1995. Available at http://gallus.tamu.edu/fsis/fsman3.html.

Krizner, Ken. ''Antibiotics Appear to Be Useless on an Emerging Strain of Salmonella.'' *Meat Marketing & Technology,* August 1998. Available at http://www.mtgplace.com.

''Newsline.'' *Poultry,* December, 1997. Available at http://www.mtgplace.com (visited 11/29/99).

Major Broiler Market Channels and Product Flow. Washington, DC: National Broiler Council. 1995.

''World Crises Affect Poultry Exports.'' *Poultry,* April, 1998. Available at http://www.mtgplace.com.

Thornton, Gary. ''Top 10 U.S. Broiler Companies.'' *Broiler Industry Magazine,* January 1997.

SIC 5145

CONFECTIONERY

This industry classification includes wholesale distributors of confectionery and related products such as candy, chewing gum, salted or roasted nuts, popcorn, soda fountain syrups and toppings, and potato and corn chips.

NAICS CODE(S)

422450 (Confectionery Wholesalers)

Confectionery wholesalers reported total sales of $21.8 billion in 1992, according to information published by the U.S. Department of Commerce. That same year, the industry employed 56,322 workers and posted an annual payroll of $1.2 billion.

According to a market study on confectionery sales conducted in the mid-1990s, supermarkets generated 40 percent of total sales in this industry. Mass merchandisers and convenience stores accounted for 15 and 14 percent, respectively. Small retailers, drug stores, vending machines, wholesale clubs, fundraising, and the military accounted for the remaining sales, each generating less than 10 percent.

Candy consumption continued to increase during the 1990s. Up from 16.0 pounds per capita in 1986, it stood at 20.7 pounds in 1990, and, according to the National Confectioners Association, reached 23.4 pounds by 1995. Candy trade products were classified in two categories: chocolate and non-chocolate. In 1995, chocolate, the top-selling category, accounted for more than 50 percent of the nation's candy sales.

Gum consumption and chewing gum sales also experienced tremendous growth in the U.S. market during the 1990s. According to statistics released by the National Association of Chewing Gum Manufacturers, total domestic factory sales increased from $716.0 million in 1980 to $1.3 billion in 1990, and sales passed $1.4 billion in 1994.

Even vending distributors, who saw a substantial loss of sales in the early 1990s, were experiencing an upward swing by the mid- to late 1990s. In 1997 total confectionery sales (excluding chewing and bubble gum) destined for vending machines increased by 14.4 percent.

In 1997, most of the businesses in this industry had a small number of employees—3,549 establishments had 1 to 4 employees, while an additional 1,276 establishments had 5 to 9 employees. Only 139 firms had more than 100 staff members.

The largest number of firms, however, were in the mid-range of sales—1,618 firms had sales between $250,000 and $499,000, while another 1,255 firms had sales between $1 million and $4.9 million. Only 78 firms had sales below $49,000.

In 1999 Vendor Supply of America (VSA) was one of the largest companies classified in this industry. A division of International Multifoods Corp. of Minneapolis, Minnesota, VSA began in 1970 and served as a specialty distributor to various food service establishments, such as vending machine operators, military units, and theaters. In 1999 the company had annual sales of approximately $360 million and employed 1,500 people.

Another leader within the confectionery classification was Sathers Inc. Founded in 1936 as a local Minnesota cookie distributor, Sathers began nationwide distribution in the early 1970s after entering into a relationship with Kmart stores. By the early 1990s, the company operated more than 300 vehicles and distributed products to all 50 states. In 1999, annual sales were reported to be approximately $360 million and the company had about 1,600 employees.

FURTHER READING

''Favorite Brands Acquires Farley, Sathers.'' *Candy Industry,* October 1996.

''Good News at the End of the Rainbow?'' *Candy Industry,* January 1997.

Lazich, Robert S. *Market Share Reporter,* Detroit, MI: Gale Research Inc., 1996.

Merrill, Ann. ''Multifoods Hires Vending Distribution Unit Head.'' *Minneapolis Star Tribune,* 18 October 1996.

National Association of Chewing Gum Manufacturers. ''The Story of Chewing Gum,'' New York, NY: NACGM, nd.

National Association of Chewing Gum Manufacturers. ''Total Domestic Factory Sales,'' Marlton, NJ: NACGM, nd.

Dun's Census of American Business 1997. Parsippany, NJ: Dun & Bradstreet, 1997.

SIC 5146

FISH AND SEAFOODS

Establishments classified in this industry are engaged in the wholesale distribution of fresh, cured, or frozen (but not canned or packaged frozen) fish and seafood products.

NAICS CODE(S)

422460 (Fish and Seafood Wholesalers)

Establishments engaged in the preparation of fresh or frozen fish and other seafood, and the shucking and packing of fresh oysters in nonsealed containers, are classified in **SIC 2092: Prepared Fresh or Frozen Fish and Seafoods.** Establishments primarily engaged in the wholesale distribution of canned seafood are classified in **SIC 5149: Groceries and Related Products, Not Elsewhere Classified,** and those distributing packaged frozen foods are classified in **SIC 5142: Packaged Frozen Foods.**

INDUSTRY SNAPSHOT

In 1997 there were 3,520 wholesale plants in the industry, up slightly from the 3,200 plants operating in the mid-1990s. Employment stood at 29,457. The Pacific Northwest, including Alaska, Washington, Oregon and California, had the highest number of operations, with 827 and employing 7,160. Per capita U.S. consumption stood at 14.9 pounds per person in 1998. That same year, frozen fishery products in cold storage stood at a low of 364.2 million pounds in May, reaching a high of 437.2 million pounds in November.

CURRENT CONDITIONS

According to statistics compiled by *Supermarket Business,* supermarkets purchased 66 percent of their seafood from specialty fish and seafood wholesalers. Another nine percent was purchased from other suppliers including grocery wholesalers. Fish sales accounted for 42 percent of supermarket fish and seafood sales. The second largest category was shrimp, representing 33 percent of sales. One of the most popular individual products was salmon.

One of the major issues facing seafood distributors during the 1990's was product safety. Some consumer groups were calling for increased FDA oversight of fish products and advocated the adoption of more stringent safety standards. Another issue was product availability. Climate changes, environmental degradation, and overfishing of stocks were being blamed for reducing the supplies of some traditional fisheries, particularly in the North Atlantic.

INDUSTRY LEADERS

Two of the nation's largest seafood distributors were Entree Corporation and Fishery Products International USA. Entree, with headquarters in Milwaukee, Wisconsin, is a subsidiary of The Diana Corporation. It distributed meat and seafood through a wholly-owned subsidiary, Atlanta Provision Company.

Fishery Products International USA, located in Danvers, Massachusetts, was a subsidiary of Fishery Products International. Fishery Products International, headquartered in St. John's, Newfoundland, Canada, harvested and marketed products, including shrimp, snow crab, sole, cod, redfish and haddock from the coast of Newfoundland and Labrador. Scallops were harvested off Nova Scotia's coast. During the first nine months of 1999, FPI recorded sales of $513.3 million, up from the $486 million reported for the same period in 1998.

FURTHER READING

Fishery Products International, Company Profile, 2000. Available from http://www.fpil.com/profile/harvesting.htm.

"Processors and Wholesalers: Plants and Employment, 1997." *National Marine Fisheries Service.* Available from http://www.nmfs.gov/trade/default.html.

SIC 5147

MEATS AND MEAT PRODUCTS

This industry consists of wholesale distributors of fresh, cured, and processed (but not canned or frozen) meats and lard. Establishments engaged in the wholesale distribution of frozen packaged meats are classified under **SIC 5142: Packaged Frozen Foods.** Establishments engaged in the wholesale distribution of canned meats are classified in **SIC 5149: Groceries and Related Products, Not Elsewhere Classified.**

NAICS CODE(S)

311612 (Meat Processed from Carcasses)
422470 (Meat and Meat Product Wholesalers)

According to projections by *Wholesale and Retail Trade USA 1995,* 3,517 establishments were engaged in the wholesale distribution of meats and meat products in 1996. Their combined sales were projected to total $61.7 billion.

As of February 1996, industry employees numbered 61,600, of whom 14,600 were women according to *Employment, Hours, and Earnings United States, 1988-96.* Shipments of red meat are forecast to rise 1 percent in 1999, while shipments of poulty are forecast to rise 3 percent.

The industry's beginning inventory in 1996 was projected by *Wholesale and RetailTrade USA 1995* to be $1.1 billion, and its ending inventory was projected to be $927.7 million. *Wholesale and Retail Trade* also estimated the industry's 1996 expenses to be $3 billion.

One of the largest meat and meat products wholesalers in the United States is Monfort, Inc. Monfort began in the 1930s near Greeley, Colorado as a family-owned cattle feeding operation and is now an international, multibillion dollar company. By the late 1990s it employed 19,000 people in the United States and, by 1999, had an annual sales revenue of $7,093 million. Monfort, Inc. is the only major meat producing company with cattle feeding, beef, pork, and lamb processing operations, national distribution and transportation, a byproducts and pet foods division, and a construction company.

In 1970, Monfort went public. It also introduced quarter-inch trim specifications, which started an industry-wide trend toward lean cuts. In 1993, in response to retailer demand for even leaner cuts of meat, the company began offering *Super Lite* cuts, trimmed to one eighth of an inch. Company officials expected demand for their products to grow as innovative packaging, value-added products, and exports helped boost sales.

In 1987, Monfort joined ConAgra, Inc. of Omaha, Nebraska, a diversified family of independent operating companies. Monfort is the major company in ConAgra Beef Companies. Australian Meat Holdings Pty Ltd and E.A. Miller are also part of ConAgra Beef. ConAgra is made of three primary groups: Refrigerated Foods, which includes meat and poultry products, is the largest of the groups. Other groups are grocery/diversified products, and frozen foods. In 1999 ConAgra had an annual growth of 1.4 percent in sales. According to *Meat and Poultry* Annual top 100 of July 1997, ConAgra was ranked the number one fastest growing meat company, with a growth of $2,197 million.

FURTHER READING

U.S. Department of Labor. *Employment, Hours, and Earnings United States, 1988-96.* Washington, DC: 1996.

Monfort. *The Monfort Story.* Greeley, CO: Monfort, nd.

Wholesale and Retail Trade USA 1995. Detroit: Gale Research, 1995.

SIC 5148

FRESH FRUITS AND VEGETABLES

This industry is comprised of wholesale distributors of fresh fruits and vegetables. It also includes establishments involved in banana ripening for the trade.

NAICS CODE(S)

422480 (Fresh Fruit and Vegetable Wholesalers)

The *1997 Economic Census* reported a total of 6,121 establishments engaged in the wholesale distribution of fresh fruits and vegetables. This was an increase from the 6,003 reported in 1992 and the 5,838 reported in 1987. Combined sales totaled $46.3 billion, up from $38.5 billion reported in 1992. California led the nation in both number of establishments (1,248) and value of sales ($14.1 billion). Florida ranked second with 666 establishments and sales totaling $4.4 billion, followed by New York, Texas, and Washington.

Most industry establishments were classified as merchant wholesalers. The remaining businesses in the classification are agents, brokers, and commission merchants.

Sales of fresh vegetables and fruits in the United States increased significantly since 1987, due in great part to nutritional awareness and promotions by national dietary-health programs such as "5 A Day—For Better Health." Increased interest in adopting a meatless lifestyle also propelled vegetable sales. By the end of the century, more than 12 million Americans considered themselves to be vegetarians.

Vegetable production in 1993 declined 1 percent, attributable to tomato crop damage in Florida and lower sweet potato production, both of which were down 8 percent. Grower receipts in 1995 were $14.8 billion—the fifth consecutive increase in receipts and a record high. Strong prices for lettuces, potatoes, carrots and melons supported the higher receipts as did broccoli and watermelon consumption. Production had increased by the end of the decade, resulting in higher wholesaling receipts. Tomato production alone totaled more than $1.0 billion in 1998.

An ongoing concern for California and Florida tomato growers impacting wholesalers has been the impact of free trade with Mexico. Tomato imports were up 22 percent in 1996. Contentions are that Mexico dumped tomatoes into the market at prices well below market value. The commerce department and the Mexican government reached an agreement in October 1996 in which Mexican tomatoes were agreed to be sold at prices comparable to U. S. products. The United States International Trade Commission discontinued its investigation as a result.

Consumer interest in ethnic foods has encouraged diversity in crops and spurred wholesalers to add variety to the traditional fruits and vegetables they carry. Mediterranean, Southwestern, and Asian cuisine stimulated sales of vegetables such as eggplant, beets, Asian cabbages, jicama, beans, and peppers. Such new interests also helped increase sales.

Citrus was one of the largest product classifications. Tree-ripe fruit of all varieties, which required special handling, helped increase profits for those able to deliver quality produce.

Sunkist Growers, Inc. was the largest marketing cooperative in the fruit and vegetable industry and one of the 10 largest marketing cooperatives of any kind in the United States. The organization's grower-owners governed the cooperative and provided direction to its subsidiaries and affiliates. Sunkist also has citrus processing facilities, fruit growers' supply warehouses, an asset management service, and a research center. Sunkist was established in 1893 by 60 citrus growers who joined together to improve their ability to deliver products to the marketplace. Bypassing commissioned agents and brokers, they bolstered grower profitability by sharing packing and marketing expenses. More than one hundred years later, Sunkist had more than 6,500 grower-owners in California and Arizona. In 1999, the cooperative generated $862.2 million in sales.

FURTHER READING

''Economic Research Service: Fruit outlook.'' M2 Presswire, 24 September 1996.

''Economic Research Service—Vegetables and Specialties, Part 1.'' M2 Presswire, 27 November 1996.

Hoover's Company Profiles, 20 March 2000. Available from http://www.hoovers.com.

Ingram, Bob. ''A Destination for 5 A Day.'' *Supermarket Business,* September 1996, 95.

Knight-Ridder Financial/Commodity Research Bureau. *The CRB Commodity Yearbook 1995.* New York: John Wiley & Sons, Inc., 1995.

Tanyeri, Dana. ''Vegetables en Vogue.'' *ID: The Voice of Foodservice Distribution,* August 1995, S22.

''U.S. & Mexico Announce Compromise Agreement on Tomato Imports.'' *SourceMex Economic News & Analysis on Mexico,* 16 October 1996.

U.S. Census Bureau. *1997 Economic Census—Wholesale Trade.* Washington, DC: GPO, 2000. Available from http://www.census.gov.

U.S. Department of Commerce, *1992 Census of Wholesale Trade: Geographic Area Series,* Washington, DC: Bureau of the Census, January 1995.

———. *1992 Census of Wholesale Trade: Subject Series.* Washington, DC: Bureau of the Census, November 1995.

SIC 5149

GROCERIES AND RELATED PRODUCTS, NOT ELSEWHERE CLASSIFIED

This industry is comprised of wholesale distributors of groceries and related products, not elsewhere classified. Some of the products included in this category are: breakfast cereals, bottled water, canned goods, coffee, cookies, cooking oils, crackers, dairy products, pet food, flour, dried fruits, health foods, honey, macaroni and spaghetti, canned or dried milk, pickles, salad dressing, sauces, soft drinks, soups, refined sugar, and yeast. Establishments primarily engaged in the wholesale distribution of beer and ale are classified in **SIC 5181: Beer and Ale.** Wine is classified in **SIC 5182: Wine and Distilled Alcoholic Beverages.**

NAICS CODE(S)

422490 (Other Grocery and Related Product Wholesalers)

INDUSTRY SNAPSHOT

Grocery wholesalers and distributors buy grocery items from manufacturers or other distributors and typically resell them to retail—including grocery and convenience stores—or other commercial enterprises—including food service establishments—that in turn sell the goods to users. The wholesaling industry also includes many firms that import foreign goods or export U.S. products. In practice many wholesalers are integrated with manufacturing and retailing of grocery products as well.

Products within this industry are subdivided into six categories: coffee, tea, and spices (representing 8.6 percent of the industry's sales volume); bread and baked goods (7.7 percent); soft drinks (13.5 percent); canned goods (23.0 percent); food and beverage basic materials (3.6 percent); and other grocery specialties (43.6 percent). During the early 1990s sales within the industry varied considerably from product to product.

CURRENT CONDITIONS

In 1997 Dun and Bradstreet listed 23,095 establishments engaged in the wholesale distribution of groceries and related products. The top 50 wholesale grocers held 38.6 percent of the market share in 1997, with each company averaging $1.62 billion in sales. The top 10 industry leaders totaled $54.2 billion in sales. Industry employment increased nearly 10 percent during the first half of the 1990s, reaching 270,000 workers with a payroll of $8.1 billion. Industry sales totaled more than $150 billion during the mid-1990s, which accounted for more than half of the broader grocery wholesaling market in the United States.

The industry faced diminished sales growth during the late 1990s. In 1997 the top 50 wholesale grocery giants reported sales of $81.1 billion, compared to $81 billion the previous year. One reason for the stagnation was competition from vertically integrated grocery retailers such as The Kroger Co. and Safeway Inc., which, because of their size, were able to buy goods directly from manufacturers—as well as to make many of their own private label products—rather than relying on other distributors. The warehouse clubs, such as Sam's Club, Costco, and BJ's also grabbed market share from traditional wholesalers by offering volume discounts to small businesses and consumers. In 1998 Sam's Club had 451 U.S. locations, BJ's had 96 U.S. locations, and Costco had 288 locations in the United States, Canada, the United Kingdom, Taiwan, Korea, and Mexico. Costco generated the most revenue in 1998, totaling $26 billion, while Sam's Club totaled $24.4 billion and BJ's $3.4 billion.

Industry Leaders

SuperValu Inc., of Minnesota, was the nation's largest grocery wholesale distributor in 1997, with more than 48,000 employees nationwide. Also a leading grocery retailer, SuperValu reported $16.6 billion in sales in that year, 71 percent of which was from its wholesale business. In 1999 SuperValu acquired Richfood Holdings Inc., of Virginia, the largest grocery wholesaler in the mid-Atlantic and the fourth largest overall, with $3.4 billion in sales during 1998. However, in 1999 Richfood lost a $600 million contract with its biggest customer, Giant Food Stores Inc., of Carlisle, Pennsylvania. The contract represented about 17 percent of Richfood's annual earnings.

Fleming Companies of Oklahoma City was the second largest U.S. grocery wholesaler in 1997, with approximately $13 billion in sales and a work force of 39,000 employees. But in 1999 Fleming announced a company-wide restructuring, cutting roughly 700 jobs and divesting itself of six supply centers and at least one retail operation. Fleming also said that it expected to lose $1 billion in sales over the next two years. The third largest national retail grocery wholesaler in 1998 was C&S Wholesale Grocers Inc. Based in Brattleboro, Vermont, C&S employs more than 2,800 workers and had annual sales of approximately $6 billion in 1998. The company provides customers with more than 53,000 food and non-food items, including meats, candy, tobacco, frozen foods, dairy, deli, and bakery products, and health and beauty aids.

Further Reading

Goldblat, Jennifer. ''Richmond, Va.-Based Food Wholesaler Loses $600 Million Contract.'' *Knight-Ridder Tribune Business News,* 24 April 1999.

''The DJ 100: The 50 Largest Tobacco/Candy/Convenience Ddistributors and the 50 Wholesale Grocery Giants.'' *U.S. Distribution Journal,* 19 September 1997.

''Sales Growth Slows For Wholesale Grocers.'' *The Food Institute Report,* 4 October 1999.

U.S. Bureau of the Census. ''Combined Annual and Revised Monthly Wholesale Trade.'' *Current Industrial Reports.* Washington, DC: GPO, 1996.

U.S. Bureau of the Census. Available at http://www.census.gov.

U.S. Department of Commerce. Available at http://www.doc.gov.

U.S. Department of Labor. Available at http://www.dol.gov.

SIC 5153

GRAIN AND FIELD BEANS

This industry classification is comprised of establishments engaged in buying and/or marketing grain, dry beans, soybeans, and other inedible beans. Also included are country grain elevators, terminal elevators, and other merchants involved in marketing grain. Establishments primarily involved in the wholesale distribution of field and garden seeds are in **SIC 5191: Farm Supplies.**

NAICS Code(s)

422510 (Grain and Field Bean Wholesalers)

A total of 6,815 establishments were classified in this industry in 1995. Their combined sales were estimated at $72.7 billion. They employed almost 60,000 workers and posted an annual payroll of $1.59 billion. Projected 1998 figures were 6,318 establishments with total sales of $66.76 billion, employing 53,647 with a total payroll of $1.57 billion.

Leading states in 1992, as measured by number of establishments and value of sales, were Illinois, Iowa, Kansas, and Minnesota. Two other states with high sales' volume, despite relatively small numbers of establishments, were Louisiana and Oregon.

Worldwide, the grain trade peaked in 1979 at 240 million metric tons. During the 1980s and early 1990s, however, both U.S. grain buyers and sellers suffered from market stagnation. Foreign policy decisions led to grain embargoes restricting the ability of U.S. merchants to peddle grains in some overseas markets. In 1992, *Fortune* reported that approximately half of the country's grain elevator and terminal capacity had been idled.

By the mid-1990s the condition of the industry had improved. The grain market of 1996 was the strongest since the 1970s, according to *The Wall Street Journal.* The failure of the winter wheat crop left supplies in storage at low levels, and high demand from importers like China pushed corn and wheat prices to record highs that year. The booming prices caused financial disaster, though, for farmers and elevators that had signed hedge-to-arrive contracts. Countrymark Cooperative Inc. of Indiana was embroiled in court cases as a result of these instruments.

The Federal Agricultural Improvement and Reform Act of 1996, or the so-called ''freedom to farm'' legislation, phased out farm subsidies over a seven-year period. It allowed farmers to grow whatever crops that were profitable on the market, rather than restricting what they could plant or forcing them to leave some of their land unplanted. Grain storage facilities anticipated changes to their operations to meet the new demands of different amounts and types of crops that would come to them.

According to data published in *Grain and Milling Annual 1996,* the top four companies as measured by total corporate grain storage capacity were: Cargill, Inc. (Minneapolis, MN); Archer Daniels Midland Co. (Decatur, IL); Continental Grain Company (New York, NY); and Bunge Corporation (St. Louis, MO). Based on annual sales, the leaders include Continental Grain, Bunge Corp., The Scoular Co., and ConAgra Trading Cos, according to Ward's Business Directory 2000.

In 1999, Cargill acquired its competitor, Continental Grain (the number 1 and number 4 grain traders, based on annual sales and total corporate grain storage capacity). This merger gave Cargill control of 15 percent of grain from farmers and at least 35 percent of America's export grain. Cargill also caused controversy when it expected farmers in Illinois to bypass country elevators. The country elevators established a boycott, sending their customers' grain to a competitor, Archer Daniels Midland.

FURTHER READING

Barshay, Jill. ''The Next Battle in the Grain Wars.'' *Minneapolis Star Tribune,* 1 August 1999.

Feder, Barnaby J. ''Grain Prices Soar on Poor Weather and Low Supplies.'' *The New York Times,* 26 April 1996.

''The Grain 100.'' *Grain & Milling Annual,* 1996.

''Grain Giant: Cargill Merger Poses Small Threat.'' *Minneapolis Star Tribune,* 16 June 1999.

''Issue: Farm Policy.'' *CQ Weekly Report,* 31 August 1996.

Heikens, Norm. ''Ag Co-Op Caught in Corn Fight.'' *Indianapolis Business Journal,* 19 August 1996.

Kilman, Scott. ''Grain Farming Boom Is Losing Steam.'' *The Wall Street Journal,* 3 October 1996.

———. ''Green Belt: High Grain Price Lifts Farmers, But Will They Overexpand as Before?'' *The Wall Street Journal,* 21 March 1996.

McCann, Nita. ''Changes in Management Commodity Mix Occur at Same Time for Farmers Grain Terminal.'' *Mississippi Business Journal,* 19 August 1996.

U.S. Department of Commerce. *1992 Census of Wholesale Trade—U.S. Summary.* Washington, DC: Bureau of the Census, 1997. Available from http://www.census.gov/epcd/www/wc92h515.html.

Wahl, Melissa. ''Grain Contracts Raise Bushel of Problems.'' *Business First-Columbus,* 21 June 1996.

Ward's Business Directory of U.S. Public and Private Companies. Detroit, Gale Group, 2000.

Wholesale and Retail Trade U.S.A. Detroit: Gale Group, 1998.

SIC 5154

LIVESTOCK

Establishments falling under this classification are primarily engaged in buying and/or marketing cattle, hogs, sheep, and goats. This industry also includes the operation of livestock auction markets. Establishments primarily engaged in the wholesale distribution of poultry are classified in **SIC 5144: Poultry and Poultry Products;** companies involved in the buying and selling of horses are in **SIC 5159: Farm-Product Raw Materials, Not Elsewhere Classified.**

NAICS CODE(S)

422520 (Livestock Wholesalers)

The marketing of livestock in the United States is conducted by a variety of businesses ranging from the order buyer who operates out of the front seat of his car to the video auction that sells cattle by beaming pictures of them to a satellite orbiting the earth. The livestock marketing business has evolved from the days when stockmen would send their livestock to a terminal market without any idea of the price they might receive. Terminal markets and commission agents still thrive in the ever-changing world of livestock marketing, but they have been joined by modern day merchants who use computers, video uplinks, fax machines, and cellular phones to market livestock.

Firms involved in the wholesale marketing of cattle, sheep, hogs, and goats include such diverse operations as stockyards, commission firms, order buyers, dealers, brokers, auction markets, and video auction companies.

INDUSTRY SNAPSHOT

Despite a plethora of new methods of marketing livestock, the auction market remained, in the 1990s, the primary agent for assisting in the transfer of title for various species of livestock. As of the late 1990s, 1,500 livestock auctions existed in the United States according to the Livestock Marketing Association (LMA); a variety of livestock were sold on a weekly and sometimes daily basis at these auctions. In addition, the United States Department of Agriculture (USDA) identified about 19,000 livestock sellers—feedlots, farmer-feeders, auctions and dealers. Combined, beef and pork accounted for 68.4 percent of the meat market, with beef controlling the largest chunk at 40 percent.

Livestock are consigned to auctions by ranchers, hog operators, sheepherders, and other stockmen to be sold by the chant of an auctioneer. Because trucking is a costly expense, most often stockmen will send their livestock to the nearest auction market. This may be ten minutes or ten hours away by truck. These auction markets are usually individually owned—only a handful were owned by conglomerates. The owner of the auction receives a commission or a per head fee for selling the livestock in addition to charging for the feed consumed while the livestock are in the auction yard. Typical commissions range from 2 to 3 percent or about $7.50 per head.

One of the largest cattle auctions in the country where the cattle are actually herded through an auction ring was located in Oklahoma City, Oklahoma. Here cattle are sold nearly every day of the week. The auction in Norfolk, Nebraska was one of the largest auctions in terms of the number of species sold. There might be a hog auction taking place in one sale ring and a dairy cattle auction in another ring on the same premises on the same day. This is an exception, however, as most of the auction yards in the country conduct sales once a week. Sheep, dairy animals, goats, hogs, horses, and cattle are sometimes offered on the same day at the same location.

Commission agents are still used at some auctions around the country—the auction at Oklahoma City being the largest. This practice is a holdover from decades ago when ranchers would send their livestock to a commission agent located at any of the larger stockyards, such as those located in Chicago. These agents would then be responsible for the care and feeding of the livestock and the selling of them once they reached the yard, and would receive a commission based on how much the animals brought at market.

Livestock is usually sold by the pound except in the case of breeding animals, which are usually sold by the head. For example, a breeding bull may bring $2,000 to $3,000, whereas a steer destined for a feedlot may sell for $60 per hundredweight. Old cows being sold for slaughter are usually sold one at a time. When a rancher sells his yearly production in the form of calves or lambs, however, the drafts may be composed of several dozen or even hundreds of head. In the latter instance the livestock are weighed and priced per pound. Steer cattle and heifers are usually sold separately, whereas a group of lambs or hogs may include both sexes.

Sitting in the auction arena are a variety of buyers who make their living attending several auction sales each week. They may be order buyers working on a per head or per pound fee, or they may be employees of a feedlot or a packing house. Order buyers may have several orders at the same auction sale. A feedlot manager may have called and wanted steers for the feedlot or a rancher may have phoned with an order for heifers suitable for breeding. Order buyers often to represent several interests at the same sale, although they usually try to avoid having more than one order for the same classification of livestock. The order buyers keep careful track of both the number of livestock they buy and the weight, which is flashed on an overhead ''scoreboard.'' Order buyers are highly skilled and are paid on a commission basis, which is usually ''fifty cents per hundred''—this means that on a purchase of a $500 animal the order buyer would be paid $2.50.

At ringside buyers convey their desire to bid by sending slight body signals to an auctioneer who has learned his chant at one of many auction schools. The livestock are sold rapidly with as many as 50,000 head per day being sold. In the case of video auctions, it is not unusual to see the ownership of 60,000 head of livestock change hands in a single day.

ORGANIZATION AND STRUCTURE

Some ranchers prefer to sell their livestock ''in the country,'' which is the popular way of saying that buyers come to the ranch or farm and purchase the animals directly from the owner rather than from an auction market. The livestock are weighed on a ranch scale that has been checked and sealed by representatives from state or county weights and measures. In most cases the same order buyers who sit in on the auction scour the country looking for livestock to buy ''in the country.''

In discussing livestock marketing, a distinction must be made between classes of livestock. Feeder cattle or calves that are just being weaned are most often sold at auction. Many feeder pigs and lambs are still sold in this manner. But most cattle, sheep, or hogs that are older and ready for slaughter are sold directly to a packer buyer. Packer buyers are given ''show lists'' from major feedyards, and they bid on the cattle either in person or over the phone.

Often cattle and hogs are actually fed by the packing plant owner. This is known as ''captive supply,'' and at times the captive supply of fed cattle in the United States exceeds 20 percent. This is cause for worry among independent livestock producers who feel that if the ''Big Three'' meat packers—IBP, Monfort, and Excel—are able to feed their own cattle, they can in some way control the market price for all classes of cattle. They would supposedly do this by withholding their cattle when supplies were large and using up their own supplies when livestock in the country were in short supply.

A growing trend in the beef business in the 1980s and 1990s was the custom feeding of cattle. This means that a rancher places his cattle in a feedlot and pays for feed and yardage expenses and then sells the cattle to a packer when they are ready for processing. In so doing, he maintains ownership of the cattle all the way through the feeding phase, which generally lasts from 120 to 200 days. The cattle are often sold on a grade and weight basis, meaning that the price per pound is determined by the quality of the meat carcass.

How livestock are marketed in the United States varies depending on what species is being merchandised. Hogs, for example, are marketed in a fashion similar to poultry—the animals are raised under contract to large packers. Although feeder pigs are still sold at auction, the tendency is toward more vertical integration and more contractual arrangements. In addition to this method there are also several hog buying stations, situated primarily in Iowa, Illinois, and Indiana, to which hogs are delivered, weighed and sold to a packer.

Purebred livestock, boars, rams, bulls, and other registered animals to be used for seedstock production are sold either at auction or by private treaty. At auction the animals are usually sold one at a time, with the auctioneer being paid 1 percent of the selling price and the sales manager receiving a commission of about 5 or 6 percent. In many farm or ranch production auctions, however, there are no sales managers, so that expense is eliminated. Private treaty sales occur when a rancher goes to the farm or ranch and purchases the animals directly from the breeder who produced them.

Legal Aspects. Many of the anti-trust laws in the United States were passed as a direct result of the problem of monopolization of the meat industry. On August 15, 1921, the Packers and Stockyards Administration was formed to police the livestock marketing industry. The P and S, as it is commonly called, works to insure the integrity of the livestock, meat, and poultry markets. This is accomplished through fostering fair and open competition and guarding against deceptive and fraudulent practices that could affect meat and poultry prices.

Producers, consumers, and the entire industry are protected by the P and S from unfair business practices which can unduly affect meat and poultry distribution and the price of meat at every level, from the ranch gate to the super market shelf. The P and S sends auditors to the various livestock marketing agents to review accounts and insure that the marketing agencies are properly bonded.

Commission firms, auction markets, dealers, and order buyers are required to be bonded as a measure of protection for livestock sellers. The size of the bond is based on the volume of business and is generally an average of two business days or a minimum of $10,000. A dealer in livestock must be bonded to legally operate.

It is the primary function of the P and S to insure that commission firms, auction markets, order buyers, and dealers remain financially solvent. The administration is also called upon to rid the industry of the unscrupulous traders who occasionally surface. Rules that livestock dealers must abide by include the prompt pay law, whereby consignors or owners of livestock must be paid promptly, usually by the close of business on the day after the transfer of possession. For example, if a cow buyer sitting on the auction seat buys a load of cattle, the livestock may be loaded and sent to the packing house but the packer must legally pay for those cattle on the day after they have been purchased. Another way the P and S insures that merchandisers remain solvent is by keeping an eye out for ''check kiting,'' which is merely swapping checks by placing them in two or more bank accounts for the purpose of creating a ''float'' or inflated balance.

The P and S also ensures that all firms engaged in livestock merchandising are playing on a level playing field. Tariffs or charges must be published, and auction markets cannot legally offer free trucking, price guarantees, or discounted commissions as an incentive for a rancher to send his or her livestock to one auction as opposed to another—doing so can result in a fine of $10,000 for each infraction.

In the intricate, competitive world of livestock marketing, no single factor is as important as the accurate measurement of livestock weight. Employees of the Packers and Stockyards Administration check the scales which are used to weigh the livestock on a regular basis. Scales must be tested by an approved weigh master for accuracy at least once every six months.

A principal trade organization for the livestock marketing sector has been the Kansas City-based Livestock Marketing Association (LMA). In addition to lobbying Congress and state legislatures, the LMA is also in the insurance business and provides bonding for the various marketing agencies. The LMA's Board of Trade issues ''hot sheets'' notifying the industry of unscrupulous dealers and firms that are no longer solvent.

Current Conditions

After experiencing declining beef demand throughout the 1980s and 1990s, the industry saw beef demand rise by 4.59 percent for the third quarter of 1999 as compared to third quarter 1998 demand, according to the National Cattlemen's Beef Association (NCBA). The annual rate of decline began to slow in the late-1980s, and started to flatten in 1996; third quarter 1999 represented the first sustained gain in beef demand, following on the heels of a significant increase during the previous quarter, as compared to the second quarter of 1998, according to the Beef Demand Index, independently tracked according to USDA data. In a presentation to the Beef Summit '99, Randy Bloch of the Denver-based market research firm Cattle-Fax attributed rising demand to increased consumer spending and per-capita consumption. A more telling revelation is the fact that consumer demand sustained growth in the face of record-high beef supplies, which drove prices up, surprisingly, in defiance of economic laws of supply and demand.

According to November 1999 projections, Cattle-Fax extrapolated yearly beef supplies to reach 27 billion pounds, a 2.5 percent increase over 1998 supplies. Simultaneously, consumer spending rose by $1.5 billion to $36.7 billion for the first 3 quarters of 1999, a 4 percent increase compared to the same period in 1998. November projections placed 1999 consumer spending at $48.56 billion, a $2 billion increase over 1998 results. Per capita spending experienced its greatest gain since 1990, according to the projected growth of $5 per capita to $178 by the end of 1999, as compared to 1998 per capita spending. The increase in beef prices by 4 cents in 1999 compared to prices the year before contributed to some of the spending increase; while increasing per capita beef consumption also contributed to some of the increase. Per capita beef consumption rose 0.9 percent in the first three quarters of 1999 compared to September 1998 figures, with projections calling for a 1.6 percent increase over the entire year, compared to 1998.

The NCBA attributed increased beef demand to several factors: increasing exports, the strong domestic economy, rising wages, low inflation, and low unemployment rates. However, NCBA CEO Chuck Schroeder cautioned against over-optimism, reminding the industry of the changing consumer profile. Increasingly, consumers were becoming less knowledgeable about the intricacies of cooking red meat properly while also calling for more convenient preparation methods, prompting the industry at the retail end to transform to more user-friendly packaging with clear cooking instructions and recipes and also packaging pre-fabricated meals and pre-cooked meats to enhance convenience.

In the 1990s, the livestock marketing industry was at something of a crossroads. Would it operate according to the rules of vertical integration, whereby livestock would no longer be sold at auction or "in the country," but instead be under contract from the day of birth to the day of processing? Or would the auction market remain intact? Though auctions have not even started to fade, contract purchases offer packers a distinct financial advantage. For example, packers spent $1.75 to $2.00 less for contract cattle per hundredweight than they did for auctioned cattle. The USDA predicted that contract purchasing would increase, especially in the cattle and hog markets.

Also, the USDA reported in a 1996 study that out the 19,000 operations selling livestock, the 152 largest sellers accounted for 43 percent of the cattle sold. The USDA noted that concentration within the livestock industry seemed to spread to the sector responsible for selling livestock just as it had to other sectors such as packing and feedlots.

In the area of sheep marketing, another problem had surfaced by the mid-1990s—the market had become extremely concentrated, and lamb raisers had only two or three buyers in the entire United States. This has caused the Western Organization Resource Council to call on the U.S. Attorney General and the Justice Department to investigate the situation and to enforce antitrust legislation.

Likewise, the beef packing industry had become increasingly concentrated at the end of the 1990s. In 1994, just three firms in the beef packing Industry—IBP, Monfort and Excel—processed 80 percent of all fed cattle and were increasing their market share cumulatively at the rate of 5 percent per year. When Upton Sinclair wrote *The Jungle,* a graphic 1906 novel that portrayed the wretched lives of workers in Chicago's meat packing plants (and the impetus behind much antitrust legislation in the food industry), the five largest meat packing firms did not control as much of the slaughter as the "Big Three" do in the modern era. The general feeling among many livestock producer groups is with fewer buyers the lack of competitive bidding will not provide true market discovery for their livestock. The USDA has persistently urged Congress to take action against the large meat-packing companies, launching study after study to reveal their effect on livestock pricing.

Research and Technology

Nearing the end of the century, one of the ways in which the livestock marketing sector has responded to increased packer concentration is through the use of video auctions. As mentioned earlier, this relatively new tool allows cattlemen to offer their livestock for sale to buyers all over the country through the use of modern day telecommunications tools. Videotaped pictures of consignments of livestock are beamed to a satellite on a predetermined sale day, and buyers can view the livestock on their own television sets, providing they are linked to a satellite dish. While they are viewing the livestock, they can call on the telephone and take part in a regular auction. This way, livestock only have to be moved once—to the new owner—thus avoiding the costly and time-consuming task of trucking animals to an auction market.

In video auction, buyers may come from down the street or across the country. The real value of video auction is the sellers have a free and open market to a much wider audience of potential buyers. The livestock are usually less stressed and healthier when sold in this manner. But descriptions of the livestock must be accurate when the buyers cannot view the animals in person. Another benefit of video auction is if a major buyer stays off the market that day, the seller does not suffer because there are plenty of other buyers to take his place.

Large video auction companies stage either monthly or biweekly sales. Western Video Market, headquartered in Cottonwood, California, is actually a consortium of auction markets that are using the video sales in combination with their own weekly, live animal sales. Superior Livestock Auction, with headquarters in Brush, Colorado and Fort Worth, Texas, on the other hand, has more than 300 agents in the country filming consignments and delivering the livestock to the new buyers. Superior was selling more than one million cattle annually by 1994; Western Video had sold more than 60,000 head in just a single day. Superior was also selling other species of livestock, including ostriches.

The marketing of livestock has come a long way from the days when cattle were herded up the Goodnight Trail in an attempt to find buyers. In the modern era the most up-to-date electronic communication tools are being used to market livestock of all species. There has also been a great deal of experimentation taking place with computer listings of livestock and computer auctions. These changes have been revolutionary for an industry steeped in tradition. One thing remains constant however; in the world of livestock marketing the transaction is bound by an honor code that has disappeared in other industries. Multi-million dollar deals are still consummated without a written contract—the marketing of livestock is still very much a handshake business between gentlemen.

FURTHER READING

Agricultural Statistics. Washington: U.S. Department of Agriculture, 1995-1996.

National Cattlemen's Beef Association. "Beef Demand Shows Improvement After 20-Year Slide," 10 December 1999. Available from http://www.beef.org/newsroom/ncba/ncba99_1102a.htm.

National Cattlemen's Association. *Cattle and Beef Handbook.* Englewood, CO, 1996.

The Packers and Stockyards Act: Program Aid Number 1374. Washington: U.S. Department of Agriculture.

SIC 5159

FARM-PRODUCT RAW MATERIALS, NOT ELSEWHERE CLASSIFIED

This industry consists of establishments primarily engaged in buying or marketing farm products that are not included in another classification. Some samples of the industry's products are animal hair, bristles, feathers, furs and hides, broom corn, raw cotton, hops, unprocessed or shelled-only nuts, tobacco leaf, raw silk, and bovine semen. Animals including chicks, horses, and mules are also industry products.

NAICS CODE(S)

422590 (Other Farm Product Raw Materials Wholesalers)

As measured by number of establishments, the leading states in the industry in the late 1990s were New York (196 establishments with sales of $1.96 billion), Texas (192 establishments with sales of $2.06 billion), North Carolina (181 establishments with sales of $1.17 billion), California (133 establishments with sales of $1.68 billion), and Kentucky (124 establishments with sales of $762.2 million).

The industry was subdivided into five categories: cotton (representing 34.7 percent of the industry's total sales volume); other farm-product raw materials (25.1 percent); hides, skins, and pelts (21.0 percent); leaf tobacco (16.2 percent); and wool, wool tops, and mohair (3.0 percent).

Universal Corp. of Richmond, Virginia led the industry with more than $4 billion in sales for its fiscal year ended June 30, 1999. H.T. Hackney Co. of Knoxville, Tennessee followed with sales of more than $1.6 billion for its fiscal year ended March 31, 1999. Syracuse, New York-based agricultural cooperative Agway Inc., which posted almost $1.6 million in sales for its fiscal year ended June 30, 1998, restructured in mid-1999 to combine sales of agricultural products with retail sales under the auspices of its newly created Agriculture and Retail Group.

Standard Commercial Corp. of Wilson, North Carolina placed fourth in the industry with almost $1.5 billion

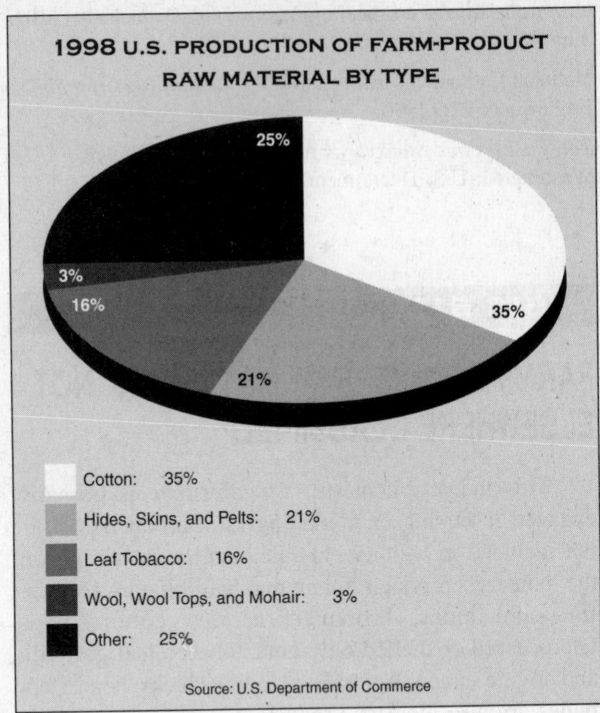

in sales for its fiscal year ended March 31, 1998. Louis Dreyfus Corp. of Wilton, Connecticut rounded out the top five industry leaders with sales of almost $1.4 billion for its fiscal year ended May 31, 1998.

The industry closely scrutinized one of its top sellers, cotton, conducting research to improve fiber quality, fiber processing, new yarns and fabrics, and dyeing and finishing. It also performed research on the consumer market by monitoring and analyzing retail sales, textile industry changes, international fashion trends, and consumer attitudes.

One of the industry's most controversial products was tobacco. An article in the November 5, 1996 issue of *Tobacco Control* compares the tobacco industry's public statements on tobacco control with its federal and state legislative agendas. The article discusses the model state bills that the industry has endorsed while also publicly opposing federal regulations requiring states to enforce laws to prohibit the sale of tobacco to minors. The authors close by saying, "As has been the case in the past, the tobacco industry is publicly endorsing a socially responsible goal while apparently taking action behind the scenes to ensure that the goal is not achieved."

Amending the 1996 tobacco regulations, the Food and Drug Administration introduced rules covering youth access—advertising, sponsorship, and promotions—and public education. Preemption and implementation were also discussed.

On a somewhat more positive note, an October 26, 1995 article in the *Wall Street Journal,* discussed the beneficial effect of the tobacco industry on local economies. The article spotlighted tobacco-related businesses in Camden, New Jersey and discussed a Price Waterhouse study done for the Tobacco Institute. The study concluded that, in 1990, 468,000 jobs—such as suppliers, wholesalers, and retailers—depended on the tobacco industry. But the article also mentioned a Michigan study which found that "without tobacco, Michigan would gain 5,608 more jobs, as smokers would spend cigarette money on other products more closely tied to the state's economy."

Wholesale and Retail Trade USA, 1995 reported that there were 1,556 establishments posting estimated sales of $21.3 billion in 1996. According to *Employment, Hours, and Earnings United States, 1988-96,* those establishments employed 10,680 workers in 1996.

FURTHER READING

"Agway combines agriculture and retail businesses." *Do-It-Yourself Retailing,* June 1999.

DiFranza, Joseph and William Godshall. "Tobacco Industry Effort Hindering Enforcement of the Ban on Tobacco Sales to Minors: Actions Speak Louder than Words." *Tobacco Control,* Summer 1966.

"The FDA's Tobacco Regulations." Rockville, Md: The Food and Drug Administration, 23 August 1996.

Infotrac Company Profiles, 18 February 2000. Available at http://web4.infotrac.galegroup.com.

"Tobacco Industry's Reach Is Wide." *Wall Street Journal,* 26 October 1995.

SIC 5162

PLASTICS MATERIALS AND BASIC FORMS AND SHAPES

This industry includes companies engaged in the wholesale distribution of plastics materials and basic forms and shapes. Industry products include unsupported plastic film, sheeting, rods, tubes, and synthetic resins.

NAICS CODE(S)

422610 (Plastics Materials and Basic Forms and Shapes Wholesalers)

A panel of 67 journalists gathered by the Newseum, a journalism museum, ranked the invention of plastic number 46 on its list of the 100 most significant news events of the 20th Century, according to a February 1999 American Plastics Council (APC) press release. *Newsweek* magazine seconded this opinion. As the APC reported in November 1999, the year-to-date plastic resin production by August 1999 amounted to 52.1 billion pounds, a 5.3 percent increase over production for the same eight-month period in 1998. August 1999 production reached 6.6 billion pounds, a 0.7 percent decrease from July 1999 production but a 4.1 percent increase over August 1998 production.

Both shipments and employment in plastics rose over the 1990s. Employment continued its annual growth rate of 3 percent since 1974, reaching 1,337,700 jobs by 1996, and shipment values continued their two-and-a-half decade growth rate of 4.1 percent, and between 1991 and 1996 alone shipment values rose 55 percent, reaching a value of $274.5 billion in 1996, according to APC statistics.

The *1992 Census of Wholesale Trade* listed 3,490 companies as wholesale distributors of plastic materials and basic forms and shapes. Their combined sales totaled $28.5 billion. At least 160 of these companies reported annual sales of $25 million or higher. The industry employed 25,504 workers and posted an annual payroll of $803.6 million. These figures can be compared to those of the 1980s, where the *1987 Census of Wholesale Trade* listed 2,744 companies in this group, with combined sales of $20.3 billion, 28,453 workers, and an annual payroll of $788.4 million.

Between 1988 and 1992, the average return on assets for the nation's plastic distributors dropped 45 percent, from 8.1 percent to 4.6 percent, although individual distributors had varying success. Mark Bogin, of Roechling Engineered Plastics in Gastonia, North Carolina, wrote in *IAPD Magazine* that "plastic distributors serve a cross-section of industry, and no two distributors serve the same market and industries in the same way." Bogin also said "there is hardly any industry that does not use our products, and regardless of general economic conditions there are always industries which are growing."

As of 1999, the largest distributor of plastics in North America was the Ashland Distribution Company of Ashland Inc., in Ashland Kentucky. For the year ended September 30, 1999, the Ashland Chemical division, located in Columbus, Ohio, generated specialty chemical sales of $1.1 billion, distribution sales of $2.8 billion, and petrochemical sales of $300 million. As of 1995, the General Polymers Division of Ashland Chemical was the highest-grossing company in this industry, with 1995 estimated sales of $650 million and 300 division employees. According to Ashland Chemical's website, "The General Polymers Division is the nation's largest source for prime, packaged thermoplastic raw materials and represents 26 major plastics producers. The division markets a broad range of thermoplastic injection molding, rotational molding, and extrusion materials to processors in the plastics industry through distribution locations in the United States, Canada, Mexico, and Puerto Rico. It also provides plastic material, bulk transfer and packaging services and less-than-truckload quantities of packaged thermoplastics."

The leading distributor of plastic sheet, rod, tube, and film was Cadillac Plastic and Chemical Company, with 1995 estimated sales of $270 million and 1,500 employees. The company, founded in 1945, began as a reseller of surplus canopies from U.S. fighter planes. By the mid-1990s, Cadillac Plastic operated in more than 147 locations around the world. Sheet products, such as Lexan and Plexiglas, were some of the company's best-known products. Lexan, made by GE Plastics, was used in safety glazing, outdoor signage, machine guards, skylights, and windows. Plexiglas, the nation's first commercially available acrylic sheet, was used in display cases and bar-code readers. M.A. Hanna Co. of Cleveland, Ohio, an international specialty plastics company, bought Cadillac Plastic in 1987.

Cadillac Plastic's line of engineering plastics included Nylon, Acetal, Teflon, Cast Acrylic, UHMW-PE, and High Performance Polymers (HPP). The company also sold tubing, lighting, adhesives, and silicones. Within the specialty film category, Cadillac Plastic provided materials used in automobile instrument panels, membrane switches, and graphic arts products. The company's Aircraft Products group marketed specialty products meeting FAA standards for commercial aircraft builders.

FURTHER READING

American Plastics Council. "Plastics and the U.S. Economy." Available at http://www.ameriplas.org/benefits/economic/ussummary.html.

———. "August 1999 Resin Statistics." Available at http://www.ameriplas.org/apcorg/newsroom/pressreleases/1999/11-2-99_resin_stats. html.

———. "Plastic Ranks As One of Century's Top News Stories." Available at http://www.ameriplas.org/apcorg/newsroom/pressreleases/1999/2-24-top_100.html.

Ashland, Inc. Ashland Chemical Homepage. Available from http://www.ashland.com.

Bogin, Mark. "Take a Good, Hard Look Around." *The IAPD Magazine,* December 1993/January 1994.

U.S. Department of Commerce. U.S. Bureau of the Census. *1992 Census of Wholesale Trade.* Washington, DC: GPO, 1995.

SIC 5169

CHEMICALS AND ALLIED PRODUCTS, NOT ELSEWHERE CLASSIFIED

This industry consists of wholesale distributors of chemicals and allied products not included in another classification. Industry products include acids, industrial and heavy chemicals, dyestuffs, industrial salts, rosin, and turpentine.

NAICS CODE(S)

422690 (Other Chemical and Allied Products Wholesalers)

Companies primarily engaged in the wholesale distribution of agricultural chemicals and pesticides are in **SIC 5191: Farm Supplies.** Companies involved in the wholesale distribution of drugs are in **SIC 5122: Drugs, Drug Proprietaries, and Druggists' Sundries.** Companies that distribute pigments, paints, and varnishes are in **SIC 5198: Paints, Varnishes, and Supplies.**

Analysts subdivide industry products into two categories: industrial gases (except liquefied petroleum) and other chemicals and allied products. During the mid 1990s, wholesalers of industrial gases represented 15.3 percent of the total number of industry firms and accounted for 3.9 percent of the dollar-value of industry sales.

According to ''The Business of Chemistry in the USA: Performance and Outlook,'' a Chemical Manufacturers Association survey released in November 1999, the value of overall domestic shipments of chemicals and allied products climbed to a record $412 billion in 1999, an increase of more than 5 percent. CMA director of economics T. Kevin Swift attributed these gains to new-product innovations in the biosciences and in specialty chemicals, as 16 percent of revenues to industrial chemical companies from 1994 through 1999 derived from new products.

Chemical exports remained flat at $68 billion through 1999, continuing a trend since 1992, when exports rose only one percent to reach $42 billion. However, the U.S. chemical industry enjoyed a $526 million trade surplus with China (1998 U.S. exports to China amounted to $1.97 billion while imports from China reached only $1.44 billion). China's proposed participation in the World Trade Organization bodes well for the chemical industry, which accumulated trade surpluses of $7.6 billion in the decade ending through 1998.

The nation's leading chemical distributor, Ashland Chemical Company of Dublin, Ohio, a subsidiary of Ashland Oil, Inc., announced in November 1999 its alliance with e-Chemicals Inc. of Ann Arbor, Michigan, to market Ashland's chemical products on the Internet. As of December 1, 1999, e-Chemicals offered 500 products available from the Industrial Chemicals and Solvents (IC&S) division of Ashland on the World Wide Web, expanding this offering to 2,500 products by spring 2000. The IC&S division of Ashland distributed more than 7,000 chemicals, solvents, additives and raw materials to industries as diverse as printing inks and industrial cleaning products. Ashland Inc.'s 1997 net income was $279 million on sales of $14.2 billion, an increase from 1996 net income of $211 million on sales of $12.9 billion.

Other industry leaders besides Ashland included Degussa Corp. of Ridgefield, New Jersey (1995 sales of $2.3 billion, with 1,800 employees), a subsidiary of the German chemical and pharmaceutical firm, Degussa AG, and, Univar Corp. of Kirkland, Washington (1995 sales of $1.9 billion, with 3,100 employees).

In 1992, according to government statistics, 10,703 establishments were wholesale distributors of chemicals and allied products, with combined sales totaling $103.89 billion. These figures were up from 1987 when 9,961 establishments existed with combined sales of $74.31 billion. The industry employed 67,922 workers in 1992 and had an annual payroll of $2.33 billion.

As a whole, the chemical industry in the United States suffered from a slow economy as the 1990s began. In 1993, however, *Chemical & Engineering News* reported the situation was improving and production of the 50 largest volume chemicals approached 656 billion pounds in 1992, compared with 632 billion in 1991.

FURTHER READING

Ashland Chemical. ''Ashland Distribution Company and E-Chemicals Inc. Announce Major Alliance.'' Available at http://www.ashland.com.

Ashland Chemical. ''Ashland Plan Bears Fruit.'' Available at http://www.ashchem.com/comm/chem2.asp.

''Hoover's Company Capsules.'' Available from http://www.hoovers.com.

Chemical Manufacturers Association. ''Chemical Shipments Rise to Record $412 Billion; Innovation Fueling Bigger Piece of Revenue Gains.'' Available at http://www.cmahq.com/newsstand.nsf/newsletterbyid/rchy-4dvt37.

U.S. Department of Commerce. U.S. Bureau of the Census. *1992 Census of Wholesale Trade,* Washington: GPO, 1995.

SIC 5171

PETROLEUM BULK STATIONS AND TERMINALS

This industry consists of companies that wholesale crude petroleum and petroleum products from bulk liquid storage facilities. Distributors of liquefied petroleum gas from bulk liquid storage facilities are also included.

NAICS CODE(S)

454311 (Heating Oil Dealers)

454312 (Liquefied Petroleum Gas (Bottled Gas) Dealers)

422710 (Petroleum Bulk Stations and Terminals)

The *1997 Economic Census-Wholesale Trade* reported 69 petroleum bulk stations and terminals companies. Sales in 1997 totaled $331.4 million, based on the NAICS code. The mid-1990s sales breakdowns for industry products were reported as: motor gasoline, $49.2 billion; no. 2 distillate fuel oil, $11.8 billion; liquefied petroleum gas, $1.8 billion; residual fuel oil, $1.9 billion; all other distillate fuel oil, $1.9 billion; jet fuel, $3.9 billion; lubricating oil and grease, $1.6 billion; crude oil, $19.7 billion; aviation gasoline, $208.0 million; and special naphtha, $94.0 million.

Analysts subdivided the industry into three categories: petroleum bulk stations, petroleum bulk terminals, and liquefied petroleum (LP) gas bulk stations and terminals. Petroleum bulk stations were defined as businesses with bulk storage capacity from 10,000 to 100,000 gallons for stations getting supplies mostly by tanker, barge, or pipeline and those with bulk storage capacity from 100,000 to 2,100,000 for stations getting supplies from other sources. Petroleum bulk terminals were those businesses whose bulk storage capacity exceeded 100,000 gallons in facilities getting supplies mostly by tanker, barge, or pipeline or exceeded 2,100,000 gallons for facilities getting supplies from other sources. LP gas bulk stations and terminals were plants selling liquefied petroleum gas to dealers, wholesale distributors, industrial users, commercial users, and government and military units.

The greatest number of companies within the industry were petroleum bulk stations and terminals. The smallest segment within the industry was liquefied petroleum gas bulk stations and terminals.

According to industry watchers, petroleum demand would rise as the U.S. economy improved after a slowdown in the early 1990s. World crude oil supplies were expected to meet demand, and forecasters predicted stable prices; this theory was disproved in the late 1990s. Improvements in fuel-consumption efficiencies, however, could slow growth within the industry.

One of the largest companies classified in this industry was Coastal Oil New England, Inc., a petroleum products marketing subsidiary of the Coastal Corporation—1999 sales totaled $8.2 billion. The Coastal Corporation, founded in 1955, was one of the nation's largest energy Companies; Coastal has the capacity for 468,000 barrels per day. In the early 2000s, the company agreed to be acquired by El Paso Energy, a natural gas leader. Another industry leader was EOTT Energy Partners, L.P. of Houston, Texas, with 1999 sales of $8.7 billion. EOTT gathered and marketed crude oil and also used third-party pipelines to deliver jet fuel, fuel oil, and unleaded gasoline. The company gathers and markets approximately 430,000 barrels of crude oil each day.

In the propane segment, one leader was a UGI Corp. subsidiary, AmeriGas Partners, LP of King of Prussia, Pennsylvania, with 1999 sales of $1.4 billion and more than 5,000 employees. Ferrellgas Partners is another propane leader, with 1999 sales of $624.1 million and 4,463 employees.

FURTHER READING

Hoover's Online. *Hoover's Company Profiles.* Austin, TX: April 2000.

U.S. Department of Commerce. Economics and Statistics Administration. *1997 Economic Census-Wholesale Trade.* Washington, D.C.: GPO, March 2000. Available from http://www.census.gov.

SIC 5172

PETROLEUM AND PETROLEUM PRODUCTS WHOLESALERS, EXCEPT BULK STATIONS AND TERMINALS

This industry class consists of wholesale distributors of petroleum and petroleum products (except those with bulk liquid storage facilities). Industry products include butane gas, fuel oil, aircraft fueling services, liquefied petroleum gases, gasoline, kerosene, lubricating oils and grease, and naphtha. Petroleum brokers are also included.

Companies that wholesale petroleum and petroleum products from bulk liquid storage facilities are in **SIC 5171: Petroleum Bulk Stations and Terminals.**

NAICS CODE(S)

422720 (Petroleum and Petroleum Products Wholesalers (except Bulk Stations and Terminals))

The number of establishments in this industry has been steadily declining throughout the 1980s (from 6,287 in 1982 to 3,826 in 1989) and the 1990s (from 3,895 in 1991 to approximately 2,400 in 1996). In 1997 the number of establishments had risen to 3607. Industry employment had been declining as well, from 56,680 in 1982 to just around 30,000 by the mid-1990s. But, again, this number increased to 35,340 in 1997. Industry sales reached a high of $133 billion in 1982 and then dropped to $95 billion in 1988. Although sales have been increasing slightly throughout the 1990s, estimates indicated that by 1996, they would begin to decline again. Indeed, they did; sales in 1997 were approximately $91 billion.

In the mid-1990s, petroleum and petroleum products wholesalers (other than bulk stations and terminals) made up 26.1 percent of the companies in the petroleum and petroleum products industry. The largest group of companies, 84.6 percent, were merchant wholesalers (wholesalers who take title to the goods they sell).

This industry is served by the Society of Petroleum Engineers (SPE), which conducts extensive research into methods of transport for oil and gas, among many other endeavors. The American Petroleum Institute (API) and the National Petroleum Council (NPC) are also crucial to industry players.

Some industry leaders include Texaco Oil Trading and Supply Co., of White Plains, New York, a subsidiary of Texaco, Inc.; Castrol North America Holdings of Wayne, New Jersey; Flying J Inc. of Brigham City, Utah; and Getty Petroleum Corp. of Jericho, New York.

Further Reading

Hoover's Online. *Hoover's Company Profiles.* Austin, TX: April 2000.

U.S. Department of Commerce. Economics and Statistics Administration. *1997 Economic Census-Wholesale Trade.* Washington, D.C.: GPO, March 2000. Available from http://www.census.gov.

SIC 5181

BEER AND ALE DISTRIBUTION

This industry includes establishments primarily engaged in the wholesale distribution of beer, ale, porter, and other fermented malt beverages.

NAICS Code(s)

422810 (Beer and Ale Wholesalers)

More than 3,000 beer and ale wholesale distributors were in operation in the late 1990s, enjoying total sales of $35 billion. While consumption patterns of alcoholic beverages tapered throughout the mid- and late 1990s, breweries' shipments totaled $19.0 billion in 1999, up from $18.0 billion the year before. Canned beer and ale constituted by far the largest share of this total, at $15.9 billion, while bottled beer and ale generated sales of nearly $1.4 billion. Wholesalers faced continuing pressure from major breweries attempting to streamline their delivery systems by integrating distributing into their business, though the nature of the competitive brewery industry opened a window whereby distributors could gain leverage. Wholesalers employed more than 96,000 individuals in 1997.

Beer Distribution Development. As long as breweries have done business in the United States, they have made continual refinements to their methods of distribution. For example, Adolphus Busch pioneered the use of refrigerated railroad cars to ship beers long distances in the late 1870s. Adolph Coors became the first brewer to develop and introduce an all-aluminum recyclable can in 1959.

When Prohibition was repealed in 1933, after 13 crime-ridden years, not only did the federal and state governments tighten controls, but brewers, distillers, and vintners adopted policies of self-regulation as well. The Federal Alcohol Administration (FAA) Act was put into place soon after Prohibition. The act still is responsible for the administration of regulations specifying who may qualify as a brewer; the collection of both brewer and wholesaler occupational taxes; and the regulation of trade practices, advertising, and labeling. Today most states have adopted various versions of the FAA Act in addition to their own statutes and rules. Different states use distribution techniques that vary from state owned to private systems.

After Prohibition malt beverages were produced in some 750 different locations throughout the country and were distributed to wholesalers and then retailers within an extremely limited geographic region, by today's standards. Beer is a relatively expensive product to transport considering its value, so any brewers wishing to expand their area of sales had to consider the freight differences involved in shipping to another market. Thus for many years after Prohibition the United States developed a number of areas that might be called "brewing centers." That is, there were several areas that contained one or more local or regional brewers.

These local or regional brewers, for competitive reasons, priced their beers at levels that would permit their wholesalers to generate the lowest consumer prices possible within their geographical areas. Any brewer desiring to sell in that area would need to consider the regional price structure, both in making their decisions about whether to enter the markets and in pricing their products. While there are fewer brewers today, this basic pricing situation still exists. Beer is priced to wholesalers by the case. It is packed in different sized packs and sometimes packed loose. Domestic brewers sell beer to wholesalers F.O.B. (free on board) the brewery, meaning the wholesalers pay the freight charges. Importers generally sell beer to wholesalers C.I.F. (cost, insurance, and freight) port of entry, although some importers also maintain warehouses from which they sell F.O.B.

In the 1930s the chief means of selling beer were in draft form and in refillable bottles. Both of these packages were expensive to ship and return and, as a result, the need for less costly containers arose. The first answer to the shipping problem came with the development of the beer can in 1935. While World War II delayed its widespread use domestically, it was used extensively by the armed forces, and after the war sales in aluminum containers started to boom. The aluminum can, along with the glass companies' response to it (the one-way bottle), enabled brewers to ship relatively more cheaply and expand their markets accordingly.

The shipping breweries, which had penetrated new markets in 1946 with minimal quantities of beer, now had product and lightweight one-way containers available to ship to these distant markets. Local breweries that had withdrawn from regional markets to protect more profitable local markets found it difficult to reenter markets they had left. In addition, many local breweries did not have the equipment to fill flat-top cans, which facilitated shipping. So, for the first time, the shipping breweries gained advantages not formerly available to them.

Beer Distribution Today. Beer and ale wholesaling has always been relatively dispersed, characterized by a large number of independent distributors. The major beer companies have periodically made attempts to purchase some of their independent distributors in an effort to vertically integrate and obtain more control over the channel of distribution. Company-owned distributors can provide an advantage in controlling the pricing and presentation of the product to the final consumer and in maintaining retailer relations to ensure availability of the product. However, for the most part, brewers have been prevented by anti-trust considerations from purchasing their distributors, and efforts to build their own distributorships risk alienating their existing distributors and losing the market penetration they have. The major breweries still maintained only a small handful of company-owned distributors in the late 1990s.

In order to maintain a modicum of control over distributors, larger breweries have often tried to replace restrictions on the ability of distributors to carry products of other brewers. However, because of Anheuser-Busch's dominating market share, competing brewers, such as Miller Brewing and Coors have been forced to relax such restrictions, allowing wholesalers to acquire each other's brands, in order to guard their market shares. However, upon the acquisition of competing brands by wholesalers in markets such as Chicago, where Anheuser-Busch's dominance is far less pronounced, brewers complained that wholesalers were taking undue advantage of their greater freedom and forsaking the very logic that lead to relaxed restrictions in the first place. Many wholesalers, at any rate, elect to stay with one brewer in order to maintain their positive relations.

Distribution is a relatively unconcentrated industry with several hundred regional independent distributors. Distributors generally remain regional since they are regulated by the state in which they do business. In most states, each distributor is awarded an exclusive sales area by the brewer and is primarily responsible for building relations with the retail and other consumer outlets to build the sales of the product. In a few states, such as Indiana, exclusive territories are not allowed and competition is fierce. In states with exclusive territories, the retail customer, including grocery chains, bars, and restaurants, has only one source of supply and is therefore at the mercy of distributor pricing. A strong dealer network is essential for brewers in order to obtain shelf space and keep the product available to the consumer. However, this is offset somewhat by the fact that there are so many distributors, so each has only limited power over the brewer.

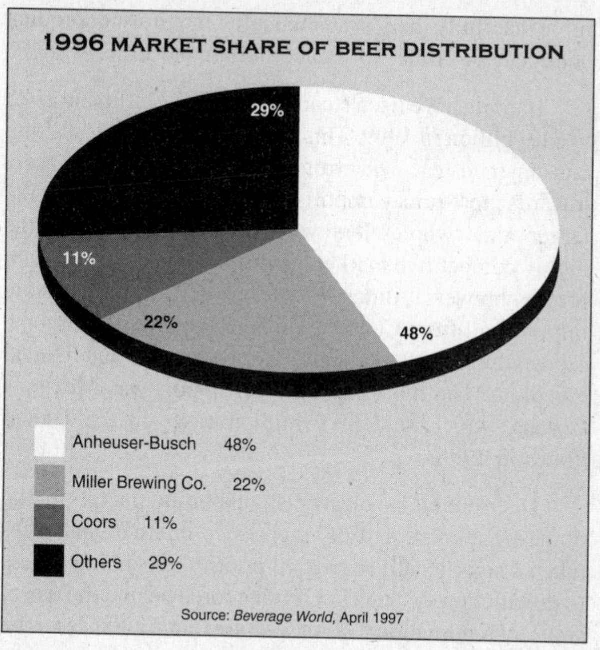

There were 1,178 breweries in the United States in 1997. Among the major breweries, there are few immediate threats to the 47 percent market share enjoyed by Anheuser Busch, who maintained a distribution network of more than 900 wholesalers. Miller Brewing, with 735 distributors, was a distant second, commanding 21 percent of the market. Coors' 600-wholesaler distribution system was only built nationally in 1986 and has not yet achieved the loyalty or presence that its larger competitors enjoy.

Imported beers, an increasingly crucial sector for distributors, have met with some difficulties regarding their products' freshness. The resulting backlash focused scrutiny on distributors, who were under pressure to reduce "inventory days," the number of days beer and ale remain on their shelves. Domestic breweries, eyeing the possible vulnerability of the burgeoning import sector, have launched a campaign advertising their own freshness as a way of marketing on the strength of this problem. While analysts hold that Eurobrews generally have a longer shelf life than domestic products, wholesalers were scrambling to streamline their operations by more carefully and systematically monitoring product code dates in order to reduce turnaround time.

Imports have risen steadily, from $1.2 billion in 1995 to $1.9 billion in 1999. This was partly driven by shifting consumer tastes away from mass-produced U.S. beers towards more pricey imports. This was good news for the larger U.S. wholesalers who invested heavily in the highly competitive market for distribution contracts with foreign brewers. Almost 95 percent of U.S. beer and ale imports hail from Canada, Mexico, and Western Europe, especially the Netherlands, Germany, and the United Kingdom. The most popular beer import was Mexico's Corona, which sold 39.9 million cases in the United States in 1998.

Distribution is clearly an important factor in the domestic market, and its importance internationally has taken a significantly increased priority. Obtaining access to distribution systems is a driving force behind the recent wave of international joint ventures and alliances. The accelerating globalization of the brewing industry has generally tended to diminish the power and influence that distributors wield, since the larger multinational breweries tend to have significantly greater ability to move into foreign markets and establish deals on their own terms.

However, declining foreign consumption of U.S. beer and ale has forced breweries to take more drastic measures. Miller Brewing, for example, contracted to maintain its German wholesaler, renaming it Miller Brands Germany. The company dropped its distribution of a variety of beverages to focus exclusively on Miller's products. Total U.S. exports of malt beverages declined significantly during the mid- and late 1990s, from $526 million in 1995 to $370 million in 1999. After the United States, the world's largest beer markets are China and Germany.

The European market differs from that of the United States and Japan in that it is more regional, with local brands dominating their regions. Very few European brands have established widespread distribution, and most have had difficulty in gaining acceptance outside their regions. Despite challenges in creating a widespread distribution system and obtaining acceptance of an American beer, Budweiser is sold in 20 European countries with an annual sales growth rate at around 25 percent, while Miller has taken enormous steps to crack the European market as well.

The overall production of malt beverages remained relatively constant since the early 1980s, and this trend continued throughout the 1990s. Total yearly output in 1998 was in excess of 190 million 31-gallon barrels, compared to 188.8 barrels in 1991. The mid- and late 1990s saw explosive growth in the number of microbreweries and brewpubs. In addition to the nation's 760 brewpubs, the mushrooming microbrewery industry boasted 400 establishments in 1999, which produced more than 6 million barrels of craft brews. These breweries generally had a very localized distribution network, though even in their small, regional markets, they had to fight hard for distribution with larger brewers who covet the smaller markets. Craft beers, brew pubs, and regional specialty beers accounted for 3 percent of all beer and ale sales in the United States and have grown nearly 25 percent since the mid-1990s. Many major brewers have now begun developing their own specialty brews.

Only a small handful of U.S. beer and ale wholesalers were able to claim a significant market share in the late 1990s. National Distributing Company, Inc., a private firm founded in 1935 with operations in Colorado, Florida, Georgia, New Mexico, and South Carolina, generated sales of $1.37 billion in 1999 while employing 1,700 people. In addition to beer and ale, the company also distributed wine and liquor. Glazer's Wholesale Distributors also enjoyed a significant presence, raking in sales of $1.08 billion and employing 2,700 people.

FURTHER READING

"The Anheuser-Busch Distribution System: A Strategic Weapon?" *Modern Brewery Age,* 14 July 1997.

Daykin, Tom. "Miller Brewing, Anheuser-Busch End Dispute Over Distributors." *Milwaukee Journal-Sentinel,* 20 May 1998.

"Industry Issues: Distribution is a Rocky Road for Craft Brewers." *Beverage Industry,* October 1997.

Khermouch, Gerry. "Miller Seen Easing Other-Brand Policy." *Brandweek,* 9 August 1999.

U.S. Department of Commerce. Bureau of the Census. *Census of Manufacturers, 1997.* Washington, D.C.: GPO, 21 December 1999.

U.S. Department of Commerce. International Trade Administration. *U.S. Industry and Trade Outlook 1999* New York: The McGraw Hill Companies, 1999.

SIC 5182

WINE AND DISTILLED ALCOHOLIC BEVERAGES

This category includes establishments primarily engaged in the wholesale distribution of distilled spirits, including neutral spirits and ethyl alcohol used in blended wines and distilled liquor. The product range includes bottled wines and spirits, brandy and brandy spirits, cocktails, liquors, wine coolers, and wines.

NAICS CODE(S)

422820 (Wine and Distilled Alcoholic Beverage Wholesalers)

Like other sectors of the wholesale industry, the wholesale wine and distilled beverages business is very fragmented, with a few large companies and many small firms. In 1997, 3,214 establishments operated in this wholesale industry, down from 3,651 in 1993. The majority of operations—1,281 distributors—were small scale, with less than five employees. 553 businesses employed between five and nine workers, 438 listed 10 to 19 employees, while another 439 employed between 20 to 49 workers. Finally, 364 establishments listed more than 50 employees on their payroll.

Most of the wholesalers operating primarily as wine and distilled beverage distributors, a total of 639, had sales in the range of $1 million to $5 million. Another 602 reported sales exceeding $5 million. 549 establishments recorded sales between $500,000 and $999,000, while 370 reported sales in the $250,000 to $499,000 range. There were 204 units that reported sales between $100,000 and $249,000, 30 between $50,000 and $99,000, and only 18 establishments that reported less than $49,000 in sales.

The top wholesaler in 1998 was Johnson Brothers Wholesale Liquor, of St. Paul, Minnesota, followed by Young's Market Co., Glazer's Wholesale Drug Company, and Sunbelt Beverage Corp.

In the mid-1990s, distilleries, losing market share in the United States to beer and wine producers, foresaw greater sales opportunities abroad. California wineries also looked to overseas suppliers to expand their product lines and provide customers with lower-priced alternatives to their premium wines. Faced with the prospect of declining wine consumption, the Wine Market Council planned an advertising campaign aimed at younger consumers. If Seagram's 1996 decision to break with the industry's self-imposed ban on broadcast advertising is any indication of things to come, the distillers may soon follow suit.

FURTHER READING

Dun's Census of American Business 1997. Parsippany, NJ: Dun and Bradstreet, 1997.

Forbes Annual Report on American Industry, 13 January 1997. Available from http://www.forbes.com/forbes/97/0113/5901160a.htm.

Shore, Teri. "More Import Perspectives: Foreign Supplies Could Help California Wineries." *Wine Business Monthly,* February 1996. Available from http://smartwine.com/wbm.1996/bm029606.htm.

Turcsik, Richard. "Wine Council Is Aiming to Fill Glasses of the Younger Generation." *Supermarket News,* 23 September 1996.

Ward's Business Directory of U.S. Private and Public Companies, 1996, Detroit: Gale Group, 1999.

SIC 5191

FARM SUPPLIES

This category covers establishments engaged in the wholesale distribution of animal feeds, fertilizers, agricultural chemicals, pesticides, seeds, and other farm supplies, except grains. Establishments primarily engaged in the wholesale distribution of pet food are classified in **SIC 5149: Groceries and Related Products, Not Elsewhere Classified;** those distributing pet supplies are classified in **SIC 5199: Nondurable Goods, Not Elsewhere Classified.**

NAICS CODE(S)

444220 (Nursery and Garden Centers)
422910 (Farm Supplies Wholesalers)
422920 (Book, Periodical and Newspaper Wholesalers)

The range of items distributed by wholesale farm supply establishments is wide, including such disparate products as alfalfa, beekeeping supplies, flower and field bulbs, harness equipment, hay, insecticides, agricultural lime, pesticides, phosphate rock, garden flower seeds, and straw.

In 1997, farmer cooperatives increased their share of overall farm supply sales to 30 percent, the highest recorded total since tracking of this data began in 1951. In the same year, co-op sales of major farm supplies totaled $21.9 billion, according to the November/December 1998 issue of *Rural Cooperatives Magazine*. These statistics, gathered by the United States Department of Agriculture (USDA) in conjunction with the Rural Business-Cooperative Service (RBS), included petroleum sales amounting to $6.8 billion, a 7.4 percent increase over 1996's total. Notwithstanding the inclusion of petroleum sales, sales of other supplies increased similarly: feed sales rose 11 percent, and crop protectant sales increased 10.5 percent for farmer cooperatives selling farm supplies. Charles A. Kraenzie, Director of the USDA/RBS Statistics Staff, attributed these increases to "the favorable crop conditions farmers had experienced in 1997."

The increasing role of farmer cooperatives in farm supply sales in 1997 continued the trend reflected in 1996 USDA statistics, when co-op farm supply sales rose to $24 billion, an increase of $2.4 billion or 11 percent. While these statistics also included a 21 percent rise in petroleum sales, sales of other supplies increased similarly, such as the 11 percent climb in fertilizer sales. As was true in 1997, favorable weather in 1996 helped fuel these increases in farm supply sales for farmer cooperatives. Net income for farm supply co-ops rose almost 17 percent, from $808 million in 1995 to $942 million in 1996, and net business volume increased from $21 billion in 1995 to $23 billion in 1997.

Just over 28,000 companies operated businesses of this nature in 1996, with overall sales of an estimated $56 billion, an increase of about 10 percent over 1993. According to *Dun's Census of American Business,* 28,481 wholesale farm suppliers were in operation, a decrease of 5,625 establishments since 1993.

In 1996 the typical wholesale farm supplier was small, with fewer than 10 employees and with sales above $250,000. More than half of the total suppliers—about 16,000—had fewer than five employees. About 9,000 suppliers employed between five and 14; 2,500 establishments employed more than 15. In 1996, there were 5,316 concerns with sales between $250,000 and $499,000; 5,257 units had sales between $1 million and $5 million; 3,318 units had sales between $500,000 and $999,000; 3,983 units had sales between $100,000 and $249,000; and roughly 1,500 had sales less than $100,000.

Leading companies involved in the wholesale farm supply business include Illinois Agricultural Association of Bloomington, Illinois; Transammonia Inc., based in New York City; and Southern States Co-op, Inc. of Richmond, Virginia.

Further Reading

Brownlee, Jim and Dan Campbell. "Farmer Co-ops Continue to Break Income and Sales Records." Available at http://www.usda.gov/news/releases/1997/08/0261.

Darnay, Arsen J., and Gary Alampi Eds. *Wholesale and Retail Trade USA.* Detroit: Gale Research, 1995.

Dun's Census of American Business 1996, Parsippany, NJ: Dun and Bradstreet, 1996.

Kraenzie, Charles A. "Co-ops Break Supply Sales Record." *Rural Cooperatives Magazine.* Available at http://www.rurdev.usda.gov/rbs/pub/nov98/break.htm

Ward's Business Directory of U.S. Private and Public Companies, 1996. Detroit: Gale Research, 1996.

SIC 5192

BOOKS, PERIODICALS, AND NEWSPAPERS

This category includes establishments primarily engaged in the wholesale distribution of books, periodicals, and newspapers.

NAICS Code(s)

422920 (Book, Periodical, and Newspaper Wholesalers)

While book, periodical, and newspaper wholesalers faced a number of daunting challenges in the late 1990s, a robust economy helped maintain sound, if lagging, industry performance. Altogether, there were 4,265 establishments engaged in this industry category in 1997, up from 4,119 the year before. Sales, however, took a fall, totaling $33.63 billion, a decline of 6.7 percent from 1996. The industry employed more than 89,300 people in 1998, down from 90,470 in 1996. Wholesalers devoted specifically to magazine distribution declined dramatically; 50 such establishments were in operation in 1999, down from 180 in 1993.

Book, magazine, and newspaper distributors tend to be small, with more than half employing fewer than six individuals; a mere 78 percent employed 100 or more people. In contrast, 622 businesses employed 100 people or more in 1987. In addition to distributing books, periodicals, and newspapers, some wholesalers carried additional product lines including photographic equipment and supplies, religious and school supplies, stationary office supplies, greeting cards, art goods (including novelties and souvenirs), toys and hobby goods and supplies, and electronic parts and equipment, and other durable goods.

The explosive growth in electronic commerce was forcing many wholesalers to close its doors in the late 1990s. The online bookstore Amazon.com established a vast network of its own distribution outlets across the United States and maintained 10 times as much distribution space in 1999 as it did in 1998. To fight back against this trend, the intensely competitive wholesaler industry has undergone immense consolidation by way of mergers and acquisitions in addition to the dropout of a number of players. The four largest magazine wholesalers, for example, control about 80 percent of all single-copy magazine sales. The industry's trade association, the Periodical Wholesalers of North America, was even forced to disband, citing lack of sufficient membership numbers.

This consolidation was driven in part by aggressive supermarkets and other large retailers, a key customer base to magazine and newspaper distributors, attempting to diminish costs by ordering product for entire regions, rather than for specific local markets. Such practices have taken their toll on smaller competitors, who were forced into alliances with their larger competitors in order to maintain their viability.

The increased centralization of the wholesale industry has produced no small amount of ire among publishers. With fewer but larger establishments, wholesalers have been able to step up their leverage in negotiating distribution deals with publishers. As overall industry sales dwindle, wholesalers seeking greater efficiency have often refused to carry less profitable titles, focusing instead on larger volume shipments of sure money makers. Mid-level sellers, meanwhile, have become less visible as wholesalers gear those titles only toward markets in which they are assured a stable customer base. Finally, wholesalers have taken advantage of their heightened bargaining power to demand higher fees and standards from publishers.

The publishing industry has not taken this lying down. Some magazine publishers have fought back against the growing power and influence of wholesalers. In 1999, rival publishers Hearst Magazines and Conde Nast formed a joint venture distribution company to bring that facet of their business under their control. Meanwhile, retail book giant Barnes & Noble attempted to purchase the wholesale industry leader Ingram Distribution Co. in 1998 for $600 million but dropped the plan to avoid an expected federal antitrust investigation.

The leaders in the book, magazine, and newspaper wholesale industry at the end of the 1990s included Ingram Distribution Co., of La Vergne, Tennessee, the world's biggest book distributor with annual revenues of $1 billion; Time Warner, Inc., of Alexandria, Virginia, whose Time Distribution Services and Warner Publishing Services generated $2 billion in revenues from wholesaling and other activities; and Baker & Taylor, of Charlotte, North Carolina, with $1 billion in revenues. Other key players include Anderson News LLC, the nation's largest magazine wholesaler; Chas. Levy, the second largest magazine wholesaler with sales of $700 million; and Hudson News.

FURTHER READING

Cooke, James Aaron. ''Clicks and Mortar.'' *Logistics Management & Distribution Report,* January 2000.

''How Some Magazines Arrive On Shelves, and Why Some Soon May Not.'' *Wall Street Journal,* 26 February 1998.

Owens, Jennifer, and Teresa Ennis. ''Latest Wholesaler Merger Shrinks Major Players to Four.'' *Folio,* February 1999.

''Single-copy Magazines: A Category in Transition.'' *Progressive Grocer,* May 1998.

U.S. Department of Commerce. Bureau of the Census. *Census of Wholesale Trade, 1997.* Washington, D.C.: GPO, September 1999.

SIC 5193

FLOWERS, NURSERY STOCK, AND FLORISTS' SUPPLIES

This category includes establishments primarily engaged in the wholesale distribution of flowers, nursery stock, and florists' supplies.

NAICS CODE(S)

422930 (Flower, Nursery Stock and Florists' Supplies Wholesalers)
444220 (Nursery and Garden Centers)
422940 (Tobacco and Tobacco Product Wholesalers)

This industry consisted of 12,586 establishments in 1997 according to *Dun's Census of American Business,* down slightly from 13,070 in 1996, continuing a downward trend that began in the early 1990s. The majority were small-scale, single-unit operations, which operated year-round and reported annual sales of less than a quarter of a million dollars. The most comprehensive study of the wholesale industry conducted in recent years, the *1992 Census of Wholesale Trade,* found that the four largest firms controlled just 20 establishments; the eight largest, 64 establishments; the 20 largest, 123 establishments; and the 50 largest wholesalers in this industry controlled 216 establishments.

Like other industries of its kind, the wholesale flowers, nursery stock, and florists' supplies industry experienced a decline in the number of establishments and only modest increases in sales, rising an average of 5 percent a year to an estimated $2.3 billion in 1996. The *1994 U.S. Industrial Outlook* attributed the decline to mergers, acquisitions, and business failures. In addition, the increase of direct manufacturer to retail agreements and the use of mail order and catalog sales negatively impacted the wholesale industry.

The largest group, comprised of 4,300 units, reported sales between $100,000 and $249,000 in 1997, according to *Dun's.* The next biggest category included slightly larger operations with gross revenues between $250,000 and $499,000 that year: 1,754 wholesalers fell into this group. More than 1,500 units had sales between $500,000 and $1 million, and about 1,700 units had sales between $1 million and $5 million. 1,202 wholesale flower and nursery stock distributors had annual sales volumes between $50,000 and $99,000; and only 366 sold between $1,000 and $50,000 worth of stock in 1997. The smallest grouping, comprised of units reporting more than $5 million in annual sales, remained relatively steady, increasing from 347 to 349 operators.

The majority of wholesale flower, nursery stock, and florist supplies distributors employed less than five workers in 1997. More than half of the total suppliers, just under 7,000 units, employed between zero and four workers. 2,538 flower wholesalers had between five and nine employees. 1,125 establishments had between 10 and 14 workers, while 517 employed from 15 to 19. There were 934 units in 1997 that had between 20 and 49 workers, and 193 with between 50 and 99 (the only category which grew). Finally, 86 stores employed more than 100 people.

Leading companies in this industry include Florimex Worldwide, Inc.; Celebrity, Inc. of Tyler, Texas; Ball Horticultural Co. of West Chicago, Illinois; and Shermin Nurseries of Ridgefield, Connecticut.

FURTHER READING

Darnay, Arsen J., and Gary Alampi, eds. *Wholesale and Retail Trade USA.* Detroit: Gale Research, 1995.

Dun's Census of American Business 1996, Parsippany, NJ: Dun and Bradstreet, 1996.

Ward's Business Directory of U.S. Private and Public Companies. Detroit: Gale Group, 1999.

SIC 5194

TOBACCO AND TOBACCO PRODUCTS

This category covers establishments primarily engaged in the wholesale distribution of tobacco and its products. Leaf tobacco wholesalers are classified in **SIC 5159: Farm-Product Raw Materials, Not Elsewhere Classified**, and establishments primarily engaged in stemming and redrying tobacco are classified in **SIC 2141: Tobacco Stemming and Redrying.** Items handled by establishments in this business include: chewing tobacco, cigarettes, cigars, smoking tobacco, and snuff.

NAICS CODE(S)

422940 (Tobacco and Tobacco Product Wholesalers)

The wholesale distribution of tobacco and tobacco products in 1997 was a relatively small but profitable industry, employing about 57,000 workers and bringing in about $50.3 billion sales. The majority of companies in this classification were small—employing less than five persons. In 1997, 638 companies had less than 5 employees; 400 had between 5 and 9 employees; 243 had between 10 and 14 employees; 161 had 15 to 19 employees; 340 had 20 to 49 employees; and nearly 200 establishments 50 or more employees.

Wholesalers of tobacco and tobacco products benefited from the explosive growth of the cigar trend in the United States in the late 1990s. The cigar emerged as a symbol of success and even celebrity. After cigar sales fell five percent annually for three decades until the mid-1990s, the industry surged on the strength of the endorsement by celebrities and pop culture generally. Glossy magazines like *Cigar Aficionado* featured movie stars and athletes sporting cigars on its famous covers. Moreover, the industry moved to acquire premium product placement in motion pictures. Premium cigars sold 370 million units, valued at $1 billion, in 1997, an almost 400 percent increase from 1992.

Continued success was not assured, however. Health concerns have intensified the examination of the cigar industry, leading to possible mandatory health-warning labels on their products, a series of printed advertisements warning against the dangers of cigar smoking, and calls from the Federal Trade Commission to prohibit cigar advertising on radio and television.

At any rate, despite the high profile of cigars, they still constitute a miniscule market sector next to cigarettes and smokeless tobacco. Throughout the entire industry, heightened regulatory scrutiny has forced wholesalers to raise their prices in order to remain competitive with increased expenses. Moreover, distributors have begun to more aggressively diversify their activities. While many have traditionally combined their cigarette shipments with the distribution of candy to capitalize on the lucrative convenience-store market, many have expanded into packaged and fresh foods as well.

Leading companies in this industry include the Eby-Brown Co. of Naperville, Illinois, with 1998 sales of $1.7 million; the Farner Bocken Co. of Carroll, Iowa; and the Imperial Trading Co. of Harahan, Louisiana.

FURTHER READING

Balu, Rekha. "Trucking Beyond Candy, Cigarettes." *Crain's Chicago Business,* 23 June 1997.

Buss, Dale. "Cigar Makers Respond to Critics." *Brandmarketing,* August 1999.

U.S. Department of Commerce. Bureau of the Census. *1997 Census of Wholesale Trade.* Washington, D.C.: GPO, 21 September 1999.

U.S. Department of Commerce. International Trade Administration. *U.S. Industry and Trade Outlook 1999.* Washington, D.C.: GPO, 1999.

SIC 5198

PAINT, VARNISHES, AND SUPPLIES: WHOLESALE DISTRIBUTION

This category covers businesses that distribute wholesale paints, varnishes, wallpaper, and supplies. Retail stores selling these items to the general public are classified in **SIC 5231: Paint, Glass, and Wallpaper Stores.** According to the Standard Industrial Classification, inventory handled by businesses in this category include calcimines, colors and pigments, enamels, lacquers, paint brushes, shellac, rollers, and sprayers.

NAICS CODE(S)

422950 (Paint, Varnish and Supplies Wholesalers)
444120 (Paint and Wallpaper Stores)

This is a relatively small industry, with just 2,791 operators in 1997—a decrease of 709 from 3,500 in 1994. Like most sectors of the wholesale trade, this industry felt the ill effects of the early 1990's recession. Although sales were down between 1988 and 1992, there were signs of a recovery by 1993, and sales grew slowly during the rest of the nineties. The majority of paint, varnish, and supply wholesalers reported sales between $250,000 and $500,000 in 1993, according to *Dun's Census of American Business;* 1,278 establishments were in this net income range, compared with 1,138 in the previous year. One thousand and ninety-three wholesalers had a sales range of between $1 million and $5 million, compared with 1,119 in 1992. One thousand and two firms had sales between $500,000 and $1 million in 1993, 31 more than in 1992; 848 outfits had sales of from $100,000 to $249,000, just one more than the previous year. Three hundred and six companies had sales of more than $5 million; 196 wholesalers earned less than $100,000; and 105 earned less than $50,000 in 1993. By the late 1990s, industry sales were projected to climb to more than $10.6 billion.

Establishments were generally productive, even with small staffs: most had fewer than four employees but a high rate of staff turnover. According to *1997 County Business Patterns* published by the U.S. Census Bureau, 1,394 companies had four or fewer employees. This represented a decrease of 2,040 in this category since 1994. There were 776 establishments that had between five and nine employees in 1997, compared with 1,827 in 1994. Four hundred and twenty-two outfits employed between 10 and 19 workers, 133 less than in 1994. Companies that employed between 20 and 49 in the industry in 1997 numbered 153, compared with 178 in this category in 1994. Of the remainder, 30 employed between 50 and 99 workers; 12 employed between 100 and 249; and only four had more than 250 workers.

The industry's leaders in the mid-1990s included the following companies: Seabrook Wallcoverings Inc. of Memphis, Tennessee, with estimated sales of $100 million and 500 employees; Thompson PBE Inc. of Clearwater, Florida, with estimated sales of $65 million and 300 employees; and Masterchem Industries, Inc. of Barnhart, Missouri, with estimated sales of $50 million and 100 employees.

The employment rate—approximately 29,000 in 1997—was predicted to grow in the wholesale paint, varnishes, and supplies industry over the next 15 years due to a rise in wholesale exports. In particular, the passing of the North American Free Trade Agreement (NAFTA) in 1994 was expected to cause export demand to rise over the long term. The paint, varnish, and supply wholesale industry should benefit from NAFTA, in terms of both job creation and sales.

FURTHER READING

U.S. Bureau of the Census. *1992 Census of Wholesale Trade.* Washington, DC: GPO, 1995.

———. *County Business Patterns 1997.* Washington, DC: GPO 1999.

SIC 5199

MISCELLANEOUS NONDURABLE GOODS

This category covers wholesalers of nondurable goods, not elsewhere classified, such as art goods, industrial yarns, textile bags, and bagging burlap.

NAICS CODE(S)

541890 (Other Services Related to Advertising)
422990 (Other Miscellaneous Nondurable Goods Wholesalers)

Just a glance at the miscellaneous nondurable goods industry shows how complex it is to place every U.S. nondurable good into a distinct group. Even if each segment of this scattered industry were given its own classification, the need for new categories would likely emerge within a few months. Items listed in this diverse category include: artists' materials, textile bags, baskets, brooms, burlap, candles, charcoal, Christmas trees, clothes hangers, tropical fish, glassware, animal and vegetable greases, hairbrushes, ice, industrial yarn, cigar and cigarette lighters, matches, paper novelties, smokers' pipes, plant food, crude rubber, sheet music, wigs, wood carvings, woolen and worsted yarns, worms, and many other items.

In 1997 *Dun and Bradstreet* listed more than 49,000 establishments in the non-durable goods industry, which reported combined sales of $491 billion, up from $468 billion in the prior year. The industry as a whole reported profits exceeding $107 billion, an increase of more than $8 billion from 1996. The sale of nondurable goods contributed more than 15 percent to the U.S. Gross Domestic Product during the 1990s. As the century came to a close, more promising figures were reported by the industry. New orders in non-durable goods rose 4 percent from August to September 1999. Sales of non-durable goods rose 6 percent in October and 4 percent in November, compared to figures for the same months in 1998.

Approximately 7.6 million workers were employed in the miscellaneous wholesale trade nondurable goods industry during 1998, according to a *Washington Post* article. In 1997 the average industry worker brought home $504.71 for 41 hours of work each week. Seventeen years earlier, the same worker brought home $255.45 for 39 hours of work each week. A November

1999 survey of approximately 16,000 U.S. companies showed that workers in the nondurable goods industries would be in high demand as the new millennium began. Conducted by Manpower, Inc., the survey also showed that the shortage of skilled workers in the industry might continue until the year 2006.

A leading company in the miscellaneous wholesale trade nondurable goods industry is Golden State Foods Corp. A privately held food-processing company based in Irvine, California, Golden State Foods had $1.5 billion in sales in 1998 and 1,750 employees. The company supplies hamburger patties, buns, tomatoes, lettuce, ketchup, and mayonnaise to 2,500 McDonald's restaurants. By 1999 it was the third-largest processor of beef patties for McDonald's and the second-largest overall supplier of products for the fast-food chain. Golden State Foods is now run by business consultant Yucaipa Companies and investment firm Wetterau Associates, who jointly acquired the food processor in 1998. Yucaipa acts as the controlling shareholder, while Wetterau manages day-today operations.

Further Reading

Berry, John M. ''Wage Gains Falling Despite Low Jobless Rate.'' *The Washington Post,* 19 November 1998.

Hoover's Company Profiles. Austin, TX: Hoover's, Inc., 1997. Available from http://www.hoovers.com.

''Manpower Inc. Says Talent Pool Is Running Dry as Firms Seek More Help.'' *St. Louis Post-Dispatch,* 23 November 1999.

The New York Times Almanac 2000: The Almanac of Record. New York: Penguin Reference Books,1999.

U.S. Bureau of the Census Web Site. Available at http://www.census.gov.

U.S. Department of Commerce Web Site. Available at http://www.doc.gov.

U.S. Department of Labor Web Site. Available at http://www.dol.gov.

RETAIL TRADE

SIC 5211

LUMBER AND OTHER BUILDING MATERIALS DEALERS

This industry consists of establishments engaged in selling primarily lumber, or lumber and a general line of building materials to the general public. While these establishments may sell primarily to construction contractors, they are known as retail in the trade. The lumber which they sell may include rough and dressed lumber, flooring, molding, doors, sashes, frames and other millwork. The building materials may include roofing, siding, shingles, wallboard, paint, brick, tile, cement, sand, gravel, and other building materials and supplies. Hardware is often an important line sold by retail lumber and building materials dealers. Establishments which do not sell to the general public and those which are known in the trade as wholesale are classified in the Lumber and Other Construction Materials industries.

NAICS CODE(S)

444110 (Home Centers)

421310 (Lumber, Plywood, Millwork, and Wood Panel Wholesalers)

444190 (Other Building Material Dealers)

INDUSTRY SNAPSHOT

The industry grew dramatically in the 1990s, due largely to the great popularity and growth of giant home improvement retailers—almost 59,000 establishments in 1997. Retail lumber and building materials outlets accounted for a large chunk of the $215 billion home improvement industry. Since its birth at the beginning of the twentieth century, the industry has grown and changed dramatically. At the start of the twenty-first century, companies across the United States strategize to find ways to keep and increase their share of this very competitive market.

ORGANIZATION AND STRUCTURE

There are several types of establishments that fall into the retail lumber and building materials category. The largest categories, by far, are lumber yards, home centers, and warehouse home centers.

Lumber yards, whether a single establishment or part of a chain, rely heavily on the industry's traditional customer base of contractors, builders, remodelers, and other professionals. Most of their business, anywhere from two-thirds to three-quarters, comes directly from the sale of lumber and building material. Most average annual sales of about $3.8 million per unit. Sutherland Lumber, Grossman's, and 84 Lumber fall into this category.

Home centers, which often sell hardware as well as lumber and building materials, generally occupy about 30,000 to 35,000 square feet. Due to their size, they greatly outsell the smaller lumberyards. Many of these sales are to do-it-yourselfers, as well as professionals. Hechinger, Lowe's Companies, and Payless Cashways are home centers.

By contrast, warehouse home centers have an average of over 100,000 square feet of floor space. They boast a wide selection of merchandise at lower prices, although they offer less frills than the smaller stores. Home Depot, Builder's Square, and HQ (Home Quarters) are warehouse home centers. At the end of 1999, annual sales reported by the U.S. Department of Commerce included totals from both home centers and warehouse home centers. The average sales per unit averaged almost $13 million annually.

Competition has driven many retailers to find new ways of attracting customers. Many outlets offer custom bath and kitchen design and installation, home decorating merchandise, garden centers, and "how to" classes. Some, such as Lowe's, have moved into even more diverse areas, such as electronics, appliances and home office equipment, accessories, and software.

Establishments in this industry purchased lumber from wholesalers or direct from factories and mills. Most of the lumber and wood products come from the Pacific Northwest and the Southeast. Other building materials, such as paints, cement, hardware, and related supplies were usually purchased through wholesalers, specialty distributors, or direct from the manufacturer. Some larger chains carried their own labels on products they sold through contractual agreement with manufacturers. Larger stores also worked with manufacturers in training employees about particular product lines.

The industry is represented in federal government policy-making processes by the National Lumber and Building Materials Dealers Association (NLBMDA.) The NLBMDA also provides educational and informational programs to meet industry needs. Some 6,800 retail lumber and building materials dealers, in all 50 states, belong to the Association. The NLBMDA also publishes the *Building Materials Retailer,* a monthly four color magazine, and maintains a site on the World Wide Web.

Background and Development

Wholesale establishments selling lumber and building materials appeared in America in the early 1900s. By the 1920s small retail operations began to develop. As the population increased, the industry followed suit. When the Great Depression hit the United States, the industry was adversely affected until public works projects gave them the boost they so desperately needed. During World War II, when home sales were down, the industry suffered another blow. However, the post war period brought tremendous growth for establishments in the industry as suburban America grew during the 1950s and 1960s.

As America grew, so did the number of retail lumber and building materials outlets. It was at this time that many companies expanded into chain stores and manufacturers began to enter the retail market. A recession in the 1970s caused a temporary decrease in new home construction which put the industry's rapid growth on hold. However, an active real estate market and an increase of home renovations in the 1980s gave the industry's sagging sales a much needed boost.

Between 1990 and 1993 expenditures in residential repairs and improvement in the United States continued to rise from $39 billion to $41 billion, an increase of 2.5 percent. Overall prices for lumber and building materials increased less than one percent between 1989 and 1991.

Enviromentalism had a serious impact on the lumber industry in the early 1990s, which, in turn, impacted those in the retail lumber business. In June 1990, the northern spotted owl was listed as an endangered species by the U.S. Fish and Wildlife Service (FWS.) As a result, about 9 million acres of timberland in the Pacific Northwest were declared off-limits to the logging industry. In addition, the ruling also targeted the areas where much of the country's old-growth trees are located. These trees are a vital part of the industry's livelihood. The lumber industry estimated that the nation's availability of lumber was significantly reduced, forcing over 200 mill closings and the loss of roughly 30,000 industry related jobs. This also drove up the price of wholesale lumber, which in turn drove up the price of lumber for lumber retailers and consumers.

President Bill Clinton, introduced what he called a "forest plan" in July of 1993. The plan was created as a way to accommodate the logging industry, while maintaining enough old-growth forest to satisfy the demands of environmentalists trying to keep the spotted owl from extinction. After input from both sides, a revised plan was approved by the federal district court in December 1994. The plan allows some logging on 693,000 of the roughly 1.5 million acres of land in national forests that contain old-growth trees.

The spotted owl controversy continued into the mid-1990s and the government continued to take steps to help the industry. Restrictions were loosened on private land-owners who agreed to use logging methods that were less damaging to the owls' habitat. Restrictions were also loosened on nonfederal lands in Washington state and northern California. In 1995, President Clinton signed a bill that called for 4.1 billion board feet salvage timber sales over the following two and a half years which included 300 million to 400 million board feet of "green timber," which had been previously deemed off limits. Also included was timber that had been burned in recent wildfires.

Despite the controversy in the early 1990s over the spotted owl and its habitat, the retail lumber and building materials industry continued to expand creating fierce competition between smaller, independent stores and chains, and the much larger home centers, or "big box" outfits as they are called in the industry. As the big box outlets sprung up all over America, many smaller chains were forced into store closings and even bankruptcy. Some of the smaller outfits merged in order to compete, while others decided to ride out the storm and hoped they could maintain their customer base with more efficient, personalized service.

The year 1995 was a rough year for retail lumber and building materials retailers. Consumers were spending less, housing starts were down by 10 percent, and lumber prices were down by 20 percent. Over 200 new stores entered the competition. There was only a 1.8 percent increase in industry sales as opposed to an 11.8 percent increase in 1994. Many companies changed their focus from the general public, back to contractors. In 1995 mixed retailers, those who sell to both markets, had an 0.6 percent drop in sales, while the top 250 companies who focused on industry professionals had a 4.1 percent increase. Competition between big box outlets and smaller chains and independents intensified into the late 1990s. The title of an August 1996 article in *Chain Store Age,* ''Home Improvement Retailing: Get Tough Time,'' summed up the industry's climate.

In 1996, there was an increase in industry sales of 6.7 percent, due in part to gains in single-unit housing starts, increased spending on maintenance, and a rise in the price of lumber. Industry leaders predicted that 1997 would be a good year for retailers who specialized in lumber and building materials, with an estimated increase of 6 to 6.5 percent.

CURRENT CONDITIONS

The NLBMDA was active in 1997 lobbying Congress for a cut in the capital gains tax, which would create a demand for building materials by encouraging construction, rehabilitation, and other investments. They also lobbied for permanent legislation to allow the salvaging of dead and dying timber, and supported full funding of the timber sale and road building program of the U.S. forest service. Another hot issue was the tariff on Canadian lumber. According to an article by NLBMDA chairman, F. Carl Tindell, ''We are the ones who have taken the brunt of the United States tariff on lumber imports from Canada. Every time the price of Canadian lumber increases, the price of its American counterpart follows suit, creating unpredictable price fluctuations.'' He then added that lumber dealers and home builders are expected to ''sacrifice so that these select producers may profit.''

As in all sectors of the U.S. economy, consolidation within the industry was endemic. Over 40 percent of all retail sales were attributable to this sector's top 500 businesses. With a total of a 6,918 locations, combined annual sales reached $89.2 billion.

INDUSTRY LEADERS

Ranked by *Fortune* magazine as ''America's most admired retailer,'' Home Depot, after being in business less than 20 years, was an outstanding leader in the retail lumber and building materials industry. With gross sales of over $38 billion in 1999, Home Depot experienced a one-year growth rate of 27 percent. The nation's second largest building supplies/home center chain, Lowe's Companies, grossed almost $16 billion in 1999. Home Depot's net profit was $2.3 billion, while Lowe's was $673 million.

Ranked number 32 by Forbes Magazine's ''1999 Fortune 500,'' Home Depot was considered the leading innovator in the home center retail industry. It operated nearly 950 Home Depot stores in the United States and Canada and employed approximately 157,000 people. The company successfully combined the economics of a warehouse store with a high level of customer service usually reserved for smaller outfits. The average Home Depot store had more than 130,000 square feet of floor space and carried 40,000 to 50,000 products, including home improvement materials, building supplies, and lawn and garden supplies.

Lowe's operated about 575 stores in 37 states, with most stores in the Southeast, and employed about 66,000 people. Most of Lowe's stores are found in small towns where they can easily offer better prices and a larger selection than smaller outlets. Lowe's strategy for the new millennium focused on expanding operations into the Midwest and West. The firm was able to greatly support that goal by adding about 40 stores in the West by purchasing the Eagle Hardware and Garden chain of retail outlets. The company sells mostly building commodities and millwork, home decorating and lighting, structural lumber, garden supplies and kitchen, bathroom, and laundry fixtures.

Founded in 1972 and headquartered in Eau Claire, Wisconsin, Menard, Inc. ranks as the third largest home improvement retailer. Its 145 outlets, largely located in the northern region of the Midwest, feature a full complement of products similar to that of its competitors, Lowe's and Home Depot. Menard, however, operated a manufacturing facility in order to maintain competitive retail pricing and increase net profits. In 2000, the company was still owned by John Menard, who headed the firm as president and CEO. It had 7,000 employees and annual sales of $4 billion.

The nation's fourth largest retail building materials company was the 84 Lumber Company. (Its president, Maggie Hardy Magerko, owned about 80 percent of the company in 2000.) The company's gross sales in 1998 were $1.65 billion. Its primary clientele, professional builders, accounted for about 75 percent of sales. With 390 locations, 84 Lumber employed about 5,100 people. The company created a market niche for itself as a no frills, low-cost retailer of basic building commodities and one-on-one personal service.

WORKFORCE

In 1997 the retail lumber and building materials industry employed more than 1.1 million people in the United States; nearly three-quarters of the employees were men. The average annual wage in the industry was $23,815. Roughly 60 percent of the industry's retail workforce comprised sales staff, while 30 percent were warehouse and shipping workers. The remaining 10 percent held positions in marketing and administration. Many of the indusry's employees held part-time positions.

Sales associates were usually trained to work with the products as well as in customer service. As the need for salespeople with rising levels of industry knowledge has increased, retailers have had to rethink the way they hire and pay their salespeople. Retailers realized that a well-informed sales staff was key to winning and keeping customers.

AMERICA AND THE WORLD

Companies in this industry no longer limit their retail outlets to the United States and Canada. Some expansion into Mexico has taken place, although the Mexican economy has not created a favorable environment for further store openings. As of 1999, Home Depot had opened 3 stores in Chile, marking its entrance into international markets. The stores were developed jointly with Falabella, which is the largest retail department store in Chile.

RESEARCH AND TECHNOLOGY

The use of technology in the industry is continually increasing. In a 1996 survey undertaken by the National Lumber and Building Material Dealers Association of 303 retailers, nearly 100 percent responded that they had incorporated the use of personal computers into their business. Some of the areas in which PCs are used are inventory, invoicing, point of sale, payroll, and accounting. The most important use for computers, however, focused on computerized inventory control; by permitting timely sales input, firms ensured that inventories remained at levels commensurate with consumer demand. Pricing was kept extremely competitive and profit margins were optimized. Most of the larger companies, such as Home Depot, Lowe's, and 84 Lumber, have extensive home pages on the Internet.

FURTHER READING

Anderson, Linnea. ''Retail and Wholesale Industry.'' *Industry Group Snapshots.* Austin, TX: Hoover's Inc., 2000. Available from http://www.hoovers.com/industry/snapshot.

''Company Information.'' North Wilkesboro, NC: Lowe''s Companies, Inc., 2000. Available from http://www.lowes.com/.

———. Atlanta, GA: The Home Depot, Inc., 2000. Available from http://www.homedepot.com/.

''Facts.'' Eighty Four, PA: Eighty Four Lumber Company, 2000. Available from http://www.84lumber.com/.

''Forest Products,'' *Standard & Poor's Industry Surveys,* 22 February 1996.

Home Depot Company Information, 10 March 2000. Available from http://www.homedepot.com.

''Home Improvement Retailing: at the Apex,'' *Chain Store Age,* August 1995.

''Home Improvement Retailing: Get Tough Time,'' *Chain Store Age,* August 1996.

Hoover's Company Capsules. Austin, TX: Hoover's Inc., 2000. Available from http://www.hoovers.com/.

Moukheiber, Zina. ''Retailing.'' *Forbes,* 13 January 1997.

''National Home Center News on the Web.'' *National Home Center News,* 1997. Available from http://www.homecenternews.com.

Pyatt Jr., Rudolph A., ''For Hechinger, Taking a Risk is Better Than Taking a Beating,'' *The Washington Post,* 24 April 1997.

The Wall Street Journal Index-Corporate News, January 1997.

U.S. Department of Commerce, Bureau of the Census. *1997 Economic Census, Retail Trade.* Washington: GPO, 1999.

SIC 5231

PAINT, GLASS, AND WALLPAPER STORES

This industry consists of establishments engaged in selling primarily paint, glass, and wallpaper, or any combination of these lines, to the general public. While these establishments may sell primarily to construction contractors, they are known as retail in the trade. Establishments which do not sell to the general public or are known in the trade as wholesale are classified in the wholesale trade industries.

NAICS CODE(S)

422950 (Paint, Varnish and Supplies Wholesalers)
444190 (Other Building Materials Dealers)
444120 (Paint and Wallpaper Stores)

INDUSTRY SNAPSHOT

In 1997 this industry operated 10,039 retail outlets. Five thousand six hundred and thirty five establishments had four or less employees; 3,198 had between five and nine employees; 983 had between 10 and 19; 209 had between 20 and 49; nine had between 50 and 99 and only five had over 100 employees. Combined, they employed nearly 51,000 workers and reported sales of over $6.3

billion. Paint, glass, and wallpaper stores accounted for nearly 43.6 percent of 1998 retail sales of paint and competed for these sales against home centers who accounted for 26.6 percent, discount stores at 15.2 percent, hardware stores at 13.6 with variety and general merchandise stores making up the remaining 1 percent. The number of retail paint, glass, and wallpaper stores grew by an annual average of 5 percent from the 1970s to the early 1990s.

ORGANIZATION AND STRUCTURE

There were two basic types of retail outlets for paints, glass, and wallpaper. The first was the independently operated store, which purchased products from manufacturers who operated distribution centers and warehouses. The second was the manufacturer operated store, which offered factory direct products and generally used its own distribution center. Both types of stores ran centralized operations from their headquarters.

Paint, glass, and wallpaper stores were also distinguished as either warehouse stores, also called discount houses, or small retail outlets. Typically, the warehouse stores purchased large quantities of products from manufacturers and sold them at discount prices. The small retail stores, many of which were owned by manufacturers, emphasized service and personalized attention. Many stores in this industry also hired contractors to provide glass installation services for customers. Small, independently run stores occasionally offered painting services.

BACKGROUND AND DEVELOPMENT

By the early 1900s, establishments in this industry were emerging on a small scale. These establishments grew steadily though as the country's population increased. In the early 1930s, many stores were adversely affected by the Great Depression. Public works projects, however, helped these small companies to boost paint and glass sales. World War II saw another decline in home sales that affected the industry. The growth of suburban America during the 1950s and 1960s, however, created a period of tremendous growth for establishments in the industry. Many small companies expanded into chain stores, and manufacturers entered the retail market. An economic recession in the 1970s caused a decrease in new home construction and a slump in paint, glass, and wallpaper sales. During the 1980s, the industry experienced another boom period in sales, engendered by an active real estate market and home renovations. The industry was projected to grow at only one to two percent per year through 2000.

The major product sold by this industry was paint. Other products sold by companies in the industry included paint supplies, wallpaper, wallpaper adhesives and supplies, varnishes for wood, anti—rust coatings for metal, glass, glass sealants, and hardware tools. Many stores in this industry also offered services ranging from decorating advice to glass window and door installation. With a greater emphasis placed on the do it yourself market in the late 1980s, paint, glass, and wallpaper stores offered painting clinics that taught customers how to paint professionally. Standard Brand stores, for instance, also had test walls for customers to see what a certain paint would look like on a wall.

The paint, glass, and wallpaper retail industry was characterized by strong brand loyalty among its customers. Most independent retail outlets relied on the manufacturers' advertising to promote their products. In response to a sales slump in the late 1980s, industry leaders started advertising campaigns to give products high visibility.

Environmental legislation affected manufacturer—owned retail outlets through hazardous waste restrictions for paint factories, which increased the cost of materials and factory produced items. In 1993, the Environmental Protection Agency (EPA) sued Sherwin Williams for failure to obtain a hazardous waste permit. This followed a two year investigation by the EPA.

CURRENT CONDITIONS

An economic recession in the late 1980s and early 1990s put an end to eight years of consecutive growth in the paint, glass, and wallpaper retail industry. This was primarily caused by a decline in new home construction.

Retailers shifted from selling to industries and the architectural market toward the do it yourself market. While the market for new home construction dropped during the recession, the industry experienced an increase in sales as a result of property renovations and rehabilitations.

From 1990 to 1992 competition intensified greatly in the industry because of higher raw material prices and the money spent by manufacturers on research and development to comply with vital organic compound (VOC) restrictions, which dramatically reduced profit margins of many small companies. In the mid 1990s, companies in the industry suffered increased competition from mass retailers, such as Sears, Home Depot and WalMart, which operated paint and wallpaper departments. Paint manufacturers were using mass retailers instead of small paint retail chains as a way of cutting distribution costs. The giant retailers' purchasing power and ability to control prices have increased sharply in recent years. As a result they now expect the manufacturers to provide low prices and to help control inventory.

INDUSTRY LEADERS

In 1998 the industry leaders included Benjamin Moore & Co. of Montvale, New Jersey, with sales of

$711 million and 2,274 employees; Ace Hardware Corp. of Oak Brook, Illinois, whose paint division had sales of $620 million and 4,672 employees; Dunn Edwards Corp. of Los Angeles, California, with sales of $238 million and 1,570 employees and Kelly Moore Paint Company of San Carlos, California, with sales of $290 million and 2,200 employees.

The industry giant was Sherwin Williams Co., recording over $4.9 billion in wholesale and retail sales in 1999 by selling paint, finishes, coatings, applicators and varnishes. The Paint Stores Segment achieved its seventh consecutive year of growth with $2.8 billion in sales. The company's products were geared toward the do it yourself market, but because of the acquisition of Cook Paint and Varnish Company in 1990, Sherwin Williams also targets industrial customers. (Sherwin Williams was founded by Henry A. Sherwin, a retail paint dealer in Cleveland, and was incorporated in 1884.) In 1992, the company also owned 12 paint plants in the United States and U.S. territories, and had subsidiaries in Brazil, Mexico, Canada, Jamaica, and the Virgin Islands. In 1999, the company owned 2,200 stores in North America and 140 in Brazil, Chile, Mexico and Jamaica.

WORKFORCE

In 1997, the industry employed 53,786 workers. Roughly 60 percent of this workforce consisted of sales staff, 20 percent was warehouse and shipping workers, and the remaining 20 percent was in marketing and administration. In independently run stores, which purchased goods from manufacturers, retail buyers and merchandise managers negotiated prices with suppliers. Most sales positions were part—time, with a starting salary of $4.25 per hour. In 1996 the industry employed nearly 5,400 non-supervisory workers averaged $9.84 per hour.

All sales staff were usually given special training in working with paints and other chemical—based products, along with training in customer service. Generally, people with backgrounds in design, professional painting, or construction work were preferred.

AMERICA AND THE WORLD

The United States maintained a favorable trade balance in paints and coatings, while glass and wallpaper had little overseas activity. In the early 1990s, American exports of paints and coatings increased 19.2 percent to $675 million in wholesale prices. Roughly 75 percent of these paints went to American owned retail outlets. Strong export growth was predicted for this industry into the mid 1990s.

RESEARCH AND TECHNOLOGY

In the early 1990s, the leading areas of research and technology emanated from paint and coatings manufacturing areas, such as research in waterborne, high solids, powder, and radiation—cured coatings. These types of coatings were geared toward increasing sales in automotive and appliance coatings and furniture finishes. Developments also were underway for new products to be sold by retailers in this industry. Titanium dioxide, which was used as a paint pigment with great covering power and durability, was being developed for the commercial market.

As a result of environmental legislation, research continued on waste management of these products, both for manufacturers and wholesalers. Another technological development for this industry intended to help protect the environment was products with no volatile organic compounds. These products were in demand because, in addition to being easier on the environment during production, they also did not emit fumes when being applied on walls. In 1998 the U.S. Environmental Protection Agency announced national VOC limits for automotive refinished and architectural and industrial maintenance coatings, effective from 1999. Eventually, these products were expected to help paint sales.

Like other retail businesses, establishments in this industry continued to increase their reliance on computers, simplifying many routine buying functions and improving the efficiency of in store sales staff. The larger paint, glass, and wallpaper retailers were relying less on sales staff for inventory counts and more on point of sales computer terminals, which provided up to date inventory and sales information.

Computerized inventory controls greatly increased the efficiency of ordering merchandise. Some systems monitored inventory levels, automatically re—ordered selected merchandise, connected chain stores to one centralized system, and calculated turnover by product, store, and sales area. For sales staff, point of sales computer systems were useful in calculating discounts, approving credit, and scheduling deliveries.

A significant development in the distribution of paints and wallpaper was the use of electronic ordering and inventory control systems, known as electronic data interchange (EDI). Replacing the use of the postal service, EDI systems enabled retailers to order paints through a computer linked directly to manufacturers and independent distributors. This facilitated quicker ordering and more accurate inventory controls.

FURTHER READING

Butterfield, John. ''Sherwin—Williams Buys Mercury Paint Stores.'' *Builder Online,* 12 June 1996.

Lazich, Robert S., ed. *Market Share Reporter.* Detroit: Gale Research, 1997.

U.S. Census Bureau. *1992 Census of Retail Trade.* Available from http://www.census.gov/epcd/www/rc92h52.html.

U.S. Department of Labor. Bureau of Labor Statistics. *Employment, Hours, and Earnings, United States, 1988—96.* Washington: GPO, 1996.

U.S. Bureau of the Census. *County Business Patterns 1997.* Washington: GPO 1999.

Company Profiles. Hoover's Online. Available from http://www.hoovers.com

Paints and Coatings: Mass Merchandisers Take Control. Chemical Week, 5 November 1997

Pointmakers Forced to Buy Market Share. Chemical Week, 19 February 1997

Paints and Varnishes. Year in Review 1998. Encyclopaedia Britannica. Available from http://www.britannica.com

Retail Paint/Glass/Wallpaper Sales, 1997. GaleNet, 2000. Available from http://galenet.gale.com/.

SIC 5251

HARDWARE STORES

This category covers establishments primarily engaged in the retail sale of a number of basic hardware lines, such as tools, builders' hardware, paint, glass, cutlery, housewares, and household appliances. Establishments primarily engaged in the sale of lumber and other building materials are classified in **SIC 5211: Lumber & Other Building Materials.** Those establishments are included in this industry analysis because of their dominant role in the hardware industry. Establishments that specialized in a particular line of hardware, such as paint or wallpaper stores, were classified in **SIC 5231: Paint, Glass & Wallpaper Stores.**

NAICS CODE(S)

444130 (Hardware Stores)

INDUSTRY SNAPSHOT

There were approximately 21,400 hardware stores in the United States in 1999. There were also roughly 10,000 home centers, which combine goods related to hardware retailing with goods related to building materials retailing. Most hardware stores are independently owned, and many retain a ''mom and pop'' image. The average hardware store has sales of more than $1 million annually. The average home center is considerably larger, with sales of about $4 million. Warehouse home centers average between $12 million and $15 million in annual sales. As a whole, the retail hardware industry reported $151.1 billion in sales in 1999, and female consumers accounted for fully half of those sales.

ORGANIZATION AND STRUCTURE

Most of the U.S. retail hardware stores are independent businesses. However, nearly all of them are affiliated with a nationwide wholesaler that offers private label brands, retail store advertising, and identification programs. Such affiliations create the appearance of a structured industry. Many of these wholesalers are actually cooperatives owned by independent hardware store owners, forming a distribution system that originated in the early twentieth century. Dealer-owned wholesalers sell only to member stores, but member stores can buy merchandise from other wholesalers or directly from manufacturers.

The largest dealer-owned cooperative is Cotter & Company, based in Chicago Illinois. It manufactures and distributes products to member-owner stores under the retail trade names of True Value Hardware and V&S Variety Stores. In 1997 Cotter merged with ServiStar, a Minneapolis-based distributor that owned Coast to Coast Stores. Together they created a $4.3 billion company that serves more than 10,000 retail outlets. Ace Hardware Corporation, based in Oak Brook, Illinois, is the nation's second largest cooperative with more than 5,100 members in 1999. Other dealer-owned wholesalers and their store identification programs include Our Own Hardware Co., of Burnsville, Minnesota (How-To Centers) and United Hardware Distributing Co., of Plymouth, Minnesota (Hardware Hank Stores).

Hardware Wholesalers, Inc., Fort Wayne, Indiana (Do-It-Best Centers) launched its own Internet web site in July 1999. Already one of the nation's largest hardware cooperatives with recorded sales of $1.9 billion in fiscal year 1998, www.doitbest.com listed 70,000 items for sale on opening day. The Web site is marketed as ''The World's Largest Hardware Store.'' But Internet hardware retailing is still rare.

Most retail hardware stores have less than 20,000 square feet of floor space. The NRHA categorizes larger formats as home centers. Home centers average more than 30,000 square feet and usually combine lumber with a greater selection of hardware products to create a one-stop shopping environment for home repair and home improvement projects. Home centers typically buy directly from the manufacturers and often sell to commercial accounts as well as individual consumers.

The home center segment also includes large warehouse-style hardware stores that average nearly 100,000 square feet and have between $12 and $15 million in annual sales. Warehouse stores began to appear in the late 1970s and have had a notable impact on the retail hardware industry. In the early 1990s industry analysts predicted that the warehouse format would revolutionize the industry. But despite attracting a great deal of attention and a significant customer base, warehouse chains such as Home Depot accounted for only about 12 percent of industry sales in the late 1990s.

Warehouse stores are able to negotiate greater discounts from wholesalers and manufacturers because of their size. Warehouse stores also base their retail business on generating a high volume of sales, rather than by pursuing high profit margins. This forces smaller, independent hardware stores and chains, which have traditionally operated on high margins, to lower their prices, become more efficient, redesign their stores, improve customer service, and bypass their wholesalers to get a better price directly from manufacturers. This new operating style has forced numerous wholesalers and retailers to go out of business.

BACKGROUND AND DEVELOPMENT

Hardware stores were among the earliest retail establishments in colonial America, selling tools imported from England. The oldest hardware store in the country is Elwood Adams Hardware in Worcester, Massachusetts. Founded by Daniel Waldo and son in 1782, it was still in business in 1999. The store was named for Elwood Adams, who purchased it in 1886. The first American manufacturer of hardware was probably John Ames, a blacksmith in Bridgewater, Massachusetts. He established a factory for making shovels in 1774. Ames' shovels became indispensable to American settlers.

The American Industrial Revolution of the early 1800s greatly increased the availability of manufactured goods and spurred the growth of general stores that stocked basic hardware. Peddlers selling hardware from the back of their wagons inundated rural areas. The industrial revolution also gave rise to factories that could supply more good than nearby communities could use. This created the need for wholesalers and distribution networks. As the U.S. economic base shifted from agriculture to manufacturing in the last half of the nineteenth century, the hardware industry began to acquire distinct manufacturing, wholesaling, and retailing segments.

National Retail Hardware Association. Many hardware stores established in the late 1800s survived for more than 100 years. These stores were largely small, family-owned businesses, and, like neighborhood grocers before the advent of supermarkets, hardware store owners knew their customers well and were important members of the local business community. Although they valued their independence, hardware store owners also recognized the need to organize. By 1900 there were 25 state hardware associations, created primarily to lobby against what retailers believed were unfair trade practices conducted by manufacturers, who sold directly to hardware store chains and mail order houses at a significant discount.

Delegates from nine of these state associations met in Chicago in 1900 to discuss their common concerns, and eventually groups from seven states formed the Interstate Retail Hardware Association. In 1901 the name was changed to the National Retail Hardware Dealers Association, which later dropped ''Dealers'' from its name. The NRHA campaigned for fair-trade laws to protect store owners from unfair pricing. Later the association offered members a broad range of management, marketing, and research services. Headquartered in Indianapolis, Indiana, the NRHA became a federation of 14 state and regional hardware associations in 1993, including the Canadian Retail Hardware Association. Five years later the entire federation voted unanimously to amend its bylaws so that NRHA could accept direct retail members from all 50 United States.

Wholesale Cooperatives. In addition to seeking legislative relief from what they perceived as unfair pricing policies, hardware store owners also began forming wholesale cooperatives to increase their leverage with manufacturers. One of the first cooperatives was the American Hardware Supply Company (AHSC), which was founded by retailers in Pittsburgh, Pennsylvania, in 1910. AHSC, the forerunner of ServiStar Corp., eventually shipped hardware to retailers throughout most of the eastern United States.

One of the most successful U.S. cooperatives has been the Ace Hardware Corporation, founded in 1924 by four Chicago retailers. The four retailers had been members of an innovative promotional program created by the E.C. Simmons Hardware Co., a St. Louis distributor providing advertising, window displays, and other store identification materials. In addition to buying directly from manufacturers on behalf of its members at volume discounts, Ace Hardware revived the Simmons promotional program. For 50 years Ace Hardware was run by Richard Hesse, a flamboyant marketer and hardware industry legend who strove to create emotional as well as economic bonds between members of the cooperative. In 1998 Ace Hardware was the second-largest hardware wholesaler with 5,100 stores and sales of $3.1 billion.

Coast to Coast Stores, though not a dealer-owned cooperative, was formed in 1928. Coast to Coast was initially both a wholesaler and a franchiser. The Minneapolis-based company assisted store owners in arranging financing, selecting store locations, and understanding the retail hardware business. In 1990 Coast to Coast was purchased by ServiStar, the Pennsylvania-based wholesale cooperative founded in 1910. At the time of the sale, Coast to Coast had about 1,100 franchisees and annual sales of $400 million. Our Own Hardware Co., is another well-known cooperative. Founded in 1913, it was originally known as the Hall Hardware Company. By 1992 Our Own Hardware Co. had about 1,000 members and sales of $185 million. The company merged with ServiStar in 1996 to form ServiStar Coast to Coast Corporation. A year later ServiStar merged with Cotter & Company, the wholesale cooperative behind the True Value chain. Together they created a $4.3 billion company with more than 10,000 retail members.

Home Centers. The boom economy that followed World War II led to a tremendous expansion of the retail hardware business. Homeowners began buying more tools, housewares, plumbing, electrical supplies, paint, building materials, and other staples of the hardware business. The do-it-yourself market was beginning to take shape. The post-war economy also gave rise to another form of competition—large, chain-owned hardware stores known as home centers. These chains were led by Lowe's Companies, Inc.; Payless Cashways, Inc.; and Builders Square, Inc., originally known as Home Pro.

Warehouse Stores. In 1979 a start-up company, The Home Depot, Inc., opened two warehouse centers in Atlanta, Georgia, sparking dramatic changes in the retail hardware industry. Home Depot's stores were greatly expanded home centers. Each store featured 60,000 square feet of space, an informal atmosphere, and low prices. Beginning with a severely limited budget, Home Depot's top shelves were often stocked with empty boxes to avoid an empty feeling in the cavernous stores. The concept, however, was an overwhelming marketing success. By 1983 Home Depot was operating 10 stores in Atlanta and southern Florida. Each store averaged 60,000 square feet in size and nearly $12 million in annual sales.

Competitors soon copied Home Depot's warehouse format. In 1983 W.R. Grace & Co. opened two House Works stores in New Orleans. Within weeks Home Depot also opened two stores in the Crescent City. This was followed by two more House Works stores. Within a span of 90 days, six warehouse hardware stores opened in New Orleans with a combined 400,000 square feet of space. Warehouse stores soon opened in other areas of the country in a confusing flood of similar sounding names, including HomeOwners Warehouse in Florida, Home-Pro Warehouse in Texas, and HomeClub in southern California. By the end of 1983, 11 companies had opened a total of 47 warehouse hardware stores.

But Home Depot was not outdone by the competition. In 1999 the Atlanta-based home-improvement giant was reporting annual sales of $30.2 billion. With 874 stores in the United States, Canada, Puerto Rico, and Chile, Home Depot was by far the largest hardware retailer in the world. According to company executives, Home Depot opens a new store every 53 hours.

In the course of this industry-wide expansion, many independent hardware stores were driven out of business. Hardware store failures were attributed largely to the success of suburban malls and discount stores, such as Kmart and Wal-Mart. For example, Wal-Mart and its growing hardware sales expanded from about 30 stores in 1970 to about about 9,000 stores in 1999. Most of these stores were typically located in stores near small communities.

The malls and discount retailers changed shopping patterns throughout the United States. Hardware stores moved away from downtown areas in both big cities and small towns where people no longer came to shop. Warehouse stores, on the other hand, actually expanded the hardware market. By one industry estimate, when the first Home Depot store opened in 1979, the do-it-yourself market was reporting earnings of about $35 billion annually. Ten years later, the market was estimated to be worth nearly $90 billion. Many retail hardware stores were able to capitalize on the expanding market by becoming more efficient and offering more personal service.

Wholesale cooperatives also helped their members deal with increased competition. Cotter & Company was credited with creating innovative store identification programs to counter the advertising campaigns and name recognition of the home centers. These programs included national advertising in consumer magazines and cost-efficient mass-produced circulars for member stores. Many such programs were copied by other cooperatives.

The chain-owned home centers may have been more adversely affected by the warehouse stores than independent hardware stores. Initially, home centers competed based on price, but competition from warehouse stores forced home centers to add services, such as installation services, and hire more qualified employees. Home Depot was an industry leader in customer innovations such as how-to clinics, bar code standards, employee training programs, and satellite communications between the chain's mainframe computer in Atlanta and point-of-sale computers in its stores nationwide.

CURRENT CONDITIONS

A 1999 NHRA report showed that the typical hardware store annually sells $104,754 per employee, while the high-profit stores(the top 25 percent of all hardware stores) annually sell $112,644 per employee. Average hardware stores sell $1,009,486 annually, while high profit stores sell $1,105,987 a year. Gross profit margin is 37.7 percent for typical hardware stores, while high-profit stores do 39 percent. Thus, while the industry as a whole grows at about 4.4 percent each year, a noticeable gulf between the high-profit hardware stores and the average store continues to exist.

Most retail hardware stores are still family-owned businesses, with many family histories extending back four or five generations. In the majority of these stores, sons and daughters worked along side their parents. But many of the present owners do not expect to pass their stores on to the next generation. Those who expect to someday sell their stores to outsiders cite hard work, long hours, an uncertain future, and the lower-class image of hardware store owners as contributing factors to the decreasing appeal of hardware store ownership. Long time employees often purchase hardware stores that are sold outside the family. In this regard, many hardware stores have established employee stock ownership programs that make it easier for employees to take over ownership.

Store owners are also more likely to cite competition from discount retailers such as Kmart and Wal-Mart as the most serious threat to their businesses. Financially, the strongest independent hardware stores are those that have staked out a variety of niche markets, such as kitchen remodeling centers and lawn and garden centers. Some wholesale cooperatives, including Our Own Hardware, have been helping members establish tool rental departments. At the same time, many store owners are reluctant to make radical changes in their businesses, and do not plan to change their product mix. Other owners are interested in bypassing traditional distribution channels to buy directly from the manufacturers.

Although none of the other warehouse hardware companies had come close to duplicating the success of Home Depot, warehouse stores continued expanding in the 1990s. Lowe's Companies Inc., which began experimenting with larger stores in 1984, made a corporate decision in 1988 to hold the line at about 60,000 square feet. In the early 1990s, however, the company decided to build larger stores and by the mid-1990s more than half of its stores were more than 60,000 square feet. Lowe's experimentation paid off. In November of 1999 it had solidified its position as the second largest home improvement store in the United States.

Another leading company with major expansion plans in the early 1990s was the Hechinger Company. Based in Largo, Maryland, Hechinger operated a chain of traditional hardware stores. In 1988 Hechinger purchased Home Quarters Warehouse Inc., and in 1991, the company opened its first warehouse-size Home Project Center. By the mid-1990s Hechinger had become the fourth largest home-improvement retailer in the nation. However, the company fell on hard times in 1997. Two years later it filed for bankruptcy protection from its creditors, and began liquidating a number of its stores.

Legislation. Among other issues of concern to the retail hardware industry as it entered the 1990s was the question of product liability. Increasingly, courts were holding retail stores liable for damages caused by defective products. Several courts had ruled that hardware stores have an obligation to ensure the safety of their products, and held them liable for money damages when they failed to fulfill this obligation. For two decades Congress has conducted hearings to determine if they should enact federal laws to insulate hardware store retailers from products liability lawsuits. Despite several pieces of proposed legislation, no bill has ever passed both houses. Thus, hardware stores continue to insure themselves against the risk of liability.

Industry Leaders

Home Depot is the largest hardware retailer in the United States. It had 849 stores in the United States, in 1997, and generated more than $22 billion in domestic sales. The Atlanta-based company controled about 6 percent of the market. It is also credited with driving the retail hardware industry to adopt newer technologies, including the use of bar codes for maintaining inventory. In the late 1990s Home Depot began to roll out a line of large-format stores called EXPO, which featured 80,000 to 100,000 square feet of space focusing on interior design materials rather than the lumber and construction offerings of its flagship chain.

North Carolina-based Lowe's Companies, Inc. is the second leading hardware retailer in the country, reporting more than $10 billion a year in sales from 484 stores. Builders Square, Inc., based in San Antonio, Texas, was the third largest retailer in 1997, with approximately $4.18 billion in sales. But two years later its parent company, Hechinger, Inc., filed for bankruptcy protection, and announced plans to close a number of stores in the Builders Square chain. Owned by John Menard (based in Eau Claire, Wisconsin) Menard, Inc. is another one the country's leading hardware retailers. It generates about $3.5 billion a year in revenue from approximately 130 stores that are located mostly in the Midwest. Founded as a single, family-owned store in Iowa in 1930, Payless Cashways, Inc. owns about 192 stores in 22 states. In 1997 it generated $2.29 billion in sales.

Workforce

The retail hardware industry employs approximately 150,000 people, with the average hardware store employing 12 full or part-time workers. Entry-level workers are usually paid at or near the minimum wage. Smaller hardware stores with a lower profit margin commonly complain about the difficulties in finding and retaining a competent staff. The problem is especially critical in small towns. Home centers typically hire away experienced employees at higher wages. They also offer employee training programs and more opportunity for advancement. Home Depot is a leader in hiring employees with a construction or building industry background to improve service. Wholesale cooperatives have attempted to help their members by instituting employee training programs.

FURTHER READING

Goldblatt, Jennifer. ''Hechinger Liquidation Puts Norfolk, Va., Employees Out of Work.'' *Knight-Ridder Tribune Business News,* 10 September 1999.

''Retailers Report December Sales Increase: Hardware Stores—1999.'' *Do-It-Yourself Retailing,* 1 February 1999.

U.S. Bureau of the Census. Current Business Reports. *Combined Annual and Revised Monthly Retail Trade.* Washington, D.C.: GPO, 1997.

U.S. Bureau of the Census. ''Estimated Monthly Retail Sales.'' Washington, D.C.: 1997.

SIC 5261

RETAIL NURSERIES, LAWN AND GARDEN SUPPLY STORES

This category covers establishments primarily engaged in selling trees, shrubs, other plants, seeds, bulbs, mulches, soil conditioners, fertilizers, pesticides, garden tools, and other garden supplies to the general public. These establishments primarily sell products purchased from others, such as plant wholesalers, but may sell some plants that they grow themselves. Establishments primarily engaged in growing trees (except Christmas trees), shrubs, other plants, seeds, and bulbs are classified in the major group for agricultural production—crops. Establishments primarily engaged in growing Christmas trees are classified in **SIC 0811: Timber Tracts.**

NAICS CODE(S)

444220 (Nursery and Garden Centers)

453998 (All Other Miscellaneous Store Retailers (except Tobacco Stores))

444210 (Outdoor Power Equipment Stores)

INDUSTRY SNAPSHOT

Retail nurseries and lawn and garden supply stores operate under a variety of names, in a multitude of consumer settings, and they offer a wide range of products to serve a peculiarly American need to cultivate, trim, embellish, and control a small plot of greenery. The robustness of a homeowner's front lawn and the pleasing visual effect provided by planted shrubs and flowers has become a status symbol in a modern industrialized society of property owners. Explaining the consumer-appeal of gardening, Seattle-based Swanson's Nursery owner Wally Kerwin said, ''Planting is therapeutic, environmentally sound and increases the value of the home . . . And it's counter-technical. Virtual gardening is not really an in thing.'' Thus, gardening did not compete against the technological revolution, but rather worked as an elixir to complement and soothe those immersed in cyberspace at work all day.

Homeowners in the 1990s came to view sprucing up their lawns and shrubbery as a relatively low-cost way to boost property values as well as spirits. According to some leisure-time experts, gardening became one of the most rapidly-developing hobbies among Americans in the 1990s. Not only did the larger, corporate-based retail nursery and garden-supply centers benefit from the boom of the 1980s, but small, individually owned firms also flourished. These latter establishments were able to provide specialty plants, rare seeds, and unusual implements and accessories for new legions of dedicated gardeners. Smaller enterprises often cultivated their own varieties of one certain plant, such as lilac or rose bushes, or geared themselves toward gardeners interested in producing their own fruits, vegetables, and herbs. Savvy consumers recognized the distinction in knowledge and expertise provided by these independents, who thrived by catering to the growing legion of buyers educated in the wares they were purchasing.

One important reason for the growth and success of the retail nursery and garden supply industry can be pinned on the demographics of the average consumer who purchases garden products. The National Gardening Association's 1994-95 survey showed that consumers of lawn and garden products tended to be college educated people in business or professional careers (or retirees) with household incomes of $30,000 and over. They were most likely to live in the Midwest and West, to be 50 years of age or older, and to be married with no children at home. Continued growth in the industry is predicted due to the country's aging population, which will provide a steady supply of both casual and committed gardeners for this segment of the retail industry.

ORGANIZATION AND STRUCTURE

Nursery and garden stores were either single-unit establishments or branches of multi-unit establishments such as Frank's Nursery. Single-unit establishments were primarily individual proprietorships, many of which concentrated on providing hard-to-find products to local or mail-order consumers, and often cultivated a variety of unique seeds and plants in-house. Multi-unit locations also situated themselves in conjunction with a larger outlet, such as Builder's Square stores alongside Kmart stores.

There are a number of professional or industry-related organizations for the nursery and garden supply business. The American Association of Nurserymen (AAN) dates back to 1875. In the late 1990s, most states had individual associations of nurserymen with member rosters that included individual owner-operators of small nurseries, growers of trees and shrubs, and plant wholesalers. They provided a multitude of small-business services to their members. The AAN's retail division is the 600-member Garden Centers of America, founded in 1972. Its stated aim is to meet the daily needs of garden center managers.

Background and Development

Retail nursery and garden supply stores have been in existence since the nineteenth century, but only in the decades following World War II did this segment of the retail economy flourish into a profitable business. To meet the postwar housing shortage, new communities filled with single-family homes grew exponentially as a result of expansion into suburban and rural areas. The availability of open acreage in the United States meant that every family could hope to own a modest plot of land surrounding their home—a front yard buffeting the home and occupants from the street, and a more private backyard for children's playtime, barbecues, and small vegetable gardens. In many of these newly created bedroom communities, a holdover from the area's more rural beginnings could be found under the awning of the local feed store. These family-owned businesses had served the needs of the area's farmers in previous decades, but with the influx of new homeowners into the community in the postwar years they soon adapted to changing demographics. They began stocking items less suitable for maintaining a large tract of cropland than for keeping a small lawn. More successful businesses purchased competitors, making major lawn and garden supply retail chains common, especially in midwestern states.

The retail nursery and lawn and garden supply industry added products and services to meet changing consumer demands over the years. It stocked chlorine and other swimming-pool maintenance items as family recreational facilities multiplied in suburban backyards in the 1960s and 1970s. Retail centers began carrying less seeds and more bedding plants in the 1990s as busy two-career households found less time to cultivate a garden plot from scratch.

The midwestern region of the United States, with its higher concentration of people who grew up on or near farmland, remains the most avid-consuming region of nursery and lawn and garden supply items. The area also boasts one of the highest rates of home ownership in the nation, and the average size of the property lot is larger than the rest of the country. The increased environmental consciousness among all consumers, but especially within the midwestern group, also positively impacted the nursery and garden supply industry. This trend is reflected in the shift toward more nature-like gardens, with an assortment of wildflowers and a less-manicured look. This transition is also evidenced by the increase in sales of organic fertilizers and the growing popularity of landscaping that appears less contrived and more natural. An example of the back-to-nature movement is seen in the use of woodland plants or prairie grasses as opposed to water-thirsty and high-maintenance trimmed lawns.

Retail nurseries and lawn and garden supply businesses witnessed phenomenal growth during the 1980s and 1990s. Most of this gain is due to changing demographics in the United States that place more consumers in the age and income category that has traditionally spent money on gardening. The overall industry has been transformed by two important trends during this period of growth. The first is the dominance of larger, multi-unit retail chains that are usually regional in scope but often provide outlets from coast-to-coast. This shift has brought a more corporate strategy to what had for many decades been a rather localized industry. Computers to track inventory and uniformed cashiers are now common in even smaller establishments. The second major change in the industry has been the increased segmentation of the nursery market.

Smaller companies, faced with the threat of competing against well-stocked chain stores whose products were bought in volume and then sold to consumers at a discount, have found that narrowing their focus has kept them afloat in the industry. Many now specialize in a certain variety of plants, which are cultivated on the premises, or aim to capture the more environmentally conscious gardener with specialized products. Another means of coping with profit losses has been the development of a segment to provide landscaping services. The industry has also been affected by the increase of large discount lawn and garden supply departments in new warehouse-style home centers such as Builders' Square and Home Depot. Such stores offer an immense selection of standard lawn and garden products, and their entry into the market has introduced greater competition.

Current Conditions

In 1996, approximately 12,000 establishments operated retail nurseries and garden stores in the United States. With the exception of the large home-centers, the majority of these were small establishments, with the average employee count per establishment at about 7, compared to the average of 12 for all retail industries. The total number of employees has increased approximately 22 percent since 1990, reaching an estimated 92,000 in 1996.

The entire retail nursery and lawn and garden supply industry generated $25.9 billion in sales in 1995, according to the National Gardening Association. That represented an increase of $3.5 billion, or 15.5 percent, over the previous year. Throughout the previous five years, sales increased about 10 percent annually. Consumers spent an average of $342 per household on their lawns and gardens in 1995, according to a Gallup Organization survey conducted for the National Gardening Association.

INDUSTRY LEADERS

One of the largest retailers of nursery plants and lawn and garden supplies is Frank's Nursery and Crafts. The company was founded in Detroit, Michigan, and in the postwar years capitalized on the area's high concentration of single-family homes in both the city and surrounding suburbs. Frank's outlets operated year-round, but switched to selling craft items such as macrame kits and artificial flowers during the lean winter months. The company has also done a brisk business as a live Christmas tree lot each December. Traditionally, Frank's Nurseries were larger than the average garden-supply store at the time and provided customers with shopping carts to traverse their many indoor and outdoor aisles. The outdoor segment, open during the temperate months, sold a variety of shrubs, bushes, vegetable plants and seedlings, and flowers to home gardeners.

The company's approach, appearing as a user-friendly, supermarket-type store accessible to not only the serious gardener but also to the more inexperienced, easily daunted neophyte, proved remarkably successful. In addition, its larger corporate structure allowed it to purchase supplies in volume at a discount and then warehouse and distribute them as needed. Frank's stocked not only plants and gardening tools but also patio furniture, lawn mowers, swimming pool products, and power tools. In 1983, the company was bought by General Host, a Stamford, Connecticut-based conglomerate. General Host soon demonstrated its strategy to make Frank's a powerhouse in the industry by divesting its other holdings. In subsequent years, General Host was rewarded by phenomenal growth in sales and revenues, in some cases achieving 15 percent increases. By 1996, the corporation reported total sales of $531 million and employed approximately 7,000 people.

In 1994, General Host closed 26 unprofitable Frank's outlets located mostly in southern states. The company closed one more store in 1995 and planned to open, relocate, or remodel eight or more stores. During 1995, Frank's tested ''In the Garden by Frank's,'' a temporary mall boutique offering gifts for gardeners. By 1996, Frank's was operating 264 outlets in 16 states, but the company lost $4.3 million on $593 million in sales for fiscal 1996. General Host assigned as Frank's new president Ernest Townshend, who helped orchestrate turnarounds at Kraft Inc. and Dole Food Co. However, fiscal 1997 sales matched those of 1996, at $530 million.

In 1993, General Host made a swap with another giant in the retail garden center industry, the Sunbelt Nursery Group. The retail powerhouse Pier One Imports, Inc., owned Sunbelt and traded its shares of the nursery group to Frank's parent company in return for General Host stock. Sunbelt's 1996 sales totaled $95.7 million. However in 1998, after moving headquarters to California, Sunbelt filed for Chapter 11, requesting a stay from the bankruptcy court allowing it to sell 15 California-based stores to generate $3 million in cash to cover its losses.

General Host also owned the 11-store Calloway's Nursery, Inc. of Fort Worth, Texas. In 1996, Calloway's operated 16 stores in Texas that sold lawn and garden products. In 1996, the company's sales totaled $24 million, an increase of nearly 7 percent over the previous year. Calloway's, in turn, acquired Houston-based Cornelius Nurseries, the other large Texas-based retail garden center in September 1999.

Also filing for Chapter 11 in 1999 was Largo, Maryland-based Hechinger's, which failed to make interest payments of $4.7 million in May after same-store sales nose-dived 20 percent in the quarter ended April 3, 1999. In desperation, Hechinger's closed 89 under-performing stores (15 Home Quarters stores, 14 Hechinger's, and 59 Builder's Squares) in 36 markets in order to buoy the 117 remaining stores in 21 states.

While the national chains suffered bankruptcies, well-run independent outfits fared well through what Nancy J. Kim called the ''big-box blight.'' One example is Molbaks Inc. in Woodinville, Washington, which enjoyed sales of $14 million in 1995, up 6 percent over the previous year.

WORKFORCE

The majority of employees in retail nurseries and lawn and garden centers tend to fit the profile of the average retail or service industry worker. They often have little more than a high-school education and hold jobs that pay poorly and lack benefits such as health care and pension. The firms that kept payroll records employed an estimated 92,000 workers in 1996. According to U.S. Department of Labor statistics, the average nonsupervisory worker in the industry worked 32.4 hours per week in 1995 and earned $263.41 at $8.13 per hour. Since many of the firms are seasonal in nature, layoffs during the winter months present additional financial setbacks to workers in the field. The nursery business is unusual in that it is extremely susceptible to negativity among employees. Low wages and a lack of benefits often correspond to a general malaise among workers in any industry, but in a retail nursery it is a relatively simple matter for one person to stealthily damage thousands of dollars worth of plants, with the undetected crime resulting in severe financial losses. Workers in the industry face additional problems from the daily exposure to pesticides. In the early 1990s, the U.S. Environmental Protection Agency (EPA) issued stringent standards for acceptable pesticide levels for farm workers.

RESEARCH AND TECHNOLOGY

In 1991, the retail nursery and lawn and garden supply industry was hit by a disaster with costly repercussions. The problem stemmed from the use of a fungicide called Benlate, manufactured by the chemical giant DuPont. The pesticide had been on the market for two decades and was known by nursery growers to be a quick-acting cure for minor blighting diseases affecting fruits, vegetables, and ornamental plants. However, nurseries and growers in 40 states soon began reporting problems in the spring of 1991, complaining that their plant stock was rapidly dying or failing to reach maturity. Apparently, Benlate was suddenly acting as a growth inhibitor, and the plants that survived the Benlate treatment fared little better in the long run. Once removed from the controlled greenhouse environment, they quickly died. The company began investigating the disaster and months later were still baffled. Scientists speculated that unknown interactions between the chemical compounds in Benlate may have created a undetectable toxic element. They believed the culprit may have been an inert ingredient that was suddenly aggravated by greenhouse conditions. Growers began treating the diseased plants with activated charcoal, which seemed to ameliorate some of Benlate's effects, but some experts believed that the wayward chemical compound lingered in the plants. DuPont began paying millions of dollars in settlements to growers faced with bankruptcy, particularly to nurseries and growers in Florida. The scandal has also raised an ethical issue among nurseries—although some owners were fully aware of the Benlate-diseased plants, they sold them anyway in an attempt to reduce some of their losses. Naturally, the plants quickly died when removed from the greenhouse setting.

FURTHER READING

1994-95 National Gardening Survey Fact Sheet. Burlington, VT: National Gardening Association, 1996.

''California-Based Sunbelt Nursery Files for Chapter 11 Protection.'' *Knight-Ridder/Tribune Business News,* 3 April 1998.

Elder, Laura. ''Calloway's Closes on Cornelius Nurseries Purchase,'' 24 September 1999.

Geer, Carolyn T. ''Pay Dirt.'' *Forbes,* 18 November 1996.

''Hechinger's Files Chapter 11.'' *Do-It-Yourself Retailing,* July 1999.

Kim, Nancy J. ''Area Nurseries a Hardy Breed.'' *Puget Sound Business Journal,* 17 May 1996.

Moody's Industrial Manual. New York: Moody's Investor Service, Inc., 1996.

Preddy, Melissa. '''Reinvented' Frank's Nursery to Shed Seasonal Image.'' *The Detroit News,* 7 August 1997.

U.S. Department of Labor. *Employment, Hours, and Earnings, United States, 1988-96.* Washington, D.C.: GPO, August 1996.

SIC 5271

MOBILE HOME DEALERS

This industry consists of establishments primarily engaged in the retail sale of new and used mobile homes and their parts and equipment. This classification excludes companies selling travel trailers or campers; these companies are discussed in **SIC 5561: Recreational Vehicle Dealers.**

NAICS CODE(S)

453930 (Manufactured (Mobile) Home Dealers)

The mobile home retail industry originated in the United States following World War II. The growth of suburbs coupled with increased demand for low-cost housing enabled mobile home dealerships to establish a foothold in the housing market. Sometimes referred to as ''trailer homes,'' mobile homes became immediately popular because they allowed families to own homes at a relatively inexpensive price. Moving was also made easier by these ''houses on wheels.'' As mobile home sales rose, mobile home parks, which leased plots of land to mobile home owners, began to offer more conveniences to their renters, including swimming pools. Mobile home owners also enjoyed the ordinary amenities offered by rental parks, like yards to mow and flowerbeds to plant.

The industry experienced steady growth until the late 1970s, when mobile home sales sagged with the rest of the economy. Even after the recession lifted and the economy improved in the 1980s, the mobile home industry lost some of its market share to traditional homes that became more affordable to consumers due to lower interest rates. Some large mobile home dealers filed for bankruptcy during this depressed market.

Mobile home retail sales began to pick up again in the late 1980s with the introduction of ''manufactured homes,'' which are steel-framed homes built in factories and driven to lots. These homes usually include at least two bedrooms and two bathrooms and cost roughly one-quarter of the price of regular houses. The mobile home industry further solidified its position during the 1990s: in 1991 total sales for mobile home dealers totaled \$5.57 billion, and by 1999 sales topped \$14 billion. Unit sales increased from around 150,000 in the 1980s to more than 350,000 in 1999.

In the late 1990s, about 20 million Americans, or 7 percent of the population, lived full-time in more than 8.5 million mobile homes. Approximately 3.3 million mobile homes were located in the southeastern United States, 1.9 million in the Southwest, 1.7 million in the Midwest, 864,000 in the Northwest, and 855,000 in the Northeast. Florida was the top ranked state with 900,000 mobile homes, followed by Texas with 722,000, North Carolina with 633,000, and California with 596,187. Most states have passed laws regulating the construction and safety of mobile homes to allay consumer concerns about their durability during storms.

At an average cost of $43,000 per unit, manufactured housing was the fastest growing sector of the housing industry. It accounted for more than 25 percent of all new single-family homes built in the United States. Mobile homes were alternatively marketed as cost-effective retirement homes, affordable housing for working folks, and seasonal housing for others.

The industry leader in mobile home retail sales in the late 1990s was Oakwood Homes Corp., a Greensboro, North Carolina, manufacturer with $1.14 billion in annual sales from 359 retail locations. Clayton Homes Inc., a manufacturer based in Maryville, Tennessee, ranked second with $535 million in sales from 273 retail locations. Fleetwood Enterprises Inc., a manufacturer based in Riverside, California, ranked fourth with approximately $250 million in annual sales from 182 retail locations. In 1999 Champion Enterprises, an Auburn, Michigan, mobile home manufacturer, acquired Care Free Homes Inc., a manufactured home retailer headquartered in Salt Lake City, Utah. The acquisition left Champion with 281 retail locations in 28 states, and sales were expected to top $1 billion in the year 2000.

FURTHER READING

Darnay, Arsen J., and Gary Alampi, eds. *Wholesale and Retail Trade USA.* Detroit: Gale Research, 1995.

Eventov, Adam. "The Fleetwood Homes in on Retailing Lead." *Business Press,* 16 November 1998

Leibs, Anthony. "Oakwood May Manufacture a Sale." *Mergers & Acquisitions Report,* 5 July 1999.

U.S. Bureau of the Census Web Site. Available at http://www.census.gov.

U.S. Department of Commerce Web Site. Available at http://www.doc.gov.

SIC 5311

DEPARTMENT STORES

This category includes retail stores carrying a general line of apparel, such as suits, coats, dresses, and furnishings; home furnishings, such as furniture, floor coverings, curtains, draperies, linens, and major household appliances; and housewares, such as table and kitchen appliances, dishes, and utensils. These stores must carry men's and women's apparel and either major household appliances or other home furnishings.

NAICS CODE(S)

452110 (Department Stores)

These products and other merchandise are normally arranged in separate sections or departments with the accounting on a departmentalized basis. The departments and functions are integrated under a single management. The stores usually provide their own charge accounts, deliver merchandise, and maintain open stocks. These stores normally have 50 employees or more.

Establishments that sell a similar range of merchandise with less than 50 employees are classified in **SIC 5399: Miscellaneous General Merchandise Stores.** Establishments that do not carry these general lines of merchandise are classified according to their primary activity.

INDUSTRY SNAPSHOT

Many retailers in 1998 had a favorable year with sales in U.S. retail operations up 5.1 percent, and as they entered 1999 the retail outlook was expected to remain stable. The economic conditions in 1994 and 1995 that left concerned retailers and resulted in price cutting, higher interest rates, and a general economic slowdown, were worries of the past. As the retail industry rebounded, consumer spending and confidence rose. As 1997 began, overcapacity of retail space in comparison to the general U.S. population was not estimated to grow as fast as it did in the early 1990s. By 1999, there were 20 square feet of retail space for each person in the United States, a decrease from past figures. This industry should see positive increases in sales growth into the early years of 2000, especially with the increasing popularity of online retailing. However, consumer spending is expected to slow eventually and the Asian economic crisis will also play a factor in international retail sales.

The department store division of the retail industry was hit particularly hard in the early 1990s by discount retailers siphoning market share away and by a drop in consumer spending. It rebounded, however in the late 1990s with sales growth of just over 6 percent since 1988, and department stores have slowly benefited from the rise in consumer spending. However, this division faces many barriers including the rising popularity of discount mass retailers. For example, Sears—one of the oldest and best-known department stores—was ousted from its number one position in sales by Wal-Mart, which had over three times more revenue in 1998. In an attempt to regain their leadership position, many department stores tried to create a new identity that would attract new customers, as well as keep existing customers happy. Department stores will remain focused on price-cutting, capturing consumer attention, and Internet retailing into the year 2000.

Part of the early allure of department stores was their atmosphere and decor, making the shopping experience a form of entertainment. At one time, these stores were the fashion monitors of the day and led the way with new trends in retailing. They were the first to provide consumer credit and to create mass-produced clothing, and they became the home for national fashion designers. They also were influential in the development of many American holiday traditions still celebrated today.

Approximately 10,000 department stores existed throughout the United States. Most operations began as a single store located within a downtown district. When customers moved to the suburbs, so did the department stores; soon branch outlets appeared throughout the country. Ownership of most department stores reverted to publicly held conglomerates. Many of these companies also owned or held interest in discount retailers or general merchandisers.

The top department stores ranked by 1999 sales and number of employees are: Sears Roebuck & Co., with sales of $41.3 billion and 324,000 employees; J.C. Penney Company, Inc. with sales of $30.6 billion and 262,000 employees; Federated Department Stores Inc., with $15.8 billion in sales and 118,800 employees; May Department Stores, with sales of $13.4 billion and 127,000 employees; and Dillard's Inc. with sales of $7.7 billion and 54,921 employees.

Department stores, along with other retailers, were quick to embrace advanced computer technology. The ability to centralize operations, have a complete and up-to-date status of inventory, and get an exact reading of items purchased are but a few pieces of information that can be generated by computerized point-of-sale systems. Retailers were also able to reduce paperwork and lead time in updating stock.

The usage of computer technology has moved from a luxury to a necessity in order for any retailer to survive in the competitive market characterizing the late 1990s. Included in this technology is Internet retailing. In *Chain Store Age,* Stephen Finn, an Ernst & Young partner, commented that, ''For sure, the Internet is changing how retailers will distribute their goods and services and interact with customers.'' The department store sector of the retail industry is taking this issue seriously, with Internet sales projected to increase to more than $40 billion by 2002. For example, Federated Department Stores put its plan in motion to buy Fingerhut Companies Inc., a catalog retailer, in Spring of 1999 in a multi-billion deal. The purchase is expected to ease Federated into a multi-distribution platform on which it could handle Internet sales, warehousing, and shipping.

Organization and Structure

Retail establishments primarily selling merchandise for personal or household consumption played a major role in the U.S. economy by providing nearly 20 percent of all jobs in the private sector in 1998. Department stores had always held a leadership position among ''traditional'' retailers, however with discount mass merchandisers chipping away at market share, department stores have seen increasing competition. The very definition of department stores changed within the industry as well, as many stores eliminated some individual departments. This new definition covered the traditional department stores, but also included the ''multi-department soft goods stores with a fashion orientation, full-markup policy, and operating in stores large enough to be a shopping center anchor,'' Penny Gill stated in *Stores.* Such stores included Lord & Taylor, Neiman-Marcus, and Saks Fifth Avenue.

Changes in how merchants sold products and in how consumers shopped led to the creation of this new division of retailers—discount mass merchandisers. This category included superstores and price clubs, which both cut into the market share of traditional retailers. Also known as off-price retailers, these stores featured a specialized merchandise line at discount prices. Superstores were large retail establishments offering discount prices on a limited product line with extensive complementary merchandise. Examples of superstores included Toys 'R' Us and Wal-Mart. Price clubs were a new type of superstore with more retail floor space and a more extensive line of merchandise at more sharply discounted prices.

Background and Development

The department store became one of the most durable creations of modern American life. Created in the heart of emerging business districts, department stores gradually became part of the landscape. The first department stores opened as early as 1846 in New York City. Although they primarily catered to the city's elite, early merchants also wanted to make themselves accessible to women of all classes. So instead of keeping goods behind the counter, they openly displayed merchandise on the floor to encourage browsing.

Stores with elaborate decor and fancy window displays created a new variety of entertainment for the masses. Even if people could not afford to buy the merchandise, they still came to the department store to peer in the windows to see what they might attain someday. The traditional department stores sold ''soft goods,'' such as apparel and linens, as well as ''hard goods,'' including furniture, appliances, and housewares. The now defunct ''notions aisle''—the place for buttonhooks, thread, sewing needles, linens, laces, and silks—was the original foundation of the department store. Notions first were sold by peddlers, who traveled by foot through the rural South and Midwest. Eventually, these peddlers obtained a horse and buggy and then graduated to a small storefront, the prototype department store.

Another innovation that emerged in the late nineteenth century was the budget floor. Filene's obtained legendary status with its Automatic Bargain Basement—selling cashmeres salvaged from a fire at Neiman-Marcus and Schiaparelli and Chanel gowns evacuated from Paris showrooms at the start of World War II. Credit began in 1911, when Sears Roebuck offered payment plans to farmers for large mail-order purchases. By the 1920s, ''layaway'' installment plans were common. The introduction of department store charge plates encouraged customer loyalty since that was the only form of consumer credit available at the time.

From the earliest days, merchants catered to women. By 1915, nearly 90 percent of all department store customers were female. Women also began to take the place of men on the selling floor, offering fashion advice and fittings.

Department stores were considered a fantasyland for toy vendors and children alike. Stores became famous for elaborate Christmas decor. No one knows exactly when Santa Claus began to show up on the scene, but in 1939, Montgomery Ward's started to give away a book featuring a character first called Rollo, then Reginald, and finally Rudolph, a reindeer with a red nose. Gene Autry recorded Rudolph's signature song in 1949, and the famous reindeer became a Christmas icon.

Department store managers also influenced other major American holidays. In the past, Thanksgiving was held on the last Thursday in November. In 1939, the holiday fell on the 30th, leaving only 24 days for Christmas shopping. Ohio merchant Fred Lazarus Jr. led a campaign to move the holiday to the fourth Thursday in November. President Franklin D. Roosevelt complied, and Thanksgiving remained on that date ever since.

After World War II, department stores began expansion into the suburbs, following the flight of their customers. By the 1950s, most department stores turned to upscale clients and merchandise, doing away with the low-end, bargain basement sales. This decision opened the way for discount operations like Kmart to enter the market. Customer loyalty quickly dissipated as the arrival of bank credit cards in the 1960s allowed consumers to shop on credit virtually anywhere. In due time, the costs of suburban expansion plus the lack of experience or interest on the part of third- or fourth-generation family members drove many department store owners to sell their operations.

By the 1980s, many department stores were in fairly poor shape. Although consumer spending was up, the stores found fierce competition from discounters, specialty stores with numerous outlets, and mail order houses, which sent out 14 billion pieces of mail annually. In an attempt to lure back customers, department stores engaged in competitive price-cutting. The result was a frenzied period of leveraged buyouts (LBOs), mergers, and acquisitions. Of the eight companies that composed the Standard and Poor's index at the beginning of 1986, four were acquired or taken private, while a fifth company undertook major restructuring.

One negative fact hanging over the industry—as well as the rest of the $3.2-trillion retail market—was that for the last 25 years, the amount of retail space per person in the United States increased by 450 percent. ''It generally is agreed that the country is already overstored, so successful operators are the ones taking market share from others. The battle for market share continues to be fought largely on the pricing front,'' William G. Barr reported in *Value Line Investment Survey.*

By the mid-1990s, department stores changed the product mix somewhat. ''White goods''—appliances such as stoves and refrigerators—were less emphasized to make room for more apparel items. Sears adopted the slogan, ''Come see the softer side of Sears,'' emphasizing that power tools and lawn equipment were not the only items you would see in the store. J.C. Penney upgraded store merchandising, also emphasizing more apparel.

However, the departure of the shop-weary consumer continued to hurt department stores' sales. In sharp contrast to the retail heyday of the 1980s, consumers in the 1990s became thriftier. Feeling financially strained, people tried to maintain their lifestyles on a smaller budget. Since consumer confidence remained relatively low, many retailers kept markups just high enough to maintain market share. As general economic conditions improved in 1996, confidence and consumer spending increased.

Changes in demographics in the early 1990s also posed challenges to department store retailers. The rate of household formations slowed dramatically in the early 1990s, and in the next two decades the percentage of young adults was projected to decline. The fastest-growing segment of the population, people between the ages of 45 and 54 years, was marked to grow 46 percent between 1990 and 2000. In other words, the baby boomers, who ''shopped till they dropped'' during the 1980s, would reach middle age by the year 2000. This age shift was forecast to have far reaching ramifications for the marketing and merchandising direction of department stores. In addition, the 65 and older segment of the American population continued to grow quickly. This group tended to spend more on health care and leisure activities and less on goods like apparel.

To top it off, research indicated that consumers no longer considered shopping ''fun.'' According to the *Lieber/Yankelovitch Monitor,* the number of consumers who described shopping for clothes as fun dropped 4 percent from 1991 to 1992. Shopping was regarded as time consuming and frustrating. However, as economic conditions improved, interest rates trended downward, and personal income slowly rose, more shoppers extended themselves on credit, bucking the earlier trend of frugal shopping. The key for retailers during the 1990s was their ability to attract new customers, regain old customers, and make existing operations more productive. Creative merchandising and keeping up with the fashion trends of the day was a crucial component to gaining sales.

There was finally a break in 1996, when department stores saw the business environment improve from the previous two years. The department stores placed more emphasis on sales of women's clothing, which was always an important item to increase store sales. The combination of better quality, higher fashion women's wear, and increased demand due to improved economic conditions in 1996 helped spur sales for department stores. Regionally, the increased economic activity in California and the Pacific Northwest also aided sales. Most large department stores also placed more emphasis on meeting the new purchasing trends—namely, that apparel, jewelry, and quality home furnishings play more of an important share of department store sales than the home improvement hard goods and home electronic products did in the past. Many department store retailers were also emphasizing their own private label brands, which had significantly improved in quality and marketing. On the operations side, these companies generally had also taken advantage of improvements in retail automation that made merchandising, accounting, inventory, and logistics functions more efficient and accurate.

The correct combination of service, customer responsiveness, and merchandise presentation was critical to the future growth of department stores. The stores would have to recreate the original pleasant, almost entertaining experience for shoppers if they were to find their space among the crowd of discount mass merchandisers.

Current Conditions

The entire retail industry realized gains in 1997, 1998, and into 1999. Department stores continued to see increases in sales and profits, although many factors deterred from those increases being even larger. The Internet, mass discount retailers, specialty retailers, and catalog shopping were competing with the traditional department store for consumer loyalty. *Chain Store Age* reported that in October 1999, ''The department store sector continues to be hot for some chains and cold for others.'' Federated Department Stores, Dillard's, and May saw increases in same-store sales, while J.C. Penney saw a slight decrease in sales and Sears remained stagnant.

In order to keep existing market share and boost sales, many department stores have adopted new ad campaigns, revamped stores, focused on high margin profit mixes, and began online retailing. Montgomery Wards, for example, is in the process of updating the floor plans of its existing stores and well as focusing on higher end merchandise. Sears, with its 'softer side' campaign, has been targeting a younger, trendier crowd with its apparel line. Although this line had a negative effect on profits in 1996-1998, sales in 1999 began to show signs of life. Sears also jumped aboard the Internet wave and began to sell appliances online. By the 1999 holiday season, it also planned sell tools. Eventually, Sears.com will offer home furnishings, lawn and garden products, and consumers will be able to request repair service online. A *Chain Store Age* October 1999 article stated that by the year 2010, at least 15 percent of all retail sales would stem from online purchasing. This apparent fact has department stores scrambling to provide the type of products that Internet savvy consumers want both online and in the stores.

Consolidation has also been a trend in the department store sector. Proffitt's, a Birmingham, Alabama-based company, purchased Parisian in 1996, and had a bid on the table for Saks Fifth Avenue in August 1998. Dillard's also bid for Mercantile Stores, an Ohio based department store chain, in 1998. Elder-Beerman took over Stone & Thomas as well. This trend has left the department store industry with a handful of larger, powerful competitors whose focus in the late 1990s was growth through acquisition.

The long-term forecast for department stores showed continued slow growth into 2000. This projection was based largely on the simple fact consumer spending would eventually slow or decline. According to a U.S. Department of Labor projection, retail sales adjusted for inflation should show an average annual growth rate of 2.5 percent from 1990 to 2005, compared with a 3.5 percent annual rate posted during the preceding 15 years. The key for retailers entering the next millennium would be the ability to attract new customers, regain old customers, and make existing operations more productive. Creative merchandising and keeping up with the fashion trends of the day would be a crucial component to gaining sales.

Whatever approach department stores decided to take with regard to merchandise mix, industry executives agreed that department stores also needed to differentiate themselves from each other. ''If individually they can find a hole not being met by their competitors, they can grow,'' Wintzer affirmed in *Stores.* ''Nordstrom has done it well with service; Saks has done it at the high end. And Macy's has done it by being a little more fashion-forward, a little trendier, while staying very promotional.''

INDUSTRY LEADERS

Sears, Roebuck & Co. Headquartered in a Chicago suburb, Sears, Roebuck & Company was the second largest retailer in the world in the late 1990s—based on its sales of merchandise and service—behind Wal-Mart. In 1999, Sears operated more than 850 department stores and 2,100 off-mall format and specialty stores across the nation, and employed approximately 324,000 people. Sears' revenues totaled $41.3 billion, with net income of $1.04 billion.

Richard Sears opened R.W. Sears Watch Company in 1886 in Minneapolis. The following year, Sears moved his business to Chicago and joined in a partnership with Alvah Roebuck, another watchmaker. In 1893 they created the corporate name Sears, Roebuck and Co. Sears began as a mail-order company, primarily providing farmers with low-cost goods delivered via the railroads and postal service. In 1895, Chicago clothing manufacturer Julius Rosenwald bought the company, and in 1906 Sears went public.

Sears' customers soon began to move from the farm into the city, so in 1925 the company decided to open a retail store. Robert E. Wood, then a vice president of Sears and later president and chairman of the board, became known as the father of Sears' retail expansion. He started with one store located in a Chicago mail-order plant, and by 1927 had 27 stores in operation. Company records indicated that during one 12-month period in the late 1920s, Sears stores opened at an average rate of one every other business day. Soon Sears began selling merchandise under its own brand names, creating the still popular brands of Craftsman, Kenmore, and DieHard.

In 1931, the retail side accounted for 53.4 percent of Sears' total sales, topping mail order for the first time. Sears continued to open stores during the 1930s despite the Depression. By the start of World War II, more than 600 stores were in operation. During the 1940s and 1950s, Sears expanded internationally with stores in Cuba, Mexico, and Canada.

In 1931, Wood also launched Allstate Insurance Company as a wholly owned subsidiary of Sears. At first, Allstate operated only by mail, but by 1933 Allstate sales booths were installed within Sears stores. In 1973, Sears completed its new headquarters in Chicago—the world's tallest building at 110 stories and 1,454 feet tall.

To combat declining market share in the 1980s, Sears initiated a restructuring of its retail division. The company acquired the 405-store Western Auto chain in 1988, introduced a new pricing policy, and added non-Sears brands in 1989. Sears also announced it was relocating from the Sears Tower to a northwestern Chicago suburb in 1992. In January 1993, Sears announced another major restructuring program to streamline its Merchandise Group. The company discontinued its U.S. catalog operations, closed unprofitable retail and specialty stores, and offered early retirement to employees. Completed in early 1994, the restructuring improved the company's net income by $300 million annually, increased cash flow, eliminated roughly 16,000 full-time and 34,000 part-time positions, and positioned Sears to compete with its discount rivals.

The company displayed a strong year in 1996—same-store sales increased 5.4 percent. Apparel, softlines, hardware, computers, and electronic product lines all recorded double digit increases. The firm achieved these increased sales while maintaining stable selling and administrative expenses. The company has successfully updated the look of the firm and its product lines. The home service businesses—along with the cosmetics, jewelry, and footwear areas—were expected to receive more attention in 1997, as well as the credit levels of Sears's 27 million cardholders. Delinquencies of cardholders rose substantially in 1996, and increases in interest rates placed demands on cardholders to watch their debt levels. Successes by Sears in ''off-mall'' areas such as Sears Hardware, Western Auto, Sears Tire, and HomeLife Furniture were also evident in 1996.

In 1997, Sears opened 275 National Tire and Battery stores across the nation. Credit operations continued to deteriorate, although fourth-quarter revenue increased 9.2 percent in comparison to 1996 figures. In 1998, the company profits fell 12 percent from 1997. In 1999, Sears' appliance and electronic sales were strong, as well as home fashions and apparel. In October of that year, total revenues were down 2.7 percent from 1998. Sears was also named one of the 'Retailers of the Century' by Lebhar-Friedman Publications.

J.C. Penney Company. In 1999, J.C. Penney was the largest general merchandise catalog retailer in the United States, as well as remaining a top department store leader, operating 1,150 department stores in all 50 states and Puerto Rico. J.C. Penney also owns Eckerd Drugstores, number four in sales in the United States. Annual sales for the company reached approximately $30.6 billion, with net income of $594 million in 1999.

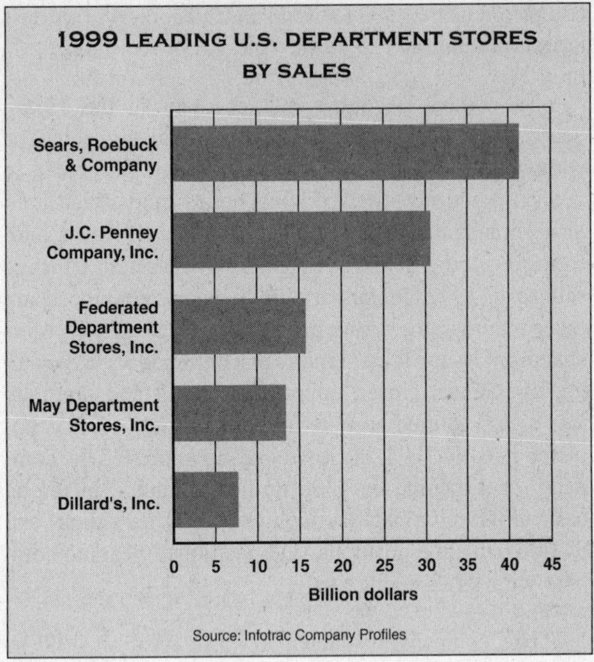

In 1902, after working for many years as a sales clerk for the Golden Rule Mercantile Company, James Cash Penney opened his first store as part owner and store manager in Wyoming. Buying out his two partners in 1907, Penney launched his own Golden Rule stores. To consolidate operations, Penney established headquarters in Salt Lake City in 1909. Although Penney moved his headquarters to New York the following year, the company's growth continued in the western portion of the United States.

J.C. Penney exploded into a nationwide organization from 1917 to 1929—growing from 174 stores to 1,395—while sales skyrocketed from $14.9 million to $209.7 million. By the 1930s, a J.C. Penney store could be found in nearly every town with more than 5,000 people, and the company continued to expand from the west to the east coast. By 1951, a J.C. Penney store existed in every state, and sales passed $1 billion for the first time.

The company entered the catalog business in 1962 and built its volume primarily through catalog sales centers located in stores. J.C. Penney Financial Services was created in 1967, including an acquisition known today as the J.C. Penney Life Insurance Company. The J.C. Penney National Bank was created in 1983 with the acquisition of the First National Bank of Harrington in Delaware.

During the 1980s, J.C. Penney closed many downtown locations or moved them to suburban malls. Stores were classified as metropolitan or geographic for those located outside metro areas. The company's real estate strategy produced hundreds of well-located stores in regional shopping centers throughout the United States.

In 1983, the company announced plans to spend more than $1 billion to modernize stores. To accommodate these changes, J.C. Penney eliminated auto service, major appliances, paint and hardware, lawn and garden merchandise, and fabrics from its stores. Upon completion, J.C. Penney began to focus on better serving the fashion needs of its customers—especially women, who accounted for more than 70 percent of apparel purchases in its stores. The composition of 1992 sales for the department store was 42 percent in women's, 29 percent in men's, 15 percent in the home division, and 14 percent in children's. The department store group accounted for nearly 75 percent of sales.

The J.C. Penney Company moved its headquarters to Dallas in 1988. J.C. Penney Telemarketing also was created that year to take catalog phone orders and provide telemarketing services for other companies. This network became the largest privately owned telemarketing system in the United States. At the start of the 1990s, J.C. Penney continued to expand stores and catalog services and also ventured into international markets such as China.

Seventy-three percent of 1995 sales was generated from department stores and 18 percent came from catalogue sales. The company acquired Kerr Drug Stores and Eckerd in 1996, which placed the total number of drug stores at 2,600—accounting for approximately one-third of total company sales. About 12 percent of pre-tax income comes from insurance and banking subsidiaries. It is estimated that 80 percent of the firm's customer base are women. Sears, Wal-Mart, and Kmart have tried to attack this base by enhancing their own private label apparel brands. With the increased use of online retailing by people using the Internet to go shopping, the catalogue business was made available online for Internet shoppers.

In 1999, J.C. Penney sold its credit business to GE Capital in an effort to reduce debt. Sales grew by 3.6 percent over 1998 and net income increased by 4.9 percent as well.

May Department Stores. The May Department Stores Company owned regional department store companies that operated more than 400 stores in 1999. These included Lord & Taylor headquartered in New York; Filene's in Boston; Hecht's in Washington, D.C.; Kaufmann's in Pittsburgh; Foley's in Houston; Famous-Barr in St. Louis; Robinsons-May in Los Angeles; The Jones Store; and Meier and Frank in Portland, Oregon. The May Company sold Payless ShoeSource Stores, accounting for 15 percent of sales and 16 percent of operating earnings, in May 1996; sold Caldor's in November 1989; and sold Venture in November 1990. May Department Stores' sales totaled $13.4 billion in 1999, with net income of $849 million, an increase of 9.5 percent over 1998.

Built on a series of acquisitions, May Department Stores Company became a leading U.S. department store operator, maintaining its independence and financial strength. German immigrant David May started with his first store in Leadville, Colorado, in 1877 and expanded into Denver in 1888. In 1892, he and the Schoenberg brothers bought The Famous in St. Louis, and in 1898 they purchased a store in Cleveland. David May moved the company headquarters to St. Louis in 1905, and in 1911 bought Barr's, creating the flagship store Famous-Barr.

While the May Company purchased other stores from 1912 to 1966, two other companies reorganized in 1916 to form Associated Dry Goods, whose principal businesses were Lord & Taylor in New York, Hahne's in Newark, and Hengerer's in Buffalo. From the 1950s to the 1970s, Associated Dry Goods also acquired various other family-owned stores. In 1986, the May Company bought Associated Dry Goods for 70 million shares of stock. Foley's and Filene's were added in 1988, purchased from Federated Department Stores for $1.5 billion. Since then, May Department Stores Company consolidated some operations and closed or sold off others. Despite the 1991 recession, the company boasted its twenty-second consecutive year of record sales and earnings per share in 1996.

The May Company has a very strong track record of earnings and dividend increases, and its return on capital is above its industry competitors. However, Federated Department Stores and Target have recently moved into many of the Northeastern markets where May Company has been strong, and they present challenges to the firm. However, 1997 was still another strong year for the company and in 1998, the company achieved its twenty-fourth year of record profits and sales.

WORKFORCE

Approximately 10,000 department stores operated throughout the United States and employed more than 1.2 million people in the late-1990s. Many of the industry's employees were under the age of 25 and worked part-time, evenings, and weekends. More than 40 percent of the people employed by department stores were retail sales workers—the people who "worked the floor" selling merchandise. Administrative support personnel were the next largest group with 15 percent of total employment. These employees provided general office skills and bookkeeping tasks, in addition to working as customer service representatives. No formal training was required for most sales and administrative support positions, although a high school education was preferred.

Management positions in department stores made up less than 7 percent of total employment. These positions included department managers, buyers, merchandise managers, store managers, and retail chain store area managers. A college degree became increasingly important for management positions, especially with large department stores. Companies preferred to hire people who earned a bachelor's degree in marketing or business to join management training programs.

Hourly workers in department stores earned two-thirds the average pay of all workers in private industry. This lower wage might be due to the high proportion of part-time and less-experienced workers. Few employees belonged to a union, and those who did generally received the same pay as nonunion workers. Department store jobs were projected to increase nearly 23 percent over 1990 through 2005 nearly as fast as the average for all industries. Large numbers of job openings should result from the high turnover rate generally found in this industry.

Advancement in computer technology should not greatly affect employment figures. However, due to computerized operations, worker productivity in the retail industry should double from 1990 to 2005, according to the U.S. Department of Labor. Although some bookkeeping and inventory control positions might be eliminated, retail sales should continue to rely upon personal interaction, even as e-commerce trends continue.

AMERICA AND THE WORLD

Most department stores had plans for some sort of international expansion by 2005. With the completion of the North American Free Trade Agreement (NAFTA) in September 1992, many stores sought opportunities in both Canada and Mexico. According to a Coopers and Lybrand survey, retailers had plans to open stores in Canada. However, those who wanted to expand in Mexico were more inclined to work through joint ventures or partnerships.

Canada has become an increasingly attractive market. The T. Eaton Co. of Toronto collapsed in the fall of 1999, leaving only Sears Canada and the Hudson Bay Co. in that market. With 64 outlets available on the auction block, players such as Federated Department Stores, J.C. Penney, Wal-Mart, and Target are expected to enter into the Canadian playing field.

Some stores have entered Mexico, and both J.C. Penney and Dillard Department Stores have anchor malls in Mexico City, Monterrey, and Guadalajara, Mexico. The Mexican malls were designed in a similar style to American malls, and Mexican retailers would occupy nearly half of the rental space. Sears also entered the Mexican market with its Homelife furniture stores.

Another possible entry into the international arena might come through catalog sales and telemarketing. In this scenario, merchandise would be sold through a partnership with a third-party national. A special catalog would be created targeting international markets, and operations would be set up similar to catalog service companies in the United States. A licensed catalog sales program would place U.S. goods in foreign markets through a licensee with little risk to the American company. All sales would be concluded domestically, with the licensee responsible for transporting goods across borders. J.C. Penney began such a program in Bermuda and Aruba, and negotiations were ongoing in Russia, Iceland, Brazil, Panama, and Argentina for additional licensed catalog sales.

''Going global'', as retailers call it, is an important issue in international commerce, especially as technology increases and trade barriers are broken. However, the Asian economic crisis is making several retailers think twice. *Stores* magazine reported in its February 1999 issue that, ''The economic turmoil in Asia left most of that region in recession, and, as a result, consumer spending contracted sharply. In rapid succession, worrisome news from Russia and several South American countries gave rise to talks of global economic meltdown.'' However, European spending was steady due a strong economy, and with the Euro expected to become the Continental currency in 2002, entering that market will appear more attractive to stores.

RESEARCH AND TECHNOLOGY

Despite the sluggish retail forecast in the mid-1990s, department store companies continued to invest in technology. Using computer technology, such as inventory management systems and point-of-sale bar code scanning, provided a tremendous advantage for stores trying to regain their competitive edge. Many stores gathered data from scanners at the point-of-sale (POS), which identified for managers peak selling periods and allowed them to better shape work schedules. This data also showed managers exactly what products were selling, which helped in keeping the stores fully stocked and in forecasting upcoming selling trends.

For example, J.C. Penney implemented a state-of-the-art, automated, merchandise replenishment system. This computerized program triggered orders based on projected sales demand so that stores were constantly stocked with basic merchandise items. Orders were processed every week instead of every two to four weeks. J.C. Penney also operated an information network based on seven large mainframe computers and 120,000 terminals, which processed about 700 million retail transactions annually.

With that technology in place, most industries, including the retail industry, came face to face with the pressures of the Internet. With the advent of online retailing—e-tailing, Internet sales are predicted to reach astounding numbers in just five years, and many department stores have begun to implement some form of online purchasing. J.C. Penney now has its catalog available for online shopping, Sears offers many products available on its site, and the May Company offers gift card purchase on its division's websites. Tom Reynolds, an Ernst & Young director, stated in a *Chain Store Age* article that, ''There will always be a need for brick-and-mortar retailers with improved buying experiences. But to succeed into the next century, they'll have to respond to what's emerging on the Internet, and even consider it as a primary way of doing business.''

Retail information technology professionals are becoming more in demand as well. As international expansion is forecast, these professionals will be called upon for technology guidance and telecommunications expertise. POS systems, among other computer systems, will have to be updated to handle foreign currency and tax issues. Their knowledge will also be required for Internet business. As technology changes quickly, stores will be faced with challenges to keep up pace with other retailers and increased competition.

In a released PR Newswire, J. Roger Friedman, CEO of Lebhar-Friedman, commented, ''We began the 20th Century with quaint downtown shops and we finish it with huge shopping malls, e-tailing and international chains featuring uniform quality standards and high customer service.''

FURTHER READING

Benston, Liz. ''Montgomery Ward's Completes Renovation.'' *Centre Daily Times,* 1 November 1999.

''Big Business Meets the E-World: Sears? Whirlpool? Now Even These Guys Want to Create E-business.'' *Fortune,* 8 November 1999.

''Braving New Worlds.'' *Chain Store Age,* September 1999.

Finn, Stephen. ''E-Commerce Will Lead to Fewer New Physical Stores.'' *Chain Store Age,* September 1999.

Moukheiber, Zina. ''Retailing: Annual Report on American Industry.'' *Forbes,* 13 January 1997.

''Penney's Sells Credit Card Division.'' *HFN,* 25 October 1999.

Reynolds, Tom. ''Retailers Must Speed Ahead With Emerging.'' *Chain Store Age,* September 1999.

Schulz, David. ''Acquisitions Set the Pace for Retail Chain Growth.'' *Stores,* August 1998.

Schultz, David. ''The Nation's Biggest Retail Companies.'' *Stores,* July 1999.

''Stellar Gains Weaken Slightly in August.'' *Chain Store Age,* October 1999.

''The Best of Century.'' *PR Newswire,* 29 October 1999.

''The Fortune 500: Retailing.'' *Fortune,* 28 April 1997.

''Retail Store Industry.'' *Valueline.* 21 February 1997.

"The Shifting Global Marketplace." *Stores,* February 1999.

U.S. Department of Labor. Bureau of Labor Statistics. *National Industry-Occupation Employment Matrix.* Available from http://www.stats.bls.gov.

Vincenti, Lisa. "Open-Door Policy: Target Canada." *HFN,* 13 September 1999.

SIC 5331

VARIETY STORES

This category includes establishments primarily engaged in the retail sale of a variety of merchandise in the low and popular price ranges. Sales usually are made on a cash-and-carry basis, with the open-selling method of display and customer selection of merchandise. These stores generally do not carry a complete line of merchandise, do not carry their own charge service, and do not deliver merchandise.

NAICS Code(s)

452990 (All Other General Merchandise Stores)

Industry Snapshot

Retailers saw an increase in sales in 1998, as shopper spending increased by 5.1 percent. This extended to the category known as discount department stores, which accounted for $306 billion in dollar volume. These firms are also known as discount variety stores, general merchandise discount stores, mass merchandisers, full-line discounters, or discount "houses." This industry is dominated by the Wal-Mart, Kmart, and Target chains. Combined 1998 revenue for these "Big Three" discount retailers was $193 billion, with Wal-Mart adding an impressive $137 billion to the total. The Big Three discount retailers began operations as individual variety stores, and by the late-1990s, evolved into chains averaging 80,000-square feet discount-selling space per store, providing: clothing; hardware, housewares, auto supplies, and small appliances; stationery and candy; sporting goods and toys; health and beauty aids; pharmaceuticals; gifts and electronics; and shoes and jewelry. Although overshadowed by the Big Three, groups of regional stores, such as Ames Department Stores, McCrory, Family Dollar Stores, and the Dollar Tree Stores, are also listed under the variety stores category. The common element among all stores in the industry is the focus on low prices.

The emergence of discounters, which relied heavily on technological advances to improve productivity and cut costs, had a tremendous impact on the financial well-being of full-price retailers. This trend was expected to continue into the next millennium, as consumers become increasingly concerned with value shopping and saving money. Other factors affecting the future of discount retailing include a consumer base of greater ethnic diversity, a heightened concern for the environment, interactive technology, and international retailing.

Organization and Structure

Variety stores can be categorized by price and level of service, and generally fall into one of the following categories: discount department stores, wholesale clubs, supercenters, hypermarts, and so-called category killers.

Wholesale clubs are no-frills stores that sell in bulk to people who pay dues to maintain membership. Originally targeted toward small businesses, which appreciated the opportunity to purchase supplies in large quantities, membership requirements have been made broader to include many segments of the general populace. Supercenters, or superstores, are large retail outlets offering general merchandise in addition to a complete grocery area. The supercenter concept evolved from the hypermart, which offers discounted merchandise and groceries, as well as ancillary businesses, such as branch banking and photo processing. Finally, category killers are specialty chain stores offering a single line of merchandise, such as T.J. Maxx, Dress Barn, and Burlington Coat Factory. While industry information related to discount retailers often includes statistics on category killers, many of these stores are formally listed under the SIC related to the merchandise in which they specialize.

Background and Development

Although discounted sales have existed since the early 1900s, the discount variety store industry picked up shortly after World War II. During this time, according to *Discount Store News,* entrepreneurs were prompted to open large variety stores due to the increasing demand for consumer goods, including such new products as record players and television sets. In the northeastern part of the country, in particular, large facilities became available to potential variety store owners when manufacturers moving operations to the South vacated several mills. Taking over such facilities for retail operations, variety store owners found that their proximity to those mills that had remained in operation facilitated the timely restocking of stores with apparel and domestic items.

By 1962, industry leaders and a standard store format were well established. Discount department stores were formed by the Dayton Company, which pioneered the Target chain, as well as Kmart stores, an offshoot of S.S. Kresge, the F.W. Woolworth Company's Woolco stores, and Sam Walton's Wal-Mart. These new stores transformed the variety store business into large, low-price, self-service stores, featuring both hard goods and apparel.

Several mergers occurred in the late 1960s and early 1970s, as chains sought to expand quickly through acquisitions. During this time, Kmart became the decided leader with more than 300 stores, which was more than double the number of the next largest chain. While over a dozen discount stores filed for Chapter 11, attributable to economic recession, Kmart and Woolco grew into national companies, while Wal-Mart expanded in the Southeast and Target in the Midwest.

During the 1970s, discount stores began exploring advances in technology, using computers, electronic registers, UPC bar coding systems, POS scanning, and satellite communication systems. Wal-Mart's explosive growth, in particular, was attributed to its successful implementation of computer technology. The company established highly automated distribution centers, which cut shipping costs and delivery time, and installed an advanced computer system to track inventory and speed up checkout and reordering. As a result, Wal-Mart increased the number of its retail establishments from 18 in 1970 to 270 in 1980.

By the end of the 1980s, Kmart, Target, and Wal-Mart dominated the industry. At the same time, other chains had filed Chapter 11, among them Woolco, FedMart, Memco, Twin Fair, Zayre, Zodys, Kings, Ames, and Hills. Regional operators experiencing moderate success included Jamesway, Caldor, and Bradlees in the East; Rose's in the South; Clover in Philadelphia; Fred Meyer in the Pacific Northwest; Fedco in southern California; and Venture, Meijers, and Value City in the Midwest.

The introduction of a full line of grocery items to the discount store format represented an important aspect of the successful supercenter in the early 1990s. Although the majority of store profits were attributable to merchandise sales, food divisions began to draw customers into the store and accounted for 40 percent of a supercenter's sales in the early 1990s. This trend was expected to have a negative impact on the traditional supermarket owner. Nevertheless, some analysts have viewed the discounters' venture into the food business with skepticism. Critics noted that since grocers earned an average of less than one penny per dollar of sales in the early 1990s, superstores faced the challenge of imposing even stricter cost controls in order to compete.

In their ongoing battle for market share, discounters also began focus on appealing to specific ethnic groups, striving to become familiar with the needs of the diversifying market in the 1990s. For example, some stores employed bilingual clerks, particularly in Hispanic communities, and featured signs and advertisements in languages other than English. Moreover, an awareness of traditions and holidays specific to certain ethnic groups helped store managers to stock seasonal merchandise.

In another effort to draw and retain loyal customers involved the promotion of environmental awareness. In addition to touting recyclable and environmentally friendly products, many discount stores attempted to cut back on lighting, heating, cooling, and other energy-draining expenses. They also began using recycled paper for printed advertisements and sign boards.

In June 1993, Wal-Mart opened an ''environmental demonstration store'' in Lawrence, Kansas. The store featured a community recycling center as well as an environmental education center. During this time, Kmart introduced programs to recycle cassette tapes, auto and truck tires, and auto and marine batteries. Target sponsored Kids for Saving the Earth, a grass roots environmental organization.

Some consolidation in the industry, particularly affecting the warehouse clubs, occurred in 1993, due to increased competition, market saturation, and a slow economy. In November 1993, Wal-Mart agreed to acquire 91 of Kmart's 113 Pace Membership Warehouse clubs for $300 million. The sale gave Wal-Mart access to five additional states and expanded its presence in California. Some of the Pace Warehouses would operate as Sam's Clubs, while others were designated for remodeling as supercenters.

Supercenters were largely considered the discount stores of the future. Kmart unveiled six supercenters, known as Super Kmart Centers, in 1992, and, by 1996, had planned to upgrade as many as 450 stores per year throughout the decade. Company spokespersons suggested that by the year 2000, Super Kmart Centers would eventually replace Kmart discount stores entirely.

Wal-Mart's supercenter business achieved annual sales of $5 billion by 1994, a substantial increase over the reported $1 billion in 1992. By 1997 there were 344 Wal-Mart Supercenters in operation, mostly in Texas and Missouri, and by 1998 that number climbed to 441.

Led by the strength of such retailers as Wal-Mart, the discount industry surpassed $200 billion in sales in the early 1990s. The Dollar General chain of discount stores was second to Wal-Mart in percentage sales growth having found a niche market in towns considered too small to support Wal-Mart stores. Kmart maintained its position as the second largest discount chain in the nation in volume, with $31 billion in 1996 sales; while Target neared $18 billion in sales in 1996. Regional discount chains that achieved strong sales growth included Connecticut-based Caldor (with $26 billion in 1996 sales) and St. Louis-based Venture Stores (with $1.5 billion in 1996 sales). The increased popularity of discount operations also led to their inclusion as anchor stores in suburban malls, a location once considered inappropriate by developers and more up-scale merchants.

CURRENT CONDITIONS

Since strong national chains originated in the 1960s, they have taken an increasing share of the market away from traditional full-price retailers, a trend that continued into the late 1990s. Discounters have seen sales rise from $2 billion in 1960 to $175 billion in 1998. The battle for market share is ongoing as traditional department stores try to fend off increased competition from these discount retailers. The August 1999 *Chain Store Age State of the Industry Supplement* stated, "discount stores continue to be in the catbird seat in the retail industry. As long as they continue to provide customers with value and quality merchandise, they will be hard to beat."

In keeping with that statement, discounters maintain top position in the market in girls, boys, and men's apparel. Traditional department stores and specialty stores still have control over the women's apparel segment, but discounters are gaining market share quickly. The stores success is attributed to meeting consumer demands, constant review of product mix, and offering higher quality, private label products. For example, Kmart began offering a "business casual" line, and Target has focused on a trendier line with its Xhileration label. Sears, Roebuck and Company's CEO Arthur Martinez stated in *Chain Store Age*, "Target and Wal-Mart have done a better job of improving and are more credible on price than Sears and mass-market retailers."

Discount stores have also seen success by diversifying product mix. In 1998, more than 36 percent of vitamins and mineral supplements were sold at discounts stores. These stores also account for the largest share of bath product sales—36 percent. In 1998, Wal-Mart took the lead over Toys "R" Us in toy sales, while Kmart and Target also saw gains in this area.

This industry has also increased focus on brand names, proprietary brands, and partnering. Kmart teamed up with Garth Brooks in 1999 to promote his new CD online. The company has also paired with Martha Stewart to offer her line of home products, sales of which exceeded $1 billion in 1998. Kmart's apparel lines—Jaclyn Smith and Kathy Ireland—have also been successful, as well as its Sesame Street line. Wal-Mart has also shared success in partnering—its Kathie Lee apparel line had more than $250 million in sales in 1998.

Along with its success however, the industry saw bankruptcies, consolidation and mergers in 1998 and 1999. Many regional chains suffered under the increasing competition from larger chains. Jamesway and Clover went through liquidations, Caldor and Venture no longer operate, ShopKo purchased Pamida, Ames bought Hills, and Bradlees filed Chapter 11.

Meanwhile, stronger, successful chains continued to grow. Both Target and Wal-Mart have increased square footage significantly from 1998 to 1999. Wal-Mart, Dayton Hudson, and Kmart have also increased expenditures in efforts to expand. At the same time, retailers invested in older store overhauls and closed stores that were not profitable.

The outlook for this industry is positive. Sales are expected to remain strong as more consumers look to the higher quality and low prices that discounters have implemented into the product mix. According to the fourteenth annual Consumer and Retailer Mood Survey conducted by Deloitte & Touche and the National Retail Federation for the 1999 holiday season, 80 percent of consumers will shop at discount department stores, up from 60 percent in 1996.

INDUSTRY LEADERS

Wal-Mart. Arkansas-based Wal-Mart was the world's largest retailer in 1998, operating more than 2,471 Wal-Mart stores—including 650 supercenters and 453 Sam's Clubs. In 1998, Wal-Mart reported $137.6 billion in annual revenue and employed 910,000 workers. Net income reached $4.43 billion. In 1998, the company's volume was larger than Sears, Kmart, Dayton Hudson, and J.C. Penney combined. Wal-Mart's founder, Sam Walton, entered the industry with a few Ben Franklin stores operating under the "Walton 5 & 10" name. When management at the Ben Franklin Company rejected the idea of opening larger discount stores, Sam Walton and his brother James "Bud" Walton opened their first Wal-Mart Discount City in Rogers, Arkansas, in 1962.

The explosive growth of the chain was facilitated by its effective use of computer technology. In the early 1990s the company invested almost $600 million in computerization and information systems, enabling it to reduce its costs to 15 percent of its annual revenues, well below the 25-percent industry average. An innovator of the wholesale club and hypermart concepts, Wal-Mart eventually came to favor the supercenter format, and in the early 1990s many Wal-Mart stores were redesigned as supercenters. In 1998, more than 40 percent of Wal-Mart's selling space went to its supercenters. During the mid-1990s the company's return on capital declined significantly due to large-scale investments in international stores, which totaled 310, with expansions mainly in Canada and Latin America. The company benefit from large economies of scale, and in 1998 foreign sales were up 63 percent to $12.2 billion.

Kmart. Michigan-based Kmart was the country's third-largest retailer in 1998, with 2,160 stores—down from a high of 4,792 in 1992. Revenues reached $33.67 billion in 1998, with a net income of $518 million. Net income increased dramatically in 1998—108 percent—from 1997 figures. The company employed 278,525 workers in 1998 and had stores in all 50 states.

Kmart's origins may be traced to 1897, when Sebastian S. Kresge and John McCrory opened their first five-and-dime stores in Memphis and Detroit. They split their partnership in 1899, and Kresge remained in the retail business. Kresge incorporated his company in 1912 as the S.S. Kresge Company, the second largest dime store chain in the United States. By the 1950s, Kresge's company had grown to become one of the largest general merchandise retailer in the nation. In 1958, company management decided to enter into discount retailing, transforming three unprofitable stores into discount operations. The first Kmart discount store was opened in Garden City, Michigan, in 1962. Americans soon grew accustomed to Kmart's ''blue-light'' specials—spontaneous sales in various departments signaled by a flashing blue light.

Growth continued in the 1970s, and the Kresge Company changed its corporate name to Kmart in 1977. During this time, the company began a series of acquisitions that included Furr's Cafeteria and Bishops Buffets, both of which were sold in 1986. Other acquisitions included Payless Drug Stores, Waldenbooks, and Builders Square. In 1988, Kmart opened its first Pace warehouse clubs as well as its first hypermart, American Fare. By 1990, Kmart had surpassed Sears, Roebuck, & Co. in retail revenue, but sales at both stores were quickly eclipsed by Wal-Mart. A major rejuvenation program, begun in the early 1990s, included the renovation or relocation of more than 2,400 Kmart stores. However, outdated inventory and old storefronts hurt sales, and the company found itself heavily discounting merchandise to retain sales. As reported in *Valueline,* ''the crucial core challenge remained the same: get customers to come back more often.'' The typical Kmart customer came in only 15 times a year, compared to 32 for Wal-Mart. Customers, in addition, often drove greater distances to avoid Kmart and go to Wal-Mart.

In 1996, Kmart introduced its Big K superstores. By 1998, Kmart had opened 165 new Big K's and remodeled 1,245 stores. With sales and net income on the rise, the company planned to remodel 575 stores in 1999 into the Big K format.

Target. Target discount stores represented the largest and most profitable division of Minnesota-based Dayton-Hudson Corporation in 1998. With 880 stores in 44 states, the Target division accounted for 76 percent of Dayton-Hudson's sales and 80 percent of its operating profit in 1998. The company had 189,000 employees in 1998 and $23 billion in sales.

By 1995, Target operated 30 Greatland stores in and around the Chicago area. The company also launched its Club Wedd bridal gift registry and the Lullaby Club baby registry. At the same time, Target also began the development of a prototype store for smaller markets, carrying merchandise similar to that in larger Target stores. Dayton Hudson, as reported in *Valueline,* earmarked 80 percent of its $1.4 billion capital budget for 1997 to add an additional 65 stores, 5 of which would include groceries. This added 8 million additional square feet to Target stores, an increase of 10 percent in 1997. Plans called for the company to expand in the northeastern part of the United States in 1998 and 1999 as well.

WORKFORCE

The retail industry was a significant source of employment in the United States, accounting for roughly 18 percent of the labor force. According to the U.S. Department of Labor, the retail industry should realize significant growth between 1998 and 2005, with more than 3 million new jobs created. Discount stores employed nearly two million people in 1999.

As larger companies relied more heavily on computer technology, lowering labor costs and increasing productivity, employees of Wal-Mart, Kmart, and other discount establishments found that job descriptions changed accordingly. With these advances, more jobs became available. According to *Discount Store News* editor Tony Lisanti, Wal-Mart is the largest employer in the United States and soon will become the largest employer in the world.

The average nonsupervisory retail worker's hourly wage was $9.17 in September 1999 and average weekly hours were 28.7.

AMERICA AND THE WORLD

While the economy remained strong in the United States and Europe in 1998 and 1999, Asia suffered. Consumer spending in that region decreased dramatically in 1998 with the economy in recession. However, international growth remained a priority in growth strategies for discount chains. The advent of the Euro has sparked interest in many European markets; Wal-Mart has forged into the German market, and Latin America remains attractive.

In 1999, Wal-Mart had operations in Puerto Rico, Canada, China, Mexico, Brazil, Germany, the United Kingdom, Argentina, and South Korea. David Toung, analyst with Argus Research, stated, ''These are very important areas for them because there is more growth opportunity for them than there is in the U.S.'' The company remains focused, along with other strong discounters, on operations abroad. By the late 1990s, several discount retailers opened stores in foreign markets, most notably in Europe and Mexico. Furthermore, companies began creating alliances with foreign operations in the form of licensing and franchising agreements, investments, and joint ventures.

Kmart began entering into joint ventures with foreign partners as early as 1968 with Coles Myer Ltd., the largest retailer in Australia. A long-time operator of stores in Canada, Kmart was also the first U.S. discount retailer to enter Eastern Europe with a 76 percent purchase of Maj, a large Czechoslovakian department store in 1992. The company had operations in Puerto Rico, Guam, and the U.S. Virgin Islands by 1996. Overall, Kmart has spent more than $100 million on the selection and renovation of department stores in the downtown areas of several foreign cities.

Success in international retailing remains linked to a company's sensitivity to cultural differences. In a *Chain Store Age* article, Ames Department Store CFO Rolando de Aguiar stated, ''Too many retailers do not pay attention to differences of doing business in different countries.'' This mistake lead to technological problems as well, as different countries use different types of communication and computer systems.

RESEARCH AND TECHNOLOGY

The Internet became a significant contributor to the retail environment with the increasing number of retailers who created web sites for general marketing information and to allow customers to purchase goods online. In 1996, Wal-Mart created two web sites for both higher and lower priced items, Kmart offered online shopping in May 1998, and Target offers online purchasing as well. With Internet sales expected to increase by the billions by 2003, discount retailers have been forced to create an online presence in order to tap into increased market share. As a result of increasing technology, information technology and information services retail professionals have been called upon and now play substantial roles in the discount stores infrastructure.

Due to the price sensitive nature of the industry, discount stores have to maintain efficient operations in order to achieve maximum profitability. The implementation of computer technology was and is, essential to store operations. Development of technology such as computer-assisted bar code scanning, online receiving, merchandise tracking, and labor management is crucial to store profitability. With the onset of computerized operations, discount stores were able to reduce inventory, speedup inventory turnover, and shorten the lead time required to move merchandise into the store.

Interactive touch screens for point-of-sale (POS) operations went into development in 1998. Graphical user interface (GUI) payment terminals are slated to become increasingly popular, despite negative feedback. Jim Dion—J.C. Williams Group senior partner—stated in a *Stores* article that, ''for some time now, retailers have made interactive kiosks, touch-screen information terminals, and similar capabilities available to customers at or near the point-of-sale. In most cases, the technology was ignored by customers over age 50 and used infrequently by 25- to 50-year-olds. Most stores and malls have backed off this technology for the time being.''

Nevertheless, vendors are pushing the new POS systems. Checkmate developed a new product, the eN-Touch 1000, which is predicted to replace existing countertop credit and debt terminals. In the same *Stores* article, Mary Lynne Campbell—Director of Business Development for Checkmate—stated, ''retail marketers can achieve 'virtual customer intimacy' through nonpayment applications such as advertising, personal messaging, instant credit, loyalty programs, cross selling, electronic coupons, surveys, managerial signoff, information kiosks, and product locators.'' Large, national retailers are expected to implement these new devices.

Use of handheld computers in the industry also increased in the late 1990s, greatly facilitating in-store communications, particularly for price verification and inventory tracking. Wal-Mart, Target, and Kmart used wireless in-store systems. The handhelds proved beneficial in maintaining stock levels and facilitating price markdowns.

Moreover, the development of spread-spectrum radio promised greater bandwidth in wireless communications, allowing stores to use wireless systems for a wide variety of tasks. Future applications for spread-spectrum radio included use as a local-area network infrastructure, which would connect handheld computers; new generations of wireless (and possibly mobile) point-of-sale (POS) systems; and electronic shelf labels, in order to provide graphs of sales trends among other information. Manufacturers of spread-spectrum radio systems continue development on graphical interfaces.

FURTHER READING

''Braving New Worlds.'' *Chain Store Age,* September 1999.

Markowitz, Arthur. ''Big Is Better in the 90s.'' *Discount Store News,* 15 February 1993.

Markowitz, Arthur. ''Retailing in the Year 2000, Fewer Players, Better Service.'' *Discount Store News,* 7 December 1992.

Murphy, Patricia. ''Interactive Touch Screens Seen Reshaping Retail Checkout.'' *Stores,* July 1998.

''Retailers of the Century Named; Wal-Mart, Walgreens, Home Depot, McDonald's, Kroger, Sears, Toys 'R' Us.'' *PR Newswire,* 29 October 1999.

Schulz, David. ''The Nation's Biggest Retail Companies.'' *Stores,* July 1999.

''The Shifting Global Marketplace.'' *Stores,* February 1999.

''State of the Industry: Discount Stores.'' *Chain Store Age,* August 1999.

''Survey Reveals Multiple Shopping Venues Spread Holiday Cheer Among Consumers and Retailers.'' *Business Wire,* 2 November 1999.

Valueline. Retail Store Industry. 21 February 1997.

''Wal-Mart Sets Growth Plans.'' *HFN The Weekly Newspaper for the Home Furnishing Network,* 26 November 1996.

Ward's Business Directory of U.S. Private and Public Companies-1996. Detroit: Gale Group, 1996.

SIC 5399

MISCELLANEOUS GENERAL MERCHANDISE STORES

This industry classification includes establishments primarily engaged in the retail sale of a general line of apparel, dry goods, hardware, housewares or home furnishings, groceries, and other lines of limited amounts. Stores selling commodities covered in the definition for department stores, but normally having less than 50 employees, and stores usually known as country general stores are also included in this industry. Establishments primarily engaged in retail sale of merchandise by television, catalog, and mail-order are classified in **SIC 5961: Catalog and Mail-Order Houses.**

NAICS CODE(S)

452910 (Warehouse Clubs and Superstores)
452990 (All Other General Merchandise Stores)

Although general goods, dry goods, feed stores, and specialty farming equipment are included in this category, catalog showroom operators have consistently dominated it. Perhaps the most recognized name in this segment of the retail industry has been Service Merchandise, with Best Products placing a distant second. Both companies operated catalog showrooms in which customers could view sample merchandise on the floor and then purchase the merchandise in-store. Currently Service Merchandise is in Chapter 11 and Best Products closed its doors to customers in 1998. Recently, competition for discount and department stores has come in the form of warehouse clubs and superstores.

Sales of consumer goods rose 7.8 percent in 1999, the largest increase since 1986. Sales in the retail industry topped $3 trillion dollars and are expected to climb in 2000, but not at the rate experienced in previous years. Retailers are keeping a close eye on the Federal Reserve, which has wanted to slow down the economy. In the United States there were 25,805 stores that comprised the general merchandise segment of the retail sector. They employed approximately 2 million employees with an annual payroll of $8 billion. While warehouse clubs and superstores made up approximately 5 percent of this category, they are responsible for 74 percent of the sales. Clubs like Costco and Sam's Club are in the forefront of a new breed of stores, called warehouse clubs or superstores. They give consumers an opportunity to purchase items at a discount and in bulk. They are typically housed in warehouses and are about 60,000 square feet larger than a regular department store or discounter.

With $3.96 billion in sales in 1996, Nashville-based Service Merchandise has been the catalog showroom innovator and industry leader. Founded in 1960 by Mary and Harry Zimmerman, the company grew to over 400 Service Merchandise stores and two Kids Central USA stores in 37 states in 1996. Service Merchandise offered fine jewelry and name brand home furnishings, luggage, electronics, cameras, sporting goods, toys, and juvenile products. The firm employed 28,836 workers. Throughout some difficult retailing times the company managed to show a profit consistently since 1986. However, a recent increase in spending, in order to alter store layouts and offer more high-end products, hurt its bottom line. Net income fell to $39.40 million in 1996, with its lowest net profit margin, 1.2 percent, since 1986. As reported in *Valueline,* company management announced plans to reduce its management ranks by 1,200 to 1,500 employees, which should help it save $15 million per year. In March 1999, Service Merchandise filed for protection under Chapter 11. It closed 130 stores and sold its subsidiary B.A. Pargh. The company is reviewing its structure and recently changed to a self-service format. In 1998 their revenue was reported at $3 billion and recent reports showed a net loss of $70 million for 1999. However, this is good news for the company since it planned for a greater loss than that reported.

In 1995 Richmond, Virginia-based Best Products operated approximately 120 catalog showrooms and 14 jewelry stores in 22 states. Best Products sold brand name merchandise including jewelry, housewares, consumer electronics, sporting goods, and toys. Sales reached $1.4 billion in 1992, most occurring during the winter holiday season. Best Products became private in November of 1988 when it was purchased in a leveraged buyout by New York-based Alder & Shaykin, an investment firm. Working under an extension for filing a Chapter 11 reorganization plan, Best Products began its expansion plan in 1993. By September of that year, the company announced its plans to pay it creditors at least 39 cents for every dollar owed and to increase the debt payments over time. The company closed 41 showrooms as part of its bankruptcy proceedings in 1992. The company emerged from Chapter 11 in June 1994 with a reorganization plan that was intended to trim the company ranks, close more unprofitable locations, and reorganize its stores into specialty outlets. But in 1998, Best Products permanently closed its doors. Unsecured creditors received 87 cents on the dollar for the amount they were owed.

Due to the continued market dominance of discount retailers and the recent introduction of superstores and warehouse clubs, the future growth of catalog showrooms appears to be flat. Customers are frequenting the new superstores on a fairly regular basis and those stores that want to stay competitive need to explore ways to improve customer service and use technology effectively in their store's operation.

FURTHER READING

''Census of Retail Trade.'' *1997 Economic Census.* Available from http://www.census.gov.

''Consumer Shopping Habits Evolve During Course of '90's.'' *Chain Drug Review,* 29 June 1998.

Cusano, Sam. ''Service Merchandise Reports High Numbers.'' *The Tennessean,* 26 January 2000.

Hoover Company Profiles. Available from http://www.hoovers.com.

''Perspectives.'' *Chain Store Age,* 1 February 1999.

Pletz, John. ''Retailers Enjoyed Steller Year in 1999.'' *Austin American-Statesman,* 18 January 2000.

''Retail Sales Edge Up, Signaling Slower Growth.'' *Los Angeles Times,* 14 February 1997.

Retailing Store Industry. *Value Line Investment Survey,* 19 November 1999.

Seckler, Valerie. ''Recasting a Colossus: The New Supercenter Versus the Discounter.'' *WWD,* 12 February 1997.

SIC 5411

GROCERY STORES

This category includes supermarkets, food stores, and grocery stores, primarily engaged in the retail sale of all sorts of canned goods and dry goods, such as tea, coffee, spices, sugar, and flour, fresh fruits and vegetables, and fresh and prepared meats, fish, and poultry.

NAICS CODE(S)

447110 (Gasoline Stations with Convenience Stores)
445110 (Supermarkets and Other Grocery (except Convenience) Stores)
452910 (Warehouse Clubs and Superstores)
445120 (Convenience)

INDUSTRY SNAPSHOT

Some 126,000 establishments comprised the U.S. retail grocery industry in 1998, a 14.9 percent decrease from 1988. Together they recorded sales of $449 billion in 1998, a 36.5 percent increase over ten years. Supermarkets themselves totaled 30,000 stores and $334.5 billion in sales.

The industry continued to consolidate in the late 1990s in response to flat sales and increased competition. Several industry leaders posted decreases in annual revenues while achieving increases in profitability from the sale or closure of underperforming stores. While targeted new store openings were part of all the major retailers' growth strategies, the total number of establishments in the industry continued to decline throughout the late 1990s. Consolidation has also meant renewed interest in both horizontal and vertical integration, and there was a wave of mergers, reorganizations, and acquisitions from the mid-1980s through the late 1990s.

The market share of the traditional grocery store has been eroding due to several trends. For one, consumer lifestyles increasingly tended toward eating outside the home, channeling cash into the foodservice industry at the expense of grocery retailers. As of 1998, U.S. consumers spent 6.7 percent of their disposable income on food-at-home, while 4.2 percent was spent on food away-from-home. According to the U.S. Department of Agriculture this margin will continue to slip as Americans dine out in record numbers. At the same time, grocery retailers faced significant threats in the late 1990s from the expansion of so-called superstores, including such chains as Wal-Mart, Kmart, and Meijer, that offered a full line of groceries in addition to extensive discount offerings in housewares, clothing, health care products, and electronics. These nontraditional competitors were able to lure customers from conventional grocery stores with their lower prices and wider selection of goods.

Grocery retailers responded with new strategies to retain their customer base and revenues. Capital investment in store refurbishment and expansion of retail space comprised part of this strategy, as did price wars. While fighting to hold existing revenues, companies in the industry also sought ways to make the most of what they had by improving efficiency of distribution and management, reducing duplication of labor, closing underperforming locations, and otherwise reducing costs. While payroll expenses and employment costs are down from past years, supplies and utilities have risen slightly.

ORGANIZATION AND STRUCTURE

Like all retail industries, the grocery industry at its most basic, functioned by obtaining goods from distributors and manufacturers, marking up the price to cover costs and to allow for profit, and reselling the merchandise to the general public. Larger grocery chains typically manufactured or prepared a limited line of goods for exclusive sale in their stores. These goods included those prepackaged under a private label, or store brand, and those offered ready-to-eat through in-house bakeries and delicatessens.

The choice of which goods appeared on grocery shelves and how many of each was often highly calculated by both manufacturer and grocer alike. Shelf space, considered a commodity, was purchased by manufacturers and distributors based on the amount of shelf space they wished to reserve for their products. According to *Sales & Marketing Management* of March 1996, the cost of shelf space, called a ''slotting fee,'' might range from $5,000 to $25,000 per product. On the retail side, grocery stores tracked their inventories—frequently using a computer system integrated with their cash registers—to determine the frequency and volume of sales for each product and ordered from their suppliers based on this data. In this arrangement, both manufacturers and retailers sought to maximize the volume of sales by giving ample shelf space to high-volume items while leaving room for lower volume and niche products. Also competing for space were the thousands of new products introduced every year. According to the Food Marketing Industry Speaks 1999, the median number of supermarket items was 40,333.

The grocery industry was dominated by supermarkets, that is, grocery stores with more than $2 million in annual sales. In 1998, there were 30,300 such units, with a total of $334.5 billion in sales and a 77 percent share of the market. This group was subdivided into affiliated independents and corporate chain supermarkets. Their differences lay in their respective financial and organizational structures.

Affiliated independents were characterized by a wholesaler-retailer interdependence. Under the terms of an agreement between the wholesaler and retailer, the retailer took advantage of the wholesaler's purchasing power and had the right to use the wholesaler's name. In return, the wholesaler maintained the retailer's business for products purchased, and also for services provided by the wholesaler. The independent retailers in the United States controlled a 15.9 percent share of the total market volume in 1998, a decrease of 5.9 percent from 1988. These stores reported $71.6 billion in combined sales in 1998.

Affiliated independents were further divided into voluntary wholesaler groups and retailer-owned cooperatives. The former were companies who bought the franchises of independently owned wholesalers. These, in turn, sponsored voluntary groups of independent retailers in their respective communities. Included in this category were supermarkets such as Supervalu and Scot Lad Foods. The retailer-owned cooperative was an association of retailers who organized for the purposes of achieving greater purchasing power and other services. Among these were the Associated Group and United Grocers.

The chain supermarkets continued to control a strong segment of the market. Their combined sales in 1998 amounted to $274.5 billion, or 61.1 percent of total industry sales. Corporate chain retail stores were company operated, and included such well-known outlets as Safeway, Kroger, A&P, Winn-Dixie, Jewel, Publix, and Acme Markets. Because of their size, these firms typically bypassed third-party wholesalers altogether and purchased in bulk directly from manufacturers. No single chain, however, dominated the national market, and none had operations in all 50 states.

Convenience stores made up the majority of units in the industry. They were defined by *Food Retailing Review* in 1993 as ''small, high margin, easy-access stores with a limited line of high convenience items, including staple groceries, nonfoods, and ready-to-heat and ready-to-eat foods.'' There were, in turn, two kinds of convenience stores: stand-alone units and gasoline station units. In the early and mid-1990s, the gas station stores, known as ''G stores,'' held significant advantage over their stand-alone counterparts. Many of the Grocery stores were newer and equipped to market a wider array of foods—including such nontraditional convenience offerings as fresh fruit in some cases—than conventional convenience marts, and all of them shared the advantage of having gasoline customers they could lure into convenience sales. In general, the G stores outperformed stand-alones, leading some stand-alones to pursue niche markets to maintain their customer base. The National Association of Convenience Stores reported that convenience outlets in the United States totaled 95,700 in 1997, up 1.6 percent from 1996. According to the Association, ''the strong shift towards urban store development continued in 1997. More than three out of every four new stores built is located in an area with a population of 50,000 or greater. While urban store development costs dropped 6.2 percent in 1997 to $1.2 million, rural store development broke the million-dollar mark. New rural stores now average $1,027,300 with land costs averaging $272,400, building costs averaging $341,000, equipment costs averaging $347,800, and inventory costs averaging $66,100.''

The industry held relatively few foreign interests outside North America in the late 1990s; however, several corporate chains were held by foreign parents. One major player was Delhaize Freres & Cie. ''Le Lion'' of Belgium, and its new holding company—Delhaize America—which held a controlling interest in the Food Lion chain in 1999. Dutch retailer Ahold NV had a sizable U.S. presence through its acquisitions of First National, Bi-Lo, Giant Foods, Pathmark, and Tops stores. Also as of 1999, a 55 percent majority of The Great Atlantic and Pacific Tea Co. (A&P) was held by Tengelmann Warenhandelgesellschaft of Germany. U.S. holdings in other countries included Safeway's Canadian operations, as well as its interest in the Mexican chain Casa Ley S.A. de C.V, which operated 80 stores in 1999. A&P also had operations in Canada. In a September 1999 press release, A&P CEO Christian Haub reported that company ''market share is also increasing in Ontario, both through internal and acquired growth. Comparable store sales in our operated Canadian stores continue to be among the strongest in the Company. The mostly franchised Food Basics format continues to do very well, including the 10 additional stores converted so far this year. Finally, we have concluded two agreements to acquire a total of 11 stores in Ontario, strengthening our positions in several markets, particularly the Hamilton/Niagara Falls area. While making these acquisitions, we improved our balance sheet during the quarter with a successful offering of 40 year bonds,'' Mr. Haub concluded.

BACKGROUND AND DEVELOPMENT

''The food supermarket was perhaps the single most important innovation in retail distributive institutions in the entire period from 1850 to the present,'' according to Malcolm McNair and Eleanor May in *The Evolution of Food Institutions in the United States.* Supermarkets, particularly chains, were able to achieve greater economies of scale than smaller outfits and were thus able to charge the consumer less while still earning a greater profit margin.

Characterized by carrying a large variety of different food stuffs, dry goods, and health and beauty products under one roof, supermarkets developed in the early 1930s. The expansion of their stock beyond essential food items was encouraged by rising operating costs, particularly rent and wages, influenced by government regulation and union bargaining. Prior to this, food was sold through local ''mom and pop'' grocery stores and chain ''economy stores.'' Faced with competition from supermarkets that undercut them by as much as a third or a half, the old style grocery store chains either converted to supermarkets, were bought out, or went out of business.

Supermarkets provided consumers with lower-priced goods during the Depression. Concentrating less on personalized service and more on bare bones cash and carry, supermarkets emphasized the utilitarian aspects of the business and let the customer do the work of selecting and handling goods. With their emphasis on high stock turnover, supermarkets benefited from the new tendency toward bulk buying, supported by the growing use of refrigeration and the proliferation of cars. The growth of automobile traffic also influenced store location, with placement for traffic convenience becoming a primary concern.

From 1930 to 1950, the industry witnessed radical and far-reaching changes in methods of food distribution. Noticeable changes included increased self-service, the wide expansion of lines, and the great increase in the number and size of stores. Consequently, consumers benefited from greater choice and convenience. Through creative marketing techniques and low competitive prices, supermarket chains, both independently affiliated and corporate, had established themselves as the leading outlet for retail food distribution by World War II.

After 1950, increased competition fostered further developments in the retail food business. The large profit margins that stores had been able to realize were undercut as supermarkets found it necessary to increase print and television advertising and initiate such promotional efforts as trading stamps, games, and contests to win business. These efforts succeeded only in pushing up supermarkets' overhead faster than they could increase gross margins. These percentages narrowed consistently throughout the 1950s and 1960s. By 1954, the United States had 288,000 grocery stores, almost 100,000 fewer than in 1948.

By 1965, supermarkets had won a 71 percent share of all retail food sales, with superettes (stores having annual sales between $150,000 and $500,000 a year) accounting for 13 percent and small stores (sales less than $150,000 annually) 16 percent. It had become evident by the 1960s that an integrated chain of self-service supermarkets could offer consumers a better deal due to their economies of scale. It was also clear, however, that cutthroat competition, which forced chains to keep their price margins low, was wiping out some of these economies.

Supermarkets sought ways to cut their costs even further and found inspiration in the new soft goods discount stores that were starting to appear. These businesses applied the same techniques pioneered by supermarkets to create low-price department stores. Supermarket managers subsequently decided to employ the discount idea in their own businesses. This necessitated abandoning their previous promotional schemes and focusing on price cutting. For consumers, the appeal was immediate, and discount pricing spread throughout the industry.

While the industry was undergoing these transformations, many supermarkets simultaneously endeavored to raise their profit margins by expanding their stock to include more general merchandise. Others bought out existing discount department stores and opened the two kinds of stores side by side or under one roof in strategically located shopping centers. Another development was the trend for supermarkets to ally themselves with discount drug stores.

The net effect of these changes was a gradual decline in the number of general food stores—although the food retailing market saw some increase in the number of specialty stores. The 1972 census recorded 194,000 supermarkets with sales per establishment more than seven times greater than in 1948. By 1996, the number of grocery stores had fallen to 130,000, but sales had grown upwards of $400 billion.

The industry enjoyed moderate sales growth during the late 1980s, although it was not shared uniformly across the industry. According to the U.S. Bureau of Census, preinflation growth between 1987 and 1992 for the industry as a whole was 23.5 percent, which included a 50 percent sales boost in the convenience segment. Supermarkets reported a 22 percent net gain in the same period, while other segments of the industry languished around 10 percent. Different firms in the industry also fared differently in this period—while some chains experienced growth in sales, others such as A&P suffered millions in losses.

Growth in that period was dampened by the recession in the early 1990s, which hit retail grocers especially hard. Already operating under low profit margins due to fierce competition, numerous chains took severe financial beatings because of the austere consumer spending climate. Fiscal weakness helped set the stage for several smaller chains to be acquired by their aggressive large-chain rivals. This consolidation trend continued into the mid-1990s. In 1993, the industry began a slow recovery from its heavy recession losses—so slow that growth was at its lowest point in the past 40 years. From a recent annual high of 7.2 percent sales gains in 1989, growth had plummeted during the recession and then leveled to between 2 and 4 percent through the mid-1990s.

By the mid-1990s the grocery industry had at least shown signs of solid recovery thanks to its ability to remain competitive. Aided by a more robust economy, the industry posted modest gains because of corporate cost savings, horizontal and vertical integration, private label expansion, and innovative marketing. Industry gains in current dollars, however, were often neutralized by inflation, according to the Food Marketing Institute (FMI), which estimated that the industry's modest 4 percent sales growth in 1995 amounted to only 0.7 percent after inflation. Despite this, the FMI noted that some measures of industry productivity had increased in 1995 following three consecutive years of decline. Average sales per labor hour in the industry, according to the FMI, were at $111.40 for 1995 compared to $106.50 in the previous year.

Current Conditions

To remain competitive with such formidable competitors as Wal-Mart, Kmart, and the wholesaler-turned-retailer Supervalu, supermarkets pursued new avenues of growth, including the expansion of private label brands, the introduction of larger stores, and the development of specialty services like delicatessens. Private labels—brands offered exclusively by a particular chain—were seen as opportunities to boost sales growth by providing lower-cost alternatives for shoppers while retaining a greater share of the profit, since private label goods were often manufactured by the supermarkets themselves or under contract by third-party purveyors. According to the Private Label Manufacturers association, ''Store brands now account for one of every five items sold every day in U.S. supermarkets, drug chains and mass merchandisers. They represent a $43.3 billion segment of the retailing business that is achieving new levels of growth every year.'' The 1998 $43.3 billion figure was up from $41 billion in 1997.

The Association also reported that consumer sentiment for private label items was high in 1998. ''For American consumers, store brands are brands like any other brands. In a recent Gallup study, 75 percent of consumers defined store brands as ''brands'' and ascribed to them the same degree of positive product qualities and characteristics—such as guarantee of satisfaction, packaging, value, taste and performance—that they attribute to national brands. Moreover, according to Gallup, more than 90 percent of all consumers polled were familiar with store brands, and 83 percent said that they purchase these products on a regular basis.''

A&P and, for example, continued a heavy push in the late 1990s for its mid- priced America's Choice label, which was offered in addition to its low-cost Savings Plus store brand. *Private Label* reported that the firm intended to offer an in-house brand to reach three separate consumer buying segments through differential branding of its private labels. Owning the manufacturing plants for private labels, however, was not always key to realizing higher profits, as Safeway reported in 1995 that it had closed several of its plants due to poor performance.

New store formats were another major component of the supermarkets' late-decade growth plan. With such competitors as warehouse clubs and the new Wal-Mart and Kmart superstores, having more physical retail space was seen as an advantage. Most of the new store introductions by the supermarket chains boasted greater retail square footage than was typical of existing units in the industry. In 1998, the median average store size was 40,483 square feet, up from 38,600 in 1996. Many of the new stores were much larger than the median, with some reaching upwards of 60,000 square feet. A typical new store in 1998 was just over 57,000 square feet, up from about 52,400 square feet in 1997.

In addition to broader nonfood selections, fresh produce and ready-to-eat dishes were often a focal point of the new stores. Enticing consumers with a wider selection of produce and high-quality, in-house delicatessens, these stores were designed to win back market share from both restaurants and discount superstores that were drawing away traditional grocery business. In the late 1990s, deli revenues were one of the fastest growing segments of total supermarket sales, with 5.79 percent of total store sales.

The larger format supermarkets maximized profits in both food and nonfood offerings. The impetus towards these combination stores was the large profit margins—in the region of 35 to 40 percent—to be made on many of the items they sold, including health and beauty items, deli food, pharmaceuticals, and bakery goods. In contrast, the markup on food and dry goods was only 15 to 20 percent, and stores devoted exclusively to grocery items were purely functional and provided less in the way of "shopping as entertainment."

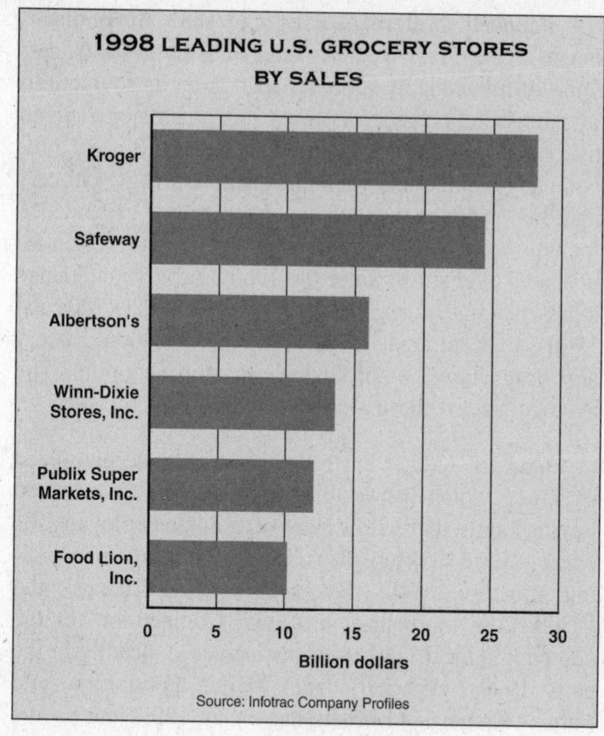

Marketing was also key to maintaining growth in the late 1990s. This did not mean, however, that chains were spending more on advertising. Several chains actually reported decreases in total advertising expenditures as part of broader cost saving initiatives. Several marketing innovations responded to consumer concerns and environmental issues. In 1995, for instance, Safeway launched an "animal welfare charter" on the meats it sold to reassure customers that the livestock had been treated humanely. On a similar note, more stores began to implement sections that contain foods that are natural or organically grown, an attempt to win consumers who are attracted to the growing natural food specialty store segment. Another tool to increase revenues was to dedicate more space to high-volume goods and focus on core product categories that earned the most money. Market research and advertising also supported major private label expansions, such as that of A&P and Kroger.

Large chains have also implemented savings cards to lure more customers. For example, Kroger began offering a "Kroger Plus Savings Card" that allows 'members' to receive special discounts on promotional items without having to clip coupons. Farmer Jack also offers a savings card and teamed up with Northwest Airlines in Michigan in 1999. Consumers now receive points towards airline travel every time they use their card.

The key to maintaining profits into the next decade will be to optimize cost awareness and attract new and existing customers. This industry has had modest growth and is predicted to have only slight growth in the future. Many larger chains have sought growth through acquisition including Albertson's, who purchased American Stores in 1999, and Kroger, who had plans to purchase 74 Winn-Dixie stores in late 1999, and bought Jay C Stores of Indiana in August 1999.

INDUSTRY LEADERS

The grocery business was dominated by the multiunit and regional supermarket chains Kroger, Albertson's, and Safeway. Other companies with a significant portion of the market share included Albertson's, A&P, Winn-Dixie, Supervalu, Publix, and Food Lion.

Kroger Co. With 2,192 supermarkets, 796 convenience stores, 380 fine jewelry stores, and 43 processing plants in 1999, the Ohio-based Kroger operated in 24 states in the West, Midwest, and South. In addition to Kroger stores, the company owned Dillon Food Stores, Fry's Food Stores, City Market, King Soopers, and Gerbes Supermarkets. Its convenience stores operated in 15 states under the names Kwik Shop, Loaf 'N Jug, Mini-Mart, Quik Stop Market, Tom Thumb Food Stores, and Turkey Hill Minit Market. Setting records for sales, operating cash flow, and earnings, the company had sales of $28.2 billion in 1998—a 6.2 percent increase from 1997 and about $4 billion more than Safeway stores, a close competitor. The company employed more than 213,000 people and net income for 1998 was $410.8 million, a slight increase over 1997.

Founded by Bernard Kroger in 1883, the company began as the Great Western Tea Company in Cincinnati, Ohio. It immediately set itself apart from its competitors by being the first grocery store to use print media advertising and to introduce an in-house bakery. By 1902, the company's name had been changedd to Kroger Grocery and Baking Company, and the operation had expanded to include 40 stores in two states. Its growth continued unabated ever since. Since the 1960s, Kroger maintained a presence in the drug store market, and in the 1980s and 1990s, concentrated on operating combination grocery and drug stores, emphasizing one-stop shopping. The average size of these stores was 48,745 square feet.

One of Kroger's strengths was its decentralized structure, which has enabled it to respond to localized buying habits. This allows it to build customer loyalty. Its decentralized structure also allows it flexibility in its pricing structure. Both ''Every Day Low Pricing'' and ''High-Low'' structures are used. Competition for the company's local market shares increased steadily in the early 1990s, especially from Meijer, Food Lion, and Publix. Kroger sold off its more than 100 Time Savers convenience stores in 1994, but as of 1995, the company reported that its convenience store sales per square foot slightly exceeded that of its supermarkets. Nonetheless, convenience sales accounted for just less than 10 percent of Kroger's total sales in 1995. The company relocated, expanded, or opened 116 stores in 1996, increasing overall store square footage by 6.7 percent. The company continued an aggressive growth strategy with plans for acquiring Winn Dixie stores in Texas and Oklahoma in late 1999, and J C Stores in Indiana. Kroger also began its foray into jewelry with its purchase of Fred Meyer Inc. in 1999. In July 1999, Kroger also announced plans with U.S. Bancorp to offer a co-branded credit card to Kroger customers.

Albertson's. The nation's second largest grocery retailer was Albertson's in 1999. Its purchase of American Stores Company in June 1999 launched it into one of the top spots in the grocery industry. The company had $16 billion in sales for fiscal 1998 and a total of 100,000 employees. In 1999, the company ran 2,400 outlets in 38 western, mid-western and southern states including Jewel Osco, Acme Markets, Sav-on, Seessel's, and Super One Foods. Many of its operations are combination food and drug stores, a strategy that Albertson's pioneered.

Albertson's was founded in 1939 in Boise, Idaho. An innovator in the grocery industry, Joe Albertson introduced such services as scratch bakery, magazine racks, home-made ice cream, and automated machines that held donuts. The first store was also the largest of its time—10,000 square feet—eight times larger than typical stores.

Alberston's continued to post profits into the 1980s. The company continued building larger stores, implemented electronic scanning, and offered personalized customer service. In 1988, it opened its first mechanized distribution center in Portland, Oregon coveringmore than 500,000 square feet.

In the late 1990s, Albertson's became one of the leading names in the industry. Withmore than $567 million in net income, plans for growth into 2004 included building 1,850 new stores, and remodeling 730 existing stores.

Safeway Inc. As the third largest supermarket chain in the United States, Safeway had 1998 sales of $24.4 billion. Its employees in 1998 totaled 170,000. Since going public in 1990, California-based Safeway has pursued a course of vigorous expansion that included its 1997 acquisition of the 320-unit California chain The Vons Companies, Inc. In 1998, Safeway operated 1,650 stores, primarily in the West, Southwest, and mid-Atlantic regions. Safeway also had substantial holdings in Canada and Mexico. Like its competitors, Safeway continued to close nonperforming stores and seek other ways to reduce costs. Its efforts succeeded, as net income was $806.7 million in 1998, an increase of 44.7 percent over 1997.

Other Leaders. Winn-Dixie Stores, Inc., Publix Super Markets, Inc, Food Lion, Inc. and the Great Atlantic and Pacific Tea Co. were leading performers for industry sales in 1998. Winn-Dixie, generated $13.6 billion in sales for fiscal 1998, while Publix posted $12.1 billion and Food Lion secured $10.2 billion in sales.

WORKFORCE

In 1998, wages and benefits represented about 13.3 percent of total industry sales. Labor, as a percent operating expense, was 57.5 percent in 1998. The average hourly earnings for nonsupervisory employees was $9.05, up from $7.79 in 1993.

There were 3.5 million workers employed by retail grocers in 1998, a slight increase over 1993 when 3.2 million workers were employed. This level of growth is roughly consistent with previous years, indicating that despite a decrease in the total number of grocery stores in the United States, the industry's workforce has remained stable. By sheer employee count, the workforce was concentrated regionally in the Southeast, mid-Atlantic, Great Lakes, and west coast states, according to the Bureau of Economic Analysis. More than a quarter of the industry's labor was located in the Southeast alone. New England, the Plains states, and the Rocky Mountain states employed proportionately fewer workers in the grocery industry; combined, these regions accounted for just 16.2 percent of the total industry workforce. Labor recruitment remained an issue in the late 1990s, due to low unemployment rates.

The labor pool is expected to decrease for grocery executives as well, due to increased jobs with Internet and other companies. According to the *Progressive Grocer*, ''a myriad of executive recruitment firms, colleges and universities, other retail channels, manufacturers, homegrown executive training programs and old-fashioned networking will become increasingly important in an industry where the shortfall in talent could reach critical proportions in less than a decade.''

Overall, unionization has declined somewhat in the industry. Although supermarket workers remained unionized at many chains, the entry into the market of nonunionized competitors, such as warehouse clubs and discount outlets, pressured the traditional chains to break the power of the unions. The industry has experienced regional strikes in most years of the 1990s. In 1995, Safeway, American's Lucky Stores, and Save Mart stores were targets of a 9-day work stoppage in northern California and Oregon. Profits in 1996 for two of the industry leaders, Kroger and Safeway, were dampened somewhat from a 44-day Colorado strike against both chains. In the same year, Safeway suffered a 40-day walkout at its Canadian stores in British Columbia, where replacement labor was against provincial law and its stores were forced to close until a labor agreement was reached. Safeway's Canadian holdings continued to experience disputes with organized labor into 1997.

RESEARCH AND TECHNOLOGY

The grocery industry is now facing challenges and increased competition due to Internet shopping. For example, according to a November 1999 *Progressive Grocer* article, ''online shoppers now will be able to name the price for their favorite name-brand grocery items. Beginning this month in New York, New Jersey, and Connecticut, Priceline.com—the Internet service that offers airline tickets and other high-priced items at consumers' bids—is licensing its business method and trademark to The Priceline WebHouse Club Inc. WebHouse club members name their grocery store of choice (including A&P, King Kullen and Gristedes) and pick products from more than 140 categories of perishables, non-perishables, canned foods and pet supplies, along with two or more of their favorite brands. Accepted requests are confirmed within 60 seconds and immediately charged to the customer's credit card. The customer then goes to the store to pick up the items.'' Another example of such a site is Homegrocers.com. Along with grocery stores offering shopper friendly sites, third party companies are looking to team up with local grocers to provide services to online shoppers.

Electronic couponing and U-Pons became available in the late 1990s. Many grocery store chains offered printable electronic coupons that are available on company websites. In September 1999, Kroger began offering U-Pons on it website. This electronic form of saving allows customers to select coupons they wish to receive. The coupons are then mailed to the customers address in 3 to 5 business days. Retailers expect that tracking coupon performance will be much easier with this process.

Research in the grocery industry has also focused on technologies to help stores reduce costs and increase efficiencies. Retailers continue to invest in technologies that will improve their accounting, ordering, receiving, and scheduling systems, particularly to integrate these operations—otherwise done on paper in some cases—into a single computer system. In 1998 for instance, Grocer Systems Support software—marketed by GSS—offered programs for inventory control, bill-back tracking, direct buy ordering, shopper tracking and analysis, direct store delivery, cashier security analysis, and accounts receivable analysis.

One of the most revolutionary of these is Efficient Consumer Response (ECR), a scanning system. The system works as follows: a customer selects a product and takes it to the cashier for checkout; the cashier runs the item through the scanner, which records the transaction; the scanner then sends a record of the sale to a central computer system, which itself is networked to the product manufacturer's computer; the manufacturer notes the sale and automatically orders a replacement on a just-in-time basis. An automatic ordering system enables the product's manufacturer to match production with demand using this information about product movement and forecasting techniques. The result is that product production becomes directly linked to consumer demand, obviating the need for the retailer to store large amounts of inventory. When the merchandise arrives at the store, the computer system acknowledges its receipt and issues a computer-generated payment for an electronic fund transfer payment. This eliminates the need for paper invoices and streamlines the accounting process.

The second phase of ECR, crossdocking—moving products from a supplier's truck through the distribution center and onto a store-bound vehicle without putting them into pick or reserve slots as defined by *Stores* magazine—was introduced to reduce warehouse costs and increase service. However, the grocery store industry has been slow to implement this process in comparison to the department store industry. Supervalu opened one of the first crossdocking facilities in 1996, one that the grocery industry looked to as a model. According to *Stores* magazine, ''in order for crossdocking to take root, retailers will need to become more adept at forecasting demand and more confident when making sourcing commitments. Expanded use of advanced ship notices (ASN) and 128 labeling, now in the early stages of implementation, are also crossdocking enablers.'' In 1998, only 15 to 20 percent of grocery items were crossdocked.

On the consumer side, several further technologies were implemented in the late 1990s. Many grocery stores installed at the point-of-sale (POS) various card-scanning devices that allowed customers to pass their credit, debit, or store-issued check cards through the scanner at the counter. Particularly for shoppers paying by check, use of store-issued magnetically encoded identification cards, or check cashing cards, represented a significant convenience over the common practice of requiring the customer to provide multiple forms of identification at the point-of-sale each visit. The results for retailers who implemented such systems were speedier checkout lines, more thorough validation of checks, and a reduction in bad checks being passed.

Stores magazine reported that in 1999 there was a, ''plethora of options—including credit, debit, electronic benefits transfer, smart cards and customer self-checkout—intiating changes in the mission critical front-end POS systems deployed by supermarkets. In an effort to improve customer service, enhance operations, keep pace with their competitors and, above all, lower costs, operators are exploring new payment technology and looking to update POS applications.''

FURTHER READING

Alberton's Inc. Home Page. Available from http://www.albertsons.com.

Food Marketing Institute Information. Available from http://www.fmi.org. ''Grocers Get a Taste of ''Net'' Profits.'' *Shopping Center World,* October 1996.

''Kroger: Earnings News Release.'' Cincinatti, OH: Kroger Co. Available from http://www.ofonews.com/kr/br012397.txt.

Lucas, Allison. ''Shelf Wars: High Priced Space Leaves Entrepreneurs Out of the Aisles.'' *Sales & Marketing Management,* March 1996.

Millstein, Marc. ''Kroger Links Networks to Wireless Technology.'' *Supermarket News,* 31 July 1995.

Reda, Susan. ''Crossdocking: Can Supermarkets Catch Up?'' *Stores,* February 1998.

Reda, Susan. ''Mission Critical: Supermarket Payments.'' *Stores,* February 1999.

Standard & Poor's Industry Surveys. New York: Standard & Poor's Corporation, 1996.

Turcsik, Richard. ''Breaking Out.'' *Progressive Grocer,* November 1999.

U.S. Bureau of the Census. *Annual Retail Trade Survey.* Washington, DC: 1996.

———. *Monthly Retail Trade Survey.* Washington, DC: 1996.

SIC 5421

MEAT AND FISH (SEAFOOD) MARKETS, INCLUDING FREEZER PROVISIONERS

This category includes establishments primarily engaged in the retail sale of fresh, frozen, or cured meats, fish, shellfish, and other seafood. Also included are establishments primarily engaged in the retail sale, on a bulk basis, of meat for freezer storage and in providing home freezer plans. Meat markets may butcher animals on their own account, or they may buy from others. Food locker plants primarily engaged in renting locker space for the storage of food products for individual households are classified in **SIC 4222: Refrigerated Warehouse and Storage.** Establishments primarily engaged in the retail sale of poultry are classified in **SIC 5499: Miscellaneous Food Stores.**

NAICS CODE(S)

454390 (Other Direct Selling Establishments)
445210 (Meat Markets)
445220 (Fish and Seafood Markets)

Individual companies in this industry generated much lower sales than most of its brethren industries. According to the most recent results on Infotrac databases, Murry's Inc. of Upper Malboro, Maryland led the industry in 1997 with sales of $180 million (most industry leaders post sales in the billions); and Detroit-based Cattleman's Inc. followed with sales of more than $125 million for its fiscal year ended April 1996. Houston-based C.B. Jackson placed third in the industry with 1998 sales of $80 million. Performance Northwest of Portland, Oregon generated sales of $78 million for its fiscal year ended June 1998. American Frozen Foods Inc. of Stratford, Connecticut rounded out the top five industry leaders with sales of $70 million for its fiscal year ended April 1998.

The retail meat and fish market industry, like other retail food markets, experienced a steady downsizing throughout the early to mid-1990s, due in large part to competition from supermarkets, superstores, and wholesale clubs that catered to consumers' desire for one-stop shopping and low prices. Total sales for this industry fell from $6.045 billion in 1993 to $5.969 billion in 1996, and sales dropped 6 percent from December 1995 to December 1996.

According to *Dun's Census of American Business,* the number of retail meat and fish markets shrunk steadily throughout the 1990s. There were 27,788 markets in 1993; by 1996 that number dropped to 20,811. The majority of these establishments remained small, employing less than five people. In 1996 about 17,000 markets had 9 or fewer employees; about 3,000 employed between 10 and 50; and roughly 450 markets had more than 50 employees.

In the early to mid-1990s, the majority of meat and fish markets had sales between $100,000 and $500,000. In 1996, 223 establishments had sales between $1,000 and $49,000; 1,572 establishments had sales of $50,000 to $99,000; 6,191 stores had sales between $100,000 and $249,000; 5,123 had sales between $250,000 and $499,000; 2,761 had sales between $500,000 and $999,000; and 3,000 stores had sales above $1 million. Independent meat and fish markets face continued competition from supermarket chains and superstores. The *1994 Industrial Outlook* interpreted the shift in some consumer segments from one-stop shopping to more of "buy as you go" attitude as beneficial to independent retailers. New retail strategies, combined with these consumer changes, could help stores hold on to and increase their market share in this industry.

FURTHER READING

Dun's Census of American Business, 1996 Parsippany, NJ: Dun & Bradstreet, 1996.

Infotrac Company Profiles, 18 February 2000. Available from http://web4.infotrac.galegroup.com.

Monthly Retail Sales and Inventories Report, Washington DC. Available from http://www.census.gov/econ/www/retmenu.html.

Ward's Business Directory of U.S. Private and Public Companies, 1996. Detroit: Gale Research, 1996.

SIC 5431

FRUIT AND VEGETABLE MARKETS

This category includes establishments primarily engaged in the retail sale of fresh fruits and vegetables. They are frequently found in public or municipal markets or as roadside stands. Establishments that grow fruits and vegetables and sell them at roadside stands, however, are classified in a range of agricultural crop production areas.

NAICS CODE(S)

445230 (Fruit and Vegetable Markets)

The retail fresh fruit and vegetable market industry, like other retail food markets, experienced declining sales throughout the early to mid-1990s, largely due to competition from supermarkets, superstores, wholesale clubs, and discount stores. An additional competitor was the newly classified "G" stores: operated by large gasoline companies, they offered a mix of items including fresh fruit and vegetables. The total number of establishments in this industry fell from 8,372 in 1996 to 8,265 in 1997.

According to *Dun's Census of American Business,* 1997, more than 70 percent of fresh fruit and vegetable markets (a total of 6,060) were small, employing less than four persons, while 1,088 establishments employed between five and nine people. At the other end of the scale, only 41 outlets employed more than 100 people.

In 1997 the majority of fruit and vegetable markets had sales in the $100,000 to $249,000 range. There were roughly 1,120 markets reporting sales under $100,000; 4,228 markets with sales between $100,000 and $249,000; 989 with sales between $250,000 and $499,000; 659 with sales between $500,000 and $999,000; and 749 markets with sales of more than $1 million. Leading companies in this industry are Fresh America, Corp., based in Houston, Texas; Capitol Foods, Inc of Memphis, Tennessee; and Norman Brothers Produce, based in Miami, Florida.

FURTHER READING

Dun's Census of American Business, 1996. Parsippany, NJ: Dun & Bradstreet, 1997.

U.S. Bureau of the Census. *Monthly Retail Sales and Inventories Report.* Washington, DC. Available from http://www.census.gov/econ/www/retmenu.html.

Ward's Business Directory of U.S. Private and Public Companies, 1996. Detroit: Gale Group, 1999.

SIC 5441

CANDY, NUT, AND CONFECTIONERY STORES

This category includes establishments primarily engaged in the retail sale of candy, nuts, popcorn, and other confections.

NAICS CODE(S)

455292 (Confectionary and Nut Stores)

According to *Dun's Census of American Business,* there were 10,176 of these kinds of stores in 1996; by 1997 the total number of establishments dropped to 9,939. In 1997, a majority of the stores in this classification (6,580) employed less than five people. Another 2,133 employed between five and nine. Only 23 stores employed more than 100 people.

In 1997, most of the businesses in this classification were small, generating sales between $100,000 to $249,000. That year, there were 2,860 such establishments, down slightly from the previous year, when 2,989 companies reported sales in this range. The next largest category was establishments reporting sales between $50,000 and $99,000. There were 2,300 stores in this range in 1997, up from the 2,200 stores with sales in this range in 1996. There were 940 with $250,000 to $499,000 in sales in 1997 while 863 reported sales of $1,000 to $49,000. In 1996, 1,103 companies reported sales of $250,000 to $499,000, while 909 reported sales of $1,000 to $49,000. Finally, the smallest categories were at the high end of the industry. In 1996, 882 stores reported sales between $500,000 and $5 million; in 1997, 795 were listed. The smallest category, however, was consistently in the $5 million plus range: only 86 businesses reported sales in this range in 1997.

Leading companies in this classification are Fannie May Candy Shops of Chicago, which reported sales of $120.0 million in 1997; Sweet Factory, Inc. of San Diego; and Candy Express Franchising of Columbia, Maryland.

Further Reading

Dun's Census of American Business, 1996. Parsippany, NJ: Dun & Bradstreet, 1996.

Dun's Census of American Business, 1997. Parsippany, NJ: Dun & Bradstreet, 1997.

U.S. Department of Commerce. *Monthly Retail Sales and Inventories Report.* Available from http://www.census.gov/econ/www/retmenu.html.

Ward's Business Directory of U.S. Private and Public Companies, 1999. Detroit: Gale Group, 1999.

SIC 5451

DAIRY PRODUCT STORES

This category includes establishments primarily engaged in the retail sale of packaged dairy products to over-the-counter customers. Ice cream and frozen custard stands are classified in **SIC 5812: Eating Places**, and establishments selling ice cream and similar products from trucks or wagons are classified in **SIC 5963: Direct Selling Establishments.** Establishments primarily engaged in processing and distributing milk and cream are classified in the various dairy products manufacturing industries.

NAICS Code(s)

455299 (All Other Specialty Food Stores)

Cheese stores, milk, butter, and other dairy products stores, as well as packaged ice cream stores, are the predominant types of retail establishments found in this group. Like other retail grocery segments, dairy markets underwent a steady downsizing as supermarkets and superstores eroded market share by offering convenience and lower prices. Overall sales plummeted from $515 million in 1992 to an estimated $141 million in 1996. According to *Dun's Census of American Business, 1997,* there were 7,459 dairy product stores that year as compared to 7,036 in 1993.

Most stores in this classification were small, private companies with less than ten employees. Of the 7,459 total establishments active in 1997, roughly 1,979 had four or less employees, and 1,406 had between five and nine employees. There were 523 establishments that employed between 10 and 14 people, and 503 that had between 15 and 49 employees. Thirty-four establishments employed between 50 to 99 people, while just 35 establishments had more than 100 employees. The largest number of establishments (1,362) had medium-range sales, between $100,000 and $249,000: in 1996, 1,439 establishments had sales in this range. The next largest category reported sales between $250,000 and $499,000. In 1997, 941 establishments were included in this group, compared with 993 units in the previous year. The third largest category was stores with sales between $50,000 and $99,000: there were 562 and 561 stores listed in this range in 1997 and 1996, respectively. A slight increase from the 280 stores in 1996, 332 stores reported sales between $10,000 and $49,000 in the next year. Finally, there were 72 stores listed in 1997 with sales more than $5 million dollars.

Leading establishments in this classification include WH Braum Inc., based in Oklahoma City, Oklahoma, which reported $350 million in sales in 1999; Farm Stores Inc. of Miami, Florida; Yogurt Ventures USA, Inc, located in Atlanta, GA; and Heritage Dairy Stores Inc., headquartered in Thorofare, New Jersey.

Further Reading

Dun's Census of American Business 1996. Parsippany, NJ: Dun & Bradstreet, 1996.

Dun's Census of American Business 1997. Parsippany, NJ: Dun & Bradstreet, 1997.

U.S. Department of Commerce. *Monthly Retail Sales and Inventories Report.* Available from http://www.census.gov/econ/www/retmenu.html.

Ward's Business Directory of U.S. Private and Public Companies, 1999. Detroit: Gale Group, 1999.

SIC 5461

RETAIL BAKERIES

This category includes establishments primarily engaged in the retail sale of bakery products. The products may be either purchased from others or made on the premises. Establishments manufacturing bakery products for the trade are classified in **SIC 2051: Bread and**

Other Bakery Products, Except Cookies and Crackers; SIC 2052: Cookies and Crackers; or **SIC 2053: Frozen Bakery Products, Except Bread.** Those purchasing bakery products and selling house-to-house are classified in **SIC 5963: Direct Selling Establishments.**

NAICS CODE(S)

722213 (Snack and Nonalcoholic Beverage Bars)
311811 (Retail Bakeries)
445210 (Baked Goods Stores)

Unlike other segments of the retail grocery industry that experienced steady loss of market share to competing supermarkets and superstores throughout the 1990s, the retail bakery industry experienced steady growth. According to *Dun's Census of American Business,* there were 30,530 retail bakeries in 1996 and 32,530 in 1997. Retail sales increased from $6.5 billion in 1995 to $6.9 billion in 1999, according to *Ward's Business Directory of Private and Public Companies, 1999.* This growth was attributed to new retailing strategies, new products, and consumers' increased demand for bakery goods. According to Peter Houstle, Vice President of the Retailer's Bakery Association, the ability to merge the independent baker with the supermarket was crucial to the industry's survival. In *Bakery Production and Marketing,* Carol Meres Kroskey wrote that a number of supermarkets opted to house bakeries of regional and national brands rather than expand in-house bakeries. Furthermore, products like the bagel experienced tremendous growth during the mid-1990s, adding significantly to the industry's overall growth.

The majority of stores in this classification are small, employing less than four persons and having sales between $50,000 and $99,000. More than 12,000 stores had sales in this range in 1997, and 2,180 stores reported sales under $50,000. 5,496 stores had sales between $100,000 and $249,000; 2,828 stores had sales between $250,000 and $499,000; and about 2,800 stores reported sales more than $500,000, including 175 that reported sales of more than $5 million.

Winchell Donut Houses of Santa Ana, California, which led the market in 1996 with $94.0 million in sales, dropped to fourth place in 1999 with similar sales. Moving up were Au Bon Pain of Boston, with sales of $237 million, Cinnabon of Seattle, Washington, with estimated sales of $155 million, and Saint Louis Bread Company, Inc. of Westgrove, Missouri, with estimated sales of $116 million.

FURTHER READING

"Can This Bakery Survive?" *Progressive Grocer,* January 1996.

Dun's Census of American Business 1996, Parsippany, NJ: Dun & Bradstreet, 1996.

Kroskey, Carol Meres "Bakery Foods are Hot, Hot, Hot" *Bakery Production and Marketing,* 15 January 1997.

Monthly Retail Sales and Inventories Report. Washington. Available from http://www.census.gov/econ/www/retmenu.html.

Ward's Business Directory of U.S. Private and Public Companies, 1999, Detroit: Gale Group, 1999.

SIC 5499

MISCELLANEOUS FOOD STORES

This industry covers establishments primarily engaged in the retail sale of specialized foods not elsewhere classified, such as eggs, poultry, health foods, spices, herbs, coffee, and tea. The poultry stores may sell live poultry, slaughter and clean poultry for their own account, and sell dressed fowls, or sell fowls cleaned and dressed by others.

NAICS CODE(S)

445210 (Meat Markets)
722211 (Limited-Service Restaurants)
446191 (Food (Health) Supplement Stores)
445299 (All Other Specialty Food Stores)

Industry leader Herbalife International Inc. of Los Angeles, which generated 1998 sales of more than $1.6 billion, foundered in the late 1990s amidst plummeting stock prices and persistent allegations of foul play. From 1985 FDA findings of unsafe ingredients in the company's diet shakes and the California Attorney General's litigation for pyramid scheme practices, to a 1999 privatization bid that has been called self-serving for the board of directors while leaving investors in the lurch, Herbalife's growth, not surprisingly, slowed considerably.

The two biggest natural foods markets, Whole Foods Market Inc. of Austin, Texas, and Wild Oats Markets Inc. of Boulder, California, both launched World Wide Web sites in 1999 to extend their in-store sales. Whole Foods, which placed second in the industry with sales of almost $1.6 billion for its fiscal year ended September 30, 1999, limited its budget for promoting this web site to $3.8 million, relying mostly on in-store ads and incentives to employees for encouraging customers to register with the site. Wild Oats, which placed fifth in the industry with sales of almost $399 million for its fiscal year ended January 2, 1999, hosted a web site featuring real-time inventory and automatic updates to accounting ledgers.

Pittsburgh-based General Nutrition Inc. placed third in the industry with sales of more than $1.4 billion for its fiscal year ended January 31, 1998. Seattle-based Starbucks Corp., placed fourth in the industry with sales of

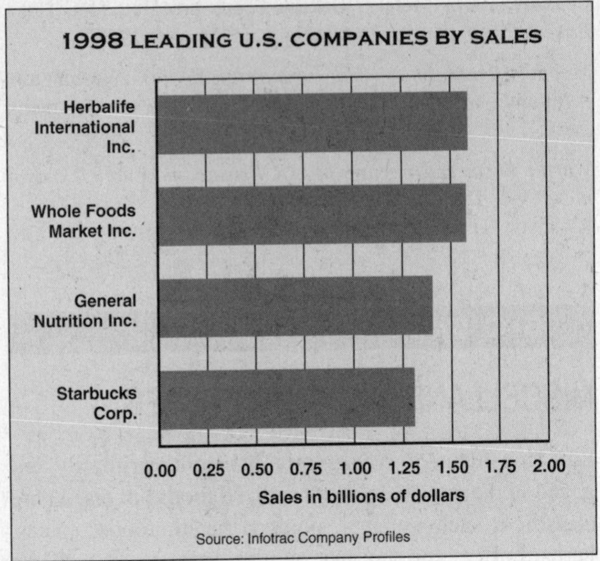

more than $1.3 billion for its fiscal year ended September 27, 1998. The ubiquitous purveyor of upscale coffee could afford to laugh at its portrayal as having taken over the world in the 1999 Austin Powers movie, ''The Spy Who Shagged Me.'' ''We thought that the movie treated our size and identity in a humorous way,'' maintained vice president of publishing George Murphy.

In the late 1990s, the fastest-growing sector of this industry was coffee stores, which typically sell coffee beans, ground coffees, and cups of brewed coffee ready to drink. Coffee stores represented the second largest segment of the industry behind health food and vitamin stores, which accounted for more than half of the estimated 7,900 establishments operating within this industry in 1996. Marianne Wilson wrote in *Chain Store Age* that the tremendous surge in self-care positively impacted the health food and vitamin industry throughout the 1990s. Also represented in large numbers were gourmet food stores and water stores. Together, these stores reported sales of an estimated $3 billion in 1996, averaging about a 4 percent annual rise in sales since 1992.

The gourmet food retail section of this industry was also profitable throughout the 1990s. These food stores are known for their more expensive lines of foods and specialty items not typically sold at regular food stores. Despite higher prices, these businesses performed well during the economic recession of the late 1980s and early 1990s. According to *Progressive Grocer,* these stores weathered the recession because their clientele were not bargain shoppers in the first place, and because, in general, people were going out less and entertaining more at home.

Further Reading

Darnay, Arsen J., and Gary Alampi, eds. *Wholesale and Retail Trade USA.* Detroit: Gale Research, 1995.

Infotrac Company Profiles, 19 February 2000. Available from http://web4.infotrac.galegroup.com.

''It's a Wonderful Herbalife.'' *Business Week,* 1 November 1999.

Karas, Jennifer. ''Wild Oats makes jump from bricks and mortar to on-line ordering.'' *Stores,* February 1999.

Orenstein, David. ''Health Store Rivals Take Different Routes Online.'' *Computerworld,* 26 April 1999.

Ward's Business Directory of U.S. Private and Public Companies, 1996. Detroit: Gale Research, 1996.

Wheat, Alynda. ''One Man's Insult Is Another Man's Publicity.'' *Fortune,* 16 August 1999.

Wilson, Marianne. ''GNC Targets Health and Wellness with Alive.'' *Chain Store Age,* April 1996.

Wold, Majorie. ''Upscale Operators: 'What Recession?''' *Progressive Grocer,* December 1991.

SIC 5511

MOTOR VEHICLE DEALERS (NEW AND USED)

This classification is comprised of establishments involved in the retail sale of new automobiles and light trucks. These establishments are franchised retail outlets for domestic and foreign automobile manufacturers. Products include passenger cars, pickup trucks, and minivans. Many establishments also sell used vehicles, replacement parts, tires, batteries, and other automotive accessories. In addition, many operate service departments.

NAICS Code(s)

441110 (New Car Dealers)

Industry Snapshot

As of January 1, 1999, Automotive News reported 22,076 total new car and light truck dealerships in the United States. Their combined sales totaled more than $300 billion, making the category one of the largest within the retail sector. The number of dealerships operating in 1998 was 22,322. The total was expected to fall below 20,000 early in the 21st century.

New auto sales for 1998 reached a total of 15.5 million units. That total included a little more than 8 million passenger cars and more than 7 million light duty trucks. The light duty truck sales reflected an increase for 1998. The increase in popularity of the light truck market benefited dealerships with higher profits.

The total number of cars in operation continued to rise. The total number of vehicles in use in 1998 was

205 million—nearly 126 million cars and 79 million trucks. Their median ages were 8.3 years and 7.6 years respectively.

The combined effects of a robust national economy and the increased age and number of automobiles on the road brought better conditions to the nation's new car dealers. In 1998, new vehicle sales had climbed to 15.5 million and used cars sales were even higher. These conditions further fueled the acquisition of dealerships by the superstores.

New car dealerships traditionally were comprised of three profit-making departments: new car sales, used car sales, and service and parts. According to the National Auto Dealers Association (NADA), the average dealership profile in 1998 was: new-vehicle department sales were a little more than $14 million, used-vehicle department sales at almost $7 million, and parts and service totaling nearly $3 million. Total dealership sales increased throughout the 1990s.

Organization and Structure

Despite the large numbers of automobiles sold in the United States, auto manufacturers had relatively few customers. Manufacturers' customers consisted primarily of their franchised dealers. Dealerships purchased cars and light duty trucks from manufacturers, and in so doing they obtained ownership of the vehicles. The millions of people who made retail auto purchases were customers of the dealerships, not the manufacturers.

Because the car-buying public made purchases from franchised, individual dealers, manufacturers had no authority to establish fixed vehicle prices. Manufacturers were able only to suggest retail prices because price fixing was forbidden by law under statutes prohibiting the restraint of trade. Dealers, who were independent businesses, were legally free to negotiate selling prices with their customers.

Many new car dealerships were members of the National Automobile Dealers Association (NADA). NADA was formed in the post-Depression era to represent dealers' interests in coping with legislative issues and in negotiating areas of concern with manufacturers. In 1988, NADA members accounted for 79 percent of the nation's dealers. NADA membership steadily increased and by 1992 accounted for 83 percent of U.S. new car dealers, representing about 19,500 franchised new car and truck dealers.

Another organization representing the interests of some automobile dealers was the American International Automobile Dealers Association (AIADA). In 1993, AIADA claimed membership of more than 10,000 American-owned businesses who sold and serviced automobiles with overseas nameplates. AIADA's mission was to represent its members' views on issues such as U.S. trade policy, domestic content requirements, taxes, fuel economy, and antipollution legislation. AIADA also undertook studies of the positive aspects of international automobile trade, focusing on its benefits to U.S. consumers, the national employment situation, and the economy.

Background and Development

Early in the twentieth century, car makers became increasingly proficient at producing automobiles. Mass production techniques necessitated mass distribution, and that developed a system of selling cars through dealers who held exclusive franchises.

During the early decades of the 1900s, market conditions—driven by excess demand and limited supply—left dealers largely unprotected against territorial infringement and forced them to accept whatever conditions a manufacturer offered. Under a typical franchise agreement, a dealer was limited to the selling of a specific line of new cars, usually the products of one company. Dealers were required to accept vehicle quotas, and the quota limit was established by the manufacturer. Dealers were required to pay for cars upon delivery, and manufacturers held the right to cancel dealer franchises.

The preexisting availability of a widespread dealer network helped some of the major automakers become established during their early years. For example, before he entered the automotive industry, William C. Durant (who went on to become the founder of General Motors Corp.) sold carriages and wagons through a network of Durant-Dort dealerships. When Durant assumed control of Buick in 1904, the Durant-Dort dealerships began to sell Buick automobiles. In 1906 they sold 1,400 vehicles, and in 1907 they sold 8,800. Studebaker, another company with prior experience selling wagons and carriages, also entered the automotive industry with a preestablished, widespread network of dealers. Other car manufacturers developed dealership networks by granting franchise rights to independent selling establishments. Most new car dealers also provided repair service for the vehicles they sold. Packard, in 1903, became the first company to offer factory training for repair personnel.

The Ford dealership network developed quickly in response to the popularity of the Model T. By 1914, the company boasted 7,000 dealers. In order to help owners keep their cars running, Henry Ford pressured his dealers to stock replacement parts. The practice became established as an industry standard that others followed.

The practice of making financing arrangements for new car purchases also began during the early decades of the twentieth century. The idea of financing was not unique to cars. Isaac Singer helped increase sales of sewing machines during the middle of the nineteenth century by offering financing. Studebaker embraced the concept in 1911, and General Motors established the General Motors Acceptance Corporation in 1919. Although Henry Ford held a personal bias against granting credit to customers, many Ford dealers offered the service.

By the middle of the 1920s, three out of four new car purchases were made on the installment plan. A typical agreement called for a down payment of one third and the remaining balance to be paid over a 12-month period. In 1925, auto dealers made an estimated $2.5 billion in loans to finance new car purchases. The repossession rate was 2.09 percent.

By the 1920s the practice of trading in an old car and using it as a down payment on a new one was also well established. By the end of the decade, approximately 80 percent of new car purchases involved trading in an old car. Profit on used cars was small, and dealers disliked used cars because they took customers away from the more profitable new car market.

Other changes also occurred within the auto market during the 1920s. While previous decades had seen demand exceed supply, the market became saturated and the supply of new cars began to exceed demand for the first time. Ford, struggling with financial restructuring and facing a depressed market for its products during 1920 and 1921, raised money by shipping unwanted vehicles to its dealers, who were required to buy them or lose their franchises. Although the practice bankrupted some dealers, most were able to sell the extra vehicles and the cash flow enabled Ford Motor Company to survive its crisis.

Ford dealers, however, continued to lose sales during the mid 1920s as Americans shopped around for cars. Other manufacturers had instituted annual model changes featuring innovations and offering speed, comfort, and styling in addition to mere transportation—which had been the Model T's claim to fame. An estimated 70 percent of Ford dealers lost money in 1926 as a result of lagging Model T sales. Ford dealers asked Henry Ford to produce a new model, and in 1927 the company announced plans bringing the Model T era to a close. The Model A appeared for the 1928 selling season.

Enthusiastic interest in Ford's new model netted deposits on 125,000 units, sight unseen. When sample models were manufactured and displayed, the American public gathered to see them. In places where no actual model was available, people lined up to see photographs. According to one estimate, 25 million Americans, about 20 percent of the nation's population, saw a sample Model A at a dealership or special showing within a week of the model's introduction. After the Model A had been offered for two weeks, 400,000 orders had been taken.

Excitement within the industry proved short-lived. The Depression years devastated auto sales. Nationwide, General Motors' dealers sold 5,810 cars during the entire month of October 1932. The figure approximated the number sold on a single weekday during 1929. Some analysts blamed the industry's reliance on credit for the severe impact it felt during the early Depression years. People were simply unwilling to go into debt when the future was uncertain.

Depression era difficulties exacerbated weaknesses in the dealer franchise system. Manufacturers put increased pressure on dealers to sell cars and canceled franchises arbitrarily. As a result of such abuses, dealers formed the National Automobile Dealers Association (NADA). Although NADA initially wielded little power because a lack of unity prevented the organization from making immediate changes, it eventually evolved into the industry's largest trade association.

During World War II, auto makers refocused their energy on providing products for the war effort. With few new cars available, dealers increased their participation in the used car market. Following the war, many people were ready to enter the new car market and demand quickly outstripped supply.

In an effort to help reduce the possibility of runaway inflation throughout the economy, the Office of Price Administration issued an order that all car selling prices had to be held to their 1942 model year levels. At the same time, manufacturers were slow to return to prewar production levels because of problems surrounding the changeover and strained labor relations. Price ceilings combined with curtailed production led to a shortage of vehicles. Dealers took full list price and offered little on trade-ins. Some dealers were criticized for taking advantage of the shortage by offering cars only with extra, high-profit accessories, demanding prices over list, and accepting bribes to make delivery. The situation improved somewhat following the end of price regulations in 1946.

In the postwar years, NADA obtained legislative victories for dealers at the state and national levels. Two principle areas concerned territorial rights and manufacturers' ability to arbitrarily cancel franchises. Prior to World War II only five states protected franchise holders: Wisconsin, Iowa, North Dakota, Florida, and Mississippi. After the war the number increased to 20 states, but enforcement remained difficult. Although franchisee protection laws theoretically safeguarded dealers from arbitrary franchise cancellation and against the practice of being required to accept and pay for unordered shipments, some abuses continued. Territory preservation also remained difficult, as manufacturers established more and more retail outlets in their efforts to increase market share.

The federal government enacted the Dealers Day in Court Act of 1956 to further protect dealerships from detrimental manufacturer actions. Although the law banned coercion and intimidation, it permitted persuasion and urging. Some automotive historians speculated that the statute's principle effect was to urge manufacturers to restructure their relationships with their dealers and avoid future, possibly more demanding, legislation.

In addition to passing laws to protect dealers from manufacturers, Congress also passed laws to protect the car-buying public from dealers. The Monroney Act, for example, required dealers to attach stickers to new automobiles when they were offered for sale. The labels were required to state the suggested retail selling price, specify items considered standard equipment, and list available options along with their suggested prices.

By 1970, 30,800 new car dealerships were operating in the United States. Their numbers, already trimmed from the 47,000 in operation in 1950, began diminishing further. Domestic makes lost market share to imports, car sales slumped during economic downturns, and dealers slashed prices and profits on new car sales in order to move their inventories. Some dealers closed and others merged. Industry-wide consolidation brought decreasing numbers and changing types of new car dealerships. In 1982, NADA reported 25,700 dealers remaining. They included 8,600 small dealers with annual new-unit sales of less than 150, and 3,500 high volume dealers with annual new unit sales in excess of 750. By 1993, the total number of dealerships had diminished further to 22,950. Of these, only 5,300 were small dealers, but the high volume category had grown to 5,700.

The changes within the industry also altered dealerships' revenue sources. Although total sales dollars from new vehicles remained the largest portion of receipts, the new vehicle department no longer represented the largest portion of profit. According to NADA statistics, in 1978 new vehicle departments had represented 74.7 percent of average dealership profit; used vehicle departments accounted for 23.7 percent; and service and parts departments 1.6 percent. By 1985 profit-making segments of dealerships had shifted. New vehicle departments still accounted for most profits, 78.5 percent, but growing service and parts departments were responsible for 14.5 percent. Used vehicle departments represented the smallest portion, 7 percent. By 1992, however, the picture had changed again. NADA statistics revealed that the service and parts department accounted for 66.5 percent of the average dealer's profits. The used vehicle department accounted for 32.5 percent, and the average dealer obtained only one percent of its annual profits from its new vehicle department. Most of that profit was attributed to aftermarket sales such as financing, insurance, and extended service contracts rather than the actual sale of a new car.

During the first two years of the 1990s, auto dealerships faced recessionary conditions. In 1990, the average dealership profit, measured as a percent of sales, stood at only 1 percent, and one out of every four dealerships lost money. NADA reported that the average dealership's new vehicle department operated at a loss in 1990 and 1991 before returning to profitability in 1992. The profits were slim, however, equaling about $3 per new vehicle sold at retail. Although conditions began improving during the end of 1992 and in 1993, industry watchers predicted profit margins would remain low.

To cope with the severe financial conditions, dealerships began restructuring efforts to make more efficient use of capital and to increase employee productivity. One measure was the increased presence of multiple-franchise dealerships. According to NADA, by 1993 more than 30 percent of dealerships belonged to chains and the average dealership had at least two franchises. Although the trend led some analysts to forecast an eventual end to the franchise system, NADA predicted its continuation and a slowing rate of dealer consolidations. At the same time, manufacturers such as Ford Motor Co. and General Motors Corp. launched efforts to shrink the number of dealerships, a move that would increase dealer profitability, allow more attention to service, and help boost brand images.

Megadealers and auto malls were two emerging forces in the industry. Megadealers were those who sold multiple kinds of automobiles either at one location or at several locations. Auto malls were large, single locations offering numerous types of cars. Two types of auto malls were ''enclosed'' and ''open air.'' Enclosed auto malls were typically comprised of the different franchises owned by one megadealer. Open air malls were typically a gathering of independent dealers on adjoining lots. In 1992, there were 117 auto malls in the United States and five in Canada. One auto mall under construction in Nevada was planned to include 20 franchises. Some forecasters estimated that 350 auto malls would be operating in North America by 2005.

Auto manufacturers did not universally accept multiple franchises at a single location. For example, Mitsubishi enforced a policy against the practice. In 1993, five Mitsubishi dealers threatened suit against the manufacturer, claiming that they would go out of business unless they were permitted to combine with other franchises. Mitsubishi claimed that dual franchises produced fewer sales.

Another factor that helped auto dealers begin to recover from the conditions of the early 1990s was falling interest rates. In 1992 new car loans dropped below 10 percent and the average loan length fell to 54.0 months, the shortest since 1987. Falling interest rates also helped dealers reduce floor plan interest expense, the interest they paid on money borrowed to finance cars in inventory.

In their own efforts to increase auto sales, car makers instituted programs that tied dealer sales incentives to Customer Satisfaction Indexes (CSI). NADA reported that dealership spending to increase customer satisfaction succeeded only in creating more demanding customers. In addition, the contests for sales incentives forced dealers to compete with other same brand dealers, thereby cutting profitability. NADA further claimed that a high CSI did not help dealers retain customers, and that 80 percent of the customers who had a loyalty to a particular make of car still shopped comparatively between dealers.

In addition to the diminished profits on new vehicle sales, auto dealers received reduced income on aftermarket items. As manufacturers offered longer warranties, fewer car purchasers opted for extended service contracts. As technology improved rust resistance, fewer buyers bought rust prevention packages. Antitheft systems, however, represented a growing aftermarket category. Systems included numbers etched into windows, starter interrupters, alarms, and radar tracking devices. Antitheft devices were especially popular among buyers using long-term financing. Under long-term financing agreements the amount outstanding during the early years of a loan was often greater than the vehicle's value. To protect car buyers from losses associated with the theft of such cars, manufacturers of antitheft systems often provided guarantees to reimburse owners for insurance shortfalls.

As new vehicle sales departments experienced falling profits and even losses, parts, service, and body departments became increasingly important. In 1992, parts and service profits accounted for almost 70 percent of total dealership profits, with profit margins of 5 to 6 percent—significantly higher than the 1 to 2 percent margins realized in vehicle sales. Because dealer service departments traditionally served vehicles less than five years old, dealers expected the sales slump of 1990 and 1991 to reduce the growth possibility within their service departments. Some losses, however, were expected to be offset by increases created through extended manufacturer warranty work and as a result of the increasingly complex electronic equipment and pollution abatement devices in cars.

To accommodate more customers and increase opportunities to provide service, many dealers were expanding their service hours. By 1992 almost half of all dealers offered hours beyond traditional workday hours. According to a NADA survey, 11.2 percent offered evening hours; 30 percent offered weekend hours; and 8.6 percent offered both evening and weekend hours. The average service department was open 51 hours per week. Some dealerships were also considering opening satellite service centers in residential areas so car owners could have their autos serviced by qualified dealer technicians without sacrificing convenience. A few even initiated home pickup and delivery for vehicles in need of service.

Used car sales provided another growing source of income to new car dealers. In 1989 new car dealerships sold more used vehicles than new ones for the first time since World War II. Used vehicle profits increased 50 percent in 1992. In that year, new vehicle dealers sold 15.1 million used vehicles and only 12.8 million new ones. Net profit on an average used car was $236, compared with an average on a new car of $3. Approximately 65 percent of the used vehicles sold were obtained from trade-ins. The remaining came from sources such as street purchases and auctions. By 1996, used cars had become even more important; new vehicle dealers sold close to 20 million used cars in that year with an average net profit of around $259 versus $77 on each new vehicle sold.

One important category of used car was the "nearly new" car. These cars, called "program cars," were sold by auto makers to rental fleets with guaranteed buy-back provisions. As manufacturers increased subsidies to daily rental companies in an effort to increase sales, the length of time cars were kept shortened. As a result, manufacturers were buying back three- and four-month-old cars with low mileage. Program cars were sold to dealers at auctions and dealers resold them to the car-buying public with warranties intact but at prices often thousands of dollars below new car list prices.

Although many dealers enjoyed the extra per-vehicle profits associated with program cars, they also complained that the practice undermined potential sales of new cars. As a result, auto manufacturers began to cut back on the number of program cars by requiring rental companies to hold cars longer. Program cars peaked at an annual volume of 1.3 million vehicles during the early 1990s and then began declining. In 1993 mileage on program cars was 10 to 12 percent higher than it had been in 1992. As the number of program cars declined, new car dealers turned to other sources to supplement the offerings on their used car lots. These included vehicles from auctions, wholesalers, repossessions, seizures, and lease returns. Lease returns, in particular, had become a primary source of used cars by the mid-1990s, as leasing spread from the corporate to the consumer markets. Franchised new car dealers were particularly well-positioned to take advantage of the boom in used car sales in spite of fierce competition from used car superstores. As NADA president, John Peterson, said at the association's 80th annual convention in February 1997, "There is still plenty of opportunity out there for us, because the future of the used car business is about supply. As franchised new car dealers, we have first access to trade-ins, first access to off-lease vehicles and first shot to buy smart at the auctions.'' A 1996 NADA report confirmed this view, noting that franchised new car dealers were taking in and selling a higher percentage of trade-in vehicles and earning higher gross margins on them than vehicles purchased from other sources. Nearly 50 percent of used car sales in the first nine months of 1996 involved a trade-in to the selling dealer, compared to 38 percent in 1982.

Industry watchers expected used vehicle departments to continue providing a significant contribution to dealership profits. Economic factors, such as slow growth, stagnating family income, and the ever-increasing price of new vehicles, were expected to keep a larger segment of the population out of the new car market. In 1996, for example, the average selling price of a new vehicle was $22,000, compared to $11,600 for a used vehicle. In addition, used vehicle certification programs, manufacturer interest in protecting residual values, and a greater emphasis on brand loyalty combined with the increasing quality and reliability of cars, served to enhance the image of used cars, and, therefore, made them more acceptable to former new car buyers in the used car market.

Another challenge facing automobile dealers was improving public perception and countering negative stereotypes based on past practices and abuses. NADA reported spending $1 million to develop a program aimed at helping dealers market themselves and their products, as well as to promote ethical and moral business practices. The program, launched at NADA's 1992 convention, provided sales training and certification in an effort to bring increased professionalism to the industry.

One area identified as a potential cause of negative impressions was the practice of bargaining over car prices. Because sales people traditionally sold cars on a commission basis, buyers sometimes felt they were being pressured to make purchases or given incorrect or misleading information. As a result, some dealers began switching to one-price selling during the early 1990s. Although one-price selling was not a new concept, its popularity flourished after it was embraced by General Motors's new Saturn division. Under one-price policies, dealers put a nonnegotiable price on a car and, theoretically, did not bargain. In practice, sticker prices fluctuated according to ever-changing market conditions and bargaining occurred over the value of trade-ins, accessories, and sometimes the actual vehicle price.

According to a report published by *Automotive News,* the number of dealers instituting one-price selling policies was increasing. In 1992, 1,665 dealers were ''no-haggle'' dealers, up 70.8 percent from 1991. Their numbers were expected to reach 2,265 in 1993. Sometimes in making the switch, dealerships replaced their commissioned sales people with salaried ''sales consultants'' or ''greeters.'' Dealers adopting one-price selling policies expected to improve customer loyalty through building better human relationships.

Another trend observed during the early 1990s was toward short-term leasing. As Richard Strauss, former president of NADA, explained in *Automotive News,* ''Retail leasing is changing the industry. Two-year leases are good for the manufacturers, dealers and the customers because they shorten the trade-in cycle. We have to find ways to make cars more affordable.'' Strauss pointed out that a 24- to 36-month lease returned customers to the dealership a lot quicker than 48- to 60-month financing plans. Off-lease cars also provided used cars for dealer-owned used car lots.

In addition to the challenges of changing economic times, dealerships confronted changing environmental regulations. The Environmental Protection Agency (EPA) provided guidelines regarding toxic wastes, emissions of volatile organic chemicals (VOCs), and the handling of chlorofluorocarbons (CFCs). In 1992, new EPA rules were adopted to exempt dealers from future liability regarding subsequent off-site oil spills. The regulations came after some dealerships who had sent waste oil to other companies for disposal or recycling were charged for cleanup costs at toxic waste sites.

New EPA rules concerning the release of VOCs from auto paints were expected to limit the availability of paint colors and increase labor and training costs. EPA rules about CFC recycling mandated technician certification to service air-conditioning units. The cost of industry compliance was estimated at $15 million. Other environmental regulations focused on proper disposal of gas, diesel fuel, antifreeze, degreasers, and brake fluids.

Current Conditions

In the late 1990s, the auto industry experienced many consolidations by manufacturers (Daimler-Benz A.G. and Chrysler Corporation, November 1998 and Ford Motor Company's purchase of Volvo Car, March 1999) and by new car dealers.

The decline in the number of franchised dealers, to 22,076 in January 1999, indicates that the dealership base was transforming to larger, well-financed companies. These modern dealerships' goals were to reach high unit volume. Since they were multifranchised dealers, they tried to increase their opportunity for a sale by lumping together different franchises on one large property.

At the close of the 20th century, the push to change the format for retailing automobiles was encouraged by U.S. manufacturers themselves. Ford Motor Company instituted *Auto Collection*, a retail venture, which they hoped to build into a national retail name. Their intentions included building multibrand superstores with large inventories, consolidating all Ford, Lincoln, Mercury and Mazda stores in a market under a single ownership group, open satellite service centers with extended hours to compete with quick-oil-change shops, and switch dealerships to one-price selling. Typically, the transformation took place by dealers selling their stores to a new company and then Ford Motor and the dealers taking shares in the new venture. One dealer was then put in charge and the others often took other positions in the company.

The Ford Retail Networks operating in the United States in early 1999 were in Tulsa, Oklahoma and Oklahoma City, San Diego, Salt Lake City, and Rochester, New York. Ford enlisted Republic Industries, Inc. as an equity partner in the Rochester, New York Auto Collection project. The retail network consisted of nine dealerships and was operated by Republic, but Ford Motor Company remained the majority shareholder.

In October 1999 General Motors announced its plan to enter the retail business. General Motors dealers thought that this was a declaration of war on independent dealers. The underlying factor behind GM's plan was to keep GM vehicles away from large dealer groups like AutoNation, Inc. GM feared their product would suffer when treated like a commodity by these superstores.

General Motors dealers felt that GM, after they analyzed the problem, came up with the wrong solution. GM looked to support from their dealers emphasizing the threat by megadealers, but the dealers saw GM as the threat. The independent dealerships believed that factory stores would have an unfair advantage over them and threatened their existence.

The National Automobile Dealers Association (NADA) planned to lobby legislators to pass or tighten state laws that restrict automakers from selling their vehicles without a licensed dealer. Laws in 26 states restrict or ban automakers from owning retailers of their vehicles. In November 1999, after GM dealerships mobilized, General Motors halted their dealership plans.

In December 1998, the first Goodwrench Service Center opened in Houston, Texas. The dealer-owned GM-sanctioned service center, was a satellite operation separate from, but located near the parent dealership. The dealers would pay for the centers, which varied in price, depending on the real estate. Dealership's service business generally consisted of vehicles that were new to five years old. The centers would specialize in light repairs and maintenance that could be completed in two hours maximum. The satellites were open nights and weekends and serviced all makes and models. Warranty work was still done at the main dealership. The centers were designed to expose dealers to a new market. According to the Motor and Equipment Manufacturers Association in 1998, the retail market for parts and service was $159 billion.

Industry Leaders

In 1998, AutoNation, Inc. was the largest automotive retailer in the United States. Their sales for 1998 included 286,179 new retail vehicles, 161,424 used, and 162,283 in fleet sales. These combined sales brought unit totals for 1998 to 609,886. In 1999, AutoNation had more than 400 automotive franchises in 23 states. Their revenue from all departments in 1998 was $13.5 billion.

United Auto Group, Inc. was ranked second in 1998, up from their 1997 ranking of fourth. Their total units sold in 1998 was 124,127. This figure was comprised of new retail units of 77,403 and used car totals of 46,724. Group revenue from all departments in 1998 was $3.3 billion. On April 12, 1999, Penske Capital Partners agreed to purchase the controlling share of United Auto Group, Inc. with Roger Penske to be the chairman.

Workforce

According to statistics compiled by the Bureau of Labor Statistics, new-car dealers employed 1.1 million workers in 1997, up 3.5 percent over 1996. At the beginning of 1999, NADA reported the average dealer employed 47 employees, while an auto group like AutoNation, Inc., formerly Republic Industries, Inc., employed 56,000 people.

Research and Technology

As the 1990s were coming to a close, the first Internet dealers were emerging. CarOrder.com planned to purchase three franchises with the intent to expand to a chain of 100 "e-dealers." Internet retailing would be the entire focus of the company, which defined "e-dealer" as a retail outlet that serves primarily as a distribution and service point for new vehicle sales.

Microsoft Corporation and Ford Motor Company, in a joint venture, said they would change the CarPoint web site into an instrument that the public could custom order and track delivery of new vehicles. Starting out, shoppers on the site would be able to check inventory at dealerships, monitor a vehicle's progress during shipment by truck or rail, and check on assembly plant schedules for the current 10-day period. The plan was to let buyers, by mid-2001, put together their vehicles under Ford guidelines, and then send the order into the automaker's sales and production banks. The system would move Ford Motor Company toward a true build-to-order manufacturing system. Ford and Microsoft claimed the new CarPoint would not eliminate dealers from the sales transaction.

Ongoing research and technological advancements within the dealerships focused on advances in computer systems to help sell and repair cars. General Motors was developing a computerized system using video, graphics, and financial data to answer questions and pinpoint products for customers based on individual preferences. The system relied on GM's Pulsat satellite network to provide daily updated information. GM began testing the program in 1993 and expected it to be available for general distribution in 1994. Other auto makers were developing similar systems.

Advanced computer technology was increasingly being used in service departments. As more vehicle functions were controlled by electronics, test equipment was needed to diagnose problems and communicate with repair technicians. Computerized information assisted in estimating repair costs, replaced bulky printed manuals, and made service bulletins more readily accessible. Another computerized diagnostic system under development was designed to be installed on a vehicle to monitor its operation and help technicians identify the causes of intermittent problems when they could not be duplicated in the service facility.

The rise of the Internet in the mid-1990s offered dealers a new marketing channel. Web sites could easily list a dealer's entire inventory, complete with color photos and full vehicle descriptions. A majority of web site customers used the Internet to gather information, but preferred to stay with a hands-on purchase.

FURTHER READING

Automotive News. ''Dealer Data.'' *1999 Market Data Book.*

Child, Charles. ''GM Taking on Used-Car Giants.'' *Automotive News,* 11 December 1995.

''Classy Used Chassis: Americans Are Becoming Big Fans of Pre-Owned Vehicles.'' *American Demographics,* July 1996.

Couretas, John. ''CarPoint Is Eager to Accept Net Orders.'' *Automotive News,* 27 September 1999.

Couretas, John. ''Trilogy's Web Buying Service Plans 'E-dealers' Chain.'' *Automotive News,* 1999. Available from http://www.auto.com

''Dealers Alive and Well and Changing with the Times, Says NADA's Peterson.'' National Automobile Dealers Asscociation (NADA) Press Release. McLean, VA: February 1997.

Detroit Free Press. ''GM Halts Dealership Plan.'' 2 November 1999.

English, Bob. ''Canada's Dealers Are at a Crossroad.'' *Automotive News,* 1 February 1999.

''Ford's Retail Network.'' *Automotive News,* 1 February 1999.

''Groups Grow.'' *Automotive News,* 1 January 1999.

Harris,Donna. ''Buyer's Market.'' *Automotive News,* 1 February 1999.

———. ''Everything to Everyone.'' *Automotive News,* 1 February 1999.

———. ''Group Struggles to Find Direction in its Response to '99's Biggest Issue: Factory-Owned Dealerships.'' *Automotive News,* 1 February 1999.

Healey, James R. ''Car Buying Sites on Net Take Turn for Best Services.'' *USA Today,* 3 September 1999.

Lira, Guillermo. ''Light Vehicle Sales Up 32 Percent in Mexico.'' *Automotive News,* 1 February 1999.

Miller, Joe. ''Dealers Vow to Fight GM.'' *Automotive News,* 4 October 1999.

Moran, Tim. ''Futurist Sees Constant Links to Net for Cars.'' *Automotive News,* 27 September 1999.

''New Car Dealerships' Revenue Tops the Half Trillion Mark, NADA Finds.'' National Automobile Dealers Association (NADA) Press Release. McLean, VA: 17 March 1997.

''New-Car Dealers Join National Effort to Improve Vehicle Air Bag Safety.'' National Automobile Dealers Asscociation (NADA) Press Release. McLean, VA: 22 November 1996.

Petersen, Scot. ''Psst! Hey, Buddy! Wanna Buy a New Car?'' *PC Week,* 30 August 1999.

Sawyers, Arlena. ''Service Centers Put GM in a New Market.'' *Automotive News,* 1 February 1999

''Trade-In Sales Up, Boosting Profitability at New-Car Dealerships, Says NADA.'' National Automobile Dealers Asscociation (NADA) Press Release. McLean, VA: 10 December 1996.

U.S. Bureau of Labor Statistics. ''New & Used Autos.'' 1997.

U.S. Department of Labor. Bureau of Labor Statistics. *The Monthly Labor Review,* August 1999.

Wernle, Bradford. ''Used Cars Will Take Bigger Bite of Market, Analyst Predicts.'' *Automotive News,* 8 May 1995.

Whitford, Marty. ''It's a Bigger World Since He Sold to UnitedAuto.'' *Automotive News,* 8 February 1999.

SIC 5521

MOTOR VEHICLE DEALERS (USED ONLY)

This category covers establishments primarily engaged in the retail sale of used cars only, with no sales of new automobiles. These establishments also frequently sell used pickups and vans at retail. Establishments who sell both new and used cars are classified in **SIC 5511: Motor Vehicle Dealers (New and Used).**

NAICS CODE(S)

441120 (Used Car Dealers)

INDUSTRY SNAPSHOT

The National Independent Automobile Dealers Association (NIADA) reported that there were 58,750 independent dealers in the United States in 1998. They went on to say that the independent dealers had 24 percent of the used car market. The average price of the used vehicles they sold was $7,172. NIADA also stated that 52 percent of the independent dealer market procures credit through finance companies and that they account for 49 percent of buyers at auctions. In the United States, retail sales of used vehicles total approximately $300 billion annually.

Many independent used-car dealers belong to NIADA, which reported that its members sold between one and two million vehicles annually and that the average used-car dealer has been in business for more than 22 years.

Background and Development

The used-car industry grew out of the automobile manufacturing industry. Technically, every new car became a used car as soon as it was driven. When manufacturers began encouraging their customers to trade in old cars and purchase new models, used cars became increasingly available. By the mid-1920s, used-car lots were a part of the American landscape.

The abundant availability of cheap used cars made car ownership within reach of almost everyone. In 1927, the average four-year-old ''basic transportation'' car sold for approximately $100, and although low income families were unable to buy new cars, even on installment, approximately 64 percent of American families did own an automobile of some kind.

During the Depression years, sales of new cars plunged, but car usage declined only slightly. In 1929, 26,704,825 vehicles were registered. The number fell to a low of 24,159,203 in 1933. People kept their cars longer and looked to the used-car market when replacement was necessary. Used cars and trucks also served to carry thousands of displaced farmers from the Dust Bowl region into California.

As the nation emerged from the Depression, car sales increased. Vehicle registrations in 1937 topped the 30 million mark. Strengthening new car sales served to fuel the used-car market. In 1938, the nation's first automobile auction was held in South Carolina; the first car auctioned was a 1932 Ford Model A.

Used cars also played an important role during World War II. During the war, production of civilian automobiles halted, and once again people held onto their cars as long as possible. Sales of parts soared, and as cars wore out, people turned to used-car dealers for replacements. Used-car prices were controlled by the Office of Price Administration, but according to automotive historian, Stephen W. Sears, ''under-the-table dealing frequently raised the price of old clunkers to more than they had cost new.''

Following the war, auto manufacturers were slow to return to full production and demand for cars was high. The shortage enabled used-car dealers to continue the brisk business they had enjoyed during the war. By 1948, the number of vehicles on American roads exceeded the number of American households.

Short supplies and heavy demand led to abuses within the industry. During the 1950s legislative efforts were made to protect buyers from unscrupulous dealers. Most states passed laws requiring dealers to give potential buyers accurate information regarding the condition of vehicles. Laws were also enacted prohibiting tampering with odometers.

To help handle the volume of used cars in the American marketplace, auto auctions expanded. During the 1970s, there were approximately 180 auctions throughout the country. Until new car dealers increased their participation in the nation's auction network during the late 1980s and early 1990s, auctions were attended almost exclusively by used-car dealers. In 1980, Americans purchased 23.1 million used vehicles.

Most new cars were eventually sold on the used-car market. According to a study undertaken by the Federal Highway Administration in 1984, average vehicle ownership was 7.2 years, but average vehicle lifetime was 12 years. A typical vehicle's lifetime mileage totaled 120,000 miles.

Federal legislation aimed at protecting used-car buyers was enacted in May of 1985, but not enforced until 1987. Under the terms of the so-called ''Used Car Rule'' dealers were required to post window stickers called ''Buyer's Guides'' describing a car's warranty. The stickers were required to state whether the car came witha full warranty, a limited warranty, or if the car was sold in ''as is'' condition with no warranty. The Buyer's Guides were legally part of the used-car sales contract and superseded any other claims. In addition, many states added protections, claiming that ''as is'' sales contracts carried implied warranties that cars were drivable.

Governmental agencies also addressed the problem of odometer tampering. In 1985, federal officials and the Pennsylvania Attorney General's Bureau of Criminal Investigation began an investigation into an odometer fraud scheme. Participants were accused of setting back mileage readings and fraudulently obtaining altered titles. The practice permitted unethical dealers to purchase low-cost, high-mileage cars and sell them at substantial profits.

During the early 1990s, as the U.S. economy experienced sluggish conditions, used-car sales surged. For the first time since World War II, sales of used cars and trucks surpassed sales of new vehicles at new car dealerships. In 1990, an estimated 32.1 million used vehicles were purchased from dealerships, used-car dealers, and through private transactions.

Legislative control over used-car sales also continued during the early 1990s at both the federal and state levels. In 1992, Congress passed a law requiring that all states use the same information on titles. One item of concern was the inclusion of permanent salvage brands on auto titles in all 50 states. The bill created a federal task force to focus on eliminating "title washing," a fraudulent procedure which cost U.S. consumers an estimated 3 billion annually. Title washing occurred when unethical used-car traders were able to purchase salvage vehicles and transfer them to a state that did not require a salvage notation on the title. Cars were rebuilt, retitled, and transferred back with clean titles.

CURRENT CONDITIONS

Used-car dealers obtain their vehicles through a variety of outlets. Chain and independent auto auctions offer vehicles retired from rental fleets. Auctions also make consignment sales on behalf of new car dealerships and insurance companies. Dealership cars most frequently came from trade-ins and insurance company offerings resulting from totaled or theft recovered vehicles. Other sources of used cars include street purchases, purchases of government owned vehicles, repossessions, and seized vehicles.

Some used-car dealers sold cars to customers who made traditional arrangements for financing. Others provided their own financing to customers who were typically unable to arrange for conventional financing either because they were unable to make a sufficient down payment or because they were judged a poor credit risk. Used-car dealers who provided financing were sometimes referred to as "note lots." Note lots charged high interest rates to cover the expenses associated with high default levels.

The popularity of leasing new vehicles provides a steady supply of cars and trucks to the used-car market. The addition of late model cars and trucks increases the public's interest to purchase a used car. The improved quality and reliability of used cars and trucks along with the monetary savings of purchasing them expanded the used-car market to 40 million transactions a year.

The strength of used-car activity brings large franchise dealers into the market. Used-vehicle superstores use a "no-haggle" one-price sales approach in their retailing philosophy. Used-vehicle retailing had been a highly fragmented industry that, historically, had no single market share leader—the megastore concept changed that.

Advanced computer technology offers many possibilities to the used-car industry. One system under development is designed to help match buyers with available cars. Called the Vehicle Information Network, the system permits used-car dealers to list vehicles for sale. Car shoppers can call a toll free number to get a list of cars matching their needs. The system is funded through a fee charged to the dealers, and although it is not expected to take the place of more traditional forms of advertising, the possibility has promise as a supplemental form of advertising.

Computers are also being used to track car inventory costs. Some dealers feel that charges for items such as detailing and repairs are easily overlooked during the negotiating process. Computer programs help ensure that all expenses associated with a particular vehicle are considered and that a sale is profitable. In addition, computer software helps determine which cars sell the fastest, which are most profitable, and which are not moving. Another specialized software package helps appraise special interest vehicles such as antiques and other collector cars.

A different type of computer technology is used to develop diagnostic equipment. Dealers can more precisely determine the mechanical condition of cars on their lots and even offer printouts of specific tests to potential customers. One diagnostic tool expected to be perfected uses ultrasound testing to determine if a car has been repaired by "clipping," a procedure in which the vehicle is cut in half and the damaged half is replaced with parts from the same type of automobile.

INDUSTRY LEADERS

AutoNation, Inc. was the largest automotive retailer in the United States in 1999. *Fortune Magazine* named it the fastest growing company in America. In 1998, AutoNation entered the Fortune 500 list at number 151 and jumped to number 83 in the 1999 Fortune rankings. AutoNation's revenue was more than $16 billion in 1998, an increase from 1997 revenues of $9 billion.

CarMax was a subsidiary of Circuit City Stores, Inc. in 1999. CarMax generated sales of $874.2 million in fiscal year 1998. In June of 1999, it had 30 used-car superstores in operation. The superstore, located at U.S. Route 1, just north of Laurel, Maryland, is the nation's largest used-car retail location.

AMERICA AND THE WORLD

The slow economic conditions in the United States during the late 1980s and early 1990s also affected other parts of the world. Just as used-car sales increased in the United States during times of economic adversity, they followed the same pattern elsewhere. In the United Kingdom, for example, sales of used cars increased 24 percent between 1988 and 1990; sales of new cars during the same period grew by only 18 percent. The increasing presence of used cars on the market in the United Kingdom earned them almost half (48 percent) of all U.K. car sales as measured by value.

In other parts of the world, political unrest coupled with ailing economies increased demand for used cars. In Eastern Europe, following the dismantling of the Soviet Union, the used-car market grew as demand for automobiles outstripped supply and new car prices rose beyond the reach of many workers.

RESEARCH AND TECHNOLOGY

General Motors was the first manufacturer to enter the used-car business and their Internet site could be a prototype for outlets nationwide. They chose Houston, Texas for this project because it was the fourth largest used-car market in the United States. Studies showed that Houston residents were also very open to Internet use. The web site contained descriptions and set prices along with pictures of the car. Customers, after giving a refundable $100 deposit, could set up an appointment to test drive the vehicle and, if desired, buy it on the spot.

FURTHER READING

ADT Automotive. *Used Car Dealer* "National Automobile Dealers Association (NIADA)." Available from http://www.niada.org

AutoNation. "About Us." Available from http://www.autonation.com

Auto Trader. "About Auto Trader." Available from http://www.autotrader.com

CarMax. "New-Car Franchise in the Washington/Baltimore Market." Available from http://www.carmax.com

Child, Charles. "GM Taking on Used-Car Giants." *Automotive News,* 11 December 1995. src]"Classy Used Chassis: Americans Are Becoming Big Fans of Pre-Owned Vehicles." *American Demographics,* July 1996.

"Fortune 500, 1999." *Fortune.* Available from http://www.fortune.com

"GM Finally Starts On-Line Retailer." *Detroit Free Press,* 18 November 1999.

Taylor III, Alex. "Driven Only on Sunday (Demand Shifts from New to Used Cars)." *Fortune,* 26 June 1995.

U.S. Bureau of the Census. "Merchandise Line Sales." *1987 Census of Retail Trade.* Washington, DC: GPO, 1990.

Wernle, Bradford, "Used Cars Will Take Bigger Bite of Market, Analyst Predicts." *Automotive News,* 8 May 1995.

Whann & Associates. "The National Independent Automobile Dealers Association." Available from http://www.niada.com

SIC 5531

AUTO AND HOME SUPPLY STORES

This classification comprises establishments primarily engaged in the retail sale of new automobile tires, batteries, and other automobile parts and accessories. Frequently, these establishments sell a substantial amount of home appliances, radios, and television sets. Establishments dealing primarily in used parts are classified in wholesale trade, **SIC 5015: Motor Vehicle Parts, Used.** Establishments primarily engaged in both selling and installing such automotive parts as transmissions, mufflers, brake linings, and glass are classified in services, industry group 753 (Automotive Repair Shops).

NAICS CODE(S)

441320 (Tire Dealers)

441310 (Automotive Parts and Accessories Stores)

INDUSTRY SNAPSHOT

As a group, auto and home supply retailers participate in what is commonly referred to as the automobile aftermarket, a term referring to all the parts and services needed by motor vehicles after they leave the manufacturing plant. This broadly defined market includes the manufacturing and sale of fuel, lubricants, tires, batteries, brakes, accessories, and a host of other products used to maintain or heighten an automobile's performance, or simply to improve its appearance. Additionally, the automobile aftermarket encompasses the installation or servicing of these products.

This multibillion dollar market includes various types of retailers other than auto and home supply stores, such as oil companies, rubber companies, service stations, discount wholesalers, and department stores, all of which control a portion of the automobile aftermarket. Moreover, auto and home supply retailers, as defined by the *Standard Industrial Classification Manual,* participate in only a portion of the automobile aftermarket. They do not generate revenue from the sale of fuel, nor do they derive the bulk of their revenue from selling and installing transmissions, mufflers, brakes, or windshield glass. These establishments generally are franchised or independent stores devoted entirely to selling, installing, or servicing a strictly limited number of automobile parts, such as the Midas brake and muffler chain, or Minit Lube, a chain specializing in lubricating automobiles.

Although consigned to a share of the automobile aftermarket, by both other retailers and the parameters of the *SIC Manual,* auto and home supply retailers generate an aggregate revenue measured in billions of dollars, the size of which is augmented by sales garnered from the industry's other focus, home supplies. These products generally consist of goods such as refrigerators, television sets, radios, or essentially any item a retailer believes consumers will purchase. Although the combination of auto parts and home appliances under one roof seems an odd mix, the inclusion of home supply products in auto parts retail stores has roots stretching back nearly to the genesis of the auto parts industry itself. Intended to complement the revenue realized from the sale of auto parts, home supply products historically have played an integral role in the performance of auto and home supply stores.

Within the auto and home supply industry, there are several types of retailers, some selling only one product such as tires, while others concentrate on one particular segment of the automobile aftermarket, such as vehicle accessories. ''Speed Shops'' are an example of the latter, offering products to increase, as their name suggests, the performance capabilities of a vehicle, which also can include an assortment of decorative merchandise. Some large tire manufacturers, such as Goodyear and Firestone, also operate retail stores devoted solely to selling their products, while the same is true of battery manufacturers.

On a broad level, the fortunes of the auto and home supply industry generally are dictated by economic factors that determine the welfare of nearly all retail, manufacturing, and service industries. Increases in the amount of disposable income held by consumers will have a favorable effect on auto and home supply retailers' business, as will appreciable increases in the nation's population, which eventually will mean more licensed drivers and more automobiles on the road. Also, significant increases in the number of new automobiles entering the market will boost retailers' sales, as new automobile owners buy products to equip their new purchases.

But auto and home supply retailers also may realize higher revenue when these same conditions worsen, lending the industry the enviable characteristic of benefitting from both the good and the bad. Reduced consumer spending can increase, in certain circumstances, the business activity of auto and home supply retailers, primarily because automobile owners will be more inclined to repair their vehicles themselves, rather than paying for the services of a professional mechanic. Similarly, fewer new automobiles on the road generally means consumers are continuing to drive their existing, older vehicles.

Positioned as such, auto and home supply retailers have enjoyed steady, and sometimes prolific growth since the emergence of the auto and home supply concept in the early twentieth century. But in the mid-1990s, various challenges portended substantial decline as the auto and home supply industry entered the twenty-first century. One concern was the increasing technological advancement and complexity of automobiles, which made them more difficult for consumers to repair themselves, thus redirecting business toward trained garage mechanics, and away from auto and home supply retailers.

A second concern was the proliferation of massive discount stores and wholesale distributorships, which led to a greater representation of these types of retailers in the automobile aftermarket, further shrinking auto and home supply retailers' customer base. To help dampen the effects of this potentially deleterious situation, more and more retailers involved in the industry began placing an emphasis on service by including additional service bays within their store format. Other concerns included the consolidation of the auto and home supply industry into just a few very large companies, and the challenges presented by computers in this industrial-age business.

ORGANIZATION AND STRUCTURE

The auto and home supply industry is a densely populated niche within the automobile aftermarket, with stores fairly evenly distributed throughout the nation. In 1980, there were 35,200 establishments in operation. That number spiraled to 46,000 in 1987. During the late 1980s, a combination of store closures and consolidations blew through the ranks of auto and home supply stores, dropping the nationwide total to some 43,000 in 1990. By the time the U.S. Census Department surveyed the industry for its 1992 *Census of Retail Trade,* the number had dropped even further, to 41,308. In 1997, the industry employed 408,300 people.

In 1980, auto and home supply retailers registered $18.0 billion in sales, a total which increased by some 40 percent to $25.2 billion in 1985, just 5 years later. The number increased dramatically again in the 3 years between 1985 and 1988, to $30.3 billion. By 1989, growth had begun to taper to $31.7 billion, which grew to $34.2 billion in 1990. The increase from 1989 to 1990 would be the last significant gain for several years, as a global economic recession negatively affected nearly all sectors of retail trade. In 1991, sales grew by a modest $0.1 billion to $34.3 billion, and by 1992 they were down to $28.6 billion.

The composition of the auto and home supply industry changed during the 1980s, as multiunit corporations increased their representation in the industry. This growth of auto and home supply chain stores followed the general retail trend toward larger stores. Larger inventories enabled retailers of all types to lower prices and, consequently, attract more customers—a concept and format auto and home supply retailers adopted with increasing frequency throughout the decade. In 1980, corporations with 11 or more auto and home supply retail outlets accounted for 26 percent of the industry's total sales, a proportional representation that increased by the decade's close, when multiunit organizations accounted for 31 percent of the industry's total sales. In 1992, firms with 10 or more establishments represented 43 percent of total sales. A poor economic climate in the 1990s exerted further negative effects on smaller independent auto and home supply retailers, forcing some to exit the business. Hence, in 1992, just 30 companies out of 27,813 (slightly more than 0.001 percent) controlled 36 percent of annual sales for the industry.

Background and Development

Auto and home supply stores date back to the early twentieth century, emerging roughly at a time when automobiles themselves were becoming a common sight on American roadways. Western Auto Supply Co., the industry's first retailer to achieve widespread success, was founded in 1909 as a mail order company, and opened its first outlet in 1913. It is fair to assume, however, that smaller, local stores were in operation before this time, though there are few existing figures for the scale of their operations.

It was a time when automobile owners purchased nearly every auto part or accessory they needed from automobile dealers. Auto parts retailers sold a limited selection of products, and only products intended for use with automobiles. It would be roughly 20 years before household merchandise began to appear on the shelves of auto parts stores, and then only to a limited extent. Instead, retailers relied on the sale of basic auto parts and supplies, antifreeze, polish, and other related items. But the growth of auto supply retailers during those fledgling years was severely restricted by the overwhelming command of the automobile aftermarket enjoyed by automobile dealers, whose only appreciable competition came from automobile repair garages.

It would be several decades before any type of retailers—service stations, garages, or repair specialists—would begin to wrest control of the automotive aftermarket away from automobile dealers. Nevertheless, the small auto supply retail market already amounted to a considerable amount of money, enough that even a small percentage represented a sufficient incentive for additional auto supply stores to join the fray. Several future auto supply empires emerged in the 1920s, particularly Pep Boys—Manny, Moe & and Jack, and Gamble-Skogmo Inc., both of which began operations in 1925. By this time, automobile dealers' control of the automobile aftermarket's distribution channels had begun to slowly lessen as the number of repair garages increased. In 1920, automobile dealers commanded 99 percent of the market; 15 years later, their share of the aftermarket had fallen to 80 percent.

In the late 1930s, auto supply retailers began to sell nonautomotive merchandise in their stores as a rudimentary marketing ploy to attract customers. Since these stores catered primarily to male consumers, the nonautomotive merchandise consisted of what then were considered traditional male products such as screwdrivers, wrenches, and other hardware items, as well as sporting goods and garden supplies. There was, however, no steadfast rule governing the selection of merchandise; retailers were merely fleshing out their display shelves to boost sales. These non-automotive products represented roughly 20 percent of the average inventory held by auto parts stores in the late 1930s, and their product mix would become more balanced in the coming years.

By 1940, the automobile aftermarket had opened up considerably. From 1935 to 1940, automobile dealers' share of the distribution channels experienced its most precipitous drop yet, falling from 80 to 66 percent. Service stations, general garages, repair specialists, and auto and home supply stores composed the balance. By 1940, auto and home supply stores accounted for approximately 10 percent of automobile aftermarket sales, twice the percentage garnered 5 years earlier.

Following World War II, the trend toward greater parity in the automobile aftermarket continued, as automobile dealers' share dropped to 56 percent by 1945 and then below 50 percent by 1950. Meanwhile, the auto and home supply industry's share in the market increased, rising to roughly 14 percent by 1950. Consumers' voracious appetite for home appliances and other hard goods during the decade further improved the position of auto and home supply retailers. Refrigerators, housewares, toys, radios, and televisions began to appear in auto and home supply stores during this postwar economic boom era. Stores also began to attract female customers in large numbers for the first time.

The product mix of auto and home supply stores' merchandise reflected an increased demand for home appliances and related products. The two elements reached equal representation in the early 1950s, and a decade later, nonautomotive products were more prevalent than automotive parts. As this trend developed, the types of home supply products offered became more diverse, and in some cases, the auto and home supply stores assisted in the design of products. In 1957, for instance, Western Auto Supply Co. (the progenitor of auto and home supply stores) helped to design a portable typewriter called the Wizard, which the retail chain featured in its approximately 400 stores. Another large retailer, White Stores Inc., offered its customers sewing machines, vitamins, and more than 1,000 health and beauty products, in addition to the more traditional home supply products.

Whereas automobile dealers' market share had slipped to 40 percent by 1955, the auto and home supply retail industry experienced tremendous growth following World War II. It generated roughly $1.5 billion in annual sales during the mid-1950s, and aggregate revenue would continue to balloon, more than doubling to $3.1 billion in 1962. The competition was higher, too. By that time there were 550 retail chains operating 6,000 stores, 4,000 independent outlets, 20,000 franchised dealers, and 3,000 wholesalers and discount stores.

The proliferation of credit sales and the addition of service bays for installing automotive parts and accessories also fueled the industry's growth. In the early 1960s, retailers began offering basic installation services for products such as automobile tires—a bid to keep customers in their stores for a longer period of time. Credit purchases increased the frequency of customers' visits. By the mid-1960s, many retailers had expanded the number of services they offered, branching into brake and ignition repair, as well as wheel alignment and balancing. The addition of these services was integral to the industry's future growth. From 1960 forward, the percentage of the market controlled by service stations shrank. The same held true for garage mechanics, who saw their presence in the market begin to ebb a decade earlier.

Other factors were contributing to the industry's growth as well, notably the rising number of consumers servicing their own automobiles. The percentage of automobile owners in the United States who tuned their own engines doubled to 20 percent between 1957 and 1966, a period during which the number of automobile owners also increased. By the mid-1960s, 40 percent of all automobile owners changed their spark plugs themselves, up from 25 percent in 1957. This growth of the do-it-yourself market was indicated by other developments in the mid-1960s, such as a significant leap in the sales of *Glenn's Auto Repair Manual,* of which 55,000 copies were sold in 1965 and another 50,000 in the first three months of 1966. When *Popular Mechanics* began running an advice column regarding auto repair, the magazine was inundated with letters. The editorial board had anticipated 50 responses a month; instead, it received 400 to 500.

Accordingly, as the auto and home supply industry entered the 1970s, the potential for profit was in place, limited mostly by the fierce competition pervading the industry. By this time the automobile aftermarket was divided fairly evenly among the major distribution channels, with auto and home supply stores controlling roughly 20 percent of the market. Recessive economic conditions in the mid-1970s, however, coupled with the effects of an oil embargo, negatively affected many industries. Consumers purchased fewer new automobiles, thus creating a national pool of vehicles that were aging and in need of repair. With less disposable income to use for professional mechanics, the do-it-yourself market, and in turn the auto and home supply industry, entered a period of invigorated growth.

But by the late 1970s, other types of retail operations had discovered automotive parts as a means to help mitigate flagging sales. Mass merchandisers and supermarkets began to stock significantly more automotive parts and accessories, frequently devoting a portion or end of a display aisle to them. Moreover, these types of retailers also began selling home appliances and other related merchandise, impinging on both segments of auto and home supply retailers' market niche. But the effect of this new breed of competition on auto and home supply retailers was partly offset by several favorable developments during this time, and others to come in the early 1980s.

Tire sales, perennially the most lucrative segment of the auto and home supply business, benefited from the introduction of small, lightweight "mini-spares" by automobile manufacturers in the late 1970s. These temporary spare tires, usable for only a limited number of miles, increased the sales of conventional tires in the aftermarket. Additionally, recreational vehicles and small pickup trucks began to emerge in greater numbers, creating a new category of vehicles that required repair and maintenance, as well as auto parts and accessories to heighten performance.

In the early 1980s, the industry's position was further buoyed by a depressed automobile manufacturing market, in which production levels descended to historic lows, and by the attrition of service stations. Due in part to the energy crises in the mid-1970s, the number of service stations (which generally sold batteries, tires, and automobile accessories) had dropped by 75,000 during the mid- and late 1970s, leaving 150,000 in existence by the early 1980s—many of which had discontinued the practice of selling automobile parts. In 1981, new automobile production plummeted to the lowest level since 1961, and in March 1982, to the lowest monthly output since 1948. As in the past, this situation meant older automobiles were populating American roads, automobiles that required more replacement parts than newer automobiles. During this time, the average age of an automobile in the United States was 6.6 years, the highest since 1952.

In the mid-1980s, a relatively new segment of the automobile aftermarket, the automobile security industry, recorded a growth rate of roughly 30 percent per year. As more and more automobile owners protected themselves against car theft by purchasing security systems and alarms, car alarms became a business estimated at $155.0 million to $200.0 million a year. This enriched auto and home supply retailers, who generally concentrated on lower-priced security systems, giving them an additional $30 million worth of business nationwide.

But technological strides in automobile manufacturing had, by the early 1980s, made the automobile a complex piece of machinery replete with electronic components, thus causing the do-it-yourself market to lose some of its vitality. By the late 1980s, this development became a pressing concern for retailers involved in the auto and home supply industry. To make matters worse for auto and home supply retailers, the same technological strides that had spawned more sophisticated automobiles also made many types of automobiles virtually maintenance-free for significantly longer periods of time. Consequently, as industry participants entered the 1990s, questions arose as to whether they could successfully compete in a dramatically changing market that threatened to keep dwindling.

Emerging from the recessive economic conditions of the early 1990s, the automobile aftermarket represented a $200.0 billion annual business, employing 2.5 million persons in approximately 500,000 establishments (Auto and home supply stores operate in only a part of the aftermarket, and thus represent a fraction of these figures). The period from 1988 to 1992 had seen a shift of $3.9 billion of product volume at the user level in the automobile market. This volume was not lost, but simply redirected into different distribution channels, such as Wal-Mart and other large nonautomotive stores that now marketed some auto supplies. Industry pundits in the early 1990s anticipated another shift between 1992 and 1996, this time of $7.3 billion.

According to predictions, by 1997 there would be dollar changes in distribution-channel volume greater than the growth of the aftermarket itself, which would mean a more intense battle among competitors for the existing market, rather than for the growth of the market. The traditional channels of distribution, in which auto and home supply retailers are included along with parts manufacturers, warehouse distributors, and jobbers, was expected to increase its aggregate sales total by $500.0 million during this four-year period. But it also was expected to cede market share to other distribution channels at the same time, giving up $2.0 billion.

Current Conditions

The predicted shifts in the market seemed to be materializing in the latter part of the 1990s. Companies were becoming bigger, and stores were increasing in size. Hence, Aid Auto Stores, a strong competitor in the New York City and Long Island markets, announced the opening of a warehouse superstore in 1996. It pioneered a new concept in auto parts sales, one that had already shown itself effective in selling items as varied as groceries and stereo equipment. Symptomatic of the fact that department stores were entering the auto parts market was the announcement by Target Stores in February 1996 that it had entered into an exclusive agreement with Car and Driver brand to sell its products, which included oil and antifreeze.

A report in *Discount Merchandiser* magazine in February of 1997 compared the numbers of outlets in various segments retailing products in the automobile aftermarket, and analyzed the shift in numbers of outlets from 1980 to 1995. According to the study, between 1992 and 1995, the automobile aftermarket had a number of losers and very few winners. Auto parts stores, for instance, had seen a decrease in their numbers, as had tire stores, service stations, and new car dealers. But discount stores, drugstores, and especially warehouse clubs had seen an increase in the number of outlets marketing auto aftermarket products. With even drugstores getting in on the act, traditional auto and home supply retailers were bound to suffer.

Companies that could not roll with the changes in the market did not last. In August 1995, one of the industry's former leaders, Nationwise, filed Chapter 11 bankruptcy and sold a large portion of its stores to Western Auto, which in 1998 was owned by Advance Holding Corp. "The automobile aftermarket is beginning to undergo dramatic consolidation," said Pep Boys CEO Mitchell Liebovitz. Even successful players such as his own company had to adjust. Thus, Pep Boys realized that it had perhaps overcorrected in accordance with market shifts, and was missing out on a large market segment who still worked on their own cars. In 1996, it opened 50 new establishments under the name Parts USA, geared toward less affluent consumers who still did their own repairs. As of 1999, AutoZone Inc. also catered to a market which performs its own repairs, as well as to professionals.

After reorganization and restructuring, the industry was stable and growing. In 1999, the industry was again on the upswing, with all of the major companies experiencing tremendous growth in both sales and number of employees.

Industry Leaders

Gone are the days when local, independent stores can generate sufficient revenue to be included in the upper echelon of their field. This holds true for many retail enterprises and particularly for auto and home supply stores, considering the enormous inventory required for them to operate successfully. The increasing number of foreign-manufactured automobiles driven by American consumers has created a commensurate increase in the number of different automobile parts and accessories an automobile owner may need, which only well-financed conglomerates are able to provide. Ranked according to sales volume, the top 5 auto and home supply retailers in the United States in 1997 accounted for roughly 23 percent of the industry's total sales, or $6.6 billion.

This top 5 in 1998 was led by AutoZone Inc. of Memphis, Tennessee, with $4.1 billion in sales in 1999, a growth of nearly 27 percent from the previous year. AutoZone reports more than 2,700 outlets and 40,500 workers. According to *Forbes,* AutoZone also had the highest per-square-foot sales ($268) of any parts seller. On the rise is Roanoke, Virginia's Advance Holding Corp., which took over former number two company Western Auto in 1998. This acquisition caused Advance to increase its sales by 44 percent to $1.2 billion, and to nearly double its workforce to 24,976 employees. In 1999, Advance was rated number two in the industry, with Advance Auto Parts, Western Auto, and Parts America stores. Genuine Parts Co. had $6.6 billion in 1998 sales (which includes other products), a 10 percent growth from the previous year, and 30,000 employees. Pep Boys took fourth place, with more than $2.3 billion in 1999 sales, a near 17 percent growth, and 27,460 employees. In fifth was Carquest Corp. of Lakewood, Colorado, which did an estimated $1.4 billion in sales in 1997.

WORKFORCE

During the 1980s, total employment by auto and home supply stores increased, keeping pace with the growth of the industry's aggregate sales. In 1980, auto and home supply stores employed 225,000 people. Then, as the number of establishments in the industry increased, the work force total responded in kind, expanding to 286,000 by 1987 and to 298,000 two years later. In 1990, 305,000 people were employed in the industry's 43,400 establishments. But by 1992, the figure had dropped to 269,069. The industry was on the upswing in late 1999 when there were an estimated 408,300 employees, of which 319,500 were production workers.

In 1980, employees involved in retail trade earned $4.88 per hour, while members of the automobile aftermarket paid their employees an average of $5.66 per hour. In 1990, employees in the retail trade earned an average of $6.75 per hour, while a typical retail employee in the automobile aftermarket earned $8.92 an hour, bringing the industry's total payroll to $5.1 billion, and reflecting a greater wage disparity between the two segments than existed a decade earlier. By 1992, whereas the average retail employee made $12,107 a year, employees in the auto and home supply industry made $17,405. In 1999, employees worked an average of 38 hours per week for an average salary of $10.41 an hour.

RESEARCH AND TECHNOLOGY

For auto and home supply retailers, particularly operators of large superstores, inventory management is of paramount importance, affecting both the internal operation of a store and the ability of a retailer to provide quick and efficient service to customers. Typically, large auto and home supply chains stock more than 10,000 products in each store, making the location of a particular product and the reordering of products a formidable task. Consequently, the emergence of computers during the 1980s as an economically viable alternative to managing the operation of a retail store on paper facilitated auto and home supply retailers' cost effective management of inventory (and nearly every other facet of retail), to an immeasurable extent. As the auto and home supply industry entered the mid-1990s, computers continued to become more sophisticated, enhancing retailers' ability to successfully function in a market that was becoming increasingly competitive. By the mid-1990s, the parts industry was in cyberspace, with sites such as Parts-In-Excess, where buyers all over the world could purchase difficult-to-find parts for a wide variety of trucks. In addition, in the late 1990s, Carquest offered hotlines to its members.

FURTHER READING

Average Hours and Earnings of Production or Nonsupervisory Workers. Bureau of Labor Statistics, 1999. Available from http://www.bls.gov.

Employment—National, Not Seasonally Adjusted. Bureau of Labor Statistics, 1999. Available from http://www.bls.gov.

Eng, Paul M. and Resa W. King. ''Cruising the Info Highway For Truck Parts.'' *Business Week,* 18 November 1996.

''Flash Report: Automobile Aftermarket.'' *Discount Merchandiser,* February 1997.

''Hoover's Company Capsules.'' *Hoover's Online,* 1999. Available from http://www.hoovers.com.

Stankevich, Debby. ''Blow Out.'' *Discount Merchandiser,* March 1996.

''Target Drives Into PL With Car and Driver Line.'' *Discount Store News,* 5 February 1996.

SIC 5541

GASOLINE SERVICE STATIONS

This category includes gasoline service stations primarily engaged in selling gasoline and lubricating oils. These establishments frequently sell other merchandise, such as tires, batteries, and other automobile parts, or perform minor repair work. Gasoline stations that include other activities, such as grocery stores, convenience stores, or carwashes, are classified according to the primary activity.

NAICS CODE(S)

447110 (Gasoline Stations with Convenience Stores)
447190 (Other Gasoline Stations)

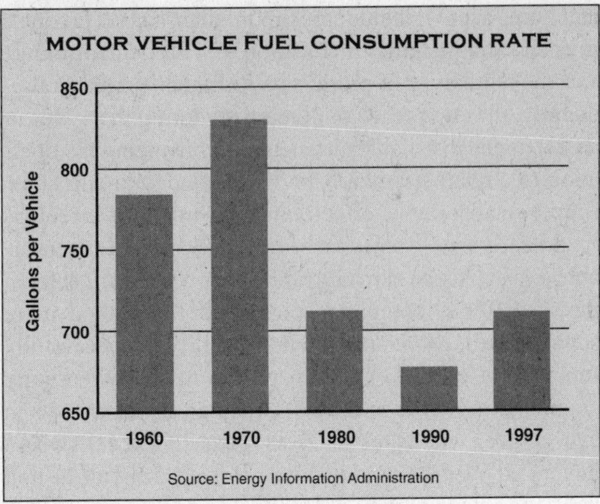

Source: Energy Information Administration

INDUSTRY SNAPSHOT

In 1997, 126,889 gasoline service stations operated in the United States. These establishments took very different forms than they had a decade before, with self-service islands and ancillary retail outlets—convenience stores, known as C-stores—creating major changes in the distribution of market share.

The total number of stations has been steadily decreasing since 1982, reflecting a trend by major oil companies to close smaller-volume franchises and concentrate on maximizing gallonage at major locations. Cost-cutting in the oil industry in general, as well as environmental legislation mandating upgrades for the gasoline service station industry, meant that most dealers were looking for ways to reduce expenses and increase sales. Traditional ''mom and pop'' style stations were frequently a casualty of market changes; consumer emphasis shifted more toward large, multi-function, automated outlets. To survive into the next millennium, gasoline service stations will continue to expand the range of goods and services they offer and emphasize convenience to the consumer through automatic pay machines, more self-service islands, and streamlined traffic flow organization.

ORGANIZATION AND STRUCTURE

The U.S. market for consumer gasoline had four major competing categories in the 1980s and 1990s: service stations, which offered service through at least one bay and had a volume greater than a set limit (typically 20,000 gallons per month); pumpers, which had more than six nozzles and had a volume exceeding a set limit (typically 50,000 gallons per month) and possibly having such ancillary services as a C-store, car wash, or remote bays; convenience stores, with a minimum of 600 square feet of retail space, the primary business of which was the sale of food items, typically with one or two islands and fewer than six nozzles; and others, facilities with gasoline volume below minimum volume for pumpers or service stations that may also include ancillary services such as a C-store, car wash, or bays. All of these competitors except convenience stores fall under this classification. Gas stations accounted for 29 percent of the total number of outlets and 26 percent of the volume of gas pumped for all U.S. stations in 1998. On average the monthly gallonage was 78,352.

Within this relatively simple categorization of outlet types, a complex web of supply sources and brand loyalties exists. More than two-thirds of gasoline service outlets were branded by major oil companies by 1992, and the trend continues into the late 1990s. Managers of branded stations, called dealers, either owned their own station or rented from the branding company—the latter were ''lessee dealers.'' Dealers bought gasoline either directly from parent companies or from branded distributors, called jobbers, who bought from parent companies. The others, independents, bought from unbranded jobbers who distributed products from a variety of companies on a surplus basis. The independents were at an obvious disadvantage in terms of purchase price and supply reliability; such factors virtually guaranteed the domination of the market by branded dealers.

Sales of accessories such as tires, batteries, oil, and antifreeze—as well as services such as carwashes, lube jobs, and tune-ups—were once considered fringe options for gasoline retailers. In the early 1990s, however, an increasing number of facilities responded to competitive pressures by incorporating these various services into their business plans, with the result that the distinction between C-stores and service stations or pumpers grew progressively tenuous. Standard delineation of industry classifications such as ''principle'' focus of business became less obvious; only income proportionality allowed pinpointing in many cases.

BACKGROUND AND DEVELOPMENT

Gasoline service stations are a phenomenon of the twentieth century. Brought into being by the simultaneous maturity of petroleum production and refinement and the invention of the combustion engine, gasoline service stations began as suppliers for a ''lunatic element'' in the population who used ''horseless carriages'' for recreational transport purposes. These early stations were actually supplied by horse-drawn tank carts; conservative petroleum refiners did not initially trust such odd contraptions as fuel-powered trucks.

The mass production of the automobile spurred mass construction of gasoline servicing facilities, with all the major oil companies staking a claim on some corner of the fledgling consumer market. Small, family-run franchises were the norm and remained the mainstay of the market in remote areas well into the 1970s.

Domestic gasoline production capacity grew with World War I and II, as did the Big Three automakers' factories. Consequently, by the 1950s, average American families had at least one car, and that car was large, gas-guzzling, and a source of intense pride. The heyday of the labor-intensive service station with several attendants in uniform to service every customer reached its peak in those post-war years.

The revolution of form which would result in modern service stations began in the 1970s, when self-service islands came into vogue. In 1975, only 22 percent of the market share went to self-service facilities; in 1992, 86 percent went to self-service, and in 1997, self-service was the mainstay, with maybe one or two pumps reserved for full serve at larger stations. There were 220,000 full service stations in the 1970s; in 1997 there are only 40,000. The number of service stations has decreased by one third since 1980. Self-service essentially ended the ''service'' orientation of gasoline retailers; consumers made it clear that lower prices were more important than uniformed attendants. Small, unbranded dealers were the first to feel the impact of this emphasis on price over service. No longer able to compete on the basis of superior, individualized attention to detail, small dealerships began to close.

In the early 1980s, department stores also began withdrawing from the gasoline retailing market. Giants such as J.C. Penney and KMart found it difficult and increasingly unprofitable to compete against major oil companies. Simultaneously, the large oil companies embarked on extensive expansion of services and renovation of facilities in branded retail outlets as their competitors forged elaborate marketing schemes to encourage brand loyalty.

Architectural homogeneity and multi-purpose stations became a chief focus for most; the Texaco ''family of buildings'' style, which basically eliminated structural clutter and revamped unplanned layouts, became a model for the industry. The trend toward having similar building structures increased with the addition of C-stores to many stations throughout the 1980s and into the 1990s.

The history of gasoline stations has been marked by trends. The first seven decades of the twentieth century saw an evolution of gasoline service stations which corresponded to consistent increases of consumer interest and disposable income; the last three decades revolutionized the industry through successive waves of automation and streamlining. If self-service was the trend of the 1970s, credit card payment was its corollary in the 1980s, and debit card machination in the 1990s was the overwhelming trend. As the twenty-first century begins, stations are experimenting with machines that will take cash at the pump. Currently the drawback of these machines is that they cannot give change and customers have to go inside to get their change.

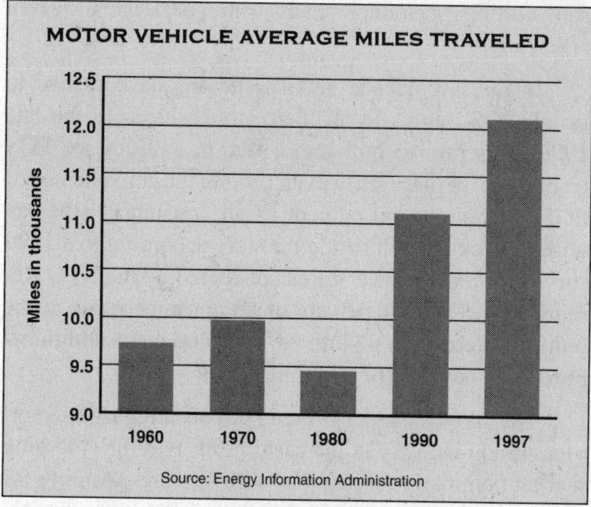

CURRENT CONDITIONS

Gasoline service stations generated $19.8 billion in sales in 1997, up from $14.5 billion in 1996, despite the decrease in the actual number of establishments. These figures illustrated an important trend—large oil companies were cutting unproductive franchises and pouring capital into strategic stations, increasing overall franchise income while reducing the number of individual franchises. The average gross profits per gallon rose 10.5 percent for C-stores in 1998. Total gasoline sales increased 3.3 percent from the previous year.

This streamlining process, a ''more with less'' motto of productivity, characterized most facets of the gasoline retailing industry in the early 1990s. Although in the 1970s, self-service sped up pumping and allowed customers to buy more gas while allowing retailers to operate with fewer employees, in the 1980s credit card payment capability sped up transactions even more and, at the same time, seemed to encourage larger sales. One survey showed that customers purchased 45 percent more fuel when using a credit card than when paying cash.

Improving on the modern self-serve, charged-with-credit tank of gas was in-pump point of sale (POS) technology, which allowed customers to purchase gasoline with credit cards without ever interacting with a cashier. Initiated in the 1980s, widespread adaptation of POS technology was anticipated to be complete by the mid-1990s. Despite the expense of installing units—POS technology costs approximately $5,000 per unit—consumer fascination with speedy, paperless transactions made it virtually mandatory for retailers to install. Self-service pumps with POS capability allowed consumers to fill their tanks without ever interacting with another person, cutting personnel needs while increasing overall efficiency.

In the last decade service stations have rushed to install POS pumps in all their service bays. In the late 1990s it is rare to pull into a station and not see POS technology in place. However, despite the convenience of POS technology, 60 percent of all consumers still pay with a check or cash inside the store according to a 1999 survey of convenience stores conducted by the NFO Research Inc. Only 21 percent of all consumers pay at the pump, preferring to go into the store and make additional purchases beyond the gasoline.

The last consumer-driven shift in the gasoline service station industry in the early 1990s was the emerging market domination of stations with C-stores. Aiming for gasoline sales of 100,000-200,000 gallons per month, major oil companies installed large numbers of branded stations with ancillary food stores in strategic locations such as major highway intersections. The investment for one of these station/superstore units was high—state-of-the-art fiberglass underground storage tanks, vapor recovery equipment, multi-product dispensers, roomy and attractive fuel islands with elaborate security lighting systems, and capacity for dispensing alternative fuels such as natural gas. Each site was a major investment and ensured that only major oil companies would be able to compete in the new C-store market.

The late 1990s is seeing an expansion of the convenience store-gasoline station in the form of multi-franchising. Known as ''co-branding,'' it refers to the pairing of two or more franchises under one roof, a move that benefits the franchisee as well as the customer. Fast food outlets, such as Burger King, McDonald's, and Subway, have become popular co-branders with gasoline stations. In Memphis, Tennessee, Mirabile Investment Corp, the area's largest Burger King franchisee, is teaming full size Burger King stores with Exxon gas stations and convenience stores. Subway has about 1,270 of its 11,000 North American outlets in non-traditional locations, co-branded primarily with convenience stores and gasoline stations. Texaco has teamed up with Burger King, Taco Bell, and Subway, and the company has plans to build or rebuild 63 outlets in the Los Angeles area in 1997 co-branding with Star Mart convenience stores and/or a fast food franchise. In 1996, Amoco Corporation shared the cost of property and maintenance costs of 50 new gas stations with McDonald's—up from 13 in 1995.

Other technology that may dominate gas stations in the next century is the return of full service, without the helpful attendant in uniform. In 1996, BMW, Mercedes-Benz, and the German oil company Aral were testing robotic gas station attendants. Drivers pull up to specially marked pumps, swipe a plastic tank card, enter a PIN number, and the unit immediately identifies the make and model of the automobile. A red laser beam then guides the robotic arm to the car's fuel door. The robots even replace the cap when finished fueling.

Adapting to consumer demand was not the only expensive challenge for gasoline service stations in the early 1990s. Environmental legislation targeted retailers in a number of ways, primarily in the arenas of gasoline evaporation, underground storage tanks, and improved refrigerants. Like C-store investment, environmental compliance spelled doom for those small independent retailers who remained in business in the early 1990s.

Stage II of the 1990 Clean Air Act stipulated that retailers use equipment that captured gasoline fumes when gasoline was discharged into a vehicle's gasoline tank. Marketers in California, New Jersey, Missouri, New York, and Washington, DC were already using Stage II equipment in 1993; marketers elsewhere may need to do the same, or the EPA may mandate on-board canisters in automobiles. Pump nozzles will most likely bear the brunt of the requirement because canisters could leak while the automobile is in motion. Estimates of costs for updating pumps ranged from $20,000 to $40,000 per station.

Underground storage tanks (USTs) came under attack by the EPA because older tanks were made of steel and many had rusted through, contaminating surrounding soil and threatening water supplies. New regulations went into effect in late 1993 and were estimated to cost $100,000 per station as individual sites seek to repair or replace existing tanks. Station remediation costs were estimated to cost an additional $155,000.

Chevron was one of the first major companies to replace the steel tanks with corrosion resistant fiberglass and has underground monitors to detect leaks of less than a quart an hour. But for the small independent stations, removing the tanks and cleaning the soil was too costly a proposition and many were forced to close in the mid-1990s.

Other environmental costs included updating refrigerant installation facilities. As chemical manufacturers phased out dangerous, ozone-depleting chlorofluorocarbons (CFCs), retailers learned to use hydrofluorocarbons as refrigerants. Hydrofluorocarbons as refrigerants and reformulated gasolines were the two major new product technologies in the early 1990s.

Alternative fuel sources such as natural gas, propane, methanol, ethanol, and electric power were making headway. In 1996 the natural gas-powered Ford Crown Victoria automobiles were on duty as law enforcement vehicles in Ventura County, California; Wixom, Michigan; and Savannah, Georgia. Ford also delivered 68 electric powered Ecostars to utilities and other customers for testing in real life driving conditions and aims to build

250,000 vehicles by the year 2001 that run on ethanol, gasoline, or a combination of the two. Chrysler Corporation was also expected to announce a major commitment to flexible fuel vehicles or FFVs, and General Motors has manufactured an electric car, the EV1. The traditional gasoline service station will continue to change to meet the needs of the new technologies.

INDUSTRY LEADERS

In 1999 Exxon Mobil was the number one integrated oil company, the result of a merger between Exxon and Mobil. In 1999 its sales topped $186 billion dollars. It currently operates over 40,000 stations in the United States. The next largest competitor is Texaco, with sales listed at $35 billion in 1999 and 38,000 gas stations in the United States. A series of recent mergers has changed the face of the industry. Just recently BP America and Amoco merged, making them the third largest integrated oil company in the United States.

WORKFORCE

In 1998, gasoline service stations employed 689,400 people, a number which had steadily increased from 1992, despite the decrease in the number of stations. This number is expected to increase 6 percent over the next ten years. Service station dealers essentially managed all aspects of the stations, from ordering supplies to supervising personnel. Typically, they employed attendants who filled tanks at the full-serve island, checked oil, and cashiered, and mechanics who attended to more complicated maintenance and repair work.

Employment prospects within the gasoline service station industry were expected to be fairly good in the 1990s. Increasingly sophisticated equipment will require more training and yield more job satisfaction for attendants. Dealers, too, will need to become familiar with more technical, sophisticated equipment such as POS units. Those dealers who can successfully juggle the managerial demands of their jobs on the larger scale that new C-store units require will be in demand.

AMERICA AND THE WORLD

The supply of gasoline and refined products is the only important aspect of the gasoline service station industry that is international in scope. In 1998 motorists used almost 8 billion barrels of gasoline per day. The United States imported 311,000 barrels of oil per day in 1998. Oil imports have fluctuated since 1991, and figures will shift as domestic production and refining capacities shrink and alternative fuels increase in both popularity and by government regulation. The possible ramifications for retailers hinge primarily on questions of supply; overdependence on foreign petroleum has historically resulted in price wars and shortages.

FURTHER READING

1997 Census of Retail Trade. Washington: U.S. Census Bureau, 1999.

American Petroleum Institute. *How Much We Pay for Gasoline: 1998 Annual Review and 1999 January-August.* October 1999.

Anderson, Robert O. *Fundamentals of the Petroleum Industry.* Norman, OK: University of Oklahoma Press.

Killeen, Barbara. ''Convenience Store Behavior Shopping: Gasoline.'' *Journal of Petroleum Marketing,* 15 June 1999.

Maynard, Roberta. ''New Strategies for Growth.'' *Nation's Business,* January 1996.

''Retail Market: SIGMA 1999 Statistical Report.'' *NPN Market Facts Supplement,* 15 July 1999.

Robertshaw, Nicky. ''One-Stop Fill-Up.'' *Memphis Business Journal,* 18 November 1996.

Standard and Poor's Industry Surveys. New York: Standard and Poor's Corporation, 1999.

Tanaka, Jennifer. ''Auto Auto-Fueling.'' *Newsweek,* 29 July 1996.

Vavra, Bob. ''It's Still for Love of Money.'' *National Petroleum News,* August 1999.

Wight, Darren. ''Prepaid Gas Cards: Are They a Help or a Hinderance?'' *National Petroleum News,* January 1999.

Woodburn, John H. *Opportunities in Energy Careers.* Lincolnwood, ILVGM Career Horizons.

Yung, Katherine. ''Ford to Sell More Vehicles that Run on Ethanol.'' *Detroit News,* 4 June 1997.

———. ''Big Three Sales Slip Due to Competition From Japan.'' *Detroit News,* 6 May 1997.

SIC 5551

BOAT DEALERS

This classification covers establishments primarily engaged in the retail sale of new and used motorboats and other watercraft, marine supplies, and outboard motors.

NAICS CODE(S)

441222 (Boat Dealers)

After a period of deep industry recession, in which boat and marine accessory sales dropped from $18.0 billion in 1988 to $10.3 billion in 1992, the boating industry at both the manufacturing and retail levels rebounded strongly during the mid-1990s. Buoyed by the strong economy, continued low interest rates, and the repeal of a 10 percent federal luxury tax on new boats prices at $100,000 and above in 1993, the industry saw retail expenditures on boating rise to $19.3 billion in 1997, although they did drop a bit to $19.2 billion in 1998.

The National Marine Manufacturers Association (NMMA), which tracks the industry, reported that overall sales of new boats (measured in units) fell by six percent to 571,100 and total retail sales dropped by one percent to 19.2 billion in 1998. Sales of the recent market-leading product, personal watercraft (or PWCs, often called ''jet skis,'' which is actually a Kawasaki Motors Corp. brand name), had almost doubled in only two years with peak sales in the mid-1990s topping at 200,000 units sold in 1995. The price of these PWCs were key to their popularity. NMMA statistics show that in 1998 the average PWC sold for $6,681, compared to $254,365 for large cabin cruisers and $23,167 for the average stern-drive power boats. However, this PWC market segment has seen a steady decline in sales into the late 1990s. The number of units sold dropped 26 percent from 176,000 in 1997 to 130,000 in 1998. The NMMA reported that the ''bread and butter'' of the retail market, outboard motor boats, held even in terms of units sold but dropped in sales figures by four percent; this was attributed to a retail unit price drop of roughly $300 per unit.

On the up side of boat sales, the industry saw an increase of nearly one third for center console and ''walkaround'' fishing boats. Sales of all-purpose deckboats rose by 20 percent. In addition, interest in kneeboarding has helped to spur sales of water ski boats. The NMMA forecast that the industry should do well into the next century.

Boat dealers in the United States are, for the most part, independent retailers. Although a retailer may choose to feature a particular manufacturer's boat, dealerships are not controlled or owned by that manufacturer. *Boat & Motor Dealer,* the leading periodical of the industry with a circulation of nearly 30,000, named as 1999's top dealerships: Lodder's Marine of Fairfield, Ohio; Baert Marine Stores of Danvers, Massachusetts; Mariner's Choice Marine of York, Pennsylvania; and Fay's Marina of LaPorte, Indiana.

According to U.S. Bureau of the Census figures, the number of people employed in the boat retail industry averaged 31,000 throughout the 1990s. Also, there were an average of 4,700 boat dealer establishments in the United States during the 1990s.

FURTHER READING

Gerdes, Wylie. ''Industry Listens to Consumers.'' *Detroit Free Press,* 3 February 1994.

U.S. Bureau of the Census. *1997 Economic Survey.* Washington, D.C.: GPO, 1999.

U.S. Bureau of the Census. *Statistical Abstract of the United States: 1998.* Washington, D.C.: GPO, 1999.

SIC 5561

RECREATIONAL VEHICLE DEALERS

This industry includes establishments primarily engaged in the retail sale of new and used motor homes, recreational trailers, and campers (pickup coaches). Establishments primarily engaged in the retail sale of mobile homes are classified in **SIC 5271: Mobile Home Dealers,** and those selling utility trailers are classified in **SIC 5599: Automotive Dealers, Not Elsewhere Classified.**

NAICS CODE(S)

441210 (Recreational Vehicle Dealers)

INDUSTRY SNAPSHOT

Retailers in this industry sell new and used recreational vehicles ranging in size from small tow-behind, pop-up camper trailers to pickup truck coaches to large, luxury motor homes. The prices for these vehicles range from around $2,000 for a new camper trailer to more than $100,000 for some motor home models. In addition to new and used vehicles, the 3,000 dealers nationwide sell parts and accessories to accompany the vehicles and trailers, as well as extended warranties and service contracts. Most dealers also operate repair centers to service the vehicles and trailers they sell. Some dealers supplement the sales operation by renting recreational vehicles on a short-term basis. Other dealers have taken on lines of related recreational products like snowmobiles to try to balance out the slightly seasonal nature of the business.

According to the Recreational Vehicle Industry Association (RVIA), manufacturers shipped 292,700 new units to dealers in 1998. The retail value of these units was $8.36 billion. In addition to new units, dealers also sell used vehicles, which account for some 30 percent of unit sales income.

The industry is dominated by smaller dealers who own single locations. However, there is a small but growing trend toward multiple location dealers, similar to that seen among dealers of new and used automobiles. Recreational vehicle dealers are more commonplace in states traditionally known as being recreation or retirement destinations, such as California, Texas, Michigan, and Florida.

The relative health of the industry is closely tied to the health of the national economy. Because of this, the fortunes of retailers of new and used recreational vehicles across the country have risen and fallen with national economic cycles.

ORGANIZATION AND STRUCTURE

The sale of new and used recreational vehicles is not a purely regional industry. New and used recreational vehicle dealers are spread across the country, although areas that attract seasonal or tourist business have greater numbers of dealerships. Almost all the dealers in the industry sell both new and used recreational vehicles, parts and accessories, while dealers also are increasingly exploring vehicle rental possibilities.

The dealers in this industry do not rely on exclusive franchises from manufacturers to carry and sell manufacturer's goods. The dealers operate on nonexclusive sales contracts, though some dealers do carry only one brand of product. Though there are a large number of manufacturers of recreational vehicles, a few produce the bulk of product sold by dealers. The various brands produced by the public company Fleetwood Enterprises (Coleman, Pace Arrow, Southwind, Cambria, Limited, Jamboree, Tioga) account for about 37 percent of the sales made by dealers in the industry. Other manufacturers like Winnebago, Jayco, Coachman, and Thor provide dealers with both vehicles and parts and accessories.

Dealers sell a wide array of products with hopes of filling as many economic or recreational needs as possible. The vehicles, supplied by about 169 manufacturers, range from folding camper trailers to luxury, self-contained motor homes. The smallest product sold is a camping trailer with collapsible sidewalls that fold for towing. Truck campers are designed to be loaded onto the bed or chassis of a truck and are designed to serve as temporary living quarters. Van conversions, a relatively new presence on dealers' lots, were the largest segment of the recreational vehicle market in 1998, with 148,600 units shipped to dealers for resale to consumers. Travel trailers, typically between 12 and 35 feet in length, made up the second largest segment of the recreational vehicle market. Self-contained motor home units, pickup truck conversions, and sport-utility vehicle conversions also were popular.

According to RVIA, 33 percent of dealers have sales between $1.5 and $3 million per year. Another 29 percent of the dealers have sales between $3 and $5 million annually, while 22 percent post annual sales of $5 to $10 million. Only 7 percent sell more than $10 million of vehicles, accessories, and repairs; 9 percent of the dealers in the industry had less than $1.5 million in sales.

BACKGROUND AND DEVELOPMENT

Even prior to the introduction of the automobile, travelers hooked trailers to their horse-drawn carriages in order to carry extra gear that would make long trips more endurable. But with the growth of motor travel, the need for easily accessible eating and sleeping facilities grew. According to Carlton Edwards' *Homes for Travel and Living: The History and Development of the Recreational Vehicle and Mobile Home Industry,* the first tent trailers were made by individuals who tired of setting up and taking down their camping gear with every stop. In 1926, the Norwich, New York-based Chenango Camp Trailer Company started up the first production line dedicated to the manufacture of recreational vehicles. By the end of the decade, a handful of entrepreneurs around the country were engaged in the production of tent campers and trailers.

The first manufacturers of trailers and motor homes sold directly to the consumer, primarily through word of mouth and referrals. As companies went into production on a larger scale, they set up regional distributorships. Distributors were responsible for selling the product by establishing dealer networks and servicing dealer accounts. Early dealers of recreational vehicles typically were already involved in the sale of automobiles or had some experience servicing them through gas/service stations. Many dealerships sold automobiles and recreational vehicles side-by-side.

By the late 1940s, regional distributorships were discontinued after manufacturers established direct relationships with their dealers. Vehicle dealers enjoyed the freedom to choose the product line they wished to carry from all those offered by manufacturers. The dealer gained the authority to discontinue lines when they weren't profitable or when the brands carried had too much product overlap. This arrangement also allowed dealers to add new lines in order to augment the selection and variety of vehicles offered.

Dealers were rocked in the 1970s by the oil embargo, recessionary conditions, and the credit crunch of the 1970s. However, sales bounced back in the early 1980s, and by the mid-1980s business was booming for manufacturers like Winnebago and Fleetwood and the dealers who sold their brands. In 1988 approximately 427,000 units were shipped to dealers.

Since the early days of the industry, dealers (along with manufacturers) have recognized the importance of camping and motor home parks to their fortunes. Availability and access to the parks was vital to the industry. The continued presence and popularity of national parks and other recreation areas have thus been a vital factor in recreational vehicle dealers' success. National parks had more than 60 million visitors in the mid-1990s, with 3.4 million overnight stays in recreation vehicles.

CURRENT CONDITIONS

The Recreation Vehicle Dealers Association of America (RVDAA) noted that, in 1995, the industry showed a 4.7 percent decrease in units shipped. This was expected, as shipments had been increasing since 1991, and reductions often occur after three or four years of increases. Even so, demand for new units in 1995 was the second highest total in at least a decade; the demand has risen since then. The retail value of those units actually hit an all-time high. The RVDAA attributed the higher value to price increases associated with features such as slide-outs, entertainment centers and electronics/communications packages.

RV manufacturers are offering a variety of high-tech amenities, which add to comfort (and price). According to RVIA, new technologies include moving walls that expand the RV's interior (sometimes doubling the available floor space) at the touch of a button; compact direct broadcast satellite antennas; global positioning systems to help travelers track their exact location; WebTV, which allows travelers access to the Internet; and space-saving appliances.

An Internet survey conducted by *RV News* offered encouraging results for the industry. Seventy-two percent of visitors to the RV American Web site already owned an RV, and 75 percent said they intended to purchase an RV within the next two years. Eighty percent were searching for parts and accessories; 75 percent were looking for dealers; 72 percent needed service facilities; and 68 percent sought information on new RVs.

About 1 household in 10 owned a recreation vehicle in 1996. Younger buyers tended to favor folding camper trailers and truck campers, while older buyers preferred motor homes and van campers. In the 1990s, the industry began courting baby-boomers, as that cohort moved into the prime RV buying age bracket of 45 to 54.

Industry Leaders

The industry is led by a few massive dealership operations. Holiday RV, based in Orlando, Florida, had 1999 sales of $78.5 million and 193 employees. Other companies include Cruise America and RV Centers. Fleetwood Enterprises, which manufactures RVs, also distributes through its own retail outlets. The company, based in Riverside, California, had 1999 sales of $3.5 billion.

Workforce

According to the U.S. Bureau of Labor Statistics, the industry employed approximately 25,600 people in the mid-1990s. Most dealerships within the industry are relatively small operations, employing a small number of people. Forty-two percent of the dealers employ between 1 and 7 people; 8 to 15 people are employed by 33 percent of the establishments. Only 11 percent of industry dealers employ between 16 and 25 people, while another 13 percent of all dealers employ 26 or more people. The number of people on the dealership payroll may fluctuate according to the season and the strength of business. Part-time, low-wage employees may be temporarily hired to clean returned rental vehicles or those taken in on trade. Temporary employees are occasionally used to prepare sold vehicles for delivery.

On behalf of dealers, the RVDAA has set up courses at a few local community colleges in the southeastern United States in an effort to improve the quality of education given to dealership service technicians. The courses are open to those interested in working as a repair technician, as well as to those already employed by dealerships.

Further Reading

"High Tech Innovations Drive RV Sales Up." Recreational Vehicle Industry Association, 1999. Available from http://www.rvia.org.

Recreational Vehicle Industry Association. *RV Shipments Data 1978-1998.* Available from http://www.rvia.org.

Second Annual Recreation Vehicle Outlook, 1996. Fairfax, VA: Recreation Vehicle Dealers Association of North America, 1996.

SIC 5571

MOTORCYCLE DEALERS

This category includes establishments engaged in the retail sale of new and used motorcycles. This classification also includes those dealers who sell motor scooters, mopeds, and all-terrain vehicles.

NAICS Code(s)

441221 (Motorcycle Dealers)

Industry Snapshot

Retail motorcycle, moped, and all-terrain vehicle dealers are divided according to whether they are engaged primarily in selling new or used vehicles. Vendors of new motorcycles, mopeds, and all-terrain vehicles own franchises to sell products of specific vehicle manufacturers. Dealers who do not operate as new vehicle franchises sell used motorcycles in addition to vehicle parts, accessories, and clothing. Almost all dealers, however, have vehicle service departments, which are also sources of significant revenue.

Motorcycling remains one of America's most popular forms of recreation and transportation. The number of people who enjoy motorcycle activities is comparable to the number of people who engage in fishing, golfing, and camping. Because there are many sizes of vehicles available, motorcycling has become a family recreational activity. In addition to providing enjoyment, motorcycles, scooters, and all-terrain vehicles are used in industry in various ways.

Whether they are used for enjoyment, utility, or transportation, motorcycles, mopeds, scooters, and all-terrain vehicles have become profitable products for dealers. New motorcycles sales (including on- and off-highway models as well as scooters) increased 23 percent through the first three quarters of 1999 as compared to the same period in 1998, according to the Retail Sales Report conducted by the Motorcycle Industry Council (MIC). This increase marked the seventh consecutive year of rising new motorcycle sales. Retail sales of new motorcycles in 1997 amounted to $2.9 billion, or 28.3 percent of the estimated $10.2 billion generated by the motorcycle industry overall from consumer sales and services, state taxes, and licensing that year. Apparel sales and accessory sales in 1998 each amounted to $1.2 billion, while repairs and parts sales contributed $1.5 billion to the combined $3.9 billion aftermarket, according to the 1998 Motorcycle Owner Survey conducted by Irwin Broh & Associates for the MIC.

As a public service and a sign of commitment to their customers, most franchise dealers have joined or formed nonprofit associations to act as advocates for their products and to provide education about the use and enjoyment of these vehicles. They provide information about safe riding practices and work to increase owners' awareness of the impact that their motorcycles, scooters, and all-terrain vehicles can have on the environment.

ORGANIZATION AND STRUCTURE

Although there were more than 7,000 nonfranchised retailers in the industry, it was the 3,400 franchised outlets that garnered more than 80.0 percent of the industry's business. According to industry statistics, the average franchised motorcycle outlet had total motorcycle related sales and services of $700,000 in the mid-1990s, compared to $122,500 for the average nonfranchised outlet. On average, sales of new motorcycles, scooters, and all-terrain vehicles made up approximately 54.0 percent of a franchised dealer's business, while 23.2 percent was attributed to sales of parts, accessories, and apparel. In contrast, 68.0 percent of nonfranchised outlet sales was parts, accessories, and apparel.

There were franchised and nonfranchised retail outlets in all 50 states and the District of Columbia. Although California had almost two times more retail outlets than any other state, the business was otherwise evenly distributed across the United States. According to MIC statistics from 1997, approximately 6.5 million motorcycles were owned in the United States, representing approximately 2.5 motorcycles for every 100 persons. In terms of rider distribution, California, Texas, New York, Florida, and Ohio accounted for more than one-third of all motorcycle ownership in the United States, while the West enjoyed the highest motorcycle penetration, with 2.9 motorcycles per 100 persons. In 1995 outlets in the Midwest generated 27.9 percent of the industry's retail sales of new motorcycles. The South was the second leading region, representing 27.2 percent of the total. Retail outlets in the East sold 22.3 percent of new motorcycles, and businesses in the West garnered 22.1 percent.

BACKGROUND AND DEVELOPMENT

The history of the motorcycle dealer industry is closely related to the development of the U.S. motorcycle manufacturing industry. The earliest motorcycles were basically bicycles powered by small engines, and the motorcycle was considered a relatively cheap alternative to the more expensive, early automobiles. Many U.S. manufacturers produced motorcycles before World War I, contributing to a dynamic, if not booming, domestic market. Literature from the Harley-Davidson company reported that by 1911, their motorcycles were among the 150 brands of vehicles vying for space on America's roads. Orient, Henderson, Cyclone, and Indian were the primary competitors of Harley-Davidson at that time. Henry Ford's affordable Model-T, however, doomed many motorcycle manufacturers. In fact, by the end of the Great Depression, the only remaining manufacturers and sellers of motorcycles were Indian and Harley-Davidson. Indian closed down production and distribution in 1953.

Harley-Davidson is one of the most recognizable brand names in the United States. The company began production in 1903 in Milwaukee, Wisconsin. By 1907, William and Arthur Davidson and William Harley had incorporated and issued their first advertising catalog. Their business grew by diversifying their product lines to include a variety of vehicles with different-sized engines, improving engine technology, and increasing sales of their motorcycles to the U.S. government for military use. Harley-Davidson watched carefully as the "motorcycle culture" developed in the late 1950s and early 1960s, often being labeled an "outlaw" lifestyle. Motorcycle gangs, in particular, prompted the public's negative opinions of cycling; in the early 1990s, however, the company maintained that fewer than 1 percent of all motorcyclists fit that category.

Competition. The late 1950s and early 1960s saw the first influx of low-priced, smaller Japanese motorcycles and scooters into the United States. Honda began U.S. distribution of its products in 1959, with the slogan, "You meet the nicest people on a Honda," to combat the negative image associated with the sport. Yamaha starting selling motorcycles in the United States during 1960; Suzuki followed in 1963; and Kawasaki joined the competition in 1967. BMW opened a U.S. distribution arm in

1975, incorporating in New Jersey. Harley-Davidson ended years of private ownership in 1965 with a public offering of its stock, and eventually merged with industrial giant AMF in 1969.

The oil crisis in the 1970s prompted the popularity of the smaller motorcycles, mopeds, and scooters that were made primarily by Japanese manufacturers. Dealers sold vehicles to those interested in conserving gas and finding cheap transportation. Harley-Davidson's market share, already dropping, was further threatened by Honda's 1969 entrance into the heavy and superheavyweight segment of the market. By the late 1970s Harley-Davidson faced severe production quality problems in addition to stiff competition. A management buyout in early 1981 set the course for the company's revitalization. It was protection under higher tariffs however, recommended by the International Trade Commission, that helped shut Honda out of Harley-Davidson's key market. In response, Japanese manufacturers evaded the tariffs by setting up assembly plants in the United States. For example, Honda built a plant in Ohio and Kawasaki opened a facility in Nebraska.

Safety Concerns. In the mid-1980s, three-wheel, all-terrain vehicle sales were negatively affected by concern over their safety. The Consumer Product Safety Commission targeted the vehicles and disabled Honda's sales efforts. *Business Week* reported that before the "crusade," 40 percent of Honda's North American business had been in all-terrain vehicles. Consequently, Honda quickly lost its market dominance to Yamaha, whose four-wheel vehicles were considered safer and therefore less controversial.

Economic Trends. The retail motorcycle, moped, and all-terrain industry is strongly affected by national economic trends. Recessionary and expansionary trends essentially dictate the retail consumption levels of vehicles. The number of new motorcycle registrations climbed until the early 1980s, but fell dramatically in the second half of that decade. Total motorcycle registrations dropped from a high of 5.7 million in 1980 to 4.1 million in 1991. The *U.S. Industrial Outlook 1994,* however, reported that this trend had bottomed out, and projected an increase in shipments from motorcycle manufacturers to dealers in the mid-1990s. After letting their inventories drop in the late 1980s, dealers began replenishing their stocks of motorcycles, mopeds, and all-terrain vehicles in the early 1990s, as buyers began shopping for new, larger motorcycles.

Harley-Davidson's resurrection and Honda's sagging sales worked to even the motorcycle market by the early 1990s. Harley-Davidson's bikes, in particular, were enjoying increasing popularity, and the company also received praise for its marketing initiatives, innovations in customer service, and improved dealer-customer communications. In 1997 the company had 340,000 members in its Harley Owners Group (HOG), 275,000 of whom were located in the United States. Members received a bimonthly magazine, a touring handbook that included city and state maps and a list of dealers in each state, and other benefits. Each authorized Harley-Davidson dealer may sponsor a local HOG chapter. In 1997 there were 590 HOG chapters in the United States and 940 worldwide.

In 1995 the industry generated approximately $4.8 billion in revenues. Sales of new vehicles accounted for about 45.0 percent, or $2.2 billion of total revenues; 30.7 percent, or about $1.5 billion, came from sales of parts, accessories, and riding apparel. Sales of used vehicles accounted for 13.8 percent, or approximately $668 million of the industry's 1995 revenues; and service labor charges accounted for 9.1 percent, or $440 million. Income from other motorcycle-related sales, primarily insurance and extended warranties, represented 1.3 percent of total industry sales, or approximately $63 million in 1995. The 53,589 industry employees earned an approximate payroll of $987 million in 1996, including owner and manager salaries and advances. Business was conducted at 10,715 retail outlets in all 50 states and the District of Columbia.

Market-share rankings fluctuated dramatically in the years leading up to the 1995 figures. While Honda remained the market-share leader, its share slipped almost 10 percentage points from 39.0 percent in 1988 to 29.2 percent in 1995. Gains made by other brands, therefore, had come at Honda's expense. In 1988 Kawasaki was the third-largest brand, holding 13.9 percent of the market. By 1995 Kawasaki actually gained market share but was in fourth place among the six major brands, with 14.1 percent of the market. Yamaha was the third-largest player, holding 15.2 percent of the market in 1995, and Suzuki accounted for 13.2 percent of new motorcycle sales. German manufacturer BMW, with 1.6 percent of the total, was sixth among the top brands. Harley-Davidson, fifth in 1988 with 9.4 percent of the market, experienced an 11-point market-share increase over four years, moving into second place in the early 1990s. In 1995 Harley-Davidson still held second place, with 23.3 percent of the market.

CURRENT CONDITIONS

The average motorcycle rider was a 38-year-old married male with a college education earning $44,250 per year, according to Irwin Broh & Associates's 1998 survey. More than a third of motorcycle owners surveyed earned at least $50,000 per year, up from 20 percent in 1990. This profile represented an increase from just two years earlier, when the average motorcycle owner was 32 years old, with a median household income of $33,100, according to the *Motorcycle Statistical Annual 1996.* These older, more affluent riders of 1998 could afford heavier, more comfortable, more expensive motorcycles. Also, the ranks of women motorcyclists continued to grow in the 1990s, rising from 6.4 percent of riders in 1990 to 8.2 percent in 1998.

The public's perception of motorcycling safety also has a large impact on the industry's prospects. In the ten years after 1988, motorcycle injury crashes dropped 47 percent and fatalities declined 42 percent. Since 1973 the nonprofit Motorcycle Safety Foundation developed motorcycle rider education courses for beginning and experienced riders. More than 120,000 riders were trained annually in these courses, most of which received state funding.

The livelihood of franchised dealers depends on the franchise they hold. In the mid-1990s, the industry was dominated by six brands of motorcycles. The MIC indicated that together, these brands accounted for 96 percent of the new motorcycles sold in 1997. Harley-Davidson's domestic motorcycle shipments broke the 100,000 unit mark in 1998, rising to 110,902 from 96,216 in 1997. Harley-Davidson's domestic shipments of 97,540 for the first three quarters of 1999 already surpassed 1997 totals. Meanwhile, Honda motorcycle sales slipped 9 percent over the second quarter of 1999, though this figure represented international sales, which were sluggish in Asia.

Industry experts suggested that dealers would see more showroom traffic from middle-aged (35 to 54-year-old males and females) consumers as manufacturers focused on designing new products targeted at this market segment. This group has historically had the highest levels of disposable income. Motorcycle dealers had success selling technologically advanced, luxury vehicles to this generation of buyers in the past and hoped to capitalize on them in future. Manufacturers also began offering improved safety features on popular heavyweight (850 cc and up) bikes.

FURTHER READING

American Motorcycle Network. ''Honda's Net Income for Q2 1999 down Almost 21 Percent.'' Available from http://www.americanmotor.com/Headlines/news/news.cfm?id=1122.

———. ''Motorcycle Sales Continue to Increase for 7th Straight Year.'' Available from http://www.americanmotor.com/Headlines/news/news.cfm?id=1124.

Harley-Davidson, Inc. ''Motorcycle Shipments.'' Available from http://www.harley-davidson.com/company/investor/inv_12.asp.

Motorcycle Industry Council. ''Media News Bureau.'' Available from http://www.mic.org/content/mediacenter/mediacenter3.html.

Motorcycle Statistical Annual 1996. Irvine, CA: Motorcycle Industry Council, Inc., 1996.

Phillips, Stephen. ''That Vroom You Hear Is Honda Motorcycles.'' *Business Week,* 3 September 1990.

SIC 5599

AUTOMOTIVE DEALERS, NOT ELSEWHERE CLASSIFIED

Establishments in this industry are primarily engaged in the retail sale of new and used automotive vehicles, equipment, and supplies, not elsewhere classified, such as snowmobiles, go-karts, dune buggies, utility trailers, and golf carts. Also included in this industry are establishments primarily engaged in the retail sale of aircraft. Not included in this classification are automobiles, light trucks, recreational vehicles, motorcycles, boats, motor scooters, all-terrain vehicles, and personal watercraft.

NAICS CODE(S)

441229 (All Other Motor Vehicle Dealers)

An estimated 1,678 establishments in the automotive dealers, not elsewhere classified, industry employing approximately 9,100 workers were in operation in 1997. These establishments brought in sales of an estimated $2.5 billion in 1997.

Businesses within this industry sell a wide range of products at the retail level. Products as different as snowmobile helmets and single-piston aircraft are sold by retail establishments that vary greatly in size and scope of business.

Snowmobile retailers sell new and used snowmobiles, parts, and equipment and are involved in the servicing of the vehicles. Dealers contract to carry the product lines supplied by the four snowmobile manufacturers worldwide. Because business depends on snow, retailers are located in the states in which winters are marked by snow accumulation that stays on the ground long enough for a respectable snowmobiling season. Dealers also often carry other types of recreational vehicles, such as all-terrain vehicles and personal watercraft, to balance out the seasonal swings in business.

The sport of snowmobiling is relatively new; the first snowmobile was mass produced about 50 years ago by Bombardier, Inc., a Canadian company. *Forbes* estimated that the market peaked in 1971 when dealers sold approximately 500,000 units. The International Snowmobile Manufacturers Association estimated that in the late

1990s, dealers were selling more than 147,000 units a year in the United States at an average unit price of $5,780. The *Statistical Abstract of the United States* estimated that, by the late 1990s, the United States purchased approximately $930 million worth of snowmobiles and related equipment.

New and used personal and business aircraft are sold by establishments that carry a small inventory of vehicles and parts. However, aircraft are more often sold by individuals or organizations who broker the sale of aircraft and related parts from one party to another. Most of the business in this sector of the industry is done in the buying and selling of used aircraft and parts. An article in *Business and Commercial Aircraft* magazine suggested that used aircraft has historically outsold new aircraft at a margin of three to one. The same article maintains that 95 percent of turbine equipment is sold to existing users of business aircraft. The National Aircraft Resale Association reported that 1,525 used jet and 1,312 turboprop sales transactions were completed in 1997. The figures were compiled by NARA's associate member, AMSTAT Corporation, a research organization that compiles statistics for the aviation business industry.

According to the Kart Marketing Group, Inc., publisher of *Kart Marketing International* magazine, go-karts generated approximately $500 million in business per year in North America in the late 1990s. There are two different types of go-karts and two types of retailers to sell them. ''Fun'' karts (recreational karts for general usage priced between $700 and $900) are sold through lawn and garden stores and hardware stores. ''Racing'' karts (those karts built especially for high-speed track usage and priced from $3,000 to $5,000) are sold through outlets dedicated to kart sales. Approximately 200,000 fun karts were sold at the retail level in the late 1990s, compared to sales of approximately 10,500 racing karts. The retail outlets selling racing karts range from individuals selling parts and equipment on a part-time basis to storefront establishments. Also, there are many Web sites dedicated to mail order of fun karts, racing karts, and accessories.

FURTHER READING

International Snowmobile Manufacturers Association. *Snowmobiling Fact Book,* 2000. Available from http// www.snowmobile.org.

U.S. Bureau of the Census. *Statistical Abstract of the United States.* Washington, D.C.: GPO, 1998.

U.S. Department of Commerce. *1997 Census of Service Industries & Geographic Area Series.* Washington, D.C.: Bureau of the Census, 2000. Available from http://www.census.gov.

SIC 5611

MEN'S AND BOYS' CLOTHING AND ACCESSORY STORES

This category includes establishments primarily engaged in the retail sale of men's and boys' ready-to-wear clothing and accessories.

NAICS CODE(S)

448110 (Men's Clothing Stores)
448150 (Clothing Accessories Stores)

INDUSTRY SNAPSHOT

The men's and boys' clothing and accessory store industry was composed of many small independently owned businesses and dozens of larger chain stores. In 1997 there were approximately 12,143 establishments engaged in the selling of men's and boys' clothing. Furthermore, roughly 180 of the larger stores generated more than $5 billion in sales, and the industry as a whole generated nearly $11 billion in sales and employed more than 100,000 people. These companies carried different product lines including tailored clothing, work clothes, and heavy outerwear.

As they entered the mid-1990s, the many businesses in this industry faced a changing retail environment. The recession of the late 1980s and early 1990s caused a conservative shift in spending behavior. In this price-conscious atmosphere, retailers of non-essentials were forced to offer goods whose price was consistent with consumer expectations of quality and value. The industry performed poorly in the early 1990s. Growth rates in men's and boy's wear apparel retailing were below the rates for the total apparel and accessory industry. Entering the mid-1990s, however, stores in the industry were reevaluating product lines and pricing strategies in an effort to improve their financial performance. Consumer demands for value priced clothing caused changes in brand name pricing and marketing. The push, beginning in the mid-1990s, toward ''casual days'' at work had an impact on the men's market; fewer suits and ties were purchased, and clothing and accessories known as ''dress casual'' began to make headway.

ORGANIZATION AND STRUCTURE

The men's and boys' segment of the apparel and accessories industry was relatively small. Historically, marketers focused on the women's market, assuming that they were more concerned about fashion than men. In 1990, the men's and boy's category generated just over 10 percent of total sales in the accessory and apparel category. At that time, the women's ready-to-wear and specialty stores commanded close to 67 percent of the category, while the family clothing stores garnered roughly 29 percent. Businesses in the industry hoped that growing fashion awareness among men and boys would increase the industry's percentage of sales.

Since they carried narrow product lines but great depth within those lines, men's and boys' apparel and accessory stores were classified as specialty retailers. Historically, retailers of men's and boys' clothing and accessories focused on particular segments of the industry. These segments usually mirrored the five divisions into which menswear manufacturers were divided: tailored clothing, including suits, overcoats, topcoats, sport coats, and separate trousers; furnishings, including shirts, neckwear, sweaters, knit tops, underwear, socks, robes, and pajamas; heavy outerwear, including jackets, snowsuits, ski jackets, and parkas; work clothes, including work shirts, work pants, overalls, and related items; and other, including uniforms, hats, and miscellaneous items.

For nearly 150 years, these categories prevailed at the retail level. Even department stores organized their men's and boys' wear departments according to these categories. Beginning in the late 1960s, however, men's and boys' wear stores moved away from specialization into more diversified retail formats that offered a variety of clothing lines.

The trend toward large diversified stores accelerated during the 1980s. By the 1990s, superstores offering huge selections at discount prices were flourishing. Companies such as S&K Famous Brands, Inc., Today's Man, Inc., and The Men's Wearhouse, Inc. that were started in the late 1960s and early 1970s enjoyed tremendous growth in the 1990s as consumers flocked to the stores in search of stylish clothing at a discount. Although these stores focused on the tailored wear segments, they also carried huge selections in all categories in an effort to provide convenient one-stop shopping for customers.

The locations of men's and boys' stores underwent changes as the superstore format became popular. Many men's and boys' wear retailers moved out of the high-rent cities and malls into less expensive, but larger, suburban locations. The new superstores, which were sometimes more than 20,000 square feet, were often located in strip shopping centers or stand-alone buildings. To avoid high rents, these superstore retailers were quite willing to locate off the beaten track.

Competitive Structure. Owing to an increase in the overall fashion consciousness of American men, the industry experienced a rapid growth stage during the 1960s. The nature and intensity of competition in this industry has varied considerably since then. During most of that decade, rising demand for men's clothing and accessories encouraged new entrants. By the 1970s, however, the number of menswear stores was decreasing. Competition increased during the 1970s as department stores and specialty retailers battled for market share in a declining market. Demand picked up again in the mid-1980s resulting in a rapid increase in the number of stores.

Throughout the 1970s, department stores, which enjoyed the advantages of location and customer recognition, appeared to have a competitive edge over the specialty stores. For this reason, many retailers that entered the industry in the 1970s were off-price stores that hoped to compete with department stores by offering low-priced merchandise. It was not until the mid-1980s that department stores were the main competition of the men's and boys' specialty retailers.

The downward economic trend of the late 1980s, however, was a boon for discounters. By 1990, many off-price specialty retailers enjoyed a competitive advantage over department stores whose merchandise was often priced 30 percent higher than that of the discounters. Heading into the mid-1990s, market conditions favored the discount retail formats. Since even affluent customers were increasingly willing to shop at off-price stores, traditional retail formats continued to decline.

Financial Structure. Businesses in this industry were often small, privately owned stores, although there were many chain stores in operation. In 1990, the smaller businesses typically generated more than $1 million on an initial investment of approximately $295,500. The sales figures for chain retailers were quite disparate owing to the varied size and success of different chains; some of the larger chains grossed upwards of $300 million in sales, while industry-leader Hartmarx Specialty Stores generated over $1 billion.

Statistics showed that men's and boys' wear stores were more expensive to operate than women's or children's wear stores; therefore, the financial structure of businesses in this category differed from other segments within the retail category. Annual payroll, for example, in men's and boy's stores averaged $13,274 per employee, while women's accessory and specialty store payroll averaged about $10,000. Inventory costs were relatively high in the men's and boy's segment as well. The short fashion cycle and resulting quick turnover of merchandise in women's apparel explains much of the disparity in inventory ratios. Men's fashions changed so infrequently that stores could carry inventory without worrying about significant changes in customer preferences.

BACKGROUND AND DEVELOPMENT

Developed in the late 1700s, the menswear industry is the oldest of the domestic apparel industries. The industry began in the northeast, where Samuel Slater built the first textile mill, and where sailors off ships needed ready-to-wear clothing when they arrived in port. As the seamen could not afford custom-tailored clothing, tailors in port cities like New Bedford, Boston, and New York made standard size suits for them to wear as soon as they arrived on land. These early garments were made of the roughest cloth and were also frequently purchased by southern plantation owners for their workers.

The industry continued to develop as the demand for ready-to-wear clothing increased. The steady stream of immigrants that arrived in the United States with few clothes of their own, the Gold Rush in 1849, and the Civil War all stimulated the industry. When the Civil War ended, opportunities in the industry continued since people moving to the newly opened land in the West purchased ready-made clothing before they departed.

In response to the growing popularity of ready-to-wear men's clothing, dry goods stores featuring men's apparel sprang up throughout the country. These early experiments in retailing were the predecessors of the modern department store and shaped the direction of the modern retail industry. Many of the stores that were started during the early 1800s continued to do business into the 1990s. Heading into the twenty-first century, Brooks Brothers, founded in 1818, was the nation's oldest clothing store still in business.

One of the pioneers in men's retailing, John Wanamaker, introduced many of the merchandising strategies that are still used in the retailing industry. Wanamaker, together with his brother-in-law Nathaniel Brown, started a men's and boys' clothing store in 1861 in Philadelphia. Wanamaker, who had almost become a minister, proclaimed that he and his brother-in-law would follow the ''Golden Rule of Business.'' Guarantees of satisfaction or money-back refunds were the hallmark of Wanamaker's businesses. So badly did Wanamaker want to get his message across that after making $24.67 on his first day of business, Wanamaker invested $24 in advertising. He was one of the first merchants to purchase a full-page newspaper advertisement. Wanamaker's, with a reputation for carrying fine clothing and accessories, became a shopping legend for all ages and both sexes. The end of an era came in 1995-1996 when most Wanamaker stores were bought out by the May Company and converted to Lord & Taylor stores. The Wanamaker's name had actually died some years earlier, although its former flagship store in Philadelphia still gives many shoppers a strong sense of the Wanamaker past.

Although many of the early men's and boys' clothing and accessory stores evolved into large department stores, the small independent shops continued to flourish throughout the nineteenth and twentieth centuries. These stores were typically conservative and specialized. Often, for example, a store would offer only tailored clothing or work clothes. For roughly 150 years, the men's and boys' wear industry retained the same selling practices.

A new segment of men's and boys' retailers developed in the 1960s: the casual and sportswear stores. Changes in lifestyle and increased demand for more variety in men's wear led to the decline of many tailored wear retailers. By the 1970s, leisure wear was the fastest-growing segment of men's and boys' retailing.

Dual Distribution. Unlike other apparel industries, the men's and boys' clothing business has been connected with dual distribution since its inception. The term ''dual distribution'' referred to the practice of selling manufactured goods on both a wholesale and on a retail level.

As the country expanded, the manufacturers in the north found themselves far away from their customers. Although the factories were located in mill towns like Lowell, Massachusetts, and New York City, the population was growing rapidly in places like New Orleans. Initially, the apparel manufacturers were willing to sell their goods to clothing stores in the South. It did not take long, however, for clothing producers to realize that owning retail stores would be profitable. By the 1830s, manufacturers operated outlet stores in large southern ports such as New Orleans and Charleston. Most factories also continued to sell apparel to independent stores at the wholesale level.

Many well-known names in this industry, such as Hartmarx Corporation, Botany Industries, and Phillips Van Heusen practiced dual distribution. In women's apparel, on the other hand, this policy was unusual. The industry watched the decline of tailored wear, especially suits. By the mid-1990s, the suit segment had been declining five percent a year since 1989. 9. The number of suits being manufactured reflected the trend: in 1990, 15.5 million men's and boy's suits were manufactured, down from 18.4 million in 1989. The suit industry was at its apex in 1979, when 25 million suits were made for the U.S. market.

In the place of the suits, the tailored separates product line was prospering. An inexpensive and flexible alternative to the traditional men's suit, tailored separates allowed customers to mix and match jackets and pants of different sizes and colors according to their needs. The separates were once considered a cheap way of selling clothes and were typically carried by bargain outlets or mass retailers like J.C. Penney. Heading into the mid-1990s, however, upscale retailers such as Brooks Brothers were carrying tailored separates as well. In fact, Brooks Brothers' separates line, called the Wardrobe Collection, represented over 30 percent of its sales by the mid-1990s.

In addition to the tailored separates, retailers in the men's and boys' clothing and apparel industry discovered that the inexpensive product lines such as ties and hats were very lucrative. Although the recession convinced many men to forgo the major purchases like suits, the lower priced items were popular. In fact, ties enjoyed faddish popularity even among teenagers. In response to increased demand, retailers of men's and boys' casual wear, such as The Gap, added ties to their merchandise in the early 1990s. Tie sales continued to grow into the mid-1990s, as new styles and fabrics continued to catch the attention of consumers. Baseball hats were also popular during this period. Sportswear stores stocked hundreds of baseball hats featuring team logos from college and professional teams that were engaged in a variety of sports.

Among the best-selling casual lines was licensed clothing. Merchandise featuring characters from popular television shows and movie releases sold extremely well in the early 1990s, as did licensed sports team apparel. The popularity of sports logos was no surprise to the men's and boys' apparel retailing business. The proliferation of new sports franchises during this period contributed to the fad. Department stores accounted for 79 percent of all licensed apparel sold in 1995.

Warner Brothers' Looney Tunes characters enjoyed tremendous popularity beginning in the early 1990s. Looney Tunes and the National Basketball League teamed up to produce apparel and accessories featuring both licenses. This line was popular with the young men's segment, especially in urban areas.

In addition to changes in the types of merchandise sold, the men's and boys' apparel and accessories industry moved more toward using private labels than it had in the past. David Feld, CEO of industry-leader Today's Man summarized the shift by noting that "years ago, retailers were representatives of manufacturers. Today, we see ourselves as the buying agent of the consumers."

Many of the large discount retailers discovered that private label merchandise was more profitable than brand-name clothing. Men's wear retailers who sold private label merchandise avoided having to mark up prices to allow for manufacturer and distributor profits. The savings was passed on to the consumer in the form of lower prices. In the value-oriented climate of the 1990s, this pricing advantage gave private label retailers a competitive advantage.

Advertising. Historically, advertising in this industry was subdued compared with other segments of the apparel and accessory category. Even men's wear manufacturers did little national advertising, preferring instead to rely on time honored reputation and brand recognition. During the 1970s and 1980s, some manufacturers provided retailers with newspaper and magazine advertisement and the necessary materials for radio and television commercials. This cooperative advertising continued to be popular into the 1990s.

By the late 1980s, however, men's and boys' retailers, especially discount chains, were aggressively advertising. Houston-based The Men's Wearhouse, for example, began advertising in local newspapers during the 1970s, but by 1993, the company spent close to $14 million on promotions, the majority of which were television commercials. Companies that focused on small to mid-size markets like Memphis, Tennessee, and Charlotte, North Carolina, valued advertising as a competitive tool. In these markets, advertising helped gain market share quickly. Discounters in these areas typically spent 5 to 6 percent of sales on advertising, though The Men's Wearhouse spent nearly 8 percent of 1992 sales on commercials.

Trade Groups. Trade groups also figured prominently in the publicity efforts of menswear retailers. Major national publicity campaigns were often organized and sponsored by a number of trade groups.

Based in Washington, DC, the Menswear Retailers of America organization drew its membership from independent menswear stores located throughout the country. The organization was originally called the National Association of Retail Clothiers and Furnishers whose principal purpose was to lobby on behalf of the menswear retail community. By the 1990s, the organization provided its members with a monthly newsletter and an annual business survey. The group also organized national conventions and seminars for industry executives.

A more niche-oriented trade association, the Big and Tall Associates concentrated on a market that represented less than 5 percent of all the nation's men. These customers were over 5'11" and/or had a chest measurement of more than 48 inches. Roughly 60 menswear manufacturers and 40 merchants were members of the association.

The importance of Father's Day for menswear merchants was underscored by the existence of the Father's Day Council, Inc. Although the council was a nonprofit organization supported by manufacturers and department stores, it provided much publicity for stores in the men's and boys' apparel accessory industry. Through various campaigns, The Father's Day Council promoted gift-giving on Father's Day. One of the organization's oldest traditions was the National Fathers of the Year awards. Each year, the recipients were chosen from various professions.

In January 2000, the American Apparel Manufacturers Association (AAMA) voted to allow retailers into their organization. The reasons for this move were related to the shifting marketplace: retailers had begun sourcing directly from overseas contractors, online commerce promised increased sales, and similarities between retailers and manufacturers were growing. Retailers had been allowed to join AAMA in the past as Associate Members, but revisions to the bylaws in January 2000 afforded them full membership status.

INDUSTRY LEADERS

Although the men's and boys' clothing and accessory industry was fragmented, a few of the companies in the industry were growing faster than the competition. These businesses were able to capitalize on the changes in consumer preferences and spending habits that were rapidly changing this traditionally conservative industry.

Traditional Retailers. The early 1990s witnessed the demise of some of the industry's well-known leaders. One casualty during this period was F.W. Woolworth Co.'s Anderson Little-Richman Brothers chain, which folded in 1992. Impacting the industry on a much larger scale, however, was the decision by Hartmarx Corporation to divest Hartmarx Specialty Stores, Inc., such as the Wallach's stores in New York.

With 1992 sales over $610 million, Hartmarx Specialty Stores, Inc. was one of the largest companies in this business. Hartmarx, however, was an example of a company that was slow to respond to changes in the industry. Like many men's wear retailers, Hartmarx's core business was in clothing manufacturing. The company built its reputation on manufacturing and selling conservative suits with labels like Hart Schaffner & Marx and Hickey-Freeman. The late 1980s were tough years for Hartmarx, when a weak economy and low demand for suits squeezed profits.

After years of consecutive losses, the company re-evaluated its competitive strengths. More than 300 retail stores were sold or closed in 1993 when the Hartmarx Corporation decided to refocus on manufacturing. In response to changing tastes, the company was emphasizing more casual looks over the traditional conservative suits.

Another industry leader involved in retail and manufacturing, and the oldest men's retail store in America, was Brooks Brothers. This company was started in 1818 by Henry Sands. Brooks Brothers was the company that invented the button-down shirt and the argyle sock. The company outfitted notable Americans like Abraham Lincoln and Franklin D. Roosevelt and continued as the last bastion of conservatism in the men's clothing industry.

According to Brooks Brothers executives, their company has been successful over the years because its name represents American style. Brooks' clothes have changed very little over time. In fact, the button-down shirt, invented by Brooks Brothers in the nineteenth century, is generally the exact same garment today. Brooks Brothers offered the stable conservative type of clothing that appealed to U.S. presidents as well as young men out of college who want to dress appropriately for a first job interview.

Although the Brooks Brothers name has been associated with conservative clothing, the company also demonstrated flexibility. Recognizing that men were buying fewer suits and were dressing more casually at work, Brooks Brothers introduced Friday Wear. The line was more relaxed than a suit, making it appropriate for casual Fridays at the office. Brooks Brothers also introduced the "Wardrobe Collection," a line of tailored separates. These and other innovations helped Brooks Brothers prosper despite that fact that many of their products have not changed since they were first introduced in the nineteenth century.

The company has been owned since 1988 by the British firm Marks & Spencer, and it has 75 retail stores throughout the U.S. It also has 65 stores in Japan and two in Hong Kong, although Marks & Spencer has considered selling the chain. Brooks Brothers sales in 1998 were $543 million.

Jos. A. Bank Clothiers, Inc., founded in 1905, specializes in suits and other business attire, although it too offers casual wear. It also sells golf wear under the David Leadbetter label. The company operates more than 100 stores in 30 states, and had sales in 1999 of $187 million.

Discount Leaders. An important departure from tradition in the men's wear businesses was the willingness of consumers to purchase tailored wear at bargain outlets. Two of the leaders in this fast growing segment were S&K Famous Brands and The Men's Wearhouse. Both of these stores used similar strategies in pricing, promotion, and location, and represented a stark contrast to traditional men's wear retailers like Brooks Brothers. The top three discount suit chains (S & K Famous Brands, Men's Wearhouse, and Today's Man) had combined sales of $1.1 billion in 1999. Industry watchers predicted that these three would hold 50 percent of the market share early in the 21st century.

S&K Famous Brands, Inc. was started in 1967 by I.J. Siegel and Abe Kaminsky as a wholesale business. The founders started their operation after retirement: they would spend their days buying one retailer's overstock and selling it to another retailer. Eventually, the volume of merchandise exceeded the space available in the car the two men used as a their base of operations. Siegel and Kaminsky rented space in a former thrift store and eventually attracted retail customers.

Siegel's son, Stuart, joined the business in the early 1970s and initiated its expansion. By 1973, S&K Famous Brands operated 5 stores; when the company went public in 1983, it had grown to 13 stores with sales of $10 million. The initial public offering generated $2.6 million, most of which was used for expansion.

Despite rapid growth, S&K Famous Brands maintained tight control of its finances. Its expansion was gradual and internally financed. Owing to this conservative approach, the company had little long-term debt as it entered the mid-1990s. By 1999 S&K had nearly 240 stores in operation in 27 states, and estimated sales total of $154.4 million.

An off-price retailer, The Men's Wearhouse had humble beginnings similar to S&K Famous Brands. The first Men's Wearhouse store was started in 1972 with a $7,000 investment by George Zimmer, an apparel salesman. Zimmer carried brand-name men's suits and sold them well below department store prices. In 1992, after 20 years of operation, the company went public.

The Men's Wearhouse battled aggressively with department stores. The company invested heavily in television advertising featuring George Zimmer attacking his competitors by name. Zimmer's ads were scathing enough to provoke Nordstrom Inc., a Seattle-based retail chain, to file a suit against The Men's Wearhouse for false and misleading advertising. Despite this challenge, by 1999 the company had grown into a 430 store chain with a presence in 40 states and Washington DC.

Today's Man was started by David Feld, the current CEO, in Philadelphia in 1971. The store expanded and in 1984 the company opened an 18,000 square foot retail superstore in the Philadelphia suburbs. The company expanded rapidly in the mid-1990s but the market for clothing became so saturated that ultimately it had to file for Chapter 11 protection. The company emerged from protection in 1997 and had 1999 sales of $213.6 million. It operates 29 stores in the Philadelphia, New York, and Washington, DC markets.

As they moved into the mid-1990s all the industry leaders were focusing on price and service as competitive priorities. Even the discounters realized that the 1990s consumer was discriminating in addition to being price-conscious. Attentive in-store service and attractive store design, therefore, figured prominently in even the most streamlined operations. The growth of the Internet has affected how virtually all businesses do their selling, and retailers are exploring the possibilities of the World Wide Web. However, as Michelle Midgette wrote in *Net-commerce* magazine, ''Comparatively speaking, the fashion and apparel industry has been slow to embrace the Net for e-commerce.'' In fact, in 1998 the industry generated just over $300 million in online sales: ''In contrast, approximately $1.5 billion were spent on PC hardware and software, and $636 million were spent on gifts and flowers.''

WORKFORCE

The U.S. Department of Labor reported that the total number of individuals employed in this industry was estimated to exceed 85,000 by the end of the 1990s. By 1997, men's clothing stores accounted for 83,000 of the industry's workers. It is difficult to gauge exact numbers because, even with the large discount stores, the industry remains fragmented. Although there are fewer and fewer of the independent specialty stores, they do still exist.

AMERICA AND THE WORLD

As the industry moved into the mid-1990s, American companies began to establish specialty retail operations abroad. Manufacturers of men's and boys' clothing and accessories were well aware of the opportunities abroad, and many had established joint ventures in foreign markets. The retailers, however, found it more difficult to penetrate foreign markets.

One company that was successful in negotiating a retail joint venture was Eddie Bauer. A division of Spiegel, Eddie Bauer was a leader in the men's and boys' wear industry in the United States with successful retail and mail order operations. In 1993, Spiegel announced that it had successfully negotiated an agreement with Otto-Sumisho in Japan to form a joint venture to sell Eddie Bauer products through retail stores and catalogs. Company executives forecasted that they would open between 75 and 100 stores in Japan and that the venture would generate from $400 to $450 million in sales.

The fact that Eddie Bauer was able to negotiate this agreement was a positive signal to other retailers. In the tailored wear sector, however, global expansion was difficult since European and Far Eastern-made suits were widely regarded as being superior to American manufactured suits. Opportunities did exist, however, in the casual wear segments, as Eddie Bauer's success indicated.

RESEARCH AND TECHNOLOGY

Inventory management became a major strategic priority in the early 1990s. Most retail environments, including the men's and boys' apparel segment, were forced to improve inventory management techniques through advanced automation. S&K Famous Brands, for example, implemented merchandising information system that tracked store inventories on a daily basis. The system improved efficiency and helped maintain the correct match of inventory to demand. Other types of state of the art technologies were sweeping men's and boys' wear retail operations and the retail industry as a whole. Many businesses invested in cash registers that could calculate discounts, approve credit, accept credit cards, and schedule deliveries. This new technology promised cost-saving in the long run, but in the short run the cost of the technology itself was prohibitive to smaller stores.

Most industry experts agreed that technology enabled retailers to react to their businesses much more quickly. Before computerized tracking systems, managers would wait until Monday morning for weekly sales figures. With the aid of technology, this information is available on a daily basis. The timeliness of this information gave retailers the ability to respond to sales by placing reorders, taking markdowns, and spotting trends on an accelerated basis.

Some apparel retailers complained about the amount of useless information the technology produced. Some industry executives pointed out that the technology revolution produced so much data, they wasted time sorting through the information. One industry analyst summarized the problem, noting that ''The technology makes it possible for retailers to be better, provided [they] also have the systems capabilities to deal with a large mass of data, to analyze and summarize, to distill what is important and what is extraneous.'' Despite these criticisms, however, industry experts agreed that automation was a prerequisite for success in the 1990s retail environment.

Using technology to enhance their businesses is critical to the success of men's and boys' apparel and accessory retailers. The intensely competitive market coupled with shifting consumer preferences made flexibility and low price important competitive weapons. The ability to enhance reaction time and to streamline operations using automation helped retailers compete in this environment.

FURTHER READING

''AAMA Votes to Include Retailers.'' *Apparel Industry Magazine,* February 4, 2000. Available from http://www.aimagazine.com/news.cfm.

Hoover's Company Capsules. Austin, TX: Hoover's Inc., 1999. Available from http://www.hoovers.com.

Midgette, Michelle. ''E-commerce is a Good Fit for the Fashion and Apparel Industry.'' *Netcommerce,* July/August 1999. Available from http://www.netcommercemag.com/july/2/html.

U.S. Census Bureau. *1997 Economic Census—Retail Sale.* Washington: GPO, 1999.

Walton, John B. *Business Profitability Data.* Dallas: Weybridge Publishing Company, 1991.

''Why Mom-and-Pop Stores Just Don't Cut It Any More.'' *Apparel Industry Magazine,* January 2000.

SIC 5621

WOMEN'S CLOTHING STORES

This industry includes establishments primarily engaged in the retail sale of a general line of women's ready-to-wear clothing. This category also includes establishments primarily engaged in the specialized retail sale of women's coats, suits, and dresses. Custom tailors primarily engaged in making women's clothing to individual order are classified in **SIC 5699: Miscellaneous Apparel and Accessory Stores.**

NAICS CODE(S)

448120 (Women's Clothing Stores)

INDUSTRY SNAPSHOT

Industry performance in the 1990s has been mixed. Apparel sales reached $113.6 billion in 1996, posting a 2.9 percent increase over 1995. According to the *U.S. Industry and Trade Outlook 1999,* slow sales could be attributed to consumers taking less time to shop and apparel purchases reaching lower financial priority than spending on investments, dining out, and vacations. Sales were expected to grow by 2 to 3 percent annually through 2002. In the women's apparel market, women opted for more practical but stylish and affordable clothing suitable for both work and leisure.

Several of the nation's retailers failed to catch onto the new trend, putting many retail stores in trouble. However, industry leaders like The Gap, Inc., with $9.1 billion in sales, and The Limited, Inc., with $9.2 billion in sales, performed quite well in 1998. The two industry giants succeeded during the slump by exploring new markets and responding to customer needs.

ORGANIZATION AND STRUCTURE

The structure of the U.S. retail industry, including women's clothing stores, has changed significantly since the early 1990s, moving from a production-driven market to a consumer-driven market. Nontraditional retailers, such as discounters, off-priced stores, and factory outlets, fared well.

Because of continuing competition from nontraditional retailers, department stores such as J.C. Penney and specialty stores such as The Limited increased their focus on private labels. For example, J.C. Penney's Arizona clothing line offered uniqueness and style that national brand labels sold by discounters and outlet stores didn't provide.

In the mid-1990s, consumers demanded more convenience and quicker service from growing no-store retailing, particularly in direct-mail order, television, and online shopping. An Internet shopping study by Ernst & Young LLP reported that the number of retailers selling online tripled in 1998 to 39 percent. The online market was estimated to reach $13 billion in sales at the end of 1999.

The relationship between larger retailers and suppliers significantly intensified because a growing number of retailers were taking on entrepreneurship roles traditionally performed by apparel producers. Larger retailers and direct-mail order companies were making decisions in areas such as product design, fabric selection and procurement, and apparel production, which in turn influenced production scheduling, pricing, and delivery dates.

BACKGROUND AND DEVELOPMENT

Women's clothing stores were introduced in Europe in the late 1700s—slightly later in the American colonies—at a time when productive capability, population, and prosperity allowed clothing production to move out of the house and into the factory, and clothes to move into retail stores. Around this time, seamstresses began opening shops offering custom-made hats, dresses, cloaks, or other garments. These garments of the latest fashion were for those who could afford to hire out the work of stitching. Trading posts in the frontier areas carried cloth and some ready-made apparel.

The invention of the sewing machine, the rise of mass production, and the proliferation of retail stores by the late nineteenth century led people first to sample and later to rely on ready-made clothing as a reliable means of obtaining fashionable clothing. In the 1890s, ready-to-wear clothing came into its own, and by the turn of the century ready-made women's wear was available in abundance in the United States. By the 1920s, it was considered more fashionable to buy clothing from a store than to make it at home.

For many years, the department store and the downtown women's shop were the mainstays of women's wear retailing. Department stores offering a vast selection of goods and specialty stores catering to unique tastes dotted the urban landscape. For those with enough money, shopping became a social event. Along with the growth of women's clothing retailing came the increasing importance of fashion.

The women's apparel industry established a voice in government through the National Retail Federation (NRF), the trade group representing the entire spectrum of the nation's retail industry. In the early and mid-1990s, the NRF lobbied the U.S. Congress on issues such as minimum wages and the proposed health care plan. The NRF was opposed to an increase in the minimum wage on the grounds that many retailers would have to close down operations or fire staff to meet expenses with a higher salary base.

In 1994, *Women's Wear Daily* reported that the NRF opposed the Clinton administration's proposed universal health coverage on the grounds that more than 700,000 jobs would have to be eliminated in all retailing. At that time only 35 percent of retail workers received health care benefits. The NRF supported a plan that emphasized offering health coverage but did not require employers to pay for that coverage and allowed for the creation of purchasing pools for group insurance.

CURRENT CONDITIONS

Posting modest returns in the mid-1990s, women's clothing sales were expected to remain strong into the twenty-first century. Dedicated women's stores, however, faced renewed competition from alternative retail venues offering specialty or general line women's apparel in addition to other product lines.

Sporting goods retailers were devising new strategies to increase women's apparel business. In 1995, women's apparel ranged from 10 percent to 40 percent of store merchandise. Sporting goods retailers saw strong potential in the women's apparel market. Retailers increased floor space to accommodate women's products; set up women's departments; increased stock of best-selling brands; and held store events to draw more female customers.

Department stores also responded to the increased demand for women's apparel and began repositioning themselves to win back the customers they had lost to more focused outlets like The Gap and The Limited. Such retailers as Bloomingdale's and Dayton Hudson Department Stores reexamined the big picture in 1995 and revamped the women's apparel collections.

The large-sized women's clothing market grabbed the attention of clothing retailers in the mid-1990s with sales reaching $20 billion and claiming 24.7 percent of the market, according to *Women's Wear Daily.* The key factors that influenced these sales were an increase in fashions featuring younger silhouettes and the use of better fabrics. Lane Bryant, a division of The Limited Inc., brought in more fashionable clothes and worked to change the perception of large-size fashion. ''Our customer wants to wear the exact same fashion her skinny friends wear,'' noted Lane Bryant's Chief Executive Jill Dean in a 1999 *Wall Street Journal* interview.

One of the hottest growth areas in retailing during the late 1990s was discounting. Clothing retailers saw an opportunity to bring fashionable clothes at reasonable prices to the masses. ''There was a time when people who shopped at department stores wouldn't shop at Wal-Mart,'' explains Kurt Barnard of *Barnard's Retail Trend Report.* ''Then it became chic to shop downscale, to shop for a bargain. People used to pay $10 and said they paid $20. Now they pay $20 and say they paid $10.'' In 1999, Target was the country's third largest discounter and a $21 billion division of the Dayton Hudson Corporation. Nearly 35 percent of Target's sales come from the clothing department. Old Navy, a division of the Gap, was launched in 1994 to compete with stores like Sears and Target with this concept in mind. *Fortune* magazine described Old Navy as ''discount shopping with an edge, discount shopping that appeals to people who can afford Gucci.''

Intimate apparel was another area with strong growth during the 1990s. From 1993 to 1998, sales of bras rose almost 50 percent, according to market research company NPD Group Inc. The *Wall Street Journal* reported in 1998 that ''although discount and department stores command a majority share of the $11 billion intimate apparel market, no single retailer has a larger chunk than Victoria's Secret stores, with 14 percent.'' In 1996, the Gap began selling intimate apparel for women in the regular Gap stores in 1996. In the fall of 1998, the Gap opened GapBody, selling bras, panties, pajamas, boxers, loungewear, and t-shirts. GapBody also sells its own fragrance, Gap Blue No. 655, and bath-related merchandise such as soap, towels, washcloths, toothbrushes and shower curtains. With five stores in 1998, the Gap planned on opening 10-15 more in 1999. With GapBody stores opening nationally, market analysts predicted some market erosion for Victoria's Secret, one of the only national retailers specializing in intimate apparel. Brian Postol, an A.G. Edwards analyst commented, ''If there is one retailer out there that's successful at going after new businesses and pulling them off, Gap is it.''

Industry Leaders

The leaders in the women's clothing store retail industry in the United States were The Gap, Inc. and The Limited, Inc. The Gap, founded in 1969 by Don and Doris Fisher in San Francisco, has become an international specialty retailer specializing in men's, women's and children's casual clothing and accessories. The Gap operated 2,237 stores in six countries in 1999, including The Gap, GapKids, Baby Gap, GapBody, Banana Republic, and Old Navy Clothing Co. Gap has stores in the United States, Japan, the United Kingdom, Canada, France, and Germany.

The Gap expanded quickly in the 1980s, purchasing the Banana Republic chain in 1983, launching GapKids, and BabyGap in 1986, and opening its first overseas store in London in 1987. By 1990 The Gap was one of the most successful apparel retailers and the second-largest clothing brand in the United States. One of the biggest successes for The Gap was the Old Navy division, launched in 1994. In less than three years, Gap opened 282 Old Navy stores and hit sales of $1 billion. Gap Online was introduced in November 1997. In 1998, the Gap reported a 28.8 percent return on capital and 17 percent average annual sales growth. The company planned to increase its international presence by opening 400 new American stores and 100 new international stores in 1999. The company budgeted $1 billion for 1999 store openings.

The Limited Inc., the top U.S. women's apparel retailer, was founded in 1963. The Limited distributes and sells women's and men's apparel. The company operated 5,400 specialty stores in 1999 under the retail names of The Limited Stores, Express, Lerner New York, Lane Bryant, Henri Bendel, and Structure.

The mid-to-late 1990s marked a number of changes for The Limited. The Limited spun off the Victoria's Secret and Bath & Body Works chains in 1995, creating Intimate Brands Inc., 84 percent owned by The Limited. In 1995, The Limited also purchased the Galyan Stores, a chain of outdoor-oriented stores. The Limited took a cautious approach to adding more stores, opening three new stores in 1996 and four in 1997. However, during the summer of 1999, The Limited sold its majority stake in Galyan's to the investment firm of Freeman Spogli & Co. The deal leaves The Limited with a 40 percent stake in the company. The Limited made Abercrombie & Fitch Co. its own public company in 1998 and in 1999, The Limited spun off The Limited Too to shareholders. According to Leslie Wexner, the founder and chairman of The Limited, ''the spin-offs will let investors better evaluate each company and The Limited can focus on developing its other brands.''

After enormous success throughout the 1980s, The Limited experienced financial difficulties in the mid-1990s. The company redesigned its women's division by re-staffing, new advertising, and improving quality. During the first quarter of 1999, Wexner announced at the company's annual meeting that ''the branding approach that made Victoria's Secret such a success is starting to take root at Express.'' Sales for the first quarter of 1999 rose 4.8 percent to $2.1 billion, compared to $2 billion in the first quarter of 1998. Wexner attributed the strong results to the company's efforts to better manage its inventories. The Limited hopes to improve profits by carrying deeper inventories of fewer styles. Lane Bryant, offering fashionable clothes for women in sizes 14 to 28, became one of the company's strongest performers, with same-store sales up 10 percent. Jill Dean, Lane Bryant's Chief Executive, estimated that revenue for the division ''could reach $1 billion in the fiscal year ending in January 2000, up from $933 million a year earlier.''

Workforce

Women's clothing stores employed an estimated 454,000 people entering the late 1990s. According to the U.S. Department of Labor, in 1992 30 percent of retail workers were less than 25 years of age and one-third of all retail employees worked part-time. Employment prospects in women's clothing were traditionally most abundant in sales, where the majority of the work force was female. Prospects for employment of women were expected to remain strong in the sector despite flat growth.

There were three basic categories of jobs in women's apparel retailing: sales associates, store management, and merchandisers. Larger chains may have also employed their own product testers, fashion consultants, and comparison shoppers. As U.S. retailing firms became more diverse and turned increasingly toward international markets, a corresponding increase in the need for multilingual personnel in all of these categories was predicted.

Sales associates are responsible for performing customer service and a variety of operational duties such as setting up displays and organizing stock. Store managers oversee sales, operations, and personnel functions. Merchandisers work with the apparel manufacturers to select apparel for the retailer and control merchandise expenses. Training for merchandisers and buyers usually includes college course work or fashion school.

Wages in the retail industry are typically lower than the average across industries, and working hours often span a seven-day week. However, the effect of the seven-day week is eased by the use of part-time employees. In some shops and departments, the sales staff received a combination of salary and commission.

AMERICA AND THE WORLD

According to *Advertising Age International,* with the success of global expansion, "the world will be a lot like a giant shopping mall by the year 2000." Expectations were that more consumers would be able to shop at the same popular retail stores anywhere in the world. In 1995, U.S. apparel retailers were occupied with expanding into Canada, Europe, and Japan.

Historically, Canada offered little market opportunity to retailers, putting restraints on size and economics, according to a survey in *Chain Store Age.* However, because the U.S. apparel retailers offered new concepts, and were more advanced in customer service, market research, and distribution, Canadian consumers were more receptive to their arrival.

Eddie Bauer, a men's and women's apparel retailer, entered into the European market in 1997, joining apparel giant The Gap. Eddie Bauer UK was expected to open two retail stores and operate a catalog division in the United Kingdom. The Gap operated stores in the United Kingdom, Canada, Japan, France, and Germany by the end of 1999.

According to *U.S.A. Today,* "U.S. mid-price apparel retailers are doing well in Japan." The new trend in the Japanese market was a push toward affordable causal clothing and convenience. Eddie Bauer operated 15 stores in Japan and planned to operate more than 50 stores by the year 2000. The Gap opened four stores in Tokyo and opened its first freestanding store in 1996.

FURTHER READING

Barrett, Joyce, "Retailers Find Health Reform Harsh Medicine." *Women's Wear Daily,* 25 January 1994.

Bastian, Lisa A. and Thomas Cunningham. "Express Makes a Turn, but Limited Stores, Structure Take Hits." *Women's Wear Daily,* 18 May 1999.

Brooklyn Public Library. *Business Rankings Annual 1999,* Detroit: Gale Group, 1999.

"Canada Attracts Many Foreign Retailers, Particularly U.S. Giants." *Chain Store Age,* December 1995.

Coleman, Calmetta Y. "The Gap Plots Panty Raid on Victoria's Secret." *The Wall Street Journal,* 1 October 1998.

Conlin, Michelle. "Mass with Class." *Forbes,* 11 January 1999.

Ethridge, Mary. "Success is Fashionably Late for Columbus, Ohio-Based The Limited Inc." *Knight-Ridder/Tribune Business News,* 2 June 1999.

"Fashion Stores Focus on No-Sweat Attitudes in Building Activewear." *Women's Wear Daily,* 4 January 1996.

Goldblatt, Jennifer. "National Retail Federation Holds Conference in New York." *Knight-Ridder/Tribune Business News,* 22 January 1999.

Hammond, Teena. "Gap Sets $1 Billion Budget for Store Openings this Year; Firm to Expand U.S., Internationally; Also Expanding On-Line Presence." *Daily News Record,* 5 May 1999.

Kletter, Melanie. "Gap, Dillard's Produce Solid First Quarters; Nordstrom Does Not." *Women's Wear Daily,* 14 May 1999.

Kletter, Melanie. "Old Navy Helps Lift Gap Net in Fourth Quarter." *Daily News Record,* 26 February 1999.

Kroll, Luisa. "Time to Kick Some Butt." *Forbes,* 11 January 1999.

Manufacturing USA 1998. Detroit: Gale Research, 1997.

Munk, Nina. "Gap Gets It." *Fortune,* 3 August 1998.

Patterson, Philana. "Lane Bryant Expects Same-Store Sales to Rise 10 Percent Due to Updated Fashions." *The Wall Street Journal,* 28 June 1999.

Pogoda, Dianne M. "Big Can be Beautiful: Large Sizes Get Hot as Fashion Takes Hold." *Women's Wear Daily,* 3 September 1996.

U.S. Department of Commerce. *U.S. Industry and Trade Outlook 1999.* New York: McGraw Hill, 1999.

U.S. International Trade Commission. "Forces Behind Restructuring in U.S. Apparel Retailing and Its Effect on the U.S. Apparel Industry." Washington, DC: 11 November 1996. Available from http://www.usitc.gov/332/ittrexmp.htm

SIC 5632

WOMEN'S ACCESSORY AND SPECIALTY STORES

This category includes establishments primarily engaged in the retail sale of women's clothing accessories and specialties, such as millinery, blouses, foundation garments, lingerie, hosiery, costume jewelry, gloves, handbags, and furs (including custom made furs).

NAICS CODE(S)

448190 (Other Clothing Stores)
448150 (Clothing Accessories Stores)

ORGANIZATION AND STRUCTURE

Stores in this industry offered a vast selection within limited product lines, and therefore were considered specialty retailers. Traditionally, these businesses were small, independently owned shops that provided distinctive merchandise and superior customer service, often at premium prices. During the 1990s, however, the women's accessory and specialty store industry experienced structural changes that paralleled changes in the retailing industry as a whole—the small, traditional retailer was being replaced by larger chains that emphasized value and convenience.

Store size was a contributing factor to a retailer's overall profitability. The size of women's accessory and specialty stores tended to be smaller than many other retail outlets. Although the size of larger chain stores in the industry averaged approximately 3,000 square feet, most accessory stores had less than 1,000 square feet of selling space. Accessory stores enjoyed relatively low overhead costs due to small store size and the low cost of goods. In fact, Claire's Stores, Inc., one of the larger retail chains, reported that new stores required an initial investment of only $85,000 for leasehold improvements and fixtures and $20,000 for inventory.

Store location often determined store size. Women's specialty and accessory stores, especially fur stores, were deliberately positioned in classy, urban retail centers such as Fifth Avenue in New York. The location of these boutiques in high-rent urban areas often encouraged the small store format. In contrast, chain stores were frequently situated in suburban shopping malls, where larger store size was financially feasible. Store size increased in the 1990s as businesses in this industry followed consumers out of the cities into suburban malls and shopping centers.

Although women's accessory and specialty stores were moving out of trendy, expensive areas, stores were designed to accommodate the fashion and status-conscious shopper. Consumers shopping at these specialty stores were interested in unique versions of basic products. With the exception of furs, the products offered by accessory stores, such as lingerie, hosiery and handbags, were not terribly expensive and were readily available at department and variety stores. A specialty accessory store, however, offered the consumer distinctive merchandise in a stylish shopping atmosphere.

Competition. Until the mid-1980s, department stores were the main competitors of women's accessory and specialty retailers. Department stores often leased space to prominent accessory manufacturers such as Crystal Brands, the Monet jewelry manufacturer, and Coach Leatherware. Like the small, independently owned accessory shops, these leased departments are staffed with knowledgeable salespeople and provide strong customer service in a pleasant shopping atmosphere. Competition in this industry shifted, however, from department stores to off-price merchandisers and discount retail stores that carried a variety of accessories and specialty items at prices well below those offered by department stores and specialty shops.

Although competition from discount stores increased in the early 1990s, the industry remained fragmented. Due to the variety of merchandise included in this category, no one company dominated the industry. Nevertheless, in the mid-1990s, the popularity of the "category killer" retail format posed a threat to the women's specialty and accessory business. The lack of market leaders and the small boutique-style store format made the industry vulnerable to attack from large retailers anxious to capitalize on the fragmented industry structure.

BACKGROUND AND DEVELOPMENT

Traditionally, the women's specialty and accessory store industry has been dominated by fur retailers. Fur coats and accessories were widely coveted luxury items and status symbols in the United States; fur retailers were tremendously successful throughout much of the twentieth century. It appeared that the fur business peaked in 1987 when sales reached $1.8 billion. In the late 1980s and early 1990s, however, cultural and economic forces caused fur sales to plummet and many fur retailers faced bankruptcy. Some large department stores such as Nordstrom's and Lord and Taylor dropped their fur departments. The industry was also adversely affected by a luxury tax imposed on furs, jewelry, and other costly nonessentials. In early 1992, a group of Senate Democrats argued that fur merchants could not withstand the combined effects of recession and additional taxation, and they sought a repeal of certain sections of the luxury tax legislation. The luxury tax on furs valued at more than $10,000 was repealed the following year.

Threats to the fur industry, however, were not only economic and legislative. Widespread negative perceptions of this business and changing cultural values also resulted in significant sales declines for fur retailers. In fact, the animal rights movement, once on the periphery of the mainstream American consciousness, saw sweeping acceptance by the mid-1980s. Heightened regard for animal rights and the growing perception that fur coats were symbols of greed and cruelty, drastically decreased demand for fur coats and accessories.

The setbacks suffered by the fur industry during the late 1980s caused changes in the mix of businesses in the women's specialty and accessory industry; however, they did not slow its development. While fur retailing suffered losses, other categories such as hats, scarves, and lingerie flourished. These categories gained popularity during the 1980s and fueled the growth of the industry in the early 1990s.

Despite a poor economic climate, the women's accessory and specialty store industry experienced solid growth in the early 1990s. While the women's clothing industry struggled to keep pace with inflation, the accessory and specialty store industry grew more than 8 percent annually during the early 1990s. The growth of specialty stores made this industry one of the few bright spots in the otherwise bleak retailing sector. Accessory retailers benefited from promotional campaigns launched by manufacturers and positive buying patterns. Some observers noted that the relative prosperity of the industry was a result of indulgence buying and pent-up demand. Additionally, national statistics revealed that specialty retail stores generally outperformed department stores during the early 1990s.

In the mid-1990s, businesses in this industry operated in a changing retail environment. The recession of the late 1980s and early 1990s caused a conservative shift in spending behavior, as consumers began to emphasize savings over consumption. Spending on intangible goods such as education and healthcare took precedence over purchases of tangibles such as new clothing. In this price-conscious atmosphere, retailers of non-essentials were challenged to offer products at prices that were consistent with consumer expectations of quality and value.

Fearing that demand would soften, sales and marketing strategies for accessories were re-evaluated in the early 1990s. In addition to improving merchandise presentation, some retailers implemented trend shop concepts, whereby merchandise was grouped into a single fashion trend and sold in one shop. At larger accessory and specialty stores, management used dedicated sales staffs to promote particular product lines. These retailer-based strategies were augmented by increased marketing efforts by manufacturers. Promotional resources, such as videos describing different ways to wear scarves, also supported salespeople's efforts. Often these sales and marketing strategies were similar to successful approaches used by cosmetics departments.

Consumer buying patterns provided another boost to accessory sales as the industry entered the mid-1990s. Some analysts observed that consumers, having endured the recession of the late 1980s and early 1990s and lacking encouraging news on the health of the economy, engaged in indulgence purchasing. Others noted that years of saving caused pent-up demand. Accessories were well suited for this purchasing mentality because they were relatively inexpensive. Industry analysts noted that the ''special occasion'' segment of the accessories business, with its glitzy holiday and party orientation, benefited most from this trend.

According to *Manufacturing USA: Industry Analyses, Statistics, and Leading Companies,* sales in the women's accessory and specialty store industry totaled more than $4.3 billion in 1996, up 16 percent from $3.6 billion in 1992. This fragmented retail segment was comprised of an estimated 9,500 small, independently owned businesses and some large chain stores. Due to the abundance of small, privately owned stores, financial data on the industry is difficult to compile. In 1995, however, the industry's top 10 companies generated more than $1.7 billion in sales, or about 40 percent of total industry revenues. These companies carried such product lines as furs, handbags, lingerie, costume jewelry, millinery, and hair accessories. The industry employs more than 50,000, most of whom are part-time sales people.

CURRENT CONDITIONS

The women's accessory industry followed similar trends as the women's clothing industry, which in the late 1990s veered toward casual wear over business wear as women found that they could fulfill their professional attire needs with casual styles. Lingerie, on the other hand, enjoyed the perennial appeal of sexuality, and the looser mores of the late 1990s allowed for more enticing advertising.

INDUSTRY LEADERS

Although the women's accessory and specialty store market was quite fragmented, a few larger companies were gaining market share in the mid-1990s. While the small, boutique-style stores competed on their superior customer service and unique product offerings, the larger companies focused on rapid expansion of their chains, enhanced store design, and national advertising.

Victoria's Secret Stores, a subsidiary of The Limited, Inc., discovered success in the 1980s by introducing a new approach to lingerie sales. The Victoria's Secret concept was originated by Roy Raymond in San Francisco. After studying the lingerie market, Raymond saw an opportunity to target men who liked to buy lingerie for their wives or girlfriends, yet were embarrassed to venture into the intimate apparel section of a department store. Victoria's Secret stores were designed to provide a comfortable and provocative environment in which men could shop.

The business was started in 1977 with $40,000 and grew quickly. By 1982, Raymond operated five stores and generated $6 million in sales. In addition to the Victoria's Secret Stores, Raymond developed a successful lingerie catalogue service. The concept saw tremendous success and rapid growth. In 1982, The Limited, Inc. offered Raymond the backing to expand the company to more than 700 stores. Raymond, however, did not want to be involved in such a large operation and ultimately sold his business for $1 million in The Limited, Inc. stock and other undisclosed benefits.

Dubbed ''The Intimate Category Killer'' by *WWD* in 1995, Victoria's Secret Stores continued to grow. Although Raymond had sold expensive designer fashions, under The Limited, Victoria's Secret Stores offered a moderately priced product line of lesser quality. The change in merchandise did not inhibit Victoria's Secret's success; its sales doubled from $600 million in 1990 to $1.2 billion in 1994, when it was The Limited's most profitable division.

Victoria's Secret diversified its advertising strategy in 1998 from just window displays and catalog distribution to a full-on media assault with commercials that aired on national television 40 of the year's 52 weeks. Victoria's Secret also hosted an Internet fashion show in January 1999 that proved so popular, attracting 1 billion viewers, that many who tried to access the event on-line got locked out.

As Victoria's Secret became more popular through the 1990s, the parent company Intimate Brands Inc. pursued a more aggressive strategy to grow Victoria's from a mainstream retailer of moderately priced lingerie to a prestigious global brand with a diversified line, adding fragrances to their menu in the late 1990s. Victoria's Secret bras sold for $14.98 on average in 1995, whereas by 1999 they sold for $30 on average, increasing the company's profit margins. Same-store sales at Victoria's Secret Stores increased 11 percent in November 1999, and Victoria's Secret Catalogue sales rose 8 percent. Intimate Brands, which also was the parent company of The Limited Inc. and Bath and Body Works stores, posted sales of $3.6 billion for the fiscal year ended Feb. 1, 1998.

Frederick's of Hollywood followed the same strategy as Victoria's Secret with a lingerie catalog, though Frederick's tended to be bolder, appealing to women who were very confident of their sexuality and adventurous in their lingerie. Frederick's generated $160 million in sales for the fiscal year ended August 31, 1998, and it employed 1,500 workers.

Claire's Stores, Inc., of Florida, a leading retailer of costume jewelry and fashion accessories typified the multi-product accessory store concept. This company operated nearly 1,500 mall stores in the United States, the Caribbean, Canada, Great Britain, and Japan under various names. The stores averaged 850 square selling feet. Although the company had relatively low overhead and a 15 percent store operating margin, it endured a period of decline in 1991.

In response, Claire's Stores underwent a reorganization which included a company-wide refocus on its core business. All non-accessory businesses were sold and stores were redesigned. The company also launched a national magazine advertising campaign targeting customers aged 13 to 40. These changes rejuvenated the chain, which grew from about 1,000 stores in 1992 to nearly 1,500 by the end of 1995. Claire's launched its European assault that same year with the acquisition of 50 stores of the bankrupt British Bow Bangles chain. In 1995, its net totaled $30.9 million on sales of $344.9 million.

Claire's approached the late 1990s by recognizing key demographic patterns: teenage girls love to shop (according to a 1997 survey by Kurt Salmon & Associates), but they didn't tend to spend much cash on their mall trips. Claire's tapped this growing demographic market by launching in 1998 its ''just nikki :)'' catalog. Teens could peruse the catalog at home and then have a parent call in an order with a credit card. Orders averaged $70, compared to the $9 average sales at stores. For the fiscal year ended January 30, 1999, Claire's garnered $661.9 million in sales. For the first nine months of fiscal year 2000, Claire's sales increased 23 percent to $539.4 million from $437.1 million for the first nine months of the fiscal year 1999.

Although no single company had significant market share, there were some signs of consolidation. Woolworth Corp. expanded its share of the accessory and specialty market in late 1993 by acquiring Melville Corp.'s Accessory Lady chain. The chain, which operated 114 stores, targeted women aged 26 to 50 and complemented Woolworth's existing chain, Afterthoughts, that focused on younger women. Moreover, the acquisition brought Woolworth's holdings of accessory-related businesses to 900 stores, a number that was competitive with Claire's Stores. Off-price merchandisers also made strong gains in this segment. Leaders included One Price Clothing Stores, Inc., with $294.7 million in sales (1995) and Deb Shops Inc., with revenues of $176.7 million (1996).

AMERICA AND THE WORLD

Fears that the domestic market was becoming oversaturated encouraged some accessory and specialty retailers to look overseas to expand in the mid-1990s. According to an August 1996 article in *WWD,* Japan and Canada were America's most fertile target markets. The magazine noted that "Japan was the fastest-growing foreign market for accessories, importing $31.4 million worth of merchandise for the year, a 95.1 percent jump." By mid-decade, Claire's Stores had acquired or established locations in Japan, Canada, Puerto Rico, and Great Britain.

The advent of electronic commerce over the World Wide Web facilitated the growth of global targeting and sales, as consumers could order online from anywhere in the world. This medium particularly aided brands such as Victoria's Secret, which was trying to globalize its name simultaneous with the e-commerce explosion in the late 1990s.

Research and Technology

Victoria's Secret went on-line Dec. 4, 1998, and sales increased 100 percent monthly, with 40 percent new customers who hadn't bought the Victoria's Secret brand previously. What's more, selling over the Internet upped the number of male customers to 30 percent from 10 percent for store and catalog sales. Apparently, the Internet fulfilled Raymond's original concept of appealing to men best, offering more comfort than Victoria's Secret stores or its catalog.

This industry lagged behind many retailers in its use of technology. Although computerized inventory management became a major strategic priority in the early 1990s, the small accessory and specialty retailers did not embrace automation. The structure of the industry accounted for the resistance to using technology. Most of the small independent business owners considered the cost of automation to be prohibitive. Moreover, since inventory was not expensive and turned over quickly, the effect of poor inventory management was not as pronounced in this industry as it was in others. Accessory and specialty retailers, nevertheless, faced increasing pressure from manufacturers and vendors to adopt automated systems to ease administrative tasks. In the competitive 1990s, retailers were forced to adopt computerized cost-saving systems.

Cost-saving systems were not the only new technologies in this category, however. In the 1990s, retailers became increasingly dependent on video marketing and computerized self-help systems. One such technology was available in Japan in the early 1990s. Developed by Wacoal, a leading Japanese lingerie manufacturer, this software package helped a woman enhance her figure by identifying her correct size of lingerie. Customers stripped down to their underwear and then stood in front of a video camera that displayed their outline on a computer screen. The screen allowed the customer to compare her figure with what the store consultants considered ideal for her age. Next, the customer tried on lingerie designed to enhance her figure and then returned to the computer screen for a look at her improved outline. Japanese stores using the system reported a 10 percent increase in lingerie sales.

Further Reading

"All Units Contribute to IBI's Sales Gains." *WWD,* 2 December 1999.

"Claire's Debuts In Europe, Acquires Bow Bangles." *WWD,* 7 February 1996, 2.

"Claire's Stores Profits Up In Quarter, Year." *WWD,* 26 February 1996, 14.

"Claire's Stores Third Quarter Earnings Up 19 percent, Sales Up 16 percent." *PR Newswire,* 11 November 1999.

"Claire's Stores Uses Catalog-Only Sales to Reach Growing Teen Market." *Knight-Ridder/Tribune Business News,* 26 February 1998.

Darnay, Arsen J., ed. *Manufacturing USA: Industry Analyses, Statistics, and Leading Companies.* Detroit: Gale Research, 1996.

"Exports Hit Their Stride." *WWD,* 7 August 1996, 28-29.

"Frederick's Mixes Old and New." *WWD,* August 9, 1999.

"IBI Giving Victoria's Secret Push into Global Prominence." *WWD,* September 29, 1999.

Moin, David. "The Intimate Category Killer." *WWD,* March 13, 1995, S12.

Parr, Karen. "New Life For Special Occasion." *WWD,* December 30, 1996, 6.

Seckler, Valerie and Robin Lewis. "Stores In A Squeeze: The Need For Growth vs. A Wary Consumer." *WWD,* March 13, 1997, 1-4.

SIC 5641

CHILDREN'S AND INFANTS' WEAR STORES

This category includes establishments primarily engaged in the retail sale of children's and infants' clothing, furnishings and accessories. Such establishments may specialize in either children's or infants' wear, or they may sell a combination of children's and infants' wear.

NAICS Code(s)

448130 (Children's and Infants' Clothing Stores)

Industry Snapshot

The infants' and children's wear business is comprised of hundreds of small independently owned shops and dozens of larger retail chains. Because many of the companies in this industry are privately owned, the exact size of the industry is difficult to determine. Total children's apparel sales for 1994 were $23.8 billion, $ 9.6 billion of which consisted of infant wear sales. There were 5,115 establishments in the industry in the latter half of the 1990s, a decrease of 9 percent since 1990.

The industry managed to grow at an annual average rate of approximately 6.6 percent in the early 1990s, despite a recessionary economic climate at the beginning of the decade. Depressed retail markets in the early 1990s caused minor consolidation of retail outlets.

Changing demographics made the children's and infants' wear industry attractive to new entrants and, therefore, extremely competitive. Large retail chains began to penetrate the market. As the industry moved into the mid-1990s the smaller shops experienced intense competitive pressure from these new industry players. Nonetheless, sales continued to grow. Fueling this growth was a rise in birth rates in the late 1980s and early 1990s, which increased demand for infants' and toddlers' wear.

In 1997, average gross sales per establishment were approximately $907,000. Total industry sales represented an estimated 4.7 percent of the total retail sales industry. Sales figures for chain retailers were quite disparate because of the varied size and success of different chains; some of the larger chains grossed upwards of $100 million, while others generated closer to $20 million.

Organization and Structure

This industry has traditionally been highly seasonal, as with other clothing businesses. Industry sales generally peak from late August through December. During this period, stores compete for precious back-to-school sales and holiday gift purchases. Stores typically generate between 30 and 40 percent of their annual sales in these months. With record high numbers of infants, toddlers, and children attending preschool throughout the year, clothing purchases for this segment are becoming less cyclical.

Because children's and infants' wear stores carry narrow product lines, they are classified as specialty retail stores. Traditionally, children's and infants' wear stores, and specialty stores in general, were small boutique-style operations. These ''mom and pop'' stores were often undercapitalized and had high overhead costs in proportion to their sales; however, they did not compete on the basis of price alone. Rather, they pursued customer satisfaction strategies, such as offering products with low turnover rates and providing more sales expertise than their competitors.

Competition. Until the mid-1980s, department stores were the main competitors of children's and infants' wear specialty retailers. As this industry moved into the mid-1990s, however, the growing popularity of off-price and discount retailers presented new challenges. By 1994, discount stores accounted for 36.5 percent of children's and infants' wear sales. These low price retailers expected to expand by outselling both specialty children's wear stores and department stores. Department stores accounted for approximately 35 percent of sales in 1994; children's and infant wear stores accounted for 13 percent.

In addition to off-price and discount retailers, smaller children's and infants' wear stores experienced increased competition from chain stores. Eager to capitalize on growth opportunities in the children's wear market, apparel chains such as The Gap, Inc. and The Limited, Inc., launched children's versions of their successful adult stores—GapKids and Limited Too. Toys 'R Us launched their children's wear stores, Kids 'R Us. All of these companies are publicly traded and have access to tremendous amounts of capital. Their entry into the children's and infants' wear industry during the mid-1980s began a shift toward consolidation in the competitive structure of the industry.

Background and Development

At the beginning of the 1990s, the industry felt the impact of a minor recession. Buyers were markedly value-oriented. Children's wear retailers noticed that consumers routinely bought basic commodity-like items such as t- shirts, but did not splurge on accessories. Although consumers resisted buying nonessentials, they were willing to purchase new and exciting children's fashions if the price was consistent with their concept of value. Some retailers speculated that infants' wear sales were not as affected by the recession as other retail markets because most items purchased for infants were essential clothing items.

Current Conditions

One trend in the industry is a continued relocation of stores to shopping malls. Working parents with limited time schedules like the convenience one-stop shopping malls provide. In the malls, children's and infants' wear stores and department stores are in close proximity. This gives customers an opportunity to comparison shop for price and quality. Price points become critical competitive priorities in the mall environment, particularly during a recessionary economic climate.

Product Lines. Casual merchandise was often carried by retailers throughout the 1990s. Customers purchased fewer frilly girls' styles and moved toward a more informal look. Denim, activewear, and fleece separates were popular fashions for both girls and boys. In the mid-1990s Osh Kosh B'Gosh, a large children's wear manufacturer, estimated that department and specialty retailers sold $500 million in fleece separates alone—a full fifteen percent of the industry's total retail sales. Throughout the 1990s, a casual look continued to be in vogue for toddlers and kids as well as teenagers.

Licensed-clothing is among the best-selling casual lines. Items featuring characters from popular television shows and movie releases sold extremely well in the 1990s. Every successful children's show or movie was released with a line of clothing to complement it. The clothing, featuring cartoon, television, and movie characters, was extremely popular. Sharing the spotlight with the ever-popular Disney characters are new characters such as public television's Barney the Dinosaur, and other commercial cartoon characters such as Power Rangers and Pokémon.

Other popular children's clothing items in the 1990s included sports apparel. The proliferation of new sports franchises during the 1990s and the fact that children who grew up with team logo apparel in the 1970s were buying this look for their own kids in the 1990s, contributed to the success of sports team clothing.

INDUSTRY LEADERS

Discount/Department Store Retailers. Although the children's and infants' wear retail market was comprised primarily of small independently owned stores, a few large retail chains dominated sales. The large retailers' competitive strategies ranged from aggressive price cutting to unique product offering. Typically, since such firms derive income from a variety of operations, sales figures are not reported by market sector (e.g., children's/infants' clothing sales), but rather as gross sales from retail operations. Regardless, total revenues reported from retail operations provides some insight regarding the presence these firms have in the children's/infants' clothing wear industry. After the close of fiscal year 1999, J.C. Penney reported $30.7 billion in retail sales; Kmart, $33.7 billion; Sears, Roebuck and Co., $41 billion; and Wal-Mart, a whopping $137.6 billion.

By 1999 Wal-Mart Stores was not only the largest retail operation in the United States, but the largest retailer in the entire world. Operating some 3,600 outlets as Wal-Mart, Sam's Club, and Wal-Mart Supercenters, the firm was larger than the combined market presence of its nearest U.S. competitors, Sears, Kmart, and J. C. Penney. As Wal-Mart approached the new century, it planned to continue its historically unchallenged growth by converting older outlets into Wal-Mart Supercenters and continuing to expand operations in Canada, Mexico, South America, Asia, and Europe.

In 1999, Sears, Roebuck and Co. was the second largest retailer in the world. Sears' year 2000 business strategy, in part, depended on promoting apparel in its 1400 specialty stores and 850 mall-based outlets in the United States. Slow to reach out into the global marketplace, Sears operated 7 department store outlets in the Americas and, through Sears International Marketing Inc. (SIMI) sought to increase sales not solely by following the industry trend of promoting discount pricing at department store retail outlets. The company strategy also depended on wholesale export of Sears brand name products.

The third largest department store retailer, Kmart Corporation, targeted low- and middle-income clientele with name-brand and private-label general merchandise. By the end of the 1990s, Kmart operated 2,160 outlets in the United States and its territories. Earlier in the decade, diversification into specialty retailing almost drove the firm into bankruptcy; but, taking its lead from the success of its largest market competitor, Wal-Mart Corporation, Kmart began a conversion program which turned old properties into superstores called Big Kmart.

J. C. Penney Company operated about 1,150 J.C. Penney department stores; a majority were in the U.S., but some were in Mexico, Puerto Rico, and Brazil (operated there as Renner department stores). Only a nominal amount of revenue from clothing sales is derived from it's 2,900 stores operated by subsidiary, Eckerd Corporation. J. C. Penney projected an increase in sales into the new millennium based on its strategy to operate boutiques within each store and by expanding private-label brands such as Arizona Jean Co., St. John's Bay, and Worthington. At the close of the 1990s, consolidation within the catalog sales sector of the industry left J.C. Penney the nation's largest general merchandise catalog retailer.

Chain-Store Retailers. Many chain retailers realize that private label merchandise is more profitable than brand-name clothing. One industry leader, The Children's Place Retail Stores, Inc., developed its own label, ''The Place,'' after years of selling branded merchandise. Children's wear retailers who sold private label merchandise did not have to mark up prices to allow for manufacturer and distributor profits; savings were passed on to the consumer. In a consumer climate that increasingly demanded retail discounting, this pricing advantage gave private label retailers a competitive advantage. Consequently, the Children's Place became popular among young mothers. The toddler and children's clothes there were modeled after adult styles. The Children's Place constantly added and updated its inventory to keep its merchandise current. In 1999, the Children's Place had revenues of $421.5 million.

One of the leaders in private label retailing was The Gymboree Corporation, a large franchise retailer whose 1999 sales were $437.1 million. That year, the company operated 600 stores and 420 franchised and company-operated play centers throughout the United States. The company was founded in 1976 by Joan Barnes, a part-time co-director of a children's recreation program at a local community center, and mother of two. Barnes developed a popular 45 minute exercise-to-music class that she ultimately expanded to other sites. Her business was a success, and in 1979, Barnes began franchising her baby-exercise classes. By 1985, she had established 204 play centers, but she was not generating profits. Forced to re-examine her business, Barnes decided that, ''Gymboree could mean more than play classes. Gymboree would mean everything significantly wonderful for kids under 5.'' In 1986, she decided to use the exercise class as a basis for selling children's clothing, which now accounts for 99 percent of Gymboree's annual sales.

The Gap introduced GapKids in 1985 to provide well-designed comfortable clothing for boys and girls aged 2 to 12. GapKids expanded its target market segment in 1990 when it opened babyGap as a department of a San Francisco GapKids store. By 1993, most of the 272 GapKids stores also offered infants' and toddlers' clothes in the babyGap department. By 1995 there were 369 GapKids stores in operation. In early 1999, 2074 Gap stores operated in the United States, Canada, France, Germany, Japan, and the United Kingdom.

A wholly-owned subsidiary of Toys 'R Us, the world's largest and fastest growing children's specialty retail chain in both sales and earnings, Kids 'R Us focused on selling brand name clothing at cut-rate prices. By 1999, the Kids 'R Us clothing store division operated 211 stores. A retail spin-off, Babies 'R Us, operated 113 outlets which not only focused on infant/toddler apparel, but infant/toddler furniture and feeding supplies. Operations were conducted in 25 countries with the largest market presence in Canada, Europe, and Japan. Kids 'R Us sales for 1995 were $11.8 billion.

America and the World

In the 1990s, the industry began to establish specialty retail operations abroad. Manufacturers of children's and infants' clothing and accessories were well aware of the opportunities overseas, and many had established joint ventures in various foreign markets. Such market penetration efforts, however, have not been very successful.

Japan and Europe were two particularly attractive markets for children's wear. In Japan, American products, especially licensed character and team logo apparel, were popular with young people. This demand, coupled with Japan's large market and high discretionary income, made the country a coveted retail market. Europe also boasted a large consumer market and historically high discretionary income. However, the stiff competition from European hypermarkets deterred smaller retailers. Nevertheless, GapKids stores were operating in the United Kingdom in the early 1990s.

Some of the barriers to global expansion in this industry were clothes sizing and fashion differences. GapKids and The Children's Place, which sold private label merchandise, controlled the manufacture of their clothing and were able to size clothing appropriately for any market. All retailers did not have this flexibility. Toys 'R Us, for example, successfully placed 167 toy stores in 11 different countries including Spain, Japan, and Malaysia by 1993. They had not, however, taken Kids 'R Us international, because the brand-name clothing that they offered was difficult to sell overseas. Despite the obstacles, children's and infants' wear retailers continued to investigate opportunities abroad, and they expanded into new markets after the implementation of the North American Free Trade Agreement.

Research and Technology

Inventory management through advanced automation was a major strategic priority in the retail environment, including the children's wear segment. Larger retailers, for example, implemented automated inventory replenishment systems management to reduce inventory ownership while ensuring that each store was supplied with the correct product mix. The system electronically linked distribution centers, inventory control, and store demand in order to determine the optimal individual store distribution. Other technologies implemented in the children's and infants' retail operations and the retail industry as a whole included cash registers that could calculate discounts, approve credit, accept credit cards, and schedule deliveries. Although this type of technology brought cost savings in the long-run, in the short run, the cost of the technology was prohibitive to smaller stores.

Further Reading

Hoover's Inc. ''J. C. Penney Company, Inc. Company Capsule.'' Austin, TX: Hoover's Online, 2000. Available from http://www.hoovers.com.

———. ''Wal-Mart Stores, Inc. Company Capsule.'' Austin, TX: Hoover's Online, 2000. Available from http://www.hoovers.com.

———. ''Kmart Corporation Company Capsule.'' Austin, TX: Hoover's Online, 2000. Available from http://www.hoovers.com.

———. ''Sears, Roebuck and Co. Company Capsule.'' Austin, TX: Hoover's Online, 2000. Available from http://www.hoovers.com.

———. ''The Gymboree Corporation Company Capsule.'' Austin, TX: Hoover's Online, 2000. Available from http://www.hoovers.com.

———. ''The Children's Place Retail Stores, Inc. Company Capsule.'' Austin, TX: Hoover's Online, 2000. Available from http://www.hoovers.com.

———. "The Gap, Inc. Company Capsule." Austin, TX: Hoover's Online, 2000. Available from http://www.hoovers.com.

———. "Toys 'R Us, Inc. Company Capsule." Austin, TX: Hoover's Online, 2000. Available from http://www.hoovers .com.

Sears, Roebuck and Co. "About Sears." Sears.com, 2000. Available at http://www.sears.com.

Standard and Poor's Register of Corporations, Directors and Executives. New York: McGraw-Hill Companies, Inc., 1997

U.S. Department of Commerce. *1997 Economic Census Retail Trade.*. Washington: GPO, 1999.

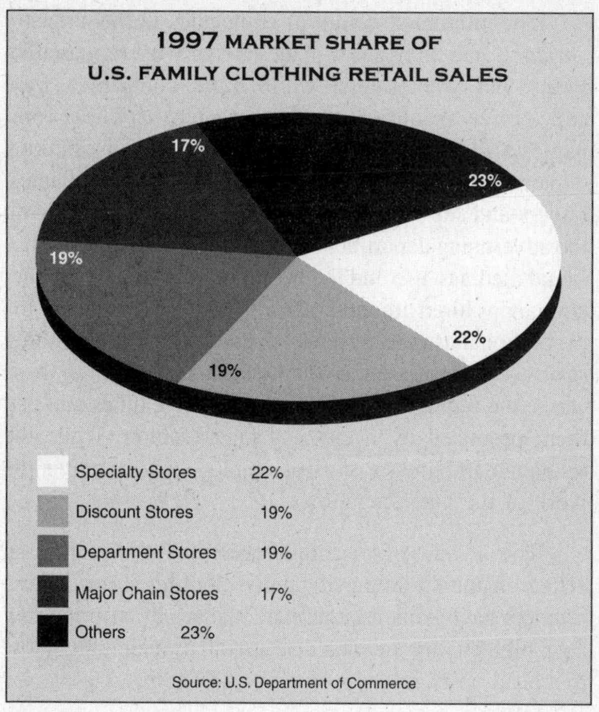

SIC 5651

FAMILY CLOTHING STORES

This industry consists of establishments primarily engaged in the retail sale of clothing; furnishings; and accessories for men, women, and children. Generally referred to as retail family clothing stores, this industry includes jeans stores and unisex clothing stores, but excludes stores targeted at one sex or age group.

NAICS CODE(S)

448140 (Family Clothing Stores)

INDUSTRY SNAPSHOT

In the late 1990s, there were 110,003 apparel and accessory stores and roughly 20,000 retail family clothing stores in the United States, represented by approximately 90 companies with sales totaling more than $45.1 billion annually. The clothing store industry was highly competitive, and marketing research, advertising, and sales promotions were central to these companies' operations. Other factors affecting sales in this industry included national economic trends, regional population growth, seasonal factors such as weather and holidays, and dramatic changes in fashions and clothing trends.

The retail industry in general should see growth from 1998 to 2003, but retail family clothing stores will be faced with a slower growth rate domestically than in previous years. Other types of retail stores—such as specialty stores, discount stores, and hypermarkets—have taken business away from this industry. In 1998, discount stores continued to strengthen market share in men's, women's, and children's apparel. However, while the number of new stores remained flat, individual stores have grown in size—on average doubling both their inventory and floor space.

ORGANIZATION AND STRUCTURE

According to the National Retail Federation, the vast majority of family clothing outlets in the late 1990s were chain stores; roughly 20 percent of these were operated as franchises. Family clothing stores were either chain stores (including department stores) or independently owned.

The large companies that owned clothing outlets across the nation generally operated distribution centers where clothes were received from the manufacturers and shipped to the outlets. Unlike warehouses, these distribution centers did not store items for a long period of time; generally goods stayed at a distribution center for only about 48 hours before being shipped to the retail stores that had placed the orders. The link between manufacturer and retailer was maintained by manufacturer's sales representatives and the retailer's merchandise buyers.

Small clothing retailers generally did not own distribution centers, though they still received items that were held at these centers. These smaller retailers tended to purchase inventory from distributors who represented several manufacturers. These retailers also ordered items solicited through distributor catalogs.

The organization of the retail family clothing store industry has changed since the beginning of the 1990s. The 1991 recession caused many firms to buy other, usually smaller, retailers. With these mergers, the decentralized purchasing practices of smaller retail chains were centralized and handled strictly by the main office, thereby cutting down on the number of buyers employed by any one company.

The internal structure of companies in this industry varied. Some companies made buying trips to manufacturers and wholesalers, while other companies were called on by manufacturers' representatives. These companies also differed in the way that the various internal departments related to one another. In some companies, buyers and merchandise managers worked closely with the advertising department in deciding the type of promotional media to use and the layout of item displays. Other companies hired autonomous advertising agencies for the promotional aspects of the business. Some retail clothing stores sold clothes under their own brand name. In these cases, the retailer typically designed the clothes and had them produced by a clothing manufacturer, while the retailer maintained a staff of employees to monitor the work of the manufacturers.

The advent of discount retailers also has had an effect on the structure of family clothing stores. These retailers have gained large market share by offering low cost, high quality merchandise as well as maintaining low overhead costs.

BACKGROUND AND DEVELOPMENT

Retail family clothing stores originated in America during colonial times. In these early days, stores were extensions of tailor shops. There were few stores relative to the size of the growing population, however, because owning a variety of clothes was considered a luxury. During the 1800s, with the expansion westward, clothing retailers were mostly manufacturers who sold their merchandise through catalogs. It was not until the late 1800s, with innovations in mass manufacturing and the growth of cities, that most retail clothing stores began operating exclusive of tailor shops.

During the twentieth century, retail family clothing stores moved from individually run small stores to regional chains, and then, in the 1990s, to nationwide chains of large stores. This consolidation trend resulted from stores moving from smaller spaces in the cities during the 1970s and 1980s into suburban shopping malls, where larger store space and new buildings were available. Such vast quantities of space also facilitated the growth of off-price retail stores, which offered discounted merchandise in large superstores, such as Wal-Mart, or in regional outlets, such as Hit or Miss.

Typically, off-price clothing outlets were in more favorable, remote suburban or newly developed areas where real estate was inexpensive, or they were in suburban shopping strips with other off-price retailers. Lower costs meant higher profits for such establishments. These outlets also kept prices down by purchasing large volumes at low prices from manufacturers; usually manufacturers were not able to profit on the items—often due to the rapid change in fashion trends—and were seeking to merely cut their losses.

Other types of stores to emerge from the growth of suburban shopping were price clubs, warehouse stores, and hypermarkets. Price clubs and warehouse stores, where customers could purchase clothes at significantly reduced prices, also resulted in part from the recession at the end of the 1980s and early 1990s. Hypermarkets also featured reduced prices, but their appeal was in the variety of stores and services offered under one roof. Often referred to as ''malls without walls,'' these stores first appeared in France. All of these larger stores carried an average of 40,000 items at any given time, compared with 25,000 items at typical retail family clothing outlets.

Despite the growth in store size, automation did little to change the basic operations in stores. Computerized cash registers allowed for more efficient management of money and inventory, but these systems were not fully employed throughout the industry. In some cases, the retailer did not have the capital to pay for point-of-sale scanners—which record the exact item sold, including color and size—and related technologies, in addition to the costs of retraining employees.

The retail family clothing store industry has also made significant changes and advances over the years in marketing. The marketing abilities of individual establishments were key within this highly competitive industry. The primary factors in the marketing mix were marketing research and promotion.

Marketing research, in the retail family clothing industry, has traditionally come from knowledge of what items sell the most, or have the fastest turnover. Sales staff and inventory workers monitored merchandise levels, and successful retailers later supplemented their employees' knowledge with electronic inventory controls, such as point-of-sale scanners. For example, Russell Mitchell of *Business Week* attributed a large part of The Gap's success as the fastest growing company in this industry during the early 1990s to ''its high-tech distribution network that keeps 1,200 Gap stores constantly stocked with fresh merchandise.'' The basics of supply and demand are quite evident in this industry.

The family clothing store industry also conducted its marketing research by surveying customers and various representative groups in the population. At the same time, this industry frequently surveyed the effectiveness of its television and radio commercials and magazine advertisements, its three main forms of advertising.

Other companies in the retail family clothing industry experimented with interactive television as a way of promoting and selling clothing. In 1994, Nordstrom, Inc., an industry leader, began an operation using catalogs and interactive television. Similar to home-shopping networks, the television portion involved displaying the items on television with call-in numbers for ordering; however, added to this was the idea of viewers calling in to see items in the catalogs and asking questions about them, along the lines of call-in talk shows. Nordstrom predicted that these types of events would bring in $50 to $100 million in sales annually in two to three years.

Low-budget marketing strategies have also worked well in this industry. For example, Wal-Mart stores spent about one third as much on advertising as their competitors; they did not run many promotional sales, but they did keep prices low at all times. In 1996 and 1997, Wal-Mart began a ''Falling Prices'' program, backed by both television and print media. The aim of the campaign was that even though Wal-Mart had low prices, they continually were going to drop them even lower. Wal-Mart also utilized employees and their family members in place of professional models in their advertisements to help lower costs and improve company image.

Another strategy was to use a sale on one product line to draw customers into a store. One company to use this approach successfully was Goody's Family Clothing Stores. As *Forbes* described the company's strategy: ''Jeans are great bait. In the past five years Goody's sales and earnings have tripled, and the number of stores it leases and operates in small towns throughout the Southeast has almost doubled. The jeans shelves are in the back of Goody's stores, meaning customers must walk as much as 35 yards past racks of merchandise on which Goody's makes its real money.''

Other marketing factors that characterized retail family clothing businesses were service and location. Consumers often formed their impressions of a store by the courtesy and efficiency of its sales staff. The Nordstrom clothing stores built their reputation on their courteous sales staff, which became part of their marketing strategy. Nordstrom knew that it was the only U.S. department store chain who had employees that would change flat tires and carry bags to customers' cars. Location was important in terms of store visibility and the relative closeness of competitors. A large shopping mall generally has at least two anchor stores for this reason. Anchor stores are those that are considered larger in both product diversity and size. Some key anchor stores are J.C. Penney, Lord and Taylor, Nordstrom, and Hecht's.

Upon entering the 1990s, family clothing retailers were affected by a weak economy and loss of their market share to other types of retailers, namely specialty stores and large department stores. The industry responded by increasing its marketing efforts, stocking more off-price merchandise, and investing in computer systems to predict market trends and reduce operating costs. Increasing marketing efforts included a trend toward scrambled merchandising—selling items normally not carried by a given retailer. This technique allowed retailers to test new merchandise and, at the same time, bring new customers into their stores to buy the standard line of apparel.

The success of off-price retailing during the recessions of the 1970s and 1980s encouraged many family clothing retailers to enter this end of the market as well. Off-price retailing also was helped by the collapse of real estate prices in the late 1980s and early 1990s. Cheaper real estate allowed this sector of the industry to acquire the large buildings it needed to move enough volume to sustain a strong profit margin on the reduced-price items.

The weak real estate market also helped to start a new trend of stores moving back into the cities, where downtown areas sought retail operations to fill locations emptied during the late 1980s. Companies with small clothing stores continued to open new stores in downtown areas. In 1992, Russell Mitchell in *Business Week* described The Gap as ''taking advantage of recessionary blues by locking up sweet lease deals, moving into downtown and urban neighborhoods, and opening on the main streets of mid-size cities.''

In 1993, retail apparel and accessory stores recorded sales of $106 billion. Although this was an increase of 7 percent (after inflation) over the previous year, it was not as great an increase as the industry witnessed during the 1970s and 1980s. This sector continued to see growth into the mid-1990s.

CURRENT CONDITIONS

In 1997, the clothing industry saw approximately $170 billion in retail sales. Women's apparel brought in $89.4 billion, men's apparel accounted for $50.8 billion, and children's wear captured $29 billion. Family clothing stores alone accounted for $45.1 billion in sales. According to the American Apparel Manufacturers Association, the breakdown on total share of retail sales was as follows: specialty stores, 22 percent; discounters, 19 percent; department stores, 19 percent; major chains, 17 percent; off-price stores, 7 percent; mail order, 6 percent; outlets, 4 percent; and other stores, 7 percent.

This industry remained quite competitive in the late 1990s. Successful advertising campaigns and Internet marketing were key in attracting new and existing customers. For example, in the first period of 1999, the Gap spent $122.5 million in advertising for its stores, including Old Navy and Banana Republic; this figure was an increase of 84 percent from the previous year.

Online shopping also became much more popular in the late 1990s. According to the National Retail Federation, Internet retail sales will surpass $17 billion in the year 2000 and reach some $40 billion in 2002. Clothing retailers have jumped aboard the superhighway and have started to use the Internet to offer online shopping and to market their products. Some retailers began offering their catalogs online as well and would even e-mail customers with updates, promotions, and fashion information.

Off-price retailing continued to play a major role in this industry in the late 1990s. With the success of Wal-Mart and the TJX Corporation, other family clothing retailers were forced to offer quality merchandise and lower costs. The Gap for instance, had seen remarkable success with its Old Navy stores; these stores offered Gap-like merchandise, at lower prices.

Successful introduction of private label brands, such as Wal-Mart's Kathie Lee line and Target's Xhileration line, have also chipped away at traditional family clothing store's market share. With clothing offered at lower prices, apparel has experienced a price deflation in the late 1990s. According to the American Statistics Index, ''apparel consumers are demanding a greater selection of good quality merchandise at low price as well as added convenience in readily finding merchandise.''

Industry Leaders

In 1998, the industry leaders in gross annual sales were Wal-Mart Stores, Inc. (owner of Sam's Clubs) with more than $137.6 billion in total sales for all departments; The TJX Companies, Inc. (owners of Marshalls and TJ Maxx stores) with $7.9 billion in 1998 sales; The Gap, Inc., with $9.1 billion in sales; and Nordstrom with $5 billion in sales.

Wal-Mart Stores, Inc. stood as the world's largest retailer in 1999. Wal-Mart was founded by two brothers, Sam and J.L. (Bud) Walton, who entered the clothing industry as owners of Ben Franklin franchises in Arkansas. In 1962 the Waltons opened their first store, Wal-Mart Discount City in Rogers, Arkansas, in order to reduce prices more than the Ben Franklin franchises would allow at the time. The brothers soon opened stores in other small towns and, by 1970, they had 18 Wal-Mart Stores in addition to 15 Ben Franklin franchises.

During the 1970s, Wal-Mart built its own warehouses to cut costs and exercise greater influence over the channels of distribution. Under this system, the company would buy in volume and store the merchandise at the warehouses and gradually build a network of stores within 200 miles of each warehouse. This system is still being used throughout the 1990s.

By the end of the 1970s, Wal-Mart owned and operated in-store pharmacies, auto service centers, and jewelry and shoe divisions. In 1980, Wal-Mart stores appeared in 11 states, taking in a total of $1.25 billion annually. The 1980s marked the company's greatest period of growth and the opening of its Sam's Clubs, which were discount warehouses, and its Hypermarket USA, a combination discount department store and grocery store with restaurants, banks, video rentals, and other services. With prices reduced by up to 40 percent, the Hypermarket USA store grew rapidly in popularity, and, by 1992, Wal-Mart had opened four of these stores. Also by 1992, Wal-Mart employed more than 28,800 workers and owned several other subsidiaries, such as Kuhn's Big K Stores Corp.; North Arkansas Wholesale Co., Inc.; and Wal-Mart Properties.

Wal-Mart has been criticized over the years for forcing small retailers out of business with its location strategies and buying practices. Wal-Mart typically dealt directly with manufacturers, bypassing their sales representatives and distributor representatives, which made it more difficult for independent retail buyers to conduct business and increased Wal-Mart's profit margin.

By 1999, the company had a store volume larger than Sears, Kmart, Dayton Hudson, and J.C. Penney combined. Wal-Mart operated 2,471 stores, including 650 supercenters and 453 Sam's Clubs. It employed 910,000 workers and was slated to become the largest employer in the world in 2000.

TJX Companies, Inc., the industry's second largest leader in sales, was considered the world's number one off-price family clothes store. In 1998, the company had $424.2 million in net income, an increase of 39.2 percent over 1997. Employees totaled 62,000.

The company was incorporated in 1962 as Zayre Corp., which was a chain of department stores based in New England. In 1969, Zayre bought the Hit or Miss chain, which moved the corporation towards the upscale off-price clothing market. During the 1970s, the Hit or Miss chain grew rapidly across the country. By 1977, Zayre decided to expand further into the off-price clothing market by opening its first T.J. Maxx store.

Both Hit or Miss and T.J. Maxx prospered during the late 1970s as a result of the recession. Zayre then expanded its off-price fashion operations into the mail-order market by forming Chadwick's of Boston. Chadwick's sold women's clothes and accessories, the same brands found in Hit or Miss, through catalogs.

The 1980s saw growth for off-price fashion retailing, but not for Zayre's department stores. Competition from Wal-Mart, Kmart, and other large department store chains forced Zayre to make large investments in its clothing stores. By 1986, the company had 420 Hit or Miss stores throughout the United States. By 1987, the company restructured, with T.J. Maxx becoming the major subsidiary, and sold 400 of its Zayre stores to Ames Department Stores, Inc.

In the early 1990s, the T.J. Maxx stores were the company's leading business, and Chadwick's of Boston was also performing well. However, Hit or Miss stores were feeling the strain of competition and a weak economy. In 1995, TJX sold both the Hit or Miss and the Chadwick's divisions, and it purchased Marshalls, Inc. for $550 million within the same year. Marshalls had been TJ Maxx's direct competition. In 1996, TJX Companies had 578 TJ Maxx stores and 454 Marshalls throughout the United States. The company employed a total of 38,000 people.

By the late 1990s, TJX operated over 620 T.J. Maxx stores. With sales and profits increasing, the company also operated Winners Apparel (a Canadian chain of family clothing stores), HomeGoods, A.J. Wright, and T.K. Maxx.

Another notable industry leader was The Gap, Inc., which has been one of the top retailers in America since its beginnings. The company was started by Donald Fisher and his wife Doris in 1969. After Donald could not find Levi's jeans in his size in a department store, he realized that market demand for jeans strongly outweighed the supply. The Gap started with a small shop near San Francisco State University, which carried only records and Levi's jeans, a combination that appealed to young people at the time. The success of The Gap concept was almost immediate, and Fisher added outlets throughout the San Francisco area.

The company grew during the 1970s with the acceptance of jeans as casual wear by people of all ages; however, baby boomers still made up the majority of Gap customers. In 1971, The Gap's sales stood at $2.5 million annually and, by 1976, sales were up to $97 million annually with 186 stores in 21 states. The company's success was also helped by Levi's, which remained the only brand Gap carried and extensively advertised.

With the recession at the end of the 1970s and the baby boomers growing out of blue jeans fashion, Gap began experiencing financial difficulties. The company reacted by changing its line of clothes to a larger variety of casual items and by selling more of its own labels. In the early 1980s, The Gap was revamped after it hired Mickey Drexler to be its new president. Under Drexler, The Gap would only carry Gap-labeled clothes and emphasize natural fibers and casual clothing styles that would appeal to both genders and a wide age range.

Upon entering the 1990s, Gap's earnings were $225 million annually, including the company's principle subsidiaries, GapKids and Banana Republic clothing stores. The Gap expanded the size of its stores to accommodate new lines of less casual, more dressy clothes. At the same time, the clothing chain converted some of its poorest performing stores into warehouse stores to compete in the discount clothing market. In 1996, Gap's sales totaled $5.28 billion, and a total of 1,854 stores were in operation.

By the late 1990s, Gap was extremely successful. With $824.5 million in net income—an increase of 54.4 percent from 1997—the company was becoming increasingly popular by its television ads and the emergence of its Old Navy stores. In 1999, The Gap had more than 1500 stores—including GapKids and babyGap—in the United States, 297 U.S. Banana Republic stores, and 442 Old Navy Stores.

Another industry leader for retail family clothing stores was Nordstrom, Inc. Founded in 1901 by the Nordstroms, a family of Swedish immigrants, in Seattle, Washington, the company started out in the shoe business and did not sell clothing until 1960, when it purchased Best Apparel, a women's clothing store. In 1966, the company purchased Nicholas Ungar, a retail fashion outlet, and soon began selling men's clothes. By 1968, under the ownership of a third generation of the Nordstrom family, the company achieved $40 million in annual sales. Within a few years, expansion allowed sales to double to $80 million. The company grew at a steady pace for the remainder of the 1970s by diversifying with a large variety of clothing departments within each store.

By the start of the 1980s, the company had expanded to offer stores in southern California, Alaska, Oregon, Utah, and Montana. Later in the 1980s, the chain starting opening stores on the East Coast. Despite diversification and growth over the years, however, shoes still accounted for 20 percent of Nordstrom's sales.

It was also during this period that the company developed its reputation for having exceptionally friendly sales people who would do things like change customers' flat tires in the parking lot, deliver merchandise to offices, and send tailors to people's homes. However, in 1989, a group of unionized employees charged that they were not being paid for providing such extra services. As a result, the government forced Nordstrom to change its compensation and record-keeping policies.

Upon entering the 1990s, the recession caused Nordstrom's sales to drop for the first time in the company's history. Despite this setback, the company continued to expand into new regional markets. In 1995, women's clothes and accessories accounted for 58 percent of Nordstrom's sales; men's clothes, 16 percent; and shoes, 20 percent.

By the end of the decade, Nordstrom's had operations in 23 states and remained known for its upscale apparel and excellent service. Net income in 1998 was $206.7 million, up 11 percent from 1997. The company operated more than 70 stores and 25 outlets and had more than 42,000 employees.

WORKFORCE

According to the National Retail Federation, nearly 1 in 5 American workers held jobs in retail in 1998. The industry's 324,900-employee workforce was made up of sales staff, including managers, marketing, and administration employees.

According to the Bureau of Labor's Occupational Outlook Handbook, employment for retail workers was expected to increase ''about as fast as the average for all occupations through the year 2006 due to anticipated growth in retail sales created by a growing population.'' Part-time positions in this industry were expected to be most available due to turnover. In addition, sales staff would continue to be hired on a temporary basis during peak selling periods, such as Christmas and tourist seasons.

Jobs in retail management were expected to remain competitive, although wages would grow slower than average throughout 2006. Other occupations supported by this industry included bookkeepers, accountants, and secretarial and clerical personnel.

AMERICA AND THE WORLD

As the American apparel market matured, international operations became increasingly necessary in the late 1990s. With little room to grow in the United States, companies looked overseas to boost revenue and income. The Gap, for instance, had penetrated certain markets abroad by 1999. The company operated—including GapKids and babyGap—121 stores in Canada, 35 stores in France, 12 stores in Germany, 39 stores in Japan, and 114 stores in the United Kingdom. Banana Republic had operations in Canada, as did Nordstroms.

The Asian economic crisis was expected to effect apparel sales abroad, as the region experienced a recession in 1998 and 1999. However, the advent of the Euro was expected to make entry into European markets more attractive. According to Wal-Mart' 1999 annual report, ''the company's foreign operations are comprised of wholly-owned operations in Argentina, Canada, Germany, and Puerto Rico; joint ventures in China and Korea; and majority-owned subsidiaries in Brazil and Mexico. As a result, the company's financial results could be affected by factors such as changes in foreign currency exchange rates or weak economic conditions in the foreign markets in which the company does business.''

The apparel industry was also seen as having a smoother entry into foreign markets compared to others. A 1998 *Stores* article stated that ''apparel retailing is one of the most viable businesses on a global scale. Several key strategic advantages set it apart from other formats, including that apparel is extremely merchandise and marketing driven, has a relatively narrow focus and can produce high gross margins sufficient to offset occupancy costs and still provide a superior profit margin.''

RESEARCH AND TECHNOLOGY

Developing technology to improve the channels of distribution remained an essential component of the future growth of the retail family clothing store industry in 1999. Like other retail businesses, establishments in this industry continually increased their reliance on computers, which simplified many of the routine buying functions and improved the efficiency of in-store sales staff. Retail buyers and merchandisers came to rely upon point-of-sale computer terminals, rather than manual on-hand counts, for up-to-date inventory and sales information. Point-of-sale data came directly from an item's bar code as it was sold and provided information regarding price, model number, color, and size.

For instance, QRS Corporation supplies the retail industry with electronic vendor communications such as business-to-business invoicing, purchase orders, and shipping notices. According to Bruce Work, Stage Store Inc.'s Senior VP of logistics, ''at this point there is no questioning that electronic retailer-to-vendor communication and information sharing is vital to staying alive and profitable in this industry.''

Another growing trend in the apparel industry was the use of the Internet to sell clothing. In 1999, Gap teamed up with America Online Inc.(AOL) to offer its clothing line in AOL's online marketplace. More than 46 million members had access to Gap apparel as a result of the deal. The company's Web site also offered online shopping in 1999, and it launched Web sites for Banana Republic and Old Navy in 1998.

With Internet sales expected to increase to nearly $30 billion by 2001, family clothing stores faced increased competition not only from large discount chains, but from Internet entrepreneurs as well. Many chains also had to add IT and IS specialists to their workforce as a result of technology trends.

FURTHER READING

''1998 Holiday Sales Data,'' 1999. Available from http://www.nrf.com/hot/holiday/dec98/.

1998-99 Occupational Outlook Handbook, November 1999. Available from http://www.bls.gov/oco/.

''America Online and Gap Inc. Announce Multi-Year Partnership.'' *Business Wire,* 26 August 1999.

Apparel Industry Trends, 1998. Available from http://www.americanapparel.org/gen_info_stats_home.html.

Apparel Sourcing Strategies for Competing in the U.S. Market, 1999. Available http://www.lexis-nexis/statuniv/.

Chandler, Susan. ''Aggressive Marketing Helps Clothing Retailers Set Fashion Trends.'' *Chicago Tribune,* 6 October 1999.

"How the Gap's Ads Got So-o-o Cool." *Business Week,* 9 March 1992.

"QRS and Stage Stores Stage E-Commerce Initiative." *PR Newswire,* 19 October 1999.

Reda, Susan. "Global Retailing." *Stores,* September 1998.

The Gap Company Information, 1999. Available from http://www.gapinc.com.

Wal-Mart Company Information, 1999. Available from http://www.wal-mart.com.

SIC 5661

SHOE STORES

Establishments in this industry are primarily engaged in the retail sale of men's, women's and children's footwear; these establishments frequently carry accessories, such as gloves, socks and hosiery.

NAICS CODE(S)

448210 (Shoe Stores)

INDUSTRY SNAPSHOT

Footwear retailers often rely less on distributors and retail buyers than those in other retail industries because many are associated with proprietary own manufacturing facilities. According to the projections by the Economic Census of the United States, the number of establishments dropped to 34,200 (down from 37,200 in 1996) with nearly 190,000 employees in the U.S. shoe retail industry in 1998. Together, they recorded more than $21.7 billion in sales that year and carried a total payroll of almost $2.4 billion. The National Shoe Retailers Association (NSRA) reported that 1998 average sales per store were $480,659.

ORGANIZATION AND STRUCTURE

Establishments in this industry are either chain stores or individually owned stores. The National Retail Federation categorizes the vast majority as franchises that belong to large chain operations. Parent company involvement varies in daily franchise operations.

This industry further divides itself into family shoe stores, which sell a broad range of sizes and styles, and specialty shoe stores, where a specific selection (such as athletic footwear or women's footwear) is offered exclusively. Athletic shoe stores were the largest specialty category, increasing market share in 1998 to 19.9 percent from 19.4 percent in 1997. Other outlets, such as department stores, apparel stores, vendor outlet mall stores, and mail-order catalogs, also generate shoe sales.

BACKGROUND AND DEVELOPMENT

Products. Products sold in this industry fall into several general categories: athletic footwear, dress shoes, casual shoes, sandals, work/duty footwear, hiking/hunting/fishing boots, western/casual boots, and "other." While athletic shoe sales dominated the marketplace for several years, SGMA reported that during the second quarter (April through June) of 1999, total spending for athletic shoes declined 10 percent, to $3.056 billion from $3.403 billion for the same period in 1998. Sales of men's models rose during that period, the association reported, but sales of women's and children's models declined.

History. This industry developed from the cobbler stores that date back to medieval times, and the mass manufacturers that emerged during the late nineteenth century. Modern stores that exclusively sold shoes began operating at that time. One of the oldest shoe retailers in the United States, Thom McAn, began when McAn opened several stores to sell his footwear.

Like other retailers that benefited from the country's growing population, shoe stores did well from the beginning of this century through the 1920s. During the early 1930s, however, they were badly hurt by the Depression and sales dropped by an average of 20 percent. The industry expanded rapidly as the economy strengthened and became highly competitive by the 1950s, when fashion trends changed and footwear styles grew more diverse. At that time, the improved post-war financial state also allowed new small-business owners to enter this industry by purchasing franchise outlets.

The retail shoe industry experienced another boom during the late 1970s and throughout the 1980s, as athletic footwear sales increased dramatically along with America's infatuation with fitness. Stores specializing in running shoes, tennis shoes, and general sport shoes spread rapidly across the country. Sales of these shoes doubled during the 1980s, and by 1990 athletic footwear became a $5-billion business as some retail price tags topped $100. The industry was impacted even further by this segment when athletic shoe leader Nike Inc. opened its own giant Niketown retail outlets; led by a 90,000-square-foot flagship store in New York City, as well as others in Japan, Germany, and the United Kingdom. During the late 1990s, the athletic footwear segment experienced a leveling off of sales due to the oversupply of retail selling space and as consumers' fashion taste moved away from athletic shoes to "brown shoes." For the first time since 1992, sales for athletic footwear declined by 8 percent in 1998 to $8.7 billion (wholesale). The Sporting Goods Manufacturers Association "1999 State of the Industry Report" noted that "many traditional athletic footwear companies expanded into the 'brown shoe' and fashion categories, enabling them to continue to increase sales and expand their market reach.''

Marketing. The shoe store industry, like other retail industries, relied heavily on marketing departments and advertising agencies to generate consumer interest. One key marketing consideration has involved store location because, by the 1980s, the majority of U.S. shoe stores were located in malls. This allowed chains to operate small stores without high overhead costs, but the operation had become increasingly competitive as many footwear retailers often compete within the same mall. In 1993, Harlan S. Byrne told *Barron's* that Famous Footwear owed its considerable success to ''its locations in strip centers, where competition is less than in shoe-happy malls.'' A NSRA survey in 1995 confirmed this, finding per-store profits were 4.1 percent at strip stores and 0.7 percent at mall stores.

Another important marketing device concerned store design. Off-price or discount shoes stores, like off-price clothing stores, typically drew bargain shoppers with large undecorated spaces filled with racks of shoes. Moderately priced and upscale shoe stores generally used simple, modern designs to attract a target audience. Seeking new ways to differentiate themselves from the competition, some innovative retailers began using additional aids to attract sales: *Footwear+* reported in 1997 that subtle use of ''sensory merchandising; the process of appealing to consumers' sense of smell, sight, sound, color and touch,'' had been shown to increase sales by up to 20 percent.

Since the U.S. fitness craze took hold two decades ago, industry advertising on television and in newspapers and magazines has grown significantly; much of this, however, highlights manufacturers or manufacturing divisions of shoe store chains. Advertising campaigns in the 1980s and 1990s that featured sports celebrities have been credited with popularizing athletic footwear among all age groups. But while younger people remain this segment's largest buying group, overall aging of the U.S. population and increasing participation in sports by women and girls has caused many retailers to refocus programs to reflect these new demographics.

One additional trend of significance reported in the mid-1990s involved the development of ''outlet malls,'' which offered huge selections of brand name products at lower prices. According to the International Council of Shopping Centers, outlet malls brought in $12.2 billion in 1997 sales. Footwear companies such as Birkenstock, Rockport, Easy Spirit, Florsheim, Naturalizer, Nike, and Reebok opened stores in outlet malls in the late 1990s. Some retailers carrying the regularly priced brands felt that outlet malls diminished the image of brands and took customers away from their stores, knowing that the same shoe brands were available at a cheaper price at the outlet stores. Manufacturers countered by saying that outlet stores carried a different mix of styles than the full-price stores, usually past-season styles and colors or factory seconds.

Current Conditions

The widespread popularity of athletic footwear helped shoe stores through the recession that impacted other retailing segments more seriously during the late 1980s and early 1990s. In 1995, SGMA measured the value of the U.S. athletic footwear market at almost $11.4 billion and said it accounted for approximately 40 percent of all shoes purchased. Additionally, this segment's overseas market expanded rapidly through the first half of the 1990s. A weakened economy and the highly competitive nature of this industry, however, forced many stores to close. Total sales in the athletic category were basically flat from 1992 through 1998. According to the 1998 *Sporting Goods Business* Year-End Survey, 19.1 percent of stores surveyed reported flat sales in athletic footwear. Many stores attributed low sales growth to the ''glut of inventory'' carrying over from 1998 to 1999 and the fashion trends moving away from sneakers and sweatpants towards casual shoes and khakis. In 1999, *Sporting Goods Business* reported Faye Landes, footwear analyst with Salomon Smith Barney, as saying that an industry-wide slowdown could be expected through-out 1999, as companies consolidated their business and closed stores. John Shanley of Van Kasper and Company estimated that there was ''20-25 percent too much store space dedicated to athletic footwear in malls'' across the United States. Second quarter results for 1999 did reflect a 10 percent decline in athletic footwear sales. ''Results for the first six months reflect what we expected going into the year, an unsettled and difficult market,'' said Gregg Hartley, executive director of the Athletic Footwear Association.

Industry Leaders

The following retail companies led the industry in sales in the late 1990s: Payless ShoeSource, Inc., which had more than $2.5 billion; Footstar Inc., reporting $1.8 billion; Brown Group, Inc., recording more than $1.5 billion; and Meldisco HC Inc., with $1.1 billion. Famous Footwear, a division of Brown, was sixth in total sales with $741 million. The late 1990s also marked a period of big changes in the footwear industry, including many store closings and acquisitions.

A private subsidiary of Woolworth Corp., Kinney topped the industry in employees as well as sales with 30,000 workers in 1996. The G. R. Kinney Shoe Corp. was a subsidiary of Brown Shoe Co. until Woolworth purchased it in 1963. However, in 1998, 15 months after closing the historic Woolworth chain stores, the Venator Group, formerly Woolworth Corp., closed all Kinney

Shoe Stores. Venator reported that its specialty footwear business had an operating loss of $35 million on $207 million in sales as of August 1, 1998. This loss compared to a $12 million operating loss on $533 million in sales in 1997. The *Tribune Business News* reported that in addition to the Kinney's store closings, Venator also closed 103 Footquarters stores and converted 60 into ''its more profitable Lady Foot Locker, Kids Foot Locker, and Colorado stores.''

Payless ShoeSource began as a private subsidiary of the May Department Stores Company in 1956. Its stores are characterized as off-price discount outlets because they use the self-service concept to offer low prices. In 1998, Payless employed more than 24,000 workers and had 4,549 stores in the United States and Puerto Rico. These stores were leased to franchise owners for a period of 10-15 years with renewal options. Payless was one of the fastest growing shoe chains in the United States during the mid-1990s, increasing 55 percent in sales, 27 percent in stores, and 33 percent in employees between 1992 and 1996. In 1997, Payless ShoeSource Inc. acquired Parade of Shoes in a deal with J. Baker Inc.

In 1998, *Footwear News* reported that the St. Louis-based Brown Group posted a loss of 54 cents per share due to the Sale of its Pagoda International business and restructuring changes. The Brown Group owned three chains: Famous Footwear, the largest branded family shoe chain in the United States with more than 800 stores in 44 states; Naturalizer stores, of which more than 400 operated in North America; and F.X. LaSalle, with more than a dozen Canadian locations. In addition to its own brands, including Naturalizer and Buster Brown, Brown also sold licensed brands like Barbie, Lion King and Dr. Scholl's. In 1995 the company acquired the upscale Larry Stuart Collection and Le Coq Sportif athletic shoes and began selling off several non-shoe operations.

Major changes took place in 1996 and 1997 at the Melville Corp., which started with a small string of shoe stores in the 1890s and within a century became one of the largest retailing conglomerates in the United States. This company created one of its most recognized subsidiaries, Thom McAn Shoes, in 1922 when it developed a method to mass produce shoes and sell them at low prices through chain stores. The Thom McAn chain grew to more than 300 stores within five years, and despite a setback during the Depression increased to more than 650 stores by the end of the 1930s. Sales of Thom McAn shoes continued to climb and in 1955 Melville owned 12 factories and 850 stores. By the end of the 1960s, Melville was America's largest shoe retailer, operating 1,400 stores.

Melville moved into other retail markets during the 1970s by purchasing drug stores, household furnishing outlets, and toy store chains. Diversification shifted the company's emphasis away from shoes and during the 1980s it closed more than one-third of its Thom McAn outlets. However, according to Subrata N. Chakravarty of *Forbes,* ''footwear has the highest return on assets of any of Melville's business groups, thanks largely to its Meldisco division, which leases and runs shoe departments of K mart's stores.'' In 1990, Melville operated more than 7,700 stores and employed 119,000 people. Two years later, Melville's three shoe subsidiaries—Meldisco, Thom McAn, and the Footaction USA athletic chain—tallied more than $2.1 billion in sales.

Footaction had become the nation's third largest athletic shoe retailer by the fall of 1996—with 438 stores and about $500 million in sales—when Melville spun it off as part of a footwear subsidiary called Footstar Inc. The parent company also converted some 85 of its Tom McAn stores to Footaction stores and closed the rest. Melville then changed its name to CVS Corp. to reflect a new emphasis on the drugstore business it had first entered in 1969, sold off Footstar and exited the footwear business.

WORKFORCE

Sales and marketing personnel comprise the bulk of the retail shoe industry's workforce. 1998 projections found it employed about 190,400 with a total annual payroll of $2.48 billion. An average of five employees worked in each store. Between 1987 and 1992, the total number of employees fell by about 10 percent as the overall number of stores decreased by nearly 6 percent. Family shoe stores employed the most workers, accounting for 54 percent of the total. Athletic stores and women's stores each employed about 18 percent, men's stores employed nearly 6 percent, and children's stores employed 3 percent.

The job outlook for retail sales and marketing staff is expected to improve faster than the average for all workers through 2005. Part-time positions in this industry have often been available due to a high turnover rate, and sales staff is often hired on a temporary basis during peak selling periods, such as Christmas and tourist seasons. Other occupations in this industry include bookkeepers, accountants, and secretarial and clerical staff.

AMERICA AND THE WORLD

American shoe retailers have performed well in overseas markets and are expected to continue to grow internationally through the remainder of the twentieth century. Mass manufacturing techniques have largely been responsible for this success. American-owned athletic footwear stores also gained a strong advantage outside the United States because of the popularity of American sports celebrities and the athletic goods they endorsed.

The SGMA ''1999 State of the Industry Report,'' reported that ''China, Asia, and Mexico will continue as preferred sourcing locations by companies planning expansion. Export sales will continue to grow, but U.S. manufacturers can no longer expect the international market to counter the sluggish growth in the United States.'' The SGMA expected that while the Asian economic crisis may be over, the economies in these regions will need time to improve. Due to high unemployment in Western Europe (about 11 percent) and tax policies, consumers in European markets will have less disposable income to spend on imported U.S. goods. According to the SGMA, the ''European trade pact and unified currency (Euro) will help contribute to an environment more conducive to growth for U.S. manufacturers.''

RESEARCH AND TECHNOLOGY

Because they simplify many routine ordering procedures and improve sales staff efficiency, establishments in this industry have continued to increase the reliance on computers. Product counts and point-of-sale data, which includes price, model number, color, and size imprinted on an item's bar code, are regularly gathered electronically to provide managers with current inventory and sales information. For sales staff, point-of-sales systems have proven useful in calculating discounts, approving credit, and scheduling deliveries.

Industry trade journal *Footwear News* declared in 1995 that all shoe stores, no matter how small, must computerize in order to stay competitive. It also reported on special software that allows footwear retailers to order directly from many major manufacturers and wholesalers, often at a discount.

According to a study conducted by Ernst & Young, the number of retailers on-line, selling products to consumers, grew from 12 percent in 1997 to 39 percent in 1998. The interactive capabilities of the Internet allow retailers to customize messages and services. In 1999, the Venator Group announced a partnership with Excite, ''a global media company which provides its Foot Locker brands a presence on Excite shopping, sports and lifestyle channels, as well as search and banner integration.'' The effect of Internet shopping for footwear on the traditional ''bricks and mortar'' stores will be seen as retailing moves into the next century.

FURTHER READING

1996 Business Performance Report. Columbia, MD: National Shoe Retailers Association, 1996.

''Athletic Footwear.'' Sporting Goods Manufacturers Association, 1996. Available from http://www.sportlink.com/afa/market/footwearmarket96/afmt96_toc.html.

''Athletic Footwear Sales Slip 10 Percent in Second Quarter, Stand Almost Equal to 1998 for First Six Months.'' Sporting Goods Manufacturers Association. Available from http://www.sportlink.com/press_room/1999_releases/afa99-004.html.

Baber, Bonnie. ''Outraged by Outlets: Vendor Outlets Continue to Pressure Retailers Selling Full-Price Comfort Footwear.'' *Footwear News,* 13 April 1998.

Carr, Bob. ''Flat Footed Sales: Retailers Have Been Spreading the Blame for Down Athletic Footwear Sales Over the Past Year.'' *Sporting Goods Business,* 8 February 1999.

Dutter, Greg. ''Sense and Sensibility.'' *Footwear+,* March 1997.

Hopper, Kathryn. ''Venator Group to Close All Kinney Stores by Year's End.'' *Knight Ridder/Tribune Business News,* 18 September 1998.

Malone, Scott. ''Payless to Add Parade of Shoes to Retail Stable.'' *Footwear News,* 20 January 1997.

———. ''Stores Report Solid Fiscal '97 Sales, Expect Double-Digit EPS Growth.'' *Footwear News,* 16 February 1998.

Tedeschi, Mark. ''Specialty Footwear Takes Cautious Steps.'' *Sporting Goods Business,* 25 January 1999.

Wholesale and Retail Trade USA. 2nd ed. Detroit: Gale Group, 1998.

SIC 5699

MISCELLANEOUS APPAREL AND ACCESSORY STORES

This industry consists of establishments primarily engaged in the retail sale of specialized apparel and accessories, such as bathing suits, belts, raincoats, riding and other sports apparel, T-shirts, umbrellas, uniforms, and wigs and toupees. This industry also includes men's and women's custom tailors.

NAICS CODE(S)

315000 (Included in Apparel Manufacturing Subsector Based on Type of Garment Produced)
448190 (Other Clothing Stores)
448150 (Clothing Accessories Stores)

In 1998, the four industry leaders brought in more than 90 percent of the industry's total sales of $275 million. The industry leader, Lost Arrow, Inc., had $170 million in annual sales in 1998 and employed 900 people at its retail chain stores. Life Uniforms and Shoe Shops Corp. of Missouri, the second largest company, took in an estimated $76 million in sales in 1998 and employed more than 1,300 people. Other industry leaders included Retail Star, with $12 million in sales; Crazy Shirts Inc., $25 million; and Norcostco Inc., $12 million. The remainder averaged less than $5 million in annual sales.

Business improved for apparel and specialty stores in October 1999 with retail sales increasing 0.9 percent from the previous month and 7.4 percent from the previous year. The industry was cautious, however, and mindful of a possible economic downturn in the future. Various apparel and accessory stores began focusing on cash rich teens as a primary market. Though discount stores and home shopping were direct competitors, smaller establishments lured back customers by repositioning themselves in the marketplace. Perhaps a greater threat was the Internet, which emerged in the late 1990s as a potent retail force. Many companies chose to fight fire with fire by establishing a presence on the World Wide Web, such as Crazyshirts.com and Sheplers.com.

The structure and organization of stores in the industry is similar to that of the retail apparel and shoe business. Establishments are either chain stores or individually owned.

Large companies own distribution centers, where merchandise is sent by manufacturers, held for a short time, then shipped to outlets or stores. Manufacturers' sales representatives and the retailers' merchandise buyers link the manufacturer and retailer. Small retailers generally do not own distribution centers. They tend to purchase inventory from distributors representing several manufacturers, including items solicited through distributor catalogs.

Unlike other stores in the fashion industry, establishments dealing in miscellaneous apparel and accessories traditionally have relied on catalogs, later the Web, and less on television and magazines for advertising and customer sales. The specialty nature of the business gave the stores a smaller share of the apparel market. Extensive use of catalogs brings service bureaus into the chain of distribution. That practice was beginning to change in the late 1990s as specialty retailers began spending more on advertising and finding ways on the Internet to gain exposure.

FURTHER READING

"Big & Tall: Major Brands Add a New Dimension." *DNR,* 10 November 1999.

Brady, Jennifer L. "Fine Jewelry Shines for Holiday." *Women's Wear Daily,* 9 January 1995.

Chandler, Susan. "Why Clothiers Are Feeling Pinched: Shoppers Are Waiting for Markdowns and Driving Hard Bargains." *Business Week,* 18 September 1995.

Lagnado, Isaac. ". . . Not a Meltdown, But Close. . . ." *Textile World,* January 1996.

Maxwell, Alison. "Apparel Sales Up .9 Percent in October." *Women's Wear Daily,* 15 November 1999.

Moukheiber, Zina. "Retailing." *Forbes,* 2 January1995.

Rozelle, Walter N. "Growth of Apparel Sales at Retail Is Strengthening." *Textile World,* November 1996.

Ryan, Thomas J. "Looking for Another Strong Year." *Women's Wear Daily,* 9 December 1999.

U.S. Department of Commerce. *Statistical Abstract of the United States 1998.* Washington, DC: GPO, 1998.

The Value Line Investment Survey (Part 3 - Ratings & Reports), 19 November 1999.

Ward's Business Directory of U.S. Private and Public Companies. Detroit: Gale Group, 1999.

SIC 5712

FURNITURE STORES

This classification covers establishments primarily engaged in the retail sale of household furniture, including beds and springs, cabinet work, juvenile furniture, mattresses, and outdoor furniture. These stores also may sell home furnishings, major appliances, and floor coverings.

NAICS CODE(S)

337122 (Nonupholstered Wood Household Furniture Manufacturing)

337110 (Wood Kitchen Cabinet and Counter Top Manufacturing)

337121 (Upholstered Wood Household Furniture Manufacturing)

442110 (Furniture Stores)

The industry is made up of both large national chains, regional stores, and small independent operations. According to data from the U.S. Bureau of the Census, consumers spent $55 billion on furniture and other home furnishings in 1997. But throughout the 1990s the fastest growing segment of the retail furniture trade has been through new retailers that offer a nontraditional approach. These new retailers, which sell household and office furniture, mattresses, and related consumer products, include large discount superstores such as Wal-Mart and Target, warehouse stores like Price Club and Office Depot, and one-stop department stores such as Sears & Roebuck and J.C. Penney. Catalog sales of furniture also have increased in recent years. This new competition has made the marketplace a much more difficult one for traditional furniture stores.

The top ten retailers of furniture and bedding in 1997 were roughly split between stores in the traditional category and those from the department/discount store segment, according to a 1999 report that appeared in *Furniture Today Retail Planning Guide, 1999.* Topping the list with sales of roughly $1.7 billion was Heilig-Meyers, a traditional furniture retailer, followed by Levitz, which

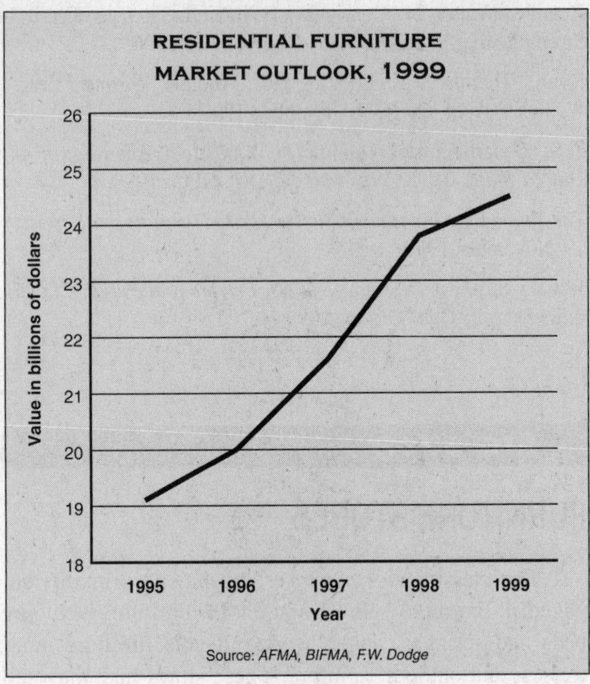

Source: *AFMA, BIFMA, F.W. Dodge*

placed second with 1997 sales of $839 million. Making up the rest of the top 10 were Office Depot ($779 million), J.C. Penney ($747 million), Federated Department Stores ($743 million), Sears ($737 million), Ethan Allen ($736 million), Wal-Mart ($673 million), Rooms To Go ($550 million), and Montgomery Ward ($547 million).

Entering the 1990s, the retail furniture industry, like many other retail industries, slumped in the face of a general economic recession. Furniture purchases are considered major, discretionary purchases that can be deferred when tough economic times hit. In 1988, the percentage of disposable income spent for household furniture was about 4.6 percent, but by 1991 this figure had dipped to about 3.9 percent. Moreover, retail sales of furniture are historically predicated on new housing construction, which slumped in the late 1980s, a dry period that lasted until 1992-93. Moving into a new home is the single most important stimulus for buying furniture, so the decline in housing starts had a direct effect on the downturn in the retail furniture trade. Studies have shown that the average consumer spends more on furniture within two years of moving into a new home than at any other time. Just as the recession of the early 1990s had dragged down sales of household furniture and bedding, the economic resurgence of the middle and late 1990s brought a noticeable uptick in these sales.

Today's furniture industry faces a more complex and dynamic distribution system than ever before. Traditional retail furniture stores continue to lose ground to their competitors among department stores and the large discount chains. As evidence of this, one need look no further than the top 10 list of furniture retailers that appeared in *Furniture Today Retail Planning Guide, 1999*. The 4 traditional furniture stores—Heilig-Meyers, Levitz, Ethan Allen, and Rooms To Go—among the top 10 retailers accounted for slightly less than 50 percent of the total sales of the top 10.

Furniture typically used to house electronic components, known as ready-to-assemble (RTA) furniture, was one of the fastest growing consumer product categories during the 1990s, according to the Electronic Industries Association. RTA furniture sales are expected to continue to grow to more than $1.3 billion annually. This type of furniture is designed to hold audio, video, and home office products. It is shipped unassembled to the store and then is either assembled by the store or the ultimate consumer. Products include home entertainment centers, television and VCR stands, home office furniture, and furniture designed to hold computers and related equipment. Due to the minimal labor in manufacturing, ease in shipping and inventory stocking, and perceived value versus price, the majority of sales of RTA furniture are made through mass merchandisers, specialty stores, and warehouse clubs. However, due to strong demand, many leading furniture stores have begun to sell RTA furniture.

Another competitive force at work in the retail furniture marketplace is the increasing number of consumers purchasing furniture and office equipment at nontraditional sites such as warehouse clubs, discount superstores, department stores, galleries, and from catalogs. Large furniture retailers, such as Levitz, and smaller furniture retailers compete with department stores, warehouse clubs, and discount superstores. Smaller retail outlets have found the resultant discount prices necessary to compete in the marketplace especially difficult to maintain.

While the economic recession of the early 1990s dealt a blow to the retail furniture industry, primarily due to the bleak performance of the housing industry, increased demand was seen throughout most of the rest of the decade. New housing construction experienced a significant uptrend during the middle and late 1990s, a development that provided a shot in the arm for the retail furniture industry. In 1997, the number of establishments in the industry was put at roughly 48,000, and sales totaled roughly $55.2 billion. As of March 1997, employment in the industry stood at about 386,600 workers.

FURTHER READING

Darnay, Arsen J., and Joyce Piwowarski, eds. *Wholesale and Retail Trade USA,* 2nd ed. Detroit: Gale, 1998.

Darnay, Arsen J., and Gary Alampi, ed. *Wholesale and Retail Trade USA.* Detroit: Gale Research, 1995.

"Largest Furniture Retailers, 1997." *Furniture Today Retail Planning Guide 1999.*

Smith, Carter. *America's Fastest Growing Employers,* Holbrook, MA: Adams Inc.

U.S. Bureau of the Census. *1997 Economic Census.* Washington: GPO, 1999.

U.S. Department of Commerce. International Trade Administration. *U.S. Industry and Trade Outlook, 1999.* Washington: GPO, 1999.

U.S. Department of Labor, *Employment, Hours, and Earnings, United States, 1988-96,* Washington: GPO, 1996.

SIC 5713

FLOOR COVERING STORES

This classification primarily includes retail sellers of floor coverings. Although companies in this industry group may also incidentally install floor coverings, contractors who primarily install floor coverings for others are in **SIC 1752: Floor Laying and Other Floor Work, Not Elsewhere Classified.**

NAICS CODE(S)

442210 (Floor Covering Stores)

The retail floor covering industry includes sellers of rugs and carpets, linoleum, asphalt tile, and ceramic tile. Floor covering retailers include specialty stores, department stores, home improvement stores, and mass merchandisers.

According to U.S. government statistics, there were just over 16,600 establishments engaged in this business in 1997, compared with 13,640 in 1992. Sales in 1997 totaled nearly $16.5 billion, compared with $9.6 billion in 1992. As of 1997, the industry employed 96,186 workers with a total annual payroll of $2.46 billion.

Reflecting the buoyancy of the U.S. economy during the mid-1990s, sales at the nation's floor covering stores surged nearly 72 percent in the five years from 1992 to 1997. This strength in sales allowed retailers to increase the number of establishments engaged in this trade from 13,640 in 1992 to 16,603 in 1997, a gain of nearly 22 percent. Employment in the industry also surged ahead of past totals during this five-year period, rising 40 percent from 1992 to 1997. Even more dramatic was the increase in the size of the industry's annual payroll, which climbed nearly 90 percent between 1992 and 1997.

At the beginning of the 1990s, the industry was struggling to shake off the effects of an economic recession, which had significantly dampened demand. A sales decline in 1991 was followed by a modest recovery in 1992. The recession hit the floor covering industry particularly hard for a variety of reasons. Among the factors affecting the sector during the slowdown was a sharp decline in residential construction, low consumer confidence, and consumer cutbacks on big-ticket home improvement expenditures. Home remodeling and new home purchases are typically the most important events spurring floor covering sales. Carpeting, in particular, is sensitive to economic fluctuations and is closely tied to the sales' rate for existing homes: most carpet sales occur in the replacement market, rather than the new home market.

In addition, as *Industry Surveys* noted, "the consolidation of the department store industry in the 1980s and the high interest charges that arose from this event forced these retailers to become more cost-conscious. As a result, they pared buying staffs and employed fewer suppliers. They also focused on carrying leaner inventories, historically their largest expense." These business conditions, coupled with competition from mass merchandisers such as Wal-Mart, J.C. Penney, and K-Mart in floor covering retail, combined to pinch floor covering retailers. The improved economy of the middle and later 1990s provided floor covering retailers with much higher sales.

Major players in the floor covering retail business in 1997 were Carpet One, which reported sales of $2 billion; Home Depot, with floor covering sales of $1.3 billion; Maxim Group, which posted sales of $1.2 billion in this sector; Abbey Carpet ($700 million); Shaw Industries ($600 million); Sears ($365 million); Lowe's ($300); Sherwin-Williams ($200 million); Hechinger/Builders Square ($150 million); and Federated ($125 million).

FURTHER READING

Darnay, Arsen J., and Joyce Piwowarski, eds. *Wholesale and Retail Trade USA,* 2nd ed. Detroit: Gale Research, 1998.

"Largest Floor Covering Retailers, 1997." *Home Furnishings News,* 20 July 1999.

U.S. Bureau of the Census. *1997 Economic Census.* Washington, DC: GPO, 1999.

U.S. Department of Commerce. International Trade Administration. *U.S. Industry and Trade Outlook, 1999.* Washington, DC: GPO, 1999.

SIC 5714

DRAPERY, CURTAIN, AND UPHOLSTERY STORES

This category covers establishments primarily engaged in the retail sale of draperies, curtains, and upholstery materials. Establishments primarily engaged in reupholstering or repairing furniture are classified in **SIC 7641: Reupholstery and Furniture Repair.**

NAICS CODE(S)

442291 (Window Treatment Stores)
451130 (Sewing, Needlework and Piece Goods Stores)
314121 (Curtain and Drapery Mills)

INDUSTRY SNAPSHOT

Curtain, drapery, and upholstery material stores were a thriving segment of the general home furnishings retail industry during the 1990s. Consumers focused on the home and personalizing their environments, and the industry recognized these lifestyle directions by providing stylish yet relatively low-priced products. Even during recessionary down times, consumers frequently replaced window treatments rather than overhauling the entire room. Reupholstering or purchasing slipcovers for existing furniture was also an alternative to redecorating a room. Furniture covers went from a specialized industry to a more mass-produced segment with many options readily available in discount and chain stores. The popularity of futons also benefited the upholstery segment because the versatile furniture can be covered with a variety of ready-made or custom-made slipcovers.

Curtain and drapery stores were adversely affected by shifting trends in home decorating fashions. Many stores changed dramatically to accommodate the new trends by adding a wider variety of merchandise both for windows and for the home itself. Chains like Blinds to Go emerged, concentrating on providing a single product. The upholstery fabric segment generally benefited from shifting trends in consumer tastes. New technological developments brought a wider range of upholstery fabrics to consumers and retail outlets, leading to increased consumer interest and increased business for retailers. Furniture stores offering custom upholstery services in a variety of prices and styles, such as Custom Expressions, emerged in major markets across the country, sparking consumer interest in upholstery, which trickled down to more established stores selling only upholstery fabrics.

ORGANIZATION AND STRUCTURE

Many of the establishments in the retail curtain and drapery industry were family-owned enterprises located primarily in commercial districts of residential areas, both urban and suburban. These establishments catered to both new homeowners with a limited decorating budget and older customers with more money to spend. The typical store offered ready-made curtains and draperies, custom-made window treatments, a selection of alternative window treatments such as miniblinds and vertical drapes, and, in some cases, kitchen and bath textiles. Kitchen and bath sales helped boost profits, compensating for flagging curtain and drapery sales. To sell their products, curtain and drapery stores relied heavily on attractive displays of merchandise. One type of store display was the vignette, or small wall-window-bed display. Designed to give a customer an idea of a how a coordinated room might look, these displays changed every few months to incorporate a new product line. The vignette's components were easily interchangeable and adaptable. The displayed products were obtained from a host of major manufacturers, who showcased their products at seasonal trade shows attended by buyers or owners of curtain and drapery stores.

A prime example of a family-owned, privately-held curtain and drapery business was Curtainland, a small chain of stores in the suburban New York area. The company was founded in 1975 by the Kanan brothers, who had previous experience in the retail furniture and appliance business. The first store, and the three subsequent Curtainland outlets, were located in areas with a recent influx of new suburban residents. The Kanans believed that the window-treatment areas of department stores did not offer as much variety as their specialty retail business. Curtainland stores aimed to combine a wide selection of products with prices even with or lower than their competitors'. The company tried to hire sales associates with some interior design experience. Curtainland's ability to provide knowledgeable and committed service helped insulate the company from downturns in the soft window-treatment business. The Kanan family played a key role as buyers for Curtainland stores, obtaining the company's merchandise from quarterly trips to curtain and drapery manufacturers' showrooms in New York City. Curtainland stores stocked miniblinds, vertical drapes, curtain and drapery rods, and pleated shades, as well as ready-made curtains, draperies, and matching bedspreads. Bath accessories such as rugs and shower curtains also accounted for some of the store's merchandise.

Prior to the 1980s formal draperies were standard fixtures in living room, dining room, and bedroom areas, while lighter-weight curtains were the primary window coverings in more informal rooms such as kitchens and bathrooms. In the 1980s the curtain and drapery store industry was dramatically affected by shifts in home decorating tastes. American window-blind manufacturers developed new technology that opened up a whole new area of hard window treatments—the aluminum miniblind. This versatile shade came in a variety of colors and styles, was relatively inexpensive, did not require drycleaning, and gave any room a modern look. Soon Taiwan restructured its lightweight plastics industry to produce vinyl imitations of the miniblind that were cheaper than miniblinds manufactured in the United States. By the 1990s miniblinds were standard window coverings in millions of households across the United States, which had a detrimental effect on curtain and drapery sales. As a result, many curtain and drapery manufacturers and retail outlets did not survive the change in style, and they were forced to exit the business or adapt their product lines to capture other segments of the home-furnishings business.

CURRENT CONDITIONS

The curtain and drapery manufacturers in operation during the 1990s offered a limited product line, with an emphasis on custom services and quick delivery. Specialty curtain and drapery stores also were damaged by competition from home-decorating areas of department stores, which employed more aggressive marketing tactics than the typical specialty curtain and drapery store. J.C. Penney was one example of a department store that invested money in its home-decorating departments to revive flagging overall sales.

On another front, the entry of discount retailers into the home-furnishings market also negatively affected the industry. Stores such as Kohl's and K-Mart began offering a wide selection of ready-made curtains and draperies in the latest styles at bargain rates. Discounters' sales thrived as they turned their domestics divisions into extremely competitive destinations. While K-Mart created its program based on sharp merchandising and the reputation of home fashions expert Martha Stewart, Target had its design staff establish a fashion direction conforming to larger style trends. *Discount Store News* noted, ''One of the big questions that remains about the domestics market isn't whether major discounters will win more share of the market but rather what share of market they will leave for other retailers.''

INDUSTRY LEADERS

In the late-1990s the leaders in the curtain and drapery industry were stores that specialized in home goods as a whole. The leader was Bed, Bath & Beyond, Inc., of Springfield, New Jersey, with $1.4 billion in sales in 1999, which represented a 31 percent sales growth from 1998. The company operated 240 warehouse-type stores in 38 states nationwide and employed 9,400 people. Linens 'n Things, Inc., of Clifton, New Jersey, held the number two spot with $1.3 billion in sales in 1999, which reflected a 22 percent increase over the previous year. Linens operated nearly 200 superstores in 38 states and had 9,700 employees in 1998. Overall, the emphasis shifted towards ''one-stop shopping'' where individuals could furnish an entire house with one trip to the store.

Otherwise, the industry was dominated by smaller, specialized companies such as Plainview, New York-based Curtains and Home, Inc. Most of its stores were along the eastern seaboard in New York, Pennsylvania, Maryland, and Virginia. The company was known as a retailer of affordable curtains, drapes, and other home furnishings, such as shower curtains and table linens. Three D Departments, Inc., based in Irvine, California, was another large retailer of curtains and draperies, as was Reiters, Inc., based in Chicago, Illinois. The company offered quality goods at a discount price. Reiters attributed much of its success and longevity in the competitive industry to its emphasis on customer service. It provided training and product education to its sales associates on a continuous basis. The stores carried an assortment of window treatments, including miniblinds. Reiters also offered shop-at-home and custom drapery and curtain services.

An innovative Connecticut-based business, the Drapery Exchange, Inc., stocked draperies on consignment and sold them to consumers at a reduced price. Local interior designers turned over their leftover inventory of custom-made drapery and window treatment ensembles, originally created for design showrooms, designer showhouses, or magazine layouts. The Drapery Exchange then sold these custom-made goods at a substantially reduced price.

Window Works, of Pompano Beach, Florida, was another aggressive participant in the curtain and drapery store industry. The company was the franchiser of over 100 custom window treatment stores across the country and relied heavily on sophisticated advertising and a contemporary look in its outlets to attract upscale but price-conscious consumers. Custom-made blinds accounted for a large part of store sales, but Window Works also stocked an array of products from drapery and curtain manufacturers.

Blinds to Go expanded from its Montreal, Canada, roots throughout the United States in 1995, opening over 40 stores by the end of the decade. The company specialized in providing customers with made-to-order window dressings quickly and at a factory-direct price.

FURTHER READING

''Bed, Bath & Beyond, Inc.'' *Hoover's Company Capsules.* Austin, Tex.: Hoover's, Inc., 1997.

''Bed, Bath & Beyond, Inc.'' 27 February 2000. Available from http://www.hoovers.com/co/capsule/3/0,2163,14933,00.html.

''Linens 'n Things, Inc.'' *Hoover's Company Capsules.* Austin, Tex.: Hoover's, Inc., 1997.

''Linens 'n Things, Inc.'' 27 February 2000. Available from http://www.hoovers.com/co/capsule/1/0,2163,5241,00.html.

''Major Discounters Squeeze Regionals' Supply Lines.'' *Discount Store News,* 10 August 1998, 61.

''Montreal Window-Dressing Chain Starts U.S Expansion in New Jersey.'' *The (Bergen, New Jersey) Record,* 2 September 1998.

U.S. Department of Commerce. *County Business Patterns 1994.* Washington, D.C.: GPO, 1996.

SIC 5719

MISCELLANEOUS HOME FURNISHINGS STORES

Establishments in this industry are primarily engaged in the retail sale of miscellaneous homefurnishings, such as china, glassware, and metalware for kitchen and table use; bedding and linen; brooms and brushes; lamps and shades; mirrors and pictures; venetian blinds; and window shades. Establishments primarily engaged in the retail sale of miscellaneous homefurnishings by house-to-house canvas or by party-plan merchandising are classified in **SIC 5963: Direct Selling Establishments.**

NAICS CODE(S)

442291 (Window Treatment Stores)
442299 (All Other Home Furnishings Stores)

Businesses involved in the sale of miscellaneous home furnishings are as varied as the goods they sell to consumers. They offer everything needed to furnish a home from kitchenware to linens, and lamps and shades to venetian blinds and window shades. Growth in sales of furniture and other household equipment remained steady during the 1990s. According to the U.S. Census Bureau, sales figures for each year between 1984 and 1997 never varied by more than 10 percent. In 1997, there were approximately 18,661 miscellaneous home furnishings stores, which employed an estimated 135,359 people and had sales of $14.3 billion.

Three factors have contributed to the steady demand of home furnishings: increased housing activity, growth in real disposable personal income, and declining consumer debt. Also contributing to the success of home furnishings sales was the fact that they could be purchased seemingly anywhere. Discount stores as well as department stores stock a wide variety of items for the consumer, and their prices vary with the brand name and the type of store that sells them. Of the several different types of retailers that sell home furnishings, one of the fastest growing was the specialty retailer that attracts upscale consumers. These stores may be independent operators or part of a chain and provide quality merchandise with moderate price tags. But price is not all that attracts customers. Specialty retailers tend to carry unusual and distinctive items that attract consumers who can't find them anywhere else.

The ten leading companies in the miscellaneous home furnishings industry made up nearly 50 percent of the industry's total sales in 1996. According to *Wholesale and Retail Trade USA,* the leading company was Dollar General Corporation. Based in Nashville, Tennessee, the company began as J.L. Turner and Son, Inc., but changed its name in 1968. The company sells general merchandise to low-, middle-, and fixed-income families at its more than 4,150 Dollar General Stores throughout the Midwest and Southeast. In addition to housewares and home furnishings, Dollar General offers health and beauty aids, cleaning supplies, and seasonal goods. Opening about 350 stores per year since 1995, the company's five-year average annual compound growth rate in net sales and income of 23 percent and 40 percent, respectively. Dollar General's net sales totaled $3.9 billion in 2000. Net income reached $219.4 million for 2000 and the company employed 29,820 people.

Bed Bath & Beyond Inc. is the leading superstore retailer in this industry classification. It operates 240 stores in 38 states and opens at least 45 more stores annually. The stores have a full line of homefurnishings including bath towels and bedding. Sales for 2000 reached $1.9 billion making for a net income of $131.2 million. In 1999, the company employed 9,400 people.

Linens 'n Things, Inc. ranks as the leading superstore retailer in the industry, behind only Bed Bath & Beyond. With 200 stores in 38 states, Linens 'n Things sold $1.3 million worth of bedding, housewares, and towels, among other things in 1999. The company had a net income of $52 million in 1999 and employed 11,900 people.

Pier 1 Imports, Inc. operates 750 stores in the United States and 80 outlets abroad. The stores offer a variety of miscellaneous household goods ranging from lamps to dinnerware. In 1999, the company generated $1.1 billion in sales and totaled $80 million in net income. The company employed 12,600 people.

Michael's Stores Incorporated, headquartered in Irving, Texas, was another industry leader in the mid-1990s. In addition to miscellaneous home furnishings products, Michael's sells general crafts, party supplies, and seasonal merchandise. Operating 453 Michael's stores and more than 70 Aaron Brothers stores in 45 states, the company reported sales of $1.4 billion in 1996.

Independently owned specialty stores, which hold the sales-per-square foot crown with a median of $339, are as varied as the products they sell—whether it's cutlery, pottery, lamps, lampshades, window treatments, draperies, or kitchenware. Consumers find such stores in shopping centers and malls, along commercial highways, or in country towns and backroad, cottage-style boutiques. Because home furnishings cover such a broad spectrum of products and prices, and because modern distribution methods bring items manufactured half-way around the world to the smallest American town, this industry continues to perform well.

FURTHER READING

Darnay, Arsen J., and Gary Alampi, eds. *Wholesale and Retail Trade USA.* Detroit: Gale Research, 1995.

"Furniture Today: 1996 Survey of Top 100 Stores." *Home Furnishings Executive,* National Home Furnishings Association, 1996.

Hoover's Company Capsule, 20 March 2000. Available from http://www.hoovers.com.

Moskowitz, Milton, and Robert Levering and Michael Katz. *Everybody's Business.* Doubleday: New York, 1990.

Statistical Abstract of the United States. Washington: U.S. Department of Commerce, 1996.

U.S. Census Bureau. *1997 Economic Census—Retail Trade.* Washington, DC: GPO, 2000. Available from http://www.census.gov.

SIC 5722

HOUSEHOLD APPLIANCE STORES

This industry covers establishments primarily engaged in the retail sale of electric and gas refrigerators, stoves, and other household appliances, such as electric irons, percolators, hot plates, sewing machines, and vacuum cleaners. Many such stores also sell radio and television sets. Retail stores operated by public utility companies and primarily engaged in the sale of electric and gas appliances for household use are also classified in this industry.

NAICS CODE(S)

443111 (Household Appliance Stores)

INDUSTRY SNAPSHOT

In 1998, the industry saw sales of $68.5 billion as consumer demand for appliances remained steady due to the stable economy, consumer confidence, and the increase of new housing developments. The majority of appliance stores were fairly small-scale operations with only a few workers in the early 1990s; however, a continuing trend toward consolidation of the market in the late 1990s led to the leadership of superstores and warehouses in this industry. Although these megastores comprise a minority of the industry's stores, the low prices that they are able to offer due to their economies of scale make it extremely difficult for smaller stores to compete against them. Due to the success of these retailers, appliance stores tended to diversify their product range. By the late 1990s, most household appliance stores offered a wide range of products—including consumer electronics and office supplies.

Towards the end of the decade, household appliances were often sold in a discount store, such as Kmart or Wal-Mart, but household appliance superstores like Best Buy and Circuit City were on par with, if not better placed than, discount stores and department stores. Household appliance stores sold everything from washers and dryers to digital satellite systems, from radios to home theater systems, from personal computers to cellular phones, and from audio cassettes and compact discs to video cassettes, DVD players, and electronic accessories.

According to the Consumer Electronics Manufacturing Association (CEMA), electronic appliances and accessories purchasing increased in the late 1990s, especially in the newer product categories. Household appliance superstores continued to deploy newer and slicker marketing strategies to keep up with the increasing competition. Sales of consumer electronics were expected to rise along with many sectors of the retail industry.

ORGANIZATION AND STRUCTURE

The appliance industry is a low-growth, relatively mature industry offering acceptable gross margins and relatively low inventory turnover. The latter, combined with the large amount of space required for storage, makes for relatively low competition compared to other sectors of the retail industry. Throughout the mid- to late 1990s, the industry experienced significant consolidation, and this is expected to continue. A number of important players have gone out of business, including Sun Television and Appliances Inc., Newmark and Lewis, Home Center and Federated Group, Crazy Eddie, Fretter, and Highland Superstores. In addition, 40 Silo stores and 110 McDuff/Video Concepts stores owned by Tandy were closed. Many other regional chains faced decreasing profits and sales as a result of competition from larger stores such as Best Buy and Circuit City.

Small stores, which sell only household appliances, were becoming increasingly rare and were being outmuscled by larger chains. The market has shifted toward superstores, which offer a comprehensive range of household wares and home office supplies, in addition to low margin consumer electronics. As in other sectors of the retail industry, there is a movement toward a no-frills warehouse-type format, which allows stores to offer a dominant selection in every category in which they compete, while creating significant cost efficiencies relative to the more traditional formats. The megastore format has the potential to generate a much higher profit per square foot. The large store size creates savings in fixed store costs—including rent, labor, service, and overhead. The idea in a mixed format superstore is to use appliances as a draw into the store. If the store can satisfy customers in what is usually the first household purchase, it can usu-

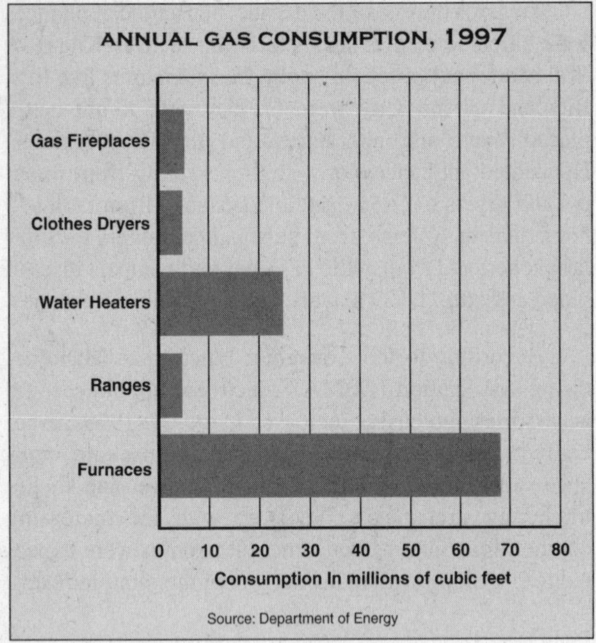

ally retain them for subsequent electronic and personal computer purchases.

In the United States, consumer home appliances and consumer electronics are an important and sizable part of total retail sales. These items together account for about $68.5 billion in sales annually. With consumer electronics, sales are usually renewed on a regular basis by the introduction of new technology that substantially widens the scope of the industry. According to P. J. Muldoon of McDonald and Company Securities, ''Over the course of the century, there has been a pattern of at least one 'revolutionary' product per decade: the gramophone (1920s), the radio (1930s), the black-and-white television (1950s), the color television (1960s), the component audio system (1970s), and the video cassette recorder (1980s). There is additional impetus to growth in this retail segment from a steady stream of enhanced forms of existing items (for example the proliferation of improved television formats—stereo, with remote, big screen, etc.). Historically, because of these factors, retail sales of consumer electronics generally grow at above-average rates relative to retail sales and consumption.''

Background and Development

The first household appliance store was established in 1827 in Salem Village, Massachusetts, by Amasa Goodyear, according to J. Leander Bishop in the *History of American Manufacturers.* She sold housewares such as coffee and tea pots, waffle irons, brass andirons, and cast iron gridirons in addition to a range of hardware goods.

The early household appliance stores usually sold a combination of housewares and hardware products, according to Earl Lifshey's *The Housewares Story.* They took shape as independent units and as departments within large stores. Of the latter, Lifshey writes: ''It was the emergence of the department stores in the latter half of the past century that spawned the housewares department as we have come to know it. The conditions and economies of those days encouraged the expansion of housewares departments. Some of the great department stores . . . had houseware departments of enormous size, owing less to the extensive assortment of items than to the practice of maintaining large stocks of goods on the selling floor. Such refinements as cost accounting and the pressure for getting maximum sales per square foot did not come until much later.''

The turning point in the industry took place around the time of the Civil War. During the early and mid-1860s, a number of key developments occurred: the electrification of peoples homes; a rise in the standard of living, improvements in transportation systems, particularly the railways; increased capital; the development of plate glass, which made store windows possible; and the rise of retail advertising. The advent of electricity, in particular, revolutionized the household appliance store industry, making possible the invention of the range of items that have become synonymous with the business, such as refrigerators, electric cookers, and vacuum cleaners.

Electricity had been around for a long time, however, before there was a significant demand for household appliances. George H. Jungen, a former vice president of the Baitinger Electric Co. in New York City, described the situation in an interview with Earl Lifshey in the December 20, 1937, issue of *Retailing Home Furnishings:* ''Electricity was first used in factories and office buildings long before being introduced into the home. Electrical appliances—such as they were at the time—couldn't be readily purchased by interested consumers from dealers simply because there were few or no such dealers around. There were only five firms (in New York City) then handling electrical goods: Stanley & Patterson; Latham; Manhattan Electric; Western Electric; and J. H. Burnell. Most of their business was done on electrical equipment. When people wanted to get an electrical appliance, it was only natural, therefore, that they should think of getting it from the people who furnished them with other electrical supplies.'' Consequently, many of the larger household appliance stores, such as Lewis & Conger and Hammacher Schlemmer, issued catalogs and mail order services to encourage sales.

As late as 1914, department stores as prominent as Marshall Fields in Chicago were debuting their ''household utilities'' departments, selling kitchen utensils, laundry requisites, refrigerators, sewing machines, vacuum cleaners, and electrical sundries. The real invasion of household appliances had yet to come. It was only in the 1940s and 1950s that many of the appliances we now take for granted became a part of the average American household. Since then, new products have appeared with increasing predictability. In the early 1980s, consumer demand for electronics led to large sales and profit growth; many companies flourished. By the mid-1980s, however, the environment became more competitive, the market for VCRs became saturated, and the recession of the late 1980s slowed overall sales.

In 1993, the overall market for home appliances improved, but remained difficult, and competition was expected to remain stiff. According to P. J. Muldoon, "From the better tone of housing markets in 1992, it appears that the trough in this segment has been reached and that demand for consumer durables will rise. The overall industry environment—namely, generally sluggish demand and the declining trend in pricing—continues to call for a strategic orientation toward grabbing more market share. Surviving operators have to properly prepare financially and strategically. Those that survive will be presented with considerable growth opportunities. This potential will be enhanced further in the more distant future when the next blockbuster is introduced."

Despite the rise and proliferation of superstores, a greater number of small stores were in the industry. According to *Dun's Survey of American Business 1993,* most stores in the industry were small or medium in size. In 1993 there were 14,201 outlets that generated annual sales between $100,000 and $250,000—more than twice as many as in any other sales' range. There were 5,669 small retail outlets that had between $50,000 and $99,000 in sales revenue, and more than 3,000 stores had sales of less than $50,000. There were progressively fewer stores in the higher revenue brackets: 6,351 outlets had sales between $250,000 and $500,000; 4,769 had sales from $500,000 to $1 million; 3,902 had revenues from $1 million to $5 million; and only 620 stores had annual sales in excess of $5 million in 1993.

The industry as a whole experienced sales growth in the first quarter of 1993. In a 1993 survey by the Salomon Brothers of 75 percent of all household appliance stores, 67 percent of stores reported unit sales growth. These figures were significantly higher than those for the third quarter of 1992, when 17 percent of stores reported flat sales and another 17 percent experienced a decline in sales. Moreover, many retailers experienced an upsurge in sales in April and mid-May of 1993. The following leading brands carried by many household appliance stores helped increase retail sales: General Electric, Whirlpool, Maytag, Roper, Hotpoint, Kelvinator, Amana, Tappan, Speed Queen, Frigidaire, KitchenAid, Sharp, and Jenn-Air. According to Russell L. Leavitt, "buyers cited manufacturer promotional activity and the financial position of consumers along with low interest rates as primary factors contributing to the stronger appliance sales."

With regard to inventory levels, the Salomon Brothers report found that 47 percent of household appliance retailers considered their inventory levels to be consistent with demand. Another 42 percent considered their stocks slightly above target levels, and 11 percent of buyers believed inventories were too low. Retailers considered their inventories of laundry, cooking, dishwasher, and microwave supplies as mostly on target, while many stated that their inventories of refrigeration equipment and room air conditioners were often high.

In terms of the range of inventory, the mix of product lines at the retail level were concentrated toward mid-priced products in the early to mid-1990s. A greater proportion of stores were stocking lower-priced refrigeration, cooking, and laundry products. According to retailers, premium brand merchandise made up 17 percent of overall appliance sales in the first quarter of 1993. The trend among appliance store retailers was to broaden product range in an attempt to increase market share.

Although personal computers were expected to be one of fastest selling products at household appliance stores through the mid-1990s, toward the end of the decade, high definition TV, consumer electronics, and digital products in all categories gained considerable market share.

Price wars, acquisitions, expansion, and slick marketing strategies were the name of the game in the mid-1990s. Household appliance superstores were carrying practically every type of electronic equipment a home would need. Household appliance stores were becoming a one-stop shop for consumers. Use of better displays, in-store catalogs, and extended service plans were helping lure customers and further boost sales at household appliance stores.

According to *HFN,* a Salomon Brothers survey found that major appliance retailers expected sales to be flat and inventories to be higher between May 1, 1995 and April 30, 1996. These forecasts were based upon sales for January through April 1995. However, the household appliance stores were ahead of the market figures with their new marketing strategies. Prices increased by approximately 2 percent. Sales softened and promotional activities expanded. Almost 55 percent of retailers reported an increase in appliance sales.

In the mid-1990s major electronics and appliances retailers were showing definite trends of expansion. Montgomery Ward's acquisition of New England based Lechmere and Circuit City's purchase of 18 former Silo store leases in the Los Angeles area validated this trend. Circuit City plans included growth by 180 stores between

January 1994 and January 1997. Minneapolis-based Best Buy Inc. had expanded in the southeastern and western United States. Best Buy introduced seven Concept III stores, the largest stores in this chain, in Los Angeles in the mid-1990s. Best Buy also opened several stores in the Washington and Cleveland areas for the first time.

Along with the expansion were new marketing strategies and promotions to increase sales. Besides opening new stores in geographically diverse areas, many companies boosted profits through employee training. The willingness of appliance superstores to reinvent themselves through product diversification was established with Best Buy's introduction of gourmet kitchen appliances at its outlets in May 1996. This also reflected the tough household electronics and appliances market of the mid-1990s.

Current Conditions

According to an article in *HFN,* the appliance industry had prospered despite increased competition. ''Notwithstanding the burgeoning of mass merchants with their capacity to slash prices, manufacturers selling directly to consumers, and the growing appeal of Internet shopping, independent electronics and appliance dealers as a whole fared reasonably well during 1997, as reflected by several key performance measures.''

Included in those measures was a lowering of wholesale cost due to retailer participation in buying groups, exciting new electronic and technological advancements, and increasing interest in home theater products. Those stores who offered appliances as well as furniture and electronics fared best, typically averaging an 18 percent gain over 1996.

Another factor encouraging the industry was the increase in housing development. The North American Retail Dealers Association (NARDA) reported that it had risen to a twelve-year high in 1999. ''January '99 housing starts jumped 3.8 percent over the robust numbers posted in December '98. This surge sets a pace for 1999 housing starts to reach 1.8 million.'' As a result, appliance and electronic sales were expected to remain strong into the next millennium as more consumers would be purchasing new items.

Demographics were also key in the success of this industry. Appliance stores in general target 35-to-64 year olds. With a 35 percent growth rate, this segment grew faster than any other in the late 1990s.

In 1998, the U.S. appliance market was also seeing a decline in prices. Due to increased importing from China, Japan, South Korea, and Mexico, increased pressure was placed on price. This resulted in lower prices for the consumer as American manufacturers were forced to provide quality, innovative products at lower costs to compete with foreign imports.

While many stores such as Best Buy and Circuit City saw gains in 1998, some smaller, regional stores succumbed to the pressure of the rising superstores. Sun Television and Appliance Inc. went bankrupt along with Fretter Inc. and Highland Superstores in the mid-1990s. Rex Stores Corp. saw sales decline in 1998, as did Tops Appliance City Inc. In 1999 though, Rex Stores did see some growth in sales.

Industry Leaders

Of the variety of companies engaged in retailing household appliances, either exclusively or as part of a range of product lines, the following two businesses led the industry in sales in 1998: Best Buy Company Inc., with sales of $10 billion; and Circuit City Stores, with sales of $10.8 billion. Heilig-Meyers Co. was also a notable company with sales of $2.4 billion.

Sears also maintained a large share in the appliance industry. Throughout the late 1990s, the company was attempting to reduce its costs and restructure itself to meet the demands of a changing market. Other major outlets for household appliances included Radio Shack, Kmart, Montgomery Ward, ABC Warehouse, and Service Merchandise.

Some of these stores emphasize one side of their business more than the other. For example, some retailers concentrated on selling more consumer electronics than household appliances. Stores selling only consumer electronics are classified separately in **SIC 5731: Radio, Television, and Consumer Electronics Stores.**

Best Buy, Inc. was the country's largest specialty retailer of brand name major appliances and consumer electronics in 1999 with sales of $10.1 billion. The company attributes its rise to the top to a concept called Concept II, which it introduced in 1989. Before implementing this new sales strategy, Best Buy's stores were much like those of competitors Circuit City and Silo—their sales were largely driven by a highly visible commissioned sales force that pushed high margin goods. Only display items were exhibited on the shop floor, and prices were not necessarily discounted. Concept II takes into account the fact that most shoppers dislike aggressive salespeople, preferring instead a self-service format, a wide selection of stock, and low prices.

F.B. Bernstein of Merrill Lynch Capital Markets explained the strategy fully. ''The Concept II prototypes have a no frills warehouse appearance, virtually all the merchandise is displayed on the sales floor, and they adhere to a lowest price policy. They feature fewer brand names than competing stores, but almost all the leading brands are carried; merchandise is displayed by vendor, rather than the more traditional merchandising by price point. They also have far more selling space than traditional consumer electronic retail stores; the additional space is mostly being utilized for expanded assortments of computers.''

Concept II had a dramatic effect on the economics of Best Buy's business. Sales increased dramatically, while gross margins and store expenses were reduced. The net effect of these changes was improved profitability. Concept II eliminated commissioned salespeople and reduced the overall number of salespeople in the store. With the success of its Concept II stores, Best Buy Inc. established a new marketing strategy with the Concept III stores in the mid-1990's. These stores, which were similar to the Concept II stores, were the largest stores in the chain. Concept IV stores were introduced in 1998. These stores were 45,000 square feet dedicated to digital displays, merchandise grouping such as Home Theater and Digital Imaging, and superior customer service. With $224.4 million in net income—a 137.5 percent increase over 1997—Best Buy employed more than 45,000 workers in 1999.

Circuit City is the nation's second largest and strongest household appliances and consumer electronics store. Its emphasis, however, is on consumer electronics. According to G. Balter of Donald, Lufkin & Jenrett Securities, ''Among the major companies that are successful today, Circuit City stands out as one that brought in professional management and invested in expensive point-of-sale technology before embarking on expansion.'' Circuit City is a public stand-alone company, based in Richmond-Petersburg, Virginia. It is classified primarily as a radio, television, and electronics store and secondarily as a household appliance store.

Founded in 1949, Circuit City employed 54,430 people and made nearly $10.8 billion in 1999—an increase of 21.8 percent over 1998. The company expected to double the number of its stores by 2001. Taking advantage of its size in the industry, Circuit City intended to open new stores, including moving back into markets in which other stores were closed.

WORKFORCE

Overall, employment in this industry rose in the late 1990s as the growth of large stores commanded a larger workforce. According to the National Industry Occupation Employment Matrix, there were 475,700 employed in the appliance store sector in 1996, a large percentage of which were part-time workers. That number was expected to grow by 13.5 percent into 2006. States that contained large metropolitan areas such as New York, New Jersey, and California had the largest concentration of electronics and appliance store employees. Overall productivity for an appliance store employee was $159,624 in median sales.

RESEARCH AND TECHNOLOGY

Like all sectors of the retail industry, household appliance stores have been strongly impacted by new technologies, particularly computerization, the Internet, and advanced electronics in the late 1990s. Computerization revolutionized the control of inventory flow and the ordering of stock and allowed more stores to move to a just-in-time system of delivery. Management information systems have made information collection and analysis faster and more accurate. Research has focused on new management techniques to keep up with the fluctuating market.

Pricing continued to be studied especially closely in the late 1990s, and an increasing number of industry retailers switched from promotional sales to every day low pricing (EDLP). According to *Standard and Poor's Industry Surveys,* ''For retailers, the benefits of an EDLP strategy versus a high/low strategy can be significant. Most important are reduced costs: advertising outlays for sales are eliminated, a more even flow of merchandise improves inventory management, and labor costs are reduced since prices no longer need to be marked down. Moreover, the equation works both ways: lower costs can be translated into lower price.'' Most of the bigger chains have undertaken detailed studies of their business and have sought ways to reduce costs, increase efficiency and productivity, control inventory, and rationalize operations.

Another change in the late 1990s was the advent of online retail shopping. While commodities such as books, CDs, and apparel were much easier to sell online, the appliance industry has not backed down from offering products online. This industry is expected to see solid growth in Internet sales by 2001. Best Buy and Circuit City offered some appliances online in 1999. The National Retail Federation expected that more than 40 million households would be shopping online by 2003.

Increased technology in the appliances themselves is also expected to have an impact on this industry. Electronics are changing how many basic appliances work. In an *HFN* article, Ron Kerber—Whirlpool Corp.'s executive vice president and chief technology officer—stated that electronics are ''going to be a huge impact on this business. They will control functionality; they will add functionality.'' Sales are expected to rise with the introduction of such innovations as: advanced cooking controls that could time the start and stop of cooking, either in an oven or microwave; advances in refrigeration, dishwashers, and clothes washers; and new products for home dry cleaning.

FURTHER READING

Beatty, Gerry. ''Best Buy Lines Up Majors.'' *HFN The Weekly Newspaper for the Home Furnishing Network,* 18 March 1996.

Beatty, Gary. ''The Laptop Refrigerator; White Goods Increasingly Will Depend on Advanced Electronic Functions.'' *HFN The Weekly Newspaper for the Home Furnishing Network,* 30 August 1999.

Bernstein, F.B. *Best Buy, Inc. Company Report.* New York: Merrill Lynch Capital Markets, 22 June 1993.

Best Buy Company Information, 1999. Available from http://www.bestbuy.com.

Circuit City Company Information, 1999. Available from http://www.circuitcity.com.

Dun's Census of American Business 1993. New Jersey: Dun and Bradstreet, 1993.

Greenberg, Manning. ''As Best Buy's Entry Nears, Tremors.'' *HFN The Weekly Newspaper for the Home Furnishing Network,* 17 October 1994.

Hartnett, Michael. ''New Gourmet Strategy Highlights Best Buy's Ever-Changing Approach.'' *Stores,* May 1996.

Lagnado, Ike. ''Circuit City, Best Buy Duel.'' *HFN The Weekly Newspaper for the Home Furnishing Network,* 23 December 1996.

Leavitt, Russell L., et al. *Appliance Industry Survey.* New York: Salomon Brothers Inc., 7 June 1993.

National Industry-Occupation Employment Matrix, 1999. Available from http://www.stats.bls.gov.

National Retail Federation Home Page, November 1999. Available from http://www.nrf.com.

North American Retail Dealers Association Home Page, November 1999. Available from http://www.narda.com.

''Retailing.'' *Standard and Poor's Industry Surveys,* 4 June 1992.

Richter, Allan. ''Add-ons on a Roll.'' *HFN The Weekly Newspaper for the Home Furnishing Network,* 9 September 1996.

''Survey Shows Softness.'' *HFN The Weekly Newspaper for the Home Furnishing Network,* 26 June 1995.

Weber, Nathan. ''Earnings, Productivity Up For Dependents.'' *HFN The Weekly Newspaper for the Home Furnishing Network,* 19 October 1998.

SIC 5731

RADIO, TELEVISION, CONSUMER ELECTRONICS, AND MUSIC STORES

This category encompasses establishments primarily engaged in the retail sale of radios, television sets, record players, stereo equipment, sound reproducing equipment, and other consumer audio and video electronics equipment (including automotive). Such establishments may also sell additional product lines, such as household appliances; computers, computer peripheral equipment, and software; musical instruments; or records and prerecorded tapes. Establishments in this industry may perform incidental installation and repair work on radios, television sets, and other consumer electronic equipment. Establishments primarily engaged in the installation and repair of these products are classified in **SIC 7622: Radio and Television Repair Shops.** Establishments primarily engaged in the retail sale of computer equipment are classified in **SIC 5734: Computer and Computer Software Stores,** and those selling electronic toys are classified in **SIC 5945: Hobby, Toy, and Game Shops.**

NAICS Code(s)

443112 (Radio, Television, and Other Electronic Stores)
441310 (Automotive Parts and Accessories Stores)

Industry Snapshot

As Americans increased spending on consumer durable goods in the late 1990s, the consumer electronic industry fared well. In 1998, $57.5 billion was spent on consumer electronics. Video products took 19 percent of the market, while mobile electronics and electronic gaming commanded 10 percent of total sales. In 1999, sales of VCRs, camcorders, audio equipment, corded telephones and laser disc players were expected to remain flat as televisions, computers, wireless telephones, satellite systems, digital cameras, and DVD players were expected to post strong gains.

According to *Chain Store Age,* ''consumer interest in all things electronic and technological has spurred purchase activity by ''technocrats'' as well as people looking for the latest toys and gadgets. The booming housing market has resulted in PC rooms to be furnished with computer equipment, virtual offices to be filled with communications tools and family rooms to be filled with audio/visual set-ups. In addition, the strong economy coupled with low unemployment and, in the case of some electronic products, deflationary prices, has resulted in an environment ripe for major purchases.''

During the late 1990s, consumer electronic retailers enjoyed sales growth of more than 5 percent. Overcoming the rocky financial situation of the early 1990s, this sector was expected to see sales gains of 6 percent in 1999.

Organization and Structure

Many radio, television, consumer electronics, and music stores were chain stores in the late 1990s. This structure enabled larger companies to purchase equipment at a sharp discount and to pass those savings along to the consumer. Chain stores have become more prevalent in the industry because smaller stores have found it increasingly difficult to compete with the chains' low prices.

One major change in the retailing strategy of consumer electronics stores has been a shift toward scrambled merchandising. This trend has been evolving since the 1970s and refers to the growing tendency for stores to become larger and to carry more diverse product lines. In 1998, there was 20 square feet of retail space per person in the United States. Most retailers expanded their merchandise lines to fill this space, and the superstore became prevalent in the industry. Radio, television, and consumer electronics stores fit into this niche nicely, because their broad scope encompassed many aspects of consumer product lines. In addition to providing a wide variety of products, most large retail outlets are able to offer their goods at substantially lower prices. Such discounters reflect changes in consumer buying patterns and the need to adapt to the reality that the largest single group of consumers, adults between the age of 40 and 50, are making purchases to replace current equipment. Consequently, as middle-aged Americans begin to save money and are more hesitant to purchase on credit, they are purchasing fewer expensive items.

Superstores typically carry an inventory of 40,000 items, compared with the 25,000 items that are carried by an average store. Because chain stores and superstores purchase such large quantities of products for their stores, manufacturers offer them substantial discounts on merchandise. For this reason, chain establishments and superstores are able to sell their merchandise to consumers at prices substantially lower than those found in small stores. Additionally, the largest chains are cutting back on sales staffs and stores display merchandise in a warehouse style without expensive displays.

BACKGROUND AND DEVELOPMENT

The Industrial Revolution of the late 1700s was the genesis of modern retailing. The mass production of saleable items began as factories started to manufacture formerly hand-crafted goods. The western frontier and the movement of railroads also created a demand for goods, and marketplaces helped to distribute merchandise to formerly remote locations. The general store was the first outlet that offered a variety of merchandise. As retail became more sophisticated in the mid-nineteenth century, the general store was replaced by specialty stores grouped together. The chain store, a configuration utilized by most modern consumer electronics outlets, had its beginnings in the late nineteenth century when the concept was pioneered by such retailers as the F. W. Woolworth Co.

The discount store became popular when the population shifted from cities to the suburbs after the end of World War II. Demand for household items increased, and new homeowners were anxious to purchase goods at less-than-retail prices. At the same time, the trend toward reducing customer services also developed. Discount stores kept their costs low by maintaining low-rent facilities and a minimum sales staff. Suburban consumers were receptive to this opportunity to save money, and discount stores grew substantially during the 1980s and early 1990s.

Technological advancements have made consumer electronics equipment available to the general public at an affordable price. Consumer electronics have proliferated in American homes and have become more reasonable as new developments drive the prices for existing technology downward. The formerly prohibitive costs for television sets and radios have become affordable to almost all households, and the development of video cassette recorders and compact disc technology has placed sophisticated electronic equipment into the hands of all interested consumers.

Retail sales of home electronics equipment continued to grow slowly and were less sensitive to changes in business conditions than were durable goods. During 1991, for example, sales of nondurable goods, such as those included in this category, increased by 2 percent. During the same period, however, total retail sales of durable merchandise decreased by more than 1 percent.

Overall, the sales increases that were once seen in this industry dropped because of market saturation. Approximately 98 percent of American households own at least one color television set, and future sales growth was expected to be seen due to replacement and upgrading. Similarly, more than 77 percent of all U.S. households that own a television set also own a video cassette recorder; consequently, this product line also was nearing saturation. Despite an abundance of electronic equipment, the sales of the top 10 best-selling consumer electronics products totaled nearly $28.0 billion in 1990. These products included televisions, car stereos, home computers, and VCRs. Potential for increased growth existed as new technology was refined and enhanced.

While sales continued to rise slowly, future growth depended upon technological improvements. Long-term growth depended on such promising innovative products as home theater equipment, compact discs, large-screen televisions, and high-quality loudspeakers. Demand for camcorders, televisions, video cassette recorders, and autosound equipment was expected to decline as these technologies reached their saturation points.

There were more than 10,000 radio, television and consumer electronics stores in the United States in the early 1990s. Many of these stores were owned by nationwide chains, such as Tandy Corp., the parent company of more than 7,200 Radio Shack stores.

A mini-shakeout of firms took place in the early 1990s as market saturation became more prevalent. Some companies began dropping out of the U.S. electronics market, and some chains were similarly closing their doors. Highland Superstores Inc., for example, pulled out of the Chicago and midwestern markets after performing as the area's largest-grossing electronics and appliance retail chain. Competition in many markets continued to pit superstores against each other and led to increased price wars.

At this time, the retail trade sector accounted for more than 20 percent of all jobs in the United States, according to *U.S. Industrial Outlook 1993.* Radio, television, and consumer electronics stores sold nondurable goods, a category that accounted for 60 percent of all U.S. retail sales in 1991. These establishments were included in the department stores category, and 1992 sales totaled $189.0 billion. Between 1987 and 1992 the industry grew slowly but steadily, with annual sales increasing an average of 5 percent.

Overall retail sales improved in the mid 1990s, after battling the recession of past years. Consumer electronics retailers reported an increase in sales during the 1993 holiday season, with the highest sales in large screen TV and CD players. Profit margins were affected by intense competition between retailers, which resulted in below-cost retailing according to *Television Digest.* Smaller retailers were the hardest hit, with the giants like Best Buy and Circuit City benefiting most.

Tandy Corp. started another trend during the mid- to late-1990s with new Gigastores. Tandy opened its sixth Incredible Universe Gigastore in Hollywood, Florida, attracting 35,000 shoppers on the opening day. This store had 185,000 square feet of retail space and featured a 40-foot magazine department, and an in-store McDonald's Restaurant. However, Incredible Universe Stores steadily lost business.

The factors that led to this included customers' dislike of the theme-park atmosphere, a nationwide consumer slowdown, and an overly aggressive expansion strategy. Tandy Corp. reorganized management, reduced expansion plans, and changed its advertising campaigns. The Incredible Universe superstore chain was redesigned with the baby boomers as the target audience rather than teenagers, focusing on products rather than the store itself. The efforts of Tandy did not pay off, as Incredible Universe was sold in the mid-1990s.

During the mid- to late 1990s, large superstores started increasing their product lines to include retail computers and related products, resulting in a growth in their clientele. Evolution of new technology resulted in a great demand for new electronics products like Web TV, Digital Satellite Television System, and home theater systems.

Current Conditions

Toward the late 1990s, consumer electronics once again were seeing profits. According to *Electronic Business*, ''consumers increased the amount of discretionary income spent on televisions, stereos, computers, telephones and emerging new technologies like digital cameras and DVD players.''

Among those consumer electronic stores reaping the benefits of the stronger economy and consumer confidence were large superstores such as Best Buy and Circuit City. Sales at Best Buy increased 21 percent in 1998 and a 25 percent growth was predicted for 1999. Circuit City increased its electronics sales by 48 percent in 1998, and the store expected to see a 20 percent gain in 1999. Tandy Corp. also was turning a profit with its Radio Shack stores. In October 1999, sales increased by 15 percent, the tenth consecutive month of double digit gains.

These profitable stores also were growing in size. In 1998, Circuit City opened 37 new superstores and also focused on targeting smaller markets. Best Buy added 28 new stores to its business—up from 13 in 1997—and planned on opening 45 in 1999. Radio Shack also was growing in size. According to Tandy Corp., 94 percent of Americans live or work within 5 minutes of a Radio Shack store or dealer.

As new technology was being introduced, many stores teamed up with high-profile electronics companies. In 1999, Radio Shack agreed to sell Sprint PCS phone service in its stores, as well as DirecTV satellite service. It also struck a deal with Microsoft in 1999 to offer Microsoft's Internet services to Radio Shack customers.

The Internet also played a role in the consumer electronics industry. Offering products online—*e-tailing*—became more popular in the late 1990s. In October 1999, Tweeter Home Entertainment Group and Outpost.com offered audio, video and consumer electronics to online shoppers. Circuit City also opened an E-Superstore in 1999. The Web site was fully integrated with its stores, allowing consumers to purchase items online and pick them up at the closest retail outlet. Radio Shack and Best Buy also were online-shopper friendly. With online sales expected to increase dramatically by 2003, consumer electronics stores focused efforts on remaining competitive with online sites that offered electronics products.

While sales gains were being seen in 1998, there was consolidation and bankruptcy as a result of the success of these larger chains. Tandy sold its Incredible Universe and McDuff Computer Chain businesses, and Campo Electronics, Lechmere, and Sun TV closed. Smaller regional stores that survived the hard economic times of the early 1990s and the onslaught of the superstores either changed ownership or have decreased in size.

Industry Leaders

Best Buy, headquartered in Minneapolis, Minnesota, was the largest retailer in this industry with sales revenue of $10 billion. Salespeople did not work on commission, and merchandise was arranged by brand name instead of by price range, both unusual practices in the superstore industry. Additionally, Best Buy limited the number of brand names it carried in order to keep costs down in the firm's more than 310 stores.

The success of this chain was largely attributed to the rollout of its Concept II, III, and IV stores. These concepts highlighted marketing features, increased store size, reduced expenses, and increased sales. In 1998, Best Buy's net income was $224.4 million, an increase of 137.5 percent over 1997. The company employed 45,000 workers as well.

Circuit City Stores Inc., the nation's second largest specialty retailer of brand name electronic equipment and consumer appliances, operated more than 512 Circuit City Superstores, 4 consumer electronics-only stores, and 50 mall-based stores. The company carried a full line of merchandise at its superstores and posted sales of $10.8 billion in 1998, an increase of 21.8 percent over 1997.

Founded in 1949, Circuit City was run by Richard L. Sharp, whose computer programming skills helped the company to design a sophisticated inventory system that provided for efficient movement of equipment in addition to trimming shrinkage losses by as much as 30 percent. By working to reduce theft to less than half of the industry average, Circuit City added as much as one percentage point to its pre-tax margin of 4.5 percent. Other strategies that contributed to the firm's success included knowledgeable salespeople and a wide product selection.

Each successful industry leader has taken a different road to success. Best Buy succeeded by using bare-bones display techniques and relying on consumer knowledge, while Circuit City focused on in-house efficiency and knowledgeable salespeople. Tandy blanketed the United States with stores that stock the company's own merchandise.

Tandy Corp. was America's third largest retailer of consumer electronics and personal computers, with a 1998 sales revenue of $5.4 billion and 38,200 employees. The company's operations included more than 7,000 retail outlets.

Tandy was incorporated in 1960 and purchased Radio Shack in 1963. The company became a leader by emphasizing the importance of gross profit margins and focusing on a small inventory of its best-selling items. In addition, Tandy worked to keep Radio Shack's prices competitive by limiting its inventory to private label items and investing in advertising. Finally, the firm paid its workers a modest salary and used bonuses as incentives to promote hard work.

Tandy had a strong history in the electronics industry despite a miscalculation in the personal computer market in the 1980s. Because Tandy's TRS-80 computers were not able to run IBM software, Radio Shack's 19 percent share of the PC market dropped to less than 9 percent in the early 1980s. Tandy built its name by focusing on improving on other's developments, rather than on innovation, and by utilizing its own in-house manufacturing divisions. However, the corporation began changing its original focus in the early 1990s by funneling money into research and development to keep abreast of new computer developments.

Additionally, Tandy reevaluated its focus on computer manufacturing and securing its roots as a retailer. Incredible Universe outlets and mini-malls that imitate the European ''hypermarkets,'' were Tandy's latest venture. The huge emporiums contained karaoke contests, child care facilities, restaurants, and extensive product lines including more than 300 types of television sets, and 40,000 audio and video titles. The stores had to sell $100 million annually at each location to be profitable, and their focus was expected to remain on maintaining the lowest prices.

Unfortunately, the concept never caught on. Tandy sold its Incredible Universe and focused on its Radio Shack stores in the late 1990s. With alliances with Sprint PCS, Microsoft and Compaq, the company's sales were seeing strong gains in 1999.

WORKFORCE

Employment was on the rise in the late 1990s. With 1 in 5 Americans employed in the retail workforce, consumer electronics stores accounted for 475,700 workers in 1996. According to the Bureau of Labor Statistics, the industry was expected to see a 13.5 percent gain by 2006.

A large percentage of the workforce included part-time workers. Productivity of workers increased in 1997—the median sales productivity of an electronics salesperson was $118,986 in 1997.

RESEARCH AND TECHNOLOGY

While technology advancements and research focused mainly on e-commerce and the Internet in the late 1990s, the need to rely on functions at a store level remained strong. According to Bruce Van Kleeck, a vice president of the National Retail Federation, ''the Internet and electronic retailing as well as other back office enhancements, are occupying a lot of attention and investment, but retailers can't afford to neglect their stores. They should be thinking about what technologies are available to beef up their store-level productivity and improve the shopping experience for the customer.''

Some technologies that retailers were taking advantage of in the late 1990s were: traffic counters, designed to analyze consumer traffic in stores; shrink reducers, which gave details on customer-employee ratios; wireless networks, which utilized ethernet systems that enhanced in-store networking and extranets, as well as simplifying upgrades and inventory checks; and digital video ITEC, a network designed for digital video and audio programming within the stores.

At a consumer level, research and development continued to drive the markets and create demand for more sophisticated electronic equipment. Prices subsequently reflected the demand, with costs for new products gradually dropping as technological advances became more widespread. Developments such as recordable compact discs became vital to the audio market as it became more saturated in the late 1990s. Overall, the market for consumer electronics is predicted to rely heavily on new innovations and technology. As market saturation of electronic items rises, innovations are expected to fuel consumer purchases of improved equipment and replacement units.

Further Reading

Ahles, Andrea. "Tandy Attributes Earnings Increase to Sprint PCS, DirecTV Sales." *Chicago Tribune,* 24 October 1999.

Bloomfield, Judy. "A Jolly Outlook: Retailers and Vendors See Yule Fueling the Camcorder Business." *HFN: The Weekly Newspaper for the Home Furnishings Network,* 21 August 1995.

Delano, Daryl. "Solid Growth For Consumer Electronics." *Electronic Business,* February 1999.

"Flourishing Economy Boosts Hard Lines Spending." *Chain Store Age Executive,* August 1999.

Forest, Stephanie Andersen. "Incredible Universe Lost in Space." *Business Week,* 4 March 1996.

Koloszyc, Ginger. "Transforming the Stores." *Stores,* May 1999.

Morgenson, Gretchen. "A Good Thing?" *Forbes,* 3 June 1996.

National Industry-Occupation Employment Matrix, 1999. Available from http://www.stats.bls.gov.

"Outpost.com Adds High-End Consumer Electronics Customer Service, Delivery Key to Tweeter Introduction to Internet." *PR Newswire,* 19 October 1999.

"Radioshack's October Total Sales Increase 15 percent." *PR Newswire,* 4 November 1999.

Tandy Corp. Company Information, November 1999. Available from http://www.tandy.com.

SIC 5734

COMPUTER AND COMPUTER SOFTWARE STORES

This industry consists of establishments primarily engaged in the retail sale of computers, computer peripheral equipment, computer printers, and computer software. The wholesale distribution of these products for business or professional use is classified in **SIC 5045: Computers and Computer Peripheral Equipment and Software.**

NAICS Code(s)

443120 (Computer and Software Stores)

Industry Snapshot

This retail industry has undergone tremendous growth in recent years with the advent of the personal computer and accessory products. Entering the late 1990s, computer superstores chains were expanding, planning to expand or changing management. Stiff competition and price deflation was restructuring this industry as well.

CompUSA for example, faced a decrease in profits in the late 1990s, along with other personal computer dealers. *Businessweek Investor* reported in June 1999 that, "as the selling price of PCs continues to decline, the revenue shortfall cuts deep into the profits of computer retailers such as CompUSA. And with the low-price and low-margin PCs becoming an ever larger slice of the sales mix, overall industry profits are hurting, too."

Industry analysts expected continued growth in the demand for home computers, especially in notebooks, due to their convenience, and easy-to-use software markets. However, they were also expecting a shift as consumers became more technically sophisticated. Replacement and upgrade products were likely to increase their portion of the market upon entering the twenty-first century.

Organization and Structure

The Office of Computers and Business Equipment (OCBE) stated that in the late 1990s, computers were "sold through most marketing channels, including corporate account resellers (22 percent), direct response telemarketers (15 percent), consumer electronics stores (12 percent), value added resellers (VARs) (11 percent), computer superstores (10 percent), computer specialty dealers (7 percent), and mail order firms (6 percent). Other outlets include direct sales forces, mass merchants, office product retailers, and systems integrators." Little market shift was expected, except of course, in terms of Internet retailing.

According to an August 1999 *Chain Store Age* article, "many changes took place in the computer retailer landscape." Large office superstores and computer superstores continued to drive down prices and strengthen their position in the market, forcing traditional stores to diversify product lines in order to keep up with competition. That segment of the market was expected to see continued growth into 2000, as was direct response and mail order sales. Small computer specialty stores and VARs were expected to decline, as many manufacturers opted to ship product to the larger store versus an independent dealer, resulting in product shortages for the smaller dealer. The increase of ''e-tailing'' also put a strain on traditional store sales.

BACKGROUND AND DEVELOPMENT

The first computers were developed in America during World War II, but it was not until 1953 that computers were sold commercially by companies such as IBM, General Electric, Honeywell, and RCA. These companies were involved in the manufacturing of computers for scientists, mostly at universities. The early commercial market was geared mainly towards large industry, which could afford the new and expensive technology. Eventually, these industry pioneers also started to market smaller and slower computers at a wider market.

By the 1960s, more than 5,000 computers were in use in the United States. During the 1960s, the number of computers doubled every two or three years to more than 40,000 by 1970. As computers grew in number, they became more reliable and faster, however, the cost for purchasing computers was still high.

Until the 1970s, the United States and Canada led the world in computer use and sales. Since then, technologies overseas have met those of North America and computers worldwide have been estimated to have grown at a rate of 20 percent per year.

The commercial sale of personal computers and easy-to-use software, developed in the 1980s boosted the retail industry. Retail sales of computers were no longer directed only at large businesses; the target market for computer and software dealers extended to small businesses, schools, and individuals for at-home use.

Personal Computer Sales. In 1990 an estimated 9.5 million personal computers (PCs) valued at nearly $28 billion were sold through retail outlets in America. Personal computers are general application computers with local programming abilities. PCs are grouped into two basic types, stationary and portable. Stationary systems are mostly desktop, deskside, or ''tower'' systems, which made up about 80 percent of PCs sold in the United States in 1993. The remaining 20 percent were portable systems such as laptops, notebooks, hand held, and pen-based systems.

The availability of PCs in a variety of retail outlets increased dramatically in the late 1980s. The furious competition spurred reduced prices for consumers. According to Link Resources, by 1993, 67 percent of small businesses (those employing less than 100 workers) had PCs. Another large market for PCs has been homeworker households; in 1993, homeworker households purchased more than two-thirds of the PCs sold to the home market.

Workstation Sales. Businesses in this industry also sold low-end workstations. Workstations are single and multiuser microprocessors, with the low end of the market very similar to PCs. Since their introduction in the early 1980s, workstations have been sold mainly for scientific and engineering use. In the 1990s, they became more popular with businesses, which use them for electronic publishing, financial services, and office automation.

Software Sales. Software products sold by retailers in this industry included word processing programs, computer games, accounting packages and software components for on-line services. In 1993, the leading software packages sold through retailers in America were: MS-DOS 6.2 Upgrade, Adobe Type Manager Font, TurboTax for Windows, Quicken 3 for Windows, and MS Works 3.0 for Windows. According to the Software Publishers Association, sales of PC applications software alone reached over $3 billion in the United States and Canada in 1993.

Software dealers rely strongly on product trends set by technological developments and software producers. Software products available on the market increasingly are concerned with meeting the needs of children, families, and small businesses. In 1993, the consumer software market was considered the fastest growing segment of this industry.

Marketing. Compared to other retailers, companies in this industry have spent relatively small amounts on advertising. This is in part due to the fact that the major computers and software manufacturers, as opposed to the retailers, carry out product advertising. Low advertising has also been a result of this industry, as a specialty retailer, advertising mainly in computer magazines and on-line services, as opposed to the more costly mediums of television and radio.

Price Wars. In the early 1990s, this industry was characterized by competitive price wars. Intense price reductions began in 1991 and set industry records the following year, with reductions for computers averaging 33 percent. In general, retail computer sales shifted from small computer dealers to the large chain computer retailers, in particular the mass merchandisers who could sell computers at discount prices. In 1992, 30 percent of personal computers sold in America were through traditional computer dealers, a fifty percent drop from only five years before.

Another channel of distribution has emerged from the price wars in this industry. Computer sales have also been made through computer flea markets, which cater to small dealers. In 1992 *Business Week* reported that computer sales at these flea markets, generally held at large convention halls, were made at discounts of up to 80 percent off of the average retail prices.

Sales through mail-order systems were the fastest growing sector of the computer retail industry in the early 1990s. According to International Data Corp., shipments in mail-order computer sales increased by an average of 75 percent among the industry leaders in 1993. The potential for profit, though, made the mail-order market an increasingly competitive one. In 1993, a previous industry leader in mail-order computer sales, CompuAdd Corp., filed for bankruptcy. According to the *Wall Street Journal,* the company had been ''stung by falling prices and an aggressive marketing war among leading vendors.''

Specialty store reaction to this shift in distribution channels was most evident in the actions of industry leaders. In the early 1990s, CompuAdd Corp., a PC manufacturer and retailer, converted several of its storefront retail operations into computer superstores. Dell Computer Corp., a PC manufacturer and mail-order retailer, began selling its computers through Soft Warehouse, Inc. a superstore operator. ComputerLand, one of the industry's top three retailers, responded to these changes in the market by converting 50 of its boutiques to larger mass-market outlets and converted most of their remaining 380 small stores into direct sales offices.

In 1993, there were 132 companies in this industry in America. These companies' total sales for that year were $4.3 billion. However, according to the International Data Corp., there were at least another 3,000 small companies, often one-person operations, dealing in computers in the United States; these companies were more difficult for industry analysts to track because entry into the business had become relatively easy with standardized technologies and such dealers constantly entered and left the business.

Unlike computers, software continued to sell mostly through specialist software retailers. However, this trend was changing as more office supply outlets and department stores carried these products, and the number of computer superstores which sold software increased. In addition, software products became easier to use and therefore did not require the specialty expertise offered at most software retailers.

Specialty software retailers were also effected by the sales of computers with software packages pre-installed by computer manufacturers, a trend which increased with the competition among suppliers. This altered purchasing habits of consumers away from the more expensive software previously necessary to operate their computers to less expensive complimentary software that adds specialized features, such as tax accounting and computer game packages.

This was a fast changing, highly competitive, and technology driven industry during the mid-1990s. Retailers were profiting a little from PC sales, and the market was becoming over-saturated. A fierce battle for market share forced prices down. The rate of returns for PCs was higher than the vendors and retailers desired. Some retailers were even treating PCs as loss leaders.

Personal computer sales dropped to 10 percent to 15 percent from 25 percent to 30 percent during 1995. Weak sales led to the bankruptcy and closure of many stores. Tandy Corporation was one of the victims, with the sale its Incredible Universe and Computer City outlets, in early 1997, due to falling sales. Nester Retail Group was another victim. This chain also reported its failure to keep up with competition from Circuit City and Best Buy.

Best Buy however, was scaling back its expansion plans unable to keep up with the increasing competition and continually declining profit margins. According to *The Wall Street Journal,* Best Buy attempted to compensate for its diminishing gross profits by offering an assortment of non-computer items that carried larger margins. This was enough indication of the financial difficulty that large computer retailers were facing.

One trend the industry adopted was to concentrate its marketing efforts on higher margin computer peripheral equipment, such as printer supplies and cables, as well as providing technical support. Add on and accessories such as, tape-drives, computer cases, cabling and joysticks were also used to make up for the low PC profit margins. Innovative means of selling these accessories were being adopted.

Software sales were also targets of innovative marketing strategies. CompUSA introduced the software sampler program in 1996 to allow customers to sample software before purchasing it. Companies like Microsoft were jumping on the innovative software marketing bandwagon and creating in-store boutiques for consumer electronics stores and computer superstores in 1996.

Retail information systems executives revealed, in an industry survey to *Computerworld,* their beliefs that the key to their success would be a stronger focus on the consumer, but the average computer shopper would be skeptical of their understanding of this concept. They felt superstores could help customers find products by installing video kiosks throughout the store to give directions.

With the focus being on consumers, computer retailers were also becoming increasingly aware that women consumers were purchasing a larger amount of the computer hardware and software that was entering homes. In 1995, women purchased 49.6 percent of the hardware and 32.0 percent of the software. Women were also influencing the design and looks of computers.

CURRENT CONDITIONS

Towards the late 1990s, the computer retail industry was growing in leaps and bounds. In 1998, sales were up 13.8 percent—PC software sales increased 15.6 percent to $4.6 billion and accessories and supplies increased by 15 percent to $5.3 billion. From a manufacturers standpoint, U.S. shipments of PCs were expected to be more than 40 million in 1999 and nearly 55 million in 2001.

While the demand for computers increased, profits and revenue were under pressure at retail outlets. With the onset of low cost home computers, bottom lines at stores such as CompUSA did not reflect the increased demand for computers and software. IBM lost $1 billion in 1998 on its PC operations. Some stores shifted gears towards higher margin goods like digital cameras and home theater equipment.

As pressure increased, stores looked to marketing and advertising campaigns to attract consumers. Circuit City for example, offered a 'Free PC' program in June 1999. By teaming up with CompuServe, the store offered the eMachine for free with mail-in rebates with the stipulation that the customer had to sign a three-year contract for CompuServe Internet Service. These rebate programs became more popular in the late 1990s and large superstores used them to entice consumers away from smaller stores.

Computer stores also faced competition from the Internet and brand name manufacturers. Companies such as Hewlett Packard, Dell and IBM offered their products online, leaving consumers the choice in avoiding the retailer all together. There were also an increasing number of online sites offering computer goods. According to a 1999 *PC Magazine* poll, 46.0 percent of Internet sales were computer related and Dell Computer Corp. was a favorite among computer shoppers. Software was also a top sales generator in terms of online sales. Software accounted for 6.7 percent of online sales in 1997.

The proliferation of manufacturers into the retail sector was driven by the saturation of the business-to-business market. As corporations and government agencies became looked upon as replacement markets, the individual consumer and small business became a target for manufacturers like Dell, Hewlett-Packard, Apple, and Compaq. In the late 1990s, these companies focused on marketing campaigns and strategies that would increase customer awareness of the products they offered.

From the consumer point of view, the increase in technology and decrease in price, was beneficial. Price dropped by 10 percent in 1998—shoppers could purchase a complete system for under $1000—and price was expected to keep falling into 2000.

INDUSTRY LEADERS

CompUSA, headquartered in Dallas, Texas, was the largest computer retailer with a revenue of $6.3 billion, 19,700 employees and more than 200 stores across the U.S. CompUSA, Inc. was founded in 1984 as a provider of software to deep discounters and corporate customers. By any measure the company has been tremendously successful, parlaying a discount sensibility and vast product holdings into a position as an industry leader. In 1988, the company opened its first superstore; by 1993, it owned 45 outlets in 28 metropolitan areas and claimed half of the superstore computer market in the United States.

CompUSA recovered from being a nearly bankrupt company it was years ago into a thriving retail chain in the mid-1990s. According to *Business Week* part of the company's success rests in it's decision to bolster services such as training and support to deal with falling margins in the retail end of the business. CompUSA recorded a $16.8 million loss on $2.1 billion of revenue in 1994. CompUSA announced record earnings of $1.2 billion for the second quarter of the 1997 fiscal year.

CompUSA bought the Computer City chain from competitor Tandy Corporation in late 1997. Increased competition in the industry led the company to weak sales in 1998, and it closed 14 stores in 1999. With profits lagging, the company remained focused on efforts to increase market share.

Consumer electronics stores like Best Buy and Circuit City, were considered some of the biggest competitors of CompUSA. As Best Buy's home office category averaged roughly 35 percent of total sales each month, its leadership in the computer market was growing as was Circuit City's. Department stores like Walmart, Sears, and Target also had competitive computer retail departments focusing on software.

WORKFORCE

More than 20 million workers were employed in the retail sector in the late 1990s. According to the National Retail Federation, in 1999, a large percentage of this industry's workforce was made up of sales staff, including managers, with the remainder of the workforce in technical support, marketing, and administration. Retail buyers and merchandise managers in this industry negotiate prices with suppliers and wholesale distributors. Technical support staff handle customers' problems with both computer hardware and software; as computer backgrounds are required for these positions, salaries ranged from $30,000 to $60,000 per year, depending on the type of products sold. Sales workers, who directly service customers, often work on a part-time basis, with a starting salary at minimum wage, plus commissions on sales, depending on the store. For retail sales workers at the managerial level, salaries averaged $450.00 per week. Stores that did not offer commissions with salaries frequently featured bonus plans as sales incentives.

The job outlook for retail sales and marketing staff is expected to increase at a healthy clip for the next several years. Technical support staff is expected to be the fastest-growing sector of this industry, as well as IT professionals. Part-time positions for non-technical sales staff have often been available due to a high turnover rate; in addition, sales staff were often hired on a temporary basis during peak selling periods, such as Christmas.

America and the World

The United States and Japan continued to be the top producers of computers and related equipment throughout the late 1990s. This dominance has been reflected in retail sales, but retail stores have not been a primary factor. Direct and mail-order sales dominate the international market for the retail sales of computers.

According to the OCBE, ''reacting to a saturating U.S. market and increasing foreign competition, U.S. suppliers continue to look abroad for sales and expanded market share, with some companies selling as much product overseas as they do domestically. Foreign vendors also seek to become global players, as reflected in the efforts of major Asian suppliers to enlarge their presence in the huge U.S. market.'' American computer exports were expected to increase to $70 billion in 2003, an increase of nearly 10 percent. Demand is expected to remain strong in Canada and Europe, with the largest PC markets being Germany, Great Britain, France, and Italy, and Latin America. Exports are expected to increase to Asia, as the economy recovers from a recession due to the Asian economic crisis. While Japan has been one of the major exporters of PCs, computers have become more popular there in the late 1990s. Skepticism about the benefits of PCs, limited office space, and the relatively higher prices when compared to the West, made it difficult for American dealers to penetrate this market, but nevertheless, the U.S. has boosted its presence in that area.

In the late 1990s, American superstores selling computers and software entered the European market, which was dominated by a few European retailers, such as Vobis Microcomputer AG of Germany. CompUSA and other major chain outlets saw Europe as a potential market for the discount computer store concept. While at first successful, *Advertising Age* noted in 1992 that ''industry observers are skeptical that the superstore concept can survive long term in Europe—at least outside the U.K.'' As many as 50 to 80 American superstores planned to operate in Europe by the end of the century.

The implementation of The Information Technology Agreement (ITA) was also expected to have a great impact on this industry. The agreement, which will eliminate tariffs on certain products, went into effect in July 1997 and the U.S. should benefit in terms of exports and as a global player. Nearly 95 percent of information technology products in world trade fall under ITA. Some countries involved in the agreement include the United States, Canada, the European Union, Japan, and Switzerland.

Research and Technology

Like other retailing businesses, establishments in this industry have continued to increase their reliance on computers at a physical store level, which have simplified many of the routine buying functions of retail buyers and have improved efficiency of in-store sales staff. Many computer and software retailers rely less on sales staff for inventory counts and increasingly on point-of-sale computer terminals, which provide up-to-date inventory and sales information. Point-of-sales data which is fed into a computer system is taken from the item's bar code and includes information such as price, model number, color and size.

These stores continued to also look for ways to make shopping easier for the consumer through advanced technology. For example, Circuit City began using Wyse Winterm Windows-based terminals in the summer of 1999. Offered by Wyse Technology, these terminals allowed for consumers to customize computer options by accessing vendor information. Chief Information Officer of Circuit City commented that the company, ''searched for a cost-effective and high-performance solution that would allow us to offer our customers high levels of customer service through our build-to-order kiosk stations and service center applications.''

Advances in Internet retailing have also changed the face of the typical computer retailer. The National Retail Federation predicts that by 2003, 40 million households will be online. In an effort to satisfy that trend, computer retailers scrambled to get their products available online in the late 1990s. Stores like CompUSA offered store branded computers in 1999.

Research and development of new products greatly effects this industry. Technological developments in the late 1990s in computers, communications, and electronics have spurred the growth of information and entertainment services. Alliances among different technologies have produced inexpensive video, sound, graphics and text services in digital form and in interactive settings. Products in this combined information and entertainment market are designed for personal, educational, and business purposes, and have included asynchronous transfer mode equipment and communications and systems software. Industry analysts expect enormous growth opportunities for this segment of the retail market upon entering the twenty-first century.

FURTHER READING

Andreoli, Teresa. ''Microsoft Readies In-store Concept Shop Campaign.'' *Discount Store News,* 18 March 1996.

Atwood, Brett. ''Holiday Multimedia Sales Slow.'' *Billboard,* 21 December 1996.

''Circuit City Enters Second Stage of Nationwide Deployment of Wyse.'' *Business Wire,* 11 June 1999.

''Circuit City Launches Free PC Program.'' *PR Newsier,* 30 June 1999.

''CompUSA Company Information,'' November 1999. Available from http://www.compusa.com.

''CompUSA Inc. Reports Record Financial Results for the Second Quarter of 1997.'' *PR Newswire,* 29 January 1997.

''Extra Points: How Accessories Can Give a Kick to the Bottom Line.'' *HFN The Weekly Newspaper for the Home Financial Network,* 6 May 1996.

''Flourishing Economy Boosts Hard Lines Spending.'' *Chain Store Age,* August 1999.

Forest, Stephanie Anderson. ''Getting the Bugs Out.'' *Business Week,* 22 July 1996.

Gottseman, Ben. ''Shopping.'' *PC Week,* 1 November 1999.

Hisey, Pete. ''CompUSA Try Before You Buy.'' *Discount Store News,* 1 April 1996.

Marcial, Gene. ''CompUSA: Set for Sweeping Change.'' *Businessweek Investor,* 21 June 1999.

Reda, Susan. ''Help Wanted: The IT Staff.'' *Stores,* June 1998.

''Retail Bankruptcy, Store Closings.'' *Television Digest,* 23 September 1996.

Ryan, Ken. ''It's a Challenge to Make a Buck: Puny Profit Margins Weaken the Appeal of PC's.'' *HFN The Weekly Newspaper for the Home Financial Network,* 5 August 1996.

Scheier, Robert L. ''Walk a Mile in the Consumers Shoes.'' *Computerworld,* 8 July 1996.

Templin, Neal. ''PC Price Wars Force Electronics Chain to Curb Expansion, Push Big Appliances.'' *Wall Street Journal,* 4 June 1996.

''The Personal Computer Market.'' *The Office of Computers and Business Equipment,* March 1998.

SIC 5735

RECORD AND PRERECORDED TAPE STORES

This industry includes establishments primarily engaged in the retail sale of phonograph records, compact discs, prerecorded audiotapes and videotapes and disks. Establishments selling computer software are covered in **SIC 5734: Computer and Computer Software Stores,** and businesses engaged in the rental of videotapes are included in **SIC 7841: Video Tape Rental.**

NAICS CODE(S)

451220 (Prerecorded Tape, Compact Disc and Recrod Stores)

INDUSTRY SNAPSHOT

In the late 1990s, many different types of establishments sold records, compact discs, and prerecorded tapes. Independent record stores, large, national and international chains, and department and variety stores were included in this sector. Several different types of distributors served the retail outlets, depending on the size and type of stores. Rack jobbers served the department stores, one-stops served the small specialty shops, and major recording company branch distributors and independent distributors served the large chains. Being essentially devoted to the sale of luxury items, the economic health of this retail industry has depended greatly on the economic health of the nation at large. The stable economy of the late 1990s along with consumer confidence boosted sales in this industry once again, after a dismal performance in the early to mid-1990s.

According to the Recording Industry Association of America (RIAA), in 1997, ''more music consumers (86 percent) shopped at retail outlets than in the past eight years. However, the gap continues to narrow between purchases made at traditional record stores versus other retail stores such as consumer electronics stores and specialty stores (51 percent versus 34 percent). The percentage of consumers who purchased from tape and record clubs (9 percent) dropped to the lowest level since 1990.'' Another shopping venue in this industry that became increasingly popular was Internet sales through sites such as Amazon.com. In 1998, 1.1 percent of music buyers used this venue to do their shopping. This percent tripled from 1997 and was forecast to grow substantially into the next millennium.

ORGANIZATION AND STRUCTURE

By far, the largest portion of industry market share went to the large national chains, such as Tower Records and Musicland in the late 1990s. Megastores, such as Tower Records, with more than 10,000 square feet of floor space in each store, cater to an eclectic public, stocking thousands of titles in each store. Variety, price, and long hours ensure the megastores' success. They offer more titles than any other single retail source, carrying esoteric items as well as current hits, and they maintain long operating hours to ensure accessibility.

Many of the larger, big city stores such as the Tower Records on Sunset Strip in Los Angeles were common post-show entertainment for young people. Because these large chain stores buy in bulk quantities, they often receive discounts, and thus frequently offer the lowest prices in town. Chain stores tend to have a strict hierarchical organization: sales clerks, buyers, and assistant managers work under a store manager, who in turn answers to company officers. Individual megastores frequently have a large degree of autonomy but rely on the buyers' and managers' knowledge of the local market to keep product returns to a minimum.

Small-store chains, like some Musicland outlets, work in much the same way, but without the variety or the long hours. While megastores tend to be free standing, smaller chain stores are usually located in shopping malls, offering customers convenience. They cater to a more general clientele then the megastores, usually centering collections on current hits and reliable standards. With fewer local employees, the smaller chains have clerks and managers but generally do not employ buyers, relying instead on the parent company for inventory selection.

Both the larger and smaller chains use both independent and record company distributors. Many of the largest record manufacturers have branch offices that distribute records locally. Independent distributors cover the smaller labels and independent record companies, as well as the larger labels in the geographical areas not covered by branch distributors. Chain retail outlets buy from these distributors in bulk, warehousing the units until they ship them to their individual stores. The advantage of this system is, as mentioned above, the price break that bulk buying allows. The disadvantage is in the lack of flexibility for the smaller chains, where individual stores frequently have no control over their own merchandise.

In many areas of the country, small and independent record stores still flourished despite the predominance of chain stores. These stores tend to carry a limited and specialized collection, catering to a specific, local clientele. Large college campuses, for instance, can frequently support stores specializing in rock, jazz, and/or classical music in addition to the local chain outlet. Independent record stores tend to buy products from one-stop distributors.

One-stops are sub-distributors who buy from the larger branch offices and independent distributors and sell to the retail outfits too small to be regular distributor accounts. Because of the smaller quantities and the markup of the one-stops, prices tend to be slightly higher than in some of the larger chains; because the floor space is smaller than the megastores, the selection tends to be less diversified, although frequently in the specialized stores (e.g., classical only) the selection within one area may be as good as the megastore and better than the small-store chain. The organization of the stores is localized and less stratified; the owners usually manage and work in their stores, and employ only a limited supplemental staff. The advantage for the shopper at these smaller stores is the personalized service the knowledgeable staff can provide.

Department and variety stores also sell a small selection of records and tapes, sold as a concession or on consignment from a distributor known as the rack jobber. Rack jobbers buy from large independent and branch distributors to fill display racks at supermarkets, department stores, variety stores, drugstores, discount houses, and bookstores. They deal in the biggest hits of the year, the most popular standards, and the cheap cut-outs and discount collections. ''Cut-outs'' are the items dropped from production and sold at greatly reduced prices; discount collections are compilations of the most popular works of the standard classical composers and jazz artists, as well as collections of older popular hits, and are designed for the general public rather than the musically-educated listener. The rack jobbers target people who might never go into a record store. They either lease retailer space, taking all of the sales in a concession arrangement, or they split the income from the sales with the retailer in a consignment arrangement.

Different types of mail order and direct-to-consumer sellers also compete with these retail outlets. Two of the biggest record labels, RCA and Columbia, sponsor record and tape clubs, in which members buy items at reduced prices through the mail directly from the company, avoiding the distributor middleman. Many small record companies sell through the mail as well as through retail outlets, as do specialty mail-order houses who sell only in a certain, usually hard to find, category. For example, *The Lady Slipper Catalogue* carries only hard-to-find recordings by women; they sell to small retail outlets as well as individuals.

BACKGROUND AND DEVELOPMENT

Thomas Edison invented phonograph recording in 1877 using wax cylinders; a few years later, Emile Berliner developed the disk format of recording. These two formats competed for a few years, but by the beginning of the twentieth century, the disk format had won. The earliest commercial recordings were sold in music stores that also sold instruments and sheet music. Classical, jazz, and popular song recordings all sold well during this period. The advent of radio provided the public with free music and, consequently, the recording industry shrank. During the Depression of the 1930s, record sales dropped 90 percent from their peak in 1927. Coming to the failing industry's aid, however, were the technological developments of the radio industry, especially microphones, amplifiers and a new electrical method of recording. In the late 1930s, when Jack Kapp of Decca cut the retail price of records from 75 cents to 35 cents, when juke boxes became the rage, and when radio began to rely as much on recorded music as live music, record sales picked up considerably. Soon small neighborhood stores devoted solely to selling records became prominent retail outlets.

The world of marketing changed dramatically in the 1950s, affecting every retail industry. Chain stores expanded and supermarkets replaced corner grocery stores; practices of bulk buying at a discount and mass advertising to sell volume business took hold. New forms of record merchandising grew to compete with, and eventually take over, the small independent record store. Initiated by Sam Goody in New York, some merchants began to sell records at discount prices with the greater volume of sales making up the profit difference. Distributors began to give major retailers discounts for buying in bulk, further fueling the war between the large and the small business. Department and variety stores began to sell a limited selection of records; rack jobbers who each handled many different stores would buy albums at bulk discounted prices and sell them at prices lower than the small retail stores were able to offer. In 1955, Columbia started the first record club, which sold items to members through the mail at discounted prices. This introduced more competition to the record store industry; consequently, many small dealers were out of business by the end of the decade.

During the 1960s, the rack jobbers and their department store accounts all but completely took over the industry. In 1961, rack sales accounted for only $47 million in sales while other retailers took in $305 million; by 1965 the two were almost equal, with rack sales pulling in $365 million and non-rack sales drawing $372 million. By 1970, rack sales accounted for 70 percent of the total sales. The rise of large chains in the 1970s, though, and especially the full-line megastore which offered unparalleled selection, brought more business back into the hands of the record stores.

During the 1980s, the new compact disc (CD) format, with its greatly enhanced fidelity, completely revolutionized the industry. While cassette tapes had existed side-by-side with records for over a decade without overtaking the record format, by the early 1990s, companies halted record album production in favor of CDs. The popularity of compact discs showed no signs of abating. The Recording Industry Association noted that almost half of all American households in 1993 had CD players. Other Association statistics indicated that shipments of CDs in 1993 increased 21 percent over the year before (to approximately 5 million total units) while cassette tape shipments dropped more than 7 percent in 1993 (to approximately 3.4 million units).

Because of the greater durability of CDs and the much higher prices (about 50 percent higher than records during the years both were sold), Wherehouse Entertainment and other major retail chains began to move into the used record business, joining small independent music outlets that commonly bought and sold used CDs and tapes. This area had been the last bastion of the independent retail store. ''Furious because they don't make any money off used CDs,'' commented critic David Browne in *Entertainment Weekly,* ''four major distribution companies—CEMA, Uni, Sony, and WEA—stopped underwriting newspaper advertising for those stores that carry them. That move alone was expected to cost the stores hundreds of thousands of dollars in lost revenue.''

It was also noted that royalties weren't paid to performers and songwriters on used CD sales. Retail outlets, however, reacted angrily instead of backing down, especially when CEMA refused to allow retailers dealing in used CDs to carry a new record by major recording artist Garth Brooks. Wherehouse Entertainment, according to *Billboard,* filed a suit, claiming that the distributors ''conspired to unreasonably restrain trade and commerce in used CDs by withholding cooperative advertising dollars from retailers who buy and sell used discs.'' Independent outlets joined the fray as well, pointing out that many observers have cited artificially high CD prices charged by the manufacturers as one primary reason for the popularity of used CDs.

The Independent Music Retailers Association, in conjunction with two small independent chains, filed a suit in August 1993, charging among other things that the four distribution companies ''violated a federal antitrust statute known as the Robinson-Patman Act, which states that businesses offering promotional allowances must offer the proportionally equivalent terms to all customers,'' according to *Billboard.* As the number of class-action lawsuits grew, the Federal Trade Commission began to investigate. Faced with a storm of legal and business turmoil, the distributors finally dropped the controversial new policies, putting an end to the matter.

During the 1980s and early 1990s, computer technology and cable television created new retail avenues for recordings. Home shopping channels began selling CDs and tapes, as did electronic department stores such as Compuserve. These new retail outlets began to have a small but definite impact on the traditional retail outlets.

While the industry continued to profit, the recession of the early 1990s still had an impact and slowed industry growth. In 1990, record producers raised the prices on both CDs and cassettes, and sales started to slide. The 10 percent growth rate of 1989, as reflected in new store openings, slowed to only 3 percent in 1990; chain acquisition and consolidation almost came to a standstill. The following year saw a shortage of hit tunes, which further depressed the market, and retailers continued to tighten their belts. New store openings decreased further, and stock orders to wholesalers were down 11 percent.

In 1992, despite sluggish sales and the slowest growth in the industry's history, down to 1.04 percent, the larger firms still showed profit, and some investors were still committed to the market. Musicland opened 109 new stores, saw income increase from $62.3 million to $69.3 million, and raised $136 million by selling 17.09 million shares of stock publicly. Blockbuster Entertainment, a video-rental chain, bought up several music retail outlets, and announced further expansion. Lynch bought the California-based Wherehouse chain. Thus, even when sales were slow, the music retail business remained a profitable venture.

The growth of the compact disc industry helped the music industry in reaching unit sales worth more than $10 billion for the first time in 1993. However, dollar and unit volume sales for album-length music cassettes declined for the same period. According to *Television Digest,* the sales increases in 1993 was considered a sign that the industry had managed to meet consumer demand for different music types.

By the mid-1990s large bookstores started retailing recorded music. Stores like Borders and Barnes and Noble added huge music sections to the bookstores while also introducing in-store music booths, where consumers could listen to the records before they bought them.

The mid-1990s were characterized by continued corporate reorganizations through acquisitions, although at a lesser rate. Also, 1994 saw the rise in manufacturers' prices of sound recordings on both CD and cassette formats. According to *Billboard,* this trend was counteracted by retailers who competed aggressively with each other in discount pricing. However, this led to the pruning of retail profits since the increase in sales as a result of lower pricing was not enough to offset the fact that there were just too many outlets selling music.

The financial troubles of the music retail industry shook up the entire sound recording business in 1996. According to *Billboard,* record labels were affected by the financial problems of retailers as well as the slowdown in the sale of catalog albums. To beef up sales, a new marketing concept was adopted in sound recording retail operations. In-store tours by the musical artists themselves was perceived to benefit both the consumers—who were honored by the presence of their favorite recording stars and the retailers—who were able to sell more records to crowds that attended such affairs.

Introduction of online retailing, the reorganization at the music distribution sector and the record-club debate were prominent concepts of the mid- to late 1990s. According to *Market News,* the annual communications industry report forecast that recorded music would be one of the fastest growing sectors of the communications industry with a five-year growth rate of 8.2 percent and gross expenditures of $14.903 billion by 1998.

CURRENT CONDITIONS

After being hit hard by lagging sales, consolidation and bankruptcy in the mid-1990s, music retailers finally recorded positive sales in 1998, the strongest year of the decade. According to RIAA, recorded music sales nearly reached $14 billion in 1998, with shipments of CDs up 12.5 percent to 847 million in 1998, and dollar value up 15.1 percent to $11.4 billion. In 1998, music videos were also hot commodity with an increase of 45.9 percent in shipments, and DVD music video shipments were worth $12.2 million. Cassettes represented just over $1 billion in sales, although shipments dropped 8.2 percent to 158.5 million in 1998, while dollar value decreased by 6.8 percent to $1.4 billion. This gain was attributed to a strong flow of top releases, renewed interest in the music sector, the stable economy and a high consumer confidence level, and advances in technology.

As well as seeing a change in sales and profits, the music retail industry saw major restructuring in the late 1990s as well. Trans World Entertainment purchased Camelot Music, and Wherehouse Entertainment acquired Blockbuster Music. In an effort to reduce debt, many large companies such as Tower Records, National Record Mart, and the Musicland Group were involved in IPOs, bond offerings, and private placements.

Online retailing also played a major role in this industry in the late 1990s. Amazon.com and CDNow encroached into the traditional music store scene, forcing retailers to offer online shopping. According to a survey held by the National Association of Recording Merchandisers, 70 percent of ''brick-and-mortar'' retail stores had an Internet site. Internet sales also accounted for 1 percent of chain stores' music sales and 3 percent of independent retailers' sales.

Aggressive marketing plans focusing on the consumer also were part of retailer's strategies in the late 1990s. For instance, Musicland launched a campaign to push its Musicland, Sam Goody, On Cue, and Media Play stores into the public eye. These stores advertised heavily in teen magazines, offered promotions on college campuses, and in some locations, presented free in-store concerts. According to Marcia Appel, senior VP of advertising for Musicland, ''the advertising is not just centered around one new release or 10 products on sale. It really is being branded to become attached to the customer's heart.''

INDUSTRY LEADERS

In 1999, Musicland Stores Corporation, MTS INC., and Wherehouse Entertainment dominated the retail music industry. The three were ranked one, two and three respectively, and together accounted for more than $3 billion in sales.

The leading music chain in 1999 was Musicland Stores. Based in Minneapolis, Minnesota, the company operated Musicland, Sam Goody, On Cue, and Media Play record stores. The company had overall sales revenue of $1.8 billion and 15,600 employees. When Jack Eugster took over Musicland stores in 1980, the chain was losing money for its parent corporation, Primerica. He installed a state-of-the-art computer inventory system, applied his merchandising expertise gained from years with Target Stores and The Gap, and turned the company's sales around. In 1988, he assisted Donaldson, Luftkin, & Jenrette in a leveraged buy out of the company and became part owner himself. He added 200 new stores and doubled sales to $1 billion, making The Musicland Group the country's largest music retailer in 1993.

In 1999, the company saw a 171.4 percent increase in net income. It also operated Suncoast Motion Picture Company stores located in shopping malls, and had a total of 1,300 stores in operation.

MTS Inc. operated 225 stores in the United States and across the world in 1999. The company owns Tower Records, Tower Books, Tower Video, and WOW! Superstores. MTS focused on online growth as well as international operations in 1999 in an attempt to combat increased competition from Internet retailers and discount chains.

Wherehouse Entertainment Inc. operated nearly 600 stores in 33 states in 1999. The company gained market share when it purchased Blockbuster Music in 1998 and saw a 51.6 percent increase in sales to $496.5 million.

Another notable company in the industry was Trans World Entertainment Corporation with sales of $698.5 million. It purchased Camelot Music Holdings in 1999 and operated more than 1,000 stores under names such as Camelot Music, Record Town, The Wall, Coconuts, Strawberries, and Spec's Music. Trans World also operated F.Y.E. stores, which offered music, videos, games and electronics, and also offered products online.

WORKFORCE

According to the National Association of Recording Merchandisers, there were nearly 35,000 workers employed in this industry in 1998. Most retail stores relied heavily on low-wage clerks for the basis of the work force, and record stores were no exception. There were nearly three times as many hourly workers compared to salaried employees. Because of the specialized nature of music, most outlets tried to employ people with some musical knowledge, but this was far from universal. The small chain stores selling standards and current popular hits have the least need and ability to hire knowledgeable staff; the best of these stores hire young people with some awareness of current popular culture.

The megastore chains depend on musically aware young people as well, and reward hard work and musical knowledge and experience with swift promotions to buyer and management levels. The best of these outlets employ knowledgeable and dependable staff that often have some sort of musical education. Frequently, the companies will hire people with musical knowledge rather than business knowledge, and provide their employees with business classes at their national meetings. The small, independent stores hire a predominantly knowledgeable staff, particularly the specialty shops. For example, many stores that sell only classical music are run by and employ musicians and others with college-level music degrees. It is not uncommon for young, struggling rock musicians to work in record stores as they try to get performing careers off the ground.

AMERICA AND THE WORLD

Music retailers looked to global expansion as trade barriers made it easier to do business abroad in the late 1990s. Tower Records for example, had successful operations in Japan and the United Kingdom. While North America represented 33.8 percent of global music sales in 1997, Europe accounted for 33.3 percent, Japan had 16.5 percent, and Latin America brought in 6.8 percent of global sales. Latin America was considered the largest emerging market with a 40 percent growth rate. With other parts of the world accounting for large portions of music sales, American-based companies looked for opportunities to expand overseas into the next millennium.

FURTHER READING

''Annual Survey Results.'' National Association of Recording Merchandisers, 1998. Available at http://www.narm.com.

Christman, Ed. ''Acquisitions Alter the Landscape of Healthy Retail Sector.'' *Billboard,* 26 December 1998.

DiCostanzo, Frank. ''In-store Tours Offer Alternative; Appearances Benefit Both Artists and Merchants.'' *Billboard,* 23 November 1996.

''Frequently Asked Questions.'' Recording Industry Association of America, November 1999. Available at http://www.riaa.com/stats.

Gillen, Marilyn. ''The Year in Business: Situation All Shook Up.'' *Billboard,* 28 December 1996.

Olson, Catherine Applefield. ''Musicland Promotions Target Personal Connections With Consumers.'' *Billboard,* 31 October 1998.

"Recording Industry Releases 1998 Consumer Profile." Recording Industry Association of America, March 1999. Available at http://www.riaa.com.

Rosen, Craig, Ed Christman, and Bill Holland. "With FTC Inquiry Under Way, Suits Mount in Used-CD Fray." *Billboard,* 14 August 1993.

SIC 5736

MUSICAL INSTRUMENT STORES

This category covers establishments primarily engaged in the retail sales of musical instruments, sheet music, and similar supplies.

NAICS Code(s)

451140 (Musical Instrument and Supplies Stores)

According to a study by *Music Trade* magazine, sales in this industry increased at an annual rate of 7 percent during the 1990s. Following a slack market in the 1980s, the industry evolved into a $6 billion dollar trade by 1999. Electronic instruments, particularly keyboards and electric guitars, generated nearly a quarter of all musical instrument sales. Musical instrument retail establishments were most prevalent in California, which reported 862 business in 1997. Second-ranked Florida had 391 stores, and Texas had 346 establishments.

Musical instrument retailers cater to a wide consumer base, ranging from parents of student musicians to professional performers. In general, the industry is dominated by independent family-run businesses; some firms in this industry succeed within a limited niche, such as sales to schools and senior citizen groups. Industry analysts predicted several prime areas of growth in retail sales of musical instruments as the 20th century drew to a close. Among the rising markets were sales of student pianos and band instruments, which were expected to increase in accordance with the annual 1.2 percent increase of the number of children between the ages of 5 and 13 in the early part of the new millenium. Additionally, nostalgic-minded baby-boomers displayed a renewed interest in traditional and acoustic instruments—especially guitars—and an estimated 62 million amateur musicians existed in the United States. Demand for electronic instruments was poised for growth also, as home computer sales increased.

The independent retail outlets that dominated the industry faced potential challenges from the aggressive marketing and low pricing of mail-order discount companies during the 1990s. Some stores dealt with these new competitors by discontinuing high-end inventories that overlapped with the mail-order products. Also during that decade, the impact of superstore-type retail outlets for musical instruments remained to be assessed. Most imposing among the superstores were Guitar Center of Agoura Hills, California; Sam Ash Music Corporation of Long Island, New York; and the Music and Recording Superstores (MARS), headquartered in South Florida. The MARS chain reported $100 million in revenues from approximately 22 stores in 1998. MARS showrooms are "... Like candy stores for any kid or adult with even the faintest glimmer of musical interest," according to Jodi Rodgers in South Florida Business Journal. MARS, established in the late 1990s, grew rapidly and went public in April of 1999. Likewise, Guitar Center experienced a swell of growth after an IPO in 1997. The stock value more than tripled within two years; and Guitar Center, which first opened its doors in Beverly Hills, California in 1964, grossed $391.7 million in sales for the fiscal year ending in 1999. At that time observers agreed that the retailer had effectively saturated U.S. markets on the Atlantic seaboard. With 1,730 employees and more than three dozen stores across the United States in 1999, Guitar Center was the largest public retailer of musical instruments and the largest among the superstore retailers.

Further Reading

Bullard, Stan. "Local Music Store Scene Tunes up for New Players." *Crain's Cleveland Business,* 18 November 1996.

Harris, Pat Lopes. "Music Giant Picks on Local Stores." *Washington Business Journal,* 25 June 1999.

Lazich, Robert S. *Market Share Reporter.* Detroit: Gale Group, 1999.

Matas, Alina. "Music Superstore Prototype Gets Ready to Rock." *Miami Herald,* 10 November 1996.

"Music Superstores on the Way." *Cleveland Plain Dealer,* 8 January 1997.

Rodgers, Jodi. "Man from MARS." *South Florida Business Journal,* 29 January 1999.

Scally, Robert. "Guitar Center Acquires a Friend." *Discount Store News,* 7 June 1999.

Speer, Tibbett L. "Marketing to Musicians." *American Demographics,* March 1996.

SIC 5812

EATING PLACES

This category includes establishments primarily engaged in the retail sale of prepared food and drinks for on-premise or immediate consumption. Caterers and industrial food service establishments are also included in this industry.

NAICS CODE(S)

722110 (Full-Service Restaurants)
722211 (Limited-Service Restaurants)
722212 (Cafeterias)
722213 (Snack and Nonalcoholic Beverage Bars)
722310 (Foodservice Contractors)
722320 (Caterers)
711110 (Theater Companies and Dinner Theaters)

INDUSTRY SNAPSHOT

According to the National Restaurant Association, Americans will spend about $354 billion at the nation's more than 815,000 eating and drinking establishments in 1999, nearly $970 million per day. Sales were expected to grow by 4.6 percent from 1998. Fast-food restaurants—the fastest growing sector of the industry—were expected to have $110.4 billion in sales in 1999, coming close to overtaking the long-time leading sector, full-service restaurants, which were expected to post sales of $117 billion. This industry was forecast to post its eighth consecutive gain in real sales growth in 1999.

The eating places industry was healthy in 1998 as were most other sectors of the retail trade due to the strong economy and high consumer confidence. Eating out continued to be on the rise as people became more pressed for time and all but the top class full-service restaurants began to stress value for money. In 1998, more than 50 billion meals were consumed in restaurants or in cafeterias. Competition increased into the late 1990s as more units crowded the market. Overall, consumers demanded convenience and value from restaurants and the industry responded. Price wars, strong marketing, and the emergence of gimmicks were used to attract customers and themes became more important in restaurant conception and design.

ORGANIZATION AND STRUCTURE

The classification for eating places encompasses a wide variety of eating establishments, including five star gourmet restaurants, roadside cafes, fast-food joints, soda fountains, casual dining establishments, pizza parlors, hot dog stands, tea rooms, and oyster bars, to name but a few. Full-service restaurants was the largest sector of the industry in 1998, with sales of $112 billion, or 33 percent of the total food service market, according to the National Restaurant Association. One of the strongest areas within this market was casual dining, that is, moderately priced dining houses offering a comprehensive menu at a reasonable price. Chains of casual dining houses, such as Olive Garden, and Red Lobster had combined sales of more than $3 billion in 1998, up significantly from 1997. This sector of the industry began to experience a slowdown in growth in the late 1990s due to maturity, competition, and consolidation.

1998 DISTRIBUTION OF RESTAURANT CUSTOMER TRAFFIC

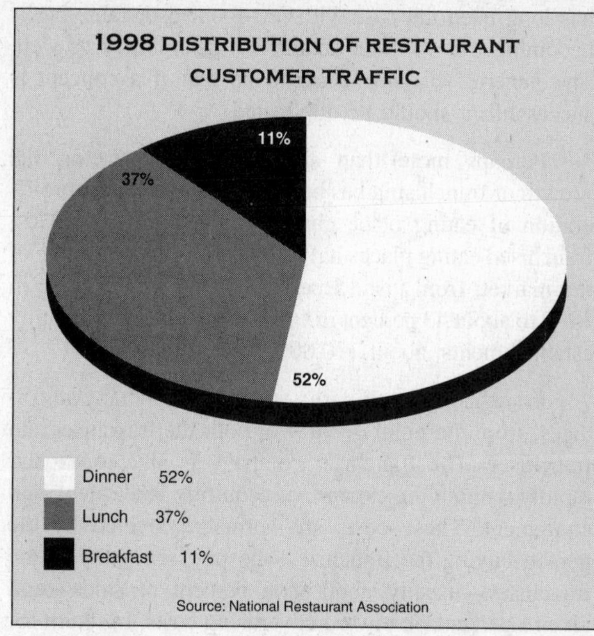

Source: National Restaurant Association

Fast-food restaurants was the second largest and fastest growing sector of the industry, with projected 1999 sales of $110.4 billion, or 31.0 percent of industry sales. Over the preceding two decades this sector's success provided much of the entire industry's growth, and in 1998, 78 percent of U.S. households used some form of fast food establishment each month.

The biggest companies operating eating places include those operating single concept chains, like McDonald's, and those operating a number of different fast food businesses, such as TRICON Global Restaurants Inc., which runs Pizza Hut, Kentucky Fried Chicken, and Taco Bell. Previously run by PepsiCo, the company spun off its restaurants division into a separate, publicly traded company—TRICON—in 1997.

Chain-owned restaurants in general have overtaken independently owned outlets in terms of number of units, possibly due to their greater stability and lower failure rate. This trend is likely to continue throughout the year 2000 through mergers and acquisitions, according to the National Restaurant Association's *Food Service Industry 2000* report.

For 1999, projected sales were as follows: eating places $238 billion, drinking places $11 billion, managed services $23 billion, hotel/motel restaurants $19 billion, and retail, vending, recreation, and mobile projected sales $30 billion.

BACKGROUND AND DEVELOPMENT

The eating place industry has grown from family-run restaurants and diners to giant chain restaurants of the 1990s. With few exceptions, the best known names in the business operate company-run or franchised chains. This has long been the case with fast-food restaurants but is becoming true in other sectors of the industry as well. The general wisdom seems to be that if a concept is successful, it should be duplicated.

Perhaps more than any other single factor, the growth of franchising has been responsible for the proliferation of eating place chains. Since the early 1970s, franchised eating places have almost tripled their share of the market, from just 15 percent of industry volume in 1970 to about 43 percent in 1995, when one in four eating establishments, about 110,000, were franchises.

Franchising's popularity stems from its many advantages, from the point of view of both the franchiser and franchisee. The franchiser company is able to expand rapidly without the expense of acquiring land, plant, and equipment. These costs are normally covered by the person buying the franchise, who pays a royalty to the franchiser—usually about five percent of sales—and gives a percentage toward advertising costs. In return for this outlay, the franchisee is assured of name recognition, which normally guarantees high sales. Although buying a franchise may increase a business person's start-up costs compared with those of an independent restaurateur, the returns render it a worthwhile investment. Franchised restaurants offer an extremely low risk, compared with independent eating establishments. Failure rates within the first year are low. Franchisees also benefit from the training and marketing support of the parent company.

The price to be paid for franchise security is a loss of flexibility. Independent restaurant owners are able to plan their own menus, avoid paying a royalty, and create and run their businesses as they see fit, whereas franchisees are restricted by the normally rigid and formulaic terms of the franchise agreement.

Though many of the best known fast food and casual dining chains are franchised, including McDonald's, Wendy's Old Fashioned Hamburgers, Burger King, and Pizza Hut, many other successful chains are not. Sales for the largest of the nonfranchised chains, the Red Lobster and Olive Garden casual dining houses, both owned by Darden Restaurants, was nearly $3 billion in 1995. Of course, even in the case of the heavily franchised chains, such as McDonald's and Wendy's, the parent company owns a considerable share of the outlets.

The exit of packaged food companies from the restaurant business, a trend that reached its peak by early 1997, created more room for franchisers. After Hershey, Sara Lee, and Ralston Purina had already jettisoned their restaurant operations, General Foods did the same in May 1995 when it spun off its Red Lobster, Olive Garden, and China Coast (which later closed) restaurant chains to form the new public company, Darden Restaurants. Similarly, in early 1997, PepsiCo announced that it would spin off its restaurants division—which included Pizza Hut, KFC, and Taco Bell—into a publicly traded company. With PepsiCo's exit, no U.S. packaged food company had a significant presence in the restaurant industry.

As the competition grew more intense in the 1990s, operators became more litigious, going to court in increasing numbers to protect their trademarks and trade dress. The easing of the burden of proof for companies filing trade dress litigation in March 1992 opened the gates for a flood of copycat suits. Defined as the overall appearance that makes a business distinctive, trade dress is becoming more of a bone of contention between competing chains. The Hard Rock Cafe, the Chicago-based Lettuce Entertain You Enterprises, Starbucks Coffee, and the Green Burrito are just a few of the many companies who have brought lawsuits against competitors, charging that their ideas have been plagiarized. Successful suits are extremely profitable and can put the competitor out of business. In 1992, the Houston-based Two Pesos chain was forced to pay $3.7 million to the Taco Cabana chain of San Antonio after a court found that it had wrongly appropriated aspects of the latter's trade dress.

CURRENT CONDITIONS

The restaurant business was healthy in the late 1990s, when more than half of the adult population visited an eating place each day. With a steady economy and high consumer confidence level, restaurant and fast-food sales have grown steadily and industry profitability is up. The National Restaurant Association's *1999 Foodservice Industry Forecast* stated that strong economic growth and soaring consumer sentiment, "helped drive stronger-than-expected growth in 1998."

The buoyancy of the industry can be traced to a number of factors: women's increased role in the workplace has left them with less time to spend preparing food at home; the proliferation of fast-food and takeout eating places has broadened consumer choice and made eating places a convenient alternative to home-cooked food; and food prices have remained low since the early 1990s, enabling the industry to offer competitive prices, although in 1998, menu prices increased 2.5 percent. More aggressive promotion by eating places of their value for money has resulted in a shift of business from food stores to eating places. According to the National Restaurant Association, "statistics indicate that restaurants have become an increasingly important part of the American lifestyle over the past few decades. About 44 percent of the U.S. food dollar is currently spent at restaurants and other foodservice operations, compared with only 25 percent in 1955. Additionally, restaurant-industry sales have increased almost eight-fold in the past three decades—from $42.8 billion in 1970 to a projected $354 billion in 1999. Meanwhile, the number of U.S. restaurants increased 66 percent from 1972 to 1996—from 492,000 to 815,000 restaurants.''

With the overall strength of the industry, competition remained increasingly fierce throughout the late 1990s. Eating places were forced to stake out a strong identity for themselves and to pay closer attention to consumers, who were becoming increasingly demanding. In 1999, convenience was nearly as important to consumers as value. More and more people simply no longer had the time, and/or the desire, to cook meals and clean up afterwards. The National Restaurant Association reported statistics indicating that, ''people would rather dine out than entertain at home. More than two out of three adults (68 percent) say that going out to a restaurant with family and/or friends not only gives them an opportunity to socialize but is also a better use of their leisure time than cooking and cleaning up, according to 1998 Association research. Furthermore, more than one out of two consumers (56 percent) report that they are not entertaining at home as often as they were two years ago.''

Emerging out of this focus on convenience was a sort of hybrid of the traditional full-service restaurant and the fast-food outlet—the home-meal replacement segment (also known as ''fast-casual''). Pioneered by Boston Chicken Inc.'s Boston Market chain, home-meal replacement offered fare reminiscent of home cooking—and higher in quality than the typical fast food—through a quick-service restaurant operation. Consumers could now take home fare closer in quality to that offered by casual dining houses. This segment of the market faced tough competition and lagging sales in the late 1990s. As a result, Boston Chicken declared Chapter 11.

An offshoot of the home-meal replacement segment emerged in the late 1990s. It was a hybrid restaurant/retail food concept, such as Brinker International's Eatzi's. Also catering to the takeout crowd, these concepts typically look like a market and often offer a wide selection of meal possibilities—some of the gourmet variety—that the customers can combine as they wish and have the onsite chef prepare for takeout. These outlets tend to offer salads, fresh breads, full-service delis, gourmet coffees, and a variety of hot items.

The theme/entertainment restaurant sector was one of the fastest growing areas of the restaurant industry in the late 1990s. In some ways the popularity of such venues was also a matter of convenience, since customers could have their appetites for both food and entertainment filled at the same time. The popular music-oriented Hard Rock Cafe started the trend, and was followed by Planet Hollywood (movies), Rainforest Cafe (tropical theme), and Official All-Star Cafe (sports). According to Katherine Paul, in an article published online by Streetnet, ''theme-based restaurants serve up side dishes

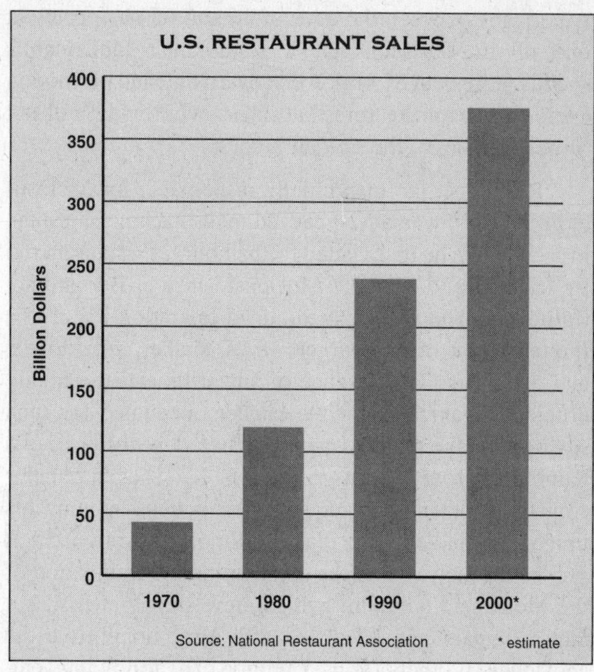

of entertainment and, in many instances, branded merchandise, along with the food.''

Meanwhile, the fast-food sector continued to be involved in price wars. McDonald's, Wendy's, and Taco Bell were emphasizing under $1 menu items. By 1999, however, increased labor, advertising, and beef costs were beginning to force the fast feeders to reevaluate their menus. Many fast food restaurants began to offer value meals, focusing on the full meal, rather than just one or two items. For instance, McDonald's—offers value meals that are numbered. A customer can order by number, and receive a sandwich, french fries, and a drink for a lower price than if they were purchased separately. Consumers also have an option to ''super size'' the meal. For a nominal fee, the meal could increase in size, an added value for the consumer. The stores also tried to lure consumers with promotional kid's meals. These stores offered popular toys in their meals, spurring intense sales increases during the promotion.

Fast food restaurant growth has slowed due to heated competition. Consolidation, the need for high return on investment, and the reduction of company-owned restaurants have all played a factor in growth development. While the outlook for sales remains strong throughout 2000, new store development is expected to decline.

INDUSTRY LEADERS

The restaurant industry may be highly competitive but it has a clear leader, the McDonald's Corporation, which recorded total sales of $35.9 billion in 1998, or roughly nine percent of the nation's total restaurant sales. According to Lebhar-Friedman, at least 96 percent of

Americans between the ages of 16 and 65 have eaten at one of 12,500 McDonald's restaurants. McDonald's spends more than $1 billion on advertising and promotion every year to make sure that diners worldwide will not forget their logo, the golden arches.

Ray Kroc, the man chiefly responsible for McDonald's success, was a 52-year old malt machine salesman in 1954 when he first visited the hamburger restaurant run by Richard and Maurice McDonald in San Bernardino, California. The highly streamlined operation featured a limited menu of hamburgers, fries, shakes, soft drinks, and apple pie. The absence of any frills and the highly efficient organization of the kitchen accounted for such savings that the brothers were able to reduce the price of a hamburger from 30 cents to 15 cents. Kroc began franchising the brothers' formula on their behalf, opening his first McDonald's in Des Plaines, Illinois, in April 1955. It proved a runaway success and became the foundation of the McDonald's empire, which grew slowly at first, but later at breakneck speed. In 1961, Kroc bought out the McDonald brothers for $2.7 million. The following year, he introduced the golden arches as the official corporate logo. McDonald's went public in 1965.

From the outset, the company set itself apart from other franchised restaurants by owning a large proportion of the real estate on which its franchised restaurants are located, and holding the leases on virtually all the rest. It selects and develops these sites, for which it later charges the franchisee rent. The upshot is that, although McDonald's invests far more capital per unit in its franchises, its returns are much higher. About 80 percent of McDonald's restaurants are franchised; the remainder are controlled by the parent company. All of the restaurants are serviced by independent suppliers.

McDonald's extraordinary success has been due in no small part to its willingness to be a trendsetter: it was the first fast-food restaurant to offer a breakfast menu (1973); to provide customers with a list of its product ingredients (1986); and to respond to consumers' environmental concerns with the scrapping of its styrofoam sandwich boxes and the introduction of more environmentally-friendly packaging. It was also first to penetrate the Iron Curtain before the fall of the communist government, opening a restaurant in Moscow in 1990. In the mid-1990s, the company was one of thirty that made up the Dow Jones Industrial Index.

In 1998, McDonald's had more than 25,000 restaurants in more than 115 countries. The company opens a new restaurant every 5 hours of every day, and 8 percent of the American population visits a McDonald's every day. Although national sales growth has slowed from a high of more than 20 percent in the 1970s to just over ten percent annually, overseas growth remains at more than 20 percent. In an attempt to retain its share of the market, management is giving franchisees more latitude to experiment with decor and menu items. It is also attempting to bolster its position through a ''made for you'' preparation program which replaced its Deluxe line in 1998.

In terms of sales, Burger King is the second largest restaurant chain in the United States. In 1998, sales were 10.3 billion. Throughout the 1980s, Burger King, then under the management of Pillsbury, suffered the consequences of high management turnover and a number of failed advertising campaigns. Burger King came under new ownership in January 1989, when it was bought by Grand Metropolitan PLC, a British company. By 1999, Burger King served nearly 1.6 billion Whoppers a year, and had more than 14 million customers daily. The company had 10,600 stores in operation in all 50 states and in 54 countries.

Three of the nation's top six restaurant chains—Pizza Hut, KFC (formerly Kentucky Fried Chicken), and Taco Bell Corp.—are owned by TRICON Global Restaurants Inc. Sales in 1998 were $20.6 billion, and the company operated 29,700 stores in more than 100 countries in 1999.

Pizza Hut is the largest pizza chain in the world, and KFC is the world's biggest fried chicken chain, while Taco Bell is the leading Mexican food chain in the United States.

Other major industry players include Wendy's, the nation's third largest chain of hamburger restaurants, with nearly 5,400 units worldwide and domestic sales of $1.2 billion in 1999; Hardee's, owned by CKE Restaurants, with 1998 sales of $1.8 billion; and Dominos Pizza, with sales of $1.2 billion in 1998 from its 6,200 U.S. units. Among nonfast-feeders, the two Darden Restaurants chains—Red Lobster and Olive Garden—are the largest in the United States. In 1998 Red Lobster, which specializes in seafood, posted U.S. sales of $1.96 billion from 635 units, while the Italian specialist Olive Garden enjoyed sales of $1.48 billion from 459 units.

WORKFORCE

The eating and drinking places industry is the largest employer in the U.S. retail business, and provided 10.2 million jobs in 1998, projected to rise to 12 million by 2006 and comprised 8 percent of the American workforce in 1999. Fifty-six percent of those employed in this sector are women, 12 percent are African-American, and 16 percent are of Hispanic origin. Although 16-to-24 year olds are this industry's main target, in recent years there has been a marked increase in the number of older workers, especially retirees, as operators adjust to a labor shortage. Restaurants are also reacting to the labor shortage by attempting to improve efficiency and productivity and by cutting back on counter service and increasing drive-throughs.

According to the National Restaurant Association, finding qualified and motivated employees was the top concern for restaurateurs in the late 1990s. Unemployment fell to just 4.5 percent in 1998, leaving this industry short of workers. The level of employment in the industry has steadied from its rapid growth during the 1980s and early 1990s. In fact, job growth in the industry slowed dramatically towards the late 1990s with a net increase of 145,200 workers in 1996 and 105,200 in 1997. Between 1990 and 2005, it is projected to slow further to 1.9 percent, according to the Bureau of Labor Statistics. In the period up to 2005, the fastest growing sector of the industry, in terms of jobs, is projected to be managerial, which is expected to increase 41 percent. Still, in the year 2005, 83 percent of workers in the industry will be employed in service occupations, including food preparation and service.

The National Restaurant Association reported that in 1999, ''the competition for labor is intense, with restaurant operators competing against one another as well as other retail and service businesses for qualified workers. Top-notch talent can take their pick of offers and frequently change jobs.''

The Association also noted that, ''research found that in 1998 executive chefs received a median salary of $40,000, plus a median bonus of $4,000; general managers and unit managers earned median salaries of $48,000 plus a $7,000 bonus, and $32,500 plus a $4,000 bonus, respectively. The research also shows that the industry offers plenty of opportunities for advancement, with three out of five salaried employees having started as hourly workers.''

The minimum wage hike in 1997 to $5.15 an hour had a dramatic effect on this industry. Job losses topped out at 150,000 in the industry as small restaurants could not afford the increase. As a result, 42 percent of restaurant owners increased menu prices on average of 5 percent.

Due to the labor shortage, the late 1990s were also a period of rising wages for workers in the eating place industry. Many restaurants tried to lure workers by offering competitive wages. In 1998, wages and benefits for full-service restaurants topped out at $40 billion, while fast-food paid out $32 billion. This labor squeeze will likely continue for several more years, as the Census Bureau reported that the number of 16 to 24 year-olds—the targeted labor market—fell in 1996 and 1997, and only began modest increases in 1998.

In addition to the labor shortage, the industry is also beset by chronic high employee turnover. A survey conducted by the National Restaurant Association concluded that unless more permanent employees came to work in the industry, high worker turnover would continue. A Department of Labor study added that ''The problem of labor turnover may be diminished by competitive pressure to reduce costs through greater use of offsite food preparation firms. Labor turnover has also been lowered by firms that offer employees improved training and occupational advancement opportunities. In addition, some firms are increasing wages and benefits to attract workers.''

AMERICA AND THE WORLD

Eating establishments are one of North America's most successful exports. McDonald's, the chain with the largest foreign presence, had more than 12,000 outlets distributed throughout more than 117 countries in 1999, accounting for 60 percent of its total worldwide sales. Ninety percent of the new store openings planned for 1999 and 2000 were overseas. Nearly all of the industry leaders have a formidable overseas presence. Restaurants such as Pizza Hut, Kentucky Fried Chicken, Burger King, and Wendy's gained a significant foothold in western Europe and the emerging eastern European markets during the late 1990s. TRICON had operations in more than 100 countries in 1999, Burger King operated in more than 55 countries, Darden Restaurants had operations in Japan and Canada, and Domino's Pizza was found in more than 60 countries.

According to *Market Share Reporter,* 27 of the 30 top leading international restaurant chains in number of units are American, a clear indicator that the American presence overseas is formidable. The North American Free Trade Agreement increased investment opportunities for U.S. restaurant companies and also increased competition in the industry, as Canadian and Mexican chains begin to penetrate the U.S. market.

The majority of restaurant chains in the United States are owned by American citizens, although the number of ethnic restaurants operated by immigrants is increasing. Overseas, the fast-food restaurants with the strongest foreign presence are generally operated by natives of the countries in which they are situated under a franchising agreement, although the parent companies retain ownership of a percentage of the foreign units.

RESEARCH AND TECHNOLOGY

Technological change is sweeping the industry, most profoundly in the area of computerization, but also in the form of devices to facilitate and speed food preparation and service. According to the National Restaurant Association, ''technology is playing an increasingly important role in restaurant operations. Operators are investing in technology to increase efficiency and productivity as well as improve customer service.'' The association also conducted a survey in which a large number of respondents were planning on increasing technology expenditures from 1998.

The most common dedicated computer systems used in the business in the late 1990s were programmed to transmit information from point of order taking to the kitchen and on to a microcomputer used by management. An electronic cash register/point of sale (ECR/POS) system transmitted customer orders to the kitchen where they were either printed out or displayed on a video display unit. The major input device in the system was a keyboard or touch screen unit, part of which was preprogrammed by the manufacturer, part of which can be programmed at the restaurant in line with its specific needs. Hand-held terminals are also in use, enabling waitpersons to key their orders at the table. Display screens are also available that allow waitpersons to monitor the progress of their orders. Printers in the kitchen issue meal checks. The data is also conveyed to a central microcomputer which uses it to keep tabs on operations and to control inventory. A number of independent ECR/POS units can be networked using a powerful microcomputer.

As well as making for smoother restaurant operation, computers produced reports and maintained files for many stores in the late 1990s. For example, says the Department of Labor report: ''Menu item files are used to monitor keyboard operations and make changes in items or prices. A labor file can produce numerous reports, including hours worked and different wage rates for each employee who may work at several different kinds of jobs during a pay period.'' Computers are especially useful in inventory control.

Large restaurant chains have found the new super microcomputers useful for monitoring their various branches. Time-consuming daily or weekly polls of each outlet's business can be replaced by a direct hookup which transmits the information automatically. These innovations not only save time but also increase efficiency and eliminate errors.

Despite these advances, compared with some other major retailing industries, the eating place sector of the food service industry remains relatively undercomputerized. However, seven out of ten tableservice restaurant operators that have computer access, utilize the Internet and use e-mail. Large national chains also have comprehensive web sites used to communicate with consumers.

Apart from computers, technology is infiltrating the restaurant business in the form of food preparation devices such as microwave ovens, automatic dishwashers, food processors, automatic beverage dispensers, and other automated equipment. A new form of vacuum cooking called ''sous vide'' is generating a good deal of interest. Although it saves on labor costs and increases efficiency, the substantial investment in special equipment that it requires, as well as the exacting safety standards that need to be observed, will probably slow its diffusion through the industry at least until the end of the 1990s, according to the U.S. Department of Labor.

Technological advancements were not confined to the kitchen in the late 1990s. A vibrating paging system for example, which costs about $5,000 and obviates the need to shout to a waiter when food is ready, was reporting great success in the late 1990s. These were also used to alert customers as to when their table was available.

Research has also shown that for fast-food restaurants eager to increase the volume and turnover of their drive-through trade, double drive-throughs are extremely successful. With one window for ordering and paying and another for food pickup, they minimize the period of stopping during assembly of orders. Fast-food restaurants operating drive-throughs also use wireless, remote control headsets worn by staff to cut back on background noise and reduce errors in order taking and are experimenting with computerized keyboards which allow customers to key in their orders; video systems; and other time saving and efficiency building devices. Restaurants on the west coast are trying out debit cards, specially coded automatic teller machine cards that are eight to fifteen seconds faster than cash transactions.

FURTHER READING

''1999 Restaurant Industry Forecast Full Service Outlook.'' National Restaurant Association. Available from http://www.restaurant.org/research/forecast/fc99-05.htm.

''1999 Restaurant Industry Forecast Limited Service Outlook.'' National Restaurant Association. Available from http://www.restaurant.org/research/forecast/fc99-04.htm.

''1999 Restaurant Industry Forecast Major Market Outlook.'' National Restaurant Association. Available from http://www.restaurant.org/research/forecast/fc99-08.htm.

''1999 Restaurant Industry Forecast Operational Trends.'' National Restaurant Association. Available from http://www.restaurant.org/research/forecast/fc99-07.htm.

Bear, Stearns & Co., Inc. ''Restaurant Review—Industry Report.'' 24 October 1996.

Darnay, Arsen J., ed. *Market Share Reporter.* Detroit: Gale Research, 1997.

''Foodservice Industry Forecast 1996.'' *Restaurants USA,* December 1995.

Papiernik, Richard L. ''Outlook: 1997.'' *Nation's Restaurant News,* 6 January 1997.

Paul, Katherine. ''Bon Appetit!'' *Streetnet,* 8 October, 1996. Available from http://www.streetnet.com/features.

''Restaurant Industry Pocket Factbook 1999.'' National Restaurant Association. Available from http://www.restaurant.org/research/pocket/index.htm.

''Retailers of the Century Named.'' *PR Newswire,* 29 October 1999.

Schroder Wertheim & Co. Inc. ''Restaurant Industry Annual Review—Industry Report.'' 7 March 1996.

Standard & Poor's Industry Surveys. New York: Standard & Poor's Corporation, April 1996.

Tejada, Carlos. ''Latest Restaurant Innovation Looks a Lot Like a Grocery.'' *Wall Street Journal,* 26 June 1996.

SIC 5813

DRINKING PLACES (ALCOHOLIC BEVERAGES)

This category includes establishments primarily engaged in the retail sale of alcoholic drinks, such as beer, ale, wine, and liquor, for consumption on the premises. The sale of food frequently accounts for a substantial portion of the receipts of these establishments.

NAICS CODE(S)

722410 (Drinking places (Alcoholic Beverages))

INDUSTRY SNAPSHOT

The drinking establishment industry—also knows as the bar and tavern industry—dates back to colonial America, which adopted the concept of a roadhouse tavern as a gathering place. The industry, however, is changing rapidly and may not exist in its traditional form by the beginning of the next century. By the late 1980s, some consultants and bar owners were predicting that the corner bar, which sells nothing but alcohol, was heading toward its demise. By way of adaptation, bars and lounges which serve food and even emphasize the sales of food items over alcoholic beverages have been gaining in popularity relative to establishments that sell beer, wine, and cocktails exclusively.

In the early to mid-1990s, the eating and drinking places industry as a whole was growing at a steady rate, averaging about five percent increase in overall sales per year. By contrast, sales from bars and taverns (including both alcohol and food receipts) were flat and in some years actually fell. According to the National Restaurant Association (NRA), for example, sales at such establishments fell from $9.4 billion in 1991 to $9.3 billion in 1993, rebounded to $10.9 billion by 1995 but then fell again to $9.4 billion in 1996 (the latter a drop of nearly 14 percent). The NRA projected 2000 sales of $11.9 billion, an increase due in large part to the rising popularity of sports bars. This expected increase amounted to a growth of 3.6 percent—a 0.5 percent increase after inflation is accounted for.

Americans' growing emphasis on healthy eating and healthy living is the primary reason for the slow growth in this category. Self-help programs designed to help people identify and end addiction to alcohol flourished throughout the 1970s and 1980s. Moreover, those who drink alcohol in moderation have become more conscious of caloric measure and the nutritive value of food and drink consumed. In addition, Americans became more disapproving of driving while intoxicated, and groups such as Mothers Against Drunk Drivers (MADD) have gained political and social clout. Rising litigation over the responsibility of drinking establishments for the alcohol consumption of patrons also acted as a force toward lower purchases of alcoholic drinks. The overall effect of this shift in thinking is that the line is blurring between full-service restaurants which serve alcohol and bars and taverns that offer full lunch and dinner menus.

This industry employed more than 2.25 million people throughout the country in 1997, either full-time or part-time, in taverns, pubs, bars, cocktail lounges, and others of the more than 52,825 establishments in this category.

ORGANIZATION AND STRUCTURE

A profile of the bar and tavern industry in terms of what percentage of the market is represented by larger concerns, such as major hotel lounges versus independently owned taverns, doesn't exist. But the leading trade association of licensed servers of alcoholic beverages boasted 20,000 members throughout the 1990s.

The small neighborhood bar, the sports bar with menu, the brew pub, and the hotel lounge are generally spread throughout urban and suburban centers in the United States. While they may differentiate themselves in image, ambiance, and type of product served (some, for instance, serve only beer), they often coexist in close proximity to one another. Many have live entertainment, such as music, or associations with celebrities, such as sports bars bearing the name of their athlete-owner.

Most eating and drinking establishments are small, independent operations. In fact in 1997, more than 70 percent of all establishments employed fewer than 20 employees. Despite the small nature of the industry outfits, drinking places generate more than $130 billion in business activity such as wages, payments, and sales. Furthermore, sales by on-premise retailers generate more than $2.5 billion in revenue for state and local government, according to the National Licensed Beverage Association.

BACKGROUND AND DEVELOPMENT

The use of fermented beverages in celebratory rituals and social gatherings has been documented in many parts of the world throughout its history. The public roadhouse was developed by the Romans in the first century A.D. as they built their infrastructure of paved roads. The word pub, in fact, is shortened from "public house," a stopping place for the traveler to rest both himself and his horse. In the fifth century, Europeans fostered winemaking. And in the tenth century an Arab physician is believed to have discovered the distillation process (for medicinal purposes).

The tavern, or pub, was an important aspect of English culture and was adopted by colonial America. Rum was prevalent at social occasions in early America, as were corn whiskey and hard cider. Tavern patrons were often entertained by performers, including ventriloquists, dancers, and musicians. The pub was also a place where the day's news was spread, as locals listened to travelers passing through from other places. This dissemination of news made the tavern a natural place for the establishment of local post offices.

The tavern owner was considered responsible for contributing to the town's orderliness. Licenses for serving alcoholic beverages dated back to 1672, and they were subject to suspension or revocation for sales to minors, slaves, servants, or intoxicated adults. Throughout the 1600s and 1700s, wine and malt liquors, as well as hard liquor or spirits, were sold. Rum was imported from the West Indies and had begun to eclipse the popularity of hard cider by the early 1700s. The colonies traded fish, tobacco, cotton, and lumber for rum and also for molasses, which was then distilled in New England as rum.

England's Molasses Act of 1733 levied a duty on products imported into the colonies. This legislation provided an impetus for independence from England. Numerous historical figures in pre- and post-Revolutionary America that were tavern owners or sons of owners included Samuel Adams, Ethan Allen, William Penn, and Abraham Lincoln.

Prohibition caused the tavern to be replaced by "speakeasies"—illegal establishments where liquor was plentiful to those who provided the correct password. Organized crime gained its foothold in America during this period, as bootlegging flourished and dealers in whiskey and other liquors protected their market with weapons. Following the repeal of the Prohibition Act thirteen years after its passage, the neighborhood tavern reemerged.

Current Conditions

Americans were increasingly doubting the healthiness of alcohol consumption in the early and mid-1990s. Medical research linked high alcohol consumption to liver cancer and other degenerative diseases. Smokers who also drink alcohol were found to have 13 times the risk of developing lung cancer as those who neither smoke nor drink. Although some research had found that widespread consumption of wine with dinner in France was responsible for their lower levels of heart disease compared with that of Americans, a 1993 study contradicted that finding. The more recent study concluded that the relative health of the French was due not to their wine consumption, but to their love of vegetables.

The bar and tavern industry has been heavily impacted by the steadily declining consumption of distilled liquor in recent decades. One bar owner in San Francisco described the environment in the late 1980s as "neo-prohibitionist." In an article in *New York Times* in 1989, Gerry E. Murphy, then executive director of the National Licensed Beverage Association (NLBA), said, "The day of the old bar which just served alcoholic beverages is past." Indeed, the *U.S. Industrial Outlook* predicted that "Domestic consumption of, and spending for, alcoholic beverages will probably continue to decline, leveling off toward the end of the 1990s."

This grim outlook for the alcohol industry as a whole does not portend well for the bar and tavern industry. Many hotel lounges have either been transformed into combination eating/drinking establishments, or eliminated altogether to be replaced by meeting rooms. Although they report that alcohol items have higher profit margins than food items, food was increasingly being emphasized more than drinks. Renewed interest in wine, martini bars, and sports bars helped stave off a continued decline at the end of the century, stopping the sales slippage with 2000 totals of $11.9 billion.

While the overall cause in this threat to the industry is the nationwide trend toward healthier living, the signposts of this shift are many. There has been, for the past several decades, a growing acceptance for the nondrinker in social settings. This has occurred in large part because of the widespread recognition of the physical and emotional health problems created by alcohol addiction. The Alcoholics Anonymous program, begun in the early 1900s by Bill Wilson and others, was created to combat the problem of alcoholism through meetings of individuals who identify themselves as having an addiction to alcohol. The number of people who have ended their consumption altogether through this mutual support program is unknown, but is believed to be in the millions. Although people who wished to abstain from alcohol consumption felt social pressure to drink at parties and public gatherings, the stigma associated with "teetotaling" faded until it was almost nonexistent in the 1990s. MADD gained political influence and helped create a stigma surrounding driving an automobile while intoxicated. In addition, several key civil actions brought by victims of auto collisions and their families resulted in increased liability of alcohol servers for intoxicated patrons that leave establishments and cause accidents.

The response of the bar and tavern industry to the liability issue has been to educate its workforce about this challenge. A program sponsored by the NLBA called Techniques of Alcohol Management (TAM) certifies bartenders and other alcohol servers in methods of curtailing the problem. The program teaches employees of taverns to identify signs of intoxication in patrons, the effect of food consumption on the rate of intoxication, how to discreetly regulate a customer's consumption, and the application of state and local laws to the sale of alcoholic beverages. The NLBA reported that over 300,000 bar and tavern employees had participated in the program. A similar program is called Training for Intervention Procedures by Servers of Alcohol (TIPPS).

Several different pieces of federal legislation either hampered the industry or threatened it in the 1990s. President Clinton signed a bill that reduced the business meals and entertainment tax deduction from 80 percent to 50 percent in 1993. The industry immediately began lobbying for repeal of that legislation through separate bills introduced in both the Senate and House of representatives.

A bill under consideration in 1999 included a provision to lower the national blood-alcohol content (BAC) level defining intoxication from .10 to .08. The NLBA opposed this measure on the basis that, of those intoxicated drivers who were killed in auto accidents, 81 percent had a BAC higher than the legal limit of .10. However, several states, including California, had already lowered the BAC to .08 while national legislation was still being considered.

While opposing legislation that was perceived to be harmful to the industry, bar and tavern owners fought back by courting consumers. The rise of sports bars in the 1980s provided an example of industry adaptation to consumer health concerns. In contrast to the dark, smoke-filled bar of past decades, sports bars are lighter, with an updated, high-energy ambiance. The vast majority of such bars, in addition to having televisions for their customers to view, serve full menus of lunch and dinner items. These types of establishment stress a casual atmosphere and efficient but unobtrusive service so that patrons may meet to watch an athletic event and enjoy gathering with friends. Sports bars also target women and families, often tailoring their menu to include light, healthy food in addition to burgers and other American fare. The celebrity element is another prominent characteristic of sports bars. Many are owned by, or named after, athletes and rely on visits by athletes to publicize and promote the establishment.

Another successful concept of the 1990s has been the brew pub. Although this is a borderline category since many brew pubs derive more than half of their sales from the food they serve, the brew pub—and microbrewed beer generally—has helped to revive both a beer industry on the decline and the drinking places industry itself. According to Michelle Dorfman, writing in *ID: The Voice of Foodservice Distribution,* "brew pubs, by definition, have an on-site brewery and more than 50 percent of the brew product is consumed on-premise." After gaining initial popularity early in the 1990s, the category has since exploded with more than 500 brew pubs nationwide by late 1996.

Posher alternatives that catered to popular fads such as swing dancing, martini bars became more prevalent and helped rejuvenate the industry. Industry entrepreneurs also embraced the cigar fad of the 1990s, and began to allow their patrons to smoke cigars on-site or created specialty cigar bars that sold a variety of cigars in addition to selling alcoholic beverages. Such innovations were signs that the industry would keep reinventing itself despite all the negative trends.

FURTHER READING

Dorfman, Michelle. "A Strong Segment Is Brewing." *ID: The Voice of Foodservice Distribution,* October 1996, 39.

Fisher, Lawrence M. "Old Standby, the Corner Bar, Falling Victim to New Values." *New York Times,* 18 November 1989.

"Foodservice Industry Forecast 1996." *Restaurants USA,* December 1995.

Krueger, Jill. "Where There's Smoke . . . Restaurants, Bars Jump on Cigar Trend, Welcome Stogies," *Orlando Business Journal,* 18 October 1996, 3.

LaFrance, Peter. "Sports Bars." *Tavern News,* June 1990.

National Licensed Beverage Association. "Tavern Statistics," 20 April 2000. Available from http://www.nlba.org.

National Restaurant Association. "2000 Pocket Factbook," 20 April 2000. Available from http://www.restaurant.org.

Papiernik, Richard L. "Outlook: 1997." *Nation's Restaurant News,* 6 January 1997, 41.

Student, John. "True Brew." *American Demographics,* May 1995, 32.

U.S. Department of Commerce. International Trade Administration. *U.S. Industrial Outlook 1994.* Washington: GPO, 1994.

SIC 5912

DRUG STORES AND PROPRIETARY STORES

Establishments in this industry are engaged in the retail sale of prescription drugs, proprietary drugs, and nonprescription medicines and may also carry a number of related lines, such as cosmetics, toiletries, tobacco, and novelty merchandise. These stores are included on the basis of their usual trade designation rather than on the stricter interpretation of the commodities handled. This industry includes drug stores that also operate a soda fountain or lunch counter.

NAICS Code(s)

446110 (Pharmacies and Drug Stores)

Industry Snapshot

The drug store industry increased sales by 7.7 percent in 1998 to $106.7 billion. Prescription sales also increased by 15 percent to $103 billion. This industry has seen rapid growth throughout the 1990s encouraging powerful supermarket and mass-merchandise chains to enter traditional drug store markets, forcing the independent drug store industry to compete with these larger companies. In addition, the drug store industry faced narrowing profit margins due to the general push to reduce health care costs in the United States and as a result, acquisitions and consolidation were prevalent in the late 1990s. These factors combined to force drug stores to concentrate on customer service, expand into niche markets, form partnerships with suppliers and health care providers, and automate operations for increased cost-efficiency.

Organization and Structure

A total of 39,754 traditional drug stores existed in the United States in 1998. There were 19,110 traditional chain drug stores, and 20,644 independent stores. The drug store industry as a whole posted a sales volume of $106.7 billion in 1998. These figures include not only prescriptions and over-the-counter (OTC) drugs sales, but also general merchandise. Prescription sales and OTCs, however, had total sales of $103 billion in 1998 and made up almost 61.5 percent of all sales in a traditional chain store. Chain drugstores accounted for 40 percent of those sales, while independents took 26 percent of the market. Mass merchandisers and supermarkets claimed 21 percent of the market, and mail order totaled 13 percent. In 1999, the independent pharmacy sales forecast is $29.7 billion. The number of retail prescriptions increased from 2.0 billion in 1992 to 2.7 billion in 1998.

As drug stores faced increasing competition from other retailers, chains and independents alike began to vary their store formats in order to differentiate themselves from competitors and strengthen their image as health care providers. As a result, five main store formats emerged within the drug store industry: independents, chain drug stores, mass merchandisers, supermarkets, and mail order.

In 1998, independents grew 10.6 percent over 1997 with $26.4 billion in perscription sales. In the same year, there were more than 20,644 outlets. According to the National Association of Chain Drug Stores (NACDS), these independent pharmacies filled almost 693 million prescriptions in 1998, an increase of 1.2 percent over 1997. Sales for OTC medications were $1.3 billion in 1998. Independent drug stores are expected to account for 24.4 percent of prescription sales in 1999.

Chain drug stores averaged 8,958 square feet and offered a wide assortment of goods. Typically, to draw traffic through, the pharmacy was placed in the rear of the store. Some well-known chains that operated conventional drug stores included Walgreen Co., CVS Corporation, Rite Aid Corporation, and Eckerd Corporation. According to the NACDS, chain pharmacies filled 60 percent of all prescriptions, more than 4 million a day and 1.6 billion per year in 1998. Prescriptions accounted for $63.3 billion in sales—61.5 percent of sales for chain stores.

Mass merchandisers accounted for 11 percent of all prescription sales in 1998, with $10.4 million in sales. The growth rate for this portion of the drug store industry is slowing somewhat, with 5,258 outlets—up from 4,914 in 1997. Prescription sales increased by 16.3 percent in 1998 and accounted for 10.1 percent of total sales. This segment dispensed 272 million prescriptions in 1998, an increase of 7.1 percent from the previous year and accounted for 10 percent of all prescriptions.

This market also includes supermarket pharmacies, which operated 6,963 oulets in 1998. These stores accounted for $11.4 billion in prescription sales in 1998, an increase of 16.4 percent from 1997. Supermarkets also controlled 11 percent of total prescription sales in this industry. These food stores dispensed 306 million prescriptions in 1998, 10.5 percent of total prescriptions.

OTC sales in supermarkets have also grown. In 1998, sales were $9.2 billion and projected to increase 7.5 percent in 1999. Mass merchandiser OTC sales were $9.3 billion and projected to increase 11.1 percent in 1999, independent sales were $1.3 billion and expected to rise by 3 percent, and traditional chain sales were $9.7 billion and forecast to be $10.4 billion in 1999.

Mail order drug stores also play an important role in this industry. In 1998, mail order constituted 13 percent of the prescription and OTC market with more than $13.4 billion in sales. Mail order dispensed 368 million prescriptions in 1998. A move that started in 1995 and continued to factor into the success of mail order was convincing federal government retirees, who are part of a managed health care program, to order prescriptions through discounted mail order outlets. By using the mail order system, retirees were able to avoid paying the usual 20 percent co-pay. If the retirees decided instead to fill their prescriptions at local drug stores, they were responsible for the co-pay.

The drug store industry relied on four core product categories for a large percentage of total sales in 1998: prescriptions, OTC medications, toiletries, and cosmetics. The chain pharmacy had sales of $135 billion in 1998 from these segments. Other categories commonly sold in drug stores included tobacco, consumables, stationery, and housewares. In general, however, drug stores responded to competition by strengthening core product areas in the late 1990s.

Total prescription sales were $103 billion in 1998, with 2.7 billion prescriptions written. By 1999, that number should increase to 2.97 billion, reflecting growth of 8 percent over 1998. Since 1992, prescriptions have grown by 23 percent. The growth in prescription sales was explained by the fact that prescription rates and prices increased. In 1998, the average cost for a brand name prescription was $53.51, an increase of 8 percent over 1997. The average cost for generic was $17.33, an increase of 2 percent over 1997. Some factors that contributed to the increase in prescriptions written included: the aging of the American population; an increase in the percentage of prescriptions reimbursed by third parties, such as insurance companies or government programs; the introduction of new products by pharmaceutical companies; and the availability of generic substitutes for brand-name drugs.

Sales of OTC medications—which included external remedies, cough/cold/flu medicines, and analgesics/digestive—was forecast to increase 8.3 percent to $32.0 billion in 1999, or just under 30 percent of drug store industry sales. In 1998, OTCs made up 27 percent of all sales in chain stores, accounting for $29.5 billion.

Sales of toiletries or health and beauty aids (HBAs) in drug store chains claimed 26 percent of their total sales, or more than $28.4 billion in 1998. The product mix for a traditional chain drug store in 1997 was as follows: prescriptions, 48.4 percent; OTCs, 12.5; consumables, 8.7; toiletries, 6.2; cosmetics, 3.8; general merchandise, 5.2; photography, 4.0; and tobacco products, 2.8 percent.

BACKGROUND AND DEVELOPMENT

The drug store industry originated in the mid-1800s, when Americans began using ''patent remedies'' to treat illnesses. Some early pharmacists operated out of village apothecaries, where they purchased chemicals in bulk and mixed them on the premises to fill prescriptions. Following the Great Depression, pharmaceutical companies grew rapidly and opened sophisticated research facilities. The number of patents issued for drug products increased from fewer than 100 before 1940 to more than 4,000 by the 1950s. Medicines began to be marketed in final-dosage form under a manufacturer's brand name rather than in bulk as generic ingredients. As a result, the number of drug stores increased, while pharmacists adopted a service-oriented role in dispensing prescriptions.

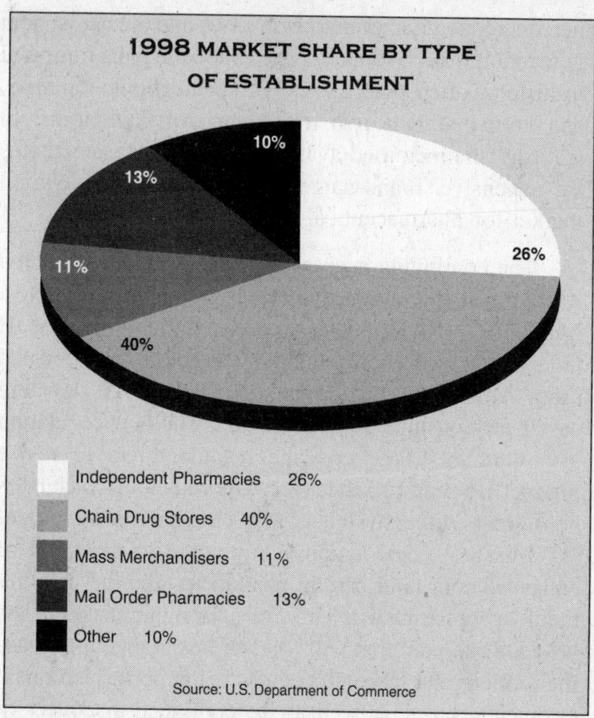

CURRENT CONDITIONS

The drug store industry more than doubled its sales volume in the past decade, and several factors pointed toward continued growth into the next millennium. For example, the two demographic groups that used the greatest amount of medication—adults over 65 and children under 10—were the fastest growing segments of the American population in the late 1990s. In fact, the number of people 65 and older increased at twice the rate of the general population, while this age group received an average of 12 prescriptions per person compared to about five for the 20 to 40 age group.

While this sector of the retail industry continued to see gains, consolidation swept through drug store chains towards the late 1990s, leaving a handful of strong players. CVS acquired Revco and Arbor Drug; Rite Aid purchased Thrifty Payless, Marco, and K&B; and JCPenney bought Eckerd Drug, merging it into its Thrift Drug operations. This merger activity was caused by increased competition to offer a variety of merchandise at low costs, and the availability of convenience in terms of pharmacy outlets.

The drug store industry also benefited from the trend toward self-medication, and a healthier attitude among consumers in the late 1990s. Drug stores controlled 44 percent of the vitamin market in 1999, and the baby boom generation, which some experts called the most informed in history, often purchased OTC medications, vitamins, and herbal remedies to treat their own symptoms. In addition, the increased availability of generic substitutes for expensive, brand-name drugs expanded the overall market for pharmaceutical products.

The continuing success of OTC products prompted regulators to get involved in that segment. According to a March 1999 NACDS press release, "Vice President Al Gore announced a new federal regulation by the Food and Drug Administration designed to make OTC labeling easier for consumers to understand. The new regulation also requires OTC medicine manufacturers to revise product labeling to reflect the importance of consumers consulting with physicians and pharmacists on proper OTC usage." This action also pointed to the trend of enhanced consumer care in pharmacies and the involvement of pharmacists in consumer purchases. The NACDS reported that with "fewer hospitalizations leading to more and more procedures being performed on an out-patient basis, as well as the continued discovery of new and more complex drug therapy, there will be an increasing reliance on community pharmacy to educate and monitor patient therapy."

Another factor that continued to affect the drug store industry into 1999 was the growing emphasis on controlling U.S. health care costs. In 1999, only 8 percent of health care costs were pharmacy related. National health care policies insured more Americans and expanded the market for drugs, but also increased pressure on drug stores to reduce costs and operate more efficiently.

While traditional chain and independent drug stores remained dominant in the late 1990s, supermarkets, mass merchandisers, and warehouse clubs posted gains in prescription sales. Attracted to the industry's growth, competition from these stores presented significant challenges to drug stores and led to a shakeup among independents and regional chains, evident by the merging or buying out of 35 chains since the early 1990s. Supermarkets continued to hold an important advantage over drug stores in consumer exposure, since the average person visited a supermarket 2.2 times per week compared to once per month for a drug store. Many supermarket chains began competing aggressively for sales of HBAs by cutting prices, increasing advertising, and emphasizing the convenience of one-stop shopping. In addition, supermarket chains opened in-store pharmacies, which they felt increased store traffic and provided a community service. Mass merchandisers such as Wal-Mart, Target, and Kmart entered traditional drug store categories—claiming a 10 percent share of prescriptions in 1998—supported by their superior distribution networks and technology.

Drug stores also faced a growing challenge to their profitability as third party payment accounted for a larger percentage of prescription sales in the late 1990s. Third parties included health maintenance organizations (HMOs), preferred provider organizations (PPOs), unions, government programs (Medicare and Medicaid), and other systems that covered costs by prearranged agreement with health care providers. Prescriptions represented the largest out-of-pocket expense for consumers, so third party payment increased substantially over the past ten years as part of the drive to control health care costs. This trend affected drug store profitability since third parties typically applied a discount of 20 percent to the average wholesale price of a drug, plus allowed dispensing fees, which covered administrative and labor costs of only $3.00 per prescription as opposed to the actual cost of $4.50. Drug stores struggled with the low margin sales and costly paperwork, but appreciated the large prescription volume third party systems could provide.

Consumer demands for lower health care costs also affected drug stores' ability to raise prices. In the past, prescription prices generally increased at twice the rate of the Consumer Price Index, and drug stores turned this trend to their advantage. Drug stores would often forward-buy inventory of pharmaceutical products at low prices and usually passed along price increases to consumers with little negative effect on sales. In 1998, brand name prescription costs increased 8 percent while generic increased by 2 percent. The average cost for a prescription was $34.43 in 1998, with 74 percent going to the manufacturer, 3 percent to the wholesaler, and 23 percent of cost being allocated to the retailer. Stores also had to remain price competitive in HBAs. Many stores focused on "Everyday Low Pricing" and beefed up advertising to lure customers.

Another challenge to the drug store industry was the advent of Internet drug stores. While Internet sales represented only 1 percent of industry sales, that number was forecast to grow along with other retail sectors. These sites, such as DrugEmporium.com, offered prescription and nonprescription drugs, cosmetics, and health and beauty aids. Many offered email access to pharmacists as well. Large drug chains have followed suit, and customers can refill prescriptions on store websites such as CVS.com. This industry, however, will see advantages from the Internet as well. In a *Drug Store News* editoral, Anthony Cuti, chairman and CEO of Duane Reade, stated that, "the bottom line is that personal medical consultations will grow more toward the individual pharmacist and less toward impersonal, less responsive communication vehicles such as the Internet. The Internet, however, will be a great provider of increased general health information that will probably promote a greater number of visits to both physicians and pharmacists to interpret and apply the technical information retrieved from the Internet.''

INDUSTRY LEADERS

As a result of the consolidation in the industry, the drug store sector was dominated by four leaders in 1999. Walgreens, CVS Corp., RiteAid Corp. and Eckerd Corp. accounted for two thirds of total chain drug store sales. American Drug Stores and Longs Drugs Stores were ranked five and six respectively in the industry.

Walgreen, the number one drug chain, steadily pursued a goal of operating 3,000 outlets by 2000. In 1998, the chain operated 2,800 stores in 39 states and Puerto Rico and posted sales of $17.8 billion, an increase of 16.5 percent over 1997. The company has expanded into new areas, both geographically and with products. In addition to adding photofinishing departments to its stores, the company started its own pharmacy benefit management firm which is actually run through the chain's mail-order business, Healthcare Plus. The store offered an online pharmacy and had 90,000 employees in 1999.

CVS Corp., the number two drug chain, had sales of $15.2 billion in 1998. The company grew with its purchases of Revco, Arbor, and Soma, an online pharmacy, and had more than 4,200 stores in operation in 1999. Net income for CVS increased more than 900 percent in 1998 to $396 million. Its subsidiary, PharmaCare Management Services provided managed care drug programs to its customers. CVS had more than 97,000 employees in 1999.

RiteAid Corp., the number 3 drug chain, had sales of $12.7 billion in 1998, an increase of more than 11 percent from 1997. The company operated more than 3,800 stores in 30 states across the United States and employed 89,900 in 1999. RiteAid also had a 22 percent interest in drugstore.com, an online pharmacy.

Eckerd Corp, the fourth largest drug chain, had sales of $10.3 billion in 1998, an increase of 69 percent over the previous year. It operated 2,900 stores in more than 25 states in 1999. Eckerd offered an online pharmacy for refills and employed 55,000 workers.

WORKFORCE

The drug store industry employed an average of 617,000 people in 1998, up 2 percent from 605,000 in 1996. The NACDS forecast that between 1998 and 2005, the number of community pharmacists will increase 6 percent, although there is a 50 percent increase expected in the number of prescriptions dispensed—2.7 billion in 1998 to 4.0 billion in 2005.

While chain drug stores employed more than 93,000 pharmacists in 1998, the major concern for this industry was the shortage of qualified pharmacists. In February

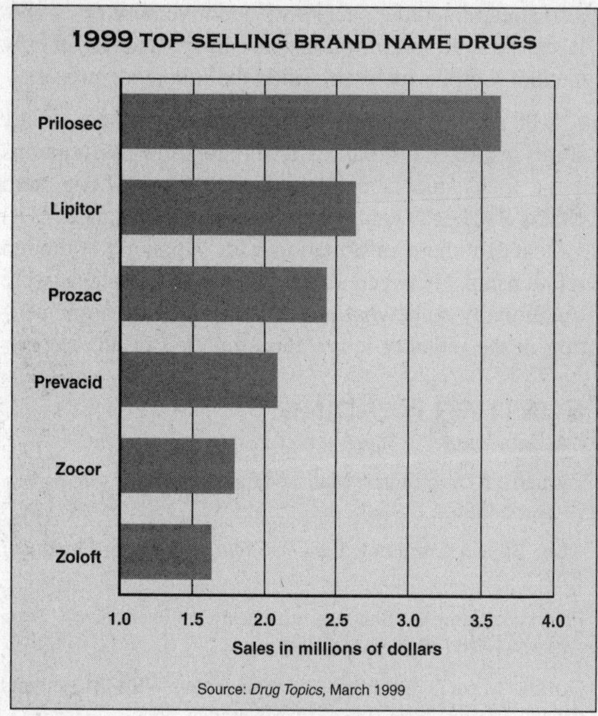

1999, there were 3,421 jobs available in this sector. Thirteen percent of drug stores were understaffed in 1999. Of the employed pharmacists, 80,000 worked full-time. Over half of those full-time pharmacists were male, while 45 percent of part-time pharmacists were female.

RESEARCH AND TECHNOLOGY

Faced with managed care and an aging population with increasing needs for prescriptions, drug stores turned to technology to increase productivity. According to *Drug Store News*, ''drug chains are turning increasingly to pharmacy technology to automate the workflow, speed the filing process, and take the guesswork out of nearly every aspect of prescription dispensing. In the process, they've poured tens of millions of dollars into high-speed pill and tablet counters, new prescription tracking software, robotic devices, work-station terminals and interactive voice response systems (IVR) for phone-in refills.''

IVRs became increasingly popular in the late 1990s. With the growing number of prescriptions, these systems allowed the pharmacy staff to concentrate on filling prescriptions and talking with in-store customers instead of taking orders over the phone. CVS, for example, has implemented these systems throughout the company's chain stores.

Some new technologies emerging in the late 1990s included: AutoScript III, which integrated robotics, labeling and pill counting into a touch screen system; QuickScript System, used for automating the entire filling process including labeling, filling and capping, and also streamlined the paperwork and inventory process—it can fill 90 prescriptions per hour; and RX-90 by Condor Corp, which simplified the inventory process.

In addition to these technological advances, many stores instituted a satellite network to allow prescriptions to be filled anywhere in the United States. Drug store chains also began using electronic data interchange (EDI) systems to share information with suppliers. Although relationships between drug stores and suppliers were traditionally somewhat adversarial, intensified competition in the industry led to the formation of alliances.

FURTHER READING

''A Cold Future?'' *Supermarket Business,* June 1996.

''American Drug Stores: Managed Care Leader.'' *Drug Topics,* 22 April 1996.

''Big Builders Building Less.'' *Chain Store Age,* December 1996.

Frederick, James. ''Shaping the Future of Pharmacy.'' *Drug Store News,* 21 September 1998.

Griffin, Marie. ''Building for Tomorrow With Bricks and Clicks.'' *Drug Store News,* 15 November 1998.

Industry Facts A-a-Glance, 1998. National Association of Chain Drug Stores. Available from http://www.nacds.org/industry/fastfacts.html.

''Mass Appeal. Rx Drug Sales to Mass Merchants Surged in '94.'' *Drug Topics,* 10 July 1995.

Mendelson, Seth. ''Win One, Lose One.'' *Supermarket Business,* November 1996.

Muirhead, Greg. ''Late Bloomer: Walgreens Brings Mail-Order Network to PBM Market.'' *Drug Topics,* 5 Feb 1996.

''Photo Focus Yields Gains for Major Chains.'' *Stores,* September 1996.

Pinto, David. ''Stage Set for Fierce Battle for Dominance in Industry.'' *Chain Drug Review,* 22 September 1997.

''Positive Sign.'' *Drug Topics,* 8 January 1996.

''Rite Aid Bails From Revco Merger,'' 24 April 1996. Available from http:www.cnnfn.com/news/9604/24/riteaid/cnnnews.

Schulz, David. ''Acquisitions Set the Pace for Retail Chain Growth.'' *Stores,* August 1998.

''Top 50 Drug Chains in Dollar Volume.'' *Drug Store News,* 27 April 1998.

SIC 5921

LIQUOR STORES

Liquor stores are establishments engaged in the retail sale of packaged alcoholic beverages, including ale, beer, wine, and liquor, for consumption off premises. Stores selling prepared drinks for consumption on premises are classified in **SIC 5813: Drinking Places (Alcoholic Beverages).**

NAICS CODE(S)

445310 (Beer, Wine and Liquor Stores)

INDUSTRY SNAPSHOT

The retail liquor store industry experienced an increase in sales from $21.7 billion in 1990 to $22.5 billion in 1995 (preinflation figures), but the industry's real income declined 10 percent during the same period. This was on top of a 17 percent drop in real income from 1980 to 1990. Real income began to revive slightly 1996, registering a growth of 2.4 percent. Factors accounting for the industry's sagging numbers included a renewed public hostility over the relationship between alcohol sales and crime, which led to prohibitions on the sales of such alcoholic products as small bottles of strong, fortified wine and single cans of beer. State efforts to curtail the growth of liquor stores, competition from alternative sources of supply, and a nationwide crackdown on alcohol-related driving offenses also contributed to the drop in sales.

Other developments in the 1990s boded well for the industry. In 1996 the Joint Committee of the U.S. Department of Health and Human Services and the Department of Agriculture issued dietary guidelines indicating that a moderate intake of alcohol among adults may be beneficial to health. That same year the American Heart Association issued a scientific advisory noting a 30 percent decrease in coronary artery disease incidence for persons who consume a moderate amount of wine. Researchers at Colombia University released a study in 1999 showing that moderate alcohol consumption can reduce the risk for stroke. Additionally, the liquor industry itself has taken action to improve sales. In 1996 national distillers voted to end their voluntary abstention from advertising liquor on broadcast media. In the first year after the ban was lifted beverage marketers spent $609 million at retail for point-of-purchase advertising. By 1998 that figure had doubled. Many liquor stores have reported increased earnings as a result of vigorous advertising. But the jury is out as to whether the liquor store industry as a whole will enjoy a resurgence.

ORGANIZATION AND STRUCTURE

The liquor store industry is made up of mom-and-pop retail outlets, independently run chains, and corporate-owned stores. While the vast majority of stores are small, family-run operations, a rapidly growing number are superstores primarily engaged in other kinds of businesses.

Among the industry's top companies, most remained independently run during the 1990s. Increasingly, however, they changed their retail strategy, consolidating multiple outlets into fewer but bigger warehouse-style stores, thus saving on overhead and payroll while still moving a large inventory. The effect has been hard on smaller neighborhood retail operations comprising the bulk of the industry. As one small retailer observed in the *New York Times* in 1996, "This is a slowly declining industry. The mom-and-pop shops just can't compete with the superstores and the discounters." State and national statistics reinforce the story. In 1970 the New York State Liquor Authority issued 5,070 licenses for new stores. By 1995 46 percent of the shops had shut down. While the traditional corner liquor store remains a fixture in most American towns, its future can no longer be taken for granted.

Background and Development

Throughout its history, the retail liquor store industry has been buffeted by changing social and political attitudes toward alcohol, and the sale of alcohol has always been highly regulated. The most severe period of regulation was the Prohibition era (1919 to 1933), during which alcohol consumption was completely outlawed by the federal government. Stores were forced to close en masse, and owners either left the business or went underground.

Liquor sales were legalized again in 1933, when it became clear that Prohibition had worsened bootlegging and facilitated the rise of organized crime. Responsibility for liquor regulation was returned to the states following Prohibition. Since then alcohol has been legally available in almost every part of the country, although a few localities remain "dry." But the nature of governmental regulation has varied markedly from state to state. Some states allow private ownership, while others restrict the sale of alcohol to state-run outlets. Some states permit grocery stores to sell wine and liquor, others do not. Some states tax liquor sales heavily, while others impose little or no taxation. In no state, however, is the production, distribution, and sale of liquor unlicensed or unregulated.

In 1978 many states deregulated liquor prices that had been set by the government. Deregulation allowed supermarkets and convenience stores to enter the business, which increased pressures on traditional corner liquor stores at a time they were already experiencing shaky profit margins. To compete, small retailers lobbied for permission to sell peanuts and other ancillary goods, such as finger foods, corkscrews, gift baskets, and lottery tickets.

State and local governments across the country have tried to address these problems. In 1994 residents of Barrow, Alaska, turned back the clock to Prohibition, voting to ban retail sales of all alcoholic products. A year later statistics showed a 70 percent drop in crime, a plunge in emergency room visits, and the virtual emptying of the town jail's "drunk tank," which usually had a full house, according to a report in the *Wall Street Journal.* Nevertheless, the ban was repealed after the one-year break, giving rise to bitter acrimony among residents (and an almost immediate refilling of the drunk tank). Some local Inupiat Eskimos and others charged opponents of the ban with a racist motivation to destroy native culture. Alcoholism, one state health official said, was the "worst problem facing native communities." Other Inupiats supported repeal, as did members of the majority community, who argued that the abuse of alcohol was an issue of individual, not social, responsibility. Pro-drink advocates also pointed to an increase in bootlegging during the dry period, as well as an increase in crime and hospital visits in neighboring communities.

Early in 1997 the Distilled Spirits Council (DSC) of the United States, a major trade group, decided to lift its self-imposed ban on television and radio advertising. The ban, included in its 1934 Code of Good Practice for Distilled Spirits Advertising and Marketing, followed the decision of the Seagram's distillery to advertise two of its scotch and bourbon brands on TV. Even before the self-imposed ban was eliminated, nine states jointly petitioned the Federal Communications Commission (FCC) in December 1996 to prohibit such commercials: Hawaii, Iowa, Kansas, Maryland, Michigan, Minnesota, North Dakota, Rhode Island, and Vermont. Alaska had made the same request a month earlier. After hearing arguments about the state's concerns, the FCC announced in 1998 that it would postpone ruling on the petition because few distilled spirits ads were actually appearing. In 1999 the DSC itself responded to the states' petition in a statement issued by its president and chief executive officer, Peter Cressy, who said that the council was "open to considering new provisions that would strengthen all beverage alcohol advertising codes."

Current Conditions

Liquor store revenues during the 1990s may have suffered from the publication of studies showing the cause-and-effect relationship between alcohol and crime. A 1996 Brookings Institution report entitled "Broken Bottles: Alcohol, Disorder, and Crime," by John J. DiIulio, Jr., found that 60 percent of convicted homicide offenders drank heavily just prior to committing the crime, the same percentage of those committing other violent felonies. The report, which observed that alcohol "acts as a multiplier of crime," also cited studies showing 30 to 90 percent of convicted rapists were drunk when they raped.

Several studies focused on alcohol abuse among youths, and on the relationship between liquor stores and poverty. A 1996 report by the National Institutes of Health concluded that ''Young adults have a higher prevalence of alcohol consumption and binge drinking than any other age group . . . Rates of alcohol abuse and dependence are disproportionately higher among those between the ages of 18 and 29 . . . Young adults are also over represented among alcohol-related traffic fatalities.''

In Atlanta a mayoral task force prepared recommendations requiring new retailers to locate at least 1,000 feet—three city blocks—away from other alcohol sellers, and at least 600 feet from libraries, schools, residences, parks, hospitals, and places of worship. Texas liquor store owners sought to limit the number of permits for retail operations to one for every 1,000 inhabitants. A few cities in the South sought to curtail permits issued for liquor stores located in poor neighborhoods. Some municipalities in other parts of the country chose to regulate liquor store hours, banning sales altogether on certain days. Other communities restricted the amount and type of gaming paraphernalia that could be sold by retail liquor stores.

In New Jersey, police officers from the state's Alcohol Beverage Control Division placed themselves in liquor stores in college towns to apprehend youths trying to purchase liquor. By August 1996 the Cops-in-Shops program had arrested 363 people, including 58 adults who had attempted to purchase alcohol for persons under age 21. In 1998 almost 200 people were arrested during June, July, and August alone, most for using fake identifications. The program ultimately expanded to Atlantic City, Avalon, Wildwood, and Seaside Heights.

Another threat facing the liquor store industry in the 1990s was the emergence of cooperatives that arranged for distributors to deliver hard-to-find microbrews directly to consumers' homes. Beer Across America was the largest such cooperative in the United States, claiming 100,000 members in 1997. But the threat posed by beer cooperatives may be waning. With assets of $3.4 million and liabilities of $7.7 million, Beer Across America filed for bankruptcy in 1998. No other business has stepped in to swoop up the insolvent cooperative's members.

Several states also toughened their laws punishing motorists who drive while intoxicated (DWI). By 1999 17 states and the District of Columbia had lowered to 0.08 percent blood-alcohol content the legal limit at which drivers could be prosecuted for DWI. The remaining 33 states allowed the higher limit of .10 percent. In July 1999 Vice President Al Gore announced that under the Transportation Equity Act for the 21st Century federal grants of more than $500 million over six years would be made available to all states that had lowered their limit to at least 0.08 percent. A number of localities went further than lowering the legal limit for DWI offenses. New York City enacted a regulation authorizing police to confiscate the motor vehicles of drivers who have been arrested for DWI.

INDUSTRY LEADERS

Major companies in the liquor store industry include Price Company, of San Diego, California, Kash-N-Karry Food Stores Inc., of Tampa, Florida, Carr-Gottstein Foods Company, of Anchorage, Alaska, Robert Mondavi Corporation, of Oakville, California, and Eder Brothers Inc, of West Haven, Connecticut. Eder Brothers is the only company whose sole business is the retail sales of alcoholic beverages. The other companies are also in related lines of business. In 1995 Price Company had profits of $7.32 billion and 20,800 employees. Kash-N-Karry had sales of $883 million and 9,400 employees. Carr-Gottstein sold more than $3 billion worth of goods with 3,300 employees, while Robert Mondavi had revenues of $200 million and 119 employees. Eder Brothers had sales of $37.1 million and employed 110 people.

Of all the top liquors stores in the country, Carr-Gottstein has done the most to expand its business. Formed in 1990, Carr-Gottstein acquired Sea Mart Supermarket and Market Place Discount Food Stores in November 1993. The next year the company acquired Hanson Trading Company, and completed its purchase of Yukon Express Service, a food service supplier. Carr-Gottstein also runs a freight transportation business under the name Delchamps, which operates a liquor store chain in Florida. In April of 1999 Safeway Co., purchased Carr-Gottstein for $330 million. At the time of the merger Carr-Gottstein was the state's largest grocery and liquor retailer with 49 stores.

Most liquor stores are privately held. Even among the top ten, only four are publicly traded: Delchamps, Carr-Gottstein, Cost Plus, of Oakland, California, and Bruno's. Based in Alabama, Bruno's owned more than 200 supermarkets in 1996, under the names Food Fair, Food Max, Food World, Bruno's Food Store, SSS Enterprises, and PS Holding Property. But in 1999 Bruno's announced that it planned to close or sell 14 stores to put the company in a stronger financial and operational position. The stores included six in Alabama, five in Georgia, and three in Florida. After shedding the 14 units, Bruno's still owned and operated 149 stores in Alabama, Mississippi, Florida, and Georgia.

Among other industry leaders, Warehouse Wines & Liquors, of Stamford, Connecticut, is typical of large liquor retailers utilizing advanced technology for both inventory control and marketing. *Inc.* magazine reported that the firm's computerized inventory management system allows it's managers to know ''exactly what has been sold as soon as it's gone,'' thereby eliminating almost all of its out-of-stock problems.

The relative ease of establishing a website and the worldwide marketing potential of the Internet has not been lost on liquor retailers. Hundreds of websites now sell wine, beer, and other alcoholic beverages over the Internet. Wine Planet has emerged as one of the Internet's most successful liquor retailers. For the September 1999 quarter the company's online sales of alcohol increased by 97 percent over the previous quarter, reaching $1.41 million. Wine Planet's revenue from online advertising totaled $98,000 during the same period. Nationwide Internet sales presently account for $500 million of the $17 billion U.S. wine industry. But alcohol regulators say that the proliferation of Internet wine and beer retailers has cost states millions of dollars in lost tax revenues. Some states have even filed lawsuits against the website operators to recoup the losses. Congress intervened in 1998 by passing the Internet Tax Freedom Act, which placed an embargo on sales taxes for Web purchases until at least 2001, while the issue is studied.

WORKFORCE

Some 117,300 people worked in liquor stores in 1996, a drop of four percent from the 122,000 in 1990. A more dramatic picture emerges in a comparison of December employment, traditionally the industry's busiest month. In December 1990 employment reached 127,400. Five years later employment was only 114,600—a decline of more than 11 percent. This drop reflected the steady falloff in the number of liquor retailers across the country. It also coincided with declining industry revenues. Concerns over workplace safety may have contributed to the declining workforce as well. The national homicide rate for liquor store employees is the highest for any industry in the country, except taxi drivers.

FURTHER READING

''Booze Flows Back Into Barrow, Alaska, After Yearlong Ban.'' *Wall Street Journal,* 15 November 1995.

Bueno, Jacqueline. ''Southeast Journal: Panel Is Expected to Present Rules on Alcohol Sales.'' *Wall Street Journal,* 10 May 1995.

Caruthers, Chrystal. ''$7 Million Debt Taps Out Beer Across America.'' *Chicago Daily Herald 1,* 2 July 1998.

''Congress Eyes Curbs on Online Wine Sales.'' *Atlanta J. & Atlanta Constitution,* 12 October 1999.

DiIulio, John J. Jr. ''Broken Bottles: Alcohol, Disorder, and Crime.'' *Brookings Review,* Spring 1996.

Dun's Census of American Business. New Jersey: Dun & Bradstreet, 1996.

Dun's Million Dollar Companies. New Jersey: Dun & Bradstreet, 1996.

''Empty Stores Still Dot the Riot-Torn Areas of L.A.'' *Wall Street Journal,* 22 May 1996.

Katz, Michael. ''Distillers Reverse Ban on Radio, TV Ads.'' *Broadcasting and Cable,* 11 November 1996.

''More Beer, Liquor Stores Found in Poor City Areas.'' *Syracuse Herald Journal,* 23 February 1995.

Quigley, Lori A., and G. Alan Marlatt. ''Drinking Among Young Adults: Prevalence, Patterns and Consequences.'' *Alcohol Health and Research World,* 1996.

Romano, Mike. ''A Brouhaha Over Beer Distribution in Colorado.'' *Restaurant Business,* 1 March 1996.

Sanderson, Bill. ''Lethal Lunatics: An Occupational Hazard.'' *N.Y. Post,* 30 July 1999.

Sebastian, Barbara. ''Business Bulletin: Special Trends in Business and Finance.'' *Wall Street Journal,* 19 October 1995.

Totty, Michael. ''Texas Journal: All For One: For the Legislature, It's the Season for Special Interests.'' *Wall Street Journal,* 24 May 1995.

U.S. Department of Commerce. ''Monthly Retail Sales.'' Various releases. *Current Business Report.* December 1996, and January 1967 to December 1985.

U.S. Bureau of the Census Web Site. Available from http://www.census.gov.

U.S. Department of Commerce Web Site. Available from http://www.doc.gov.

U.S. Department of Labor Web Site. Available from http://www.dol.gov.

U.S. Department of Labor. *Employment, Hours, and Earnings.* Washington, DC: GPO, 1996.

SIC 5932

USED MERCHANDISE STORES

This category includes establishments primarily engaged in the retail sale of used merchandise, antiques, and secondhand goods, such as clothing and shoes, furniture, books and rare manuscripts, musical instruments, office furniture, phonographs and phonograph records, and store fixtures and equipment. This industry also includes pawnshops. Dealers primarily engaged in selling used motor vehicles, trailers, and boats are classified in the Automotive Dealers and Gasoline Service Stations industries, and those selling used mobile homes are classified in **SIC 5271: Mobile Home Dealers.** Establishments primarily selling used automobile parts and accessories are classified in **SIC 5015: Motor Vehicle Parts, Used.** and scrap and waste dealers are classified in **SIC 5093: Scrap and Waste Materials.** Establishments primarily engaged in automotive repair are classified under Automotive Repair Shops industries.

NAICS CODE(S)

522298 (All Other Non-Depository Credit Intermediation)

INDUSTRY SNAPSHOT

The used merchandise business, a branch of the retail industry, boomed in the early 1990s, benefiting from the economic recession. According to *1997 Economic Census,* an estimated 17,990 used merchandise stores operated in 1996, employing 97,965 people. Once havens for bargain-hunting students, used merchandise stores now appeal to people from all walks of life. Between 1987 and 1995 retail grew 52 percent, while the resale industry grew 92 percent. One barometer of the rising popularity of such stores was recorded by *New York Times* reporter Felicity Barringer, who noted that young Washington, D.C. insiders no longer shunned used clothes. ''With the cost of dressing for success rising faster than the cost of housing, secondhand clothes are losing their stigma for a growing crowd of legislative aides, lobbyists, journalists, and consultants.'' Greta Bonaparte, owner of the Washington, D.C.,-based used clothing store A Man for All Seasons, told Barringer ''Attitudes have changed. There's no doubt about it. It's become a kind of in thing, the bargain of it.'' The mid-1990s brought with it a new style of dressing. The look, ''retro,'' was epitomized by music videos and rock stars dressing in fashions from the all ages of the twentieth century. Teenagers latched onto the retro look, and shopping at used clothing stores was one way to go in order to achieve it.

ORGANIZATION AND STRUCTURE

In the late 1990s, the vast majority of used merchandise businesses were privately owned and family run. The industry was attractive to small businessmen and women because of its relatively small capital investment and relatively high returns. Consumers liked used merchandise stores because they could realize 50 to 85 percent savings off the cost of new goods, yet the profit margin for the retailer was often higher than that realized with new goods. The cost of purchasing merchandise to sell in such operations was extremely low, and operators typically sold used products for double their cost. Used merchandise sellers buy their inventory from the public, offer goods on consignment, or receive goods for free—at very low cost—from charities. Both not-for-profit and for-profit used merchandise stores buy their inventory from charities that collected door-to-door for as little as $8 per three cubic feet of goods. ''Thanks to the low cost of goods, pretax profits are around ten percent, roughly double Wal-Mart's,'' wrote Lisa Gubernick in *Forbes.*

Women, especially, were attracted to the used merchandise business, particularly for clothing. Many owned and operated used merchandise stores out of their homes. *Nation's Business* reporter Sharon Nelton profiled two women who typified the kind of entrepreneur who is attracted to the used merchandise business. Karen Lynch, a former flight attendant, founded Children's Orchard in 1980. The store specialized in quality used children's clothing, which it sold for 50 to 80 percent less than new clothing. The store paid cash for its stock, which had to be clean and in mint condition. By 1996, Lynch's business had grown to include more than 70 franchises in nine states. Used apparel accounts for two-thirds of the sales and makes up 80 percent of the store,'s inventory.

At the other end of the scale was Judy Bradford, who operated I Do—I Do, a used bridal wear consignment store, out of her home. Consignees acted as agents for people wishing to sell used items, displaying used merchandise and splitting the price with the consignor after it had been sold—usually 50/50. The advantage of selling on consignment is that the risk of being left with immovable goods is virtually eliminated. The disadvantage is that consignment stores offer lower profit margins and little control over merchandise, at least where a store relies on donations and drop-offs.

Many used merchandise operations mixed their means of sale between resale, consignment, and initial sale. Bradford and Lynch offer new merchandise that compliments the shops' main lines. Offering new merchandise alongside used ''serves an important marketing purpose by upgrading the entire store's image, bringing in customers that might otherwise never go into a secondhand store,'' Gubernick commented. When people look at used clothing stores as their own, favorite ''specialty'' shop, it is wise to have a little of everything for sale. A new area of retail that was taking off was selling used office furniture. According to a 1999 article in the magazine *Office Systems*, the stigma of displaying used furniture had diminished because more business were decorating with a so-called retro look. In 1999, used furniture was a $1.2 billion segment of the $12 billion office furniture inustry. Sales of used furniture were projected to represent 25 percent of the industry in 2000, according to the article. This is especially good news for small to medium sized companies, which can't always afford brand new furniture.

An important, though declining, segment of the used merchandise industry was the pawn industry. Very popular during the Depression, pawn shops were sometimes the only way for people to get money for food and essentials. Pawnshops loan money on the security of a personal property. The item pawned is then offered for sale in the pawnshop. Unsold items may be redeemed by the pawner for the same price originally given by the pawnbroker. Pawnshops deal in all used merchandise, from household items to musical instruments to jewelry. Pawnshops were once quite common in economically depressed urban areas, where they acted as a sort of bank, ''lending'' money at grossly inflated rates. Though their shady reputation led to their decline, pawnshops were reportedly staging a minor comeback in the 1990s. In 1998 there were 13,000 to 15,000 pawnshops throughout the United States, compared with 6,800 when the National Pawnbrokers Association was founded in 1986. Pawnshops were still mostly found in large, urban areas.

Antique shops comprise another important segment of the used merchandise business. Antique shop owners act as dealers of old and often valuable furniture, ornaments, coins, rare manuscripts, etc. Sometimes the dealers pay outright for the used merchandise, but just as operated on consignment. The number of antique shops grew in the 1980s, mainly at the lower end of the market, with the rise of cottage industry style antique/junk shops.

Used merchandise stores generally have been marketed by appealing to working-class consumers in need of inexpensive merchandise or by positioning themselves as dealers in rare items prized for their investment value, as is true of antique shops. A third kind of marketing became evident in the 1990s: shops geared toward middle-class but price-conscious buyers. TVI, a company that ran ''thrift department stores,'' used television advertising to lure customers—an unusual tack for thrift stores.

CURRENT CONDITIONS

Used merchandise stores were doing a brisk business in the 1990s as more and more middle-class consumers who were short of disposable income and looking to save a buck turned to resale goods.

More than half the customers at Washington, D.C.-area Goodwill stores earned between $25,600 and $51,200 annually, more than 60 percent had full-time jobs and were women between 22 and 45, according to a 1996 survey by the industry leading Goodwill Industries. More than 62 million people shopped at Goodwill stores each year. In 1996 some Goodwill stores opened ''computer shops'' in the backs of larger stores, a move estimated to draw in even more customers.

Joan Schindel, owner of a Virginia Play It Again Sam, said the store's typical customer is a professional or middle class family with children. A used sporting goods store, Play It Again Sam sells merchandise for at least half what it would cost new. ''Because there isn't unbounded optimism in the future, people are more aware of the choices they make,'' Schindel added. Even people who could afford to buy new products shopped in used merchandise stores for the thrill of finding a bargain or because their children quickly wore out or grew out of their clothes.

Throughout the 1990s, the used merchandise industry also benefited from increased environmental consciousness. ''People are more conscious in the '90s of recycling and not wasting,'' Amy Helgren, co-owner of a Chicago children's resale shop told *Newsweek* in 1992. Karen Lynch, owner of Children's Orchard boutiques, noted, ''We see the resale business as recycling at its very best.''

Because of this and other factors, the number of for-profit resale shops increased an estimated 10 to 15 percent each year during the early to mid-1990s, according to the National Association of Resale and Thrift Stores. There were more than 65,000 used merchandise stores in 1996, up from 55,068 in 1992. The greatest number of shops in the 1990s specialized in women's clothes, followed by children's clothes, bridal wear, and men's wear.

Dun's Census of American Business, which categorized used merchandise stores according to sales volume, reported that approximately 87 percent of the stores surveyed had less than $250,000 in annual sales. In 1993, 26,955 stores (45 percent) reported annual sales between $100,000 and $249,000; 13,799 (23 percent), less than $50,000; and 11,574 (19 percent), between $50,000 and $99,000. A very small proportion showed higher sales volume: 3,613 stores (6 percent) had sales between $250,000 and $499,000; 1,912 (3 percent), between $500,000 and $999,000; 1,248 (2 percent), between $1 and $5 million; and 131 (0.2 percent), more than $5 million.

INDUSTRY LEADERS

The used merchandise industry was dominated by Goodwill Industries International, Inc. a private, not-for-profit company based in Bethesda, Maryland. It operated a chain of secondhand stores and provided vocational training for young people. Founded in 1902, the company employed 60,000 people and generated more that $1 billion in revenues in 1998. One of its closest competitors was Cash America International, Inc. a public, stand-alone pawnshop chain based in Fort Worth, Texas. It employed 3,035 people and earned $342 million in 1998. Another major player was the franchise Grow Biz , based in Minneapolis, Minnesota. Besides selling clothing, the company sold used sports equipment, musical instruments and tools. In 1998, merchandise made up 76 percent of its total revenue at $73.3 million dollars.

WORKFORCE

Nearly 90 percent of used merchandise stores in 1995 employed fewer than five people. According to *Employment and Wages Annual Averages 1996,* 106,177 people were employed in the industry in 1996, an increase of 6,156 from 1995. The average weekly wage was $283 in 1996. The U.S. Department of Labor reported that non-supervisory-worker average hourly wages were $7.13 in 1995.

FURTHER READING

Alexander, Karen. ''What's Old is New Again.'' *Office Systems,* January 1999.

Barringer, Felicity. ''The Dress for Success a Second Time Around.'' *The New York Times,* 11 January 1990.

Buck, Genevieve. ''More Credence Lent as Pawnshops Grow.'' *Chicago Tribune,* 18 July 1998.

Darnton, Nina. ''I Can Get It for You Resale: Secondhand Shopping Is Chic as Well as Thrifty.'' *Newsweek,* 3 June 1991.

U.S. Department of Labor. *Employment and Wages Annual Averages 1996.* Washington, DC: GPO, 1996.

Gubernick, Lisa. ''Secondhand Chic.'' *Forbes,* 26 April 1993.

Hoover's Company Capsules. Hoover's Inc., 1999. Available from http://hoovers.com.

National Association of Resale and Thrift Shops. Available from http://www.narts.org.

Nelton, Sharon. ''Where Frugality Is Fashionable.'' *Nation's Business,* April 1992.

Stoughton, Stephanie, and Sarah Schafer. ''Used Clothing as Gift Gains Trend Status.'' *Fort Worth Star Telegram,* 17 December 1998.

Goodwill Industries Inc. *Goodwill Industries Information.* Available from http://www.goodwill.com.

SIC 5941

SPORTING GOODS STORES AND BICYCLE SHOPS

This category consists of establishments primarily engaged in the retail sale of sporting goods, sporting equipment, and bicycles, bicycle parts, and accessories. Retail establishments primarily engaged in selling motorized bicycles are classified in **SIC 5571: Motorcycle Dealers.** Those engaged in the retail sale of athletic footwear are classified in **SIC 5661: Shoe Stores.** Establishments primarily engaged in repairing bicycles are classified in Services, **SIC 7699: Repair Shops and Related Services, Not Elsewhere Classified,** while those renting bicycles are classified in **SIC 7999: Amusement and Recreation Services, Not Elsewhere Classified.**

For information on the industry that produces durable goods for athletic competition, exercise and recreation, see **SIC 3949: Sporting Goods Equipment.**

NAICS CODE(S)

451110 (Sporting Goods Stores)

INDUSTRY SNAPSHOT

The advent of e-commerce via the Internet transformed the sporting goods industry, as it did with other retail industries. The revolution, however, had only just begun by the turn of the twenty-first century. In an April 1999 National Sporting Goods Association *NSGA Retail Focus Magazine* article, both Tim Harrington, CEO of Fogdog Sports, and Jim Medalia, CEO of justballs!, pointed out that immediate profitability was not the goal of e-commerce. Harrington stressed that web retailers should analyze ''market size, long-term profitability, barriers to entry and points of differentiation,'' while Medalia admitted that his e-commerce business was not yet profitable, but ''It *shouldn't* be profitable at this stage.'' Medalia stressed the importance of analyzing costs versus potential income.

The potential profitability of e-commerce in the sporting goods industry was staggering. Sales of sporting goods in 1998 over the World Wide Web amounted to approximately $56 million, according to Forrester Research, but projections called for 1999 e-commerce sales to triple in this category, reaching an estimated $137 million. Industry analysts expected Internet sales to snowball to $1.9 billion by the year 2003. One indication of the infancy of e-commerce in this industry was the fact that the market leader, the Sports Authority, Inc., of Fort Lauderdale, Florida, didn't establish its presence on the Web until November 1999.

ORGANIZATION AND STRUCTURE

The types of firms listed in this classification include department and discount stores, franchise chains, specialty shops (bicycles and athletic equipment), mail-order businesses, and e-commerce businesses.

A 1996 survey conducted by Kurt Salmon Associates determined that 56 percent of the consumers polled in the United States preferred to shop at sporting goods chains. E-commerce, however, transformed this profile. A September 1999 buy TRACK study, commissioned by SBR Net, revealed that active participants in sports such as in-line skating, golfing, and fishing were more likely to purchase sports equipment online than less active participants in these sports. Brick-and-mortar stores retained their appeal for certain types of purchases, though, especially those requiring fitting, such as apparel and footwear sales.

Bicycles are sold in department stores, specialty bike shops, and discount, variety, and hardware stores. The typical American bicycle shop served a customer base of approximately 9,000 persons. Approximately 40 percent of the bicycle shops in the nation were single proprietorships and were primarily ''home-owned'' facilities. A small percentage of bike shops were business partnerships. Only about 25 percent of U.S. bike shops were as large as corporations in terms of average sales, according to the U.S. Department of Commerce industry profile.

Bicycle shops stocked four major classifications of bicycles: single-speed cruiser bicycles (the average price was $100-$250); contemporary utility bicycles ($100-$300); lightweight 10- to 18-speed bicycles (from $300 to more than $2,000); and specialty bicycles, such as mountain bikes, sports models, touring bicycles, folding bicycles, and all-terrain bicycles ($300-$3,000).

BACKGROUND AND DEVELOPMENT

The fitness craze of the 1980s led to an increased demand for sporting goods and bicycles in the early 1990s. By 1996 there were more than 23,000 sporting goods stores and bicycle shops serving the nation. Retail sales of sporting goods more than doubled from $7.49 billion in 1983 to $17.3 billion in 1996. The 1996 sales figure represented a 4.8 percent increase from the industry's 1995 sales of $16.5 billion. While adults between the ages of 25 and 44 constituted the mainstay of purchasers, industry leaders recognized a need to focus their marketing strategies on the inclusion of both younger as well as older consumer groups.

As the fitness industry sparked consumer appeal for exercise equipment, accessories, and athletic wear, trends gradually shifted from sporting goods stores, which were typically sole proprietorships and small ''pro shops,'' to franchises and eventually sporting goods chains. Bicycle shops even began changing their names to ''bicycling and fitness'' shops and expanded their product mixes to include exercise bicycles, treadmills, climbers, and weight machines to capitalize on the craze. These types of stores appealed to a growing number of consumers who were exercising in their own home gyms.

Consumers started turning to discount chains and stores because they knew what equipment to purchase. According to an East Coast buyer in *Discount Merchandiser,* in the early days of the fitness craze, customers felt the need to talk to experts before making a major purchase. As consumers used more types of exercise equipment and became more knowledgeable about fitness, however, they became much more familiar with the type of equipment they needed. Consequently, store managers were changing their store displays to enable customers to ''test drive'' a product before taking it home. Such ''hands-on'' displays often proved helpful in alleviating customers' anxiety about assembly. Seeing the assembled product in the store could convince them that it was easy to set up at home.

According to *Chain Store Age,* the fitness craze leveled off in the late 1980s. Traditional recreational activities such as golf, team sports, fishing, and camping all made comebacks in the 1980s, though retail sales in these categories slowed by approximately 4 percent in 1987. Camping was pinpointed as the strongest growth category in sporting goods sales in 1987, experiencing a 15.5 percent increase in sales that year. Fishing was the second-highest growth category during 1987 according to *Chain Store Age.*

Sales of American-made bicycles also remained relatively flat in the late 1980s. This was due in part to delivery delays that kept popular models out of shops, according to Ken Howard in *Sport Style* magazine. The European mountain-bike boom drained American supplies and left many dealers in the United States with unfilled orders. All in all, bicycle shops reported spotty sales on some popular bikes in 1990. East Coast bicycle shop dealers reported flat sales in 1990, but their counterparts on the West Coast reported an 8 percent sales increase.

Firearms, ranging from handguns to hunting rifles to assault weapons, had long been available from sporting goods stores with virtually no guidelines. In 1993 and 1994, however, that changed. The Brady Bill, a piece of legislation championed by the Clinton administration that mandated a five-day waiting period before purchasing a gun, was ratified into law over the objections of the National Rifle Association and others. A ban on the manufacture and sale of 19 types of assault weapons also passed in May 1994. MCI Communications Corp. developed an automated system that enabled the registration approval process to be completed within the mandatory 10-day waiting period. The former, and less expedient, postal process required up to 20 days for completion.

The early 1990s were prosperous for privately owned Herman's Sporting Goods Inc. as they posted $570 million in yearly sales. The effective marketing strategy by Sports Authority, of providing the consumer with a wide selection of in-stock merchandise and low prices, however, reduced Herman's sales by more than $230 million. This paralyzing situation caused the 117-store, octogenarian chain to file for Chapter 11 protection in April 1996.

CURRENT CONDITIONS

Exercise, golf, and hunting represented the strongest segments of the sporting goods industry, though sales in all three categories dipped down slightly in 1998 as compared to 1997, though rebounds were projected in all three categories for 1999. Sales of golf equipment fell from $3.70 billion in 1997 to $3.64 billion in 1998 before rebounding to projected 1999 sales of $3.71 billion; sales of exercise equipment dropped from $2.97 billion in 1997 to $2.85 billion in 1998, but sales were projected to increase to $3.08 billion in 1999; similarly, sales of firearms and hunting equipment fell from $2.56 billion in 1997 to $2.20 billion in 1998, and then regained ground to a projected $2.31 billion in 1999.

October sales for the market leader Sports Authority dropped 5.2 percent, from $119 million in October 1998 to $106.2 million for the same period in 1999. The retailer attributed 1 percent of this slide to its decision to limit its assortment of hunting rifles and suspend its handgun sales altogether. Although these decisions affected the retailer negatively in the short term, long-term gains could compensate, as consumers tended to look favorably on socially responsible decisions by companies.

Rapid sales gains of in-line skates and equipment in the early 1990s reflected the U.S. consumers' urge to become part of the vastly popular West Coast sport. In-line skate sales increased 200 percent from 1990 to 1991. In-line equipment sales escalated to an estimated $742 million in 1995, reflecting a 50 percent increase from 1994. This trend reversed, however, in the late 1990s, as sales of in-line skates fell to $561.7 million in 1997 and continued to plummet to $514.6 million in 1998. National Sporting Goods Association projections placed 1999 sales at $504.3 million in 1999.

In terms of bicycles, imports were projected to increase by 8 percent to meet an ever-growing U.S. demand for foreign mountain-bike brands. Baby boomers, now the parents of the current baby boom, would be more likely to purchase bicycles for their children during the next five years. The use of bicycles as an alternative to pollution-causing automobiles was also expected to increase demand for the product.

Industry Leaders

Sports Authority, with 1998 sales of $1.6 billion, clearly controlled the sporting goods market. It operated 196 stores in 32 states across the United States, plus five in Canada. The Sports Authority also licensed Mega Sports Co., Inc. to operate 17 more store in Japan, which accounted for $7.6 million of 1998 sales. The Sports Authority's $870 million in sales in 1996 easily outdistanced their nearest competitor by more than $300 million. This 1994 brainchild of Kmart, the Sports Authority's venture into the Northeast proved to be a primary factor in the demise of Herman's Sporting Goods.

Other leaders in this vastly overcrowded industry included Sports and Recreation Inc., Recreational Equipment Inc., Oshman's Sporting Goods Inc., Bass Pro LP, Sports Town Inc., Dunham's Athleisure Corp., and Sport Chalet Inc. By the mid-1990s, the industry had 24,500 establishments dealing in the retail sporting goods trade. More than 15,000 of these businesses employed fewer than 5 individuals, and only 47 employed more than 100.

Workforce

Smaller sporting goods stores usually employed a small staff (one to two people), whereas medium-sized firms had staffs of up to 10 employees. Staffs at medium-sized sporting goods shops increased by 7 percent annually from 1972 until 1979, and by about 4 percent from 1979 until 1986. The U.S. Department of Labor projected an annual increase in employment of about 3 percent at these firms from 1986 through the year 2000. The 10 most successful industry giants (based on yearly sales) accounted for 90 percent of the industry's workforce. In the mid-1990s, 157,000 individuals were employed in this industry.

America and the World

In *Discount Merchandiser,* SGMA president John Riddle noted that the industry had several growth markets: Canada, Germany, Japan, and France. Demand for American bicycles was also increasing in Argentina, Hong Kong, and Venezuela, where U.S. exports increased by 263 percent, 125 percent, and 114 percent respectively in 1992. The approval of the North American Free Trade Agreement also expanded trade in Mexico and Canada and could contribute to increased sales in this category.

Meanwhile, bike manufacturers—such as Schwinn—were revived and remained competitive with foreign companies on American turf. Schwinn, which was once the most popular bicycle brand sold in the United States, went bankrupt in 1989. By the early 1990s, however, Schwinn was getting back into the market by heavily marketing its popular mountain bikes. Other manufacturers, such as Cannondale, were trying to break into foreign markets. This Connecticut-based company specialized in high-performance mountain and racing bikes. Cannondale had success selling American-made bicycles in Japan by working directly with bicycle shop dealers. Capitalizing on the tremendous popularity of mountain bikes and sport utility vehicles, several bike companies and automotive manufacturers were teaming up to provide a new line of off-road bikes that they hoped would appeal to the adventurous. Such ''partnerships'' included: Chrysler's Jeep/Ross Bicycles, Subaru/Specialized Bicycles, Volkswagen/Trek, Volvo/Cannondale, Mercedes/AMP, and Toyota/Schwinn.

Research and Technology

Today's sporting goods are more streamlined and are made with lightweight, but durable, metals and plastics. Developments in materials manufacturing made these sleek and colorful designs possible. Technological advances also gave rise to all-terrain bicycles, mountain bikes, high-tech athletic shoes, all-in-one weight machines, aerobic stair steppers, and computerized treadmills, stair climbers, and stationary bicycles. Similarly, sporting goods retailers were using sophisticated multimedia techniques to enhance store environments and make sports involvement more appealing to men, women, and children.

FURTHER READING

"Another Retailer Bites the Dust." *Editor & Publisher, the Fourth Estate,* 25 May 1996.

"Brand Loyalty Rules Sporting Goods Market." *Stores,* April 1996.

Darnay, Arsen J., and Gary Alampi, eds. *Wholesale and Retail Trade USA.* Detroit: Gale Research, 1995.

"eData." Available from http://www.esports-report.com.

Epstein, Joseph. "Sports Authority: Home Run." *Financial World,* 16 September 1996.

"Gun Dealers Get a Shot in the Arm." *Computerworld,* 20 January 1997.

Harris, Kelley. "Three's a Charm for Internet Panel." *NSGA Retail Focus Magazine,* April 1999. Available from http://www.nsga.org.

"In-Line Skate Retailers Hit First Bump in the Road." *Stores,* July 1996.

National Sporting Goods Association. "Consumer Purchases." Available from http://www.nsga.org.

"The Sale of the Year: Great Retail Stocks." *Money,* January 1996.

Sporting Authority. "The Sports Authority Announces October Sales." 4 November 1999. Available from http://www.sportingauthority.com.

"Subaru Outbacks onto Slopes, Trails." *Brandweek,* 7 October 1996.

Ward's Business Directory of Private and Public Companies. Detroit: Gale Research, 1997.

SIC 5942

BOOK STORES

This category includes establishments primarily engaged in the retail sale of new books and magazines. Establishments primarily engaged in the retail sale of used books are classified in **SIC 5932: Used Merchandise Stores.**

NAICS CODE(S)

451211 (Book Stores)

INDUSTRY SNAPSHOT

For the first half of fiscal 2000 (January through June 1999), sales at the four largest bookstore chains were up about 10 percent. The four largest chains in the United States were Barnes & Noble, Borders Group, Books-A-Million, and Crown Books. Total sales for the industry from January through June 1999 was $6.2 billion, up 3.9 percent from 1998 sales of $6 billion. The big four accounted for $14.9 billion—24 percent—of the industry's sales. For the first nine months of 1999, sales rose 2.8 percent industry-wide, compared to a sales increase of 8.8 percent for the entire retail industry.

ORGANIZATION AND STRUCTURE

The retail bookstore industry was dominated by several large Chains, including Borders Group, Inc.; Barnes & Noble, Inc.; and Crown Books Corporation. The rest of the market was shared by about 10,000 independent bookstores. Chain stores, many of which opened during the 1970s, were generally located in shopping malls and usually carried between 15,000 and 20,000 of the most popular titles targeted for a broad consumer market. Independent bookstores often carried a greater variety of titles, between 30,000 and 40,000 per store. With 900,000 books in print, independent bookstores often specialized, offering a wider variety of titles than the chain stores for niche markets such as religion, science and technology, hobbies, or children's books.

In the 1990s, chain store operators began opening dozens of "superstores." These large freestanding bookstores carried between 50,000 and 150,000 titles, offered substantial discounts, and provided a variety of customer amenities such as reading rooms and coffee bars. Superstores prompted speculation that independent booksellers would be driven out of business. However, other industry analysts noted that there were similar dire predictions in the 1970s during the rapid growth of mall-based chain stores. While chain stores did siphon business from the independent bookstores, they also greatly expanded the total market. In fact, market research showed that the presence of a superstore increased the local market for books by 50 to 60 percent.

Another type of bookstore also began appearing in the early 1990s. These were multimedia stores that carried books, audiotapes, videotapes, and computer programs. While other bookstores had sections devoted to electronic information media, multimedia stores mixed different media by category rather than by format, placing the printed works of Shakespeare alongside videocassettes of his plays. WGBH Learningsmith stores in Massachusetts were leaders in the area of multimedia bookstores. The company licensed the use of "WGBH" from the award-winning public television station in Boston.

Virtual bookstores also gained popularity in the mid-1990s, thanks to the possibility of online commerce offered by the Internet and World Wide Web. Of these, Amazon.com was by far the most popular and most successful, offering more than 1 million titles.

BACKGROUND AND DEVELOPMENT

The first bookstores appeared in the American colonies as early as 1640, with Boston becoming a pre-Revolutionary War center for both book selling and publishing. By the time Benjamin Harris, who published the first newspaper in the colonies, opened a bookstore in 1686, there were already seven other booksellers in Boston. By 1700, there were as many as 30 book sellers in the town, which then had a population of about 10,000. Although a fire swept through the bookseller district in 1711, destroying all the bookstores but one, within a few years there were more bookstores in Boston than ever before.

In addition to importing books from England, most early booksellers were also publishers. For example, Hezekiah Usher, who may have opened the first bookstore in Boston in 1642, published *Spiritual Milk for Boston Babes in Either England,* the famous catechism by Puritan minister John Cotton, in 1656. Bookseller and newspaper editor Benjamin Harris published the first edition of the *New England Primer.* In fact, book selling as a profession independent of publishing did not begin to emerge until about 1800.

Early bookstores were also more like variety stores than bookstores in the modern sense. For example, Andrew Bradford offered his customers merchandise ranging from feathers to pickled sturgeon. Thomas Fleet, a publisher of children's books in Boston, sold slaves from his bookstore. Moreover, colonial bookstores often carried a remarkable variety of books. In 1766, Boston shop owner John Mein published a catalogue listing more than 1,700 titles. Religion and philosophy dominated the early book trade. The widespread availability of books by John Locke and other philosophers who wrote about natural rights helped set the stage for the American Revolution and booksellers were often among the intellectual leaders of the colonies. However, novels were also popular, including many with highly suggestive titles such as *Married Libertine* and *Suspicious Lovers. Memoirs of a Woman of Pleasure,* originally published in England in 1748 and better known as *Fanny Hill,* also was available in many bookstores.

The first post-Revolutionary War advancement in book selling came in the 1840s, when an American, Richard Hoe, invented the rotary press. The first Hoe presses were able to print 8,000 sheets an hour, which was later increased to 20,000. This technology made possible a mass market for books. It also hastened the differentiation between publisher and bookseller and greatly increased competition. The technology also led to the creation of the paperback industry. The first paperbacks were pirated reprints of English novels printed as supplements to newspapers. Eventually they were sold as separate publications.

Bookstores flourished between 1845 and the beginning of the Civil War. However, book selling began to change dramatically about the time the war ended. In the late 1860s, most large publishers were operating their own bookstores in competition with independent booksellers. In addition, publishers began offering volume discounts to large dry goods stores that opened up book departments. Volume discounts eventually cut bookstores out of the textbook trade altogether and would remain an issue of contention between publishers and bookstores up until the present time, especially with the development of chain stores in the 1970s.

Perhaps even more significantly, in the years following the Civil War publishers' agents began crossing the country selling books door-to-door by subscription, taking prepublication orders for delivery direct to the customers. Publishers often sold books direct for less than they sold them to bookstores and even offered to pay for postage. In 1872, *Publishers Weekly* warned that "The retail book trade cannot live against the competition of manufacturers and either the competition or the retailers must cease to be." John Wanamaker, whose legendary Philadelphia department store was able to undercut bookstores, flatly declared "book selling is a decaying business."

Book Sellers vs. Publishers. The first attempt to organize American booksellers occurred in 1802, when 50 publishers and booksellers met in Philadelphia to form the American Company of Booksellers; that association lasted only four years. In 1872, publishers and booksellers again got together and formed the American Book Trade Association (ABTA). This time they agreed to limit wholesale discounts to no more than 20 percent. However, the public viewed the ABTA as a cartel organized to keep prices high, and newspapers attacked the plan vehemently. Many publishers also failed to live up to the agreement, and the ABTA only lasted five years. In 1890, the publishers formed their own association aimed at forcing bookstores to sell books at a retail price set by the publisher. The publishers agreed that they would continue offering discounts, but they also agreed to blackball stores that violated the "net price" system.

In 1900, six booksellers announced plans to form the American Booksellers Association (ABA) to lobby on behalf of bookstores. The ABA, which held its first convention in 1901, endorsed the publishers' net price system wholeheartedly, since it would eliminate price-cutting by department stores and so-called "book butchers," who bought quantities of discontinued or surplus books and sold them at a fraction of what other bookstores charged. However, in 1890, Congress also passed the Sherman Antitrust Act, designed to prevent unfair restraint of trade. In 1902, Macy's Department Store in New York filed suit under the Sherman Antitrust

Act against the American Publishers Association and the American Booksellers Association. Eleven years later, in 1913, the U.S. Supreme Court declared the publishers' actions illegal and let stand $140,000 in damages awarded to Macy's by a lower court.

A near heroic figure in the case, from the department store's perspective, was Miss E. L. Kinnear. Kinnear was Macy's book buyer who managed to keep the store's book department stocked while the suit was heard, despite being blacklisted by the publishers. She used surrogates as far west as Denver to buy books and secretly ship them to Macy's. Macy's would continue to be a thorn in the side of New York book sellers, according to a *Publishers Weekly* retrospective: "During the '30s, the great crusade of the retailers was against price-cutting. The department stores were the chief discounters and books were high on the list of loss leaders. Macy's especially was the hated enemy."

The American Publishers Association disbanded in 1914, following the Supreme Court decision. However, the ABA survived and remained concerned with price stability. *Publishers Weekly* noted that while the Supreme Court made it clear that the publishers had acted illegally, the case also made clear "that unwarranted 'cut prices' are a stupendous merchandizing blunder, if not immoral or illegal." For a while, fair trade laws passed by several states in the early twentieth century allowed manufacturers to established minimum retail prices on trademarked products, achieving the same results the publishers had wanted. The Miller-Tydings Act, passed in 1937, legitimized these state laws by setting aside federal antitrust laws. However, the consumer interest groups eventually won out and most of the fair trade laws were repealed between 1950 and 1970. Congress eliminated the last of them in 1975.

Book Clubs. The first book clubs were formed in the 1920s and immediately became the target of opposition from retail bookstores. The Literary Guild and the Book-of-the-Month Club were both denounced at the ABA's convention in 1927. By the 1940s, book clubs had become such a concern that the ABA complained to the Federal Trade Commission (FTC) about violations of fair trade laws then in effect. The ABA also complained that publishers were leasing printing plates to the book clubs for low-cost reprints of popular books, but refusing the same privilege to members of the ABA. In 1951, the FTC charged several publishing houses with unfair trade practices. The most significant outcome of the case was that publishers were not allowed to require bookstores to adhere to minimum retail prices if book clubs were not bound by the same requirement.

During the 1980s, book club sales did not keep pace with the burgeoning retail bookstore industry. While total book sales grew about 8 percent per year in the 1980s, and retail bookstores nearly doubled, book club sales grew about half as fast. With the increase in bookstore competition, readers often received discounts equal to or greater than the discounts offered by book clubs and did not have to wait for delivery.

By the early 1990s, book club sales were decreasing, and clubs were beginning to change their marketing tactics to emulate successful mail-order clothing outlets. This included greater market segmentation and direct-mail advertising, deeper discounts, and faster service through 24-hour telephone ordering. The Literary Guild was experimenting with a "900" telephone number. Callers to the 24-hour Home Previewline could listen to one or several recordings by popular authors who either discussed their works or read selections. Callers could then order the books they wanted.

Perhaps the most significant change was that many book clubs were abandoning negative-option selling, in which members would receive monthly club selections unless they mailed in an order card saying no. In 1993, *The Wall Street Journal* reported that the Book-of-the-Month Club planned to begin a new club drawn from millions of former members who quit because of the negative option. More than half of all Book-of-the-Month Club members quit every year.

Chain Stores. The Walden Book Co., which had operated rental libraries, opened its first retail bookstore in Pittsburgh in 1962. Four years later, the Dayton Hudson Corp., a department store conglomerate, opened the first B. Dalton Bookseller store in suburban Minneapolis, in the nation's first multi-level enclosed shopping mall. Waldenbooks and B. Dalton Bookseller, which became the two largest bookstore chains in the United States, transformed the book selling industry. Prior to Waldenbooks and B. Dalton Bookseller, bookstores tended to be small, crowded, and situated in out-of-the-way locations. Waldenbooks and B. Dalton Bookseller bookstores positioned themselves in high-traffic malls and created colorful displays that invited the general public to browse. John Pope, then advertising director for B. Dalton, told *Saturday Review* in 1979, "What we've done is taken the awesomeness out of the book-buying experience." John Dessauer, author of the annual *Book Industry Trends,* was less complimentary, especially about the selection of titles: "I think of the chains as doing for reading what the fast-food operations have done for eating. You can preach to the chain stores about cultural obligations, but with their economics, they really can't afford to mess with pate de foie gras."

The chain stores, led by Waldenbooks and B. Dalton with hundreds of outlets each, were so successful that by the early 1970s, some industry analysts were predicting the end of independent bookstores. They also predicted that the chain stores would have a harmful effect on publishing. Victor Navasky, writing in the *New York Times Book Review,* warned that volume-buying chain stores would force publishers to abandon books of limited appeal and focus solely on mass-market best sellers.

ABA executive director G. Roysce Smith countered such complaints in *Publishers Weekly,* arguing that as long as there were readers for books, somebody would publish them and some bookstore would sell them. The literary, social, or political value of a book would determine its success, he claimed, not the chain stores. Although many independent bookstores closed during the 1970s, often due to chain store competition, Smith also noted that the total market for books was expanding. So even while the market share for chain stores was increasing, there was still a growing market for independent bookstores. Book sections in department stores, especially those located in malls with chain-owned bookstores, suffered more than independent bookstores.

The same fears reappeared in the late 1970s with the growth of discount stores. Crown Books, founded in 1977, was one of the first and most aggressive discounters, selling best sellers for as much as 40 percent off the publisher's suggested retail price. ''How to deal with a discounter'' was a popular topic at ABA conferences in the 1980s. But by 1988 even discounters were seen as good for business, as the ABA acknowledged the value that competition brought to the bookseller industry. In the organization's report for the Bowker Annual, Allan Marshall, then director of professional development and education, wrote that ''sellers of books at retail are enjoying an increasing market share as more and more people are either returning to or discovering for the first time the joys of shopping in bookstores, having originally been introduced to the concept of book ownership through book clubs, direct mail, or discounters.''

Censorship. Bookstores were often at the center of controversy regarding censorship, obscenity laws, and the First Amendment guarantee of free speech, which to booksellers also meant the right of adults to read uncensored material. Periodically, especially in the 1920s, 1950s, and 1970s, police departments raided bookstores, arresting clerks and store owners and confiscating books they felt violated obscenity laws or were otherwise bad for the community, including books about religion and politics. Community organizations also tried to force bookstores to quit selling books or magazines they found objectionable through boycotts, picketing, and occasional violence.

The first federal obscenity law was the Tariff Act of 1842, which made it illegal to bring ''indecent and obscene'' material into the country. The Comstock Law, passed in 1873, made it illegal to use the U.S. Post Office to distribute obscene materials, along with information about birth control and abortion. In 1957, the Supreme Court ruled that the First Amendment does not protect pornographic material. In 1964, the Supreme Court specifically ruled that Henry Miller's *Tropic of Cancer,* written in 1934 and perhaps the most censored book in American history, was not obscene. In *Miller v. California* in 1973, the Supreme Court ruled that whether something was obscene depended on ''local community standards.''

The first official notice the ABA took of censorship was conciliatory. Despite the politically motivated book raids of the 1920s, which resulted in the arrest of many booksellers, in 1923 the ABA passed a resolution deploring the sale of ''unclean'' books. In 1925, the ABA issued a statement opposing publication and distribution of ''salacious'' books. The ABA sponsored a discussion on censorship at its convention in 1930, but did not change its official position opposing publication, and therefore approving censorship, of ''obscene'' books.

In the 1950s, however, there was another rash of book bannings inspired by the investigations of the House Committee on Un-American Activities, and the anticommunist crusade led by Senator Joseph R. McCarthy. Libraries and bookstores were forced to remove books such as John Steinbeck's classic *The Grapes of Wrath,* which was seen as a communist polemic.

The Supreme Court's ''local community standards'' ruling in 1973 set off another round of police raids and prosecutions for selling obscene books. At its convention that year, the ABA protested the ruling and issued a statement in support of the President's Commission on Obscenity and Pornography, which in 1970 had recommended the repeal of laws restricting the sale of obscene or pornographic materials to adults. In 1973, the ABA also helped form the Media Coalition, an organization of publishers, booksellers, and motion picture producers that circulated information on censorship laws and activities. In *Bookselling in America and the World,* Chandler B. Grannis wrote that joining the Media Coalition marked the ABA's full commitment against censorship.

In the 1980s and early 1990s, the ABA became more proactive in its opposition to censorship. Beginning in the early 1980s, the ABA co-sponsored an annual Banned Books Week to draw attention to the many books that different groups were trying to ban or remove from library shelves. The group also filed suit against ''minor's access'' laws that would force bookstores to remove books from shelves or store displays. Through the Media Coalition, the ABA opposed efforts to declare pornography a form of sexual discrimination.

In 1986, the ABA publicly opposed the nomination of Robert Bork to the Supreme Court because it believed his views on the First Amendment would be detrimental to bookselling. Ironically, some bookstores were accused of engaging in censorship themselves for refusing to stock *The Tempting of America,* written by Bork.

In 1989, when Iran's Ayatollah Ruhollah Khomeini called for the assassination of author Salman Rushdie, several bookstores, including Waldenbooks, B. Dalton Bookseller, and Barnes & Noble, pulled copies of his controversial book, *The Satanic Verses,* from their shelves. However, other bookstores used the incident to call attention to the ongoing struggle against censorship by promoting the book and the ABA took out ads protesting Iran's attempt at intimidation. The chain stores reversed their policies within a few days, in part because of a consumer demand for the book. Two bookstores in the United States were firebombed apparently because of the book, but there were no injuries.

In 1990, the ABA took out full-page ads in major newspapers nationwide to protest censorship of all forms, from the banning of *Little Red Riding Hood* by a California school system because it was deemed too violent to anti-pornography groups that were trying to force bookstores to stop selling Playboy magazine.

CURRENT CONDITIONS

In the mid-1990s, superstores continued to dominate the market, with Borders Group, Inc. the undisputed leader. The market is changing, however, with a new form of competitor rapidly gaining market share—the online bookstore.

Of these, Amazon.com claims to be not only the largest online bookstore, but the ''Earth's biggest bookstore.'' The company offered 2.5 million titles in its Web-based store in early 1997. With infinite shelf space and no retail rent, overhead can remain low resulting in lower prices to consumers. Conceived by former hedge-fund manager, Jeff Bezos, Amazon.com offers online chats with authors and reader reviews in addition to its superb list of titles. A new service—MatchMaker—was announced in early 1997. Using sophisticated collaborative filtering technology the service will recommend books that customers are likely to enjoy. The Amazon.com model of ''sell-source-ship'' means little inventory to buy or track and no returns to publishers. Instead the company orders products after receiving customer orders.

The surge in online sales forced drastic changes in the industry. In 1996, Encyclopedia Britannica has turned to direct mail, television advertising, and its own Web site. In turn, the company completely eliminated its sales force of 550 people. In November 1998 Barnes & Noble acquired Ingram Book Group, a major book distributor, to better serve its online customers. This only exasperated

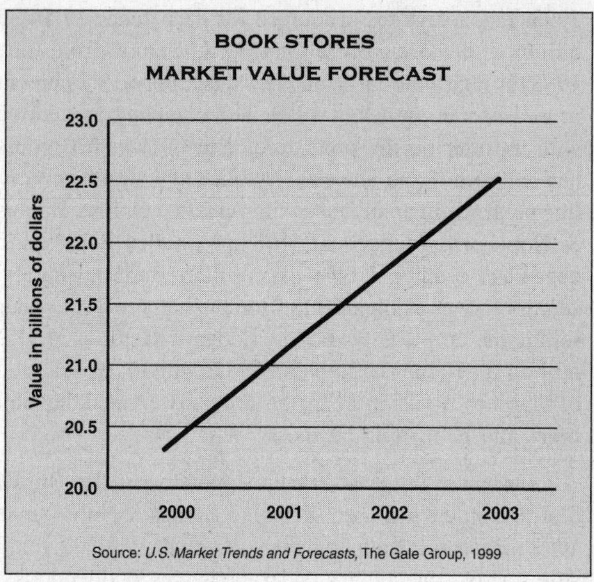

independent booksellers who are fearful that already large chains are getting better deals from publishers and distributors than the smaller stores. In March 1998, the ABA and 26 independent booksellers filed suit against Barnes & Noble and Borders saying the chains receive favorable terms and secret discounts not available to all in the industry. The trial was set for 2001.

Independent booksellers are fighting the encroachment of superstore chains and online services. A group of independent booksellers in California protested to the state government in December 1999 that the online services should be collecting sales tax. Not charging sales tax gives the online seller an advantage over brick and mortar stores. The group says the law states tax can be collected if the company has a physical presence in the state. They argue that Borders and Barnes & Noble both have stores in California and that Amazon.com has affiliate programs with companies in the state.

Some independent booksellers are turning to the Internet to supplement their sales. Some find it challenging because it's hard to get up and running and some don't have the staff to maintain a site. Online sales accounted for only 3 percent of book sales in 1998, but it is expected to increase from $630 million in 1998 to $3 billion in 2003. Some smaller bookstores, especially those specializing in a narrow field, are getting out of storefront operations altogether and opening up on the Internet.

INDUSTRY LEADERS

Barnes & Noble is the largest bookseller in the United States. In 1999 the company operated 520 Barnes and Noble stores, 470 B. Dalton bookstores and barnesandnoble.com. The company had sales of $1.5 billion in the first six months of 1999, up from $1.3 billion in

1998. Its superstores accounted for 83 percent, or $1.25 billion, of the sales. B. Dalton closed 66 stores from June 1998 through June 1999, and its sales dropped 9.2 percent in the second quarter of 1999. The company is credited with introducing the superstore concept (which Borders has embraced) and has also established a significant online presence in an alliance with America Online. Barnes & Noble was founded in 1873 by Charles Barnes and began as a used book business. William Barnes, Charles' son, took over as president of the business in 1902, later selling the firm to C.W. Follett. Leonard Riggio paid $1.2 million for Barnes & Noble in 1971; with the acquisition of Marboro Books in 1979, the company entered the mail order and publishing business.

Once the largest bookstore operator in the United States, Borders has been second to Barnes & Noble since 1992. Borders Group operates more than 1,100 retail stores across the country under the names Waldenbooks, Borders, and Planet Music (CDs). In 1993, Kmart Corporation was the nation's second largest bookseller, owning two of the largest bookstore chains, Walden Book Company, Inc. and Borders, Inc. In early 1994 Kmart combined Borders and Walden into the Borders-Waldenbooks Group. As part of the restructuring, Walden closed 187 under-performing outlets. The downsizing at Walden was in marked contrast to Borders, which experienced rapid expansion and went public after a 1995 buy back of stock by the original Border brothers from Kmart, consolidating its three divisions in Ann Arbor, Michigan. Changes related to the spin-off led to a $211 million loss in 1996. Borders Group continues to focus on its superstores, which average 30,000 square feet. In 1999 Borders had 288 superstores, 894 Waldenbooks outlets, and an online presence with borders.com. The company posted sales of $1.3 billion in the first six months of 1999, up 14.5 percent from 1998's $1.1 billion.

Walden Book began as a small rental library in Bridgeport, Connecticut, in 1933 by Larry W. Hoyt, who leased space in a department store. He rented books for three cents per day. By 1948, the company was operating 250 rental libraries and had begun to sell books as well. In 1962, the company opened its first retail bookstore in Pittsburgh. It was named The Walden Bookstore, a reference to Walden Pond, the lake near Concord, Massachusetts, where author Henry David Thoreau lived from 1845 to 1847. The company opened 50 more Walden Bookstores in less than seven years.

In 1969, Walden Book was purchased by Carter Hawley Hale Stores, Inc., parent company to several leading department stores. The store names were changed to Waldenbooks nationwide in 1972, and in 1981, Walden Book became the first company to operate retail bookstores in all 50 states. The company also opened a central warehouse, the first in the industry, and linked all 750 of its stores to a nationwide computer system that tracked sales and inventory. In 1984, Walden Book was purchased by Kmart, then the second largest retailer in the United States. Walden Book acquired Brentano's, a chain of upscale bookstores, the same year. The first Waldenbooks & More superstore opened in Levittown, New York, in 1985. Walden Book opened the first Waldensoftware and Waldenkids stores in 1987.

Borders, which started the industry's return to large, comfortable, well-stocked bookstores with knowledgeable workers, was founded in 1971 by brothers Louis and Tom Borders in Ann Arbor, Michigan. By 1976, they had developed a computerized inventory and ordering system that made their Borders Book Shop one of the most profitable and best-run bookstores in the country. While the industry average for unsold books returned to their publishers was about 40 percent in 1990, Borders returned just 8 percent, despite offering five to ten times as many titles as the average mall bookstore. Borders also sponsored book signings, poetry readings, literary discussions, and storytelling sessions.

In 1985, Borders expanded to Birmingham, Michigan, and Indianapolis, Indiana. When it was purchased by Kmart in October 1992, Borders was operating 19 superstores. Kmart opened three more Borders Book Shops in 1992 and shifted responsibility for its nine Basset Bookstores from Walden Book to Borders. The Basset stores were to become Borders Book Shops in 1993. In 1992, Borders also added espresso bars and larger children's book sections to several stores and opened the first two Borders Books and Music stores, which offered 70,000 musical selections and 9,000 videotape titles in addition to books. The stores targeted the musical tastes of book buyers in the 35 to 54 age group. Kmart opened one new Borders Book Shop and 13 more Borders Books and Music superstores in 1993. Plans were for the new stores to have at least 22,000 square feet of floor space, compared to about 15,000 square feet in the older stores. In July 1995, two labor unions (IWW and UFCW) attempted to organize workers at Borders locations. By year-end, two Borders stores unionized, but union drives at other bookstores failed.

Chairman Herbert H. Haft, and his family, owned a controlling interest in Crown Book Corporation, which was founded in 1977. The leading discount bookstore chain, Crown Books sells bestsellers for as much as 40 percent off the publisher's suggested retail price. In 1993, the company operated 247 Crown Bookstores, each of which carried 3,000 to 4,000 titles. In 1990, the company opened its first Super Crown Bookstore, which offered about 30,000 titles; in 1993 there were 32 Super Crown Bookstores. In 1992, the publicly owned company had approximately 2,300 employees and $232 million in sales. In the mid-1990s power struggles in the Haft family created problems within the business. Herbert ousted his son Robert and replaced him with his other son, Ronald. Robert sued and won a jury award of $34 million. Ronald stepped down in 1995, leaving the company in the hands of CEO Steve Stevens.

In mid-1998 Crown Books declared bankruptcy, filing Chapter 11, citing downward sales and losses that continued to mount. Crown broke free of bankruptcy protection in November 1999, with 92 stores in Washington, Chicago, San Francisco, and Los Angeles, down from a high of 179 stores. The company was projecting sales of $190 million for 1999. The company said it would remain a deep discount bookseller, pointing out that their prices were lower than online sellers when shipping costs were taken into account. In the spring of 2000, the company was expected to announce plans for online retailing, new stores, and the remodeling of old stores.

FURTHER READING

Delaney, John J. "Bookselling in New York: 1930s-1970s." *Publishers Weekly,* 19 May 1997.

"Bookstore Sales Ahead Through June." *ABA Industry Newsroom,* 3 September 1999. Available from http://www.bookweb.org.

"California Booksellers Demand Level Playing Field for E-Commerce." *ABA Industry Newsroom,* 14 December 1999. Available from http://www.bookweb.org.

Milliot, Jim. "ABA Adds Chains' Subsidiaries to Lawsuit." *Publishers Weekly,* 29 November 1999.

———. "Chain Sales Up 100/0 in First Half of Year." *Publishers Weekly,* 4 October 1999.

———. "Scaled-Down Crown Books Emerges from Bankruptcy." *Publishers Weekly,* 22 November 1999.

"Monthly Retail Trade Survey." *U.S. Census Bureau,* 15 December 1999. Available from http://www.census.gov.

Mutter, John, and Jill A. Tardiff. "For Indies, Ho-Hum Holidays on the Whole." *Publishers Weekly,* 18 January 1999.

Royal, Weld. "Death of Salesmen." *Industry Week,* 17 May 1999.

"September Store Sales Fall 3 Percent." *Publishers Weekly,* 29 November 1999.

Verrier, Richard. "Online Booksellers Cutting into Independent Book Stores' Business." *Knight-Ridder/Tribune Business News,* 23 December 1998.

SIC 5943

STATIONERY STORES

This industry consists of establishments primarily engaged in the retail sale of stationery, such as paper products (including printing and engraving), postcards, school and office forms, legal forms, and supplies. Those establishments primarily engaged in selling office forms and supplies are discussed in **SIC 5112: Wholesale Trade,** and those primarily engaged in the retail sale of greeting cards are discussed in **SIC 5947: Gift, Novelty, and Souvenir Shops.**

NAICS CODE(S)

453210 (Office Supplies and Stationary Stores)

INDUSTRY SNAPSHOT

Sales in the retail stationery industry were somewhat erratic in the 1990s. The total sales volume was stagnant or declining slightly in the early 1990s. However, it recovered and grew slightly in the mid-1990s and continued to grow in the later part of the decade. Industry sales rose significantly in the late 1990s; sales of office supply superstore chains Staples, Office Depot, and OfficeMax together had estimated sales of $13.2 billion in 1997. Staples reported sales of $7.1 billion for 1998, while Office Depot's sales reached $8.9 billion. OfficeMax, the smallest of the three superstores, had sales of $4.3 billion in 1998. These superstores nonetheless are discussed in this category since they sell the same goods as smaller stationery stores and have a dramatic impact on those stores. While office superstores have become immensely popular, discounters, supermarkets, and drug stores all have seen significant growth in stationery sales.

The stationery store industry underwent a dramatic change in the 1980s and 1990s. As computers began to revolutionize the business world in the late 1970s, suppliers to businesses changed as well. Stationers have had to shift their focus away from stationery products toward the ever-growing demand for office products. Greeting cards, which are not part of this industry, are still sold in many stationery stores. Likewise, large office products, such as office furniture and computer equipment, are often carried by stationery stores but are not covered in this industry.

Office products have become the central component of many stationery stores. This change also has affected the kinds of stationery stores that control the market. Many smaller, independent dealers have been merged or acquired, while several large retailers have grown even larger. An indication of the depth of the shift is that the trade association formerly known as the National Stationers Association is currently known as the National Office Products Association (NOPA).

ORGANIZATION AND STRUCTURE

According to the U.S. Bureau of the Census, establishments that sell to the general public are classified as retail traders, even if the material they sell is not used in a household. Establishments that sell exclusively to businesses, institutional and industrial establishments are classified in wholesale trade. Most retail stationery stores categorized in this industry have fixed addresses, advertise to attract buyers, and buy merchandise in addition to selling it. Commodity classifications are assigned according to the primary source of an establishment's receipts. In the case of the stationery store industry, this means that a stationery store may sell office supplies but must derive most of its receipts from stationery sales.

The supply chain to stationery stores begins with manufacturers that produce office supplies. These firms sell some products directly to retail dealers, and other products are sold first to a wholesaler and then to a dealer. A growing number of manufacturers have begun to follow the practice of selling their merchandise directly to dealers. Warehouse clubs (such as Sam's Club), superstores (such as Office Depot), and discount stores (such as Kmart) buy almost exclusively from manufacturers.

In the 1980s, new channels for stationery and office products emerged. These included superstores such as Staples and Office Depot, warehouse clubs such as Sam's Club, and mass-market stores such as Wal-Mart. Sales of stationery products and office products through these outlets were expanding in the 1990s. No other mass-market retail channels have come close to office superstores and discount stores in stationery sales.

Background and Development

In 1775, pioneer papermakers of the now-legendary Crane family produced the paper used for the first currency of the young colonies. That paper was engraved by Paul Revere. The Crane family drew on the European tradition of making paper from cotton fibers and sold its products at the finest stores. Crane stationery and papers are sold at Tiffany's and fine department stores, but as businesses grew in the nineteenth century, more typical mass-market quality papers were developed. Early stationers sold business stationery as well as other products that could be used in an office.

During the twentieth century, business supplies shifted from typing paper, envelopes, and writing utensils to electronic products. Each of these products had replaceable parts: inkwells and cartridges for pens, ribbons for typewriters, and later, computer supplies such as printer ribbons, diskettes, and computer-appropriate paper and labels. The stationery stores responded by expanding and changing their inventories to supply all of the needs of the new business world.

Current Conditions

Perhaps the biggest development in this industry in the mid-1990s was the proposed acquisition by Staples Inc. of Office Depot Inc., a combination of two of the largest U.S. office supplies superstore chains. Announced in September 1996, the proposed merger was seen by stock market analysts as a positive development for both the companies and the industry, largely because it would help to avoid ''destructive'' price competition as the superstore market becomes saturated with stores.

This merger was blocked by the U.S. Federal Trade Commission (FTC). The FTC charged that the proposed merger would result in less competition and higher prices. The FTC previously had raised serious objections to the merger but Staples responded to the FTC's objections by agreeing to sell 63 Office Depot and Staples stores to OfficeMax Inc. for $108.8 million. The group of stores included some of the two chains' most profitable stores. Despite Staples' vow to fight the FTC challenge, the merger effort was eventually aborted in 1997.

Stock market analysts had expected the merger to be a very positive development, both for Staples and its principal competitor, OfficeMax. By combining resources and management, the merged company was expected to save more than $400 million in costs over three years.

Besides the growth of office product superstores and the consolidation of smaller stationery store chains, one trend that both small and large establishments in this industry were watching in the 1990s was the increase in the number of home offices. For stationery stores, this meant that more consumers would purchase items individually rather than for entire staffs. Special needs of the home office user include convenient hours and locations, good return policies, broad selection, and products offered in small quantities.

In addition to the growing number of home businesses, stationery stores were affected by consumers' increasing environmental concerns. After the Federal Resource Conservation and Recovery Act was implemented, Stuart Hall was among the first recycled paper products sold in stationery stores. However, many consumers did not want to compromise on price or quality, and some environmentally friendly paper products were more expensive than those made from virgin material. Consequently, the growth of recycled paper in the market has been slower than expected.

For the future, many sources predicted that independent dealers would be fewer in number and the surviving units would likely combine into new associations and groups. National distribution networks and more partnering relationships between manufacturers, wholesalers and dealers were expected to introduce more efficiencies to the stationery distribution system.

At one time, stationery retailers marketed their products to all of their prospective customers in the same way.

However, the multitude of customers and their diversity of needs has forced dealers to develop sophisticated sales strategies that enable them to sell parts of their inventories to specifically targeted consumers. They have had to develop sophisticated and focused marketing plans, recognizing that people who buy stationery and office supplies can choose among catalog dealers, warehouse clubs, commercial stationers, superstores, and retail stationers.

INDUSTRY LEADERS

The stationery and office products retail business is divided into two dramatically different segments: the office supply superstore segment and the smaller stationery stores. Due to the failed Staples/Office Depot merger, the industry has three leaders, the third being OfficeMax.

While Staples is considered to be the leader among the office superstores, Office Depot is larger and had greater sales than both Staples and OfficeMax in 1998. Staples has the youngest store base in the industry and has implemented a strategy of building smaller stores and saturating a market aggressively.

The growth of these retail superstores has been dramatic. Office Depot opened 100 stores in 1998 and planned to expand its store count by 15 percent annually through 2003. Staples plans to open 170 stores in 2000, which would eclipse Office Depot's proposed number by almost 20.

These superstores carried office supplies and products at prices that often were far below those of their competitors. They carried brand-name products and serviced small and medium-sized businesses with stores conveniently located in both suburban and urban areas. Most of the stores have high-volume operations and carry top stationery brands.

Among the chains of smaller stationery stores, leaders include Fay's Inc., Liverpool, Ohio; Franklin Quest Co., Salt Lake City, Utah; Beckley-Cardy Inc., Duluth, Minnesota; B.T. Miller, Arlington, Texas; and J.L. Hammett Co., Braintree, Massachusetts.

WORKFORCE

Smaller stationery stores employed about 32,000 people in 1996 with a payroll of about $454 million. By comparison, the combined Staples and Office Depot would employ about 53,000 people. Among the smaller stationery stores, about 49 percent of the employees were cashiers; 8 percent were marketing and sales worker supervisors; 7 percent were store clerks; 6 percent were general managers; and the remaining 22 percent were spread across a number of job categories.

AMERICA AND THE WORLD

The American stationery and office supplies industry is one of the world's largest. With the introduction of superstores and competitive pricing, the U.S. industry saw further recognition of its leadership in the international market. Distributors of office supplies began doing more business abroad in the early to mid-1990s, while prices for technologically advanced items in the U.S. market dropped significantly. Staples has tapped into the overseas market; in 1999 the company boasted 63 stores in the United Kingdom, 45 in Germany, 21 in the Netherlands, and 6 in Portugal. In early 1999 Office Depot had a total of 87 locations in Mexico, France, Israel, Poland, Columbia, Japan, Hungary, and Thailand. As of late 1999, OfficeMax did not operate any stores in Europe.

RESEARCH AND TECHNOLOGY

Modern technology has had a profound influence on the products sold by stationery and office supplies stores. Dealers in office supplies used to sell calculators and electric staplers, while office machines dealers sold copiers, word processors, fax machines, and computers. However, the distinction has blurred in the 1990s. For instance, technological expertise and after-care service requirements became a must for computerized equipment. Calculator prices declined to the point that they became replacement items like typewriter ribbons. Typewriters themselves were almost completely replaced by word processors and computers. As more information was conveyed electronically from one terminal to another, more steps involving paper were eliminated. Again, the effect on the stationery store industry was a loss in net sales.

All three of the major office superstores have established a presence on the Internet, offering their products and services online.

FURTHER READING

Avery, Susan. "Can Consolidation Continue?" *Purchasing,* 17 October 1996.

Cohen, David, et al. "Office Equipment and Supplies Industry." *The Value Line Investment Survey.* (Part 3-Ratings & Reports), 27 January 1995.

Darnay, Arsen J., and Gary Alampi, eds. *Wholesale and Retail Trade USA.* Detroit: Gale Research, 1995.

"Discounters, Superstores Dominate." *MMR.* 15 November 1999.

"Industry Trends Debated at Leadership Council Meeting." *Business Product Industry Association (BPIA) Industry Report,* 15 March 1997.

"More International Alliances Seen from Dealer Groups." *Business Product Industry Association (BPIA) Industry Report,* 15 March 1997.

"School/Home Office." *MMR.* 20 September 1999.

Specialty Retail Update: Industry Report. New York: Sanford C. Bernstein & Co., Inc., 24 October 1996.

Troy, Mike. "Office Depot Flying High with Internet, Store Gains." *Discount Store News,* 3 May 1999.

———. "Office Depot's 2-for-1 Stock Split Comes on Heels of Record Results." *Discount Store News,* 8 March 1999.

———. "Staples Gleans Growth From Base." *Discount Store News,* 21 June 1999.

———. "Staples Maintains its Momentum." *Discount Store News,* 8 November 1999.

———. "Staples To Open 20 in Key Florida Market." *Discount Store News,* 13 December 1999.

Wilke, John, and Joseph Pereira. "Staples Agrees to Extending FTC Review of Buyout." *The Wall Street Journal,* 3 March 1997.

———. and Joseph Pereira. "FTC Votes to Bar Staples' Bid for Rival." *The Wall Street Journal,* 11 March 1997.

———. "Staples Sets Store Sales to Rescue Merger." *The Wall Street Journal,* 13 March 1997.

Young, David. "FTC Again Rejects Plan for Office-Supply Chain Merger." *The Chicago Tribune,* 5 April 1997.

SIC 5944

JEWELRY STORES

This industry consists of establishments primarily engaged in the retail sale of jewelry, such as diamonds and other precious stones mounted in precious metals and sold as rings, pins, or bracelets; sterling and plated silverware; and watches and clocks. Establishments primarily engaged in the retail sale of costume jewelry are classified in **SIC 5632: Women's Accessory and Specialty Stores.**

NAICS CODE(S)

448310 (Jewelry Stores)

The retail fine jewelry industry is divided into two types of enterprises: chain stores and independents, with chain stores predominate. The cyclical nature of the business had ushered in a recessionary era of poor sales and bankruptcies in the early 1990s, but the industry had regained valuable footing by mid-decade. By the end of the decade, U.S. annual fine jewelry and watch sales totaled $40 billion. A strong economy and low unemployment had served to boost the sale of luxury goods, including jewelry, as the industry headed into 2000. However, since the jewelry industry is cyclical in nature, retailers know that if the economy turns down and consumer discretionary spending slows, they will be hit first.

For retailers, 1999 proved to be a stellar year for sales of watches and related products, and this trend was expected to continue. Watch sales were predicted to rise due in part to the influence of fashion designers who in the late 1990s made watches a status symbol. Technology was also expected to fuel sales with the advent of watches that connect to the Internet.

In the independent jewelry retail business, participants have fought a tough battle to maintain their identity in the competitive jewelry business of the 1990s. One such tactic has been the introduction of in-house credit cards, engineered by retailers and their banks. Such lines of credit boost sales and often provide the customer with a much lower interest rate and better terms.

Among the chains, the retail jewelry industry is led by some well-known names: Zale Corp., Sterling Inc., and Tiffany and Co. Founded in 1924, the Irving, Texas-based Zale Corp., which holds the number-one spot in the industry, posted sales of $1.25 billion in 1997 and in 1999 increased sales by 14 percent to $1.43 billion. That same year it posted a net income of $80.9 million, up from $31.5 million in 1995. Zale has 1,345 outlets in the United States and Canada and controls about 5 percent of the nation's $40 billion jewelry industry. Stores operate under the names Zales Outlets; Peoples Jewelers; Zales Jewelers, which carries lower-priced items; Gordon's Jewelers, which carries mid-priced items plus regional fashion jewelry; and Bailey, Banks & Biddle, which carries the upscale product lines. In 2000, Zale expects to open 85 more stores.

Zale's hegemony was all the more impressive given that it had emerged from bankruptcy in 1993. With a new chair, Robert DiNicola, the company was showing a revitalized strategy by the mid-1990s. DiNicola lowered prices on best-selling items considerably, which increased sales. Another strategy was to "make Zales the McDonald's of the jewelry business," wrote Amy Feldman in *Forbes,* "with national ads and standardized goods." Due to changing markets, Zale's increased spending on advertising (particularly television), incorporated a toll-free number in its newspaper inserts and direct mail catalogs, and expanded into the mail order catalog business late in 1996. By the late 1990s, it was selling merchandise direct on its Web site at www.zales.com. In 1999, DiNicola, who was credited with turning the company around, stepped down as the chief executive turning over the reins to the president and chief operating officer, Beryl Raff.

Meanwhile, what has become perhaps the most famous name in the history of American jewelry stores, Tiffany, opened two new stores in the United States and posted record sales for the 1996 holiday season. A new marketing strategy that aimed to lure Americans of a wider strata of income levels into Tiffany stores seemed to work well. The Fifth Avenue-headquartered firm's net sales for fiscal 1998 hit $1.17 million.

As retail jewelers entered the twenty-first century, they faced heavy competition from mass merchants, such as home shopping channels, mail-order firms, and discounters. These mass merchants, which were not even in existence 30 years ago, have snatched up 25 percent of the estimated total $40 billion U.S. annual fine jewelry and watch sales market. Jewelers are not worried, however, believing it easier to turn a sale with the product in hand.

Another change in the industry will be Internet sales. Online sales, which now make up less than 1 percent of total retail sales, are projected to increase exponentially well into the next century. Jewelers will have to get online to be competitive, but several, including Zale and Tiffany, already offer direct online sales.

FURTHER READING

Beres, Glen A. ''The Jewelry Goliaths Grab Market Share.'' *Jewelers Circular-Keystone,* February 1999.

Canedy, Dana. ''In Expanding Its Luxury Appeal to a Mass Market, Tiffany Tries Television for the First Time.'' *The New York Times,* 24 December 1996.

''How Tiffany's Took the Tarnish Off.'' *Business Week,* 26 August 1996.

Janowski, Ben. ''Mall Stores: How Strong a Future?'' *Jewelers' Circular-Keystone,* January 1996.

LaHood, Lila. ''CEO of Texas-Based Jewelry Retailer Zale Corp. Resigns.'' *Fort Worth Star-Telegram,* 8 September 1999.

LaHood, Lila. ''Irving, Texas-Based Jewelry Firm Zale Corp. Continues Growth Trend.'' *Fort Worth Star-Telegram,* 13 November 1999.

''Shaking Things Up.'' *Forbes,* 23 October 1995.

''Silver Linin.'' *Forbes,* 11 September 1995.

Tiffany & Co. ''Financial Highlights.'' Available from http://www.shareholder.com/tiffany/annual98/fianacial.htm.

''Timekeepers Worth Watching.'' *Jewelers Circular-Keystone,* March 1999.

Ward's Business Directory of U.S. Public and Private Companies. Detroit: Gale Research, 1996.

Zale Corporation. ''Financial Highlights.'' Available from http://www.zalecorp.com/relations/zale99ar/intro.html.

SIC 5945

HOBBY, TOY, AND GAME SHOPS

This industry consists of establishments primarily engaged in the retail sale of toys, games, and hobby and craft kits and supplies. Establishments primarily engaged in selling artists' supplies or collectors' items, such as coins, stamps, and autographs, are classified in **SIC 5999: Miscellaneous Retail Stores, Not Elsewhere Classified.**

NAICS CODE(S)

451120 (Hobby, Toy, and Game Shops)

INDUSTRY SNAPSHOT

According to the *1997 Economic Census,* the sales volume for the hobby, toy, and game shop industry was $14.4 billion. Stores ranged from independent shops to national chains, which sold toys and hobby supplies exclusively. Other types of stores carrying toys as part of their retail offerings include discounters, department stores, warehouse clubs, home supply stores, catalog houses, and drug stores.

In 1998, the Toy Manufacturers of America (TMA)—a trade organization founded in 1916—noted that, due to holiday shopping, approximately two-thirds of toy industry sales occurred in the fourth quarter. Christmas 1999 found shoppers pursuing such products as ''Pokemon'' and ''Star Wars'' action figures.

In response to the increasing dominance of large toy chains, specialty toy store owners formed the American Specialty Toy Retailers Association (ASTRA) in 1992. ASTRA created a forum for store owners to exchange ideas, and attempted to create a unified voice that would enable the industry to promote the sale of educational and high-quality toys. Specialty stores were estimated to have about 5 percent of a $14 billion market in the 1990s.

ORGANIZATION AND STRUCTURE

Manufacturers of toys and games sell their products either to wholesalers, or directly to retailers, although some manufacturers sell to both retailers and wholesalers. Retailers with multiple outlets require efficient delivery systems from their manufacturers. Toy manufacturers with outdated systems have thus found it difficult to convince large retailers to carry their products.

In the hobby and craft industry, manufacturers sell products through independent sales representatives or through their own salespeople. Wholesalers and distributors often play the role of middleman. Pre-packaged craft kits are increasingly sold in non-traditional outlets. Independent craft and toy retailers now compete with nationwide chains of specialty stores as well as with large discount stores carrying craft products. HIA estimated that nearly 20,000 stores could be considered toy and hobby outlets if sewing and other craft-related fields were included.

During the 1980s and 1990s a consolidation of retail toy stores led to the dominance of five top retailers—Toys ''R'' Us, Inc.; Kay-Bee Toy and Hobby Shops, Inc.; Wal-Mart Stores, Inc.; Kmart Corporation; and Target Stores Inc. In 1999, these stores accounted for 52 percent of toy sales in the United States. Many industry observers, however, believe that specialty toy stores can still thrive in this marketplace. Those emphasizing convenience, top-notch service, and quality products are most likely to succeed.

Background and Development

With the opening of the first Toys ''R'' Us in the 1950s, retailing of toys in the United States changed forever. The vast retail chain began as a bicycle shop, was transformed into a juvenile furniture store, and finally became a toy store. Additional Toys ''R'' Us stores were soon opened; these outlets emphasized deep discounts and wide selections.

Another key factor in the growth of the retail sale of toys was the increase in the use of television advertising. In the late 1950s and early 1960s, television promotions reached into many homes where toy purchasing decisions were made.

In the 1970s many parents expressed concern about toy safety. Several consumer groups began to lobby on behalf of toy safety, as well as in search of manufacturers and retailers who would support limitations on television advertising. The National Advertising Division of the Council of Better Business Bureaus was established in 1974. It included the Children's Advertising Review Unit (CARU), which promoted responsible children's advertising.

Many toy manufacturers helped toy stores sell items by licensing products that were perceived as popular, or ''hot toys.'' One emerging trend was the production of licensed promotional items by the retailers themselves, though this practice was limited to larger retailers who could make the investment of time, money, and space in their stores.

The late 1970s and early 1980s also saw the introduction of electronic games and toys. While retailers were enthusiastic about the tendency of buyers to purchase these items year-round, they suffered from a glut of products left on their shelves. These unsold items became so costly for some retailers that losses forced them to close in the late 1980s. This led to the consolidations that occurred in the 1990s.

Current Conditions

Toy Retailers. Manufacturers' shipments of toys, not including video games, increased from $11.4 billion in 1992 to $14.4 billion in 1996, and reached $29.9 billion in 1999. Retail sales rose from $17 billion to $24 billion in the same period. The retail industry as a whole is looking healthier following a difficult recession in the late 1980s and early 1990s. This recovery, coupled with the continued popularity of discount chains such as Wal-Mart, Kmart, and Target, had strong effects on the toy store industry. Some of the toys sold at small independent stores were available at a lower cost on the discounters' shelves because of the inventory advantages such large chains enjoy. Meanwhile, catalog houses, which have made inroads in a number of areas of retailing, have yet to establish themselves as a significant force in the toy retail sector. Toy and hobby catalog purchases still account for only a small share of the total toy market.

Retailers also examined the effect of the increasing numbers of mothers in the workforce, as well as the increasing buying power of the children themselves. Children not only influence their parents in the choice of school items and toys, but, outfitted with greater amounts of disposable income than ever before, also comprise a significant target market by themselves.

Another measurable asset to the toy industry was the sale of video games. David Miller, president of TMA, noted that the success of video games showed that a steep price was not a barrier to the profitable sale of any particular toy. Much of the burden of selling these toys fell on the retailers, whose marketing efforts showed parents and other buyers that the play value of these items was high enough to justify the price. These video games did not fit neatly into retail stores and their existing toy categories. A combination of home entertainment and toy, the video game needed its own space on the retail floor; those retailers who realized this found tremendous profits in video games.

Hobby and Craft Retailers. Retail sales of hobby and craft items increased in the early 1990s as well. In the crafts sector in 1996, general crafts made up 31 percent of purchases ($2.95 billion), while florals and naturals made up 16 percent ($1.53 billion). Frames accounted for 9 percent ($.91 billion), needlecrafts made up 6 percent ($.59 billion), and art materials accounted for 10 percent ($.96). The remainder of sales was in the area of sewing and notions ($2.73 billion).

Statistics in the early 1990s showed that consumers preferred to buy their model kits from hobby and toy stores rather than discount stores because of the service they received from the former. Moreover, hobby retailers cite low prices as another factor in their ability to withstand the competition from discounters and catalog sales.

Jockeying With Toy Manufacturers. The Kmart Corporation made an unusual request of toy manufacturers in the summer of 1993—to sell toys on consignment. This meant that the toys would be considered inventory of the manufacturer until their arrival at Kmart stores. Kmart did not want to pay for toys until they went to stores even if they sat in distribution centers for long periods of time. The practical result of this request would be that a poorly-selling toy would be the responsibility of the manufacturer. Some large toy manufacturers have refused to comply with Kmart's request, mindful that other retailers were watching Kmart's bid with interest. Other manufacturers, though, have less leverage and are heavily dependent on Kmart to get their products into the marketplace.

This bid came as Kmart, Toys ''R'' Us, and Wal-Mart, the three largest toy retailers in the United States, sought to convince manufacturers to assume a greater risk in the toy business. The retailers urged a system wherein toys would be replaced immediately by the manufacturers as stocks were depleted. Manufacturers, concerned about the potential for excess inventory such a system would create, have balked at this as well.

INDUSTRY LEADERS

Industry leaders in 2000 included Wal-Mart, which had a 17.4 percent share of the market; Toys ''R'' Us, which had a 15.6 percent share of the market; Kmart, 7.2 percent; Target, 6.8 percent; and Kay-Bee Toy Stores, 5.1 percent. Other significant toy retailers included Ames and J.C. Penney with just over 1 percent market share each.

Wal-Mart Stores, Inc., the leading retailer in the world, operates approximately 3,600 Wal-Marts and Sam's Clubs throughout North America, South America, Asia, and Europe. Primarily through wide-scale expansion, the company was able to increase its share of the toy market to become the leading retailer in the industry in 2000.

Toys ''R'' Us, the world's largest toy retailer, had sales of $11.9 billion in fiscal year 2000. It operated discount toy stores in the United States, the United Kingdom, Canada, France, Japan, Spain, and other countries. Kay-Bee Toy Stores, the second-largest toy retailer in America—Kmart, Wal-Mart, and Target are general merchandise discount retailers—operates more than 1,300 toy stores. A division of Consolidated Stores, the company placed most of its stores in shopping malls. Besides these chains, there are an estimated 3,000 specialty toy stores in the United States.

WORKFORCE

An estimated 111,757 people were employed in the U.S. toy industry in 1997. Almost 49 percent of the workforce in this industry was taken up by salespersons. The rest of the workforce was split among various other jobs such as cashier, stock clerks, executives, and shipping and receiving clerks. Every field within this industry was expected to grow going into the next century, some by as much as 40 percent, and some by only 7 percent.

AMERICA AND THE WORLD

The United States has the largest market for toys in the world. Other successful toy markets include Japan, Germany, France, and the United Kingdom, and global toy sales amounted to $67.8 billion in 1998. Domestic toy manufacturers in 1998 were riding a crest of increased exports that began in the mid-1980s, with exports totaling $1.0 billion. Imports have risen just as steadily, bringing that total to $14.3 billion. Many American toy stores have tried to capitalize on the changing face of the world. Toys ''R'' Us was one of the first U.S. retail stores to open in Japan. In the early 1990s the company projected that sales there could reach $1.5 billion by the year 2000. It planned to open ten stores each year beginning in 1993. When Toys ''R'' Us began to expand into Australia, it met with heavy competition from Australia's own retailer, Coles Myer. In the mid-1990s, Coles Myer planned to open large stores called World 4 Kids (W4K) that would go head to head with Toys ''R'' Us in each market.

A growing concern for consumers is the conditions under which toys, and other personal products, were produced. William J. Holstein, in a *U.S. News and World Report* article entitled ''Santa's Sweatshop,'' points out that many of the most popular toys are made in sweatshops around the world by overworked, and in many cases, underpaid workers, toiling in unhealthy conditions. The toys mentioned ranged from F.A.O. Schwarz's Bernie St. Bernard to Mattel's Barbie, to a range of Disney products. Holstein also points out that a ''Made in America'' label is no longer a guarantee of non-sweatshop production, particularly in the garment industry.

RESEARCH AND TECHNOLOGY

In the competitive toy store industry, the latest technological advances have always been sought. Scientific progress has for many years been mirrored in toy development and sales. Independent retailers of toys, mindful of maintaining good relationships with their manufacturers, try to get early shipments of these new toys.

Video games changed the face of toy stores in the 1970s and 1980s. That craze was followed in the 1990s by excitement in toy stores over advanced software, such as computer games that incorporate CD-ROM technology.

Electronic Learning Aids, or ELAs, accounted for large sales increases in many toy stores in the early 1990s. Unlike video games, the electronic toys appeal to parents as well as children. They are age-specific and can be used even by very young children. Some ELAs require no more technology than batteries. Some, however, require purchase or rental of CD players, televisions, or VCRs. Milt Schulman wrote in *Playthings* that industry executives expect to see interactive technology increase its presence in toy stores. ''These new, interactive toys will challenge retailers to take innovative merchandising approaches that help explain what these advanced toys are capable of doing.''

New technology also helped toy retailers keep track of their inventories and increased sales. Even smaller toy retailers were moving from manual inventory tracking to computerized systems that hinged on the point-of-sale computer register.

The Internet has also helped bolster the retail toy industry. While sites offering books, movies, and music grew by 17 percent in 1998, toy sites grew by 86 percent. This trend served as a signpost for a bright immediate future for the industry. Amazon.com, Inc, an online shopping company that generated sales of $1.6 billion in 1998, entered the toy-retailing market in the late 1990s and was expected to have a large impact on the industry.

FURTHER READING

Crispell, Diane. ''Hawking The Hunchback.'' *American Demographics,* November 1996, 22-23.

Holstein, William. ''Santa's Sweatshop.'' *U.S. News And World Report,* 16 December 1996, 50-60.

Hoover's Company Capsule, 20 March 2000. Available from http://www.hoovers.com.

Meltzer, Stephanie. ''A Bear Market For Teddies.'' *American Demographics,* February 1996, 8-9.

Miller, Annetta. ''Santa's Surly Toy Peddlers: Chains Slash Prices in Preholiday Clash.'' *Newsweek,* 11 November 1991, 54.

Mogelonsky, Marcia. ''Butterfly Barbie Affect.'' *American Demographics,* May 1996, 8.

Toy Manufacturers Association. ''2000 Toy Industry Fact Book: The Year in Review,'' 20 April 2000. Available from http://www.toy-tma.com.

Toy Manufacturers Association. ''Industry Statistics,'' 20 April 2000. Available from http://www.toy-tma.com.

U.S. Census Bureau. *1997 Economic Census—Retail.* Washington, DC: GPO, 2000. Available from http://www.census.gov.

SIC 5946

CAMERA AND PHOTOGRAPHIC SUPPLY STORES

This industry consists of establishments primarily engaged in the retail sale of cameras, film, and other photographic supplies and equipment. Establishments engaged primarily in the retail sale of video equipment are categorized in **SIC 5731: Radio, Television, and Consumer Electronics Stores;** those primarily engaged in photofinishing are covered in **SIC 7384: Photofinishing Laboratories.**

NAICS CODE(S)

443130 (Camera and Photographic Supply Stores)

Fifty-three percent of households in the United States buy their cameras and photography supplies at discount chains such as Kmart and Target. Drug stores and supermarkets hold second and third place with 32 percent and 27 percent, respectively. Camera specialty stores only account for 6 percent of U.S. household purchases. (Total equals more than 100 percent because consumers named multiple sources.)

The retail photographic supply industry has historically been a competitive one. Large manufacturers such as Kodak trained their sales representatives to go to retail stores to help sell their equipment. This has been especially important for retailers as new technologies became available. Photo CD technology, for instance, demands that retailers be trained by manufacturers and their sales representatives to ensure that new products can be explained to prospective customers. Photo CD allows consumers to take pictures with regular cameras and film. The film is then transferred onto compact disc for display on computers and televisions where the image can be manipulated.

The industry has several major associations. In the 1940s, the Photo Finishers Association of America (founded in 1924) expanded to include photographic dealers and was renamed the Master Photo Dealers' and Finishers' Association. At that time, photographic dealers became more closely aligned with photographic equipment manufacturers and photofinishers. In 1974, recognizing that marketing was central to photo retailing as well as photo finishing, the association became the Photo Marketing Association International (PMAI).

The industry thrives on new technology. Many consumers only shop at photographic supply stores when there is a new lens, camera, or film type that they have heard about and are eager to try. Retailers are eager to remain on the cutting edge of photographic technology and to sell the latest equipment. They also service repeat customers who buy add-ons as well as replacement items such as filters and film.

Single-use cameras were the fastest-growing category with sales increasing by 25 percent annually. Sales of digital cameras also rose substantially in the latter half of the 1990s, from 500,000 in 1995 to 3 million in 1999. Digital camera prices also continue to fall as well; 900,000 of such cameras bought in 1999 were sold for under $200.

The industry benefited from the Advanced Photo System, or APS, a format introduced in April 1996. As a bridge between digital and standard photographic techniques, the 24mm system used a high-quality emulsion for its film and a new small hand held camera. With a magnetic strip on the film, the camera could record, as well as give, information. The film was loaded with a simple drop-in method, and the camera automatically extracted the film from the container and read the film type, ISO, speed, and the current exposure. The film could also record the camera setting, date, format (ranging from 4x6 to panoramic), and even any special input from the user such as a title or description, to be printed on the back of the photo. In addition, the camera could read the last exposure taken and rewind the film in the event the user wants to change the film in the middle of the roll. When the original roll was reloaded, the camera automatically advanced past the last photo taken, thereby eliminating double exposure and film ruined by light exposure. The format also produced prints with a higher quality than standard 35mm film, due to the new emulsion. By the end of the 1990s, APS had captured a 30 percent share of all cameras sold.

A marketing strategy gaining popularity at the end of the twentieth century was co-branding. A number of the larger film and camera makers agreed to sell their products to specialty stores at substantial discounts. In return, the stores agreed to showcase that manufacturer's products. Eastman-Kodak planned to have more than 500 co-branded sites by 2005.

Most of the leading companies in this retail industry are privately owned. Some of the more successful camera and photographic equipment stores include Kits Cameras, Inc. of Kent, Washington ($42 million in sales); Inkley's, Inc. of Salt Lake City, Utah ($20 million); Samy's Camera, Inc. of Los Angeles ($20 million); Southwest Camera of Houston, Texas ($19 million); and Comgraphics of El Paso, Texas ($18 million). These retailers, as well as others in the industry, have benefited from the efforts of domestic and foreign camera and film manufacturers to secure a share of the U.S. consumer marketplace.

Ritz Camera, the industry's largest participant, generated $650 million in sales for 1998. Employing 6,500 people in 1,000 stores in 47 states, Ritz offered cameras and photographic supplies. Ritz stores also operated under the name ''Camera Shop.''

Wolf Camera of Alpharetta, Georgia, generated an estimated $500 million in sales for 1998—nearly doubling the previous year's sales.

FURTHER READING

Beardi, Cara. ''Argus Camera Turning Attention to Mass Retail.'' *Advertising Age,* 31 January 2000.

Radice, Carol. ''Imaging: Ready to Roll.'' *Progressive Grocer,* February 1998.

White, Larry, ''APS . . . It's Finally Here! The Advanced Photo System: Will It Change Photography Forever?'' *HyperZine,* 10 February 1997. Available from http://www.hyperzine.com.

SIC 5947

GIFT, NOVELTY, AND SOUVENIR SHOPS

This industry consists of establishments primarily engaged in the retail sale of combined lines of gifts and novelty merchandise, souvenirs, greeting cards, holiday decorations, and miscellaneous small art goods.

NAICS CODE(S)

453220 (Gift, Novelty and Souvenir Stores)

Charles Gordon, writing in the Canadian newsmagazine *Maclean's,* stated ''We live in a souvenir society, a world in which everything we do, everywhere we go, has to be commemorated.'' This attitude has encouraged the growth of gift, novelty, and souvenir shops, which have expanded from limited operations in airports and near tourist destinations into a multimillion dollar industry of its own, with specialty stores opening up in shopping malls and retail centers around the country. Many different kinds of stores, including discounters, drug stores, and supermarkets, sold gifts and novelties. However, specialty retail shops marketing exclusively in gifts and souvenirs had become a distinct billion dollar industry by the mid-1990s.

The Walt Disney Company was the leader in the field of specialty shops. Consumer product revenues were $3 billion in 1999, a 5 percent drop from 1998, due to declines in worldwide merchandise licensing and sales from the Disney Stores. Declines were partially offset by increases at Disney Interactive (Disney's software and publishing operations). While this downward trend reflects a move toward online merchandising, Disney pledged in 2000 to invest up to $750,000 in revamping its 715 retail stores worldwide in an effort to reverse the profit slump.

Other leaders in this field included Spencer Gifts Inc., Cracker Barrel, Marriott Hotel Shops, Matthews Inc., Spains Gifts, Museum Shop, and South of the Border Shops. These stores were located in shopping centers, near tourist destinations such as monuments or resorts, or even in museums, zoos, hotels, and airports.

Seasonal and temporary carts, kiosks, and stores gained prominence in the novelty shop industry, ballooning into a $10 billion business in 1999. Virtually every enclosed mall had a temporary retail program; this allowed major retailers to explore new concepts, artists to peddle handmade items, and entrepreneurs to capitalize on hot trends.

Retail outlets that specialize in the sale of greeting cards are also classified in this industry. Not classified with other stationery products, greeting cards are a cornerstone of the gift and souvenir shop retail industry. The greeting card industry diversified considerably since its beginnings in the 19th century. Mass-produced Christmas cards were first sold in England by Sir Henry Cole in the 1840s, and Louis Prang introduced such cards to the United States not long afterwards. Some of these lines of cards were sold through stationery stores, but other lines were a better match for contemporary gift and novelty shops. Souvenir stores in tourist destinations often carried greeting cards that targeted travelers.

Greeting cards are commonly purchased for a variety of special events, from birthdays to weddings to holidays. The perennial popularity of such items provided retail outlets with a steady source of income throughout the year, regardless of economic factors that might have devastating effects on other industries.

Hallmark Cards Inc. remained the undisputed leader in the retail sales of greeting cards by virtue of its huge presence in both the manufacturing and retailing of greeting cards. The long-time card manufacturer opened the first of its many retail outlets in the 1950s, establishing a dominant position in the industry. The other two market-share leaders were American Greetings and Gibson Greetings. American Greetings, the largest publicly held greeting card company, was in the process of acquiring Gibson Greetings in early 2000.

Hallmark and American Greetings were in steep competition with some relative newcomers to the industry, as gift and souvenir shops that specialized in the sale of greeting cards faced a vastly changing market. Distributors of gifts and novelties increasingly utilized large warehouse clubs and superstores that carried many product lines at reduced prices. Also, many card manufacturers sold their products through discount stores and grocery stores such as Wal-Mart and Kmart. In some cases, smaller gift and novelty stores were forced to restructure their businesses radically to compete. Buying patterns shifted; in the 1970s and 1980s the card market began moving away from card shops toward one-stop shopping establishments, such as discounters, grocery stores, and drugstores. While half of all cards purchased 20 years ago were sold at specialty shops, that figure shrank rapidly through the 1990s.

Hallmark and American Greetings both began to sell over the Internet. Their sites allowed customers either to design and personalize their own cards or to order traditional cards, all from their home computer. Customers can also send electronic greetings as e-mail messages. This online trend saw tremendous growth in the late 1990s. The number of Hallmark e-cards sent on a daily basis in November 1999 increased more than 600 percent over November 1998. *Discount Store News* noted the danger of this technological revolution: ''The increasing use of e-mail poses a long-term threat to category profits by offering consumers an alternative that is often free, and in some respects superior to paper cards.'' A survey conducted by American Greetings revealed that 95 percent of e-mail users prefer to keep in touch with friends and relatives electronically, and about 75 percent of these people receive and send cards online. Companies such as Blue Mountain Arts and Egreetings.com became very popular card sites on the Internet, offering free electronic greetings with animation and sound.

The Greeting Card Association in 1999 estimated the greeting card business to be a $7.1 billion industry. Growth in recent decades was attributed to societal trends, as greeting cards took the place of letter writing in the modern world, and niche marketing was successful due to society's diversity.

FURTHER READING

''American Greetings Extends Tender Offer for Gibson Greetings' Stock.'' *PRNewswire,* 4 January 2000.

Bawden, Tom. ''Disney Stores in GBP300m Overhaul.'' *Marketing Week,* 18 November 1999.

Business Rankings Annual. Detroit: Gale Research, 1997.

Cooke, Bethany. ''Card-Bored Greetings.'' *Information Week,* 24 January 2000.

Disney Press Release, 4 November 1999. Available from http://disney.go.com/investors/earnings/q499.html.

Forkan, Jim. ''Disney Shuts ESPN Stores, Touts Web.'' *Mulitchannel News,* 6 September 1999.

''Giftware News Greeting Card Gazette.'' Available from http://www.giftwarenews.net/NewIssue/Pages/052Gaz.htm.

Ginsburg, Janet. ''They're Looking Better and Better as Holiday Sales Venues.'' *Business Week,* 13 December 1999.

Gordon, Charles. ''Christmas Shopping at the Beer Store.'' *Maclean's,* 16 December 1991.

''Greeting Cards and Stationery Reach $12.1 Billion in Sales.'' *Business Wire,* 28 May 1999.

Hallmark Press Release, 18 January 2000. Available from http://hotnews.hallmark.com/1312199901.html.

Lazich, Robert S., ed. *Market Share Reporter.* Detroit: Gale Research, 1997.

Taylor, Dennis. ''Very Best Not Good Enough.'' *The Business Journal,* 18 November 1996.

Troy, Mike. ''E-Greetings Break the Mold, Redefine the Industry.'' *Discount Store News,* 13 December 1999.

Ward's Business Directory of U.S. Private and Public Companies. Detroit: Gale Research, 1997.

SIC 5948

LUGGAGE AND LEATHER GOODS STORES

This category includes establishments primarily engaged in the retail sale of luggage, trunks, and leather goods.

NAICS CODE(S)

448320 (Luggage and Leather Goods Stores)

There are 1,977 luggage and leather goods stores in the United States, according to U.S. Census Bureau statistics. Luggage and leather goods stores employed more than 12,000 persons and generated net sales of $1.3 billion in 1998. As specialty retailers, all of these businesses carried narrow product lines but many offered deep selection within those lines. Often, luggage and leather goods stores specialized in either leather apparel or gift items. Many of these stores were found in discount malls and airports.

The industry is served by the National Luggage Dealers Association. Founded in 1925, this trade association continues to represent retailers of luggage and leather goods around the country. The association's primary function is to produce promotional material and relevant industry information for its members. Through the efforts of both this organization and the leather producers, the retail luggage and leather goods industry is well organized on a national level, staying in constant contact with the leather producers and manufacturers.

Retailers maintain close relationships with the leather producers to gain a better understanding of customers' desires. Often, the producers hire fashion experts to advise retailers in future fashion trends in leather. The leather producers also provide promotional material and samples to retailers well before the leather articles are available to the public.

As they entered the late 1990s, luggage and leather goods stores faced a challenging business environment. Although people traditionally viewed fine leather as a luxury, the 1990's consumer placed a premium on value. Therefore, in an effort to remain competitive, industry leaders focused on providing customers with good values without compromising quality. Some businesses used strict cost control and streamlining as a means to this end, while others relied on competitive leather sourcing from China, India, and Brazil since these countries supplied quality leather goods at low cost. In 1999, 53 percent of the leather and leather products sold in the United States were imported. Since labor costs represented a high proportion of total production cost for leather goods, it was more cost-effective to import leather goods from developing countries with lower wage rates.

Like most retail segments, luggage and leather goods retailers use technology and automation to improve efficiency. Retailers also needed to attend to customer demands and desires because U.S. consumers in the 1990s shunned hard-side luggage, preferring lighter and less expensive soft-side goods.

Changes in the regulations concerning the use of carry-on baggage in air travel provided yet another challenge to the luggage industry in the late 1990s. Anne DeCicco, President of The Luggage and Leather Goods Manufacturers of America, stated, "Luggage producers must be certain to accurately and truthfully label products within the parameters of the new carry-on baggage environment that has resulted from the Federal Aviation Administration's 1998 Advisory Circular on Carry-on Baggage and from changes the domestic airlines have implemented in their respective carry-on programs. Luggage manufacturers that use terms such as approved carry-on bag or approved by the FAA or that use incorrect sizes can be charged with fraudulent or misleading advertising by the Federal Trade Commission." How this will impact industry practice is one area of interest that will certainly be carried into the new millenium.

FURTHER READING

Leib, Jeffrey. "Excess Baggage? Major Changes Are Planned for Samsonite, But What Will They Be?" *Denver Post,* 30 September 1996.

DeCicco, Anne L. "Carry-On Baggage: The Next Steps." *SHOWCASE International,* December-January 1999.

"Poised for a New Millennium, Luggage and Leather Goods Trends are Y2K Compatible." *AOL Newswire,* 16 April, 1999.

Luggage and Leather Goods Manufacturers of America. Available from http://www.llgma.org/.

SIC 5949

SEWING, NEEDLEWORK, AND PIECE GOODS STORES

This category includes establishments primarily engaged in the retail sale of sewing supplies, fabrics, patterns, yarn, and other needlework accessories.

NAICS CODE(S)

451130 (Sewing, Needlework, and Piece Goods Stores)

INDUSTRY SNAPSHOT

Although this industry was dominated by a few large national chains, hundreds of small shops were scattered throughout the country. Because many of these small businesses were privately owned, the size of the industry was difficult to determine. In 1999, the two largest companies in this sector, Jo-Ann Stores, Inc. and Hancock Fabrics, Inc., generated approximately $1.76 billion in sales—one-fourth of industry totals.

An increase in the popularity of arts and crafts and a surge in home decorating prompted renewed growth in the sewing, needlework, and piece goods industry during the 1990s. Although the industry demonstrated enviable vitality, competition was intense. The attractive growth rate encouraged new entrants to the industry and convinced discount retailers to devote more resources to craft items. Retailers in this industry also competed with some hobby retailers classified in **SIC 5945: Hobby, Toys, and Game Shops,** that carried craft supplies such as yarn and fabric.

As the industry emerged from the mid-1990s, the business environment was changing. Small shops were experiencing increasing competitive pressure from the larger craft/fabric super stores. Consumers, moreover, were attracted to the enormous variety offered by such stores. Consequently, several smaller chains were acquired by bigger firms during this period. Consolidation was typical as many large fabric chains closed small shops and operated fewer but more expansive stores.

In the late-1990s, many firms reported increased profits with fewer but larger outlets. Significantly expanded inventories and retailers' emphasis on home decorating fabrics added a much-needed boost to the lackluster sales figures of earlier years. In 1997, the 6,590 establishments in this industry totaled $6.6 billion in sales and employed 45,351 people.

ORGANIZATION AND STRUCTURE

Since all the stores in this industry carried limited product lines, albeit deep selection within those product lines, they were classified as specialty retailers. Within the broad category of specialty retailers, the sewing, needlework, and piece goods industry was populated by two different retail formats. In the sewing and fabric category, large ''super stores'' were the norm. The needlework stores, on the other hand, were usually small boutique-like shops.

Although these two types of stores often carried similar products, they had different competitive priorities. While the large fabric retail chains, such as Hancock Fabrics and Jo-Ann Stores, carried large inventories of varying quality, the small independent shops focused on providing high quality products and services. Rather than competing on the basis of price, they pursued customer satisfaction strategies with low turnover rates and more sales expertise than the large chain stores. The small stores, moreover, usually carried products related to only one or two segments of the industry, such as quilting or knitting. The local stores, therefore, exuded distinctive competence in service and quality, while the national chains emphasized selection and price.

Like most retail industries, the popularity of discount retailers changed the competitive structure of the sewing, needlework, and piece goods industry. By the early 1990s, department stores, once the industry's primary competitors, had virtually eliminated their fabric and craft departments. In their place, however, emerged discount retailers such as Wal-Mart.

In the sewing, needlework, and piece goods industry, the influence of off-price retailers was particularly strong because the arts and crafts trend of the 1990s encouraged discounters to augment their craft departments. Shifts in consumer preferences, moreover, favored discounters. A 1996 Hobby Industry Association (HIA) nationwide consumer study revealed that the key consumer motives in the craft industry were price, merchandise selection, convenient store location, and merchandise quality, in that order. Consequently, the well-stocked discounters found themselves with an advantage over niche-oriented shops with limited selections.

By the mid-1990s, however, consumer needs and the popularity of discount retailers encouraged the national chains to reevaluate store size and location. Hundreds of stores in this industry were moved out of malls and into strip shopping centers. The new locations, which were usually 10,000 to 12,000 square feet in size, were more accessible and expansive than the traditional mall-based stores. The dizzying pace of store conversions lasted nearly a decade.

These structural and organizational changes were not unique to this industry, however. These developments were typical of the retail industry overall. Competitive pressure in the sewing, needlework, and piece goods industry was, however, unusually strong.

BACKGROUND AND DEVELOPMENT

Many of the businesses in this industry opened in the 1940s and early 1950s as basic fabric outlets. Carrying garment-oriented sewing supplies, these stores catered to the post-World War II mother who sewed a large percentage of her family's clothing. Throughout the 1950s and into the early 1960s, businesses in the home-sewing industry prospered. Some businesses, such as Fabri-Centers of America (now Jo-Ann Stores), were able to grow from small local enterprises into national chains by acquiring or merging with other fabric retailers. In the late

1960s, however, the home-sewing market began to decline.

Two factors influenced the demise of home sewing: the increase in affordable ''off the rack'' clothing, and an increase in the number of working mothers. In the first case, the influx of inexpensive clothing, especially from Southeast Asia, virtually eliminated the cost savings associated with sewing. This cost factor, coupled with the fact that a working mother barely had time to cook and clean, made sewing a costly alternative to buying clothes. As demand for home-sewing related fabrics and notions declined, fabric retailers were forced to search for new product lines.

Fortunately for these retailers, the decline of home sewing was succeeded by a series of fads in other sewing and needlework segments. Entering the 1970s, the yarn and needlework crafts fared better than garment sewing. These types of crafts, such as knitting, typically involved less time than sewing and were convenient for time-pressed women. One critical difference between garment sewing and needlework was that sewing required a person to sit at a sewing machine, while crafts such as knitting or needlepoint were portable. Working mothers could work on these portable needlework projects while commuting or during their lunch hours. Many large fabric retailers diversified into yarn crafts in response to growing demand.

The popularity of these types of crafts, especially knitting, caused a boom period in the number of small yarn shops during the 1970s. These knit shops carried full lines of yarn, knitting and crocheting supplies, and usually offered classes. Unlike the large fabric retailers that stocked average-quality acrylic yarn, the small knit shops sold a wide variety of expensive natural fibers such as mohair and cotton. While fabric chain stores targeted price-conscious customers, small shops catered to the quality-oriented consumer. This customer segmentation continued throughout the 1980s and into the 1990s.

The industry continued to evolve as different sewing and needlework segments gained and lost popularity. Successive waves of craft trends dictated store inventories. In the late 1980s, for example, quilting became popular, immediately followed by fabric painting. The 1990s saw a revival of cross stitch and embroidery popularity. Though the colors changed year after year, the different crafts required the same raw materials like fabric, yarn, and notions.

CURRENT CONDITIONS

As the sewing, needlework, and piece goods industry emerged from the mid-1990s, earnings had begun to show signs of recovery from a slump earlier in the decade. Competition among the larger chains was somewhat reduced through massive store closures and the recessionary period of the early 1990s. Conditions improved as retailers' expanded craft inventories. An increase in consumer demand for home decorator fabrics and supplies also contributed to the rise in sales. By this time, many of the large chains finished consolidating stores and the industry outlook began to brighten.

Fueled by continued growth in crafts, the industry saw a surge in home decorating as well. The Hobby Industry Association's nationwide consumer study for 1996 revealed that in 84 percent of U.S. households, one or more persons participated in crafts or hobbies. Moreover, the average number of different craft activities engaged in was 4.5 among the households surveyed.

The explosion in the number of customers meant rising profits for companies in this business. During 1999, Hancock Fabrics, Inc. reported a sales increase of 2.7 percent over the previous year. Jo-Ann Stores, Inc.'s sales were up 11.2 percent from 1998.

Retailers in the industry responded to the increased demand for craft supplies by building bigger stores and by increasing selection. In 1999, Hancock Fabrics had about 460 stores in 40 states, while Jo-Ann Stores operated approximately 1,050 stores in 49 states. These stores were mainly located in strip shopping centers.

In addition to expanding inventories, retailers in the sewing, needlework, and piece goods industry changed the type of goods and services they offered during the mid-1990s. Fabric retailers reduced the apparel-type fabrics in favor of decorator fabrics and quilting supplies, while many yarn shops stocked more needlecraft kits than in previous years. Most notably, however, classes and in-store consultations, once the hallmark of small stores, were offered by most retailers. The addition of these services reduced the competitive advantage enjoyed by the small shops and increased the popularity of craft specialty chains.

Evidence of competitive pressure in the sewing, needlework and piece goods business could be seen as the industry entered the post-1995 period. The proliferation of new and bigger stores coupled with competition from discounters created a difficult operating environment. Retailers responded by using promotional pricing tactics, television advertising, and more creative direct-mail circulars and catalogs.

Jo-Ann Stores partnered with Martha Stewart Living Omnimedia in 1999 to bring a line of 89 home decorating fabrics to its stores nationwide. The partnership was seen by Jo-Ann Stores to signify an important growth opportunity for them. Chairman, president and CEO of Jo-Ann Stores Alan Rosskamm was quoted in the *Akron Beacon Journal* as saying: ''The new collection reflects our strategy to develop partnerships with highly respected, nationally known entities to further build our brand identity.''

INDUSTRY LEADERS

The sewing, needlework and piece goods industry was dominated by two companies: Hancock Fabrics and Jo-Ann Stores (formerly Fabri-Centers of America).

With 1999 sales of $1.38 billion, Jo-Ann Stores was the leading company in the industry. The company was started in 1943 as a single fabric store in Cleveland, Ohio and was incorporated in 1951 as Cleveland Fabric Shops, Inc. The name Fabri-Centers of America was adopted in 1968.

Fabri-Centers grew by acquiring fabric and craft stores throughout the country. These acquisitions included Sewing Shops, Inc., a ten-store chain in Washington, DC; Giltberg's Fabrics of northern Florida, Alabama, and Georgia; New York Fabrics of San Francisco; and Missouri-based Cloth-World. The company continued to operate stores in selected markets under the name New York Fabrics, though most stores used the name Jo-Ann Fabrics. Fabri-Centers acquired the 261-store House of Fabrics chain in 1998, and officially became Jo-Ann Stores to more closely align its corporate identity with that of its retail locations.

Fabri-Centers of America adopted its strategy of super store conversion in 1988, after years of ceding sales and market share to large discounters. By 1996, nearly all of Fabri-Centers 916 stores had been converted to super stores, and the total retail space had nearly doubled, from 3.2 million square feet in 1988 to more than 7.4 million in 1996. According to Jo-Ann Stores, these super stores produced higher revenues and profit margins than the mall-based stores and were entrusted with the future of the company.

Jo-Ann Stores operates all of its stores under either the name Jo-Ann Fabrics and Crafts or Jo-Ann etc. The Jo-Ann etc. stores are fabric, craft supply, and home decorating megastores where customers are offered demonstrations, classes, and specialized customer service. The Jo-Ann etc. stores debuted in 1996.

Following Jo-Ann Stores was Hancock Fabrics, the Michigan-based fabric specialty store. Formerly a division of Lucky Stores, Hancock Fabrics became independent in 1987. By 1999, the company operated almost 500 stores averaging 14,000 square feet. Hancock Fabrics' 1999 sales totaled $381.6 million.

Although they dominated industry sales, leaders in the sewing, needlework, and piece goods business were not lacking for competition, as many stores in different retail categories offered similar products. One extremely successful competitor classified in **SIC 5945: Hobby, Toys, and Game Shops** was Michaels Stores, Inc., a hobby and craft retailer that enjoyed tremendous growth in the 1990s.

Faced with this competitive pressure and the threat of new entrants, industry leaders worked hard to maintain market share. As they entered the new millennium, businesses in the sewing, needlework, and piece goods industry were searching for new ways to gain a competitive edge. Super store conversion, increased customer service, more creative marketing, and expanded inventories were high on the agenda for these companies.

FURTHER READING

Brammer, Rhonda ''A Great Notion?'' *Barron's,* 13 February 1995.

Conroy, David ''Paring Stores, Building Profits; Fabric Chains Accent Home as Part of Growth Strategy.'' *HFN—The Weekly Newspaper for the Home Furnishing Network,* 30 December 1996.

''Creative Marketing Efforts Offer Hope to Struggling Craft Chains.'' *Discount Store News.* 1 July 1996.

Croghan, Lore. ''Shakeout at the Strip Mall.'' *Financial World.* 23 May 1995.

''Fabri-Centers Chooses New Name.'' *Discount Store News,* 22 June 1998.

Fabri-Centers of America, Inc. Company Profile. Information Access Corporation: Company Profiles Database. 9 August 1996.

''Fabric Stores' Varied Appeal.'' *HFN—The Weekly Newspaper for the Home Furnishing Network.* 23 September 1996.

Glover, Kara. ''House of Fabrics Secures New Financing, Updates Operations.'' *Los Angeles Business Journal.* 17 April 1995.

Hancock Fabrics, Inc. Company Profile. Information Access Corporation: Company Profiles Database, 1 October 1996.

Hobby Industry Association. ''1996 Nationwide Craft/Hobby Consumer Study,'' 23 February 1996. Available from http://www.hobby.org/hia/cons.html.

House of Fabrics, Inc. Company Report. Information Access Corporation: Investext Database, 9 July 1996.

Howell, Debbie. ''Hancock Fabrics Buys 24 Mae's Units in Move to Offset Underperforming Stores.'' *Discount Store News,* 6 September 1999.

———. ''Jo-Ann Forms United Front, Surges Ahead.'' *Discount Store News,* 25 January 1999.

''Hudson, Ohio-Based Fabrics Retailer Signs Up Martha Stewart.'' *Akron Beacon Journal (OH),* 28 July 1999.

Levenson, Maurice. ''Fabri-Centers.'' *The Value Line Investment Survey.* 22 November 1996.

———. ''Hancock Fabrics.'' *The Value Line Investment Survey.* 22 November 1996.

———. ''Michaels Stores.'' *The Value Line Investment Survey,* 22 November 1996.

Musselman, Faye. ''Jo-Ann Stores Inc. Keeps On Keeping On.'' *HFN,* 30 August 1999.

Pfaff, Kimberly. ''Home Fabric Surge; Stores Credit Custom Decorating Trend.'' *HFN—The Weekly Newspaper for the Home Furnishing Network,* 21 August 1995.

———. ''Independents Focus on Service Selection.'' *HFN—The Weekly Newspaper for the Home Furnishing Network,* 28 August 1995.

U.S. Census Bureau. ''1997 Economic Census—Retail Trade,'' 18 April 2000. Available from http://www.census.gov.

SIC 5961

CATALOG AND MAIL-ORDER HOUSES

The catalog and mail-order house industry, or nonstore retail industry, is comprised of establishments primarily engaged in the retail sale of products through television, catalog, and direct mail. Such organizations include companies that sell book club memberships, magazines, and retail consumer and business products. These establishments deliver products and services through the mail. This classification does not encompass direct-mail advertising firms or stores that are operated by catalog companies for the purpose of on-site retail sales.

NAICS Code(s)

454110 (Electronic Shopping and Mail-Order Houses)

Industry Snapshot

Catalog and mail-order selling is a vibrant industry, especially as technological advances make the process easier and more cost-effective. The industry experienced great growth during the 1980s when mail-order selling activity leapt more than 300 percent. From 1990 to 1996, mail order sales grew at a rate of more than 9.9 percent per year, about 1.7 times the average growth of general merchandise, apparel, and furniture store sales. Sales continued to increase at similar rates during the latter half of the decade. Total mail order sales were $318.5 billion in the United States as of 1997. Consumer sales accounted for $159.5 billion of the total, while sales to businesses were $85.3 billion. The remainder went to direct mail solicitations from charities. Consumer mail order sales represented 2 percent of the Gross National Product and 4 percent of total retail sales.

The catalog industry saw renewed opportunity with the growth of Internet shopping in the late 1990s. This market arena began to blossom in 1997. While some new Internet sales companies seemed to pose a threat to established non-store retailers, the industry soon reacted by adopting the new technology. As of 1999, an estimated 90 percent of catalog sellers who were members of the Direct Marketing Association were online in some way, and 60 percent of them were selling over the Internet. Catalog retailers' Internet sales represented a high growth area in the late 1990s, with some major companies reporting the doubling and tripling of online sales growth annually.

Catalog and direct-mail sellers also saw some blurring of the lines in the industry in the late 1990s, as retailers launched catalogs, catalog sellers opened stores, and many merchants explored the option of selling via the Internet. The industry also went through a period of consolidation through a host of mergers and acquisitions between 1997 and 1999. And a new line of business opened as some direct marketers found they could sell management expertise to newer companies, especially Internet merchants who lacked the know-how to distribute products smoothly.

Organization and Structure

The catalog and mail-order house industry encompasses companies that sell products through all ''nonstore'' retail channels, including radio, television, and computers. Although larger retailers, such as J.C. Penney, typically maintain an inventory warehouse, most industry participants keep little, if any, inventory on hand. When a customer orders a product, the retailer contacts a wholesale company that ships the product to the retailer or directly to the customer.

Because they refrain from traditional retail purchasing, manufacturing, and inventory management activities, many nonstore retailers are essentially marketing companies. Some catalog companies, for instance, simply assemble a group of complimentary products manufactured by other companies and try to market those items in a catalog to the customers they think would be most interested in them. Similarly, many direct mail and broadcast media retailers essentially act as middlemen, selling products that are manufactured and stored by wholesalers.

The three major categories of nonstore retailing include business, consumer, and charitable sales. Throughout the 1990s, consumer sales accounted for approximately 50 percent of industry revenues, while business and charitable sales each garnered about 25 percent of the market. About 60 percent of consumer nonstore sales were products, while the remaining 40 percent were services. Of nonstore consumer product sales, more than 80 percent were derived from specialty items that were not commonly available in stores. The remaining approximately 20 percent came from sales of general merchandise. Of nonstore sales of consumer services, about 40 percent of revenues were garnered from financial services.

One tremendous advantage that companies in this industry enjoy, however—whether they secure sales via catalogs, direct mail, the Internet, or television home shopping—is the elimination or severe curtailment of two expenses that have a tremendous impact on the bottom line of traditional retailers: rent and sales workforce. And another advantage is that even small to mid-size companies can use mail order to grow the business and/or give current business a larger presence in the market without expanding overhead costs.

The primary disadvantage of mail and broadcast retailing is high advertising costs. The cost of producing and delivering catalogs, fulfilling orders, and servicing customers often leaves retailers with slim profit margins, or losses, if the response to a promotion is poor. The cost of mailing a simple letter and brochure typically ranges from 40 to 65 cents per piece, and the retailer often expects only .5 percent to 3 percent of the recipients to actually purchase a product. In fact, a 2-percent response rate is considered highly successful in the mail-order business. Although response to a catalog is often higher, usually between 3 percent and 6 percent, production costs often exceed $3 per catalog. Mean response rates from catalogs peaked at 8 percent in 1996, and the drop to 5 percent by 1998 was seen as a possible portent of slowing in the industry.

Nonstore Consumers. Nonstore retail industry consumers differ from store customers in several ways, which affects the method companies use to reach the target market. Catalog shoppers, for instance, are better educated, are more likely to work in professional and managerial capacities, earn more money, are more conservative and traditional, and are more comfortable with modern technology and financial instruments. Catalog shoppers are also more likely to be women—58 percent to 42 percent, versus an even percentage of store shoppers. A greater percentage of nonstore customers are also divorced and middle-aged. For example, 25 percent of catalog shoppers are 35 to 44 years old, versus only 17 percent of store customers.

Many demographic differences bode well for nonstore merchandisers. Dual-income households, for example, are more likely to shop through catalogs. As a result, more than 50 percent of households that regularly shopped through mail-order earned $30,000 to $99,000, versus 38 percent in that range that never shopped by mail. Catalog shoppers are also more likely to listen to media advertisements, and typically expose themselves to more news and financial media. Catalog patrons also spend more money on grocery items ($65 per week versus $55 per week for non-catalog patrons), and are more likely to develop brand loyalty.

Background and Development

The history of mail-order is said to go back to the 1490s, just after Gutenberg's invention of movable type. The first known catalog dates from 1498 when Aldus Manutius of Venice offered 15 books by Greek and Latin authors for sale. Mail-order operations have existed in the United States since colonial days. In fact, Benjamin Franklin is believed to have initiated the industry with the first direct-mail offer ever presented to the public. Not until the latter part of the nineteenth century, however, did mail order assume a significant role in the economy. The main impetus for merchandisers to offer products through the mail was the inaccessibility of the massive rural consumer market. Companies knew that they could benefit by getting product information to farmers, who represented the majority of the population.

Although a few firms successfully promoted products to the rural population through catalogs and mail, Richard Sears achieved the most notable success. In 1886 Sears began selling watches in the mail. Eventually, the Sears Roebuck, & Co. catalog became a staple of American life, delivering access for millions of Americans to general merchandise that was locally unavailable.

During the late 1800s and early 1900s, several developments contributed to the emergence of a nonstore retail industry. Most importantly, the construction of a continental rail network provided a vital distribution channel for East Coast mail-order houses. In addition, the U.S. postal service began offering special rate structures for mail-order businesses that encouraged the dissemination of advertising papers and catalogs. Furthermore, in 1913 the postal service developed the parcel post system. These factors provided a relatively inexpensive alternative to products sold by controversial middlemen, who often garnered huge profit margins from the sale and delivery of goods to rural customers.

Three of the largest mail-order houses that gained prominence in the early 1900s were: Sears, Montgomery Ward and Company, founded in 1872, and Spiegel, Inc. These companies, like others of that era, generated huge profits by offering general merchandise at low prices. They often made their own products and benefited from large-scale advertising and high-quantity sales.

Although mail-order houses continued to experience sales growth throughout the mid-1900s, particularly during the post-war economic boom of the 1950s and 1960s, the role of catalog and mail-order sales in the U.S. economy was changing. As the population shifted from primarily agricultural to predominantly urban and suburban, the importance of delivering general merchandise to remote consumers waned. Instead, mail-order companies began emphasizing shopping convenience and access to specialty products.

Despite industry growth, nonstore shopping still represented less than 1 percent of all retail sales by 1960. Even by 1967, U.S. mail-order sales had only reached $2.4 billion. During the 1970s, moreover, mail-order houses realized only modest gains in combined sales.

The 1980s. A variety of developments in the 1980s combined to result in explosive growth in the catalog and mail-order house industry. Technological advances, demographic changes, and more efficient financial markets were the predominant forces behind this phenomenal growth.

Technological advances that catapulted many competitors to success in the 1980s included computers and software, which increased marketing efficiency and improved customer service. The computer systems that became popular in the early 1980s allowed companies to manage and manipulate large amounts of consumer data. As a result, companies were able to cull from a customer list only the best prospects for a particular product or catalog, thereby reducing unnecessary marketing expenditures. Furthermore, by storing customer information in databases, companies were able to efficiently market new products to existing customers.

Computers were also used to track and manage inventory. When a customer ordered a product, the mail-order house could electronically alert its warehouse, or its supplier, and ship the product quickly. Similar information management systems allowed merchandisers to integrate money-saving, just-in-time inventory control, and customer service systems. Furthermore, inexpensive desktop computer systems allowed small, specialty nonstore retailers to compete more easily with larger firms on a national scale.

In addition to computer technology, the nonstore retail industry benefited in the 1980s from pivotal demographic changes affecting American buying patterns. One of the most important changes was a rise in the percentage of working women and dual-income households. Between 1980 and 1990, the percentage of women involved in the labor force climbed from 42 percent to 46 percent, or from 107 million to about 125 million. Because dual-income households did more shopping by mail, this change increased nonstore merchandising revenues. A rise in the number of elderly Americans, who were also more likely to shop through the mail, prompted industry growth as well.

Another factor boosting mail-order growth in the 1980s was the development and public acceptance of new methods of paying for and financing products purchased through the mail. Credit cards allowed both retailers and consumers a safe and efficient means of paying for mail-order items. By the mid-1980s, more than 600 million credit cards were held by Americans. The proliferation of toll-free ''1-800'' (and after 1996, ''1-888'') numbers also generated a large increase in sales. Many catalog companies reported increases of more than 60 percent in sales as a direct result of utilizing toll-free order numbers.

The effect of these and other advances was a 300 percent increase in nonstore retail sales between 1980 and 1990. Indeed, from just $72 billion in 1980, sales in mail-order houses skyrocketed to $211 billion by 1990, representing average annual growth rate of more than 11 percent. By the end of the decade, catalog and mail-order shipments were responsible for about 10 percent of all merchandise sales, more than 3 percent of retail sales, and 1 percent of consumer services sales. Furthermore, trade in the industry represented nearly 2 percent of U.S. gross domestic product.

However, U.S. mail-order sales growth declined in the early 1990s as a sluggish economy suppressed revenues in all retail sectors. By 1992, industry participants faced heightened price competition that reduced profit margins. In addition, many analysts believed that the catalog and mail-order industry was maturing and had passed its stage of high profits and dynamic growth. Several trends supported this theory: the industry was becoming more consolidated; sales growth was leveling off; advertising costs were escalating; and failure rates were up. A major cause of higher advertising costs was media saturation. Because consumers were being bombarded by increasingly larger amounts of mail-order advertising, response rates for promotions, on average, were declining. The average consumer received more than 21 pieces of mail per week in 1995. Households that regularly purchased items through the mail, however, often received much more.

In addition to declining sales growth and slimmer profit margins, catalog and mail-order houses were battling state and federal regulatory efforts that sought to eliminate an important industry advantage—the absence of sales taxes on products sold to out-of-state consumers. Companies narrowly averted disaster in 1992 when the Supreme Court ruled that states could not force mail-order retailers to collect or remit state sales taxes unless they were physically present within the state. An opposite decision would have cost the industry at least $3 billion, in addition to lost sales. Many states continued to seek methods of taxing out-of-state sales, however.

In response to the relatively inclement business environment of the early 1990s, catalog and mail-order houses scrambled to increase sales and profit margins. Companies emphasized customer satisfaction by gathering data on preferences and wants, and then carefully tailoring products and promotions accordingly. Companies also eliminated large, general audience catalogs and relied instead on specialty niche promotions. In 1992, for instance, Fingerhut Companies Inc. joined forces with Montgomery Ward and Co. to develop a set of 10 specialty catalogs.

Part of the customer satisfaction strategy included the integration of advanced database management techniques. By gathering and storing consumer information on a computer database, retailers were able to determine what, when, and how to market to each of their customers. For many companies, database marketing became an exact science that allowed them to maximize the efficiency of every advertising dollar. Indeed, many companies offered products to potentially new customers at a loss so that they could gather information on the consumer and generate profits from follow-up sales.

In the mid-1990s, the business-to-business division of Dell Computer Corporation spent more than $1 million to clean up its database, using a comprehensive telemarketing campaign to add more than 150 fields of information to its database; at the same time, the company eliminated more than 50 percent of its existing list. As a result of this $1-million expenditure, Dell doubled the response rate from its remaining customers, and by reducing printing and postage costs realized an approximate $4 million in annual savings.

Firms also beefed up inventory control systems in the early 1990s. Just-in-time management techniques, whereby warehousers kept minimum stock on hand and relied on prompt delivery by suppliers, became standard for most successful large mail-order houses. Value pricing, too, became an important strategy for many firms. By improving the quality of merchandise, increasing service, and reducing prices, many successful competitors were able to overcome reduced margins by increasing market share and sales volume, and taking advantage of follow-up sales opportunities.

In addition to internal efforts, a flurry of mergers and acquisitions characterized the industry in the early 1990s, as companies sought the benefits of economies of scale and greater access to investment capital. Aaron's Furniture Warehouse, Donnelly Marketing, Burpee, Ticketron, and Conde Nast were just a few of the companies that were absorbed by other mail-order houses. One of the largest mergers involved the sales of Murdoch Magazines to K-III holdings for $650 million.

The Rise of Electronic Retailing. Although the Home Shopping Network was founded in the late 1970s, this retail medium was stagnant for a number of years. Dismissed ''as a downscale medium whose average viewer was a far cry from the urban and suburban sophisticates that merchants hanker after,'' as *Business Week* observed, electronic retailing was given little attention by major retail companies. The arrival of former FOX Network executive Barry Diller as a part-owner of QVC, however, lent the concept increased credibility.

At the same time, retailers increasingly recognized that, given the moribund performance of many of the stores, electronic retailing had its charms. As an analyst at UBS Securities observed in *Business Week,* electronic home shopping is ''a low-cost distribution system. You don't need thousands of stores, and you don't need thousands of pieces of inventory in each location.''

The Direct Marketing Association reported that in 1995, 77 percent of the U.S. population had viewed direct response television in an infomercial, a direct response television spot, or a home shopping program. More than 22 million adults had watched home shopping programs, and approximately 8 million bought merchandise from a television offer. One of the fastest growing areas of television sales was the infomercial (an in-depth promotion of a product, replicating a television show), which increased from $350 million in 1988 to $1 billion in 1994.

The next big event in the history of nonstore shopping was the arrival of the Internet. Though some commerce had been tried over the Internet earlier, on-line shopping became a recognized presence on the American scene in 1997. The success of some early on-line ventures, such as 1-800 Flowers and Amazon.com, led to a plethora of on-line sales sites. Many of these were small start-up ventures without the marketing sophistication of brand identity of either traditional retailers or catalog vendors. But by 1999 the majority of catalog houses had some presence on the Internet, and many traditional retailers also published online catalogs. Major sellers on the Internet were books, computer products, recorded music, gifts, and financial services.

CURRENT CONDITIONS

In the late 1990s, the catalog and mail-order industry was both growing and changing. The doldrums of the early 1990s ended, and sales grew at levels hovering around 8 percent annually at the end of the decade. Though earlier analysts had thought the mail-order industry was saturated, by the late 1990s it seemed that the traditional retailing industry was saturated too, and catalogs were an easy way to expand. The president of the Direct Marketing Association, H. Robert Wientzen, explained in a September 22, 1999 *New York Times* article, ''[T]here aren't a whole lot of places left to put stores.'' So for example Federated Department Stores bought venerable direct-marketer Fingerhut in 1999, and Fingerhut then ran the catalog and online divisions of Federated's stores. Staples, a giant chain of office supply stores, acquired the catalog office supply vendor Quill in 1998, and Office Depot, another sprawling retail office supply chain, also acquired a catalog vendor, Viking. Yet this trend worked in reverse at the same time, as catalog marketers decided to open stores in the late 1990s. L.L. Bean, which had had only one retail store in its almost 90-year history, announced in 1999 that it would begin to open a chain of stores. These mergers and changes showed the catalog and mail-order industry was still volatile at the end of the 1990s. In many cases, this volatility meant lower profits. Many major direct marketers had flat or declining sales as they struggled to adjust business strategies. For example, in 1998 sales remained level or shrank for Lillian Vernon, J.C. Penney, and Land's End, all industry leaders.

Catalog and mail-order sales as a whole expanded in the late 1990s, but the area of the most explosive growth was Internet sales. Some major catalog retailers reported rapid expansion of their Internet sales, even if overall sales were flat. Online sales for J.Crew, a major apparel catalog, quadrupled in 1998, reaching $20 million. Total sales for J. Crew were $816 million, so Internet sales represented only a small percentage. But Internet sales at the company continued to rise over the next year. Though Land's End, another apparel catalog company, reported a steep drop in earnings in 1998, its Internet sales nevertheless grew from only $18 million in 1997 to $61 million a year later. The stagnating company planned to move more aggressively into Internet selling, while abandoning some of its retail stores. But Internet selling seemed unlikely to replace catalog selling in the industry as a whole. According to a survey of major catalog retailers in the *New York Times*, direct-mail advertising and large catalog mailings were still considered the best way to reach new customers in 1999.

Some of the highest growth mail-order companies in the late 1990s were computer retailers. Dell had sales of $18 billion in 1998, an increase of 33 percent over the previous year. CDW did almost as well, with an increase of 26 percent in 1998, leading to sales of $1.7 billion. Gateway was another stellar computer retailer, with $7.5 billion in sales, and revenues increasing 16 percent.

Another new development in the industry in the late 1990s was the introduction of the hybrid magazine/catalog. These "magalogs" or "catazines" were mostly given away as store promotions. Leading retailers Abercrombie & Fitch, Nordstrom, and Neiman Marcus were early on the magalog scene. J.C. Penney created *Noise*, a free magazine for teens, in 1999. These publications were a skilful blend of feature articles and photos that touted store brands without explicitly saying so. The appeal of this kind of catalog seemed to be that it stood out from other mailings. As the number of catalogs mailed increased in the late 1990s, the hybrid version was hoped to be more arresting than the run-of-the-mill direct mail offering.

INDUSTRY LEADERS

The largest catalog retailer in the United States in the late 1990s was J.C. Penney, the department store chain. The catalog has always figured heavily in its retail mix, but that was not the sole source of the company's business. Fingerhut Companies, Inc., of Minnetonka, Minnesota moved up from being the ninth-largest mail-order firm in the country in 1995 to being the second-largest firm in 1999. Fingerhut sold more than 15,000 different products, including various housewares, electronics, and domestic items, to a customer database of more than 13 million people. In 1999 Federated Department Stores, a conglomerate that owned several department store chains including Bloomingdales and Macy's, bought the company. After the acquisition, Fingerhut found a new niche for itself handling the catalog and online sales of some of Federated's divisions. In 1999 it inked a contract with the world's largest retailer, Wal-Mart, to manage its Internet sales.

Damark International was another consistent leader in the catalog and mail order industry in the 1990s. The company's 1998 sales stood at $484.4 million. Damark ran a massive catalog operation, mailing out some 150 million catalogs annually. It offered computers, home office equipment, sporting goods, electronics, and other consumer goods at discount prices. Damark also ran direct mail shopping clubs. In the late 1990s it had nine such clubs with approximately 1.7 million members. Club members paid roughly $60 a year to join and were then able to buy Damark's discounted entertainment, travel, health and fitness and restaurant services.

One of the fastest growth mail-order companies in the late 1990s was Dell Computer Corporation. It was one of the largest catalog operations by revenue in the late 1990s, and led the world in direct mail sales of personal computers, software, and peripheral equipment. Being a computer corporation, it was natural for Dell to move heavily into Internet sales, and almost half its business transactions were expected to take place on the web by the end of the twentieth century. Dell's sales of $18 billion in 1998 increased 33 percent from the year before. By the late 1990s Dell had organized into a three-tier structure to handle further growth. Its segments were Domestic Dell, International Dell, and Internet Dell.

And the phenomenon of the late 1990s nonstore retailing world was Amazon.com. It was arguably the company that made Internet shopping a comfortable option for American consumers. By the close of 1998, more than 6 million customers had purchased books, music, or videos from its online store. Sales were $610 million that year, profits were zero, yet sales growth was more than 300 percent. It branched out from its position as a virtual bookstore to essentially become a virtual shopping mall. Amazon.com did this by acquiring the online auction house e-bay and stakes in a host of other online vendors including drugstore.com, HomeGrocer.com, and Pets.com. The *Wall Street Journal* named Amazon.com as its best one-year performer in 1999, and for the direction of Internet retailing, it was clearly the company to watch.

The largest foreign mail-order company in the world in the late 1990s was Otto Versand (Spiegel), of Germany. With 1999 general merchandise, sporting goods, and apparel mail-order sales of about $18.6 billion, this European giant dwarfed overseas competitors. The company overcame sluggish sales in the early 1990s by tightening inventory controls, reducing costs, and intensifying target marketing efforts. Otto Versand subsidiaries included Eddie Bauer, Honeybee, and Spiegel.

WORKFORCE

Employment in the catalog and mail-order house industry was expected to grow faster than employment in most other U.S. retail sectors in the 1990s and early 2000s. Advances in automation and information systems, however, could curtail job growth as companies eliminate labor-intensive positions. Despite expected growth, the catalog and mail-order industry offered relatively meager employment opportunities in relation to businesses with similar sales volumes. The greatest job growth was expected to occur among computer programmers and information systems professionals, who were needed to integrate and streamline customer, inventory, and financial information. Most computer positions required little prior training, allowing opportunities for many entry-level information specialists.

Jobs in sales, photography, layout, and design were likely to increase between 50 percent and 65 percent. Labor and blue-collar positions were forecast to expand as well—by about 50 percent. Positions in management, finance, and information systems were also expected to realize growth rates of 50 percent to 60 percent by 2005.

AMERICA AND THE WORLD

The U.S. catalog and mail-order industry is the largest and most advanced in the world. There are two basic reasons for this industry's continual growth: a large population and a relatively high income level. Although other countries may be more densely populated, they lack a large enough number of people who have the income to buy.

Mail-order retailers in the United States benefit from several other advantages. Most importantly, U.S. retailers enjoy access to the largest industrialized, relatively homogenous market in the world. As a result, multiple economies of scale exist for domestic merchandisers. An entire U.S. mailing list industry has emerged, for example, allowing retailers to efficiently attack specific market niches.

Another very important advantage for the U.S. mail-order industry is relatively low postal rates. U.S. bulk and first-class postal rates are the lowest in the world—much lower, in fact, than rates in most of Asia, Europe, and South America. Postal rates in much of Europe, for instance, are twice as high as U.S. rates, making it difficult for companies to successfully promote products through the mail. Higher shipping charges further dilute profit potential in overseas markets.

In addition to these factors, most foreign mail-order markets are characterized by: relatively limited media availability; much tighter government regulation of advertising content and product approval requirements; a lack of public understanding and acceptance of mail order; language and cultural barriers; low credit card penetration; and a lack of toll-free numbers. Furthermore, in some European countries many types of mail promotion are banned for environmental and social reasons. The European Community mail-order industry also suffers from a lack of uniform postal and business standards. Some of these mitigating factors were disappearing in the late 1990s, and the growth of the Internet also served to break down geographical barriers.

Cross-Border Sales. Foreign sales by domestic catalog and mail-order houses have traditionally been limited by language and cost barriers. Despite the inefficiency of nonstore retailing in many overseas markets, however, several U.S. and foreign firms have successfully penetrated other markets. Cross-border sales between the United States and European Community (EC), particularly steadily increased throughout the 1990s, spurred in part by increasingly uniform EC markets.

The most exportable mail order products in the 1990s, in order of revenue size, were information, education, and collectible products. In addition, several U.S. firms successfully marketed specialty American products in some Asian countries. Some of the most successful offshore U.S. mail-order enterprises included Hanna Anderson, Austad's, Eddie Bauer, L.L. Bean, Black Box, Inmac, Myron Manufacturing, and Recreational Equipment Incorporated (REI).

RESEARCH AND TECHNOLOGY

The most successful catalog and mail-order houses increasingly moved computer systems toward client/server architecture with relational databases and distributed processing. Information databases would eventually allow companies to produce highly specific catalogs and marketing materials tailored to smaller groups, or even individuals. A company might be able to print a set of catalogs, for instance, each of which contained a different product mix and marketing message. Just-in-time inventory practices would assume a primary role in helping companies to maintain profit margins through lower fixed costs and better customer service.

New advertising media increasingly complements traditional broadcast, print, and telephone channels. The burgeoning multimedia environment will eventually integrate video, telecommunications, optical disk technology, and personal computers. Advertisers will be forced to adjust marketing techniques as consumers gain more control in choosing which ads and media they internalize. Advancements in recycled paper, printing technology, and ink would likely help the industry move toward reduced waste and lower production costs. At the same time, the proliferation of specialty cable television channels that reach more homogenous niche markets is expected to increase the efficiency of broadcast advertising.

The importance of new Internet technology was amply demonstrated by the catalog and mail order industry as it embraced online selling in the late 1990s. Some innovations included Catalog City, a web site consumers could visit to request any of 17,000 catalogs. Partially owned by Bear Creek Corporation, parent of the mail-order fruit and gift firm Harry and David Orchards, Catalog City allowed small vendors without much Internet expertise to have a presence on the Web. Internet shopping also offered new opportunities for interaction between the consumer and the catalog. For example Land's End offered a "virtual fitting room" where women could construct a three-dimensional model of themselves on screen to find clothes that flattered their build.

FURTHER READING

Anders, George. "Best- and Worst-Performing Companies". *Wall Street Journal,* 25 February 1999.

Antonucci, Mike. "Is It a Magazine? A Catalog? Retailers Combine the Two". *Knight-Ridder/Tribune News Service,* 2 September, 1999.

"Catalog". *Chain Store Age Executive,* August 1999.

Fishman, Arnold. "The Annual "Monster" Mail Order Guide." *Direct Marketing,* September 1998.

Geller, Lois K. *Response! The Complete Guide to Profitable Direct Marketing.* New York: The Free Press, 1996.

Niemira, Michael. "Are Nonstore Sales a Threat to Traditional Store Business?" *Chain Store Age,* September 1996.

Patterson, Philana. "Catalog Firms Are Expected to Report Lackluster Profits as Industry Changes". *Wall Street Journal,* 23 April 1999.

"Nonstore Retailing Performance." *Chain Store Age Executive,* August 1998.

"Nonstore Retailing Performance". *Chain Store Age Executive,* August 1999.

Ray, Debra and George Reis. "Catalog Sales Projected to Reach $74.6 Billion by Year End." *Direct Marketing,* August 1996.

Stamler, Bernard. "Direct Marketers Find Some Familiar Ground." *New York Times,* 22 September 1999.

SIC 5962

AUTOMATIC MERCHANDISING MACHINE OPERATORS

This industry consists of establishments primarily engaged in the retail sale of products by means of automatic merchandising units, also referred to as vending machines. This industry does not include the operation of coin-operated service machines, such as music machines, amusement and game machines, and lockers and scales. Insurance policies sold through vending machines are classified in **SIC 6300: Insurance Carriers** or **SIC 6400: Insurance Agents, Brokers, and Service.** Establishments primarily engaged in operating music machines, amusement and game machines, lockers and scales, and most other coin-operated service machines, are classified in services, Division I.

NAICS CODE(S)

454210 (Vending Machine Operators)

The U.S. government issued the first vending machine patent in 1886, and in 1888 the Thomas Adams Company installed similar machines on the train platforms in New York City to sell gum. Less than 100 years later, the vending machine phenomenon had permeated American culture, becoming more commonplace than the corner mailbox. The number of vending machine operators declined during the 1980s, as larger companies—including food service and beverage suppliers—bought out smaller companies. Yet more than 8,000 vending machine operators maintained services in the United States in 1999, and the industry dispensed $30 billion worth of products. By 2000, ingenious entrepreneurs had transformed the machines into veritable mini-malls, vending everything from video games to underwear. Sales in this industry grew by 428 percent between 1995 and 1999.

Establishments in this retail industry typically rent space for their coin-operated machines in office buildings, large stores, subway and train stations, airports, and places of entertainment. At the turn of the twenty-first century, vending machines were located in every mainstream location, from office buildings to grade schools. An estimated 85 percent of vending machine sales involved food or beverage. Other common merchandise sold in vending machines includes toiletries and other personal items. Automatic merchandising machine retailers fill and service the machines regularly with products from a range of manufacturers and food packagers.

Important factors in the operation of these types of non-store retail businesses are vending machine locations, turnover of products at each location, and the quality of service personnel who fill and repair machines. Computerized systems monitor vending machine sales and usage and facilitate maintenance for the operator as well. By the end of the twentieth century, machines equipped with radio transmitters and small antennas allowed machine owners to count the money in the machines and take inventory from remote locations. Remote control systems could also alert operators to malfunctions such as coin jams and other mechanical problems. Larger companies in the industry used highly sophisticated inventory control systems and study market research data in order to optimize product inventory and machine placement. Additionally, the National Automatic Merchandising Association (NAMA), headquartered in Chicago, Illinois, assists vending machine operators by providing access to educational services, information, and technical support.

Innovations in vending machine technology and design developments improved the quality and scope of vending machine services during the 1900s, enabling a wider selection of products to be sold via the machines. Snack food machines were adapted to handle a greater variety of package shapes and sizes, and to support hot and cold food and beverage, including ice cream and freshly brewed Cappuccino. Electronic improvements contributed to the ability of modern machines to provide digital readings and push-button functionality and to accept credit cards, thus enhancing the convenience for consumers. In 1999 industry leader Canteen Service Company of the British Compass Group PLC expanded its vending machine operation through agreements with popular restaurant chains to sell name brand fast food. Canteen, founded in 1931, operates restaurants as well as automated merchandising apparatus.

FURTHER READING

''About Vending,'' 1999. Available from http://www.vending.org/about_vending.

Ho, Rodney. ''Vending Machines Make Change—Now They Sell Movie Soundtracks, Underwear—Even Art.'' *Wall Street Journal,* 7 July 1999.

McCright, John S. ''To Order Coffee, Press 1.'' *PC Week,* 1 November 1999.

Richey, Warren. ''It's Vendors' Turn to Try to Get Money Back.'' *Christian Science Monitor,* 3 February 2000.

SIC 5963

DIRECT SELLING ESTABLISHMENTS

Retail companies that sell merchandise door-to-door, from trucks and wagons or from other temporary locations, make up the direct selling industry. Included are individuals who sell products by these methods and are not employees of the organizations they represent, as well as establishments that are retail sales offices from which employees operate to sell merchandise by house-to-house canvassing.

NAICS CODE(S)

722330 (Mobile Caterers)
454390 (Other Direct Selling Establishments)

Although direct selling has been a staple method of distribution for retailers in the United States since colonial times, the industry has undergone major changes since the 1970s. This industry, which for years included just a few mainstays such as books, household appliances, and cosmetics, now encompasses an enormous variety of products, from household goods to gourmet foods.

For most of its history, the direct selling industry relied on door-to-door sales. Indeed, many organizations built large retail empires based primarily on home sales methods. Avon Products Inc., Tupperware Corp., and AB Electrolux are a few of the organizations traditionally associated with house-to-house canvassing that generated huge profits during the post-World War II economic boom.

Despite past successes, the effectiveness of some forms of direct selling waned in the 1970s and 1980s as new retail channels emerged. As a greater proportion of women entered the work force, salespeople found it increasingly difficult to find prospects at home during the day. Moreover, because two-income families had less time to shop at stores, they began to purchase more goods through direct mail, catalogs, and the Internet. The increased popularity of consumer goods shows, warehouse stores, television shopping networks, and other selling techniques further reduced direct sales to the remaining one-income families. Finally, increased crime rates caused many potential customers to refuse strangers' entry into the home, and some municipalities banned door-to-door sales altogether.

Responding to this trend, in 1992 both Avon and Tupperware started marketing their products for the first time through mail-order catalogs and direct mail. AB Electrolux, also shifted its focus from door-to-door sales to catalog showrooms and warehouses in the late 1980s.

In 1996, after 60 years of selling door-to-door, Encyclopedia Britannica Inc. laid off its entire sales force in the United States and Canada. Sales had declined from $650 million in 1990 to $405 million in 1995, mainly due to the advent of CD-ROM encyclopedias. In June 1996, Collier's Encyclopedia followed suit. According to Linda Corman of *Sales & Marketing Management,* Britannica's decision to eliminate door-to-door selling marked the ''end of an era in sales,'' and noted that it was probably a ''harbinger of what lies ahead for the sales profession, as selling and marketing in the information age become more sophisticated, more targeted, and more driven by technology.''

The largest growth area in the direct selling industry in the 1980s and 1990s was the direct selling organization (DSO), also known as network or multilevel marketing (MLM). With MLM, one person becomes a product distributor and then makes a commission on the sales made by other distributors he or she signs up. The first network marketing company, founded in the 1940s, was Nutrilite (now part of Amway), a maker of nutritional supplements. By 1997, almost every kind of product was being sold through DSOs, including cosmetics, art, time management systems, tires, kitchen tools and appliances, lingerie, long-distance phone services, and computers.

Many DSOs use the party plan, in which the seller invites friends to a party where goods are displayed and sold, or else they build sales through networking. In 1996, Christina Gold, Avon's chief for North America, told *The New York Times* that since 1994 she had expanded her sales force from 45,000 to 445,000. Explaining that more than one-half the company's sales are made or arranged at work, Gold stated that ''We train people in how to connect at the office and factory. . . . It's a high touch business.''

According to the Direct Selling Association, worldwide retail sales in U.S. dollars reached approximately $68 billion in 1995. There were 17 million distributors worldwide, covering at least 44 countries, with the 6.3 million U.S. distributors producing $16.5 billion in sales.

In 1999, there were an estimated 364,800 employees in all non-store retailing industries. Most worked slightly more than 30 hours a week for an average wage of $10.33 per hour.

Direct selling, or doorstep marketing, also was growing overseas by the mid-1990s. In 1995, Brazil became Avon's largest market outside of the United States, with 478,000 sales representatives. Amway, introduced to Brazil in 1991, had increased its number of distributors to 200,000 by 1995. The Direct Selling Association reported that other countries with a strong selling presence included Japan, where sales reached $30.3 billion; Taiwan, with sales of $1.7 billion; and Korea, with sales of $1.3 billion.

Some of the leading direct selling companies in 1999 included Amway Corp. ($6 billion); Avon ($5.2 billion); and Nikken ($1 billion).

FURTHER READING

Anderson, Duncan Maxwell, and Michael Warshaw. ''The New Elite.'' *Success,* December 1995.

Brooke, James. ''Who Braves Piranha Waters? Your Avon Lady!'' *The New York Times,* 7 July 1995.

Bureau of Labor Statistics. *Employment Statistics.* 2000. Available from http://www.bls.gov.

Corman, Linda. ''Closing the Book.'' *Sales & Marketing Management,* September 1996.

''Ding Dong.'' *PC Week,* 23 September 1996.

''Hoover's Company Capsules.'' *Hoover's Online.* 2000. Available from http://hoovers.com.

Myerson, Allen R. ''The Death of Some Salesmen.'' *The New York Times,* 28 April 1996.

''P.F. Collier to End Door-to-Door Sales of Its Encyclopedias.'' *Wall Street Journal,* 24 May 1996.

Roha, Ronaleen R. ''Want to Buy a Potato Peeler? Wanna Sell a Bunch of 'Em?'' *Kiplinger's Personal Finance Magazine,* March 1997.

Ward's Business Directory of U. S. Private and Public Companies, Detroit: Gale Research, 1999.

SIC 5983

FUEL OIL DEALERS

This classification covers companies primarily retailing fuel oil. Companies that primarily sell fuel oil burners are in **SIC 5074: Plumbing and Heating Equipment and Supplies (Hydronics);** those that install and service fuel oil burners are in **SIC 1711: Plumbing, Heating and Air-Conditioning;** and those that repair and service fuel oil burners are in **SIC 7699: Repair Shops and Related Services, Not Elsewhere Classified.**

NAICS CODE(S)

454311 (Heating Oil Dealers)

Dun and Bradstreet listed 8,391 establishments doing business under this industrial classification in 1997. Companies in this industry sell motor oil for vehicles and fuel oil for heating buildings, with the largest earnings coming from heating oil sales. Residential customers are the primary consumers of heating oil. In 1999 the U.S. Department of Energy reported that 16 million American homes use a total of 11 billion gallons of heating oil each year, which represents 700 gallons per household. Schools, hospitals, businesses, and industry account for the bulk of non-residential heating oil sales. Similar figures for motor oil consumption are not updated regularly. Retail sales of motor oil in the U.S. reached $4.2 billion in 1995, the last year statistics were available.

Industry sales of heating oil vary with the season and geographic market. Demand is normally higher in northern states during the winter, causing oil prices to rise. But price is also affected by regional climatic changes. Nearly the entire continental United States experienced a series of mild winters in the late 1990s. In the fairly typical winter of 1996 the average price of heating oil reached $1.14 per gallon. But two unseasonably warm winters caused a 34-cent per gallon dip in price. By February 1999 heating oil prices had fallen to 66 cents per gallon. Nine months later heating oil distributors were bolstered by forecasts of a bitterly cold winter for the northern states. Industry experts predicted that the average price of heating oil for the year 2000 winter might hit $1.06 per gallon.

Fuel oil dealers can also be affected by international conflict and domestic politics. The 1970s energy crisis inflated the price of crude oil (which sets the pace for heating and motor oil prices) and reduced profitability for gasoline and fuel oil dealers. Gasoline prices peaked again in January 1981 shortly before the Iran-Iraq oil embargo. Oil prices collapsed in 1985 and 1986, when Saudi Arabia and Kuwait launched an oil price war in OPEC. In 1993 the industry successfully launched a campaign against President Bill Clinton's proposed 60 cents BTU (British Thermal Unit) tax on heating oil. The tax was eventually lowered to the same level as tax increases on other forms of energy. Both motor and heating oil prices have been affected by the ongoing crisis between the U.S. and Iraq. Dating back to the 1991 Persian Gulf War, fuel oil prices have ebbed and flowed with tensions in the Middle East. In November 1999 Iraq suspended exports, forcing crude oil to its highest level since Operation Desert Storm.

Two of the largest heating oil distributors in the 1990s were Petroleum Heat and Power Company, Inc. and Star Gas Partners L.P., both of Stamford, Connecticut. Petroleum Heat and Power was widely considered the largest heating oil distributor in the United States, with 340,000 customers in the Northeast and Mid-Atlantic states, and $548.1 million in sales in 1997. Star Gas reported more than 166,000 customers in 1997 and $161.4 million in sales. In 1999 Star Gas purchased Petroleum Heat for $368 million. It also purchased Maryland-based Diamond Fuel, New Jersey-based Foreman Hardware Co., Inc., and Ohio-based Mohrfeld Inc. in 1999, adding about 1,800 accounts to their customer base. Another industry leader was Warren Equities Inc. of Providence, Rhode Island. The privately held company owns Extra-Mont gas station/convenience stores, in addition to selling fuel oil. In 1997 it reported sales of more than $900,000 and a payroll of 2,100 employees.

In 1998 the three best-selling brands of motor oil were Pennzoil, Quaker State, and Valvoline. Pennzoil held 21.8 percent of the market, Quaker State had 15.9 percent, and Valvoline had 14.2 percent. In 1999 Pennzoil Co. acquired Quaker State Co. for about $1 billion and formed the Pennzoil-Quaker State Co. The merger will join Pennzoil's 1,516 Jiffy Lube centers with Quaker State's 600 Q Lube oil change stores. Pennzoil-Quaker State is expected to have about $2.7 billion in assets, about $1 billion in equity, and annual sales of about $3 billion by the year 2000.

Further Reading

Hoover's Online. *Hoover's Company Profiles.* Austin, TX: 1999. Available from http://www.hoovers.com.

U.S. Department of Commerce. *1997 Economic Census.* Washington, D.C.: Bureau of the Census, 1995.

SIC 5984

LIQUEFIED PETROLEUM GAS (BOTTLED GAS) DEALERS

This industry consists of companies that primarily sell bottled or bulk liquefied petroleum (LP) gas, which is used mainly for heating homes and businesses in rural areas. This classification includes other byproducts of crude oil, such as bottled butane gas, used as an additive in gasoline and for lighters, and bottled propane gas, which is most often used to produce LP gas.

NAICS Code(s)

454312 (Liquefied Petroleum Gas (Bottled Gas) Dealers)

This industry arose from the industrial revolution, when manufacturers sought plentiful, easily transported fuel. In the twentieth century, dealers of liquefied petroleum and propane and butane gases had customers in commercial, industrial, and residential markets. Industry sales rose with population growth and industrial expansion. However, profitability varied due to changes in demand and production costs, both of which were affected by such factors as economic conditions and the price of crude oil imports used to make these products.

In 1997, the fuel industry employed 98,400 workers, most of whom worked 37 hours a week for an average wage of $13.26 per hour.

As of 1999, the industry leader in this category appeared to be AmeriGas Partners, L.P. of King of Prussia, Pennsylvania, with sales of $872.5 million and 5,026 employees. In addition to selling engine fuels, AmeriGas sold propane to more than 950,000 residential, industrial, agricultural, and commercial users, and possessed a fleet of 3,400 vehicles. The company is a wholly owned subsidiary of UGI Corp.

Second in this industry was Ferrellgas Partners, L.P. of Liberty, Missouri, with 1999 sales of $624 million and 4,463 employees. Ferrellgas also owned its own delivery fleet, which included 4,000 vehicles, most of which ran on propane gas. Another industry leader was Suburban Propane Partners, L.P. of Whippany, New Jersey, with 1999 sales of $544 million and 3,179 employees. Suburban Propane was spun off from the British conglomerate, Hanson PLC, which still owns 24 percent of the business. The company operated 350 stations in 44 states, and owned its own storage units, railroad tank cars, and trucking fleet. Cornerstone Propane Partners, L.P., of Watsonville, California, another industry leader, employed 2,396 workers.

Liquefied petroleum gas dealerships were also secondary businesses for companies in related industries, such as dealers in **SIC 2869: Industrial Organic Chemicals** and businesses in **SIC 4925: Mixed, Manufactured, or Liquefied Petroleum Gas Production and/or Distribution.** In 1989, Quantum Chemical Corp., a retailer in industrial organic chemicals and propane gas, made news when it purchased Petrolane, Inc. in a partnership deal with First Boston. According to *Chemicalweek,* the purchase was "in line with the company's strategy to grow its propane business through acquisitions." Though a secondary business for Quantum, the propane operations of the company held about 15 percent of the propane market in 1989.

In the 1990s, demand for liquefied petroleum and other petroleum products grew at roughly 1.5 percent annually. However, demand for commercial and residential use declined while transportation use rose.

FURTHER READING

Hoover's Company Profiles. Available from http://www.hoovers.com.

U.S. Bureau of Labor Statistics. *Employment Statistics,* 2000. Available from http://www.bls.gov.

U.S. Department of Commerce. *1992 Census of Retail Trade,* Washington, DC: U.S. Bureau of the Census, 1995.

Ward's Business Directory of U.S. Private and Public Companies, Detroit: Gale Group, 1999.

SIC 5989

FUEL DEALERS, NOT ELSEWHERE CLASSIFIED

Establishments in this industry primarily sell coal, wood, and other fuels, not elsewhere classified.

NAICS CODE(S)

454319 (Other Fuel Dealers)

The United States produced 1.1 billion tons of coal in 1998, with 940 million tons going for domestic use and the remainder being exported. Over 87 percent of U.S. coal was sold to utilities in 1998. Approximately 3 percent was sold to the industrial, residential, commercial, and transportation sectors. Americans are projected to consume 580 million cubic meters of wood and wood products in the year 2000. Most U.S. fuel wood is sold to electric companies. But this could change if the U.S. becomes a leading exporter of fuel wood in the next millennium. In 1998 the U.S imported $9.4 billion dollars more of forest products than it exported. U.S. wood exports have dropped 20 percent since 1994, while foreign wood imports have increased 33 percent. At the same time, developing countries burn nearly 2 million tons of wood fuel each day. Wood fuel supplies are up to 95 percent of domestic energy in these countries and also contributes to commercial and industrial needs.

Companies in this industry are affected mainly by production levels of the products they sell and by customers' use of competing fuel sources, such as petroleum and natural gas. Coal was the leading source of fuel used in America until the 1920s, when the growing popularity of automobiles and developments in the aviation industry introduced new fuels. Meanwhile, the coal industry overexpanded, which led to intense competition among coalmines and a decline in coal prices, both wholesale and retail. By the 1940s, the coal industry lost one of its largest markets after railroads converted to diesel-powered systems. Coal consumption rose again in the 1970s and 1980s due to the oil crisis, which prompted new coal-processing technologies. At the start of the 1990s coal production rose 4 percent annually with increasing demand from electrical utilities.

In 1997 Dun and Bradstreet listed 1,287 establishments doing business under this industrial classification. Leaders in the industry ranged from big companies with large payrolls to smaller companies that still generated significant revenue. Do-All Gas Company of Benson, North Carolina, reported $790,000 in miscellaneous fuel products sales during 1997, while employing less than 20 workers. Clonch Industries, Inc. of Belva, West Virginia, generated $3.7 million in wood-related sales in 1997, while employing 50 workers. Southern Appalachian Coal Sales, Inc. of Knoxville, Tennessee, reported more than $23 million in revenue during 1997, and a staff of several thousand employees.

FURTHER READING

"U.S. Coal Production." *Coal Week,* 18 October 1999.

"The New York Times Almanac 2000: The Almanac of Record." New York: Penguin Reference Books 1999.

U.S. Bureau of the Census Website. http://www.census.gov. December 1999.

U.S. Department of Commerce Website. http://www.doc.gov. December 1999.

U.S. Department of Labor Website. http://www.dol.gov. December 1999.

"Value of U.S. Wood Exports"*The Journal of Commerce,* 11 January 1999.

SIC 5992

FLORISTS

This category covers establishments primarily engaged in the retail sale of cut flowers and growing plants. Establishments primarily engaged in the retail sale of seeds, bulbs, and nursery stock are classified in **SIC 5261: Retail Nurseries, Law and Garden Supply Stores.** Greenhouses and nurseries primarily engaged in growing seeds, bulbs, flowers, and nursery stock are classified in **SIC 0181: Agriculture.** Establishments primarily engaged in the retail sale of artificial flowers are classified in **SIC 5999: Miscellaneous Retail Stores, Not Elsewhere Classified.**

NAICS CODE(S)

453110 (Florists)

INDUSTRY SNAPSHOT

According to the American Floral Endowment Consumer Tracking Study, conducted between June 1998 and May 1999, projected 1999 retail sales of floriculture items would reach $15 billion. Retail florist shops still dominated the industry, numbering 27,341 and averaging annual sales of $209,182 per shop. However, these traditional outlets faced increasing competition from floral departments in supermarkets, which numbered 23,000 at the time of the study, and 10,857 retail nurseries and lawn and garden supply stores. The industry imported about 60 percent of the cut flowers sold in the United States, with 64 percent of these imports originating from Colombia. Ecuador held a distant second with 12 percent of cut flowers imported to the United States. California controlled the domestic growing of cut flowers, with 65 percent of the market; Florida came in a distant second, growing a mere 7 percent of cut flowers.

The traditional image of men buying women cut flowers for a date does not correlate with consumer sales trends tracked by the study, which tracked only personal consumer purchases, not business purchases. The study revealed that cut flower sales accounted for only 28 percent of florists' business; outdoor bedding and garden plants accounted for almost half (49 percent) of their sales; and flowering or green houseplants accounted for almost a quarter (23 percent) of sales. Also, women predominantly purchased flowers. Women made 81 percent of overall floral sales, though men caught up some in cut flower sales with one third of purchases. What's more, individuals purchased flowers for themselves a majority (64 percent) of the time, leaving only 36 percent of purchases as gifts. Cut flower sales turned this statistic on its head, though, with only 31 percent of purchases for the self, compared with 69 percent as gifts. Finally, calendar events accounted for only 15 percent of overall floral sales; Mother's Day accounted for 23 percent and Valentine's Day for 16 percent of these sales. The majority of floral sales (85 percent) marked no calendar occasion; only 4 percent of these purchases commemorated love or an anniversary, with exactly half of these sales marking no special occasion and 21 percent of these purchases for home decoration.

ORGANIZATION AND STRUCTURE

Florists either design arrangements per customer request or sell and design arrangements according to standard designs. Their job also entails floral decoration of buildings, cost and price consulting, and training others in floriculture. Most traditional retail florists are affiliated with national wire services that handle long-distance orders by telephone. The receiving florist gets a commission from the sending florist depending on the size of the order. Often, customers are charged an additional service fee by the sending florist.

Wire services play an important role in the industry. According to Bram Cavin, in his book *How to Run a Successful Florist and Plant Store,* the number of wire orders increased from 4 million in 1947 to 10 million in 1965. FTD, a cooperative of 20,000 florists in the United States and 52,000 florists in 140 countries worldwide, reported 20 million wire orders in 1992. FTD is the only member-owned floral cooperative of its kind. The Society of American Florists estimates the flower-by-wire business accounts for 20 percent of a traditional florists' sales. Most florists belong to one or more of the 11 flower-by-wire services serving the floral industry.

In order to increase service, computers were used to send customers' orders to other towns. Some consumers used toll-free numbers to reach the florist who actually sent the product. Others used various florists, who in turn used various wire services like Florist Transworld Delivery, Teleflora, and AFS to send the flowers. Wire services offering memberships give florists advertising and promotional materials and assistance, as well as training in management, marketing, and point-of-purchase aids.

Standard arrangements were designed to make it easier for the customer to order. Other factors that helped this industry included telephones and credit cards. These allowed direct contact between retailers and growers—unlike the old days of telegrams—and provided a better way to pay, thereby protecting both parties even though they did not know each other.

While technology made it easier for florists to communicate, it also brought in heavy competition. Traditional florists lost market share because of the proliferation of ''nonflorists''—supermarkets, discount retailers, department stores, and nurseries—selling the same products. According to *Flowers* magazine, in 1992 traditional florists held 56 percent of the market compared to nonflorists who held 44 percent.

BACKGROUND AND DEVELOPMENT

The Society of American Florists formed in 1884 to represent retail florists and all segments of the industry. Unfortunately, association officials have no records of the first retail floral establishments in the United States. Florist Transworld Delivery (FTD) of Downers Grove, Illinois, was the first floral wire service to standardize order placement among florists nationwide. Originally, 15 florists banded together in 1910 in Rochester, New York, as the Florists' Telegraph Delivery Association to exchange orders for out-of-town deliveries by telegraph. Before the formation of FTD, floral arrangements were shipped out of town via train or mail. FTD was the first to create a standard special bouquet order with its member florists and was also the first such company to publish floral arrangement catalogs to help consumers select the proper arrangements.

A green plant boom in the 1970s, coupled with a big demand for imported cut flowers, prompted a rapid nationwide expansion in the number of florists. The Floral Index, Inc., a Chicago-based marketing and consulting service reports overall retail sales of floral items were slowing after unprecedented growth between 1982 and 1989. Between 1989 and 1990, growth slowed to less than $500 million or one-half the rate of previous years. Americans purchased floral products at about $49.33 per capita in 1992, more than double the amount purchased in 1982, but 3 percent less than in 1991. According to *Flowers* magazine, this figure represents the first decline in per capital sales in 17 years.

Individual floral shop sales also experienced a 3 percent decline from $185,200 in 1991 to $180,000 in 1992, based on estimates from some 40,480 shops in the United States. American consumers paid an average of about $16.15 per unit for their floral items in the early 1990s. Imports of fresh cut flowers such as, carnations and roses were forcing prices down, causing some retail flower shops to lose market share to nontraditional shops with low overhead.

Close to 70,000 retail florists and supermarket flower departments sold cut flowers and growing plants in the early 1990s, compared to about 20,000 such shops in the early 1970s. U.S. retail sales of floral products remained steady at about $13 billion from 1990 to 1993, in part due to a sluggish worldwide economy. In the mid-1990s, the United States had 26,757 florists, which employed about 120,000 workers. In 1996, nonsupervisory workers earned about $8.76 per hour.

Roses remain the number one selling flower and were grown domestically and imported from 26 countries. Per capita purchases of roses were 4.1 stems per person in 1992, nearly double the amount purchased between 1975 to 1980. Sixty-five percent of all roses sold were red, and the majority, some 64 million, were sold around Valentine's Day. An increase in corporate gift giving was also helping to expand the floral market. Plants and flowers, according to a Gallup poll commissioned by the American Floral Marketing Council in 1990, were the ''most convenient gift'' and the best ''I love you gift.'' Green plants, while losing market share, continued to be a $1 to $2 billion industry segment.

CURRENT CONDITIONS

Growth continued to be divided among retail outlets and traditional florists. Supermarkets not only continued to sell flowers, but many were expanding their floral departments. According to a survey conducted by *Supermarket News,* 9 percent of the surveyed operators planned to expand their floral departments and over 15 percent planned to add full service floral departments. According to *Supermarket News,* the expansion was fueled by higher profit margins.

Increasing competition between the traditional and nontraditional florists spurred uses of new technology such as flowers-via-computer and toll-free numbers to make floral item purchases more accessible to the public. Advertising campaigns were also focusing on non-occasion uses for flowers and plants. In the late 1990s, television commercials promoting gifts of flowers were becoming very common. The Internet played a substantial role in setting a new trend at the turn of the century. Many traditional florists were resorting to the Internet to sell flowers, and others only sold flowers via Web sites.

INDUSTRY LEADERS

As the largest flowers-by-wire cooperative, FTD was the industry leader in the early 1990s. With its recognizable winged Mercury—messenger of the gods—logo in a yellow and black circle, FTD was estimated to have 60 to 70 percent of the flowers-by-wire market. The company made florists accessible by placing ordering outlets in gas stations, car dealerships, fast-food franchises, and even pizza parlors. It also distinguished itself from other floral wire services with its 100 percent satisfaction guarantee. FTD members pay 7 percent of the value of their transactions in return for advertising support from FTD.

In May 1999 FTD announced increased sales for the third quarter (as well as for the first nine months) of its fiscal year. Third quarter net sales increased by $10.2 million or 21.1 percent, to $58.5 million from $48.3 million in the third quarter of fiscal 1998. Net sales for the first nine months of fiscal 1999 increased by $22.7 million or 16.8 percent, to $157.6 million from $134.9 million for the first nine months of fiscal 1998. The explosion in e-commerce pushed sales up dramatically, as FTD not only hosted its own World Wide Web site, but also inked an agreement with CompuServe in July 1998 making FTD the exclusive floral sales organization on this computer network.

The March 1999 acquisition of Florafax International, Inc., by Gerald Stevens, Inc., exemplified the diversity of the floral industry in the Late 1990s. Gerald Stevens was already a geographically diverse company, with 94 stores in 13 U.S. markets: 62 free-standing retail shops and 32 supermarket locations. Florafax represented the fourth-largest wire service in the floral industry, serving all 50 states by 5,300 member-florists. Gerald Stevens acquired the Florafax subsidiary National Flora, a company that generated more than 500,000 floral-product orders in 1998, increasing its net revenues by 24 percent over 1997, to $13 million. At the same time, Gerald Stevens acquired Internet Services, LP, parent of the oldest e-commerce company in the industry, FlowerLink, which experienced order increases of 60 percent for the first six weeks of 1999 as compared to the same six-week period in 1998.

Clearly, the Internet represented the biggest opportunity for growth in the floral industry, just as e-commerce was bolstering most every other business segment. 1-800-FLOWERS.com announced in October 1999 impressive growth in its first quarter of 2000, with online revenues increasing by 88.1 percent to $11.8 million and telephonic revenues increasing 9.5 percent to $37.6 million; total revenue climbed 22.1 percent to a record $58.1 million. What's more impressive is the fact that these increases occurred in the slowest quarter of the fiscal year for the floral industry, the summer, with fewer calendar events prompting consumers to purchase flowers.

AMERICA AND THE WORLD

Foreign countries are stepping up their efforts to gain more of the U.S. market by flooding the market with exports and establishing retail stores, thus driving prices down. In the early 1990s, imports of Latin American roses accounted for 40 percent of the roses sold in the United States, compared to 2 percent sold in 1971. American rose specialists protest that this will only devalue the rose and have launched campaigns emphasizing the rose as a strictly American product. More than $325 million worth of fresh cut flowers had been imported from overseas producers at the end of 1991, compared with less than $5 million in 1971.

FURTHER READING

1-800-FLOWERS.com. ''1-800-FLOWERS.com Reports Online Revenues Rise 88 percent in Fiscal 2000 First Quarter.'' Available from http://www.1800flowers.com.

Cavin, Bram. *How to Run a Successful Florist & Plant Store.* New York: David McKay Company, 1977.

Florafax International, Inc. ''Florafax Announces Acquisition by Gerald Stevens,'' December 1999. Available from http://www.florafax.com/Floranews.htm.

''The Floral Industry and How it Works.'' *Jindra Floral Design,* 1997.

Society of American Florists. ''Floral Stats,'' December 1999. Available from http://www.aboutflowers.com/floralstats.html.

U.S. Department of Labor. Bureau of Labor Statistics. *Employment, Hours, and Earnings, United States, 1988-96.* Washington, D.C.: GPO, 1996.

SIC 5993

TOBACCO STANDS AND STORES

This entry includes establishments primarily engaged in the retail sale of cigarettes, cigars, tobacco, and smoker's' supplies.

NAICS CODE(S)

453991 (Tobacco Stores)

In 1998 a reported 5,204 tobacco stores operated in the United States, with sales totaling $460,757 according to *Smokeshop* in the ''1999 Industry Report.'' Eighty-eight percent of sales came from tobacco-related merchandise.

Tobacco specialty stores, often called ''smokeshops,'' were traditionally located in malls or downtown business districts. The mall shops were often part of a chain, while the downtown shops tended to be independents that also sold other items such as magazines and newspapers. Historically, tobacco manufacturers subsidize some of these endeavors in an effort to ensure a constant retail outlet for their products. The largest domestic concentration of smokeshops appears in the southern United States, with 1,516 establishments reported. Although the total number of establishments declined by 23 percent in 1998, the states of Montana, South Dakota, Wisconsin, Oklahoma, and the District of Columbia reported an increase in the number of shops. Across the United States, the number of shops declined at a rate of 8 to 1, with the most significant decline in the western states with 35 percent reduction in stores. Total sales dropped by 14 percent, although employment in smokeshops increased from an average of five employees per store in 1997, to 7.4 employees in 1998, with 43 percent of smokeshops offering employee fringe benefits.

The number of tobacco stands decreased steadily in the United States during the latter half of the twentieth century. Declines were attributed to a change in life-style for many Americans as businesses moved out of the downtown areas where support for smokeshops was high. With less pedestrian traffic, the smokeshops suffered a loss of clientele. Many of the smokeshops that were located in malls in the 1970s slowly disappeared in the 1980s as rents climbed too high for small businesses to endure. Additionally, the steady decrease in consumption of most tobacco products, due in part to the dissemination of information about the dangers of tobacco use, factored into the decline. Meanwhile, an increasingly wide array of stores added smoking supplies to their inventories. Distributors reported that many of the specialty tobacco shops lost sales to other less specialized retail outlets, including drug stores, grocery stores, and convenience stores. Discount department stores and supermarkets became popular second-tier distributors, even for pipe tobacco. The overall convenience and the lower prices offered at these outlets increased their attraction for consumers as an alternative to smokeshops.

At the end of the 1990s, pharmacies discontinued sales of tobacco products in response to negative public sentiment towards the tobacco industry, and convenience stores began to pose serious competition to tobacco specialty shops. In 1997, a particularly large number of non-specialty retail outlets joined the trend and backed away from the tobacco business in response to efforts by the U.S. government to regulate the tobacco industry. The FDA—backed by President Bill Clinton—passed several regulations, among them a mandate that retailers verify the age of cigarette buyers at the risk of steep fines for those retailers in violation of the law. Remarkably, the anti-tobacco onslaught contributed in part to a limited revival of smokeshop businesses. In anticipation of these stricter regulations, new cigarette outlet stores—small smokeshops selling low-priced products at high volume—opened for business nationwide. In fact, the number of cigarette outlet stores in the United States jumped 36 percent, to about 3,600, between March of 1995 and April of 1996. In 1998, 67 percent of tobacco shops listed themselves as tobacco-only retailers. Analysts predicted a growing trend if government regulators prevailed, and if supermarkets, drugstores, and convenience stores continued to abandon the tobacco consumer.

In 1998, the largest form of retail tobacco consumption came from increased sale of premium cigars—cigars that sell for $2 or more. These accounted for 39.7 percent of tobacco sales at smokeshops. The escalating popularity of premium cigars prompted many department stores, such as Saks Fifth Avenue and Macy's, to add cigar accessory shops in order to profit from the modern fashion trend. So popular were the cigars that, even as President Clinton signed bills hindering cigarette advertisements during the 1990s, he refused to abandon his own habit of enjoying an occasional smoke. Restaurants and liquor stores across the country added fine cigars to their retail mix, further reducing the clientele at traditional smokeshops. Statistics from the Cigar Association of America, reprinted in *Market Share Reporter* in 1999, revealed that only 16 percent of cigar sales transpired at cigar stores in 1998. During that time, smokeshops in rural sites remained stable, yet urban sites declined by 10 percent. Of existing establishments in 1998, 95 percent were independent, 75 percent existed at only a single location, and 9 percent of businesses operated three or more stores.

Among the largest businesses listing tobacco stands and stores as their primary business were Burley Tobacco Growers Cooperative Association and A. Fader and Sons. Other businesses in this industry included Nazareth's Fine Cigars of Beverly Hills, California; Smoke and Snuff Shops of Clearwater, Florida; and Smoker's Den of Bennington, Vermont.

FURTHER READING

"1999 Industry Report." *Smokeshop,* August/September 1999.

Barry, Susan. *U.S. Industry & Trade Outlook '99.* New York: McGraw-Hill, 1999.

Curan, Catherine. "Big Stores See Cigars Puffing up Yule Sales." *Daily News Record,* 8 November 1996.

"Fader's Tobacconists, Smokers Accessories, Cigars, Pipes, Tobacco Lounges." Available from http://www.faderstobac.com/aboutfaders.htm.

Lazich, Robert S. *Market Share Reporter.* Detroit: Gale Group, 1999.

Osterholm-Cox, Nancy. "Tobacco Specialty Stores Taking Root in Colorado Springs." *Knight/Ridder Tribune Business News,* 3 April 1997.

Romell, Rick. "Discount Cigarette Stores Have Smokers Puffing for Bargains." *Milwaukee Journal Sentinel,* 29 August 1996.

"Smokeshope Magazine's 1999 Industry Report." *Smokeshop Online.* Available from http://www.gosmokeshop.com/0899/report.htm.

U.S. Distribution Journal. November-December 1997.

Vaughan, Vicki. "Cigars Are Back from the Ashes." *San Antonio Express-News,* 17 November 1996.

Ward's Business Directory of U.S. Private and Public Companies. Detroit: Gale Research, 1996.

SIC 5994

NEWS DEALERS AND NEWSSTANDS

This category covers establishments primarily engaged in the retail sale of newspapers, magazines, and other periodicals. Home delivery of newspapers by other than printers or publishers is classified in **SIC 5963: Direct Selling Establishments.**

NAICS Code(s)

451212 (News Dealers and Newsstands)

Industry Snapshot

Newsstands and news dealers occupy a nostalgic corner of modern urban history in the United States. A majority of such businesses are located in heavily populated areas, and are owned and operated by a single proprietor. The 1997 Economic Census reported 2,313 active news dealers and newsstand establishments. Sales figures for the same year were $853 million, with 9,770 people employed in this field.

Some news dealers and newsstands are seasonal and shut down in winter months. The small kiosks often lack insulation, and space heaters may not provide enough warmth during the most frigid weeks of the northeastern seaboard. Most, though, stay open throughout the year. As mentioned, most of the businesses classified in this industry are small single-proprietor establishments. However, larger chain and franchise operations are becoming more common. According to industry watchers, the number of street-based news dealers and newsstands has been steadily dwindling over the past several decades. The industry is dominated by enterprises with five or fewer employees.

Organization and Structure

A typical newsstand derives its profits from volume sales of newspapers and magazines. Ancillary items such as cigarettes and chewing gum also play an important part in its financial success. A typical day for a newsstand operator or dealer begins in the pre-dawn hours of the morning, when a distribution service drops off bundles of periodicals that come out on that particular day of the week. Newspaper trucks deliver the morning dailies, and may return later with a p.m. edition. Each delivery requires employees to audit and verify the shipment invoice, remove the unsold prior editions from display, and stock either all of the new delivery or store part of it until needed later. Historically, Monday was the busiest day for both deliveries and sales with the arrival of weekly magazines. However, in the 1990s *People* magazine started delivering on Friday, and the resulting increase in sales prompted many other weekly publications to follow suit.

Morning patrons generally limited their purchase to a single newspaper or periodical. Later lunch-hour and afternoon customers lingered over the magazine racks and often made impulse purchases. Many larger newsstands also acted as local bookstores, stocking popular paperbacks and sometimes even hardcover editions. A typical newsstand drew its sales primarily from the sales of daily newspapers, but in cities such as New York or Los Angeles, with many citizens transplanted from other areas of the country or globe, foreign newspapers and magazines were also big sellers. There, the *International Herald Tribune,* the *Times of London,* as well as European weeklies such as *Paris Match* and the German magazine *Stern,* sold well.

In the late twentieth century, the industry shifted toward more standard business practices as a result of corporate ownership. For example, cash registers appeared at newsstands even though most customers on their way to a job or commuter train did not want to be held up for the few seconds longer these machines require.

A news dealer or newsstand typically made a small profit from every item their establishment sold. A dealer would typically receive a maximum of 20 percent for each daily newspaper sold. Magazines had a higher profit margin because the intense competition between magazine titles and publishing houses resulted in courting the retailer. In addition to the 20 percent sellers received from the sale of each magazine, they would often obtain an additional 10 percent in the form of a retail display allowance. This premium came most often from larger magazine publishing corporations, such as Conde Nast or Time-Warner, as an incentive to keep their magazine titles prominently displayed near the transaction counter. Additional incentives could be paid to the news dealer for positioning a certain magazine overhead above the counter or for allowing poster displays of current issues. Such premiums could become a large part of revenue for major newsstands in New York City, where competition for display space was fierce. The monthly fees could sometimes reach into the thousands of dollars.

BACKGROUND AND DEVELOPMENT

For much of its history, the newsstand industry has been operated by new immigrants, especially in the decades following World War II. European families originally dominated the business, while Arabic and Asian entrepreneurs entered the field in the 1980s and 1990s. In New York City alone, 1,325 newsstands were in business in 1950, a figure that can be compared with the 2,313 newsstands operating in the entire United States in 1997. By then, New York City was home to only 330 street vendors of newspapers and magazines.

While street newsstands continued to be a presence in large metropolitan areas, other forms of newsstands emerged in the late 1990s. One development was the emergence of ''superstores'' devoted almost entirely to periodicals. Because these stores had more space than a traditional street stand, they could offer a larger selection of titles to their customers—up to 4,000 in some cases. Some firms have also experimented with opening newsstands in shopping malls, areas with the high pedestrian traffic that traditional street vendors have relied on for their business.

CURRENT CONDITIONS

The number of news dealers and newsstands has increased only slightly since 1992, when 2,260 newsstands were in operation. The industry is increasingly dominated by larger multi-unit organizations such as Eastern Lobby Shops. These corporate entities have brought modern business methods to what were mom-and-pop type establishments—cash registers were implemented in order to keep an eye on sales, and computer-aided stock tracking helped keep sufficient copies on the racks. Yet in major urban areas like New York City and Chicago, small one-person operations could still be found on many major thoroughfares.

In the late twentieth century, street dealers became increasingly restricted by laws regulating all urban street vendors, while a rise in crime has also played a decisive role in their dwindling numbers. A lone owner-operator, having worked up to an 18-hour day, makes an easy robbery target at closing time when he or she heads to the bank with the day's receipts. Small newsstands, like all other stationary objects in a large city, have also been the target of graffiti.

Street newsstands have also faced community pressure to clean up both their appearance and their merchandise in some large cities. In New York City, the mayor's office has pushed for regulations that would limit the amount of adults-only material that dealers could sell or display. The mayor's office has also proposed that dealers' license fees be proportional to the value of the property their stands occupy. Under this proposal one dealer's annual fee would increase from $538 to $3,750.

In Philadelphia, which has around 300 street news dealers, a 1999 regulation required that stands be built from durable materials instead of wood. The city developed a standardized stand for this purpose. Some vendors opposed the change, though, because of the $10,000 they would have to pay for the new stands.

Several marketing changes had also put pressure on newsstands and news dealers by the late 1990s. These pressures stemmed from publishers' and distributors' practices and from new outlets for periodicals. While the number of magazine titles published increased at a rate of nearly ten per week in 1998, this larger selection did not bring an increase in single-copy sales. The Audit Bureau of Circulation reported combined sales of approximately 367 million magazines per issue, but only 18 percent were purchased as single copies instead of by subscription. Furthermore, only 3 percent of the single copy sales occurred at newsstands.

There are many reasons for newsstands' small share of this market. Circulation departments began aggressively pursuing subscription customers, rather than single-copy readers who purchased magazines at newsstands, because retail sellers could return unsold copies for a refund. Other outlets for periodicals have also cut into newsstands' sales. Mass-market bookstores have proliferated, offering extensive magazine sections in an enclosed space for perusing the numerous titles. The rise in cafes and coffee houses in urban areas also had a negative effect on newsstand sales. Many such enterprises began selling magazines and newspapers to attract customers who wanted to sit and read for a while over a cup of coffee. Publishers also began targeting specialty stores as retail outlets for magazines—placing *Vegetarian Times* at health-food store check-out counters or *Rolling Stone* in record stores. Technological innovation has also cut into a market that had long been a staple of newsstands: the out-of-town newspaper. With many newspapers available on the Internet, customers have become less inclined to visit a newsstand for a publication that is at least a day old when they can get the news from afar more immediately on their computers.

INDUSTRY LEADERS

Although most newsstands are singly owned establishments, a few companies have a fairly large presence in the industry. Hudson News Company has a large presence in the New York City area. While primarily a magazine distributor, the company also owned and franchised several newsstands and had total sales of $508 million in 1998. Healy News Store, Inc., of Wakefield, Rhode Island, is a small firm that managed to earn $1.2 million in sales with only nine employees in 1998. A company with more of a national presence is Eastern

Lobby Shops, which has 120 newsstands around the country.

FURTHER READING

Bernstein, Elizabeth. ''New Magazine Superstore Sells Books as 'Auxiliaries'.'' *Publishers Weekly,* 24 November 1997.

Bishop, Todd. ''Extra! Extra! Newsstands Redesigned.'' *Philadelphia Business Journal,* 3 September 1999.

Darnay, Arsen J., and Gary Alampi, eds. *Wholesale and Retail Trade USA.* Detroit: Gale Research, 1995.

Garigliano, Jeff. ''New York Newsstands in a Two-front Battle.'' *Folio: The Magazine for Magazine Management,* June 1998.

''Hudson News Company.'' Austin, TX: Hoover's. Available from http://www.hoovers.com.

Lowenstein, Joanna. ''Q&A: Barnes & Nobles' Richard Lawton—Leader of a Retail Power Shift.'' *Folio: The Magazine for Magazine Management,* 1 April 1999.

———. ''Rich Jacobsen.'' *Folio: The Magazine for Magazine Management,* 15 April 1999.

The Magazine Handbook. New York: Magazine Publishers of America, 1999. Available from http://www.magazine.org.

''Raising Roof Over Newsstand Rates: Council May Revoke Rudy's Right to Hike Charges as Street Furniture Hangs Fire.'' *Crain's New York Business,* 24 August 1998.

Strupp, Joe. ''Out-of-Town News Blues: Online Newspapers Hit Niche Newsstands Where They Live.'' *Editor & Publisher,* 11 September 1999.

Tanner, Lisa. ''Read All About It. . . .'' *Dallas Business Journal,* 2 July 1999.

U.S. Bureau of the Census. *1997 Economic Census: Retail Trade, Geographic Area Series.* Washington, DC: U. S. Bureau of the Census, 1999.

Ward's Business Directory of U.S. Private and Public Companies 1997. Detroit: Gale Research, 1997.

SIC 5995

OPTICAL GOODS STORES

This entry includes establishments primarily engaged in the retail sale of prescription eyeglasses and contact lenses for individuals. Establishments primarily engaged in the retail sale of binoculars, telescopes, and opera glasses are classified in **SIC 5999: Miscellaneous Retail Stores, Not Elsewhere Classified.**

NAICS CODE(S)

339115 (Ophthalmic Goods Manufacturing)
446130 (Optical Goods Stores)

INDUSTRY SNAPSHOT

U.S. retail eyewear stores generated $15.8 billion in sales during 1998, a 2.6 increase over 1997. Independent opticians (vendors of eye wear prescribed by ophthalmologists or optometrists), optometrists (graduates of optometry school who are trained to detect eye diseases, but not to treat them), and ophthalmologists (medical doctors who can treat eye diseases, prescribe medication, and perform surgery) accounted for two-thirds of that total. National chains like Pearle Vision Inc. and LensCrafters accounted for the rest. Industry observers expect annual earnings to hit $19.5 billion by 2002. In 1999 Dun and Bradstreet listed more than 18,000 U.S. establishments under this industrial classification, with more than 65,000 employees on their payrolls.

BACKGROUND AND DEVELOPMENT

The eyeglasses and contact lens retailing industry has been increasingly crowded, as opticians, optometrists, and ophthalmologists compete for the same market. Ophthalmologists and optometrists examine eyes and write eyewear prescriptions. Traditionally, both ophthalmologists and optometrists have offered to fill the eyeglass and contact lens prescriptions they write. But independent opticians can also fill these prescriptions. In the late 1960s optical stores and some small regional chains began offering eye exams along with glasses and contacts. Retail giants began to spring up, and an industry that was once considered strictly a ''health-care'' field became a competitive retail market.

Two 1978 legal decisions further opened the door for retail competitors. In one decision the Federal Trade Commission (FTC) ruled that optometrists and ophthalmologists must give patients their prescriptions, making it possible to shop around for glasses rather than rely exclusively on the doctor who wrote the prescription. In the second decision the FTC unanimously approved a rule preempting state law and prohibiting states and professional organizations from banning advertisements for eyeglasses, contact lenses, and eye examinations. Four years later the FTC issued an order prohibiting the American Medical Association from placing a ban on advertising by its member physicians. The Association appealed to the United States Court of Appeals for the Second Circuit, which approved enforcement of the Commission's order. American Medical Association v. FTC, 638 F.2d 443 (2d Cir. 1980), aff'd, 456 U.S. 966 (1982).

These rulings transformed eyeglasses into a marketable consumer product. Retailers began advertising fast turnarounds, low prices, and convenient hours and locations. They promoted eyeglasses and contacts as fashionwear and convinced the public of the need for more than one pair—in part by offering special deals when two were purchased. Retailers introduced lighter and thinner lenses and more attractive frames, which stimulated sales. Retailers began offering contact lenses in a variety of colors, and many consumers bought several pairs because they liked the idea of changing their eye color. In recent years, the emergence of less-expensive daily ''disposable'' contacts has opened further marketing opportunities.

CURRENT CONDITIONS

At least 150 million people—or more than half of all Americans—require vision correction, and the incidence increases with age. Nearly two-thirds of all women in the U.S. wear corrective eyewear. About 26 million Americans wear contact lenses. The industry's growth rate has slowed through the 1990s from steady annual increases of around 10 percent to yearly gains as low as 4 percent, but sales are expected to rise as the population continues to age. In the late 1990s corrective laser eye surgery provided competition to optical goods retailers. At a cost of between $1,800 and $2,500 per eye, laser surgery provided a permanent solution to impaired vision for approximately 1 million Americans each year.

In the 1980s emerging retail eyewear chains grabbed a third of the market from optometrists, ophthalmologists, and independent optical goods establishments—which previously had dominated the entire market—but their total share has since remained constant. Cole Vision Corp. was the nation's largest eyewear retailer in 1998, with approximately $1 billion in sales, 2002 stores, and a 7 percent market share. Based in Ohio, Cole Vision expanded its business in 1996 by purchasing Pearle Vision, Inc., for $165 million.

In 1998 National Vision Associates, Ltd., moved to second place among national retail eyewear chains, when it purchased New West Eyeworks Inc. and Frame-n-Lens Optical. The acquisitions gave the Georgia-based eyewear chain 919 stores in 45 U.S. states and Mexico. The next year National Vision Associates changed its name to Vista Eyecare, and looked into expanding its business further. Company executives predicted revenues in excess of $1 billion for the year 2000. With only 858 stores LensCrafters led all U.S. retail eyewear chains in sales during 1998, reporting more than $1.1 billion in earnings. The Ohio-based company reported more good news for the first three quarters of 1999, when sales increased 14 percent to $965.3 million. Founded by Procter & Gamble Co. executives 17 years ago as a profoundly team-driven company, LensCrafters has always been family-friendly. In 1999 LensCrafters parent company, Luxottica SpA, the Italian eyeglass frame company, purchased Bausch & Lomb's sunglass business for $640 million.

FURTHER READING

''National Vision Associates, Ltd. Completes Acquisition of Frame-n-Lens Optical, Inc.'' *PR Newswire,* 29 July 1998.

''National Vision Associates, Ltd. Announces Extension of Offer to Purchase all Common Stock of New West Eyeworks, Inc.'' *PR Newswire,* 8 August 1998.

''Cole National Completes Acquisition of Pearle, Inc.'' *PR Newswire,* 18 November 1996.

U.S. Bureau of the Census Website. http://www.census.gov. December 1999.

U.S. Department of Commerce Website. http://www.doc.gov. December 1999.

U.S. Department of Labor Website. http://www.dol.gov. December 1999.

SIC 5999

MISCELLANEOUS RETAIL STORES, NOT ELSEWHERE CLASSIFIED

This category includes establishments primarily engaged in the retail trade of specialized lines of merchandise that are not included elsewhere, including art and architecture supplies; autographs, sets of coins, and related supplies; finished monuments and gravestones; cake decorating supplies; baby carriages; cosmetics; awnings and banners; candles; fireworks; rough gemstones and rock and stone specimens; home swimming pools (not installed); hearing aids; and trophy shops. It also includes ice dealers; hot tub and whirlpool bath dealers; orthopedic and artificial limbs stores; pet shops; rubber stamps stores; art dealers; auction rooms; typewriter stores; religious goods (other than books); telephone stores; and tent shops.

NAICS CODE(S)

446120 (Cosmetics, Beauty Supplies, and Perfume Stores)
446199 (All Other Health and Personal Care Stores)
453910 (Pet and Pet Supplies Stores)
453920 (Art Dealers)
443111 (Household Appliance Stores)
443112 (Radio, Television and Other Electronics Stores)
448310 (Jewelry Stores)
453998 (All Other Miscellaneous Store Retailers (except Tobacco Stores))

The industry also includes establishments primarily engaged in selling a general line of their own or consigned merchandise at retail on an auction basis. Establishments primarily engaged in auctioning tangible personal property of others on a contract or fee basis are classified in **SIC 7389: Business Services, Not Elsewhere Classified.**

As part of the more than $2 trillion retailing business in the United States, these businesses are wide-ranging in size of operation and revenue generated. While many of the enterprises in this category can be classified as small business, their impact on the U.S. economy is substantial, accounting for as much as 30 percent of the gross domestic product. These businesses sell everything from light bulbs to sunscreen to mailing supplies to cat toys. The products are not always glamorous, but for many, they are necessities.

Depending on the segment of retailing being examined, the profit margin for these businesses hovers around the 2 percent range nationwide. In the late 1990s, some enterprises in this classification (e.g., typewriter stores, ice dealers) no longer enjoyed the same prominence or level of enterprise that they did 20 or more years ago. On the contrary, other enterprises like religious goods stores and pet stores have enjoyed healthy activity, even during difficult times.

The growth of discount stores and price clubs that carry a wide variety of durable and nondurable goods (e.g., Wal-Mart and its sibling operation Sam's Club) have seen an increase in popularity. Wal-Mart is by far the best known of these stores; with 910,000 employees in 3,600 stores and 1999 sales of $138 billion, it is larger than Sears, Kmart, and JC Penney combined, according to the Hoovers' Business Information Service.

It is difficult to predict future trends for this segment of the economy, given all of the variables involved and the ''scrambling'' of merchandise among the businesses. Some experts predict gloomy times ahead, despite the fact that consumer confidence has been up and the stock market has been at record highs. Although various individual businesses may have posted double-digit sales increases, retailing as a whole posted less impressive numbers. Indeed, economic predictions are hard to make, but it is a fact that, in the mid- to late 1990s, thousands of retail companies sought protection from creditors in bankruptcy courts. Reports of bankruptcies, voluntary consolidations and hostile takeovers still occupy a regular place in business news columns.

One effect of retailing failures is the growth of liquidator-type stores. A liquidator will either purchase a store's inventory or run a going-out-of-business sale when a merchandiser cuts back its operation or closes down. In the late 1990s, liquidators moved billions of dollars' worth of inventory: Boston-based Gordon Brothers Group LLC alone estimates that it moves $2 billion of merchandise annually. Besides Gordon Brothers, the Schottenstein Bernstein Capital Group is another big name in the liquidation business. These companies have worked with Jamesway, Woodward & Lothrop, along with selected Kmart, Edison Brothers, and Petrie Stores.

Home-based shopping in the form of catalog offerings (e.g., Spiegel and Fingerhut) and broadcast-based presentations (like QVC and the Home Shopping Network) are also part of this diverse retailing segment, although their sales have slowed in the 1990s.

This general slowdown might be attributed to another trend that will surely have a long-term impact on retailing: the Internet. In less than five years, the Internet and the rise of electronic commerce has become an important, if not integral, part of many people's lives; and, often, it is these people who possess the most buying power. It is difficult to find businesses that have no presence on the Internet: moving companies, restaurants, and bakeries all seem to have their own web sites. Sites that began with one specific product now sell a variety of items; Amazon.com, which started as a book dealer but now sells a variety of retail goods over the Internet, is the best known example.

Still, the Internet is subject to hype, and many of the companies that try to establish a presence on the web will fold, or sell out to competitors. Moreover, there are still a number of glitches in computerized retailing. The 1999 Christmas season was supposed to revolutionize how people bought gifts. Although more people shopped online than ever before, they also found themselves having to contend with overloaded web sites that could not handle the volume. Besides, the products purchased online need to be delivered offline—and that step has to be done by ground or air transportation. Despite advances in security systems, a number of people are still leery about submitting their credit card information while online, and, consequently, many people search for the product they want on the Internet and then order it by telephone. This is expected to change as the technology becomes more trustworthy in the eyes of consumers.''Once secure transactions become more prominent, the Web will be for people of this century what the Sears Roebuck catalog was for consumers in the last century,'' according to Robert Marczak, an Internet marketing specialist and president of Marczak Business Services of Sharon Springs, New York.

FURTHER READING

''Internet-Based Businesses.'' *The Futurist,* July-August 1996.

Bongiorno, Lori. ''Everything Must Go to the Liquidators.'' *Business Week,* 15 January 1996.

Changler, Susan. ''Gloomy Days Are Here Again.'' *Business Week,* 8 January 1996.

Moukheiber, Zina. ''Retailing: Hard Goods Were Relatively Weak Last Year, but the Rag Business Was Pretty Good.'' *Forbes,* 13 January 1997.

Rotenier, Nancy. "Want to Sell Consumer Products, from Bleach to Barbie? Better Know Which Buttons to Push." *Forbes,* 13 January 1997.

Vaughan-Nichols, Steven J. "On-Line Shoppers: 'Just Looking, Thanks.'" *Byte,* March 1996.

Finance, Insurance, & Real Estate

SIC 6011

FEDERAL RESERVE BANKS

This classification includes the Federal Reserve Banks and their branches, which serve as regional reserve and rediscount institutions for their member banks.

NAICS Code(s)

521110 (Monetary Authorities-Central Banks)

Industry Snapshot

While U.S. banks were experiencing greater autonomy as restrictions were relaxed in the late 1990s, the U.S. banking structure was still heavily regulated by the U.S. Federal Reserve System. The Fed, as it is popularly called, also greatly influences the U.S. financial markets and monetary supply, to which banks must continuously react. At the end of 1998, there were 3,041 member banks of the Federal Reserve System, with 46,112 branches. This included 39 percent of all commercial banks and 74 percent of all banking offices. The total net income of the 12 Federal Reserve Banks was $26.25 billion in 1999, of which $25.4 billion was deposited into the U.S. Treasury. Most of this income was derived from the interest earned on federal government securities, which The Fed acquires on the open market. The twelve banks spent $1.9 billion on operations and had a combined budget of $2.3 billion.

Banking institutions can be regulated by as many as four major, independent federal agencies as well as state agencies. Historically, there have been two distinct types of financial institutions in the United States: commercial banks and savings banks. Commercial banks are depository institutions with investment and broad lending powers for short- or intermediate-term purposes. Savings banks include thrift institutions, which hold passive deposits and investments in long-term real estate mortgages, and credit unions, which are owned by the members and provide short term personal loans. Either of these types of financial institutions may be state or federally chartered.

The Federal Reserve banks enforce Federal Reserve Board regulations, clear and collect checks for depository institutions, extend credit to depository institutions, and act as the fiscal agent of the United States. In addition to the Federal Reserve, the banking industry is regulated by several other agencies. The Federal Deposit Insurance Corporation (FDIC) insures deposits in commercial banks and thrifts, and also regulates these institutions. The Office of Thrift Supervision has a role in overseeing thrift institutions. The Office of the Comptroller of the Currency supervises national banks. Finally, each state has a banking office to regulate state-chartered banks. The Resolution Trust Corporation (RTC), which had managed thrifts with conservators, completed its work and disbanded in the mid-1990s.

Banks and savings institutions chartered under state law are subject to the laws and regulations of that state, as are nationally chartered institutions where the state provisions are not preempted by federal laws. The resulting combination of federal and state regulation and charters has created an interrelated system under which most state banks are subject to some federal supervision and state laws are often applicable to national banks.

The Federal Reserve is the primary federal supervisor and regulator of all United States banks and of state-chartered banks that are members of the Federal Reserve System. In its supervision of the general operations of these financial institutions, the Federal Reserve seeks to promote the soundness of these institutions and ensure their compliance with relevant laws and regulations. The Federal Reserve is also responsible for reviewing the participation of these institutions in electronic data processing, fiduciary activities, government securities dealing and brokering, municipal securities dealing and brokering, and securities underwriting.

The Federal Reserve greatly influences the amount of money circulating through the country's financial system. By purchasing and selling Treasury bills, the Federal Reserve causes fluctuations of the rates charged to banks for short-term loans to other banks. These open-market transactions can also raise or lower interest rates throughout the economy, since higher rates force banks to set a higher bar for lending practices, thus leading them to favor more expensive funds. In addition the Federal Reserve can alter the interest rates charged to member banks for loans involving government securities. These discount rates more or less monitor the pulse of the United States bond market. Conversely, the Federal Reserve can create printed money with which to purchase securities, increasing its reserve supply and lowering interest rates. In the late 1990s, the Fed hedged the economy against inflation through a series of interest-rate hikes, thereby limiting the available supply of credit.

ORGANIZATION AND STRUCTURE

The Federal Reserve banks are an integral part of the Federal Reserve System and were created under Section 4 of the Federal Reserve Act.

The Federal Reserve System is composed of four parts: a board of governors, known as the Federal Reserve Board, which is an independent government agency; the Federal Open Market Committee (FOMC); the Federal Advisory Committee (FAC); and 12 Federal Reserve banks, each with their own board of directors, which are independent instruments of the government.

The Federal Reserve Board. The Federal Reserve Board is made up of seven members appointed for 14-year terms. The president names the chairman and vice-chairman to four-year terms. The Federal Reserve Board supervises and examines the Federal Reserve banks; state-chartered member banks, bank holding companies and nationally chartered commercial banks; international operations of domestic banking organizations; and the U.S. operations of foreign banks. The Federal Reserve Board also has the authority to act on bank mergers involving member banks and to review changes in control over state-chartered banks and bank holding companies.

The Federal Reserve Board implements U.S. monetary policy. The board seeks to maintain low unemployment, price stability, and economic growth. The board exercises this authority through open market operations, the review and determination of discount rates, and the prescription of specific reserve requirements of financial institutions.

The supervisory role of the board includes prescribing rules and regulations governing advances and discounts by Federal Reserve banks to member banks; open market purchases by Federal Reserve banks; acceptance by member banks of drafts or bills of exchange; legal reserve requirements; purchase of warrants by Reserve banks; accounting and disclosure requirements of member banks; extension of securities credit by lenders other than banks, brokers, and dealers; eligibility requirements for membership in the Federal Reserve System; issuance and cancellation of stocks of Federal Reserve banks; collection of checks and other items by Federal Reserve banks; regulation of foreign banks operating in the United States; loans to executive officers of member banks; regulation of interlocking relationships under the Clayton Act; prescription of minimum security devices and procedures for member banks; regulation of interest on time and savings deposits; relationships with securities dealers; extension of credit for margin purchases; bank service arrangements; loan guarantees for defense procurement; regulation of bank holding companies; and the regulation of a variety of consumer-related functions.

The above does not exhaust the range of supervisory powers assigned to the Federal Reserve Board. It is also active in the regulation of mergers, consolidations, or acquisitions of assets by state member banks, a responsibility it shares with the FDIC, the Comptroller of the Currency, and the attorney general. The board is empowered to fix for each Federal Reserve district the percentage of individual bank capital and surplus that may be represented by security loans. The board may take punitive action toward member banks and Reserve Bank employees for the violation of regulations or laws relating to the bank or engaging in unsound practices.

The board's supervisory powers also include the oversight of the implementation of the international credit guidelines under the Voluntary Credit Restraint Program, permitting Federal Reserve banks to rediscount paper for one another at rates approved by the board, allowing Federal Reserve banks to make four month advances to adequately secured member banks and to make loans to groups of five or more banks that are inadequately secured, and requiring the writing off of worthless assets from the books of the Federal Reserve.

Finally, the board's powers include the operation of the Interdistrict Settlement Fund, the examination of Federal Reserve banks and member banks, the production of various reports on the Federal Reserve banks and member banks, suspension of reserve requirements for 15 days (renewable), imposition of penalties for deficiencies of reserves of member banks, supervision and regulation of the issuance and retirement of Federal Reserve notes, and the appointment of the three Class C directors of each Federal Reserve bank, as well as selection of the chairman and vice-chairman from these directors.

The Federal Open Market Committee. The Federal Open Market Committee (FOMC) consists of seven Federal Reserve Board members and five Federal Reserve bank representatives. The FOMC sets monetary policy by selling government securities to influence the credit supply and interest rates. The FOMC has centralized direction and control of the open market operations of the Federal Reserve System.

The FOMC was organized under the Banking Act of 1935. Each Federal Reserve bank is required to participate in the FOMC's operations and may not engage in market operations on their own without the committee's approval. Policy directives of the FOMC are issued to the Federal Reserve Bank of New York for the execution of transactions on the open market. The individual Federal Reserve banks are authorized to engage in open market transactions in foreign exchange, subject to the direction and regulation of the FOMC.

The Federal Advisory Council. The Federal Advisory Council (FAC) consists of one member from each Federal Reserve District. The FAC meets regularly with the Federal Reserve Board to discuss general business conditions and make recommendations regarding the Federal Reserve System. The FAC has a purely advisory and consultative function.

The Federal Reserve Banks. The 12 Federal Reserve Banks are located in each Federal Reserve District, and include numerous branches and regional check processing centers. The 12 district banks are located in Boston, New York, Philadelphia, Richmond, Atlanta, Cleveland, Chicago, St. Louis, Dallas, Minneapolis, Kansas City, and San Francisco. Each of the 12 banks has its own distinct organization and serves its own district. The minimum capital for each district bank is $4 million in subscribed capital; most of the banks hold significantly more capital than this.

Each of the Federal Reserve banks is overseen by nine directors divided into three lettered classes: A, B, and C. Class A and B directors are elected by the member banks of the district, while Class C directors are appointed by the Federal Reserve Board of Governors. The Class A directors are intended to represent the member commercial banks and are usually bankers by trade. The Class B and Class C directors are intended to represent the public. Directors may not be member of Congress, while Class B and C directors may not be employees of any banks, and Class C directors may not be stockholders of any bank. All directors are expected to exercise discretion and to avoid participation in partisan political activities. These directors are elected for three-year terms on a staggered basis. The Class A and B directors are elected by mail by the member banks of the district. The banks of the district are divided into three categories, based on capitalization, and each category may nominate three directors for each Class.

One of the Class C directors, armed with significant banking experience, is appointed by the Board of Governors as the chairman of the Federal Reserve Bank and as the Federal Reserve agent. A second Class C director is appointed vice-chairman and the final Class C director presides at meetings of the bank's board of directors. The Federal Reserve agent may appoint experienced assistants, with the approval of the Board of Governors, to assist the agent in the performance of his duties and to act in his place during absence or disability.

Despite the fact that the member banks are the sole stockholders and elect two-thirds of the investors, policy control lies with the Board of Governors. The district banks are required to participate in the programs of the FOMC. Discount rates set by the district bank directors are subject to the review and acceptance of the Board of Governors, which makes the final determination as to reserve requirements and has broad control of operational matters through its regulations.

The responsibilities of the Federal Reserve banks include: enforcing Federal Reserve Board regulations, clearing and collecting checks for depository institutions, extending credit to depository institutions and acting as the fiscal agent of the United States.

Federal Reserve banks are actively involved in the enforcement of Federal Reserve Board Regulations. The breadth of these regulations is comprehensive, spanning the full authority of the Federal Reserve System. One example of the Federal Reserve's enforcement efforts recently gained significant media attention. In the early 1990s the Federal Reserve banks became involved in the investigation of the Bank of Credit and Commerce International (BCCI) and other institutions and individuals that aided BCCI in illegally gaining control of shares of U.S. banking organizations. Amidst the booming economy of the late 1990s, an upswing in risky lending activity among commercial banking institutions forced the Fed to step up evaluation procedures, working to help banks establish internal risk grades by which to weigh potential lending options.

The district banks are responsible for providing an efficient system of collecting out-of-town cash items such as checks. Each district bank acts as a regional clearinghouse for the depository institutions in its district. The Board of Governors acts as the national manager for clearing debit and credit balances among the Federal Reserve banks through the Interdistrict Settlement Account.

Regional Check Processing Centers (RCPC), located in Boston, New York, Philadelphia, Cleveland, Richmond, Atlanta, Chicago, St. Louis, and Minneapolis, are responsible for collecting checks overnight. These RCPCs are operated by the Federal Reserve banks to expedite check collection. The RCPCs sort, clear, and deliver checks deposited by commercial depository institutions.

The Federal Reserve banks offer credit to depository institutions by accepting eligible paper for rediscount or by offering secured loans to the institution with eligible paper or government securities as collateral. The depository institution may choose to receive the proceeds in Federal Reserve notes or other forms of currency to meet deposit withdrawals or as credit to its reserve account. These institutions may also return excess currency to the Federal Reserve bank for credit to its reserve account. To maintain the stability of this arrangement, the Federal Reserve bank must meet collateral requirements for Federal Reserve notes. These notes must be fully secured by gold certificates, special drawing rights, eligible paper, or U.S. government obligations, tendered to the Federal Reserve agent at the district Federal Reserve bank.

The Federal Reserve banks act as the fiscal agent of the United States, supplying currency and coin to over 9,700 institutions. Each of the 12 Federal Reserve banks carry an account for the U.S. Treasurer and undertakes transfers of treasury balances, handles issuance and redemption of U.S. government obligations, and performs other functions for the federal government. The banks are also responsible for the replenishment of currency to the member banks and the issuance of new currency to replace worn and mutilated bills and coins.

The Federal Reserve banks maintain 25 branches, 37 automated clearinghouses, 46 regional check processing centers, and nine check clearing offices in the major commercial centers of the United States. The largest is the New York bank, employing 3,826 individuals. The branch offices perform many of the functions of the district banks for their territories. Each branch is directly supervised by a board of either five or seven directors, the majority being appointed by the district bank and the remainder by the Board of Governors. These directors are subject to the regulations of the Board of Governors and the general supervision of its district bank.

National banks are required to become members of the Federal Reserve System. State-chartered banks may become members if they wish. In the early 1990s slightly less than half of all banks in the United States belonged to the Federal Reserve System. Those banks with membership, however, held nearly three-quarters of the country's total deposits.

Each member bank is required to hold stock in its district's Federal Reserve bank in an amount equal to 3 percent of the bank's capital and surplus. Access to Federal Reserve credit facilities and to Federal Reserve services, including check clearing and transfer of funds, is open to both member and nonmember institutions.

Lastly, the Federal Reserve brings all of the nation's diverse financial activities into a tight statistical relationship with each other via the flow of funds (FoF) system. This system identifies, tracks, and monitors the influences on financial markets of nonfinancial activities. The FoF system divides the economy into basic sectors, including households, governments, nonfinancial businesses, financial businesses, and all foreign activity, in order to make sure the all the sectors' transactions balance with each other. In so doing, the FoF system tracks the proliferation of financial claims and the size of capital stock throughout the economy.

BACKGROUND AND DEVELOPMENT

The history of banking in the United States is characterized by a tension between a reluctance to give the federal government control over monetary policy and the concept of Federalism. Alexander Hamilton secured the establishment of a strong central bank to give stability to the fledgling republic's currency. The First United States Bank was authorized to stabilize United States currency for a period of 20 years. However, a bill to renew its charter was defeated by one vote in both the House and Senate in 1811. The ensuing chaos led to the establishment of the Second Bank of the United States in 1816. In 1836 the charter of this second bank was not renewed and financial chaos followed once again.

The National Banking Act of 1863, coupled with the National Banking Act of 1864, established the contemporary banking system through the authorization of national bank charters and the creation of the Office of the Comptroller of the Currency. This was a major improvement to the ad-hoc system that was in place between 1836 and 1863. However, this system was still inadequate for the growing country's economy.

The Federal Reserve Act of 1913 created the Federal Reserve System. This act created the Federal Reserve Board, an independent government agency, and 12 regional banks. On 2 April 1914, 100 days after President Woodrow Wilson signed the Federal Reserve bill into law, the Organization Committee released its report naming the cities of Boston, New York, Philadelphia, Richmond, Atlanta, Cleveland, Chicago, St. Louis, Dallas, Minneapolis, Kansas City, and San Francisco as locations for the Federal Reserve Banks. On 16 November 1914, the 12 Federal Reserve Banks opened for business.

During World War I, the Federal Reserve banks extended loans to the member banks to help them buy U.S. securities. Although this move aided the treasury it also aggravated price inflation. The Federal Reserve's tightening of credit to halt gold outflows in the aftermath of the war exacerbated the economic recession of 1920-1921. This experience helped formulate the Federal Reserve's later policy of raising the discount rate to curtail credit in periods of expansion and lowering it to stimulate economic growth.

The system was faced with even greater challenges during the Depression era. As panicking depositors withdrew currency from member banks in response to the number of bank failures, the volume of Federal Reserve discounts declined. The depletion of commercial bank reserves led to reductions in new lending, which further aggravated the Depression. In response to this crisis, the Federal Reserve was later given greater regulatory powers, including the power to regulate margins in stock purchases and the power to vary reserve requirements of member banks.

In World War II the Federal Reserve was also involved in helping the treasury borrow at low interest rates. The Federal Reserve banks purchased around $20 billion dollars of U.S. securities and provided member banks with additional reserves so that they could also buy treasury securities. Despite rigorous price controls and aggressive sales of savings bonds, inflation increased sharply in the late 1940s. The Federal Reserve Board was criticized sharply for not using open market operations more aggressively to curb inflation.

To increase lending, the member banks sold treasury securities during the Korean War, forcing the Federal Reserve banks to buy these securities to keep the prices stable. The increased inflation, financed by credit, presented a new set of problems for the Federal Reserve. In response, the Federal Reserve Board asserted its independence and reached an accord with the Treasury in 1951 that agreed that Federal Reserve policy should not be subordinated to treasury financing.

After 1951 the policies of the Federal Reserve were more focused on domestic economic stabilization than funding the Treasury. In the early to mid-1960s, the Reserve's focus was on price stability and the restriction of monetary growth; in the late 1960s the emphasis was on full employment and growth of output. The late 1960s also marked the beginning of the concern with international trade deficits and the outflow of gold, the latter culminating in the repeal of the gold-reserve requirements for the Federal Reserve by Congress in 1968 and the end of the Gold Standard under the Nixon administration on 15 August 1971.

The events of the 1970s were difficult for the Federal Reserve. The discount rate tripled, the federal debt more than doubled, gasoline prices increased ominously, and inflation was seemingly out of control. Congress began looking for ways to limit the independence of the Federal Reserve or, at minimum, force it to reveal its policies and goals in specific terms. The bank was also becoming bogged down in the sheer number of transactions that it had to complete, including check collection and shifting deposits. Pressure was mounting to make significant changes to the Federal Reserve as well as to the overall financial structure of the United States.

In 1980 Congress passed the Financial Institutions Deregulation and Monetary Control Act. This act was to have a significant impact on the Federal Reserve. It required all depository institutions that maintain transaction accounts or nonpersonal time accounts to maintain reserves with the Federal Reserve to the extent necessary for the conduct of monetary policy. It opened the facilities of the Federal Reserve to all banks, including savings and loan associations and credit unions. Finally, it required the Federal Reserve to charge fees for its services to banks in order to cover the costs, including taxes and interest, incurred by the Reserve for providing these services. The implementation of this new legislation was difficult and costly. By 1984, however, the goal of breaking even on services had been achieved.

The Federal Reserve's role in bank regulation was changed by the Federal Deposit Insurance Corporation Act of 1991. This act came in the aftermath of the savings and loan crisis of the late 1980s when the viability of the banking system was in question. This legislation significantly modified the Federal Reserve Act in response to these uncertainties. The Federal Reserve also assumed greater responsibility for consumer protection in the 1990s. The Division of Consumer and Community Affairs addressed concerns about fair lending practices in urban areas, access to credit by minorities and low-income households, possible discrimination in mortgage lending, and the need to match its consumer regulations to industry developments. In 1995, the Board joined in issuing revised interagency regulations under the Community Reinvestment Act that included the publication of two proposals. The new rules emphasized performance in lending; they will help promote consistency in assessments and reduce compliance burdens for many banks. In fair lending, the Board adopted streamlined procedures for referring discrimination complaints to the Department of Justice. In 1995, the Board also completed its first full year of operating a specialized fair-lending school for Federal Reserve examiners. The two-week school covers an extensive range of conceptual topics and practical, hands-on classwork. A total of 109 examiners attended the three sessions offered during the initial year. By the early 1990s the Truth in Lending Act, the Fair Credit Billing Act, and the Equal Credit Opportunities Act involved the Federal Reserve in the protection of individuals rights in obtaining consumer credit. The Fair Credit Reporting Act, the Consumer Leasing Act, the Real Estate Settlement Procedures Act, and the Home Mortgage Disclosure Act involved the Federal Reserve in requiring and monitoring the disclosure of crucial financial information to consumers involved in credit transactions. The Electronic Funds Transfer Act provided a basic framework regarding the rights, responsibilities, and liabilities of consumers who used electronic funds transfer as well as those of the institutions granting them. Finally, the Federal Trade Commission Improvement Act authorized the Board of Governors to identify and implement legislation to prohibit unfair or deceptive bank practices.

CURRENT CONDITIONS

Perhaps the most profound event affecting the Federal Reserve during the late 1990s was the passage in 1999 of the Gramm-Leach-Bliley Act, which repealed the Glass-Steagall Act and thus began to dismantle the distinction between commercial and investment banks. The legislation was expected to overhaul the entire financial-services landscape. Lobbyists for the financial industry had campaigned for over 20 years to bring down the Depression-era law. Overall, the legislation lifts a broad range of restrictions on the range of financial institutions' activities, allowing them to offer insurance products, run travel agencies, and a host of other previously prohibited business areas. Among other features, the Glass-Steagall Act prohibited commercial banks from dabbling in the stock market. The Gramm bill knocks down that law, and allows banks to directly underwrite municipal revenue bonds.

The Federal Reserve's responsibilities under Gramm-Leach-Bliley center on the risk management and capitalization of holding companies. By dismantling provisions of the Bank Holding Company Act of 1956, barriers between banks, securities firms, insurance companies, and other institutions will crumble, leading to extensive merger activity. The resulting firms will form financial holding companies, thereby preserving the regulatory muscle of the Federal Reserve, who will determine the validity of those holding companies on the basis of their capitalization. Requirements include a relatively high level of capital relative to risk-based assets and a satisfactory rating under the Community Reinvestment Act.

Analysts note, however, that while the Gramm bill is certainly a landmark piece of legislation, banks' nonbanking activities have been extensive for years. The Bank Holding Company Act was filled with loopholes, particularly Regulations K and Y, which allowed banks to invest in nonbanking institutions through small business investment companies (SBICs). Nonetheless, the Gramm bill was expected to lead to unprecedented consolidation in the financial-services industries.

In the mid- and late 1990s, the Federal Reserve was occupied with keeping a sharp watch out for inflationary pressures. During the economic expansion of these years, the Fed held off raising interests for two years until early 1997, when it instituted the first of what was expected to be a series of rate increases to ward off inflation. The Fed's action to cool off a booming economy temporarily upset the stock market and resulted in political criticism from those who believed the Fed's tight control would weaken the employment outlook. Since then, the Fed implemented a series of adjustments, including four rate increases in 1999 and early 2000, with more expected in the near future.

While the U.S. enjoyed unprecedented economic growth during the late 1990s, the rising number of weak or potentially weak loans at some institutions alarmed the Fed, which issued a guidance to banks warning them against the relaxation of credit discipline, including the over-reliance on the borrower's promise to pay. The Fed attributed the development to overconfidence in clients' portfolios. The Federal Reserve hoped to stave off a trend toward laxity before its potentially ill consequences rippled through the financial markets.

In foreign affairs, the early 1990s saw the Federal Reserve begin to implement the Foreign Bank Supervision Enhancement Act of 1991. In conjunction with this act, the Federal Reserve Bank began to strengthen its supervisory role with respect to the operation of foreign banks in the United States. By the end of the decade, the Fed was working on a series of information-exchange agreements with the financial supervisory authorities in countries around the world, with the purpose of opening information channels regarding the banking activities of the respective nations. With the continued international face of finance, such agreements were set to allow U.S. banks to make further inroads into foreign markets, and vice versa.

WORKFORCE

The Federal Reserve employed approximately 22,650 employees at 12 district facilities in 1998. These employees were recruited and hired by each of the Federal Reserve district banks.

The training of Federal Reserve System staff emphasized analytical and supervisory themes common to the four areas of supervision and regulation: examinations, inspections, applications, and surveillance. The training stressed the interdependence of these areas.

AMERICA AND THE WORLD

There was heavy interaction between Federal Reserve policies and international economic developments. The Fed engages in foreign-exchange transactions, which involves the purchase of foreign currencies and maintaining them in reserve. The exchange value of the dollar relative to foreign currencies is a primary instrument by which the Federal Reserve engineers U.S. monetary policy. By raising interest rates in the United States, the dollar rises in value relative to foreign currencies, thereby raising the cost of U.S. goods on the world market and decreasing exports. The reverse, of course, is true when the Fed lowers interest rates. Furthermore, after the Asian financial crisis and Russian bond default in 1998 sent shockwaves through financial markets, the Federal Reserve has focused its international efforts on tallying the extent of U.S. banks' exposure to volatile economies.

Since the early 1970s, the Federal Reserve and other central banks have developed a reciprocal, or swap, network by which central banks may access each other's currencies. In this way, central banks can intervene to prop up their local currencies. The New York Federal Reserve Bank handles swap transactions, transferring dollars to a foreign central bank in exchange for that country's currency, at the same time agreeing to reverse the transaction a few months later.

The concept of central banking was developed in response to the recurrent British financial crises of the 19th century. Modern market economies are subject to frequent economic fluctuations. The causes of these fluctuations are diverse; however, there is general agreement that the ability of banks to create money may exacerbate them. This raises the need for an independent monetary authority able to view economic and financial developments objectively and to exert control over the activities of the banks.

Central banks have four major functions: the maintenance of a sound commercial bank structure; the management of international trade and financial relationships; to ensure the adequacy of banking capacity and services for the community; and, finally, to act as financial advisor to and take responsibility for the financial affairs of the government.

To maintain a sound commercial banking structure, central banks are often called upon to offer support to financial institutions in times of crisis and to avoid such crises. The Federal Reserve System examines the books of commercial banks and sponsors various educational programs. In some developing countries such as India and Pakistan, the central banks continually scrutinize commercial bank operations. The Bank of England plays a crucial role in the United Kingdom's banking system, ensuring that banks have a steady supply of cash, even during periods of credit restrictions.

Central banks also manage the international financial relationships of its country. Central banks normally manage the foreign exchange activities of its country. This role often requires coordination and cooperation with other central bank and international financial institutions, such as the International Monetary Fund (IMF) and certain regional super-national organizations.

Another responsibility of a central bank is the assurance of the availability of banking services. In rural areas of India and Norway, the central banks have been active in ensuring that the banking needs of these areas are met. In France, this concern has led to the expansion of the central bank's activities to France's territories. Central banks are also active in assuring that the quality of banking services is adequate. In India and Pakistan, as in the United States, the central banks inspect and audit bank operations. In other countries, such as France and South Africa, this function is delegated to a separate authority.

Finally, central banks are often called on to act as the government's financial agent and advisor. The Bank of England developed into a central bank from its original role as the banker to the government. The Federal Reserve, as well as the Bank of France and the German Bundesbank, has historically been involved in granting credit to the government on a direct or indirect basis. However, many banks are severely restricted in engaging in these activities.

Currently, many of the world's central banks are nationalized. These banks have taken a role as a public institution that exists to serve the community as a whole. Most of these banks, however, do garner significant profits.

Most central banks at the turn of the century were, like the Federal Reserve, trying to guard against inflation. The European Central Bank, the Bank of Korea, the Bank of England and others were raising key interest rates, though in areas where the spectacular financial performance the U.S. has enjoyed was lacking, such as continental Europe, such moves were widely viewed as an attempt to prop up local currencies and make assets more attractive.

Research and Technology

The Federal Reserve Bank has been aggressive in implementing new technology. In 1999 the Fed revised Regulation CC to allow broader validity for check images as substitutes for physical checks. The ruling opens greater opportunities in electronic checking, a technology that was somewhat restricted by Regulation CC's vague passages regarding the handling of returned items. The revised ruling clarifies that images are in fact an acceptable replacement for paper wherever the two parties, or a consortium of parties, agree to it.

In 1991 the Philadelphia Federal Reserve adopted the DISC Global Payment System for transferring and receiving Federal Reserve payment instructions. This system provided customer initiation, service delivery, and payment processing in a single product operating a comprehensive electronic wholesale banking system on the same platform.

The Fedline personal computer software was upgraded to offer greater flexibility in electronic transaction services. The upgraded software offered improvements that allow banks to make electronic bids for treasury securities, treasury security transfers, and automated clearinghouse and wire transfer transactions and currency orders.

In addition to decreased processing time and improved service, the Federal Reserve also cut costs through the implementation of new technologies. One of the most important of these cost-saving methods was the consolidation of 12 general purpose data processing centers into three regional operations located in Dallas, Richmond, and the New York Bank's East Rutherford, New Jersey, facility.

Finally, the Federal Reserve has implemented measures to shore up the Banks' security systems, particularly in the growing area of electronic funds transfer. To ensure the $1.5 trillion in funds transferred daily through the Federal Reserves's bank network, the Fed has implemented the Triple DES (data encryption standard) method. Nearly ready for application in 2000 was the Advanced Encryption Standard (AES), which uses 256-bit key lengths to encode electronic data, compared with DES's 56-bit key lengths.

FURTHER READING

Anason, Dean. "Welcome for Reform Law Gives Way to Uncertainty." *American Banker,* 16 December 1999.

"Canada Set to Sign Agreement With Fed." *International Banking Regulator,* 11 May 1998.

"Federal Reserve Banks To Use Triple DES Security." *American Banker,* 16 April 1998.

Garver, Rob. "FDIC Is the Only Regulator With Plans to Tighten Belt." *American Banker,* 3 January 2000.

"Landmark Financial Services Legislation for the U.S." *Reactions,* December 1999.

Marjanovic, Steven. "Fed Rule Revision to Allow Wider Use of Electronic Returned-Check Images." *American Banker,* 23 December 1999.

Moore, Carl H. *The Federal Reserve System: A History of the First 75 years.* Jefferson: McFarland & Company, Inc., 1990.

Rehm, Barbara A. and Dean Anason. "Fed Opens Fast Lane for 1-Stop-Shop Applications." *American Banker,* 20 January 2000.

Snow, David. "New Banking Laws Prompt Yawns and Cheers." *Buyouts,* 22 November 1999.

U.S. Board of Governors of the Federal Reserve System. *85th Annual Report 1998.* Washington, 1999.

U.S. Board of Governors of the Federal Reserve System. *The Federal Reserve in the International Sphere.* Washington, 1998.

SIC 6019

CENTRAL RESERVE DEPOSITORY INSTITUTIONS, NOT ELSEWHERE CLASSIFIED

This classification includes central reserve depository institutions, other than federal reserve banks, primarily engaged in providing credit to and holding deposits and reserves for their member commercial banks, thrift and loan associations, credit unions, insurance companies, and other federally insured financial institutions who hold at least 10 percent of their assets in residential mortgage loans.

NAICS CODE(S)

522320 (Financial Transactions Processing, Reserve, and Clearing House Activities)

The Federal Home Loan Bank System (FHLB System) was established by Congress in 1932 with the passage of the Federal Home Loan Bank Act. The FHLB System's intended role was to provide readily available, low-cost funds to federally insured savings institutions.

As it was originally constituted, the FHLB System acted as regulator and supervisor of federally chartered savings institutions and federally insured state-chartered savings institutions.

Coming on the heels of the savings and loan debacle of the 1980s was the creation of The Financial Institutions Reform, Recovery and Enforcement Act of 1989 (FIRREA) and the dissolution of the Federal Home Loan Bank Board (FHLBB).

FIRREA eliminated the FHLBB and transferred those powers to the Federal Housing Finance Board (FHFB). Thrift institutions that were members of the FHLB System continued, as before, to be regulated by the Office of Thrift Supervision, which is part of the U.S. Treasury.

FIRREA simultaneously expanded member eligibility in the FHLB System to include commercial banks, credit unions, thrift and loan associations, and other federally insured financial institutions.

Since the dismantling of the FHLBB, the 12 regional governing banks in the system now act as wholesale banks only, providing their shareholders with an important link to the U.S. capital markets. As of 1999, more than 7,200 member banks composed the FHLB System.

Today, it is the banks' mission is to provide access to housing for all Americans and to improve the quality of credit by raising funds for their lender institutions/shareholders through the Office of Finance which, in turn, issues and services debt for the banks—the FHLB System is one of the three largest issuers of debt in the world. The system's consolidated debt rating is the highest rating available from Standard and Poor's and Moody's rating services. The United States Government is neither responsible for nor guarantees these obligations.

The FHFB has regulatory authority and supervisory oversight responsibility for the 12 FHLB banks and the Office of Finance. According to its Web site, the finance board "ensures the safety and soundness of the Bank System, establishes policy for the Community Investment Cash Advances programs (including the Affordable Housing and Community Investment programs), oversees the Banks' financial performance and operations and evaluates their attainment of public policy mission as a government-sponsored enterprise (GSE)."

The FHLB System is regulated by the FHFB, an independent agency of the executive branch responsible for ensuring that the banks carry out their housing finance mission, remain adequately capitalized, raise funds in capital markets and be fiscally solvent. The finance board also establishes policies and regulations governing the operations of the banks.

The FHFB is comprised of a five-director board, one of whom is the secretary of housing and urban development. The four other directors are appointed by the president and are subject to senate confirmation. The FHFB's directors are chosen from a pool of people who have extensive experience in housing and community development finance or with a commitment to representing consumer or community interest in services, credit needs, housing, or consumer protection.

The FHFB is supported by assessments from the 12 FHLB banks. The banks finance their own operations through investments, the sale of collateralized obligations, and by charging for credit products and services they provide to member institutions. No tax dollars or other appropriations are used to support the operations of the FHFB or the bank system.

FURTHER READING

1998 Annual Report of the Federal Home Loan Bank of San Francisco, 12 February 2000. Available from http://www.fhlbsf.com.

Federal Home Loan Banks System, 12 February 2000. Available from http://www.fhlBanks.gov.

Federal Home Loan Finance Board, 12 February 2000. Available from www.fhfb.gov.

Office of Finance, 12 February 2000. Available from http://www.of.gov.

Office of Thrift and Supervision, Department of Treasury, 12 February 2000. Available from http://www.ots.treas.gov.

SIC 6021

NATIONAL COMMERCIAL BANKS

This classification includes commercial bank and trust companies (accepting deposits) chartered under the National Bank Act. Trust companies engaged in fiduciary business, but not regularly engaged in deposit banking, are classified in **SIC 6091: Nondeposit Trust Facilities.**

NAICS CODE(S)

522110 (Commercial Banking)
522210 (Credit Card Issuing)
523991 (Trust, Fiduciary, and Custody Activities)

INDUSTRY SNAPSHOT

The U.S. commercial banking industry was voraciously healthy in the late 1990s, though its ranks were thinning rapidly. Indicative of the massive consolidation of financial services in the United States, there were 8,817 commercial banks in operation in 1998, dramatically down from 18,769 at the end of 1975. Throughout the 1980s and early 1990s, as merger and acquisition activity reached record levels, so did bank failures. In the late 1990s, however, most of the continued consolidation was due to merger deals between banks. Between 1993 and 1997, 2,839 banks, or 21 percent of all commercial banking institutions, were acquired by other industry players. Much of this activity was sparked by the poor credit qualities among mid-sized players. Commercial banks held about $5.4 trillion in assets in 1998, registering an increase of 20 percent from 1996, and 64 percent from 1989. Keeping in mind the shrinking number of banks, the average bank's assets leaped 138 percent during the 1990s. Nine U.S. banks maintained assets over $100 billion in 1998, accounting for banks accounted for more than 52 percent of total banking industry assets.

Analysts do not expect the consolidation mania to subside anytime soon; indeed, most expect that it will accelerate, not only between banks, but between banks and other financial institutions, such as securities brokers and insurance companies. Landmark legislation passed in late 1999 opens the door to such deals, which were prohibited since the Great Depression.

Commercial banking was among the first industries to develop in the United States. Subject to a convoluted set of regulations at the state and federal levels, the banking industry is broad in scope and complex in nature. Modern commercial banks provide both individual and corporate customers with an increasing number of financial services. Recent innovations in this industry include the introduction of credit cards, accounting services for corporate firms, factoring, leasing, trade in Eurodollars, lock box banking, and security investment. Banks are constantly seeking to improve service to customers by expanding the quality and number of their services.

Commercial banks perform at least eight major functions in the U.S. economy. First, banks facilitate the elastic credit system that is necessary for economic progress and steady growth. Second, they allow the efficient transfer of money between firms and individuals. Third, they encourage the pooling of savings, making these savings available for lending. Fourth, banks extend credit to credit worthy borrowers, increasing production and capital investment. Fifth, banks facilitate the financing of foreign trade by converting various currencies. Sixth, they act as trust administrators and advisors. Seventh, they aid in the safekeeping of valuables. Finally, banks have recently been allowed to engage in brokering activities, buying and selling securities for customers.

Despite the increasingly relaxed regulatory climate, the banking industry is one of the most regulated parts of the U.S. financial system. The industry operates under the supervision of three regulatory agencies: the Federal Reserve System, the Office of the Comptroller of the Currency (OCC), and the Federal Deposit Insurance Corporation (FDIC). The Federal Reserve System, created in 1913, is the central bank of the United States and is responsible for monetary policy. Its operations are carried out by its 12 regional banks. The OCC has wide discretionary authority, which it uses in routine examinations of all national banks' books to identify unsafe or unsound banking practices. This agency is the most involved with national bank regulation. The OCC has the authority to take any actions necessary to correct the conditions resulting from violations of law or sound and safe banking practices. Finally, the FDIC was created to reduce the risk of making deposits by insuring the deposits of member banks, both national and state.

ORGANIZATION AND STRUCTURE

The National Bank Act of 1863 created the basis for the first national U.S. banking system and continues to serve as the basic banking law for American national banks. The act was originally created to provide a uniform national currency backed by U.S. Government bonds that would replace the various currencies issued by state banks and other forms of exchange that were then in use. The original plan for the national banking system was outlined by Salmon Chase, the Secretary of the Treasury, in 1861.

National banks are chartered and supervised by the Comptroller of the Currency of the United States. The charters issued by the comptroller are of indefinite duration. Upon the submission of an application, a national bank examiner in the region where the proposed national bank will be located initiates an investigation of the bank, focusing on the character and experience of the organizers, existing banking facilities, and prospects for success. A national bank must meet certain capitalization requirements depending upon its location, and can not begin operation until it has paid-in surplus equal to 20 percent of its capital. The examiner puts the capital and paid-in surplus of each bank to an ''adequacy'' test that subjects each potential bank to criteria based on established minimal capitalization levels and analysis of local conditions. If the application is accepted, the Comptroller of the Currency issues the necessary documentation to the bank and, eventually, a certificate to commence business.

All national banks are required to be members of the Federal Reserve bank of their district and to invest in the capital stock of the bank as required by the Federal Reserve Act of 1913, which requires that six percent of the national bank's capital and surplus must be pledged and three percent deposited as payment. National banks are further required to be insured by the Federal Deposit Insurance Corporation (FDIC).

National banks have 20 enumerated, general powers, which are effective upon the execution and filing of the articles of association and the organization certificate. Such powers include the obvious—receiving and loaning money—as well as the obscure—providing travel services for customers. National banks are granted general corporate powers, which include making contracts, suing and being sued, electing and appointing directors, and prescribing by-laws, and are allowed to establish branch offices in the United States and abroad, under specified conditions. They are also allowed a range of activities involving real estate, U.S. government securities, the establishment of trusts, and other financial activities. Such broadly construed powers enable national banks to engage in far more than strictly commercial banking.

Commercial banks may be classified as either unit or branch banks. In the United States, unlike other countries, banks of both types exist. Historically, however, unit banking has been the most common. Under unit banking, services are provided by a single office or institution. The system of unit banking is the product of an earlier American social and economic structure in which a single local bank could service the needs of a relatively small and insular town. As communication has become more efficient and the economic environment has become more complex and interdependent, however, branch banking has become dominant in many areas of the country. Branch banking is a system under which a single banking firm operates at two or more locations. There are different degrees of branch banking across the country. In general, the more densely populated areas, such as the East and West Coasts, have adopted branch banking, while more sparsely populated areas have maintained unit banking.

BACKGROUND AND DEVELOPMENT

The first incorporated commercial bank in North America was opened in Philadelphia on 7 January 1782, one week after the Continental Congress had granted a perpetual charter to the Bank of North America. This bank was intended to be a pillar of American credit that would play a significant role in the financial management of the fledgling republic. The number of banks in the United States grew exponentially in the early nineteenth century. By 1816, there were 246 banks in the United States and, by 1840, there were three times as many as there had been in 1820. Between 1840 and 1860, this number again doubled, to 1,500.

By the outbreak of the Civil War, both the North and the South had well developed banking, but the systems were decentralized. Before the war, banking policy was controlled by the individual states. But the war strengthened the central government and began a new era in banking. In 1863, the government crafted legislation giving the federal government powers to regulate banking. For the first time, the nation had a uniform bank currency controlled by a central authority. This marked the beginning of what is called the "dual banking system," which consists of banks chartered by the states and other banks chartered by the federal government.

The existence of a strong federal banking structure after the Civil War, underlay the explosion of productive capability that characterized the United States in the late nineteenth century. Yet, while a dependable money supply aided economic expansion, it also prompted distrust of those controlling the flow of money. By the end of the nineteenth century, reformers looked to further banking legislation to smooth economic turmoil. In 1913, the Federal Reserve Act created the system of Federal Reserve banks. The Federal Reserve Act was created to bring stability to commerce and industry, prevent financial panics, make commercial credit available, and to discourage speculating by banks. Although this legislation was initially opposed by bankers, the Federal Reserve since developed into a cornerstone of the current banking system.

Despite improved supervision and economic prosperity, nearly one quarter of the banks operating in the mid-1920s had closed by the end of the decade. Between 1921 and 1929, more than 5,700 banks closed, far exceeding the total for the previous 56 years. After the stock market crash in 1929, banks continued to close at an alarming rate. The rampant failure of banks led to the implementation of a deposit insurance program created by the Banking Act of 1933, or the Glass-Steagall Act. One important part of this legislation was the establishment of the Federal Deposit Insurance Corporation, which guaranteed the deposits of investors up to a certain limit. The Glass-Steagall Act also created the distinction between commercial and investment banking. Commercial banks were prohibited from underwriting securities, engaging in the stock market, and a host of other activities that legislators felt had contributed to the financial crisis. Commercial banks were to focus on accepting deposits and providing commercial loans. The act also built on long-standing distrust in the United States of centralized monetary institutions by regulating and restricting bank branching.

After 1945, U.S. banks began to expand their operations to encompass a wide range of financial services. In the 1960s, banks began to represent themselves as "full-service banks," indicating their involvement in a growing range of financial activities as regulatory constraints were relaxed. This trend toward deregulation continued throughout the second half of the 20th century. After 1965, banks began to expand into foreign markets, while foreign banks also began to gain footholds in the United States.

Commercial banking assumed an increasingly international posture through the late twentieth century. In 1965 13 U.S. banks maintained operations abroad, controlling $10 billion in assets; by 1980 the number had grown to 159, holding assets of $340 billion. However, U.S. creditors began to realize in the early 1980s that they had overextended themselves in emerging markets as foreign borrowers failed to service their debts, resulting in massive losses. Not until the early 1990s were commercial confident about lending in such markets again. U.S. bank assets held $861 billion in foreign assets in 1998, while 82 banks maintained foreign branch offices, down significantly from the 162 in 1985. This decline was primarily reflective of the intense consolidation of U.S. commercial banking; the number of branches in foreign markets was at a record high of 935 in 1998.

In February 1993, during the first few months of the Clinton Administration, the General Accounting Office announced that despite the extensive bureaucracy, the federal government did a poor job of examining the books of banks and thrifts. The Comptroller of the Currency, Charles Bowsher, indicated he felt that the regulatory agencies did not adequately ensure that unsafe banking practices were uncovered. Although these sentiments were not uncommon, many felt that there was no reliable evidence about what was happening in the banking industry.

The Treasury Department suggested that the fundamental changes needed in the banking industry required thorough reconsideration of the foundations of the financial system, including the scope and operation of the federal deposit insurance system, the nature of bank supervision and regulation, and bank and non-bank affiliations. Four broad principles to guide the reform process were proposed by the Treasury Department, which suggested that banks should: preserve deposit insurance for small depositors, but protect taxpayers by exposing large depositors to some risk; create a system of incentives and sanctions that encourages higher levels of capital; allow banks to engage in a broader range of business activities and to operate nation wide; and make the regulatory structure more efficient to strengthen the banking system.

By 1994 banking institutions had become far less restricted by geographical boundaries. That year the Riegle-Neal Interstate Banking and Branching Efficiency Act eliminated most of the remaining regulatory barriers impeding interstate banking activity. The act unleashed a massive reorganization of banking structures. Previously, banks maintained separate subsidiaries in states other than those in which they were headquartered. With the passage of Riegle-Neal, banks could organize all their operations under one institution with separate branches across state lines, enabling more streamlined networks and diversification of product lines. In the first six months after the bill's passage, the number of interstate branches of U.S. commercial banks more than doubled.

CURRENT CONDITIONS

With the continued relaxation of the U.S. financial regulation climate, the reach of large national commercial banks expanded rapidly, moving across state and national borders and swallowing smaller banks who found it increasingly difficult to remain profitable in the face of competition from their more leveraged competitors. The fiercely competitive market forced banking institutions to offer a greater range of services and to ''out-local'' the national banks, ''out-national'' the local banks, or both. By 1998 25 percent of all commercial banking assets were controlled by institutions with operations in more than one state; only a small handful of banks were engaged over state lines in 1980. The control of assets likewise gravitated toward the largest national banks. The largest 100 commercial banks maintained about 70 percent of domestic banking assets in 1998, up from 50 percent in 1980. Small community banks, however, were not among the primary victims of this consolidation, managing to hold their own in their own localized markets where they can market their service to and shared interests with the community.

The financial industry prepared for a complete transformation entering the 2000s as the passage of the Gramm-Leach-Bliley Act, also known as the Financial Services Modernization Act, repealed the Glass-Steagall Act, capping a 20-year effort by lobbyists. The new law allows banks to engage in a range of activities prohibited since the Great Depression. By establishing financial holding companies, banks may establish brokerages, insurance operations, and a other financial service offerings in addition to their traditional banking activities all under one institution. The ruling was expected to unleash even more merger activity, especially across financial sectors. Bank of America, for instance, took advantage of the opening to become the first bank to reorganize its insurance operations from an operating subsidiary to a financial subsidiary, relocating it to the bank's headquarters. Analysts predicted that the new rules would eventually lead to ''financial supermarkets,'' whereby customers will increasingly place most or all of their financial business with a single organization. In order to establish a financial holding company, national banks must meet the following criteria: they must be considered well capitalized, determined by a ratio of at least 10 percent total capital to risk-adjusted assets, as evaluated by the Federal Reserve; they must receive a satisfactory rating under the Community Reinvestment Act; and aggregate consolidated assets of all banks' financial subsidiaries must amount to either less than $50 billion or 45 percent of the banks' total assets, whichever is lower.

While the Financial Services Modernization Act is certainly a landmark piece of legislation, banks' nonbanking activities have been extensive for years. The Bank Holding Company Act of 1956 was filled with loopholes, particularly Regulations K and Y, which allowed banks to invest in nonbanking institutions through small business investment companies (SBICs). Moreover, in the years leading up to the new law, Federal regulators had become so lenient in interpreting legal loopholes that the Glass-Steagall Act, meant specifically to prevent combinations between banks that lend money and Wall Street brokers in the business of offering corporate securities to the public, was nearly meaningless. Nonetheless, the Gramm bill was expected to lead to unprecedented consolidation in the financial-services industries.

Such changes did little to quiet fears (deemed irrational by many banking executives) that the U.S. banking system was unsound and might experience a disaster similar to that experienced by the savings-and-loan industry in the mid- and late 1980s. Bank deregulation under the Reagan administration was blamed for the failures of hundreds of savings-and-loans which would cost American taxpayers as much as $500 million in repayments to depositors. Those seeking lessons from the fiasco tended to suggest that banks needed more rather than less regulation.

Perhaps validating many such fears that the dramatic surge in financial performance masked an unsound foundation was the alarming increase in consumer bankruptcies, which reached a record 1.35 million in 1997, up 20 percent from the year before, even in the midst of the strongest U.S. economy in years. The blame for this development was hurled at everything from short-sighted and aggressive creditors luring customers into spending beyond their means to relaxed bankruptcy laws that invited debtors to escape the consequences of their financial activities by filing for bankruptcy. Whatever the cause, the issue shocked the otherwise-euphoric industry, and spurred the Federal Reserve to issue a guidance to banks warning them against the relaxation of credit discipline, including the over-reliance on the borrower's promise to pay. The Fed attributed the development to overconfidence in clients' portfolios. The Federal Reserve hoped to stave off a trend toward laxity before its potentially ill consequences rippled through the financial markets.

Overall, however, banks did not seem worried by such developments. Commercial and industrial loans expanded 13 percent in 1998, reaching $847 billion as bankers remained confident in the sound fundamentals of U.S. companies. Total deposits at commercial banks were also in good shape at $3.3 trillion, up 11 percent from 1997, while 95 percent of all bank assets in 1998 were held by banks considered well-capitalized by the Federal Reserve.

Industry Leaders

While the number of national banks is quite large, there are several recognized leaders in terms of size of deposits and range of services. These industry leaders include Citibank Inc., BankAmerica Corp., Chase Manhattan Corp., and Bank One Corp.

Citibank was originally organized in New York in 1812 and was chartered under the National Banking Act in 1865. The bank conducts general banking business including retail and wholesale operation, and operates an extensive international network covering over 100 countries. Citibank is one of the nation's largest bank issuers of credit cards. At the end of 1998, it reported total assets of $667 billion, more than double the total from 1996, and employed 166,500 people.

BankAmerica Corp. was organized in California in 1930. The bank is heavily involved in commercial banking, savings, trusts, safe deposit, and installment credit. The bank has several foreign subsidiaries in Europe and Latin America. BankAmerica controlled assets of more than $633 billion in 1998 while maintaining a payroll of 155,900 workers.

The Chase Manhattan Corporation emerged when Chemical Bank purchased Chase Manhattan. At the time of its merger in 1996, the combined entity was the largest commercial bank in the United States with approximately $300 billion in pro forma assets. By 1998, the firm's assets reached $366 billion while posting revenues of $18.65 billion and employing 72,000 workers.

Bank One Corp., based in Chicago, was formed via the merger in 1998 between Banc One Company and First Chicago NBD Company. The firm's business includes commercial and retail banking, and various investment activities. Bank One was the top bank card issuer in 1998, with $70 billion in outstandings, and is also a leading manager of mutual funds. The company reported total assets of $262 billion in 1998 and employed 91,300 people.

America and the World

Despite the intense consolidation, the U.S. banking industry remains highly fragmented when compared with other industrialized nations. However, even among those nations that already rely heavily on central banking institutions, U.S. style consolidation is the order of the day. The globalization of financial markets is largely responsible for this development, since typically only larger, more leveraged institutions are able to compete in overseas markets. The increasingly liquid global financial markets invite the deregulated industries to tap into new markets abroad.

The most popular entity for international banking among U.S. national banks is the foreign branch office, which maintains full access to its parent bank's capital when making lending decisions, rather than being restricted by its host country to its own balance sheet. In 1998, 82 U.S. commercial banks maintained foreign branch offices, controlling assets of $704.5 billion. Almost $350 billion in assets was held by branches based in Europe, though that figure declined somewhat in the late 1990s. The Latin American market experienced the most pronounced growth for this type of foreign entity during the 1990s; at the start of the decade about 250 foreign branches held a total of $10 billion in assets in this region, while by 1998 $32 billion was controlled by 350 branches.

However, in many cases foreign tax laws or other considerations relating to the host country favor the establishment of foreign subsidiaries, legally separate entities that are responsible for, and limited to, their own asset holdings, even though they are wholly or partially owned by the parent bank. Foreign subsidiaries also shield the parent bank from liabilities accrued by the foreign operation. U.S. banks owned 1,133 foreign subsidiaries in 1998, controlling assets of $717.9 billion. About half of these assets were held in the United Kingdom.

The lending of currency in the host countries' denomination creates what is known as ''transfer risk,'' which measures the exposure of a U.S. banking operation to that country's financial market. Foreign-currency lending is among the most tightly concentrated sector of the U.S. banking industry, with the six largest banks accounting for more about 83 percent of transfer risk. By the late 1990s, the strength of the dollar relative to foreign currencies had begun to slow the demand for such lending, however, as dollar markets emerged in many countries and emerging markets experienced dramatic volatility in their currency valuations.

The Japanese financial system was in the midst of sweeping reform, known as the ''Big Bang,'' in 2000, which will completely overhaul the banking system in an effort to mitigate the country's decade-long economic woes. Most significantly, the reforms will open Japanese financial markets to foreign players and, like the United States, break down restrictions against banks' engagement in other financial activities such as securities underwriting.

Meanwhile, the European financial markets continue to integrate. In 1999 all European Union members with the exception of the United Kingdom, Sweden, and Denmark officially chained their currencies to the euro, with the United Kingdom expected to jump on board within a few years. The European Union thus constitutes the largest economic area in the world, with banking policy administered by the European Central Bank, which has worked to open its market to more liquid financial flows.

WORKFORCE

The entire banking industry employed about 1.5 million people in the late 1990s, including 550,000 bank tellers, who earned an average annual salary of $16,300. However, the year 1998 witnessed a record number of layoffs in the financial sector. The top handful of banks eliminated more than 70,000 positions due to merger activity and the attempt to remain competitive by cutting costs. As banks become increasingly connected to the performance stock and other financial markets, the temptation to downsize a bank's labor force to mitigate sagging stock prices will likely intensify.

RESEARCH AND TECHNOLOGY

As the banking industry became ever more complex in the mid 1990s, banks around the world began to adopt new technologies and automation. Much of the investment was for Automatic Teller Machines (ATMs), teller work stations, check processing equipment, and related software. Electronic check presentment (ECP), which involves check processing via electronic transfer and which was expected to save the industry some $2.8 billion in paper costs, was beginning to take firm hold in 1999, as was online banking. With increased emphasis on the electronic transfer of funds, however, banks were forced to invest heavily in security systems. Security spending for electronic systems was projected to skyrocket from $1.2 billion in 1996 to $7.4 billion by 2002, mainly for firewalls and encryption systems.

FURTHER READING

Anason, Dean. ''Welcome for Reform Law Gives Way to Uncertainty.'' *American Banker,* 16 December 1999.

''Banking.'' *Business Week,* 10 January 2000.

Bomfim, Antulio A. and William R. Neslon. ''Profits and Balance Sheet Developments at U.S. Commercial Banks in 1998.'' *Federal Reserve Bulletin,* September 1999.

''E-cheques Move a Stage Closer.'' *Electronic Payments International,* 30 November 1999.

Fraser, Katharine. ''Big Banks' Fees Keep Going Up, Study Says.'' *American Banker,* 1 September 1999.

Garver, Rob. ''Bank of America Is First To Seek Approval to Move Insurance Unit to HQ City.'' *American Banker,* 29 December 1999.

Hill, Sidney. ''Web Banking's New Fledglings.'' *Financial Services Online,* 20 January 1999.

Klebaner, Benjamin J. *American Commercial Banking: A History.* Boston: Twayne Publishers, 1990.

''Landmark Financial Services Legislation for the U.S.'' *Reactions,* December 1999.

Marjanovic, Stevem. ''Fed Rule Revision to Allow Wider Use of Electronic Returned-Check Images.'' *American Banker,* 23 December 1999.

O'Connell, Brian. ''Plugging IT Security Leaks.'' *Bank Technology News,* December 1999.

Reed, Edward W., Richard V. Cotter, Edward K. Gill, and Richard K. Smith. *Commercial Banking,* 3rd ed. Englewood Cliffs, NJ: Prentice-Hall, 1984.

Rehm, Barbara A. ''OCC Issues New-Powers Rules for National Banks.'' *American Banker,* 21 January 2000.

Rehm, Barbara A. and Dean Anason. ''Fed: Consumers Flocking to Nonbank Lenders.'' *American Banker,* 19 January 1999.

———. ''Fed Opens Lane for 1-Stop-Shop Applications.'' *American Banker,* 20 January 1999.

Snow, David. ''New Banking Laws Prompt Yawns and Cheers.'' *Buyouts,* 22 November 1999.

U.S. Department of Commerce. International Trade Administration. *U.S. Industry and Trade Outlook 1999.* New York: The McGraw Hill Companies, 1999.

SIC 6022

STATE COMMERCIAL BANKS

This category includes commercial banks and trust companies (accepting deposits) chartered by one of the states or territories. Trust companies engaged in fiduciary business, but not regularly engaged in deposit banking, are classified in **SIC 6091: Nondeposit Trust Facilities.**

NAICS CODE(S)

522110 (Commercial Banking)
522210 (Credit Card Issuing)
522190 (Other Depository Intermediation)
523991 (Trust, Fiduciary, and Custody Activities)

INDUSTRY SNAPSHOT

Commercial banking in the United States rushed toward consolidation throughout the 1990s. Between 1993 and 1997, 2,839 banks, or 21 percent of all commercial banking institutions, were acquired by other industry players. Much of this activity was sparked by the poor credit qualities among mid-sized players. Commercial banks held about $5.4 trillion in assets in 1998, registering an increase of 20 percent from 1996 and 64 percent from 1989. This trend invariably favored larger, more well capitalized banking institutions, particularly regional and super-regional banks, while squeezing state and local commercial banks.

As interstate banking restrictions gradually disappeared, the reach of large national commercial banks expanded rapidly, moving across state borders and swallowing smaller banks who found it increasingly difficult to remain profitable in the face of competition from their more leveraged competitors. By 1998 25 percent of all commercial banking assets were controlled by institutions with operations in more than one state; only a small handful of banks were engaged over state lines in 1980.

Landmark financial legislation at the close of the 1990s was expected to exacerbate many of these trends, but it also was expected to offer many potential avenues for state commercial banks to grow. The challenge remains for state banks to prove capable of providing a range of new financial services in conjunction with their traditional operations while fending off competition from super-regionals and foreign bank branches seeking to take advantage of more open financial markets to encroach on state banks' customer bases.

Despite the increasingly relaxed regulatory climate, U.S. state commercial banks were subject to a range of regulations at the state and federal level. In addition to the federal regulatory bodies which oversee national banks, each state has a system of supervisory bodies charged with the chartering and regulation of state commercial banks. These diverse structures and organizations are responsible for regulating the state's banking industry in a manner which is most appropriate for the financial, economic, and social environment of the state.

Historically, there were advantages to be found for banks in the multiplicity of rules and regulations state to state. At one time, for example, Minnesota was among the few states to allow its banks to sell insurance. Meanwhile, Texas once barred branch banking, so that any bank building had to exist as its own corporation with its own board of directors. While such differences have smoothed out to a great extent thanks to interstate banking deregulation in the 1980s and 1990s, enough perceived differences remain, in the form of tax incentives and loose restrictions, to convince many banks that it is still advantageous to be chartered by a state rather than by the federal government.

Organization and Structure

Commercial banks, which are organized primarily to conduct general banking business, are most often state or national banks. State banks are organized under a charter granted by the state government, while national banks are organized under charters issued by the Comptroller of the Currency of the United States. Many institutions that are chartered as trusts offer services which are generally considered commercial banking while many banks also offer trust and savings services. These institutions and operations are also included under the commercial banking category.

The regulation of banks on the state level is delegated to a banking authority in each state. These bodies exercise primary and additional regulatory powers. There are four primary bank regulatory powers: new bank charter approval, new branch or separate facility application approval, cease and desist orders, and officer removal orders. There are also four additional state bank regulatory powers: power to fine, power to order affiliate examinations, power to order special examinations, and power to issue regulations. Such regulatory powers are exercised by either the state's primary banking authority or by the state's banking board, depending upon the structure of the state's system. Most states maintain a banking board comprised of between 5 and 17 members who are generally appointed by the governor for three to six year terms. Some states, however, regulate banking without a banking board.

The specific type of institutions which are regulated by the state banking authorities can also vary. Normally, the state authorities will regulate commercial banks, trust companies, money order companies, loan production offices, and foreign bank branches. The states may also regulate other entities such as travelers check issuers, currency exchanges, and collection agencies. State banks may voluntarily join the Federal Reserve system, in which case they are required to adhere to the regulations which apply to all national banks, including those which apply to the purchase, sale, underwriting, and holding of investment securities and stock for national banks.

Background and Development

Among the first institutions created by the administration of President George Washington was the Bank of the United States. Washington's Secretary of the Treasury, Alexander Hamilton, insisted that a national bank was necessary to give the fledgling democracy stability and legitimacy. Centralized banking remained a politically divisive issue for over 70 years, as those fearful of a powerful federal government attacked the power vested in the bank. President Andrew Jackson made the Second Bank of the United States one of the primary issues in his presidential campaign of 1832, launching what is known as the Bank War, which left the nation with no central banking agency by 1834. Nearly 30 years later, the Federal Banking Act of 1863 brought banking under federal control and created a uniform bank currency controlled by a central authority for the first time in the nation's history.

The existence of a strong federal banking structure after the Civil War underlay the explosion of productive capability that characterized the United States in the late 19th century. Yet, while a dependable money supply aided economic expansion, it also prompted distrust of those controlling the flow of money. Important steps were taken during the administrations of Woodrow Wilson (1912-1920) and Franklin D. Roosevelt (1932-1944) to further curb the power of bankers and provide equal access to and protection from the U.S. banking system. The Federal Reserve Act of 1913 established 12 regional banking districts and made the district banks answerable to regional as well as national concerns, thus addressing the historical dominance of eastern bankers. The creation of the Federal Deposit Insurance Corporation (FDIC) in 1933 ensured Americans that their deposits were safe in accredited banks, thus calming concerns over bank instability caused by the Depression.

The U.S. banking system is thus the product of two centuries of adjustment designed to make banks serve the interests of the widest number of people operating in a capitalist economic system. Banking regulation proceeds downward from the Federal Reserve Bank through a variety of national regulations to state regulations crafted to suit the needs of particular localities. The ''dual'' banking system created by the actions of independent national and state regulatory agencies has allowed innovation in local banking, while ensuring continuity in banking between the states.

The stock market crash of 1987 came at the worst time for commercial banks. After investing heavily in infrastructure to make them competitive in the investment banking industry, the banks were faced with a much smaller and more competitive market in the wake of the crash. Equally troubling to the banking industry was the failure of hundreds of savings-and-loan institutions. While these institutions were insured, the administration of President Ronald Reagan left them largely unregulated, and taxpayers were left to pay the roughly $500 million needed to repay depositors. In the aftermath of these two disasters, broad skepticism about the stability of the financial system brought the banking system under closer scrutiny. However, booming profits in the mid-1990s and a looser regulatory environment were leading to a blurring of the regulatory borders between various branches of the financial services world.

CURRENT CONDITIONS

In 1999 there were 8,011 commercial banks in the United States, about 60 percent of which were state chartered. All of these institutions were subject to multiple layers of oversight. Moreover, 994 state-chartered banks were part of the federal reserve system, representing 11.4 percent of all U.S. commercial banks and 24.2 percent of all commercial bank assets.

Throughout the 1990s banks were granted greater freedom to focus on other activities, such as investment banking. Following a series of concessions by regulatory bodies, state banks strived to court wealthier clients by delving into the surging hedge fund industry, acting as management custodians, lenders, and brokers. Furthermore, commercial banks increasingly participated in the lucrative investment-banking sector, a practice forbidden commercial banks since the Great Depression. Thus the industry continued to chip away at the long-standing regulatory climate restricting the range of banks' activities. By the end of the decade, however, bankers finally achieved the sweeping legislation they were hoping for.

As U.S. banks enjoyed record revenues, the financial industry geared for a long-awaited overhaul as a result of the Gramm-Leach-Bliley Act in November 1999. Also known as the Financial Services Modernization Act, this legislation repealed the Glass-Steagall Act, capping a 20-year effort by lobbyists. The new law allows banks to engage in a range of activities prohibited since the Great Depression. By establishing financial holding companies, banks may establish brokerages, insurance operations, and a other financial service offerings in addition to their traditional banking activities all under one institution. The ruling was expected to unleash even more merger activity, especially across financial sectors.

Analysts predicted that the new rules would eventually lead to ''financial supermarkets,'' whereby customers will increasingly place most or all of their financial business with a single organization. In order to establish a financial holding company, banks must meet the following criteria: they must be considered well capitalized, determined by a ratio of at least 10 percent total capital to risk-adjusted assets, as evaluated by the Federal Reserve; they must receive a satisfactory rating under the Community Reinvestment Act; and aggregate consolidated assets of all banks' financial subsidiaries must amount to either less than $50 billion or 45 percent of the banks' total assets, whichever is lower.

The precise effects these new rules would have on state banks was uncertain, though analysts agree that banks at all levels will be forced to take greater strides to expand their product lines and cultivate effective niches and relationships with customers. Many state banks, however, were expected to merge with larger competitors.

The U.S. banking industry weathered image problems in the late 1990s. A 1999 study by the National Community Reinvestment Coalition found that more than 40 percent of Americans felt that banks engaged in racial, gender, or other forms of discrimination in their lending practices. Among blacks, 32 percent responded that they knew someone who had been subjected to discrimination when applying for loans. Forty-nine percent also felt that a white man would be more likely to be approved for a loan than an equally qualified black man, and 51 percent felt a white man would receive the nod over a Hispanic man.

AMERICA AND THE WORLD

In 1998, 33 state banks maintained 188 foreign branches. Branches are the most popular mechanism by which U.S. commercial banks engage in operations overseas. These entities maintain full access to their parent banks' capital when making lending decisions, rather than being restricted by their host countries to their own balance sheets.

Foreign banks, while operating under what seem to be very different regulatory frameworks, nevertheless share a number of regulatory concerns with the American banking system. These include regulation of market entry, capital and liquid adequacy, permissible business activities, foreign currency exposure, concentration of loans and country risk exposure, and bank examination. These regulatory concerns transcend national boundaries. In contrast to the U.S. ''dual'' banking system, most countries regulate their banking systems exclusively on the national level. This means there is generally no equivalent of a state commercial bank outside of the United States.

Globally, patterns have generally followed the U.S. trend toward relaxed regulation of financial services. Specifically, banks worldwide are being allowed to offer a broader range of financial services, contrary to past practices. The European Union's financial liberalization program has been a catalyst, encouraging the liberalization of American and Japanese policies to keep pace with their European competitors. In 1999 all European Union members with the exception of the United Kingdom, Sweden, and Denmark officially chained their currencies to the euro, with the United Kingdom expected to jump on board within a few years, as the E.U. worked to open its market to more liquid financial flows. The Japanese financial system, meanwhile, was in the midst of sweeping reform, known as the ''Big Bang,'' in 2000, which will completely overhaul the banking system in an effort to mitigate the country's decade-long economic woes. Most significantly, the reforms will open Japanese financial markets to foreign players and, like the United States, break down restrictions against banks' engagement in other financial activities such as securities underwriting.

RESEARCH AND TECHNOLOGY

Changes in computer technology have radically altered the role of banks in American society. The most profound change was the capability of processing automated transfers of money between banks, companies, and consumers. Electronic funds transfers, or EFTs, are computer-based payment systems which substitute electronic and digital transfers for movements of cash and paper checks. EFTs have virtually eliminated manual paper handling in payments between institutions. Direct deposit has also eliminated some of the paper transfers between institutions and individuals. The trend has been toward more and more automation of payments systems.

Similarly, it was estimated that by 2002, 20 percent of all U.S. households will engage in online banking. An expected 15,850 banks offer online services by 2003. In 2000, over 3,000 banks maintained their own Web sites. There has also been increased use of intranets for staff conference, communication, and data management. The heightened emphasis and dependence on electronic information and funds transfers was expected to lead to an explosion in bank spending on information technology security systems and software, particularly electronic encryption systems, to generate a $7.4 billion market by 2002.

More visible to the consumer are automated teller machines, or ATMs, which are the ubiquitous computerized terminals from which consumers can access their savings, checking, or credit accounts. The ATM revolution began in 1969, when Chemical Bank in New York City installed one of the first cash dispensers in the country. There were 187,000 ATMs in 1998, up 13.3 percent from 1997. In contrast, only 72,000 ATMs existed in 1990. Most ATMs allow access to accounts at institutions other than those of the bank which owns the machine, and allow the consumer to process account balance inquiries, cash withdrawals, deposits, fund transfer between accounts, and transfer-to-house accounts.

These new technologies have made a number of significant changes to the American market place, including: changes in the methods of personal finance and in the process of purchasing consumer goods and services; changes in the structure of financial and retail organizations and their methods of operation; changes in the flow of funds in the marketplace; increased potential for the invasion of personal privacy and new avenues for the occurrence of fraud and theft; and changes in the regulatory and competitive balance among financial institutions. These and other technological changes radically altered the American commercial banking industry in the late 1980s and early 1990s.

FURTHER READING

Anason, Dean. ''Welcome for Reform Law Gives Way to Uncertainty.'' *American Banker,* 16 December 1999.

''Banking.'' *Business Week,* 10 January 2000.

Bomfim, Antulio A., and William R. Neslon. "Profits and Balance Sheet Developments at U.S. Commercial Banks in 1998." *Federal Reserve Bulletin,* September 1999.

Garver, Rob. "2 In 5 People Think Lenders Are Biased, a Survey Finds." *American Banker,* 17 December 1999.

Hill, Sidney. "Web Banking's New Fledglings." *Financial Services Online,* 1 September 1999.

Klebaner, Benjamin J. *American Commercial Banking: A History.* Boston: Twayne Publishers, 1990.

"Landmark Financial Services Legislation for the U.S." *Reactions,* December 1999.

Marjanovic, Steven. "Fed Rule Revision to Allow Wider Use of Electronic Returned-Check Images." *American Banker,* 23 December 1999.

"Online Banks: Mixed Messages." *Interactive Week,* 20 September 1999.

Rehm, Barbara A., and Dean Anason. "Fed Opens Lane for 1-Stop-Shop Applications." *American Banker,* 20 January 1999.

U.S. Department of Commerce. International Trade Administration. *U.S. Industry and Trade Outlook 1999.* New York: The McGraw Hill Companies, 1999.

SIC 6029

COMMERCIAL BANKS, NOT ELSEWHERE CLASSIFIED

This category includes commercial banks (accepting deposits) that do not operate under federal or state charter.

NAICS CODE(S)

522110 (Commercial Banking)

The 1990s have been characterized by dramatic consolidation in the commercial banking industry. The number of commercial banks fell 18 percent between 1993 and 1999, due primarily to mergers and acquisitions. In general, commercial banks are involved in financing the production, distribution, and sale of goods and services by acting as a source of short-term funds for the producer. Funds are acquired by the banks from the deposits of individuals who earn interest on these deposits. The vast majority of these institutions are either national or state banks. National banks are organized under the National Bank Act of 1863 and overseen by federal agencies. State banks are organized under similar state regulations and overseen by state banking authorities. Organizations created under these regulations charter the banks and give them access to depositors' insurance.

Industry leaders in commercial banking include: Citibank of New York; Bank of America National Association of Charlotte, North Carolina; Chase Manhattan Bank of North America; First Union National Bank of Charlotte, North Carolina; Morgan Guaranty Trust Company of New York; Bank One National Association of Chicago; Wells Fargo National Bank of Chicago; and Chemical Bank of New York.

The nation's 8,011 commercial banks maintained assets of $5.4 trillion in 1999. In a reversal of a trend that had characterized the national commercial banking sector since the mid-1980s, the number of commercial banks losing money has escalated in the late 1990s. While 17.1 percent of banks were losing money in 1985, that figure dropped to 3.6 percent in 1995, largely reflecting the declining number of banks as smaller and less profitable firms were forced out of business or swallowed by larger competitors. In 1998, 5.8 percent of commercial banks were unprofitable, due in part to relaxed lending regulations that allowed many banks to enter into risky loans.

A small minority of commercial banks are private—neither federally nor state chartered. These banks are sometimes owned by a small group of partners who assume unlimited liability, in effect insuring the bank themselves. These banks tend to focus on global custody and private banking, two growth sectors of banking in the 1990s.

Traditional global custodian services include paying for a security in local currency, minimizing settlement problems; collecting dividends and interest; handling safekeeping and tax reclamation; and taking care of bookkeeping for stock splits and rights issues. As this industry continues to grow, at an estimated rate of 30 percent, bankers have had to develop new, high value-added services. These services include analytics, performance measurement, and full master trust reporting.

The repeal of the 1933 Glass Steagall Act with the passage of the Gramm-Leach-Bliley Act in 1999 broke down many of the restrictions on the kinds of activities banks are permitted to engage in. By allowing financial services firms to offer lending, insurance, and brokering services under one company, it was expected that customers would increasingly begin to place all their financial business with a single firm. Thus, banks will be forced to find ways to make quick and efficient inroads into other financial sectors to secure or maintain a sound customer base.

Private banking involves offering banking services to very wealthy customers. These services are generally more personalized and flexible than services offered by other types of commercial banks. Private banks usually set net worth or minimum deposit requirements that vary from $250,000 to $2 million.

One reason that banks in the United States are chartered is to impose discipline on the individual banks. In private banks, discipline is imposed by the need for consensus, the unlimited liability of the partners, and the limitation of capital. This structure also has the benefit of allowing the partners, who often serve for many decades, to take a long-term view of their business. Perhaps the most important of these banks is Brown Brothers Harriman, the oldest and largest private bank in the United States, founded in 1818. In 1999, it employed more than 2,000 people nationwide and had total assets of $2.6 billion, up from $1.95 billion in 1997.

FURTHER READING

American Banker. Washington: American Banking Association, 5 August 1996.

"The Fragmented Bank Industry Consolidates." *Standard & Poor's Industry Surveys,* 13 May 1999.

Rehm, Barbara and Dean Anason. "Fed Opens Fast Lane for 1-Stop-Shop Applications." *American Banker,* 20 January 2000.

U.S. Department of Commerce. International Trade Administration. *U.S. Industry and Trade Outlook 1999.* Washington, D.C.: GPO, 1999.

SIC 6035

SAVINGS INSTITUTIONS, FEDERALLY CHARTERED

This category includes savings and loan associations operating under federal charter and savings banks operating under federal charter. Both savings and loan associations and savings banks fall under the general term "thrifts." Thrifts are financial institutions that exist primarily to hold retail deposits and make residential mortgage loans. About half of all residential mortgage debt, or dollars lent to individuals for the purpose of buying a home, is held by thrifts, though this market share has declined with the rise of mortgage bankers and the shrinking of the thrift industry. The thrift industry is the second largest type of financial institution, after commercial banks. This article deals only with federally chartered institutions; **SIC 6036: Savings Institutions, Not Federally Chartered** discusses state chartered institutions.

NAICS CODE(S)

522120 (Savings Institutions)

INDUSTRY SNAPSHOT

As of December 31, 1996, there were more than 1,900 thrift institutions in the United States. These thrifts held more than $1.0 trillion in assets (compared to about $4.5 trillion held by commercial banks), employed about 250,000 people, and operated from some 14,500 offices. Of these thrifts, 1,334 were federally chartered, with total assets of $789 billion. The remaining 590 thrifts were state chartered and held $259 billion in assets. The number of thrifts declined from nearly 2,500 just five years earlier. This trend reflected regulatory changes that caused some thrifts to become commercial banks. It also reflects the wave of mergers and acquisitions that continued to alter the nation's entire financial services world. Of the nation's thrifts, more than 1,500, including virtually all the federally chartered institutions, were insured by the Savings Association Insurance Fund (SAIF). The remaining few hundred thrifts were insured by the Bank Insurance Fund (BIF). Of the industry's total $1.028 trillion assets on December 31, 1996, $502 billion, or 50 percent, were in one to four family mortgages. That was a sharp decline from the 76 percent level for these small mortgages just five years earlier—another reflection of the growing diversification of the financial services industry. Of thrifts' other assets, some $262 billion were held in securities, while $59 billion were in multifamily residential properties and $50 billion were in commercial real estate loans. Although the number of institutions continued to shrink, the industry's level of assets, deposits, and other measures stabilized in the mid-1990s after undergoing major restructuring and shrinkage in the early 1990s.

In the late 1990s the banking industry was characterized by mergers, resulting in fewer and bigger institutions. The thrift industry also experienced an influx of previously nonbanking companies who were determined to capture a market share in financial services such as home mortgages, auto loans, and deposit services. Thrifts changed organizational structure, advanced their technology, and recreated job descriptions in order to deal with fewer and larger institutions over an interstate area. In the *Forbes* 1999 "Platinum List" which looks at all industries in the coming year, magazine experts predicted that financial institutions most likely to succeed in 1999 would have a good proportion of noninterest income, and would be prepared to deal with the year 2000 computer problem.

ORGANIZATION AND STRUCTURE

Of the federal savings and loan associations in existence in December 1996, roughly half were owned through the issuance of capital stock traded on the stock exchanges, just like any other corporation. The others were mutually owned. Mutually owned savings and loans, or "mutuals," do not issue stock and are owned by the customers of the institution. Any customer who opens an account at a mutual becomes a part owner of the institution. The type of ownership—stock or mutual—and the type of institution—S&L or savings bank—is specified in the thrift's charter. Thrifts were prohibited from having branches in more than one state until 1992.

Federal Home Loan Bank System. The Federal Home Loan Bank (FHLB) System is to thrifts what the Federal

Reserve is to banks. It provides liquidity to federally chartered savings and loans, which must join it, and to any state chartered institutions that wish to join. Members are affiliated with 1 of the 12 regional FHLBs from which they may borrow. Such borrowing is not long term; a thrift does not go into debt to a FHLB for any extended period of time, only for a short period, often overnight. To fund such borrowing, FHLBs have credit with the U.S. Treasury and issue government agency debt bonds, much the way that the Federal Reserve sells Treasury bills. The 12 regional FHLBs were managed by the Federal Home Loan Bank Board until that board's abolition in 1989, after which they were managed by the U.S. Department of Treasury.

Regulation: The Office of Thrift Supervision. The many failures in the thrift industry, beginning in the late 1980s, brought the industry under great scrutiny and regulation. The Office of Thrift Supervision (OTS), an agency within the U.S. Treasury Department, became the chief regulator of the thrift industry with the bailout law of 1989. Since the bailout law, thrifts are tightly regulated, mainly because the deposits of their customers are federally insured. It is to the taxpayer's advantage that thrifts be profitable. The OTS decides if a thrift is healthy and profitable enough to do normal business. The OTS charters, regulates, and examines the operations of federally chartered savings and loans.

The OTS classifies thrifts by capital levels and profitability. There are four such classifications, each of which corresponds to a particular level of capital: Group I thrifts are healthy institutions, fully capitalized, and profitable; Group II comprises those institutions that do not quite meet the capital guidelines for Group I, but are expected to; Group III thrifts have poor earnings and low capital; and Group IV consists of those thrifts whose assets will be transferred to the Resolution Trust Corporation. As of November 1992, 37 percent of all assets of the federally chartered thrift industry were held by Group I thrifts. Thirty-five percent of the industry assets were in Group II, 24 percent in Group III, and only 4 percent in Group IV. This meant that 72 percent of all assets in federally chartered thrifts were in institutions that were considered either healthy or expected to meet the healthy capital guidelines. By December 1996, the health of the industry improved even further. The FDIC estimated that there were only 35 problem thrifts at that time, compared to 71 just two years earlier and 480 at the end of 1990.

For a thrift to be in OTS Group I, it must pass the following tests. First, 1.5 percent of assets must be in tangible capital. Tangible capital is stockholder's equity minus investments in activities that were legal before the bailout law but are no longer legal for thrifts to undertake. This condition existed because the thrift industry was in a period of transition in the early 1990s, with tighter regulations being phased in to minimize losses. Second, 3 percent of assets must be in leverage capital. Leverage capital is tangible capital plus the value, as judged by the OTS, of the firm's goodwill and intangible assets. Goodwill is defined as an asset equal to the market value of another institution a thrift purchases minus the value of its liabilities. The 1989 bailout law calls for goodwill to be phased out as part of the capital a thrift reports. Third, 7.2 percent of a thrift's risk-weighted assets must be in total capital. Risk-weighted assets are obtained by assigning a weight to each kind of asset. For example, the amount of cash and government securities is multiplied by zero, while the amount of higher-risk assets are multiplied by as much as two times the face-value of the asset. Total capital includes leverage capital less items being phased out, such as nonresidential construction loans, plus an allowance for general loan loss.

In addition to these capital guidelines, during at least three-quarters of each year, thrifts must invest 65 percent of assets in certain investments. Among these acceptable investments are residential mortgages, car loans, Fannie Mae loans, home equity loans, and investment in the Resolution Trust Corporation. The idea behind this last requirement, known as the Qualified Thrift Lender Test, is that none of these acceptable investments are of the high-risk venture capital or commercial real estate variety that became popular areas for thrift investments during the years after the 1980 deregulation.

If a thrift does not comply with the above guidelines for Group I, it must submit a plan to the OTS saying how it will meet them and comply within 60 days. If this does not happen, the OTS will place restrictions on the thrift such as limiting the growth in the amount of future loans, and further limits on the kinds of loans the thrift may make. The delinquent thrift also may not purchase an interest in any other company.

Other Regulators. The Federal Deposit Insurance Corporation (FDIC) is the provider of deposit insurance for all depository institutions. The FDIC controls the Savings Association Insurance Fund and the Bank Insurance Fund. Therefore, the FDIC has an interest in assuring that thrifts stay profitable so as not to pose a threat to the insurance fund. Whereas the OTS is the chief regulator of thrifts and is concerned with overall operations, with an emphasis on the asset side of the balance sheet, the FDIC regulates deposits at thrifts and conducts investigations to the effect of securing deposits. The FDIC works closely with the Resolution Trust Corporation (RTC) in administering the affairs of failed thrifts. The RTC seizes the assets of Group IV thrifts and attempts to either sell the institutions or liquidate them and pay off depositors with federal insurance money, as provided for in the 1989 bailout law.

The thrift industry is also under the same depository regulations of the Federal Reserve System as all other depository institutions. As of 1993, all depository institutions, including thrifts, must hold a certain amount of deposits as reserves. The current reserve requirement is 3 percent of all savings deposits up to $42.2 million in deposits, and then 10 percent of all savings deposits above $42.2 million. The Federal Reserve imposes this ''reserve requirement'' in order to insure that at least some deposits remain in the vaults of depository institutions as a hedge against bank runs.

BACKGROUND AND DEVELOPMENT

Savings and Loans Versus Savings Banks. The nineteenth-century origins of savings and loan associations and savings banks were separate. Savings and loans were first created primarily with the goal of fostering home ownership among members of the association. These ''building societies'' were originally designed to exist only until all members received a home loan. But inevitably some societies would continue to accept new members and exist in perpetuity. Savings banks, on the other hand, were designed to encourage thrift and personal savings, and from their origins intended to be permanent institutions. Yet savings banks also found mortgage lending a sound investment of depositor funds. In this way, savings and loan associations and savings banks came to have similar functions.

The first federal charters for savings and loans were granted in 1933. Savings banks were not federally chartered until 1980. Thus, before 1980 savings and loan associations and savings banks were distinct segments of the thrift industry because all savings banks were state-chartered mutuals. Savings and loans focused on residential mortgage lending, which made up more than 75 percent of their assets. Savings banks also were heavily into mortgage lending, but without federal regulation they were able to have much greater shares of assets in other kinds of consumer lending.

Historically, all savings banks were mutually owned and state chartered, thus the name ''mutual savings bank.'' With the Depository Institutions and Monetary Control Act of 1980, mutual savings banks could easily obtain federal charters and change their ownership to stock form. In 1982, with the Garn-St. Germain Act, federal savings banks could convert to federal savings and loans and vice versa. As the thrift industry entered the 1990s, virtually the only difference between savings and loan associations and savings banks was that the FDIC administered insurance funds; the SAIF and the BIF are kept separate to make it easier to have separate insurance premiums for the two segments of the industry.

Postwar Favoritism. After World War II, savings and loans enjoyed less deposit regulation than commercial banks because housing was a national priority. The Federal Reserve's Regulation Q prevented commercial banks from paying greater than 3 percent on deposits from 1933 to 1962. As such, savings and loans typically offered one-quarter percent higher interest than banks, easily attracting deposits. In 1966, Regulation Q was extended to place a deposit interest ceiling on thrifts as well, but in such a way that thrifts always paid one-quarter to one-half percent higher than commercial banks. The Federal Reserve would periodically make adjustments in the rate ceilings, but the Fed could not cope with the skyrocketing and erratic interest rates of the late 1970s, and an important deregulation law passed in 1980 removed all deposit interest rate ceilings from all depository institutions.

Deregulation. The Depository Institutions Deregulation and Monetary Control Act (DIDMCA) changed the regulatory environment for both banks and thrifts. It deregulated the thrift industry by allowing thrifts to acquire more nonmortgage loans, eliminating interest rate ceilings on both loans and deposits, and eliminating some geographical lending restrictions on thrifts. Prior to this act, federally chartered savings and loans could only make non-mortgage consumer loans if they were for home-improvement, mobile homes, education, or if the loans were secured by deposits. DIDMCA allowed savings and loans to make a broad range of consumer loans, just like state-chartered savings banks. DIDMCA also allowed savings banks to get federal charters and to convert ownership to stock form, and opened the Federal Reserve's discount window to all depository institutions, both federally and state chartered, banks and thrifts. This act allowed federally chartered savings banks and savings and loans to switch charters from one to the other and gave both segments of the thrift industry power to make commercial loans. Thrifts responded by trying to become more full-service financial institutions, making commercial real estate loans, buying commercial paper, and making direct commercial loans. It was the mismanagement of many individual thrifts trying to become more like commercial banks that led to the rash of thrift failures later in the 1980s.

Crisis and Bailout. From 1986 through the early 1990s, hundreds of thrift institutions became insolvent. A comparison of asset holdings of solvent and insolvent thrifts as of December 31, 1987, showed that insolvent thrifts differed from solvent ones in several aspects of asset structure: lower percentage of residential mortgages (31.3 versus 46.3), higher percentage of commercial real estate (14.5 versus 9.9), higher percentage of repossessed real estate (9.9 versus 1.3), and lower levels of cash and government securities (11.5 versus 13.3). Simply put, many thrifts, when presented with their new lending powers under deregulation, experienced bad judgment and made many bad loans.

The regulators of thrifts made the problem worse. The Federal Home Loan Bank Board (FHLBB) was established in 1932 as the chief regulator of thrifts. The FHLBB oversaw the Federal Savings and Loan Insurance Corporation (FSLIC), which insured thrift deposits up to $100,000 per account. The insurance money for the FSLIC came from premiums paid by member thrifts. But unlike other regulators, the FHLBB was more of an advocate for its members and as such kept the premium very low. So the FSLIC was underfunded, and by the end of 1987 so many thrifts had failed that the FSLIC itself became insolvent. Also, throughout the 1980s the FHLBB allowed the FSLIC to practice creative accounting to hide the depth of member problems. The FHLBB was so under the influence of the industry itself that a whole new regulatory environment was needed.

The Bailout Law. The Financial Institutions Reform, Recovery, and Enforcement (FIRRE) Act of 1989 eliminated the FHLBB, an independent agency, and replaced it with the OTS, which would be under direct control of the U.S. Treasury Department. Meanwhile, FIRRE took the insurance fund out of the hands of regulators and put it under the control of the FDIC, in the form of the Savings Association Insurance Fund. The FDIC was considered to be more sound and with stricter examination standards than the insolvent FSLIC. FIRRE also strengthened capital-to-asset ratio requirements and phased out forms of intangible assets from the counted capital levels. The act also established the Resolution Trust Corporation to oversee and administer the sale or liquidation of failed thrifts.

Bad loans continued to haunt the thrift industry in the early 1990s, as nearly 2 percent of loans were delinquent in the first quarter of 1992. Twelve percent of construction and land loans were delinquent at this time, demonstrating why such loans were discouraged in the new regulation following the 1989 bailout law. In accordance with the OTS capital guidelines, and as a result of closing troubled thrifts, the industry-wide level of tangible capital as a percentage of total assets rose through the early 1990s from 3.5 percent in March 1990 to 5.2 percent in March 1992.

Recovery and Profits. Despite the continuance of some bad loans, profits in the thrift industry steadily climbed in the early 1990s. Losses from 1987 to 1990 totaled $30 billion, but by 1992 profits were up to $5.14 billion, one of the industry's best years ever. Profits were aided in the early 1990s by the widest interest rate spreads in decades, that is, a wide gap between the rates charged on loans and paid to depositors. One reason for the wide spread at thrifts was simply a reaction to some of the widest gaps ever between the 30-year Treasury bill and the short-term T-bills. Long-term T-bill rates are usually higher than short-term rates, but this gap was exceptionally large through the early 1990s. The gap grew from 2.91 percent in March 1991, to 3.33 percent by December 1992.

Another reason for the wide spreads at thrifts was the Federal Reserve's easing of interest rates in response to a sluggish economy. Thrift profits tend to be higher when interest rates are low. Mortgages are long-term commitments while deposits are relatively short-term. Therefore, when interest rates rise, thrifts lose profits, with rates to depositors rising while revenue from fixed-rate mortgages stays level. The high interest rates of the late 1970s were responsible for thrift failures at that time, encouraging the deregulation in the early 1980s, which ultimately and ironically led to the failures of the late 1980s.

Falling rates, likewise, reduce costs of thrift liabilities to depositors while mortgage revenues fall more slowly, increasing profits. Lower interest rates in the early and mid-1990s made the industry's recovery during this period much easier.

Profits were also aided by a decline in the amount of troubled assets. The ratio of noncurrent assets plus real estate owned to all assets fell from 3.98 percent at the end of 1990 to 1.10 percent at the end of 1996. Moreover, the number of failed or assisted institutions fell to 1 during 1996 from 223 in 1990. These healthy declines can be attributed to several factors. First, falling mortgage rates combined with an economy no longer in as deep a recession, helped consumers pay their mortgages on time. Second, the real estate market in general was improving in the early 1990s; the major slowdown in home sales experienced in 1989 and 1990 was over. Finally, the strict regulation following the 1989 bailout law found many thrifts writing down their bad assets. Many of these write-downs were in commercial and out-of-state loans, the worst sources of thrift troubles in the late 1980s.

Profits were also aided by higher capital-to-asset ratios. The ratio of leverage capital (as discussed above) to total assets industry-wide grew from 4.06 percent in March 1990 to 7.77 percent at the end of 1996. This strengthened net worth base allowed more thrifts to engage in profitable ''equity financing'' (funding new loans without taking on any new liabilities in the form of deposits). Equity financing is pure profit, and the amount of equity financing increases with the capital-to-asset ratio.

Types of Loans. There are two kinds of loans that thrifts offer: fixed-rate loans and adjustable-rate mortgages (ARMs). About 30 percent of the thrift industry offers mainly fixed-rate loans, most of which are the traditional 30-year mortgage, though some other time periods are available. About 30 percent of thrifts offer both kinds of loans, and 40 percent of the industry offers mainly ARMs. Many thrifts prefer to offer ARMs because they pose less risk to the institution by not locking into a low rate. ARMs are adjusted either monthly or yearly and may be tied to either the Office of Thrift Supervision's cost-of-funds index for monthly adjustments, or to the rate of the one-year Treasury bills for annual adjustments.

The relative preference of consumers for fixed-rate mortgages or ARMs depends, of course, on the prevalent level of interest rates. At low rates, such as in the early 1990s, consumers want to lock in to a low fixed rate, while at high rates ARMs will be more popular in hopes that rates will fall. Yet the willingness of thrifts to offer one versus the other is the exact opposite; thrifts prefer ARMs when interest rates are low so that revenues from loans will rise with interest rates. ARMs first became legal for thrifts to use in 1981. Thrifts began to lobby for ARMs in the late 1970s, spurred by the pioneering usage of ARMs in the mid-1970s by some California state-chartered institutions.

There are few differences between thrift institutions with respect to what their products look like. The only differences are in the kind of loan as described above, or in the interest rates offered for loans or savings and checking accounts. The large number of firms in the industry tends to keep interest rates, both on assets and liabilities, pretty close from one savings institution to another. After all, with so many institutions and so little difference in the kinds of product, thrifts will be very careful to keep their interest rates competitive.

Refinancing. One phenomenon thrifts faced in the early 1990s was refinancing of mortgages. Falling mortgage rates allowed many consumers to lock in to lower fixed rates. The average rate on a 30-year mortgage fell from 10.2 percent in 1990 to 7.5 percent by 1993, a 20-year low. Refinancings lower thrifts' profits in the long term because of the lower fixed rates, but in the short term they contribute to profits, as they did in the early 1990s. Refinancing brings in new business. Refinancing also brings in up-front fees such as application fees and points.

Charter Flips. The 1982 Garn-St. Germain Act allowed thrifts to change over from savings and loans to savings banks and vice versa. The number of such charter flips, plus changes from a federal to a state charter, went from zero in 1989 to 29 in 1990, 54 in 1991, and 114 in 1992. Some of these institutions were seeking a name change to avoid the stigma of being called a savings and loan. Others were looking to continue pursuing the commercial banking activities discouraged of thrifts under the 1989 bailout law. State-chartered thrifts are exempt from OTS rules regarding capital-to-asset ratios, and also need not pass the Qualified Thrift Lender Test, which forces federal thrifts to keep 65 percent of assets in housing-related areas. It is not clear that charter flips are always advantageous, as the downside includes loss of access to the Federal Home Loan Bank system, as well as the administrative costs of the flip.

Takeovers by Banks. A residual phenomenon of the thrift bailout in the early 1990s was the great extent to which the commercial banking and thrift industries were merging through the acquisition of thrifts by banks. In 1992 alone, banks bought 16 percent of the assets held by thrifts, up from 4 percent in 1991 and 1 percent in 1990, according to *Standard and Poor's Industry Surveys.* The FDIC Improvement Act of 1991 made thrift acquisition easier for banks, and banks were enjoying record high stock prices in the early 1990s. Banks tend to have a stronger balance sheet than thrifts, and bankers already have the skills needed to manage a thrift.

Current Conditions

During the mid- to late 1990s many businesses aggressively pursued the financial services market. Such businesses used the federal thrift charter as a loophole to offer virtually unregulated financial services all over the United States. Such services included trust funds, deposit service, loans, and almost everything that a bank could offer, with the exception of corporate banking and bond trading. Under the federal charter, thrifts were able to offer nearly the same services as commercial banks, but with less regulation.

In 1998, OTS approved 43 charters, and more than 33 percent of these were given to companies not in the banking business, such as State Farm Mutual Automobile Insurance Company. In 1999 OTS was faced with applications for charter from more nonbank companies such as Ford Motor Company and the Farm Bureau. While an OTS director (Ellen S. Seidman) claimed in *Business Week* (22 March 1999) that the OTS used discretion in granting charters to applicants, industry banking commissioner Catherine A. Ghiglieri of Texas called the trend a ''recipe for disaster'' and stated that ''you have traditional bank products being sold through nontraditional means by people who haven't been in the business before.''

Although Congressional reform could make it more difficult for nonbanks to obtain thrift charter status, such reform had been unsuccessfully attempted for the last three decades, according to an article in *Business Week* (7 December 1998). In 1998 the House Banking Committee Chairman (James A. Leach, R-Iowa) led unsuccessful reform to completely eliminate savings and loans. In 1999, Leach concentrated on initiatives that would slow or block nonbanks from purchasing new thrifts. But the new players in the thrift arena made sure that they didn't face the same fate of Savings and Loans in the 1980s. The new thrifts focused on loan origination only, followed by a sale of the loan to investors to reduce the risk of holding bad assets.

Industry Leaders

The thrift industry really has no industry leaders in the sense of most industries, although there are a handful of large institutions. Several savings and loans have more than $10 billion in assets, all of them based in California. Yet even combined, these institutions hold only 22 percent of all assets in Federal savings and loans and only 16 percent of assets in all Federal thrifts. Including state-chartered thrifts, and considering that thrifts only account for less than half of the market for mortgages, we see an industry characterized by perfect competition nationwide. In an industry with $1 trillion in assets, 92 percent of thrifts hold less than $1 billion in assets.

However, since thrifts do most business inside their respective states of origin, some states may have a handful of thrifts dominating the market. Most thrifts try to keep operations in a limited geographic area so as to give the impression of saturating the market. Nothing prevents a consumer from patronizing a thrift in another geographic area except convenience of banking at a local branch. Yet with the 1992 ruling legalizing interstate branches or thrifts and the emergence of electronic banking, even greater competition lies on the horizon for thrifts.

From an advertising perspective, one thrift directed efforts in the late 1990s toward making sure that its sheer size in the industry didn't scare away potential customers. Washington Mutual, called the ''nation's largest thrift'' by *Advertising Age* (13 July 1998), spent $30 million in 1998 to launch an advertising campaign that portrayed it as a ''big bank with a small town feel'' and empahsized personal service. After consolidating and folding two California thrifts (American Savings Bank and Great Western Bank), Washington Mutual reported assets of $103.1 billion in 1998.

Kiplinger's Personal Finance Magazine (December 1998) reported on 24 thrifts across the country that they considered excellent investment possibilities. Criteria for selection included assets of more than $50 million, a good return on assets, and a low portion of nonperforming loans. Among the selections: Continental Savings Bank in Milwaukee, Wisconsin; Yakima Federal S&L Association in Yakima, Washington, and Benjamin Franklin Savings Bank in Franklin, Massachusetts.

WORKFORCE

The industry group America's Community Bankers, based in Washington, D.C., estimated that in mid-1998 there were 244,925 people employed in savings institutions in the United States, 1,713 institutions, and 14,434 branches.

The Bureau of Labor Statistics (BLS) provides breakdowns of occupations within an industry only by broader industrial classifications. The following breakdown of occupations is for all commercial banks, savings institutions, and credit unions. In 1990, 23.4 percent of employees were tellers, 6.1 percent clerical supervisors, 5.6 percent financial managers, and 5.5 percent loan officers and counselors. Clerical positions combined, including tellers, general office clerks, secretaries, and other kinds of clerks made up 63.2 percent of the workforce.

Accoriding to the BLS, trends in the industry such as the advent of insterstate banking will impact the workforce in this industry. Tellers, for example, are expected to find little or no change in employment through the year 2006, even though rapid turnover will continue in this position. The BLS suggests that interstate banking will diminish the total number of banks, but change the job responsibilities in a new type of financial institution which is larger than its counterpart of the past. BLS predicts that the financial industry will cut costs in order to more effectively offer an expanded network of interstate services. Among changes that impact the workfoce: the hiring of part time rather than full time tellers and the use of customer service representatives who can also perform teller duties and who are housed in all-service locations such as bank branches in grocery stores. Such a workforce would need to perform more tasks, so thrifts have started to train employees using computerized tutorials on the job, right at the thrift branch itself, rather than sending employees to a traditional training center.

AMERICA AND THE WORLD

Most industrial countries have financial institutions to provide mortgages and house personal savings similar to the thrift institution in the United States. Because the thrift institution is segmented locally, with no institutions owning branches outside of the state where headquartered until 1992, most business done by thrifts is local. Since thrifts serve a domestic market, serving the local needs of individual savers and borrowers, thrifts do not have the international business that many commercial banks and brokerage houses have. Thrifts do not have to compete in world markets as do some commercial financial institutions. The major impact of international finance on thrifts is that of interest rates, because the interest rates that affect thrift profitability are highly influenced by world markets. But thrifts are no different in this respect than any financial institution.

RESEARCH AND TECHNOLOGY

As thrifts entered the 1990s, technology played an increasing role in how they did business. Thrifts were becoming more sales oriented in the wake of the bailout crisis, moving away from higher-risk ventures and back to consumer-oriented banking; for this reason, customer relations became a prime area for the application of technology. A variety of media was being used by thrifts to improve their services, both salesperson-activated and customer-activated. Salespeople could use the latest software to access all kinds of information on the thrift's rates and products. As time constraints on consumers increased, thrifts responded by having loan representatives use automated credit scoring, allowing consumer loans to be approved by telephone in minutes.

Thrifts also introduced technology to reduce risks when making loans. Thrifts hoped to use artificial intelligence systems to assist in various decision-making processes, such as loan applications and deciding which financial services to offer. *Bankers Monthly* in 1990 quoted Tom Lester, then first vice-president and manager of information systems at San Diego's Great American Bank, as saying "Thrifts are slowing down and choosing carefully which services to offer in order to meet capitalization requirements. We expect things to be cool for the next couple of years, and we'll be focusing on maximizing core earnings while reducing general and administrative costs."

ATMs, voice/audio response systems, and "smart cards" became widespread during the 1990s. These cards accessed accounts like ATMs, contained a microchip with information about the customer's accounts, and could be used as a debit card. In 1990 Connecticut-based People's Bank became the first financial institution to offer a three-way card combining a credit card, telephone calling card, and debit card. By networking the computer systems at a bank and a telephone company such a card could be used by the consumer to interact with hardware systems at both companies. The consumer could also access interactive video technology to use the thrift as a financial supermarket, getting visual information about different rates, loans, and investment products before speaking with a customer service representative. With the completion of the electronic superhighway, consumers would be able to do this at home for thrifts all across the country, reducing the local saturation of some thrifts.

As the amount of free time available to Americans declined, thrifts responded to the demand for faster service through electronic banking, phone banking, and direct deposit. In addition to a hope of improved service, thrifts looked ahead to cutting costs by using smaller, better-trained staffs supported by high-tech automation. By the late 1990s, other means to cut costs using technology included creating bank branches consisting of ATMs and kiosks. Kiosks added a new dimension to an ATM transaction; the kiosk allowed the bank customer to communicate with bank personnel via remote and interactive video.

FURTHER READING

America's Community Bankers 1996 Annual Report and Related Research Statistics. Washington, DC: 1996.

America's Community Bankers Industry Profile, 1998. Available from http://www.acbankers.org/About/Profile.htm.

Arndorfer, James B. "Washington Mutual Kicks Off $30 Mil Ad Effort in California, Florida; McCann Work Touts Big Thrift's Personal Service." *Advertising Age,* 13 July 1998.

"The Forbes Platinum List: Banking," *Forbes,* 11 January 1999.

Fox, Justin, "The Irresistible Glamour of Federal Savings Bank Charters." *Fortune,* 8 June 1998.

"It's a Wonderful Loophole." *Business Week,* 22 March 1999.

Lankford, Kimberly. "How to Rob a Bank." *Kiplinger's Personal Finance Magazine,* December 1998.

McNamee, Mike, and Owen Ullmann. "Hear the Banks Howling? The S & Ls are Back." *Business Week,* 7 December 1998.

U.S. Bureau of Labor Statistics. *1998-99 Occupational Outlook Handbook: Bank Tellers,* 29 January 1998. Available from http://stats.bls.gov/oco/ocos126.htm.

SIC 6036

SAVINGS INSTITUTIONS, NOT FEDERALLY CHARTERED

This category includes savings and loan associations operating under state charters and savings banks operating under state charters. Both savings and loan associations and savings banks fall under the general term "thrifts." Thrifts are financial institutions that exist primarily to hold retail deposits and make residential mortgage loans. The thrift industry is the second largest type of financial institution, after commercial banks. Thrifts can be either federally chartered, and regulated by the Treasury Department's Office of Thrift Supervision, or state-chartered and subject to regulation varying by state. This article discusses state-chartered thrifts and is intended as a supplement to **SIC 6035: Savings Institutions, Federally Chartered.** Much information pertinent to both federally and state chartered institutions is included in that article.

NAICS CODE(S)

522120 (Savings Institutions)

INDUSTRY SNAPSHOT

As of December 31, 1998, there were more than 1,600 thrift institutions in the United States. These thrifts held more than $1.0 trillion in assets (compared to about $5.4 trillion held by commercial banks) and operated from some 14,138 offices. Of these thrifts, 952 were federally chartered, with total assets of $1,327 billion. The remaining 735 thrifts were state chartered and held some $330 billion in assets. The number of thrifts declined from nearly 2,800 in 1990. This trend reflected regulatory changes that saw some thrifts convert to commercial banks. It also reflects the wave of mergers and acquisitions that continued to alter the nation's entire financial services world. Of the nation's thrifts, more than 1,300, including virtually all the federally chartered institutions, were insured by the Savings Association Insurance Fund (SAIF). The remaining few hundred thrifts were insured by the Bank Insurance Fund (BIF). Of the industry's total $1.08 trillion assets on December 31, 1998, some $518 billion, or 50 percent, were in 1 to 4 family mortgages. That was a sharp decline from the 76 percent level for these small mortgages just seven years earlier, another reflection of the growing diversification of the financial services industry. Of thrifts' other assets, some $269 billion were held in securities, while $54.5 billion were in multifamily residential properties and $47 billion were in commercial real estate loans. Although the number of institutions continues to shrink, the industry's level of assets, deposits, and other measures stabilized in the mid-1990s after undergoing major restructuring and shrinkage in the early 1990s. By the end of the decade thrifts were returning record earnings.

Since the mid-1980s, the state-chartered portion of the thrift industry has been characterized by a greater rate of insolvencies. Because they were governed by fewer regulatory safeguards than federal thrifts, state thrifts were able to make risky investments with depositors' funds. Also, there was increasing defection to federal charters among savings and loans, with similar but less widespread charter flipping among savings banks. Some of the healthiest federal thrifts began to go against this trend and switch to state charters in the early 1990s. The industry strengthened in the 1990s, with 1997 being the first year since 1959 with no thrift failures.

ORGANIZATION AND STRUCTURE

Thrifts can be classified in three ways: by type of ownership (stock or mutual), by type of institution (savings and loan association or savings bank), and by type of charter (state or federal). The type of ownership and institution is specified in each thrift's charter, and distinctions between the different types of ownership and institutions are discussed in **SIC 6035: Savings Institutions, Federally Chartered.** The distinctions between the organization and structure of state-chartered versus federal-chartered thrifts are discussed below.

Depository Insurance. All thrifts, both federal and state, have federal depository insurance. Savings and loan associations are insured by the Savings Association Insurance Fund (SAIF), and savings banks are insured by the Bank Insurance Fund (BIF). Both of these funds are administered by the Federal Deposit Insurance Corporation (FDIC), an independent federal agency, which originally was formed to provide depository insurance for commercial banks, but assumed the role of insurance provider for thrifts with the passage of the 1989 bailout law. Savings banks have always been insured by the FDIC; savings and loans were insured by the now defunct Federal Savings and Loan Insurance Corporation (FSLIC) until 1989. The two funds are kept separate to justify higher insurance premiums at the SAIF, though there have been ongoing discussions in Congress regarding their merger, which was proposed to take place in 1999. A more thorough discussion of depository insurance is found in article **SIC 6035: Savings Institutions, Federally Chartered.**

In all states, federal deposit insurance coverage is a necessary condition to obtain and keep a state charter. Those state institutions that opt for federal insurance must comply with any rules of the particular insurance fund, but are not subject to most federal regulatory rules in general, with some important exceptions as explained below. The situation of all state-chartered thrifts having federal insurance that has existed since the 1980s did not occur by law, but simply because most of the individual state-sponsored insurance funds failed by then.

State Regulation. States can regulate many aspects of state-chartered thrifts. For example, California and Texas each have a separate agency that regulates thrifts. In other states, such as New York, thrifts and commercial banks are regulated by the same agency. Historically, states could regulate the kinds of assets thrifts may acquire; however, the Financial Institutions Reform, Recovery, and Enforcement Act (FIRREA) of 1989 forced state regulation to conform more closely with federal requirements pertaining to asset acquisitions.

States can regulate locations of thrift branches, whether thrifts may have branches in other states, and whether branches may exist for out-of-state thrifts. When a state-chartered thrift becomes insolvent, the state may appoint a conservator or receiver to handle the thrift's assets, though disposition of assets may also be carried out by the Federal Resolution Trust Corporation. (See **SIC 6035: Savings Institutions, Federally Chartered.**)

Since the passage of FIRREA, state-chartered thrifts must meet net worth and capital to asset ratio standards identical to federally chartered thrifts. Before the 1989 act, state thrifts did not have to meet any federal standards outside of the few imposed by the FSLIC for those thrifts that chose to obtain deposit insurance there. But some leeway still exists for state-chartered thrifts, as those that do meet the net worth standards are free to invest deposits in assets that federal thrifts may not, or in certain assets to a greater extent than federal thrifts are allowed. However, the FDIC has the right to veto any asset acquisition of state thrifts if it determines that the asset may pose too much risk for the insurance fund. Since FIRREA, there are fewer distinctions between the types of ventures that are permissible for state versus federal thrifts.

Office of Thrift Supervision. The OTS System, and its predecessor agency, the Federal Home Loan Bank System, is to thrifts what the Federal Reserve is to banks. It provides liquidity to federally chartered savings and loans, which must join it, and to any state-chartered institutions that wish to join.

Reserve Requirement. State-chartered thrifts are also under the same depository regulations of the Federal Reserve System as all other depository institutions (both state and federal and including thrifts) and must hold a certain amount of deposits as reserves. As of 1998 the reserve requirement is 3 percent of all savings deposits up to $47.8 million and then 10 percent of all savings deposits above $47.8 million. The Federal Reserve imposes this ''reserve requirement'' as a hedge against bank runs.

BACKGROUND AND DEVELOPMENT

Savings and Loans Versus Savings Banks. Savings and loan associations and savings banks both have origins in the nineteenth century. Savings and loans were first created primarily with the goal of fostering home ownership among members of the association. Savings banks, on the other hand, were designed to encourage thrift and personal savings, but also found mortgage lending to be a sound investment of depositor funds. In this way, savings and loan associations and savings banks came to have similar functions, and their differences in the twentieth century stemmed from variances in regulation and chartering.

Regulation. Chartering and regulation of savings and loans by individual states was all that existed until the creation of the Federal Home Loan Bank System in 1932. From this time, savings and loans could obtain a federal charter and could have either stock or mutual ownership, but savings banks were only state chartered and mutually owned until 1980. After 1932 state savings and loans willing to pay the premiums could receive federal insurance from the Federal Savings and Loan Insurance Corporation (FSLIC). Aside from FSLIC standards, these state thrifts were exempt from federal regulations. Since state-chartered savings and loans historically held a smaller portion of the industry's assets than federal ones, dual regulation sometimes served as a testing ground for new concepts. Because particular states in the 1970s allowed adjustable rate mortgages (ARMs), notably California and Wisconsin, ARMs became popular enough to convince Congress to allow federal thrifts to offer them. State regulations were for the most part little different from federal ones, perhaps slightly more liberal, until federal deregulation in the early 1980s provided inspiration for many states to allow massive experimentation by thrifts with minimal regulation.

Deregulation. The Depository Institutions Deregulation and Monetary Control Act (DIDMCA) of 1980 and the Garn-St. Germain Act of 1982 were the two acts that deregulated federally chartered thrifts. However, these acts had a profound effect on state-chartered thrifts as well. Because federal thrifts were now able to pay higher deposit rates and could now invest those deposits in a much wider variety of consumer and commercial loans, it gave state governments incentive to deregulate their own thrift industries. In an effort to allow their state-chartered thrifts to remain competitive with the newly deregulated federal thrifts, several states made regulations much more lenient than even the newly eased federal regulations, with Texas and California leading in leniency followed by Florida and Arizona. In California, the state with the largest number of state-chartered thrifts, the Nolan Bill became law at the beginning of 1983, allowing almost anyone to own a savings and loan, with unlimited deposits and no rules pertaining to what those deposits may be invested. All of these deposits, for a very small premium, were insured by the FSLIC. Other states passed laws almost as lenient.

It would be oversimplifying to say that deregulation caused savings institutions to fail. Deregulation was a response to the inflation-induced insolvencies of the 1970s, and in the early years of the 1980s, it appeared as if deregulation was helping the industry recover from the previous decade's slump. Yet the facts show that failures of thrifts were more widespread at the state level than in federal thrifts in the mid-1980s, so it can be said that the industry, especially at the state level, grew too fast, accumulating vast quantities of federally insured deposits, which were badly invested without regulation. Deregulation caused a huge increase in new thrift start-ups, mostly at the state level. From 1982 through 1986, 139 new state charters were granted with only 67 new federal charters. Compared to the new federal thrifts, the new state thrifts had a higher variance of returns on assets, riskier asset portfolios, and were more likely to pay higher than competitive rates on deposits in order to grow more quickly.

Shrinkage of the State-Chartered Segment. From 1980 to 1986 state-chartered savings and loans declined from 50 percent of all savings and loans to 46 percent, and then down to only 42 percent by 1989. The share of all savings and loan assets held by state-chartered institutions from 1980 to 1986 fell from 44 percent to 36 percent, and then down to only 26 percent by 1989, the level it still roughly held in the mid-1990s. Most of this shift away from state to federal charters happened in the last part of the 1980s because of the realization in the mid-1980s that state-chartered thrifts were more likely to be insolvent. The FIRREA of 1989 reduced the advantages of holding a state charter, leading to more charter flips in the 1990s. Savings banks could not obtain federal charters until 1980, and since the crisis of failures and insurance insolvency did not affect savings banks as harshly, only a handful of savings banks made the switch.

Tax law changes in 1996 made it more cost effective for commercial banks to acquire thrifts, and in 1997, 77 savings institutions were acquired, an industry record.

CURRENT CONDITIONS

Both state and federal thrifts began recovering in the early 1990s. Lower interest rates and loan refinancing had positive effects on both state and federal thrifts. These issues are all discussed in the **Current Conditions** section of **SIC 6035: Savings Institutions, Federally Chartered.** At the turn of the twenty-first century there were over 7,000 state-chartered banks with at least 70 percent having assets under $100 million. Most state banks are still small community banks.

Charter Flipping. The rapid switching of state thrifts to federal charters in the mid-1980s resulted from the extra problems of state thrifts. Yet by the early 1990s, some federal thrifts were healthy enough to make the opposite switch. These thrifts tended to be among the healthier and better capitalized institutions. These healthier thrifts found it possible and advantageous to pursue the few regulatory perks of a state charter that still existed post-FIRREA. Having met the federal capital to assets requirements, these institutions found it advantageous to switch to state charters so that they could invest in a broader variety of assets. By the late 1990s Congress was considering legislation to deregulate the governance of financial services that may be offered by all depository institutions in the areas of securities, insurance, real estate, and similar nonbanking services. President Clinton signed the Gramm-Leach-Bliley Act into law on November 12, 1999. The act is predicted to accelerate combinations among banks, brokerages, and insurance companies.

During the mid- to late 1990s many thrifts converted their charters to commercial bank charters. Between 1990 and 1997, 135 thrifts made this change. This is an astoundingly high number considering that only 8 thrifts made this change during all of the 1980s. This was in large part due to favorable tax legislation enacted in August of 1996. Also in 1996 there was legislation easing restrictions that allowed commercial banks to qualify for a thrift charter if they wished. This legislation included increasing the amount of credit card loans and student loans a thrift could hold. From 1996 to 1998, 14 commercial banks converted to savings institutions.

There are also an increasing number of community banks, both commercial and thrift. While the total number of community banks in the United States is decreasing due to consolidation, new community banks are proliferating. Independent Community Bankers of America reported in 1999 that the highest number of new or ''de novo'' community banks formed in nearly a decade, with 205 new charters reported during the year. The last record was in 1989 when 192 new banks were formed.

FURTHER READING

America's Community Bankers 1996 Annual Report and Related Statistics. Washington, DC, 1996.

America's Community Bankers Web Site, 1999. Available from http://www.acbankers.org.

Coyle, Tom. ''Thrifts set record earnings in 1998.'' *America's Community Banker,* April 1999. Vol. 8, No. 4, 38.

Federal Deposit Insurance Corporation. ''The Banking Crisis of the 1980s and Early 1990s.'' *FDIC Banking Review,* 1998. Vol. 11, No. 1. Available from http://www.fdic.gov.

———. ''Banking Industry: Statistical,'' 20 March 2000. Available from http://www.fdic.gov/bank/statistical/index.html.

———. *A Brief History of Deposit Insurance.* September 1998. Available from http://www.fdic.gov/bank/historical/brief/index.html

———. ''Historical Statistics on Banking,'' 20 March 2000. Available from http://www2.fdic.gov/hsob/.

Federal Deposit Insurance Corporation Web Site, 20 March 2000. Available from http://www.fdic.gov.

Giannone, Joseph A. ''Banking Bill Expected to Spur More Mergers.'' *The Columbus (Ohio) Dispatch.* 13 November 1999. Business Section, p. 2G.

Independent Community Bankers of America Web Site, 1998. Available from http://www.icba.org/.

Office of Thrift Supervision. *1998 Fact Book: A Statistical Profile on the United States Thrift Industry.* June 1999. Available from http://www.ots.treas.gov/docs/48080.pdf.

Office of Thrift Supervision Web Site, February 2000. Available from http://www.ots.treas.gov/.

''Thrifts Set Record Earnings in 1998.'' *America's Community Banker,* April 1999, 38.

U.S. Department of Commerce. *U.S. Industry & Trade Outlook '99.* Washington, DC: GPO, 1999.

''U.S. Thrifts Earn $1.4 Billion in the Fourth Quarter.'' *SNLSecurities.* Press Release of 6 February 1998. Available from http://www.snl.com/press/19980206b.html.

SIC 6061

CREDIT UNIONS, FEDERALLY CHARTERED

This industry classification includes cooperative thrift and loan associations (accepting deposits) organized under Federal charter to finance credit needs of their members.

NAICS CODE(S)

522130 (Credit Unions)

INDUSTRY SNAPSHOT

Credit unions spent the late 1990s diversifying their range of services in order to attract new members and maintain current ones amidst intensifying competition from commercial banks. By the end of the decade, the repeal of the Depression-era Glass-Steagall Act prepared the way for ''financial supermarkets,'' under which financial services will increasingly consolidate as banks expand into and merge with insurance operations and securities brokerages. Customers were expected to begin conducting most or all of their financial business with a single firm. Credit unions thus faced the complicated pressure of promoting the unique benefits offered by credit unions while simultaneously assuming more of the character of commercial banks.

A credit union is a collective, cooperative financial institution created and owned by its members for their own benefit. Credit unions collect members' savings and make loans to members from these accumulated savings. Unlike commercial banks, credit unions are non-profit organizations. The formation of credit unions was encouraged by a broad cooperative movement in the early years of the industrial revolution that focused on providing affordable financial services to people of modest means.

Membership in a credit union is limited to individuals or groups who are members of the organization (employer, association, residence, etc.) specified in its charter. These membership criteria are collectively known as the common bond provisions. Individuals qualified under these provisions may submit an application and, if approved, become members with voting rights similar to those of shareholders in public corporations. In 1999, about 78 million members, or 28 percent of the U.S. population, belonged to 11,000 credit unions nationwide. The median U.S. credit union in the late 1990s controlled assets of $5.65 million and boasted 1,725 members. A number of credit unions served very small, localized communities; 25 percent of credit unions possess less than $2 million in assets, with an average membership of 638. While these institutions often benefit from close-knit relationships among their members, larger credit unions are generally better leveraged to diversity their services, and thus are likely to become increasingly prominent as financial services markets open more widely.

The system of credit unions in the United States is quite extensive. In 1999, 6,700 credit unions were chartered under federal law, with membership ranks totaling 44 million and accounting for $240.1 billion in assets and $148.0 billion in outstanding loans. The remainder were charted under state or Puerto Rican laws.

The market for credit union loans stood at $500 million in 2000. However, credit unions increasingly were trying to tighten their belts by moving loans off their books. Those credit unions wishing to remain in the market have sought syndication with others to pool resources.

ORGANIZATION AND STRUCTURE

Credit unions are organized according to a general philosophy called the Rochdalian Principles. This doctrine emphasizes self-help, a mutual form of organization, and ''one-man, one-vote'' democratic rule.

The credit union industry is supported by the Credit Union National Association (CUNA), the professional society for credit union executives, which collects, processes, and disseminates information on credit unions and engages in advocacy and publicity for the industry as a whole.

A number of bodies are charged with ensuring the financial soundness of the nation's credit unions, including at least one state regulator and an array of local regulators in each state. The National Credit Union Administration (NCUA), created in 1970, oversees the system of federally charted credit unions. It has six major functions:

- to promote self-help security through privately owned and democratically controlled federal credit unions
- to stimulate systematic savings to provide capital and cash reserves for credit union members
- to make credit available to individuals with modest means for reasonable purposes
- to help stabilize the U.S. economy by promoting sound thrift, savings, and personal financial management practices
- to study the financial problems of individuals with modest means to determine the benefits of cooperative savings and loans and to publish the results
- to insure the accounts of members of all federally chartered credit unions and those of state credit unions that apply for insurance and are qualified.

These goals are achieved through four primary means: chartering, supervising, and examining credit unions, as well as providing an insurance system for federal and state use.

Credit unions encourage savings on the part of their members. The board of the credit union then creates guidelines for loaning these accumulated savings back to the credit union's members. These board members are elected by the credit union's members at an annual meeting that is similar to a shareholders meeting. Each member has one vote regardless of the number of shares owned. This board then elects the credit union's officers from its own membership and also appoints a supervisory committee. The board, officers, and supervisory committee usually serve on a volunteer basis.

Any net earnings realized are distributed to the members in the form of dividends. In 1996 more than $8 billion was paid in dividends by federal credit unions nationwide. The average annual rate was 3.5 percent.

Background and Development

Credit unions first began operating in Germany in 1848 and were promoted by Hermann Schulze-Delitzsche and Friedrich Wilhelm Raiffeisen. The idea spread to Italy and then to North America by 1900. Credit unions were first popularized in the United States in Boston by a local merchant named Edward E. Filene.

The Federal Credit Union Act of 1934 established federally chartered credit unions in the United States. Initially, the administration of the act was the responsibility of the Farm Credit Administration. In 1942 Executive Order 9148 transferred the administration of the act to the Federal Deposit Insurance Corporation (FDIC). In 1948 Congress gave all responsibilities for credit unions to the Bureau of Federal Credit Unions, which was part of the Federal Security Agency. This bureau became a department of the Social Security Administration. Finally, the oversight of credit unions was charged to a new independent agency of the executive branch, the National Credit Union Administration (NCUA), in March 1970, just as the number of credit unions peaked at 23,900 nationwide.

In 1980 the Depository Institutions Deregulation and Monetary Control Act brought all depository institutions under the control of the Board of Governors of the Federal Reserve System. This act created the Depository Institutions Deregulation Committee (DIDC), which included the Chairman of the NCUA Board as one of its members. The mission of the DIDC was the elimination of limitations on dividend rates and interest paid by deposit institutions.

The Monetary Control Act of 1980 allowed depository institutions to offer negotiable order withdrawal (NOW) accounts for individuals and certain non-profit organizations. Credit unions were authorized to charge a maximum of 15 percent annually on loans, and the NCUA was authorized to increase this rate for a period not to exceed 18 months. Credit unions that were federally insured were authorized to offer share draft accounts. Federal deposit insurance was raised to $100,000 per account for all depository institutions.

Through the 1980s, the Interstate Banking and Branching Act and other moves toward deregulation led to large-scale encroachment of commercial banks on credit unions' business. Credit unions responded by consolidating in order to pool resources and offer more services. The median U.S. credit union's membership grew by 45 percent in the 1990s, while asset-holdings increased 105 percent. The number of credit unions with less than $5 million in assets, meanwhile, fell 53 percent in the 1990s, as those with over $200 million in assets increased by 93 percent.

Current Conditions

While fending off intensifying competition from commercial banks, the expansion of the variety of services offered by credit unions mirrored the expanding size of credit unions themselves. The 285 credit-union mergers in 1999 represented an increase of 33 percent from 1998; most of those credit unions absorbed maintained less than $5 million in assets. The NCUA further reported that 1999 also delivered near-record low numbers of liquidations (15) and failures (23), of which the majority also involved credit unions with under $5 million in assets.

Many credit unions, meanwhile, have opened several branches and offer ATM (automated teller machines) and other sophisticated customer services. According to the NCUA, 45 percent of all credit unions offered credit cards in late 1999; 47 percent offered ATM cards; 40 percent provided first mortgages; and 30 percent maintain debit-card programs. The late 1990s also saw credit unions begin to integrate online services into their operations, including loan applications and approval and check imaging.

As credit unions move to expand the services offered to their customers, some conflicts arose. This was especially true among those institutions that offered financial planning and brokerage services. Some of the concerns included: the tension between increased service portfolio and the possible loss of credit union savings; the fear of taxation; and member-trust issues. Resolving these conflicts will be one of the primary challenges facing the industry in the early 2000s as the line between credit unions and other financial service institutions dissolves following the passage of the Gramm-Leach-Bliley Act, also called the Financial Services Modernization Act, in November 1999. By the end of the decade the major difference between credit unions offering these services and commercial banks in the same field was the former's emphasis on service as opposed to profit.

The CUNA responded to competition from the increasing power of commercial banks with a national public relations campaign, in which all 10,000 CUNA members participated, to promote credit unions as favoring "people over profits." The campaign featured a logo with hands linked together in the form of a star to emphasize the participatory environment of credit unions, underscored by the slogan: "Where people are worth more than money."

In keeping with the relaxed regulatory environment throughout the financial services industries, the federal government prepared a relief package in 1999 for federally chartered credit unions that exhibited financial soundness and healthy business practices, a description that applies to perhaps half of all federally chartered credit unions. The package mandates fewer regulatory examinations and permits heightened discretion in credit union investment activities.

INDUSTRY LEADERS

Federal credit unions vary in size from the very large, with assets in the billions and employees numbering in the thousands, to smaller institutions with only a few employees. The size of a credit union depends on the size of the organization that it represents. Not surprisingly, the largest credit unions represent federal government workers, state employees, or the employees of large corporations.

In 1999, the largest credit union in the United States was the Navy Federal Credit Union in Merrifield, Virginia, which represents U.S. Navy employees and personnel. Chartered in 1947, it controlled nearly $11 billion in assets and boasted 1,810,466 members. Other leading federal credit unions include the Pentagon Federal Credit Union of Alexandria, Virginia, chartered in 1935, with $3.15 billion in assets; and the United Air Lines Employees Credit Union in Chicago, also chartered in 1935, which held $2.47 billion in assets in 1999.

WORKFORCE

One distinctive feature of the employees of credit unions is that they are often also members of the organization that they represent. Many credit unions depend upon the volunteer efforts of these workers to remain in operation. Credit unions employ anywhere from four to 3,700 workers. Nationally, credit unions employ an average of 45 workers per $100 million in assets, though that number is expected to decrease with consolidation. U.S. credit unions currently employ 163,230 full-time workers, 33,460 part-time workers, and 140,260 volunteers.

AMERICA AND THE WORLD

Cooperative savings banks are common financial institutions around the globe. These institutions were created to address the credit needs of workers who were ignored by commercial banks during the industrial revolution. The World Council of Credit Unions, Inc. (WCOCU) reports that the international credit union movement is growing steadily, despite strong competition from commercial banks as they focus increasing attention on consumer services. The United States is by far the leader in credit-union membership. Financial industries in Europe and other industrialized economies tend to be far more centralized than in the United States. Nonetheless, the WCOCU reported that the movement grew about 5 percent in 1998, reaching total membership of ranks of about 101 million, with 37,620 participating credit unions. The total assets of these institutions equaled $451.4 billion.

Germany. The concept of cooperative banking originated in Germany during the mid-nineteenth century under the guidance of Friedrich Raiffeisen and Hermann Schulze-Delitzsche. Currently its system is one of the most sophisticated in the world. The cooperative banks have tended to merge into larger institutions and increase their branch office network. These banks tend to make loans to agricultural customers, small and medium sized companies, and local cooperative societies.

France. The cooperative banking system is highly developed in France. Some of France's largest financial institutions, including Credit Agricole, Credit Mutuel, and Banques Populaires, are co-operative banks. These banks are capable of offering services similar to those offered by commercial banks.

Eastern Europe. In all of the East European countries there is one major institution to handle the banking system for the population as a whole. In general, with the exception of Poland, co-operative banks have been unimportant in Eastern Europe. Major changes can be expected in this region as these countries make the transition to market-based economies.

Japan. There are three types of co-operative banks in Japan, each stringently regulated by the Japanese authorities: Sogo banks, which conduct business for small and medium sized factories, wholesalers, and retail stores; Shoko Kumiai Chuo Ginko banks, which facilitate the finance of co-operatives of small and medium sized enterprises; and Norin Chukin banks, which service agriculture and forestry.

The Developing World. Savings banks in the newly industrialized countries, or NICs, have experienced a number of unique problems. For example, the habit of saving may not be as established as it is in developed nations. Some banks have developed non-traditional means to overcome these problems. Caixa Economica Federal in Brazil operates the state lottery as well as the national soccer pool, channeling the revenues into socially positive projects.

In general, co-operative banks in developing countries face four similar challenges: poor infrastructure, difficulty in mobilizing funds, inadequate resources, and a shortage of qualified managers. Despite these challenges, co-operative banks have made some progress in these areas over the last three decades.

FURTHER READING

Barancik, Scott. ''Regulator Preparing Relief for Federal Credit Unions Exemplifying Soundness.'' *American Banker,* 4 January 2000.

''Credit Unions Introduce Nationwide Brand.'' *Bank Advertising News,* 4 October 1999.

Diekman, Frank J. ''Five Big Trends Affecting Lending.'' *Credit Union Journal,* 20 October 1999.

———. ''Reconciling What CUs Do With What Members Want.'' *Credit Union Journal,* 24 November 1999.

Edmonson, R.G. ''Debit Cards Finally Catching On In a Big Way.'' *Credit Union Journal,* 4 August 1999.

''NCUA Approves Mergers.'' *American Banker,* 10 December 1999.

Rick, Steven W. *Credit Union Restructuring: A Response to the Developments in the International Finance Industry.* Madison, WI: World Council of Credit Unions, 27 February 1998.

Roberts, Ed. ''Loan Quality Improves Among Largest CUs.'' *Credit Union Journal,* 5 January 2000.

SIC 6062

CREDIT UNIONS, NOT FEDERALLY CHARTERED

This industry classification includes cooperative thrift and loan associations (accepting deposits) organized under other than a Federal charter to finance credit needs of their members.

NAICS CODE(S)

522130 (Credit Unions)

A credit union is a collective, cooperative financial institution created by its members for the benefit of these members. These members share a bond of employment or affiliation, which the credit union is designed to serve. In 1997, there were 11,629 credit unions in the United States, of which about 4,100 held assets in excess of $10 million. According to industry data, credit unions serve 70 million Americans, but hold less than 2 percent of each member's total financial assets. Credit union loans to consumers were mainly in the auto and credit card sectors.

Credit unions are owned by their members. Typically, these institutions collect the savings of their members and make loans to members from these accumulated savings. Unlike other financial institutions, such as commercial banks, credit unions are non-profit organizations that focus on serving their members. The primary objective of a credit union is not profit maximization, as no individual can claim any residual profit. Instead, credit unions attempt to maximize the economic and social interest of its members. The formation of credit unions was encouraged by a broad cooperative movement in the early years of the industrial revolution.

Membership in a credit union is limited to individuals or groups who are members of the organization (employer, association, residence, etc.) specified in the charter. These credit union membership criteria are collectively known as the common bond provision. An individual who is qualified under these provisions may submit an application and, if approved, becomes a member with voting rights similar to those of a shareholder in a public corporation.

The common bond provisions of credit unions have a number of operational benefits. These include lower information costs, lower collective loan default risk, operating subsidies, and mitigation of the borrower verses saver conflict. It has been argued, however, that the deregulation that took place in the late 1980s will erode some of these benefits. Indeed, in February 1997, the U.S. Supreme Court agreed to hear a case that tested whether credit unions could serve multi-occupational memberships without violating common bond requirements. The attempt by some credit unions to broaden their membership base beyond a single occupation stems from a search for greater liquidity in an increasingly competitive financial marketplace.

State credit unions are chartered under the state's credit union provision. In general, these laws are similar to the federal law, premised on the Federal Credit Union Act. The federal act was largely based on the preceding state provisions.

Leading state credit unions include the Food Lion Credit Association, headquartered in Salisbury, North Carolina; and State Employee's Credit Union, based in Raleigh, North Carolina. Other large state credit unions include the Golden 1 Credit Union of Sacramento, California; Granite State Credit Union in Manchester, New Hampshire; Patelco Credit Union of San Francisco, California; and Delta Employees Credit Union of Atlanta, Georgia.

Credit unions, by nature, tend to be small. In 1997, there were 1,990 with less than 5 employees, 1,296 with 5 to 9 employees, and only 57 with over 100 employees.

FURTHER READING

Aaron, Kris. ''The Credit Union Year in Review.'' *Credit Union Management,* December 1992, 9-10, 22. Available from http://www.callahan.com.

Hagaman, T. Carter. ''Credit Unions: A Force for Today.'' *Management Accounting* 74, no. 3 (March 1993): 51.

Dun's Census of American Business 1997. Parsippany, NJ: Dun & Bradstreet, 1997.

Ward's Business Directory of U.S. Private and Public Companies, 1999. Detroit: Gale Research, 1999.

SIC 6081

BRANCHES AND AGENCIES OF FOREIGN BANKS

This industry category includes establishments operating as branches or agencies of foreign banks that specialize in commercial loans, especially in trade finance. They typically fund themselves via large denomination interbank deposits, rather than through smaller denomination retail deposits. Federally licensed agencies of foreign banks may not accept deposits. Federal branches may accept deposits; however, if they choose to accept deposits in denominations of $100,000 or less, federal deposit insurance is required. Establishments that are owned by foreign banks but primarily engaged in accepting retail deposits from the general public in the United States are classified as commercial banks.

NAICS CODE(S)

522293 (International Trade Financing)
522110 (Commercial Banking)
522298 (All Other Non-Depository Credit Intermediation)

INDUSTRY SNAPSHOT

Historically, banks that were chartered in a particular country conducted most of their business in that domestic market. The long period of prosperity in the 1960s and early 1970s, however, led to substantial increases in global operations of industrial and commercial companies. This, in turn, caused an increase in international banking activity, since banks tend to follow their customers. Since the early 1980s, however, financial institutions in the United States and in other nations have rapidly expanded their overseas offices.

By the end of 1998, foreign banks had assets totaling $1.16 trillion in the United States, a 1.4 percent decline from the June 1998 level. The drop, however small, represents the first downturn in the industry in over two years. Since 1996, assets at foreign banks and their subsidiaries in the United States experienced steady growth, with levels climbing from $996 billion to $1.18 trillion by June 1998, which represents an 18 percent hike. In *International Banker,* Laura Mandaro attributed the drop to the ongoing impact of the 1997-98 emerging markets crisis and to corporate restructuring. At the same time, however, foreign banks accelerated their investments in U.S. offshore sites, such as the Cayman Islands; growth during the period was 5 percent.

The U.S. offices of Japanese banks had the largest aggregate assets of all foreign banks operating in the United States at the end of 1998. But Mandaro reported that structural weaknesses and bad loan problems of Japanese banks had a negative impact on their U.S. operations. Due to financial pressures, Japanese banks closed some of its U.S. subsidiaries, notably Sumitomo Bank Ltd., which sold its $4.7 billion-asset retail bank in California. The total number of Japanese branches and agencies in the United States fell from 88 to 82 from mid-1998 to year's end. Japan also lost its ranking in another category: ABN AMRO of Netherlands supplanted Japan's Bank of Tokyo-Mitsubishi Ltd. to become the largest foreign bank in the United States.

Other significant industry news included Deutsche Bank's takeover of Bankers Trust in New York in 1999, which reflected the worldwide industry trend toward mergers and consolidation. Foreign banks operating in the United States benefited from a relaxed regulatory environment. In 1997, the Federal Reserve Board widened the scope of so-called Section 20 companies, allowing more banks in its system to deal in securities underwriting activity. Nancy Jacklin reported in the *International Financial Law Review,* "This important streamlining of the regulatory regime for U.S. securities affiliates of banking organizations, coupled with the substantial expansion in the scope of their permitted securities underwriting and dealing activities, adds up to a significant enhancement of the investment banking opportunities available to U.S. and foreign banks in the U.S. market."

However, in the 1990s money laundering scandals spawned new regulatory zeal in the United States. In the mid-1990s, Citigroup, Inc., allegedly violated its money laundering guidelines when it transferred some $125 million in suspicious funds on behalf of Raul Salinas, brother of former Mexican president Carlos Salinas. And in 1999, investigators discovered that Bank of New York Co. washed billions of dollars in dirty money on behalf of Russian companies. To thwart future money-laundering efforts, the Clinton administration and Congress proposed new legislation—dubbed the 1999 National Money Laundering Strategy—that would require new financial disclosures about customers and banking activities.

ORGANIZATION AND STRUCTURE

Foreign banks operate in the United States through five types of banking offices: branches, agencies, investment companies, "edge" or "agreement" corporations, and commercial banks.

Foreign Branches. Historically, foreign banks have opened limited branches in more than one state with relative ease, and nearly half of the foreign banks with U.S. offices have established multi-state banking facilities. To enter the U.S. financial markets, most foreign banks initially opened offices in New York City; the institutions then opened offices in other parts of the country, particularly in places where a bank's home-country customers had trade or financial relationships. The International Banking Act (IBA) and the Foreign Bank Supervision Act of 1991 govern the establishment of branches at the federal level (licensed by the Comptroller of the Currency), in any state that does not prohibit such a branch. Foreign banks may also obtain branching licenses from certain states. These states usually require the foreign banks to have their deposits insured by the Federal Deposit Insurance Corporation (FDIC). State law also generally requires the foreign bank's home country to offer reciprocity to U.S. banks seeking to branch into that nation. The IBA grandfathers existing multi-state branching networks of foreign banks; however, establishing branches in more than one state is prohibited. State banking regulators supervise almost 95 percent of all the U.S. assets of foreign banks. In 1996, New York accounted for more than 58 percent of all foreign branch and agency assets in the United States. California accounted for about 27 percent, with the remaining foreign assets scattered primarily in Florida, Louisiana, Maryland, and Illinois.

Foreign Agencies. A more limited type of banking than that provided by a branch may be engaged in by a foreign bank through an agency. For the most part, agencies and branches offer similar services and enjoy similar powers; however, agencies are not permitted to accept domestic deposits. They can accept credit balances of customers in connection with international activities. While agencies may not accept domestic deposits, they have more flexibility than branches because they are not subject to reserve requirements or to loan limits to a single borrower. Federal agencies would be subject to loan limits to a single borrower, and they would be required to keep on deposit with a member bank investment securities and deposits equal to the amount of capital that would be required if the agency were being established as a national bank at that location.

Unlike the other types of U.S. offices, which are separate institutions, agencies and branches are integral parts of their parent banks. Both agencies and branches may conduct full-scale lending operations. Agencies and branches generally are wholesale banking offices; that is, their customers are chiefly banks and other nonbank businesses rather than individuals, and they compete primarily with large U.S. banks. By year-end 1996, agencies and branches of foreign banks held almost 83 percent of all assets held by foreign banks in the United States. Nearly half of the credit extended by the agencies and branches was in the form of business loans, with about one-quarter of these loans representing lending to non-U.S. residents.

U.S. Investment Companies. New York State permits the organization of investment companies by foreign banks. Investment companies, like agencies, may not accept domestic deposits, but can hold customers' credit balances. They are subject to neither reserve requirements nor limits on loans to a single borrower, and operate essentially as commercial finance companies.

Edge or Agreement Corporations. The International Banking Act (IBA) allowed foreign banks to own, with the prior approval of the Board of Governors of the Federal Reserve System, a majority of the stock of an edge corporation. Furthermore, the IBA repealed the stipulation that edge corporation directors be U.S. citizens. Edge Corporations are similar to agencies in that they may not accept domestic deposits, but may hold credit balances pursuant to international business. They are chartered by the Board of Governors of the Federal Reserve System and may be domiciled anywhere in the United States. Additionally, a bank may establish more than one edge corporation in more than one state. Agreement corporations are state-chartered corporations that have entered an agreement with the Federal Reserve Board to limit their activities to those of an edge corporation.

Commercial Banks. In contrast to the agencies and branches, many of the commercial bank subsidiaries are retail banks whose customers include many individuals and smaller businesses. Unlike agencies and branches, these banks are engaged in consumer and real estate lending in about the same proportions as domestically owned commercial banks. In California and New York in particular, foreign banks have acquired subsidiary commercial banks with large retail branch networks. Large U.S. banks acquired by banks from other industrial countries in the late 1970s and early 1980s include Bank of California, Harris Trust and Savings Bank, LaSalle National Bank, Marine Midland Bank, National Bank of North America, and Union Bank. Chicago-based LaSalle, for example, is a subsidiary of the Dutch ABN AMRO Bank N.V., one of the world's top 20 banks. In 1996, ABN AMRO Bank had 1,800 locations in more than 60 countries. In the early 1990s, a number of banks from developing countries also sought to acquire or establish banks in the United States.

The Bank Holding Company Act (BHCA) regulates the foreign ownership of a United States bank. Any company—including partnerships, but excluding individuals—that owns 25 percent of a U.S. bank is considered a bank holding company, and must apply, pursuant to the terms Section 3 of the BHCA, for permission from the Federal Reserve System to acquire that bank. The tests required by the BHCA relate to competition and the public interest. These requirements are less likely to present problems for a foreign bank holding company, because an application to acquire a U.S. bank is not likely to have an anti-competitive effect unless the holding company already owns another U.S. bank, is in a consortium or joint venture with U.S. banks, or unless the bank to be acquired is active in international banking.

Other Alternatives. There are several other ways in which foreign banks or individuals can participate in a less direct way in U.S. banking markets. For example, they can purchase less than a controlling interest in a U.S. bank merely as an investment. Another way for interested parties to participate is through a correspondent relationship, whereby a U.S. bank will perform various services for the foreign institution. A final approach available to foreign banks and individuals is the representative office. A representative office is merely an office of a representative of the foreign bank. Technically, such an office cannot engage in banking, and is supposed to be used only for making contacts and promoting the parent bank. As such, no regulatory approval is needed under present law to establish such an office, although under the IBA all such offices must be registered with the Secretary of the State. These offices are frequently used as forerunners to either a branch or agency after the representative has surveyed the landscape and cultivated a client base.

Background and Development

Foreign banks typically establish offices in the United States for several reasons: to conduct trade financing activities, to service U.S. activities of home-country operations, to participate in the U.S. interbank market, to manage the dollar assets and liabilities of their parent organizations, to engage in foreign exchange trading, and in some cases to develop a retail banking business. A number of the larger foreign banking institutions have used the contacts and expertise developed through their initial presence in the United States to compete for the business of large U.S. companies. By the 1980s, however, many of these banks had already captured their most natural U.S. business from large national and international companies, and they found establishing a credit business with medium-sized U.S. companies more difficult. As a result, a number of U.S. offices es of foreign banks have become actively engaged in new areas of banking and finance, such as merger-related lending, or have begun to place more emphasis on specialized financial areas in which they have expertise.

The activities of U.S. offices of foreign banks grew dramatically in the 1970s, as they tried to establish a foothold in the U.S. market through aggressive price competition. The industry's growth slowed during the early 1980s, but it began to pick up during the latter part of the decade. During the early 1990s, the industry was subjected to increased regulation and supervision. The extraordinary growth in the presence of foreign banks in the United States since the early 1970s, however, has complicated the review and supervision procedures of U.S. regulators. This bureaucratic confusion has contributed to the underlying problem of the international banking industry—the lack of a consolidated supervisory process. However, The Riegle-Neal Interstate Banking and Branching Efficiency Act, signed into law by President Clinton on September 29, 1994, was structured to transform the U.S. banking system particularly in regards to interstate bank activity and mergers. The Act allowed a foreign bank, subject to certain regulatory approvals, to establish de novo branches in states outside the foreign bank's ''home state'' if a U.S. bank headquartered in the same home state could establish such branches.

By the end of 1996, there were more than 870 foreign banks in the United States with aggregate assets in excess of $994 billion, or 21 percent of total U.S. banking assets. Foreign banks had 493 branch and agency offices, 99 U.S. bank subsidiaries, and 11 Edge Act and Agreement Corporations. Indeed, banking transactions have become increasingly global, setting the stage for even greater transnational financial activities in the late 1990s. In 1996, the commercial and industrial loans made by foreign-owned U.S. banks amounted to $461 billion—around 34 percent of all business loans to U.S. borrowers. By comparison, selected assets and liabilities of domestically owned commercial banks and U.S. offices of foreign banks having less than 25 percent foreign ownership totaled more than $3,804 trillion in 1996 with a total of $2,390 trillion in loans. This figure includes assets and liabilities on the books of International Banking Facilities.

Total deposits in 1996 by U.S. offices of foreign banks was $529 billion, representing nearly 17 percent of all deposits made in the United States. Domestically owned commercial banks, U.S. agencies and branches of foreign banks, and commercial banks and New York investment companies with more than 25 percent foreign bank ownership (but not Edge or Agreement Corporations) had a total of $4,795 trillion in assets in 1996. Loans for this group totaled nearly $2,851 trillion. Of these, the total assets of U.S. offices of Japanese banks totaled nearly $362 billion in 1996 with total business loans at nearly $127 billion and deposits nearly $198 billion. This significant cross-border presence of banks, though, has the disturbing potential to increase the risk of bank failure and reduce the soundness of the international banking system. Major branches and agencies of foreign banks in the United States included French American Banking Corp., Israel Discount Bank Ltd., and Nippon Credit Bank of Los Angeles.

This surge in foreign banking has been accompanied by a variety of questions and concerns on the part of the public, legislators and regulators, and U.S. bankers. Many of these concerns have been addressed by the passage of the International Banking Act of 1978 (IBA) which tightened federal and state control over foreign bank operations in the United States. International bank scandals, most notably the closure of the worldwide operations of the Bank of Credit and Commerce International (BCCI), illustrate the disastrous effects of deficient supervision of the international banking system. The Federal Reserve responded to the corruption with the promulgation of the Foreign Bank Supervision Act of 1991 (FBSEA). The FBSEA greatly expanded the supervisory authority contained in the International Banking Act of 1978 and placed the bulk of this authority in the hands of the Federal Reserve Board. As a result of this act, the entry of foreign banks in the United States slowed down considerably in the early 1990s. In 1992, for example, no foreign bank opened a new branch, agency, or representative office anywhere in the United States. This was attributed to administrative delays in processing the applications required to be submitted to the Board of Governors of the Federal Reserve System for such offices.

As far as Federal Deposit Insurance Corporation (FDIC) deposit insurance was concerned, most federal branches and agencies of foreign banks were not covered. As a result, uninsured U.S. federal branches and agencies were not permitted to accept retail deposits under $100,000. An exemption existed for certain minimal (so-called de minimis) deposits up to 5 percent of branch deposits. The Riegle-Act required the Office of the Comptroller of the Currency (OCC) and the FDIC to reduce that exempted amount from 5 percent to 1 percent of branch deposits. In other words, it could accept retail deposits under $100,000 limited to 1 percent of the daily average of deposits of the last 30 days of the most recent quarter. In 1995, the OCC made a proposal for a transition period of up to 5 years to phase out deposits held in the existing 5 percent de minis accounts.

Another objective of the Riegle-Neal Act was to ensure the competitive equality of foreign and domestic banks, as well as credit availability to various sectors of the U.S. economy, including trade finance. The OCC proposed to adopt the exemptions cited in the Act, with some modifications and additions. As a result, uninsured federal branches would be allowed to accept deposits under $100,000 from individuals who are neither U.S. citizens or residents; foreign individuals employed by a foreign bank, business, or government, or a recognized international organization; foreign businesses and large U.S. businesses; U.S. and foreign governmental units and international organizations; persons to whom the branch or the foreign bank has extended credit or provided other non-deposit services in the past year, or has agreed to provide credit or non-deposit services in the next year; persons who deposit funds in connection with transmitting funds; and persons who may deposit funds with Edge corporations, such as persons engaged in certain international business activities.

The OCC's proposed rule also clarified the permissible activities for agencies of foreign banks. For instance, the proposed rule would implement the provision for the Riegle-Neal Act that addressed the ability of a federal branch or agency of a foreign bank to manage the activities of the bank's offshore offices. The Act permitted a federal branch or agency to manage the same offshore activities permissible for U.S. banks to manage offshore.

Legal/Regulatory Framework for U.S. Operations of Foreign Banks. Bank regulation in the United States can be viewed on three levels. The first level involves examination and supervision of individual banking institutions and rules designed to ensure that each banking organization is being operated in a sound manner. The second level of regulation is concerned with competitive conditions and expansion within the banking industry. Its focus is on maintaining not only soundly operated banks but also a competitive banking system that balances economic efficiency with certain political and economic goals. These goals are reflected in legislation governing bank mergers and acquisitions, intrastate and interstate expansion of banking organizations, and monetary control. The third level of regulation involves ownership and other relationships between organizations and other financial, commercial, industrial, and service enterprises operating in the United States. While this level of regulation includes elements of bank safety and soundness and competitive concerns, its primary focus is on broader policy objectives such as maintaining a separation between banking and commerce. This type of regulation is embodied in the Bank Holding Company Act (BHCA), the Glass-Steagall Act and the Riegle-Neal Act.

Examination and Supervision. State and federally chartered banks that are subsidiaries of foreign banks are supervised and examined by appropriate federal and state banking authorities and are treated the same as other state or federally chartered banks in virtually all respects.

The examination and supervision of U.S. agencies and branches of foreign banks, however, differs in many respects from that of subsidiary banks, because these offices are not separately incorporated legal entities but rather are integral parts of their foreign parent banks. As a result, examination and supervision of a U.S. agency or branch of a foreign bank is generally aimed at ensuring that the office is operated in a safe and sound manner and that local depositors and creditors are protected in the event of any problem with the parent banking institution. Because an agency or branch must rely on the resources of its parent bank for support, lending limits and similar prudential controls applied to branches and agencies are generally based on the capital and surplus resources of the foreign parent bank.

Since the passage of the Riegle-Neal Act, the Institute of International Bankers—a New York association that represents foreign bankers—recommended that the

Act permit international banks to change their home state more than once, clarify the procedures under which international banks could acquire additional branches or agencies outside of their home states, permit the ''upgrade'' of existing limited branches and agencies to wholesale branches where permitted under state law, and clarify that a branch or agency can act as an agent for an affiliated depository institution to the same extent that U.S. banks can perform that role.

Regulation of U.S. Banking Activities of Foreign Banks. To open an agency or branch in New York City, for example, a foreign bank must obtain approval from both the New York State banking authorities and the Comptroller of the Currency. Similar conditions apply in other states, although some states permit only agencies, some permit only branches, and some permit neither. While the IBA gives foreign banks the option of establishing federal agencies or branches, the act also defers to the states by allowing state comptrollers to approve the establishment of a branch or agency by a foreign bank according to state law. If a state does not prohibit foreign bank agencies or branches, but merely sets conditions for their establishment (such as requiring that the state banks have reciprocal privileges in the foreign bank's home country), the comptroller may approve the establishment of a federal branch or agency in that state without regard to such requirements. Thus, as long as there is not an outright prohibition in state law, the foreign bank has the dual-banking system option of proceeding under the more favorable regulatory climate.

Before the IBA was passed, foreign banks were free to establish deposit-taking operations in more than one state as long as state laws permitted such operations. Because Congress determined that this gave foreign banks a competitive advantage over domestic banks, the IBA subjected foreign banks to interstate banking prohibitions on deposit taking designed to parallel those applied to U.S. banks. However, Congress also provided foreign banks with liberal grandfather treatment and permitted the establishment of limited interstate branches. These branches may only accept deposits that are incidental to international or foreign banking activities.

As a result of the IBA enactment, foreign banks are required to designate a home state and may only change their home state designation one time, subject to certain conditions. A foreign bank may not establish outside its home state a branch that takes domestic deposits and may not acquire more than 5 percent of the voting shares of a domestic bank outside its home state if such an acquisition would be prohibited under Section 3(d) of the Bank Holding Company Act (BHCA). The interstate banking restrictions of the IBA do not apply to state or federally licensed agencies, to limited branches, or to investment company subsidiaries of foreign banks, because these operations do not accept domestic deposits. Section 3(d) of the BHCA generally prohibits the Federal Reserve Board from approving interstate bank acquisitions by bank holding companies unless such acquisitions are permitted by the law of the state in which the acquired bank is located. Although state laws are increasingly being amended to permit bank holding company acquisitions across state lines on a regional and even national basis, foreign banks are not always able to take full advantage of these opportunities.

A foreign bank seeking to expand in the United States by establishing a *de novo* subsidiary, branches in states outside the foreign bank's ''home state,'' or by acquiring an existing bank may do so under the Riegle-Neal Act. Like any other bank holding company, a foreign bank's acquisitions must be consistent with interstate banking restrictions, with restrictions on nonbanking activities, and with competitive safety and soundness, and other public interest criteria.

In addition to placing restrictions on the geographic expansion of deposit-taking activities of foreign banks, Congress also decided to subject such activities to Federal Reserve Board requirements. The purpose was to promote competitive equality between domestic and foreign banking institutions in the United States and to ensure that the effectiveness of monetary policy would not be impaired by the existence of a rapidly growing segment of the banking industry not subject to federal requirements. Subsequent to the enactment of the IBA, Congress extended federal reserve requirements to all depository institutions in the United States in the Monetary Control Act of 1980.

The Foreign Bank Supervision Act of 1991. Although the Federal Reserve Board possessed some form of supervisory authority over foreign banks since the 1978 adoption of the International Banking Act, it had never before been authorized to approve the opening of foreign bank branches, agencies, or representative offices. The enactment of the IBA gave foreign banks the option, similar to that enjoyed by domestic banks, to establish a banking office in the United States by obtaining either a federal license from the Office of the Comptroller of the Currency or a license from the appropriate state regulator. The Foreign Bank Supervision Act of 1991 provided the mechanism for consolidated supervision over such a dual banking structure. The Federal Reserve was given this umbrella supervisory authority. The following issues are the main areas of supervisory concern: the entry of foreign banking institutions into the American market; the application of regulations to foreign banks; and the extent of supervision and examination.

The regulation is applicable whenever a foreign bank seeks to establish an office in the United States. This criterion applies to the first U.S. office opened by a foreign bank, as well as any additional branch, agency, or representative office set up by a foreign bank having a previous U.S. presence. In addition, the regulation requires the submission of an application whenever an existing office is upgraded in status or relocated to another state. In certain limited circumstances, however, an application need not be filed. These situations include the establishment of a branch, agency, commercial lending company, or representative office merely as a by-product of one foreign bank's acquisition of another, without any merger or organic change occurring in the organization.

Another significant mandatory requirement for approval is that a foreign bank applicant must be engaged directly in banking in its home country and be subject to supervision by the appropriate authorities in that country. Because of this requirement, the Federal Reserve Board has been compelled to study in detail the initial application it receives from each country with respect to the adequacy of the country's supervision.

The board has indicated that a determination of the adequacy of a particular supervisory scheme will be based on a variety of factors, including whether the home country supervisor performs the following duties: verifying the existence of procedures for monitoring and controlling worldwide risks and operations; obtaining consolidated information on a periodic basis; obtaining information concerning transactions among affiliates; analyzing periodic consolidated financial reports; and evaluating prudential standards on a worldwide basis.

And yet another requirement is that foreign banks must furnish the Federal Reserve Board with such information as the board deems necessary for the application. Additionally, the board has the prerogative to assess whether an applicant has provided it with adequate assurances that it will continue to make available additional information that the board deems necessary. The board is concerned that the prospect of foreign secrecy laws may hamper its supervisory efforts. Therefore, an applicant is required to disclose in its application any laws that may inhibit the board's access to pertinent information.

In evaluating branch and agency applications, the regulation provides the board with the power to assess the following additional issues that are similar to those previously considered by most states: whether home country authorities have consented to the new office; the financial and managerial resources of the applicant, including its experiences and capabilities with respect to international banking; and whether the foreign bank and its U.S. affiliates are in compliance with applicable U.S. laws. The regulation also identifies other relevant factors that the board may consider. The regulation notes that the size of the applicant should not be the sole factor determining approval, and states that the board is permitted to consider the needs of the community, the applicant's history and relative size in its home country, and whether the regulator in the applicant's home country shares information with U.S. supervisors.

Regulation of Nonbanking Activities of Foreign Banks. A foreign bank that has a controlling interest in a U.S. bank, whether state or federally chartered, is a bank holding company under U.S. law and is subject to both the banking and nonbanking prohibitions of the BHCA with regard to its activities in the United States. Foreign banks that have established branches, agencies, or investment company subsidiaries in the United States but do not control a domestic bank are not considered bank holding companies. However, they are still subject, under the IBA, to the nonbanking prohibitions of the BHCA and are thereby subject to the regulation by the Federal Reserve Board with regard to their nonbanking activities and investments in the United States.

In an attempt to eliminate unfair competitive advantages in the industry, federal and state agencies require that foreign banks with a branch, agency, commercial bank, or investment company subsidiary in the United States comply with the same binding legislation that applies to domestic holding companies attempting to diversify into nonbanking activities. However, many foreign banks enjoy grandfather privileges with respect to activities or investments in the United States that the banks had initiated before enactment of the IBA. For example, some European banks have grandfathered investment banking subsidiaries in the United States that would otherwise be prohibited under the BHCA.

Moreover, when the IBA was being considered for ratification, Congress was also faced with the problem that many foreign banks were linked through stock ownership in their home or other foreign markets with foreign nonbanking companies that were expanding into the United States. Strict application of BHCA rules in such situations would have either required foreign banks with U.S. banking operations to divest themselves of many non-U.S. stock holdings or blocked investment in the United States by foreign companies in which foreign banks have substantial ownership interests.

Congress decided that neither of these options was in the political or economic interests of the United States, and thus granted certain exemptions in the IBA. In general, foreign banks that are principally engaged in the banking business outside the United States are permitted to maintain both their banking operations in the United States and certain investments in foreign nonbanking enterprises that also conduct activities in the United States. The exemption permits foreign banking organizations to own a foreign nonbank company that engages in the same commercial nonbanking activities in the United States that it conducts abroad. Financial nonbanking activities in the United States require prior approval by the Federal Reserve Board and are generally permitted only to the extent that U.S. bank holding companies are allowed to engage in the activities.

Legislative proposals before Congress in 1996, however, raised the issue of international banks' ability to expand into new securities and other activities comparable to what U.S. banking organizations are allowed to do even if they do not maintain FDIC insurance.

Policy Issues Affecting Future Entry and Expansion. Despite enactment of the IBA in 1978 and the FBSA in 1991, the role of foreign banks in the U.S. banking system continues to be a subject of much attention and debate. Three issues in particular could have a significant impact on future foreign bank entry and expansion in the United States.

In late 1983, for example, legislation was proposed in the U.S. Senate that would have required the comptroller to consider the home country's reciprocating policies regarding U.S. banks before approving the establishment of a federal agency or branch. This proposal reflected a judgment that, at least in some countries, U.S. banks were not being given equal competitive opportunities with local banks and that reciprocity would be a useful means for opening banking markets abroad to U.S. banks. Although limited in scope and ultimately never enacted, the bill became the focus of considerable debate as to whether reciprocity should be a consideration in U.S. policy toward foreign bank entry and expansion.

Reciprocity is typically used to refer to efforts to assure a precise balancing of the treatment countries accord to each other as trading partners. For example, under a policy of reciprocity, if a foreign bank country limited the presence of U.S. banks to agencies, banks from that country would be able to establish only agencies in the United States. Such "mirror image" reciprocity has been consistently opposed by the U.S. government on the grounds that it would be almost impossible to administer in the United States, would remove flexibility, and would interfere with the role of the United States as a major international financial center. Instead, in order to attack the problem of discrimination against U.S. banks abroad, the U.S. government has used both bilateral and multinational channels to promote greater liberalization and equality of competitive opportunities in banking markets abroad. The Riegle-Neal Interstate Banking and Branching Efficiency Act was intended to transform the American banking system and remold it to be more in line with those of other industrialized nations.

In addition to establishing the various prudential standards for international lending, the International Lending Supervision Act of 1983 (ILSA) required U.S. bank regulatory authorities to establish minimum capital ratios for U.S. banking institutions. The establishment of such ratios focused increased attention on perceived disparities between U.S. and foreign bank capital requirements, with the larger U.S. banks claiming that many foreign banks enjoy competitive advantages due to lower capital ratios. The Federal Reserve Board addressed these concerns in Section 3(c) of the BHCA. This section requires the board to ensure that foreign banks establishing banking operations in the United States meet the same general standards of strength, experience, and reputation required of domestic banking organizations. Foreign banks are also expected to serve on a continuing basis as a source of strength to their banking operations in the United States. In this regard, the board has initiated consultations with foreign bank supervisors and has begun work on developing more fully the concept of functional equivalency of capital ratios for banks of different countries. The overall goal is to achieve broader international comparability of capital standards; this emphasis suggests that U.S. authorities may increasingly try to assess the capital adequacy of foreign banks according to functionally equivalent international standards.

Interstate banking in the United States has been growing rapidly as a result of the enactment of laws by a number of states that permit acquisitions of in-state banks by bank holding companies in other states. However, many of these state laws permit interstate acquisitions only among states with regional or historical ties. For example, laws in many northeastern states restrict acquisitions to bank holding companies headquartered in those states. Under the principle of national treatment embodied in the IBA, it would seem that a foreign bank might be treated as if it were a local bank headquartered in the state the foreign bank has chosen as its home state. For example, a Canadian bank with Connecticut as its home state could be treated as a Connecticut bank for purposes of regional interstate banking statutes. Delaware stands out as a particularly progressive state in this regard. In 1999, Governor Tom Carper signed a bill to let foreign banks establish Delaware as their home state, giving banks another economic incentive to open shop in a state that already has an extremely favorable tax environment. However, in some states, regional interstate banking laws have either expressly or implicitly excluded foreign banks or their U.S. bank subsidiaries from taking advantage of regional acquisition opportunities.

Foreign banks have expressed the view that such state laws deny them equal competitive opportunities and are thus inconsistent with national treatment. Prior to the passage of the Riegle-Neal Act, Congress largely deferred to the states in the area of interstate banking and would not address this issue of possible discrimination against foreign banks. With the Riegle-Neal Act, however, a bank holding company in one state became able to acquire a bank in another state after Sept. 29, 1995, without regard to the law of the other state. Under the more recent Act, the only significant restriction a state could impose was to restrict the acquisition of a bank that has not been in existence for a specified period of time (up to five years). The purpose of this requirement was to preserve the value of existing banks by discouraging the start-up of new banks merely for the purpose of facilitating entry into a state.

While foreign banks still enjoyed considerable flexibility in the United States in the early 1990s, a regulatory framework at the federal level began taking shape. That framework eliminated certain advantages foreign banks possessed relative to domestic banks, but also opened the possibility of operating through edge corporations, obtaining funds from the Federal Reserve System, and obtaining deposit insurance. International banks could change their home state more than once and acquire additional branches or agencies outside of their home state.

AMERICA AND THE WORLD

Analysts expected that foreign banks interested in securing a significant presence in the United States, both as a source of dollar funding and with a view to active participation in international lending, would focus on establishing a branch or subsidiary bank in a home state and combining it with edge corporations in several other states.

Banks from Group of 10 countries operate about half of the U.S. offices of foreign banks but account for a majority of the assets. The G-10 countries are the 11 participants in the General Arrangements to Borrow of the International Monetary Fund; namely, Belgium-Luxembourg, Canada, France, Germany, Italy, Japan, the Netherlands, Sweden, Switzerland, the United Kingdom, and the United States. Japanese banks with offices in the United States had nearly $362 billion in assets in 1996, or 7.5 percent of the total assets held by ''Domestically owned'' commercial banks and U.S. offices of foreign banks. Japanese banks alone accounted for six of the 10 largest foreign branches in New York ranked by total assets. Japanese banks with U.S. offices in New York had nearly $241 billion in assets. Japanese banks with branches and agencies in New York had nearly $223 billion in assets. In California, Japanese banks with offices there had more than $85 billion in assets; those Japanese banks with branches and agencies in California had $41 billion. The size of Japanese banks' U.S. activities reflected, in part, their role in financing the increasing trade deficit between the United States and Japan and in servicing the growing number of U.S. subsidiaries of Japanese corporations. Although banks from non-G-10 countries, particularly in Latin America and Asia, have also opened many U.S. offices since the early 1980s, they represented a relatively small segment of the industry in the early 1990s.

After the introduction of International Banking Facilities (IBFs) in the United States in December 1981, foreign banks established IBFs at many of their U.S. offices. An IBF is a segregated set of asset and liability accounts that may be established at a banking office located in the United States for the purpose of conducting transactions with foreign residents without being subject to federal reserve requirements or to deposit insurance coverage and assessments. At the end of 1992, about half of the total assets of U.S. agencies and branches of foreign banks were booked as their IBFs. The agencies and branches accounted for more than two-thirds of IBF activity.

The U.S. international banking industry faced a plethora of problems and opportunities at the dawn of the twenty-first century. As transnational financial services have increased, the significance of national borders has decreased. Globalization has also accelerated the speed at which financial transactions take place. While this has triggered explosive growth in emerging economies, it has also made these states vulnerable to financial crises. The rapid capital outflows made possible by globalization triggered the 1997 Asian meltdown that spread to Brazil and Russia. Banking regulators both within the United States and abroad were called upon to coordinate efforts and to cooperate with their international counterparts to deal with these situations. Foreign banks have played a large role in the development and stability of the U.S. banking and financial system. This role, coupled with the growth of international financial services, presents foreign banks with significant growth opportunities in the United States well into the next century.

FURTHER READING

Blanden, Michael. ''Business as Usual,'' *The Banker,* March 1999.

Institute of International Bankers. *International Banking Focus,* January 1997.

Jacklin, Nancy. ''Fed Expands Role of Section 20 Companies,'' *International Financial Law Review,* April 1997.

Kraus, James R. ''U.S. Bankers Fear Laundering Proposals Will Lock Them Out,'' *American Banker,* 23 November 1999.

Mandaro, Laura. ''Foreign Bank Assets Decrease for First Time in More than Two Years,'' *International Banker,* 5 July 1999.

McTaggert, Timothy R. ''With New Law, Delaware Opens Door Wider to Foreign Banks,'' *American Banker,* 23 July 1999.

Seltzer, Mark D. ''Fighting Money Laundering,'' *Boston Globe,* 2 November 1999.

SIC 6082

FOREIGN TRADE AND INTERNATIONAL BANKING INSTITUTIONS

This category covers establishments of foreign trade companies operating in the United States under federal or state charter for the purpose of aiding or financing foreign trade. Also included in this industry are federal or state chartered banking institutions that only engage in banking outside of the United States.

NAICS CODE(S)

522293 (International Trade Financing)

The deregulated posture of the United States financial sector in the late 1990s resulted in a more international banking market. While for much of the twentieth century the regulatory environment was aimed at restraining banking concentration and bank involvement in other financial activities, such restrictions had given way to more liberalized capital flows and a more relaxed attitude toward consolidation and foreign involvement, both by U.S. banks operating overseas and by foreign banks in the United States.

The number of foreign banks with offices in the United States totaled approximately 700 in 1999, controlling assets totaling over $1.2 trillion. Of these, 305 were branch banks; 81 were agencies; and 90 were subsidiaries more than 25-percent owned by branch banks; 211 were U.S. representative offices of foreign banks; 12 Edge Act and Agreement Corporations; and 3 New York investment companies in which a majority is owned by foreign banks.

In 1919, the U.S. government adopted a federal law called the Edge Act named for its sponsor, Republican Walter E. Edge of New Jersey. The Edge Act of 1919 allowed the Federal Reserve to charter foreign and domestic banks to permit them to participate in international trade finance and investment through what became known as Edge Act banks. These banks were allowed to expand their offices in more than one state without the usual non-banking restrictions.

An Edge corporation offers foreign banks and their affiliates ways to expand operations in the United States without being subject to the nonbanking restrictions set by the Bank Holding Company Act of 1956. Edge banks can accept deposits and engage in a broad array of financial activities, without necessitating a foreign office to purchase international loans or process credit.

The late 1970s witnessed a great expansion of Eurobanks, which acquired an increased share of the U.S. banking market, generating heated political debate in the U.S Congress. This resulted in the International Banking Act of 1978, implemented to equalize regulatory treatment of foreign and U.S. banks doing business in the United States. This Act, along with revisions to Regulation K (International Banking Operations), gave foreign banks and affiliates the right to own a majority of shares in these Edge corporations.

Prior to revisions to the Edge Act in 1984, the Fed used the ''transaction-by-transaction'' approach, which imposed fairly stringent constraints on the U.S. operations of the Edge banks. This approach required that all deposits to Edge corporations be related to international transactions and that all transactions with domestic residents be related to identifiable international transactions. With the debt crisis in the 1980s, combined with a flood of consolidations and bank mergers, many Edge banks disappeared.

In 1984, three major revisions were made. Two of the revisions expanded the U.S. activities of the Edge banks, while the third closed a loophole in the Edge banking statute that permitted three nonbanking firms to enter the Edge banking field.

The first revision expanded U.S. activities to provide full banking services—deposit-taking, lending, and other services—to any entity that engaged in international business. These companies included international airlines, shipping lines, and export trading companies that were engaged exclusively in international activities and that were restricted to international business by their charters or licenses.

The second revision permitted an increase from $2 million to $15 million in the amount an Edge bank could invest or lend in permissible activities without prior approval from the Federal Reserve.

The third revision to Regulation K closed a loophole in the existing Edge banking laws, which allowed nonbank financial service companies to acquire the charters of existing Edge banks without the requirement of prior approval of the Federal Reserve. The new statute required any persons to give 60 days of notice before acquiring 25 percent or more of the voting shares of an Edge corporation. This allowed the Fed to impose conditions necessary to prevent adverse effects such as conflicts of interest, undue concentration of resources, or unsound banking practices.

Although subject to capital restrictions and the limitations of the Edge Act, an Edge corporation could engage in contracts to finance activities involving projects performed substantially abroad, importing or exporting goods, assembly or repackaging of goods imported or exported, issuing long-term debt, and financing the costs of production of goods and services for export. In addition, the Edge was involved in buying and selling spot and forward foreign exchange, issuing securities to finance foreign activities, guaranteeing debts of customers, acquiring participation in extensions of credit, and holding securities or buying and selling securities upon the order of the customer.

An Edge possessed certain limited powers as a corporation. It had the power to maintain its corporate existence for 20 years, to sue and be sued, to make contracts, to appoint officers and employees, to elect directors, and to adopt by-laws. The banking powers of an Edge corporation with a final permit included borrowing and lending money, issuing letters of credit, and effecting transactions in coin, bullion, exchange, and securities.

U.S. banks, which are bound by law to focus foreign investment only in other banks, are able, by investing in Edge corporations, to spread their portfolios into just about any foreign company. By 1998, 70 percent of U.S. banking assets of foreign subsidiaries was channeled through Edge corporations.

While restrictions from interstate banking have diminished substantially, the benefits for foreign activities remain attractive to some firms. As of 1998, there were still more than 30 Edge branches, concentrated primarily in New York and Miami, with assets of $18 billion.

International banking facilities (IBFs), a legal classification created in 1981, differ from Edge corporations in that they have no separate organizational identity, but merely constitute separated accounts established by host banks, including both U.S. banks and U.S. branches of foreign banks. IBFs are compelled by law to limit their activities to international transactions that demonstrably do not directly affect U.S. markets. Such facilities offer several incentives, such as the exemption from reserve requirements and, in some states, favorable tax status. In 1998, such facilities possessed $46 billion in assets for U.S. banks and $169 billion for U.S. branches of foreign banks.

The passage in 1999 of the Gramm-Leach-Bliley Act, also known as the Financial Services Modernization Act, paved the way for new conglomerations of financial services formerly prohibited by the Glass-Steagall Act of 1933. Among other provisions, the Financial Services Modernization Act allows for the creation of financial holding companies, by which banks may combine diverse financial operations, such as insurance firms, brokerages, securities underwriters, travel agencies, and others under one establishment. It thus opens the door, for instance, to mergers between U.S. insurers and foreign banking operations as well as between foreign and domestic banking concerns, without necessitating the divestiture of one party's operations by the merged company. For a foreign banking firm operating in the United States to establish a financial holding company, the Federal Reserve must bestow a sound rating on the firm's capitalization and management based on an evaluation of accounting and lending practices, the nature of the firm's capital exposure, and its reliance on federal support to meet capital standards, among other considerations.

The further deregulation of the U.S. financial sector has spurred the increased centralization of foreign firms' U.S. banking operations. While relaxed restrictions on interstate banking led to substantially increased merger and consolidation activity among U.S. banks, foreign banks have likewise recognized the need for greater efficiency and centralization in order to compete with U.S. players. Fuji Bank Ltd. and Sanwa Bank Ltd. closed down many of their U.S. branches in order to shore up and expand the operations of regional headquarters. Meanwhile, some U.S. states, such as Delaware, have gone to great lengths to attract foreign banks through the relaxation of tax laws. In 1999 Delaware Governor Tom Carper signed into law the Foreign Banking Amendments, which allows foreign banking concerns to establish Delaware as their home state, thereby allowing them to maintain branches with full banking capabilities equal to those of out-of-state U.S. banks.

Total U.S. banking assets of foreign banks increased sharply from $27 billion in 1972 to $1.1 trillion in 1998, accounting for 23 percent of the U.S. market share. Leading foreign banks operating in the U.S. included the Bank of Tokyo-Mitsubishi Ltd. of Japan, Societe Generale of France, Fuji Bank Ltd. of Japan, Bank of Nova Scotia, and the Bank of Montreal.

Of all the foreign banks, Canada, France and the United Kingdom have the largest number of bank offices in the United States. The U.S. cities with the greatest numbers of foreign bank offices include New York, Los Angeles, Chicago, Miami, and San Francisco.

FURTHER READING

''Fuji Joins Other Banks in Shrinking U.S. Ops.'' *International Banking Regulator,* 15 June 1998.

International Activities of U.S. Banks and in U.S. Banking Markets. U.S. Federal Reserve, December 1999.

McTaggart, Timothy R. ''With New Law Delaware Opens Door Wider to Foreign Banks.'' *American Banker,* 23 July 1999.

Rehm, Barbara A. and Dean Anason. ''Fed Opens Fast Lane for 1-Stop-Shop Applications.'' *American Banker,* 20 January 2000.

Structure Data for U.S. Offices of Foreign Banks. U.S. Federal Reserve, 31 September 1999.

SIC 6091

NONDEPOSIT TRUST FACILITIES

Establishments in this classification are primarily trust companies engaged in fiduciary business, but not regularly engaged in deposit banking. Some of these establishments occasionally hold limited amounts of special types of deposits, and their uninvested trust funds are usually classified as deposits. These nondeposit trust facilities may have either National or State charters. This industry does not include establishments operating under trust company charters, which limit fiduciary business to that incidental to real estate title or mortgage loan activities, which are classified in **SIC 6361: Title Insurance.**

NAICS Code(s)

523991 (Trust, Fiduciary, and Custody Activities)

A trust company is primarily involved in establishing trusts, mechanisms under which the company manages assets for the benefit of a third party. In the establishment of these trusts there are typically three parties. The first is the trustor, who is the party creating the trust and also may be known as the settlor, grantor, or donor. Second is the beneficiary for whose benefit the trust is established. Finally, the third party is the trustee, who is responsible for the management and preservation of the property of the trust estate.

Trust arrangements have become more popular in recent years. They are often established to provide for the education of children and provision for old age. Once the trust is created, it is irrevocable, even by the trustor himself, unless there is express provision for revocation or the purposes of the trust have been accomplished. Trusts allow an individual to guard against the dissipation of wealth while still allowing for the necessary use of available funds.

A trust is a fiduciary relationship in which one person or entity is the holder of the legal title to property, subject to the equitable obligation to keep or use the property for the benefit of another. The trust company must use the assets entrusted to it in the best interest of the beneficiary of the trust.

A trust company is a company organized for the purpose of executing such arrangements. The functions of these companies can be divided into two broad categories: individual trusts and corporate trusts. Individual trusts act in several capacities including executor, administrator, trustee, guardian, conservator, custodian, and conservator in lunacy. Corporate trusts act as fiscal agents, registrars of stock, transfer agents, trustees under deed of trusts, depositary for protective committees, reorganization committees, and escrow agents.

Individual trusts are often established for individuals with lack of business experience, people in poor health, absentee property holders, the elderly, and persons traveling or residing in foreign countries. In these cases the trust company will take complete charge of the assets and property of the individual and collect all income due the estate. The trust company must also make all payments required by the estate, such as property taxes, etc.

Corporate trusts are often established to act as a trustee under a mortgage securing an issue of bonds, as a financial or fiscal agent of a municipal or private corporation, as a transfer agent and registrar, as a depositary for protective and reorganization committees, and as an escrow agent. These functions tend to be more specialized and complex than those associated with individual trusts.

The history of the trust can be traced to feudal concepts of property and have become a part of American law through the common law of England. From this early point in time, trusts served the purpose of preserving property so that the beneficiary could benefit as recipient of income from the principal of the trusts.

Many different fields of endeavor are represented in this industry classification. Financial professionals play a key role, just as their supporting functions have played a role in the development of these new financial services. In addition to these, lawyers are heavily represented because this field is so tightly constrained by the principles of property and banking laws.

During the 1990s, the trust field was as competitive as the rest of the financial services marketplace when the Baby Boom generation discovered trusts as a way to safeguard wealth realized during the soaring stock markets of those years. In 1996, 148 nondeposit trust companies managed 560,058 accounts valued at $1.1 trillion. Many banks operated nondeposit trust companies as subsidiaries. Representative nondeposit trust facilities include Amalga Trust Company Inc., which had 1997 assets of $6.1 billion; First of America Trust Co., with 1998 assets of $14.4 billion; Imperial Trust Co., with 1997 assets of $9.3 billion; and Mercantile Trust Company N.A., with 1997 assets of $28.7 billion.

Further Reading

Company profiles in General BusinessASAP database.

Statistics compiled by the Federal Deposit Insurance Corporation. Available from http://www2.fdic.gov/structur/trust/tables/table_a1.txt.

SIC 6099

FUNCTIONS RELATED TO DEPOSITORY BANKING, NOT ELSEWHERE CLASSIFIED

This category includes establishments primarily engaged in performing functions related to depository banking, not elsewhere classified.

NAICS CODE(S)

522320 (Financial Transactions Processing, Reserve, and Clearing House Activities)
523130 (Commodity Contracts Dealing)
523991 (Trust, Fiduciary, and Custody Activities)
523999 (Miscellaneous Financial Investment Activities)
522390 (Other Activities Related to Credit Intermediation)

This industry comprises several types of functions related to depository banking including the transmittal of financial information between institutions and electronic payment services. Some of the primary functions that constitute this category are automated clearinghouses, check cashing agencies, check clearinghouse associations, deposit brokers, electronic funds transfer networks, escrow institutions other than real estate, fiduciary agencies other than real estate or trust, foreign currency exchanges, money order issuers, smart card issuers, representative offices of foreign banks, safe deposit companies, tax certificate sale and redemption agencies, and traveler's check issuers. Each of these functions is organized and operates differently.

Automated Clearinghouses. An automated clearinghouse processes and delivers electronic debit and credit payments among participating institutions, usually commercial and savings banks, savings and loan associations, and credit unions. The electronic debits include preauthorized mortgage payments and insurance premiums that are deducted from a customer's account. The electronic credits include pre-authorized direct payment of paychecks and dividends that are added to a customer's account. Automated clearinghouses are similar to check clearinghouses, in that all of the obligations are sorted and payment instructions are recorded electronically.

There are typically five steps in an automated clearinghouse transaction. First, the customer authorizes an electronic entry to their account. Second, the company introduces the electronic payment data through its bank. Third, the originating institution receives electronic payment data from the company. Fourth, the automated clearinghouse receives the electronic entry from the originating institution, processes it, and delivers the electronic payment to the appropriate institution. Fifth, the receiving institution posts the electronic entry to the customer's account.

In 2000, there were four automated clearinghouses that serviced some 13,000 financial institutions grouped into 24 regional associations. This system facilitated efficient clearing of accounts and reduced costs for participating institutions. There is no question that electronic payment systems continue to grow in popularity. To highlight one indicator, by 2000, 60 percent of all paychecks in the non-governmental sector were directly deposited via automated systems, up from a mere 8 percent 15 years ago.

Check Cashing Agencies. Check cashing agencies are small organizations that cash checks for a fixed fee. They do not require that a customer have an account to cash a check.

Clearinghouse Associations. A clearinghouse association is a voluntary group of banks located in the same city and having a mutual agreement to facilitate the daily exchange of checks, drafts and notes among themselves. The New York Clearinghouse Association is a good example of just such a group. It's computerized communications network, called CHIPS, allows for large sums of money to be electronically transferred among members, thereby eliminating the need for official bank checks.

Electronic Funds Transfer Networks. Electronic funds transfers (EFT) describe any transfer of funds not initiated by a written instrument that originates through an electronic terminal, telephone, computer, or magnetic storage device and authorizes a financial institution to debit an account. Examples include point-of-sale transfers, automated teller transactions, direct-deposit of funds, and transfers initiated by telephone pursuant to a pre-arranged plan.

EFT transactions can be divided into two broad categories: commercial transactions and consumer transactions. The former arise when an originating institution uses an automated clearinghouse to collect payments from or make payments to consumers and corporate entities. The latter encompass all retail banking services, such as deposits, withdrawals, and queries. These retail transactions are facilitated by point-of-sale systems and automated teller machines, or ATMs.

Escrow Institutions, Other Than Real Estate. Escrow institutions hold written agreements entered into among three parties and deposited for safekeeping with the third party as custodian. It can be delivered to the receiving party only upon the performance or fulfillment of some pre-arranged condition. The escrow institution is legally obligated to adhere to the terms of the agreement with respect to the involved parties.

Fiduciary Agencies, Other Than Real Estate. A fiduciary agency is an organization entrusted with certain property of a principal for a specified purpose. The fiduciary agency is required to act in the best interests of the principal in achieving the goals outlined in the trust instrument.

Foreign Currency Exchanges. Foreign currency exchanges convert one type of currency into another at a given exchange rate. That rate is determined by the supply and demand of the desired currency plus processing fees and/ or commissions charged by the retail institution. Commissions are either fixed or a percentage of the total amount of currency purchased. Many of these agencies are affiliated with banks or travel agencies and are usually located in areas frequented by tourists.

Money Order Issuance. Money orders are a type of credit instrument that allow the payment of money to the named payee through a safe means without the use of a checking account. Money orders can typically be issued by commercial and savings banks, as well as other institution such as the U.S. Postal Service and American Express Company.

Regional Clearinghouse Associations. Automated clearinghouses are assembled in regional networks to facilitate the clearing of accounts within and between regions. All of the automated clearinghouses participate in an interregional network that enable them to exchange electronic payments with others throughout the United States. The Automated Clearing House (ACH) Network is a nationwide batch-oriented electronic funds transfer system governed by the NACHA operating rules. The rules provide for the interbank clearing of electronic payments for participating depository financial institutions. The American Clearing House Association, the Federal Reserve system, Electronic Payments Network, and Visa are central clearing facilities through which financial institutions transmit or receive ACH entries. In 1998, 5.3 billion ACH transactions were processed with a total value exceeding $16 trillion.

Representative Offices of Foreign Banks. A representative office is a facility set up with an agent or officer of the foreign bank who is empowered to act on behalf of the bank. A representative office typically handles only a limited amount of business, serves to maintain contacts and look for new business opportunities. They generally do not process financial transactions or perform similar activities handled by branches or at the main office.

Safe Deposit Companies. Safe deposit companies are institutions organized to provide facilities for the systematic safekeeping of securities, contracts, wills, insurance policies, jewelry, and any other valuable documents and property. These organizations exist alone or as a part of a larger institution such as a bank or trust company. A customer leases a box for a fixed period, usually on an annual basis. The customer is then assigned a box that can only be unlocked when two keys are used. One of these keys is given to the individual, and the other is retained by the company. The institution becomes responsible for the safety of the stored goods. The box is kept in a large vault, entry is strictly controlled, and positive identification is required. Safe deposit companies are state-chartered, similar to state banks.

Travelers' Check Issuance. Travelers checks are international checks that are not drawn on any specific bank, but are payable at virtually all banks worldwide. These checks are guaranteed by well-known institutions, such as international credit card companies like American Express or Visa. These instruments offer a convenient and safe form of currency and can be purchased from most banks for a 1 percent fee. If travelers' checks are lost or stolen, no loss is likely to be incurred since only the payee could cash them and the counter signature has to be written in the presence of the person cashing them. The owners of travelers' checks are typically reimbursed for their loss, as long as the second signature was not written.

FURTHER READING

Downes, John and Jordan Elliot Goodman. *Dictionary of Finance and Investment Terms.* Happauge, NY: Barron's Educational Services, 1987.

Munn, Glenn G., F.L. Garcia and Charles J. Woefel. *Encyclpedia of Banking and Finance.* Detroit: St. James Press, 1991.

National Clearing House Association. ''The Electronic Payments Association,'' 20 March 2000. Available from http://www.nacha.org/.

U.S. Census Bureau. *1997 Economic Census—Finance and Insurance,* 20 March 2000. Available from http://www.census.gov.

SIC 6111

FEDERAL AND FEDERALLY SPONSORED CREDIT AGENCIES

This classification includes establishments of the federal government and federally sponsored credit agencies primarily engaged in guaranteeing, insuring, or making loans. Federally sponsored credit agencies are established under authority of federal legislation, but are not regarded as part of the government. They are often owned by their members or borrowers.

NAICS CODE(S)

522293 (International Trade Financing)
522294 (Secondary Market Financing)
522298 (All Other Non-Depository Credit Intermediation)

INDUSTRY SNAPSHOT

The federal government has created several organizations to provide services to communities where they otherwise would not be available, or would not be affordable. It also created entities to encourage activities that are seen to be in the national interest. Most of these services are targeted at rural communities. Due to the sparse populations in these areas, as well as the instability of local income producing enterprises, it is often not profitable for private firms to provide services such as credit and telephone services. In other cases, such as student loan financing, the government has an interest in promoting and encouraging the continued vibrancy of this field.

Rural lending in particular is often affected by peripheral circumstances in the industry. The consolidation of banks in the 1990s (commercial banks decreased between 1990 to 1995 from 12,729 to 10,149) caused one business periodical to note that such mergers often resulted in a decrease in rural lending, particularly if a rural bank was consolidated into a larger urban bank. A study by the Kansas City Federal Reserve Bank found that rural lending dropped by 23 percent in the three years after such a consolidation trend.

The organizations in this industry classification, while government sponsored, should not be strictly interpreted as government organizations. In fact, they are typically more private than public. The board and chief executive officer is typically appointed by the president of the United States, and its operations are nominally overseen by a cabinet-level secretary; however, the day-to-day operations of the organization are left to the staff. Furthermore, these agencies operate under the assumption that they are accountable for their continued financial well being. The operational details of these organizations can vary greatly.

ORGANIZATION AND STRUCTURE

A wide variety of agencies are included under this classification. These agencies are described below.

Banks for Cooperatives. The first banks for cooperatives in America were established in Massachusetts. A law was passed May 14, 1877, authorizing the establishment of cooperative savings fund and loan associations. These associations later became known as Cooperative banks. Cooperative banking takes on several forms: building and loan associations; credit unions; federal land bank associations; labor banks; savings and loan associations; and savings banks.

Commodity Credit Corporation. The Commodity Credit Corporation (CCC) was originally incorporated in Delaware in 1933, and was operated and managed in close affiliation with the Reconstruction Finance Corporation. In 1939 the CCC was made a part of the Department of Agriculture, and in 1948 the CCC was made an agency of the United States under a permanent federal charter.

The amended charter authorized the CCC to support prices of agricultural commodities through loans, purchases, payments, and other operations; support production and marketing of agricultural commodities; procure agricultural commodities for sale to other government agencies, foreign governments, and domestic, foreign, or international relief or rehabilitation agencies; dispose of surplus agricultural commodities; and establish policies to increase domestic consumption of agricultural commodities through the development of new markets, marketing facilities, and uses.

The CCC normally uses the customary conventions and mechanisms of trade and commerce to pursue its purchasing and selling operations and in storing, transporting, processing, and handling commodities. This often entails contracting the use of plants and facilities. The CCC has authority to acquire equipment, as well as to rent or lease office space. The CCC is not allowed to acquire real property or any interests in real property except to protect its financial interests and for providing adequate storage facilities. Cold storage facilities may only be built or bought when Congress has approved money to do so.

The operations and activities of the CCC are administered by the Agricultural Stabilization and Conservation Service (ASCS). The ASCS is an organization within the Department of Agriculture. The operations of the CCC are governed by the Food Security Act of 1985. This act extended CCC support of sugar beets and sugarcane and continued the soybean loan support program and quotas for peanuts. The Farm Act also authorized the CCC to offer commodity marketing loans to enhance U.S. competitiveness abroad, make rental payments to producers to move erodible land form production, intervene in dairy markets to support prices, and make payments to dairy producers to eliminate excess capacity. Finally, the act continued the previous ''target price'' system to augment commodity loans in supporting farm income and prices. ''Target prices'' are the basis for which agricultural subsidies are calculated. These subsidies, applied to wheat, feed grain, cotton, and rice producers who conform to specified standards and are eligible to receive subsidy payments, are equal to the difference between the target price and the higher of the market or the CCC loan value of the commodity.

To finance its activities, the CCC borrows from the U.S. Treasury, as well as from private lenders. The CCC is managed by a board of directors, which is chaired, *ex officio,* by the Secretary of Agriculture. The remainder of the board consists of six directors who are appointed by the President with the advice and consent of Congress. Not more than three of the directors may be of the same political party. The board is required to meet at the Secretary's convenience at least every 90 days.

Export-Import Bank. The Export-Import Bank (Eximbank) was incorporated in 1934 under the laws of the District of Columbia. The receipts and disbursements of the bank were removed from the budget of the United States by the Export Expansion Finance Act of 1971. The Export-Import Bank Act, as amended by legislation in 1968, provides for a board of directors consisting of five members. The members, appointed by the president with the advice and consent of Congress, consist of the president of the Eximbank, who serves as the board's chairman, the vice president, and three others. Of these, not more than three may be of the same party.

The primary objective of the bank is to aid in financing exports and imports as well as to facilitate international trade and the exchange of commodities between the United States and foreign countries. The Export-Import Bank Act was designed to encourage the use of private capital for trade purposes, but considers other factors in making loans not typically associated with corporate lending, including human rights considerations, adverse effects on U.S. industry, scarcity of materials, and domestic employment.

The Eximbank offers several programs. These include direct credits to borrowers outside the United States, export credit insurance, and export credit guarantees. The Eximbank also participates in the Foreign Credit Insurance Association (FCIA) with the insurance industry. The FCIA was established in 1961 to provide credit protection for U.S. exporters. The policies issued by the FCIA insure repayment in case of default by foreign buyers. These policies cover medium and short-term transactions. The Eximbank also guarantees repayment to those commercial banks that finance these types of transactions as well as insuring service contracts and leases. Eximbank loans carry the lowest interest rate allowed by the Organization for Economic Cooperation and Development (OECD).

Farmers Home Administration. The Farmers Home Administration (FHA), a division of the Department of Agriculture, operates under the Consolidated Farmers Home Administration Act of 1961; Title V of the Housing Act of 1949; and Part III, Title A, of the Economic Opportunity Act of 1964. It was originally established under the Farmers Home Administration Act of 1946.

The Farmers Home Administration operates primarily in rural areas of America and takes applications for loans in a wide range of areas. The applications are reviewed and approved by a local committee, which is composed of three people, at least two of which must be farmers. The money for the loans and grants made by the Farmers Home Administration come from appropriations from Congress and private lenders who make loans, which are guaranteed by the agency. Most of the loans offered are of the latter type.

Loans made by the Farmers Home Administration include operating loans to small family farmers who cannot get the credit needed to make improvements and adjustments needed for successful farming, recreation, and non-farm enterprises. Operating loan borrowers are expected to refinance their operating loans as soon as it is feasible to do so. Other loans available to farming families from the FHA include farm ownership, individual soil and water conservation, and recreation loans; these loans allow farmers to buy or extend their existing farms or ranches. Individual soil and water conservation loans help farmers in developing, conserving, and making proper use of their land and other resources, while recreation loans allow farmers to convert part of their existing land to income producing recreational land.

The FHA also is empowered to make additional loans for various purposes. These include loans to Indian tribes and tribal corporations for the acquisition of lands within the reservation or community; loans to farming associations to develop communal resources such as irrigation projects; rural housing loans to families of low and moderate income in areas with a population of not more than 20,000 where there is a lack of housing mortgage credit; emergency loans to farmers in areas affected by natural disasters to resume farming operations; watershed protection and flood prevention loans to local communities to finance projects that protect and develop land and water resources in small watersheds; loans for natural resource conservation and development in specified areas; emergency livestock guarantees to lenders making loans to ranchers to continue operations during difficult periods; and rural industrialization and development loans to local community organizations for the purpose of improving the economic and environmental climate in the community.

Federal Home Loan Mortgage Corporation. The Federal Home Loan Mortgage Corporation (FHLMC), or Freddie Mac, was established in 1970 under Title II of the Emergency Home Finance Act of 1970. This agency was established to strengthen the secondary markets in residential mortgages insured by the FHA or guaranteed by the Veterans' Administration. The agency also helps develop secondary markets for non-federally insured or guaranteed residential mortgages. The agency buys mortgages from members of the Federal Home Loan Bank System and other financial institutions that are insured by agencies of the U.S. government. The agency then repackages and sells these loans.

The capital stock of the FHLMC consists of one class non-voting shares of common stock, which are only issuable to the 12 Federal Home Loan Banks. The board is composed of three members of the Federal Home Loan Bank Board, whose chairman is also the chairman of FHLMC.

The FHLMC was created to encourage the growth of secondary markets for residential mortgages to increase the effective supply of these mortgages by making these investments more attractive. The agency developed a standardized home loan application and single-family appraisal report, as well as uniform documents for mortgages. The agency introduced an automated underwriting system in 1972 and the guaranteed mortgage certificate (GMC) in 1975. Although the Federal Home Loan Mortgage Corporation is an organization created under the auspices of the U.S. government, it is not considered a federal agency. It is taxable under relevant federal laws.

Federal Intermediate Credit Bank. Title II of the Federal Farm Loan Act of 1923 established the 12 Federal Intermediate Credit Banks (FICBs). These banks were created to discount or buy short-and medium-term notes from commercial banks and other financial institutions holding notes of farmers and ranchers. The capital stock of the FICBs are owned by production credit associations, local credit cooperatives organized under the Farm Credit Act of 1933.

The FICBs work closely with the various production credit associations (PCAs). PCAs are primary lenders that provide rural communities with short- and medium-term credit for operating, capital, and other needs. These loans vary in maturity length from a few months to seven years. The PCAs often work in conjunction with commercial banks to provide these services to rural customers. As primary lenders, the PCAs sustain losses to the extent of available resources. The PCAs adopted mutual loss sharing, participating loan plans, or both to spread the risk. The borrowers of the individual PCAs elect the board of directors.

The FICBs loan money to farmers, ranchers, producers and harvesters of aquatic products, operators providing farm services, and rural residents. They make loans to discount commercial paper for local financial institutions. The FICBs also help the production credit associations make sound credit available in rural areas. FICBs issue stock and sell participation certificates to raise capital. While the majority of their loans are made for production purposes and mature within one year, farm and rural home loans may have extended terms of up to 10 years and loans to producers and harvesters of aquatic products may be made for up to 15 years.

Federal Land Banks. The Federal Land Banks complement the mission of the Federal Intermediate Credit Banks by offering long-term farm mortgage loans. The Federal Land Banks were created by the Federal Farm Loan Act of 1916. This act also created the Federal Land Bank associations—local farmer borrowing associations through which the Federal Land Banks make loans. The stock of the Federal Land Banks is owned by the Federal Land Bank associations whose stock is owned by farmers and ranchers who are members of the association as well as borrowers.

Federal Land Banks mortgage loans may not exceed 85 percent of the appraised value of the property (97 percent if the loan is guaranteed by a government agency) on terms of five to 40 years. The majority of the loans have a 20-year maturity. Each borrower is required to buy stock in the local association equal to 5 percent of his loan and the association is required to buy an equal amount of stock in the district's Federal Land Bank.

Federal National Mortgage Association. The Federal National Mortgage Association (FNMA), or Fannie Mae, was created by the Reconstruction Finance Corporation in 1938. The FNMA became a government-sponsored private corporation through Title VIII of the Housing and Urban Development Act of 1968. It is responsible for secondary mortgage operations for home mortgages.

As a government-sponsored organization, the FNMA is accorded certain advantages not normally accorded to business corporations. The Secretary of the Treasury may buy FNMA obligations at any time, although the corporation's management tries to conduct its business so as to avoid the need to use this option. Another advantage the FNMA enjoys is that it's common stock and other securities are exempt from Securities and Exchange Commission (SEC) Laws and regulations to the same extent as U.S. government securities. The FNMA, however, does voluntarily disclose the same information as required by the SEC. Finally, the FNMA is exempt from state and local taxes, except real property taxes.

The corporation's obligations are issuable through the facilities of the Federal Reserve banks. Since the obligations of the FNMA are classified as federal agency securities, they are given favorable consideration by the financial markets. Technically, however, the FNMA's issues are not federal government obligations nor are they federally guaranteed by the U.S. government. While FNMA is not an agency of the U.S. government, it is subject to federal supervision and oversight from the offices of Housing and Urban Development and Treasury.

Government National Mortgage Association. The Government National Mortgage Association (GNMA), or Ginny Mae, was created in its current form in 1968 after being originally chartered under Title III of the National Housing Act of 1938. It is a corporate organization of the U.S. government with no capital stock or board of directors. The GNMA operates under the supervision of the Secretary of the Department of Housing and Urban Development.

The GNMA is involved in several programs related to residential mortgage finance. These projects include: 1) Special assistance in the financing of federally underwritten mortgages. Typically the GNMA buys the mortgages from private lenders at below market prices and sells them to private investors at market prices. 2) Management and liquidation of the portfolio of existing mortgages. 3) Management of the Government Mortgage Liquidation Trust, Small Business Obligations Trust, Federal Assets Liquidation Trust, and Federal Assets Financing Trust. 4) Guaranty of the timely payment of principal and interest on trust certificates and other securities issues by the Federal National Mortgage Corporation, as well as its own mortgage backed securities and those of other approved organizations.

National Consumer Cooperative Bank. The National Consumer Cooperative Bank was established in 1978 by the National Consumer Cooperative Bank Act. The mission of the bank is to encourage new and existing consumer and self-help cooperatives in the areas of health care, housing, consumer goods, and other public interests. The bank helps improve the quality of available goods and services to consumers. To accomplish this goal the bank makes loans to credit-worthy cooperatives at market interest rates. Institutions that do not qualify for credit may receive special financial and technical help from the Bank's Office of Self-Help Development and Technical Assistance.

The bank is governed by a board of directors that consists of 15 members who are appointed by the president. Eight of these members are appointed from the ranks of the executive department heads and the remaining seven are experienced members of the public. The bank is an independent financial institution raising capital through the sale of its bonds, debentures, notes, and other instruments. The U.S. government is not responsible for any obligation of the bank

Rural Electrification Administration. The Rural Electrification Administration (REA) was created in 1935 as an emergency relief program. It was later authorized to continue as a permanent program by the Rural Electrification Act of 1936. The REA was established as a lending agency with responsibility for developing a program for rural electrification. It later expanded its involvement in modernizing rural areas by extending telephone service to rural areas. In 1973 the REA began guaranteeing loans made by private lenders. Since its founding, about 1,000 electric and 900 telephone utility systems have received loans from the REA.

The REA administrator, its chief officer, is appointed by the president subject to U.S. Senate confirmation. The REA operates under the supervision of the Under-Secretary of Agriculture for Small Community and Rural Development.

REA loans are made from a revolving fund in the U.S. Treasury, which is replenished through collections on outstanding and future loans, borrowings from the Treasury, and sale of financial instruments. The REA also guarantees loans for large-scale projects. Guarantees are considered for projects if REA loans could have been made to the project. The loan itself may be obtained from any organization qualified to make, hold, and service the loan. All of the policies and procedures of the REA are applicable to the loan.

Student Loan Marketing Association. The Student Loan Marketing Association (SLMA), or Sallie Mae, is a private corporation created in 1972 by amendments to the Higher Education Act of 1965. The mission of the SLMA is to expand the money available for student loans by providing liquidity to educational lenders involved in the guaranteed loan program. As of June 30, 1996, Sallie Mae managed $37.4 billion in guaranteed student loans, representing about a third of all such loans outstanding, and had $47.4 billion in total assets.

The SLMA offers three programs under its student loan program: a loan purchase program; a warehousing advance program; and commitment programs. To provide liquidity for institutions involved in educational loan programs, the SLMA offers a program of loan consolidation, purchase of auxiliary loans, and a program of loan participation. The SLMA is also engaged in a health education assistance program for students. Loans originated under the SLMA's loan programs are either insured or reinsured by the federal government.

Sallie Mae enjoyed steady growth during the mid-1990s. Its average student loan portfolio rose from $28.6 billion in 1994 to $33.3 billion in 1996. Its net income rose $53 million between 1995 and 1996 to a total of $419 million as a result of its increases in student loans managed. Sallie Mae employs approximately 4,625 people in its corporate office in Washington, D.C., and in its 10 sales and loan servicing centers.

Background and Development

While each of these separate entities included under this industry classification has a distinct history and development, there are themes that are common to all. Many of the programs were created or are the result of legislation passed in the wake of the Great Depression. The need for these services was most apparent in rural regions of the country, which were some of the hardest hit by the economic downturn of the 1930s. This legislation is collectively known as ''New Deal'' legislation passed during the Franklin D. Roosevelt administration.

The recession of the late 1980s and early 1990s soured the public's support of government expenditures in all areas, including federally sponsored organizations. This diminished public support led to more intense government scrutiny of proposed spending programs. However, since the organizations in this industry classification are largely self-supporting, they escaped some of the difficulties faced by other purely government programs.

The need for the services provided by these organizations continued into the 1990s. Many rural communities remain in desperate financial conditions. The recession also caused a general tightening of credit, making many rural borrowers ineligible for credit through other credit agencies.

CURRENT CONDITIONS

While rural community issues are not limited to subjects of agriculture, certain farming trends may affect this industry. In 1998 the United States Department of Agriculture (USDA) reported that farm debt was expected to stabilize in 1999, following increases which tapered from 6 percent in 1997 to 4.5 percent in 1998. The USDA anticipated that farmers would use government emergency assistance payments (which were disbursed at a record high in 1997) to pay down debt. Farmers, who had faced reduced income during the second half of the 1990s, were expected to be less apt to incur more debt, according to the USDA. The USDA reported that anticipated farm debt by the end of 1999 would be $169 billion. The USDA also predicted that guaranteed loans would have $2.7 billion available during 1999, and that under $2 billion of these funds would be available for uses other than the purchase of real estate.

In 1997, the top five issuers of Ginnie Mae mortgage-backed securities included Norwest Mortgage Inc. ($15.5 billion), Countrywide Home Loans ($13.8 billion), Chase Manhattan Mortgage Corporation ($7 billion), HomeSide Lending ($6.6 billion) and Resource Bancshares Mortgage Corporation ($4.2 billion).

Regarding home mortgage trends in the industry, both Freddie Mac and Fannie Mae announced increased limits for single family mortgages for 2000. The new limit of $252,700 per single family mortgage represented an increase of 5.3 percent over the 1999 ceiling for single family mortgages of $240,000.

INDUSTRY LEADERS

The public companies Freddie Mac and Fannie Mae are industry leaders in the sense that they do a relatively larger portion of business in the industry than other lender brokers. One of every six mortgages in the United States is indirectly financed by Freddie Mac. Private competitors in the industry have objected to the unique business hybrid existence of a company like Fannie Mae, complaining that Fannie Mae has a competitive advantage in the lending market. Fannie Mae had sales of $31.4 million in 1998 with a 1998 sales growth of 13.4 percent. Fannie Mae's net income in 1998 was $3.4 million, an increase of 11.9 percent. Freddie Mac had $18.0 million in sales during 1998 and a 25.3 percent growth in sales that year. The company had net income in 1998 of $1.7 million, a 21.9 percent increase from the previous year.

WORKFORCE

Organizations covered in this industry classification range in work force size from 11,000 to 225,000 employees. These employees represent all of the disciplines found in the private lending sector, including secretaries, financial analysts, managers, and clerks. These organizations are affiliated with the government to some degree and thus have many employees in the greater Washington, D.C., area. Similarly, many of the organizations serve rural constituencies, so many employees involved with those organizations live in communities of less that 50,000.

FURTHER READING

''Fannie Mae.'' 1999. Available from http://www.hoovers.com/co/capsule/3/0,2163,10553,00.html.

''Farm Debt Stabilization Anticipated in 1999; with Farm Debt Expected to be $172.7 Billion.'' Economic Research Service, United States Department of Agriculture, 23 September 1999. Available from http://www.econ.ag.gov/briefing/farmincome/fbs/debt_text.htm.

''Freddie Mac.'' 1999. Available from http://www.hoovers.com/co/capsule/4/0,2163,13944,00. html.

Looker, Dan. ''Farms and Ranches Should Form Long Term Relationships with Well Managed Banks and Farm Credit Services Instead of Seeking the Services of Captive Finance Companies.'' *Successful Farming,* March 1997.

''Lower Interest Rates to Benefit Farmers.'' Economic Research Service, United States Department of Agriculture, 23 September 1999. Available from http://econ.ag.gov/briefing/farmincome/def_ccc.htm.

''NAR Applauds Freddie Mac and Fannie Mae Announcement.'' *PR Newswire,* 30 November 1999. Available from http://finance.individual.com.

SIC 6141

PERSONAL CREDIT INSTITUTIONS

This category covers establishments primarily engaged in providing loans to individuals. Also included in this industry are establishments primarily engaged in financing retail sales made on the installment plan and financing automobile loans for individuals.

NAICS CODE(S)

522210 (Credit Card Issuing)
522220 (Sales Financing)
522291 (Consumer Lending)

INDUSTRY SNAPSHOT

''Credit'' is derived from the Latin word ''credo,'' which means ''I believe.'' It typically refers to a purchase or the power to make a purchase of goods for enjoyment in the present while deferring payment to a future date. Thus, the transaction consists of a transfer and delivery of goods in the present in exchange for a promise of future payment.

The granting of credit depends upon three factors: character, capacity, and capital. Each of these factors introduces some risk into the transaction. The risk of lending on character is called "moral risk." The risk of lending on capacity is called "business risk." The risk of lending on capital is called "property risk." An ideal borrower will meet a minimum of requirements set for evaluating each of these three risks.

Since it is impossible for most companies to determine how their credit applicants are ranked in each of these categories, they must obtain their information from centralized sources. These sources are credit reporting agencies. Credit reporting agencies keep files of information on all consumers who have made credit transactions at some point in their lives. Credit granting institutions may purchase these files to evaluate the "credit worthiness" of individual applicants. Since misuse or abuse of these files can be financially detrimental to the consumer, the credit reporting industry is heavily regulated. Adverse information must be removed within seven years—except bankruptcy, which remains in a credit file for ten years. Disputed information that cannot be verified must be removed, and access to the file must be granted for the individual concerned. Finally, the information may only be given to authorized users.

The personal credit industry encompasses many diverse organizations. These participants range from General Motors Acceptance Corp. (GMAC), with 1998 sales of $20.2 billion and 23,619 employees, to tiny one-office credit firms with a handful of staff and assets under $1 million.

ORGANIZATION AND STRUCTURE

Personal credit transactions are regulated by the Uniform Commercial Code (U.C.C.) and the Uniform Consumer Credit Code (U.C.C.C.). Additionally, a number of pieces of legislation are designed to protect the consumer, including the Fair Credit Reporting Act. Each of the various entities that constitute this category have varying organizations and structures.

Automobile Loans. Since automobiles are too expensive for most individuals to purchase with cash, most new car purchases are made with the assistance of automobile loans; these types of loans are typically made by banks and finance companies. This type of consumer lending typically has a maturity of 8 months, although maturities of 60 months and longer are not uncommon.

Automobile loans may be either direct or indirect. Direct automobile loans are made to the consumer to purchase an automobile and are secured by a chattel interest in the auto. Indirect automobile loans are made by the auto dealer. Under this arrangement the dealer collects the required information from the consumer and furnishes it to the bank. The bank then either accepts or rejects the applicant. Usually the dealer packages the loans in bundles and sells them to banks; these loans tend to have higher delinquency rates than direct loans.

The automobile loan is the most common type of consumer loan, accounting for more than 40 percent of all consumer credit. Normally consumers spend about 5 percent of their income on automobiles, down from nearly 7 percent in the 1970s. Banks, however, make less than 40 percent of all automobile loans. The remainder of the loans are made by auto manufacturers' financing divisions. These financing entities offer below market rates as well as more flexible financing options to stimulate the sales of their products.

Banks also offer "floorplan" financing to support dealers' leasing programs. "Floorplan" financing, or trust receipt financing, is a form of inventory financing under which the bank holds title to the automobile inventory. The automobile dealer is considered the borrower in these transactions and is loaned funds to buy the inventory from suppliers. The dealer holds the inventory in trust for the bank and then sells inventory to consumers. Subsequently, these proceeds are paid to the bank, but the dealer keeps the mark-up of the retail price over the payments due the bank. When the sale is made on a credit basis, the dealer often sells the obligation to the bank.

Consumer Finance Companies. Consumer finance companies are small loan companies that specialize in personal loans under the small loan laws of the various states. These establishments are often called personal finance companies.

Financing of Automobiles, Furniture, Appliances, Personal Airplanes, etc., Not Engaged in Deposit Banking. The financing of personal property is included under the general title of consumer credit. Consumer credit is the short- and medium-term debt owed by individuals to financial institutions, retailers, and other distributors for financing consumer purchases of goods and services, but not including real estate mortgages and insurance policy loans. In 1995 the total consumer installment credit outstanding was $1.02 trillion. Of that, $353.3 billion was for automobile loans, $395.2 billion was for credit card loans (plus bank overdraft privileges and the like), and $276.2 billion was for other types of loans.

Due to the disparate positions of the creditor and consumer in negotiating credit terms, the government regulates this industry very heavily. The Consumer Credit Protection Act of 1968 assures that every consumer with a need for credit is given meaningful information with respect to the cost of that credit. This means that the dollar amount of the finance charge, as well as the annual percentage rate computed on the unpaid balance, must be disclosed. Other information must also be disclosed to allow the consumer the opportunity to readily compare the various credit terms offered by different sources.

The Consumer Credit Protection Act and other related regulations apply to banks, savings and loan associations, department stores, credit card issuers, credit unions, automobile dealers, consumer finance companies, hospitals, and any other organizations that extend or arrange credit to which a finance charge is added. Residential mortgage brokers, craftsmen, doctors, dentists, and other professionals are also subject to these regulations. The Act does not apply to business and commercial credit (governed by the U.C.C.), credit to government entities, transactions covered by the SEC, and credit over $25,000 except for household and agricultural uses.

Interest on consumer credit transactions is typically computed in one of two ways. For open-end credit accounts with credit cards and revolving charge accounts in retail stores, finance charges are imposed on unpaid balances each month. To determine the monthly finance charge rate, the annual rate is divided by 12. For example 1.5 percent might be applied per month for an annual rate of 18 percent. For other forms of credit, including loans and sales credit, the total amount, number of payments, and due dates are negotiated with the consumer. Examples of these transactions include an automobile loan or the purchase of a large appliance on department store credit.

Installment Sales Finance, Other Than Banks. Installment sales are sales of goods under a definite schedule of payments, which involve a specified cash outlay as a down payment with the balance payable in agreed upon periodic installments until the item is paid for. This type of sale is a relatively recent phenomena. Before 1922, installment sales were confined to a small number of retail outlets, typically those specializing in lower quality merchandise. In the late 1920s, this type of transaction became more popular after its success in the automotive industry and intense promotion by consumer finance companies. Automobile sales have been the most prevalent form of installment sales through the present day.

Installment sales are based on one of two legal documents. The first is a conditional sales contract under which the title, or ownership, of the item remains with the seller. The second is the chattel mortgage under which the buyer holds title subject to a lien in favor of the seller. As the various states have detailed and complex legislation on conditional sales, most creditors favor the chattel mortgage, which is governed by Article 9 of the U.C.C. Under this process, the buyer signs a promissory note, secured by the product, that constitutes a promise to repay the debt. The mortgage will typically contain an acceleration clause (causing the entire debt to come due upon certain conditions that indicate default) and a power of sale clause (allowing the seller to repossess the item and sell it subject to certain conditions that indicate default).

Other terms may also be present in chattel mortgages. A "balloon" installment plan is one under which the initial payments are small but a later one is very large, usually requiring refinancing. Another financing plan is the "open end" type of chattel mortgage under which additional purchases may be made on an installment basis. Under this arrangement the seller retains a lien on all of the purchased goods whether they have been paid for or not. If the buyer defaults on a later purchase, the seller may repossess all of the items purchased. While many of these provisions still exist, the current trend is towards consumer-oriented legislation that renders such excessively punitive practices illegal or non-binding.

The following are some of the most important pieces of federal legislation regulating consumer credit:

The Consumer Credit Protection Act of 1968. The key provisions of this act are: Title I, the Truth-in-Lending Act, which provides for consumer credit cost disclosure; Title II, which contains penalties for extortionate credit transactions; Title III, which contains restrictions on garnishments; and Title IV, which provides for the establishment of the National Commission on Consumer Finance to report and make recommendations to Congress on consumer credit topics. Title V pertains to the issuance of credit cards, liabilities of credit card holders, and the fraudulent use of credit cards. Title VI contains provisions relating to credit information and credit reports and gives credit consumers the right to confront the preparers of credit reports and correct any misstatements of facts contained in such reports. The Act also prohibits unwarranted disclosure of the information contained in these reports, requires the elimination of erroneous information, and protects against unfair credit reporting practices.

The Fair Credit Billing Act, an amendment to the Truth-in-Lending Act, states that consumers shall have fair methods available for the correction of billing errors.

The Equal Credit Opportunity Act declares that creditors cannot discriminate against consumers seeking credit on the basis of sex or marital status.

The Real Estate Settlement Procedures Act requires that a standard real estate settlement form be developed in compliance with the provisions of the Truth-in-Lending Act for use in all transactions involving federally funded or secured mortgage loans. This form includes a clear and conspicuous itemization of all settlement charges imposed upon the buyer and seller as well as greater disclosure of the nature and costs of real estate settlement charges.

The Home Mortgage Disclosure Act requires that mortgage lending be free of discriminatory bias and requires that depository institutions with offices in metropolitan areas and with assets of over $10 million identify the geographic distribution of their home mortgage loan.

The Consumer Leasing Act, another amendment to the Truth-in Lending Act, requires that consumers be provided with full information regarding the terms of their leases of personal property, including open-end and closed-end vehicle and furniture leases.

The Fair Debt Collection Practices Act makes abusive and deceptive debt collection practices illegal for those the Act defines as debt collectors, as opposed to the primary lender.

The Truth-in-Lending Simplification and Reform Act exempts all extensions of credit for agricultural purposes from the disclosure provisions of the Truth-in-Lending Act, eliminates disclosure requirements calling for periodic statements from lenders in connection with closed-end credit transactions, and allows an exception to the ''cooling off'' period for consumers who pledge their homes as collateral in open-end credit arrangements.

The Installment Sale Revision Act liberalizes the rules for postponing tax on property that is sold on the deferred payment basis.

Most of this legislation was passed between the late 1960s and mid-1970s in response to a broader concern for consumer protection. Currently, the consumer credit industry is one of the most heavily regulated segments of the economy.

As installment selling has become more established, commercial banks have also become involved in this industry. To remain liquid, finance companies and retailers often sell these obligations, or chattel paper, to banks or factors. The bank pays cash, normally at a discount, to the seller who turns the buyer's obligation over to the bank.

In the late 1970s, the Carter Administration attempted to restrain consumer credit to curb inflation. The Board of Governors of the Federal Reserve System implemented several programs in compliance with this broader policy, including a voluntary credit restraint program; a program of restraint on specified types of consumer credit, including credit cards, check overdraft plans, unsecured credit, and secured credit, where the proceeds are not used to finance the collateral; an increase in the marginal reserve requirement on managed liabilities of Federal Reserve member banks and a decrease in the base amount on which these charges applied; a 10 percent deposit requirement on managed liabilities of non-member banks and 15 percent deposit requirement on any increase of money market funds over the March 14, 1980, base period; and a surcharge on frequent discount borrowing by large Federal Reserve member banks.

Morris Plans Not Engaged in Deposit Banking. Morris Plans are named after Arthur J. Morris who founded a system of personal loans in 1910 at the Fidelity Savings & Trust Co. of Norfolk, Virginia. Morris Plan loans are made on a monthly repayment basis, with the first month's installment deducted from the face value of the loan and the remaining balance. This arrangement makes the effective interest rate about twice the nominal rate. Because of the permissive banking laws effective at the time, the plan evolved as a loan for the amount desired, nominally to purchase an investment certificate, to be paid for in monthly installments with the credit for the payments going to the certificate rather than the loan account. A variation on this scheme credited the monthly payments to a deposit account. Thus, under either scenario, the effective rate of interest, about twice the nominal rate, did not violate usury laws. Currently, several states have modified their banking laws to allow Morris Plans, avoiding the need to resort to legal actions.

In addition to providing loan funds, Morris Plans also provide life insurance for borrowers. Borrowers can purchase life insurance policies for the full amount of their loans; if the borrower dies while the loan is outstanding, the insurance would be applied to the full amount of the loan and the remainder would be paid to the family or estate.

Mutual Benefit Associations. Mutual Benefit Associations, or Mutual Associations, are savings banks, savings and loan associations, insurance companies, and credit unions that are not organized under state corporation laws as stock corporations but are owned by their depositors, policyholders, or members. In the mid-1990s, these included mutual savings banks, savings and loan associations, and credit unions. Savings and loan institutions are either state or federally chartered and deposit insurance is available from state and federal insurance agencies for these institutions.

Mutual savings banks, savings and loans, and credit unions are permitted to sell federal mutual certificates, which allow these institutions to efficiently build their net worth and reserves. These certificates are obligations that are subordinated to savings accounts, savings certificates, and debt obligations of the mutual benefit association. The target net worth-to-resources ratio is 3 percent and the desired net worth-to-liability ratio is 6 percent.

Personal Finance Companies, Small Loan: Licensed. These organizations specialize in personal loans, which are cash loans to individual borrowers for such purposes as refinancing payments on medical bills, taxes, and insurance premiums. These companies also provide cash for transactions that will permit cost savings for borrowers.

The industry is very closely regulated. Personal finance companies are subject to related statutes in all 50 states, the District of Columbia, and Puerto Rico. Most of the loans made by these companies are subject to a state version of the Uniform Small Loan Law or the Model Consumer Finance Act. These institutions are also subject to state laws that regulate sales financing and revolving credit, insurance premium financing, home repair financing, second mortgagees on homes, and usury laws. Personal finance companies must also comply with the Uniform Consumer Credit Code and the Federal Consumer Credit Protection Act.

Personal loan companies operate either as chains with many locations or as independent offices. The primary customers of these institutions are wage earners in the lower income bracket. To target these customers, most personal loan companies are located in industrial centers and urban areas where they can generate sufficient volume or in jurisdictions that allow them to charge the high interest rates necessary to maintain profitability.

Most of the receivables of these companies are unsecured. They are most concerned with the ability of the borrower to repay the obligation out of monthly income as opposed to the ability to repossess and liquidate security. Because of the frequently urgent nature of such loans, the application process tends to be simplified and streamlined.

Personal finance companies, also known as consumer credit companies or small loan companies, have been instrumental in educating consumers in the management of personal finance, particularly in advising against over-borrowing and improper management of personal finances.

BACKGROUND AND DEVELOPMENT

While each of these separate entities included under this industry classification has a distinct history and development, there are issues that are common to all.

As the American economy has become more consumer oriented, many options that allow consumers easier access to products have been created. Most of these fall under the personal finance industry. By the mid-1990s, personal finance was one of the largest and most aggressive sectors of the broader finance industry.

From the late 1960s to the mid-1970s, a wave of regulations were passed by Congress in response to the public's demand for greater protection from unfair practices by the government. This wave of regulation was designed to protect the consumer from unfair credit collection practices and unconscionable credit terms by requiring creditors to adhere to stricter standards and fully disclose consumer credit terms.

Many personal credit institutions sell their loans to other companies. This frees money for new loans and investments. While this practice is not new, it intensified during the early 1990s. In other cases, the loans are serviced for a fee by companies other than the lender, which allows the loan originator to free resources normally used in processing loan-related paperwork. The booming economy of the mid-1990s allowed credit companies to prosper. GMAC, for example, saw its total assets rise by $8 billion from year-end 1995 to year-end 1996. The company operates from nearly 600 offices worldwide and services 7.2 million customer accounts. GMAC's primary business remains what it has always been, financing consumer purchases of new cars. But the widely diversified company also finances home mortgages, home equity loans, various insurance products, and other lines of business. Since its founding in 1919, GMAC extended $870 billion in credit to help finance more than 138 million vehicle purchases.

The competition between credit card companies intensified in the late 1980s and early 1990s, as consumer confidence decreased and the public grew more reluctant to buy on credit during the prolonged recession. In 1993, MasterCard International Incorporated had the largest change in volume, with a 23 percent increase, compared with 16 percent for Visa International and 10 percent for American Express Company. Most of this difference was attributed to Mastercard's aggressive co-branding program. In co-branding, a card issuer joins with another organization, a car manufacturer for example, to offer a card jointly with benefits from both companies including rebates on purchases from the co-branding company. By the end of 1993, Mastercard issued 25 million co-branded cards to consumers.

CURRENT CONDITIONS

By the end of 1997, *U.S. Banker* reported that consumer debt was on the rise again. The American Bankruptcy Institute of the Administrative Office of the United States Courts reported that consumer debts during the 1990s grew twice as fast as mortgage debt, which grew 60 percent faster than consumer earnings. The personal loan industry was also challenged by the trend of increasing personal bankruptcy; in 1996, for example, $30 billion of consumer debt in the United States was discharged in bankruptcy, leaving credit agencies with nothing. Bankruptcies peaked in 1998 and the first quarter of 1999 was close to the previous record for a quarter. Credit agencies took preventative measures to try to slow the trend, including raising interest rates and putting more effort into collections.

Personal credit agencies also looked to form new alliances with credit counseling agencies in an attempt to stave off the effects of consumer bankruptcy. Visa, for example, ran 70,000 radio information spots in 1997 to persuade debt-ridden customers to consider working with credit counseling agencies. The National Foundation for

Consumer Credit reported in 1997 that it expected to counsel 1.5 million consumers, a 20 percent increase from the previous year.

INDUSTRY LEADERS

The following companies in the industry distinguished themselves in various rankings. *Forbes* ranked Green Tree Financial a ''Most Profitable Lease and Finance Company'' based on the company's 24.4 percent average return on capital over five years. A *Fortune* survey of executives ranked American Express the ''Most Admired Consumer Credit Corporation,'' with a score of 7.56 out of 10 points. In the credit card sector of the industry, Visa captured 50.8 percent of the market share in the first quarter of 1999, according to the *Wall Street Journal.* As of April 1999 Bank One/First USA led credit card issuers with number of cards issued (44.1 million), according to the *New York Times.*

WORKFORCE

This industry classification includes many diverse employers who employ anywhere from 20 to 20,000 workers. The employees in this field represent diverse backgrounds in the finance industry and its related support services. These workers include bankers, tellers, loan officers, secretaries, and security personnel.

RESEARCH AND TECHNOLOGY

In the late 1990s, credit companies that had been forced to downsize adopted the use of new technology to compensate for previous staff functions. According to *Business Credit,* such technology allowed personal credit agencies to maximize efficiency and increase productivity. The technology that the industry adopted generally included software that addressed accounts receivable functions or addressed task-specific applications. According to a 1999 survey by *Business Credit,* companies generally spent amounts ranging from a few hundred dollars to $100,000 for such software. The survey noted that the personal credit industry would be expected to interface increasingly with the Internet. An example of such an interface is provided by the Internet company Creditland, which was founded in 1998 and directs consumers to good matches for personal loans, auto loans, mortgages, or credit cards.

FURTHER READING

''Annual Report on American Industry.'' *Forbes,* 12 January 1998.

''Creditland Announces $15 Million in Second Round Financing.'' *PR Newswire,* 8 December 1999. Available from http://finance.individual.com/display_news.asp?doc_id=PR19991206SFM083.

''Good Debts: Consumer Loans.'' *Economist,* 5 July 1997.

Henwood, Doug. ''Going for Broke.'' *Nation,* 19 July 1999.

''Leading Credit Care Issuers, 1999.'' *New York Times,* 25 April 1999.

Marshal, Jeffrey. ''Calling all Counselors: In a Time of Soaring Bankruptcies, Credit Counseling Agencies are Key Allies in Helping Lenders Get Repaid.'' *U.S. Banker,* December 1997.

''Nilson Report.'' *Wall Street Journal,* 11 June 1999.

Ochs, Joyce R., and Kenneth L. Parkinson. ''Software for Credit Managers.'' *Business Credit,* July-August 1999.

U.S. Department of Commerce. *Statistical Abstract of the United States.* Washington, D.C.: GPO, 1996.

SIC 6153

SHORT-TERM BUSINESS CREDIT INSTITUTIONS, EXCEPT AGRICULTURAL

This industry includes establishments primarily engaged in extending credit to business enterprises for relatively short periods. Private establishments primarily engaged in extending agricultural credit are classified in **SIC 6159: Miscellaneous Business Credit Institutions.**

NAICS CODE(S)

522220 (Sales Financing)

522320 (Financial Transactions Processing, Reserve, and Clearing House Activities)

522298 (All Other Non-Depository Credit Intermediation)

INDUSTRY SNAPSHOT

Credit generally refers to a purchase, or the power to make a purchase, of goods for use in the present—with payment deferred to a future date. Granting credit typically depends upon three factors: character of the borrower, capacity to repay, and capital used as collateral. Each of these factors introduces some risk into the transaction. The risk of lending on character is called ''moral risk,'' the risk of lending on capacity is called ''business risk,'' and the risk of lending on capital is called ''property risk.'' An ideal borrower will combine a minimum of each of these three risks.

Lenders are often not in a position to evaluate a business against these criteria as easily as they could with an individual. Consequently, they may contact either general or special mercantile agencies to find needed information. General agencies, such as Dun & Bradstreet, collect information on a wide range of business enterprises nationwide. Special agencies limit their coverage to one or few business areas and may operate nationally or locally.

General agencies furnish general and special reports. General reports are leased by subscribers on a quarterly basis and contain information on capital (based on financial statements), and credit, denoting the grade of credit ratings. Special reports are limited to specific businesses or companies and are obtained under contract. These reports are more extensive than the general reports, and contain background as well as general information. Credit reporting agencies collect their information from several sources, including direct investigation, trade creditor and banking connections, insurance records, and public records. The lenders usually pay an annual fee to these agencies in exchange for an unlimited amount of information.

A large portion of modern business is conducted on a credit basis. The need for credit arose from a complex system of manufacturers, suppliers, distributors, and retailers in the modern market economy. Credit allows the smooth operation of such a system. A cash-only business is virtually impossible in the 1990s.

ORGANIZATION AND STRUCTURE

Business transactions, including credit transactions, are regulated by the Uniform Commercial Code (UCC). The UCC is a standardized commercial law effective in most U.S. jurisdictions whose goal is to simplify interactions between businesses. The numerous entities that constitute this category have varying organizations and structures.

Purchasers of Accounts Receivable and Commercial Paper. Accounts receivables are promises from customers to pay for goods or services that have already been rendered. Commercial paper is any form of short-term negotiable instrument that arises out of a commercial transaction, to be distinguished from speculative, investment, real estate, personal, or public transactions. Many companies receive financing by using their accounts receivable as collateral, or selling the accounts outright at a discount.

Factors of Commercial Paper. Factors provide financing on accounts receivable by discounting accounts receivable on a non-recourse basis. Upon buying the accounts, the factor assumes the position of the seller—including the risk of default and credit losses—and may not hold the original seller liable in the event of loss. The factor then pays the entity that sold the account, paying upwards of 85 percent of the face value of the account receivable. The remaining amount is considered a discount fee, which is the factor's payment. In short, factors buy the accounts on an ''as is'' basis. Customers then pay factors. Factors often are also engaged in inventory financing, secured loans against fixed assets and other resources, as well as unsecured loans. They may also offer financial advisory services.

Sellers benefit from using factors because they are able to avoid tying up working capital in accounts receivable for the full credit period, which may be several months. Another advantage enjoyed by sellers using factors is that they may eliminate their in-house credit and collection departments.

Financing of Dealers by Motor Vehicle Manufacturers' Organizations. Automobile manufacturers offer ''floor plan'' financing to support dealers' sales and leasing programs. ''Floor plan'' financing, or trust receipt financing, is a form of inventory financing under which the bank holds title to the automobile inventory. The dealer is loaned money to buy the inventory from the original equipment manufacturer and holds the inventory in trust for the manufacturer. As the borrower sells inventory to consumers, he pays these proceeds to the manufacturer. The dealer keeps the mark-up of the retail price over the payments due the manufacturer. When the sale is made on a credit basis, the dealer often sells the obligation to the manufacturer. This practice is used in other industries as well as the automobile industry.

Mercantile Financing. Mercantile financing is typically done through the sale of mercantile paper. Mercantile paper is a note, acceptance, or bill of exchange made or endorsed by concerns engaged in jobbing, wholesaling, or retailing of commodities.

Working Capital Financing. Working capital refers to an entity's net current (or liquid) assets, or current assets minus the current liabilities (those expected to mature within one year). This excess, called free working capital, is the cash available to meet a company's liabilities as they mature over this one-year period. This liquidity is achieved by a number of means including trade credit, bank loans, factoring, and sales of accounts receivable.

BACKGROUND AND DEVELOPMENT

As the U.S. economy became more complex and competitive in the 1980s and 1990s, businesses needed increasingly flexible short-term financing to remain competitive. This flexibility is provided by a business credit market that offers a variety of financing options.

Co-branding led business credit institutions to get involved in other services. General Motors (GM), for example, has always been involved in financing the sale of its cars to consumers and floor plan financing. In the early 1990s, GM got involved in credit card financing in a co-branding arrangement with MasterCard, thus providing automobile and credit card financing to its customers. By 1994, GM had earned $9.4 billion from financing. Ford Motor Credit has also been involved in this type of co-branding financing, earning $21.3 billion in 1994.

CURRENT CONDITIONS

Throughout the 1990s, most business credit institutions broadened the range of services offered. In the late 1990s, the major credit card companies began to offer purchasing or procurement cards in addition to typical business credit cards. These cards were designed to make the purchase of small items cheaper and more efficient. The average company conducts 90,000 transactions—typically individual purchases of $10,000 or less—annually. The cost of each of these transactions is about $80, but can be minimized through the use of procurement cards.

All three major credit card providers—MasterCard International Incorporated, American Express, and Visa USA—adapted their services in the late 1990s to facilitate electronic commerce conducted business-to-business. In late 1999, MasterCard and American Express expanded their alliances with e-commerce businesses: MasterCard allied itself with Commerce One, which tailored its BuySite and MarketSite to accept online payment with the MasterCard Corporate Purchasing Card; American Express increased the number of affiliations with e-commerce companies in its portfolio to 10, adding Clarus, Extensity, Sun-Netscape Alliance, and Trilogy to its affiliations with Ariba, Commerce One, Concur Technologies, Intelisys, Remedy, and tradex Technologies.

At the same time, Visa USA focused its efforts on tailoring its procurement cards toward the newly-defined global commodity code standards merging the United Nations' Common Coding System (UNCCS) and Dun and Bradstreet's Standard Products and Services Codes (SPSC) to create UN/SPSC Codes specifically for electronic commerce. SAP ag, Visa's ally in e-commerce, adopted this coding system to streamline its purchasing systems, paving the way for other affiliates such as Ariba.

All of the major international credit card companies—American Express, MasterCard International and its affiliates Europay and Mondex, Visa International, and JCB of Japan—joined forces in the Smart Card Security Users Group (SCSUG) to create a standardized system, called Common Criteria, for evaluating the security of smart cards. The astronomical increase in online credit card use brought with it the inherent fraud enabled by transactions conducted in such a public forum. Credit card security thus became a key issue, not only in terms of real protection, but also in terms of consumer perceptions of security.

WORKFORCE

The short-term business credit industry includes many diverse companies, employing anywhere from 2 to 50,000 employees. These occupations include bankers, tellers, loan officers, secretaries, and security personnel.

FURTHER READING

Brunelli, Mark A. ''Card Companies Create Alliances and New Services.'' *Purchasing,* 4 November 1999.

Kutler, Jeffrey. ''Global Heavyweights Form Group to Set Smart Card Security Standards.'' *American Banker,* 10 November 1999.

Small Business Exchange, 20 March 2000. Available from http://www.americanexpress.com.

SIC 6159

MISCELLANEOUS BUSINESS CREDIT INSTITUTIONS

This industry covers establishments primarily engaged in furnishing intermediate or long-term general and industrial credit, including the finance leasing of automobiles, trucks, and machinery and equipment. Also included in this industry are private establishments primarily engaged in extending agricultural credit. Federal and federally sponsored credit agencies primarily engaged in extending agricultural credit are classified in **SIC 6111: Federal and Federally-Sponsored Credit Agencies.** Establishments primarily engaged in other types of leasing of passenger cars and trucks are classified in various automotive rental and leasing industries.

NAICS CODE(S)

522220 (Sales Financing)
522293 (International Trade Financing)
522298 (All Other Non-Depository Credit Intermediation)

BACKGROUND AND DEVELOPMENT

Modern business is frequently conducted on a credit basis. The need for credit developed as market economies became more complex and included many players: manufacturers, suppliers, distributors, and retailers. Credit facilitates smooth operations.

The decision to extend credit depends upon three factors: character, capacity, and capital. Each factor introduces risk to the transaction. The risk of lending on character is called moral risk. Business risk involves lending on capacity. The risk of lending on capital is called property risk. An ideal business borrower will combine a minimum of each.

Lenders are often not in a position to evaluate a business against these criteria. To verify a credit applicant's creditworthiness, a lender may contact either general or special mercantile agencies to find needed information. General agencies, such as Dun & Bradstreet, collect information on a range of business enterprises nationwide, while special agencies limit their coverage to one or a few business areas and may operate either nationally or locally.

General agencies furnish two types of reports. General reports are leased by subscribers on a quarterly basis and contain capital ratings, based on financial statements, and credit ratings, denoting the grade of credit. Special reports are limited to specific businesses or companies and are provided under contract. These reports are more extensive than the general reports and contain background as well as general information. Credit reporting agencies collect their information from several sources including direct investigations, trade creditor and banking connections, and public and insurance records.

Business transactions, including credit transactions, are regulated by the Uniform Commercial Code (UCC) The UCC is a collection of modernized, codified, and standardized laws that apply to all commercial transactions, except real property. The code is binding in most U.S. jurisdictions and has standardized most commercial law.

Automobile Finance Leasing. As automobile purchases require significant capital investment, most new car purchases are made with the help of automobile financing typically made by banks and finance companies. Under a lease arrangement, the financier keeps the automobile's title. The customer usually makes monthly payments and has an option to buy the vehicle at the end of the lease period.

Banks also offer floor plan financing to support dealers' leasing programs. Floor plan financing, or trust receipt financing, is a form of inventory financing under which the bank holds title to the automobile inventory. The dealer is loaned money to buy the inventory from suppliers and holds the inventory in trust for the bank. As the borrower sells inventory to consumers, he pays the bank. The dealer keeps the mark-up of the retail price over the payments due the bank. When the sale is made on a credit basis, the dealer often sells the obligation to the bank.

Agricultural Credit Institutions. There are two types of agricultural credit institutions: federal and commercial. Federal institutions include the Federal Land Banks and Land Bank Associations, the Federal Intermediate Credit Banks, Production Credit Associations, District Banks for Cooperatives, the Commodity Credit Corporation, Agricultural Stabilization and Conservation Service, Federal Crop Insurance Corporation, Farmers Home Administration, Rural Electrification Administration, and the Rural Telephone Bank.

These federal institutions were created to provide credit opportunities to communities in which financial services otherwise were neither available nor affordable. The federal government has also created organizations to encourage activities that are in the national interest. Most of these services are targeted at rural and agricultural communities. For example, the federal government is deeply involved in the financial structure of the agricultural industry because of the former's interest in protecting the nation's ability to produce food. In many communities, sparse populations and an unstable agricultural business creates a nonprofitable environment for private firms to provide credit.

These organizations, while government sponsored, are typically more private than public. The board and chief executive officer are typically appointed by the president and the institution's operations are nominally overseen by a cabinet level secretary; however, the day-to-day operations of the organization are left to the staff. Furthermore, these agencies operate under the assumption that they are accountable for their continued financial well-being.

Many commercial organizations provide agricultural credit with the support of federal institutions. Commercial lenders may extend credit to an agricultural endeavor that is secured or guaranteed by the federal agency involved. The type of financing may be short-, medium- or long-term, depending upon the terms of the agency's support and the needs of the borrower.

Farm Mortgage Companies. Farm mortgage companies provide credit for farm and home purchases. These mortgages may be private or backed by government institutions such as the Farmers Home Administration (FHA).

The Farmers Home Administration helps farmers get mortgages for homes or personal farms. The agency, a division of the Department of Agriculture, operates under the Consolidated Farmers Home Administration Act of 1961, Title V of the Housing Act of 1949, and Part III, Title A of the Economic Opportunity Act of 1964. It was originally established under the Farmers Home Administration Act of 1946.

The Farmers Home Administration operates primarily in rural areas. Offices, located in county-seat towns, accept applications for loans that are designed to provide enough income to raise families' living standards to allow them to make payments on their debts. The applications are reviewed and approved by a local committee that is composed of three people, at least two of which must be farmers. The money for the loans and grants made by the administration come from appropriations from Congress and private lenders who make loans guaranteed by the agency.

Finance Leasing of Equipment and Vehicles. The acquisition of equipment and vehicles represents a significant capital investment. Therefore, most equipment and vehicle purchases are made with the help of some type of financing, often leasing. Lease financing is typically made by banks and finance companies. Under a lease arrangement the financier retains the title to the equipment. The customer typically makes monthly payments and has an option to buy the equipment at the end of the lease period.

Intermediate Investment Banks. The twelve Federal Intermediate Credit Banks (FICBs) were created by Title II of the Federal Farm Loan Act of 1923. These banks were created to discount or buy short- and intermediate-term notes of agricultural business from commercial banks, savings and loans, and other financial institutions.

The FICBs work closely with Production Credit Associations (PCAs). PCAs are primary lenders that provide rural communities with short- and medium-term credit for a variety of needs. The loans they offer vary in maturity length from a few months to seven years. The PCAs often work in conjunction with commercial banks to provide these services to their rural customers. As primary lenders, the PCAs sustain all losses to the extent of available resources. The PCAs have adopted mutual loss sharing, participating loan plans, or both, to spread their risk. The borrowers of the individual PCAs elect that institution's directors.

The FICBs loan money to farmers, ranchers, producers and harvesters of aquatic products, operators providing farm services, and rural residents. They make loans to and discount commercial paper for local financial institutions. The FICBs also help the Production Credit Associations in making sound credit available in rural areas. The FICBs issue stock and sell participation certificates to raise capital. The majority of their loans are made for production purposes and mature within one year. Farm and rural home loans, however, may have extended terms of up to 10 years. Loans to producers and harvesters of aquatic products may be made for up to 15 years.

Small Business Investment Companies. Investment companies are typically involved in three activities: investing, reinvesting, or trading securities; issuing face amount certificates of the installment type; and holding investment securities having a market value exceeding 40 percent of the issuer's total assets.

In the United States, investment companies are a relatively new phenomenon. They did not become commonplace until after 1923, and grew quickly through the 1960s, leading to increased regulation. Investment companies are regulated by the Securities and Exchange Commission (SEC). In general, there are five areas of regulation: registration, adequacy of capital, conservatism of capital structure, investment policies, and management practices and procedures. The SEC periodically inspects investment companies to ensure compliance with their regulations.

Livestock Loan Companies. Livestock loan companies are sanctioned by the Federal Reserve Act as companies organized for the purpose of lending credit to cattlemen and ranchers for the purchase, raising, and marketing of cattle and other livestock. They may be either independent institutions or affiliated with local banks. As affiliates, livestock loan companies are exempted from the restrictions outlined in Section 23-A of the Federal Reserve Act.

There are several steps in making a livestock loan: the borrower provides a sworn statement of his/her financial condition, the cattle are inspected, a search of public records to determine the status of any liens is completed, a chattel mortgage is executed, usually at 25 percent above the amount of the loan, and the note is executed.

Livestock loan companies relieve commercial banks of the burden of carrying cattle paper, which often amounts to several million dollars. These companies frequently act as intermediaries between borrowers and money center banks. They may also be involved in rediscounting some classes of cattle paper for purchase by the Federal Reserve Banks.

Machinery and Equipment Finance Leasing. Since machinery and equipment represent a significant expenditure of cash, most businesses finance these purchases. Leasing is one type of financing arrangement. As with automobile leasing, the financier keeps the title to the equipment, while the customer typically makes monthly or quarterly payments and has an option to buy the equipment at the end of the lease period.

INDUSTRY LEADERS

In a March 1999 issue, *American Banker* listed the top 10 finance companies based on commercial receivables and total receivables for 1998. Atop both lists was General Electric Capital Services of Stamford, Connecticut, with $77 billion in commercial receivables and $122 billion in total receivables, up 17.12 percent from 1997. Ford Motor Credit Co. of Dearborn, Michigan came in second place in commercial receivables with $28 billion, but it outpaced GE Capital in total receivables with $131 billion, up 12.45 percent over 1997. General Motors Acceptance Corp. of Detroit rivaled Ford in commercial receivables with $27 billion, but GM lagged behind Ford in total receivables with $99 billion, up 16.46 percent from 1997.

Rounding out the top 10 were the following companies: Associates First Capital Corp. of Irving, Texas, with $24 billion in 1998 commercial receivables and $61 billion in total receivables, up 10.37 percent from 1997; IBM Credit Corp. of Stamford, Connecticut, with $14 billion in 1998 commercial as well as total receivables, down 5.33 percent from 1997; CIT Group Holdings Inc.

of New York City; Heller Financial Inc. of Chicago; FINOVA Group Inc. of Phoenix, Arizona; Caterpillar Financial Services Corp. of Nashville, Tennessee; and Philip Morris Capital Corp. of Stamford, Connecticut.

WORKFORCE

Each of the organizations covered in this industry classification are small or medium-sized companies employing between one and 25,000 employees as loan officers, secretaries, financial analysts, managerial staff, and clerks, to name a few.

These organizations are spread throughout the country. Some of these organizations are government related and have employees concentrated in the greater Washington, D.C., area. Similarly, since many of the organizations serve rural constituencies, a significant portion of the industry's workforce lives in communities of less that 50,000 inhabitants.

FURTHER READING

"Annual Report on American Industry." *Forbes,* 3 January 1994, 144.

Lazich, Robert S., ed. *Market Share Reporter.* Detroit: Gale Research, 1997.

Standard and Poor's Register of Corporations, Directors, and Executives. New York: Standard & Poor's, 1996.

SIC 6162

MORTGAGE BANKERS AND LOAN CORRESPONDENTS

This industry covers establishments primarily engaged in originating mortgage loans, selling mortgage loans to permanent investors, and servicing these loans. They may also provide real estate construction loans.

NAICS CODE(S)

522292 (Real Estate Credit)

522390 (Other Activities Related to Credit Intermediation)

INDUSTRY SNAPSHOT

The mortgage loan industry differs from other industries in its passivity: whereas new products and services can create new markets in other industries, the mortgage industry remains at the mercy of home owners and buyers, who almost never buy on impulse. Instead of creating new markets, mortgage bankers must respond to existing markets and anticipate marketplace changes, transforming their services in reaction to larger societal forces, such as population demographics and interest rates. This passivity forces the industry to be dynamic, constantly shifting to meet new demands, such as rising rates of first-time home buyers, and take advantage of new opportunities, such as e-commerce. At its core, the mortgage industry remains solid because home ownership represents an enduring aspect of American life.

The mortgage financing industry experienced record-high results for combined purchase and refinancing transactions of $1.02 trillion in 1993; 1998 results surpassed this high-water mark, with projections calling for continued growth in mortgage-banking activities through 2000. Double-digit interest rates still existed in 1993, thus refinancing fueled that year's record transactions. In 1998, refinancing still accounted for some transactions, as borrowers took advantage of low interest rates to decrease their mortgage payments from above 8 percent to below 7 percent, with predictions calling for the rate to drop to 6.5 percent. These low interest rates also fueled unprecedented growth in new transactions, particularly by the growing segments of first-time home buyers, low-income buyers, minorities, and immigrants. Lenders realized that fair and affordable lending not only made ethical sense, but also made very good business sense.

The advent of electronic commerce via the Internet in the late-1990s significantly transformed the mortgage financing industry. Janina Pawlowski and Christina Larsen, co-owners of the Palo Alto Funding Group, spent the mid-1990s trying to finance an online version of their mortgage firm with little success, as potential backers could not conceive of selling mortgages through a Web site. However, the pair found financial support to launch E-Loan, their web-based mortgage company, in 1997. Over the next two years, the concept of transacting mortgages online gained credence, prompting other major lenders to set up their own Web sites. While online lending will never fully replace in-person mortgage sales, as the Internet cannot provide the kind of personalized service and comfort of individualized service by a mortgage expert, e-commerce has radically transformed the shape of the mortgage services industry in the late-1990s.

ORGANIZATION AND STRUCTURE

As liaisons, mortgage bankers are more than just loan brokers, because they maintain a responsible presence from the time mortgage loans are created until they are paid in full. The mortgage banker functions in a continuum extending from the seller/builder of the property to the seller's agent, to the mortgage borrower, to the mortgagee (the mortgage banker), and to the mortgage investor. Mortgage bankers specialize in the origination or production of mortgage loans for sale to the secondary mortgage market. Many mortgage lenders make or buy loans, while some sell loans, and others service loans. Mortgage bankers link the three functions.

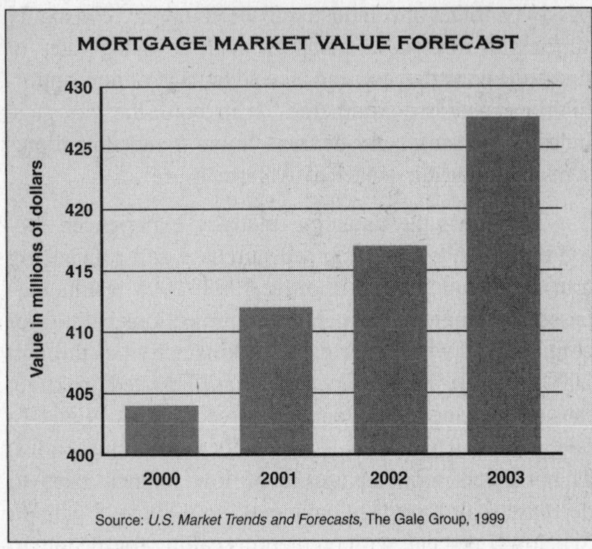

Source: *U.S. Market Trends and Forecasts*, The Gale Group, 1999

The housing finance system in the United States includes many private and public institutions and several levels of market activity. The mortgage lending/investment process involves the provision of housing credit to borrowers by institutions and individuals who hold housing loans in their portfolios. However, a number of institutions may come between the ultimate investors, and the characteristics of the mortgage asset may be transformed along the way as insurance and guarantees are attached and as securities replace the original mortgage loans.

Residential mortgage loans are made (originated) in primary markets where lenders and borrowers conduct business. Borrowers get mortgage credit in these markets mainly from depository institutions or mortgage banking companies. Since the 1930s, mortgage loans made in primary markets typically have been long-term, fixed-rate instruments with level payments that pay off (amortize) the principal balance over the term of the loan. However, new types of mortgage instruments emerged recently to serve the various needs of borrowers and investors. Most of the new mortgage instruments provide for adjustable interest rates, graduated payment schedules, or some combination of these features.

Institutions operating in primary mortgage markets may hold the mortgages they originate, adding them to their asset portfolios. In many cases, however, originators sell their loan production on secondary markets, thereby replenishing their supplies of loanable money. Transfers of outstanding mortgages among mortgage investors also take place in secondary markets.

Sales of mortgage loans from originators to investors inevitably involve some cost, but such transfers are often necessary for the effective functioning of the housing finance system. Secondary market transactions may be needed to correct interregional imbalances in the supply of and demand for mortgage credit, or to move mortgage assets from one type of institution to another within the same market area. The latter need arises within a system characterized by specialization and division of labor. One type of institution may perform a mortgage banking function, specializing in mortgage origination and servicing and selling assets to investors who choose not to perform these functions. Such a division of functions can be encouraged by federal or state regulations governing the activities of various types of institutions.

There are several types of loan instruments available to individual and institutional investors:

Fixed-rate Mortgages. Historically, 30-year fixed-rate mortgages have been the loan instrument of choice for many borrowers. The changing conditions in the mortgage market, however, coupled with sharp fluctuations in interest rates, have increased the demand for shorter maturities, more interest-sensitive loans, and nontraditional mortgage instruments.

Adjustable-Rate Mortgages (ARMs). Because of the thrift crisis in the late 1980s, lenders began offering adjustable rate mortgages. Lenders, buffeted by interest rate risk, looked to shift the risk to the borrower. In exchange, they offered borrowers a lower initial rate. What was once an instrument designed to keep housing affordable during periods of high interest rates turned into an interest rate gamble for a growing number of borrowers. Borrowers that opt for fixed-rate loans anticipate stable or increasing interest rates. If they are wrong they can refinance later. Borrowers that choose adjustable plans believe that rates will decline. The ARM in its brief history has shown resilience as a loan product and unexpected risk for borrowers and lenders.

Convertible ARMs. These instruments have been available for years, but have been marketed aggressively only during high interest rate periods. This type of mortgage vehicle gives the borrower the benefit of a low initial rate with the option to refinance to a fixed-rate mortgage at about half the typical refinance cost. The convertible ARM may be attractive to lenders with loan-servicing portfolios, since they would be less likely to see refinance business go elsewhere. If the borrower switches to a fixed-rate mortgage when rates are low, however, the lender will have a portfolio of low-rate, fixed-rate loans.

Shorter Term Mortgages. Fixed-rate mortgages with terms shorter than the traditional 30-year instruments have become tremendously popular since the early 1980s. They are expected to become increasingly popular as borrowers see the value of their mortgage interest deductions decline as they move into lower tax brackets. Moreover, during periods of low inflation, borrowers can pay down their principle in cheaper dollars. The 15-year loan historically had rates between 40 and 50 basis points (a basis point is equal to 0.01 percent) below the 30-year loan, and has lower overall financing costs. The higher monthly costs make the 15-year loan available mainly to affluent borrowers. This has helped keep default rates low, making it a good intermediate term asset for portfolio lenders and attractive to investors. Industry estimates place default rates on 15-year loans at about half that of 30-year mortgages.

Bi-Weekly Mortgages. Bi-weekly mortgages are similar to 15-year or 30-year mortgages except that the borrower pays half of the scheduled monthly payments every two weeks. This creates the equivalent of 13 monthly payments a year, resulting in a much faster pay-off. A 30-year mortgage would be paid off in 19 years with this instrument. Virtually all bi-weeklies are fixed-rate loans, and much of the bi-weekly volume is generated by refinancing. Borrowers take advantage of declining rates to lock in a fixed-rate, shorter term loan with slightly lower monthly payments. Lenders target sophisticated, second- and third-time home buyers for this product. The loan usually is tied to a checking or deposit account from which payments are debited directly. Delinquency rates on this instrument are extremely low, especially in cases in which the financial institution requires one or two payments to be kept in the deposit account at all times.

Home Equity Loans. Since the passage of 1986 tax reform legislation, home equity loans have become increasingly popular. These loans generally are tied to the prime rate, and may be tax deductible. They are usually revolving lines of credit with little standardization. Because of this, there is not an active secondary market for home equity loans. Investors are wary of potentially high default rates, as well as how legislators will respond to the collection process.

Portable Mortgages. A loan for movers, the portable mortgage traveled to the United States from Canada (as did the bi-weekly). With a portable loan, the lender hopes to keep the mortgage loan even in the event of relocation by the borrower. A borrower who moves to another house may take this loan with him without paying additional points. In the event that a borrower needs additional money, they are added to the loan at the prevailing rates, making a portable blend.

BACKGROUND AND DEVELOPMENT

For most of its history, the mortgage banking business was comprised of a relatively small number of independent firms who acted as intermediaries between borrowers and permanent mortgage investors. The major part of their activities concentrated on residential loan origination, and most of that consisted of Federal Housing Administration (FHA) and Veterans Administration (VA) loan production. Savings and loan associations dominated most of the conventional residential market and there were few sources of mortgage capital besides such traditional mortgage investors as thrifts and life insurance companies. It was, for the most part, a private market where available capital disappeared when interest rates rose and capital availability tightened.

Before 1970, the Federal National Mortgage Association (Fannie Mae) provided one of the few national secondary markets through its whole-loan purchase and sale program. Even that program, however, was limited to government loans. The establishment of the Federal Home Loan Mortgage Association (Freddie Mac) in 1970 and the entrance of Fannie Mae and Freddie Mac into the conventional secondary market in 1972 initiated the expansion and rise in importance of secondary market activities for all mortgage lenders. This factor manifested itself through the standardization of loan documentation and underwriting criteria and a consistent market presence that the private secondary market had never achieved.

The 1980s were a transitional period for mortgage bankers. The first great challenge was the high level of interest rates that all but shut down origination volume. Creative lenders took advantage of liberalized lending regulations, and the result was a vast expansion in the menu of mortgage banking products, including more than 200 types of adjustable rate mortgages and a sometimes bewildering profusion of graduated payment, growing equity, shared equity, wrap, and second mortgage loans. As so often happens, the wishes of consumers and investors were diametrically opposed: investors demanded loans that would adjust immediately to the market, while consumers sought out loans that looked as fixed as possible (with lower interest rates of course). For a long while mortgage bankers despaired as thrifts dominated the origination market with teaser rate Adjustable Rate Mortgages.

The marketplace eventually winnowed the product menu down to a few manageable choices, and the lower interest rates of the late 1980s increased the popularity of fixed rate loans. The competitiveness of mortgage bankers was enhanced not only by the return of a fixed rate environment, but also by two other factors that dramatically changed the industry: the savings and loan crisis and the rise to dominance of Mortgage-Backed Securities (MBS).

The thrift industry was at once a blessing and a bane: while thrift investors were primary outlets for whole loan products, thrift originators were frequently unbeatable competitors. However, the same short-sighted impulse that led thrifts to aggressively push market teaser rate ARMs (some of which had caps below the prevailing level of fixed rates) led to a multitude of other dubious business decisions that sealed their fate. At the same time that thrifts were diminishing in importance as investors, the MBS was coming into its own. By the late 1980s, even ARMs and jumbo loans were being packaged into generic MBS and resold through Wall Street to institutional investors, many of whom would never dream of investing in a whole loan product. Early fears that the thrift investor base could never be replaced proved groundless. The MBS products provided an ongoing source of capital.

By the mid-1980s, government deregulation, lax underwriting standards, and some of the more dubious products offered earlier in the decade were producing catastrophic results. Lenders passed on risks to mortgage insurers, many of which failed to adequately monitor the situation. Losses mounted because of the growing number of loan defaults. Industry analysts pointed to payment shock or equity erosion or other factors as the reason. It eventually became clear that equity was the single most important determination of credit risk. As underwriter ratios were tightened, many underwriters complained that the insurance companies were punishing them for the borrowers' sins. Gradually, insurers analyzed the delinquency and default experience of millions of loans and arrived at sensible standards that protected the interests of borrowers, lenders, insurers, and investors.

Just as the early 1980s were dominated by the effects of high interest rates, the second half of the decade was strongly influenced by declining interest rates. This had several profound effects. Origination and refinance volume soared, and this opened up many profitable opportunities for mortgage bankers. As a result, new products began increasing the investor base for mortgage loans while at the same time dampening the volatility of most mortgage bankers' earnings.

As a result of economic fluctuations of the 1980s and early 1990s, mortgage banking and the mortgage finance industry began to undergo fundamental changes that altered the role of traditional participants, opened the market to new players, saw Wall Street emerge as a major provider of mortgage capital, and radically changed the nature of the secondary mortgage market.

The dramatic changes in mortgage banking have been driven by a series of developments that have affected all financial services. Each development would have been significant in its own right, but in combination, have altered mortgage financing beyond recognition.

Mortgage Securities and Wall Street. Mortgage lenders recognized long ago that the original secondary market lacked the ability to consistently provide mortgage capital in the amounts needed or the geographic distribution required to adequately meet the housing needs of the nation. With no central marketplace, an awkward and unliquid investment vehicle, and nonstandard documentation, mortgages could not compete in the capital markets when demands for capital exceeded the available supply from thrifts and other portfolio lenders.

Mortgage-backed securities, which offered access to the broad investor base and capital formation abilities of Wall Street, were revived with the creation of the Government National Mortgage Association (GNMA, or Ginnie Mae) in 1968 and the issuance of the first GNMA pass-through securities in 1970. Mortgage-backed bonds had once been widely used in the 1920s, but had a dismal record in the depression of the 1930s. With the government guarantees on the underlying mortgage collateral and on the securities themselves, GNMA securities traded on Wall Street began to attract nontraditional mortgage investors. At about the same time, Freddie Mac initiated pass-through securities backed by conventional residential mortgages. By the mid-1970s, residential mortgages, government and conventional, had been accepted as viable security collateral by the investment community. The result was a rapid growth in the volumes and types of mortgage securities in the marketplace.

In addition to reaching a huge investor base and new sources of capital, the securities markets offer a speed of execution and efficiency of pricing that the traditional secondary mortgage markets cannot match. As a result, the securities markets have been outlets for increasingly large percentages of residential mortgage production. Securities markets drive mortgage pricing nationwide, heavily influence mortgage product design, and reduce the mortgage finance industry's reliance on mortgage portfolio lenders.

Economic Influences. Since the early 1980s, as mortgage securities were assuming a major role in mortgage financing, changes occurred in the basic economics of all financial markets that have forced major alterations in the way mortgage banking operations are planned and managed. The magnitude of interest rate movements and the speed with which they occur have reached levels unknown and unanticipated before the 1980s. The collapse of mortgage security prices in the spring of 1987 illustrated the potential volatility of the market, which can be influenced by factors unrelated to mortgage rates or the housing capital markets.

This volatility made the mortgage banker's job of risk management much more complex and difficult. Mortgage bankers put together strategies and operating procedures, which include sophisticated reporting systems, to monitor and control the risk exposure of their operations.

Further complexities have been added to the business with the wider variety of mortgage products offered to borrowers, whose preferences often shift from one loan type to another as the economic climate and expectations change. This tendency is illustrated by the changing market share of originations by fixed-rate, adjustable-rate, and balloon loans. As mortgage rates fall, fixed-rate products and balloon loans tend to dominate the market. As rates rise, lower initial rates bring adjustable products a larger share of the market. The mortgage banker's risk position changes with each shift, and swift action is required to maintain prescribed risk exposure limits.

As the economics of the marketplace changed, so have the economics of mortgage banking. The industry has become a complex financial services business requiring analytical skills and financial modeling and forecasting abilities far beyond the levels necessary in the past. The resources required to compete effectively made it challenging for the small, independent firm to survive and nearly all of the medium and large mortgage banking operations are now subsidiaries of larger diversified institutions.

With the dominant role of mortgage securities and the impact of economic changes felt in all sectors of the mortgage finance industry, the composition of the participants in the industry has also changed. Wall Street firms, commercial banks, nonfinancial corporate giants, and traditional portfolio lenders are playing a part in mortgage banking with various degrees of influence and success.

Securities dealers have become the primary market makers as the bulk of residential mortgage originations are used to collateralize mortgage securities, primarily through secondary loans originating from Freddie Mac, Fannie Mae, and Ginnie Mae. Many major Wall Street firms ventured into primary, or direct, mortgage banking activities in the 1980s, establishing their own mortgage banking operations, and buying and selling mortgages and loan servicing rights. Most of these ventures disappeared or are serving small, specialized markets and Wall Street's emphasis returned to mortgage securities and the derivative securities that developed as the mortgage security markets matured. Some of the industry leaders in this area include: Goldman Sachs, Salomon Brothers, and The First Boston Corporation.

In 1996, Fannie Mae held a portfolio of more than $286 billion in secondary home mortgages and Freddie Mac held a $610 billion portfolio. Countrywide Credit Industries, Inc. led the primary lending market in 1996 with roughly $22 billion in loans concentrated in California.

Thrift institutions and the thrift industry have been decimated by the consequences of the excesses, incompetence, and fraud of the 1980s. They are no longer the major source of mortgage capital and their market share dropped from 41 percent of the loan origination market in 1987 to 24 percent in 1992. About 2,000 viable institutions remained after the cleanup was completed, but their presence in the market has been severely diminished. Most thrifts will continue to maintain a mortgage loan portfolio, but not on a scale that will make them primary sources of mortgage money as they had been before the 1980s.

Commercial banks, particularly such large national banks and bank holding companies as Fleet National, Chase Manhattan/Chemical, and Bank of America, emerged as major players in mortgage banking. Many of the nation's largest mortgage banking operations are subsidiaries of these institutions. The banks view mortgage banking as a natural extension of their mortgage lending operations and as a cross-selling opportunity, while the mortgage banking operations benefit from the credit facilities and financial presence of the parent institution in the marketplace.

Nonfinancial corporations and holding companies acquired or built some of the largest mortgage banking operations in the country with mixed results. Some operations have done very well and continue to prosper, but others have struggled. As in the case of commercial banks, the parent organization has to understand the business of mortgage banking and the operating disciplines that it requires if the mortgage banking operation is to succeed.

Life insurance companies and pension funds have long been viewed by mortgage bankers as prime sources of mortgage funds, but tapping these sources has not been easy. Life insurance companies returned to residential mortgage investment in the 1980s, after effectively leaving the field 20 years earlier, but most did so by setting up their own mortgage companies. Like Wall Street's venture into mortgage banking, most of these operations have been closed or shut down, although several life insurance companies, such as Prudential Home Mortgage and Metropolitan Life, have had success in the mortgage banking segment. Pension funds rarely provide mortgage bankers with direct access to money and tend to invest in mortgages through mortgage securities.

Investment in mortgages by individuals has grown faster than all expectations. Individuals generally prefer Ginnie Mae securities and often invest through mutual funds. As with pension funds, individual investors funnel money directly to the mortgage market. In doing so, individuals receive a higher yield on their investment than they would by depositing their money in savings institutions.

Like the broader financial services industry, the mortgage industry continued to be swept by changes during the 1990s. These changes were driven by deregulation, competition, and technological advances. Since the 1980s, private mortgage companies that do little but originate loans have become the main source of mortgage lending. There were approximately 4,000 of these companies in the United States in 1996 (out of about 12,000 total organizations making mortgage loans) and they accounted for nearly 60 percent of all new mortgage loans, or originations. This is nearly double the share that mortgage companies had in 1987. The next largest source by volume of mortgages was commercial banks, followed by the thrift industries, which as recently as 10 years earlier had domi-

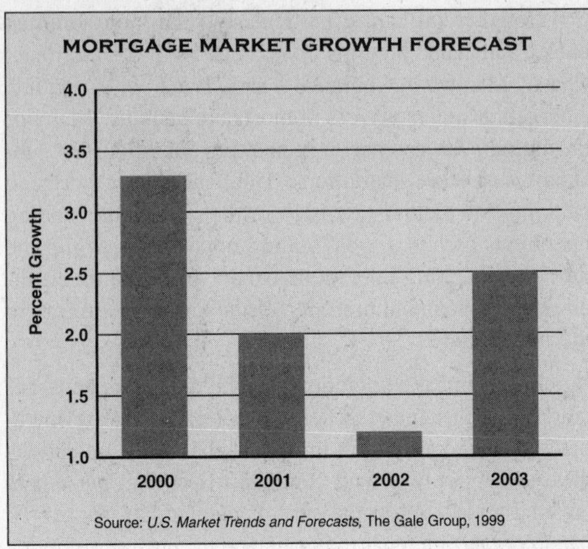

Source: *U.S. Market Trends and Forecasts*, The Gale Group, 1999

nated the industry. Other mortgage lenders included credit unions and life insurance companies. During 1996, some $784 billion in one-to-four-unit residential mortgage loans were originated in the United States. That is somewhat below the peak of just over $1 trillion worth of loans originated in 1993, but the record year had been strongly influenced by a wave of refinancings as mortgage rates dipped to their lowest point in years.

While the cost of entry into loan origination continues to be low, the financial sources necessary to compete and succeed as a full service mortgage banker increased dramatically. As a result, the industry is increasingly dominated by the largest players, behemoths like General Motors Acceptance Corporation (GMAC), which in 1996 originated more than $3.4 billion of new residential loans representing more than 30,000 home loans.

Although there may always be a profitable niche for small originators, that niche may be in mortgage brokerage, and the outlook for the medium-sized mortgage banking firm that services its own loans is much less certain.

A number of the largest mortgage bankers grew very quickly in the late 1980s and early 1990s through bulk purchases of loan portfolios. The secondary market for mortgage loan securitization fueled the growth in origination volume. Although the volume of mortgages sold into the secondary market tends to vary with changes in the volume of fixed-rate lending (as opposed to variable rate loans) the percent of home loans sold through the secondary market in 1996 was 56 percent. That was down from a peak of 65 percent during 1993, but it represents a sizable increase over the 33 percent level of 1988, when the market was not as mature.

CURRENT CONDITIONS

Consolidation transformed the mortgage loan industry in the 1990s. Since 1980. 7,000 banking institutions have merged, though few of these mergers centered around mortgage financing. However, the consolidations did affect the industry: in 1990, 28 percent of home loans originated from 25 lenders; as of September 1998, the top 25 lenders accounted for 53 percent of home loans. In October 1999, Intuit Inc. of Mountainview, California, paid $370 million in stock to buyout market leader Rock Financial Corp. of Bingham Farms, Michigan, which generated 1998 revenues of $90 million and closed more than $2.3 billion worth of residential loans in 1998. Intuit merged Rock's Web site, RockLoans.com, with its own loan site, QuickenMortgage.com. In addition to consolidations, the industry experienced spin-offs: in 1998, for example, Ford Motor Co. spun off Associates First Capital Corp., which earned $387 million in the third quarter of 1999, a 22 percent increase over third quarter 1998, thus signaling the success of this spin-off.

The process of consolidation did not always create more efficiency, though; often, newly-consolidated companies experienced growing pains, and the quality of their service declined. In this climate, niche lenders and small, local specialists thrived. For example, companies responsive to the Hispanic market stood to gain from the demographic and economic growth of this sector. Whereas Hispanics made up 11 percent of the population in the late 1990s, this population accounted for 18 percent of all new homeowners from 1996 through 1998. In the first half of the decade, Hispanic owner-occupied housing units increased 34 percent. The U.S. Bureau of the Census forecasted the Hispanic population to grow to 15 percent of the total U.S. population by 2015 and 25 percent by 2050. Companies such as Countrywide Home Loans, Inc., of Pasadena, California, benefited from these demographics by employing bilingual employees and translating loan literature into Spanish.

Another niche market in the late 1990s was the emergent trend of the so-called money-back home loan, which allowed borrowers' monthly payments to be placed in an insurance policy rather than against the principal of the loan. At the end of the term, the value of the policy could potentially exceed the principal of the loan and provide the borrower with a cash payment of the surplus. This method was common in international markets such as the United Kingdom but was still relatively new in the United States.

Forecasts called for the continued growth of the total outstanding mortgage debt, which would increase by 7 percent to 9 percent annually, according to Fannie Mae. The Board of Governors of the Federal Reserve pegged the total outstanding mortgage debt at $4 trillion at the end of 1997; according to projections, this figure would reach almost $6 trillion by 2002.

FURTHER READING

Bove, Richard X. "Mortgage Industry: Boom or Bust?" *The Journal of Lending & Credit Risk Management,* September 1998.

Habal, Habal. "Intuit in $370M Deal for Rock Financial; To Sell Loans at QuickenMortgage Site." *American Banker,* 8 October 1999.

"In Brief: Associates 1st Reports 22% Rise in 3Q Profits." *American Banker,* 13 October 1999.

Mozillo, Angelo R. "Emerging Opportunities: Growth Through New Market Development." *Mortgage Banking,* October 1998

———. "Mortgage Milestones in the Year Ahead." *Mortgage Banking,* 1 January 1999.

Wise, Christy. "Three Strategies." *Mortgage Banking,* April 1998.

SIC 6163

LOAN BROKERS

This category covers establishments primarily engaged in arranging loans for others. These establishments operate mostly on a commission or fee basis and do not ordinarily have any continuing relationship with either borrower or lender.

NAICS CODE(S)

522310 (Mortgage and Other Loan Brokers)

INDUSTRY SNAPSHOT

The loan brokers industry is comprised of firms principally engaged in arranging loans between borrowers and lenders. Such enterprises commonly earn a fee or commission for their services. The industry is dominated by mortgage brokers, though loan agents also arrange miscellaneous business, farm, and personal loans.

Although loan agents and brokers have existed for centuries, the industry received little respect or attention before the 1980s. In fact, as late as the mid-1980s, brokers were relatively insignificant players in the multibillion dollar mortgage lending business. In the late 1980s and early 1990s, however, several factors combined to propel the industry to unprecedented stature. Low interest rates, a trend toward outsourcing and contracting by financial institutions, and a shift in the structure of U.S. financial markets were the most prominent forces boosting industry success.

In 1996, mortgage brokers were originating more than $400 billion in loans annually. This was equivalent to about 50 percent of all mortgages originated in the United States and was an increase from 20 percent in 1987. Furthermore, firms in this industry were reaping healthy profits in the early 1990s. The average mortgage brokerage firm owner earned more than $100,000 in profit during 1993, while staff originators earned more than $60,000. Although the business is cyclical, prospects for long-term growth in this unique cottage industry were positive going into the mid-1990s.

Mortgage loan brokers in late 1997 began offering a variety of mortgage options for customers, including the adjustable rate (ARM) mortgage (designed to help customers take advantage of low rates but placing the risk on the customers' shoulders should rates suddenly climb) and hybrid or two step mortgages. Two step mortgages offered customers an initially low five to seven year rate, with the rate then climbing above the market rate. These loans served to let customers borrow with a lower outlay and the hybrid mortgage qualified buyers for more money than under traditional mortgage qualifying means. 1997 also saw the continued popularity of second mortgages and mortgage lender like Green Tree Financial and First Plus Financial made an estimated $10 billion worth of these loans in 1997, twice the amount made in 1996.

In late 1999 at least two lenders were preparing to retain customers with good credit in anticipation of future mortgage refinancing trends. Although rates began to rise again in December 1999, City Line Mortgage, of San Diego, California, and Service Savers, of Fairfax, Virginia, offered fixed rate mortgages that featured rates that dropped when the interest rate dropped, and rates that didn't rise if the interest rate rose. At least for this segment of the industry, the cost of such loans were outweighed by the chance to retain good customers.

ORGANIZATION AND STRUCTURE

Although loan agents and brokers serve other markets, mortgage loans comprise the vast majority of industry sales. The four-step mortgage lending process includes: originating the loan, which entails approving and selling a mortgage to a customer; funding or underwriting the loan; selling the mortgage in the secondary mortgage market, which supplies lenders with cash to make new loans; and servicing the loan, which involves collection, reporting, and administrative management duties. Most mortgage brokers are concerned only with the first step of the process, mortgage origination. However, some brokers facilitate the buying and selling of mortgages in the secondary market.

A broker, by definition, acts as an intermediary between a buyer and a seller in a transaction. He may represent either party, and he does not take possession of goods or property or deal on his own account. The broker receives a fee or commission from one or both of the parties that is usually based on a percentage of the value of the transaction. Brokers differ from dealers in that dealers are transacting on their own account and may have a vested interest in the transaction. Brokers fill an important marketing need by bringing buyers and sellers together. They also facilitate transactions by providing expertise and advice to buyers and sellers.

The two basic types of mortgage brokers are retail and wholesale. A retail broker, or third party originator (TPO), takes a loan application from a potential buyer and submits it to a lender. The lender reviews the application to determine whether or not to grant the loan. If the lender makes the loan to the applicant, the broker secures a commission, usually between 1 percent and 2 percent of the loan amount. Some lenders also pay a fee to the broker for rejected applications.

Wholesale mortgage brokers represent a smaller segment of the industry. They arrange the purchase and sale of mortgages that have already been originally funded. They help bankers find investors for their mortgages, so that the bank will have money to make new loans, for example. They also solicit retail brokers and mortgage originators that are seeking the most beneficial mortgage terms for their clients.

Mortgage brokers can deliver many benefits to lenders and borrowers. For instance, because brokers are able to efficiently search several institutions to find the best terms, they save time for consumers and help them get the lowest rates and closing costs. In addition, brokers often act as their customers' advocate, walking them through the application process and helping them to avoid delays caused by minor technicalities. Sometimes they are even able to reduce closing costs or waive special fees. Brokers commonly speed up the mortgage process by providing a candid preliminary assessment of what a buyer can afford before the consumer applies for a loan. Brokers are also able to offer several different mortgage options to buyers, whereas individual lenders usually have a more limited selection of lending instruments.

Mortgage brokers benefit the lending industry by providing a more flexible and less costly channel for originating mortgages. Brokers can alleviate a bank's or saving and loan's need to hire and support a sales staff, for instance. By outsourcing their origination activities, banks are able to eliminate many management and administrative costs, education and training expenses, facility expenditures, and salaries and benefits required by an in-house mortgage origination staff. Brokers also allow lenders to geographically diversify their lending operations and to enter and exit different markets very quickly.

Types of Brokers. Most mortgage brokers can be classified into one of four different categories, though "full-service" firms may participate in two or more areas of the business. Traditional mortgage brokers are typically lenders of last resort. Consumers sometimes turn to this type of broker when they are unable to secure a market rate loan through a lending institution. As a result, these agents usually deal with high-risk, high-interest loans, and often participate in the fractionalization of mortgages, meaning that more than one investor is involved with a single mortgage.

Conventional residential mortgage brokers represent 70 to 90 percent of the industry. These professionals work with consumers to secure the best possible loan terms for their particular needs. They represent products offered by the largest financial institutions that are indirectly supported by government sponsored secondary market institutions, such as Fannie Mae and Freddie Mac. Wholesale brokers are also included in this group.

Commercial mortgage brokers arrange loans for nonresidential or multifamily properties. This market differs in that it is not supported by secondary market agencies, and it is not subject to the state and federal regulation imposed to protect residential consumers. Commercial brokerage fees are often three or four times greater than residential mortgage commissions. However, lucrative fees can be elusive because commercial loans are much more difficult to close. Commercial brokers also deal with a wider variety of lenders, including insurance companies, pension funds, and foreign investors.

A fourth sector of the industry is made up of firms that broker government and miscellaneous loans. Federal Housing Administration and Veteran's Administration loans make up most of this market.

Competitive Structure. In 1997, the National Association of Mortgage Brokers (NAMB) boasted a membership of 5,000, one-third the number of total brokers in the country. They also had chapters in 38 states. The industry is difficult to track because many of its participants overlap into other lending, banking, and brokerage activities, and because it was growing very quickly in the early 1990s.

Most brokerage firms are very small shops with between one and 10 employees. Some firms have as many as 50 workers. Though they are self-employed, some brokers act as agents, working only for a single lender. Such agents and brokers usually operate on 100 percent commission, but may also receive health benefits or application fees. Other brokerage arrangements include franchise operations which maintain chains of mortgage brokering shops on a regional or national scale.

The industry is regulated primarily through state laws that are designed to protect consumers against fraud and to discourage financial misconduct. Although some states, such as Mississippi, have few constraints, others have more advanced regulatory structures. Florida, for instance, required brokers to take 24 hours of classes on mortgage finance before applying for a license in the early 1990s, and required brokers to disclose all fees that they received. In Illinois, brokers are licensed annually and tested every other year, their loans are spot-checked, they must be bonded, and they must prove a net worth of $25,000. The American Association of Residential Mortgage Regulators (AARMR), which served as a clearinghouse for reports of industry fraud in the industry, was trying to encourage more uniform state legislation in the early 1990s.

BACKGROUND AND DEVELOPMENT

Mortgage lending in the United States was limited before the 1930s. Savings institutions and life insurance companies were the primary lenders for home buyers. They often relied on mortgage bankers to originate and service their loans. These lenders typically required a 50 percent down payment on a piece of property, and usually offered a loan term of only five years. Because lenders placed themselves at significant risk in these transactions, they charged high interest rates. As a result, the market for mortgage loans was negligible in the early part of the twentieth century.

The Great Depression, which catapulted large numbers of mortgages into foreclosure and bankrupted many lenders, gave birth to a new lending system in the United States. Realizing the need for a stable and accessible mortgage market, the federal government created the Federal Home Loan Bank (FHLB) system in 1932, the Home Owners Loan Act in 1933, and other programs that sought to reduce the risk of mortgage lending and enforce industry standards. These initiatives, along with FHA and VA programs, served to insure mortgages with government funds and to protect consumers.

The mortgage banking industry flourished in the postwar economic boom. Banks and other financial institutions, which bought many mortgage banking operations, integrated origination and servicing activities into their organizations. As mortgage lending ballooned, the secondary mortgage market evolved as a place for lenders to sell their loans to investors. Wholesale mortgage brokers emerged to unite these investors and lenders.

Although some retail brokers also served the industry in the 1960s and 1970s, loan origination remained an activity provided almost solely by mortgage banks and savings and loans. Loan brokers, in fact, were often viewed as seedy money lenders that charged excessive fees and rates to arrange loans for problem borrowers. Rather than relying on sound credit analysis, brokers usually protected themselves by insuring that the borrower had a substantial amount of personal equity in a property.

Several developments in the 1980s served to radically alter the mortgage brokering industry, as well as most other U.S. financial services industries. High bond rates and the term structure of interest rates in 1981 caused a massive shift of money from thrift institutions to money market funds. Because they had no money to make loans, mortgage lending institutions laid off thousands of loan originators to whom they paid salaries. Many displaced originators became self-employed mortgage brokers who worked off commissions or on contract, rather than salary.

In 1982, money market rates plummeted and institutional lenders were again prepared to lend. Rather than hiring new originators, however, many institutions continued to look to brokers to supply their mortgages. As mortgage activity accelerated in the early and mid-1980s, an identifiable, respectable mortgage brokerage emerged to service the origination function. Many brokers expanded their services, and even began franchising their businesses. Savvy lenders, meanwhile, concentrated on underwriting, funding, and service activities, causing many organizations that retained the retail origination function to become less competitive.

Increasing the importance of the mortgage brokers role in the 1980s was the introduction of hundreds of financial instruments that lenders began offering to potential borrowers. Adjustable rate mortgages (ARMs), for example, grew in popularity as hundreds of new ARM options allowed buyers to access a plethora of interest rate structures and payment terms. Before the 1980s, mortgage lenders offered a relatively homogenous product. Borrowers basically had to choose only between government or conventional loans. Inundated with financing options in the 1980s, borrowers began to seek the aid of brokers that could identify the best product for their individual needs.

In addition to increased outsourcing of originations and the development of new mortgage products, a third advancement affected the brokerage industry during the 1980s—the rapid proliferation of new mortgage securities. Among other consequences, these new securities succeeded in luring short- and intermediate-term investors to the market, and in lubricating the flow of money for new loans. Although retail mortgage brokers indirectly benefited from these developments, many traditional wholesale brokers found themselves displaced by securities trading and brokerage firms that sold securitized mortgages on over-the-counter markets.

Although changing financial markets gave birth to a respected mortgage brokering industry in the early and mid-1980s, it was not until the late 1980s and early 1990s that the industry rocketed to prominence. Historically low interest rates, which caused massive mortgage refinancings and spurred new originations, contributed to trends started earlier in the decade and pushed industry revenues to all-time highs.

While brokers originated a negligible share of all mortgages before 1981, by 1988 brokers had captured about 20 percent of the market. By the early 1990s, the industry was selling about 45 percent of the more than $800 billion worth of mortgages originated annually in the United States, resulting in total fees and commissions of between $10 and $14 billion. Some of the most successful individuals were generating as much as $500,000 per year in fees.

Massive growth in the mortgage brokering industry is reflected in NMBA membership growth. Started in 1973, the NMBA had just a few hundred members by 1980. Membership jumped to about 440 by 1988. By 1991, more than 1,200 brokers belonged to the Phoenix organization. Furthermore, the NMBA estimated that about 16,000 companies were providing mortgage brokering services in the early 1990s that were not association members. Likewise, in 1988, more than 85 percent of all applicants to the Mortgage Bankers Association (MBA) were classified as brokerage companies—up from a minute fraction of that amount in the early 1980s.

Mortgage brokers had grown to dominate entire regions in some areas of the United States. In California, for instance, more than 70 percent of all mortgages were originated by brokers in 1991. ''In 1984 there were not five mortgage brokers in the state of New York,'' said Ralph LoVuolo, Sr., President of LoVuolo & Company, Inc., in *Mortgage Banking.* ''Now there are almost 2,000.''

As interest rates continued to fall in the early 1990s, the mortgage brokering industry expanded. Lenders were seeking increasingly faster processing times, high volume, geographic diversity, and lower overhead that they could achieve by outsourcing their origination activities. Consumers were also becoming more comfortable with the concept of using mortgage brokers rather than traditional lending institutions. By 1993, brokers were originating about 50 percent of all U.S. mortgages. The percentage remained the same through 1996, with mortgage brokers originating approximately $405 billion worth of loans.

Though the industry faced few obstacles to continued growth, one imminent threat promised to snuff out massive profit opportunities that characterized the 1980s and early 1990s—rising interest rates. Rates on long-term mortgages dipped below 7 percent in the early 1990s, at the same time that ARMs fell to less than 4 percent. Homeowners subsequently rushed to refinance their mortgages or to buy new homes. By 1994, though—after reaching 30-year lows—interest rates appeared to have stabilized and were even inching back up. In early 1997, the average mortgage rate for a 30-year loan was approximately 8.25 to 8.5 percent, while a 15-year loan was around 7.75 to 8.0 percent.

Brokers who had been involved in the mortgage industry for long periods of time were well aware of the cyclical nature of the business. In fact, many brokers left other jobs to participate in the industry during the refinancing boom of the late 1980s and early 1990s. Many of those same workers planned to exit or reduce their dependence on the industry as rates climbed. They would go back to real estate appraisal, commercial brokerage, insurance underwriting, or some other job and wait for the next industry upswing.

Despite the expectation of higher interest rates and waning mortgage activity, industry participants were generally optimistic about the future. The recent surge of growth had served to establish respect for brokers. Once viewed suspiciously by most lenders, brokers were now viewed as potentially excellent sources of originations. Even federal secondary marketing organizations, such as Freddie Mac, were buying brokered mortgages in 1997, and extolling the advantages of such purchases. Greater respect and acceptance of brokers by financial institutions meant that brokers would likely increase their share of the mortgage market in the mid- and late 1990s, thereby reducing the negative effects of rising interest rates.

Other factors were also expected to buoy industry earnings during the inevitable down-cycle. One such influence was a lending practice called ''warehousing.'' Warehouse lenders provide loans for other lenders to use to underwrite new mortgages. In 1993, about 25 domestic banks and a dozen foreign banks were making warehouse lines of credit available to mortgage banks and even mortgage brokers. Many more organizations were expected to begin making warehouse loans.

In the long term, the mortgage brokerage industry should proliferate as lenders increasingly outsource their originations. Because the origination business is localized and service-oriented by nature, small mom-and-pop shops will continue to dominate. Companies that underwrite, sell, and service the loans which brokers originate, however, will consolidate. Only the largest, most efficient, technologically advanced lenders will remain competitive. Smaller lenders will be consumed by their larger competitors as the industry consolidates. As a result, brokers will supply increasingly fewer lenders in the 1990s and into the twenty-first century.

As the industry matures, brokers can expect to experience greater competition and lower profit margins. Fluctuating interest rates and housing starts, however, will insure periods of high profitability. Increased regulation will also play a role in the industry's evolution.

Fraud and Regulation. While most mortgage brokers in the mid-1990s were legitimate, lax industry regulation contributed to widespread abuse by some brokers. Second-mortgage scandals, particularly, were marring the industry's reputation in the late 1980s and early 1990s. In one type of scheme, for example, dishonest brokers offer to provide home improvement services to prospects.

They convince homeowners to take out a second mortgage on their home to pay for the repairs. Besides charging interest rates as high as 20 or 30 percent, the brokers may also deliver shoddy construction. Such brokers typically operate in low-income neighborhoods where their prospects don't have access to normal bank credit. In 1996, California was trying to pass a measure that would regulate this kind of high-interest, high-fee loans. A federal law went into effect in 1995 which addressed some of the problems. Other scams involve fraudulent documents and embezzlement of lenders' funds.

Broker fraud lawsuits have been filed in Alabama, California, Georgia, Virginia, and many other states. In 1996, the state of Idaho, for the first time, passed legislation regulating mortgage brokers in an effort to protect consumers. According to FBI and mortgage professionals, 10-15 percent of all loan applications involve some kind of fraud.

In an effort to stem fraud and protect the reputation of legitimate operators, several states were scrambling to regulate the fast growing industry. New regulation was aimed at requiring brokers to prove a minimum net worth and to secure bonding. Some states in the mid-1990s were also striving to develop fee limits and to mandate written agreements between brokers and customers. In general, regulators were seeking increased disclosure requirements, for borrowers and investors, and stricter licensing requirements.

Many legitimate brokers were wary of what they viewed as federal and state government intrusion. Some observers believed, for example, that a lack of uniformity in state regulations would severely impede the efforts of some lenders to establish national networks of brokers. Other brokers believed that regulation would squelch profits. In 1993, brokers in Illinois, one of the more heavily regulated states, were already spending an average of $4,000 to $8,000 annually on license and audit fees, examinations, and state spot-checking programs. Likewise, brokers in Arizona were required to pass a course, two exams, and post a $10,000 bond before they could operate.

Regulation also occurred at the federal level in the mid-1990s. Fannie Mae, for instance, required participating lenders to spot-check 10 percent of all the mortgages they produced, and revise discretionary samplings of brokered loans. Likewise, the Department of Housing and Urban Development was pressuring the industry to disclose its fees. Other brokers welcomed new regulations as a way to exterminate illegitimate operators.

CURRENT CONDITIONS

Mortgage interest rates remained low in the late 1990s and reforms instituted by Freddie Mac and Fannie Mae helped loan brokers offer the customer more for their mortgage loan dollar. In 1999, Freddie Mac created options to lower the cost of mortgage insurance, required for homeowners with less than 20 percent of a down payment for the total mortgage amount. Such reforms could save a customer with a 30 year $100,000 mortgage anywhere from $1,302 to $2,800. For larger mortgages, loan brokers could offer customers savings of several thousand dollars.

Fannie Mae worked with loan brokers to make mortgages available to underserved customer populations, under the institution's Trillion Dollar Commitment, an endeavor with the goal of "pledging a trillion dollars in housing finance to serve underserved families, and offering lenders cutting-edge mortgage products and technology," according to Fannie Mae CEO and Chairman Franklin D. Raines. Between 1994 and 1999 the initiative targeted $700 billion to fund such mortgages. Fannie Mae worked with the loan brokering industry under the initiative by creating partnerships with lenders and making use of technology to provide flexibility to the lending process.

INDUSTRY LEADERS

The loan and mortgage brokering industry is highly fragmented. Because of its localized nature, no firms dominate the industry on a national, or even regional, scale. For example, the largest firm in the industry in 1992, DMC Financial Corp., of California, employed fewer than 100 people and maintained assets of less than $2 million. DMC, like virtually all other top companies in the industry, is a privately held company. Because most participants are privately held and are not required to publish operating results, little financial data exists about firms within the industry.

Industry leaders in 1996 included: Manhattan Mortgage Co., of New York City, with under 1,000 employees, but more than $27 million in operating revenues; Homes for South Florida, Inc., of Miami, Florida, had $21 million in operating revenues, and also employed under 1,000 employees; NBR Mortgage Co., of Santa Rosa, California, with $19 million in total assets; and Randall Mortgage, Inc., of Maitland, Florida, with $9 million in operating revenues.

In 1996 Norwest Mortgage Inc. was a leader in mortgage origination, leading competitors with $55.27 billion in originated loans. Norwest was also the top servicer of residential mortgages (205,841) for investors during 1996. Norwest merged with Wells Fargo in 1998 to become Wells Fargo and Co. Wells Fargo and Company had 1998 sales of $20.4 million and a one year sales growth of 112 percent. The company had net income in 1998 of $1,950 million. In 1998 retail lending was headed by Lehman Brothers at $5 billion (1998 total sales were $19.8 million with a one year sales growth of 17.8 percent), followed closely by Credit Suisse First Boston at $4 billion.

WORKFORCE

Although the mortgage brokering industry lacks statistical data that is available for most industries of its size, a study released in 1992 by the NMBA indicated that the average brokerage firm had six employees, had been in business for five years, and had a net worth of $75,000. A NMBA survey released one year later, though, showed that the median broker originated $26 million in mortgages in 1992—a 65 percent increase over 1991.

Many brokers earn in excess of $200,000 or even $500,000 per year, and the average industry income is very high at peak times. Brokers also enjoy independence and flexibility in comparison to many salaried employees. The business has its drawbacks, however. For instance, mortgage brokering is a highly cyclical business. During periods of rising interest rates many brokers experience rapid and significant declines in income levels. In addition to cyclical downturns, brokers usually work long hours and spend many nights and weekends meeting with prospective clients at their convenience.

Also frustrating brokers is the fact that 50 percent of all the loan applications that they assemble for their clients are rejected by banks, resulting in zero fees for the broker. Furthermore, most brokers spend their first few years on the job making cold calls to attorneys, CPAs, and real estate brokers to build a referral base for future business. Finally, mortgage brokering can be very stressful. "You're the primary contingency whether a deal flies or not," said Karen Dell, loan consultant for First Federal, of California, in the *Los Angeles Business Journal.* "People have a lot of money at stake, so their tempers can be short."

Employment prospects for the industry were positive going into the mid-1990s. Besides general growth in the demand for brokers and originators, the demand for support staff should also rise. The Bureau of Labor Statistics estimates that jobs for secretaries and clerical staff in the industry should rise by more than 40 percent between 1990 and 2005. Positions for bill and account collectors should jump by 54 percent. Management support and credit analysts positions should increase by more than 50 percent as well.

RESEARCH AND TECHNOLOGY

The mortgage brokering industry is highly dependent upon modern office technology and, in effect, is a corollary of the information age. There are 0.8 laptop computers per originator in the industry, according to the 1992 NMBA survey, much more than almost any other U.S. industry. Almost all brokers are heavily dependent on fax machines to send and receive loan and credit information. Nearly half of all brokers are part of a computer network, and 13 percent access a computerized loan origination system that lists rates among real estate agents. About four-fifths of all brokers used some form of mortgage processing software in 1993.

In addition to creating an environment which allowed brokers to efficiently originate loans, information technology was also driving increased efficiency of the financial markets, on which mortgage brokers depend to buy their originations and pay their fees. Successful lending institutions were using complex information systems and software to eliminate overhead and reduce administrative costs. Such advances were a driving force behind lender consolidation.

New systems were already being implemented in the mid-1990s that sought to provide a better link between lenders, brokers, real estate agents, and even consumers. New Mortgage Bankers Association of America and American National Standards Institute standards had been developed regarding electronic communications. Countrywide Funding Corp., for example, offered its brokers access to DirectLine Plus, a system which allows brokers to find current data on loans-in-process 24 hours a day. Mortgage companies were moving toward delivering brokers full access to their integrated processing systems.

Advances in technology continued to expedite the mortgage lending process in the late 1990s for lenders and customers. Newly developed software tools such as Desktop Underwriter allowed lenders to use flexibility in evaluating individual loan applications. Fannie Mae CEO Raines estimated that such software increased the amount of low down payment loans that the institute was able to buy, as well as decreasing delinquency among its borrowers.

Loan brokers continued to be served by advances in Internet technology in the late 1990s. In late 1999, IMX(r) Exchange, an online commerce resource for loan brokers, collaborated with Byte Enterprises and Contour Software to improve the efficiency of services available to loan brokers. The collaboration produced the online feature XpressPost(TM), which would allow loan originators to post applications online in real time and receive immediate bids for loans from brokers that were part of the IMX(r) network.

FURTHER READING

Caplin, Joan. "A Loan That Lets You Cut Your Rate Later." *Money,* 1 December 1999.

Carlson, Brad. "New Mortgage Broker Law Said a Benefit to All Parties Involved." *Idaho Business Review,* 29 April 1996. 1A.

Darnay, Arsen J., ed. *Finance, Insurance, and Real Estate USA,* 3rd ed. Detroit: Gale Research, 1996.

"Freddie Mac Reduces Homeownership Costs for Low-Downpayment Borrowers." *Today's News,* PR Newswire, 15 March 1999. Available from http://www.prnewswire.com.

Goldwasser, Joan. ''Jim Palmer's Pitch: Easy Money—Second Mortgages that Exceed Your Equity May be More Costly than You Think.'' *Kiplinger's Personal Finance Magazine,* February 1998.

''In the Hopper: Pending Legislation.'' *Business Journal-Sacramento,* 24 June 1996, 22.

''IMX(r) Exchange Announces Expanded Strategic Alliances with Major LOS Software Providers Byte and Contour to Integrate Seamless Posting Feature in Next Software Release.'' 7 December 1999. Available from http://www.individual.com/browse/.

''Industry Overview.'' The Mortgage Mart, 1997. Available from http://www.mortgagemart.com/oview1.html.

''Largest Retail Lenders, 1998.'' *Shopping Center World,* April 1999. Available from http://www.galenet.com/.

''Lehman Brothers Holdings, Inc.'' 1999. Available from http://www.hoovers.com/.

''Merlin's Market Update.'' April 1997. Available from http://www.mortgagemart.com/.

National Association of Mortgage Brokers Homepage. 20 March 2000. Available from http//www.namb.com/press.htm and http//www.namb.com/member.htm.

Salder, Robert J. ''Mortgage Fraud.'' The Mortgage Mart, 1997. Available from http://www.mortgage-mart.com/gaps.html.

Shaffer, Rick. ''Farewell to ARMs: Why Fixed Rate Mortgages are Still Your Best Bet These Days.'' *Financial World,* November 1997.

''The 1990s Marks the Greatest Decade Ever for Home Buyers: Fannie Mae's Raines Says Company is on Track to Fulfill its Trillion Dollar Commitment by End of Year 2000.'' *Today's News,* PR Newswire, 15 March 1999. Available from http://www.prnewswire.com.

''Top Servicers of Residential Mortgages for Investors, 1997.'' *American Banker,* 24 April 1998. Available from http://www.galenet.com/.

''Top Mortgage Originators, 1997.'' *Mortgage Market Statistical Annual, Inside Mortgage Finance.* Available from http://www.galenet.com/.

''Wells Fargo and Company.'' 1999. Available from http://www.hoovers.com/.

SIC 6211

SECURITY BROKERS, DEALERS, AND FLOTATION COMPANIES

The securities industry is made up of establishments primarily engaged in the purchase, sale, and brokerage of securities. This industry also encompasses investment bankers, which originate, underwrite, and distribute issues of securities. Firms in this industry essentially serve as financial intermediaries, matching investors with entities that need money. They also provide a pricing mechanism for the investment market, and furnish a vehicle for the liquidation of investors' assets. Although many of these firms also provide investment consultation, companies engaged predominantly in advisement are classified in **SIC 6282: Investment Advice.**

NAICS CODE(S)

523110 (Investment Banking and Securities Dealing)
523120 (Securities Brokerage)
523910 (Miscellaneous Intermediation)
523999 (Miscellaneous Financial Investment Activities)

INDUSTRY SNAPSHOT

In 1995 there were 981 companies with revenues of $176.26 billion and 429,900 employees. In that year U.S. corporate stock and bond sales rose to $709.3 billion from $705.7 billion in 1994, due to a robust calendar of common-stock offerings. Behind the strong financing activity was a blend of lower interest rates and higher stock prices, which together spurred more and more individual investors to buy common stock. One of the most vibrant areas of the common-stock underwriting market was the initial public offering, as 572 companies came to market for the first time in 1995. Total debt sales, including convertible offerings, slipped to nearly $611 billion in 1995 from $628.8 billion in 1994. But asset-backed offerings jumped 42 percent to $107.1 billion.

Major U.S. stock markets smashed an array of trading records in 1995. Average daily volume on the over-the-counter NASDAQ (National Association of Securities Dealers' Automated Quotations System) stock market reached 400 million shares, up 36 percent from 1994. Average daily volume on the New York Stock Exchange (NYSE) totaled a record 346 million shares, up 19 percent.

In a dramatic recovery from record losses that bludgeoned dealers and brokers in 1990, the industry realized its highest revenues in history in 1995. While the future of the highly volatile securities market is nearly impossible to predict, economic and demographic trends—such as the aging of baby boomers—offered hope for continued healthy security markets throughout the 1990s.

ORGANIZATION AND STRUCTURE

Securities firms have three major functions in financial markets: they provide a mechanism that links people who have money with those seeking to raise money; they deliver a means of valuing and pricing investments; and they offer a vehicle that investors can use to liquidate their investments. Entities in the market that are served by securities firms include individuals, corporations, and governments.

Securities firms typically serve the first function, raising capital, through investment banking and brokerage activities. By acting as an intermediary between those with and those without capital, the firms channel funds between various sectors of the economy. The second function, pricing, is served when companies provide timely information to the marketplace about investments. The essential ability of securities firms to deliver this information quickly has made U.S. capital markets the world's most efficient. Liquidity, the third function, is served as brokers and dealers buy and sell securities for investors as efficiently as possible to avoid losses not related to market conditions.

Although not considered an integral function in the financial market, advisement and product development services offered by many full-service securities firms are significant factors in the dynamics of the industry. Companies continually strive to develop and refine financial instruments specifically tailored to customer needs. These instruments are designed to accomplish myriad investment goals including sheltering taxes, maximizing dividends, or increasing capital gains. Firms that engage in investment counseling provide extensive research for potential investors. These activities entail: obtaining information on the customer's investment strategy and goals; providing information on various investment vehicles; offering advice on specific market trends and forecasts; providing information regarding government initiatives such as tax laws; and recommending investments that match the customer's needs.

Types of Securities. Firms buy and sell an enormous variety of securities for their customers. These securities generally can be categorized as either equity or debt instruments. Equity instruments, most often stock, represent ownership interest in a firm and entitle the owner to a portion of the company's profits. Debt instruments, on the other hand, signify a promise on the part of the issuing entity to repay, at a specified time, a sum of money and an amount of interest for use of that money. Created as a means of raising capital, both debt and equity vehicles are often purchased and sold numerous times through various securities markets.

In addition to trading in traditional corporate stocks and bonds, securities firms were selling increasing amounts of alternative investment vehicles in the 1990s. These vehicles included municipal (state and local) bonds, junk bonds, options, mutual funds, asset and mortgage-backed securities, futures, and real estate investment trusts.

Two vehicles that continued to receive increased emphasis in security markets in the 1990s were derivatives, such as futures and options. An option is a contract to purchase or sell shares of a particular stock. The contract specifies the security, the purchase or sale price, the life of the option, and the number of shares that the contract represents. A ''put'' option gives the owner the right to sell a security, while a ''call'' option allows the owner the choice of buying a security. In contrast to an option, a future is a commitment to receive or deliver a specified quantity and quality of a commodity by a specified future date. A future can be used to insure a transaction price at a date prior to the actual exchange.

Types of Firms. Many securities firms serve as both brokers and dealers in the market. A broker is an agent who buys and sells securities on behalf of a client for a commission or fee. A dealer is a principal that buys and sells on its own account with the intention of making a profit. Firms that serve as broker-dealers typically have a headquarters office supported by numerous branch offices. The branch offices sell and market the company's services, while the main office handles administrative activities, research, and product development. Depending on the type and extent of services offered beyond brokerage and dealing activities, securities firms fall into one of several categories.

For instance, national full-line firms provide a range of services for both retail and institutional customers. These companies usually have many offices nationwide. Examples of such firms include Merrill Lynch and Paine Webber. Investment banking firms, such as Goldman Sachs and First Boston, primarily provide institutional customers with services related to underwriting new securities issues, and mergers and acquisitions. They may also act as brokers and dealers. Regional firms offer full lines of securities products to customers within a particular geographic area. Large firms of this type are Robert W. Baird, Wheat First Securities, and Alex Brown.

In addition to full-service, investment banking, and regional firms, the marketplace also includes discount brokers. These companies allow retail customers to buy and sell securities for less than they would have to pay to a full-service broker. Because discount brokers usually do not offer investment advice, have sales staffs, or act as marketers for financial products, they are able to charge lower commissions. Popular firms in this category include Charles Schwab and Olde Discount.

Industry revenues remained highly concentrated among the top-tier firms, as they have been since the inception of the industry. In the early 1990s the top 25 brokers garnered over 80 percent of all industry revenues. Furthermore, the top 10 brokers amassed nearly 70 percent of all industry revenues.

Primary Marketplaces. Industry participants buy, sell, and issue securities in three primary markets: exchange, over-the-counter (OTC), and money. Exchange markets provide organized trading facilities for stocks, bonds, and/or options. These facilities act as auction houses, where securities brokers and dealers essentially bid for securities. Organizations must meet requirements set forth by the exchange in order to have their securities listed, or made available for trade, on the exchange. The New York Stock Exchange (NYSE) is the best-known exchange, but others include the American Stock Exchange (AMEX), Midwest Stock Exchange, and the Chicago Board Options Exchange.

OTC markets, in contrast to organized exchange facilities, consist of a network of brokers and dealers that represents customers in the purchase or sale of securities. No central location exists for this type of market. Trading departments of securities firms negotiate price with customers or their agents over the telephone. OTC markets usually trade in securities of companies that are small in comparison to those on organized exchanges.

The money market trades mostly in short-term securities that have a maturity of one year or less. These instruments are characterized by high liquidity and typically trade in high denominations. Examples of securities traded in this market are U.S. treasury bills, certificates of deposit, and commercial paper. As with OTC markets, money markets do not have central trading places, and the market is composed primarily of banks and firms that borrow or invest large amounts of money for a short term.

BACKGROUND AND DEVELOPMENT

The U.S. securities industry gradually evolved from a mix of financial services available as early as 1800. These services, and the subsequent development of a sophisticated industry, mimicked financial markets that developed in Europe in the eighteenth century. In fact, much of the early investment banking activity in the United States, which was responsible for issuing the first securities, was conducted through joint ventures between Europeans and Americans. Many of the famous families that helped to shape the American securities market are still well known, such as the Rothschilds, Warburgs, and Barings.

Throughout the nineteenth century the development of the American securities industry lagged several decades behind that of Europe. However, the Civil War and the construction of the U.S. railroads created a demand for financial services that spurred the growth of the investment banking and securities industry. In fact, government securities sold during the Civil War represented the first successful security offering made to the general public on a large scale. This opened the way for sales and distribution systems that would be used by securities firms throughout the twentieth century. Some of the larger investment banking houses that dominated the nineteenth-century securities industry in the United States included Kuhn Loeb, Morgan, Lehman Brothers, and Goldman Sachs.

The securities industry rapidly expanded after World War I, as the prosperity of the 1920s caused an almost insatiable appetite for securities. Despite massive growth in the popularity of municipal and utility issues, for the first time in 1929 the volume of even more popular stock issues surpassed the amount of bonds issued. Throughout the 1920s investment bankers raced to meet the demand for new securities. Even an influx of foreign securities was insufficient to satisfy consumers.

The immense success of the securities industry, however, foreshadowed its rapid decline and the subsequent transformation of its structure. The industry that had evolved by 1930 was loosely regulated and was dominated, many people at that time believed, by an exclusive network of power brokers. In addition, banks were allowed to participate in both commercial and investment banking activities, which created a conflict of interest for many firms.

The Industry Crash and Reformation. The stock market crash of 1929 confirmed the suspicions of many that the securities industry was in need of reform. A variety of New Deal legislative orders quickly transformed the industry into one of the most regulated sectors of the American economy. In 1934 Congress established the Securities and Exchange Commission (SEC) to protect investors against fraud and mismanagement by securities firms and other investment entities. The Securities Exchange Commission (SEC) performs legislative, judicial, and executive functions. The most inclusive and far-reaching piece of legislation enacted by the SEC in the 1930s was the Glass-Steagall Act. Other laws included the Revenue Act, the Securities Act, and the Securities Exchange Act. These laws required stricter standards of disclosure and erected a barrier between investment and commercial banking. They were also used to strengthen the banking industry and to reduce speculative risks that threatened the health of the U.S. economy.

The result of the industry transfiguration was a relatively stable securities market throughout most of the remainder of the twentieth century. After 1930 the industry gradually grew and prospered under SEC regulation until the late 1960s, when demand for new business boomed. The amount of new common stock issued increased from about $10 billion in 1965 to a peak of over $40 billion by 1968. New issues of bonds reflected a similar pattern. Although the dynamics of the industry had changed significantly after 1930, the industry remained dominated by several of the larger brokerage houses until the late 1970s, when the increased volume allowed smaller companies to begin to establish a presence in the market.

One of the greatest developments in the securities industry occurred in 1975, when commissions that securities firms charged were deregulated, and negotiated rates were allowed. Since this time, market volume has increased dramatically, and new service offerings have increased. For example, the volume of common stock issued skyrocketed from about $40 billion per year in 1975 to over $75 billion by 1985. During the same period, the amount of new bond issues leapt from $40 billion to over $110 billion per year.

The 1980s. Deregulation of commission rates, a strong market demand for new issues of securities in a vibrant economy, and the increase in the volume and number of new financial instruments all contributed to the growth of the securities industry in the mid-1980s. Between 1982 and 1986 combined industry commissions on securities rose from $6 billion to over $12.6 billion, and total industry revenues jumped from $23.2 billion to $50 billion. Industry employment soared from about 170,000 in 1980 to a peak of 262,000 in 1987. In addition, merger and acquisition activity by American companies, which securities firms handled, proliferated throughout most of the decade, peaking at over $250 billion of completed deals in 1988. Leveraged buyouts and junk bond issues, both of which were high margin activities for securities firms, also added to industry growth and profitability.

Just as the boom of the 1920s foreshadowed the fall of securities markets in the 1930s, the mid-1980s were a prelude to industry setbacks in the late 1980s and early 1990s. The stock market crash on Black Monday, in October of 1987, significantly diminished activity and profits for securities firms during the next few years. As equity and debt trading declined, and mergers and acquisitions decreased between 1987 and 1990, pre-tax income for the entire industry plummeted from $8.3 billion in 1986 to $3.2 billion in 1987 and only $800 million by 1990. As industry employment fell to less than 210,000 in 1990, Wall Street posted its worst year on record.

As if economic woes were not enough, the industry was also rocked by scandals in the late 1980s. Arrests and indictments of executives from some of the largest brokerage houses in the United States shook up Wall Street. Charges by the SEC ranged from insider trading, or trading while in possession of non-public information, to concealing stock ownership. Charges against Dennis Levine, of Drexel Burnham Lambert Inc., and Ivan Boesky in 1986 led to subsequent investigations of a number of prominent Wall Street figures. Boesky received three years in prison and a $100 million civil penalty. Levine was sentenced to serve four years in prison and was fined $362,000.

Increased Competition. At the same time that the securities industry was experiencing its volatile rise and fall during the 1980s, it was also undergoing structural changes. The initiation of negotiated competitive commissions in 1975 gradually reduced the percentage of company revenues created by commissions. In fact, commission income as a percentage of total industry revenues plummeted from over 40 percent in 1976 to 16 percent by 1990.

Other regulatory changes also jostled the market. Some of these laws were prompted by scandals that tarnished the industry's image during the 1980s, while others were a result of a changing marketplace. For instance, the Glass-Steagall Act was essentially dismantled, as regulators tried to make the U.S. banking industry more competitive in global markets. Additionally, the Tax Equity and Fiscal Responsibility Act (TEFRA) and Rule 415 also affected the industry. TEFRA, which increased reporting requirements for securities companies, compelled firms to invest in costly information technology. Rule 415 allowed multiple security offerings to be covered by one underwriting, thereby increasing fee competition in the industry.

Besides regulatory changes, three major factors increased the competitiveness of the industry. First of all, the pool of investment dollars grew because of large increases in the size of pension funds, a trend that was expected to accelerate through the end of the twentieth century. Secondly, interest-rate volatility was partly responsible for growth in the trading of fixed-income investment products, which increased opportunities for commissions in the industry. Finally, rapid growth in the federal deficit resulted in a large increase in the available pool of U.S. government investment instruments, causing increased trading in bonds.

One effect of these changes was the entrance of new players in securities markets. Banks, insurance companies, and investment advisors, among others, all began competing for a piece of the securities market pie in the late 1980s, placing downward pressure on securities firms' profits. Furthermore, discount brokers, many of which charged as much as 90 percent less than full-service firms, cornered 20 percent of the individual investor market during the 1980s.

Securities firms reacted to increased competition and reduced commission income in two ways. First, they emphasized the services side of their business, relying less on income from buying and selling securities and more on money management and advisory services. Secondly, the number of firms in the industry declined, as companies merged to benefit from economies of scale. Besides mergers between securities firms, several large firms also merged with insurance companies and other institutions that complemented their role in the market. For example, Kemper Insurance Company merged with five regional broker-dealers. The number of securities firms fell from a peak of 9,515 in 1987 to 7,610 in 1992.

Despite significant setbacks for securities firms triggered by the 1987 stock market crash and aggravated by increased competition, the industry staged an amazing recovery by 1991 and 1992. Following one of its worst years on record in 1990, industry pre-tax income rose to historical highs of $8.6 billion in 1991 and over $10 billion in 1992. Low interest rates and high stock prices sparked much of the activity. Lower rates increased the amount of new debt offerings and encouraged corporations, municipalities, and homeowners to refinance their existing debt. Because stock prices were high in relation to company earnings, corporations tended to issue more new equities.

However, the bond market crashed in 1994 as a result of an unexpected rise in interest rates. Furthermore, brokerage companies experienced slowdowns in underwriting and trading. Firms became stuck with unwieldy cost structures that outstripped revenues. Thus, Wall Street firms curtailed expansion plans and eliminated more marginal businesses.

In 1995 pre-tax profits of NYSE-member securities firms soared. Virtually all revenue components posted increases led by trading gains. Commissions and asset management fees also hit new highs. In 1995 securities firms took in $6.58 billion in disclosed underwriting fees, making 1995 Wall Street's third best year ever. Triggering the surge in fees was robust activity in stock sales, the most lucrative underwriting sector. Stock sales yielded $4.02 billion in fees alone, or nearly two-thirds of all underwriting fees.

Another positive factor in 1995 was the volume of mergers and acquisitions activity. In 1995 all records for mergers and acquisitions activity in the United States and abroad were broken. An unprecedented $458 billion in deals was announced by U.S. companies, up 32 percent from the old record of $347 billion reached in 1994. Globally, a record $866 billion in transactions was reached, up 51 percent from the $572 billion announced in 1994. However, investment bankers took a back seat in a number of the transactions. Some of the biggest deals were hammered out by chief executives. Even though deal volume was 35 percent above 1988, the best year of the 1980s, many of 1995's deals were crafted without all the complicated financial arrangements, such as junk bonds and bridge loans, that can generate large fees.

In late 1996 the Federal Reserve Board loosened the cap on banks' underwritings from 10 percent to 25 percent of the revenue in their securities' affiliates. Furthermore, during 1996, industry firms continued to diversify their revenue bases. A generally favorable environment for financial assets continued to provide a backdrop for impressive profits postings in the industry. Mutual fund inflows and trading volumes increased.

During 1997 there was an increasing pace of consolidation among Wall Street firms. For example, in January 1997 Morgan Stanley announced a $10.2 billion merger with Dean, Witter, Discover & Co.

CURRENT CONDITIONS

The late 1990s saw the advent of online trading, a trend that revolutionized and changed the industry. According to an article in *The Economist* (8 May 1999), one of every six shares traded during 1999 was traded through the Internet, or 500,000 shares per day. In 1994 there were no online brokerage accounts; by 1999, 5 million of these accounts were active. Online brokerage firms were typically discount brokerages, with an average commission of $15.00 per trade, much less than the full-service brokerage fee of $100 to $300 per trade. Traditional brokerages such as Merrill Lynch appeared not to be concerned with the rising competition—arguing that the discount online brokerage model was not sustainable in a business sense. Online brokers in 1999 continued to shape their niche in the industry by offering additional services and products such as insurance or online research on companies. The CEO of Prudential Securities, a traditional firm without online trading, suggested that the value for consumers in sticking with a traditional firm lay with the advice that the firm could provide, rather than the actual execution of the trade, which online providers excel at, and offer at a cheap price.

Performance among online brokerages varied as these companies evolved in the late 1990s. A *Kiplinger's* article (November 1999) surveyed the performances of online brokerages and found a disparity in the quality of service provided. Among the disadvantages of online brokerages were long phone waits (one investor lost $5,000 because he couldn't get through to the firm), computer crashes, or difficulty logging onto the brokerage site. Advantages included low brokerage fees from some companies (good for frequent traders) and information available on a brokerage site. Using several criteria for ranking online brokerages (including commissions, responsiveness, margin rates, availability of initial public offerings [IPOs], broker knowledge, and web site), Kiplinger's ranked Accutrade and Ameritrade highly. Web Street Securities received the lowest overall rating. *Forbes* 1999 Annual Report (11 January 1999) noted that Charles Schwab, a traditional brokerage firm, had done well both in establishing dominance in the mutual fund market and in online brokerage services.

INDUSTRY LEADERS

The largest security broker-dealer in the United States in 1991 was Merrill Lynch and Company, Inc. of New York. The firm is the world's largest equities underwriter, providing financing, investment, and insurance services to clients worldwide. Merrill Lynch is one of the few financial services companies to have achieved strength in both the retail and institutional markets at home and abroad. Despite the unprecedented bull market in the United States, the company has made significant acquisitions overseas, such as Smith New Court PLC, a global securities firm based in Great Britain. In 1996, Merrill Lynch had total worldwide revenues of more than $25 billion.

Morgan Stanley, a premier institutional brokerage firm, employed more than 12,000 individuals in 1996. In that year the firm was ranked number one in global announced mergers and acquisitions transactions and number three in worldwide common stock underwriting, according to Securities Data Co. Morgan Stanley's network of offices spans 22 countries, and the firm's Morgan Stanley Capital International indices serve as benchmarks for international investors. In 1996 the firm generated net revenue of $5.8 billion.

Merrill Lynch remained the largest U.S. securities firm in 1998, with 49,800 employees. Fidelity Distributors retained the greatest market share (as of February 1999) for a mutual fund at 12.84 percent. The Fidelity Magellan Fund had the greatest market share of mutual funds (during the first quarter of 1999) at $85.86 billion dollars.

WORKFORCE

Since 1980 the securities industry has, on average, grown faster than other industries. However, employment in the industry has been highly volatile compared to other segments of the economy. Tasks performed by workers in many occupations in the security brokerage industry have been transformed, as global markets have expanded, and computerized trading has increased. The industry has increased employment in highly technical professional occupations such as computer scientists and statistical financial analysts and has streamlined managerial and internal analysis jobs. The increase in the professional share of the industry's employment has largely offset a decrease in the managerial share.

With more commercial banks gaining their Federal Reserve approval to open securities affiliates, the demand for experienced research, sales, and trading people is greater than the supply. Money-center banks, such as Chemical Bank and Chase Manhattan, have hired dozens of experienced professionals in these areas.

Employment in the field typically requires knowledge of finance and investments, although many brokers in the past have started their careers with little of either. Jobs usually are available in one of five basic functional areas: sales and marketing, where securities or financial products are sold directly to customers; investment banking; research; trading, which often entails buying and selling on an exchange floor; and finance and administration. Although salaries in more traditional business functions are similar to other industries, salaries in commission-based positions in brokerage or sales can vary greatly depending on the market and the success of the worker.

One of the most glamorous and high-paying areas, and the most difficult to break into, is investment banking. Although employment in the field declined after the mid-1980s, the industry remains cyclical, and economic growth could open more opportunities in this field. Successful investment bankers typically work long hours, have a master's degree in business administration, and work in one of a few large metropolitan areas, particularly New York.

The greatest job growth in the securities market during the 1990s is expected to be in financial services and operations. Money management, financial consulting, and other fee-based services are expected to grow. Likewise, operations positions in the industry should increase faster than average throughout the 1990s. Operations departments are basically responsible for maintaining customer accounts, updating records, and handling cash and securities receipts and deliveries. As companies struggle to keep costs down, and securities markets increasingly become electronic, firms will continue to invest in advanced information processing and delivery systems.

During the consolidation, merging, and downsizing of Wall Street brokerages in the 1990s, many brokers became independent. Between 1992 and 1997 independent brokers across the United States increased by 23 percent, though that amount tapered slightly in 1998, when large, traditional brokerage firms attempted to woo independent brokers back to their firms. In 1998, 96,000 independent brokers offered services nationwide. Independents cited an ability to offer flexibility to customers, since these brokers were not limited to offering products from a parent company.

Regional securities brokers also took advantage of Wall Street downsizing to beef up their own staff. While firms like Merrill Lynch and Company planned to cut its staff by 5 percent (or 3,400 people) in 1998, smaller regional firms like Piper Jaffray of Minneapolis, Minnesota, used funds of $730 million to hire additional staff.

Brokerages in the late 1990s attempted to better reach untapped potential customers by hiring women and minority brokers. According to the Securities Industry Association, nearly 800,000 potential customers represent untapped women or minority markets in the country. But CEO Joseph Grano of PaineWebber Inc. (*American Banker,* 2 June 1998) admitted that the industry had a long way to go in hiring minorities, claiming that the industry had a difficult time attracting them and retaining them. Other executives cited industry consolidation and resistance to change as barriers in hiring more women or minority brokers.

AMERICA AND THE WORLD

Securities firms in the United States, as well as in other countries, often deal in foreign markets to access untapped capital, among other reasons. By issuing a security in a foreign market, a company can increase the success of its offering simply by increasing the size of the potential market. A second important impetus for buying and selling overseas securities is to achieve greater returns and asset diversification. Although the United States maintains the largest and most efficient securities industry and markets in the world, foreign securities industries were becoming increasingly competitive, and overseas markets more attractive, in the early 1990s.

The international securities market began to realize explosive growth in 1983. U.S. purchases and sales of foreign stocks skyrocketed from $15.7 billion in 1982 to $320.3 billion in 1992. Purchases and sales of bonds during the same period bounded as well, from $61 billion to $824 billion. At the same time, foreign purchases and sales of U.S. stocks and bonds increased at an even greater pace. Combined sales and purchases of U.S. stocks and bonds spiraled from $296 billion in 1982 to $5.1 trillion by 1992, a 17-fold increase.

Although new technology was the greatest reason for the emergence of the global securities market, as discussed later, regulatory reform on all continents was also an important factor. This has resulted as governments have discovered that globalized financial markets encourage flows of capital to regions offering the best returns. They also recognized that open markets have allowed investors to achieve greater portfolio diversification, thus creating more stable markets.

The United States has been a leader in the opening of markets for foreign investment. During the 1980s the SEC revised many of its rules to assure that capital raising in the United States by foreign issuers was not unnecessarily hampered. In 1990 the SEC adopted Rule 144a, which made it easier for large institutions to trade certain securities among themselves, thereby encouraging foreign issuers to invest in U.S. markets despite U.S. disclosure requirements. In 1991 the SEC acted again by allowing certain Canadian firms to issue securities prepared in accordance with Canadian requirements, rather than under U.S. laws. Furthermore, in the 1990s foreign companies increasingly issued American Depository Receipts (ADRs) in the United States in order to obtain additional sources of equity capital.

Similar breakdowns in barriers of overseas markets in the 1980s and early 1990s were encouraging U.S. securities firms to venture abroad as well, often despite less efficient overseas markets. For instance, surplus countries—such as Japan—have opened their markets as a result of pressure from other nations seeking a greater balance of world capital flows. In fact, Japan and England both led other Asian and European nations to deregulate their markets when both countries abolished many of their controls in 1979. Further reorganization of financial markets by the European Community promises more efficient markets in the future.

The ramifications of global markets for the U.S. securities industry include the potential for a broadened role in world financial markets, more investment alternatives and financial products, greater access to capital, and a greater volume of transactions. As markets continue to become more efficient, and foreign securities industries become more advanced, however, the global market will also mean greater competition for U.S. firms.

RESEARCH AND TECHNOLOGY

Advances in technology continued to have a marked impact on the securities industry in the 1990s. Technology was rapidly changing the entire structure of the industry in several ways. Companies were relying increasingly on computer automation to reduce costs and to meet federal reporting requirements. In addition, markets and exchanges in the United States were becoming more ''electronic'' each year, allowing various trading functions to be conducted by computer. Finally, computer technology was quickly creating a global securities market in which investors and capital seekers around the world could collaborate.

Successful securities firms in the 1990s were those that had made, or were making, the technological leap from transaction processors to information processors. Firms were coordinating sales, trading, and financial advisory services through advanced information system networks. This was allowing companies to reduce transaction costs, make better investment decisions, and deliver new products more quickly, thereby increasing customer service and lowering overhead costs. Advanced information systems were also becoming vital as a result of increased SEC reporting requirements.

Besides making companies within the industry more productive, information technology was also altering the way that securities were bought and sold in the marketplace. For instance, programmed trading allows brokers and dealers to complete transactions by computer, rather than from the floor of an exchange. Although critics of this system argue that it creates excessive market volatility, increased regulation of the system following the 1987 market crash has alleviated resistance.

Automated trading techniques will increasingly influence the market, as they continue to deliver greater cost benefits. For instance, in 1988 the average cost of executing an order on the floor of the NYSE for a firm was $12.87 using one of its own brokers, and $24.32 for an independent broker. Using Designated Order Turnaround (DOT), the automated system, the cost fell in the range of

$4.84 to $8.67 per transaction, depending on the number of daily transactions a company made on the system.

In addition to changes it has prompted in the way firms and markets operate, information technology has had the most notable impact upon global securities markets. Advancements in telecommunications and satellite systems allow investors and capital seekers to monitor and participate in world markets on a minute-by-minute basis. By the mid- to late 1980s, however, issuing procedures had been simplified and accelerated to the point that borrowers could offer issues in several national markets simultaneously. Indeed, all market participants now have access to information allowing them to swiftly orchestrate complex financing techniques that simultaneously integrate multiple national markets.

While great strides have been made in uniting international markets with new technologies, there was still enormous room for improvement going into the mid-1990s. Industry leaders in participating nations were still in the process of developing a central or global depository/clearance system, which would essentially settle trades of securities made by members of separate nations. A system of this type, similar to the one that exists for trades made in the United States, would make markets more efficient. Furthermore, many nations were still overcoming their reluctance to allow computerized access to their financial markets.

FURTHER READING

Darnay, Arsen J., ed. *Finance, Insurance, and Real Estate, USA.* Detroit: Gale Research, 1995.

———, and Marlita A. Reddy, eds. *Market Share Reporter.* Detroit: Gale Research, 1996.

Dillon, Jim. ''Centerville, Ohio, Securities Brokers See Benefits of Independence.'' *Knight-Ridder/Tribune Business News,* 14 October 1999.

''The Forbes Platinum List: Financial Services.'' *Forbes,* 11 January 1999.

Goldberg, Steven T. ''Online Brokers GROW UP.'' *Kiplinger's Personal Finance Magazine,* November 1999.

Graff, Brett Illyse. ''Employment Trends in the Security Brokers and Dealers Industry.'' *Monthly Labor Review,* September 1995.

''Largest Mutual Fund Groups, 1999,'' 30 April 1999. Available from http://www.mfcafe.com/market/msp_top50.html or http://www.galenet.com/servlet/GBR/hits?c = 18&seg = 0&t = KW&s = 6&r = d&o = DocTitle&n = 25&l = dm&DT = Market + Share + Report&SE = ''6211 + - + Security + Brokers + & + Dealers''.

''Largest Mutual Funds, 1999.'' *Christian Science Monitor,* 12 April 1999. Available from http://www.galenet.com/servlet/GBR/hits?c = 21&seg = 0&t = KW&s = 6&r = d&o = DocTitle&n = 25&l = dm&DT = Market + Share + Report&SE = ''6211 + - + Security + Brokers + & + Dealers''.

''Largest Securities Firms, 1999, Dun & Bradstreet's Business Rankings, 1998.'' *Industry Week,* 18 January 1999. Available from http://www.galenet.com/servlet/GBR/hits?c = 24&seg = 0&t = KW&s = 6&r = d&o = DocTitle&n = 25&l = dm&DT = Market + Share + Report&SE = ''6211 + - + Security + Brokers + & + Dealers''.

Lipin, Steven. ''1995 Year-End Review of Markets and Finance: Review of Finance; Let's Do It—Disney to Diaper Makers Push Mergers and Acquisitions to Record High.'' *Wall Street Journal,* 2 January 1996.

Merill Lynch Annual Report, 1996.

Monahan, Julie. ''Recruiting Minorities, Women: Brokers Say They're Trying.'' *American Banker,* 2 June 1998.

Morgan Stanley Annual Report, 1996.

Raghavan, Anita. ''1995 Year-End Review of Markets and Finance; Review of Underwriting: Underwriters Revel In a Robust Year as Interest Rates Drop.'' *Wall Street Journal,* 2 January 1996.

''The Real Virtual Business.'' *The Economist,* 8 May 1999.

Standard & Poor's Industry Surveys. New York: Standard & Poor's Corporation, July 1996.

Tarquino, J. Alex. ''Regional Securities Brokers Hiring as Wall Street Cuts Back.'' *American Banker,* 16 October 1998.

''Why Old-Line Firms Need New Online Tricks.'' *Business Week,* 24 May 1999.

SIC 6221

COMMODITY CONTRACTS BROKERS AND DEALERS

This industry classification includes establishments primarily engaged in buying and selling commodity contracts (futures) on either a spot or future basis for their own account or for the account of others. These establishments are members, or are associated with members, of recognized commodity exchanges. Establishments primarily engaged in buying and selling commodities are classified in wholesale trade. However, the Chicago Board of Trade doesn't trade, it just provides facilities for members to trade future and options contracts.

NAICS CODE(S)

523130 (Commodity Contracts Dealings)
523140 (Commodity Brokerage)

In 1997, 2,044 establishments operated under this industry classification, most of which were commodity contracts brokerages. The industry employed 17,763 people and generated $5.3 billion.

In general, brokers are independent traders who bring together buyers and sellers of the same commodity and execute their orders. The broker receives a commission on each of these transactions. These brokers are agents of their clients and are, therefore, subject to the law of agency in their dealings with their clients. In contrast to the broker's role as an agent, a dealer acts as a principal in relations with customers. This is the only difference between commodities brokers and dealers.

Commodities brokers and dealers are engaged in the trade of commodities on either a current, "spot," or a future basis. Commodities are typically agricultural, mineral, or other basic products and financial futures that are traded on a commodity exchange. The products are generally substitutable. This means that the purchaser is unlikely to differentiate between one unit of the product and another. Agricultural products such as wheat, corn and soybean contracts are written with certain grade and other specifications as standardized contracts stating the quantity and quality of the product.

The commodity exchanges are organizations that are owned by their members for the purpose of bringing buyers and sellers together. The transactions made by these parties can be performed on a spot basis, in which the commodity is sold for cash and immediate delivery, or on a future basis, under which the purchaser has the right to buy a commodity at a future time at a fixed price. There are a number of these exchanges throughout the country, all of which are supervised by the federal government under the Commodity Exchange Act administered by the Commodity Futures Trading Commission.

Commodity prices are quoted on either a spot or future basis on an electronic board each time they change. Future prices are quoted based on the date of delivery of the contracted commodities. Prices are quoted as they occur based on trades in trading pits during specified hours. Trades are only made by members. There has been a trend in the commodities futures markets to move away from traditional commodities. As the type and number of commodity futures contracts have increased, brokers have handled ever higher volumes.

Commodity brokers and dealers range in size from large operations to small businesses. Industry leaders include Smith Barney, Andersons Investment Service Corporation, Archer Daniel Midland Company, Bank America Corporation, Bankers Trust New York Corporation, Bunge Corporation, Citicorp, Credit Lyonnais, Rouse USA Ltd., Dean Reynolds, Inc., First Chicago Corporation, Goldman Sachs Company, J.P. Morgan Futures Inc., Merrill Lynch Futures Inc., and Yamaichi International.

FURTHER READING

Commodities Traders Manual. Chicago: Chicago Board of Trade, 1997.

Troy, Leo, *Almanac of Business and Industrial Financial Ratios.*

U.S. Census Bureau. *1997 Economic Census—Finance and Insurance,* Washington: GPO, 2000. Available from http://www.census.gov.

SIC 6231

SECURITIES AND COMMODITIES EXCHANGES

This category includes establishments primarily engaged in furnishing space and other facilities to members for the purpose of buying, selling, or otherwise trading in stocks, stock options, bonds, or commodity contracts.

NAICS CODE(S)

523210 (Securities and Commodity Exchanges)

INDUSTRY SNAPSHOT

This classification is divided into two distinct industries: stock exchanges and commodities exchanges. Each of these industries has its own structure, history, and participants. Modern securities exchanges in the United States are voluntary entities organized for centralized trading. These organizations' constitutions, bylaws, rules, and regulations govern the members and the trading of issues listed by the exchange. These organizations do not trade the listed securities themselves, rather, they provide the facilities required for organized trading. Stock exchanges also aid the marketability of their listed issues by providing the facilities required for high volume trade and by requiring the firms listed on the exchange to observe standards in accounting and reporting. These functions make the issues accessible and enhance public confidence in the exchange and its listed securities.

The Securities Exchange Act of 1934 regulates the trade of securities in the United States. This act created the Securities Exchange Commission (SEC) and required any brokers or dealers engaged in the exchange of securities to report these transactions to the SEC, unless the exchange was registered as a national securities exchange, was specifically exempted, or was not practicable and necessary nor in the public interest for the protection of the investors to require such registration.

In addition to these formal exchanges, the over-the-counter market is also very significant. Over-the-counter transactions do not have a central market in which they are executed. Instead, they are negotiated over the phone or, more commonly, electronically. The NASDAQ (National Association of Securities Dealers Automated Quotation), in particular, has grown in importance, gaining market share of stock listings over the regular exchanges.

Bonds, too, are an exception. While various stock exchanges list bonds, they are traded primarily by bond houses and major commercial banks. The bond market is primarily institutional, with commercial banks as the primary investors. It is not heavily regulated, and there is no federal agency dedicated to overseeing the bond market other than the SEC.

Commodities exchanges are typically organizations that are owned by trading members and are organized to facilitate transactions between buyers and sellers of various commodities. These exchanges are regulated by three different acts. First, the Commodity Exchange Act of 1922 established the Commodity Exchange Commission, which consisted of the U.S. Secretary of Commerce, Secretary of Agriculture, and the Attorney General. Second, the Commodity Exchange Act of 1936 attempted to limit fraud, manipulation, and excessive speculation. Finally, The Commodities Futures Trading Commission Act of 1974 created the Commodities Futures Trading Commission, which succeeded the Commodity Exchange Commission.

Organization and Structure

Securities exchanges are governed by the Securities Exchange Act of 1934 and regulated by the SEC. The SEC has three major responsibilities: ensuring the provision of full and fair disclosure of all material facts concerning securities offered for public investment, pursuing litigation for fraud when detected, and registering securities offered for public investment. The SEC's activities are similar to judicial proceedings, and appeals from its decisions are taken to the U.S. Court of Appeals. Structurally, the SEC is composed of five commissioners appointed by the president for five-year terms. No more than three of these commissioners may be from the same political party. The chairman is also designated by the president.

Commodities exchanges are regulated by the Commodities Futures Trading Commission subject to the Commodities Exchange Act of 1922. This act, along with its later amendments in 1936 and 1975, subjects commodities, commodity futures, and option trading to federal supervision and restricts trading to futures exchanges designated and licensed by the Commission. The Commodity Exchange Commission, was originally established by the Security Exchange Act of 1922 to supervise commodity exchange, but the Commission was succeeded by the Commodity Futures Trading Commission upon the passage of the Commodity Futures Trading Act of 1974.

In general, both the stock and commodities exchanges are governed by a board of directors who are elected from the membership of the exchange. In some cases board members are also selected from outside the exchange's membership to represent the public. The members are individuals or other legal entities who own a "seat" on the exchange. Seats are generally acquired by purchasing existing seats from previous members. The individual exchanges derive their income from membership dues, listing fees, and specialized services. This income is used to cover the operational expenses of the exchange.

Background and Development

Prior to 1934, the exchange of stocks in the United States was unregulated. The exchanges that existed at the time were only limited by a sense of duty to their members and concern for their reputation. This system was sufficient through the bull market of the 1920s; however, the 1929 stock market crash and resulting Great Depression brought this system under renewed scrutiny.

In 1933, the Congress passed the Securities Act, establishing disclosure requirements. This act was followed by the Securities Exchange Act in 1934, which brought stock exchanges under federal regulation. The act created the SEC and required all transactions to be completed on exchanges registered with the SEC. This registration required the exchange to file a registration statement containing various information and documents. Every corporation listed on the exchanges was also required to register with the SEC and to file annual reports and other periodic updates.

In 1975 amendments to the Securities Exchange Act mandated the creation of a National Securities Market by the SEC. This system is composed of automated linking of various stock exchanges. The links were created to stimulate competition in the market. These changes were implemented due to the increased volume of trading, as individual investors were slowly being replaced by institutional investors. The exchanges adjusted to this new market by altering their rules and adopting automation. From 1975 to 1987 the yearly volume of trade on the New York Stock Exchange increased ten-fold.

Despite comprehensive automation, the market strained to handle the volume of transactions caused by the market collapse on Black Tuesday, October 19, 1987. That crisis led to the adoption of circuit breaker mechanisms, which halt trade when prices fall too quickly. The exchanges have also increased floor space, computer system capacity, and raised specialists' capital requirements. Many experts believe that these changes have made the U.S. exchanges more reliable and resilient.

One major development during the 1990s was the advent of communications technology that enabled trading to be conducted off exchange floors. Electronic Communications Networks (ECNs) are alternative trading systems that function much like stock exchanges—collecting, displaying, and automatically executing customer orders. In 1994, charges were made that NASDAQ market makers were charging excessive markups on trades they executed. In response, the SEC effectively forced the adoption of Order Handling Rules in 1997. The rule requires dealers to post customers' orders on NASDAQ's screen or send them to an electronic communications network that would post them for everyone's viewing. ECNs were thus inadvertently allowed into the exchanges.

Day-trading firms, which for years had sought greater market access to NASDAQ, soon rushed in to set up ECNs. The oldest and largest of the ECNs is Reuter Group PLC's Instinet. ECNs, which are regulated by NASDAQ's parent, the National Association of Securities Dealers (NASD), accounted for nearly 30 percent of NASDAQ's share volume in 1999.

Competition from the ECNs also caused the exchanges to expand the hours of trading. Since ECNs are set up to offer round-the-clock trading, exchanges would have to do the same to protect their market from eroding. Most of the world's largest stocks already trade in three major time zones, namely, the United States, London, and Tokyo. Related changes as a result of continuous trading would mean further growth for discount brokers and Internet trading. Newspapers and television networks would adjust their financial reporting to fulfill the demand, and more people would be added to the workforce to cater to the trading activities.

In 1999, a new SEC rule commonly known as "Reg ATS" (Alternative Trading Systems) took effect. This regulation allows ECNs and other electronic trading systems to actually become stock exchanges. ATSs are small, private systems that are lightly regulated and are able to make quick innovations. They serve to drive down the cost of trading and to spur innovations such as extended trading hours and online trading via the Internet.

The rise of the Internet as a revolutionary new form of interactive communication has also affected the delivery of financial information by providing investment tools or executing securities transactions. By the end of 1996, Internet technology had made stock quotes available on dozens of Web sites, and most suppliers were giving the data away. This change in the delivery of securities data has contributed to the boom in online trading.

According to Forrester Research, there were about 4 million online brokerage accounts at the end of 1998. It also projected 9.2 million online brokerage accounts by the year 2001. The largest discount brokers, such as Charles Schwab, have witnessed their online account share of their total account base jump from 5 percent 5 years ago to 60 percent in 1999.

Online brokers grew from 1 to 100 in just 3 years as reported by Gomez Advisors in 1998. Most Internet brokers are the online offspring of traditional financial service firms. Coupled with the online account growth of traditional service firms offering online access was the growing account base of the predominately online-only brokerage such as E*Trade, Ameritrade, and Datek Online.

The number of online trading individuals also grew 53 percent to 6.1 million in a year from 1998 to 1999, according to reporting by Cybercitizen Finance. Given this lightening-fast growth, the exchanges are confronted with the question of what constitutes an exchange and the role it will play in the future.

Prior to 1922, commodities exchanges were unregulated. In 1922 the Grain Futures Act was passed, beginning the regulation of commodities exchanges. In 1936 this act was amended to include commodities other than grain, and in 1975 an independent federal agency was created to administer the provisions of this act. In addition to the trend towards more regulation, the commodities exchanges have also mirrored the stock exchanges' move towards greater automation.

Early in the 1990s futures exchanges started to seek alliances to boost business. In 1992, the Chicago Mercantile Exchange (CME) launched Globex, with the Singapore International Monetary Exchange (Simex) and France's Matif as partners. In 1993, the New York Mercantile Exchange (NYMEX) opened its Access system in London listing its own energy contracts. The quest for listing on international exchanges thus continued.

Setting up global networks to create a globally linked marketplace that provides cross-border opportunities for investors worldwide has become the goal of the exchanges. By 1999 an alliance between Eurex, the all-electronic German/Swiss derivatives exchange, and the Chicago Board of Trade (CBOT) was announced. Soon after, CME and the London International Financial Futures & Options Exchange (Liffe) were to link up their electronic platforms, Globex2 and Liffe Connect, to allow members to trade each other's short-term interest rate contracts electronically. Liffe chairman Brian Williamson believes that the partnership brings to their customers international access to a wide range of products, lower transaction costs, and a more efficient use of capital.

CURRENT CONDITIONS

The New York Stock Exchange (NYSE) is the largest equities marketplace in the world with 3,025 companies worth more than $16 trillion in global market capitalization. As of year-end 1999, the NYSE had 280.9 billion shares worth approximately $12.3 trillion listed and available for trading. Over two-thirds of the roster of NYSE companies has listed with the Exchange within the last 12 years.

Since its inception in 1971, NASDAQ has steadily outpaced the other major markets to become the fastest-growing stock market in the United States—and ranks second among the world's securities markets in terms of dollar volume. The NASDAQ difference is in its market structure. In contrast to traditional floor-based stock markets, NASDAQ has no single specialist through which transactions pass. NASDAQ's market structure allows multiple market participants to trade stocks through a sophisticated computer network linking buyers and sellers from around the world. This successful model has pushed other exchanges to reinvent themselves. For instance, the London Stock Exchange, the Singapore Stock Exchange, and Japan's JASDAQ all adopted NASDAQ's screen-based, floorless electronic market system.

As the NYSE continues to face stiff competition from alternative trading systems, it has announced several plans to modernize and to transform its operation. The main plan is to list itself as a public company. Like any other for-profit companies, the quickest way to modernize itself is to find an Internet business partner and in this case, an ECN. For NYSE, it will set up its own electronic communications network to automatically match small orders of up to 1,000 shares. Coupling with this initiative, the NYSE might also increase the free time that specialists have to give member firms coming over the NYSE's electronic routing system without charging. These initiatives mean less income for its specialists and floor brokers but offer its Wall Street member firms better service at reduced cost. NASD is also planning to spin off the NASDAQ Stock Market as a for-profit entity. The Pacific Exchange has likewise taken action to reinvent itself as the nation's first for-profit stock exchange.

When an exchange goes public, institutional investors will be able to buy a large enough stake in it to affect the rules that govern listed companies. The question becomes whether the exchanges can both trade on and regulate the exchanges. The NASD's plan is for the regulatory portion to retain its not-for-profit status. However, there are increasing numbers of shares traded over electronic networks that are not governed by any self-regulating organizations. Of course one would assume that the institutional investors with equity in the exchange would act in the best interest of the exchange with respect to rules governing it. Otherwise the listed companies can leave the exchange and take their business elsewhere.

At the same time the exchanges were protecting their stakes, the SEC was completing Market 2000 in 1993, its first review of the U.S. equity market for 20 years. This SEC paper asked respondents to identify regulatory anachronisms and called for comments on rules 390 and 500. Rule 390 bans member firms from trading issues listed on the exchange prior to 1979 off the exchange's floor while it is open. Rule 500 requires a two-thirds majority vote of shareholders in favor to delist a company. By the end of 1999, the board of the New York Stock Exchange voted to repeal Rule 390, moving into line with the wishes of the SEC. With the rule eliminated, firms could transfer more of their customers' orders from public markets into their own trading rooms.

In the options market, the exchanges are competing to list big companies. The Chicago Board Options Exchange (CBOE) listed Dell Computer Corp. in August 1999, a major contract that before had been listed solely by the Philadelphia Stock Exchange (PHLX). The unwritten rule was that certain marquee contracts are listed by one single exchange. Since CBOE ignored this agreement, PHLX listed CBOE's Coca-Cola and Amex's Apple Computer Inc. to position themselves accordingly. By September, CBOE listed 29 other previously single-listed contracts, notably Microsoft Corp., Sun Microsystems Inc., and 3Com Corp.

The competition is favored by the SEC and the Commodities Futures Trading Commission (CFTC), which have taken steps to encourage multiple listing of equity options and approve the applications of screen-based systems as contract markets.

The growth of information technology and the rise of NASDAQ and Internet trading have changed the landscape of the securities industry. The information that was once privileged to bankers and Wall Street elites is now at everyone's fingertips, more changes will occur as the Internet matures.

INDUSTRY LEADERS

Securities Market Centers. At the end of 1999 there were eight major stock markets operating in the United States, including seven stock exchanges and NASDAQ, the first floorless, screen-based market center in the world. The two largest of these market centers by far are the New York Stock Exchange (NYSE) and the NASDAQ stock market. Other major exchanges include: Boston Stock Exchange, Chicago Stock Exchange, Chicago Board of Options, Cincinnati Stock Exchange, Pacific Stock Exchange, and Philadelphia Stock Exchange.

The ''Buttonwood Agreement'' established the New York Stock Exchange in 1792. Today the NYSE is generally recognized as the world's most prestigious and influential stock exchange, although beginning in 1994 the NASDAQ has regularly surpassed it in annual trading volume. Over 3,000 companies are traded on the NYSE, and the aggregate market value of these companies was approximately $9.4 trillion at the end of 1997.

The NASDAQ stock market was created in 1971 as the world's first electronic market listing small companies. In the 1980s, NASDAQ experienced substantial growth as hundreds of new technology firms rushed to have their shares listed in this high-tech marketplace.

Even as NASDAQ enjoyed almost uninterrupted growth, however, the American Stock Exchange (Amex) suffered from a steady decline in its company listings and trading volume. At the end of 1997, over 5,400 hundred companies were listed on NASDAQ, compared to 771 for the Amex. Although finding itself unable to compete effectively with NASDAQ's tech-heavy appeal or the Big Board's blue chip prestige, the Amex did develop into the country's second-largest options market behind the Chicago Board Options Exchange.

The National Association of Securities Dealers, Inc. (NASD) and the American Stock Exchange merged at the end of 1998 to maximize the efficiencies of both organizations. NASDAQ and Amex continue to operate as separate markets under the NASDAQ-Amex Market Group, a subsidiary of the NASD that oversees both market systems and explores technological efficiencies and international opportunities. Since the merger, one area of growth for the Amex has been in the area of Index-Based Products or Exchange Trade Funds (ETFs) such as Standard and Poor's Depositary Receipts (SPDRs), World Equity Benchmark Shares (WEBs), and NASDAQ-100 Index Trading Stock (QQQ or ''Cube''). These increasingly popular investment instruments provide investors with an alternative to index-based mutual funds as a way to achieve ''instant'' diversification in the stock market.

Commodities Exchanges. There are 13 major commodities exchanges currently operating in the United States. Of the 13, 4 are the most significant. The Chicago Board of Trade (CBOT), founded in 1858, is the most important grain exchange in the United States. Approximately 90 percent of the world's grain futures are traded on its floors. In addition to commodities, CBOT is also involved in the financial futures and options markets as well as precious metals. CBOT is regulated by the Commodities Futures Trading Commission subject to the Commodities Exchange Act.

The Chicago Mercantile Exchange (CME), founded in 1919, provides a national market for transactions in spot and futures contracts for commodities. The CME is also a leading exchange for futures trading in financial instruments and foreign currencies. The CME is regulated by the Commodities Futures Trading Commission subject to the Commodities Exchange Act.

The Commodity Exchange (COMEX), created by the post-Depression merger in 1933 of four exchanges, is one of the largest and most active commodities exchanges in the world. COMEX provides an organized, centralized market where commodities contracts of precious metals are traded. In 1994 COMEX was bought by the New York Mercantile Exchange (NYMEX), which trades futures in precious metals, oil, and gas. COMEX maintains its name as a division of NYMEX.

Commodities exchanges of lesser importance include: Amex Commodities Exchanges, Inc., Chicago Rice and Cotton Exchange (CRCE), Coffee, Sugar & Cocoa Exchange (CSCE), Kansas City Board of Trade (KCBOT), Mid-America Commodity Exchange (MACE), Minneapolis Grain Exchange (MGE), New York Cotton Exchange (CTN), New York Futures Exchange (NYFE), and Philadelphia Board of Trade (PBOT).

WORKFORCE

According to the Securities Industry Association, the securities industry employed over 612,000 people in 1997. This figure represents a 36 percent increase in 5 years, reflecting the growth in investment activities that began in the earlier part of the decade. By the end of 1999, the industry employed approximately 700,000 individuals.

AMERICA AND THE WORLD

One major trend in the securities industry that came to the fore in the 1990s and is certain to continue on in the 2000s, is globalization. More than ever before, U.S. investors poured money into foreign stocks during the 1990s, with over $1.4 trillion worth of foreign stocks being traded in 1997 alone. Similarly, foreign investors found much to attract them in the U.S. stock market.

The continued strength of the U.S. equity market, and global mergers and acquisitions, have attracted international companies to list their stocks on the U.S. exchanges. About 200 foreign companies per year list in the United States, and the number has been rising. NYSE has experienced substantial growth in this sector over the years since 1985. As of July 1999, 382 non-U.S. companies were listed, more than triple the number in 1994.

At the end of 1998, the NASDAQ listed over 440 foreign companies, compared to 4,600 U.S. firms. Overseas, the London Stock Exchange listed over 500 foreign companies (85 of which were U.S. firms), to go along with the 2,400 British firms included on the Exchange. Foreign companies were also particularly well represented on the exchanges in Switzerland, Amsterdam, and Brussels.

The most compelling globalization trend for the past few years, however, is the move towards cooperative undertaking among exchanges both regionally and worldwide, and the related move towards 24-hour-a-day continuous trading of stocks.

NASDAQ has ambitious plans for global expansion, with plans to set up a European equity exchange that eventually will be electronically linked both with its established U.S. market and with NASDAQ-Japan. The latter is scheduled to be launched in late 2000, to be co-run by the NASD and Japan's Softbank.

Along with NASDAQ's plans there is a drive towards the creation of a pan-European stock market that was launched in early 1999—spearheaded by the London Stock Exchange and the Deutsche Borse. Of course, even prior to the emergence of true worldwide markets and platforms for stocks and derivatives, most of the world's largest stocks already trade in a nearly full-day environment, as they are listed on exchanges in the United States, Europe, Japan, and elsewhere in Asia.

RESEARCH AND TECHNOLOGY

In a world of ECNs, discount brokers, instantaneous online access to investment information and trading opportunities (and the resultant growth of day trading), the North American securities industry as a whole spends billions of dollars per year on information technology. Eleven and a half billion dollars were spent in 1996 alone. Like securities firms, stock markets are faced with an on-going need to keep themselves technologically current—especially given the rush towards instigating continuous around-the-clock securities trading in a truly global market.

NASDAQ, which is already an electronic trading system, is in many respects best positioned to respond to current trends in technological change. Indeed, by the end of 1999, fully 30 percent of all NASDAQ transactions were being handled by ECNs.

NASDAQ has taken several steps to assure its technological infrastructure will be able to keep up with the demands of the marketplace. In late 1997, NASDAQ and MCI began working to develop a new telecommunications infrastructure for the stock market. The system is designed to be able to handle up to 8 billion shares being traded per day. Also in 1997, NASDAQ introduced a trio of new Web sites: NASDAQ Online, NASDAQ Newsroom, and NASDAQ Trader. Following the merger with the Amex in 1998, NASDAQ Online—designed to provide executives of NASDAQ-listed companies with up-to-the-minute market intelligence—was renamed NASDAQ-Amex Online. The merger between the two also provided Amex with access to a new electronic limit order book, order routing, and transaction system, intended to allow investors and market professionals to electronically execute orders from both on and off the trading floor.

For its part, the NYSE is looking for ECNs to begin trading NYSE-listed stocks sometime in 2000. In the meantime, the Exchange spent $2 billion on new technologies during the 1990s. By the end of 1999 NYSE's communications system had been upgraded so that it could handle systemic traffic of up to 1,000 messages per second—double the capacity of just two years earlier.

In a move to enhance productivity, the NYSE rolled out Smart Report in 1998, a new feature of its specialist display book designed to help free up specialists to focus on maintaining an orderly market. Another recent focus of technological improvements by the NYSE has been its Broker Booth Support System (BBSS), which provided member firms with direct electronic links from upstairs desks to the trading floor, to points of sales, and, ultimately, to the customer. Begun in 1993 with 16 terminals in use, the BBSS had grown by 1998 to having more than 700 terminals in use.

FURTHER READING

Barrett, William P. "End of an Era." *Forbes,* 11 October 1999.

Carey, Theresa W. "The Electronic Investor: This Was the Year of the Internet." *Barron's,* 30 December 1996.

Cavanaugh, Katherine. "NASDAQ Chief Reveals His Global Plan." *Wall Street and Technology,* December 1999.

Codding, Jamey. "Exchanges Break Unwritten Rule." *Futures,* October 1999.

Garrity, Brian. "Global M&A Boom Creates Glut of U.S. Listing Hopefuls." *The Investment Dealers' Digest: IDD,* 6 September 1999.

"HighTech Trading: the Market's New Landscape." *Wall Street Journal Europe,* 28 July 1999.

"Index Shares." 2000. Available from http://options.nasdaq-amex.com/indexshares/index_shares_over.stm.

"Key Statistics 1998." *London Stock Exchange Web Site.* Available from http://www.londonstockexchange.com/about/keystatistics/comparisons.html.

"Let Markets Multiply." *The Economist,* 16 January 1993.

Mosser, Mike. "Liffe and CME Form Partnership." *Futures,* September 1999.

"NASD and Amex Merger Completed: the NASDAQ-Amex Market Group Formed." NASDAQ news release, 2 November 1998. Available from http://www.nasdaq.com/reference/sn_day1PR.stm.

"NASDAQ's Parent in Talks to Take Over American Stock Exchange." *Dow Jones Business News,* 3 March 1998.

The NASDAQ Stock Market. *The NASDAQ Stock Market 1998 Fact Book & Company Directory*, 1998, p. 6.

NASDAQ Web Site. Available from http://www.nasdaq.com.

New York Stock Exchange. *Fact Book for the Year 1997, 1998.* New York: 1997, 1998.

New York Stock Exchange Web Site, 1999. Available from http://www.nyse.com.

"NYSE IPO Threatens Corporate Governance of Listed Companies." *Investor Relations Business,* 6 September 1999.

Securities Industry Association. "Securities Industry Trends." 6 May 1998.

Securities Industry Association. "Securities Industry Trends." 12 May 1999.

Securities Industry Association. ''Technology Trends in the Securities Industry: Spending Strategies, Challenges and Changes-1997.'' *Securities Industry Association Report*, 1997.

Securities Industry Association Web Site. Press Release of December 28, 1999. Available from http://www.sia.com/html/pr858.html.

''Stock and Derivatives Exchanges.'' *Financial Times*, 23 March 1999.

''U.S. Market Size for Internet Usage with Number of Online Consumers, Purchasers and Users by Financial Function at July 1998 vs. July 1999.'' Available from http://www3.xls.com/cgi-bin/tblsuite.exe.

Vinzant, Carol. ''Do We Need a Stock Exchange?'' *Fortune*, 22 November 1999.

Wipperfurth, Heike. ''Pacific Exchange Tours New York in Search of Partners.'' *The Investment Dealers' Digest: IDD*, 18 October 1999.

———. ''Beset by Rivals, the NYSE Considers Two Broad Electronic Trading Counterattacks: One Could Cost Specialists up to $100 Million in Lost Commissions.'' *The Investment Dealers' Digest: IDD*, 8 November 1999.

Wolf, Barnet D. ''Extra Dividends: Expanded Trading Hours Will Continue to Change Landscape; Does a Longer Trading Day Mean Companies Will Start Making Big Announcements at 1 a.m.?'' *The Columbus (OH) Dispatch*, 6 June 1999.

SIC 6282

INVESTMENT ADVICE

This category covers establishments that participate in the investment advisement industry and are predominantly engaged in furnishing information and advice to companies and individuals concerning securities and commodities. These firms serve their clients on a contract or fee basis. Establishments that provide advice but also act as brokers or dealers are excluded from this category.

NAICS CODE(S)

523920 (Portfolio Management)
523930 (Investment Advice)

INDUSTRY SNAPSHOT

A broad spectrum of advisory firms make up the industry and are responsible for managing billions of dollars of U.S. and foreign assets every year. Mutual fund assets alone, of which investment counselors in the industry manage a significant portion, totaled more than $6 trillion by 1999. Mutual funds controlled more U.S. money than banking institutions.

Going into the mid-1990s, investment counselors were experiencing varying degrees of success depending on the market segment that they served and how they had positioned themselves in an increasingly competitive market. Companies that managed mutual fund dollars, for instance, were facing increasing competition from banks and other financial institutions that were making forays into nontraditional markets. Futures advisory services and investment research companies continued to realize solid growth. All firms in the industry were grappling with a general metamorphosis of financial markets, advancements in technology, and a gradual shift toward a global economy.

ORGANIZATION AND STRUCTURE

Futures and investment advisory firms, investment counseling services, research organizations, and mutual fund managers compose the investment advice industry. Several companies offer a multitude of services for all segments of the market, serving as ''one-stop shops'' for their clients' every need. Other organizations provide expertise in just one area, such as real estate investment research, indexing, or international hedging. Many of these firms form alliances with other specialty companies to deliver a package of client services. Although many firms exist solely to meet the market demand for these services, numerous industry participants offer advisory services only as a sideline. For instance, much of the advice and management of funds in the United States and abroad is provided by insurance companies and banks that are engaged primarily in other industries.

Futures and investment advisory firms typically provide advice and manage pools of funds for institutional clients. On a fee or contract basis, these firms seek to minimize their clients' exposure to risk in relation to the level of return that a client is seeking. Advisory firms that manage large pools of funds often seek the services of specialty firms that can provide expertise in a single area, such as real estate. In addition, many of these firms are often employed by larger players in the industry, such as mutual fund managers.

Investment counseling services may also assist institutions and provide services to larger firms. These firms, however, may also offer portfolio management services to individuals. Counselors will develop and manage an investment strategy that is specifically tailored to one individual's financial goals. Counselors consider the client's tax status, retirement plans, and other factors in an effort to protect and increase the client's resources. Though many firms require a minimum account size of at least seven figures, customers benefit from the individual attention. Money managers often charge between 1.5 and 3 percent of the account per year for their services.

Mutual Fund Managers. The largest single segment of the investment advice industry belongs to mutual fund managers. In mid-1999, there were 7,521 mutual funds. A mutual fund is effectively an investment company that

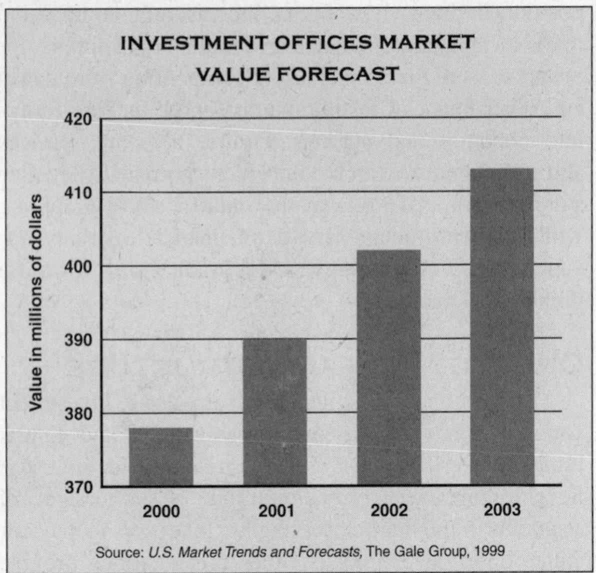

pools the money of many individual investors. Investors buy shares in the fund and the company invests the shareholders' cash for them. The company hires an adviser, or management company, to develop an investment strategy and to manage the fund.

Mutual fund investors do not benefit from individualized service as they might from a personal counselor. Mutual funds, however, allow small investors access to professional investment advisers who would otherwise be inaccessible—and at a relatively low cost. Furthermore, a wide variety of funds exist that are tailored to the needs of specific types of investors, allowing people with smaller accounts to place their money in funds that match their financial needs.

Most fund advisers receive a fee for stock selection and portfolio management activities based on the average value of the assets under management. Depending on the type of services provided and the category of fund managed, fees typically range from .20 percent (for index funds) to more than 1 percent of average annual fund assets. The management fee is usually set on a declining scale relative to fund size. The management company may administer and pay for some or all of the following: office space and personnel; portfolio managers and traders; regulatory compliance activities; preparation and distribution of prospectuses, advertising, and shareholder documents and reports; bookkeeping, accounting, and tax services; and bonding and insurance.

As of 1999 the six largest investment managers by total assets directed 93 percent of the $6 trillion in assets. Banks and insurance companies managed a large portion of those assets, however. In fact, four bank and trust companies and one insurance company were included in this elite group. The typical U.S. pension plan had about 39 percent of its assets in U.S. stocks, 20 percent in bonds, 14 percent in the company's own stock, 9.5 percent in international stocks, and 7.2 percent in guaranteed investment contracts.

Background and Development

The history of individual segments of the investment advisory industry is varied. Most advisory services and financial markets in the United States were originally derived from European markets—particularly those in the United Kingdom. After their inception, however, U.S. financial markets were more heavily influenced by domestic market conditions and regulatory developments.

The roots of U.S. futures trading, for example, date back about 200 years, when supply and demand imbalances in regional cash markets and agricultural commodities arose. Following the creation of organized futures exchanges between 1850 and 1900, hedging with futures eventually became an integral component of portfolio management theory. Investment advisers and fund managers found that they could use futures, as well as other instruments such as options, as tools to reduce risk and increase overall portfolio returns for their clients.

Opportunities for firms that offered futures advisement services proliferated in the 1980s and early 1990s as growing numbers of individual speculators began putting trading decisions in the hands of professional money managers who specialized in futures. Between 1980 and 1992, the number of commodity futures pool operators registered with the Commodity Futures Trading Commission grew 28 percent, to 1,350. The amount of money under management by these pools increased during the same period from $675 million to about $20 billion.

Growth in Mutual Fund Management. In contrast to futures, the first American mutual fund was not organized until 1924, when Massachusetts Investors Trust was started. The stock market crash of 1929 and World War II both served to hamper development of this industry throughout the late 1940s, when fewer than 100 funds representing only about $2 million existed. Opportunities for investment advisers who managed mutual funds remained relatively meager throughout the 1970s, although several new types of funds were developed during the mid-1900s.

In the late 1970s and early 1980s the demand for mutual fund advisers, as well as for investment consultants who served these managers, began to escalate. A combination of economic and regulatory factors made mutual funds more appealing to both individuals and some institutional investors. Furthermore, the increase in the number of no-load funds, which did not charge an entrance fee, made mutual funds more attractive until the mid-1980s. As assets in the mutual fund industry soared during the 1980s for a variety of reasons, the demand for fund advisers swelled. Mutual fund assets under management skyrocketed between 1986 and 1996 from about $700 billion to about $3.5 trillion dollars by 1996 and to $6 trillion in 1999. Growth in individual retirement accounts helped swell mutual fund assets. By 1999, retirement accounts held one-third of mutual fund assets.

Increasing Fees. The fees that advisers were charging to investment companies also escalated in the 1980s. Contracts that had traditionally been set at a fee of about .5 percent of managed assets jumped to an average of between .75 percent and 1 percent for funds organized during the late 1970s and 1980s. Another implication of growth in the 1980s that managers of some of the more popular funds realized was a loss of investment flexibility. As managers of these funds saw their fees jump as assets inflated into the billions of dollars, they found that they could not achieve investment returns similar to what they had generated prior to the rapid growth of assets. As a result, some larger funds struggled to keep market share from smaller competitors.

Pressures to hold down investment management fees were growing and alternative pricing arrangements were gaining favor. Managers handling international equity assets were reaping higher fees for their work than their colleagues managing domestic assets. Also, the fees on domestic equity categories easily outdistanced the charges on domestic fixed-income securities.

Competition Increases. Despite the growth in the amount of assets under management by firms primarily engaged in the investment advisement industry, the share of the total money management market served by these companies fell in the early 1990s. Banks and insurance companies increased their advisory services in an effort to offset losses in their core businesses. In addition, large publicly traded brokerage firms, such as Salomon Brothers Inc., Merrill Lynch & Co., and Prudential Securities Inc. moved into money management as they diversified from transaction-based businesses into fee-based ones. Furthermore, regulatory developments supported this trend by reducing the traditional distinctions between financial institutions. The result was more homogenous, though increasingly competitive, financial markets.

CURRENT CONDITIONS

Going into the late 1990s, the investment advice industry continued to experience both growth and turbulence in most market segments. Strong securities markets, shifting demographics, increased competition, changes in the structure of financial industries, and expanding global markets were all having a marked impact on industry activity.

Despite the recession of the late 1980s and early 1990s, futures and investment advisers, investment counselors, and mutual fund managers all enjoyed steady growth rates. Firms that managed mutual funds or provided expertise used by mutual fund managers realized the greatest gains. Aside from strong securities markets, fund advisers benefitted from an infusion of capital into long-term funds, as money continued to flow out of banks and long-term insurance instruments into more flexible mutual funds that provided higher returns. The growth in defined contribution pension plans, such as the 401(k), imbued large amounts of cash into the funds. Particularly benefitting from growth in mutual fund assets were money management firms that capitalized on expertise in a specific asset class, such as mortgage-backed securities.

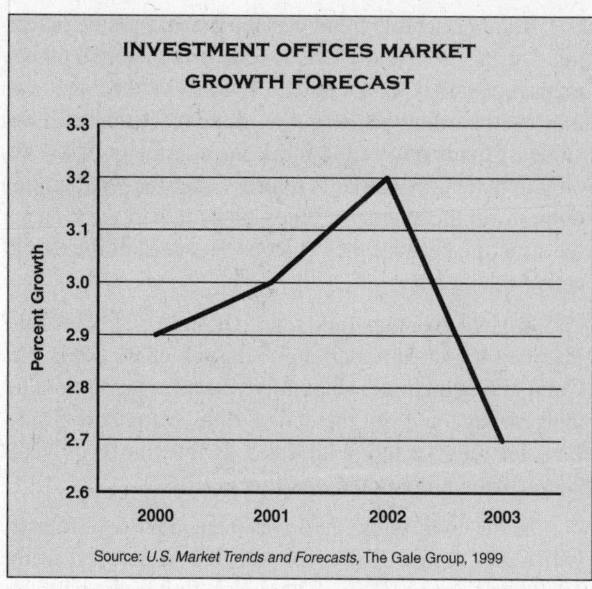

Source: *U.S. Market Trends and Forecasts*, The Gale Group, 1999

Another trend expected to continue into the year 2000 and beyond was industry consolidation. To achieve greater economies of scale and to offer one-stop-shop services to larger institutional clients, investment management firms began acquiring or merging with their competitors in the late 1980s. The consolidation trend accelerated in the mid-1990s. In 1994 Mellon Bank paid the equivalent of $1.8 billion to the stockholders of mutual fund manager Dreyfus. Also, Swiss Bank announced the purchase of institutional asset manager Brinson Partners, whose principals would receive $750 million for payment in an 11-year earn-out. In 1995 the acquisition of Wells Fargo Nikko Investment Advisors by Barclays PLC created one of the largest institutional money managers in the world, with $205 billion in assets. By 1999, former giants Scudder, Dreyfus, Founders, Stein Roe, Invesco, and Mutual Series had all merged with banks and other financial institutions.

Growth continued as of 1999, but slowly. There were 654 fund managers and only 52 new funds that year. Overall, sales fell 40 percent from 1998 to 1999. The slow growth rate continued to cause greater competition industry wide. Of the 654 fund managers, the top six companies controlled 93 percent of the industry.

Another notable trend was the rise of passive investing. During 1995 and 1996, the majority of active money managers failed to match the returns of the S&P 500 index. Accordingly, there was dramatic growth in the value of funds devoted to indexing, a strategy that seeks only to match the market's returns (after fees) rather than outperform the averages. Index funds thwart the existing fee structure because they charge less than half the fees of active managers.

In 1999 the index fund rose to prominence. This fund intended to match a market index such as the S&P 500. Competitive on price, index funds cause lower returns for their managers. As of the end of 1999, Vanguard Group, Inc., led this sector, with sales double those of FMR Corp., known commonly as Fidelity Investments.

In the long term, the investment advisory industry will likely realize slower growth than it enjoyed in the 1980s and early 1990s. Although aging baby boomers will be investing larger amounts of money in preparation for their retirement years, banks and insurers will continue to accrue greater shares of the money management market. Furthermore, costs associated with managing mutual funds will likely increase at a faster rate than advisory fees, placing downward pressure on company profit margins. Unfavorable economic developments could also deliver an unforeseen blow to the industry.

Industry Leaders

In 1999, 6 companies managed 93 percent of mutual fund assets, with the remaining 648 companies dividing the leftover 7 percent. Vanguard led the group with 35 percent, followed by Janus Capital Corporation with 20 percent, Fidelity with 17 percent, and PIMCO, Alliance, and MFS each with 7 percent.

Vanguard, of Malvern, Pennsylvania, reported 1998 sales of $1.2 billion, a 33 percent growth from the previous year. Janus, of Denver, Colorado, reported 1998 sales of more than $626 million, a 39 percent growth. Fidelity, based in Boston, reported 1998 sales of $6.7 billion.

PIMCO Advisors Holdings L.P., of Newport Beach, California, reported 1998 sales of $90.7 million, a 62 percent growth. Alliance Capital Management Holding L.P., of New York City, reported 1998 sales of $1.3 billion. MFS Investment Management, of Boston, reported 1998 sales of $849 million.

Workforce

Job growth in the advisement industry was projected to be greater than the average for all U.S. industries throughout 2005. Much of the growth would occur in firms that were principally engaged in other industries, such as banks and insurance companies. Besides clerical and support positions, the industry employed large numbers of portfolio managers, financial analysts, and other investment professionals. In 1992 the total number of portfolio managers employed by the 500 largest money managers rose 2.8 percent to 7,432. Analyst positions with those firms rose 5.8 percent to 5,723.

Other growth fields in the industry were expected to be in the areas of computer and information systems, which could experience over 80 percent growth between 1992 and 2005, and in sales. Positions in financial services sales would be likely to increase more than 60 percent by 2005. The greatest number of jobs would arise in larger metropolitan areas, particularly in Boston, Los Angeles, and New York.

America and the World

According to *Pensions & Investments* annual survey, the top 50 international and global money managers grew by 27.4 percent in the year that ended March 31, 1996, to $357.3 billion. A year earlier, the top 50 managed a total of $280.48 billion and in 1994, the top 50 managed $240.14 billion.

As fund managers continue to increase foreign investment to achieve greater returns and to reduce risk, the demand for international investment expertise should accelerate at the start of the twenty-first century. The demand for services by foreign investors will also likely increase as other countries increase investment abroad and seek respected U.S. financial expertise.

Although sales of U.S. fund shares was negligible prior to 1993, interest by foreign investors in U.S. funds was growing as financial markets became more globalized. In fact, in 1993 the Securities and Exchange Commission was actively working to liberalize international fund sales and to create uniform global investment regulations that would eventually result in nearly seamless world financial markets. Although these events could increase competition from foreign firms, U.S. advisement firms will likely benefit from integrated markets.

Research and Technology

Technological innovation affected the investment advice industry in two notable ways in the mid-1990s. First, smaller firms formed alliances that allowed them to compete with larger one-stop shops. And second, global and domestic markets became more integrated and efficient.

Driving both industry developments were advanced information systems that allowed people to access and exchange information almost instantaneously. For instance, small specialty firms found that they could forge partnerships with other firms using information systems. While each member of the alliance retained their expertise, the groups were often able to deliver a comprehensive service package for a lower fee than that charged by many institutional advisers.

As information systems permeated every corner of the global marketplace, investment advisers benefitted from instant access to global financial markets. Electronic trading and satellite information networks provided the information that was necessary for the industry to efficiently take advantage of global investment opportunities. Furthermore, new reporting and service delivery systems allowed advisement and management firms to reduce labor costs and errors and to maintain profit margins in the face of increased competition.

Competition was also expected to continue into the year 2000 from the wave of online investing. Unhappy with the industry's small growth, many people were beginning to manage their own money. Forecasters expected the trend to continue only in the short run, because the general public was not trained or knowledgeable about the industry.

FURTHER READING

Association for Investment Management and Research Homepage, 1999. Available from http://www.aimr.com.

Cardona, Mercedes M. ''Pressure on Fees Mounts.'' *Pensions & Investments,* 29 April 1996.

Dorfman, John R. ''Bigger Firms and Fatter Assets Dominate World of Money Managers.'' *Wall Street Journal,* 2 January 1997.

Perrit, Gerald W. *Mutual Funds Made Easy,* Chicago: Dearborn Financial Publishing, 1995.

Price, Margaret. ''Managers See Assets Increase 27.4 Percent.'' *Pensions & Investments,* 24 June 1996.

Standard & Poor's Industry Surveys. New York: Standard & Poor's Corporation, 1995.

Teitelbaum, Richard. ''Look Who's Beating Fidelity: Putnam.'' *Fortune,* 10 June 1996.

U.S. Department of Commerce. *U.S. Industrial Outlook, 1995,* Washington, DC: GPO, 1995.

U.S. Department of Labor. Bureau of Labor Statistics. *Occupational Outlook Handbook,* 1998-99 ed. Washington, DC: GPO, 1998. Available from http://stats.bls.gov/ocohome.htm.

Whitford, David. ''Where Have All the Geniuses Gone?'' *Fortune,* 11 October 1999.

SIC 6289

SERVICES ALLIED WITH THE EXCHANGE OF SECURITIES OR COMMODITIES, NOT ELSEWHERE CLASSIFIED

Services allied with the exchange of securities and commodities, not elsewhere classified, include companies that support financial markets. This industry excludes firms that provide investment advice or offer investment research and management services. Encompassed are a wide variety of companies that offer expertise in a broad variety of miscellaneous activities.

NAICS CODE(S)

523991 (Trust, Fiduciary, and Custody Activities)
523999 (Miscellaneous Financial Investment Activities)

Commodity and security clearinghouses are corporations established by an exchange in order to facilitate the execution of trades. This is accomplished by transferring funds, assigning deliveries, and guaranteeing the performance of all obligations. Member firms regularly submit statements to clearinghouses that indicate a net balance in each security or commodity on the exchange, along with the net amount to be paid or received, in order to balance the member's account.

A securities' custodian is a company, usually a commercial bank, that holds someone's assets for safekeeping in an account. For a fee, the custodial institution may collect dividends, interest, and proceeds from securities' sales, and disburse funds according to a customer's instructions. A quotation service is a firm that provides statements or listings of the prices at which securities trade. These quotes are often the last prices at which trades took place, but they may also be the current bid or asking price.

Transfer agents are another type of company in this industry. These organizations are usually banks or trust companies and are appointed by a second party to transfer its securities. The agent may also maintain current records of securities owners for transmitting dividends, reports, or securities distributions.

This industry originated in the United States in the early to mid-1800s, during the emergence of various U.S. financial markets. The establishment of the Securities and Exchange Commission (SEC), soon after the Great Depression in 1929, boosted many services. The SEC established various regulations that encouraged, and often mandated, the use of many of the miscellaneous services that now exist. The industry realized rapid growth during the post-World War II economic expansion.

Strong securities markets in the 1990s enabled most sectors of the industry to benefit from very active markets through the end of 1999. The Dow Jones Industrial Average continued to reach new heights throughout the late 1990s, zooming well past the 10,000 mark.

The major challenge facing the industry in the mid-1990s is the proliferation of discount trading via the Internet. As of 1998, online trading leaders, in terms of market share, were Schwab at 27.4 percent, Waterhouse at 12.4 percent, E*Trade at 11.8 percent, Datek at 10.0 percent, Fidelity at 9.4 percent, and Ameritrade at 7.6

percent. While many securities dealers offer online trading—such as Merrill Lynch, Quick and Reilly, Charles Schwab, Jack White—new companies like E*TRADE, which typically have very low trading charges and convenient online account services 24 hours a day, provide serious competition for established industry leaders. According to *Fortune,* "Market share is difficult to measure because players like Schwab and American Express don't break out their numbers . . . it appears that E*Trade is the leading Internet trading firm, with more than 6,000 Internet-based transactions a day."

As reported by *U.S. Banker* in their April 1999 edition, top clearinghouse firms in terms of market share were Bear Stearns at 10 percent, Pershing at 9 percent, Fidelity at 6 percent, CSC at 4 percent, Southwest Securities at 4 percent, and U.S. Clearing at 4 percent.

Further Reading

Business Rankings Annual 1997. Detroit: Gale Research, 1996.

Clarke, John M., Jack W. Zalaha, and August Zinsser III. *The Trust Business.* Washington, DC: American Bankers Association, 1988.

"E*TRADE: Is This Investing's Future?" *Fortune Online,* 3 March 1997.

Market Share Reporter 2000. Detroit: Gale Group, 1999.

Moody's Investors Service. *Moody's Industry Review.* New York: The Dun & Bradstreet Corp., January 1997.

"Number of Web Users Doubled From Year Ago." *Reuters Limited,* 25 April 1997.

Standard & Poor's Industry Surveys. New York: Standard & Poor's Corporation, October 1996.

SIC 6311

LIFE INSURANCE

This classification provides coverage of establishments primarily engaged in underwriting life insurance. These establishments are operated by enterprises that may be owned by stockholders, policyholders, or other carriers.

NAICS Code(s)

524113 (Direct Life Insurance Carriers)
524130 (Reinsurance Carriers)

Industry Snapshot

The insurance industry in America, particularly the life insurance industry, is considered a pillar of the economy. Its sales, assets, and investments are in the multibillion dollar range. Tied as it is to the public interest, the life insurance industry has been subject to governmental scrutiny and legislation almost since its inception more than two centuries ago. There were about 1,700 companies that underwrote life insurance and annuities in 1996, with premiums totaling $104.6 billion. The premiums are invested and accounted for 10.8 percent of funds in financial markets in 1996. Not uniform by any means, the industry is marked by a number of corporations selling the same product in a variety of ways, and earning varying amounts of money.

Organization and Structure

Although insurance companies may operate according to similar principles, the life insurance industry is hardly homogeneous. Companies do not charge the same amount for premiums, do not charge for expenses the same way, do not pay the same amount of commission to sales agents, do not provide the same kind or amount of training, do not sell the same products, and are not equally solvent. The one commonality throughout the industry is that licensed life insurance salespeople act as agents for their companies. These agents write several different kinds of life products, or policies, that the company offers.

Companies usually have a number of field offices, or branches. Large insurance organizations strategically place these around the country so that agents may market to as many potential clients as possible. Agents order or issue policies, collect premiums, renew and change existing coverage, and help clients with questions or problems related to coverage. Many agents who previously worked for large life insurance organizations branch out on their own and become independent agents. They will often continue to retain the company they worked for to underwrite the policies they sell.

Nearly all life insurance is issued by either mutual or stock life insurance companies. Mutuals have no stockholders, only policy holders, and the policyholders elect the board of directors who run the company. In this way, mutual policyholders participate in the fiscal management of the company and share in decisions regarding mortality expense, overhead costs, and investment rate of return. With $5.2 billion worth of life insurance in force, mutuals accounted for 35.7 percent of all the life insurance in force with U.S. life companies in 1995. Stock companies, on the other hand, are owned by their stockholders. They provided $9.4 billion worth of life insurance, or 64.3 percent of the total. Other sources of life insurance include fraternal societies and the federal government. Taking all of these sources into account, there was $12.9 trillion of life insurance in force at the end of 1995, or an average of $131,600 per American household.

There are four major categories of life insurance: ordinary, group, industrial, and credit. Ordinary life insurance accounted for approximately 60 percent of all life insurance in force at the end of 1995. More than doubling from 1985 to 1995, there was $7.5 trillion of ordinary life insurance in force in the United States at the end of 1995, with whole life insurance accounting for more than half of that total. Most of the rest of the ordinary life insurance in force was accounted for by some type of term life insurance. From 1985 to 1995 the amount of group life insurance increased from $2.6 trillion to $4.8 trillion, with term life accounting for nearly all group life insurance in force. Industrial life insurance decreased over the decade from $28.2 billion in 1985 to $20 billion in 1995. The amount of credit life insurance, which is designed to pay the balance of loans in case the borrower should die, increased from $199.5 billion in 1993 to $231.3 billion in 1995.

Half of all full-time workers in commerce and industry in the United States are enrolled in retirement plans other than Social Security. Private pension plans are established by private agencies such as commercial, industrial, labor and service organizations, and nonprofit organizations. Individual Retirement Accounts (IRAs) or Keogh Plans are set up by individuals. Pension plans can be administered by the holder of the plan, placed with banks or trust companies, or insured with life insurance companies. At the end of 1995, life insurance companies covered plans with 65.4 million people and provided retirement income to 6.4 million people. More than 24 million people were covered by government-administered plans at the end of 1995. The federal Old-Age and Survivors Insurance (OASI) system, part of the Social Security program, remained the most comprehensive government retirement program offered. There were 173 million people eligible for Social Security benefits at the end of 1995.

BACKGROUND AND DEVELOPMENT

Life insurance companies in the United States can be traced back to 1759, when ''The Corporation for Relief of Poor and Distressed Presbyterian Ministers and of the Poor and Distressed Widows and Children of Presbyterian Ministers'' was founded by the Synod of the Presbyterian Church. The oldest insurance company in the world, the firm is still fully operational as the Presbyterian Ministers' Fund. The industry began to take on a more formal, mathematics-based foundation when, in 1789, Professor Edward Wigglesworth at Harvard prepared a modified table of mortality. This was the first crude attempt to scientifically predict the probability of risk, or to compute premiums and reserves on a scientific basis. Comparing the probability of risk to revenues generated from policy sales and the size of claim settlements has been the formula the industry has relied on to establish itself as a viable business.

In 1794, the Insurance Company of North America became the first general insurance company to sell life insurance in the nation, but the company sold only six policies and discontinued its operations in 1804. Nevertheless, the Pennsylvania Company for Insurance on Lives and Granting Annuities was incorporated in 1812 and became the first company formed to issue life insurance policies and annuities. Soon after this the New York Life Insurance and Trust Company formed and became the first company to employ life insurance agents. By the late 1840s, general insurance laws began to come into effect, and in 1851 the state of New Hampshire established the first regulatory body to examine the affairs of insurance companies.

The insurance industry became more structured as the nineteenth century progressed, a result of governmental legislation and self-regulation. Around 1857, the first pension funds for government employees were established, and in 1861, Massachusetts required nonforfeiture values as part of life policies. These and other covenants of the industry began to materialize when publications such as the *American Experience Table of Mortality* were issued (1868). Covering experiences from 1843 to 1858, this document remained the most frequently consulted mortality table used by American companies until the 1940s. Whether or not the industry should have been granted national jurisdiction and been compelled to abide by national or state regulations was a hotly debated issue. It was not until 1869 that the U.S. Supreme Court held that insurance is not a transaction in commerce, thus affirming the validity of state regulation of insurance.

Insurance agents, the backbone and front-line of the industry, were first organized in Chicago in 1869. The issuance of life insurance is transacted by selling the client an insurance policy. In 1873, the first weekly premium policy was issued, and the first industrial insurance agency system was introduced in the United States. The American Express Company played a very active role in formulating employer pension plans, as did the Baltimore & Ohio Railroad Company, which set up the first formal pension plan supported by employer and employee contributions in 1880. This was followed by the establishment of cash surrender values mandated by law in Massachusetts in 1880, and the adoption of pension plans for professors at age 65 with a minimum of 15 years service. This represented the first private college retirement plan in the country. Later, the first pension plan for public school teachers was established in Chicago, and the Steel Company set up the first pension plan in a manufacturing company.

In 1911, the first group life insurance for employees was introduced. World War I prompted the federal government to get involved in insurance as well. Life insurance for servicemen was offered under the War Risk Insurance Act of 1917, subsequently known as U.S. Government Life Insurance. Soon after, the Federal Civil

Service Retirement and Disability Fund was created by Congress. Another major advance in the insurance industry occurred in 1921, when Metropolitan Life Insurance Company issued the first group annuity contract. The Revenue Act of 1921 deemed employer contributions to profit sharing trusts to be tax-exempt. Provisions were extended to pension trusts in 1926. The first examinations of life underwriters, those who actually underwrite and issue policies as representatives of insurance companies, were held seven years later.

Regulation. As the industry developed, the federal government continued to enact legislation with far-reaching effects on the insurance industry. The Temporary National Economic Committee was charged with investigating the industry and making regular reports to Congress regarding its structure and development. Contrary to its previous decision, the U.S. Supreme Court held in 1944 that insurance is commerce and that, when conducted across state lines, is interstate commerce and subject to federal laws. In 1945, the McCarran-Ferguson Act declared that the regulation of insurance by states is in the public interest and granted an exemption from the antitrust laws to the extent that business is regulated by state law.

A major step for federal employees was achieved when the Federal Employees' Group Life Insurance Act of 1954 was introduced. This act ensured that federal employees would be provided group life insurance and accidental death and dismemberment insurance through private insurance companies. In 1965, the Servicemen's Group Life Insurance Act was introduced, providing members of active duty in the uniformed armed services with group life insurance underwritten by private insurance companies with the Veterans Administration. In 1976, the first individual variable life insurance policy was issued, followed by the first ''universal'' life insurance policy in 1977.

A lot federal regulation was aimed at insuring equal access to insurance regardless of age and sex. The Supreme Court decided in *Norris vs. Arizona* that employee retirement benefits based on contributions made after August 1, 1983, must be calculated without regard to the sex of the employee. The Retirement Equity Act of 1984 lowered the minimum age for vesting and participation purposes, insured that written consent of the spouse would be required before joint and survivor coverage may be waived under pension plans, and required the payment of a survivor annuity in case of a vested participant who dies before the annuity starting date.

The taxation of life insurance companies has always been a strongly contested issue. The Tax Reform Act of 1984 included universal life insurance within the definition of life insurance, thus preserving its favorable tax treatment. Two years later, the Tax Reform Act of 1986 eliminated the tax deductibility of IRA contributions for highly paid people who are covered by pension plans. Also reduced was the maximum contribution to salary reduction, or 401(k) plans; the deductibility of interest paid with respect to loans on corporate-owned life insurance policies was also limited. A year later, the Revenue Act of 1987 established, more expedient funding requirements for underfunded pension plans, a variable rate premium, and a lower full-funding limitation for qualified plans. Finally, in 1988, the Technical and Miscellaneous Revenue Act created a class of life insurance contracts, the policy loans and surrender payments of which are subject to taxation rules similar to deferred annuities and made many changes related to 401(k) plans.

The Bull Market. Assets of U.S. life insurance companies reached a record high of $2.1 trillion in December 1995. This represented an increase of 10.4 percent, or $201 billion, over 1994. Assets of U.S. life insurance companies were invested in corporate bonds, government securities, stocks, mortgages, real estate, policy loans, and other assets. U.S. life insurance companies increased their holdings in stock by 32 percent over 1994.

Managers of insurance company investment portfolios were rewarded with a fairly stable year in 1996, after 1995 when interest rates rose dramatically. In November 1996 the Dow Jones Industrial Average broke 6500 for the first time. In the bond market, life and health insurers increased their holdings of below-investment grade bonds to 6.1 percent of their fixed income portfolio, still well below the levels maintained during the late 1980s and early 1990s. Insurance investment in mortgage-backed securities continued to decline in 1996 as a percentage of fixed income portfolios, reaching 26 percent after being reduced to 30 percent in 1995 and 33 percent in 1994. Overall, the financial stability of the industry continued to improve.

CURRENT CONDITIONS

Continuing its record-setting trend, life insurance in force reached a record high in 1995 of $12.6 trillion, an increase of 7.7 percent over 1994. Life insurance remained by far the largest segment of all insurance sold. Purchases of individual and group life insurance in 1995 were $1.6 trillion. Traditional whole life and combination insurance accounted for 55 percent of policies sold, a decrease from 58 percent in 1993. Universal and variable life insurance accounted for 21 percent of new sales. Approximately 78 percent of all U.S. households owned some form of life insurance in 1994, and the average amount per insured household was $159,100.

The average size of life insurance policies sold also continued to increase. In 1995 the average new individual policy was $82,310, compared to $79,710 in 1994 and $75,350 in 1990. Approximately half of all new policies bought in 1994 were for people between the ages of 25 and 44, with 38 percent of those insured buying term policies and 22 percent buying universal or variable life policies.

Total premium receipts for 1995 totaled $339.2 billion for life insurance companies. This represented an increase of 3.9 percent over 1994. Receipts came from three sources: $98.9 billion from life insurance, $159.9 billion from annuities, and $80.4 billion from health insurance. Benefit payments reached a record $165.7 billion from life insurance policies and annuities during 1995, an increase of 11.4 percent over 1994. Of that total, more than $85.8 billion was paid to life insurance policyholders, $46.4 billion to annuitants, and $33.5 billion to beneficiaries.

The top 20 ordinary life companies accounted for 49.67 percent of the U.S. market share in December 1995, with the remaining 50.33 percent spread among 846 other ordinary life companies. The top 10 U.S. life insurance companies, ranked by direct premiums, were Prudential Insurance Company, Northwestern Mutual, Connecticut General Life, Hartford Life Insurance, Metropolitan Life, New York Life, State Farm Life, AIG Life Insurance Company, American Life Insurance Company, and Massachusetts Mutual Life Insurance. Together, they accounted for 36.77 percent of the life insurance market, with Prudential alone claiming a 6 percent market share at the end of 1995.

In 1999 the life insurance industry continued the trend of consolidation, not only within the industry, but also with similar industries. The Financial Services Modernization Act, S.900 of 1999 allowed for these mergers between banks, stockbrokers, insurance and other similar companies. More companies in the future will sell directly to consumers, instead of using agent/brokers; in 1999 agents sold about 80 percent of life insurance products in the United States—that figure is expected to continue downwards. Banks that buy insurance companies will make full use of current customers for direct-mail, advertising, and telephone sales for leads and sales.

An alternate to buying (or being bought) is for companies to set up alliances with companies in similar industries. Putnam Investments began selling Allstate Life Group's variable annuities exclusively through a joint venture set up in February 1999. In the same month, MetLife and American Express signed an agreement whereby MetLife's 401k product will be sold by AMX's financial planners.

Many life insurance companies set up as mutual companies have taken the step towards demutualization as a means of capitalizing on the bullish stock market. Some companies have opted to move to a mutual holding company first; this allows the company to sell-off subsidiaries in anticipation of becoming stockholder owned.

From 1993 through 1997 a frenzy of consolidation in the industry led to high earnings. In 1998 operating earnings for the industry were 18 percent lower than in 1997. Higher costs were associated with compliance for the year 2000 (Y2K) and cross-marketing of products.

The life insurance industry is gradually letting go of the safest investment mentality, left over from bad real estate investments in the 1980s. More companies are looking to pump up the returns in their portfolios, usually consisting of common equities, public bonds, and commercial mortgages. The portion of stock holdings are expected to rise and there will be more companies holding commercial mortgages directly. A slow, but steady decline in the acceptable rating of public bonds is expected to happen—from AA to AA− or AA− to A+, for example.

The Internet has changed how many industries conduct business, yet the life insurance industry was entering the Internet slowly in 1999. Some companies have had early success in this direct-selling environment; yet the industry as a whole spent only 3.5 percent of it's revenue on information technologies and only 25 percent of the companies in the industry were selling on the Internet. This was expected to increase in 2000 and beyond as customers become accustomed to 24-hour-a-day, 7-day-a-week shopping opportunities.

Some analysts believe consumers will want to have one-stop shopping for all of their financial services needs. But since consumers are becoming more financially savvy and have access to more products and information, some analysts believe the trend will be to buy where the deals are. They believe consumers will not have brand loyalty and prefer to spread their risks.

WORKFORCE

There were approximately 1,700 U.S. life insurance companies in operation in 1996. The number has decreased steadily since 1988, when there were 2,343 companies. Overall, the U.S. insurance business employed some 2.24 million people in all of its branches in 1995. Of that total, there were approximately 1.54 million home office insurance personnel, 575,100 of whom were in life insurance. There were approximately 696,800 insurance agents, brokers, and service personnel employed in 1995. While the number of home office personnel engaged in life insurance declined from 581,100 in 1994 to 575,100 in 1995, the number of insurance agents, brokers, and service personnel has steadily increased from 663,300 in 1990 to 696,800 in 1995. Approximately 30 percent of all insurance agents were self-employed.

Agents usually receive some sort of financial assistance from the companies they are affiliated with while they build a client base. They are also usually placed on a stipend or retainer, which is often replaced by straight retainer to cover monthly expenses. Life insurance companies often help agents with basic expenses such as office furniture and supplies, though most agents cover their own travel, telephone, entertainment, and other expenses. Agents may receive commissions in two ways: a first-year commission for making the sale (usually 55 percent of the total first-year premium), or a series of smaller commissions paid when the insured pays his or her annual premium (usually 5 percent of the yearly payments for nine years). Most companies will not pay renewal commissions to agents who resign.

Incomes of insurance agents vary greatly. Income depends on the agents' own skill and knowledge of the industry, as well as the strength of the industry and market. Each year, about 20,000 agents qualify for the "Million Dollar Round Table" by selling policies with a face value of more than $1 million. Agents in their first five to 10 years on the job earned an average of $42,000 in the early 1990s. Those with 10 or more years selling life insurance averaged $65,000 a year. The median annual earnings of salaried insurance sales workers was $31,620 in 1994, with a middle range of $22,050 to $46,380. The top 10 percent earned more than $69,990, while the lowest 10 percent earned $15,500 or less.

America and the World

Widely varying economic conditions, personal income levels, living and health standards, and other circumstances make it difficult to make direct comparisons of national levels of life insurance ownership between countries. One statistical measure that reduces the influence of these diverse factors is the ratio of life insurance in force to national income. This ratio has generally shown improvement in most countries since 1984. In the United States, for example, that ratio was 191 percent in 1994, indicating that the amount of life insurance in force in the United States equaled 191 percent of U.S. national income. In 1994, Japan led all nations, followed by Korea (349 percent), South Africa (250 percent), Canada (245 percent), Ireland (233 percent), and the Netherlands (220 percent). Other countries whose life insurance in force exceeded their national income included Australia, France, Sweden, Norway, Denmark, and Germany.

Beyond 2000, U.S. life insurers face the prospect of having increasingly larger global competitors operating in their own market. At the end of 1995, there were only three U.S. life insurers ranked among the top 10 insurers globally based on assets. Prudential ranked fifth in the world, followed by Teachers Insurance Annuity Association (TIAA/CREF) at eighth, and Metropolitan Life at tenth. Three of the top four largest insurers were based in Japan. Since 1950, when 74 percent of all insurance premiums originated in North America, the percentage of total premiums have shifted away from the United States. By 1994, only 32 percent of all insurance premiums originated in North America, and 68 percent came from the rest of the world.

U.S. life insurers have established international operations largely through acquisitions and joint ventures. New opportunities were expected to open up in Europe toward the end of the 1990s, as European countries began to dismantle their welfare states and privatize such areas as pension coverage, health, and unemployment insurance. Latin America was a hot market for U.S. life insurers in the mid-1990s, as companies were attracted by stabilizing economies, growing middle classes, and the privatization of some state-run pension programs. Aetna Inc., for example, was expected to invest as much as $390 million for a 49 percent stake in a joint venture with Brazil's largest insurer, Sul America Seguros. Other life insurers with expanded operations in Latin America included Metropolitan Life, ITT Hartford Group, New York Life, and Principal Financial Group. The expansion continued in the late 1990s, when Aetna set up a joint venture with a Polish bank in 1999 to sell retirement products in Poland and Prudential formed a new life insurance company in Argentina.

While U.S. companies looked overseas to expand sales, many European companies looked to the United States as fresh markets for their products. In 1999 two European companies announced plans to acquire U.S. insurers—Transamerica by Aegon and Life USA by Allianz.

Further Reading

1996 Life Insurance Fact Book. Washington, DC: American Council of Life Insurance, 1996.

Albanese, Michael L. and Cynthia J. Crosson. "Gap Widens Between Haves and Have-Nots." *Best's Review: Life/Health Edition,* January 1997.

Brostoff, Steven. "Analysts See Fin'l Services Reconfiguration." *National Underwriter Life & Health-Financial Services Edition,* 29 November 1999.

"Insurance." *U.S. Industry & Trade Outlook '99.* New York: McGraw-Hill, 1999.

King, Carole Ann. "A Brief History of Key Events Leading to S.900." *National Underwriter Life & Health-Financial Services Edition,* 22 November 1999.

Mayewski, Larry G. et al. "The New Value Proposition." *Best's Review: Life/Health Edition,* January 1997.

Occupational Outlook Handbook, 1996-97 Edition. Washington, DC: U.S. Department of Labor, 1996.

Scism, Leslie. "Aetna Joins the Crowd of U.S. Insurers Making Investments in Latin America." *Wall Street Journal,* 4 February 1997.

Standard & Poor's. "Life Insurance Industry Stable, According to Standard & Poor's." *The Consumer Insurance Guide,* July

1999. Available from http://www.insure.com/ratings/analysis/99q2life.html.

Upton, Thomas S. and Michael L. Albanese. "Sharpening the Focus on Investment Management." *Best's Review: Life/Health Edition,* January 1997.

SIC 6321

ACCIDENT AND HEALTH INSURANCE

This category covers establishments primarily engaged in underwriting accident and health insurance. This industry includes establishments that provide health insurance protection for disability income losses and medical expense coverage on an indemnity basis. These establishments are operated by enterprises that may be owned by stockholders, policyholders, or other carriers. Establishments primarily engaged in providing hospital, medical, and other health services on a service basis or combination of service and indemnity bases are classified in **SIC 6324: Hospital and Medical Service Plans.**

NAICS CODE(S)

524114 (Direct Health and Medical Insurance Carriers)
525190 (Other Insurance and Employee Benefit Funds)
524130 (Reinsurance Carriers)

INDUSTRY SNAPSHOT

More than 1,000 companies provided accident and health insurance in the United States in the late 1990s, writing more than $100 billion in premiums. Commercial carriers faced earnings pressure due to higher medical claims and higher expenses. The increasing growth of managed care companies (see **SIC 6324: Hospital and Medical Service Plans**) forced many carriers to suppress necessary rate increases in the face of intense price competition. While the outlook remained stable-to-positive for commercial carriers that made strong local market adjustments, small-to-medium sized indemnity carriers faced a less promising outlook. Fewer competitors were expected to exist in the future, as companies would exit markets and product offerings and others would be absorbed in mergers and acquisitions.

ORGANIZATION AND STRUCTURE

Accident and health insurance is provided on an indemnity basis by commercial carriers and Blue Cross & Blue Shield plans. Under indemnity insurance, the insurer pays the insured directly for any hospital or physician costs for which the insured is covered. Other providers of accident/health insurance include specialty health insurers, self-funded employer plans, and government plans. The accident and health line consists of the following categories: group, credit, collectively renewable, non-cancelable, guaranteed renewable, nonrenewable, and other individual health and accident lines.

Accident/health insurance companies may also provide service plans in connection with health care providers. Insurance companies arrange to pay health care providers for any service for which an enrollee has coverage. Under the service plan, the insurance company effectively agrees to provide the insured with health care services, rather than reimbursement dollars. Service plans offer the advantages of reduced paperwork and reduced financial liability for the insured.

In addition to voluntary insurance, a second type of private health insurance is managed care. Managed care plans, or prepaid health plans, have increased in popularity during the 1980s and the 1990s. By the mid-1990s, managed care plans had proven their ability to control medical costs more effectively than traditional fee-for-service insurance plans. Under a managed care plan, a person can enroll in an organization that charges a monthly fee. In return for this monthly fee, the enrollee receives access to health care services from the organization. Organizations that offer such prepaid plans include Health Maintenance Organizations (HMOs), Preferred Provider Organizations (PPOs), and Exclusive Provider Organizations.

BACKGROUND AND DEVELOPMENT

Accident and health insurance, like other lines of insurance, serves to spread the consequences of a loss that would normally fall upon a single individual over the members of a large group. It also ensures that health care providers will be paid for services that an uninsured individual would otherwise not be able to afford.

Although the concept of insurance dates back more than 2000 years, the first form of health insurance in the United States can be traced back to the 1800s, when merchant seamen paid a modest premium to obtain health care as they traveled from port to port. Health insurance as it is known today, however, is a relatively new concept that has its roots in the Great Depression of the 1930s.

The most popular form of health insurance is major medical expense protection, which insures a person for a maximum amount of loss. The insured pays a deductible, usually $100-$500. This plan of insurance is favored because it protects against catastrophic losses yet avoids administrative burdens associated with smaller claims below the deductible amount. Critics of this type of insurance, though, believe it discourages preventive treatment and encourages inflation of health costs.

Growth of the Industry. It is only since the 1960s that the accident/health industry has grown massively in proportion to other types of insurance. One of the greatest reasons for the explosion in the popularity of health insurance during this time has been the increase in benefits offered by employers.

After World War II, health insurance became a popular benefit for employees. Health insurance premiums were, and remained in the early 1990s, tax-deductible to the employer and were not taxable to the employee. Therefore, it became a cost-effective form of compensation. Also, as unions began to find it more difficult to gain wage increases for their members, health care benefits became an increasingly popular bargaining tool.

One of the primary reasons for the growth of the accident/health insurance industry was the advent in the 1970s of modified agreements that shifted a greater amount of health care risk to the employers that offered employee insurance plans. Under these agreements insurers, employees, and health care providers had little reason to control health care costs because the employers, as policyholders, were paying the insurance bill. In fact, one result of these agreements was that insurance company profits increased in proportion to the rise in the cost of medical care. These circumstances resulted in an unprecedented rate of growth in group health insurance, an average of 15 percent per year in the 1970s and early 1980s.

Industry Stagnation. By 1983, changes in the American economy began to dictate a need for change in the accident/health insurance industry. Employers began to shift more of the insurance burden to their employees, as economic stagnation exerted downward pressure on company profits and a new corporate cost-consciousness developed. At the same time that employers were trying to reduce their insurance expenses, insurance companies were battling new economic and regulatory forces. Skyrocketing inflation, deregulation of banks and financial institutions, and public pressure to cap rising insurance rates all contributed to a decline in industry profitability. In response to the new business environment, insurance companies changed their products, marketing objectives, underwriting goals, and investment strategies. The end result of these changes by the early 1990s, however, was reduced industry stability, record financial losses, and company insolvency.

In addition to other problems in the industry, health care costs continued to spiral upward much faster than inflation throughout the 1980s and early 1990s. This trend helped to open the door to accident/health insurance alternatives such as HMOs and other managed care alternatives. Moreover, the current system excludes millions of Americans, a situation that threatens to change the structure and dynamics of the entire accident/health insurance industry.

Legislation. Accident/health insurers in the United States are subject to regulation at both the state and federal levels. Many of the regulations are designed to require that insurers maintain sufficient reserves to cover future liabilities. Other regulations require that companies not discriminate against certain customers or raise premium rates above certain levels that are deemed competitive by the governing body. Additional legislation that has had a significant impact on the industry relates to Medicare and Medicaid, which ensure coverage for elderly and poor citizens.

Investment Income. With a pool of large reserves to invest, insurance companies can offset some of their underwriting losses with investment income. Managers of insurance company investment portfolios were rewarded with a fairly stable year in 1996, after 1995 when interest rates rose dramatically. In November 1996 the Dow Jones Industrial Average broke 6500 for the first time. In the bond market, life and health insurers increased their holdings of below-investment grade bonds to 6.1 percent of their fixed income portfolio, still well below the levels maintained during the late 1980s and early 1990s. Insurance investment in mortgage-backed securities continued to decline in 1996 as a percentage of fixed income portfolios, reaching 26 percent after being reduced to 30 percent in 1995 and 33 percent in 1994.

Spiraling Health Care Costs. Rising health care costs made underwriting profits difficult to obtain for insurers. As costs escalate, so do claims by policyholders. Insurers have been unable to raise premium rates at the same rate as health care inflation rates. Some critics maintain that the current insurance system is partly to blame for escalating health care costs because it provides little incentive for providers to control costs. In fact, some observers believe that the current system provides an incentive for providers to perform superfluous tests, procedures, and services. Many other factors, though, have contributed to the rise in costs. They include: the burgeoning elderly population that requires additional health care, increased reliance on expensive medical equipment and technology, the shift of some costs from the government to private insurers, the costs of long-term illnesses such as AIDS and cancer, and an overall greater demand for health care services. Moreover, the meteoric rise in the cost of medical malpractice insurance has also taken its toll.

Medical savings accounts (MSAs), given improved tax status as part of the Health Insurance Reform Act of 1996, also known as the Kassebaum-Kennedy Bill, promised to offer employers a chance to reduce their healthcare costs. As envisioned, MSAs would combine a high-deductible catastrophic health insurance plan with an employer-paid account that employees could use to pay their regular medical expenses. Commercial carriers were prepared to join the MSA market in 1997, should they prove to be popular.

Industry Reform. Accident/health insurers are under increasing pressure from both state and federal governing bodies that seek to regulate the industry. After President Clinton's national health-care reforms failed in 1994, state initiatives dominated the reform agenda in 1994 and 1995 and continued into 1996. The political realities of election year 1996 again forced Congress to address the issue of health-care reform at the national level. The result was the passage of the Kassebaum-Kennedy health insurance reform package.

Key elements of the Kassebaum-Kennedy bill of 1996 included portability, guaranteed coverage, group purchasing for small groups, and medical savings accounts (MSAs). While the impact of this legislation has yet to be determined on accident and health insurers, some companies left states that had enacted similar reforms concerning community rating, guaranteed issue, and similar measures.

Future Expectations. No line of insurance faces a more uncertain future than accident/health, especially regarding health care reform, changing demographics, and potential tax reforms. Managed care alternatives experienced explosive growth in 1995 and 1996 and were expected to continue gaining market share at the expense of commercial carriers. Additional competition may come from banks, mutual funds, and other financial institutions that may start offering plans that compete directly for traditional health insurance dollars.

Despite these threats, several long-term considerations offered promise for a stronger accident and health insurance industry. Demographic influences, such as income growth, wealth accumulation, population and workforce changes, and increased home ownership could all serve to increase the demand for certain types of insurance products. The aging of the baby boom population should also increase demand for health care insurance products.

CURRENT CONDITIONS

Life insurance companies, which underwrite accident and health plans as well, had 1,700 companies in the industry in 1996 and took in a total of $354 billion in premiums. About 21 percent, or $73 billion, came from underwriting health insurance. The continued move to managed care plans is responsible for the slowdown in premiums—it accounted for almost 23 percent of premiums for life insurance companies in 1986.

Accident and health insurers remain under growing pressure to maintain profitability. Higher medical claims and higher expenses increased earnings pressure in 1996. Intense price competition dramatically affected the medical loss ratios of accident and health insurers. With HMOs and other managed care organizations aggressively increasing their enrollment, some well-known commercial carriers left the health insurance business in 1996. Those leaving the field included Massachusetts Mutual Life Insurance Co. and John Hancock Mutual Life Insurance Co. Uncertainties about health care reform, changing demographics, and potential tax reforms on nonqualified products were expected to continue to pressure accident and health insurers.

Accident and health insurers are constantly looking for ways to rehabilitate employees and get them back on the job. In 1997 The Hartford introduced ''Ability'' insurance. The insurance spreads the costs and follow-up care responsibilities more evenly between insurer, employer, and employee. The Hartford provides the injured worker and employer with a team consisting of a nurse, vocational rehabilitation counselor, and claims adjusters. The goal is to focus on what the employee can do, instead of what he can't, and to help the employer make adjustments to accommodate the injured or disabled employee.

INDUSTRY LEADERS

Prudential Insurance Company of America is the largest provider of accident and health insurance in the United States. In 1997 it underwrote $6.2 billion of all premiums sold, down 2.4 percent from $6.3 billion in 1996. Prudential holds a 7 percent market share. Prudential began in 1873 under the name Widows and Orphans Friendly Society. It quickly became a major innovator in the life insurance industry and slowly added other lines of insurance throughout the twentieth century. Prudential is now active in all lines of insurance and is the largest insurer, and one of the largest financial institutions, in the world. The company also operates in securities, investments, real estate, employee benefits, mortgages, and corporate relocation.

After Prudential, the top insurers in 1997 were Northwestern Mutual Group, with $6.2 billion and a 7.0 percent market share; Metropolitan Group, with $6.1 billion and a 6.9 percent share; New York Life Group, with $4.9 billion and a 5.5 percent share; and Hartford Insurance Group, with $3.6 billion and a 4.1 percent market share.

WORKFORCE

Employment in the accident/health insurance industry is representative of employment in the overall insurance industry, which also encompasses life and property/casualty insurance. In fact, most people employed in accident/health insurance work for multi-line insurers.

Employers in the insurance industry consist mainly of either insurance carriers or insurance agents and brokers. In 1996 there were 322,100 people who sold primarily health insurance, up from 306,100 in 1995. The growth in managed care was a large factor in employment growth.

Jobs in the accident/health industry include administrative support, sales, executive, and managerial positions. More than half of all employment in the insurance industry is in the area of administrative support, which includes secretaries, word processors, and bookkeepers. Other occupations in this category include insurance policy processing clerks, claims clerks, and claims examiners and investigators.

Twenty percent of insurance employees have executive, administrative, or managerial jobs. Many of these workers are underwriters that evaluate applications to determine the risk involved in issuing a policy. Underwriters gather information on applications, review associated risks, and apply underwriting standards to reach a decision about whether or not to cover applicants for insurance. Typical career progression is from underwriter to senior underwriter to underwriting manager. Because many underwriting managers progress into general management, this occupation is popular for those seeking access to upper level management opportunities.

Other administrators and managers are employed as accountants, investment managers, or policy managers. Statistically, one of the most lucrative and rewarding opportunities in this category is that of actuary. Actuaries use mathematical models and statistical techniques to analyze risk and to create and price accident/health products. Candidates for managerial positions usually have a college degree as well as knowledge of finance, economics, or accounting.

America and the World

The U.S. accident and health insurance industry is the largest and most advanced in the world, with premiums of $359.5 billion in 1995. Although it was originally modeled after the British health insurance system, the industry in America differs from that of many other industrialized nations because it is one of the most privatized in the world. While most other nations, such as Canada and Britain, have already addressed rising costs and inaccessibility of health care with nationalized plans, the United States has maintained a relatively competitive and private system, with the notable exceptions of Medicare and Medicaid.

U.S. life insurers have established international operations largely through acquisitions and joint ventures. New opportunities were expected to open up in Europe toward the end of the 1990s, as European countries began to dismantle their welfare states and privatize such areas as pension coverage, health, and unemployment insurance.

Sales of non-life insurance products by foreign affiliates of U.S. insurance companies rose 52.4 percent, from $22.9 billion in 1990 to $34.9 billion in 1995. The largest non-life insurance markets in the world, after the United States, are Japan, with premiums of $126.8 billion in 1995; Germany, $92.8 billion; the United Kingdom, $55.2 billion; France, $48.4 billion; and Italy, $24.3 billion.

Research and Technology

As markets became more competitive and profit margins continued to narrow during the 1990s, successful insurers were those that best utilized the efficiencies that automation and innovation could provide. A 1996 study of 25 top life/health insurers revealed that key success factors included efficiency in information technology, policyholder service, and underwriting.

With narrower margins and intense price competition, cost reduction continued to play an important role in achieving profitability for accident/health insurers. Besides reorganization and downsizing, the most effective way to achieve these ends was through computer automation. By implementing information technologies already proven effective in manufacturing industries, insurers hoped to significantly improve customer service, reduce errors, improve new product delivery time, and reduce human intervention.

By integrating all their company information into one system, insurers were able to synthesize efforts in product development, marketing, sales, and customer service. In addition, many companies were putting new litigation management systems to work for them that allowed law departments to accelerate access to legal research data, internal company information, and client data. This information is used to protect company interests and combat fraud.

Examples of new technology that accident/health insurers were integrating into the industry in the 1990s included open-systems architecture computer systems, network computing, computer-aided software-engineering tools, multi-media training tools, and information management and delivery systems that use satellites. Industry regulators were also using this new technology to identify potentially insolvent insurers.

Another facet of research and technology, and one that has hindered the accident/health insurance industry, relates to the technological innovation that characterizes the health care industry. Although new medical technology has saved lives and improved the quality of health care in the United States, it has also created a financial burden for health insurers and has increased the likelihood of federal intervention that may negatively impact the industry.

On the other hand, the industry is seeing an increased emphasis on medical technology that serves to create more efficient procedures and services. These advances could help pave the way toward reduced costs as well as improved service in the future.

FURTHER READING

"'Ability' Insurance." *Life Association News*, 5 January 2000. Available from http://www.insure.com/life/lan/dis797-2.html.

Bond, Michael T., et al. "Medical Savings Accounts: the Newest Medical Cost Reduction Tool for Employers." *Business Horizons*, July-August 1996.

"Insurance." *U.S. Industry & Trade Outlook '99*. New York: McGraw-Hill, 1999.

Lenckus, Dave. "Efficiency a Common Trait of Top Life/Health Companies." *Business Insurance*, 26 August 1996.

Natarajan, Kartik. "European Health Insurance Market Emerges," *National Underwriter Life & Health-Financial Services Edition*, 28 October 1996.

Nowacki, Manfred J., et al. "Prognosis: Guarded." *Best's Review, Life/Health Edition*, January 1997.

Occupational Outlook Handbook, 1996-97 Edition. Washington, D.C.: U.S. Department of Labor, 1996.

Sweeney, Patrick M. "A&H Underwriting Loss More Than Doubled, Again," *Best's Review, Life/Health Edition*, December 1996.

"Top 100 Individual Life Insurers." *Insure.com*, July 1999. Available from http://www.insure.com/ratings/analysis/99indlife100.html.

Upton, Thomas S., and Michael L. Albanese. "Sharpening the Focus on Investment Management." *Best's Review: Life/Health Edition*, January 1997.

SIC 6324

HOSPITAL AND MEDICAL SERVICE PLANS

The hospital and medical service industry, also commonly referred to as the managed care industry, is comprised of establishments providing hospital, medical, and other health services to enrollees or members of a prearranged plan or agreement. Many of these establishments also provide traditional health insurance vehicles. Managed care plans typically arrange to provide medical services for members in exchange for subscription fees paid to the plan sponsor. Members receive services from physicians or hospitals that also have a contract with the sponsor. Thus, managed care plans integrate the financing and delivery of appropriate health care services to covered individuals.

NAICS CODE(S)

524114 (Direct Health and Medical Insurance Carriers)
525190 (Other Insurance and Employee Benefit Funds)
524130 (Reinsurance Carriers)

INDUSTRY SNAPSHOT

Although they serve the same basic function as traditional insurance plans, managed care plans differ because the plan sponsors play a greater role in administering and managing the services that the health care providers furnish. For this reason, advocates of managed care believe that it provides a less expensive alternative to traditional indemnity insurance plans.

Managed care grew rapidly in popularity beginning in the early 1980s, as health care and related insurance costs skyrocketed. Following some financial setbacks for managed care companies in the late 1980s, enrollment in managed care plans increased dramatically throughout the 1990s. Membership in managed care escalated rapidly throughout the 1990s. In 1994, more than 100 million people were enrolled in one of four types of managed care plans: health maintenance organizations (HMOs), preferred provider organizations (PPOs), exclusive provider organizations (EPOs), and point-of-service plans (POS). In 1995, about 74 percent of the U.S. population participated in some type of managed care plan. In 1997, only 15 percent of covered employees remained in traditional health plans, and by 1999, there were 107.3 million Americans who were members of managed care groups. These included 85 percent who were enrolled in managed care plans as part of their employee coverage. Factors that contributed to the rapid growth of managed care included the improved benefits with lower premiums and deductibles. Analysts attributed the slow growth in the cost of health care during the 1990s to the rise of managed care plans.

The industry became highly competitive at the turn of the twenty-first century. Several issues surfaced that affected the managed care market and contributed to the competitive atmosphere as plan members placed growing emphasis on the quality of care received and expressed concerns over access to treatment. In 1999, *U.S. Industry & Trade Outlook* projected that managed care would dominate 90 percent of the health care market by 2002. Premiums, according to projections, would increase up to 8 percent per year through the year 2001.

ORGANIZATION AND STRUCTURE

Managed health care plans, or pre-paid plans, exist in various forms yet all plans serve the same basic function—to spread the risk of extensive losses suffered by one individual across an entire membership group that is exposed to similar risk. By pooling the health care dollars of many subscribers, individual enrollees are assured of receiving care that they otherwise might not be able to afford. Managed care differs from traditional insurance in that members of managed care programs typically have less freedom to choose their health care providers thus limiting the plan member's control over the quality and delivery of care in a managed system. Members of managed care plans usually must select a ''primary care physician'' from a list of doctors provided by the plan sponsor.

As managed care plans evolved into the twenty-first century, competing plans offered innovative health care delivery in response to the preferences of consumers. Still all plans retained certain elements in common. Common factors included arrangements with selected providers to furnish a set of health care services to members, definition of explicit standards for the selection of health care providers, maintenance of ongoing quality assurance standards, and the utilization of review programs. Additionally, significant financial incentives were set in place to discourage members from using providers and procedures not covered by the plan. In 1999, 181.4 million Americans were enrolled in managed care plans. Many of these people participated in plans offered through their employer. Statistically, 85 percent of U.S. workers covered by company insurance plans participated in some form of managed care, in keeping with a trend for increasing numbers of employers to offer a managed care option as part of their health benefits package. An estimated 89.1 percent of all commercially insured Americans were members of managed care plans by the year 2000.

How Managed Care Works. Managed care plan administrators act as middlemen by contracting with health care providers and enrollees to deliver medical services. The enrollees pay a set fee that entitles them to services. The plan administrator then supervises the health care providers. Subscribers benefit from reduced health care costs, and the health care providers profit from a guaranteed client base.

Enrollment in managed care plans appeals to members because it can provide savings over traditional indemnity insurance plans which typically serve the singular function of claims reimbursement. Contrary to traditional insurance plans, managed care sponsors are highly motivated to suppress health care costs and deliver quality services. Indemnity insurance in contrast offers little incentive to control the cost of health services. The savings of managed care result from an active role taken by the plan sponsor in determining the most cost-efficient means of delivering care to its members. Sponsors of managed care, for example, work with health care providers to increase outpatient care, reduce administrative costs, eliminate complicated claims forms procedures, and minimize unnecessary tests. Plan sponsors accomplish these tasks by reviewing each patient's needs before treatment and requiring a second opinion before authorizing doctors to administer care. Likewise hospitalization of a plan member requires prior authorization, and services performed by specialists cannot proceed in the absence of approval. Some managed care plans offer bonuses to doctors for avoiding expensive tests or costly services performed by specialists, and some sponsors employ award bonuses to doctors in return for shortening the time a patient stays in the hospital. Practices such as these, according to critics of managed health care, can easily lead to under treatment.

Managed care instead places emphasis on preventive medical techniques that help patients avoid serious future health problems, which, in turn, reduce cost. For instance, managed care plans typically authorize regular physicals and checkups at little or no charge to their members, to prevent or detect long-term complications at an early stage. Many plans offer cancer screenings, stress reduction classes, programs to help members stop smoking, and other services that save the sponsor money in the long run by keeping the plan member healthy. Some plans offer financial compensation to members who lose weight or achieve fitness goals. For example, one plan offered $175 to overweight members who lost 10 pounds and gave $100 to members who participated in fitness programs.

Managed care plans exist in many forms. Most popular are Health Maintenance Organizations (HMOs) and Preferred Provider Organizations (PPOs). Other plans that combine elements of HMOs and PPOs include Exclusive Provider Organizations (EPOs), Point of Service plans (POS), Third Party Administrators, and Competitive Medical Organizations. In addition to these established plans, many employers and organizations offer hybrid plans that combine various forms of insurance and managed care into programs that offer multiple options for members of their group. In 1999, 79.3 million Americans were covered by HMOs, 89.1 million by PPOs, and 13 million by EPO plans.

Health Maintenance Organizations. The most popular plan, the basic HMO, characterizes the description of managed care plans provided above. HMOs, with 70 million enrollees in 1999, boasted a 30 percent market share among managed care providers, up from just under 60 million people at the end of 1996.

Four organizational models exist for the HMO; these define the respective relationship between plan sponsors, physicians, and subscribers. Under the first model, called *independent practice associations (IPA),* HMO sponsors contract with independent physicians who agree to deliver services to members for a fee. Under this plan, the sponsor pays the provider on a per capita, or fee-for-service, basis each time it treats a plan member. Under the second model, the *group plan,* an HMO contracts with a group of physicians to deliver client services. The sponsor then compensates the medical group on a negotiated per capita rate. The physicians determine how they will compensate each member of their group. Another model, called the *network model,* is similar to the group model but the HMO contracts with various groups of physicians based on the specialty that a particular group of doctors practices. Enrollees then get their service from a network of providers based on their specialized needs. In a fourth model, the *staff arrangement,* doctors practice as employees of the managed care plan sponsor. The HMO owns the facility and pays salaries to the doctors on staff. This type of arrangement allows the greatest control over costs but also has the highest start-up costs.

Preferred Provider Organization. A PPO is a variation of the HMO and combines features of indemnity insurance and HMO plans. A large insurer or a group of doctors or hospitals typically organizes a PPO. Under this arrangement, networks of health care providers contract with large organizations to offer their services at a reduced rate. The major difference from the HMO is that PPO enrollees retain the option of seeking care outside of the network with a doctor or hospital of their choice. They are usually charged a penalty for doing so, however. Doctors and hospitals are drawn to PPOs because they receive prompt payment for services; also PPOs provide access to a large client base. PPOs held a 30 percent share of the market in 1999, an equivalent amount to that held by HMOs.

The PPO industry tends to be more fragmented than HMOs, with numerous independent firms providing regional and local services. Some of the larger PPOs have started providing programs and designing products that are similar to those offered under HMO plans. One type of plan that has emerged is the Exclusive Provider Organization (EPO), which is essentially a smaller PPO provider network offering higher discounts. Most EPO plans provide few, if any, benefits when an out-of-network provider is used.

Point of Service. POS plans have a 20 percent market share. These combine characteristics of HMOs and PPOs. Like PPOs, POSs use a network of providers. Covered individuals select a primary care physician who controls referrals to specialists. As long as the covered individual uses a plan provider, there are few or no out-of-pocket expenses. If care is received from a provider not in the plan, then the covered individual pays higher copayments and deductibles, and the provider is reimbursed by the plan.

Demographic Influences. The type and magnitude of managed care offerings varies significantly with age, region, and the size of the employer delivering the managed care plan. HMOs and PPOs tend to appeal to younger families with children, yet traditional insurance plans are most popular with elderly people. Only 25.7 percent of the Medicare segment rely on managed care, while 61 percent of Medicaid recipients turn to managed care. Managed care plans also tend to be more popular with large employers, although the growth rate of managed care offerings in smaller companies is greater. According to *OR Manager* in 1998, more than one-half of HMOs were located in the Pacific regions or in the Northeast, with HMOs most prevalent on the Pacific Coast. California had 14 million enrollees by 1997, and HMOs in the Pacific Northwest held a market share of 47 percent, the highest in the United States. Enrollments were highest in New York and California in the latter half of the 1990s, while the growth rate of HMOs in Mississippi, at 103 percent, was the highest across the nation. HMO penetration at that time was lowest in the southeastern United States. While population density may also be a factor in attracting managed care plans, the demographic variances in managed care popularity are mainly the result of differences in the rate at which health care costs have escalated for different segments and regions of society.

BACKGROUND AND DEVELOPMENT

The use of managed care in the United States coincides with the use of health care insurance itself. It was first used by the U.S. Public Health Service to provide medical treatment for merchant seamen who traveled from port to port. In the 1800s, managed care expanded to cover some corporate employees and some government employees, including railroad workers. Henry J. Kaiser and Dr. Sidney Garfield, to provide medical care for San Francisco shipyard workers, started the first major plan in the 1930s. This plan was offered to the public at large in the 1940s.

Although plans similar to the Kaiser plan were formed during the 1950s and 1960s, managed care did not become available to the population until the 1970s, when society began to address spiraling health care costs. The Federal Health Maintenance Organization Act of 1973 stimulated the growth of the industry by providing grants and loans that expanded plans and spawned new HMOs. Although a few companies, such as Kaiser and Group Health of Puget Sound, offered managed care plans in 1973, less than 3 percent of Americans were enrolled in them.

Spiraling Health Care Costs. The greatest reason for the advent and popularity of managed care has been spiraling health care costs, which many critics blame on the traditional indemnity insurance system. Throughout the 1980s and much of the 1970s, average health care costs in the United States jumped an average of 15 percent per year. Furthermore, between 1965 and 1992, health care expenditures, as a percentage of the Gross Domestic Product (GDP), soared from 6 percent to more than 15 percent. Between 1988 and 1993, health care expenditures rose 63 percent, reaching $889 billion.

As health insurance costs skyrocketed, so did the cost of all types of health insurance. From 1989 to 1991, for example, the average employee contribution to company sponsored health insurance plans increased 50 percent while the amount of services diminished and deductibles went up. As employers began to scale back their insurance offerings to save money, the number of uninsured Americans rose to nearly 35 million by 1992. Many smaller businesses were forced to terminate their health benefits.

These considerations caused employers and individuals to seek new forms of insurance in the 1980s and 1990s—such as HMOs and PPOs—that could contain costs while still providing satisfactory service. Others, including some government regulators, were advocating a nationalized health care plan similar to those in Canada or Great Britain. In the early 1990s, the United States remained one of the only industrialized countries in the world that relied on a privatized system of health care.

Industry Growth. During the 1970s, the HMO industry grew by approximately 25 percent, serving about 4 percent of the U.S. population by 1980. The HMO industry achieved its greatest period of growth during the 1980s. During this decade, the number of HMOs soared to about 700 in 1987, and enrollment jumped to include approximately 15 percent of the population.

In addition to rapid growth in the number of people enrolled in HMOs, PPOs became a popular form of care and grew at a faster rate than HMOs during the mid-1980s. Between 1984 and 1993, the number of PPOs bounded from 115 to nearly 900, with almost 40 percent of the population having the choice to enroll in PPOs through their employer. The PPO industry tended to be more fragmented than the HMO industry, with numerous PPOs offering regional or local services.

HMO industry profits began to sag in 1986. The number of people enrolling in HMOs began to decrease in 1988, with the number of HMOs falling from 707 in 1987 to about 546 by 1993. These trends reflected increasing start-up costs, increased mergers and acquisitions, and concerns by some people that HMOs would not be able to control costs as well as first hoped.

The effect of increased start-up costs was demonstrated in the growth rate of new HMOs between 1988 and 1991. In 1991, only four new HMOs were formed, compared with seven in 1990, 19 in 1989, and 34 in 1988. The sluggish economy and lack of start-up capital that was common in the late 1980s and early 1990s contributed to the fall in newcomers to the market. Many of the very large companies that had entered the industry in the 1980s remained unprofitable into the 1990s.

Increased economic pressures were also responsible for the merger and acquisition trend that reduced the number of HMOs in the late 1980s and early 1990s. While overall industry profits continued to grow in the early 1990s, many underfunded HMOs experienced financial difficulty.

The dramatic growth of the managed care industry can be seen by comparing the market share of managed care plans in 1988 and 1993 to that of traditional indemnity health insurance. In 1988, conventional health insurance held a 71 percent market share. The managed care share of the market was split between HMOs with 18 percent, and PPOs/POSs at 11 percent. By 1993, managed care accounted for 51 percent of the market, and conventional health insurance had fallen to 49 percent. Within the managed care industry, HMOs accounted for a 22 percent market share, the fast-growing PPOs accounted for 20 percent, and POSs took 9 percent. In 1996, HMOs replaced traditional indemnity plans as the primary choice for health care coverage by employers. Of the 1,151 firms with 200 or more employees surveyed, HMO enrollment rose during 1995. Memberships, which were at 29 percent at mid-year in 1995, rose to 33 percent in the first half of 1996. Meanwhile, enrollment in conventional health plans fell from 31 percent to 26 percent over the same time period. The survey showed that enrollment in some type of managed care reached 74 percent—a dramatic increase from 29 percent in 1988.

After experiencing financial problems in the late 1980s, managed care industry profits recovered during the early 1990s. Rapid growth, reduced medical costs, and the promise of stable premium rates characterized results in 1995. Some larger HMOs reduced premiums to boost enrollment. One of the largest and most profitable publicly traded HMOs, United HealthCare Corporation, announced it would sacrifice its 1995 profits by cutting premiums to increase enrollment. In 1999, United HealthCare Corporation ranked fifth largest in the United States.

Mergers and Acquisitions. Before 1996 there was little blending of HMO companies and traditional insurance companies, but that quickly changed with a series of well-publicized acquisitions. United HealthCare Corporation acquired MetraHealth Companies, Inc. toward the end of 1995. MetraHealth was formed earlier in 1995 by combining the group health care operations of Metropolitan Life Insurance Company and The Travelers Insurance Group. At the time of the acquisition, MetraHealth served more than 10 million individuals, 5.9 million of whom were in network-based care programs. Other mergers included the entry of Humana, Incorporated into the traditional finance and insurance industry with the acquisition of Emphesys Financial Group and one of its subsidiaries called Employers Health Insurance Company, and a major acquisition that involved the takeover of WellPoint Health Network.

Government Reform. Managed care companies were poised to benefit from political changes in 1993 that promised to promote the industry. The most crucial development was the election of Bill Clinton as President. Clinton promised in his campaign to deliver a national health care plan within his first 100 days in office. He promised a plan that would reduce costs and provide some type of care for all Americans. In 1993, First Lady, Hillary Rodham-Clinton orchestrated the development of a national health care reform package that promised sweeping changes. However, by 1994 it was clear that Clinton's health reform initiatives were dead.

State initiatives dominated the reform agenda in 1994 and 1995 and continued into 1996. In November 1996, two anti-managed care referendums failed in California and Oregon, an indication that consumers remained concerned with the higher costs associated with traditional indemnity insurance. The political realities of election year 1996 again forced Congress to address the issue of health-care reform at the national level. The result was the passage of the Kassebaum-Kennedy health insurance reform package.

Key elements of the Kassebaum-Kennedy bill included portability, guaranteed coverage, group purchasing for small groups, and medical savings accounts (MSAs). This legislation impacted managed care companies by increasing expenses due to regulations requiring upgrading and evaluating care. Federal and state regulations concerning 48-hour hospital stays for new mothers, for example, put increased pressure on profit margins by increasing costs for managed care companies.

While some large organizations experimented with health care cost controls that forced competitive pricing, many individuals and small businesses sought ways to participate in managed care systems. One solution advocated by government reformists in the early 1990s was health insurance purchasing cooperatives (HIPCs). HIPCs allowed individuals or small groups to pool their buying power and negotiate cheaper managed care.

Although some groups found ways to control their health care costs through managed care and managed competition, critics of managed care accused HMOs of ''shadow pricing,'' a technique used to keep premiums just below the level of expensive indemnity plans. They also argued that some managed care providers were engaged in competitive practices that would eventually hurt the overall quality of the U.S. health care industry.

CURRENT CONDITIONS

Profitability. In 1996, the managed care industry experienced falling margins resulting in less profitability. It was a combination of aggressive rate reduction and unrealized medical cost savings that contributed to many managed care companies losing favor with Wall Street. Another factor that put pressure on profit margins was the banding together of doctors and hospitals to negotiate higher provider fees. As a result, enrollment increased by an average of 19.2 percent in 1996, while margins declined to 0.2 percent, down from 2.4 percent in 1995. As a result of falling margins, the industry changed its focus from enrollment growth to one of managing medical costs to achieve profitable margin levels.

According to a study by Weiss Ratings of Palm Beach Gardens, Florida, and reported in *Healthcare Financial Management,* managed care premiums rose by 3 percent to 4 percent in the mid-1990s and continued the slow rise, or else remained flat, through the end of the decade. These single-digit increases in premiums were commensurate with the rate of inflation, yet more than 50 percent of HMOs failed to achieve profitability by 1997 and again in 1998 as margins remained under 1 percent. It was provider-owned plans that suffered most severely from the ominous economic conditions of the managed care industry, with average losses estimated at $19 million.

In devising plans to curb escalating health care costs through managed care, regulators looked to examples of HMOs in the relatively new managed care industry. Although many HMOs were successful in the 1990s, others had failed. Furthermore, many of the new arrangements and innovations involving HMOs indicated that, as the federal government prepared to implement comprehensive reforms, the free market was beginning to deal effectively with spiraling health care costs. Managed care plans offered employers a chance to save on their medical expenses. According to the A. Foster Higgins survey, it cost employers an average of $3,739 to insure each indemnity member in 1996, an increase of 2.4 percent over the previous year. That cost compared with $3,185 for each HMO member, a decrease of 2.2 percent. With increasing numbers of indemnity plan participants converting to managed care membership, the market for managed care became saturated, which intensified competition between providers.

The volatility of HMOs in the 1990s was seen when Humana Corp. experimented by vertically integrating its hospital business with its HMO start-up operation during the 1980s. Although the strategy met with initial success, it eventually alienated many physicians and competing HMO networks. Doctors who were not a part of the Humana network started directing their patients away from Humana hospitals and facilities. As a result, Humana split the HMO and hospital businesses into separate divisions in 1993. The splintered corporation grew to be the sixth largest managed care provider in the United States, with 6.2 million enrollees by 1999.

One successful example of the implementation of HMOs to curb costs involved a plan implemented by Xerox Corporation using the managed competition concept. Like many companies, Xerox offered a combination of indemnity and HMO plans to its employees. However, the company also used a ''benchmark'' system that limited company funded premiums per employee to the level of premiums charged by the least expensive HMO plan. This caused HMOs competing for Xerox employees to reduce their premiums and subsequently served to keep the rising cost of premiums in check. The program allowed employees to pocket the savings offered by the more efficient plans or pay extra for choosing indemnity plans that offered more freedom in choosing physicians. Xerox distinguished itself among employers over the well-publicized situation, through the practice of closely monitoring the HMOs that serviced the corporation, to ensure that its employees received satisfactory care. Similarly, through an innovative administrative policy, Minnesota became the first large employer to base its health care contributions for employees and dependents on the lowest-priced HMO in each county.

Customer Satisfaction. In 1999, *American Medical News* quoted Employer Benefit Research Institute statistics indicating that 49 percent of Americans expressed satisfaction for their PPOs, while only 35 percent of HMO members were satisfied with their respective plans. The largest positive response, however, came from fee-for-service plan participants, of whom 64 percent were satisfied. This was in direct contrast to a report issued seven years earlier by the National Research Corporation indicating that people were most satisfied with HMOs and least satisfied with fee-for-service plans. Additionally, the earlier survey indicated that while 85 percent of the people were at least somewhat satisfied with their health plan, younger respondents reported the least amount of contentment. Furthermore it was the younger respondents who were also the most likely to convert from traditional to managed care plans. As a result of the findings of the later survey, the managed care industry contracted Waylon Advertising of St. Louis, Missouri, to create an advertising campaign to help shed a more positive light on the industry. Along with the American Association of Health Plans, other members of the coalition that contracted the advertising campaign included Aetna U.S. Healthcare, Blue Cross and Blue Shield Association, and CIGNA Healthcare.

U.S. Industry & Trade Outlook for '99 has forecasted a decline in the 1990s trend toward merger between health care organizations as the smaller corporations fall prey to acquisition and disappear from the marketplace. Increased member premiums for managed care programs combined with expanded contracting of medical specialists by plan providers are other strategies predicted for the early 2000s.

INDUSTRY LEADERS

In 1999, Blue Cross and Blue Shield System/HMO-USA was the largest provider of managed care (by enrollment) in the United States with 47.7 million members, more than twice the enrollment of the second largest provider, Aetna U.S. Healthcare. Blue Cross/Blue Shield surpassed Kaiser Permanente as the largest HMO organization at the end of 1995, according to rankings published in *The New York Times.* Throughout the United States, the 62 member plans of the Blue Cross and Blue Shield Association reported that 52 percent of their members were covered by POS contracts, PPO plans, or HMO plans in March 1996. That translated into one-sixth of the U.S. population that were covered by the Blues' managed care plans.

Aetna Incorporated, with 18.1 million enrollees and 1999 revenue of $26.4 billion was the second largest managed care provider. CIGNA Corporation, with 9.3 million enrollees and sales of $18.8 billion was the third largest managed care provider.

Kaiser Foundation Health Plan was the largest non-profit managed care provider in the industry, with 8.6 million enrollees. Kaiser, founded during the 1930s, remained the oldest managed care provider in the United States at the end of the twentieth century. The organization had sales of $15.5 billion in 1998, to grow by 6.9 percent over the previous year.

The merged conglomerate of Minnesota's United HealthCare—a part of the UnitedHealth Group—increased its membership to cover an additional 10 million individuals through acquisitions. Among United HealthCare's expanded membership, 5.9 million individuals were members of network-based care programs. The group's sales were a reported $19.3 billion in 1999, which comprised a growth of 13.1 percent. With 6.4 million enrollees, United HealthCare Corporation was the fifth largest managed care plan provider in the United States.

Humana, Incorporated was the sixth largest managed-care provider in the United States, with 6.2 million enrollees and 1999 revenue of $10.0 billion.

Pacific Physicians Services of California, a fledgling managed care organization during the 1980s, grew rapidly in the early 1990s. The HMO increased revenues from $17 million in 1987 to more than $100 million in 1992. The company relied on energetic young doctors to drive the company's success. Doctors were drawn to Pacific Physicians in particular because the company offered free medical malpractice insurance, bonuses for productivity, and a starting salary of $108,000.

WORKFORCE

The increase in the popularity of managed care, in conjunction with an aging U.S. population requiring more care, ensures a stable employment market within the industry well into the twenty-first century. The jobs in the managed care industry parallel the positions that existed previously within the health care and health insurance industries. The basic difference, however, is that organizational structures within the managed care industry are subject to an excessively bureaucratic management environment. Additionally, employee and practitioner compensation trends within managed care organizations call for lower wages than health care providers such as doctors, nurses, and facility administrators have traditionally commanded.

Managed care offers similar positions in the insurance and health care fields: jobs in finance, accounting, sales, and administrative support. Managed care health professionals are equivalent to those in other health care environments: physicians, nurses, physical therapists, lab technicians, and occupational therapists. Nurses, who were in particular demand during the 1990s, reported greater job satisfaction in the managed care fields than within the traditional hospital structure.

In 1998, Blue Cross and Blue Shield Association employed 150,000 workers, and Kaiser Foundation Health Plan employed 100,000, although neither corporation showed employee growth for the year. The largest employee growth for that year was at Aetna; with 33,500 employees the company realized an employee increase of 16.9 percent for one year. Nearly as large was the employee growth at Humana, which realized an increase of 16.4 percent for one year count of 16,300 employees. Third-ranked CIGNA grew to 49,900 employees for 4.6 percent growth, while UnitedHealth Group increased its staff to 29,200, a 1.4 percent increase.

RESEARCH AND TECHNOLOGY

The managed care industry has been a major innovator and implementor of advanced research and technology. This is partly because the industry is focused on cost containment. Another reason is most companies in the managed care industry are relatively new and more open to change. In fact, indemnity insurers and hospitals later implemented many of the advances first developed in the managed care industry.

The managed care industry has become increasingly competitive, with HMOs and PPOs vying—and sometimes actually bidding—for contracts to serve the employees of different companies and organizations. As a result, managed care companies with the most advanced information systems and the most effective automation have excelled. Many companies are using new technology to help them provide a ''one-stop-shop'' for employers seeking efficient managed care benefits for their employees.

Kaiser Foundation Health Plans signed a 10-year $70 million contract, to run through 2002, with an IBM subsidiary for the development and management of information systems in its expansion regions. Other managed care companies used information systems to integrate data about clinical and support services, medical staffs, and enrollees with data from internal operations such as cash management, human resources, and strategic and financial planning. These ''seamless'' health care delivery systems monitored and lowered treatment costs, reducing human error and intervention in the administrative process, thus speeding treatment. These advances also spilled over into the areas of ambulatory services and medical legal functions.

In 1999, the health care industry invested $19.9 billion dollars in research and development, not including research by drug manufacturers and medical equipment suppliers.

FURTHER READING

''Aetna Inc.,'' *Hoover's Online,* 1 January 2000. Available from http://www.hoovers.com/co/capsule/9/0,2163,10039,00.html.

Barry, Susan, Ed., *U.S. Industry & Trade Outlook '99,* McGraw-Hill, New York, 1999.

Bell, Allison. ''Health Cost Inflation Uptick Expected.'' *National Underwriter: Life & Health/Financial Services Edition,* 27 January 1997, 1.

———. ''Managed Care Covers Over Half of Blues' Members.'' *National Underwriter: Life & Health/Financial Services Edition,* 2 September 1996, 64.

''Blue Cross and Blue Shield Association,'' *Hoover's Online,* 1 January 2000. Available from http://www.hoovers.com/co/capsule/7/0,2163,40067,00.html.

''CIGNA Corporation,'' *Hoover's Online,* 1 January 2000. Available from http://www.hoovers.com/co/capsule/.

Geisel, Jerry. ''Benefit Costs Continue Slide.'' *Business Insurance,* 16 December 1996, 1.

''Humana Inc.,'' *Hoover's Online,* 20 March 2000. Available from http://www.hoovers.com/co/capsule/.

Jacob, Julie A., ''Managed Image,'' *American Medical News,* December 6, 1999.

''Kaiser Foundation Health Plan, Inc.,'' *Hoover's Online,* 20 March 2000. Available from http://www.hoovers.com/co/capsule/.

Lazich, Robert S., Ed. *Market Share Reporter.* Detroit: Gale Research Inc., 1999.

''Managed Care: Managed Care Fact Sheet,'' *Managed Care On-Line,* 20 March 2000. Available from http://www.mcareol.comfactshts/.

McCarthy, Edward J. ''Provider-owned Health Plans: El Dorado or Armageddon?'' *Healthcare Financial Management,* November 1999.

Niedzielski, Joe. ''Health Premiums Now Only Inching Upward: Study.'' *National Underwriter: Life & Health/Financial Services Edition,* 21 October 1996, 34.

———. ''HMOs Hike Premiums after So-So 1996.'' *National Underwriter: Life & Health/Financial Services Edition,* 17 March 1997, 1.

1996 Business Rankings Annual. Detroit: Gale Research, Inc., 1996.

Nowacki, Manfred J., et al. "Prognosis: Guarded." *Best's Review, Life/Health Edition,* January 1997.

Occupational Outlook Handbook. Washington, D.C.: U.S. Department of Labor, 1996.

"United Health Group," *Hoover's Online,* 20 March 2000. Available from http://www.hoovers.com/co/capsule/.

SIC 6331

FIRE, MARINE, AND CASUALTY INSURANCE

This classification covers establishments primarily engaged in underwriting fire, marine, and casualty insurance. These establishments are operated by enterprises that may be owned by stockholders, policyholders, or other carriers.

NAICS Code(s)

524126 (Direct Property and Casualty Insurance Carriers)
525190 (Other Insurance and Employee Benefit Funds)
524130 (Reinsurance Carriers)

Industry Snapshot

In 1994, there were 19,915 establishments in the United States providing fire, marine, and casualty insurance and an estimated 3,800 companies, which were mainly organized as stock companies or mutual companies. Together these companies generated $23 billion in after-tax earnings, with net written premiums of $244.9 billion. Perhaps a more significant indicator of the importance of this industry to the U.S. economy is the amount of investment assets it controls. Between 1992 and 1997, insurance companies and banks accounted for almost 20 percent of all net business investments.

Although the industry recorded steady increases in revenues in the early 1990s, profits and financial fortitude deteriorated. A combination of low interest rates, a decrease in the growth of demand for insurance coverage, and a series of catastrophic events contributed to this decline. For example, four natural disasters in 1992 cost the industry a combined total of over $22 billion dollars in claims. A snow storm in early 1993 added another $1 billion to that total. An earthquake in 1994 caused $12 billion in damage, and two hurricanes, one in 1995 and one in 1996, cost a total of $1.6 billion each.

In addition to these problems, the industry was also beset in the late 1980s and early 1990s by an increase in the number of company insolvencies, which resulted from general mismanagement and fraud, as well as increased regulatory action. These insolvencies prompted an increase in government regulation which changed the face of the property/casualty industry in the mid-1990s.

Organization and Structure

The fire, marine, and casualty insurance industry, commonly known as the property/casualty industry, is part of the larger primary insurance industry, which also encompasses both life and health insurance. In addition to these three types of primary insurance, the reinsurance industry serves life, health, and property/casualty companies. Some companies participate in more than one primary industry segment.

Companies within the property/casualty industry provide financial protection for businesses, individuals, and other entities against property loss or losses by third parties for which the insured is liable. The two major segments of the industry are business and personal insurance, each of which accounts for almost 50 percent of the total dollar amount of property/casualty insurance premiums written.

Within all segments of the property/casualty industry, several types of insurance are available. Although most property/casualty insurance traditionally has been written to cover homes, automobiles, and other property, other types of coverage include workers' compensation, product liability, and medical malpractice. Of all the available lines, automobile insurance is the largest segment of the industry, accounting for over 45 percent of property/casualty insurance premiums written in 1992. Automobile insurance accounted for the largest increase in premiums, up $5.6 billion. Several other market segments account for the remainder of premiums in existence.

Workers' compensation insurance is the second largest segment of the individual market. A study released in early 1996 stated that insurers paid out $16 billion in asbestos losses alone between 1993 and 1995. Premiums for workers' compensation dropped 5 percent to $29.7 billion and accounted for just 13 percent of the property/casualty premiums written in 1992. Furthermore, fire and marine insurance combined represented less than 7 percent of all premiums written for individuals during that same year.

The entire insurance industry, including life, health and property/casualty, is comprised of four functional groups: insurers, who carry the risk of their clients; field organizations, which provide client services such as settling claims and writing insurance; intercompany associations or bureaus that, among other things, establish standards of practice, influence legislation, and determine rates; and associations of agents and brokers that promote the interests of the field organizations.

Financial Structure. Insurance companies generate profits by selling, or underwriting, policies to customers and then investing these revenues in income producing assets. Therefore, insurers may derive revenues, or losses, both from collecting premiums on insurance and from investment income. Insurers are in the precarious position of selling products and services before they are sure how much these products and services will cost to provide.

One factor distinguishing the property/casualty industry from other primary insurance industries is the nature of its investment activities. Future liabilities tend to be short term, compared to the life or health insurance industries, and are much less predictable. In addition, most property/casualty policy claims are settled quickly. Therefore, insurers must invest predominantly in assets that they can quickly convert to cash. For instance, bond holdings alone typically constitute over 70 percent of property/casualty industry assets, and stocks account for about 20 percent. These figures contrast the life insurance industry, which usually invests about 20 percent of its assets in relatively liquid mortgage loans and real estate.

Competitive Structure. Although industry growth stagnated in 1989 and throughout the early 1990s, the number of U.S. property/casualty insurers jumped 34 percent between 1979 and 1988. Of the nearly 20,000 companies that comprised the industry by 1994, 85 had 1,000 or more employees, and 275 had between 250-500 employees. Employment deceased in the early 1990s as insurers moved to streamline operations and dropped to 545,400 in 1993. Employment was up again in 1994 to 610,368. Advertising and customer service are also important elements of competition within the industry, since the industry is characterized by relatively homogeneous products which are difficult to differentiate from company to company.

BACKGROUND AND DEVELOPMENT

The concept of insurance developed in response to society's desire to spread the consequences of a loss that would normally fall upon a single individual over the members of a large group exposed to the same hazard. Through a system of equitable contributions, members of a large group can reduce the risk of disastrous personal loss. The result is an atmosphere of certainty, rather than uncertainty, regarding accidental or disastrous occurrences.

One widely cited definition of insurance emanated from a court case in Great Britain in 1806: "Insurance is a contract by which the one party, in consideration of a price paid to him adequate to the risk, becomes security to the other that he shall not suffer loss, damage, or prejudice by the happening of the perils specified to certain things which may be exposed to them."

Insurance companies concern themselves only with pure risk, which involves only the negative possibility of loss. Conversely, insurers must avoid insuring business risk, or speculative risk, which involves the chance of both loss or gain. In addition, the clients insured by companies must stand to lose by the happening of the event contemplated. Otherwise, the arrangement would amount to little more than a wager and would be unenforceable or illegal.

Other conditions that must be met in order for a group to be insured against an event are: the insurer must be able to quantify the risk of the event occurring; persons exposed to the risk must feel a sense of responsibility for the loss; the insurer must be capable of shouldering the burden of loss; and the events involved must be purely subject to chance.

Property/casualty insurance is limited to loss or destruction of property by fire, windstorm, hazards of the sea, earthquake, water leakage, explosion, riot and civil commotion, vandalism, theft, forgery, and vehicle collision. In addition, loss of property can result from liabilities related to compensation of injured workers, property damage caused to others, and negligence concerning the use of personal property.

Evolution. Organized systems of fire, casualty, or marine insurance have existed since at least the fifteenth century when a marine insurance industry emerged to serve Italian traders. The industry did not develop into a form resembling what exists today until the seventeenth century in England, following The Great Fire of London in 1666. This event prompted the development of a sophisticated fire insurance industry, which helped to lay the groundwork for the gradual development of a broader property/casualty industry. Rapid industrialization in the western world during the nineteenth and twentieth centuries sped the industry's development, as a decrease in individual independence magnified the benefits of insurance.

In the United States, it was not until early in the twentieth century that the hazards of wind, water, damage, and explosion were added to the established lines of fire insurance. Other forms of insurance followed, such as personal accident, which covers costs related to illness and accident; liability; and workers' compensation insurance. A turning point occurred in the U.S. property/casualty industry in 1948, when states began allowing insurance companies to write policies on several lines of insurance, rather than limiting companies to just one segment of the market. This practice, called multiple-line underwriting, had long been in practice in the rest of the world. Significant trends shaping the industry as it entered the 1990s included an increased emphasis on computers and automation in virtually all aspects of the market and the continued globalization of the industry. The trend continues into the late 1990s.

Regulation and Legislation. One aspect of the U.S. property/casualty industry that separates it from insurance industries in most other countries, aside from its sheer size, is its detailed system of government regulation. Until the 1940s, regulation was the exclusive province of state and local governments. However, in 1944 the Supreme Court, in *United States v. South-Eastern Underwriters Association,* ruled that insurance is commerce—commerce that is conducted between state lines. By redefining its scope, the Court made the entire insurance industry subject to the powers of Congress under the Commerce Clause of the Constitution. Congress then gave states until 1948 to revise their regulatory structures to meet certain standards laid down by the Act. State revisions enacted during that time were sufficient to preclude excessive federal intervention. However, events in the early 1990s again threatened the authority of states to regulate the industry, and increased federal regulatory action seemed likely.

Another legislative event with a significant impact on the industry is California's Proposition 103, legislation which California residents voted to enact in 1989. The proposition required property/casualty insurers to reduce, or rollback, automobile insurance rates by 20 percent. Enforcement of the proposition was postponed until 1992. This legislation reflected growing consumer discontent with escalating insurance costs nationwide and provided a testing ground for states considering similar legislation. Many insurers responded by reducing, or stopping, business in California.

Record losses from catastrophes, a lack of good investment alternatives, and a sluggish economy were the three predominant factors which converged to make 1992 a historically dismal year for the property/casualty industry. Small improvements over 1991 in the dollar value of premiums written, combined with capital gains realized from the sale of assets, were the only factors which kept earnings positive for that year.

By the late 1990s, federal regulators argued that the state regulatory system was inefficient and had contributed to the financial instability of the industry. By requiring more stringent regulations concerning financial health, federal regulators hoped to strengthen the fiscal soundness of the industry and force companies to operate responsibly.

In 1997, an effort to reduce unnecessary regulatory burdens on casualty insurance is making strong headway in many states. NAIC invited insurance industry representatives, including the American Insurance Association, to present proposals for reducing regulations for large purchasers of commercial insurance. In March 1997, NAIC outlined several regulatory relief proposals, and the industry anticipates more action to follow.

Catastrophes. Catastrophes were the single greatest affliction for the industry in the early 1990s, resulting in over $22 billion in combined losses. Of all the catastrophes during 1992, Hurricane Andrew was the most expensive. Its damage in Florida and Louisiana in August 1992 racked up record claims topping $15 billion for the industry. Less than one month after Andrew, Hurricane Iniki blasted the Hawaiian Islands, wreaking an additional $2 billion in destruction. In addition, tornadoes ripped through the South and Southwest of that same year, causing $130 million in damage, and the Chicago floods reaped another $300 million in claims. A few months after the Chicago floods, riots in Los Angeles amounted to $750 million in damage. In early 1993, a heavy snowstorm on the East coast dealt a $1 billion blow to property/casualty insurers. These catastrophes contributed to a staggering loss in underwriting income of over $34 billion in 1992, compared to the past record high loss of $25 billion in 1985. In comparison, underwriting losses from 1989 to 1991, which were also burdened by exorbitant catastrophic claims, averaged about $20 billion.

Investment and the Economy. A second factor contributing to financial stress within the industry during the early 1990s was excess capital and comparatively poor investment opportunities in the sluggish economy. Property/casualty insurers began to rely increasingly on investment income to shore up their earnings in the 1980s. However, low interest rates and limited investment returns began to limit this source of revenue by the early 1990s. By liquidating $9 billion in assets to realize capital gains, insurers were able to boost their income in 1992, but at the expense of weakening the economic strength of the industry.

A third problem for insurers in the early 1990s was the sluggish economy. The dollar amount of premiums written increased just 3 percent in 1992—well below the 6 percent growth rate which some analysts had predicted, but slightly greater than the growth in 1991. Stagnant growth in premium rates, partly because of regulatory rate suppression, compounded financial difficulties for insurers.

Insolvency. Besides catastrophes, a sluggish economy, and low interest rates, the property/casualty industry continued to suffer from a relatively high rate of company insolvency. Between 1984 and 1992, over 370 companies failed, compared to a total of only 141 in the 15 years prior to 1984. Most of these insolvencies involved smaller companies. But despite the 1992 catastrophes, there were only nine insolvencies during the first half of 1993.

Although the root cause of many failures was mismanagement or fraud, a more aggressive regulatory environment resulted in a greater number of company failures than would have otherwise occurred. In addition, Hurricane Andrew alone was a major cause of at least nine of the failures. Some industry observers believe that the number of insolvent companies peaked in 1990 and may have been decreasing since that time. Nevertheless, insolvency has been a major contributing factor to the increase in federal and state industry regulation.

Democratic Michigan Representative John Dingell addressed the regulators' interests when he introduced a controversial bill in April 1992. The Dingell Bill was designed to enforce uniform capital requirements for insurers. Industry reactions were mixed, and many industry leaders opposed the bill. In response to federal regulatory attempts such as the Dingell Bill, the National Association of Insurance Commissioners (NAIC) tried to strengthen state requirements and avoid increased federal entanglement in the industry. Pressures to increase federal regulation mounted in 1992 when there were congressional efforts to reform the McCarran-Ferguson Act, which exempted insurers from Federal antitrust laws. Reform of this act would mean the loss of an important defense for insurers against federal involvement in the regulatory process.

Increased Competition. The second significant long-term challenge for industry participants in 1997 was increased competition. This challenge meant a reduction in the work force and consolidation, by merger and acquisition, for many property/casualty companies. In 1997, the Providian Corporation announced that its shareholders approved the merger of the company's insurance operations with AEGON USA, a subsidiary of Netherlands based AEGON, NV, one of the largest listed insurance organizations worldwide.

Insurance giant Aetna sold its Casualty and Surety Company to the Travelers Group for $4.1 billion in 1997, creating the largest writer of personal automobile insurance through he independent agency system. Sagging industry profits, foreign expansion into the United States, and market segmentation were a few of the factors driving this trend.

Limiting their participation in the industry to specific market segments in which they had developed expertise is one way companies sought to increase their chances of maintaining profitability in the 1990s. Companies wanting to compete effectively also were learning to become more efficient through automation and customer focus. Many companies, especially smaller ones, were seeking to merge with other companies to strengthen their capital position. In addition, many companies were looking into ways to streamline operations and reduce the size of their work force. Expansion into foreign markets offered another opportunity for property/casualty insurers to shore up profit margins. "Companies must downsize, consolidate divisions, reduce their employee base, and enhance their capital spending . . . to compete globally," according to Robert M. Demichele, President of the Reinsurance Corporation of New York, in *Best's Review, Property/Casualty Edition.* In June 1997, the American Insurance Association (AIA) urged Congress to support tax legislation that would help to make the U.S. property/casualty insurance industry more competitive in the global marketplace.

Current Conditions

In the first nine months of 1998, the industry had a net income of $23.2 billion, down 15 percent from the $27.4 billion posted in 1997. The catastrophes, especially hurricanes in the Atlantic, mounted in the first half of 1998 making it the fifth worst year since 1950. The losses from the claims accounted for about 75 percent of the decline in income. By the end of 1998, the industry's policyholder surplus rose only 7.5 percent, compared to the rise of 22.2 percent in 1997. The catastrophic losses totaled $10 billion for the year, compared to only $2.6 billion in 1997. The losses, combined with reduced investment yields and year-to-year capital gains, accounted for this decline. In 1999 the catastrophes did not let up; with tornadoes and other weather-related phenomenon, 1999 was predicted to be the second worst year since 1994 in terms of catastrophic losses.

Some analysts predict a continued decline for the industry. The strong stock market may not be able to support the overcapitalization of the industry nor the pricing policies. The industry is absorbing higher costs due to favorable loss cost trends, catastrophic losses, and harvesting of past loss reserves. All these factors contributed to a downward trend in the industry from 1998 through the middle of 1999. As the industry is highly competitive, premium increases are expected to remain flat.

To survive, many companies are merging, buying related companies, and finding alternative outlets for sales. Some companies are offering fee-based services and others are becoming facilitators, consultants, and managers, in addition to their traditional roles as risk retainers. Mergers continued in 1999 as insurance companies looked to diversify and expand their offerings. In mid-1999 Allstate announced it would buy the personal lines from CAN, a transaction worth $1.2 billion. The Hartford bought Omni to augment their product line and was expanding the non-standard auto operations.

Regulation continues to plague the industry. In the late 1990s, the minimum workers compensation rate law was repealed, commercial lines were deregulated, and there was a move to repeal the Glass-Steagall Act. In addition, in 1999 OSHA proposed regulations to protect workers suffering from musculoskeletal problems. The agency proposed ergonomic standards that had insurers and businesses up in arms. The insurance industry stated it didn't oppose worker safety, but felt the OSHA proposals discouraged worker/employer relations in discussing workplace safety; proposed coercive regulations without thought to employer motivation; and added significant costs with provable benefits.

In addition to regulation and increased competition, environmental liability posed a potential major threat to profitability in the distant future. Large environmental claims typically are made many years after the cause of the claim occurs, making it difficult for insurers to predict cleanup cost liability. One study estimated that cleaning up the known hazardous waste sites could cost over $750 billion over 30 years, excluding litigation costs which could double that figure. Because property/casualty insurers could potentially be stuck with the entire bill, companies needed to consider building reserves of assets to address those future claims.

INDUSTRY LEADERS

Of the top 10 companies writing 40 percent of the property/casualty premiums in the United States, the State Farm Group of Illinois was the largest as of 1998. They service 65.8 million policies, employing 69,000 people and enlisting the services of 17,000 agents. One in five cars in America is insured by State Farm, and they are the largest insurer of automobiles, homes and pleasure boats. In 1998 they had $25.7 billion in premiums, down 1.6 percent from 1997. The net income was $1.1 billion, down from $2.5 billion in 1997. In 1998, State Farm Fire and Casualty, a subsidiary of The State Farm Group, had a policyholder protection fund of $3.2 billion, down slightly from the $3.3 billion in 1997 and an investment fluctuation reserve of $2.4 billion, up from $1.9 billion in 1997. They employed more than 11,000 people, and has no history of employee layoffs since its inception in 1935.

Allstate Insurance, also of Illinois, is the nation's largest publicly held property and casualty insurance company. They have over 14,000 agents and 20 million customers in the USA, Canada, and Japan. The company offered multiple lines of insurance and was started in 1931 by Sears Roebuck & Company. The company had increased revenues for 1998—up 3.3 percent over 1997 to $21.8 billion.

Several companies with sales in the $5 to $7 billion range vied for third place in size in 1997, including Travelers Insurance Company, ITT Hartford Insurance Group, and Liberty Mutual—the number one workers compensation insurers in the United States. Most of these companies also provided health and life insurance.

WORKFORCE

Even in companies that were not adding jobs, more opportunities were available through attrition and shifts in the work force than were available in most other industries. With a strong economy and many companies showing increased sales and profits in the mid-to-late 1990s, the job market is strong. Opportunities existed in five functional areas, including sales, claims, underwriting, accounting/finance, and professional staff support positions.

The greatest number of jobs in existence in the insurance industry, by far, are sales positions, and this field is also the most accessible for people trying to enter the industry. Sales positions are available at the tens of thousands of local insurance offices scattered throughout the United States and Canada.

Although a career in sales involves more risk than many salary positions, it can be one of the most rewarding jobs in the industry, combining personal freedom with an income in excess of over $100,000 per year. Success in the field typically requires an outgoing, entrepreneurial, and persistent personality. The profession can also be quite demanding, requiring 60 or more hours of time per week during the first few years of selling. Another significant drawback for property/casualty salespeople is industry cycles, which usually mean periods of low income.

A position in claims in the property/casualty industry involves assessing the dollar value of damage a policyholder has sustained and authorizing payment by the parent company. Claims adjusters combine knowledge with experience to judge how much damage the company will cover. In comparison to sales, claims positions are highly detailed-oriented and structured. Claims adjuster is a responsible position, which can lead to promotions within the company to a claims examiner, who handles complex claims, or a claims supervisor, who manages claims adjusters and examiners.

Underwriters are faced with the task of determining which applicants for insurance the company will reject or accept and how much coverage the applicant may receive. This assignment involves gathering information on applicants, reviewing associated risks, and applying underwriting standards to reach a decision. Underwriters specialize in either personal or business lines of property/casualty insurance, although most underwriters start out in personal lines. In 1994, underwriters held 96,000 jobs, with 38 percent in fire, marine, and casualty. The median earnings of full-time wage and salaried underwriters was about $30,800.

Insurance accountants are typically charged with auditing functions, examination of policyholders financial records as part of the underwriting process, or enforcing underwriting guidelines prescribed for underwriters by the parent company. Finance professionals, on the other hand, are usually more involved with financial and investment analysis, marketing research, and sales forecasting. Employers of both accounting/finance and underwriting professionals usually seek applicants with analytical backgrounds in economics or business administration.

Property/casualty insurers hire large support staffs to administer important functions that support the revenue producing activities within the company. These disciplines include actuaries, lawyers, marketers, and others. Actuaries use mathematics to determine insurance rates and policies and to establish pricing and investment guidelines, which will increase profits. The actuarial field involves complex mathematical modeling and most actuaries endure years of examinations before becoming fully designated within their profession. This occupation is also ranked among the highest in worker satisfaction and pay.

Insurance law provides excellent opportunities for attorneys, especially in the litigation arena. Because every insurance policy is a binding legal contract, attorneys receive more emphasis in the industry than they do in most other industries. Although salaries are typically below those found in the top law firms, they are similar to other corporate law positions. Other opportunities exist in public relations, customer service, and loss control. Loss control is a relatively new specialization which involves finding ways to prevent injury, theft, and damage—mostly by educating policyholders.

AMERICA AND THE WORLD

The United States has the largest and most advanced insurance industry in the world. During 1992, over $276 billion, or 43 percent, of the $649 billion in non-life insurance premiums in the world were written in the United States. Europe followed closely with about $237 billion, and Asia made up the third largest market at $95 billion. The Latin American market lagged far behind at just $7.1 billion in premiums. The United States leads the world market for non-life insurance, with 42.3 percent of the premiums. Next is Japan with 12.3 percent, followed by Germany, with 9.5 percent and the United Kingdom with 5.8 percent. The size of the U.S. market is due primarily to health and casualty insurance, and private insurers rather than the public sector, provide most of the health insurance.

During the mid-1980s, the surge in multinational companies and international trade and investment encouraged the growth of many international insurance companies. Insurers, including property/casualty insurers, from the United States, Asia, and Europe expanded internationally through avenues such as branches, subsidiaries, joint ventures. Although global expansion in the property/casualty markets slowed after 1988 as world markets recessed, it continues to offer opportunities for insurers.

From the viewpoint of United States insurers, global expansion has two sides—U.S. expansion and investment abroad and foreign expansion and investment in the United States. U.S. insurers are becoming increasingly active in foreign expansion either through cross-border trade, in which foreign customers are covered by a company in the United States, or subsidiaries, which are located in the country where the customer is located. Sales by U.S.-owned insurance companies in other countries topped $36 billion in 1991, mostly from non-life insurance operations including income from investments. The majority of these sales occurred in Europe ($11 billion).

Regulatory developments in the European Community (EC) have been directing its members to liberalize their markets for insurance and offers new opportunities for U.S. property/casualty insurers in the 1990s. These developments include countries that were opening their insurance markets to foreign investment for the first time, EC efforts to standardize accounting and reporting practices, and EC directives that made it easier for companies to transact business across country borders. Several EC countries, especially in Southern Europe, have opened this insurance sector to foreign investment.

New opportunities also existed in Latin America and Asia. Latin governments were deregulating the insurance industry and allowing foreign investment for the first time. The North American Free Trade Agreement (NAFTA) has opened up the small Mexican property/casualty market, allowing U.S. insurers to operate equally with Mexican insurers. Asian countries offered an even larger potential for U.S. expansion abroad as incomes in this region continued to grow. Taiwan and Korea continued to be particularly attractive to U.S. insurers.

The newest opportunity exists in the People's Republic of China, where in 1995, a national insurance law was enacted. For 30 years after the founding of the present republic, the country had only one insurer, the State-owned People's Insurance Company of China. Few Chinese had insurance, but in an era of increasing opportunity and risk, more than 100 million took out property coverage in 1995. Competition is slowly growing, and foreign insurance firms are seeing a potentially lucrative market. Since 1992, China has only permitted two foreign firms, one of them the American International Group, licenses to sell insurance, first in Shanghai and more recently in Guangzhou. While it waits for a license, the U.S. firm Chubb Insurance has committed $1 million over the next five years to set up a school in Shanghai to train regulators and agents.

Foreign Involvement in the United States. Although opportunities existed for U.S. insurers abroad in the mid-1990s, many property/casualty insurers felt that significant barriers still existed for U.S. companies trying to compete overseas. Conversely, the American market was very open to foreign competition. An opportunity to create a more level playing field for the industry existed, however, under the Uruguay Round Group of Negotiations on Services under the General Agreement on Tariffs and Trade (GATT) during 1993. These rules could allow U.S. insurers to enter and operate in foreign markets on an equal basis with domestic insurers in the future.

Foreign insurance company investment in the U.S. market surpassed U.S. activity abroad during the 1980s. Foreign owned insurers had sales of $72.9 billion in 1991, up sharply from $62.6 billion in 1990, primarily due to foreign acquisitions. They captured more than 11 percent of the market in 1991 and sold non-life insurance policies worth more than $39 billion. These companies expanded into the U.S. property/casualty industry by acquiring American companies, buying interests in U.S. companies, or by creating new subsidiaries in the United States.

U.S. insurers have become more active overseas in recent years, with sales of $36.2 billion in 1991. The key markets for U.S. insurers are Canada, Europe, and Japan, primarily in non-life operations. Cross border trade in insurance is a small but important part of the U.S. insurance market. U.S. based insurers received more than $5.5 billion of premiums from overseas in 1992, and premiums of $11.9 billion went to foreign based insurers to cover risks in the United States. Most premiums sent abroad went to Europe or the offshore centers like Bermuda for reinsurance. Reinsurance premiums sent abroad represented about one-third of the reinsurance market in the United States. Foreign-owned insurers from all lines in the United States had sales of $72.9 billion in 1991.

The most significant investments included Germany's Allianz Holding Company's acquisition of Fireman's Fund Insurance Companies in 1991 and BAT Industries (UK) acquisition of Farmers Insurance Group in 1988. These two deals amounted to over $5 billion of foreign investment. In addition to a share of the U.S. insurance market, foreign investors have benefited from access to superior technology related to automation, claims adjusting, risk management, actuarial methods, investment practices, and information technology. In 1997, AEGON NV of the Netherlands acquired the insurance section of the Providian Corporation.

Research and Technology

Companies in the property/casualty industry have been slower than their U.S. counterparts to integrate advanced research and technology into their operations. However, two of the most important keys to success in the industry during the 1990s will be increased use of market research and customer focus, along with integration of advanced automation technologies that can reduce costs and improve service.

As they entered 1997, insurers were striving to become more customer focused in response to the increasingly competitive property/casualty environment. Part of this strategy included finding out exactly what the customer needs and fulfilling that need, often with very niche-oriented insurance products. Insurers were continuing to increase their efforts in the research and development of new and more specialized insurance products that could be offered at competitive prices. The purpose of these new products was to either bring new customers into the market or to cause customers already in the industry to switch from competitors' products.

Even more important than new product development and research, however, was the implementation of automation technologies, which will improve customer service, reduce errors, improve delivery time, and reduce human intervention in the entire insurance process. Insurers that had already implemented computerized automation were enjoying increased speed of new product delivery to the market, as well as reduced personnel expenses.

Examples of new technology, which property/casualty insurers were integrating into the industry in the late 1990s, included open-systems architecture computer systems, network computing, computer-aided software-engineering tools, multi-media training tools, and information management and delivery systems that use satellites. Industry regulators were also using this new technology to identify potentially insolvent insurers. Several companies have realized significant cost reductions and improved customer service through comprehensive automation programs.

Further Reading

"AEGON: Providian Shareholders Approve Merger with AEGON USA." M2 PressWire. 9 June 1997.

"Alliance Very Disappointed in OSHA's Proposed Ergonomic Standard; Says Failure to Change Approach Will Hinder Effectiveness." *Alliance of American Insurers,* 23 November 1999. Available from http://www.allianceai.org/cgi-bin/Hsrun/web.../PrintBulletin?FileName=NEWSo164-99.HTML.

"Allstate Posts Fourth Consecutive Record Profit." *Allstate,* 10 February 1999. Available from http://www.allstate.com/media/news/pr_1999/pr_1999_02_10.html.

"A.M. Best Upgrades Allstate Insurance Co. to A+ (Superior) from A (Excellent)." A.M. Best Company Press Release, 1997.

Johnston, Stuart. "Unix, OS/2 Hold Their Ground Against NT." *Computerworld,* 26 February 1996, 54.

Kerin, Roger. "Largest Property and Casualty Insurance Companies." *Birmingham Business Journal,* 29 January 1996, 20.

"NAIC Again Slams Administration Plan for Financial Services Modernization." *BestWeek,* 1997.

"Property/Casualty Companies Post Smaller Profits." *The Consumer Insurance Guide,* 10 December 1998. Available from http://www.insure.com/gen/pclosses1298.html.

"Property/Casualty Insurer's Surplus Growing More Slowly." *The Consumer Insurance Guide,* 21 July 1999. Available from http://www.insure.com/gen/pcsurplus799.html.

Sanchez, Jesus. "State Farm to Cap Replacement Payments on California Policies." *Los Angeles Times,* 9 January 1997, D-1.

Simms, Larry L. "China's Insurance Law." *China Business Review,* 1 October 1996, 30.

Standard & Poor's. "Outlook for Property/Casualty Industry Remains negative." *The Consumer Insurance Guide,* July 1999. Available from http://www.insure.com/ratings/analysis/99q2pc.html.

"State Farm Announces Financial Results for 1998." *State Farm Press Release,* 24 February 1999. Available from http://www.statefarm.com/media/release/firesult.html.

"Underwriting the Year 2000 Problem." A.M. Best Press Release, 1997.

SIC 6351

SURETY INSURANCE

This classification provides coverage of establishments primarily engaged in underwriting financial responsibility insurance.

NAICS CODE(S)

524126 (Direct property and Casualty Insurance Carriers)

524130 (Reinsurance Carriers)

INDUSTRY SNAPSHOT

Surety insurance, sold in the form of a surety bond, is a tool used to guarantee the performance by one party of an obligation to another. It differs from other types of insurance in several ways—including the number of parties involved, the way companies determine premium rates, and in the way that the burden of risk is apportioned. The most common type of surety insurance is construction bonding, which insures that contractors will be able to complete a construction contract and pay their suppliers and subcontractors. Other common types of surety insurance include bonding of employees (fidelity insurance), license and permit bonds, and court bonds.

ORGANIZATION AND STRUCTURE

Surety insurance can cover almost any contractual agreement, whether the contract is written or implied. Although it is often classified as a line of property/casualty insurance, surety is similar to other types of insurance only in that it is a form of risk management. Because it is different in other ways, surety bonding is usually offered through a separate division or department within an insurance company and is governed under a different set of laws from other insurance lines.

Surety insurance involves three parties: the principal, the obligee, and the surety (insurer). The principal is the party who agrees to perform an obligation. For example, a builder may contract to construct a building. The obligee expects the principal to fulfill a contract. In the example above, the obligee would be the party with which the builder agreed to construct the house. The surety, then, is the party which guarantees that either the principal will perform adequately or the obligee will be compensated for the principal's failure. For instance, if the principal finished building only part of the house and then quit, the surety might compensate the obligee for any losses incurred in getting another builder to finish the home. In the example, and in most cases, the surety is not necessarily responsible for fulfilling the broken contract, but only for the obligee's losses related to completion of the contract. For this reason, surety insurers do not necessarily cover risks associated with devastating losses, but only with varying degrees of default risk.

Another major difference from other types of insurance is that surety insurers look to the insured party for repayment of losses it incurs. In the example, the surety would be entitled to recover its losses from the principal, unless the principal was insolvent. For this reason, the risk associated with writing bonds has traditionally been very low. In fact, theoretically the surety anticipates no losses if the underwriter has used the necessary information about the principal required to determine whether or not to write the bond.

Surety insurance also differs from other insurance lines in the methods insurers use to determine premium rates. Because the risk to the surety is usually very low, premium rates for surety bonds are primarily service fees and are less influenced by the risk of loss. Fidelity insurance, which covers a company against losses caused by dishonest performance by its employees, is a major branch of the surety industry. In 1995, fidelity bonds constituted about 31 percent of all direct surety premiums written.

Company Structure. The surety market is divided into the standard market and the specialty market, each of which is served by different types of surety companies. The standard market represents the more traditional approach to surety bonding and is served primarily by large national agency companies. These companies tend only to underwrite clients which have a very sound financial history and represent little risk of insolvency or contract default. In addition, many national agency companies only underwrite contracts which assure $25,000 to $50,000 in gross premiums per year. In 1995, national agency companies wrote nearly 60 percent of all surety premiums, with about 30 percent written by regional companies and 11 percent by direct writers. Of these premiums, the 20 leading surety writers accounted for $1.87 billion in premiums—69.1 percent of the $2.71 billion surety market. National agency companies wrote 68 percent of all fidelity premiums in 1995, with 10 percent written by regional companies and 22 percent by direct writers. The top 20 fidelity writers accounted for $843.6 million in premiums written, or 91 percent of the $927.5 million fidelity market.

The specialty market, on the other hand, is served primarily by regional agency companies. These companies are less strict in their underwriting requirements and will generally bond contractors that the standard market may have rejected. Regional companies are able to serve these clients because they require collateral of 20 percent to 30 percent of the bond obligation for each contract they insure. In addition, regional companies are more likely, and able, to vigorously pursue recovery from their clients in the event of default.

The biggest expense for surety underwriters involves qualifying applicants, not providing loss compensation. Surety writers do not expect losses, and they focus their efforts on screening out risky applicants. Premium rates reflect the cost of providing a credit-based guarantee rather than loss compensation. In 1995, surety writers showed an improved operating ratio, indicating they were controlling costs such as commission and brokerage expenses and other underwriting expenses associated with screening applicants.

Market share in the surety industry is split between national agency, multi-line companies, which serve the standard surety market, and regional agency companies, which serve the specialty market. In 1995, national agency companies wrote nearly 60 percent of all surety premiums and 68 percent of all fidelity premiums. Regional companies wrote about 30 percent of surety premiums and 10 percent of fidelity premiums, and direct writers wrote 11 percent of surety premiums and 22 percent of fidelity premiums. Of the surety premiums, the 20 leading surety writers accounted for 69.1 percent of the surety market. The top 20 fidelity writers accounted for 91 percent of the fidelity market.

Major Products. Surety products can be separated into two categories: those that are easy to obtain, and those that are more difficult. Bonds that are relatively easy to obtain typically involve small amounts of money or present a low level of risk to the surety. Bonds in this category include license and permit bonds, which protect city or state governments against claims that arise because of a license which the government body issued to some party. Court fiduciary bonds, which bond a person named to handle money for an estate, and judicial bonds, which ensure that a plaintiff will pay damages to a wrongly charged defendant, also fall into this category. Public official bonds, which bond officials against losses resulting from their failure to conduct their duties within the confines of the law, are also easy to obtain. Bonds that are difficult to obtain include construction-related bonds such as performance, payment, and bid bonds.

Legislation. Surety companies benefit from state and federal legislation that requires bonding of various types of contracts. These laws require, for instance, that employers who self-insure employee benefits are bonded. Similarly, many states require automobile owners who have been in an accident to post a bond of financial responsibility before they allow them to operate their vehicles again. One of the most prominent pieces of legislation in this regard is the 1935 Federal Miller Act, which requires prime contractors in the United States to provide a performance bond for any construction contract which exceeds a certain amount. In 1992, this amount was $25,000 in total construction costs.

Background and Development

Although the concept of suretyship dates back more than 2,000 years to ancient Babylon, the commercial surety industry in the United States did not begin until 1884 with the incorporation of the American Surety Corporation of New York. Since that time, the industry has grown steadily and, until recently, has had comparatively high profitability. The industry realized its greatest growth and profitability during the rapid national expansion that occurred between the end of World War II and the early 1970s. During this time, the construction industry was not very competitive, a booming economy created demand for all lines of bonds, and profit margins were high. During the past 20 years, however, increased competition, as well as an overall decrease in demand for construction, has reduced profit margins for insurers and increased the risk of default and insolvency for those insured or bonded. Surety and fidelity underwriters showed profitable underwriting results in the late 1980s and 1990s, with surety lines being profitable from 1989 through 1995 and fidelity lines being profitable from 1986 through 1995. Surety premiums written increased steadily from 1987 through 1994. Premiums written for fidelity bonds, after double-digit increases from 1985 through 1987, declined from 1988 through 1992, then began increasing slightly from 1992 through 1995.

There were $2.8 billion in direct premiums written for surety and fidelity bonds in 1995, with $2.71 billion for surety bonds and $927.5 million for fidelity lines. For surety lines, that represented the third straight 9 percent or better annual increase, while fidelity lines posted a 2.1 percent increase in net premiums written. Surety and fidelity underwriters showed profitable results in the late

1980s and 1990s. In 1995, surety underwriting profits nearly doubled to $276.9 million, while fidelity underwriting profits were flat—up only 1.9 percent to $232.9 million. By comparison, most other lines in the property and casualty insurance industry experienced underwriting losses from 1979 through 1995. In 1995, the overall property/casualty industry posted underwriting losses of $18.1 billion.

Although distinctly different, the surety industry is considered a small part of the overall property and casualty insurance industry. In 1995, surety and fidelity insurance accounted for about $2.8 billion in premiums written—a small amount compared to the $250.7 billion in net premiums written by property and casualty insurers in 1994. Surety and fidelity underwriters showed profitable results in the late 1980s and 1990s. In 1995, surety underwriting profits nearly doubled to $276.9 million, while fidelity underwriting results were flat, up only 1.9 percent to $232.9 million. In terms of premiums written, surety bonds recorded a 9 percent annual increase from 1993 to 1995. Premiums written for fidelity bonds decreased steadily from 1988 to 1992, then began showing small percentage gains through 1995.

CURRENT CONDITIONS

In some ways, the surety insurance industry works opposite to the rest of the insurance industry, thus acting as a counterbalance for integrated companies. For example, the overall industry chalked up 1997 as a banner year, in part due to the mild weather attributed to the influence of El Niño, which resulted in low catastrophe losses for the insurance industry. By comparison, 1998 represented a worse year, with more catastrophic weather requiring more insurance-financed construction. The surety industry experienced 1997 and 1998 conversely: the mild weather of 1997 meant less catastrophe-based construction, hence less surety bonds; on the other hand, the more catastrophic weather of 1998 created more construction work requiring more surety bonds, thus bolstering the surety industry.

Since a large part of surety and fidelity insurance is related to the construction industry, the industry tends to follow the cycles of the overall economy. The industry has been helped by good economic conditions in the 1990s, including low interest rates, low inflation, and stable oil prices. Other factors influencing the industry's performance include federal initiatives to build infrastructure and natural disasters that increase demand for construction bonds.

Legislation passed by Congress in 1991 was expected to expand the role of surety insurers in the cleanup of environmental waste sites. The laws free sureties from liabilities for tort claims related to default by bonded contractors. This could be an important development for sureties during the next few decades and beyond because of the potential for increased environmental cleanup costs and the billions of government dollars already earmarked for the Superfund cleanup. On the other hand, legislation that could raise the minimum cost for federal construction contracts, which must be bonded from the current level of $25,000 to $100,000, could hurt the industry. This legislation would allow contractors to bid on and complete smaller construction jobs without having to buy a bond under the Federal Miller Act.

In reality, the Superfund did not produce the kinds of results expected because its funding got bogged down in Congressional debate. Only one-third of the sites covered by the Superfund were cleaned up as of 1998. However, that year Congress tried to jump-start the Superfund by allocating $650 million of expedited funds.

INDUSTRY LEADERS

Of the companies that primarily provide surety insurance, the industry leaders include Travelers Surety and Casualty Co. of Hartford, Connecticut, whose 200,000 employees generated $27 billion in sales for 1998. MBIA of Armonk, New York, with 46 workers, a mere fraction of Travelers', created more than $12 billion in sales for the same fiscal year. In comparison, MBIA's sales represented $268 million per employee, while Travelers generated only $135,000 per employee. AMBAC Financial Group Inc. of New York City garnered more than $11 billion in sales for the same fiscal year on the work of 340 employees, each of whom generated almost $33 million. Although many surety companies began by providing only surety or fidelity insurance, many of the companies in this industry now provide multiple lines of insurance.

WORKFORCE

The entire property and casualty insurance industry employed about 616,000 people in 1994, while non-property/casualty insurers employed about 935,000 people. Of the approximately 6,000 insurance companies in the United States, about 3,300 sell some form of property and casualty insurance. Many of the property/casualty companies offer multiple lines of insurance, including surety insurance. However, about 900 national property/casualty companies account for most of the sales. Surety insurance accounted for approximately 1.1 percent of property/casualty sales in 1995 and accounted for a similar proportion of the jobs within the industry.

Job opportunities in the surety industry mimic those available in the larger property/casualty insurance industry. Positions in the surety industry, as in the property and casualty industry, are available in sales, underwriting and accounting, legal, and staff support.

Job opportunities also exist at regional agency companies, most of which do not provide other lines of insurance. Because these regional companies emphasize collateralized contracts and tend to vigorously pursue losses from bonded clients that default, positions with these companies require fewer credit and underwriting skills and more legal knowledge related to subrogation.

America and the World

Although it had a late start, the surety industry in the United States is the largest and most sophisticated in the world. However, its organization and structure closely parallels the surety industry of Great Britain, after which it was modeled. While the fire, marine, and casualty insurance industry in the United States experienced an influx of foreign investment and participation during the 1980s, the surety industry remained relatively local. This is due in part to the advantage which regional companies have when pursuing losses in court from clients that default on bonds.

Another factor responsible for a lack of cross-border activity within the industry is the nature of surety insurance compared to other lines of insurance. Surety bonding more closely resembles a fee-based service than it does typical insurance underwriting. Therefore, the investment advantages gained through foreign ventures are diminished.

Research and Technology

Because its basic function has changed little since its inception in 1884, the U.S. surety industry has been slow to realize the advantages of efficiency available through increased automation. The industry is just beginning to implement automated systems to ease workload. The types of automation include computer networking, information delivery and management systems, and multi-media training tools. Automation is especially important as the industry continues to become more price competitive.

Another important technical development for surety insurers in the early 1990s was a corporate interest in the use of surety bonds as a tool to obtain low-cost financing. Firms with strong credit ratings found that they could issue debt using company assets as collateral and then obtain surety bonds that guaranteed payment of the debt. By doing this, the firm which bought the bond could eliminate the risk of company insolvency related to the insured debt. This technique allowed companies to obtain low-cost financing during the credit crunch of the early 1990s. It also provides a potential new market for sureties throughout the 1990s.

Further Reading

Bowers, Barbara. ''1997: A Year of Profits, Mergers and Regulation Tussles.'' *Best's Review—Property-Casualty Insurance Edition,* January 1998.

Farinella, Michael A. ''Lower Claims Boosted 1995 Underwriting Profits.'' *Best's Review, Property/Casualty Edition,* September 1996, 26.

Gilbert, Evelyn. ''1995 Surety and Fidelity Results Called 'Excellent'.'' *National Underwriter: Property & Casualty/Risk & Benefits Management Edition,* 24 June 1996, 13.

Gorke, Thomas P. ''Guaranteeing Performance: The Role of Surety Bonds.'' *Risk Management,* November 1996, 22.

Infotrac Company Profiles, 20 March 2000. Available from http://web7.infotrac.galegroup.com.

May, Ronald A., et al. ''Annual Survey of Fidelity and Surety Law.'' *Defense Counsel Journal,* January 1996, 86.

1996 Property/Casualty Insurance Facts. New York: Insurance Information Institute, 1995.

Sclafane, Susanne. ''Insurers Report Fortune Reversals in 1998.'' *National Underwriter Property & Casualty-Risk & Benefits Management,* 1 March 1999.

''Surety Bond Industry Grows Modestly in 1995—Mixed Projections for '96.'' *ENR: Engineering News Record,* 25 March 1996, S3.

SIC 6361

TITLE INSURANCE

This classification covers establishments primarily engaged in underwriting insurance to protect the owner of real estate, or lenders of money thereon, against loss sustained by reason of any defect of title.

NAICS Code(s)

524127 (Direct Title Insurance Carriers)
524130 (Reinsurance Carriers)

Typical title defects result from liens and encumbrances on a property related to unpaid taxes, land use and zoning restrictions, unsettled contractor disputes for work done on the property, and unrecorded deeds. Title insurance also protects the buyer and lender from fraud perpetrated by the seller.

Title insurers must carefully analyze government records and legal documents to determine the risk of defects for a title on a given parcel of property. The insurer must then underwrite an insurance policy for the buyer that reflects the character of the property title under consideration. Although title searches and warranty deeds have been used to assure title validity in the past, title insurance grew in popularity during the 1980s and early 1990s because it was the most absolute form of protection.

The 1990s were a turbulent period for the industry, which experienced one of its worst years in 1991, when operating losses exceeded $190 million. Business stabilized in 1992 as demand for title insurance increased and many companies reported operating profits for the first time in many years. A large drop, however, in the number of refinancings in 1994, due to higher interest rates, placed more financial pressure on companies that carried over into 1995. Large companies such as Chicago Title and Trust Co. and Lawyers Title Insurance Corp. tried to reverse their decline in profits by instituting staff cutbacks and salary reductions.

To combat downward pressure on profits, title insurance companies tried to increase efficiency by automating, laying off employees, improving services, and increasing lines and regions of service through mergers and acquisitions of smaller companies. In addition, many companies were able to find work in the foreclosure industry, serving law firms and banks, and by offering new real estate services (e.g., loan servicing and appraisals). By the late 1990s the industry had ridden out the serious financial hardship that occurred because of problems and rapid fluctuations in the real estate resale and new construction market.

Between 1986 and 1999 the number of companies providing title insurance in the United States fell from 85 to fewer than 70, and the market became increasingly controlled by several large companies. During this time a number of title companies failed; many of the companies that were left merged so as to pool resources and capital. In late 1999 Fidelity National Finance announced the purchase of number-one-ranked Chicago Title Corp. in a $1.2 billion merger. With combined 1998 revenues of $3.4 billion, this merger created the largest title insurance company in the United States.

The industry was using new developments in computer technology to aid in the underwriting process. Several companies were leading the way with artificial intelligence systems designed to predict the likelihood of default by a mortgage borrower and other automated services. PMI Mortgage Insurance Co. instituted an advanced system employing statistical predictive models to aid in the underwriting process. United Guaranty Residential Insurance Co. collaborated with IBM Corp. to develop an expert system that could render underwriting decisions in less than 10 seconds, and Stewart Title began a similar electronic document preparation service as well as a flood determination company.

Despite their use of computer technology, the title insurance industry was finding it much more difficult to streamline the records search process using computers and automation. Except for major metropolitan areas, most county governments charged with collecting title records were still maintaining them just as they did 100 years ago, according to Chicago Title. Although checking the ownership of a parcel of land was a straightforward process, in order to ensure the validity of title for a buyer, title insurance companies had to also track prior owners of the land and determine if the land had any easements, liens ,or other encumbrances. Title insurance companies were limited in that they could be only as efficient as the county in which the records were kept. For most counties, there was only a limited amount of information maintained in a computerized database, and this information was typically indexed in only one way, usually either by seller or buyer. Rarely were property records indexed by legal description, address, or type of document. This significantly hampered the investigation required to underwrite a policy of title insurance.

FURTHER READING

Collins, Brian. ''Two Top Mortgage Bankers Developing Title Insurance.'' *National Mortgage News,* 29 July 1996.

Darnay, Arsen J., ed. *Finance, Insurance, and Real Estate, USA.* 3rd ed. Detroit: Gale Research, 1996.

Finkelstein, Brad. ''Title Insurer Revenue Jumps 20%.'' *National Mortgage News,* 9 December 1996.

Frantz, James. ''Title Industry Goes Tech.'' *National Real Estate Investor,* September 1999.

Jones, John A. ''First American Financial Adds More Real Estate Services.'' *Investor's Business Daily,* 22 July 1996.

Lawyers Title Insurance Corp. ''Lawyers Title Corporation, General Motors Form Joint Venture.'' 4 March 1996. Available from http://www.ltic.com.

Paire, Jennifer. ''It's All about the Ratings.'' *National Real Estate Investor,* May 1999.

Richards, Geoffrey. ''NREI Presents: Who's Who in the Title Insurance Biz.'' *National Real Estate Investor,* May 1997.

———. ''Rating Title Firms: A Trend That Keeps Growing.'' *National Real Estate Investor,* May 1998.

Sclafane, Susanne. ''$1.2B Deal Creates Largest U.S. Title Insurer.'' *National Underwriter,* 9 August 1999.

''Title Insurance: An Industry on the Verge of Transformation.'' *Best's Review (Property/Casualty),* May 1996.

U.S. Department of Labor. Bureau of Labor Statistics. *Occupational Outlook Handbook,* 1998-99 ed. Washington, DC: GPO, 1998. Available from http://stats.bls.gov/ocohome.htm.

SIC 6371

PENSION, HEALTH, AND WELFARE FUNDS

Establishments primarily engaged in managing retirement, health, and welfare funds comprise what is commonly called the pension fund industry. Companies owning pension funds are called fund sponsors. Sponsors maintain funds for the purpose of meeting future obligations, such as benefit payments to retired employees. Some sponsors manage their own funds, or reserves, while others hire fund managers or consultants to conduct their investment activities.

NAICS CODE(S)

523920 (Portfolio Management)
524292 (Third Party Administration for Insurance and Pension Funds)
525110 (Pension Funds)
525120 (Health and Welfare Funds)

INDUSTRY SNAPSHOT

Total pension fund assets in the United States amounted to $8.01 trillion in 1998, up from $7.03 trillion in 1997, while 56 million people, about 20 percent of the U.S. population, were invested in some sort of retirement plan. The industry was characterized by the scramble for increasingly diversified investment strategies, as fund managers attempted to safeguard long-term stability while registering strong short-term yields in the powerful surging U.S. financial markets. Private funds continue to assume a greater proportion of all pension fund assets, accounting for 71.5 percent in 1998 versus 49 percent in 1995. This was attributable to a number of factors, including uncertainty regarding the future of the public pension system, a relaxed regulatory environment in the financial sector, and the strong economy. According to the Federal Reserve Board's *Flow of Funds Accounts of the United States,* 29.1 percent of all U.S. household assets were held in pension funds in 1998, continuing a long trend; the figure stood at 14.7 percent in 1980 and 23.3 percent in 1990. Pension funds held $3.8 trillion in corporate equities. Pension funds were expected to grow at an increasing rate through the turn of the century as the baby-boomer population ages.

ORGANIZATION AND STRUCTURE

Pension funds are essentially vehicles by which workers can save income generated during their productive years to help them maintain a reasonable living standard when they retire. More than 80 percent of employers offer some type of savings plan that will provide pension or retirement benefits to at least some for their employees. In addition, workers can invest in pension vehicles such as life insurance or various tax-deferred annuities that act as funds.

Pension funds operate under the assumption that money, which the employer or employee places into the fund, will earn interest income at a rate greater than inflation. The more interest and savings that accrue over a period of time, the more money will be available to provide benefits for the employee at retirement. Pension funds are generally favored over most other long-term savings plans because they benefit from a favorable tax status. These tax laws allow employees to defer taxes on both their savings and the interest income that those savings produce.

Government Agencies. Federal, state, county, and municipal governments all provide pension plans for their employees. Publicly owned corporations, such as the Tennessee Valley Authority, also fall into this category. In addition, the federally funded Old Age Survivors' Insurance (OASI) fund is included in this group. These public funds constitute approximately 29 percent of all pension assets. Old Age Survivors' Insurance (OASI) is the largest, by number of members, of all government pension funds. This national program of social insurance is designed to cover all persons employed in the United States with the exception of clergy, some state employees, and most federal workers. Unlike national insurance programs in other countries, OASI entitlements are not based on need but rather on previous individual contributions. In 1999 more than 175 million Americans were covered under OASI and the fund maintained about $350 billion in assets.

Most federal employees who are not covered by OASI are included in the Civil Service Retirement System (CSRS) or Federal Employees Retirement System pension funds, which provide retirement, survivorship, and disability benefits to career employees of the federal government. Participation in these plans is compulsory. In 1999 these plans covered a combined 5 million workers and maintained approximately $430 billion in assets.

State and local pension funds, which cover public employees, together covered an estimated 18 million employees in 1998, with assets of $2.34 trillion.

Private Plans. Private plans that employ fund managers exist in both the nonprofit and commercial sectors. These funds (exclusive of funds managed by insurance companies) accounted for approximately 71.5 percent of all pension assets. Organizations in the nonprofit sector include churches and service associations, while commercial entities include for-profit establishments. Together, these pension funds accounted for about $5.73 trillion in assets in 1998. Funds sponsored by insurance companies include persons covered by Keough or other self-employment plans, Individual Retirement Accounts (IRAs), and various tax sheltered annuity savings plans. Pension assets sponsored by insurance companies amounted to $1.4 trillion, or 17.5 percent of all pension assets, in 1998.

Pension funds in the private sector, as well as some funds in the public sector, can be classified as either ''defined benefit'' or ''defined contribution'' plans. Defined benefit plans, once the most popular type, promise annuities—beginning at retirement—that are usually based on the worker's years of service and average wage during the last few years of employment. With a defined contribution plan, firms effectively contribute to an employee's savings account. The accumulated tax-preferred savings belong to the worker, who usually receives a lump sum at retirement. In 1998, private defined benefit plans carried about $2.13 trillion in assets, with 62 percent invested in equities; while defined contribution plans held about $2.2 billion, with 69 percent in equities.

In order to receive tax-preferred status for their private pension funds, managers must comply with Internal Revenue Service (IRS) regulations and guidelines. The Federal Employee Retirement Security Act (ERISA) of 1974 is the principal legislative tool used to govern pension funds. It imposes minimum funding requirements, primary fiduciary responsibilities, and disclosure criteria. For instance, a fund manager must show that its reserves cannot be diverted prior to the satisfaction of all liabilities and that it will not discriminate in favor of its more highly paid employees. Details about the fund must also be made known to employees or members.

An important element of the private pension fund market is the Pension Benefit Guaranty Corporation (PBGC). This government agency insured the pensions of 42 million Americans in about 44,000 defined benefit pension plans during 1999. If a company defaults on its retirement benefit obligations to its members or their dependents, the PBGC assumes liability.

Fund Management Structure. Pension fund management entails two basic activities: serving members or employees covered by the plan and directing investment and management of asset reserves. The fundamental provisions of any pension plan sets forth rules of eligibility, conditions for the receipt of pensions, a pension benefit formula, and a source of contributions. Companies that sponsor funds usually place control of the funds with a corporate trustee. Trustees, or custodians, oversee the funds to ensure that they comply with federal regulations. Trustees also supervise investment decisions made by fund managers.

While many fund sponsors hire outside consulting and investment firms to assist with investment of their pension reserves, most also have fund managers in-house, or within their organization. The fund manager may, in turn, hire several other managers or consultants who specialize in various investment activities. Administration activities, such as handling fund members' needs and delivering payment services, are often handled separately by the fund sponsor.

A pension fund manager is charged with three basic duties: developing a financial profile of the fund, developing investment policies, and formalizing an investment program. The financial profile essentially describes the plan's funding structure. The funding structure consists of existing assets such as cash and investments, obligations for currently retired employees, obligations for future retirees, and expected future contributions by both employees and the fund sponsor. The plan's funding structure is influenced by several factors, including the growth stage of the company, estimates for future employee and profit growth, expected future investment returns, and future tax rates.

When developing investment policies, managers must adopt return objectives, risk constraints, and asset diversification requirements. These components, when properly synthesized, serve to minimize the risk of investment losses and ensure that the minimum return necessary to meet future obligations is realized.

Finally, the formalization of the investment program requires selection of an investment committee to review strategy; definition of an asset allocation plan; creation of a detailed investment portfolio strategy; and the determination of an effective means of monitoring, evaluating, and reporting investment results. For example, the manager must determine the proportion of assets that are placed into stocks, bonds, real estate, international assets, or other investment vehicles. A common method that fund managers use to gauge the performance of their funds is comparison with standard indexes. Market indexes, such as the Standard & Poor's 500 stock index, serve as benchmarks to judge the effectiveness of the manager's strategy.

Financial Structure. Although thousands of pension plans served both the public and private sectors in 1998, the control of assets was steadily gravitating toward the largest funds. The top 200 funds maintained assets of $3.7 trillion that year, amounting to 38 percent of all pension-fund assets. The top 100, moreover, controlled $3.1 trillion, up from a mere $270 billion in 1979.

BACKGROUND AND DEVELOPMENT

Pensions for military personnel have existed for centuries. The pilgrims of Plymouth Colony enacted a crude pension system for their soldiers in 1636. The first pension law in the United States, however, was implemented in 1789 and promised benefits to those who enlisted in the colonial army.

The concept of providing pensions for retired employees did not begin until the nineteenth century in Europe and did not significantly spread to the United States until the early twentieth century. One of these first pension plans set up a fund for teachers in New Jersey in 1896. Similar plans soon followed. One of the first federal pension funds was the Federal Civil Service Retirement and Disability Fund, established in 1920. Public plans that followed set up funds to benefit retiring policemen, firemen, and congressmen.

Just as it helped to establish public pension plans, legislation has been a great impetus for the advancement of the private pension industry. The Revenue Act of 1921 provided the first major private pension catalyst. This act laid the foundation for the basic tax rules governing private pensions in the 1990s. It allowed pension contributions to be deducted from the firm's taxable income, permitted tax-free accumulations within pension funds, and allowed deferral of personal income taxation on pensions until retirement.

The pension movement gained additional strength during World War II, when government wage and salary restrictions caused workers to seek more fringe benefits. A few years later, in 1949, pensions were classified by the court as acceptable tools for union bargaining. This development vastly increased the number of U.S. laborers in pension plans.

Growth of Pension Funds. Despite their origins in the first half of the twentieth century, private and public pension funding did not realize widespread popularity until the 1950s. Prior to 1950, pension plans were largely viewed as a discretionary benefit offered by an employer as a token of appreciation for a worker's efforts. After that time, however, several factors began to reshape society's views toward pensions. Companies began to use pensions as a form of compensation because of the tax advantages associated with them. In addition, an aging population was seeking ways to ensure a stable future.

In 1974 the Employee Retirement Income Security Act allowed for substantially greater diversification of pension fund investments. The act stressed that investments needn't be examined individually by regulators, but in the context of an entire portfolio, thus granting much greater leverage to and placing more emphasis on fund managers.

Between 1950 and the end of the century, the number of people covered by Social Security insurance alone increased from 23 million to more than 175 million. Fund assets for all pension plan types during this period swelled from about $31 billion to $8.01 trillion in 1998. During the 1980s alone, pension-fund assets grew by more than 300 percent. The bull market of the mid- and late 1990s also boosted pension-fund assets.

Aside from changing public attitudes and legislation, an aging population is a root cause of the growth in pension fund assets. The percentage of the U.S. population over 65 years of age more than doubled between 1920 and 1980 to about 12 percent. The fantastic growth in the number and percentage of aged persons in the United States reflects birthrate declines, an increase in life expectancies, and the curtailment of immigration.

The 1980s. Pension fund management during the 1980s was affected by several trends and developments that continued to shape the industry in the early 1990s. Two of the most significant trends included an increase in popularity of defined contribution plans in comparison to traditionally popular defined benefit plans, and stricter regulations regarding fund reserves.

The increase in the popularity of defined contribution plans in the private pension market resulted in part from the economic boom of the 1980s, as well as the more appropriate benefit structure of contribution plans in the new business environment. Defined contribution plans also benefited from a comparatively liberal set of regulations and tax laws. As a result, they provided a higher rate of return than defined benefit plans.

Besides increased investment returns, one reason for the popularity of defined contribution plans during the 1980s was that employees had a better feel for exactly what they were getting back from their investment. Workers also felt as if they had more investment control than defined benefit plans offered. Contribution plans were also viewed as more mobile—an important consideration for people that expected to change employers.

Many employers also preferred defined contribution plans because they were easier and less expensive for the company to maintain than traditional defined benefit plans. In addition, employers were able to shift more administrative costs to their employees.

Rapid growth in defined contribution plans began to wane slightly in the late 1980s as the economy slowed and new regulations diminished their benefits. Nevertheless, total investment in contribution plans by fund sponsors exceeded assets in defined benefit plans in the mid-1990s.

A second development that fund managers encountered in the 1980s was stricter federal reserving requirements for their funds. Regulators began to question whether many private pension funds had adequate reserves to meet their future obligations. Amplifying their concerns were company failures in the late 1980s, which placed stress upon PBGC reserves. Furthermore, the stock market crash of 1987 reduced the value of many pension funds. The failures of Pan Am and Eastern Air Lines alone cost the PBGC $1.6 billion. As a result, several regulations and initiatives were enacted that affected pension funds.

Three efforts, in particular, served to change the industry. The Omnibus Reconciliation Act (OBRA) of 1987 and Financial Accounting Standard (FAS) No. 87 both served to enforce adequate reserves in pension funds. In addition, the Tax Reform Act of 1986 effected changes reducing some of the employer and employee gains derived from both defined contribution and defined benefit plans.

Besides increasing their use of defined contribution plans and having to adapt to new regulations, fund managers also started becoming actively involved in the management of the companies in which they invested. As some pension fund managers became concerned about what they felt were unsound business practices, they began to put pressure on the companies in which they owned significant shares to improve their operations. Typical suggestions for improvements related to better boardroom practices. The California Public Employees' Retirement System (CALPERS), for example, began targeting 12 companies each year for improvements. In 1992, CALPERS published the names of some companies that refused to meet with its representatives regarding changes; the companies subsequently agreed to meet with fund managers. Other trends in the pension fund industry that accelerated in the 1980s included activity by fund managers in alternative investments and foreign assets.

In contrast to solid investment returns realized by fund managers during most of the 1980s, investment performance diminished in the late 1980s and early 1990s as the U.S. economy stagnated. Regulators became concerned that many pension plans were underfunded and might not be able to meet their future obligations. Therefore, legislation was enacted to help ensure the financial stability of private funds. Meanwhile, the future success of the federal social insurance pension fund remained doubtful.

The 1990s. Going into the 1990s, pension fund sponsors and managers were struggling to overcome the stagnating effects of low interest rates combined with lackluster returns on their investment portfolios. They were also striving to improve the ratio of assets to liabilities in their funds in the face of a sluggish world economy. Many of them were also grappling with increased fund liabilities brought about by premature employee layoffs from downsizing. General Dynamics Corp., for instance, reduced its workforce by almost 67 percent in two years, requiring it to raise at least $1 billion in payments to companies that purchased some of its divisions. As another example, Texas Utilities Co.'s fund assets plummeted 50 percent, to $785 million, as its workforce shrank 30 percent and assets were consumed to meet unexpected benefit obligations.

The pension fund industry in the mid-1990s also prepared to manage a rapid influx of capital during the coming decade, a result of aging baby-boomers saving for their retirement. Hotly contested political debates over the future of the Social Security System also portended strong growth in private pension funds. With the help of the bull market in stocks, pension funds enjoyed strong asset growth in the mid-1990s. Assets allocated to foreign investment, real estate equity investments, and alternative investments showed significant growth, while popular alternative investments included private equity and buyouts, venture capital investments, private debt, and non-investment grade bonds. In foreign investments, allocations remained far larger in foreign equities than in foreign bonds.

New legislation promised to change the face of the pension fund industry as the Democratic Clinton administration took office in 1993. By the end of his first term, Clinton had proposed or signed into law more legislation and pushed for more regulatory changes than any administration since the passage of the Employee Retirement Income Security Act of 1974 (ERISA).

Two major pieces of legislation affecting pension plans were the Retirement Protection Act of 1994 (RPA) and the Small Business Job Protection Act of 1996 (SBJPA). The RPA resulted in several new regulations for pension plans covering areas such as minimum funding requirements, liquidity, payouts, and reporting requirements. The SBJPA contained provisions revising the Internal Revenue Code and ERISA that were billed as "pension simplification." These provisions included new tax rules covering individuals, retirement plan distribution rules, and a new tax-favored retirement plan for small businesses called the Savings Incentive Match Plan for Employees (SIMPLE). It was expected that the SIMPLE plan would replace the current SAR/SEP plan being used by small businesses by the end of 1997.

Among the major policy changes embedded in these pieces of legislation was the reduction of the salary cap used for calculating pension benefits. By reducing the salary limitation from $225,000 to $150,000, the new law had the effect of reducing the maximum pension benefits for high-paid executives. Another major change concerning Individual Retirement Accounts (IRAs) allowed nonworking spouses to receive favorable tax treatment for contributions of up to $2,000.

CURRENT CONDITIONS

An estimated 18 percent of private pensions were underfunded in 1999, down from 55 percent in 1980. Moreover, the majority of those pension funds that are fundamentally sound were particularly well insulated to weather potential minor stock-market plunges. Analysts surmise that it would require about a 30 percent decline in the stock market before surplus assets would be depleted among the healthy funds, a cushion that was markedly thicker among the largest funds. As a result, fund managers were likely to see their contributions and expenses decline well into the 2000s. Contributions by the top 200 funds totaled $38.1 billion in 1999, down from $44.1 billion in 1997. Meanwhile, assets among the top 200 were outpaced liabilities by a margin of 20 percent, a gap not enjoyed since the end of the last economic-boom cycle in 1989. Assets jumped 13.4 percent in 1999, while liabilities dropped 13 percent.

The most pronounced growth among the top 200 funds was due in large part to mergers and acquisitions. High-profile pension-fund mergers occurred between SBC Communications and Ameritech Corporation, resulting in the fifth-largest corporate fund, as well as between BP America and Amoco Corp. The consolidation in the asset-management industry mirrored the increasing concentration of the financial-services sector as a whole, resulting in a tightening supply of institutional investors with burgeoning buying clout. It also intensified the growing international flavor of the pension-fund industry; fifty-four mergers or acquisitions in 1999 were between domestic funds, while 51 involved international deals

Investment Strategy. Restrictions on investment strategies have relaxed considerably since the early 1980s, leading to increased exposure to equities by the leading public funds. A total of 61 percent of these funds' assets were invested in public securities in 1999, up from 22 percent in 1979. Moreover, fund managers were leaning toward more proficient employment of alternative investment exposure by way of real estate and venture capital. Finally, with the fantastically high ratio of assets to liabilities, a strategy that has gained favor with fund managers is the splitting of portfolios into two distinct parts that focus on separate goals. While one half can focus on covering liabilities, the other can chase immediate returns. Still, amidst the raging economy and bull market, many fund managers were reluctant to forego potentially lucrative short-term gains in favor of shoring up their risk-management schemes, out of fear of losing investors.

Pension plan sponsors may choose to manage their assets internally or use outside money management services. In 1995, internally managed equity assets surpassed internally managed fixed income investments for defined benefit plans. In 1996, that was reversed, with internally managed bond portfolios surpassing those of stocks. Among the top 200 pension funds, $1 trillion in assets invested in defined benefit plans were managed internally in 1998; for defined contribution plans, of course, the figure was much lower, at only $103 billion.

Several factors were at play affecting the choice of internal versus external management. It was generally recognized that it was cheaper to purchase investment services externally than internally. Some funds experienced trouble retaining good money managers, who could find higher salaries at money management firms. Some funds have grown so large that they began to feel it would be more effective to have their funds managed externally. One factor working in favor of internal management was the trend among larger plan sponsors to index their core equity assets rather than have them actively managed.

Various investment strategies are available to pension plan sponsors. Among the top 200 funds, more than 100 funds utilized such strategies as equity index funds, foreign equities, and real estate in their investment strategies. Defined benefit plans tend to more heavily invested in U.S. equities, which totaled $501 billion held by the top 200 in 1998 and are generally associated with asset allocation in stable long-term funds. Defined contribution plans focus more on the current performance levels. Thus, the heightened popularity of defined contribution plans in the mid- and late 1990s was in large measure related to the booming financial markets.

Pension funds with a social conscience also began to establish themselves in the late 1990s. After laws were clarified allowing trustees to offer pension funds the option of employing socially responsible investment (SRI) schemes in their portfolios, the use of SRI criteria jumped 13 percent in 1999, following a 9-percent incline the year before. Overall, approximately $2.1 trillion in funds run in accordance with SRI principles, which take into account social issues ranging from human rights to environmental friendliness in screening for sound investment options. Recently, the performance of such portfolios has outpaced the industry average, which, along with heightened popular concern over social issues, is expected to result in even greater SRI application in coming years.

Social Security Insolvency. Another major pension issue potentially affecting all fund managers in the 1990s was the gradual demise of the Social Security pension system. The long-term viability of this system was in serious doubt, as pension analysts predicted that the plan was underfunded to such a degree that it would be insolvent by 2036, leaving private pension funds and individual savings plans to make up the shortfall. Furthermore, the fund will likely require federal reimbursements by the year 2016. By the end of the 1990s, debates were raging on Capitol Hill regarding the possible privatization of Social Security.

INDUSTRY LEADERS

The top pension fund sponsors in 1999 were California Public Employees ($155.7 billion in assets), New York State Common ($111.4 billion), California State Teachers ($98.4 billion), Florida State Board ($93.2 billion), General Motors ($90.0 billion), New York State Teachers ($81.5 billion), and Texas State Teachers ($79.4 billion).

Some of the largest fund management consultants that serve many of the larger funds, such as those just mentioned, include the Frank Russell Company, Callan, Wilshire, and Evaluation Associates. These firms offer specialty services to pension fund clients such as real estate investment or index counseling.

The largest trustee company in the pension fund industry was Bankers Trust New York Corporation. Other large trustees include Northern Trust, State Street Bank, Mellon Bank, and J.P. Morgan. These trustees, or custodians, monitor and effectively account for pension funds to ensure that sponsors and managers comply with federal regulations.

WORKFORCE

The pension fund industry workforce is largely comprised of professionals with the financial or legal knowledge necessary to properly oversee and invest fund assets. Seven employment functions within the industry include administrative staff, attorneys, actuaries, investment advisers and money managers, accountants and auditors, custodians or trustees, and performance monitors. Each of these functions also requires support staff. Administrative employees are responsible for keeping track of existing fund assets, current and future obligations, and future contributions. Positions in this field require financial and accounting skills.

Attorneys help fund managers to follow both federal and state regulations governing fund management and administration. Actuaries are responsible for predicting future pension fund obligations and contributions; they also determine investment return requirements. Actuaries rely on advanced mathematical and statistical techniques to accomplish these tasks and often must train for several years to become fully designated in their profession.

Money managers provide portfolio investment services for fund sponsors and managers. They buy and sell securities and other assets in accordance with prevailing investment strategies and market conditions. Various companies may provide these services, including bank trust departments, money management firms, specialty management firms, and index fund managers. Index fund managers administer funds in which pension fund sponsors and managers can place assets. Index funds, which became popular during the 1980s, derive returns from a broad market portfolio that serves to minimize transactions costs and management fees and to reduce market risks. Pension funds typically pay mangers a percentage of the assets managed. Corporate fund managers earned an average annual salary of $118,632 in the late 1990s. Jobs in money management typically require at least business or economics degree, and often an M.B.A. or other advanced degree.

Accountants and auditors, usually Certified Public Accountants, assist in the financial reporting process. They also provide technical assistance with data processing and financial analysis.

Employment opportunities in most areas of the pension fund industry are expected to grow much faster than average, as assets placed in funds proliferate during the 1990s and 2000s. Particularly, the demand for specialty consultants who can provide detailed investment advice about alternative investment assets should increase. The demand for services related to defined contribution plans should also grow faster than average.

AMERICA AND THE WORLD

The pension fund industry in the United States is similar to and was originally modeled after the British pension system. While most other industrialized countries have pension systems similar to the United States and Britain, some countries rely more heavily on government-sponsored pension plans.

Besides the fact that the United States has more pension fund assets than any other country in the world, American pension funds also differ from funds in many countries in the way that their assets are allocated. Britain, which has the second largest pension fund industry, places much more of its assets in both domestic and international equities than in bonds. Pension plan managers in the Netherlands, on the other hand, are far more likely to place more of their assets in bonds and international assets than are U.S. managers.

Foreign Investment. Although U.S. pension managers have been investing internationally since the 1970s, it was not until the 1980s that investment in overseas assets accelerated. In 1980, the largest U.S. pension funds were devoted almost exclusively to U.S. investment. By 1998, more than 69 percent of U.S. companies offered international equity, compared with 39 percent in 1994. In fact, the dollar value of foreign assets held by U.S. pension funds skyrocketed during the 1980s and early 1990s to more than $125 billion by 1991 and more than $300 billion by 1994. By 1999, nearly $960 billion in assets were invested overseas. Moreover, six of the ten most expensive merger or acquisition deals in 1999 were between U.S. and foreign funds.

Fund managers sought foreign investment assets in the 1990s because they provided higher yields. For instance, since 1971 foreign bond returns have outperformed U.S. bonds by a margin of 5 percent. Foreign investments also increase investment-portfolio diversity, which reduces the risk of losses caused by regional economic downturns.

Part of the reason for the influx of investment into foreign countries has been a reduction in the barriers to entry for fund managers. The development of the European Union and its common currency along with a pan-European investment market in the late 1990s opened up the market to increased foreign investment. Multilateral investment deals negotiated at major world financial institutions have accelerated this process.

Despite reduced investment barriers, many restrictions still exist in most countries that limit pension fund activity. For instance, local and regional restrictions place limits on the amount foreigners can invest in various assets classes. Localities in some nations, such as Spain and Portugal, require that funds invested in their precinct be managed by local organizations.

Public pension systems in all industrialized nations were under increasing strain throughout the 1990s, which was expected to lead to greater emphasis on private pension funds. The nations of continental Europe were likely to experienced the most pronounced privatization boom due to the historically high reliance on state provision in those countries.

While increased returns and diversification have lured U.S. pension managers particularly to industrialized Asian and European countries, the emerging markets in Latin America, the Pacific Rim, and China are beginning to offer some of the greatest opportunities for investors. While these less-developed markets remain riskier, they offer the potential for comparatively high returns as well as diversification for many pension fund portfolios.

RESEARCH AND TECHNOLOGY

The pension fund industry, like most other service industries in the United States, has lagged behind manufacturing sectors in the implementation of advanced automation and technology. In the late 1980s and early 1990s, however, an increasingly competitive business environment forced pension fund managers to find new ways to cut costs and increase the quality of their services. Pension fund portability also put pressure on fund sponsors and managers to deliver faster and better services to fund participants.

In the 1990s, pension sponsors were using advanced information systems to reduce their administrative work forces and improve efficiency. Similarly, fund managers implemented systems allowing more efficient reporting and monitoring of investments. These systems were used to integrate the sponsors general pension fund strategies with the investment activities of its managers and consultants. Consultants were under pressure, as well, to improve their record-keeping systems to compete with larger investment management companies.

Advances in computer technology and software continued to deliver significant advances in the actuarial investments fields. Professionals used new mathematical models and statistical techniques that were previously unavailable.

Pension funds were also scrambling to catch up to banks and stock brokerages in establishing an online presence. The extent of online financial services will grow exponentially in the early 2000s, and consumers will perform a greater share of their investing through the World Wide Web. As relaxed regulations allow financial institutions to perform a wider range of activities, analysts expect a growing number of customers will place most or all of their financial business with a single firm. As a result, pension funds were rapidly entering the online world to snare potential customers through this exploding medium before they develop relationships with other, more Internet-savvy firms.

FURTHER READING

Barreto, Susan. ''Top 1,000 Funds Grow 13 percent for Year.'' *Pensions & Investments,* 24 January 2000.

Burr, Barry B. ''Contribution Holiday: Pension Surpluses Big Enough to Weather Fall.'' *Pensions & Investments,* 24 January 2000.

Chernoff, Joel. ''It's a Different World for Institutional Managers.'' *Investment News,* 24 January 2000.

''Fund Management: Japan's Investment Revolution.'' *Euroweek Japan Supplement,* August 1998.

Jacobius, Arleen. ''DC Equity Exposure Tops DB Plan Levels.'' *Pensions and Investments,* 7 February 2000.

Kelly, Bruce. ''Banner Year: U.S. Pension Funds Finish the Decade in Tiptop Shape.'' *Pensions & Investments,* 10 January 2000.

Kennedy, Mike. ''Few Wane: Mergers Move Funds in Top 200.'' *Pensions & Investments,* 24 January 2000.

Lansing, Kevin. ''Social Security Fix Becomes More Difficult as Time Passes'' *Bridge News,* 20 December 2000.

''Pension Reform Ahead.'' *Life Insurance International,* February 1999.

U.S. Board of Governors of the Federal Reserve System. *Flow of Funds Accounts of the United States.* Washington, D.C.: GPO, 15 December 1999.

''U.S. Warms up to SRI Schemes.'' *Financial News,,* 15 November 1999.

Williamson, Christine. ''The Marrying Kind: More Money Than Deals in 1999 Mergers; European-U.S. Partnerships Top the List.'' *Pensions & Investments,* 10 January 2000.

Woolsey, Christine. ''Nest Eggs are Hatching Online.'' *Insurance Networking,* November 1998.

SIC 6399

INSURANCE CARRIERS, NOT ELSEWHERE CLASSIFIED

Establishments providing insurance coverage but not covered by any other insurance category make up the industry classification entitled Insurance Carriers, Not Elsewhere Classified (NEC). Federally supported organizations providing insurance for financial institution deposits make up most of this industry. Other miscellaneous insurers, however, cover everything from pets and trademarks to body parts and automobile warranties.

NAICS CODE(S)

524128 (Other Direct Insurance Carriers (except Life, Health, and Medical))

The Federal Deposit Insurance Corporation (FDIC) is the largest organization in this industry. Created by the Banking Act of 1933 following the failure of more than 8,000 banks during the depression, the FDIC promotes and preserves public confidence in U.S. financial institutions by insuring bank and thrift deposits up to the legal limit of $100,000 per account. In 1999 the FDIC insured more than $3 trillion of U.S bank and thrift deposits at approximately 11,000 institutions. But the FDIC has other responsibilities besides acting as an insurer. It examines state-chartered banks that are not members of the Federal Reserve System for safety, soundness, and compliance with consumer protection laws. The FDIC may liquidate the assets of failed institutions to reimburse the insurance funds for the cost of failures. It also has the power to set interest rate limits and approve bank mergers.

An independent government agency within the executive branch, the FDIC is run like a private company by a five-member board of directors that includes the Comptroller of Currency, the Director of the Office of Thrift Supervision, and three presidential appointees. The Corporation does not operate on funds appropriated by Congress. Its income is derived from assessments on deposits held by insured banks and from interest on the required investment of its surplus funds in government securities. It also has authority to borrow from the Treasury up to $30 billion for insurance purposes.

Congress passed the FDIC Improvement Act (FDICIA) in 1991. The law instituted a number of agency reforms and gave the FDIC increased power over foreign banks active in the United States. The agency has also been affected by a number of federal laws relating to the downsizing of the federal government. The FDIC cut $143 million or 8 percent from budget between 1996 and 1997. Employee compensation was reduced the most during that period, 8.9 percent to $867 million. The agency' payroll shrunk from more than 17,000 workers in 1995 to just 7,241 in 1998. In 1997 the FDIC approved a budget of $1.62 billion, down $221 million or 12 percent from the $1.84 billion authorized in 1996. In each of the next two years the agency operated on a $1.2 billion budget.

The Savings Association Insurance Fund (SAIF) is the second major federal depository insurance organization. Administered by the FDIC, SAIF insures deposits at the nation's savings and loan institutions up to $100,000 per account. Concerned with sagging funds at SAIF in the mid-1990s, Congress passed the Deposit Insurance Funds Act of 1996, which directed the FDIC to take immediate steps to recapitalize SAIF and change the basis on which funds were raised. In response the FDIC levied a $4.5 billion special assessment (equal to nearly a year's earnings on SAIF-insured deposits) to fully fund SAIF. As a result of recapitalization, deposit insurance premiums for SAIF-insured thrifts were approximately $800 million lower in 1997 than in 1996. Meanwhile, SAIF's earnings were on the rise, increasing from $550 million in 1997 to $584 million in 1998. Almost all revenue for both years was derived from interest on investments in U.S. Treasury securities and deposit insurance assessments. By 1999 SAIF had an unrestricted fund balance of $9.2 billion and $978 million in the restricted Special Reserve.

In 1999 Dun and Bradstreet listed more than 900 insurance carriers doing business within this industrial classification. Other industry leaders included Veterinary Pet Insurance Co., a subsidiary of California Veterinary Services, Inc., which underwrites health insurance for pets. It generated $5.5 million in revenue during 1997, and employed 55 workers. Warrantech Consumer Product Services Inc., a Connecticut-based insurer of warranties, employed 100 workers in 1997 and reported revenue of $23 million. General Star Management, a commercial specialty risk insurer based in Stamford, Connecticut, employed 281 workers in 1997 and generated $14.4 million in revenue. Travel Guard International, Inc., an underwriter of travel insurance based in Stevens Point, Wisconsin, employed 99 workers in 1997 and reported earnings of $7.8 million.

FURTHER READING

Hoeschen, Brad. "SAIF bet: Last year's insurance fund charge pays off in higher rates, earnings." *Business Journal-Milwaukee,* 14 November 1997.

"The New York Times Almanac 2000: The Almanac of Record." New York: Penguin Reference Books 1999.

U.S. Bureau of the Census Website. http://www.census.gov. December 1999.

U.S. Department of Commerce Website. http://www.doc.gov. December 1999.

U.S. Department of Labor Website. http://www.dol.gov. December 1999.

"The United States Government Manual." The Office of the Federal Register, National Archives and Records Administration. 1998-1999 edition.

SIC 6411

INSURANCE AGENTS, BROKERS, AND SERVICE

This industry includes agents primarily representing one or more insurance carriers, or brokers not representing any particular carriers who are primarily engaged as independent contractors in the sale or placement of insurance contracts with carriers, but not employees of the insurance carriers they represent. This industry also includes independent organizations concerned with insurance services. Establishments engaged in searching real estate titles are classified in **SIC 6541: Title Abstract Offices**.

NAICS CODE(S)

524210 (Insurance Agencies and Brokerages)
524291 (Claims Adjusters)
524292 (Third Party Administrators for Insurance and Pension Funds)
524298 (All Other Insurance Related Activities)

INDUSTRY SNAPSHOT

Agency and brokerage firms selling and servicing insurance policies constitute the majority of the insurance agency, brokerage, and service industry. These companies are primarily engaged in representing one or more insurance carriers as independent contractors in the sale or placement of coverage. The industry also encompasses various specialty entities that offer services to insurance companies and to policyholders, such as independent claims adjusters, information bureaus, pension and retirement planning services, and research organizations.

By the late 1990s, the insurance industry underwent some adjustments itself, which affected the roles of agents and brokers. While most agents and brokers continued to specialize in life insurance, a growing number began selling policies that cover life, property/casualty, and health and disability. Moreover, agents and brokers are adopting e-business strategies to service their clients. In 1996, insurance agents and brokers held about 409,000 jobs in the United States, accounting for 44 percent of the entire insurance-related workforce. About 30 percent of agents and brokers were self-employed. The Bureau of Labor Statistics projects a sluggish job outlook through 2006.

The fortunes of insurance brokers and agents reflect larger trends in the industry. Demographic changes, notably the graying of the boomer generation, increased premium sales in 1999. In a 1998 study, A.M. Best, an insurance research company, reported that net written premiums reached $299.4 billion by September 1998, representing a 15 percent hike from the previous year. However, new competition in the insurance industry, by banks and other financial firms, will affect the long-term prospects of policy-writers. Industry experts predict that U.S. firms will continue to consolidate in the next century and expand their international activities, with the goal of becoming global players. Finally, demutualizations, the conversion of ownership status from mutual to stock form, are expected to rise.

ORGANIZATION AND STRUCTURE

Insurance agents and brokers serve the function of bringing insurers and people or companies needing insurance together. They help their clients select the right policy for their particular needs. Although their primary function is to sell policies offering financial protection against loss, agents and brokers may also help their clients plan for personal, family, or business financial security. In addition, they often provide advice about various insurance products, prepare reports and maintain records, and help policyholders settle insurance claims.

Insurance agents typically represent an insurance carrier under a contract arrangement. The agreement furnishes the agent with a small salary, fringe benefits, and commissions. The agent relies primarily on commissions for compensation, which are earned by selling new insurance policies and by renewing and servicing in-force or existing policies. An important characteristic of the agency relationship is that the agent is under the authority of the principal, or insurance carrier, and has the ability to make decisions as a representative of the carrier. Therefore, the principal can be held legally liable for the agent's business actions. Additionally, the agent is bound to place all business which he or she solicits with the principal.

Brokers, in contrast to agents, do not necessarily work under the authority of an insurance company. Rather, brokers place insurance policies for their clients with the carrier offering the most appropriate rate and coverage. The broker is remunerated by the carrier, though typically at a rate lower than that paid to the carrier's agents. Brokers may also charge clients who purchase insurance fees for services not compensated by the carrier's commission. Brokers serve an especially beneficial role for organizations with large and varied insurance needs requiring professionals to represent their interests. Some brokers also act as agents in certain areas of their business.

Commercial insurance in the United States is organized into four principal parts: insurers, who bear risk and manage surplus capital for their clients; field organizations, including agents and brokers, that maintain public contact, sell policies, and settle claims; intercompany organizations that establish standards, devise rates, and represent the political interests of insurers; and associations, or boards of agents and brokers that influence legislation, conduct research, and establish standards for the agency and brokerage industry. The American Insurance Association (AIA) is an example of an entity representing the interest of the industry and helping to establish professional standards. Many other organizations offer professional designation programs and lobby for agents' and brokers' interests.

Agents and brokers serve four basic types of insurers: national companies, regional insurers, mutual companies, and reinsurers. While many agents represent only one company's products, an increasing number of agents in the 1990s were selling policies for all industry types of insurers or tiers. The first tier, national companies, includes such massive organizations as The Prudential and The Equitable Life Assurance Society. These companies typically offer multiple lines of insurance for both individuals and businesses, and they support hundreds or thousands of agencies in cities throughout the United States. Agents who represent these companies benefit from such factors as public familiarity with the insurer, national advertising programs, and geographic diversity, which strengthens the carrier. The second tier, regional insurers, support agencies in a limited geographic area. Although some regional companies offer multiple lines of insurance, many emphasize one line of coverage, such as auto or home insurance.

The third tier, mutual insurance companies, in contrast to stock corporations, differs from most national and regional firms since mutual insurance's clients own a part of the company. Mutual agents essentially sell a membership to a cooperative, allowing each member to simultaneously become insurer and insured by purchasing a policy. The fourth tier, served mainly by brokers, is the reinsurer. Reinsurers provide coverage for insurance companies against unforeseen losses that could devastate the organization.

Products. Agents and brokers sell various forms of life, health, accident, property, and casualty insurance, each generating approximately equal amounts of annual revenue from premiums. Many of them also market financial instruments that complement their product offerings. Many agents and brokers sell policies in both the life/health and property/casualty divisions, although more agents specialize in selling life policies than any other line of coverage.

Life insurance differs from many other forms of insurance because it is usually considered a long-term investment and offers significant tax advantages. Typical products offered by agents in this market include: whole life products; term products, such as universal, variable, and universal variable life insurance; and annuities, which are effectively tax-deferred investment instru-

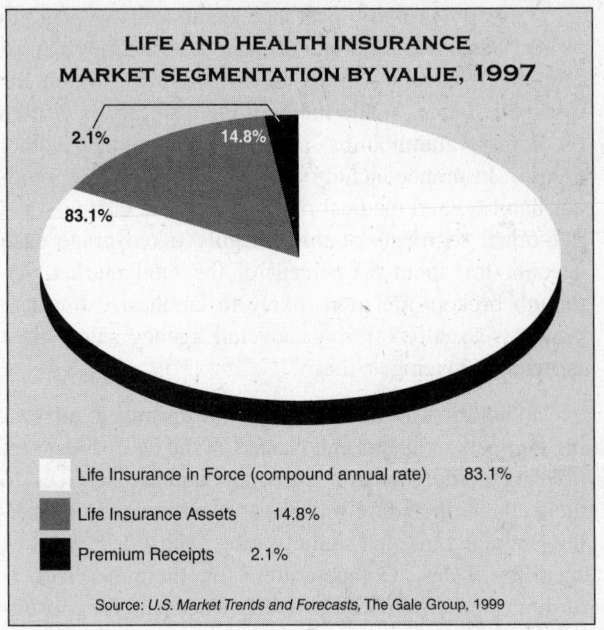

ments. In 1999, life insurers faced stiff competition from other financial services firms, making only modest gains in capturing savings dollars. While traditional life insurance products showed flat sales, fee-based products, such as annuities, grew in the late 1990s. But the shifting portfolio has also meant narrower profit margins for insurers, causing them to adopt cost-cutting measures.

Whole life policies combine a death benefit with a forced savings plan. In other words, the insured effectively overpays during the early years of his or her coverage when the risk of death is small. The interest earned on the savings is used to build the policy's cash value so that in the future the insured can borrow against the savings at a low interest rate. The policy also carries a redeemable cash value that can be withdrawn at once or used for retirement income. Term coverage differs from whole life in that the customer can avoid the forced savings plan, thus reducing his or her total investment. Products such as universal life insurance combine term and whole life advantages. Annuities, in contrast, do not provide a death benefit. The agent is essentially selling investment instruments that offer potentially higher returns than are available in whole life products, yet retain tax advantages.

Life insurance can also be divided into group and individual, or ordinary insurance. Group policies offer advantages related to economies of scale and provide greater bargaining power for some organizations through their employees.

Health and accident insurance represents nearly 70 percent of the American population. In contrast to life insurance, health coverage is not viewed as an investment instrument. It does provide important tax benefits, however—especially for employers.

Property/casualty insurance agents sell coverage to protect businesses, individuals, and other entities against property loss or losses by third parties for which the insured is liable. While much of the coverage is written on homes, automobiles, and business property, other types of insurance include worker's compensation, product liability, and medical malpractice. The business and individual segments of this category of coverage each account for about 50 percent of the total market. Although brokers are more likely to emphasize business property/casualty offerings, overall agency sales stress individual coverage.

In addition to traditional lines of insurance, increasing numbers of agents and brokers in the late 1990s were offering comprehensive financial planning services to their clients including retirement planning and counseling, mutual fund and annuity sales, and other types of securities sales. Compensation for these services is through commissions or an hourly wage paid for consulting services.

Company Structure. Approximately 30 percent of agents and brokers are self-employed, and their companies are typically very small. In 1994, only eight establishments employed more than 1,000 people, versus the 92,000 companies that employed four or fewer individuals. Only 15 firms had between 500 and 1,000 employees.

For an agent to qualify to represent a carrier, he or she must often meet volume and production requirements. For instance, smaller mutual insurers may require agents to produce $25,000 to $50,000 worth of sales per year. Large national carriers, on the other hand, generally require agents to commit to $500,000 to $1 million in annual sales.

Background and Development

The nature of the insurance industry of the 1990s emanated from fifteenth-century Italian ports where marine insurance became an effective technique of spreading individual losses over a large number of merchants. The structure of the U.S. industry, however, was derived from the English system that originated in the seventeenth century. The concept slowly spread to North America during industrialization in the nineteenth and twentieth centuries. During these early periods a formalized agency and brokerage system was not established. Most insurance was sold directly by the insurer from the office headquarters. In fact, the first reference made to an informal agent/broker industry was in the British case of *Power v. Butcher* in 1830, where brokers were referred to as ''those that arranged policies of insurance.''

Establishment of the U.S. agent/brokerage industry lagged far behind the development of the British system. In fact, not until 1949, when Congress permitted sales of coverage across state borders, could a single company in the United States offer multiple lines of insurance on a wide scale. As insurers became more widely dispersed and began to increase offerings to many market segments, the need for an effective means of joining buyers and sellers became paramount. Furthermore, larger companies found the need to develop local customer services such as claims adjustment and underwriting. Thus emerged the expansive network of sales organizations supported by main or branch offices that shapes the insurance industry of the 1990s.

As the insurance industry experienced rapid expansion in the post World War II era, the insurance agency, brokerage, and service industry flourished. Property/casualty agents prospered as individuals began to accumulate and insure greater amounts of personal wealth and possessions. Likewise, the surge of giant corporations with large and varied property and liability protection needs stimulated the brokerage industry.

Life insurance, too, experienced unprecedented growth. Aided by favorable tax laws and an aging population with dependents, sales skyrocketed from the 1950s through the 1970s, creating a boon for agents. Furthermore, health insurance agents and brokers benefited from massive growth, particularly in the 1970s, as large companies began to offer health insurance as a tax deductible benefit. Spiraling health care costs fueled industry profit growth as well. For example, throughout the 1970s and early 1980s, agents' revenues from health insurance commissions grew at a rate in excess of 15 percent per year.

The 1980s. Although many companies in the industry languished in a recession during the late 1970s and early 1980s, agents and brokers enjoyed fairly strong sales and increased demand for new products in most lines of coverage during the mid-1980s. The volume of property/casualty premiums written by stock companies, for instance, rose from $74.5 billion in 1983 to over $140 billion by 1989. In 1994, the net premiums written for this segment were $244.9 billion, up from $217 billion in 1990. Health insurance lines realized bullish growth too, increasing from a volume of $38 billion in premiums written in 1983 to about $61 billion by 1991.

Premiums for life insurance agents experienced more steady increases in the 1980s, with the exception of annuities. More customers switched from whole life to less expensive term life insurance in the 1980s. As a result, term life holders were looking for new vehicles in which to invest their money. Agents and brokers responded by marketing a profusion of annuities and other financial products that could lure those dollars. As the volume of whole life insurance premiums written grew steadily from about $50 billion in 1983 to $79.3 billion in 1991, annuities sales skyrocketed over 400 percent in the same period, from $30.5 billion to over $129 billion. The consequence was a boon of commissions for agents that rode the financial products wave. In 1994, $1.1 trillion worth of life insurance was purchased in the United States, while $11.6 trillion was currently in force. More than one-half of all policies were ordinary, and the average American household in 1994 had $118,700 worth of life insurance.

Industry Turbulence. Solid growth in many sectors of the agency and brokerage business in the mid-1980s was made bittersweet by changes transforming the overall insurance industry. Increased governmental regulation, rising insurance costs, and escalating public pressure were all constraining insurance company profit margins. Consequently, carriers were looking for ways to cut expenses, including costs related to agents, brokers, and service. At the same time, new entrants to the market such as banks and other financial institutions were competing for agency and brokerage sales dollars.

Although sales remained relatively strong throughout most of the 1980s, problems for property/casualty agents in some areas wreaked havoc. Public pressure, for example, was leading some states to enact laws that suppressed premiums on automobile and workers' compensation insurance. In 1989, for instance, California voters passed Proposition 103, requiring insurers to eventually reduce, or rollback, automobile insurance rates by 20 percent. As a result, many insurers were terminating business in regulated states and abandoning their agencies.

Also burdening property/casualty agents and brokers was insurer insolvency, caused by a combination of mismanagement, fraud, and a more aggressive regulatory environment. As over 370 carriers failed in the mid-1980s and early 1990s, agents representing them were left scrambling to maintain their operations. Although carrier failures had subsided by the early 1990s, the situation created the likelihood of increased federal regulation in the future, which could affect sales professionals.

In the mid-1990s, the 123,998 establishments in the industry employed 661,685 people—nearly 40 percent of the entire insurance-related work force. The insurance companies served by this industry generated a combined total of about $500 billion in premiums from customers in 1993. This total represented the culmination of steady growth occurring in the insurance industry since 1982, when approximately $250 billion in premiums were written.

Demand for insurance grew sluggishly in the early 1990s, but became more robust as the economy recovered in the second half of the decade. Although the economy was improving, agents and brokers in general were experiencing reduced income and profit—a trend which began in 1989. Reduced margins for most companies were the result of lower commissions, ceding markets in some highly regulated states, increasing operating costs, and escalating competition. In response to the inclement economic environment, agents and brokers started diversifying into new lines of business, working harder to maintain revenues, expanding into overseas markets, and relying on new technology to automate their operations and become more efficient.

Health reform legislation in 1996 provided a boon to health insurance agents. Self-employed people would be able to deduct 40 percent of health premiums from their 1997 taxes; in 1998-2002 the amount would increase to 45 percent and gradually keep rising to 80 percent in 2006. This ruling would encourage the self-employed to purchase health insurance. The 1996 health initiative also encouraged consumers to finance their own long-term health care by including a provision that most of those benefits would not be taxed. In 1995, in anticipation of the health reform bills, 517,000 new long-term care policies were sold, more than any year since records began to be kept in 1987. In total, 4.35 million such policies were sold between 1987 and 1995, with an average growth rate of 23 percent.

A development that was cutting into profits for agents and brokers in all lines was the increased popularity of direct insurance sales, or sales of coverage made directly by the carrier. By advertising and selling insurance themselves, even on a national scale, many carriers were successfully bypassing agents and delivering policies at lower costs to the market. In addition to these and other problems causing turbulence for agents in all lines was increased competition. This challenge meant a reduction in the work force and consolidation, by merger and acquisition, for many property/casualty companies. In 1997, the Providian Corporation announced that its shareholders approved the merger of the company's insurance operations with AEGON USA, a subsidiary of Netherlands based AEGON, NV, one of the largest listed insurance organizations worldwide.

Insurance giant Aetna sold its Casualty and Surety Company to the Travelers Group for $4.1 billion in 1997, creating the largest writer of personal automobile insurance through the independent agency system. Sagging industry profits, foreign expansion into the United States, and market segmentation were a few of the factors driving this trend.

Limiting their participation in the industry to specific market segments in which they had developed expertise was one way companies sought to increase their chances of maintaining profitability in the 1990s. Companies wanting to compete effectively also were learning to become more efficient through automation and customer focus. Many companies, especially smaller ones, were seeking to merge with other companies to strengthen their capital position. In addition, many companies were looking into ways to streamline operations and reduce the size of their workforce. Expansion into foreign markets offered another opportunity for property/casualty insurers to shore up profit margins. ''Companies must downsize, consolidate divisions, reduce their employee base, and enhance their capital spending . . . to compete globally,'' according to Robert M. Demichele, President of the Reinsurance Corporation of New York, in *Best's Review, Property/Casualty Edition.*

One of the largest acquisitions that provided evidence of these trends is General Re Corporation's (GEC's) acquisition of the Swiss reinsurance operations of Allstate Insurance Company in early 1992. This move strengthened GEC's European position. In June of 1997, the American Insurance Association (AIA) urged Congress to support tax legislation that would help make the U.S. property/casualty insurance industry more competitive in the global marketplace. Two tax law changes, H.R. 1783 and S. 843, would treat the active business income of U.S. financial services industries, including insurance, like the active business income of non-financial businesses.

CURRENT CONDITIONS

In the late 1990s, many life insurance agents and brokers struggled with decreased commissions and greater competition. This was largely a result of the switch to term life policies, which offered less commission than traditional whole life policies, and the increased popularity of the annuities. These changes signaled an industry-wide shift from a commodity-based market to a service-intensive market. In *National Underwriter Life & Health,* Samuel H. Turner identified three trends in today's market: buyers forcing lower loads, meaning they make one purchase at a time; buyers forcing the unbundling of products and services, which has given rise to the fee-based services; and buyers collectively demanding more choices, such as variable insurance and indexing.

Along with these changes came new competitors in the marketplace. In 1998, the $82.5 billion merger of Citicorp, a major commercial bank, and Travelers Group, Inc., an insurance firm, sent ripples through the industry. The move dissolved the traditional wall separating banks and insurers and ushered in a new trend called bancassurance, the distribution of insurance products through banking channels. By 2010, the consolidated bank expects to service a customer base of 1 billion people worldwide. The merger has hastened the restructuring of the U.S. insurance industry. Congress and state legislatures were considering new laws that would allow banks and other financial services firms to sell insurance. The process began with the Supreme Court's 1996 Barnet Bank decision, which allowed banks to begin selling insurance in small towns in the United States. Soon it became a national trend, presaging the giant mergers of today's market. For small independent agents, the consolidations intensified the pressure to join large organizations in order to survive.

The late 1990s has witnessed the rapid growth of distribution channels in the insurance industry. New companies, such The Direct Response Insurance Co., allow customers to circumvent traditional agents and brokers. Moreover, the Internet offers customers the opportunity to buy insurance online. In *Best's Review Life/Health Edition,* Mark L. Gardner says independent agents are poised to enter the twenty-first century in an awkward position. ''Although the agent may be quite knowledgeable about the insurance products he offers, and he may be located near the policyholder, and he may even be in control of a large clientele,'' says Gardner, ''economic forces over which he has no control will compel him to radically adapt to compete.''

Other Challenges. In addition to regulation and increased competition, environmental liability posed a potential major threat to profitability in the distant future. Large environmental claims typically are made many years after the cause of the claim occurs, making it difficult for insurers to predict cleanup cost liability.

Another key trend affecting the property-casualty insurance industry today, according to *Standard & Poor's Industry Surveys,* is excess underwriting capacity. The economic boom of the late 1990s has placed downward pressure on the insurance industry, driving down the price of premiums—and driving up risks for insurers. The Insurance Services Office (ISO) reported that premiums written-to-surplus ratio as of December 31, 1998 reached a record low of 0.84-to-1. The normal surplus leverage is 2-to-1, meaning that there are $2 of premiums written for every $1 of surplus.

Also affecting the industry were new mental health parity laws. In 1999, 10 states passed legislation to give patients who suffer from depression, schizophrenia, and other mental health illnesses equal coverage to those who suffer from physical conditions. The Clinton administration put mental health in the spotlight, commissioning a new study by the Surgeon General, which detailed the economic costs of mental illness for the national and pushed for insurance coverage of treatment and medication costs.

INDUSTRY LEADERS

Of the top 10 companies that write 40 percent of the property/casualty premiums in the United States, The State Farm Group of Illinois was the largest in 1997. The State Farm Group began in 1922 by providing auto insurance to Illinois farmers. They serviced 65.8 million policies, employ 69,000 people and enlisted the services of 17,000 agents. One in five cars in America was insured by State Farm, and they were the largest insurer of automobiles, homes, and pleasure boats. In 1996 they had $42.78 billion in sales. State Farm Fire and Casualty, a subsidiary of The State Farm Group, had assets of $12.9 billion in 1996, and employed more than 11,000 people; the subsidiary has no history of employee layoffs since its inception in 1935.

Allstate Insurance, also of Illinois, was the nation's largest publicly held property and casualty insurance company. They had over 14,000 agents and 20 million customers in the United States, Canada, and Japan. The company offered multiple lines of insurance, including life and health, and was started in 1931 by Sears Roebuck & Company. In 1997, the company had assets of $17.8 billion net premiums written. They had $28.5 billion in assets in 1996. A.M. Best Company, America's oldest and most widely recognized insurance rating and information source, raised Allstate's rating in 1997 from A (excellent) to A+ (superior).

In addition to capturing the lion's share of the property/casualty insurance market, State Farm and Allstate also experienced the greatest exposure to catastrophic losses in 1992. The two companies expected to pay a combined total of over $4 billion in claims for Hurricane Andrew. State Farm was especially hard hit by the disasters, because it did not carry reinsurance to offset losses, as do many other large carriers. In January of 1997, State Farm announced it would stop offering unlimited replacement coverage on California home ownership policies and would transfer its 1.5 million home ownership insurance customers in the state into a separate policy. State Farm covers one in four insured California homeowners, and the announcement spurred opposition from consumer groups who stated that the insurer was reducing its risk and putting more of a burden on the policyholders.

The third largest property underwriter in 1997 was CNA, with $10 billion net worth of premiums written, followed by American International, which wrote $9.3 billion worth of policies, and Farmers Insurance, in fifth place with $8.5 billion worth of policies written.

WORKFORCE

Insurance agents and brokers comprised a 409,000-strong workforce in 1996. Due to intense industry competition, however, the job outlook for insurance agents and brokers was not good. Experts predicted slower-than-average growth through the year 2006, with most new entrants to the field replacing agents and brokers who retire. Opportunities existed in five functional areas, including sales, claims, underwriting, accounting/finance, and professional staff support positions.

Sales. The greatest number of jobs in the insurance industry, by far, are sales positions; this field is also the most accessible for people trying to enter the industry. Sales positions are available by the tens of thousands through local insurance offices scattered throughout the United States and Canada. Each of these offices represents products from a parent company.

People just entering the sales field usually do not receive a salary, but instead depend on commissions. As the salesperson's list of clients grows, he or she benefits from commissions on repeat business from previous sales, in addition to any new business he or she generates.

Although a career in sales involves more risk than many salary positions, it can be one of the most rewarding jobs in the industry, combining personal freedom with an income in excess of over $100,000 per year. Success in the field typically requires an outgoing, entrepreneurial, and persistent personality. The profession can also be quite demanding, requiring 60 or more hours of time per week during the first few years of selling. Another significant drawback for property/casualty salespeople is industry cycles, which usually mean periods of low income.

Claims. A position in claims in the property/casualty industry involves assessing the dollar value of damage a policyholder has sustained and authorizing payment by the parent company. Claims adjusters combine knowledge with experience to judge how much damage the company will cover. In comparison to sales, claims positions are highly detail-oriented and structured. A claims adjuster position can lead to promotions within the company to a claims examiner, who handles complex claims, or a claims supervisor, who manages claims adjusters and examiners.

Underwriting and Accounting. Underwriters are faced with the task of determining which applicants for insurance the company will reject or accept and how much coverage the applicant may receive. This assignment involves gathering information on applicants, reviewing associated risks, and applying underwriting standards to reach a decision. Underwriters specialize in either personal or business lines of property/casualty insurance, although most underwriters start out in personal lines. Typical career progression is entry-level underwriter, senior underwriter, and finally underwriting manager. Many underwriting managers progress into general management, which is one reason this is a very popular route for professionals seeking executive level positions within the industry.

Accounting/finance positions can also provide a route to senior level positions within the industry. Insurance accountants are typically charged with auditing functions, examination of policyholders financial records as part of the underwriting process, or enforcing underwriting guidelines prescribed for underwriters by the parent company. Finance professionals, on the other hand, are usually more involved with financial and investment analysis, marketing research, and sales forecasting.

Professional Staff Support Positions. Property/casualty insurers hire large support staffs to administer important functions that support the revenue producing activities within the company. These disciplines include actuaries, lawyers, marketers, and others. Actuaries use mathematics to determine insurance rates and policies and to establish pricing and investment guidelines, which will increase profits. The actuarial field involves complex mathematical modeling, and most actuaries endure years of examinations before becoming fully designated within their profession. This occupation is also ranked among the highest in worker satisfaction and pay.

Insurance law provides excellent opportunities for attorneys, especially in the litigation arena. Because every insurance policy is a binding legal contract, attorneys receive more emphasis in the industry than they do in most other industries. Although salaries are typically below those found in the top law firms, they are similar to other corporate law positions. Other opportunities exist in public relations, customer service, and loss control. Loss control is a relatively new specialization which involves finding ways to prevent injury, theft, and damage—mostly by educating policyholders.

AMERICA AND THE WORLD

The forces of globalization are transforming the insurance industry. The mergers of the late 1990s, which greatly expanded the international reach of insurance companies and banks, built upon the trend set in the mid-1980s, when a surge in multinational companies and international trade and investment encouraged the growth of many international insurance companies. Insurers, including property/casualty insurers, from the United States, Asia, and Europe expanded internationally through avenues such as branches, subsidiaries, and joint ventures.

From the viewpoint of United States insurers, global expansion has two sides—U.S. expansion and investment abroad and foreign expansion and investment in the United States. U.S. insurers are becoming increasingly active in foreign expansion either through cross-border trade, in which foreign customers are covered by a company in the United States, or subsidiaries, which are located in the country where the customer is located.

Regulatory developments in the European Community (EC) have been directing its members to liberalize their markets for insurance and offers new opportunities for U.S. property/casualty insurers in the 1990s. These developments include countries that were opening their insurance markets to foreign investment for the first time, EC efforts to standardize accounting and reporting practices, and EC directives that made it easier for companies to transact business across country borders. Several EC countries, especially in southern Europe, have opened insurance sectors to foreign investment.

New opportunities also existed in Latin America and Asia. Latin governments were deregulating the insurance industry and allowing foreign investment for the first time. The North American Free Trade Agreement (NAFTA) has opened up the small Mexican property/casualty market, allowing U.S. insurers to operate equally with Mexican insurers. Asian countries offered an even larger potential for U.S. expansion abroad as incomes in this region continued to grow. Taiwan and Korea also continued to be particularly attractive to U.S. insurers.

The newest opportunity exists in the People's Republic of China, where a national insurance law was enacted in 1995. For 30 years after the founding of the present republic, the country had only one insurer, the State-owned People's Insurance Company of China. Few Chinese had insurance, but in an era of increasing opportunity and risk, more than 100 million took out property coverage in 1995. Competition was growing slowly, and foreign insurance firms were seeing a potentially lucrative market. Since 1992, China has only permitted two foreign firms licenses to sell insurance—first in Shanghai and more recently in Guangzhou. One of those foreign firms was the American International Group. While it waits for a license, the U.S. firm Chubb Insurance has committed $1 million over the next five years to set up a school in Shanghai to train regulators and agents.

By 1998, several firms provided political risk insurance for investments in China. These include the Multilateral Investment Guarantee Agency (IGA), an affiliate of the World Bank, the People Insurance Company of China, and the U.S. Overseas Private Investment Corporation (OPIC), whose activities were suspended because of the 1989 Tiananmem Square incident, but which continued to honor its outstanding contracts.

Foreign Involvement in the United States. Although opportunities existed for U.S. insurers abroad in 1993, many property/casualty insurers felt that significant barriers still existed for U.S. companies trying to compete overseas. Conversely, the American market was very open to foreign competition. An opportunity to create a more level playing field for the industry existed, however, under the Uruguay Round Group of Negotiations on Services under the General Agreement on Tariffs and Trade (GATT) during 1993. These rules could potentially allow U.S. insurers to enter and operate in foreign markets on an equal basis with domestic insurers in the future.

Foreign insurance company investment in the U.S. market surpassed U.S. activity abroad during the 1980s. Foreign owned insurers had sales of $72.9 billion in 1991, up sharply from $62.6 billion in 1990, primarily due to foreign acquisitions. They captured more than 11 percent of the market in 1991 and sold non-life insurance policies worth more than $39 billion. From 1991 to 1992, they added another $6 billion to that figure. These companies expanded into the U.S. property/casualty industry by acquiring American companies, buying interests in U.S. companies, or by creating new subsidiaries in the United States.

U.S. insurers have become more active overseas in recent years, with sales of $36.2 billion in 1991. The key markets for U.S. insurers were Canada, Europe, and Japan, primarily in non-life operations. Life insurance companies have also moved aggressively into Asia. Cross-border trade in insurance was a small but important part of the U. S. insurance market. U.S.-based insurers received more than $5.5 billion of premiums from overseas in 1992, and premiums of $11.9 billion went to foreign-based insurers to cover risks in the United States. Most premiums sent abroad went to Europe or the offshore centers like Bermuda for reinsurance. Reinsurance premiums sent abroad represented about one-third of the reinsurance market in the United States. Foreign-owned insurers from all lines had 1991 sales of $72.9 billion in the United States. This figure was almost double the amount of sales by U.S. companies abroad and was up from $54 billion in 1989. Companies from the European Community made up more than half of all foreign insurance investment activity in the early 1990s. Canada was the largest investor with $14.9 billion in sales, followed by the United Kingdom with $13.8 billion.

The most significant investments included Germany's Allianz Holding Company's acquisition of Fireman's Fund Insurance Companies in 1991 and BAT Industries' (UK) acquisition of Farmers Insurance Group in 1988. These two deals amounted to over $5 billion in foreign investment. In addition to a share of the U.S. insurance market, foreign investors have benefited from access to superior technology related to automation, claims adjusting, risk management, actuarial methods, investment practices, and information technology. In 1997, AEGON NV of the Netherlands acquired the insurance section of the Providian Corporation.

RESEARCH AND TECHNOLOGY

Companies in the property/casualty industry have been slower than their U.S. counterparts to integrate advanced research and technology into their operations. However, two of the most important keys to success in the industry during the late 1990s were increased use of market research and customer focus and integration of advanced automation technologies to reduce costs and improve service.

As they entered the new century, insurers strove to become more customer focused in response to the increasingly competitive property/casualty environment. According to Tim Pease in *National Underwriter,* new technology will level the playing field between insurers. "With the right technology and strategy," says Pease, "any company—whether an independent agency, insurer, reinsurer, direct marketer or direct writer—can win in the new game." In addition to upgrading their technological capacity, insurers seek to identify customer needs, often fulfilling them with very niche-oriented insurance products. The implementation of automated systems served to improve customer service, reduce errors, improve delivery time, and reduce human intervention in the entire insurance process.

Examples of new technology that property/casualty insurers were integrating into the industry in the late 1990s included open-systems architecture computer systems, network computing, computer-aided software-engineering tools, multimedia training tools, and information management and delivery systems that used satellites. Industry regulators were also using this technology to identify potentially insolvent insurers. Several companies have realized significant cost reductions and improved customer service through comprehensive automation programs.

FURTHER READING

"AEGON: Providian Shareholders Approve Merger with AEGON USA." *M2 PressWire,* 9 June 1997.

"Alliance of American Insurers." Available from http://www.allianceai.org.

"American Insurance Association." Available from http://aia.com.

"A.M. Best Upgrades Allstate Insurance Co. to A+ (Superior) from A (Excellent)." A.M. Best Company Press Release, 1997.

Bowers, Barbara. "Banking on Insurance." *Best's Review,* Property/Casualty Insurance Edition, June 1998.

"China: Foreign Investments in China-II: Developments in Related Areas." *East Asian Executive Reports,* 15 July 1998.

"NAIC Again Slams Administration Plan for Financial Services Modernization." *BestWeek,* 1997.

Darnay, Arsen J., ed. *Finance, Insurance, and Real Estate USA.* Detroit: Gale Research, 1996.

Gardner, Mark L. "Pressure to Sell Out." *Best's Review* Life/Health Edition, October 1999.

"Insurance: Life & Health," *Standard & Poor's Industry Surveys.* New York: Standard & Poor's Corporation, 8 April 1999.

"Insurance: Property-Casualty," *Standard & Poor's Industry Surveys.* New York: Standard & Poor's Corporation, 8 July 1999.

Johnston, Stuart. ''Unix, OS/2 Hold Their Ground Against NT.'' *Computerworld,* 26 February 1996.

Kerin, Roger. ''Largest Property and Casualty Insurance Companies.'' *Birmingham Business Journal,* 29 January 1996.

Occupational Outlook Handbook. Washington: U.S. Department of Labor,1998-99.

Pease, Tim. ''Technology Will Level the Playing Field.'' *National Underwriter,* 12 July 1999.

Pintar, James. ''Insurance: Insurers Need to Make Up Ground in E-Business.'' *American Banker,* 20 July 1999.

Sanchez, Jesus. ''State Farm to Cap Replacement Payments on California Policies.'' *Los Angeles Times,* 9 January 1997.

Simms, Larry L. ''China's Insurance Law.'' *China Business Review,* 1 October 1996.

Turner, Samuel H. ''UL Future Hinges on Service-Intensive Sales.'' *National Underwriter Life & Health,* 5 July 1999.

Unsworth, Edwin. ''More Consolidation, Demutualization Expected..'' *Business Insurance,* 26 July 1999.

SIC 6512

OPERATORS OF NONRESIDENTIAL BUILDINGS

The commercial real estate operation and leasing industry consists of establishments primarily engaged in the ownership and operation of nonresidential real estate. These companies own and operate properties such as retail establishments, shopping centers, marinas, theaters, and commercial and industrial buildings. The industry does not include owners of hotels, campgrounds, or other establishments that are classified as service operations.

NAICS CODE(S)

711310 (Promoters of Performing Arts, Sports and Similar Events with Facilities)

531120 (Lessors of Nonresidential Buildings (except Miniwarehouses))

INDUSTRY SNAPSHOT

Hammered by a depression in the real estate industry that began in the late 1980s and continued into the early 1990s, commercial property owners and operators were beset with high vacancy rates, a severe shortage of capital, and dismal earnings. Many companies were not able to meet their mortgage obligations and were forced into bankruptcy. Companies that survived the shakeout learned to operate more efficiently and to compete by providing better customer service. (See **SIC 6531: Real Estate Agents and Managers**).

After a continued slump in 1993, the industry bottomed out and vacancy rates in many sectors began to stabilize. The dramatically improved economic climate through 1996 was reflected in an equally dramatic recovery of the office and industrial segments, especially in suburban areas. However, the retail segment was an exception. New construction continued unfettered, so the retail market was oversaturated by 1996. Slow retail sales and numerous retail bankruptcies threatened to worsen the situation even more.

The unprecedented longevity of the late-1990s economic boom spilled over into the nonresidential real estate market. Although forecasts called for a decided slowdown in demand in this sector in 1999, the unexpected continuing strength of the U.S. economy managed to keep tenant demand relatively strong, particularly in the office and shopping center segments of the market.

Industry analysts were predicting the industry would see a wave of restructuring—much as has been seen in the banking, insurance, auto, and steel industries—in the early years of the new millennium. Management and technological innovations may well prove to be the key to restructuring in the real estate market as they have in other key industries.

ORGANIZATION AND STRUCTURE

The entire real estate industry is highly fragmented and has traditionally been characterized by low barriers to entry. Therefore, companies that own, lease, and operate commercial properties range from small mom-and-pop firms to large national corporations. In addition, many of the largest owners and operators of real estate emphasize other business operations and thus are not primarily engaged in the industry. For instance, some of the largest commercial property owners are insurance companies that invest some of their reserves in real estate, which they may or may not actively manage. Other owners and operators include large corporations such as General Motors or IBM, which operate properties that serve their core businesses.

Specialization. Companies that are primarily operators and lessors of commercial properties often specialize either by region or by property function. Those that specialize by property function benefit from an acute understanding of the market segment that they serve. Through experience, they learn how to streamline their operations and reduce costs while generating maximum revenues from a given number of square feet, or dollars invested, in a project. For example, some companies specialize in the operation and leasing of shopping malls, while some other companies focus on self-storage facilities or office buildings.

Because the real estate industry has traditionally been highly localized, many industry participants specialize in just one geographic region or locale. For a company to own and operate a property that effectively competes for tenants, it must have an intimate understanding of the local market characteristics. These attributes include demographics, location, surrounding facilities, vacancy rates, zoning restrictions, local taxation, and future economic expectations. For this reason, very small firms that concentrate in their own community benefit from a shrewd understanding of their local market. They are also more likely to take advantage of business relationships that give them an edge in their community. Property owners that do not specialize regionally will often contract with third party management firms that are familiar with the community in which their property is located.

Institutional Investors. Aside from the large and small property owners, operators, and lessors who have traditionally dominated the commercial market, another type of owner/operator includes subsidiaries of large institutional investors. These companies specialize in real estate ownership and operation for their parent investment company. They typically invest in many properties in various regions, often worth millions of dollars. Asset managers employed by these companies oversee the properties and are ultimately responsible for their financial performance. In many cases the asset managers contract with, and directly supervise, local property management firms that perform on-site maintenance and lease tenant space.

Also falling into this category are lending institutions. Many of these institutions became property owners/operators by default as the developers to which they loaned money during the 1980s failed to meet their debt obligations.

Professional and Trade Organizations. There are several professional and trade organizations involved with this industry. The Building Owners and Managers Association International was founded in 1908 and currently is headquartered in Washington, D.C. Its activities include lobbying on legislative and regulatory issues, conducting training programs for property administrators, and establishing industry standards, such as the Standard Method of Floor Measurement (last revised in 1996). The International Facility Management Association, located in Houston, TX, focuses on the management of the work environment. It conducts research, provides educational services such as facility manager certification programs, and sponsors international conferences and networking. The Institute of Real Estate Management, which includes both residential and nonresidential real estate, also provides educational services such as property manager certification and began establishing international partnerships with developing nations in the mid-1990s.

BACKGROUND AND DEVELOPMENT

Commercial real estate ownership in the United States is made possible by real property laws that govern land and property rights and conveyances. These laws were originally based upon English property laws that developed between the tenth and the twentieth centuries, and were mimicked in America as early as the seventh century. U.S. real property laws differ from English law, however, in that they vary significantly from state to state and even from city to city.

An important feature of real property laws in the twentieth century has been the emergence of social control, which has limited the freedom of property owners to use and develop land in a manner that does not serve the public good. Social control has manifested itself in eminent domain, zoning laws, and police regulations. The concept of eminent domain implies that an owner's land may be taken away by government decree, against the owner's wishes, for a use that serves the public. Similarly, zoning laws restrict the functions for which owners can use their property. The 1926 case *Village of Euclid v. Ambler Realty Co.* established the first zoning laws. The third form of social control is police regulation, by which a property owner can be directed by the state to take a specified action regarding his property. This concept gained momentum in the case of *Miller v. Shoene* in 1928.

Industry Growth. The commercial real estate operation and leasing industry became a force in the American economy beginning in the 1950s. The rapid expansion of the U.S. economy, population, and work force generated an unprecedented demand for office buildings, retail centers, commercial recreational facilities, and other types of real estate developments. Throughout the 1960s and early 1970s the amount of nonresidential property owned and operated for commercial profits continued to grow at a brisk rate, often averaging more than one billion square feet in new space per year.

Just as important to the industry as the demand for new properties however, was the availability of capital for new ventures. In fact one distinguishing characteristic of the U.S. real estate industry is that its growth has traditionally been driven by the amount of capital available to fund new projects, rather than by market demand. This phenomenon is largely a result of favorable tax laws that have artificially boosted returns on commercial real estate investments.

The 1980s Boom. The commercial real estate industry realized the greatest expansion in its history in the mid- and late 1980s. Owners and operators of real estate, as a group, rapidly expanded their holdings and attained enormous profits during this period. The total square feet of new commercial space developed, owned, and managed increased from an average of about 700 million per year from 1981 to 1983 to more than one billion between 1984 and 1989.

This boom occurred despite only a moderate surge in the market demand for new real estate developments.

Several factors accounted for the massive growth. Financial reasons included: the deregulation of U.S. savings and loan associations (which ultimately ended in disaster when many of these associations folded after poor investment practices); an absence of bank investment alternatives, tax shelters, pension fund growth, and investment in real estate; and an influx of foreign investment dollars. Nonfinancial factors that encouraged overbuilding in the 1980s included: the growth of office-based employment, increasing employment of women outside the home; the growth in office space required per worker; the oil price bust in the mid-1980s; and explosive population growth in several states.

The 1990s Bust. By 1989, investment capital dried up, tax laws had changed, and the U.S. economy had stagnated. Property owners and operators started to suffer from the consequences of overbuilt markets. By 1990 the amount of new real estate developed fell from a six-year average during 1984 to 1989 of 1 billion square feet per year, to less than 600 million square feet in 1990. High vacancy rates and diminished profits plagued owners and operators who were struggling to meet mortgage payments on their distressed properties. In addition, owners were often unable to sell their Properties—even for a moderate loss—because property values had collapsed. As a result of these problems, many owner/operators were forced out of business as lenders took over their bankrupt properties.

Four major implications for the commercial property ownership and operation industry resulted from the 1980s boom and subsequent bust. The first was an increase in the ownership of properties by large institutions and a decrease in ownership by local companies that had a personal interest in management of their property. The second was the emergence of owners who sought short-term investments rather than long-term profitability. A third outcome was overbuilding, especially in office space, and the ensuing fall in effective rent rates. Finally, the collapse of lending institutions strained by nonperforming real estate loans left the industry with reduced access to capital for development and renovation, projects that the market demanded in the early 1990s.

In 1993, commercial real estate remained one of the weakest sectors in the U.S. economy. In 1992, vacancies had reached record highs, averaging more than 19 percent in the nation's business districts. As a result, owners continued to charge less rent. For instance, rent per square foot for Class A office space fell from an average $21.81 in 1991 to $21.44 in 1992. In addition, many owners offered large incentives to lure and keep tenants, such as several months of free rent, free parking spaces, and free space renovations. Most large institutional investors continued to receive poor investment returns from their real estate portfolios.

Owners sustained their search for capital to renovate or develop properties. Under a provision of the Federal Deposit Insurance Corporation Improvement Act, which became effective December 19, 1992, many lending institutions were pressured to avoid any loans that could be construed by regulators as risky. Other regulations, such as the risk-based capital standards, were tightened early in 1993, further constricting the flow of capital available to owner/operators.

Property owners also started to recognize the financial implications of the Americans with Disabilities Act, which became effective in 1992. This act mandated that owners of most newer buildings provide reasonable access to their properties for disabled people. The Act included thousands of regulations stipulating such details as elevator button heights, bathroom sink dimensions, door widths, and the type of locks that could be used on door handles.

In response to these and other market forces that were exerting downward pressure on profits in 1993, owner/operators sought ways to reduce operational costs, increase their marketing effectiveness, and improve customer service. They used more advanced financial reporting methods, hired more highly educated and experienced property managers, and developed customer service programs.

Current Conditions

By 1997, the overall market for nonresidential real estate had changed drastically. At that point the market could be viewed in three different segments: the office segment, the industrial segment, and the retail segment. Of the three, the office and industrial segments made great strides toward recovery; only the retail segment continued the slump of the early 1990s.

As the U.S. recession began to end in 1992, the economy responded by producing 8.7 million new jobs from 1993 through 1995, many of them in high technology and corporate services firms. As a result, by the beginning of 1997 office space occupancy stood at the highest level in a decade. Financially solid investors (unlike many in the 1980s) began to pour capital into new construction, particularly in suburban areas where costs of operation are lower, traffic and parking are less troublesome, and safety and quality of life are more appealing for many employees. Grubb & Ellis' 1996 Real Estate Forecast estimated that suburban office space accounted for 75 percent of the office demand since 1990. Suburbs around cities like Boston, Atlanta, Houston, and Los Angeles began to blossom with new office construction. Even Phoenix, which was devastated by the savings and loan crashes, increased its office occupancy rate from 70 percent in 1990 to almost 90 percent by the beginning of 1997.

The industrial segment likewise saw a great resurgence by 1997. Industries producing goods experienced a surprising rebirth during the economic upturn of the mid-1990s. As a result, demand for warehouses, research and development facilities, and similar facilities jumped. A new generation of investors emerged, including real estate investment trusts (REITs), which entered this market along with private investors, corporate owners of property, and pension fund investors. Dallas, Portland, and Chicago led in the warehouse market; the ''Sunbelt'' led the light assembly market; and Boston and Seattle led the research and development market. The trend was toward larger, consolidated facilities, although many existing small facilities were being taken over by startup companies. Industrial parks also began to grow in both size and number.

The one segment unable to recover in the mid-1990s was the retail segment. Reasons for this depressed condition were numerous: slow retail sales; retail bankruptcies and consolidations; poor management; overly leveraged investments; and a general oversupply of retail properties. Companies as diverse as Barney's and Caldor's reached a crisis point in 1996, although some chain operations such as Staples and Wal-Mart continued to prosper and plan for expansions. There was an increase in urban retail development because many suburban markets had become overbuilt.

The closing years of the 1990s saw even the retail segment of the nonresidential market sharing in the good times fueled by the long-running economic boom.

Data from the U.S. Bureau of the Census showed that lessors of nonresidential buildings generated revenues of more than $38.1 billion in 1997. The bureau reported in its 1997 Economic Census that more than 31,000 establishments were actively involved in this market in 1997. They employed a workforce of 145,317 and had a total annual payroll of $3.8 billion.

The growing popularity of electronic commerce presented the nonresidential real estate market with new challenges as the new millennium dawned. It became increasingly clear that management companies would have to adapt to e-commerce to survive. Analysts predicted that for those who were quick to make the transition, the rewards would likely be stronger growth, increased market share, and new business opportunities. The key to success would be the ability to be more flexible, innovative, and nimble than their competitors.

INDUSTRY LEADERS

Among the major players in the nonresidential real estate market in the late 1990s were Simon Property Group Inc. (formerly known as Simon DeBartolo Group), Rouse Co., General Growth Properties Inc., Trammell Crow Co., Kimco Realty Corp., Security Capital Group Inc., and Urban Shopping Centers Inc.

Simon, based in Indianapolis, is North America's largest operator of shopping malls, including among its properties the massive Mall of America in Minnesota and the Forum Shops at Caesar's Palace in Las Vegas. With 6,300 employees, Simon posted 1998 revenue of more than $1.4 billion. Another major force in the retail real estate market is Rouse Co. of Columbia, Maryland, which has been responsible for the development of such retail centers as Faneuil Hall Marketplace in Boston and New York's South Street Seaport. As of late 1998, Rouse employed just over 4,100 and reported 1998 sales of $768.3 million.

The nation's second largest owner/operator of shopping malls after Simon Property Group, General Growth Properties Inc. is headquartered in Chicago. The company, which employs a workforce of more than 3,200, posted 1998 revenue of $470.5 million. Dallas-based Trammell Crow Co. is one of the country's most successful commercial real estate management companies. With more than 5,000 employees, Trammell Crow posted 1998 revenue of $459.7 million.

Kimco Realty Corp., headquartered in New Hyde Park, New York, had interests in more than 450 properties in 41 states as of late 1999. Kimco reported 1998 sales of $353.6 million. Security Capital Group, based in Santa Fe, New Mexico, reported 1998 revenue of $342.3 million, while Urban Shopping Centers of Chicago posted 1998 sales of $210.2 million.

According to *Shopping Center World*'s March 1998 ranking of leading shopping center managers, the top five were Simon Property Group, which at the time managed approximately 138.7 million square feet of retail space, followed by General Growth Properties (90.1 million), Urban Shopping Centers (56.9 million), Rouse Co. (44.3 million), and Kimco Realty (43.3 million).

WORKFORCE

Despite the gloomy state of the commercial real estate market in the early 1990s, jobs in property operations and leasing were a bright spot in the industry as the decade proceeded. Because owners focused on efficient management and customer service, jobs and salaries in property management were expected to grow as fast or faster than most other industries in the United States throughout the 1990s. Many of the new jobs, however, were initially filled by real estate professionals from other disciplines, such as development and sales, who were displaced during the recession of the early 1990s.

The best locations for employment by owners and operators of nonresidential real estate in the late 1990s was in suburbs of large cities with thriving office and industrial markets, such as Boston, Atlanta, and Dallas.

Property managers, who work directly for property owners or for consulting firms that contract with owners, usually are between the ages of 35 and 45. These positions often require a college education. According to data from the Department of Labor's Bureau of Labor Statistics, approximately 271,000 were employed as property managers in 1996. The median annual salary for all property manager was $28,5000 in 1996. About 10 percent of all managers earned more than $60,700 annually, while another 10 percent earned less than $12,000 a year. Employment in this sector was expected to grow between 10 and 20 percent in the decade from 1996 to 2006, according to BLS projections.

Asset managers usually have at least a college degree, and often an MBA, and are typically between 45 and 55 years old. Senior level asset managers earned between $100,000 and $250,000 in 1992 depending on their geographic region and the types of property they managed.

Leasing professionals, who market and lease space to tenants, averaged salaries ranging from $50,000 to $100,000 in the early 1990s. Because these positions are usually complemented by commissions, salaries vary according property type, experience, and region.

In the early 2000s candidates with the best chance of finding a position in the industry will be those with financial and computer skills. The industry is increasingly requiring skills in advanced computer software and automated systems that will allow reduced operational costs, precise financial/investment analysis and reporting, and improved customer service. Key professionals such as finance officers, acquisitions specialists, and asset managers are likely to receive the premium compensation packages.

AMERICA AND THE WORLD

Few, if any, foreign property owner/operators in the early 1990s were reeling from the same magnitude of problems caused by overbuilt U.S. markets. This is because the supply of commercial properties is influenced more by demand than by available capital in most industrialized countries. The world real estate industry in general, however, was recessed and lacked capital for new projects and renovations.

In light of the global slowdown, many American property owners and operators sought to enter potential growth markets in emerging European, Asian, and Central American countries. For instance, Trammell Crow Co., Tishman Speyer, and other large real estate firms pursued new projects in Berlin. Athens and Brussels also offered potential for American investment in European properties. Mexico was another bright spot for American real estate companies in the early 1990s. Markets in developing economic areas such as the former Soviet Union and China presented great potential for the early 2000s.

The most significant international factor affecting property owners/operators in the United States was the decline of foreign investment in U.S. real estate, which began in 1991. This contributed to the plummeting real estate values, which destroyed much of the equity that owners had in their properties. Although foreign investment peaked in 1990 at $34 billion, it fell to a fraction of that amount in 1991. The Japanese, for instance, invested $16.5 billion in U.S. real estate in 1988, compared with just $5 billion in 1991. Even a rise in the dollar against European currencies in 1992 was not enough to buoy the market for foreign capital.

As the decade progressed, foreign investors became more interested in re-entering the U.S. market, particularly in suburban areas. For example, P.P.M. America, Inc., which is associated with Prudential of the United Kingdom, bought a 305,000 square foot suburban Atlanta office building in 1996 for $32 million.

The North American Free Trade Agreement (NAFTA) and General Agreement on Tariffs and Trade (GATT) also affected certain U.S. industries. The textile industry in the southeast was adversely affected when companies moved operations outside of the country and closed production facilities in the United States. New business, however, has been generated in cities bordering Canada and Mexico, such as Detroit and El Paso, thus increasing the need for nonresidential space.

FURTHER READING

BOMA International Home Page, 1997. Available from http://www.boma.org/.

Brown, Steve. ''Looking Ahead: Challenges Coming for Commercial Real Estate.'' *Dallas Morning News,* 25 December 1998.

Bruno, Carl, and Patty Mitchell. ''Maximizing Compensation Through Value Creation.'' *National Real Estate Investor,* September 1996.

Ciandella, Donald R. ''Lagging New Supply, Rising Demand Invigorates Office Sector.'' *National Real Estate Investor,* July 1996.

Hoover's Online, 1999. Available from http://www.hoovers.com.

IFMA Home Page, 1997. Available from http://www.ifma.org/.

Kane, Carl. ''2000 & Beyond: Oldies But Goodies.'' *Naitonal Real Estate Investor,* 30 September 1999.

''Leading Shopping Center Managers.'' *Shopping Center World,* March 1998.

Litke, Ronald. ''The Institute of Real Estate Management Delves into International Markets.'' *National Real Estate Investor,* September 1996.

Richard, Geoffrey. ''Industrial Market Leads the Pack to Recovery.'' *National Real Estate Investor,* April 1996.

———. ''Office Market Finds Short Cut to Recovery—Through the Suburbs.'' *National Real Estate Investor,* October 1996.

Ross, Stan. ''2000 & Beyond: Making the 'Offer.''' *National Real Estate Investor,* 30 September 1999.

''The Industrial Market . . . 1997 Landauer Real Estate Market Forecast.'' *National Real Estate Investor,* January 1997.

''The Office Market . . . 1997 Landauer Real Estate Market Forecast.'' *National Real Estate Investor,* January 1997.

''The Retail Market . . . 1997 Landauer Real Estate Market Forecast.'' *National Real Estate Investor,* January 1997.

''Top Property Manager Survey.'' *National Real Estate Investor,* November 1995.

U.S. Bureau of the Census. *1997 Economic Census.* Washington: GPO, 1999.

U.S. Department of Labor. Bureau of Labor Statistics. *Occupational Outlook Handbook, 1998-1999 Edition.* Washington: U.S. Department of Labor, 1998.

SIC 6513

OPERATORS OF APARTMENT BUILDINGS

This category includes establishments primarily engaged in the operation of apartment buildings. Apartment buildings are defined as those containing five or more housing units.

NAICS CODE(S)

531110 (Lessors of Residential Buildings and Dwellings)

Operators of apartment buildings are responsible for a valuable asset: income-producing real estate. Their goal is to preserve the asset and increase its value over time through proper management techniques, while generating current income. It is a common misconception that operators of apartment buildings merely collect rent, show apartments, and sign leases. In reality, the operation of an apartment building is far more complex. This is why many owners of apartment buildings contract with a professional property management firm to oversee management of their property and maximize its value.

Property managers act as the agent of the owner of the property and have a wide variety of responsibilities. They market vacant apartments to prospective tenants and establish rental rates in accordance with local conditions. They negotiate and prepare leases, collect rents, hire maintenance personnel, and handle the bookkeeping (taxes, mortgages, insurance) for the property. The property manager must also prepare reports for the owner concerning all aspects of the apartment property. Effective management of apartment buildings, from small buildings to very large apartment complexes, thus requires expertise in business management, real estate, finance, and accounting.

Early Apartment Operators. The demand for effective management of apartment buildings began in the late nineteenth century, in large measure because of two inventions that would change the face of urban real estate. Creation of the steel frame building and the electric elevator made possible the advancement of high rise apartment and office buildings, changing the urban landscape forever. Construction of multi-family apartment buildings certainly contributed to this transformation.

The depression of the 1930s had a profound effect on the evolving property management profession. Numerous failures and foreclosures during this era placed much of the nation's real estate in the hands of institutions: trust companies, insurance companies, banks, and other organizations. A large number of income-producing properties thus fell into the hands of corporations. While some of these corporations formed their own property management firms, many quickly realized that responsibilities involved more than simply collecting rent payments and selecting tenants. As the need for more specialized expertise emerged, the industry gained strength in numbers and stature.

CURRENT CONDITIONS

Today the professional apartment management firm must have a comprehensive understanding of the economic forces at work in the real estate market. Operators must be able to realistically evaluate the property in light of the real estate market, forecast its potential for the future, and construct a management plan to maximize the building's potential market value, while remaining flexible to the demands of the ever-changing real estate market.

Most property managers handle several buildings simultaneously. Managers also negotiate contracts for security, trash removal, landscaping, and janitorial services for common areas. If the building has other facilities, such as a swimming pool, tennis courts, health facilities, parking areas, or a golf course, maintenance and repair contracts for these areas must also be secured. Managers oversee all repairs and maintenance of the property. At a larger property, they hire personnel to maintain the facility's heating, ventilation, and air-conditioning systems and perform routine maintenance and repair work.

In 1999, investing in apartments was considered low risk. The market was evenly split between those interested in selling and those interested in buying. The relative stability of the apartment marketplace made it an attractive investment for those interested in purchasing real estate. The demographics of the renter's marketplace are shifting towards older couples who want less responsibility than required of a house and more childless couples who do not always need a large house. Also, there is money to be made in ancillary services, such as allowing companies to use rooftops for transmission antennas or making a deal with local cable operators.

In 1999 there were 59,718 establishments in the United States, employing 267,784 employees. Annual sales for this industry was approximately $36 billion. Prominent companies involved in apartment building operation in the late 1990s included Wilmac Corp., a private company out of Pennsylvania; its annual sales figures were nearly $1.2 billion. Holding the number two spot was Connecticut-based Avalon Properties Inc., with annual sales at $1 billion. The third largest company, in sales, was Forest City Enterprises of Cleveland Ohio, in 1999 its sales were $633 million.

FURTHER READING

"Amber Waves of Gain." *Journal of Property Management,* September-October, 1996: 56.

"Changing Demographics Stymies Apartment Demand." *Building Design & Construction,* January 1997.

Palmieri, Christopher. "My Partner, Your Landlord." *Forbes,* 20 May 1996.

Sinderman, Martin."Apartment Market: Too Good to be True?" *National Real Estate Investor,* June 1999.

Ward's Business Directory of U.S. Public and Private Companies. Detroit: Gale Research, 1999.

U.S. Bureau of the Census . *1997 Economic Census.* Available from http://factfinder.census.gov.

SIC 6514

OPERATORS OF DWELLINGS OTHER THAN APARTMENT BUILDINGS

This industry includes establishments primarily engaged in the operation of dwellings other than apartment buildings. By definition, such dwellings contain four or fewer housing units. This industry does not include hotels, rooming and boarding houses, camps, and other lodging places for transients. Hotels and motels are classified in **SIC 7011: Hotels and Motels;** rooming and boarding houses are classified in **SIC 7021: Rooming and Boarding Houses;** and camps are covered in **SIC 7032: Sporting and Recreational Camps.**

NAICS CODE(S)

531110 (Lessors of Residential Buildings and Dwellings)

Bixby Ranch Co. of Seal Beach, California, which placed second in the industry with 1998 sales of $82 million, found itself embattled with residents in its home town who opposed a 218-acre development that started out as a golf course plan and grew into a combined housing and shopping center plan. Residents expressed concern over increased traffic and pollution resulting from the commercialization of its community, preferring a housing-only development. Bixby pointed out several compelling arguments defending its position: first, the Bixby family owned the land since 1875; second, the project passed the scrutiny of a thorough environmental impact review as well as city council approval; and third, that the commercial interests will bring in revenue and create jobs in the depressed economy.

Gertrude Gardner Inc. of Metairie, Louisiana led the industry with sales of $222 million for its fiscal year ended September 30, 1998. Indianapolis-based Gene B. Glick Company generated 1999 sales of $74 million, and New York City-based Time Equities Inc. placed fourth in the industry with 1998 sales of $28 million.

This segment of the real estate industry is a small—worth an estimated $3.5 billion by the mid-1990s—primarily populated by individual owners of rental properties (generally houses). Large chains or companies are a relatively small presence, typically limited to regional influence. As an established, albeit minor, element of the larger real estate industry in the United States, establishments involved in this industry are influenced by the same economic and social factors that impact the largest real estate property management firms. The U.S. Census Bureau estimated some 9,000 establishments in this category in the early 1990s.

As the U.S. economy surged, beginning in 1992 and continuing into the new millennium, rental properties in general became more appealing to small investors, both companies and individuals. Individual investors began to put more capital into investment properties even though federal tax changes in the late 1980s had limited deductions on investment property. Many of these individuals sought small properties in which to invest so that mortgages would be manageable or not necessary.

An example of a company that capitalized on this trend in the late 1990s is the Burnett Financial Group, headquartered in Edina, Illinois, near Chicago. Burnett was ranked as the country's fourth largest real estate brokerage in 1995. In early 1997, Burnett opened a subsidiary, Burnett Property Management, which had several functions. It handled traditional rental properties, particularly for small investors who did not want to perform all of the management functions such as screening tenants and making emergency repairs. It also provided property management services for people who were temporarily leaving the area or who had to move before they could sell their single-family residences.

FURTHER READING

DeNitto, Emily. ''Eighties Redux? Invested Interest: Individual Investors Taste Past Glories in Newly Profitable Residential Market.'' *Crain's New York Business,* 13 January 1997.

Gendler, Neal. ''Burnet Financial Group Announces Creation of Property Management Group.'' *Star Tribune,* 19 February 1997.

Infotrac Company Profiles, 19 February 2000. Available at http://web4.infotrac.galegroup.com.

''1996 Executive Summary; Real Estate Industry Forecasts; 1996 Landauer Real Estate Forecast.'' *National Real Estate Investor,* January 1996.

Segura, Joe. ''Calif. Homeowners Complain about Commercial Devlopment.'' *Knight-Ridder/Tribune Business News,* 6 May 1997.

''The Residential Market; Real Estate Forecasts; 1996 Landauer Real Estate Forecasts.'' *National Real Estate Investor,* January 1996.

Tuinstra, Rachel. ''Proposed Seal Beach, Calif., Development Builds Up Anger.'' *Knight-Ridder/Tribune Business News,* 19 December 1998.

SIC 6515

OPERATORS OF RESIDENTIAL MOBILE HOME SITES

This category covers establishments primarily engaged in the operation of residential mobile home sites. Establishments primarily engaged in the operation of sites for overnight or transient use for travel trailers are classified in **SIC 7033: Recreational Vehicle Parks and Campsites.**

NAICS CODE(S)

531190 (Lessors of Other Real Estate Property)

INDUSTRY SNAPSHOT

Mobile homes account for about 6 percent of the total U.S. housing stock. There are an estimated 50,000 income-producing properties and manufactured-home communities throughout the United States and Canada. Of these, approximately 24,000 consist of at least 50 to 75 rental home sites per property.

Increasingly, mobile homes are approaching the average size and amenities of conventional housing units, as the share of mobile homes consisting of multiple sections has grown. Mobile homes are coming into direct competition with conventional units, especially as more doublewide units are built.

The industry remained generally unsophisticated in the 1980s in comparison to other sectors of the housing ownership and operation industry. However, during the 1990s, it underwent a transformation based on its significant affordability advantage over single-family, site-built housing. As a result, the manufactured housing industry accounts for about a 33 percent share of new homes.

ORGANIZATION AND STRUCTURE

Land owners who get permission from local zoning authorities can develop a mobile home park with a relatively small investment. The only significant costs involve bringing utilities—including water, gas, sewerage, and electricity—into each site and developing automobile access within the park. For parks that are unpaved, improvement costs are negligible compared to the costs associated with traditional site-built housing communities. Because there are so few barriers to entry, the mobile home operation industry has traditionally been dominated by small companies. According to the 1996 Allen Report on the Largest Community Owners, 500 major multiple-property portfolio owners control about 15 percent of the total property count and one-third of the investment-grade manufactured-home communities.

How the Industry Operates. Mobile home buyers can choose ''singlewide'' homes that average 980 square feet in size, or ''doublewide'' multisectional homes, averaging 1,440 square feet. Some new multisectional homes also allow ''triple-wide'' structures. Although residents usually rent their lots, most buy their dwellings. The standard purchase agreement allows the dealer a markup of 20 percent to 25 percent over the wholesale price of the home. The dealer sometimes arranges financing of the home through the manufacturer, though banks finance most mobile homes. Additionally, the dealer usually assumes responsibility for delivering the home to a community and installing it on a lot.

Many local authorities have used zoning laws to ban mobile home parks, restrict their size, or relegate them to the least desirable parts of a community. With supply constrained, occupancy rates have historically remained above 90 percent, which compares favorably with apartment buildings.

Turnover of mobile home residents is very low—only 5 percent for the actual homes and 10 percent among homeowner-renters who generally sell their homes in place before relocating. Turnover is so low because today's larger single-section and multisectional homes are quite difficult and expensive to move. Rent in manufactured housing communities is typically one-third that of nearby townhouse apartments.

In addition to mortgage payments to the manufacturer of their home, most mobile home park residents pay rent to their community owner/operator. Monthly rent typically ranges from $100 per month, although high-end developments with amenities usually charge more than $200 per month. In about 30 percent of communities being developed in the early 1990s, operators also arranged to sell lots to residents as part of a condominium. Some offered 99-year leases on lots, which effectively amounted to buying the parcel.

One reason park owners and operators do not allow residents to buy lots is that they may be able to sell the land for higher prices in the future. In fact, many land owners operate mobile home parks with the specific intent of eventually converting, or selling, the property for a more lucrative purpose as it becomes more valuable.

Regional and Demographic Variations. Profiles of typical mobile home parks differ principally by region and by the age and economic status of its residents. For instance, some communities cater to retirees, offering smaller lots for smaller homes. Other communities cater to families and provide big yards, more parking, and amenities that appeal to children such as swimming pools and playgrounds. Developments designed to appeal to low-income residents offer small lots, few amenities, and unpaved streets. Conversely, most communities aimed at the upscale segment of the market provide paved streets and sidewalks, recreational facilities, large lots with lawns, wooded public areas, off-street parking, and adequate outdoor lighting.

Regional differences result from variations in housing prices, as well as demographics. Parks in the Midwest, Southeast, and Northeast are characteristically traditional. They are usually arranged in grid patterns, are more apt to appeal to low-income residents that are elderly or childless, and charge monthly rents for lots. Mobile home communities in western states and in Florida, on the other hand, are more likely to appeal to families and middle-income residents. These developments also are more likely to have curved, paved, and wooded streets. They also offer more financing options to their tenants, such as condominium or lease-to-buy arrangements.

The migration of population to the Sunbelt has been one of the most significant factors that affect mobile home output and sales. More than 50 percent of mobile homes sold in the 1990s were in the South. The Midwest and West absorbed 20 percent and 16 percent, respectively, while the Northeast accounted for only 8 percent of home placements. Western states had the highest proportion of multiwide units as well as the highest average unit price.

Background and Development

Uniquely American, the mobile home operation industry emanated from the invention of recreational trailer-coaches in the 1930s. During this early stage, mobile home parks were designed to serve temporary guests who needed a place to park their trailer for a short time. By 1940, more than half of all trailers were being built for permanent housing, and parks began serving permanent, as well as overnight, tenants. The industry gained public recognition when the government bought large numbers of mobile homes to house servicemen and defense workers during World War II. This led to mobile homes becoming an acceptable housing alternative in the 1950s when a national housing shortage left many people out of the housing market. As site-built houses caught up with demand in the 1960s, mobile home operators began offering facilities for larger, comparatively luxurious homes.

In the 1970s, two factors spurred growth of mobile home parks. First, productivity advances in manufactured housing technology allowed mobile homes to become increasingly price competitive with other types of housing. For instance, the average price of a manufactured house, including land development costs, increased from $18,000 in the mid-1970s to $27,800 by 1990. During the same period, the average cost of a site-built house jumped from $44,000 to $150,000. Second, the development of larger, more luxurious homes changed the public perception that mobile homes were temporary housing trailers. Many newer mobile homes in the 1970s offered central air-conditioning, covered parking, and garbage disposals. Also, since 1976, manufactured homes have been required to meet a federal preemptive building code known as the National Manufactured Housing Construction & Safety Standards Act. This code ensures a high level of product quality and allows manufactured housing to cross state lines for siting in almost any locale.

A number of changes have occurred within the manufactured-housing industry during the past two decades. In the early 1970s, nearly 80 percent of manufactured homes were in manufactured home communities. Today, half of the new, larger manufactured homes are placed on privately owned, scattered building sites and into housing subdivisions. Second, few new manufactured-home communities were developed in the past two decades, and existing ones are nearly full—averaging a 94 percent occupancy in 1995. Furthermore, where vacant rental sites exist, they often can't accommodate today's larger manufactured home.

New manufactured-home production has gone through a boom and bust cycle. In 1973, the industry shipped 579,960 homes. This fell to only 212,690 home shipments in 1975. In 1994, 303,932 homes were shipped—the first year since 1974 to top 300,000 homes. In 1995, 339,601 homes were produced.

The Allure of Mobile Home Communities. The greatest appeal of manufactured housing for most residents is that it offers many of the advantages of home ownership at a cost comparable to renting an apartment. Most residents in manufactured housing communities have their own yard and parking space. They also are allowed to add personal amenities to their property—such as shrubs, covered parking, decks, and storage sheds—that would not be allowed at most apartment complexes.

Mobile homes are comparatively inexpensive in comparison to traditional site built homes because they are built entirely in factories. With drywall construction, brand-name appliances, and other quality features, multisectional manufactured homes are often indistinguishable from site-built, single-family houses. These multisectional houses have increased from 28 percent of total manufactured home shipments in 1980 to 50 percent in 1996. In 1994, multisectional manufactured housing cost $27.41 per square foot. The average cost of site-built houses was almost twice as much, $54.65. Mobile home community residents also benefit from low maintenance, attractive financing terms, and tax advantages. Manufactured homes are usually easy to trade-in, move, or sell.

The traditional residents of mobile home communities are either first-time home buyers, between the ages of 25 and 44, or elderly retired people. While these groups benefit from cost advantages, disadvantages entail limited appreciation in property values and minimal land use rights. Insurance rates for manufactured homes are typically 10 percent to 20 percent higher than those of site-built homes because of increased wind and fire risks. Furthermore, residents of mobile home parks often are alienated from surrounding communities because of the negative image associated with manufactured housing.

In more recent years, demand for manufactured housing has been boosted by considerably more favorable public regard for the units, as well as by various economic and demographic factors. After suffering for many years from a poor public image, manufactured home builders have upgraded the quality of their product offerings.

The industry has been focusing on selling manufactured homes and sites as a unit. The Federal National Mortgage Association (Fannie Mae) buys and secures residential mortgages on manufactured housing, as long as the house and land are sold together in a single transaction.

Another factor making manufactured homes a more desirable living alternative has been the long-term trend toward producing larger multisectional units. Twenty years ago, 80 percent of new manufactured homes produced were single-section—12 to 14 feet wide by 50 to 60 feet long. At the century's close, only a slight majority were single-section, and even these were larger than they previously were at 16 to 18 feet wide and 70 to 80 feet long.

Rising consumer acceptance, favorable demographics, readily available credit, and a slowdown in low- to middle-income apartment construction should keep demand relatively strong. The relative affordability of manufactured housing is helping the group to build market share versus conventional, site-built homes. Manufactured housing represents almost one-third of all homes built in the United States. Furthermore, the industry has significant growth possibilities due to the replacement of the large number of older manufactured homes coming to the end of their useful lives.

Industry Trends. Although many mobile home operators still catered to traditional buyers in the mid-1990s, most newer developments tried to attract more sophisticated residents. As a result, manufactured housing developments grew larger and more expensive and began to resemble site-built communities, rather than traditional trailer parks.

Trend-setting states, including Washington and California, broke new ground in the industry, and operators in other states hurried to follow their lead. California operators lured residents with larger developments, larger lots, aesthetic neighborhood designs with woods and lakes, and recreational amenities. These changes reflected the fact that in 1990 fewer than 20 percent of Californians could afford site-built housing, compared to 50 percent who could afford manufactured housing in a park.

Between 1980 and 1990, the average density of mobile home communities in California fell from 10 to 6 units per acre and the average lot size nearly doubled to 4,800 square feet. During this same period, the number of larger multisectional units in California housing parks increased 100 percent, to nearly half of the market. Furthermore, 80 percent of new mobile home sites being developed in the 1990s were "family projects." Most of the homes in these new projects had three or more bedrooms, a site-built two-car garage, a large front lawn and back patio, and used traditional building materials such as roof shingles and aluminum siding.

An important change taking place in trend-setting markets like California has been the profile of the mobile home operator. While most manufactured housing site operators in traditional markets such as the South are small operations, site owner/operators of newer developments are more likely to be larger, traditional tract housing developers. These developers use manufactured homes to reduce costs and speed product delivery in an effort to lure more traditional, and wealthy, home buyers. These communities differ from traditional mobile home parks because the homes are more permanent and are usually sold on-site.

Financial Markets. One factor expected to increase the popularity of mobile home communities during the 1990s is financial market activity that will provide easier financing for manufactured home buyers, as well as more capital for community owner/operators.

In the 1980s, The Government National Mortgage Association, The Federal National Mortgage Association, and the Federal Home Loan Mortgage Corporation all offered secondary markets where lenders could sell portfolios of mobile home loans. The secondary markets were only available for loans on houses that were permanently attached to their lot and were sold as one transaction. Throughout the 1990s, these secondary markets were expected to increase the popularity of larger, more modern mobile home parks that sell homes on-site.

Another source of financing for the mobile home park industry in the capital starved economic environment of the 1990s was locally sponsored tax-exempt bonds. Recognizing the need for affordable housing and the advantages that properly planned manufactured housing communities could deliver, cities increasingly tried to create a friendly political environment for mobile home operators. One way of doing this was to help owner/operators finance new developments that would serve the local community. Beside issuing tax-exempt bonds to finance new projects, some cities also eased zoning restrictions and created agencies to help residents in buying units and lots in mobile home developments.

A third source was the real estate investment trust (REIT). In 1992, real estate mogul Sam Zell arranged to sell a 64 percent stake in Manufactured Home Communities Inc., a Chicago operator of 40 mobile home parks in 16 states, as part of an REIT. Three other major operators of mobile home parks followed Manufactured Home Communities in forming REITs: ROC Communities Inc. of Englewood, Colorado; Sun Communities of Farmington Hills, Michigan; and Chateau Properties Inc. of Detroit, Michigan.

INDUSTRY LEADERS

Chateau Properties is a self-administered, self-managed real estate investment trust that owns, manages, and leases 47 manufactured-home communities with 20,003 sites in Florida, Michigan, Minnesota, Illinois, and North Dakota. Chateau also owns lands next to some of its communities containing an additional 1,495 expansion sites yet to be developed. Of the 43 properties, 36 have 200 or more sites, with the largest having 1,423 sites. Occupancy rates average more than 90 percent, with monthly rents averaging about $265.

In 1996, Chateau merged with ROC, forming the largest company in the manufactured-housing communities industry. Chateau executives said one the advantages of the merger would be geographic diversity, making the combined company less vulnerable to regional economic shifts. Also, ROC owned a lot of land that could be developed, allowing for expansion of the consolidated company. The merger was approved despite a lawsuit by Manufactured Homes trying to block the deal. Manufactured Homes had earlier bid $400 million for Chateau.

Sun Communities, Inc., a real estate investment trust, owns and operates 79 manufactured housing communities containing about 28,800 sites in eight states, primarily in the Midwest and Southeast. In addition, the company has nearly 2,000 potential expansion sites. The overall occupancy rate is more than 90 percent, with average rents of about $220 per site.

Other industry leaders included Ellenburg Capital Corp. of Clearwater, Florida, which generated sales of $52 million for the fiscal year ending June 30, 1995, according to the most recent information available on Infotrac. Outdoor Resorts of America Inc. of Nashville, Tennessee, generated $15 million in sales for its fiscal year ending March 31, 1999. Outdoor Resorts created its own niche in the market by catering to mobile vacationers traveling in recreational vehicles. Company president and CEO E. Randall Henderson Jr. predicted in 1996 that motor home resorts would grow 250 percent over the next decade. Outdoor Resorts already operated 16 such resorts, including its premiere $55 million Outdoor Resorts Palm Springs RV Country Club.

FURTHER READING

Crist, Dean. "Mobile Home Characteristics." *Housing Economics,* October 1995.

Easton, Thomas. "Real Estate for Bargain Hunters." *Forbes,* 17 June 1996.

Gargaro, Paul. "Home Free . . . Almost." *Crain's Detroit Business,* 30 September1996.

Goldenberg, Sherman. "Henderson Sees Growth in Motorhome Resorts." *RV Business,* June 1996.

Hoover, Gary, Alta Campbell, and Patrick J. Spain, eds. *Hoover's Handbook of American Business.* Emeryville, Calif.: Publishers Group West, 1995.

Infotrac Company Profiles, 22 December 1999. Available from http://web2.infotrac.galegroup.com.

Shilling, Gary A. "Home Sweet Factory-Built Home." *Forbes,* 12 February 1996.

SIC 6517

LESSORS OF RAILROAD PROPERTY

Establishments in this classification are primarily engaged in leasing railroad property.

NAICS CODE(S)

531190 (Lessors of Other Real Estate Property)

This industry consists of lessors of new and used rail car equipment (both single and double-stack), locomotives, and often, as part of the lease agreement, the refurbishment and maintenance of these items. Rail cars are categorized as grain cars (covered hopper cars most often carrying grain), boxcars, gondolas, and intermodal cars, which carry products in a trailer or container. Three types of leases are common: short (which includes per diem), middle, and long term.

Rail property lessors primarily provide transport of such commodities as grain; farm products; metallic ores; coal; crushed stone; nonmetallic minerals; grain mill products; food and kindred products; primary forest products; lumber and wood products, pulp, paper, and allied products; stone, clay, and glass products; military equipment; and waste and scrap materials.

The railroad industry is subject to complicated safety, environmental, structural, and financial regulations. A deregulation movement in the 1980s resulted in loosened restrictions that had a positive impact on the vigor of the leasing industry. Deregulation permitted negotiated, rather than statutory, freight rates and terms. This trend culminated in the abolition of the Interstate Commerce Commission (ICC) effective January 1, 1996; in the process some regulatory functions were eliminated altogether. Prior to 1996, the ICC was a key regulatory agency overseeing the industry; in its demise the remaining functions—those that were not abolished—reverted to the U.S. Department of Transportation. The Federal Railroad Administration within the Department of Transportation deals with safety issues surrounding the industry, rehabilitation of rail passenger services, consolidation of federal funding, and support of research and development. The Association of American Railroads, a trade organization, represents the interests of the vast majority of Class I railroads, including the leasing of railroad property, through legislative activity and support. The Equipment Leasing Association of America represents the equipment leasing and finance industry in general, including many railroad lessors.

Railroad property leasing is highly competitive, as lease agreements are often sought by several lessors. Competitive pricing strategies, technological advancements in equipment, and issues of the compatibility of advanced information systems are areas of competition among lessors. At the center of the financial health of railroad property leasing is a lively debate about whether railroads should lease or buy their own railcars and locomotives. Opponents of leasing tout the tax advantages of owning rail property. Lease proponents, however, cite the ability to use equipment without incurring additional long-term debt, as well as the lack of maintenance costs. Valuation issues also influence the industry; end-of-lease and early-buy-out prices determine if lease offerings are competitive against full purchase. A poor economy generally bodes well for railroad property lessors because railroads do not invest capital to buy new equipment in lean times. Primary competition to railroad property lessors comes from direct railroad equipment purchases, as well as from aircraft lessors, who experienced vulnerability to competition at the end of the 1990s because of failures on the part of the airline companies. Additionally, at the turn of the twenty-first century, expansion into foreign markets remained an option not fully explored. The passage of the North American Free Trade Agreement (NAFTA) combined with the privatization of the Mexican railroads presented fresh opportunity for a slumping U.S. railway economy to experience renewed growth.

A cyclical atmosphere propels the economy of the entire railroad industry. Thus, despite NAFTA, poor airline performance, and a vigorous U.S. economy in 1999, a cyclical downturn plagued the railroads. The normal tendency toward slowdown, combined with poor performance at the customer level brought the entire industry to an economic low. Blame for the situation went largely to poor on-time service by all major railroad lines. Yard congestion and disruptions of service attributed to persistent merger activity by the railroad companies, and poorly integrated computer systems contributed to the downturn. Loadings remained stagnant throughout 1998 and 1999. Only the rail fleet remained stable at 1.17 million cars in 1999, just under the 1996 peak of 1.2 million. Mergers characterized the industry at the turn of the century. Among the industry leaders, Westinghouse Air Brake and MotivePower merged late in 1999. The two corporations combined to offer a diverse assortment of railcar and locomotive component services. Two months later, in mid-January of 2000, The Greenbrier Companies Inc. of Lake Oswego, Oregon, expanded its European operations with the acquisition of the Freight Wagon Division of DaimlerChrysler Rail Systems GmbH of Berlin (Adtranz). The Greenbrier fleet included 33,000 cars, and the addition of DaimlerChrysler introduced an $82 million (U.S. dollars) catalog of wagons to Greenbrier's European selection.

Other prominent rail car and locomotive lessors include Chicago Freight Car Leasing Company of Rosemont, Illinois; First Union Rail, also of Rosemont; and GE Capital Railcar Services of Chicago.

FURTHER READING

''CFCLC History,'' 18 February 2000. Available from http://www.crdx.com/history.htm.

''Equipment Leasing Association of America Home Page.'' Equipment Leasing Association of America. March 1997. Available from http://www.elaonline.com/.

''Federal Railroad Administration Home Page.'' Federal Railroad Administration. March 1997. Available from http://www.fra.dot.gov/.

"First Union Rail," 18 February 2000. Available from http://www.firstunion.com/rail/.

"Freight Car Fleet Grew During Third Quarter." *Association of American Railroads Press Release,* 19 December 1996. Available from http://www.aar.org/.

"GE Capital Rail Services," 18 February 2000. Available from http://www.ge.com/capital/rail/whoweaare/rcwho.htm (February 18, 2000).

"Greenbrier Reports Increased Revenues, New Orders, and Purchase of Minority Interests." *PR Newswire,* 8 January 1997.

ICC Termination Act of 1995. Pub.L. No. 104-88, 109 *Stat,* 1 January 1996, 803.

Kruglinski, Anthony D. "1996 Guide to Equipment Leasing." *Railway Age,* July 1996.

"Railway Supply Industry," 18 February 2000. Available from http://www.rpi.org/supply.htm.

"Todays News—Greenbrier Completes Acquisition of Adtranz Freight Wagon Division." 24 January 2000, available from http://www.prnewswire.com/cgi-bin/stor...STORY=/www/story/01-24-2000/0001121434.

"Wall Street Transcript Publishes Special Railroad Stocks Report." *Yahoo! Finance,* 12 January 2000, available from http://biz.yahoo.com/prnews/000112/ny_twst_ra_1.html.

SIC 6519

LESSORS OF REAL PROPERTY, NOT ELSEWHERE CLASSIFIED

This category covers establishments primarily engaged in leasing real property, not elsewhere classified.

NAICS CODE(S)

531190 (Lessors of Other Real Estate Property)

The lessors of real property industry encompasses companies that own and lease, or only lease, to other organizations land used for airports, sports facilities, commercial timber operations, some types of lodging, and natural resource excavation. Industry participants typically do not engage in the enterprise conducted on their land. More than 12,000 establishments were engaged as lessors of real property in 1997. They employed some 37,620 employees and generated $5.54 billion in revenue.

Real estate lessors bring together owners of land and people who are looking for property on which to conduct a certain business activity. They benefit their clients by providing expertise about locating, appraising, and conveying legal rights to property. In contrast to real estate brokers, lessors arrange the conveyance of property rights for a limited time rather than permanently transfer ownership; however, lease agreements are often made for as long as 100 years.

Lessors in this industry are typically entrenched in a specific market niche. A company that specializes in leasing timberland, for example, would have knowledge of timber rights, tax codes, logging practices, and other factors specific to that industry. When it matches a land owner with a compatible lessee, the leasing company helps the two parties negotiate terms and secure a legally binding agreement. Land holding companies often find clients and handle lease arrangements themselves.

In addition to specializing by property function, many real estate lessors focus on one locale or region where they accrue an in-depth knowledge of local zoning codes, demographics, and land values. As a result of geographic and functional diversification, the industry is highly fragmented. In fact, most companies classified in this industry had fewer than 100 employees and sales of less than $10 million in the mid-1990s.

The real estate leasing industry saw rampant growth during the mid-twentieth century. Besides general economic expansion that boosted leasing activity, the emergence of eminent domain and other real property controls vastly increased the complexity of land rights and transactions. Likewise, property lessors enjoyed an unprecedented business boom during the mid-1980s. By the late 1980s, however, a virtual depression in most real estate sectors pummeled many industry participants. Going into the mid-1990s, most segments of the leasing industry were still trying to recover from continued economic malaise.

As the economy rebounded and interest rates remained low from 1993 through 1996, the real estate market in general also improved. Demand for most positions in the real estate industry increased and was expected to rise by 10 to 20 percent between 1994 and 2005, according to the Bureau of Labor Statistics. Demand was expected to be greatest for leasing agents with financial and computer skills. Although salaries varied by region and specialty, experienced property lessors in the mid-1990s typically earned commissions of $50,000 to $100,000 per year.

In 1995 and 1996, a series of large-scale leasing transactions reflected the positive economic outlook. When Denver opened its new $5 billion international airport, the older Stapleton Airport became the target of redevelopment that included short-term leasing agreements. The airport's 60 existing buildings (including offices, hangars and the terminal itself) were put on the leasing market in 1995, and a third of the 1.5 million square feet of space was quickly rented to new lessees. Incentives by the city, such as options for extensions of the short-term leases (limited to five years) and credits to tenants for making improvements, were a major enticement to potential tenants.

In 1996, the Cross Timbers Oil Company sold its Tyrone gas plant (spanning a field in Oklahoma and Kansas) to NationsBank Corporation and BancBoston Leasing Investments, Inc. for $28 million. The leasing companies then leased the plant back to Cross Timbers under an eight-year renewable lease. Cross Timbers seized on this lucrative opportunity in order to reduce the debt level it had accumulated earlier in the decade. Also in that year, Bethlehem Steel Corporation sold a major West Virginia coal mine to A.T. Massey Coal Company of Virginia. The sale to Massey, the fourth-largest U.S. coal producer, included mineral rights to the West Virginia mine as well as the leasing of other mining facilities. Another owner of mining land, United Park City Mines Company of Utah, no longer conducts mining operations itself but instead develops, leases, and sells Utah real estate. Over half of its 8,300 acres of surface land is leased to ski facilities.

A brief run-down of several companies indicates the breadth of the industry in the late 1990s. Airport Group International Inc. of California leases airport real estate and generated $250 million in operating revenue in 1998. Calcasieu Real Estate and Oil Company Inc. of Louisiana is a lessor of oil and gas mining property that garnered $897 million in operating revenue in 1998. Real estate leases generated $397 million in operating revenue for Miller-Valentine Group of Ohio in 1998. Leasing of coal fields generated $28 million in operating revenue for Pocahontas Land Corp. of West Virginia in 1997. Tulsa Metal Processing Co. of Arizona generated $15 million in sales in 1998 through the leasing of industrial land and offices.

FURTHER READING

"Beth Steel Sells West Virginia Coal Mine." *The Baltimore Sun,* 4 September 1996.

Byrd, Edward W. "Some Early Progress in the Long-Term Task of Putting Denver's Old Airport to New Uses." *The New York Times,* 30 August 1995.

Company profiles in General BusinessFile ASAP database.

"Cross Timbers Completes Sale-Leaseback of Hugoton Field Gas Gathering and Processing Facilities." *Southwest Newswire,* 3 April 1996.

Darnay, Arsen J., ed. *Finance, Insurance, and Real Estate, USA.* Detroit: Gale Research, 1996.

Occupational Outlook Handbook, 1996-1997 Edition. Washington: U.S. Department of Labor, 1996. Available from http://stats.bls.gov.

"Real Estate and Rental and Leasing—1997 Economic Census." U.S. Department of Commerce. Bureau of the Census. December 1999. Available from http://www.census.gov/prod/ec97/97f53-us.pdf.

"United Park City Mines Company." *Hoover's Company Capsules.* Available from http://www.hoovers.com.

SIC 6531

REAL ESTATE AGENTS AND MANAGERS

This classification includes establishments primarily engaged in renting, buying, selling, managing, and appraising real estate for others.

NAICS CODE(S)

531210 (Offices of Real Estate Agents and Brokers)
813990 (Other Similar Organizations)
531311 (Redidential Property Managers)
531312 (Nonresidential Property Managers)
531320 (Offices of Real Estate Appraisers)
812220 (Cemeteries and Crematories)
531390 (Other Activities Related to Real Estate)

INDUSTRY SNAPSHOT

Real estate agents and managers assist people who are purchasing, selling, leasing, financing and building places to live. The industry also includes agents and managers who work on commercial real estate, including high-rise office buildings, shopping centers, industrial plants, ranches, medical centers, museums, and theaters.

The real estate industry employs hundreds of thousands of full- and part-time workers in the United States, including real estate agents who assist buyers and sellers of property, mortgage brokers who assist with financing, leasing agents who lease residential and commercial real estate, property managers who manage the property of others, appraisers who analyze the fair market value of property, and developers who build new structures. In 1996, 124,500 establishments were involved in the area of real estate agents and managers, and 688,700 people were employed in the field in 1997.

The overall health of the real estate industry is closely intertwined with swings in the economy. As businesses grow, they generally acquire more real estate to expand their plants and hire more workers. The supply and demand of available homes, office buildings, and other real estate are strongly influenced by the availability of financing for developers who develop land into residential and business properties. Thus, during periods of tight credit and declining economic activity, real estate activity is low. Changes in tax laws and interest rates also have a great impact on the real estate industry.

ORGANIZATION AND STRUCTURE

Real estate is a service business involving a variety of professionals who act in concert to bring about the purchase, sale, financing, leasing, or construction of property. It could involve residential real estate, commercial real estate, industrial property, agricultural land, or vacant lots.

Real estate brokers or agents generally earn their income from commissions on the purchase, sale, or leasing of real estate. In most states, a real estate broker holds an advanced license and manages an office of real estate agents. The agents have less experience and work under the supervision of a broker. When the agent earns a commission, it is usually split between the agent and the supervising broker. The term ''realtor'' is a registered term belonging to the National Association of Realtors, and only brokers and agents who belong to the organization may use the term.

Homeowners usually consult one or more real estate agents when trying to sell a home. The agents will then discuss the price at which the property might sell, develop their plans for marketing the property, outline the strengths and weaknesses of the property, and determine how the property compares to other homes on the market. The seller will then select one agent to market the property and represent the seller's interests when it comes to negotiating a contract of sale. The agent and the seller will sign a contract authorizing the agent to act on behalf of the seller and market the property, in exchange for a specified commission upon the sale of the property. If a buyer is not found for the property, the agent will not receive any commission.

Likewise, buyers of residential real estate generally contact one or more agents to scout neighborhoods for homes fitting the buyers' requirements in terms of size, price, location, and amenities. The agent then represents the buyer in negotiating a contract and assists in obtaining inspections of the property by experts, such as structural and termite inspectors, and may assist the buyer in obtaining a mortgage loan.

Some real estate agents are relocation specialists and work primarily to assist individuals who are relocating to another geographic area. They must have extensive knowledge of school facilities and other neighborhood attributes in order to properly serve their clients. They are sometimes paid by an employer that is relocating its employees.

Commercial real estate agents work in a similar fashion when the purchase or sale of commercial property is contemplated. This could include nearly any type of property used in a business. But their knowledge must include those things of special concern to businesses, including available housing for employees, school facilities for employees' children, and the availability of an appropriate labor force.

Leasing commercial real estate is another area in which many real estate agents are employed, particularly in major metropolitan regions. The leasing agent's purpose is to keep the building fully occupied, while obtaining the highest possible rental rates. This job requires the agent to have a thorough knowledge of the rental rates in the local market and to keep abreast of anything that may affect the market. Local laws affecting real estate development and rent control laws have significant impact on the real estate market, and agents must also be knowledgeable of any changes in such laws.

Leasing procedures vary, but the agent generally receives a commission based on the total value of the lease. The longer the lease term the higher the commission. Office leases generally are for longer time periods than residential leases, often having a term of three to 15 years. The leasing agent must advertise the property and use every possible sales tool when leasing a brand new property, as it is important to the owner that the building be rented as quickly as possible without long exposure in the marketplace.

A large branch of the real estate industry involves managing property owned by others. Leasing commercial property is often one of the functions of a property manager. The modern-day property manager acts as an adviser and agent of the owner, and is primarily concerned with establishing rental rates, advertising and leasing the property, and negotiating leases. Property managers also collect rents; make sure that mortgages, taxes, insurance premiums, and other bills are paid; act as liaisons to tenants; and make sure the building is maintained in good working order. They supervise and hire the building staff and may contract for janitorial, engineering, security, and refuse services. They often do the bookkeeping for the property and prepare periodic financial reports for the owner. Owners of office buildings, shopping centers, apartments, and other income-producing properties usually hire a real estate firm to manage the property.

The appraisal of real estate values is a specialized segment of the real estate industry. An appraisal might be done to determine the value of a home that an individual wants to sell, or it may be done at the request of a lending institution which is considering providing a mortgage loan to a prospective buyer. Appraisers use accepted methods to determine the value of a piece of property and generally express an opinion on the fair market value, insurable value, or investment value of the property. Real estate appraisers visit the property, search public records and interview those with knowledge about the property and the surrounding community, taking into consideration the structural quality and overall condition of the property. Any trends in real estate or imminent changes in the community that could influence the value of the property are also taken into account when appraising the property. Many appraisers specialize in particular types of property, such as residential properties, commercial office buildings, or shopping centers.

CURRENT CONDITIONS

The real estate industry experienced strong growth during the last half of the 1990s, spurred by low interest rates for real estate loans. From the beginning of 1997 until the middle of 1998, home sales grew each quarter. More than 16 million existing single-family homes were sold in 1997. However, confidence in both the residential and commercial segments of the market began to drop in the second quarter of 1998. According to a survey by the Federal Deposit Insurance Corporation (FDIC), this change was largely attributed to assessments that conditions were unchanged from the previous quarter, rather than improving, as had been the case throughout the previous year. Expansion in the field responded to these trends, with 13 percent of residential real estate firms opening new offices in 1998, whereas only 3 percent shut down an office.

Like many other industries in the 1990s, the field of real estate agents and managers saw its share of acquisitions and mergers among the larger firms in the industry. Still, small local establishments remained the norm. In 1999, 83 percent of the firms in the field operated from only one office, and 60 percent of them had five or fewer agents. Only 22 percent of real estate establishments were affiliated with a regional or national franchising operation.

There also has been a strong move toward diversification of business activities, as well as toward providing services beyond those of the traditional agent/broker roles. Many of the largest real estate firms began offering their clients title insurance, mortgage loans, and similar extended services. Brokers and agents who represent only buyers of real estate also have been growing in numbers and are represented by the National Association of Exclusive Buyer Agents.

Real estate brokers have also benefited from using the latest in computer technology. Basic information about all of an agency's listings are routinely placed on office computers. In addition, real estate advertisements, complete with photographs and listing information, began to appear routinely on Internet sites in the mid-1990s. About 64 percent of residential real estate agencies had listings on REALTOR.COM, sponsored by the National Association of Realtors, in 1999.

INDUSTRY LEADERS

While real estate agencies tended to be local operations, a few national and multinational firms generated a large volume of business. Cendant Corporation was by far the largest corporation involved in the field, owning both Century 21 and Coldwell Banker, the number one and number three agencies in the field. Cendant generated $456 million in revenue through its real estate operations in 1998. RE/MAX Realty, based in Denver, also had a large presence, with more than 3,400 offices around the world.

WORKFORCE

Every state and the District of Columbia require that real estate brokers and agents be licensed. They must complete educational courses in the fundamentals of real estate and pass a written examination. Appraisers of property financed by federally regulated lenders must be certified within their states.

The real estate industry employed 408,000 agents, brokers and appraisers nationwide in full- and part-time employment in 1996. Most of these people worked on a commission or fee basis rather than as employees. Many real estate agents begin working part-time because of the intermittent income the work provided. Though agents were essentially independent contractors, most were affiliated with a nationally known or local brokerage firm.

As sales commissions can be high on many properties, successful real estate agents can earn large amounts of money. However, only a small percentage of agents actually do so. The median annual income for full-time agents, brokers, and appraisers was $31,500 in 1996. Half of these workers received between $20,500 and $49,700. The number of agents, brokers, and appraisers employed was expected to grow more slowly than other occupations through 2006. Still, 778,500 people were expected to be working in the field by then, an increase of nearly 90,000 from 1997. Opportunities also exist in this area due to the high turnover, which is characteristic of the profession.

There were approximately 271,000 real estate managers in 1996, most working for property management firms, development companies, banks, government agencies, and other entities. There also was a large group of self-employed developers, owner-managers of buildings, and operators of building management firms. Approximately 40 percent of property managers were self-employed in 1996. No formal certification or licensing was required except for managers of federally subsidized housing, who had to be state-certified. Many other managers completed training programs that included certification by the sponsoring organization, such as the Institute of Real Estate Management (IREM).

Median annual earnings of all property and real estate managers were $28,500 in 1996. Half of these people had an annual income of between $19,000 and $39,800. Growth in this field was expected to be average through 2006. Increased demand for managers was expected in commercial and residential real estate, as trade continued to expand and new housing construction continued the trend of creating homeowner associations for residents. Employers of real estate managers were expected to increasingly turn to hiring college graduates with degrees in business administration and fields related to real estate.

AMERICA AND THE WORLD

The U.S. real estate industry was tapping the market within the former Communist countries of eastern Europe, such as Russia and Hungary, where ownership of private property became legal. Beginning in 1993, the IREM began to enter into partnerships with real estate associations in those countries to help in training of real estate personnel and adoption of national standards. By mid-1996, there were 28 such partnerships in effect. The IREM also had partnership arrangements in Canada, Mexico, Singapore, and Spain. The National Association of Realtors was conducting similar activities in eastern Europe, and entered into agreements with five countries—Bulgaria, the Czech Republic, Hungary, Poland, and Russia—at its annual convention in 1996. In addition to industry-wide efforts such as these, individual firms were entering the real estate markets of other countries. In 1998 Coldwell Banker began entering into franchise arrangements with brokers and agencies in Mexico.

FURTHER READING

Bivins, Ralph. ''Texas Coldwell Banker to Lead Expansion Into Mexico.'' *Knight-Ridder/Tribune Business News,* 27 March 1998.

Bureau of Labor Statistics, U. S. Department of Labor. *Occupational Outlook Handbook, 1998-99 Edition.* Washington, DC: U. S. GPO, 1998.

''Cendant Corporation.'' *Hoover's Online.* Austin, TX: Hoover's, 1999.

Cremeans, John E., ed. *Handbook of North American Industry.* Washington, DC: Bernan Press, 1999.

Heath, Tracy, and Carrie King. ''Brokers Speak Out: Sixty Professionals Tell Us How the Business Is Changing.'' *National Real Estate Investor,* April 1996.

''Is Bigger Better for Brokerages?'' *Chain Store Age Executive with Shopping Center Age,* August 1997.

Lazich, Robert S., ed. *Market Share Reporter 1997.* Detroit: Gale Research, 1997.

Litke, Ronald. ''The Institute of Real Estate Management Delves into International Markets.'' *National Real Estate Investor,* September 1996.

National Association of Realtors. *The 1999 National Association of Realtors Profile of Real Estate Firms.* Washington, DC: The National Association of Realtors, 1999. Available from http://www.onerealtorplace.com.

Timmons, Heather. ''No Toes Too Tender for This Lobbyist; Former HUD Official Battles Curbs to Realty Alliances.'' *The American Banker,* 24 January 1997.

———. ''Realtors Looking Abroad for Growth Opportunities.'' *The American Banker,* 20 November 1996.

U. S. Bureau of the Census. *Statistical Abstract of the United States: 1999.* Washington, DC: U. S. Bureau of the Census, 1999. Available from http://www.census.gov.

''You May Save Big Bucks by Hiring a Buyer-Broker.'' *Money,* June 1996.

SIC 6541

TITLE ABSTRACT OFFICES

This category covers establishments primarily engaged in searching real estate titles. This industry does not include title insurance companies, which are classified in **SIC 6361: Title Insurance.**

NAICS CODE(S)

541191 (Title Abstract and Settlement Offices)

Title examiners, also known as title abstractors, are responsible for researching, analyzing, and evaluating the legal ownership or title to real property. Whenever real estate is bought, sold, or financed, a search of title records is required to ascertain all persons who may claim legal ownership in the property. A title search may also be required to fulfill the terms of a will in distributing property, to subdivide land into smaller parcels, or to obtain a building permit. Persons who acquire land generally want to purchase property that is free from competing claims of ownership, delinquent taxes, and other legal headaches that can devalue the investment. Even buyers who purchase land despite such potential problems generally want to be made aware of any defects in the chain of title when making a bid. Title examiners review the chain of title for a number of defects, including liens on the property, easements, rights of way, water and mineral rights, and other encumbrances. Title examiners are typically employed by title insurance companies, land development companies, and state and local governments.

The common practice of recording real estate transactions with an official recorder or registrar began in colonial Massachusetts and quickly spread across the country. Every state now keeps some form of public record that identifies formally documented property rights. In some states county governments are charged with the duty of maintaining official property records, while in other states municipal governments have been given the responsibility. But almost every locality categorizes and indexes the information in a slightly different fashion. Title abstracts are prepared to reflect these public records, often by the examiner himself. Title examiners then usually search the chain of title from the most recent owners to the oldest. When there is a gap in the public records, examiners must do additional investigative work to complete the chain of title.

Additional investigation may include a search through miscellaneous public filings that could cloud title to land, including records relating to marriage, divorce, birth, adoption, and other legal proceedings. Plat drawings, metes and bounds descriptions, land books, and zoning ordinances may also help title examiners in completing a chain of title and removing possible defects. After the search has been completed and all documents reviewed, title examiners prepare a title report that describes the property's legal title and lists any existing encumbrances, competing rights, or conflicting claims. Title examiners occasionally assist in preparing a legal description for property as well.

The total number of title examiners and searchers was approximately 28,000 in the mid-1990s. The employment outlook for title examiners is expected to experience little change through the year 2005. The number of real estate sales and increasingly complex real estate transactions is also expected to fuel an increased demand for practitioners. Training is typically acquired on the job, and lasts between one and two months. Despite this seemingly short apprenticeship, the industry has been under pressure to improve standardization.

The American Land Title Association (ALTA) is the primary professional organization in the industry, with more than 2,400 members, sales of approximately $3.7 million, and a net worth of $6.2 million in 1997. ALTA members include title insurance agencies, title examiners, and attorneys. Based in Washington, D.C., ALTA and its members are also involved in numerous other aspects of the residential real estate business. They provide credit reports, escrow services, flood certifications, and relocation services.

All four of the nation's leading title insurance companies have created title examination divisions: First American Title Insurance Co., LandAmerica Financial Group, Chicago Title Corp., and Fidelity National Title each reported profitable title examination operations in 1999, which contributed to the strength of the industry as a whole as it entered the new millennium. These title companies were also searching for other ways to expand their businesses, developing profit centers for a better bottom line, adding appraisal services, and increasing automation.

But not all expansion in the industry has been encouraged by the government. Certain proposed mergers and acquisitions have raised federal antitrust concerns. In 1996 Commonwealth Land Title Insurance Company proposed to consolidate its title plant operations in the District of Columbia with those of First American Title Insurance, its only competitor in the market. The next year Commonwealth terminated existing contracts with customers and required them to sign interim deals under which they would pay higher prices for title services. In 1998 the Federal Trade Commission (FTC) issued an order in response to the proposed joint venture. The FTC compelled Commonwealth to rescind all the interim deals, make refunds to customers who were overcharged, and provide services to customers based on the prices, terms, and conditions available before November 1997. Commonwealth was also required to relocate its operations and maintain them as a fully functional title plant in competition with First American.

FURTHER READING

Adams, Susan. ''Backlash.'' *Forbes,* 25 March 1996.

Cohn, Steven. ''NC State Bar May Set New Limits for Independents.'' *Legal Assistant Today,* January/February 1996.

Federal Trade Commission News Release. ''Washington, DC-Based Title Plant Agrees to Settle FTC Charges,'' 26 August 1998.

Jennings, Marianne M. ''The Evolving Nature of Title Insurance as a Contract: Removing the Notions of Panacea.'' *Real Estate Law Journal,* Winter 1997.

———. ''Title Insurers Embrace Change for a Better Future.'' *National Real Estate Investor,* December 1996.

———. ''Will Economy, Politics Spell Better in 1996?'' *National Real Estate Investor,* May 1996.

Selinger, Marc. ''Joint Venture of Title Plants Dissolved to Satisfy FTC''.*Washington Times,* 27 August 1998.

U.S. Bureau of the Census Web Site. http://www.census.gov. December 1999.

U.S. Department of Commerce Web Site. http://www.doc.gov. December 1999.

U.S. Department of Labor Web Site. http://www.dol.gov. December 1999.

SIC 6552

LAND SUBDIVIDERS AND DEVELOPERS, EXCEPT CEMETERIES

This category includes establishments primarily engaged in subdividing real property into lots, except cemetery lots, and in developing it for resale on their own account.

NAICS CODE(S)

233110 (Land Subdivision and Land Development)

INDUSTRY SNAPSHOT

Real estate development is a multifaceted industry. It includes the purchase of vacant or raw land, its subdivision into small parcels, and the construction of residential single-family houses, condominiums, or apartment buildings. It includes construction of retail shopping centers, industrial plants and warehouses, office buildings, schools, prisons, hospitals, and almost any type of structure. Additionally, it includes the renovation or restoration of warehouses to loft apartments or offices and the construction of parking garages. Generally land development and subdivision falls into three categories: rural, urban, and suburban.

In the twenty-first century, land developers coordinate a battery of activities necessary to carry out the development of land into useable space. Developers typically purchase a tract of land, devise a building program, obtain government approvals and financing, and then set about to have the structures built. After the building is complete, the developer may sell all or part of the property, or keep it on account and manage the property by leasing space to tenants. There are nearly as many different scenarios as there are developers. Successful development firms operate under a variety of paradigms, including that of niche developer, such as Francesco Galesi of the Galesi Group. Galesi, a global corporation, developed 900 million square feet of space in the twentieth century. Galesi purchased the land from the General Service Administration (GSA) of the United States government and developed the acreage into strategically located distribution centers for military supply depots, some capable of holding 20 or more railroad cars. The company's operating cash flow exceeded $12 million annually by the end of the 1990s. Likewise, industry leader Simon Property Group grew to lead the real estate industry in North America by the end of the twentieth century through extensive investment in the shopping mall arena.

Among the leading developers' associations, the 15,000-member Urban Land Institute encourages effective urban planning and studies new area development.

BACKGROUND AND DEVELOPMENT

Real estate development in the 1990s underwent a dramatic change from previous decades. Several factors spurred long-range change in the real estate development industry, including a severe economic recession in the early 1990s that affected many geographic regions of the United States. In 1991 a Census Bureau study found that 57 percent of all families were unable to afford a median-priced home in their community, a circumstance that led developers to increase construction of apartments and other multiple dwellings over single-family residences. Beginning in 1993 an overall surge in the American economy and growth in housing starts enabled developers to obtain financing and accomplish this purpose. Also at issue were the overbuilding of office and commercial space in many U.S. markets and tax changes stemming from the Tax Reform Act of 1986 affecting the desirability of real estate as an investment vehicle. A crisis in the savings and loan industry, associated with a record number of bank failures aggravated the situation. Restrictive lending policies emerged as a result of government intervention. New policies and increased government regulation affected the time and cost involved in obtaining government approvals.

Thus, land subdivision and development is a highly speculative industry involving complex processes. Subdividers and developers incur both fixed and variable costs in the process of creating single-property lots for individual sale from large parcels of acreage. It is the ability of the developer to absorb all costs within a reasonable margin that determines the success of each respective venture. Developers fund not only the variable development costs to prepare the individual lots for retail sale, but also the many fixed costs associated with the building of streets, sewage conduits, and other elements critical to the infrastructure of the development. Additionally there are government levies for extended infrastructure costs. These assessments, called development contributions or ''impact fees,'' contribute further to the cost of development.

For assistance with crucial cost determinations, subdividers turn to professional appraisers, yet the element of risk cannot be underestimated. Through careful analysis of the total costs of development in comparison to the potential retail value per lot, development firms speculate on an amount of land to purchase—based on salability—and develop accordingly, in order to maximize profit. Market survey results often provide indicators of the potential retail sale price of each. Surveys and investigations provide additional data regarding the existence of competing projects in the immediate geographical area, along with the potential impact of such projects. Overall, the timeliness of a proposed construction project figures keenly into the risk assessment, as does the creativity of the developer in designing a salable residential or business community. After comprehensive appraisal of risk and cost factors, the subdevelopment process moves into the hands of lenders. With appropriate financing, the subdivision project becomes a matter of civic and legal issues, and the process of obtaining approvals and licensing ensues before construction begins.

Construction and Sale as a Function of Property Development. The actual construction of the subdivided lots is crucial to the development process. Subdividers and land developers commonly include home and office construction within the scope of their respective business operations. Likewise many developers support sales, leasing, and property management services for convenience and to expedite the development process. In a report in *Appraisal Journal,* Professor Robert Owens of Southeast Missouri State University in Springfield intimated that the developer's ability to presell lots and to build a significant proportion of the developed lots might be a crucial factor contributing to the success of a development. Marketing is a key aspect of the development process. Most states do not require developers to hold real estate licenses, but marketing of the property, particularly to out-of-state buyers, must conform to state guidelines regardless. According to Owens, convenient access to a sales force frequently enhanced the developer's potential for success on a venture.

Syndication. Some development arrangements, called syndication, involve groups of individual investors who pool their money. Investors sometimes contribute to a development venture in exchange for part ownership of the developed property, while others act strictly as lenders. A real estate specialist, called a *syndicator,* sponsors or manages the syndicate and maintains an active role in overseeing development of the project. The function of syndication commonly overlaps with the role of the developer.

CURRENT CONDITIONS

Causes for Concern. In the late 1990s, ongoing expansion by developers into rural areas raised concerns about the rapid conversion of rich farmland into "tar and cement," especially in the American Northeast where American Farmland Trust, an activist group, attracted media attention to the circumstance. Also of concern was the alleged destruction of historic Iroquois villages in order to claim land for residential subdivisions in New York and Canada. In defense of developers, the Ohio Home builders Association refuted such claims, noting that the amount of land taxed at agricultural rates actually increased for four years during the 1990s. A mounting crisis condition, called urban sprawl, nonetheless plagued communities and developers alike. Such growth was typified at Sioux Falls, South Dakota, which experienced rapid growth during the late twentieth century. The population increased from 72,000 in 1970 to 116,000 in 1996. During the same period the total urban area increased from 27 square miles to 50 square miles, and by the year 2015 projections held that the community would grow to support a population of 156,000.

Increasingly commonplace as a means to combat the rapid encroachment of urbanization on farmland was the implementation of urban growth boundaries (UGB) that confined developers to operate within strict geographical boundaries. The UGB system, originally supported by the National Association of Home Builders (NAHB), lost favor in time, as the practice led to tight housing markets,

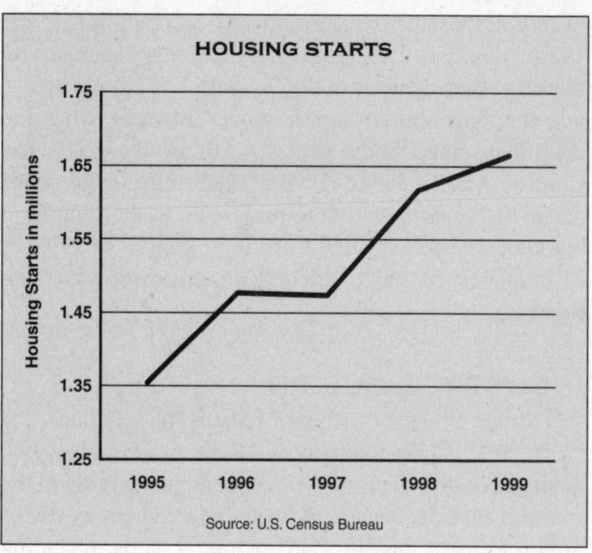

with skyrocketing costs for new homes. As land prices tripled in some urban areas, while UGB restrictions remained firm, buyers moved into outlying areas, exacerbating rather than alleviating the condition of sprawl, and generating long-range traffic congestion in the process. The development community responded to the crisis with smaller lot sizes, increased pressure to expedite boundary expansion, and increased cooperation toward devising new solutions. Also active in the ongoing efforts to find new solutions are the California Building Industry Association (CBIA) and American Planning Association (APA). Areas of particular concern to NAHB in the late 1990s as a result of UGB restrictions included Portland, Oregon; Washington, D.C.; and Boulder, Colorado. Likewise, in California, builders reported that only 130,000 homes could be built each year in a market capable of supporting 250,000.

Also of concern was significant overdevelopment of property, both commercial and residential, throughout the 1990s. Of greatest concern were specific situations in Texas, Georgia, and Illinois. In Dallas, Texas, developers continued with new expansion, despite rising office vacancies that approached 20 percent in mid-1999 along the Dallas North Tollway, up from 9 percent in the prior year. Also, in Illinois, one Chicago suburb reported new construction vacancy rates as high as 15 percent. Analysts expressed similar apprehension regarding specific locations in Atlanta, Georgia, and Houston, Texas. Concerns in Atlanta focused on a reported 17 percent office vacancy rate along a major highway corridor near the northern suburb of Buckhead. Additionally, the Houston, Texas, district known as the "energy corridor" suffered from waning demand for office space through the end of the 1990s, as an ongoing reaction to an earlier oil bust in the 1980s.

Optimistic Prognosis. Ongoing issues notwithstanding, building conditions in the 1990s and at the turn of the twenty-first century were improved over conditions in the 1980s. Based on U.S. Bureau of the Census statistics on housing starts, January of 2000—with 1,775,000 starts—was the third highest month in over 20 years, when the monthly average for the year was 2,020,000 in 1978. The Housing Market Index (HMI), which reflects the confidence of the home-building profession in the long-term market, increased steadily from 38 in January of 1995, to 71 in January of 2000, with only minor slowdowns along the way.

Industry Leaders

Simon Property Group of Indianapolis, Indiana, the largest real estate company in North America in 1999, managed over 240 properties, concentrated largely in the states of Florida, New York, and Texas. The majority of Simon Property holdings are shopping malls, including the largest mall in the United States, Minnesota's Mall of America. Simon purchased Corporate Property Investors in 1998 for 33.5 percent growth and that year reported revenues of $1.433 billion. Prior to 1998 General Growth Properties was the largest development company, following as the result of its acquisition of Homart.

Another major force in real estate development, with 11 percent ownership of Simon Property Group, is the Edward J. DeBartolo Corporation. This firm, started in 1948 by Edward DeBartolo in Youngstown, Ohio, is a leading builder and operator of enclosed shopping malls across the nation. DeBartolo's 76 million square feet of mall space makes up nearly 10 percent of all mall space in the country and is visited by 40 million customers each week. In addition, the company develops and operates office buildings, hotels, and office parks. Other holdings include the San Francisco 49ers football team, the Pittsburgh Penguins hockey team, and horse racing tracks in Ohio, Oklahoma, and Louisiana. DeBartolo had a keen foresight with regard to real estate trends. He foresaw the exodus to the suburbs in the 1950s and capitalized on it by developing suburban shopping centers. In the 1960s he anticipated the coming real estate boom in Florida and purchased large tracts of land there. When the boom hit, the company had one-third of its holdings in Florida. DeBartolo Realty pursued a strategy of developing one mall every year, diversified further into entertainment ventures, and went public with its real estate investment trust (REIT) in 1994. Upon his death in December of 1995, founder Edward J. DeBartolo Sr. left a diversified corporation of malls, race tracks, river boat casinos, and sports teams, although future growth was temporarily stymied over matters of probate that endured into the twenty-first century.

Trammell Crow Company, based in Dallas, Texas, is one of the nation's largest real estate developers. Its $14 billion portfolio of owned and managed properties approaches 300 million square feet of commercial properties in the United States, with 350 office buildings in 50 cities, 90,000 residential units, 35 hotels, and 160 shopping centers. Crow began his illustrious real estate career in Dallas shortly after World War II. An accountant who earned his degree in night school, he became successful when he joined with the Stemmons brothers, and together they built more than 50 warehouses in Dallas in the 1940s. Crow had a knack for anticipating the needs of the market and adding building amenities that appealed to his tenants. He formed partnerships with other developers and shared incentives and rewards generously with his partners. In fact, the Trammell Crow Company built a reputation not only as a skilled developer, but also as an incubator for smaller developers. Nonetheless, in the early 1990s the depressed real estate market affected even Trammell Crow Company. Problems in the Southwest forced the company to refinance 150 properties in 1990, and new construction totaled only $500 million in 1991, down from $2.2 billion in 1985. By 1999 the company rebounded, maintaining 158 offices worldwide, including Canada, Europe, Asia, and South America. With 5,100 employees in 1999, Trammel Crow Company earned revenues totaling $628.4 million for a 36.7 percent sales growth.

Catellus Development Corporation headquartered in San Francisco, California, is the largest private landholder in that state. Catellus's holdings are spread throughout the western United States. The company oversees its holdings under its property management firm, Catellus Commercial Group, and separately operates the Catellus Residential Group as a development corporation, under the auspices of a REIT. Catellus holds an estimated 15.5 million square feet of income property, 5,400 acres of land leases, and 854,000 acres of land. In 1999 Catellus reported $172.3 million in sales, for a growth rate of 15.3 percent.

Workforce

Land subdivision and development requires complex entrepreneurial skills and a solid knowledge base in many disciplines. Developers work with experts in many fields, including architects, builders, planners, financiers, attorneys, urban government and inspection personnel, community representatives, and investment partners. Developers must additionally acquire a thorough knowledge of every local community associated with a development venture, including the local political machinery, local economy, and local real-estate markets. Local policy shifts and economy swings might effect any development project to a dramatic degree; successful developers respond with flexibility, shifting strategies abruptly in order to insure the ultimate viability of any project. Successful developers must be skilled at problem solving, which is the essence of development. They must have a clear vision and a penchant for minute details—the omission of appropriate soil tests or the wrong clause in a title insurance policy can devastate an undertaking. As master planners, developers absorb ultimate responsibility for any mistakes associated with a development project.

AMERICA AND THE WORLD

Foreign real estate investment in the United States in the late 1900s was partly to blame for the overbuilding of commercial office space. Experts agreed that the U.S. economy might be several years in absorbing the many vacant office buildings in U.S. metropolitan areas, a situation further aggravated by the increasing number of U.S. companies that shifted manufacturing operations overseas, further reducing demand for domestic facilities.

Elsewhere in the world, global real-estate development occurred rapidly. Currency, regulatory, and logistics—as opposed to market demand—comprised the most significant obstacles for developers, as market risk virtually vanished. Sites in North Africa and Asia were among the more lucrative markets for land development at the turn of the twenty-first century, with the Asian nations among the most accommodating to foreign investment. In Hong Kong, residential prices rose 25 percent in the late 1990s, causing the government to seek promises from developers to concentrate on residential development over commercial sites. In the Philippines, a rapidly expanding economy resulted in a proliferation of U.S.-style residences in a near risk-free market. Capital infusions from the International Monetary Fund (IMF) to alleviate financial crises on the Asian continent further contributed to a growing interest in the Far Eastern economies on the part of astute developers. Continued restrictions meanwhile prevailed in the Arabian countries in the form of strict licensing controls on the construction and engineering trades, a condition that served to enhance the appeal of the less restrictive Asian sector.

South Korea, which revitalized its economy during the second half of the twentieth century, grew to constitute the eleventh-largest economy worldwide, but subsequently fell prey to the vestiges of a monetary crisis in nearby Asian countries at the end of 1996 and throughout 1997. In an effort to encourage long-term capital flow into the country and to revitalize the waning won, South Korea, like other Asian nations, embraced liberal trade policies and opened development arenas to foreign investment. Early in 1998 the seaport city of Inchon, near Seoul, announced its intent to establish an international free-trade city, open to foreign development, for the purpose of increasing industrial and distribution complexes. Also the ancient city of Taegu in South Korea's North Kyongsang Province announced in mid-1998 a plan to encourage foreign development at industrial sites within the city limits. The program permitted foreign investors to purchase and develop land for subsequent sale or lease. Taegu further proffered subsidy guarantees to foreign investors who might undertake tollways and highway bridge-construction projects.

Also hit hard by the financial crisis of the late 1990s, Malaysia rebounded late in 1999 and into the year 2000 with an upsurge in development on a variety of fronts. Sunway Masalam Sdn Berhad, a subsidiary of Sunway Holdings Incorporated, signed an agreement on December 30, 1999, to build an expansive golf resort in Selangor, including both residential and commercial property developments, to be known as the Serendah Golf Resort. The planned development, to be surrounded by condominiums and commercial areas, was scheduled for completion in 2007. Rapid growth in nearby Kuala Selangor on the Strait of Malacca led that town to adopt a program of planned progress, in order to ensure that new development in that arena might proceed over a widespread area, and in particular to abate imminent overdevelopment in the valley town of Kelang. The city's planned growth allowed development to proceed throughout various locations in Kuala Selangor, Bukit Belimbing, Puncak Alam, and other locales. SAP Holdings Berhad and Golden Hope Berhad were among the prominent developers named as participants in the project. Also scheduled for controlled development were certain locations in the vicinity of Penang. In nonurban development, Kwantas Corporation announced an undertaking early in 2000 in conjunction with Indonesian PT Agronesia Makmur Sentosa, to develop oil-palm plantations from existing timberland on both the Indonesian and Malaysian sections of the large island.

RESEARCH AND TECHNOLOGY

In Houston, Texas, the Land Tejas Company, in collaboration with IBM Corporation, made bold strides into the age of computers by creating ''intelligent neighborhoods.'' In developing new communities such as its Stone Gate development, Land Tejas and IBM took technology one step father than simple prewired Internet access for the new homes. Instead, the development partners designed the building specifications to include the installation of Category 5 telephone wire and RG6 cabling at the subdivision, in order to connect the homes via a professionally architected community intranet. The intranet at Stone Gate, scheduled to go live early in 1999, provides homebuyers with on-line access to immediate traffic conditions for their neighborhood, as well as with weather and communications links to local school administrations. After work and school, and during inclement weather, Stone Gate residents ''camp in'' with video-on-demand and Internet access through their neighborhood backbone cable. Home owners at Stone Gate make restaurant reservations online, collect electronic coupons for use at local retailers, and enjoy other conveniences at an estimated cost of $1,000 per home for the cabling, plus an additional $1,000 per home for the IBM Internet connector center.

FURTHER READING

"1998 Country Reports on Economic Policy and Trade Practices," submitted to the Congress by the U.S. Department of State, 31 January 1999. Available from http://www.state.gov/www/issues/economic/trade_reports/98_toc.html.

"A City of the Future." *Business Korea,* July 1998.

Bady, Susan. "Urban Growth Boundary Found Lacking." *Professional Builder,* September 1998.

Bangsbert, P. T. "South Korea Plans Free-trade City to Draw Foreign Capital to Inchon." *Journal of Commerce and Commercial,* 29 April 1998.

Barker, Heather. "Trammell Crow Scored with Complex Buy." *Archive: Atlanta Business Chronicle,* 10 March 1997. Available from http://www.amcity.com/atlanta/stories/031097/focus36.html.

"Call for Council to Develop Wakaf Land." *New Straits Times,* 9 November 1999.

"Catellus Development Corporation." *Hoover's Online,* 2 March 2000. Available from http://www.hoovers.com/co/capsule/6/0,2163,14176,00.html.

"Edward J. DeBartolo Corporation." *Hoover's Online,* 25 February 2000. Available from http://www.hoovers.com/co/capsule/9/0,2163,40142,00.html.

Encyclopedia of Associations. 32nd ed. Detroit: Gale Research, 1997.

Fagan, Brian. "A Finite Iroquoian Legacy." *Archeology,* September 1996.

Fischel, William A. "Limit the Size of Residential Lots." *American Enterprise,* November 1996.

Fitch, Stephane. "The Great Suburban Overbuild." *Forbes,* 6 September 1999.

"Growth Explodes in Rural Colorado." *Knight-Ridder Newspapers,* 21 March 1997.

Hazel, Debra. "Megamergers Hit the Mall." *Chain Store Age,* May 1996.

"Housing Starts: 1978-1999." *National Association of Home Builders,* 23 February 2000. Available from http://www.nahb.com/facts/forecast/starts.htm.

Johnson, Ben. "Simon DeBartolo Merger: The Start of Something Big?" *National Real Estate Investor,* May 1996.

"Join the Queue." *Economist,* 18 January 1997.

"Kwantas to Develop Land in Indonesia." *Business Times,* 14 February 2000.

"Lessons from the New No. 2." *National Real Estate Investor,* May 1996.

Marriott, Cherie. "Developers Turn to Lucrative Mass Housing Market." *Asia Money. The Philippines Back in the Spotlight Supplement,* March 1996.

McCrary, Ernest. "The New Land Rush." *Global Finance,* September 1996.

McLeister, Dan. "With 854,000 Acres, Catellus Becomes a Big Player in California." *Professional Builder,* September 1996.

———. "Builders sell technology." *Professional Builder,* 1 January 1999.

Owens, Robert W. "Subdivision Development: Bridging Theory and Practice." *Appraisal Journal,* July 1998.

"Reforestation in Amazon Revealed by Satellites." *Futurist,* September 1996.

"RM20bil to Develop Land in Selangor." *New Straits Times,* 12 September 1999.

Robbins, Anthony W. "Historic Preservation and Planning." *Journal of the American Planning Association,* Winter 1995.

Satchell, Michael. "To the Rescue at Yellowstone." *U.S. News & World Report,* 26 August 1996.

"Simon Property Group, Inc." *Hoover's Online,* 25 February 2000. Available from http://wwww.hoovers.com/co/capsule/2/0,2163,16582,00.hml.

"Sioux Falls is Growing Like a Tree, But Does It Need Pruning?" *Fedgazette,* October 1996.

Stodghill II, Ron. "Simon Says: Grow." *Business Week Industrial/Technology Edition,* 15 April 1996.

"Trammell Crow Company." *Hoover's Online,* 3 March 2000. Available from http://www.hoovers.com/co/capsule/9/0,2163,40469,00.html.

U.S. Department of Commerce. Economics and Statistics Administration. Bureau of Economic Analysis. *Statistical Abstract of the United States 1996.* 116th ed. Washington, D.C.: GPO, 1996.

Voight, Joan. "EvansGroup Offices Share Mall Client." *Adweek Western Edition,* 18 November 1996.

Watkins, Andrew R. "Impacts of Land Development Charges." *Land Economics,* August 1999.

Yamin, Mary S. "Galesi Group Finds Success with Industrial Parks." *Archive: Capital District Business Review,* 3 March 1997. Available from http://www.amcity.com/albany/stories/030397/focus3.html.

SIC 6553

CEMETERY SUBDIVIDERS AND DEVELOPERS

This industry includes establishments primarily engaged in subdividing real property into cemetery lots, and developing it for resale on their own account.

NAICS CODE(S)

812220 (Cemeteries and Crematories)

According to industry estimates, there are 75,000 to 100,000 cemeteries in the United States. These vary in size from small plots in churchyards to huge national military cemeteries. Cemeteries may be run on a profit or not-for-profit basis. Traditional cemeteries have upright monuments, usually made of stone, and may also include private mausoleums for above-ground internment. Memorial parks, in contrast, have no tombstones, but rather bronze memorials placed level to the ground; they often have fountains, sculpture, or memorial architecture.

Natural preserve cemeteries protect and restore land, and offer natural burials also known as ''green'' burials. According to Memorial Ecosystems, Inc., they established their first nature preserve cemetery, Ramsey Creek Preserve, in South Carolina in 1998. According to Pam Kelley of the *Charlotte Observer*, Memorial Ecosystems offers ''green'' burials and only allows biodegradable caskets made of wood or cardboard and does not allow embalming.

In 1997, a small but growing percentage of cemeteries were run by large, publicly traded firms known as ''consolidators,'' which have operations in many states and several countries. These firms benefit from economies of scale that result from owning several funeral homes and cemeteries in a single area—a central embalming location, a limousine motor pool, and a team of personnel that can serve facilities in a given region. The companies have also built some funeral homes in or near cemeteries, which offer customers greater convenience.

The largest of the consolidators is Service Corporation International (SCI), which in 1996 had 331 cemeteries and 2,832 funeral homes, with total revenues of $1.6 billion. The second largest, Loewen Group, Inc., had 265 cemeteries and 814 funeral homes, and total revenue of $600 million. Both firms have been the target of strong criticism by some consumer groups, who question their prices and business practices. The companies claim that errors are no more likely to be made by consolidators than other funeral operations, and that their prices are reasonable.

The financial community views the industry more favorably. As Susan R. Little, an analyst with Raymond James & Associates, told *National Real Estate Investor* in 1996, ''There's amazing opportunity in death care because it is very fragmented, and there are sufficient barriers to entry.'' She added that the industry is recession resistant, and that death rates are expected to climb with the aging of the ''Baby Boomers.'' Since the six largest death care facilities own fewer than 20 percent of the funeral homes and cemeteries in the United States, the opportunity to acquire businesses that have been typically family-owned and operated is substantial.

Much of the growth of the large firms has come from the sale of ''preneed'' contracts, where customers make funeral and burial arrangements for themselves. At the end of 1995, SCI alone had $2.3 billion in contracts for prearranged funerals. In some states, preneed policies were tax-exempt, and thus practically served as tax shelters. Cemetery owners were also becoming more aggressive in their marketing of cemetery plots, with campaigns like the ''buy one plot, get a second one for a penny,'' mounted by one owner.

FURTHER READING

Cemeteries and Memorial Parks. Falls Church, VA: American Cemetery Association.

Ciandella, Donald. ''Investors Take Swings at Unusual Property Niches and Expect Home Runs.'' *National Real Estate Investor,* July 1996.

Kelley, Pam. ''A Simpler Way to Go.'' *The Charlotte Observer,* 6 July 1999. Available from http://www.charlotte.com/observer/0706family.htm.

Larson, Erik. ''Fight to the Death.'' *Time,* 9 December 1996.

''Memorial Ecosystems Establishes Ramsey Creek Preserve.'' *Memorial Ecosystems, Inc.,* 21 February 1998. Available from http://www.memorialecosystems.com/Rcpressrelease.htm.

Service Corporation International, 1995 10-K. Houston, TX: Service Corporation International, 1996.

SIC 6712

OFFICES OF BANK HOLDING COMPANIES

Offices of bank holding companies are primarily engaged in holding or owning the securities of banks for the sole purpose of exercising partial or complete control over the activities of those organizations. Companies holding securities of banks, but which are predominantly operating the banks, are classified according to the kind of bank operated.

NAICS CODE(S)

551111 (Offices of Bank Holding Companies)

INDUSTRY SNAPSHOT

Holding companies have played a relatively minor role in the U.S. banking industry throughout most of the twentieth century. During the 1980s and early 1990s, however, the bank holding industry experienced rapid growth and became a force in the country's financial markets. In fact, the number of multibank holding companies (MBHCs) in the industry jumped from 284 in 1980 to more than 950 by 1992, with total employment surpassing 1.3 million for the top 100 companies alone. As a testament to the significance of the industry, the top 300 companies had assets of $2.8 trillion in 1992—nearly 90 percent of the assets of the entire banking industry. In 1996, the top 10 companies employed over half a million people and had combined assets of $1.7 trillion.

The emerging dominance of MBHCs reflects serious problems in the overall banking industry, however, as well as a basic restructuring of U.S. financial markets. Increased competition from less regulated financial services firms, stagnant growth in loans and deposits, and general shifts in monetary policy have contributed to the decline of banks. In fact, the percentage of U.S. assets held by commercial banks declined from nearly 40 percent in 1970 to 24.5 percent by 1993. In 1994, federally insured depository institutions held $5 trillion in assets, up slightly from the from the previous year. In 1995 $2.7 trillion was held in American bank deposits, but the future still remained uncertain for commercial banks. Depositors realized they could get better returns than those offered by low-interest savings accounts. Nonbank lenders such as GE Capital offered cheaper credit than banks, for example. Bank loans have dropped from 50 percent of all corporate debt to less than 30 percent, from 75 percent of banks' total business to less than 60 percent. According to the 1997 Federal Reserve Bank bulletins, commercial banks had a good year in 1996, with reported strong growth, preserving high levels on return of equity and return on assets. There was strong growth of interest earning assets and delinquency, and charge-off rates stayed low for business loans but climbed throughout the year for consumer loans.

In response to an increasingly threatening environment, bank holding companies in the 1990s took advantage of their size and invested in new lines of business, expanded nationally, and increased income from service fees. They also relied on favorable legislation, implementation of new technology, and foreign markets to increase profits. Online banking influenced the industry, allowing customers new and quick access to markets. The United States banking industry in the late 1990s was estimated to be worth $520 billion.

In 1997, the Census Bureau estimated that this industry contained 2,390 establishments and employed 26,921 people. Revenue totaled $21.3 billion.

Organization and Structure

Bank holding companies are essentially corporations whose assets are comprised of controlling shares of stock in one or more banks. The two principal types of companies are ''one-bank'' and ''multibank'' holding companies, which together encompass nearly all large banks. Although the majority of bank holding companies in the United States are classified as ''one-bank'' holding companies, most of these companies were organized to directly operate a bank, and are not, therefore, included in the bank holding company industry. The multibank corporations that make up the industry exercise varying degrees of control over the subsidiaries they own.

MBHCs earn money by increasing the scope, diversity, and efficiency of banks and bank branches. Banks and their branches, in turn, earn money by paying interest at rates lower than that charged on loans. Banks also generate revenue from such services as asset management, investment sales, and mortgage loan maintenance. Because of regulatory constraints, banks not associated with holding companies must operate under restrictions that often put them at a disadvantage compared to other financial institutions.

To overcome regulatory restraints, banks often use holding companies to circumvent legal restrictions and to raise capital by otherwise unavailable means. For instance, many banks can indirectly operate branches in other states by organizing their entity as a holding company. Banks are also able to enter and often effectively compete in related industries through holding company subsidiaries. In addition, holding companies are able to raise capital using methods that banks are restricted from practicing, such as issuing commercial paper.

Another important advantage that MBHCs have over individual banks is economies of scale. Many subsidiary banks benefit from operational efficiencies such as centralized and computerized bookkeeping, auditing, advertising, marketing, purchasing of supplies, research, personnel recruitment, group insurance and retirement programs, tax guidance, investment counseling, and other advisory services. In addition to greater access to capital, holding companies also facilitate mobility of money among their subsidiaries and allow them to spread gains and losses over all members of the holding corporation.

Background and Development

MBHCs first appeared in the United States around 1900, when they were used to develop banking networks that were otherwise prohibited by law and custom. Most of the organizations were relatively small Midwestern operations. During the 1920s and 1930s the number of holding corporations increased as the population shifted to urban areas and rural banks sought to pool their resources. At the same time, banks in the Midwest, West, and South increased the use of holding companies to combat the threat of eastern and western banks that were expanding nationally. By 1929 bank holding companies and a few chains that resembled holding companies, controlled about 8 percent, or 2,103, of all U.S. banks. They also held more than 12 percent, or $11 billion, of all loans and investments.

Regulation Defines the Industry. After the Great Depression, the banking and bank holding industries came under intense scrutiny. Initially, the federal government regulated both industries in an effort to create a division between banking and investment activities. Later, however, regulations were used to influence the competitive structure of financial markets. In general, regulatory measures that shaped banking activities were responses to financial crises rather than the result of constructive economic planning.

Loose government regulation of holding banks ended with the Banking Act of 1933. In response to thousands of bank failures during the Great Depression, this act led to increased legislation between 1930 and 1960 that limited bank holding activity and expansion. The Bank Holding Company Act of 1956 required bank holding companies to refrain from all nonbanking related operations. It also required companies to seek state permission before acquiring banks in other states. In 1956 a total of 53 MBHCs represented 428 banks with 783 branches. They controlled about $14.8 billion in deposits. By 1965 the number of companies participating in the industry remained at 53, although total deposit assets had nearly doubled to $27.5 billion.

Prompted by the Federal Reserve Board, Congress enacted laws in 1966 that were designed to revive the bank holding industry by eliminating many of the restrictions enacted in 1933. These laws resulted in favorable tax provisions as well as massive industry growth between 1965 and 1970. During this period, the number of MBHCs rose to 121 and deposits in holding company banks skyrocketed to more than $78 billion, or 16.2 percent of all U.S. bank deposits.

In 1970 new legislation was enacted that established a list of permissible activities in which holding companies could participate. One facet of these amendments to the 1956 act gave multibank companies an avenue for significantly broadening their operations. It allowed industry participants to operate nonbanking subsidiaries across state lines even though those subsidiaries engaged in some of the prescribed bank related activities. The result was that by 1974 about 275 MBHCs controlled approximately $359 billion in assets.

The Late 1970s and 1980s. Before the 1970s, most bank holding companies were competing against organizations within the banking industry—all of which were subject to the same legal restrictions. However, the dynamics of banking began to change in the 1970s in three principal ways that had a profound effect on the multibank holding industry: monetary policy shifted, new industries and products competed for traditional banking dollars, and new technology changed the way banks conducted business.

The shift in monetary policy was partly a result of failed regulatory policies of the 1950s and 1970s. Because the government limited rates that banks could pay depositors, banks were placed at a competitive disadvantage in relation to government securities and instruments offered by financial institutions. New investment vehicles that offered higher rates than bank deposits, such as Merrill Lynch's Cash Management Account, began acquiring deposits that would have been made to banks.

Certificates of deposit became a popular way for banks to attract more money, though at a higher cost. As the cost of money increased for banks, profit margins narrowed. To offset increased costs, banks were forced to charge higher interest rates on loans, which meant that they were assuming more risk. Furthermore, in 1979 the Federal Reserve reacted to rising inflation rates by keeping the money supply stable and allowing interest rates to vary. The net result of this move was that many banks experienced higher costs of money, or deposits, than they could earn on their loans.

The 1980s was a decade of rapid foreign expansion for U.S. and foreign banking industries. Between 1980 and 1990 the number of foreign-owned banks on U.S. soil increased from less than 400 to more than 700, including branch banks. The number reached 747 in 1992, falling slightly to 720 in 1993. Foreign banking assets in the United States also climbed during that period, from $198 billion to about $850 billion, accounting for approximately 25 percent of total U.S. banking assets by 1990. The majority of this expansion was concentrated in New York, California, Illinois and Florida, and was principally conducted by Japan, Canada, France, and the United Kingdom. U.S. expansion abroad mimicked the pace set by foreign banks throughout much of the 1980s. In 1992, 120 Federal Reserve member banks were operating 774 branches in foreign countries and overseas areas of the United States, a decline from the 916 branches at the end of 1985. Of the 120 banks, 88 were national banks operating 660 branches and 32 were state banks operating the remaining 114 branches.

In the late 1980s and early 1990s, a sluggish world economy and an ailing global banking industry slowed expansion of most holding companies. Beginning in 1988, expansion by foreign banks slowed and continued to lag into the 1990s. Many U.S. banks, in contrast, deliberately reduced activity abroad. By 1991 the number of U.S. branch banks operating abroad had fallen to 793. Of the 123 banks operating those branches, 92 were national banks that represented 674 branches; the other 120 branches were owned by 31 state banks.

The overall slowdown in global expansion by MBHCs reflected slim profit margins typically offered by overseas markets. Companies tried to compete outside of their national borders saw lower profit margins and stiffer competition for a variety of reasons. In 1991, for instance, MBHCs in the largest industrialized nations generated domestic interest margins (net interest income as a percentage of average interest-earning assets) of 4 percent, compared to interest margins of only 2.1 percent in foreign markets. While some banks tried to improve international margins by investing in technology and consolidating operations, other competitors retrenched.

Another way in which the banking environment began to change in the 1980s was through the increase in the number of products and industries competing with banks. For economic and regulatory reasons, banks suddenly found themselves competing with pension funds, insurance companies, mutual funds, and private finance companies. Manufacturing companies with finance subsidiaries, such as General Electric and Ford Motor Company, were also vying for traditional banking dollars. These new competitors often enjoyed many of the advantages that bank holding companies offered to individual banks, such as the ability to engage in interstate activities.

New technology changed the face of banking forever in the 1980s. Electronic fund transfer systems, automatic teller machines, and computerized home banking services all transformed the way in which banks conduct business. These advances, in addition to increased automation of normal operations, reduced labor demands and hastened the trend toward larger and more centralized banking organizations. They also diminished the role that banks had traditionally played as personal financial service organizations.

Changes in monetary policy, increased competition, and new technology resulted in the general decline of the banking industry. At the same time, insurance companies increased their percentage of assets to nearly 18 percent, and pension fund holdings jumped from 13 percent to more than 20 percent of all U.S. assets. Most strikingly, mutual funds increased their share from about 2 percent to more than 10 percent.

As competition in financial markets heated up, bank holding companies became an increasingly important factor because of the regulatory advantages favoring individual banks. Also driving MBHC growth was the erosion of restrictions on interstate banking in 1985. Legislation in that year allowed states to decide whether to allow interstate banking. By 1992, 950 MBHCs controlled more than 90 percent of all bank assets. Furthermore, the total number of individual banks declined 30 percent from 1983-92 to about 10,000. In the mid-1990s, with deregulation, the largest national banks are able to move into any state and buy smaller banks to establish their presence. This trend has added to the shrinkage of individual banks. In a 1994 survey of European banks by Gemini Consulting, it was predicted that within the next decade, 15-20 retail banks would dominate Europe. Edward Crutchfield Jr., chairman and CEO of First Union Corporation believes that at the decade, eight to 10 institutions will account for 50 percent to 80 percent of the nation's banking business.

In addition to consolidating operations through MBHCs, banks also began exposing themselves to more risk to maintain traditional profit margins. Although the Depository Institutions Deregulation and Monetary Control Act of 1980 (DIDMCA) and other legislation was enacted to correct many of the restrictions that limited the industry's freedom, banks continued to increase their exposure to risk throughout the 1980s.

Deregulation of banks in the early 1980s through DIDMCA and other legislative measures, in combination with higher lending risks assumed by many banks, culminated in a banking crisis in the late 1980s and early 1990s. In 1989, 206 banks failed, and another 168 failed the following year as the U.S. economy sank into recession. In response to troubles within the industry, legislators passed laws designed to impose more vigilant government monitoring of bank activities. The Federal Deposit Insurance Corporation Improvement Act (FDICIA) of 1991 was one example of this legislation.

A poor economy increased the acute profit pressures most banks faced. Holding companies became the focus of the banking industry. Many smaller and mid-sized banks found they simply could not compete in the financial environment that had developed by the early 1990s. Commercial bank loans fell slightly from $2.3 billion in 1990 to $2.28 billion in 1991, and dropped by 20 percent in 1995 to corporate clients. Although deposits and assets continued to increase slightly throughout the early 1990s, rising costs were placing downward pressure on profit margins. The percentage of U.S. assets held by the banking industry continued to decline to 24.5 percent by 1993. As a result, increasing numbers of banks were merging with, or being acquired by, MBHCs to compete effectively.

Analysts suspected that relaxed federal regulation of bank-brokerage companies would lead to more traditional bank mergers in 1997. According to Michael Ancell, a financial services industry analyst at Edward D. Jones & Co., a St. Louis brokerage firm, bank mergers would be fueled "by the need to compete and the difficulty in growing earnings and investing for the future at the same time." The 1933 Glass-Steagall Act restricted banks' ownership of brokerages, but under the latest revision of the act, banks could derive up to 25 percent of their revenues from brokerages, up from 10 percent.

MBHCs' Competitive Response. MBHCs were taking measures aimed at allowing their members to compete more effectively in financial markets. Some of these measures included orchestrating cost-cutting programs, centralizing and automating operations, exploring new markets, emphasizing fees from services, and trying to initiate legislation that was more favorable to their industry.

Perhaps the most important change that MBHCs brought to the industry in the early 1990s was centralized organizational control and consolidation of assets. Two-thirds to three-quarters of the banks that had merged with holding companies in 1990 and 1991 had already consolidated some or all of their systems, operations, and technical management by 1992. MBHCs were finding that they could reduce operating costs of the individual banks they had acquired by an average of 30 percent.

Much of the consolidation activity occurred among mid-sized and larger banks. It involved the transfer of a significant amount of the industry's cumulative technology base to bigger corporations, which resulted in a major shift of management and asset control from banks in the $250 million to $2 billion deposit range to MBHCs with more than $4 billion in deposits. By mid-1992 the top 150 MBHCs controlled 15 percent of all banks, 30 percent of all branch offices, and 50 percent of all deposits in the banking industry.

In addition to consolidation of assets and management, MBHCs took advantage of increased asset bases to invest in labor saving technology and to increase customer service. As banks became more consolidated, especially during the 1980s and early 1990s, the number of employees shrank. For instance, despite an increase in the dollar value of assets, loans, and investments held by banks, the number of employees in the banking industry declined from 1.54 million in 1987 to 1.5 million by 1993.

MBHCs also allowed increased activity by member banks and subsidiaries into new markets and financial products, many of which were off limits to individual banks. Partial deregulation of MBHCs and reduction of some interstate trade restrictions were largely responsible for the new activities. Many banks positioned themselves for future success by replacing income from interest streams with fee income streams. For instance, some banks were expanding fee-based financial advisory services related to underwriting debt and equity, loan securitization, underwriting commercial paper, and treasury management. Banks also entered mortgage banking, asset management, and investment sales—activities traditionally relegated to other financial sectors.

One of the greatest areas of growth in new markets in the early 1990s was in mutual and money market fund sales, which became a viable market for banks following legislation enacted in 1987. By 1993 more than 90 percent of all banks with more than $1 billion in assets offered mutual funds, and all banks combined accounted for 30 percent of all money market fund sales. In 1995 $2.2 trillion was held in American mutual funds, nearly as large as the amount held in bank deposits. Few MBHCs managed funds, instead deriving fee income through leasing arrangements with broker-dealers operating on a bank's premises. An increasing number of larger MBHCs, however, were managing their own funds—allowing them to also earn custodial, transfer agent, and advisory fees.

Despite generally favorable legislation implemented in the late 1980s and early 1990s, MBHCs still sought to remove competitive barriers many industry participants felt were outdated holdovers from the Depression era. Furthermore, some analysts believed that new federal legislation handicapped MBHCs.

Restructuring Strengthens Industry. Industry consolidation and subsequent efforts by MBHCs to strengthen the banking industry began to pay off in 1991. According to one survey of the top 300 MBHCs, the banking industry was healthier than it had been in several years. MBHCs in particular showed signs of renewed strength and stability. Banking industry profits captured by the top 300 of the 950 MBHCs jumped from 63 percent in 1991 to 76 percent in 1992. During the same period the total assets of these companies increased from $2.6 trillion to $2.8 trillion. Moreover, these MBHCs controlled nearly 90 percent of all industry assets. Profits, too, were up. In 1996 the top five MBHCs alone had assets of $1 trillion.

Importantly, the survey indicated that increased earnings and financial performance were the result of cost-cutting measures and market positioning, rather than the effect of temporary economic factors. Some of the nation's largest MBHCs, for instance, had jettisoned hundreds of millions of dollars worth of real estate and other nonperforming assets. Improved margins were largely a result of strengthened capital positions, geographic expansion, increases in fee-based income, and heavy investments in technology. The survey showed, for instance, that nine of the 20 highest rated MBHCs derived at least 40 percent of their income from fees—a trend that was gaining momentum.

Future Expectations. In addition to strengthened market conditions, MBHCs in the mid-1990s were expected to benefit from a moderate rebound in overall residential and commercial lending, and increased competition, particularly from nonfinancial corporations entering the banking field through subsidiaries. The most successful MBHCs were expected to be those with innovative products and delivery systems, creating new securities by converting assets into marketable certificates, and expanding into foreign markets.

Although it was unclear what effect the Clinton administration would have on MBHCs, some companies expressed concern over specific administration policies. For example, President Bill Clinton advocated reducing or eliminating the role that private banks played in the student loan program. On the other hand, he was likely to seek a reduction in barriers to small business lending by banks and was pursuing a favorable regulatory reform package in early 1993. In 1995 the Riegle-Neal Interstate Banking and Branching Act gave national banks authority to open interstate branches by merging with existing banks or opening offices.

CURRENT CONDITIONS

In the late 1990s, past deregulation initiatives continued to spur mergers and a drive by MBHCs to offer more one stop shopping services to customers. Industry giants such as Nationsbank and BankAmerica merged in 1998, creating a new BankAmerica that exceeded Chase Manhattan in size and revenues. In the late 1990s, the banking industry had a value of $520 billion and included 9,100 commercial banks and 1,800 thrift institutions. Though actual numbers of banks and thrifts had declined during the 1990s (due in part to consolidation and mergers), the rising prevalence of large national banking chains spurred competition in the industry to meet the needs of customers who disliked the impersonal feel of the new mega banks. Banks continued to forge ventures and to offer formerly untraditional services such as brokerage, securities underwriting, and insurance.

In 1997, changes to the 1993 Glass-Steagall legislation allowed MBHCs to own securities subsidiaries, which could contribute as much as 25 percent of sales revenue. The opportunity created more mergers; including those between Sun Trust Banks and Equitable Securities, Fleet Financial and Quick and Ready, and Bankers Trust and Alex Brown.

Online banking developments also promised to influence the industry. In 1997 it was estimated that 4.5 million households would have access to online banking. By the late 1990s, 66 percent of the top 50 banks in the United States offered computer banking from home and electronic bill paying services. The advent and increasing popularity of online banking caused one industry expert (*Knight-Ridder/Tribune News Service,* 22 April 1998) to speculate whether the megamergers so characteristic of the industry in the 1990s were really in the public's best interest. According to this expert, the heralded "one stop shopping" advantage of these mergers (according to the banks doing the merging) was rendered moot by the fact that customers could achieve instant access to many markets, via online home access.

INDUSTRY LEADERS

After a $43 billion merger in 1998, Bank of America Corporation (resulting from the combination of BankAmerica and NationsBank) emerged as the industry leader. Bank of America was, as a result of the merger, situated in locations nationwide. The company included 11,500 branches in almost all of the 50 states and in 40 countries. Bank of America had 1998 sales of $51.8 billion (a 138 percent annual increase) and employed 170,975 employees.

Citicorp was one of the largest MBHCs in 1996 and the largest banking company in the United States in terms of revenues. In the late 1990s Citicorp merged with Travelers Group to form Citigroup. Citigroup offered banking, investment, insurance, and credit card services in 100 countries. The company ranked seventh among Fortune 500 companies and had 1999 sales of $57.2 billion (a 25 percent annual sales growth). Citigroup employed 173,700 employees during 1998.

Norwest Corporation of Minneapolis was listed in *Business Week's* 1996 "BW 50," a new ranking of all S&P 500 companies based on eight criteria, including revenue and earnings growth and return on equity. Norwest's development is representative of many successful MBHCs in the early 1990s. In the late 1980s the bank found itself inundated with nonperforming high-risk loans, while its profit margins diminished. Management launched a reorganization program to improve productivity, credit quality, and stability. The company increased the portion of its fee-based business to 40 percent by diversifying into mortgage, finance, and technical services, and by offering new investment products. It also expanded its operations into 50 states and all 10 Canadian provinces. Norwest posted record earnings in the first quarter of 1997, up 18.6 percent from last year during the same period. In 1997 they also acquired a series of companies: First Valley Bank Group of Texas, which had $447 million in assets and 18 branches throughout the state; Continental State Bank also of Texas, with $125 million in assets; and Packers Bank and Trust, with $166 million in assets and four branches in Omaha, Nebraska. In 1996 Norwest had $72.1 billion in assets, employed 53,369 people, and had sales of $8.8 billion. Norwest merged with Wells Fargo in the late 1990s, and was slated to formally assume the new name of Wells Fargo and Company during 2000. At the end of 1998, the company was the sixth largest in the industry and offered 6,000 statewide locations. Wells Fargo and Company had 1998 sales of $20,482 (a 112 percent annual increase) and employed 92,178 people in 1998.

WORKFORCE

Some analysts predicted that by 2000 20 percent of industry jobs would be eliminated through consolidation and automation by MBHCs. An example of this trend, is the merger of MBHCs BankAmerica and Security Pacific in the early 1990s, which resulted in the elimination of more than 15,000 jobs. Likewise, the merger of Chemical Bank and Chase Manhattan in 1996 eliminated 12,000 jobs. There are 1.5 million people employed in banking, a decline of 70,000 over the past decade. While mergers accounted for a decline in the number of employees, the sharp rise in the number of ATMs also accounts for the drop in employment. ATMs have contributed to the number of people needed to process checks and a reduction in the number of customers who enter a bank. The number of bank tellers decreased by 41,000 between 1985 and 1995. For the industry, the Bureau of Labor Statistics projected a 0.9 percent decline in employment, specifically among bank tellers, annually between 1994 and 2005.

In 1995, according to a survey by Robert Half International, high-paying jobs in the industry included commercial loan officers, who typically earned between $36,100 and $82,500, depending on skill and the size of the institution. CEOs of larger MBHCs, on the other hand, earned an average of $237,000 in 1994, while chief financial officers at large institutions earned between $60,000 and $295,000. The outlook for job growth is good through 2005, according to the U.S. Occupational Outlook.

Growth opportunities with MBHCs in the 1990s will likely be in technical areas as information systems and data processing, and for securities sales representatives. Growth for this specialty is forecast as excellent through 2005, with earnings of approximately $37,000 in 1994. The top 10 percent of securities sales representatives earn $120,700 or more. Positions may increase for financial professionals who can bring expertise relating to financial products and investment vehicles that are new to the banking industry. Bank information system (IS) staffing levels are expected to remain stable at 6 percent of total bank employment through 1997. IS professionals with C++ and object-oriented programming skills are in big demand in the banking industry.

AMERICA AND THE WORLD

Long-term growth markets for U.S. banks will likely include the Pacific Rim and Europe. Western Europe's evolution toward unified financial markets is expected to eliminate many of the trade barriers faced by North American competitors in the mid-1990s. Although many MBHCs are avoiding European markets, Citicorp already maintained an extensive network throughout Europe and hoped to gain from unification. Unfortunately for U.S. MBHCs, the large Japanese banking market remained impenetrable in 1993, despite relatively open U.S. financial markets and strategic alliances attempted by a number of U.S. firms with Japanese counterparts.

Competitive Structure of Global Markets. In 1996 the largest bank in the world was the Tokyo-Mitsubishi bank, with 19,300 employees and $19.633 billion in sales. The world's second largest bank, Sumitomo Bank, is also based in Japan. In 1996 they had assets in excess of $500 billion, with 360 offices in Japan and 74 branches overseas. Their American subsidiary, the Sumitomo Bank of California, is the fifth largest in the state. Other large Japanese banks include the Dai-Ichi Kangyo, the fifth largest bank in the world, with assets of $500 billion, 400 offices in Japan, and 77 branches in 31 countries; the Fuji Bank; and Sanwa Bank. Despite the size and strength of the many banks in Japan, the industry there was not immune to the global slowdown in the early 1990s. In fact, the Japanese banking industry was especially hard hit by a sinking stock market, falling property values, and bad loans incurred during the 1980s.

Other large multinationals include Credit Agricole of Paris, the number one commercial bank in France, with 1995 sales of $32.34 billion and 72,607 employees; the Credit Suisse, the largest bank in Switzerland, with most of its business conducted outside the country (American subsidiary is Credit Suisse First of Boston); and the Union Bank of Switzerland, the second largest in the country, with two-thirds of its assets coming from overseas operations.

Because they play different roles in different countries, a true comparison of banks throughout the world is difficult. For instance, although no U.S. banks placed in the top 25 in terms of capital, the U.S. MBHC industry accounted for 200 of the 1,000 largest banks in the world. In comparison, Japan had the second largest number of banks, with 100. Italy, which has a diversified banking industry similar to Japan's, also had about 100 establishments in the top 1,000. Furthermore, some countries, like the United States, still maintain highly fragmented banking industries with thousands of banks serving the market. Japan, by contrast, has 150 banks, while Canada and the United Kingdom have 65 and 550 banks, respectively.

Regulation. The Foreign Bank Supervision Enhancement Act of 1991 (FBSEA) established federal standards for the entry and expansion of foreign banks in the United States. The act also increased the role of the Federal Reserve System in the supervision and regulation of foreign banking operations in the United States. The act requires foreign banks competing in U.S. markets to engage directly in the business of banking outside the country and to be subject to comprehensive supervision or regulation on a consolidated basis by its own domestic authorities. The act also requires that the banks furnish information to U.S. authorities, allowing the latter to assess the bank's application filed under the Bank Holding Company Act.

RESEARCH AND TECHNOLOGY

Although most financial payments are still being made with cash, checks, and credit cards, electronic funds transfer (EFT)—including transactions made with automated teller machines (ATMs)—is an important aspect of MBHC branch operations. By 1995, 9.7 billion transactions were processed at 123,000 ATM terminals in the United States. Although ATM growth had slowed in the United States, expansion of that technology in world markets was increasing at a rapid pace. (About 200,000 ATMs were serving customers in Japan and Europe.)

In addition to ATMs, debit cards are becoming an important part of electronic banking. Debit cards are used for withdrawals from ATM machines as well as for transactions made at point-of-sale (POS) terminals. The POS allowed for the transfer of money from a buyer's account to a seller's account through either an on-line transaction or through an automated clearinghouse (off-line transaction). For instance, consumers could buy groceries using debit cards that removed money from their personal accounts and transferred them to the store.

Another advance in technology that was slowly gaining stature in U.S. markets was the 'smart card.' Widely used in France and Japan, the smart card contained a microprocessing chip, rather than the standard magnetic stripe on most credit and ATM cards. The chip was more difficult to counterfeit—an advantage to MBHCs battling a $1 billion a year fraud problem. Until late 1995, the smart cards had only been tested in specific regions and test market groups. NationsBank started offering smart cards to Atlanta consumers in preparation for the 1996 summer Olympics. It is predicted that by 2000, there would be 100 million smart cards in the he United States.

Home banking also became more popular in the United States, as more advanced home computer technology allowed consumers more complete and less expensive access to their money. Also, about one-third of all American households conducted a banking transaction over the telephone at least once a month. The latest trend is Internet banking, and U.S. banks are competing with each other to provide content via online services. More than 100 banks have created home pages on the Web, and spending on electronic banking has grown at a compound annual rate of 150 percent in recent years.

Some of the greatest growth in electronic services was in the corporate customer market. Banks located a growing number of end-user banking devices on the premises of banks' corporate customers, increasing the number of wholesale banking customers who have on-line access. A survey by Ernst & Young and *American Banker* found that banks expected to continue to invest in technology to cut costs, reduce labor and increase customer service.

An important technological development that affected the internal operations of MBHCs and their members in the early 1990s was image technology and CD-ROM storage devices. This technology allowed banks to electronically scan incoming paper and route information to the appropriate department or bank location. Technological advances also allowed banks to electronically capture and route telephone conversations and faxes.

FURTHER READING

Ball, Robert. ''Global Agenca Banking the Business That Will Never Be the Same Again.'' *Time International,* 13 March 1995, 46.

''Bank of America Corporation.'' *Hoovers Online.* Available from http://www.hoovers.com/co/capsule/4/0,2163,58444,00.html.

''Citigroup Inc.'' *Hoovers Online.* Available from http://www.hoovers.com/co/capsule/5/0,2163,58365,00.html.

Hoffman, Thomas, and Neal Weinberg. ''Big Mergers, Big Layoffs.'' *Computerworld,* 4 September 1995, 1.

Hoover's Company Capsules. Hoover's, Inc. 1997. Available from http://www.hoovers.com.

Houlder, Vanessa. ''High Street Dinosaurs Wake Up (Online Banking).'' *Financial Times,* 29 January 1996.

Korobow, Leon. ''Are Mega-Mergers By U.S. Banks in the Public Interest?'' *Knight-Ridder/Tribune News Service,* 22 April 1998.

Mullins, Robert. ''Forget Bank-Broker Marriages, as More Banks Merge in '97.'' *Business Journal,* 28 February 1996, 5.

Spain, Barbara. ''Banks and Banking Institutions Industry.'' *Hoovers Online.* Available from http://www.hoovers.com/industry/snapshot/0,2204,7,00.html.

U.S. Census Bureau. *1997 Economic Census.* Washington, D.C.: Bureau of the Census, 1999.

''Wells Fargo and Company.'' *Hoovers Online.* Available from http;//www.hoovers.com/co/capsule/0/2163,58450,00.html.

SIC 6719

OFFICES OF HOLDING COMPANIES, NOT ELSEWHERE CLASSIFIED

Offices of holding companies, not elsewhere classified, include firms that primarily hold or own securities of other companies to exercise control over the activities of those organizations. This industry classification excludes bank holding companies, but includes investment, personal, and public utility holding companies. Corporations that operate the entities whose securities they hold are classified in their respective industry.

NAICS CODE(S)

551112 (Offices of Other Holding Companies)

Holding companies have several functions. They may be used to achieve financing goals or to circumvent certain federal or state regulations. Most often, however, a holding company allows a corporation to achieve economies of scale as well as geographic or market diversification. The holding company also allows a corporation, through its subsidiaries, to integrate both horizontally and vertically. For instance, an automaker may vertically integrate by buying a steel mill that can make steel for its cars without a mark-up in price. The same automaker might also integrate horizontally by acquiring or merging with another automaker, thereby providing new manufacturing technologies, a broader market, or complimentary product lines.

The first U.S. holding companies were in New Jersey, after that state passed the New Jersey Holding Company Act. This allowed corporations to bring previously independent firms under unified control. Holding companies were an alternative to trust organizations, which often allowed monopolies to form. Although the goal of the Public Utility Holding Company Act of 1935 was also passed to prevent such monopolies in the electric power industry, electric companies serving a group of states or a single state still operated in such a manner.

The New Jersey Act generated so much tax revenue that other states soon followed its lead. The rise of holding companies allowed many corporations to reach national markets. Intense U.S. merger activity occurred periodically, from 1898 to 1902, during the 1920s, from 1951 to 1955, in the 1960s, and during the mid-1980s.

Mergers and acquisitions fell during the late 1980s and early 1990s, as heavy debt, the late 1980s recession, and a lack of capital slowed holding company growth. Furthermore, many industries dominated by large holding companies had lackluster revenues in the early 1990s.

By the end of the 1990s, however, mergers and acquisitions were on the rise, especially in the public utilities area, as electric and natural gas companies merged. The percent of utilities that owned natural gas distribution companies increased from 40 percent to 55 percent by the end of 1998. Since then, 11 mergers have united companies involved predominantly in electricity with natural gas companies. For instance, SCANA Corporation of Columbia, South Carolina, an energy-based holding company, announced it was merging with Public Service Company of North Carolina, Inc. (a natural gas utility) in that same year.

From 1996 to 1998, gas distribution assets and revenues grew by 59 and 29 percent, respectively, for electric utility holding companies; however, international assets still exceed those of gas distribution as the leading form of diversification. These increased a whopping 173 percent the same period, with revenues doubling. Another huge growth was seen in telecommunications assets, which rose 658 percent with a similar increase in revenues.

The amount of oil and gas exploration and processing assets rose by 51 percent for the same period, whereas pipeline assets jumped by 89 percent. Electric utility holding companies are also acquiring trading organizations, with revenues growing from $7.6 billion in 1996 to $47.7 billion in 1998. Industry experts also believe independent power revenues will see a significant increase between 1999 and 2000.

Other utility companies are either reorganizing into a holding company structure or acquiring competitors. In 1999, for example, one natural gas holding company, Southern Union Co. of Austin Texas, acquired its rival, Valley Resources Inc. Public Service Company of New Mexico, an electric and gas utility, split its business into two subsidiaries under a new holding company that same year. Washington Gas Light Company also announced it was forming WGL Holdings, Inc., so that it and its subsidiaries could operate separately under the holding company.

Other types of holding companies, both foreign and domestic, were expected to diversify internationally throughout the 1990s. Analysts thought horizontal and vertical integration would allow more firms to reach new markets and to produce goods and services more efficiently. Many holding corporations should also benefit from advanced information systems that allow more efficient centralized control of their enterprises.

FURTHER READING

Cashin, John and Esquivar, Joan. ''Financial Review: What's the Holding Company Holding?'' *Electric Perspective,* November/December 1999.

Hoover's Company Profiles. Hoover's Inc., 1997. Available from http://www.hoovers.com.

Leibowitz, Alissa. ''The Utilities Economy: The Next Big Thing.'' *Venture Capital Journal,* 1 January 2000.

''PNM Seeks to Form Holding Company.'' PR Newswire, 17 November, 1999.

''SCANA & PSNC to Close Merger on February 10, 2000'' PR Newswire, 29 December 1999.

''Washington Gas Announces Intention to Form Holding Company.'' PR Newswire, 30 December 1999.

SIC 6722

MANAGEMENT INVESTMENT OFFICES—OPEN-END

The open-end management investment industry is comprised of investment companies that sell shares in open-end mutual funds. Open-end funds require the issuing company to redeem the shares upon request by the security holder. Often referred to as the mutual fund industry, the open-end fund industry comprises about 95 percent of the mutual fund market. Unit investment trusts, face-amount certificates, and closed-end mutual funds are excluded from this classification. Mutual fund management firms that work for investment companies are part of the investment advice industry **SIC 6282: Investment Advice.**

NAICS Code(s)

525910 (Open-End Investment Funds)

Industry Snapshot

The mutual fund industry experienced explosive growth in the 1980s and early 1990s, as investors transferred assets from other financial sectors into mutual funds, and investments in general increased. U.S. open-end mutual funds controlled more than $1.7 trillion in assets by 1993, making them a major force in the country's economy. In 1992, 27 percent of all U.S. households owned shares in mutual funds—up from 6 percent in 1980. In 1993, assets in funds continued to grow at a rate of more than $1 billion per day. More than 2,700 such open-ended funds are in existence. According to 1997 statistics, there were 1,489 establishments engaged in this industry. The industry reported 1997 revenues of $16.6 billion.

Following unprecedented industry growth throughout much of the 1980s, mutual fund assets continued to increase rapidly in 1996. A strong securities market, as well as an influx of new dollars from other financial sectors, contributed to the surge. Although mutual funds nourished the U.S. economy in many ways, such as providing capital to some thinly traded securities markets, the growing industry was also cited by some observers as a leading cause of stock market volatility.

Organization and Structure

A mutual fund is a corporation chartered by a state to operate as an open-end investment company. The company invests in a portfolio of assets and obtains capital by selling shares in its own securities. Capital is, in turn, reinvested in the portfolio. Income from investments is disbursed to shareholders or is used to compensate fund managers and expenses. The price investors pay for a share of the company is based primarily on the market value of the securities in the portfolio. The distinguishing characteristic of an open-end fund, in relation to a closed-end fund, is that the investment company must redeem an investor's shares upon his or her request. Mutual fund investors also benefit from professional management of their money which they might otherwise be unable to afford. One disadvantage of mutual fund investing is that mutual funds are not tailored to the specific investment needs or tax status of individual shareholders. The shares in the fund are valued at their net asset value (NAV), and share prices fluctuate every day.

Many mutual funds provide investors with many services. Shareholders may elect to have money automatically withdrawn from their accounts on a periodic basis for investment in a mutual fund. Many funds also offer check-writing privileges and automatic reinvestment programs that pour dividends and capital gains back into new shares. The reinvestment option has proven to be very popular due to the tax saving advantages of not withdrawing dividends.

Types of Funds. The two primary types of mutual funds are ''no-load'' and ''load'' funds. No-load funds do not require investors to pay fees or sales commission, and the price of a share in a no-load fund is identical to its net asset value. The investment company typically acts as the distributor for its funds, and therefore bypasses brokerage fees and commissions. Investors in no-load funds do, however, usually incur some indirect costs related to marketing and other advertising expenses.

Shares in load funds, on the other hand, are usually sold through separate distributorships. The distributors sell fund shares through dealers and brokers, such as banks, insurance companies, or financial planners. The front-end load, or commission, is often about 8.5 percent, of which the distributor keeps 1.5 percent, and the dealer and broker receive the remaining 7 percent. Therefore, of $1,000 invested in an 8.5 percent load fund, $915 would actually be invested in the fund—resulting in an effective fee of 9.3 percent.

Commissions are often scaled down as the size of the purchase increases, and although investment performance on average is the same for no-load and load funds, total returns are usually higher on no-load funds because of their lack of fees. During the 1990s, about 30 percent of all funds were considered true no-load funds, although many ''low-load'' funds charged commissions as low as 2 percent or 3 percent.

Mutual funds can also be categorized according to the contents of their portfolios or their investment objectives. Although a plethora of funds serve diverse market segments, the three major categories of funds are common stock, bond, and money market.

Aggressive growth funds, also known as capital appreciation, seek to maximize capital gains, rather than current income. This type of fund is considered relatively risky and more volatile than many other funds because it typically focuses on securities of companies or industries with unproven potential for strong growth. Managers of aggressive funds may also make use of options or short-term speculative trading techniques. In the 1990s, more than 200 aggressive growth funds were available on the U.S. market.

On the other hand, the objective of a balanced fund is to conserve the investor's principal, pay a high level of income, and promote long-term growth. Assets in this type of fund are usually invested in a combination of conservative bonds, preferred stock, and common stock. Corporate bond funds try to achieve a similar objective by investing in a combination of corporate debt, U.S. treasury bonds, or other federal bonds. In 1999, there were approximately 100 balanced and corporate bond funds each.

Money market funds are low-risk investment vehicles holding short-term, high-grade securities such as treasury bills, certificates of deposit, and commercial paper. This type of fund is popular because it maintains a very stable net asset value. Tax-exempt money market funds differ in that they invest in municipal securities with short maturities. In the late 1990s, nearly 1,000 money market funds were available to investors.

Global equity and bond funds maintain a portfolio of securities and debt instruments traded worldwide. These funds offer American investors access to diverse financial markets and companies that would otherwise be difficult, or impossible, to capitalize on. The investment of the fund is in stocks of U.S. and foreign companies. Other popular open-end mutual funds include income-mixed, municipal bond, high-yield bond, precious metal, and income-equity funds.

Mutual Fund Owners. Although mutual funds are usually initiated and often indirectly managed by investment companies, shareholders own the funds. Shareholders include large numbers of individual investors with financial backgrounds ranging from modest to wealthy. In addition, many pension plans, profit-sharing funds, and other institutional investors also place portions of their assets into mutual funds. As Americans embraced mutual funds during the 1980s, the diversity of shareholders increased. For instance, in 1980 only 6 percent of all American households held shares in mutual funds. This jumped to nearly one-third by 1997.

Of the households that owned funds, 72 percent owned equity funds, 41 percent held bond and income funds, and 50 percent were shareholders of money market funds. The average household held shares in two funds. Eighty-four percent of these customers bought their shares through a sales force of some type, such as a financial planner, bank, brokerage firm, or insurance agent. Thirty-seven percent of the households invested directly through the investment company. The median mutual fund owner was 46 and earned $50,000 per year in the early 1990s. Fifty-six percent of all shareholders were male, 50 percent had college degrees, and 72 percent were married. Employed investors represented 72 percent, while 24 percent were retired.

The Industry's Role in Financial Markets. Because of its popularity with investors, the mutual fund industry is a major means of financial intermediation in the U.S. economy and has a decisive impact on formation of domestic capital markets. During the 1990s, money market funds regularly controlled more open-market paper in the United States than any other industry segment. Furthermore, mutual funds provided an efficient tool to help finance everything from corporations and start-up companies to mortgages and governments.

Mutual fund companies were also the largest institutional purchasers of corporate equities, buying approximately one-quarter of all corporate bonds that were issued. Moreover, the amount of discretionary assets that U.S. households invest in mutual funds was estimated at nearly 16 percent in the mid-1990s.

In comparison to other U.S. financial institutions, mutual fund investment companies have become serious contenders in terms of controlling assets. All mutual funds combined contained more than $1.6 trillion in assets in 1992. Insurance companies, by comparison, controlled about $1.6 trillion, and commercial banks held more than $2.4 trillion.

Regulation. Investment companies operating mutual funds are regulated by the Securities and Exchange Act of 1934 and the Investment Company Act of 1940. The 1934 act was established to maintain fair and honest securities markets, and it also enforces other laws requiring investors to have access to information about the underlying condition of companies in which they invest. The Securities and Exchange Commission (SEC) administrates federal regulation of the industry. The 1940 act provides for the registration and regulation of companies that are primarily engaged in the business of investing in securities.

Among many other requirements, the 1940 act stipulates: A company must redeem shares duly offered by shareholders within seven calendar days at per-share net asset value; the maximum load cannot exceed 9 percent of the share's offering price; and shareholders must be sent complete financial reports at least semiannually. Furthermore, a fund must have at least 75 percent of its funds invested such that: Not more than 5 percent are invested in any one issue and not more than 10 percent of the voting securities of any corporation are held by the fund. Mutual funds must also comply with regulations of each state in which its shares are held.

BACKGROUND AND DEVELOPMENT

Mutual funds, in one form or another, have been functioning in financial markets since the nineteenth century. Funds in Great Britain, for instance, helped to finance reconstruction of the post Civil War U.S. economy by investing in farms, railroads, and businesses. British mutual funds heavily influenced the U.S. industry's development, and the first American open-end mutual fund, Massachusetts Investors Trust, was started in 1924.

The Great Depression and World War II hampered asset growth in mutual funds. The period from 1929-40 did, however, serve to establish the regulatory infrastructure that would influence the industry throughout the twentieth century. For instance, in 1940 the Investment Company Institute (originally called the National Association of Investment Companies) was established to develop industry standards and to influence mutual fund legislation.

Fewer than 300,000 shareholders, representing about $450 million in accounts, were participating in the industry in 1940. By 1945, however, mutual funds held more than $1 billion. The industry continued to realize vibrant growth throughout the postwar expansion as a surplus of investment dollars flowed from all sectors of the financial markets. In 1951, mutual funds represented more than 1 million accounts. This amount grew to about $17.4 billion in 1960.

Before 1960, mutual funds were viewed as a relatively conservative and placid investment instrument—much like trusts and endowment funds. In the late 1960s, however, a new breed of mutual fund company began to develop. Focusing on investment performance, these new companies offered maximum capital appreciation and high risk. Several of the new funds also practiced speculative trading techniques, such as short selling and options, in the hope of raising profits. Sophisticated investors began to find the new breed of aggressive funds attractive, and many people felt these funds offered the hands-on investment management they were seeking. In fact, 96 new ''maximum capital gains'' funds were launched in 1968 and 1969 alone. By 1970, about 400 funds of all types held more than $50 billion. Although the new aggressive funds took a beating in the 1970 bear market, they helped to expand the role of mutual funds and increase public awareness of mutual funds.

Until 1970, mutual funds were viewed as an efficient means of investing primarily in the stock market. The industry was transformed by the advent of the first money market mutual fund (MMMF) in 1971, called the Reserve Fund. This product allowed small investors to participate in high short-term interest rates in the money market that had previously been accessible only to the relatively wealthy. People suddenly had a viable alternative to bank deposits with substandard government regulated interest rates. Municipal bond funds followed MMMFs in 1977, and tax-exempt MMMFs debuted in 1979.

As interest rates surged past 17 percent in the 1970s and early 1980s, massive amounts of funds shifted from bank deposits to higher paying MMMFs. As a result, the mutual fund industry controlled about $300 billion in assets by the early 1980s. Furthermore, nearly 75 percent of all mutual fund assets were held by money funds in 1982. Nevertheless, the 1980s would be the industry's most pivotal decade for change and growth.

Since 1982, several factors have induced a major shift in the allocation of assets within the mutual fund industry. Falling interest rates reduced the popularity of money funds in comparison to other types of mutual funds. Strong securities markets brought more money into bond and equity funds. Also, a general increase in public familiarity with mutual funds, combined with the deregulation and metamorphosis of U.S. financial markets, increased the amount of money invested in mutual funds. By the early 1990s, the percentage of industry assets held by MMMFs had fallen to about 34 percent. Equity and bond funds each held about 36 percent and 30 percent, respectively.

While the composition of the industry was shifting, mutual funds continued to realize dynamic asset growth throughout the 1980s. Many new funds and investment vehicles brought more investors into mutual funds. The public's awareness and familiarity with mutual funds was another factor that boosted industry assets. Even many institutional investors, such as pension funds and bank trust departments, were investing increasing amounts in mutual funds to cut costs and increase returns on their portfolios.

Basic fund categories that were experiencing the greatest proliferation of new entrants in the late 1980s and early 1990s included taxable MMMFs, growth, state municipal bond, and international funds. Expansion of new funds had slowed, however, for income-mixed, high-yield bond, precious metal, and aggressive growth funds.

By 1990, 3,105 different mutual funds held more than $1 trillion in assets and represented more than 60 million shareholder accounts. These figures represented steady, stunning growth throughout the decade. While in 1980 only about 12 million shareholders participated in 564 accounts controlling $300 billion in assets, five years later the industry encompassed about $500 billion in assets, 35 million shareholders, and 1,528 different funds.

Mutual fund growth continued at a rapid pace throughout the 1990s, increasing from more than $1 trillion in fund assets in 1990 to more than $1.7 trillion by mid-1993. An influx of bank and pension assets into mutual funds was responsible for much of the growth. Other trends taking place in the industry in 1993 included an increase in the popularity of specialized mutual funds, shifts in the distribution channels used to sell shares, and escalating international activity.

Fund asset growth in the 1990s was largely a result of strong securities markets combined with an infusion of new investment dollars. Despite economic recession, the Dow Jones Industrial Average shot up past a record high 3,500 in 1993, resulting in a boon for equity funds. At the same time, new money was shifting to the mutual fund industry from other financial institutions. Although maturing certificates of deposit were sending assets from banks to fund companies, a diversion of retirement savings from traditional pension management institutions—banks, trusts, and insurance companies—was the greatest reason for the deluge of cash.

Various social and economic changes in the 1970s and 1980s had created an environment that was leading growing numbers of pension plan sponsors and participants toward mutual funds. By investing 401(k) and other pension assets into mutual funds, sponsors and participants were realizing greater diversification of assets and participation in retirement plans. Furthermore, many participants favored mutual funds over other investment vehicles because they felt they had more control over their savings and a better understanding of how their funds were being invested. Although the share of U.S. assets held by pension funds was nearly double that held by mutual funds in 1992, mutuals were gaining quickly.

The impact of mutual fund growth was also evidenced in the stock market. In the early 1990s, for the first time, mutual funds bought more stock market equity than pension funds. Mutual fund dominance of equity markets was causing some observers to question whether the trend was a positive one for the stock market, which was increasingly susceptible to fund-induced volatility. Mutual fund equity purchases shot up 87 percent in 1992, to $80.5 billion—beating the 1991 record high of $43 billion in equity purchases. Indeed, in 1991 and 1992 mutual funds bought more equities than all private pension funds combined had bought between 1960 and 1989.

Long-term mutual funds, which invest for long-term gains, were responsible for much of the industry growth in the early 1990s. As the percentage of industry assets invested in short-term funds fell to less than 35 percent by 1993, long-term fund assets grew to more than 65 percent.

Other Trends. Contributing to the growth and competitiveness of the mutual fund industry were new distribution routes. To survive in a more competitive economic environment, caused in part by the strength of the mutual fund industry, banks and other financial institutions were selling mutual fund shares to generate fee income.

The banking industry, in particular, plunged into mutual fund sales in 1987—the year that banks were deregulated to act as full-service brokers. By 1992, more than 3,500 banks had entered the mutual fund fray and were selling 30 percent of all shares. James Shelton, executive director of the Bank Securities Association, commented in a June 1993 article in *ABA Banking Journal,* ''Banks will soon become the major source of distribution for mutual fund products.'' In addition to selling shares, 700 banks managed proprietary funds in 1993, accounting for about 10 percent of the mutual fund market.

Prospects for regulatory changes in the early 1990s boded well for the industry's future in general. The SEC's Division of Investment Management recommended numerous changes in 1992 that would potentially affect the industry, such as deregulation of sales fees and commissions, registration exemptions for transactions involving sophisticated investors, and provisions for the globalization of mutual fund sales. A notable proposal advocated cross-border marketing of fund shares with countries that have safeguards similar to those in the United States.

In addition to new distribution routes, an abundance of new specialty funds were appealing to investors with unique needs in the mid-1990s. At this time, the number of categories into which mutual funds were divided had grown to 21, up from seven in 1975. Furthermore, at the end of 1996 there were more than 2,700 funds operating. This category had expanded to include funds emphasizing securities in utilities, biotechnology, aviation, telecommunications, real estate, and other niche markets.

In the long run, analysts speculated that demographic changes should boost industry assets, as aging baby-boomers save for retirement and investor-directed retirement programs continue to shift to mutual funds. Distribution channels and new products were expected to continue to evolve and increase the efficiency of the industry. Banks were expected to increase their sales role, and the division between load and no-load funds could eventually become obscured. As the industry matured, companies were expected to seek cost-efficiency through labor-saving automation, by streamlining marketing programs, and by merging with, or acquiring other mutual fund companies.

CURRENT CONDITIONS

By the late 1990s, it was estimated that 40 percent of households in the United States had stock investments. The overall favorable market conditions in the 1990s for the United States resulted in an average growth in fees and commissions for securities companies of up to 30 percent annually. Online stock trading resulted in consumers who could trade in real time, and in over only a few years time during the late 1990s, the financial services industry rose to a value of about $6 billion. The flurry of activity and increase in interested individual investors caused many financial services to offer new mutual funds at an increasing rate. Some of these funds grew so large that it impaired their ability to post outstanding returns.

The continued globalization of the world economy also affected the financial market and mutual fund offerings and performance. In a 1998 industry periodical article, experts suggested that investors take advantage of world market volatility by trading United States open-ended mutual funds. The authors outlined a strategy that included buying open ended, international mutual funds when the S&P index rose by a substantial amount; and switching back to a U.S. index fund on the day that the S&P declined significantly. Apparently, the strategy had proven effective because of foreign markets' tendency to show correlation among returns, and because this correlation appeared to travel from the United States to foreign markets.

INDUSTRY LEADERS

Because open-end investment companies are actually owned by the shareholders that belong to the mutual fund, the shareholders elect board members and approve various operating policies, such as selection of the investment advisor and the basic contents of the portfolio. Because of the way that funds are structured, the day-to-day management and operation of mutual funds is typically handled by a separate fund management company (see **SIC 6282: Investment Advice**). In fact, most funds are established by members of the board of directors, which owns a management company. Indeed, the purpose of starting a fund is often to allow those members' management company to earn fees as the investment advisor for the fund.

Leading companies typically manage a family of funds representing various investment focuses. Fidelity Investments, led by its flagship Magellan fund, was the leading fund management company by 1997 asset size. Its fund assets—representing nearly 200 individual funds—totaled more than $360 billion in 1997. Magellan alone commanded more than $105 billion in net assets by the year 2000. Fidelity was ranked the number one mutual fund at the beginning of 2000. It closed to new investment in 1997. The fund featured stock from domestic companies operating in the United States and overseas.

Vanguard managed the second-largest asset base, with $238 billion, followed by Capital Group/American Funds ($191 billion), Putnam Mutual Funds ($122 billion), and Franklin Templeton Funds ($119 billion). Vanguard's Index Trust 500 Portfolio fund was ranked the second best mutual fund at the beginning of 2000 for performance. In early 2000, the number three mutual fund was PX Washington Mutual Investors Fund, a fund managed for principal growth.

The mutual funds delivering the highest returns throughout the late 1980s and early 1990s were also some of the riskiest funds in which to invest. A $10,000 investment in 1988 in the Kaufmann Fund, for instance, would have grown to $43,658 by 1992. Similarly, a $10,000 investment in the Financial Strategic Health Sciences fund would have delivered $38,513. The same investment in the Fidelity Select Biotechnology mutual fund would have jumped to $37,155 during the same period. Few mutual funds delivered the performance offered by these successful high risk funds. Nevertheless, a $10,000 investment in 1983 in the American Capital Bond fund would have grown to $28,758 by 1992—a relatively healthy return for that sector of the industry.

WORKFORCE

Most of the jobs created by the open-end investment industry are with investment advisement firms, insurance companies, and other institutions that handle the daily management of funds and develop portfolio investment strategies. Management firms employ large numbers of portfolio managers, financial analysts, and other investment professionals. In 1997, a total of 35,271 people were employed in this industry. Further information may be found under **SIC 6282: Investment Advice.**

AMERICA AND THE WORLD

U.S. mutual funds conduct negligible cross-border sales of their shares because of domestic and foreign regulations. In fact, foreign ownership of U.S. funds is estimated at less than 1 percent. Rather than combat barriers to cross-border sales, many mutual fund companies were expanding their sales to other countries in the 1990s by opening foreign subsidiaries that operated and advised overseas mutual funds. This tactic allowed companies to tailor their funds to meet regulatory, tax, and investment needs of the shareholders in a particular country.

International financial markets, furthermore, were steadily becoming a more important aspect of fund management. Fund managers were finding that they could increase their diversification and often boost investment returns by buying securities in foreign markets—despite risks inherent in overseas investing. In the early 1990s, there were more than 130 global bond and equity funds with combined U.S. and foreign assets of $48.7 billion. In addition, about 140 international funds, which invested solely in foreign securities, boasted growing assets of $23.1 billion. These figures were up significantly from 1989, for example, when the combined total of global and international funds was about $26.5 billion. In 1985, moreover, both types of funds held less than $8 billion in overseas assets.

Foreign Mutual Funds. As in the United States, mutual fund industries in many other industrialized countries were realizing rapid growth rates. Mutual fund assets in nine foreign countries studied in 1987, for instance, grew more than 55 percent by 1992, to $1.2 trillion. Total assets of 18 countries that had mutual fund industries totaled $1.5 trillion in the early-1990s. Worldwide, it was estimated that all non-U.S. mutual funds had grown to the approximate equivalent of assets held by U.S. funds.

As the middle class continues to expand, particularly in emerging industrial nations, the amount of foreign assets invested in mutual funds will likely accelerate. Furthermore, as financial markets become more globalized and integrated, opportunities for cross-border sales by U.S. companies could skyrocket. Although the large Japanese financial market remained closed to U.S. competitors, European and South American markets were showing promise. The passage of the North American Free Trade Agreement (NAFTA), for instance, will likely boost opportunities in Mexico for U.S. firms.

The European Community (EC) was striving to implement Undertakings for Collective Investment in Transferable Securities (UCITS) in the mid-1990s. This directive would effectively facilitate cross-border marketing of mutual fund shares within the EC. Several holes existed in the plan, however. For example, many tax issues and questions about marketing and distribution needed work. Nevertheless, the plan does take significant steps toward integrated investment policies, public disclosure guidelines, and other industry controls. When U.S. companies gained access to European consumers, they would gain access to mutual fund markets that topped $1 trillion in the late 1990s.

The U.S. mutual fund industry and the SEC were cooperating to liberalize fund sales during the 1990s. The SEC advocated a proposal that would allow foreign funds to sell shares in the U.S. market if they abided by certain guidelines. The objective of this strategy was to lead other nations into allowing U.S. companies to conduct sales on their soil. The SEC, along with U.S. mutual fund industry representatives, eventually sought to adopt a global system that mimicked the EC initiative.

RESEARCH AND TECHNOLOGY

Technological advances in information systems and computer automation were having a significant impact on open-end investment companies throughout the 1990s. By implementing state-of-the-art systems, mutual funds and their management companies were achieving more efficient customer service, reducing errors in record-keeping and reporting, and reducing labor costs. As the industry becomes increasingly price competitive, automation will offer a critical edge for industry leaders. The proliferation of computers in households makes tracking mutual funds an easy task, since computers have made information on mutual funds and the stock market available on demand.

Mutual fund companies were also benefiting from technological advances affecting foreign and domestic securities markets. With advanced satellite communications networks and on-line trading systems, investment companies were increasing their access to up-to-the-minute investment information from markets around the world. At the close of the 1990s, for instance, it was possible to track, and to buy or sell, securities on several Asian markets. Mutual funds were also using these computer advances to integrate and synthesize their reporting and investment operations.

Interestingly, larger mutual fund companies were experiencing stiffer competition from smaller competitors that were using the new technology to level the playing field. By forming alliances with fellow companies that offered complimentary services, specialty investment and consulting companies were delivering high quality packaged services for prices at or below those commanded by the large ''one-stop-shop'' mutual funds.

Information technology that allowed allied companies to integrate their reporting and investing data provided the crucial link necessary to fuse their services. The alliances had been especially successful at capturing and managing investment dollars from retirement plans that would have otherwise been invested with large mutual funds. The trend toward alliances proliferated in the mid-1990s.

FURTHER READING

Bharagava, Rahul, Ann Bose, and David A. Dubofsky. ''Exploiting International Stock Market Correlations with Open End International Mutual Funds.'' *Journal of Business Finance and Accounting,* June-July 1998.

Fidelity Magellan. Yahoo Fund Profile, 10 February 2000. Available from http://biz.yahoo.com/p/F/FAMGX.html.

Spain, Barbara. *Financial Services Industry. Hoovers Online.* Available from http://www.hoovers.com/industry/snapshot/o,2204,18,00.html.

U.S. Census Bureau. *1997 Economic Census.* Washington, D.C.: GPO 1999.

U.S. Department of Commerce. Economics and Statistics Administration. *County Business Patterns 1994.* Washington: GPO, September 1996.

Vanguard 500 Index. Yahoo Fund Profile, 10 February 2000. Available from http://biz.yahoo.com/p/V/VFINX.html.

Washington Mutual Investors. Yahoo Fund Profile, 10 February 2000. Available from http://biz.yahoo.com/p/A/AWSHX.htm.

SIC 6726

UNIT INVESTMENT TRUSTS, FACE AMOUNT CERTIFICATE OFFICES, AND CLOSED-END MANAGEMENT INVESTMENT TRUSTS

The closed-end investment industry consists of investment offices primarily engaged in issuing closed-end funds, unit investment trusts, or face amount certificates. For related information on investment industries, see **SIC 6722: Management Investment Offices, Open-End** and **SIC 6282: Investment Advice.**

NAICS CODE(S)

525990 (Other Financial Vehicles)

INDUSTRY SNAPSHOT

Unit investment trust (UIT) and closed-end fund (CEF) companies sell shares in securities portfolios. These shares must be purchased when they are initially issued—or afterwards on the open market—and are not redeemable before a designated date. Face amount certificates are essentially obligations of the issuing company to pay a fixed sum at a specified maturity date, and often require periodic payments by the purchaser.

Because shares in this industry's portfolios must be held until a set date, they are not as popular as open-end, or mutual, funds, although they may generate greater earnings. With a stable pool of money, portfolio managers can take more risks in search of profits, often investing in volatile countries and emerging markets. In 1999, there were 85 CEFs specializing in regions of specific countries. Many closed-end funds, which are traded on stock exchanges, are bargains, since they sell for less than the value of the stocks or other investments that they hold. Funds may also sell for more than their value. UITs do better than CEFs in garnering new assets. In 1998, UITs added 60 percent in assets and held $94.6 billion. On the other hand, CEF assets increased 1 percent to $151.6 billion. Fund managers included major brokerage houses as well as investment companies.

ORGANIZATION AND STRUCTURE

CEFs. Closed-end fund companies are similar to open-end mutual companies in that they both sell shares in a portfolio of actively managed securities. Shareholders benefit from efficient access to professional investment management and from portfolio diversification that they likely would be unable to achieve on their own. Unlike open-end funds, however, CEFs issue a fixed number of shares, which are sold through initial public offerings (IPOs). The money collected through this initial offering is invested in securities. After the IPO, shares may not be redeemed until a predetermined date. They must be sold and purchased through a broker on an exchange or through over-the-counter markets.

An important characteristic of a CEF share is that its price is determined by market demand and supply, rather than by the net asset value of the securities represented by the share. CEFs usually trade at a discount to their net asset value, which can vary widely for several reasons. While most CEF shares are traded on the New York Stock Exchange (NYSE), the American Stock Exchange (AMEX), and the National Association of Securities Dealers Automated Quotation (NASDAQ) systems trade CEFs as well.

After an investment company initiates a CEF, it employs a fund adviser to manage the investment of the shareholders' assets, to conduct research, and to handle administrative tasks. The fund advisory firm is often a subsidiary of the investment company. In fact, the CEF is often established for the purpose of allowing the investment company's directors to earn fees from managing the fund. The adviser's management fee is usually based on the amount of assets in the fund and is commonly set on a sliding scale that declines as total assets increase. Fees of 0.3 to 1.0 percent of fund assets are common, although some funds offer incentives that are linked to performance. When combined with other fund management costs, operating expenses can consume 10 percent or more of a fund's total income.

Several types of CEFs are offered by investment companies, including equity, bond, and specialty funds. Some portfolios are highly diversified while others emphasize a particular industry or security type. In the early 1990s, about 70 percent of all CEF assets were invested in bond funds. That percentage decreased slightly, to 66 percent, by the end of 1997, when $97.9 billion of the total $149 billion invested in closed-end funds was invested in bond funds. While the primary objective of a CEF that emphasizes bonds is to produce high yields, stock fund advisers seek capital gains. Specialty funds include nondiversified CEFs that focus on precious metals, venture capital, utilities, single or multiple countries, single industries, or other investments.

UITs. Like CEF companies, UIT investment firms issue shares in a fixed portfolio of assets that cannot be redeemed until a specified date, which is usually between 20 and 30 years after issuance. The shares are traded in the open market until their redemption. Unlike CEFs, however, UITs represent an undivided interest in a unit of specific securities—usually bonds. The trust does not have a board of directors and the pool of assets is fixed. The portfolio is, therefore, left mostly unmanaged for the trust's duration. The trust distributes the bonds' interest to shareholders until all the bonds mature or are called. UITs are often called defined or focused portfolios.

Because most UIT assets are invested in bonds, UIT participants purchase shares with the expectation of earning a steady, monthly income and then receiving most of their principal back when the shares expire. Investors theoretically get the benefit of holding bonds until maturation without the volatility and risks inherent in short-term trading. Unlike CEFs, or mutual funds for that matter, UIT shareholders know exactly what they are buying. One drawback, however, is that UIT portfolios are unresponsive to changing market conditions. In addition, many UIT holders find that their shares are difficult to liquidate in the open market.

BACKGROUND AND DEVELOPMENT

In Belgium, 1822, the first closed-end fund was created by King William I. In the 1860s, similar investment trusts were formed in Great Britain. In fact, the Foreign and Colonial Investment Trust, formed in London in 1868, was still operating in the early 1990s. In the 1880s, British CEFs began investing in the United States to achieve higher returns and diversification. These funds were instrumental in providing capital to finance Civil War reconstruction and to build railroads.

British CEFs led to the development, in 1893, of the Boston Personal Property Trust, the first American CEF. Excess capital generated during the 1920s caused a boom in CEFs, or investment trusts as they were referred to at that time. Several hundred new funds were formed, including the oldest CEF still in existence today—General American Investors, founded in 1927. Some 265 new funds were established in 1929 alone, many of which invested in stocks, and were highly leveraged.

When the stock market crash of October 1929 rocked financial markets, CEF investors took a beating. One dollar invested in a leveraged CEF index fund fell to a value of about five cents overnight. A positive outcome of the Great Depression for CEFs, however, was critical legislation that served to shape and promote the industry throughout much of the 1900s. The Securities Exchange Act of 1934 and the Investment Company Act of 1940 became the basis for regulation of both open- and closed-end funds.

Although asset growth in CEFs waned during the 1940s and 1950s, investors began to steadily reinvest during the 1960s and 1970s. Furthermore, the industry began to diversify its offerings. The Japan Fund, for example, became the first American CEF investing in a foreign country in 1962. Convertible funds and corporate bond funds also originated in the 1960s and early 1970s. By 1960, CEFs held about $2 billion—compared to only $613 million in 1940. However, by 1970, the industry had expanded its holdings to more than $4 billion. Total assets doubled again during the 1970s, reaching more than $8 billion by 1980.

Even though they were not introduced to U.S. markets until 1961, UITs enjoyed a growth pattern similar to that experienced by CEF companies during the 1960s and 1970s. The first UIT was a municipal securities fund. The industry expanded to include corporate and debt funds in 1972, and government securities funds in 1978. As investors increasingly sought the benefits touted by the UIT industry, assets poured into funds.

The 1980s. The boom in most financial markets during the 1980s contributed to growth for the closed-end investment industry. At the same time that securities and financial markets were benefiting from increased investment capital, investors were shifting their assets from government regulated bank deposits in an effort to garner higher returns. Often, these assets ended up in closed-end instruments or face amount certificates.

Also contributing to the growth of the industry was a variety of new fund offerings that lured new investors. For instance, ''personality funds,'' developed in the mid-1980s, maintained CEF portfolios that reflected the distinctive investment style of the portfolio manager. Gabelli Equity Trust, the Zweig Fund, and Z-Seven (Barry Ziskin's funds) were all popular personality funds in the 1980s and were still in existence in the late 1990s.

Single-country funds also proliferated in the 1980s. Funds that specialized in investing in Mexico, Korea, Australia, Indonesia, Germany, Turkey, and other countries experienced solid asset growth. The number of convertible bond funds also increased. UITs expanded into new financial vehicles as well, investing in junk bonds, zero-coupon bonds, and real estate.

Industry growth was evidenced by the number of public offerings for new CEFs in the late 1980s. Many of these IPOs were made following the stock market crash of 1987, when weak securities markets pushed many investors into bond funds. Although in 1980 there were no IPOs, and the following year there was only one, there were 26 in 1986, as well as 35 and 62 new issues in 1987 and 1988, respectively. Furthermore, total assets held in CEFs soared from less than $8 billion in 1985 to more than $55 billion by 1990. The number of CEFs grew from just 54 in 1985 to 209 by the end of the decade. UITs grew at a similar pace, encompassing about $130 billion in assets by 1989.

To the Mid-1990s. Many closed-end investment offices experienced steady asset growth in the early 1990s. The amount of money invested in CEFs, for instance, increased nearly 25 percent between 1991 and 1992. Weakened equity markets in the late 1980s, as well as an influx of assets from other financial institutions and investment instruments, were partly responsible for overall industry growth. Despite the success of CEFs and UITs, many investment professionals cautioned against them due to their difficulty to liquidate, lackluster returns, and the high risk involved. However, by the mid-1990s, 18 of the 150 CEFs available had returns on investment of 100 percent or greater.

Although open-end investment offices eclipsed the popularity of closed-end investment instruments, a significant portion of U.S. assets were held by UITs and CEFs in the mid-1990s. For instance, more than $85 billion was invested in CEFs, and about $200 billion in UITs had been sold. The 268 establishments in the United States selling UITs and CEFs were drawing in $388.3 million in revenue and employing 1,104 workers.

But the industry experienced a slowdown in asset growth during the same period. The saturation of CEF and UIT markets, stronger securities markets that were pushing investments into equity instruments, and the growing popularity of open-end mutual funds all contributed to the slowdown. For instance, UIT deposits fell in January 1993 to $819 million, down 12 percent from January 1992. Furthermore, while CEF assets climbed a healthy 35 percent between 1990 and 1992, this was well below the 70 percent growth experienced between 1987 and 1989.

The growing popularity of open-end mutual funds was seen as a threat to many closed-end investments. Many analysts felt that open-end funds, particularly no-loads, offered better returns. In addition, investors' open-end funds benefited from greater liquidity and more active portfolio management than with UITs. Indeed, assets in open-end funds had grown about 92 percent between 1980 and 1993, to more than $1.7 trillion—compared to the approximately $285 billion held by UITs and CEFs combined.

In the mid-1990s, the largest company in the industry was Meditrust SBI, of Massachusetts. This company had assets of $820 million and employed fewer than 100 people. The second largest company was RYMAC Mortgage Investment Corp. based in Maryland. RYMAC had assets of $564 million in 1992. Likewise, Source Capital Inc., the third largest based on its assets, had no employees and maintained capital of $286 million. The top 10 companies in the industry, in fact, employed fewer than 200 people in 1992.

Current Conditions

In the late 1990s, the industry was seeing only modest growth in new assets deposited. Closed-end fund assets increased 5 percent between 1996 and 1997, from $142.3 billion to $150.1 billion, but only 1 percent in 1998, to $151.6 billion. Assets were held by 476 U.S. funds. In 1999, 532 closed-end funds traded on U.S. stock exchanges held $123 billion in assets.

According to the Investment Company Institute, 2.3 percent of all U.S. households owned CEFs in 1998; 80 percent of them also owned open-end funds. The typical investor had $12,000 in two closed-end funds. Domestic equity and high-yield bond funds were the most popular types. In 1998, for the first time since 1994, investments in foreign securities declined to 18 percent of all CEF assets from 21 percent the previous year.

The value of unit investment trusts fared somewhat better than CEFs, increasing 10 percent per year in the late 1990s. Outstanding UITs had a market value of $78 billion in 1996, $86 billion in 1997, and $94.6 billion in 1998. Between 1997 and 1998, UITs added 60 percent in assets, while mutual fund assets dropped 12 percent. In the late 1990s, some UIT companies were extending their product lines by joining with insurance companies to offer defined portfolios with the advantages of tax-free annuities. For example, in 1999, Nike Securities and Ohio National Life Insurance Company began offering Nike's Dow 10 UIT as part of Ohio National's ONcore Series of variable annuities.

Industry Leaders

Familiar names in the financial services industry offer UITs and CEFs. Among those firms are Morgan Stanley, Paine Webber, Prudential Securities, Smith Barney, and Van Kampen. In addition, numerous investment companies offer the products. Tri-Continental Corporation, with more than $4 billion in assets, is the largest publicly traded, diversified closed-end investment company in the United States. Petroleum and Resources Corporation has approximately $475 million invested in some 80 stocks in the only closed-end fund specializing in oil and gas and other natural resource stocks. Adams Express Company, with $1.69 billion in total assets, and General American Investors Company, with $1.02 billion in total assets, also are major closed-end fund companies. The John Nuveen Company, which sells UITs as well as other investments, had 1999 sales of $349 billion.

Further Reading

Charski, Mindy. ''Bargains Down in the Basement.'' *U.S. News & World Report,* 12 April 1999.

Garrity, Mike. ''Closed-End Shareholders Invest Long-Term.'' *Mutual Fund Market News,* 3 May 1999.

''Hoover's Company Capsules.'' *Hoover's Online.* Austin, TX: Hoover's Inc., 1999. Available from http://www.hoovers.com/.

''Industry Stats.'' Kansas City: Closed-End Fund Association, 1999. Available from http://www.closed-endfunds.com.

Investment Company Institute. *A Guide to Closed-end Funds.* Washington, DC: Investment Company Institute, 1999. Available from http://www.ici.org.

Investment Company Institute. ''U.S. Household Ownership of Closed-End Funds in 1998.'' *Fundamentals: Investment Company Institute Research in Brief.* 8, no. 3 (April 1999). Available from http://www.ici.org.

Pizzani, Lori. ''Unit Investment Trusts Make Foray into Variable Annuities.'' *Annuity Market News,* 1 July 1999.

SIC 6732

EDUCATIONAL AND RELIGIOUS TRUSTS

The charitable trust industry is comprised of companies that manage educational, religious, and charitable trust funds and foundations. The industry also encompasses the trust operations of not-for-profit research institutes.

NAICS Code(s)

813211 (Grantmaking Foundations)

INDUSTRY SNAPSHOT

In the late 1990s, more than 4,000 organizations employing nearly 42,000 people managed charitable trusts. In addition, about 4,000 banks provided trust administration services. Employment by trust companies was up from about 28,600 in 1987, reflecting a trend toward an increase in assets in the trust industry during the 1980s. Between 1980 and 1986, for example, total assets in all trust funds increased from $571 billion to more than $1 trillion. Even the economic slowdown of the late 1980s and very early 1990s did little to inhibit U.S. charitable giving. And when economic good times returned in 1992 and 1993, U.S. contributions to charities showed a sharp jump. In an economic upturn of unprecedented length, sharply higher levels of charitable giving were observed even as the new millennium dawned.

Although banks provided most of the management services for charitable trusts, other institutions were competing with banks in the 1990s for control of the endowment management industry. In addition, trust departments at all financial institutions were facing rising management costs, the threat of federal tax laws, which could potentially diminish some benefits associated with charitable trusts, and decreased investment returns resulting from economic recession.

ORGANIZATION AND STRUCTURE

A trust is defined as a legal relationship in which one party holds title to property for the benefit of another. The arrangement involves the transfer of property by a "trustor" to a "trustee," who manages the property and issues benefits to the "beneficiaries." Although some companies, or trustees, specialize in trust management, most trustees are banks. Beneficiaries of a charitable trust may include any not-for-profit concern, such as churches, research institutes, schools, museums, governments, social or professional associations, and charity organizations.

In addition to cash, beneficiaries may receive such gifts as income-producing property, business inventory or equipment, securities, life insurance, works of art, real estate, or jewelry. Although the trustor typically donates property out of a sense of altruism, the trustee relationship may also provide a trustor with a reduction in tax liabilities. Charitable contributions are also sometimes used as an indirect means of transferring wealth among the trustor's family members, as well as to the beneficiary. A critical advantage that most trusts offer the contributor over other means of gift giving is the control a trustor can retain over the use of the donated property.

Trustee Responsibilities. A financial institution or trust company acting as a trustee for a charitable contribution assumes many legal duties. A trustee is expected to exhibit skill and care in administration and management of property. It is also expected to be loyal to the beneficiaries and to protect the trust property from outside attack. Other responsibilities include keeping accurate records and reporting to the beneficiary when required to do so by the trustor. Most importantly, the trustee is obliged to carry out the wishes of the trustor in good faith.

Unlike all other forms of trusts, the conditions placed on a charitable trust are usually enforced by the federal government on behalf of U.S. citizens. In fact, the entire trust industry is closely regulated by the federal government. If the trustee violates his trust, by making an unlawful investment for instance, the beneficiary may reclaim the property.

In return for assuming responsibilities associated with trusteeship, the bank or trust company retains compensation from the property based on the amount of assets under management. For many banks, fees from trust services are of vital importance.

Types of Charitable Trusts. Donors used a variety of trusts to transfer their wealth to nonprofit causes in the 1990s. Each type of trust offered different advantages pertaining to the amount of control that the trustor could exercise over the gift, various tax benefits that could accrue to the trustor, and the method of compensation bestowed upon the beneficiary.

In the charitable remainder annuity trust (CRAT), a fixed amount of property is periodically distributed to noncharitable parties, often including the grantor of the trust. After a recipient dies, the remainder of the CRAT then passes to a charitable organization. Among other advantages, the CRAT allows the grantor to receive charitable income tax deductions equal to the present value of the remainder interest ultimately received by the charity. These deductions are used to offset income from the trust during the grantor's life.

The wealth replacement trust is used in conjunction with a charitable gift. This complex type of trust is used to replace assets given to a charity while at the same time benefitting specific noncharitable parties—often family members of the grantor. The grantor may receive valuable tax benefits related to capital gains, gift, and estate taxes. Furthermore, survivors of the grantor's estate often benefit from reduced inheritance taxes.

Charitable lead trusts distribute income to charitable entities for a fixed term. At the end of the term the remainder of the trust is transferred to a noncharitable beneficiary, such as a spouse or child. One benefit of the charitable lead trust is that the grantor avoids estate taxes on the value of assets that defaults to the beneficiaries.

A pooled income fund is a trust maintained by a charitable organization. Each donor that transfers income to the pool may be eligible to receive significant income tax and gift tax deductions, as well as estate tax benefits.

Charitable gift annuities, which became popular in the 1980s, bestow similar benefits upon donors. This type of trust, however, is arranged so that the grantor receives a specified sum of money each year for the remainder of the donor's life.

Other charitable trusts include "bargain sales," in which a donor sells property to charities for below market prices, and "charitable stock bailouts," in which a donor contributes closely held stock to a charity and derives various tax and business benefits.

Background and Development

Trust officers, or their equivalent, have been holding, managing, and caring for the property of others since around 4000 B.C., when the practice was common in Egypt. Various prototypes of trust institutions were later developed in second-century Rome, some of which involved the use of property for charitable purposes. The industry began evolving into its present form in eighth-century England, where clergymen served as executors of wills and trusts. Throughout the Middle Ages and the sixteenth and seventeenth centuries, trusts developed under English common law into a semblance of their present form.

The trust business in the United States may be traced back about 150 years, when trusts began to serve the estates of wealthy businessmen and were used to transfer the wealth of some farmers. The first institution chartered to engage in the trust business was Farmer's Fire Insurance and Loan Company, founded in 1822. By 1840, several life insurance companies and financial institutions were involved in the industry. In 1906, Congress elected to allow banks to enter the trust business, and by 1920, about 1,300 banks were offering trust services.

After the Great Depression, federal laws began to have a significant impact on the trust industry. The amount of money in trusts during this time escalated, despite the initial inconsistency of U.S. regulations pertaining to trusts. Also affecting trusts in the twentieth century were periods of inflation. For instance, a long period of inflation during the 1970s produced demand for higher returns on trust funds by beneficiaries and donors. As a result, many trustees began investing funds in riskier and shorter-term investment vehicles in an effort to remain competitive with other financial products and services.

The 1980s. The greatest growth in charitable trusts occurred during the early and mid-1980s, when assets in non-employee benefit trust accounts jumped from $342 billion in 1980 to more than $614 billion by 1986. During much of this period, higher returns on market investments as well as tax advantages made trusts more attractive. The Tax Reform Act of 1986, however, proved a pivotal piece of legislation for trustees. The Act created increased paperwork for many trustees, resulting in greater confusion and management expenses.

The increase in the number of available investment products also increased management expenses. Although trustee revenues climbed during the 1980s as charitable assets grew, increased costs outpaced income growth for many companies. Even a massive industry investment in computer automation during the 1970s and 1980s did not allow many trustees to maintain traditional profit margins.

To make matters worse, many banks began to experience severe financial distress in the late 1980s as economic recess and general mismanagement culminated in reduced profits from lending activities. Banks were increasingly relying on income from services, such as trust management, to buoy income. As the industry became more competitive, profit margins on trust services were reduced for many companies. Trust managers knew that if they could not deliver competitive investment returns and deliver good service that they risked losing valuable trust clients to more efficient investment vehicles and tax shelters.

The 1990s. In the early 1990s the charitable trust industry was benefitting primarily from two circumstances. First, Americans began donating more money than ever before to charitable causes. While 1987 saw donations of more than $93 billion to charities, donations in the 1990s were estimated at well over $100 billion per year. This level of spending continued into the new millennium, with a growing portion of this spending directed to science-oriented projects, according to the American Association for the Advancement of Science (AAAS). The organization estimated that U.S. private foundations poured about $20 billion into charitable trusts in 1999.

Second, increases in taxes on the wealthy and a reduction in tax loopholes, a result of the Tax Reform Act of 1986, were causing many people to consider charitable contributions as tax shelters. The results of growth in the industry following the Tax Reform Act of 1986 are reflected in employment by firms that specialize in managing charitable trusts. Despite hefty company investments in labor-saving automation, the number of people employed in the industry rose from about 22,000 in 1986 to about 40,000 by 1990. Similarly, the annual payroll of these firms increased from about $383 million to more than $726 million—a 90 percent increase.

Although greater amounts of money flowing into charitable trusts was creating a boon for many firms in the industry, trustees in the 1990s were also facing potential obstacles. For instance, charitable trusts were threatened by such legislation as the generation-skipping transfer tax (GST). Although the GST had been in existence since the early 1980s, its impact was not realized until the 1990s, when families trying to transfer wealth through charities were penalized. Among other effects, the GST increased taxes on wealth passed to nonprofit beneficiaries through charitable trusts. Furthermore, in 1996 certain sections of the Income Tax Assessment Act 1936 were amended to restrict distribution of funds outside the United States. The amendment was applied to charitable trusts established after August 1996, and became effective after their 1996-97 income year. Apparently, this was a move by the government to prevent charitable trusts from being used as a means to recycle funds back to the trustor's beneficiary without tax penalty. Therefore, it was expected to have little impact on genuine charities.

In addition to a variety of legislative issues, some trustees were also fighting beneficiaries who began to contest the traditional fee structure employed by most managers. Plaintiffs in lawsuits alleged that banks charging fees of one-half to one percent were receiving excessive compensation for what amounted to a few administrative duties. Beneficiaries of larger accounts, in particular, were suffering, and, according to the plaintiffs, the trustees were not acting in the interest of the beneficiary. Indeed, many heirs and beneficiaries of charitable trusts favored a free and competitive trust marketplace where accounts could be switched to trustees of their preference—a practice forbidden by federal regulations in the early 1990s.

In an effort to combat downward pressures on profit margins, trustees were applying several tactics going into the mid-1990s. In addition to reducing labor costs through automation, trustees were stepping up their marketing efforts. Many were also combining accounts to achieve economies of scale and to reduce transaction fees related to purchasing securities. Also, many companies were experimenting for the first time with tying trust officers' compensation to portfolio and department performance.

INDUSTRY LEADERS

Throughout the 1990s, Bankers Trust New York Corporation was one of the largest providers of trust services in the nation. The corporation managed more than $200 billion of non-employee benefit trust assets for more than 350 clients. The company's trust department offered a wide range of services, including performance measurement; portfolio management, analysis, and review; record keeping and benefit disbursement; tax accounting; and international investment services. At the end of the decade, this major New York banking institution was acquired by Germany's Deutsche Bank A.G. in a move that made the latter the largest bank in the world.

Chemical Bank of New York was another major trustee in the 1990s. It managed non-employee benefit trust assets of more than $65 billion for 469 clients. Later in the decade, Chemical Bank purchased the Chase Manhattan Bank Corporation, which managed some $62 billion in non-employee benefit trust assets, and took the Chase name as its own. Other large trustees included Citicorp of New York, which managed $38 billion in nonemployee benefit trust assets, Comerica of Detroit ($41 billion), State Street Bank and Trust Company of Boston ($160 billion), and Northern Trust Company of Chicago ($148 billion).

WORKFORCE

During the 1980s, most of the firms that specialized in managing trusts for religious, educational, and other nonprofit trusts were small companies; in the early 1990s, more than 3,000 of the 4,000 companies that served the industry had fewer than 20 employees. However, as companies in the industry followed a pattern of consolidation through merger and acquisition, the number of large companies began to increase in the 1990s as the percentage of smaller companies declined.

Jobs in the charitable trust industry exist primarily with banks and trust companies. Trust departments hire trust officers and support staff to manage investments, handle reporting and record keeping activities, market trust services to potential grantors, and distribute benefits. In the 1990s, trust officers at large banks earned $35,000 to $45,000 on average, while their counterparts at small and midsize banks earned about $28,000 to $38,000. Trust support staff earned $20,000 to $30,000 on average. Senior trust officers average approximately $100,000 per year, and trust investment officers averaged about $47,000.

Positions in the charitable trust industry are expected to increase faster than the average for all U.S. industries through the year 2005. Although new tax laws may diminish advantages associated with transferring wealth to nonprofit beneficiaries through charities, a generally inhospitable tax environment will likely keep charitable trusts attractive. The general increase in charitable giving should also expand the industry. Growth should occur in computer programming and information systems jobs, which are projected to increase more than 100 percent by 2005. Sales and marketing positions for trust services should also realize disproportionate increases.

RESEARCH AND TECHNOLOGY

As the cost of managing charitable trusts has grown with increased regulation and investment requirements, trust managers have turned to automation and advanced information systems to hold profit margins steady. In the late 1970s and 1980s companies were reducing costs related to such labor as data entry and basic accounting tasks. By the late 1980s and going into the 1990s, advanced systems were automating more detailed tasks, such as maintaining asset inventories, making disbursements to beneficiaries, calculating dividend payments and printing checks, trading securities, and filing tax information.

New image technology was beginning to be used in banks and trust departments in the 1990s. Using these advancements, trust administrators were able to reduce paperwork and reporting tasks by scanning forms and reports into their computer. The images were then automatically filed and processed by the computer system and made available for easy access at a later date.

FURTHER READING

Cohen, Jon. "Science Funding: Philanthropy's Rising Tide Lifts Science." *Science,* 8 October 1999.

Computer Law Services. "Measures to Reduce Avoidance Through Charitable Trusts." Available from http://www.cls.com.au/tax/budget/28.htm.

Darnay, Arsen J., ed. *Finance, Insurance, and Real Estate USA,* 4th ed. Detroit: Gale Research, 1998.

Hermann, William. "Arizonans Glad to Aid Charities; Report Tracks Giving Around Country." *Arizona Republic,* 20 December 1999.

"Hoover's Company Capsules." *Hoover's Online.* Austin, TX: Hoover's Inc., 2000. Available from http://www.hoovers.com/.

SIC 6733

TRUSTS, EXCEPT EDUCATIONAL, RELIGIOUS, AND CHARITABLE

The trust industry is comprised of companies that manage trust funds and foundations, excluding those whose beneficiaries are educational, religious, and charitable organizations.

NAICS CODE(S)

523920 (Portfolio Management)
523991 (Trust, Fiduciary, and Custody Services)
525190 (Other Insurance and Employee Benefit Funds)
525920 (Trusts, Estates, and Agency Accounts)

INDUSTRY SNAPSHOT

In the late 1990s, approximately 6,000 organizations, employing more than 30,000 people, managed noncharitable trusts. Approximately 4,000 banks that competed in the industry, however, provided the bulk of trust administration services in the United States.

The decline in the growth of funds invested in trusts reflected a recessed economy in the late 1980s that persisted into the early 1990s. Contributing to the decline was competition for U.S. investment dollars between banks, trust companies, and other financial institutions. In addition, trust departments at all financial institutions were facing rising management costs, the threat of federal tax laws that could potentially diminish some benefits associated with trust funds, and decreased investment returns caused by the recession. Although employment in the industry remained below its peak levels of the late 1980s, the flow of money into noncharitable trusts showed an increase in the mid- to late 1990s as the U.S. economy experienced unprecedented growth. By the close of the century, the economy had strengthened and so had growth of trust funds.

ORGANIZATION AND STRUCTURE

A trust is a tool that an individual or institution uses to transfer property to a beneficiary. The entity that grants the property is called the trustor. The trustor gives the property to the trustee, which is charged with the task of disbursing the property to a beneficiary according to the instructions of the trustor. One advantage that a trust has over a simple gift is that the trustor can exercise control over the disposition of the property over time, providing stipulations that must be adhered to even after an individual trustor has died or an institution acting as trustor has dissolved. A second and perhaps more important advantage is that trusts can often be used to minimize tax burdens incurred when transferring wealth.

Trustee Duties and Benefits. Although trust companies and banks expect to make a profit by acting as trustees, they have a legal responsibility to act in the best interest of the beneficiary and the trustor and to conduct their activities with skill and care. Responsibilities include: protecting trust assets from attack by outside parties; dispensing property to beneficiaries; investing trust assets in a prudent manner; keeping accurate records; and accounting to the beneficiary as specified by the trustor.

In return for their services, trustees are compensated by one of several methods. One pricing schedule delegates a percentage of the market value of assets under management to a trust account. Under this arrangement, trustees typically charge from 0.1 to 0.5 percent, and in some cases as much as 1 percent per year of the total value of assets in the trust. For example, a $2 million trust fund might yield $5,000, or 0.25 percent, in annual fees.

Similarly, some trustees charge a "gross income receipts fee," which is a percentage of income collected from interest and dividends on the account. For instance, if the trustee earned interest and dividends of $50,000 by investing account assets for a period of one year, the trustee might receive 5 percent of those proceeds—or $2,500. In addition to these charges, some trustees charge minimum annual management fees and activity fees for special services.

Types of Trusts. Noncharitable trust accounts managed by banks and trust companies are categorized as either individual or institutional accounts. Individual accounts can be further classified into personal agencies or trusts.

Personal agency accounts are different from ordinary trust accounts in that property does not actually change hands. Instead, the trust company simply manages assets under the direction of its client, often acting as a safekeeping agent, custodian, manager, or escrow agent. The company may provide complete investment management and reporting services as well.

Individual trust accounts involve a beneficiary. The trustor establishes an account with a trustee that manages, invests, and distributes the property. Income from the assets is then used to benefit dependents, organizations, children, or other people or entities. The trust may also be used to benefit the trustor. A multitude of trust structures exist allowing a trustor to achieve various tax benefits and to retain varying degrees of control over account assets.

Two types of individual trusts are guardianships and estate settlement accounts. Under a guardianship arrangement, the trustee acts as a guardian of a minor or mental incompetent, caring for the property that benefits that person. Estate settlements, on the other hand, involve securing and valuing a client's assets, distributing assets in accordance with a will, and otherwise representing the client's wishes at death. Individual trusts are also classified as either revocable or irrevocable. Revocable trusts are used to distribute wealth while the grantor is still living and can be amended at any time. In an irrevocable trust, the trustor relinquishes all control over account assets.

Like individual trusts, institutional trusts can also be broken down into agency and trust accounts. Institutional trusts, however, exist to raise capital for businesses, to reward employees, or to provide income for retired employees. The two most common types of corporate agencies are transfer agencies and registrarships. Trustees in these agency relationships serve to transfer and register stocks and bonds.

Under a corporate trust, the trust company acts as a trustee for a group of people that lends money to a corporation through bonds or other obligatory instruments. Employee benefit accounts are another form of corporate trust. These trusts provide full custody services, compliance reporting, investment management, and special record keeping of each participating employee's interest in pension, profit-sharing, and other benefit accounts.

BACKGROUND AND DEVELOPMENT

In the United States, the trust business got its start in 1822. That year, Farmer's Fire Insurance and Loan Company of New York became the first institution chartered to engage in the trust business. Besides serving the needs of wealthy individuals, the company pioneered the concept of corporate trusts in 1830, to help raise money for business ventures. Over the next 50 years, the number and types of institutions engaged in the trust business rose rapidly. Most of these entities maintained a separate department that was devoted exclusively to trust services, which was removed from the firm's other business concerns.

In 1906, Congress elected to allow banks to begin engaging in the trust industry. As a result, about 1,300 national banks were offering trust services by 1920. After the Great Depression, the industry was rattled by legislation that essentially restricted institutions other than banks and trust companies from serving as trustees. Legislation also established what became known as the ''Chinese Wall''—referring to measures that forbade commercial and trust departments of a bank from sharing customer credit or investment information.

Furthermore, as a result of the ways in which the Depression brought about new attitudes toward saving and investing for the future, the industry began to encompass more diverse segments of the American population. Employee benefit trusts, for example, became popular in the 1940s. Since that time, employee benefit trusts proliferated so rapidly that Congress enacted the Employee Retirement Income Security Act (ERISA) in 1974 to define the responsibilities of trustees managing those funds. By 1986, employee benefit trusts represented more than 40 percent of all U.S. trust assets.

Investments in individual trusts also escalated after the Depression. Wealthy individuals, in particular, increasingly used trusts as a way to invest their savings and to transfer wealth. Increases in tax benefits that allowed trustors to avoid estate and gift taxes also boosted the trust industry.

The 1970s and 1980s. In the late 1970s and early 1980s the trust industry began to undergo changes caused by a number of economic and regulatory influences. For instance, high interest rates and deregulation of certain sectors of the financial markets prompted trust departments to invest their assets in new instruments. Instead of traditional T-bills and commercial paper, trustees began putting money into certificates of deposit, money market funds, variable-rate notes, and other more risky investments. In addition, a strong economy in the mid-1980s generated an influx of investment dollars, much of which went into trust funds. Between 1980 and 1986, the total amount of money invested in trusts jumped from $571 billion to $1.065 trillion.

Although industry assets under management continued to climb throughout 1987, trustees began to suffer in the late 1980s. The Tax Reform Act (TRA) of 1986, for instance, increased paperwork for trustees and created some confusion, serving to discourage the use of trusts and estates as devices to accumulate wealth. The act's provisions also added to the already rising costs associated with managing trusts.

The TRA and other regulatory measures, in addition to the recession of the late 1980s, began exerting downward pressure on trust department profit margins. Investment in trust funds slowed in the late 1980s at the same time that investment returns were shrinking. Even a massive industry investment in labor-saving technology during the 1980s was not enough to buoy profits for many companies. Between 1987 and 1989, the number of trust companies dropped from 6,285 to 4,283, and total employment fell from 32,491 to 25,853. The total payroll of those companies also fell—from $666 million to $574 million. At this time, approximately $229 billion in employee benefit trusts and $342 billion in other types of trusts were being managed by trust companies.

Current Conditions

In the 1990s, the trust industry was facing the promise of asset growth throughout the decade. The most important reason was the increased amount of personal savings by aging baby boomers and their need to arrange means to transfer wealth was likely to elevate opportunities available to trust companies and banks. The trust industry had grown in importance in the late 1980s and 1990s, as well, because service fees from trusts had become an important stream of revenue for many banks that were suffering losses on loan portfolios.

Despite the expectation of a recovery in the industry, trustees were still struggling to maintain profits in an increasingly competitive marketplace. Mutual funds, defined-benefit contribution plans like the 401(k), and other investment vehicles were competing for investment dollars that might otherwise go to banks and trust companies. Trust departments were also battling rising costs associated with reporting, accounting, and investment activities.

However, Congress passed the Taxpayer Relief Act of 1997 that raised the amount of total assets permitted in a trust without tax penalty to $1 million by 2006. The passage of this legislation was expected to cause some to use trusts more in estate planning.

Cutting Costs. To remain competitive and sustain profit margins, most banks and trust departments continued their efforts to reduce administrative costs, improve investment performance, and improve service in the 1990s. The most potent weapon to cut costs was new technology. In addition, many trustees were actively marketing their services for the first time, rather than waiting for business to come to them. Some banks, for instance, were giving their trust officers specific client-contact goals that encouraged them to initiate new business.

Another important change that many trust departments were experimenting with was performance-based incentives for investment personnel. Indeed, some trust departments were realizing productivity gains by linking the performance of their investments to portfolio managers' compensation. Trustees were also achieving savings by grouping accounts with similar investment objectives, allowing them to operate more efficiently and to obtain leverage in their investment purchases and sales.

Cost-cutting efforts were likely paying off, according to at least one study conducted by the American Bankers' Association. The study indicated that commercial bank trust departments outperformed nonbank investment managers over a 10-year period ending in 1992. The study showed that bank trusts produced higher yields than mutual funds, insurance companies, and equity fund advisors. Furthermore, bank trusts exhibited more consistent results, according to the study, because they had lower risk profiles.

In 1997, the trust, fiduciary, and custody services section of the industry was composed of 2,286 establishments and generated $6.9 billion. This subsection employed 47,843 people.

Industry Leaders

Although banks provide most of the trust services in the United States, the non-bank trust industry is dominated by small firms. In the early 1990s, for instance, 94 percent of the 4,283 trust companies that served the market employed fewer than 20 people. Furthermore, only five companies had more than 250 employees. The largest trust company in 1992, according to the amount of total company assets, was Continental Auxiliary Company of San Francisco. Although it employed fewer than 100 people, Continental had more than $90 million in assets. Detroit Heritage Fund Limited Partnership of Michigan was a distant second, with approximately $3 billion in assets.

One of the largest bank trust departments in the United States in the 1990s was Bankers Trust Company of New York, which in mid-1999 was acquired by Germany's Deutsche Bank A.G. This acquisition made the German bank the largest banking institution in the world. Late in the 1990s, this company managed more than $750 billion in trust assets. Another major player among the banks managing trust assets during the 1990s was State Street Bank and Trust Company of Boston.

Research and Technology

Advanced computer systems and information technology had become a vital link to survival for many trustees by the 1990s. By implementing labor-saving information systems, trustees were reducing costs, eliminating errors, and improving the efficiency of their reporting operations. The systems were used to maintain inventories of account assets, determine when and to whom disbursements should be paid, calculate dividend payments, print checks, and handle tax accounting and reporting tasks.

For trust departments that wanted the advantages of high technology without having to manage the investment and implementation, outsourcing became a popular option in the 1990s. By outsourcing many of their trust operations to third party vendors, trustees reaped the benefits of automated accounting, control, and reporting systems that were completely integrated with their investment and customer service activities. Many trust departments were quickly reducing operations costs by 15 percent to 40 percent, while at the same time having more predictable and less-risky cost outlays that would be required by in-house automation.

FURTHER READING

"Could the Unified Credit Be Going Up Again?" *SaveWealth.Com,* 28 September 1998.

Darnay, Arsen J., ed. *Finance, Insurance, and Real Estate USA,* 4th ed. Detroit: Gale Research, 1998.

Hoover's Online, 2000. "Bankers Trust Corporation." Available from http://www.hoovers.com/premium/history/9/0,2156,10179,00.html.

U.S. Census Bureau. *1997 Economic Census.* Washington: GPO 1999.

SIC 6792

OIL ROYALTY TRADERS

This industry classification includes establishments primarily engaged in investing in oil and gas royalties or leases, or fractional interest therein.

NAICS CODE(S)

523999 (Miscellaneous)
533110 (Owners and Lessors of Other Non-Financial Assets)

Companies in the oil royalty trading industry invest in oil and gas royalties and leases. Besides investing for third parties, they may also buy and sell interests for themselves. In the mid-1990s, there were 746 establishments engaged in this activity, but the number has increased, hitting 973 by 1997, according to *Dun's Census of American Business.* These are mostly small operations—78 percent (or 767) of these operations had less than five employees. Thirty of these establishments, however, posted revenues over $5 million each in 1997.

An oil and gas lease is a contract between a mineral owner and the company that wants to extract oil and gas deposits. The lease specifies the length of time that the company is allowed to mine the mineral owner's deposits, rental payments, advance compensation for exclusive drilling rights, and other terms of the agreement. A typical rental payment is usually a relatively small amount, ranging from $1 to $10 annually per acre. This rental payment, which is also called a deferred drilling payment, serves to legally maintain the lease contract when the company is not actively drilling. This rental payment is not what generates high income for the mineral owner. The big money comes if oil or gas is actually found on the land.

The mineral lease also specifies royalties. The royalty is the percentage of revenues that the company pays to the mineral owner in the event that gas and petroleum is actually extracted from the land. Royalties vary from 10 percent to as high as 25 percent of total oil and gas revenues before any associated drilling expenses are subtracted.

Because the true value of a royalty interest is unknown before the company drills for oil and gas, investing in royalties and leases can be a highly speculative endeavor. Royalty owners often sell part of their interests to reduce their exposure to risk or to generate cash. Royalty investment companies that buy and sell such royalties are trying to either gain a return on their investment or generate commissions by investing for their clients.

Investors have been trading oil and gas rights in the United States since the early 1800s. Between 1859 and 1870 more than 10,500 new oil and gas wells were drilled. Between 1871 and 1900, an additional 135,000 wells sprang up. It was during first two decades of the twentieth century, however, that investments in oil and gas ventures started to boom. More than 400,000 new wells were drilled during that period. The number of new wells drilled annually continued to rise through the 1950s to more than 50,000 by 1959.

The royalty investment industry, which is largely driven by drilling activity, sagged between 1960 and 1979 in comparison to the first half of the century. Skyrocketing foreign oil prices in the late 1970s and early 1980s, however, spurred renewed U.S. drilling. The number of new wells drilled jumped past 90,000 per year, and U.S. oil production surged to nearly 9 million barrels per day in the early- and mid-1980s. Growth was short-lived, however, as falling crude and gas prices plummeted in the late 1980s. By 1990 the United States was producing about 7 million barrels of oil per day. That number has declined in the 1990s. In December 1999, the U.S. produced 5.9 million barrels a day, down slightly from a year earlier when production stood at 6 million barrels per day. During this same time, liquid natural gas production stood at 1.8 million barrels per day, up from 1.6 million the previous December.

Oil and gas drilling in the United States, however, ended 1999 on a strong note. According to *Petroleum Finance Week,* during the fourth quarter of 1999, completions of oil and gas wells and dry holes hit 5,442, a 5 percent increase from 5,188 completions during 1998's fourth quarter. The number of U.S. drilling permits increased in 31.2 percent in December 1999 to 2,445, as compared to 1,864 a year earlier. There was, however, a 32 percent decrease in the total footage drilled, from 139.5 million feet in 1998's fourth quarter, to 19.5 million feet in 1999.

Going into the mid-1990s, royalty investment firms were still suffering from the effects of low energy prices and reduced drilling activity. Revenues dropped more than 13 percent to around $70 million. Likewise, the number of royalty trading companies slipped from 600 to 550. The industry continued its decline in the early 1990s as the number of active U.S. oil wells continued to drop. Contributing to the continued lull in U.S. oil and gas royalty trading activity was an increase in drilling overseas, particularly in South America and Australia.

U.S. oil and natural gas drilling expenditures, however, have increased in the late 1990s and in 1998 hit the highest level they had been since 1985. In 1998, total drilling expenditures rose 9.6 percent from 1997 and were estimated at $17.6 billion, up from $16.0 billion the previous year, according to the ''1998 Joint Association Survey on Drilling Costs''.

Despite a slowdown in the 1980s and 1990s, the long-term prospects for the oil and gas royalty investment industry are bright. Crude and gas prices, which are rising as a result of multiple factors, should boost investment activity and profits. Industry employment was expected to jump significantly between 1990 and 2005, according to the U.S. Bureau of Labor Statistics. Jobs for executives, which make up 10 percent of the industry work force, should climb by more than 50 percent. Management support positions should rise similarly, and sales and legal positions will likely leap more than 70 percent.

FURTHER READING

American Petroleum Institute. ''1998 Drilling Expenditures.'' 9 November 1999. Available from http://www.api.org/release.cgi.

———. ''Energy Facts & FAQs.'' January 2000. Available from http://www.api.org/faqs/.

Darnay, Arsen J., ed. *Finance, Insurance, and Real Estate, USA.* Detroit: Gale Research, 1996.

Dun's Census of American Business, 1997. Bethlehem, PA: Dun and Bradstreet, 1997.

''U.S. Oil and Gas Drilling Showed Strength Toward the End of Last Year.'' *Petroleum Finance Week,* 7 February 2000.

SIC 6794

PATENT OWNERS AND LESSORS

This classification includes establishments primarily engaged in owning or leasing franchises, patents, and copyrights that they in turn license others to use.

NAICS CODE(S)

533110 (Owners and Lessors of Other Non-Financial Assets)

The patent owners and lessors industry deals with the sale of intangible rights in property. This business has often become controversial, as it is sometimes difficult to determine who created the property, and thus who is entitled to transfer rights in it. Another problem has been making a distinction between similar examples of intangible property, like two similar songs or books, for instance.

This industry covers three forms of intangible property: copyright, franchise, and patent. Copyright generally refers to literary or artistic products of an intangible nature; franchise deals with the trademark and goodwill of a business enterprise; and patents concern products and industrial processes.

In general, licensing entails granting permission to perform a specified activity. In the case of this industry, it constitutes permission to use someone else's intellectual property. Copyright, patents, rights in music, and performance rights are all aspects of intellectual property. Rights in these forms of intangible property are protected by law to a similar extent as rights in real property. These licenses are personal to the licensee and thus are not transferable or assignable except by express agreement. They are also generally revocable at any time.

Franchising entails granting rights to operate a business of a uniform type to a franchisee by permission of the franchiser. In general, the franchiser grants an individual, the franchisee, the right to operate a business under its name. In exchange for a substantial portion of the individual business' revenues and support from the franchiser, the franchisee pays an up-front fee and a portion of revenues and agrees to use specified products and procedures in the operation of the business. According to the U.S. Department of Commerce, 40 percent of all retail sales are from franchise businesses. Predictions place that figure up to more than 50 percent by the year 2000. In 1995 there were 540,000 franchise businesses in the United States, employing more than 8 million people. The franchise industry generated $758 billion in sales in 1995 alone.

The major components of the patent owners and lessors industry include: copyright buying and licensing; franchise selling and licensing; music licensing to radio stations; sheet and record music royalties; patent buying and licensing; and performance rights licensing. Each of the various entities that constitute this industry have different organizations and structures.

Copyright Buying and Licensing. Under copyright law, the writer or originator of literary or artistic productions receive sole and exclusive privilege of the making and sale of copies for a prescribed statutory period. This right could be bought, sold, and licensed, just as any other rights in property. For example, the rights to copy and sell the recording of a song could be sold by the writer to another party. This party might license the rights to the song to a third party, allowing this party to produce and sell copies of the recording in a specified area, such as another country.

Franchise Selling or Licensing. Under a franchising arrangement, the franchisee receives the exclusive right to use brand names, trademarks, patents, as well as the right to engage in the manufacture, sale, or provision of products or services owned by the franchiser in a specified area for a fee. After the business begins operation, the franchiser continues to provide support in the form of supplies, advertising, and managerial aid in exchange for an operational fee based on the franchisee's revenue. This relationship allows the franchiser to expand its operation quickly without directly investing large amounts of capital. It also allows the franchisee to start a business under the sponsorship of an established firm, capitalizing on its business goodwill, product line, and operating ideas and methods.

This form of enterprise first became popular in the 1960s and was especially important in the growth of the fast food industry. In 1998, McDonald's Corporation had the greatest total annual sales at $12.4 billion and the second largest number of units at 25,000—80 percent of which are franchised. TRICON Global Restaurants, which owns KFC (formerly Kentucky Fried Chicken), Pizza Hut, and Taco Bell, was second in sales at $8.4 billion and first in number of units at 29,700 combined.

The 1980s and 1990s saw a proliferation of the types of industries utilizing the franchise structure. Some examples include video rental outlets, private postal services, early childhood education facilities, and health food stores. Despite this trend toward a wider range of franchised business, most of the market has still been in fast food.

Music Licensing to Radio Stations. The owner of a copyright in music has the exclusive right to perform the work. However, it would be very difficult for an individual owner to police and enforce this right against the numerous radio stations, nightclubs, and other music sources in the United States. Similarly, it would be very difficult for an individual radio station to negotiate directly with the several hundred copyright owners whose works they use each day. These difficulties have been overcome by performing rights societies, which act as clearinghouses for performance rights on behalf of many copyright owners. Thus, the individual stations could buy a blanket license for all of the music represented by a given society for a fixed fee. The society then pays the music creators.

The three most important societies in the United States were the American Society of Composers, Authors, and Publishers (ASCAP); Broadcast Music, Inc. (BMI); and SESAC, Inc., formerly the Society of European Stage Authors and Composers. These organizations together represented more than 90,000 writers and 50,000 publishers in 1999.

Sheet and Record Music Royalties. A royalty describes the payment made to the holder of the right to use patented or copyrighted property. Royalties are calculated as a percentage of income arising from the commercialization of the owner's rights or property. For each copy of printed or recorded music sold, the copyright owner receives a fixed percentage of the revenues.

Patent Buying and Licensing. A patent entails granting an individual the privilege of exclusive rights to make and sell an invention for a term of years. The difference between a patent and a copyright is that the former protected the right to exploit a particular process or design in making a physical product and was usually industrial in nature. The latter pertains to ideas and purely intangible creations of the mind and is usually artistic in nature.

As with other property rights, patents can be sold or licensed. For example, an inventor could patent the design of a transmission system and then sell the right to produce the system to a major automobile manufacturer. The manufacturer could in turn allow one of its suppliers to produce the system for a limited time or for limited purposes by granting it a license. Just as patent rights could be bought, sold, and licensed, they could also be leased—given for use for a fixed period for a fixed sum. In 1998, the United States granted 260,889 total patents. Of that amount, 93 percent were utility patents (those for the invention of a new or improved item).

Performance Rights Publishing and Licensing. Certain performances of copyrighted material are exempt from copyright protection. For example, performance of copyrighted work without any commercial purpose and without the payment of any fee—as long as there is no admission charge or such revenues are donated for educational, religious, or charitable purposes—are exempt. All other performances require permission of the creator. This permission is obtained by requesting a license—the right to perform the work for certain purposes and with certain restrictions. Similarly, printed material could not be copied and used by any party, except the creator, unless a license is granted allowing the use of the material for specified purposes.

Copyright and patent were well-established concepts, tracing their history to the common law of Great Britain. The explosive development of technology and popular culture in the mid-1900s led to the increased importance of this field. Franchising was relatively new, but flowed logically from the concepts of intangible property embodied in copyright and patent. This field grew steadily beginning in the 1960s and was significant in the development of certain consumer-related industries, especially fast food.

FURTHER READING

About ASCAP. *The American Society of Composers, Authors, and Publishers,* 1999. Available from http://www.ascap.com.

Hoover's Company Capsules. *Hoover's Online: The Business Network,* 1999. Available from http://www.hoovers.com.

U.S. Patent Statistics. *U.S. Patent and Trademark Office,* 1999. Available from http://www.uspto.gov.

Wright, John W., ed. *The Universal Almanac.* Andrews & McNeel, 1997.

SIC 6798

REAL ESTATE INVESTMENT TRUSTS

This industry covers establishments primarily engaged in closed-end investments in real estate or related mortgage assets operating so that they could meet the requirements of the Real Estate Investment Trust Act of 1960 as amended. Such trusts include mortgage investment trusts, mortgage trusts, realty investment trusts, and realty trusts. This act exempts trusts from corporate income and capital gains taxation, provided they invest primarily in specified assets, pay out most of their income to shareholders, and meet certain requirements regarding the dispersion of trust ownership.

NAICS CODE(S)

525930 (Real Estate Investment Trusts)

INDUSTRY SNAPSHOT

After coming of age in the early 1990s and flourishing in the mid-1990s, the investor-driven REIT (pronounced ''reet'') industry languished at decade's end. Dragged down by tightened credit and waning investor interest, publicly traded REITs coped with falling share prices by selling properties and buying back shares. Despite these measures, total market capitalization of U.S. REITs sank $16 billion between 1997 and 1999, according to statistics published by the National Association of Real Estate Investment Trusts (NAREIT), the industry's leading trade organization. Figures from NAREIT showed that industry market capitalization fell from $141 billion in 1997, the industry's best year, to $124 billion for the 203 REITs on record at year-end 1999.

The industry's troubles stemmed from a few sources. Since REITs depend heavily on investor goodwill to raise capital for real estate acquisitions and development, the industry suffered when investors poured money into Internet and other technology stocks that offered higher returns than REITs. The problems for REITs were only compounded by a mid-1990s run-up in real estate prices, signaling to some investors that REITs were paying too much for their properties and that a downward correction was imminent. Historically the real estate sector has gone through boom cycles with heavy development and escalating prices, followed by bust cycles notorious for oversupply and falling prices. In addition, international economic crises in 1997 and 1998 led to credit tightening at many banks, and as a result, less money available to REITs to finance new growth.

By 2000, some analysts believed that the industry was poised for recovery, arguing that it had hit bottom in 1999. Indeed, in late 1999 and early 2000, indices of REIT shares staged somewhat of a comeback, although the average share price was still well below its 1999 peak, let alone historical highs. Still, these analysts were encouraged by the industry's underlying value—REITs' assets were worth more than their market capitalization—and by the overall health in the U.S. real estate market. Other observers remained wary, though, and predicted a round of REIT consolidation and privatization as a remedy for the industry's market woes.

ORGANIZATION AND STRUCTURE

REITs are corporations, trusts, or associations that pool investor money to purchase and manage real estate and sometimes related investments such as mortgages. A corporation or trust that qualifies as a REIT generally is not required to pay federal income tax. In most states, REITs are also exempt from state income taxes.

U.S. tax laws specify exacting standards for what qualifies as a REIT. Among other requirements, a REIT must have:

- a board of directors or trustees
- at least 100 shareholders
- at least 75 percent of its total assets in real property
- at least 75 percent of its gross income from real estate operations
- no more than 30 percent of gross income from the sale of real property held for less than four years or from securities held for less than six months

- shareholder dividends equal to at least 95 percent of its taxable income

Most REITs issue shares that are traded publicly on an exchange such as the New York Stock Exchange (NYSE), the American Exchange (AMEX), or the NASDAQ. The NYSE is home to about three-quarters of all REITs. These vehicles pool investors' money, using professional managers to supervise a portfolio of properties, mortgages, or both, depending on the business objective. REITs thus provide liquidity to investors wishing to participate in the real estate market, while providing capital for real estate managers and developers to develop new revenue streams from real estate holdings.

REITs characteristically have high dividend yields, which recently have been about the same as yields on 10-year Treasury notes. High yields make REITs interest-rate sensitive like utility stocks and other financial companies, since high-yielding equity investments compete with fixed-income securities for investor money.

Types of REITs. There are three basic types of REITs: equity trusts, mortgage trusts, and hybrids. Most REITs belong to the equity category. These REITs invest directly in real property; they receive rental income and lease payments and occasionally realize capital gains from selling properties. Equity trusts are typically organized as blind pools for the purpose of investing in several unspecified rental income-producing properties to be held for an indefinite period to produce cash flow from rents, which could be distributed as dividends to shareowners.

A fully specified REIT invests in properties or in mortgages detailed in its offering statement; these investments do not change over time. As a result, investors can attempt to evaluate the quality of the underlying real estate prior to investing in the REIT. A blind-pool trust, in contrast, raises capital initially and then searches for real estate properties or mortgages in which to invest the proceeds raised from the offering.

Some equity trusts are organized as specified funds or specified trusts. Sale-leaseback trusts, in contrast to blind-pool trusts, invest in nondepreciable land underlying buildings and then lease the land back to the sellers from which they were purchased. Because these trusts offered tax advantages to the seller-lessee, they typically attempt to obtain higher rental returns by sharing in the gross receipts of the lessees or the proceeds from refinancing the respective buildings.

Mortgage REITs are established to invest the proceeds from the sale of their shares in mortgages secured by real estate holdings or mortgage-backed pass-through certificates. These trusts are sensitive to the credit quality of the borrower. Some mortgage trusts limit their investments to construction and other short-term mortgages; others invest only in long-term or permanent mortgages, and some invest in both types of mortgages.

Another type of mortgage trust—a dedicated trust—is organized to provide mortgage financing to a particular real estate developer for a given project. Hybrid trusts are organized to invest in both equity properties and mortgages. In recent years, several mortgage trusts have started issuing collateralized mortgage obligations (CMOs) at interest rates below the interest rates received on the mortgages, or the mortgage-backed pass-through certificates, acquired by the REIT and pledged to the respective CMOs. In the late 1980s, REITs were organized to invest in mortgage securities called ''CMO residuals''—real estate mortgages offering potentially high risks and yields.

Within these categories, REITs may be classified by other characteristics, such as closed-end or open-end. Under a closed-end REIT, the number of shares issued to the public at the initial offering are limited in order to protect shareholders from future dilution of their equity interests. This practice results in more predictable projected returns and reduces the price volatility of the shares themselves. Open-end REITs, in contrast, create and sell new shares as they discover new opportunities for investment. Although the new shares dilute the interests of existing shareholders, management representatives and shareholders believe that the total value of each share will ultimately be increased by the additional investments.

Term. REITs may also be distinguished on the basis of whether they are finite. A finite life trust is established as a self-liquidating investment vehicle; it must dispose of its assets and distribute the proceeds to shareholders by a specified date. In such cases, properties will be acquired for various periods, usually between 4 and 15 years, after which the properties will be sold and the proceeds distributed to the shareholders when the trust is liquidated. In theory, the advantage of a specified investment lifetime is that REIT's share prices should closely match its current asset values because investors can presumably make fairly accurate estimates of the residual values of the respective properties. Non-finite life REITs have a perpetual life and typically reinvest any sale or financing proceeds in new or existing properties. To retain their status as real estate investment trusts, perpetual REITs must distribute most of the cash flow from rental or interest payments to shareholders.

Leverage. REITs may be further distinguished on the basis of leveraging. When a leveraged REIT acquires properties, it seeks mortgage financing to fund the acquisition. In general, the financing may pay up to 90 percent of the value of the purchased assets. Unleveraged REITs do not utilize debt financing in their acquisitions, but they instead purchase properties for cash or invest their funds in mortgages.

BACKGROUND AND DEVELOPMENT

Contemporary REITs are an outgrowth of the so-called Massachusetts Trusts—early business trusts formed by nineteenth-century corporations to avoid certain legal constraints imposed by states on corporate holdings of real estate. Under the standard form of real estate trust organization, investors were permitted to pool their funds and obtain equity interests in real estate with centralized management and the safety of diversification without incurring the personal liability associated with partnership interests. Funds established through the trust form of organization were largely responsible for the development of Boston in the nineteenth and early twentieth century, as well as for the early development of such cities as Detroit, Chicago, Minneapolis, St. Paul, Kansas City, Omaha, Duluth, and Seattle.

From 1913 to 1935, common law business trusts, as distinguished from corporations, were not taxed on trust income distributed to owners. However, in 1935, the U.S. Supreme Court held that business trusts should be taxed as corporations in *Morrissey v. Commissioner.* In the aftermath of World War II, fueled by large amounts of capital and heavy demand for new construction, real estate syndicates began to expand, primarily in the larger Eastern cities. To reduce the impact of the corporate tax, many of these syndicates were formed as ''thin'' corporations, whereby the investor would invest as little as 20 percent of funds as capital, with the remaining 20 percent of the total investment being accounted for in bonds or debentures signifying the corporation's debt.

In the decades following the *Morrissey v. Commissioner* decision, no new substantial REITs were formed as common law business trusts. Instead, pooling of real estate investments was undertaken under either the corporate or partnership form of business organization.

In 1960 President Eisenhower signed into law the Real Estate Investment Trust Act of 1960, which granted special tax concessions to REITs and qualified REITs for tax-exempt status. The law limited the tax benefits of REITs to common law business trusts; corporations could not qualify. It sought to extend to REIT owners substantially the same type of tax treatment they would receive if they invested directly in the real estate equities and mortgages held by the trust.

The law also aimed to encourage the growth of such investment trusts and to increase the funds available for financing real estate developments. This equated the treatment of investors in REITs with that accorded investors in regulated investment companies (such as mutual funds). In both REITs and investment companies, small investors can enjoy advantages that before were available only to institutions or the wealthy. These advantages include spreading the risk of loss by the greater pooling of investments, sharing the opportunity to obtain the benefits of management by real estate experts, and sharing in projects that the investors could not undertake individually. The special tax status provided by the law was intended to be limited to passive investors in real estate, not to entities that actively operated a real estate business.

After a few other technical changes to the tax code, REITs grew rapidly in the late 1960s, raising through public offerings significantly more capital than did traditional sources of real estate financing. However, as the volume of capital increased, REIT managers found it increasingly difficult to find real estate projects in which to invest those funds. According to analyst Menachem Rosenberg, as the supply of funds began to exceed the number of quality projects available, property prices increased dramatically, and many REITs paid too much for projects, particularly development projects. A number of REITs invested their funds into high-risk construction and development loans, and REITs that specialized in mortgage lending tended to become careless in their underwriting practices. For 24 consecutive months beginning in April 1973, REITs posted negative total returns.

When the 1974-75 recession caused many real estate projects to fail, the REIT industry suffered a severe downturn. In 1975, provisions were amended to provide for the treatment of property acquired by a REIT through foreclosure on a mortgage or as a result of a default on a lease, and in 1976 the requirements for qualifying as a REIT were modified and penalties in lieu of disqualification were enacted. In 1978, safe harbor rules for determining when sales of property of a REIT would not be taxed as a ''prohibited transaction'' were added, and the grace period on foreclosure property was extended. The Tax Reform Act of 1986, as amended by the Technical and Miscellaneous Revenue Act of 1986, made further changes to federal tax law affecting REITs.

During the 1980s, equity REITs outperformed the Standard & Poor's 500—with fewer vicissitudes in returns. In 1985 investors began to take a renewed interest in REITs when it appeared as though the limited partnerships would lose most of their tax shelter under proposed tax reforms. The Tax Reform Act of 1986 significantly limited the tax advantages associated with real estate limited partnerships, providing a boost to the REIT industry. Overall, 33 REITs were established in 1985.

During the 1980s, the rapid increase in the supply of new commercial real estate space greatly exceeded the growth of aggregate space demand. This, in turn, resulted in market imbalances and downward pressure on rental rates and real estate asset values. As a result, real estate developers came under significant financial pressures.

Major changes were also occurring in the real estate capital structure. Previously, real estate investment was dominated by institutional investors such as banks, savings and loans, insurance companies, pension funds, and foreign investors that supplied private capital for both equity and mortgage investments. Around 1990, these institutional investors faced higher costs of capital, more conservative investment guidelines, and reductions in portfolio allocations to real estate. The result was a vacuum in the capital market, which could potentially be filled by real estate investment trusts.

However, the U.S. tax code still made it difficult for large investors like pension funds to participate in REITs. The law, designed to prevent individuals from sheltering private real estate holdings under a corporation to avoid taxes, meant that a large investment by a U.S. pension fund could force a REIT to pay corporate taxes. This, in turn, would diminish investors' returns and make the REIT a less efficient and less profitable investment channel. The problem was solved in 1992 by the creation of the Umbrella Partnership REIT (UPREIT) structure. In an UPREIT, the investors don't own the REIT's properties directly. Instead, they hold shares in the umbrella partnership, which in turn owns the company's real estate.

Between 1992 and 1997, investors poured money into REITs at an unprecedented pace. Based on NAREIT statistics, REIT market capitalization soared from less than $16 billion in 1992 to more than $140 billion by the end of 1997. The number of REITs tracked by NAREIT also surged nearly 50 percent, from 142 to 211. REITs achieved such growth in part because of strong interest in REITs as lower-risk, higher-yield investments in the traditionally volatile real estate sector. Investors' perceptions of REITs were also boosted by favorable market trends in real estate, including rising property values and relatively high occupancy rates.

But by 1998 the REIT industry's fortunes reversed. Investors worried that REITs were bidding up real estate prices too fast, potentially setting the stage for a downturn. Currency and debt crises in Asia, Russia, and Latin America left major international banks reeling from bad loans and caused many to tighten their lending policies, making it harder and more expensive for REITs to borrow. Meanwhile, skyrocketing technology stocks lured investors away from real estate. To make matters worse, a glut of new REIT shares were issued in late 1997 and the first half of 1998. As these pressures converged, investors began to pull out of REITs and share prices tumbled. By the end of 1998, REITs had collectively shed 18 percent of their share value for the year. In 1999 the picture was largely the same, although average declines weren't as bad as in the year before.

CURRENT CONDITIONS

Although as of early 2000 REITs were worth $122 billion in market capitalization, they held less than 10 percent of all commercial real estate in the United States. The largest REIT segment that year was office and industrial properties, representing nearly a third of the industry in terms of market capitalization. Second were retail REITs (ones that own shopping centers), which accounted for more than one-fifth of REIT capitalization. Other large segments included residential REITs, which mostly own apartment buildings, and diversified REITs, which have significant holdings in multiple segments.

In spite of REITs' poor showing in the late 1990s and early 2000s, a number of analysts believed that the underlying picture wasn't as bleak as it seemed. Unlike during the 1980s, they argued, there was no building spree creating an overabundance of commercial real estate. Indeed, the economic fundamentals of the real estate business appeared quite sound with a growing economy, low inflation, moderate interest rates, and high occupancy rates. Moreover, with REIT shares trading so low, in many cases the trusts' properties were worth more than their capitalization reflected. In other words, if a typical REIT sold all of its assets, the proceeds would be worth more than its stock valuation. Uncommon in other stock investments, this hidden value could make REITs attractive to investors seeking quality.

In 2000 the most vulnerable REIT segment was hotels and resorts. Among other troubles, the lodging business suffered from oversupply and tepid revenue growth. However, the 15 U.S. hotel REITs amounted to just 5 to 6 percent of the industry in terms of market capitalization.

INDUSTRY LEADERS

The largest U.S. REIT is Equity Office Properties Trust. In 2000 this Chicago-based trust owned some 291 office buildings totaling 76.6 million square feet. Headed by billionaire real estate tycoon Sam Zell, Equity Office owns property in most major U.S. metropolitan areas and, as of January 2000, had a market capitalization of $6.4 billion. The firm announced in 2000 plans to acquire Cornerstone Properties Inc., a New York-based REIT, in a transaction that would add 90 properties and almost 20 million square feet to Equity Office's portfolio. The merger was seen by some as a precursor to further consolidation among REITs. Equity Office's sister company, Equity Residential Properties Trust, also controlled by Zell, is one of the largest owners and lessors of apartments, with more than 1,000 properties throughout the country.

Another leading REIT is Simon Property Group, Inc. The largest of the retail REITs, Simon Property specializes in regional malls and other types of shopping centers primarily in suburban settings. The Indianapolis-headquartered REIT has a 50 percent interest in Minneapolis' Mall of America, one of its best-known holdings. All together, in 1999 the company had an interest in 259 sites with 184 million square feet of gross leasable area. Its market capitalization in January 2000 stood at $4.2 billion.

FURTHER READING

Brody, Michael J, and David S. Raab. ''A Primer on Real Estate Investment Trusts and Umbrella Partnership Real Estate Investment Trusts.'' *Real Estate Finance Journal,* winter 1994.

Hamilton, Kathryn. ''REITs: No Need to Abandon Hope.'' *Buildings,* March 1999.

Morrissey, Janet. ''REITs Battle Investor Tide in 2000.'' *Wall Street Journal,* 10 December 1999.

National Association of Real Estate Investment Trusts. ''Real Time Index.'' *NAREIT Online.* Washington: February 2000. Available from http://www.nareit.org.

Rich, Motoko, and Peter Grant. ''For Commercial Real Estate, It Was a Year of Joy—and of Discontent.'' *Wall Street Journal,* 29 December 1999.

SIC 6799

INVESTORS, NOT ELSEWHERE CLASSIFIED

This classification covers establishments primarily engaged in investing, not elsewhere classified. Businesses covered in this industry include investment clubs, commodity contract pool operators and trading companies, and venture capital companies.

NAICS CODE(S)

523910 (Miscellaneous Intermediation)
523920 (Portfolio Management)
523130 (Commodity Contracts Dealing)
523999 (Miscellaneous Financial Investment Activities)

Investment Clubs. An investment club is a group of individuals who meet regularly, usually once or twice a month, and pool their money, time, knowledge, and efforts to discuss and invest in securities. The investment club is a method whereby individuals are able to gain experience and acquire knowledge about stocks, financial statements, and securities markets. It is a proven means of learning and profiting by doing with others what an individual cannot accomplish alone. The primary goals of an investment club are: to educate the individual members; to make a profit on the money invested; and to encourage social harmony among the members for greater productivity. Investment clubs also serve a vital national function in that they create many new investors trained in successful investment techniques, and in so doing, provide a substantial and regular flow of capital for the needs of growing industries.

The purpose of the National Association of Investment Clubs (NAIC)—a division of the National Association of Investors Corporation, a nonprofit organization owned by its membership—is to encourage the creation of investment clubs for the purpose of becoming successful operations. Founded in 1951, the NAIC has grown to a level wherein the total new monthly money invested through NAIC membership investment exceeds $14 million. The total holdings of NAIC members' portfolios exceed $466 million. According to National Association of Investors Corporation statistics, there are nearly 25,400 investment clubs worldwide with an estimated 500,000 members.

An investment club must file tax returns like any other business entity. When the club adopts the partnership format, the individual members pay taxes on dividends and realized capital gains even though the members leave their money in the club for many years. The partnership must also file the partnership information return form, which informs the Internal Revenue Service of the financial distributions made to individual partners. The investment club may request an exemption from filing this form by writing to the U.S. Treasury Department. If an exemption is granted, the partners must still file their share of club income on their personal tax forms. If the club is a corporation, it must pay taxes on its earnings, with no tax liability accruing to the members until a distribution is made. In 2000, investment club members were required to file a Form 1065 (U.S. Partnership Return of Income) and a Schedule K-1 (Partners Share of Income, Credits, and Deductions) on individual tax returns. While the club does not have to pay federal income taxes, it must report to the IRS the portfolio results, including each member's share of the account.

Commodities Markets. While stocks, bonds, and mutual funds are the most common investment vehicles for individual investors, they are by no means the only ones. Two other types of investments, futures and options, have become increasingly popular for the individual investor. In the futures market, investors trade futures contracts, which are agreements for the future delivery of designated quantities of given products for specified prices. Until 1972, this market was linked exclusively with commodities, such as soybeans, cocoa, silver, or pork bellies. Since that time, the fastest growing part of the futures market has been that of futures contracts on financial instruments, such as treasury bonds or stock indexes. While traditional commodities still trade actively, the divergence between the two branches has grown increasingly wide in recent years. In 1999, for instance, there were 390 million contacts traded concerning financial instruments, while there were only 32.7 million grain contracts traded.

In many ways futures trading is simpler than securities trading. For one thing, there are less than 100 actively traded American commodities, compared with many thousands of different common stocks. Margins, short sales, and tax considerations are far less complicated than in securities trading. Accordingly, a futures trader chooses investment opportunities from a very small sample and trades are affected with generally more simple mechanics than those associated with securities. It is also considerably easier to follow news and market developments that might have an impact upon a given commodity (such as wheat prices) than it is to follow the complex details that surround any individual stock, such as dividends, earnings, the competition, interest rates, the overall market, and other national and international factors.

A futures contract is a standardized, exchange-traded contract calling for the delivery of a specified amount of a specified commodity in a specified month in a specified location. Unlike a securities transaction, no transfer of property is involved unless and until delivery actually occurs. In fact, analysts estimate that fewer than 5 percent of all contracts actually result in a delivery of the actual commodity. Money does not change hands between the buyer and seller of a futures contract, although each is required to post a margin deposit to ensure responsibility for the entire contract in the delivery month. Unlike an options contract, if a futures contract is held through the last trading day in the delivery month, the holder of the contract must accept delivery and the seller must deliver. Also, futures contracts never result in a delivery prior to the appointed month, whereas an option on a security may normally be exercised and delivery demanded at any time from the trade date to the expiration date.

While most futures contracts used to be agricultural in nature, now people trade futures contracts for a variety of items, including interest rates, stock indexes, manufactured and processed products, nonstorable commodities, precious metals, and foreign currency. Proposals for new kinds of contracts are made all the time.

Futures Exchanges. There are nine major future exchanges in the United States. Trading is conducted by open outcry in ''pits'' or ''rings.'' The former term is commonly used in Chicago, which is by far the world's leading commodities market. While trading futures bear a number of similarities to stock trading, there are notable differences. For example, futures exchanges put a limit on the maximum daily price changes, a practice not undertaken by stock exchanges. Futures trading is regulated by the Commodity Futures Trading Commission (CFTC), an independent federal regulatory commission established by Congress in 1974. The CFTC regulates the industry and the industry's employees. The Commission was set up to prevent abuse, neglect, fraud, and to promote competition.

The CFTC is Based in Washington, D.C. According to its 1999 annual report, it regulates the activities of 45,593 sales people, 9,482 floor brokers, 1,409 floor traders, 1,534 commodity pool operators, 2,806 commodity trading advisors, 211 futures commission merchants, and 1,609 introducing brokers.

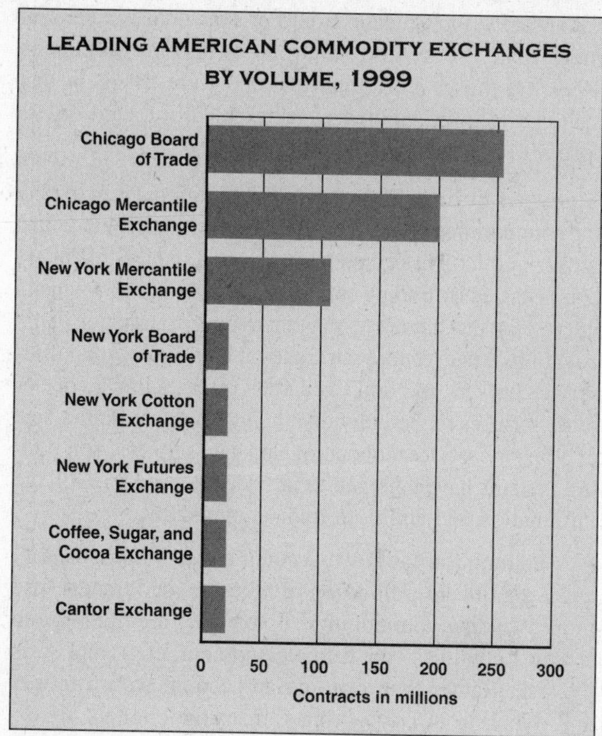

There were a total of 614.2 million contracts traded in 1999, down 1.7 percent from 1998's fiscal year volume. The leading American commodity exchanges and their trading volume for 1999 included: the Chicago Board of Trade, which posted 254.5 million contracts; the Chicago Mercantile Exchange, with 200.7 million contracts; the New York Mercantile Exchange, with 109.5 million; the New York Board of Trade, New York Cotton Exchange, New York Futures Exchange, the Coffee, Sugar and Cocoa Exchange, and the Cantor Exchange, 21.2 million; the Kansas City Board of Trade, with 2.5 million contracts; the Minneapolis Grain Exchange, with 1.2 million contracts; and the MidAmerica Commodity Exchange, with 31,262 contracts.

The Chicago Board of Trade (CBOT) continues to be the world leader, posting more than 200 million contracts in the six consecutive years ending in 1999. The Chicago dominance results not only from its original agricultural preeminence, but also from its innovations in the realm of financial futures. It should be noted that not all commodities contracts succeed, and that once-popular contracts often fall out of favor.

At the dawn of the twenty-first century, technology played a major role in boosting total trading volume as more investors began trading electronically. In January 2000, electronic trading on the Chicago Mercantile Exchange's GLOBEX2 system increased more than 94 percent from the previous year, topping 2 million contracts.

Likewise, at the Chicago Board of Trade, customers sent more than 2.1 million electronic orders to brokers in 1999. Of those, more than 660,000 were filled. In that same period, the volume of electronically routed orders rose 300 percent from 1998.

Managed Futures Industry. The traditional way to play the commodities market has been to open an account with a broker and let that person trade your account. Brokers are compensated by trading commissions and have no financial interest in the outcome of your trading transaction. Discount brokers execute your trades at a lower cost than full-service brokers, but don't generally offer trading advice or other services to the individual investor. As a result, a host of advisory services, quotation and data services, and trading systems have emerged to provide the investor with the information and ability to trade commodities.

Trading for your own account is a risky proposition, and a significant proportion of investors and traders lose money trading commodities. Fixed costs are high (quote screens, commissions, office equipment, etc.), and so is the risk. Rather than opening an account with a broker and dabbling in commodities, many individuals are allowing professional managers to trade futures for them. Managed futures offer individuals several choices: individual managed accounts, private futures funds, and public futures funds. Many new programs that were launched throughout the 1990s entice people to trade their own commodities from home. With personal computer ownership and usage at an all-time high, it is more conceivable that individuals may begin to become their own brokers.

Hiring an advisor to manage an individual trading account is similar to using a broker, but with one key difference: the commodity trading advisor (CTA) isn't usually compensated on commissions. Rather, advisors most often participate in the profits of the money they manage through management fees and profit incentive fees. Management fees are charged as a percentage of the equity in the account. Profit incentive fees vary per CTA, but are calculated as a percentage of new trading profits. If the advisor does not make money trading the investor's money, then no fees are charged. At the start of 2000, there were 2,806 CTAs, according to the CFTC.

CTA's organize client trading in two ways: individual client accounts or a single, pooled account from which all client money is traded. A CTA who does the latter is a Commodity Pool Operator (CPO). From 1980 to 1996, the number of commodity pool operators registered with the Commodity Futures Trading Commission grew from 1,055 to 1,350. By 2000, the CFTC was regulating 1,534 commodity pool operators.

According to International Traders Research Inc., the top-ranked managed futures program fund manager for the 12 months ending in December 1999 was Mangin Capital Management, based in Basking Ridge, New Jersey, with a compounded rate of return of 121.89 percent and $1.4 million in equity.

Venture Capital. Venture capital is a private source of financing for high-risk business endeavors. It is one financing alternative among many sources of capital that are available to growing companies. Venture capital is generally invested in equity ownership of a company or new venture. The investment is usually in the form of stock, or sometimes in the form of convertible debt, which is a loan that becomes a stock holding at some point. Offsetting the high risk the investor takes is the promise of a very high return on investment.

Between 1992 and 1994, 417 venture-backed companies went public. In 1993, venture capital-backed companies raised $4.2 billion, up 19 percent from 1992. The number of venture capital entities, however, has dwindled in recent years. During the third quarter of 1998, for instance, only 19 companies funded principally with venture capital went public, raising $1.13 billion, bringing to 68 the total number of IPOs. Their offering size was $3.38 billion. During the same period in 1997, however, 98 companies raised $3.35 billion. The average offering size, though, increased from $34.2 million in 1997 to $49.7 million in 1998. During this time, the software and services industries had the most number of IPOs. The telephone and data communications industry came in second. The lead underwriter for this time period was BankBoston.

FURTHER READING

Brown, Carolyn M. "Your Club in Dollars and Sense: Good Record-Keeping is Vital to a Club's Longevity." *Black Enterprise,* February 1997.

Chicago Board of Trade. *About the Exchange,* 2000. Available from http://www.cbot.com/about_exchange/overview.html.

Chicago Board of Trade. *An Overview.* 1997. Available from http://www.cbot.com.

———. *CBOT 1999 Volume at 254,561,215 Contracts.* 2000. Available from http://www.cbot.com/points_of_interest/pressbox/pressreleases/p0001041.html.

Commodity Futures Trading Commission. *About the CFTC.* 2000. Available from http://www.cftc.gov/annualreport99/about99.htm.

———. *CFTC at a Glance.* 1997. Available from http://www.cftc.gov.

———. *Futures and Options.* 1999. Available from http://www.cftc.gov/.

International Traders Research Inc. *CTA Rankings Reports.* 25 January 2000. Available from http://www.managedfutures.com/12month.html.

Securities Exchange Commission. *Average Offer Size Up $15.5 Million from 3rd Quarter '97.* 1 October 1998. Available from http://www.secdata.com.

SERVICE INDUSTRIES

SIC 7011

HOTELS AND MOTELS

This industry comprises commercial establishments known to the public as hotels, motor hotels, motels, or tourist courts, primarily engaged in providing lodging, or lodging and meals, for the general public. Hotels that are operated by membership organizations and open to the general public are included in this industry. Hotels operated by organizations for their members only are classified in **SIC 7041: Organization Hotels and Lodging Houses, on Membership basis.** Apartment hotels are classified in **SIC 6513: Operators of Apartment Buildings;** rooming and boarding houses are classified in **SIC 7021: Rooming and Boarding Houses;** and sporting and recreational camps are classified in **SIC 7032: Sporting and Recreational Camps.**

NAICS CODE(S)

721110 (Hotels (except Casino Hotels) and Motels)
721120 (Casino Hotels)
721191 (Bed and Breakfast Inns)
721199 (All Other Traveler Accommodations)

INDUSTRY SNAPSHOT

The hotel and motel industry played a vital role in the development of trade, commerce, and travel in the United States. In supplying everything from a cheap night's accommodation on the road, to meeting and convention spaces and coordination for large corporate events, the remarkably diverse services that American hotels provide have made the hotel industry significant. According to the American Hotel & Motel Association (AH&MA), the industry's revenues total about $93.1 billion annually.

In the United States, there are 3.9 million rooms at approximately 51,000 properties, or about one hotel room for every 80 U.S. citizens. Roughly one-third of these are at suburban locations, and another third are situated along highways. The rest are located in cities (14 percent), resort sites (12 percent), and alongside airport strips (7 percent). The room supply is rising most significantly in suburban areas, and new construction is focused primarily on limited-service facilities—an increasingly popular option for cost-conscious travelers not inclined to frequent more elaborate full-service properties.

The AH&MA reports that 64 percent of all properties are occupied on any given night. About 24 percent of lodging industry customers are leisure travelers, and another 21 percent are staying in a hotel for personal or family reasons. Among leisure travelers, 45 percent spend one night, 26 percent stay for two nights, and the remainder spend three or more nights. The typical leisure-related visit is by two adults (50 percent) who are traveling by auto (78 percent), and who pay about $74 per room night. The typical business-related visit is by a male (74 percent) who is a white-collar worker (52 percent), paying $83 per room night.

Tracking the industry by region shows huge variability, depending on location and regional economic factors. The southern California market as a whole has been depressed, while Florida continues to experience gains in room sales—Orlando has become the largest hotel market in America, with about 85,000 rooms. Los Angeles, Las Vegas, Chicago, Washington DC, and New York each have between 65,000 and 80,000 rooms.

In recent years, modest gains in occupancy and the average room rate have resulted in higher revenues and profits for all types of hotels. According to the AH&MA, the industry reached record profitability in 1998, grossing

$20.9 billion in pretax profits, up from a loss of $5.7 billion in 1990. Likewise, industry revenues increased from $62.8 billion in 1990 to $93.1 billion in 1998.

Today, demand is strong in most parts of the country. Construction has increased at the low and middle ends of the market, largely in franchised properties of large hotel chains. However, the full service side of the market is seeing little new construction.

Organization and Structure

Most analysts classify the industry into full- and limited-service enterprises. Full-service hotels constitute the majority of all properties, although this ratio is dwindling. Typically, they are large properties—averaging about 280 rooms—that often generate about 30 percent of their operating income from food, beverage, and such services as restaurants, room service, and meeting spaces. Limited-service hotels, by contrast, are smaller establishments—averaging about 130 rooms—that do not offer food and beverage services or extra facilities. They rely on room sales for nearly 95 percent of their revenue base.

Vast differences exist in the expenditures that each type of hotel incurs for various services, including room maintenance, food and beverages, and telephones. These costs can diminish profit margins considerably in years with low occupancy rates, especially given that hotels must also keep room rates low in such years to compete for a reduced number of customers. Full-service hotels with significant departmental expenses have, in general, been hurt far more by the oversupply of the industry. Their occupancy rates have not been markedly different from those of limited-service hotels, but room rates have been kept far too low to pay for the cost of servicing them.

All-suite hotels came to prominence in the late-1980s and, because their segment's demand growth remains healthy, continue to capture attention. Such hotels—most of which are branches of specific brand chains—conventionally offer consumers both a living and a bedroom area. While most all-suites offer both food and beverage services, this is not always the case. Indeed, limited-service all-suites often report substantially more attractive profit margins—again, as a result of much lower departmental expenses—and have subsequently attracted increasing interest. Their occupancy rates have been higher than those of their full-service counterparts, relative to the rest of the industry, without a tremendous dropoff in room rates.

Resorts, hotels with gambling facilities, and conference/convention center hotels represent three smaller but important industry categories. Like all-suites, their demand growth and occupancy rates have generally been higher than the average and will probably remain so, simply because they are so capital intensive to build and maintain. Casino hotels have grown in popularity due to the expansion of legalized gambling, and the convention center has become a popular component of efforts to reinvigorate urban infrastructure.

The casino segment of the hotel industry currently remains clustered in Las Vegas and Atlantic City. In Las Vegas, several new spectacular destination resorts, such as the Luxor and the Bellagio, were constructed in the 1990s. In contrast to convention center hotels and resort hotels, most hotels with gambling ventures tend to offer low room rates; the gambling activity of the hotel patrons is thus central to the establishment's success. In recent years, the gaming industry has attempted to market its lodging to entire families.

The resort phenomenon is also highly regional and, inasmuch as they have had to become more price competitive, resort hotels perhaps rely more on overall regional promotion than anything else. The South Atlantic (primarily Florida) has grown into the country's most lively resort region. Even after a number of years of steady growth, its occupancy rates are still the highest of any region in the country, regularly upwards of 75 percent. The second largest resort market in revenue, the Mountain and Pacific region, has steadily lost market share in recent years.

Industry Strategies. There are essentially three forms of participation in the hotel and motel industry: straight ownership of properties, management agreements, and franchising or licensing a brand name. Most large hotel companies are active in all three categories, keeping themselves flexible to utilize varied strategies as the market dictates. Owning a hotel is a capital-intensive endeavor, yet it imparts control and can be very lucrative in an expanding market when asset values show sizable appreciation. Since the 1980s, managing other people's hotels has become a widespread activity.

The trend away from straight ownership, and its inherent risks, has given franchising a greater appeal. Large franchise chains are first and foremost based on the benefits of brand name recognition, for which an operator either pays a straight fee or gives up a percentage of revenue. The name represents a specific concept and standard, consistent at every location. This familiarity appeals to many consumers. It also provides the company a greater efficiency in the use of resources, especially as the chain grows. Through license or franchise agreements, hotel companies can generate revenues from limited capital investments and can market their product more pointedly. In an attempt to segment the market, some companies have successfully developed a variety of chains that are advertised aggressively and provide varying levels of service.

Eager to expand their lodging chains, many companies have turned to conversions of existing hotels rather than new construction in an already bloated market. The scope of industry conversions has more than doubled since 1988, with approximately half of these involving the switching of chain affiliations.

Affiliations and Partnerships. As the travel industry became increasingly sophisticated and global in nature, hotel operators have developed competitive advantages through agreements of various kinds with other industries that serve travelers. Frequent-flyer/guest/renter programs have been developed in cooperation with airline and car rental companies. These programs offer ''points'' for air travel, hotel visits, and car rentals that can be redeemed for upgrades and awards through any of the three partners. These programs are geared towards fostering brand loyalty, both in the individual leisure traveler who receives regular statements and in the corporate traveler who, through side agreements with certain companies, is often given corporate rates or some other preferred-customer benefits.

Relationships with travel agencies and tour operators are also an integral element in the success of many hotels. Agencies, which book approximately 40 percent of the hotel rooms in the United States, are a crucial sales mechanism for the industry, and many hotels operate centralized commission payment systems to make agents more confident about prompt and accurate payments of commissions—generally between 5 to 10 percent. Many hotels also feature toll-free travel agent help-desks to answer questions about commissions and to assist in solving reservation system problems. Agreements with tour operators to offer substantial room discounts on bulk bookings are ubiquitous in the hotel and motel industry, as properties benefit not only from the added business but also by the free publicity from appearances in tour operator brochures.

Associations. The American Hotel and Motel Association (AH&MA) is the major trade association of the industry. It works in partnership with 51 member state associations representing more than 11,000 member properties. The AH&MA conducts surveys and industry analysis, and keeps its members up to date on industry trends through newsletters and educational conferences. Primarily, however, it serves as a promotional mechanism for the industry, both in publicity campaigns and in lobby efforts aimed at national and regional governments. AH&MA member properties account for 75 percent of total revenues generated by the industry.

BACKGROUND AND DEVELOPMENT

The earliest versions of hotels were tiny, single-room dwellings that traveling merchants used in the sixth century B.C.. The first such American lodging was the colonial inn, counterpart of the English inn, which flourished during the late 1700s. Colonial inns and taverns dotted the seaport towns and stagecoach roads. They became popular not only with travelers but also with locals, who came to use them as public gathering places for town meetings, schools, and even courts of law.

Hotels as we know them today arose quickly as the major cities grew. The very first, the 73-room City Hotel at 115 Broadway in New York City, was completed in 1794, and similar establishments were soon constructed in Philadelphia, Boston, and Baltimore. The number of hotels increased dramatically in the 1800s as hotels moved westward. With each new hotel, it seemed, some new service was added, thereby forcing existing hotels to change or face obsolescence. The City Hotel became so outdated that it was converted into an office building only 38 years after it opened. Behind many of the transformations of the industry was a trend towards luxury accommodations that was sparked by the Tremont House in Boston, which was the first to offer such amenities as private guest rooms, locks on doors, a washbowl with free soap, bellboys, French cuisine, and an annunciator that enabled the front desk to communicate with guests in their rooms. Ironically, the Tremont House itself later fell prey to the very trend it had initiated, as it closed for major renovations after just 20 years and was regarded as an outdated establishment toward the end of its 65-year history.

In the mid-1800s, hotels followed the railroads further west, and the properties became increasingly lavish in such cities as Chicago, St. Louis, and San Francisco. Often the hotels' capacities far exceeded potential demand. Curiously, the industry continues in its third century to suffer from many of the same ills that these early development tendencies demonstrated: propensity towards overdevelopment and rapid obsolescence as a result of constant changes in transportation patterns, customer preferences, and new competition.

The First Boom and Bust. Many nineteenth-century American travelers, unable to afford accommodations at the luxury hotels, were forced to lodge in threadbare rooming houses. Medium-range accommodations were rare, but with the growth of the middle-class and the increasing affordability of rail travel, a sizable market for comfortable yet affordable lodging emerged. The first to recognize and serve this market was E.M. Statler, who built the country's first truly modern commercial hotel. The revolutionary Buffalo Statler opened in Buffalo, New York, in 1908 with such conveniences as circulating ice water and a free morning newspaper. Its slogan was ''A room and a bath for a dollar and a half'' and, in making cleanliness and comfort accessible to so many, the Statler, and its imitators, contributed greatly to the middle-class travel bug.

As the American economy flourished in the 1920s, the hotel industry was poised for its first major boom. Occupancy rates were close to 90 percent as the decade opened, and hoteliers were encouraged to expand exist-

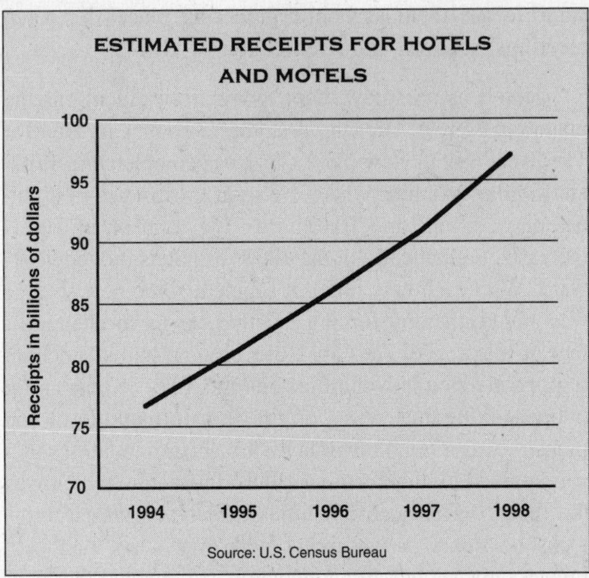

ing properties and build many new, larger ones. At the height of the activity, in 1927, Chicago's Hotel Stevens—now the Conrad Hilton—was hailed as the world's largest hotel, and remained so until the 1960s. The Depression brought an abrupt halt to the industry's expansion and sent many hotels into foreclosure or receivership as occupancy rates fell to around 50 percent. At the same time, however, the economic crisis provided the initial impetus to develop hotel chains because it allowed those hoteliers who survived the collapse to increase their holdings inexpensively.

World War II rewarded the aggressive buyers of the 1930s by refilling the existing hotels with transient defense industry workers and military personnel. Occupancy rates approached 90 percent. The 1950s witnessed the beginnings of a complete transformation of the industry. Hotels increasingly catered to a more affluent and mobile society. Americans embraced the convenience of highways and airplanes, making the railway system a less important factor in travel.

Motels, Budgets, and Another Boom. The early ''no-frills'' motels were put up quickly and cheaply on large plots along highways. These enterprises, which appealed to lower-income vacation travelers, salesmen, and middle-management businessmen, competed effectively with hotels in the 1950s. The initially significant differences between the two types of lodging—size, start-up costs, operating ratios, and management needs—began to diminish in the 1960s as motels franchised, grew in size, and started offering more amenities and services. At the same time, a sector of the hotel industry modified itself to compete with motels. Eventually, these hybrid properties came to be known as motor hotels.

Lodging at motor hotels was priced somewhat higher than at the original motels, once again creating a void at the low end of the rate scale. This was soon filled by so-called budget motels. Budget motels were essentially larger, more standardized motels that operated on the same principles as their predecessors—lower initial investments and fewer frills—but were more consciously part of an overall plan to profit by fitting more beds in less space and filling them.

The commotion over the introduction of budget motels to the market coincided with the creation of the real estate investment trust (REIT), which enabled small investors to hold real estate mortgages and equities. This resulted in an unprecedented availability of financing for ambitious builders. Large hotel chains had also started to pursue further expansion through franchise agreements. As a result, the industry became overextended and fell into disarray in the mid-1970s amid the oil crisis, which reduced travel overall; deepening inflation, which caused construction costs and interest rates to soar; and the recession, which forced businesses to cut back on travel and convention spending.

In the 1980s, the hotel industry completed yet another full cycle of growth and retrenchment. As room occupancies reached record levels by the end of the 1970s as a result of an improving economy, the usual losses by attrition, and the suspension of building activity, the industry was poised for a new phase of construction in 1979. The subsequent postponement of expansion, the result of the Federal Reserve's tightening of the money supply, only made the expansion more dramatic when the Reagan Administration began easing these lending constraints and creating tax incentives for developers. In total, the extraordinary building activity added about 7,000 hotels and 900,000 rooms to the industry, priming the industry for yet another oversupply condition.

While the growth during this period was remarkable in itself, transformation of the industry's structure remains its more enduring legacy. Although the market had undergone some segmentation previously with the introductions of motels and budgets, the proliferation of such new lodging concepts as all-suites in the 1980s is unparalleled. The acquisitions that companies made were often diversification measures, which provided their customer base with an assortment of property-types from which they could choose. Segmentation also allowed companies to plan more specifically and apply their resources more efficiently.

Current Conditions

During the 1990s, the industry had finally absorbed the overcapacity created by the phenomenal building activity of the 1980s. Lodging industry profits have improved dramatically in recent years, boosted by stronger consumer demands and the absence of significant new capacity. According to the AH&MA, the industry's pretax profits reached $20.9 billion in 1998, a 23 percent increase over the previous year and nearly twice the profitability of 1996. This represents a dramatic turnaround from the $5.7 billion loss suffered by the industry as recently as 1990.

A number of noticeable trends occurred during the 1990s. Construction has increased, as companies increasingly look to develop new chains by building new facilities. Increased automation of labor-intensive functions, such as hotel check-in and checkout, reduces long-term operating costs and increases customer satisfaction. An emphasis on business-related amenities, such as voice mail, fax, and computer services, appeals to business travelers. Involvement by hotel companies in time-sharing projects provides a means to leverage their expertise in real estate and financing. Finally, extended-stay enterprises, which offer such amenities as separate living room areas and kitchen facilities, enjoy growing popularity.

INDUSTRY LEADERS

Starwood Hotels & Resorts Worldwide, based in New York, is the world's largest lodging company. With more than 700 properties in 75 countries, the firm owns and operates such brands as Westin, Sheraton, St. Regis, The Luxury Collection, Four Points, and Ciga. Starwood was founded in 1991 as a real estate investment firm, and throughout the decade expanded into the lodging industry through the acquisition of such hotel companies as ITT Corp., owner of Sheraton, Caesars, Four Points, and Ciga Hotels. Starwood's revenues in 1998 reached $4.9 billion.

Cendant Corporation was formed through the December 1997 merger of CUC International and HFS Inc. With more than 6,000 properties, Cendant is the world's largest hotel franchiser. CUC International, founded in 1973, was a direct marketer and provider of home-shopping and discount wholesaling clubs; it later acquired operations in online apartment rental, value-added tax refunds, and software publishing. HFS was founded in 1992 as the holding company of the Howard Johnson, Ramada, and Days Inn hotel chains. Several years later, HFS diversified into real estate through the acquisitions of Century 21, Coldwell Banker, and Electronic Realty Associates; into car rental through the purchase of Avis; and into tax preparation through the acquisition of Jackson Hewitt. With a 22 percent share of the economy- and mid-priced hotel market, Cendant's properties include Days Inn, Howard Johnson, Knights Inn, Ramada, Super 8, Travelodge, Villager Lodge, and Wingate Inn. The company's revenues reached $5.3 billion in 1998.

Owned by the British company Bass PLC, Atlanta-based Bass Hotels & Resorts has about 450,000 rooms at more than 2,700 properties in some 90 countries. Formerly known as Holiday Inn Worldwide, the company holds a portfolio of such lodging brands as Holiday Inn, Holiday Inn Express, Crowne Plaza, Inter-Continental, and Staybridge Suites. Bass reports that they have approximately 150 million customers annually.

WORKFORCE

The AH&MA reports that the hotel and motel industry employs more than 1.16 million part- and full-time workers. Its work force is highly diverse. It often includes minimum-wage restaurant staff, room and building maintenance workers, middle-income administrative and marketing positions, and high-salary upper management personnel. The primary union in the industry is the Hotel Employees and Restaurant Employees International Union, based in New York City.

AMERICA AND THE WORLD

Since increasing numbers of U.S. travelers are leaving the country for both business and leisure, many U.S. chains are expanding oversees. Most of the major U.S. hotel companies have already expanded into Europe, and are likely to continue to increase their global presence to accommodate the growth of international travel. The opening of Eastern Europe, coupled with the relaxation of trade barriers between European countries, has given further momentum to the enthusiasm for developing international operations.

FURTHER READING

"The 1998 Lodging Industry Profile." Washington, DC: American Hotel & Motel Association, 1999. Available from http://www.ahma.com/infocenter/lip_98.htm.

Bass Hotels & Resorts, Inc. Home Page. Available from http://www.basshotels.com.

Cendant Corp. Home Page. Available from http://www.cendant.com.

Hoover, Gary, Alta Campbell, and Patrick J. Spain. *Hoover's Handbook of American Business 1995.* The Reference Press, 1996.

"Hotels Increase in Value." *Hotel & Motel Management,* 19 February 1996.

Johnson, Ben. "PKF Study: Light is On For Investors in U.S. Hotels." *National Real Estate Investor,* January 1996.

Lloyd-Jones, Anne R., and Stephen Rushmore. "Recent Trends in Hotel Management Contracts." *Real Estate Finance Journal,* Summer 1996.

SIC 7021

ROOMING AND BOARDING HOUSES

This category covers establishments primarily engaged in renting rooms, with or without board, on a fee basis. Rental of apartments, apartment hotels, and other housing units are classified in Real Estate Operators (Except Developers) and Lessors industries. Rooming and boarding houses operated by membership organizations for their members only are classified in **SIC 7041: Organization Hotels and Lodging Houses, on Membership Basis.** Homes for the aged, children, and the handicapped that also provide additional services, other than nursing care, are classified in **SIC 8361: Residential Care,** and homes that provide nursing care are classified in Nursing and Personal Care Facilities industries.

NAICS Code(s)

721310 (Rooming and Boarding Houses)

Industry Snapshot

Rooming and boarding houses provide generally low-cost lodging on either a temporary or long-term basis. Although the distinction between rooming, boarding, and lodging houses is not always clear, a rooming house is typically an establishment that provides only for the rental of rooms, while a boarding house provides meals and may offer such amenities as maid service and laundry service. At one time, rooming and boarding houses were a common, and often desirable, form of housing that catered to members of a wide range of social classes and professional occupations, but this sector of the lodging industry has generally been in decline. A 1985 *Engineering News-Record* report on a housing alternatives symposium characterized rooming and boarding houses as "bygone housing styles." Commercial rooming and boarding house establishments, while not "bygone," have undeniably become associated with the less fortunate classes. Nonetheless, rooming and boarding houses play an important role within the lodging industry and, as New Jersey architect Michael Mostoller argued in the course of the *Engineering News-Record* symposium, "the boardinghouse and roominghouse . . . must be reconsidered" as an economical and potentially convivial form of commercial congregate housing.

Organization and Structure

The rooming and boarding house sector of the lodging industry includes non-organizational rooming houses, lodging houses, boarding houses, and dormitories that do not provide for such special services as nursing or personal care. Rooming and boarding houses can offer single rooms, shared double rooms, efficiencies, or suites; private, shared, or communal living and eating areas; and private, shared, or communal bathrooms. Approximately two-thirds of commercial rooming and boarding house establishments are owned by sole proprietors or partnerships, rather than by corporations. Most rooming and boarding houses are relatively small-scale operations. The average establishment had only five employees and an annual revenue of only $181,849.

Rooming and boarding house establishments are subject to Department of Housing and Urban Development, Federal Housing Administration, and other federal or local building codes and standards, which effectively limit design options for new establishments, plus state and/or local licensing and inspection. A related concern for rooming and boarding house owners is insurance, which can be difficult to obtain for multi-family dwellings.

Background and Development

In a study published in the *Journal of Marriage and the Family,* John Modell and Tamara K. Hareven assessed the nineteenth century heyday of lodging in both domestic and commercial establishments, noting that "these two categories (from the point of view of the lodger) essentially competed within a single market." Modell and Hareven found that the nineteenth century prevalence of rooming and boarding can be associated with rapid industrialization, urbanization, and population growth, coupled with increases in the number of manufacturing employees, of young, unmarried working men and women in the cities, and of foreign-born urban residents—though the authors stressed that lodging was far more characteristic of American and migrant cultures than of foreign cultures, who generally turned to lodging only as an expedient. Modell and Hareven proposed that "in an industrializing, rapidly urbanizing society," rooming and boarding "was so widespread as to be reasonably considered indispensable."

Mark Peel, in an article published in the Winter 1992 *Journal of American History,* focused on the lodging house in Boston in the second half of the nineteenth century. Peel elaborated on the cultural distinctions between the often genteel boarding house and the generally working- or lower-class rooming house, which was less socially structured and less supervised by landlords or hosts. Peel concluded that the rooming house "was not just a place where thousands of migrants and immigrants first met the American city," but a potentially radical housing alternative where "some urban dwellers explored a very different social trajectory from those who entered through the boardinghouse, the tenement, or the suburban home."

Commercial rooming and boarding house establishments could readily adapt to such variant and shifting "social trajectories." Lisa F. Fine, in a study published in the *Journal of Social History,* described five particular boarding houses in Chicago that catered to women. These boarding houses, in the first three decades of the twentieth century, "provided safe, respectable, home-like, low cost housing, and a vast array of social services that allowed white-collar women to lead relatively independent lives." In 1915, among the residents of these boarding houses, 233 were classified as stenographers, clerks, bookkeepers, or secretaries; 132 were listed as students; and 32 were teachers.

During the course of the twentieth century, however, the rooming and boarding house sector of the lodging industry has gradually been eroded. In an article published in the Winter 1992 *Journal of Social History,* Richard Harris summarized the scholarly consensus on the factors that led to the "social marginalization of lodging." By the late nineteenth century, increasing levels of prosperity, along with essentially middle-class concerns about a lack of space and privacy in congregate housing, gradually made boarding or lodging in private residences less common, although it persisted as a source of supplemental household income well into the twentieth century. As the economic tie between homeowners and lodgers was broken, and single-family housing became entrenched as a cultural ideal, lodging became less respectable. This led to the decline of boarding arrangements for the economically prosperous, whether in domestic or commercial establishments. Inexpensive rooming houses, with lodgers eating, socializing, and securing such services as laundry outside of the rooming establishments, became the predominant form of lodging house. Beginning in the 1920s, a boom in urban housing construction and the proliferation of inexpensive apartment blocs undermined the already narrowed market for rooming houses. In addition, beginning in the 1930s, the gradual establishment of the welfare state further lessened some of the economic bases of the rooming and boarding house sector of the lodging industry.

By the second half of the twentieth century, commercial rooming and boarding house establishments had become associated with housing for new workers or for the transient, poor, aged, or disabled. Of particular note was a 1977 incident in Sea Bright, New Jersey, in which four mentally retarded boarding house lodgers were killed in a fire that may have been set off by hostile neighbors. This incident created a national scandal and triggered congressional initiatives for the licensing and regulation of rooming and boarding house establishments.

The above developments contributed to a steady drop in the number and profitability of these establishments through the 1990s. Nonetheless, rooming and boarding houses have proven their flexibility in the past. Still, the fate of this segment of the lodging industry remains subject to fluctuations in cultural, political, economic, demographic, and regional factors.

CURRENT CONDITIONS

The total number of commercial rooming and boarding houses nationwide was 1,620, down from 1,781 in 1987. The states with the highest number of rooming and boarding house establishments continued to be large states with high numbers of transient residents, such as California (280 establishments), New York (175 establishments), Florida (83 establishments), and Pennsylvania (79 establishments). Many states (Alaska, Arkansas, Delaware, Hawaii, Idaho, Kentucky, Louisiana, Montana, Nebraska, Nevada, New Hampshire, New Mexico, North Dakota, Rhode Island, South Dakota, Utah, West Virginia, and Wyoming) had 10 or fewer commercial rooming and boarding house establishments.

The national revenues for the rooming and boarding house sector of the lodging industry amounted to approximately $294.6 million. This figure represented an increase of 19.6 percent over 1987, but it was far less than the average 56 percent increase in revenues during that period for taxable service industries in general.

During the 1990s, the industry experienced negative publicity that focused on initiatives for the inspection, regulation, and reform of substandard or illegal rooming establishments. The *New York Times* reported on the "growing number of one-family homes illegally converted to single-room occupancy." In such cities as Chicago, neighborhood associations were organized to combat illegal conversions in areas zoned for one-family or two-family homes. These neighborhood associations protested the loss of neighborhood integrity and the decline of property values. They also feared—both for themselves and for the occupants of illegal rooming houses—problems related to congestion, security, fire, pollution, sanitation, and noise. Further, some establishments also became centers of drug activity, as allegedly happened in the case of Peck's Row, a historic row house in Milwaukee that had been converted into a rooming house and became the subject of controversy over its preservation.

As in the past, many illegal rooming establishments are inhabited by recently immigrated populations, whose vulnerability to exploitation may be aggravated by a lack of language and cultural skills and/or by illegal immigration status. The *New York Times* article quoted Bill Apgar of the Harvard University Joint Center for Housing Studies on this specific problem: "There are a lot of illegal conversions where . . . people are being allowed to live in unsafe conditions while paying rent which is disproportionate to the service they receive. . . . The fear of being deported is the leverage that the landlord holds over the tenant." Even so, city inspectors are often reluctant to take action against illegal rooming establishments. The landlords may be subject to only limited and temporary penalties that provide little deterrent, while the socially and economically disadvantaged tenants might suffer greatly from attempts at governmental intervention or control. Some municipalities have taken a more positive approach to this problem by considering conversion of rooming houses into low- and moderate-income housing units.

Despite this generally gloomy outlook, the industry does offer some positive aspects. Located in New York

City, the Katherine House, one of the last surviving traditional boarding houses for women, has a waiting list of 18- to 25-year-old women who wish to obtain a private room with two daily meals for a mere $135 per week. A hybrid form of housing, ''extended-stay lodging,'' provides hotel-like accommodations for travelling businesspeople for periods of weeks or months, sometimes with meals included, and became increasingly popular in the mid-1990s.

Workforce

The rooming and boarding house sector of the lodging industry created only a limited number of employment opportunities. Rooming and boarding house employees included janitorial and housekeeping staff and food service, laundry, and maintenance workers. The total number of people employed in the industry was approximately 8,000, with an average of five employees per establishment.

Further Reading

''1997 Industry Quick Reports.'' Washington, D.C.: U.S. Census Bureau, 26 November 1999. Available from http://factfinder.census.gov.

Gould, Whitney. ''Bid for Historic Status on Hold.'' *Milwaukee Journal Sentinel,* 18 March 1997.

Modell, John, and Tamara K. Hareven. ''Urbanization and the Malleable Household: An Examination of Boarding and Lodging in American Families.'' *Journal of Marriage and the Family,* August 1973.

Murphy, Shelby L. ''Austin Becoming Hotbed for Extended-Stay Lodging.'' *Austin Business Journal,* 24 January 1997.

O'Brien, Miles, Joie Chen, and Janine Sharell. ''Katherine House Provides Young Women Affordable Housing.'' *CNN Saturday Morning News Transcript,* 22 February 1997.

Tabachnik, Sheri. ''Hotel Conversion Would Fill Avon Housing Mandate.'' *Asbury Park Press,* 29 January 1997.

SIC 7032

SPORTING AND RECREATIONAL CAMPS

This industry consists of establishments primarily engaged in operating sporting and recreational camps, such as boys' and girls' camps, and fishing and hunting camps. Establishments primarily engaged in operating sports instructional camps, such as baseball, basketball, football, or karate camps, and those operating day camps are classified in **SIC 7999: Amusement and Recreation Services, Not Elsewhere Classified.**

NAICS Code(s)

721214 (Recreational and Vacation Camps)

Industry Snapshot

In 1999 nearly 9 million people attended one of the nation's 8,500 camps, according to the American Camping Association (ACA). About 5,500 of those camps were resident camps, 2,200 were day camps, and the remaining 750 offered both day and overnight programs. Although the majority of camps were of the conventional summer camp variety, specialty camps that operated year-round and focused on one of a diverse range of subjects (such as accounting or space travel) were appearing in growing numbers. Camps catering to adult participants were on the rise as well and ranged from dude ranches to nudist camps. The camp industry employed 500,000 primarily full-time seasonal workers, usually college students, teachers, and health care professionals. The cost of attendance varied greatly from one facility to the next. Day camps typically cost between $10 and $50 per day, while the daily rate for resident camps ranged from $15 to $120.

Organization and Structure

About 75 percent of the 8,500 camps in the United States are operated by nonprofit groups or agencies. These include religious institutions, scouting organizations, and such well-known groups as Camp Fire, Inc., YMCA, and Boys and Girls Clubs of America. The remaining 2,125 camps are operated privately by families or individuals. In the United States there aren't any companies that operate large chains of commercial camps.

Establishment Size and Distribution. Nearly 40 percent of the establishments in the sporting and recreational camp industry are tax-exempt, a figure that is considerably higher than the 9.6 percent across all service industries. The tax-exempt segment of the industry accounts for only about 35 percent of the revenue generated by the industry, while employing 41 percent of its workers. Whether tax-exempt or not, camps are generally small operations in comparison to the rest of the service sector. Nonprofit camps employ, on average, only six people per establishment compared to 39 per establishment in other nonprofit operations in the service sector.

Geographically, camps are usually found where one finds the two necessary ingredients—people and space. New York and California, which have plenty of both, have the most sporting and recreational camps, with well over 200 ACA-accredited establishments each. States in the northern part of the Midwest, particularly Michigan, Minnesota, and Wisconsin, are also strongly represented in this industry, as are Pennsylvania and Texas.

Accreditation. A voluntary accreditation program has been administered by the American Camping Association (ACA) since the late 1940s. By 1999 roughly 2,200 U.S. camps were accredited by the ACA. Accreditation of a camp is established through an evaluation process based on up to 300 national standards. Trained volunteers visit the camp and, using a set of established guidelines, grade the facility in a variety of areas, including site and facility, administration, transportation, personnel, programs, health care, and activities. Site and facility criteria cover such basics as sanitary arrangements and food service. Standards for administration include safety regulations and emergency procedures. Vehicle safety and maintenance are examined for compliance with transportation standards. Personnel standards apply to the training, qualifications, and supervision of staff members. Qualifications of activity leaders are among the topics covered by program standards. Health care standards include the availability of first aid care and emergency transportation.

The list of standards used in the ACA's accreditation program has evolved over the course of several decades, beginning as the ''Suggested Tentative Standards'' adopted in 1935. The first set of official camp standards was adopted at the ACA's National Convention in 1948, after several years of study and debate and with financial support from the Chrysler and Kellogg foundations. In the 1950s, the standards for camp personnel and programs were adopted, as well as the methods by which conformity to these standards could be ascertained. Further research and development of the standards took place in the 1960s, including the formation of a Standards Rewrite Committee. In the 1970s and 1980s, standards were adopted that incorporated the needs of campers with disabilities and special medical conditions, such as diabetes. In 1990 a new set of standards was adopted that emphasized health and safety issues over the business-related issues that had been emphasized in the past.

BACKGROUND AND DEVELOPMENT

The roots of the camping movement are often traced to the second half of the nineteenth century. In the summer of 1861 Frederick William Gunn, a Connecticut schoolmaster, took his class of 40 boys for a two-week campout to Long Island Sound, where they simulated the lifestyle of Civil War soldiers. The outing was so successful that it became an annual event known as Gunnery Camp. The next notable camp experiment was begun in 1881 by Ernest Balch, an undergraduate at Dartmouth. Seeking a summer alternative for children of wealthy families, Balch founded Camp Chocorua in New Hampshire. At Chocorua, boys from 12 to 16 years of age received a taste of wilderness, which Balch theorized was a healthier way to spend the summer than accompanying their parents to the swanky resorts of the day. In the following years new camps were founded on the Chocorua model.

Fresh Air and Other Programs. Late in the nineteenth century the Fresh Air movement arose out of concern for the needs of poor children in urban areas. Camps were established near cities where growing immigrant populations were living in overcrowded conditions, which were perceived as unhealthy and conducive to delinquency. Some camps that were founded in the early days of the Fresh Air movement are still in existence, including Camp Algonquin, founded by Chicago's United Charities in 1907, and Incarnation Camp, Inc., an Episcopal center that began as early as 1886. Around 1875 Country Week programs were established in Philadelphia and Boston. The Philadelphia program was started by Eliza Turner, who invited 12 girls to spend two weeks at her farm; by 1910 3,000 children were participating. In New Jersey the publisher of *Life Magazine* founded what became known as Trail Blazer Camps in 1887; by 1918 40,000 children had participated in two-week sessions at the camp.

Private girls' camps began to appear in greater numbers around 1902. That year, three such camps opened: Kehonka in New Hampshire; Pinelands of Centre Harbor, Maine; and Wyonegonic Camps in Bridgton, Maine. Another camp, Camp Arey, which was founded years earlier as a natural science camp for boys, also became a girls' camp. By 1915 100 private girls' camps were in operation. These camps offered girls from sheltered backgrounds a chance to wear comfortable clothing and engage in activities that were more rugged than those in which they were usually allowed to participate.

YMCA and YWCA. The Young Women's Christian Association (YWCA) was first formed in Philadelphia as a sort of resource center for women employed in industrial occupations. The first YWCA camp, called Sea Rest, was set up in 1874 in Asbury Park, New Jersey. Its purpose was to enable overworked young women to take a low-cost vacation from their 60-hour-per-week jobs. It received an enormous amount of publicity from the start, including a dedication speech by President Ulysses S. Grant.

The Young Men's Christian Association (YMCA) appeared in the 1850s as a support program for teenaged boys and young men who lived on their own. The YMCA's camping program was founded by Sumner Dudley in 1885. That year, Dudley took seven YMCA boys camping at Pine Point on Orange Lake, only six miles from their home in Newburgh, New York. The program grew rapidly over the next few summers. The camp that Dudley founded was still operating 100 years later and now bears his name.

Camps operated by nonprofit organizations began to proliferate in the early part of the twentieth century. Among the groups that joined this trend were the Boy Scouts and Girl Scouts of America, Camp Fire Girls, and a wide variety of religious, labor union, and other types of organizations. Like their predecessors, these camps were mainly concentrated in the northeastern portion of the nation.

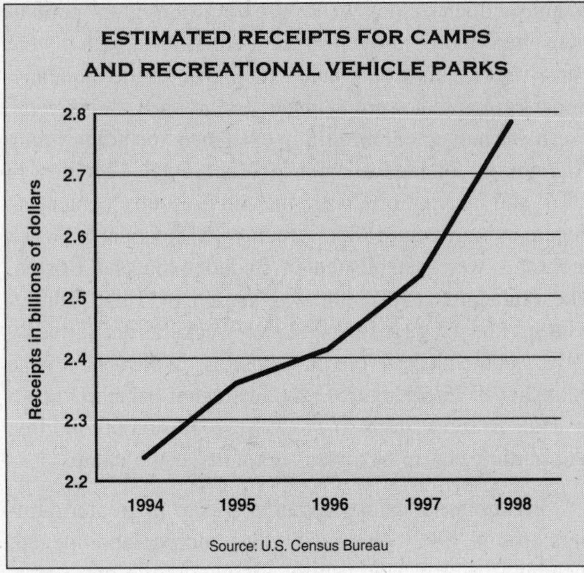

Government Involvement. Historically, government agencies have not played an important role in the development of the camp industry, at least not in the sense of operating camps of their own. It is estimated that the percentage of camps operated by public agencies at any given time has never exceeded five percent. Government agencies have contributed to the growth of camps in other ways, however. During the 1930s the National Park Service, which was established in 1916, developed a number of organized camping facilities for lease to camping groups that did not possess their own camping areas.

State parks have also been a source of camping facilities for a variety of groups since the early 1900s. New York, for example, established a camping department as early as 1917. By 1950, there were 296 organized camping facilities in state parks throughout the United States. City parks and recreation departments began setting up camp programs around the same time. Los Angeles, Detroit, and Kansas City had municipal camping programs by 1920.

Emergence of the American Camping Association. In 1910 the directors of several private boys' camps got together to form the Camp Directors Association of America (CDAA). The CDAA merged in 1924 with the National Association of Directors of Girls' Camps, which had formed in 1916. The combined group was called the Camp Directors Association (CDA). With an organization in place that could establish communication among camp administrations and articulate the goals of the industry, new areas were found on which to place emphasis. In particular, facilities for people with disabilities began to multiply in the 1930s and 1940s. Industry-wide publications such as *Camping* (the official CDA journal) and *Camp News* (a commercial venture) began to appear. In 1935 the CDA evolved into the American Camping Association (ACA), which remains the most widely recognized voice of the camp industry.

Current Conditions

According to the ACA, enrollment in the U.S. camping industry grew nine percent in 1998. Females accounted for 55 percent of the nation's total enrollees. This was the seventh consecutive year that enrollment increased by eight to ten percent.

An ACA survey conducted in the late 1990s discovered that parents and campers desired shorter camping sessions, a view that contributed to the popularity of the one-week camp over the two-week or one-month sessions. This desire was likely to be fueled further by the concept of year-round schooling. This emergent trend, which was opposed by the ACA, had implications for the camping industry nationwide and was the subject of study among educators and other interested parties. Dr. Peter Scales of the Search Institute, a Minneapolis-based institution that conducted research on youth development, was quoted by the ACA: "The biggest plus of camp is that camps help young people discover and explore their talents, interests, and values. Most schools don't satisfy all these needs. Kids who have had these kinds of (camp) experiences end up being healthier and have less problems." In July 1998 the New York City Board of Education launched a pilot program to provide an alternative to 12-month schooling. *Break-Aways: Partnership for Year-Round Learning* combined a nine-month school session with up to 28 additional days in a camp environment in which campers were exposed to both traditional academic lessons and camp activities.

A number of popular activities had been added to many camping programs by the late 1990s. These new areas of interest included adventure activities, such as mountain biking, rock climbing, and boating; fine arts, including performing arts, photography, and jewelry making; and organized sports, such as in-line skating, gymnastics, soccer, volleyball, and golf.

At the same time, various special purpose camps had also arisen. Some of these were instructional sports camps, which are classified under **SIC 7999: Amusement and Recreation Services, Not Elsewhere Classified.** In addition to these, recent entries have included NASA's U.S. Space Camp, ornithology camps, adult band camps, Breakers Etiquette Camp for teenagers, a circus camp called Circus Smirkus, and a host of camps with environmental themes.

Despite the trends of increased enrollment and the inclusion of popular activities, some 2,500 camps have closed since the mid-1970s. A disproportionate number of these had been run by nonprofit agencies. One of the chief reasons for these closures was that camps located near urban areas, especially those on the water, had become extremely attractive to real estate developers. Moreover, the prohibitive cost of liability insurance had become a problem for small camps that lacked significant financial resources.

WORKFORCE

Summer youth camps account for about 500,000 full-time jobs in the United States. However, most of these jobs are seasonal. The ACA reports that the typical salary for a camp counselor is between $1,000 and $3,000 for the camp season. Counselors with special skills, such as trained lifeguards, are often paid as much as $4,000 for the same period. Most camps also provide their employees with room and board, and health care and laundry services are often available. A large percentage of camp counselors are college students on summer break. In some programs, college credit can be earned for camp experience.

In addition to counselors, camps also employ clerical workers, administrators, cooks, drivers, and other specialists. The vast majority of these workers are not represented by unions. In general, salaries for camp workers are fairly low compared to those of their counterparts in other service industries. Private camps usually pay higher wages than camps operated by nonprofit agencies. One unique characteristic of the sporting and recreational camp work force is its international composition. Each year, about 75 nations are represented on the staffs of American camps, accounting for as many as 18,000 foreign counselors in the 1990s.

AMERICA AND THE WORLD

Organized camping, particularly of the summer camp variety, is very much an American phenomenon. One possible reason for this is the relative abundance of open landscape close to large cities. The United Kingdom, however, experienced a dramatic upswing in the popularity of summer camps in the 1980s. Between 1983 and 1988 the number of children attending ''multi-activity holidays for children'' doubled to 75,000. Unlike in the United States, the industry in the United Kingdom is highly concentrated, with a handful of companies accounting for a large share of the market. PGL Travel Ltd., for example, was the United Kingdom's leading operator of youth summer camps in 1999, hiring more than 2,000 workers annually.

FURTHER READING

''ACA Fact Sheet.'' *American Camping Association Web Site,* 28 November 1999. Available at http://www.acacamps.org/media/factshet.htm.

Darnay, Arsen J., ed. *Service Industries USA,* 3rd ed. Detroit: Gale Research, 1996.

''Dispelling the Myths about Summer Camp.'' *American Camping Association Web Site,* 28 November 1999. Available at http://www.acacamps.org/media/myths.htm.

Eels, Eleanor. ''History of Organized Camping: The First 100 Years.'' *American Camping Association Web Site,* 28 November 1999. Available at http://www.acacamps.org/media/history.htm.

''More Than a Summer Job.'' *American Camping Association Web Site,* 28 November 1999. Available at http://www.acacamps.org/media/sumjob.htm.

''Summer Camps Professionals Speak out Against Year-Round Schooling.'' *American Camping Association Web Site,* 28 November 1999. Available at http://www.acacamps.org/media/yearscho.htm.

SIC 7033

RECREATIONAL VEHICLE PARKS AND CAMPSITES

This industry classification includes establishments primarily engaged in providing overnight or short-term camping sites for recreational vehicles, trailers, campers, or tents.

NAICS CODE(S)

721211 (RV (Recreational Vehicle) Parks and Campgrounds)

INDUSTRY SNAPSHOT

In the late 1990s more than 40 million Americans went camping every year. Additionally, 30 million recreational vehicle (RV) enthusiasts were in possession of 9.3 million recreational vehicles (a general designation for motorized or towable vehicles that provide temporary living quarters). According to the Recreational Vehicle Industry Association (RVIA), nearly 10 percent, or 8.6 million, of vehicle-owning households in the United States owned at least one RV. By the year 2010 the number of RV-owning households was expected to reach 10.4 million. The average RV owner was 48 years old with a household income of $47,000. RV trips were less expensive—50 to 80 percent cheaper—than comparable vacations based on other forms of transportation and lodging.

Commercial recreational vehicle parks and campsite establishments (i.e., campgrounds) typically provide RV owners and campers with inexpensive outdoor, recreation-oriented accommodations located near scenic and water recreation areas, national parks and forests, historic sites, theme parks, or major travel routes. The basic features of campgrounds are RV sites (ranging from rustic clearings to ''pull-thru'' concrete pads with utility hookups for water, sewage, electricity, and propane gas), tent sites, rest rooms, and shower facilities. Other typical amenities include cabins to rent, convenience stores or snack bars, picnic areas and grills, coin-operated laundry facilities, garbage and sewage disposal stations, swimming pools or natural swimming areas, fishing and boating facilities, recreation halls, playgrounds, sports facilities, nature and biking trails, movies, cable TV hookups, telephones, and motorcycle accommodations. Moderately expensive resort and membership establishments also feature such ''country club'' amenities as 18-hole golf courses, tennis courts, and spa facilities.

Recreational vehicle parks and campsites are frequented by a wide range of the population, including middle-aged or senior citizen couples, often on prolonged trips with wide-ranging travel itineraries; families with young children; and young people or couples. Establishments may cater exclusively to such demographic groups.

Individual campgrounds may contain anywhere from one dozen to several hundred RV pads and/or tent sites. Establishments may be open seasonally or year-round, depending on climate and the nature of the surrounding tourist attractions. Rates may vary by season. Senior citizen, RV club member, and other discounts are typically available, and longer-stay rates may also be discounted.

By the 1990s the RV and campgrounds industries had given rise to a wide array of affiliated businesses and services. Companies such as Cruise America and the Canadian-based Go Vacations International furnished motor homes and travel trailers on a rental basis to both domestic and international tourists. Various international, national, regional, and state directories (including computerized databases) were being marketed, along with such ''lifestyle'' magazines as *RV Times* and *Trailer Life.* Specialty RV storage facilities, RV equipment and accessories retailers, and RV emergency road services were also available.

Organization and Structure

By the late 1990s there were approximately 16,000 campgrounds and RV parks in the United States, of which approximately two-thirds were commercially owned. Public camping facilities were also operated by the National Park Service (440 campgrounds), the USDA National Forest Service (4,000 campgrounds), the Bureau of Land Management, the U.S. Army Corps of Engineers (53,000 campsites), the U.S. Fish & Wildlife Service (504 National Wildlife Refuges), state park and forest systems, and county and city governmental bodies. These public campgrounds typically offered few amenities and some did not accept reservations, or did so only on a limited basis. Public campgrounds were free of charge or very economical; typical rates ranged from free-of-charge to $12 per night for tent sites and $10 to $20 per night for RV sites with hookups.

In comparison to public campgrounds, commercial campgrounds were more easily accessible, more predominantly oriented to RV camping, and more concentrated in the East and the upper Midwest. These commercial campgrounds, numbering approximately 8,500 in the late 1990s, typically offered more amenities (including reservation services) and were slightly less economical, although rates were still inexpensive in relation to the lodging industry as a whole.

The National Association of RV Parks and Campgrounds (ARVC), founded in 1967 as the National Campground Owners Association, has provided networking, advocacy, convention, and information services for commercial campground owners. The ARVC, with approximately 3,500 members in the late 1990s, sponsored the Go Camping America Committee to promote campground tourism, as well as the RV Park & Campground Industry Education Foundation to provide educational programs and publications to commercial campground owners. Many states established campground associations affiliated with the national ARVC. Government bodies that have promoted campground tourism include the U.S. Travel and Tourism Administration and the Rural Tourism Development Foundation, which was established in 1993.

Chain Campgrounds. Chain campgrounds, despite the connotations of this label, are often distinctive, independently-owned businesses that are affiliated under varying arrangements with commercial campground organizations in order to take advantage of national or international marketing and reservation services. In the late 1990s the largest chain was Kampgrounds of America (KOA), based in Billings, Montana. KOA held a network of more than 550 franchised campgrounds in the United States and Canada. While many of these establishments were roadside facilities with few amenities, others were destination resorts. Best Holiday Trav-L-Park Association, a non-franchise chain founded in 1982, included 71 independent parks that shared a central reservation service. Yogi Bear's Jellystone Park Camp Resorts, established in 1969 and geared to families with children, consisted of 72 member campgrounds with a theme based on ''Yogi Bear,'' the Hanna-Barbera cartoon character. Chain campgrounds typically offer rate discounts for repeat customers within the campground network.

Independent Campgrounds. In the 1990s establishments in the independent campgrounds category varied widely in size and quality, ranging from small-scale, modest operations to such destination resorts as Disney's Fort Wilderness Resort in Florida. Many independent campgrounds were registered with the nation's leading RV owners club, the Good Sam Club, as Good SamParks.

Other independent campgrounds were older facilities that weren't equipped to handle the parking and hookup requirements of the newer, larger, and more luxurious recreational vehicles.

Membership Campgrounds. In the 1980s and 1990s, membership campgrounds were destination resorts typically operated on one of two membership bases. One form of membership campground offered RV pads and campsites free of charge to members who paid a membership fee and annual dues. A second form of membership campground offered access to RV pads and campsites on a time-share basis. Both forms of membership campgrounds often belonged to networks, whereby members could extend their privileges to affiliated membership campgrounds for nominal fees. Membership campgrounds were often oriented toward golf, tennis, water-recreation and/or boating, and provided clubhouses and restaurants. Initiation fees for membership campgrounds started at $5,000 (although memberships were often resold at discounted rates), with annual fees starting at $100 or more.

BACKGROUND AND DEVELOPMENT

Several cultural forces provided the impetus for the commercial recreational vehicle parks and campsites industry. The central factors, of course, are the national enthusiasm for camping, which has been ranked by the U.S. Census Bureau's *Statistical Abstract of the United States* as the fourth most popular participatory sport/activity in the country, and the American passion for automobiles and recreational vehicles. America's camping tradition can be traced to the desire for an affordable form of travel and tourism, particularly given the geographical expanse of the United States; the nation's scenic diversity and natural endowments, which give weight to such tourism slogans as ''See America First'' and ''Discover America;'' a national ambivalence about city life, with its crowds, pollution, and noise (conditions, unfortunately, sometimes reproduced within busy campgrounds); an idealization of nature and the ''frontier,'' and a corresponding adoption of Native American traditions; the conservation and ecological awareness movements; the country's outstanding interstate highway system; and the development, dating from the last quarter of the nineteenth century, of the national park and forest systems. The prestige and popularity of national parks at the Grand Canyon, Yellowstone, Yosemite, and California's redwood forest have played no small role in making camping one of the most popular leisure activities in the country.

''Sagebrushing,'' as the first wave of automobile- or RV-based camping was called, became a cultural phenomenon in the 1920s and 1930s, continuing even throughout the Depression. Such camping became even more popular after World War II, particularly among the burgeoning suburbanite population, and it utilized wartime technology such as four-wheel drive. By the 1960s recreational vehicles became increasingly prominent on the camping scene, spurring the development of private campgrounds featuring utility hookups and a new level of amenities. The 1970s and 1980s marked the development, initially in the Pacific Northwest, of membership campgrounds. In the 1980s record crowds at the most popular public campgrounds, in conjunction with Reagan-era federal budget cutbacks, created further growth opportunities for the commercial campground industry.

CURRENT CONDITIONS

According to the RVIA, the RV industry hit a 20-year high in 1998, as measured in shipments of RVs to dealers nationally. That year's total of 292,700 RVs represented a 15 percent increase over 1997. Results for the first three quarters of 1999 suggested a continuance of the upward trend, as the 251,000 in shipments was a 9.5 percent increase over the same period in 1998. ''These robust numbers confirm that RV travel has entered a new era of growth,'' said David J. Humphreys, president of the RVIA, in a press release. ''The industry is now benefiting from an influx of baby boomers into the RV ownership ranks, long projected by market analysts.''

Demographic studies confirm the industry's positive outlook. The University of Michigan Survey Research Center predicted that the number of RV-owning households in the United States would rise to 10.4 million by the year 2010, a 21 percent increase over the 8.6 million such households in the late 1990s.

This study also found that RVs were increasingly appealing to younger consumers. Although Americans aged 55 and older owned approximately one-third of the total RVs on the road in the late 1990s, the segment experiencing the most growth in the industry was baby boomers. RV ownership by Americans aged 45 to 54 increased 25 percent in the mid-1990s. By 1999 approximately 45 percent of the nation's RVs were owned by boomers between the ages of 35 and 54, compared to the 40 percent owned by those aged 55 and older. The University of Michigan study also determined that nearly 25 percent of boomers intended to purchase an RV sometime in the future. A study by Louis Harris and Associates found a similar buying pattern—more than half of all likely RV buyers fell in the 30- to 49-year-old range.

This demographic trend indicates a positive outlook for leisure activities, such as RV camping, that are favored by middle-aged and older populations. As *Business America* noted, ''The progression from tent camping to RV camping as campers grow older is evident.'' Therefore, the aging of baby boomers should ensure a phase of renewed growth for an industry that achieved peak profits in the late 1980s but experienced a slight downturn at the beginning of the 1990s.

A separate trend affecting the campground industry in the 1990s was the growing ecological and environmental awareness that was reflected in the international tourism industry by the advent of ''ecotourism.'' Some campers and campground owners, increasingly concerned about minimizing their negative impact on natural and wildlife environments, had turned to environmentally sensitive camping methods and products, including the recycling or careful disposal of garbage, food waste, and sewage. The *New York Times* reported that ''operators of private campgrounds, while still eager to draw customers and make profits, are more aware that the lure of the outdoors means preserving the outdoors.'' Public campgrounds also responded to this trend; in 1993 Yosemite became the first national park to develop a comprehensive garbage and food waste reduction strategy.

Industry Leaders

Thousand Trails, Inc., founded in 1969, had $67.9 million in revenues in 1999. That year, the firm's 106,000 members had access to a network of 53 private campgrounds in 17 states and British Columbia. Its subsidiary, Resort Parks International, is a network of affiliated, private RV and condominium resorts.

Kampgrounds of America, Inc., (KOA) is the world's largest system of franchised campgrounds. Established in 1962 to offer overnight amenities for cross-country travelers, KOA was comprised of about 550 locations in the United States, Canada, Mexico, and Japan by 1999. About 90 percent of the campgrounds were franchised, with the remaining 10 percent company-owned. KOA recorded revenues of $26.6 million in 1998.

Workforce

Traditionally, many commercial campgrounds were modest, owner- or family-operated establishments. Therefore, only a limited number of seasonal or permanent positions were created by the industry. These positions were typically for registration clerks, convenience store clerks, janitors, groundskeepers, and recreation-related employees.

America and the World

The United States has historically been dominant in the recreational vehicle parks and campsites industry, and American RV owners and campers have fueled the commercial campground industries in Canada, Mexico, and other popular international camping destinations. By 1999 Kampgrounds of America had established several franchises in Canada, Japan, and Mexico. International visitors to the United States comprise a significant percentage of KOA's customers, and vacationers from Japan, Australia, New Zealand, Germany, and the United Kingdom, in particular, have increased the U.S. RV rental market.

Vacationing in ''caravans,'' as recreational vehicles are generally called abroad, is popular in Australia, New Zealand, and Europe, notably, in Germany, Switzerland, Austria, Scandinavia, and the United Kingdom. As in the United States, campgrounds abroad have been established by both government bodies and commercial interests. In the 1990s international campground operators included EuroCamp and Eurosites. National campground operators included Big 4 Tourist Parks (Australia), Azur Camping (Germany), The Best of British (Great Britain), Top 10 Holiday Parks (New Zealand), Club Caraville (South Africa), and DomanTurist AB (Sweden).

Further Reading

Bellafante, Gina. ''The Sedate Outdoors.'' *Time,* 19 August 1996.

Hoeffel, John. ''Where RVs Dare Not Go.'' *American Demographics,* February 1996.

Kampgrounds of America, Inc. Web Site. Available at http://www.koa.com.

National Economic Survey of Campgrounds & RV Parks. RV Park & Campground Industry Education Foundation (bi-annual).

National Standards for RV Parks and Campgrounds. American National Standards Institute.

''Research Reveals Larger, Younger RV Market.'' *Recreational Vehicle Industry Association Web Site.* Available at http://www.rvia.org.

''RV Fast Facts.'' *Recreational Vehicle Industry Association Web Site.* Available at http://www.rvia.org.

RV Park & Campground Report. National Association of RV Parks and Campgrounds (monthly).

''RV Shipments at a 21-Year High.'' *Recreational Vehicle Industry Association Web Site.* Available at http://www.rvia.org.

''RVs in High Gear.'' *Advertising Age,* 10 July 1995.

Thousand Trails, Inc. Web Site. Available at http://www.thousandtrails.com.

Trailer Life's Campground & RV Services Directory. (directory of the Good Sam Club).

Ward's Business Directory of U.S. Private and Public Companies, 1997 ed. Detroit: Gale Research, 1997.

''Woodall's Market Facts.'' *Woodall's Campground Directory,* 1997.

SIC 7041

ORGANIZATION HOTELS AND LODGING HOUSES, ON MEMBERSHIP BASIS

This category covers lodging houses and hotels operated by membership organizations for the benefit of their constituents, and not open to the general public. Commercial hotels operated by such organizations are classified in **SIC 7011: Hotels and Motels** and commercial rooming and boarding houses are classified in **SIC 7021: Rooming and Boarding Houses.** Residential homes for the aged and handicapped are classified in **SIC 8361: Residential Care.**

NAICS CODE(S)

721110 (Hotels(except Casino Hotels) and Motels)
721310 (Rooming and Boarding Houses)

The organization hotels and lodging houses industry included establishments such as: boarding houses for members of organizations; fraternity and sorority houses; residence clubs; and rooming houses operated by private clubs. Commercial hotels, public boarding houses, and residential homes for the aged were classified elsewhere.

Membership lodging establishments existed in the United States from the founding of the nation. For example, the first fraternity, Phi Beta Kappa, was founded in 1776 at William and Mary College. The first sorority, Kappa Alpha Theta, was instituted in 1870 at Depauw University. A plethora of other not-for-profit organizations that offered boarding facilities emerged during the twentieth century. The Young Men's Christian Association (YMCA), for instance, started its U.S. chapter in 1851 and grew to more than 13 million members by the early 1990s. Likewise, Youth Hostels Inc. of America, which provided inexpensive travel lodging nationwide to its members, had over 100,000 members. With the population aging, organizations like Elderhostel have also become popular. Here people 55 or older pay a fee to join, then take advantage of numerous study trips around the United States and the world. Most of these trips involve a classroom or field trip environment.

In addition to not-for-profit membership lodging facilities, the fastest growing sector of this industry during the 1980s was commercial vacation travel clubs. Members of these organizations often paid an annual fee and received access to private vacation facilities or special travel packages. A proliferation of travel and vacation membership clubs during the 1980s boosted the number of industry participants to about 2,500 by the late 1980s with revenues reached about $350 million. The industry suffered during the recession of the late 1980s and early 1990s, however, as vacation and travel industry revenues plummeted. Several companies folded and industry profitability withered.

In 1998, There were an estimated 1655 establishments in this industry with 10,200 employees. In 1999, $490 million in revenue was reported, an almost 9 percent increase from the previous year.

Timeshares were developed in Florida in the mid-1970s. Investors buy a week's time at a particular resort, then pay extra to join an ''exchange'' club. The ability to exchange vacation time with other affiliated resorts heightened the appeal of the timeshare concept. In 1998, the largest timeshare club was Fairfield Communities of Orlando, with $407.9 million in sales, 4,700 employees, and 270,000 owners. Second was Santeria Corp., also of Orlando, with $359.4 million in sales, 6500 employees, and 260,000 owners. Third was Trendiest Resorts of Redmond, Washington, with sales of $197.9 million, 1,549 employees, and 50,000 owners. Another leader was Silverleaf Resorts, Inc., of Dallas, Texas, with $138.4 million in sales, 2,347 employees, and 78,000 owners.

Despite setbacks during the recession of the early 1990s, hotel and lodging industry job opportunities were expected to increase significantly between 1990 and 2005, according to the Bureau of Labor Statistics, with most occupations growing in number by 20-40 percent by 2005. Although most of the growth would likely occur in low-paying labor jobs, such as those for janitors and waitresses, positions for trained hotel managers should leap by more than 50 percent.

FURTHER READING

Darnay, Arsen J., ed. *Service Industries U.S.A.* Detroit: Gale Research, 1999.

Hoover's Company Capsules.*Hoover's Online,* 2000. Available from http://www.hoovers.com.

Occupational Outlook Handbook, 1996-1997 Edition, Washington, DC: U.S. Department of Labor, 1996.

U.S. Department of the Census.*Economic Census 1997,* 2000. Available from http://www.census.gov.

Ward's Business Directory of U. S. Private and Public Companies, Detroit: Gale Research, 1999.

SIC 7211

POWER LAUNDRIES, FAMILY AND COMMERCIAL

This category includes firms that primarily operate mechanical laundries powered with steam or other means. Companies that primarily supply laundered work clothing on a contract or fee basis are classified in **SIC 7218: Industrial Launderers.**

NAICS CODE(S)

812321 (Power Laundries, Family and Commercial)

Projections based on U.S. Bureau of the Census County Business Patterns show a decline in the industry over the course of the late 1990s, with 1,422 establishments remaining by 1998, down from a peak of 1,853 in 1992. The industry grossed a high of $932 million and employed 26,700 workers in 1995, with a decline of $5.5 million projected by the end of the decade. Most of these businesses were sole proprietorships or family-operated. Employment averaged 13 workers per establishment.

The laundry industry grew steadily from 1990-1992 as it underwent significant change. New technology altered the way clothes were laundered, dried, and finished, and laundry automation made for greater speed, efficiency, and productivity. Two major industry areas currently getting attention are automation and environmental issues. The latter concerns the use of certain detergents deemed damaging to the environment—such as those containing phosphates—and the safe disposal of waste products. Phosphates, considered to be the most effective laundering compound, may accelerate alga growth in water and deprive it of oxygen. Attempts were made to restrict their use. The impetus came from within and outside the industry. Some laundry managers turned to alternative products, anticipating future regulations against phosphates.

As power laundries grew more automated, industry observers anticipated a reduction in labor requirements, and despite a 7 percent surge in the labor force in 1992 a pattern of workforce reduction persisted throughout the end the decade. Industry projections for 1998 indicated that employment levels would continue to decrease to 81 percent of 1992 figures, despite payroll and revenue growth. Automation increased productivity and reduced the need for workers by cutting down on the number of manual tasks. For instance, networking washers, dryers, and finishing machines eliminated manual handling of loads between different laundering phases. Computerization also reduced labor requirements for office tasks, such as data entry. According to *Laundry News,* ''Computer systems and automated machinery allow laundries which might have previously operated two shifts with 100 people to operate one shift with 70 people.'' Automation may also reduce the number of accidents in power laundries and alleviate employees' health concerns. Laundry workers commonly suffer back injuries from heavy lifting, muscle strains from stretching, carpal tunnel syndrome from repetitive motions, skin diseases from contact with heavy duty detergents and chemicals, and heat stress conditions.

In 1999, the leading family and commercial power laundry business in the United States was Unifirst Corporation of Wilmington, Massachusetts, a public company with annual sales of $419 million and an estimated 7,000 employees. Pride Cleaners Incorporated of Kansas City, Missouri was second, with $37 million in sales.

Further Reading

Darnay, Arsen J., ed. *Service Industries USA.* 3rd ed. Detroit: Gale Group, 1999.

Lazich, Robert S. *Market Share Reporter.* Detroit: Gale Group, 1999.

U.S. Department of Commerce, *1992 Census of Service Industries.* Washington: GPO, 1995.

SIC 7212

GARMENT PRESSING, AND AGENTS FOR LAUNDRIES AND DRYCLEANERS

This industry category includes establishments that primarily serve as agents for launderers and drycleaners. Companies in this industry may do their own pressing or finishing work but have the laundry and dry cleaning work done by others. Businesses operating their own laundry plants are classified in **SIC 7211: Power Laundries, Family and Commercial,** and those operating their own dry cleaning plants are classified in **SIC 7216: Dry cleaning Plants, Except Rug-Cleaning.**

NAICS Code(s)

812391 (Garment Pressing and Agents for Laundries)

The average work force for industry firms consisted of 13 employees; most companies were privately owned, according to U.S. census figures. The *Journal of Commerce and Commercial* noted the total dry cleaning industry was ''dominated by immigrant small-business owners and families with limited means.'' According to U.S. government statistics, there were 3,159 establishments in this category in the mid-1990s, with negligible fluctuation expected through the end of the decade. The industry was otherwise projected to grow in the late 1990s, with revenues exceeding $606 million, employment of approximately 13,900 workers, and anticipated total payroll of $148.7 million. The garment pressing and cleaners' agents industry is concentrated most heavily in the midwestern United States, with a secondary concentration in the New England states.

Environmental Regulations. In 1993 the Environmental Protection Agency (EPA) amended the Clean Air Act of 1990, adding new rules to reduce atmospheric levels of the most common dry cleaning chemical, perchloroethylene. *Journal of Commerce and Commercial* noted the chemical was ''the most effective cleaning agent'' in the industry, ''but the government has identified it as a probable human carcinogen.'' The EPA estimated about 30 percent of U.S. drycleaners would be affected by the new regulations. Industry observers said drycleaners would have to invest at least $7,000 to meet the necessary standards, a heavy burden for many small operations.

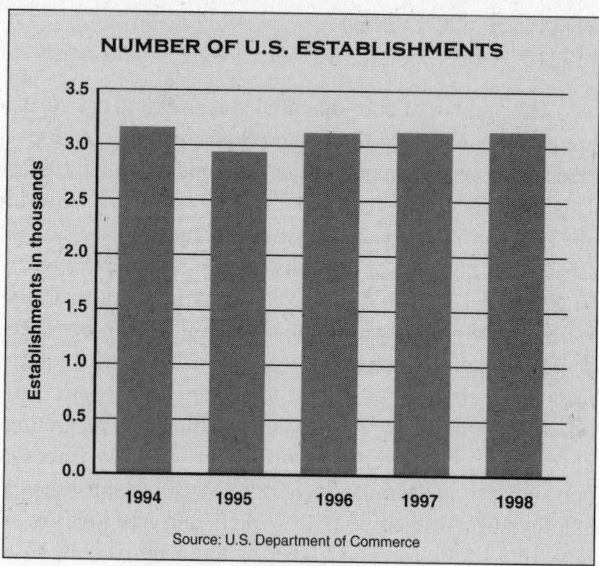

Anticipating the implementation of the new EPA standards, chemical producers set out to find replacement substances for perchloroethylene, including solvents based in carbon dioxide and silicone. Yet, by 1999 an estimated 85 percent of drycleaners continued to use the chemical, with cost and cleaning quality of major concern. Other methods of chemical vapor reduction were devised. Five states—Illinois, Kansas, North Carolina, Oregon, and Wisconsin—have adopted legislation to mandate closed-loop delivery systems for the substance. Conversion to closed-loop required installation of a valve—at an estimated cost of less than $50 per system in 1999—and typically resulted in cost reduction in equipment maintenance and solution refill costs. The closed loop systems enhanced worker safety by minimizing human exposure to the chemical.

FURTHER READING

Childers, Everett. ''A New Cleaning Solution.'' *American Drycleaner,* June 1999.

Darnay, Arsen J., ed. *Service Industries USA*. 4th ed. Detroit: Gale Group, 1999.

Eng, Sherri. ''Environmental Concerns Catch Up With the Dry-Cleaning Industry.'' *Journal of Commerce and Commercial,* 13 July 1993.

Lazich, Robert S. *Market Share Reporter.* Detroit: Gale Group, 1999.

Matas, Alina. ''New Federal Rules Combat Air Pollution from Dry Cleaning.'' *Journal of Commerce and Commercial,* 7 October 1993.

''Making Perc Manageable,'' *American Drycleaner,* October 1999.

Santaniello, Neil. ''Drycleaner Pushes Non-Toxic Methods to Laundry Industry.'' *Journal of Commerce and Commercial,* 5 February 1993.

Tullo, Alex. ''Dry Cleaning Alternatives Emerge but Chemical Makers Stand by Perc.'' *Chemical Market Reporter,* 15 December 1997.

U.S. Bureau of the Census. *1994 County Business Patterns.* Washington, DC: 1996.

U.S. Department of Commerce. *1992 Census of Service Industries & Geographic Area Series,* Washington, DC: Bureau of the Census, 1995.

Ward, Mark. ''Greener Dry Cleaners.'' *MIT's Technology Review,* November-December 1997.

SIC 7213

LINEN SUPPLY

This industry classification covers businesses that primarily supply or rent to commercial establishments or household users the following laundered items: uniforms, gowns, and coats used by doctors, nurses, barbers, beauticians, and waitresses; table linens, bed linens, towels and toweling; and similar various items. Companies included in this industry may or may not operate their own laundry facilities. Companies that primarily provide diaper service are in **SIC 7219: Laundry and Garment Services, Not Elsewhere Classified.**

NAICS CODE(S)

812331 (Linen Supply)

According to U.S. government statistics, there were 1,267 establishments in this category in the late 1990s, down from 1,338 in 1987. A continued decline in number of businesses was anticipated into the start of the new century. Industry sales, in contrast, were expected to increase in 1998 to reach a projected $2.86 billion, compared with $2.39 billion in 1990. Industry employment held steady throughout the last half of the 1990s, with around 54,000 workers estimated in the industry and a total payroll slightly more than $1 billion.

Among the dominant corporations in the industry, Aratex Services Incorporated and National Linen and Uniform Company reported more than $500 million in sales for 1998. Uniform giant, Cintas Corporation, based in Mason, Ohio, also designs, manufacturers, and rents work uniforms, in addition to its dry cleaning services. The company serves businesses ranging from small shops to large corporations. Cintas's clientele exceeded 150,000 business customers in 1996. The company acquired Unitog in 1999, and, largely as a result of the merger, Cintas doubled its 1996 customer base. Cintas reported $1.75 billion in sales in 1999, a growth of 46 percent over a 12-month period.

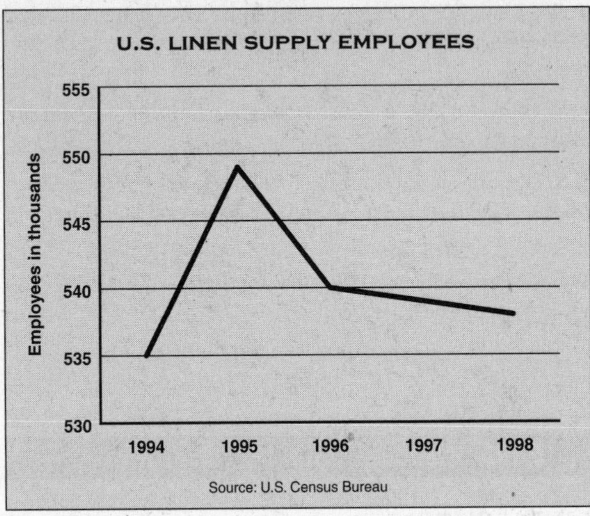

Other industry leaders included: privately held Steiner Corp. of Salt Lake City, Utah, with 6,900 employees and reported sales of $370 million in 1998; American Linen Supply Co. of Minneapolis, Minnesota, also privately held and with 5,500 employees, reported sales of $290 million in 1998.

Further Reading

''Cintas Corporation.'' *Hoover's Online.* Available at wysiwyg://5/http://www.hoovers.com/co/capsule/o/9,2163,12868,99.html.

Darnay, Arsen J., ed. *Service Industries USA.* 4th ed. Detroit: Gale Group, 1999.

Lazich, Robert S. *Market Share Reporter.* Detroit: Gale Group, 1999.

U.S. Bureau of the Census. *1994 County Business Patterns.* Washington, DC: 1996.

U.S. Department of Commerce. *1992 Census of Service Industries Geographic Area Series.* Washington, DC: Bureau of the Census, 1995.

SIC 7215

LAUNDRIES AND DRY CLEANING, COIN OPERATED

This industry classification covers establishments primarily engaged in the operation of coin-operated or other self-service laundry and dry cleaning equipment either for use on the premises, or in apartments, dormitories, and similar locations. These include establishments known as laundromats, launderettes, and self-service dry cleaners. It also includes establishments primarily engaged in installing and operating coin-operated laundry equipment in apartments, dormitories, and similar locations.

NAICS Code(s)

812310 (Coin-Operated Laundries and Drycleaners)

The number of coin-operated laundries and dry cleaning establishments in the United States declined and leveled off to approximately 12,500 for much of the 1990s. This followed a one-year peak of 13,002 establishments in 1992, according to U.S. Census Bureau figures. Prior to 1992, the number of establishments hovered between 11,000 and 12,000. Of these, the overwhelming majority were primarily engaged in the operation of coin-operated or similar self-service laundry and/or dry cleaning equipment on their own premises; less than 1,000 were estimated as primarily engaged in installing and operating coin-operated laundry equipment in apartments, dormitories, and similar locations. These establishments employed more than 50,000 workers and had total revenues of $3.5 billion and higher as the century drew to a close. Revenue projections showed a consistent increase through the end of the decade, reaching 3.9 billion in 1998.

Although the coin-operated laundry and dry cleaning industry is highly fragmented, the clear industry leader is Roslyn, New York-based Coinmach Laundry Corporation, with more than 760,000 machines in the United States. In April of 1995, Coinmach acquired its former competitor and industry giant Solon Automated Services, Incorporated; and, in January of 1997, Coinmach acquired Dallas-based Kwik Wash Laundries, Incorporated, one of the largest companies in the industry. The 1997 combination of Kwik Wash and Coinmach earned total revenues of $248 million for the twelve months ending September 27, 1996. Prior to its acquisition of Kwik Wash, Coinmach's market share—with 245,000 units—was less than 10 percent; in fiscal year 1999 the company grew at a rate of 55.5 percent, with sales of $505.3 million, and 2,045 employees, which represented a growth of 10.5 percent.

This industry has been quick to embrace technological innovations. The former Solon Automated Services, Incorporated pioneered the use of IBM's Application System/400 Model B50 to link each of its sites to a centralized data bank. The system slashed accounting errors with the use of a bar-coding system that tracked the number of coins taken in by each machine and provided useful information about the machines—including usage and maintenance records.

Other new technologies include machine-readable cards that operate laundromat washers and dryers in lieu of coins. The cards, produced at Arthur D. Little, Incorporated's Center for Technology and Product Development, hold magnetically encoded data with patrons' monetary balances. Patrons use the cards to operate laundry machines, and the machines automatically read and deduct the charges from the card balance.

FURTHER READING

"Coinmach Laundries Corporation." *Hoover's Online.* Available from wysiwyg://20/http://www.hoovers.com/co/capsule/1/0,2163,51271,00.html.

Darnay, Arsen J., ed. *Service Industries USA.* 3rd ed. Detroit: Gale Group, 1999.

Lazich, Robert S. *Market Share Reporter.* Detroit: Gale Group, 1999.

SIC 7216

DRY CLEANING PLANTS, EXCEPT RUG CLEANING

This category includes establishments primarily engaged in dry cleaning or dyeing apparel and household fabrics other than rugs. Press shops and agents for dry cleaners are classified in **SIC 7212: Garment Pressing, and Agents for Laundries and Dry Cleaners.** Establishments primarily engaged in cleaning rugs are classified in **SIC 7217: Carpet and Upholstery Cleaning.**

NAICS CODE(S)

812322 (Drycleaning Plants)

INDUSTRY SNAPSHOT

Most companies in this industry provide general dry cleaning, although some specialize in treating drapery, carpeting, or fire-damaged materials. The majority of dry cleaning plants are single-proprietor firms that gross an average of less than $200,000 annually. Based on a U.S. Bureau of the Census report, an estimated 20,794 plants were expected to be in operation in the United States during 1998. This figure, however, indicated a decline in the number of firms in this industry, following a peak in 1995 when 20,856 establishments were in operation. Revenues, on the other hand, maintained a steady upward trend and were anticipated to surpass $6.1 billion in 1998.

BACKGROUND AND DEVELOPMENT

Regarded as a mature industry, dry cleaning has proven resilient in difficult economic times, benefiting from the tendency of patrons to care for old clothes rather than purchase new ones in such periods.

The later decades of the 1900s witnessed the introduction of legislation that shaped the industry. The Care Labeling Rule, instituted by the Federal Trade Commission in 1972, made it easier for dry cleaning establishments to determine the proper mode of clothing care. Additionally, in September of 1993, the U.S. Environmental Protection Agency issued national regulations to control possibly harmful air emissions from dry cleaners due to perchloroethylene, a dry-cleaning chemical suspected to cause ill health effects to those with which it came in contact. As a result, the industry was forced to change the traditional dry cleaning method known as the transfer system—washing clothes in perchloroethylene inside a machine and then transferring them to a separate dryer. In response, chemical companies raced to develop new, less toxic cleaning formulas. Meanwhile, five states instituted regulations that outlawed all but closed-loop perchloroethylene systems for dry cleaning. Conversion to closed-loop systems was both environmentally safer and relatively inexpensive, at approximately $45 per machine in 1999.

WORKFORCE

Employment in the industry, which does not have a meaningful union presence, fluctuates. The industry employed an estimated 169,500 workers in 1998. The annual turnover rate, according to the International Fabricare Institute, ranges from 20 to 40 percent. Annual industry payroll increased from $1.49 million in 1987 to an estimated $2.17 million in 1998. About 17 percent of employees in the dry cleaning industry worked as counter and rental clerks in the mid-1990s. Laundry and dry cleaning machine operators accounted for 14 percent of employees while pressing machine operators accounted for 13 percent. Counter and rental clerk positions were expected to increase by more than 15 percent from the mid-1990s to the year 2006. Positions for both laundry and dry cleaning machine operator and pressing machine operator were also expected to increase through the year 2006, by 5 and 15 percent respectively.

INDUSTRY LEADERS

Among the largest dry cleaners in 1999 was Johnson Group Management of Cincinnati, Ohio, with sales of $160 million and 3,000 employees. Dryclean U.S.A., Incorporated, also of Cincinnati and a subsidiary of the Johnson Group, had a nationwide market and employed approximately 550 workers in 1998. Established in 1976, the company had $25 million in sales in 1998.

Other major companies in the industry included Pride Cleaners, Incorporated of Kansas City, Missouri, with sales of $37 million and 700 employees in 1998; and Swan Cleaners Inc. of Columbus, Ohio, with sales of $26 million and approximately 500 employees.

FURTHER READING

Childers, Everett. "A New Cleaning Solution." *American Drycleaner,* June 1999.

Darnay, Arsen J. *Service Industries USA.* Detroit: Gale Group, 1999.

International Fabricare Institute. Silver Spring, MD: IFI, 1994.

"Making Perc Manageable." *American Drycleaner,* October 1999.

Tullo, Alex. ''Dry Cleaning Alternatives Emerge but Chemical Makers Stand by Perc.'' *Chemical Market Reporter,* 15 December 1997.

SIC 7217

CARPET AND UPHOLSTERY CLEANING

This category includes establishments primarily engaged in cleaning carpets and upholstered furniture either at a plant or on customers' premises. Establishments primarily engaged in rug repair are classified in **SIC 7699: Repair Shops and Related Services, Not Elsewhere Classified,** while those primarily involved in reupholstering and repairing furniture are classified in **SIC 7641: Reupholstery and Furniture Repair.**

NAICS CODE(S)

561740 (Carpet and Upholstery Cleaning Services)

The advent of nailed-down (wall-to-wall) carpets in the 1950s fueled growth in the industry after a period of economic stagnation during World War II. Previously, people rolled up their carpets and took them to the dry cleaners or to other facilities. The shift to in-home services enabled new businesses to establish themselves more easily. Instead of maintaining a commercial location with a public counter for transacting sales, prospective dry cleaners needed only transportation and the necessary equipment and chemicals to get started in business. Consequently, the number of service providers swelled during this time. By 1998, there were an estimated 9,112 estimated carpet and upholstery cleaning establishments in operation in the United States, employing 45,900 workers and earning total revenues of $2.85 billion. These figures reflected the decade's continual upward trend, which, overall, represented an increase of more than 68 percent from 1990, when 5,629 carpet and upholstery cleaning establishments constituted a $1.69 billion industry.

In the late 1990s, the industry was dominated by small businesses, with approximately one-third of the total industry establishments and one-quarter of employees operating under the representation of the Institute of Inspection, Cleaning, and Restoration Certification (IICRC). Most firms in the industry appeared in metropolitan areas, employed an average of five people, and offered cleaning services exclusively, according to Cleaning Management Institute. Increased demand for additional services characterized the carpet cleaning industry in the 1990s, according to professional rug cleaner, Larry Cooper. He was quoted in the industry journal, *Cleanfax,* stating that ''Companies [in the 1990s] . . . are expected to be experts in many areas in addition to the normal carpet and upholstery cleaning services, including: water damage restoration, fire damage restoration, odor control, carpet installation, and repairs etc. . . . [reflecting a change from the past when] . . . carpet cleaning companies cleaned mostly carpet and occasionally upholstery.'' Very few of the larger companies, however, offered carpet and upholstery cleaning as part of a range of disconnected services in the 1990s, during which time residential cleaning accounted for the majority of revenue. Throughout those years, commercial customers constituted the fastest growing segment of clientele in the carpet and upholstery cleaning industry. Increasingly, schools, stores, restaurants, and offices switched from hard, washable flooring to soft floor coverings that required professional cleaning services. Additionally, concern with ''sick building syndrome'' fueled increased business on the commercial side.

In 1999 *Service Industries USA* listed Hagopian and Sons, Incorporated of Oak Park, Michigan as the industry leader in carpet and upholstery cleaning, with estimated revenues of $21 million in 1998. The second largest firm, BMS Enterprises, Incorporated of Fort Worth Texas, earned $7 million.

FURTHER READING

Darnay, Arsen J. (Ed.). *Service Industries USA.* Detroit: Gale Group, 1999.

''Environment and Health Issue.'' *Cleanfax Magazine,* June 1993.

Institute of Inspection, Cleaning, and Restoration Specification Materials. Vancouver, WA: IICRC, 1997.

Lazich, Robert S. *Market Share Reporter.* Detroit: Gale Group, 1999.

Stanley Steemer International. Available from http://www.stanley-steemer.com.

SIC 7218

INDUSTRIAL LAUNDERERS

This industry category includes establishments that primarily provide laundered or drycleaned industrial work uniforms and related work clothing, such as protective apparel (flame and heat resistant) and clean room apparel; laundered mats and rugs; dust control items, such as treated mops, rugs, mats, dust tool covers, and cloths; laundered wiping towels; and other selected items to industrial, commercial, and government users. These items often belong to the industrial launderer who rented them to users—who may or may not have operated their own laundry or drycleaning facilities.

NAICS CODE(S)

812332 (Industrial Launderers)

According to U.S. government statistics, the number of industrial laundering businesses fell from 1,435 businesses in 1992 to an estimated 1,368 in 1998. Total industry sales for 1998 were projected at $5.08 billion, which would be a 41 percent increase over the 1992 figure of $3.6 billion. Industry employment forecasters estimated a total of 71,900 workers, with a combined industry payroll of $1.5 billion. Although many firms in this industry are small-scale operations, the majority of these companies employed ten or more workers. Not surprisingly, industrial laundering businesses were most prevalent in densely populated states. California had the most, with 165 firms; followed by Texas, with 124; then Ohio and Pennsylvania, with 79 and 63 firms respectively.

As of 1999, the foremost industrial laundering company in the United States was the Cintas Corporation of Cincinnati, Ohio. The company earned $840 million in sales' revenues for 1998, and employed a workforce of 12,000. Cintas had a 15 percent share of the market for industrial uniform rentals, and boasted a clientele of 150,000 customer firms. More than 1.7 million uniformed employees wear apparel serviced by Cintas. Another prominent industrial launderer was Aratex Services, Incorporated of Burbank, California. Aratex, a privately owned firm, had 10,000 employees and reported sales of $550 million in 1998. National Linen and Uniform, headquartered in Atlanta, Georgia, ranked as the third largest firm in this arena, with 1998 sales totaling $540 million and a staff of 11,2000 employees.

FURTHER READING

Darnay, Arsen J., ed. *Service Industries USA.* Detroit: Gale Group, 1999.

Hoover's Company Profiles. Available from http://www.hoovers.com.

Lazich, Robert S. *Market Share Reporter.* Detroit: Gale Group, 1999.

U.S. Department of Commerce. *1992 Census of Service Industries,* Washington, DC: Bureau of the Census, 1995.

SIC 7219

LAUNDRY AND GARMENT SERVICES, NOT ELSEWHERE CLASSIFIED

This industry category includes establishments that perform laundry and garment services, not elsewhere classified, such as the repair, alteration, and storage of clothes for individuals and for the operation of hand laundries. Custom tailors and dressmakers classified in **SIC 5699: Miscellaneous Apparel and Accessory Stores;** fur shops making fur apparel to custom order are classified in **SIC 5632: Women's Accessory and Specialty Stores;** and press shops are classified in **SIC 7212: Garment Pressing, and Agents for Laundries and Drycleaners.**

NAICS CODE(S)

812331 (Linen Supply)

811490 (Other Personal and Household Goods Repair and Maintenance)

812399 (All Other Laundry Services)

Establishments in this category provide diverse services, ranging from diaper laundering to pillow cleaning and renovation to general tailor shops (except custom or merchant tailors) to textile mending services. Of these miscellaneous services, the diaper services are most common and have the biggest economic impact in the United States. Due to rising birth rates and environmental concerns over disposable diapers, the diaper laundry segment remained a healthy one through the 1990s.

Forecasts based on U.S. government statistics estimated that 4,462 establishments existed in this industry in 1998, nearly double the number of firms in 1988. Total industry revenues doubled to $652.8 million between 1987 and 1992, and in 1998 the top five companies in the industry earned a total of $703 million collectively.

The industry employed an estimated 26,600 workers in 1998, with total payroll costs of $325 million. Laundry and drycleaning machine operators, and pressing machine operators combined totaled 28.2 percent of the industry workforce, while 17.4 percent of employees in this industry worked as counter and rental clerks.

Diaper services dominated the leading companies in this category. Additionally, major firms such as Angelica Corp. and Kahler Corp. had a significant presence in the industry, although they were better known for their services in other areas of the laundry industry. Other leading moneymakers in this category in 1998 included Enterprise L.L.C. of Detroit, Michigan; Rezex Corp., of Los Angeles, California; and Baby Diaper Service, Inc. of Greensboro, North Carolina.

FURTHER READING

Lazich, Robert S. *Service Industries USA.* Detroit: Gale Group, 1999.

U.S. Bureau of the Census. *1994 County Business Patterns.* Washington, DC: 1996.

U.S. Department of Commerce. *1992 Census of Service Industries Geographic Area Series.* Washington, DC: Bureau of the Census, 1995.

SIC 7221

PHOTOGRAPHIC STUDIOS, PORTRAIT

This category covers establishments primarily engaged in still or video portrait photography for the general public. Establishments primarily engaged in commercial photography are classified in **SIC 7335: Commercial Photography;** those engaged in video tape production other than portrait are classified in **SIC 7812: Motion Picture and Video Tape Production;** and those engaged in film developing or print processing for the trade or the general public are classified in **SIC 7384: Photofinishing Laboratories.** Establishments primarily engaged in processing film for the motion picture production industry are classified in **SIC 7819: Services Allied to Motion Picture Production;** and those engaged in computer photography are classified in **SIC 7299: Miscellaneous Personal Services, Not Elsewhere Classified.**

NAICS CODE(S)

541921 (Photographic Studios, Portrait)

The photographic portrait studio industry serves the general public with a range of portrait services. The industry includes portrait photographers, school photographers, home photographers, passport photographers, and video photographers. Specific portrait services include family portraits, wedding photos, passport photos, glamour photos, school photos, and team photos.

There were 12,436 portrait studio establishments in operation in the mid-1990s, according to the U.S. Census Bureau. These establishments employed roughly 75,000 people and earned nearly $3.2 billion in revenues.

The professional portrait industry is segmented into two major categories and numerous subcategories of portraits. The first group is school portraits, which are further divided among kindergarten to grade 11 students, high school seniors, high school prom, and college. The second group, nonschool, encompasses wedding, family, adult, daycare/nursery school, sports/team, children outside of school, glamour, class/family reunion, pet, hospital baby, church directory, and executive.

The general portrait studio provides services ranging from passport photos to family portraits. The studio offers these services at rates according to the size of the prints or the number of photographic print copies sold in a package. The studio keeps the negatives because, by law, they own the copyright, although proofs may be given to the purchaser for reordering purposes. Because of many studios' reliance on the school market, the industry is often a cyclical one, with peaks in the fall (yearly student pictures) and the spring (prom and graduation portraits).

Professional portraits may be taken in a variety of locations including a professional studio, a chain studio, a department store, a school, a church, an outdoor setting, a day care center, or an individual's home.

History of the Portrait Studio. The camera has been used as an artist's instrument for portraiture since its invention (the earliest known form of camera was originated by Leonardo da Vinci in 1482) and the subsequent advances made in the early 1800s. A French inventor named Louis J.M. Daguerre made improvements on another French inventor's work to create the earliest examples of portrait photography. Known as daguerreotypes, these photographs were dark and grainy, with little or no background.

It was an American, Samuel F.B. Morse, inventor of the telegraph, who opened one of the first portrait photography studios in America. Because Morse was a portrait painter, the primary purpose of this first studio was to make portrait studies for his paintings. Later, armed with an increasingly sophisticated process, Morse opened a second studio (in New York) devoted primarily to taking daguerreotype portraits. Other studios soon followed.

There were many problems facing these early studios, one of which was the fact that the process of taking a subject's portrait was a time-consuming one. There was not enough light available in the studios, and exposures sometimes took 30 minutes or longer to be completed. As time progressed, portrait photographers utilized new methodologies to bring additional light into the studio, resulting in reduced exposure time.

Soon, the photographic portrait studio business was on its way to becoming a profitable industry. Portrait studios developed in cities across America while photographers set up their operations, including somewhat crude studios in the rural areas of the West. Studios were usually located on the top of buildings in order to make the best use of available sunlight. Many of these new portrait studios were ornate and large, with several rooms for portrait taking.

Discoveries in the 1850s enabled photographers to eradicate some of their lighting problems, thus reducing the amount of time a portrait subject was required to sit while the picture was being taken. The most prominent discovery that led to these advances was the positive-negative system of photography. Other advances enabled the backgrounds in the portraits to become more detailed. Lush, detailed paintings were often used as backdrops behind the subject being photographed.

In 1851 the wet-plate process was introduced, enabling photographers to further reduce exposure time, and thus, the subject's sitting time. In 1871 a dry-plate process was developed, which eventually reduced exposure time to a fraction of a second. As a result, cameras could now be held in the hand, giving the photographer greater mobility and creativity. The dry-plate process also produced higher-quality prints.

Professional portrait studios matured and diversified in the 1920s. As the advertising industry grew and began to use more photographs, portrait studios began to cater to commercial needs. Soon, many studios were devoting their time entirely to commercial enterprises like advertising, while others concentrated exclusively on glamour portraits, passport photographs, and other specialized portraits. The general portrait studio that provides all of these portrait services continues to exist.

According to the Photo Marketing Association International (PMA), overall, the photographic portrait studio industry was profitable in 1995, with more than one-half of all portrait services reporting an increase in sales. The survey indicated that in 1995, by portrait type, K-11 schools had the best sales performance, followed by wedding, sports/team, high school prom, high school seniors, and reunion photos. According to the *PMA 1996 U.S. Consumer Photo Buying Report,* 40 percent of all U.S. households had a professional portrait photo taken in 1995, a slight decrease from 1994. Of these households, 19.8 percent were K-11 school photos; 10.4 percent were non-school photos of a child or children; 9.3 percent were family portraits; 7.5 percent were sports/team photos; 5.5 percent were church directory photos; 3.7 percent were nursery/day care photos; 3.9 percent were high school senior photos; 2.9 percent were wedding photos; 2.5 percent were glamour (image salon) photos; 2.2 percent were class/family reunion photos; and 4.9 percent fell into another category of professional photos (hospital baby, pet, or executive).

A study in the *PMA 1996 U.S. Consumer Photo Buying Report* indicated that in 1995, 19.5 percent of all portraits were taken at a school, 11.6 percent at a department store, 5.3 percent at a chain portrait studio, 6.6 percent at a church, 6.1 percent at a professional studio, 5.2 percent in an outdoor setting, 2.4 percent in a day care center, and 1.2 percent at an individual's home.

In 1995 K-11 school photos, sports/team photos, church directory photos, high school senior photos, wedding photos, and class/family reunion photos saw an increase in portrait sitting shares. Conversely, child/children (non-school), family portrait, nursery/day care photos, and glamour photos saw a decline in sitting shares.

In the most lucrative industry segment, K-11 portraits, the PSPA 1995 School Photography Survey showed that despite an increasing annual number of enrolled students, the percentage of parents purchasing portrait packages has been declining at an overall average rate of 1.4 percent per year. Thus, without an increase in package prices, school photo revenue would decline (an average package price in 1995 was $17.19, compared to $16.20 in 1994). Studies also indicated that although school photos are convenient in terms of location and methods of payment, compared with department or professional studio photos, school photos are disadvantaged in terms of package flexibility, number of poses taken, types of poses, number and type of backdrops, quality, proofs, and speed of delivery. According to the Photo Marketing Association International, to achieve success in the sales of all types of portraits, photographers need to implement marketing strategies.

Established in 1932 in Selma, Alabama, and named after its founder, Olan Mills Inc. is the world's leading producer of family portraits. Through more than 700 studios in the United States, Canada, and the United Kingdom, Olan Mills provides portraits to individuals, families, churches, clubs, and businesses. Since the mid-1990s, the firm had been forced to close hundreds of studios due to increased competition from studios operated by retail stores. At the same time, however, it began installing Olan Mills studios in KMart retail locations. The company also discontinued serving the school portrait market in order to focus on other business areas.

Lifetouch Inc. is one of the leading school portrait photographers in the United States, producing some 16 million school portraits each year. Founded in 1936 as National Schools Studios, Lifetouch also operates studios in such retail establishments as JCPenney and Target throughout the United States and Puerto Rico. It also produces family portraits, yearbooks, church directories, and identification cards, and offers such services as event imaging and video production.

FURTHER READING

Lifetouch Inc. Web Site, 30 November 1999. Available from http://www.lifetouch.com.

Olan Mills Inc. Web Site, 30 November 1999. Available from http://www.olanmills.com.

PMA 1996 Industry Trends Report. Photo Marketing Association International, 1996.

PMA 1996 U.S. Consumer Photo Buying Report. Photo Marketing Association International, 1996.

U.S. Census Bureau. *1997 Economic Census.* ''Professional, Scientific, and Technical Services.'' Washington, D.C.: GPO, December 1999. Available from http://www.census.gov.

SIC 7231

BEAUTY SHOPS

This category encompasses establishments primarily engaged in offering beauty or hairdressing services. It includes unisex salons as well as combination beauty and barber shops. Beauty and cosmetology schools are also covered in this category. Information concerning only barber shops can be found under **SIC 7241: Barber Shops.**

NAICS Code(s)

812112 (Beauty Salons)
812113 (Nail Salons)
611511 (Cosmetology and Barber Schools)

Industry Snapshot

The service industry that has developed around haircare has long been dominated by small, single-owner neighborhood establishments. Only in more recent decades has this industry seen the growth of chain salons, which are usually part of larger, diversified parent corporations. Such corporate entities often operate outlets on a franchise basis. These chain- and franchise-based hairdressing establishments are most often located in shopping malls.

There were 82,768 establishments in this industry, generating $9.9 billion in revenues, according to 1992 U.S. Census Bureau statistics. These beauty shops employed 387,249 cosmetologists and other workers. In 1997 there were 1,805 cosmetology and barber schools employing a total workforce of 10,289 and generating revenues of nearly $454 million.

For several years, Glemby International and Essanelle dominated the national chain-operated salon industry. Such outlets were commonly found in major American department stores under a variety of other names. In the late 1980s, however, such companies as Supercuts gained a significant foothold in this industry segment by offering discounted, no-frills services. The industry as a whole saw growth rates ranging between 15 and 20 percent during the late 1980s, as smaller salons targeted working women and larger companies opened numerous outlets that provided fast and low-budget hairstyling services.

Since the 1980s the industry has diversified to target specific consumer trends, and companies filling these niche markets have grown considerably. A prime example is the Hair Club for Men, which offers non-surgical hair replacement.

Organization and Structure

In a beauty salon run as a sole proprietorship, the principal is most likely female and is often an active hairdresser in the establishment. Such salons are typically geared exclusively toward women and offer a range of additional services, including manicures, facials, and massages. These auxiliary services provide an important part of the income generated by the smaller salons. Both owners and employees of these beauty shops are usually licensed cosmetologists who have attended state-certified cosmetology schools and passed standardized exams before receiving their licenses. Stylists are typically compensated on a commission-only basis or through a salary-plus-incentive plan.

Hair salon chains generally market their services toward families; consequently, they report a larger number of men and children among their clientele. These salons staff a larger number of stylists and primarily offer only the basic services of cutting, perming, and coloring. Stylists in these establishments generally receive a straight salary without any further compensation.

Franchised salons, which are commonly found in such high-traffic areas as strip malls, may be started up by a single entrepreneur or by a group. The franchisee pays the franchise holder an up-front fee, typically between $10,000 and $25,000, and continues to pay a 10 percent royalty on sales. In turn, the franchise holder pays for advertising costs and avails other resources to the franchise unit.

Background and Development

The service industry of hairstyling dates back to ancient Egypt, Rome, and Greece. Not until the late nineteenth century, however, did establishments geared toward the public begin to flourish. Their popularity was aided by the development of technological innovations that created new demands for hairstyles. These novelties included the use of synthetic and organic hair coloring products in 1883 and the invention of a chemical method of permanent waving around 1927.

Schools of cosmetology were first established in the late 1890s to train students, primarily women, for the burgeoning profession. For many years, small sole proprietorships were standard in the industry. As the purchasing power of working women rose rapidly during the 1970s and 1980s, the industry began to expand and the number of corporate-owned salons increased dramatically.

Current Conditions

Hairdressing services have proven to be virtually recession-proof, as consumers traditionally cut back on other discretionary expenses before decreasing their spending on personal grooming. The industry experienced a promising annual growth rate that ranged between 10 and 20 percent until the early 1990s, when it fell drastically to only three percent. Since then smaller, privately-owned salons and no-frills unisex establishments have focused on filling specific niches in the market rather than competing against one another. Some corporate-owned salons focus on providing fast service at inexpensive prices. These entities have concentrated on capturing market share through a large number of outlets spread among densely populated communities. The older and more established sole proprietorships often market their fuller range of personal care services not as luxuries, but rather as accompaniments to a more healthy and vivacious lifestyle. These salons offer their clients such services as tanning facilities, relaxation massages, and seaweed body wraps. Industry analysts have theorized that an aging class of baby-boomers will freely spend extra income on such services that make them feel youthful, and they forecast success for salons offering these amenities in addition to traditional beauty services.

INDUSTRY LEADERS

Regis Corporation is the world's largest owner and franchiser of hair salons, with more than 5,000 salons in the United States, Canada, Puerto Rico, and the United Kingdom. It operates the chains Regis Hairstylists, Supercuts, MasterCuts, Trade Secret, and SmartStyle (located in Wal-Mart stores). Despite its position as world leader, the firm holds only a two-percent share of the highly fragmented U.S. salon market. Regis traces its roots to a single barbershop founded in 1922, which grew to an enterprise of 60 shops over the next three decades. During the 1960s it began establishing salons in shopping malls, a strategy that fueled rapid growth. It also began acquiring competitors, including its purchase in 1999 of the 980-salon chain The Barbers, Hairstyling for Men & Women. Regis' revenues that year exceeded $927 million.

Opal Concepts, Inc., is the nation's second-largest salon company, with 1,660 salons in more than 40 states. Its largest chain is Fantastic Sams, which operates more than 1,300 salons in five countries. Opal's other salons operate under such names as Jose Eber Salons, Pro-Cuts, Carlton Hair International, Linear Hair, American Hair Force, and Haircuts Plus. Founded in 1990, the firm is owned by Japan-based Shiseido Company, several investment firms, and a management group.

The Hair Club for Men serves the market niche of men's hair replacement. Founded in 1976, the firm had 80 locations throughout the United States and Canada by 1999. Hair Club specializes in adding a customized, human hair blend to a client's existing hair, and then offers the client hairstyling services in the months and years following the procedure.

WORKFORCE

Women are generally the owners of and principal stylists in privately-owned and -operated salons. Smaller salons have an average staff of five employees, most of whom are fully-licensed cosmetologists. Often these stylists work full-time, but many salons also hire part-time employees. Larger firms often employ a receptionist, a greater number of stylists, and a shampoo crew. Employees in a salon's shampoo crew are usually students in cosmetology programs who work in salons on an apprenticeship basis.

According to the *1998-99 Occupational Outlook Handbook,* approximately 586,000 hairdressers, hairstylists, and cosmetologists were employed in the United States in 1996, with another 43,000 jobs held by manicurists and 13,000 by shampooers. About 40 percent of cosmetologists were self-employed, working in a privately-owned and -operated salon. The remaining 60 percent leased workspace from the owners of such salons, with their income coming from either commissions or wages. The median weekly income for cosmetologists was $290 in 1996, far below the national median of $490 across all industries. Factors that contribute to income include size and location of the salon, the number of hours worked, and the ability to attract and maintain clientele.

All states require the licensing of cosmetologists, a process that typically entails graduation from an accredited cosmetology school and successful completion of written and practical examinations. Licensed cosmetologists are often required to attend additional classes to keep abreast of new styles and techniques.

The *Occupational Outlook Handbook* expects employment in the cosmetology industry to increase as fast as the national average for all professions through 2006. Manicurists are expected to experience the fastest growth, as are other such specialists as estheticians, who provide skin treatments, and electrologists, who remove unwanted hair through electrolysis.

FURTHER READING

"Barbers and Cosmetologists." *Occupational Outlook Handbook.* 1998-99. Washington, DC: Bureau of Labor Statistics, 1999. Available at http://stats.bls.gov/ocohome.htm.

Fantastic Sams Web Site. Available at http://www.fantasticsams.com.

Hair Club for Men Web Site. Available at http://www.hairclub.com.

Regis Corporation Web Site. Available at http://www.regiscorp.com.

U.S. Bureau of the Census Web Site Available at http://www.census.gov.

SIC 7241

BARBER SHOPS

This category covers establishments primarily engaged in providing barber and men's styling services. It also includes barber colleges.

NAICS CODE(S)

812111 (Barber Shops)
611511 (Cosmetology and Barber Schools)

This industry is primarily focused on furnishing hair care services for men and has undergone dramatic changes in the latter half of the twentieth century. In 1996 there were 41,340 barber shops in the United States, a drop of 14 percent from 1991. By comparison there were more than 210,000 beauty salons, an 8 percent increase over the same period. Many of those salons cut men's hair as well. Barber shops earned an estimated $1.8 billion in revenues in 1996 and employed about 12,800 barbers and other workers. The majority of the establishments in this industry are sole or joint proprietorships that hark back to a bygone era when most consumer's needs were met by shops in the town square. As the new millennium approached, barber shops faced stiff competition from a growing number of no-frills unisex facilities whose sales continue to increase annually.

Most barber shops are located in older commercial districts of both urban areas and small towns. They serve an almost exclusively male clientele and are generally owned by a single person, the proprietor, who is usually a middle-aged male. All barbers must attend a barber college for a specified training period that varies from state to state, and they must pass a state licensing examination.

The service of providing men's grooming is more than 2,000 years old. The practice of trimming men's hair and beards began in the Macedonian area around 400 B.C. and then spread to Egypt and other countries. The word ''barber'' is derived from the Latin word for beard, ''barba.'' The first persons to hold themselves out as experts in the trade appeared in Rome about 296 B.C. However, in both ancient Greece and Rome, barber shops were seen as places of ill repute because men from the upper classes were groomed privately by servants. Throughout the centuries, men's beards were seen as symbols of intelligence and strength and were sometimes cared for quite meticulously. In Elizabethan times, for example, they were often dyed various hues and trimmed into unusual shapes.

For centuries barbers were highly skilled in the unusual adjunct profession of medical surgery, which they learned from monks during the Middle Ages. Barbers performed work that surgeons refused, such as bloodletting, leech attaching, and teeth extracting. After a papal decree in 1163 forbade clergy from letting blood while engaging in surgical tasks, barber shops gained a monopoly over the service. Organizations that regulated the profession first appeared in France in 1096 and later in England in the thirteenth century. The traditional red-, white-, and blue-striped pole outside modern barber shops is a remnant from this era—the red stripes represented blood, the blue stripes represented veins, the white stripes represented clean bandages, and the spiral pattern represented washed bandages twisting in the breeze to dry. By the nineteenth century, however, the two professions of barbering and surgery had become completely separated.

The modern barber shop industry in the United States was established in the early twentieth century. In the 1920s two organizations—the Associated Master Barbers of America and the National Association of Barber Schools—were formed to regulate the profession. A barber's speed and efficiency have been improved by technological advances, including the use of appliances such as electric hair clippers and blowdryers.

Single proprietor barber shops providing personalized service to a family of clients have become increasingly rare. Larger shares of young men are patronizing a new breed of corporate-owned unisex hairstyling establishments. These no-frills salons offer a quick haircut as well as access to the latest styling tools and hair care products. They are often targeted at busy families and are located in such high-traffic areas as malls and strip retail centers, offering convenience to a wide range of price-conscious consumers. Additionally, full-service salons that traditionally only provide hair care services to women have been attracting more male customers. This development has been attributed to a heightened style consciousness among men and a greater social acceptance for men to patronize traditional bastions of femininity.

In 1998 the two biggest providers of retail hair cutting services for men were two Minnesota-based companies, Regis Corp. and The Barbers. Regis generated about $800 million in sales nationwide from approximately 3,600 unisex hair salons, including franchises operating under the names City Looks, We Care Hair, Cost Cutters, and Supercuts. The Barbers operated about 980 salons across the country, generating about $26 million in sales. The two competitors merged in 1999, when Regis acquired The Barbers for $58.7 million. Executives from the two companies said that the newly merged business would continue to expand. Prior to the deal, The Barbers had 190 Wal-Mart salons and was adding about 40 a year, while Regis had 320 Wal-Mart salons and was adding about 80 a year. Regis predicted that revenue for 2000 would exceed $1.5 billion. Minnesota-based Great Clips Inc. is now in second place among national unisex hair salons, with more than 1,100 establishments that generated about $200 million in 1998.

Further Reading

Higgins, Amy. ''End of a Barber Shop Era.'' *Journal & Courier,* 2 June 1997.

McCartney, Jim. ''Owner of Minnesota-Based Regis Hair Care Has Big Plans for Company.'' *KRTBN Knight-Ridder Tribune Business News,* 20 December 1998.

Nolin, Robert. ''Era on the Edge: The Old-Fashioned Razor Shave, Once The Closing Act of Barbershop Rituals Everywhere, Has Become a Dinosaur.'' *Sun-Sentinel Ft. Lauderdale,* 29 November 1997.

SIC 7251

SHOE REPAIR SHOPS AND SHOESHINE PARLORS

This category covers establishments primarily engaged in repairing footwear or shining shoes. Also included are establishments engaged in cleaning and blocking hats.

NAICS CODE(S)

811430 (Footwear and Leather Goods Repair)

INDUSTRY SNAPSHOT

Shoe repair and shoe shining is a small industry that provides a moderate living for the craftsperson/entrepreneur. The shoe repairman has survived for many years in a constantly changing marketplace, but is struggling to find ways to maintain a profitable business in the modern era. Those business owners who have been able to adapt to the changes in the industry brought on by improved technology, manufacturers' emphasis on disposable goods, and changing consumer expectations have survived. Those who have not adapted or who have maintained old methods of business operation have slowly vanished. Many shoe repair and shoe shining establishments are small retail stores usually owned and/or operated by a craftsperson who, with the help of skilled employees, performs services for a certain rate. U.S. Bureau of Labor Statistics (BLS) figures indicated that shoe repair workers held approximately one-half of the approximately 21,000 jobs in the leather goods industry at the end of the twentieth century, although increasingly, traditional services offered by the industry have been combined with other modern amenities. Additionally, some shoe repair companies are part of a larger franchise, and shoe repair shops appeared with greater frequency in retail malls and in shopping centers—locations deemed essential to the survival of the industry. Among the largest establishments in operation in the year 2000, Shoe Doctor Incorporated of Dover, New Hampshire, had sales as high as $7 million during the previous decade and employed approximately 100 workers.

BACKGROUND AND DEVELOPMENT

The business of repairing shoes has been in existence as long as the shoe itself. Until advancements made in the twentieth century, shoes were expensive and difficult to manufacture, most times taking the shoemaker the better part of a day to create one pair. Therefore, it made economic sense to have shoes repaired when necessary, rather than purchase new ones.

The evolution of the shoe repairman can be traced back to the Middle Ages, with craftsmen called cobblers. Cobblers bought old, worn shoes, repaired them, and resold them. Eventually cobblers stopped selling repaired shoes and concentrated entirely on repair as a business. Meanwhile, many shoemakers stopped repairing shoes and concentrated exclusively on manufacturing.

In the early part of the twentieth century, the Industrial Revolution in the United States put an emphasis on manufacturing. Shoe styles changed quickly, and the consumer, in an effort to remain fashionable, began to ignore the benefits of shoe repair. But other circumstances began to harm the shoe repair industry as well. According to the journal *Shoe Service,* widespread economic hardships led to do-it-yourself repairs that became prevalent in the 1930s. Also, many unskilled shoe repairmen would fix and sell shoes at lower prices to retailers outside of the industry. Dissatisfaction with the level of craftsmanship was also cited as a reason for the industry's difficulties.

World War II had a significant effect on the shoe industry. Manufacturers and repairers found raw materials increasingly harder to come by, and the government urged the public to take better care of their shoes. After World War II industrial advances made shoes cheaper. As shoes wore out, it was easier for the consumer to buy a new pair than to have an old pair repaired. Manufacturers were also increasingly using nonrepairable materials such as rubber and plastic in their products. The introduction of these innovations has continually challenged the shoe repair industry.

The number of shoe repair shops plummeted by 40 percent in the 1960s. Since that time the shoe repair industry has constantly tried to find ways to combat the effects of mass shoe production, nonrepairable materials, and ever-changing fashion trends. Overall the industry experienced a continued slow decline for several decades leading into the twenty-first century. The number of establishments decreased by approximately 16 percent, and the number of employees dropped about 11 percent during the 1990s alone.

CURRENT CONDITIONS

In the 1990s, with the average payroll per establishment at $26,811 and average revenue per establishment at approximately $102,000, many shoe repair shops and shoeshine parlors remained very small, employing an average of just two people. BLS reported minimum wage conditions for new workers in the late 1990s, along with projected declining employment for the industry through the year 2006. The consensus among experienced industry members was that the key elements to the survival and growth of the industry included the ability to guarantee quality and convenience (the speed with which repairs are made). Shoemakers, when queried about conditions in the year 2000, concurred that the evolution of shoe styles throughout the final decades of the twentieth century resulted in designs that were effectively irreparable, because of a molded all-in-one structure that precluded heel or sole replacement. One craftsman in Grand Prairie, Texas, who was quoted in *Arlington Morning News,* suggested that by the year 2000 approximately 75 percent of new shoes were of the molded design. Another shoemaker in Colorado made similar comments and added that the high cost of service proved a further deterrent to repairs, in that replacement often provided the more cost-effective solution.

In the midst of diminished demand for shoe repair, one promising technology for insole replacement emerged late in 1999. The method employs a computerized fitting system, which utilizes a computerized scanner to record sole measurements, including pressure points where the footstep makes the heaviest contact with the ground. The technology enabled shoe repair personnel to fit custom insoles easily through the use of the digital measuring system, at a cost of under $50 per pair. The ability of some shoemakers to adapt to such new techniques lies at the basis of the continued existence of this industry. Other factors for survival involve combining shoe repair service with other services and products, relocating shops into high-traffic areas such as retail mall outlets, and changing the consumer's traditional notions of the shoe repair store by means of aggressive advertising.

FURTHER READING

Darnay, Arsen J. *Service Industries USA.* Detroit: Gale Research, 1999.

Flores, John W. ''Heart and Sole: Family Keeps Old-fashioned Shoe Repair Craft Alive.'' *Arlington (Texas) Morning News,* 20 February 2000, 5A.

Jackson, Bob. ''Shoe Shop Grew from Ground up.'' *Denver Rocky Mountain News,* 16 January 2000, 60A.

Liddane, Lisa. ''Computer Crafts Foot Fixer-uppers.'' *Dallas Morning News,* 20 December 1999, 7C.

U.S. Bureau of Labor Statistics. *Occupational Outlook Handbook,* 26 February 1999. Available from http://stats.bls.gov/.

SIC 7261

FUNERAL SERVICE AND CREMATORIES

This classification includes establishments primarily engaged in preparing the dead for burial, conducting funerals, and cremating the dead.

NAICS CODE(S)

812210 (Funeral Homes)
812220 (Cemetaries and Crematories)

INDUSTRY SNAPSHOT

The U.S. Bureau of Census projects deaths to grow at the approximate rate of 1 percent per year from 1990 to 2010. Gains in industry revenue have slowed, with some stock prices dropping, despite continued consolidation by corporations and improved business practices by independent funeral homes. The steady rise in the cremation rate, as well as a trend towards personalization, continues to turn the industry toward finding creative ways to market its services.

ORGANIZATION AND STRUCTURE

More than 22,200 funeral homes are in the United States. Of this number, almost 87 percent are family owned and operated. Funeral homes in the United States average 47 years in business; however, it is not uncommon to find firms that have been in operation for 100 years or more.

Since intervention and subsequent regulation by the Federal Trade Commission (FTC) in 1984, there have been major shifts in the way that funeral homes deal with the general public. No longer was the consumer to be kept in the dark concerning funeral cost. By forcing each funeral home in the United States to provide consumers with a copy of their general price list upon request, it was possible for the consumer to make cost comparisons for like services among competitors. This price list includes the various services that the funeral home provides, a description of those services, and the cost of each individual service. By presenting these items in an itemized fashion, the consumer may select and pay for only those services desired. Prior to the FTC ruling, it was common practice among funeral homes to use unit pricing. The cost shown on the casket selected generally included all the services requested by the consumer. Most funeral homes, however, did not allow for reductions in services.

The general price list, while possibly the most important consumer tool, is not the only requirement that directly affected the funeral purchaser. Telephone disclosure of prices is also required, as well as disclosures concerning local laws and cemetery regulations concerning the practice of embalming and cemetery merchandise.

BACKGROUND AND DEVELOPMENT

The practice of preparing the dead for burial has been recorded throughout human history, with the ancient Egyptians being the most famous example. Funeral services, as they are known in the United States today, originated in the late nineteenth century. Prior to that time, responsibility for the burial of the dead was assumed by the family of the deceased. The preparation and viewing of the body was usually done at home, a practice that continued into the 1960s. Funeral services were generally held in the community church with the burial following in a grave prepared by friends and family. Caskets were obtained from local carpenters and, later, from local furniture merchants.

In no other country in the world is the practice of embalming bodies as widespread as it is in the United States. Embalming gained popularity during the Civil War when arrangements were made with the families of soldiers killed in battle to embalm the bodies and return them home for burial. Eventually, the practice gained such popularity that it became the basis for the funeral industry.

Embalming was usually performed at home using crude hand pumps. These pumps were used to introduce the embalming fluid into the arterial system of the body, thereby temporarily preserving it. These same pumps were used in reverse to remove any unwanted fluids or gases from the body. It eventually became impractical for families to use their homes for the preparation of the body and for the funeral service; this practice moved away from the home and came to be performed at the undertaker's establishment, the funeral parlor.

Sensing an opportunity for additional income, furniture merchants began to set aside space in their stores for the display of caskets and other funeral merchandise. From this arrangement, the modern funeral home industry was born as the merchants took over the role of coordinating the various aspects of the funeral service, such as scheduling funerals, preparing newspaper notices, arranging for transportation of the body, preparing the grave, and preparing the body.

Initially the practice of funeral directing and embalming was virtually unregulated. To become an undertaker, all that was required was the desire to do so. Embalmers generally acquired an embalmer's ''certificate'' after attending a short seminar on embalming and, in some cases, purchasing a required amount of fluid. This part of American tradition evolved into the funeral industry and the undertaker; the professional title later became funeral director.

By 1957, the average cost of a funeral service was $646. While the average funeral cost has increased around 3 percent a year, profit margins have declined as a result of higher merchandise cost to the funeral home and an increase in the cost of providing services. Funeral homes have been slow to pass these cost increases on to consumers, resulting in a decrease of 4.8 percent in the profit margin from the years 1980 to 1998.

CURRENT CONDITIONS

In the summer of 1999, the FTC's Funeral Industry Practices came up for review. The Funeral & Memorial Societies of America (FAMSA) requested that the regulations be broadened to include third party sellers, cemeteries, and other providers of funeral goods and services. The change was supported by the National Funeral Directors Association (NFDA) and the American Association of Retired Persons (AARP), but it is opposed by the International Cemetery & Funeral Association (ICFA).

According to the Federated Funeral Directors of America (FFDA), the average funeral in the United States cost $4,605 in 1999, with the average number of funerals per establishment per year being approximately 182. This cost included nondeclinable professional service charges, embalming, other preparation of remains, visitation, the funeral service itself at the funeral home, funeral car, a service car, acknowledgment cards, and a mid-range casket. Cost of the funeral service increased with the addition of items such as family limousines and outer burial containers.

The concept of pre-planning or pre-funding funerals in advance of need became popular due to the rising cost of funeral services. Various programs existed for this purpose. The most popular programs offered consumer protection against cost increases over time. In 1998, the NFDA conducted a state by state survey of pre-need regulations. They found that pre-need funds were primarily placed into trusts with nearly 50 percent of the states requiring 100 percent trusting level. In addition, funds must be deposited in a time specified by the state, and all parties must be notified when a withdrawal occurs. There must be a mechanism to revoke a pre-need contract, and some states require a fee paid to a state guaranty fund, while others require bonds to be posted.

Nontraditional Alternatives. Various alternative groups exist throughout the United States to provide consumers with options to reduce their funeral costs. These groups, generally referred to as memorial societies, attempt to offer their members savings over the cost of using traditional funeral establishments. In some cases, they negotiate with funeral directors to provide discounted costs to members. By not having the higher overhead associated with operating a full service funeral establishment, these organizations are generally able to provide lower costs to the consumer. However, in most cases this results in a reduction of attendant services normally associated with a traditional funeral.

Cremation has seen a steady rise in acceptance in the United States. Even areas such as the tradition-minded South saw an increase in cremations. In 1998, cremation was selected in 24 percent of deaths nationally, and it was projected to reach 36 percent by 2010. Regional cremation projections for the year 2010 vary from 10 percent in the central southeastern United States (Alabama, Kentucky, Mississippi, and Tennessee) to a high of 65 percent in the Mountain Region (Arizona, Colorado, Idaho, Montana, Nevada, New Mexico, Utah, and Wyoming), an increase of more than 20 percent over 1997 levels.

In 1998 the average cost of a direct cremation by a funeral home was $1,200, using a container for the body provided by the funeral home. Cremation societies, similar to memorial societies in mission, tended to offer their members a less expensive alternative to traditional funeral homes. Again, the lack of overhead facilitated this. The rising cost of traditional funeral services and merchandise, coupled with the consumer's desire to save money, greatly contributed to the increase in acceptance of cremation. A less economically associated factor, but still one of great importance, was societal education regarding cremation. Many consumers also looked for a more simplistic way to dispose of the body. A simple cremation met this desire. Funeral homes offered more cremation-related services, such as urn niches and alternative memorializations.

In addition to the rising cremation rate, another obstacle challenging the funeral home operator was the appearance of the retail casket store. While common in Europe, these stores only began to appear in the United States in the 1990s due to an FTC ruling preventing funeral homes from charging special handling fees to consumers for providing their own caskets. Most retail casket suppliers advertised their goods at 40 to 60 percent below funeral home cost. They offered caskets in showrooms and catalogs, and some even took advantage of the World Wide Web and offered their caskets on the Internet. The retail casket suppliers forced the industry to rethink the way funerals traditionally were priced, with the casket making up the bulk of the service cost. The industry moved toward itemized pricing, which reflected the cost of each item or service. Package discounts also minimized any cost differential between the casket store and the funeral home.

Industry Leaders

The family-operated funeral home was still the most common form of ownership. However, citing changes in tax laws and the increase in federal regulations and monitoring, not to mention inflated offers to purchase, a growing number of independent funeral homes began to sell to corporations. These corporations specialized in the operation of funeral homes, crematories, and cemeteries. In 1998 the top seven U.S./Canadian companies owned 14 percent of the funeral homes and accounted for 25 to 30 percent of the volume. Industry analyst Susan Little saw future consolidations dealing with facilities rather than administration, with consolidation continuing at a slower pace as less capital became available due to lower stock prices.

The largest corporate operator of funeral homes in the United States was Service Corporation International, headquartered in Dallas, Texas. In 1998 SCI operated 2442 funeral homes, 433 cemeteries, and 191 crematoria in 20 countries across five continents. In 1998, SCI acquired 308 funeral homes, 47 cemeteries, and 118 crematoria. Revenues from funeral home operations for the year ending 1998 were $2.9 billion, an increase of 13.4 percent over 1997. However, 1999 started with a decline in revenue, and the company took cost cutting actions. SCI continued to expand into Europe, with Paris being their largest cluster worldwide with 6 percent of total company profits. Steve Saltzman, industry analyst, expected SCI to expand into Western Europe.

The Loewen Group, based in Burnaby, British Columbia, Canada was the second-largest provider of funeral services in the United States. However in 1999, Loewen filed for Chapter 11 bankruptcy in the United States and creditor protection in Canada. At that time, the Loewen Group totaled 1100 funeral homes in the United States, Canada, and the United Kingdom. Revenues from the funeral home operations reached $136 million in 1998, an increase of 1.9 percent from 1997. After filing for Chapter 11, Loewen planned to place all its efforts into its funeral homes and larger cemetery operations.

A third industry leader, Stewart Enterprises, Incorporated, is based in Metairie, Louisiana. In early 1999 Stewart operated 558 funeral homes and 140 cemeteries in 28 states, Puerto Rico, Mexico, Australia, New Zealand, Spain, France, Belgium, Holland, and Canada. Revenues for 1998 were $648.4 million, an increase of 22 percent over 1997. Approximately 50 percent of domestic revenues come from their cemeteries, with 70 percent of revenue reported as preneed.

On a much smaller corporate scale is Carriage Services, Inc., based in Houston, Texas. Carriage Services operated 167 funeral homes and 27 cemeteries in 30 states in 1998. Revenues for Carriage Services in 1998 were $110 million from funeral operations, an increase of 50 percent over 1997.

A common theme among the corporations was to bring the benefits of corporate knowledge and practices to generally small business operations while maintaining a feeling of local flavor. Using this formula, corporations hoped to become the dominant force in the funeral industry.

By incorporating a practice called cloistering, the corporations sought to increase revenues by decreasing operating cost. Cloistering is a practice that allows funeral homes in the same area, owned by the same corporation, to use the same people and same equipment in their daily operations. By utilizing the buying power of several different cloisters, the corporations also decrease cost by buying in bulk. In theory, this works well, but in actual practice has been known to create difficulties. Personnel are sometimes required to travel great distances between assignments and, often, the need for rolling stock exceeds the inventory. A large number of these firms generally operate with a minimal number of employees to increase profits, sometimes resulting in a situation where the employees struggle to handle their assigned case loads.

Personnel expenses made up 48.0 percent of total industry expense; facilities, 28.8 percent, various business expenses, 6.9 percent; automotive equipment, 8.2 percent; promotions, 5.5 percent; and supplies, 2.9 percent.

WORKFORCE

While not unique to corporate funeral homes, poor working conditions such as a lack of benefits, poor pay, and demanding schedules have resulted in increased turnover of funeral home employees.

In 1998, the funeral industry employed approximately 35,000 licensed professionals and 89,000 unlicensed workers. Licensed positions include apprentices, embalmers, and funeral directors. Non-licensed staff includes secretaries, bookkeepers, hostesses, and maintenance workers. The occupational growth rate is expected to remain constant through 2005. The average funeral home employs four full-time and four part-time employees.

Presently almost all states have some type of educational requirement for funeral directors and embalmers. Examinations for licensing are usually administered by a state board. Apprenticeships and continuing education requirements vary from state to state. There are more than 40 schools specializing in funeral service education throughout the United States. Some of these are standalone facilities, some are located on community college campuses, and a small number are part of university curriculums. Educational awards include diplomas certifying completion of educational requirements, associate's degrees, and bachelor's degrees in funeral service.

FURTHER READING

Acorn, Linda. ''Online Casket Sales: Boom or Bust?'' *ICFM,* July 1999.

Batesville Casket Company. ''Has a Casket Store Opened in Your Neighborhood Yet?'' *Batesville Source,* March 1997.

''CANA: 1998 Cremation Rate is 23.75 percent.'' *CFSA Newsletter,* September 1999.

Cremation Association of North America. ''1994 Projection to the 2010.'' Chicago, 1998.

Cronley, Joe. ''Mergers & Acquisitions 1999.'' *Alliance,* May 1999.

''Federated: $4604.66 is Funeral Price.'' *CFSA Newsletter,* June 1999.

Gilligan, T. Scott. ''Caveat Emptor Unnecessary.'' *The Director,* March 1999.

''Industry Statistics.'' *American Funeral Director,* June 1999.

National Funeral Directors Association. ''Funeral Price Information from the NFDA 1996 General Price List Survey.'' Milwaukee: 1997.

Saltzman, Steven. ''Death Care Industry Still Riding Consolidation Wave.'' *AFD,* June 1998.

SIC 7291

TAX RETURN PREPARATION SERVICES

This category covers establishments that primarily provide tax return preparation services without also providing accounting, auditing, or bookkeeping services. Establishments engaged in providing income tax return preparation services that also provide accounting, auditing, or bookkeeping services are classified in **SIC 8721: Accounting, Auditing, and Bookkeeping Services.**

NAICS CODE(S)

541213 (Tax Preparation Services)

INDUSTRY SNAPSHOT

The latest available figures by the U.S. Census Bureau counted 12,830 tax return preparation service establishments in operation in 1997, generating nearly $2.1 billion in revenues, and employing 147,698 people. Tax return preparation services primarily operate during the first four months of the calendar year, since April 15 is the standard due date for federal tax return filings.

Preparer Responsibilities. According to *Tax Return Preparer's Liability,* a number of Internal Revenue Service (IRS) regulations govern the preparation of tax returns that must be followed by members of this industry. All tax preparers are required to sign their clients' returns and provide additional identifying information, including the names of all persons assisting sufficiently in return preparation to qualify as preparers themselves. Because the IRS might contest only a portion of a complex return, it requires exact identification of the preparers responsible for each portion. In addition to furnishing clients with copies of their returns, preparers are required to keep copies on file for subsequent inspection. They are not, however, allowed to disclose personal information kept on file to other parties.

Preparers are penalized for negotiating the amount of a refund on a return or for accepting a refund as payment. This regulation arose because of unscrupulous preparers who had accepted refund checks as their preparation fees and then, without the clients' knowledge, increased the amount of the refund and pocketed the extra income. This form of abuse not only cheated customers but also put these tax payers at risk of penalization by the IRS.

Any falsification of the tax amount owed or to be refunded is unacceptable, although tax return preparation services are not expected to make independent verification of the truth of a client's claims. Preparers are, however, expected to raise questions about uncertainties or apparent irregularities and cannot ignore a suspected mistake or falsehood.

False reporting and knowingly understating a client's true tax liability can result in penalties by the Internal Revenue Service. The government, however, assumes innocence in the case of certain errors, such as clerical or mathematical mistakes. The incorrect handling of elements of tax law does not incur penalty if the IRS judges those elements sufficiently technical or uncommon as to excuse the preparer.

Background and Development

Taxation Creates an Industry. Temporarily necessitated by the Civil War, federal income tax did not become a permanent fixture in the United States until February 1913, when it was ratified as the Sixteenth Amendment to the Constitution. Subsequent revenue acts were codified in 1939 and again in 1954 as the Internal Revenue Code, which was recodified in 1986 after passage of the 1986 Tax Reform Act.

The 1913 income tax produced a degree of chaos because of the haste with which it was introduced and the lack of guidance offered to those preparing returns. As late as 1939, fewer than 6 percent of the population was affected by federal tax. By the end of World War II, more than three quarters of the population were subject to federal tax. This major increase in scope set the stage for tax return preparation services to assume a heightened importance and presence. In a fairly short period of time, a service industry of rapidly growing dimension took shape.

Current Conditions

Traditionally, tax returns have been filed through U.S. postal mail. Indeed, as midnight draws near on April 15, post offices are congested with long lines of last-minute filers rushing to mail their returns before the tax deadline. A paper tax return received by the IRS through the mail is processed through what the IRS calls ''pipeline processing.'' Once received, the return must go through sorting, batching, numbering, coding, data entry, error resolution, and storage. The entire process can take between six to eight weeks to complete. Not until this process is completed can a return be processed for refund. During peak filing periods, refunds can take as long as eight weeks to be returned to the taxpayer. While paper filing is still common today, the age of computers has introduced electronic filing of tax returns.

Championed by the IRS, the trend toward electronic filing is growing. Electronic filing reduces the amount of time it takes for a taxpayer to receive a federal tax refund and provides a greater guarantee to the taxpayer that the return is mathematically correct. An electronically filed return eliminates the initial steps of ''pipeline processing.'' Electronic filing uses automation to replace most of the manual steps needed to process paper returns, resulting in faster and more accurate processing. Tax preparers who are registered with the IRS as Electronic Filing Originators (EFOs) can file returns electronically to the IRS for a fee—typically $15 to $25. Using this method, a refund takes about three weeks to be returned; refunds may be received sooner if a taxpayer options to directly deposit the refund into a savings or checking account.

An eligible electronic filing customer may also apply for a Refund Anticipation Loan, or RAL. Within one week after the date of filing, the filer receives a check in the amount of the loan, less the bank's transaction fee and any tax return preparation fee. The IRS then directly deposits the filer's actual federal income tax refund into a designated account at the bank in order for the loan to be repaid. The bank charges interest on the loan.

1040-EZ taxpayers may file their tax return using a touch-tone telephone. The simplicity of these returns, however, may preclude the tax payer from using a tax preparation service.

Industry Leaders

With sales of more than $1.5 billion in 1999, H&R Block easily outpaced its nearest competitors. In 1997, H&R Block served about 18 million tax payers in the United States, Canada and Australia. H&R Block has approximately 4,640 corporate offices located throughout the United States, in addition to the 4,500 franchises currently in operation. H&R Block is the largest seasonal white-collar employer in the United States. It has approximately 1,200 regular full-time employees and hires about 72,000 seasonal employees. In order to maintain its work force, H&R Block offers good pay, stock options, and commissions that range from 20 to 30 percent. Customers may have a loyal following with H&R Block for good reason: in 1996 the average refund for H&R Block customers was $1,408, compared to the $1,225 the IRS states as the average taxpayer refund. In the late 1990s H&R Block started to expand from its traditional operation, offering investment, tax planning and mortgage services. It also bought eight accounting firms to start its own U.S. accounting firm.

Further Reading

1997 Economic Census. Available from http://www.census.gov.

''H&R Block Adopts Inrise Corporation for Key Tax Preparation System.'' *PR Newswire,* 11 May 1998.

''H&R Block 10-K Edgar Filings.'' Available from http://www.sec.gov/Archives/edgar/data.

Hoover Company Profiles. Available from http://www.hoovers.com.

SIC 7299

MISCELLANEOUS PERSONAL SERVICES, NOT ELSEWHERE CLASSIFIED

This industry covers establishments primarily engaged in providing personal services, not elsewhere classified. Establishments primarily engaged in operating physical fitness facilities, including health fitness spas and reducing salons, are classified in various lodging industries depending on the type of lodging provided; if they do not provide lodging they are classified in **SIC 7991: Physical Fitness Facilities.**

NAICS CODE(S)

624410 (Child Day Care Services)
812191 (Diet and Weight Reducing Centers)
532220 (Formal Wear and Costumes Rental)
812199 (Other Personal Care Services)
812990 (All Other Personal Services)

This industry encompasses a wide array of niche industries that provide personal services in one realm or another. Diverse establishments such as dating services, costume rental shops, massage parlors, scalp treatment services, tuxedo rental, escort services, baby sitting bureaus, and valet parking outfits all are placed in this miscellaneous industry classification.

An estimated 19,037 miscellaneous personal service establishments were in the United States in 1996. In 1998, some of the leading companies in this industry were Philadelphia-based ARAMARK Corp., with $6.7 billion in 1999 sales; Weight Watchers International, headquartered in New York, with estimated sales of $1.5 billion; GE Capital Mortgage, of Cherry Hill, New Jersey, with $1.3 billion in sales, and Unifirst Corp., of Wilmington, Massachusetts, with 1999 sales of $487.1 million.

Among the largest business segments of this industry classification are dating services, weight loss centers, and formal wear rental outlets. In 1999, the two most successful weight reducing companies that used the classroom method were Weight Watchers International and Jenny Craig, Inc., with $321 million in sales. In an effort to expand into the non-overweight consumer market, the diet industry is expected to incorporate products and services geared toward total wellness on into the next century.

The miscellaneous personal services industry, including tax return preparation services, which are also discussed in **SIC 7291: Tax Return Preparation Services,** employed an estimated 149,300 workers in late 1999, according to the *Bureau of Labor Statistics.*

FURTHER READING

Employment—National, Not Seasonally Adjusted Data. Bureau of Labor Statistics, 1999. Available from http://www.bls.org.

Hoover's Company Capsules. Hoover's Online: The Business Network, 1999. Available from http://www.hoovers.com.

Pollack, Judann. "Fed Up With Promoting Diets, Weight-Loss Rivals Branch Out: Marketers Find Wellness, Fitness Tantalizing, Too." *Advertising Age,* 29 March 1999.

SIC 7311

ADVERTISING AGENCIES

Includes establishments primarily engaged in preparing advertising (writing copy, artwork, graphics, and other creative work) and placing such advertising in periodicals, newspapers, radio, and television, or other advertising media for clients on a contract or fee basis. Establishments that either place advertising with media but offer no creative services, or provide creative services but do not place the advertising with media, are excluded from this industry.

NAICS CODE(S)

541810 (Advertising Agencies)

INDUSTRY SNAPSHOT

Advertising agencies are primarily responsible for two functions. The first is the production of advertising materials in the form of written copy, art, graphics, audio, and video. The second is the strategic placement of the finished creative product in various media outlets, such as periodicals, newspapers, radio, and television. Agencies generally receive compensation for production costs from the client, plus a standard 15 percent commission from the media source for the ad placement.

Advertising agencies can be found throughout the United States, with the greatest percentage located in large cities. Many have headquarters in New York and field offices in Chicago, Los Angeles, San Francisco, Atlanta, Detroit, and other major areas of commerce in order to be close to clients.

Although the larger agencies are more frequently mentioned in the media and in trade publications, the industry is actually predominately comprised of smaller agencies, many with only one or two principals. Industry observers credit lower overhead, diversified services, willingness to accommodate change, and an entrepreneurial attitude for the success of smaller, boutique agencies.

As many clients have begun to focus on a variety of forms of marketing communications, advertising agencies have had to look beyond conventional media-based advertising. Advertising budgets reflect this shift, with additional dollars being earmarked for point-of-sale promotions, public relations, and a major entry into the media mix—the Internet. Changing demographics and a savvy American consumer were the driving forces behind these alternative forms of marketing communications.

Some industry leaders have projected that advertising agencies will not only need to augment their primary line of work, but also change their long-standing compensation system based on commissions. Realizing the need for ''integrated marketing services,'' many agencies have responded by offering public relations, direct mail, promotional, and Internet services.

Organization and Structure

The activities within an advertising agency are typically divided into four broad groups: account management, the creative department, media buying, and research. These divisions are usually physically separated from each other, although all four areas work closely together to produce an advertising campaign in its entirety. Account managers usually have daily interaction with a counterpart at the client's office and coordinate the activities of the other departments according to the client's wishes. The creative department designs original themes or concepts for ads, while the media department places finished ads within the media in which they will receive the most exposure to a target audience. The research department provides data about consumers to help the agency and the client make informed advertising decisions.

Recently added to advertising agencies' roster of services are public relations, direct marketing, and promotional services. Other activities that used to be completed by outside vendors, such as photography and high-tech print work, have been brought in-house in many agencies.

Background and Development

Advertising agencies began in the mid-1800s, when independent agents sold newspaper space. Later these agents took on the added responsibilities of writing and designing the actual advertisements. Such advertising agents could be found in major industrial areas such as Philadelphia, New York, and Boston. Volney Palmer opened offices in 1841 in Philadelphia. Representing a selected list of newspapers, Palmer sold space to advertisers and received a 25 percent commission from the newspapers. After his death, Joy, Coe & Co. took over the business and renamed the firm Coe, Wetherill & Company. This agency later was absorbed by N.W. Ayer & Son, the oldest American advertising agency still in existence.

By 1860 roughly 30 agencies in the United States sold newspaper space by offering exclusive representation in selected periodicals. As new agents entered the scene, the principle of exclusive representation ended because publishers accepted anyone who brought in advertising. Most agents soon became independent brokers or middlemen, selling space to advertisers and then buying from publishers to fill their orders.

Increased commercial and industrial activity following the Civil War facilitated the growing acceptance of advertising as a sales tool. A new type of advertising agent also appeared on the scene at this time. Space wholesalers, including industry leader George Rowell, purchased space in bulk from publishers at a discounted rate and then resold the space to advertisers. Some agents went as far as purchasing all the advertising space in the publications they represented, thereby essentially controlling selected periodicals.

Advertising legend J. Walter Thompson had his start in the industry at this time. Thompson persuaded several literary magazines to carry advertising, something not previously done. Thompson thought magazines should accept advertising because their widespread circulation could be a powerful selling medium. By 1900 his ''List of Thirty'' represented most of the popular women's and general monthly periodicals. This transformation of magazines into an advertising medium had an enormous impact on the entire advertising industry, because magazines were the first publications with nationwide distribution.

George Rowell took an early step toward changing the advertising business into a modern-day agency. In 1875 Rowell announced that he would act on behalf of his clients, rather than the newspapers and periodicals in which their ads appeared. He was the first to offer a full line of services to advertising clients: to ''act as their agent, working only in their interest, dealing to their best advantage . . . making up schedules, checking insertions, and paying bills,'' according to *Advertising: Today, Yesterday, Tomorrow*.

Shortly after Rowell's announcement, Ayer began what was considered to be a revolutionary plan—the open contract, plus commission. This arrangement created a long-term relationship between the advertiser and the agent. At first, commissions fluctuated from 12.5 percent to 8 percent to 15 percent. Although not immediately embraced by the rest of the industry, Ayer's rate of 15 percent soon became the norm. The commission system has remained the traditional method of payment to an agency.

By the 1890s the advertising industry had gained momentum due to the increased use of brand names and trademarks, the growing distribution of newspapers, the talent of experienced copywriters, and the success of earlier advertisers. For instance, only 121 trademarks were registered with the United States Patent Office in 1871. By 1875 that number had grown to more than 1,000 and by 1906 to more than 10,500. In addition, free newspaper delivery to rural areas exposed the entire country to national advertising campaigns.

The result was the creation of a relatively homogenous marketplace, perfect for selling mass-merchandise items. By 1897 more than 2,500 companies had large-scale advertising campaigns, including many brands still known today. Kodak, Coca-Cola, Ingersoll, Prudential, Waterman, Quaker Oats, Hire's, Cream of Wheat, and numerous other goods became commonly known by their brand names.

By the 1920s advertising agencies had become professional entities in their own right. Agencies were organized into departments or operating units that served numerous clients. They offered specialized services in both campaign research and development and media placement. Copywriting staffs were augmented with art departments, and research departments were established.

Perhaps the most significant indicator of the increasing prevalence of the advertising industry was soaring ad budgets. For instance, Coca-Cola spent $11,000 on advertising in 1893; by 1928 its ad budget had grown to $5 million. Campbell's Soup spent $4,000 on advertising in 1899 and $2.5 million in 1928. Wrigley started advertising its chewing gum with only $32; ten years later its ad budget had reached $3 million.

Radio became a significant advertising medium during the 1920s with the formation of NBC in 1926 and CBS in 1927. Early radio stations only sold empty time, not time slots related to programming, as became common with television advertising. However, most of the big, nighttime radio programs were actually created by advertising agencies and were used as a way to communicate their client's message. Advertising agencies also created daytime radio dramas. The Blackett-Sample-Hummert agency produced such programs for its client, the consumer products giant Procter & Gamble, and aptly named the programs ''soap operas.''

The second revolution in advertising occurred in 1948 with the advent of television. This new form of entertainment came with large billings and even larger agency commissions. Combined with the healthy postwar economy, the advertising industry boomed during the 1950s. ''Staffs were again enlarged, new agencies formed, mergers strengthened existing organizations. Branch offices proliferated, and small agencies formed networks to provide reciprocal services for their clients in cities across the country,'' Paul Harper recalled in *Advertising: Today, Yesterday, Tomorrow.*

As new product categories proliferated, the overwhelming reliance on television advertising made millions for ad agencies. From 1976 through 1988 total U.S. ad spending grew faster than the economy as a whole. Meanwhile, the three television networks, which completely dominated the market, demanded and received continual advertising rate increases.

An industry downturn began in 1988. Industry observers suggested that the recession of the early 1990s only emphasized the diminished power of traditional advertising to sell products and services. ''Even before the recession, the industry began lagging behind gross national product growth. Total ad spending grew just 5 percent in 1989 and 3.8 percent in 1990—well below nominal GNP growth,'' reported Mark Landler in *Business Week.*

Industry analysts suggested several explanations for the apparent loss of effectiveness of advertising. First of all, consumers became less receptive to the continual assault of commercials, and also became more price conscious and less brand loyal. The days of a ''Colgate family'' or a ''Crest family'' effectively ended, as large numbers of shoppers bought primarily on the basis of price.

At the same time, technological advances and the proliferation of alternative communication tools transformed the way advertisers reached their customers. For example, computerized market research allowed manufacturers to collect detailed information about their customers. Direct marketing increased in usage and popularity, along with in-store promotions and price discounts. ''Companies now spend 70 percent of their marketing budgets on promotions, leaving just 30 percent for ads,'' Landler stated in *Business Week.*

Advertising agencies responded to these changes by expanding their services into new areas and developing new specialties like direct marketing or, later, Internet services. Some also expanded their reach by absorbing smaller shops located in strategic cities.

The proliferation of television viewing options also took its toll on the advertising industry. The networks of ABC, CBS, and NBC used to account for 93 percent of the U.S. homes watching TV. By 1993, however, the big three maintained only a 60 percent share, while cable television and alternative networks claimed the difference. In 1997 network commercials accounted for about $13 billion in advertising revenues, or about 29 percent of total television advertising. During the early 1990s network television stations responded to the increased competition of cable TV by cutting their ad rates in an attempt to draw back advertisers. But since agencies obtained

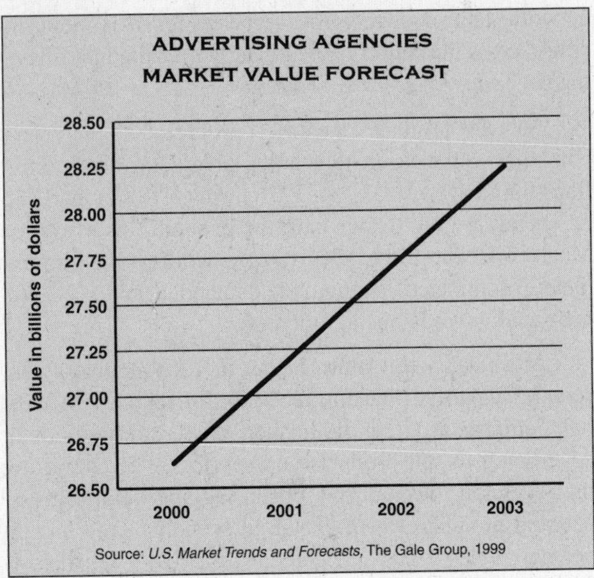

Source: *U.S. Market Trends and Forecasts*, The Gale Group, 1999

most of their commissions from placing media ads, this meant they lost money with the implementation of rate reductions.

In addition, as clients searched for greater creativity and lower costs, many advertisers divided their ad jobs by assigning media and creative work to different agencies. Larger companies even began to bring some of their marketing, advertising, and promotional work in-house. Smaller advertising agencies appeared to be more capable of adjusting to the evolving marketing needs of their clients. A lack of bureaucracy and emphasis on creativity helped smaller agencies become the fastest-growing segment of the industry by capturing large accounts. Some large advertisers demanded that main line agencies change their work habits and entrenched processes to accommodate all aspects of a marketing campaign, including packaging, in-store promotions, direct mail, direct response, toll-free comment lines, database marketing, coupon redemption programs, and cable programming.

Current Conditions

According to the Television Bureau of Advertising, the total dollar value of U.S. advertising spending rose by seven percent in 1997 to reach $187.5 billion. This figure seemed to indicate that the advertising industry had fully recovered from its depression in the 1980s, a recovery that began in the early 1990s. By segment, television accounted for the greatest share of the industry, with 23.8 percent, accounting for more than $44.5 billion in ad revenues. Newspapers, despite their declining readership, recorded advertising revenues of $41.7 billion, or a 22.2 percent share. Direct mail posted $36.9 billion, or 19.7 percent, of total ad revenues. Radio brought in $13.5 billion, or a 7.1 percent share; the Yellow Pages sold $11.4 billion in ads for a 6.1 percent share; and magazines drew $9.8 billion, or 5.2 percent. The remaining revenues were generated by farm publications, business papers, outdoor ads, and miscellaneous media.

If television was the second revolution in the advertising industry, few would argue that the Internet represented the third revolution. In 1996 *Advertising Age* reported in its own online forum that the dollar size of the Internet segment of the interactive industry had grown from $366 million in 1994 to $771 million in 1995 and $1.5 billion in 1996. Projected sizes for 1997 and 1998 were $2.4 billion and $3.7 billion, respectively.

Industry Leaders

Omnicom Group Inc. was the world's largest advertising agency in 1998, posting revenues of $4.1 billion that year. This New York-based holding company operated three of the top ten global advertising networks—BBDO Worldwide, DDB Worldwide, and TBWA International. It also operated various smaller advertising agencies as well as Diversified Agency Services, which is a global public relations/direct marketing network of more than 75 companies, and Optimum Media Direction, an independent media-buying service. Omnicom, which ranked as the world's third-largest advertising agency as recently as 1994, credits its growth to an aggressive acquisition campaign enacted in the mid-1990s. Among such acquisitions were Ross Roy Communications, one of the largest full-service marketing communications services companies; Ketchum Communications Holdings and Fleishman-Hillard, two top public relations firms; and London-based GGT Group. Omnicom offers its services to clients worldwide on a local, national, pan-regional, or global basis.

The Interpublic Group of Companies, Inc., was the world's second-largest advertising group by the late 1990s. Based in New York, this holding company operated Universal McCann, Lowe Lintas & Partners Worldwide, and Western Initiative Media Worldwide. These subsidiaries actually served rival clients while using the resources of the parent. While Interpublic had, historically, focused on advertising services, in the mid-1990s it expanded into such new areas as interactive technology and brand consultancy.

Interpublic traces its roots to 1911, when Harrison McCann established a small advertising firm to serve Standard Oil of New Jersey. Through a 1930 merger, this firm became McCann-Erickson Co. After acquiring a variety of strategic companies, McCann-Erickson reorganized itself in 1961 as a holding company that provided resources for its separately operating subsidiaries. Acquisitions continued through the 1990s as the company, then known as Interpublic, strengthened its advertising operations while venturing into such markets as public relations, direct marketing, film production, sports management, and Internet services. Interpublic gained $1.5

billion in new billings in 1998, contributing to its $3.8 billion in revenues that year.

WPP Group PLC, a marketing conglomerate built by takeovers, was the world's third-largest advertising company by 1998. Comprising 60 companies in 950 global offices, WPP recorded 1998 revenues of nearly $3.2 billion. Included in this London-based collection of companies were the large advertising agencies J. Walter Thompson Company and Ogilvy & Mather. In addition to advertising services, WPP had operations in media planning, buying and research, information and consultancy, public relations and public affairs, and specialist communications.

WPP began in 1958 as Wire and Plastic Products, a small manufacturing firm. During the late 1980s the company, renamed WPP, ventured into advertising by acquiring several small marketing firms. In 1989 it became the world's largest advertising company by purchasing Ogilvy Group in a transaction that nearly crippled the company by overloading it with debt during an industry-wide recession. After recovering by the mid-1990s, WPP turned to fueling growth through the establishment of international offices rather than through large acquisitions. By 1997, however, the firm reverted to its acquiring ways and purchased a number of firms throughout the remainder of the decade, among them Batey Holdings, Management Ventures, and Goldfarb Consultants, as well as acquiring stakes in Asatsu and AGB Italia Group.

Young & Rubicam Inc., based in New York, operated in five primary areas in the late 1990s: advertising, database marketing and customer relationship management, perception management and public relations, branding identity consultation and design services, and healthcare communications. It was comprised of such companies as Young & Rubicam Advertising, Dentsu Young & Rubicam, The Bravo Group/Kang & Lee, Wunderman Cato Johnson, KnowledgeBase Marketing, Brand Dialogue, The Media Edge, Burson-Marsteller, Cohn & Wolfe, Landor Associates, and Sudler & Hennessey.

Founded in 1923, Young & Rubicam achieved several decades of steady growth by fostering an unencumbered, creative atmosphere. The firm made history during the 1960s by producing the first television commercials in color. The 1970s were marked by acquisitions, a strategy that proved unwise when the industry hit a recession in the 1980s. The early 1990s also provided a challenge for the firm, which pled guilty to bribery charges in connection with a Jamaican tourism account. In 1993 the company announced its fourth restructuring in eight years. In 1994 one of the company's top executives, Thomas Mosser, was killed by a bomb attributed to the Unabomber. In 1995 the company's luck seemed to turn around when it landed the Colgate-Palmolive worldwide brand advertising account valued at an estimated $200 million. Still, the company suffered from a heavy debt load. To ease this burden Young & Rubicam ended its 75-year tradition as a private company by holding its initial public offering in May, 1998. Sales that year surpassed $1.5 billion, an increase of more than 10 percent over the previous year.

WORKFORCE

According to the U.S. Census Bureau, 13,879 advertising agencies were located in the United States in 1992 and they employed a total workforce of 132,042. New York accounted for a huge portion of that workforce, employing 29,775 workers that year. California was a distant second with 15,938 employees, followed by Illinois (11,601), Michigan (6,497), and Florida (5,111).

Similar to other industries, the field of advertising was traditionally dominated by large, public corporations, many a collection of independent agencies. However, most professionals who worked in the industry were employed at small agencies. In fact, the average firm had only 11 employees, and nearly 4 out of every 5 agencies employed fewer than 10 people. Advertising agencies varied greatly in size and scope of activities. Workers in smaller agencies might be responsible for a variety of tasks, while those in larger agencies would find their job duties to be more defined.

The advertising industry was highly competitive in terms of entry. Most entry-level applicants had earned at least a bachelor's degree and many had participated in internships or gained some kind of previous advertising work experience. Managers, executives, sales people, and administrative support workers accounted for nine out of every ten jobs in the industry.

AMERICA AND THE WORLD

As major U.S. manufacturers of consumer products ventured into overseas markets, American advertising agencies followed. Marketers and ad agencies viewed international expansion as an essential part of their future growth. Compared to the mature U.S. market, such international markets as Asia and Latin America offered tremendous growth possibilities. Other promising regions included China, the former Soviet Union, and Eastern Europe.

Some agencies forayed into Vietnam, a country touted as the next boom market in Asia. With 68 million people—half under the age of 19—Vietnam held tremendous potential for marketers of consumer goods. Agencies that had established a presence by the mid-1990s included J. Walter Thompson, Backer Spielvogel Bates Worldwide, Ogilvy & Mather Worldwide, and Saatchi & Saatchi.

''Many Asian countries offer a predominately young and hungry marketplace,'' A. William Deval, senior vice president, Asia-Pacific, for Grey Advertising told *Advertising Age.* "In addition to new-found prosperity and a growing population of younger consumers, changing political forces are opening Asian markets to greater numbers of foreign goods." Japanese firms set up 26 joint ventures after Vietnam relaxed its foreign investment law in 1988. U.S. companies, however, were restricted by a trade ban from investing in Vietnam.

Latin America also was expected to be an increasingly popular destination for marketers. This region provided a sizeable market of young consumers, as 65 percent of its population of 450 million was under 30 years old, and 37 percent was between the ages of 10 and 29. These age groups are successful target markets for consumer products.

Further Reading

Harper, Paul. "The Growth of Advertising—the Past." *Advertising: Today, Yesterday, Tomorrow.* New York: McGraw-Hill, 1963.

The Interpublic Group of Companies, Inc., Web Site. Available at http://www.interpublic.com.

Landler, Mark, Walecia Konrad, Zachary Schiller, and Lois Therrien. "What Happened To Advertising?" *Business Week,* 23 September 1991.

Omnicom Group Inc. Web Site. Available at http://www.omnicomgroup.com.

Standard & Poor's Industry Surveys. 20 July 1995.

Trends in Advertising, Volume 1995-1997. Television Bureau of Advertising. Available at http://www.tvb.org.

U.S. Bureau of the Census Web Site. Available at http://www.census.gov.

WPP Group PLC Web Site. Available at http://www.wpp.com.

Young & Rubicam Inc. Web Site. Available at http://www.yr.com.

SIC 7312

OUTDOOR ADVERTISING SERVICES

This industry includes establishments primarily engaged in the preparation of poster displays and painted and electronic spectacular displays on billboards, panels, bulletins, and frames, principally outdoors. Such establishments may construct, repair, and maintain display boards and may post advertisements. Establishments primarily engaged in manufacturing electrical, mechanical, or plate signs and advertising displays are classified in **SIC 3993: Signs and Advertising Specialties.**

NAICS Code(s)

541850 (Display Advertising)

Industry Snapshot

Outdoor advertising was the first, and at one time the only, form of advertising in the world. By 1997, with the competing advertising media of television, radio, magazines, newspapers, and cable television, outdoor advertising—primarily billboards—made up less than five percent of total advertising expenditures in the United States.

Historically, outdoor advertising agencies have relied heavily on tobacco and alcohol advertising—at one point these accounts provided more than 50 percent of their revenue. However, in the past few decades outdoor advertising of these products has dropped substantially because of the public's increasing concern for health and safety.

With the decline in tobacco and alcohol advertising, outdoor agencies began to focus on attracting new business. Some advertisers were quite successful in doing so as the most popular billboard spaces, once dominated by long-standing tobacco contracts, became available. According to the Outdoor Advertising Association of America (OAAA), advertisers spent more than $4.4 billion in 1998. Billboards alone generated the lion's share—$2.3 billion, an increase of 9.1 percent over 1997. This increase marked the sixth consecutive year of growth in the industry. This trend was expected to continue during 1999 and 2000, when the OAAA projected spending on billboards would increase by ten percent each year.

In an attempt to win new clients in the 1990s, outdoor advertising agencies began to use such technologically advanced equipment as computerized painting and mapping services. These tools allowed outdoor ad companies to provide high-quality images and to target specific geographic and demographic markets. Additionally, outdoor agencies promoted the cost effectiveness of their medium. Outdoor advertising, which in 1999 cost about 81 cents CPM (cost per thousand), was relatively inexpensive compared to other media. A 30-second television ad averaged $10.40 CPM on prime-time network and $18.90 CPM for a prime-time spot. A 60-second radio ad during drive-time cost $5.57 CPM. A quarter-page newspaper ad averaged $11.03 CPM, while a four-color magazine ad cost $9.14 CPM.

Marketers of apparel, packaged goods, financial services, entertainment, and other consumer products and services began to increase their usage of outdoor advertising in the early 1990s. For example, in 1992 McDonald's launched its first outdoor campaign with the introduction of its Value Meals program. Unlike McDonald's, however, most marketers do not use outdoor advertising for product launches but instead work the medium in conjunction with television and radio. By 1995 such marketers as fashion designers Calvin Klein, Ralph Lauren, and Donna Karan started using outdoor advertising as a major part of their ad campaigns—a move many in the industry took as a sign of the medium's growing strength. "The fashion industry has definitely brought respectability to the medium," Terry McGrath, a partner at the PGR Media ad agency, told *Marketing News.* "It's bringing in advertisers that wouldn't have even considered it before."

ORGANIZATION AND STRUCTURE

The outdoor advertising industry can be divided into two major classifications: on-premise and off-premise. On-premise advertising basically entails the use of signs to identify a business establishment. Off-premise advertising is a service in which outdoor displays are erected and maintained on property owned, leased, or controlled by a third party.

Off-premise outdoor advertising has generally been geographically subdivided—rural versus urban. The rural road sign tends to the immediate needs of the traveling public, such as food, fuel, and lodging. In urban settings, three kinds of off-premise advertising have historically been found. The first two, transit advertising and neighborhood point-of-purchase, have historically produced only a small volume of business, although by the late 1990s the industry had begun to fully utilize advertising on mass transit buses, subways, taxicabs, and more. The third category of off-premise advertising—called a standardized medium, but better known as a billboard—has dominated the outdoor industry.

Bulletins are the largest kind of billboards and can be found in three sizes: 14 feet by 48 feet, 10.5 feet by 36 feet, and 20 feet by 60 feet. Usually these boards are found on interstate highways. The traditional billboard, sometimes called a 30-sheet, runs 12 feet by 24 feet and has been used for niche marketing. Relatively new to the industry has been the eight-sheet billboard, measuring 6 feet by 12 feet. Previously found in highly dense areas with limited space, eight-sheets are being used in suburban communities and have been especially popular for regional and ethnic marketing. At an average price of $100 to $150 per board in the 1990s, eight-sheets were significantly less expensive than the traditional posters, which sold for an average of $500.

New, technologically advanced boards have also begun to show up in outdoor advertising. One example has been the Premier panel, created by Patrick Media Group. This type of board offers improved graphics by printing ads on vinyl using computer technology. The Premier panel also has 30 percent more space than a traditional 30-sheet because it stretches the advertisement around the board rather than containing it inside the frame.

BACKGROUND AND DEVELOPMENT

The history of outdoor advertising can be traced to the development of mass communication. Until the fifteenth century, public posting was the only means (other than the town crier) of disseminating information. In 1450, when Johannes Gutenberg invented printing from moveable type, messages could be duplicated on a widespread basis and advertising in its infancy took the form of a handbill. Around 1480 William Caxton introduced a new type of printing in England and the first poster was printed. When German Alois Senfelder perfected the lithographic process in 1796, he provided the means for merging the all-type handbill with graphics, creating an illustrated poster.

The printing press made possible the development of two other media: the handbill and the circulated bill. The handbill was popular because it could be distributed in quantity. The circulated bill was the forerunner of newspapers and magazines.

At first, bill-posting consisted of sticking advertisements on walls and fences around London and hoping that the competition would not tear them down or cover them with postings of their own. Eventually, standards were developed to ensure exposure for a set period of time, which required gaining the exclusive rights for posting. As the areas with the most traffic grew, bill-posters soon began to build their own surfaces. Due to the tendency to use fences for posting, these new structures took the name of "fences." Bill-posting spread overseas with the development of the colonies in North America, and the new structures built in America soon were referred to as "billboards" or "boards."

Early poster advertising in the United States consisted of notices selling farm stock and equipment and announcing county and state fairs, theatricals, circuses, horse races, community parades and celebrations, carnivals, and medicine shows. Since a large portion of the posted material was used to advertise the theater, the local theater manager was often in charge of the outdoor advertising in the city. It also was a common practice to ensure the protection of a posting by giving a present, such as tickets to the circus, to the owner of the billboard.

Outdoor advertising broadened its scope with the advent of the automobile and the U.S. highway system. From the 1920s to the 1960s outdoor advertising was considered one of the best ways to reach consumers outside the home, especially in areas not covered by the major daily newspapers or magazines. The unchecked growth of outdoor advertising subsided by the early 1970s as environmentalists began to complain about the "clutter," especially in rural communities. Through the work of Lady Bird Johnson, the Highway Beautification Act, which set limitations for billboards in rural areas, was passed in the mid-1960s. December 1991 saw the passage of the Intermodal Surface Transportation Efficiency Act (ISTEA), which banned the construction of new billboards along scenic highways. Despite these and other local restrictions, U.S. cities remain covered with out-of-home advertising opportunities.

Tobacco marketers were the largest outdoor advertisers in 1992, spending $123 million. At the same time, however, the category posted the greatest decline in spending—33.5 percent. To illustrate, TDI, a large outdoor advertising agency, received 23.5 percent of its total revenue from tobacco companies in 1991, but that percentage had dropped to less than 5 percent by 1994.

Because the outdoor ad industry relied so heavily on alcohol and tobacco advertising, it was hit hard by the continual drop in outdoor spending by alcohol and tobacco producers. These reductions can be credited to health considerations and legal restrictions—such as those adopted by many states that forbade liquor, beer, and tobacco billboards from being within 500 feet of places where children spend a significant amount of time.

Current Conditions

Annual spending for out-of-home or outdoor advertising has remained relatively small, accounting for less than five percent of all media billings in 1997. Although agency executives do not foresee outdoor advertising surpassing, or even approaching, the reach of broadcast television, they do acknowledge that the industry has gained popularity with their clients since it has become a cost-effective and timely medium. Advertisers use billboards to support primary media plans, and some major accounts have stepped up their outdoor coverage.

By the late 1990s, as outdoor advertising by alcohol and tobacco companies waned, other categories increased their spending in this medium. According to the OAAA, in 1998 the category of local services and amusements was the greatest spender, accounting for $190.9 million, or 10.6 percent, of all outdoor advertising revenues. Public transportation, hotel, and resorts, was a close second, with $176.8 million, or 9.9 percent of total spending. Retail accounted for $162.7 million, or 9.1 percent; miscellaneous merchandise for $161.7 million, or nine percent; restaurants for $158.1 million, or 8.8 percent; and media and advertising for $143.5 million, or eight percent. A relatively sharp decline preceded the seventh-place category, automotive dealers and services, which accounted for $120.3 million, or 6.7 percent of outdoor ad dollars. The remaining top ten categories were insurance and real estate, with $94.6 million, or 5.3 percent; automotive, with $90.2 million, or five percent; and financial services, with $73.6 million, or 4.1 percent.

Industry Leaders

Outdoor Systems, Inc., was the largest outdoor advertising firm in North America in 1999, generating revenues of $705.9 million in 1998. The company had 112,500 bulletin, poster, mall, and transit advertising displays in the United States, Canada, and Mexico, and about 125,000 subway advertising displays in New York City alone. The company operated in each of the 50 largest U.S. markets, 13 of the 15 largest Canadian markets, and 44 of the largest 45 Mexican markets. Founded in 1980, the company served the local Phoenix market until it went public in 1996. With that influx of capital, the company expanded rapidly, purchasing Gannett's outdoor advertising operations before acquiring Mediacom, Van Wagner Communications, and dozens of other competitors by the late 1990s. In May 1999, the company agreed to be acquired by Infinity Broadcasting Corporation in an $8.3 billion transaction.

Following that purchase, Infinity Broadcasting Corporation would become the nation's leading outdoor advertising company. Outdoor Systems' 235,000 displays will be folded into Infinity's outdoor advertising subsidiary, TDI Worldwide, which operates in the United States, the United Kingdom, Ireland, and the Netherlands. Infinity was founded as a small collection of radio stations in 1973, but aggressively began increasing its holdings during the 1980s. By the mid-1990s it was the largest radio group in the United States. The controversial antics of such radio personalities as Howard Stern and Don Imus generated publicity for Infinity—and fines from the Federal Communication Commission. Westinghouse Electric (later renamed CBS) purchased Infinity in 1996, then spun it off two years later.

By 1999 Lamar Advertising Company was the largest U.S. outdoor advertising company in terms of the number of displays. Operating in 42 states, the firm had erected approximately 125,600 billboards and signs as well as 23,600 Interstate logo signs and 6,100 transit ads. The company has grown steadily since its formation as a bill-posting company in 1902. Beginning in the 1970s, Lamar fueled its diversification and geographic expansion through acquisitions. In 1998 the firm acquired about 40 companies, contributing to its annual revenues of $288.6 million. In September 1999 Lamar paid $1.9 billion for the outdoor advertising business of AMFM Inc.; as part of that deal, Lamar was required to divest itself of approximately $30 million worth of billboards.

Workforce

The work force of outdoor advertising agencies is relatively small. According to the U.S. Bureau of the Census, more than 1,300 establishments operated in this industry in the mid-1990s. This figure was expected to increase to more than 1,400 by the late 1990s. The number of employees in the mid-1990s totaled approximately 13,500 and was expected to reach 14,000 by the late 1990s. According to the U.S. Department of Labor, these figures represented less than 25 percent of the work force for the entire advertising industry.

RESEARCH AND TECHNOLOGY

Technological developments such as computer painting, 3-D effects, weekly changes of boards, and geographic and demographic mapping have transformed outdoor advertising into a timely, targeted, and cost-effective medium. One of the most significant technological advancements has been the creation of computerized painting, which has eliminated the quality problems associated with traditional painting methods. Computerization allows advertisers to see their ads beforehand on a computer screen, easily make changes, speed delivery time, and assure consistency in reproduction.

The introduction of computerized mapping and tracking systems has been another important technological development for the out-of-home advertising industry. In late 1995 the OAAA established voluntary industry standards involving the use of bar coding and geocoding technologies. Global Positioning Systems (GPS) are used by many outdoor companies to track the precise location of billboards, as well as to incorporate other geographic and demographic data in order to devise customized marketing solutions. Standards for bar coding facilitate the tracking of advertising copy for all interested parties, including advertisers, printers, and outdoor companies.

Another innovation came with the invention of Poster Audience Research (Postar) in 1996. The system uses both demographic research and neural network technology to estimate the traffic passing billboards in a specified location and the relative visibility of the advertisement. Advertisers can use this information to manipulate other technology, such as rotating billboards that stay fixed during certain times of the day. For instance, advertisers seeking to reach businesspeople can have their signs appear during rush hour, while consumer goods appear during the middle of the day.

In July 1996 the Federal Highway Administration reversed its ban on off-premise changeable message signs. This technology enables a single structure to display to three different messages or images. While still subject to state regulations, this federal decree has given outdoor campaigns a boost in competing for the advertising dollar, particularly since consumers have increasingly come to expect flashy and otherwise high-tech ad campaigns.

FURTHER READING

"Billboard Business Remains Hot." *The Outdoor Advertising Association of America Web Site,* 12 March 1999. Available at http://www.oaaa.org.

Darney, Arsen J., ed. *Service Industries USA,* 3rd ed. Detroit: Gale Research, 1996.

Gray, Robert. "Putting the Show on the Road." *Marketing,* 20 June 1996.

Hudis, Mark. "Keeping the Message Out Front." *Mediaweek,* 18 September 1995.

"Industry Snap Shot." *The Outdoor Advertising Association of America Web Site,* 29 November 1999. Available at http://www.oaaa.org.

Lamar Advertising Company Web Site, 29 November 1999. Available at http://www.lamar.com.

"Outdoor Gets a Makeover: Hippie Look Includes Fashion and Movie Ads." *Marketing News,* 10 April 1995.

Outdoor Systems, Inc., Web Site, 29 November 1999. Available at http://www.outdoorsystems.com.

Shaw, Russell. "Outdoor: Ban or No, Say Good-bye to Tobacco." *Adweek,* 9 September 1996.

SIC 7313

RADIO, TELEVISION AND PUBLISHERS' ADVERTISING REPRESENTATIVES

Establishments primarily engaged in soliciting advertising on a contract or fee basis for newspapers, magazines, and other publications or for radio and television stations. Separate offices of newspapers, magazine, and radio and television stations engaged in soliciting advertising are classified as auxiliaries.

NAICS CODE(S)

541840 (Media Representatives)

INDUSTRY SNAPSHOT

Companies included in this industry are called "rep firms." They sell advertising time or space on radio, broadcast television, cable television, and in print. Most rep firms specialize in a single medium. Company leaders per medium dominated their respective industries, as rep firm consolidation occurred throughout the 1990s.

According to the Radio Advertising Bureau (RAB), radio advertising reached a record $15.4 billion in 1998, a 13 percent increase over the previous year. Approximately $2.8 billion came from national spots, $11.9 billion from local spots, and the remaining $720 million from network advertising. Despite these results, radio comprised only about 7 percent of the $188 billion advertising industry in 1997.

In contrast, television—broadcast and cable—brought in about $47.5 billion in annual advertising revenue in 1998, accounting for a 23.5 percent share of all advertising. Networks (ABC, CBS, NBC, and FOX) garnered approximately 29 percent of broadcast television's annual advertising revenues.

Meanwhile, newspapers and magazines achieved more than $51.8 billion in annual advertising revenue—approximately 27.6 percent of the market in 1997. Direct mail and other media sources accounted for the remaining percentages.

Of the $188 billion spent for advertising in the United States in 1997, approximately $110 billion was spent on national spots. This represented about 59 percent of all expenditures. The media rep firms listed in this industry are responsible for the placement of these national ads, which can run in any market or combination of markets.

Organization and Structure

Most television stations, radio stations, and newspapers have their own personnel to handle sales within their respective markets. However, national media representatives are called in to sell commercial time or print space to clients outside a local market. This sales arrangement has been based on economy, since it would be too costly for every television station, radio station, and newspaper to have its own sales staff in every major market across the country.

Radio networks are arranged in a fashion similar to their television counterparts, such as ABC, CBS, and NBC. The network provides programming to stations throughout the country and receives advertising time in exchange. Unlike national spots, network ads run simultaneously on a particular network throughout the country.

Media reps sell national spots that can be placed in any market in any combination of U.S. markets. Other kinds of advertising include local spots and network ads. Local spots are advertisements that usually are solicited by the local staff of a television station, radio station, or newspaper. Network advertising refers to those ads that run on network television or network radio.

Background and Development

The media rep business began with the original form of mass communication in the United States, the newspaper. Emanuel Katz started one of the first rep companies in 1886. At the request of William Randolph Hearst, Katz went to New York to convince advertisers to purchase ads in Heart's newspapers in San Francisco. When this venture proved successful, Katz opened his own media rep firm in 1888, the E. Katz Special Advertising Agency.

Media rep firms like Katz's expanded their client lists to include radio and television during the late 1940s and early 1950s. Many rep firms decided to specialize in one kind of medium. For example, Katz dropped all newspaper representation in 1969 in order to focus on broadcast media. Others, like The Interep Radio Store, later known as Interep National Radio Sales, remained loyal to their traditional medium.

In 1996 President Clinton approved the Telecommunications Act, which had great implications on many industries, including that of media representation. Some key provisions of the Act included: discontinuation of limits on television station ownership; removal of barriers to ownership of TV stations and cable systems serving the same market; relaxation of limits on radio station ownership; and de-regulation of cable service rates.

Current Conditions

Radio. Recently rising from the shadow of television, radio advertising continues to increase in annual revenue. September 1999 marked the 85th consecutive month of sales growth in the radio industry. Radio stations and networks reached a record $15.4 billion in advertising revenue in 1998, a 13 percent growth rate over the previous year.

Industry experts have attributed "dot-com" advertising as the impetus for much of this growth. Radio is an effective means of publicizing web sites, both at the national and local level. Gary Fries, CEO of the RAB, identified this segment as an area of growth for radio. Quoted in an April 1999 press release, he remarked, "Dot-com advertisers are using Radio overwhelmingly—more than 80 percent of their ad budgets in many cases—to build brand identity and to tell people where they are located."

Television. The Television Bureau of Advertising (TVB) reported that total advertising expenditures for local, national, and syndicated television reached $47.5 billion in 1998, accounting for 23.5 percent of the nation's total advertising. That year, 98.3 percent of the nation's households had at least one television, compared to 87.1 percent in 1960, 64.5 percent in 1955, and 9.0 percent in 1950.

Network advertising accounted for the largest share of television's total, $13.7 billion. Local spot was the second largest generator of advertising revenue, accounting for $12.2 billion. It was followed by national spot ($10.6 billion), cable ($8.3 billion), and syndication ($2.6 billion).

Consolidation marked the media rep industry during the 1990s. However, an obstacle to this trend has been client stations that continue to object to dual representation—having the same company represent competing stations within a market. Yet some stations have started to reconsider the parameters of dual representation, opening the door to the possibility of future structural changes. For example, NBC decided to seek outside representation for its national spot business, and rep firm Petry tried to win the entire $230 million NBC account. The firm already represented Fox stations in New York, Los Angeles, and Chicago, where NBC also has stations. To avoid direct confrontation between Fox and NBC, Petry suggested that the firm create a separate division for NBC. In the end, Fox opposed the arrangement, and Petry was awarded only a portion of the NBC account.

One possible explanation for TV broadcasters' willingness to explore alternative sales representation could be the emergence and growing strength of cable television. More than 65.8 million or 67.2 percent of the nation's total, households in the United States had basic cable in 1997. Cable television's share of total TV advertising rose from 3.4 percent in 1985 to 6.3 percent in 1990 and to about 17.0 percent in 1998. Between 1990 and 1998, total advertising revenues on cable television have grown from $2.4 billion to an estimated $8.3 billion. Yet the growth of cable television itself may be slowed due to competing services, such as direct-broadcast satellite (DBS) and alternative access into the consumers' homes through telephone lines or computer modems.

Newspapers. The newspaper industry began to recover from the poor showing of the late 1980s and early 1990s as the total dollar value of advertising placed in the nation's newspapers started growing in 1993. In 1997, newspaper-advertising revenues approached $41.7 billion, accounting for a 22.2 percent share of the nation's total advertising. However, many industry experts believe that some advertising will never return to the newspaper. Beyond a sluggish economy and poor consumer spending, the changing dynamics of the marketplace may have affected newspaper advertising permanently.

Most major department stores have shifted some of their newspaper advertising dollars into local television and radio spots. Packaged goods marketers have traded newspapers ad dollars for coupons and other kinds of promotions. And large discounters that have taken the lead from department stores and specialty retailers do not buy much advertising. Moreover, the existing purchasing system—one lacking in standard advertising billing and rate practices—has made it difficult for newspapers to retain national and retail chain advertisers.

Perhaps more significant, however, is the decline in newspaper readership by the late 1990s. According to the RAB, newspapers experienced a decline in some 5.5 million readers between 1986 and 1996. Part of this decline is attributable to the availability of news, classified ads, and employment ads on the Internet.

Magazines. Magazines, particularly consumer publications, suffer the same competition from the Internet as do newspapers. Still, like newspapers, magazine advertising revenues continue to grow, even though readership has largely stalled. The TVB reports that magazines posted more than $9.8 billion in ad revenue in 1997, at a 9 percent annual increase.

INDUSTRY LEADERS

New York-based Katz Media Group, Inc., a subsidiary of AMFM Inc. (formerly Chancellor Media), is the oldest media representation firm in the United States. Operating in the United States and the U.K., it sells advertising time for more than 2,100 radio stations, 300 television stations, and 1,645 cable systems, as well as Internet sites. In 1888 Emanuel Katz established the nation's first media representative firm. Initially operating in the newspaper market, the firm expanded into radio advertising during the 1930s and into television in 1949. By 1969, these later ventures proved more lucrative than print media did, so Katz abandoned newspaper representation to focus on electronic media. In 1992 the company became the nation's largest media rep organization when it acquired Seltel, a rival television representative. Also in 1992, Katz ventured into cable television by purchasing a stake in Cable Media Corp., which was merged with National Cable Advertising in 1994 to form National Cable Communications, the nation's largest cable rep firm. The following year, Katz began selling advertising on web sites. In 1998, Katz, having been purchased by Chancellor Media the previous year, posted revenues of $192.8 million.

Interep National Radio Sales, Inc. was the nation's largest representation firm devoted solely to radio by the late 1990s. The firm sold radio advertising time for nearly 2,300 stations through its eight subsidiaries—ABC Radio Sales, Allied Radio Partners, Caballero Spanish Media, Cumulus Radio Sales, Infinity Radio Sales, Clear Channel Radio Sales, D&R Radio, and McGavren Guild Radio. The company was founded when Daren McGavren purchased a regional rep firm with radio stations in the Pacific Northwest. The Daren McGavren Company was established during the 1950s, when radio's identity was in flux due to the arrival of television. As other radio rep companies ventured into television during the 1960s, the Daren McGavren Company stuck with radio. McGavren soon expanded his company with the acquisition of Ralph Guild and his radio stations. Throughout the 1980s, radio rep firms consolidated through mergers and acquisitions, and by 1984, only two mega rep firms were in place—McGavren Guild and Katz Radio Store. McGavren Guild was renamed The Interep Radio Store in 1988, and adopted its current name in 1997.

RESEARCH AND TECHNOLOGY

The introduction and usage of software packages in all aspects of the media representation industry has produced increased productivity, efficiency, and ease in purchasing. Examples of computer software usage can be found in the cable TV and radio rep business. Turner Broadcasting Sales, along with other cable networks, began to use CableXchange, a software system created by Jefferson

Pilot Data Service. This program provides up-to-the-minute information on inventory availability, generates sales proposals, and covers post-analysis work such as monitoring airtime and tracking audience guarantees.

"CableXchange is designed to take our entire sales process electronic, from proposal through post-analysis," says Rick Sirvaitis, executive vice president and chief operating officer for Turner Broadcasting Sales. "It will save not only time but also cut down on errors from re-inputting orders."

Radio rep firms also have been relying upon computer technology to automate their sales operations. Interep introduced an exclusive software package that can identify radio stations whose listeners are likely to purchase specific brands of consumer products. The BrandNET software program can localize a brand's consumer profile and then identify the radio station whose audience has the most similar profile and would have the highest purchase potential.

The Internet and World Wide Web sparked interest in the mid-1990s when Katz created Millennium Marketing, a subsidiary dedicated to selling advertising and sponsorship on the Internet. Initial clients included the Sci-Fi Channel, Better Homes and Gardens Live, and Car Talk. By the late 1990s, the Internet had become a force to be reckoned with in virtually every advertising segment. Some media, such as radio and television, experienced notable increases in ad revenues from web marketers publicizing their sites. In a single year, television drew an 81 percent increase in Internet advertising revenues, from $120.3 million in 1997 to $217.2 million in 1998. Likewise, radio drew $44.5 million in Internet advertising revenue during the first nine months of 1998, compared to $15.6 million for the full-year 1997.

Further Reading

Advertising Expenditures. Radio Advertising Bureau, 1 December 1999. Available at http://www.rab.com/station/mgfb99/fac28.html.

"Broadcasting & Cable." *Standard & Poors Industry Surveys,* 1 August 1996.

Interep National Radio Sales, Inc., 1 December 1999. Available at http://www.interep.com.

Katz Media Group, Inc., 1 December 1999. Available at http://www.katz-media.com.

"The Radio Industry Will Evolve More in the Next Five Years Than We Did in the Past Fifty." Radio Advertising Bureau, 23 April 1999. Available at http://www.rab.com/pr/gf99snab.html.

Taylor, Cathy. "The Repping of the Web." *AdWeek,* 26 February 1996.

Trends in Advertising Volume, 1995-1997. Television Bureau of Advertising, 1 December 1999. Available at http://www.tvb.org/tvfacts/trends/advolume/1995_1997.html.

TV Basics. Television Bureau of Advertising, 1 December 1999. Available at http://www.tvb.org/tvfacts/tvbasics.

U.S. Bureau of the Census, 1 December 1999. Available at http://www.census.gov.

SIC 7319

ADVERTISING, NOT ELSEWHERE CLASSIFIED

This classification covers establishments primarily engaged in offering advertising services, not elsewhere classified, such as aerial advertising, circular and handbill distribution, distribution or delivery of advertising material or samples, and transit advertising. Establishments primarily engaged in direct mail advertising are classified in **SIC 7331: Direct Mail Advertising Services;** those that write advertising copy, but do not place the advertising with media, are classified in **SIC 8999: Services, Not Elsewhere Classified;** and those that provide services in commercial art, graphics, or other creative advertising services, but do not place the advertising with media, are classified in **SIC 7335: Commercial Photography** or **SIC 7336: Commercial Art and Graphic Design.**

NAICS Code(s)

481219 (Other Nonscheduled Air Transportation)
541830 (Media Buying Agencies)
541850 (Display Advertising)
541870 (Advertising Material Distribution Services)
541890 (Other Services Related to Advertising)

The advertising services offered by this industry include coupon distribution; display service, except outdoor; independent media buying services; poster advertising, except outdoor; distribution of product samples; shopping news advertising and distribution; and sky writing. Approximately 2,246 establishments operated in this industry in 1998, employing 45,500 workers. Leaders by sales volume in 1999 included LM Berry and Company, SFM Media Corporation, and Heritage Media Corporation.

Historically, one of the most active sectors of this industry has been media buying services. These companies are independent of traditional advertising agencies and serve their clients only by purchasing media. Responsibilities of media buyers include monitoring media space and purchase availability; verifying the accuracy of ads placed; and calculating rates, usage, and budgets. These services charge 3 to 5 percent of the cost for the ad, as opposed to the traditional 15 percent charged by agencies.

As clients have become more cost-conscious, many have bypassed the traditional advertising agency and moved to independent companies to make their media purchases. For instance, more than 22 percent of the 201 agency executives responding to a 1992 *Advertising Age* Beta Research Corp. survey reported that their clients use independent media services. As of 1998, media buying services handled 6 percent of all advertising.

Western International Media led this industry with more than $2.3 billion in media billings in the mid-1990s. Since 1989, many accounts have moved to independent media services like Western International. These include the $90-million American Isuzu Motors account, the $90-million Nike account, the $70-million Reebok International account, and the $50-million Bally account. In 1996, this trend continued when Bell South Corporation awarded its $185-million plus account to Western International Media. Efficiency of service and the power of media buying consolidation have been two reasons cited for the switch to independents.

Promotional items and services make up another active segment in this industry. This segment has been especially successful in grocery stores. In the past, marketers of packaged goods have used kiosks that dispense coupons, along with advertising on supermarket floors and shelves to promote their products. The industry, however, has been developing a new generation of promotional services that capitalize on technology. In 1997, for example, J.C. Penney, Toys ''R'' Us, and Boston Market offered coupons from an Internet site called CoolSavings. Developed by the Interactive Coupon Network (ICN), customers retrieved proprietary printing software that allowed them to customize and print their own coupons locally. Encoding assured that coupons were authenticated. McDonald's and Domino's participated in another online experiment called SmartSave in 1997. Using the Internet and a ''smart'' card, consumers visited the SmartSave site, browsed for coupons, and transferred the information to the ''smart'' card for later use.

Transit advertising was expected to be another growth area for the industry. Gannett Outdoor Group operates transit displays in six major markets including New York and Los Angeles. Gannett's subsidiary in Canada, Toronto-based Mediacom, also has predicted a growing market for transit advertising and recently added about 500 new travel shelters throughout Canada. In 1996, Outdoor Systems of Phoenix agreed to buy Gannet Outdoor Group for $690 million. Meanwhile, Patrick Media Group operates bus shelters in Orange County, California and Miami. The company also provides transit advertising in the Bay Area Rapid Transit (BART) system throughout the San Francisco Bay area. Patrick Media was sold in 1995 to Eller Media for $518 million.

Advertising employment was expected to grow rapidly through the year 2006, due to increased competition between other industry competitors and the need for more effective marketing.

FURTHER READING

Bugge, Bary. ''Media Buying Services.'' *Screening for Profit Digest,* 3 July 1998.

Cleland, Kim, and Chuck Ross. ''BellSouth Makes $185 Million Call to Western International Media.'' *Advertising Age,* September 1996.

Darnay, Arsen J. *Service Industries USA.* Detroit: Gale Research, 1999.

Dun's Census of American Business 1995. Bethlehem, PA: Dun & Bradstreet Corporation, 1995.

Hudis, Mark. ''All the Signs Point Up.'' *Mediaweek,* July 1996.

LaMonica, Paul R. ''Double Discount.'' *Financial World,* June 1996.

Media Buying Services. *Cool Fire Technology,* 2000. Available from http://www.cftech.com.

Scally, Robert. ''Cybercoupons Open the Door to One-On-One Marketing.'' *Discount Store News,* November 1996.

U.S. Department of Labor. Bureau of Labor Statistics. *Employment Statistics.*2000. Available from http://www.bls.gov.

———. Bureau of Labor Statistics. *1998-99 Occupational Outlook Handbook,* 2000. Available from http://stats.bls.gov.

SIC 7322

ADJUSTMENT AND COLLECTION SERVICES

This category covers establishments primarily engaged in the collection or adjustment of claims other than insurance. Establishments primarily engaged in providing credit card service with collection by a central agency are classified in **SIC 6153: Short-term Business Credit Institutions, Except Agricultural;** those providing adjustment services are classified in **SIC 6411: Insurance Agents, Brokers, and Service;** and those providing debt counseling or adjustment services to individuals are classified in **SIC 7299: Miscellaneous Personal Services, Not Elsewhere Classified.**

NAICS CODE(S)

561440 (Collection Agencies)
561491 (Repossession Services)

INDUSTRY SNAPSHOT

Debt collectors are businesses acting as third-party agents to recover outstanding debts from consumers and businesses. Most credit grantors initially attempt to collect the money due using their in-house collection departments. At some point, however, it becomes more economical to hand over past-due accounts to a collection company. In turn, the agency works to recover the amount still owed and is paid a percentage of the amount received. According to the American Collectors Association (ACA), in 1997 more than $32.2 billion in outstanding debt was collected—out of the $247.4 billion in new accounts turned over that year to third-party collection agencies.

The debt collection industry has grown from small, localized businesses to nationwide companies. The industry has also become more regulated with the implementation of the Fair Debt Collection Act of 1977. This legislation mandates behavioral guidelines for creditors. Violations of the act are reported to the Federal Trade Commission (FTC). In addition, the majority of states also regulate debt collection agencies through state licensing, registration, or certification of the right to conduct business within a particular state.

Debt collection industry leaders have been large, computerized agencies, such as the NCO Group and Outsourcing Solutions. Beyond the few major national corporations such as these, the remaining companies in the industry are small, local, private companies.

ORGANIZATION AND STRUCTURE

Collection and accounts receivable management agencies are third-party agents that assist in recovering delinquent or written-off debt. Although most large corporations have their own internal collection departments, a creditor will typically release the debt to a collection agency after the account is 180 to 240 days in arrears. Third-party agents can generally provide more effective service at a lower cost than in-house personnel. Collection agencies usually are compensated by commission, based on the percentage of debt recovered.

Some collection agencies market a prepaid letter service that includes dunning notices and related reporting and collecting services. This type of service generally has been used by smaller businesses and organizations. With a letter service, the client prepays a flat fee rather than paying through a percentage of the money collected. The more traditional collection service operates through the activities of the contingency collection agencies, working on commission and earning 25 to 35 percent of the amount collected.

The debt collection industry can be divided into four main groups: health care, including hospitals and doctor's offices; retail businesses, including department stores and credit-card companies; utilities; and commercial accounts, or businesses owing money to other businesses. Hospitals and bank cards have provided the greatest amount of overdue debt collection placements. Various health services and utilities also have become large users of collection agencies. Education and government-backed loans, both relatively new categories, have also grown. Previously, debt collectors lacked the staff or expertise to handle these kinds of accounts.

BACKGROUND AND DEVELOPMENT

The debt collection industry, often called accounts receivable management, was traditionally characterized by small, local businesses with shady reputations at best. However, since the late 1970s, the collection agency industry has transformed into nationwide companies with ''hundreds of closely supervised collectors and computerized operations,'' reported Clifford J. Levy in a 1991 issue of *The New York Times.*

Changes in the appearance and activities of the debt collection industry have been due to two factors: the growth of national companies demanded that debt collectors operate on a national basis and have highly computerized facilities; and the implementation of the Fair Debt Collection Act of 1977. Administered by the Federal Trade Commission (FTC), this legislation has determined specific rules of conduct for debt collectors. According to the act, debt collectors cannot threaten debtors, lie to them, or call them at inappropriate times. Conversations and correspondence with debtors are to be confidential, and debtors can tell collectors to stop contacting them. As a result of the act, less-than-professional operators have been pressured to upgrade their practices or have been forced out of business.

Despite the Debt Collection Act, complaints have been on the rise in the early 1990s. In fact, consumers filed 2,000 debt-collection complaints with the FTC in 1992, double the amount filed in 1991. However, this figure remains well below the 5,000 complaints received annually before 1977. One example of debt collection harassment has been the case that the FTC brought against Payco American in August 1993. The company was charged with using abusive language, falsely threatening arrest, and improperly revealing personal financial information to outsiders. All of these charges are in violation of the Debt Collection Act.

Due to government regulations and the emergence of national, commercial, institutional, and government accounts, the debt collection industry experienced consolidation between the 1970s and 1990s. The result was a decline in the number of debt collection agencies in operation, from about 6,500 at the end of the 1970s to approximately 5,500 to 6,000 in 1994. Industry revenues grew from roughly $2.5 billion to around $5.5 billion during the same time period. Higher revenues fueled more growth in the number of collection agencies in 1995 to 7,400 nationwide, again increasing the number of establishments in this industry.

CURRENT CONDITIONS

The American Collectors Association (ACA) compiles and publicizes statistics on the nation's consumer debt. By the late 1990s, the average consumer debt was $300. Outstanding consumer installment debt totaled $1.3 trillion as of March 1999. There were nearly 152 million credit card holders in 1998, with total outstanding credit card debt reaching $538 billion. About 1.4 million consumers, or 8 percent of Americans, filed for bankruptcy in 1998. In 1996 more than $13 billion in bounced checks were written, a total projected to rise annually by 2 to 4 percent through 2020. Additionally, 496 million fraudulent, or forged, checks were written in 1997, valued at $9.9 billion.

Aside from commerce-based debt, Americans owe large amounts of money in other markets. The ACA reports that the U.S. General Accounting Office totals child support delinquencies in excess of $56 billion, although other estimates place the total closer to $200 billion. Only about 22 percent of such debt is currently recovered by state governments, but that percentage is anticipated to improve with the utilization of private collection agencies. Private agencies are also employed by the government in collecting its own outstanding debt in the form of taxes, fines, fees, overpayments, and student loans. By the end of 1997, about $259 billion in nontax debt was owed to the federal government, while the Internal Revenue Service was owed another $110 billion. Due to steadily increasing college tuition costs, the amount of student loan debt has skyrocketed. During 1995 the U.S. Department of Justice filed about 1,140 student loan default cases in federal court—in 1998 it filed 14,080 such cases. As of September 1997, the U.S. Department of Education was owed $44.7 billion.

One of the strongest factors in determining the collectability of a debt is the timetable for turning an account over to a collection agency. Generally, the rule has been ''the sooner, the better.'' When a loan is 90 days overdue, a 75 percent chance of collecting exists, but the odds fall .5 percent with each passing day. By the time a loan is 180 days or six months past due, the chance for recovery has dropped to 30 percent. After a year, it is less than 10 percent.

INDUSTRY LEADERS

The NCO Group, Inc. was the world's largest provider of accounts receivable collection services, a position that it claimed through its August 1999 acquisition of Compass International Services Corp. The Pennsylvania-based firm had grown rapidly by acquiring rivals, adding some 15 companies to its stable since the mid-1990s. In addition to bad debt recovery, NCO also offered such services as billing, customer service and support, delinquency management, and marketing strategy, research, sales, and fulfillment. The firm operated from call centers throughout the United States and the Caribbean, as well as in Canada and the United Kingdom, where it operated under the name Financial Collection Agencies (FCA). NCO's revenue for 1998 reached $179 million; this increase of 109.9 percent over the previous year was principally attributable to the acquisition of such companies as MedSource Inc. and FCA International Ltd.

By the late 1990s, Outsourcing Solutions Inc. was a leading provider of debt collection and accounts receivable management services. Founded in 1995, the Missouri-based company operated more than 60 call centers in the United States, generating nearly $480 million in revenue in 1998. The privately held company also offered such services as billing, contract management, portfolio purchasing, customer service, and market research.

WORKFORCE

The *1998-99 Occupational Outlook Handbook* reports that approximately 260,000 Americans were employed as bill and account collectors in 1996. About 16 percent worked for third-party credit reporting and collection agencies, with the remainder employed directly for institutions, such as banks and retail stores, that extend credit. Employees typically worked on commission, earning a percentage of what they collect from past-due accounts. Agency employees usually are paid a salary and commission, which varies among companies. In 1996 the median salary was $410. The *Occupational Outlook Handbook* projects that employment in the industry is expected to grow significantly faster than the national average through 2006, as the amount of consumer debt increases. In an attempt to produce a more professional and well-trained workforce, the ACA conducts 250 seminars a year for its members and their employees and administers certification and degree programs for advanced training in professional collections.

RESEARCH AND TECHNOLOGY

Computer technology has provided tremendous assistance in making debt collection companies highly automated. Prior to the introduction of computers, debt collectors conducted their business entirely by paper. By the start of the 1980s, collectors started using computers to maintain files, call debtors, and search for addresses.

By the mid-1990s, large national debt collection agencies had turned into giant data processing centers. Computerized services common to the debt collection industry include automated phone dialing and file retrieval, access to national databases for address information, and customized collection methods. One example of an automated agency has been Atlanta-based Nationwide Credit. Nine hundred collectors work out of 11 offices using an automatic dialing service. This computerized system calls debtors until the phone is answered. Immediately, the call is sent to a collector while the debtor's credit history simultaneously appears on the collector's computer system. Collectors also are able to access national databases of addresses, information collected from telephone directories, subscription houses, and voter registration records.

Another example of the advances in computer technology is the development of *Payment,* a PC-based software program developed by GE Capital Corp. This program devises custom-made debt collection per debtor. First the software program downloads the debtor's credit and repayment history from a mainframe to the collector's PC. With this information, the software program calculates the best method for getting each debtor to pay the outstanding amount due. Using this program, GE Capital handled 300 private label credit cards, including R.H. Macy & Co., Montgomery Ward & Co., and Apple Computer Inc.

Further Reading

''Adjusters, Investigators, and Collectors.'' *1998-99 Occupational Outlook Handbook.* Washington, D.C.: Bureau of Labor Statistics, 1999. Available from http://stats.bls.gov/ocohome.htm.

Collection Fact Sheets. Minneapolis: American Collectors Association, Inc., 2 December 1999. Available from http://www.collector.com/news/fact.

NCO Group, Inc. Web Site, 2 December 1999. Available from http://www.ncogroup.com.

Siwolop, Sana. ''Spending It: Nasty Calls at 6:00 a.m.: Dunners Who Go Too Far.'' *New York Times,* 14 July 1996.

Wagenbrenner, Anne. ''Collection Agencies, Attorneys to Help IRS Collect Tax Debts.'' *Journal of Accountancy,* June 1996.

SIC 7323

CREDIT REPORTING SERVICES

This industry includes establishments primarily engaged in providing mercantile and consumer credit reporting services. Examples of such establishments include consumer credit reporting bureaus, credit bureaus and agencies, credit clearinghouses, credit investigation services, and mercantile credit reporting bureaus.

NAICS Code(s)

561450 (Credit Bureaus)

Industry Snapshot

The U.S. credit reporting industry was valued at $3.76 billion in 1998, with only five companies accounting for 92 percent of the market. The U.S. Bureau of the Census counted 1,658 credit reporting establishments in operation in 1992. It was estimated that this number had decreased to approximately 1,528 by 1996. As an industry, these agencies generate several billions of dollars in annual revenues. Most credit bureaus are either owned by or under contract agreement with one of the United States' three major consumer credit reporting agencies: Equifax, Experian, and Trans Union. These national agencies maintain centralized computer databases that contain the credit records of more than 170 million Americans. Similarly, agencies such as Dun & Bradstreet Information Services provide credit information on more than 10 million U.S. businesses. Credit bureaus generate more than a half-billion credit reports every year and 2 billion pieces of information about consumer trade activities are entered into consumer credit records each month.

Credit reporting services are a prime source of credit information for both consumer and mercantile (business) markets. Although there are numerous credit reporting agencies operating all over the United States, with most specializing within specific industries, the services they offer are usually limited to reference books, ratings, recommendations, and reports. Some agencies, such as Dun & Bradstreet, provide all these services, while other agencies may offer only one or two. While reference books, ratings, and recommendations are primarily used by credit managers, credit bureau reports can be used by others to verify that individuals or firms have listed all of their debts and provide valuable clues about individuals' or firms' payment behavior. Marketers may also use such information to effectively segment their markets based on credit performance criterion.

Organization and Structure

Consumer and mercantile credit are the two broad categories of services that are offered by the credit reporting agencies in the United States. Consumer credit is the medium of exchange that an individual consumer may offer to a seller of goods or services or to a lender of money. Consumers use credit to obtain items in the present and pay for them at some future time. Despite the fact that virtually every person in America eventually has contact with some phase of consumer credit, the extent to which consumers use credit varies. Consumer credit reporting services provide information on retail, service, and cash credit. These services gather and evaluate information on a consumer's credit activities for his or her lifetime. Based on this information, agencies provide a consumer's credit rating to the party seeking credit information.

Consumer Credit. Retail credit is sought before processing retail sales to consumers. The sale may take place as a revolving credit, an installment credit, or an open charge transaction. Credit reporting services are critically important to the business of retail credit. For example, credit reporting services provide information on each consumer that applies for retail credit cards such as American Express, Visa, or MasterCard. Credit reporting agencies are also extensively used to check the credit status of mortgage applicants. Many retail outlets that provide installment credit, which is a plan that allows a customer to pay in several installments, also use credit reporting agencies in a similar credit-check fashion.

Service credit consists of credit provided to consumers for services rendered, such as those by doctors, dentists, and lawyers, or for the use of gas, electric, or water utilities. The credit reporting services provide credit ratings for consumers of these service organizations.

Cash credit involves lending money directly to consumers. Organizations such as consumer finance companies (sometimes called personal finance companies or small loan companies; commercial or industrial banks (personal or consumer loan departments); credit unions; insurance companies; and other types of lenders seek the service of the credit reporting establishments. They request advice from these companies before approving the loan and consequently providing money to the consumer.

Mercantile Credit. Business credit is one of the principal means by which business executives can translate opportunities into productive ventures. Credit reporting establishments provide two types of services to the organizations seeking business credit information: commercial and cash credit.

Commercial credit is extended when a manufacturer or supplier provides goods to another party (an intermediary, wholesaler, or final retailer) for resale to the consumer. Credit reporting services are used extensively in this area due to the volume and the value of goods exchanged. This is especially true when a supplier is conducting new business with an unfamiliar party. In this case, credit reporting services are used to provide information in the form of a credit rating that contributes to the critical final credit evaluation.

Cash credit allows businesses to borrow cash to acquire both current and fixed assets, which it agrees to repay on a long (over five years); intermediate (one to five years); or short (less than one year) term basis. Organizations such as commercial banks, investment companies, insurance companies, commercial finance companies, and even individuals seek credit information about businesses before lending them cash.

Types of Consumer Credit Reporting Agencies. Information about the credit position of individuals and families may be purchased from many sources. Since credit investigations have become extremely specialized, organizations usually rely on specialists. Credit information in the files of specialized credit reporting agencies can be used more than once. In fact, multiple use of the same information is the principal on which a consumer credit reporting agency is founded.

There are several types of consumer credit reporting agencies. Some agencies serve a wide geographic area with their own computer database. The primary source of their data is accounts receivable tapes of credit grantors and public record information. The four major credit reporting firms in the United States are Equifax, Experian (formerly known as TRW Information Services), Trans Union, and CSC Credit Services.

Some agencies operate by contract arrangement with the large computerized reporting firms. Such agencies pay a monthly fee for the access to the file data. Any credit bureau has access to the records of all other bureaus. The credit file of an individual who moves from one area of the country to another is available to credit businesses in a new community through inter-bureau reporting arrangements. Therefore, computerized bureaus have instant access to the credit histories of millions of people.

There are three types of commercialized sources of credit information. The general mercantile agency, Dun & Bradstreet Inc., reports on any business enterprise in response to subscribers' credit inquiries. The Business Credit Reporting Service of the National Association of Credit Management operates for the systematic exchange of ledger information among members. And the Specialized Mercantile Agencies reports on business enterprises in particular lines of trade at subscribers' request.

An annual or monthly fee is usually charged for credit reporting services, and is billed to all members according to the membership contract. A per report cost is also charged, which varies depending on the type of report required and the format in which it is received.

Operation of Consumer Credit Bureaus. Credit bureaus must maintain control of the data they collect. To comply with the Fair Credit Reporting Act, credit bureaus must carefully check on the identity of all that request credit information. Individuals or firms that are not members of the bureau can purchase reports if they have a legitimate need and are properly identified. The Fair Credit Reporting Act lists permissible purposes for obtaining consumer credit reports.

The information needed to create a credit report is gathered from a variety of sources, located in one or more trading areas that are willing to exchange information. Credit bureaus try to secure data from as many creditors and other sources as possible. Bureaus obtain ledger information from credit grantors, verify employment with employers, and collect credit-related public records from courthouses. The present status of the consumer is of most importance, but the reader of a credit report is usually greatly interested in the historical status as well (i.e. how often the consumer was significantly late in paying bills).

Credit bureaus check public records regularly to gather credit-related data. A bankruptcy, lawsuit, judgment, or divorce may affect a consumer's paying habits regardless of his or her previous record. Also, as the population becomes more mobile, consumers make many purchases outside their local trading areas. Under these circumstances one credit bureau must request a credit report from another bureau. Through an inter-bureau reporting system, the record of an individual in other markets is readily available.

In using multiple sources of credit information, credit bureaus distinguish between facts and statements of opinion. According to Associated Credit Bureaus, Inc., consumer credit reports contain personal information such as: person's name, last reported address, Social Security Number, date of birth, marital status, spouse's name, number of dependents, previous addresses, and employment information; a listing of the consumer's credit information, including credit account numbers, the creditors' name, the amount of last payment, the credit limit of the account and the timeliness of the credit payments; a listing of public record information, such tax liens, court judgments, and bankruptcies; and an inquiry section that lists all creditors who have reviewed a copy of the credit report. This final section is particularly important for consumers to examine when they receive a copy of their report because it acts as an audit trail to ensure that no unauthorized parties have accessed the report.

Credit reports once included opinions of credit grantors and even comments about the subject's parents. But now credit bureaus refuse to place any information other than verifiable, factual data in their files. Credit reports do not contain any information about a person's character, lifestyle, race, national origin, religion, medical history, political affiliation, sexual preference, friends, or relatives.

Legal Aspects of Credit Reporting Business. Section 602 of the 1971 Fair Credit Reporting Act regulates the credit reporting industry. The Act established, among other things, the length of time that adverse information may remain in a credit file. This legislation bars the inclusion of ''bankruptcies . . . which antedate the report by more than 10 years . . . , suits and judgments which . . . antedate the report by more than seven years or until the governing statute of limitations have expired . . . , paid tax liens which . . . antedate the report by more than seven years . . . , accounts placed for collection . . . which antedate the report by more than seven years, . . . any other adverse item of information which antedates the report by more than seven years,'' according to section 605 of the Fair Credit Reporting Act. The Federal Trade Commission (FTC), which is responsible for enforcing the act, has announced interpretations that have affected credit reporting organizations' mode of operation. For instance, if a credit grantor declines credit privileges to an applicant based on information in a consumer credit report, the credit grantor must advise the applicant and provide the name and address of the credit bureau.

Since the Fair Credit Reporting Act became law, credit grantors have been extremely conscious of the definition of a credit reporting agency. Legally, if a credit grantor relays third party data as distinguished from its own ledger information, it becomes a credit reporting agency itself. For example, if an electronics appliance store calls a clothing store about a consumer's paying habits and the clothing store provides secondhand information learned from a utilities company, the clothing store is then deemed to be a consumer reporting agency and is liable for all the record-keeping and interview procedures required in the Fair Credit Reporting Act.

One of the most important provisions of the act is the right to know the contents of one's own credit records. The law provides that every consumer reporting agency reveal, upon request and proper identification of the consumer, the contents of all file information on the consumer, the sources of the information, and any recipients of reports on the consumer. Furthermore, the law states that a consumer cannot be charged for a report if, within the past 30 days, the consumer has been denied credit because of a report from a credit bureau or has received a notice from a collection department affiliated with a credit bureau. The Act also allows individuals the right to challenge the accuracy of information and have it reverted, updated, or removed. Individual states also have their own laws that deal with credit reporting.

Background and Development

Local credit bureaus are primarily a twentieth-century development, though credit has long been a feature of American business. The first credit bureau was founded in the middle of the nineteenth century, but the growth and development of credit bureaus was slow prior to World War II. For a long time, retailers who sold on credit either operated their own system of checking a consumer's financial resources or, in the case of small retailers, advanced credit to neighbors who they knew from daily interactions. As cities grew and merchants could no longer keep up with the demands of either knowing or checking on their customers, they increasingly turned to credit bureaus for assistance. Credit bureaus have become the main clearinghouses for information provided by their subscribers, members, and other outside sources. Furthermore, credit bureaus are the quintessence of close cooperation within businesses serving the American population.

In the nineteenth century, the possibility of securing organized and factual data on business organizations was extremely remote. Credit decisions were usually hit-or-miss affairs. As a result, business experienced large credit losses that had to be offset by greater margins of profit. The impetus for developing the first organized sources of credit information grew out of the uncertainties and losses experienced during the economic panic of 1837, the rapid changes in the country's economic structure, and the expansion of trading areas. Manufacturers and suppliers needed credit to trade over wide geographic areas. This implied that credit judgment could no longer be based on personal relationships, nor could adequate information be gathered in the immediate vicinity of the creditor. Consequently, a system of organized credit reporting evolved to eliminate some of the major uncertainties of trade.

In 1841, Lewis Tappan, widely acknowledged as an excellent judge of a credit risk, organized the Mercantile Agency to collect and disseminate information for the benefit of creditors. Though the agency had its headquarters in New York City, Tappan developed a branch office system to penetrate major trade centers. R.G. Dun, an employee of the Mercantile Agency, became the sole proprietor of the company in 1859 and changed the name to R. G. Dun & Co. In 1849, John M. Bradstreet, an attorney in Cincinnati, founded the Bradstreet Company, which operated in a manner similar to the Mercantile Agency and served the same areas of trade. In 1933, the two firms merged to form Dun & Bradstreet, Inc.

Another commercial credit reporting agency includes the Business Credit Reporting Service of the National Association of Credit Management (NACM). The NACM was organized in 1896 to cope with the growing problems of fraud, misrepresentations, interstate commerce, absence of a uniform federal bankruptcy law, and increasing demand for credit. From a humble beginning of less than 600 members, NACM represented 30,000 member companies by the late 1990s.

Origin and Growth of the Credit Association Bureau. The organized exchange of consumer credit information between local regions started in the early 1900s. In 1906, William H. Burr, owner of a credit company in Rochester, New York, had the managers of several other consumer credit reporting agencies meet with him and discuss the possibility of forming a national association of credit bureaus. Their cooperation gave birth to the sole national organization of credit bureaus, then called the National Association of Retail Credit Agencies, now known as Associated Credit Bureaus, Inc. (ACB).

Today ACB is one of the most active trade associations in the credit reporting industry, representing more than 1,450 consumer credit, mortgage reporting, and collection service companies, and offering its members such varied benefits as interbureau reporting rosters, standardized reporting forms, trade publications, educational services, credit bureau research, and annual meetings and conferences. ACB also operates a comprehensive certification program leading to the designations ACB Certified Credit Reporter, ACB Certified Collector, and ACB Certified Credit Interviewer.

INDUSTRY LEADERS

By 1998, five credit reporting companies controlled about 92 percent of the $3.76 billion industry.

Equifax Inc. surpassed Dun & Bradstreet as the industry's leader in 1998, generating $1.1 billion in revenues. This 19.1 percent annual revenue gain is expected to continue in upcoming years as the firm increasingly pursues the Internet as a delivery channel. Equifax was founded in 1899 to provide local Atlanta businesses with individuals' credit histories. The young firm diversified into the investigation of insurance applicants' backgrounds, and later expanded into other industry segments. By 1973 the company had grown so large that the Federal Trade Commission filed an antitrust suit against its consumer credit division; the suit was dropped in 1982. During the 1980s and early 1990s Experian facilitated growth through acquisitions in the United States and across Europe. By the end of the decade, it sought to establish a beachhead in the fertile Latin American market.

Dun & Bradstreet, Inc. ranked second in 1998, posting $985 million in revenues. The company is one of the world's largest providers of business, commercial-credit, and business-marketing information services. Founded in New York in 1841 as one of the first commercial credit-reporting agencies, the firm expanded overseas in 1857. Two years later it launched the *Dun's Book,* containing information on 20,000 businesses; that number surpassed one million three decades later. Since the 1960s Dun & Bradstreet has pursued a strategy of growth through acquisitions, including that of Moody's Investors Service. By the late 1990s it had operations in 37 countries and a global database that covered more than 57 million businesses in more than 200 countries.

Experian Information Solutions Inc., the third-largest player, supplies consumer and business credit, as well as direct marketing and real estate information services. During 1998 the firm began shifting its focus from consumer credit operations to marketing information and services, causing credit information revenues to stagnate at $576 million in fiscal 1999, a relatively small portion of the firm's total revenues of $1.5 billion. Experian was formerly known as TRW Information Systems & Services, the group of information businesses previously owned by TRW Inc. In November 1996, U.K.-based Great Universal Stores PLC purchased Experian for $1.7

billion. Headquartered in both Orange, California, and Nottingham, England, Experian maintains a database of some 780 million customers and had offices in 16 countries in 1999. It also holds a minority interest in Central Communication Bureau, Japan's third-largest consumer credit information agency.

Founded in 1969, Trans Union LLC is the youngest of the national consumer credit reporting services. In 1970 it introduced Cronus (Credit Reporting Online Network Utility System), the first online information storage and retrieval data-processing system to complement the automated techniques used by credit grantors. In 1980 the firm was acquired by the Marmon Group, a global association of manufacturing and service companies. By the late 1990s, Trans Union offered such products as credit reports, credit and insurance risk scoring models, target marketing systems, pre-employment evaluation reports, skip tracing and search tools, collection services, customized lists, and transaction services. It operated in the United States, Canada, Botswana, Chile, Hong Kong, Italy, Kenya, Mexico, Namibia, Peru, Puerto Rico, South Africa, and Spain. Its credit information revenues in 1998 reached $536 million, an annual increase of 5 percent.

CSC Credit Services was the nation's fifth-largest credit information provider in 1998, although its $257 million in revenues was less than half of fourth-placed Trans Union. Owned by Computer Sciences Corp., the consumer reporting firm is an affiliate of Equifax, which holds an option to acquire CSC at some later date.

Workforce

According to the U.S. Bureau of the Census, the credit reporting industry provided employment to 26,585 people in 1992. The state of California had the highest number, 4,430, of credit reporting employees, followed by Texas (2,511), New Jersey (1,488), and New York (1,480). Types of workers included bill and account collectors, office clerks, sales workers, credit checkers, general managers, top executives, secretaries, computer operators, credit analysts, computer programmers, financial managers, marketing managers, and accountants. The industry has also attracted a large number of entrepreneurs due to the ease of starting operations provided by computer technology.

Research and Technology

The explosion of using the Internet during the late 1990s has impacted the credit reporting industry significantly. In 1997 QSpace Inc. became the first provider of online consumer credit reports, available for a fee at www.qspace.com. This revolutionary move was quickly adopted by the industry's major players. By 1999 the Internet had become a convenient, fast, and inexpensive delivery channel of mercantile credit information, and similar delivery of consumer credit information is expected to become widespread in 2000.

Equifax, the industry's leader, began utilizing the Internet for delivery of both business and consumer credit information in late 1999. It also entered into an alliance with the portal Lycos to offer its products and services on a new co-branded web site. Also in 1999, Experian launched several Internet-based products, including a verification-enhancement service.

Because of the ease and convenience of Internet delivery of credit information, the issue of consumer privacy has become an important consideration for credit reporting agencies. The sensitive nature of the information, as well as the strict regulations of the Fair Credit Reporting Act, has prompted these companies to foray cautiously into new technologically driven delivery mechanisms. It is likely that the U.S. government and consumer watchdog groups, which have been scrutinizing various Internet-related privacy issues during the late 1990s, will keep a close watch on such practices by credit reporting agencies.

Further Reading

Associated Credit Bureaus, Inc., 4 December 1999. Available at http://www.acb-credit.com.

Dun & Bradstreet, Inc., 4 December 1999. Available at http://www.dnb.com.

Equifax Inc., 4 December 1999. Available at http://www.equifax.com.

Experian Information Solutions, Inc. 4 December 1999. Available at http://www.experian.com.

"Leading Credit Info. Providers Look to Retain Growth in 1999." *Electronic Information Report,* 17 September 1999.

National Association of Credit Management. 4 December 1999. Available at http://www.nacm.org.

QSpace, Inc., 4 December 1999. Available at http://www.qspace.com.

Trans Union LLC, 4 December 1999. Available at http://www.transunion.com.

U.S. Bureau of the Census, 4 December 1999. available at http://www.census.gov.

SIC 7331

DIRECT MAIL ADVERTISING SERVICES

This category includes establishments primarily engaged in creating, producing, and mailing direct mail promotional pieces for clients. This industry also encompasses establishments primarily employed in compiling and selling mailing lists. Establishments primarily engaged in reproducing direct mail copy on order, but performing none of the other direct mail advertising services, are classified in manufacturing, industry group 275 if they print the copy, and in **SIC 7334: Photocopying and Duplicating Services** if they duplicate the copy by photocopying or similar reproduction methods.

NAICS CODE(S)

541860 (Direct Mail Advertising)

INDUSTRY SNAPSHOT

In 1999, direct mail advertising was a $230 billion industry. In 1998, it generated $421.2 million in sales, an increase of 8 percent from $390 million in 1997, and a jump of 62 percent from $260.2 million in 1992. The Direct Marketing Association, the industry's trade organization, reported the average compound annual growth rate of direct mail at 8.2 percent from 1992 through 1997. This rate was expected to accelerate to 8.6 percent from 1997 through 2002.

North American advertisers spent $162 billion on direct marketing, of which direct mail represented a $29 billion market. Direct mail expenditures were projected to grow to $40 billion in 2003 and $52 billion in 2008, according to a recent study published by the Graphic Arts Marketing Information Service (GAMIS). This represents a much slower growth rate compared to the 1993-98 period.

Direct mail's expenditures were expected to grow at 6 percent per year from 1998 to 2008, at the same rate projected for total advertising. Advertisers are seeking to replace mass media marketing with more focused and targeted marketing activities, which serve to increase response rates and reduce unproductive mail. As a result, new opportunities are opening up for database marketers, companies that gather and manage purchase history and personal information.

Concerns about privacy are affecting the industry. More consumers are choosing to remove their names from mailing lists, and new laws regulate the companies' use of personal information. The Internet is also exerting an influence over the industry. While web research complements direct mail efforts by providing new ways to gather information, it also competes with traditional print media for limited advertising dollars. E-commerce is relatively cheap compared to direct mail packages. As with direct mail packages, unsolicited commercial e-mail, a practice known as "spamming," has come under fire with consumer advocates, prompting new legislation.

ORGANIZATION AND STRUCTURE

Direct mail, like other forms of advertising, plays an important role in the American economy by informing consumers about products and services. By expanding information and distribution channels, advertising is thought to benefit both businesses and customers with a more efficient market. Direct mail is part of the larger direct marketing industry, which also includes specific types of ads that are found in newspapers and magazines, on television and radio, and in telephone marketing. By 1995, direct marketing generated 12 percent of total U.S. consumer sales, with predictions of a full-point percentage increase by the year 2000.

Like other forms of direct marketing, direct mail ads differ from more traditional general advertising in several ways. The most important distinction, though, is that direct mail advertising typically solicits a direct response from the consumer. General advertising, on the other hand, usually seeks to promote a company or product image, inform consumers, or sway public opinion. While direct mail may also attempt some or all of these goals, its primary purpose is to elicit a tangible, measurable reaction.

Besides prompting consumers to take a specific action at a certain time, direct mail also differs from general promotional mail in that each advertisement is usually targeted at a specific individual at his or her address. For this reason, direct mail is often referred to as a form of target marketing. It is also unique because customers respond directly to the company that placed the ad, so the marketer maintains control of the offer throughout its delivery. In contrast, companies that use general advertisements lose control of their message—at the moment an ad enters a distribution channel, consumers are left to decide when, where, and how they will react to the promotion. Direct mail ads are also more likely to stress benefits and features of a product or service. Furthermore, direct mail commonly contains repetitive messages within each ad, whereas general advertisements rely on repetition over time.

Although some advertising firms were engaged solely in providing direct mail services, most companies in the industry were active in all aspects of direct marketing. Moreover, many of the largest companies that offer direct marketing also provided general advertising services. In addition to actually printing, assembling, and mailing promotional pieces, most direct mail firms provided services related to strategic planning, research and development, results tracking and reporting, and database management.

Types of Ads. Direct mail promotionals can be categorized as lead generation, mail order, traffic building, subscription marketing, and fundraising. According to a 1996 Gallup survey, about 89 percent of direct mail advertisers employ lead generation mailers. These ads simply ask recipients to exhibit an interest in the company's offer. For instance, the consumer may indicate a desire for more information by returning a response card requesting that the company call or write them with more data. Lead generation ads are often used to build a list of prospects on which the company can focus its future marketing efforts.

Direct mail advertisers are also varying the contents of their packages. The traditional format includes an outer envelope, cover letter, product brochure, order form, and sometimes a separate reply envelope. The 1999 study conducted by the Graphic Arts Marketing Information Service (GAMIS) says that direct marketers are now using co-op packs, card decks, ride-alongs, statement stuffers, and self-mailers. The new models tend to be si simpler in design, and therefore cheaper to produce. Direct mail advertisers are also using more four-color printing and specialty papers to attract potential customers.

Almost all direct mail campaigns fall into one of three market categories: charitable contributions, business ads, or consumer promotions. According to the 1996 Gallup survey, companies used many different forms of direct mail to generate leads and sales. The survey reported 86 percent used brochures; 80 percent, direct mail letters; 77 percent, flyers; 69 percent, newsletters; 55 percent, postcards; 35 percent, catalogs; 25 percent, invoice inserts; and 22 percent used package inserts. Average mid-sized and large companies' direct mail production was 672,100 pieces each year.

Benefits and Disadvantages. Among the reasons that organizations seek services from direct mail companies are selectivity and personalization. By carefully selecting the group of consumers that will receive an ad, and carefully tailoring the message to that group, a direct mail company can maximize the efficiency of a client's marketing dollars. For this reason, direct mail advertising is the most cost effective means of advertising for many types of products. In addition to savings related to marketing expenditures, direct mail allows many manufacturers to completely bypass costly retail centers and distribution facilities by delivering products through the mail.

Direct marketing companies also offer the benefit of being able to measure and test the effectiveness of a company's advertising efforts. In fact, direct marketing firms commonly test multiple offers and formats before distributing an ad on a broad scale. This important feature allows an organization to exercise more control over its promotion than is allowed by almost any other type of media. A related advantage, in comparison to other forms of advertising, is that direct advertising campaigns are more difficult for competitors to monitor and track.

A major disadvantage of direct mail is that it can be very expensive. Direct mail firms typically charged at least 40 cents per piece to print, assemble, and mail even a relatively simple promotion. In addition, clients often pay for creative services, tracking, and strategic planning. In comparison, a full-page advertisement in a trade magazine that reaches 50,000 readers may cost as little as $2,000 to $3,000. Another disadvantage of direct mail is mailbox competition. In the *New York Times,* Stuart Elliot reported that direct mail climbed to 44 percent of all pieces of mail handled by the post office in 1998, up from 41 percent a decade ago and 32 percent in 1978.

Consumer perception is another pitfall. Most consumers commonly refer to direct mail as ''junk mail,'' and hold in low regard the more cost-efficient mail-merge packages that combine pieces from a number of different advertisers in one envelope. More than 50 percent of direct mail envelopes end up in the garbage. And many consumers—the DMA reported more than 3 million—were exercising their right to have their names removed from mailing lists. Fewer consumers take the time to clip and redeem coupons the way they once did, making it difficult to track the effectiveness of direct mail campaigns. Despite a general rise in coupon face values, the overall coupon redemption rate has fallen throughout the decade—6 percent in 1993, 9 percent in 1994, 6.5 percent in 1995, and 8.6 percent in 1996.

Mailing Lists. Mailing lists, the backbone of the direct mail advertising industry, constituted about $1.3 billion, or more than 5 percent, of all direct mail expenditures in 1992. Regardless of how competent and alluring an offer may be, the success of any direct mail promotion is contingent upon the quality of the mailing list used to distribute the piece. To avoid unnecessary expenses, list providers must insure that address lists are up-to-date, devoid of duplicate names or addresses, and accurate. Mailing lists were commonly sold on labels for anywhere from $7 to $80 per thousand for one-time use, and about twice that amount for computerized lists that could be used more than once.

Mailing list companies offer the critical advantage of market segmentation by tailoring a list to include only the consumers to which it would be profitable for a company to advertise. For instance, a luxury Japanese car dealership may wish to send an advertisement to all residents in Southern California that earn more than $150,000, have two or more children, own a three-car garage, and currently drive a German car. Using computer database management techniques, list companies in the early 1990s were able to extract even the most unique niches, such as that just described, from a list of names and information.

In the early 1990s, list companies offered more than 10,000 different lists, most of which could be tailored to suit specific requirements. The four major types of lists were response, compiled, consumer, and business. Response lists were made up of people that had previously responded to a direct marketing promotion. Because these lists typically provided higher response rates and were more difficult to create, they commonly cost $50 to $80 per thousand. Furthermore, these lists accounted for approximately 60 percent of list industry sales.

Compiled lists were usually created using mass listings from voter registrations, telephone books, licensed driver listings, or other common groups. These lists typically cost $25 to $30 per thousand. Consumer lists were compiled from the general U.S. population, and were segmented by various demographic factors. Because these lists often were not proprietary and are sold in huge volume, they usually cost $7 per thousand. In 1992, more than 90 percent of the U.S. population was accessible through more than 6,000 consumer mailing lists. Business lists (13 percent of sales) contained addresses of more than 9 million different enterprises from more than 4,000 lists in 1992. Prices in this segment ranged from $35 to $40 per thousand names.

By the late 1990s, however, a fundamental shift had occurred regarding the perception of information. For decades, information collected about or from consumers was regarded as the property of the organization that collected it, to be used at that organization's discretion. But another consensus developed that said the information was the property of consumers, whose consent should be required before information about them was used. Privacy protection laws, which seek to limit the transfer of personal information, especially medical histories and other sensitive data, have been enacted or were under consideration in the United States.

BACKGROUND AND DEVELOPMENT

Direct mail advertising was invented by Benjamin Franklin in 1744. He produced a mail order catalog bearing this promise: ''Those persons who live remote, by sending their orders and money to said B. Franklin, may depend on the same justice as if present.'' About 100 years later in Philadelphia, in 1841, the first advertising agency was opened. In 1863 congress authorized the issuance of a discount stamp for mailers of ''printed matter and manuscripts,'' known as second-class mail. It also issued a third-class stamp for ''bulk mailers.''

Direct mail advertising in the United States did not became a popular marketing tool until the beginning of the twentieth century. Although still not considered an important information and distribution channel in the early days of the industry, several large companies relied heavily on direct mail to promote their businesses. Sears, Roebuck, and Co., which marketed heavily through its innovative mail catalogs in the early 1900s, became a notorious early example of direct marketing. The Montgomery Ward, Aldens, and Spiegel companies also mailed large numbers of catalogs.

In addition to the large catalog retailers, store-based retailers and industrial advertisers helped expand the industry. In fact, these organizations accounted for the bulk of direct mail sent out by the 1910s. National Cash Register (NCR), for instance, attained legendary results by using mail order to generate leads and to support its sales force. On the cutting edge, NCR mailed tens of thousands of advertisements targeted specifically at niche markets, such as butchers and grocery store owners. Fundraisers, particularly politicians, were also beginning to realize the benefits of direct advertising.

In response to the growing volume of direct mail advertising, lettershop owners and their customers formed the Direct Mail Advertising Association (now called the Direct Marketing Association, or DMA) in 1917. The organization was established to help advance the fledgling industry, and grew throughout the 1920s from its initial membership of around 500. The 1920s also saw the emergence of several companies devoted solely to providing direct mail services. For example, DIMAC Direct of St. Louis, Missouri, was founded in 1921 and remained an industry leader in the early 1990s.

Despite immense setbacks during the Great Depression of the 1930s, when DMAA membership fell to under 300, the industry continued to progress. The post-World War II economy spurred the success of direct mail companies, which were using their increasing political clout to influence postal rates. By the late 1950s, the DMA had about 2,500 members and the direct mail industry represented a multi-million dollar business. The industry maintained steady growth in the 1960s and 1970s, spawned in part by new catalog retailers like L.L. Bean, Inc., J.C. Penney, and Lillian Vernon. Also boosting industry growth in the 1970s was the advent of postal zip codes, which allowed companies to more easily target their mailings.

By 1980, U.S. companies were spending more than $7.6 billion per year on direct mail advertising, and total mail order sales had risen to $72 billion. Furthermore, direct mail accounted for nearly 15 percent of all advertising expenditures. During the coming decade, these figures were destined to rise substantially, for both technological and demographic reasons.

One of the greatest reasons for the proliferation of direct mail advertising during the 1980s was the metamorphosis of American lifestyles. More women working outside the home meant that households had more expendable income but less time to spend it. As a result, many consumers adopted direct mail advertisements, such as mail order catalogs, as an alternative to conventional shopping patterns. Moreover, personal selling through direct marketing became more popular, which put a pinch on traditional retail outlets. The average cost of a business-to-business phone sale, for instance, had grown from $57 in 1971 to $137 in 1979 to more than $250 by

1987. Technological advances also increased the power and decreased cost of computers, allowing direct mail advertising firms to achieve almost exponential efficiency gains. By 1990, computers dominated every step of the direct mail process, from program planning and list development to order fulfillment and response tracking.

The proliferation of new niche products and services boosted industry profits in the 1980s. A dominant market trend since the 1980s was highly specialized offerings that targeted individual needs. Because direct mail provides efficient access to niche market segments, it became the medium of choice for growing numbers of companies. These companies also benefited from toll-free telephone numbers and private mail services, which further increased the efficiency of direct mail advertising efforts.

Other factors that contributed to the growth of the direct mail industry in the 1980s included: greatly expanded use of credit cards; the availability of computerized mailing lists; an aging population that shopped at home more often; and a rise in single households. By 1990, expenditures on direct mail topped $23 billion, representing a more than 300 percent rise since 1980. Furthermore, mail order sales grew to more than $200 billion by 1990. Direct mail expenditures also had grown to represent nearly 20 percent of all advertising dollars and had grown faster than any other segment of the advertising industry during the 1980s. In addition, industry employment leapt from 44,000 in 1983 to approximately 90,000 by 1990.

The growth of the direct mail advertising industry, which averaged well over 10 percent during much of the 1980s, continued in the early 1990s, despite a sluggish economy that reduced overall advertising activity. The industry remained healthy and billings for direct marketing services rendered by ad agencies surpassed $4 billion. Direct billings increased 15 percent in 1990, and 13 percent in 1991. Furthermore, total expenditures on direct mail increased 4.5 percent in 1992, versus a 2.9 percent increase in 1991 and a 7 percent increase in 1990. In fact, total direct mail expenditures climbed from $11.8 billion in 1983 to more than $25.4 billion by 1992.

By 1993 the direct mail advertising industry had firmly established itself in almost every sector of the economy. Once considered ''junk mail'' by some large corporations, direct response ads had become an important form of advertising for even the most elite and sophisticated corporations. IBM, General Motors, Nieman Marcus, and similar organizations were using direct response ads to promote their products and services. Small companies, too, were increasingly turning to direct mail to increase sales and to compete with larger companies.

According to a Gallup study in 1996, 77 percent of U.S. companies used direct mail, and marketing executives considered it the most effective technique in reaching their objectives. The survey reported that marketing executives credit direct mail sales with an average of 5 percent of their company's revenue. Compared to other media, however, direct mail continued to trail telephone marketing by volume of sales generated.

By 1997, sales generated by direct mail surpassed an estimated $421 billion per year, according to the DMA. As further evidence of the upward trend, approximately 100 million Americans were making shop-at-home purchases each year in the early 1990s, and 70 percent had used a toll-free number to purchase an item. About 68 percent of all magazine subscriptions were sold through mail order in the early 1990s, accounting for more than $190 million in sales. Also, insurance premiums totaling more than $10 billion per year were earned through mail order. In 1991, the average American spent $425 as a result of mail order advertisements. Furthermore, about 25 percent of all charitable contributions were obtained through mail solicitations, totaling about $50 billion.

Current Conditions

In the late 1990s, the direct mail industry was thriving. In 1998, direct mail advertising accounted for 4 out of every 10 pieces of U.S. mail and generated more than $421 million in sales. Industry experts projected moderate growth into the next decade. Yet, the volume of incoming mail has not affected consumers' response rate. Most direct mail marketers considered a 2 or 3 percent response rate to be successful. Up to 98 percent of the people who receive unsolicited mail reject the offers, most tossing the direct mail unopened. The United States Postal Service (USPS) says that consumers are just as likely today to respond to direct mail as they were 10 years ago.

What has changed is the sophistication of the direct mail packages. An important shift in marketing has occurred in the last few years—a move away from mass marketing and towards a more information-led, targeted audience. Advertisers and agencies strive to increase the relevance of—and decrease customer annoyance with—direct mail by customizing the pitches they send to customers.

Database companies provide sophisticated information about customers by overlaying generic information, from phone lists and driver records, for example, with specific information about customers' spending patterns and family size. The Internet provides direct marketers with a powerful new information-gathering tool. ''The consumer technology that makes the Internet possible,'' says Stuart Elliot in the *New York Times,* ''is also helping direct marketers in their quest for the grail of relevancy by making it easier than ever to compile extensive information about consumers before any mail is sent.''

The direct-mail techniques have also become more sophisticated. A USPS study estimated that more than 20 percent of advertising mail was thrown away unread, partly because it looked unprofessional. To offset this image, the industry has developed new printers that add color, personalize addresses with special fonts to look hand written, and which can add personal touches like deliberately crossed-out names. Direct-mail envelopes are sometimes designed to look like express mail and next-day delivery packages to imply urgency.

Consumers are not the only targets of direct-mail advertisers. The GAMIS study reported a rising trend of business-to-business direct-mail marketing. In 1998, business-to-business expenditures represented 39 percent of direct mail expenditures according to the GAMIS study; by 2009, they were expected to hit 45 percent. Consumer direct mail, which accounted for a 61 percent share in 1998, was expected to shrink to 55 percent by 2008.

Industry Challenges. Despite strong growth, the direct mail industry was not without its problems in the late 1990s. Postal rates increased in 1996, increasing the costs of and reducing the efficiency of direct mail ads. This led direct mail agencies and their clients to streamline their lists to reduce the size of mailers and customize their pitches. Moreover, as the cost of mailing grew, more companies moved toward telephone marketing. By 1995, the telephone marketing industry had seized 40 percent of the total direct marketing expenditures, surpassing direct mail by 17 percent. But by 1999, the tide had again changed. In a Pitney Bowes ''Mail vs. Telemarketing'' survey, U.S. customers stated a preference to mail by a 4-to-1 margin.

Industry success was leading to another problem—overcrowded mailboxes. Because direct ads were competing with increasing numbers of other mail promotions for consumer attention, the response rate and profitability of sending out direct mailers was beginning to decline. Like the increase in postal rates, this problem encouraged more precise market segmentation.

Environmental waste, created by approximately 65 billion direct mail pieces sent out every year, represents a continuing challenge to the direct-mail industry. Each year, those direct ads and catalogs consume more than 1 million acres of forest. According to a study by Carnegie Mellon University, bulk mail was responsible for 5 percent of all paper pollution in 1996. The study concluded that companies could also find equal response and sales using the Internet. Consumer environmental awareness has negatively impacted the public's perception of mail ads. In an effort to reduce waste, the DMA reported that direct mail advertisers now use more recycled materials.

By 1997, the direct mail industry faced some competition from Internet marketing. Termed ''spam'' in Internet jargon, bulk e-mail grew with the number of subscribers. In 1996 the difference in cost was 99 percent less to send bulk e-mail instead of direct mail. Philadelphia-based Cyber Promotions, Inc., would send an e-mail ad to more than a million computer users for as little as $59 in 1996. This controversial practice was far from becoming commonplace entering the late 1990s, though, and faced potential government regulation in several states despite the general ''hands-off'' approach to Internet commerce promoted by the Clinton administration.

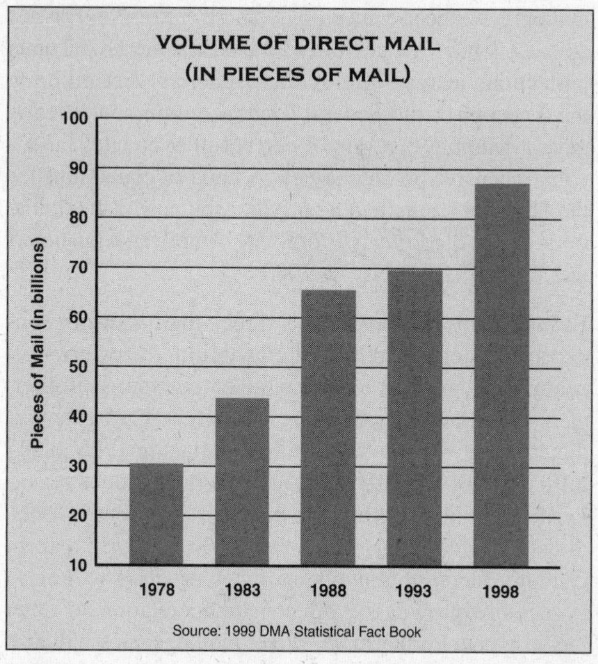

Source: 1999 DMA Statistical Fact Book

However, by 1999, new synergies were emerging between the direct mail and Internet industries. A study commissioned by Pitney Bowes, Inc., Mailing Systems Division, ''The Role of Mail in E-commerce Study,'' analyzed the relationship between direct mail and the Internet. It concluded that direct mail was considered the most effective tool for getting customers to go to a web site and place an order, and it was nearly as powerful as Internet advertising in encouraging website visits, or ''hits.'' Mail could help develop awareness, sales and customer relationships, which, combined with the reach of the Internet, could create a powerful sales medium. In December 1999, Big iDeals, Inc., a Silicon Valley-based direct marketing services company, launched the Big iDeals Internet Guide, a 16-page booklet featuring multiple advertisers in a single publication that targeted women aged 25-54 who had an Internet connection. *PR Newswire* says the new publication signals a new trend among marketers toward using traditional direct marketing in conjunction with online marketing.

And at the end of the century, the direct-mail industry experienced strong consumer backlash. The efforts of direct-mail marketers targeting customers and perfecting mailers have been viewed by some as intrusive. Privacy advocates have successfully lobbied for more consumer protections against information gatherers. According to the *Economist*, the Federal Trade Commission recently gave a warning that only 2 percent of Web sites have a comprehensive privacy policy. A flood of complaints led the DMA to strengthen its privacy policies, with stipulations called the Privacy Promise to American Consumers due to take effect July 1, 2000.

Future Expectations. The direct mail industry was expected to enjoy continued growth into the twenty-first century as the trend toward targeted marketing proliferated. Advertising expenditures for direct mail were predicted to grow from $31.2 billion dollars in 1995 to $47 billion by 2001. While the entire advertising industry was expected to increase billings by about 4 percent in 1993, direct mail ad billings were expected to rise by 15 percent or more. Increasing numbers of new products will mean even more growth for direct mail in relation to other media types. Furthermore, direct mail agencies will also be the greatest beneficiaries of advances in computer and print production technology.

Direct mail advertising methods will continue to become more sophisticated. For instance, more advertisers will stress database marketing, which entails maintaining computerized information about customers and leads generated from previous ad campaigns. Such databases are used to market new, or ''add-on,'' products and to establish a relationship with the consumer that will lead to a pattern of sales. By 1992, 54 percent of advertisers were using database marketing, and 23 percent planned to begin doing so in the near future. Many direct mail agencies already offered database management services to their clients.

Direct advertisers will also practice greater media integration, which involves running direct mail ads as part of a larger multi-media promotion. Sophisticated campaigns will coordinate the image, message, and timing of multiple marketing channels to increase their overall effectiveness. According to Joanna Lowenstein in *Folio,* one method that might improve direct-mail response is telesurveying in advance of a direct-mail campaign. New technology and international marketing will also play a role in future growth.

Industry Leaders

In 1996, one of the largest U.S. companies engaged primarily in direct mail advertising was DIMAC Direct of St. Louis, Missouri. The company generated 100 percent of its revenue from services related to direct mail. From $107 million in direct mail volume in 1990, DIMAC had grown 28 percent in 1991 to generate more than $134 million worth of direct mail pieces. During 1992, DIMAC produced the equivalent of one day's volume of the U.S. Postal Service. By 1995, the company's revenue dropped down to $126 million with 1,198 employees. In addition to direct mail fulfillment services, DIMAC also offered results tracking, creative, and list services.

Wunderman, Cato, and Johnson Worldwide of New York held the second top direct response agency position in 1996 with $101 million in 1995 revenue and 569 employees. Barry Blau & Partners, Inc., of Connecticut was the second largest direct response agency in the early 1990s, but dropped to number seven in 1996. In 1991, this firm produced $127 million worth of direct mail, a 26 percent rise over 1990. In 1995, revenues had decreased to about $50 million. Other industry leaders included Rapp Collins Worldwide, of New York, with about $80 million in direct response volume in 1995, and Bronner, Slosberg, and Humphrey, of Boston, which produced $67 million in direct response volume.

The largest mailing list company in the 1990s was Donnelley Marketing, Inc., of Connecticut, which specialized in consumer lists. The company was purchased by First Data Corp. of Houston in 1996 for $185 million. This diversified media company estimated list sales at between $75 million and $100 million in 1995. In 1996 Donnelly Marketing maintained a factual and behavioral database on 96 million households and 170 million consumers. Dun & Bradstreet of New Jersey was the second largest list producer in 1991, with list sales estimated at $55 million to $75 million. Other large list companies include American Business Information, R.L. Polk, Metromail, and Database America.

In the mail-order catalog division of the direct mail industry, Dell Computer held the top spot for catalogers in 1999, followed by IBM, J.C. Penney, Office Depot, and Micro Warehouse, according to *Direct Marketing*.

The company that generated the greatest amount of worldwide sales of its products and services through mail order advertising in 1991 was United Services Automobile Association. This insurance company generated more than $4.8 billion dollars in sales through direct mail promotions. Time Warner, the second largest seller through direct mail, garnered about $3.47 billion by marketing its books, magazines, and cable TV subscriptions. Sears Roebuck placed third in total mail order sales, with $3.45 billion, and J.C. Penney was fourth, with $3.17 billion in direct mail sales. Other large direct mail advertisers in the early 1990s included American Association of Retired Persons ($2.8 billion in worldwide mail order sales), Tele-Communications ($2.7 billion), Readers Digest ($2 billion), and GEICO ($1. 1.8 billion).

Workforce

Approximately 82,000 workers were employed by direct mail firms in the mid-1990s. This figure was down slightly from the late 1980s. Despite increased automation, employment for specific professions within the industry was forecast to grow faster than average, according to the U.S. Bureau of Labor Statistics. For example, jobs for duplicating and mail processing machine operators, which account for about 11 percent of the industry work force, were likely to grow by 64 percent between 1990 and 2005. The total employment for direct response agencies, in-house, and service bureaus was expected to grow from 1.9 million in 1995 to 2.2 million by 2000. The total work force affected by direct marketing was expected to increase to 23.1 million by the year 2000, with a growth rate of 3.9 percent per year from 1995.

Even jobs for managers and executives, which made up 5.7 percent of the direct mail work force in 1990, were expected to grow by 46.5 percent by 2005. Jobs in sales, photography, layout, and design, which accounted for a total of about 18 percent of the work force, were expected increase between 50 percent and 65 percent. Labor and blue collar positions were forecast to expand as well, by about 50 percent. Positions in management, finance, and information systems were also expected to realize growth rates of 50 percent to 60 percent by 2005. The greatest employment growth in the industry was predicted to occur in marketing, advertising, and public relations positions, where job opportunities would likely increase by about 80 percent.

Although job growth will continue to occur with advertising agencies, an increasing number of direct mail advertising positions will open up with product and service companies that are moving their direct mail operations in-house. In addition, direct mail ad occupations will become increasingly blurred with other advertising positions, as the trend toward multimedia and integrated marketing proliferates.

AMERICA AND THE WORLD

Direct mail advertising originated and developed in the United States, and America still leads the world in the use of direct advertising. In fact, while nearly 45 percent of all global advertising dollars are spent in the United States, a much larger proportion of global direct mail dollars are spent domestically. For instance, the average American receives about 290 pieces of direct mail per year, far more than citizens in any other country. Canadians, who receive the second largest number of mail ads, get only about 130 pieces per year, and much of that is mailed by U.S. companies.

Germans, in contrast, receive about 70 pieces per year, and Britons get about 40 direct mail ads each year. People in Australia only see about 15 mail ads every year. Even in Japan, which has a relatively advanced direct mail industry by world standards and a very high per capita GNP, companies only spend about $14 billion per year advertising through the mail. Furthermore, many direct mail agencies in that country lag far behind American firms in automation and information technology.

Besides the fact that other countries lag behind the comparatively advanced U.S. advertising industry, direct mail is popular in the United States for several reasons. For instance, the American lifestyle is more suited to mail advertising than most foreign societies. The U.S. marketplace imposes fewer language barriers than marketers in Western Europe, for example, might encounter. Finally, the lowest postal rates in the industrialized world make the United States a haven for direct mail advertisers. While a first-class letter could be mailed for only 33 cents in the United States, Germans and Italians paid the equivalent of about 63 cents per letter. First-class letters in Japan and Norway cost about 50 cents, and most European Community nations charged more than 40 cents per piece.

Many Americans have become jaded by some less-than-honest direct-mail practices. Scandals involving Publishers' Clearinghouse, in which some elderly Americans lost their savings, served to tarnish the industry's image. However, direct mail was considered a new phenomenon in many parts of the world. While many Americans toss direct mailers in the trash unread, recipients in the Czech Republic and Russia, for example, pore over their mailings and pass them along to others. Higher postal rates and language barriers have not dissuaded many American companies from launching direct mail campaigns overseas, and many increased their efforts by 1998.

However, other overriding political and economic factors radically changed the international investment landscape—and the prospects for successful advertising campaigns. The 1997-98 financial crises that toppled economies from Asia to Russia and Brazil posed challenges to direct-mail marketers, including reduced demand, increased protectionism, and the deterioration of infrastructures, according to William J. McDonald in *Direct Marketing.*

RESEARCH AND TECHNOLOGY

Direct mail advertising companies continue to benefit from advances in automation and information technology that increase the value of their services. Advances in computer technology were already allowing companies to make mailings more personalized and specific. For example, many catalog producers were working toward developing personalized catalogs that would be tailored to certain demographic profiles. The same company's catalog, for instance, might be tailored during printing to emphasize different products or offers for a variety of different customer types.

Direct mail advertisers may also be impacted, perhaps negatively, by multimedia technology which will eventually integrate video, optical disk storage devices, and personal computers. Multimedia will increase the trend toward consumer controlled advertising by allowing consumers more power in choosing which ads and media they internalize. Advancements in recycled paper, printing technology, and ink will likely help the industry move toward reduced waste and lower production costs.

FURTHER READING

Behrens, John C. "Direct Mail Still a Good Buy." *American Printer,* July 1996.

"Big iDeals Launches Offline Internet Guide for Online Businesses." *PR Newswire,* 1 December 1999.

"Business: Direct Hit." *Economist,* 9 January 1999.

"Direct Mail Is King." *American Salesman,* July 1996.

Elliot, Stuart. "You've Got Mail, Indeed." *New York Times,* 25 October 1999.

Endicott, R. David. "Direct Ads Spur 12 Percent of Consumer Sales." *Advertising Age,* 9 October 1995.

Hatch, Denison. "Direct Mail: The Workhorse of Direct Marketing." *Target Marketing,* August 1995.

Lowenstein, Joanna. "Telesurveys: A Direct Mail Tune-Up Technique." *Folio,* 1 April 1999.

McDonald, William J. "International Direct Marketing in a Rapidly Changing World." *Direct Marketing,* March 1999.

Michaels, Abraham. "Junk Mail." *Public Works,* May 1996.

Miller, Samantha. "Spam Wars." *People Weekly,* 18 November 1996.

Mitchell, Alan. "Data Access Shake-up for Direct Marketing." *Marketing Week (London),* 19 August 1999.

"New Study Reveals That Mail Plays a Critical Role in the Internet Economy; Companies Selling on the Web Say Mail Is Best for Generating E-Commerce." *Business Wire,* 10 November 1999.

Quittner, Jeremy. "1st Data to Buy Donnelley, a Direct Marketing Firm." *American Banker,* 12 September 1996.

Roth, Jill. "The Good, the Bad, and the Uncertain." *American Printer,* August 1999.

Schmid, Jack. "State of the Union for Catalogs." *Target Marketing,* April 1996.

Smith, Wilson. "How To Get Rid of All Your Junk E-Mail." *Money,* July 1996.

"Top Agencies by U.S. Direct Response Revenue." *Advertising Age,* 10 July 1995.

"Top Catalogers List Released." *Direct Marketing,* October 1999.

"The Top 10 Direct Response Agencies." *AdWeek,* 15 April 1996.

"U.S. Consumers Like Mail Better Than the Telephone When It Comes to Buying Products and Services." *Business Wire,* 11 November 1999.

U.S. Department of Commerce. *U.S. Industrial Outlook 1993.* Washington, DC: GPO, January 1993.

Whitelaw, Kevin. "Shopping Around for Help; Big Paper and Postage Costs Hurt Catalogs." *U.S. News & World Report,* 18 December 1995.

SIC 7334

PHOTOCOPYING AND DUPLICATING SERVICES

This category covers establishments primarily engaged in reproducing text, drawings, plans, maps, or other copy, by blueprinting, photocopying, mimeographing, or other methods of duplication other than printing or microfilming. Establishments primarily engaged in printing are classified under **SIC 2752: Commercial Printing, Lithographic; SIC 2754: Commercial Printing, Gravure;** and **SIC 2759: Commercial Printing, Not Elsewhere Classified.** Those companies engaged in providing microfilming services are classified under **SIC 7389: Business Services, Not Elsewhere Classified.**

NAICS CODE(S)

561431 (Other Business Service Centers (including Copy Shops))

INDUSTRY SNAPSHOT

The photocopying and duplicating services industry did not really win full recognition from the U.S. Department of Commerce until the 1990s. In fact, sales figures/estimates were not even collected and reported until 1995. By then, according to the *Service Annual Survey: 1997* (U.S. Census Bureau), the photocopying and duplicating services industry had "suddenly" appeared as an industry that generated $5.7 billion in sales per annum.

Industry profitability is between 9.4 percent and 12.5 percent depending on the nature of the shop. Franchise operations profitability is 11.7 percent; franchises, largely but not exclusively, represented the majority of firms with annual receipts of $1 million or more. Of those firms, average sales per employee grew 14 percent in just three years, from $84,000 in 1997 to $98,000 in 1999. Interestingly, receipts were directly proportional as a function of total dollar volume—the shops with the highest dollar volume had the highest sales per employee. The industry generated $6.8 billion in receipts in 1997.

The quick printing industry represents a relatively new dimension of both the commercial printing and graphic arts industries. Most companies in the photocopying industry began as printers offering while-you-wait service dubbed "quick printing." What began as a small segment of the printing market experienced phenomenal growth beginning in the 1970s, changing the printing industry forever. In 1969, 1,000 quick printers were operating in the United States, and by 1974 that number had reached 6,000. From 1975 to 1992, the quick printing industry exploded, and an estimated 30,000 were operational by the early 1990s. By 1997, these quick printing shops were run by 5,780 distinct establishments. According to industry expert Franklin Printing, at the end of the decade over $4.5 billion was spent annually on quick printing alone.

ORGANIZATION AND STRUCTURE

The quick printing industry generally provides two types of services: convenience and commercial. With storefront locations in strip malls and downtown shopping districts, the convenience quick printer serves the needs of small businesses and consumers. Convenience quick printers include both independent and franchised operations that rely largely on copiers and paper plates on 11' x 17' presses. The commercial printer typically provides services similar to those of the convenience shop, with larger facilities and several added capabilities for serving the needs of larger businesses.

BACKGROUND AND DEVELOPMENT

The quick printing industry emerged from the development of the Itek camera/platemaker, acquired in the early 1960s by Bill LeVine, a commercial printer. This machine produced black ink on 8'' x 11'' paper with photocopiers or electrostatic plates, forming images in powdered or liquid ink directly on the surface to be printed.

In the 1970s, quick printing generally produced black-and-white or one-color offset prints on flat surfaces using photomechanical plates or paper mats. By the end of the decade, however, the industry was augmented by the introduction of high-speed copiers, which produced one-color prints.

By the 1980s, many quick printers were able to offer a variety of paper sizes and two- and four-color copies. Furthermore, high-speed copiers became more common in the industry, as did large document copiers. During this time, copier technology advanced, and some quick printers offered desktop publishing systems, camera and darkroom facilities, and advanced bindery equipment. The 1990s have been dominated by the growing adoption of digital technology, new products and services, Web pages and publishing, and transmission of data to the quick printer electronically. Regardless of a business's development, continued growth and perhaps survival will be dependent on adaptation to and adoption of digital imaging and electronic communication.

The historic paths to becoming a giant in the industry have been to open multiple small sites and build volume, open a facilities management site within a large corporation, or to migrate steadily from quick printing only to graphic arts services.

Some of the challenges to the industry have been the cost of paper, which seems to have stabilized; keeping up with technology; and the increasing demands for shorter turn around time. Printing and copying is divided into three major areas: multicolor copying (26 percent), copying (25 percent), black and white (17 percent), and rapidly growing digital printing (6 percent).

Toner-based copying dramatically changed the nature of quick printing, especially for high volume work. High-speed copying, able to produce quality halftones and two-sided copies, set the standards for the quick printing industry. Wide format or folio printing has also continued to grow with close to 200,000 printing devices installed 1996.

In order to strengthen the scope of their service, quick print shops began to expand into areas outside of copying and printing. For example, according to a 1990 National Association of Quick Printers (NAQP) member survey, 81 percent of its membership provided fax services and 53 percent offered desktop publishing. Some shops even rented computers and sold office supplies. While not the source of major profits, such diversifications offered customers value-added service.

Many quick print shops tested the market for color copying and further automation in desktop publishing. By 1992, over 60 percent of NAQP's membership offered full-color copying. Moreover, a joint study conducted by the NAQP and *Quick Printing* magazine indicated that the companies widely regarded as industry leaders had offered color copying services since at least 1987.

The growing popularity of desktop publishing has also augmented the industry. Some quick printers began offering disk conversion services in which computer files are reproduced in a hard copy format. Neal Lorenzi, contributing editor at *American Printer,* commented in a July 1989 article that ''The very nature of quick printing places it on the edge of the desktop publishing revolution. Simply put, more print customers are using personal computers in their daily operations and finding quick printers to be a convenient source for outputting files on laser printers and other image setters.''

As early as 1991, a study by Printing Industries of America predicted that quick printers would represent the largest segment of the printing industry, measured by the number of establishments, by the year 2000. Much of this growth was attributed to the introduction of franchise operations during the mid-1970s. The prediction proved true—franchisers became an integral part of the quick printing industry—the top four companies had roughly 1,000 shops each.

The future of the quick printing industry depended on the timely and cost-effective use of technology. Future developments were expected to include advances in desktop publishing, increased use of two- and four-color copies, and the availability of ancillary services, such as faxing, binding, proofreading, and translating.

Acquisitions and mergers were prevalent in 1996. There were 85,000 high speed copiers operating in the United States with 45 percent of them in the print-for-profit sector. Quick print shops derived 35 percent of their revenue from copiers that are easier to operate than presses and incorporate finishing productions such as binding and/or stitching or gluing.

Current Conditions

With the market for photocopying and duplication services booming, retailers in related industries saw the opportunity for expansion. Their distribution infrastructure was already in place via an established chain of retail outlets. Office superstores found easy entrance to the market by establishing quick print sites in their stores. Office superstores such as Office Depot, OfficeMax, and Staples, actively sought a chunk of the traditional quick print market. For example, by the mid-1990s, OfficeMax carved out 5,000 to 7,000 CopyMax quick print shops within their stores.

Video capturing, a process in which individual frames can be pulled from videotape and incorporated into printed materials, represented another area for growth in the industry. The ability to generate art and assemble pages electronically also remained a lucrative service. According to Bob McKarney, of the quick print franchise Sir Speedy, ''In the near future, quick printers will be able to go directly from computer to press. PC color software and filmless platemaking systems were developed before the century ended. For short runs (300 to 500), an operator could direct graphics directly from computer to color copier.'' By 2000, this proved to be true.

In spite of predicted shakeup in the quick print industry, which experienced its first ever decline in sales in 1991, the industry recovered and continued to grow throughout the decade. Observers had predicted up to a 25 percent reduction of shops in the mid-1990s, claiming that only those capable and willing to keep up with technology would survive. Tom Carnes, president of PDQ Printing, observed in *American Printer* that ''the market is over saturated with quick printers. Many are good at putting ink on paper but not at running a business.'' Elwood Smith, past president of NAQP, agreed: ''Many quick printers won't make it,'' he noted in *American Printer,* adding that ''Those that do will have to provide extra-good service and quality products. They will have to be customer oriented and market driven.''

A growing number of quick printers are turning to the Internet for advertising. For example, displaying initial color proofs for review by clients, StarNet provides an on-demand fully digital printing service running Docutechs and Indigo E-Print 1000 machines. Another company, Dave's World, was set up exclusively for Internet and Intranet work. Targeting audiences and specializing may become more important than generalizing and diversifying in the future.

Industry Leaders

Among the leading companies including private and franchise are Kinko's, Inc., with $1.8 billion in sales, and TRM Copy centers. The top franchises in the industry at the century's close in terms of dollar volume were Sir Speedy, Kwik Kopy, AlphaGraphics, American Speedy, Insty-Prints, Proforma, LazerQuick, and Signal Graphics.

Founded in 1981, TRM Corporation had 593 employees and $56.2 million in annual sales in 1999. Rather than owning and operating retail copying centers, TRM Copy Centers placed its 31,000 TRM Centers in small, independent retail establishments such as pharmacies, gift shops, and convenience stores throughout 56 metropolitan areas in the United States, Canada, and the United Kingdom. This mode of operation allowed the company to maximize its market potential and more effectively compete with regional shops. Host locations of TRM copiers—including convenience stores, hardware stores, and pharmacies—collected the usage fees for the copiers and were billed by TRM on a monthly basis. TRM's inventory of copy machines consisted largely of copiers that the company rebuilt to better-than-new condition and serviced through a highly trained field staff. Most customers used TRM machines for convenient, low volume copying at reasonable prices.

With over 1,000 centers throughout United States, Canada, Mexico, and 20 other countries, Sir Speedy, Inc. was one of the world's largest franchisers of copying centers. Headquartered in Laguna Hills, California, the Sir Speedy franchise network generated $400 million in sales in 1998. The annual average sales revenue for a typical Sir Speedy center exceeded $500,000; of those franchises, the top 25 averaged over $1 million in sales.

Sir Speedy has adapted to cash in on the computer created document and electronic duplication now prevalent with digital technology. Sir Speedy acquired PIP Printing near the end of 1996. Toronto-based Moore Corporation sold its chain of quick print and copy centers in Europe to Sir Speedy in 1996. Sir Speedy president Don Lowe recently signed an agreement with Eastman Kodak to launch Kodak's Photo Portfolio CD to create multimedia presentations for customers. SpeedNet, a bulletin board, lets franchisees create and send documents in minutes to any one of 880 copy centers. It targets the 41 million Americans who work at home.

Kinko's Copies—a non-franchised corporation that is controlled by Paul Orfalea, the 32 percent owner of Kinko's, Inc.—became a $400 million plus chain in 1995. By 1999, sales were an estimated $1.8 billion. In a major move possibly precipitated by a copyright infringement lawsuit, Kinko's decided to shift from a college student clientele toward small and medium size businesses, including self-employed people working from home. At the end of the 1990s, Kinko's operated over 1,000 business centers. It has also equipped its stores with self-service desktop publishing computers. Voice and video services, allowing customers to conduct video conferencing for $75 an hour, began in 1996. Most centers now offer Internet access for its customers. With its copying and computer supplemental services, it caters to executives, small business owners, and home office workers. Nearly all Kinko's shops are open 24 hours a day and market themselves as the customers' branch office. An investment fund injected $200 million into Kinko's in exchange for a minority stake in order to help finance expansion. Going into the new millennium, Kinko's planned to go public.

Kwik Kopy Corporation, a $372.7 million empire based just outside of Houston, Texas, is among the oldest quick print shops in the industry. Founded in 1967 as an offshoot of Bud Hatfield Printers, Kwik Kopy had 25 printing centers by 1970. In 1972, when franchising became the leading trend in the quick printing industry, Kwik Kopy's business flourished, and by 1977, the company had established 170 printing centers in 18 states. Posting an 18 percent growth rate annually in the early 1990s, Kwik Kopy had 735 centers in 13 countries, including Canada, Australia, South Africa, Israel, and the United Kingdom, by 2000. Kwik Kopy rewards its franchise owners for timely submission of reports and other behaviors it wants to reinforce. Their Stars program allows franchisees to mentor their peers by visiting each other's shops, suggesting changes, and submitting feedback to corporate headquarters. Kwik Kopy's target customers are volume repeat corporate accounts.

AlphaGraphics, which operates 340 stores world wide, offered AlphaLink Direct, allowing customers to electronically transmit documents and graphics from their home, office, or lap top computer directly to local AlphaGraphics sites around the world. The company was founded on the principle of combining high technology with sound business practices. System wide sales for 1996 were $246 million. AlphaGraphics strategy going into the new millennium called for acquisitions internationally and a projected goal of 700 stores by 2000.

WORKFORCE

Nearly 160,000 owners, managers, and other employees work at the 33,000 quick printing centers throughout the United States. In 1997, the total number of employees involved strictly in photocopying and duplicating services was at 87,221, roughly three-quarters of whom were production workers. The latter group worked an average of 36.5 hours a week and earned an average of $10.80 per hour in 1996. Growth in the industry was projected to continue into the 2000s. According to Printing 2000, the quick printing industry could expect an annual growth rate of between 5 and 8 percent during this time.

By 1999, the photocopying and duplicating services industry was dominated by large franchise operations and operations linked to office superstores. Nonetheless, average sales for *all* establishments, many of which were single-owner, small shops, were an estimated $888,000. An average of 8.6 employees worked in each shop and accounted for about $103,000 in sales per employee. According to PrintImage International, the premier professional industry association, management positions (i.e., production, customer service and general managers and bindery supervisors) averaged $10.56 to $20.76 per hour with $675 to $6,500 average yearly bonuses. Wages for professional employees, (i.e., graphic artists, press and copier operators, strippers, and mailing service technicians), averaged from $9.15 to $14.64 per hour and received $575 to $1,062 in yearly bonuses. Also, a new trend in the industry was to engage outside sales representatives. Average compensation, based on average sales of $303,577, was generally about $52,000.

AMERICA AND THE WORLD

Quick copy centers expanded internationally in two ways. Some particularly well-financed franchise operations opened shops abroad. Others, including independent operations, added services geared toward international business communications needs.

Franchises such as AlphaGraphics and Sir Speedy established operations in Russia, Hungary, Australia, Bahrain, the United Arab Emirates, Canada, and Mexico. AlphaGraphics planned to build a network of 40 printing franchises in Mexico by the year 2000 and expected to open 40 shops in Spain.

Some expansion plans took the form of joint ventures, such as the union of American Speedy Printing Centers of Bloomfield Hills, Michigan, with a British printing shop to create EuroSpeedy Printing Centers in the United Kingdom. Kinko's Copies branched out into the Japanese market with services based in Nagoya under the name Kinko's Japan KK.

Smaller, independent quick printers found that exporting services was not the only way to take advantage of the growing global economy. Many quick printers began offering foreign language word processing, page layout, and typesetting computer programs; translation and proofreading services; and an increased awareness of foreign standards for paper and envelope sizes and business forms.

Research and Technology

The most dramatic technological developments in the 1990s involved desktop publishing. Elwood Smith claimed that ''Desktop publishing represents the next step in the evolution of quick printing—the most important innovation since the Itek camera/platemaker.'' Given the increased amount of work based on disk conversion, some industry observers even predicted that quick printers would eventually become desktop publishing experts.

Offering one-stop service for all printing needs, AlphaGraphics was one of the first quick printers to become involved in publishing, referring to itself as a desktop publishing retailer. Several other shops made complete conversions to computerized service—including Laser Image in Durham, North Carolina, which operated a completely automated shop, including computerized page layout, high-speed copiers, high-speed laser printing, and electronic color copying.

Computers were also used increasingly for managing shop operations in the industry. By the end of the 1990s, utilizing software for estimating needs, tracking orders, and updating inventory had become the industry standard.

A new class of multifunction peripherals combining printing, copying, scanning, and/or faxing into a single system have emerged. Xionics Document Technologies, Inc, is the leading supplier of these embedded systems whose technology has been adopted by Hewlett-Packard, IBM, Seiko, Epson, and Panasonic. RISO furthered the trend towards multi-function systems by making it possible to incorporate once separate, after-print operations such as perforation, slitting, scoring, folding, and stapling. Another innovation is Electronics for Imaging's Fiery Xje embedded controller that turns digital copiers into high-speed network printers such as the Ricoh Corporation's Aficio 2000 series.

Mopy, the practice of making multiple copies of originals to take to the printer can cut costs in some cases. The HP LaserJet 5SiMopier is touted as the first printer designed to make multiple copies; this method could save two cents a page.

New ''gapless'' printers pioneered by Heidelberg-Harris have been followed by other versions from Mitsubishi, KBA, and MAN Roland. The technology eliminates or minimizes the blanket and cylinder gaps and makes it feasible to build wide-format color quality offset presses that run at high speeds and take a digital image and print it on paper, film, canvas, or adhesive backed material for large format jobs is providing new sources of revenue. Once limited to pen plotters it is now 85 percent of the inkjet market. Changes in plotters have resulted in applications in quick print shops with large format color printing solutions.

Further Reading

Allerton, Haidee. ''One-Stop Shopping.'' *Training & Development,* July 1996.

''AlphaGraphics Credits Its Success to Strategy.'' *Graphic Arts Monthly,* September 1996.

''AlphaGraphics Makes Major Overseas Gains.'' *Graphic Arts Monthly,* June 1996.

''Around the World.'' *Franchising World,* September/October 1996.

Bates, Karl. ''Video Conference is Next Best Thing to Being There for That Special Day.'' *Detroit News,* 10 May 1996.

''Clients Linked to Franchises.'' *Graphic Arts Monthly,* January 1997.

Company News Archives. ''Corporate Profile for Sir Speedy, Inc., dated Oct. 22, 1999.'' New York: Business Wire, October, 1999. Available from http://www.businesswire.com/.

Currid, Cheryl. ''Better to 'Mopy' or Copy?'' *Informationweek,* 25 November 1996.

Dilger, Karen Abramic. ''Selling Smarts.'' *American Printer,* April 1996.

Ducey, Michael J. ''Wide-Format Catches Fire.'' *Graphic Arts Monthly,* December 1996.

Esler, Bill. ''Copier/Duplicators Meet the Press.'' *Graphic Arts Monthly,* April 1996.

———. ''The Quick Print Giants.'' *Graphic Arts Monthly,* December 1996.

Falck, Susan. ''PIP's Presses Roll with the Flow.'' *Franchising World,* November/December 1996.

Ferris, Fred. ''Super Threat?'' *American Printer,* July 1996.

Franklin's Printing. ''About Franklin's.'' Cypress, TX: International Center for Entrepreneurial Development, 2000. Available from http://www.franklins-printing.com/about.htm/.

Gilhooly, Rob. ''Kinko's Duplicating Firm's Success in Japan.'' *Japan Times Weekly International Edition,* 13 November 1995.

Johnson, Greg. ''A Pressing Matter: The Quick Print Business is Undergoing a Revolution.'' *Los Angeles Times,* 26 January 1997.

Hoover's Company Capsules. Austin, TX: Hoover's Inc., 2000. Available from http://www.hoovers.com/.

''Industry News.'' *Network.* December, 1999.

''Investment Fund Plans to Inject $200 Million Into Kinko's Chain.'' *New York Times,* 11 June 1996.

Kemper, Matt. ''Kinko's Offers Internet Access for Customers.'' *Atlanta Constitution,* 20 September 1996.

''Kwik Kopy Printing Corp., Cypress, Tex.'' *Inc.,* November 1995.

Larson, Polly. ''Small Business—Big Ideas.'' *Franchising World,* January/February 1997.

Lorenzi, Neal. ''Quick Printers Find Their Niche.'' *American Printer,* May 1996.

''Moore Corp.'' *New York Times,* 4 January 1996.

Moukheiber, Zina. '''I'm Just a Peddler.''' *Forbes,* 17 July 1995.

National Association of Quick Printers. ''Online.'' 1997. Available from http://www.naqp.org/index.html.

———. ''1997 NAQP Industry Pricing Study.''Available from http://www.naqp.org/resources/pristudy.html.

Noel, Jeffrey. ''Spinning a Web.'' *American Printer,* January 1997.

''Quick Printers on Demand.'' *American Printer,* September 1996.

Sanderson, Rhonda. ''Staying One Step Ahead.'' *Franchising World,* July/August 1995.

Schmitz, Barbara. ''Plotting Along with Inkjets.'' *Computer-Aided Engineering,* December 1996.

Smith, Richard. ''More Than a Copy Shop.'' *American Printer,* July 1996.

''Survey indicates Quick Printers Bullish, Plan to Expand.'' Chicago: Print Image International, February, 2000. Available from http://www.printimage.org/indNews/11.html/.

''The Business Services Boom.'' *Success,* March 1995.

Toth, Debora. ''Multiple Media Spur Wide-Format Imaging.'' *Graphic Arts Monthly,* January 1997.

U.S. Census Bureau. *1997 Economic Census* Washington, DC: GPO 2000. Available from http://www.census.gov.

U.S. Department of Commerce, Bureau of the Census. *Service Annual Survey: 1997.* Washington: GPO, 1999.

U.S. Department of Labor. Bureau of Labor Statistics. *Occupational Outlook Handbook.* Washington: GPO, 1996.

Wilken, Earl. ''Look, Its's a Printer, It's a Copier: No, Its a Mopier.'' *Graphic Arts Monthly,* January 1997.

D & B Business Rankings 1999, Bethlehem: Dun & Bradstreet, 1999.

SIC 7335

COMMERCIAL PHOTOGRAPHY

This category includes establishments primarily engaged in providing commercial photography services to advertising agencies, publishers, and other business and industrial users. Establishments primarily engaged in still and video portrait photography are classified in **SIC 7221: Photographic Studios, Portrait,** and those primarily engaged in mapmaking are classified in **SIC 7389: Business Services, Not Elsewhere Classified.** Establishments primarily engaged in producing commercial video tape or films are classified in **SIC 7812: Motion Picture and Video Tape Production.**

NAICS CODE(S)

481219 (Other Nonscheduled Air Transportation)
541922 (Commercial Photography)

Commercial photographers provide the images for American business. Whether those images are as simple as a daytime photograph of a small town ice cream shop for a newspaper advertisement, or as complex as a carefully lit, elaborately staged still photo of an ice cream sundae for a nationally distributed magazine advertisement, they are created by commercial photographers. Commercial photographers also provide photos for annual reports, brochures, catalogs, and a range of other business needs. ''Commercial work means: You make it. We photograph it,'' photographer Bud Hjerstedt told the *Northeastern Wisconsin Business Review.* ''You can't think of a single thing, a single company, that cannot use photography.''

The commercial photography industry is remarkably eclectic, with few boundaries in terms of business size or activity. Large cities may provide employment for hundreds of commercial photographers, some working out of shops with several thousand square feet of studio space and sophisticated film processing facilities, some working freelance with their own equipment and facilities. In larger markets, many commercial shops develop specialties in some area of photography, such as food, fashion, or industrial photography. Small towns, on the other hand, may have just a few commercial photographers who shoot an advertising layout one day, a senior picture the next, and a wedding on the weekend. At the time of the last industry census in 1992, there were just over 4,200 commercial photography establishments with combined revenues of $1.5 billion operating in the United States. By 1997, the Bureau of Census estimated that sales rose to $2.2 billion.

Salaries for commercial photographers depend on the region and how hard the photographer is willing to work. Ken Bourdon of Bourdon & Bourdon Studios told the *Tribune Business Weekly* that a small town photographer may charge between $600 and $1,200 a day for his or her work, while a photographer working in a large city can charge from $2,000 to $3,500 a day. Such per day charges include all the lighting, staging, and assistants that the photographer may employ. The U.S. Bureau of Labor Statistics indicated that there were over 154,000 people employed as photographers and camera operators in 1996; 4 out of 10 of these photographers were self-employed. Larger commercial photography shops also employ photo processors and lab technicians. Self-employed commercial photographers have the potential to earn much more than the salaried studio photographer, but the potential risk for failure is greater. An established freelancer with many jobs and contacts can make $350,000 in an average year. By contrast, median annual income for salaried photography/camera professionals was about $30,000—the top and bottom 10 percent earned $75,000 and $14,500 respectively.

The commercial photography industry has traditionally been open to self-starters who learned the trade in the armed services, at one of many photographic schools scattered throughout the country, or from a more experienced photographer. With some technical expertise and a flair for visual images, one could set up shop. As the industry becomes more sophisticated and more dependent on complex digital equipment, additional training will be required.

The leading technological development in the industry is digital image processing, which was revolutionized by the 1992 introduction of the Leaf Digital Studio Camera, made by Leaf Systems Inc. of Southboro, Massachusetts. The Leaf Camera, which sells for a base price of $29,000, converts visual images to computer pixels immediately. This allows the photographer to instantly view and manipulate the ''photograph'' on a computer screen. No film processing is required.

The cost of digital equipment remained stagnant through 1996 and into 1997. The cost of Leaf Systems equipment had not dropped since 1993. However, the equipment was expanding and improving at a phenomenal rate; new digital cameras and computer photography software, as well as new digital printers, were being developed that could make high resolution images on photographic paper almost as good as standard photographic prints. By the close of the century, Kodak, Ricoh, and Sony had all developed small, handheld compact digital cameras in the $300-$500 price range, including software. However, digital cameras with resolution comparable to standard photographic methods still sell at prices as high as $20,000.

For those studios that could afford the high price of going digital, it was a profitable transition. Infinite Photo & Imaging, an Arlington, Virginia full service lab, equipped itself with state-of-the-art cameras, computers, and printers to become a fully digitized lab in 1996. Their new equipment produced high quality 4x8 foot prints, the most requested size, with any style of paper needed for commercial, trade show, corporate, and museum printing. By the beginning of the year 2000, they were capable of producing the world's largest, seamless photograph (48 inches by 67 feet) and large-scale reproductions up to 80 feet in length.

A watershed for the industry came when Warner Bros. publicists for the 1994 film *Batman Forever* used some of the latest digital technology. Warner credited the technology with helping the film break summer box office records. Publicists used standard color negative cameras, but used digital scanners and printers to make the posters and publicity photographs. The digital printer used could create a print every 75 seconds, greatly speeding up their production. These images were also scanned onto CD-ROM for delivery to New York for processing onto the movie Web site. At the premiere of the movie in California, photos of Jim Carrey's arrival were taken on digital cameras, stored on a memory card that could hold up to 84 images, then sent via modem to New York. They were placed on the Web site before the premiere was over.

Digitizing has also changed the industry in unexpected ways; for example, it introduced companies to stock photographs kept on CD-ROMs. By 1997, stock photographs sold for $250 to $1,500, depending on quantity and demand. With a CD-ROM, a company could buy a disc containing thousands of stock images for a cost of $10 to $250.

Even as digital equipment becomes increasingly prominent, traditional cameras and films will remain a part of commercial photography for many years.

FURTHER READING

Curtin, Dennis. ''Choosing a Digital Camera.'' Marblehead, MA: ShortCourses Web Site, 2000. Available from http://www.shortcourses.com/.

Darnay, Arsen J., ed. *Services Industries USA.* 3rd ed. Detroit: Gale Research, 1996.

Hoover's Company Capsules. Austin, TX: Hoover's Inc., 2000. Available from http://www.hoovers.com/.

Lee, Mie-Yun. ''Stock Photographs Can Make Your Work Picture Perfect.'' *Business First of Buffalo,* 10 February 1997.

Rinowitz, Allen. ''High Tech Publicity Sets the World's Most Famous Crime Fighter Apart From the Crowd.'' *Photo Digital Imaging Magazine* 38, no. 8.

''The Cool to the Second Power Awards.'' *Photo Digital Imaging Magazine* 39, no. 2.

U.S. Department of Labor. *Occupational Outlook Handbook 1996-97.* Washington: GPO, 1996.

U.S. Department of Commerce, Bureau of the Census. *Service Annual Survey: 1997.* Washington: GPO, 1999.

Wilheim, Henry. ''Continuous Tone Prints are Now Possible in Jumbo Sizes.'' *Photo Electronic Imaging Magazine* 39, no. 5.

SIC 7336

COMMECIAL ART AND GRAPHIC DESIGN

This industry includes establishments primarily engaged in providing commercial art or graphic design services for advertising agencies, publishers, and other business and industrial users. Establishments primarily engaged in art, except commercial and medical, are classified in **SIC 8999: Services, Not Elsewhere Classified;** those engaged in medical art are classified in **SIC 8099: Health and Allied Services, Not Elsewhere Classified;** and those providing drafting services are classified in **SIC 7389: Business Services, Not Elsewhere Classified.**

NAICS CODE(S)

541430 (Graphic Design Services)

INDUSTRY SNAPSHOT

The commercial art and graphic design industry encompasses the business of selling artwork for business (promotional) purposes, rather than for strictly aesthetic purposes. The artwork can be produced using a myriad of techniques, including handpainting, computer-aided design software, and video cameras. Commercial art and graphic design can be found on posters, packages, films, and television.

Commercial art remains subject to many of the same standards of ''high art,'' regardless of its ultimate use or intended purpose. Therefore, a graphic designed for an advertisement may not be as significant as the Sistine Chapel murals, but the difference between them is one of degree rather than kind. Commercial art is similar to other art in that it is custom made, and it requires time, skill, judgment, taste, and background on the part of the artist to produce it; it is usually purchased before it is produced; and there are few fixed standards for evaluating the end-product. Personal taste and opinion determine the effectiveness of commercial art.

Commercial art differs from other art in value. According to *Forbes,* the value of commercial art diminishes quickly. For example, LeRoy Neiman's limited edition sports prints sold at commercial galleries for $2,000 to $20,000 when they were first produced. At an auction in 1992, Neiman prints sold for 5 to 20 cents on the original dollar price. In contrast, the value of paintings by Pablo Picasso or Vincent Van Gogh greatly appreciates over the years.

ORGANIZATION AND STRUCTURE

The structure of the commercial art industry is characterized by individual freelance artists and corporations who produce commercial art graphics as well as the businesses who buy the art. In the 1970s, this industry was characterized by many individual freelance artists who sold their work to agents—middlemen—who then found the ultimate buyer of the art work.

Due to vertical integration and advances in technology in the 1980s and 1990s, many companies, such as advertising agencies, have created their own art and graphics departments. These departments have allowed firms to exercise more control over the commercial art process. Moreover, an abundance of commercial art and graphic design firms have entered the industry. The number of freelance artists has declined as the number of specialized design departments and firms has increased.

Artists have been using high-technology equipment such as computers, plotters, and printers since the 1960s, but the technological revolution of the 1980s has made such devices as color copiers, scanners, still video cameras, and desktop publishing software widely available for use as artistic tools. In commercial art and graphic design, high-tech equipment has all but replaced paint brushes and drawing pens at magazines, newspapers, and advertising agencies.

Desktop publishing (DTP) is a good example of how technology has changed this industry. DTP has become one of the most widely used forms of creating commercial and graphic art. DTP can produce attractive, artistic pages using different typefaces and graphic elements in harmony. The advantage of DTP is that even the smallest firm can cost-effectively publish in-house.

The basic requirements to engage in DTP are a computer with the appropriate software package, a mouse, a scanner, and a color printer. In the late 1990s, the cost of a small, high-end desktop computer dropped to under $1,000 while a production system cost about $10,000. Due to these relatively low startup costs, desktop publishing has allowed magazines, newspapers, and advertising agencies to create in-house graphics departments. Moreover, smaller entrepreneurs have emerged to create spectacular art and graphics with little investment in capital compared to other businesses.

Frequently, situations arise where the law plays an important part in commercial art and graphic design. In most commercial art and graphic design businesses, a legal counsel is hired for nearly all actual and potential legal problems. The services of a knowledgeable lawyer can save time, money, and misery. The major issues in commercial art and graphic design include contracts, agents, copyrights, royalties, patents, bailments, and ownership of artwork.

Each time an artist accepts an assignment for artwork, he or she enters into a contract. For contracts to be considered valid, a contract must have three common elements: offer, acceptance, and consideration. An offer may be made orally, in writing, or by conduct. For example, if a publisher from *Time* magazine delivers a story manuscript to an artist who is aware of the prices paid by the magazine, the assumption is that delivery constitutes an offer to the artist to illustrate the story at those prices. Acceptance also may be communicated verbally, in writing, or by conduct. In the *Time* example, the retention of the manuscript by the artist may be construed as acceptance of the offer. However, a written document stating the artist's acceptance would give the artist greater leverage in the court system and greater protection. Consideration is defined by the publisher's implied promise to pay at the known rates and by the artist's implied promise to illustrate the story. The consideration constitutes one party promising to pay a certain sum in exchange for the other party's promising to perform a certain act.

An agent is someone who acts on behalf of another—the principal—in dealing with a third party. The types of agents most commonly found in the art business are salespeople, advertising agencies, representatives, galleries, and studios. Agents are used by commercial artists and firms to allow their art to reach may outlets—buyers—who may be interested in the work. Agents, therefore, are middlemen who find the parties who will purchase the artists' or firms' work.

The relationship between the artist/firm and the agent may be created by an oral understanding, by written agreement, or by implication. The law states that a true agent may not serve two masters. Therefore, the agent for the artist may not serve a third party—another artist—who has negative competitive ramifications for the artist.

Copyrights protect artistic works against unauthorized copying. In certain circumstances, an artist is wise to gain a copyright or royalties for a work instead of an outright sale of the artwork. A copyright is a limited monopoly granted by the government to an artist. A copyright allows an artist to sell limited reproduction rights to several parties that would not conflict with one another in the use of the work. The duration of the copyright is 28 years and can be renewed for another 28 years. Specific artistic works that may be protected by copyright include works of art, models or designs for works for art, and reproductions of works of art.

A royalty arrangement with the manufacturer or publisher guarantees an artist a fee for each piece of his or her work that is sold. A royalty agreement may be most applicable when an unknown quantity of a product may be sold, such as in the sale of calendars, maps, greeting cards, and children's books. The royalty arrangement provides protection for both the publisher and the artist.

Design patents may be secured for new, original product designs that are novel and considered an invention. A piece of art is considered patentable if it has not been previously known or used by others in the United States, has not been patented in the United States or abroad, and has not been in public use for more than one year prior to the application for a patent, unless it is proven to be abandoned.

When an artist delivers a painting to an individual or studio for use as a sample of his or her work, the legal relation of bailment will ordinarily be created. The title to the material remains with the bailor, or the artist. The liability of the bailee, or the studio or individual, will vary. However, generally speaking, bailees' liabilities are in direct proportion to the extent of the benefit they are expected to derive from the bailment. Therefore, if the artwork is lost or damaged, bailees are liable for greater damages if they had been using it to procure work for profit, than if they had held the artwork for safekeeping without compensation.

In the absence of an oral or written agreement, the full rights of ownership belong to the purchaser. An artist can legally protect him or herself by presenting a specific written agreement. The artist can write into the purchase order any retention of rights or additional compensation requirements.

Background and Development

In terms of revenues and number of employees, commercial art and graphic design establishments are smaller institutions than other service industry establishments. Interestingly, the average payroll per employee in commercial art and graphic design establishments was in the mid $20,000, compared to $17-$20,000 for other service industries. These figures demonstrate that the higher salaries were justified by the significantly higher profitability of the commercial art and graphic design industry when compared to other service industries.

In the mid-1990s, the industry had an estimated 13,184 establishments, which employed about 51,300 people. Revenues for that year were estimated to be slightly less than that of 1995—$6.12 billion, as compared to $6.2 billion in 1995.

California and New York had the most establishments, with 1,765 and 1,618, respectively. Other states with high numbers of establishments included Illinois (940), Florida (637), Texas (598), and New Jersey (507). Wyoming and Alaska had the lowest number of establishments, with 10 and 5, respectively.

Current Conditions

Computers continue to change the face of the commercial art and graphic design community. Hard copy mechanical art has been replaced by electronic mechanicals and film-based photography has been replaced by digital photography. In fact, at the beginning of 2000, digital proofing represented 25 percent of the market. Additionally, the increased use of color printers by advertising agencies, corporations and design firms also has impacted the industry.

In the late 1990s, the Graphic Communications Association of the Printing Industries of America developed

GRACoL, General Requirements for Applications and Commercial Offset Lithography. GRACoL is a series of specifications that ensures uniformity of color.

Another concern facing small, independent commercial art and graphic design firms was their ability to compete in the job market. A human resources survey conducted by the Printing Industry of America found that more than 60 percent of firms with less than 10 employees do not offer benefit programs.

According to the Bureau of Labor Statistics, jobs in desktop publishing are expected to increase by 72.6 percent in the decade ending in 2008. A 27.1 percent increase is expected for designers; 25.7 percent for commercial artists; 23 percent for advertising and marketing sales; and only .2 percent for printing jobs.

INDUSTRY LEADERS

Most of the top 10 companies in the industry were privately held. The top 2 companies sold more than twice their nearest competition. Continental Graphics Corp. and Applied Graphics Technologies were the leading companies in the industry, with each posting in the neighborhood of $250 to $300 million in sales annually. Applied Graphics Technology is part of the communications empire headed by Mort Zuckerman, owner of *U.S. News and World Report.*

The other industry leaders were Creative Associates with $86 million in sales; Avionics Research Corp. ($80 million); GML Inc. ($17 million); Stanford Blaine Design Inc. ($10 million); Desktop Graphics Inc. ($9 million); T-Square Express Inc. ($9 million); King Graphics Inc. ($9 million); and United Letter Service Inc. ($8 million).

FURTHER READING

Darnay, Arsen J., ed. *Service Industries USA. 3rd ed.* Detroit: Gale Research, 1996.

Drury, Tracey. ''Graphic arts companies struggle to find benefits.'' *Business First of Buffalo,* 18 October 99.

Gruman, Galen. ''Graphics and Publishing.'' *Macworld,* February 1996, 100-101.

Robertshaw, Nicky. ''Constant Change.'' *Memphis Business Journal* 10 December 1999

Roth, Jill. ''Proofs for all reasons.'' *American Printer,* October 1999.

Sentinery, Robert. ''How To Get Great Design With Desktop Publishing.'' *Source Book Supplement* 1996, 211.

Siklos, Richard. ''Sweetheart, get me rewrite.'' *Business Week,* 30 November 1998.

Stoller, Peter M. ''Should You Fire Your Service Bureau?'' October 1996, 122-126.

SIC 7338

SECRETARIAL AND COURT REPORTING SERVICES

This category covers establishments primarily engaged in providing secretarial, word processing, typing, editing, proofreading, resume writing, letter writing, stenographic, or court reporting services.

NAICS CODE(S)

561410 (Document Preparation Services)
561492 (Court Reporting and Stenotype Services)

Many governmental bodies, businesses, and individuals have discovered that by outsourcing tasks like word processing, proofreading, and document transcription to specialized secretarial and court reporting services, they can save time and money, avoid adding to or straining their staff and equipment, and focus on their own core functions.

By the late 1990s, there were approximately 18,000 commercial establishments offering secretarial and court reporting services nationwide.

An official court reporter traditionally produces a court transcript containing such information as witness testimony, attorney arguments and examination of witnesses, and judicial comments and instructions. A freelance court reporter typically transcribes pre-trial depositions arranged by attorneys. In 1999, the National Court Reporters Association maintained approximately 31,000 members and sponsored various certification programs. Court reporting agencies generally provide some training to employees in the form of specialized shorthand reporting. Ranging from two to four years in length, these training programs focus on computer operation, grammar, law, and attaining at least 225 words per minute on a stenotype machine. Typically, employee benefits such as health insurance and pension plans are not offered.

While secretarial services perform a large portion of contracted work on their own premises, services are also provided on-site and in ''satellite offices'' set up within larger businesses. A contributor for *Home-Office Computing* reported word processing rates of $2 to $4 per page and secretarial labor rates of $15 to $20 per hour.

A vital question facing participants in this industry is how technology will alter it. Some industry observers have predicted the demise of professional services such as proofreading, editing, and court reporting due to advances in computer technology and software. For example, the use of computer software programs capable of spell checking has caused a decline in the need for proofreading services. Still, automated editing programs that can identify an ungrammatical or awkwardly constructed sentence remain unable to identify illogical or libelous assertions. High error rates still existed with the use of such voice and speech systems by 1999.

Despite the advances in computer-aided transcription and voice-activated computer transcription, the profession of court reporting has flourished rather than suffered a decline. According to the National Court Reporters Association, more than 90 percent of all court reporters used some form of computer-aided transcription (CAT) in 1999. New advances in realtime reporting, where notes are converted into text and projected on monitors or screens as they are recorded, allow synchronized video testimony. Realtime reporting has complied with the Americans With Disabilities Act by making testimony available to the vision and hearing impaired. James Stith remarked in *Career World* that while the use of videotape recording equipment has increased, it will not replace human reporters. He noted that ''the technology is not as reliable as the human ear. It breaks down, and it takes longer for a person to listen to a tape than to read a transcript.''

By 1999 approximately 25 percent of all court reporters were using the Internet to e-mail, research, network, and advertise. It is predicted that during the first few years of the new millenium, court reporters will be using the Internet for nearly every aspect of their job. Transcripts are predicted to become available ''on-demand.'' Furthermore, new software was developed to enable reporters, attorneys, and litigation staff to review and transcripts more efficiently.

By the end of the century, the courts and attorneys were able to search transcripts using key words and phrases to reexamine testimonies. Realtime text has made it possible for the court reporter to provide an instant transcript to be displayed on computer monitors or projection screens for viewing. Besides its use for television captioning, this technology made it possible for the hearing-impaired to participate in trials, and it also extended the length of a career for judges suffering hearing loss.

Industry Leaders

In 1999, the largest U.S. court reporting firm was Esquire Communications. Although law firms made up the majority of its clients, the company also provided service to insurance companies and various corporations. Total sales for 1998 equaled $111 million, up 108 percent over 1997. Esquire owns the subsidiary DepoNet, which is a referral network consisting of 400 independent contracted firms providing court reporting and related services. Since 1997 Esquire has acquired more than 40 new companies, thus continuing to strengthen its presence in the legal field.

In 1997, the Bureau of Labor Statistics reported estimates sales receipts at $3 billion for the industry. Nationwide, freelance court reporters earn an average yearly income of $45,000, but 25 percent were able to make more than $64,000 annually. Earnings were based on the reporter's education, experience, and geographic location. Budget cuts in the courts were expected to decrease the number of reporters working directly for them, but the need for freelancers and reporters willing to provide services was predicted to increase through the first decade of the new century.

Further Reading

Encyclopedia of Careers and Vocational Guidance. Chicago: J.G. Ferguson Publishing, 1997.

Hoover's Company Capsule. *Esquire Communications.* 1999.

''Realtime FACTS.'' National Court Reports Association, March 1997. Available from http://www.ncraonline.org/rtfacts.html.

U.S. Department of Commerce. *Census of Service Industries 1997.* Washington, DC: GPO, 1997.

''Verbatim Reporters Center.'' National Court Reporters Association. 1999. Available from http://www.ncraonline.org.html.

SIC 7342

DISINFECTING AND PEST CONTROL SERVICES

This industry covers establishments primarily engaged in disinfection and in termite, insect, rodent, and other pest control, generally in dwellings or other buildings. Establishments primarily engaged in pest control for lawns or agricultural production are classified in various agricultural service industries.

NAICS Code(s)

561720 (Janitorial Services)
561710 (Exterminating and Pest Control Services)

Industry Snapshot

The building disinfection and pest control industry is a multibillion dollar industry that overlaps with the building cleaning and maintenance service industry (see **SIC 7349: Building Cleaning and Maintenance Services, Not Elsewhere Classified**). For example, ServiceMaster LP, a leader in the building cleaning and maintenance field, owns Terminix, Inc., one of the nation's largest pest control concerns.

Disinfecting and pest control companies are either independently owned enterprises, franchises, or part of a national company. Two of the largest franchise companies in the United States are Terminix, Inc. and Orkin Exterminators.

CURRENT CONDITIONS

Current research targets development of new types of pesticides, cleaning products, and other compounds for everyday use that are earth-friendly and non-toxic to humans and other animal life. But while development continues, the first choice among commercial establishments is to use those chemicals that have been formulated for the industry. Most products in use today are still toxic to the pests they are designed to eliminate, but toxicity is relative to exposure. While the level of toxicity of many of these products has been diluted in recent years, they still present a hazard to humans and domestic animals if used improperly. The industry recognizes the need for less toxic materials and such materials are in the development stages.

Types of Non-toxic Pest Control. Several methodologies other than the toxic chemical method of pest control are available. Preventive measures include sanitation and moisture control that aim to maintain unattractive environments for pests to dwell and reproduce. Mechanical means include caulking, screening, and traps. Insecticidal soaps are most effective against insects such as fleas. Insect Growth Regulators (IGRs) and pheromones are both hormonal methods for treating pest infestations. IGRs are laboratory-made growth hormones naturally found within insects. Their application prevents the insects from reaching maturity and thus reproducing. Pheromones—scent hormones—are used to bait traps and trick male insects into thinking they have found a female. Thus, that particular male does not achieve his reproductive goals. Repellents include citronella, eucalyptus, wormwood, and other commercially prepared compounds. They do not kill but rather repel the targeted pest with no ill effects to the pest or the user. Biological controls are probably best known by those in agriculture. It is the intentional use of ''good'' organisms against ''bad'' ones. For example, trichogamma wasps can be used to control meal moths. A more common example is the use of cats to catch mice. While environmentally these non-toxic methods may have merit and some degree of effectiveness in certain situations, toxic chemical products are more often used for reasons of efficiency, speed, expense.

INDUSTRY LEADERS

In 1999, the national leaders in sales among companies with interests in this industry were Service Master of Consumer Services LP, of Memphis, Tennessee, the owner of Terminix, with $910 million in revenue; and Orkin Extermination Company of Atlanta, Georgia, with $555 million in revenue.

WORKFORCE

In 1999, there were 91,800 employees in this industry, of which 73,300 were in production. Employees worked an average of 37.9 hours per week for a salary of $11.93 per hour. Employment prospects were expected to increase through 2006 due to higher standards of living and increased regulation of pesticides, requiring more intensive, inclusive, and proactive treatments.

FURTHER READING

Bureau of Labor Statistics. *Employment Statistics,* January 2000. Available from http://www.bls.gov.

Dun's Census of American Business 1995. Bethlehem, PA: Dun & Bradstreet, 1995.

Encyclopedia of Career and Vocational Guidance. Chicago, IL: J.G. Ferguson Publishing, 1997.

''Pest Controller.'' *Occupational Outlook Quarterly.* Washington, DC: Winter 1998.

Ward's Business Directory of U.S. Private and Public Companies. Detroit: Gale Research, 1999.

SIC 7349

BUILDING CLEANING AND MAINTENANCE SERVICES, NOT ELSEWHERE CLASSIFIED

This classification covers establishments primarily engaged in furnishing building cleaning and maintenance services, not elsewhere classified, such as window cleaning, janitorial service, floor waxing, and office cleaning.

NAICS CODE(S)

561720 (Janitorial Services)

INDUSTRY SNAPSHOT

The building cleaning and maintenance industry provides services to a wide range of clients—private homes, multifamily residences such as apartment buildings and housing projects, schools, libraries, museums, nursing homes, hospitals, government offices, hotels/motels and resorts, restaurants, churches and synagogues, community and senior citizen centers, airports, bus stations, railroad stations, marinas, and other commercial buildings and businesses.

In 1998 there were about 58,220 cleaning and maintenance businesses not elsewhere classified in the United States. The industry as a whole generated an estimated $31 billion in sales, an increase of over 14 percent from the previous year. The industry employed 912 million cleaners and janitors in 1999. Of that number, about 20 percent were employed by cleaning and janitorial service companies. About a third of those employed worked on a part-time basis (less than 35 hours a week). The other 80 percent were employed by schools, hospitals, or other institutions or businesses as in-house cleaning staff.

Organization and Structure

Service industries are an increasingly important element of the American economy. One of the fastest growing service industries is the cleaning and building maintenance business. Some analysts estimate that the number of employees in the industry in the year 2005 could well exceed five million.

With changes in needs and technology, the old view of the janitor as someone who only swept out a basement has changed dramatically. While today's custodians or cleaners may still employ brooms, they also make use of a variety of other machines, tools, and skills to keep buildings clean and well maintained. For the most part, custodians and building maintenance employees work indoors, in heated and air-conditioned environments. Work shifts vary tremendously, and some establishments, such as hospitals, large hotels, or transportation companies may employ such personnel on a round-the-clock basis. Entry-level janitors can earn between $12,500 and $14,000 annually while experienced janitors may earn $15,000 to $20,000 per year, and college-educated managers can earn $37,000 or more.

The types and sizes of cleaning and maintenance businesses range from the single-person enterprise to franchises and large, nationally recognized companies that employ thousands of people. Smaller companies tend to service residential dwellings primarily because of the fewer demands on resources (employees, skills, and time.)

For the most part, larger companies service commercial buildings, schools, and apartment houses because larger numbers of employees with varied skills are needed to do the job and because fees are higher for such establishments. This facet of the industry has become highly organized; more than 1,400 building service contractors belong to a national organization, the Building Contractors Association.

The number of such service companies has grown over the last few years because they have developed increasingly efficient and economical ways to accomplish cleaning and maintenance tasks. Part of that efficiency results from the ways in which a contractor contracts its services with the specific need of a particular client in mind: individual assignment, crew assignment, specific cleaning assignment, and general assignments.

In individual assignment, one person is responsible for a specific area. That person must know how to do all the different kinds of cleaning required, as well as basic maintenance. In a crew assignment, a team is responsible for an area, usually larger than a single area. Among them, they have all the skills required for the proper cleaning and maintenance required.

Specific cleaning assignments are different in that each member of the team has specific skills for a particular area. The team as a whole performs a wide range of jobs. Finally, the general assignment jobs provide almost limitless variety. There may be enough work for one person or a whole team of people. The responsibilities, as well as how many people will be assigned, vary according to needs.

Industry Leaders

The top three companies in this industry by sales volume in 1999 are International Service Systems, Inc. ($2 billion), American Building Maintenance Industries Inc. (ABM) ($629 million), and Unicco Service Company ($522 million). Founded in 1909 by Morris Rosenberg who invested $4.50 in a bucket, mop, sponge, broom, and brush, ABM and its divisions posted sales in 1999 of over $600 million. In addition to the usual janitorial services for owners of commercial, industrial, and institutional buildings, the company offers a wide range of services that includes: cleaning; elevator maintenance; air conditioning, heating, engineering, and energy conservation services; lighting and electrical sign maintenance; building security; parking garage management; and janitorial supplies. One small portion of its business also included pest control. However, since the company's focus had been to provide services to commercial, industrial, or institutional clients, the residential nature of the pest control business seemed inappropriate. ABM therefore sold this division to Terminix in October of 1991.

Two other large cleaning and building maintenance companies in the country are both franchise chains: JaniKing and ServiceMaster. JaniKing had 5,500 units in 1997. ServiceMaster, in business since 1947, had more than 4,306 franchise units in 1997. Both companies offer services that include residential and commercial cleaning services, disaster restoration, and specialized services such as window and carpet cleaning. In addition, ServiceMaster offers pest control and lawn care, and provides management services to health care facilities, schools, and factories.

In November 1986 ServiceMaster purchased Terminix International, the nation's second largest pest control company. At the time, the company owned 164 outlets and 150 franchises nationwide. Merry Maids, a home-based cleaning business founded in 1980, came into the ServiceMaster fold, as did a Memphis-area home appliance maintenance and plumbing service with a client list of approximately 400. Then in 1990, ServiceMaster purchased two divisions of Waste Management, Inc., a pest control business and a lawn care service, further diversifying beyond its core building maintenance niche.

WORKFORCE

In 1999 there were 912 million workers employed by this industry, most of whom worked under 30 hours a week for an average wage of $8.68 per hour. The U.S. Bureau of Labor Statistics predicted the residential cleaning industry would have the second largest job growth rate through 2005. In the mid-1990s a projected 9.4 million households paid a professional to clean their homes (9 percent of all homes).

FURTHER READING

Darnay, Arsen J., ed. *Service Industries USA.* Detroit: Gale Research, 1999.

Dorch, Shannon. "Tomorrow's Markets." *American Demographics,* November 1996.

Dun's Census of American Business 1995. Bethlehem, Penn.: Dun & Bradstreet Corporation, 1995.

Encyclopedia of Career and Vocational Guidance. Chicago: J.G. Ferguson Publishing, 1997.

"Hoover's Company Capsules." *Hoover's Online,* 2000. Available from http://www.hoovers.com.

Smyth, Julie Carr. "Franchise Wants to Clean Up the Capital Region." *The (Albany, N.Y.)Times Union,* 2 January 1997.

U.S. Bureau of Labor Statistics. *Employment Statistics,* 2000. Available from http://www.bls.gov.

———. *1998-99 Occupational Outlook,* 2000. Available from http://stats.bls.gov.

Ward's Business Directory of U. S. Private and Public Companies. Detroit: Gale Research, 1999.

SIC 7352

MEDICAL EQUIPMENT RENTAL AND LEASING

This classification comprises establishments primarily engaged in renting or leasing (except finance leasing) medical equipment. Establishments included within this industry may also sell medical supplies. Those establishments primarily engaged in finance leasing are classified in **SIC 6159: Miscellaneous Business Credit Institutions.**

NAICS CODE(S)

532291 (Home Health Equipment Rental)
532490 (Other Commercial and Industrial Machinery and Equipment Rental and Leasing)

The medical equipment rental and leasing industry provides an alternative to purchasing equipment outright and had significant growth for much of the 1990s. For many individuals and health care institutions, the advantages of renting or leasing expensive, high-technology equipment—subject to obsolescence as advances in medical technology spawned new, improved equipment—outweighed the advantages of purchasing such equipment. These advantages included preserving cash flow, increased flexibility to replace old equipment, and improved timeliness in acquiring the newest technologies. In the early 1990s, the industry generated roughly $1.5 billion in sales, representing 5.1 percent of the total yearly leasing volume in the United States. According to a 1995 survey, approximately 63 percent of hospitals used some from of lease financing for medical equipment. A similar 1992 study indicated only 14 percent of hospitals used lease financing. Volume of medical equipment leasing is affected by increased cash reserves, attractive bond financing, and the growing market for refurbished equipment. In 1997, sales of refurbished medical equipment were estimated at $240 million; total business activity in this industry was estimated at $3.9 billion, a 3 percent increase since 1993.

Revenues in the medical equipment leasing and rental industry were expected to grow from $5.6 billion in 1999 to $8.3 billion by 2003. In 1998, a marketing study by Finova Copelco Capital and DVI estimated that 25 percent of all medical equipment was leased. Of that, an estimated $2.5 billion of new medical equipment was purchased through leasing. Markets for the industry in 2000 and beyond were hospitals, diagnostic imaging centers, chronic disease treatment centers, and physician group practices/clinics.

The medical equipment rental and leasing industry was comprised of a majority of relatively small businesses. The typical service establishment in the early 1990s employed 13 people, while on average a medical equipment rental and leasing establishment employed only 8. However, by the end of the decade, larger corporate players dominated the market. In 1998, sales leaders in this industry included Apria Healthcare Group Inc. with 8,175 employees and revenues of $933.8 million; MEDIQ, Inc. which posted almost $181 million in sales with 1,271 employees; and Universal Hospital Services, Inc., 462 employees and sales of $69 million.

Nearly 85 percent of the medical equipment rental and leasing establishments in the late 1980s were owned by corporations, compared to about a 60 percent average for other service industries. This preponderance of corporate ownership is due largely to the expensive nature of medical equipment, which at once predicated the industry's existence and limited entry to those individuals or corporations possessing substantial cash reserves. Sole proprietorships constitute 10 percent of industry establishments, compared to over 30 percent in other service industries. The remaining 5 percent are controlled through partnerships.

Despite the large number of establishments located in Texas, the greatest regional concentrations of medical equipment rental and supply businesses are located in the eastern United States, particularly New York, New Jersey, and Pennsylvania, which have 732 establishments. The rest of the medical equipment and rental businesses are scattered throughout the United States.

Further Reading

Darnay, Arsen J., ed. *Service Industries USA.* 3rd ed. Detroit: Gale Research, 1996.

Dun's Census of American Business 1995. Bethlehem, PA: Dun & Bradstreet Corporation, 1995.

"Financing Capital Equipment: Leasing Looking Better and Better." *Hospital Materials Management,* June 1995.

Hoover's Company Capsules. Austin, TX: Hoover's Inc., 2000. Available from http://www.hoovers.com/.

"The U.S. Medical Equipment Leasing and Rental Industry: the Status of the Industry in 1999." Tampa, FL: Marketdata Enterprises, Inc., 1999. Available from http://library.northernlight.com/CK19991221010001774.html?cb=0&sc=0#doc/.

U.S. Department of Commerce, Bureau of the Census. *Service Annual Survey: 1997.* Washington: GPO, 1999.

Ward's Business Directory of U.S. Private and Public Companies 1997. Detroit: Gale Research, 1997.

SIC 7353

HEAVY CONSTRUCTION EQUIPMENT RENTAL AND LEASING

This classification covers establishments primarily engaged in renting or leasing (except finance leasing) heavy construction equipment, with or without operators. Establishments primarily engaged in financial leasing are classified in **SIC 6159: Miscellaneous Business Credit Institutions.**

NAICS Code(s)

234990 (All Other Heavy Construction)

532412 (Construction, Mining and Forestry Machinery and Equipment Rental and Leasing)

Industry Snapshot

The U.S. Census Bureau estimated that $3.8 billion was directly attributed to heavy construction equipment rental and leasing firms in the early 1990s. By 1999, sales in the equipment rental industry were projected to reach nearly $20 billion dollars. The number of establishments in this industry grew from 4,390 in 1988 to 5,790 in 1995. However, in 1997 the number of establishments had fallen to 4,961 as larger companies were buying up smaller ones and consolidating their operations. In 1997, the heavy construction equipment rental and leasing industry had a total average annual payroll of nearly $1.9 billion, and employed an estimated 53,700 individuals.

The heavy construction industry remained in a slump in the early 1990s, but showed signs of an upturn by the mid-1990s. Throughout 1996, industry sales and activity experienced a slow growth at 3 percent overall. As a result, leasing and rental of heavy construction equipment registered a slight, corresponding increase. By 1999, the demand for equipment rentals continued to be very strong. Industry analysts estimated that overall revenues had grown by about 20 percent per annum over the last ten years.

Organization and Structure

This industry is concerned only with equipment rental and leasing arrangements that qualify as "operating" leases. Operating leases are generally short-term arrangements that allow contractors to acquire equipment for a fraction of the asset's useful life. "Financing" leases, on the other hand, are longer term arrangements that allow contractors to acquire equipment over a period of steady payments.

Construction contracting companies (lessees) lease or rent heavy equipment from leasing companies (lessors) under the assumption that higher productivity and profits are derived from equipment use, rather than from ownership of the equipment. In other words, companies that lease and rent equipment believe that they can generate greater returns by investing capital in business ventures other than equipment ownership. In contrast, firms that rent or lease equipment to contractors do so under the assumption that they can garner greater returns by investing their resources in, and managing, equipment—not building with the machinery.

One advantage accorded the lessee is flexible terms. Arrangements can be adjusted to the user's unique market conditions, cash flow expectations, equipment needs, and tax situation. Leasing or renting also allows the lessee to defer the risk of losses caused by obsolescence inherent in the purchase of heavy equipment. Furthermore, leasing frees the lessee's capital for investment in other ventures that would normally be consumed by the hefty down payment and debt burden usually required by purchase agreements.

Lessors benefit from the leasing arrangement because they typically have greater expertise in the equipment market than their clients and can more efficiently manage investments in expensive equipment. In most cases, lessors can offer equipment to the lessee for a price that is highly competitive to what the lessee would have to pay if it financed a purchase. Advantages that lessors cultivate include greater bargaining power when purchasing equipment, an increased ability to liquidate used equipment, lower financing costs, and lower equipment maintenance fees. Lessors can also benefit more than many lessees from various tax laws that apply to leasing, such as depreciation allowances.

In a study conducted by the CIT Group in 1996, 62 percent of contractors who intended to lease equipment in 1997 cited "limited need" as a major reason for leasing equipment. For the fourth straight year, "cost" continued to decline as a reason for leasing equipment. However, "unexpected need" gained popularity as a frequently cited reason for leasing equipment in 1997. By 2000 there was also a growing realization by contractors that it was more economical to rent than buy, unless the equipment could be utilized more than 75 percent of the year. By leasing, they were also able to access more and different types of equipment while taking advantage of the best technology available.

Equipment and Projects. The principal types of equipment leased and rented by firms included bulldozers, cranes, and earth moving equipment. Earth moving equipment includes a wide range of machinery such as tractors, trenchers, scrapers, graders, and crawlers. Miscellaneous pieces of construction machinery such as tunneling equipment, well drills, loaders, cutters, compactors, excavators, oversized trucks, and portable mixers rounded out the industry's offerings. While some companies owned and leased many types of equipment for various heavy construction activities, other firms specialized in renting equipment for a specific line of work.

The largest manufacturer of the leasing industry's equipment in 1999 was Caterpillar Inc., which was also the largest supplier in the world. Other large manufacturers included CNH Global, Terex Corp., and John Deere. These companies, along with 700 others in the United States, accounted for most equipment sales to leasing companies, as well as 70 percent of all worldwide equipment sales.

The two basic divisions of the market for which leasing companies provided equipment were public and private. Private heavy construction activities included commercial and industrial projects that were completed with the intent of generating a profit for the owner of the project. Examples of private heavy construction projects include office buildings, manufacturing facilities, hotels and other commercial buildings, golf courses, oil wells, private electric utilities, hospitals, and private prolonged care institutions. In 1999, total U.S. expenditures for new private non-residential construction were $175.2 billion.

Public heavy construction activities for which equipment was rented or leased were completed with public dollars, and not necessarily with the intent of generating a profit. Examples of such projects include schools, highways, water works, public utility plants, dams, railroads, canals, prisons, hazardous waste site clean-ups, and landfills. Indeed, real public works construction expenditures had been on a nearly uninterrupted upward trend since hitting bottom at $78.9 billion in 1982 and 1983. At $131.3 billion, real public works spending in 2000 was forecast to be 66 percent above the lows of the early 1980s.

BACKGROUND AND DEVELOPMENT

The heavy equipment rental and leasing business in America emerged as a recognizable industry during the U.S. construction boom of the 1960s. Although little of the construction equipment used during this time was rented or leased, some contractors began to realize advantages related to borrowing specialty equipment for short-term uses. Construction markets in the United States remained relatively strong in the 1970s and early 1980s, despite cyclical downturns, and leasing activity increased as a result of regulatory changes that made leasing more appealing to some companies. For instance, investment tax credits conveyed benefits to lessors of equipment that invested in new machinery. Furthermore, depreciation allowances were modified at various times and became particularly beneficial for most heavy equipment lessors during the early and mid-1980s. These allowances permitted lessors to deduct from their tax burden larger amounts of expenses associated with equipment depreciation. Depending on the type of equipment being depreciated, some lessors were able to increase their profits by completely depreciating pieces of machinery long before their economic, or useful, life was complete.

In addition to favorable federal policies, the renting and leasing industry was helped by the construction boom of the mid-1980s. During this time, the total value of new construction soared from $332 billion during 1983 to nearly $420 billion by 1987. But while the amount of heavy equipment rented increased during this period, most companies continued to prefer to purchase their machinery; lessors thus enjoyed only a minor share of the entire equipment market. In fact, throughout the 1980s, contractors owned more than 90 percent of the equipment used for heavy construction.

The industry began to experience difficulties in the late 1980s. In 1987, the commercial construction market began plummeting into a virtual, and prolonged, depression. New commercial construction, not including maintenance and rehabilitation, fell from about $87 billion in 1985 to $67.5 billion in 1988 and $53.8 billion by 1992.

In addition to the recessed market, regulatory changes had an impact on industry profits. The Tax Reform Act of 1986 eliminated investment tax credits the industry had previously enjoyed and reduced the benefits available through deduction of depreciation expenses. It also reduced corporate tax rates and strengthened the minimum corporate tax. All of these factors combined to reduce tax advantages that assisted firms in the industry.

Heavy construction equipment lessors benefited from a recovery in construction markets that began in 1992, when the value of new construction jumped four percent over 1991 to about $373 billion. In addition, the election of President Clinton in 1992 meant that the public sector market for equipment would likely grow since Clinton had proposed increased federal spending on infrastructure of $80 billion over four years. The Clinton administration also advocated adoption of new investment tax credits that helped lessors. Furthermore, $155 billion was earmarked for construction spending under the Intermodal Surface Transportation Efficiency Act (ISTEA) during the 1990s, which served to increase demand for the rental of heavy equipment.

Although the construction market was expected to partially recover in the 1990s, regulatory constraints affecting heavy equipment lessors showed signs of increasing. Some state and local governing bodies that were seeking ways to increase revenues were mulling over tax rule changes that would increase taxes on leasing and rental transactions. For instance, Florida tried, but failed, to institute a proposal that would have allowed the state to collect sales tax up front on leases, rather than on a periodic basis as rental payments came in. Multistate Tax Commission (MTC) proposals, which attempted to shift the source of leasing income in multi-state transactions, were also an important issue facing the industry in the mid-1990s. In 1996, an industry survey conducted by the CIT Group reported that firms in this industry cited governmental regulation as the single most serious problem facing the industry.

While the industry generally improved in the mid-1990s, firms continued to face stiff competition as a result of lackluster demand compared to the mid-1980s. Firms like Hertz, Prime, and Home Depot aggressively entered this industry. A capital crunch made it difficult for lessors in the industry to secure financing to buy new equipment or expand into different market segments. Furthermore, lessors were not able to rely on expanding international markets to boost sales as other segments of the construction and equipment industries. In fact, only a negligible amount of international trade occurred in the industry in the early 1990s. This was a result of the obvious impracticality of transporting heavy machinery long distances for short-term applications. In fact, most firms in the industry were characteristically localized. At the time (1996), Fred Anderson of the American Rental Association posited that ''while major players like Prime and Hertz have equipment rental divisions, the predominant number of players are still locally-based independents.''

Other factors that determined the health of the industry in the 1990s included: interest rates, which reached lows in the mid-1990s and were remained relatively friendly to borrowers on into the new millennium; high commercial vacancy rates, which kept the lid on new office and retail development; and demographic factors that impacted school and hospital construction spending.

Current Conditions

According to Robert J. Merritt, President and CEO of the CIT Group, ''In 1996, the construction industry expanded by nearly 3 percent in inflation-adjusted dollars.'' Another bright spot in this industry was the 6 percent growth rate for commercial construction activities during that same year. By 1999 the $619 billion construction industry was growing at an annual rate of about 4 percent.

In 1999, a Buyers' Intentions study conducted by the Associated Construction Publications asked contractors if they rented or leased equipment. The responses showed that on a national level, 46 percent rented or leased equipment; only 6 percent said they exclusively leased. It was evident that the rental market was growing at a brisk rate, while leasing seemed to be on the decline. Contractors indicated that they were only interested in buying equipment that they would use on a regular basis, such as trucks and backhoe loaders then filling-in with rental units when they had jobs that required more equipment. Crawler dozers and cranes topped the list of popular equipment rentals.

Industry Leaders

In 1997, Beco Construction Power Co. was the largest competitor in the industry with sales of about $41 million. Morrow Equipment Company, of Oregon, was the second largest firm in the industry, realizing sales of $38 million. Rounding out the top ten companies in 1997 were Rental Tools and Equipment Co., S and R Equipment Company Inc., McLean Rentals Inc., Ferdon Equipment Co., Brown Rental Equipment Company Inc., Strawn Merchandise Inc., United Crane and Shovel Service, and Bat Rental Inc.

By 1999, however, the industry had changed. It was a large, fragmented market that was undergoing a major consolidation process—there were more than 20,000 small and medium-sized equipment rental equipment companies doing business in North America. United Rentals had become the number one equipment rental company by merging with U.S. Rentals and buying dozens of smaller rental firms. With more than 600 locations in Canada, Mexico and the United States, 1998 sales totaled $1.2 billion and they employed 8,501 workers.

Hertz Equipment Rental Corporation (HERC), a division of Hertz, emerged as the number two company with sales of $631.3 million. Rental Service Corporation, who had been bought by Atlas Copco in 1999, had more than 280 locations and recorded sales of $578 million. Other leading companies were Neff Corp. with sales of $324 million and NationsRent, Inc. with sales of $236 million.

WORKFORCE

Positions in the heavy construction equipment renting and leasing industry entailed a variety of jobs in the mid-1990s. The greatest number of jobs was clerical, representing about 18 percent of the work force. Equipment operators and mechanics accounted for about 14 percent and 8 percent of all employees, respectively. Management and executive jobs accounted for 12 percent of industry employment. Other positions included work supervisors, bookkeepers and accountants, and sales people. Although the industry was expected to grow at an average rate in comparison to other sectors of the U.S. economy throughout the 1990s, above average growth was likely to take place in some occupations.

Forecasting to the year 2005, the U.S. Bureau of Labor Statistics identified the highest growth jobs in the miscellaneous equipment rental industry as counter or rental clerks. In the early 1990s, almost 10 percent of the workforce in this industry were counter or rental clerks.

RESEARCH AND TECHNOLOGY

As the construction industry became increasingly competitive in the late 1980s and 1990s, contractors were seeking advanced technology that would give them an edge in completing jobs faster and easier. Continuous technological advances in construction equipment were shortening the practical life span of some types of machinery, quickly rendering earlier models of equipment obsolete. As a result, in order to avoid ownership risks associated with obsolescence, the incentive to rent heavy machinery increased in the 1990s. By 2000 some of the larger companies were also planning for e-commerce in order to reduce costs and improve customer service. Catalogs were available on CD-ROM, customers had online access for electronic payments and many companies paid their suppliers electronically.

FURTHER READING

''CIT/Equipment Financing: Anticipate Sustained Construction Growth in '99.'' Construction Equipment Distribution, 1999. Available from http://www.aednet.org/ced/jan99/cit.htm

''Construction Activity to Continue at a Healthy Pace into the Next Millennium.'' Construction Equipment Distribution, 1999. Available from http://www.aednet.org/ced/aug99/cit.htm

Hertz Corporation. ''1998 Hertz Annual Report.'' Hertz Corp., 1999. Available from http://www.hertz.com

''Hoover's Company Capsules.'' *Hoover's Online.* Austin, TX: Hoover's Inc. Available from http://www.hoovers.com/.

Johnson, John R. ''Revenue for Rent: Renting Tools and Equipment.'' *Industrial Distribution,* November 1996.

Manfredi, Frank E. ''Best Guess for '97? CE Markets Probably Up.'' *Construction Equipment Distribution,* December 1996. Available from http://www.aednet.org/ced/dec96/market.htm.

Sitek, Greg. ''Contractors Renting More—All Over U.S.'' American Rental Association, Rental Management, 1999. Available from http://www.ararental.org/rm/ARCHIVES/featurecontractors4.html

U.S. Bureau of the Census. *1997 County Business Patterns.* Washington, DC: GPO, 1999.

''U.S. Construction to Maintain Modest Growth in 1997.'' Livingston, NJ: CIT Group, 1996. Available from http://www.citgroup.com.

SIC 7359

EQUIPMENT RENTAL AND LEASING, NOT ELSEWHERE CLASSIFIED

This category covers establishments primarily engaged in renting or leasing (except finance leasing) equipment, not elsewhere classified. Establishments primarily engaged in finance leasing are classified in **SIC 6159: Miscellaneous Business Credit Institutions.** Establishments renting and leasing automobiles and trucks without drivers are classified in **SIC 7514: Passenger Car Rental;** those renting automobiles with drivers are classified in **SIC 4119: Local Passenger Transportation, Not Elsewhere Classified;** those renting trucks with drivers are classified in **SIC 4212: Local Trucking Without Storage;**those renting personal items such as lockers (other than refrigerated), clothes, and pillows are classified in **SIC 7299: Miscellaneous Personal Services, Not Elsewhere Classified;** those renting amusement and recreation items, such as bicycles, canoes, and beach chairs and accessories are classified in **SIC 7999: Amusement and Recreation Services, Not Elsewhere Classified;** and those renting commercial boats are classified in **SIC 4499: Water Transportation Services, Not Elsewhere Classified.** Establishments producing machinery and equipment (including computers and other data processing equipment) which lease or sell their products are classified in the manufacturing industries. Manufacturers' sales branches or offices leasing or selling the machinery and equipment of their manufacturing plant are classified in the wholesale trade industries. Establishments primarily engaged in leasing computer time, including time sharing services, are classified in **SIC 7374: Computer Processing and Data Prepara-**

tion and Processing Services; and those renting or leasing computers or data processing equipment are classified in **SIC 7377: Computer Rental and Leasing.**

NAICS Code(s)

532210 (Consumer Electronics and Appliances Rental)
532310 (General Rental Centers)
532299 (All Other Consumer Goods Rental)
532412 (Construction, Mining and Forestry Machinery and Equipment Rental and Leasing)
532411 (Commercial Air, Rail, and Water Transportation Equipment Rental and Leasing)
562991 (Septic Tank and Related Services)
532420 (Office Machinery and Equipment Rental and Leasing)
532490 (Other Commercial and Industrial Machinery and Equipment Rental and Leasing)

Industry Snapshot

Companies in the miscellaneous equipment rental and leasing industry made short-term equipment loans to their customers for a fee. The industry, in general, garnered annual sales of approximately $21 billion in 1992. According to the U.S. Census Bureau, 18,182 companies employed a work force of 143,741 in 1997. That same year industry sales were estimated to be $14.7 billion.

Although rentals of some products slumped in the late 1980s and early 1990s, economic recovery and strong growth in selected segments, such as furniture, gradually revived the industry as the last decade of the twentieth century came to a close. Demographic and financial trends generally boded well for long-term growth, but the business was strongly influenced by unpredictable tax laws and other legislation.

Organization and Structure

The miscellaneous equipment leasing industry encompassed the rental of numerous specialty products, such as portable toilets, video recorders, tools, pianos, and party supplies. The major product segments were airplanes, business machines (except computers), and furniture. Airplanes constituted about 16 percent of all equipment leased under nonfinance arrangements in 1991. An estimated 17 percent of all business machines in use in the United States were leased in the early 1990s, and office machines accounted for over 5 percent of all equipment rented. According to the Equipment Leasing Association, a trade organization, almost 80 percent of companies leased some or all of their business equipment in 1995. Approximately 6 percent of all office furniture was leased, and a growing number of individuals rented their home furnishings in the mid- to late 1990s.

Leasing offered numerous advantages for both lessors and lessees. Many companies that leased equipment believed higher productivity and profits were derived from product use, rather than equipment ownership. An airline company, for example, might benefit from investing its limited resources in marketing or ticketing operations, rather than in jets. In turn, companies that leased equipment to others believed that they could do a better job of buying, financing, servicing, and selling equipment than could their customers .

Numerous financial and tax motivations were behind leasing. Companies that leased equipment avoided the risk of investing in an office machine, for example, that might soon become technologically obsolete. Or they might need the equipment for only a short time. In any case, the company was able to deduct its lease payments from its taxable income, rather than having to deduct equipment depreciation. In addition, companies could reduce their apparent debt burden by leasing. Finally, many individuals leased goods, like furniture, simply because they could not afford to obtain credit or buy.

Companies that leased equipment also benefited in several ways. Compared to their lessees, they were often able to acquire equipment at a low cost, liquidate it efficiently, and obtain acceptable financing terms. Lessors were also better positioned to take advantage of some tax laws, like depreciation allowances and investment tax credits.

Lease Types. The two primary types of leases were operating and finance (capital). Finance leasing companies, the lessors, which were excluded from this industry, essentially sold equipment to their customers, the lessees. The lessee typically rented the item for its entire useful life or agreed to eventually pay for and own the item through a lease-to-own arrangement. About 80 percent of all equipment leased in the United States during the early 1990s were finance leased.

Operating leases encompassed in this industry constituted short-term equipment loans. Lessors usually rented an item more than once during its useful life, and lessees did not commit to purchase the equipment in the lease. However, several types of operating leases were actually hybrids of finance and operating leases. The dollar-out lease and the bargain lease, for example, both allowed the user to acquire the equipment for a negligible or undetermined amount at the end of the lease. Under a sale-leaseback arrangement, a company sold its own assets and then leased them back from the buyer. Each type of lease combined different financial and tax advantages.

Background and Development

Phoenician traders rented ships from the Egyptians around 500 B.C., but it was not until the latter half of the twentieth century that a recognizable leasing industry emerged. The introduction of numerous office machines contributed significantly to industry growth during the 1960s and 1970s. Plus, entirely new specialty leasing sectors emerged, such as airplanes, portable toilet rentals, refrigerated freight trailers, and cargo containers.

During the 1980s, the industry flourished in the wake of new tax laws implemented early in the decade. Lessors were able to take advantage of hefty new investment tax credits and higher depreciation allowances. Likewise, lessees benefited by writing off lease payments and, in many cases, reducing their effective tax burden. As a result, leasing of all types of equipment surged. Office equipment rentals, for instance, grew more than twice as fast as overall business investment in new equipment during the 1980s. By 1998 equipment leasing was estimated to be a $207 billion industry.

The industry was hammered in the late 1980s. Many of the tax advantages that boosted industry profits were quashed by the Tax Reform Act of 1986. Furthermore, a U.S. recession during the late 1980s and early 1990s thwarted demand. Importantly, the sizable aircraft leasing business suffered from airline industry infirmity, as airline traffic decreased, and some major carriers filed for bankruptcy. Airline leasing rebounded between 1992—2,155 aircraft under lease—and 1994—4,500 aircraft under lease. By 1996, 58 percent of all domestic operating aircraft were under lease while, worldwide, 44 percent of all global operating aircraft were under lease.

Despite major setbacks, some companies benefited from declining interest rates, which allowed them to purchase new equipment at a lower cost. In addition, a lack of investment capital forced a number of firms to lease rather than buy. Nevertheless, overall U.S. leasing industry revenues declined more than 4 percent between 1989 and 1991 and rose only slightly in 1992. According to the American Rental Association's 1997 ''Cost of Doing Business Report,'' operating revenues rebounded 8.2 percent from 1994 to 1995 for firms within the **SIC 7359: Equipment Rental and Leasing, Not Elsewhere Classified** industry.

Miscellaneous equipment rental and leasing companies profited from a moderate U.S. economic upswing in 1993 and 1994. Office machine rentals increased an estimated 6 percent, and airline-operating leases continued to rebound from depressed 1990 levels. Furthermore, economic and demographic trends suggested at least modest growth through the mid-1990s, barring unforeseen federal entanglement. Relatively low interest rates, a greater general acceptance of leasing options, and the increased risk of equipment obsolescence all appeared likely to contribute to heightened leasing activity.

An industry bright spot in the early 1990s was the furniture rental business, most of which was not classified in this industry as of 1994. Indeed, the furniture rent-to-own business experienced rampant growth during the 1980s and early 1990s, culminating in a $3.9 billion business with over 3.6 million customers by 1994. Many of these companies achieved huge profits by charging finance rates of between 40 and 400 percent compared to the 1993 national average rate of 111 percent.

Although most rent-to-own furniture rentals were classified as finance leases, they closely resembled operating leases. In fact, the majority of customers, unable to meet the terms of the lease, never took ownership of the furniture. As a result, federal initiatives in 1993 and 1994 were aimed at reclassifying the leases as operating, which could add billions of dollars to this industry group. At least two federal court decisions in the early 1990s corroborated those efforts.

CURRENT CONDITIONS

The industry received a boost from new leasing innovations that gained favor in the mid-1990s. Some office equipment lessors, for example, offered one-stop-shopping programs for corporate customers, whereby a single master lease was arranged to cover equipment and furniture for an entire office facility. In addition, Trans Leasing International of Illinois offered the LeaseCard, a credit card that allowed business owners to effectively purchase and finance goods at below-market interest rates.

In the long term, industry growth was largely influenced by the economic growth rate; interest rates and the supply of financing for new equipment; the stability of the credit environment, which affected the breadth of the market that lessors served; and federal legislation, which could easily bolster or deflate industry profits. In 1996, 30 percent of the estimated $563 billion spent on productive assets was acquired through leasing, with an estimated 80 percent of all U.S. companies leasing some or all of their equipment. In December of 1999 the Equipment Leasing Association stated that the industry had an overall growth of 12 percent since the same time in 1998.

INDUSTRY LEADERS

In 1997, 18,182 companies competed in the miscellaneous equipment rental and leasing industry. According to the *County Business Patterns,* from the U.S. Census Bureau most were extremely small enterprises. Only 6 companies had more than 500 employees, 12 had between 250 and 500 employees, 60 had 100 to 249 employees, 201 had 50 to 99 employees, 1,081 had 20 to 49, 2,235 had 10 to 19, 5,577 had 5 to 9 and 9,010 companies had under four employees. The largest company in 1999 was Rent-A-Center Inc. with $809 million in sales, with Rent-Way, Inc. at number two with $494 million in sales. Other industry leaders included Aaron Rents, Inc. ($370 million), CORT Business Services ($319 million), Globe Business Resources, Inc. ($147 million), Connell Equipment Leasing ($125 million) and PLM International, Inc. ($59 million).

WORKFORCE

Approximately 30,000 workers served this industry going into the 1990s. According to the U.S. Census, this number rose to 143,741 in 1997. Counter and rental clerks comprised 12 percent of the work force, as did employees in sales and related positions. Truck drivers accounted for 10 percent of employment, and general managers and executives represented 8 percent of the work force. Long-term employment prospects were generally positive for this sector. In fact, opportunities in most occupations should escalate more than 50 percent between 1990 and 2005, according to the Bureau of Labor Statistics. Positions for clerks and sales workers, for example, appeared likely to rise between 60 and 70 percent.

FURTHER READING

''Ask Professor Lessor.'' Equipment Leasing Association, 1997. Available from http://www.elaonline.com/PROFLESR.HTM.

''CODB Reflects Higher Operating Profits.'' American Rental Association, 1997. Available from http://www.ararental.org/codb.htm.

''Company Profiles.'' *Hoovers Online,*, 1999. Available from http://www.hoovers.com.

Darnay, Arsen J., ed. *Finance, Insurance, and Real Estate USA.* Detroit: Gale Research, 1996.

''ELA Online Facts About the Equipment and Leasing Industry.'' Equipment Leasing Association, 1997. Available from http://www.elaonline.com/INDFACTS.HTM.

1999 Equipment Leasing Performance Indicators Report Illustrates Growth. Equipment Leasing Association. Available from http://www.elanonline.com/pressrealeases.

''U.S. Rentals IPO.'' *Standard & Poor's Emerging and Special Situations,* 18 February 1997.

U.S. Census Bureau. *1997 County Business Patterns.* Washington, D.C.: GPO, 1997.

Willen, Janet L. ''Should You Lease Office Equipment?'' *Nation's Business,* May 1995, 59-60.

SIC 7361

EMPLOYMENT AGENCIES

This category pertains to establishments primarily engaged in providing employment services, except theatrical employment agencies and motion picture casting bureaus. Establishments classified under this code may assist either employers or those seeking employment. Establishments primarily engaged in operating theatrical employment agencies are classified in **SIC 7922: Theatrical Producers (Except Motion Picture) and Miscellaneous Theatrical Services;** those operating motion picture casting bureaus are classified in **SIC 7819: Services Allied to Motion Picture Production;** farm labor contractors are classified in **SIC 0761: Farm Labor Contractors and Crew Leaders;** temporary help services are discussed in **SIC 7363: Help Supply Services.**

NAICS CODE(S)

541612 (Human Resources and Executive Search Consulting Services)

561310 (Employment Placement Agencies)

INDUSTRY SNAPSHOT

According to government figures, the total dollar volume for employment agencies in 1998 (SIC 7361) was $14 billion. Help supply establishments (SIC 7363) had total volume of some $80 billion. *Executive Search Review* pegged the combined 1997 revenues of the six top executive search firms at $1.3 billion

In late 1999, the employment picture was excellent. Unemployment stood at a 30-year low of 4.1 percent, a remarkable achievement when coupled with continued low inflation. Long-term prospects were bright as well. The U.S. Bureau of Labor Statistics predicted employment would increase 14 percent between 1998 to 2008, a gain of more than 20 million jobs. All of the job growth was expected in the services sector. In the goods-producing sector, a rise in construction employment was projected to offset declines in manufacturing and mining. Health, business, and social services, coupled with engineering, management, and related services, were expected to account for almost half the jobs added to the non-farm sector from 1998 to 2008. By occupation, the greatest growth was expected for computer engineers and support specialists. One government estimate pegged the number of vacant IT (Information Technology) jobs at 346,000.

The 1998-2008 forecast called for the number of jobs in the personnel supply industry to increase by 1.4 million. While at this rate annual growth would still be a respectable 3.7 percent per year, it would be substantially below the 9.1 percent clip recorded from 1988-98.

An employment agency's major function is to place people into short- or long-term positions. The industry has been positively affected by the boom in technology, the government's efforts to get more people off welfare and into employment, the shift from corporate paternalism to the independent portability of employment skills, and the growing need for professionals on short-term bases. One cannot discount the role of temporary employment firms as a try-before-you buy means of finding full-time employees. Employment agencies are also beginning to offer retirement and health care benefits.

The situation is not unlike the first industrial revolution. Today's high-tech society is as much a transition to a new breed of worker that is leaner, more productive, and more highly educated as it is an elimination of positions. On the other hand, there is an increase in the number of service industry jobs.

Staff reductions induced by restructuring and corporate mergers continued to hurt workers in the late 1990s. Despite the tight labor market, corporations announced more than 680,000 job cuts in 1998, the highest number for any year in the 1990s. Many of the cuts stemmed from the economic crises in Asia, Latin America and Russia, which hurt manufacturing export markets, and also caused increased competition from imports. Mergers and acquisitions also contributed to the layoffs.

At century's end, however, the economy was producing so many jobs that laid-off workers usually found new employment, albeit not always at prior salary levels. Older workers had more to fear than the young, who moved easily into technology-related employment stemming from the rise of the Internet. But workers from every segment of society—including inner-city youth who have often been locked out of private-sector employment—were benefiting from strong growth and low inflation.

As employers scrambled to find qualified workers, even small businesses were turning to executive recruiters—formerly the preserve of major corporations—to staff their companies. Much of the new business was coming from high-tech start-ups, generously supplied with venture capital to acquire the talent they needed. In the booming equity markets for new companies in the late 1990s, these firms were also able to offer headhunters stock options in lieu of cash for conducting the search.

The outlook for employment firms was mixed. On the one hand, the booming economy created an enormous need for workers, a need that often could only be satisfied with the use of professional employment firms. On the other hand, the technologies of the Internet and database management were making it possible for some companies and job seekers to bypass staffing firms altogether. Employers could post job descriptions at their company web sites or in newsgroups and have workers from around the world respond. New specialized employment web sites appeared daily, concentrating on employment in fields like accounting and software.

Indeed, online job-matching became one of the fastest-growing businesses on the Internet, generating $105 million in 1998. That figure should expand to $1.7 billion by 2003, according to Forrester Research, an Internet consultant. Many employment firms were creatively using the Internet to attract clients and find hires. The Internet broadened and sharpened the tools available to agencies for researching and reaching potential job candidates.

Even in the Internet age, recruiters served important functions. They could still make the argument that the best candidate for the job is probably not looking for a job at all, and that the recruiter was best placed to find him and make the initial overture. Recruiters can also act as go-betweens in salary negotiations, which is often the toughest part of bringing a candidate onboard.

Search firms faced one unhappy statistic: some 25 percent of all searches don't result in a hire. Sometimes the search firm just doesn't do a good job of finding and holding candidates, rather than merely passing resumes around. Other times, though, the client was at fault. As executive recruiter Christopher Hunt told *Business Week*, "[They] may not have provided a clear strategy to the search firms; that's common with entrepreneurs with a lot of money."

ORGANIZATION AND STRUCTURE

Employment agencies are defined by the National Association of Personnel Consulting as "offering an orientation of finding jobs for people; building a back log of screened candidates by consistent advertising and by referrals from satisfied candidates and employers." Placement fees are paid by either the job-seeking candidate or the employer and are contingent upon an offer by the employer and acceptance by the job seeker. Fee structures vary, but are generally based on a percentage of the annual salary of the job being filled. These fees are also known as contingency fees.

Employment agencies are also called personnel placement firms, personnel consulting firms, and personnel service firms. Executive search, recruiting services, "head hunters," and other firms that help employers fill higher level executive and management positions and place qualified candidates for these particular jobs are sometimes also known as employment agencies. Private agencies are more likely to combine career counseling and placement as one service. Applicants are more "job-ready," whereas public agencies deal with people who are deemed in great need of supportive services before being considered job ready, according to Tomas Martinez in *The Human Marketplace.*

According to Donald A. Levenson in *Personnel,* licensed employment agencies are paid by job seekers who come to them for placement. These agencies generally serve hourly workers, first line supervisors without degrees, clerical workers, and entry level technical and professional workers. Recruiters locate candidates for positions. Professional search consultants conduct in-depth searches for potential candidates to fill specific job openings.

Search consultants can work on either a contingency or retainer basis. A contingency search typically costs 20 percent to 30 percent of the hire's salary, paid once the search is completed. Retained searches, usually for top-level jobs, cost a third of the placement's first year pay package, a third of which must be paid up front. For both types of searches, however, other fee arrangements are possible. Some firms will cut their fees if they're guaranteed several assignments. Other recruiters have begun charging on a per-hour basis. With so many start-up firms looking for talent, recruiters, like accountants and lawyers, before them, have received equity stakes in lieu of cash compensation.

The staffing industry has consolidated significantly. According to a study by Staffing Industry Report, in 1997 the staffing and IT services industry recorded 356 mergers and acquisitions, up 16 percent from the previous year.

Background and Development

The business of serving as a broker between employers and those seeking employment has existed throughout history, perhaps as early as the fifteenth century. The English practice of indentured servitude would fall under this definition because it involved men acting as employment brokers or agents of free men. These brokers acted on behalf of employers who did not have easy access to laborers. They negotiated the contracts that bound these free people to work for a specified period. Indentured servants agreed to work in exchange for benefits that ranged from free passage to the New World to food and lodging.

The first known private employment agencies were called ''intelligence offices,'' and some historians note their existence dating to the early nineteenth century. In his book, Martinez cites the ''Employers and Servants Protestant Agency''—established in 1819 for the ''better regulation of Domestic Servants''—as the earliest reference to a bona fide employment agency. Martinez also notes that the first large scale employment agency appeared in 1863 as the American Emigrant Company, created to ''secure laborers and skilled workers for a number of American employers.'' Fees were collected from employers and registration fees exacted from European job seekers. The agency paid for transportation to America then was reimbursed via future deductions from the immigrant worker's wages.

Private employment agencies appear with more frequency in the latter nineteenth century as evidenced by classified advertising in newspapers of the period. Before World War I, private employment agencies recruited manual laborers or female domestics. Almost anyone could be an employment agent—the middleman and often the only source of information between employers and prospective workers.

Immigrants were valuable commodities to employment agencies because they provided cheap, capable, and, to their detriment, naive labor. Because of this, many immigrants were abused by unscrupulous employment agencies. Employment agencies were often located in poor neighborhoods, saloons, and pool halls, usually as part of patronage systems in big cities like Chicago and New York. People who ''got out the vote'' were rewarded with jobs.

Agencies specializing in hiring women as domestic servants also concentrated on hiring African American and immigrant women. But there was a difference, states Martinez: ''Male employment agents sold jobs to the applicants, while the domestic employment agents sold servants to the housekeepers. In each case, the object being sold was scarce and the buyers were plentiful. Thus the buyer or the party paying the fee was not given as much service as the more precious marketable commodity.''

Private employment agencies often had less than stellar reputations. Besides instituting a form of legalized indentured servitude, many often trafficked in providing houses of ill repute with immigrants and minority women who were often unaware of what type of employment to which they were actually applying.

Specialization in the industry did not occur until after the turn of the century, when agencies began serving teachers, nurses, barbers, and engineers. But the generic employment agency of today evolved from what was termed the ''white collar'' agency that placed clerks, secretaries, and managers in office positions.

In the late nineteenth century, white collar workers primarily obtained work on their own. But by the early years of the twentieth century, employers found it increasingly difficult to find qualified office help and became increasingly dependent on employment middlemen to bail them out. After World War II, this type of agency multiplied rapidly.

Regulation. Government supported agencies, on the other hand, existed as state and municipal agencies as early as 1834 to alleviate unemployment, according to Anna Y. Reed in *Occupational Placement.* A federal employment agency was established by the U.S. government in reaction to the economic crisis of 1907—its focus being the employment of newly arrived immigrants.

This action paved the way for another federal initiative in 1913 when the Department of Labor separated from the Department of Commerce to ''foster, promote and develop the welfare of wage-earners of the United States, to improve their working conditions, and to advance their opportunities for profitable employment.''

Between 1914 and 1917, specialized services such as the National Farm Labor Exchange, Marine Placement, and youth services were attempts to establish a national employment agency. The U.S. Employment Service was created in 1918 but was deemed ineffective in resolving unemployment because after the war ended, so did the worker shortage. Placement work for soldiers, sailors, and other civil service government workers pressed into service during the war was also discontinued by the fall of 1919.

It would take the Great Depression for the U.S. Employment Service to be resurrected under the Wagner-Peyser Act in 1933. The agency's principle focus was to find jobs for the millions of unemployed by overseeing the functions of labor recruitment under the National Recovery Act and state employment services. Access to employment services as a right of American citizenship were formalized under this act's passage.

The emergence of a federal agency appeared to threaten those in the private sector. Private employment agency leaders charged the government with spending taxpayers' money to find jobs for people who were already employed. Instead, they supported using tax dollars to only pay for training and employment of the unemployed and called for restricting federal employment programs to people who qualified for unemployment insurance.

Widespread abuse of job seekers by private employment agencies, however, had prompted attempts by state governments to regulate the industry. At issue was whether individuals had a right to full employment for free or whether they had to pay for it. The prevailing view at this time was that private agencies exploited workers by charging exorbitant fees and not guaranteeing job openings, especially when work was scarce. Private employment agencies also inhibited the free flow of labor during times of high unemployment. By 1914, 24 states had tried to directly regulate private employment agencies, and 19 states had created free public employment agencies. By 1928, all but nine states had instituted some form of legislation to regulate private agencies, either directly or indirectly. Canada and several European countries were also in the process of banning such agencies and establishing nationalized employment services.

Reform. After World War II, private employment services underwent tremendous specialization in response to the changes affecting American industry, whereas public employment agencies have remained relatively less specialized along occupational lines. In the 1940s people sat around and went out on day jobs. From 1947-60, the employment placement fees were paid by the employee.

The private employment agency industry earlier had created its own trade association, the National Employment Association, which was renamed the National Association of Personnel Consultants in the 1970s. As a trade association, it set out to abolish abuses and end discriminatory hiring practices as well as lobby for its member agencies. The National Association of Personnel Consultants in 1988 represented close to 2,000 member employment agencies nationwide, including regional, state, city, and local private employment agencies. In addition to representing its member employment agencies, the Association, based in Alexandria, Virginia, also conducts annual seminars and supervises the certification of employment agency professionals.

The debate over whether employment agencies should be run by the government or by privately held continues to this day. Both types of agencies exist either as state and municipal-run public employment services or as private personnel consulting (employment) agencies. Public and private employment agencies provide services to the public. A 1991 *Current Population Survey* by the Bureau of the Census noted, however, that ". . . Job seekers using private employment agencies had the highest likelihood of finding employment in 1991; almost one-fourth of them found jobs. In contrast, job seekers placing or answering ads or using public employment agencies were among those least likely to find a job in the second month." The survey also noted that "almost 28 percent of the women who used private employment agencies were employed by the second month. In contrast, private employment agencies were the least successful for men—less than 23 percent of them found jobs" in that time period.

Around 1,992 companies requested the staffing industry to supply quality applicants and reduced their number of staffing corporation relations to one or two. The staffing industry has maintained a growth rate of 10 percent to 14 percent in the mid-1990s. Technology has become a hot field of outsourcing. Companies are requesting more workers in the computer, health care, legal and finance fields as they focus on job flexibility.

A small but possible significant factor in voluntary unemployment may be the number of people whose interest in managing their own career transcend the old company paternalism idea as the growing concern for their dispensability creates greater anxiety. Some people may leave by taking advantage of voluntary or involuntary "buyouts" or because of changes in lifestyles where other factors become of greater importance.

New demand for just-in-time temporary workers is being created by temporary work surges. In 1995, a record 2.26 million temporary employees worked daily. Challenges in finding people with appropriate skills are derived from demands for highly skilled workers and a shrinking labor force stemming from an aging population.

CURRENT CONDITIONS

In 1998, revenues for the 59 public staffing firms tracked by Staffing Industry Report grew 27 percent, while net income was up 20 percent. These results were down slightly from 1997 levels, owing to soft demand in some sectors and tight recruiting markets.

On the one hand, the government's emphasis on employing the unemployed is fostering the growth of placement agencies. At the same time, declining government involvement in the job search process is fostering the process of self-placement. The unemployed prefer direct job applications and networking over more formalized methods. The shift in jobs out of the manufacturing sector has in part eroded government placement as well.

Growth of the Industry. Rapid growth in what is known as the private personnel consulting/employment agency industry has occurred within the past 25 years in response to a fluctuating economy, according to the National Association of Personnel Consultants. Double-digit increases in revenues throughout the 1970s and 1980s made executive recruiting a booming business, according to John A. Byrne in *Business Week.* Some industry leaders attributed the slowed growth in revenues in the 1990s to the fact that the industry as a whole was maturing. Nonetheless, with rapid growth came calls to reform.

Private employment agencies are market-driven, money-making businesses. Some professionals are advocating that agencies should concentrate more on developing relationships with employers to generate business. Employment agencies are being forced to provide a higher level of services such as reference verification, computer testing, and consulting to justify the fees they charge, stated Paul Falcone in *HR Focus* magazine.

Other professionals are calling for revamped fee schedules and better working arrangements between clients and consultants. For example, Donald A. Levenson stated in *Personnel* magazine that recruiting fees should no longer be based on ''rigid fee schedules,'' but on ''the value of the job, the degree of difficulty anticipated in recruiting candidates and the level of service desired by the client.''

An increasing number of managers in the publishing industry are using professional search firms. Many companies are using the Internet. National Personnel Associates, Inc., founded in 1956 to provide leading edge support to executive level contingency placement firms, maintains a web site for the public and its members.

A growing number of employment agencies are using employee benefits to recruit workers. Benefits including paid vacations and holidays, bonuses, health care insurance, computer training, stock purchase discounts, 401(k) pension plans, and advancement potential started to be offered by major temporary help services in 1995. In a survey of 2,000 temporary workers by the National Association of Temporary and Staffing Services, 56 percent received holiday pay, 46 percent free skills training, and 39 percent had paid vacation days. Kelly Services provides a week's paid vacation after working 1,500 hours in a 12-month period and six holidays for qualified workers. Manpower Inc. offered the same, plus two weeks of vacation after 1,800 hours.

The ''executive-for-rent'' concept is gaining in a business world concerned with re-engineering and downsizing. Paul Dinte, one of the first to capitalize on the idea, formed a leading executive firm that provides executives on a temporary basis.

Industry Leaders

The largest public staffing companies are Adecco SA, Manpower Inc., Olsten Corp., Kelly Services, and Staff Leasing Inc.

Adecco is the largest employment agency in the world, with more than 200,000 clients and 3,200 offices in 52 countries. It was formed by the merger of Switzerland's Adia and France's Ecco. Adecco's places temporary and permanent personnel in many industries. In 1998, fiscal revenues grew 34 percent to $10.6 billion, while net loss was cut slightly to $134 million.

Manpower has about 3,200 owned and franchised offices in 50 countries, primarily France, the United Kingdom, and the United States. Most of its revenue comes from placing staff in offices and light industrial settings. Sales in 1998 were up 21 percent to $8.8 billion, while net income fell 54 percent to $75 million.

Olsten has 1,400 offices in the United States and more than a dozen other countries. Most Olsten offices are company-owned, but it also has franchises and licensees. The Olsten family owns about 15 percent of the firm but controls a majority of its voting shares. It primarily provides office and clerical staff, and also has a health-care division. In 1998, sales were up 12 percent to $4.6 billion, while net income fell 95 percent to $4.3 million.

Kelly Services, formerly known for its ''Kelly girls,'' has expanded from its female secretary roots to be come the second-largest temporary agency in the United States. Kelly has about 200,000 customers in 19 countries. Chairman and CEO Terence Adderley owns slightly more than half the company. Revenues were up 6 percent in 1998 to $4.1 billion, while net income rose 5 percent to $85 million.

Staff Leasing loans out its 127,000 employees to do tasks like payroll administration, risk management, and benefits administration for some 10,000 clients. The firm's main customers are small businesses with two to 100 employees, primarily in construction and service industries like auto repair, beauty salons, etc. In 1998, the company's sales rose 28 percent to $2.4 billion, while net income fell 24 percent to 23.4 million. Chairman Charles Craig owns about 21 percent of the firm.

Among the biggest Internet employment sites were Monster.com, HotJobs.com, CareerPath.com, and CareerMosaic. Yahoo was prominent in local and regional job listings. In the college market, JobWeb and Jobtrak were the top names.

WORKFORCE

The total number of workers in the personnel supply services industry was expected to rise from 3.2 million in 1998 to 4.6 million in 2008. The median average wage for employment interviewers in 1998 was $14.33 an hour.

More than 30 million contingent employees are working in the United States, a trend fostered by the globalization of business and re-engineering. Only 29 percent were covered under any employee sponsored defined benefit plan. Only 11 percent were covered under a defined contribution plan. Express Personnel Services began offering immediate participation in the firm's 401(k) plan in July 1996.

Most agencies, public and private, prefer to hire college graduates for interviewer jobs. Expansion of the personnel supply industry, especially in the private sector, is expected to continue. In addition to private personnel firms there are a number of positions in state employment agencies. Earnings vary because private personnel firms tend to pay workers on a commission basis with total earnings dependent upon the volume and value of the business they bring in. Commission rates are usually 30 percent of whatever the client is billed. Some pay on a salary plus commission.

RESEARCH AND TECHNOLOGY

According to Internet Business Network, there was expected to be a total of 28.7 million Web job postings in 1998 alone. Surveys in 1999 indicated that the Internet was second only to newspapers as a tool for recruiters and job seekers.

The use of computer databases and online services to track potential employees and job openings is increasing among employment agency professionals, who consider computer and the Internet as a low cost alternative to traditional search methods. A computer database contains information on likely candidates and can be compiled by an employment agency, search firm, or government office.

In a matter of minutes, a candidate's resume can be accessed from the database according to the qualifications, areas of expertise, and training specified in a search. Employment agency professionals can either use one of the estimated 159 recruitment databases on the market or develop their own, according to Rod Willis in *Personnel* magazine.

Some databases are open to the general public, but most corporate job banks and other privately held recruitment databases are confidential and are restricted to employment agency personnel. Recruiting databases include the Bank Executives Network, Corporate Organization and Research Service, College Recruitment Database, First International Personnel Consultants, and the National Insurance Recruiters Association. According to Willis, "recruiting firms are doing more 'targeted searches' for middle-management positions, making effective use of computerized databases." Because companies are turning to employment agencies to find managers and specialists with more sophisticated skills, they are more likely to use employment agencies using the latest technology. Employment agencies, in turn, are able to charge a flat fee based on the difficulty of the job search via a computer database, instead of charging employers a contingency fee based on a candidate's salary.

FURTHER READING

"1996 Industry Report: Trends." *Training,* October 1996.

Adhikari, Richard. "Managing a Mountain of Paper." *Informationweek,* 14 October 1996.

Allan, Peter. "Downsizing Strategies that Minimize Layoffs." *American Business Review,* January 1997.

Anderson, Keisha. "Job Feast or Famine?" *Black Enterprise,* February 1997.

Balch, B.W. "Declining Government Involvement in Job Search and the Rise of Self-Placement: A Macroeconomic Explanation." *American Business Review,* January 1997.

Brandstrader, J. R. "It's an Ill Wind . . ." *Barron's,* 25 March 1996.

Calvacca, Lorraine. "How to Hunt for a Headhunter." *Folio: The Magazine for Magazine Management,* Special source book issue for 1997 supplement.

Cone, Edward. "Back to Work." *Informationweek,* 18 November 1996.

"Creating a Key Personnel Player." *Mergers & Acquisitions,* July/August 1996.

Croghan, Lore. "Escaping the Cycle." *Financial World,* 18 July 1995.

Demery, Paul. "Building a Temporary Staffing Unit In-House." *Practical Accountant,* September 1996.

Defoe, Deborah. "Diverse Staff Brings Benefits" *InfoWorld* 23 February 1998.

Dyson, Esther. "futurespeak." *Sales & Marketing Management,* February 1999.

Epstein, Joseph. "Staying Power." *Financial World,* 16 December 1996.

"Executives for Rent." *Success,* October 1996.

Falcone, Paul. "Maximize Your Recruitment Resources" *HR Magazine,* February 1999

Flipczak, Bob. "Training Co-Opts a Video Network." *Training,* February 1996.

Gallagher, Leigh, "Wired Hires" *Forbes* May 17, 1999.

Gianatasio, David. ''A Healthier McKay.'' *Adweek,* 20 January 1997.

Gottesman, Alan. ''A Bright Future, For a Change.'' *Brandweek,* 9 September 1996.

Greenwood, Judy. ''Temp Agencies Offering Full-time Benefits.'' *Business Insurance,* 9 December 1996.

''Grow, Survive, Thrive.'' *Success,* November 1996.

Haddon-Grant, Hugo. ''Targeting the Hiring Squad.'' *Director,* September 1996.

Haeksley, Flavia. ''Prowess to the People.'' *Accountancy,* June 1996.

''Headhunters: Search and Destroy''*Economist* 27 June 1998

''Invasion of the Body Snatchers''*Business Week* October 11, 1999.

Lee, Chris. ''Trust Me.'' *Training,* January 1997.

Leonard, Bill. ''Manpower Inc. Signs Youth Jobs Agreement with France.'' *HR Magazine,* January 1997.

Levenson, Donald. ''Needed: Revamped Recruiting Services.'' *Personnel,* July 1988.

McCarthy, Joseph L. ''Riding the Boom in Staffing Services.'' *Chief Executive,* December 1995.

Melcher, Richard A. ''Manpower Upgrades Its Resume.'' *Business Week,* 10 June 1996.

''Opening a Window to Work.'' *Business Week,* 13 January 1997.

''Policy and Practice in Recruitment: An IRS Survey.'' *IRS Employment Review,* September 1996.

Reed, Anna Y. *Occupational Placement, Its History, Philosophies, Procedures and Educational Implications.* Ithaca, N.Y.: Cornell University Press, 1946.

Risher, Howard. ''Behind the Big Picture: Employment Trends in the 1990s.'' *Compensation & Benefits Review,* January/February 1997.

Rosen, Evan. ''Videoconferncing Revolutionizes Training and Recruiting.'' *Telemarketing & Call Center Solutions,* January 1996.

Rubis, Leon. ''Benefits Boost Appeal of Temporary Work.'' *HR Magazine,* January 1995.

Sacco, Samuel R. ''Temporary Help and Staffing Services: Wave of the Future.'' *Managing Office Technology,* December 1996.

Sherter, Alain L. ''Personnel Firm's Sec. 401(k) Plan Offers Measure of Permanence to Temporary Workers.'' *Employee Benefit Plan Review,* October 1996.

''Still Growing.'' *Barron's,* 2 September 1996.

''Temporary Staffing's Still Growing, But a Little Slower.'' *Managing Office Technology,* September 1996.

The, Lee. ''HR App Meets Critical Needs.'' *Datamation,* 15 June 1996.

''The Year Downsizing Grew Up.'' *Economist,* 21 December 1996.

Verespej, Michael A. ''Skills on Call.'' *Industry Week,* 3 June 1996.

Worsham, James. ''The Flip Side of Downsizing.'' *Nations's Business,* October 1996.

SIC 7363

HELP SUPPLY SERVICES

This classification includes establishments primarily engaged in supplying temporary or continuing help on a contract or fee basis. The help supplied is always on the payroll of the supplying establishments, but is under the direct or general supervision of the business to whom the help is furnished. Establishments providing both management and staff to operate a business are classified according to the type of activity of the business. Also excluded from this industry are establishments primarily involved in furnishing personnel to perform a range of services in support of the operation of other establishments, which are classified in **SIC 8744: Facilities Support Management Services.** Establishments supplying farm labor are classified in **SIC 0761: Farm Labor Contractors and Crew Leaders.**

NAICS Code(s)

561320 (Temporary Help Services)
561330 (Employee Leasing Services)

Industry Snapshot

In a decade of phenomenal growth—with industry revenue tripling between 1990 and 1999—the help supply industry was slowed, ironically, by the booming U.S. economy. Tight labor markets in the late 1990s stunted growth of help supply services, which mainly consist of temporary staffing agencies, by making recruiting more difficult and leaving job openings unfilled. Still, for a slow year the $80 billion industry was able in 1999 to boost temporary placements by 3.9 percent to an average of 2.89 million U.S. workers on temporary agency payrolls.

Temporary staffing prospered in the 1990s as mass layoffs displaced workers and corporate outsourcing gained favor as a way to control costs. Staffing agencies also made the work more attractive, offering benefits and other perks that weren't traditionally associated with temporary employment. Though the industry's core markets lay in clerical and light industrial personnel, in the course of the decade sizable markets emerged for technical and professional temps—everything from programmers and engineers to accountants and lawyers. Altogether, average temporary employment soared 150 percent from 1990 to 1999.

Beyond welling demand for temporary workers, the industry has also been able to build revenues faster than net placement levels. Several trends contributed, including rising wages, greater numbers of higher-skilled placements, and most recently, value-adding human resources services offered by staffing firms. For example, the use of vendor-on-premises services, where the agency places a coordination staff on a large customer's site to manage temps in person, grew from 2,000 worksites in 1995 to 4,500 in 1999. The same year, even though average placement levels edged up just 3.9 percent, industry revenue increased 9.5 percent.

ORGANIZATION AND STRUCTURE

Companies contract with staffing agencies to obtain personnel on a contingency basis. Typically the temp earns less than his or her in-house counterparts and receives benefits, if any, from the agency rather than the host employer. The company requiring temporary help usually pays anywhere from 25 percent to 50 percent of a temp worker's hourly wage to the agency to cover its fees. Although this may make temps more expensive than in-house workers on an hourly basis, in the long run companies figure they save from the flexibility and reduced administrative burdens of having a smaller in-house labor force.

More than 23,000 temporary employment establishments in the United States were in operation in 1997, more than twice the number that were operating in the early 1980s. The companies managing these operations were primarily small, independent, one-office concerns, with a handful of companies operating on a national, and sometimes international, level. The relatively low investment required to establish a temporary employment business has encouraged small operators to enter the industry since its inception, and accounted for the large representation of such companies in the 1990s.

Compared to the average number of employees per establishment in all service industries, the average number of employees per establishment in the temporary employment industry is significantly larger because of the nature of the business. In 1997 the typical administrative service industry establishment employed 26 workers, while temporary employment establishments employed an average of about 111 workers. Revenues per establishment were also higher in the temporary employment industry than the average recorded by all other service industries, with the typical administrative service entity posting just over $1 million in revenues compared to the average of $2.43 million per establishment in the temporary employment industry.

Geographically, temporary staffing agencies are fairly evenly distributed throughout the United States. They tend to be located near their customers, and thus agencies are clustered in large metropolitan areas with strong white-collar employment bases.

BACKGROUND AND DEVELOPMENT

The need for temporary or emergency employment presumably has existed ever since industry and commerce in the United States reached substantial proportions; employees have always fallen ill, businesses have always experienced surges of growth and spasms of decline, and a certain percentage of the national labor pool has always been idle. On a theoretical level, therefore, the maturity of the U.S. economy should have induced the emergence of a class of workers willing to satisfy the sometimes fleeting employment needs of corporate America.

The genesis of the temporary employment industry, however, lagged far behind the establishment of the national economy. Although distant progenitors of the industry began emerging as early as 1910, the basic, modern structure of the industry as it exists in the 1990s did not develop until after World War II. Undoubtedly, businesses and industries had relied on temporary help in some form much before this time, but the industry, as a definable and organized entity, did not appear until the immediate post-war years when two temporary employment companies, integral to the industry's organization and growth, first formed.

Signaling the advent of an industry that would eventually develop into a multi-billion dollar business, William Russell Kelly created Kelly Girl Service Inc. in 1946 to capitalize on the need for temporary office workers by small business owners. Initially, Kelly and his "Kelly Girls" performed typing and machine tabulation tasks for companies financially unable to hire full-time permanent workers to execute such chores. Kelly quickly realized that many businesses surrounding his Detroit office had a variety of positions that could be filled by temporary workers, so his company, defined as a "service bureau" by Kelly, began supplying temporary workers to assume an assortment of clerical positions.

Two years after Kelly started his business in 1948, two Milwaukee law partners, Elmer Winter and Aaron Scheinfeld, opened their own temporary employment agency called Manpower Inc. Born out of a need for temporary help by the two founders themselves, Winter and Scheinfeld created Manpower after searching for a temporary replacement for a sick employee of their own. Unable to readily locate a temporary replacement, the two attorneys persuaded a former secretary to return and, consequently, became convinced that other businesses suffered from the same difficulty. Recruiting workers and reassigning them on a temporary basis, Manpower provided the same types of workers as Kelly Girl, but supplied industrial temporaries as well.

Once a need for temporary employees had been identified by these two early entrants in the industry, other similar business were formed in rapid succession. Entry into the industry required little capital investment, with costs incurred from recruiting, advertising, and rent standing as the only significant financial exigencies for the would-be owner of a temporary employment agency. Consequently, with virtually no initial need for fixed investment, and the latent demand for the type of service provided, a majority of the companies that would lead the industry for the next 20 years—Olsten based in New York, Employers Overload in Minneapolis, and Western Girl in San Francisco, in addition to Manpower and Kelly Girl—were already established by the early 1950s.

As the number of industry participants proliferated during the early 1950s, by infiltrating new, untapped markets, the range of services offered by the industry also broadened. Initially, temporary employment agencies provided employees to perform primarily office and clerical duties, the one notable exception being Manpower's industrial niche, but other companies began operating in the early 1950s that focused on providing technical workers, such as engineers, designers, and draftsmen, on a temporary basis. This trend prompted the creation of a new breed of temporary employees that would prove to be a highly lucrative component of the industry. Moreover, some temporary help companies added sales divisions during the decade to perform marketing and promotional assignments, further widening the scope of the industry's services.

The industry received its greatest surge of growth, however, from geographical expansion, as companies already established in the industry extended their reach across the country. Manpower, for example, had opened 21 company-owned branch offices in 13 cities by 1954, six years after it first opened its doors. That same year, Manpower also began offering a franchising program, followed by Kelly Girl Services, which enabled franchise ownership under the Kelly name a year later, in 1955. Expansion was not restricted to domestic markets, but stretched overseas, when Manpower opened offices in London and Paris in 1956. By the end of the decade, the temporary employment industry generated annual revenues of approximately $100 million.

For the industry, which essentially had been in existence for only 10 years, these initial developments—the broadening range of services it provided, the proliferation of new companies, and the dramatic growth of existing companies—established a firm foundation for the industry's future, validating the assumptions of the industry's founders that, indeed, American business and industry had a large appetite for temporary employment help.

As the industry headed into the late 1950s and 1960s, a period during which temporary help companies, on the whole, enjoyed phenomenal success, its clients began utilizing temporary help for different reasons. Originally, the demand for temporary personnel stemmed almost exclusively from the need to replace sick or vacationing employees, but gradually employers began using temporary employment agencies to fulfill more strategic needs. Historically, companies experiencing an upturn in business hired additional labor on a permanent basis to meet deadlines during peak periods of activity, but once business activity returned to normal levels, the added employees remained, saddling the company with excess staff. By utilizing temporary employees, however, companies could quickly hire and dismiss a portion of their staff according to the dictates of their business cycle. This payroll fluidity enabled personnel managers to incorporate temporary employees into management plans, rather than relying on them only in panic situations, which underscored the necessity of the temporary employee in the American workplace.

In the 1960s, the temporary employment industry flourished, as the benefits accorded to companies utilizing interim help dovetailed with favorable market conditions on the whole to exponentially increase the industry's revenues. Aside from the personnel flexibility that temporary employees provided, client companies also profited from reductions in unemployment compensation costs, the creation of investment tax credits, and an increase in consumer spending. Although hiring a temporary worker generally cost more per hour than hiring a permanent employee, savings were realized by not having to pay for fringe benefits, which typically averaged 30 percent of an employee's total wage. Also, the use of temporary labor could dramatically reduce the amount of unemployment tax a particular company was forced to pay. Companies are taxed a certain percentage of their total payroll for unemployment compensation, the amount of which is determined by the layoff record of a particular company. For example, if a company hires additional staff to meet increased production demands and subsequently releases those employees, then the company's compensation percentage is increased. By using temporary employees, however, companies can still respond to various business cycles, but their unemployment compensation percentage is not affected, since temporary employees are not considered part of the regular workforce.

Benefiting from these advantages that temporary employment gave to businesses of all types, the industry's participants thrived during the 1960s. Manpower, by 1963, operated more than 300 offices nationwide, and its penetration of foreign markets had deepened considerably from the two offices it opened in 1956 to a total of 45. Revenues for the company exceeded $30 million, excluding the billings recorded by Manpower franchises, which totaled an additional $29 million, and the company had added a technical division to supply specially skilled employees on a temporary basis. Kelly Girl at this time was also diversifying its services, initiating a pilot program to lease out industrial laborers.

The bulk of the industry's growth, however, occurred after 1963 into the late 1960s. The industry's ascension was attributable, in part, to the diminished labor force of the nation as a whole. Unemployment dropped during the middle of the decade due to the overall health of the nation's business community and government programs specifically designed to winnow unemployment levels. Additionally, the Vietnam War began to drain an appreciable portion of the country's work force, while at the same time infusing more money into the economy. The effect of these circumstances tightened the nation's labor supply, which improved the temporary employment industry's position. Growing at a 25 to 30 percent annual rate, the industry's leading companies, those founded in the early 1950s, helped push the industry's revenues to $500 million by 1967, more than twice the amount recorded four years earlier.

By the beginning of the 1970s, however, the industry's growth had slowed. Geographic expansion had fueled, in large part, the growth of the industry, with small, independent companies sprouting up in cities bereft of temporary employment companies and the larger, national companies opening offices at a rapid rate. Manpower, a useful benchmark of the industry's breadth, had more than 550 offices in operation by 1968 and had nearly tripled the number of its foreign branches in five years to 127 offices. But after 1966, the rate of geographic expansion began to decline, as fewer untapped markets remained to be exploited. By the end of the 1960s, geographic expansion, the former driving force of the industry's growth, had ceased to significantly increase the industry's revenues.

Concurrent with the near saturation of the sundry temporary employment markets, the nation's economy soured in late 1969, causing the temporary employment industry, for the first time, to falter. Lacking new markets to move into, companies involved in the industry were left with no way to offset the slackening demand for their services and the industry, consequently, suffered a decline in revenues.

The damage to the industry, however, was only short-lived and the effects negligible, as temporary employment companies in their recovery demonstrated a characteristic unique to the industry—as general economic conditions worsened, the temporary employment industry's position improved. When the economic downturn of 1969 and 1970 developed into a full-fledged recession in the early and mid-1970s, businesses began to lay off workers to combat soaring inflation and depressed business activity. While personnel managers reexamined staffing needs, sometimes discharging too many workers, or discovering certain positions did not warrant full-time employment, temporary employees were often sought to fill particular employment gaps, which helped mitigate the awkward process of arriving at an efficient number of employees. Moreover, the difficult financial conditions forced individuals that voluntarily excluded themselves from the nation's work force, housewives in particular, to seek part-time, temporary employment. Buoyed by these depressed economic conditions, temporary employment companies began to focus on broadening the range of services they provided to other industries. Since geographic expansion could no longer be relied on to stimulate sales, companies began concentrating on recruiting professional temporaries and specially trained laborers.

The result of these changes, both outside and within the industry, protected, to a large extent, temporary employment companies from the pernicious economic conditions affecting the rest of the nation. In 1974, while many industries struggled to generate profits, the approximately 2,000 companies involved in the temporary employment industry recorded more than $1 billion in revenues. However, the deleterious financial conditions did take their toll on the industry; total temporary payroll, for example, dropped 18.3 percent in 1975, but the industry demonstrated an ability to quickly recover from a downturn. The industry by this time supplied nearly 3 percent of the nation's total labor force, with Manpower alone drawing from a reservoir of 500,000 temporary workers.

Throughout the remainder of the decade, the industry's sales growth rate was somewhat less than the prolific pace enjoyed during the 1960s, but it was still an enviable 10 percent to 15 percent. By 1978, the industry employed roughly 2.5 million temporary employees for 500,000 customers and had annual revenues in excess of $1.5 billion. By the late 1970s, 8 of 10 American companies used temporary employees to fill an assortment of positions, including such markets as health care, corporate management, marketing, and science—although secretarial and clerical business still accounted for 70 percent of the industry's placements. The movement away from using temporary workers only in emergency situations had gained momentum since the late 1950s, accounting for 40 percent of the industry's business in the late 1970s compared to the 90 percent figure that once represented the use of temporary employees in earlier panic situations.

By the early 1980s, the temporary employment industry was the third-fastest growing industry in the country. Revenues eclipsed $5.1 billion in 1982, while over 90 percent of American companies used temporary workers on a regular basis. Despite, or perhaps due to this pervasive presence in the nation's business community, recessive conditions struck the industry once again in the early

1980s. However, at this time the industry was insulated by the diversity of services it offered and temporary payroll fell by only 1 percent.

By the mid-1980s, temporary employees filled more than 700,000 jobs a week, considerably more than the 470,00 per week recorded in 1983. According to the National Association of Temporary and Staffing Services (NATSS, later renamed the American Staffing Association), the number of temporary employees on any given day in 1995 was over 2 million. Low initial investment coupled with the tremendous success the industry had enjoyed over the past 40 years continued to attract more and more competition, raising the specter of market overcapacity, but the bulk of the recent additions to the industry consisted of small, one-office operations, only serving customers in close proximity. By 1985, there were 2,300 companies engaged in the industry, operating nearly 7,500 offices, up from the 2,000 companies and 5,000 offices in existence three years earlier. Ten years later, in 1995, more than 16,000 help supply offices were operating in this industry nationwide.

Revenues mushroomed throughout the mid-1980s, nearly tripling from 1982's volume to more than $15 billion in 1987, as other industries increased their use of temporary employees with specialized skills. This trend led not only to significant increases in sales, but also widened the profit margin earned by temporary employment companies. From 1986 to 1989, the industry recorded an annual growth rate of 18 percent and stood, by the beginning of the 1990s, as an industry inseparably woven into the employment structures of an overwhelming majority of American businesses. Between 1990 and 1993, the industry experienced a 25 percent increase in growth. And, in the one year period between 1994 and 1995, temporary help receipts rose by 12.9 percent.

According to the observations of one economist, a rise or decline of 50,000 temporary employees usually augurs a parallel shift of roughly one million permanent, or payroll employees a month or two later. This portentous characteristic of the industry became apparent once again in the late 1980s and early 1990s as a global recession quaked the foundations of a majority of industries. Temporary employee placements peaked in 1988 at slightly over one million, remaining flat through 1989, then rebounded in 1990, becoming for client companies an effective way to combat vacillating production demands. During the ensuing months of the recession, while other industries floundered, the industry fared comparatively well. The industrial component of the industry demonstrated particularly strong growth, with daily temporary placements for manufacturing positions rising from 224,000 in early 1992 to 348,000 by the end of the year.

As temporary employment companies charted their course toward the mid-1990s, the dynamics of the industry were changing, echoing the changing relationship between employers and employees in general that was prompted by mounting global competition and the concerted push for more efficiency in the American workplace. Increased pressures on American businesses to assiduously monitor expenditures persuaded many companies to reexamine their personnel needs in the wake of the recession of the early 1990s. As a result of this introspection, business operations were streamlined nationwide, leaving a considerable number of companies with reduced payrolls and convincing some observers of the national economy to prognosticate that the focus on efficiency and trend toward smaller staffs may not be just a temporary answer for depressed economic conditions, but may reflect a permanent shift in management philosophy. Manufacturers, for example, once produced an excess of goods, holding the surplus in storage, or building up sizeable inventories, but after the deleterious economic climate of the early 1990s, they preferred to manufacture products only when quantifiable demand could be measured.

Current Conditions

In 1998 the help supply industry generated more than $80 billion in revenues, according to Census Bureau statistics. Quarterly agency surveys by the American Staffing Association suggest that of that amount, about $58.7 billion, or 73 percent, came from temporary staffing services. The rest came from employee leasing services, which involve longer-term co-employer contracts, and other minor staffing-related activities. In 1999 the temporary segment was estimated at $64.3 billion, a 9.5 percent gain over the year before, and temporary staffing revenue was expected to climb another 8 percent in 2000.

Looking further ahead, a number of observers expected continued, albeit slower, growth for the industry in the early 2000s. In its ten-year projections published in 1999, the Bureau of Labor Statistics predicted the broader personnel supply services industry, which includes help supply as well as executive recruitment and other forms of employment agencies, to expand by 43 percent between 1998 and 2008. By the end of the period, the industry group was expected to employ a total of 4.62 million people, up from 3.23 million as of 1998.

In the late 1990s the industry went through a spell of significant consolidation. Mergers and acquisitions were fueled in part by slowing growth in the overall market, but also by two strategic trends. For one, large clients seek single-vendor relationships with comprehensive service providers that can fill niches that formerly several different agencies might have. Second, with labor in tight supply and companies increasingly doing business across international borders, large international temp agencies can better meet the needs of multinational firms by having access to labor pools in many different places. At least one analyst expected consolidation activities to continue unabated through at least 2000.

Part of the shift toward providing integrated, comprehensive services has been the growth of so-called vendor-on-premises (VOP) services. Under these arrangements, staffing agencies provide management or coordination staff and other resources at the customer's worksite. Used primarily in large contracts, VOP services ease the administrative burden of using temps for the customer and can make the agency more responsive to the client's needs—the agency assumes some of the risk in the deal. Although the practice isn't necessarily more profitable for staffing agencies, it is part of the industry's strategic thrust toward providing more value-added and comprehensive solutions to customers' needs. It also makes staffing agencies more important when the job market is tight, as it was in the late 1990s, because they are serving additional functions besides simply finding enough bodies to meet the customer's quota. Customer reactions have been largely favorable.

VOP services have been around for a while, but they became much more prevalent from the mid-1990s on. From 1994 to 1999, the number of U.S. workplaces using VOP programs more than quadrupled, reaching 4,500 in 1999. Revenues associated with such sites using VOP rose accordingly, from $2 billion to $8.75 billion (those figures include the salaries of all the temps placed at a VOP site). At that level, VOP programs were linked to about 13.5 percent of total U.S. temporary staffing revenues as of 1999.

INDUSTRY LEADERS

Two of the industry's founders, Manpower Inc. and Kelly Services Inc., helped spark interest in the use of temporary employees by businesses both domestic and foreign. These companies pioneered many of the industry's developments in service and maintained consistent growth throughout the industry's history.

Manpower. Initially more aggressive than Kelly, Manpower rapidly expanded during the 1950s through company-owned offices and through its franchise program. Manpower set the tone for the industry's future by supplying industrial temporaries in its first year of operation and then diversifying its services later to include salespeople. By the early 1960s, Manpower had established a technical division to provide architects, engineers, and draftsmen to its clients, and operated more than 300 offices. At this point in the company's history, three of every four offices were franchise operations, bringing total revenues to $56.8 million in 1963, with 159,500 temporary workers on its payroll serving 105,000 customers.

Four years later, Manpower opened its 500th office and served 160,000 customers with 270,000 temporary employees. Its international presence by this time had greatly increased, and now included 100 offices located in Europe, Asia, South America, Australia, Mexico, and Canada. To further capitalize on its foreign involvement, Manpower created its ''Push Button Global Service'' program that enabled traveling businesspersons to be met by a secretary or interpreter on arrival in a foreign city.

By the early 1970s, Manpower had established a considerable lead in the industry, with temporary employment offices in 31 countries. The company's Paris office was the largest of its offices and the heart of its total global presence. Domestically, Manpower had created an assortment of programs to train temporary employees for particular jobs and catered to a diverse clientele, supplying workers trained in marketing, data processing, and a variety of other skilled and unskilled occupations.

Toward the end of the 1970s, Manpower created a petroleum division to supply gas-pumping attendants for approximately 700 service stations in the United States. Through its 750 worldwide offices, the company generated $383 million in revenues in 1977, more than twice as much as its nearest competitor, Kelly Services. By the mid-1980s, with revenues totaling $1.5 billion, Manpower continued to increase its presence domestically and internationally, operating 650 offices in the United States and 450 offices abroad. In 1999, Manpower operated 3,300 offices in 52 countries. As of that year, the company recorded a 9 percent annual gain in revenue, making $11.5 billion worldwide. Net income was also up 13 on the year, reaching $150 million.

Kelly Services. Slower to diversify its services than Manpower, Kelly Services initially supplied only one type of temporary employee—female office workers. By the early 1960s, however, Kelly Services, originally Kelly Girl Service Inc., had begun a pilot program of providing male temporaries for industrial jobs. The company was also slower in establishing additional offices, especially in international markets, taking until the early 1960s to even consider foreign expansion, and then did so only on a limited scale in Canada. Despite these differences, Kelly Services' revenues roughly approximated Manpower's revenues throughout the 1950s and 1960s, the first full decades both companies were in operation. By the close of the 1960s, Kelly Services had nearly 300 offices in operation, a majority of which were franchises like Manpower, and had annual revenues of nearly $80 million.

The company eventually broadened its line of temporary employees, establishing marketing, labor, and technical divisions within its operations during the 1960s; and by the early 1970s, Kelly supplied a selection of temporary workers as diverse as Manpower's. Its clerical workers, still the company's specialty, were trained in

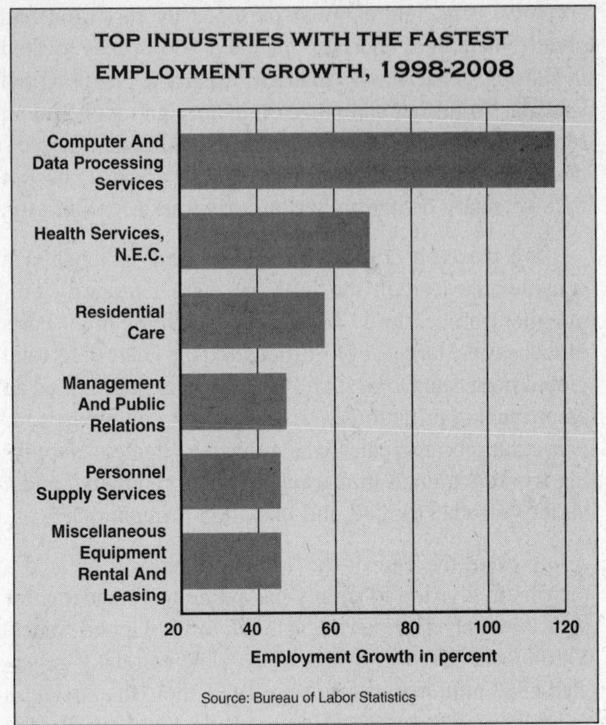

125 skill classifications, blanketing the full spectrum of office and clerical temporary needs, one of which was supplying businesses with data processing workers.

In the late 1970s, Kelly Services, with annual revenues hovering around $160 million, branched out into the health care field, supplying licensed practical nurses and hospital orderlies on a temporary basis. This foray into providing temporary health care workers proved to be a lucrative and prudent move by Kelly Services, enabling the company to carve a niche in a market that would become a boon for temporary employment companies in the 1980s and early 1990s. The company continued acquiring smaller providers throughout the 1990s, including a number in Europe, where it also aggressively opened its own branches in the late 1990s. By 1999 Kelly supported 1,800 offices in 19 countries. Kelly Services had revenues of $4.3 billion in 1999, marking a 4.3 percent rise, while net income was flat at $85 million.

WORKFORCE

In 1999 the temporary employment industry employed an average of 2.89 million people on any given day. According to U.S. Bureau of Labor statistics from the mid-1990s, secretaries and general office clerks were the most widely employed temporary workers at that time, with each representing 8.7 percent of the total temporary employment labor force. Typists and word processors trailed closely, composing 8.4 percent of the industry total; while the fourth largest category of temporary employees were industrial workers classified as helpers, labors, and material movers, which accounted for 7.9 percent.

Wages were generally lower for temporary employees than for permanent workers. In 1996, the median weekly earnings for temporary employees was $295 compared to $416 for permanent workers. Benefits were offered less frequently to temporary employees. Only 20 percent of temporary workers had employer-provided health insurance while more than 60 percent of permanent workers enjoyed this benefit. In 1995, however, between 33 percent and 41 percent of all companies including help supply firms offered access to some form of benefits. Temporary employees, on the whole, are most likely to be female, African-American, young, and enrolled in school.

AMERICA AND THE WORLD

Since the genesis of the modern temporary employment industry following World War II, American temporary employment companies have maintained a strong presence in international markets. Manpower Inc., the first U.S. company to aggressively pursue foreign business, paved the way for other industry participants to follow, leading to a broad global representation of American temporary employment companies in the 1990s.

The business today is thoroughly internationalized. All the major U.S. firms have extensive operations in other countries, particularly Europe, which is the second-largest regional market for staffing services behind the United States.

Particularly in the wake of mergers in the mid- and late 1990s, European firms rank alongside U.S. agencies in terms of size and global reach. Indeed, the world's largest staffing agency as of the late 1990s was Switzerland-based Adecco S.A., which was the product of several key mergers and acquisitions. In the late 1990s Adecco obtained 30 percent of its revenue from North America, and that proportion was expected to rise because of its purchase of some U.S. based Olsten Corp. staffing units in 2000.

FURTHER READING

American Staffing Association. "Staffing Facts." Washington, 2000. Available from www.natss.org.

Boudette, Neal E. "Tempted by Temps." *Industry Week,* 7 August 1989.

Carrns, Ann. "Contingent Workers: The Trend That Wasn't." *Working Woman,* February 1996.

"Contingent Employment." The Conference Board: New York, 1995.

Davidson, Linda. "Temp Workers Want a Better Deal." *Workforce,* October 1999.

Flynn, Gillian. ''Number of Contingents Is Smaller Than Thought.'' *Personnel Journal,* January 1996.

Hipple, Steven. ''Earnings and Benefits of Contingent and Noncontingent Workers.'' *Monthly Labor Review,* October 1996.

Leeson, Fred. ''Staffing-Firm Employment Rises Nationwide.'' *Oregonian,* 7 November 1999.

McNerney, Donald J. ''Contingent Workers: Companies Refine Strategies.'' *HR Focus,* October 1996.

Mullins, Robert. ''Manpower's New Man.'' *Business Journal—Milwaukee,* 24 September 1999.

Polivka, Anne E. ''Contingent and Alternative Work Arrangements, Defined.'' *Monthly Labor Review,* October 1996.

———. ''A Profile of Contingent Workers, Defined.'' *Monthly Labor Review,* October 1996.

Risher, Howard. ''Behind the Big Picture: Employment Trends in the 1990's.'' *Compensation and Benefits Review,* January/February 1997.

Thomson, Allison. ''Industry Output and Employment Projections to 2008.'' *Monthly Labor Review,* November 1999. Available from www.bls.gov.

SIC 7371

COMPUTER PROGRAMMING SERVICES

This industry consists of establishments primarily engaged in providing computer programming services on a contract or fee basis. Establishments of this industry perform a variety of additional services, such as computer software design and analysis; modification of software; and training in the use of custom software. Mass-produced software development is discussed under **SIC 7372: Prepackaged Software.**

NAICS CODE(S)

541511 (Custom Computer Programming Services)

INDUSTRY SNAPSHOT

With 2000 revenues estimated at more than $80 billion, the custom programming services industry is one of the largest segments of the broader information technology (IT) services sector. Though it receives much less attention than the packaged software segment, custom software development is usually somewhat larger in terms of annual revenues.

The industry has grown rapidly as businesses have upgraded and expanded their computer systems. Although annual growth was uneven from 1990 to 1998, ranging from as low as 6.8 percent in 1992 to more than 28 percent in 1998, the industry's gross receipts climbed during the period at a compound average of 13.6 percent a year, based on U.S. Census Bureau data. However, the surge in the late 1990s was due in part to one-time Year 2000 (Y2K) compliance services, and thus, growth was expected to ease to a more moderate pace in the early 2000s.

Still, a host of corporate development projects were set aside for Y2K preparedness, and these were expected to drive new custom programming business in 2000 and beyond. One of the biggest growth areas in custom programming was in developing and deploying Web-enabled applications, especially for e-commerce.

ORGANIZATION AND STRUCTURE

Among the industry's top players such as IBM and EDS, custom programming services are only one of a multitude of IT services offered ranging from consulting and training to systems integration and facilities management. Indeed, the broader IT services industry has increasingly evolved toward a one-stop solution model, where a single contractor provides a comprehensive set of computer services to its clients. As such, many non-government statistical sources, and often the companies themselves, don't separate custom programming from these other activities.

Custom programming services are used primarily as an alternative to using packaged software unmodified, and hiring in-house programming staff to write custom software. The first use is noteworthy as a reminder that packaged software is often modified by third-party vendors for specific businesses; not all custom software work begins from scratch. The second use highlights that the industry is closely associated with outsourcing technical functions. In fact, it's sometimes described as the IT outsourcing industry.

A separate and popular way for companies to obtain programming services without committing to maintaining an in-house staff of programmers is to contract for leased or temporary programmers and consultants. Several large national agencies have special units devoted to placing experienced technical workers. However, unless the contracting firm is itself a programming services provider, such activities are considered outside the scope of this industry.

A variety of trade and professional organizations represent the industry. Among others, the National Association of Computer Consultant Businesses (NACCB) and Independent Computer Consultants Association (ICCA) have members involved in contract programming. These trade associations represent their members in different ways. NACCB, headquartered in Washington, D.C., lobbies government officials on behalf of member businesses. ICCA is based in St. Louis and offers certification exams. Successful completion of a computerized test allows a member to be designated a Certified Computing Professional.

Background and Development

As computer systems became commonplace in businesses and other organizations, the need for custom programming and other computer programming services increased. From the 1950s through the 1980s technology made huge leaps forward. Computer programmers were very hard to find in the early years, so many companies did not bother to hire them. By the late 1980s and early 1990s, very sophisticated computer equipment needed equally sophisticated code to handle growing amounts of information at rapidly increasing speeds.

Computer service companies were originally hired to automate record-keeping tasks such as payroll. Later, they expanded into customer-related areas such as fund transfer systems, just-in-time inventory systems, and customer information systems. Many companies could only hire these service firms in the best of financial times given the high cost of the services. Early programming was highly customized, but the needs of businesses by the 1990s necessitated more standardization.

Computer programming companies grew in part by presenting themselves as a cost-saving alternative to in-house programming departments. According to the prevailing logic, they were specialists and could save corporations money by programming systems and software on a contract basis. Although there's been the occasional backlash against service firms when their clients aren't satisfied with the outside service's performance—sometimes spurring the disgruntled customer to bring the project back in-house—custom programming services are still widely seen as being more cost-efficient than internal development.

Current Conditions

Revenues from custom programming and related services have grown swiftly as businesses seek higher levels of automation and efficiency, greater control over internal and external information, and the ability to conduct business transactions electronically, particularly over the Internet. From 1990 to 1998, industry revenues more than tripled from $21 billion to $64 billion, according to government statistics, yielding a 13.6 percent compound annual growth rate. Projections for 1999 and 2000 showed annual receipts expanding to $73 billion and $83 billion, respectively. Census Bureau data suggests that industry firms typically bring in around three-quarters of their gross revenues from programming services; the rest come from activities classified under other industries, such as systems integration and maintenance services.

In the late 1990s, the Census Bureau estimated that more than 32,000 U.S. establishments provided custom programming services as their primary line of business. The lion's share—more than 95 percent—had fewer than 50 employees. Those figures didn't include firms that offer custom programming as secondary activities.

In the late 1990s, the industry enjoyed a surge in business related to Year 2000 (Y2K) computer conversion. The entire process, which involved checking and modifying software to ensure it would work properly after the date change, cost businesses worldwide anywhere from $280 billion to $600 billion by various estimates. Only part of that money went for programming, though, as a great deal was also spent on other preparedness measures such as keeping extra staff and special supplies on hand in the event of a major crash. Although January 1, 2000 proved an uneventful day for most computer systems—provoking sharp criticism of computer consultants who some believe overstated the risks—residual spending on Y2K problems was expected to total another $20 billion during 2000.

Traditional custom-developed applications and utilities face rising competition from packaged software, which has grown more powerful, flexible, and cost-efficient, particularly since the mid-1990s. Indeed, some package vendors, notably SAP and Oracle, have increasingly tooled their high-end applications like the popular enterprise resource planning (ERP) suites to enable relatively fast customization. Such packages come with a range of standard functions as well as a development environment that allows individual businesses—usually mid- to large-sized ones—to adapt the software to their own needs and existing systems. SAP, for example, has been at the forefront of working with customers to build hybrid applications that are in large part custom, but then are generalized and resold to other customers with similar needs. In effect, customers enjoy benefits of customization without as many costs and uncertainties as with all-out custom development.

Some believe the emerging application service provider (ASP) model, where businesses rent software applications over the Internet instead of installing and running them on their own machines, will further change the competitive dynamic in the custom software business. Under this scenario, ASPs may well go beyond hosting and maintaining software and actually perform customization for individual clients. Depending how this plays out, it could spell either an opportunity or a threat to the conventional custom programming industry.

Industry Leaders

Custom programming services are furnished by a diverse group of companies, including several multinational firms that provide a comprehensive set of IT services to large businesses and government agencies. Some of the biggest include IBM Global Services, Electronic Data Systems Corp., Computer Sciences Corp., Andersen Consulting, and Compaq Computer Corp. (including the service arm of the former Digital Equipment Corp. acquired by Compaq in 1998).

On the second tier is a collection of service vendors that focus on national or regional customers, and often on a more limited range of systems and technologies. Examples of companies in this group include American Management Systems., Inc.; Analysts International Corp.; Cambridge Technology Partners; Ciber, Inc.; Keane, Inc.; and Modis Professional Services.

WORKFORCE

Employment in the industry has soared as companies adopt and upgrade information technology in all facets of their businesses. Throughout the 1990s the industry added new workers at an average of almost 12 percent a year. By 1999, the industry employed about 405,000 people, more than double the count only six years earlier. Indeed, the U.S. labor market for programmers and others with IT skills has been exceptionally tight. Acute demand for high-tech employees has led to worker shortages, aggressive recruitment of foreign workers, and rising salaries for individuals with highly sought skills. By some calculations, in the late 1990s there were tens of thousands more positions available than qualified personnel to fill them.

In 1999 the industry's average hourly wage for nonsupervisory workers was $25.36, according to Bureau of Labor Statistics estimates. This greatly exceeded the 1999 national private-sector average of $13.24 an hour. Computer services companies are likewise considered better than average places to work in terms of working conditions and fringe benefits.

Professionals employed by computer programming firms often receive ongoing education and training in new technologies. More programmers are needed in software maintenance than in software development, and these maintenance programmers must be familiar with many types of hardware and software. They need to understand Internet and networking technology and to be flexible enough to work as development programmers. Many employers are interested in technical staff who not only have a strong understanding of prevailing languages and technologies in their field, but also are willing to quickly develop new skills as corporate needs change. Programmers with broad training and in-depth knowledge of several fields have the greatest potential for success.

Computer services jobs are predominately white-collar positions. Unlike workers in telecommunications equipment, who are more likely to find jobs as precision workers, computer services workers are more likely to work as professionals, technicians, or managers.

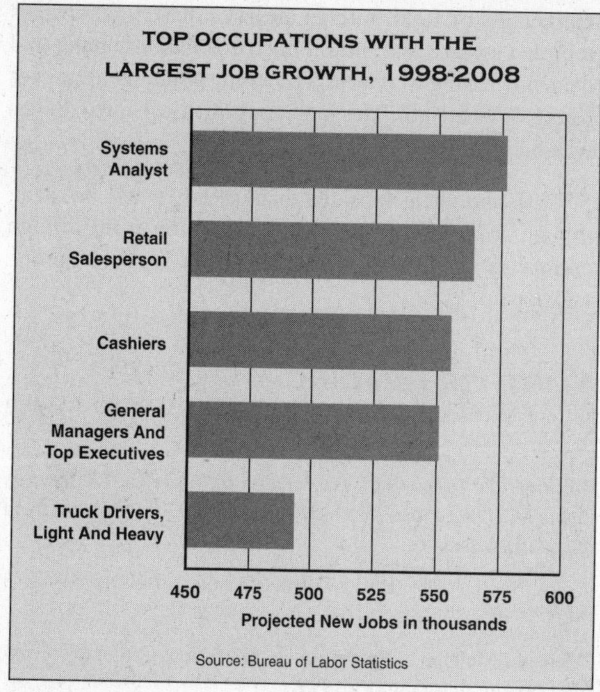

AMERICA AND THE WORLD

The United States is a leader in computer programming as well as in other computer professional services. Because of the U.S. high-tech worker shortage, however, the U.S. industry has grown more dependent on skilled contract workers overseas to keep pace with the steep demand for IT services. (The shortage has also spurred U.S.-based IT services companies to lobby for higher immigration rates of technically skilled workers into the United States.) Non-U.S. programmers often earn somewhat less than their U.S. counterparts and, according to some studies, are more productive, making international labor at times more cost-efficient. Important international labor markets for U.S. firms include India, Ireland, and Israel.

Computer professional services such as programming were encouraged by the passage of the North American Free Trade Agreement (NAFTA) and the expansion of the General Agreement on Tariffs and Trade (GATT). The U.S.-Canada Free Trade Agreement of 1989 led some U.S. computer services companies to expand into other markets by buying Canadian firms. Some U.S. companies also had subsidiaries in South America and Europe.

Custom programming remains an area of vigorous cross-border trade. According to the Bureau of Economic Analysis, exports of U.S. computer and data processing services, which include custom programming along with a variety of other services, totaled $2 billion in 1998—this compares with imports of just $365 million that year. However, most international trade in computer services is realized through affiliate organizations based in the target market. As of 1996, foreign affiliates of U.S. companies reported some $28.8 billion in receipts for computer and data processing services. The corresponding figure for foreign-owned affiliates operating in the United States was $4.7 billion.

Despite their lopsided market advantage to date, though, U.S. firms face stiff competition from foreign companies, particularly those located in Western Europe and Japan.

FURTHER READING

Caton, Michael. "The Next-Generation App." *PC Week,* 3 January 2000.

Information Technology Association of America. *IT Services Division Home Page.* Washington, D.C.: 2000. Available from http://www.itaa.org.

Leibs, Scott. "The 'Build-vs-Buy' Debate." *Industry Week,* 3 May 1999.

Menagh, Melanie. "Programmers for a New Century." *Computerworld,* 1 November 1999.

Stedman, Craig. "SAP Taps Users to Build Software; Firms Get Near-Custom Industry Applications." *Computerworld,* 31 January 2000.

"Top 50 U.S. IT Services Firms." *IT Services Business Report,* June 1999. Available from http://www.itreport.com.

SIC 7372

PREPACKAGED SOFTWARE

This industry classification covers establishments primarily engaged in the design, development, and production of prepackaged computer software. Important products include operating, utility, and application programs. Establishments of this industry may also engage in services such as preparation of software documentation, installation of software, and training users in the use of software. Businesses primarily engaged in preparing software documentation or installing software on a contract or fee basis are classified under **SIC 7379: Computer Related Services, Not Elsewhere Classified.** Businesses primarily engaged in training users in the use of computer software are classified in **SIC 8243: Data Processing Schools.** Those primarily engaged in buying and selling prepackaged software are classified in trade industries; those offering custom computer programming services are classified under **SIC 7371: Computer Programming Services**; those developing custom computer integrated systems are classified in **SIC 7373: Computer Integrated Systems Design.**

NAICS CODE(S)

511210 (Software Publishers)

334611 (Software Reproducing)

INDUSTRY SNAPSHOT

A key growth engine in the information economy—and the U.S. economy in general—the packaged software industry roared through the latter half of the 1990s with 15 percent-a-year sales growth. Industry profits and employee ranks swelled by similar rates. Conservative estimates placed domestic sales in 2000 at $65 billion, but some analysts reckon that figure closer to $80 billion. Worldwide, International Data Corp. predicted that packaged software sales in 2000 would surpass $175 billion, a 13.5 percent gain over 1999. Most observers expect comparable growth in the early 2000s, spurred by new product launches and rising e-commerce sales.

Factors Influencing Growth. Software demand has risen steadily as computer hardware and software innovations have improved business productivity and information management. Sales of desktop computers and higher-end hardware, which rose strongly throughout the 1990s, directly fuel new demand for packaged software. Strong PC shipments, for instance, create a fertile market for standard desktop software packages like operating systems and productivity suites.

New product categories, especially ones aimed at the business market, can also stimulate brisk growth. Emerging business software categories include enterprise resource planning (ERP), customer relationship management (CRM), sales force automation, knowledge management, and e-commerce suites.

Meanwhile, version upgrades drive repeat sales. Microsoft's release of Windows 2000, the most comprehensive overhaul of the operating system since 1995, was expected to usher in a new wave of upgrade sales, particularly by corporate users.

New Delivery and Pricing Options. The most fundamental changes in the software industry, however, will be how and when end users obtain new software—and under what pricing terms.

Software for rent, delivered by so-called application service providers (ASPs) over the Internet, poses a serious challenge to conventional software distribution and pricing. Instead of buying a static version of a program to run on their own computers, users log onto network-based applications that reside on the ASP's hardware. This means the current version is always on tap and users aren't saddled with installation and maintenance chores. What's more, rather than paying a fixed license cost, users pay either a flat monthly fee or a per-use fee. By some estimates, renting can save 20 percent or more over conventional licensing. These savings can be found not only in less money and time put into owning the software itself, but also in reduced or eliminated costs of buying and maintaining servers to run network applications.

ORGANIZATION AND STRUCTURE

Software Categories. Packaged software is a major segment of the broader software industry, which also includes custom software development and systems integration services. The term ''packaged'' is thus in contrast to customized software. It is typically mass-produced with standard functionalities that are expected to work across a given class of computers, such as PCs running Windows 98 or network servers running Unix. Some high-end business software straddles the packaged and custom classifications; it comes with standard functions and interfaces, but requires customization for a particular company's needs.

From a functional standpoint, there are three basic types of software:

- operating systems software, which controls how a computer operates;
- applications software, such as word processing or spreadsheet programs; and
- utility software, designed to perform support tasks for operating systems or applications.

Many software companies sell products in each of these categories.

Software Markets. In broadest terms, the software industry serves two markets, consumers and businesses. There's some overlap, though, particularly between consumers and small, home-based businesses. Productivity suites and operating systems, for example, are common to both homes and businesses.

The U.S. consumer market represents less than 10 percent of industry sales. Important subcategories within it include operating systems, financial and tax applications, games (including ones for game consoles like Nintendo's Game Boy and Sony's Playstation), educational software, and virus detection utilities. Software publishers like Microsoft, The Learning Company, Symantec, Intuit, Havas Interactive, and GT Interactive lead the consumer market.

Much larger and more fragmented, the business market is the software industry's bread and butter. Aside from the ubiquitous desktop operating systems and productivity packages, business software includes categories such as

- application development software
- systems management utilities
- network operating systems and utilities
- database management systems
- storage management systems

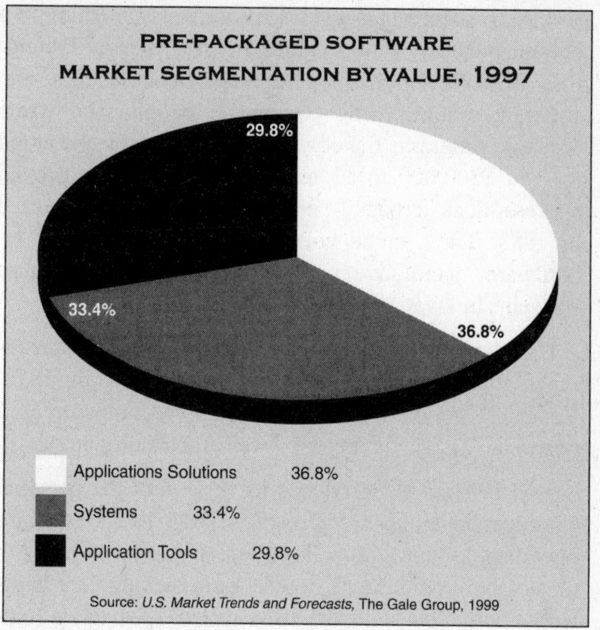

- workgroup applications (groupware)
- function-oriented applications for areas such as finance, sales, manufacturing, logistics, human resources

Leading vendors in these areas include BMC Software, Computer Associates, IBM, Oracle, PeopleSoft, and SAP.

BACKGROUND AND DEVELOPMENT

The packaged software industry has its origins in a 1969 U.S. Justice Department settlement that forced IBM to sell software for its mainframe computers separately from the hardware. IBM had included basic software with the computer and additional programming was generally done in-house. With this decision, individual entrepreneurs were finally able to compete with IBM. Small software companies sprang up, usually to offer a single program or utility. Most mainframe software was leased, however, rather than sold.

Early Products Flourish. The rise of the packaged software industry was a direct result of the appetite for software for personal computers. PCs got off the ground in the late 1970s as computer enthusiasts bought machines by Apple Computer, Inc., Tandy Corporation, Atari, and Commodore. Software publishers such as Microsoft emerged to write programming languages for them, and soon these languages were being sold to the public through retail outlets. By the end of 1979, Microsoft had already sold 1 million copies of its version of the BASIC programming language. Primitive spreadsheets and other applications began to appear as well, all of them created by small, relatively unknown companies.

At this stage packaged software was something of a cottage industry, with programs often written by individuals at home in their spare time. Because authoring software requires little equipment, people who wrote software programs risked only their own time, and stood to gain $200,000 to $1 million if the program proved successful, as perhaps 1 percent were, as *Forbes* reported in 1983. These small companies were encouraged by hardware manufacturers, particularly Apple, because software innovations helped sell hardware.

Considered revolutionary, Visicalc, the first spreadsheet for microcomputers, was introduced in 1979. Visicalc's popularity sold many Apple computers and raised the public awareness level of PCs in general.

In 1981 IBM introduced its version of the personal computer and chose Microsoft's DOS as its standard operating system. Other hardware manufacturers, with the notable exception of Apple, began making their hardware compatible with the IBM system, providing standardization for the industry. Standardization meant that software which ran on one manufacturer's equipment would run on all with minimal modification.

IBM's prestige also changed the image of the PC in the business world from that of a toy to that of serious equipment, and sales of software and hardware rose accordingly. In 1980, 300,000 people owned microcomputers; by 1983 nearly ten times that number did.

More than 21,000 PC software packages were available by 1983. Packaged software had garnered about $2.7 billion worth of retail sales a year as early as 1981, and the industry grew at a rate of nearly 50 percent a year. Given this record of tremendous growth, the packaged software industry and PCs began to attract a great deal of attention from the press and investors, and a number of successful software firms soon went public. Over $180 million in venture capital was raised by about 90 software firms in 1983, and 20 firms went public. As the computer hardware business became less profitable, many investors switched to software companies.

By the end of 1983, 500,000 copies of MS-DOS had been sold, carrying Microsoft's annual sales to $69 million. Other software publishers picked up steam as well. Lotus Development Corporation introduced its 1-2-3 spreadsheet in 1983 and was immediately successful; some businesses even bought computer hardware just so they could run the Lotus software. Software houses that had been tiny entities only a few years earlier racked up huge sales.

One of the most frequent complaints about early software was that it was too hard to use. Making software easier to use became an important goal. A defining advance came in 1984 when Apple introduced the Macintosh. It was the first popular system to employ a graphical user interface (GUI), a computing environment that relies heavily on images and visual tasks rather than text-based commands and keywords to control the computer. Apple also issued rules for companies writing Macintosh software to ensure all software for Apple systems would look and behave similarly.

Microsoft followed in 1985 with its first release of Windows, a GUI that ran on top of MS-DOS. Early versions were slow and cumbersome; sales were poor. Microsoft worked to upgrade Windows, but it and IBM also began work on an operating system to replace the aging DOS. Called OS/2, the new operating system was envisioned as a more powerful graphical interface than Windows. Other software developers began adapting their applications for OS/2, but few of these versions were ready by the time OS/2 was released at the end of 1987. Initial reviews and sales of OS/2 were disappointing. By the mid-1990s IBM all but abandoned OS/2, as Windows grew firmly entrenched as the dominant PC operating system, commanding as much as 90 percent market share.

Competition Mounts. With sales of PC software booming, software developers quickly branched into new markets and ratcheted up competition. It became much harder to launch new companies on a shoestring. Prices fell wherever similar programs existed, while the cost of marketing new software rose dramatically. VisiCorp, which had introduced Visicalc in 1978 on a $500 budget, spent more than $10 million by 1984 developing its VisiOn computing environment.

Meanwhile, competition mounted as software packages for spreadsheets, word processing, databases, and graphics proliferated. Software companies escalated the competitive frenzy by offering discounts and upgrade and trade-in deals. To make switching brands easier, software publishers introduced conversion utilities that could read competitors' file formats. Some even offered on-screen tutorials specifically aimed at migrating users from a competitor's program, as when Microsoft Word added special help screens tailored for WordPerfect users.

Competition also led to a price war—the first in an industry that had been largely immune to serious pricing battles. Some observers groused that prices of individual productivity applications, which could easily reach $500 per user, were exorbitant. Packaged software prices were also hard to justify given the falling prices of computer hardware; no one wanted to spend $500 on an application for a $1,000 computer. Discounting, often tied to attempts to win over customers from competitors' programs, resulted in savings of as much as 80 percent off a package's list price. Larger publishers like Lotus and Microsoft also introduced collections of three or four programs, known as suites, at a much lower per-unit price. Some industry analysts took the price war as a sign that the packaged software business was beginning to mature.

Businesses Connect. As corporations invested in personal computers instead of mainframes and minicomputers, methods for linking computers to share information became increasingly important. Packaged software could often be shared only when the computers all ran the same operating system, but businesses often wanted to link computers that used different operating systems. This forced software companies to make heavy use of consultants and, sometimes, to design custom solutions. Networking forced software firms accustomed to mass production of software to pay increasing attention to service. As market growth for PC software slowed to 15 percent by 1990, down from 40 percent in 1988, network applications, which run on network servers and facilitate sharing of storage space and resources such as network printers, also provided a new and lucrative niche for software publishers.

Until the mid-1990s, Novell, Inc.'s NetWare dominated the PC networking market without close rival. However, as elsewhere, Microsoft began edging market share away from Novell with its 1993 launch of Windows NT. Windows NT gained ground quickly by having the power of Microsoft's immense marketing engine behind it, by integrating easily with other Microsoft products, and by embracing innovations and new technologies. For example, Microsoft beat Novell by almost a year in adding Internet technology and a World Wide Web server to its network platform.

Alternatives to Windows. Tight integration with its ubiquitous DOS and Windows operating systems and aggressive marketing and distribution tactics enabled Microsoft to dominate the applications and operating-system market, but other firms cast about for ways to break that hold.

IBM tried with OS/2 and failed. In a separate effort, Apple and IBM announced in 1991 an alliance to create the next-generation operating system, running on newer, more powerful hardware. Dubbed the PowerPC, the move was an attempt to win market share from Microsoft, but also had potential to finally unite the IBM and Apple platforms. IBM floundered, however, and delayed promoting the product and developing software for it. This left its future almost entirely in Apple's hands. By the time the PowerPC was released in the mid-1990s, Apple was far too weak to compete head-on against Windows. Instead of becoming the next-generation PC, it quietly became the next-generation Macintosh.

In the meantime, Unix had proven a more viable alternative to Windows in some contexts. Originally designed in the 1960s by AT&T for telecommunications networks, Unix gradually became the standard for high-powered scientific and technical computers working on networks. As workstations from Sun Microsystems and Silicon Graphics caught on in the 1980s, Unix slowly entered the mainstream. Among its strengths was the ability to run several programs simultaneously and display them on large monitors with crisp graphics. Indeed, few operating systems matched Unix's power and stability.

One disadvantage of Unix, though, was a lack of standardization. Many companies had released variations on it, and often applications written for one version didn't work on another. Moreover, while a great deal of Unix software existed for science and engineering applications, few packages were available for the wider market.

In 1991, AT&T created Unix Systems Laboratories (USL) to manage the Unix operating system. The following year Novell bought USL from AT&T in a bid to take control of Unix. Another salvo in Novell's growing battle with Microsoft, the acquisition gave Novell an operating system of its own. Novell quickly moved to widen the program's appeal, trying to standardize its competing versions and link it with NetWare.

Fearing Microsoft's impending release of NT, a half-dozen major Unix companies—IBM, Hewlett-Packard, Sun Microsystems, Santa Cruz Operation, USL, and Univel—agreed in 1993 on a standardization scheme. The alliance released specifications for the Unix interface and other key elements of the operating system, while allowing companies to pursue their own variations. In the months leading up to Windows NT's debut, many of these companies released new versions of Unix.

Despite such countermeasures, Windows NT enjoyed qualified success. It failed to displace Unix and other networking platforms, but developed a user base on small and medium-sized networks. The workstation version likewise generated modest sales as a more robust and stable flavor of Windows for desktop machines. By 1998, some market watchers estimated that NT was the operating system of choice on more than a third of new servers. Still, worldwide it was believed to hold less than 14 percent of the server market, where Unix versions continued to prevail.

Internet Changes Industry. While Windows NT made headway in corporate IT departments in the mid-1990s, a vastly more visible contest emerged over the Internet. The public computer network stemmed from a 1969 project of the U.S. Defense Department and had been used by scientists and researchers for years. The Internet gained popularity with its ease of exchanging text messages and files, and more importantly, with its expansive collection of linked graphical pages known as the World Wide Web.

It all required software. In 1994 Netscape Navigator was released as the first commercial Web browser. Developed by Marc Andreesson, a computer science undergraduate who masterminded the noncommercial Mosaic browser, Netscape was distributed mostly as a free download. This proved a shrewd tactic to gain market share and draw attention to the fledgling company's Web server products. Within a year, Netscape controlled some 80 percent of the burgeoning browser market. Other firms, including many start-ups, released software for Internet tasks like managing e-mail, browsing news groups, and authoring Web pages.

Microsoft countered Netscape in 1995 with the launch of its Internet Explorer, based primarily on licensed Mosaic code. Like Netscape, Internet Explorer was given away online and bundled free with other Microsoft programs. Widely seen as an inferior product, Explorer caught on slowly at first. Six months into its release, it held just 7 percent of the market.

Then, in a stunning feat, Microsoft reached an accord in 1996 with America Online, the largest online consumer service, to feature Internet Explorer as AOL's preferred browser. The deal surprised most observers because AOL already had an alliance with Netscape. AOL's collaboration and Microsoft's clout with PC makers helped the software giant pry its way into the browser market, claiming 20 percent at the end of 1996. It went on to capture more than 40 percent by late 1998, when, in another unexpected turn, AOL agreed to buy Netscape.

Elsewhere in the industry, Internet functions were increasingly integrated into many types of applications. On the simplest level, developers made common programs like word processors and spreadsheets more Internet friendly by allowing Web content to be imported and exported. More profoundly, heavy-duty corporate packages like databases and enterprise applications were infused with e-commerce capabilities.

Current Conditions

Technological advances and changing market sensibilities continue to recast this ever-changing industry. For consumer and business market alike, software publishers strive increasingly to deliver smart, integrated solutions that empower users and make them more productive—while minimizing or eliminating the hassles associated with ramping up new software applications.

Take enterprise resource planning (ERP) software. ERP packages are used by large companies to integrate diverse business functions, say, finance, logistics, and human resources, under a common, powerful, Internet-enabled interface. The software improves corporate information management and provides timely, high-level, organization-wide information for top management. In the late 1990s, it was one of the fastest-growing categories in the industry.

However, in 1999 ERP sales faltered. Growth that year slipped to 12.5 percent, an otherwise healthy level for many industries, while individual companies' revenues and profits sank well below expectation. Some observers pronounced ERP dead. That was premature, but ERP, despite its promise, was notorious for long, problematic implementation cycles before executives could bask in the real-time corporate intelligence these systems were supposed to deliver. Fears about computer glitches in the changeover to the year 2000 only aggravated ERP's problems. While the category was expected to recover and continue broadening its appeal, ERP's woes demonstrated the software market's rising aversion to uncertainty and imperfection.

Indeed, end users are becoming more sophisticated and demanding more value from each new piece of software; studies suggest, moreover, that brand loyalty in the software market is weak. While improvements to software are generally welcome, many customers, especially businesses, have grown wary of software upgrades that seem to be driven more by the vendor's marketing schedule than its product development feats. Many large companies, for instance, have stated policies not to buy a new version of a widely used program until it's been on the market at least several months and they can evaluate what impact—positive or negative—the upgrade is having at other firms. Many also wait for software developers to release service packs, which are bundles of software fixes and tweaks that correct some of the most egregious flaws in new programs.

The wisdom of such precautions is borne out by statistics on upgrade costs. For Windows 2000, the research firm Meta Group, Inc. estimated a typical large firm would spend $700-$800 per workstation to upgrade. The majority of that amount wouldn't be spent on the software license, but on staff time for upgrade-related activities like training, fielding user questions, and troubleshooting. Though high, this wasn't bad by historical standards: the conversion from Windows 3.1 to Windows 95 cost an estimated $1,500 per user.

Linux. Since the mid-1990s a swell of attention has been paid to the Linux operating system. It achieved much of its popularity simply by being an alternative to Microsoft's operating systems—an alternative that undermines Microsoft's traditional closed-code licensing paradigm. Inspired by Unix, Linux is an open-source (public domain) operating system for individual PCs and network servers. As such, different Linux packages are offered by a number of vendors, including Caldera Systems Inc., Corel Corp., and Red Hat Software Inc., and the software is inexpensive or even free. This means Linux generally isn't subject to the same kinds of licensing restrictions as most commercial programs.

While the Linux mystique helped drive a steep run-up in share prices for several publicly traded companies with Linux ties, the software's technical merits and true market potential aren't clear-cut. Various software researchers have concluded that each operating system's effectiveness differs by the task the computer is performing. For instance, a controversial benchmarking study found Linux to run faster on desktop PCs than Windows NT. Microsoft disputed the methodology and sponsored further testing. A few separate studies—some independent of Microsoft's feedback—later showed Windows NT performed significantly better than Linux on multiprocessor servers under heavy traffic. Indeed, there appears to be a growing consensus that commercial versions of Linux thus far lack the speed and management tools necessary for large corporate servers.

Although the idea of a Linux-Windows horse race may be compelling, in business settings Linux isn't likely to be a full replacement for Windows. Instead, early adopters have harnessed Linux for lightweight jobs like departmental networking and low-volume Web serving. Linux performs well in these settings and can save thousands of dollars even in a small deployment. Corporate IT departments, in fact, have grown used to running multiple operating systems for different functions. Just as NT often proved to supplement, rather than supplant, NetWare and Unix systems, so, too, is Linux likely to find a place alongside one or more other operating systems in a typical company network.

Still, as the software attracts new attention, Linux sales are expected to rise sharply in the early 2000s. International Data Corp. predicted sales would jump by an average of 25 percent a year through 2003.

Application Service Providers. More broadly, ASPs are expected to upset the software industry's status quo by pushing software distribution and hosting to the Internet and by overturning pricing conventions. The end result: software applications, especially for business, will likely be cheaper and easier to manage.

Under the traditional model, users buy software licenses at a set price per user and install the programs, typically from CD-ROM, on their machines. Usually licenses cover only the current version; when a new version comes out, the cycle begins anew.

To be sure, the shift toward ASPs will be gradual. Yet even Microsoft, which previously derided the notion, announced in fall 1999 guarded intentions to offer its market-leading Office suite for rent. The software giant has favored electronic distribution of conventional licenses. Competitors like Sun Microsystems, Oracle, and a cadre of start-ups have unveiled more sweeping plans for Internet-only packages. Such firms have much more to gain—and much less to lose—than traditional players. A 1999 Dataquest study projected global ASP revenues to surge tenfold between 1999 and 2003, topping $22 billion by 2003.

INDUSTRY LEADERS

Although monopoly allegations have captured countless headlines, the industry as a whole is nonetheless fairly fragmented. In one of the most comprehensive studies of its kind, each year *Software Magazine* ranks the world's leading 500 software producers by their estimated software revenues (thereby excluding sales of hardware, integration services, and other nonsoftware products and services). Based on the 1999 results (calendar 1998 sales), several figures illustrate the industry's competitive breadth:

- 11 firms boasted a billion dollars or more in annual software sales
- 102 firms weighed in with more than $100 million in sales
- 344 firms had sales of $10 million or greater

According to *Software Magazine*'s report, the ten largest software vendors were as follows: Microsoft Corp., IBM Corp., Oracle Corp., Computer Associates International Inc., Hitachi Ltd., SAP AG, Hewlett-Packard Company, Sun Microsystems, Inc., Compaq Computer Corp., and PeopleSoft Inc. These producers collectively sold in 1998 more than $50 billion in software worldwide, amounting to less than half of global software sales that year.

Below are profiles of some of these and other companies that have led various segments of the U.S. software industry either in sales or in influence.

Microsoft. The world's largest software company, Microsoft was founded in 1975 by Bill Gates and Paul Allen. The software leviathan got its first major break in 1981, when IBM chose it to supply an operating system (MS-DOS) for IBM's pathbreaking first PC. As IBM's desktop computer became accepted as the industry standard, so did Microsoft's operating system. Microsoft quickly began offering application packages as well, and became a major player in the Macintosh software market during the 1980s. Microsoft's Windows graphical interface, which partly emulated the Macintosh interface, became another standard in the IBM-compatible market, lifting the firm's sales to $1 billion by 1990. As Microsoft shored up its applications software line, which would eventually be united under its flagship Office productivity suite, the firm grew increasingly aggressive with hardware manufacturers about licensing its software according to its exacting terms. This later became fodder for the antitrust litigation that dogged Microsoft.

Microsoft's aggressive tactics and phenomenal profit margins during the early and mid-1990s kept it lumbering forward in the software markets. The company developed a knack for neutralizing competitors through a combination of product innovations, application integration and bundling, strategic alliances, and marketing prowess.

By 1998 Microsoft had unseated IBM as the world's largest software maker and held a commanding lead in the markets for PC operating systems, desktop productivity applications, and Internet browsers, and was zeroing in on categories like software development applications, e-mail applications, and business diagramming applications. In calendar 1998 it recorded an estimated $16.3 billion in software sales, which included a tantalizing 31 percent profit margin. For its fiscal year ending June 1999, Microsoft's corporate revenues topped $19.7 billion, with the vast majority coming from applications and operating systems.

In spite of its being declared a de facto monopoly by the judge in its antitrust case and despite widespread rumors it would be broken up, Microsoft lunged ahead in 2000 with ambitious plans to release new versions of a few of its most popular programs, most notably its Windows 2000 upgrade, in a bid to unify its divergent Windows NT and 95/98 operating systems and stave off new competition from Linux.

IBM. Historically the world's largest packaged software producer, venerable IBM fell to second place in 1998 as it redirected its strategic focus and as Microsoft's sales steamed ahead full throttle. In 1998 software represented about 15 percent, or $11.9 billion, of the computer giant's $81.7 billion in global revenues. Big Blue's main packaged software offerings include operating systems for its popular S/390 mainframes and AS/400 midrange systems; DB2 and IMS database management systems and other packages for transaction processing and system management (including Tivoli Systems); and groupware and desktop applications from its Lotus division, including Lotus Notes and Domino. However, it has faced mounting competition from Microsoft in the groupware and database server markets.

Oracle. Oracle Corporation, incorporated in 1977, is the world's biggest vendor of database management systems software, which is used to run high-end corporate data systems. IBM, Microsoft, and Informix are among its database software competitors. Oracle's products also include customer relationship management software and other large enterprise-oriented packages, where it competes with vendors such as SAP, PeopleSoft, and Baan. The firm is also noteworthy for its outspoken CEO, Larry Ellison, a sharp-tongued critic of Microsoft.

Though it's battling encroachment on its core database server business by Microsoft's SQL Server line, Oracle made a strong showing in 1999 on both sales and profits as it introduced new software and positioned its products as e-commerce tools. Oracle databases are generally viewed as more stable and reliable for high-volume, mission-critical business functions, where Microsoft databases are weakest; however, Microsoft has been closing the gap by improving its software and its SQL Server 2000 upgrade was threatening to make further inroads.

Oracle's 1998 software sales reached an estimated $5.3 billion, and for the fiscal year ended May 1999, company-wide sales surpassed $8.8 billion on a 14.6 percent net margin.

Computer Associates International. Computer Associates International began offering utilities for mainframes in 1976 and grew by buying programs from other software firms. In the mid-1980s it pushed into the market for PC applications software. At the beginning of the 1990s the firm, best known for its Unicenter system management package, beefed up customer support and began implementing a plan to link different types of computer systems and allow all its programs to communicate with each other. In 1998 software sales for the company approached $4.9 billion. Computer Associates reported a modest 11.9 percent net margin for that period.

Sun Microsystems. Best known for its speedy workstations and low-end servers, Sun is both a sizable producer of packaged software and, since the mid-1990s, a rising force for change in the industry. Headed by Chief Executive Scott McNealy, another would-be Microsoft slayer, Sun has embarked on a multi-tiered attack on conventional industry practices.

In 1996 it introduced the Java programming language, geared toward delivering platform-independent programs and functions over the Internet. In theory, this would make operating systems and even Web browsers irrelevant details because Java programs would be compatible with all kinds of systems and devices, including noncomputing devices.

In a bolder foray, Sun bought in 1999 Star Division, a relatively minor business productivity software vendor. The significance was this: Sun planned to distribute the Star Office suite freely over the Internet—broadsiding the pricing and distribution paradigm Microsoft thrived on.

However, thus far Sun's software revenue, which totaled $1.4 billion in 1998, comes largely from much more traditional software, such as its Unix-based Solaris operating systems and other midrange systems software. As of 1998, software represented less than 10 percent of Sun's annual revenue.

PeopleSoft. PeopleSoft is one of the top three major enterprise resource planning (ERP) vendors, along with Germany's SAP AG and the Netherlands' Baan, although it faces increasing competition from Oracle and others. ERP packages like PeopleSoft's, which came into vogue in the latter half of the 1990s, automate and integrate diverse organizational functions at large companies under a common software umbrella. Such functions might include finance and human resources, operations, and supply chain management. As corporate interest in ERP systems surged, PeopleSoft's revenue more than doubled between 1996 and 1998. In 1998 its software revenue totaled just over $1 billion. However, a 1999 slowdown in ERP sales threatened to dampen PeopleSoft's exuberant growth. The company also earns a small portion of its revenue from customization services, which most ERP packages require. PeopleSoft's net margin in 1998 approached 11 percent.

Compuware. Software testing and implementation are Compuware's specialty, as it offers applications to assist developers of high-end applications in mainframe and client/server environments. Compuware's core products help software developers identify errors and debug software, but it also provides software for high-end file and data management. The firm has capitalized on recent trends in the high-end corporate market by positioning its products as complements to large companies' deployment of ERP and e-commerce applications. With revenues more than doubling between its fiscal 1996 and 1998, Compuware was cited as the world's 15th-largest software company in the 1999 *Sofware Magazine* study. Its software revenues in calendar 1998 were $929 million and, for the 12 months ending in March 1999, it enjoyed a 21.4 percent net profit margin.

Adobe Systems. Ranking at number 16 on the 1999 *Software Magazine* list, Adobe Systems Inc. is a leading provider of desktop graphics and document publishing software. Among its best-known titles are Illustrator, PhotoShop, and PageMaker, which supplied the majority of its $895 million in 1998 software sales. Adobe is also known for its ubiquitous Acrobat Reader, which displays and prints highly formatted documents, and its PageMill Web authoring suite. In 1999 Adobe launched a major new desktop publishing title, In Design, aimed squarely at the high-end market dominated by Quark Inc.'s Quark-Xpress. Adobe's sales in 1999 sailed past the $1 billion mark, yielding a robust 23.4 percent net profit.

WORKFORCE

The packaged software industry's vibrant growth has demanded a steady influx of new employees. Indeed, industry employment nearly tripled during the 1990s, rising from around 112,000 in 1990 to more than 290,000 by 1999, the Bureau of Labor Statistics estimated. Private-sector analysts reckon the count at more than 800,000, based on a looser classification. On average, according to government figures, the industry boosted its labor ranks by about 12 percent each year from 1990 to 1999, and the employment outlook remains upbeat for the 2000s.

Major occupational groups represented in the industry include programmers (also called software engineers), project/product managers, graphic designers, technical writers and editors, and technical support staff. In addition to its regular employees, the industry also relies heavily on contract programmers and technical consultants, whose work may be classified under other industries for statistical purposes.

The industry's fast expansion, coupled with a tight labor market, has also yielded above average compensation for many of its workers, who tend to be highly skilled and educated. Rank-and-file application developers, for instance, earned in 1999 a median annual salary of $60,000, while their managers on average made closer to $80,000, reported a yearly *InformationWeek* survey. According to a separate study, in 1998 the average worker in the software industry took home around $68,900, more than twice the average U.S. salary.

Still, pay varies considerably by workers' experience and skills, as well as by what kind of company they work for. For example, starting salaries for recent computer science graduates are typically in the low $40,000s. Senior technical and managerial positions, on the other hand, often garner $100,000 or more. Meanwhile, programmers who use the Java and C++ languages tend to earn 15-20 percent more than those using Visual Basic, which is easier to learn but less versatile. Employees at publicly traded software companies, especially small firms, may also receive shares of company stock or stock options as compensation, a practice famous for making young and relatively low-level employees wealthy if the firm does well in the stock market. Well-funded start-ups may likewise offer more generous salaries to attract top talent from established outfits, whereas large companies tend to splurge more on benefits packages, on-site amenities, and other kinds of perks.

Working conditions for programmers and other industry employees are generally good. Because they require concentration do to their jobs, most programmers working in quiet office settings and work alone. However, as in other professions, programmers are working increasingly out of their homes. The hours at some firms are the traditional nine-to-five, but from its earliest days, the software industry has been known for its long hours.

AMERICA AND THE WORLD

The United States is the world's largest producer, exporter, and consumer of packaged software, but there are important industry players around the globe. According to *Software Magazine*'s analysis, 18 of the world's top 20 software concerns in 1999 were headquartered in the United States. The two non-U.S. leaders were Hitachi Ltd. and SAP AG, heralding from Japan and Germany, respectively.

Behind the United States, Western Europe is the second-largest regional software market, representing about 30 percent of global purchases. The United Kingdom, Germany, France, Italy, and the Netherlands are the biggest consumers; they account for more than two-thirds of the Western European market.

Third-largest, Asia makes up 15 percent of the world's software market. It is led by Japan, which alone commands almost two-thirds of the Asian market. Japan's market is served by a strong domestic industry. Other large Asia-Pacific software markets include Australia, China, and South Korea. India, a major exporter of programming services, has a sizable and fast-growing market as well. Continued economic recovery in Asia was expected to revive growth in the early 2000s.

Latin America is another promising growth market for packaged software. Though some countries in the region were broadsided by economic and currency troubles in the late 1990s, the longer-term outlook remains upbeat. Software sales in Latin America are low compared to elsewhere in the world, estimated at $3 billion as of 1999, but they were expected to more than double within five years.

Piracy Persists. A major hurdle facing the global industry is piracy. In 1998, it was estimated that more than $11 billion was lost to piracy worldwide. Throughout the world, it is believed that more than a third of all business applications in use are illegal copies. But the piracy rate varies drastically by region. In places like Russia piracy was as high as 92 percent; in Latin America, the average was closer to 62 percent. China, a perennial target of U.S. intellectual property gripes, weighed in at 95 percent. Ironically, though the United States had the lowest piracy rate in the world at 25 percent, the industry's greatest monetary losses to piracy occur in the United States. The economic value of piracy in the United States is twice that of China, which is second worst in terms of monetary losses. This is because the U.S. market is so vast, representing around 43 percent of global software demand.

Anti-piracy advocates argue that reducing piracy will boost industry revenues, lower software prices, and yield other economic benefits such as increasing government tax revenues and creating more skilled jobs.

Further Reading

1998 Global Software Piracy Report. Washington, D.C.: Business Software Alliance, May 1999. Available from www.bsa.org.

Boston, William. "Business-Software Sales Expected to Surge after Y2K Moratorium." *Wall Street Journal,* 3 January 2000.

Business Software Alliance. *Forecasting a Robust Future: An Economic Study of the U.S. Software Industry.* Washington, D.C.: 1999. Available from www.bsa.org.

Clark, Don. "Customers' Upgrade Fatigue Could Threaten PC Profits." *Wall Street Journal,* 14 May 1998.

———. "The End of Software." *Wall Street Journal,* 15 November 1999.

Hamilton, David P. "Sun to Challenge Microsoft's Office with Purchase of Software Maker." *Wall Street Journal,* 31 August 1999.

Hamm, Steve. "Industry Outlook 2000: Software." *Business Week,* 10 January 2000.

Favell, Andy. "Hard Sell." *Wall Street Journal,* 6 December 1999.

PC Data, Inc. "PC Data Releases 1998 U.S. Software Sales Statistics." Reston, VA: 27 January 1999.

"The Software 500." *Software Magazine,* June/July 1999. Available from www.softwaremag.com.

Taylor, Roger. "Microsoft Counters Sun with Plan to Rent Out Software on Internet." *Financial Times,* 30 September 1999.

SIC 7373

COMPUTER INTEGRATED SYSTEMS DESIGN

Establishments in this industry are primarily engaged in developing or modifying computer software and packaging or bundling the software with purchased computer hardware—computers and computer peripheral equipment—to create and market an integrated system for a specific application. Establishments in this industry must provide each of the following services: the development or modification of the computer software; the marketing of purchased computer hardware; and involvement in all phases of systems development from design through installation. Establishments primarily engaged in selling computer hardware are classified in **SIC 5045: Computers and Computer Peripheral Equipment and Software,** and **SIC 5734: Computer and Computer Software Stores;** those manufacturing computers and computer peripheral equipment are classified in **SIC 3570: Computer and Office Equipment.**

NAICS Code(s)

541512 (Computer Systems Design Services)

Industry Snapshot

Spurred by e-commerce development and other trends, systems integration revenues took a sharp upswing in the mid-1990s and healthy growth was expected to continue into the early 2000s. E-commerce integration, which involves linking Internet-based data and applications with corporate databases and other non-Internet applications, has been one of the fastest-growing segments, rising by some estimates at more than 100 percent a year in the late 1990s. Other growth drivers have included corporate migration to large enterprise application environments like enterprise resource planning (ERP) and supply-chain management (SCM) systems, mergers and acquisitions that require marrying the separate data systems of the merged entity, and the ongoing need to share business data and applications across diverse platforms and software environments.

From 1996 to 1998 alone, according to government statistics, U.S. systems integrators' revenues vaulted 50 percent, approaching $32 billion, including consulting and related work. The industry as a whole was not expected to sustain that rate, but even the most conservative estimates placed growth in the late 1990s and early 2000s at 10 percent a year or better.

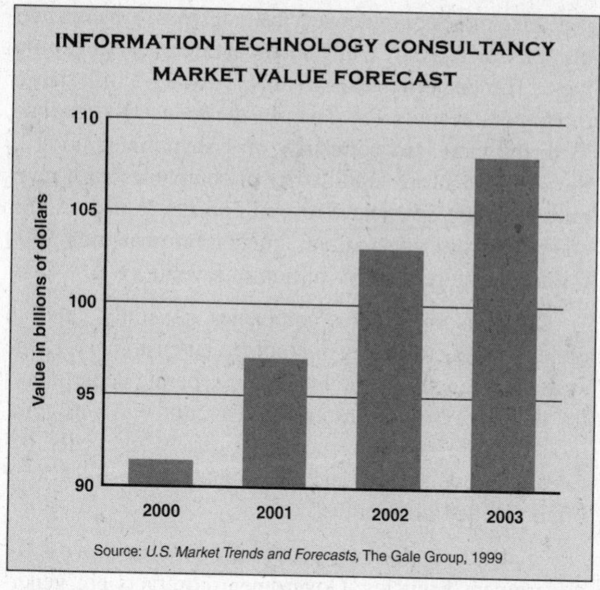

Source: *U.S. Market Trends and Forecasts*, The Gale Group, 1999

ORGANIZATION AND STRUCTURE

Once a company identifies the specific design, operational, or management functions it wants its information system to perform—and the level of that performance—a systems integrator creates a system to meet those objectives. Systems integration services combine expertise in hardware, software, and communications to deliver complete information systems, including their design and development, the management of vendor contracts, the purchase of equipment and its technical integration, the implementation of the system, and any training necessary for the company to run its new or modified system.

The Information Technology Association of America, a trade group for the computer hardware and services industries, used the following analogy to explain systems integration: "In construction industry terms, the systems integrator would compare to the general contractor who interfaces with the electrician, the plumber, the mason, and any other trades that are necessary for the job, and who may undertake part of the task (for example, the role of architect). In systems integration, this general or 'prime' contractor responsibility may be assumed by an outside vendor or by the user, who may also wish to provide some of the core skills."

Integration services are, in practice, commonly offered as part of a broader package of services, many of which aren't considered integration. These activities range from consulting to application development to system management. Indeed, few, if any, large systems integrators practice integration exclusively.

Companies wishing to establish or upgrade an information system turn to systems integrators for a variety of reasons. In an industry where knowledge about computers is not central to the business—such as health care, insurance, automobile manufacturing, and numerous others—engaging the services of a systems integrator gives companies access to cutting-edge skills and technologies. Having a single contract with a systems integrator, rather than separate contracts with numerous separate vendors, gives companies a fixed price and delivery date for an entire system and assurance that the system will meet their stated needs. In addition, the integrator protects the user from problems that are typical when engaging multiple vendors—including incompatible platforms, interfacing difficulties, and contract loopholes.

Like most computer service industries, systems integration has attracted many entrepreneurs. In the past, relatively little capital was needed, compared to the computer hardware industry. Agreements with equipment manufacturers for the products to be placed in the system are made on a current-period basis. Cash outlays increase as contracts increase; there is no need to manufacture anything in anticipation of growth. The majority of the investment is made in highly specialized staff with experience in several complex fields—systems and applications software, hardware, telecommunications products, and networks. In addition, experts are needed to oversee the entire process and work with customers. When selling a service, marketing also proves an important component in the structure of the business.

Systems integration companies generally grow geographically at first, simply providing their service to a wider range of customers. Because profits do not need to be invested in increased manufacturing or in research and development, systems integration companies generate a positive cash flow more easily than manufacturers. Cash flow makes acquisitions a common method of expansion, particularly into new service fields. Many systems integration companies have expanded into other computer or business services in order to avoid becoming overly dependent on one service, which might allow a competitor to undercut them or new products or regulations to jeopardize their business.

Like most computer service industries, systems integration is offered by many small, entrepreneurial companies. The majority are privately owned. Still, larger integrators account for much of the industry's revenue. With the increased popularity of systems integration in the 1990s, a strong middle tier of companies with revenues between $50 and $100 million developed. A few companies offering systems integration generated $500 million to more than $1 billion in revenues.

Systems integration companies generally cater to either federal customers or commercial customers. Large systems integration firms maintain separate departments for the two types of customers. This division was common because soliciting contracts differs markedly between the two sectors and the projects themselves were often fulfilled differently.

Federal regulations dictated the bidding process for government agencies. Government contracts are generally longer term, whereas commercial ones might be either long or short term and tend to be more dynamic. Government agencies frequently contract with systems integrators in order to avoid lengthy procurement cycles and still keep up with technological advances. A systems integrator may be hired to design and buy a whole system so that no competitive bidding is required for each separate component of the network or system. The contract might also stipulate that the systems integrator will update the system as necessary to meet the agency's functional specifications. Recent revisions in federal procurement policies, however, have made government contracts more like commercial ones in some respects.

Commercial companies contract with systems integrators because they see a competitive advantage. For instance, incorporating new technologies could improve their efficiency, save them money in the long run, or help them match their competitors.

BACKGROUND AND DEVELOPMENT

Systems integration was traditionally dominated by original equipment manufacturers, who bought equipment, components, and software from various suppliers to produce a complete computer system that it then sold to end-users. In the early 1980s, the industry boomed and computer service firms began to compete in this area. Industry revenues in 1980 were $2.2 billion; in one year they rose 36 percent to $2.9 billion.

The federal sector contributed significantly to the growing popularity of systems integration in the 1980s. Government agencies previously approached the development of their information systems in a technical manner, prescribing the individual technical components to be included in the vendor's bid. Because the federal procurement process was lengthy, an overly technical approach meant that technical specifications could become outdated even before the bidding process was over. To keep up with the rapidly changing computer industry, agencies began using functional specifications rather than technical ones, and systems integrators to simplify the procurement process. Several large federal contracts in the early 1980s caught the commercial world's attention and helped popularize systems integration services. For example, EDS won a contract in 1982 to computerize administrative functions in 47 U.S. Army bases, generating revenues of $1 billion over 10 years. Around the same time, the Planning Research Corporation won a similar contract from the U.S. Patent Office.

The advances in mini and microcomputers in the late 1980s opened up the market for systems integration. Smaller companies, for whom mainframe systems were unfeasible, began establishing in-house computer systems and turned to systems integrators for assistance. In addition, larger companies continued to need help integrating new technologies.

Revenues in the systems integration industry grew at a healthy rate through the late 1980s and early 1990s, averaging 7.5 percent per year. However, a survey conducted by the Information Technology Association of America of predominantly public systems integration companies showed that their average net profit margin fell from 6.1 percent in 1988 to an average net loss of 0.09 percent in 1992. According to the U.S. Department of Commerce, revenues rose 8.7 percent between 1993 and 1994 and were expected to continue to rise between 1994 and 1997 at an annual rate of 8.1 percent.

The steady rise in revenues despite a general economic downturn in the early 1990s was spurred by various factors. Industry downsizing helped value-added resellers, who once handled predominantly low-cost products from small companies. Many began handling sophisticated, expensive design automation products from manufacturers who reduced or eliminated their dedicated sales forces in an effort to cut costs. Approximately 1,800 companies provided systems integration services in the United States in 1993. Their revenues totaled an estimated $19.3 billion that year and were expected to reach $20.9 billion in 1994.

Networking services were a strong portion of the systems integration industry's growth in the early 1990s. Centralized mainframe computing, once the mainstay in the business world, was gradually supplemented, sometimes even replaced, by distributed networks of minicomputers, workstations, and personal computers. The many options available and the constant introduction of new products discouraged companies from designing systems themselves. Analysts expected this trend toward open system architectures to affect the systems integration industry through the 1990s. Rapid advances in telecommunications technology also contributed to the increasing reliance on systems integrators. The advantages of remote connectivity to geographically dispersed companies was only partly realized by the mid-1990s, creating strong demand for network integration services.

Services for computer-aided design (CAD), computer-aided manufacturing (CAM), and computer-aided engineering (CAE) were not growing as quickly as the systems integration services industry as a whole in the early 1990s as the incorporation of these technologies slowed. Despite the already high installed base, the ever-increasing complexity of designs and the advantages of automation for the mechanical, architectural, engineering, construction, and mapping industries was expected to sustain the growth of CAD/CAM/CAE technology and services.

CURRENT CONDITIONS

Amid strong demand, in 1998 industry revenue approached $32 billion, according to the U.S. Census Bureau; this was up from just $20 billion as of 1996 and about $13 billion in 1990. Growth from 1992 to 1995 was languid, averaging 3-7 percent a year. By 1996, annual growth shot up to almost 16 percent and in 1997 it approached a frenzied 30 percent. Although it slowed to about 22 percent in 1998, annual growth was expected to continue between 10 percent and 20 percent a year into the early 2000s, with industry revenues likely to exceed $40 billion in 2000.

E-Commerce Integration. Web and e-commerce integration have been the focal point for the industry. Brisk demand for these services emerged in the mid- and late 1990s as companies embraced the Internet as a sales and marketing channel. Typical e-commerce integration projects include linking a Web site and its supporting applications to existing corporate systems for storing product information, recording orders, managing transactions, and storing customer information. Because e-commerce initiatives are seen increasingly as vital to a company's competitive strategy, the market for e-commerce integration can be particularly demanding, requiring fast turnaround and extensive knowledge of different systems—new and old.

Enterprise Application Integration. Another important growth driver, especially in the large corporate market, has been the widespread adoption of enterprise applications aimed at unifying data storage and management across broad swaths of corporate activities—from human resources and payroll to manufacturing and logistics. Many also have industry-specific components intended for, say, telecommunications providers or financial services. These applications, offered by vendors like Oracle, PeopleSoft, and SAP, come with many preconfigured functions and tools, but generally require customization and integration for specific users. Thus, systems integrators often sell, install, and customize them for individual clients.

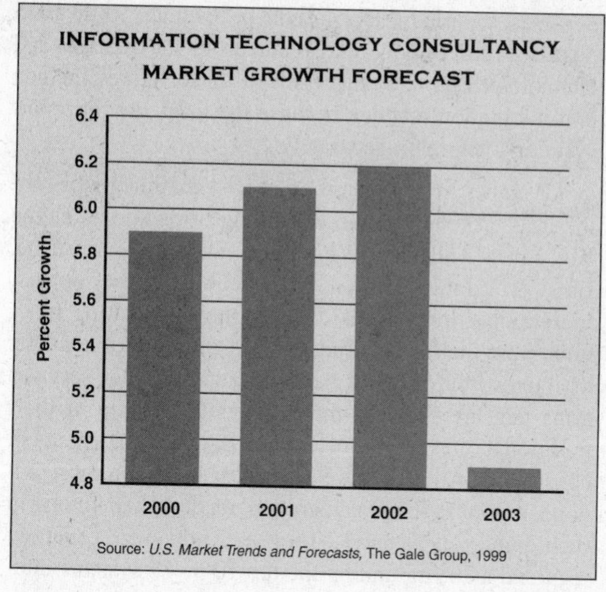

Source: *U.S. Market Trends and Forecasts*, The Gale Group, 1999

Some applications like enterprise resource planning (ERP) systems, which saw dramatic growth in 1997 and 1998 only to face a slowdown in 1999, have gained an unfavorable reputation for having long, disruptive deployment schedules and not always living up to customers' expectations. Still, demand for ERP and others like supply-chain management systems and customer-relationship management systems was expected to remain strong in 2000 and for the next few years.

Competitive Environment. The competitive landscape for integrators has changed as demand has surged. Some smaller firms, for instance, have an advantage in the market for rapid e-commerce integration, where they may be seen as more flexible, more responsive, possibly more knowledgeable, and better able to meet tight deadlines. Meanwhile, large integrators like EDS and IBM Global Services bring tremendous resources and bargaining power to the table, and are able to win larger, more complex contracts through their name recognition and stable brand image—even though they may subcontract the actual work to smaller, less-well-known firms. The industry has also seen a wave of mergers and acquisitions as companies seek the right mix of competencies and market access to best meet new demand.

INDUSTRY LEADERS

By revenue size the two largest firms in the industry, both in the United States and the world, are IBM Global Services of Somers, New York, and Electronic Data Systems of Plano, Texas. Both are massive service organizations that provide a complete range of computer services like outsourced management and consulting in addition to systems integration. In 1999 IBM Global

Services recorded $32.2 billion in revenue, while EDS posted $14.8 billion in revenue from its systems and technology services unit. Both of those figures include non-integration revenue because the firms do not report systems integration separately.

Another important group of systems integrators are the large accounting and consulting firms known as the Big Five: Andersen Worldwide, Deloitte & Touche, Ernst & Young, KPMG, and PricewaterhouseCoopers. Increasingly these firms distance their consulting functions from their accounting business, for fear of conflicts of interest, but they all have vibrant computer services arms that are growing much faster than some of their traditional businesses of accounting and management consulting. All five have revenues in the billions, but none report systems integration receipts separately in their public disclosures. They are, however, generally regarded as being among the top 10 or 15 systems integrators in the world.

Additional players that rank in the industry's top ten include the integrated hardware-services providers Compaq Computer Corp., Hewlett-Packard Co. (HP), and Unisys Corp. Each of these has a thriving hardware business (although less so for Unisys, which has focused mainly on services) in addition to its professional services organization. All of them provide a full array of services, including consulting and applications development. Including all service income, Compaq was the largest of the three in 1999, with $6.6 billion in service revenues. It was followed by HP, with $5.9 billion, and Unisys came in close behind with $5.4 billion.

Other major systems integrators include Computer Sciences Corp., American Management Systems Inc., Computer Associates International Inc., and Perot Systems Inc., all of which had 1999 revenues of $1 billion or greater.

Workforce

The number of systems integration employees has grown dramatically along with the general growth of the industry. In 1980, systems integration employees numbered 35,000; by 1990 the count had nearly tripled to 97,500. By 1999 the industry's employee count more than doubled again, reaching 197,600. From 1990 to 1999, the industry added each year a compound average of more than 8 percent to its employee ranks. More growth was expected in the early 2000s.

The majority of jobs in the systems integration industry were white collar, and many required specialized knowledge. Functional area specialists had considerable expertise in a particular industry, such as financial services or health care, and used that knowledge to help the systems integration team tailor solutions to the specific needs of a company. Project managers coordinated entire projects, including planning, budgeting, training, the initial operation of new systems, and selecting products, services, and vendors. The transmission of information between people, computers, and locations was handled by communications specialists who analyzed and designed networks that carried data, voice, and video traffic.

Software specialists analyzed software requirements and designed software to meet client needs, created ''blueprints'' for systems integration projects, and were often involved in the development and implementation cycles. Hardware specialists designed optimal hardware configurations and managed the operation of hardware for systems in use. Supporting staff marketed and sold services, negotiated contracts, or worked in finance or accounting.

By the mid- to late 1990s, there was a great demand for systems integrators, especially those with a strong understanding of the Internet, intranet, and web-based application design. The demand was for people with skills in Java programming, security and firewall experts, and people who could connect presentation-level interfaces with databases and legacy systems, according to the *Computer Reseller News.*

America and the World

The U.S. systems integration industry is the world's largest, with the domestic market amounting to as much as 45 percent of world demand, and many of the largest integrators are U.S. firms. According to a study by market researcher International Data Corp., all of the world's top ten integrators in 1998 were U.S. firms.

Western Europe is the second-largest market for systems integration and many U.S. integrators have built sizable businesses there. Large companies like IBM, EDS, the Big Five, and Computer Sciences Corp. obtain a significant portion of their revenues from Europe and elsewhere outside the United States.

Meanwhile, the fastest-growing markets for integration services have been in Asia and the Pacific Rim and Latin America. Economic downturns in these areas reduced demand for some services in the late 1990s, but as they recovered emerging economies like those of China, South Korea, Argentina, Brazil, and Mexico were expected to provide ample growth opportunities.

Firms based in Europe, Japan, and India, which has a well-developed and flourishing technology services industry, were well placed to compete with U.S. firms in Asia and elsewhere.

Research and Technology

Technical standardization increased in the computer, telecommunications, and CAD/CAM/CAE industries in the late 1980s and early 1990s, influencing the work of systems integrators. The Computer Framework Initiative, Inc., a consortium dedicated to the development of industry standards, developed guidelines for CAD/CAM/CAE software, making it easier to integrate software from different suppliers. Other industry standards with which producers began to comply included electronic data interchange (EDI) protocols, integrated systems digital network (ISDN) protocols, and the ISO 9000 series of quality-system technical standards. Analysts expected the number of producers complying with these and other standards to increase throughout the 1990s.

In the mid-1990s, computer systems and telecommunications networks continued to grow more complex, and engineering, manufacturing, and front-office automation grew more common. In the face of these changes and the rapid rate of technical advances, companies increasingly depended on systems integrators to maintain their competitiveness.

FURTHER READING

Caton, Michael. "The Great Systems Integrator Search." *PC Week,* 21 June 1999.

Dunlap, Charlotte. "Open Market Woos Web Integrators." *Computer Reseller News,* 5 August 1996.

Edelman, Russ. "Application Integration a Hands-On Job." *Information Week,* 17 March 1997.

Elgin, Ben. "Be Sure to Watch Your Back." *Sm@rt Reseller,* 27 September 1999.

Girishankar, Saroja. "Integrators Turn Their Attention to E-Commerce." *Information Week,* 21 May 1999.

Information Technology Association of America. *The U.S. Information Technology Industry Profile.* Arlington, VA: 1998. Available from www.itaa.org.

Klinger, Linda. "Fed Downsizing Sends Work to Systems Integrators." *Washington Business Journal,* 22 January 1999.

Longwell, John. "Taking Clients to the Next Level: The World Wide Web." *Computer Reseller News,* 25 November 1996.

Madden, John. "Changing of the Guard." *PC Week,* 17 May 1999.

———. "CSC, EDS Jump into Web Hosting." *PC Week Online,* 2 March 2000. Available from www.pcweek.com.

Maney, Kevin, and Julie Schmidt. "Sun's Network Line May Spark Low-Cost Revolution." *USA Today,* 29 October 1996.

Violino, Bob, and Bruce Caldwell. "Analyzing the Integrators." *Information Week,* 16 November 1998.

Vowler, Julia. "Contemplate a Mammoth Investment." *Computer Weekly,* 30 September 1999.

Zarley, Craig. "Integrators—A New Breed of Competitor Joins the Ranks of Traditional Integrator Companies." *Computer Reseller News,* 3 June 1996.

SIC 7374

COMPUTER PROCESSING AND DATA PREPARATION AND PROCESSING SERVICES

This category encompasses establishments primarily engaged in providing computer processing and data preparation services. The service may consist of complete processing and preparation of reports from data supplied by the customer or a specialized service, such as data entry or making data processing equipment available on an hourly or time-sharing basis. Subgroups within this entry include computer calculating services, computer service bureaus, computer tabulating services, computer time-sharing, data entry services, data processing services, data verification services, keypunch services, leasing of computer time, optical scanning data services, and rental of computer time.

NAICS CODE(S)

514210 (Data Processing Services)

INDUSTRY SNAPSHOT

Serving a diverse array of industries, data processing services allow companies to outsource some or all of a data management process, be it payroll, electronic transaction processing, or some other task. Data processing firms offer specialized knowledge and technologies as well as economies of scale, making them efficient and often cost-effective alternatives to handling such data in-house. As a result, demand for data processing services rose sharply in the 1990s. From just 1994 to 1998, according to government statistics, industry revenue swelled 50 percent, topping $45.8 billion by 1998.

The largest segments of the industry include payroll processing, employer tax reporting and filing, credit-card transaction processing, billing services, insurance claims processing, and general data-center services. Many of these functions have been outsourced for a decade or more, but market penetration is still relatively low for some, leaving considerable room for growth. Small companies, for example, are increasingly a target for payroll-processing firms because the small business market is the least saturated for such services.

One of the most important growth trends affecting the industry has been a shift toward Internet-based bill payment and presentment. Under these services, a third-party processor packages billing information for another company, say, an electric utility or a long-distance carrier, and presents it to the customer, often a consumer or small business, in a unified environment. A service might also allow users to pay bills electronically. In the late

1990s the field was wide open for competitors and had attracted both traditional data processing firms as well as many nontraditional players. Revenues from online bill payment and presentment services were predicted to climb quickly in the early 2000s as more consumers and businesses engage in e-commerce.

Organization and Structure

In 1989, firms that provided data processing services totaled 6,811, and employment totaled 217,900. By 1996 the number of firms had increased to more than 7,000, and employment was estimated at 250,400. The industry ranged from small family-type operations to large multinational companies. Several of the biggest firms are publicly traded, independent companies, but many others are subsidiaries, joint ventures, divisions, or affiliates of larger corporations like banks.

Background and Development

The data processing services industry has evolved greatly since the 1950s, when computers became more prevalent in business. The computer services industry developed when companies purchased systems and needed assistance to effectively use them. Other niches developed as other firms saw the benefits of computerizing certain business functions but could not afford to install and operate systems. Computer time-sharing developed as an alternative to purchasing and maintaining an expensive system and allowed clients to purchase time on a computer as needed and avoid personnel and equipment costs. Calculating, keypunch, optical scanning, and tabulating services were used by corporations that saw the value of automating large batch jobs but could not maintain these systems in-house.

Many computer service companies became successful because they could offer useful services at lower prices than it would cost companies to install and maintain similar systems. The costs were divided among all users, making data processing services an attractive option. Often costs were determined by the number of transactions, instead of simply a flat rate.

Many of the segments of the industry, such as keypunch service and computer time-sharing, have decreased substantially since the 1970s. Keypunch services became outmoded for general applications when computer disks and magnetic tape were developed. Disks and magnetic tapes, the storage materials of choice, are less sensitive than cards and contain thousands of bytes of memory capacity. Computer time-sharing decreased as an industry segment when hardware prices decreased in the 1970s and 1980s and software became more adaptable. Many corporations have invested in computer hardware and have hired in-house staffs to maintain and program their computer systems.

As computer capabilities increased, companies looked to the computer service industry to provide either more sophisticated services or to reduce their record-keeping costs. Data entry services that have typically been maintained in-house became candidates for outsourcing as employee benefit costs increased. Access to the most sophisticated computer systems may become important for specific tasks, which would be prohibitively expensive if companies had to purchase a computer and customize the software.

Outsourcing represents the segment of this industry with the greatest growth potential. Outsourcing is the practice of turning over a portion of the company's data processing to an outside vendor. Eastman Kodak was the first major corporation to sign a ten-year contract with International Business Machines (IBM) in 1989. Other companies soon followed Kodak's lead, and outsourcing was projected to expand by 25 percent annually to become a $21-billion business by 1996.

Economic conditions in the early 1990s forced companies to re-examine the resources devoted to data processing. Competition intensified in business, placing an additional burden on information systems. Many companies opted to use outside computer service firms for various tasks in order to tap into the most precise and timely information. By using computer service firms, companies could reserve expensive personnel and capital resources for other portions of their business.

Time-sharing and transaction processing are the two main categories within processing services. Time-sharing involves purchasing time on a large computer that otherwise would not be accessible to the company. Few companies use time-sharing any longer because most basic corporate processes can be performed in-house with the abundance of inexpensive hardware and sophisticated software. Companies that do use time-sharing do so because they can access accelerated computer power that would otherwise be too expensive; the purchase makes a computer upgrade transition period more smooth; and a company's computer resources are taxed beyond their capacities during certain seasons.

Back-office tasks, or routine, high-volume clerical tasks such as payroll processing, have long been completed by computer service vendors. Payroll duties include generation of checks and journals, employee earnings statements, departmental earnings summaries, and withholding tax reports, as well as pension fund and profit-sharing reports, according to *Standard & Poor's Industry Surveys.* The future of payroll processing is tied to the economy: when unemployment increases, the number of paychecks decreases, as does the number of small businesses because some fail during an economic downturn. While payroll processing remains the largest single application, the industry is evolving and being utilized for more sophisticated applications in banking, finance, insurance, and medical industries.

Transaction processing vendors process routine, high-volume applications. Computer services have primarily automated back office functions. Because most companies have completed this automation, many data processing services are focusing on areas that enable companies to win business from customers, or front office functions, according to *Standard & Poor's Industry Surveys.* Computerization can aid in automating customer information systems, providing electronic funds transfer systems, and other decision support tools. These applications rely on real-time, or immediate, activities and cannot be batch processed, unlike credit card or medical claims. The future growth in this area will be slower than previous outsourcing revenue.

Traditionally, companies providing data processing services have utilized their own extensive computer facilities and proprietary software. This practice enables them to divide the cost among many users, which makes the services more affordable for each company. Trends are developing, however, that include placing the contractor's hardware in the client's site or utilizing existing client hardware. This practice reduces the vendor's costs, as well as their revenues, while placing an increased burden on the client. The contractors generally welcome the chance to exclude hardware costs and to make their clients responsible for computer maintenance and upkeep. Instead of focusing on hardware, the vendors are able to provide software applications to industries such as health care or insurance. Duplicating such sophisticated information applications in-house would be technologically and financially impossible. The data processing services industry is adapting to technological advances by seeking ways to assist computer owners to more efficiently utilize their resources.

CURRENT CONDITIONS

In 1998 data preparation and processing service revenues were valued at $45.8 billion in the United States and $59.5 billion worldwide. Globally, according to estimates by International Data Corp., the market for processing services was forecast to total $67 billion in 2000 and upwards of $80 billion by 2003, growing at a modest 6 percent a year.

Despite relatively slow growth expected for the industry worldwide, some segments were predicted to expand much faster. Payroll processing services, for one, were expected to build annual revenues at closer to 15-18 percent in the early 2000s, driven by broader market penetration. Among businesses with 100 or fewer employees, for example, payroll outsourcing services had at most a 20 percent penetration rate in the United States during the late 1990s. Even among companies with more than 100 employees, the penetration rate was barely over 50 percent. Firms like Automatic Data Processing, Ceridian, and Paychex stand to gain substantially as smaller companies opt for outsourcing their payroll functions.

Electronic bill payment and presentment is likely to be another major growth vehicle for some industry firms. However, they will compete with a more diverse swath of other companies that have been positioning themselves in that business. In 2000 CheckFree Holdings Corp., already a contender in the electronic billing space, was poised to take a definitive lead with its purchase of TransPoint, a joint venture between longtime data processing player First Data Corp. and Citibank and Microsoft. Meanwhile, financial software publisher Intuit Corp. held a stake in CheckFree. With such weighty backing, the merged company was expected to provide formidable competition to various other online billing entrants. Some of those include Internet Payment Exchange, The Exchange, Billserv.com Inc., and Princeton E-Com Corp. Other banking and credit-card concerns were expected to enter the fray, as well, in what was forecast to be a multibillion-dollar enterprise in the early 2000s.

INDUSTRY LEADERS

One of the largest firms in the business, Automatic Data Processing, Inc. (ADP) is the biggest independent payroll processor in the United States. In the late 1990s it had as its clients an estimated one-third of the payroll processing market among companies with 100 or more employees. With more than 450,000 business customers, the publicly traded firm had sales in fiscal 1999 of $5.5 billion. In additional to payroll processing, ADP provides government and tax filing services, benefits management, automotive insurance claims processing, automotive dealer services, and securities transaction processing.

Electronic Data Systems Corp. is a major integrated technology services firm and a major processor of medical insurance claims and financial data. EDS signed its first long-term contract in the medical area in 1966, when legislation establishing Medicare was passed. EDS organized claims processing support across the country, and by 1968 Medicaid and Medicare contracts represented 25 percent of Electronic Data Systems' revenues. Data processing today, however, represents only a small part of EDS's revenue. In 1999 its business process management unit reported sales of $2.6 billion out of the entire company's $18.5 billion in total revenue.

Catering to the small business market, Paychex, Inc. is considered the second-biggest U.S. payroll service, with 340,000 customers and $1.2 billion in sales as of 1999. The firm held an estimated 7 percent share of the payroll processing market for companies with fewer than 100 workers. Like ADP, Paychex offers a package of related human resource services like benefits management and tax filing.

Ceridian Corp. is another leading contender in payroll processing and human resource services. With $1.3 billion in 1999 sales, the company ranked as the United States' third-largest payroll service, but it was the leading provider in Canada and the United Kingdom. In 1999 the firm had 100,000 customers worldwide.

First Data Corp. tops the credit-card transaction processing side of the business, with $5.5 billion in 1999 sales. First Data is one of the backers of the CheckFree/TransPoint electronic bill payment and presentment service. The company also operates the Western Union cash transfer network and is involved with merchant credit-card processing services and check authorization. Despite its overall financial health, First Data announced layoffs in 2000 aimed at controlling costs and keeping its profits strong.

Workforce

As of 1999 the industry employed about 277,000 people in the United States. Some industry segments, such as data entry and keypunch services, did not require a college or university education, but could be filled by high school or technical school graduates. Most segments preferred workers with college educations despite the training that they provided; in-house education at specific companies enabled workers to learn their duties. An interest and background in computer science was typically desirable for this industry.

America and the World

The U.S. data processing services industry is the world's largest. Most American service providers operate internationally and strive to function within vertical markets to tailor their services as business conditions changed.

In the 1990s the data processing industry received approximately 20 percent of its income from foreign sources. The percentage should continue to increase as electronic data interchange activity grows throughout multinational corporations. The United States faced less competition from Japanese companies in data processing services than in the hardware industry.

The industry operated with a favorable trade balance and will focus on foreign markets as U.S. companies operate internationally. Many U.S. companies were expanding overseas and seizing the opportunity to upgrade underdeveloped information industries, especially in Europe and Asia. Few foreign firms operated in the United States, but the number was growing.

North American expenditures on information services stood at $104 billion, or 52 percent of the world's total of $201 billion. European expenditures totaled $61 billion, and the Asian/Pacific expenses were $32 billion. In 1995, the expenditures were projected to be $193 billion by the United States, $143 billion by Europe, and $76 billion by Asia and the Pacific. The United States is projected to grow 13 percent, while the other two markets will each increase 19 percent. Foreign markets should continue to be plentiful as developing nations privatize their industry and modernize their businesses.

Research and Technology

The future of the industry depends upon overcoming barriers, including ''unfair competition, industry regulation, taxation, high telecommunication costs, and inefficient telecommunication infrastructure,'' according to the *U.S. Industrial Outlook 1993.* Electronic data interchange services and outsourcing will remain the brightest spots in the computer processing and data preparation and processing services industry.

Focusing on vertical markets and responding to customers' perceived needs will be essential in the future. The hardware industry continues to evolve rapidly, and data services firms will be able to produce information for their customers at a lower cost than if the companies brought the systems in-house. As outsourcing continues to become a major market segment, some of the smaller corporations that provide this service will be usurped by the major players, such as Electronic Data Systems and International Business Machines. Fewer corporations will find investing in the large-scale systems necessary for complete data processing outsourcing to be fiscally viable, and the larger outsourcing firms will prosper. Companies will be inclined to take advantage of fixed costs for data processing procedures, instead of the variable costs that are associated with maintaining a system in-house. The economy will encourage other companies to pursue outside data processing and computer services, and this industry will continue to grow.

Prosperous firms will be those that continue to expand the front-office, or customer-related, services that they offer to their clients. Computers will become more prevalent for electronic funds transfer, inventory control, and customer information systems. Front-office needs will continue to be time-sensitive, and data processing service providers will need to focus on innovations that allow corporations to supplement personnel with computer services.

Further Reading

Posch, Robert. ''Database Marketing Has a Good Year.'' *Direct Marketing,* February 1996.

Russo, Ed. ''Omaha, Neb.-Based Banking Processor Axes 400 Jobs, with More to Come.'' *Knight-Ridder/Tribune Business News,* 3 March 2000.

Tangwall, Doug. ''The Online Billing & Payment Race.'' *Credit Union Executive,* November-December 1999.

U.S. Bureau of Labor Statistics. *National Employment, Hours, and Earnings.* Washington, D.C.: 2000. Available from www.bls.gov.

U.S. Census Bureau. *Service Annual Survey 1998.* Washington, D.C.: 2000. Available from www.census.gov.

SIC 7375

INFORMATION RETRIEVAL SERVICES

Companies in this industry are primarily engaged in providing online information retrieval services on a contract or fee basis. The information generally involves a range of subjects and is taken from other primary sources such as the original publishers of the materials. Establishments primarily engaged in performing activities, such as credit reporting, direct mail advertising, and stock quotation services, and who also create databases are classified according to their primary activity. Establishments primarily engaged in collecting databases from primary sources and reformatting or editing them for distribution through information retrieval services are classified in **SIC 7379: Computer Related Services, Not Elsewhere Classified.**

NAICS CODE(S)

514191 (On-Line Information Services)

INDUSTRY SNAPSHOT

Demand for electronic information has skyrocketed with the growth of the Internet, but the resulting low-cost competition has wreaked havoc with traditional subscription information services. The information retrieval business, which usually charges customers either by the amount of information retrieved or at a flat subscription rate, has traditionally served corporate and academic researchers and librarians—audiences that were used to paying a premium for professional-quality information. This stable market has been undermined, however, as similar information has come available on the Internet, often free.

With newspaper and magazine articles routinely available for free on the Internet, old-line full-text database services like Lexis-Nexis and Dialog have witnessed customer flight to cheaper services. As a result, competition has gotten tougher and, in many cases, revenues at traditional providers have stagnated or fallen. Mergers, acquisitions, and partnerships were frequent in the late 1990s as information providers adapted to the new marketplace. Nearly all have likewise embraced the Internet in some form, as demand has weakened for proprietary software, dial-up database connections, and CD-ROM subscriptions.

In spite of some providers' woes, however, government statistics suggest that the industry had an influx of new revenue in the mid- and late 1990s. In 1998 industry revenue was estimated at nearly $12.3 billion, up more than 100 percent from 1995. Indeed, in 1998 alone sales spiked 35 percent.

ORGANIZATION AND STRUCTURE

Online information services, increasingly over the Web, are the leading means of delivering electronic information. Other methods include CD-ROM, diskette, and magnetic tape. Online services are trademarked services that may or may not bear the same name as the companies that own and operate the services.

Online service companies may be considered the vendors, distributors, resellers, or retailers of informational databases that are often developed by third-party database publishers. The database publishers, often considered part of the broader ''information services industry,'' are not part of the online services industry, however, and are usually classified by the type of publishing they perform. The data in the databases may be numeric (such as financial statistics), bibliographic (citations to periodical literature), full-text documents, directory or dictionary entries, patents, images, or even digital audio recordings. Most online services provide multiple databases. Specialized online services may also produce one of the databases themselves. Increasingly, there are online services that provide a combination of databases that they have developed along with others that they have licensed to redistribute.

Online services can be categorized as either business/professional research services or personal online services. Business/professional online services may be highly specialized by offering only a single set of related databases to a niche market, such as the Sabre airline reservation system or the Bridge financial securities information service. They may be somewhat specialized but offer multiple databases from different sources on a similar broad subject, such as the legal online services LEXIS-NEXIS and Westlaw or the scientific service STN International. Finally, professional online services may be very general and offer up to hundreds of databases on all different subjects, such as the Dialog, LEXIS-NEXIS, or Dow Jones Reuters Business Interactive. Such distributors of multiple databases are most often referred to as ''database vendors,'' and their clients are usually corporate librarians.

The largest business segments are legal and investment. Marketing, intellectual property, scientific, and credit information service needs also comprise a large portion of this market. The remainder of the industry serves a variety of niche markets. For instance, many databases are tailored specifically to one industry or profession, such as chemical, health care, civil engineering, agricultural, banking, insurance, or food service. In addition, many niche services are managed by nonprofit industry service organizations.

While the business/professional services encompass both the specialized online services and the general-subject online services, consumer information services tend to be general, offering a wide variety of databases in order to appeal to a wider market. With the emergence of the Internet, however, consumer information services have largely become indistinct from other businesses such as electronic publishing, Internet access services, and search engines.

Indeed, by far the most pervasive form of information retrieval system, both for businesses and consumers, is the Internet search engine. Far different from the traditional information service revenue model, popular search engines are completely free to users. They instead earn money through selling advertising on the site and through electronic commerce partnerships with other firms.

Although parts of information retrieval industry are relatively young, and therefore entrepreneurial in nature, each segment of the market tends to be dominated by one or two large firms that pose formidable barriers to smaller competitors. For instance, the market for legal information is dominated by just two competitors, LEXIS-NEXIS and Westlaw—and even they have been struggling. Even niche markets tend to favor the single competitor that is first to establish a presence and to acquire ongoing access to essential copyrighted information. As a result, firms in the industry typically diversify and grow through mergers, acquisitions, or joint-ventures with other companies.

Online services allow customers using computers or computer terminals to access a remote, central computer storing databases, by connecting through a telephone/telecommunications network. If the customer is using regular analog phone lines—historically the most common method and still the most common means for home and small office customers—the customer's computer is then connected to the phone line with a modem, a device which converts between digital computer signals and analog phone signals. Business customers are increasingly using digital phone lines, such as ISDN, for online service access, because they enable higher speed and quality of data transfer. Customers access a central data bank of information by calling a local, or sometimes long-distance, telephone number, and information is then transferred to the user over the phone lines. Online services can offer local dial-up numbers throughout the country to a faraway data bank by making use of any one of various data communications networks. An alternative way to connect to the online service's computer is via the Internet, especially the Web. If a customer's organization has a host computer directly on the Internet, then its users can connect to the Internet through a local area network and no modems are needed.

Online services, which manage the databases, may charge the customer a flat monthly rate for unlimited access to the data bank. In other cases, customers pay according to the length of time they access the databases, the amount of information that they access and print, and/or the type of information that they use. Professional online services may charge as much as $300 per hour to access certain databases—and additional fees for printing records—because collecting timely information, paying copyright royalties, providing telecommunication connections, and supporting sophisticated data storage equipment generate immense overhead. Customers who access large amounts of tax and legal information may pay tens of thousands of dollars per month in online charges. In comparison to business information services, personal systems are typically inexpensive because the data is less costly and the volume of users in the market is large.

The advantage that online systems have over other forms of electronic information services is timeliness. The medium is especially appropriate for customers that require up-to-the-minute information. Database managers can continually update information related to stock quotes and other financial data, legal rulings and court proceedings, sporting events, world news, and other timely matters. Online systems are also advantageous because they allow access to massive amounts of information is cumbersome for customers to access via print or other media. In fact, the most popular online services offer simultaneous searching of multiple databases.

Background and Development

The electronic information services industry was born during the post-World War II information explosion. The advent of computers during this period formed the basis for channeling large amounts of data to scientists, engineers, businesses, and government agencies. Government investment in new information technologies in the 1950s and 1960s was supplemented by increased private sector spending on research and higher education. The result was that, for the first time, skilled professionals could create, store, and quickly access large amounts of data.

The purpose of the earliest retrieval systems was simply to store and print information—mostly for technical endeavors. As the number and size of the databases grew, however, systems engineers began to focus on searching capabilities that could filter out unneeded data. Eventually, users were able to type commands into a computer that would search and display information containing specific keywords or phrases.

The first computerized bibliographic databases stemmed from the federal government's need for the efficient application of research dollars and the desire to eliminate duplicate analyses. Some of the more popular databases developed in this period included MEDLINE and ERIC. The government also subsidized nonprofit efforts, such as the American Chemical Society's Chemical Abstracts database.

In addition to supporting nonprofit services, government investment in the 1960s initiated many of the private information retrieval services that dominated the market in the 1980s and early 1990s. For instance, DIALOG sprung from a venture between the National Aeronautics and Space Administration (NASA) and Lockheed Corporation called Project RECON. ORBIT Online was developed as a result of System Development Corporation's work with the National Library of Medicine. Industry giant Mead Data Central (now called LEXIS-NEXIS) got its start from seed money provided by U.S. Air Force projects.

The federal government also played a vital role in developing telecommunications networks that made online services possible. Networks that essentially provided affordable access for database online users through local telephone lines stemmed from Department of Defense efforts. The network of all networks, the Internet, also began as a Department of Defense project.

As more efficient telecommunications networks arose and computer technology advanced in the late 1960s and 1970s, the market for online information services began to proliferate. Companies and libraries were increasingly relying on technical and legal information to provide a competitive edge in the marketplace or to make their research efforts more efficient. Furthermore, many users were finding electronic information access to be an important tool for increasing productivity.

As electronic markets began to grow, many publishing houses began to experiment with electronic publishing as a means of delivering their information. H. W. Wilson and Company, for instance, began offering access to Wilson indexes and abstracts online through WILSONLINE. Likewise, McGraw-Hill and other periodical publishers began offering their publications online. One of the greatest commercial uses of electronic information retrieval was for legal publications.

By the end of the 1970s, the emerging information retrieval industry was beginning to establish itself in many sectors of government, academia, and industry. Because of technical limitations, however, retrieval systems remained extremely costly. Furthermore, most systems were complicated and required professional research skills for effective use. As a result, estimated industry revenues were still well under $500 million by 1980.

Technological breakthroughs in personal computer and data storage devices fueled rapid industry growth through the 1980s and early 1990s. At the same time that microcomputers were becoming faster and less expensive, users were becoming accustomed to working with modems, networks, and other communications devices which allowed large numbers of people to gain access to reservoirs of data. For the first time information retrieval companies were able to expand their services to the end-user, or the person that would actually use the information, rather than professional researchers.

As end-users increasingly became the market for information providers, companies began to emphasize user-friendly system interfaces that allowed easier data searching and access, such as providing menus instead of requiring the user to memorize arcane commands. Firms were also quick to take advantage of retrieval technologies. For instance, online services were able to make use of faster modem communication speeds, including high-speed, always-on network connections that are now common in businesses and, increasingly, in homes.

As new markets emerged, companies began to expand their offerings. Online information ''supermarkets'' such as DIALOG evolved where users could access hundreds of specialized databases covering thousands of publications. Information ''boutiques'' that offered simultaneous online access to multiple databases and services for one particular industry or profession also resulted. Individual niche services flourished as well. Between 1987 and 1992 the number of electronic databases available in the industry leapt nearly 300 percent, from 3,369 to more than 10,000.

In the late 1980s the emergence of CD-ROM technology, for storing and accessing large amounts of data by a personal computer, appeared as a competitive threat to online aggregators. Many database publishers who had previously been distributing their electronic databases exclusively through online services began to publish and distribute that same data themselves on CD-ROM. By the early 1990s, however, it became clear that the information market was growing fast enough to accommodate both online and CD-ROM media and that the two could exist side by side serving different customer needs.

CURRENT CONDITIONS

The Internet's Impact. In many ways the Internet has turned the traditional information retrieval business model on its head. In a few short years, for example, a consumer-oriented indexer/search engine like Yahoo! Inc. could dramatically outpace in revenue established indexers and aggregators like Dow Jones and Dialog—all without charging end users a dime. Such economics have put severe pressures on old-style subscription services, and some have begun to crack under the strain.

Dialog, one of the oldest and most revered subscription databases for professionals, has been one casualty. In 1997 the troubled service was purchased from Knight Ridder, a newspaper publisher, by an obscure British concern known as Market Analysis Information Database (MAID). Renamed Dialog Corporation plc, the service continued to flounder with flat revenues and fleeing customers. In a controversial move, the company ratcheted up its search fees drastically when it learned many users were identifying information sources (newspapers, periodicals) with its powerful search engine but then retrieving the articles more cheaply from the sources' Web sites. This alienated more users. Although the company managed to turn a slim profit in 1998, it was strapped with debt and faced an uncertain market. Finally, in 2000 the Dialog service and trade name was sold to Thomson Corp. of Canada, and Dialog Corp. ceased to exist.

Still, all of this doesn't spell doom for traditional fee-based providers. According to an estimate by LEXIS-NEXIS, in 2000 the Web contained just 40 million unique documents, compared to LEXIS-NEXIS's 2.5 billion documents. For professional researchers, the power of such retrieval systems also far exceeds that of a Web search engine, allowing more versatile search options and often more efficient indexing and classification. A database like LEXIS-NEXIS or Dialog is also usually more stable than many Web pages, an important feature for historical research. Hence, for the time being, many researchers believe there is vital need for both free and low-end subscription services over the Internet as well as proprietary database systems, whether accessed through the Web or other means. The main problems for vendors of traditional services will be pricing and market share, as some of their business is lost or relocated because of newer Internet sources.

Market Conditions. In 1998, according to Census Bureau figures, the information retrieval industry took in $12.3 billion in sales. The total market for electronic information services is tricky to gauge, however, because it depends on how they are defined. Private-sector estimates are usually quite a bit higher. For example, Veronis, Suhler & Associates, a communications market research firm, estimated that the market for business information services alone reached $33.5 billion in 1998.

Most sources agree that demand for information services grew rapidly in the 1990s. Based on the Census Bureau's revenue estimates, the industry grew at an average of nearly 18 percent a year between 1992 and 1998. That growth was heavily weighted toward the end of the period, when industry sales surged 30 percent or more each year. Using the six-year compound growth rate as a predictor, industry sales were likely to top $17 billion in 2000.

Legislation and Legal Issues. The main type of legislation that affects the information services industry is copyright law. Most of the information contained in databases distributed by online services is copyrighted, yet because it is in electronic form it can be easily reproduced. By 1996 the U.S. Congress debated whether online services should be held fully responsible for copyright infringement by their customers, and infringement suits based on online content were already circulating in the U.S. court system.

To fulfill copyright law obligations, online services must monitor the distribution and customer access of each copyrighted database record to ensure that proper royalty fees are paid. Thus, the computer systems of online services automatically tally how many times a specific record is accessed to determine how great the licensing fees should be that are paid to the database producer. (Database producers, in turn, pay royalty fees based on this tally information to the original publishers.) For the fairest, most accurate payment of royalties, the end-user customer must also be charged for each record accessed and perhaps at a different rate for different kinds of records. This system has worked well for certain professional and business customers, but the home consumer market prefers flat-fee pricing. Through careful historical analysis of database access statistics, database producers and online services have in many cases been able to derive revenue projections that have enabled them to begin charging flat fees for the customers and still honor royalty agreements.

Online services have not felt any need to challenge existing copyright law, but challenges from others have touched their industry. Original authors of published articles and artists of creative works have sued database producers and vendors for electronically distributing their articles without permission.

INDUSTRY LEADERS

General Professional Database Services. LEXIS-NEXIS, a division of Reed Elsevier Inc., is the largest general-purpose database for professionals, with 1998 sales of approximately $1.2 billion. The company, founded in 1970 and based in Dayton, Ohio, was known as Mead Data Central, until its parent, the Mead Corporation, sold it to the European publishing joint venture Reed Elsevier plc in 1994. The company's two services are called LEXIS, the market leader in providing legal databases and accounting for about 60 percent of revenues, and NEXIS, a collection of news databases. NEXIS is the largest provider, and often exclusive provider, of full-text U.S. newspapers, with almost 19,000 sources. LEXIS-NEXIS had 1.8 million subscribers in 1999. To ensure LEXIS-NEXIS and its other services remained competitive in the Internet age, Reed Elsevier announced plans in 2000 to invest $1.2 billion in its Web business, even while it cut staffing.

Thomson Corp., Toronto, Canada, is parent to scores of general and industry-specific information retrieval services and is a major information provider worldwide. Its largest general-purpose database is Dialog. The Dialog service was the pioneer in online retrieval services when it was founded in 1972. It was sold in 1988 for $353 million by its parent Lockheed Corp. to the newspaper publishing and news service company Knight-Ridder Inc. Under Knight-Ridder Information Services, Dialog was also linked in the mid-1990s with DataStar, a European information service. However, amid sluggish sales, Knight-Ridder sold its information services in 1997 to U.K.-based Market Analysis Information Database (MAID) for a steep $420 million. The new company, called Dialog Corporation plc, failed to effect a turnaround; sales languished as the company was slow to embrace the Internet paradigm. MAID sold Dialog to the deeper-pocketed Thomson Corp. in 2000 for $275 million. Dialog's sales in 1999 were estimated at $280 million. In addition to Dialog, Thomson's other major electronic retrieval systems include Infotrac, a periodical index and full-text database provided by the Gale Group (publisher of this encyclopedia), and Westlaw, a legal database provided by the West Group.

Business and Finance. Among the online services that serve specialized business markets, the largest companies are those that provide real-time securities and other financial information services. The largest companies, which have been in the business for some time, not only provide information services but some also continue the practice of leasing proprietary computer terminals to access the information.

Bridge Information Systems, Inc., a closely held subsidiary of Welsh, Carson, Anderson & Stowe, emerged in the late 1990s as one of the top three financial information vendors through two key acquisitions by its parent company: Knight-Ridder Financial in 1996 and Dow Jones Markets (Telerate) in 1998. The company provides terminal and Web-based financial news and data in real time to brokers, traders, and analysts in the securities business, and offers a variety of databases and related services.

Reuters Group PLC of London is another major player in financial and news information services. It has long been the biggest provider of financial news to businesses, but its position is being challenged increasingly by Bridge. The company also operates a massive global news wire and news gathering business, and since 1999 it's run an information retrieval joint venture with Dow Jones Interactive called Factiva (formerly Dow Jones Reuters Business Interactive) that features a full-text newspaper and journal database. In 1998 the Reuters Group had more than $5 billion revenue.

The other leading competitor is Bloomberg L.P. of New York. Like Reuters, it provides an extensive line of financial and news information products, including information terminal service to the financial industry. Bloomberg also has media and publishing ventures. The company's revenue in 1998 was estimated at $1.5 billion and it has more than 100,000 information terminals installed worldwide.

Internet Search Engines. Web-based universal search engines have had profound impact on the rest of the information retrieval business. Unlike other services, they rely on advertising almost exclusively for revenue. Although most search engines have struggled to turn a profit, as of 1999 leaders like Yahoo! Inc. were in the black for the first time and their revenues exceeded those of many veteran retrieval services.

Yahoo! Inc. is the world's largest Web search engine based on number of users. From its inception Yahoo! has taken a value-added approach to collecting Web site information: it classifies all sites in a hierarchy for ease of searching. While this has meant that Yahoo! doesn't always list as many sites as competing search engines, users have been pleased with its approach. In 1999 the company's sites recorded more than 120 million unique visitors. In February 2000 alone, the service attracted over 45 million unique viewers. Yahoo! brought in $589 million in revenue for 1999, more than double the total from a year earlier, and posted a healthy profit of $61 million. The vast majority of its revenue comes from advertising, although the company is trying to diversify its sales base by partnering with e-commerce merchants. In addition to its search engine, the Yahoo! Web portal includes news, financial data, classified ads, and a variety of other content.

Lycos Inc. was the second-largest independent Web search engine service in 2000. Its core site attracted over 27 million unique visitors as of February 2000. As with Yahoo!, Lycos has forged content and e-commerce relationships to bolster its advertising-driven Internet search business. Advertising represented 69 percent of sales in 1999. For its fiscal 1999 the firm posted revenues of $135.5 million but a heavy net loss of $52 million.

Other Leaders. Other specialized professional online services include Northern Light, Quotron Systems Inc., and Primark Corp., the latter through its subsidiaries Data Stream International Inc., Disclosure Inc., I/B/E/S International Inc., Ovid Technologies Inc., Chemical Abstracts Services, which provides the STN International service, and Questel-Orbit Inc.

WORKFORCE

In 1999 information retrieval services employed 115,700 workers in the United States, according to the U.S. Bureau of Labor Statistics. This was more than twice the number employed as of 1994. Because growth will likely continue or accelerate, prospects for employment in the industry are forecast to be much better than average well into the twenty-first century. Positions in the information retrieval services industry include: computer programmers; system analysts; information processing and delivery professionals; sales representatives; management; clerical and office management; writers and editors; and research analysts.

Occupations which will likely experience the greatest growth in the next decade are related to computer programming and system development. Jobs for sales professionals in all computer and data processing fields are projected to grow at a healthy clip as well, while significant increases in the number of writers, editors, and technical writers employed in the industry are also anticipated.

America and the World

The U.S. electronic information retrieval industry is the largest and most advanced of any nation in the world. It is also acknowledged by foreign markets as the provider of the most comprehensive and highest quality information services. Acceptance of the English language as the standard for information services has helped U.S. companies compete abroad. As a result of these factors, U.S. firms have found major growth opportunities in overseas information markets. The fact that online services specialize in transferring data over long distances has made the expansion into international markets a logical step.

The largest market for online service outside of the United States is Western Europe. Both the major U.S. business and consumer online services have subscribers in Europe. The liberalization and privatization of telecommunications services in Europe was also expected to lower the telecom rates paid by businesses and consumers and consequently encourage the use of online services.

The Asia/Pacific region, and Japan in particular, is another fast growing market. The number of online and Internet subscribers in the Asia/Pacific region was projected to increase from 9 million in 1995 to 24.3 million in 2000. Asia/Pacific (including Japan) online and Internet revenues are projected to increase from $2.9 billion in 1996 to $10.8 billion in 2000. Almost 30 percent of the households in the highly developed economies of Japan, Taiwan, Australia, South Korea, Singapore, and Hong Kong will subscribe to Internet or online services by 2001, according to the Strategis Group Consumer Research.

In the late 1990s even greater opportunities for growth will likely arise in Latin America and Eastern Europe. Foreign investors from all countries are seeking information about these markets, and these countries and regions will all demand increasing amounts of business, legal, and financial information about the United States and other developed markets.

Another aspect of the globalization of the online services industry is not merely the export of the services, but also the internationalization of the databases being offered. U.S. database vendors are increasingly contracting database providers in Europe and Japan to provide the content for databases on their respective industries, which in turn are offered back to the European and Japanese markets in addition to the U.S. market. For example, NEXIS began offering BizEkon, a Russian business directory, and Comline Corporate Directory, which contains profiles of Japanese firms. DataTimes, a full-text online newspaper service, started delivering ''China Daily'' and several other Chinese publications. Similarly, U.S. database producers are licensing their databases to foreign database vendors for distribution abroad.

Research and Technology

The electronic information retrieval industry is heavily influenced by technological advances and is, in effect, a corollary of recent advances in computer and telecommunications technology.

Developments in the computer industry have made more powerful computers and database management software available at lower costs. This has permitted online services to expand their database offerings without technical limitations and has lowered the entry barrier to smaller companies to get into the business of online services.

Computer software developments have led to the growing use of graphical user interfaces for accesses online services. The software then permits users to organize the data on their own computer hard drives without spending additional costly time being connected to the online service. The most recent trends in software have made access to external data appear as a seamless part of working on one's own computer desktop. This is particularly the case for computer users whose computers are directly linked to the Internet through an organization's local area network. Lotus Notes groupware software and Microsoft Office 97 software offer features of integrating online accessed data with desktop applications.

The development of telecommunications technologies are of particular importance to online services, which rely upon phone lines to transmit data to their customers. Even though modems may enable data transmission speeds of up to 433,600 bps, whether such speeds are actually attained depends on the bandwidth of phone lines—and usually the optimal speeds cannot be reached. While telephone networks are being improved with fiber-optic lines, the capabilities of a phone line are only as good as its weakest link, typically the final connection to the individual office or residence. Business are investing in their own high-bandwidth dedicated lines, leased lines, and wide area networks. Residences, too, now have the opportunity to use high band-width ISDN lines for additional charges. Wireless communications technologies, such as cellular modems for portable computers, are also being further developed, so that users can access online services in remote locations. It was also expected that by the end of the 1990s the use of direct broadcast satellites for Internet and online connections would be commercially viable.

Finally, the combined developments in computer hardware, software, and telecommunications services are enabling the transmission of more complex kinds of data through online services. Advancements in data compression technologies have enabled at least limited transmission of full-motion video and accompanied sound through online services; new compression schemes were on the horizons in the late 1990s to better provide this functionality. At this point the distinction between online information services and interactive cable television broadcasters becomes blurred. The difference may merely depend on whether the data is defined as information or entertainment or whether it is viewed through a computer monitor or television screen.

FURTHER READING

''Business Information Market Expands.'' *Online,* March 1999.

Computer Industry Forecasts. Data Analysis Group, 1997.

''Congress Debates Online Liability.'' *Information Law Alert: A Voorhees Report,* 9 February 1996.

Davis, Joel, et al. ''Dutch Giant Sinks Teeth into Web.'' *Editor & Publisher,* 28 February 2000.

''It's All Happening on the Web.'' *Online User,* January-February 1997.

''LEXIS-NEXIS Breaks the Billion Mark.'' *Information Today,* November 1996.

Lubove, Seth. ''Dial-a-Mess.'' *Forbes,* 24 January 2000.

Milliot, Jim. ''LEXIS-NEXIS Is Bullish About Future of Online.'' *Publishers Weekly,* 1 April 1996.

Pemberton, Jeff. ''An Industry Analysis with Outsell Inc.'' *Online,* July-August 1999.

Plummer, James C. ''Decent Information?'' *Consumers' Research Magazine,* August 1996.

Tenopir, Carol. ''Getting What You Pay For?'' *Library Journal,* 1 February 2000.

———. ''Unlikely Partnerships.'' *Library Journal,* July 1999.

Tenopir, Carol, and Jeff Barry. ''Data Dealers Forging Links.'' *Library Journal,* 15 May 1999.

U.S. Census Bureau. *Service Annual Survey 1998.* Washington, D.C.: 2000. Available from www.census.gov.

U.S. Department of Labor. *Occupational Outlook Handbook, 2000-01 Edition.* Washington, D.C.: GPO, 2000. Available from www.bls.gov.

Veronis, Suhler & Associates. ''Business Information Services.'' *Communications Industry Report.* New York, 1999. Available from www.veronissuhler.com.

SIC 7376

COMPUTER FACILITIES MANAGEMENT SERVICES

This category includes establishments primarily engaged in providing on-site management and operation of computer and data processing facilities on a contract or fee basis. Establishments primarily engaged in providing computer processing services at their own facility are classified in **SIC 7374: Computer Processing and Data Preparation and Processing Services.**

NAICS CODE(S)

541513 (Computer Facilities Management Services)

INDUSTRY SNAPSHOT

One of the oldest of the computer services industries, facilities management includes interactive and batch data processing, data storage and retrieval, system diagnostics and maintenance, and network management. Customers hire facilities management companies to perform any or all of these services at computer facilities located on their own premises, much as they would hire a concessionaire to run a company cafeteria. Because relatively little capital is needed for equipment or buildings, facilities management initially attracted many entrepreneurs, the vast majority of who were small, privately owned enterprises.

Once a mainstay of the computer services industry in its own right, in the 1990s facilities management evolved into just one of many services offered by companies specializing in ''outsourcing.'' Although companies whose primary offering was facilities management still do a substantial amount of business, many companies arrange complex service agreements to include combinations of facilities management, remote computing (doing the client's data processing off-site), contract software programming, systems integration, communications network management, and software maintenance.

Because the profit margin for facilities management fell slowly but steadily over the years, its combination with more lucrative services had a growing appeal to companies in that industry. In addition, corporations with large in-house computing facilities began looking for service companies who not only could handle day-to-day processing but could also update aging computer systems. In the late 1980s, several large corporations arranged long-term contracts for computer services valued at more than $100 million. By the early 1990s, such megacontracts exceeded $1 billion. For an increasing number of computer services companies, facilities management became just a single component of complex service agreements.

Strategic outsourcing had become the trend of the 1990s. Besides smaller corporations that hired contractors to manage their facilities and information technology (IT) needs, even the larger corporations hired contracting firms to manage their information systems. Strategic outsourcing consists of placing a company's computer budget and operations in the hands of another company in return for the assurance that operational savings and other improvements would result.

Organization and Structure

Many companies found that their data centers, distributed networks, and related facilities could be handled more efficiently by others than by themselves. Programmers and experienced staff were difficult and expensive to hire. For this reason—particularly in industries where wages were generally low and data processing needs were high, such as the insurance industry—facilities management services were frequently used. In addition, running computers was often outside the realm of expertise of a particular company. Managing the operations of complex computer systems tended to distract management from the primary focus of the business, whether it was banking, utilities, or health care. To eliminate this distraction and to cut costs, many companies hired a facilities management company to run their computer facilities on a contract or fee basis.

Facilities management companies generally charged a fixed annual amount to maintain a data center, then added fees based on processing volume. An in-house operation entailed a large fixed cost; with facilities management, data processing became a variable cost. Data processing costs increased when the company's business activities increased, and decreased when business slowed. This pricing schedule allowed more efficient use of the company's funds.

A facilities management company needed little capital to begin operations. Unlike a company specializing in remote data processing, which required sizable data centers and extensive communications capabilities, a facilities management company had few equipment and building requirements.

Specialized personnel, however, were a crucial component for facilities management firms, not only for the obvious technical areas, but in marketing as well. Knowledge and skill was needed to sell an intangible service to repeat customers. Facilities management companies competed not only with others who offered the same service, but also with those who offered remote processing and with the customers themselves, who could revert to in-house handling of their computer facilities. This need to constantly cost-justify their service in the face of increasing numbers of competitors led to a steady erosion of profit margins in this industry.

Facilities management companies generally began by specializing in one field of business, such as banking, health care, or government agencies. They developed an expertise in the particular needs of that industry and drew new customers from within that niche. The division between companies providing facilities management to commercial customers and those catering to the government was especially strong. A company required extensive knowledge of the bidding process for government contracts and needed to meet particular government regulations to qualify as a vendor.

Companies that began by providing specialized service in a niche market first expanded geographically, providing that same service over a wider area. Many then expanded into new service areas, gaining new expertise through mergers or acquisitions of companies in different fields. In an industry that changed as rapidly as the computer industry, it was often risky for companies to provide only one service. Such specialization made them vulnerable to price cuts by competitors and to new products, laws, or regulations that made services obsolete or difficult to provide. The leading service vendors then expanded into multiple fields. They combined multiple services into a package tailored to individual company needs.

This increased packaging of services led to the trend of ''outsourcing,'' in which facilities management played a significant role. The most basic definition of outsourcing in the computer industry was simply the purchase of outside IT services, such as hiring a firm to handle payroll processing or manage a network; however, it often referred to the reduction or dismantling of in-house operations and the sale of fixed assets—like a data center or a telecommunications network—to a company specializing in information technology. The IT company then agreed to provide the services connected to those assets back to the client. Frequently, outsourcing deals of this sort also involved the transfer of personnel to the IT company. In addition to relieving themselves of the burden of running and maintaining their computer facilities, companies gained access to significant cash resources that had been tied up in their computer equipment. Other companies entered outsourcing agreements without selling their facilities because they wanted an escape in case they regretted the decision, since it was easier to rebuild in-house operations if the company still owned its computer facilities.

Facilities management was also integral in the development of transformational outsourcing. Companies that purchased mainframe computers and established their computer operations in the 1970s faced updating aged and outmoded computer facilities. Many companies saw advantages in open architectures that incorporated client/server computing and local area networks (LANs), but did not have the expertise to design new systems for themselves and coordinate the shift from the old system to the new. Transformational outsourcing placed the responsibility on others' shoulders. An IT company agreed to take over the client's existing system, design a new one, and handle all operations during the transition, be it gradual or abrupt. Such a contract involved facilities management, systems integration, and perhaps off-site data processing and other services.

BACKGROUND AND DEVELOPMENT

Facilities management services began to be offered not long after mainframe computers and data centers became more common in the 1960s. At first, computers and the in-house operations associated with them were a matter of pride for companies profitable enough to afford this cutting-edge technology. However, it soon became apparent that specialists who could bring economies of scale to the activity could often operate these facilities more efficiently than those who owned them.

From its infancy, the facilities management industry was composed of small, entrepreneurial companies. Even after more than a decade of growth, 47 percent of data processing firms had revenues of less than $1 million, and 47 percent had revenues between $1 and $10 million. Of the remaining 6 percent, only half had revenues of more than $25 million.

By the late 1970s, it was already increasingly difficult to distinguish between companies that offered remote computing, software services, and facilities management. Major vendors offered several services that blended in various ways, depending on the needs of the customers.

From the late 1960s to the early 1980s, the data processing industry, including facilities management, fluctuated with the economy. The annual rate of revenue growth declined by approximately 10 percent during periods of recession in the early 1970s and 1980s. The following periods of economic acceleration produced a corresponding increase in the growth rate. Although the data processing industry was affected by the general health of the economy, it maintained a healthy growth rate throughout the 1970s and early 1980s. The lowest growth rate in that period was in 1982, when the industry grew by only 11 percent—a rate that nevertheless compared favorably to other industries at that time. Although facilities management individually had the smallest share of data processing revenue in early 1980s, its annual growth rate at times exceeded the average for the industry. Revenues were $989 million in 1980 and grew an average of 13 percent annually to reach $1.4 billion in 1983.

In 1981, the market researcher INPUT projected a 21 percent compounded growth rate for the facilities management industry over the next five years. However, in the early 1980s, several developments in the hardware and software industries threatened the strong growth of the facilities management industry. International Business Machines Corporation (IBM) software became increasingly standardized, making computers easier to use and leading more companies to manage their facilities themselves. In addition, cheaper, more user-friendly minicomputers became common, adding to the do-it-yourself trend. However, declining prices and the need to keep up with competitors who had computerized led many more companies to buy computers, enlarging the overall market for computer services. Although the facilities management industry did not meet that 21 percent growth rate, it continued to grow steadily.

By 1992, revenues in the facilities management industry reached $3.8 billion, almost double the revenues of 1988. The rate of growth was approximately 18 percent per year between 1990 and 1992. Firms also became increasingly productive—average sales per employee rose from $110,000 in 1990 to $135,000 in 1992. By 1997, the facilities management industry's revenues had nearly quadrupled from its 1992 level to $15.1 billion.

Facilities management remained a strongly entrepreneurial industry throughout the 1990s. The vast majority of facilities management companies were privately owned and had revenues under $2 million. Private companies composed 99.3 percent of the computer services industry in 1992, though the remaining publicly held companies dominated the higher end of the revenue scale. Large information technology services firms, such as Electronic Data Systems (EDS) and Computer Sciences Corporation, continued to make inroads in the desktop-technologies and networking markets in 1995, while companys' internal IT departments continued to feel more secure in their ability to build client/server applications. As a result, smaller and more specialized client/server integrators were forced to respond by thinking up new value added services.

The facilities management industry also remained a highly fragmented one, with companies specializing in providing services to a particular industry. According to *Business Week,* specializing often acted to a company's advantage, as long as the services it provided to a particular industry were comprehensive enough: "Profit margins are tightening in the generic outsourcing field, where they simply run existing systems for less money than customers can. But to broaden their scope, those giants will have to invest heavily in industry-specific software—or buy established specialty outsourcers. Either way, it seems, the specialists can win.''

Current Conditions

According to data from the U.S. Census Bureau, computer facilities management was a $15.1 billion business in 1997, and it showed little sign of slowing down as the new millennium approached. Census figures showed that more than 1,400 establishments with a total of nearly 72,000 employees were actively engaged in this business in the United States in 1997. The industry's annual payroll totaled almost $3.4 billion in 1997. Although facilities management companies had incentive to develop into full-service outsourcers, given the growing market and the improved profit margin involved, only a few had the resources necessary to offer that extended range of services. In addition to expertise in facilities management, an outsourcing vendor needed to understand systems integration, network operations, communications, and software development. Capital requirements were also higher. Frequently, a remote data center for off-site processing was required, along with an extensive communications network to transfer the data to the remote site. Additional capital might be needed to purchase the customer's existing computers or data center facilities and hire their information systems personnel. Only the larger IT service companies possessed the resources to accept such contracts. In an industry traditionally composed of small, entrepreneurial companies, only a minority were expected to take full advantage of this trend.

For those companies that did evolve into outsourcing vendors, many are turning to ''enterprise resource planning'' (ERP) applications and e-commerce. A major new growth area in outsourcing—applications-rental—is expected to be a $6 billion business by 2002, according to Forrester Research, a consultancy in the information technology field. Some of the large software companies that specialize in ERP applications are creating a dynamic new business opportunities from the ground up. Working with Internet service providers (ISPs) and major hardware manufacturers, these outsourcing vendors want to make the latest business software applications available on a subscription basis. They are targeting companies with annual revenue of less than $500 million.

In perhaps an extreme example of outsourcing, the U.S. Chamber of Commerce in 1998 struck a deal with Cap Gemini America to handle not only its information systems but Internet access, telephone switches, its Web site, a virtual private network, along with its data and voice wide-area network services. The 10-year agreement carried a price tag of $75 million, according to a spokesman for the Washington-based Chamber. Prior to striking its agreement with Cap Gemini, the Chamber had an annual information systems (IS) budget of nearly $7 million and an IS staff of 60.

Industry Leaders

No one particular company dominated the facilities management industry. As they grew, most facilities management companies added services outside of the industry. EDS, headquartered in Plano, Texas, was a major player with 1998 revenue of $16.9 billion. Besides computer facilities management for businesses and government, EDS was involved in consulting services, data processing, and computer network systems integration. EDS, which had about 120,000 employees in 1998, was founded in 1962.

Computer Sciences Corporation, with 50,000 employees and fiscal 1999 revenue of $7.6 billion, was founded in 1959 and is headquartered in El Segundo, California. The company began by working in a niche market, like many facilities management companies, and gradually became one of the largest of the IT services companies. Computer Sciences derived the majority of its business from state, local, and federal government work—much of it involving facilities management—and developed long-standing relationships with NASA, the Navy, and other defense contractors. Although it was considered one of the primary outsourcing firms, it no longer lists facilities management as one of its primary activities.

Workforce

The growth in outsourcing at the turn of the century was phenomenal and the demand for skilled workers was very high. The industry was booming, and many jobs such as programmers and systems analysts were available with very few skilled workers to fill these positions.

Although the nation's workforce of computer operators declined throughout the 1990s and was expected to continue to shrink well into the new millennium, all other occupations in this industry continued to grow at impressive rates. Data from the U.S. Bureau of Labor Statistics (BLS) showed that computer operators numbered 291,000 in 1996 and were expected to continue to decline sharply through 2006. Jobs in computer programming, which totaled 568,000 in 1996, were expected to increase between 21 and 35 percent by 2006, according to BLS projections. Employment in the ranks of computer scientists, computer engineers, and systems analysts, numbering 933,000 in 1996, was expected to increase 36 percent or more by 2006, according to BLS. Of the 933,000 jobs in this category, 506,000 were held by systems analysts, 216,000 by computer engineers, and 211,000 by other computer scientists, including database administrators and computer support specialists. More than three-quarters of the jobs in the computer services industry were classified as white collar.

FURTHER READING

Collins, Tony. ''Why Strategic Outsourcing Carries a Far Greater Risk.'' *Computer Weekly,* 11 January 1996.

''Computer Outsourcing: For Rent.'' *Economist,* 9 January 1999.

Darnay, Arsen J., ed. *Service Industries USA* 4th ed. Detroit: Gale Research, 1998.

''Hoover's Company Capsules.'' *Hoover's Online.* Austin, TX: Hoover's Inc.. Available from http://www.hoovers.com/.

Scrupski, Susan. ''The Future is Now.'' *Datamation,* 15 January 1995.

U.S. Bureau of the Census. *1997 Economic Census.* Washington, DC: GPO, 1999.

U.S. Department of Commerce. Bureau of Economic Analysis. *Survey of Current Business,* October 1999.

U.S. Department of Labor. Bureau of Labor Statistics. *Occupational Outlook Handbook.* 1998-1999 ed. Washington, DC: U.S. Department of Labor, 1998.

Wallace, Bob, and Julia King. ''Rare Deal: Self-Funded Outsourcing.'' *Computerworld,* 23 February 1998.

SIC 7377

COMPUTER RENTAL AND LEASING

This industry consists of establishments primarily engaged in renting or leasing computers and related data processing equipment on the customers' site, whether or not also providing maintenance or support services. This industry does not include establishments engaged in both manufacturing and leasing computers and related data processing equipment. Establishments primarily engaged in finance leasing of computers and related data processing equipment are classified in **SIC 6159: Miscellaneous Business Credit Institutions.** Establishments primarily engaged in leasing computer time are classified in **SIC 7374: Computer Processing and Data Preparation and Processing Services.**

NAICS CODE(S)

532420 (Office Machinery and Equipment Rental and Leasing)

INDUSTRY SNAPSHOT

Companies in this industry bought, sold, and leased new and used high-technology equipment. These companies included maintenance companies, refurbishment/reconfiguration firms, transportation companies, financial institutions, original-equipment-manufacturer (OEM) finance companies, software distributors, and industry consultants.

The success of computer rental and leasing companies evolved from the strong urge among U.S. industries to remain on the cutting edge of technology. While many companies wanted to upgrade their computer equipment, few were ready to invest the necessary money up front, and many decided instead to turn to rental and leasing companies. By leasing equipment, companies could experiment with new computers and peripherals, upgrading as they felt necessary.

Sales volume in the computer leasing and remarketing industry was between $15 billion and $25 billion annually in the early 1990s. By 1998 equipment leasing had grown to a $183 billion industry, according to the Equipment Leasing Association. The second half of the 1990s proved to be a profitable environment for the computer leasing industry, despite dramatically reduced purchase prices of new computers. Some computer leasing companies responded by adding services to their leases, such as computer maintenance and insurance.

ORGANIZATION AND STRUCTURE

The two main types of leases used in the industry were finance leases and operating leases. In direct finance leases, which were excluded from this industry classification, the lessor provided the financing. In leveraged leases, other investors provided debt financing. Operating leases were considered the best option for companies trying to avoid depreciation deductions. In an operating lease, the lessor owned the equipment and took the depreciation, so the user incurred no liability. The cost of leasing was considered an expense on a company's income statement but did not show up on its balance sheet. There were four typical lessors: banks, captives (usually manufacturers' subsidiaries), independents, and financial services organizations.

Other kinds of leases included the purchase option lease, in which a business owned the equipment but did not carry the balance-sheet debt; the sale-leaseback, in which a company sold its own computer equipment to a lessor to remove it from the balance sheet and then leased it back; and the dollar-out lease, in which the business could acquire the equipment at the end of the lease for one dollar. In some cases the purchase price was determined at the end of the lease based on the fair market value of the equipment at that time, and in other cases the price was determined at the lease negotiation.

Computer rental and leasing companies selected their clients carefully. They considered credit ratings, as well as the type of company they were dealing with, before structuring the lease. Some lessors required several payments up front. Others took their first payment upon delivery of the equipment. They also offered various levels of service that accompanied the lease. The industry is tied to the client's ability to obtain credit approval and money lending institutions' willingness to fund computer leases. This ability fluctuates with the economy.

Rentals were attractive to corporate buyers who were not ready to commit to a purchase or a long-term lease while personal computer (PC) prices were falling. On the other hand, rental rates needed to reflect the cost of PCs, and rental firms suffer smaller margins when the prices are low. The key to survival for theses rental firms is service. Many offer delivery, installation, and maintenance along with the rental.

Some companies rented or leased computers until they decided what kind to buy. Others rented or leased in order to save enough money to buy equipment. Still others used rental or leasing as a way to upgrade their existing computer systems without the immediate output of money. Monthly payments for leased equipment were usually lower than monthly payments on loans taken out to buy computer equipment.

With high-tech equipment, companies kept an eye on evolving technology by leasing computers and trading up when they were ready for the latest development. The drawback of leasing was that it cost more in the long run and did not provide companies with ownership of new computer equipment. Vying for customers, companies in the computer leasing and rental industry approached the twenty-first century with attractive rates as well as promises of service and support.

Two associations of companies involved in the U.S. computer leasing industry were the Information Technology Resellers Association (ITRA) and the Equipment Leasing Association of America (ELA). ITRA was formed in 1998 by the merging of the Computer Dealers and Lessors Association (CDLA) and the Digital Dealers Association (DDA). The CDLA was created in 1981 from the Association and the Computer Dealers Association. The member companies signed a Code of Ethics that was backed up by a standing committee formed in 1974. ITRA advertised on behalf of its member companies, emphasizing their flexibility, concern with ethics, and ability to save clients money.

ELA, which was organized in 1961, helped introduce information-sharing among its members. As a nonprofit trade association, ELA worked with Dun & Bradstreet to create a database with credit histories of lessees while also tracking industry statistics and creating educational programs for members. ELA is a nonprofit organization headquartered in Arlington, Virginia, representing more than 800 member companies, which provide a variety of asset-based financial products, primarily equipment leasing.

Background and Development

Rental and leasing had a continuous history from ancient times through the present. In the 1980s, leasing grew twice as fast as business. According to a CDLA survey conducted in late 1994, 70 percent of computers and peripherals were leased versus 30 percent which were purchased. These included desktop computers, large and small servers, and telephone systems.

The rapid rise of technology after World War II caught many businesses unprepared. In 1956, after the U.S. Justice Department decided a complaint against IBM, a Consent Decree paved the way for companies to purchase IBM machines that would be leased to users. IBM had previously rented its own equipment to businesses and received the equipment back at the end of the rental term, which prevented a secondary market from developing. The Consent Decree was still in effect in the 1990s, and it offered maintenance to IBM owners, replacement parts, and training for independent companies.

Equipment leasing and remarketing reported industry-wide volumes of $138 billion in 1998. As a rule, the computer rental and leasing industry was strongest when the computer industry was healthy and strong. When the economy suffered, so did this industry. Like the retail computer industry, the rental industry went through a period of consolidation. Some smaller leasing companies specialized in particular products, services, and support, marketing themselves as being knowledgeable and quick. Some offered special equipment for their customers.

In 1992 computers replaced aircraft as the most frequently leased item in the United States. According to *Equipment Leasing* magazine, total new business for the second quarter of 1999 was $7.2 billion, up 4.3 percent from the previous year. Computer leasing companies either leased their merchandise directly or arranged the lease and provided some or all of the financing. Many different lease terms were offered, although most customers chose three- to five-year leases for computers, computer peripherals, and related equipment. By comparison, furniture was often leased for as long as ten years.

Leasing made sense for many businesses partially because lease payments were fully deductible for tax purposes, and sales taxes and interest payments used when purchasing equipment were not deductible. In 1986 the Tax Reform Act removed the investment tax credit while stretching out depreciation schedules. But companies unable to use their depreciation were able to transfer tax benefits to lessors in exchange for reduced equipment costs. For tax purposes, leases were required to be short enough so that 20 percent of the estimated useful life of the equipment remained after the lease term. Options to buy the equipment at the end of the lease were required to specify how the price would be determined after the lease was over.

Current Conditions

The equipment leasing industry is continuing to enjoy growth into the twenty-first century. With the growth of e-commerce and e-tailing, the need for current technologies in the workplace is growing. Although the cost of computing equipment continues to fall, the issues of maintenance and support are significant, and lessors are often bundling training, software, maintenance and support into their contracts to make leasing more attractive. A Gartner Group study quoted in *Information Week* stated that $4 billion in desktop PCs were leased in 1998 and predicts more than $6 billion worth will be leased in 2002.

In the mid- to late 1990s, computer equipment manufacturers and computer leasing and remarketing firms had a symbiotic relationship. By working together, each tried to maximize its success, but the first step to a successful relationship was for manufacturers to develop policies and practices that permit and maintain healthy secondary markets in their equipment. ITRA (previously the CDLA) played the role of watchdog to ensure that the computer leasing and remarketing industry had a strong, unified voice through effective working relationships with major manufacturers of computer and telecommunications equipment.

Industry relations between computer equipment manufacturers and computer leasing and remarketing firms evolved with the industry, according to ITRA. As the companies focused on a greater diversity of equipment, they also established working relationships with a number of manufacturers. Independent computer dealers and lessors provided a valuable service to the end user and a steady source of additional sales and maintenance revenue for the manufacturer.

Roberta Furger, in a 1998 article in *PC World,* suggested that the straight math for leasing PCs didn't make sense when compared to outright purchase or purchase on credit. With the decreased cost of purchase, the industry may well need to continue to provide the extras of reliable support in order to maintain their markets.

INDUSTRY LEADERS

Many of the industry's firms were small and operated by entrepreneurs, while a handful of larger firms dealt in equipment leasing worldwide. Most leased both new and used computer equipment and remarketed pre-owned computer systems. Some also provided extra services, such as systems integration, installation, and maintenance.

Most major computer manufacturers, such as Dell, Hewlett-Packard, and Compaq, also dealt in leasing and remarketing. However, since those companies were also engaged in manufacturing, they were classified separately.

Comdisco, Inc., formerly a computer leasing leader with revenues of $4.159 billion, was the largest company in the industry in the mid-1990s. In 1999 Comdisco restructured and sold its mainframe leasing to IBM. Comdisco is now focusing on providing high tech e-services to corporations.

Larger lessors were able to create leases that included computer equipment as well as other supplies, while specialty lessors were able to help their clients choose appropriate equipment by suggesting such options as combining new and used equipment to save money.

IBM Corp., based in Armonk, New York, with 1999 sales of over $87 billion, has a financing division, IBM Global Financing, that deals internationally in computer leasing and financing. Symix Systems, Inc., based in Columbus, Ohio, recently partnered with IBM Global Financing and EAB Leasing Corporation's Softech Financial division to offer a comprehensive technology leasing program, according to a September 1999 Symix press release.

Other industry leaders included General Electric Capitol Information Technology Solutions, located in Stamford, Connecticut; El Camino Resources International, located in Woodland Hills, California, with 1999 sales of $668 million; GENICOM Corporation, located in Chantilly, Virginia, with 1998 sales of over $452 million; and Leasing Solutions, Inc., located in San Jose, California, with 1998 sales of nearly $300 million.

WORKFORCE

The major companies in the computer rental and leasing industry had a combined total of 9,647 employees in 1997. The total payroll for the 972 establishments doing business in the industry was $604 million, according to the U.S. Census County Business Patterns. In a 1999 article in *Equipment Leasing*, it was indicated that the total number of employees in the industry is leveling off after several years of growth, most likely due to an increase in acquisitions and mergers which have consolidated the work force.

Changes in state and federal tax codes affected salespeople in the rental and leasing business. They needed to understand the tax implications of their leases for potential customers. Customers served by this industry were also more knowledgeable about the equipment itself and looked for rental and leasing companies that offered equipment plus several lease options and a high level of service.

AMERICA AND THE WORLD

The U.S. market for rental and leasing of computer equipment was quite self-sufficient. While few of the leasing companies not affiliated with computer manufacturers had a large presence overseas, there was very little competition from foreign firms. In fact, the only leasing business run by European or Asian companies came from several large banks. New business opportunities for U.S.

firms in Canada and Mexico have also resulted from the passage of the North American Free Trade Agreement (NAFTA).

RESEARCH AND TECHNOLOGY

The computer rental and leasing industry was vitally connected to technology, and only the companies that remained on top of the most recent trends and industry changes were successful. Automated reservation systems were used effectively by even the smallest computer leasing or rental companies to avoid delays or inventory problems for customers. Companies in the industry spent money and time developing protocols for leasing such technologies as Internet servers and parallel-processing mainframes.

The rapid growth of e-commerce is also a driving force in the need for current computing power, though much of this technological need is being outsourced by smaller companies who contract for web hosting and on-line shopping cart services rather than maintain the hardware and software in-house. However, these web based services, which are often offered business to business, are requiring companies to update employee desktop computers to support the client software needed for access.

Service on computers and peripherals is increasingly done remotely, via dial-in diagnostic tools, Internet connections, and automated web-based support centers. This type of troubleshooting service saves the lessor and the lessee the expense of sending someone out personally. As service becomes more central to the financial success of computer lessors, the prices of hardware and software continue to drop. Therefore, the lessors are also expected to lease lower-priced items more frequently.

FURTHER READING

''1994 Survey of the Computer Leasing & Remarketing Industry.'' *Information Technology Resellers Association,* 1999. Available from: http://www.itra.net.

Comdisco Company Web Page, 1999-2000. Available from: http://www.comdisco.com.

El Camino Resources International, Inc. Web Page. Available from: http://www.elcamino.com.

Equipment Leasing Association Web Page. 2000. Available from: http://www.elaonline.com/.

Funger, Roberta. ''Look Before You Lease''. *PC World.* March 1998. V. 16, N.3 P 33-36.

GE Capital Information Technology Solutions Web Page. 2000. Available from: http://www.gecits.ge.com/.

GENICOM Corporation Web Page. 2000. Available from: http// www.genicom.com.

''IBM to Fund E-Business Leases.'' *Information Week,* 13 December 1999, 34.

''Industry Overview.'' *CDLA,* April 1997.

Information Technology Resellers Association Web Page. 1999. Available from: http://www.itra.net/.

International Business Machines Corporation Web Page. Available from: http://www.ibm.com.

Mclean, Bethany. ''Comdisco: From Computer Leasing to Venture Capital.'' *Fortune,* 22 November 1999. V. 140, N. 10, P. 408-410.

''Mixed Results: Report Shows Rise in Portfolio Growth, Decline in Credit Approval.'' *Equipment Leasing,* October 1999. V. 18, N. 10, P. 5.

Muhammad, Tariq K. ''Rent-a-server: the Latest Trend in Business Software.'' *Black Enterprise,* December 1999. V. 30, N. 5, P. 48.

''Symix Introduces Midmarket-Focused Leasing Porgram to Support Customers' E-Business, ERP Advancements.'' *Symix* press release, 29 September 1999. Available from: http://www.ibm.com/finance.

U.S. Department of Commerce. Census Bureau, 2000. *County Business Patterns.* Available from: http://tier2.census.gov/cbp/index.html-ssi.

''Who Are They, What They Do.'' *CDLA,* April 1997.

SIC 7378

COMPUTER MAINTENANCE AND REPAIR

This category covers establishments primarily engaged in the maintenance and repair of computers and computer peripheral equipment.

NAICS CODE(S)

443120 (Computer and Software Stores)

811212 (Computer and Offices Machine Repair and Maintenance)

Two main types of companies operated in the computer maintenance and repair industry: third-party maintenance (TPM) companies, which performed service contracts on equipment from various manufacturers; and original equipment manufacturers (OEM), which both manufactured and serviced computers and peripheral equipment. This distinction was less pronounced in reality, however, because OEMs often subcontracted their service agreements to either affiliated or unaffiliated TPM firms.

The computer maintenance and repair industry grew dramatically in the 1980s and 1990s as computer sales skyrocketed. From total shipments of less than 2,000 units and $600 million in 1960, the computer industry topped 900,000 units and $16 billion by 1980, and reached 7 million units and $44 billion by 1990. By 2003, this number was expected to double to more than 15 million units annually. This rapid growth, along with a shift from mainframes to PCs, introduced opportunities for small, independent TPM companies to compete against the large OEMs. Nonetheless, in the late 1990s OEM companies were reported to hold as much as 80 percent of the maintenance and repair market in some categories, such as high-end system and mainframe services.

Leading OEM firms included many of the nation's best-known technology companies, such as IBM Corp., Sun Microsystems, Compaq, Electronic Data Systems, and AT&T Corp. While the majority of TPM firms were smaller local and regional providers, several service firms operated on the national level, including the Cerplex Group, ENTEX Information Services Inc., and Inacom Corp.

The U.S. Census Bureau estimated revenues specific to this industry at $15.4 billion in 1998, up more than 50 percent from $7 billion in 1990. The total U.S. market for services performed by this industry was estimated at much more—$62 billion for 1998. Less than one-quarter of this market, however, was served by firms primarily engaged in computer maintenance and repair. Instead, the bulk of maintenance and repair revenues were generated by larger, diversified companies like IBM and AT&T that had a presence in many industries. The *New York Times* reported that the lucrative PC segment of the computer repair market was worth $28 billion alone in 1995, based on a Dataquest study, and was expected to grow at 14 percent annually in the late 1990s. Within the PC segment, the home PC repair market was considered an emerging—but largely untapped, according to Dataquest—customer base for this traditionally business-focused service industry.

As demand for computer maintenance and repair surged in the 1980s and 1990s, TPM companies developed new strategies to address the lower cost and increased reliability of computer hardware. First, TPM firms reduced repair time by replacing components instead of repairing them. Next, they developed remote diagnostic software to minimize the need for costly on-site service. Finally, they expanded their services to include installation and software maintenance, including virus protection, Internet connectivity, and site-authoring services by the late 1990s.

OEMs also changed their strategies as computers became increasingly similar. They began to differentiate their products by enhancing their maintenance services. Many even started supporting competitors' equipment. As the industry entered the late 1990s, several discount or "clone" manufacturers reduced their support and forced customers to handle their own maintenance. This provided a new opportunity for TPM firms, which offered disaster-recovery services and started supporting software and multimedia to satisfy more demanding customers. At the same time, corporate emphasis on outsourcing—the practice of hiring external firms to perform specialized functions formerly done in-house—translated into new business for TPM providers. Cerplex, for example, actively branded itself as an outsourcing solution.

"The increasing complexity of software and interactive multimedia made hardware troubleshooting a more complex task that required a different kind of TPM," said David Glascock, president of the North American Computer Service Association (NACSA). As computer and communication technologies merged in the late 1990s, Glascock believed that TPM companies would expand their services to include supporting high-definition computer displays and wireless communication devices.

Growth in the industry is often dependent upon external trends and events, such as new software releases and technological change. The release of Microsoft's Windows 95 operating system, for example, led to increased demand for system maintenance—particularly upgrades—as home and corporate users coped with new demands on memory and other system resources. Similarly, one-time events, such as converting older systems to process calendar dates past the year 1999, created new business for the short term.

Employees in the computer service industry generally possessed a high school degree and technical training in computer science, electronics, and circuitry. Training programs were offered by computer manufacturers, TPM companies, and vocational-technical schools. Some study programs took 3-6 months, but formal programs required 1-2 years. Continuous education was required to keep up with fast-paced technology improvements.

Job prospects for computer equipment servicers were excellent. According to the Bureau of Labor Statistics, in the late 1990s there were more than 80,000 workers in this industry. This number represented an increase of 67 percent since 1995 and was projected to increase steadily. Overall, the number of data-processing machine repairers was anticipated to rise another 36 percent by 2006. In the late 1990s, the median annual earnings for computer repairers was just over $32,000. The highest earners made $50,000 or more a year.

In the opening years of the new millennium, the mostly small firms in the computer repair business may be facing competition from a brand new quarter. Wal-Mart Stores, which has given mom-and-pop retailers around the country a real run for their money, in the fall of 1999 launched a test to see whether it could interest its customers in getting their computers repaired at the same place they shop for clothing and toiletries. The company contracted with Computer Doctor to open computer repair shops inside ten of the giant retailer's Midwest Supercenters. Computer Doctor, headquartered in Aberdeen, South Dakota, opened its first Wal-Mart repair shop on Sept. 15, 1999, in Ankeny, Iowa. If the experiment proves successful, Wal-Mart is likely to expand the service to all of its Supercenters, which numbered more than 600 in late 1999.

Another novel experiment in computer repair was launched in the Cincinnati area in the latter half of the 1990s. Entrepreneur Steve Pollak's mobile computer repair service, PC On Call, started with a single service van but by early 1999 had expanded to 16 vehicles and 30 employees. PC On Call had also set up shop in Columbus, Ohio, and had its sights on Dayton as well. According to Paul Cashen, the company's chief executive, PC On Call was planning to expand into up to 10 new markets by the end of 2000 and hoped eventually to serve 40 cities nationwide. Cashen said the company usually responds within 24 hours to service calls, of which it receives between 100 and 150 daily.

FURTHER READING

Boyer, Mike. "Mobile Computer Repair Business." *Gannett News Service,* 25 March 1999.

Darnay, Arsen J., ed. *Service Industries USA.* 4th ed. Detroit: Gale, 1998.

Glascock, David. Interview by Rolandò Hernandez. February 1994.

Lohr, Steve. "Stock Prices Aside, The Smart Money May Be in PC Servicing." *The New York Times,* 28 March 1996.

U.S. Bureau of the Census. *1997 Economic Census.* Washington, D.C.: GPO, 1999.

U.S. Department of Labor. Bureau of Labor Statistics. *Occupational Outlook Handbook, 1998-1999 Edition.* Washington, D.C.: 1998.

"Wal-Mart Teaming with Computer Doctor: Discount Retailer Testing PC Upgrade, Repair Shops in 10 Midwest Supercenters." *Dallas Morning News,* 21 September 1999.

SIC 7379

COMPUTER RELATED SERVICES, NOT ELSEWHERE CLASSIFIED

This category covers establishments primarily engaged in supplying computer related services, not elsewhere classified. Computer consultants operating on a contract or fee basis are also classified in this industry. Establishments primarily engaged in producing prepackaged software are classified under **SIC 7372: Prepackaged Software;** and those engaged in offering data processing courses or training in computer programming and in computer and computer peripheral equipment operation, repair, and maintenance are classified under **SIC 8243: Data Processing Schools.**

NAICS CODE(S)

541512 (Computer Systems Design Services)
541519 (Other Computer Related Services)

INDUSTRY SNAPSHOT

More than a decade ago, a handful of companies like IBM Corporation and some smaller rivals dominated this industry. Corporate downsizing and reengineering in these companies forced economic power to shift from a handful of monopolies to hundreds of smaller high-tech specialists, according to the *Dallas Business Journal.* The power in the marketplace also shifted during the 1990s from those making the computers to those using the computers. A direct and striking result of this trend was the explosion in demand for computer services.

The computer related services industry was only a small part of the computer professional services industry. According to the International Trade Administration of the U.S. Department of Commerce, the computer professional services industry had 1997 revenues of nearly $109 billion—an increase of more than 63 percent from $66.7 billion in 1994. Within this computer services category, the single biggest component was computer system design services, accounting for $51.2 billion of revenue. Computer facilities management services brought in another $15.1 billion. Bringing up the rear within the computer services sector were computer related services, not elsewhere classified, which produced revenue of approximately $4.3 billion.

The growth of firms in the computer related services industry was in double digits toward the end of the twentieth century. Companies increasingly turned to computer specialists to handle their disk conversions, database developments, or troubleshooting. The popularity of the information superhighway and its effects on U.S. companies meant a larger role for consultant services. Although many companies developed extensive in-house computer centers from the 1960s through the 1980s, in the 1990s they turned to computer service firms in increasing numbers, particularly to handle special assignments. Some found that it was more cost effective to lay off or reassign their own computer personnel while using third-party data processors, systems integrators, or computer consultants. Computer services firms made it their responsibility to stay on the cutting edge of technology and to offer services that most in-house departments could not match.

ORGANIZATION AND STRUCTURE

Those computer related services not classified under other SIC codes included hardware and software requirement analysis and diskette conversion services. Some consultants marketed themselves to businesses as experts in a particular area. Those who performed hardware requirement analysis thrived in the computer-centered economy by recognizing the need for business to select the best computer equipment for its goals. These analysts were usually hired on a contract basis to spend several weeks or months working with a company to select the company's computer hardware. Often they discovered that existing equipment was not satisfactory and that either upgrades or complete overhauls were necessary to bring the company up-to-date. At the opening of the twenty-first century, these computer consultants and analysts were in a good position to succeed financially.

The National Association of Computer Consultant Businesses (NACCB) is a nonprofit trade organization, based in Washington, DC, whose members include skilled professional consultants or programmers. Founded in 1987, NACCB supports legislation, provides job fairs and model legal contracts for members, and encourages professional standards among its members. NACCB also lobbies Congress to consider the needs of independent contractors and employees in the industry.

The Independent Computer Consultants Association (ICCA) is a nonprofit trade association based in St. Louis that was founded in 1976. Its members are experts in hardware and software. ICCA publishes tips for hiring computer consultants as a support for its members. It also compiles industry statistics, offers insurance programs for member companies, and develops standard consulting contracts.

Computer related services consultants perform tasks similar to those performed by other computer professionals. Many work for large computer firms before going off by themselves or joining consulting firms. The consulting firms tend to be small to medium in size and can be found in every kind of community in the United States, from large metropolitan areas to rural communities. Those consultants working in the smaller areas commute to their clients' offices, often working there for the duration of a project.

BACKGROUND AND DEVELOPMENT

As computers and computer systems became commonplace in the working world, the necessity for computer related services increased. From the 1950s through the 1980s, technology made huge leaps forward. As costs fell in the 1970s and 1980s, more businesses came on line for straightforward tasks. By the late 1980s and early 1990s, very sophisticated computer equipment needed equally sophisticated specialists who could handle disk conversion, database development, and recertification of disks and tapes. These consultants worked to make a niche for themselves among businesses of all sizes and types.

Computer service companies were originally hired to automate such record-keeping tasks as payroll. They expanded into such customer-related areas as fund transfer systems, just-in-time inventory systems, and customer information systems. Many companies could only hire these service firms in the best of financial times given the high cost of the services. Early programming was highly individualized, but the needs of business by the 1990s necessitated more standardization.

New tax laws and proposed health care changes were some of the areas of concern to the computer consulting industry. The National Association of Computer Consultants Businesses (NACCB) wanted computer systems analysts and other computer consultants to be considered professionals exempt from overtime rates. Their staff members worked with the U.S. Department of Labor to create laws that dealt fairly with NACCB's members. The 1986 tax law's Section 1706 indicated that only technical services firms could deduct the use of independent contractors. NACCB actively tried to repeal this part of the law. President Clinton proposed to repeal Section 1706 as part of his health care reform bill, saying that more workers needed to be treated as employees.

Pennsylvania enacted a 6 percent sales-and-use tax for computer related services. It met with strong resistance from the industry, whose leaders said that computer services firms were in the early stages of development and could be harmed by the steep tax. At the same time, these firms were contending with an influx of products that were designed to be operated by average office personnel without the assistance of specialists.

Prepackaged software also took away some of the steam of these companies, as more users of computer hardware and software became familiar with their equipment, needing less support from computer services professionals. There was also a longer lag between the purchase of computer equipment and the need for computer professional services, which forced these companies to operate ''leanly.'' As more companies integrated computer systems into their operations, new additions to the installed base increased slowly because many purchases were just upgrades.

By the mid-1990s, an increasing connection existed between the computer and telecommunications industries, especially in Europe and Japan. This was expected to help computer professional services firms as consultants were called in to connect changing technologies so that performance was seamless.

The Independent Computer Consultants Association (ICCA) encouraged its member consultants to use formal contracts that outlined such details as payment terms,

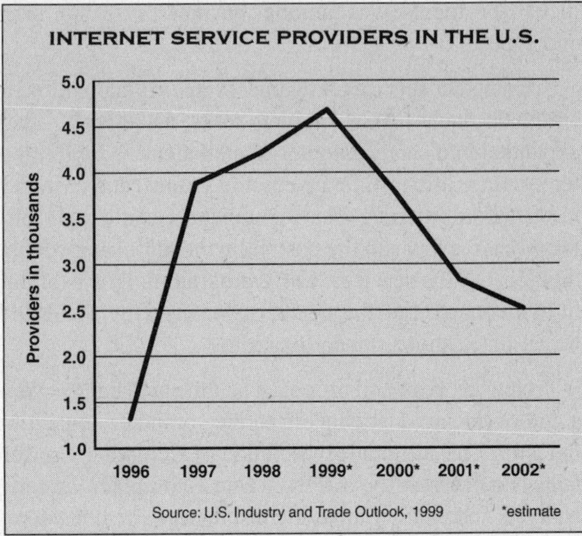

Source: U.S. Industry and Trade Outlook, 1999 *estimate

length and scope of the project, and copyright information on the finished project. Custom software developers, for example, usually held the rights to the computer code they developed, and the customer was allowed to use the system, but not to sell it.

Beginning in 1988, the Internal Revenue Service (IRS) penalized companies for calling employees independent contractors and not paying taxes for them. The IRS used several factors to determine whether a part-time worker was an employee or an independent contractor. These included employee training, working hours, payment practices, and the company's right to discharge the worker or the worker's right to terminate the working relationship. As long as the employer controlled what the work was and how it was to be done, the worker was considered an employee.

Many in the industry were also concerned about competition from foreign computer experts. NACCB fought the abuse of immigration laws that allowed foreign workers to do computer consulting work at illegally low rates and without proper visas.

Current Conditions

Worldwide revenues of the information technology industry rose to more than $1 trillion in 1998, up from $688 billion only three years earlier, according to the Information Technology Industry Council (ITIC). These revenues represented sales of computers and related equipment, software and services, business equipment, and telecommunications equipment and services.

U.S. Census Bureau data put revenues of the U.S. computer services industry at nearly $109.0 billion in 1998. Spending for computer-related services, not elsewhere classified, accounted for a little over $4.3 billion of this total.

Industry Leaders

More than 80 percent of the companies in this industry were smaller, entrepreneurial firms with annual sales below $2 million. Many of these computer services companies were owned by minority Americans, according to a 1987 Census Bureau survey of minority-owned enterprises. Many non-computer firms joined the industry by adding divisions or by acquiring computer services companies. Banks, publishers, airlines, and telecommunications companies were among those whose information technology divisions were involved in this industry.

There was much industry consolidation in the 1980s and early 1990s. Larger firms laid off workers, and some smaller firms merged, while large firms acquired computer related firms to enhance their position in the industry. Many U.S. companies attempted to meet all of their computer needs with one large contract. This trend forced some smaller computer-related services firms to join forces with other small firms in order to get the bigger projects.

Computer professional services included custom software, system design, and outsourcing services. Among the major players in this industry in the late 1990s were Automatic Data Processing (ADP), Ceridian Corp., and Perot Systems Corp. Acxiom Corp. ADP, headquartered in Roseland, NJ, employed 37,000 workers worldwide and posted sales of $5.5 billion in fiscal 1999, the twelve months ended June 30, 1999. Based in Minneapolis, MN, Ceridian employs a workforce of nearly 10,000 and reported 1999 sales of $1.3 billion. The employer of 6,000 people, Perot Systems Corp., based in Dallas, TX, posted 1998 sales of $993.6 million.

Workforce

The Information Technology Association of America (ITAA), looking forward to 2005, predicted that computer services would have the largest increase in personnel among information technology fields—including computer hardware and telecommunications industries. According to the Information Technology Industry Council, export and employment statistics forecast were also strong. The information technology industry employed 2.06 million Americans in 1997, according to a study commissioned by the Computer Research Association. That was up more than 63 percent from an IT workforce of 1.26 million in 1988. The composition of the IT workforce, however, changed considerably over those nine years. In 1988 computer programmers made up 45 percent of all IT employees, against computer scientists at 38 percent. In 1997 computer scientists made up 60 percent of the IT workforce, compared with 30 percent for programmers.

Those consultants and analysts who took advanced training in new technologies and who had a broad base of knowledge were better placed to succeed in the competitive world of computer services. The ICCA had its own certifying organization known as the Institute for Certification of Computer Professionals. This institute administered a standard computerized examination at more than 140 sites around the world. Those who passed the exam were designated Certified Computing Professionals and could market themselves as experts in computer systems.

AMERICA AND THE WORLD

The United States comprised the largest market for computer services, with almost half of the information services used by consumers worldwide used in the United States. Computer consultants and consulting firms, therefore, were on solid ground in the U.S. market. Many foreign companies used U.S.-based computer related services as they tried to enter U.S. markets or as they concentrated on their own markets.

Overall, U.S. computer professional services were highly successful abroad. Computer related services were encouraged by the passage of the North American Free Trade Agreement (NAFTA) and the expansion of the General Agreement on Tariffs and Trade (GATT). The 1989 U.S.-Canada Free Trade Agreement led some U.S. computer services companies to expand into other markets by buying Canadian firms. As an export, computer related services thrived in Canada, which was the major importer of U.S. computer services as well as of computer software, hardware, and telecommunications services. Some U.S. companies also had subsidiaries in South America and Europe.

Computer related services were being exported by U.S. firms at an increased rate in the 1990s. The U.S. Department of Commerce described the industry as having outstanding prospects for exporting success. According to the Bureau of Economic Analysis, the export of U.S. computer services was $2.04 billion in 1998, while imports were only $365 million. This represented an increase of more than 97 percent in exports from a level of $1.03 billion in 1990. Imports, on the other hand, climbed more than seven-fold from $44 million in 1990. The Information Industry Association (IIA) and ITAA both supported the efforts of U.S. firms overseas.

As countries around the world began to allow corporations to operate privately, computer services firms stood to gain new entry into foreign markets by helping the companies bring their operations up-to-date. Many consulting operations increased their marketing campaigns abroad in response to waning interest at home.

The European Community encouraged mergers and acquisitions among Western Europe's computer professional services firms. This trend had potential to create steep competition for U.S. companies. At the same time, a few Japanese, Canadian, and British computer services firms bought U.S.-based computer services firms in the early 1990s.

RESEARCH AND TECHNOLOGY

Such new technologies as computer-aided software engineering, or CASE, allowed some companies to handle their own computer programming without bringing in consultants. Some consulting companies fought this trend by offering skilled specialists who could perform computer tasks at rates far below the company's cost to do the work in-house.

In the early 1990s, an increasing proportion of computer related services was in electronic mail systems and services. This technology included the proliferating voice mail systems as well as electronic messaging systems that traveled across computer networks. Other telecommunications areas were expanding into computer consultants' territory as well. Integrated services digital networks, or ISDNs, provided computer professionals with another field in which their services could be used. The key for companies in the computer related services industry was to stay ahead of the corporate world and to continue offering services that enabled corporations to focus on their business while the consultants took care of their computer needs.

In the late 1990s, as the dawning of the new millennium neared, computer consultants reaped a bonanza as American businesses, large and small, spent heavily to have their computer systems safeguarded against the so-called Y2K bug. The widespread fear was that computer systems would fail to recognize the arrival of the year 2000 and would either stop functioning altogether or would malfunction. As it turned out, perhaps because of the billions spent on preparations or perhaps because the threat was never so big as it was reported to be, the new millennium arrived with virtually no dislocation in the computer sector. However, as long as bugs in software continue to pose a problem, computer consultants will have plenty of business trying to track down and eliminate them. Examples of the damage such a bug can cause are numerous. In January 1990, AT&T's long-distance switching system crashed because of such a bug. Sixty thousand customers lost service for the nine hours it took to get the system up and running again. In another case, the results were deadly when a Therac-25 radiation therapy machine produced a ''Malfunction 54'' error message. Unaware that the message meant ''radiation overdose,'' the machine's operator reset the machine and continued to treat patients, several of whom later died.

The new uses of the Internet, especially the potential for e-commerce, promises to spur further growth in this industry. Since Web site errors have the potential to drive customers into the arms of competitors, the explosive growth in the Internet undoubtedly will produce a wealth of business for computer consultants. In a mid-1999 example of the new opportunities for computer consultants, Neal N. Gibbons Services Plus+, a computer consultancy based in Magnolia, Texas, announced a new service for auto dealers with Web sites. The product, called AutoDIA (Auto Dealer Internet Audit) monitors the Web sites of new car dealers continually for errors, ensuring smooth operation.

Further Reading

Behr, Peter. ''By the Numbers: Why It's Not Easy to Get a Tech Job.'' *Washington Post,* 14 June 1999.

Brown, Joseph. ''Y2K Isn't the Last Word in Computer Bugs.'' *Tampa Tribune,* 9 January 2000.

Byrne, Harlan S. ''Golden Days: Business is Booming for the Computer-Service Companies.'' *Barron's,* 9 December 1996.

Darnay, Arsen J., ed. *Service Industries USA,* 4th ed. Detroit: Gale, 1998.

Gumucio, Marcelo. ''High-Tech Specialists Take Over Computer Industry.'' *Dallas Business Journal,* 19 August 1994.

''New Service Monitors Auto Dealer Web Sites for Costly Problems.'' *Business Wire,* 15 July 1999.

''Record U.S. IT Industry 1994 Revenues Exceed Expectations.'' *Information Technology Industry Council,* 18 April 1995.

U.S. Bureau of the Census. *1997 Economic Census.* Washington: GPO, 1999.

U.S. Department of Commerce. Bureau of Economic Analysis. *Survey of Current Business,* October 1999.

U.S. Department of Labor. Bureau of Labor Statistics. *Occupational Outlook Handbook, 1998-1999 Edition.* Washington: U.S. Department of Labor, 1998.

The U.S. Information Technology Industry Profile 1992. Arlington, VA: Information Technology Association of America, 1993.

''U.S. IT Industry 1995 Revenues Top $688 Billion.'' *Information Technology Industry Council,* 1 July 1996.

SIC 7381

DETECTIVE, GUARD, AND ARMORED CAR SERVICES

This category covers establishments primarily engaged in providing detective, guard, and armored car services. Establishments primarily engaged in monitoring and maintaining security systems devices, such as burglar and fire alarms, are classified in **SIC 7382: Security Systems Services.**

NAICS Code(s)

561611 (Investigation Services)
561612 (Security Guards and Patrol Services)
561613 (Armored Car Services)

Industry Snapshot

Some establishments in this industry have been the subject of scandal or, at the very least, controversy. Armored car robberies grab headlines, and many of these crimes are abetted by employees of the company. Companies that provide security services face little regulation and often hire guards with dubious, if not outright criminal, backgrounds. Detective services seldom make the news—discretion, after all, being a key attraction of their service—but when they do, it is most likely because they have committed some breach of common ethics, perhaps by intruding on a celebrity's privacy or committing questionable acts to obtain information. In one instance, private detective Tony (the Pelican) Pellicano was accused of staging the surreptitious exhumation of producer Michael Todd's bones in 1977. He was attempting to lead Chicago police, based on information from an alleged informant, to the location of the missing remains hidden under some leaves about 75 yards from the grave. In spite of all this, the demand for detective, guard, and armored car services remains strong.

Organization and Structure

Detective agencies provide investigative services. The area of investigation can vary widely, from uncovering corporate espionage to uncovering an unsavory episode in the background of a courtroom witness for the purpose of discrediting that witness. These enterprises range in size from small independent agencies to larger corporate businesses.

Business, industry, and government agencies all use guard services. Uniformed guards are hired to protect client property against theft, trespassing, vandalism, or to protect clients from physical harm. Some companies that provide guard services also provide security systems services (**see SIC 7382: Security Systems Services**). There are over twice as many security guards in the United States as police officers.

There are approximately 150 armored car services in the United States, some of which are subsidiaries of large corporations, while others are independently operated and may belong to the Independent Armored Car Operators Association. In addition to providing armed transport of cash between banking locations (for example, between the Federal Reserve Bank and bank branches), armored car companies also have what they call commercial accounts. These include food stores, restaurants, fast-food chains, department stores, and, potentially, any business that needs to move large sums of cash off-site to a bank.

Many armored car companies also have a money room, where money is stored temporarily and where services such as auditing deposits and processing orders for change are performed for client banks. In some cases, the cash may even move from a retailer to a money room, and then straight to the Federal Reserve, bypassing the retailer's bank altogether.

The money-courier industry is largely unregulated. There are no federal regulations covering who may transport money, or how. Although the top companies use armored vehicles and try to screen out employees with criminal records, other companies may use ordinary minivans and do little to screen employees. Law enforcement officials, as well as officials within the industry, have charged that the lack of a government regulated licensing process, one which would require a thorough background check of potential employees, has bred an industry in which robberies are all too frequently ''inside jobs.''

CURRENT CONDITIONS

U.S. manufacturers, in an attempt to prevent theft and counterfeiting of their patented products and ideas, are turning to private investigation firms for undercover operations. In one case, a female private detective was hired to apprehend those responsible for the theft from two major U.S. companies of proprietary plans for industrial compressors. A spokesman for the American Society for Industrial Security (ASIS) estimated that theft of proprietary information costs U.S. and Canadian firms $20 billion each year. A survey of ASIS members revealed that theft of manufacturing process technology is on the rise. Another area of concern to U.S. industry is protection of pharmaceutical trade secrets.

An emerging field for private detective work is the investigation of environmental crime. This might involve tracing illegal industrial sewage discharge to the guilty party, or doing research to determine which companies had in the past disposed of toxic waste at a particular site. Another unfortunate field of opportunity for detective work is urban terrorism. This was the case in 1991 when Laidlaw Transit, in Seattle, Washington, received three letters warning that school buses operated by Laidlaw would be blown up on Friday the thirteenth. (Private investigators, working with the Seattle police, determined the threat to be a hoax.) Other developing areas include: computer and communications crime detection, and forensic accounting, where a firm's books are examined for instances of in-house fraud.

In 1997, detective, armored guard, and armored car services was a $14.5 billion industry. It remained an industry that enjoyed growth in the recent past; industry sales in the early 1990s were seven times what they were in 1956. Twenty years ago there was concern within the industry that the use of credit cards would eliminate the need for armored car services. These fears have yet to become a reality, though, and credit card companies have themselves become major users of armored car services. Transportation of food stamps has provided another growth area for the armored transport industry as has the use of ATM machines. However, there are those who believe that all cash transactions eventually should be replaced by a federally operated electronic money system, which would eliminate many criminal activities. If such a system were to be implemented in the future, armored car companies could expect a drastic decline in demand for their services.

The industry may be approaching maturity, however; as banks consolidate and close branches, demand for armored car services is lessened. It has been speculated by Jim L. Dunbar, the chief executive of Federal Armored Express, that in the future there will be increased emphasis on money-room services as a source of revenue for armored car companies. The industry has also attracted new entrants who are competing based on price. Some companies are able to offer price reductions by cutting back on such security precautions as well-fortified vehicles. And if the courier is insured to protect the client against loss or theft, the client may be persuaded by the cost savings offered to forego optimal security.

The demand for security guards, on the other hand, enjoyed steady, rapid growth through the 1990s. During the 1990s, the industry experienced average annual growth of eight percent. Fueled by public perceptions of increasing crime, a growing schism between the haves and have-nots, the rise of gated communities, and an apparent willingness on the part of federal, state, and municipal authorities to leave public security to private firms, employment opportunities in the security guard industry were expected to grow rapidly in the coming decade.

The climate of fear that proved so hospitable to the security guard sector was heightened by the terrorist bombing in Oklahoma City in 1995. On the day after the bombing, the stock price of Wackenhut Corporation, America's third largest provider of security guards, jumped 20 percent. Though the panic was short-lived, demand for security guards continued to grow.

Guard companies, on the other hand, struggled during this period, facing what one analyst described as unacceptably high guard contract turnover. The reason for this was the conservatism and traditionalism of guard company management. Instead of assessing and reacting to changing levels in the customers risk profile, most companies made operational changes only in response to customer criticism. By the mid-1990s, security firms began to take tentative steps to enhance the effectiveness, scope, and productivity of security officers with information-related technology. These technologies made it possible for a guard company to upgrade its customer service by tracking client asset changes and making the corresponding changes in guard services automatically. Online central information processing allowed direct management of the guard force, while three-dimensional modeling programs and high-speed portable equipment made it possible to create customized security plans on a daily basis rather than working from specifications that changed infrequently, if at all.

INDUSTRY LEADERS

Borg-Warner Corp. (BWC) was formed in 1928 through the merger of four firms engaged in the manufacture of auto parts. Throughout subsequent years, this Chicago-based firm diversified into other areas such as chemicals, industrial equipment, air conditioning, and, with the purchase of Baker Industries in 1978, protective services. After being bought out by Merrill Lynch Capital Partners in 1987, BWC divested itself of all operations except for the automotive and protective services businesses. Principal subsidiaries in the protective services group, in addition to Baker Industries, which provides a wide range of protective services, were: Wells Fargo Guard Services, providing detective and guard services to institutional and residential clients; Burns International Security Services, providing security guard and investigative services to industrial and institutional clients throughout the United States, Canada, the United Kingdom, and Columbia; and Wells Fargo Armored Service Corp., providing armored car service as well as ATM servicing and cash services.

Burns underwent a restructuring and this resulted in a change of name to Burns International Services Corporation which, in turn, was the result of combining Wells Fargo Guard Services and Burns International Security Services. Burns International Services had 73,000 employees and recorded sales of almost $1.4 billion in 1999.

The Pittston Company was created by the Alleghany Corporation (which operated the Erie Railroad and Pennsylvania Coal Company) in 1930 as a means of dodging antitrust regulations in the U.S. coal market. (Pittston leased mines from the Erie Railroad and sold the coal through its own distributors.) Alleghany again faced the antitrust issue when it purchased the New York Central Railroad in 1954. This time, the solution for Alleghany was to divest itself of Pittston, leaving the latter an independent company. In 1956, Pittston, which had already diversified into trucking and warehousing, diversified further with its purchase of a 22 percent interest in the Chicago-based security transportation company, Brink's, Inc. Brink's was founded in Chicago in 1859 as a delivery company, and began making payroll deliveries in 1891. By 1956, it was the world's largest company providing armored car services. In 1962, Pittston completed its purchase of Brink's, but in 1976 Alleghany's legacy of antitrust confrontation fell upon Pittston: a federal grand jury indicted Brink's with antitrust violations. The charges cost the armored car company millions in settlements, the last of which was $2.7 million paid in 1980 to 12 Federal Reserve Banks. In spite of this, Brink's grew during the 1980s even as Pittston's older oil and warehousing operations were sold off. In 1998, the Pittston Brink's Group employed 41,800 people and had sales of approximately $1.45 billion.

The Wackenhut Corporation, founded in 1954 by ex-F.B.I. agent George R. Wackenhut, is another leading U.S.-based security company. It provides a broad range of security services at home and abroad, including executive protection and security for embassies and international airlines. The company's primary business is in uniformed security guard services, but Wackenhut is also involved in the business of private investigations, as well as activities under other SIC classifications such as correctional facilities management, classified in **SIC 8744: Facilities Support Management Services** and security systems implementation, classified in **SIC 7382: Security Systems Services.** In July of 1993, Wackenhut acquired U.K.-based International Maritime Services, Ltd., a company that provided security systems to the maritime industry. Wackenhut had sales of approximately $2.2 billion in 1999, and employed 70,000 people.

The country's first detective agency was established in 1850 by Allan Pinkerton, an immigrant from Scotland. Today, Pinkerton's, Inc., based in Westlake Village, California, is one of the largest U.S. companies providing security and investigative services. It has clients in the United States, Canada, Mexico, and the United Kingdom. In 1999, about 85 percent of revenues came from security guard services. Pinkerton's guards were used by hospitals, governmental units, special events promoters, and other industrial, commercial, financial, and retail customers to provide security, access control, traffic control, theft prevention, and related services. Pinkerton's also offered design and consulting services, conducting on-site analyses and making recommendations to design or improve systems. In 1998, this publicly held company employed 48,000 people and had sales of just over $1 billion. Pinkerton's enjoys strong name recognition; capitalizing on this, Sun Coast Merchandise Corp. licensed the Pinkerton's name in 1992 to apply to a line of emergency lighting—Pinkerton Home Security & Safety Products.

Another leading firm providing investigative services is Kroll Associates. J. Kroll Associates was formed in the early 1970s by Jules Kroll to offer companies a service that would audit their purchasing process to prevent devious practices by the company's employees, such as receiving kickbacks or charging payments to fictitious suppliers. Kroll's services have expanded considerably since then. During the 1980s, Kroll's company provided investigative services to Wall Street financial institutions, such as tracing money through foreign banks, analyzing the credit of a principal in a takeover deal, determining the true financial value of a targeted acquisition, and detecting illegal insider trading. Kroll also provided services to U.S. and foreign governments. For example, Kroll assisted in the Federal Deposit Insurance Corporation's investigation of the savings and loan scandal, and was asked in 1992 by the Republic of Russia to locate money believed to have been taken out of the country by directors of state run enterprises who feared the advent of privatization.

In 1997, J. Kroll Associates merged with another firm to become The Kroll-O'Gara Company. The new venture expanded the company's capabilities; in addition to Kroll's range of services, the new firm conducts personnel background checks and provides both (security) driver and security training. A Kroll-O'Gara subsidiary modified vehicles for private, corporate, military, and government clients. Another subsidiary, Laboratory Specialists of America provided employee drug-testing. In 1998, Kroll-O'Gara had 2,446 employees and sales of $264.8 million. (Note: At the beginning of 2000, The Blackstone Group, an investment firm, began arrangements to purchase Kroll-O'Gara.)

WORKFORCE

Anyone can hang out a sign and claim to be a detective, and there appears to be no single career route which one follows to become a private eye, although a prior career in law enforcement is common. Anthony Pellicano, who has made a name for himself by providing detective services to Hollywood stars, is a high school dropout and former bill collector for Spiegel; Jules Kroll, on the other hand, has a law degree from Georgetown Law School, and worked for the Manhattan District Attorney's office. Kroll operatives include a former security chief for IBM, a former CIA station chief, a former Green Beret and international crime and terrorism expert for Rand Corporation, and a former New York City Police Commissioner. The company has 40 investigators, 10 of whom are women. Kroll also uses the services of behavioral researchers and independent private investigators, many of the latter being ex-police officers.

FURTHER READING

''Burns International Services Corporation.'' Hoover's Company Capsules, 23 March 2000. Available from http://www.hoovers.com/co/capsule.

''Burns Int'l Services Corp,'' Market Guide, 23 March 2000. Available from http://cnnfn.marketguide.com/mgi/snap/A03E1.html.

Hoover's Company Capsules. Austin, TX, Hoover's Inc., 2000. Available from http://www.hoovers.com.

''Living on the Defensive.'' *Advertising Age,* 24 April 1995.

''Profits of Doom.'' *The Economist,* 13 May 1995.

''Standard & Poor's Industry Surveys.'' New York: McGraw-Hill, 1996.

U.S. Department of Commerce, Bureau of the Census. *Service Annual Survey: 1997.* Washington: GPO, 1999.

Van de Mark, Donald. ''Head of P.I. Firms Talks About His Success.'' *Business Unusual (CNNfn),* 29 August 1997.

SIC 7382

SECURITY SYSTEMS SERVICES

This classification includes establishments primarily engaged in monitoring and maintaining security systems devices, such as burglar and fire alarms. Establishments of this industry may sell or lease and install the security systems which they monitor and maintain. Establishments primarily engaged in the sales and installation, or installation only, of such devices are classified in **SIC 1731: Electrical Work.**

NAICS CODE(S)

561621 (Security Systems Services (except Locksmiths))

INDUSTRY SNAPSHOT

Simple onsite burglar alarms, which may deter an intruder with their noise and attract the attention of a passerby, are usually insufficient for the higher security needs of many businesses and some residences. Security systems services provide added security by continuously monitoring property alarms for multiple clients through their own offsite central station. Accordingly, these companies often are referred to as central stations.

Central station-monitored alarms, when triggered, send a silent alarm signal to the station through a leased telephone line, a coaxial cable (television) line, or a reserved radio frequency. Unless contacted by the subscriber within a few minutes to cancel a false alarm, the station then calls the police, possibly dispatches its own guard, and notifies the client. The monitoring agreement may involve keeping the central station notified of the business' regular hours and when the alarm is turned on or off, thus sharing the responsibility for and the control of operating the alarm system.

Most of the commercial alarm monitoring businesses deal with burglar alarms. Only a small number of police stations are willing to directly monitor alarm systems themselves because of the high incidence of false alarms and limited police resources. Alarm systems connected directly to police stations usually only exist when no private central station is operating within a particular area. Private monitoring companies are considered to have greater security advantages than police station monitoring systems. Fire alarm systems, on the other hand, generally are monitored directly by fire departments, since false alarms occur less frequently.

Burglar alarm systems typically include both door and window trip switches to detect break-ins and sensors to detect motion. Both kinds of devices are linked by wires or short-range radio transmitters to a central console, where the system is switched on or off. Different detection systems provide varying levels of security. Alarm systems are rated by Underwriters Laboratories (UL), an independent product testing organization that serves insurance underwriters.

UL not only tests alarm equipment, but also inspects and rates the firms installing and monitoring the equipment. UL also certifies alarm service companies upon approval. Central stations are graded according to the length of time they take to dispatch a guard to the property, and whether the line that runs from the property to the central station is protected from electronic tampering. Other than UL's services, the industry is relatively self-regulated. Not every state requires the licensing of alarm installers.

Central stations often install the alarm systems, a service the manufacturer of the system usually does not perform. As for the maintenance of alarm systems, installers typically provide a one-year warranty on parts and labor. Thereafter, annual maintenance contracts usually cost around 10 percent of the original installation price.

Organization and Structure

There were approximately 2,000 establishments in the United States engaged in security systems services. These included both private and publicly held companies and a number of unincorporated individual proprietorships or partnerships. The majority of firms concentrated on the monitoring of burglar alarms. Most provided only local service, although several were national in scope. Central stations served both residential and business clients, and occasionally specialized in particular types of clients. Many central stations were specialized in the business of security service monitoring, but some companies also offered onsite security guard services, other electrical equipment installation contracting, and other building maintenance activities, such as janitorial services.

Background and Development

In the 1920s, crime increased significantly in the United States, and new burglar alarm systems were devised as a response. Originally, most alarms were monitored directly by the police, but police stations gradually became overwhelmed by false alarms. In some cities, they responded only to alarms owned by special permit holders or only to alarms protecting businesses requiring high security, such as banks and jewelry stores. Private enterprise central stations gradually took over for the police.

In the 1980s and 1990s, private central stations began monitoring fire alarms as well. Fire alarm monitoring, however, tended to be contracted out by municipal fire departments, rather than directly by property owners. A number of cities were beginning to privatize their fire alarm monitoring services to save money, to avoid having to make continuous investments to keep up with the latest technology, or to avoid having to compete against private companies. Often, central stations that already handled other types of alarms, such as burglar alarms, took on fire alarm monitoring as well.

The number of alarm monitoring companies in the United States declined because of a number of acquisitions. The industry was originally very fragmented and localized, but began to consolidate in the late 1980s, a trend which accelerated in the early 1990s. Larger companies took over smaller ones by offering limited partnerships. Alert Holdings Inc., for example, acquired close to 400 companies between 1985 and 1991. Smaller companies found it difficult to compete with larger ones that offered lower priced installations. The alarm monitoring business easily benefited from economies of scale. National companies could monitor clients in other states through one central station.

In the late 1980s, alarm monitoring services began to target their marketing efforts more seriously toward private home owners. The residential market was not as well penetrated as the business market because home owners usually took care of their security needs with simple on-site siren systems they had installed themselves. Decreasing alarm-system installation prices and rising crime, however, boosted the residential business of central stations. Installation costs of centrally monitored systems fell from around $3,250 in 1970 to $1,250 in 1993. Occasionally, installations were offered at no charge as part of a multi-year monitoring contract. Residential monitoring services also began to offer other security services, including the monitoring of medical alert signals, possible water pipe and gas leaks, and thermostat controls. Consequently, centrally monitored alarms represented the fastest growing segment of the home alarm business in the early 1990s.

About 1 million home systems were installed in 1992, for roughly $1.4 billion in service fees and equipment expenses. About 75 percent of these professionally installed systems were connected to central stations for

$1.9 billion in annual revenue from monthly residential security monitoring and maintenance fees.

In 1990, alarm monitoring represented the third largest use of information services over telephone lines, after database services and transaction processing, and ahead of telephone answering services and 900 telephone number services. Alarm monitoring through telephone lines accounted for about $2.5 billion worth of services.

CURRENT CONDITIONS

In 1987, the security systems services industry recorded $2.21 billion in revenue. Growth was fueled not only by an increasing fear of crime, but also because some property insurance underwriters required their clients in high risk businesses to obtain security services before a policy was issued. The security systems services industry experienced steady growth; total revenues increased markedly due to continued public concern over security issues. The industry had an average yearly growth pattern of over 6 percent from 1993 to 1997. Most notably, during the intervening decade, total industry annual receipts more than doubled by 1997 to $5.9 billion.

Some commercial alarm monitoring services were broadening their services in response to client requests, including drive-by spot-checks and the dispatching of guards. In the wake of the Oklahoma City bombing in 1995, demand for security systems and equipment was expected to boom. Fear of crime was at an all-time high—though actual crime statistics failed to support public perceptions—and security companies tooled up for an anticipated surge in demand. As it turned out, while demand for more security remained strong, that sector of the industry involved in reselling, installing, and monitoring remained unsettled.

Alarm monitoring brought in about 20 percent of all dollars in 1996, with equipment and installation accounting for most of the rest. Greater consolidation also continued within the industry in 1996, as the largest national and regional firms bought up smaller firms and accounts. The trend was expected to continue as cash-rich utilities, Wall Street investors, telephone companies, and powerhouse retailers had all bought their way into the security industry. Companies also showed less interest in the home security market, an amorphous area that was overly price-sensitive and whose needs were difficult to gauge. Also worrying was the growing do-it-yourself (DIY) business. The sale of home computers with home automation bundled in, and the sale of DIY sensors, detectors, and even CCTV components posed a serious threat to alarm installation and monitoring firms. As a result, many companies turned their attention to the large commercial market where they were able to offer systems integration services, reap higher profits, and build longer-lasting client relationships.

INDUSTRY LEADERS

As the twentieth century ended, the security services industry became a microcosm of widespread globalization of markets and trends towards acquisitions by conglomerates in related businesses. As a result, total revenues reported for most firms in the industry were not solely derived from security services activity and operations. Two of the largest companies in the industry were Burns International Services, with sales of almost $1.4 billion and ADT Security Services, Inc. (operated as a subsidiary of Tyco International Ltd.), with sales of $5.5 billion. The largest electronic security services company in North America, ADT provided electronic security monitoring services to business customers in retailing, financial services, manufacturing, and to the public sector in North America and Europe.

At the beginning of the new millennium, other viable competitors operating in the security services industry were also subsidiaries or divisions of conglomerates. Pinkerton's, Inc., with total reported sales of $1 billion structured operations with company units Pinkerton Securities, Inc. (primarily security officers/staff), a systems integration division, and security consulting services. With $1.4 billion in revenue, Pittston Brink's, Inc. operated in two related security operations, Brink's (armored transport) and Brink's Home Security. The Wackenhut Corporation offered even more diverse security services and recorded total revenue of almost $2.2 billion. Perhaps most illustrative of the continuing trend of leading security systems industry firms to operate as part of a consolidated corporate structure comprising a variety of security services, Wackenhut engaged in private prison management, (security) employee staffing, and security services (which included security systems) in sensitive markets such as background investigations and facilities in airports, nuclear power plants, and embassies.

RESEARCH AND TECHNOLOGY

Central stations benefited from technological advancements achieved during the 1980s and 1990s, particularly those emanating from the telecommunications industry. To prevent criminal tampering of leased telephone lines that carried the alarm signal, alarm services developed a computerized method of sending signals, made up of thousands of signals sent at random, that burglars could not duplicate. There also was progress in wireless communications, including tests that used cellular telecommunications, rather than regular phone lines.

Computer software for alarm monitoring became more sophisticated. There were improvements in installed alarm systems. In particular, efforts were made to reduce the incidence of false alarms through more advanced sensoring devices and better consumer and dealer education. One innovation on the technological side was the introduction of shock glass break sensors tuned to the frequency of the glass. Unlike acoustic sensors, these responded only to changes in the glass itself, resulting in significantly fewer false alarms.

Further Reading

Bowman, Eric J. ''Security Tools up for the Future.'' *Security Management,* January 1996.

Hoover's Company Capsules. Austin, TX: Hoover's Inc., 1997. Available from http://www.hoovers.com/.

''Integrated Security Systems Inc.'' Pricewaterhousecoopers Technology Centre, 15 March 2000. Available from http://edgarscan.pwcglobal.com/servlets/getCompanyDetail?Name=INTEGRATED+SECURITY+SYSTEMS+INC.

''Living on the Defensive.'' *Advertising Age,* 24 April 1995.

''Profits of Doom.'' *The Economist,* 13 May 1995.

''O'Toole-Zalud Report.'' *SDM* Magazine. *SECURITY* Magazine, 1996.

Tyco 1999 Annual Report. Exeter, NH: Tyco International Ltd., 1999.

U.S. Department of Commerce, Bureau of the Census. *Service Annual Survey 1997.* Washington: GPO, 1999.

SIC 7383

NEWS SYNDICATES

This category covers establishments primarily engaged in furnishing news, pictures, and features and in supplying news reporting services to newspapers and periodicals. Separate establishments of newspaper and periodical publishers that are engaged in gathering news are classified as auxiliaries.

NAICS Code(s)

514110 (New Syndicates)

As of 1997, there were 527 establishments classified as news syndicates employing more than 9,400 people, with combined industry sales reaching $1.4 billion. In addition to the broad coverage of mainstream wire services, organizations within the news syndicates category cover specialized areas such as regional news services (Panafrican News Agency and Macedonian Press Agency), industry-specific services (ComputerWire and International Business News Service), and government information (Federal News Service and Capitol Newswire), to name a few.

The genesis of U.S. news syndicates can be traced to the construction of the first successful telegraph line in 1844. When completed, the line connected the cities of Washington and Baltimore and was immediately utilized by newspapers in Washington as a means of receiving news of the Maryland State Convention in Baltimore. As more lines were constructed, more and more newspaper publishers recognized this new communications technology as a valuable means of receiving news from distant locations. It was through the effort by newspaper publishers to share access to the telegraph lines, and to share the costs associated with using this new technology as a news gathering tool, that news syndicates came into being.

The National Associated Press (AP) was a collective formed in 1897 from various city, state, and regional Associated Press units. AP bylaws allowed its members to refuse association membership to applicants whose newspapers were located in the same city as those members (a practice which the U.S. Supreme Court in 1945 held to be an illegal restraint of competition). By 1907, there was a growing pool of newspapers that had been denied membership into AP, including most of the newspapers owned by E.W. Scripps. That year, Scripps challenged the AP monopoly on national news brokering by establishing the United Press Association, a commercial venture which, after taking over William Randolph Hearst's International News Service in 1958, would go on to become United Press International (UPI).

During the 1960s and 1970s, the number of competing newspapers declined, leaving many cities with only one newspaper. Newspaper publishers who had felt competition-driven pressure to subscribe to both the AP and UPI services now felt that it was safe to let one of them go. In the ensuing fight to retain its subscribers, AP fared better than its rival. Although UPI was still one of the four major news syndicates serving the international market—along with AP, London-based Reuters, and France's Agence France-Presse—and was second only to AP domestically, it reported a pre-tax loss of $12 million in 1980. Financial difficulties continued on through the decade, and, in June 1992, UPI was acquired in bankruptcy court for $3.95 million in cash by Middle East Broadcasting Center Ltd. (M.B.C.), a London-based television news and entertainment company owned by a group of Saudi businessmen. At the time of the sale, UPI employed about 450 people full-time, and another 2,000 part-time. Its new comeback strategy as a privately held company focused on small-market newspapers and radio stations. In the area of new media, UPI provides national news online to The Microsoft Network.

The Associated Press was the world's largest newsgathering organization during the late 1990s, with more than 235 news bureaus in about 70 countries around the world, providing news, photos, graphics and audiovisual services to more than 1,700 newspapers and 5,500 television and radio stations.

Founded in 1865, Reuters relayed news and financial information from more than 340,000 computer terminals in 158 countries in 1995. It also provided data feeds to financial markets and sold software for analyzing bonds, currencies, futures, options and stocks. Information was gathered from 267 exchanges and over-the-counter markets, from 4,700 subscribers who contributed data directly to Reuters, and from a network of about 1,936 journalists, photographers and camera people.

In addition to providing reports of general-interest news for the print and broadcast media, the news syndicates have expanded into areas of specialized interest. One area that has experienced significant growth is business news services. In 1967 AP joined with Dow Jones & Company to create a worldwide economic news service to foreign subscribers. In addition to the AP-Dow Jones News Service, Dow Jones also operates the Dow Jones News Service in both the United States and Canada. This service provides business information to brokerages, banks, corporations, and investment houses.

The 1990s also saw the Internet gain prominence for news syndicates, with Reuters entering the fray aggressively, providing news to all major on-line services, including The Microsoft Network. At AP, officials had also committed to increase their role in cyberspace and formed a new-media department, offering services such as new multimedia Internet "pages" via member newspapers' on-line services.

FURTHER READING

Albers, Rebeccca Ross. "Wires Get Wired." Newspaper Association of America, 1995.

Badaracco, Claire. "Dow Jones & Company, Inc." *International Directory of Company Histories,* Chicago: St. James Press, 1991.

U.S. Bureau of the Census. *1997 Economic Census.* 1999.

———. *1997 NAICS Definitions.*

SIC 7384

PHOTOFINISHING LABORATORIES

This industry classification includes establishments primarily engaged in developing film, making photographic prints and enlargements, or retouching photographs for businesses or for the general public.

NAICS CODE(S)

812921 (Photo Finishing Laboratories (except One-Hour))

812922 (One-Hour Photo Finishing)

INDUSTRY SNAPSHOT

The photo finishing laboratories industry group includes establishments whose core business is developing and printing film (except for commercial motion picture film); duplicating, enlarging, or retouching photographs; developing and processing home movies; and providing transfer and other film photography services related to digital imaging, photo CD, and other forms of electronic photography. Many retail stores, discount stores, drugstores, supermarkets, camera stores, photography studios, and other businesses also offer commercial photofinishing services, whether through onsite (or "captive") labs or through commercial wholesale laboratories; such ancillary photofinishing services are the primary competition of the photofinishing laboratory businesses that fall within this category.

According to the *1997 Economic Census,* the number of photofinishing laboratories showed a slow but steady decline throughout the 1990s. From 1992 to 1997, the number of labs in the United States declined by 10 percent to 7,055 establishments. Conversely, annual receipts rose steadily from $4.4 billion to $7.7 billion. Consolidation within the industry was largely attributable to a growing trend for the public to have their rolls processed by wholesale and mail order labs. As discount stores and supermarkets continued to equip themselves with minilabs, dominance by central labs was expected to disappear by the year 2000, when the number of minilabs finally would likely outnumber central labs.

ORGANIZATION AND STRUCTURE

In the 1990s, photofinishing laboratories relied primarily on automated equipment that reliably produced quick results. Photographic laboratories could be classified as minilab outlets, mail order laboratories, or wholesale laboratories.

Minilabs Outlets. Photofinishing laboratories featuring onsite minilabs could be independent or affiliated with photofinishing chains, and physically autonomous or situated within larger businesses. Minilab systems, which consisted of compact automated photoprocessing equipment, often required less than 1,000 square feet of floor space. Minilab outlets specialized in fast photofinishing (with photographs processed in as little as 30 minutes to an hour) and commanded relatively high photoprocessing rates. Leading minilab chains included Moto Photo; CPI Photo Finish; Fox Photo 1-Hr Labs; and Fotomat Express.

Mail Order Laboratories. Mail order laboratories, often with nationwide markets, generally provided amateur photographer customers with envelopes and instruction forms for mailing in photoprocessing orders. Mail order laboratories generally relied on repeat orders from established customer bases, often enclosing additional mailing envelopes for customer use when returning photoprocessing orders. Some mail order laboratories distributed mailing envelopes through camera stores or methods such as direct mail campaigns and newspaper inserts. Some mail order laboratories sold ''prepaid'' mailers through outlets such as camera stores. Mail order laboratories generally offered convenience (orders could be sent from anywhere and received at any mailing address) and relatively low prices. However, some mail order laboratories were premium operations emphasizing customized services and rigorous quality control. Photoprocessing through mail order laboratories generally took one to two weeks. Leading mail order laboratories included Clark Color Labs; Custom Quality Studio; Kodalux (formed through the merger of the former Kodak photofinishing laboratories and Fuqua Industries); Mystic Color Lab; PhotoWorks (formerly Seattle FilmWorks); and Skrudland Photo.

Wholesale Laboratories. Wholesale laboratories, often with nationwide markets, generally processed commercial orders and/or orders dropped off by amateur photographers at supermarkets, discount stores, drugstores, and other locations. Wholesale laboratories often operated anonymously behind the imprimatur of such retailers. Drop-off boxes provided for amateur photographers were often very simple affairs; in the early 1990s, however, IBM manufactured an automated drop box developed by Delphi Technologies, whereby membership card or credit card customers could drop in photoprocessing orders and key in instructions through computer screens. Wholesale laboratories, which processed thousands of rolls of film daily, generally offered less-expensive rates than minilab outlets and a turnaround of one day to one week. Leading wholesale photofinishing laboratories included Allprints Quality Photo Services, Dean's Photo Service, Guardian, Fuji TruColor (established in 1993 by Fuji Photo Film USA), Qualex, TruColor Photo, True Color, and United Photo.

The primary association related to commercial photofinishing and the photography industry as a whole was the 16,000-member Photo Marketing Association (PMA), which was established in 1924. The PMA, previously known as the Master Photo Dealers' and Finishers' Association, was formed by the merger of the Master Photo Finishers of America (founded in 1924) and the National Photographic Dealers Association (founded in 1933). The PMA sponsors several important industry publications and maintains a photofinishing and photography retailing reference library and hall of fame at its Jackson, Mississippi, headquarters.

Current Conditions

According to the Photo Marketing Association's *Industry Trends Report 1995-96,* photo processing held the largest share of the revenue in the amateur market with 43.1 percent. Within the amateur market, 710 million rolls of film were developed in 1995. Total rolls were down slightly from the 1994 figure of 716 million, but higher than the 1993 total of 694. Sales in the amateur market continued to remain fairly stagnant since 1988. In that year sales totaled $5 billion, rising by $200 million every year until 1991. From 1992 to 1994 sales remained at $5.5 billion every year, and dropped slightly to $5.4 million in 1996.

Drugstores continued to lead the market of photofinishing with 23.8 percent of total sales and 24.8 percent of total rolls processed in 1995. Drugstore share was down slightly from 24.5 percent in 1994 as discount sores continue to gain more share but drugstores continued to lead. Stand-alone minilabs had 22 percent of the photofinishing market in 1995, also down from 1994. However, minilab statistics do not include minilab equipment used in other stores. Only 40.5 percent of minilab equipment was used in stand-alone minilabs. Almost 21 percent were in discount stores, 17 percent in camera stores, 13 percent in drugstores, and 7 percent in supermarkets. Discount stores held 21.9 percent of the total market in 1995, one of only two retail channels to show growth from 1994 when it had 18.8 percent of photofinishing sales. Supermarkets accounted for 12.6 percent, the other retail channel to grow from 1994 when it held 11.8 percent. Mail order held 5.4 percent, down slightly from 5.6 in 1994. Other outlets accounted for the remaining 3.2 percent of 1995 photofinishing sales. According to the PMA, in 1997, 65.1 percent of photoprocessing was done by wholesale, captive, or mail order labs; the remainder was done by retail labs.

Minilab equipment has become increasingly common in the photofinishing industry, accounting for 33.5 percent of the amateur market photofinishing dollar sales in 1986, 40.3 percent of dollar sales in 1988, 43.4 percent of dollar sales in 1990, 44 percent of the amateur market photofinishing dollar sales in 1992, and 44.4 percent in 1995. The estimated number of minilabs nationwide increased from 5,200 laboratories in 1984 to 11,900 laboratories in 1986 and 15,300 laboratories in 1988. After that year, growth in the number of minilabs leveled off to a degree. In 1991, the estimated number of minilabs nationwide was 17,200, and grew by only about 150 per year to 17,500 in 1993. But in 1994 minilabs began to grow quickly again, shooting up to 18,900 in that year and 20,500 in 1995.

Within the various film formats, 35mm film increasingly dominated the market, accounting for 57 percent of exposures in 1984, 65 percent of exposures in 1986, 75.4 percent of exposures in 1988, 83.1 percent of exposures in 1990, and 88 percent of exposures in 1992. With the introduction of the disposable camera, 35mm dropped slightly to 80.5 percent of exposures in 1995, with disposable cameras filling in with 6.9 percent of exposures. Conversely, 110/126 film accounted for 18 percent of exposures in 1984, 17.6 percent of exposures in 1986, 15.1 percent of exposures in 1988, 12.3 percent of exposures in 1990, 9.6 percent of exposures in 1992, and only 6.5 percent of exposures in 1995. Disc camera film dropped off quickly as the novelty and excitement for the product dropped off. Disc accounted for 22 percent of exposures in 1984, 14.5 percent of exposures in 1986, 7.4 percent of exposures in 1988, 3.8 percent of exposures in 1990, only 1.6 percent of exposures in 1992, and nearly disappeared in 1995 with only .8 percent of exposures. The rest of exposures in 1995 were taken by instant film with 2.7 percent, and slide film with 2.6 percent of exposures.

Camera stores and stand-alone minilabs had strong commercial sales increases in 1995, especially from commercial sources such as graphic arts and advertising. With 35mm's slight drop in share (it's first ever), large format film types from these commercial sources helped fill in the gap along with disposable cameras. As Advanced Photo films, introduced in April 1996, take on more of the market (it took an estimated 7 to 8 percent of the share in 1997), it will also take some of the 35mm share.

While roll volume decreased by just under 1 percent, total exposures fell even more with a 3 percent decline. The total number of exposures per roll sold decreased in 1995, bringing about the decline in total exposures. Enlargement volume as a percentage of total photofinishing sales also continued to decline to 5.4 percent, down from the high of 7.5 percent in 1991. Although volume sales are increasing—mostly through labs developing online ordering services—pricing competitions keep the total percentage of revenues down.

INDUSTRY LEADERS

In 1991, the end of a photofinishing retail era was marked with the acquisition by CPI Corporation of Fox Photo, a pioneer in photofinishing retail "kiosks." This acquisition added more than 250 retail sites and 50 minilabs outlets to CPI's base of approximately 1,360 photofinishing retail sites, including almost 1,000 outlets situated within Sears stores. In the early 1990s, Fuji Photo Film U.S.A. and its sister company Fujifilm Photofinishing U.S.A. acquired or gained controlling interest in Allprints Quality Photo Services, Dean's Photo Service, McJohn Inc., Northern Photo, and TruColor Photo, all wholesale photofinishing laboratories. The Photo Marketing Association's *Industry Trends Report 1992-93* indicated that "continued consolidation among central labs produced double-digit dollar expansion for those firms."

CPI Photo placed first in the industry with 2000 sales of $319.1 million, and 8,178 employees. Other industry leaders include PhotoWorks (formerly Seattle Film-Works) with 1999 sales of $89.6 million and 690 employees, and Moto Photo with 999 sales of $36.6 million and 478 employees.

WORKFORCE

In 1982, there were approximately 71,700 photofinishing laboratory employees nationwide. By 1987, this figure increased to 82,500. In 1992, however, the number had dropped to 69,300, and by 1994 there were only 57,000 jobs as photographic processors. By 1997, this number had rebounded to 71,991 employees, 15,123 of whom worked in one-hour photofinishing labs. In 1995, the states with the greatest number of photofinishing laboratory employees were California (12,671 employees, or 17.1 percent of the national total), New York (6,461 employees), and Texas (5,079 employees).

In 1982, the total national photofinishing laboratories payroll was $813.8 million. By 1987, the total payroll had increased to $1.12 billion. And in 1993, payroll had increased again to $1.28 billion. The states with the highest total photofinishing laboratories payroll were California ($177.3 million) and New York ($106.8 million). In 1992, the national average payroll per establishment was $154,531 (compared to $314,133 per establishment for service industries as a whole); the average payroll per photofinishing lab employee was $17,330 (compared to $23,335 per employee for the service industries as a whole). The states with the highest average payroll per employee were Maine ($20,145) and New York ($16,533). The average payroll per employee was lower in Texas ($14,491) and California ($13,922); and among the states with the lowest average payroll per employee were Arizona ($10,504), Tennessee ($10,535), and Vermont ($10,710).

AMERICA AND THE WORLD

Internationally, film sales per household are highest in Germany (165.0 million units, or 6.5 units per household), Austria (15.8 million units, or 5.6 units per household), and France (106.4 million units, or 5.5 units per household). In 1992, photo processing accounted for 53 percent of $3.7 billion in photographic expenditures in Germany; 47 percent of $1.56 billion in amateur photographic expenditures in Australia; 42.9 percent of photographic expenditures in Canada; and 40 percent of $58 million in photographic expenditures in the United Kingdom.

RESEARCH AND TECHNOLOGY

Microlabs are scaled-down photofinishing laboratories that are less expensive than minilabs—and they require as little as 7 square feet of floor space for equipment and 18 square feet of total working space. Systems such as the Fuji Mini 27 and the Konica Nice Print are also waterless, and thus do not require special plumbing. In the early 1990s, Photogo launched a chain of microlabs based on the P135 system in the United

States, Europe, and the Far East. The microlabs' features have encouraged retailers and other businesses to set up in-store photofinishing booths.

The emergence of computer-based digital imaging technology and photo CDs are particularly suited for media, publishing, and other commercial uses that rely on fast electronic processing, transmission, and reproduction. While digital imaging is not expected to replace film photography, photofinishing laboratories have increasingly offered digital imaging and photo CD services.

Some of the biggest retail photo labs across the country, including Wolf Cameras and Konica Photo Services USA, Inc., were developing digital imaging in the form of photos over the Internet. In late 1996 and early 1997, these labs would process the film normally, and if desired, would scan the pictures into digital format and place them on a Web site. The customer was given a highly secure access code and password. From a home computer the customer could view, download, and manipulate the photos, even giving access codes to friends and family who could order reprints online. Early statistics showed that customers ordered five times as many reprints and enlargements over the Internet than through standard procedures.

Local environmental regulations, which were often the most strict, were sometimes enforced through the processing of annual permits for photofinishing laboratories. Photofinishers have made efforts to recycle chemical drums, toner cartridges, single-use cameras, film cartridges, film canisters, and film spools. They have attempted to reduce the use of toxic chemicals such as photoreceptors, recover the silver used in photoprocessing, and to reduce or capture waste effluent.

FURTHER READING

International Photo Processing Industry Report 1996-97. Bonita Springs, FL: Photofinishing News, Inc.

International Photo Processing Industry Report 1997-98. Bonita Springs, FL: Photofinishing News, Inc.

Omura, Glenn. *Minilabs: Strategies for the Future.* Jackson, MS: Photo Marketing Association, 1994.

Photo Marketing Association International. *The 1995-96 PMA Industry Trends Report: U.S. Markets Report,* Jackson, MS: 1997.

Photo Marketing Association International. *The 1996-97 PMA Industry Trends Report: U.S. Markets Report,* Jackson, MS: 1998.

U.S. Department of Commerce. *County Business Patterns 1994.* Washington: GPO, 1995.

U.S. Department of Commerce, Bureau of the Census. *Census of Service Industries 1992.* Washington: GPO, 1997.

———. *Economic Census, Other Services (Except Public Administration).* Washington: GPO, 1999.

SIC 7389

BUSINESS SERVICES, NOT ELSEWHERE CLASSIFIED

This group covers establishments primarily engaged in business services, not elsewhere classified, such as bondspersons, drafting services, lecture bureaus, notaries public, sign painting, speakers' bureaus, water softening services, and miscellaneous auctioneering services, on a flat fee or commission basis.

NAICS CODE(S)

512240 (Sound Recording Studios)
512290 (Other Sound Recording Industries)
541199 (Other Legal Services)
812990 (All Other Personal Services)
541370 (Surveying and Mapping (Except Geophysical) Services)
541410 (Interior Design Services)
541420 (Industrial Design Services)
541340 (Drafting Services)
541490 (Other Specialized Design Services)
541890 (Other Services Related to Advertising)
541930 (Translation and Interpretation Services)
541350 (Building Inspection Services)
541990 (All Other Professional, Scientific and Technical Services)
711410 (Agents and Managers for Artists, Entertainers and Other Public Figures)
561421 (Telephone Answering Services)
561422 (Telemarking Bureaus)
561439 (Private Mail Centers)
561431 (Other Business Service Centers)
561491 (Repossession Services)
561910 (Oackaging and Labeling Services)
561790 (Other Services to Buildings and Dwellings)
561599 (All Other Travel Arrangement and Reservation Services)
561920 (Convention and Trade Show Organizers)
561591 (Convention and Visitors Bureaus)
522320 (Financial Transactions, Processing, Reserve and Clearing House Activities)
561499 (All Other Business Support Services)
561990 (All Other Support Services)

The miscellaneous business services industry encompasses a broad range of specialties, ranging from baby shoe bronzing services and yacht brokers to window trimmers and playwrights. Establishments classified in this industry are generally engaged in providing services that do not generate a sufficient amount of national revenue for the U.S. government to track alone.

Roughly 212,000 firms were engaged in this industry during 1995. Government statistics indicate that about two-thirds of the companies classified in this industry are corporations, with the remainder being either sole proprietorships or partnerships.

According to government sources, the industry generated $32 million in sales in 1992. Notable industry statistics for 1992 included sales for sign painting shops ($523,000), interior designing ($2.3 million), and phone answering services ($1.0 million). The average company engaged in this industry generated annual revenues of $450,000, for an industry total of about $20 billion.

While the employment outlook varies by segment, overall industry employment is expected to rise over the course of the next decade. A few major occupational groups, however, such as switchboard operators and telephone message specialists, were expected to diminish in size during this period. The corporate and management training industry, as one example of the specialty services provided in this category, benefited from the $58 billion corporate budget dedicated to training in 1996. In 1995, 93 percent of all organizations offered some form of basic computer training.

Sears, Roebuck and Co. of Hoffman Estates, Illinois led the industry in 1999 with sales of more than $41 billion. Sears employed 324,000 workers, creating a sales-per-employee standard of $126,762. Houston-based Waste Management Inc. followed with 1998 revenues of more than $22.7 billion, employing 68,000 workers who generated $334,047 each. New York City-based Time Warner Inc. employed 675,000 who each contributed $216,030 toward the company's 1998 sales of almost $14.6 billion. Unisys Corp. placed fourth in the industry with 1999 sales of more than $7.5 billion, behind the strength of 33,200 employees who each generated $7,545 toward that total.

Among the myriad of other companies that are involved in providing miscellaneous business services, leaders include such diverse firms as RGIS Inventory Specialists, VIP Event Services Inc., Sotheby's Inc, Freeman Decoration Co., and Michael Fox Auctioneers Inc.

FURTHER READING

"1996 Industry Report: Training budgets." *Training,* October 1996.

Dun's Census of American Business 1995. Bethlehem, PA: Dun & Bradstreet Corporation, 1995.

Flynn, Gillian. "Training Industry Report Highlights: 1995's Big Trends." *Personnel Journal,* January 1996.

Infotrac Company Profiles 19 February 2000. Available from http://web4.infotrac.galegroup.com.

U.S. Department of Labor. Bureau of Labor Statistics. *Industry-Occupation Matrix.* Washington: GPO, 1994.

U.S. Department of Commerce. *Census of Service Industries 1992.* Washington: GPO, 1992.

U.S. Department of Commerce. International Trade Administration. *U.S. Industrial Outlook 1993.* Washington: GPO, 1993.

U.S. Department of Commerce. International Trade Administration. *U.S. Industrial Outlook 1994.* Washington: GPO, 1994.

SIC 7513

TRUCK RENTAL AND LEASING, WITHOUT DRIVERS

This category covers establishments primarily engaged in short-term rental or extended-term leasing (with or without maintenance) of trucks, truck tractors, or semitrailers without drivers. Establishments primarily engaged in finance leasing of trucks are classified in Finance, **SIC 6159: Miscellaneous Business Credit Institutions;** those renting trucks with drivers are classified in various trucking and courier service industries; and those primarily engaged in renting and leasing, except finance leasing, of industrial trucks are classified in **SIC 7359: Equipment Rental and Leasing, Not Elsewhere Classified.**

NAICS CODE(S)

532120 (Truck, Utility Trailer and RV (Recreational Vehicle) Rental and Leasing)

INDUSTRY SNAPSHOT

Growth in the truck rental market slowed in the mid-1990s after an expansive period in the late 1980s and early 1990s. By 1999 the industry continued to grow, and 35 percent of all trucks in service in the United states were owned by rental or leasing companies. The industry leader, U-Haul International Inc., continued to dominate, owning well over half of all the rental trucks in service in the United States and owning 52 percent of the market. The Budget Group, with Budget Truck Rentals and Ryder TRS comprised 27 percent of the market. The remaining 21 percent was made up of a few other midsized players, such as Rollins Truck Leasing Corp. and Penske Truck Leasing, plus thousands of small operators. The industry generated 1997 revenues of $10 billion, employed 46,566 workers, with an annual payroll of $1.4 billion.

CURRENT CONDITIONS

Growth in the truck rental market slowed in the mid-1990s after the expansive period of the late 1980s and early 1990s, as U-Haul and Ryder competed for expansion of dealer locations and market share in the consumer truck market. Ryder sold its Ryder Consumer Truck Rental division during 1996, but the Budget Group, the new owners, have indicated a commitment to their current name and market identity as Ryder TRS.

In 1999 U-Haul International led the industry with some 190,000 trucks for rent from over 15,000 dealerships. It reported U.S. rental revenues of over $1.5 billion and employed 14,400 workers. U-Haul's business consisted entirely of rentals to do-it-yourself movers.

Ryder TRS owned a fleet of 33,500 trucks from 3,500 dealer locations. It reported 1999 U.S. rental revenues of $550 million. Some 70 percent of its business was on the consumer side, the remainder coming from business rentals.

Among important trends affecting the industry in the 1990s were changing tax laws, stricter environmental regulations, and efforts by large corporations to keep trucking assets off their books. These all seemed to indicate a strong future for the leasing industry. Larry Miller, then president of Iowa-based Ruan Transportation Management Systems, the third largest truck-leasing company with about 10 percent of the market, told *Commercial Carrier Journal* in 1990, "Pride of ownership is a luxury. It's the old way of doing business." Among newer regulations affecting fleet ownership were federal laws that required commercial vehicles over 10,000 pounds gross weight to undergo an extensive safety inspection every 12 months; in addition, there were new Environmental Protection Agency regulations regarding underground storage tanks, and the federal Clean Air Act required vehicles to meet tougher emission standards.

Amtralease, a network of independent leasing companies, estimated that 30 percent of all commercial trucks in the early 1990s were leased, compared to less than 20 percent in the 1980s. However, Amtralease also reported that profits for truck-leasing companies were flat despite the increase in market share. Although some companies leased large fleets, *Commercial Carrier Journal* reported that the typical customer leased three to four trucks.

In the late 1980s many companies with transportation needs began moving to full-service leasing, with the leasing firm assuming responsibility for all matters relating to the vehicle, including purchase, fuel, taxes, licenses, and hauling permits. Don Estes, then president of Ryder Truck Rental, told *Beverage World* that "full service leasing is basically turning truck transportation problems over to the leasing company." Although drivers sometimes complained about the quality of maintenance with full-service leasing, surveys indicated that repair and maintenance operations at larger lease companies often were better managed and their mechanics better trained than with private fleet operations.

By 2000 the larger companies had developed web sites and launched Internet on-line booking. Internet access allowed customers to communicate directly with the companies, receive instantaneous confirmation of booking, and make payments on-line.

Industry Leaders

Ryder System, Inc. was founded in 1933 by James A. Ryder. In 1996, in addition to its full-service truck leasing and rental operations, Ryder also provided a variety of aviation and other transportation services, including automobile transport.

In 1932 James Ryder was a high school student in Florida working as a summer laborer for 25 cents an hour when he learned that another student was making 35 cents an hour to drive a truck. The next summer Ryder purchased a 1931 Model A Ford and went into business as a commercial hauler. Ryder struggled through the Depression, slowly building a fleet, and by 1937 the Ryder Trucking Co. owned 37 trucks. In 1938 Ryder learned that a Miami beer distributor was interested in leasing five large trucks. Ryder presented the distributor with a proposal, and Champagne Velvet Beer became the company's first lease account.

Ryder continued as both a local leasing company and an over-the-road transport service for several years. Then in 1945 two businessmen from Tampa, who had acquired the Anheuser-Busch beer distributorship for Florida, contacted Ryder. The beer was beginning to arrive from the brewery in St. Louis, and the distributors needed trucks in a hurry. Ryder met the need by pulling trucks from its over-the-road fleet. Overnight, Ryder became the largest truck leasing firm in Florida. By the end of the 1940s, Ryder's leasing operations topped $1 million and far exceeded its over-the-road trucking business. Ryder also signed a lease agreement with the Minute Maid Corporation, which gave Ryder national exposure. By 1949, when the company changed its name to the Ryder Truck Rental System, the leased fleet had grown to more than 500 trucks.

In 1955 Ryder reorganized and went public, creating Ryder System, Inc., a holding company that owned the Ryder Truck Rental System and the Great Southern Trucking Company, which Ryder acquired in 1952. In 1956 Ryder initiated a corporate identification program, and by the following year, the entire leased and over-the-road fleet carried the familiar red and black "Big R" trademark. The leasing division also became known as Ryder Truck Rental.

Between 1956 and 1959, Ryder acquired 21 more companies, including the Denver-based Baker Truck Rental, which was then the largest truck leasing firm west of the Mississippi River, and the Alabama-based Dixie Drive-It-Yourself System. Although the "Big R" trademark created some uniformity, the rapid growth left Ryder with trucks painted almost every color imaginable. In 1962 Ryder adopted a common color scheme for all its trucks: bright lemon yellow with a black undercarriage. In 1965 Ryder sold its motor carrier division to International Utilities and focused on the growing truck leasing business. International Utilities continued to operate the trucking business under the Ryder name until 1982.

In 1968 Ryder formed a consumer truck-rental operation known as Ryder One Way. Initially, Ryder planned to purchase 300 trucks for consumer rental; however, a market test in six southern states indicated a greater demand, and Ryder began operations with 1,000 trucks and vans. By the end of the year, Ryder One Way had dealers in 325 cities across the country and ordered another 2,000 trucks. In the mid-1970s Ryder secured a contract with the Department of Defense to provide rental trucks for military personnel at 110 bases in the United States. By 1987 Ryder had surpassed U-Haul as the largest consumer truck-rental operation in the United States. However, U-Haul regained the lead in the early 1990s. In June of 1998 the Budget Group purchased Ryder's truck rental division and ran it under the name it Ryder TRS. Ryder maintained 25,000 rental trucks at 80 locations, but its primary area of business was full-service commercial leasing with 109,000 trucks. Ryder had also become a major supplier of integrated logistics services in the United States.

U-Haul International, Inc., was founded in 1945 by L. S. Schoen. Today U-Haul is the largest consumer truck-rental business in the world. U-Haul is a subsidiary of AMERCO, one of the largest privately owned companies in the United States. The company entered the self-storage industry in 1975 and is now the second largest operator of self-storage in the United States, with 232,000 rooms, over 19 million square feet of space, and 800 company-owned storage locations. U-Haul reports that more than 98 percent of the American public recognize the name U-Haul, making it among the most recognizable registered trademarks in the world.

In 1945 L. S. Schoen slipped out of a military hospital to move his wife and newborn son from Los Angeles to nearby Corona, California. He rented a beat-up utility trailer from a service station, and that night he made a notation in his diary: "I am intrigued by the business potential of this idea especially from the standpoint of one-way rentals." He was discharged from the military later that year and moved his family to Portland, Oregon. Within two weeks, he had purchased his first trailer and painted "U-Haul Co.; Rental Trailers; $2.00 per day" on the sides.

By 1946 Schoen had a fleet of 70 trailers spread out from Seattle to Los Angeles, and in 1948 he decided to go national. He offered one-way rentals from the West Coast to anywhere in the United States. The only catch was that customers had to find service station managers at the end of their trips who were willing to become Schoen's agents. The plan worked, and by the end of the year, U-Haul had a fleet of 200 trailers and a network of agents nationwide.

In 1951 U-Haul launched a low-risk program for fleet ownership of its trailers as a way to raise money and expand the network even faster: investors would purchase trailers from U-Haul, which would assume full responsibility for insurance, maintenance, and distribution. Each month, fleet owners would receive a report and payment for rental activity on their trailers. The fleet-ownership plan raised $2 million in the first two years. By 1955 there were more than 10,000 U-Haul trailers in 200 fleets scattered around the country, and U-Haul was adding 600 trailers a month.

U-Haul began renting trucks in the late 1950s and dominated the consumer truck-rental industry into the 1970s. However, in 1970, U-Haul acquired A to Z Rental and began a transition from renting trucks and trailers to renting everything from garden tools to dinnerware. In 1974, U-Haul opened more than 100 U-Haul Rental Centers. The transition was hastened by the Arab oil embargo in 1973, which eventually resulted in the closing of many independent service stations that had been the backbone of U-Haul's rental network. In the late 1960s U-Haul trucks and trailers were available at more than 14,000 service stations, but by the mid-1970s more than 6,000 had gone out of business.

By the early 1980s there were more than 1,100 U-Haul Rental Centers. However, while it was expanding into new rental businesses, U-Haul was paying less attention to its aging fleet of trucks and trailers. Ryder, whose trucks were air conditioned and featured automatic transmissions, began cutting into U-Haul's market share and overtook U-Haul in 1987. The year before U-Haul was knocked out of first place in consumer truck rentals, two of Schoen's sons gained control of the company and forced their father to resign. They began closing the rental "supermarkets" and refocused on renting truck and trailers. U-Haul eventually regained the market lead it had lost to Ryder. In 1999 U-Haul controlled 52 percent of the truck rental market.

FURTHER READING

"1997 Fact Book." *Auto Rental News.* Redondo Beach, Calif.: Bobit Publishing Company.

"1998 Annual Report." *Budget Group, Inc,* 2000. Available from http://www.bgi.com.

"Company Profiles." *Hoover's Online.* Available from http://www.hoovers.com.

U.S. Census Bureau. *1997 County Business Patterns.* Washington, D.C.: GPO, 1997.

SIC 7514

PASSENGER CAR RENTAL

This category covers establishments primarily engaged in the short-term rental of passenger cars without drivers.

NAICS CODE(S)

532111 (Passenger Cars Rental)

INDUSTRY SNAPSHOT

The passenger car rental industry in the United States generated nearly $15 billion annually during the 1990s, with almost 1.6 million cars available for daily rental at more than 22,000 locations. Airport and near-airport rentals accounted for about 80 percent of the rental car market. Approximately 70 percent of the airport and near-airport rentals were for business trips. The leisure market accounted for the other 30 percent of rentals. Most of nonairport car rentals were to motorists whose own cars were being repaired, although there was a growing weekend market among urban residents who did not own their own cars. In the early 1990s there were more than 100 million rental car transactions in America every year, although only about 20 percent of all adults in the United States have ever rented a car. About 2.5 million frequent business travelers accounted for nearly half of all airport and near-airport car rentals. In 1999, the industry employed an estimated 1.4 billion workers.

Despite booming levels of business, the passenger car rental industry underwent some difficult times in 1996 and early 1997. Discrimination lawsuits challenged some major companies' policies on both race and age. Meanwhile, changes in corporate ownership continued to realign the industry. Finally, issues such as whether to accept bank debit cards in payment generated an unexpected share of controversy.

BACKGROUND AND DEVELOPMENT

The car rental industry—better known as the ''Drive-Ur-Self'' business in the early years—had its beginnings not long after the Ford Motor Company introduced the Model T automobile in 1908. An entrepreneur named Joe Saunders is known to have begun renting a secondhand Model T in Omaha, Nebraska, in 1916. He affixed a mileage meter to the left front wheel and rented the car for 10 cents a mile. His first customer was a traveling salesman who had a date with a local girl. By 1925 Saunders had car rental operations in 21 states. The Chrysler Company ran full-page ads boasting that Saunders had purchased $1 million worth of Chrysler automobiles. Saunders went bankrupt, though, during the Great Depression of the early 1930s.

In the early days of the industry most Drive-Ur-Self cars were rented by local residents. The industry gained a shady reputation because rental cars were often used by bootleggers, bank robbers, and prostitutes. In 1952, *The Saturday Evening Post* estimated that as many as 90 percent of the cars rented during Prohibition were used for illegal purposes. The industry began to gain more respectability after the Eighteenth Amendment that outlawed alcohol was repealed in 1933.

In 1940 the loss of passengers to private automobiles prompted a group of railroads to form Railway Extension Inc., which franchised car rental dealerships in cities stretching from Chicago to New Orleans. The railroads provided space for car rental booths in stations and free telegraph service so passengers could wire ahead and reserve cars, which would be waiting for them when they arrived. The railroads also paid for the advertising. The American Drive-Ur-Self Association, controlled by Hertz, negotiated a less favorable relationship with railroads east of Chicago. Under the Hertz plan, car rental dealerships paid for their own advertising and telegraph service, and cars were not available on-site at the train stations.

During World War II, the U.S. Office of Defense Transportation (ODT) limited rental cars to 1,500 miles per month to conserve gasoline. The limit was cut to 650 miles per month in the Miami area when the ODT discovered that local residents were using rental cars to circumvent gas rationing in the use of private automobiles. Rental car dealers also were not allowed to buy new or replacement cars for their fleets during the war and were required to maintain a record of each rental, including the person's name, address, occupation, and purpose of trip. Rates were frozen at 1942 levels, which averaged between 14 and 18 cents per mile for the first 50 miles. Government agencies and industries with war material contracts often monopolized available cars.

Airline Service. After the war, the car rental industry grew rapidly, carried along by the expanding economy. The railroads revived their car rental plans in 1947, establishing dealers in some 300 cities. But the real growth coincided with a boom in airline passenger service. In 1947 the Hertz Drive-Ur-Self System, then with about 2,300 rental cars nationwide, opened operations at airports in Atlanta and Milwaukee. That same year, Warren Avis, then president of Frost-Avis Inc., a Ford dealership in Detroit, formed the Avis Airline Rent-A-Car System.

Avis was a former Army Air Corps flyer who recognized that airplanes would soon replace passenger trains as America's favorite form of travel. He started with car rental booths at airports in Detroit and Miami, and by 1949 had licensed use of the Avis name to rental agencies in New York, Chicago, Dallas, Washington, D.C., Los

Angeles, and Houston. More aggressive than Hertz, Avis also arranged for American Airlines and Eastern Airlines to include information about Avis in passengers' ticket envelopes. In 1949, *Business Week* reported, "this kind of business is operated on an exclusive franchise basis; the first firm in has a big advantage. At present, Avis seems to have a substantial lead."

Hertz, however, was not long in responding. By 1952 Hertz and its franchised dealers were operating at more than 120 airports. In 1953 General Motors Corp. sold the business back to John Hertz, then chairman of the Omnibus Corporation, which had shed itself of bus operations to concentrate on car and truck rentals. The price was $10.8 million. The following year Hertz opened operations in 50 additional airports and 20 more railroad stations. The company also began buying up franchised dealers. By 1955 the Hertz Rent-A-Car System encompassed nearly 1,000 company-owned or licensed dealers with total revenues of $90 million. Avis had 850 dealers and $35 million in revenues.

In 1956, Hertz and National Rent-A-Car, then the third largest rental car operation in the country, cracked the exclusive franchise that Avis had held with the Miami International Airport for eight years. This opened up the lucrative Florida vacation business.

Price Wars. By the early 1960s, Hertz, Avis, and National were entrenched as the industry leaders. However, there were hundreds of independent companies, many with only a few cars, eager to cash in on the growing market. In 1965 there were more than 135,000 rental cars available in the United States. The industry at that juncture was a $450-million-a-year business, an increase in value of 80 percent from only three years previously.

The average Hertz or Avis rental in a resort city such as Miami or Las Vegas was $10 a day, but the frugal renter could find rates as low as $1. These discount companies often purchased used cars or replaced new cars less often. They also saved by locating their businesses near targeted airports, thus avoiding fees the leaders paid for on-site locations. Budget conscious vacationers didn't seem to mind the inconvenience. Many discount companies, however, were fly-by-night operators and managed to give the car rental industry a bad name before dropping by the wayside. But the success of reputable companies such as Budget Rent-a-Car eventually forced the industry leaders to cut their rates. Avis began offering compact, British-made Ford Cortinas for $3.95 a day and 9 cents a mile. Hertz and National also began offering lower rates on smaller cars. The price wars lasted until 1985, when car rental companies suffered through one of the worst financial years in industry history. After a few years of uneasy truce, the price wars were revived in the early 1990s.

Energy Crisis. The industry was detoured by the energy crisis in the early 1970s. In 1973, federal regulations limited the amount of gasoline available to car rental companies to 1972 levels. This forced rental companies to replace full-size cars with more fuel-efficient vehicles. Even then, many rental cars were sent out with half-empty gasoline tanks. Hertz survived by buying a fleet of ten tanker trucks to shift supplies of gasoline from city to city to deal with local shortages.

The industry also moved into the used-car business in the early 1970s. When it came time to update their fleets, rental companies had traditionally sold their cars to wholesalers, who auctioned them off to used car dealers. However, the rising cost of new cars and a decision by automakers to curtail fleet discounts made it more attractive for rental car companies to sell their cars directly to the public. In 1975, Kenneth Krabbe, then vice president of Dollar-Rent-a-Car, told *Business Week,* "You've got to run a rent-a-car business on what you can sell. If you don't make money there, you're through."

Hertz was the first rental car company to move into retailing in a serious way. Hertz opened its first small showroom in Southern California in 1971, and by 1974 the company had more than 100 used car outlets across the country. By 1980 Hertz had become the largest used car dealer in the United States, selling 70,000 cars at 139 locations. Frank Olson, then chairman of Hertz, told *Forbes* that the auto makers "did us a favor. They put us out of a lazy man's business." Avis, which unlike Hertz had previously leased most of its cars to reduce financial risk, began buying its cars outright in 1978 so they could then be sold in the used car market. By 1987 Avis was selling about 50,000 used cars annually. In 1992 rental car companies sold more than 1.5 million used cars.

Unfair Practices. In 1975 the Federal Trade Commission (FTC) accused Hertz, Avis, and National of conspiring to monopolize the airport car rental market. The FTC said the companies, then armed with 96 percent of the airport business, pressured airport authorities into establishing requirements for on-site operations that smaller companies could not meet, such as offering a nationwide reservations system. Off-airport car rental companies were not even allowed to advertise in some airports. An executive at the Philadelphia International Airport told *Business Week,* "If you're getting 10 percent from one company and 0 percent from another, you don't want to hurt those giving you the money." The FTC also accused the major car rental companies of illegal price fixing.

The case was settled out of court in 1976, without any of the companies admitting guilt. However, they agreed not to engage in any predatory practices in the future. As a result, smaller car rental companies found it easier to negotiate on-site locations at major airports.

Budget was especially aggressive, more than doubling its share of the airport car rental business from about 7 percent in 1976 to 17 percent in 1982. In 1983 Olson told *Fortune,* ''Short-term we have to worry about Avis. Long-term it's Budget.''

The increased competition also led rental car companies into a battle of give-away programs. The leaders—Hertz, Avis, National, and Budget—offered everything from athletic equipment and luggage to televisions and airline tickets for repeat customers who piled up points. In 1983 *Fortune* reported, ''Unintentionally but predictably, the industry has imprisoned itself in a campaign that is horrendously expensive, poisonous to profits, and difficult to stop.'' By 1985 the companies were financially battered and bruised, but market share had stayed about the same. The companies called an unofficial truce.

Restructuring. The 1980s also saw a major restructuring of the car rental industry, as automobile makers purchased controlling interests in the leading companies. In 1987, an investment group headed by Ford Motor Co. paid $1.3 billion to buy Hertz from the Allegis Corporation, which also owned United Airlines. Ford later sold a 20 percent share to Volvo North America Corporation, retaining a 60 percent interest. Ford purchased Budget in 1988. Avis was sold five times between 1983 and 1987, finally ending up in the hands of an employee stock ownership plan (ESOP). In 1989 General Motors Corp. purchased a 25 percent share of Avis. General Motors also purchased a 45 percent share of National in 1988, later increasing its share in that company to 80 percent. The Chrysler Corporation owned Pentastar Transportation Group, which operated General Rent-a-Car, Dollar Rent-a-Car, Thrifty Rent-A-Car, and Snappy Car Rentals.

The manufacturers' interest in the rental car industry stemmed from the fact that rental companies were their biggest single customers and purchasing the company locked in sales. Each of the four major rental companies agreed to purchase 70 percent or more of their fleets from their auto company owners. In 1988, Ford sold more than 100,000 cars to Hertz; GM sold about 85,000 cars to Avis and National; Chrysler sold about 75,000 cars to its car rental firms. When Mitsubishi Motor Sales of America purchased Value Rent-A-Car in 1991, it replaced the fleet's 25,000 mostly Ford automobiles with its own. Car rental companies accounted for about 10 percent of all domestic auto sales in the early 1990s.

Rental cars also provided manufacturers with an effective marketing tool. Millions of potential buyers were exposed to the car makers' newest models every year. Renters also helped eliminate glitches in new cars by providing feedback to the manufacturers. Car makers generally offered to buy their cars back from the rental companies after four to six months and often shared the cost of advertising if the ads mentioned the manufacturer. In the early 1990s car makers began to request that rental cars be kept in service longer, from six to nine months, because the ''almost new'' fleet cars were cutting into sales of new automobiles.

Issues in the 1990s. The booming economy of the mid-1990s erased any lingering effects of the previous recession, which had limited air travel and, thus, airport car rentals. Industry-wide revenues jumped from $13 billion in 1995 to nearly $15 billion in 1996. The industry closely watched the economic indicators for any signs of a new recession, but several more immediate issues dominated the headlines in 1996-97.

In March 1997, New York state's highest court ruled that rental-car companies can't refuse to rent cars to young drivers solely because of age. As the *Wall Street Journal* reported in its story, most of the major car companies, including Hertz, Avis, and National, routinely refused to rent to drivers under 25 years old, citing higher accident rates. The decision by the New York Court of Appeals was the first major ruling on what had been an industry-wide practice for decades, legal experts said. The rental car companies criticized the decision, saying it made them too vulnerable to a dangerous group of drivers. Consumer advocates, however, praised the decision. It is now standard practice for rental companies to rent to ''under-age drive,'' but to compensate their risk by charging a higher rate.

Avis also faced a barrage of bad publicity over a race discrimination case involving one of its franchise owners in the South. The franchisee, who owned several Avis outlets, had allegedly instructed his workers to refuse rentals to African-Americans. When the practice was exposed, it received widespread publicity on the television program *60 Minutes* and elsewhere. Avis vowed to end the practice immediately, although bad feelings lingered because the practices had reportedly been continuing for several years before Avis moved to halt them.

In early 1997 there arose another controversy, this time over bank debit cards. Hertz, Avis, and other companies decided not to accept debit cards as payment, despite their similar appearance to credit cards. As *The New York Times* reported, for years the rental companies used possession of a credit card as a crude way to weed out potentially risky renters. But this test no longer works with debit cards, since—because no loan is involved in a debit card transaction—banks will now give them to nearly everyone with a bank account. Hertz spokeswoman Lisa LoManto told the *Times* that Hertz was entitled to a certain level of confidence because in car rental, unlike almost any other business, the customer is given total control of a vehicle worth $20,000 or more.

Still, it is certain that with more than 60 million bank debit cards now in circulation, the decision not to accept them will lead to some confusion and frustration at rental agency counters.

Meanwhile, auto makers are also expected to continue playing a major role in the development of the industry. Auto makers influence what makes and models of rental cars are available, how long they stay in service before being replaced, and the direction of car rental advertising. During 1996, automakers sold almost 1.5 million vehicles to the rental companies, a volume equivalent to about 10 percent of total production by "the Big Three." In 1991 Vincent A. Wasik, then chairman of National, told *Automotive News,* "With the substantial ownership positions in the major rental car companies (GM, Ford and Chrysler) the game is really being played at a different level. Customer satisfaction through superior service is now the 'product' that makes the difference."

The mid- to late 1990s also saw another wave of ownership changes and consolidation. In 1996 HFS, Inc., a New Jersey-based company with significant holdings in lodging and real estate, took over ownership of Avis, Inc. Republic Industries announced that its intention to purchase Alamo Rent-A-Car for $625 million. In 1994, Ford Motor Co. went from 49 percent ownership in Hertz to 100 percent. That same year, Chrysler sold Snappy Car Rentals to company management and the Jacobson Partners. As Jon LeSage, executive editor of the trade journal *Auto Rental News* wrote in his *1997 Fact Book,* "Car rental is a mature industry . . . dominated by a small number of major companies. While it is not the most profitable industry in the world these days, there are several advantages in controlling part of the market for the companies and investors who are buying car rental companies."

Overall, the industry was expected to remain very competitive, with many of the leading companies becoming more aggressive in the leisure market. Unlimited mileage offers became a common promotional weapon in the leisure market. There also were increasingly fewer distinctions between on-airport and off-airport car rental companies. Major airports had become so congested—and rental fleets had become so large—that on-site rental companies were forced to shuttle customers to distant car lots. Off-airport companies were able to offer similar service by running shuttle buses between airport terminals and their own locations. Conversely, off-airport rental companies began to lose their financial advantage, as airports introduced access fees for airport shuttle buses.

INDUSTRY LEADERS

In 1998 the car rental industry was dominated by six companies: Enterprise Rent-a-Car Inc. (20 percent with a 1999 fleet of 370,000 cars); Avis Rent A Car, Inc. (19 percent, 205,000 cars); The Hertz Corporation (16 percent, with a 1996 fleet of 250,000 cars); Budget Group, Inc., (11 percent, 1996 fleet of 128,000 cars); Alamo Rent A Car, Inc., (8 percent with a 1998 fleet of 150,000 cars); and National Car Rental System, Inc., (8 percent with a 1996 fleet of 135,000 cars). These companies accounted for more than 90 percent of the airport and near-airport car rentals. Hertz, Avis, and Budget also had strong international presences. Hertz alone had 500,000 cars for rent in 140 nations.

Enterprise Rent-a-Car, Inc. represented the greatest growth story of the past few years. It had nearly doubled the size of its fleet since 1993. Its strategy was to leave the highly competitive airport rental market to the other companies and concentrate on the non-airport market. It operates more than 2,600 outlets (Hertz operated about 1,200), many near auto repair shops, so that Enterprise could rent to customers whose vehicles were in the shop for work. With the exception of Alamo, many of the major airport and near-airport car rental companies were owned wholly or in part by auto makers, although the amounts of ownership continued to vary as firms bought or sold controlling interests. In 1999, Enterprise had sales of $47.3 billion and employed 40,000 workers. It offers lower rates than its competitors and is the only company to target local rentals.

Avis. With the rise of Enterprise, Avis, Inc. has slipped from its long-time position as second largest car rental company in the United States to third. In 1999 Avis was owned by Cendant Corporation. Avis, with a fleet of 205,000 automobiles, had sales of $2.3 billion in 1998 and employed 19,000 workers. With the majority of its 1998 business comprised of business rentals, Avis made plans to draw more of the leisure market.

Originally known as Avis Airlines Rent-A-Car System, the company was founded in 1946 by Warren Avis, who owned an automobile dealership in Detroit. Avis started with rental operations at Detroit's Willow Run Airport and Miami International Airport. He then licensed the Avis name to independent car rental companies to serve airports in New York, Chicago, Dallas, Washington, D.C., Los Angeles, and other cities. In 1948, Avis began to open offices near hotels and business districts and dropped "airlines" from the company name.

Avis sold Avis Rent-A-Car System in 1954 to Richard S. Robie, operator of a car rental business in New England, for $8 million. At the time, there were 185 Avis locations in the United States and Canada, and working agreements had been established with local companies throughout Europe. Under Robie, the company developed the first nationwide plan for one-way rentals and introduced its own credit card. Robie sold the business in

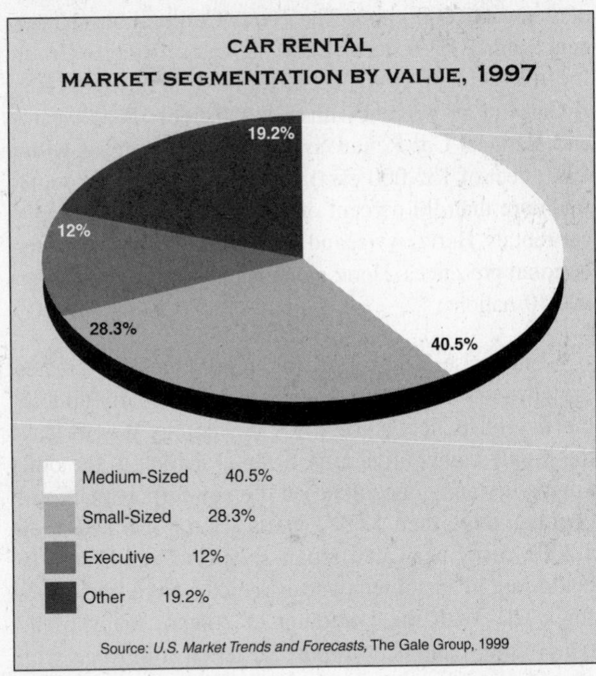

Source: *U.S. Market Trends and Forecasts,* The Gale Group, 1999

1956 to the Amoskeag Company, which created a holding company—Avis, Inc.

Avis grew rapidly in the late 1950s and early 1960s, expanding its fleet from 1,200 to 7,500 vehicles, but the changes in ownership that would characterize Avis continued. Amoskeag sold the business in 1962 to Lazard Freres & Co., a New York investment banking firm. In 1965 Avis was purchased by the International Telephone & Telegraph Corporation (ITT). Under ITT's leadership, Avis strengthened its presence in Europe, where it became the leading car rental company. Avis also created the first online computerized car rental reservation system in 1972 with the introduction of the Wizard System. ITT was ordered to divest Avis in 1972 as part of federal antitrust proceedings. When ITT was unable to find a buyer, Avis became a public company in 1974, with 52 percent of the stock held by a court-appointed trustee.

In 1977 Norton Simon, Inc. purchased control of Avis for $174 million. Revenues had grown to more than $673 million, with Avis accounting for about 25 percent of the car rental market. Under Norton Simon, Avis was riddled by dissension from its licensed dealers. The dissension became public in 1982 when Avis launched an advertising campaign with Norton Simon Chairman David Mahoney as spokesman. The franchise group took its $5 million advertising budget to a different agency and created its own ads promoting low rates. In the confusion, Hertz widened its lead over Avis. National and Budget also gained market share. Avis posted a $50 million loss in 1982.

Changes in ownership continued in the 1980s. In rapid succession, Esmark, Inc., purchased Norton Simon in 1983, and Beatrice Company acquired Esmark in 1984. In 1985 Kohlberg Kravis Roberts & Company acquired Beatrice in a leveraged buyout. A year later, a management group and the Wesray Corporation purchased Avis for $265 million and the assumption of $1.34 billion in debt. In 1986 Wesray disposed of about half of Avis' European rental operations and its leasing operations in America. In 1987 Wesray sold the rest of Avis to an employee stock ownership plan for $750 million and the assumption of $1 billion in debt. General Motors purchased its 25 percent share of Avis in 1989. These changes continued with the HFS deal in 1996.

Hertz. The Hertz Corporation is an industry leader in terms of revenue. In 1998, Hertz operated a worldwide fleet of 500,000 vehicles at 6,000 company-owned or licensed car rental locations in 140 countries and reported sales of $4.1 billion and 24,800 employees. In 1998 the majority of Hertz's sales came from the airport rental market, both business and leisure.

Hertz had its beginnings in 1908, when Walter L. Jacobs founded the Rent-a-Ford Co. in Chicago. By 1923 Rent-a-Ford had a fleet of 200 cars and $1 million in revenue. That same year Jacobs sold the business to John Hertz, then president and owner of the Yellow Cab and Yellow Truck and Coach Manufacturing Co. Hertz renamed the business the Hertz Drive-Ur-Self System. Hertz converted the rental fleet to the oversized sedans used by Yellow Cab, but customers balked at renting the bulky automobiles, and the fleet was switched back to regular passenger cars. General Motors Corp. purchased Hertz in 1926 and sold it to the Omnibus Corporation, then headed by John Hertz, in 1953. Omnibus changed its name to The Hertz Corporation in 1954. The RCA Corporation purchased Hertz in 1967.

In 1985 Hertz was purchased by UAL, Inc., the owner of United Airlines, which planned to expand into other travel-related services. UAL, however, which changed its name to the Allegis Corporation, abandoned the strategy within months. Allegis sold Hertz in 1987 for $1.3 billion—more than twice what it paid in 1985—to the Park Ridge Corporation, a holding company created by Ford and Hertz management.

In 1988, Hertz pleaded guilty to defrauding insurance companies and motorists by inflating the cost of repairs—or charging for repairs that were never performed—after cars were damaged in more than 100,000 accidents between 1978 and 1987. Hertz was ordered to pay a fine of $6.85 million—the largest fine ever imposed at that time in a criminal consumer fraud case. The company was also ordered to pay restitution of more than $13 million to the motorists and insurance companies.

In 1999, Hertz announced plans to offer a navigation system in 50,000 of its rental vehicles. The system, being installed on into the year 2000, is offered in several different vehicle makes and models.

Budget. Budget Group was the fourth largest car rental company in the United States by revenue in 1996 with a U.S. fleet of 126,000 cars, 1998 sales of $2.6 billion, and 14,500 employees. Budget had car rental operations at more than 1,000 locations in America, including more than 300 airports. Ford was a minority owner in the company.

Budget Rent-a-Car was founded in Los Angeles in 1958 by Morris Mirkin, who started with a fleet of 10 cars. The Budget Rent-a-Car Corporation was started in 1960. Initially, the company focused on the discount leisure market with its off-airport locations, but its image also appealed to economy-minded small business travelers. Budget began pursuing corporate accounts aggressively in 1989. Budget promoted its cars with the advertising tagline "The Smart Money Is On Budget."

Hoping to increase sales and visibility, Budget began offering its cars for price bidding online in late 1999. In this way, consumers can comparison shop without going to another rental company.

Alamo. Alamo Rent A Car, Inc., with U.S. rental revenues of $1.3 billion, was the fifth largest car rental company in the United States by revenue in 1996, behind Hertz, Enterprise, Avis, and Budget. Alamo was also the leading car rental company in Florida and the largest independent car rental company in the country. In 1998, Alamo had a fleet of 150,000 automobiles in 550 locations worldwide. Leisure customers account for 75 percent of Alamo's market share.

Alamo was founded in 1974 with a fleet of 1,000 cars and operations in Miami, Fort Lauderdale, Tampa, and Orlando. The name "Alamo" was chosen because it placed the company ahead of its major competitors in the telephone directory. Alamo initially focused on the discount rate leisure market, cultivating relationships with travel agents, and operated solely at off-airport locations. Travel agent referrals continued to account for more than 50 percent of Alamo's business in 1993.

Alamo opened its first on-airport site in 1981 in Atlanta and began moving into business rentals aggressively in the mid 1980s. In 1983 the company also opened a 77,000-square-foot rental plaza near Orlando International Airport. Alamo claimed that the plaza was the largest car rental facility in the world.

The crimes against tourists in Florida in 1993 rocked Alamo, the rental leader in the state. The family of a slain German tourist eventually sued Alamo for $10 million, charging that the company had been negligent in complying with the Florida governor's executive order concerning the removal of identifying marks from rental vehicles.

Alamo set its sights on international markets in 1997. In 1998 Alamo focused on electronic reservations and billing. As of 1999, Alamo offered a 24-hour risk-free money-back guarantee.

FURTHER READING

Beirne, Mike. "Hertz Ads Zero In on Navigation." *Brandweek*, 23 August 1999.

"Cmon, Drive Happy with Alamo." *Association Management*, September 1999, A4.

Diederich, Tom. "Budget Rent A Car Joins Online Bidding—Customers Can Pick Price They Will Pay." *Computerworld*, 3 May 1999.

"Employment—National, Not Seasonally Adjusted Data." *Bureau of Labor Statistics*, 20 March 2000. Available from http://www.bls.gov.

Hansell, Saul. "Not All Plastic Is Created Equal When It Comes to Renting a Car." *New York Times*, 2 April 1997.

"Hertz Cars to Carry NeverLost Service." *RCR-Radio Communications Report*, 20 September 1999.

"Hoover's Company Capsules." *Hoover's Online: The Business Network*, 20 March 2000. Available from http://www.hoovers.com.

Lazich, Robert S., editor. *Market Share Reporter 2000*. Detroit: Gale Research, 1999.

Miller, Lisa. "Young Drivers Can Rent Cars, New York Rules." *The Wall Street Journal*, 28 March 1997.

"Our History." *Alamo Rent A Car*, 20 March 2000. Available from http://www.goalamo.com.

SIC 7515

PASSENGER CAR LEASING

This category covers establishments primarily engaged in extended-term leasing of passenger cars without drivers. Establishments primarily engaged in finance leasing of automobiles are classified in **SIC 6159: Miscellaneous Business Credit Institutions.**

NAICS CODE(S)

532112 (Passenger Cars Leasing)

INDUSTRY SNAPSHOT

The passenger car leasing industry was comprised primarily of companies that provided corporate clients with a range of fleet management services in addition to automobile leasing. About 30 percent of all "company cars" in the United States were leased. According to *Consumers Research* magazine, a third of all cars were leased in 1996 and one in four persons who bought a new car leased it. That figure represented an increase of 400 percent from 1984, and many industry analysts predicted that more than 50 percent of all vehicles would be leased by 2000.

Fleet management services could be classified broadly as vehicle acquisition, maintenance management, fleet disposition, and fleet support services, which ranged from fuel credit cards to driver safety programs. The National Association of Fleet Administrators reported that the most popular services were vehicle ordering, delivery to individual drivers, insurance subrogation, and accident repairs. Most companies in the industry also leased light trucks and utility vehicles.

Leasing of cars to individuals boomed during the early 1990s, and many automobile manufacturers began to coordinate more closely with their financing arms and dealer networks to capture a share of this growing market. The auto makers' efforts lured some customers away from banks and independent finance companies.

Background and Development

The automobile leasing industry developed in the 1940s as companies looked for affordable ways to provide their sales and service personnel with reliable transportation. Petrolager, a large pharmaceutical company in Chicago, was an early case in point. Petrolager began by paying part of the cost for employees to purchase their own cars, but that became a losing proposition when the employees left for other jobs and took the automobiles with them.

In 1939, Zollie Frank, a car dealer in Chicago, suggested that Petrolager lease five automobiles for its salesmen instead of purchasing them. The benefits were twofold. Petrolager would retain control of the vehicles and also avoid large cash outlays. Petrolager agreed, and soon afterward Frank and his brother-in-law Armund Schoen founded the Four Wheels Co., which many in the industry identified as the first automobile leasing company. In 1954, the company became known as Wheels, Inc. It remained one of the largest fleet management companies in the United States in 1997 with more than 160,000 automobiles under lease.

The industry developed slowly, however, especially after the United States entered World War II and wartime restrictions made it almost impossible for leasing companies to purchase new automobiles or replacement parts. However, the industry began to grow in the late 1940s during the post-war economic expansion.

Finance Leasing. In 1946, three former servicemen—Duane L. Peterson, Harley W. Howell, and Richard M. Heather—formed a partnership in Baltimore, Maryland, to counsel companies on fleet management. But by 1954, Peterson, Howell & Heather had incorporated and moved into the leasing business.

The company was credited with developing the industry's first ''finance lease.'' Under the PHH Car Plan, Peterson, Howell & Heather would purchase automobiles and lease them to a client for a set monthly fee. When the lease ended, the company would sell the cars to pay off the balance on its original loan. Any surplus was returned to the client, but the client was billed if the resale failed to cover the loan. In a ''closed'' or ''walk-away'' lease, by contrast, the lessee had no financial obligation at the end of the lease period.

In 1981, a U.S. District Court ruled that finance leases were conditional sales contracts, which eliminated many of the tax benefits of ''open-ended'' leasing. However, although the percentage of closed or ''operating'' leases increased, open-ended leasing remained popular even after the court ruling. Automobiles were often sold to the client's employees when the lease expired.

Competition. The car leasing business grew rapidly in the late 1950s. In 1963, *Time* described the industry: ''In the past five years, the number of cars under lease has doubled to more than 600,000 and created a new industry that takes in $750 million a year. The market for leasing looks so promising that some 3,000 companies have gone into the business.'' *Time* added that ''competition among lessors has become so stiff that some companies make only about $6 a year per car; whether they show a profit at all depends on what they can get for their autos on the used-car market after the lease has run out.''

Car makers were also beginning to take note of the industry. In 1962, Chrysler Corp. formed its own leasing company, the Chrysler Leasing Corp., which was phased out in 1968. Ford Motor Company and General Motors also announced special financing programs in the early 1960s to encourage car dealers to offer fleet leasing. By 1970, more than 11,000 car dealers were involved in leasing and the total number of automobiles under lease in the United States exceeded one million.

Restructuring. Rising interest rates, as high as 21 percent in 1980, forced many smaller companies out of the industry. However, the Economic Recovery and Tax Act of 1982, which gave vehicle leasing companies substantial tax benefits, attracted several powerful new players. In 1987, for example, General Electric Company purchased GELCO Fleet Management Services, and Ford Motor Company purchased United States Fleet Leasing, Inc. GELCO was later renamed GE Capital Fleet Services.

Impact on Detroit. Because leasing represented a major share of the domestic automobile market, leasing companies had a major influence on U.S. car makers. Clients generally followed their leasing company's recommendations, from broad suggestions about size and optional equipment to specific models.

Until the 1960s, most leasing companies recommended standard six-cylinder automobiles with manual transmissions and very limited optional equipment. But in the 1960s, companies began recommending bigger cars with automatic transmissions, power steering, air conditioning, and radios. By the end of the decade, most corporate fleets consisted of full-size, eight-cylinder automobiles.

In the early 1970s, leasing companies began recommending intermediate-sized cars for better fuel economy. Intermediates accounted for 16 percent of the leased fleets by 1973, and 80 percent by 1977. In 1981, Peterson, Howell & Heather (later PHH FleetAmerica) became the first major leasing company to recommend compact cars. More than half the fleet automobiles leased in 1981 were 4-cylinder cars. The most popular cars leased in 1995 were midsized: Ford Taurus, Honda Accord, and the Ford F-Series Pick-up. Until the late 1980s, leasing companies almost never recommended foreign makes of automobiles, even if they were built in the United States.

CURRENT CONDITIONS

Corporate downsizing and cost-cutting in the early 1990s also affected the automobile leasing industry. Fleets were reduced either because corporations had fewer employees or because they eliminated benefits such as company cars. The number of car leasing establishments decreased significantly from 1,144 in 1990 to 531 in 1996. The number of industry employees also decreased, from 10,800 in 1990 to 5,700 in 1996; a decline of almost 50 percent. However, the largest leasing companies gained business during the same period.

In late 1999, the decline of personal use leasing continued, with leased cars accounting for 31.8 percent of the new car market, down 3 percent from the previous year. Industry analysts expect the rate of decline to continue for new vehicles, primarily because of the growing economy and lack of dealer lease training. However, the rate of used car leasing was expected to surge into the year 2000.

In general, leasing companies that also provided fleet management services were optimistic about the future, since more corporations began to contract for services that previously were provided in-house or new services that offered better control of costs. Many corporations with large fleets also looked to leasing companies for help in meeting federal regulations regarding fuel efficiency.

Some analysts also predicted that more companies would begin dealing directly with car makers. But A. Warren Feirer, then president of the National Association of Fleet Administrators, told *Sales & Marketing Management* in 1991 that most companies preferred working through knowledgeable specialists, ''and as long as they do, leasing companies that stress service are probably the easiest middlemen to deal with. But as of 1999, fewer manufacturers were taking on fleet costs, creating a smaller group of fleet dealers.''

The Uniform Consumer Leases Act is expected to be in force by the year 2000. This Act is expected to harm automobile lessors, primarily because it is a largely one-sided document, emphasizing consumer needs. It includes language regarding lease rate disclosure, open-end lease restrictions, GAP coverage provisions, and limitations on determination of excess wear and tear.

Automobile manufacturers found that leasing increased brand loyalty and provided dealers with a steady stream of good used cars. However, some analysts worried that as leasing gained in popularity, the resulting flood of used cars could deflate prices and detract from new car sales. The trend toward used vehicle leasing is expected to combat such issues. In addition, some car makers found that short-term leases meant that products needed to be updated more quickly, or else consumers would likely switch to a competing product. In order to distinguish themselves in the increasingly competitive leasing field, manufacturers developed innovative programs, including a 12-year lease with replacement every 2 years, and a weekend-only lease for urban residents. In 1999, fleet dealers were focusing on customer service and marketing segments to retain their competitive edge.

INDUSTRY LEADERS

The largest vehicle leasing company in the United States, GE Capital Fleet Services, based in Eden Prairie, Minnesota, was founded in 1957 as the General Leasing Co. General Leasing, which changed its name to GELCO Corporation in 1972, acquired six other companies between 1968 and 1974, including Interstate Vehicle Management; the Interstate Fleet Corp.; Selig Leasing Co.; Lease Plan, Inc.; and the Valley Leasing Co. In 1987, the company was purchased by GE Credit Corporation, which formed GE Capital Fleet Services. In 1996, the company acquired the JMJ Fleet Services and now offers fleet management services to corporate and governmental customers throughout Australia. GE Capital Corporation had sales of more than $41.4 billion in 1997.

PHH Vehicle Management Services, a subsidiary of Avis Rent A Car, based in Hunt Valley, Maryland, was the second-largest automobile leasing company in the United States. PHH Vehicle Management also provided a full range of fleet management services. In 1998, PHH Vehicle Management had sales of $10.9 billion and employed 9100 workers. The company was founded in 1946 as Peterson, Howell & Heather, Business Consultants, with the intention of advising companies on fleet management. The business was incorporated in 1954 and moved into leasing with the industry's first finance lease program. In 1975, Peterson, Howell & Heather also became the first major leasing company to recommend compact cars to its clients.

The company became the PHH Group, Inc., in 1978. The fleet management division retained the name Peterson, Howell & Heather until 1986, when it became PHH FleetAmerica. PHH FleetAmerica also acquired the domestic operation of Avis Car Leasing, Inc. in 1986. In 1972, PHH offered vehicle managing and leasing operations in the United Kingdom, expanded to Germany in 1987, and extended service to clients in France, Italy, and Belgium in the mid-1990s. In 1988, PHH Group became the PHH Corporation. In addition to vehicle leasing and fleet management, the PHH Corporation provides international relocation, real estate services, and mortgage banking services. The real estate services division helps companies relocate employees with home buying and selling and moving services. In 1997, PHH was acquired by HFS, Inc., and in 1999 was sold to Avis Rent A Car.

Among automobile manufacturers, Ford entered leasing most aggressively. According to R.L. Polk registrations, they leased more cars and trucks in the industry in 1996, and has overall sales of more than $144 billion in 1998. Some luxury car makers, like Jaguar, leased up to 70 percent of the vehicles they sold in the United States. Japanese auto makers found leasing to be an ideal way to camouflage price increases caused by the strong yen.

FURTHER READING

''1999 Industry Forecast.'' *Vehicle Leasing Today,* Winter 1999.

Buss, Dale D.. ''On A Roll: F & I Experts Expect Used-Vehicle Leasing to Become More Popular This Year.'' *Automotive News,* 22 March 1999.

Candler, Julie. ''Leasing's Link to Efficiency.'' *Nation's Business,* 5 January 1995.

Cavallaro, Peter I.. ''Uniform Consumer Leases Act Nears Completion.'' *Vehicle Leasing Today,* Summer 1999.

Darnay, Arsen J., ed. *Service Industries USA.* Detroit: Gale Research, 1995.

Edgerton, Jerry. ''Price of New Cars Up.'' *Money,* March 1996.

Harris, Donna. ''Personal-Use Leases Begin to Slack Off.'' *Automotive News,* 25 October 1999.

Hoffer, James A. ''Selecting a Fleet Dealer in the New Millennium.'' *Vehicle Leasing Today,* Summer 1999.

Hoover's Company Capsules. 1999. Hoover's Inc. Available from http://www.hoovers.com.

Peters, Eric. ''On Auto Leasing.'' *Consumer's Research Magazine,* April 1996.

———. ''Small Fleets Get New Lease on Life.'' *Nation's Business,* May 1996.

U.S. Department of Commerce. *County Business Patterns 1994.* Washington, DC: GPO, 1996.

SIC 7519

UTILITY TRAILER AND RECREATIONAL VEHICLE RENTAL

This category covers establishments primarily engaged in daily or extended-term rental of utility trailers and recreational vehicles (RVs). Establishments primarily engaged in renting motorcycles, bicycles, golf carts, go-carts, or recreational boats are classified in **SIC 7999: Amusement and Recreation Services, Not Elsewhere Classified;** and those engaged in renting airplanes are classified in **SIC 7359: Equipment Rental and Leasing, Not Elsewhere Classified.** Establishments primarily engaged in the rental of mobile homes on site are classified in Real Estate, **SIC 6515: Operators of Residential Mobile Homes Sites.**

NAICS CODE(S)

532120 (Truck, Utility Trailer and RV (Recreational Vehicles) Rental and Leasing)

The utility trailer and recreational vehicle (RV) rental industry is comprised of two distinct operations. Utility trailers are rented generally by establishments that also rent trucks for the consumer market, such as U-Haul International. Most of those establishments are automotive service centers or centers affiliated with a major truck rental company. Recreational vehicles generally are rented by establishments that focus exclusively on renting RVs for the vacation market, or by RV dealers for whom the rental market is a sideline to RV sales and service. Some establishments rent utility trailers and camper-trailers, considered the low-end of the RV rental business. In 1996, an estimated 450 establishments rented utility trailers, recreational vehicles, or both. These establishments had sales of $294 million and employed 1,800 people. Annual payroll was $52 million. According to the Census Bureau, in 1997 there were 5,296 establishments engaged in truck, utility trailer, and RV rental and leasing; they generated revenues of more than $10.3 billion and employed about 47,000 people.

Most of the larger establishments renting recreational vehicles belong to the Recreation Vehicle Rental Association (RVRA), a division of the Recreation Vehicle Dealers Association (RVDA). In 1992, 56 percent of RVRA members reported having 10 or fewer recreational vehicles available for rent, while 35 percent said they had fleets of 11 to 50 vehicles. About 8.5 percent had fleets larger than 50 vehicles.

Utility Trailers. L. S. Schoen, the founder of U-Haul International, generally is credited with turning the haphazard rental of utility trailers into an organized industry. In 1945, Schoen, then in the military, rented a beat-up trailer from a service station to move his family's belongings from Los Angeles to Corona, California. That night he made a notation is his diary: "I am intrigued by the business potential of this idea especially from the standpoint of one-way rentals."

Schoen was discharged from the military later that year and moved his family to Portland, Oregon. Within two weeks he had bought his first trailer. He painted "U-Haul Co.—Rental Trailers—$2.00 per day" on the sides. By 1946, Schoen had a fleet of 70 trailers stretching from Seattle to Los Angeles, and in 1948 he decided to go national. He offered one-way rentals from the West Coast to anywhere in the United States. The only catch was that customers had to find service station managers at the end of their trips who were willing to become Schoen's agents. The plan worked, and by the end of the year, Schoen had a fleet of 200 trailers and a network of agents nationwide.

In 1951, Schoen launched a low-risk program for independent fleet ownership as a way to raise money and expand the U-Haul network even faster: investors would buy trailers from U-Haul and would assume full responsibility for insurance, maintenance, and distribution. Each month, fleet owners would receive a report and payment for rental activity on their trailers. Schoen raised $2 million in the first two years. By 1955, there were more than 10,000 U-Haul trailers in 200 fleets scattered around the country, and Schoen was adding 600 trailers a month.

In the late 1960s, U-Haul trailers were available at more than 14,000 service stations. Although the number of outlets declined during the 1970s, when many service stations closed, U-Haul remained the leader in utility trailer rentals. U-Haul also began renting trucks in the late 1950s, and came to dominate the consumer truck-rental industry as well. For 1997, U-Haul had revenues of $1.2 billion. AMERCO became the holding company of U-Haul International in 1997.

In 1999, U-Haul rented its trailers, trucks, and tow dollies through 1,100 company-owed centers and 15,000 dealers in the United States and Canada, and sales topped $1.5 billion. This wasn't enough to top industry leader Ryder System, Inc., who had 199 sales of $5 billion. Penske Truck Leasing placed second with 1998 sales of $1.8 billion. Other utility trailer rental companies include Transamerica Leasing Inc., which had 1997 sales of $734 million, and XTRA Lease Inc., which had 1998 sales of $300 million.

Recreational Vehicles. Recreational vehicles became widely popular in the United States during the 1960s, and, in 1970, RV dealers formed the RVDA. The RVDA worked to enhance the image of RV dealers and to improve warranty programs offered by RV manufacturers. By 1982, RV rentals had emerged as a separate industry, which led to the formation of the RVRA. The group later became a division of the RVDA. In 1988, the RVRA began publishing *Rental Ventures* (now called *RVRA Rental Directory*), a consumer guide to renting recreational vehicles. That was followed in 1991 by the *Rental Operations Manual,* which provides guidelines and marketing suggestions for RV rental dealers. The RVRA also publishes an annual membership directory.

In the late 1990s, baby boomers, who liked to rent or lease all types of products, were boosting demand for RV rentals and causing the traditional rental season to lengthen. Their most common rental choice was a Class C RV, or mini-motor home. In 1998, fleet owners planned to expand their fleets by 11 percent, as RV rentals were expected to increase 24 percent.

The largest RV rental establishment is Cruise America of Mesa, Arizona, with more than 100 company-owned facilities and satellite rental centers in the United States. The company, as part of Budget Group, Inc., has a fleet of more than 4,300 vehicles, including self-contained RVs, motor homes, camper homes, truck campers, and motorcycles. In 1997, Cruise America had revenues of $95.6 million. Cruise America operates a joint venture with Thor Industries, Inc., a leading maker of RVs, for renting to the public.

FURTHER READING

Hoover's Online Company Capsules, 20 March 2000. Available from http://www.hoovers.com.

"Real Estate and Rental and Leasing—1997 Economic Census." U.S. Department of Commerce. Bureau of the Census, 20 December 1999. Available from http://www.census.gov/prod/ec97/97f53-us.pdf.

Watkins, Ronald J. *Birthright: Murder, Greed, and Power in the U-Haul Family Dynasty.* New York: William Morrow and Company, Inc., 1993.

SIC 7521

AUTOMOBILE PARKING

This classification covers establishments primarily engaged in the temporary parking of automobiles, usually on an hourly, daily, or monthly contract or fee basis. Establishments primarily engaged in extended or dead storage of automobiles are classified in **SIC 4226: Special Warehousing and Storage, Not Elsewhere Classified.**

NAICS CODE(S)

812930 (Parking Lots and Garages)

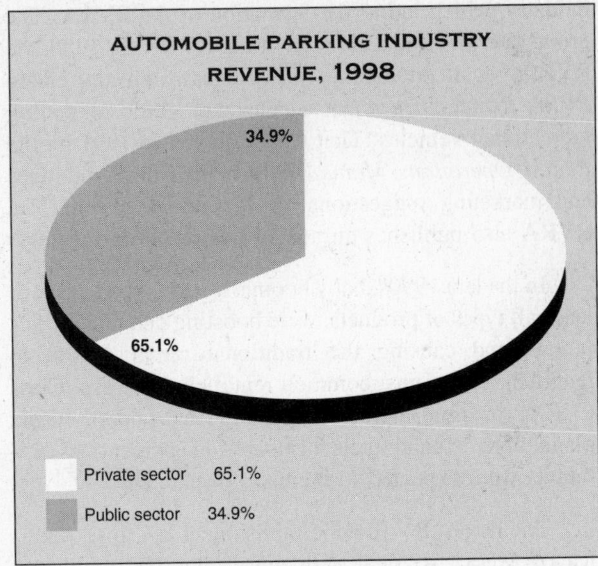

Industry Snapshot

According to International Parking Institute sources, the automobile parking industry generated $43 billion in 1998, with $28 billion coming from the private side and $15 billion coming from the public side. This was a substantial increase over figures reported in previous years. The financial success of the automobile parking industry is tied to commercial real estate growth—a boom in new office buildings (and high occupancy rates within them) requires more lots to house the cars of commuters, clients, and related service industries in the area.

The International Parking Institute also reported that there were roughly 18,500 parking establishments in the United States in 1998. Approximately half of them were owned by municipalities, and the rest were privately held. There were about 105 million parking spaces in the United States with a 2 to 1 ratio of off-street versus on-street parking.

The industry employed about 73,400 workers, the majority of which were parking lot attendants and cashiers. Other positions included enforcement officers, maintenance personnel, office personnel, and information managers. According to the U.S. Bureau of Labor Statistics, the outlook for these jobs looked excellent through the year 2008, with the expected growth at 24 percent, industry-wide.

Organization and Structure

Often, parking lot operators do not own the land on which their businesses sit. Arrangements with the real estate holder are primarily of the fixed-fee management contract type, which does not require an outlay of capital from the operator; the parking company simply contracts to run a parking lot on the land and then collects a percentage of the parking revenues. Fixed-fee management contracts usually run one to three years. In another, less common type of contract, known as a lease arrangement, contracts run three times longer but provide a greater profit potential. In leasing a lot, a parking-lot operator is required to invest their own capital in the expansion or improvement of the lot, but receives a greater share of the profits.

The National Parking Association (NPA), founded in 1951 and based in Washington, D.C., had a membership of more than 1,000 private and public parking professionals. The association organized annual conventions and trade expositions, and published *Parking*, a trade periodical. The NPA also lobbied for industry concerns and reported on its activities in periodic *Legislative Updates* and *Issue Alerts*. The NPA's Parking Consultants Council, formed in 1972, was a professional and technical advice group within the association concerned with design issues, economic analysis, financial counseling, and analysis and maintenance of off-street parking facilities. The NPA also operated a foundation, the Parking Industry Institute, which granted scholarship awards to employees of member organizations and their families.

The International Parking Institute (IPI) was founded in 1962. It has a company member base of more than 1,300. Its mission is to provide leadership, technical resources, and information to the parking profession and related fields. The IPI provides professional training, holds an annual conference and publishes a monthly magazine called *The Parking Professional*,among other services and activities.

Background and Development

The growth of the parking industry has, of course, coincided with the growth of the automobile industry itself. According to the International Parking Institute, the first parking garage was built out of timber in 1909 in Columbus, Ohio. In 1912, the city of Chicago developed municipal parking lots in an effort to relieve the heavy downtown traffic congestion. The first parking meter was displayed in 1935 in Oklahoma City. Over the years, the number of off-street and on-street parking spaces and facilities has grown rapidly in response to the popularity of the automobile and the development of public roadways. Parking equipment has also grown more sophisticated, including automated gates and machines that accept money, calculate fees, and print tickets with and without the aid of an attendant.

Industry Leaders

Ranked according to sales volume, the three largest automobile parking companies in the United States in 1999 were Standard Parking Corp, based in Chicago, Illinois, with $450 million in sales and 3,800 employees; APCO, Inc. based in Cleveland, Ohio, with $350 million in sales and 3,500 employees; and Central Parking Corp, based in Nashville, Tennessee, with $232 million in sales and 9,300 employees.

FURTHER READING

International Parking Institute, 27 November 1999. Available from http://www.parking.org.

Parking Design Guide.. Detroit: Federal APD, Inc., 1997.

U.S. Bureau of Labor Statistics. *National Industry-Occupation Employment Matrix.* Washington, DC: GPO, 1999. Available from http://stats.bls.gov/oep/nioem/empior.asp.

Ward's Business Directory of U.S. Private and Public Companies. Volume 5. Detroit: Gale Group, 1999.

SIC 7532

TOP, BODY, AND UPHOLSTERY REPAIR SHOPS AND PAINT SHOPS

Firms in this category repair automotive tops, bodies, and interiors, or engage in automotive painting and refinishing. This includes non-factory customizing of vans, trucks, and automobiles. Firms building custom-designed vehicles on a factory basis are classified in **SIC 3716: Motor Homes.** Franchise operations are classified under **SIC 6794: Franchises, Selling or Leasing.**

NAICS CODE(S)

811121 (Automotive Body, Paint, and Upholstery Repair and Maintenance)

INDUSTRY SNAPSHOT

For almost as long as there have been cars, ''scratch and dent'' shops have been in business to rejuvenate them. Not long after cars became affordable for most of the public, car owners began looking for ways to ''jazz up'' their vehicles to suit their individual tastes. Such customizing uses the technology and expertise of the body and paint shop to convert mass-produced cars, vans, and trucks into special-use vehicles.

As the cost of new cars escalated, increasing numbers of Americans were extending the life of their current vehicle with a little paint and body filler. According to the *1998 Statistical Abstract of the United States* published by the U.S. Census Bureau, automotive repair shops of all kinds took in $65.3 billion in 1997, up from $62.0 billion in 1996. In 1997, car owners spent $19.8 billion on auto body repair and paint services, nearly one-third of total industry revenues, up from $18.7 billion in 1996.

ORGANIZATION AND STRUCTURE

Most firms in the industry were relatively small; many were owner-operated ''mom-and-pop'' shops. Individual proprietors ran 15,977 firms in 1993, partnerships accounted for 1,757 establishments, and corporations and other business groups accounted for operation of the remaining 17,734. According to the U.S. Census of Service Industries, in 1993 there were 35,074 establishments, a slight increase from 1992. The number of establishments was projected to reach 36,815 in 1998.

Although the operations must be physically separated, many body shops also had onsite painting facilities. Generally, these shops strive for a craftsman image, emphasizing quality rather than speed of delivery. Consumers, however, chronically placed auto repair shops in general, and body shops in particular, high on their complaint lists. Many firms adapted an assembly-line system to the repainting process. These shops performed only minor body repair, concentrating instead on a high-volume business in quick paint jobs. In the 1990s, franchising became an important segment of the industry, combining the small, personal craftsman image with the impact of nationally recognized trademarks.

In 1987, more than 3,000 converters supplied specialty vans to car dealers and individual buyers. However, the product was often unacceptable to consumers, prompting Ford, General Motors, and Chrysler to establish ''consignment pools'' of preferred converters. That policy and increasing competition for a dwindling market share drove the number of active converters down to between 300 and 600 by the early 1990s. It was predicted that this number would decrease even further as larger, better-capitalized conversion firms such as the Starcraft Corporation (the holding company for Starcraft Automotive Group) forced out the craft-shops through intense price and service competition. Posting almost $53.1 million in sales in 1999, Starcraft was the largest company in the industry. Firms manufacturing for the consignment pool are classified under **SIC 3716: Motor Homes.**

BACKGROUND AND DEVELOPMENT

In 1937, the price of painting a car ranged between $85 and $350 and took from six days to two weeks to complete. Then came the assembly-line paint job, pioneered by Earl Scheib Inc. of California, offering the same job for $19.95 and same-day service with a three-year guarantee. Scheib's technological innovation led to a basic division in the paint and body shop industry that continues to persist.

Small shops provided detailed precision work using high-grade materials and tools developed for the modern automobile. In the 1980s, the major auto manufacturers switched to unibody construction and metallic paint finishes. Consequently, frame straightening and quality

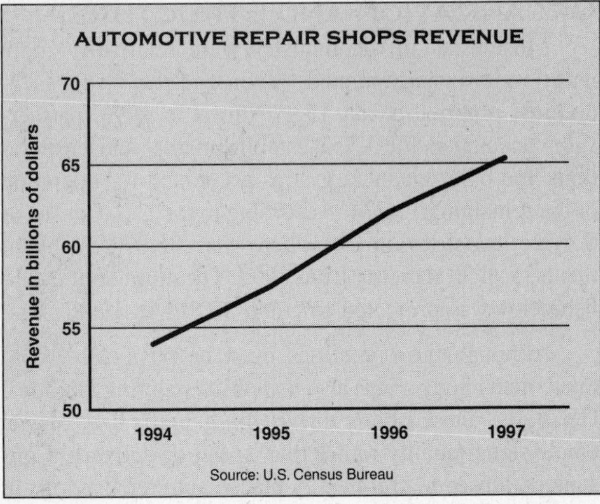

paint application began to require specialized equipment costing hundreds of thousands of dollars. Those shops, which could not afford the massive capital investments in this technologically advanced machinery, became non-competitive.

Assembly lines also provided quality work by specializing in repainting and confining their body work services to surface preparation and minor repairs. During the early 1970s, MAACO Enterprises Inc. of Pennsylvania combined the best of both systems with its franchising concept. Instead of creating a chain of company-owned shops, MAACO used its name and national image to tie together a system of 553 independently operated facilities in 1999. A 1997 issue of *Entrepreneur* magazine ranked MAACO number one in auto appearance services. MAACO claimed that they painted and repaired more vehicles than anyone else in North America. In March 1997, MAACO painted its 10 millionth car in a special promotion commemorating their 25th year in business.

Other firms, like One-Day Paint and Body and Econobake followed. The national clout of these chains and their access to sophisticated tools and training forced many of the marginal craft shops out of business. These franchise operations are covered in **SIC 6794: Franchises, Selling or Licensing.**

Current Conditions

Increased environmental protection legislation brought additional challenges to paint shops in the 1990s. Paint and body shops were primary sources of air and water pollution and contributed significantly to toxic waste stocks. To address this problem, the industry attempted to reduce and recycle waste thinners, solvents, and paints. The Federal Clean Air Act of 1990 mandated a reduction in volatile organic compounds (VOCs); consequently, paint shops had to invest in a major retooling of their facilities. The industry warned that it possibly would not be able to meet the new standards, and if it could, prices would soar and quality would plummet. Paint shops were faced with higher handling costs for chemicals, particularly for disposal, in addition to increased retooling and re-education costs. Major assembly plants had been able to reduce their VOC emissions by 60 to 90 percent over the decade preceding the Clean Air Act, thanks to multimillion dollar investments in ever changing technology, but small shops lacked the capital to invest in modern innovations. In 1990 the switch from oil-based to water-based paints began successfully, but painting processes still produced toxic sludge that often ended up in waste dumps. Studies in the early 1990s found that up to 40 percent of sprayed paint was wasted in this manner.

Environmental regulations also made companies legally liable for toxic contamination in waste containment facilities. One of the largest companies in the industry, Earl Scheib, faced two such lawsuits in 1992 for solvents dumped at landfill sites during the 1960s and 1970s. Clean-up costs for these violations reached an estimated $988,000.

Chrysler Corporation began using a method developed by Haden Environmental Corporation of Troy, Michigan, to combat toxic waste produced by auto paint. According to *Ward's Auto World,* the process recycled the over-spray into a powder, which was then used for under-body paint on Dodge trucks.

Automotive manufacturers introduced water-based paints into their assembly line process with reasonable success in 1982, but these paints required a high-temperature ''bake,'' making them impractical for most aftermarket paint shops. In 1993, Imperial Chemical Industries PLC (ICI) of Britain began preparations to market a new version that eliminated the need for high temperature treatment. The acrylic polymer compound produced an excellent film at 60 degrees Celsius. In England, the new paint commanded a premium of only 5 percent, but in Germany and Italy, it increased the price of a can of paint by as much as 30 percent. Some American paint shop operators estimated that the paint and associated equipment could increase their costs between 10 percent and 40 percent, but their main customers, the insurance companies, were not responding quickly to the suggestion of an increase. According to ICI, tests on the process in Germany and Italy found that no major equipment or retraining investments were necessary. Moreover, the system was expected to improve conditions for painters by making the work environment healthier and cleaner. A water-based paint produces 72 percent less VOC emissions than the industry's standard solvent-borne metallic paints, which contain as much as 85 percent solvent. By some estimates, metallic paint spray accounted for one half of all industrial solvent emissions. Powder coatings emit zero VOCs, and were the fastest growing product in the paint and coatings industry.

Acrylic powders were being used in the late 1990s in primer surface applications. In 1992, General Motors started using an acrylic-based primer and an acrylic trim coating at its Shreveport, Louisiana, plant, and has since started using acrylic based powder primer surfacer at two other plants. Most producers, however, were aiming to develop clearcoats. In the late 1990s, Ferro—one of the world's largest paint suppliers—developed a powder coating that greatly reduced waste and solvent emissions. Their sales grew much faster in North America than in Europe, where powder coatings have been commercialized for a longer period. It was predicted that most primers and clearcoats would eventually be converted to powder, while the color coats were likely to be converted to waterborne coatings, which retain better color consistency and depth than powder.

In addition to reducing their VOC emissions, auto body shops must also recycle and capture refrigerants whenever a car's air conditioning system is repaired or scrapped. Before topping up systems, workers are required to check for leaks. Various pieces of equipment, from leak detection gear to recycling/recovery devices are necessary to complete this process. This equipment, all combined, can cost several thousand dollars.

Image also became an issue for body shops. Shedding the gritty, junkyard image, new shops stressed customer service in clean, friendly environments with easy main-street access. Some firms used central major repair centers to handle the ''heavy-hitters,'' vehicles that needed more than $2,500 in body repairs. This practice kept the ''wrecks'' out of the public eye, improving the body shop's good-neighbor image.

Industry Leaders

In 1999, the paint and body portion of the industry was dominated by the Starcraft Corporation of Goshen, Indiana. Specializing in aftermarket van conversions, Starcraft posted $53.1 million in sales and employed 555 people. Other industry leaders included Earl Scheib Inc. of Beverly Hills, California, with sales of $50.8 million and 1,600 employees; CSI Holdings Inc., with $40.2 million in sales and 190 employees; 1-Day Paint and Body Centers Inc., with $30 million in sales and 520 employees; and Dealers Truck Equipment Company Inc., with $26.4 million in sales and 120 employees.

Workforce

Traditionally, the industry has used a skilled work force trained by apprenticeship. The federal government's Bureau of Apprenticeship and Training worked through state and territorial agencies to promote cooperative programs with employers.

Even so, the average body shop employee stayed with one employer for only two years. Between 1987 and 1996, the total number of employees in the industry increased from approximately 162,800 to 168,800, although there were fluctuations in the labor force during the nine-year period. Most of that increase was in the labor-intensive body repair and van conversion segments. The paint shop segment showed a 2.3 percent decline between 1982 and 1987, with employment dropping from 18,488 to 15,050. This reflected an ongoing trend toward automation, mechanization, and the consolidation of small shops into larger units. According to the U.S. Census Bureau, 186,000 people worked as paint and coating operators in the 1998, in a variety of industries including automotive.

A 1999 survey sponsored by *Auto Body Repair News* revealed that independent repair shops made up 82 percent of the industry and were staffed by craftsmen who were often the shop owners.

Since the average shop had less than five employees, most workers performed tasks with materials and components used for jobs other than grinding and sanding, body repair, or detailing and painting. They might also work on suspensions and electrical systems, replace glass, or do minor mechanical repairs anywhere on the vehicle. Most workers were paid a flat rate, based on an industry standard for the number of hours required to perform the repair. In 1998, employees had gross payroll wages in excess of $4.7 billion.

Research and Technology

In an *Automotive News* article, Emil Hassan, vice president of engineering for Nissan Motor Manufacturing Corp. USA, reported, ''Paint plant technology has progressed faster in the past 10 years than in the previous 30 years.'' This technological revolution would inevitably impact the small aftermarket paint and body shop in the late 1990s. Small shops would have to find capital to invest in new materials and costly equipment to remain competitive in the industry.

Clearcoat paints were introduced in the early 1990s. These paints cover color coats, provide a glossy finish, and reduce acid-etching from today's high pollution levels in cities. In 1995, Dupont was working to produce a one-coat clearcoat system to replace the cumbersome and expensive multi-coat process that was widely used in the industry. It used the process of group transfer polymerization to achieve 3 percent to 4 percent higher solids, solvent-based coating, while reducing VOC content and yielding better color. Dupont was the first company to introduce waterborne finishes to a U.S. OEM assembly plant. Powder clearcoats soon became wide spread throughout the industry.

The ''green'' evolution was also progressing at manufacturer paint facilities in the 1990s. At the Subaru-Isuzu plant in Indiana, managers were pushing for a 95 percent reduction in VOCs, rather than the 72 percent expected elsewhere, by combining the use of water-based paint applied electrostatically along with a paint-solvent after-burner. In 1995, the U.S. Council for Automotive Research, a consortium including Ford, General Motors, and Chrysler, built a $20 million test facility at Ford's Wixom, Michigan, assembly plant to develop standards, materials, and process equipment for powder coatings. The demand and popularity of powder coatings increased rapidly due to their zero-VOC content and durability.

In 1996, the National Paint and Coating Association announced its coatings CARE Program, which was a progressive initiative that enabled companies to follow a common, effective management approach for their health, safety, and environmental programs. Participation was voluntary, but because the program offered expanded resources, improved communications, and opportunities for heightened industry performance in health, safety, and education, the NPCA believed that participation was vital to an organization's future. They believed that the industry, regardless of size, product or specialty, would have to adopt to new technologies and respond quickly to keep pace and satisfy growing consumer demands.

New materials being used by automobile manufacturers also impacted the paint and body shop industry in the 1990s. Automakers, intent on reducing car weight to improve gas mileage, began using more plastic, fiberglass, and aluminum in place of steel. These materials require specialized paint application processes that must be performed by trained professionals.

Such new technologies as laser wheel-alignment machines, hydraulic frame straighteners, and high-temperature bake ovens were becoming common at many body shops in order to comply with the consumer demand that the repaired car look just as good as it did when it rolled off the manufacturer's assembly line. Auto repair and paint shops were also making use of another new technology—the computer.

Further Reading

Clark, Mark. ''Paint Missing Foes 90s.'' *Body Shop Business,* May 1996.

D & B Business Rankings 1999, Bethlehem: Dun & Bradstreet, 1999.

Darnay, Arsen J., ed. *Service Industries USA,* 3rd ed. Detroit: Gale Research, 1995.

Earl Scheib Inc. 1996 Annual Report. Beverly Hills, CA: Earl Scheib Inc., 1996.

Earl Scheib Paint and Body. '' Corporate Information.'' Available from http://earlscheib.com/.

Fattah, Hassan. ''Paints & Coatings.'' *Chemical Week,* 10 November 1995.

Green, David. ''Using Acrylic Powder Coatings in Automobiles.'' *Paint and Coatings Industry,* September 1995.

Phelan, Mark. ''Heavy Breathing in the Paint Shop.'' *Automotive Industries,* September 1996.

Starcraft. ''Press Releases and Financial Information.'' Goshen, 1999. Available from http://www.starcraftcorp.com/.

U.S. Census Bureau. '' Domestic Trade and Services.'' *Statistical Abstract of the United States: 1999..* Washington, DC: GPO, 1999.

U.S. Department of Commerce. Bureau of the Census. *County Business Patterns 1994.* Washington: GPO, 1995.

U.S. Department of Commerce. Bureau of the Census. *Service Annual Survey 1995.* Washington: GPO, 1996.

SIC 7533

AUTO EXHAUST SYSTEM REPAIR SHOPS

This industry classification includes establishments primarily engaged in the installation, repair, or sale and installation of automotive exhaust systems. The sale of mufflers, tailpipes, and catalytic converters is considered to be incidental to the installation of these products.

NAICS Code(s)

811112 (Autmotive Exhaust System Repair)

Industry Snapshot

This industry covers exhaust system repair which primarily involves the sale, installation, and repair of mufflers, tailpipes, and catalytic converters. It is distinct from businesses engaged in the overall repair of automobiles. Such businesses are primarily categorized in **SIC 7532: Top, Body, and Upholstery Repair Shops and Paint Shops** and **SIC 7538: General Automotive Repair Shops.** Businesses engaged in specialized automotive repair, such as fuel service, brake repair, wheel alignments etc., are classified in **SIC 7539: Automotive Repair Shops, Not Elsewhere Classified.**

Organization and Structure

Car exhaust system service is typically provided by dealership garages and auto exhaust repair shops. Besides the existence of numerous ''mom and pop'' auto service businesses, the industry was led by a few relatively well-known repair shop chains. Among them were Monro, Meineke, and Speedy International Inc. No single company has dominated the industry.

According to the U.S. Census Bureau, the auto exhaust repair industry consisted of 6,237 establishments in 1998, up from 6,071 in 1997. Employment figures showed that 28,800 people were employed in the industry in 1998. Revenues totaled $2.63 billion. In the same year, the industry had a $665.5 million payroll.

Exhaust Systems. The exhaust system of every modern automobile requires frequent care and repair. Condensation in the typical exhaust flow, coupled with ordinary wear, will often result in the necessary replacement of the car's muffler and exhaust pipes. The result is a vehicle with minimal engine noise and an exhaust system that more effectively funnels toxic fumes produced by the vehicle away from the car's interior. When owners determine that their exhaust systems may need repair, they typically avoid do-it-yourself (DIY) replacements and seek the services of exhaust system repair shops. These repairs are also necessary for the owner to maintain car emissions that meet Environmental Protection Agency (EPA) standards. Auto exhaust repair shops install, repair, and inspect the proper pollution control devices.

A car's exhaust system consists mainly of an exhaust pipe, a muffler, and a tailpipe. The exhaust pipe collects the exhaust of a car through a series of exhaust ports in the internal manifold of a car engine. This exhaust is funneled to a downstream pipe and moved through the muffler. The tailpipe discharges the car's exhaust into the atmosphere after it has passed through the muffler.

The muffler is the main component of the exhaust system. It is basically a device that reduces the noise produced by the movement of gas and internal combustion of the car's engine. The typical shell of an automobile muffler is shaped like an oval that measures roughly 20 inches long, 10 inches wide, and 6 inches high. Its internal architecture is comprised of perforated steel tubes and a number of chambers separated by steel partitions. This combination of filters and tubes acts as a honeycomb that acoustically filters the exhaust sound. The typical muffler can reduce the sound pressure of a car's exhaust from 90 to 60 decibels, a 1,000-fold decrease. More expensive dual exhaust systems have four or more mufflers.

Federal regulations require that motor vehicles be fitted with emissions control devices. Therefore, a mechanism such as a catalytic converter has become an addition to a car's exhaust system. Since their initial requirement in 1975, catalytic converters have served to reduce harmful exhaust. Improved emissions allow the owner to comply with standards mandated by the Environmental Protection Agency.

Legislation to control automobile pollution is in the Clean Air Act, which was passed in 1956 with significant amendments in 1970 and 1977. Regulation of mobile pollution sources was considered controversial. In fact, an EPA study in 1979 attested to the difficulty involved with getting automobile owners to comply with state and federal standards requiring the installment and maintenance of properly functioning pollution control equipment, specifically the catalytic converter. The converter cleans up the car's exhaust gases to meet those standards created by the EPA. Today's converters are made of a honeycomb-like material that is lightly coated with palladium and platinum. These two elements, when in the presence of oxygen, aid in the reduction of hydrocarbons and carbon monoxide.

The emissions control system of a car does not become the responsibility of the owner until the manufacturer's warranty expires. At that point, problems with the catalytic converter usually lead the car owner to an auto exhaust repair shop that provides emissions control work. The most common difficulties with the converter are clogging and melt down. These two problems typically occur in high-mileage engines and result in exhaust problems. Converter failures can also be symptomatic of other problems.

The technicians at auto exhaust repair shops who are faced with converter problems have a number of options for diagnosis of the converter and accompanying emissions systems. Technicians may begin with a visual examination of the mechanism to discover any evident rust destruction, leaks, or broken connections. More complicated methods of testing the system include thump, temperature, and back pressure tests. These tests detect difficulties of the converter caused by circumstances such as build-up of phosphorous on the surface of the converter due to burning oil, foreign matter plugging the interior of the converter, excessive sulfur content in the fuel, antifreeze leaks into the engine which pollute the converter, or broken or ineffective exhaust air pumps.

Current Conditions

Overall, the industry expanded its sales throughout the late-1990s. In 1998, auto exhaust repair shops earned $2.62 billion, up slightly from 1997's $2.57 billion.

The industry outlook for auto exhaust repair shops was quite promising in 1999. Advancing technology (particularly in the area of mufflers and catalytic converters) and increased automobile emissions regulations promised to create more work for exhaust repair shops. Also, an increase in the number of older cars on the road (mainly the result of high car prices and a prolonged recession) meant that more car owners were maintaining and repairing their cars rather than simply replacing them. Because most gas stations began exiting the repair industry in the mid- to late-1980s, and many new specialty shops did not perform exhaust repair, there appeared to be a shortage of exhaust repair service providers in the mid-1990s. In fact, since 1975, a 70 percent decline in the number of repair outlets resulted in remaining repair shops increasing their average number of repair jobs per year from 398 in 1980 to 460 in 1988.

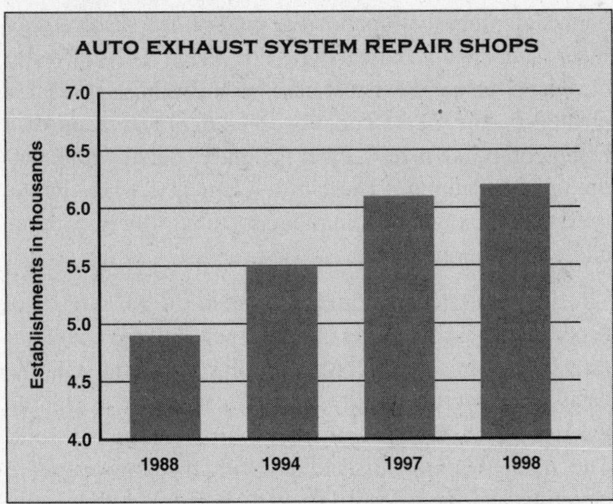

Although there was some fluctuation in exhaust repair business from year to year—largely a result of weather (salt on snowy and icy roads causes corrosion) and the amount of technological change—the overall market for automotive aftermarket repair was large, fragmented, and growing. Acting as factors in favor of the industry were the declining ability of car owners to perform their own repairs because of more complex vehicles (particularly the dramatic increase in electronic components), less leisure time, and increasingly stringent emissions regulations that made more exhaust system inspections necessary. Likewise, the increase in vehicles on the road, vehicle miles driven, and the average age of cars contributed to the strength of the industry.

The greatest threat posed to industry participants going into the mid-1990s was new entrants. In 1992, General Motors entered the auto exhaust repair industry by offering such repair work to its dealers' service and parts operations. General Motors dealers began the Goodwrench Exhaust Program, which provided them with mufflers, resonators, pipes, accessories, and service tools necessary for exhaust system repair. Dealers were allowed to decide the extent of the inventory they would maintain (from $3,000 to $40,000), while stocking racks and service tools were provided free. The new program was General Motors' attempt to muscle in on a growing and lucrative industry. The program was backed by substantial marketing and advertising efforts. The automaker's move threatened the current leaders in the industry and forced them to develop better marketing and service programs.

Industry Leaders

One of the most successful competitors in the early 1990s was Monro Muffler Brake Inc., which began as a Midas International Corp. franchise in the 1950s. Founder Chuck August added brake shops and took the company public in 1991. In 1984, a group led by Wall Street executive Peter J. Solomon bought a controlling interest in the company; the group owned about 20 percent of the company in 1996.

Between 1987 and 1992, the company more than doubled its sales. Since the early 1990s, the company aggressively opened new shops. In 1992, the company had 167 shops in eight states, predominantly in the Northeast. Overall, Monro's rapid expansion has added 15 percent to square footage every year. Substantial growth occurred between 1991 and 1996, when sales climbed from $21.5 million to $117 million. By 1996, the company owned and operated 274 muffler and brake repair shops. Monro also came close to doubling its number of stores again in 1997. In 1999 Monro achieved sales of $154.3 million and employed 2,138 people.

Monro's management strategy relied on advanced inventory control systems and exceptional customer service. The focus on customer service gave the company an advantage over its larger franchise competitors. The strategy manifested itself even in chairman Jack Gallagher's policy of personally replying to all customers' letters. This strategy tended to create a focus on customer satisfaction even at the shop level. The end result was a 77 percent repeat customer rate in the mid-1990s. This approach appeared to be successful as business continued to grow in the late-1990s.

The typical Monro outlet and repair shop had six service bays and 4,500 square feet. Monro organized its stores around one key outlet, which carried a larger inventory and acted in a support role for smaller satellite shops. Monro improved its overall service ability when it implemented measures designed to result in more effective inventory management. Since the 1989 installment of a point of sale (POS) inventory tracking system, the company dramatically increased its ability to meet customer needs with on-hand inventory. This system improved customer satisfaction and increased gross margins, and allowed Monro to react more efficiently and effectively.

Monro repair shops were staffed by four to six mechanics who reported to a store manager. The company retained its quality mechanics by providing them with career growth opportunities. In fact, most regional and store managers began their careers with the company as service technicians. Also, the company paid a premium hourly wage to its mechanics who received an Automobile Service Excellence award. This emphasized the company's desire to insure quality service and acted as an incentive for employees to become certified mechanics.

A standard Monro repair shop broke even after only its first year of operations. This required achieving an average in first year sales of $300,000. Nearly all stores opened in the mid-1990s met this goal. The success attested to Monro's strategy of placing shops in high-visibility and well-traveled locations.

Besides Monro, significant players in the industry included Toronto-based Speedy International Inc., which not only replaces and repairs mufflers but also provides tire, suspension, oil, and alignment services. Founded in 1956 by Fred Karp, Speedy became a private, multinational company with operations in Canada and the United States (through CarX Muffler and Brake). Although he sold it to Tenneco Inc. in 1968, Karp bought the chain back in 1988 when Tenneco underwent a major restructuring. In 1999, Speedy posted third quarter revenues of $41.3 million, 76.3 percent lower than the same period in 1998. This dramatic decline resulted from Speedy's sale of its European operations in early January 1999 and the sale of its stores operating under the Speedy brand in the United States in September 1998.

RESEARCH AND TECHNOLOGY

Technological threats to the exhaust repair industry have occasionally appeared in the form of improved components that require less repair. For example, in the late 1980s a stainless steel muffler was introduced that promised less erosion. Many of these advances acted to improve business. In 1992, the EPA proposed tougher rules for checking vehicle emissions. The change was expected to cost Americans $1 billion, much of which would go to repair shops required to perform the work. The proposed rules subjected 100 million cars to the tougher, costlier testing.

Advancements in muffler and converter technology have taken the shape of improved efficiency. Researchers at the Noise Cancellation Technology Labs in Connecticut invented a new electronic muffler that utilized computer generated ''anti-noise'' to further muffle engine noise. The new muffler, which can be produced for the same cost as conventional mufflers, improves engine power and fuel efficiency. Meanwhile, Corning Inc. developed a catalytic converter that would not require a car to warm up before operating effectively. These and similar developments for improvement to automobile exhaust systems did not appear to threaten the industry's steady increase in size and revenues.

FURTHER READING

D & B Business Rankings 1999, Bethlehem: Dun & Bradstreet, 1999.

Darnay, Arsen J., ed. *Service Industries USA,* 3rd ed. Detroit: Gale Research, 1992.

Hitchcock, A. ''Mufflers Promote Clean, Quiet Pneumatics.'' *Hydraulics and Pneumatics,* December 1992.

Jewett, Dale. ''GM Adds Exhaust Program.'' *Automotive News,* 27 July 1992.

Speedy Auto Service. ''Speedy Announces Third Quarter Results.'' Toronto: 1999. Available from http://www.speedy.com/.

Templeton, Fleur. ''Corning Cooks Up Cleaner Catalytic Converters.'' *Business Week,* 16 March 1992.

U.S. Census Bureau. ''Service Annual Survey.'' Washington, D.C.: GPO, 1995. Available from http://www.census.gov/prod/2/bus/cbp94/cbp94-6.pdf.

SIC 7534

TIRE RETREADING AND REPAIR SHOPS

This classification covers businesses that primarily repair and retread automotive tires. Industry firms either retread customers' tires or retread tires for sale or exchange.

NAICS CODE(S)

326212 (Tire Retreading)
811198 (All Other Automotive Repair and Maintenance)

Tread increases a tire's traction, particularly on wet roads. The forward portion of a tire's contact area wipes away water so the rest of the contact area will grip a dry surface. Continuous channels from the center to the edge of the tread propel water outward, eliminating potentially dangerous ''aquaplaning.'' Snow tires and off-road tires have deeper treads designed to grip through snow and dirt. After tire treads wear down, tire retreading and repair shops repair the tires by cutting or stamping new treads into the rubber on the tire.

Because about 70 percent of a new tire's cost is in its body rather than its tread, tire retreading shops provide a valuable and cost-effective service, especially for companies running a large vehicle fleet. A typical retreaded tire costs about 50 to 70 percent less than a new tire. And retreads typically offer service, mileage, dependability, and warranties comparable to new tires. Most truck tires can be retreaded two or three times, resulting in up to 750,000 miles of service.

Although pneumatic automobile tires—invented in 1888—were used in the United States during the early 1900s, treads, which reduced ''sideslip,'' were not introduced until 1910. Soon after, treads became standard on all types of tires. The massive expansion of the automobile industry, combined with the development of a national highway system, generated a strong demand for tires and retreading services during the mid-1900s. By the early 1980s, tire retreading industry revenues topped $935 million.

Because of advances in technology and gains in manufacturing productivity during the 1980s, automobile tire retreading became more cost-effective than it was during the 1960s and 1970s. Still, industry revenues grew meagerly, to about $1.1 billion by the late 1980s as the incidence of truck tire retreading slowly increased. Eventually the industry disproved consumers' perceptions that retreaded tires were not as durable as new tires and that they ''unraveled,'' so that by 1995 retreaded tires outsold new tires in the replacement market. The industry also benefits the environment. It takes 7 gallons of oil to retread a truck tire compared to 22 gallons to manufacture a new one. Overall, retreading conserves more than 400 million gallons of oil a year. Further, the new tread applied can contain up to 10 percent recycled, reprocessed rubber. In addition, retreading tires reduces solid waste disposal problems by up to 75 percent. Because of these environmental benefits, President Clinton signed an executive order in 1998, which superseded one issued in 1993, that mandated the use of retreaded tires on all federal government vehicles.

In addition to government vehicles, nearly all off-the-road, heavy duty vehicles, and all of the world's airlines use retreaded tires, as well as school buses, trucking fleets, taxis, race cars, and emergency vehicles. Marvin Bozarth stated: ''Aircraft tires routinely receive 12 or more retreads; haulage and local pickup and delivery truck tires are often retreaded five times or more; and high-speed long haul truck tires generally receive two or three retreads. Passenger tires are usually retreaded only once.'' Safety standards developed by the U.S. Department of Transportation govern the manufacture of retreaded passenger car tires, and manufacturers of retreaded truck tires must comply with industry standards. The Federal Aviation Administration approves commercial aircraft retreads, while the military branches approve military aircraft retreads.

During the 1990s, the industry underwent considerable consolidation. According to government statistics, there were 1,845 companies in this category in 1992, down from 1,930 in 1987. Most of these were small, local tire repair shops. Total annual receipts for the industry were $1.3 billion in 1992, a 19 percent change from the 1987 sales total of $1.1 billion. In 1997, there were 632 companies, operating 754 establishments. Their shipments were valued at $983 million. The top five states, in terms of establishments, were Texas, Ohio, Pennsylvania, North Carolina, and Illinois. In 1992, 12,898 workers served the tire retreading and repair shop industry, down from 13,808 in 1987. By 1997, the number of workers had dropped to 7,939. The Tire Retread Information Bureau reported in its *1999 Fact Sheet* that ''Approximately 30.9 million retreaded tires were sold in North America (produced by some 1415 plants in the United States and Canada) in 1998, with sales totaling more than 2 billion dollars.'' Most plants were independent owner/operator businesses; others were owned by new tire manufacturers and a major tread rubber supplier.

Two industry leaders are Treadco Inc., of Fort Smith, Arkansas, and Bandag, Incorporated of Muscatine, Iowa. Treadco, which retreads more than 500,000 truck tires annually at its 26 production facilities, had 1998 sales of $181.3 million. A subsidiary of Arkansas Best Corporation, Treadco also sells new tires at 29 stores strategically placed by interstate highways. Bandag supplies about 15 percent of the market for light and heavy-duty truck retreaded tires; the company had 1998 sales of $1.06 million. New tire manufacturers, including Goodyear, Michelin, Bridgestone, and Marangoni, also participated in retreading, albeit to a lesser extent.

According to The Tire Retread Information Bureau, ''Because of the competitive nature of the retreading industry, [customers] can expect to see continuous improvement in quality, durability, and reliability, as the major retread suppliers annually invest millions of dollars in research and development.''

FURTHER READING

Bozarth, Marvin. ''Retreads - Best Buy in Recycling.'' Tire Retread Information Bureau. Available from http://www.retread.org/packet/index.cfm?ID = 10.

''Current Industrial Reports: Tire Retreading—1997.'' U.S. Department of Commerce. Bureau of the Census. August 1999. Available http://www.census.gov/prod/ec97/97m3262b.pdf.

Darnay, Arsen J., ed. *Service Industries USA.* 3rd ed. Detroit: Gale Research, 1996.

Deierlein, Bob. ''Retreading Has Finally Been Accepted.'' *Beverage World,* 15 June 1997.

Hoover's Online Company Capsules. Available from http://www.hoovers.com/.

Tire Retread Information Bureau. ''Fact Sheet'' and other documents.1999. Available from http://www.retread.org.

SIC 7536

AUTOMOTIVE GLASS REPLACEMENT SHOPS

This category covers establishments primarily engaged in the installation, repair, or sales and installation of automotive glass. The sale of the glass is considered incidental to the replacement.

NAICS CODE(S)

811122 (Automotive Glass Replacement Shops)

INDUSTRY SNAPSHOT

Automotive glass replacement shops catered to such common problems as windshields that were cracked or punctured—either by stones and other debris thrown up by the road—or by the sharp difference in temperature between the interior and exterior surfaces during the winter. They also repaired damage to other glass areas found on automobiles, as well as stopped leaks—traditionally one of the most challenging problem areas to correct. None of these repairs was of a type that drivers were likely to attempt for themselves.

ORGANIZATION AND STRUCTURE

Three types of businesses were available to fix and install automotive glass: those undertaking various kinds of glass repairs; those specializing in automotive glass; and those working on all parts of a vehicle body, including glass. Many repair businesses specializing in automotive glass were franchises connected to large chains.

BACKGROUND AND DEVELOPMENT

The earliest automobiles were open bodied and traveled at such low speeds that windshields were hardly necessary. Only when automobiles became significantly faster and featured closed construction did the windshield and windows become significant features of automotive design, and hence of automotive repair.

Windshields were first introduced as an option on Ford's Model T in 1909, but became standard on all automobiles within a couple of decades. Windshields were originally flat, mounted at a right angle to the body of the vehicle, and upon shattering, would fly apart in numerous sharp fragments. As Caleb Hornbostel noted in *Construction Materials,* "Laminated glass was evolved as a result of developments within the automobile industry and to a lesser extent the plastic industry. The tremendous demand for shatter-proof glass for the closed automobile (in the late-1990s, over 90 percent of the total production of automobiles were closed cars) stimulated the glass industry into producing laminated glass."

Another important innovation occurred in 1932 when the French developed tempered glass. Although it eventually became the standard for side and rear windows, "tests demonstrated that tempered glass wouldn't work in windshields. While its resistance was great, it broke into patterns on impact that were so dense that vision was impaired," according to James L. Polak in *Automotive Engineering.* In addition, the very toughness of tempered glass represented a hazard when windshields were struck by the head of a driver or passenger in the event of an accident or sudden stop. Unlike laminated glass, it was too hard to give way, and thus could thus potentially cause severe injuries.

Though laminated glass would yield under such circumstances and could also be cracked more easily than tempered glass, its construction guaranteed that even the severest shattering would not lead to dangerous fragmentation—the plastic interlayer that was bonded between two sheets of glass to create the laminate adhered so strongly that no particle of glass could break free. The first laminated glass had celluloid interlayers, which proved apt to discolor in certain climates. Toward the end of the 1930s, the introduction of a polyvinyl butyryl (PVB) interlayer overcame this problem. The durability of PVB was further enhanced in the mid-1960s with a quadrupling of its impact resistance.

One-piece curved windshields—an expensive Chrysler option in 1934—became a Nash standard feature in 1949 and, like wraparound rear windows, spread quickly thereafter. General Motors applied the wraparound design to windshields in 1954. The increased use of curved glass complicated installation and repair, requiring greater levels of care and precision, but also made possible improvements in styling and, ultimately, aerodynamic efficiency. With the advent of the oil crisis of the 1970s, streamlining became an economic, as well as aesthetic, priority. This was partially accomplished not only by curving windshields, but also by safely thinning (and thereby reducing the weight of) all automotive glass, and by flush glazing the joints between glass and body parts that had once required obtrusive metal trims.

Some manufacturers introduced green-tinted windshields in the 1940s, which soon became somewhat controversial. According to Polak, "Critics claimed that the shading would diminish night vision. Tests showed, however, that the night vision reduction would be negligible while the cut in glare from the day's sun and the night's headlights would be a significant improvement." Overcoming that controversy paved the way for such further refinements as the introduction of sun strips in the 1950s and, near the end of the next decade, of polarized windshields that were nonreflective and glare eliminating. In the 1980s, automotive designers took an important step toward overcoming the hazards of snow and frost with the introduction of electrically heated windshields.

Safety standards governing automotive glass durability and impact resistance were introduced by the American Standards Association (ASA) in the 1930s. Initially subject to voluntary compliance, these standards shortly became part of state and federal regulation, and thereafter were made more rigorous when the ASA became the American National Standards Institute (ANSI).

Another area of regulation of critical concern to automotive glass replacement shops was the possibility of instituting standards in relation to levels of windshield hazing. As explained in *Automotive Engineering,* "This phenomenon results from small craters created by salt, sand, and pebbles as they strike the glass, in addition to streaking caused by windshield wipers, ice scraping, and cleaning with abrasive substances. Haze caused by these factors not only tends to obscure drivers' vision of the road, but also contributes significantly to driver fatigue and impairs concentration." The institution of such standards seemed likely to generate a significant amount of business for automotive glass repair services, given that an estimated one percent of vehicles on the road had windshields with excess haze.

Current Conditions

Recent trends in automobile design have created an even greater need for replacement glass accessories: glass makes up more than 30 percent of a car's exterior surface area, an increase of approximately 30 percent from the early 1990s.

As of 1998, 5,542 operations made up the industry, employing 26,400 workers. The industry also had a total payroll of $681 million, and posted revenues of $3.68 billion. Of the total, 3,272 establishments in the industry staffed under 5 employees, 1,171 employed under 10 workers, and only 112 had over 20 employees.

Industry Leaders

As of 1999, the leaders in the automotive glass replacement industry were Harmon Glass Company, Inc. with $259.8 million in sales and 1,532 employees; Lear Siegler Holdings Corporation, posting $190.7 million in sales and 3,400 employees; Auto Glass Specialists Inc. with $56.1 million and 540 employees; Diamond/Triumph Auto Glass, Inc., with $31.2 million and 624 employees; and Diversified Glass Services, Inc. with $25.0 million and 500 employees.

Workforce

Automotive glass installers and repair personnel received training either from classes in glazing or by learning on the job. They had to exercise care and precision in the removal of broken and sharp-edged glass, in cutting and fitting sheets of glass with the requisite degree of accuracy, and in fitting such strips and seals as were necessary to achieve a weatherproof finish.

Beginning in the late 1980s, the efforts taken to ease factory installation of increasingly large and complex glass shapes had obvious advantages to those repair businesses also engaged in the installation of such glass. The major breakthrough came with the introduction of modules, because these "provide almost a perfect seal in the vehicle since each module is precisely produced in the same mold and fits almost perfectly into the sheet metal opening," according to Joseph M. Callahan in *Automotive Industries.* "It's estimated that about a quarter of all windows in U.S. cars are now modular, with the expectation that it will reach 75 percent or more in the next several years," Callahan continued.

America and the World

As the foremost car culture in the world, the United States generated a great volume of general maintenance and repair business. In the area of automotive glass in particular, one key difference between the United States and Great Britain lay in the fact that windshields in the latter country were commonly made of tempered glass. In addition, European designers were leading the way with experiments in automotive double glazing. As Peter J. Mullins explained in *Automotive Industries,* "Two layers of glass, very precisely made with an air gap of a few millimeters between them, help to reduce . . . noise amplifications and also cut road and engine noise. One maker has even connected a small vacuum pump to the gap to evacuate the air and improve performance; another is circulating dry air to cut condensation."

Research and Technology

The overall trend in U.S. automotive design near the end of the twentieth century toward using increased expanses of technologically complex glass could only prove beneficial to businesses specializing in glass repair and installation. However, a problem associated with such an emphasis on glass in vehicle body design was the material's heavy weight, and hence its tendency to impair fuel economy and overall performance. *Ward's Auto World* reported that the amount of glass in American-made cars increased from 83.5 pounds in 1980 to 97.0 pounds in 1999. Polycarbonates were increasingly being considered as lighter alternatives to glass in automotive design, but no plastic had attained the resistance to scratching and discoloration that glass possessed. Another alternative was the use of thinner glass, about 70/1000ths of an inch thick compared to the conventional 88/1000ths. Eisenstein claimed that this change would reduce the weight of an average windshield by 3 pounds.

In addition to increasing weight, larger expanses of automotive glass also raised interior temperatures. In fact, about 71.7 percent of the typical sources of passenger compartment heat were attributable to glass. Moreover, the increased heat on plastic interior trim could lead to the release of vapors, which would tend to settle as a film on interior surfaces of the glass. Higher temperatures from greater reliance on glass were a particular cause of concern in the automotive industry because of impending legislation requiring the replacement of traditional air-conditioning systems with more environmentally friendly but generally less efficient alternatives.

In response, automotive designers experimented with various kinds of films and tintings capable of reflecting or absorbing greater quantities of temperature-raising infrared light and with photochromic materials darkening or lightening in automatic response to the amount of sunshine. They also sought comparable methods of reducing the damage to interior plastics created by ultraviolet light. As Callahan pointed out, however, any new developments along these lines had to take into account that "the government requires that automotive glass transmit at least 70 percent of the visible light striking it.''

Other innovations focused on overcoming problems associated with bad weather: devices not only for rapid melting of ice or snow on glass but also for defogging more efficiently and for controlling windshield-wiper operation through moisture sensitivity.

FURTHER READING

D & B Business Rankings 1999, Bethlehem: Dun & Bradstreet, 1999.

Eisenstein, Paul. ''More Glass!'' *Automotive Industries,* September 1989.

Hornbostel, Caleb. *Construction Materials.* 2nd ed. New York: John Wiley and Sons, 1991.

Mullins, Peter J. ''European Glass: Double Glazing.'' *Automotive Industries,* September 1989.

Plumb, Stephen E. ''Safer Vision.'' *Ward's Auto World,* June 1989.

———. ''Beating the Heat.'' *Ward's Auto World,* January 1990.

U.S. Census Bureau. ''1997 Economic Census—Service.'' Washington, DC: GPO, 1999. Available from http://www.census.gov.

Ward's Automotive Yearbook 1999. Detroit: Ward's Communications, 1999.

''Windshield Wear.'' *Automotive Engineering,* September 1988.

Winter, Drew. ''New Glasstech Process Gives Windshields the Bends.'' *Ward's Auto World,* December 1991.

SIC 7537

AUTOMOTIVE TRANSMISSION REPAIR SHOPS

This category covers establishments primarily engaged in the installation, repair, or sales and installation of automotive transmissions. The sale of transmissions and related parts is considered incidental to the installation or repair of these products.

NAICS CODE(S)

811113 (Automotive Transmission Repair)

INDUSTRY SNAPSHOT

By the late 1990s, developments in U.S. automotive technology and design ensured that both manual and automatic transmissions were among the most reliable parts of an automobile. But the complexity of the transmission as a system of many precisely interrelated components, as well as the difficulty of diagnosing and correcting faults, meant the problems that did occur were unlikely to be tackled by drivers in their own garages. Instead, this situation created a market for professional mechanics specializing in transmission repair.

ORGANIZATION AND STRUCTURE

In 1998, 10.7 percent of new cars sold in the U.S. came with a manual transmission. This reflected a major shift from the 1970s, when, because of sharp increases in oil and gas prices, manual transmissions dominated the new car market. Manual transmissions were far more fuel efficient, and were standard on small foreign imports, which became popular during the efficiency-aware '70s. But as prices settled and automatic transmissions became more fuel-efficient and increasingly advanced, they rose in again in popularity through the 1980s and into the 1990s.

Routine maintenance demanded the periodic checking and changing of automatic transmission or transaxle oil, and possibly the replacement of the transmission filter. As with engine oil, transmission fluid could be checked by means of a dipstick. The detection of signs of contamination of the transmission fluid, by metal, dirt, moisture, or friction material from internal parts, was an important step because such contamination could lead to rapid wear of parts and to premature transmission failure.

Inspection of the transmission fluid also provided an invaluable guide to the diagnosis of existing or potential problems. Fluid that was milky typically became intermixed with the engine coolant; fluid that was blackened or had a burnt odor indicated serious damage to the transmission; and fluid with a light brown color usually had broken down, which led to a wide variety of further problems.

Manual transmissions required the operation of a clutch mechanism subject to high levels of wear and tear. Among the problems tackled by transmission specialists working on manual transmissions were pulsating or stiff clutch pedals; clutches that grabbed, chattered, dragged, or slipped because of improper clutch adjustment; a binding clutch release mechanism; a broken engine mount; or oil or grease on a clutch disc. Repairs to the clutch often required the removal of drive axles, transaxles, and even entire engines. Other problems found in manual transmissions were noise, leaks, grinding of gears during shifting, difficulty in making gear shifts, or transmissions locked in one gear or jumping out of the gear selected.

In automatic transmissions, the most common adjustments that could be made with the transmission still in place were adjustments to the transmission band, the shift linkage, or the neutral safety switch. More major internal problems required the removal of the entire transmission. In the removal and disassembly of all kinds of transmissions, the utmost care had to be taken to avoid damaging the component parts. In addition, any worn or damaged parts needed to be replaced, or else the reassembled transmission would soon require another disassembly for a future problem.

Background and Development

The earliest automobiles required constant but low-level maintenance. The earliest drivers were either enthusiastic enough to perform the necessary minor adjustments themselves or wealthy enough to employ a mechanic for this purpose. The earliest automobiles were also slow. Only with the advent of faster vehicles did transmission technology—designed specifically to maximize engine efficiency by adjusting performance in coordination with changes in speed—become an important feature of automotive design, and thus a sophisticated mechanism requiring expertise to maintain, repair, or replace.

The first transmissions were manual. Easier to drive but harder to fix, automatic transmissions began appearing in the United States in significant numbers after World War II. At first, auto manufacturers were reluctant to adopt what they considered to be an overly complex gadget, but its popularity with consumers soon convinced them.

By the early 1970s, transmission repair specialists were a solidly established sector of automotive mechanics. However, at this time the automotive repair industry became the number one source of consumer complaints about incompetence and dishonesty. In the field of transmission repairs, the heavily advertised AAMCO chain suffered from bad publicity due to the number of franchises found guilty of some form of systematic abuse of their customers. Some franchises offered free diagnoses, on the basis of which transmissions were dismantled and then not rebuilt until the consumer consented to the performance of repairs that often proved to be both unnecessary and expensive. Many AAMCO franchise holders were not experienced mechanics, so there was no guarantee that the work performed would be competent. All franchise holders were also pressured to achieve an assigned average repair order—something they could not do without performing unnecessary repairs at least some of the time.

Consumer protection groups and changes in legislation curbed the grossest of these abuses, but the entire automotive repair industry in the United States remained largely unregulated toward the end of the 20th century. In the case of transmissions, consumers had little choice but to trust that a given mechanic performed repairs in a conscientious and competent way. As Arthur P. Glickman noted in *Mr. Badwrench,* "The unknowing motorist whose car won't shift or shifts badly can easily believe that his car is in need of $250 to $600 worth of repairs, though the problem may actually be minor." Conversely, however, the complexity of transmission systems presented acute difficulties for mechanics who had to produce honest estimates before probing for problem areas among many interrelated parts.

Current Conditions

The automobile repair and service industry had a total revenue of $69.6 billion in 1998, while the automobile transmission repair sector accounted for $2.9 billion of the market.

In 1997, there were a total of 6,768 establishments performing automotive transmission repairs, an increase of nearly 12 percent over an estimated 6,060 in 1996.

By the mid-1990s, automatic transmissions appeared in more than 85 percent of new American cars, although a gasoline price spike could again bring manual transmissions back into fashion as they were in the 1970s. While the new automatics of the late 1990s were smoother shifting and more fuel-efficient than their predecessors, manuals were still more fuel-efficient than even the best automatic.

Industry Leaders

In 1999 the leader in automotive transmission repair was AAMCO Transmissions Inc., a franchise with $40.9 million in sales and 225 employees. AAMCO was rated as the ninth largest franchise in the United States by the *1999 Business Rankings Annual.*

Workforce

Transmission specialists were generally regarded as among the most extensively trained and knowledgeable of all automotive mechanics. To perform their job adequately, they needed to be familiar with all features of transmission technology, including electronic, hydraulic, and computer systems. In addition, they had to understand automotive fundamentals outside their chosen area of expertise in order to distinguish between transmission-related problems and those stemming from some other source. In fact, transmission specialists had to achieve much the same level of coverage as National Institute for Automotive Service Excellence (NAISE or ASE) certified "master mechanics" in order to perform repairs on what was arguably the most sensitive and complicated area of an automobile.

The many interrelated components of a transmission, and the different technologies regulating their functioning (hydraulics, electronics, and computers, for instance), means that transmission specialists have to be able to wield a wide variety of tools, including micrometers and telescoping gauges, special pullers, electronic stethoscopes, and transmission jacks. Transmission repair experts also face a variety of dangers on the job, from the weight and bulk of transmissions, the hot transmission fluid, and the asbestos from which clutch disc linings or friction material is made.

Approximately 29,500 employees worked in this industry in 1997. This was a substantial 19 percent increase from 1993's 24,800 employees. Total payroll in this industry reached over $709 million.

AMERICA AND THE WORLD

Transmission specialists outside the United States were likely to encounter a significantly higher proportion of manual transmissions than their American counterparts. In addition, one important new design concept seen in some foreign cars was the continuously variable transmission (CVT), which featured an infinite number of driving ratios rather than the three, four, or five forward speeds found in traditional types. As James E. Duffy explained in *Modern Automotive Mechanics*, the CVT was ''capable of increasing fuel economy approximately 25 percent because it keeps the engine at its most efficient operating speed. Engine RPM can be kept relatively constant. The engine does NOT have to accelerate through each gear, resulting in an almost smooth increase in vehicle speed.'' In the late 1990s, automatic transmissions were beginning to make some headway in Europe, where most drivers still preferred manuals. But a new generation of high-tech, smoother shifting and more fuel-efficient automatics—not to mention congested roadways that make frequent shifting a hassle—has made the automatic transmission more popular overseas.

RESEARCH AND TECHNOLOGY

Key areas of concern for the U.S. automotive industry in the 1990s included the wider use of electronics in conventional vehicles and the development of electric cars. As a result, transmission repair shops prepared themselves to work on increasingly sophisticated systems. As Stephen Plumb explained in *Ward's Automotive Yearbook 1993*, ''In 1991, electronic transmissions accounted for less than 20 percent of all gearboxes installed on domestically produced cars. This figure is expected to rise to over 80 percent by the late 1990s, which means virtually all automatic transaxles will be electronically controlled. Electronic transmissions help improve drivability, shift smoothness, and fuel economy.'' Plumb's estimate was not far from reality. In 1997, one car in nine came with a stick shift—most being sportscars and ultra-economy compacts. And for the manual-shift enthusiasts who wanted the best of both worlds, in 1996 Chrysler introduced the Autostick, a transmission that's part automatic and part manual. It had no clutch, but drivers could drop the shifter out of automatic and change gears.

FURTHER READING

1999 Business Rankings Annual. Farmington Hills: The Gale Group, 1999.

AAMCO Website. Available from http://www.aamco.com.

D & B Business Rankings 1999. Bethlehem: Dun & Bradstreet, 1999.

Darney, Arsen J. ed. *Service Industries USA.* Detroit: Gale Research, 1995.

Duffy, James E. *Modern Automotive Mechanics.* South Holland, IL: Goodheart-Willcox, 1990.

Glickman, Arthur P. *Mr. Badwrench.* New York: Seaview Books, 1981.

McGinn, Daniel. ''Death of the Stick?'' Newsweek, 14 October 1996.

Plumb, Stephen. ''Vehicle Electronics Set to Blast Off.'' *Ward's Automotive Yearbook 1993,* Ward's Communications, 1993.

U.S. Census Bureau. U.S. Department of Commerce. *1997 Economic Census.* Washington, D.C.: GPO, 1999.

———. *County Business Patterns.* Washington, D.C.: GPO, 1995.

———. *Service Annual Survey: 1995.* Washington, D.C.: GPO, 1995.

SIC 7538

GENERAL AUTOMOTIVE REPAIR SHOPS

This category covers establishments primarily engaged in general automotive repair, including those specifically engaged in repairing engines. Establishments primarily engaged in industrial truck repair are covered in **SIC 7699: Repair Shops and Related Services, Not Elsewhere Classified.**

NAICS CODE(S)

811111 (General Automotive Repair)

INDUSTRY SNAPSHOT

The general automotive repair industry, once dominated by small, independent service stations offering personal attention, evolved toward heated competition between manufacturers, dealer networks and large, chain service centers. The rapidly increasing complexity of vehicles in the mid-1990s led to greater specialization among automotive mechanics. In some cases, however, the abundance of electronic engine components facilitated the diagnosis of problems.

ORGANIZATION AND STRUCTURE

Four types of businesses in the United States offered general automotive repair services: full-service gasoline stations, independent garages, automotive dealerships, and chain automotive centers. In the mid-1990s, full-service gasoline stations and independent garages experienced a decline due to the trend toward specialization in automotive mechanics and the competition offered by automotive dealerships and chain automotive centers. Results of a study conducted by Lang Marketing Resources, Inc., a consulting and analysis firm, showed a decrease in the service station and garage population from 227,000 to 155,000 between 1980 and 1996. Many of those stations were light vehicle repair locations. The Lang study showed that in 1980, they installed nearly half of the aftermarket products in the United States, but by 1996, these service stations and garages installed only 35 percent of the product volume. According to the 1998 Statistical Abstract of the United States provided by the U.S. Census, the number of automotive repair services had risen to 192,000 by 1997.

Some owners of independent service stations complained that auto manufacturers reduced the repair options available to consumers by limiting availability of factory manuals and instruction to their own dealer networks. Other concerns about dealer repair centers focused on the expense of parts and repairs, as well as the conflict of interest involved when the same companies that sold new vehicles also provided most repairs. On the positive side, dealerships did offer a greater number of specialists with up-to-date training than most independent repair shops.

Because of their size, chain automotive centers garnered high levels of general automotive repair business and typically charged lower rates than dealerships. In the absence of any comprehensive regulatory standards, they also appealed to consumers because of their name recognition. Disturbingly, however, there were numerous cases where such centers were found guilty of undertaking unnecessary repairs, and even of punishing employees who failed to maintain a set sales target for parts and service. In his book, *Mr. Badwrench,* Arthur P. Glickman quoted a study conducted at the University of Alabama at Huntsville in 1972 that found five major chains guilty of unnecessary repairs ranging from 22 percent to 47 percent of the total number performed. Similarly, in 1993 both Sears and Kmart faced charges of making unnecessary repairs in their automotive service centers. Problems of this nature continued to arise with other companies through the late-1990s.

In a 1995 independent study conducted by Wiese Research Associates, Inc., independent neighborhood automotive repair shops scored higher than all other automotive service centers in five out of seven categories. They rated highest in the categories of honesty/integrity, pricing fairness, responsiveness, answer questions, and friendliness. The categories receiving lower ratings than the other shops were cleanliness/appearance, and management.

By 1997 had become apparent that automotive dealers and service stations had addressed customer service issues. In a survey conducted by Medical Economics, independent service facilities ranked seventh in customer satisfaction—behind Lexis and Infiniti, Saturn Corp., Shell Oil Co., Audi, Acura, Mobil, and Buick.

Common performance problems addressed by engine repair mechanics were no-start, hard starting, stalling, misfiring, vacuum leak, hesitation, surging, backfiring, run-on, pinging, vapor lock, gas line freeze, poor fuel economy, and lack of engine power. In many cases, these problems were easy to identify but hard to diagnose, given the wide range of causes that led to them.

Engine analyzers typically combined methods of checking the battery, charging, and starting systems, ignition systems, engine condition, fuel systems, and emission control systems into one unit. Alternatively, engine repair mechanics tested facets of engine performance with dozens of specialized instruments, including tachdwell meters, exhaust gas analyzers, and volt-ohm-milliammeters.

The performance of tune-ups was necessary in the case of gasoline engines to limit exhaust pollution and to maintain engine power and acceleration, economical fuel consumption, smoothness of engine operation, ease of starting, and engine service life. Diesel engines did not require the same level of tune-ups because they did not contain spark plugs or an ignition system.

Common mechanical problems addressed in engine repairs included leaking gaskets, worn piston rings, burned and leaking valves, loose or worn engine bearings, worn timing chains, and cracked, broken, or scored engine parts. Stethoscopes aided in the detection of abnormal noises. Color of exhaust smoke was often useful in diagnosis, as well. But mechanics above all had to refer to service manual troubleshooting charts covering specific makes and models of engines.

Background and Development

The earliest automobiles were driven by wealthy enthusiasts who could either perform their own repairs or afford to employ a personal mechanic. The advent of the affordable, mass-production, assembly-line automobile created many more drivers, but was based on a simple design and required easy repairs. As the number of drivers and roads in the United States grew, and as vehicles became more varied and complex, gasoline stations offering not only fuel but also routine maintenance and repair services proliferated. These full-service gasoline stations were augmented by independent garages capable of working on more difficult mechanical problems.

At this stage, the United States enjoyed what many analysts of the automotive repair industry described as a golden age. Full-service gasoline stations offered an ideal mode of apprenticeship for would-be mechanics who learned on the job as they went from pumping fuel to routine maintenance and repairs. However, oil companies began replacing full-service, independent gasoline stations with their own self-service stations offering no repairs. Consumers welcomed the cheaper fuel prices, even if they did not fully appreciate what they lost in terms of personal service.

In the late 1980s, smaller operations were also threatened by environmental legislation dictating insurance coverage for possible leaks in underground gasoline storage tanks and replacement of old units. The industry also anticipated further, expensive renovations to accompany the increasing emphasis on alternative fuels causing less damage to the environment. However, some small service stations planned to retain their repair facilities even if they were forced to discontinue selling fuel.

CURRENT CONDITIONS

According to the National Automobile Dealers Association (NADA) the service and parts department in the average franchised car dealership reported $2,676,572 in revenue during 1996, a 10 percent increase in dollar sales over sales in 1995, and an increase profit margin to 5.9 percent from 5.3 percent in the previous year. In a survey conducted by AutoInc. Magazine, ''37 percent of responding Automotive Service Association (ASA) mechanical repair shops listed total annual revenue in 1996 as between $250,000 and $500,000; 17 percent indicated between $500,000 and $750,000; 15 percent were from $100,000 to $250,000; and 14 percent listed between $750,000 and $1 million. Eleven percent showed revenues greater than $1 million.''

INDUSTRY LEADERS

The most successful automotive repair shops during the late-1990s were dealerships and franchises. Among the leaders at this time were Jiffy Lube International, Inc.—ranked as the fifth most successful franchise of 1998 by Entrepreneur Magazine—with 1390 franchises nationwide; AAMCO Transmissions, Inc.; Speedy Transmissions Centers; Group 1 Automotive; and United Auto Group.

WORKFORCE

A 1999 survey conducted by Cahners Research for ABRN Magazine of 2000 automotive repair shops (1800 independent franchises, 200 dealerships) indicated that the average hourly rate for frame/structural services was $40.60 per hour for frame/structural services, while $46.70 per hour was the average charged for mechanical services.

According to the survey, $44,378.50 was the average starting base salary for a shop owner. The salary for foreman/managers began at $34,744.10. Thirty-percent of Foremen/Managers were between 41 and 45 years of age, while the average shop owner was 45.6 years old.

Approximately half of the repair shops surveyed employed between four and seven body repair technicians and painters. Approximately half of shop owners paid employees an hourly rate—the average shop paid $19.50 per hour for paint labor, $19.90 per hour for collision labor, and $21.90 per hour for mechanical labor. Technicians were provided an additional commission by over one-third of these shops. Four out of seven shop owners provided employees with a raise in 1998; the average increase was 4.5 percent. A majority of these shops also offered paid vacations and company-paid training.

The number of jobs available for automotive mechanics was anticipated to increase through the year 2005 at about the average rate for all occupations, with continued declines in employment at full-service gasoline stations balanced by growth in employment at dealerships and elsewhere. This growth was attributed in part to the increasing average age of automobiles. With the aging of the vehicle comes the need for service and repairs. The average age of cars in the U.S increased to 7.8 years old in the mid-1990s from 5 years old in 1970.

Mechanics engaged in general automotive repairs had to wield a variety of tools, and to work methodically through a checklist of important parts to isolate a problem area or to guarantee that all areas of an automobile were being adequately maintained. Working conditions varied from business to business, but in general much of the work performed was necessarily dirty, greasy, and uncomfortable, with strenuous lifting of heavy equipment often required and minor injuries common.

Whereas automotive electronics and electrical systems had once been the province of specialists, by the late-1990s they had become so much a feature of automotive design that mechanics in general had to become increasingly familiar with them. As a result, employment opportunities favored those mechanics who had completed some training in the area of electronics. The overall trend toward heightened technological complexity also stressed the need for greater levels of training and made specialization an increasingly probable step for mechanics.

AMERICA AND THE WORLD

The lack of regulation involved in the performance of automotive repair and maintenance in the United States, especially compared to the stringent standards enforced in other parts of the world, drew harsh criticism from some analysts. For instance, Monty Norris observed in *Auto Repair Frauds* that, ''In Europe and Canada, all mechanics must complete a rigorous training program, pass tough exams, and serve under a certified mechanic from three to five years. No one is permitted to serve as an auto mechanic without earning either an A, B, or C certificate issued by the automobile trade governing body. . . . The result is a highly respected trade of skilled repairmen—in sharp contrast to the many blundering parts changers that dominate the industry here.'' These differences generally became less extreme by the late-1990s, as increased automotive complexity led to demand for skilled mechanics worldwide.

Research and Technology

With fuel economy and environmental concerns of paramount importance to the automotive industry, engine repair specialists expected changes in engine design, with a particular emphasis on new technologies taking advantage of alternative fuels. The overall increasing sophistication of all areas of automotive design had mixed consequences for automotive mechanics. New technologies made available a variety of electronic and computer systems for increasingly swift and accurate measurement of aspects of automotive performance, which facilitated the diagnosis of problems. On the other hand, the growing importance of electronic and computer systems in the actual running of most parts of a vehicle ensured that mechanics would need to become ever more highly skilled and specialized.

Further Reading

AutoInc. Magazine, 2000. Available from http://www.autoinc.org/.

Automotive Service Association. ''AutoInc. Stat Corner.'' July 1996. Available from: http://www.asashop.org.

Cahners Research. ''Career Survey'' June 1999. Available from http://www.abrn.com/.

Glickman, Arthur P. *Mr. Badwrench.* New York: Seaview Books, 1981.

''Occupational Outlook Handbook: 1996-1997.'' U.S. Department of Labor. Bureau of Labor Statistics. Available from http://stats.bls.gov/oco/ocos181.htm.

SIC 7539

AUTOMOTIVE REPAIR SHOPS, NOT ELSEWHERE CLASSIFIED

This category covers businesses that primarily do specialized automotive repair, not elsewhere classified, such as fuel service (carburetor repair), brake relining, front-end and wheel alignment, and radiator repair. Businesses that primarily do automotive welding are in **SIC 7692: Welding Repair.**

NAICS Code(s)

811118 (Other Automotive Mechanical and Electrical Repair and Maintenance)

Miscellaneous services done by automotive repair shops included automotive tune-ups, automotive electrical repair, battery and ignition repair, fuel system conversion, generator and starter repair, and brake work. This broad classification had 9,674 businesses in 1997, many of which were sole proprietorships or partnerships. These shops employed 42,234 people and had annual sales of nearly $3.5 billion in 1997.

As cars became a staple of American life during the mid-1900s, demand for specialized repair services rose. When annual car sales peaked at about 11.5 million annually in the late 1980s, repair shop revenues in this industry reached $2.23 billion in 1987 and industry employment swelled to 40,302. Although most automotive-related industries suffered during the U.S. recession in the late 1980s and early 1990s, repair shops were less affected. As consumers put off buying new cars, they spent more on maintenance and repair, so the industry's sales remained steady. Automotive repair services benefited from the mid-1990s economic recovery as well.

Industry firms generated average revenues of $10 million during 1990s. The majority of shops were local and privately owned, but there also were regional chains that surpassed that median, such as Brake Centers of the Southwest, which had sales of $34.1 million and had 550 employees. In addition, there were industry giants, (many of which were franchises) that generated hundreds of millions of dollars in income, such as Monro Muffler Brake, a Rochester-based company that employed more than 2,100 people and earned $193 million in 1997. Several of these industry giants had products and services that crossed over into other business categories, such as Pep Boys, which offered not only automotive repair services, but also sold auto parts. Pep Boys had sales of $2.3 billion and employed more than 27,000 people in the late 1990s.

Automotive repair jobs were expected to rise at the same rate as the average for all occupations through 2006, according to the Department of Labor. New job openings for mechanics, however, would most likely be filled by technicians with advanced technical or vocational training—especially those with knowledge of electronics and emissions control equipment. Competition would be more intense for entry-level positions.

More than 100 community colleges offered two-year degrees sponsored by the major automobile makers. In addition, the National Automotive Technicians Education Foundation (NATEF) certified quality training programs offered by high schools and technical schools. In the mid-1990s, mechanics earned a median income between $333 and $667 weekly. Less-skilled mechanics earned less than $250 per week. Master mechanics can earn between $70,000-$100,000 annually.

FURTHER READING

Dun & Bradstreet Directory of Service Companies 2000. Murray Hill, NJ: 1999.

Information Please Almanac. Boston: Houghton Mifflin, 1993.

U.S. Department of Commerce. *1997 Census of Service Industries & Geographic Area Series.* Washington, D.C.: Bureau of the Census, 1999.

U.S. Department of Commerce. U.S. Census Bureau. *1997 NAICS Definitions.* Available from http://www.census.gov/epcd/naics/NDEF811.htm.

U.S. Department of Labor. *Occupational Outlook Handbook, 1998-1999 Edition.* Washington, D.C.: GPO, 1999.

SIC 7542

CARWASHES

This category covers establishments primarily engaged in washing, waxing, and polishing motor vehicles (including automobiles, trucks, and buses), or in furnishing facilities for the self-service washing of such vehicles.

NAICS CODE(S)

811192 (Car Washes)

INDUSTRY SNAPSHOT

An estimated 97 percent of Americans take their automobiles to commercial carwashes. In 1998, the International Car Wash Association estimated that there were 9,570 full-service carwashes in North America, approximately 4,546 exterior-only carwashes, nearly 30,000 self-service carwashes, and about 30,000 rollover/high pressure washes, the majority of these being affiliated with gas stations or convenience stores. Together these carwashes generated more than $14 billion in annual revenue.

The carwash industry grew rapidly from 1977 to 1987, but its growth began to slow in the decade following 1987. In 1977 there were 5,785 carwash establishments nationwide classified in SIC 7542. It was a business oriented to small-scale proprietors: these establishments were owned by 5,290 firms, of which 5,091 operated only one carwash. Approximately 45 percent were incorporated, another 42 percent owned by individual proprietors, and just 3 percent by partnerships. The total receipts for carwash establishments nationwide came to $668.6 million in 1997. Forty-two out of 5,290 carwash firms and 243 out of 5,785 carwash establishments reported annual receipts of $1 million or more.

Just ten years later, there were 9,132 commercial carwash establishments nationwide, an increase of almost 60 percent. The proportion of incorporated establishments had risen to just over 50 percent (but still a low figure for the service industries as a whole, in which 60 percent of all establishments were incorporated). The number of sole proprietors had dropped to 37 percent (compared to 32 percent for all service industries), and partnerships had jumped to almost 13 percent, nearly double the overall service industry figure of 7.3 percent. The total national revenues for the carwash sector had reached $1.8 billion, with California and Texas together representing more than one-quarter of nationwide revenue. Nationally, the average revenues per establishment were just over $197,000 a year (only 34 percent of the average for the service industry as a whole.) But because carwashes tended to be less labor-intensive than many other service industries, average revenues per employee for carwash establishments ($23,534) were slightly more than 50 percent of the service industry average.

In 1992, the number of carwash establishments in the nation had risen to 11,589, an increase of 27 percent. This indicated a slight leveling off in the rate of increase compared to the 1977 to 1987 period. The proportion of incorporated establishments had increased to 56 percent while the service industry average remained at 60 percent; individual proprietorships had dropped another two points, to 35 percent (slightly more than the service industry average), and partnerships accounted for only 9 percent. The leading state in the nation remained California (1,408 establishments), followed by Texas and New York. National revenues had increased by 47 percent to $2.64 billion, or $228,158 per establishment; but this was still only about 35 percent of the service industry average. Revenues per employee had increased by 21 percent, to $28,407; a mere 46 percent of the industry average.

The carwash industry is heavily affected by such issues as weather, climate, and time of day. A May 1996 survey by *Auto Laundry News* reported that Saturday was overwhelmingly the best day for business, with an 82 percent vote. February, with 19 percent, was chosen the best month of the year, and November (0.5 percent) the worst. Not only did carwash owners have a favorite season (winter, with more than half the votes, as opposed to fall, with only 3 percent), they even had a favorite time of day. Just over 40 percent of respondents said the majority of their business was conducted between 1:00 and 3:00 p.m.

ORGANIZATION AND STRUCTURE

The carwash segment of the SIC 7540 industry group (which also includes Automotive Services, Except Repair) covers commercial establishments primarily offering car washing; car cleaning, polishing, and detailing; and bus and/or truck washing. These services are provided both to private individuals and to automotive dealers, automobile rental establishments, automobile fleet owners, and other businesses. Although carwash establishments may offer a combination of facilities and options, carwashes generally can be classified as coin-operated, self-service facilities, automatic facilities, full-service conveyorized facilities, or automobile detailers.

Coin-Operated Self-Service Facilities. In these self-service facilities, which generally do not require full-time supervision, customers clean their cars in drive-through bays equipped with ''wand'' type high-pressure spray nozzles and other car-cleaning accessories. Coin-activated controls determine the length of spray nozzle operation and allow the customer to switch among presoak; engine cleaning; tire cleaning; and foam, rinse, and wax sprays. In addition, these facilities generally provide coin-operated vacuums for the cleaning of car interiors and may have car care products such as towels and polishes available though coin-operated dispensers. In 1996, an average customer spent $1.50 for a five-minute cycle at a coin-operated self-service carwash. In 1998, average in-bay pricing for a self-serve carwash was about 32 cents per minute. The typical self-service carwash bay grossed $1,100 per month. Of the 98 percent of self-serves that had vacuums on the premises, the average monthly revenue per vacuum was $169. The average self-serve location has 5.4 vacuums.

Automatic Facilities. Like self-service washes, automatic facilities do not require full-time supervision, and they can service approximately 20 vehicles an hour. Here customers activate the automatic system by driving their cars onto platforms within open-ended bays. Rollover carwashes are based on guide wheels that follow a vehicle's contours with horizontal overhead brushes and vertical ''wraparound'' brushes that clean the car in presoak, undercarriage, foam, rinse, and wax spray cycles, followed by a hot-air dryer. Customer concerns about vehicle and paint finish damage have led to the development of ''brushless'' soft-cloth systems, and subsequently to the marketing of ''frictionless'' spray-only systems controlled by electric eyes and robotics technology. Like self-service facilities, automatic carwashes generally provide coin-operated vacuums for the cleaning of car interiors. In 1996, the average cost of a basic automatic carwash (as opposed to one offering extra cycles) was $3.40.

Full-Service Conveyor Facilities. Full-service facilities not only require more space than self-service or automatic systems, they are also more labor-intensive. In these facilities, full-time workers service 60 or more cars per hour as an automatic conveyor carries the vehicle through an open-ended service tunnel. In 1990, the International Car Wash Association reported that among full-service conveyorized facilities, 59 percent used cloth-only systems, 20 percent used friction/frictionless wash combinations, and 8 percent used frictionless washes only. On-line services typically provided by conveyorized facilities include exterior wash, rust-inhibiting undercarriage wash, tire and whitewall cleaning, various waxing options, and the scenting of interior air. Off-line services typically include cleaning and polishing of exterior and interior vinyl and leather, shampooing of carpet and upholstery, cleaning floor mats, cleaning ashtrays, cleaning the engine, and applying a polymer protectant. In the early 1990s, the typical cost of a customized car cleaning package at a full-service conveyorized system was approximately $30. In 1998, a full-serve carwash had an average wash volume of 65,113 vehicles. The average 1998 price for a full-service wash was $9.93. The average gross revenue per car was $11.21. The average gross income for a full-service carwash is approximately $730,000. Meanwhile, the average annual operating costs were $527,900, of which 46 percent was on-line labor costs.

Automobile Detailers. In these facilities, the focus is on manual cleaning of cars both inside and out, using hoses and brushes as well as hand-held tools rather than high-technology carwashing equipment. The ''detailing'' of an automobile is an exhaustive process. A September 1993 *Harper's* magazine article described detailing as the ''cleaning of a car beyond all reason.'' In addition to essentially manual versions of the on-line and off-line services provided by full-service conveyorized systems, detailing operations focus on such car parts as hood interiors and spare tires and on ''details'' such as shining the interior of gas caps and dusting the spaces between radio buttons. In 1996 the typical cost for detailing was $131.10 for complete interior/exterior services.

The cost of carwash equipment may vary regionally, based on such factors as water availability and water quality and area soils or pollutants. According to the International Carwash Association, in 1998, annual operating costs for a five-bay self-service carwash were $56,500, whereas the cost of operating a full-service wash were more than ten times as much, or $527,900. The leading professional trade organization was the 5,000-member International Carwash Association, which publishes a semiannual directory and a monthly management report both in print and on the Internet. Chief among industry trade publications was *Professional Carwashing and Detailing.*

Background and Development

An article in a 1923 edition of *Literary Digest* discussed the ''first automobile wash-bowl that has been built in this country,'' a carwash located in St. Paul, Minnesota. For this three-minute carwash, ''the owner drives his car in and around the bowl until he is satisfied that the mud has been cleaned from the chassis and wheels . . . at the exit door there is a spray with forced water which cleans the body . . . an electric drier completes the job.'' Three years later the same magazine described a seven-minute ''Automobile Laundry,'' a carwash relying on two pitmen; hoses of hot, cold, and soapy water for car exteriors; and a compressed air hose for car interiors. The article predicted that the carwash would become ''one of the largest specialized industries in the country.''

The modern carwash industry began in 1946 in Detroit with the opening of Paul's Auto-Matic Car Wash, the ''first automatic autowash in the world.'' The establishment was a conveyor-style carwash in which the car was pulled through by a moving chain. Twelve years later the first full-service Jax Kar Wash opened in Detroit. This pioneering operation serviced 280,000 cars in its first year of business. Coin-operated self-service facilities and automatic rollover carwashes emerged in subsequent decades.

In the early 1990s, the carwash industry was in a dynamic phase. Important trends in the carwash industry included a customer preference for soft cloth or frictionless carwashes over automatic brush rollovers and the emergence of detailing operations and growth in the high-quality carwash segment. The adoption of sophisticated computer software for business planning, customer service, and bookkeeping needs, and an industry focus on environmental issues were other important trends.

At the beginning of the 1990s, *Forbes* magazine had described carwashes as ''one of the largest small businesses in the United States and one that's growing at five to ten percent a year.'' But conditions began to change by the latter part of the decade, and while the industry continued to grow at a rate of six percent, new forces—particularly environmental laws and competition from service stations offering free carwashes with a fill-up—had begun to encroach.

CURRENT CONDITIONS

States and communities have passed sewage, water conservation, and water reclamation codes that affect or are directed at commercial carwash establishments, and individual businesses are increasingly turning to a combination of fresh and reclaimed water in the operation of their car cleaning systems. In addition, the federal Environmental Protection Agency has begun to regulate the underground tank storage systems and to analyze the chemicals, detergents, and wax products used by the carwash industry.

Establishments in this industry sector have also faced increasing competition from service stations, convenience stores, and other facilities that offer washes as one of several on-site profit centers. Some of these utilize innovative technology such as a television, which customers view while pumping gas. On the screen they see an advertisement for a carwash, which they can purchase when they pay for their fuel. Others give away free washes with a gas fill-up.

INDUSTRY LEADERS

The leading carwash chains, as reported in *Ward's Business Directory of U.S. Private and Public Companies* (1997) are National Pride Car Wash Systems, based in Forth Worth, Texas; Stanton Corp. of Virginia Beach, Virginia; Buffs-N-Puffs Ltd. of Murray, Utah; Hollingshead Industries Inc. of Sacramento, California; and Wash on Wheels Inc. of Sanford, Florida. Other national leaders included Tankar Stations, McKinley Car Wash, Car Salon Inc., White Glove Automatic Care Inc., and Gateway Waterworks Inc.

WORKFORCE

Employees of the carwash industry include vehicle washers; equipment operators and maintenance workers; secretaries, bookkeepers, and general office clerks; cashiers; and laborers and helpers. In the early 1990s, ''revolving door'' workers became an industry concern, in part due to the negative impact of employee turnover on customer service. This concern has prompted more careful hiring and training of employees and the implementation of incentive and commission programs, particularly in full-service conveyorized carwashes and in automobile detailing operations.

FURTHER READING

Abcede, Angel. ''Automation Links Up Car Washes.'' *National Petroleum News,* June 1995.

———. ''Car Wash Owners Seek Edge as Competition Heats Up.'' *National Petroleum News,* January 1995.

''The Flivver's Bathtub.'' *Literary Digest,* 13 January 1923.

''International Carwash Association Start-up Kit.'' Chicago, IL: International Carwash Association, 1996.

SIC 7549

AUTOMOTIVE SERVICES, EXCEPT REPAIR AND CARWASHES

This category covers establishments primarily engaged in furnishing automotive services, except repair and carwashes. Establishments primarily providing automobile driving instructions are classified in **SIC 8299: Schools and Educational Services, Not Elsewhere Classified.**

NAICS Code(s)

811191 (Automotive Oil Change and Lubrication Shops)
488410 (Motor Vehicle Towing)
811198 (All Other Automotive Repair and Maintenance)

Examples of miscellaneous automotive service providers include emissions testing centers, inspection services, do-it-yourself garages, diagnostic centers, lubricating and oil change shops, emergency road services, rustproofers, window tinting shops, and towing services. The industry consisted mostly of small repair shops. The average number of employees per establishment, for example, was 6 in the mid-1990s, while the average for all service industries was 13. In addition, only the top 10 companies in the industry generated annual revenues of more than $10 million. The majority of establishments within this classification had sales that fell within the $100,000 to $249,000 range.

The automotive services industry grew out of America's love affair with the automobile. Immediately after Henry Ford's introduction of the Model T in 1905, car sales boomed. From just 2.2 million in 1920, annual automobile production rocketed to more than 8 million by 1950. As auto output fluctuated around 8 million annually throughout the mid-1900s, the automotive services industry ballooned. Importantly, federal safety and emissions regulations developed in the mid-1960s bolstered demand. By the early 1990s, the miscellaneous auto services industry generated $3.4 billion in revenues each year and employed 67,400 workers. By 1996, revenues and employment were expected to reach almost $4.4 billion and 86,300 workers, respectively.

Demand for miscellaneous automotive services expanded during the 1980s, due to a surge in car sales to almost 11.5 million per year in 1986 and 1987. Furthermore, the rapid proliferation of quick and convenient oil change and lubrication shops allowed the industry to encroach on traditional service stations.

A U.S. recession in the late 1980s and early 1990s hampered growth in most segments of the industry. Markets for some fast-growth services, such as quick oil changes and window tinting, became saturated. Nevertheless, the demand for general automotive services was forecast to rise in the 1990s and early 2000s. The U.S. Environmental Protection Agency significantly boosted local demand for services with its IM 240 emissions testing legislation, even though many states resisted its regulations.

The largest company in the industry in 1999 remained Envirotest Systems Corp. of Phoenix, Arizona, with assets of $141 million. Other industry leaders included Q Lube, Industrial Powder Coatings, Interstate national Dealer Services, Inc. and Grease Monkey.

Job prospects for miscellaneous automotive service providers were promising going into the late 1990s. In fact, most occupations were expected to increase by over 40 percent between 1990 and 2005, according to the U.S. Bureau of Labor Statistics. Positions for coating and decorating workers, for example, appeared likely to rise by about 30 percent. Jobs for miscellaneous mechanics were anticipated to jump by about 50 percent. Wages in this industry, however, were low in relation to most other service industries, including automobile-related sectors. Because most positions required a relatively low level of skill and training, the average industry employee earned about 72 percent as much as the average service industry worker in the early 1990s.

Further Reading

Dun's Census of American Business 1996. Bethlehem, PA: Dun & Bradstreet, Inc., 1996.

Dun's Census of American Business 1997. Parsippany, NJ: Dun & Bradstreet, 1997.

Occupational Outlook Handbook. Washington: U.S. Department of Labor, 1992.

Service Industries USA. Detroit: Gale Research, 1996.

Ward's Business Directory of U.S. Private and Public Companies, 1999. Detroit: Gale Research, 1999.

SIC 7622

RADIO AND TELEVISION REPAIR SHOPS

This classification covers establishments primarily engaged in repairing radios, televisions, phonographs, stereo equipment, and tape recorders. Also included are establishments engaged in installing and repairing television, amateur, and citizens' band antennas, or in installing and servicing radio transmitting and receiving equipment in homes, offices, boats, automobiles, or other vehicles. Establishments primarily engaged in installation, repair, or maintenance of radio and television broadcast transmitting antennas and towers are classified elsewhere.

NAICS Code(s)

811211 (Consumer Electronics Repair and Maintenance)
811213 (Communication Equipment Repair and Maintenance)
443112 (Radio, Television and Other Electronic Stores)

Industry Snapshot

Television and radio repair in the United States is performed by many service centers operated by the manufacturers of electronic equipment or by appliance, department, electronics, or specialty stores. Only about 25 percent of the firms participating in the industry are independent repair shops; for government classification purposes, only the independents are considered part of this industry.

The radio repair segment of the industry has diminished significantly as technology has changed. However, when the industry emerged in the 1930s, radios were the only consumer electronic equipment requiring servicing. All that changed as broadcasting came into its own and households acquired television receivers. Depending on their area of specialization, establishments classified under the radio and television repair shops category install and service household and citizens' band (CB) antennas; they also repair aircraft radio equipment, automotive radios, intercommunications equipment, stereos, hi-fi's, tape recorders, phonographs, compact disc players, digital video disc players, public address systems, stereophonic equipment, electronic organs, home security systems, microwave ovens, slide and motion picture projectors, and video recorders or players.

In 1998, there were an estimated 4,678 establishments in this industry. About half of the establishments were corporate entities and half sole proprietors/partnerships. The establishments were concentrated in the Northeast, Southeast, and Great Lakes regions of the United States. The top seven companies by sales in 1998 were: ABC Appliance Inc., Contec L. P., Electra-Sound Inc., Technicar Inc, Markey's Audio-Visual Inc., Audiovisual Inc., and Electronic Maintenance. According to the U.S. Census Bureau, collectively all firms in the industry brought in $2.8 billion in 1998.

BACKGROUND AND DEVELOPMENT

Principles discovered in the nineteenth century were the basis for the wizardry of current audio and video home and mobile electronics. Heinrich Geissler first demonstrated in the 1850s that electricity discharged in a vacuum tube caused small amounts of rare gases in the tube to glow. In 1898, Karl Braun produced the first cathode ray tube that could control the glow caused by the freeing of electrons in a vacuum. In 1907, Lee De Forest, known as the father of radio, developed the first amplifying tube capable of strengthening electronic signals.

A few more years would elapse before new developments would make it possible to combine the basic elements of television transmission into a system. In 1922, teenager Philo Farnsworth developed a practical electronic scanning system. The following year, Vladimir Zworykin developed the iconoscope and kinescope, which are the respective basic elements of the television camera and the television receiver. The first public demonstration of Zworykin's all-electronic television system was in 1929.

Radio also developed from technology discovered in the 1800s and gradually perfected in the twentieth century. The infant radio and television medium did not develop enough to warrant a sales and service industry until regular commercial broadcasting began and people started to purchase receivers. Stations KDKA in Pittsburgh and WWJ in Detroit launched commercial radio broadcasting in 1920. Six stations initiated regular television broadcasting in 1946. Both broadcast industries grew rapidly, but television's growth was phenomenal. The United States had 6 million television sets by 1950 and more than 100 million by 1989. In the 1990s, almost every U.S. household had at least one television, while almost two-thirds had two or more.

The need for repair technicians was low when commercial broadcasting first hit the airwaves. Early radio sets were simple, with only a limited number of things that could fail and cause reception problems, so owners made most of their own repairs. But as new developments and improvements occurred in the broadcasting industry, the receivers became more complicated. Trade and technical institutes were founded to train technicians capable of fixing radio sets. During the Great Depression of the 1930s, a number of people seeking new careers or ways to supplement their incomes took correspondence courses in radio repair.

After World War II, trade and technical schools flourished to meet the burgeoning demand for trained television service technicians. Aided by the GI Bill's educational benefits, many ex-servicemen who had been communications or electronics technicians in the armed forces entered the field. The invention of the transistor, stereophonic sound, color television, and other innovations ensured the job security of those in the repair industry who kept current with technology. These innovations meant that only trained technicians with the proper testing equipment and tools could repair the resulting television sets, radios, and other home electronics equipment.

The number and variety of electronic devices for home and business use proliferated throughout the 1970s, 1980s, and 1990s. Miniature and super screen projection televisions, video cameras and videocassette recorders (VCRs), and other new electronics equipment sustained a continuing need for trained technicians to install, maintain, and repair what had become essential household items for most Americans.

WORKFORCE

Radio and television service technicians diagnose and repair malfunctions in electronic home entertainment equipment, including radios, television sets, stereos, VCRs, video cameras, compact disc players, audio recorders, video games, and related electronic equipment. Outside technicians make service calls on customers, while bench technicians use test equipment and hand tools in a shop setting to fix problems.

Workers in this industry use their knowledge of electrical and electronic circuits to service and install equipment. Most enter the field by graduating from an accredited technical training program and working for at least a year under shop supervision. Junior colleges and correspondence, private, and vocational schools offer training programs. In addition, technicians may learn the field through apprenticeships or on-the-job training. The latter option generally is limited to existing service shop employees who display a basic understanding of electronics. Because of the constantly changing technology of electronics devices, successful service technicians attend short courses given by manufacturers to learn about special areas and current developments.

Some 33,000 electronic home entertainment equipment repairers held jobs in the late 1990s, out of 120,800 employed in electronic repair shops. Of those, about one in seven were self-employed, more than in most other repairer occupations. The level of employment is expected to decline by the year 2006 as continuing improvements in electronic devices and advances in component technology make equipment more reliable and easier to service. Those entering the field will mainly be replacing those service technicians who transfer to other occupations.

Further Reading

Darnay, Arsen J., ed. *Service Industries USA.* Detroit: Gale Research, 1999.

U.S. Department of the Census. *Employment Statistics.* Washington: GPO, 2000. Available from http://www.census.gov.

U.S. Department of Labor. *Occupational Outlook Handbook.* Washington: GPO, 1998-99. Available from http://www.bls.gov.

SIC 7623

REFRIGERATION AND AIR-CONDITIONING SERVICE AND REPAIR SHOPS

This classification covers establishments primarily engaged in servicing and repairing household and commercial electrical refrigerators and air-conditioning and refrigeration equipment. Establishments primarily engaged in servicing and repairing gas refrigeration equipment are classified in **SIC 7699: Repair Shops and Related Services, Not Elsewhere Classified;** and those repairing automotive air-conditioning equipment are classified in **SIC 7539: Automotive Repair Shops, Not Elsewhere Classified.**

NAICS Code(s)

443111 (Household Appliance Stores)

811310 (Commercial and Industrial Machinery and Equipment (except Automotive and Electronic) Repair and Maintenance)

811412 (Appliance Repair and Maintenance)

Industry Snapshot

In the past 50 years, refrigeration and air-conditioning products have evolved from luxury items primarily offering comfort and convenience to vital components of many industries. Today, virtually every scientific and technological industry relies on cooling systems and equipment that control the temperature, humidity, air movement, and air quality of enclosed environments. Commercial, residential, and other buildings also rely on climate control systems.

Refrigeration and air-conditioning service and repair shops employ the mechanics and service technicians who keep self-contained and split-system air-conditioner units, electric refrigeration equipment, and electric refrigerators in good repair. In 1998 there were an estimated 3,658 establishments in this category. Typically these firms were small, employing an average of 6 employees and generating a total of $3 billion.

Organization and Structure

The three main employers of refrigeration and air-conditioning service and repair technicians are manufacturers of environmental control equipment; distributors or dealers who sell and service equipment; and firms involved in air-conditioning, heating, and refrigeration, among other fields. Some technicians also establish themselves as entrepreneurs, opening up their own repair businesses.

The majority of establishments operating in the refrigeration and air-conditioning service industry—some 67 percent—are corporate entities. Of the remaining establishments, 31 percent are sole proprietorships and 2 percent are partnerships. Industry establishments are located throughout the United States.

Small appliance products serviced by industry technicians include home refrigerators and freezers, room air conditioners, packaged terminal heat pumps, dehumidifiers, under-the-counter ice makers, vending machines, and drinking water coolers. Industry service technicians also work on complex customized appliances used in the chemical, pharmaceutical, petrochemical, and manufacturing industries, as well as in industrial ice machines and ice rinks.

BACKGROUND AND DEVELOPMENT

The earliest climate control systems—piped steam installed to heat factories, churches, assembly halls, and other large buildings—eventually led to ventilation systems that combined heating with circulation of fresh air. About the same time heating systems were being developed, experimentation with artificial refrigeration began. By the mid-1800s, inventors understood the principles on which mechanical refrigerators operated. Dr. John Gorrie applied those principles when he invented a cold-air machine to relieve the suffering of yellow fever patients in a Florida hospital in 1842. After the Civil War, several companies in southern states applied them in ammonia-absorption machines to make artificial ice. Still, until the early part of the twentieth century, refrigeration continued to rely on ice cut during the winter and stored for later use.

While the technology to cool and circulate air was developed by the turn of the century, nothing was known about regulating its moisture content, or humidity, until Willis Carrier carried out a scientific study on air-conditioning. In the summer of 1902, he designed the first system to control the temperature, humidity, and circulation of indoor air. Soon afterward he devised a way to cool using an artificial fog instead of coils. The two methods became the basic ones involved in all later air-conditioning equipment. Industry after industry adapted Carrier's invention for controlling humidity to their particular production purpose. Because of his pioneering research and inventions, Carrier became known as the father of air-conditioning.

In 1914, Carrier developed the first residential air-conditioning system. Seven years later he created the centrifugal refrigerating machine. This machine had a refrigerant that made it possible to produce safe, dependable, large-capacity cooling devices. By the 1930s, air-conditioning spread from industry to become common in stores, theaters, and other large buildings.

In the early days of the industry, manufacturers and distributors trained most technicians and mechanics in how to repair air-conditioning and refrigeration equipment. The equipment had limited capacity to cool and regulate air quality, and thus the systems and the skills needed to maintain them were relatively simple. Over the years the equipment became increasingly sophisticated, and the knowledge and skills required to maintain cooling systems became more specialized. Modern equipment utilizes a wide variety of synthetic refrigerants, depending on the cooling job to be done and the types of evaporators, condensers, and compressors in the system. In addition, components are being installed with microcomputer controls. Because of the high-technology aspects, modern refrigeration service and repair workers generally receive training at community colleges, vocational-technical schools, and trade associations. Preparatory courses include electronics, chemistry, physics, mathematics, drafting, and writing. According to Marvin M. Kaplan in "Keeping Cool Is Hot," females comprise up to 20 percent of training programs, and "each year, more than 30,000 new graduates are hired."

Stratospheric Ozone Protection. The biggest challenge facing refrigeration and air-conditioning service and repair technicians in the 1990s and the early part of the next century was compliance with rules and regulations governing refrigerants. During the early 1970s, scientists identified the use of chlorofluorocarbons (CFCs)—a common refrigerant—as a primary cause of the depletion of the ozone layer of the earth's atmosphere, which protects life from harmful radiation. The U.S. Environmental Protection Agency (EPA) and the Food and Drug Administration (FDA) banned the use of CFCs in all but a few essential applications in 1978.

In 1986, further research showed a connection between CFCs and global warming. Scientists also found an opening in the ozone layer over Antarctica. Recognizing the global nature of the problem, 24 nations and the European Economic Community (EEC) convened in Canada in 1987. As a result of the meeting, in 1992 most of the major CFC and HCFC (halon) producing and consuming nations signed the Montreal Protocol on Substances That Deplete the Ozone Layer. The Montreal Protocol, along with later amendments, called for a gradual reduction in worldwide consumption of eight chemicals and, ultimately, their complete phase-out. The agreement also encouraged countries to recover, recycle, and reclaim controlled refrigerants.

The United States drafted additional regulations regarding CFC and HCFC substances as part of the 1990 Amendments to the Clean Air Act. The act contained regulations affecting mechanics repairing or servicing an appliance or industrial process refrigeration. As of July 1, 1992, a service technician could not knowingly release or dispose of any substance used as a refrigerant in a manner which permitted the substance to enter the environment. Furthermore, effective November 1995, the prohibition applied to substitutes for CFCs and other banned refrigerants, unless the EPA specifically determined the substances posed no threat to the environment. By 2000, CFC production was completely banned. The penalties and fines for violating the act's provisions could be severe.

In 1993, the EPA published additional regulations for refrigerant recycling and emissions reduction. The regulations provided guidelines designed to minimize release of CFC and HCFC refrigerants into the environment during the service, maintenance, repair, and disposal of appliances. Technicians were required to follow the act's required practices and use equipment certified for the type of appliance opened for service. These guidelines applied not only to technicians, but to refrigerant reclaimers, appliance owners, and manufacturers of appliances and recycling and recovery equipment.

CURRENT CONDITIONS

Air-conditioning and refrigeration are essential in all segments of modern society. Nearly every newly built home has central air conditioning installed, and many existing buildings are retrofitted with air-conditioning equipment. Carefully controlled temperature and humidity conditions are crucial to the manufacture, transport, and storage of numerous products. Numerous chemicals, pharmaceuticals, explosives, solid state electronic devices, and oil products require refrigeration during their production. Fully 95 percent of food production depends on refrigeration, including some half-billion tons of perishable food each year. In addition, refrigeration supports surgery by safely storing drugs, blood, bone, and tissue, and by supplying clean, pure ice for such purposes as frigid anesthesia.

Each refrigeration and air-conditioning application represents a different segment of the large and very diverse service industry. Each segment requires engineers and technicians who can keep the equipment and systems operational. Opportunities for establishments that service and repair refrigeration and air-conditioning equipment should increase as the number of applications increases.

WORKFORCE

Most of the refrigeration and air-conditioning repair industry's employees worked for cooling and heating contractors. Others worked in large buildings, schools, and factories. Approximately one out of eight technicians was self-employed. The average wage was $13.95 per hour in 1999. Analysts predicted that jobs in the air-conditioning and refrigeration service field would increase into 2006.

Apprentices usually start out at half the wage rate of experienced workers. Approximately 20 percent of the technicians are union members, most belonging to the Sheet Metal Workers' International Association and the United Association of Journeymen and Apprentices of the Plumbing and Pipefitting Industry of the United States and Canada. Many employers provide such benefits as health insurance, pension plans, work-related training, uniforms, company vans, and tools.

Technicians learn the trade through technical school, apprenticeship training, or occasionally, informally on the job. Six-month to two-year programs in air-conditioning, heating, and refrigeration are offered by secondary and post-secondary technical and trade schools, junior and community colleges, and the armed forces. Besides the basics of installation, maintenance, and repair, students study theory, design, equipment construction, and electronics. Frequently sponsored by trade and union organizations, formal apprenticeship programs usually run three or four years and combine classroom instruction and on-the-job training. Those who learn the trade informally usually begin by helping an experienced technician and performing tasks that gradually become more difficult.

All technicians who purchase or handle refrigerants must pass a written certification examination administered by organizations approved by the EPA. They may become certified in three possible areas: Type I, servicing small appliances; Type II, high pressure refrigerants; and Type III, low pressure refrigerants. Some trade organizations provide training programs to prepare technicians for the examination, as well as general skills improvement training and self-study courses.

FURTHER READING

Darnay, Arsen J., ed. *Service Industries USA*. Detroit: Gale Research, 1999.

Kaplan, Marvin M. ''Keeping Cool Is Hot Work.'' *Career World,* October 1995.

U.S. Bureau of Labor Statistics. *Employment Statistics.* 2000. Available from http://www.bls.gov.

U.S. Department of Labor. ''Heating, Air-Conditioning, and Refrigeration Technicians.'' *Occupational Outlook Handbook 1998-99.* 2000. Available from http://stats.bls.gov.

———. ''Heating, Air-Conditioning, and Refrigeration Technicians.'' *Occupational Outlook Handbook 1996-97.* Washington: GPO, 1996.

SIC 7629

ELECTRICAL AND ELECTRONIC REPAIR SHOPS, NOT ELSEWHERE CLASSIFIED

This industry category includes establishments that primarily repair electrical and electronic equipment, such as electrical household appliances and electrical and electronic industrial equipment.

NAICS CODE(S)

443111 (Household Appliance Stores)
811212 (Computer and Office Machine Repair and Maintenance)
811213 (Communication Equipment Repair and Maintenance)
811219 (Other Electronic and Precision Equipment Repair and Maintenance)
811412 (Appliance Repair and Maintenance)
811211 (Consumer Electronics Repair and Maintenance)

Specialized electronic repair emerged as an industry after electrical devices appeared in the late 1800s and early 1900s. The development of electronic standards and measuring devices in the 1890s was pivotal to the industry's birth. The profusion of new electrical and electronic goods after World War II pushed miscellaneous electrical repair industry revenues to nearly $2 billion by the end of the 1970s.

Widespread semiconductor use during the 1970s and 1980s in turn expanded the use of electronics in American homes and businesses. Miniaturized electronics were integrated into traditional items, such as home appliances and razors. They also created new product categories, such as microwave ovens and fax machines. As sales of that equipment doubled to reach more than $6 billion during the late 1980s and early 1990s, demand for repair of new semiconductor manufacturing equipment went up.

The growth of new applications boosted electrical repair industry billings to about $3.5 billion by 1987—a 60 percent increase from early 1980s revenues. As sales rose in the 1980s, industry jobs went from 41,000 in 1982 to about 56,000 in the late 1980s. The number of companies in the industry expanded from 6,800 to 8,600, although a recession in the late 1980s and early 1990s stalled industry growth. Slowly recovering markets in the mid-1990s allowed many companies to boost sales and strengthen margins. In 1996, the industry as a whole had approximately 11,295 establishments and estimated revenues of $8.17 billion. In 1997, the industry had 12,490 establishments and receipts of $13.02 billion.

The leader in this sector is Sears Roebuck & Co. In 1997 Sears had a 10 percent share in the appliance/electronics repair market, with some $2 billion in revenues. Other successful companies engaged in this sector include Black and Decker Corporation's Products Service Division in Hampstead, Maryland, with 1997 sales of $172.7 million; Barfield, Inc., which repairs aircraft flight instruments, with 1997 sales of $35 million and 300 employees; and Tandy Corporation's RadioShack.

About 396,000 electronic equipment repair specialists held jobs in 1996. According to the Bureau of Labor Statistics, overall employment of these repair people was expected to grow slowly through 2006. Although demand for computer and office machine repairers, commercial and industrial electronic equipment repairers, and communications equipment mechanics is expected to expand, jobs for electronic home entertainment equipment repairers and telephone installers and repairs are forecast to plunge.

Jobs in this industry pay well compared to other service industries. The payroll per employee in the early 1990s was about $20,000 per year, compared to about $18,000 for other service sectors. In 1996, the average service technician made $9.03 to $15.48 per hour, according to a private industry survey. Most electrical repair people earned $500 to $600 per week, but these jobs required a more educated worker. Most entry-level positions required completion of a one- or two-year vocational training program, or on-the-job training in the U.S. armed forces.

FURTHER READING

Darnay, Arsen J., ed. *Service Industries USA.* Detroit: Gale Research, 1996.

Hoover's Online Company Capsules. Available from http://www.hoovers.com/.

Occupational Outlook Handbook. 1998-99. U.S. Department of Labor. Bureau of Labor Statistics. Available from http://stats/bls.gov/oco/ocos183.htm.

"Other Services (Except Public Administration)—1997 Economic Census." U.S. Department of Commerce. Bureau of the Census. December 1999. Available from http://www.census.gov/prod/ec97/97s81-us.pdf.

Service Dealer's Newsletter. 1997 Press Release Summary from The Electronics Technicians Association International.

SIC 7631

WATCH, CLOCK, AND JEWELRY REPAIR

This category covers businesses that primarily repair watches, clocks, or jewelry. Companies that primarily assemble watches from purchased parts are in **SIC 3873: Watches, Clocks, Clockwork Operated Devices, and Parts.**

NAICS CODE(S)

811490 (Other Personal and Household Goods Repair and Maintenance)

The watch, clock, and jewelry repair industry consists of a few large industry leaders and many small local shops. Most watch, clock, and jewelry repair shops are small, privately owned firms, often affiliated with local jewelry retailers. Large watch, clock, and jewelry makers may also have divisions devoted solely to repairing their products.

Watch, clock, and jewelry repair firms fix malfunctioning and broken timepieces and jewelry. The industry's repair technicians (called horologists) replace broken or worn parts mainly with factory replacement parts. Technicians are able to repair both older mechanical and newer battery-operated quartz timepieces. When working with older timepieces, however, technicians often make replacement parts themselves.

Approximately 80 percent of the watch repairers in the United States are self-employed. They operate their own repair shops or have contracts with jewelry retailers and department stores. Many new horologists found jobs with jewelry retail stores or department stores. Furthermore, many large clock, watch, and jewelry makers employed horologists in their repair departments. Most repair technicians were members of the American Watchmakers Institute, the national watch, clock, and jewelry repair trade organization.

New York City-based SMH Inc. led the industry with sales of $200 million for 1997, according to the most recent results available from Infotrac databases. That year, SMH entered into a joint agreement with Calvin Klein to manufacture CK branded watches. Second in the industry, Mayor's Jewelers Inc. of Sunrise, Florida was bought out in early 1998 by Jann Bell Marketing, which decided to retain the "Mayor" name for its subsidiary. Mayor's generated $120 million in the year before the buyout, and sales rose to $140 million for 1998, the year of the buyout.

Two Toledo companies placed third and fourth in the industry. Peoples Jewelry Company Inc. garnered revenues of $78 million for its fiscal year ended September 30, 1999, and Time Service Inc. generated sales of $20 million for its fiscal year ended August 31, 1999. S. Joseph and Sons Inc. of Des Moines, Iowa rounded out the top five industry leaders, with sales of $16.5 million for its fiscal year ended January 31, 1999.

In the early 1990s, the United States had a shortage of qualified repair technicians. Analysts estimated that nine out of ten Americans owned watches, and watch and jewelry sales rose consistently throughout the 1990s. Widespread sales of inexpensive electronic watches reduced business for repair shops, because these watches are cheaper to replace than repair. The decrease, however, has been offset by higher replacement battery sales.

Watch, clock, and jewelry repairers trained for one or two years at vocational schools, technical institutes, or junior colleges. Some states require repair technicians to be licensed. Repairers generally worked 40 to 50 hours per week and earned between $200 and $400 per week. Self-employed repairers generally worked more hours and had larger salaries.

According to U.S. government statistics, there were 1,662 businesses in this category in 1992, a tiny increase from the 1,661 in 1987. Total industry sales for 1992 were $274 million, an 18.8 percent increase from the $231 million in sales for 1987. In 1992, the industry employed 5,141 workers, with a total payroll of $78 million. According to Dun & Bradstreet's *Industry Norms,* the average watch, clock, and jewelry repair firm had total assets of $94,072, net sales of $199,043, and net profits after taxes of $21,298 in 1992.

FURTHER READING

Careers in Watch/Clock Repairing. Cincinnati, OH: American Watchmakers Institute.

Curran, Catherine. "Calvin sets watch introduction; designer in joint venture with SMH Group." *Daily News Record,* 14 July 1997.

Infotrac Company Profiles, 19 February 2000. Available from http://web4.infotrac.galegroup.com.

"Jan Bell to Acquire Mayor's, Create Two-Tier Florida Jeweler." *Knight-Ridder/Tribune Business News,* 24 February 1998.

U.S. Department of Commerce. *1992 Census of Service Industries & Geographic Area Series.* Washington: Bureau of the Census, 1995.

SIC 7641

REUPHOLSTERY AND FURNITURE REPAIR

This classification covers businesses that primarily reupholster and repair furniture. Companies that primarily sell upholstery materials for personal or household use are in **SIC 5714: Drapery, Curtain, and Upholstery Stores;** and those making furniture and cabinets on a custom basis are in **SIC 5712: Furniture Stores.**

NAICS CODE(S)

811420 (Reupholstery and Furniture Repair)

Furniture making became more automated after water- and steam-powered tools were introduced early in the nineteenth century. The artisan's role was largely eliminated in the mainstream furniture industry, and inexpensive furniture produced by high-volume manufacturers reduced demand for labor-intensive repair services.

Renewed interest in antiques and corporate cost-consciousness during the late 1980s hiked industry activity. Many refinishing and repair shops found new demand for refurbishing high-quality case goods, seating, and other pieces designed in classic, popular styles and produced by reputable makers. Corporate buyers could save up to 70 percent over the cost of new furniture by having their office furniture and equipment revitalized, or they could buy used furniture. By 1996, total U.S. furniture repair industry sales were an estimated $1.2 billion, up from $980 million in 1992.

Despite a U.S. recession in the late 1980s and early 1990s, the furniture repair industry grew. The market for refurbished and used furniture grew at 15 percent annually going into the 1990s, leading most other furniture industry segments. Demand for on-site refurbishing services was strong and growing in the late 1990's. Such companies replaced laminated desk- and counter-tops, repainted file cabinets and other metal equipment, and refurbished wall panels. Companies also repaired and refurbished antiques and other furniture on-site for non-business customers.

Trends through the mid-1990s included more partnering, where furniture dealers and refinishing/refurbishing services teamed up to provide long-term, one-stop shopping services for clients. Another trend was more government regulation. Due to strict federal mandates from the Clean Air Act Amendments of 1992, refinishers and painters were forced to follow sometimes costly procedures related to indoor air quality and waste disposal.

The U.S. reupholstery and furniture repair industry was diverse and fragmented in 1997, with 6,598 firms offering services ranging from antique furniture repair and home furniture reupholstery to refurbishing office furniture. Most firms were small, local, and provided a range of services. The industry generated $1.2 billion in receipts in 1997.

Furniture Medic was the largest franchiser in furniture repair and restoration in the late 1990s. Furniture Medic was founded in 1992 and acquired by ServiceMaster in 1996. Based in Memphis, Tennessee, it had 600 franchised locations across the United States, as well as locations in Canada and Europe.

Industry firms employed an estimated 22,315 workers in 1997, up from 21,200 in 1992. The total industry payroll for 1997 was $389 million, up from $311 million in 1992. According to the Bureau of Labor Statistics, industry jobs may grow 20 to 40 percent between 1990 and 2005.

FURTHER READING

U.S. Bureau of the Census. *1997 Economic Census.* Washington, 1999.

U.S. Department of Commerce. *1992 Census of Service Industries.* Washington: Bureau of the Census, 1995.

SIC 7692

WELDING REPAIR

This classification covers businesses that primarily do general repair work by welding, including automotive welding.

NAICS CODE(S)

811490 (Other Personal and Household Goods Repair and Maintenance)

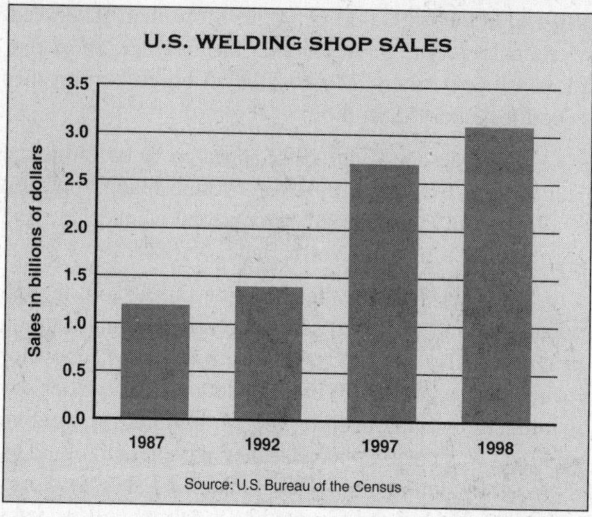

Welding joins materials by applying heat, and sometimes pressure, with or without the use of a filler metal. The process joins metals by melting, fusing, and then solidifying the joined area. Welding is used to make structural components, aircraft, cars, ships, and most other metal industrial products. Industry firms do general repairs in their own shops on welded items, such as motor vehicles. Welders that travel to construction sites are in **SIC 1799: Construction, Industry.**

There are eight major welding techniques used for different applications. One of the most common is shielded metal-arc welding, which uses an electric arc to quickly weld a point. Cold welding, a more specialized technique, uses pressure alone to join metals without any heat. Explosion welding uses a controlled blast to pressure two metals. Other welding techniques include: diffusion, which uses heat and pressure; laser-beam; ultrasonic, which utilizes high-frequency vibration; and variations of electric arc welding.

Massive U.S. industrial expansion during the mid-1900s created an identifiable welding repair industry. Post-World War II car and truck sales also caused demand for welding repair shops. By the end of the 1970s, welding repair revenues approached $1 billion and industry jobs surpassed 24,000. Although U.S. industrial output, particularly for cars, rose during the 1980s, inflation-adjusted welding repair revenues stagnated. The development of new welding techniques, which increased durability, was one reason for a decline in repair work. Also, increased use of synthetic metal substitutes reduced demand for future welding repairs.

There were an estimated 5,629 welding repair shops in 1998, down from 5,985 in 1987. Sales for 1998 totaled $3.1 billion, up from $1.2 billion in 1987, and a 14 percent increase from 1997. In 1998 the industry employed 26,600 workers. The total industry payroll for 1998 was $626 million. Most industry firms averaged sales of about $200,000 per year. More than 50 percent were sole proprietorships, and the average shop employed four workers. Most of the 25 biggest companies billed less than $5 million.

The largest firms in 1999 appeared to be Industrial Hardfacing Inc. of Elk River, Minnesota; Crookston Welding and Machine of Crookston, Minnesota; and Vopalensky's Inc., of North Bend, Nebraska.

Many welders got their training on the job, though vocational and technical schools offered formal training programs. Also, the U.S. military ran welding schools for its enlisted personnel. While the demand for welders by manufacturers may decline, the job outlook for welding repairers was positive because they were less likely to be replaced by automation. The Bureau of Labor Statistics estimated the demand for welding repairers will increase 25 percent by the year 2005. Unfortunately, industry workers were paid relatively low wages, an average of $13.95 per hour.

Further Reading

Darnay, Arsen J., ed. *Service Industries U.S.A.* Detroit, MI: Gale Research, 1999.

U.S. Bureau of the Census. *Economic Census 1997,* 2000. Available from http://www.census.gov.

U.S. Department of Commerce. *1992 Census of Service Industries & Geographic Area Series.* Washington, DC: Bureau of the Census, 1995.

U.S. Department of Labor. *Employment Statistics,* 2000. Available from http://www.bls.gov.

Ward's Business Directory of U.S. Private and PublicCompanies. Detroit: Gale Research, 1999.

SIC 7694

ARMATURE REWINDING SHOPS

This category covers businesses that primarily rewind armatures and rebuild or repair electric motors. These companies may either repair customers' equipment, or repair or rebuild for sale or exchange to users or the trade.

NAICS Code(s)

811310 (Commercial and Industrial Machinery and Equipment (Except Automotive and Electronic) Repair and Maintenance)

335312 (Motor and Generator Manufacturing)

A generator, or dynamo, converts mechanical energy into electrical energy by rotating an armature through a magnetic field. Most electricity used in cars, homes, and industry is made by generators. The armature—usually made of copper wire wound around a laminated core of soft iron—is the rotating or stationary assembly in the generator, and is the main current-carrying conductor. A steel shaft is fitted through the center of the core to which the two ends of the copper wire connect.

Companies in the armature rewinding business rewind damaged coils or stators, fix hermetic seals on electric motors, and generally restore electric motors and components. They fix everything from small automotive generators to giant industrial and utility devices. The industry consisted of 2,119 companies in 1998, most of which were small service centers.

Englishman Michael Faraday and American Joseph Henry developed the generator during the 1830s after discovering they could make a magnet produce electric current. Generators became widely used during the late 1800s, which, in turn, created a demand for repair shops to service them. After World War II, the industry benefited from U.S. economic expansion, which increased electricity consumption and generated a need for motor vehicle generators. Throughout the twentieth century, the basic design of the generator and armature have hardly changed.

By the early 1980s, armature rewinding shops billed $1.8 billion annually and employed a work force of 31,000. Industry revenues climbed at a rate roughly equivalent to inflation during the 1980s, pushing sales to $1.9 billion by 1987. Total sales for 1992 were $2.3 billion. There were 2,498 industry firms in 1992, down from 2,830 in 1987. There were 26,607 industry workers in 1992, down from 27,255 workers in 1987. This job decline may have been due to increased automation and efficiency within the industry. A recession weakened some firms in the early 1990s, but by the mid-1990s the both the industry and the economy began to recover. In 1998, this industry reported $2.8 billion in sales, a 10 percent increase from the previous year.

Some of the largest armature rewinding shops in 1999 were Brithinee Electric of Colton, California and Southwest Electric Company of Oklahoma City, Oklahoma. Even the top 25 competitors in the mid-1990s, however, had sales of less than $15 million and employed fewer than 100 workers.

Although efficiency gains reduced industry jobs during the 1980s, positions for armature rewinding industry workers were expected to rise between 1990 and 2005, according to the Bureau of Labor Statistics. Jobs for general repairers were predicted to climb as much as 35 percent by 2005, and electrical equipment positions were expected to increase by at least 9 percent. In 1998 there were an estimated 22,700 employees in the industry.

Further Reading

Darnay, Arsen J., ed. *Service Industries USA.* Detroit, MI: Gale Research Inc., 1999.

U.S. Bureau of the Census. *Economic Census 1997.* 20 March 2000. Available from http://www.census.gov.

U.S. Department of Commerce. *1992 Census of Service Industries & Geographic Area Series.* Washington, DC: Bureau of the Census, 1995.

U.S. Department of Labor. *Employment Statistics.* 2000. Available from http://www.bls.gov.

Ward's Business Directory of U. S. Private and Public Companies. Detroit: Gale Research, 1999.

SIC 7699

REPAIR SHOPS AND RELATED SERVICES, NOT ELSEWHERE CLASSIFIED

This category covers establishments primarily engaged in specialized repair services, not elsewhere classified.

NAICS CODE(S)

561622 (Locksmiths)
562991 (Septic Tank and Related Services)
561790 (Other Services to Buildings and Dwellings)
488390 (Other Support Activities for Water Transportation)
451110 (Sporting Goods Stores)
811310 (Commercial and Industrial Machinery and Equipment (except Automotive and Electronic) Repair and Maintenance)
115210 (Support Activities for Animal Production)
811212 (Computer and Office Machine Repair and Maintenance)
811219 (Other Electronic and Precision Equipment Repair and Maintenance)
811411 (Home and Garden Equipment Repair and Maintenance)
811412 (Appliance Repair and Maintenance)
811430 (Footwear and Leather Goods Repair)
811490 (Other Personal and Household Goods Repair and Maintenance)

Miscellaneous repair shops service a plethora of items such as motorcycles, bicycles, leather goods, lawn mowers, window shades, camping equipment, pianos and organs, septic tanks, surgical instruments, surveying equipment, and bowling pins. This industry also encompasses taxidermists, locksmiths, and other miscellaneous services. While many companies, such as furnace cleaning firms, specialize in one type of activity, other industry participants are general maintenance companies that supply a variety of repair and related services. The largest single occupational group is welders and metal cutters.

General maintenance workers are jacks-of-all-trades, and they work as plumbers, carpenters, and mechanics. They repair and maintain machines and equipment, for example, and fix air-conditioning systems, repair roofs and floors, maintain cafeterias, restore tools, refurbish furniture, inspect mechanical systems, and perform many other services. They are often self-employed, will travel to a work site, and work for governments, institutions, and private industry. Although earnings vary widely by industry, geographic area, and skill level, general maintenance personnel earned around $9.40 per hour in the mid-1990s, according to the U.S. Department of Labor's *Occupational Outlook Handbook.*

The demand for miscellaneous repair and related services mimicked U.S. economic expansion during the mid-1900s. By the early 1980s, about 24,000 companies and 130,000 employees were classified in this industry, and total revenues approached $6.5 billion. General economic growth boosted industry billings to about $10 billion by the late 1980s, reflecting a 35 percent increase over early 1980s levels. In 1998, there were an estimated 36,584 repair shop establishments employing 232,800 people, with aggregate receipts of $19.8 billion.

The business is extremely fragmented. The average industry participant employed only five workers in the late 1980s and generated billings of about $340,000 per year. The average establishment in the mid-1990s had 6 employees and receipts of $441,585. In terms of annual sales, in 1999 the largest company in the industry was Insituform Technologies Inc. Other leaders were Roto-Rooter, Inc., of Cincinnati, Ohio; Leamco-Ruthco of Texas; and Siemens Power Corp., of Milwaukee, Wisconsin. There were only 17 companies with annual sales above $10 million, and only four had more than 1,000 employees.

Future employment prospects in the miscellaneous repair industry are generally positive. Most occupations will realize growth of 20 percent to 30 percent between 1990 and 2005, according to the Bureau of Labor Statistics. Jobs for welders and cutters, for instance, will likely rise about 23 percent. General management jobs, which account for approximately 7 percent of the work force in this category, will increase about 17 percent by 2005. Openings related to machinery and automotive repair will rise 35 percent, as will miscellaneous service positions related to construction.

FURTHER READING

Darnay, Arsen J., ed. *Service Industries U.S.A.* Detroit: Gale Group, 1999.

Occupational Outlook Handbook 1996-1997. Washington, DC: U.S. Department of Labor, 1996.

U.S. Bureau of Labor Statistics. *Employment Statistics.* 2000. Available from http://www.bls.gov.

U.S. Department of Commerce. *1992 Census of Service Industries.* Washington, DC: GPO, 1995.

Ward's Business Directory of U.S. Private and Public Companies. Detroit: Gale Group, 1999.

SIC 7812

MOTION PICTURE AND VIDEO TAPE PRODUCTION

This category covers establishments primarily engaged in the production of theatrical and nontheatrical motion pictures and videotapes for exhibition or sale, including educational, industrial, and religious films. Included in the industry are establishments engaged in both production and distribution. Producers of live radio and television programs are classified in **SIC 7922: Theatrical Producers (Except Motion Pictures) and Miscellaneous Theatrical Services.** Establishments primarily engaged in motion picture and videotape reproduction are classified in **SIC 7819: Services Allied to Motion Picture Production** and those engaged in distribution are classified in **SIC 7822: Motion Picture and Video Tape Distribution.**

NAICS CODE(S)

512110 (Motion Picture and Video Production)

INDUSTRY SNAPSHOT

The U.S. motion picture and video production industry serves as a major supplier of entertainment and information to the world by producing videos, television programs, and movies that can be seen in more than 100 countries.

Despite hefty profits, some segments of the industry felt the effects of the recession in the early 1990s. Fewer people went to the movies in 1992 than during any single year in the 1980s. Following the recession, box-office revenues climbed again, but competition from cable television and video sales continued to erode the theatrical audience. A 1997 report by the American Film Marketing Association stated that just 43 percent of motion picture sales came from television, while theatrical releases accounted for nearly 31 percent and video sales brought in about 26 percent.

Several media conglomerates dominated the industry through the 1990s. In 1995, five companies had a combined U.S. box office market share of more than 80 percent: Walt Disney Co., Paramount Pictures Corp., Warner Brothers Inc., Sony Corp., and Universal Studios. By the end of the 1990s, global revenues for American film companies totaled more than $5 billion dollars.

ORGANIZATION AND STRUCTURE

Motion picture and videotape production is one element of a larger three-part industrial structure. After a movie or a video has been produced, it is usually transferred to a distributor, who in turn arranges to make the product accessible to the consumer through movie theaters, video rental and/or sale outlets, and television broadcasts. In the case of movies, the distribution company and the theater usually split the box office receipts. The financial and management structures of a production company often depend on the company's relationship to the distribution arm of the industry, which in turn often depends on a company's size.

Production companies can be classified according to three major categories: the ''majors,'' the ''mini-majors,'' and the ''independents.'' The majors include large conglomerates such as Warner Bros., Disney, Sony (owner of Columbia Pictures and Tri-Star), and Viacom (owner of Paramount). In the case of the majors, a single corporate structure often controls both the production and distribution of films, as well as an array of related operations through which the corporation can market movie soundtracks, toys, and other promotional tie-ins. Warner Bros., whose merger with Time, Inc. in 1989 dramatically strengthened its distribution system, presented one of the most striking examples of coordinated production and distribution. Some major film corporations have also invested in movie theaters, despite the history of antitrust actions against theater chains owned by studios. Time Warner and Paramount, for example, share Cinamerica, and Sony owns Loews Theatres. Slightly smaller companies, often called ''mini-majors'' (Orion Pictures Corporation, for example), may have weaker distribution powers and may specialize in a specific segment of the film market, such as art films or action films. Small independent filmmakers may have no distribution capability at all and must depend entirely on outside distribution companies.

Because success in the film production industry depends largely on a wide distribution network and access to the substantial capital required for film production, major film companies have obvious advantages over smaller companies. In addition to distribution capabilities, many of the major studios have been operating long enough to build up sizable film libraries, which provide revenue through video sales or through sale or rental to television stations. These well-established companies are likely to wield substantial financial leverage and control physical production facilities. In fact, small production companies and independent filmmakers often rent the production facilities of the larger companies.

During the studio era, which lasted from 1920 to 1950, major studios considered their stable of stars, directors, and other talent under long-term contract as assets. Movie companies in the 1990s, however, were more likely to sign contracts with artists for a single project. Such one-shot contracts have given talent agents considerable power over the production process. Often agents will assemble a "package" including a script, a director, and a star and sell the whole project to a studio. By performing much of the preproduction work on a project themselves, agents give clients greater control over the kinds of projects they undertake. This sort of arrangement limits the movie company's artistic involvement to that of an investor who simply provides the money, facilities, and equipment required to complete the project.

The explosion of new television technologies since the late 1970s has had a significant impact on the financial structure of film production and has helped to encourage independent production. Developments such as cable TV, videocassettes, and pay-TV services like Home Box Office (HBO) have stimulated demand for new films and created new options for film financing. These ancillary markets allow movie companies to sell distribution rights before production has even begun on a movie. HBO, for example, has helped to finance new movies in order to ensure the steady supply of films necessary to fill its programming schedule. Video rentals have proven to be an even greater source of revenue for motion picture companies. A 1997 report by the American Film Marketing Association stated that slightly more than 43 percent of motion picture sales were derived from television, while video contributed nearly 26 percent and theatrical releases a little more than 31 percent. By the time a feature film has been fully exploited, it will have been released in a theater, on home video and pay-per-view channels, on cable television, and on the major television networks—most likely in that order.

Ancillary markets have been a boon to production companies of all sizes, but independent producers have had special cause to celebrate their rise. Lacking the financial leverage of the majors, small movie companies have often had to struggle to gather the capital required to make a film. The ability to sell ancillary rights to pay cable and video companies has expanded the financial resources available to independents, resulting in a healthy growth of independent film production since the mid-1980s. By the mid-1990's a growing network of satellite broadcasting systems, the arrival of an exciting new high-quality, low-cost consumer digital video system (DVD), and the latent potential of the emerging Internet were creating an ever-widening range of distribution channels, all hungry for new content.

In addition to producing a steady supply of feature films, many movie studios also provide programming for television. Telefilm productions range from made-for-TV movies to half-hour situation comedies. Major movie studios accounted for approximately half of all prime time programming for the networks during the early 1980s, with gaps filled by independent telefilm producers such as Mary Tyler Moore's MTM Enterprises. Prior to 1991, the Federal Communications Commission (FCC) actually restricted the amount of programming that networks could produce for themselves and prevented networks from owning a share in the syndication rights of the shows they exhibited. These restrictions were designed to prevent the networks from developing a monopoly over television programming and to maintain a competitive environment for the program production industry. On June 15, 1991, the FCC altered some of these restrictions, permitting networks to hold the syndication rights for 40 percent of the programming that they run during prime time.

BACKGROUND AND DEVELOPMENT

The U.S. film industry was born in Thomas Edison's laboratories in West Orange, New Jersey, when William Kennedy Laurie Dickson successfully devised a motion picture camera and the kinetiscope, a device that allowed a single viewer to watch a short film through a peephole. Dickson's invention enjoyed a period of brief profitability as consumers paid a nickel to enjoy the novelty of moving pictures, but widespread commercial success of motion pictures did not materialize until projectors made it possible to show a movie to more than one viewer at a time. The Vitascope, invented by C. Francis Jenkins and Thomas Armat, became the first movie projector to be publicly exhibited in the United States on April 23, 1896. The Cinematographe of Louis and Auguste Lumiere ran a close second, debuting in New York City on June 29, 1896—several months after its unveiling in France. Former Edison employee Dickson introduced his own Biograph projector on October 12, 1896.

Early manufacturers of cinematic equipment were also the first motion picture producers, who made the films to be shown on their own hardware. Before the advent of movie houses, production companies had to provide projectors, projectionists, and films to exhibitors. Employees of movie companies or owners of franchises purchased from movie companies would take the company's equipment and movies on the road, showing the films in vaudeville houses, empty storefronts, and a wide variety of other makeshift venues. Films for the Vitascope projector were produced by the Edison Manufacturing Company in a crude black-painted shack known as the "Black Maria," while Biograph filmed its motion pictures on a movable outdoor stage with a camera which could be moved back and forth on wheels. The Biograph filmmakers and the Lumiere brothers gained a competitive edge by producing travel and documentary films on location in addition to studio productions. In all of these cases, the cameraman served as the chief creative intelligence behind each short film and was responsible for the subject matter, photography, printing, and editing.

This system was well adapted to a relatively low volume of production. A number of developments in the first decade of the twentieth century, however, worked dramatically to expand the market for new motion pictures and encourage the application of mass-production techniques to movie making. As more movie companies began selling movies outright to independent exhibitors, the number of exhibitors increased, and the need for an improved distribution system became clear. In order to be cost-effective, film exhibitors had to have access to a greater number of films than they could afford to buy. Harry and Herbert Miles solved this problem in 1903 by organizing a ''motion picture exchange'' that bought a large stock of films and then rented them to exhibitors. Other such exchanges followed, and the increased film supply fostered a proliferation of ''nickelodeons''—makeshift theaters named for the price of admission—equipped with seats, a projector, and a piano. Many nickelodeons were originally installed in working-class neighborhoods, but around 1905 exhibitors worked hard to widen the movie-watching market to include the middle-class. Demand soon escalated, and movie companies adapted by developing better mass-production and techniques.

Mass production entailed a transition from the cameraman system of creative control to the director system, and initiated an industry-wide shift away from documentary films toward narrative films. Under the director system, production labor was divided between a director, who coordinated and managed all aspects of production from scenario development to editing, and the cameraman, who handled the nuts and bolts of the photography and film developing. Narrative fiction became the budding industry's genre of choice because it offered producers greater control and efficiency than was possible for documentary films, which depended on the uncertain supply of newsworthy events. Edwin S. Porter's film *The Great Train Robbery,* filmed for Edison in 1903, broke new narrative ground in its length (around 15 minutes) and its depiction of a multi-scene story, complete with close-ups and an unprecedented use of editing to build suspense.

Thomas Edison initiated the movie industry's long tradition of corporate struggle for monopolistic control. Patent infringement suits were Edison's first weapon against his competitors. With aggressive litigation, Edison sought to preserve exclusive rights to all motion picture devices, and he did manage to intimidate some companies from the U.S. market for a while. But Biograph held its ground and won an appeal of an important test case that Edison had won in a lower court. Before the legal battle could reach its conclusion, however, Edison changed tactics and began making pacts with his competitors. The final result was the Motion Picture Patents Company (MPPC), an organization formed in 1908 for the purpose of preserving the patent rights of all of its members, which included Biograph and other major producers. Through a system of licenses and fees for the use of motion picture equipment, the MPPC managed to exclude newcomers to the industry while sewing up the market for the technologies and films owned by its members. Ultimately, the MPPC, known informally as ''the Trust,'' bought out almost all of the distributors to which it had granted licenses and formed its own distribution organization: the General Film Company.

The power of the Trust was eventually challenged by independent companies. Some independents confronted the Trust head-on by offering theaters a full program of short subjects that could rival those marketed by the MPPC. Carl Laemmle's Independent Motion Picture Company, for example, bypassed the Trust's distribution system by banding together with other independent filmmakers to create Eastman Kodak.

Other filmmakers, such as Adolph Zukor, avoided direct competition over the market for one-reel short subjects by pioneering the multiple-reel feature film and creating the distribution and exhibition system necessary to market the new form. Producers of feature films aggressively promoted products and, starting with small-time vaudeville houses, gradually built up a network of exhibition venues that could generate the revenues required to pay for the high production costs of long features. The expansion of the feature film market led to the construction of palatial theaters dedicated solely to the exhibition of motion pictures. This sort of movie theater served the needs of the feature film producer much more effectively than the nickelodeons, which could accommodate only small audiences. Feature films also encouraged the development of the star system. By promoting individual actors and actresses, movie companies could guarantee a market for risky high-cost features. Performers like Charlie Chaplin, Mary Pickford, and Douglas Fairbanks quickly became hot commodities and commanded enormous salaries.

Competition and an antitrust suit, *United States v. Motion Picture Patents Co.,* ultimately broke the hold of the MPPC over the industry. Other companies, however, were already integrating production, distribution, and exhibition operations on an unprecedented scale. This process of cohesion soon left the industry in the hands of a few massive studios known as ''integrated majors'' and ushered in the ''studio era'' of movie history. In 1916 Adolph Zukor executed a takeover of Paramount, a national distribution company that was created in 1914 to fill the distribution needs of feature film producers. Paramount then became a subsidiary of the new corporation formed by the merger of Zukor's own Famous Players company with the Jesse L. Lasky Feature Play Company. By the time the restructuring was completed in December of 1917, the Famous Players-Lasky Corporation had set a new standard of scale for the motion picture industry. In 1919, Zukor set about acquiring theaters, and in 1926 he inaugurated the Publix Theater Corporation. By controlling the production, distribution, and exhibition of its films, Zukor's organization became the first fully integrated movie company. Marcus Loew achieved a similar integration starting from the exhibition end of the industry, adding producer-distributor Metro to his theater chain in 1920. His company went on to acquire Goldwyn Pictures Corporation and Louis B. Mayer's production company, creating the studio that would eventually be known as Loew's Metro-Goldwyn-Mayer. By 1925 four companies held most of the power in the industry: Zukor's Paramount, Loew's, First National, and Twentieth Century Fox.

In the early twenties, the major movie companies set about consolidating their gains and securing the place of movies in American culture. Financial institutions began to see the prospering movie industry as a legitimate investment. While bank loans for movies were unheard of before the 1920s, in 1926 $1.5 billion of the industry's capital came from outside investment. To combat attempts by outside groups to censor movies, industry leaders created the Motion Picture Producers and Distributors of America (MPPDA) and hired prominent republican Will Hays to head the organization and enhance the industry's respectability.

Just as the industry was settling into a stable status quo, the advent of sound technology upset the balance and resulted in two new major competitors: Warner Brothers and RKO Corp. Warner Brothers paved the way for the ''talkies'' when *The Jazz Singer,* using Western Electric's Vitaphone system, set off a national craze for movies with sound in 1927. Riding the flood of profits from the breakthrough, Warner was able to finance a massive expansion effort that put it in the ranks of the industry giants. Meanwhile, RCA had been working on a sound system to rival Vitaphone, which it called Photophone. In October of 1928 RCA created the Radio-Keith-Orpheum (RKO) Corporation, a fully integrated major studio from the very moment of its birth, in order to make use of its new technology. A slightly altered hierarchy of industry leaders emerged from the talkie revolution, with Warner Brothers, MGM, Twentieth Century Fox, Paramount, and RKO dominating the field as integrated majors. Columbia and Carl Laemmle's Universal (a later version of his Independent Motion Picture Company) controlled powerful production and distribution arms, but lacked theater chains and were relegated to the status of ''major minors.''

Most majors and major minors employed similar systems of production in the late 1920s and early 1930s. The owners and corporate officers of a company were typically based in New York City, while most production took place in sprawling studio complexes in Hollywood, California. Hollywood's colony of movie studios had been growing since the early 1910s as more and more producers took advantage of the area's sunny weather and diverse scenery for movie-making. In a studio's West Coast operation, a central producer served as an intermediary between the financial concerns of the New York office and the creative concerns of Hollywood, overseeing such aspects of the process as script development, casting, and the production schedule in order to ensure that the studio produced marketable films as quickly and economically as possible. At MGM's Culver City studio, for example, central producer Irving Thalberg oversaw the production of one-third of the studio's projects himself (usually the big budget features that used the studio's most popular stars), while the rest were handled by supervisors nicknamed ''Thalberg men'' who answered directly to Thalberg. Thalberg shared the upper ranks of the Culver City management with studio boss Louis Mayer, who handled the studio's talent (the stars and directors), and E.J. Mannix, who handled the physical production facilities.

Censorship continued to be an issue during this period as reform groups pressured the industry to adopt stricter standards of decency in movies. Will Hays and the MPPDA responded in 1930 by replacing the trade organization's relatively informal list of ''Don'ts and Be Carefuls'' with a more comprehensive document entitled *The Motion Picture Production Code.* While the new guidelines provided a more rigorous standard of decency for film producers, it made no provision for its own enforcement. Producers began to ignore the code when the economic pressures of the Great Depression made them resort to more controversial material to attract viewers, and the Legion of Decency waged a bitter protest in response. In 1934 the MPPDA created the Production Code Administration, a censorship board empowered to prevent offending films from reaching audiences in theaters affiliated with the MPPDA. This form of industry self-censorship proved to be acceptable to champions of moral decency and remained intact for decades.

The Depression dealt a heavy blow to the movie industry, but with the help of President Roosevelt's National Industrial Recovery Act (NIRA), the industry was able to regain its footing quickly and maintain a healthfulness unusual for the era. Between 1930 and 1931 the total profits of the eight leading movie companies fell from $55 million to $6.5 million. NIRA, enacted in June 1933, loosened restrictions on monopolistic business practices in hopes that the increased freedom would help large corporations lead an economic recovery. When NIRA was ruled unconstitutional in 1935, it had already helped the major studios strengthen their hold on the movie industry and get back on their feet. The latter half of the decade marked the beginning of a new period of creative fertility and financial prosperity for the film industry.

The 1930s also marked the transformation of the central-producer system of production management. While the central producers of the 1920s had helped the majors develop production methods, it eventually became clear that these methods had become so ingrained in the studio system that they no longer required the guidance of central producers like Thalberg. The middleman between the administrative and creative branches of the typical corporate structure disappeared, widening the split between the New York corporate headquarters and the production process and allowing individual artists greater control over film production. The central management teams at the Hollywood studios came to assume a more purely administrative character, backing away from the sort of hands-on approach they had taken in the past. The unit production system that came to replace the central-producer system dispersed production authority over a number of ''unit producers.'' These unit producers were essentially ''Thalberg men'' without a Thalberg—supervisors who oversaw a relatively small number of projects without having to report constantly to a central supervisor.

In 1938 the U.S. Justice Department began the campaign of anti-trust litigation that would eventually result in the demise of the studio system. By controlling the production, distribution, and exhibition of movies, the integrated majors had been able to use strategies such as block booking, the practice of forcing theaters to book movies in blocks, which included a few quality films with several B-grade productions. As a result of the 1938 court battle, the integrated majors consented to curtail block booking and other tactics that took advantage of the integrated structure.

Before the final demise of the integrated studio system, however, the majors enjoyed a boom brought about by World War II. The wartime economy gave Americans the money they needed to go to the movies, and the movies satisfied their hunger for morale-boosting entertainment. The prohibition of block booking forced studios to de-emphasize B-movie production, which led to an increase in the quality of films that ultimately benefited the majors. Following recommendations issued by the Office of War Information, Hollywood fed America a steady diet of war movies and other patriotic fare. This boom lingered for several years after the war ended.

In the late 1940s, however, the Justice Department resumed its anti-trust campaign against the majors, and with the advent of television, the end of the studio system was drawing near. The consent decrees forced out of the integrated majors by the 1938 court battle had expired toward the end of the war. In May 1948, however, the Supreme Court upheld a decision against Paramount that restricted block booking, admission price fixing, and other practices classified by the decision as illegal restraint of trade. The battle continued as the Justice Department pursued its ultimate goal of forcing the integrated majors to give up theater chains. In order to avoid further legal conflict, Paramount and RKO signed consent decrees requiring them to divest all theater holdings, and Loew's MGM, Twentieth Century Fox, and Warner Bros. soon followed suit. The five integrated majors became producers and distributors but lost exhibition powers. Independent producers soon took advantage of the increased access to theaters created by this divestment. The number of independents doubled between 1946 and 1956. Divestment also weakened the power of the Production Code Administration. Without the theater chains, the five majors who dominated the MPPDA could no longer threaten to deprive offending movies from exhibition.

The year 1948 also marked the beginning of the television era. Americans owned 172,000 television sets in that year, compared with 14,000 the previous year. Combined with the post-war trend toward suburbanization, the rise of television ate into movie companies' profits. Between 1946 and 1956 the combined profits of the top 10 movie companies fell 74 percent. As companies tightened their belts, they discarded the practice of maintaining a stock of actors and directors under long-term contract. As a result, talent agencies assumed a more important role in the industry, frequently operating as ''packagers'' who sold the studios a preassembled combination of star, director, and story scenario or script. In order to provide consumers with entertainment they could not get on a small black and white television screen, moviemakers produced more color films and blockbuster epics and experimented with gimmicks like 3-D and the wrap-around screen of Cinerama.

At the same time, some movie companies tried to exploit the television market. While a number of independent companies like DesiLu Productions were created specifically for the purpose of producing television programming, established movie companies also began to explore the possibilities of ''telefilm'' production. Columbia led the way in 1949 by converting its Screen Gems subsidiary into a telefilm outfit. The Walt Disney Co. combined program production with advertising when it created its *Disneyland* television series, complete with plugs for its current movies. By 1963 almost 70 percent of prime-time television programming was being produced in Hollywood. Some of the leading Hollywood telefilm outfits were run by old major movie studios, while others like MCA (originally a talent agency) became major production operations only after the advent of television.

Movie companies also took advantage of the new market created by television by selling old films to television stations. In December of 1955 a programming syndicate bought RKO's library for $15 million; Warner's library went for $21 million the following February. Before long all of the major studios were capitalizing on this type of asset, and they soon realized the true value of old films to television networks hungry for programming. By the 1960s an amicable relationship had developed between Hollywood and the networks, with Hollywood-based companies providing both new programming and old products.

Federal action further solidified the role of the major studios and other non-network producers of network programming. Fearing that the networks could gain monopolistic power over television communication, the Department of Justice filed an antitrust suit in 1972. As a result, the networks signed consent decrees limiting the amount of program hours a network could produce for itself and stipulated that networks could gain no financial benefit from the syndication of programming. The Federal Communications Commission (FCC) altered this rule 19 years later to allow networks to own up to 40 percent of the syndication rights of their prime-time programming.

Having experienced the benefits of diversification into television, the majors diversified into other entertainment markets, such as music recording, by acquiring or creating new companies. Some production companies became a part of diversified corporate structures through a different route: by being acquired themselves. In 1966, for example, Gulf + Western took over Paramount. Hotel developer Kirk Kerkorian acquired MGM in 1969, and the same year Kinney National Services took over Warner Brothers. By the end of the 1960s the heavily diversified media conglomerate had become the standard corporate structure in the movie and telefilm production business.

In 1969 this trend toward expansion was interrupted by an industry-wide crisis. The heavy emphasis on high-grossing films had placed many movie companies in risky financial positions, and the advent of three new major production companies (ABC, CBS, and National General) created a glut of big-budget pictures. At the same time, the market for feature films on television also became saturated. Television audiences could watch a feature film on network television every night of the week, and the networks had accumulated a stock of films that would last for several years. Hollywood had come to rely on the television ancillary market as a way to stabilize risky productions, and this crutch was suddenly no longer secure. As movie studios tried to cope with the losses created by over-production, they trimmed corporate structures and began to emphasize low-budget films. Although the success of *The Godfather* in 1972 quickly revived the credibility of the blockbuster strategy, movie companies had learned to be cautious. They realized that the market could support only a few big hits a year, and they began to capitalize on the reliable profitability of sequels to popular films like *Rocky* and *Jaws*.

The next revolution in television and film production took place in the 1980s, as new television technologies became commonplace. Videocassette recorders allowed consumers to do their own television programming, and cable television and satellite broadcasting popularized such programming innovations as pay TV services and 24-hour music video stations. While some analysts feared that these new technologies would threaten the motion picture industry, they actually had the opposite effect of providing new ancillary markets for feature films. Home Box Office (HBO) led the way for pay television by using satellite broadcasting at a time when few cable companies had the equipment to receive such broadcasts. The gamble paid off as more and more cable companies bought receiving dishes. After HBO successfully fought FCC regulations designed to protect free television, other premium channels such as the Movie Channel and the Disney Channel debuted. Not only did these channels need films to fill programming schedules, they also occasionally financed the production of new movies in order to supplement their supply.

Home video similarly affected the financing of movies. Producers could sell video rights before production on a film even started and apply the proceeds toward the cost of the film—an arrangement particularly useful for small independent producers. Videocassettes provided yet another arena in which filmmakers could exploit products. At the same time, however, videocassette rental and home taping of movies from television decreased the power of studios to garner profits from every exhibition of a film. Once a rental store or home viewer had its own copy of a movie on tape, that tape could be shown repeatedly and the production studio would gain nothing. MCA and Disney had tried to nip these practices in the bud in 1976 by accusing Sony, the manufacturer of the Betamax Videocassette Recorder, of copyright infringement. By 1981 the *Betamax* case had reached the Supreme Court, which ruled that neither taping a broadcast for home use nor purchasing a cassette for the purpose of rental constituted copyright infringement. Although the Betamax machine itself eventually became extinct due to the popularity of the VHS cassette format, cassette rental and home taping became everyday practices.

In addition to these new ways of exploiting the feature film, new technology also brought a new form of film and video art—the music video. Music videos originated in the United States as a programming strategy for the Warner Cable Corporation (WCC), a division of the giant media corporation Warner Communications Inc. By April of 1979, WCC had two satellite-broadcast channels available for cable systems: Nickelodeon and Star, a pay channel that later became The Movie Channel. When

John A. Lack became executive vice president of WCC, the operation was losing money, and he attempted to turn WCC around by expanding the preschool audience of Nickelodeon to include teenagers. The centerpiece of Lack's new format was a show called *Pop Clips.* Produced by Mike Nesmith, formerly of the rock group the Monkees, and his Pacific Arts Corporation, *Pop Clips* consisted of a half-hour of short video clips accompanying pop songs. The idea caught on, and Lack went on to create Music Television (MTV), a 24-hour cable channel composed entirely of such clips or ''videos.'' The new channel debuted on August 1, 1981.

Initially, a scarcity of programming material posed a problem for the network. The videos were provided at no charge by recording companies and were originally produced as promotional material for distribution to European television networks. MTV's original library of videos numbered no more than 125. Only when the value of MTV as a promotional medium started to assert itself did the recording industry invest in large-scale video production. Companies continued to provide videos free of charge until competing video music programs like NBC-TV's *Friday Night Videos* entered the market, creating a potential demand for exclusive rights to exhibit videos. NBC broke the ice by offering to pay for the right to premiere a video and have exclusive access to it for two days. By the time this ''pay for play'' policy became common practice, however, it became obvious that MTV had the competitive advantage in bidding for exclusivity. Recording companies valued the access offered by a 24-hour station to acts that might not make it onto a two- or three-hour video show, and MTV threatened to withhold this access from labels which favored other video programs with exclusive deals. Using tactics like these, MTV fiercely defended its status as the nation's primary source of video music entertainment. Rival 24-hour music video channels, such as the Discovery Music Network and Ted Turner's short-lived Cable Music Channel, challenged MTV's reign and failed.

With undertakings like MTV, Warner and other leaders of the motion picture and video production industry continued to diversify, expand, and set new standards of scale for media conglomerates. For many corporations, this sort of expansion could not continue indefinitely. Gulf + Western jettisoned many of its non-communications holdings in order to concentrate its corporate structure on the entertainment industry, and in 1989 renamed itself Paramount Communications Inc. to reflect this newly found focus. Similarly, when the popularity of Atari collapsed in 1982, Warner sold its video game operation along with many of its other ventures, including MTV. Nevertheless, Warner went on to merge with Time Inc. in 1989, and Time Warner became a media conglomerate of unparalleled size.

In the shadows of these giants, smaller film and video producers continued to make their voices heard. The new options for film financing offered by home video and other ancillary markets fueled a boom in independent production during the mid-1980s. Mini-majors and independents increased production by 100 movies per year between 1984 and 1987. In the late 1980s and early 1990s this boom resulted in a glut that damaged some independents.

In the early 1990s the motion picture industry suffered from the effects of the recession. While movies brought in a record $5 billion at U.S. theaters in 1989, box office receipts declined in the following two years, totaling approximately $4.8 billion in 1991. Box office receipts rose to about $4.9 billion in 1992, but increased ticket prices accounted for much of this rise. Admissions actually declined from 1.1 billion in 1990 to about 977 million in 1992, sinking below the lowest levels of the 1980s. Decreasing attendance seemed to translate into a decreased volume of production. In the first half of 1992 production started on 173 films, down from the 224 films that were started in the first six months of 1991. Independent production companies accounted for 150 of the 1991 film starts and 122 of the 1992 starts.

Increasing video sales softened the blow of falling box office figures. In 1992 an estimated $12.2 billion in revenues were gained from home video sales at retail outlets, up from $11.5 billion in 1991 and $10.8 billion in 1990. The demand for videotapes has been stimulated by a steady increase in the number of households with video cassette recorders (VCRs). According to the Electronic Industries Association, 77 percent of U.S. homes owned a VCR at the beginning of 1992, up from 72 percent in 1991. Just six years earlier less than 20 percent of U.S. homes were equipped with VCRs.

The demand for movies, television shows, and other forms of filmed entertainment has grown over the last 15 years as cable and home video have made it easier to deliver a wide variety of programming to consumers in their homes. In coming years the continued growth of movie and video production may depend on new innovations in delivery systems. Pay-per-view (PPV) systems may offer one such direction for growth. U.S. consumers paid a total of $350 million for PPV programming in 1992. This amount represents 3 percent of total spending on videocassettes.

By 1995, box office sales were back up over the $5 billion mark, but profits continued to erode in spite of increasing sales to the video an TV markets. Much of the decline could be attributed to the rapidly inflating costs of production and the industry's increasing reliance on ''blockbuster'' films as a primary source of revenue. After the release in the early 1990s of such films as *Jurassic Park* and *Terminator 2,* Hollywood movies became special-effects extravaganzas, with each new film upping the ante in an attempt to dazzle an ever-more jaded audience. Each year saw a new record set for production costs, with 1995's *Waterworld* totaling $150 million. While some of these films—like 1996's *Independence Day*—were hugely profitable, they seldom brought in enough to cover less successful films. Not surprisingly, profit margins shrank, pressuring film producers to focus even more on producing sure-fire hits. So-called ''big-event'' films became the mainstay of Hollywood. In addition to pumping out a seemingly endless stream of sequels, the industry turned to old television shows and comic books in search for product with a built-in audience. Major films of the 1990s, including *The Flintstones, The Addams Family, The Beverly Hillbillies, The Brady Bunch, Mission Impossible, The Saint,* and *The Prisoner,* were all based on television programs from the 1960s and 1970s. Comic book heroes such as *The Phantom* and *Judge Dredd* were also turned into film stars, though with less success.

Hollywood inflation was also fueled by the studios' need to grab attention in a crowded marketplace. Marketing costs rose dramatically through the early part of the decade, jumping 20 percent between 1995 and 1996 alone. Talent fees also rose rapidly through this period, with actors such as Tom Cruise, Tom Hanks, Jim Carrey, and Arnold Schwartzenegger routinely getting anywhere from $10 to $20 million per picture. With costs leaping out of control, even major studios found it increasingly difficult to come up with the funds necessary to produce a ''big-event'' film. One solution was collaboration. In 1996, for example, Tri-Star teamed up with Disney to produce *Starship Troopers,* a big-budget science fiction film directed by *Robocop* 's Paul Verhoeven. Even without any major stars, this film was still expected to cost more than $100 million.

CURRENT CONDITIONS

The trend in the motion picture industry at the close of the 1990s was the belief that the bigger the budget, the more successful the film. As the production costs for more and more motion pictures reached or exceeded $100 million, the studios were in the perilous position of trying to recoup costs at a box office that was increasingly being threatened from cable television, video sales, and the Internet and other new communication technologies. For every mega multi-million dollar hit like 1997's *Titanic* and 1999's *The Phantom Menace,* there were scores of underachievers that further depleted the coffers of the major studios.

In 1998, in an attempt to increase revenue sources, the motion picture companies increased the amount of money cable companies had to pay them for the rights to air pay-per-view movies. Motion picture companies were asking for a 5 percent increase in revenues that would bring up their cut of the pay-per-view fee to one half. Cable operators were fighting this increase as the decade ended. The revenue sharing agreement between the studios and video rental chains was also revised, although this revision was a bit more amenable to both participants. Previously, the studios charged a costly fee, sometimes $50 per copy of a rental video cassette to the video stores because the stores kept the income generated from each rental of the tape. As a result, stores would often purchase only a few copies of a popular title because of the prohibitive cost involved. The studio began to change that practice in the late 1990s as they set up revenue sharing agreements with the video chains where the studios would cut the cost of the rental cassette and share in the profits from the rentals of the tape.

Late 1999 saw the addition of the newest player in the motion picture distribution arena, Amazon.com, the Internet book and music superstore. Amazon.com has gotten involved in the distribution of independent films that may not have had a chance to be released any other way. Amazon touted independent distribution outlet as a new avenue for acclaimed and underground filmmakers.

INDUSTRY LEADERS

If one measures success in terms of box office market share, five large producer-distributors consistently lead the film entertainment industry: Warner, Disney, Universal, Sony, and Paramount. Competition is fierce, and rarely does a single company hold the top position for long. The multi-media conglomerate known as Time-Warner was the industry leader in 1998, while the Walt Disney Company was not too far behind. Paramount, Sony and Universal round out the top five. Together these companies accounted for more than 80 percent of domestic box office sales in the mid- to late 1990s.

Warner and Paramount have both continued to rank as major studios since the studio era. Warner first achieved major status with the success of its sound technology. Paramount was, in fact, a division of the first studio to become fully integrated. Universal, a descendent of Carl Laemmle's Independent Motion Picture Company (a rival to Edison's ''Trust''), was classified during this period as a ''major minor'' studio in spite of its major production and distribution capabilities, primarily because it lacked an exhibition arm.

Unlike these three studios, Disney operated as an independent studio specializing in animation during the studio era. Only when it began producing live action movies in 1953 did it attain major status. Throughout the 1950s and 1960s, Disney blazed the trail for diversification into a variety of entertainment markets. With its ''Disneyland'' network series it became one of the first movie studios to explore the promotional possibilities of television. The company's theme park in California provided 60 percent of its profits in 1969. Universal later followed suit with its Universal Studios theme park, and in 1992 Paramount bought into five theme parks. Disney's other early diversification efforts included publishing, recording, and merchandising. Throughout its development as an entertainment corporation, Disney has specialized in the family market. Not until the 1984 release of *Splash* under its new Touchstone division did Disney try to break into the adult market. Since then, the company has increasingly entered the adult market, but its target audience remains the family.

The entrance of the Sony Corporation into the film market in 1989 with its acquisition of Columbia Pictures and Tri-Star brought another major player into the business. Sony's vast resources and eagerness to integrate its hardware and software divisions with its new entertainment arm helped spur the explosion of production costs that occurred in the 1990s. Other Japanese electronics giants like Matsushita Electric (Panasonic) and JVC followed Sony's lead, briefly leading to fears that Hollywood would fall under foreign control. But Matsushita's 1992 purchase of Universal Pictures soon proved a bust and the company sold 80 percent of its shares to Seagram's Co.

Research and Technology

Just as home video and cable technologies have shaped the movie and video production industry by heightening the demand for programming, further advances in technology could stimulate production in the future. Pay-per-view, for example, has the potential to open up the market, but presents consumers with limited program choices and gives them less scheduling flexibility than a videocassette. Fiber optic cables and other techniques for compressing information could overcome these limitations by offering the viewer more program options and greater freedom of choice over when to watch them.

While improved pay-per-view technology would create new ways to deliver the same kinds of programs, other advances might create altogether new forms of filmed entertainment. By allowing viewers to play a movie on computers, CD-ROMs make it possible for viewers to interact with a movie as they watch it. In a CD-ROM version of *A Hard Day's Night* developed by the Voyager Company, the viewer can use the computer to access relevant articles, read the script, or search for a particular part of the film while the movie plays in a 2-inch-by-3-inch window on the monitor. However, because of CD-ROMs limited storage capacity (and low-grade picture quality), the format has been unable to climb out of its niche market status and is likely to soon be supplanted by DVD (an acronym variously said to stand for Digital Video Disc and Digital Versatile Disc), a CD-like system offering enormous storage capacity, picture quality superior to any conventional consumer video systems, and compatibility with both computer and television systems. Backed by all the major electronics manufacturers and supported by movie producers, all expectations are that DVD will establish itself as the leading consumer video standard by the end of the decade. Also, in the works are such things as video-on-demand, whereby consumers could download a movie via the Internet or a similar delivery system. Such a system could ultimately eliminate the need for storage media such as video discs or tapes altogether, as well as dramatically changing the nature of traditional broadcasting. Such interactive multimedia combinations of text and film have the potential to blur the line between the publishing industry and the entertainment industry, thereby opening up new aesthetic possibilities and new markets.

The tremendous growth of the Internet in the mid- to late 1990s has also brought about the concept of cyber cinema in Europe. Orbiting satellites transmit digital motion pictures to cinemas that are specially designed for the purpose of showing these films. These digital film copies are less costly than the traditional film copies and as a result more places can afford to show first run films in a more cost efficient manner as the digital technology and hardware is less expensive than the traditional equipment. Also in late 1998, the United States had its first satellite digital broadcast. This innovation in motion picture distribution and exhibition has lead to the concept of Internet films. Paying customers link into a specified site on the Internet and view, via personal computers, films specifically produced and created for the Internet. In short, the motion picture industry has come full circle in the century or so since its birth from nickelodeons to massive megaplexes and then on to the home computer.

Further Reading

Carver, Benedict. "Tube Triumph." *Variety,* 22 February 1999.

Conlin, Michelle. "Sam Goldwin on $900." *Forbes,* 14 December 1998.

Dempsey, John. "Pay-Per-View Fight: Studios vs. Cable Ops." *Variety,* 8 June 1998.

"Filmed Entertainment." *Standard and Poor's Industry Surveys.* New York: McGraw Hill, January 1997.

Hoovers Online. Austin, TX: November 1999. Available at http://www.hoovers.com.

Klady, Leonard. "Studios Fixated by Numbers Game." *Variety,* 12 July 1999.

Meza, Ed. "Cyber Project Tries to Redefine Cinema." *Variety,* 8 June 1998.

Quittner, Joshua. "Amazon Goes to the Movies." *Time,* 6 September 1999.

Schlosser, Joe. "The B—as in Broadcast—List?" *Broadcasting and Cable,* 1 January 1999.

Spaulding, Jeffrey. "Life With the Charts." *Film Comment,* March/April 1998.

Time. "Movies Hit the Net."6 September 1999.

SIC 7819

SERVICES ALLIED TO MOTION PICTURE PRODUCTION

This category includes establishments primarily engaged in performing services independent of motion picture production, but allied thereto. These include motion picture film processing, editing and titling, casting, wardrobe and studio property rental, motion picture and video tape reproduction, and stock footage film libraries.

NAICS CODE(S)

512191 (Teleproduction and Other Post-Production Services)
561310 (Employment Placement Agencies)
532220 (Formal Wear and Costumes Rental)
532490 (Other Commercial and Industrial Machinery and Equipment Rental and Leasing)
541214 (Payroll Services)
711510 (Independent Artists, Writers, and Performers)
334612 (Prerecorded Compact Disc (Except Software), Tape, and Record Manufacturing)
512199 (Other Motion Picture and Video Industries)

INDUSTRY SNAPSHOT

This highly fragmented industry covers a range of services and products geared toward the production of motion pictures. Usually, firms engaged in this sector focus mainly or exclusively on a specialized operation and generally contract their services to motion picture producers or distributors. As small, relatively unleveraged firms, these hired guns are often forced to compete with each other on pricing in order to attract major Hollywood studios as well as independent filmmakers, who typically work with a tight budget.

By the late 1990s, major studios, such as Disney and Twentieth Century Fox were investing in large facilities to house equipment for post-production activities such as editing and sound mixing that can be accomplished on site. Some, like Twentieth Century Fox, boast complete ground-up digital integration, bypassing the need for analog sound conversion. Others include wardrobe and scenery stocks and tape reproduction facilities; thus, the firms engaged in services allied to motion picture production were scrambling to maintain their viability in this increasingly consolidated marketplace, often positioning themselves as an attractive purchase for major studios.

The hottest sector of the industry in the late 1990s was the production of special effects and animation. The astounding success and proliferation of films and movies featuring computer-generated special effects led to a rapid expansion and enhancement of these technologies. Film studios were engaged in competition to dazzle audiences with the most amazing visual images. By the end of the 1990s, 16 of the 20 largest all-time box-office hits had sold themselves primarily on special effects.

ORGANIZATION AND STRUCTURE

The overall structure of the services allied to motion picture industry is distinguished by a heavy reliance on subcontracting and freelance talent. Firms rarely enjoy movie-gross percentages and remain fixed on jumping from one short-term contract to another. As a result, these companies are usually in a poor bargaining position with studios, a feature that is exacerbated by the highly fragmented nature of the industry. They are continually forced to monitor the contracts competitors enter into in an effort to out-price them and attract studios.

The key players in the industry—directors and producers—develop strong relational networks based on previous successes and reputations. The production team, which is composed of primary and allied production services, brings together a diverse group of professionals, services, and capital equipment. These relationships are temporary, created for the single purpose of producing a particular film. However, such temporary organizations are reassembled with the production of each new film; a service provider's reputation is a paramount factor in his/her ability to facilitate membership in the new network.

Motion picture production is a highly complex business that involves an interplay of commercial and creative considerations. There are a number of interrelated activities that may be broken down into four phases: development, pre-production, production, and post-production.

Development. The development stage involves acquiring literary rights, writing and developing a screenplay, and hiring key creative personnel such as the director and the cast. Key allied services during the development stage include those offered by literary agents and talent and casting services.

Literary agents represent writers and directors. Agents negotiate for their clients and review scripts. They make determinations regarding what projects constitute good film property and then convince producers and actors to take on these projects. Most literary agents are involved in the development of potential deals, concept development, and the provision of creative and practical advice on translating a script into a motion picture.

Casting for a motion picture is usually the result of interaction between the casting director and casting consultants or services. The casting director is responsible for casting roles and maintaining an ongoing relationship with talent and casting consultants. Casting consultants are hired on an individual-project basis. They function as an actor clearinghouse for the director. Casting consultants seek out and hire actors, negotiate salary and billing issues with the actors' agents, prepare contracts for all actors, and make ''first work'' calls. In the late 1990s, the key player in the casting service business was the Casting Society of America. Most other major casting service firms were located in and around the Los Angeles/Hollywood area.

Pre-production. During pre-production, the remaining creative personnel are hired, a budget is developed, shooting schedules and locations are planned, and other necessary steps are taken to prepare the motion picture for primary photography. Key allied services during the pre-production stage include studio and production facility rental services.

The most prominent studio facilities are the mainstream producers of large-scale release motion pictures. These include Twentieth Century Fox, Warner Brothers, Columbia/Tri-Star, Universal Studios, Paramount, Disney/Buena Vista, Sony, New Line, Miramax, and MGM. However, the industry is really a continuum ranging from mainstream studies to true independent producers. The mainstream studios control nearly 90 percent of the revenue in theatrical rentals but are responsible for only 42 percent of the production starts. There are many small productions, then, that utilize small, independent production facilities; this is especially true of productions filmed outside of the Los Angeles/Hollywood area.

Production. This phase of motion picture development includes the actual filming. Key allied services include animation, camera-equipment rental and operation, costume design and rental, lighting equipment rental and operation, and property and scenery design, rental, and maintenance.

It is during the production stage that the division between equipment rental/provision and operation is manifested. Equipment provision services are conducted by a number of independent firms; equipment operation, on the other hand, is conducted by union employees. The most prominent entertainment unions in this area is the International Alliance of Theatrical Stage Employees (IATSE) and Moving Picture Machine Operators of the United States and Canada.

Animation is the process of exposing film by individual frames while introducing a slight change in the photographed object or drawing following each exposure. By linking hundreds or thousands of frames, the materials become animated, moving in accordance with the intention of the individual creating the film. Other animated files are created by single frame exposures of models or objects. Film special effects are increasingly dominated by digital animation. Technological advances have allowed lower production costs in animation, allowing increased use of animation in motion picture openings, commercials, and special effect simulations. Animation and special effects are dominated by a small number of firms, unlike most sectors of this industry. This sector generates estimated revenues of $600 million each year, a figure that has more than doubled since 1993, as more movies incorporate or feature animation and special effects. Prominent players include George Lucas' Industrial Light & Magic, James Cameron's Digital Domain, Sony Corp.'s Imageworks, Hanna Barbera, Rankin/Bass Productions, and Walt Disney Studios.

Camera equipment and personnel are an important aspect of motion picture production support. Such elements include the actual photographic device for shooting film; camera-hauling vehicles; the director of cinematography and associated camera crew; and individuals responsible for lighting, setting up, and composing shots. Although camera supply houses do not provide operators, they usually offer ancillary services such as equipment repair.

Costume design is a vital part of the film production process. Costume rental firms exist in virtually every major city, due to demand not only from motion picture production, but local theater and private costume rental.

Lighting equipment rental and operation is another important service. Although setting the position of lights on the set is the responsibility of the director of photography (cinematographer), the cumbersome nature of film lighting equipment makes actual implementation both difficult and time consuming. There are more than 100 lighting equipment firms in both Los Angeles/Hollywood and New York. Lighting technicians, repairmen, and lighting operators all fall under this category.

Property and scenery design, rental, and maintenance is an important production element as well. Property (or ''props'') includes any moveable item seen or used on a motion picture set. Scenery includes any background or backdrop used in a studio. There are several key professionals engaged in prop design and maintenance. A ''prop maker'' is frequently a member of the construction department (usually a carpenter) who is responsible for making the necessary props. A prop master is responsible for maintenance, availability, and placement of props on the actual set. Scenic artists are responsible for production of all illustrations, scenery and set designs, scale models, props and other set dressings. More than 90 percent of property and scenery rental firms make their homes in the Los Angeles and New York areas.

Post-production. In post-production, the picture is edited into its final form; music, dialogue, and sound effects are synchronized with the picture, and special effects are completed, resulting in the negative from which release prints are produced for distribution. Key allied services include computer colorization, cutting rooms, editing equipment and services, film processing and preservation, music libraries and cutting services, sound and recording services, special effect services, subtitle services, and trailers.

Editing equipment and services are essential to the post-production process. Editing involves joining together the various pieces of film shot by the cinematographer into a single, cohesive, and dramatic whole. The autonomy experienced by the editor depends on the director. For some films, the editor and director will work closely in selecting each shot and determining where to cut, splice, and edit. Accordingly, some directors shoot a large quantity of footage, allowing the editor a great deal of choice; other directors shoot less footage, providing the editor with less autonomy.

As is common in this fragmented industry, editing equipment, editing services, and editing personnel are provided by three different groups of organizations. There are more than fifty editing equipment firms, the majority of which are located in Los Angeles and New York. More than 100 firms, represented equally between New York and Los Angeles, provide film editing services.

Other major post-production services include: (1) Cutting rooms—specially designed facilities equipped with editing equipment where the editor and assistants can put the final film together. (2) Film processing and preservation—the actual development of the film into a negative and subsequent processing, copying, and preservation. Technicolor was an industry leader for this service. (3) Music libraries and cutting services; sound and recording services—these services include the process of recording sound during production and subsequently editing and adding sound to the final product. Some producers use stock music by anonymous composers to develop a sound track, while others utilize commissioned musicians. Again, this segment of the industry is highly fragmented, with more than 100 firms engaged in music cutting and music libraries and more than 100 firms that provide sound and recording services. Sound technicians include: production mixers who are responsible for sound equipment and recording on set; boom operators who operate the microphones to pick up actor's dialogue; re-recording mixers engaged in combining sound in the studio; and sound effects mixers, responsible for sound effects both on the set and in the studio. (4) Special effect services—special effects include a wide variety of creative photographic and sound effects. There are more than 50 special effects firms, which operate primarily in Los Angeles and New York, but also in such locations as Las Vegas, San Francisco, and Orlando. Prominent firms include Buena Vista Visual Effects Group in Burbank, California; Lucasfilm, Ltd., in San Francisco; and Walt Disney/MGM Studios in Orlando. (5) Subtitle services—subtitles refer to titles that appear at the bottom of the screen of foreign language films or to narrative titles in silent films.

CURRENT CONDITIONS

Firms engaged in services allied to motion picture production are intimately tied to the success of the film industry as a whole and, as such, keep a close eye on box office receipts. The late 1990s did not disappoint. Box office receipts finally emerged from their stubborn mid-1990s stagnation, increasing from $5.9 billion in 1996 to $7.0 billion in 1999. Foreign sales showed an even faster growth in the last 1990s, rising more than 10 percent annually between 1996 and 1999.

As major studios attempt to streamline their production operations and limit costs, they increasingly integrated operations covered by this industry into their organizations. Firms specializing in the various sectors of services allied to motion picture production were purchased by large film and telecommunication firms, such as when AT&T's Liberty Media Corp. purchased the California-based Four Media Co. in 1999. The effects company Digital Domain was likewise purchased by chip-manufacturer Intel. Such moves were indicative of the overall trend toward integration of high-level technological platforms for use in both entertainment and communications.

There was tremendous concern in the late 1990s in the film industry over the loss of jobs to runaway production, in which film producers take production to Canada and other foreign countries, largely to capitalize on the favorable exchange rates that make production in those countries significantly cheaper. In 1998 U.S. film and TV production conducted out of the country cost the U.S. economy $10 billion, an increase of 500 percent since 1990, according to the Screen Actors Guild and Directors Guild. Legislators in California and other states, and at the federal level, responded by introducing bills that offered tax breaks to production that was conducted in the U.S. Despite the growth of runaway production, however, over the same period employment in California's film industry nearly doubled.

For consumers, Hollywood's budget problems meant more sequels and increasingly formulaic films. For businesses involved in providing support to motion picture production, it meant a shrinking market in which relationships with studios were a top priority.

RESEARCH AND TECHNOLOGY

A relatively recent technological advance in the film industry has been the colorization of old films. Colorization is the process by which black-and-white films are transformed into color. The process involves breaking down each frame into 525,000 dots. An art director examines the first and last frame of each scene and programs the colors for each object. There are two primary firms engaged in colorization, American Film Technologies and Color Systems Technology, both of which are located in the Los Angeles area.

Undoubtedly, the most significant technological developments in the film industry in the 1990s occurred in the special effects sector, where computer-generated images quickly became a staple of Hollywood films in the, thrusting firms like George Lucas's Industrial Light and Magic and James Cameron's Digital Domain into the national spotlight. Increasingly, the level of special effects assumed a primary selling characteristic for blockbuster films, such as *Titanic,* which featured a special effects budget of $40 million.

Though computer-generated images have been making tentative forays into films since 1984's *Tron,* manipulating images this way requires vast amounts of memory due to film's superior picture quality. Since the powerful technology needed for this process was too expensive, few movies made in the 1980s used computer-generated images. By the late 1990s, however, cheap, powerful workstations and a wide range of versatile graphics software made computer graphics a viable alternative to the models traditionally used for special effects. The widespread transfer of high-end digital production to computer platforms, which offer tremendous cost benefits, especially in computer animation, afforded allowed major studios to invest more heavily in attracting the top graphic artists and less on expensive equipment. Moreover, small, independent filmmakers were able to process high-level special effects in-house.

The film industry also made aggressive moves toward the use of digital cinema as a replacement for film, a move that has been discussed in the industry for several years. To date, no technology can deliver digital results without sacrificing quality. Digital cinema is like to be incorporated into use with DVD-ROM, a physical distribution that, in the meantime, seems more attractive than satellite and cable due to the increased delivery control afforded by the physical format.

In a development not likely to prove popular among actors, industry observers noted that digital technology had reached a point where just around the corner waited the implementation of virtual actors into major motion pictures, one of the primary foci of the digital animation industry. By combining scores of photographs in a data memory bank, graphic artists can shape features and movements tailored to the needs of the director. While the technology has yet to reach a stage in which the actors appear truly real, analysts note that it is simply a matter of time. Such moves take selective casting of actors to the next level, by literally creating actors from the ground up, allowing directors to get the precise features and capabilities they desire. Such actors could pull off physical stunts beyond the capacities of live stunt actors—without necessitating elaborate set designs.

FURTHER READING

Carey, Patricia M. ''Group Shoots for More Special Effects: Producers Vie With L.A. for Work.'' *Crain's New York Business.* 14 September 1998.

Deneroff, Harvey. ''An Expanding Universe.'' *Hollywood Reporter,* 5 March 1999.

Katz, Judith A. *The Business of Show Business.* New York: Barnes & Noble Books, 1981.

La Franco, Robert. ''Profit Disaster.'' *Forbes,* 21 September 1999.

''New Technicolor Acquisition, A Step Toward Digital Cinema.'' *Emedia,* October 1999.

Parisi, Paula. ''Fox Sound is Taken to the Next Stage.'' *Hollywood Reporter,* 15 November 1999.

''The State of Production.'' *Hollywood Reporter,* 20 July 1999.

''Two Oakland, Calif.-Area Companies Work to Create Digital Actors.'' *Contra-Costa Times,* 26 August 1999.

U.S. Department of Commerce. International Trade Administration. *U.S. Industry and Trade Outlook 1999.* New York: The McGraw Hill Companies, 1999.

SIC 7822

MOTION PICTURE AND VIDEO TAPE DISTRIBUTION

This classification covers establishments primarily engaged in the distribution (rental or sale) of theatrical and non-theatrical motion picture films or in the distribution of video tapes and disks, except to the general public. Establishments engaged in both distribution and production are classified in **SIC 7812: Motion Picture and Video Tape Production.** Establishments primarily engaged in renting video tapes and disks to the general public are classified in **SIC 7841: Video Tape Rental.** Those businesses engaged in the sale of video tapes and disks to individuals for personal or household use are classified in **SIC 5735: Record and Prerecorded Tape Stores.**

NAICS CODE(S)

421990 (Other Miscellaneous Durable Goods Wholesalers)

512120 (Motion Picture and Video Distribution)

INDUSTRY SNAPSHOT

The U.S. motion picture distribution industry in the 1990s was stratified into two distinct categories: majors and independents. Major studios, such as Twentieth Century Fox and Buena Vista, control the lion's share of movie-distribution revenues and show films in large multiplexes and community theaters alike, while independent distributors, such as Artisan, rely more heavily on smaller art houses and rarely achieve the box-office blockbusters enjoyed by the majors. Through the 1990s, majors invested heavily in purchasing many of the leading independent distributors, such as Miramax and New Line Cinema, in a massive trend toward vertical integration. Those independents that remained so in the late 1990s benefited from the unexpectedly robust box-office success and critical acclaims of a string of high-profile independent films, breathing new life into this struggling market sector.

In 1999 domestic box office returns equaled $7.5 billion, up 8 percent from the previous year's record; this represented the eighth consecutive year of box-office expansion. Admissions, however, dipped slightly from the 39-year high of 1.48 billion in 1998 to 1.47 billion tickets sold. The difference was covered by rising ticket prices. Over the course of the current expansion, ticket prices increased 20 percent—8 percent in 1999 alone.

A total of 345 films were released in 1999, down from 368 the previous year. Major studios produced 146 of these, 9 fewer than in 1998, while independent distributors released 199 films, a significant decline from the 213 in 1998. While these numbers seem to favor independent distributors, those films generally maintained very limited reach; nearly 90 percent of all ticket sales were accumulated by the handful of leading major distributors. The number of wide releases—defined as those that play in at least 600 theaters simultaneously—totaled 145 in 1999, up a bit over the previous year, though below the 1996 decade peak of 155. These figures include both independent and major releases, though the total is obviously tilted heavily in favor the latter. Another landmark was surpassed in 1999 when for the first time two distributors, Buena Vista and Twentieth Century Fox, topped $1.0 billion in box office receipts. The video rental market grossed a record $8.5 billion in 1999.

World markets for films and television programs have long been critically important to U.S. producers and distributors. Over the last thirty years, foreign markets have generally accounted for about one-half of major U.S. producers' total sales in these industries. The success of American films and television productions in world markets is indicated both by industry trade balances and by comparisons with other film and television exporting nations. The United States has historically exported more than three times the total television programming exports of the next three leading exporting nations combined. The overseas market for U.S. motion pictures in theaters, video tape, and television totaled $7.6 billion in 1999. The 130 independent distributors that comprise the American Film Marketing Association reported foreign film sales of $1.8 billion in 1997. Though overseas markets remain lucrative for U.S. distributors, theatrical revenue growth was not expected to match that at home in the early 2000s, as foreign film markets continue to build their local industries. Europe receives nearly two-thirds of U.S. film exports, while other major markets include the Far East, particularly Japan. For years limited significantly by a variety of barriers to trade in foreign markets, U.S. studios welcomed the relaxation of such restrictions in the mid- and late 1990s as a result of free trade agreements enforced by the World Trade Organization.

ORGANIZATION AND STRUCTURE

The organization and structure of the motion picture industry has become concentrated in the major Hollywood studios who have taken control over its three major divisions: production, distribution, and exhibition. The organization of the industry into companies which have become fully integrated producers/distributors/exhibitors represents a structure that existed in the 1920s and 1930s, but was disbanded under antitrust regulation and then rekindled during the Reagan Administration. This structure has hurt film distributors without established alliances or reputations, known in the industry as ''independents,'' because many of the nation's prime theater venues have relationships with the major distributors who book the larger theaters months in advance.

Typically, a motion picture studio distributes or licenses the rights to its film to an independent distributor, who in turn sells these rights to theaters or exhibitors across the country and abroad. The distributor licenses films to exhibitors by either bidding or negotiation. To obtain the maximum revenue from motion pictures, they are released in a series of runs to theaters across the country. ''First run'' indicates a picture's initial widespread release to ''high gross'' theaters across the country. Subsequently, the films are released to lower gross theaters across the country until the earning capacity of the film is finally depleted in the exhibitor market. The film is then marketed abroad by foreign distributors and then released in video format and offered on cable television before it is syndicated to the television broadcast network.

When an independent distributor pays for the rights to market a specific film from a Hollywood studio, that company then forms a contract with the exhibitor market to show the end product. These contracts take many forms, but normally include several key features. The distributors create ''zones'' or geographic boundaries for their pictures. Normally, within each zone a distributor would only release a particular motion picture to one theater for exhibition. This practice ensures that the distributor will obtain the largest audience for a film and it prevents other theaters in close proximity from competing for the same customers who might wish to see that particular movie. There is usually a clearance clause in the contract that relates to the amount of time that must elapse between the end of the first run of a motion picture and the beginning of its subsequent runs. Longer clearances provide more first run revenues for a picture. Finally, many of the distributors of ''A'' rated films also practice block booking. Block booking is the practice of offering for license one feature, or a group of features, upon a condition that the exhibitor also license another feature, or group of features, released by a distributor during a given period. Block booking ensures outlets for a motion picture regardless of its quality or box office potential. The practices of block booking and blind bidding (requiring an exhibitor to bid for a film before reviewing it) by distributors are now regulated in approximately half of the states in the United States. These statutes, while primarily concerned with curbing the practice of blind bidding, also regulate the whole bidding process.

Background and Development

Since the formation of the motion picture industry by individuals such as Thomas Edison, Louise and August Lumiere, C. Francis Jenkins, and Thomas Armat in the 1880s, movie producers and distributors have attempted to control the industry by engaging in a multiplicity of tactics. Originally, monopolies were attempted through the ownership and protection of patents on the equipment and technology needed to produce and exhibit motion pictures. As technology advanced, the power that these patents could provide decreased. In an attempt to maintain control, industry leaders, led by Edison, merged their companies and formed a cartel, The Motion Picture Patents Company (MPPC).

At first, the MPPC wielded its power by pooling all of the licenses and patents that its individual members held. It defended its position by bringing numerous lawsuits against those who infringed on their rights. At the same time, motion picture exchanges developed to distribute the movies that the MPPC was producing. These entities purchased or leased films from producers and rented them to theater owners. These exchanges became quite profitable and the MPPC purchased most of them in a vertical integration marketing strategy. As the MPPC purchased exchanges, they instituted practices that were designed to increase their bargaining power and their ability to control the exhibitors who needed their product. Using their patents to force compliance from the exhibitors, the MPPC imposed restrictions on these exhibitors, including stipulations that implemented a system of distribution based on theatrical runs, geographic zones, and clearances (the amount of time contracted for between the first run of a motion picture and subsequent runs). The MPPC's successful control over distribution was short lived. A motion picture antitrust action brought by one of the few exchanges that MPPC did not operate resulted in the dissolution of the trust arrangement. The first attempt by movie producers at organized distribution had failed.

Although this decision brought an end to the MPPC, it was not successful in curtailing the control that motion picture producers and distributors had now gained. In 1916 Paramount Pictures Corporation, a fully integrated production and distribution company, arose from the ashes of the MPPC. Paramount, as a producer, had contracts with many popular film stars. It was able to use the appeal of the stars together with their distribution capabilities to create a new mechanism for control through block booking. While Paramount was a dominant force in the industry, other companies gained similar control by engaging in similar practices. Block booking, along with the established run-zone-clearance system, effectively put the exhibitors at the mercy of the producer/distributor companies.

In response to these practices, the exhibitors gained bargaining power by forming chains and circuits. In 1917 the First National Exhibitors Circuit was formed. This group of exhibitors gained power and market domination through anti-competitive practices of their own. As a consequence of the power that these exhibitors had gained in their circuits, control of these cinemas meant control of the entire industry, and they became targets for purchase by the big producers. The studios' purchasing was influenced by the realization that if they could control every level in the motion picture industry, from production to distribution to exhibition, they would not only be able to control prices and ensure access to screens for the exhibition of their own pictures, but they would also be able to prevent competition from independent producers and gain control over the entire industry. The studios began to purchase exhibitors to make this complete control a reality. As a result of these monopolistic activities, with studio-owned circuits gaining control over entire exhibition markets, the government felt it was necessary to intervene.

By 1930 the government had filed numerous lawsuits against the circuits and distributors in an attempt to curtail these practices. The industry was clearly dominated by a group of eight major studios. The top five vertically integrated firms—all with a major presence in distribution, exhibition, and production—were Warner Brothers Inc., MGM Inc., Paramount, Twentieth Century Fox Film Corp., and RKO. The other three included Universal Studios and Columbia Pictures (involved solely in production and distribution) and United Artists (distribution only). The majority of these suits charged the defendants with illegally restraining trade by adopting various anti-competitive practices including the use of arbitrary clearances, discriminatory zoning methods, and block booking. Although the government succeeded in forcing the studios to restrict their conduct, they ultimately lost the battle as the anti-competitive atmosphere had taken over the industry. By the end of the 1930s, the majority of the most powerful circuits had been purchased by the major studios.

In 1938, as a result of these anti-competitive practices, the U.S. government filed a case against the major studios, which has come to be known as the ''Paramount Case.'' The suit alleged that the motion picture producer defendants had attempted to monopolize and had monopolized the production and distribution of motion pictures. Although the case never went to trial, the major defendants signed a three year consent decree which enjoined them from: block booking more than five pictures, blind bidding, and requiring unreasonable clearances from exhibitors. The agreement also stifled forced rentals and limited the defendants in their quest to purchase exhibitors. This decree was unsuccessful in bringing about change in the industry because the government did not require the separation of production and distribution from exhibition.

In the late 1940s and early 1950s, the government reopened the Paramount case. The final result of this action was that all major motion picture studios were required to license motion pictures on a picture by picture basis, solely upon the merits and without discrimination in favor of affiliated theaters, circuit theaters or others. In addition, the government forced the five major companies to divest specific theaters and theater circuits. This action dismantled the fully integrated motion picture industry. The grip that studios had once held over the industry had finally been loosened. By eliminating the domination of vertically integrated studios, the hold over motion picture distribution was sufficiently weakened to give independent producers and distributors access to screens and a chance to prosper in the industry. The number of independent producers grew from 70 in 1946 to nearly 170 in 1950. In early 1953, the U.S. Justice Department concluded that the industry had become ''demonopolized'' and that competitive bidding and negotiations had become the dominant method of film licensing and distribution. In this environment, independent theaters were given the chance to compete equally for the right to exhibit first run movies.

The industry operated under this format until 1980, when President Reagan allowed studios to once again become vertically integrated by giving them the right to own movie theaters. This new application of the antitrust doctrine under President Reagan was used by the studios to reshape the motion picture industry. Under the Reagan Administration's policies, the Paramount consent decrees were not enforced and the movie studios once again reassembled the vertical integration path abandoned in 1948. By 1985, the studios were overcome with acquisition fever and were purchasing theaters at a record pace. Although some studios waited with cautious observance to analyze the Justice Department's response to these acquisitions, it raised no objections. Between 1985 and 1988, movie companies spent more than $1 billion to purchase independent movie theaters. The entire motion picture industry reverted back to the structure that existed before circuit divorcement and theater divestiture in 1948.

CURRENT CONDITIONS

With the increasing popularity and mainstream critical acclaim of independent hits in the late 1990s, the motion picture distribution industry has experienced an ever-tightening link between independent producers and Hollywood distributors, who see in the former's products a lucrative and refreshing break from the increasingly formulaic, sequel- and budget-driven Hollywood market. In that spirit, major distributors have entered into revenue-sharing agreements with independents, in which the majors take a share of the receipts in exchange for wider exposure. This practice encapsulates the decade-long efforts of major studios to reach into the independent market.

Meanwhile, rising advertising costs made it more difficult for independents to turn a profit, and were likely to result in fewer films in an attempt to scale back budgets, with advertising and exposure efforts devoted to the more hopeful products. While few independent distributors could expect to reap Hollywood-scale rewards at the box office, some were able to break into the major-studio stratosphere in the late 1990s. Independent films enjoyed spectacular revenues at theaters from wide-scale features like *The English Patient, Shakespeare in Love* (both of which won several Oscar Awards, including Best Picture), *Good Will Hunting,* and *The Full Monty.* Meanwhile, the unlikely runaway success of the independent Artisan's ''The Blair Witch Project,'' with $140 million in box office revenue, generated a record in profitability, since the documentary-style film was produced for less than $60,000.

The major independent studios include October, Fine Line, Fox Searchlight, and Artisan. The number of independent films released doubled between 1995 and 1998. The bread and butter of independent films are the smaller art houses, which have diminished in number with the trend toward enormous multiplexes, which are dominated by the major distributors. Along with the rising numbers of independent film productions, this has created a fiercely competitive distribution market among independents. As a result, this market has become internally stratified as distributors concentrate their production and promotional budgets on those films likely to achieve the greatest success. Sixty-eight independent films grossed $1 million in 1998, compared with 48 million in 1997, but far fewer earned more than $20 million.

For the independent exhibitors, distributors, and producers, one of the most unsettling aspects of the resurgence of major studio involvement in distribution and exhibition was that the studios hoped to guarantee their access to screens. Although the Paramount decree required divestiture and mandated that motion pictures be distributed theater by theater solely on merit and without discrimination, the reintegration of the industry has removed these safeguards altogether. As affiliated and nonaffiliated circuits continued to grow in size, independent circuits have been virtually eliminated from the competition to obtain first run motion pictures. While there is no evidence of collusive or discriminatory behavior by distributors or affiliated circuits, the market power of the large affiliates has been allowed to resurface.

In an attempt at rectifying the imbalance of bargaining power that distributors have maintained over exhibitors in the licensing of motion pictures, many states have passed statutes to regulate motion picture licensing. The majority of these statutes regulate the licensing of motion pictures and the bidding practice used to gain control of a motion picture. Motion-picture licensing usually occurs under a competitive bidding, competitive or noncompetitive negotiation, or track system. With competitive bidding, distributors send exhibitors solicitation letters informing the exhibitors of the release of new films. This correspondence contains a minimum amount of information about the film, possibly the stars and a brief plot synopsis, and suggested terms for the licensing of the film. If the distributor is unhappy with the bids that they receive, they will either solicit new bids or negotiate directly with the exhibitors. Lastly, the track system is used when there is an established relationship between an exhibitor and a distributor.

Exhibitors themselves have also attempted to obtain some bargaining strength against the major studio distributors with the use of "split agreements." Split agreements are the practice whereby exhibitors in a given market split the rights to negotiate for the rental of upcoming films. These agreements ensure that each split member has an initial right to bid or an opportunity to negotiate for certain films without competition from other split members. Because other split members agree not to submit bids for films that have not been designated to them, participants in split agreements initially face competition only from exhibitors who are not members of the split. Distributors have tried to fight these agreements in court, in order to maintain their bargaining strength.

The nature of motion picture distribution was dramatically altered by the rise of home video in the 1980s and 1990s. Distributors increasingly relied on small-screen revenues to recoup their costs. With box office receipts shared between distributors and theater operators, the home video market came to be an important part of the distribution system. In 1998, movie distributors earned about $8.5 billion in video rentals from U.S. and Canadian theaters and a similar amount overseas. On the other hand, video sales and licensing films for television broadcast brought in more than $12 billion. Nevertheless, while home video has become the leading source of profit for distributors and offers many movies a new lease on life—films that would otherwise go straight into the company vaults are now routinely released on video without a theatrical run. Box-office performance remains critical to a film's future success in the home video and television markets. Another growing market for film runs in the late 1990s was in satellite broadcasts. By 1999 made-for-satellite films constituted a $543 million distribution market. There were approximately 10 million pay-per-view subscribers in the United States, a figure that was expected to increase with the further proliferation of DirecTV service. Furthermore, satellite broadcasters were leaning increasingly toward on-demand video service, in which customers could download any film licensed to the broadcaster directly to their homes. Several major Hollywood directors, including Francis Ford Coppola and John Landis, boosted the satellite movie market by producing made-for-satellite films, in which producers contract directly with satellite broadcasters for exclusive rights to show the films.

Industry Leaders

Nearly 90 percent of the U.S. film market was dominated by a small group of major Hollywood distributors in 1999. At the box office, Buena Vista topped the list, controlling 16 percent of the U.S. market, followed by Paramount (15.8 percent), Warner Brothers (10.9 percent), Sony Corporation (10.9 percent), Twentieth Century Fox (10.6 percent), and Universal Studios (5.5 percent).

In overseas markets, the leading distributors were Twentieth Century Fox, with $1.95 billion in foreign box office receipts; Buena Vista, with $1.17 billion; and Sony Corporation's Columbia and Tri-Star divisions, with a combined $1.07 billion.

Home video rentals were led by Warner Brothers, with revenues of $2.6 billion; Buena Vista, with $1.6 billion; Twentieth Century Fox, with $755.1 million; and Paramount, with $710.5 billion.

AMERICA AND THE WORLD

Twenty U.S. films exceeded $100 million in foreign box office receipts in 1999, while the total revenue from overseas theaters reached a record $5.7 billion in the sixth consecutive year of growth in this crucial market sector. By 2000, however, Hollywood distributors faced growing challenges in many staple markets as their local film industries experienced robust growth.

World markets for films and television programs have long been critically important to U.S. producers and distributors. During the past 30 years, foreign markets have generally accounted for about one-half of major U.S. producers' total sales in these industries. The success of American films and television productions in world markets is indicated both by industry trade balances and by comparisons with other film and television exporting nations. The United States has historically enjoyed tremendous advantages in these areas.

Motion picture and video tape distribution to other countries is, however, hindered by several factors. Trade problems encountered in the media industries fall into two general classes: government-imposed non-tariff barriers and various forms of film and video piracy. These problems greatly reduce American industries' revenues in many markets. Non-tariff barriers include various quantitative restrictions, limitations on the repatriation of earnings, and discriminatory taxes, usually aimed at protecting domestic markets from foreign competition. Perhaps even more important in terms of its effect on export earnings is video piracy. Producers' and distributors' losses due to piracy have increased enormously as a result of the growth of new copying and distribution technologies. Copyright enforcement problems of varying degrees are encountered in all markets throughout the world. Moreover, the nature and severity of copyright infringement differs among individual markets and channels of distribution. Copyright infringement problems fall into four broad categories: unauthorized public exhibition, print theft, videocassette piracy, and theft of broadcast signals.

The first of these activities, unauthorized public exhibition, has been reported to occur primarily in more developed countries. Unauthorized presentations of copyright protected films often occurs in hotels, cafes, homes, and theaters around the globe.

A second, related category of copyright infringement is the actual theft of film prints themselves. Copies of prints can be stolen at various stages of distribution, and the negatives can subsequently be used to produce unauthorized prints.

The third, and perhaps most widespread, form of copyright infringement is videocassette piracy, which has become a global phenomenon. Analysts estimate that hundreds of millions of dollars are lost to videocassette piracy each year. These copyright infractions, coupled with other forms of piracy such as the theft of broadcast signals, has resulted in poor relations between U.S. producers and distributors and foreign agencies. As motion picture technology converts to a purely digital format, as it is expected to during the 2000s, film distributors are hoping to outpace pirates in establishing safeguards against illegal copying with the new technology. In that spirit, a number of telecommunications and film companies joined forces in 1998 to implement a restrictive encryption standard on digital films and music to prevent piracy.

In Europe, Germany represents a particularly lucrative market, especially for major distributors in the late 1990s. The independent circuit is generally more devoted to German films, which have made a notable comeback in recent years.

The surge in the long-depressed British film industry has helped turn the U.K. into a miserable market for independent U.S. distributors. However, major U.S. distributors maintain a 90 percent share of the U.K.'s foreign theater market.

The notoriously proud French film industry has likewise made it difficult for U.S. independents to gain much of a footing there. Hollywood films, however, have made substantial inroads into the French television market.

Italy is generally more open to independent U.S. distributors than its northern neighbors. Successful Hollywood films, meanwhile, have been the prime victims of the growing Italian film market.

Hard-hit by economic woes, Japan enthusiastically welcomes Hollywood films, but displays little enthusiasm for independents. Japan has a $5 billion video-rental market, which represents 45 percent of the total U.S. export market.

China's restrictive market was loosened considerably in 1999, as the country continued to open toward market economics and prepared to enter the World Trade Organization. As part its WTO-admission agreement with the Clinton Administration, China agreed to double the number of U.S. films it imports annually to 20.

Hollywood was particularly eyeing emerging economies in the late 1990s. The market for U.S. films in Latin America increased 20 percent in 1998; continued market reforms in Eastern Europe also represent strong potential for film distributors. The Middle East, in contrast, continues to provide only a small market, though it also increased 30 percent in 1998.

RESEARCH AND TECHNOLOGY

Advancements in technology in the multi-media marketplace are being incorporated into the motion picture industry and are changing the way traditional products are being developed, licensed, and distributed. Film is becoming a digital media and is acquiring many of the similarities found in software products such as video games. Conventional film companies are exploring the opportunities in interactive transmission and technology. Companies are digitizing their film libraries and exploring new ways to make this product available to distributors and consumers. Already, first run motion pictures are being shown outside the customary movie theater and are available in motorcoach bus tours. The transformation of the motion picture industry to a digital format and the increase in new technologies available to cable companies, the broadcast networks, and consumers will provide the public with an array of viewing possibilities.

Improved technology is also being developed to make the World Wide Web a film-viewing medium, thus creating an inexpensive outlet for film makers without significant financial backing. With decreased production costs and inexpensive computer software, these film makers only need space on a Web server to bring their films to public exposure. Fees for such films will likely be covered by advertising on Web servers, perhaps supplemented by an online pay-per-view system. Major distributors are, of course, eyeing these developments carefully.

By the 1990s, distributors and producers were far less wary of new technologies than they had been. The arrival of home video recording in the late 1970s, once viewed as a threat, had proven to be a vastly lucrative new source of income. Hence, the arrival of the new DVD digital video format—which allowed an entire film to be stored on a disc similar to a CD—in late 1996 was widely supported by the industry. Copy protection systems and a regional coding system that prevented discs manufactured in one country from playing on players manufactured in another country assuaged fears that a given country would be flooded with high-quality digital copies of a motion picture before its actual theatrical release. By the end of the 1990s developers were still working to manufacture affordable DVD technology without sacrificing image quality. Digital cinema is like to be incorporated into use with DVD-ROM, a physical distribution that, in the meantime, seems more attractive than satellite and cable due to the increased delivery control afforded by the physical format.

Further Reading

"5 Companies to Join in Anti-Piracy Pact." *New York Times,* 20 February 1998.

Boliek, Brooks. "China to Allow More U.S. Films." *Hollywood Reporter,* 16 November 1999.

Fuson, Brian. "7-Year Rich at the Box Office: 1998 Continues Streak With Another Record." *Hollywood Reporter,* 4 January 1999.

Fuson, Brian. "'99 B.O. Reels In $7.5 Billion." *Hollywood Reporter,* 3 January 2000.

Geier, Thom. "Hopes for Hits Broken by Fractured Audiences (Year End Wrap 98: The Indies)." *Hollywood Reporter,* 7 January 1999.

Hettrick, Scott. "Buena Vista is Happiest on Video Shelves." *Hollywood Reporter,* 4 January 1999.

Hollinger, Hy. "Territory Roundup." *Hollywood Reporter—Special American Film Market Issue,* February 1998.

"It's 'Witch' Craft." *Hollywood Reporter,* 6 January 2000.

Litwak, Mark. *Reel Power: The Struggle For Influence and Success In The New Hollywood.* New York: William Morrow, 1986.

Matthews, Regina. "Exclusive! (Sort Of . . .)." *CableVision,* 19 July 1999.

McClintick, David. *Indecent Exposure: A True Story of Hollywood and Wall Street,* New York: William Morrow, 1982.

Sporich, Brett. "Hollywood Makes Rev-Sharing Deal on Collection of Indie Films." *Video Store,* 19 December 1999.

Stevens, Tracy and Patricia Nicolescu, eds. *1999 International Motion Picture Almanac.* New York: Quigley Publishing Co., Inc., 1999.

Talacko, Paul. "Web Gets a Slice of the Action." *Financial Times,* 22 December 1999.

"U.S. Exports Hit $5.7 Billion." *Hollywood Reporter,* 31 August 1999.

Woods, Mark. "More Players Split O'Seas Pie." *ariety,* 10 January 2000.

SIC 7829

SERVICES ALLIED TO MOTION PICTURE DISTRIBUTION

This classification includes establishments primarily engaged in performing auxiliary services to motion picture distribution, such as film delivery service, film purchasing and booking agencies, and film libraries.

NAICS Code(s)

512199 (Other Motion Picture and Video Industries)
512120 (Motion Picture and Video Distribution)

Industry Snapshot

Services allied to motion picture distribution faced challenges on a number of fronts in the late 1990s. Shifting patterns in the theater market threatened to undercut film booking and purchasing agencies; film technology was forcing film carriers to rethink their operating strategies to accommodate emerging trends; and major motion picture distribution companies were quickly encroaching on the traditional film-library market.

Businesses in this industry are allied to the process of film distribution, instead of directly providing services to film distribution companies. In other words, these firms contract with companies in the film exhibition industry, including theater houses, rather than with the distributors. Industry players tend to specialize in their particular market segments, which include film booking and purchasing agencies, film libraries, and film delivery services. Companies in this industry tend to be small; many serve only regional areas.

ORGANIZATION AND STRUCTURE

Film Booking and Purchasing. Film booking and purchasing agencies were contracted by movie theaters to act on their behalf in the process of acquiring and negotiating the terms to rented feature films from motion picture distribution companies. (The terms ''purchasing'' and ''buying'' do not mean the actual sale of films, but a form of rental). Traditionally the term ''booking'' referred to agreeing which films to play, while ''buying'' referred to negotiating the payment for the film and its length of run. Both activities, however, were performed by the same agencies. Accordingly, booking and purchasing agencies were synonymous designations. Agencies also helped theaters select films by screening them first when possible. Booking agencies occasionally offered additional business services to theaters, such as market research, consulting, accounting, and bookkeeping. Booking agencies were hired by a majority of independently owned theaters, whereas larger chains of theaters tended to perform their own booking.

Booking agencies tended to be very small companies, many serving only a handful of theater clients operating a total of 20 to 30 cinema screens. While most booking agencies employed few workers, some were simply self-employed agents. Larger agencies occasionally operated branch offices and served theaters in different parts of the country but rarely employed more than a dozen workers.

Especially with the move toward megaplexes, large movie houses featuring a number of screenings simultaneously, film booking agencies are likely to play a diminishing role in the U.S. film industry. The number of movie screens has increased by about 4,000 since the mid-1990s; however, during the same period, theaters housing 16 or more screens grew by 400 percent. Leading theater operators like Carmlike Cinemas and Regal Cinemas, Inc. typically negotiate with distributors directly.

Film Libraries. There were several different types of entities that were all called film libraries. Film libraries that were independent companies involved in renting out films tended to serve the non-theatrical market, namely educational institutions and other non-profit organizations. They differed from the film exchanges that distribution companies used by holding their collections for longer periods of time, and having complete control over their distribution and rates. Since they served a non-profit market, film libraries charged a relatively low flat rental fee, instead of requiring a share of the profits, as did commercial distributors. Film libraries increasingly offer film on videotape in addition to reels. In addition to film library companies, there are also non-profit organizations that rent film free of charge to educational institutions.

The term film library also was used to designate the film collection held by a motion picture production company or distributor. These film libraries, however, were not independent enterprises, but represented the assets of the companies. Theaters showing older films contracted with the company whose library contained the desired film. For films dating back several decades, the owner was not necessarily the original producer, since film studios and distribution companies have at times acquired the rights to each others' older films. In fact, the term ''film library'' did not necessarily correspond to the physical location of the films, but referred to the ownership of the copyrights.

The issue of film copyrighting came into play when copies of film were to be sold, rather than rented. A market for the sale of film, especially shorter film clips, existed among the producers of television programs, commercials, and videos, which incorporated the old clips into their new productions. When producers were unable to purchase film clips directly from the film libraries of the studios or distributors, they turned to a third type of film library. Stock-shot and archival footage film libraries owned and licensed film clips of interest to other producers.

Finally, there were film archives. These tended to be non-profit organizations that preserved original prints of films for posterity. Some exhibited their films on a limited basis, while others did not exhibit them at all, in order to preserve the films' quality. Thus, archives were not involved in the distribution process.

The 1990s witnessed a large-scale rearrangement of the ownership structure of the film-library market, as libraries were rapidly bought and sold, often in merger deals. Independent film libraries, meanwhile, have been swept up in the rapid consolidation of the major film studios. The film-library market has thus been characterized by the scramble to find buyers.

Film Delivery. Film delivery services, also known as film carriers, were usually classified under the transportation services industry, in particular **SIC 4213: Trucking Except Local,** but belonged under both classifications because of their unique services. Film carriers were specialized transportation companies serving the needs of motion picture theaters by delivering and picking up rented theatrical films. Film was transported between the cinemas and the national network of film exchanges (also known as film depots), or directly between theaters, based on their booking schedules. Metal canisters of 16 mm or 35 mm film were delivered to the theaters, usually on a weekly basis. Unlike other delivery services, film carriers had keys to the theaters they supplied so they could drop off and pick up film when the theater was closed. Most delivery was done by truck or van because of the heavy weight of the film canisters, which made them impractical for air freight, except in rush circumstances. Film carriers served only theaters, since other organizations that screened films tended to use the more easily transportable videotape format, or else had only occasional film needs, which could be handled by any non-specialized delivery service.

There were fewer than 30 major film delivery companies throughout the country that served nearly the entire theater market. Most served up to a couple hundred theaters, some covering a region comprising several states. There were also a commensurate number of smaller film carriers that exclusively served single theater chains of around 15 to 20 theaters. Films generally weigh about 62 pounds, and are often accompanied by large cardboard stand-up displays and other promotional items theaters place in lobbies.

Background and Development

Film Booking and Purchasing. The greatest developments in film booking and purchasing occurred in the booking process itself, and in the terms negotiated. Issues of negotiation in film rentals included the percentage of the gross income paid back to the distributor during consecutive weeks of a film's play, and the sum excluded the percentage that was turned over to the distributor to cover the theater's expenses. Other issues included the amount of the non-refundable guarantee paid by the theater up front to secure the film, the amount of the refundable advance, and the guaranteed extended playing time for the film.

In the past, block booking was common practice, in which the larger studios would rent out a block of good and mediocre films at an all-or-nothing deal to theaters. A proportion of the films would be rented at a flat rate while others would be paid for in a percentage of the profits. The practice was banned between 1921 and 1932, but continued again until the Supreme Court outlawed it in 1948.

An old practice of blind bidding resurfaced in the 1970s. Distributors convinced theaters to buy films before production was completed, and thus theaters could not view the film before deciding they wanted to purchase it. Studios had turned to blind bidding to cover their growing expenses, but states began to outlaw it. When nearly half the states forbade blind bidding, the practice was discouraged by the late 1980s.

To avoid competitive bidding among theaters in the same region, theaters devised a practice called ''product splitting'' by which they agreed among themselves how they would divide the upcoming films. This practice was made illegal following an anti-trust lawsuit in 1977.

Film Delivery. Film carriers quickly became a specialized service within the transportation industry with the emergence of the motion picture theaters in the 1920s. By 1933 the trade association Film Carriers Conference (later renamed National Magazine and Film Carriers Inc.) was formed. Later, film carriers gradually began to diversify into magazine transportation, beginning with services to *Time* magazine in the 1940s, as the film carriers' routes and delivery schedules fit well with the needs of magazine wholesalers. Film carriers diversified into delivering other theater supplies, including popcorn and candy sold at theater concession stands.

Current Conditions

The effect on the services allied to motion picture industry of digital film, and the expected introduction of digital film projectors, is yet to be determined. The new technology, which analysts expect to overtake the film industry in the 2000s, poses a particular concern regarding the control of delivery networks. Eventually, digital films could be transmitted electronically or even by satellite, though in the short term it seems likely that theater operators will favor physical distribution precisely because of the greater degree of delivery control afforded the theaters. Meanwhile, film libraries can expect to reap rewards from the conversion of their collections to digital format.

Equally nebulous was the impact of emerging technology aimed at delivering quality film footage over the Internet. Technology was rapidly developing to turn the World Wide Web into a film-viewing medium, thus creating an inexpensive outlet for filmmakers without significant financial backing. With decreased production costs and inexpensive computer software, these filmmakers only need space on a Web server to bring their films to public exposure. The electronic distribution of film over the Web would of course render delivery companies unnecessary. Meanwhile, online entrepreneurs have put out the word that they are in the market for film libraries. While Web film distribution will face legal hurdles in the form of licensing formalities for transmitting films over the Internet, this development could prove attractive to independent film libraries, which have the greatest difficulty finding consistently stable distribution networks.

The segment of film libraries renting for non-theatrical exhibition was being seriously hurt by the conversion of film to videotape and the subsequent growth of video rental outlets. Although it was technically illegal, teachers saved money by renting videos from a consumer video shop instead of renting the film through a film library.

Smaller booking agencies also felt the pinch of new technology and rapidly-consolidating Hollywood's growing concern for the bottom line. An intensified focus on first releases or "event" films in major markets squeezed out many smaller exhibitors, putting pressure on the companies who served them. Theater business was rapidly ushered into large multiplexes throughout the 1990s. At the same time, satellite-distributed digital movies and home videos were reducing the number of trips to the cinema. Over the long term, continuation of this trend was expected to reduce the cultural diversity of film product and downgrade the market to only a few thousand screens, charging exorbitant prices for exclusive runs of event-scale films; ticket prices increased more than 20 percent between 1992 and 1999—8 percent during 1999 alone.

In an effort to reverse this trend, innovative new companies sprang up that took advantage of the rapid development of computer networking technology in the mid-1990s to offer low-cost booking and promotional services via the Internet. Companies like Maine-based Cinema Links used computer technology and computer networks to link hundreds of exhibitors and distributors nationwide, promising to significantly lower the costs associated with booking and promoting films and thereby to increase profit margins. Plot summaries, screeners' advisory notes, release schedules, distributor terms, and other critical booking information were available daily via modem, telephone, or FAX. Box office reports were uploaded daily, computerized, and then forwarded to the distributors.

The number of stock-shot and archival-footage libraries, on the other hand, increased significantly in the early 1990s. There was a continued drive to archive and restore classic films, interviews, and footage for use in documentary materials and revived screenings. This segment also felt the impact of the World Wide Web; an enormous stock footage library called Footage.net cropped up online. The site is linked to dozens of film libraries around the world, and acts essentially as an online intermediary between the physical libraries and consumers. There also was a growing foreign market for stock footage. The growth of the field was attracting innovative newcomers to the stock footage film library business. Many such film libraries have also started producing their own stock footage to complement their collections by shooting city scenes and natural vistas. Meanwhile, the Film Department at the University of California at Los Angeles allied with Robert Redford's Sundance Institute to initiate a project devoted to archiving, preserving, and presenting independent films. It will be incorporated into the Sundance collection and make films available to film makers and educational programs.

INDUSTRY LEADERS

The leading film delivery company was Airborne Express, which held exclusive deals with Universal Studios, Miramax, Disney/Buena Vista, and a host of other major and minor film distributors through its partnership with Technicolor Entertainment Services. The firm delivered to more than 8,000 studios nationally and generated $25 million in revenue from its Technicolor-related operations in 1998, registering annual growth of 30 percent since its formation in 1993. Another major film carrier was Benton Express Inc. of Atlanta, Georgia with $35 million in revenues, some of which derived from its trucking operations.

A leading non-theatrical film library was Films Inc. of Chicago, with 120 employees and 1998 revenues of $10 million. Leading stock footage film libraries include Film Search Inc. of New York with $11.0 million in revenues and a payroll of 340 employees, and Archive Films Inc. of New York, which employed 120 and garnered sales of $14.3 million.

FURTHER READING

Carver, Benedict. "Indies Throw Cash at Pix Stash." *Variety,* 22 February 1999.

Dempsey, John. "Turner, Cash Returns Spur Pic Preservation." *Variety,* 5 October 1998.

Krause, Kristin S. "Moving the Movies." *Traffic World,* 6 July 1998.

"Multiplexing America." *Plain Dealer,* 8 March 1998.

Peers, Martin and Dan Cox. "The Internet Logs Onto Showbiz." *Variety,* 5 April 1999.

"A Preview of Coming Attractions: Digital Projectors Could Bring Drastic Changes to Movie Industry." *New York Times,* 22 February 1999.

Stevens, Tracy and Patricia Nicolescu, eds. *1999 International Motion Picture Almanac.* New York: Quigley Publishing Co., Inc., 1999.

"Sundance, UCLA Declare Independents Partnership." *Hollywood Reporter,* 18 November 1997.

SIC 7832

MOTION PICTURE THEATERS, EXCEPT DRIVE-IN

This category covers commercially operated theaters primarily engaged in the indoor exhibition of motion pictures.

NAICS Code(s)

512131 (Motion Picture Theaters, Except Drive-In)

Industry Snapshot

Motion picture theaters are part of an increasingly complex film industry that has been characterized by large initial capital investments and long revenue streams. Movie theaters are one aspect of the film industry that also includes movie studios, broadcast and cable television, and videotape sales and rentals.

Motion picture theaters remain a significant contributor to the film industry. Although videos have surpassed theaters as the biggest contributor to film industry revenue, the United States' 35,000 movie screens create the initial market for a film's future formats. The industry, along with the rest of the U.S. economy, endured a recession in 1990 and 1991, but box office receipts rose from $4.8 billion in 1991 to a record $6.95 billion in 1998. Admissions reached 1.48 billion in 1998, a 40-year high.

The industry's nearly 6,000 establishments employed 123,045 people and generated receipts of $7.5 billion.

Organization and Structure

The movie theater industry is represented by the National Association of Theatre Owners (NATO). NATO was formed through the 1966 merger of the Theatre Owners of America, which was founded in 1920, and the Allied States Association of Motion Picture Exhibitors, which was created in 1939. The organization compiles and publishes statistical and historical information on the economics of theater and concession operations, film producers and distributors, theater equipment, box-office sales, and attendance.

Throughout the movie theater industry's history, entrepreneurs have had to make high up-front investments. Film rental fees are usually negotiated in terms of box office revenue in which movie studios charge a percentage of the box office receipts. Payroll only constituted a small percentage of annual revenues in the early 1990s.

Total theater receipts are derived from three sources: admissions, concessions, and screen advertising. In 1996 admissions generated $5.8 billion in revenue for U.S. theaters. Concessions brought in more than $1 billion more. Although a smaller percentage than ticket sales, concession income is a favorite of cinema operators because it commands a high profit margin that is not split with movie studios. In the early 1990s, concessions and screen advertising, a relatively recent phenomena, were considered potential avenues for growth. On-screen ads included live-action spots and slide-show-type reels that promote local businesses. The advertising concept was not particularly well-received by patrons and some distributors, and by the late 1980s several studios rebelled against the practice. In fact, Walt Disney Company and Warner Bros. banned on-screen advertising in theaters showing their films.

Background and Development

The motion picture theater industry was born at the dawn of the twentieth century following the 1903 release of *The Great Train Robbery,* which is widely regarded as the first feature film. Previously, movies were given second billing in deference to live vaudeville acts, but as the films' technical quality and popularity grew, they became attractions in and of themselves. The first building devoted exclusively to movies was built in Pittsburgh in 1905, and the first movie house opened in Manhattan, New York City, in 1913.

Theaters became the United States' primary source of entertainment during the 1920s, and some theaters boasted full houses three or four times each day. During this decade, elaborate venues seating as many as 5,000 were built in cities and towns across the country. These theaters sometimes upstaged their featured films with architectural styles that ranged from baroque, Greek, and Spanish to Egyptian, Byzantine, and Aztecan. Details included imported marble columns, crystal chandeliers, and gold-painted figures; huge pipe organs were built for many theaters to provide music for silent films. Services included immaculately uniformed doormen, ushers, and lounge attendants.

The 1927 release of *The Jazz Singer,* the first film with synchronized sound, revolutionized the motion picture industry. Millions of dollars were spent to upgrade film production facilities and buy equipment for movie houses. Within three years the transformation to sound was complete—silent films, pipe organs, and many movie stars of the silent film era faded from the limelight.

Many theaters were able to convert efficiently to sound because they had the backing of major movie studios. The motion picture theater industry of the first half of the century was dominated by a handful of companies known as ''the five majors:'' Paramount, Twentieth Century Fox, Warner Bros., MGM, and RKO Pictures. The five produced, distributed, and exhibited films in company-owned theaters. Columbia, Universal Pictures, and United Artists Corporation, known as the ''little three,'' were primarily film distributors. Ironically, it was one of the ''little three''—United Artists—that became the motion picture theater industry's biggest player by the end of the twentieth century.

The five major studios controlled the exhibition of movies throughout the 1920s, 1930s, and 1940s. Together they produced 95 percent of all big-budget features released before 1950 and owned 70 percent of the first-run theaters in the United States' 92 largest cities.

Each studio gave the others access to its first-run theaters in exchange for reciprocal privileges. They also enforced ''block booking,'' whereby independent theater owners wanting to run a big-name movie had to agree to run several of the studio's lesser pictures. The five majors even dictated admission prices.

The Depression took its toll on movie attendance in 1931 and 1932, and the five majors gained even more control over the remaining market. Even the architectural style of newly-constructed movie theaters reflected the tough times. One author surmised that the streamlined art deco look grew popular ''as an economy measure of sorts, an attempt to maintain a richness of design without spending quite so much.''

In the 1930s and 1940s, attendance fluctuated from lows of 60 million per week to highs of 90 million per week in the late 1940s, before a significant period of decline set in. From 1946-53, 853 indoor theaters were built, but 4,696 were permanently closed as television siphoned off theater's audiences. Many in the indoor theater industry blamed booming drive-in attendance for their declining fortunes, but historical analysis has concluded that drive-in theaters actually kept the movie industry alive during the 1950s in the face of bruising competition from television.

In 1949 the federal government ordered the five majors to divest their theater holdings. The industry had been the object of scrutiny by the government since the 1920s, when the major studios emerged, but it took a 1938 lawsuit to get the wrecking ball rolling. Loews and MGM resisted the trust-busting the longest, and it was not until 1957 that the breakup was completed. The percentage of chain-owned theaters dropped from 70 percent to 46.8 percent by the time of the final dissolution.

The breakup of the theater trust exacerbated the film industry's decline, because it eliminated the major studios' guaranteed revenue. This loss of revenue in turn limited production budgets, resulting in fewer and less extravagant films. The court order also compelled movie distributors to negotiate theater-by-theater, movie-by-movie contracts, as opposed to block booking and other agreements that had previously given the dominant theater chains advantages over their independent counterparts.

The flight of affluent city dwellers to the suburbs was the final blow for traditional downtown theaters. Shopping center cinemas with free, abundant parking were closer to the burgeoning suburban population. Nevertheless, weekly attendance at films continued to spiral downward through the 1950s from 60 million per week in 1950 to a decade low of 39.6 million per week in 1958 before bottoming out in the low 40 million range. Because of the country's population boom, these figures represented even lower percentages of moviegoers than during the Depression. Box office receipts, employment, and the number of establishments also fell steadily from 1954-63. Industry-wide box office revenues fell from $1.17 billion in 1954 to $803.46 million in 1963. During that same period, the number of movie houses declined from 14,716 to 9,150.

The number of theaters continued to decline throughout the 1960s to just over 8,300 in 1972. Annual ticket sales dropped steadily as well, but ticket prices increased by 110 percent from 1963-74. Despite these factors, industry revenues grew 43 percent to $1.4 billion from 1963-72.

Multiplexing, the grouping of several relatively small screening rooms in one facility, began in the 1970s. The multiplex attracted more patrons with more films to choose from while using fewer employees. From 1972-77, industry revenues increased by 50 percent to $2.13 billion as the motion picture industry and the theater business rebounded.

The theater industry recorded consecutive annual gains from 1981 through 1984, with box office sales peaking at more than $4 billion in 1984. But admissions fell 11.9 percent and box office receipts dropped 7 percent in 1985, as construction glutted the market with screens. During the early 1980s, Hollywood produced plenty of films, but there were not enough screens to accommodate them. This resulted in over-construction in the theater industry; from 1980-87 the number of screens increased from 17,675 to more than 23,500. An opposing industry trend found Hollywood releasing fewer and fewer feature-length films; the number of films produced annually peaked in 1987 at 515 but sunk to about 470 in 1989. The net result of these two trends was that theater owners had to offer larger cuts of the box office revenue to movie studios to remain competitive and book top films.

The mid-1980s industry recession combined with a relaxation of some regulatory restraints resulted in a revival of the distributor-owned movie theater. Four of the top six distribution companies made sizable gains in theater ownership, including Matsushita Electric Industrial Ltd., which acquired about half of Cineplex Odeon; Sony, which bought the Loews Theatres chain; and a joint venture between Paramount and Time Warner, which bought the Cinamerica theater chain. These four distributors had a stake in about 9 percent of the United States' theater screens, enough to attract the attention of federal regulators, who seemed to indicate that they would keep their distance as long as the distributors did the same. Strengthened by new corporate ties, the top 10 exhibition chains captured 55 percent of the United States' theaters by 1990, up from 27 percent in 1985.

''Expansion madness'' gripped the U.S. theater industry in the early 1990s. The number of screens in-

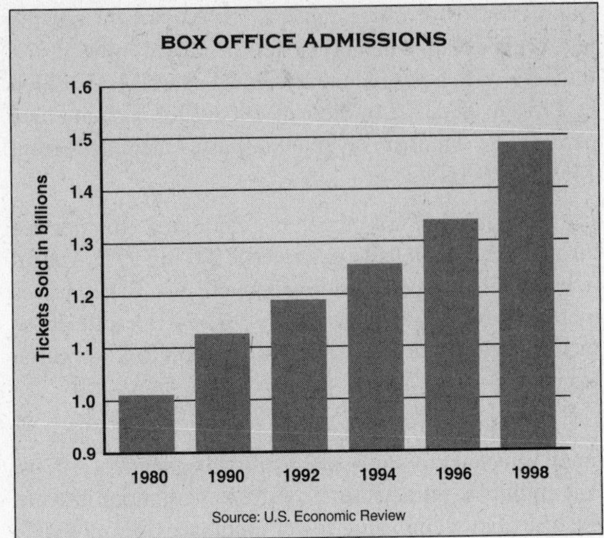

creased from about 24,000 in 1991 to nearly 30,000 by the end of 1996, up 7 percent (about 1,900) in 1996. By the end of the year, there was one screen per 9,000 people. The boom was driven in part by an increase in the number of movie releases from Hollywood, which was generating upwards of 300 feature films each year. The advent of the ''megaplex'' (16-plus screen complex) increased the number of screens exponentially with each new construction project. Mid-decade, this trend showed signs of migrating to international markets.

Current Conditions

The number of movie screens in the United States increased from 30,000 in 1996 to 35,000 in 1998. The market is expected to peak at about 40,000. Large format cinema remained first in annual growth rate among attraction/entertainment businesses, second only to the gaming industry. In 1998, there were approximately 160 large format screens operating in the United States. By 1999, there were 29 large format films in production, with another 19 in development by 2001.

The 1999 summer box office season broke all records. In just 17 weeks, box offices took in $3.1 billion, a 19 percent increase from 1998. Additionally, 10 films grossed more than $100 million each. Admissions increased from 1998's 533 million to near 610 million in 1999, a 14 percent increase.

Industry Leaders

The leaders in the motion picture theater industry at the close of the 1990s were Regal Cinemas, Loews Cineplex Entertainment, Carmike, and AMC. Somewhat smaller but also significant were Cinemark, United Artists Theatre Circuit, and GC Companies. Regional markets were influenced by a number of other chains, including Edwards Theatres Circuit, headquartered in California, and Clearview Cinema Group, with theaters in suburban communities around New York City.

Based in Knoxville, Tennessee, Regal Cinemas became the country's largest theater chain in 1998 when it merged with the Act III chain. It operates more than 4,100 screens at about 405 theaters in 30 states, mostly in medium-sized cities and suburban areas east of the Mississippi River. Most of its theaters are less than 8 years old.

Regal Cinemas posted 1998 sales of $707 million, a 47.6 percent increase over the previous year. About 12,000 people worked for Regal Cinemas as of 1998.

The second-largest theater chain in the United States was also created in 1998 as the result of a merger. Loews Theatres joined forces with Canada's Cineplex Odeon Corporation to form Loews Cineplex Entertainment, with headquarters in New York and Toronto. It is owned primarily by Sony Pictures Entertainment (51 percent) and Universal Studios (26 percent). The company operates approximately 2,900 screens in more than 450 theaters mainly in major U.S. and Canadian cities, as well as having a moderate international presence. In addition, Loews Cineplex Entertainment is a partner in Magic Johnson Theatres and Loeks-Star Theatres.

Sales for Loews Theatres in fiscal year 1999 were $851.2 million, more than doubling the previous year's total. The large jump in sales resulted in a net income of $5.9 million. More than 16,000 people worked for Loews Cineplex Entertainment as of 1999.

Carmike Cinemas, with headquarters in Columbus, Georgia, operates more than 2,750 screens in about 490 theaters across 36 states. Carmike has traditionally concentrated on secondary markets (cities and towns with populations of less than 100,000), although it is beginning to make some tentative forays into larger metropolitan areas. Before 1998, it grew mostly by acquiring existing theaters and circuits. It then launched an effort to build screens and expand smaller complexes as well as renovate its older theaters. Carmike's sales for 1999 were $486.9 million. Its net income for the year was $18.9 million. The number of employees in 1998 was 10,234.

Based in Kansas City, Missouri, AMC Entertainment Inc. in 1999 operated about 2,800 screens in some 240 theaters in the United States, Canada, Spain, Portugal, Hong Kong, and Japan. Additional projects were planned for Asia and Europe. Since 1995, AMC has specialized in building megaplexes containing 20 or more screens. These entertainment complexes feature stadium seating with plush, high-backed seats, AMC's own High Impact Theatre System (HITS) with wall-to-wall and floor-to-ceiling screens and unique speaker configuration, and state-of-the-art computer systems to monitor everything from ticket and concession sales to the theater's temperature.

In the fiscal year ending March 1999, AMC realized the highest sales in its history—$1 billion, up 21 percent from 1998. Its net income was $16 million and it employed 12,300 people.

WORKFORCE

Motion picture theaters employ more than 110,000 workers, a majority of them part time. Each theater averaged about 13 employees total, a far cry from the 1920s, when elaborately uniformed workers met the patron's every need; a New Orleans theater during that period boasted a corps of 100 ushers who were called ''The Soldiers of Service''. Ushers, lobby attendants, ticket takers, and food servers still comprised two-thirds of the industry's work force. Requiring up to one month of on-the-job training, projectionists were the only skilled members of the industry. They were also often union members

AMERICA AND THE WORLD

The European theater industry of the 1980s was reminiscent of its U.S. counterpart in the 1950s and 1960s: run-down and shrinking fast. A recovery of the industry abroad that commenced in the mid-1980s reflected the resurgence of American movie houses a decade before. The European renewal started in 1985 in Britain, when American Multi-Cinema Inc. opened a U.S.-style multiplex. As the new theaters spread, British movie attendance nearly doubled.

The movement emigrated to the mainland during the 1990s. The first movie theaters to be built in Germany's Ruhr Valley in decades were opened in 1991. One was a joint venture of Paramount and Universal (United Cinemas International), and the other was built by Time Warner. Both players hoped to revive the Spanish and Italian movie markets in the early 1990s. Although U.S. exhibitors stimulated the overseas theater renaissance, several European chains played a part in the rejuvenation as well.

In 1997, 37 percent of large format screens were in Asia, 12 percent in Europe, 4 percent in Latin America, and 2 percent each in Southeast Asia and Australia.

RESEARCH AND TECHNOLOGY

When television pirated the country's movie audience during the 1950s, Hollywood looked for new ways to get people into theaters. CinemaScope and stereo sound were introduced by Twentieth Century Fox in the 1950s. Cinerama's giant concave screen and Paramount's Vista-Vision big-screen system tried to capitalize on a movies' visual impact, which television could not equal. Other gimmicks, like three-dimensional films, were unique but often less technically impressive and proved to be passing fads.

Movie house owners worked to redefine the ''theater experience'' in the early 1990s to compete with the public's plethora of entertainment options. Expanded concessions included pastries, cappuccino, mineral water, and frozen yogurt. Credit-card and phone-ahead ticket sales, first introduced chain-wide by Cineplex Odeon Corp. in 1991, added convenience. Advance ticket sales and reserved seating followed in 1992 when United Artists Entertainment Co. began testing the service. Movie boutiques stocked with film-related t-shirts, posters, stuffed toys, and other paraphernalia capitalized on the rising popularity of movie licensing.

Motion simulation theaters were developed by Omni Films International Inc., Imax Corp. and Iwerks in the 1990s. Previously, these panoramic, curved screens, designed to give audience members the sensation of being in the film, had been limited to amusement parks, planetariums, museums, and science centers. Omni hoped that its 50-seat motion theaters, which incorporated hydraulically mobilized seats and a computer control unit to synchronize seat movements with the film, would become attractions at shopping malls. The newest theaters also used state-of-the industry digital sound and high definition projection systems.

FURTHER READING

Bielski, Lauren. ''Coming Soon to a Theater Near You: HDTV Digital Movie Transmission.'' *Advanced Imaging,* April 1995, 30-31.

Crowe, Kenneth C. ''Movie Projectionists Protest Cuts In Jobs, Lower Wages.'' *Newsday,* 3 March 1996, 6.

Darnay, Arsen J., ed. *Manufacturing USA: Industry Analyses, Statistics, and Leading Companies.* Detroit: Gale Research Inc., 1996.

Eisenberg, Daniel. ''It's Theaters Galore.'' *Time Canada,* 13 September 1999, 35.

Hoover's Company Capsules, 17 March 2000. Available from http://www.hoovers.com.

''In a Time Warp.'' *Newsweek,* 18 January 1999, 6.

Klady, Leonard. ''Heat Wave at Summer Box Office.'' *Daily Variety,* 7 September 1999, 1.

La Franco, Robert. ''Coming Soon: A Megaplex Near You.'' *Forbes,* 12 August 1996, 132-133.

———. ''My Megaplex Is Bigger Than Your Megaplex.'' *Forbes,* 24 February 1997, 50-52.

''Large Format Cinema Has Bright Future, Price Tells LFCA Members.'' *Amusement Business,* 7 June 1999, 19.

''Muliplex Theater Entertainment Centers.'' *Encyclopedia of Emerging Industries.* Gale Group, Detroit, 2000.

Peers, Martin. ''Headless United Artists Feeling The $ Squeeze.'' *Variety,* 23 December 1996, 9-11.

Philips, Chuck. ''Theater Firm's Chairman Quits.'' *Los Angeles Times,* 10 December 1996, D10.

Reingold, Jennifer. ''Carmike Cinemas: It Always Plays in Peoria.'' *Financial World,* 14 March 1995, 20-21.

Schoolcraft, Lisa. ''AMC Ready to Open Curtain on Latest Theater Technology.'' *Business Journal: Serving Jacksonville & Northeast Florida,* 12 March 1999, 3.

Tanzer, Andrew and Robert La Franco. ''Luring Asians From Their TV Sets.'' *Forbes,* 3 June 1996, 40-41.

Ward's Business Directory. v.5, Detroit: Gale Research Inc., 1997.

U.S. Census Bureau. *1997 Economic Census.* GPO: Washington, D.C.: 1999.

SIC 7833

DRIVE-IN MOTION PICTURE THEATERS

This category covers commercially operated theaters, commonly known as drive-ins, primarily engaged in the outdoor exhibition of motion pictures.

NAICS Code(s)

512132 (Drive-In Motion Picture Theaters)

Industry Snapshot

The drive-in theater industry is a phenomenon that peaked in the 1950s, then declined precipitously in the 1970s and 1980s. According to the Motion Picture Producers Association (MPPA), there were 847 drive-in theaters, or ''ozoners,'' as they were sometimes called, in the United States in 1996. This industry has greatly dwindled from its peak in 1952 when it surpassed the traditional theater industry in attendance. The number of drive-in theaters has, however, remained stable since the late 1980s. The affordability and convenience of an evening at a drive-in, the desire to get out of the house during pleasant weather, plus nostalgia for the 1950s, which many drive-ins are playing up, has kept the drive-in from total extinction. ''A trip to the drive-in is a movie-going paradox. It's more social than any indoor theater (where you're not even allowed to talk, much less walk your dog or throw a Frisbee with the guy down the row) . . . Likewise, drive-ins combine the best of commercial-theater scale with home-theater indulgence: No home entertainment system gives you a 2,600-square foot screen, and in no multiplex can you eat, smoke and drink yourself silly,'' said reporter Steve Hendrix in the *Washington Post.*

In 1997, the industry was estimated to employ 1,996 people. Total receipts were $110.3 million.

Organization and Structure

The drive-in theater industry was comprised largely of independent operators and a few regional chains. During the late 1940s, chains owned 31.9 percent of establishments and controlled 39.8 percent of car capacity. Some of the larger chains included General Cinema Corporation, which ranked as a top indoor and Park-In Theatres, Inc., both in the eastern United States; Pacific Drive-In Theaters; and Paramount-Richards Theatres, Inc., in the southern United States.

Since the drive-in industry was considered a competitor of the traditional theater industry for many years, their owners were not welcomed into such associations as Theatre Owners of America or Allied States Association of Motion Picture Exhibitors. However, since many drive-in operators were so successful in their early years, they did not perceive a need for professional affiliation or the information-sharing and lobbying services that such an association could provide until the industry reached its demise.

Financial Structure. Like traditional theaters, drive-in theaters derived profits from two primary activities: admission fees and concessions. Most drive-ins were seasonal operations open an average of eight months each year. During their most prosperous years, 88 percent of drive-ins charged admission on a per-adult basis, admitting children for free. As the industry declined in the 1980s, operators desperate for patronage switched to a per-car admission. During the 1950s, annual profits ranged from 15 percent to 30 percent of invested capital—a very high margin compared to indoor theaters, which averaged about 10 percent at the time. Concessions usually contributed 35 percent to 40 percent of a drive-in's gross receipts.

Drive-ins required a relatively high initial investment. It is estimated that the first drive-in theater cost about $30,000 to build. After World War II when the industry reached its zenith, the average initial investment was about $100,000, not including the land. Although high, this capital outlay was only about 30 percent of the average cost of an indoor theater at the time.

Regular expenses included film rental, energy consumption for projection and food preparation, payroll, and real estate. Payroll typically constituted about 28 percent of a drive-in's operating expenses.

Background and Development

The concept of the drive-in theater was first patented and introduced by Richard Milton Hollingshead, Jr. in 1933. Known as ''the father of the drive-in,'' Hollingshead opened the first establishment in Camden, New Jersey, in June of that year. The ''Automobile Movie Theatre'' featured rows of inclines on which patrons would park their cars; a large, central screen; three loudspeakers atop the screen to project the movie's soundtrack; and a barricade around the perimeter of the lot to prevent would-be viewers from sneaking in.

Hollingshead had trouble enforcing his patent, and he watched his idea spread unauthorized to Pennsylvania, Texas, California, Massachusetts, Ohio, Rhode Island, Florida, and Michigan by the end of the decade. Many of the new businesses were unlicensed, and Hollingshead was obligated to spend time and money trying to enforce his patent. He eventually petitioned the U.S. Supreme Court in an attempt to uphold his patent, but in 1949 it was declared invalid on the basis that it ''lacked invention.''

The industry as a whole faced other problems that prevented it from catching on until the late 1940s and early 1950s. Some were technical: poor sound quality and faulty synchronization of image and soundtrack along with distortion of the picture at some vantage points hampered the viewing experience. In addition, neighbors of these early drive-ins protested the loud broadcast of movie soundtracks throughout the evening hours. Other obstacles were rooted in Hollywood studio politics. Many big-budget movie producers, who controlled production and distribution of films throughout the 1940s, refused to circulate their best movies to drive-ins.

These problems were partly alleviated in the late 1930s, when the major Hollywood studios began to make their films available, in later runs, to drive-ins. Improvements in projection technology permitted patrons in drive-ins with a 1,000-car capacity to see a movie more clearly. And the development of individually-controlled, in-car speakers solved the sound problem in 1941. But just as the drive-in industry was poised to erupt into a full-fledged craze, World War II's gasoline rationing, rubber shortages, and building restrictions prohibiting ''unnecessary construction'' postponed the movement.

In 1942 there were 95 drive-ins in 27 states. The average lot held 400 cars, took up seven or eight acres, and had one screen. The number of establishments remained relatively constant until the end of the war when it exploded. By the end of the 1940s, almost three new drive-ins were opening daily.

Kerry Seagrave, author of *Drive-in Theaters: A History from Their Inception in 1933,* attributed the craze to two social factors: America's love affair with the automobile and the postwar baby boom. Kerry noted that ''ozoners were an ideal place for a young family with children—no baby-sitter needed, no parking problems, dress as you like, and (they provided) relatively cheap entertainment.'' In keeping with the family orientation of drive-ins, free admission for children under 12, playgrounds, and even bottle warmers soon became industry standards.

The industry reached an apex in August 1952, when the average weekly attendance at outdoor theaters surpassed that of traditional theaters by 1.3 million. By 1955 there were more than 3,700 drive-in theaters in the United States. That number peaked in 1958, when more than 4,000 drive-ins brought in $230.42 million. Despite the technological limitations that dictated a 1,300-car maximum capacity, some operators built 2,500-car theaters to capitalize on the trend. During this peak decade, it did not seem to matter whether the patron could see the film clearly; most of the films shown were still the ''table scraps'' of the indoor theater industry anyway.

Drive-ins lured return patrons by offering several added attractions. A ticket might entitle the bearer to a free door prize for each child; or a theater might have a live band, dance troupe, or acrobatic act before the show. Some venues offered free milk and diapers for babies, a children's playground, or even a miniature golf and a driving range.

Although many operators of indoor movie theaters blamed the precipitous decline in their attendance figures during the 1950s in part on drive-ins, Seagrave maintained that drive-ins kept the movie industry afloat during the 1950s. But, growth of the industry began to stagnate by the end of the decade. The shakeout between 1958 and 1963, when the number of drive-ins decreased from 4,063 to 3,502, probably eliminated the most inefficient operators from the industry. The industry declined significantly in the early 1960s then leveled off until the late 1970s. Another steady decline began in the late 1970s and continued into the early 1990s as the drive-in theater neared extinction. This decline occurred for a variety of societal and economic reasons.

Family patronage, which Seagrave called ''the backbone of the drive-in,'' dropped off in the 1960s and 1970s. Some drive-in playgrounds were eliminated due to the fear of lawsuits resulting from possible injuries. Once the sidelight attractions were eliminated, all drive-ins had left to offer was the film itself, which was still too often second-run or second-rate. Also, the content of films began to change significantly in the late 1960s, hastened by the elimination of the Production Code in 1966, which had restricted the use of potentially offensive material. The introduction of nudity, profanity, excessive violence, and explicit sexuality made going to films less likely to be a regular family activity.

By the 1980s, cable television and VCRs had firmly supplanted the economy and convenience of drive-ins. Rising land values further eroded the viability of drive-ins: it became more cost effective to develop the land, rather than try to maintain outdoor exhibitions for a few months of the year.

Seagrave summarized the demise of the industry in his 1993 book: ''Drive-ins today sit poised on the edge of extinction. The last handful may be around yet for decades. A few may be kept alive as sort of living museums, perhaps subsidized. But they are finished as a part of the American landscape. New ones will never be built.''

Bob Wagner, owner of the Bel-Air Drive-In Theater in Churchville, Maryland, agrees. In 1996, he told the *Washington Post,* ''We'll be around for awhile longer, I think. I don't see anybody ever building a new drive-in. But we'll keep this one going by doing whatever we can think of.''

No longer venues for low budget B-pictures and second runs of top level films, drive-ins offer the same features that are shown at indoor theaters. As with indoor theaters, the amount of business done by drive-ins depends upon the general popularity of film releases. In the summer of 1996, some drive-ins were filled to capacity during showings of the science fiction blockbuster *Independence Day.*

In addition to being dependent on the appeal of current films, a drive-in's business depends on good weather. ''Weather is the key. On a good Friday or Saturday we can get 1,500 to 2,000 people in here. But even the prediction of rain keeps people away,'' Memphis drive-in owner Larry Pankey explained to the *Memphis Commercial Appeal.*

A new problem for drive-ins is the changing style of automobiles. Designed for the low and wide sedans that were prevalent in the 1950s, drive-ins must contend with vans, trucks, jeeps, and recreational vehicles which can block the view of customers in regular cars. Relegating high and bulky vehicles to the back row is not always possible due to the increasing number of them.

CURRENT CONDITIONS

There was only a slight decline in operating drive-in movie theaters in the United States from 1996-98: down from 847 to less than 800 (although one statistic places the number at 530). Those that have weathered the decline stand to do well: nostalgia and pseudo-nostalgia are at all-time highs. The Drive-In Theater Fanatic Fan Club (www.driveintheater.com/fanclub) and the American Drive-In Movie Theatre (www.americandrivein.com) represent two groups of followers helping to stave off extinction. The status of the remaining drive-ins is expected to remain at a plateau for several years.

In 1998, America's oldest remaining drive-in movie theater celebrated its 65th anniversary. Shankweiler's Drive-In, in Orefield, Pennsylvania, is open from April to September. Although few drive-ins turn a profit, many are able to maintain business by appealing to family audiences. By combining playground equipment, ''diners'' serving old-fashioned hamburgers, and programs featuring general audience films, many drive-in owners hope to carry a fleeting image of Americana far into the millennium.

AMERICA AND THE WORLD

Unlike the traditional movie theater, the drive-in never amounted to more than a novelty in other countries. Until the 1990s, only Canada and Australia came close to rivaling America's drive-in industry. As Seagrave noted, this was because most foreign countries did not have the prerequisites to establish such an industry: high personal income; cheap, vacant, and accessible land; ubiquitous automobile ownership; and inexpensive gasoline.

One of the only countries that possessed these requirements, however, was Japan. As the U.S. industry declined, almost 20 drive-ins were built in Japan from 1983-93. A country renowned for its expensive real estate, Japan built low-budget drive-ins that used parking lots and other locations that were not used at night by simply installing a screen, a projector, and an office. Rather than being a product of a booming economy like their U.S. counterparts, Japanese drive-ins were money-making ventures spawned by the country's worst recession since World War II.

FURTHER READING

Atkin, Ross. ''Drive-In Movies: Featuring Families.'' *Christian Science Monitor,* 5 August 1998, B1.

Hendrix, Steve. ''Fields of Screens.'' *Washington Post,* 26 July 1996, N6.

Lucas, John. ''Back to the Drive-Ins.'' *Memphis Commercial Appeal,* 14 June 1996, 1C.

Palmer, Joel. ''More Than a Movie Theater.'' *Des Moines Business Record,* 13 July 1998, 30.

Seagrave, Kerry. *Drive-In Theaters: A History from Their Inception in 1933.* Jefferson, N.C.: McFarland & Company, Inc., 1992.

''The Lost World of Drive-Ins.'' *Time,* 26 May 1997, 94.

SIC 7841

VIDEO TAPE RENTAL

This category covers establishments primarily engaged in renting video tapes and disks to the general public for personal or household use. Establishments primarily engaged in renting video recorders and players are classified in **SIC 7359: Equipment Rental and Leasing, Not Elsewhere Classified.** Establishments primarily engaged in selling recorded video tapes and disks to the general public are classified in **SIC 5735: Record and Prerecorded Tape Stores;** those engaged in the wholesale distribution of recorded video tapes and disks are classified in **SIC 7822: Motion Picture and Video Tape Distribution.**

NAICS CODE(S)

532230 (Video Tapes and Disc Rental)

INDUSTRY SNAPSHOT

Under assault from alternative entertainment media like pay-per-view television and video-on-demand services, video stores in the early 2000s face a mixed future. After rapid growth in the 1980s and early 1990s, video rentals in the United States stalled in the mid-1990s as the market grew saturated and as competing modes of entertainment chipped away at home video rental. Sales of videos at mainstream retail outlets like Wal-Mart and drugstore chains have also cleaved market share away from video stores. The industry staged a modest recovery in the late 1990s, aided by new revenue-sharing agreements with movie studios, but some observers see slow growth at best in the early 2000s.

Although the video rental business is fairly fragmented compared to other industries, with the top five video chains claiming only 41 percent of the U.S. market, large chains continue to edge market share away from smaller, independent video stores. Thousands of independents have been forced out of business as big chains moved in; others have been relegated to niche markets. This pattern was expected to continue in the early 2000s.

ORGANIZATION AND STRUCTURE

Film studios and distributors sell videotapes and DVDs to rental outlets, which then rent the videos to consumers. Under traditional pricing, rental outlets pay $50 to $80 per videocassette, which they then rent to customers for typically $1 to $4 per night. Under this arrangement the video store keeps all the rental revenues for itself. Increasingly, however, video stores have pursued revenue-sharing deals with studios. These contracts dramatically reduce stores' initial cost of buying videos—sometimes eliminating up-front costs all together—and convert those into variable costs by paying the studio a percentage of rental income each time a movie is borrowed. Revenue sharing, which came into widespread use in 1998, benefits not only video stores' cash flow, but also frequently helps boost overall revenue because stores are able to stock—and rent out—more product.

Typically, video stores earn the bulk of their sales (about 70 percent at large chains like Blockbuster) from video rental fees. The rest come from sell-through videos, where tapes and discs are sold as new, gaming software rentals (such as for Nintendo and Sony game consoles), snack food sales, and miscellaneous sources like sales of musical recordings and used videos.

Video specialty stores compete directly with supermarkets, drugstores, and other mainstream retail outlets that also sell or rent videos. Often mainstream stores sell videos at deep discount, creating pricing pressure on video stores.

The number of video stores has fallen significantly as large chain stores and so-called superstores have expanded. From 31,000 in 1990, the number of video stores had dropped below 25,000 by 1999. The decline was expected to continue.

Videos vs. Theaters. Video stores have always had a complex relationship with movie theaters. Early on, conventional wisdom held that video rentals cannibalized theater admissions because a typical consumer, the theory goes, would watch a movie either in a theater or at home, but not both. This pattern seemed to hold in the late 1980s and early 1990s, when box-office receipts began to decline as video rentals surged.

The relationship between video rental and movie-going grew murkier in the mid-1990s; however, rentals stagnated while business at the box office swelled. Indeed, Census Bureau statistics reveal that in 1996 theater revenues surpassed video store revenues for the first time since 1993, the year rentals first pulled ahead of theaters. To further complicate matters, by the late 1990s both video stores and theaters posted healthy gains side-by-side. In sum, analysts believe that video stores and movie theaters do vie for the same audience some of the time—especially when the economy is sluggish—but also that each can create demand for the other.

Video Rights. Owning video rights to films is an important source of revenue for film studios. For example, in 1995, 47 percent of movie revenue in the United States came from home video, according to a study by Veronis, Suhler and Associates and Smith Barney, Inc. By contrast, revenue from theatrical exhibition accounted for 33 percent, and television showings contributed 20 percent.

DVD Format. In addition to videocassette, laser discs such as the DVD format are also available for home video viewing. Many view DVDs as the eventual replacement for VHS-format tapes. Images stored on laser discs are sharper than videotape images, and viewers can move more easily to different places on the recording. Discs can also provide digital stereo audio, which makes them especially attractive for programs involving music. The drawback is that laser disc players usually can't record programs like VCRs can. Nonetheless, DVD rentals and sales have become a sizable and fast-growing revenue stream for many video stores.

BACKGROUND AND DEVELOPMENT

Although videocassette recorders and players have been available since the mid-1970s, pay-TV services were more popular early on. At the top was the cable network Home Box Office (HBO), which financed films

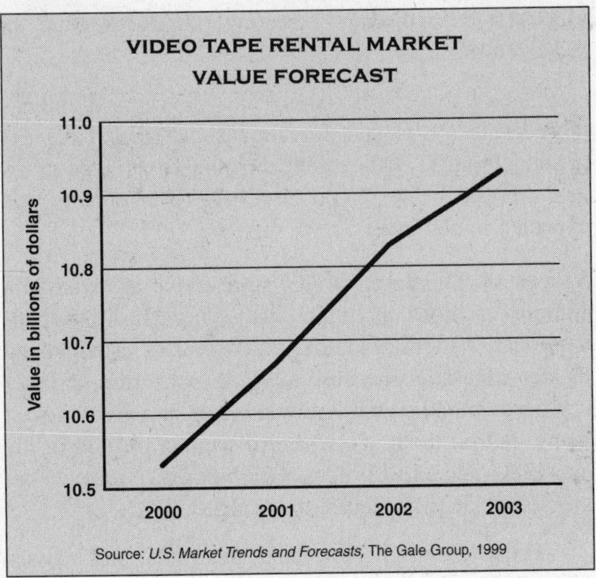

Source: *U.S. Market Trends and Forecasts,* The Gale Group, 1999

in exchange for pay-TV rights and thus secured exclusive deals on very profitable movies.

By the mid-1980s, pay-TV viewers grew increasingly disenchanted with programming just as home video technology became more affordable and more widely available. Videos offered far more variety and flexibility in viewing for the customer. The cost of VCRs continued to fall—from $300 to $400 in the industry's early days for lower-priced models to $150 to $250 in 1993—further contributing to the rise in popularity. By the late 1990s, 84 percent of U.S. households owned at least one VCR.

Entering the mid-1990s, consumer demand for video rentals began to stabilize somewhat as sales of VCRs began to slow. In 1995 revenues from video rentals and sales actually declined, and rental business was essentially flat for the next two years. Though statistics vary, annual figures compiled by Alexander & Associates, a market research firm for the industry, portrayed video unit rentals falling in all but one year between 1995 and 1999. According to the same research, rental revenues managed to stay afloat largely through price hikes.

On the other hand, sell-through videos performed the best in the mid-1990s. One explanation for this trend was the decreasing cost of buying videos. In 1995, according to *Billboard,* Disney-owned Buena Vista Home Video began pricing quality features at $9.99. Other studios followed suit with similar programs.

Current Conditions

The industry's 1998 shift toward revenue sharing with film studios, allowing video stores to stock more titles at lower up-front costs, helped lift industry-wide revenues out of their mid-1990s doldrums. According to widely cited figures from Paul Kagan Associates, rental revenue in 1998 totaled $8 billion and sell-through sales reached $9 billion, bringing industry revenues to $17 billion for the year. Though estimates vary, this translated into somewhere between three and four billion videos rented, and some 676 million sold. The media research firm predicted sales would surpass $20 billion by 2002.

Though lauded by many as a major breakthrough, revenue sharing appears to further entrench a few large chains at the expense of smaller outfits, according to both statistical and anecdotal evidence. One reason is that the large chains have been able to secure more favorable deals with studios, and thus the playing field is far from level. Big chains negotiate with studios directly, whereas small stores usually go through intermediaries. Because small stores get worse pricing, so far at least, they often opt out of revenue sharing. Meanwhile, their large competitors are able to stock more videos and more copies of each (known as copy depth), and have seen a rise in revenue as a result.

Besides revenue sharing, another factor contributing to growth has been the popularity of DVD-format videos. In 1998 the number of DVD players topped 1 million units, and the number was estimated near 3 million in 1999. Indeed, by 2007, more than 40 million units were forecast to be in use. Sales of DVDs have been strong, and more recently, the rental market has picked up. In 1999 DVD only accounted for around 4 percent of one leading chain's sales, but that proportion was expected to grow rapidly in the early 2000s.

The conventional video store business competes increasingly with other services that can deliver movies directly to the home, such as pay-per-view and direct-broadcast satellite television. In 1999 pay-per-view was a $1.1 billion business and growing rapidly. Thus far it's unclear how much of this market has been taken away from video stores, but many observers believe the clash is inevitable.

A relatively undeveloped technology, however, poses perhaps the greatest threat. Video-on-demand services, which allow consumers to receive broadcast movies of their choice at any time, have the potential to lure a large portion of the market away from video rentals and sales. Under testing by various cable systems, movies would be served up from the cable provider's digital network at the viewer's discretion. Pricing would be similar to pay-per-view—and comparable to rental fees—only the movies could be started at any time, could be paused or fast-forwarded, and the consumer would never have to leave home. By some estimates, such services could garner $3 billion by 2005, most at the expense of video rental.

Industry Leaders

Blockbuster. The undisputed leader of the video store industry is Blockbuster Inc., owned since 1994 by the media conglomerate Viacom. In 1999, according to

VidTrac data, Blockbuster controlled 32 percent of the U.S. video market, up from 27 percent the year before. The company planned to boost its share to 40 percent by 2002.

Despite its dominance, Blockbuster's corporate performance has been spotty. From 1997 to 1999, although its revenue grew significantly, it ran net losses and racked up heavy debt. Blockbuster's weakness was also an ongoing source of friction with its parent, Viacom, which was under pressure from investors to spin the video unit off as a separate entity. After long delays, the first steps were taken in 1999 with a public offering of part of Blockbuster's stock. When they finally came, however, the new shares weren't warmly received by the market, and in following months Blockbuster's shares largely hovered below their offering price.

In 1999 Blockbuster pulled in $4.5 billion in worldwide sales but posted a moderate net loss of $69 million. At year end, the video leader operated 7,153 stores throughout the world, including 3,970 domestic outlets. The worldwide count also included 1,274 franchised or joint-venture stores. Around 25 percent of Blockbuster's sales originated outside the United States.

Hollywood Video. The second-largest U.S. video store operator, Oregon-based Hollywood Video held in 1999 an 11 percent market share. Owned by Hollywood Entertainment Corp., the chain consisted of 1,615 outlets at year-end 1999. The parent company also owns one of the Internet's most popular film sites, Reel.com, which it acquired in 1998.

The company has expanded aggressively as it battles with Blockbuster for market share. In 1999 Hollywood Entertainment's revenue was expected to top $1 billion for the first time, up from $760 million in 1998. Video rentals accounted for 84 percent of revenue.

In 1999 Hollywood and Blockbuster engaged in talks about merging their online offerings to better compete in the emerging electronic film delivery business. Those talks mushroomed into full-blown merger discussions, but the Federal Trade Commission quickly doused any such plans by expressing antitrust concerns. An Internet collaboration remained in the offing, though.

Movie Gallery. With 961 stores, Movie Gallery ascended to the industry's third place in 1999. Focusing on smaller cities and rural areas, Movie Gallery recorded sales of $277 million in 1999. That figure was only up slightly from the year before. The firm was believed to be suffering growing pains from its rapid acquisitions in the late 1990s, including the purchase of BlowOut Entertainment in 1999. The retailer planned to add another 100 stores in 2000.

Video Update. Video Update, Inc. was number four in the video store business in 1999. It acquired its position in part through the 1998 purchase of Moovies stores, following a string of smaller acquisitions. In 1999 Video Update's 700 stores brought in more than $250 million in sales, but the company suffered heavy losses related to the merger.

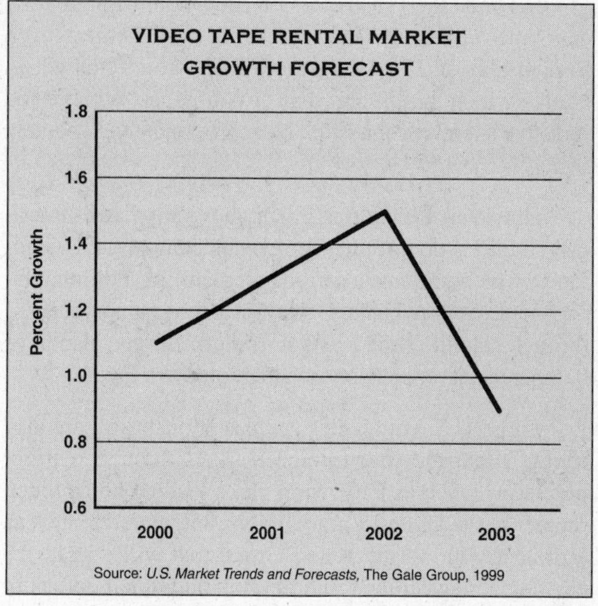

Source: *U.S. Market Trends and Forecasts*, The Gale Group, 1999

AMERICA AND THE WORLD

The United States leads the world in video rentals and in the number of households owning VCRs (84 percent). Australia, Canada, Japan, and the United Kingdom approach the U.S. level, while the countries of Western Europe vary considerably in their video tape rental practices. For example, 30 percent of Italian households owned VCRs, as compared to 40 percent in France, and 59 percent in Switzerland. In Latin America, Mexico and Argentina led with more than 33 percent each, followed by Colombia having approximately 28 percent and Brazil at 26 percent.

In much of Western Europe, purchasing videotapes was more popular than renting them. For example, in France in 1991, four times as many tapes were bought as rented, which reflected a 40 percent increase over the previous year. In Spain, 40 percent of the $350-million retail-sales total was due to purchases by consumers, and in the Netherlands the figure climbed to 50 percent. In the United Kingdom, however, there was a 10 percent drop in both rental and purchase revenues.

In Japan, an especially lucrative market in which U.S. films account for nearly one-half of all feature films shown, the number of rental outlets also fell since 1987 and average monthly revenues also have dropped approximately 3 percent per month since 1989. Part of the reason may be increased taping of movies from satellite television.

In Brazil the 1991 recession and a bout with inflation sent videocassette revenues plunging by 43 percent, even though almost 25 percent more titles were released. In Chile, which has more than 1,000 video outlets, the industry's total revenues fell by approximately 30 percent in 1991.

However, the figures given above for Latin American countries do not include revenue from pirated videotapes, which remains a serious problem. In addition, taping of U.S.-copyrighted television programs received through satellite broadcasts in Eastern Europe also have hampered the expansion of video markets there.

Large U.S. companies such as Blockbuster are also trying to expand into foreign markets through outright purchases (such as Cityvision plc, a leading home video retailer in the United Kingdom) or joint ventures, such as a project with Virgin Retail Group that will operate 15 existing ''megastores'' and develop additional outlets in Europe, Australia, and the United States.

RESEARCH AND TECHNOLOGY

Although the Internet may be one of the industry's most important development frontiers, leading video store chains were slow to adapt to an e-commerce model. As a result, regional upstarts like Kozmo.com pose a serious challenge to the traditional leaders. Kozmo.com operates a Web-based order and delivery service in large metropolitan areas such as New York, San Francisco, and Seattle. Indeed, in 1999 it claimed 30,000 customers in New York alone. The site offers videos for rent as well as a limited selection of snack foods and other products for purchase. What's more, the company delivers the video to the customer's door within an hour. In a similar vein, a number of Internet start-ups have made inroads in the DVD-for-sale market, offering wide selections of digital videos for purchase from the convenience of home.

However, a more radical use of the Internet is to skip the physical delivery altogether—by allowing videos to be downloaded. In the short term, connection speed and bandwidth constraints will prevent the Internet from being a viable delivery point for most users. However, as cable and DSL high-speed Internet services proliferate, growing video content is being offered on the Internet. In 2000, this was mostly limited to short previews and animations, as opposed to full-length movies that tend to be rented on video. Nonetheless, analysts expect that pay-per-view Internet distribution services will begin to draw consumers away from traditional video rental as the network infrastructure improves in the early 2000s. Major video retailers like Blockbuster, as well as independent start-ups like iFilms.com, are gearing up to compete in this space.

FURTHER READING

Alexander & Associates. ''Historical Data.'' New York, 2000. Available from www.alexassoc.com.

Carricaburu, Lisa. ''Independent Video Stores Feel Brunt of Slowdown, Increasing Competition.'' *Salt Lake Tribune,* 16 March 1998.

Feuerstein, Adam. ''Will Web Rival Send Video Stores Reeling?'' *San Francisco Business Times,* 17 September 1999.

Heller, Laura. ''Revenue Sharing Rocks Rentals.'' *Discount Store News,* 12 July 1999.

Jeffrey, Don. ''Revenue-Sharing: Once Derided It's Now Seen By Many as Video Distribution's Future.'' *Billboard,* 11 July 1998.

Mullins, L.K., et al. ''Blockbuster Inc.'' New York: Salomon Smith Barney, 9 September 1999.

Pringle, David. ''Video-on-Demand Will Transform Pay-Per-View, Rental Businesses.'' *Wall Street Journal,* 11 November 1999.

Scally, Robert. ''VSDA Turnout Mirrors Industry: Mass Rules.'' *Discount Store News,* 26 July 1999.

Sweeting, Paul. ''Home Screen Feeds Big Green to Plexes.'' *Variety,* 6 December 1999.

———. ''Top Vid Chains Nurture Net Eggs.'' *Variety,* 8 November 1999.

SIC 7911

DANCE STUDIOS, SCHOOLS, AND HALLS

Establishments in this industry are primarily engaged in operating dance studios, schools, and public dance halls or ballrooms. Establishments primarily engaged in renting facilities used as dance halls or ballrooms are classified in **SIC 6512: Operators of Nonresidential Buildings.** This category includes ballroom operation, children's dancing schools, dance hall operation, dance instructors, dance studios and schools, discotheques (except those serving alcoholic beverages), and professional dancing schools.

NAICS CODE(S)

713990 (All Other Amusement and Recreation Industries)

611610 (Fine Arts Schools)

This approximately $500 million industry constitutes a very small portion of the overall recreation category. It is dominated by small, independent schools run by sole proprietors, usually owner-operators. The two major nationwide dance school chains, Arthur Murray International and Fred Astaire Dance Studios, cater to adults. Independent studios, which are primarily involved in teaching ballet and tap dancing to children, outnumber franchises by about six to one.

The dance school industry in America has had an uneven history. Dancing as a leisure activity was forced underground by the dominant Protestant culture that declared dancing socially unacceptable and linked it with drinking and lewdness. Even when European immigrants brought traditional dances to America during the nineteenth century, they were limited to celebrations at ethnic social halls.

Dancing became more mainstream after the turn of the century, when music and more organized bands earned enthusiastic followings. The advent of prohibition in 1920 separated dancing and drinking to a certain extent, and made dancing more socially respectable. Many commercial dance palaces were set up during this period, and in New York City alone, dance halls had revenues of $8 million in 1920.

Arthur Murray and Fred Astaire, the namesakes of the twentieth century's two largest dance schools, got their starts during this period. Murray opened his first dance studio when he was just 18 years old. Murray's career reflected the fortunes of the dance school and hall industry, crescendoing in the 1940s, when the song, ''Arthur Murray Taught Me Dancing in a Hurry'' was penned by Johnny Mercer. A request by a hotel manager to have Arthur Murray dance instructors in all Statler Hotels was just the beginning of what has become a $111 million company. Headquartered in Coral Gables, Florida, the company has locations in North America, Europe, and the Middle East.

Fred Astaire and Ginger Rogers inspired young men and women to emulate their moves in such popular films as *Top Hat, Swing Time, and Shall We Dance.* The Fred Astaire Dance Studios, headquartered in Boca Raton, Florida, were established in 1947 and have locations throughout North America.

A combination of social, economic, and demographic factors contributed to the decline of ballroom dancing and the dance school industry in the 1950s and 1960s. Fewer extravagant, romantic movie musicals were filmed. The advent of counter-culture rock-and-roll music was accompanied by alcohol use, transferring much social dancing into another industrial category. Moreover, the mass exodus to suburbia during this period resulted in a decreasing number of couples visiting urban dance halls. During the 1960s and 1970s, improvised singles dancing grew increasingly popular, and organized couples dancing became reserved for weddings and other special occasions.

Ballroom dancing regained popularity in the 1980s, spurred by a modest revival of music from the first half of the century. As the decade of conspicuous consumption progressed, ballroom dancing provided an outlet for prosperous men and women to dress up and spend money. Dance studios and halls also benefited from the fitness craze, as people danced for exercise and to relieve tension. Some observers even cited the increasing fear of both AIDS and romantic commitment as reasons for the industry's upswing, noting that individuals could get to know each other without having a formal date. The return of traditional formal weddings also contributed to this industry's growth in the 1980s. Dance teachers also credited the Public Broadcasting Service, which carried major ballroom dance competitions beginning in 1981, for promoting the activity. Dance studios began to coordinate more competitions, which encouraged students to take more lessons in preparation for competition.

The International Dancesport Federation (IDSF, formerly the International Council of Amateur Dancers) spent the latter half of the twentieth century working toward the acceptance of ballroom dancing as an Olympic event. In 1987, IDSF designated the United States Amateur Ballroom Dancers Association as the sole governing body for amateur ballroom dancing in the United States. Ten years later, the International Olympic Committee gave full recognition to the IDSF and its affiliates. As the twenty-first century began, the dancesport community was awaiting inclusion as a medal sport. Should this occur, it is expected to have a significant and positive effect on the dance industries.

Even without this inclusion, the growing popularity of recreational dance was evidenced by the number of Web sites devoted to ballroom, folk, Latin, swing, and country/western dancing. These sites offer directories of schools, dance halls, and competitions.

As popular dance boomed, however, professional dance lagged. Rehearsal space in New York City, always rare, has been taken away from professional dancers and college students and used for more lucrative activities. A sizable number of professional dancers supplemented their incomes by working as aerobic instructors. In addition, dance companies were licensing fitness centers to use their names, choreography and techniques.

Although college dance students were being urged by their professors to prepare for alternative careers, dance schools at the University of Utah, University of Hartford, Rutgers University, University of Iowa, and Hunter College of the City University of New York still provided professional dancers for smaller companies. A growing concern for dancers' health was responsible for the inclusion of nutrition classes in these curriculums.

Music copyright collections was a prominent issue for dance schools. Schools are required to pay fees for the use of music registered with ASCAP, BMI, and SESAC.

Although there appeared to be agreement in the dance community that composers should receive royalties when their music is used during public performances, the status of many schools as non-profit institutions was a cause for controversy.

Further Reading

Goldman, Phyllis. "Can College Dance Departments Prepare Students for the Future?" *Back Stage,* 15 November 1996, A32.

Horosko, Marian. "Don't Pay SESAC Music Fees—Yet!" *Dance Magazine,* July 1999.

"IDSF and DanceSport now fully recognized by IOC." The International Dance Sport Federation, 10 February 2000. Available from http://www.rullens.colm/idsf/press97.

Solomon, Gus, Jr. "Movement with Martha: Depreciating Dance." *The Chronicle of Higher Education,* 29 October 99.

Trager, Cara S. "Ballroom Studios Know the Score." *Crains New York Business,* 11 March 1996.

United States Amateur Ballroom Dancers Association, 10 February 2000. Available from http://www.usabda.org/.

SIC 7922

THEATRICAL PRODUCERS (EXCEPT MOTION PICTURE) AND MISCELLANEOUS THEATRICAL SERVICES

This category includes companies engaged in providing live theatrical presentations, including road companies and summer theaters. This industry also includes services allied with theatrical presentations, casting agencies; booking agencies for plays, artists, and concerts; scenery, lighting, and other equipment services; and theatrical ticket agencies. Also included in this industry are producers of live and taped radio programs and commercials and producers of live television programs. Establishments primarily engaged in the production of taped television programs and commercials are classified in **SIC 7812: Motion Picture and Video Tape Production.** Theaters that are normally rented to theatrical producers and stock companies are classified in **SIC 6512: Operators of Nonresidential Buildings.** Motion picture theaters and motion picture service industries are classified in the major group for motion pictures. Establishments primarily engaged in operating dinner theaters are classified in **SIC 5812: Eating Places.**

NAICS Code(s)

561310 (Employment Placement Agencies)
711110 (Theater Companies and Dinner Theaters)
711410 (Agents and Managers for Artists, Athletes, Entertainers, and Other Public Figures)
711120 (Dance Companies)
711310 (Promoters of Performing Arts, Sports, and Similar events with Facilities)
711320 (Promoters of Performing Arts, Sports, and Similar Events without Facilities)
512290 (Other Sound Recording Industries)
532490 (Other Commercial and Industrial Machinery and Equipment Rental and Leasing)

Industry Snapshot

New York City, particularly Manhattan, has always been the undisputed center of the U.S. theater scene. The late 1990s did nothing to change this, though developments somewhat altered the internal dynamics of New York's theater market. At all levels, the theater industry was characterized by rising production costs, which have focused efforts on more tested and proven productions that can more readily assure profits. This trend is most pronounced among the large Broadway theaters with the most to lose—one reason for the proliferation of revivals on Broadway, which are more reliable than new productions.

The scope of theater nationwide is so broad and varied that a snapshot of its size, as measured by revenues, does not currently exist. Broadway productions are fairly well documented; off-Broadway and off-off-Broadway are significantly less so. Regional touring companies, community theaters, summer stock (where one ensemble performs several plays each season), and their contributing entities such as agencies and scenery design and building are so fragmented as to render a comprehensive overall picture nearly impossible to draw.

Throughout the nineteenth and early twentieth centuries, the New York theater district along Broadway kept moving north as new theaters were built and old ones were abandoned or torn down. After World War II, as construction of new theaters became rare, "Broadway" stabilized in an area that can be roughly defined as the section of Broadway between Times Square and 53rd Street. Most of Broadway's 32 theaters are not actually on Broadway but clustered on side streets.

The New York theater market surged in the late 1990s at all levels, generating about $1.6 billion in ticket sales. Although Broadway enjoyed record box office returns, the biggest gains, both in attendance and in prestige, occurred at off- and off-off-Broadway venues, most of which have theater capacities of 75 to 400 seats.

Broadway. The 1998-99 New York Broadway attendance reached a record 11.7 million, according to information provided by the League of American Theaters and Producers, Inc. This represented a 23 percent increase from the 9.45 million Broadway attendees in 1996. Box office receipts also achieved unprecedented heights in 1999, totaling $588.5 million, up 5.5 percent from the year before. Thirty-nine Broadway productions opened in New York, four more than in 1998. However, the total playing weeks of Broadway shows fell slightly to 1,440. Major successes of the late 1990s included ''Art,'' which turned a profit of $4.5 million from its 600 performances; Disney's ''The Lion King,'' a box office smash indicative of Broadway's heightened attempts to draw young and other non-traditional audiences into its; as well as the revivals of ''Cabaret'' and ''Chicago.''

Although the numbers seem encouraging, there is serious concern about Broadway's future. Ticket prices have gone up with the cost of production. In 1957, top price orchestra seats at a Broadway musical could be had for $8.05. By 1970, the price nearly doubled to $15.00, and by the early 1980s soared to $45.00. In 1999, orchestra seats were going for $75.00. According to the League of American Theaters and Producers, Inc., the average paid admission to a Broadway production was $50.30, up from $48.58 in 1998, and could reach as high as $85.00. In 1987 the average stood at $28.66. Ticket prices for Broadway road companies follow a similar pattern. The rising costs are attributed to a strong U.S. economy, the increasing wealth of the typical theater audience, and, most particularly, rising production costs. Unless production costs diminish, it seems unlikely that ticket prices at commercial theaters will decrease.

In the mid- and late 1990s, the minimum cost of mounting a Broadway production was $750,000 for a play, and $3.5 to $6 million for a musical. Some musicals have had budgets in the $10 million range. Increased costs have made turning a profit more difficult, and shows can run for well over a year without moving to the plus side financially. Investors are increasingly reluctant to back risky ventures—those which do not have the potential for a lengthy run. This situation has led to a preponderance of revivals of past successes, especially musicals. *Carousel, Damn Yankees, Show Boat, The King and I,* and *How to Succeed in Business Without Really Trying,* are just a few of the older works that have returned to Broadway in the 1990s. According to the *New York Times,* about half of the productions that opened on Broadway in the 1995-96 season were revivals. Though revivals are a normal and necessary part of the theater, such a large number of them is unprecedented and problematic. Meanwhile, one of the lynchpins of the late 1990s Broadway market, ''The Lion King,'' had already proven itself as a fantastically successful animated Disney motion picture, thus constituting another relatively safe investment.

Soaring production costs further sparked increased focus on marketing campaigns as a competitive field for Broadway producers. A typical Broadway production spends between $300,000 and $1 million on pre-opening marketing campaigns and maintains publicity with about $50,000 per week after the production hits the theater. Meanwhile, the League of American Theaters and Producers has entered into a number of promotional contracts with major companies, including Schweppes, which agreed to launch a Broadway sweepstakes campaign advertised on its beverage bottles. Similarly, the First USA Bank-Broadway credit card features Broadway-related consumer incentives. Broadway shows have advertised on McDonald's French fries containers, while youth-oriented productions such as ''Rent'' and Disney productions have placed products such as coloring books in schools.

An extension of Broadway are road companies, which bring streamlined, though still often extremely elaborate, versions of Broadway productions to major cities around the United States and Canada. In the 1998-99 theater season, 14.8 million people attended Broadway shows outside of New York, down 20 percent from 1996. The box office take equaled $716 million, also down from $721 million. The declining number of touring productions largely accounts for sagging receipts; only 25 Broadway shows took to the road in 1999, down 30 percent from 1996.

Off-Broadway. Re-staging of material that has already proven itself Off-Broadway or in London is also a current feature of Broadway. The conservative reluctance to exhibit new and untested work has somewhat diminished Broadway's status as the center of the American theater. The pressure to come up with a long running crowd pleaser has also turned away creative personnel. Off-Broadway, a term applied to a wide variety of smaller theaters in New York located away from the major theatrical district, is becoming more important as a place to showcase original material. Once considered a training ground for Broadway, Off-Broadway is now accorded as much prestige as Broadway, as a venue in which audiences can glimpse the latest, most innovative works before they explode on the commercial scene, as was the case with the late 1990s hit ''Bring in 'da Noise, Bring in 'da Funk.'' Having a success Off-Broadway has even come to be seen as an end in itself. Many playwrights and theater composers, including well-established ones such as Stephen Sondheim, Neil Simon, and Edward Albee, have taken some of their works Off-Broadway in the 1990s.

Eight million people attended non-Broadway shows in New York during the 1997-98 season, representing an increase of 8 percent from the previous year. The commercial possibilities of Off-Broadway have increased along with its prestige. Although the vast sums brought in by ''megahit'' Broadway shows are not possible in Off-Broadway's small to moderate size theaters and lower profile atmosphere, handsome profits are still being made. Some long-running Off-Broadway successes, such as *Tony and Tina's Wedding,* have franchised lucrative duplicate productions in other cities. Off-Broadway's appeal has increased so much that, by the mid-1990s, there was a clamor for space in its handful of larger size theaters. Some analysts view the increased status and popularity of off-Broadway productions with some caution; the trend spurred theater construction at a pace of nearly one-and-a-half new theaters per month in 1999, sparking fears of a possible glut in coming years—especially should the newfound success of off-Broadway prove only a fad.

Demographics. The League of American Theaters and Producers notes that the average theater attendee belongs to a household with more than $80,000 in annual income. Moreover, about 88 percent of audiences are white, though that figure diminishes among the growing youth audience.

The increase in ticket sales enjoyed by theaters in recent years is often attributed to an overall increase in the adult population due to the post World War II ''baby boom,'' rather than increased interest in the theater. Though the number of tickets sold has gone up, the percentage of Americans who say they have attended a theatrical production in the last year has declined steadily to about 11 percent in 1999. Various reasons have been put forth for the waning popularity of theatergoing, including the greater availability of home entertainment; high ticket prices; and the trend towards late-in-life parenthood, which has left many people with child care obligations well into middle age.

For many years, the theater industry was most disturbed by the strikingly low attendance rates among younger audiences, suggesting that the theater's future lifeline was sorely thin as younger people showed little interest in theater shows as an entertainment form. Toward the end of the 1990s that long-standing trend began to change somewhat. The percentage of Broadway audiences composed of people younger than 18 years of age grew from 1.3 percent in 1990 to 4.7 percent in 1998. The 18-24 sector, meanwhile grew from 3.6 percent to 5.9 percent over that period. While in the late 1990s many attributed this sudden turnaround to the massive popularity youth-directed productions, such as the Generation-X-angst production ''Rent,'' some analysts suspected that long-running intensive marketing efforts geared toward younger audiences were finally paying off.

Notable developments on the road included a considerable gender gap in Broadway audiences, particularly among younger attendees. Women comprise 70 percent of the touring Broadway audience; moreover, they purchase 75 percent of the tickets for those shows. A demographic study by the League of American Theaters and Producers concluded that approximately 30 percent of theater goers are ''apparently dragged to the theater by their wives or girlfriends.''

Tourists constituted an increasing proportion of Broadway audiences through the 1990s, equaling roughly 60 percent of Broadway attendees at the end of the decade, up from 50 percent just three years earlier. For long running hits such as *Les Miserables* and *Cats,* (which prepared to shut down production in 2000 after 7,397 performances since its opening in 1982) the percentage of tourists can be as much as 80 percent. There is great concern that the theater in New York, and elsewhere, is losing its base of regular patrons whose interests go beyond an occasional visit to a hit show. Observers surmise that tourists tend to be drawn to the traditional glamour and mystique of Broadway, while more hardened New York locals have grown weary of its increasing conservatism and reliance on lavish revivals.

Background and Development

Theater in America dates back to the Revolutionary War period, which saw the formation of the first professional company in Williamsburg, Virginia, in 1752. The company was led by Lewis Hallam and was a profit-sharing venture. This financial structure called upon the actors to pay a percentage of company expenses and to receive a share of the profits. This organizational structure was adopted from Elizabethan England and also existed in the first known company in the Americas, which began in Peru in 1599. The general manager of the company was also generally a leading actor and would both invest more, and receive a greater share of the profits than, the other performers in the company. Playwrights and musicians would also participate in this type of ensemble. Not only did the performers often make a meager living from this arrangement, but they also faced the barrier of resistance from Quaker and Puritan colonists. But theaters began to open in the late 1700s and were well established by the turn of the century.

The era of profit-sharing theater companies gave way to one of independent stock companies, which lasted through the 1870s. The independent stock company would instead have a fairly permanent stable of actors and a fixed supply of scenery and props. These companies would stage a variety of current works and classics, and would either tour or present shows in a fixed venue. Most actors remained relatively obscure, although audiences made tours of celebrity performers from England popular during this time.

The impetus for the next major change in the structure of theater was the development of the railroad system, which led to the ''combination company''—the ensemble that toured by train from one major city to another, stagehands, scenery, and the like in tow. Most combination productions were organized in New York, and this led to centralization of the American theater in that city (Philadelphia and Boston had offered some rivalry to New York in earlier decades). The combination system required a complicated booking system to insure that large ensembles of performers and scenery would move smoothly through lengthy tours. As a result, theater ownership became centralized into a small number of circuits, which monopolized booking rights in various geographical areas. In 1896, three theater owning circuits joined forces to create the "Theatrical Syndicate," which dominated the theater for the next two decades. Producers who wanted to use a Syndicate-owned theater in a certain city were forced to book their entire tours in Syndicate theaters. Thus, theaters owned by non-Syndicate members languished and competition was minimal. Syndicate members, most notably Charles Frohman, were also producers and reserved the best routes and best theaters for their own productions. Theatrical offerings of this era focused on star performers in vehicles suited to their talents, such as Maude Adams in *Peter Pan* and David Warfield in *The Music Master*. Road tours, which made one-night stops in small cities as well as playing for lengthier engagements in large cities, were more profitable than playing in New York and only a handful of major successes ran on Broadway for more than two or three months. Eventually, the Theatrical Syndicate declined, and the chain of theaters owned by the Shubert brothers became the nation's most powerful theatrical landlord. The Shubert Organization still thrives, owning sixteen of Broadway's thirty-two theaters, with a half interest in a 17th, the Music Box. Theater owners hold an important position in the commercial theater since they control what goes in their venues.

In the 1920s, the once lucrative road dissolved as many theaters were converted into movie houses which are inherently more profitable than legitimate theaters since operating costs are lower. Theatergoers in many medium and small cities were left with no theater to attend. According to Jack Poggi in *Theater in America,* the number of legitimate theaters outside major metropolitan centers dropped from 1,549 in 1910 to 400 in 1928. Motion pictures had begun to capture the imagination of public, especially that segment that had patronized second tier theatrical comedies and melodramas. This left the theater with a smaller but more sophisticated clientele.

The stock market crash of 1929 and subsequent Great Depression hurt the theater but, unlike in other industries, improvement in the economy did not bring a recovery. The level of Broadway activity in the prosperous post-World War II era, sometimes considered Broadway's heyday since so many works from that period still enjoy popularity, was actually no higher than during the depths of the Depression.

A burgeoning number of non-profit resident theaters, or repertory companies, began operating in cities outside New York in the 1970s, though a number of them, such as the Pasadena Playhouse in California and the Arena Stage in Washington, D.C., have existed for much longer. These companies, which have lower ticket prices and a wider range of offerings than the commercial theater, depend to a great extent on government grants and private sector donations. Reduced levels of support from these sources imperil many resident companies. The budget of the National Endowment for the Arts was slashed by 40 percent in fiscal 1996, and while its budget was squeezed tightly throughout the remainder of the decade, debate raged on Capitol Hill and elsewhere often calling for the endowment's dissolution altogether.

Even more important, in the opinion of some analysts, is the dramatic drop in private philanthropy. Younger people are patronizing art organizations at a decreasing rate and, consequently, they are not supporting such organizations with generous donations. Charitable donations to the arts declined by about half between the mid-1980s and mid-1990s, and registered a further 2.5-percetn drop in 1998, despite a booming U.S. economy and increased income among the largest traditional arts-patronage demographic. To deal with this situation, many resident theaters are restructuring their finances, making longer range economic plans, and producing works that appeal to a wider audience. There is also greater acceptance of the idea that some resident theaters, especially those that cannot put themselves on a stronger financial footing, will have to be disbanded. This situation is troubling to many people since producing highly commercial material is not viewed as the purpose of non-profit theater, and companies with sound finances are not necessarily those of the greatest artistic merit.

FURTHER READING

Bernstein, Paula. "'Year of the Play' Brings Record Broadway Revenue." *Hollywood Reporter,* 1 June 1999.

"Broadway Finally Has its Promotion Act Together." *Entertainment Marketing Letter,* May 1998.

"Fewer Broadway Musicals Hit the Road." *Wall Street Journal,* 9 December 1999.

"Forget the Stereotype: America Is Becoming a Nation of Culture." *Wall Street Journal,* 17 September 1998.

Gener, Randy. "Theaters Enter Big Growth Stage: Venues Burgeon; Is Glut In Offing?" *Crain's New York Business,* 18 January 1999.

"The Great Hyped Way." *Business Week,* 3 May 1999.

"The Magic Is In the Marketing." *New York Times,* 19 November 1998.

"Market Fact 1998: Tourism." *Crain's New York Business,* 6 July 1998.

"A New Season Shines." *Travel Agent,* 6 September 1999.

O'Brien, Tim. "Youth Increases at Touring Broadway Shows." *Amusement Business,* 12 April 1999.

Peterson, Kyle. "Disney Fans First, Then the Highbrows." *Advertising Age,* 1 February 1999.

Poggi, Jack. *Theater in America: The Impact of Economic Forces, 1870-1967.* Ithaca, NY: Cornell University Press, 1968.

Siebert, T.W. "Raleigh Little Theater Flyers Play for Big Laughs." *Washington Post,* 2 February 1997.

SIC 7929

BANDS, ORCHESTRAS, ACTORS, AND OTHER ENTERTAINERS AND ENTERTAINMENT GROUPS

This category covers establishments primarily engaged in providing entertainment other than live theatrical presentations; these establishments include bands, orchestras, and entertainers.

NAICS CODE(S)

711130 (Musical Groups and Artists)
711510 (Independent Artists, Writers, and Performers)
711190 (Other Performing Arts Companies)

Music. The pop music concert circuit reached record levels in the late 1990s, deriving its success from seasoned veterans as well as trendy new acts. The top ten acts managed to bring in $414.3 million, up substantially from sagging mid-1990s receipts. Internationally, concert receipts totaled $1.3 billion in 1999, up 12 percent from 1998, while in North America revenues reached $1.23 billion, representing an increase of 11 percent. Some of the top performers in popular music in the late 1990s included genre stalwarts The Rolling Stones, who raked in $89.2 million in 1999; Bruce Springsteen, whose reunion tour with the E-Street Band generated $53 million in box office receipts; hip hop stars Master P and Sean Puffy Combs, who in 1998 earned $56.5 million and $53.5 million, respectively; the Dave Matthews Band, whose concerts brought in sales of $44.5 million; pop diva Celine Dion, with $55.5 million in 1998; and 'N Sync, the top new act in 1999, earning $44.3 million to edge out their boy-band competitors The Backstreet Boys, who made $24.5 million. Barbara Streisand, meanwhile, broke the box-office record for a single show with her New Year's Eve 1999 performance in Las Vegas, which generated ticket sales of $14.7 million, topping the Three Tenors' New Jersey show in 1996, in which Luciano Pavarotti, Placido Domingo, and Jose Carneras raked in $13.4 million.

Festivals continued to play a vital role as a way to excite concert goers, with touring shows such as the Lilith Fair designed to showcase a particular niche market, in this case the female pop singer-songwriter genre, in a forum that draws greater numbers than promoters surmise the artists could draw on their own, while fetching a higher ticket price in the meantime. Following the same logic while drawing on pop culture mystique, the Woodstock '99 concert in upstate New York drew 186,963 fans to its three day festival, generating ticket sales of $28.86 million. The show managed to arouse controversy, a staple of the rock and roll scene, as the kids took to destroying the venue and, disturbingly, committing over a dozen sexual assaults. From a financial standpoint, however, the show was indicative of the year's success in rock and pop music. Gimmickry was also alive and well on the concert scene. The Christian rock band The Newsboys planned a U.S. tour in 2000 featuring their own portable arena, a 3,500-seat blow-up model that could be set up in 90 minutes and transported from city to city.

Country music, however, failed to enjoy such good news; attendance was down about 20 percent in 1999 after dramatic growth through the mid-1990s. Total receipts for country music shows fell 16 percent to $116 million, with two acts, Shania Twain and George Strait, accounting for more than half of that total, at $36.6 million and $32.0 million, respectively. Observers attributed a large share of this decline to the absence of country star Garth Brooks from the concert scene in 1999. Long the brightest star in country music, Brooks was among the top entertainers in 1998 with concert sales totaling $54 million.

One of the most notable popular-music trends at the close of the 1990s was the voracious market for teen pop acts. The boy-band craze of 1999, featuring acts such as The Backstreet Boys, 'N Sync, and 98 Degrees, along with other artists such as Britney Spears, jumped on the youth fan base stirred up in preceding years by The Spice Girls to create the most visible and lucrative niche market in popular music. Despite the notorious track record of here-today, gone-tomorrow youth acts such as New Kids on the Block, some record executives were banking on such artists for the long haul; in 1999 Jive Records signed The Backstreet Boys to a five-album, $60 million contract, one of the biggest music deals ever.

Other trends in popular music relied less on teen innocence and more on parental shock. Acts such as Marilyn Manson and Insane Clown Posse incorporated explicit lyrics and often-graphic sexual or gory imagery into their live performances, arousing parental ire and even leading to talks in state and local legislatures of implementing a ratings system for live shows. Analysts estimated that about 25 percent of pop-music concert revenues were generated by acts that engage in some type of obscenity on stage. By including warning labels on tickets or rating shows in the manner of motion pictures, proponents hoped to keep children away from such concerts unless accompanied by an adult. Some artists, however, considered these proposals an act of censorship; high-powered acts such as Pearl Jam and R.E.M. announced that they would refuse to play in any state that passed a concert-rating law.

Another musical genre making an unexpected surge in the mid- and late 1990s was opera, which *Forbes* labeled "one of the hottest sectors in the entertainment business." The 18 to 24-year-old crowd attendance grew by 15 percent between 1989 and 1999, while the number of opera companies has gone from 60 in the late 1970s to 170 in 1998. Opera's popularity rested on its traditional styles as well as on cross-over collaborations between opera stars like Luciano Pavarotti with pop acts such as U2. Meanwhile, some corporations paid as much as $75,000 for an opera star to sing for as little as half an hour at a company event, quite a bit higher than the $15,000 top fee for singing at the New York Metropolitan Opera.

Symphony orchestras continued to struggle in the 1990s, often going to great lengths to court younger audiences. The Philharmonic Society of Orange County, California, for instance, devised a multimedia performance for their concerts incorporating video footage and live theater in accompaniment with the musical performance. The Dallas Symphony Orchestra (DSO), meanwhile, invested in a World Wide Web site to showcase both technological and symphonic music, often in hybrid form, and to transmit live Web-casts of DSO performances.

One reason cited for frustrating sales figures is the high price of tickets for symphonic performances, which averaged $112 in 1999. Personnel costs made up nearly half of an orchestra's budget. Minimum starting salaries for new orchestra members in "major orchestras" (orchestras with a $5 million or higher budget) were approximately $74,360 annually, with highs of $130,000 reported by the New York Philharmonic and the Chicago Symphony. Salaries in most orchestras range from $25,000 to $100,000. There were more than 800 symphony orchestras in the United States in the late 1990s.

Magic Shows. Other live entertainment that has recently regained popularity has been the age-old industry of magic. Some of the highest paid entertainers are magicians, or illusionists. David Copperfield, long the reigning illusionist, generated sales of $49.5 million in 1999. Las Vegas has been the hot spot for the rebirth of the illusionist, with all the major casinos touting their own acts. The business community has also tapped into illusionists, using them at trade shows and sales meetings, with fees running as high as $2 million for Siegfried & Roy to appear at a German theme park opening.

Comedians. Comedians were also laughing their way to the bank, with comedy clubs cropping up around the country. Jerry Seinfeld topped the 1998 *Forbes* list of the highest-paid performers, taking in $225 million. Meanwhile, comedy records registered a huge upsurge in the mid- and late 1990s, with comedians such as Seinfeld and George Carlin releasing highly successful recordings of their live performances.

Actors. Although musicians and actors have differing talents, the most successful ones end up looking rather similar. They are wealthy and powerful, and have national, if not international, name recognition. Talk-show host Oprah Winfrey continued her reign as the highest-paid television performer, raking in $125 million in 1999, Tim Allen followed with $77 million. Winfrey's syndicated talk show faced challenges in this period from Jerry Springer's notoriously volatile program.

Screen actors are generally the most high-profile and glamorous personalities in entertainment. Leading actors include Harrison Ford, who pulled in more than $58 million in 1998; Robin Williams, with $56 million; and Mel Gibson, with $55 million.

The lingering wage disparity between actors and actresses was a growing concern to the acting community in the late 1990s. The Screen Actors Guild (SAG) noted that men typically earn about twice as much as women in the profession, while leading actresses could command anywhere near the top-dollar salaries of their male counterparts. Furthermore, SAG reported in 1999 that 63 percent of all movie roles are written for men, a gap that has held steady since 1992. Most of the difference is accounted for in the heavily male-dominated supporting role field. When combined with age demographics, the disparity was even more pronounced. While about two-thirds of all acting roles were awarded to people under 40 years of age, only 27 percent of all female roles went to women over 40, compared with 37 percent for men.

Meanwhile, the television and film industries fell under scrutiny in 1999 as disproportionately few roles were awarded to minorities. According to SAG reports, only 19 percent of all roles were awarded to minority actors in 1998. Latinos were the most under-represented, accounting for only 3 percent of all roles despite constituting 10 percent of the U.S. population.

Many actors and actresses spend the majority of their careers in live theatrical productions. Many reasons can be found for this interest in the theater. The stage is regarded by many actors as a demanding, exhilarating venue from which to practice their craft. In 1997, the minimum weekly salary for Broadway actors was about $1,040, while off-Broadway actors commanded about $$600 per week. The uncertain future of governmental arts subsidies could have dramatic consequences for actors and actresses in this field.

FURTHER READING

"1999 Top 100 Boxscores." *Amusement Business,* 27 December 1999.

"Actors and Actresses." *Direct,* January 1999.

"Dallas Symphony Plays Internet." *Newsbytes News Network,* 1 February 2000.

Emmons, Natasha. "Eclectic Orange Fest Aims to Attract Younger Audience." *Amusement Business,* 20 September 1999.

"Newsboys: Have Venue, Will Travel: Band Hits Roads With Its Own 'Dome'." *Amusement Business,* 17 January 2000.

Pappas, Ben. "Forget Ring-A-Ding-Ding. For Today's Musical Moneymakers, the Word is 'Yo'." *Forbes,* 21 September 1998.

"R-Rated Rock Shows? Take Mom to Hear Marilyn Manson?" *New York Times,* 1 December 1997.

"Stones Are Highest Rollers in '99." *Hollywood Reporter,* 28 December 1999.

"Top 40 Entertainers." *Forbes,* 21 September 1998.

Waddell, Ray. "News Both Good and Bad On Country Music Scene." *Amusement Business,* 27 December 1999.

SIC 7933

BOWLING CENTERS

This industry includes establishments known to the public as bowling centers or bowling alleys. Such establishments frequently sell meals and refreshments.

NAICS CODE(S)

713950 (Bowling Centers)

INDUSTRY SNAPSHOT

Approximately 53.3 million Americans visited a bowling alley at least once in 1997, making tenpin bowling the most popular indoor participation sport in the United States, based on participation of once or more per year. There were also 8 million "frequent bowlers," or those who bowled more than 25 times per year.

Bowling boomed following the invention of the automatic pin setter in the early 1950s. By the mid-1960s, approximately 12,000 bowling centers were built in mostly blue-collar, urban areas of the United States. Due to demographic and lifestyle changes, however, the bowling market collapsed during the 1970s. As of 1998, there were only 6,542 certified bowling centers in the United States, the lowest total since 1954. In response, the bowling industry tried to redefine its image, with the hopes of attracting the affluent middle class and their children. New centers have been built in better market locations with state-of-the art facilities. Operators renovated their existing centers to include computerized scoring, upscale dining, entertainment, and even child care.

ORGANIZATION AND STRUCTURE

Many forms of bowling existed, but tenpins became the most widely played version in the United States and throughout most of the world. According to rules specified by the American Bowling Congress (ABC), tenpin bowling is played indoors with 15-inch pins arranged in a triangle at the end of a wooden or synthetic lane. The game consists of ten frames with two rolls of the ball per frame. The goal is to knock down all ten pins with the first ball, which earns a strike. If pins are left standing after the first roll, the fallen pins are removed and a second delivery attempted. Knocking over all the remaining pins earns a spare. A perfect game totals a score of 300 and consists of 12 strikes in a row (two additional rolls are granted on the final frame).

The traditional strength of the bowling center industry was its highly organized, competitive league structure. Men's and women's leagues consisted of teams with up to five players each. The total number of teams per league depended upon the number of lanes per bowling center. Three bowling associations determined the rules of league play. They also handled the prize money collected from bowlers' entry fees.

Most bowling alleys relied upon the steady revenue of league bowling instead of walk-in traffic. Approximately two-thirds of revenues came from bowling fees, so it was critical for centers to attract large numbers of customers to their lanes. Demographic and lifestyle changes triggered a decline in bowling leagues. In response, some operators instituted flexible leagues, while others shortened their seasons to 20 weeks, or offered league play every other week.

BACKGROUND AND DEVELOPMENT

The modern game of bowling probably originated in ancient Germany as a religious ceremony. As early as the third or fourth century, most Germans had kegels, or clubs, that they used for both sport and self-defense. Some Germans would take their kegels to church in an attempt to rid themselves of sin. They would place the kegels at the end of a long lane, similar to the modern bowling alley, and roll a stone toward them. If the kegels were knocked over, the owners were absolved of sin.

Dutch settlers brought ninepin bowling to the United States in the seventeenth century. The game quickly grew in popularity but was soon taken over by gambling interests. So strong was gambling's hold on bowling, some states outlawed the game altogether. In fact, some sources claimed that the tenth pin was added to the game in the early eighteenth century to circumvent the prohibition of bowling, which applied only to the ninepin game.

The popularity of tenpin bowling spread as German immigrants moved to Chicago, Milwaukee, St. Louis,

Cincinnati, and Detroit. However, the lack of uniform rules and equipment stunted the development of the sport. In 1875, intending to establish standardized rules and regulations, nine bowling clubs in New York City and Brooklyn organized the National Bowling Association.

Despite this initial attempt, disagreement over game rules persisted. In 1895 a second group, the American Bowling Congress (ABC), was organized in New York City. ABC succeeded in establishing standard regulations and became the governing body for men's bowling, sponsoring its first national tournament in 1901.

ABC's counterpart, the Women's International Bowling Congress (WIBC), was founded in 1916 and began its annual national championship in 1917. Although they remained separate organizations, these two groups shared equipment testing and research facilities. In an attempt to attract a younger audience, the Young American Bowling Alliance (YABA) was established in 1982. This group worked with bowlers from childhood through college age. All three organizations combined to serve about 4.5 million members.

The invention of the automatic pin setter in the early 1950s revolutionized bowling and acted as a catalyst for the growth of alleys and league play. Between 1955 and 1963 the number of bowling alleys in the United States grew from 6,600 to 11,000, while the number of organized league bowlers jumped from less than 3 million to 7 million.

During the same time period, the Professional Bowlers Association of America (PBA) was established. Similar to professional golf, the PBA quickly developed a star system complete with professional tournaments. With the advent of television, PBA members became household names and earned millions in prize money.

Following its boom in the 1950s and 1960s, bowling centers were overbuilt in the 1970s. During the same time period, bowling's primary clientele—blue-collar workers—moved from the inner city to the suburbs. While demographics and lifestyles changed, the industry failed to adapt.

Since the late 1970s, the bowling industry has participated in a collective reconstruction and repositioning campaign. Many operators shut down their inner-city facilities while renovating suburban locations. Companies invested in computerized lane operations and added other recreational activities and eating establishments, turning bowling alleys into entertainment centers. One consequence of this regeneration was the demise of small, family-owned bowling alleys, especially those located within inner cities.

Despite a 25 percent drop in league bowling from 1980 to 1987, bowling remained one of the largest indoor participation sports in the United States in the early 1990s. However, the growth of the industry continued to be slow. In 1998 the total membership in the American Bowling Congress, Women's International Bowling Congress, and Young American Bowling Alliance decreased 5.7 percent, the twenty-second consecutive year it had decreased. There has also been a 28 percent decline in ''frequency'' of play since 1987.

Demographic data indicated that bowlers gradually increased in income level and were predominantly male. Between 1987 and 1995, the number of male bowlers grew 13 percent to represent about 53 percent of the total, while the number of female bowlers increased only 8 percent. In addition, the number of bowlers with an annual household income above $50,000 increased 52 percent over the same time period, while those with incomes under $25,000 fell 15 percent.

CURRENT CONDITIONS

Despite downward trends through the mid-1990s, some industry analysts said the bowling industry was poised for a comeback. In 1998 bowling manufacturers sales' were up 3 to 5 percent on average. To take advantage of this trend, bowling center operators continued to diversify their image by renovating their alleys into entertainment centers and marketing to upscale adults as well as their children. Operators began to attract younger customers by including video games in their centers and promoting programs such as ''rock and roll bowling'' and Brunswick Corp.'s Cosmic Bowling, which integrated music, laser lights, and fog machines. As of 1998, teenagers accounted for only 15.9 percent of current bowlers, but those in the bowling industry looked for an increase in this figure over the next decade, as the teenage population itself was expected to grow 15 percent. For small children, bowling operators began offering ''bumper bowling,'' in which the gutters were filled with plastic tubes to keep balls on the lane. In 1996 American Recreation Centers (ARC) introduced the ''Family Entertainment Center'' (FEC) concept with Fun Fest, a 49,000-square-foot facility in Addison, Texas. Many bowling proprietors viewed this kind of facility as the prototype for the future of the industry.

INDUSTRY LEADERS

As of 1997, AMF Bowling Centers, Inc. was the largest owner and operator of bowling centers in the world. It has been a leader in the bowling industry consolidation, acquiring Bowling Corp. of America in 1996 and American Recreation Centers, Inc. in 1997. As of 1998, AMF Bowling Worldwide owned and operated 490 bowling centers, with more than 100 in the United States. It also was buying more of them, at a rate of 13 a month. After aggressively researching new prototype designs for its centers, AMF conducted a $1.6-million renovation job at its East Meadow Bowl on Long Island. The establishment included an AMF automated scoring system, an updated color scheme, and a 20-foot outdoor sign. Another AMF project was a $10-million recreational complex in Franklin, New Jersey. This property included a bowling center, movie house with ten screens, video arcade, billiard parlor, and restaurant. AMF Bowling Worldwide conducted approximately 60 percent of its business in 70 international markets.

Brunswick Recreation Centers owned and operated more than 125 ''fun centers'' in the United States, Canada, and Europe, featuring bowling, billiards, and restaurants. Brunswick introduced Glow-in-the-Dark Cosmic Bowling in the mid-1990s, which increased open play revenues in more than 20 of its locations. In 1996 Brunswick began offering Cosmic Bowling to other proprietors. Brunswick Corp. is a major manufacturer of bowling equipment, from balls and bags to computerized scoring systems and pin setters. Brunswick Corp. also manufactures fitness equipment, camping and fishing equipment, boats, marine engines, and bicycles.

Alexandria, Virginia-based Bowl America operates more than 20 bowling centers (15 in the Baltimore-Washington, D.C. area, 3 in Richmond, Virginia, and 4 in Jacksonville and Orlando, Florida. Unlike other operators that also manufactured bowling equipment, Bowl America's principal source of revenue was bowling fees and the sale of food and beverages consumed on premise. The company's most noteworthy property was its Gaithersburg, Maryland, center that opened in early 1994. Dubbed ''America's most modern center,'' the 45,000-square-foot property featured 48 computer-controlled lanes and dining capacity for 170. Bowl America has attempted to attract younger bowlers through promotions such as ''Extreme Bowling'' (bowling accompanied by stereo sound and a laser show).

America and the World

The modern game of tenpin bowling became popular in Great Britain during World War II, when lanes were installed on U.S. military bases. Since then, the business of bowling in Great Britain followed its American counterpart, peaking in the 1960s and decreasing continuously ever since. However, British companies such as First Leisure Corporation were so successful in shedding the poor image of bowling that American operators toured facilities in Great Britain looking for pointers. Bowling also became popular in Asian countries, including Japan, Hong Kong, Thailand, Singapore, and Indonesia. The Professional Bowlers Association (PBA) expanded its international presence as it held the first Korea Cup in Seoul in 1996. The PBA anticipates that this event will grow to the popularity level of the Oronamin C Japan Cup, which has had a successful annual run since the mid-1980s. The PBA also plans to expand and exploit growing markets in Europe, Mexico, and Taiwan.

In 1997 U.S. bowling exports increased by 27 percent, with sales to China accounting for almost one-third of the total sales. This generated a great deal of optimism about the possibilities of the growing Chinese market. However, the Asian financial crisis, combined with market saturation and the low average income of the Chinese population, has resulted in a halt in expansion in this area. In addition, U.S. bowling exports decreased more than 50 percent in 1998. Manufacturers will likely need to be patient in order for the international markets to grow.

Research and Technology

Although technological innovations affected all aspects of bowling, some of the most dramatic changes occurred in the makeup and design of bowling balls and alleys. In addition, computerized operations brought in the use of automatic scoring and video coaching.

Modern bowling balls made from synthetic materials were completely different than their predecessors, which were made from hard rubber. In 1981 AMF took the lead by producing the first computer-designed bowling ball made from urethane. Using a computer-aided design, AMF found that urethane balls with different finishes could alter a player's performance. Likewise, bowling lanes were increasingly made from synthetic materials. These new lanes required less oil than wooden lanes and never needed resurfacing.

Computerized scoring systems were introduced in the early 1980s, making manual scoring obsolete. Most systems not only tallied the score of a game, but also kept track of handicaps and the scores of league players. Along with AMF, Brunswick Corp. was a leader in the research and development of computer systems for bowling alleys. In 1989 Brunswick introduced BowlerVision, a computer video that enabled players to set up practice shots.

Another notable attraction was the world's first bowling stadium, located in Reno, Nevada. The $47.5-million National Bowling Stadium had 80 lanes, a pro shop, gift shops, exhibit space, meeting rooms, restaurants, a giant-screen movie theater, valet parking, general seating for about 1,000 spectators, and video monitors displaying instant replays. The American Bowling Congress used the stadium in 1995 to celebrate its one-hundredth anniversary and to house its annual championship tournament—an event with nearly 100,000 participants.

Further Reading

American Recreation Centers. *American Recreation Centers Inc. 1996 Annual Report.* Rancho Cordova, CA: 1996.

Kina & White Advertising. *The Complete Bowling Index.* Irvine, Calif., 1997. Available from http://www.apc.net/kinawhite/bowling.

Young, David. ''Brunswick Pins Down a Strategy.'' *Chicago Tribune,* 28 May 1996.

SIC 7941

PROFESSIONAL SPORTS CLUBS AND PROMOTERS

This category covers establishments primarily engaged in operating and promoting professional and semi-professional athletic clubs. It also covers establishments engaged in promoting athletic events, including amateur athletics, and in managing individual professional athletes. Stadiums and athletic fields are included only if the operators are actually engaged in the promotion of athletic events. Otherwise, establishments engaged in operating stadiums and athletic fields are classified in **SIC 6511: Operators of Nonresidential Buildings.** Amateur sports and athletic clubs are classified in **SIC 7997: Membership Sports and Recreation Clubs.**

NAICS CODE(S)

711211 (Sports Teams and Clubs)
711410 (Agents and Managers for Artists, Athletes, Entertainers, and Other Public Figures)
711320 (Promoters of Performing Arts, Sports, and Similar Events without Facilities)
711310 (Promoters of Performing Arts, Sports, and Similar Events with Facilities)
711219 (Other Spectator Sports)

INDUSTRY SNAPSHOT

Sports is one of the fastest growing and most complex industries in the United States. According to the latest figures available from the U.S. Census of Service Industries, more than 300 professional and semi-professional sports teams were in the United States, with almost 20,000 employees and combined revenues of more than $2 billion. In addition to established sports like baseball, football, basketball, and hockey, professional clubs also were springing up across the country in sports such as volleyball, soccer, roller hockey, and lacrosse. The industry additionally supported approximately 775 sports management and promotion firms, with about 14,000 employees and total revenues of more than $1 billion. As of 1998, the total number of sports clubs and promoters was approximately 1,300 with close to 40,000 employees and revenues of more than $4 billion.

Some 50 cities hosted professional sports teams, while more than 100 cities were home to minor league franchises. Salaries paid to top professional athletes have increased dramatically in the 1990s, even as team owners continually expressed desire to stem the tide. For example, in 1998 National Basketball Association star Michael Jordan made in excess of $30 million for a single season of work. In 1999, the Los Angeles Dodgers of Major League Baseball signed Kevin Brown to a seven-year, $105-million contract. A decade earlier, players in both baseball leagues averaged less than $500,000 in annual salary.

ORGANIZATION AND STRUCTURE

Most professional sports teams are organized into leagues that establish rules and regulations controlling nearly every aspect of the business—from competition to player compensation. The three most influential professional sports organizations in the United States are Major League Baseball (MLB), the National Football League (NFL), and the National Basketball Association (NBA). Another large professional sports organization, the National Hockey League (NHL), has franchises in both the United States and Canada, as do MLB and the NBA.

Major League Baseball. As of 2000, MLB consisted of 30 franchises organized into 6 divisions within 2 leagues: the National League of Professional Baseball Clubs and the American League of Professional Baseball Clubs. MLB is controlled by the team owners who appoint a president for each league and a commissioner of the entire sport. Bud Selig, formerly of the Milwaukee Brewers, was appointed commissioner in 1998 after acting in that role for several years. Players in the league are legally represented by the Major League Baseball Players Association. Sales for 1998 totaled $3.2 billion, an increase of 43.2 percent from 1997.

National Football League. As of 2000, the NFL consisted of 31 professional football teams organized into 6 divisions and 2 conferences: the American Football Conference and the National Football Conference. The NFL is controlled by the team owners and the commissioner of football, who is appointed by the owners to oversee the league's operation. The former NFL Players Association was decertified after a strike in 1987. In 1999, sales increased by 33.6 percent from the previous year to reach $3.3 billion.

National Basketball Association. The NBA includes 29 professional basketball teams organized into 4 divisions and 2 conferences: the Eastern Conference and the Western Conference. The NBA also is controlled by the team owners, who appoint a commissioner of basketball. The players are presented by the NBA Players Association. Two professional basketball leagues for women, one of which was affiliated with the NBA, began operations around the United States in the mid-1990s, though by 1998 the NBA-operated league was the only one still in operation. Sales for the NBA in strike-shortened 1999 were $955.5 million.

National Hockey League. The NHL includes 30 professional teams and, like the NBA, they are organized into 4 divisions and 2 conferences: the Eastern Conference (Northeast and Atlantic Divisions) and the Western

Conference (Central and Pacific Divisions). The NHL was formed in 1917, and the players are represented by the National Hockey League Players Association (NHLPA). In 1999, sales reached $1.5 billion, an increase of 10.5 percent

Background and Development

Baseball. An American game that evolved in the early 1800s, baseball is thought to be a derivative of the English game ''rounders.'' Rules for rounders, including the number of players and bases, varied widely by locale. Sports historians believe that sometime in the late 1830s or early 1840s, players in New York decided to stop throwing the ball at base runners, an aspect of the rounders game, and begin tagging them out. A commission established by Major League Baseball in 1906 gave credit to Abner Doubleday for inventing the game in Cooperstown, New York, in 1839. However, the commission's findings were most likely rooted in a patriotic desire to brand baseball as a purely American sport. Historians later disputed whether Doubleday did any more than organize a game of rounders.

During the Civil War, baseball was a favorite pastime for northern troops, who sometimes taught the game to their southern prisoners. When the war ended, the game's popularity led to rivalries between towns, and baseball clubs began enticing the best players with offers of jobs or money. James Creighton, a pitcher for the Excelsior Club of Brooklyn, purportedly became the first professional player in 1860 when his team agreed to pay his lost wages so he could join them on a road tour. When the National Association of Base Ball Players was founded in 1858, the organization had restrictions against professionalism. By 1868, however, the association had more than 300 member clubs in 17 states and officially recognized two classes of players, professional and amateur.

By the late 1860s, promoters were building enclosed ball parks and charging spectators for admission. To attract the best teams to their fields, the promoters shared a percentage of the gate receipts. In 1871, players from 10 professional baseball clubs from New York formed the National Association of Professional Base Ball Players. Nine clubs eventually paid a $10 membership and competed for the first national baseball championship.

National League. In 1876, the Cincinnati Red Stockings and seven other teams formed the National League of Professional Base Ball Clubs. The league set ticket prices, agreed to pay umpires, and prohibited playing games on Sundays and selling alcoholic beverages in the ball parks. The league granted the Chicago-based sporting goods company of A.G. Spaulding & Brothers the exclusive right to supply baseballs to the league; the company remained the exclusive provider of baseballs to the league for 101 years. Albert G. Spaulding was a former baseball player in Boston and Chicago who broke ranks with the players' association because he believed baseball needed to be run by businessmen. He later became league president.

In 1878, the National League created the League Alliance to cover minor league baseball. For a $10 membership fee, the National League would recognize a minor league's territorial rights and player contracts. It was the first working agreement between Major League Baseball and the minor leagues. The most controversial act by the young league, however, was its adoption of the ''reserve rule'' in 1879. The reserve rule, at first a secret agreement among team owners, gave each club the exclusive right to re-sign players from one season to the next. Only if a club gave up that right could a player be signed by another team. In Spaulding's words, the rule was ''to prevent competition for the best players.'' The reserve clause was challenged many times before baseball players won the right of limited free agency in 1976.

American League. Hard hit by the depression of 1893, the National League struggled along with 12 teams until 1900, when the owners voted to eliminate financially weak franchises in Baltimore, Washington, Louisville, and Cleveland. The Western League, a minor league that actually operated in the midwest, saw this as an opportunity to expand. Changing its name to the American League, it claimed major league status and established teams in Boston, Philadelphia, Chicago, and the four cities abandoned by the National League.

The American League received support from the newly formed Ball Players Protective Association, which urged its members not to sign contracts with National League teams unless the salary cap was lifted. The American League signed several top National League players and in its second season in 1901, surpassed the National League in attendance. When the American League then set its sights on expanding into New York, the National League capitulated by acknowledging the American League as a second major league. The two leagues agreed to honor each other's contracts, enforce the reserve clause, and respect each other's playing territories. The American League was also allowed to establish a franchise in New York that eventually became the Yankees.

In 1903, the National and American leagues signed another agreement which established a three-member commission consisting of the league presidents and a chairman elected by the club owners to set policy. The two year old National Association of Professional Baseball Leagues, which then represented 13 minor leagues, also signed the agreement. Under the agreement, major league baseball clubs, which had been created, moved, reorganized, sold, and disbanded with regularity for the past 20 years, achieved some stability.

Labor Movement. Major League Baseball players were without a labor organization from the time the Ball Players Protective Association folded in the early 1900s until 1946, when the eight-year-old Congress of Industrial Organizations convinced the players to form the American Baseball Guild. In August 1946, the Pittsburgh Pirates debated on striking for better pay and working conditions. Although there was no strike, the threat was sufficient to win some concessions for the players from the owners, including a $5,000 minimum salary, a limit of 25 percent on pay cuts from year to year, and a pension plan.

Decline of the Minor Leagues. The 1950s and early 1960s were turbulent years for organized baseball. Although the minor leagues enjoyed record crowds in the early 1950s, major league attendance fell 25 percent between 1948 and 1952. By the mid-1950s, the minor leagues were also having financial trouble, which was blamed on the emergence of television. Television provided plenty of entertainment at home, which kept people away from both major league and minor league ball parks. Major league teams compensated by negotiating broadcast rights with local television stations, although the results were mixed. In 1959, for example, the New York Yankees received $1 million in television rights fees. In contrast, the Washington Senators received only $150,000; the minor league teams, however, received nothing.

At first, organized baseball tried to protect the minor leagues from the effects of television by restricting broadcasts to within 50 miles of the home ball park, as it had done for many years with radio. But a Congressional investigation prompted organized baseball to lift the restrictions in 1953, and millions of Americans saw their first major league baseball game. When given this choice of watching baseball on television or going to a ball park, the fans chose television. Although national television exposure gave baseball a boost in the late 1950s and early 1960s, the sport began to slump again in the mid-1960s when interest in professional football rose dramatically. By 1965 baseball games were among the least watched programs on television, and to attract fans to the stadiums, team owners resorted to rule changes, colorful uniforms, exploding scoreboards, and offbeat promotions that were reminiscent of minor-league ball parks.

Labor Relations. Labor relations between the owners and the players also came to the forefront in the mid-1960s. In 1966, Sandy Koufax and Don Drysdale, then all-star pitchers for the Los Angeles Dodgers, presented salary demands to owner Walter O'Malley and forced him to negotiate with their agent, attorney J. William Hayes. Hayes negotiated $60,000 raises for both players, more than doubling Koufax's salary and tripling Drysdale's.

Also that year, the Major League Baseball Players Association (MLBPA), which had carried little influence since it was created in 1954, hired Marvin Miller, a former United Steelworkers of America union official, as its first full-time executive director. Within a year, Miller had negotiated an agreement with the owners that increased the players' minimum salary by more than 50 percent, from $6,000 to $10,000, and increased the owners' contributions to the players' pension plan. When the first agreement expired in 1969, the MLBPA used the threat of a strike to force the owners to recognize the union as the sole bargaining unit for all major league players in everything but salaries. For the first time, the owners also agreed to deal with the players' agents on matters of salary.

The first strike in organized baseball occurred after the second agreement expired in 1972 and the players voted 663 to 10 to walk out of spring training camps. The strike lasted one week past the scheduled opening day and cost club owners about $5 million in lost ticket revenues. The players lost about $1 million in salary. The strike ended when the owners agreed to contribute another $500,000 to the players' pension fund; however, the two sides did not reach a new labor agreement until the next year.

In 1973, the owners agreed that players with 10 years of major league experience and five years with the same team could veto trades. They also agreed to binding arbitration in contract disputes involving players who had been in the majors at least two years—a concession that was to cost the owners millions of dollars in later years. The reserve clause, however, remained intact, especially after the Supreme Court reaffirmed baseball's antitrust exemption in 1972 by ruling against former St. Louis Cardinal outfielder, Curt Flood.

Free Agency. Baseball regained favor with sports fans during the 1970s. The dramatic World Series between the Boston Red Sox and the Cincinnati Reds in 1975 was the most watched sporting event in history. However, the most crucial event for baseball that year came after the season ended. On the advice of their agents, pitchers Andy Messersmith and Dave McNally had played the entire 1975 season without signing their contracts. When the season ended, the two pitchers claimed that the reserve clause, which had guaranteed clubs the right to re-sign players since 1879, did not apply to them because they were not under contract. They were, they said, free agents.

The issue went to arbitration, and Messersmith and McNally's position was upheld by a professional arbiter, Peter Seitz, who was promptly fired by Major League Baseball. The decision, however, forced the owners to face the question of free agency. In the spring of 1976, the owners shut down training camps and threatened to cancel the season until the MLBPA agreed to restrictions on the movement of players between teams, but commissioner Bowie Kuhn interceded and the season began on time. That summer the MLBPA and the league ownership signed their fourth contract, in which they agreed that players could become free agents after six years in the major leagues. Technically, the players became part of a re-entry draft, and the clubs who lost players were entitled to compensation in the form of an additional pick in the amateur draft.

With free agency, players' salaries began to escalate rapidly. The average professional baseball player's salary more than doubled in a short period of time, from $45,000 in 1976 to more than $100,000 in 1979. The owners also began to issue dire predictions that wealthy teams would prosper, while less affluent teams, especially teams in small urban markets without large local television contracts, risked bankruptcy. The MLBPA's response was that television revenues would more than cover rising costs.

In 1979, baseball club owners decided that any team losing a player to free agency should be entitled to compensation in the form of a player from the free agent's new team. Teams would be allowed to protect either 15 or 18 players, depending on the quality of the free agent, but all other players would be at risk. The MLBPA objected and when negotiations between the owners and the union broke off in April 1980, the players again walked out of camp. The season, however, started on time when the negotiations resumed. When the two sides ultimately failed to reach an agreement, the owners unilaterally declared that the compensation plan would become effective in 1981. That led to the most damaging strike in major league history. The players struck on June 11, 1981, shutting down a baseball season that was already in progress. The strike lasted 50 days. It cost the owners an estimated $116 million, and cost the players an estimated $30 million. Polls taken during the strike showed that fans supported the owners over the players, whose average annual salary had by then climbed to $130,000. Eventually, the players and owners compromised on a player-compensation plan. Despite the labor problems, baseball enjoyed a renaissance throughout the 1980s, with record-setting attendance at major league ball parks. Salary levels rose as well, as did debate about the economics of the game.

By the time the players' average annual salary reached almost $1.2 million in 1994, things had taken a serious turn for the worse. ''Realizing they are unable to control themselves, or each other, in holding the line on players' salaries, the owners . . . asked the players to split all revenue 50-50 and accept a salary cap,'' according to the *Detroit Free Press.* The relationship between owners and the players' union continued deteriorating in an escalating war of words until August 12, 1994, when players who had refused to accept a new collective bargaining agreement with the salary cap provision walked out of the nation's ballparks and went on strike. They did not return to work for 234 days, which canceled the 1994 World Series for the first time in 90 years and delayed the start of the 1995 season. They went back when forced to by a federal judge. Fan interest was initially slow to rebound, and average salaries declined for the first time in 30 years. MLB responded by adding new franchises (in Tampa and Phoenix), scheduling regular-season interleague play, and embarking on various marketing and public relations efforts designed to boost interest and attendance. In November 1996, owners and players brought the unrest to an official end by finally ratifying a collective bargaining agreement that held into the next century. Significant recovery was evident by 1997, when both attendance and salary figures again began to climb. The recovery was further fueled in 1998 by a chase of the single season home run record, held by Roger Maris. St. Louis Cardinal Mark McGwire and Chicago Cub Sammy Sosa were able to break the record and draw fans back to the ballparks in record numbers.

Football. American football evolved from rugby in the late 1800s. In 1874, Harvard University, whose students played a form of soccer, accepted a challenge from McGill University, a Canadian school that played rugby. The schools played one game of each sport. Afterwards, Harvard switched to playing rugby and introduced the sport to other Eastern colleges in the United States. Walter Camp, who played on and later coached the rugby team at Yale University, is credited with developing many of the rules in the early 1880s that eventually made American football a sport distinct from rugby. For example, he created the center snap and the system of yards and downs. The first professional football game was played in 1895.

National Football League. Professional football remained generally disorganized until the American Professional Football Association was founded in 1920, with the Chicago Cardinals and the Staleys of Decatur, Illinois, as the original charter members. The Green Bay Packers joined the league a year later. In 1922, George Halas and Dutch Sternaman purchased the Staleys for $100 and moved the team to Chicago where it was renamed the Bears. The American Professional Football League also changed its name in 1922 to the National Football League (NFL). The New York Giants made it a three-team league in 1925. Additional clubs joined the NFL throughout the 1930s and 1940s, but, as is the case with many young leagues, the early years of the NFL were characterized by the rise and fall and relocation of many of these franchises.

Rival Leagues. The first of several leagues formed to challenge the NFL was the All-America Football Conference. Founded in 1944, the league played four seasons and folded in 1950. The next challenger was the American Football League (AFL), formed in 1960, which proved to have greater staying power and fan appeal. The AFL began play with teams in New York (Titans), Dallas (Texans), Los Angeles (Chargers), Denver (Broncos), and Houston (Oilers). The Buffalo Bills, Boston Patriots, Oakland Raiders, and Miami Dolphins joined the league over the next five years. The Chargers would move to San Diego after only a year in Los Angeles, and the Texans moved to Kansas City in 1963, where they became the Chiefs, but none of the original AFL teams folded.

The NFL and AFL battled over fans, players, and television revenues for six years before agreeing to merge in 1966 under the banner of the NFL. The first Super Bowl, pitting the AFL champion against the NFL champion, was played in 1967. Regular season play between the realigned National Football Conference and the American Football Conference began in 1970.

There have been two other challenges to the NFL since the American Football League, although neither has lasted long. The World Football League was formed in 1974 and played only a season and a half before folding. The United States Football League (USFL) was organized in 1983 and enjoyed a brief, three-season existence. The USFL played its first two seasons as a spring and early summer league and enjoyed modest acceptance from football fans, even though all of its teams lost money. However, in 1985, the league switched its schedule to the fall and went head-to-head with the NFL, a strategy that proved faulty. Still, the USFL did have a significant impact on the NFL. In 1983, the average NFL salary was $126,000. With the USFL bidding for top college players, the NFL average increased to $205,000 by the 1986 season.

The USFL also filed an antitrust suit in 1984, charging the NFL with conspiring to block a national television contract, deliberately expanding its rosters to prevent the USFL from signing players, tampering with players under contract to the USFL, and refusing to allow USFL teams to play in stadiums that were either owned or controlled by NFL teams. The USFL won the lawsuit, although by then the league had ceased to field any teams. In addition, instead of the $400 million the league had asked for in damages, which would have been increased to $1.2 billion under antitrust laws, the jury awarded only $1.

Union Representation. The NFL Players Association was formed in 1956, and even though the NFL owners refused to acknowledge the organization as a union, the first basic agreement was negotiated in 1957. It covered minimum wages, preseason pay, and medical care and salaries for injured players. The owners formally recognized the union in 1968.

When a contract negotiated with the NFL in 1982 after a 57-day strike expired, the players called another strike during the 1987 season. The owners, however, hired replacement players from the ranks of semi-pro and former NFL players and continued play. The strike ended after 24 days. Afterwards, in a strategic move, the union voluntarily decertified itself as the players' collective bargaining unit and became a self-described trade association. The move opened the door to antitrust suits by individual players since technically there was no longer a collective bargaining agreement or ongoing negotiations with a union. The union was recertified to represent NFL players in 1993.

Free Agency. Like baseball and basketball players, professional football players achieved a degree of free agency only after a lengthy series of legal challenges. The first significant case involved William Radovich, a former Detroit Lion who jumped to the All-America Football Conference in 1946. The NFL blacklisted Radovich and, in 1948, the NFL prevented him from playing for a team in the Pacific Coast League. Radovich sued and, in 1957, the Supreme Court ruled that unlike baseball, football was subject to antitrust laws. The court awarded damages to Radovich.

Then in 1971, John Mackey, president of the NFL Players Association, and 15 other players challenged the Rozelle Rule, named for the late NFL commissioner Pete Rozelle. The Rozelle Rule gave the commissioner absolute authority to order teams that signed free agents to give up other players in compensation, effectively stopping almost all free-agent signings. In 1976, a Federal District Court in the Mackey case ruled that the Rozelle Rule was unreasonable and had been unfairly forced on the players during labor negotiations.

The NFL draft of college players was also challenged in the 1970s as a violation of antitrust laws. In the key case, James ''Yazoo'' Smith, who had been drafted by the Washington Redskins, suffered a career-ending injury in the last game of the season. Smith, who did not have a guaranteed contract with the Redskins, claimed that the draft, which limited him to dealing with a single team, prevented him from negotiating a better contract. The court ruled that the draft was unreasonable restrictive and awarded Smith $276,000 in damages.

Armed with favorable decisions in these and other cases, the players association signed a new agreement with the NFL in 1977 that sanctioned the draft and allowed for some restrictions on player movements in return for financial incentives for the players. In another antitrust case that went to court in 1978, the court ruled that antitrust trust laws did not apply because the players had voluntarily given up certain rights when they agreed to the contract with the NFL.

After an abortive strike in 1987, the players association claimed in 1989 that it was no longer a union, and therefore, the expired labor agreement no longer protected the NFL from antitrust suits. The association also claimed that all players would become free agents as their individual contracts expired. NFL team owners argued that the players association was continuing to operate as a union despite its self-decertification.

In the absence of a negotiated contract, team owners also unilaterally instituted a free-agency plan in 1989 that came to be known as ''Plan B,'' as in ''let's go to Plan B'' when the initial plan fails. Plan B allowed teams to ''protect'' 37 of their 47 players after each season. The remaining 10 unprotected players were free to negotiate with whatever team they wished. A protected player whose contract had expired could also enter the free agent market; however, his former team had the right to match any offers or to receive draft picks as compensation. Several players challenged Plan B in court, and late in 1992, an eight-member Federal District Court jury in Minneapolis found Plan B was overly restrictive and, therefore, in violation of federal antitrust laws. However, the jury also agreed with the NFL that some restrictions on free agency were necessary.

Finally, observed the *Monthly Labor Review,* ''the National Football League and the National Football League Players Association reached a collective bargaining settlement in 1993 that the parties hoped would auger a more progressive, cooperative relationship, instead of the contentious and litigious one that had existed since the 1980s. In the end, the parties had a seven-year agreement with free agency, and the union was recertified to represent National Football League players.'' Salary cap figures and free agency restrictions were included in the agreement, and in 1999 the cap was increased to $58 million.

Basketball. The game of basketball was invented by James A. Naismith, a physical education instructor at the former International YMCA Training School in Springfield, Massachusetts, who needed a game that would keep the school's rugby and football players occupied during the winter months. Naismith's game became so popular that professional basketball teams were formed by 1895, although modern fans would hardly recognize the game.

National Basketball Association. Most early professional teams were touring squads that would challenge a local community's best players for a share of the gate receipts. There were, however, early attempts to organize professional basketball into leagues. The first league was probably the National League. Founded in 1898, it lasted only until 1903. The next major attempt to organize professional basketball was the American Basketball League (ABL). Players on most NBL teams worked for their corporate sponsors during the day and played basketball at night. Teams were often named for their sponsors' products, such as the Zollner Pistons of Fort Wayne, which later became the Detroit Pistons. In 1946, the owners of several professional hockey teams formed the Basketball Association of America (BAA) to help keep their arenas filled during hockey's off-season. The more established NBL boasted better players and more competitive play, but the East Coast-based BAA played in larger cities and better facilities. In 1948, the two strongest teams in the NBL, the Minneapolis Lakers and the Rochester, New York, Royals, bolted to the BAA.

The loss of its two best teams and its fiercest rivalry nearly devastated the NBL. In a desperate attempt to survive, the NBL signed all the graduating starters from the NCAA champion University of Kentucky team and assigned them to a new franchise in Indianapolis. The college stars had all played on the Gold-medal winning U.S. Olympic team in 1948, and the franchise was named the Olympians. The team gave the NBL enough leverage to force a merger with the BAA in 1949. The combined league, which sported 17 teams, was named the National Basketball Association.

Modern Basketball. Professional basketball in the early 1950s was a plodding game characterized more by pushing and shoving than by scoring. In 1954, the NBA instituted two rule changes designed to speed up the game and increase fan interest. The first was to award free throws after a team had accumulated five personal fouls in a quarter. This eliminated much of the rough play and intentional fouling that had bogged down the games. The second rule change had an even greater impact. Stalling occurred when one club held possession of the ball for long periods of time without attempting a shot and it was a common tactic in basketball. But Danny Biasone, owner of the Syracuse Nationals, proposed giving teams 24 seconds to shoot or lose the ball to the other team. Biasone chose 24 seconds because that would allow each team about 60 shots a game, which was considered an optimum pace. In addition to raising scores so that 100-point games became common, the 24-second clock also had a dramatic impact where it counted most—at the box office. Basketball closed out the 1950s as the fastest growing professional sport in the United States.

Union Representation. The NBA Players Association (NBAPA) was formed in the early 1950s, but it operated more as a fraternal organization than a labor union until the early 1960s. In 1964, however, the union threatened to boycott the All-Star Game unless the owners agreed to improve pensions. The players literally refused to leave the locker rooms until the owners capitulated. In 1967, the union negotiated the first basic labor agreement in professional basketball.

American Basketball Association. The American Basketball Association (ABA) was formed in 1967 and introduced several innovations, such as the three-point shot. Billing itself as "the Lively League," the ABA also drove up salaries by competing with the NBA for the best players. However, the league never achieved financial stability. After a decade of playing with its signature red, white, and blue basketball, the ABA was merged into the NBA in 1976. ABA franchises in Denver, New York, San Antonio, and Indiana each paid $3.2 million for the privilege of joining the NBA. The three remaining ABA franchises in Kentucky, St. Louis, and Virginia folded.

Free Agency. The NBAPA attempted to stop the league from merging with the ABA by filing an antitrust suit in U.S. District Court. The union also challenged the NBA's option clause, which, like baseball's reserve clause, gave teams the exclusive right to re-sign players when their contracts expired. Although the players failed to stop the merger, they did receive a preliminary ruling that cast doubt on many of the NBA's labor practices. Armed with the ruling, the NBA Players Association negotiated an agreement in 1976 that did away with the option clause and league rules, which provided for compensation for teams that lost players to free agency.

The players negotiated further concessions on free agency in 1987. Under the old agreement, players became free agents when their contracts expired, but their old teams had the right to match any offers they received. Since teams were seldom willing to lose star players, bidding on free agents drove up salaries, but few quality players actually changed teams. In 1987, the owners agreed to give up the right of first refusal for veteran players whose contracts had expired. In the first year of the agreement, the liberalized rules applied to players with seven years of experience, but that dropped to four years in 1989.

Salary Cap. The merger between the NBA and ABA eased the pressure of escalating salaries, but the long fight for players, a series of drug scandals, and sagging attendance left professional basketball with serious financial problems. Pro basketball was then the least-watched sport on television, trailing even golf, and the NBA was the only major professional sports league without a national television contract.

By the early 1980s, 16 of the 23 NBA teams were losing money, and four teams were on the verge of bankruptcy. To save the league, the NBAPA agreed to a limit on the total amount that teams could pay in salaries. In return, the owners promised that team payrolls would never fall below 53 percent of the leagues' gross revenues. While NBA teams were still free to offer multimillion dollar contracts to their superstars, the salary cap slowed the overall growth of salaries and helped put the league back on firm financial footing. These fiscal steps, coupled with the emergence of a number of particularly popular star players and an upswing in marketing savvy, enabled the NBA to reverse its fortunes. By 1987, almost every NBA club was profitable.

The growth of the league continued unabated into the mid-1990s, as evidenced by increasingly lucrative television contracts and attendance records. Player salaries surged as well. By 1994, the average NBA player made $1.4 million. In 1998, the NBA owners put a stop to the salary surge by putting a cap on the amount that could be played to individual players. This amount increased based on a player's experience in the league. It is felt that this system may well be a model for other professional leagues to follow.

Hockey. Ice Hockey was originally known as ice hurley in the early 1800s, and was started in northern Europe. By 1950, it was commonly called hockey. In 1873, J.G.A. Creighton became known as the father of organized hockey after he introduced the sport in Montreal. In 1892, the English Governor General of Canada, Lord Stanley of Preston, bought a trophy that was given to the best amature team in Canada. By the 1900s, the game was rapidly expanding across the United States and Canada and professional leagues were created in 1904 and 1910. In 1914, two leagues were in existence, the National Hockey Association (NHA) and the Pacific Coast League (PCL). The NHL opened in 1917 with five teams, and the winner played the PCL champion for the Stanley Cup. The PCL folded in 1926 and the NHL was the only remaining professional league.

Approximately 700 players are represented by the National Hockey League Players Association (NHLPA), which is headed by Trevor Linden. The association even had its own television show in the late 1990s—"Be a Player! The Hockey Show," which profiled players and presented trivia challenges. The Stanley Cup is now awarded to the best professional team in the NHL.

CURRENT CONDITIONS

Professional sports have assumed ever greater economic importance over the past three decades and the rise of mega-dollar contracts, powerful sports agents, dominant player organizations, fashionable superstar personalities, rewarding product endorsements, and lucrative broadcast deals has mirrored their growing popularity. In the early 1990s, professional sports were arguably more popular than ever before. The NFL and NBA were selling more than 90 percent of all available seats for their games, while MLB was enjoying record attendance. The NHL was steadily increasing in popularity. Television networks were willing to spend billions of dollars to broadcast sports events. Cities were willing to spend millions of dollars to build new stadiums or provide incentives to keep or attract professional sports teams. Sports franchises were escalating in value. In 1997, 52 public companies owned part of the 113 MLB, NBA, or NHL franchises; they were being viewed as "brands" that could be used in many profitable ways.

But in the midst of plenty, most professional teams also faced serious financial challenges due to operating costs, most of it tied up in spiraling player salaries that were rising far more rapidly than revenues. In many instances, teams were faced with declining revenues without any expectation that the incredible growth in salaries would slow.

Revenues. Heady bidding among the major broadcast and cable television networks, plus the sale of local broadcast rights, provided professional sports with steadily increasing revenues throughout the 1980s. Each NFL team, for example, received about $5.9 million from national broadcast rights in 1980; by 1990 that amount had increased to more than $26 million per team. Television revenues for MLB increased from about $3.3 million per team to $14 million. The NBA saw television revenues increase from $1.2 million per team to $5 million. In 1997, football brought in revenues of more than $160 million; basketball garnered close to $120 million; baseball brought in approximately $110 million; and hockey garnered more than $70 million.

In the 1990s, however, fees for sports broadcast rights began to reflect a glut of TV programming and a dearth of advertising revenue. The NBA, the only major sports league with increasing television viewership, signed a four-year, $750 million contract with NBC in 1993 that represented a 25 percent increase over its previous contract. But two years later and with many of its teams already operating at a loss, MLB accepted an unusual $516 million joint contract with NBC and ABC that paid each team only $4.6 million—about one-half of what they received in the final year of the previous deal with CBS. MLB's continuing rebound was reflected in a new national deal in 1996 that put total broadcast revenue at $730 million. Around the same time, the upstart Fox network jumped into the picture and helped up the ante by paying $395 million to broadcast NFL games and $31 million to bring NHL contests to a national audience. The NHL now has a $600 million television deal with ABC and ESPN, and the NFL has a $2.2 billion television contract with 4 networks through 2006.

The broadcast issue is more complicated for MLB than for other sports, because its teams also negotiate individual fees with local outlets. Owning to their location in the nation's top media market, the New York Yankees reportedly received almost $60 million in 1997 in total broadcast revenues—more than every other franchise and about three times the league average of $20 million. Baseball teams in smaller markets generally fare far worse, which was one of the prime rationales for the rich team/poor team revenue-sharing program included in the long-delayed collective bargaining agreement accepted in late 1996.

With traditional revenue sources no longer guaranteed, sports franchises in the late 1990s were developing new income sources. Chief among these are new or renovated stadiums with more seats, higher ticket prices, private "skyboxes" and "club sections" that command premium prices, and a widening array of commercial licensing opportunities that range from jumbo electronic scoreboard advertisements to naming rights for the stadiums themselves. Some teams have also struck previously unheard-of endorsement deals with major sponsors; others have been purchased outright by corporations that also control broadcasting properties or other avenues for peripheral profit. Additionally, in the late 1990s all of the major professional leagues were looking to increase their international operations.

Salaries. The greatest cost involved in operating a sports franchise is the salaries paid to the professional athletes. In the 1980s, free agency, player unions, and seemingly unlimited television revenues combined to drive salaries ever higher. In 1995, according to *Financial World,* they represented 68 percent of revenues in the NFL, 62 percent in MLB, 49 percent in the NBA, and 41 percent in the NHL. All of the major leagues have tried to reign in these escalating salaries, with different results.

The NBA system has been the most successful in limiting salaries, but having only been around since 1998, the results will need to be analyzed over longer periods of time. The NFL-implemented salary cap has been somewhat successful, although it has increased from $37 million in 1995 to $57 million in 1999. An average increase in salaries of $5 million per year per team is not what NFL owners hoped for.

Baseball owners initially tried to stem the rising tide of player salaries by simply agreeing among themselves in the late 1980s not to bid on free-agent talent. But the MLBPA filed suit against the owners, charging collusion. The owners lost the court battle, were ordered to pay $280 million in damages, and saw salaries begin to rise again. In 1992, the average salary for a major league baseball player was slightly more than $1 million and at least 30 players earned more than $3 million annually; in 1997, according to Associated Press figures, the average had climbed to nearly $1.4 million and about 130 players were in the $3 million club.

Industry Leaders

Within the industry, the top five companies in sales in 1996 were the Boston Celtics Limited Partnership

($52.3 million); St. Louis Rams Football Co., Inc. ($43.8 million); St. Louis National Baseball Club ($40 million); Pacers Basketball Corp. ($31 million); and WJA Realty Limited Partnership (28.8 million), which operates jai-alai frontons.

Driven by multimillion-dollar television contracts, the value of professional sports franchises ballooned in the 1980s, increasing an average of 20 percent per year. However, as television contracts and other revenues became less certain in the early 1990s, franchise values began to fall. In 1992, the value of the New York Yankees baseball club had fallen to about $160 million from more than $200 million several years earlier. Renewed public interest and stronger media deals, however led to a rebound, and the Yankees value rose to $491 by 1998. Other top MLB franchises that year included the Cleveland Indians, $359 million; Atlanta Braves, $357 million; Baltimore Orioles, $351 million; Colorado Rockies, $311 million.

The most valuable NFL franchises by 1997, according to *Forbes,* were the Dallas Cowboys, $413 million; Washington Redskins, $403 million; Carolina Panthers, $365 million; Tampa Bay Buccaneers, $346 million; Miami Dolphins, $340 million. The most valuable NBA franchises in 1998 were the Chicago Bulls, $303 million; New York Knicks, $296 million; Los Angeles Lakers, $268 million; Portland Trail Blazers, $245 million; Phoenix Suns, $235 million. The top hockey franchises in 1998 were the New York Rangers, $195 million; Philadelphia Flyers, $187 million; Boston Bruins, $185 million; Detroit Red Wings, $184 million; and the Washington Capitals, $178 million.

Gaining entry into the world of professional sports ownership has consistently become more expensive. In 1996, *Financial World* said it would cost at least $150 million to start up a new baseball or football team and $100 million for a team in basketball or hockey. As of 1999, the cost for new professional teams was steadily moving towards $500 million.

FURTHER READING

Alexander, Charles C. *Our Game: An American Baseball History.* New York: Henry Holt and Company, 1991.

Atre, Tushar, et al. "Sports: The High-Stakes Game of Team Ownership." *Financial World,* 20 May 1996.

Bjarkman, Peter C. *The History of the NBA.* New York: Crescent Books, 1992.

Business Rankings Annual. The Gale Group, 2000.

Hoover's Company Capsules, 20 March 2000. Available from http://www.hoovers.com.

"In The Money." *The Denver Post,* 3 April 1997.

"National Hockey League." *LCS: Guide to Hockey, 1997.* Available from http:www.lcshockey.com.archive/nhl.asp.

National Hockey League Players Association. "Player Compensation, 1997." Available from http://www.nhlpa.com/nhlpa/comp/index.html.

National Hockey League Players Association. "What is the NHLPA?" 30 November 1999. Available from http://www.nhlpa.com/about_nhlpa/nhlpa.htm.

"NFL Salary Cap to Increase." *Sportsline USA NewsWire,* 11 February 1997. Available from http://www.cbssportsline.com.

Saporito, Bill. "Stars' Salaries: Swish!" Time, 29 July 1996.

U.S. Census Bureau. *1997 Economic Census—Arts, Entertainment, and Recreation.* Washington, DC: GPO 2000.

Zimmerman, Paul. "Strapped." *Sports Illustrated,* 18 January 1999.

SIC 7948

RACING, INCLUDING TRACK OPERATION

This classification covers promoters and participants in racing activities, including racetrack operators, operators of racing stables, jockeys, racehorse trainers, and race car owners and operators.

NAICS CODE(S)

711212 (Race Tracks)

711219 (Other Spectator Sports)

INDUSTRY SNAPSHOT

The thrill of competition and the overall excitement of racing drew millions of American spectators to the wide variety of events in the racing industry, including horse races, dog races (greyhound), automobile races, and motorcycle races. The industry generated close to $5 billion in revenue in 1995.

Thoroughbred horse racing alone attracted 60 million spectators to racetracks in 36 states. On a total of 8,000 racing dates, visitors bet more than $13 billion at the tracks and at off-site locations. In the late 1980s, however, the horse racing industry began to fall behind more publicized and simplistic forms of legalized gambling, particularly the state lotteries. Unprepared for the influx of competition, track operators scrambled to make their courses more inviting to spectators in order to attract new and younger customers.

ORGANIZATION AND STRUCTURE

Horse Racing. In the horse racing sector of the industry, most U.S. racetracks were privately owned, and racing operations were governed by state commissions where the tracks were located. Most tracks were operated for a profit, as were the horses, while the trainers and jockeys worked as independent contractors. Some U.S. tracks, such as the ones operated by the New York Racing Association, were non-profit organizations. By contrast, racetracks in some other countries were owned and operated by the national government.

All horse racing, except quarter horse racing, involved thoroughbreds, usually three-year-olds. A racehorse achieves peak ability at age five, but few races included horses older than four due to increases in purses, breeding fees, and sale prices. Owners of thoroughbreds tried to produce superior horses through complex mating strategies, with the most desirable horse being one that performed well during long races. But as Patrick Cunningham, a professor of animal genetics at Trinity College in Dublin, claimed in *Fortune,* "only 35 percent of the differences between horses is attributable to genetic factors; the other 65 percent reflects diet, training, and random health-affecting events around the barn."

Early horse races featured a simple system of wagering in which spectators tried to pick the winner. In modern horse racing, however, spectators placed their bets on the first three horses, and most of the purse money was provided by the stakes fees of the horse owners. This practice, called pari-mutuel betting, created a common betting pool and paid off numerous winners. Those who wagered on horses finishing in the first three places (win, place, or show) shared the total amount betted, minus a percentage for the track management. Most purses allocated 60 percent to the winner, 20 percent to second place, 10 percent to third place, and 5 percent to fourth place. The system always provided the operator a profit and allowed any number of bettors to win.

Racetrack management began to offer pari-mutuel betting with the invention of the totalizator in the 1920s. The totalizator collected all bets and provided an instantaneous picture of the betting pools, displaying the approximate odds to win on each horse. Computerized totalizators at modern tracks flashed these totals to spectators at regular intervals, as well as displayed race results, payoff amounts, and running times.

Dog Racing. The dog racing sector of the industry consisted of events featuring a group of greyhounds chasing a mechanical rabbit around an enclosed track. Based upon an older sport where dogs hunted by sight rather than scent, the first greyhound race was held in Emeryville, California, in 1919. In U.S. races, eight dogs competed per run, with up to 11 quarter-mile races per program. Similar to horse racing, dog racing in the United States included wagering and was governed by state commissions. The 1990s saw animal rights groups start wide spread lobbying efforts to secure homes for retired greyhounds.

Car Racing. In the 1900s, many cities and states began banning car racing on public roads, which led to the advent of closed circuit courses built specifically for the purpose of auto racing. The automobile racing sector of the industry included several different types of events. Stock cars—American production cars with some modifications to their bodies and engines—generally raced on oval tracks with banked corners. Stock car racing was governed by the National Association of Stock Car Auto Racing, or NASCAR. Formula One or Grand Prix cars—open-wheeled, race-prepared cars—competed at a number of tracks and street courses in the United States and around the world. Formula One racing was governed by an international authority. The American version, often called Indy cars, raced on both oval and road courses around the country. Indy car racing was governed by the United States Auto Club (USAC) at the Indianapolis 500 and by Championship Auto Racing Teams (CART) at all other venues. Dragsters—which included a wide variety of cars with significant modifications to their tires and engines—generally raced for a quarter mile in a straight line. Drag racing was governed by the National Hot Rod Association (NHRA). Various other professional and amateur auto racing series existed, including sports cars, dirt-track racers, and go-carts.

The Daytona International Speedway, known as the "World Center of Racing," became one of the best known racetracks in the United States and featured stock car, sports car, and motorcycle events. The track's most popular race, the Daytona 500, began in 1959 and remained the premier event and opening race of the NASCAR Winston Cup Series. The Daytona 500 was started in February of 1959 when prize monies totaled $67,000. By 1999, that figure had jumped to over $3.6 million.

The Indianapolis 500 became the main event of the 12-race USAC drivers' championship. For many years following its inaugural running in 1911, the race took place on a surface of paving brick, which gave rise to the speedway's nickname, "the Brickyard." The modern track, however, featured an all-asphalt surface except for a 36-inch strip of the original brick at the starting line. The 500 was the only annual race at the speedway until 1994, when the first Brickyard 400 race for NASCAR Winston Cup stock cars was held. In 1999, the combined winnings for the Indianapolis 500 was more than $9 million.

Motorcycle Racing. The motorcycle racing sector of the industry included two main types of events, road-bike races and dirt-bike races. In road-bike races, professionals and amateurs rode low, sleek racing motorcycles on asphalt tracks. In dirt bike racing, participants rode all-terrain motorcycles with knobby tires and special shock absorbers on dirt tracks. Street and off road racing has become more and more popular, with regular appearances on the popular sporting television channels such as ESPN and ESPN2.

BACKGROUND AND DEVELOPMENT

Horse racing was one of the oldest sports known to mankind. Some of the earliest races, both chariot and bareback, were held at the Olympic Games in Greece from 700 B.C. to 40 B.C.. England's King Charles II, who ruled from 1660 to 1685, inaugurated the first races that offered prizes to winners, which were called the ''King's Plates.'' The original King's Plates were standardized four-mile heat races for six-year-old horses carrying 168 pounds. A horse had to win two heats to be declared the winner. Although heat racing continued in the United States well into the 1860s, dash racing took over in Europe. A dash was any race decided by one heat, regardless of distance.

Thoroughbred breeding began in the 1700s, and all of the 500,000 Thoroughbreds born since that time were said to have descended from the same small group of Arabian and English horses. In fact, Cunningham proved that modern Thoroughbreds drew half of their genes from only ten horses. A famous horse known as the Godolphin Arabian, born about 1725, contributed 14.6 percent of the genes.

In North America, horse racing began in 1665 at Hampton Plains, Long Island. Richard Nicolls, governor of the colony of New York, offered a silver cup as the prize—the first known North American racing trophy. During the modern era, horse racing evolved from an activity to amuse the leisure class into an enormous business providing public entertainment. The three best known American races were the Belmont Stakes, inaugurated in 1867, the Preakness Stakes, first run in 1873, and the Kentucky Derby, which began in 1875; these races together were dubbed the Triple Crown.

Americans began racing automobiles virtually as soon as they were invented in the late 1800s. The first racetracks generally formed either where people gathered to race their cars—like on the flat sand beaches at Daytona—or where manufacturers tested their new products—like the facility in Indianapolis. Speeds increased dramatically over the years, as did the stakes. Prize money for the Indianapolis 500 topped $9 million in 1999, and the race was won by driver Kenny Brack.

CURRENT CONDITIONS

While the gambling industry in general soared 67 percent from 1982 to 1988 to reach $253 billion, the annual amount betted on horse racing climbed barely 17 percent during the same period to $13.7 billion a year, according to *Business Week.* Horse racing faced intense competition from other forms of legalized wagering, including riverboat gambling, casinos, and state lotteries—which alone drained about 11 percent of potential bettors from horse races. Many analysts claimed that racetracks became complacent in their marketing efforts and were unprepared for this new competition. Because illegal horse racing bets are still taken throughout the country, the exact amount of money wagered on such events is hard to pin point.

Even off-track betting (OTB) shops presented a threat to the racetracks. Although the tracks received a percentage of OTB commissions, customers watched simulcasts of live races at off-track sites rather than coming to the racetrack. So while total wagering on thoroughbred racing nationwide increased, paid admissions fell. According to *Business Week,* ''From 1986 to 1990, nationwide betting from off-track sites soared 86 percent, to $4.1 billion, while on-track wagering fell 36 percent to $6.1 billion.'' The drain caused by simulcast races magnified the need for track management to attract new spectators to their venues. By the early 1990s, many tracks began to market themselves more diligently, adding customer relations departments and special services.

However, several industry analysts felt that the horse racing industry suffered from a more fundamental problem: Many Americans simply did not understand the sport. For example, Ken Alhadeff, executive vice-president of Longacres Race Course near Seattle, told *Business Week,* ''Kids grow up with football, but horse racing remains a mystery to most of us. The savior of racing will be our ability to attract new fans by ripping down the intimidation factor.'' Longacres' attempts to retain spectators included handing out ''First Timer's Kits,'' which explained how to read the Daily Racing Form, and offering a ''New Comer's Corner,'' which taught betting techniques.

Several track operators also began hedging their bets by adding other gambling venues, like video poker machines. Hollywood Park in Los Angeles, for example, opened a card club, and Louisiana Downs planned to run a riverboat casino. Moreover, some racetracks began adding non-racing entertainment, such as restaurants, video arcades, music theaters, and parks.

In 1998, there were finally signs that horse racing was making a comeback. The average purchase price for horses of all ages increased, with an impressive 35 percent increase in the sale price of yearling horses, the most popular age. Television ratings were up as well, thanks in no small part to the near Triple Crown performance of the horse Real Quiet. A strong 1999 season by the horse Charismatic continued this trend. Though the horse racing industry is still not where it once was, it is now making positive strides.

INDUSTRY LEADERS

The leading companies in the racing industry included: New York Racing Association, Inc. of Jamaica, New York; Hollywood Park Inc. of Inglewood, California; Anita Operating Company of Arcadia, California; International Speedway Corp. of Daytona Beach, Florida; Los Angeles Turf Club, Inc. of Arcadia, California; and Churchill Downs Inc. of Louisville, Kentucky.

A non-profit organization, the New York Racing Association (NYRA) owned and operated the three largest racetracks in New York—Aqueduct, Belmont Park, and Saratoga. Established in 1955, the NYRA was a non-dividend-paying corporation governed by a board of trustees.

Races at NYRA's tracks brought in the highest on-track attendance and daily wagers throughout the United States. NYRA tracks averaged 9,800 fans per race day, with nearly 130,000 more watching at OTB shops or at inter-track simulcast facilities. Approximately 2.5 million people attended the races at NYRA tracks in 1998. The Saratoga track led the country in on-track attendance. The average amount bet on NYRA races, including OTB wagering, of more than $9 million per day, far exceeds any other racing organization in the United States.

Hollywood Park Inc. was the ninth-largest organization in the racing industry. Accommodating more than 50,000 spectators at facilities that opened in 1938, Hollywood Park was the site of the Breeder's Cup and the Hollywood Gold Cup. After losing $30 million in four years, the shareholders of Hollywood Park elected a new CEO, R. D. Hubbard, in early 1991. As a result, Hollywood Park showed a profit that year and more than tripled its earnings in 1992.

Most recently the company operated eight riverboat and land-based casinos in the states of Louisiana, Mississippi, and Nevada, as well as the country of Argentina. In 1998, Hollywood Park, Inc. reported $408 million in sales. In 1999, the company sold its namesake, Hollywood Park, to Churchill Downs, Inc.

Workforce

The labor pool in the horse racing sector of the industry included jockeys, grooms, and exercise riders, along with other skilled and unskilled workers. Approximately 2,800 jockeys were licensed throughout the country, nearly 20 percent of whom were women. Approximately 53,900 horse owners and 4,440 trainers were registered with the national office of the Horsemen's Benevolent and Protective Association (HBPA). The group also posted nearly 5,400 combined owners and trainers.

The number of other workers at U.S. racetracks was difficult to determine because the work was seasonal. Moreover, illegal aliens were often used for labor at the tracks. In fact, in 1985, more than 400 illegal aliens were seized at Southern California tracks. When track management complained that they could not find U.S. citizens willing to perform such work, the U.S. Immigration and Naturalization Service granted H-2 visas that permitted temporary work status for skilled employment. Certification for unskilled workers was declined.

America and the World

As of 1997, Japan had 40 racetracks, 30 public courses and 10 owned by the Japan Racing Association (JRA). The JRA is the sports governing body in Japan, and is a non-profit organization that operates on a 15 percent share of betting turnover. This organization severely restricts Japan's horse racing industry to outsiders.

As Karen Lowry Miller explained in *Business Week,* ''Only 114 of Japan's 6,000 registered thoroughbreds are foreign-born. Just two annual races, the Japan Cup and the Fuji Stakes, allow foreign horses that have raced before. And just 35 percent of the 6,000 races held by the JRA allow foreign-born horses at all, even if they're trained in Japan.'' Representatives of both the United States and Great Britain urged Japan to reduce its trade restrictions, especially to lower its barriers against imported racehorses. Since the U.S. industry had declined, foreign markets like Japan became increasingly important. American horse owners were especially interested in the Japanese market because of its bettors. The Japanese eventually conceded to a plan to allow foreign-born horses to run in 65 percent of JRA-sanctioned races by 1996 and to open 15 more events to foreign owners.

Horse racing also became wildly successful in Hong Kong, with an average racing day bringing 50,000 spectators to the tracks. These spectators, along with 1.5 million off-track bettors, wagered $170 million per racing day. And due to its ever-increasing purse size, Hong Kong's races began attracting more international entries.

Research and Technology

The United States began moving toward high-tech horse racing in the 1990s. As with simulcasting, these technological advances were expected to bring additional bettors to the racing world, but not necessarily to the tracks. One program was interactive betting, a system used at home via a ''black box'' cable program. Wagering via telephone also appeared to be destined for the future of racing.

The NYRA set up computerized personal betting accounts for its patrons. Using a special debit card, a user could place a bet at terminals located throughout the track. Money was added or subtracted from the account as the bettor won or lost. The bettor could wager over the phone and even electronically transfer funds from a MasterCard or Visa credit line to their account. Following a test run at Belmont, the system moved into full operation at all three NYRA racecourses in late 1991.

In the automobile racing sector of the industry, research centered around increasing speed and driver safety. Often, technological advances originating in race cars became standard equipment for passenger cars within a few years. Some early examples included four-wheel brakes, turbo charged engines, and aerodynamic designs.

FURTHER READING

"Champ Brack Earns $1.4 million of Record '500' Purse," 17 December 1999. Available from http://www.indy500.com/press/1999/purse-053199.html.

Cooke, Bill. "Equestrian History and Culture," 1 December 1999. Available from http://www.imh.org/imh/jp/jp3.html.

Daytona International Speedway Information. Daytona, Florida: Daytona International Speedway, March 1994.

Infoseek. "Company Capsule: Hollywood Park, Inc.," 22 November 1999. Available from http://infoseek.go.com/Content?arn=15018&qt=HOLLYWOOD+PARK,+INC&col=HV&svx=lhscaps.

Nack, William. "On the Money," *Sports Illustrated,* 28 September 1998, Accessed 17 December 1999. Available from http://www.britannica.com/bcom/magazine/article/print/0,5746,49388,00.html.

Wright, John W., ed. *The Universal Almanac 1997.* Andrews and McNeel, 1997.

SIC 7991

PHYSICAL FITNESS FACILITIES

Establishments in this industry are primarily engaged in operating reducing and other health clubs, spas, and similar facilities featuring exercise and other active physical fitness conditioning, whether or not on a membership basis. Also included in this industry are establishments providing aerobic dance and exercise classes. Sports and recreation clubs are classified in **SIC 7997: Membership Sports and Recreation Clubs** if operated on a membership basis, and in **SIC 7992: Public Golf Courses** or **SIC 7999: Amusement and Recreation Services, Not Elsewhere Classified** if open to the general public. Health resorts and spas providing lodging are classified in **SIC 7011: Hotels and Motels** and **SIC 7041: Organizational Hotels and Lodging Houses, on Membership Basis.** Establishments that promote physical fitness through diet control are classified in **SIC 7299: Miscellaneous Personal Services, Not Elsewhere Classified.**

NAICS CODE(S)

713940 (Fitness and Recreational Sports Centers)

INDUSTRY SNAPSHOT

In 1998 fitness and health centers in the United States generated combined revenues of more than $5 billion. The vast majority of these operations were sole proprietorships and single-unit endeavors. Approximately 70 percent of the industry's centers concentrated on fitness alone, while the remainder were multipurpose facilities.

In the 1990s health clubs emphasized all three aspects of physical fitness: cardiovascular conditioning, strength, and flexibility. Some even added nonprofessional mental health services like stress reduction and counseling programs. Full-service health clubs featured aerobic conditioning equipment, resistance equipment, dance and exercise classes, swimming pools and spa areas, and sometimes even tanning and massage.

Membership and enrollment (or initiation) fees from the industry's 22.5 million members constituted the vast majority of club revenues in the late 1990s. Although these fees have long been the mainstay of industry income, other revenue sources like children's programs, personal training, exercise classes, physical therapy, and aquatic programs started contributing a growing proportion of health club revenues in the 1990s.

ORGANIZATION AND STRUCTURE

The fitness center industry is self-regulated through several professional organizations that were formed in the mid-1970s. The two most influential of these are the Association of Physical Fitness Centers (APFC) and the International Racquet Sports Association (IRSA). The APFC was founded in 1975 to provide the burgeoning industry with information, education, and public relations advice. This organization is concerned with the public's perception of the fitness industry, and it has led the way in self-regulation. The APFC's *Code of Ethical Practices* was one of the first and, until the early 1990s, only attempt to establish and enforce industry guidelines. Member facilities had to agree to honor the *Code,* but the APFC had no legal authority over its members. IRSA, which has since changed its name to the International Health, Racquet & Sportsclub (IHRSA), was formed when the National Tennis Association and the National Court Club Association consolidated in 1981. As its name indicates, the majority of IHRSA's membership (about two-thirds) consists of multipurpose clubs that combine fitness and racquet facilities. IHRSA's most valuable contributions to the fitness industry include its statistical surveys and its professional journal, *Fitness Management.* Fitness centers are geographically concentrated in high population areas. Consequently, California leads the nation, followed by New York, Texas, and Florida. The vast majority of these businesses were privately-held, with notable exceptions being industry leaders Bally Total Fitness Corp., Sports Club Company Inc., and Health Fitness Physical Therapy Inc.

BACKGROUND AND DEVELOPMENT

Health Spas. Known early in their history as health spas, fitness centers sprung up in the early 1960s, by which time increasing automation had negated the need for most people to perform daily physical labor. At the time, some experts predicted that physical health in the United States in general would deteriorate, but some Americans made a concerted effort to encourage physical fitness. This "fringe movement" of enthusiasts and entrepreneurs started a trend that led to a fitness boom.

Spas were the first establishments of the fitness center industry. They emphasized relaxation with a European flavor, featuring whirlpools, steam rooms, and massage services. The following were the most prominent of these spas: Europa, European, Scandinavian, Grecian, and Olympic. These early facilities also had some fitness equipment, including manual joggers, stationary bicycles, standard resistance machines for men, and passive resistance equipment for women. Most spas focused on a single sex and had only one locker room. Some clubs tried to maximize their facilities by alternating women and men on particular days of the week. In 1972, however, the New York Health and Racquet Club ushered in co-ed fitness when it built its first facility that had both a men's and women's locker room. The vast majority of fitness clubs constructed since that time also have locker rooms for both men and women.

Self-regulation. An appreciation of professionalism was also spawned in the early 1970s. In the decade prior to that time, health spas were largely isolated from one another and were characterized by "inexperienced, inefficient and insincere" management, according to *The Complete Health Club Handbook.* Rising concerns about providing consistent quality led to the creation of affiliate organizations like the APFC and, later, the IHRSA.

But these early attempts at professionalization were not sufficient to stem the rising tide of consumer complaints that precipitated public Federal Trade Commission (FTC) hearings in the late 1970s. The government's investigation identified several industry-wide problems, including: false, deceptive, and misleading advertising and sales presentations; high-pressure sales tactics; bait advertising; deceptive pricing; misrepresentation of membership benefits and staff qualifications; and unfair cancellation and refund policies. Despite the large number of complaints, Dr. Jimmy Johnson, then executive director of the APFC, convinced the FTC that the industry was "well on its way to being self-policing." Johnson's protestations and his association's laudable efforts at self-regulation prevented the FTC from bringing the industry under government regulation. Although the problems cited in the 1970s continued to crop up over the next two decades, the fitness center industry managed to avoid government control throughout the 1980s and early 1990s by steadily increasing self-regulation.

Nevertheless, abuses continued. In 1994 Bally's Health & Tennis (later Bally Total Fitness Corp.) was fined $120,000 and ordered by the FTC to refund thousands in membership fees in connection with charges of improper billing and collections practices.

Certification of individual employees began in the mid-1980s, but stringent evaluation and certification of facilities was not undertaken until 1989, when the American College of Sports Medicine (ACSM) began a feasibility study of the proposition. After determining that facility certification was necessary "to elevate the credibility of the health and fitness industry to the purchasing public, as well as to ensure the safety of the public when exercising at a facility," the ACSM laid out three phases for the project. They first developed standards and guidelines for facilities, then published a 16-page booklet targeted to the public titled, *The ACSM Guide to Selecting a Health and Fitness Facility.* Released in 1992, the publication helped educate potential fitness facility members and determine which facilities offered safe, high-quality services. The ACSM started its third phase, actual certification, in mid-1993.

The Fitness Boom. An enormous number of adult exercisers generated a sport and fitness boom in the 1970s and 1980s, which caused rapid growth in the fitness center industry. In 1961 less than one-quarter of Americans, when asked, said that they did something aside from work to promote their own physical fitness. But throughout the 1970s and 1980s, more than 45 percent responded affirmatively to that question.

It was during this period that many of the best-known fitness center chains (including Bally's, Holiday Universal, Inc.; President's Health & Racquet Clubs, Inc.; Vic Tanny International, Inc.; and Scandinavian Health Spa) experienced dramatic growth. The aerobics and running craze of the late 1970s and early 1980s launched a general fitness boom, and by the early 1990s more than two-thirds of Americans claimed to participate in some form of exercise. Health clubs were even celebrated as smart singles spots in the 1980s, but this social orientation faded in the 1990s.

Legal Aspects. The fitness center industry has not been able to escape the tidal wave of litigation that has overwhelmed the United States. Fitness center managers have needed to employ waivers and releases, risk management services, and liability insurance to protect themselves from financial disaster at the hands of an unhappy member and his or her lawyer. The most exacting claims seemed to occur in three primary categories: slip-and-fall or wet area accidents, injury to participants engaged in athletic activity, and claims involving health center employees.

David L. Herbert asserted in *Fitness Management* magazine that "one who merely rents space for a particular activity owes no duty to those utilizing the space to supervise its use." But as fitness centers in the 1990s offered more services like health and fitness appraisals, weight training, smoking cessation programs, and stress management, they incurred more liability. Herbert emphasized that "once a facility does more than merely rent space, it is likely that it will be required to exercise due care to protect users from unreasonable risk of harm or to insure compliance with safety-related game rules." Fitness centers and their employees who did not properly screen or test participants before exercise, improperly prescribed activities, and improperly or negligently supervised activities opened themselves to lawsuits, according to Herbert.

The Americans with Disabilities Act (Public Law 101-336), which went into effect in January 1992, added another legal challenge to fitness center management. The law, which prohibited discrimination by places of public accommodation against those with disabilities, compelled architectural and program changes, such as the addition of ramps and changing screening systems, for example. Again, Herbert warned that, "Health and fitness facilities that presently utilize screening systems to admit or exclude individuals to particular exercise or recreation programs may have to modify their policies to accommodate the provisions of the law." On the other hand, however, prospective members whose medical histories forbade particular activities would not be able to gain access to those programs, regardless of the law's stipulations.

Top Challenges. In 1993 IHRSA members claimed that the following issues were the five most pressing external challenges to the industry: local economy, price sensitivity of the market, competition from clubs, taxes, and unfair competition from non-profit establishments like YMCAs. The same survey respondents specified member retention, personnel management, advertising and marketing, cost control, and sales management as their top five internal priorities. Although home exercise was farther down the list of external threats, some industry analysts have noted that "the boom in home fitness is cutting into the health club business." The National Sporting Goods Association reported that sales of home fitness equipment in the United States more than tripled over the course of the 1980s, from $54.17 million in 1980 to $1.79 billion in 1990. Home exercisers cited convenience and privacy as advantages, but most consumers conceded that they could not recreate the variety of activities possible in a multipurpose fitness center.

CURRENT CONDITIONS

America's recessionary economy of the late 1980s and early 1990s challenged fitness center managers. Conventional wisdom predicted that consumers who had less discretionary income would eliminate health club memberships from their personal budgets. But performance of the fitness industry in past economic downturns showed that people often focused more on their health during stressful economic periods. Membership in virtually every age group rose continuously throughout the 1990s. Memberships for those over the age of 55 and those under the age of 18 were particularly active areas of growth during this time. Women were also a major area of growth for the industry. By 1997 women made up 57 percent of health club patrons, almost triple the amount of 1981.

During the economic downturn, fitness centers that were already weak or questionable were "shaken out." One analyst said, "Recessions are grand opportunities for the strong," because the healthy businesses would be able to capture their failing competitors' members. Industry statistics supported that commentator's view: the total number of commercial clubs decreased for the first time in the history of the industry, from about 13,500 in 1990 to 12,000 in 1991 and remained at that level through 1995. By 1997, though, the number had climbed again, numbering more than 13,000.

The fitness center industry continued to grow throughout the decade. The number of adult users of clubs increased from 18 million in 1995 to 22.5 million by 1998. Despite dire predictions, there was no "credit crunch," and, in fact, low interest rates helped boost the average pretax net income of fitness centers by 41.2 percent. This increase was due in large part to debt restructuring. Great potential for increased membership remained—only 8.5 percent of the population were members of health clubs in 1998.

INDUSTRY LEADERS

With more than 4 million members and 360 clubs in 27 U.S. states and Canada, Chicago-based Bally Total Fitness Holding Corp. (BFIT) was by far the nation's largest fitness chain. In fact, BFIT was more than three times larger than its next nine biggest competitors combined. BFIT was the fitness-center division of parent company Bally Manufacturing Corporation. In 1998, Bally Total Fitness had revenues of $742.5 million. The fitness centers were spun off from their parent company in 1996, and had a public stock offering in 1997. Two other fitness center chains followed Bally into the public realm in the 1990s. Los Angeles-based Sports Club Company Inc. ($81.9 million in 1998 sales) and Minnesota's Health Fitness Corporation ($25.6 million). Both of these companies have been successful, but on a much smaller scale than Bally.

Other leading companies in the industry included: Women's Workout World Inc.; Northwest Racquet Swim and Health Clubs Inc.; Australian Body Works; and Beverly Hills Weight Loss and Wellness.

WORKFORCE

Composition. The fitness center industry employs more than 600,000 full- and part-time workers, and part-time employees outnumbered full-timers by a ratio of five-to-one in the late 1990s. The work force was predominantly composed of fitness and dance instructors, who are paid hourly, by the session, or per student. More than 80 percent of aerobics instructors have some college education, and most clubs require certification of instructors. Front desk employees made up the second largest segment of industry workers. These unskilled, entry-level workers were paid an hourly wage. Owners constituted the third-largest group of fitness center workers. Fitness centers also employed maintenance engineers, tennis instructors, racquetball/squash instructors, sales and marketing personnel, and administrators. An increasing number of clubs hired independent contractors as sports trainers, physicians, and physical therapists. Approximately 85 percent of the industry's clubs provided some level of employee health benefits for full- and/or part-time workers. An across-the-industry hiring and pay freeze in the 1990s helped hold down operating expenses.

Certification. Throughout most of the history of the fitness center industry, employees were not required to have any formal training. The only exceptions were lifeguards, who were required by law to be certified. Several public and private universities had health, physical education, and recreation programs, but most employees of physical fitness centers were not required to have such training. That changed in the early 1980s, when knowledgeable consumers began to demand more than just enthusiasm from fitness instructors.

Certification tests and programs proliferated in the 1980s from such professional organizations as: the American College of Sports Medicine (ACSM), the American Council on Exercise (ACE), the Association for Fitness in Business (AFB), the National Strength and Conditioning Association (NSCA), and IDEA-The Association For Fitness Professionals (formerly the International Dance-Exercise Association). IDEA's certification examination for aerobic dance instructors, first administered in 1986, is a good example of such tests. It consisted of 175 multiple choice questions on: exercise physiology, anatomy, kinesiology, programming skills, leadership techniques, nutrition, weight loss and control, emergency training, health screening, and legal issues. Those seeking certification were required to be at least 18 years old and have current CPR certification. Notwithstanding the prevalence of certification, there were no national or state accrediting standards in the late 1990s.

AMERICA AND THE WORLD

The American fitness center industry is generally regarded as being a decade ahead of its European counterpart. Reasons cited for the disparity focus on costs and professionalization. For example, high energy costs make standard swimming pools very expensive for European businesses to operate. Consequently, they have tried to compensate with expanded whirlpool and sauna areas. Moreover, high real estate costs have forced most fitness center owners to lease their facilities. As far as professionalism is concerned, the European industry appeared to be in a ''pre-association'' state in the 1990s: club owners didn't share information and, consequently, many of their management practices, promotional ideas, and marketing tactics were accomplished by trial and error. The ''pay-as-you-play system'' that characterized America's fitness industry in its early years was the norm in European clubs of the 1990s.

RESEARCH AND TECHNOLOGY

Research and technology have played an important, but sometimes dubious, role in the fitness center industry. Fleeting trends have sometimes brought sweeping transformations in equipment and training methods at fitness centers. In the late 1980s and early 1990s, everything from stationary bicycles to resistance equipment became computerized. Much of the technologically advanced equipment simulated other sports, like downhill and cross country skiing, rowing, and even rock climbing. And while some practitioners, like Augie Nieto (president of Life Fitness, Inc.), predicted increasing computerization, other observers, like Douglas Garfield (of Bodyguard, Inc.), foresaw ''less high-tech and more high-touch'' activities in health clubs of the future.

Demographics Influence Trends. As a mass of ''baby boomers'' entered middle age, the health and fitness center industry rushed to meet their needs. The industry had to make a critical transition from an almost exclusive focus on the young adult market, toward the ''40-somethings'' and their families. Some club owners asserted that ''family-oriented health programs are the fastest-growing segment of the health club industry.'' Programming gained popularity as a source of member recruitment and retention and increased revenue. Convenience-oriented services included food service, salons, child care, laundry facilities, car washes, ATMs, and sporting goods shops. Bally even began offering a line of vitamins and nutritional supplements.

Enrollment fees, long considered a powerful inducement to member retention, were proven to have no power to ensure member longevity. More and more clubs have dropped enrollment fees, partly in response to consumer demands. This trend is predicted to continue in coming years. Although some industry observers decried the return to old-fashioned ''pay-as-you-play,'' fitness services, other entrepreneurs viewed them as ''a valuable option for wooing customers into joining.''

Other trends for the future include the growth of more all-female health clubs, the development of ''ultraluxe fitness centers,'' and a continuing focus on attracting more baby boomers. As of 1997, only 5 percent of health clubs were single-sex, and the industry felt it could capitalize on women who didn't want to ''mingle'' while they were working out. ''Ultraluxe'' clubs feature services as varied as plush surroundings, gourmet meals, business centers, and dry cleaning. They have sprung up in major cities such as Chicago and New York and cater to an extremely wealthy clientele. As baby boomers approach retirement, they will have more free time, and the industry hopes to capitalize on this extra time by drawing them in as new customers.

FURTHER READING

Atlas, Riva. ''Shape Up.'' *Forbes,* 20 May 1996.

''Bally's Fitness Unit Agrees to Refunds in FTC Settlement.'' *Wall Street Journal,* 15 April 1994.

Dietrich, John, and Susan Waggoner. *The Complete Health Club Handbook.* New York: Simon & Schuster, 1983.

''For Members Only.'' *WWD,* 12 September 1996.

Green, Kathleen. ''Leading the Fit Life.'' *Occupational Outlook Quarterly,* Summer 1995.

Gubernick, Lisa. ''Sagging.'' *Forbes,* 19 June 1995.

Hoover's Online. *Hoover's Company Profiles,* 1999.

Jackson, Lisa. ''Exercise: All-Female Health Clubs a Big Hit.'' *The Detroit News,* 5 November 1997.

Oleck, Joan. ''Health Clubs: Sweating in Elegant Places.'' *BusinessWeek,* 28 May 1998.

''Pre-boom a Boom to Gyms.'' *American Demographics,* January 1999.

Stoneman, Bill. ''Weighty Trends for Fitness Marketers.'' *American Demographics,* April 1999.

SIC 7992

PUBLIC GOLF COURSES

This industry includes establishments primarily engaged in the operation of golf courses open to the general public on a contract or fee basis. Membership golf and country clubs are classified in **SIC 7997: Membership Sports and Recreation Clubs.** Miniature golf courses and golf driving ranges are classified in **SIC 7999: Amusement and Recreation Services, Not Elsewhere Classified.**

NAICS CODE(S)

713910 (Golf Courses and Country Clubs)

By definition, public golf courses are open to the public on a contract or fee basis. According to The National Golf Foundation, there were 16,365 golf courses in the United States as of December 31, 1998. Of those, only 4,708 were private facilities. The remaining 11,657 courses were privately owned facilities open to the public or city-owned municipal courses. In 1999, 387 more courses in the United States were finished with construction. Florida, California, Michigan, New York, and Texas boast the greatest number of total courses in America; in all of those states, the number of daily fee and municipal courses available far outnumber those of private club courses.

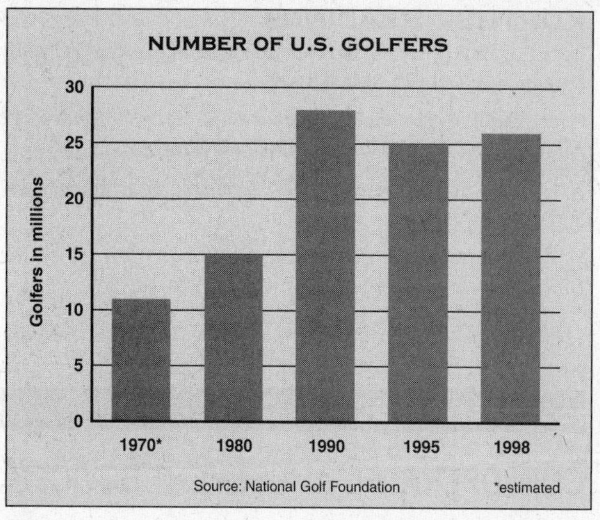

Until recently, the game of golf had enjoyed a steady growth in popularity that spanned the last few decades. In 1970 most estimations placed the number of golfers in the United States at approximately 11 million. By 1980, that number had increased to more than 15 million. According to the National Golf Foundation, however, the number of golfers in the United States peaked at 27.8 million in 1990 and settled at 25 million in 1995. By the close of 1997, the number climbed to 26.5 million, with Americans playing a total of 547 million rounds of golf during that year.

Although the number of golfers had gone flat, the number of golf courses in the United States continued to grow. In the past, the game of golf was practiced predominantly at country clubs and other membership and recreation clubs. Over time, however, that has changed: the number of private courses increased by only ten in 1998, while 86 percent of the courses built that year were open to the public. All of this growth had some adverse effects on the industry as a whole: what some believe may have been overbuilding has forced many real estate developers and municipalities nationwide to grapple with unexpectedly high debt burdens.

Still, the often expensive fees and dues associated with membership clubs has led many of the sport's practitioners away from traditional country clubs to public golf facilities. Moreover, with the growing number of courses offered and continued enthusiasm to build, many golfers are finding public courses rivaling private clubs in terms of aesthetics and level of skill.

FURTHER READING

Gargaro, Paul. ''Michigan Is at the Forefront of Golf.'' *Crain's Detroit Business,* 25 March 1996.

Geer, Carolyn T. ''Gold Mine or Sand Trap?'' *Forbes,* 12 August 1996. Available from http://www.forbes.com.

National Golf Foundation, 1999. Available from http://www.ngf.org.

U.S. Department of Commerce. *Statistical Abstract of the United States.* Washington, DC: GPO, 1996.

SIC 7993

COIN-OPERATED AMUSEMENT DEVICES

This industry includes establishments primarily engaged in operating coin-operated amusement devices, either in their own or in other places of business. Such amusement devices include jukeboxes, pinball machines, mechanical games, electronic games, pool tables, shuffle alleys, electronic darts, video games, kiddie rides, prize dispensing machines, and slot machines. Amusement (including video game) arcades and parlors are also included in this industry.

NAICS CODE(S)

713120 (Amusement Arcades)
713290 (Other Gambling Industries)
713990 (All Other Amusement and Recreation Industries)

Coin-operated amusement devices can be found in a variety of locations. Primary locales include taverns and bars, restaurants, retail stores, and shopping malls, which often include one or more video arcade establishments. Other locales in which coin-operated amusement devices can be found include bus terminals, hotels, grocery stores, and truck stops. In 1997 there were 2,737 amusement arcades across the country, with another 2,668 operators of coin-operated, non-gambling, amusement devices.

The 1990s have seen a dramatic proliferation of indoor amusement facilities, known as ''family fun centers,'' which vary greatly in size and in the activities they offer. The indoor facilities often include bumper car rides, bumper boats, basketball machines, and a variety of video arcade equipment. Many of the family fun centers start small—often with an outdoor miniature golf course—and when they develop inside, sometimes bumper cars become a new attraction, and almost invariably some type of ''video arcade'' devices are introduced.

The International Association of Family Entertainment Centers (IAFEC) reported 350 members in 1999. Although this group owned establishments at nearly 2,800 locations, 70 percent of their membership owned only one site. These locally owned establishments faced competition from chains. One of the most ambitious chains to emerge in the late 1990s was Gameworks, a joint venture between Dreamworks, Universal Studios, and the video-game giant Sega. When the first Gameworks opened in 1997, the company announced plans to have 100 locations within five years.

The proliferation of legalized gambling has produced dramatic growth for some participants in another segment of the coin-operated amusements industry. Slot machines have become so popular that they provide 75 percent of casino revenues. Besides the more than 700 casinos operating in the United States in 1997, there were another 328 operators of slot machines. Based on an average cost of roughly $5,000 each, slot machines provide a huge return on investment.

Slot machines have not changed much since the 1980s when electronic mechanisms were added inside the machines. In the United States alone, players fed an estimated $16 billion per year into the machines. Slot machines were the fastest growing segment of legalized gambling.

Another popular coin-operated gambling device is the video lottery terminal (VLT). VLTs are slot machines that display video games, such as video poker and bingo, for low-stakes gambling. In states where these machines are operated, they are part of the state lottery system. The VLT terminals are the same as the video poker machines in Las Vegas, Nevada, except for the payment devices. Money is fed into the machine, and winnings and losses are electronically calculated and printed out for the player. State lottery revenues have slacked off, and the video lottery is a means for states to increase revenues. Video lottery terminal machines offer the gambler the opportunity to play video poker, blackjack, keno, or bingo for a nickel to $2.50 a bet.

With the increase in slot machines and the easy access to VLTs, another gambling industry—horse racing—has felt the affects of competition. In response, racetracks have lobbied for permission to operate slots on their premises. States such as Delaware, Iowa, and West Virginia, among others, have passed laws allowing such operations. Many of these laws contain regulations to ensure that the primary focus stays on the races and does not shift to slot machines at these establishments.

The leader in the gambling segment of the industry is International Game Technology (IGT), the world's largest manufacturer and designer of gaming machines and software. IGT currently controls more than 75 percent of the U.S. slot machine market and had 1998 revenues of $824 million. Its products include progressive slot machine systems like Fabulous Fifties, High Rollers, and Megabucks; reel-type slot machines like S-Plus; video gaming products; and video gaming terminals for government-sponsored state run lotteries. IGT has benefited from the legalization of gambling on riverboats and Indian reservations and is betting on an increased consumer interest in gambling for future profits. IGT also has an international presence, with nearly 25 percent of its revenue coming from sales to other countries.

State regulation of coin-operated amusement devices varies from state to state. Some are very strict regarding every aspect of the industry, including use and location of the machines. For instance, in the state of Texas, regulations determine the percentage operators may pay to the owner of the establishment in which their machine in located. Operators must also keep records of income from individual machines. By contrast, some other states regulate less strictly and allow operators wider parameters.

FURTHER READING

Emmons, Natasha. ''Slot Machine Status Main Focus of World Gaming Congress & Expo.'' *Amusement Business,* 29 November 1999.

Guier, Cindy Stoohsbury. ''Family Entertainment Centers.'' *Amusement Business,* 18 March 1998.

———. ''Mom & Pops Holding Their Own.'' *Amusement Business,* 3 May 1999.

''International Game Technology.'' Austin, TX: Hoover's, 1999. Available from http://www.hoovers.com.

Lubove, Seth A. ''One-Armed Bandits Brawl.'' *Forbes,* 11 March 1996.

Turner, Dan. ''Here Comes the Super Arcade; Hollywood Studios Debut Digital Thrill Park.'' *Los Angeles Business Journal,* 10 March 1997.

U.S. Bureau of the Census. *1997 Economic Census: Arts, Entertainment, and Recreation; Geographic Area Series.* Washington, DC: U. S. Bureau of the Census, 1999. Available from http://www.census.gov.

SIC 7996

AMUSEMENT PARKS

This category covers theme parks, kiddie parks, amusement piers, centers, and parks, and other establishments (excluding fairs, circuses, and carnivals) that operate in part or whole such attractions as mechanical rides, amusement devices, refreshment stands, and picnic grounds. Amusement concessionaires operating within these establishments are generally covered in **SIC 7999: Amusement and Recreation Services, Not Elsewhere Classified.**

NAICS CODE(S)

713110 (Amusement and Theme Parks)

According to *The Great American Amusement Parks,* the earliest amusement parks were the European pleasure gardens of the seventeenth and eighteenth centuries. But only with the technological advances of the Industrial Revolution did the mechanical rides of the modern amusement park come into being. In this area of development, American parks led the way.

Jones's Wood in New York City, established in the early nineteenth century, was probably the first major U.S. amusement park. But its humble attractions—including billiards, bowling, and donkey rides—were soon eclipsed by Coney Island. This legendary resort first began to expand dramatically in the 1870s when a railway line to it was constructed. In 1920 the extension of the New York subway system to Coney Island put city residents a nickel away from the resort's attractions. Indeed, before the advent of the automobile, ease of travel played a crucial role—''trolley parks'' acquired their name from the system of transport that brought customers to them.

Mechanized rides of the kind taken for granted in modern amusement parks reached Coney Island in 1884, with the advent of LaMarcus Adna Thompson's Switchback Railway, the first roller coaster. From their inception, roller coasters proved the most popular attractions, as well as the largest and most expensive to build and maintain.

The first ferris wheel—named for George Ferris not because he invented the concept, but because his engineering talents produced the first such ride made of steel rather than wood and built on a huge scale—made its appearance at the 1893 Chicago World's Fair Columbian Exposition. Coney Island, and the many other amusement parks that sprang into being in response to its success, faced hazards from fire and water. Rainy weather discouraged attendance because most of the attractions were outdoors. Initial reliance for construction on such cheap but highly flammable materials as lath and staff—a combination of plaster of Paris and hemp fiber—meant that fires were frequent and caused great damage.

Other problems such as noise, dirt, and criminality often found in the early amusement parks became more apparent as larger numbers of middle- and upper-class Americans owning cars gained the freedom to seek their entertainment elsewhere. The formation of the International Association of Amusement Parks and Attractions in 1920 was motivated in part by the industry's concern over its reputation. Individual parks, such as Cincinnati's Coney Island and Playland, in Rye, New York, also sought to create a more family-oriented image by making sure that structural damage, litter, and graffiti were swiftly removed from sight.

Disney was the most significant creator of wholesome amusement in its innovative theme parks. The first of these, Disneyland, opened its doors in 1955. An instant success, the park initially proved hard to imitate. But Six Flags Over Texas, opened in 1961, found another winning formula, leading to the construction of additional Six Flags complexes. Other Disney competitors also began to find new angles on the theme park concept.

CURRENT CONDITIONS

American Demographics estimated that more than 50 million people over the age of 18 visited one of North America's theme parks in 1998. This obviously does not account for the large number of children who visit these parks as well. The magazine further projected a 4.5 percent increase in this attendance by 2005 and a 10.4 percent increase by 2008. Motion picture tie-ins and high-tech rides were the big draws, with simulator rides growing in popularity. Start-up costs for a new theme park were estimated at $500 million on the low end, with a single simulator ride costing upwards of $40 million. According to *Amusement Business,* Disney properties continued to lead the present-day amusement park industry. Disney World's Magic Kingdom, Epcot Center, and Disney-MGM Studios Theme Park, both located in Lake Buena Vista, Florida, brought in more than 35.7 million customers in 1998. Disney's newest park in the Florida region, Animal Kingdom, attracted 6 million further visitors in 1998. Tokyo Disneyland and Disneyland Paris have also become popular tourist attractions, resulting in Disney's plan for further international expansion.

Six Flags parks, which are partly owned by Time Warner, uses Warner movie tie-ins to boost their attendance. The fact that there are currently 25 Six Flags theme parks across the United States makes location another important strategy for the company. Paramount Entertainment also uses the movie strategy in operating its six theme parks, including Paramount' Great America in Santa Clara, California, and Paramount's Kings Island in Cincinnati, Ohio. More than 13 million people visited one of these parks in 1998. The amusement parks of MCA/Universal Studios, located in Orlando, Florida, and Hollywood, California, combined to serve 8.9 million in 1998. Anheuser-Busch operates parks such as Busch Gardens and Sea World. These parks attracted 20 million guests in 1998 and generated $116 million for the company.

Just as the tourist appeal of California and Florida aided Disney in the development of its domestic amusement parks, so location offered a crucial advantage to competitors in Las Vegas, where Circus Circus Enterprises, MGM Grand, and Mirage Resorts were developing a line of casinos angled toward the family, with kiddie parks to keep children happy while parents gambled. Other operators looked to complexes combining amusement parks with retail outlets, such as the Mall of America in Bloomington, Minnesota—the largest mall in America. The mall's anchor attraction is Knott's Camp Snoopy Indoor Theme Park.

Europe and Asia were the new growth areas for amusement and theme parks. With old parks being renewed and new parks opening up, Europe has seen a 10 percent increase in attendance, as reported in *Newsweek.* In Asia, according to *The Economist,* more free time and increased income was spurring a leisure revolution. Shopping malls have become theme parks, with more than 40 opened in China alone during the past decade. Unlike their American counterparts, these often tend toward a cultural, historical, or environmental theme. Bangkok, Singapore, and Kuala Lumpur all would like to become hubs of tourism, and theme parks have figured into that future.

Future industry challenges will be devising ways of bringing out the aging populations. Viacom Inc. has started opening adult playgrounds featuring virtual reality games, while Disney has started marketing ads to retired couples.

FURTHER READING

''Asians at Play.'' *The Economist,* 21 December 1996.

Blank, Christine, and Shannon Dortch. ''Parking it for Fun.'' *American Demographics,* April 1998.

''EuroDisney Posts 77 Percent Surge in Yearly Earnings.'' *New York Times,* 20 November 1996.

Frankel, Mike. ''Welcome to Euro-World!'' *Newsweek,* 12 June 1995.

Kyriazi, Gary. *The Great American Amusement Parks.* Secaucus, NJ: Citadel Press, 1976.

McGraw, Dan. ''America's Theme Parks Ride High.'' *U.S. News & World Report,* 26 June 1995.

SIC 7997

MEMBERSHIP SPORTS AND RECREATION CLUBS

This industry classification covers sports and recreation clubs that are restricted to use by members and their guests. Country, golf, tennis, yacht, and amateur sports and recreation clubs are included in this industry. Health clubs and other fitness facilities are classified in **SIC 7991: Physical Fitness Facilities.**

NAICS CODE(S)

713910 (Golf Courses and Country Clubs)
713940 (Fitness and Recreational Sports Centers)
713990 (All Other Amusement and Recreation Industries)

An estimated 15,100 membership sports and recreation clubs were in operation in 1998, generating revenues of more than $7.5 billion. These numbers represent a

15.5 percent growth in the number of clubs and a whopping 61 percent increase in revenues from 1990. Employment grew nearly 23 percent since 1990, totaling about 297,300 in 1998.

American country clubs were born in the late 1880s—a creation of the wealthy upper class as an exclusive social setting in which to enjoy various athletic and recreational endeavors. The clubs flourished until the late 1920s, when the Depression forced many of them to close. A renaissance took place in the late 1940s and 1950s, spawned by post-war affluence and the increased interest in golf (a sport that has enjoyed a tremendous amount of growth across the nation for the past several decades); and, as a direct result of this heightened popularity, many country clubs were built during this period. In the late 1990s, private country clubs have become a major pastime for many Americans, with nearly 12,000 such facilities in operation.

Golf Clubs. The National Golf Foundation estimated that more than 26 million golfers played roughly 520 million rounds of golf in 1998, up about 6 percent from the 490 million rounds played in 1994. The United States boasted nearly 16,400 golf courses by the end of 1998, the majority of which were either municipal or private courses that were open to the public. Many private golf courses offered a variety of different memberships, with the most sought-after and expensive membership being a full-equity membership, in which members have full use of the golf course and share of stock in the club and with which they are able to share with any approved member. Other, more restricted memberships included dining room privileges only, while some full memberships gave members use of all facilities except the golf course.

Because of new tax laws passed in 1994 eliminating the business deduction for club dues and reducing deductions on business meals, many of which were eaten in private clubhouse dining rooms, clubs struggled in the mid-1990s to retain current members and to attract new members.

ClubCorp International, headquartered in Dallas, Texas, is the world's largest private club and resort operator. In 1999 ClubCorp owned or managed approximately 230 clubs, resorts, public fee golf courses, and real estate developments worldwide. In 1998 the company garnered revenues of more than $850 million.

Other Membership Sports and Recreation Clubs. Americans support a wide array of athletic and recreational clubs offering a variety of sports and recreational activities, such as yachting, archery, and tennis. Many of these establishments are independent clubs with no other affiliations, privately owned by the club membership. Others operate as subsidiaries of larger corporations.

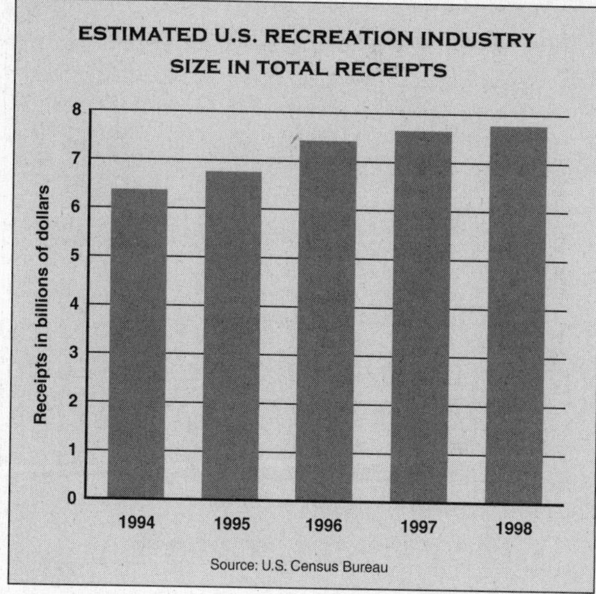

In the late 1990s, other major players in the industry included American Golf Corp., the world's largest golf management company, and Golf Trust of America. American Golf, based in Santa Monica, California, operates more than 250 public and private golf courses and country clubs. The company reported 1998 sales of more than $575 million. Golf Trust, headquartered in Charleston, South Carolina, has a stake in more than 30 upscale U.S. golf courses, the bulk of them located in the Sunbelt. It posted 1998 revenues of $44.5 million.

FURTHER READING

Darnay, Arsen J., ed. *Service Industries USA,* 4th ed. Detroit: Gale Research, 1998.

National Golf Foundation, 1999. "Frequently Asked Questions." Available from http://www.ngf.org/faq/.

Tuscana, Joe. "It's a Buyer's Market Out There." *Executive Report,* 1 March 1996.

U.S. Bureau of the Census. *1997 Economic Census.* Washington, D.C.: GPO, 1999.

U.S. Department of Commerce. *Statistical Abstract of the United States.* Washington, D.C.: GPO, 1996.

SIC 7999

AMUSEMENT AND RECREATION SERVICES, NOT ELSEWHERE CLASSIFIED

This industry covers establishments primarily engaged in the operation of sports, amusement, and recreation services, not elsewhere classified, such as bathing

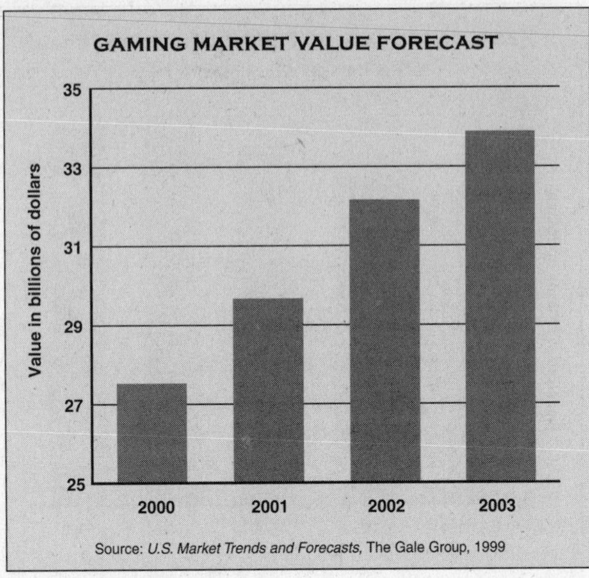

beaches, swimming pools, lottery operations, riding academies and schools, gaming establishments, carnival operations, exposition operations, horse shows, picnic grounds operation, ski resorts, and shooting galleries. Establishments primarily engaged in showing or handling animals at shows or exhibitions are classified in **SIC 0752: Animal Specialty Services, Except Veterinary.**

NAICS Code(s)

561599 (All Other Travel Arrangement and Reservation Services)
487990 (Scenic and Sightseeing Transportation, Other)
711190 (Other Performing Arts Companies)
711219 (Other Spectator Sports)
713920 (Skiing Facilities)
713940 (Fitness and Recreational Sports Centers)
713210 (Casinos (except Casino Hotels))
713290 (Other Gambling Industries)
712190 (Nature Parks and Other Similar Institutions)
611620 (Sports and Recreation Instruction)
532292 (Recreational Goods Rental)
487110 (Scenic and Sightseeing Transportation, Land)
487210 (Scenic and Sightseeing Transportation, Water)
713990 (All Other Amusement and Recreation Industries)

Americans entertain themselves with a broad spectrum of amusements and recreations that include participatory and spectator sports, tourism, and other activities. Members of this broad industry range from athletes to bowling instructors and from fortune tellers to fireworks operators. The U.S. population's traditional interest in a rich and varied range of recreational activities has supported the growth of an enormous, sprawling industry to capitalize on the continued popularity of such activities.

Spending on recreational activities has grown dramatically since 1990, even in the absence of more free time. It was projected that spending by Americans on recreational activities would increase more than 30 percent between 2000 and 2005. Entertainment spending was dramatically higher in affluent and well-educated households.

While this industry classification covers many establishments, several areas of the industry have particular economic significance in the United States.

Ski Resorts. Skiing is one of America's favorite recreational sports, but with the number of skiers leveling off and operational costs such as snowmaking and workers' compensation rising, resorts were forced to hike prices and even explore consolidation opportunities. Many younger outdoor enthusiasts were taking up snowboarding, further contributing to the downhill skiing slump. In 1996, flashy new ski designs were introduced to appeal to skiers over 35, who make up an increasing share of the market. The new skis claim to allow ordinary skiers to cut smooth turns at slow speeds and with little effort.

Vail Resorts Inc., the nation's largest ski resort operator, currently owns the nation's three most popular resorts: Vail Mountain, Breckenridge Mountain Resort, and Keystone Mountain. Vail Resorts Inc. has been an active participant in the consolidation trend.

Tourism. The tourism industry includes such items as air, bus, cruise ship, and rail travel; hotel and motel accommodations; camping; food and drink; retail purchases; and amusement and recreation service. Across the United States, cities and counties have found success by using tourism to attract industry. The tourism industry ranks among the top 3 employers in a majority of the 50 states. Travel spending in the United States is responsible for millions of jobs generating hundreds of billions of dollars in wages and salaries.

As concern for the environment has grown, the so-called ''eco-trip'' or adventure travel, has become a popular vacation alternative. These eco-tours, which include such excursions as white water rafting, watching sea lions, or visiting a rain forest, are not new, but they have become a growth area of the travel industry.

Gaming Establishments. Until the late 1980s, only Nevada and New Jersey permitted casinos. But with states and localities hard-pressed to generate jobs, tourism, and tax dollars, the gaming industry has increasingly been viewed as a vehicle for economic growth. Today, some form of legal gambling is available in 47 states and the District of Columbia. In 1996, 56 percent of Americans gambled at least once, generating more than $50 billion in gross revenues.

Based on revenue, Las Vegas and Atlantic City remain the two largest centers of the U.S. gaming market. In

1995, Nevada's total wagerings grew almost 6 percent to $112 billion, the smallest gain in 6 years. While Las Vegas has been enormously successful at attracting new visitors, they are gawking more and gambling less. The amount of money and time spent gambling has decreased in recent years, while spending on shows, sightseeing, and other activities outside the casinos has more than tripled.

In contrast to Las Vegas, which is more of a resort and business convention destination, about 30 percent of the visitors to Atlantic City arrive by charter bus and stay for less than a full day. Ten of Atlantic City's gaming facilities are located on or near the Boardwalk.

During the early 1990s, casino-type activity become increasingly accessible to U.S. consumers. The geographic expansion of legalized gaming broadened the industry's customer base. People who had never traveled to Las Vegas or Atlantic City were being lured to local riverboats or Native American casinos. As of 1996, there were approximately 65 riverboat casinos open in Iowa, Illinois, Mississippi, Louisiana, Missouri, and Indiana. In addition, a number of states had authorized video gaming terminals (VGTs), which resembled slot machines.

The 1990s also witnessed the expansion of Native American gaming facilities. Under the Indian Gaming Regulatory Act of 1988 (IGRA), Native Americans can operate whatever form of gambling legally exists in a given state. Typically, a tribe seeks an agreement, or compact, with the state, detailing the gambling activity for which it seeks approval. Currently 24 states have permitted Native American gaming sites, with the most active being Connecticut, Minnesota, and Michigan.

More recently, however, there has been a slowdown in the number of new jurisdictions adopting legalized gambling. Concerns about social and moral issues may continue to restrict the spread of legalized gambling, and Congress established the Gaming Impact and Policy Commission in 1996 to study the effects of the industry on the public. The Commission found that while the gambling industry has entertained and provided decent jobs for some, it does have significant problems. The main problems cited were the effect on those with a pathological gambling problem and their families, and the fact that in many cases, the revenues from gambling that were supposed to go into causes like education or the environment, have simply not gone there. The Commission recommended that a ''pause'' was necessary before further legalization of gambling was allowed.

INDUSTRY LEADERS

Mirage Resorts is one of the largest casino operators in Las Vegas. Its major U.S. properties include the Mirage, a tropically themed 95,000 square-foot casino and 3,000 room hotel; Treasure Island, a pirate-themed 75,000 square-foot casino and 2,900 room resort; and the Golden Nugget, a 38,000 square-foot casino with 300 hotel rooms located in downtown Las Vegas. In 1998, Mirage opened the $1.6 billion Bellagio casino/hotel in Las Vegas. Future plans included resorts in Atlantic City.

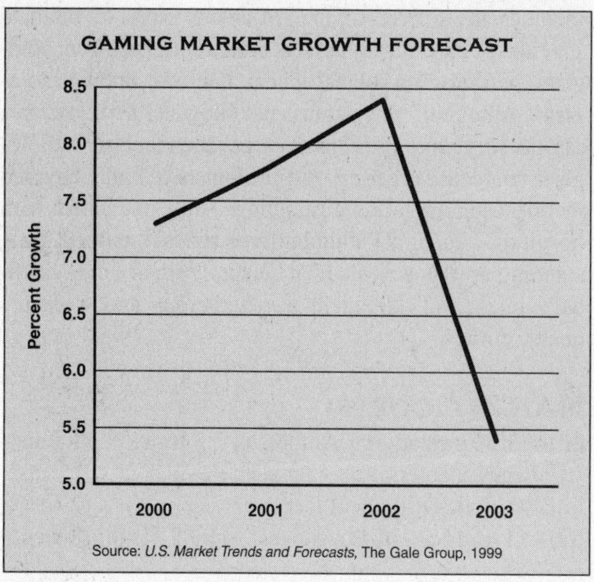

Source: *U.S. Market Trends and Forecasts,* The Gale Group, 1999

Hilton Hotels owns, manages, and/or franchises more than 260 hotels around the globe. With its $2 billion purchase of Bally Entertainment in 1996, Hilton became the nation's largest gambling business. Its U.S. gaming assets include casino hotels in Las Vegas and Atlantic City, a riverboat casino in New Orleans, and an interest in a Canadian casino. Among the most well known Hilton properties are The Waldorf-Astoria, Hilton Hawaiian Village, and Palmer House Hilton.

FURTHER READING

Kacapyr, Elia. ''Jumping for Joy.'' *American Demographics,* June 1996.

Lubove, Seth. ''Snake Eyes?'' *Forbes,* 15 July 1996.

Wilke, John R. ''Vail Of Fears: Colorado Ski Area Starts To Snowball; The Owners' Plans To Acquire Other Resorts In The State Alarm Skiers And The Feds.'' *Wall Street Journal,* 17 December 1996.

SIC 8011

OFFICES, CLINICS OF DOCTORS OF MEDICINE

This industry consists of offices and clinics of licensed medical doctors, excluding doctors of osteopathic medicine (covered in **SIC 8031: Clinics of Doctors of Osteopathy**). These establishments are engaged in general or specialized medicine or surgery. This category includes the offices of the following types of medical specialists: anesthesiologists, dermatologists, gynecologists, neurologists, obstetricians, oculists, ophthalmologists, orthopedic physicians, pathologists, pediatricians, plastic surgeons, psychiatrists, psychoanalysts, radiologists, medical surgeons, and urologists. Clinics covered in this category are freestanding—not associated with hospitals—such as ambulatory surgical centers, freestanding emergency medical centers, primary care medical clinics, and outpatient psychotherapy and women's health clinics.

NAICS CODE(S)

621493 (Freestanding Ambulatory Surgical and Emergency Centers)
621491 (HMO Medical Centers)
621112 (Offices of Physicians, Mental Health Specialists)
621111 (Offices of Physicians (except Mental Health))

INDUSTRY SNAPSHOT

According to the American Medical Association (AMA), there were more than 756,000 licensed physicians (excluding doctors of osteopathy) in the United States as of December 31, 1997. Of these, approximately 685,000 were practicing medicine, with the remainder employed as teachers, hospital and clinic administrators, and researchers. Of physicians practicing medicine in 1997, more than 458,000 were based in offices and clinics. The number of practicing physicians in the United States was expected to increase between 21 and 35 percent by the year 2005.

In 1996, 166 physician practice management companies in the United States owned and operated doctors' offices and clinics, generating more than $6.1 billion in sales. Although this segment of the industry appeared to be on the leading edge of the health care business in 1996, only two or three years later a number of companies were abandoning the field. According to some observers, the practice management companies were feeling the effects of ineffective cost controls in a capitated fee environment. Under a capitated fee system, health maintenance organizations pay medical providers a set monthly per-patient stipend for the treatment of each patient's medical needs.

Additional sales in the industry were obtained by self-employed doctors, although no figures were available for this segment of the market. It was estimated that Americans paid nearly $218 billion for all physician services in 1997. The industry grew rapidly and was predicted to continue to grow with the expansion of the overall health care industry. At the same time, the nature of this industry's growth was expected to undergo tremendous change in the twenty-first century as the government instituted health care reforms.

ORGANIZATION AND STRUCTURE

This industry is organized mainly according to the type of practice or medical specialty performed at an establishment. Of the 458,000 physicians in office- and clinic-based practice in 1997, more than 85 percent were involved in specialties outside the field of general/family practice. Leading fields of specialty included internal medicine with more than 81,000 doctors, pediatrics (36,800 doctors), obstetrics/gynecology (30,100), general surgery (27,900), and anesthesiology (25,600).

The 1980s introduced another classification within this industry based on whether a doctor was working completely independently or through a group, such as a health maintenance organization (HMO) or a preferred provider organization (PPO). According to Lani Luciano in *Money* magazine, 50 percent of all American doctors earned some or all of their incomes through HMOs and PPOs or similar provider networks in 1990.

Managed care also cultivated the increase of practice consolidation by putting added pressure on solo and small group practices. Smaller practices did not have the ability to negotiate favorable enough managed care contracts to keep them in business. The proportion of physicians with managed care contracts increased from 56 percent in 1986 to 83 percent in 1995, with little variation between specialties.

In the past, most physicians were self-employed and ran their offices in a partnership or group, sharing office help and medical assistants. During the 1980s, some physicians started to franchise; this involved paying a franchiser to handle administration, such as billing and insurance claims. By 1995 the number of self-employed patient care physicians in solo practices dropped from 40.5 percent in 1983 to 26.3 percent in 1995. The number of self-employed physicians in group practices fell from 35.3 percent in 1983 to 28.3 percent in 1995. The number of physicians employed by a health care company, however, rose from 24.2 percent in 1983 to 45.4 percent in 1995.

Of those physicians employed by an outside agency in 1995, 31 percent worked for physician groups and 8 percent for staff-model HMOs. Many staff-model HMOs were quite large in 1996, with as many as several thousand physicians. By the late 1990s, many physicians either merged with larger medical groups or sold their practices to hospitals. This trend led to the development of physician-hospital organizations (PHOs) and management services organizations (MSOs).

PHOs far outnumbered MSOs in 1995, creating a partnership between physicians and hospitals with equal management weight to each. Also a hospital partnership, MSOs require physicians to purchase shares in the MSO, which provided management services and equitable management to both hospitals and physicians. In MSOs, physicians could later sell their shares in the organization for profit.

Physicians who sold their practice in 1995 received generous compensation. Specialty and multispecialty practices had the highest median value per physician at $244,000, plus a base salary. More than 80 percent of the physicians who sold their practices could also receive bonuses in future years. The largest number of physicians who sold their practices in 1995 were primary care physicians, especially family physicians and internists.

Doctors' offices and clinics play an important role in the overall operation of the health care industry. Doctors usually work with one hospital and refer patients to that hospital for tests and treatment. For this reason, the relationship between doctors and hospitals is often regarded as a buyer-seller relationship, where hospitals approach local doctors for their patients. In addition, doctors are also buyers in their relationship with pharmaceutical companies. According to *Money,* doctors controlled 80 percent of the costs of medical care in 1990.

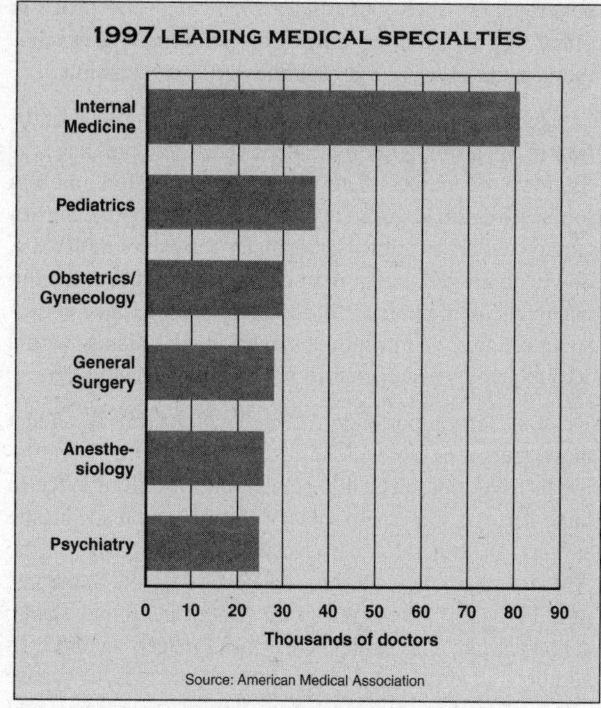

BACKGROUND AND DEVELOPMENT

While the convention of doctors working in some institutional or hospital-like establishment dates back to ancient Egypt, doctors' offices as independent establishments emerged in the Middle Ages with barber-surgeons. These independently employed doctors worked in their offices or in patients' homes and received payment for their services as they were provided. Doctors who cared for patients in hospitals received no payment from their patients or the hospital. In the nineteenth century, however, hospitals began paying doctors, and the profession grew rapidly.

During the twentieth century, the role of the physician changed with economic, government, and societal pressures, along with technological advances. In the early part of the century, doctors in the United States were a highly autonomous group, which was held accountable to the standards defined by the profession itself and not the general public, according to Harold M. Swartz and Ann Barry Flood in *Money, Power, and Health Care.*

The gap in salaries between primary care physicians and specialists grew significantly in the twentieth century. As a result, there was a general shift from primary care physicians to specialists. The use of HMOs and provider networks to cut medical costs also changed this profession from wholly self-employed doctors to those working on salaries for hospitals, HMOs, and provider networks. By 1995 the average share of physicians' revenues from managed care rose from 11 to 27 percent, with a higher proportion going to primary care physicians.

Technical advances in this industry were abundant during the twentieth century. From 1900 to the 1950s, the development of antibiotics and public health initiatives—such as water treatment—increased physician effectiveness in many parts of the country, and simultaneously decreased the need for doctors in many respects. Wars and increases in population and fatal crimes offset this, however.

During the second half of the twentieth century, technical developments increased doctors' roles in health care; many diseases, such as Hodgkin's disease and leukemia, were now treated through chemotherapy. Moreover, detecting disease became more practiced with new technologies for diagnosis. The development and use of these technologies, however, was regulated by governmental bodies and insurance companies.

The second half of the twentieth century also witnessed a growth in freestanding clinics. By the end of the 1980s, there were 23,000 licensed clinics in the United States, according to the General Accounting Office (GAO). These included outpatient ambulatory care facilities, outpatient surgical centers, psychiatric and psychotherapy clinics, and obstetric/gynecological clinics.

The rapid proliferation of clinics posed problems for state regulators of these facilities. According to a 1989 GAO report, state health regulators were concerned about the complex appeals systems between patients and clinics and were disturbed to find that roughly one-half of the states did not have any means of resolving patient complaints against clinics.

The government acknowledged the growing need for psychiatric outpatient care in 1989 when it increased its coverage for such care under Medicare. The program opted to provide more types of psychiatric and psychotherapy care and to increase the caps on payments.

In the 1980s physicians broke with a long-held tradition by advertising their services. This new practice was the focus of much debate within the profession and was initially regarded by many physicians and other health care providers as unprofessional. By the end of the 1980s, however, advertising in newspapers, television, and radio became common. By 1992 doctors' offices and clinics spent roughly $50 million annually in advertising, with a 13.7 percent growth rate in advertising expenditures.

Jon Berry reported in *AdWeek's Marketing Week* that plastic surgeons spent an estimated $30 million on advertising in 1990; this was a 400 percent increase from 1985. In large part this was due to societal changes that made plastic surgery in general more acceptable. According to the American Society of Plastic and Reconstructive Surgeons, in 1987 nearly 50 percent of all Americans found plastic surgery acceptable, compared with 35 percent in 1982. In addition, advertising by plastic surgeons increased because a larger number of doctors went into plastic surgery and had consequently increased competition.

Due to increased health care costs and rising competition among doctors seeking business, the late 1980s witnessed a surge in consumers seeking medical information outside of doctors' offices. Nurse-call lines, self-help medical books, and educational videotapes started to compete with doctors' offices. Some offices and clinics, however, adapted to this trend by showing videotaped programs as a way of educating patients about procedures and the treatment options available.

Company Clinics. By the end of the 1980s, large companies across a variety of businesses greatly expanded their company clinics in response to rising health care costs. By 1990 about 12 employers sponsored clinics for their employees. Many of these clinics were operated by the companies themselves and others were operated by medical management companies. One of the primary ways in which these clinics brought down medical costs was through the hiring of doctors on salaries on the assumption that salaried physicians did not have incentives to perform any unnecessary tests, according to Jerry Geisel in *Business Insurance.*

In 1992 John Deere was the first company in the United States to set up a primary care clinic for their employees in conjunction with a third-party hospital, the Mayo Clinic of Rochester, Minnesota. The largest company clinic in the country was operated by Southern California Edison Company, which had 10 medical clinics and first-aid stations, employing a staff of 70 and facilitating more than 100,000 patient visits annually. Similarly, the Gillette Company and Goodyear Tire & Rubber Company sponsored corporate primary care clinics and offered incentives for employees to use them.

Medicare and Medicaid. Medicare and Medicaid are government programs providing financial assistance for medical treatment. The Medicare program is designed for individuals at least 65 years old and for the disabled, while Medicaid helps families with low incomes. Government funds for these programs come from both federal and state sources and primarily through Social Security payroll taxes.

In 1997 more than 55 million people received Medicare and Medicaid payments. Medicare payments for doctors, clinics, laboratory services, end-stage renal disease treatments, and continuous-use medical equipment—such as wheelchairs—totaled $51.7 billion in 1997, with $38.2 billion going to physicians. Medicaid payments going to both hospitals and doctors and other health care facilities and providers totaled $123.6 billion in 1997.

Though Medicaid expenditures nearly doubled between 1990 and 1997, growth dropped to 2.8 percent from 1995 to 1997. In 1997 Medicare paid for 20.7 percent of the 787.4 million patient-visits to office-based physicians, while Medicaid financed another 8.1 percent of total visits. Private insurance covered 53.1 percent of 1997 visits to office-based physicians.

Medicare and Medicaid greatly affected this industry by increasing administrative duties involved in handling paperwork and by setting costs for medical services. Since the late 1980s lawmakers have tried to reduce Medicare and Medicaid financing by shifting coverage to promote outpatient treatment over extended hospital care.

In 1991 the Medicare program was reduced by $43 billion as part of the federal government's economic budget changes. In 1992 the Health Care Financing Administration, which managed Medicare, started a plan to change how doctors were paid by the government. Under the new plan, doctors' fees were based on resources and the doctors' time in consultations, rather than on procedures performed by the physicians. This was set up to attract primary care physicians who felt the old system was unfair. The American Medical Association (AMA) opposed total use of this system, pointing out that some unfairness to specialty doctors needed to be worked out of the system before private insurers adopted it for their payment plans. At the end of the 1990s the cost of Medicare was still a hot topic for political debate in the goal to balance the budget and create health care reform.

Malpractice. The Insurance Information Institute (III) reported that the number of medical malpractice claims filed against doctors peaked in 1985 at 17.8 per 100 doctors and then trended downward for the rest of the decade, dropping to 8 claims per 100 doctors by 1989. During the

1990s the rate of increase in the number and size of claims tended to fluctuate, according to the III. The malpractice insurance market attracted new entrants in many states, increasing competition and holding down rates.

Due to the proliferation of malpractice suits, the practice of defensive medicine increased considerably. Defensive medicine refers to excessive precautions doctors take in order to safeguard themselves against possible malpractice suits. Precautions that doctors often took in treating patients included ordering duplicate tests, requesting additional diagnostic procedures, and using consultants. According to the AMA, in 1992, defensive medicine added $15 billion to the cost of health care nationwide. In 1991 medical malpractice represented $9.1 billion of total tort costs in the United States; of that total, 58 percent was incurred by physicians. In 1993 the number of malpractice claims had been reduced by state health regulators imposing caps on suit awards and by the insurance industry and medical profession—represented by more than 30 medical associations—together advocating tort system reforms.

Obstetricians and gynecologists were among the doctors most commonly sued for medical malpractice in the early 1990s. According to a study conducted by the American College of Obstetricians and Gynecologists, in 1992 about 27 percent of all claims against gynecologists were for failure to diagnose a medical condition, usually breast cancer. The average payment for claims won against gynecologists was reported at $92,500 in 1990. Approximately 33 percent of all obstetric complaints were for infant brain damage. The average payment for obstetric claims was $311,400 in 1990. Given the frequency and costs of these claims against obstetricians and gynecologists, their average insurance premiums were $36,946 in 1991, while the average for all physicians was $15,900. Insurance payments and claims awards, however, varied considerably from state to state.

Malpractice cases also strained the relationship between physicians and hospitals. Hospitals had higher insurance coverage and more general funds to cover malpractice cases; consequently, many claims involving doctors were directed at hospitals in order to receive higher awards.

According to a 1993 study by the Health Research Group of Public Citizens, the most common complaints against doctors were for negligence, misprescribing drugs, and substance abuse by the physicians. The study also showed that 150,000-300,000 medical negligence cases were not disciplined by such measures as revoking or suspending licenses. The AMA responded to this study by pointing out that physicians as a group acted as a self-correcting organization, whereby doctors did not refer patients to doctors with reputations for such practices. Moreover, as pointed out at the time of the study, many states did not had the funds to investigate the many claims against doctors.

One measure taken to protect patients from consulting negligent doctors began in 1990 with the establishment of the National Practitioners Data Bank. Owned by the federal government, this computer data bank stored and provided information about physicians who had their licenses suspended or who faced disciplinary action for negligence, and helped to prevent these physicians from setting up new offices.

Other ways of dealing with malpractice cases and the costs they placed on health care included placing caps on the size of awards for personal suffering; this system was used in California since the late 1970s. Under health care reform programs discussed at the federal level in 1993, most of the cost of malpractice awards would be paid by HMOs and other health management organizations.

Self-Referrals. In the mid-1980s, consumer groups drew attention to physicians who referred patients to laboratories totally or partially owned by the doctors, a practice known as ''self-referrals.'' In 1992 a study conducted by the Health Care Financing Administration estimated that at least 25 percent of independent laboratories were financially tied to individual physicians. The same study reported that Medicare patients who were referred by physicians to laboratories they owned received 45 percent more lab tests than other Medicare patients. Some sources estimated that the annual excess in costs as a result of self-referrals were roughly $140 million; others estimated the costs in the tens of billions.

Legislation was expected to be drafted on the federal level to prohibit physicians from making self-referrals for Medicare patients. State legislators had been adopting similar laws to cover patients on private insurance.

Doctors' Offices Dispensing Medicine. Since the early 1900s, when licensed physicians gained the legal right to prescribe drugs, doctors' offices and clinics had dispensed drugs in limited numbers to patients. Originally, this practice was not done for profit; during the 1980s and into the 1990s, however, drug dispensation began to increase rapidly. This increase was prompted by high profits and persuasive marketing by the pharmaceutical repackaging industry. Pharmaceutical repackagers purchase drugs in bulk and repackage them in small units, allowing doctors to maintain a stock of a large variety of drugs at their offices. In 1987 about 5 percent of doctors' offices and clinics routinely dispensed these repackaged drugs; by 1993, nearly 50 percent of doctors' offices and clinics were dispensing repackaged drugs.

The dispensing of drugs out of doctors' offices and clinics caused friction between the pharmaceutical industry and medical doctors. Moreover, this practice raised ethical issues within the medical community. Health care

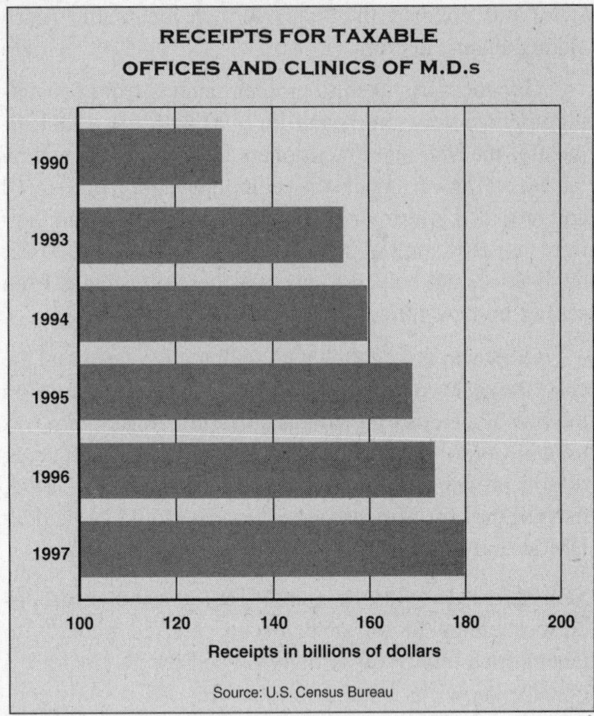

professionals disagreed as to whether doctors should engage in competition with pharmacists and whether doctors, who were generally not as well trained in medicines as pharmacists were, had the qualifications to routinely dispense drugs.

In 1988 the federal government tried to amend the Food, Drug, and Cosmetic Act to restrict doctors from selling drugs out of their offices, with the exceptions of emergencies or cases in which patients would have difficulties getting to a pharmacist. The amendment did not pass, and the federal government has since prohibited states from passing similar laws that restrict doctors from dispensing drugs.

Current Conditions

According to the National Center for Health Statistics, the number of people who used the services of doctors' offices and clinics gradually increased throughout the 1980s, with the largest increases occurring in cities. This industry also benefited from the aging population, which was reflected in the growth in geriatric medicine and the offices of ophthalmologists—where technical innovations provided eye surgery for the elderly.

In the 1990s this industry faced challenges to its organizational structure and its means of making a profit. The economic needs of employers and the expected government reforms have changed the industry's structure from individual practices to group care. The rising costs of health care also introduced new ways of pricing services provided by doctors. In addition to the new system adopted by Medicare, which attempted to establish salary parity between primary care doctors and specialists, private insurers and health provider networks imposed caps on the costs of doctors' services. Government efforts at health care reform were also expected to reduce the time doctors' offices spent in handling paperwork; according to the Lewin-VHI health consulting firm, 20 percent of health dollars spent in 1993 went to administrative costs.

Organizational changes also occurred in this industry as health care moved from inpatient to outpatient surgery. Ambulatory surgical centers, ophthalmology clinics, and gynecology clinics were the fastest growing of these outpatient centers, estimated at nearly 1,500 in 1991. The growth of managed care has promoted the trend toward practice consolidation and significantly reduced the number of self-employed, solo practice physicians.

This industry experienced a shortage of primary care physicians, particularly in rural areas. The more lucrative specialists' salaries drove medical students away from primary care. Rural areas were even less desirable for primary care physicians because salaries were generally smaller than those offered in cities, and physicians preferred to live in metropolitan areas. From 1985 to 1994, the number of physicians in relation to the population increased 11 percent in nonmetropolitan areas compared to 16 percent in large metropolitan areas (populations over 1 million) and 19 percent in small metropolitan areas. Rural hospitals attempted to attract more primary care physicians by offering income guarantees for doctors who joined local practices, and state governments helped rural practices in recruiting new doctors.

Industry Leaders

Since many doctors were self-employed or in small group practices, this industry's leaders during the 1990s were companies that owned and managed large groups of doctors' offices and clinics. In 1996 there were 166 of these physician practice management companies, employing more than 40,800 medical and nonmedical personnel. Most of these companies were privately held, while a handful were publicly traded and a few others were subsidiaries of hospitals. As the decade neared an end, however, this segment of the industry found itself under increasing financial pressure, and a number of companies bailed out of the business. Originally set up to relieve physicians of such nonmedical concerns as mushrooming paperwork, capitated payments, and the rise of managed care, the practice management companies began foundering because of ineffective cost controls.

Three of the major players in the physician practice management field in the late 1990s were PhyCor Inc., PhyAmerica Physician Group Inc., and Caremark Rx Inc. In 1999, PhyCor, headquartered in Nashville, Tennessee, operated more than 45 clinics with nearly 3,000 doctors in 24 states. The largest company in the physician practice business, PhyCor in 1998 reported a net loss of $111.4 million on revenue of $1.5 billion. Also experiencing financial pressure as the millennium ended was PhyAmerica, which was forced to sell off some of its assets. Headquartered in Durham, North Carolina, PhyAmerica suffered a net loss of $20.1 million on sales of $294.2 million. Caremark Rx, formerly known as MedPartners, was in the process of extricating itself from the physician practice management industry as the 1990s ended. Headquartered in Birmingham, Alabama, Caremark Rx suffered a net loss of $1.26 billion on revenue of $2.63 billion in 1998.

Other companies in the physician practice management business included United American Healthcare Corp. and American Physicians Service Group Inc. Headquartered in Detroit, Michigan, United American managed to turn a profit in fiscal 1999, the 12 months that ended June 30, 1999, earning $600,000 on revenue of $93.5 million. American Physicians Service Group, based in Austin, Texas, ended 1998 in the black, reporting net income of $1.5 million on sales of $16.4 million.

WORKFORCE

Of the 458,200 doctors working out of offices and clinics in 1997, roughly 62,000 were in general and family practice. The major medical specialties in this industry employed 36,800 pediatricians; 24,500 psychiatrists; 30,100 obstetricians and gynecologists; and 25,600 anesthesiologists. In other common specialties, there were 15,100 ophthalmologists; 10,200 pathologists; 8,200 neurologists; 7,400 dermatologists; and 5,300 plastic surgeons.

Other positions in doctors' offices and clinics include medical assistants, medical secretaries, nurses, physician assistants, and medical laboratory technicians. Medical assistants provide office and medical assistance for physicians, such as basic bookkeeping and clinical procedures. It is one of the few health occupations open to individuals with no formal training. Usually one medical assistant works with one or two doctors.

In 1997 there were about 225,000 medical assistants in the United States. Medical assistants earned varied amounts depending on experience. Those with less than two years of experience earned between $8.07 and $10.90 per hour. Those with more than five years of experience earned between $10.38 and $13.46 per hour. The number of medical assistants was anticipated to increase 36 percent or more by the year 2006.

Medical secretaries work in offices of physicians and medical scientists. They have job duties similar to those of other secretaries, such as typing and keeping track of appointments; in addition, they need to be knowledgeable of medical terms and the health care industry. To meet this additional requirement, medical secretaries train in medicine for one or two years. As of 1997, there were 239,000 medical secretaries in the United States. The average salary for medical secretaries was $23,200. The number of medical secretaries was expected to grow 21 to 35 percent by the year 2006.

Registered nurses working in doctors' offices and clinics assist physicians by administering medications and treatments and by performing routine laboratory and office work. They receive their training through bachelor and associate degree programs in nursing or through three-year diploma programs in hospitals. They must pass a licensing examination to obtain a nursing license. Nurses working in doctors' offices and clinics reported annual salaries of roughly $36,200 in 1997. Registered nurses held about 1.97 million jobs in 1997, with two-thirds employed by hospitals. Forecasts predicted the number of registered nurses would increase 36 percent or more by the year 2006.

Physician assistants support physicians and provide routine diagnostic, therapeutic, and preventive health care services under the supervision of a physician. Physician assistants take medical histories, examine patients, order and interpret laboratory tests and X rays, make preliminary diagnoses, and treat minor injuries. Physician assistants must complete an accredited, formal education program. Most states require physician assistants to pass a certifying exam. In 1997 about 64,000 physician assistants worked in the United States, earning a median annual salary of $53,284. Roughly two-thirds of these physician assistants worked in the offices and clinics of physicians, dentists, or other health practitioners.

Medical laboratory technologists work under the direction of a pathologist. There are three types of medical laboratory technologists with different levels of training: medical technologists, with four years of specialized training; medical laboratory technicians, with two years training; and medical laboratory assistants, with one year of training. Of these three, only the medical technologist carries out supervisory and administrative duties. In 1997 the median salary for medical technologists was $35,100, while medical laboratory technicians earned an average of $26,500 annually. Employment in these areas was projected to grow 10 to 20 percent by the year 2006.

Jobs for physicians and other positions in doctors' offices and clinics were generally expected to grow through the year 2000, along with the overall growth in the health care industry and the aging population. Government reforms, however, were expected to address the shortage of medical doctors in primary care by reducing the demand for and income of specialists. Moreover, due to cost controls enforced by HMOs and government programs, physicians' incomes were predicted to level off by the end of the century, curtailing their considerable annual growth rate. Under government reforms, the need for medical support staff such as nurses and medical assistants was expected to increase, while the number of secretaries would be reduced as reforms reduced paperwork and doctors left their individual practices to join HMOs and other group practices.

America and the World

American doctors and health care companies faced an expanding market for their services outside the United States—in places such as Western Europe, Mexico, and Japan—where aging populations grew. In addition, these countries began developing HMO services for non-state-run care.

In order for foreign doctors to practice medicine in the United States, they had to be licensed in the United States. Given that American doctors earned more than their foreign counterparts—in 1990, German doctors earned $120,000 a year, Japanese doctors earned $78,000, and British doctors earned $65,000—practicing medicine in America was highly desirable for foreigners entering this profession. As a result, however, of an influential study by the U.S. Department of Health and Human Services, which predicted a large surplus of doctors by the end of the century, the U.S. government passed legislation in 1976 restricting foreign doctors from practicing in America. The laws prohibited foreign doctors who had completed their residency programs in the United States from practicing in the United States for two years after obtaining their degrees.

The laws restricting the practices of foreign doctors in America had a strong impact on Canadian doctors in particular. Prior to these laws, Canadian doctors could easily obtain five-year permits using their Canadian credentials. The 1976 laws required Canadian doctors to have a full-time resident's green card if they wanted to practice in the United States. This was often difficult to acquire and greatly reduced the number of Canadian doctors working in the country.

Research and Technology

Upon entering the 1990s, new technology fueled the shift from inpatient hospital care to outpatient surgical clinics. Technologies, such as laser surgery, decreased the invasiveness of many medical procedures, allowing them to be performed in outpatient facilities. Technological advances also decreased complications related to the administering of anesthesia, which often required overnight hospitalization.

The trend away from prolonged hospitalization also gave rise to the development of in-home monitoring devices. These devices were used by patients who left hospitals for financial reasons, but who also had conditions requiring observation, such as congestive heart failure. The monitoring devices were electronically linked between the patient's home and a doctor's office or health care agency.

Advances in information technology were slowly used in this industry, particularly by self-employed doctors, but became important to the operation of these establishments by the 1990s. In order to reduce office paperwork and maintain more accurate patient records, doctors started using desktop systems for such routine functions as accessing patients' medical histories and insurance records and placing prescriptions with pharmacists.

Doctors also began using information technology to assist them in making diagnoses. Computers provided doctors with sorted information and success ratios on treatments and procedures. According to Reed Abelson of *Forbes,* this type of information was especially valuable to doctors who needed data on rare diseases and conditions. Researchers in this area were continuing to develop software able to handle the massive amounts of information required by doctors.

Further Reading

Cleverley, William O., Carson F. Dye, and Patrick J. Knott. "The Price of a Physician Practice." *American Medical News,* 25 March 1996.

"Could Equity-Model MSOs Supplant PHOs?" *Medical Economics,* 10 April 1995.

Darnay, Arsen J., ed. *Service Industries USA.* 3rd ed. Detroit: Gale Research, 1996.

Fogarty, William A. "Trends in Physician Practice Consolidation." *AMA Report of the Council on Medical Service.* American Medical Association, 1996. Available from http://www.ama-assn.org/meetings/public/i96/reports/cms9i96.htm.

Jarman, Max. "Heyday of Physician Practice Management Firms Has Passed." *Arizona Republic,* 17 January 1999.

Johnson, Julie. "MedPartners, Caremark Merge into $4.4 Billion Firm." *American Medical News,* 3 June 1996.

"Summaries." *American Medical News,* 22-29 April 1996. Available from http://www.ama-assn.org/sci-pubs/amnews/amn_96/summ0422.htm.

"Summaries." *American Medical News,* 13 January 1997. Available from http://www.ama-assn.org/sci-pubs/amnews/amn_97/summ0113.htm.

U.S. Bureau of the Census. "Statistical Abstract of the United States: Health and Nutrition." 1999. Available from http://www.census.gov/prod/www/statistical-abstract-us.html.

U.S. Department of Labor. Bureau of Labor Statistics. *Occupational Outlook Handbook,* 1998-99 ed. Washington, DC: GPO, 1998. Available from http://stats.bls.gov/ocohome.htm.

SIC 8021

OFFICES AND CLINICS OF DENTISTS

This industry consists of offices and clinics of licensed practitioners of dentistry with the degree of D.M.D., D.D.S. or D.D.Sc. Included in this industry are the offices of dentists, dental surgeons, pediatric dentists, endodontists (root canal specialists), oral pathologists (specialists in mouth diseases), orthodontists (specialists in straightening the teeth), periodontists (gum specialists) and prosthodontists (artificial teeth and denture specialists).

NAICS CODE(S)

621210 (Offices of Dentists)

INDUSTRY SNAPSHOT

In 1997 Americans spent almost $51 billion on dental services from the nation's 150,090 professionally active dentists, more than 138,000 of whom worked in private practice in an independent office or through a group practice or clinic. Nearly 20 percent of all active dentists in the United States were specialists, with the two largest groups being made up of orthodontists and oral surgeons. The total number of board-certified dentists in 1997 exceeded 150,090, but many of those not actively practicing were involved in dental education or research projects.

According to the 1997 Survey of Consumer Attitudes and Behaviors Regarding Dental Issues, conducted by the American Dental Association (ADA), most American adults reported that they had visited a dentist within the past year. Nearly 60 percent of adult Americans reported that they had visited a dentist in the previous 6 months, while another 16 percent said they had seen a dentist between 6 and 11 months ago. For most Americans, the factor most influential in making a decision to visit a dentist was the elimination of pain, according to the ADA survey.

Throughout the 1990s, this industry expanded to meet the needs of two growing sectors of the population: the aged and babies. During this period, pediatric dentistry became the fastest-growing sector of the industry. Additional growth had occurred as an increasing number of Americans acquired dental insurance.

ORGANIZATION AND STRUCTURE

The dental profession is divided into eight types of practices carried out at dental offices and clinics: general dentistry, oral and maxillofacial surgery, endodontics, orthodontics, pediatric dentistry, periodontics, oral pathology, and dental public health.

Prior to the 1980s, establishments in this industry that were owned by self-employed dentists were operated by the dentist and a small staff. During the 1980s, dentists began running their offices like small businesses, by employing the outside services of managerial consultants and dental office advisers. These organizational changes continued throughout the industry in the 1990s. With the health care industry moving toward managed care, dental maintenance organizations (DMOs) grew rapidly; at these organizations, participating dentists were paid fixed monthly rates. In 1989, only 10 percent of dentists worked with DMOs. By 1992, 15 percent of all dentists participated in these organizations, and analysts forecasted that 40 percent would be participating in such plans by the year 2000. Another reason that DMOs were seen as necessary was because the dental inflation rate had started to exceed the medical inflation rate in the mid-1990s. In 1995, approximately 18 percent of Americans were enrolled in a DMO. In fact, a total of 100 million people (including 52 percent of adults) were in a dental plan that covered part or all of their dental expenses.

BACKGROUND AND DEVELOPMENT

Modern dentistry began in the sixteenth century with the European revival of arts and sciences. According to dental historians, dentistry was being practiced independently from general medicine and surgery as early as 1544. Dentistry and medicine had been united for centuries because both sciences were practiced by barbers. The sixteenth century saw the important developments of dental instruments designed for cleaning and filling teeth.

In the seventeenth century, dentistry developed into an area of scientific inquiry in the way medicine had for many centuries. In Europe and America, academic and scientific articles began to appear on dentistry topics. During this time, the occupation of the barber-dentist evolved into that of tooth puller, while a separate practice of dental surgeons began to develop. The practices of periodontics and dental pathology began to develop during the eighteenth century.

Dentistry saw tremendous growth in the twentieth century. Preventive dentistry and public education on the importance of dental health and hygiene paid off for this industry. The number of patient visits rose significantly, especially for preventive measures. Moreover, elderly patients, unlike previous generations, did not lose their teeth and therefore went to dentists regularly.

Advances in fluoride treatments and dental technology have decreased the number of cavities Americans have had. In 1990 Americans had 151 million fillings, only half the number of fillings in 1959, even though the population had doubled during that time. The number of root canals, however, tripled.

Income levels play a significant role in the number of times a person visits the dentist. In 1997, approximately 59 percent of people with household incomes between $10,000 and $19,999 indicated they had visited a dentist within the past 12 months, while 84.9 percent of people with annual household incomes of $55,000 or more said they had been to a dentist.

Technological Advances. The expansion of this industry during the twentieth century was also due to numerous technological advances. During the 1940s and 1950s, new methods of anesthetics greatly reduced pain during clinical procedures. The 1960s saw the development of bonding, whereby a liquid resin is applied to a tooth, then shaped as it hardens, providing a better fitting and more attractive cap, or crown.

In the late 1980s, orthodontists' offices increased as new types of braces and appliances were developed that were suitable for adults. Clear plastic braces and more cosmetically appealing appliances that fit inside the mouth were marketed toward adults undergoing orthodontic treatment. Similarly, dental surgeons provided services for an increasing number of adults wanting to have their jaws realigned for both medical and cosmetic reasons.

Perhaps the most significant technological development for modern dentistry has been the surgical laser, which came into common use at the end of the 1980s. In 1997 the International Academy of Laser Dentistry estimated that across the world 5,000 lasers were in use, often shared by several dentists.

The Nd:YAG laser has been the laser most commonly used by dentists. This laser is used for soft-tissue procedures to heal inflammation and reduce bleeding. Since 1987, Nd:YAG has been studied for its use in hard-tissue cutting procedures, such as working with enamel and metal for orthodontic dentistry. The CO2 laser was the first to be approved by the Food and Drug Administration (FDA) and is the second-most widely used laser in dentistry. It is employed for soft-tissue surgery, such as removing lesions, and like Nd:YAG, has been experimented with for hard-tissue applications. The third major type of laser is the argon laser, which has been used for soft-tissue procedures, such as curing tissue. All three lasers also have uses for sterilizing dental instruments and are expected to undergo further developments.

Other significant technological innovations for this industry have been in intra-oral television and T-Scan devices; both have been utilized to educate patients on the condition of their teeth and the work involved in various procedures. Intra-oral television, as its name indicates, shows patients an enlarged view of their teeth and gums on a television screen. T-Scan uses a computer screen to show patients the static and dynamic contacts on their teeth. Both of these types of visual aids have helped dentists explain procedures to their patients and make them feel more comfortable.

Dental Office Hazards. Working with nitrous oxide (commonly known as ''laughing gas'') has long been a concern of dental office workers. In 1993 this gas was used by nearly 50 percent of all dentists in the United States, primarily by general dentists. While the government recommends that dentists take in under 25 parts per million of this gas, most dentists get 250 times this amount, according Elise Tanouye in the *Wall Street Journal.* Realizing possible health hazards, this industry has tried to lower the amounts that escape by using special types of masks, known as ''scavenging systems,'' that are worn by the patient.

Although the risks of nitrous-oxide exposure are not fully known, the increase in the number of female dentists, dental assistants, and hygienists has drawn attention to reduced fertility among women working in dentists' offices and clinics. A 1992 study showed that women exposed to high levels of nitrous oxide were 60 percent less fertile than women who had not been exposed to the gas, according to Tanouye in the *Wall Street Journal.* The Dental Assistants Association suggested that nitrous oxide exposure could be linked to miscarriages, liver disease, and neurological problems. As the twentieth century drew to a close, the topic was still being hotly debated.

Another cause of concern in dental offices has arisen with the frequent use of lasers. Lasers could be harmful to both patient and staff if misdirected to the wrong tissue, especially toward the eyes. Given the risks, dentists have taken precautions, such as the use of eye protection and surgical masks specially developed for laser surgery.

Costs of Infection Control. In 1990 a Florida dentist who had AIDS had allegedly transmitted the HIV virus that leads to AIDS to at least three of his patients. While it is not certain that the patients contracted the virus from their dentist, these cases received much public attention and national publicity. As a result of this, dentists' offices and associations received thousands of inquiries from concerned patients. Throughout this industry, dentists responded to these new concerns by investing in more infection-control measures. Moreover, the Occupational Safety and Health Administration has enforced additional regulations for the safety of dental office workers, who are believed to be at greater risk of getting AIDS from their patients than vice versa.

Infection control includes the use of more disposable items, disinfectants, sterilizers, and ultrasonic cleaners. According to a 1993 study by Clinical Research Associates, infection control cost an average of nine dollars per patient visit, adding more than $30,000 annually to a dentist's overhead costs, according to Gordon J. and Rella P. Christensen in the *Journal of the American Dental Association.* These costs have been handed down to patients, with some dentists adding an extra fee to their bills and labeling it ''infection control.''

Dental Fraud. With an overall increase in dental benefits insurance plans starting in the 1980s, this industry was noted for significant amounts of billing fraud. Though exact numbers are not available, according to Nancy Coe Bailey in *Business and Health,* one large insurer reported 88 dental fraud cases in 1989, while another insurer was investigating claims of $300,000 in billing fraud from one dental group alone.

There are basically three types of dental fraud: double-billing, where dentists charge both a patient's insurer and the insurer of the patient's spouse for the same procedure; billing for services not rendered; and manipulating billing codes by ''unbundling'' a procedure and billing it under several codes. Partially in response to the growing amount of billing fraud in the health care field in general, the Department of Health and Human Services enacted the Health Insurance Portability and Accounting Act of 1996. This act established a national bank to take reports of fraud and abuse and issue regular reports on the issue.

A related problem for this industry has been the concern that insurance companies have been ''downcoding'' dentists' bills. In downcoding, insurance companies price a procedure based on less-complex and lower-costing procedures than that reported by the dentist. This is part of a larger problem facing dentists' offices and clinics, where insurance companies have started to play an important role.

Marketing. According to the American Dental Association (ADA), less than 1 percent of income from dentists' offices and clinics was spent on advertising in 1993. Traditionally, this industry has taken a nonaggressive approach to advertising because most patients go to a dentist who has been referred to them by other patients or to the dentist their parents sent them to as children. This industry has benefited, however, from indirect advertising. The ADA recognizes that public health programs as well as toothpaste and mouthwash advertisements promote preventive dentistry and indirectly advertise for dentists' offices and clinics.

CURRENT CONDITIONS

Throughout the 1990s, dentists' offices and clinics were faced with new challenges related to industry reforms and the rise of managed care. Dentists sought changes in managerial practices and human resources to bring down high overhead costs. With inflation rates for dental care exceeding those for medical care, DMOs were becoming more popular. Growth in DMOs, however, has been slow, with only about 25 percent of people enrolled in one by the end of the 1990s.

INDUSTRY LEADERS

By the close of the 1990s, the industry boasted more than 109,000 dental offices and clinics. A 1996 report by

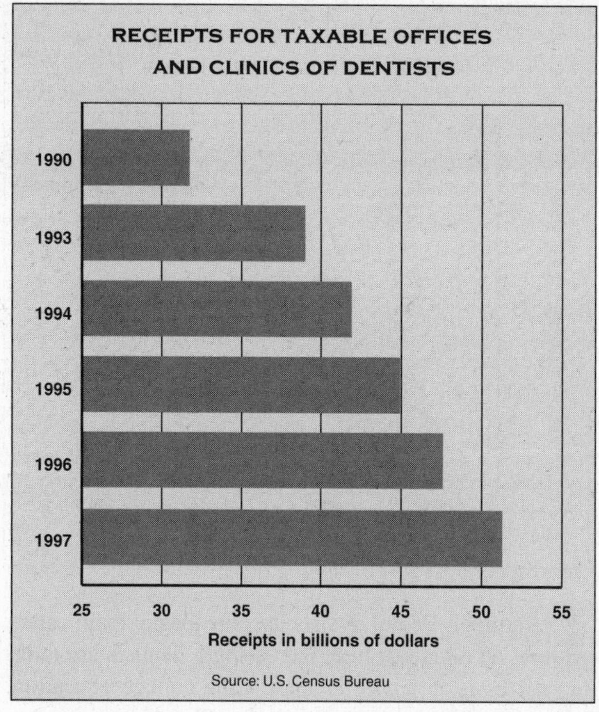

Inc. magazine listed dental offices as the third-highest category of start-up businesses that were likely to survive. The industry leaders were companies that owned several dental clinics and/or group offices. In the late 1990s, the industry leader was SafeGuard Health Enterprises, Inc., a publicly held company headquartered in Anaheim, California. In 1999 the company provided dental services to well over 1 million employees in both the private and public sectors, as well as multiple-employer trusts. SafeGuard offered dental care through a force of about 16,000 dentists practicing in some 14,000 independent offices. The states in which SafeGuard did the most business included California, Florida, Texas, Missouri, and Colorado. In 1998 the company posted revenues of $97.4 million, a 2 percent increase over its sales in 1997.

WORKFORCE

The American Dental Association (ADA) reported that in 1997 there were more than 150,000 dentists and approximately 100,000 dental hygienists. Additionally, the industry in the late 1990s employed more than 200,000 dental assistants. Companies operating large dental offices and clinics employ additional office personnel, including insurance claims specialists and managers. According to the 1996-97 edition of the *Occupational Outlook Handbook,* a publication of the Bureau of Labor Standards (BLS), the average dentist in 1996 employed four staff members, two of whom were full time and two of whom were part time. The average number of personnel employed by general dentists rose from 3.3 in 1986 to 4.2 in 1996.

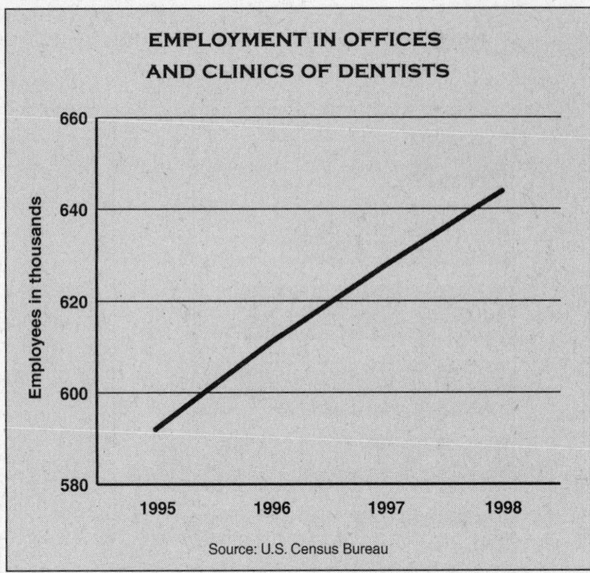

Although dental assistants may begin their career without a college degree, increasingly dentists are looking for assistants with at least some college education. Most dental assistants are employed by dentists in general practice, although dental specialists, including endodontists and periodontists, employ assistants as well. In 1996, almost 80 percent of general dentists employed at least one assistant working chairside. With many areas of the country reporting shortages of dental assistants, employment growth in this area is expected to be at least as rapid as that for all other jobs through the year 2005, according to the BLS handbook. The average hourly wage for dental assistants was $11.70 in 1996.

The employment outlook for dental hygienists was even brighter than that for dental assistants in the late 1990s. The *Occupational Outlook Handbook* predicted employment of hygienists would grow much faster than the average for occupations through the year 2005. As of 1996, almost 70 percent of all general dentists employed at least one dental hygienist, either full or part time. Hygienists must have a minimum of two years of college in an accredited dental hygiene program. Hygienists conduct clinical dental procedures and educate patients about dental health and hygiene. Some of the common clinical tasks of hygienists include cleaning teeth, developing x rays, and preparing model impressions of teeth for study. In addition to working with dentists, hygienists work on their own at public health agencies, industrial plants, and at small clinics; about half worked part time—less than 35 hours a week. The average hourly wage for hygienists in 1996 was $22. The wage for part-time hygienists averaged $27 per hour in 1996.

In 1997, according to the ADA, dentists working in private practice enjoyed an average net income of $133,430 annually, while those in specialty practices (approximately 20 percent of dentists) earned $197,720. Of the dentists not in private practice, most were in research and teaching; a small percentage worked for the government in hospitals and clinics of the Veterans Administration or the U.S. Public Health Service.

Even though the need for dental health was expected to continue to grow in the twentieth- first century, most of the increase in the work force is expected to come from dental hygienists and assistants. The number of dentists in the field should remain stable.

America and the World

According to the American Dental Association, this industry is not characterized by its international market. While foreign dentists come to the United States to study procedures related to the latest technology, American dentists tend to practice and perform research in the United States.

Research and Technology

In the realm of dental health, periodontal (gum) disease remained the biggest concern among dentists in 1998, according to the American Dental Association (ADA)/Colgate Oral Health Trend Survey. More than half of the dentists surveyed reported that periodontal disease was the one area of dental health about which their patients seemed inadequately concerned. Nearly three-quarters of the dentists surveyed reported they planned to step up educational efforts about the dangers of periodontal disease, particularly in view of the recently discovered links between gum disease and heart problems. According to Dr. Timothy Rose, president of the ADA, ''it's possible to have periodontal disease and not recognize the warning signs. That is why regular dental check-ups and periodontal examinations are important.''

According to Howard Glazer, president of the Academy of General Dentist and associate clinical professor at the Albert Einstein College of Dentistry, new techniques being considered in the dental industry included ''digitized x rays, laser techniques for painless drilling, osseointegrated implants to replace bridges and other nonpermanent artificial teeth, and synthetic tooth enamel.''

Other advances in research were predicted in the development of new procedures and materials, such as techniques used to perform tooth implants and substances used for bonding and repairing teeth.

Further Reading

American Dental Association. ''Dental Assisting.'' Available from http://www.ada.org/prac/careers/fs-dass.html.

———. ''Dental Care Usage Rates Higher among Women; Race, Education, Income, and Age Also Studied.'' Available from http://www.ada.org/newsrel/9904/nr-02.html.

———. ''Dental Hygiene.'' Available from http://www.ada.org/prac/careers/fs-dhyg.html.

———. ''Dentists View Gum Disease as Primary Oral Health Issue; Survey Also Reveals Patients Show Little Concern.'' Available from http://www.ada.org/newsrel/9812/nr-01.html.

———. ''Fact Sheet—Dental Hygiene Today.'' 1997. Available from http://www.ada.org/pra/carers/fs-dhyd.html.

———. ''Fact Sheet—Dentistry Today.'' 1997. Available from http://www.ada.org/pra/careers/fs-dent.html.

———. ''Fraud/Abuse.'' 1997. Available from http://www.ada.org/washrpt/970218/wr-04.html.

———. ''Frequently Asked Questions.'' Available from http://www.ada.org/p&s/sc/sc-faq.html.

Book, Ester Wachs. ''Mouth Makeovers.'' *Forbes,* 25 March 1996.

Callahan, Dan. ''Managed Dental Care: Delta Dental's Minnesota Program.'' *Compensation & Benefits Management,* Winter 1995.

Mogelonsky, Marcia. ''Dentists Are Forever.'' *American Demographics,* August 1996.

Peterson, Carolyn. ''Dental Plan Industry Showing Fluctuations.'' *Managed Healthcare,* July 1995.

U.S. Bureau of the Census. *Statistical Abstract of the United States, 1996.* Washington, DC: GPO, 1996.

U.S. Department of Labor. Bureau of Labor Statistics. *Occupational Outlook Handbook,* 1998-99 ed. Washington, DC: GPO, 1998. Available from http://stats.bls.gov/ocohome.htm.

SIC 8031

OFFICES AND CLINICS OF DOCTORS OF OSTEOPATHY

This industry consists of offices and clinics of licensed doctors of osteopathic medicine (D.O.) and engaged in the practice of general or specialized osteopathic medicine and surgery. Establishments operating as clinics of osteopathic physicians are included in this industry. Like medical doctors, doctors of osteopathic medicine are complete physicians with at least four years of medical school training; however, they differ from medical doctors by focusing on structural derangement, especially that of the spinal cord, as the chief cause of disease.

NAICS CODE(S)

621111 (Offices of Physicians (except Mental Health Specialists))

621112 (Offices of Physicians, Mental Health Specialists)

According to the American Osteopathic Association (AOA), in 1998 there were 44,000 doctors of osteopathy (DOs) in the United States, making up about 5.5 percent of all physicians in the United States. Of these doctors, nearly 60 percent practice in the primary care fields. Although DOs represent less than 6 percent of all physicians, they account for 15 percent of all physicians practicing in rural areas with populations of 2,500 or less. Their fields of specialty include surgery, obstetrics and gynecology, pediatrics, psychiatry and neurology, and internal medicine.

This branch of medicine has grown considerably since 1970, when there were just over 14,300 DOs practicing in the United States. Ten years later, that number had jumped to 18,800, and by 1990 the number of osteopathic doctors practicing had climbed to 30,000, with only 2 percent of those DOs working in hospitals and another 2 percent teaching. By 1998, the total number of DOs had grown to 44,000 and is expected to top 45,000 by the year 2000. The AOA estimates that DOs receive some 100 million patient visits annually. The greatest demand in the future for DOs will be in rural and suburban areas. Employment is expected to grow faster than average, with the best prospects being in primary care fields such as family practice, geriatrics, and preventive care specialist.

While exact figures on the revenues in osteopathy as a whole are not available, doctors of osteopathic medicine in private or group practice earned annual salaries of roughly $85,000 to $150,000 in the late 1990s, depending on whether they were general practitioners or specialists. Beginning osteopathic physicians who practice in Veterans Hospitals earn an average of $47,500 a year.

There has been a sharp jump in the number of students pursuing studies in osteopathic medicine, according to the AOA: enrollment increased nearly 41 percent between 1990 and 1998. The National Center for Health Statistics projected that the 19 U.S. colleges of osteopathic medicine would graduate nearly 2,000 DOs in the year 2000. The 1980s and 1990s have also seen a sharp jump in the number of minority and female students enrolling in programs of osteopathic study. Between 1980 and 1996, minority students and female students in osteopathic programs increased 15 percent and 17 percent, respectively.

In 1996 there were more than 500 approved osteopathic sites, offering more than 3,800 residency programs. There were also more than 200 osteopathic health care systems in the United States, and that number was expected to grow.

In 1995 three out of four DOs practiced in twelve states, each state being one with osteopathic schools and hospitals. Michigan had the greatest number of DOs, followed by Pennsylvania, Ohio, Florida, New Jersey, and Texas.

Overseas, American doctors of osteopathic medicine have operated clinics and trained staff but typically have not set up private practices for themselves, as salaries are not as high as those in the United States. The United States is the only country in the world that has osteopathic medicine integrated with a physician's degree. In other countries, practitioners generally earn certification after one to two years of schooling and hold less prestige than their American counterparts.

In 1998, about 60 percent of all DOs were involved in primary care, providing about 9 percent of all primary care available in the United States; primary care physicians, including both family and general practitioners, are the first to see a patient. More importantly for this branch of medicine, DOs' services account for 15 percent of primary care in rural areas, where primary care physicians have been in increasing demand since the 1980s, when more and more physicians (MDs and DOs) either went into specialized medicine or preferred to work in the cities. Given this expanding niche in the health care market, doctors of osteopathic medicine are expected to become more recognized and earn higher revenues in the future.

Further Reading

American Osteopathic Association. ''National Facts and Future Trends.'' Available from http://www.aoa-net.org/government/relations/facts.htm

———. ''Osteopathic Medicine.'' Available from http://www.am-osteo-assn.org/Consumers/omed.htm

———. ''Unity Summit II.'' Available from http://www.aoa-net.org/executive/unitycampaign/summit2.htm

Lidz, Richard and Linda Perrin, eds. ''Osteopathic Physician.'' *Career Information Center.* 6th ed. Vol. 7. New York: Macmillan Library Reference, 1996.

''Osteopathic Health care System.'' American Osteopathic Health care Assn. Web page. Available from http://www.aoha.org/ostins.htm.

SIC 8041

OFFICES AND CLINICS OF CHIROPRACTORS

This category includes establishments of licensed practitioners having the degree of Doctor of Chiropractic and engaged in the practice of chiropractic medicine. Operations serving as clinics of chiropractors are also covered in this industry.

NAICS Code(s)

621310 (Offices of Chiropractors)

Industry Snapshot

The central element of chiropractic is the belief of practitioners that the nervous system holds the key to maintenance of a healthy balance in the body. Practitioners believe that their manipulations of the spine can prevent disease and promote well-being. Doctors of chiropractic (DCs) believe that a patient's susceptibility to disease increases when homeostasis, or a healthy balance, in the body is disrupted by the misalignment of vertebrae. Chiropractors use gentle manual pressure to correct such misalignments, or subluxations. Chiropractors also use muscle massage and ultrasound stimulation of deep tissue.

Although doctors of medicine, as represented by the American Medical Association, long have suggested that chiropractic is something that falls far short of medicine, in recent years, anti-chiropractic rhetoric from the AMA has diminished significantly. Indeed, some medical doctors today grudgingly acknowledge that there definitely is a place for chiropractic, particularly in the treatment of chronic back and neck pain and headaches. For their part, most chiropractors unhesitatingly refer certain patients to medical doctors if they feel the latter are best equipped to deal with those patients' ailments.

Although the Federation of Chiropractic Licensing Boards (FCLB) reported in 1998 that there were nearly 80,000 active chiropractic licenses in the United States, the American Chiropractic Association (ACA) estimated that the real number of practicing doctors of chiropractic (DCs) was probably somewhere between 55,000 and 70,000. FCLB maintains data on the total number of DC licenses granted by all state licensing boards in the United States, but some DCs operate in more than one state and need to carry multiple licenses. Others may maintain their licenses even though they are not in active practice. Some of the DCs not currently in active practice on their own may teach, conduct research for chiropractic colleges, or work in hospitals. According to the ACA, the average annual gross income of a practicing DC in 1999 was $230,000, of which $130,000 was required on average for operating expenses.

Based on a poll conducted by the Gallup organization in the early 1990s, ACA estimates that about 10 percent of the adult American population visits a chiropractor every year. Assuming that this figure has remained relatively static, that would mean that 27 million to 28 million Americans use chiropractic services each year.

Organization and Structure

Chiropractors must be licensed before setting up practices. Regulations differ regionally, but all 50 states grant licenses to doctors of chiropractic who have passed state-mandated medical exams and educational requirements. Generally, state licensing boards require that doctors of chiropractic complete a four-year course in chiropractic after two years of college, while others call for a bachelor's degree.

Chiropractors must have a license to practice and can only practice in the states where they have licenses. According to the *Occupational Outlook Handbook,* all states recognize chiropractors trained by colleges accredited by the Council on Chiropractic Education. The majority of State licensing boards require at least two years of undergraduate college education, followed by the four-year training course at a chiropractic college, while others require a bachelor's degree.

Most states accept part or all of the National Board of Chiropractic Examiners three-part test. Some states ask chiropractors to take an additional basic science proficiency exam. Those who complete a chiropractic education are awarded the degree of Doctor of Chiropractic (D.C.). Almost all States require chiropractors to complete a specific number of hours of continuing education every year to keep their licenses current. Some chiropractic associations provide courses to obtain specialty certification, called ''diplomate'' certification. Areas of specialty include: orthopedics, sports injuries, nutrition, radiology, thermography, neurology, internal disorders, and occupational and industrial health.

About 70 percent of licensed chiropractors open solo private practices. Some join established practices on a salary basis to earn enough money to open their own clinics. Although many chiropractors are self-employed, most work about a 40-hour work week and vary schedules to accommodate patients' needs. Chiropractors on average employ about three office staff and their salaries constitute a practitioner's largest operating expense. The geographical location ratios of chiropractors are imbalanced, since many open their practices near chiropractic colleges.

Financial Structure. Average gross revenue for chiropractors totaled about $230,000 in 1999, down about 2 percent from 1990. Chiropractors had about 132 patient visits per week in 1999, up from 128 per week in 1990, and received 40 percent of their payments from private insurance; 29 percent from cash; 15 percent from worker's compensation (the lowest level since 1987); eight percent from Medicare; seven percent from personal injury, auto, no-fault insurance; and one percent from Medicaid.

According to the American Chiropractic Association, chiropractors had a median annual income of $86,000 after expenses in 1999. The variance from the lowest 10 percent (median net income $28,000) varied greatly from the highest 10 percent (median net income $150,000). A chiropractor's income may be influenced by a number of factors, including experience, characteristics, qualifications, and geographic location.

BACKGROUND AND DEVELOPMENT

The chiropractic method was first developed in America in 1895 by Daniel David Palmer, a teacher, spiritualist, and magnetic healer from Davenport, Iowa. Magnetic healing was based on a theory by Austrian physician Anton Mesmer. Mesmer believed that the body had magnetic poles that facilitated a natural flow of fluid. Any obstacle that interrupted this flow resulted in sickness. Healing could thus be obtained by massaging the body's poles to restore this natural flow.

In search of an alternative to traditional medicine, Palmer made his first discovery by manipulating the spine of Harvey Lillard, a deaf janitor who worked in his Davenport office building. Palmer had learned that Lillard had become deaf upon wrenching his back. An examination later demonstrated that Lillard's vertebra had moved. By ''racking his spine into position'' Palmer was able to eventually restore Lillard's hearing. It was from this ''first adjustment'' in 1895 that the field of chiropractic medicine was born.

Palmer, however, was soon dismissed as a heretic and a charlatan for his belief in healing through magnetism and spinal manipulation. According to J. Stuart Moore in *Chiropractic in America,* ''Palmer was determined that his new brainchild, chiropractic, would acquire the scientific respectability that his earlier career in spiritualism and magnetic healing had lacked.''

Palmer based chiropractic on the theory that a misaligned spine (subluxation) caused illness. By readjusting the spine and thus restoring full nervous system function, all illness could be prevented and or cured. By 1897, Palmer had founded the Palmer Infirmary and Chiropractic Institute (the Palmer School of Chiropractic) in Davenport. Palmer in 1910 became affiliated with the Pacific College of Chiropractic in Portland, Oregon. It was there that he wrote the textbook and primer for beginning chiropractors, *The Chiropractor's Adjuster: A Textbook of the Science, Art, and Philosophy of Chiropractic for Students and Practitioners.* His son, Bartlett Joshua (B.J.), became a practitioner. B.J. Palmer founded the first chiropractic association and helped establish chiropractic colleges nationwide. Early practitioners of chiropractic were defiant in the face of skepticism from the established medical community.

Theories of chiropractors often put them in direct conflict with medical doctors. The practice of chiropractic was often entwined in mysticism and unorthodox religious beliefs during the profession's early development. Some chiropractors were even jailed for practicing 'medicine' without a license.

Other practitioners would eventually refine spinal adjustments and use X-rays to make better diagnoses. But the development of the industry was often clouded. Chiropractors of the latter twentieth century come from a wide range of beliefs and theories and many do not base their practices on single chiropractic doctrine. For example, chiropractors who use chiropractic with other theories like iridology, hair analysis, and colonic irrigation, are termed ''mixers,'' and represented by the American Chiropractic Association. ''Straights,'' represented by the International Chiropractic Association, base their practices solely on correcting subluxation in the tradition of Palmer. Then there are chiropractors who believe in manipulating a certain area of vertebrae (National Upper Cervical Chiropractic Association) instead of merely readjusting the spine at the site of pain.

By the mid-1990s, chiropractors followed a standard routine to diagnose and determine the treatment necessary. The data includes: the patient's medical history; results of physical, neurological, and orthopedic exams; posture and spine analysis; and sometimes X rays and other laboratory tests. Chiropractic treatment had expanded so much that some practitioners specialized in select areas, such as sports injuries, neurology, orthopedics, nutrition, internal disorders, and diagnostic imaging.

Chiropractors of any kind, however, encountered fierce resistance to the profession in America throughout the mid-1990s. While chiropractic enjoyed increased recognition in many regions of the world at this time, the American Medical Association was adamant in its opposition to the practice. Nonetheless, chiropractic care was included under Medicare coverage in 1973, while in 1974 Mississippi became the last state to establish a review board for licensing chiropractors.

Growth of Chiropractic. Current statistical surveys, including a Gallup poll commissioned by the American Chiropractic Association, indicate that roughly 10 percent of adult Americans visit chiropractors annually. The profession is gaining in popularity. With just 30 percent of back care patients using chiropractic treatment, the potential for growth is enormous. Chiropractors in the 1990s are the third largest medical profession behind dentists and medical doctors. Although chiropractors cannot administer or prescribe drugs or perform surgery, they may counsel patients about nutrition, exercise, and stress management.

One avenue that the chiropractic profession has pursued to secure acceptance in the medical community has been via the legal system. In 1976 a lawsuit was filed by four chiropractors against the American Medical Association (AMA) for anti-trust violations. The chiropractors in *Wilk v. AMA* alleged that the AMA and other health providers conspired to put them out of business. The AMA said it was trying to protect patients from methods they saw as ''unscientific and deleterious,'' reported the *University of California Wellness Letter.* In the 1960s, the AMA had told its members that it was unethical to associate with chiropractors.

The AMA dropped its ethical ban in 1980 after modifying it years earlier. In 1981, charges were dismissed against all defendants, but the federal appellate court ordered a new trial. In 1987 the Federal Court of Appeals ruled in favor of the chiropractors by issuing a permanent injunction against the AMA, the American College of Surgeons, and the American College of Radiology that prevented them from denying chiropractors entry to labs and hospitals and access to insurance reimbursement. The court dismissed charges against several other defendants.

Another lawsuit ensued in December of 1993, when three New York chiropractors again sued the AMA, along with state and county medical societies, four national insurance trade groups, and a dozen insurers and managed care plans. In this suit, the plaintiffs claimed that ''physicians and insurers have conspired to keep them from taking part in New York managed care panels,'' and that many of the defendant plans do not cover chiropractic services, according to *American Medical News.* The AMA intended to file a request to have the case dismissed for lack of merit in 1994. According to a study in 1995, nearly half of all HMOs covered chiropractic treatments. In June of 1995, the AMA and two other medical societies were dismissed as defendants in the case, but the plaintiffs continued the suit against the remaining defendants.

In a report from *The Back Letter* in 1995, many hospitals began giving clinical privileges to chiropractors across the country. Hospitals recognized chiropractic treatment as more cost-effective than surgery in some cases, and the chiropractors would provide another source of revenue. The number of chiropractors reporting to chiropractic departments in hospitals doubled from 1993 to 1995, according to the American Chiropractic Association.

Current Conditions

Recent studies have suggested that chiropractic care may even be more effective for back and neck pain than regular medical care. Treating back pain is estimated to cost from $8 billion to $24 billion annually in the United States. A report by the RAND Corporation found that chiropractic care is ''effective in treating acute back pain when no serious neurological symptoms are present,'' and that patients with low-back pain did better with chiropractic treatment, often at less cost than medical treatment. The *British Medical Journal* found that ''spinal manipulation was more effective for relieving low-back aches for up to three years after diagnosis.'' However, those with nerve disorders, sciatica and chronic low back pain did not benefit as much from chiropractic treatment.

Industry Reform and Renewal. According to Robin Kamen in *Crain's New York Business,* chiropractors are increasingly turning to modern marketing techniques to maintain their businesses, using advertising and sales promotional literature to educate the public about the benefits of chiropractic.

A renewed interest in alternative medicine has contributed to an increasing public interest in chiropractic theory. Slowly, medical doctors are discovering they can benefit from referring their patients to chiropractors because they request ''natural treatment'' and non-invasive techniques. Chiropractors in turn, refer patients who need medical treatment they cannot provide.

However, chiropractors nationwide are finding that they are losing patients because their insurance or worker's compensation either restricts visits to chiropractors or does not cover chiropractic altogether. Medicare does cover some services but is limited. Trade and state chiropractic associations in Oregon, New York, and Colorado, have been conducting extensive lobbying efforts to garner more extensive insurance benefits for chiropractic patients, although without much success. For example, New York lawmakers in 1993 approved a bill requiring unlimited insurance coverage for chiropractic clients, but withdrew the legislation after Governor Mario Cuomo threatened to veto it.

Efforts also are underway to provide cost-containment strategies to reduce chiropractic costs, as reported in *Risk Management.* Excessive treatment, at times because of criminal motives, has been cited as a key factor in the price of chiropractic care. *Risk Management* magazine cited a study by National Medical Audit, Inc., where a four-part chiropractic review program was used and helped reduce chiropractic costs by 25 percent. The American Chiropractic Association in 1992 issued guidelines to set parameters on the frequency and duration of care and ''more appropriate and realistic reimbursement systems,'' reported *National Underwriter Life & Health.*

Chiropractors won an important victory in November 1999 when President Bill Clinton signed into law legislation that will make chiropractic care more accessible to U.S. veterans. The Veterans Millennium Health Care Act (H.R. 2116) requires the Veterans Administration to develop a policy covering the use of chiropractic treatment within the VA's health care system. Successfully lobbying for the chiropractic provision were the ACA and the Association of Chiropractic Colleges. The legislation gave the VA 120 days to develop a chiropractic care policy.

Chiropractors and other alternative health care service providers (nurses, optometrists, podiatrists, midwives, acupuncturists) are fighting, via political action committees and other means, to establish their piece of the future health care establishment. These groups hope that health care reform legislation in the mid-1990s will enable them to gain access to more patients who would receive expanded health coverage that would include ''nontraditional'' medical treatments.

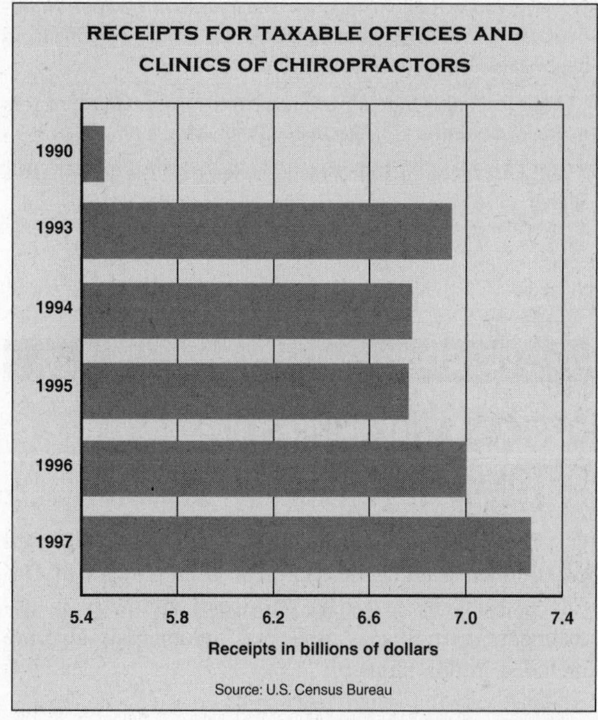

WORKFORCE

The job outlook appeared very favorable for chiropractors in the late 1990s. The number of chiropractic graduates increased ''fourfold since the early 1970s,'' according to *U.S. Occupational Outlook Handbook.* In 1999, between 55,000 and 70,000 chiropractors practiced in the United States, according to the American Chiropractic Association. Employment growth will depend on the need to replace retired chiropractors, the continued popularity of the practice, and the ability of patients to pay for services under health insurance plans. In addition, as the population of elderly people increases, so will the need for treatment of mechanical and structural difficulties. The growth of chiropractors is expected to accelerate faster than the average for all occupations through 2005.

FURTHER READING

American Chiropractic Association. ''Frequently Asked Questions.'' Available from http://www.amerchiro.org/about_chiro/faq.html.

———. ''New Law Makes Chiropractic More Accessible to Veterans.'' Available from http://www.amerchiro.org/media/120899.html

———. ''What Is Chiropractic?'' Available from http://www.amerchiro.org/about_chiro/index.html.

U.S. Bureau of Labor Statistics. *Occupational Outlook Handbook 1996-1997.* Washington, DC: GPO, 1996. Available from http://stats.bls.gov/oco/ocos071.htm.

"U.S. Hospitals Granting Clinical Privileges to Chiropractors in Record Numbers." *The Back Letter,* May 1995.

"Will Utilization of Chiropractic Increase?" *The Back Letter,* March 1996.

SIC 8042

OFFICES AND CLINICS OF OPTOMETRISTS

This category covers establishments of licensed practitioners having the degree of O.D. (Doctor of Optometry) and engaged in the practice of optometry. Establishments operating as clinics of optometrists also are included in this industry.

NAICS Code(s)

621320 (Offices of Optometrists)

Industry Snapshot

According to the Association of Schools and Colleges of Optometry (ASCO), there were nearly 30,000 full-time equivalent practicing doctors of optometry in the United States during the late 1990s. These optometrists served in 7,084 communities across the country and in more than 4,300 of those communities were the only primary eye-care providers. Doctors of optometry examine, diagnose, and treat a variety of diseases and disorders of the vision system, the eye, and associated structures. Services rendered by optometrists include the prescription of glasses and contact lenses, rehabilitation of the visually impaired, and the diagnosis and treatment of ocular disease. According to ASCO data, the mean net income for optometrists in the late 1990s was $88,690.

Figures supplied by the American Optometric Association indicated that approximately $17.5 billion was spent in 1995 on vision care and prescription eyewear. That figure did not include costs for eye surgery or treatment for eye injuries and disease. ASCO statistics showed that in 1995 some 86 million Americans had their eyes examined and more than half of all Americans wore either glasses or contact lenses.

Organization and Structure

Sixty-eight percent of optometrists worked out of their own clinics or offices and were self-employed. They, unlike ophthalmologists, are not medical doctors. Optometrists examine the eyes to evaluate eye health and visual acuity and to diagnose eye diseases and eye conditions. Optometrists are not qualified to perform eye surgery, but they can prescribe corrective treatment: glasses, contact lenses, vision therapy, and low-vision aids. As of June 1996, 48 states had passed legislation that authorized optometrists to use drugs to treat diseases of the eye, allowing them to compete with ophthalmologists who have traditionally performed this service. Industry experts predicted that all doctors of optometry (ODs) would soon be given this right. Optometrists are also lobbying for the right to perform photorefractive keratectomies. Most states require that a licensed doctor perform the surgery, but Idaho allows optometrists to do the procedure.

Some optometrists held more than one job or worked out of more than one office or clinic. Commercial vision-care centers serve as another option for optometrists establishing their practices. According to the *Occupational Outlook Handbook,* optometrists were increasingly buying franchises from large retail optical chains and operating them as independent businesses. Younger optometrists also tended to join partners or form group practices. The *Handbook* noted that working optometrists also earned salaries as employees of health maintenance organizations (HMOs), health centers and eye clinics, public and private health agencies, insurance companies, or schools of optometry. The majority of optometric practitioners worked full time.

Like others in the health care profession, some optometrists worked in a general practice, while others chose to specialize. Some areas of specialty in the field of optometry include geriatrics, contact lenses, low-vision services, occupational vision, pediatrics, sports vision, and vision therapy. Still other doctors of optometry chose to devote their careers to teaching or scientific research.

All 50 states and the District of Columbia require optometrists to be licensed upon obtaining a doctor of optometry degree from an accredited school or college. Doctors of Optometry must either pass a state board examination or the National Board of Examiners in Optometry exam. There is some reciprocity between states concerning licenses; 46 states, however, require that optometrists complete a specified number of continuing education hours to renew their licenses.

Training consists of a four-year undergraduate degree and two-to-three years of pre-optometric study at an accredited school. As of the late 1990s, there were 17 colleges of optometry in the United States and Puerto Rico accredited by the Council on Optometric Education of the American Optometric Association. Those applying to an optometric program must take the Optometry Admission Test, which measures academic ability and scientific comprehension. Competition to gain admittance to these schools is fierce.

Optometrists wishing to teach or do research may study for Master's or Ph.D. degrees in visual science, physiological optics, neurophysiology, public health, health administration, health information and communication, or health education. One-year postgraduate clinical residency programs are available for optometrists who wish to specialize in family practice optometry, pediatric optometry, geriatric optometry, vision therapy, contact lenses, hospital based optometry, primary care optometry, or ocular disease.

BACKGROUND AND DEVELOPMENT

The practice of optometry began with the invention and subsequent refinement of eyeglasses in the early nineteenth century. Optometry guilds were formed at this time, and the practice eventually was regulated under statutory law. Jewelers were actually some of the first professionals to use eye charts and sell glasses to the public.

The industry in the United States expanded during the Civil War when the government purchased large quantities of binoculars and microscopes for the war effort. Eyeglasses became plentiful and, by the end of the nineteenth century, schools were teaching the science of optics, often in combination with instruction in watch repair.

Door-to-door peddlers, jewelers, and optometrists all sold eyeglasses in the late 1800s. At the beginning of the twentieth century, however, physicians conducted most of the eye examinations. "Refracting opticians," who provided the same service, later became known as the present-day optometrists. In some fairly fundamental ways, optometry practices have operated the same way for decades. That is, clients still visit optometry offices to secure eyeglass prescriptions, which are sent to an optical laboratory. The lab makes the glasses according to specifications and sends the frames to the officiating optometrist, who subsequently fits them to the client.

In the late 1960s, however, mass marketing of optical products and services changed some optometry practices. Vision-care chain stores emerged, but many states prohibited doctors from working in them. Some chain stores such as Sears and Kmart circumvented these restrictions by leasing space to optometrists, who worked independently but were able to lease space at below market rates. Doctors often profited from discounted rent and equipment. This partnership enabled chain stores to advertise that they provided full-service vision care at their facilities.

Competitive Structure. The advent of vision-care chain stores contributed to a loss of market share for private doctors of optometry. Private practitioners sell their businesses on the quality care and services they provide and emphasize personal service and attention. Often this is communicated by word of mouth and not through the aggressive marketing techniques that chain stores use. According to the *Journal of Commercial Lending,* "Repeated surveys have also shown that people feel they get a 'better' examination from a private OD compared with one received in a 'commercial environment.'"

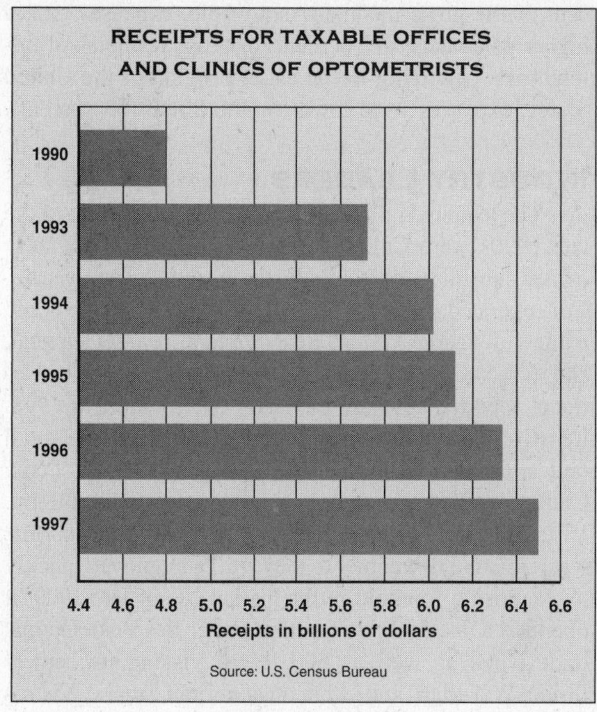

The *Journal* also cited a study conducted by Robert R. Nathan Associates, Inc., a Washington, D.C.-area private economics consulting firm that found that "vision problems other than routine nearsightedness were detected almost twice as frequently by noncommercial ODs than commercial ODs." Optometrists in the study also spent an average of 30 minutes per exam compared to their commercial counterparts, who spent an average of 15 minutes in examining a patient.

Vision-care chain stores have resorted to coupons and other special deals to attract customers. Some also promoted their quick turnaround time in filling eyeglass and contact lens prescriptions. Private practitioners also began to reduce the waiting time for glasses and contacts, in an effort to remain competitive. They also expanded their private practices to include lab services, which enabled them to fill prescriptions in a shorter time.

Financial Structure. Overhead costs for maintaining an optometric practice increased since the mid-1980s. According to the "State of the Profession 1996" in *Optometric Economics,* the ratio of net income to gross income declined. Expenses for staff totaled 14.7 percent of gross income, while total laboratory expenses made up 28.9 percent. Other costs included rent and utilities (6.6 percent), contributions to retirement plans (1.7 percent), and miscellaneous office expenses (15.9 percent). The average net percentage for a practitioner was only 32.2 percent of the gross income. As a whole, expenses took a higher percentage (77 percent) of gross revenues of optometrists practicing in the eastern region of the United States; expenses were lowest in the South (63 percent).

Industry Leaders

The leading U.S. vision-care services chains as of the late 1990s were Cole National; LensCrafters, a wholly owned subsidiary of Italy's Luxottica; and Vista Eyecare. Cole operated some 2,800 retail locations under the brand names of Pearle Vision, Sears Optical, Target Optical, and B.J.'s Optical. With 13,100 employees, Cole National reported revenue of nearly $1.1 billion in 1998. LensCrafters, as of March 31, 1999, operated 853 retail outlets throughout the United States and Canada. LensCrafters' 1998 revenue was estimated at $1.1 billion. Vista Eyecare, headquartered in Lawrenceville, Georgia, was a relative newcomer to the field, but it moved quickly to establish a foothold in the market. As of late 1999, it operated some 300 retail outlets under the Vista Optical trade name as well as 600 leased vision-care centers inside Wal-Mart and other major retail stores. Vista's 1998 revenue topped $245 million.

Workforce

Optometrists earned an average of about $27,000 in their first full year of practice in 1984. By the mid-1990s, the mean net income for optometrists had risen to almost $89,000. Optometrists who were self-employed earned an average of $95,707 in 1994. That same year female ODs reported a median net income of $59,500, while male ODs reported $83,500. This discrepancy was partly due to the length of time in the field, but even accounting for that, females, in general, earned 16 percent less than males. The *Occupational Outlook Handbook,* however, noted that salaries were also dependent upon specialization and location of the practice.

Increasingly, more optometrists joined HMOs and managed-care organizations. In 1996 more than two-thirds of optometrists were providers for some managed-care program. Medicare, too, began to cover examinations, treatment of eye diseases, and postoperative eye care services provided by optometrists to cataract surgery patients.

The American Optometric Association (AOA) was the largest trade association in the industry, representing more than 32,000 optometrists, students of optometry, and optometric technicians in the United States. Founded in 1898, the association aimed to make available and improve the quality of eye and vision care for all. The group focused on helping their members achieve the highest standards of efficiency and patient care. It also represented the industry to government and other health care organizations.

Future Expectations. As the AOA pointed out, 54 percent (145 million people) of all Americans needed prescription eyewear. Employment of optometrists was expected to grow about as fast as the average for all occupations through the year 2005 in response to the vision-care needs of a growing and aging population. By the year 2000, estimates suggested that there would be 32,000 optometrists in the United States (2,000 more than in 1998). The maturing of the baby-boom generation, together with rapid growth in the oldest age group would drive this growth. As baby boomers reached the age of 45 they would be more likely to visit optometrists and ophthalmologists because of the onset of vision problems in middle age. The demand for optometric services would also increase because of growth in the oldest age group, with their increased likelihood of cataracts, glaucoma, diabetes, and hypertension. Employment of optometrists would also grow due to greater recognition of the importance of vision care, rising personal incomes, and growth in employee vision-care plans.

Employment of optometrists would grow more rapidly were it not for anticipated productivity gains that will allow each optometrist to see more patients. These gains would result from greater use of optometric assistants and other support personnel, and the introduction of new equipment and procedures.

Replacement needs were low. In this occupation, replacement needs arose almost entirely from retirements. Optometrists generally remained in practice until they retired; few transferred to other occupations.

Further Reading

Association of Schools and Colleges of Optometry. ''What Is a Doctor of Optometry?'' Available from http://home.opted.org/asco/faq2.html.

Bennett, Irving, Richard Edlow, and Farrell Aron. ''State of the Profession 1996.'' *Optometric Economics,* Winter 1996.

''Facts and Figures About . . .'' Media Information Kit. American Optometric Association, 1996.

''LCA-Vision and Cole National to Make Available Laser Vision Correction to 50 Million Members of Cole Managed Vision.'' *Business Wire,* 12 July 1999.

''Luxottica Group Completes Purchase of Bausch & Lomb's Sunglass Business.'' *Business Wire,* 28 June 1999.

U.S. Department of Commerce. Bureau of the Census. *Statistical Abstract of the United States.* Washington, DC: GPO, 1995.

U.S. Department of Labor. Bureau of Labor Statistics. *Occupational Outlook Handbook,* 1998-99 ed. Washington, DC: GPO, 1998. Available from http://stats.bls.gov/ocohome.htm.

Wandycz, Katarzyna. ''Seeing-Eye Ads.'' *Forbes,* 17 June 1996.

SIC 8043

OFFICES AND CLINICS OF PODIATRISTS

This category pertains to establishments of licensed practitioners having the degree of D.P. (Doctor of Podiatry) and engaged in the practice of podiatry. Establishments operating as clinics of podiatrists are included in this industry.

NAICS CODE(S)

621391 (Offices of Podiatrists)

The podiatry industry is gaining increasing public recognition as a health profession. Podiatrists work at private or group practices, health maintenance organizations (HMOs), hospitals, public health services and departments, and podiatric schools of medicine. The majority of podiatrists work in their own private practices and set their hours of business accordingly.

Approximately 14,000 podiatrists practiced in the United States in 1997, up from 11,000 in 1996. These doctors averaged a 42.5-hour workweek, primarily occupied with patient visitation. Their income ranged from $56,000 for most inexperienced, to $138,000 for experienced doctors with over 30 years of practice. While the majority of podiatrists work in major metropolitan areas, they are not evenly distributed geographically. Since the 1970s the northeastern United States has been the site of the highest concentration of podiatrists. Many podiatrists set up practices near the seven colleges of podiatric medicine—in California, Florida, Illinois, Iowa, New York, Pennsylvania, and Ohio. There are also two podiatric hospitals—in Pittsburgh and San Francisco. The south and southwestern portions of the United States and nonurban areas have fewer podiatrists. Less than 200 podiatrists practice in Washington State, where doctors report a saturated market.

The U.S. Bureau of Labor Statistics (BLS) maintains that podiatry is a well-paid profession, with projected growth at a par with the average growth rate for all occupations through the year 2006. In 1997 the American Podiatric Medical Association (APMA) estimated that 5 percent of the population visited podiatrists, and according to the California College of Podiatric Medicine, demand for podiatrists is projected to reach 80 million visits per year in the twenty-first century. BLS further advises that opportunities for this profession are most lucrative in group practices or within medical networks, as opposed to individual private practice.

Podiatry involves the study of movement and medical care of the foot and ankle. Doctors of podiatry diagnose and treat diseases and disorders of the foot, but they also can diagnose other maladies such as arthritis, diabetes, and heart disease because the foot is often the first part of the body to manifest the signs of serious illness. Orthopedists specialize in foot surgery, orthopedics, children's problems (podopediatrics), or foot problems of the elderly. The major focus of a podiatrist's practice, however, is the treatment of corns, bunions, calluses, ingrown toenails, and nail diseases, along with *palliative* care (to ease pain). Women of middle age comprise as much as 80 percent of some podiatrists' clientele, a situation attributed to the poor design of women's shoes.

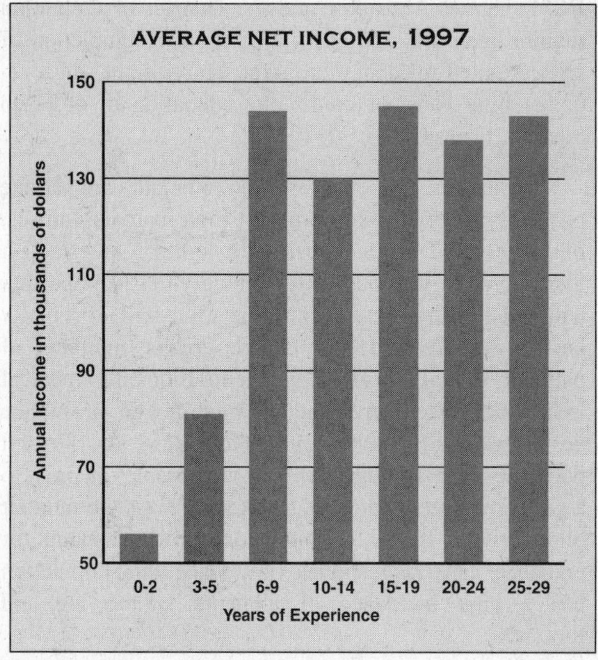

The industry has experienced steady growth in the number of trained podiatrists who establish practices. Younger podiatrists, though, saddled with college-aid debt, often elect to work in partnerships to earn enough money and experience to open their own practices.

To gain admission into one of the seven colleges of podiatric medicine, prospective students must first complete at least 3 years or 90 semester hours of college credit at an accredited undergraduate institution, according to the American Podiatric Medical Association. Over 90 percent of the students entering a college of podiatric medicine have bachelor's degrees. Applicants must take the Medical College Admissions Test (MCAT). Podiatrists must be licensed to practice podiatric medicine after earning a doctor of podiatric medicine (DPM) degree from an accredited college of podiatry. Training for the DPM degree requires study in the basic and clinical sciences—anatomy, chemistry, pathology, physiology, pharmacology—and inpatient care. Graduate study entails a residency of one to three years in length after the

DPM degree. All states and the District of Columbia require licensure, and another 32 require completion of an accredited residency program. Thirty-eight states require some form of continuing education in order to renew a license.

Podiatrists, like other alternative health care service providers such as chiropractors, optometrists, nurses, midwives, and acupuncturists are fighting to establish themselves in the medical community. They hope that national health care reform legislation will eventually become reality and will enable greater numbers of patients to gain access to ''nontraditional'' medical treatments. Medicare and private health insurance do not normally cover routine foot care. As a result podiatric care is dependent on disposable income to a greater degree than other medical care. As the number of elderly in the U.S. population grows, demand for podiatric care also should rise, since this population has a high incidence of ailments in the leg and foot area.

Managed care also has raised serious concerns within the profession. In early 1997 an investor-owned Florida company, Consolidated Health Corporation, purchased the Podiatry Hospital of Pittsburgh, one of only two such hospitals in the United States. The hospital, which has about 70 affiliated podiatrists, had seen dwindling admissions in the era of managed care. It was converted to for-profit status, and a private management firm was hired by Consolidated. Faced with such developments, in 1996 podiatrists organized the first national labor union for doctors, the First National Guild for Health Care Providers of the Lower Extremities, which will be affiliated with the AFL-CIO. Among the issues of concern to podiatrists is the change in podiatrist fee schedules associated with managed care, whereby only services are reimbursed, to the exclusion of supplies.

Further Reading

Freeman, Paul. ''Managed Care Keeps Podiatry Population Down. . . .'' *Puget Sound Business Journal,* 23 May 1997.

Japsen, Bruce. ''Florida Firm in Podiatry Via Deal.'' *Modern Healthcare,* 24 February 1997.

''News at Deadline Column.'' *Modern Healthcare,* 28 October 1996.

''The Rewards of Podiatric Medicine.'' California College of Podiatric Medicine, 2000. Available at http://www.ccpm.edu/About/rewards.html.

Schuler, Burton S., D.P.M. ''Podiatry.'' *Foot Care 4 U,* 1997. Available at http://www.footcare4u.com/podiatry.html.

U.S. Bureau of Labor Statistics. *Occupational Outlook Handbook,* 24 February 1999. Available from http://stats.bls.gov/.

SIC 8049

OFFICES AND CLINICS OF HEALTH PRACTITIONERS, NOT ELSEWHERE CLASSIFIED

This industry consists of establishments of health care practitioners engaged in the practice of health fields not elsewhere classified. Practitioners may or may not be licensed or certified, depending on the state in which they practice. Establishments operating as clinics of health practitioners, not elsewhere classified, are included in this industry. Specific health care practitioners included in this industry include: acupuncturists (except M.D.s), audiologists, Christian Science practitioners, dental hygienists, hypnotists, respiratory therapists, midwives, naturopaths, nurses (except home health service nurses), nutritionists, occupational therapists, paramedics, physical therapists, physician's assistants, psychiatric social workers, clinical psychologists, psychotherapists (except M.D.s), speech clinicians, and speech pathologists.

NAICS Code(s)

621330 (Offices of Mental Health Practitioners (except Physicians))

621340 (Offices of Physical, Occupational, and Speech Therapists and Audiologists)

621399 (Offices of All Other Miscellaneous Health Practitioners)

Industry Snapshot

The offices and clinics of health care providers in this industry are characterized by their contrast and competition with offices and clinics of medical doctors. While in America many sectors of this industry have not enjoyed the public acceptance given to medical doctors. As a whole this industry has become more accepted during the latter part of the twentieth century as a result of various social and economic factors.

This industry earns income from the tens of thousands of health providers in private practice who are either self-employed or employed through health maintenance organizations (HMOs).

Since the mid-1980s, the ''graying'' of America has helped to fuel the growth of offices and clinics of respiratory therapists, physical therapists, and nurses, with a substantial number employed by home health care services.

Organization and Structure

Offices and clinics in this industry belong to either hospitals, where the practitioners may be employed by the hospital or those that work independently of hospitals. Occupational and physical therapists, psychologists, and acupuncturists often work, to some extent, with hospitals. Occupational and physical therapists are frequently employed by general and rehabilitation hospitals, and many psychotherapists work at psychiatric hospitals treating the mentally ill.

Unlike the offices of medical doctors and dentists, establishments in this industry do not rely on payments made through insurance companies or government programs like Medicare and Medicaid as their main source of income. However, occupational and physical therapists receive the largest portion of their incomes from employee compensation plans. Practitioners in this industry use referral services, such as those of profession associations, as a tool to ensure a steady flow of self-funded patients.

BACKGROUND AND DEVELOPMENT

Common to the background of many of the professions represented by this industry, such as acupuncturists, is their long global history. Many of these practices, however, have gained acceptance in the United States only during the twentieth century. Another common feature of these professions has been their rapid growth since the 1970s, when ''natural'' and Eastern medicine gained popularity; at the same time, the rising costs of traditional health care spurred patients to seek new approaches to health care.

Acupuncturists. Acupuncture is a system of medicine that uses needles on nerve and ''energy'' points to cure disease and modify certain behaviors. Developed in ancient China, acupuncture was not widely practiced in America, outside Chinese communities, until the 1960s. Today acupuncture and other forms of Oriental medicine are among the fastest growing segments of health care in America. According to the National Acupuncture and Oriental Medicine Alliance, as of late 1999, thirty-eight states and the District of Columbia had recognized the practice of acupuncture, and legislation had been introduced in eight additional states. The number of licensed acupuncturists in the United States from 5,525 in 1992 to 10,512 in 1998. Nearly all full-time acupuncturists in the United States are self-employed. Others, mostly medical doctors, have been trained in acupuncture and use the technique mostly as a form of anesthesia.

Audiologists and Speech-language Pathologists. Audiologists work in the diagnosis and treatment of hearing problems; in addition, these practitioners work in public health, providing instruction and counseling for the hard of hearing. By 2005, a doctoral degree may be required to enter audiology practice. This sector of the health care industry has grown steadily since the 1970s, in part because of a maturing patient base and in part because of technological advances that allow increasingly effective treatment of patients with hearing difficulties.

Speech-language pathologists treat and counsel people with communication disorders caused from hearing loss, brain injury, learning disability, mental retardation, or emotional problems. These practitioners are mostly self-employed and work at rehabilitation hospitals and clinics and out of private offices. In 1993 the American Speech-Language-Hearing Association reported that nearly 58,000 speech-language pathologists were established in the United States. In 1992 it was estimated that nearly eight million Americans sought treatment from speech-language pathologists. Of those, more than three million were children undergoing therapy for speech impairments, primarily stuttering.

In 1997 there were about 87,000 speech-language pathologists and audiologists practicing in America. The median annual salary in 1997 for speech-language pathologists was $44,000 and $43,000 for audiologists. One half provided services in preschool, elementary, secondary schools or in colleges and universities; 10 percent worked in hospitals. Both of these fields are expected to grow because of the aging population and also federal laws that guarantee special education for all eligible children.

Christian Science Practitioners. These practitioners, in following the Christian Science faith, use spiritual healing to cure ailments. This form of healing, which relies on prayer and Bible reading, dates back to the start of the Christian Science religion, founded by Mary Baker Eddy in 1866. Throughout this profession's history, efforts have been made, mostly by governing bodies, to prohibit this form of health care; however, laws guaranteeing the right to religious practices have continually fought this opposition. Some states have passed laws specifically designed to protect the rights of this profession.

Nationally, this profession suffered negative publicity in the 1980s following several incidents where children died under the care of a Christian Science practitioner; in these cases, medical experts testified that the children would not have perished under the care of a medical doctor. These incidents were highlighted by legislation brought about in 1983 that drew the public's attention to spiritual healing. That year the federal government defined a parent's failure to provide medical care—which excludes spiritual healing—for a child as child neglect. Additionally, the government had the right to intervene if a parent's actions prohibited medical treatment. Consequently, the parents of children who died under the care of Christian Science practitioners faced criminal charges.

Most of these cases were dismissed on the basis of lack of due process, while another case was dismissed due to freedom of religion acts; other cases remain in the appeals system. In 1993, however, a landmark decision was made against the Christian Science Church itself that returned a $5.2 million wrongful death judgment to the biological father of a diabetic boy who died under a Christian Science practitioner's care. This decision was important to this industry as it placed the blame upon the practitioners and not the parents. Legal battles continue in this area, which involves issues ranging from children's rights to religious rights.

Dental Hygienists. Dental hygienists provide treatment and education for oral hygiene and prevention of gum disease. The offices and clinics of dental hygienists, independent from employment by a dentist, involve working for public health agencies, industrial plants, and independent dental clinics. In 1996 there were approximately 133,000 dental hygienists working in America, of which the majority worked for general dentists.

Hypnotists. The practice of putting a person into a trance, or sleep-like state, in order to influence their actions and behaviors, was long regarded as a form of trickery. Its origins are unclear, although the first reliable form of hypnotic induction was reported in the eighteenth century. Research continued during the nineteenth century and the hypnotic state came to be increasingly attributed to physiological and psychological factors. By 1893 the British Medical Association "officially recognized hypnotism in a report that found the hypnotic state to be real and of value in relieving pain and alleviating certain functional ailments. The report was not approved by the American Medical Association until 1958, and acceptance of it among medical doctors continues to be slow," noted the *New Age Encyclopedia.* Modern hypnosis is used for treating smoking, alcoholism, weight control, disorders related to stress, and many phobias.

According to the American Association for Professional Hypnotherapy, in 1997 nearly all of the 13,300 hypnotists practicing in America were self-employed, and a considerable number were licensed in other health fields, such as psychotherapy or medicine; hypnotherapy has been developing as a treatment used in conjunction with more traditional health practices. However, even when hypnosis is used by a medical doctor, it is rarely covered by insurance; this factor has hindered the growth of this profession within the medical community.

Midwives. Midwifery, the profession providing care and assistance for delivering babies, has a long history. The dominance of obstetrics in America, however, has significantly diminished this profession from the role it enjoyed earlier in the country's history. However, the practice enjoyed something of a revival in the late 1980s and 1990s. Midwifes delivered 3.7 percent of all births in 1989, but eight years later in 1997 that figure had nearly double to 7 percent. As of 1999, the American College of Nurse-Midwives reported its membership had topped 6,700, of whom about 5,700 were in clinical practice. Of these, less than 500 were self-employed, while the majority of midwifes worked at birth centers or clinics or as nurses to medical doctors.

Historically, midwives were not licensed to use instruments, such as forceps, and they had to call upon a medical doctor if there were any complications with a birth. Despite these restrictions, prior to the seventeenth century midwifery was a lucrative profession for women. In Europe during the seventeenth century, a male-dominated medical profession sought to include childbirth as part of their practice. Since then, the scientific advances available to women through the established medical profession has kept pregnant women away from the natural methods of childbirth usually employed by a midwife.

In colonial America, midwifery was still a prosperous profession and remained so until the expansion of medical schools and specialties in the nineteenth century, and the consequent development of the field of obstetrics. It was also during this time that European immigration to America had a negative impact on the midwives' profession. In Europe, midwives usually belonged to the middle classes, and since the Europeans who immigrated to America belonged mostly to the lower classes, midwives were left behind. According to the 1910 census, after a wave of European immigration, 50 percent of births in America were carried out by midwives, a precipitous drop from an estimated 90 percent during colonial times.

Midwifery in America was to see another major setback during the 1920s and 1930s, as medical procedures for childbirth in hospitals improved dramatically, as did medical training in the field of obstetrics. It was also during this time that some states decided to prohibit the practice of midwifery, while many other states enforced strict supervision. Many historians (of medicine and women's studies) have explained this change from midwifery to obstetrics as a male takeover of the profession of assisting childbirth.

Midwives practicing in America cared for less than 10 percent of childbirths by 1960. However, during the 1960s and 1970s, interest in women's rights and the women's liberation movement brought renewed interest in natural childbirth and the services of a midwife. Between 1975 and 1980 the number of American babies delivered by midwives doubled. In 1993, CNMs attended 188,370 deliveries, which accounted for 4.5 percent of all U.S. births. By 1997, midwife-assisted births had climbed to 7 percent of total U.S. births.

Naturopathic Physicians. Naturopathic physicians specialize in the use of natural therapeutics and are primarily concerned with overall health instead of alleviating specific symptoms or illnesses. The types of treatments and medical practices used by these physicians include herbology, acupuncture, natural childbirth, and homeopathy (which employs drugs that reproduce the symptoms of a disease as a way of canceling it out). Naturopathic physicians are only licensed in eleven states: Alaska, Arizona, Connecticut, Hawaii, Maine, Montana, New Hampshire, Oregon, Utah, Vermont, and Washington.

Their offices and clinics are operated in ways similar to those of primary care physicians, with the assistance of medical secretaries and medical assistants. These health care providers routinely perform physical examinations, lab tests, and minor surgery. In 1997, there were an estimated 2,300 offices and clinics of naturopathic physicians in the United States.

Nurses. The offices and clinics of nurses, independent from medical doctors, have had long histories in institutions and large industrial sites where first aid facilities are needed. This role has evolved since the 1960s into the job of occupational health nurse. In addition to administering first aid, occupational health nurses develop health promotion programs related to fitness and well-being, as well as safety regulations for the work site. Regulations passed by the Occupational Safety and Health Administration (OSHA) during the 1980s have greatly expanded the roles of occupational health nurses, whose responsibility it is to see that regulatory standards are met.

Establishments of nurse practitioners outside of institutions and industrial work sites have also evolved into new, more challenging roles. With the rise in health care costs and the shortage of family doctors, nurses have been providing primary care previously serviced by medical doctors. According to *Business Week,* registered nurses with advance training can provide 60 to 80 percent of all primary care. Given that nurses' salaries are considerably less than those of doctors, these services are provided at a savings and are filling a niche in the health care industry. A study by the American Nurses Association found that primary care provided by a nurse practitioner cost an average of 60 percent less than that provided by a medical doctor. For these reasons nurses are expected to benefit from government imposed health care reform designed to expand primary care and cut costs.

However, the move into primary care for nurses has been challenged by the medical profession and state governments. These groups have expressed concern over the qualifications of nurses seeking to expand their roles into primary care. Moreover, in some states, such as California, controversy has arisen over whether nurses should legally be allowed to fill prescriptions.

In 1994, there were about 1.97 million registered nurses practicing in the United States. Of those, nearly two-thirds worked in hospitals, while the remaining third worked in nursing homes, home health care agencies, schools, government agencies, and the offices and clinics of physicians. The median annual salary for a RN was $36,240. In 1996 there were roughly 700,000 licensed practical nurses (LPNs) with a median annual salary of $24,336.

Nutritionists and Dietitians. Nutritionists plan and supervise meals in state and government health departments, social service agencies, residential care facilities, and at schools. They may also counsel individuals on aspects of nutrition and ways to prevent diseases. In 1996, there were 58,000 dietitians and nutritionists. According to a Hay Group survey of acute care hospitals, their median annual salary was $34,400 in early 1997.

Occupational Therapists. Occupational therapists treat people with physical or emotional illnesses that affect their abilities in a day-to-day work or home environment; this type of therapy emphasizes treatment of work-related behaviors and skills. According to the American Occupational Therapy Association, the most common problems among patients of occupational therapy in the 1990s were strokes, developmental disabilities, arthritis, hand injuries, depression and schizophrenia. In 1996 there were roughly 57,000 occupational therapists practicing in the United States, earning a median base salary of $40,560 a year. Most occupational therapists worked in hospitals, with school systems being the second largest employer. A small but rapidly growing segment works in private practice.

The offices and clinics of occupational therapists originated in Europe and America after World War I with the emergence of rehabilitation hospitals for the long-term disabled. By 1925, the Council on Physical Therapy was created by the United States federal government. This governing body reviewed occupational therapy programs and established accreditation standards for therapists and their assistants.

This sector of the health care industry witnessed steady growth from the 1930s through the 1970s. Since the 1980s, growth in occupational therapy has accelerated with the aging population and increased efforts to integrate more disabled people into the workforce.

The profession has changed in recent years in the types of services offered. Fewer occupational therapists have been working with mental health patients and patients with cerebral palsy and arteriosclerosis; these trends can be explained in part by the increase in the number of psychotherapists and psychiatric social workers and by the development of better medications. At the same time, following increased public awareness of learning disabilities (such as dyslexia and slow cognitive processing), occupational therapists have increasingly turned to patients with learning disabilities.

Paramedics and Emergency Medical Technicians (EMTs). Paramedics and EMTs are medical technicians who give on-site medical treatment in place of a physician. These health care practitioners provide treatment most commonly for heart attack and accident victims. Paramedic services were introduced in the United States in the 1960s. During the late 1990s, there were about 150,000 paramedics and EMTs working in the United States. One-third of them worked with police, fire, and rescue squad departments; two-fifths worked for private ambulance companies and one-fourth in hospitals. The average salary of a paramedic was $30,407, while an EMT made $25,051. Many work on a voluntary basis.

Physical Therapists. Similar to the work of occupational therapists, physical therapists provide treatment for the physically or developmentally disabled; their patients include victims of strokes and accidents and the elderly. These practitioners carry out programs of testing, massage, exercise, and other therapeutic treatments to increase their patients' muscular strength and range of motion and to relieve pain.

In 1996, there were roughly 115,000 physical therapists working in the United States, earning a median base salary of $39,364 a year. Most of these therapists worked in general hospitals, rehabilitation hospitals, and nursing homes. Since the mid-1980s the aging population has resulted in an increase in the number of physical therapists working in patients' homes or out of their own private practices.

Psychotherapists and Clinical Psychologists. The offices and clinics of psychotherapists and clinical psychologists began with the emergence of psychotherapy in the late 1800s in Europe. Like psychiatrists, psychotherapists and clinical psychologists treat patients with mental disorders and emotional problems. According to *American Demographics,* 76 percent of the patients of psychotherapists (including clinical psychologists who practice psychotherapy) were being treated for emotional conditions such as anxiety disorders, neuroses, and relationship problems. However, unlike psychiatrists, psychotherapists and clinical psychologists do not prescribe medication and are not licensed as medical doctors. Another notable difference between these two related professions is that psychoanalysis requires more frequent patient visits and treatment outcomes are less predictable than those of psychiatric treatment.

These differences have made it more difficult for psychotherapists and clinical psychologists to gain wide acceptance in America. The insurance industry traditionally limited its coverage for mental health patients not under a psychiatrist's care. The role of the insurance industry has played a large part in the growth of this industry. It was not until after World War II that this industry was given a boost by commercial insurance companies offering coverage of mental health care for the first time. At first such insurance coverage provided for psychiatric and nonpsychiatric care; however, by the 1970s insurers started restricting coverage of non-psychiatric mental health care, mainly because of the difficulty of diagnosing such ailments and the uncertain amount of time needed to treat disorders. In 1989 federally funded insurance provided through Medicare expanded its coverage policy to include treatment by psychotherapists and clinical psychologists; this prompted private insurers to offer wider coverage again—a key factor in the industry's recent economic improvement.

In addition to increased insurance coverage, this sector of this industry has been aided by employers' increased awareness of work-related psychological disorders such as stress and fatigue. Many companies have set up Employee Assistance Programs (EAP). The involvement of psychotherapists and clinical psychologists in treating such problems in corporate environments has seen rapid growth since the mid-1980s. Many government agencies also mandated the set up of EAP programs for their employees.

The offices and clinics of psychotherapists and clinical psychologists compete for business with the establishments of psychiatrists, psychiatric social workers, and primary care physicians who counsel their patients. In 1989 there were a considerably greater number of clinical psychologists than psychiatrists; however, psychiatrists held a considerably larger portion of the mental health market.

In 1997, there were about 143,000 psychologists employed in the United States. Nearly 40 percent of them worked in educational institutions while 30 percent were employed in health services, and one-sixth worked in government agencies. The U.S. Department of Veterans Affairs and the Department of Defense used 80 percent of the federally employed psychologists.

Respiratory Therapists. Respiratory therapists treat patients with cardiopulmonary (heart and lung) problems that obstruct breathing. These health care practitioners work primarily in hospitals and nursing homes, but have also filled a growing need in home health services. Out of the 82,000 respiratory therapists working in 1996, more than 9 out of 10 worked in hospitals.

Current Conditions

Like other sectors of the health care industry, establishments in this industry entered the 1990s expecting growth due primarily to the maturing American population, but at the same time held concerns about health care costs and government reforms affecting the management and insurance coverage of their services.

The needs of the aging population of the United States have contributed to the rapid growth of home health services, which primarily employ physical and occupational therapists, respiratory therapists, and nurses. Other sectors of this industry which entered the 1990s to service the needs of the elderly include audiologists and paramedics.

According to *Business Insurance,* the changes expected with more managed care have been of particular concern to psychologists and psychotherapists, as these professions have been negatively affected by existing managed care systems; which have favored the use of psychiatric social workers over psychotherapists and clinical psychologists as the least expensive outpatient mental health provider. By 1996, some managed care organizations were beginning to cover certain alternative treatments, including acupuncture and hypnosis.

With cost-cutting changes in health care moving the health care industry away from inpatient treatment and toward more outpatient treatment, the offices and clinics of occupational and physical therapists have increasingly moved from hospital settings to more private offices and outpatient clinics.

INDUSTRY LEADERS

Some of the leaders in this industry in the late 1990s included HEALTHSOUTH Corp., NovaCare Inc., Comprehensive Care Corp., and Tenet Healthcare Corp.

HEALTHSOUTH, headquartered in Birmingham, Alabama, is the largest provider of outpatient surgery services and rehabilitative health care in the United States, operating nearly 2,000 health care facilities in this country, Australia, and the United Kingdom. With more than 51,000 employees worldwide, HEALTHSOUTH posted 1998 net income of $46.5 million on sales of $4 billion. Although the company's sales were up more than 32 percent from 1997, net earnings were nearly 86 percent below the level achieved the previous year.

NovaCare, one of HEALTHSOUTH's leading competitors in the field of rehabilitative health care, was in the process of extricating itself from the business in late 1999. The company suffered a net loss of $189.5 million on revenue of $1.48 billion in fiscal 1999, the 12 months ended June 30, 1999. NovaCare, which provided rehabilitation services to nearly 3,000 hospitals and nursing homes, employed 54,800 worldwide as of late 1999.

Comprehensive Care Corporation provides inpatient and outpatient mental health and substance abuse therapy and counseling. It contracts with hospitals and also operates free-standing facilities. Its subsidiary, Comprehensive Behavioral Care Inc., provides the same care for employers, HMOs, PPS, government organizations, third party administrators, and other group purchasers of healthcare. Headquartered in Tampa, Florida, the company posted net income of $42.0 million on revenue of $46.1 million in fiscal 1998, the 12 months ended May 31, 1999.

Although its main business is the operation of hospitals, Tenet Healthcare Corp. also runs a number of outpatient surgery centers and rehabilitation centers. With more than 125,000 employees worldwide, Tenet posted net income of $249 million on revenue of $10.9 billion in fiscal 1999, the 12 months ended May 31, 1999.

WORKFORCE

The various professions represented by this industry are on the whole expected to grow well into the end of the century. The fields that involve home health care and health care conducive to managed care systems are expected to do best; nurses and physical and occupational therapists represent three of the fastest growing areas of the health care industry. According to the U.S. Bureau of Labor Statistics, by the year 2005, there will be a 55 percent increase in the number of self-employed nurses and occupational therapists; the job market for physical therapists is expected to grow by more than 25 percent.

During the latter half of the 1990s, the average salaries for practitioners in this industry were as follows: audiologists and speech-language pathologists, $43,000 and $44,000, respectively; dental hygienists, $39,468; registered nurses, $36,244; licensed practical nurses, $24,336; occupational therapists, $40,560; occupational therapy assistants, $27,442; paramedics, $30,407; physical therapists, $39,364; psychiatric social workers, $35,000; psychotherapists, hospital/clinic, $51,000; psychotherapist, government, $62,120; and respiratory therapists, $32,500.

With the exceptions of midwives and occupational therapist assistants, the occupations listed above require at least four years of training, usually in conjunction with a bachelor's degree. Midwives can practice with two years of training and certification in the state they work. Occupational therapist assistants undergo two years of training through an associate's degree program and have to be certified by the American Occupational Therapy Association.

AMERICA AND THE WORLD

Many of the professions represented by this industry have had larger and often more profitable markets overseas, especially practitioners of "alternative medicine," such as acupuncture and natural therapies. Acupuncture is not only a standard form of medicine in China, but is also widely practiced all over the world. In Great Britain and Germany acupuncture is covered by the government-run health programs. Hypnosis, naturopathy, and various forms of spiritual healing have also been more widely accepted overseas than in the United States.

America's approach to midwifery has also been significantly different from approaches overseas. In most other industrialized countries, midwifery has been blended into the medical profession, while in the United States, the use of obstetricians and gynecologists has taken precedence. Midwives from overseas, unlike many other nurse-practitioners in the health care industry, do not tend to seek employment or set up practices in the United States.

However, the better salaries offered in the United States for nurses and physical and occupational therapists have brought many practitioners in these professions to the United States. Nursing professionals, in particular, are apt to secure work overseas because their credentials are easily transferable and because of the worldwide shortage of nurses.

Research and Technology

Like other sectors of the health care industry, establishments in this industry are greatly affected by medical research and technology. Technological developments since the mid-1980s such as computerized infusion therapy and smaller physical therapy apparatus have helped home health care services grow. In addition, at-home monitoring devices for the elderly have increased the efficiency and use of paramedics.

Information technology has brought about new developments in computer-assisted health care, including psychotherapy. Computer systems, such as the Therapeutic Learning Program, developed by a California psychiatrist, provide therapeutic advice to employees at their work site, meeting the concerns of employers over employees' psychological well-being. Such systems can be operated by the patient, although mental health practitioners see such systems as working in conjunction with services provided by a practitioner for personalized diagnoses.

The National Institutes of Health have also begun research on alternative therapies, such as naturopathy and hypnotism. The institute is offering grants for private studies on such therapies. The outcome of these studies will either help promote or reduce the number of people interested in using these kinds of healing methods.

Further Reading

American Association of Naturopathic Physicians, 1996. Available from http://www.infinite.org/naturopathic.

American College of Nurse-Midwives. ''A Brief History of Nurse-Midwifery in the U.S.,'' 1996. Available from http://www.acnm.org/HISTORY.HTM.

———. ''Basic Facts About Certified Nurse-Midwives.'' Available from http://www.midwife.org/press/basicfac.htm.

American Dental Association. ''Fact Sheet—Dental Hygiene Today,'' 1997. Available from http://www.ada.org.

Meckler, Laura. ''The Doctor's Still In.'' Associated Press, 2 December 1999.

National Acupuncture and Oriental Medicine Alliance. ''Quick Facts About Acupuncture and Oriental Medicine in the U.S.'' Available from http://aacuall.org/usaccept.htm.

U.S. Department of Labor. *Occupational Outlook Handbook.* 1996-97. Washington, D.C.: GPO, 1996.

SIC 8051

SKILLED NURSING CARE FACILITIES

Establishments primarily engaged in providing inpatient nursing and rehabilitative services to patients who require continuous health care but not hospital services. Care must be ordered by and under the direction of a physician. The staff must include a licensed nurse on duty continuously with a minimum of one full-time registered nurse on duty during each day shift. Included are establishments certified to deliver skilled nursing care under Medicare and Medicaid programs. Skilled care facilities include the following: Convalescent homes with continuous nursing care; extended care facilities; mental retardation hospitals; and skilled nursing homes.

NAICS Code(s)

623311 (Continuing Care Retirement Communities)
623210 (Residential Mental Retardation Facilities)
623110 (Nursing Care Facilities)

Industry Snapshot

In 2000, according to the Health Care Financing Administration, the United States would spend $1,295,226 trillion on health care. Of this, nursing home care would cost $96.4 trillion, or 7.4 percent of total health care expenditures. In the year 2005, estimated total national health care expenditures were projected to increase to $1,841,003 trillion, with nursing home care at $130.8 trillion (7.1 percent). These figures represent significant increases from 1996, when total health care spending was $1,035,080 trillion. Of that amount, $78.5 trillion (7.6 percent) went to nursing homes; $202.5 trillion (19.5 percent) went to physicians' services care; $358.5 trillion (34.6 percent) went to hospital care; $62.2 trillion (6.0 percent) went to prescription drugs; and $30.1 trillion (2.9 percent) went to home health care.

In 1995, 16.5 percent of the population was estimated to be over 60 years old—2.2 million were between the ages of 85 and 90, 1.2 million were between 90 and 99, and 53,000 were 100 or older. By 2000, 35.3 million Americans will be over 65, 12.3 million will be between 75 and 84, and 4.2 million will be over 85. Also in 1995, sub-acute care—where convalescing patients received care at lower costs—was already a $4 billion business and was predicted to grow to $20 billion by 2000.

During the next 25 years, the number of Americans aged 85 and over is expected to grow by 94 percent, compared to a general population growth rate of 25 percent. By the year 2050, the current elderly nursing home population of 1.5 million patients could increase to as many as 5.0 million. The over 50 population will increase from 76 million in 1995 to a projected 96 million in 2010. The number of people over 65 was expected to double between 1996 and 2016, but the number of available beds in nursing homes would not. In addition, 4 percent of all children under age 21 suffered from a chronic disease or a severely limiting disability, and an estimated 3.9 percent of all spinal cord injury patients resided in nursing homes.

Smaller families with fewer children to share responsibilities for the aged will mean a greater need for medical health companies. Medicare funds are estimated to dry up by 2001. However, the nursing home and long-term care industry will continue to grow. Funding will be the dilemma, although the recent availability of private sector long-term care insurance is promising.

Essentially, these figures sketch the scope and populations served by the skilled care nursing industry. Over the course of the past decade, innovative reallocation of resources has expanded options for long-term care, but few, however, match the optimum level of skilled nursing care provided for populations with chronic and multiple disablement. Skilled nursing care, similar to custodial or convalescent care conceptually, represents a long-term vehicle for meeting the comprehensive medical, personal, and social service needs of chronically disabled persons.

Skilled nursing care services differ in terms of the levels of services provided, patient admission criteria, staffing, and reimbursement mechanisms. Each aspect of the skilled nursing care environment reflects the high level of intensive care. All skilled care facilities provide continuous 24-hour care that is prescribed, directed, and executed under the supervision of a medical doctor. Professional performance and supervision by licensed personnel also apply to the provision of ancillary services such as physical therapy and other such prescribed services.

One of the trends affecting health care is integration or integrated delivery systems—a system that tracks patients over time and spans all levels of care and fosters alliances among the various care givers. Nursing home regulations, the need for new managers, standards, and managed care contracts were among some of the challenges facing the industry.

ORGANIZATION AND STRUCTURE

Skilled nursing care facilities primarily operate under three categories of ownership: for-profit, nonprofit, and government. For-profit skilled care nursing encompasses tax-paying structures operating under proprietary or investor/shareholder ownership by licensed administrators or as a subsidiary of a corporation. Nonprofit ownership includes both non-secular, church-related nonprofit organizations and secular, fraternal or other membership group, ownership. Government, or public ownership, includes establishments operated by city, state, or federal governments.

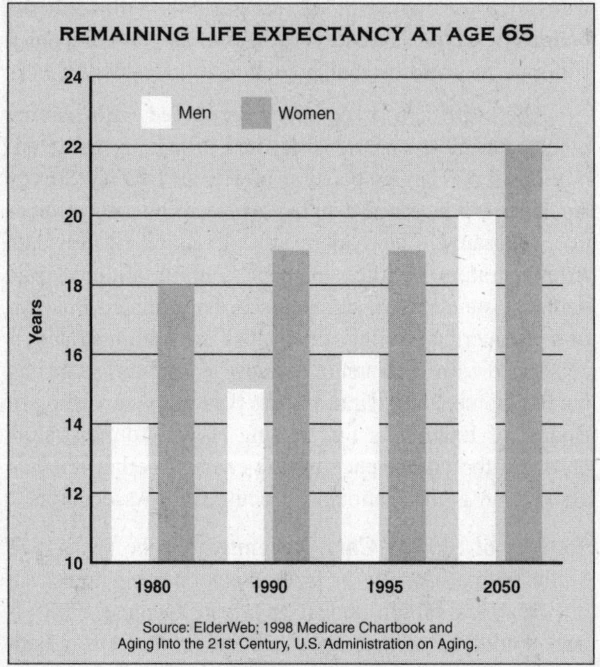

All three types of ownership may operate single homes or a chain consisting of multiple nursing homes. Ownership may be on an owned, leased, or managed basis. For-profit operators constitute the largest group, while nonprofit organizations own or manage less than one-third the number of facilities operated by for-profit establishments. Of the total number of U.S. beds utilized for skilled nursing care purposes, for-profit facilities maintain the highest number of beds at 58 percent, followed by nonprofit facilities with 22 percent, and government-owned facilities with 13 percent. In both for-profit and nonprofit facilities, skilled care ranks as a priority component; for-profit facilities often offer the greatest variety of such services, while church-sponsored facilities, dogged by budgetary realities, may provide the least amount of skilled care services. However, many skilled nursing care facilities are operated by religious organizations offering premier care services.

In the mid-1990s, nonprofit nursing homes, which were either self-financed via retained earnings of through tax exempt debt, began facing a bigger challenge from the for-profit sector. For-profit organizations can raise funds through stock offerings and retain managers through stock option plans. The non-profit sector is challenged to manage as efficiently and effectively as the for-profit group. Seventy-three percent of nursing homes were investor-owned in the early 1990s. Although the nonprofit sector is relatively stable, larger companies continue to acquire smaller long-term care facilities.

There are 296 associations concerned with nursing homes and 59 associations devoted to nursing home administration. The Association of Health Facility Survey Agencies is concerned with facility licensing and certification programs. The American College of Health Care Administrators certifies member's ability to meet and maintain standards of competence. Its affiliated Foundation of American College of Health Care Administrators is concerned with scholarship to improve long-term care and nursing home administration. The National Association of Boards of Examiners for Nursing Home Administrators produces the competence testing exam. Another relevant association is the National Subacute Care Association.

Sources of Skilled Care Revenue. Of the nearly $78 billion spent nationally for private sector nursing home care in 1995, $32.6 billion came from private sources, or out-of-pocket and private insurance, and $45.3 billion from Federal and State government sources. Analysis of revenue trends based on facility ownership also reveals that, for government and for-profit homes, Medicaid accounted for more than 60 percent of revenues. Private pay revenue was highest for church-related and secular homes.

Medicaid. Medicaid is the largest insurer of long-term care for all Americans, including the middle class, and covers 68 percent of nursing home residents and over 50 percent of nursing home costs. Medicaid expenditures for health care assisting 11.6 million persons totaled $152 billion (Federal and State) in 1995.

Medicaid is a federal/state funded program administered by individual states. Originally designed for poverty-level women, children, and the elderly, increased utilization by the elderly has converted long-term care to a majority component of Medicaid. All long-term care patients, however, are not automatically eligible for Medicaid assistance. Ineligibility may be decided either because a prospective patient's assets exceed the normal $2,000 limit or the patient's monthly income exceeds state limitations.

Several legislative changes in Medicaid reimbursements have created tensions between the state government officials and nursing home providers. Specifically, the Boren Amendment enacted in 1980 and the broad nursing home reform provisions mandated by the Omnibus Budget Reconciliation Act (OBRA) of 1987 have been problematic for providers.

Prior to the Boren Amendment, nursing homes were reimbursed on the basis of reasonable, cost-based expenses. The Boren Amendment changed the system by granting the states greater freedom and latitude in determining the amount of Medicaid reimbursements considered to be ''reasonable and adequate.'' Because of budgetary and other fiscal problems, the amount of Medicaid reimbursement paid by states to nursing home providers frequently did not cover basic costs of patient care. Nursing home operators understandably objected.

Elimination of the Boren Amendment was the only Medicaid reform jointly agreed upon by the Republicans, the Clinton Administration, and the governors in 1996 and was viewed as unlikely to survive any rewrite of Medicaid by either party. This amendment provides for equitable reimbursement of nursing homes.

Nursing home operators were also concerned with the effects of OBRA. Among other things, OBRA regulated the purpose, nature, and use of restraints in long-term care facilities to ensure they were for the patient's benefit and not the provider's convenience. Nursing homes, however, did receive some relief from governmental actions. A 1990 Supreme Court ruling gave providers the right to challenge states regarding reimbursement levels. As a result of this ruling, states must now adjust Medicaid payments sufficiently to assist providers to meet compliance costs associated with OBRA.

Still another integrity issue surrounding Medicaid emerged from a recent U.S. Census Bureau report that claimed Medicaid, as the principal payer for almost two-thirds of nursing facility resident days, was plagued by fraudulent claims from ineligible applicants who did not meet poverty guidelines. To curb these practices, which potentially threaten Medicaid's fiscal base, the American Health Care Association (AHCA) called for action designed to: enforce existing statutory prohibitions against transferring or otherwise disposing of assets used in determining Medicaid eligibility; and identify and amend statutory provisions encouraging implementation of Medicaid Estate Planning.

Medicare. Only a small percentage of homes accept Medicare patients. About 58 percent of Medicare patients occupy for-profit homes. Medicare Hospital Insurance, under Part A, assists in covering costs for skilled nursing home care, excluding convalescent or custodial homes. Skilled nursing facilities generally are reluctant to utilize Medicare reimbursement for several reasons: First, complexities associated with Medicare reporting guidelines frequently result in losses because of disallowance of patient and patient-related skilled care costs. Secondly, under the current reimbursement system, hospitals receive a higher rate of compensation than nursing facilities for providing the same type of skilled care nursing services. As a result of this inequitable system, the higher rates allow hospitals a significant competitive edge. One proposed solution for payment equity calls for hospitals and nursing facilities to receive the same rate for providing the same type of skilled nursing care.

Another contentious issue between skilled nursing facilities and Medicare focuses on the three-day hospital stay requirement for admission to skilled care facilities. Intended to function as a measure to protect against unnecessary admissions, skilled nursing care facilities argue that the ruling leads to unnecessary hospital stays resulting in further delays of essentially needed skilled nursing care for patients. Providers prefer total elimination of a pre-hospital stay admission requirement. Based on the government's analysis, elimination of this requirement would increase Medicare spending by an estimated $3 billion over five years. Based on the AHCA's analysis, however, elimination of the three-day requirement would save $1 billion over five years because savings in Medicare hospital expenditures would more than offset expenditures of skilled nursing facilities.

In the 1990s, the conversion of beds into "subacute" care beds has emerged as one trend in the nursing home industry, in part because the latter offers much greater levels of Medicare revenue. For example, the average Medicare payment per diem in the nursing home setting was $98 in 1990, as compared to $292 in 1996, with almost all of the increase due to ancillary services.

Under the present payment system for skilled nursing facilities, Medicare will pay for up to 100 days of nursing home care, subsequent to an acute care hospital stay of at least three days. Rates are determined in terms of "reasonable" costs, which fall into three categories: routine costs (including daily expenses that a skilled nursing facility incurs); ancillary service costs (including rehabilitation therapy, nonroutine medical care, and radiology services); and capital costs (including depreciation, amortization, and interest).

Before passage of the Balanced Budget Amendment, skilled nursing providers were anticipated to receive $83 billion during the period from fiscal year 1998 through fiscal year 2002. However, after the implementation of BBA, that total decreased to only $74 billion over the same period.

Almost 70 percent of all nursing home residents have at least part of their care paid for by Medicaid. The Kassenbaum-Kennedy health insurance portability law makes long-term care expenses and premiums tax deductible. State governments were concerned about their one-third share of spending on Medicaid, which they felt was going to the middle class rather than the poor.

Respiratory therapy is currently provided in approximately 35 to 40 percent of all nursing homes, but it is not a reimbursable cost in skilled care facilities unless certain conditions are met. One condition for Medicare reimbursement for respiratory therapy requires a transfer agreement that specifies that the hospital provide respiratory care personnel to the skilled nursing facility. As it now stands, patients transferring from hospitals to skilled nursing facilities are likely to discover Medicare disallowance of respiratory therapy payment.

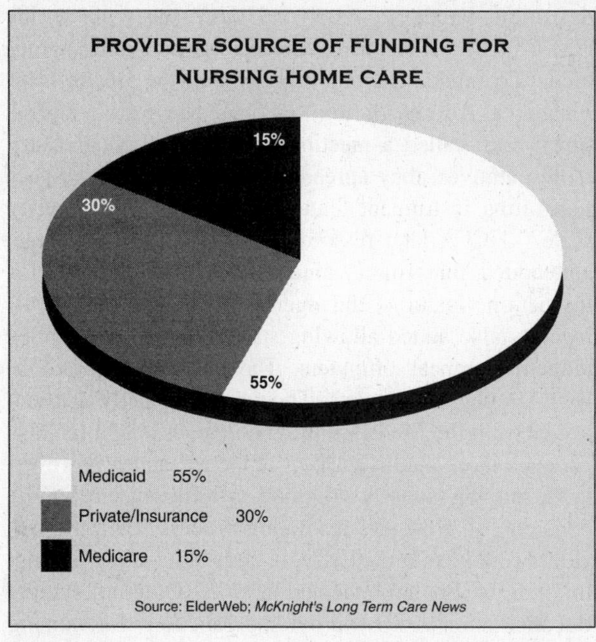

Source: ElderWeb; *McKnight's Long Term Care News*

Reimbursement for Medicare and Medicaid requires certification of nursing facilities by the funding agencies. The certification process, normally accomplished via inspection, assesses the total spectrum of the facility's capacity to provide optimum skilled care. The certification process has always represented a challenge for nursing facilities and proven to be a significant hurdle for a significant number of facilities. The 1987 Omnibus Budget Reconciliation Act's (OBRA) impact is changing the course of nursing home enforcement. This federal law was created in response to increasing concern about the industry in the 1980s that arose out of a series of well-publicized accounts of neglect and ill treatment at nursing care facilities. As a committee of the Institute of Medicine noted, "a stronger federal leadership is essential because not all state governments have been willing to regulate nursing homes adequately unless required to do so by the federal government." OBRA provided new federal regulations that were implemented "to improve nursing home conditions by giving patients a stronger voice in their care, requiring facilities to document treatment and specifying how surveyors should inspect nursing homes to see whether the new standards are being met," according to the *New York Times.*

One major change affected by OBRA is the survey inspection procedure. Pursuant to OBRA, the Department of Health and Human Services was directed to enter agreements with state survey agencies for assessing nursing facilities' compliance with OBRA's requirements. The results of on-site inspections subsequently determine whether to enter into, deny, renew, or terminate a facility's Medicare/Medicaid participation agreement. To implement this requirement, the Health Care Financing Administration (HFCA), Medicare's operational arm, called a meeting of nursing home industry representatives; they agreed on utilization of an inspection rating instrument featuring a ''scope and severity scale.'' HCFA later revised the plan, deleted the scale, and added fines of as much as $10,000 per day for inspection violations endangering a patient's life. A ruling was also added allowing state takeover of facilities judged as repeat offenders. The industry objected to HCFA's new regulations. Though infrequently applied, ouster from the Medicare program can cripple a facility. An even more punitive aspect of the measures, however, in the nursing industry's opinion, is the absence in HCFA revisions of a dispute resolution process whereby providers could explain, clarify, or contest a survey finding. In 1995, HCFA implemented the 1987 Omnibus Budget Reconciliation Act by providing sanctions for nursing home violations. Support surfaces that were previously considered routine costs, such as mattress replacements, became considered ancillary costs. HCFA plans to revise its survey and clarify conditions for civil monetary penalties when the moratorium is lifted.

OBRA also granted nursing homes funds for correcting inspection violations. Rectification of inspection deficiencies would be completed in adherence to a state designed timetable. If facilities did not rectify deficiencies, then federal law required the state to repay the federal government the amount of funds given to the nursing facility. Rather than be saddled with such repayment obligations, states sometimes choose to decertify facilities deemed incompliant.

While the other 49 states implemented the 1987 Omnibus Budget Reconciliation Act, California openly and blatantly rebelled. California refused to adhere to federal guidelines for inspections on the basis that federal requirements would impose an additional $500 million annual cost to the Medicaid program. Tit-for-tat actions ensued. California sued the federal government. The government withheld $24 million of $5 billion in Medicaid contributions. After a few months of bitter controversy, a satisfactory resolution was finally reached when the government attributed problems to a misunderstanding and accepted California's proposed inspection changes. Several other issues regarding compliance with OBRA remain in various discussion stages. Some felt that OBRA was an overregulation that harmed those it was intended to protect.

In the mid-1990s, nursing homes were also governed by Occupational Safety and Health Administration (OSHA) regulations, with fines of up to $2,000 per violation. Most frequent violations were lack of a written program, lack of employee training, lack of proper labels for containers, and failure to make material safety data sheets available.

Rehabilitation Skilled Nursing Homes. Patients of these homes include accident victims who enter for shorter extended stays needing care and rehabilitation services connected to head injuries, strokes, spinal cord injuries, amputation, orthopedic and neurological impairment, arthritis, or war-related trauma. The recent proliferation of highly specialized trauma centers concentrates on services for single injury-related rehabilitation such as head, spinal cord, or other types of disablement. Growth of the rehabilitation industry can in part be attributed to medical science advances. Because of these advances, the potential of rehabilitation has expanded options for all ages of patients.

Skilled Nursing Care Facilities for AIDS Patients. AIDS morbidity, as the newest escalating group of nursing home patients, creates yet another challenge for the nursing home industry. Skilled care needs of AIDS patients differ from those of other nursing home patients. Provision of optimum care means comprehensive reallocation of nursing home staffing and other resources. One study found that 20 percent of AIDS patients experienced difficulty with placement in skilled nursing facilities. A survey of 54 Illinois homes related the most salient reasons for this difficulty related to cost, staff abilities, or resistance, due to concerns regarding mixing AIDS patients with other patients.

Skilled Nursing Care Facilities for Children. Children under the age of six who are victims of traumatic accidents, congenital defects, and chronic diseases such as cystic fibrosis and other ailments, are a fast-growing long-term care group in America. The combined total of children's facilities in the United States includes 47 freestanding or independently operated children's hospitals, with the remainder affiliated with other types of institutions. Although many children's facilities are backed by large endowments, several conditions contribute to extreme financial conditions. Because these facilities often care for seriously ill patients, about one-third of their beds are allocated for intensive care, comparable to skilled nursing care. Many admissions consist of transfers from community hospitals that were unable to provide the prescribed level of intensive care. Despite the fact that Medicaid reimbursement covers an average of more than 80 percent of the care cost and disproportionate share payments cover the difference, children's facilities frequently face financial crises. One reason stems from frequent delays of Medicaid reimbursements. This state of affairs can impose significant financial strain and conceivably threaten the survival of children's facilities. More problems can be anticipated if future payment rate allowances fail to consider the high numbers of Medicaid and uninsured patients served by children's hospitals.

Subacute Skilled Care Nursing Facilities. For the most fragile patients, many long-term care facilities have developed a subacute level of care, described by the American Health Care Association as intensive, licensed, skilled nursing care provided in a distinct part/skilled nursing facility. Many subacute level patients are ''heavy care'' elderly with respiratory ailments requiring ventilator or intravenous therapy. Because of inadequate Medicare reimbursement for this type of treatment, nursing homes are unwilling to accept these patients.

CURRENT CONDITIONS

Crime is a growing concern for the industry. A national Senior Crime Stoppers program was designed to help long-term care providers deter crime within health care facilities by providing 24-hour access to a toll-free number for reporting thefts or other crimes.

The average cost of a nursing home in 1996 was $40,000 a year and was expected to continue increasing at about 7.5 percent per year, but the industry's current fiscal status is regarded as somewhat flat. While expansion capital may not be readily available to the industry, neither is the concept of expansion an overwhelming objective for most of the industry. Nursing home chains still recall the heady conditions of an expansive period during the 1980s. Ballooning profits and expansions contributed to an enthusiastic appraisal of the industry's future.

As companies felt the impact of Medicare price changes, however, members of the industry scaled back expectations. Precariously slim profit margins, due in part to an overload of unprofitable and unnecessary relics from the expansion period, forced companies to scale back to survive. What followed was an austerity phase characterized by budget cutting and dumping of unprofitable entities. Many of the innovative strategies of restructuring, diversification, and other cost-saving measures continue as industry foundations today. Humana, one of the larger chains, added an insurance entity that is today proving to be a profitable strategy. Other organizations diversified by adding specialized services as well, and a new association was also in 1995—The Health Resources Alliance—to act as a contact point for long-term care clients needing a variety of specialized care facilities.

According to Irving Levin Associates Senior Care Acquisition report in the March 1996 issue of *Modern Healthcare,* the average price for retirement housing increased 9 percent during the two years prior to 1995—to $59,000; the average price per nursing home bed rose 21 percent—to $39,000—in the same period.

Although nursing homes may be designated as skilled care nursing care facilities, occupancy patterns for most facilities combine a mix of skilled and unskilled care patients. To meet federal and state requirements for skilled nursing care, facilities thus maintain distinctly separate beds, staffing, records, and other services. Statistically, this organizational pattern, in addition to other factors, determines the demographic approach for documenting the skilled nursing care industry. First, more accurate indicators regarding the skilled care nursing industry emerge from enumeration of the number of beds rather than the number of facilities. Second, because Medicare or Medicaid reimbursement of skilled nursing care depends on certification by these mechanisms, this method allows still another means of documentation. Finally, while the predominant elderly population of skilled care nursing homes formulates a valid sample, the universe of skilled care nursing includes all ages of adults, children, and even infants suffering from chronic illness. The National Governors' Association approved a compromise in nursing home coverage for the poor and disabled elderly that would give states greater authority of payments and eligibility.

Non-profit nursing homes, self-financed via retained earnings or tax exempt debt, face challenges from the for-profit sector, which can raise funds via stock offerings or use stock-option plans to retain managers or staff. This creates a growing challenge to manage effectively and efficiently. Small providers are banding together to compete for managed care business. The for-profit sector threatens to provide nursing facilities at lower costs and with more services, including assisted living and home care, than nonprofit sectors. According to the National Center for Assisted Living, in the late 1990s, about 13 percent of all assisted living residents were in nursing facilities.

Continuing Care Retirement Communities (CCRCs) nursing homes sometimes lose residents to HMOs when they are discharged from the hospital and told they must go to an HMO provider. In the middle and late 1990s, CCRCs were seeking their own contracts with HMOs.

The under-age-65 nursing home population totaled about 173,100 in the mid-1990s, with admissions due to disablement by reason of mental retardation, chronic disease, or illness incidental to congenital defects, trauma, or accident. With the exception of purely age-related conditions, manifestations of chronic illness and disability are practically the same for both the elderly and younger groups.

Future nursing homes resources will need to be expanded to accommodate the projected volume increase of elderly patients presenting these manifestations. Advances in medical science have enabled people to live longer lives, but higher costs trail longevity. U.S. Census reports project that by the year 2025, the number of people over age 85 will climb to 7 million—from the 3.4 million in the mid-1990s. Because frailty and deterioration intensify with age, future nursing homes will find a majority of patients in need of more intensive care. Preparing to offer no less than optimum care for this patient segment means expansion of industry resources with accentuation on intensive care exclusively offered by skilled nursing systems.

There is a growing interest in substituting skilled nursing facilities (SNF) for extended hospital care among the managed care plans. In 1996, 12 percent of all Medicare beneficiaries, 4.5 million persons, were enrolled in managed care plans. Major cost savings are achieved by switching patients from hospitals to SNF for convalescing.

HMOs and MCOs can slow the growth of health care costs although they may not be able to reduce them. The number of HMOs continues to decline while the number of enrollees continues to climb.

The new trend toward expansion will require new financing that is becoming increasingly easier to obtain because of the excellent profit potential. It serves the fastest growing segment of the population. Nursing homes are among the most cost-effective providers of health care services. Honesty and accuracy in reporting fiscal, regulatory, management, and marketing portions of a home will improve loan approval.

About 1,500 of the 17,000 nursing homes are financed or owned by real estate investment trusts (REITs). Thirteen REITs invest exclusively in health care, with Meditrust's 1.8 billion portfolio being the largest. Advantages of REIT financing include long-term loans, better rates than banks, and the potential for operators to have a sales/leaseback option.

Late 1990s Changes. The Balanced Budget Act of 1997 (BBA) mandated the phase-in of a prospective payment system (PPS) for nursing homes over a four-year period starting on January 1, 1999. Under PPS, which went into effect in July 1998, Medicare pays nursing homes a fixed per patient-day based on the acuity level of the patient. Traditionally, the "cost-plus" reimbursement approach reimbursed nursing homes for actual service cost, in addition to a percentage based on capital expenditures and other operating expenses.

In this transitional period, the nursing home industry has had many difficulties coping with the new changes. Small nursing homes, in particular, have suffered because attempts to control costs below the per-diem rates have resulted in operating margin erosion. Generally, nursing facilities with relatively more numerous, sicker residents are operating less profitably, a situation that potentially threatens their ability to provide patients with adequate care.

The nursing home PPS legislation has contributed to a significant decline in many service areas, especially rehabilitation and respiratory therapies and pharmaceutical services.

Consolidated revenues and profits did not rebound in the late 1990s and are not anticipated to do so in the near future. Reflecting these changes, the *Standard & Poor's Health Care (Long-Term Care) Index* decreased 31 percent in the first four months of 1999, following a 54 percent freefall in 1998.

Industry Leaders

For-Profit Homes. According to a Agency for Health Care Policy and Research (AHCPR) survey, 65 percent of nursing homes operated for profit in 1996. About 68 percent of those for-profit homes (45 percent of all nursing homes) are part of a chain. Beverly Enterprises, an Arkansas-based, for-profit nursing home chain, was the industry leader in ownership of 637 facilities comprising 71,375 licensed beds, according to the *Hoechst Mario Roussel Managed Care Digest Series 1997*. Beverly Homes and Vencor, the two largest long-term care operators, sold some of their holdings to smaller operators in the mid-1990s. Long-term care providers are experiencing pressure to revamp the delivery of services and broaden their range of services. Beverly Enterprises was one of seven nursing home chains to receive a multi-state contract for veterans care as part of the Veterans Affairs' (VA) attempt to cut administrative costs. Other chains receiving contracts included Vencor, Sun Healthcare Group, Genesis Health Ventures, Integrated Health Services, Unicare Health Finances, and Harmony. All told this will give the VA access to 1,100 homes in 43 states.

Integrated Health Services acquired five home care companies in 1996, signed a merger agreement with Coram Healthcare, and acquired a rehabilitation provider. Hill Haven Corporation, Manor Care, Inc., Continental Medical Systems, Health Care & Retirement, Unicare Health Facilities, and Living Centers of America are among some the other leading companies in the industry. In 1995, Sun Healthcare Group acquired Golden Care, the largest privately held respiratory service in a $55-million transaction.

Non-Profit Nursing Homes. According to a Agency for Health Care Policy and Research (AHCPR) survey, non-profit nursing homes are more apt than for-profit homes to be affiliated with non-nursing units, such as personal care or independent living. Nonprofit nursing homes are more likely to be hospital-based than for-profit nursing homes.

Rehabilitation Skilled Nursing Homes. Rehabilitation facilities, similar to other industries, face the usual cost strategies involving restructuring, takeovers, and other measures. Although rehabilitation operations enjoy a lucrative investor status in the 1990s, public officials view its growth status with less enthusiasm. Public health officials charge that these facilities shun the indigent and make treatment decisions in deference to the patient's ability to pay. Several other problems surrounding rehabilitation facilities have dented the industry's integrity.

Public or Government Owned/Leased Skilled Care Facilities. According to the Medical Expenditure Panel Survey of the Agency for Health Care Policy and Research, in 1996 almost 66 percent of nursing homes were operated for profit, about 26 percent were nonprofit facilities, and the remaining 8 percent were owned by Federal, State or local governments. Nonprofit and government-owned nursing facilities were more apt to be a part of a hospital-based nursing home than were for-profit nursing homes. The United States Department of Veterans Affairs is the largest of the government-owned facilities. In some instances, Veterans Affairs delivers long-term care services via service contracts with other nursing homes, as mentioned previously.

The *Hoechst Mario Roussel Managed Care Digest Series 1998*, as reported in the Standard & Poor's Industry Profile, *Healthcare: Facilities*, ranked the 15 largest nursing home chains in the United States in 1997. They were, in order of largest to smallest in terms of number of facilities: Beverly Enterprises; Vencor Inc.; Integrated Health Services; Sunrise Healthcare Group; Living Centers of America; ManorCare Health Services; Life Care Centers of America; Genesis Health Ventures; Evangelical Lutheran Good Samaritan Society; Extendicare Health Services; GranCare Inc.; Health Care & Retirement Corp.; Texas Health Enterprises; Mariner Health; and Centennial Healthcare.

The *Hoechst Mario Roussel Managed Care Digest Series 1998* also reported that the largest 33 nursing home chains operated 3,062 facilities and comprised about 24 percent of all nursing homes in 1997, as compared to 3,369 (about 22 percent) in 1996. Licensed beds at these facilities increased 6.0 percent in 1997, to 416,495, totaling nearly 25 percent of such beds nationwide.

WORKFORCE

According to the *1998-99 Occupational Outlook Handbook*, there are more about 1.9 million registered nurses (RNs)in 1996. It is also one of the five occupations projected to have the largest numbers of new jobs. Median weekly earning of full-time registered nurses were $697 in 1996. The lowest 10 percent earned less than $415; the highest 10 percent earned more than $1,039. According to the Buck Survey conducted by the American Health Care Association, staff RN's in chain nursing homes had median hourly earnings of $15.85 in 1996. The middle 50 percent earned between $14.03 and $17.73.

Statistically, the highest number of employees per set-up beds characterized nonprofit, Medicare-certified

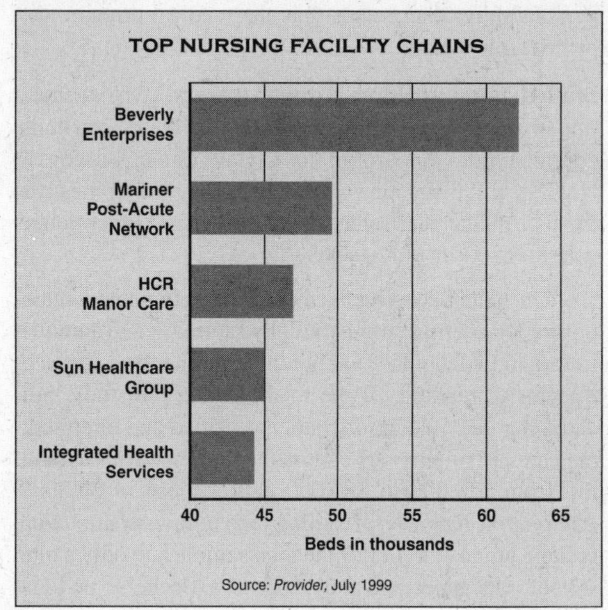

facilities. For-profit homes consistently maintain the fewest number of employees per bed.

The employment of registered nurses (RNs) is expected to increase 24.8 percent from 1994 to 2005; nurse's aides will increase 30.6 percent, and licensed practical nurses (LPNs) will increase by 28 percent. Employment in nursing and personal care facilities is expected to grow at an annual rate of 3 percent.

Compared to other industries, nursing homes bear an unusually weighted portion of labor problems emanating from high turnover, staff shortages, and volumes of unskilled workers. Scattered stories of physical and sexual abuse, fraud, injuries, drug abuse, mistreatment of patients, and incompetence in the 1980s and 1990s marred the image of nursing homes as havens of care and security for the disabled. Over the last few years, particularly post-OBRA, labor conditions are beginning to change. In addition to mandating reimbursement changes, OBRA also mandates comprehensive changes in staff training. Evidence of these changes even now stimulates a work environment that, proponents say, encourages more creative recruitment and retention strategies. Most of the more than two-thirds of all nursing homes with OBRA violations in July 1995 had complied by October 1995. In 1996, a seven-state initiative to help 1.6 million nursing home workers in over 5,000 nursing homes reduce injuries and illnesses through focusing on common hazards was initiated by Labor Secretary Robert Reich.

Skilled nursing home staffing patterns primarily divide into three categories: administrative, nursing, and patient and facility maintenance. All skilled nursing care is supervised or under the direction of a medical director. Patients have the option of selecting their primary physician. Most nursing home patients, however, choose their personal physician rather than the medical director as a primary physician.

Skilled Nursing Home Administrators. Management of daily facility operations is directed by the skilled home administrator. According to a Hay Group survey of HMOs, group practices, and hospital-based clinics, the median annual base salary of full-time nurse practitioners was $66,800 in May 1996.

One study constructed a profile of a typical, contemporary long-term administrator by sampling 226 administrators in Oklahoma. Functioning as owner, president, or director of nursing, of the total sample, the study indicated that the 19 administrators of skilled and intermediate care nursing homes earned the highest salaries, ranging from $28,000 to $80,000 with a mean of $43,000. Although a majority of skilled care administrators were college graduates, 111 of the total sample had only a high school education, and only 66 had a Bachelor or Master's. Implementation of OBRA will address the educational needs of administrators through development of standards of education, additional training requirements, and licensure.

Skilled Care Nursing Staff. Within the nursing staff, turnover rates have remained relatively stable in the early and middle 1990s. Turnover rates for RNs and LPNs remained at a constant low rate of around 21 percent in the mid-1990s. The industry does suffer from tremendously high turnover rates for nursing aides, particularly in church-related and Medicare-certified facilities.

Starting salaries for nurses in this industry vary a great deal geographically. For example, in 1995, the median salary of a registered nurse in Atlanta, Georgia, with little or no experience would be about $27,560; whereas one in similar circumstances in New York would start at $38,584. A much dimmer picture characterizes nurses' aides' starting salaries, which are often less than half of their RN and LPN colleagues'.

Prior to OBRA, little attention was given to the training or career needs of nurses' aides. For the first time ever, OBRA introduced a requirement for newly-hired nurse assistants in long-term care facilities to receive at least 75 hours of state-approved training and competency testing. The statute also requires that Medicare and/or Medicaid reimburse nursing facilities for the costs of conducting nurses aide training programs. The American Health Care Association goes a step further in proposing legislation that would create and fund career ladders for nurses' aides under a "pay back system."

Change is permeating every facet of long-term care according to the American Association of Homes and Services for the Aging's (AAHSA) Annual Meeting in 1996. Obvious changes are those currently forthcoming in Medicare and Medicaid, increased fiscal and regulatory scrutiny, declining public money, challenges from the for-profit sector, and continuing challenges to non-profit status are some other issues.

America and the World

In 1998, national health expenditures exceeded $1.1 trillion, with per capita spending of approximately $4,000. This represented about 13.5 percent of the gross domestic product (GDP) in the United States. In this context, most major countries such as Sweden, Canada, France, and the United Kingdom had a higher ratio of government to private spending.

In Canada, public and private health care spending totaled about $55 billion in 1996, with an additional $1.0 billion used to purchase health care services in the United States. With the Canadian Government depending more on the private sector for health care needs, there are more opportunities for U.S. firms specializing in medical matters.

Latin America is providing more opportunities for U.S. health care businesses. Many Latin American companies in the late 1990s were beginning to incorporate parts of a managed care system, including capitation and salaried medical specialists. Such Latin American countries as Columbia have demonstrated the desire for better health care; in 1993, health care spending there represented about 2 percent of the GDP, and in 1998 it was 5 percent.

Research and Technology

The health industry is embracing computerized health care systems at a rapid rate. The current estimated market of $15 billion for health care systems is expected to grow to $50 billion by the year 2000. Computerization will facilitate quantification of data and comparison of nursing home services. Health Outcomes Management, Inc. began developing a shared database for it—Assurance Long-Term Care System software.

HMOs and managed care organizations can slow the growth of health care costs. The health care industry is embracing computerization at a rapid rate. The market for health care information systems is estimated to be $15 billion and is expected to grow to $50 billion by 2000.

Further Reading

Addleman, Robert B. "Eldercare: Out of the Institution and Into the Community." *Healthcare Forum,* May/June 1995.

———. "Advance Care Plans 1999." Available from http://www.penpages.psu.edu/penpages/reference/21600/216001250.html

Bailis, Susan S. "Prospective Payment for Skilled Nursing Care." *Nursing Homes,* November/December 1996.

Barber, Patrick. "Financing Growth: More Necessary, Less Difficult." *Nursing Homes,* November/December 1995.

Benson, David. "Health Care REITs." *Nursing Homes,* November/December 1995.

Berger, Susan. "The Only Time to Buy Insurance for Long-Term Care." *Money,* September 1996.

Bloom, Alana. "Support Surface Coverage: Why You're Confused." *Nursing Homes,* November/December 1996.

Bonn, Karen L. "What Is a Restraint?" *Nursing Homes,* October 1995.

Bruck, Laura. "Employment Legislation Update." *Nursing Homes,* October 1996.

———. "What's Ahead: The Long-Term Care Network." *Nursing Homes,* November/December 1995.

———. "N.M. Nursing Home Chain Buys Respiratory Therapy Group." *Modern Healthcare,* 8 May 1996.

"CCCRs and Managed Care: A Perfect Marriage?" *Nursing Homes,* June 1996.

Cleary, Allison. "The Long View on Long-Term Care." *Hospitals & Health Networks,* 20 March 1995.

Cole, Linda. "Getting Ready for Today's Bank Financing." *Nursing Homes,* November/December 1995.

Darnay, Arsen J., ed. *Manufacturing USA.* 5th ed. Detroit: Gale Research, 1996.

Day, Bill. "Not Just Patients Anymore." *Business Record-Des Moines,* 2 March 1998.

Dugan, Joan M. "Is That Nursing-Home Loan Terminal or Just Doing Poorly?" *ABA Banking Journal,* May 1996.

Encyclopedia of Associations. 32nd ed. Detroit: Gale Research, 1997.

Epstein, Joseph. "License to Steal." *Financial World,* 26 September 1995.

Erisckson, Jenean M. "There Ought to Be Some Common Sense." *Nursing Homes,* November/December 1996.

"Exploring Change." *Nursing Homes,* September 1996.

Ford, Douglas S. "Beginnings of an Integrated Delivery System." *Nursing Homes,* October 1996.

Gardner, Jonathan. "VA Nursing Home Contracts Go to Long-Term-Care Giants." *Modern Healthcare,* 23 September 1996.

———. "Governors' Proposal Urges Coverage for Poor Elderly." *Modern Healthcare,* 19 February 1996.

———. "HCFA Nursing Home Report Revives Debate on New Rules." *Modern Healthcare,* 11 September 1995.

Goldman, Jonathan. "Health Care: The Giant That Keeps on Growing." *Institutional Investor,* December 1996.

Griggs, Ted. "Health Care Trends." *Advocate-Baton Rouge,* 1 March 1998.

Haddon-Grant, Hugo. "Care Turns Bullish." *Director,* February 1996.

Hall, Carl T. "Nursing in Turmoil." *San Francisco Chronicle,* 16 February 1998.

"Healthcare: Facilities." *Standard & Poor's Industry Profile,* June 1999.

"Health Care: Our Forecast." *Business Record-Syracuse,* 15 February 1998.

Health Care Financing Administration. *Guide to Choosing a Nursing Home,* Baltimore, MD: U.S. Department of Health and Human Services.

———. "1996 Statistics at a Glance." Available from http://www.hcfa.gov/stats/stathili.html.

———. "The Medicaid Program." Available from http://www.hcfa.gov/medicaid/mcdsta95.html.

"Healthcare: Managed Care." *Standard & Poor's Industry Profile,* June 1999.

Kendrick, James. "OSHA Offers to Help Nursing Home Owners." *Occupational Health & Safety,* October 1996.

Kerr, Tom. "GOP Plan Threatens Eldercare." *Food Management,* November 1995.

"Managed Care: The Easy Money May Have Already Been Made." *Institutional Investor,* December 1996.

"Market Watch: Nursing Home Trends 1999." Available from http://www.demko.com./min1222.html

Meyer, Harris. "Egging People On." *Hospitals & Health Networks,* 20 October 1996.

Moore, J. Duncan, Jr. "Union Attacks Beverly's VA Contract." *Modern Healthcare,* 21 October 1996.

"New Law Lightens Nursing Homes' Administrative Burden." *Healthcare Financial Management,* December 1996.

"New Resource Available for Nursing Home Data." Press Release, June 28, 1999. Agency for Health Care and Policy and Research. Available from http://www.ahcpr.gov/news/press/pr1999/chbk3pr.htm.

Novack, Janet. "Old Age Security—1995 Money Guide." *Forbes,* 19 June 1995.

Patterson, David. "Here Come the Outcomes." *Nursing Homes,* March 1996.

Pham, Alex. "Independent Nursing Homes Form Network." *Boston Globe,* 13 January 1998.

———. "HCFA's Software Pans." *Nursing Homes,* January 1996.

———. "The Future: Is Scandinavia Showing Us the Way?" *Nursing Homes,* February 1996.

Senior Living Alternatives. Winter/Spring 1997.

Shriver, Kelly. "Senior-Care Market is on the Upswing." *Modern Healthcare,* 4 March 1996.

Snow, Charlotte. "One-Stop Shopping." *Modern Healthcare,* 25 November 1996.

———. "Rivals Aly to Net Managed-Care Pacts." *Modern Healthcare,* 5 August 1996.

———. "Vencor, Beverly to Sell Some Facilities." *Modern Healthcare,* 9 December 1996.

Stahl, Dulcelina A. "1995 Leadership Challenges for SNFs." *Nursing Management,* March 1995.

Steffen, Teresa M. "Satisfaction with Nursing Homes." *Journal of Health Care Marketing,* Fall 1996.

Swisher, C. Lynn. "OSHA Update." *Nursing Homes,* September 1995.

"Trends in Medicare Skilled Nursing Facility Utilization." *Health Care Financing Review: Medicare and Medicaid Statistical Supplement,* February 1995.

"Two to a Bed." *Journal of Financial Planning,* April 1996.

Ukens, Carol. "No HCFA Surprise." *Drug Topics,* 9 January 1995.

Ullery, Judy. "A New Attack on Nursing Home Crime." *Nursing Homes,* October 1996.

U.S. Department of Commerce. Economics and Statistics Administration. Bureau of the Census. *Statistical Abstract of the United States 1996.* 116th ed. Washington, DC: GPO, 1996.

U.S. Department of Labor. Bureau of Labor Statistics. *E&E: Employment and Earning,* December 1996.

U.S. Department of Labor. "12. Employment of Workers of Nonfarm Payrolls by Industry, Monthly Data Seasonally Adjusted." *Monthly Labor Statistics,* November 1996.

"Valuation of the Nursing Home Industry." *The Corporate Growth Report,* 23 September 1996.

SIC 8052

INTERMEDIATE CARE FACILITIES

Establishments that provide inpatient nursing and rehabilitative services, but not on a continuous basis. Designated in particular are facilities certified under the Medicaid program to deliver intermediate care to the developmentally disabled.

NAICS Code(s)

623311 (Continuing Care Retirement Communities)
623210 (Residential Mental Retardation Facilities)
623110 (Nursing Care Facilities)

Industry Snapshot

The *Code of Federal Regulations* (4-1-93 Edition) has defined an ICF as "a proprietary facility or a facility of a private nonprofit corporation or association licensed or regulated by the State . . . for the accommodation of persons, who, because of incapacitating infirmities, require minimum but continuous care but are not in need of continuous medical or nursing services. The term also includes additional facilities for the nonresident care of elderly individuals and others who are able to live independently but who require care during the day."

ICFs provide inpatient nursing and rehabilitative services, predominantly to individuals with developmental disabilities. Though they operate 24 hours a day, services are not provided on a continuous basis. Personnel in ICFs must include 24-hour staff in addition to a licensed nurse on duty full-time each day. The term "developmental disabilities" generally refers to mental retardation. Therefore, ICFs often are designated as ICF/MRs—Medicaid-funded facilities which provide residential care and services for individuals with developmental disabilities. ICF/MR services were used primarily by the aged (34.9 percent) and the disabled (6.9 percent), and not by low-income children or low-income adults.

Approximately 2.5 percent of the national population can be classified as mentally retarded. While the majority of individuals with mental retardation or related conditions are able to live with their families or other adults in ordinary homes, other individuals with developmental disabilities are cared for in ICFs. Alternatively, individuals with developmental disabilities who require continuous medical or nursing care can be placed in nursing facilities. Many patients reside in ICF/MRs from youth until old age.

ICFs also can provide care to individuals with cerebral palsy, epilepsy, or other severe impairments of the central nervous system, not attributable to mental illness, that result in physical, mental, and behavioral disabilities comparable to those caused by mental retardation.

Medicaid spent $8.3 billion or 7.7 percent of its $108.3 billion budget for ICFs for the mentally retarded in 1994, according to the *Health Care Financing Review* statistical supplement published in October 1996. ICF/MR costs rose $6 per aged person from $13 to $19 during the period 1987 to 1994. In 1994, Medicaid served 159,000 ICF/MR persons, up an average of 4.5 percent per year for each year during the previous decade.

In 1993 there were 58,790 private and 1,765 state residential facilities for persons with mental retardation housing a total of 299,039 residents. The average daily maintenance expenditures per day per resident was $225 in state facilities, including all salaries, wages and operating costs. In 1994 there were 159,000 mentally retarded recipients in ICFs for which medical vendor suppliers received a total of $8.3 billion dollars in Medicaid payments. The average rate of expenditure per person was $52,497. In 1995 there were 2 million ICF mentally retarded recipients for whom $10.4 billion were paid by Medicaid to vendors. This amount represented 9 percent of the total payments to all Medicaid vendors for all Medicaid services.

ICF/MR's share of total Medicaid expenditures has continually declined in recent years from a high of 12.6 percent in 1984 to the current 7.7 percent. Payments for the disabled were $7.7 billion, or 13 times greater than the $585 million spent for the aged.

The individuals with developmental disabilities in ICFs typically require both health care and special services due to limited capabilities for self-care—housekeeping, language, social, and vocational skills. The health care offered by ICFs must include: a consultation by a registered nurse at least once a week on the delivery of health care to individual inpatients; and a licensed nurse on full-time duty for each day shift. Other services that ICFs provide include habilitation (training) in daily living, self help, socialization, pre-vocational skills (such as focusing on tasks and observing time schedules), and vocational skills. ICF programs also can sponsor sheltered workshops (whereby disabled individuals receive less than minimum wages, calibrated to individual productivity, for economic output) and supported employment (whereby disabled individuals join nondisabled persons in work settings). ICFs also can provide recreational activity centers for inpatients and respite care (temporary care of individuals with developmental disabilities who generally reside with and are cared for by their families).

ORGANIZATION AND STRUCTURE

Licensed ICFs are categorized into three types by the California Department of Developmental Services (CDDS): Larger facilities (more than 16 beds) that provide developmental, training, habilitative, and supportive health services to adults and children who have a primary need for developmental services, but intermittent need for skilled nursing services; smaller, habilitative units with 4 to 15 beds that provide the aforementioned services, plus personal care in the least restrictive community setting to the above, who also have an ongoing and but predictable need for intermediate care for skilled nursing services; and finally, smaller units that provide the same services outlined above, except that they include nursing supervision, and require recurring but intermittent nursing services not available above.

The Medicaid program, which is federally supported but state administered, is the primary source of economic aid for the ICF population, although other funds also are available. In general, individuals with developmental disabilities qualify for Medicaid benefits by meeting the disability and financial criteria established for the Supplemental Security Income (SSI) funding, must meet federal standards intended to ensure that residents live in a safe environment, are supervised by qualified staff, and receive appropriate habilitation and medical treatment. Individuals who meet the disability criteria for Medicaid funding generally must be both mentally impaired (with an IQ of 50 or less) and functionally disabled (incapable of performing the ordinary activities appropriate for persons of their age). Financial eligibility is based upon the economic resources of the developmentally disabled individual and, if the developmentally disabled individual is a child less than 21 years old and living in the family household, on the economic resources of that individual's parents. Once a developmentally disabled child has been institutionalized for a month or more in an ICF or a comparable Medicaid institution, only income actually provided by the parents is considered in determining that child's financial eligibility for Medicaid.

BACKGROUND AND DEVELOPMENT

Prior to the development of ICFs, care of individuals with developmental disabilities had been the responsibility of individual states. Most individuals with developmental disabilities who did not live with their families were placed in large state facilities, generally in rural and isolated locations, which emphasized custodial care rather than treatment. By the 1950s, parents and advocates of individuals with developmental disabilities began to push for the reform of such large state institutions and for the development of community-based services, whereby individuals with developmental disabilities could receive special services but continue to live at home. In 1962, a panel appointed by President Kennedy recommended that only developmentally disabled individuals whose specific needs were appropriately met by institutional services should be placed within state facilities. This panel also recommended that federal and state agencies and local communities cooperate in the establishment of community services for individuals with developmental disabilities. In the 1960s and 1970s, with the press reporting on the often harsh conditions to which institutionalized individuals with developmental disabilities were subjected, the movement to reform and provide alternatives to large custodial facilities gained momentum.

Until the 1970s, individual states bore the economic burden of providing for individuals with developmental disabilities. In that decade, however, Congress began enacting legislation to provide federal funds for the treatment of developmentally disabled individuals. In 1971, Congress authorized the use of federal Medicaid funding for the services to be provided by ICFs. The purpose of Congress' substituting federal for state funding was to encourage reform by imposing federal standards on state facilities. Throughout the 1970s, federal expenditures on ICFs rose rapidly, initially due to an increase in the enrollment of individuals with developmental disabilities who qualified for Medicaid benefits. In 1981, the congressional Omnibus Budget Reconciliation Act authorized home and community based waivers whereby states could apply Medicaid funding for individuals with developmental disabilities to services provided in noninstitutional settings. Since that time, increasing numbers of individuals who otherwise would have been directed to ICFs are being treated within their homes and communities. In 1981, the Health Care Financing Administration published guidelines for small ICFs/MR (defined as facilities with 15 or fewer beds). In 1990, the congressional Omnibus Budget Reconciliation Act gave further impetus to community-supported living arrangement services for developmentally disabled individuals.

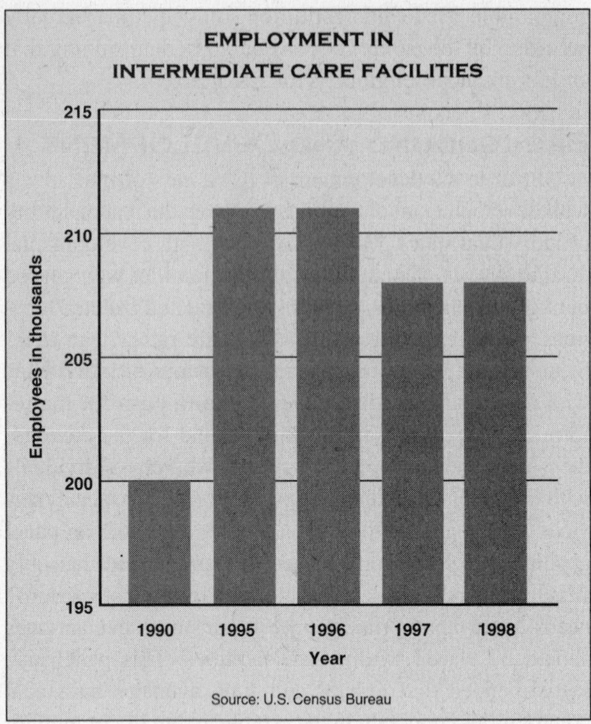

In 1975, the approximate number of Medicaid recipients in ICFs/MR was 69,000. This total reached 121,000 in 1980 and 147,000 in 1985. This increase in ICFs/MR Medicaid recipients represented an 11.3 percent average annual increase for the years 1975 to 1980, but only a 4.0 percent average annual increase for 1980 to 1985, and a 0.2 average annual decrease for 1985 to 1991. In 1977, 43 states provided for ICF/MR services for individuals with developmental disabilities; in that year, there were 547 ICFs/MR nationwide. The total number of ICFs/MR climbed to 1,853 in 1982, to 3,456 in 1986, to 4,562 in 1988, and to 5,405 in 1990. Per capita spending for Medicaid recipients in ICFs/MR grew from approximately $16,000 in 1980 to $50,000 in 1990. By 1990, all states provided for ICF/MR services.

In 1991, almost 150,000 individuals with developmental disabilities relied on ICF/MR services, with federal and state Medicaid funding of such services totaling $7.7 billion. The proportion of federal and state Medicaid spending for ICFs/MR stood at more than 10 percent, although this population represented less than 1 percent of the overall Medicaid beneficiaries. However, home and community based services and day programs for individuals with developmental disabilities may increasingly supplement or provide alternatives to residential ICFs. While ICFs/MR funding accounted for 21 percent of the growth in spending on the developmentally disabled between the years 1975 and 1984, and for 48 percent of such growth between the years 1980 and 1985, this figure fell to 18 percent for the years between 1985 and 1991. Conversely, spending on home and community based services has risen from less than 2 percent of the growth in spending on the developmentally disabled between the years 1975 and 1980, to 6 percent of such growth between the years 1980 and 1985, to 10 percent of such growth for the years 1985 to 1991. This trend reflects the movement away from institutionally based health care that has characterized national initiatives for health care cost containment and reform. The average rate of expenditure per person was $52,497. In 1995 there were 200,000 ICF/MR recipients for whom $10.4 billion were paid by Medicaid to vendors. This amount represented 9 percent of the total payments to all Medicaid vendors for all Medicaid services.

Current Conditions

By 1996 the total of Medicaid recipients in ICFs/MR had receded to 100,000.

The value of integration of services was illustrated by a significant decrease in the number of doses per resident in one 475 bed residential ICF/MR when clinical pharmacy services were instituted. This resulted in pharmacy budget savings, decreased nursing time and resulted in fewer antipsychotic episodes for some patients.

A wave of mergers is expected among the nursing home industry at large, which is likely to impact the ICF segment as well. As is generally the rule, a fragmented industry with generally weak management is a prime candidate for growth by acquisition.

Industry Leaders

According to 1996 *Services Industries USA* the national leaders in sales among companies with interests in ICFs were Genesis Health Ventures, Multicare Companies Inc., Carondolet Health Corp., United Health Services Inc., RehabCare Corp., and Turtle Creek Health. Eger Lutheran, Charter Care Corp., Penninsula United Methodist, Waterfront Health Care Center, and Dover Nursing were some of the leaders in the early 1990s.

Genesis Health Ventures Inc. provides basic and specialty health care services for the elderly. Under the Genesis ElderCare name, the company owns or manages 325 geriatric care facilities, including primary care physician clinics, pharmacies, medical supply distribution centers, rehabilitation clinics, and infusion therapy services. Revenues for fiscal year 1999 were $1.9 billion, up from $1.4 billion in fiscal 1998.

RehabCare Group Inc., a major provider of contract rehabilitation services, provides services for more than 3,000 hospitals, long-term care units, and outpatient facilities across the United States. RehabCare's subsidiary Health care Staffing Solutions provides temporary therapist and nurse staffing services to nursing homes and hospitals. RehabCare announced fiscal 1999 net earnings of $15.1 million.

United Health installed a private ATM and Sonet network to increase communications efficiency between its hospitals, its corporate headquarters, and 25 physicians throughout its region. United Health evolved rapidly into a comprehensive delivery system by using a variety of methods to bring about real integration between physician and non-physician leaders. One S&P health care analyst cited United Health Care as one of the superior stocks in 1996.

Genesis Health Ventures used computer-assisted learning and values clarification training in interpersonal skills to better prepare its staff for the work place. Chief Financial Officer George V. Hager, Jr., was awarded the 1996 Cain Brothers Award for communicating the company's story while keeping a firm hand on its finances and capital decision plans. In 1994 Genesis was 1 of 8 stocks analysts forecast to gain 22 percent to 75 percent in 1995. Integrated Health Services acquired 5 home care companies and a rehabilitation provider in the Carolinas. It also signed a merger agreement with Coram Health care in 1996.

WORKFORCE

ICF employees include administrators and managers; nursing aides, orderlies, and attendants; licensed practical nurses and registered nurses; food service workers; cleaning supervisors, janitors, maids and housekeepers; laundry and dry cleaning workers; maintenance personnel; and recreation workers.

ICFs employed 220,700 persons earning an average of $8.51 and worked an average of 31.8 hours a week in November 1996.

In 1992, the average number of employees per establishment was 45 (compared to 13 employees per establishment for service industries as a whole). In proprietary establishments, the average number of employees was 50; in tax exempt establishments, the average number was 46. In 1995, ICFs accounted for a total of 212,800 employees, of which 191,400 worked in nonsupervisory positions. The states with the greatest concentration of ICF employees were Ohio (23,402 employees, or 9.3 percent of the national total), Illinois (20,656 employees, 8.2 percent of the national total), and New York (16,789 employees, or 6.6 percent of the national total). By 1999, ICFs in the United States employed 202,200.

In 1992, the total ICF payroll was $3.5 billion, of which 43 percent was tax exempt (compared to 28.5 percent for service industries as a whole). The states with the highest total payroll were Ohio ($311.4 million), Illinois ($252.3 million), and New York ($269.3 million). The average payroll per establishment was $388,205 (compared to $314,133 per establishment for service industries as a whole). The average payroll for proprietary establishments was $317,927; the average payroll for tax exempt establishments was $616,822. The average payroll per employee was $13,702 (compared to $23,335 per employee for the service industries as a whole). In proprietary establishments, the average payroll per employee was $13,153; in tax exempt establishments, the average was $14,732. The state with the highest payroll per employee was Alaska ($21,861), followed by New Jersey ($16,793). This figure was lower for New York ($16,040), Ohio ($13,307) and Illinois ($12,215), and significantly lower for states such as North Dakota ($8,618).

Preliminary estimate of the total ICF workforce for October 1996 was 219,700, up from 214,600 in 1995. The average weekly hours was 32.7 in 1995 and 31.6 in 1996, with hourly earnings of $8.13 and $8.47 respectively. Using the above figures, weekly earnings were $265.85 and $267.65.

FURTHER READING

Darnay, Arsen J. ed. *Service Industries USA*. 3rd ed. Detroit: Gale Research, 1996.

Drawbaugh, Kevin. ''Merger Wave Expected Among U.S. Nursing Home Firms.'' Available from http://biz.yahoo.com/bin/jump?/finance/97/02/13/bev_etmi_1.html.

''Genesis Health Ventures, Inc.'' Available from http://biz.yahoo.com.profiles/ghv.html.

Gerard, Roger. ''A Marriage Saved.'' *Health care Forum,* September/October 1995.

Green Book: Overview of Entitlement Programs (updated annually), Washington: U.S. House of Representatives, Committee on Ways and Means.

Health Care Financing Administration. ''Table 4. Medicaid Recipients by Type of Service.'' Available from http://www.hcfa.gov/medicaid/495.html.

———. ''Table 5. Medicaid Vendor Payments by Type of Service.'' Available from http://www.hcfa.gov/medicaid/595.html.

———. ''The Medicaid Program.'' Available from http://www.hcfa.gov/mcdsta95.html.

McKee, Jerry R. ''Clinical Pharmacy Services in an Intermediate Care Facility for the Mentally Retarded.'' *Hospital Pharmacy,* March 1994.

Pallarito, Karen. ''A Capital Offense.'' *Modern Health care,* 7 October 1996.

Rendleman, John. ''Health Care at 155 Mbps.'' *Communications Week,* 8 July 1996.

''RehabCare Group, Inc.'' Available from http://biz.yahoo.com/profiles/rhbc.html.

Scherreik, Susan. ''These Survivors Could Gain 24% to 35% as Rivals Go Extinct.'' *Money,* May 1996.

Snow, Charlotte. ''One-Stop Shopping.'' *Modern Health care,* 25 November 1996.

State of California. Department of Developmental Services. ''ICFs.'' Available from http://www.dds.cahwnet.gov/icf001.html.

Tschop, Carol A. ''Back to Basics.'' *Nursing Homes,* November/December 1996.

U.S. Department of Commerce. Economics and Statistics Administration. Bureau of the Census. *Statistical Abstract of the United States 1996.* 116th ed. Washington: GPO, 1996.

U.S. Department of Health and Human Services. ''Medicare and Medicaid Statistical Supplement, 1996.'' *Health Care Financing Review,* October 1996.

U.S. Department of Housing and Urban Development, Office of Housing Production and Mortgage Credit. *Administrative Procedures for Nursing Homes and/or ICFs.* Washington: GPO, n.d.

U.S. Department of Labor. Bureau of Labor Statistics. *E&E: Employment and Earnings,* January 1997.

U.S. House of Representatives, Committee on Energy and Commerce, Subcommittee on Health and the Environment, Congressional Research Service. *Medicaid Source Book: Background Data and Analysis.* Washington: GPO, n.d.

SIC 8059

NURSING AND PERSONAL CARE FACILITIES, NOT ELSEWHERE CLASSIFIED

This classification covers establishments primarily engaged in providing limited nursing and health-related or personal care to individuals who do not need the degree of care and treatment that a skilled or intermediate care facility provides.

NAICS Code(s)

623311 (Continuing Care Retirement Communities)
623110 (Nursing Care Facilities)

Industry Snapshot

Facilities in this category are used mainly by the elderly and to a much lesser extent by psychiatric patients and the mentally retarded. These individuals may be healthy or require only a minimum of nursing care such as the administration of medicine or supervision of self-administered medications prescribed by a physician. These live-in facilities run the gamut from nursing homes and board-and-care facilities to affluent retirement villages. Convalescent homes for psychiatric patients and group homes for the mentally retarded also fall in this category. Nursing homes in this category are classified as residential care facilities, but some are housed in skilled or intermediate nursing homes. Assisted living, congregate care, domiciliary care, and other arrangements also are in this classification.

Residential care facilities represent the second largest component of health services in this country because of the need to provide care for the growing number of elderly, but the concept of the nursing home is becoming outdated as a place for residential care. It has ''become out of sync with the needs and expectations of our elderly population who require long term care,'' wrote Martin S. Valins in *Nursing Homes.* Valins is an architect specializing in the design of long-term care. He adds that ''the root cause of the problem is that nursing homes were originally conceived out of a hospital model of care—an environment best suited to short-term medical treatment. Only recently did the nation begin to distinguish old age from illness. Becoming old does not necessarily imply that one will become ill or need constant medical supervision.''

One of the most significant associations in the industry, the Assisted Living Federation of America, was founded in 1991 as the Assisted Living Facilities Association of America. The non-profit organization is a trade association devoted to the assisted living industry and the population it serves, and is comprised of more than 6,000 members, including providers of assisted living; state associations of providers; and others interested in promoting awareness, standards, and the interests of the industry. The American College of Health Care Administrators (ACHCA) is a professional society for 6,300 administrators in long-term care, assisted living, and subacute care. The ACHCA's mission to be ''the premier organization serving as a catalyst to empower administrators who will define professionalism throughout the continuum of care.'' The American Health Care Association (AHCA) is a federation of 50 state health organizations and represents nearly 12,000 non-profit and for-profit assisted living facilities, nursing facilities, and subacute care providers.

Organization and Structure

While this category consists of group homes for the mentally retarded and convalescent homes for psychiatric patients, the largest segment and fastest growing area was the assisted living component. ''Nursing and personal care'' are frequently lumped together in statistical charts under nursing homes in general. This broader category was a $11.1 billion industry in 1996, up from $2.8 billion in 1990. As a bundled group, it contained 1.75 million workers in November 1996, an increase of about 46,000 from November 1995.

The projected population of those 65 and older was expected to increase to 35 million by the year 2000, and to 40 million by 2010. More than 6,000 Americans turn 65 each day. The increase in the 85-plus population was predicted to grow by 94 percent in the next 25 years compared to a general population growth of 25 percent, according to Jonathan Goldman in a special supplement on health care in the *Institutional Investor*. Life expectancy for those who have reached 85 has increased 24 percent from 1960 to 1990 and was expected to increase another 44 percent by 2040. A growing percentage of those over 65 were employed from 1990 to 1995, and there was an increase in those 75 and over who were living alone.

More than 1.5 million persons spend between $10 billion and $15 billion annually to live in 40,000 assisted living communities in the United States. The assisted living industry was expected to grow from $8 billion to nearly $25 billion by 2000.

Assisted-living free-standing residences are easy to build and less risky than other entries into the retirement market, according to 80 percent of the respondents to a survey of 326 senior housing executives published in *Commercial Investment Real Estate* in 1995. They also require less capital investment and lower operating costs.

It was estimated that between one-fourth and one-half of nursing home residents could be in assisted-living at substantially less cost. With 90 percent of assisted-living funds coming from private individuals, nursing homes could house only Medicare/Medicaid patients. Average costs for assisted living are $60 per day versus $80 to $100 for nursing homes. Nearly all assisted-living expenses are funded privately. However, 46 percent of all persons leaving assisted care do enter a skilled nursing facility.

Assisted living can provide a sense of independence and dignity. One of the problems is that Medicare or Medicaid funds nursing home stays, but does not cover assisted living. In some cases, this may foster upgrading or overstating a condition to become a nursing home resident. Oregon passed legislation allowing unlicensed staff to perform selected nursing duties. This has cut assisted-living costs to two-thirds of those for nursing homes. The primary objective of managed care is to move patients to the most appropriate and least expensive level.

During the first half of 1994, more than 25 assisted living retirement facilities with a total value of $400 million were financed by Real Estate Investment Trusts (REITs). The evolution of national assisted living chains have accelerated the role of REITs.

Until recently, residential nursing care for the elderly was not reimbursed by payments from Medicaid, the federal and state health care insurance for low-income individuals. However, many states are seeking waivers so that Medicaid can fund a variety of residential care settings.

Residential care units often exist in skilled or intermediate nursing facilities that are funded primarily by the government. Every state has its own licensing regulations and its own methods of enforcing regulations. About 68 percent of total nursing home expenditures in 1997 were funded by Medicaid. Private insurers paid for 23 percent of costs. Assisted living facilities have higher operating margins because they are developed with private capital and their clients pay privately, allowing them to adjust charges accordingly.

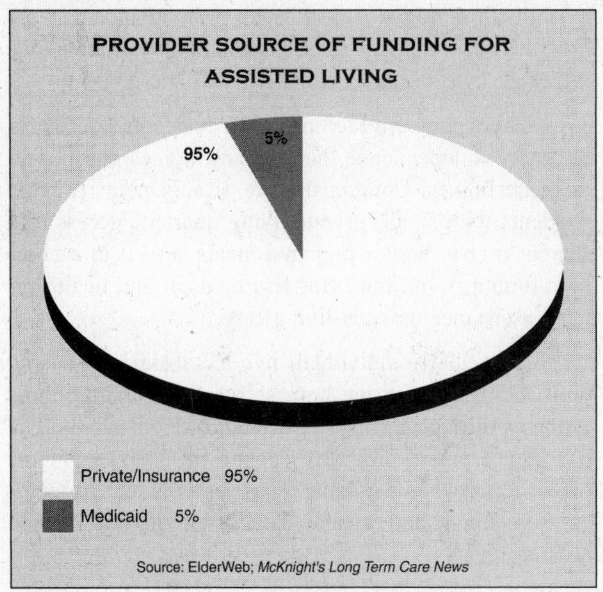

Source: ElderWeb; *McKnight's Long Term Care News*

Total nursing home industry revenues were estimated at $74.3 billion in 1993, most of it from government reimbursement for patients requiring skilled or intermediate level nursing care. During 1997 there were approximately 17,000 nursing facilities with 1.8 million beds. The industry was projected to increase to 2.2 million beds by the year 2000. According to Social Security Administration projections, the number of individuals 75 and older will increase by 31 percent between 1991 and 2010.

There is a continuum of care among the types of facilities in this category, ranging from retirement villages and assisted living arrangements to nursing homes. Retirement villages offer gracious living in private homes or town houses, often with hotel-type services and recreation. Many of these developments offer medical backup, medical alert systems, and sometimes a connection to a nursing home. The most expensive retirement villages offer continuing care and a guarantee of increasing nursing care as needed for life. Less expensive retirement communities provide only short-term nursing care. More and more facilities offer a choice of care in a campus setting or in different wings of the same building.

Assisted living is based on the European model of residential long-term care. Residences are in homes, apartment buildings, or studio or one-bedroom apartments. Transportation, housekeeping, meals, personal care, and often other services such as adult day care, vision clinics, rehabilitation programs, and health promotion centers are provided. The number of such communities nationwide increased over the last decade from 277 to 1,000.

Congregate-care facilities offer residents considerably more independence than nursing homes and board-and-care homes. Congregate-care arrangements provide residents with small, private-living quarters, access to a shared kitchen and/or prepared meals served in a common dining room, but offer less medical and health related assistance assisted-living care.

Some elderly individuals live in subsidized housing units built by nursing homes, on the nursing home grounds, through a U.S. Department of Housing and Urban Development program. Though these arrangements offer access to some nursing home services such as medical screenings and meals, they often do not include nursing care.

Residential-care nursing offers a supportive and protective living environment for ambulatory residents, usually those older than 50, who have difficulty taking care of themselves but who do not require skilled nursing on a routine basis. Medicare has not paid for those in residential care, nor has Medicaid, though attempts are underway to change this. Medicaid traditionally has gone to licensed nursing homes providing skilled or intermediate care.

Increasingly, many facilities are choosing to offer a combination of all of these services, enabling residents to move through the system as needed. At the Ida Cuber House in the state of Washington, many options are available and there is considerable movement within the facility. Some residents want a permanent home and the option of progressing through levels of care as needed. Others are admitted for short-term stays and are expected to return to their homes.

At the Ida Cuber House, the nursing care center and assisted living program accommodate short-term care, with supportive therapies to return residents to the lightest level of care possible. Other residents who have initially come to the facility's nursing care center from the general community have been discharged to assisted living or to an independent living facility. On the other hand, as some residents become more functionally or cognitively impaired, they move to assisted living or to the nursing care center.

Board-and-care facilities, sometimes known as rest homes, provide little more than housing and meals. These facilities can house as few as four or five residents boarding in someone's house, to several hundred residents. In 1989, the U.S. General Accounting Office (GAO) estimated that there were 41,000 licensed homes of this type with 563,000 beds and additional unlicensed beds. The GAO also found that many failed to provide medical care, hygiene, and nutrition.

New York was among the first states to expose such abuse and fraud. It created a permanent special prosecutor to investigate such matters. In 1974 information was uncovered that millions of Medicaid dollars earmarked for the care of elderly indigent patients was instead going into the pockets of certain New York nursing home owners and operators. By 1977, with the federal government spending $16 billion a year on Medicaid, a Senate investigating committee found a substantial portion of the total was the result of ''rampant fraud and abuse,'' brought about by state indifference. In 1977, Congress passed legislation establishing the State Medicaid Fraud Control Unit Program, which enabled qualifying states to become eligible for reimbursement of 90 percent of their expenses for fraud control expenditures.

Background and Development

By the year 2000, ''assisted living was expected to grow from $8 billion to $25 billion—an annual rate of 25 percent,'' according to John Goldman.

Continuing-care retirement communities' (CCRCs) assisted living beds rose 12.8 percent to a total of 13,584. In 1994, 526 CCRCs had 68,895 independent living units, 12,369 assisted-living beds, and 20,360 nursing beds.

Current Conditions

Despite increasing demands for residential care, fewer people are winding up in nursing homes than had been predicted. Healthier lifestyles and improved medical technology are allowing seniors to recover from strokes, broken hips, and other pitfalls of the aging process so that they do not need to live in a skilled nursing facility.

For that reason, the days of the skilled nursing home as the preferred model of long-term care may be numbered, as nursing home industry leaders warned their colleagues. They recommended that nursing homes either be converted to apartment-like facilities providing assisted living or to sub-acute institutions caring for the seriously ill, as part of a managed care network. Since the proposed health reforms in the mid-1990s were calling for moving health care delivery away from hospitals and into community-based satellite health care facilities, nursing home leaders suggest that homes serve the needs of non-resident seniors in their community as well as residents. Assisted living units built in conjunction with single-family homes and condominiums in a planned unit development or adjacent to a health center, are a newer concept that would allow older persons the opportunity to mingle with their children, relatives, or other young people in a neighborhood.

In the meantime, nursing homes continued to search for revenue and ways to reduce costs, hoping to become integrated into health care networks of hospitals and clinics. Medicaid was the fastest growing state expenditure. At a time when the states were in financial distress, many tried to hold down expenses by not issuing permits for the construction of new nursing homes. In 1997, changes in the nation's health care system cut back on Medicaid reimbursement for elder care providers. By late 1999, some of the leading providers of care had filed for bankruptcy protection.

Prejudices about the elderly among health care professionals and other staff, plus attitudes that favor high-tech over low-tech treatment, may also interfere with advances in residential care. Worse than prejudices are the repeated instances of neglect among residential facilities caring for the elderly, leading to complaints that the residents are merely being "warehoused." Reports of such instances have continued to prompt investigations. Nursing home inspections have become more stringent, leading to the discovery of more abuses. In 1996 there were investigations of nursing homes in nationwide. Nursing home abuse has led states such as New York to propose criminal checks on nursing aides and stringent penalties for convicted abusers. Nursing homes continued to be plagued by accusations of mistreatment into 2000.

The "hottest niche for the future," according to Sandy Lutz in *Modern Healthcare,* appears to be assisted living and low-intensity medical services housing. Residential care was number one on the U.S. Small Business Administration's list of fast growing markets, with most of the growth coming from assisted-living facilities.

INDUSTRY LEADERS

Leaders were not without challenges in the late 1990s and into 2000, facing bankruptcies and a continuing stigma toward the nursing home industry. Many organizations sought to change the public's concept of nursing homes from dull, sterile places to elegant manors with delicious food, fun activities, and home or resort-like atmospheres.

At the end of 1999, leading public companies were: Sun Healthcare Group Inc., Beverly Enterprises Inc., Assisted Living Concepts Inc., Manor Care Inc., Marriott Senior Living Services, and Mariner Post-Acute Network Inc.

Changes are rapidly occurring in the insurance industry to provide for long-term care coverage. TIAA, a major retirement fund for college teachers, began to offer such insurance for family, including parents, in 1997. Other retirement systems and private insurers will most likely follow. There also is a movement to obtain federal assistance for assisted living as a lesser-cost alternative to nursing homes.

WORKFORCE

Personnel at residential care facilities will vary according to the number of residents and services provided.

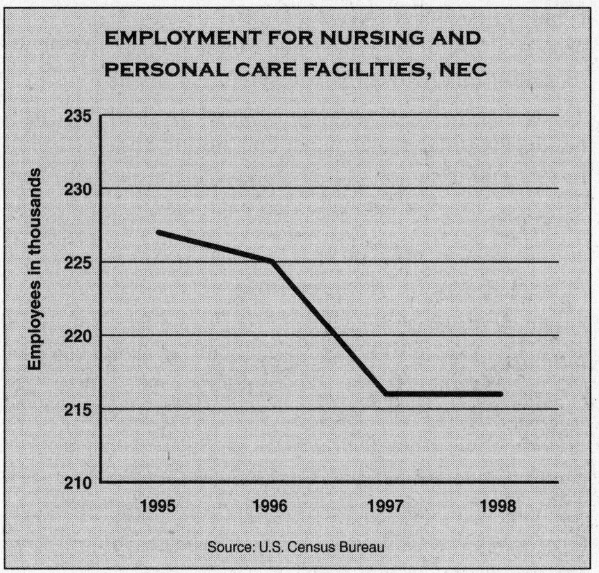

Staff may be employed by the facility or in cooperation with an outside agency. In nursing and convalescent homes, there is a manager or administrator, plus personal care attendants on staff who assist residents with personal needs (such as feeding, dressing, and bathing), nurses who assist residents with education and the administration and supervision of medication, physical therapists, activities coordinators, food service managers, and maintenance staff.

Many states require the administrator or manager of nursing homes to complete a state-approved certification program within one year of being hired and require them to take continuing education courses annually from a state board of nursing, social work, or other such agency.

Employment in residential care facilities in general represents 18 percent of the jobs in the health services. Jobs in this sector increased by 3.9 percent during the 1980s, adding a 550,000 employee increase to the industry. Today, nursing homes and personal care facilities employ about 1.6 million workers at approximately 21,000 work sites. By 2005, this figure is expected to rise to 2.4 million workers. Employment in this industry has been affected little by the changes in the economy.

One new and possible trend is the movement toward a holistic or universal work attending to all the daily needs of a resident. The same person will assist with meal services, light housekeeping, and laundry. Retraining staff from task orientation to resident orientation is a major challenge. Employment strictly in this industry was 229,000 in 1995, an increase of 7,000 from 1994. If the average workweek and wage is the same as that for the broader category of nursing and personal care, it is 32 hours and $9.06 per hour, respectively.

FURTHER READING

American College of Health Care Administrators (ACHCA). Available from http://www.achca.org/.

Assisted Living Federation of America (ALFA). Available from http://www.alfa.org/.

Bruck, Laura. ''Assisted Living Snapshot.'' *Nursing Homes,* April 1996.

Calbria, Mark A. ''Elderly Migration, a Study of Major Cities.'' *Housing Economics,* November 1996.

Goldman, Jonathan. ''Long-Term Care and Assisted Living.'' *Institutional Investor,* Bonus supplement. December 1996.

Guyton, Kate. ''Just Like Home.'' *Washingtonian,* October 1996.

''Long-Term Care Alternatives. A Special 1997 Update.'' New York: Teachers Insurance and Annuity Association, 1997.

Lutz, Sandy. ''Wall Street's Ills Infect Healthcare IPOs.'' *Modern Healthcare,* 29 July 1996.

McCune, Jenny. ''The Face of Tomorrow.'' *Journal of Business Strategy,* May/June 1995.

McLean, Bethany. ''Promising Industries for 1997.'' *Fortune,* 23 December 1996.

N.Y. State Special Prosecutor for Medicaid Fraud Control Unit. ''New York State Special Prosecutor for Medicaid Fraud Control Unit.''

''National Data on Nursing Facilities.'' American Health Care Association. Available from http://www.ahca.org/who/profile4.htm#1.

''Nursing Homes: Bad Medicine for Elderly.'' *USA Today: The Magazine of the American Scene,* July 1996.

Nursing Homes. Occupational Safety & Health Administration/ U.S. Department of Labor. Available from http://www.osha-slc.gov/SLTC/nursinghome/.

''Oregon Keeps Assisted-Living Costs Down.'' *Public Health Reports,* May 1996.

Pallarito, Karen. ''Assisted Living Leads Growth.'' *Modern Healthcare,* 20 May 1996.

———. ''Hospitals Turn Attention to Assisted Living.'' *Modern Healthcare,* December 1995.

Patterson, David. ''When Is a Chair not a Chair?'' *Nursing Homes,* May 1996.

———. ''REITs and Assisted Living.'' *Nursing Homes,*April 1996.

Peck, Richard L. ''Private LTC Insurance: Still a Budding Resource.'' *Nursing Homes,* April 1996.

'''Practical' Research: Assistive Technologies.'' *Nursing Homes,* November 1996.

Rotenier, Nancy. ''Old Folks Welcome.'' *Forbes,* 17 July 1995.

Roth, Dennis. ''Golden Opportunities in Assisted Living.'' *Commercial Investment Real Estate Journal,* Spring 1995.

Rowe, Megan. ''Assisted Living: Hospitality's Horizon Expands.'' *Lodging Hospitality,* November 1996.

Schless, David S. ''Challenging 10 Commonly Held Assumptions About Seniors Housing.'' *National Real Estate Investor,* November 1996.

Schwartz, Ronald. ''LTC Organizations Split on Assisted Living Guidelines.'' *Nursing Homes,* July 1996.

''Today's Nursing Facilities and the People They Serve.'' American Health Care Association. Available from http://www.ahca.org/who/profile.htm.

U.S. Department of Commerce. Economics and Statistics Administration. Bureau of the Census. *Statistical Abstract of the United States 1996.* 116 ed. Washington: GPO, 1996.

U.S. Department of Labor. Bureau of Labor Statistics. *E&E: Employment and Earnings,* December 1996.

———. *Monthly Labor Review,* November 1996.

Weaver, Peter. ''Opportunity Knocks as America Ages.'' *Nation's Business,* August 1996.

Widdes, Tal. ''Assisted Living's Universal Worker.'' *Nursing Homes,* April 1996.

Wise, Kathryn O. ''Making the Choice to Carpet.'' *Nursing Homes,* July 1996.

SIC 8062

GENERAL MEDICAL AND SURGICAL HOSPITALS

This industry consists of establishments primarily providing general medical and surgical services and other hospital services in a hospital setting. This grouping excludes specialty hospitals classified in **SIC 8069: Specialty Hospital, Except Psychiatric** and psychiatric hospitals covered in **SIC 8063: Psychiatric Hospitals.**

NAICS CODE(S)

622110 (General Medical and Surgical Hospitals)

INDUSTRY SNAPSHOT

According to the 1996 *Statistical Abstract of the United States,* the United States had about 6,400 general and surgical hospitals. Made up of both non-profit and profit-making establishments, they employed slightly more than 5 million workers and took in about $410 billion in annual gross revenues. This accounted for nearly one-half of the nation's total annual health care employment and health care expenditures, placing hospitals at the center of the health care industry.

In recent years, hospitals in America have been increasingly under pressure by government and businesses to provide higher quality service at lower costs while increasing access and preserving patient choice. A move to emphasize outpatient over inpatient care, and efforts to use health maintenance organizations (HMOs) and other cost-cutting measures implemented by employers, has dramatically altered the business over the past several decades. One result is a trend toward more academic medical centers, more ambulatory surgery, and fewer community hospitals, which have declined in total number by 17 percent since 1981. As pressure to enact such changes continued, general medical and surgical hospitals were approaching the end of the twentieth century with persistent uncertainty about the direction and shape of their industry's future.

ORGANIZATION & STRUCTURE

General and surgical hospitals are generally categorized as non-profit, profit-making, and both state and local government establishments. The 1996 *Statistical Abstract of the United States* reported 3,139 non-profit, 719 profit-making, and 1,678 government hospitals in the United States. About 82 percent, providing 3.6 beds for every 1,000 U.S. residents, were further described as ''community hospitals,'' meaning they were facilities and services open to the public, which therefore excluded federal, long-term hospitals, psychiatric and special hospitals, and hospitals of institutions such as prisons. During the 1990s, community hospitals have increasingly become part of multihospital systems, where one owner or an ownership group owns more than one hospital. The Public Citizen Health Research Group found that 1 in 12 community hospitals across the United States was involved in merger activity in 1995 alone. The leading example that year was the $5.6 billion acquisition of Healthtrust by Columbia/HCA Healthcare Corp., itself the product of a 1994 merger between Columbia Healthcare Corp. and Hospital Corp. of America. In 1995, Columbia/HCA Healthcare was the largest operator in this category with 318 hospitals and $17.7 billion in annual revenues. Still the largest hospital chain in the U.S., Columbia/HCA ended 1999 with 100 fewer hospitals and surgery centers.

Hospitals receive their revenues from different sources for the services they provide to patients. The largest source of income to community hospitals in the 1990s came from Medicare and Medicaid programs, but tightening restrictions and the ongoing possibility that massive additional cutbacks will be enacted have increasingly impacted these two income sources since the 1980s. The remainder of all hospital revenues came primarily from third-party payers like private health insurance plans and, to a much smaller extent, directly from patients.

Hospital expenses are strongly affected by legislation, costs of medical technology, and trends in medical practice. As they continually rose throughout the 1990s, on-site administrative, food service, maintenance, and laundry support often were streamlined or contracted out in response. To counteract rising costs, many hospitals also attempted to expand their revenues by increasing their role in community health maintenance efforts beyond traditional emergency, obstetrics, and inpatient care to include disease prevention and patient education programs such as weight reduction, drug rehabilitation, prenatal care, and pediatric wellness.

Internally, hospitals are structured around an administrative staff that oversees nursing and administrative functions and separately operated medical staff and ancillary services—such as a pharmacy and the services of various therapists.

BACKGROUND & DEVELOPMENT

Early hospitals were established by governments and religious groups for care of special segments of the population, such as the poor, the military, and slaves. In Europe, doctors and other medical staff were not paid for their services in hospitals, as such services were regarded as Christian charitable work. Records show that during the Middle Ages, medical staffs of charity workers were divided into two groups which rotated their work each month.

Starting in the thirteenth century, hospitals greatly increased in number throughout Europe. With this, hospitals gradually became more secular and began paying their medical staffs. At this time, and up until the eighteenth century, private patients in a hospital ward were virtually nonexistent. Hospitals were still regarded as places for the poor, while wealthy patients were usually treated in their homes by hired physicians.

By the late eighteenth and early nineteenth century, another form of hospital emerged. ''Voluntary'' institutions were developed with the idea of providing charitable treatment for all segments of the population. These hospitals grew into the ''non-profit'' U.S. establishments of the twentieth century.

Early hospitals in America followed the pattern of their European predecessors; most hospitals developed out of houses and treatment centers for special groups of the population. Many of these early American hospitals were often quickly built in order to confine the spread of contagious diseases. The first hospitals in America were Bellevue Hospital founded in New York in 1658, and Philadelphia Hospital, founded in 1713. Both institutions were originally intended for the insane, the aged, and the poor.

In 1752, the Pennsylvania Hospital was founded as a voluntary hospital to serve both the poor in large public wards and other patients in private rooms; these affluent patients paid both the physician and the hospital for their services. However, hospitals in Europe and America were still viewed as places for the poor until the nineteenth century, when medical technology made large advances. During this period, hospitals became equipped with anesthesia (considered by experts to represent a turning point for hospitals), new medicines, and more sterile environments, making hospitals safer places for treatment.

The nineteenth century brought about other significant developments for hospitals. Hospitals became the centers of medical education and research. In addition to doctors, other medical staff, most notably nurses, became professionals in their own right, developing their own professional standards and certifications. It was also during this century that the health insurance industry started. Patient insurance began in Germany in 1883 and was operated and paid for by the German government; in America the idea was taken over by private insurance companies.

The twentieth century has witnessed remarkable changes in this industry. Technological advances in radiology have meant earlier diagnosis of many fatal ailments—in particular cancers—and treatment of those conditions. As many fields in medicine have developed, such as obstetrics, pediatrics, and transplant surgery, so too have departments providing these services in hospitals.

In response to the post-war baby boom, the 1950s saw a large growth in the number of hospitals throughout the country. At this time, medical schools and teaching hospitals grew to meet the demands of the new generation. From 1970 until 1990, the role of hospitals in American society and their function within the larger health care industry has changed significantly. During this period, the number of hospitals in America began to decline from 7,123 with 1.6 million beds, to 6,400 with 992,000 beds. Additionally, the rate of occupancy in hospitals also dropped from 80 percent in 1970 to 66.1 percent in 1994. The following year, the *Journal of the American Medical Association* projected hospital admissions would decline an additional 26 percent and average length of stay would dip another 11 percent by the end of the century.

This ongoing reduction in the number of hospitals and the drop in occupancy rates reflected a general trend away from traditional inpatient care to procedures that can be done just as effectively but even more economically on an outpatient basis. Outpatient visits at all U.S. hospitals accordingly rose from 181 million in 1970 to 454 million in 1994. Much of this movement resulted from government legislation and health insurance plans offering more coverage for less costly treatments that did not require overnight stays. Additional growth was spurred by technical advances in outpatient surgical procedures, which permitted the number of all surgeries performed outside of a traditional hospital setting to rise from 24 percent in 1983 to 55 percent in 1993.

Since the 1970s the industry has also seen proprietorship of hospitals shift from a climate in which the ownership of individual establishments was predominant to one in which chains of hospitals now prevails. This has enabled hospitals to share technology and management resources across their chains of establishments and cut costs due to economies of scale. Moreover, it has allowed hospital owners to begin specializing their ownership services by dividing hospitals into the three main industry groups: general medical and surgical, psychiatric, and other specialties. The consolidation has not been without problems, however, especially as it changed some nonprofit institutions into for-profit enterprises, which do not always stand in high regard.

Services Offered by Hospitals. General medical and surgical hospitals provide a variety of hospital-based health services. According to the 1996 *Statistical Abstract of the United States,* more than 92 percent of hospitals in the United States had emergency departments. For AIDS sufferers, nearly 74 percent of hospitals offered general inpatient care (up from 61 percent in 1992), while 6.7 percent offered specialized outpatient AIDS programs. Therapy services also made up a large portion of services provided by general medical and surgical hospitals: 91.2 percent of these hospitals offered respiratory therapy services, 85.5 percent had physical therapy programs, and 55.5 percent assisted with occupational therapy. Addressing the needs of the aging population, American hospitals increased their geriatric services during the 1980s and 1990s. By the mid-1980s, nearly two-thirds of all hospitals offered one or more geriatric services. These included geriatric response, which monitors elderly patients in their homes and links them with hospitals in case of emergency; respite care facilities; and geriatric acute care units. A small number of hospitals developed Alzheimer's diagnostic and assessment services and adult day care facilities. However, the fastest growing field within geriatric care is psychiatric services; in 1992, 27 percent of general hospitals offered geriatric mental heath programs. According to Paula Eubanks in *Hospitals,* the majority of geriatric mental health programs were only available at non-community hospitals like large university hospitals and hospitals run by the Department of Veteran Affairs.

According to the American Hospital Association, 87 percent of general medical and surgical hospitals in the United States had an official outpatient department in 1993, while almost 94 percent offered at least some outpatient surgery services. That year, outpatient surgical procedures accounted for 55 percent of all surgeries performed in community hospitals. About 85 percent of all hospitals had blood banks, more than 66 percent had birthing rooms, and nearly 85 percent had ultrasound. Approximately 21 percent offered alcohol/chemical dependency care and 23 percent had psychiatric services. In the 1990s, many hospitals also opened outpatient centers that specialized in the treatment of pain. These outpatient pain clinics varied in size and the specific types of treatments offered. With the growth in managed care and patients seeking alternatives to costly inpatient stays, these clinics were expected to increase in the late 1990s. Another significant growth area for outpatient services is in home health care; in 1993, 41.5 percent of all community hospitals offered home health care services.

Another growing service provided by general medical and surgical hospitals is inpatient and outpatient care for victims of domestic violence. In 1992, a study compiled by *Hospitals* estimated that $44 million of the nation's annual medical costs went to hospital treatment for over 21,000 cases of domestic violence.

In the 1990s, community hospitals also provided a growing array of health promotion services. In 1993, the American Hospital Association reported that more than 88 percent had patient education programs. Approximately 60 percent of all hospitals offered worksite health promotion programs.

Medicare and Medicaid. Medicare and Medicaid are federally funded health insurance programs that provide assistance to patients over 65 years of age and patients with end-stage kidney disease, low incomes, or disabilities. In 1993, Medicare paid for 51 percent of all inpatient hospital visits and 8 percent of outpatient hospital costs; Medicaid paid for 27 percent of inpatient stays and 6 percent of outpatient charges. The Hospital Insurance (HI) program within Medicare pays for care given at hospitals, home health agencies, hospices, and skilled nursing facilities. In 1997, HI payments totaled $137.8 billion for 38 million enrollees.

The introduction of Medicare and Medicaid programs in the early 1970s significantly impacted this industry. In 1970, Medicare and Medicaid accounted for just over 6 million patient admissions to general medical and surgical hospitals and paid for $5 billion of their hospital charges; by 1993, Medicare alone paid $76.3 billion in inpatient hospital charges. Between 1980 and 1990, the number of Medicaid recipients receiving inpatient treatment rose by 913,000 annually, while the number of Medicaid patients receiving outpatient care rose by 2.6 million annually. By 1995 Medicare was the largest single insurer in the United States, covering about 14 percent of the entire population. As the population continues aging and additional advances are made in medicine and technology, Medicare funds for people over 65 years of age have become the largest portion of all hospitals' government-funded health coverage.

Medicare and Medicaid programs have also affected hospital management, requiring greater training in non-medical matters in order to deal with paperwork regulations and various service requirements. But cutbacks and changes in the payment systems in Medicare and Medicaid during the 1980s and early 1990s had their largest impact on the industry's bottom line. In 1991 alone, $43 billion was cut from the Medicare budget, and in 1996 President Clinton vetoed a Republican balanced budget plan that would have mandated Medicare cuts of $270 billion and Medicaid cuts of $163 billion by the year 2000; the President's own alternative called for $124 billion in Medicare reductions, so even though no compromise was immediately reached, the hospital industry readied itself for even more changes.

As part of the overall realignment, the Health Care Financing Administration (HCFA), which manages Medicare, had proposed fixed-rate pricing on many medical services. This new pricing system was projected to bridge the gap between the salaries of specialist physicians and general or family practitioners and was expected to improve the accounting involved in ambulatory care services.

Mergers. Mergers and joint ventures have played important roles in this industry as a way of sharing the costs of needed technology and trimming redundant costs. Moreover, as the occupancy rate increases in hospitals across the country, joint ventures open means of sharing liabilities to reduce the impact of financial downturns on individual hospitals.

In the late 1980s, the federal government imposed antitrust rulings in two highly publicized cases prohibiting the merger of certain hospitals. Following this, a few mergers per year were investigated by federal agencies. As a result, the American Hospital Association ran a campaign to have antitrust laws relaxed, believing such laws hindered mergers and joint ventures between hospitals. The government has not reversed any of its rulings concerning antitrust laws over hospital mergers. However, this issue remains important to this industry as it enters the twenty-first century.

Malpractice. By the 1990s, the American Medical Association was estimating that $15 billion of the nation's health costs went towards ''defensive medicine,'' that is, additional tests and diagnostic procedures carried out to protect doctors from malpractice claims. For this reason, the increase in malpractice cases, particularly during the mid-1980s, has increased the use of hospital laboratory facilities. However, malpractice cases have been more noted for negatively affecting this industry. Because hospitals have more insurance and larger revenues than individual doctors, they are often the targets of such suits. In the early 1990s, hospitals responded to malpractice cases by increasing medical staff decisions and reviews of doctors' procedures. Hospitals have also started protect-

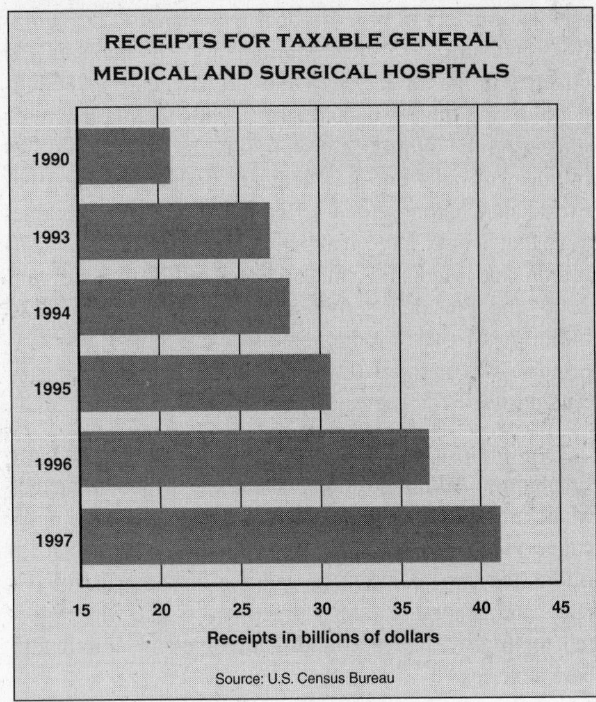

ing their assets by placing them in separate corporations or endowments.

Hospitals and Pollution. Establishments in this industry have long dealt with the problem of waste disposal. Not only do hospitals generate large amounts of general waste, such as paper and food, but they also have to dispose of chemical and pathogen waste. The AIDS epidemic has increased concern over waste containing live pathogens, which could be contaminated with the AIDS virus.

Until the late 1980s, hospitals in America disposed of medical wastes by using on-site incinerators, which were effective in burning wastes, but polluted the air. In 1988, nine states passed medical-waste disposal legislation, and in 1989 an additional 22 states passed these types of laws. By 1990, new government standards, mostly at the state level, affected an estimated 6,000 hospital incinerators. Complying with the new standards imposed costs of between $500,000 and $1 million on each hospital.

To avoid the direct financial burden of upgrading incinerators, small hospitals, especially those in rural areas, banded together to share regional incinerators which met the new air pollution standards. However, this approach has introduced new costs related to hauling waste to the incinerator.

Current Conditions

As a result of overexpansion of facilities in the 1970s and the economic recession at the beginning of the 1990s, hospitals have been struggling without easy access to capital and charitable funding. Between 1985 and 1995, according to *Modern Healthcare,* approximately 600 acute care hospitals closed and eliminated about 180,000 beds. Even so, some believed that with the ongoing fiscal belt-tightening as many as 447,000 unnecessary beds still remained—enough to fill almost 2,500 hospitals.

In order to deal with the various financial problems they faced some companies in this industry have been increasing their psychiatric units and rehabilitation clinics, both of which are high-profit facilities. Nearly all hospitals have been expanding their outpatient services, which generally bring in lower profits than inpatient units but yield continuous revenues. Many are automating routine administrative tasks.

According to *Hospitals,* this industry also entered the 1990s suffering from a public image problem that affected the non-profit status of most hospitals in America. This had resulted from public criticisms of hospital pricing practices, the growing number of malpractice cases, and the way in which hospitals have taken on a more business-like approach to managing their establishments. The decision by 447 formerly single-unit community hospitals to merge with larger corporations in 1995, along with the conversion that year of 58 non-profit hospitals to for-profit status, did not help the industry's overall public image.

The business-like approach that now generally marks the entire industry has been characterized by ''quality management.'' Instead of leaving the quality of care in the hands of individual practitioners, hospitals have begun instituting measures to prevent faulty processes from occurring. According to Julia Flynn Siler and Sandra Atchison in *Business Week,* quality management was originally adopted by hospitals to improve food service and lower the length of patient stays; however, in the 1990s this approach was also used for clinical decisions and processes.

The shift towards more outpatient care also has affected hospital management. Although hospitals account for outpatient care separately from inpatient treatment, management of the two types of services has traditionally been under one supervisor. However, in the 1990s hospitals started moving towards specialized management, which would unite the various types of outpatient services while keeping them separate from inpatient care.

Industry Leaders

In 1999, industry leaders were Columbia/HCA Healthcare Corp., Vencor Inc., Tenet Healthcare Corporation, and Ascension Health.

Columbia/HCA Healthcare Corp., created by the 1994 merger of Columbia Healthcare Corp. and Hospital Corp. of America., became the largest hospital company when it merged again with Healthtrust in 1995. The new $17.7 billion-enterprise controlled 318 hospitals, staffed

62,277 acute care beds, and employed 240,000 workers. *Standard & Poor's* reported that the 1994 merger enabled the company to save $130 million annually through consolidation and lower purchasing costs; the 1995 merger, it predicted, would lead to an additional $125 million in savings each year.

In 1993, before the mergers, Hospital Corp. of America (HCA) owned 96 hospitals in 21 states. Despite sales of over $4 billion in 1991, this company recorded a loss in that year of $5.4 million. However, in 1992, it rebounded with earnings of $28.2 million on $5.13 billion in sales revenues.

The following year, it received public attention as part of the Government Accounting Office (GAO) report on hospitals found to be overbilling Medicare. According to the report, in 1991, Hospital Corp. of America sought Medicare payments for over $1.1 million in questionable non-medical costs. The company's account for these overbillings was $75,000, pointing out that it was a small fraction of the $114 million the hospital received from Medicare in 1991.

Columbia/HCA Healthcare Corp. sought to reinvent itself in the late 1990's by halting its expansion plans and trimming operations. By 1999, after the sale of 100 hospitals and its prescription benefit unit, Columbia owned and operated 214 hospitals and 84 ambulatory surgery centers, and employed 184,000.

Vencor, Inc. operates 60 acute care hospitals, 300 skilled nursing facilities, and pharmacies, and is the nation's second-largest provider of long-term health care. After a 1998 split into two separate companies, Ventas, Inc. owned and managed all of Vencor's real estate assets and Vencor operated the nursing home and hospital businesses. Soon after, Vencor sold its health and hospice divisions to focus on its main lines of business. In mid-1999, Vencor filed for bankruptcy after struggles with lenders, dipping profits, and lower federal reimbursements.

Tenet Healthcare Corporation is the second largest hospital chain in the U.S., owning or operating 130 hospitals in 17 states and an additional hospital in Barcelona, Spain. Ascension Health, the number one Catholic hospital system as well as the largest not-for-profit healthcare system in the U.S., operates a network of nearly 80 Catholic hospitals, nursing homes, psychiatric wards, and other facilities in 15 states and the District of Columbia. Ascension was formed in 1999 by the merger of Daughters of Charity National Health System and the Sisters of St. Joseph Health System.

WORKFORCE

In 1995, general medical and surgical hospitals employed slightly more than 5 million workers. Nearly 3.7 million had been employed in 1993, which itself represented a 2.4 percent increase from 1990. This total was comprised of salaried staff—including administrators, clerical workers, laboratory technicians, physical therapists, dietitians, and allied health personnel who are independent clinical workers assisting physicians and medical specialists—as well as physicians and nurses. According to the Bureau of Labor Statistics' *Occupational Outlook Handbook,* general medical and surgical hospitals employed about 1.3 million registered nurses (RNs) and 223,680 licensed practical nurses (LPNs) in 1996. Approximately 112,000 physicians worked in general hospitals in 1996. Physician Assistants (PAs) held 12,800 jobs in hospitals.

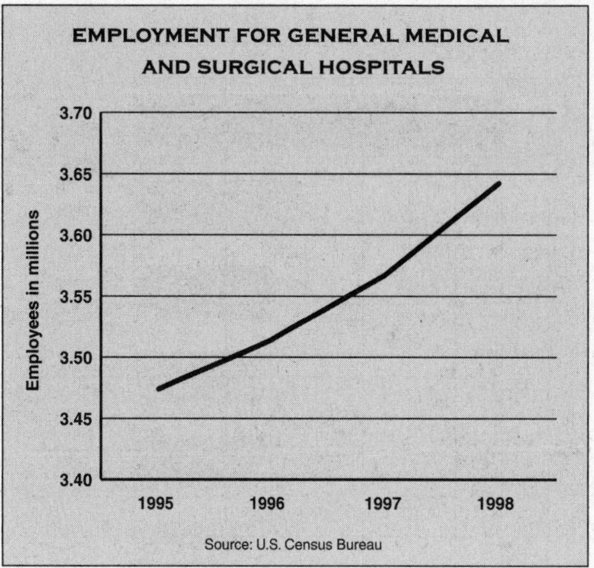

The overall job outlook for people working in hospitals is not as good as it was at the start of the 1990s when community and non-community hospitals were experiencing severe worker shortages. According to James C. Franklin in *Monthly Labor Review,* hospital staffs are expected to expand but at the slowest pace of all industries in the health care sector through 2005 as consolidations and cost-cutting efforts continue.

Since the 1970's growth in hospitals, there has been a shortage of nurses. Job prospects for them are expected to remain favorable through 2005, although it is anticipated that hospital employment will grow slowly and more nurses will go to work in home health, long-term, and ambulatory care facilities. In 1996, the median annual salary for RNs was $36,244. Licensed practical nurses work under the direction of physicians and registered nurses. Their duties include taking temperatures and blood pressures, changing dressings and bathing patients. In 1996, the median annual salary for LPNs was $24,336.

Job prospects for PAs are expected to be high through 2006. Due to an emphasis in the industry on cost containment, PAs will be looked upon as a favorable

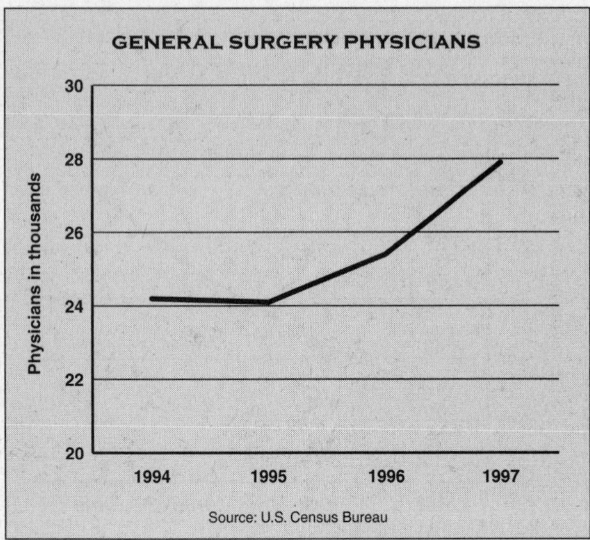

alternative to hiring more expensive physicians. PAs can assist in medical and surgical procedures as well as provide primary care to patients. In 1996, the median income for full-time physician assistants in clinical practice was $60,700.

The increase in hospital paperwork generated by private insurance companies and government insurance programs has created growth for specialized occupations, such as medical record technicians. These workers are responsible for patient records and for providing statistical reports to insurers and hospital administrators. In 1994, medical records technicians held about 40,000 jobs in hospitals and had median annual salaries of $36,700.

In 1996, approximately 112,000 physicians, both M.D.s and D.O.s, were based in hospitals. In 1995, median net income of allopathic physicians was approximately $160,000, with the middle 50 percent earning between $115,000 and $238,000. Salaries for specialists were generally much higher; for example, median net income after expenses for radiologists was $230,000, and for anesthesiologists, $225,000. Due to the better salaries offered in specialties, the number of general practitioners has been decreasing.

America & the World

This industry as part of the larger health care industry is expected to experience considerable growth in overseas markets as countries in western Europe expand their privatized services and countries in eastern Europe seek to fill shortages in general medical services. Only since the late 1970s have American hospitals sought business overseas, and at first they opened only a few hospitals in Canada, Great Britain, and Spain. *Business America* reported that American health care providers were increasingly looking toward countries in Europe and Asia, as well as in the Middle East, for expansion opportunities in 1996. U.S. enterprises also had established more than 12 arrangements with local providers in the former Soviet Union and eastern Europe.

Research & Technology

Technological advances since the 1970s have largely contributed to the number of outpatient surgeries available in hospitals. Less invasive procedures have been made possible by radiology and new surgical instruments and techniques.

In inpatient treatment, the last half of the twentieth century has witnessed tremendous advances in transplant surgery. In 1990, over 10 percent of community hospitals performed organ transplants. With over 20,000 patients on waiting lists for transplants, continued research and technological developments were expected to address the increasing needs. AIDS treatment and research was another area in which growth was expected to continue. Services for AIDS patients are likely to change with advances in drug treatments, such as AZT and Pentamidine. Moreover, research continues in specialized physical and respiratory therapy for AIDS sufferers.

Larger hospitals have traditionally had an easier time investing in sophisticated medical technologies and gathering the expertise necessary to utilize them.

Further Reading

''Brief Summaries of Medicare & Medicaid, Title XVIII and Title XIX of The Social Security Act as of June 25, 1998.'' Available from http://www.hcfa.gov/medicare/ormedmed.

Levy, Doug. ''Group Claims Mergers Hurt Health Care.'' *USA Today,* 7 June 1996.

''Market Forces Tame Health Care Inflation.'' *Standard & Poor's Industry Surveys,* 7 September 1995.

Plock, Ernest. ''The Global Healthcare Services Market is Growing Fast As Foreign Consumers Look for Better Medical Care.'' *Business America,* July 1996.

Voelker, Rebecca. ''Outpatient Trend Continues.'' *Journal of the American Medical Association,* August 1995.

SIC 8063

PSYCHIATRIC HOSPITALS

This industry consists of establishments primarily engaged in medical services for the mentally ill. Hospital establishments primarily engaged in providing health care for the mentally retarded are classified in **SIC 8051: Skilled Nursing Care Facilities.**

NAICS Code(s)

622210 (Psychiatric and Substance Abuse Hospitals)

INDUSTRY SNAPSHOT

Psychiatric hospitals are primarily inpatient, acute care units. A growing public awareness of mental disorders between 1970 and 1992 led to a significant increase in the number of these establishments and in the range of services they provided. U.S. Bureau of Census figures revealed the total number of psychiatric hospitals in the United States peaked by 1992, with 919 establishments in operation—an increase of nearly 17 percent over the 1987 figure. Between 1984 and 1991 individual hospital admissions rose by 27 percent until the number of psychiatric hospital beds reached approximately 121,000 in the United States, according to the American Hospital Association. Regardless, this period of rapid escalation did not reflect solid growth, and employment within the industry increased by a disproportional 5.1 percent.

Even as private insurance companies and government sources came forward with increased psychiatric coverage for patients, the industry markedly recoiled between 1992 and 1998. Total revenues declined from $4.4 billion in 1992 to $3.5 billion in 1996, and forecasters projected declines to $3.3 billion by 1998. State hospitals ceased operations at an unprecedented rate between 1990 and 1997, with the number of closures tripling the rate of the previous 20 years. The reorganization of many public psychiatric hospital systems accounted for a large number of the reductions, as 77 percent of U.S. states reorganized their hospital systems. The ratio of state-housed psychiatric beds to private beds dropped inversely—from a proportion of 4-to-1 in 1970, state-owned accommodations fell to comprise slightly over 1-in-4 by 1994. From 1994 to 1996, 11 states closed 18 state psychiatric hospitals, while 8 other states announced intentions to close 10 more. Additionally, 4 states planned to merge two or more hospitals by 1998. Most of the closures occurred in the Midwest and Northeast.

In conformance with a prevailing trend among many types of hospitals during the 1990s, psychiatric hospitals reduced inpatient facilities and increased outpatient services in their stead. The inpatient count at state hospitals fell from 470,000 in 1965 to fewer than 60,000 by the end of the century. Due to the reduction in facilities, the average occupancy rate in all psychiatric hospitals remained consistently high and declined by less than 5 percent during the 1980s and into the 1990s. By the mid-1990s the occupancy rate for psychiatric hospitals continued in excess of 80 percent. General hospitals in comparison reported only 60 percent occupancy, and lower rates were reported in other specialty hospitals.

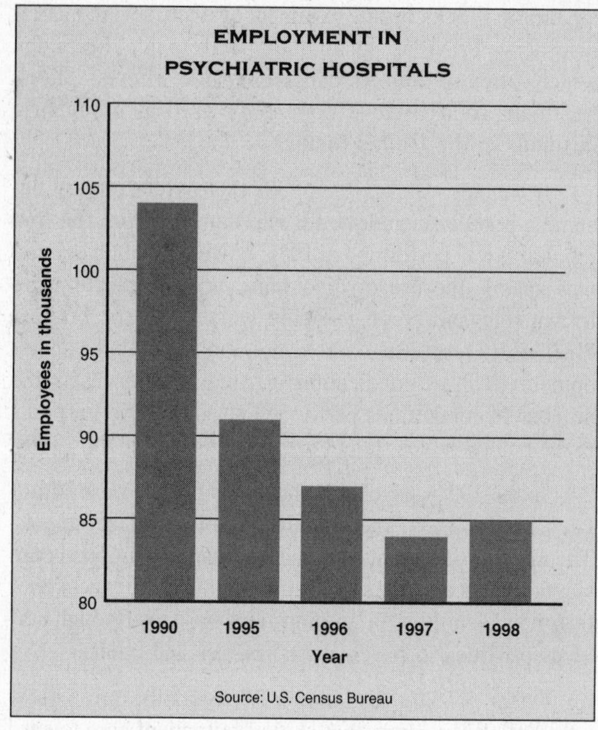

ORGANIZATION AND STRUCTURE

Psychiatric hospitals fall into one of two categories: non-profit, or profit making. Non-profit entities include government-administered facilities and charitable institutions. In the mid-1990s, nearly one-half of the nation's psychiatric hospitals were either non-profit or government entities. In keeping with this configuration, the standards and revenues of the industry are largely shaped by government legislation.

BACKGROUND AND DEVELOPMENT

Historical Evolution. The first psychiatric hospital founded in the United States was the Eastern Lunatic Asylum in Williamsburg, Virginia in 1772. It was around this time that Dr. Benjamin Rush had introduced a medical and humanistic approach to mental illness in the United States. However, mental illness was regarded, as it had been for centuries, as the result of physiological disorders. Connecting neurotic or hysterical behaviors with the mind did not develop until the late nineteenth century, with the origin of psychoanalysis.

The development of psychoanalysis altered the patient treatment at psychiatric hospitals as the psychoanalytical methods better explained diseases and offered more cures. However, psychoanalysis programs took years for patients to complete and were not suitable for most hospital settings. Eventually, psychoanalysis began to take place mostly in doctors' offices and clinics.

The 1920s marked significant change for psychiatric hospitals in the United States, as a result of developments in psychiatric medicine. In the 1920s, the connections between bacterial infection and brain functions were identified. Moreover, techniques for treating neurosis symptoms and deep-seated psychoses were also developed. In 1938, a neuropsychiatrist in Italy began using electronic shocks for the treatment of many severe mental disorders. Previous techniques used toxic chemicals, which often produced dangerous side effects. Shock treatment soon became commonly used at psychiatric hospitals in the United States.

It was also during the 1930s that psychosurgery became a popular technique for altering behavior. The first lobotomy was performed in 1935; however, public opinion was against the use of lobotomies because results were irreversible and were generally worse than the original illnesses. In response to public opinion and with the development of more medications to treat severe cases, the number of lobotomies performed at psychiatric hospitals in the United States started to drop at the end of the 1940s.

In the 1950s psychiatric hospitals began to use stimulants, tranquilizers, and vitamin therapies to treat patients. The number of patients confined to hospitals dropped considerably, because these therapies allowed patients to control their disorders on an outpatient basis or through services provided at psychiatrists' offices and clinics.

After 1970 the use of psychotherapy grew substantially, a move that shifted outpatient care toward more group-oriented psychotherapy programs, either with family or other individuals. Psychiatric hospital care shifted from emphasizing a cure to helping patients cope with their mental illnesses and disorders. Drug therapy augmented psychotherapy as a standard means for dealing with the majority of mental illnesses and disorders. Along with psychotherapy, drug treatment programs played a major role in the overall services offered by psychiatric hospitals.

Modern Services. By the late 1900s, psychiatric hospitals in the United States expanded services and offered a variety of inpatient and outpatient services. The nature of mental illnesses and its treatment dictated that inpatient care at psychiatric hospitals be linked to routine outpatient treatments, which typically continued after the patient's release from inpatient care. Follow-up treatment habitually involved psychosocial services in addition to medical treatment. Over 50 percent of psychiatric hospitals offered outpatient services. In addition to psychotherapy conducted as part of patient treatment, other therapy programs were incorporated into the services provided at psychiatric hospitals after 1970.

Most prevalent among the outpatient services offered at psychiatric hospitals was substance abuse treatment, or dependency outpatient clinics, with over 40 percent of all psychiatric hospitals having such clinics. Also by the 1990s 67 percent of psychiatric hospitals in America offered occupational therapy to help patients maintain daily living and work skills. Nearly 90 percent of psychiatric hospitals used recreational therapy as an integral part of treatment; physical therapy and speech therapy were both employed in over 25 percent of psychiatric hospitals. In contrast to other types of hospitals, psychiatric hospitals do not perform many surgeries; during the peak facility year of 1992, psychiatric hospitals performed less than 10,000 surgeries.

Some industry growth was attributed to increases in patient insurance coverage for mental health care and came as a result of changing social attitudes during the 1980s when the image of mental health care lost much of its stigma. Demand for many services increased, and insurance companies expanded coverage of these services in response to public pressure. Consequently, many people who previously avoided psychiatric treatment for financial reasons sought to obtain assistance. Between 1985 and 1990, the number of insurance providers for mental health care increased 500 percent, a trend projected to continue into the 21st century.

Psychiatric hospitals in the United States also developed comprehensive health promotion services. In the 1990s, more than 62 percent of psychiatric hospitals offered patient education services. Outside of the hospital establishments, 35 percent of psychiatric hospitals were engaged in community health promotion and an additional 37 percent in work-site health promotion.

Key among the expanded service roster developed by psychiatric hospitals were programs that addressed the psychiatric and psychological problems of children and adolescents. In 1986, over 20 percent of the patients in psychiatric hospitals were under 18 years old, and by the 1990s, more than 70 percent of psychiatric hospitals offered programs specially designed for this age group. Such programs emphasized outpatient care, in an effort to encourage teens to seek treatment without the fear of inpatient hospitalization.

Modern psychiatric hospitals implemented specialized services for geriatric patients as well. In the 1990s, nearly 20 percent of psychiatric hospitals in America had comprehensive geriatric psychiatric assessment facilities. More than 12 percent had Alzheimer's diagnostic programs and 11 percent offered geriatric acute care units. Psychiatric hospitals met the needs of the aging population with adult day care programs and geriatric clinics.

Since the discovery of the AIDS virus in the mid-1980s, psychiatric hospitals strived to meet the needs of the growing number of AIDS victims with special psychiatric ailments. By 1992, nearly 13 percent of psychiatric hospitals in America offered special inpatient services for AIDS patients.

Industry Setback from Fraud. In the early 1990s eight insurance companies sued National Medical Enterprises, Incorporated (now a part of Tenet Health Care) for providing unnecessary hospitalization and costly treatments. In addition, the company was accused of admitting patients based on health care coverage and not genuine need. Over 130 lawsuits were filed against NME by patients. In 1994, the company paid almost $375 million in fines to the Justice Department for violations. As a result of this case, similar reports surfaced concerning other private psychiatric hospitals. Some hospitals allegedly sought to acquire new patients by paying police, student counselors, and probation officers for referrals. Other accusations maintained that certain hospitals altered patient fees to collect inflated insurance reimbursements. Government investigations ensued. Some of the charges were adjudged to be true, and the resultant negative publicity affected hospitals that were not involved in the scandals. According to *Employee Benefit Plan Review,* other private hospitals suffered from drops in occupancy rates and diminished stock prices as a result of the scandal.

The Citizens Commission on Human Rights accused the industry of further collecting $600,000 to $900,000 a year on nonexistent or bogus treatments. Additional charges held that the industry employed ''patient brokers'' who accepted finder's fees—payments as high as $3,000—for the successful solicitation of prospective patients. Statistics revealed that psychiatrists comprised a disproportionately high percentage of the health care practitioners banned from the Medicare program for reasons of fraud. According to Gary Null, Ph.D., an investigative reporter and author of several books, ''Last year [1995], $411 million was paid to the government in fines and penalties for health care fraud and 90 percent of that was paid by psychiatrists or psychiatric institutions.''

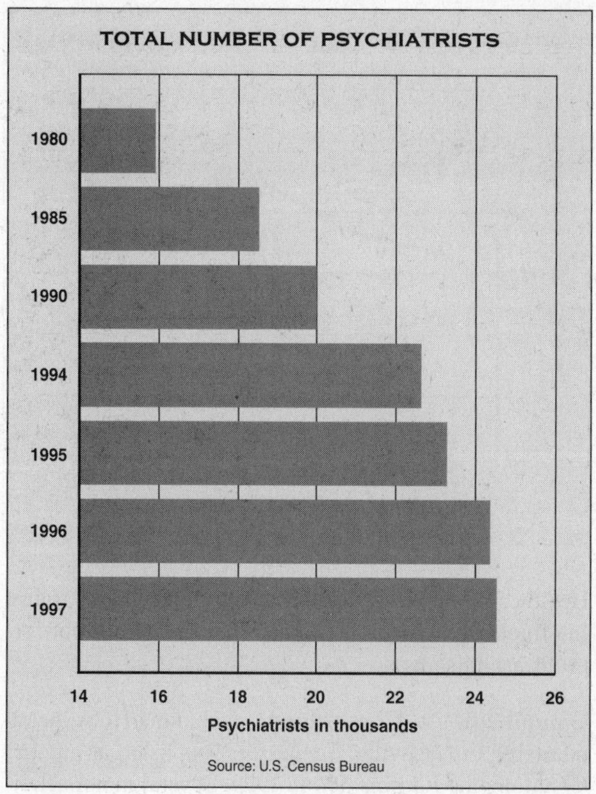

CURRENT CONDITIONS

Social Obligations. The rapid reduction in psychiatric hospital accommodations after 1992 raised concern over the continued funding and profitability of these institutions. The issue loomed as a crucial factor in the preservation of these mental health resources for the American public.

In 1999 the U.S. Surgeon General released a report wherein it directed criticism toward the private insurance sector for its failure to provide adequate coverage for inpatient care at psychiatric hospitals. *Washington Post* in reporting the matter refuted the charges and chastised instead the government bureaucracy for its own latent failure to provide hospitalization benefits for psychiatric disorders under the Medicaid system. The *Post* cited the hundreds of thousands of mentally ill people in the United States who fall within the jurisdiction of the Medicaid system for reasons of incarceration or homelessness, yet fail to receive appropriate medical attention for their psychiatric problems due to government failure to provide coverage.

Economic Viability. Restrictions imposed by the Health Care Financing Administration (HCFA)—a government body that manages Medicare—placed potentially detrimental restraint on the profitability of the mental health care industry. In 1992 HCFA undertook the implementation of a system to impose caps on the amount that health care providers could charge patients. Anticipation that similar systems would spread beyond Medicare as the federal government assumed a larger role in the nation's health care system generated new concerns over government reform of the mental health care industry.

Despite cutbacks and restrictive governmental action, the annual cost of psychiatric care reached $12.3 billion by the mid-1990s. The cost increase more than doubled the 1980 total of $5.8 billion, yet the producer price index for the psychiatric hospital industry increased at a rate that was generally slower than other medical industries. Following 0.1 percent growth in 1995, the supplier index rose by 5 percent in 1996 but fell by 6.7 percent in 1997. In 1998 the rise of 0.5 percent was low in comparison to 1.3 percent for general medical and surgical hospitals and 2.3 percent for other specialty hospitals. Ellen Paris in *Forbes* suggested that future cost controls for psychiatric hospitals might focus on inpatient services, where the highest profit margins endured.

INDUSTRY LEADERS

In 1999 according to *Service Industries USA*, the two leading providers of psychiatric hospital services in the United States were publicly traded companies: Columbia/HCA Healthcare Corporation and Tenet

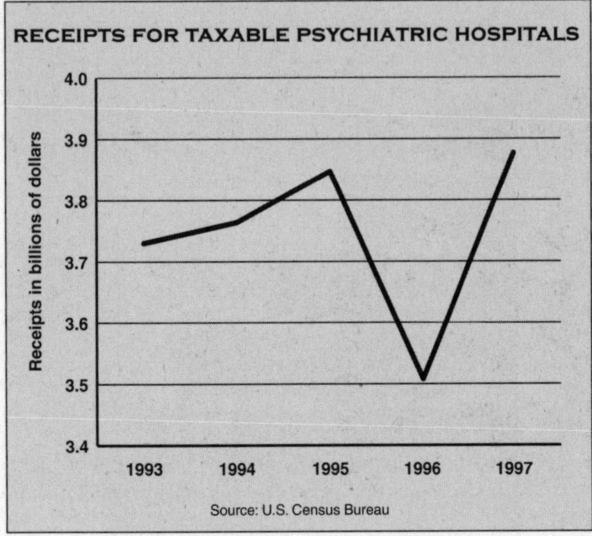

Healthcare Corporation respectively. The third largest, Intermountain Health Care, Incorporated was a not-for-profit establishment.

Columbia/HCA Corporation. Columbia/HCA, headquartered in Nashville, Tennessee, was listed at number 69 among the *Fortune 500* in 1999. Several major acquisitions and mergers in the 1990s allowed the company to grow overall, despite internal upheaval in the wake of an investigation into the company's potentially unethical referral procedures and possible Medicare fraud. Columbia/HCA, with operations in the United States, Switzerland, and the United Kingdom, reported sales revenues of $18.7 billion for a revenue growth of 0.7 percent in 1998. The corporation operated a total of 220 hospitals and freestanding surgery centers at the end of the century.

Tenet Healthcare. As the second-largest hospital chain in the United States, Tenet Healthcare Corporation of Santa Barbara, California operated over 120 hospitals and offered general hospital, psychiatric, surgery, and neonatal services. Tenet's subsidiaries and holdings include home health care centers, an health maintenance organization, and a managed care insurance company. The Tenet employee count in 1999 totaled 125,950 workers, an increase of 7.8 percent for the year. Tenet reported a one-year sales growth of 10 percent in 1998, with sales of $10.9 billion in 1999.

Intermountain Health Care. Intermountain Health Care of Salt Lake City, Utah ranked third in size in 1999. Intermountain is a not-for-profit organization established in 1975 as the result of donations to local communities in behalf of the Mormon Church. The organization serviced over 425,000 members in the western states of Utah, Idaho, and Wyoming and reported a sales growth of 7.3 percent in 1998.

Further Reading

''CMHS Releases Biennial Report on Mental Health Data.'' *Mental Health,* 19 April 1999.

Darnay, Arsen J., ed. *Service Industries USA.* 4th ed. Detroit: Gale Group, 1999.

''Financial Information.'' Tenet Healthcare Corporation, 1997. Available from http://www.tenethealth.com.

Jaffe, D. J., and Mary Zdanowicz. ''Federal Neglect of the Mentally Ill.'' *Washington Post,* 30 December 1999.

National Association of State Mental Health Program Directors. ''State Mental Health Agency Profile. System Highlights,'' November 1996. Available from http://www.nasmhpd.org/nri/SHSP_RPT.HTM.

Null, Gary. ''The Hidden Side of Psychiatry.'' *Townsend Letter for Doctors and Patients,* 1996. Available from http://www.tidp.com/162psych.htm.

SIC 8069

SPECIALTY HOSPITALS, EXCEPT PSYCHIATRIC

This industry consists of establishments primarily engaged in providing hospital services for specialized categories of patients, except for the mentally ill (see **SIC 8051: Skilled Nursing Care Facilities** and **SIC 8063: Psychiatric Hospitals.** Hospitals in this industry classification include facilities that treat alcoholism and drug addiction, cancer, children's illnesses, chronic disease, maternity, orthopedic, and tuberculosis.

NAICS Code(s)

622110 (General Medical and Surgical Hospitals)
622210 (Psychiatric and Substance Abuse Hospitals)
622310 (Specialty (except Psychiatric and Substance Abuse) Hospitals)

Industry Snapshot

Establishments in this industry provide hospital services for patients who have usually already seen a physician at a general hospital or medical office. Specialty hospitals appear most densely in the mid-Atlantic United States, including New York and Pennsylvania, with the second greatest concentration in Texas, Oklahoma, and Louisiana. Many are located along the southern Atlantic seaboard as well. This industry, as part of the broader health care industry, saw overall growth throughout the 20th century, with certain areas experiencing distinct growth in the final years of the century. Specific specialty hospitals, such as those treating tuberculosis and cancer, grew as a response to the increase in the number of people diagnosed with these ailments. Maternity hospitals conversely decreased in number as technology and social change brought about an increase in birthing facilities at general hospitals.

Throughout the 1990s, these hospitals, like other establishments in the larger health care industry, were faced with cost-cutting measures imposed by economic factors and anticipated government reforms targeted at health care. *Service Industries USA* reported 577 specialty hospitals in the United States in 1992, up from 505 in 1987, an increase of 14.3 percent; yet viable projections suggested a continued revenue decline beginning in 1997.

ORGANIZATION AND STRUCTURE

Several distinct types of hospitals are classified in this industry group—each with a unique history and status. Like other hospitals, specialty hospitals are either non-profit or profit making and have competition from government-owned hospitals. In 1990, the U.S. government owned the vast majority of tuberculosis and chronic disease hospitals in the United States. Alcohol and drug abuse rehabilitation hospitals and cancer hospitals tended to fall under private ownership. Of the total number of specialty hospitals in the 1990s, 64 percent fell into the category of non-taxed (government operated or non-profit) institutions.

Specialty hospitals include both long-term and acute (short-term) facilities. Long-term specialty hospitals (where patients usually stay for 30 days or more) include alcohol and drug abuse rehabilitation hospitals, (physical) rehabilitation hospitals, chronic disease hospitals, and cancer hospitals. Short-term specialty hospitals (where patients usually stay for 30 days or less) include maternity (obstetric) hospitals and children's hospitals.

BACKGROUND AND DEVELOPMENT

The evolution of specialty hospitals is best understood through an examination of the diverse histories and services offered by each respective hospital type.

Tuberculosis Hospitals. Tuberculosis, an infectious disease that usually affects the lungs, was the leading killer of Americans at the turn of the century. This disease, also referred to as consumption, gave rise to hundreds of sanitariums in the early 1900s. It was thought that rest and isolation, along with treatments using temperature extremes, were ways of curing the disease. It was not until the 1940s that antibiotics were used successfully to cure the disease, turning many of the sanitariums into tuberculosis hospitals. Preventive treatments were developed and, during the 1950s, hundreds of tuberculosis hospitals in the United States closed.

In 1985, the federal government reduced funding for preventive treatments, thinking that tuberculosis was under control. In the 1990s, however, documented cases of tuberculosis began to rise again for the first time in more than 50 years. At that time, there were reportedly only four tuberculosis hospitals in the United States. The total of these facilities included 470 beds at 66.4 percent occupancy rate. Additionally, the hospitals provided services for more than 16,800 non-emergency outpatient visits. (These hospitals did not provide emergency services.) Observers forecast the conversion of selected general hospitals into tuberculosis hospitals to meet the potential demand.

Maternity Hospitals. In the early 1990s, there were 12 maternity hospitals, with a total of 1,894 beds, in operation in the United States. During that time, these hospitals had a 57.4 percent occupancy rate and performed duties for more than 55,000 births. In addition, maternity hospitals serviced more than 60,000 surgeries, 58,000 emergency outpatient visits, and 223,000 non-emergency outpatient visits. By the mid-1990s, approximately 135 licensed birth centers invaded the market in 34 states, with 90 additional centers slated to open before the end of the century.

Eye, Ear, Nose, and Throat Hospitals. There were 12 eye, ear, nose, and throat (otolaryngology) hospitals in the United States in the mid-1990s. These facilities together offered 669 beds and a 32 percent occupancy rate. During that time, they performed more than 79,000 surgeries, and provided services for more than 78,000 emergency outpatient visits and 458,000 non-emergency outpatient visits.

Rehabilitation Hospitals. Rehabilitation hospitals provide medical services for patients suffering from physically debilitating ailments, usually as a result of an injury. In the 1990s, most patients admitted to these establishments suffered from head or traumatic spinal cord injuries. More than 140 rehabilitation hospitals maintained operation in the United States, with a total of 19,079 beds and an average 73.6 percent occupancy rate. These facilities performed more than 5,300 surgeries, and serviced more than 29,000 emergency outpatient visits and more than 2.2 million non-emergency outpatient visits.

Rehabilitation centers dedicated to the treatment of addiction encountered a serious challenge in the mid-1990s with the rise of managed care insurance programs. Managed care plans in general afforded their members little or no coverage in the area of substance abuse and addiction treatment, and hospitals that specialized in the treatment of these ailments suffered subsequent loss of revenue. "The number of inpatient treatment programs has declined precipitously," Monica Oss, editor of the behavioral health industry newsletter, *Open Minds,* told *Time.* "Between 1988 and 1993, the average number of patient bed days dropped from 35 to 17." Rehabilitation facilities countered the circumstance by offering a variety of treatment options, including outpatient therapy.

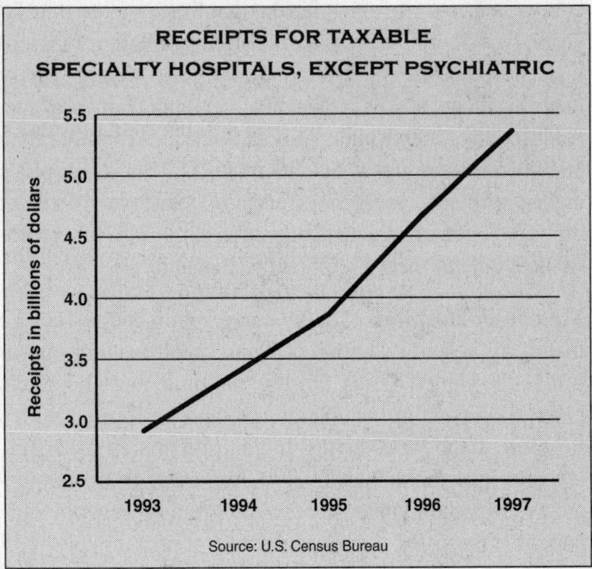

Orthopedic Hospitals. In the 1990s, there were approximately 30 orthopedic hospitals in operation in the United States. These facilities treated patients with physical deformities; often these patients are children. These hospitals had a total of more than 2,000 beds and a 55.5 percent occupancy rate. They performed more than 58,000 surgeries and serviced nearly 40,000 emergency outpatient visits and more than 570,000 non-emergency outpatient visits.

Chronic Disease Hospitals. More than 30 chronic disease hospitals operated in the United States in the 1990s. These hospitals most commonly provide long-term inpatient care facilities for patients with chronic illnesses, such as chronic respiratory infections. Chronic disease hospitals had a total of 10,870 beds and a 90.3 percent occupancy rate. During that time, they performed just over 1,000 surgeries and provided services for more than 4,500 emergency outpatient cases and 118,000 non-emergency outpatient cases. Chronic disease hospitals do not treat cancer and tuberculosis patients.

Children's Hospitals. Among other specialty hospitals in the United States, the leading establishments are children's hospitals and cancer hospitals. In the mid-1990s, children's hospitals were in high demand, and administrators commonly resorted to the use of waiting lists as a method of prioritizing admittance into the facilities. One crucial factor that contributed to the growing need for children's hospitals was the increase in the number of children in the United States who required care for illnesses related to poverty.

The demand for cancer hospitals increased during the 1990s. *Hospitals* noted that, "The American Cancer Society . . . estimates that one in three Americans now living will develop cancer at some point in their lives. Each year of this decade, more than 1.1 million people will be diagnosed with the disease." Accredited cancer programs proliferated at general hospitals across the country in response to the need, even as cancer treatment specialty hospitals increased in number.

Prognosis. In 1998 HCIA, Incorporated reported that a renewed upsurge of specialty hospitals in certain geographic areas stimulated cooperative efforts between those hospitals and the physicians of the region. The collaborations resulted in the formation of mutual partnerships between the two factions. Survey results suggest that the entry of a specialty hospital into any given market place might potentially drain as much as 35 percent of revenues from traditional programs within the respective locale. Findings were based on a study that focused on effects of cardiac specialty facilities on the disbursement of Medicare dollars within a given area.

Industry Leaders

According to *Service Industries USA,* in 1999 the three industry leaders for specialty hospitals in the United States were Columbia/HCA Healthcare, with $18.7 billion in revenue in 1998; Tenet Healthcare Corporation, with 1999 revenue of $10.9 billion; and Beverly Enterprises, Incorporated, reporting $2.8 billion in revenue.

In 1994, Columbia Healthcare Corp. of Kentucky, merged with Hospital Corporation of America. In April of 1995, Columbia/HCA formed yet another merger—with HealthTrust Incorporated, of Tennessee. The 1995 merger was the largest hospital chain merger in U.S. history. The $5.6 billion merger resulted in a huge chain of 318 hospitals. In the mid-1990s, Columbia/HCA Healthcare owned and operated approximately 220 facilities. Tenet Healthcare involved more than 120 facilities across 18 United States, plus operations overseas in Barcelona, Spain.

Another merger in this field combined the next two leaders in the industry in March of 1995. National Medical Enterprises merged with American Medical International to form Tenet Healthcare Corporation, of California. In 1997, Tenet challenged Columbia/HCA Healthcare as the largest hospital operator when it acquired OrNda HealthCorp for $3.1 billion. According to *Modern Healthcare,* Tenet Healthcare anticipated the new acquisition would add $2 billion to its $9 billion annual revenues in 1997. American Medical International owned and operated 8,853 beds in 36 facilities; National Medical Enterprises had 6,671 beds in 33 facilities; and OrNda had 8,423 beds in 47 facilities. However not all facilities were strictly specialty hospitals. Already impressive, Tenet reported revenue growth of 10 percent in 1999, as compared to Columbia/HCA which grew by only 0.7 percent in 1998.

Industry leaders among the non-profit segment of the industry in 1999 were City of Hope National Medical Center in Duarte, California; Spaulding Rehabilitation Hospital Corporation in Boston, Massachusetts; and Bethesda Hospital Association of Zanesville, Ohio—each with more than $50 million in reported earnings. Greenery Rehabilitation Group, Inc., which operated rehabilitation hospitals for young adults with neurological impairments was nexr in earnings, followed by Children's Hospital of Orange County, and Women and Infants Hospital of Rhode Island.

WORKFORCE

In the mid-1990s, approximately 270,000 people were employed in specialty hospitals in the United States. The distribution of the work force included registered nurses (RNs) comprising 25 percent of the total, aides and orderlies made up 6.2 percent, and licensed practical nurses (LPNs) comprised 4.6 percent. Non-medical personnel, such as maintenance and clerical workers, totaled 11.6 percent of the work force, while professionals, administrators, and physicians comprised 8.1 percent, not including 5.1 percent categorized as technicians. Other professions included therapists, social workers, psychiatric staff, and medical secretaries.

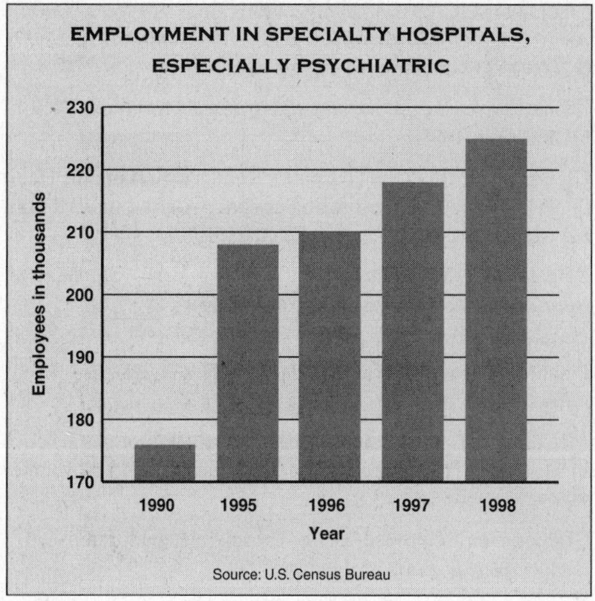

RESEARCH AND TECHNOLOGY

This industry, which can be regarded as primarily one for specialists, relies strongly on developments in research and technology. Research in biotechnology is expected to have a tremendous impact on cancer treatments provided by cancer hospitals and general hospitals. *Hospitals* noted that such research advances could mean that "biotech will shift the site for treatment from inside to outside—from external, systemic treatments like radiation and chemotherapy, to targeted, tumor-specific drugs that strengthen and then deploy the body's immune system to destroy cancer cells." The Pharmaceutical Manufacturers Association cited numerous cancer-treating biotechnology drugs under development, and biotech drugs may replace radiation and chemotherapy, which have been the main forms of cancer treatment since the 1970s. Additionally, the emerging field of gene therapy holds promise in the field of cancer research. Researchers at the Karolinska Institutet in Stockholm, Sweden, announced advancements in 1999 of the development of enhanced methods of delivering tumor-killing genes. Investigators observed that the technology performed effectively in vitro (in test tubes) and expressed promise for the potential of a genetically based offensive against cancer.

Another significant development in cancer treatment, which will also expand the use of outpatient services, has been in bone marrow transplants. Traditionally, bone marrow transplants have required long hospital stays ranging from a few weeks to a month, and from the hospitals' viewpoint, extensive staffing for the follow-up care and related administrative duties. In the early 1990s, advances in the use of laser technology and other less-invasive procedures allowed many types of bone marrow transplants to be performed on an outpatient basis. New changes in cancer treatment clearly hold the potential to effect the nature and duration of treatment at cancer hospitals. Advanced technologies hold the promise of shifting emphasis from long-term inpatient facilities such as those required for radiation and chemotherapy treatment to minimized inpatient care and outpatient care of shorter duration. Indeed a trend in the direction of expanded outpatient care for cancer patients was underway by the end of the 20th century, independent of molecular biological research, as a result of cost cutting by many hospitals.

Research in the 1990s has led to the development of a number of prosthetic and other devices related to orthopedics. Developments in biotechnology and biomaterials, as well as research and development with carbon composite prostheses and thermoplastic prostheses will also affect orthopedics.

Technological advances in computer systems have also assisted many specialty hospitals by providing networks of information, which can be linked among hospitals throughout the country. Throughout the 1990s, these hospitals increasingly shared information on treatments through the use of treatment registries available on computer networks.

FURTHER READING

"Beverly Enterprises, Inc." *Hoover's Online.* Available from http://www.hoovers.com/co/capsule/1/0,2163,10211,00.html.

"Columbia/HCA Healthcare Corporation." *Hoover's Online.* Available from http://www.hoovers.com/co/capsule/7/0,2163,15237,00.html.

Darnay, Arsen J., ed. *Service Industries USA.* 4th ed. Detroit: Gale Group, 1999.

Gleick, Elizabeth. "Rehab Centers Run Dry: Kicking the Habit of 30-Day Inpatient Treatment, Substance Abuse Clinics Retool for Managed Care." *Time,* 5 February 1996.

"Healthcare: Hospitals Drugs, and Services." *Standard & Poor's Industry Surveys,* 7 September 1995.

Japsen, Bruce. "Tenet Gains Ground: OrNda Deal Creates a Financially Powerful No. 2 Chain." *Modern Healthcare,* 3 February 1997.

McCormick, Louis H., and Bruce R. Korf. "Editorial: Genetics in Medicine: The Future Is Here." *Patient Care,* 15 November 1998.

"Reports on Improved Gene Therapy Method Published." *Cancer Weekly Plus,* 25 January 1999.

Service Industries USA. 3rd ed. Detroit: Gale Group, 1999.

"Specialty Hospitals Disrupt Local Markets." *Findings,* 12 December 1999. Available from http://www.hcia.com/findings/981230_competitivethreat.htm.

"Tenet Healthcare Corporation." *Hoover's Online.* Available from http://www.hoovers.com/co/capsule/5/0,2163,11055,00.html.

SIC 8071

MEDICAL LABORATORIES

This category covers establishments that provide professional analytic or diagnostic services to the medical profession or to patients upon prescription of their physician.

NAICS Code(s)

512199 (Other Motion Picture and Video Industries)

Industry Snapshot

The laboratories in this classification are independent, commercial enterprises that provide bacteriological, biological, histological, blood, chemical, and pathological analysis; urinalysis; and medical and dental x-rays. While demand is high due to the increased health care needs of the c country's aging population and the outbreak of new and serious diseases, intense competition, cost-cutting measures implemented by managed care organizations, and a lack of skilled workers presented challenges to the industry's continued growth in the twenty-first century.

Laboratory companies have met these challenges by growing through mergers and acquisitions and by continually developing faster, cheaper, and less invasive testing procedures.

Backround and Development

Medical laboratories are governed by the Clinical Laboratory Improvement Act of 1988 (CLIA '88). These regulations, implemented in 1992, increased requirements for proficiency testing, thereby raising costs. The cost of proficiency materials tests went up by 67 percent in the first eight months of 1992. While the new regulations caused the cost of materials to go up, the regulations also simplified administrative costs by unifying separate rules that had been established under previous programs.

National health care expenses more than doubled between 1980 and 1990 from $250 billion to $666 billion per year. Because of these huge increases, employers and insurers sought to control costs. They took steps to substitute outpatient treatment for hospitalization when possible. Insurers and employers wanted to see laboratory tests and x-rays to determine if hospitalization recommended by physicians was really necessary. Hospitals also had a stake in making sure that unnecessary hospitalizations were not occurring. After 1983, hospitals were reimbursed for Medicare patients at a modest rate as determined by federal "diagnostic related groups (DRG)"—standard rates determined by a patient's diagnosis, age, sex, treatment modality, and discharge status. If costs exceeded DRG prices, the hospitals were required to absorb the cost. Ironically, the new emphasis on tests caused the cost of diagnostic procedures to skyrocket. Insurers and employers sought to hold down costs for these as well.

One of the most vigorous debates in medicine in the mid-1990s centered around clinical laboratories owned by doctors. In 1989, the federal government passed a law prohibiting doctors from referring Medicare or Medicaid patients to clinical laboratories in which they had invested, but critics wanted to ban doctors from referring *any* patients to such laboratories. Self-referral, they argued, leads to unnecessary diagnostic procedures. Government studies indicated that 10 percent of the nation's doctors had invested in a business to which they sent their patients, and that these doctors made more such referrals than doctors who had not invested in the facilities to which they referred patients.

Other legal issues that haunted the industry during the early '90s included fraud and charges of unsafe practices. In 1993 state and federal officials subpoenaed the Medicaid and Medicare records of at least five of the country's largest medical labs in an effort to stop suspected fraud, such as unallowable overhead Medicare charges, overcharging, and false claims. The owner and president of Diagnostic Technology Inc. and New York Blood Components was convicted of a felony and misdemeanors and fined $25,000 for sending lab test kits containing HIV- and hepatitis B-contaminated blood through the mail. In the late 1990s, industry observers were concerned with the future direction of EPA rulings governing lab waste disposal.

CURRENT CONDITIONS

Total revenues for all clinical laboratory services in the United States in 1999 were $39.2 billion, with revenues for 2000 forecasted at $40.7 billion. Commercial laboratories, which are represented by this SIC, were responsible for more than one-third of those totals, with 1999 revenues of $14.9 billion and projected 2000 revenues of $15.9 billion. Other providers of clinical laboratory services were hospitals and physicians' offices. Of these types of laboratories, commercial labs showed the most growth, with a compound growth rate of 5.4 percent, compared to 2.5 percent for hospitals and 1.2 percent for physicians' offices. Hospitals have been reducing the number of laboratories they operate.

The increasing presence of managed care in the health care industry has been a major influence on the continued consolidation of medical laboratories. As in other sectors of the economy, large national chains dominated and often drove out independent laboratories. While there were fewer large chains in the late 1990s, those chains in existence increased dramatically in size. Some analysts suggest that only large chains—or laboratories that join to form ''purchasing groups''—can afford to provide services at the extremely low costs managed care firms demand. Some managed care groups have also negotiated a ''subscription'' rate with laboratories so that they pay one total annual fee for all services rather instead of paying for each test individually. The trend toward managed care has also compelled physicians to order fewer tests to cut costs, and to take fewer samples for testing.

INDUSTRY LEADERS

The medical laboratories industry underwent significant reorganization during the late 1990s. In 1998, industry leaders ranked by sales included SmithKline Beecham ($9.61 billion), Horizon/CMS Healthcare ($1.80 billion), Quest Diagnostics ($1.53 billion), and Laboratory Corporation ($1.43 billion). SmithKline Beecham's sales figures were inflated by its pharmaceutical division.

In February 1999, however, SmithKline Beecham announced an agreement to sell its laboratory division to Quest Diagnostics (formerly MetPath/Corning Clinical Laboratories, until Corning sold it off in 1997). The division was sold for $1.02 billion and a 29 percent equity interest in Quest (estimated worth, $245 million). Quest announced 1999 revenues of $2.2 billion, making it the largest medical laboratory company in the United States.

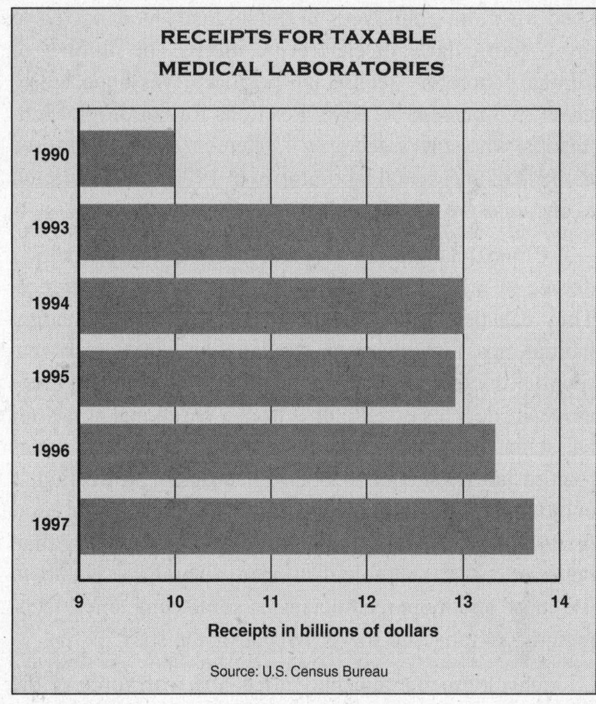

Its acquisition of SmithKline Beecham's lab operations also made it the industry leader in drug testing services for employers. In early 2000, Quest announced a joint venture with online health services provider Caresoft Incorporated to make patients' lab results available through Caresoft's Web site.

Horizon/CMS struggled with legal problems in the mid-1990s before resolving them so the company could be acquired by HealthSouth Corp. In early 1997, the company settled a federal investigation into its billing practices for $5.8 million. It later settled another case that alleged securities fraud for $20. With those cases out of the way by the end of 1997, HealthSouth purchased Horizon/CMS for over $1.6 billion.

Despite its high sales ranking, Lab Corp. also faced serious difficulties in the second half of the 1990s, starting with its guilty plea to accusations of criminal fraud in 1996. The company lost $166 million between 1996 and 1997. Some company officials, as well as some industry observers, suggested that the government was partially to blame for the fraudulent billing because it lacked clear billing guidelines. Nonetheless, some financial analysts maintained that Lab Corp. was in a good position to grow, given the trend toward large businesses shutting independent firms out of increasingly competitive markets.

WORKFORCE

Employment in this industry has grown steadily through the 1980s and 1990s. In 1990, there were 118,400 employees in this field, while in 1998 there were a projected 180,400—an increase of 52 percent. The need for more employees in this industry is expected to grow, particularly in clerical positions. The number of clinical laboratory technician positions was expected to grow 23.8 percent by 2006. Positions for radiologic technicians, who comprised only 4.8 percent of the workforce at medical and dental laboratories in 1996, were expected to increase by 85.7 percent by 2006.

Clinical laboratory technologists have a bachelor's degree in medical technology or in another life science. They can perform a variety of complex tests. In larger laboratories, they generally specialize in a particular area, such as microbiology or immunology. Technicians have associate degrees or a diploma from a vocational or technical school and perform more routine tests. Some states require lab personnel to obtain licenses. Certification is another way that individuals in this field prove their competence. Because technicians are cheaper to employ than better-educated technologists, many labs have begun to use more and more technicians; at some companies, technicians comprise up to 75 percent of the staff.

Developments that may affect the workforce in the twenty-first century include increasing automation, a growing number of products that allow patients to self-test at home, and more ''point-of-care'' testing (testing that does not need to be performed at a central laboratory site). In 1999, the Medical Automation Research Center reported that 50 percent of tests performed at central laboratories could be performed at the point of care using only existing technology. The center predicted that by 2004, 80 percent of tests will be performed ''at the patient's bedside.'' Others suggest, however, that the need for manually obtained specimens and the increasing number of lab tests available will ensure continued job growth in this field.

Research and Development

An important trend in the development of new clinical testing procedures is the increase in early-stage testing procedures that can find disease much sooner than tests used in the past could. These procedures are often less invasive and quicker than older methods. Examples include a test that more accurately determines one's risk of heart disease by ''listening'' to fats in the blood, thus allowing a more precise reading of cholesterol levels. Researchers have also developed an instrument that analyzes the breath to detect diseases, including kidney problems and diabetes. This device was expected to be available by 2005.

Testing for cancer is another growth area—early testing could mean thousands of lives saved each year. New technologies in 1999 included a less invasive test for prostate cancer that more precisely measured the amount of prostate-specific antigens. A test that detects unusually high amounts of certain DNA elements in the urine—a potential sign of cancer—was in the early trial stage. Genetic testing is also a major area of research for the detection and prevention of cancer, but as of 1999, over 90 percent of this type of testing was performed in university hospitals—an indication that this technology is still at a very early stage of development.

Other areas of expected development included the miniaturization of laboratory devices, allowing them to fit in the hand; and molecular biotechnology, an example of which is applying knowledge gained from the sequencing of the human genome, a project expected to be completed by 2003.

Further Reading

Felder, Robin, Sean Graves, and Theodore Mifflin. ''Reading the Future: the Increased Relevance of Laboratory Medicine in the Next Century.'' *Medical Laboratory Observer,* July 1999.

Gray, Tim. ''False Positive.'' *Business North Carolina,* Sept. 1997.

Manning, Margie. ''Quest in Quest of Partners After Spinoff from Corning.'' *St. Louis Business Journal,* 13 January 1997.

Medical and Healthcare Marketplace Guide. Philadelphia: Dorland's Biomedical, 1999-2000.

Occupational Outlook Handbook 1996-1997. Washington: U.S. Department of Commerce, 1996.

Plunkett, Jack W. *Plunkett's Health Care Industry Almanac 1999-2000.* Houston: Plunkett Research Ltd., 1999.

''Positive Results in Workplace Drug Testing Index Extend Dramatic Decline of Past Decade.'' 19 October 1999. Available from http://www.questdiagnostics.com/news/press991019.

''Quest Diagnostics and Caresoft Announce Agreement to Provide Personalized Lab Information Service to Consumers Over the Internet.'' *PR Newswire,* 24 January 2000.

''Quest Diagnostics Announces Improved Operating Performance in Fourth Quarter and Full Year 1999.'' *PR Newswire,* 27 January 2000.

Rice, Berkeley. ''How an HIV Diagnosis Can Get You Sued.'' *Medical Economics,* 13 January 1997.

Service Industries USA. 4th ed. Detroit: Gale Group, 1998.

Snow, Charlotte. ''Assembly Required: HealthSouth Decides Which Horizon/CMS Pieces Fit.'' *Modern Healthcare,* 19 May 1997.

———. ''Selling After Settling: Post-Acute Firms Ending Litigation Before Wooing Buyers.'' *Modern Healthcare,* 1 December 1997.

Statland, Bernard E. ''Tumor Markers: Testing for Cancer.'' *Medical Laboratory Observer,* July 1997.

Trundle Ott, Diana. ''Learn to Deal with the Work Force of 2000 and Beyond.'' *Medical Laboratory Observer,* June 1997.

Wilcox, John B. ''Medical Waste Disposal Hinges on New Regs.'' *World Wastes,* April 1996.

SIC 8072

DENTAL LABORATORIES

This classification comprises establishments primarily engaged in making dentures, artificial teeth, and orthodontic appliances to order for the dental profession. Those establishments primarily engaged in manufacturing artificial teeth, except to order, are classified in **SIC 3843: Dental Equipment and Supplies**, and those providing dental x-ray laboratory services are classified in **SIC 8071:Medical Laboratories**.

NAICS CODE(S)

339116 (Dental Laboratories)

INDUSTRY SNAPSHOT

According to the U.S. Census Bureau, there were approximately 7,500 dental laboratories providing almost $3 billion worth of services in 1997. These businesses produced custom-made prosthetic appliances for the dental profession. By 1997, this fragmented industry employed roughly 41,000 people domestically. Entering the mid-1990s, the industry had been expected to experience some growth based on continuing ''advances in dental techniques, increased cosmetic dentistry, and increased dental insurance coverage.'' Advances in preventive dental care, however, were also predicted to have a negative impact on the pace of that anticipated growth. In fact, the number of businesses declined from 1993 to 1997 while the dollar value of sales increased. Computer technology played an increasing role among dental laboratories, from the standpoint of both research and business management. Advances in computer technology weeded out businesses that were unable to keep up, and may have accounted for the decline in the number of employees. But technological advances also accounted for the rise in sales and profitability for businesses on the leading technological edge.

ORGANIZATION AND STRUCTURE

About half of all individual dental laboratories are owned by corporate bodies, while the balance are owned and operated through sole proprietorship and partnerships. The Census figure of nearly $3 billion in revenues for 1997 agrees with data from economic conditions surveys sponsored by the National Association of Dental Laboratories. According to the survey, ''dental laboratory sales represented only about two-tenths of a percent of the nation's total expenditures on health care'' for 1994. The survey also indicated that 77.4 percent of dental labs with sales of no more than $50,000 were sole proprietorships; conversely, 82.3 percent of dental labs with sales volumes exceeding $1 million were owned by ''regular corporations.'' National Dented Corporation, considered the largest operator of dental laboratories in the United States, experienced sales of over $44 million for fiscal 1995 alone, while Senate Corporation—the second largest owner of dental laboratories domestically—posted sales of $43 million for the same year.

Most of the country's dental laboratories are found in large metropolitan areas. Dental laboratories are spread throughout the United States; in 1997, each state contained at least 34 establishments. California was the leader, containing almost twice as many labs as any other state. With about 1,100 laboratories in 1997, California employed a work force of 6,000 people in this industry, and accounted for over $400 million of the industry's sales. Ranking directly behind California were Florida, with over 600 establishments, and New York, with almost 500.

Customarily, in creating an actual dental prosthesis (for example, full or partial dentures, a bridge, or a crown), laboratories follow instructions provided by the individual dentist and use a wax or plastic impression of the patient's mouth that had been made in the dentist's office. In some cases, dental laboratory technicians work directly for dentists and are present in the dental office setting itself to facilitate such procedures. Dental laboratory technicians working in actual laboratories may also have contact with patients in preparing and fitting the individual prostheses, but more commonly have no contact with patients at all. Dental laboratories typically purchase their materials from companies that manufactured products specifically for the health care industry (see**SIC 3843, Dental Equipment Manufacturers**).

By the mid-1990s, dental laboratories were expected to comply with certain standards as set forth by the federal Occupational Safety and Health Administration (OSHA) and were subject to inspection by that body. According to the National Association of Dental Laboratories in 1996, a relatively small percentage of laboratories was actually inspected by the OSHA and the manner in which OSHA standards were applied to the industry's specific procedures and instruments was considered problematic due to inconsistency.

Qualifying dental laboratories were eligible to apply for certification from the National Board for Certification of Dental Laboratories (CDL), which had established specific standards for ''personnel skills, laboratory facilities, and infection control in dental laboratories.'' According to the CDL, certification was potentially ''invaluable in establishing credibility with outside third parties, including courts of law, insurance companies, and government.'' To receive certification, a laboratory is required to employ certified dental technicians in supervisory positions, document facility compliance with accepted health and safety standards, and maintain high levels of training and practice in infection control.

Background and Development

Restorative dentistry, as outlined by Bonnie L. Kendall in *Opportunities in Dental Care,* traced its beginnings to the Etruscan people of central Italy, who made bridges and crowns. In the Roman Empire, numerous processes were developed for the restoration of teeth by artificial means. Few dental advances were made in the Middle Ages, when the main antidote to toothache was extraction of the offending tooth. It was not until at least the sixteenth century that anatomical study led to new discoveries about teeth.

Restorative dentistry in the American colonies consisted of tooth transplants, false teeth, and a hygienic dentifrice. Such items were generally fashioned by the same individuals who treated toothaches. As the population of the United States grew, "dentists" began to establish permanent rather than itinerant practices. According to Kendall, silversmiths and goldsmiths periodically assisted in the creation of artificial teeth, working either independently or with dentists. By the nineteenth century, the majority of dentists made such prostheses themselves or employed apprentices to assist in their production. With the 1840 opening of America's first dental college in Baltimore, students began to receive training not only in dental procedures but also in the preparation and setting of artificial teeth; nationally, by 1986, there were 58 accredited training programs for the education of dental lab technicians. The precise date when independent laboratories first appeared is not known; by 1920, approximately 2,000 laboratories were in operation in the United States.

In 1933, according to Kendall, the government ruled that the dental laboratory industry should be operated by "a code of fair practices," and a group was established to formulate these guidelines. In 1951, the American Dental Laboratory merged with the Dental Laboratory Institute to form the National Association of Dental Laboratories (NADL). In 1952, the NADL opened its offices in Washington, D.C., and by 1958 had set up its Certified Dental Technician (CDT) program. The NADL's voluntary national program for laboratory certification (the National Board for Certification of Dental Laboratories) was instituted in 1977.

One of the most significant developments in the course of the dental laboratory industry's existence, aside from a gradual movement toward an increased emphasis on dental care, was the utilization of orthodontic appliances in a widespread fashion. Attributable in part to the growing affluence of the nation as a whole during the 1960s, this increase in use was also a result of technological advances made in the same decade. Prior to that period, in an era when only the most financially secure could afford orthodontia, dental surgeons had to adhere each metal band to individual teeth, one at a time, pinching the band around a tooth, then soldering it permanently in place—an arduous and time-consuming task. By the 1960s, however, significant advances had been achieved in the manufacture of metal braces, taking orthodontics into mass-production and eliminating the need for the piecemeal application of braces.

With these developments, the number of patients opting for orthodontia increased, eventually creating one of the primary market segments that would support dental laboratories in years to follow.

In the mid-1990s, health-related issues were of particular importance to the dental laboratory industry as a whole. Topics of concern included such items as infection control guidelines, occupational risk of exposure to HIV and other blood-borne diseases, and occupational lung diseases. There was a significant increase among all areas of dentistry in the hygienic precautions regularly taken to reduce the risk of exposure to blood.

Infection control guidelines from the U.S. Centers for Disease Control and Prevention applied not only to workers in dental offices, but to employees in dental laboratories as well. Occupational lung diseases, caused by exposure to a variety of dusts, also presented a risk to dental technicians, according to *Infection Control Weekly.* According to a study by French researcher D. Choudat, several respiratory and non-respiratory ailments were identified as being possibly related to the inhalation of dusts present in dental laboratories, specifically silica, alloys, and acrylic plastics. Although this was more of a concern in small independent labs than in large establishments, and more of a problem abroad than domestically, dental laboratories were encouraged to install and maintain adequate ventilation systems to reduce potential exposures for all employees. Choudat noted that these risks appeared cumulative, manifesting themselves to a greater degree and at a higher incidence among employees who had worked in dental laboratories for many years. Additionally, employees who smoked were considered at greater risk of contracting these occupational illnesses.

Current Conditions

The dental laboratory industry makes about three-fourths of its income from the production of artificial teeth, dentures, and other orthodontic appliances specifically based on prescriptions and orders from dentists. Laboratories provide record-keeping services that account for the remainder of its income. The industry's finished products add over $2 billion to the materials, energy, and other consumables used in manufacture.

Industry Leaders

According to revenue figures posted by the individual companies, the following companies lead the dental laboratory industry: National Dentex Corp. of Wayland, Massachusetts, with sales exceeding $63.8 million in 1998, 1,211 employees, and a dollar value in sales per employee of $52,684; Recigno Laboratories, Inc., of Willow Grove, Pennsylvania, with sales of $39 million in 1995, 500 employees, and sales per employee of $78,000 for 1995; Sentage Corp., with sales of $43 million, and 1,000 employees; James R. Glidewell Dental Ceramics, with sales of $26.5 million, and 400 employees; Americus Dental Labs LP, with sales of $14 million, and 200 employees; Dentalcare Partners Inc., with sales of $12 million, and 125 employees; and Dental Arts Laboratory Inc., with sales of $10.4 million, and 250 employees. As of 1996, National Dentex served an active customer base of 8,000 dentists via 24 full-service and five branch dental labs in 20 states and offered a full range of dental prostheses.

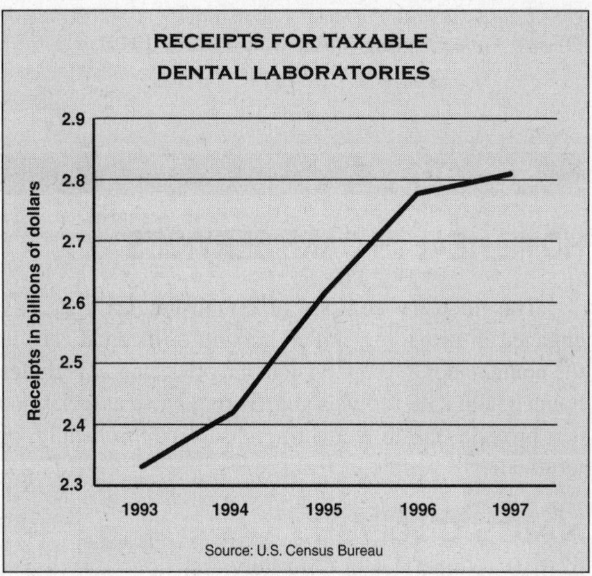

WORKFORCE

The industry employed about 41,000 people in the late 1990s, down from roughly 44,000 people in the mid-1990s and from 49,000 in the early 1980s. Employment opportunities were expected to remain fair through the year 2005, according to *Career Information Center*. According to the 1997 Census, over 6,000 labs employed less than 10 people. Only the four largest labs employed more than 250 people.

The formal training of many dental laboratory technicians may begin as early as high school, through specific vocational courses, or via apprenticeship. Trainees normally work under the guidance of experienced practicing technicians, and generally gain skills over a period of at least three years. Individual technicians seeking to gain professional credentials as a Certified Dental Technician apply to the NADL's appropriate governing board for certification.

According to the U.S. Department of Labor, dental lab technicians, in the course of their daily work, may engage in the following sorts of tasks: employing a variety of hand tools for extremely detailed work; reading dentists' prescriptions and examining dental impressions and models; displaying expertise in grinding, polishing, and soldering of dental appliances; attempting to resolve problems in the design and setup of dentures; consulting with individual dentists for problem resolution, when necessary; and fabricating full or partial dentures and crowns.

Trainees in dental laboratories, according to the 1995 NADL survey, may have earned between $5.50 and $7.00 per hour to start. Wages for technicians with at least 10 years of experience earned at least $12 an hour, with $19 capping the hourly range.

RESEARCH AND TECHNOLOGY

As one example of technological advances in the field, in 1995, Dr. Anthony Chillura wrote in *Newsweek* magazine that ''technological breakthroughs promise to revolutionize the way . . . crowns . . . are created and fitted.'' Chillura noted that crown production in the past was a ''time consuming multi-step process that began with alginate impressions of the tooth and continued through fabrication in a dental laboratory and subsequent fitting (and adjustment) to the patient in the chair.'' Using the new computerized crown manufacturing machine ''the prototype system rapidly scans the tooth image and then computer-guided cutting hardware creates the crown.'' Gold or porcelain crowns that once took hours to prepare could henceforth be fashioned in about half an hour.

According to *Business Wire* in November 1996, Automated Products Incorporated (API), a Texas-based developer of such technology, indicated that by using this type of system one technician could ''produce up to one hundred or more crown copings per day.'' Planned enhancements to API's system were expected to include ''the ability to produce multi-unit bridges, inlays, onlays and laminates.''

FURTHER READING

Business Wire, November 1996.

Career Information Center. 6th ed. Indianapolis, IN: Macmillan Library Reference USA,1996.

Chillura, Anthony E. ''High-Tech Dentistry.'' *Newsweek,* 23 October 1995.

Journal of Dental Technology, December 1996.

Macht, Joshua. ''Together at Last: Communications.'' *Inc.,* 19 March 1996.

''Occupational Risk: Occupational Exposures Among Dental Workers.'' *AIDSWeekly,* 30 October 1995.

Report on the NADL 1995 Economic Conditions Survey of the Commercial Dental Laboratory Industry. Alexandria, VA: National Association of Dental Laboratories, 1995. Available from http://www.nadl.org.

U.S. Census Bureau. "Dental Laboratories." *1997 Economic Census: Manufacturing Industry Series.* July 1999.

SIC 8082

HOME HEALTH CARE SERVICES

This industry consists of establishments primarily engaged in providing skilled nursing or medical care in the home under the supervision of a physician. It includes home health care services and visiting nurse associations that provide care to recovering, disabled, chronically, or terminally ill people.

NAICS CODE(S)

621610 (Home Health Care Services)

INDUSTRY SNAPSHOT

Home health care services mostly target respiratory therapy programs, which provide complete air support for patients suffering from many respiratory ailments, including asthma, bronchitis, and cystic fibrosis. Other homecare services include delivery of nutrients intravenously or through feeding tubes; the intravenous infusion of antibiotics to treat infectious diseases; and infusion therapies for patients with fully or partially dysfunctional digestive tracts.

In 1995, there were 18,874 certified home health care organizations, including 9,120 Medicare-certified home health agencies, 1,857 Medicare-certified hospices, and 7,897 home health agencies. By 1999, the National Association for Home Care (NAHC) counted more than 20,000 providers of home care services to approximately 8 million people suffering from acute illness, long-term health problems, disabilities, or terminal illness.

For 1996, about $30,192 billion was spent on home health care, only about 2.9 percent of the total spent on all national healthcare expenditures, according to the Health Care Financing Administration. By 1997 expenditures had risen to $40 billion and 1998 to $42 billion.

According to a Congressional Budget Office (CBO), it was estimated that the effect of The Balanced Budget Act of 1997 would decrease health care expenditures by $16 billion between fiscal year 1998 and fiscal year 2000. With CBO revisions, the reductions seem more likely to exceed $47 billion. Due to these cutbacks, more than 2,000 home health agencies shut down between 1997 and 1999.

ORGANIZATION AND STRUCTURE

Home health care services are categorized by ownership: government, hospitals, privately owned companies, and nonprofit organization or visiting nurse associations, all of which provide these services. In 1998, nearly private companies owned 46 percent of all home health care agencies in America. In the same year, around 12 percent were owned by nonprofit organizations or visiting nurse associations, hospitals more than 27 percent, and the government owned 12 percent. Local health care providers owned roughly 75 percent of establishments not owned by the government as franchises.

While there has been a trend toward consolidation, the home healthcare industry was still somewhat fragmented in the late 1990s. The total number of home health care agencies operated by the 38 largest homecare chains increased from 3,649 offices in 1996 to 3,984 offices in 1997, an increase of 9.2 percent. These chains represented about 26 percent of the homecare industry in 1997.

The impact of The 1997 Balanced Budget Act (BBA) on homecare cannot be underestimated. In addition to capping the amount of annual reimbursement that a homecare agency could receive per patient, the act required home health agencies to obtain surety bonds. Regulated by the Health Care Financing Administration (HCFA), only certain types of surety bonds qualify, complicating the process for many homecare agencies.

BACKGROUND AND DEVELOPMENT

The first home care agencies were established in the 1880s, and by 1963 more than 1,100 such agencies existed. The dramatic increase in home health care providers between 1965 and 1999 was propelled by the 1965 Medicare enactment making home care services available to the elderly as long as the services were for "nursing and therapy of a curative or restorative nature," according to the NAHC. In 1973, these benefits were also made available to the younger population. Between 1967 and 1985 the number of Medicare-certified agencies participating in the Medicare program rose from 1,753 to 5,983. The industry leveled off temporarily in 1985 as Medicare paperwork and policies made regulatory compliance difficult and payments were not made reliably. In 1987, consumer groups, the NAHC, and members of Congress successfully sued the Health Care Financing Administration (HCFA). Medicare home care policies were rewritten, annual Medicare outlays were increased, and the number of Medicare-certified agencies again rose, this time to 10,000. That number is again on the decline (9,655 at the end of 1998), this time as a result of the Balanced Budget Act's changes in Medicare home health reimbursement.

Home health care has increasingly been regarded as one of the essential components of comprehensive health care. The high costs of hospital and nursing home care have helped this industry to become one of the fastest growing sectors of the larger health care industry in America.

Home health care services provide a variety of services for patients in the home. In 1996, the three most common services offered by home health agencies were skilled nursing, personal care for the elderly and disabled, and home infusion therapy. Of patients using home health services, 30 percent had diseases of the circulatory system, while 20 percent had some form of heart disease. Other services included administering antibiotics, providing rehabilitation services, and aiding chemotherapy. Generally, these services were provided by a team of health care professionals.

Home infusion therapy has been one of the fastest growing services offered by companies in this industry. Home infusion therapy provides initial patient evaluation, compounds and dispenses drugs, solutions, and nutrients, and provides ongoing clinical monitoring. According to the National Alliance for Infusion Therapy, in 1995, the most common treatment given through home infusion therapy was antibiotic therapy, relying mostly on pumps for drug delivery. This was followed by enteral nutrition, chemotherapy, and pain management. In the same year, the most common diagnoses of patients using home infusion therapy were AIDS, Lyme disease, and colon cancer.

Medicare, the federally funded health insurance providing assistance to the elderly and disabled, has played an important role in the growth of this industry. It was the largest single payer of home care services, accounting for more than one-third of total home care expenditures in 1995.

In 1997, Medicare financed $214.6 billion in spending for 39 million aged and disabled enrollees, according to HCFA. By spending category, the largest one was hospital care (57.6 percent of total expenditures), as compared to home healthcare at 6.0 percent. In 1996, roughly 3.9 million of the 37 million Medicare enrollees received home healthcare services, about twice the number of people who received such services in 1990. However, annual growth in Medicare spending decreased from 12.2 percent in 1994 to 7.2 percent in 1997. Home healthcare growth has also decreased, mostly due to the public sector's desire to restrain the boom in home healthcare services in the middle and late 1990s.

During the 1990s, this industry was marked by mergers among industry leaders. In 1993, Abbey Healthcare Group, which specialized in rehabilitation and respiratory therapy equipment, purchased Total Pharmaceutical, which dealt mainly in intravenous drug and nutritional therapy. In the same year, Olsten Corporation, which owned Olsten Health Care Services, purchased Lifetime Corp., along with its subsidiary, Kimberly Quality Care. This merger ended a highly publicized takeover battle between Abbey Healthcare and Olsten Corporation; Abbey offered to purchase Lifetime for $220 million, yet this offer was rejected for Olsen's offer of $449 million.

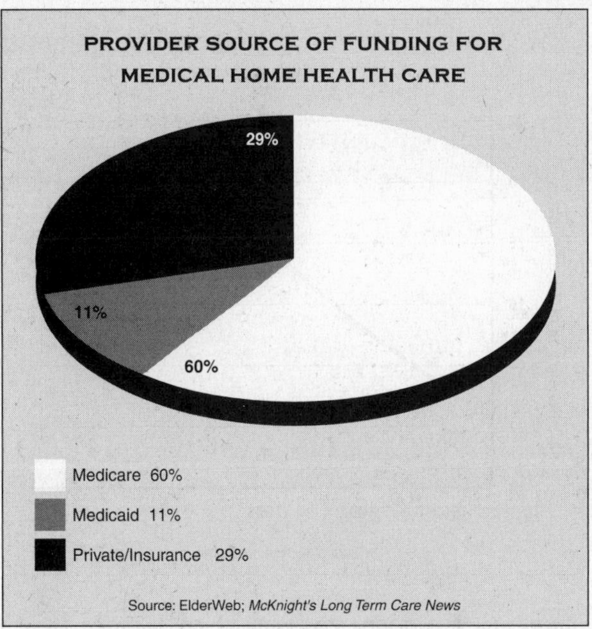

In 1995, Abbey and Homedco, two of the largest home health care providers in the United States, merged to form Apria Healthcare Group, Inc., making it the largest provider in this field.

Also in the early 1990s, the public's attention was drawn to the ethical practices of home infusion therapy services. One ethical issue arose when some home infusion agencies paid physicians a weekly stipend for each patient they referred to the agency. Concerns were raised over whether the payment of such stipends would influence physicians' judgments in using home infusion services. Another ethical controversy for home infusion therapy companies arose when these companies bought a practice from a physician and later hired the physician as an employee; this suggested that the physician was bought to write prescriptions for the company. Both of these ethical issues have been addressed by legislators at the state and national levels, and by the mid-1990s, a few states had already enacted legislation prohibiting physicians from being financially linked to clinics or certain types of home health services.

INDUSTRY LEADERS

Olsten Corporation. Among the largest of the homecare chains is the Olsten Corporation. Olsten is one of the largest temporary services agencies in the world, known best for providing office, clerical, and accounting staff. Olsten is also a leading provider of health care workers to hospitals and home care agencies through Olsten Health Services, operating more than 400 health care offices and employing more than 22,000 people

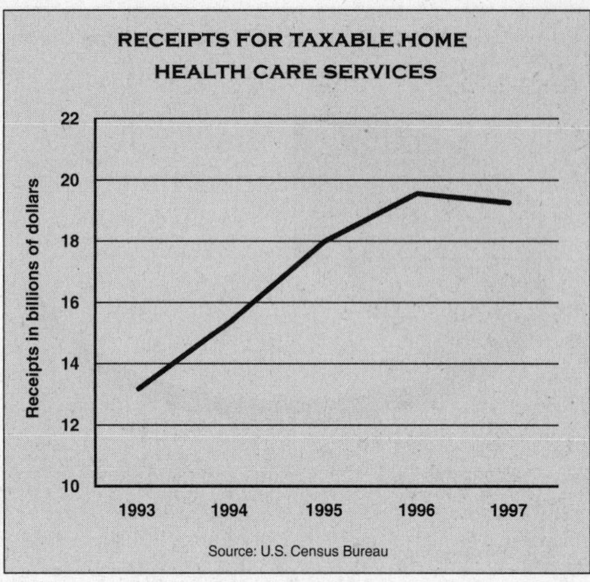

during the late 1990s. The Olsten Corporation earned $4.6 billion in 1998 and employed 700,850 people.

Integrated Health Services. Based in Owings Mills, Maryland, Integrated Health Services is one of the largest health care companies in the country with 1998 revenues of $2.9 billion and 84,000 employees. Integrated Health offers rehabilitative and diagnostic services and operates nursing homes around the United States.

Caremark Rx. Caremark International, Inc. was started in 1992 by Baxter International, which purchased Caremark Inc. in 1987. Caremark International Inc. reported gross sales of $1.5 billion in 1993; by 1995 gross sales exceeded $2.3 billion. In 1996, MedPartners acquired Caremark for $2.5 billion. This merger combined the nation's two largest managers of doctor practices. Now named Caremark Rx, the company focuses on its prescription services, disease management, drug therapy, physician support, and education services. Caremark earned $2.6 billion in 1998 and had 19,636 employees.

Apria Healthcare Group, Inc. Apria Healthcare Group, Inc. was formed in 1995 when Homedco and Abbey Healthcare merged. These two companies showed a combined revenue of $1 billion in 1994. This merger created the largest home healthcare company in the United States. The bulk of its revenues (53 percent) came from its respiratory therapy. By 1999, Apria (headquartered in Costa Mesa, California) operated 350 branches across the country. The company earned $933.8 million in sales during 1998 (20.9 percent growth over 1997 earnings) and employed 8,175 people.

Coram Healthcare Corporation. Based in Denver, Colorado, Coram Healthcare Corporation was formed in 1994 by a four-way merger of Curaflex Health Services, HealthInfusion, Medisys, and T2 Medical. Coram acquired HMSS in 1994 and Caremark, International in 1995. (Note above that Caremark was sold in 1996 to MedPartners). Coram now provides services ranging from infusion to anti-infective chemotherapy, clinical research, and medical informatics services. 1998 sales were $526.5 million, 13.4 percent growth over 1997, and the company had 3,600 employees. Coram is Apria's greatest competition.

Lincare. Lincare, with headquarters in Clearwater, Florida, was one of the nation's largest providers of oxygen and other respiratory therapy services. They reported more than 180,000 customers in 42 states. Lincare earned $487.4 million in 1998, showing 10 percent growth for the year. The company's net income in 1998 was $85.3 million and it employed 4,200 people. In 1995, Lincare considered merging with Coram Healthcare Corporation, but those plans were abandoned.

National HealthCare Corporation. National HealthCare of Murfreesboro, Tennessee, manages assisted living centers and retirement centers as well as providing in-home patient care. They offer nursing and rehabilitative care through their 110 long-term care centers and 36 home health care programs. In 1998, the company earned $441.2 million and had more than 16,000 employees.

American HomePatient, Inc. American HomePatient, Inc. of Brentwood, Tennessee, is one of the largest home care companies in the United States. In August 1997 it acquired five companies with combined annualized revenues of $10.3 million. Those companies were Central Home Medical Supply, located in Enid, Oklahoma; Ameriquipt Corporation Inc., in Leesburg, Florida; Homecare Medical Equipment, Inc., in Whitely City, Kentucky; Downeast Medical Shoppe, in Bangor, Maine; and the reparatory and medical equipment divisions of Headley Home Care Medical Services, based in Fransville, Wisconsin. The company provides health care services and medical equipment through its 300 branches in 35 states. In 1998, American HomePatient earned revenues of $403.9 million and employed 4,766 people.

WORKFORCE

In 1996, the BLS counted 665,400 employees in home health care agencies, excluding hospitals and public agencies. And in 1998, the HCFA reported 372,453 full-time employees of certified home health agencies (down 43,000 from 1997). While both agencies generate figures differently, both counts illustrate some of the same employment trends. The largest numbers of employees in both figures were home care aides and registered nurses (RNs), followed by licensed practical nurses (LPNs). Employment growth more than doubled in the home care industry from 1988 to the late 1990s. During 1993-1997, BLS statistics showed that home care employment rates grew 7.9 percent annually, but declined by 7.2 percent in 1998.

The largest segment of this workforce was registered nurses. RNs, who work with more seriously ill patients and administer medications, earned a median salary of $697 weekly in 1996. Licensed practical nurses, who provide services such as bathing patients and sometimes doing light housework for the disabled, earned $468 per week on average in 1996.

With the growth of home infusion therapy, pharmacist practitioners were predicted to be in high demand through the end of the century. Pharmacist practitioners earned $992 weekly on average in 1996. In addition, home health aides would be one of the fastest growing occupations through the year 2005; home health aides' salaries varied greatly, with an average annual income of $16,600 in 1995 for HCA II and $15,000 for HCA III.

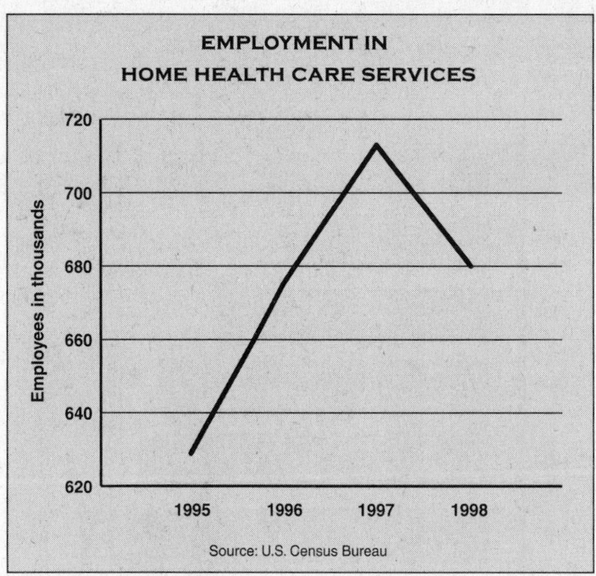

RESEARCH AND TECHNOLOGY

New drugs, drug pumps, and home infusion equipment have helped the home health care industry to expand by offering more services, previously only available in hospitals or nursing homes, in the home. Future technological developments can only be expected to benefit this industry, which has grown in the wake of soaring health care costs at the end of the twentieth century.

FURTHER READING

Balinski, Carol. "Patients Stand to Lose: Medicare Regulations Stunt Home Health Care Growth." *Eastern Pennsylvania Business Journal,* 9 February 1998.

"Basic Statistics About Home Care." Washington, DC: National Association for Home Care, 1999.

Boyles, Peg. "Health Care in the Home Is Under Fire." *New Hampshire Business Review,* 24 October 1997.

Conklin, Michele. "New Regulation May Force Home Health Firms to Close." *Rocky Mountain News,* 24 January 1998.

Ferguson, Lisa. "Apria Healthcare." *April Healthcare,* 27 November 1995. Available from http://www.insite.uci.edu/knowledge/profiles/APRIAH-1.htm.

Griggs, Ted. "Health Care Trends." *Advocate-Baton Rouge,* 1 March 1998.

"Health Care: Our Forecast." *Business Record-Syracuse,* 15 February 1998.

Healthcare: Facilities. "Standard & Poor's Industry Surveys." June 1999.

Hoovers Company Capsules. Austin, TX: Hoovers, Inc., 1999. Available at http://www.hoovers.com.

"Lincare Holdings Inc. Announces Fourth Quarter and Year End 1996 Financial Results." *PRNewswire,* 11 February 1997. Available from http://biz.Yahoo.com:80/news/lncr.html.

"MedPartners Acquiring Caremark for $2.5 Billion." *San Diego Daily Transcript,* 14 May 1996. Available from http://autos.thesource.net/files/librarywire/96wireheadlines/05_96/DN96_05_14/DN96.

Morel, Mitch. "AMEDISYS Inc. Acquires Alliance Home Health." *PR Newswire,* 7 January 1998.

National Association of Home Care. "Basic Statistics About Home Care 1996." Available from http://www.nahc.org/Consumer/hcstats.html.

Russell, Judi. "Home Health Companies Face a Burdensome New Deadline." *New Orleans City Business,* 2 February 1998.

Walsh, Bill. "Home Care Budget Cuts Patients Start to Feel the Pinch as Medicare Brings Down Costs." *Times Picayune New Orleans,* 17 February 1998.

Wissing, Edward K. "American HomePatient Acquires Five Companies with 13 Centers and $10.3 Million in Annualized Revenues." *Business Wire,* 13 August 1997.

SIC 8092

KIDNEY DIALYSIS CENTERS

This industry consists of establishments primarily engaged in providing kidney or renal dialysis services. Establishments operating as clinics of physicians are covered in **SIC 8011: Offices and Clinics of Doctors of Medicine.**

NAICS CODE(S)

621492 (Kidney Dialysis Centers)

INDUSTRY SNAPSHOT

An aging population and a growing health care sector were reflected in the continued growth of the dialysis center industry, which is composed of approved independent and hospital-based or affiliated facilities. All

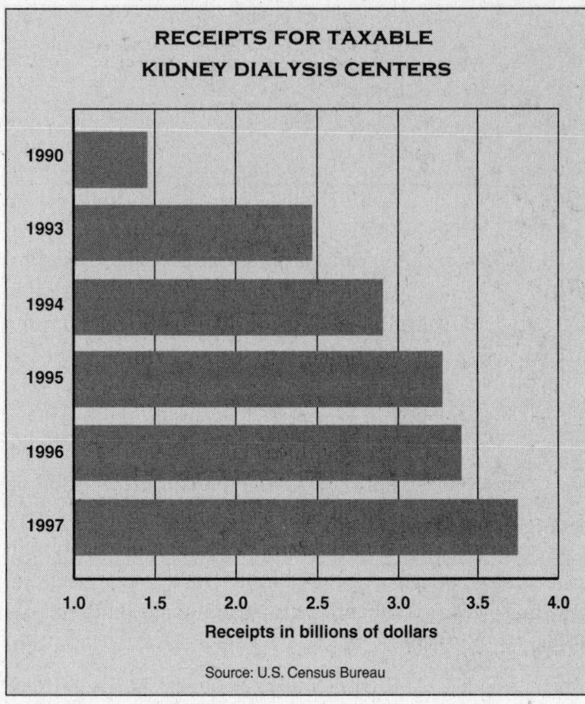

kidney dialysis centers are regulated and subsidized by the federal government, which grants exclusive licenses to providers to supply long-term dialysis within a designated territory. The facilities are reimbursed through the Health Care Financing Administration (HCFA) with Medicare funds.

As in many other sectors of the economy, trends toward mergers, acquisitions, and nationwide chains influenced the growth of this industry. Investors have grown increasingly interested in this area, attracted by an increase in revenues of nearly 190 percent during the 1990s.

Background and Development

The process of dialysis was invented about 1854 by a Scottish chemist named Thomas Graham, who would later become the first to employ dialysis to prolong life. The procedure was not widely used until after 1945, when Dr. Wilhelm Kolff used it to save the life of a patient in active renal failure, demonstrating that the process not only could prolong life for a short time, but could actually increase survival rates for renal failure.

Most users of dialysis in the late twentieth century were victims of end-stage renal disease, which requires either dialysis or transplant for survival and is not reversible. Two kinds of dialysis are used: hemodialysis and peritoneal dialysis. Hemodialysis is generally performed three times a week in two- to four-hour sessions, removing waste though an artificial kidney machine outside of the patient's body. Peritoneal dialysis uses the peritoneum, a membrane in the abdomen, to remove the waste, using a procedure that can be performed at home by the patient. The amount of patients receiving peritoneal dialysis is expected to increase, as it is a cost-saving measure that keeps patients out of the hospital. As of 1999, however, the technology for peritoneal dialysis was not sufficiently advanced to allow all patients to use it, particularly those with severely impaired renal function. In 1999, less than 15 percent of kidney patients were treated at home.

Since 1972, the number of chronic dialysis patients has increased a hundredfold. In 1996, an estimated 214,000 Americans received dialysis. The HCFA predicted that the number of these patients will increase by at least 9 percent per year. HCFA reimbursements accounted for the majority of payments to kidney dialysis centers. Scarcity of funds caused the federal government to cut back on its reimbursement rates, making it difficult for many hospital-based centers to keep operating. Some hospitals have responded by referring patients to free-standing centers.

In the mid-1990s, however, that cost-cutting proved deadly. A National Kidney Foundation report published in 1995 found that American dialysis patients faced a much higher mortality rate than dialysis patients in other countries. Figures for 1992 showed that nearly 24 percent of U.S. dialysis patients died, compared with a mortality rate of 9.7 percent in Japan, 10 percent in Germany, and 11 percent in France. Because cost incentives built into the system may have limited dialysis treatment times and frequency, and the reuse of supplies, the number of end-stage renal disease patients—and mortality rates—went up. The for-profit nature of dialysis centers seemed only partially to blame. The National Kidney Foundation study found that cost-cutting in the form of poorly trained staff and inefficient use of dialysis machines also seemed to be a factor in the 45,000 American deaths. As Dr. Neil Kurtzman told the *Journal of the American Medical Association,* "The government pays for visits to a facility. We believe it should change this and pay for the actual care a patient receives."

A campaign was launched in 1995 by the National Kidney Foundation to improve patient care at dialysis centers and decrease deaths. The licensing of a new, relatively lightweight, and easy to use home-dialysis machine was also expected to bring changes to the industry.

Current Conditions

The number of patients receiving kidney dialysis in the United States was expected by some analysts to hold steady at close to 214,000, given the increasing number of kidney transplants being performed and the expectation of improved transplant success in the future. The HCFA, however, predicted in 1996 that the number of patients would continue to grow at the rate of 9 percent annually until at least 2001, and possibly until 2006. The aging of the American population was also expected to contribute to an increase in patients. In 1999, the United States was the world's largest market for kidney dialysis, followed by Japan, the rest of Asia, and Latin America.

A treatment trend of the late 1990s was daily hemodialysis. Estimates suggest that in 1998, 12 centers worldwide were providing daily treatments for more than 100 individuals with renal failure. This treatment plan was not for the general public, however; at that time, such frequent treatments were not covered by Medicare, which paid for any patient with end-stage renal disease.

As an industry, kidney dialysis centers grew steadily throughout the 1990s, from revenues of $1.45 billion in 1990 to $3.38 billion in 1996. Projected revenues for 1998 were $4.19 billion, reflecting a growth of nearly 190 percent. Employment in this industry, like many other health care industries, was also forecast to increase significantly. Most positions—such as nurses, physicians, and lab technicians—were expected to increase by close to 50 percent by the year 2006. Rapid increases in employment opportunities have made adequate training a problem for the work force in this industry.

Growth of individual businesses has been limited in some areas by the requirement for a Certificate of Need (CON). The certificate demonstrates that "the communities they're targeting for additional dialysis services need more service, that their proposed projects are the best way to meet those needs, that they're financially feasible and that they will deliver high-quality service," according to a 1997 article in the *Puget Sound Business Journal.* This system has tended to favor smaller, local, or nonprofit businesses already in place at the expense of national or worldwide firms seeking to expand their territory. Larger companies have complained that the regulation is anticompetitive. Some states have phased out this requirement. In Ohio, prior to the elimination of the CON rule, the state foresaw a need for 40 new dialysis stations. Once the rule was lifted, 571 new ones were added. Current dialysis providers in Washington fear the frenzied competition created by lifting the CON rule will drive several existing companies out of business, particularly independent providers.

INDUSTRY LEADERS

As of 1998, the largest companies in this industry, ranked by sales and number of employees, were Fresenius National Medical Care, Gambro Healthcare Inc. (with its subsidiaries COBE Laboratories Inc., Vivra Inc., and REN Corporation), and Total Renal Care.

Fresenius National is the U.S. subsidiary of Fresenius Medical Care, based in Germany. In 1998, Fresenius National reported $2.2 billion in sales—a figure that also reflects its interests in home health care service and other medical products, although in mid-1998 the company sold off its U.S. holdings not related to its core business of kidney dialysis. In 1999, Fresenius claimed to serve 23 percent of dialysis patients in the United States. In the late 1990s, Fresenius was the subject of two major lawsuits charging false claims; the company settled in both cases without acknowledging any wrongdoing.

Gambro Healthcare posted $1 billion in sales in 1998, and its subsidiaries also did well: COBE Laboratories reported $1.7 billion in sales; Vivra, $517 million, and REN, $132 million. Gambro acquired Vivra in 1997, making the company second only to Fresenius as a worldwide provider of dialysis products and services. In 1999, Gambro announced plans for a joint venture with Baxter Healthcare, a pioneer in hemodialysis technology. Baxter created the first commercial artificial kidney machine in 1956 and was also a leader in developing home-based dialysis products. Gambro also announced plans to reorganize the company significantly in 1999, possibly selling COBE Labs and consolidating worldwide operations by moving offices from Sweden into its Colorado headquarters.

Gambro's closest competitor for second place was California-based Total Renal Care, which acquired Renal Treatment Centers Inc. in 1997. Total Renal Care Holdings Inc. claimed $1.2 billion in revenues for 1998. Total Renal Care stock was popular with investors until mid-1999, when its CEO and chief financial officer both stepped down and the company posted a second-quarter loss of $21 million. The interim CEO blamed a billing backlog—uncollected moneys from both patients and hospitals—for the financial setback.

FURTHER READING

Donahue, Ann. " Total Renal Care Seeks to Reassure Troubled Investors." *Los Angeles Business Journal,* 23 August 1999.

"Fresenius Reaches Settlement with U.S. for Medicare Billing." *The Wall Street Journal,* 18 May 1999.

"Home Dialysis Makes Patients Independent." *USA Today,* February 1996.

Medical and Healthcare Marketplace Guide. Philadelphia: Dorland's Biomedical, 1999-2000.

Neurath, Peter. "Kidney Centers Rekindle Certification Debate." *Puget Sound Business Journal,* 28 November 1997.

Plunkett, Jack W. *Plunkett's Health Care Industry Almanac 1999-2000.* Houston: Plunkett Research Ltd., 1999.

Service Industries USA. 4th ed. Detroit: Gale Group, 1998.

Snow, Charlotte. "Renal-Care Biggies Plan Merger." *Modern Healthcare,* 24 November 1997.

Taylor, Mark. "False Claims Suit Settled for $16.5 Million." *Modern Healthcare,* 21 June 1999.

"Total Renal Care Announces Appointment Of David Barry as President and Chief Operating Officer." *PR Newswire,* 26 January 2000.

"Total Renal Care Announces Estimated Fourth Quarter Charges." *PR Newswire,* 19 January 2000.

"Vivra Stock Falls on News of Federal Investigation." *New York Times,* 28 December 1996.

Ward's Business Directory of U.S. Public and Private Companies. Detroit: Gale Research, 1996.

SIC 8093

SPECIALTY OUTPATIENT FACILITIES, NOT ELSEWHERE CLASSIFIED

This grouping covers establishments primarily engaged in outpatient care of a specialized nature with permanent facilities and with medical staff to provide diagnosis, treatment, or both for patients who are ambulatory and do not require inpatient care. Offices and clinics of health practitioners are classified according to their primary health care activity.

NAICS Code(s)

621410 (Family Planning Centers)

621420 (Outpatient Mental Health and Substance Abuse Centers)

621498 (All Other Outpatient Care Facilities)

Industry Snapshot

Facilities in this category are diverse and include outpatient centers offering alcohol or drug treatment, biofeedback, family planning, mental health services, rehabilitation centers, outpatient surgery, kidney dialysis, lithotripsy (therapy that reduces kidney stones into small pieces so that they can be voided), and diagnostic imaging environments. Efforts to cut huge medical costs starting in the 1980s led to a movement away from inpatient treatment that continued to the 1990s, resulting in a number of different outpatient services. Growth was expected to continue into 2006 in new areas, most of which are less than 10 years old because of technology that further reduced the cost of providing these services and allowed them to be offered in outpatient facilities.

In the early 1990s these outpatient and office locations were less regulated and utilized third-party reimbursement. Many were owned by physicians or physician groups and were not subjected to the same oversight as inpatient procedures. This changed in the middle of the decade with the introduction of government legislation to reduce abuses by physicians referring patients to self-owned laboratory services. The Stark Amendment created a list of 11 designated services to which physician owners could not refer Medicare or Medicaid patients. Combined with pressures from managed care companies, many physicians sold their interests in facilities, resulting in many publicly owned companies entering this specialized marketplace offering multiple services at a lower cost.

Organization and Structure

Drug and Alcohol Treatment. The trend of using specialized outpatient facilities is especially evident in substance abuse treatment. Drug and alcohol treatment is increasingly being done on an outpatient basis. The 17 percent growth rate for the service market for inpatient drug and alcohol treatment centers was at its height in 1989, bringing in $3.9 billion in revenues. This area has remained at this economic level through the 1990s.

The industry had been built on inpatient care. But in a cost-cutting environment, reimbursement requests for substance abuse treatment were being subjected to greater scrutiny by insurance companies. More co-payments were required, and lifetime caps were set on reimbursement. Outpatient care was less costly as well, and treatment methodologies changed as a result of all these factors. Now patients are typically treated for only a brief period in a hospital before moving on to outpatient centers, where treatment typically lasts four weeks.

The shift to outpatient care is apparent in the declining numbers of days that patients receive inpatient substance abuse treatment. Formerly the length of stay was 28 days. In the 1990s inpatient stays averaged 15 to 19 days. The number of treatment beds was also down and, according to industry statistics, substance abuse facilities were operating at about 65 percent capacity, a decline from 80 to 90 percent capacity levels posted in the late 1980s.

Increased regard for civil liberties has also decreased compulsory inpatient treatment. In addition, community-based support groups have become an integral part of drug and alcohol abuse treatment enabling drug abuse patients to avoid hospitalization. Another factor discouraging the use of inpatient facilities for substance abuse is the increasing number of young people with alcohol abuse problems who are seeking treatment. These clients typically have fewer medical problems related to their addiction and are less in need of hospitalization to treat such related problems.

Psychiatric Outpatient Care. Insurance companies and other third-party payers are also taking a harder look at claims for inpatient psychiatric care today, prompting hospitals and other health care providers to set up less expensive outpatient facilities. According to a survey from the National Association of Psychiatric Health Systems (NAPHS), nearly 67 percent of psychiatric centers provided outpatient services. The average length of an inpatient psychiatric stay has gone down, according to the

Health Care Institute of America, a health care consulting firm. The average stay in a psychiatric hospital went down to 11.5 days in the late 1990s from 25.7 days in 1987, while total patient rates increased. The number of outpatient admissions rose nearly 21 percent to over 1,200. The number of each patient's visits declined during that time.

Family Planning Clinics. These free-standing centers practice measures designed to assist pregnant women (and families) in making various decisions regarding their condition. Such clinics have a unique history and are at the center of a controversial ethical debate. Abortions are one of the services provided by these clinics since the Supreme Court's *Roe v. Wade* decision that legalized abortion in the United States. Since that decision, however, debate has raged about the practice. Protests outside family planning clinics of abortion services have grown increasingly frequent in recent years. The fortunes of such clinics have thus changed with shifts in political power at the national level. Under the Bush administration, which did not favor abortion rights, regulations were passed preventing federally funded family planning centers from providing abortion counseling. That regulation was rescinded by the Clinton administration.

Family planning clinics not only provide contraceptive methods but also offer screening services to contraceptive clients since the services are required for prescribing birth control pills. Almost all such establishments provide pelvic examinations, blood pressure tests, PAP smears, and breast examinations.

Planned Parenthood-World Population, formerly the Planned Parenthood Association, is a leading family-planning network, and one which brought organized family planning to the United States. It was founded in 1921 and has centers throughout the United States. Many Planned Parenthood affiliates also offer services such as colposcopy (examination of the vagina and cervix) and HIV testing.

Prospective Payment System In the 1980s a movement away from retrospective payment for inpatient care began. When Medicare was initiated in 1965, it reimbursed hospitals and physicians based on bills submitted after treatment. But in 1983 that type of payment for hospital inpatient treatment was replaced with the Prospective Payment System. Yet charges for physicians and outpatient services continued to be reimbursed retrospectively, encouraging a shift to outpatient therapy.

The Prospective Payment System for the first time rewarded hospitals for holding down costs and allowed hospital administrators to know before treatment how much a hospital would be reimbursed for illness at rates determined by geographic region as well as by specific procedures and medical problems.

CURRENT CONDITIONS

Today, each medical problem is classified by a specialized group of health professionals into a Diagnostic Related Group. If a hospital spends less than is allotted under prospective payment it makes a profit, but if it spends more, the hospital must make up the difference. As a result many believe that doctors may be admitting fewer patients and referring more to outpatient settings not subject to peer review or prospective payment. Indeed, the incidence of outpatient treatment rose dramatically following introduction of the Prospective Payment System.

Many Clinton administration officials expressed determination to eliminate what they viewed as the insurance industry's discrimination against the mentally ill. Both Medicaid and private insurance policies severely restrict coverage of mental health care. Generally the elderly and disabled beneficiaries must pay 50 percent of the bills for outpatient mental health services, a stark contrast with the 20 percent contribution generally required for treatment of physical ailments. Currently the federal government pays for a quarter of the $67 billion spent annually for mental health care, with private insurers and patients paying the balance. Proposed plans for alleviating this problem included the creation of incentives for community-based care and outpatient services rather than hospitalization.

Yet there have been problems with treating the mentally ill as outpatients. During the 1980s, in an effort to cut costs, several states deinstitutionalized mental patients and made plans for them to continue their treatment in outpatient settings. New York hospitals, for instance, made elaborate plans for treatment of mentally ill patients after their release, but those plans fell through. According to a 1993 study of the New York State Commission on the Quality of Care for the Mentally Disabled, 40 percent of the discharged mental patients whose cases were reviewed ended up being rehospitalized within six months of their discharge because they were unable to make their way through the complicated government and health care bureaucracies they needed to help them. The released patients were rehospitalized at an average cost of $30,750. Nine of ten patients had abused drugs or alcohol and received no services for the mental illness or addiction.

In 1998, total industry revenue was reported to be nearly $5.9 billion, with expenses of $5.5 billion. This represented a 1.4 percent decrease in revenue, and a 1.1 percent decrease in expenses from the previous year.

Family Planning. Financial strains on family planning facilities have increased in recent years. There has been less public funding, while expenses have gone up. New contraceptive methods such as the contraceptive implant are expensive. To meet these expenses many agencies

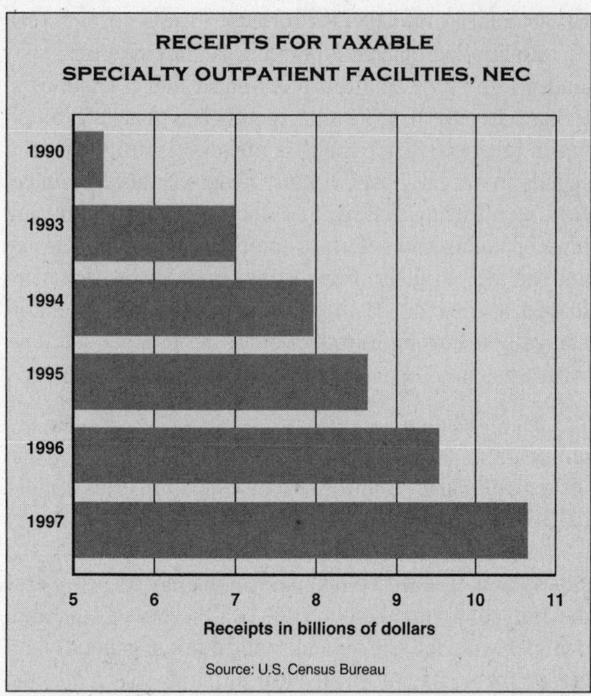

have had to raise fees. While the Clinton administration is friendly to these clinics, in contrast to the previous administration, clinics face long-term economic insecurity. Without public funds, family planning leaders say, their clinics will have to merge with managed care organizations or offer primary care to remain financially viable—and providing primary care would force these clinics to narrow the range of contraceptive care they offer.

Hospital Outpatient Treatment. Outpatient facilities are also being set up by hospitals. Anxious to preserve their traditional centrality in health care, hospitals are establishing health care networks with a variety of outpatient services in addition to the traditional inpatient care. The Berlin Memorial Hospital in central Wisconsin, for example, links women's heath clinics in three separate towns with anesthesiology centers, internal-medicine centers, an extended-care facility, and a nursing home. Information systems in such cases are integrated for ease of handling by insurers and participating physicians. The effort by hospitals nationwide to assume a more important role for outpatient centers is part of the overall trend advancing outpatient care at a time when the nation is taking a critical look at its traditional health care system.

Workforce

The employment pattern for miscellaneous outpatient services underwent accelerated growth during the period from the 1980s through the 1990s and proved to be basically immune to recessionary pressures. This is due, in part, to the large increase in the numbers of middle-aged and elderly in the population. An aging population typically brings an increased incidence of disease and need for outpatient services. For example, employment of radiology technologists is expected to grow faster than average through 2006 because of the vast clinical potential of diagnostic imaging and therapeutic technology. In the late 1990s, the average starting salary was just under $29,000. Department heads' salaries were $68,500.

Further Reading

''Health, United States, 1998.'' *National Center for Health Statistics,* 20 March 2000. Available from http://www.cdc.gov/nchs.

''NAPHS Survey Documents Changing Hospital Care Driven by Market.'' *Psychiatric News,* 3 October 1997.

Neuer, Anne. ''Long-term Healthcare Looks Good, as Long as Washington Behaves.'' *STREETnet,* 27 February 1997.

———. ''Specialized Service Providers Keep Costs Low for Patients and Managed Care.'' *STREETnet,* 27 February 1997.

''Radiology Technologists.'' *Occupational Outlook Handbook,* 1 April 1996.

U.S. Bureau of Labor Statistics. *1998-99 Occupational Outlook Handbook,* 20 March 2000. Available from http://stats.bls.gov.

U.S. Bureau of the Census. *Service Industry Census,* 20 March 2000. Available from http://www.census.gov.

SIC 8099

HEALTH AND ALLIED SERVICES, NOT ELSEWHERE CLASSIFIED

This classification is comprised of establishments primarily engaged in providing health and allied services, not described under other classifications.

NAICS Code(s)

621991 (Blood and Organ Banks)
541430 (Graphic Design Services)
541922 (Commercial Photography)
621410 (Family Planning Centers)
621999 (All Other Miscellaneous Ambulatory Health Care Services)

Industry Snapshot

This segment of the health services industry includes an array of services and occupations that most often do not involve the provision of direct care. Rather they provide diagnostic services or facilitate the work of physicians and other health care providers.

Despite the extreme diversity of establishments in this classification, all enjoy the economic advantages of offering services that are in great demand regardless of economic climate. The establishments include blood banks; hearing testing services; childbirth preparation classes; health screening centers, except by physicians; sperm banks; osteoporosis centers; medical illustration; oxygen tent services; and plasmapheresis centers. In 1997, the industry had total revenues of just under $23 billion; by 1998 the industry employed 339,000 people.

The classification contains a notable mix of profit and non-profit organizations. Blood banking, for example, is a multi-billion dollar industry in which the purified products, though donated, command a high price if sold. Hearing testing services may be available for free at schools or for a fee at private commercial establishments. Most hearing testing is done in schools and colleges, with 10 percent in hospitals and the rest in private offices and speech, language, and hearing centers. Similarly, childbirth preparation classes are often available through schools, community groups, and other nonprofit organizations, but they are also available from commercial childbirth preparation centers. Health screenings are done by municipal health departments as well as independent commercial establishments. Unlike the rest of the activities on this list, medical equipment like oxygen tents are profit-making ventures, while medical art and photography may be provided by independent entrepreneurs contracted by medical textbook publishers or others engaged in medical education.

The state of the nation's health has had a great impact on two of the health services in this group—the collection and production of blood. Combined, this sector, the most lucrative in this classification, has been much affected over the last decade by the need to test for hepatitis and AIDS. The same concerns hold true for sperm banks.

ORGANIZATION AND STRUCTURE

Since there is such a diversity of activities within the health and allied services group, there is no overall industry structure. Rather, different structures govern each activity. For example, in the case of blood banks, three nonprofit organizations preside over the $3 billion U.S. whole blood market.

In 1999 the leading blood market organization was the Red Cross, which had 38 regional blood centers that collected blood from more than 4.5 million donors, and supplied more than half of the nation's blood supply. The number of blood centers the previous year was 45, however, the organization was forced to restructure their blood bank operations after questions arose regarding their quality standards. The 1996 restructuring cost approximately $162 million.

The Red Cross was estimated to have $1.9 billion in revenue in 1997. A majority came from biomedical services (the collection, testing, and distribution of blood and blood components); revenue derived solely from these activities accounted for $1.1 billion.

Second to the Red Cross is America's Blood Centers (ABC), a nation-wide network of independent blood centers in 46 states at over 450 sites. Their mission also included blood diagnostic and therapeutic services. In 1999, ABC collected approximately 47 percent of the blood used in the United States.

Industry Divisions. The miscellaneous services provided in the health and allied services industry can be subsumed into two general groupings: first, services provided to physicians and hospitals; and second, services provided to health care consumers.

The services provided to physicians and hospitals include medical photography and art and blood and blood products from blood and plasmapheresis centers. Medical or biological subjects may be illustrated for teaching purposes through photography, graphics, paintings, and three-dimensional models. Medical art and photography appears in books, films, videotapes, and computer graphics. Blood banks provide whole blood and some derived components that are processed, typed, and stored until needed for transfusion. Blood should be used as soon as possible since the number of red blood cells decline significantly after 14 days. At plasmapheresis centers, blood is removed from the body, centrifuged, and the red cells suspended in a solution. They may be re-injected into the donor or into a patient who requires red cells rather than whole blood.

Examples of services provided to health consumers include health screening, hearing testing, child birth preparation classes, sperm banks, and osteoporosis centers.

Health screening centers, whether private or public, are likely to focus on particular problems such as cancer detection; sexually transmitted diseases; or nutrition, diet, and weight control.

Hearing centers diagnose hearing problems and prescribe treatment. An audiologist uses an audiometer and other testing devices to measure the loudest sound at which a person begins to hear. The audiologist also measures the ability to tell the difference between sounds and the extent of any hearing loss. The results of the tests may be correlated with other medical, psychological, and education test results and a course of treatment determined.

Childbirth preparation classes often follow the principles of the French obstetrician Fernand Lamaze, who advocated avoiding highly medicated childbirth. The method stresses the active participation of the mother through muscle control and breathing, with encouragement and massage given to her by her husband. In this method, also known as pyscho-prophylaxis, the husband is prepared to act as his wife's labor coach.

The fact that sperm can be kept alive for long periods of time in cold temperatures has enabled banks of human semen to be maintained for use in artificial insemination. Licensed sperm banks are members of the American Fertility Society. The society has revised its guidelines for therapeutic donor insemination of sperm several times in recent years to improve selection of donors and decrease the potential hazard for transmitting infectious agents.

Current Conditions

As in general medical professions, there are controversies within this classification regarding the right of physicians to refer patients to establishments in which they have invested. In 1993, the Federal Trade Commission used antitrust legislation to challenge two oxygen and oxygen equipment businesses owned by doctors who referred their patients to them. According to the Federal Trade Commission, 60 percent of the lung specialists in two California counties, Contra Costa and Alameda, had invested in the medical equipment companies. The Commission stated that such ''self-referrals,'' as they are called, exclude competitors from the market in violation of the law since the doctors can control the referral of patients who need these services. Since other home oxygen companies may not be able to get referrals from doctors, they were unable to compete in the market regardless of the quality or prices. The commission and the companies agreed on a settlement, stipulating that some of the lung specialists would have to sell their shares in the company so that no more than 25 percent of the lung specialists in the area would have a connection with the company.

The need to protect the blood supply against hepatitis and AIDS has made the work of blood banks and plasmapheresis centers increasingly complex. To screen against the two diseases, blood centers have added five tests since 1985. Commercial companies and nonprofit blood centers have acquired computer systems to track donors throughout the country. The American Blood Resources Association is setting up a nationwide donor referral registry, so that a blood center can call an 800 number to find out if the donor has ever tested positive for the AIDS virus or another condition that would rule them out as a donor. Aware of public concern over the safety of the blood supply, the American Association of Blood Banks in 1993 mounted a public relations program designed to increase public awareness about the general safety of the blood supply.

Plasma, in particular, is the fastest growing sector of the blood products industry. There is a worldwide market for blood plasma. A pint of whole blood has a $100 price tag, but its components add up to $190 a pint. Plasma lasts longer than blood and $55 worth of plasma can be extracted from a pint of blood. The technology and training for processing plasma requires a significant investment. Obtaining plasma may often involve paying donors. Plasma can be separated into albumin, which is necessary to keep blood vessels from collapsing after an injury; factor VIII, an important blood clotting agent; and immune globulins, which can protect against several diseases.

With 30 percent market share, the leader in the industry is Armour Pharmaceutical Company (of Bluebell, Pennsylvania), a subsidiary of Rhône-Pulence Rorer, the French government-owned pharmaceutical company. Next, with 25 percent of the market, is Hyland Therapeutics (of Glendale, California), a subsidiary of Baxter International Inc. The Red Cross became involved in the commercial market in 1978 when it took donated plasma from its supplies and used the Hyland manufacturing facilities to turn it into its marketable components. That move brought the Red Cross approximately $100 million of tax-exempt revenue in 1990. By 1996, the Red Cross had become a $1.9 billion organization.

The blood and blood products sector is the most highly regulated sector within this classification. The U.S. Food and Drug Administration (FDA) licenses plasmapheresis firms as well as the firms that ship their products from state to state. The problems that were uncovered at a Tacoma, Washington plasmapheresis center illustrate the risks involved when this type of firm does not adhere to regulations. The firm, AVRE Plasma, received a four-month suspension of its establishment and product licenses in 1992 as a result of operating practices that the FDA termed ''dangerous.'' AVRE sells source plasma to pharmaceutical firms for processing into serum albumin, immune globulins, and other medical products.

Workforce

The training required to carry out the duties of the health and allied services listed here varies greatly. Medical illustrators generally have a four-year bachelor's degree, and often from one of the six accredited schools in the United States that offer a degree in medical illustration. Audiologists also have four years of training, but with a master's degree, may acquire the Certificate of Clinical Competence offered by the American Speech and Hearing Association. They must also have 300 hours of supervised clinical experience in a 9-month, postgraduate internship, and pass an examination. In contrast to the extensive training required by others in this category, phlebotomists can be trained to draw blood in from one to three months. However, much more extensive training is required for the technicians who analyze blood to determine if there are abnormalities; hence, the medical director of a blood bank is often a pathologist with a full medical degree.

Research and Technology

The blood industry will require huge infusions of money over the next decade to purchase new equipment for research and employ more staff. The commercial blood products companies have invested $50 million for research into new blood products; the Red Cross has invested $7 million alone.

The advent of the AIDS epidemic has also resulted in people storing their own blood in preparation for operations or emergencies. The first autologous blood storage was done by a sperm bank owned by the Daxor Corporation, based in New York. The blood can be stored for 10 years, and storage charges vary from $12 a month for a pint of fragile red cells to $8 for plasma. Autologous blood banks have not been a good investment, according to Dr. Joseph Feldschu, who founded Daxor. Acceptance of this approach has been slow. Traditional blood banks also consider that autologous blood threatens the system of voluntary blood donations for others.

Reports at the 1994 American Association of Blood Banks Conference showed how new technologies could reduce or even replace the need for blood transfusions. One such technology involves the transplantation of purified peripheral blood progenitor cells, which are collected through an immunoabsorption system. In tests at the University of Colorado Cancer Center in Denver, patients showed improvements in their recovery rate. ''Patients are recovering faster, doing better, and getting out of the hospital more quickly, which translates into reduced costs,'' Shelly Heimfeld, director of biological research at CellPro in Washington, told *JAMA*. ''Peripheral blood also dramatically reduced the number of red blood cell and platelet transfusions needed.''

In 1999, under the auspices of the Federal Drug Administration's Investigational New Drug (IND) application process, the blood community began Nucleic Acid Amplification Testing (NAT). This new technology specifically sought increased protection of the nation's blood supply by detecting genetic material that marked HCV and HIV viruses.

The medical illustration industry benefited greatly from computer technology innovations in the mid- to late 1990s. By 1997, illustrators had access to more techniques, such as three-dimensional scientific imaging, surface modeling, and animation. In addition, medical illustrators could use laser scanners and digitizers to enhance detail and accuracy. Illustrators could also manipulate three-dimensional information using the virtual reality modeling language (VRML) to put biological models and data on the World Wide Web for examination by medical students, patients, and consultants.

FURTHER READING

''ABC Foundation.'' Washington: America's Blood Centers, 1999. Available from http://www.americasblood.org/.

Darnay, Arsen J., ed. *Service Industries USA,* 3rd edition. Detroit: Gale Research, 1996.

Finkelstein, Katherine Eban. ''Blood Money: Liddy Dole's Red Cross Runs Amok.'' *The New Republic,* 12 August 1996.

Hansen, David J. ''New Computer Techniques for Medical Illustration and Scientific Visualization.'' *JAMA,* 5 February 1997.

''Industry Report-Health and Allied Services, Not Elsewhere Classified.''*National Industry Operation Matrix.* Washington: Bureau of Labor Statistics, 1999. Available from http://stats.bls.gov/asp/oep/nioem/.

Scott, Lisa. ''Red Cross Touts Its Broad Restructuring.'' *Modern Healthcare,* 13 November 1995.

True Stories: 1997 Annual Report. Washington: American Red Cross, 1997.

U.S. Department of Commerce, Bureau of the Census. *Service Annual Survey: 1997.* Washington: GPO, 1999.

SIC 8111

LEGAL SERVICES

This industry consists of establishments that are headed by members of the bar and are primarily engaged in offering legal advice and/or services. Such establishments include attorneys, counselors at law, law offices, lawyers, legal aid services, legal services, patent solicitors' offices, and referees in bankruptcy.

NAICS CODE(S)

541110 (Offices of Lawyers)

INDUSTRY SNAPSHOT

The legal service industry is the second largest professional service industry in the nation, second only to health services. The industry collects more than $132 billion in annual revenue—more than 5 times the annual revenue collected by advertising firms, almost 3 times the revenue collected by accounting and auditing firms, and approximately one-third less than the amount of revenue generated by the automobile industry. The legal services industry employs more than 1.3 million people, with approximately 70 percent of the workforce comprised of practicing attorneys.

ORGANIZATION AND STRUCTURE

An attorney, also known as a lawyer, is an agent, a person appointed to act on behalf of another. As indicated by noted attorney Karl Llewllyn in the *ABA Journal* in 1942, ''. . . the essence of our craftsmanship lies in skills and wisdom; in practical, effective, persuasive, inventive skills for getting things done . . . We are the trouble-shooters.'' The right to assume this agency relationship is granted by state statutes dictating admission to the state bar. Admission to the bar confers the authority or license to practice law. Requirements for admission usually include three years of college, graduation from an American Bar Association (ABA) accredited law school, residency requirements, and successful completion of the bar examination. Some states such as California have varying practices regarding study requirements and allow apprenticeships in lieu of academic study. In addition, some states rely entirely upon their own bar examinations while others utilize a ''multistate'' examination. Attorneys admitted to the bar in one state may not practice in another without permission of the other state's authority. Practicing law without proper accreditation is a punishable and sometimes criminal offense. While there has never been a nationwide bar exam, 46 states require that the applicant pass the MBE (multi-state bar exam) as part of the admission process.

Lawyers are admitted to the bar for life; however, misconduct can bring suspension or disbarment as well as other appropriate punishment. As a general axiom, any conduct that would have prevented admission to the bar also would be sufficient to suspend or disbar an attorney. The general criterion is whether or not the attorney is deemed fit for the confidence and trust required in the attorney-client relationship.

The bar review industry is an extremely concentrated and competitive industry wherein 5 firms control most of the market. The 5 major players in the industry—Bar/Bri, PMBR, SMH, Barpassers, and Reed—aggressively pursue the limited market of 58,000 annual exam takers, which generates $50 million in revenues. Founded in 1967, Bar/Bri is the leader among such reviewers, with more than 600,000 students having taken their course.

Legal Service Providers. Four broad categories of legal service providers in the United States, each having subcategories of their own, are public legal assistance, government, nonprofit, and private.

Public Legal Assistance. According to the Sixth Amendment to the U.S. Constitution and affirmed by the landmark Supreme Court case *Gideon v. Wainwright,* all individuals are entitled to legal services regardless of ability to pay. Due to the high cost of legal counsel, public legal assistance programs have been established for people who cannot afford it.

In 1963, Clarence Earl Gideon, an uneducated gambler and petty thief, insisted on his right to legal counsel. The Supreme Court and Justice Hugo Black upheld this right, indicating: ''Any person hauled into court who is too poor to hire a lawyer cannot be assured a fair trial unless counsel is provided for him . . . This seems to us to be an obvious truth.'' The courts have expanded the ruling in *Gideon* to apply to all criminal cases. This has led to the establishment of two types of public legal offices: public defenders and legal aid offices.

Public defenders represent criminal defendants. A criminal case is distinguished from a civil case by two primary elements. In a civil suit, someone has sustained a loss or harm as the result of some act (or failure to act) by another. The individual filing the act is seeking compensation (either monetary or performance) rather than seeking punishment, as in a criminal case. Secondly, an individual party usually files against another in a civil case; a criminal case is filed by the state against an individual. The current state of public defense has been enormously strained by caseloads that have overwhelmed defense attorneys, as well as a paucity of funds. Legal aid offices represent the civil counterpart of public defenders. These organizations represent those who cannot afford legal counsel in civil matters such as tort litigation (i.e. lawsuits resulting from negligence, etc.). Eligibility guidelines for access to public legal services vary depending on location, family size, and household income.

Government Lawyers. Supported by tax dollars, hundreds of attorneys work for the government at each of the three levels: local, state, and federal. Government attorneys are primarily engaged in legal problems concerning government service (e.g., Bureau of Consumer Protection, Human Relations Commission, or Department of Environmental Resources) or government-regulated industries (e.g. Public Utilities Commission).

Nonprofit Organizations. These types of organizations provide free representation to individual cases that relate to the organization's unique interests. Special interest organizations such as the Environmental Defense Fund, the National Association for the Advancement of Colored People (NAACP), and the American Civil Liberties Union (ACLU) are engaged in the provision of legal services.

In addition to career nonprofit lawyers, charitable legal services or pro bono work is becoming increasingly prevalent as a mandatory part of legal education. Several law schools have public service requirements for graduating students. Tulane University School of Law requires that graduating students perform at least 20 hours of public service law. Beginning with the class of 1996, Columbia University School of Law required its students to complete 40 hours of pro bono work over a period of two years. At other schools, nonprofit work is voluntary—New York University's entering class pledged to perform 95 hours of community service work apiece during their three-year tenure. In addition, more than 50 law schools have initiated programs to ease the debt burden of graduates who go into nonprofit practice.

Private Lawyers. The most prevalent form of legal service provider is the private attorney. There are two basic types of private attorney: individual or sole practitioners, and group practitioners or law firms. Group practices fall into three primary categories: informal arrangements in which two or more lawyers share office space and support services, partnerships, and legal corporations. Partnerships and legal corporations are designated as law firms. An American Bar Association (ABA) survey indicates that practices with five or fewer attorneys comprise 25 percent of the industry. Approximately 31 percent of lawyers engage in practice as partners or as associates of law firms with 20 or more practitioners. Law firms range in size from two practitioners to large, multidivisional firms engaging more than 100 associates. Large corporations employ an additional category of private lawyers as house counsel.

A recent survey of ABA membership indicated that 4 out of 5 (80 percent) attorneys work in private practice with law firms and another 10 percent work in corporate law departments. Thus, approximately 90 percent work in private practice. The remainder is divided between government, judiciary, and academia.

Economic Structure. Most of the $132 billion annually collected by lawyers and law firms is collected through direct billing of legal fees. There are four fee arrangements generally utilized within the industry: contingent fees, hourly rates, retainers, and fixed fees.

Contingent Fees. A large percentage of civil case fee arrangements are structured so that the attorney is only compensated if they are successful in obtaining a settlement on the client's behalf. The fee usually is a percentage of the amount of the settlement. Some contingent-fees can range as high as 60 percent of an eventual settlement, with the industry standard hovering around 30 to 35 percent of the amount of the settlement.

Contingent fee arrangements also require the client to cover the expenses accrued in filing a complaint, engaging in discovery, and either negotiating a settlement or trying the case in court. These expenses are the responsibility of the client, whatever the outcome. There are two basic contingent fee arrangements: expenses off the top and expenses after the deduction of fee.

Hourly Rates. An hourly rate is assessed based on the amount of time an attorney invests in a case. However, trends within the industry toward increased client accountability have led to modifications in the traditional practice of ''billable hours.'' Consulting firms that advise both law firms and clients about billing practices have become more common. These firms have assisted law firms in assessing their service provision costs and investments and allocating these costs to clients in the form of equitable fee setting. Fee-consulting firms also have been able to save clients from 10 to 30 percent on their legal bills.

Retainers. A retainer is an advance payment estimated to cover the cost of legal services. Retainers are based on an estimate of the time spent by the lawyer, the complexity of the legal issues in question, and the potential amount of money involved in the action.

Fixed Fees. Fixed fees usually are assessed for simple legal tasks, such as deed preparation, no contest divorce, consumer bankruptcy, etc. Fixed fees are those in which the client pays in advance a fixed amount for a certain legal service—for example, $100 for preparation of a deed—regardless of the length of time it takes the attorney to complete the task.

CURRENT CONDITIONS

The legal industry in the United States is facing a number of contemporary issues regarding internal firm structure, external competition, and diversified growth.

Career Progression. Fueled by increased competition between law firms, the traditional ''partnership track'' is changing within the industry. Previously, there was an unspoken promise among major law firms that a summer job between the second and third year of law school was a practical guarantee of a permanent position after graduation, with a relatively safe period of tenure as an associate for at least one year and up to five years. Those attorneys completing the five years as an associate usually were offered a partnership position. However, the partnership path has become more arduous, with the apprenticeship period prior to ''making partner'' lasting 10 years or longer. Further, employers simply have rejected many candidates with partnership potential.

To keep revenues ahead of costs, law firms have had to increase the ratio of associates to partners from a one-to-one ratio to five partners for every six associates, according to an *ABA Journal* report.

This change in the dynamics of legal career progression has led to two internal innovations within the industry. The first is an increased use of paralegals to do the work now assigned to associates. The second strategy is to develop a new position, the ''career attorney.'' Law firms offer those individuals who have little or no chance of making partner a higher salary than other associates make for staying with the firm.

Firm Size. Another structural innovation to maintain competitiveness is the increased use of branch offices and acquisitions. According to a report in the *ABA Journal,* 30 percent of the lawyers in the nation's 250 largest firms practice in branch offices. The *ABA Journal* notes that ''branches have become a major weapon in many law firm's arsenal to fight for new business and increased market share.'' Many large U.S. law firms are looking overseas to international opportunities as well. As Ward Bower, a consultant with the Philadelphia office of Altman, Weil and Pensa, said, ''The costs of overseas expansion are very heavy, so the downside can be great, but so is the potential.''

Some within the industry feel a trend is emerging toward increased size and concentration among the largest firms. According to the ABA, by 2001 approximately 20 to 50 law firms will dominate the legal profession while mid-sized firms will become increasingly specialized in an attempt to carve out niche markets. In addition, the report speculated that the largest law firms will double in size, employing 3,000 or more attorneys.

Small firms will continue to handle issues such as landlord-tenant disputes, traffic violations, and a variety of criminal matters that have been the traditional province of the small firm. However, increased competition from legal chains such as Hyatt Legal Services, coupled with spiraling overhead costs, will force the small or solo practitioners to be better organized and more efficient.

Professional Management. The trend toward increased size in law firms has led to an increasing need for professional management. The law firm is faced with dual pressures: the need for increased responsiveness to client needs and demands counterbalanced by the need to generate revenue. Furthermore, increased size is creating an additional impediment to effective management; firms with 200 or more partners cannot run a firm as a democracy. The trend is toward creating a new position, an executive director, who will function as a chief operating officer. This individual will have minimal legal responsibility and perhaps will not even be a lawyer. In fact, nonlawyers may be established as partners at even the most prestigious law firms.

In addition to professional management, law firms are (and will continue) adopting other accouterments of more traditional business organizations. These include practice managers (similar to product managers) who augment service delivery and expedite performance appraisal in diverse sub-disciplines (e.g. tax, litigation, etc.) within the profession.

External Competition Issues. Lawyers are facing increased competitive pressure from paralegal firms offering low-cost legal services. Independent paralegals increased from approximately 200 individuals in 1985 to an estimated 6,000 in the mid-1990s. These nonlawyer practitioners are offering legal services in such areas as will and living trust preparation and child-support arrangements. Concerns expressed by the American Bar Association regarding the ancillary businesses include creating a danger of loss of confidentiality and conflict of interest, and distracting lawyers from their duties of law practice and their professional responsibilities. In contrast, members of the legal community indicate that full-service law firms allow attorneys the opportunity to better serve their clients. Furthermore, proponents of ancillary businesses indicate that professional diversification already is practiced by accounting firms that do tax law and banks that engage in estate planning. Diversification, supporters argue, allows law firms to remain competitive.

Industry Leaders

The legal industry is highly atomistic, with the top 10 law firms accounting for only 3.5 percent of total industry revenues. The leading firm (in terms of revenue) in the industry—Baker & McKenzie of Chicago, the largest firm in the nation with more than 2,000 lawyers in the firm's multinational network and $503.5 million in 1995 revenue—also controls only 0.5 percent of the market. Skadden, Arps, Slate, Meagher & Flom, in New York, is another industry leader, with 652 lawyers and $440 million in revenues. Although only 4.5 percent of the nation's attorneys work for the largest 100 law firms, those firms take in 16 percent of the industry's revenue.

Chicago's Baker & McKenzie firm built its position in the industry in a different fashion. The firm has been engaged in legal practice for more than a century. The growth of the firm primarily is attributed to expertise and growth in international law, with a substantial portion of the firm's almost 1,600 lawyers located in overseas branch offices. The firm has more than 45 international branch offices to complement 9 domestic offices. The international offices are located in more than 25 different nations, including the People's Republic of China (Beijing, Guangzhou, and Shanghai), Russia (Moscow), and Saudi Arabia (Riyadh).

Skadden Arps is another firm with a large market share, revenue, and productivity. Its ascension to the top of the profession primarily is a function of the diligence and expertise of partner Joseph Flom. Flom joined the five-lawyer firm in 1948 after graduating from Harvard law School. He developed an expertise in helping shareholders challenge the management of their companies. In 1974 Flom successfully represented International Nickel Corporation (INCO) and won control of a target company, ESB Inc., in a takeover attempt that was to set the tone for the merger and acquisition activity prevalent in the 1980s. In 1975 Flom represented Chicago's Marshall Field's and saved it from a takeover attempt by Carter Hawley Hale. Flom employed a unique strategy—he encouraged Marshall Field's to begin building stores in towns where Carter Hawley Hale already had outlets. The strategy created such complicated antitrust implications that Carter simply dropped the takeover attempt.

By the mid-1980s, Skadden Arps was a part of many major deals. According to Kim Eisler's book *Shark Tank,* Flom's instinct for acquisition and defense skills were so expertly developed that many active players in the mergers and acquisitions market paid Flom a retainer to ensure that a potential raider couldn't use his skill against them.

WORKFORCE

The workforce in the legal services industry was approximately 1.34 million in the mid-1990s. The majority of the workforce—more than 950,000 employees—is composed of practicing attorneys. The remainder of the industry's workers are primarily support staff personnel such as paralegals and clerical support personnel.

Wages in the industry continue to rise at a rate above that set by most other industries. In the early 1990s the average beginning lawyer earned $36,600 per year, and top graduates from top law schools started out at around $80,000 per year. Since then, the current economic climate has induced law firms to take a more conservative approach to hiring. Despite this ''soft'' market for recent law school graduates, average starting salaries have continued to accelerate. In the mid-1990s, graduates from prestigious law schools such as Yale University, Columbia University, New York University, and Georgetown University Law Center received average starting salaries in excess of $70,000. This demand for higher salaries is fueled in part by rising tuition costs at major law schools and heavy student loan burdens faced by recent graduates. Average associate salaries for young New York attorneys exceed $82,000.

Lawyers on salary receive increases as they assume greater responsibility. Lawyers starting their own practice may need to work part time in other occupations during the first years to supplement their income. Their incomes usually grow as their practices develop.

Lawyers who are partners in law firms generally earn more than those who practice alone, although a majority of associates and others polled considered partnership to be less of a necessary step toward career advancement. According to the National Association for Law Placement, only about half of all associates (56 percent) perceive partnership as an incentive for their careers in private practice.

The field of law makes a difference, too. Several areas of the legal profession are currently regarded as ''hot'' practice areas. These include bankruptcy and corporate reorganization, environmental law, alternative dispute resolution, and technology law. Environmental and technology practices will remain strong practice areas. These areas are fueled by growing concerns and increasing legislation in regards to the environment and ubiquitous high-technology issues such as computer fraud and electronic funds transfer. In addition, firms operating in the increasingly competitive pharmaceutical and biotechnology businesses are seeking to protect their innovations through patents, accelerating the demand for patent attorneys and attorneys with technical training. Patent lawyers generally are among the highest paid attorneys. Finally, the litigious nature of modern American society is expected to ensure a continued emphasis on legal mediation and arbitration.

In support services, paralegal work represents the area with the greatest employment potential. Law firms, rather than pay top salaries to law school graduates, are utilizing increasing numbers of paralegals to do routine work traditionally performed by new associates.

Although there has been a marked fall-off in merger and acquisition and real estate practice, New York remains the strongest job market, according to the National Association for Law Placement. The next largest legal job market is Washington, D.C.

RESEARCH AND TECHNOLOGY

The practice of law has and will continue to become increasingly automated. Law office automation is becoming a necessity to improve office productivity and efficiency, to maintain cost controls and competitiveness, and to meet minimum standards of professional practice.

The evolution of the personal computer and the phenomenal growth of the Internet beginning in 1998 represent the primary focal points of automation and instant communication in the legal industry. ''On-line'' databases made available through vendor services such as LEXIS-NEXIS or Westlaw allow the practitioner to expedite research. The LEXIS-NEXIS service features both legal reference sources and news publications, from *The American Lawyer* to *USA Today* to transcripts of CNN and The PBS Lehrer Report. A report issued by the ABA Legal Technology Research Center in Chicago predicted that individual law firms will create their own in-house databases to draw on their past work and handle new matters more expeditiously. Furthermore, firms will create ''expert'' software that allows the entire firm to tap into a specialist's knowledge.

FURTHER READING

Bucholz, Barbara B. ''When Firms Branch Out.'' *ABA Journal,* March 1991, 49-51.

Eisler, Kim. *Shark Tank: Greed, Politics & the Collapse of Finley Kumble, One of America's Largest Law Firms.* New York: St. Martin's Press, 1990.

Gibbons, Thomas, F. ''Law Practice in 2001.'' *ABA Journal,* January 1990, 69-74.

Goldberg, Stephanie B. ''More than the Law: Ancillary Business Growth Continues.'' *ABA Journal,* March 1992.

Morse, Robert J., et. al. ''America's Best Graduate Schools.'' *U.S. News and World Report,* 22 March 1993.

National Association for Law Placement, The premier source for information for legal career planning and recruitment. Copyright, 1999.

U.S. Occupational Outlook Handbook 1994-1995, U.S. Bureau of Labor and Statistics, 1996.

SIC 8211

ELEMENTARY AND SECONDARY SCHOOLS

This category includes elementary and secondary schools furnishing academic courses, ordinarily for kindergarten through grade 12. It includes both public and private institutions and encompasses parochial schools, boarding schools, vocational high schools, and schools providing special services for physically and mentally handicapped students.

NAICS CODE(S)

611110 (Elementary and Secondary Schools)

INDUSTRY SNAPSHOT

By the close of the twentieth century, elementary and secondary education in the United States was characterized by the growing emphasis on technological access and education in order to boost the educational quality and attainment levels of U.S. students and to prepare them for a future in a rapidly evolving technological work environment. While the public-school system continued to receive its share of criticism, alternatives such as charter schools were enjoying increased popularity.

About 53 million students attended elementary and secondary schools in the United States during the 1997-98 school year. The previous year, a total of 86,058 U.S. public schools served 45.6 million students. This represented an increase of 1.7 percent over the number of students reported for the previous school year, though the number of schools increased only 1.1 percent. Public elementary schools totaled 50,205 in 1997-98, while public middle and junior high schools numbered 12,425 and public high schools totaled 14,560. By the late 1990s, according to the National Center for Education Statistics (NCES), enrollment in public elementary and secondary schools rose 16 percent between 1985 and 1996. The fastest growth continues to occur in the elementary grades where enrollment rose from 27.0 million in 1985 to a record high of 33.5 million in 1998, an increase of 24 percent. Enrollment at public high schools grew from 11.3 million in 1998 to 13.3 million a decade later. High schools account for 19 percent of all public schools and 27 percent of enrollment.

More than 5.6 million students participated in programs for the disabled in 1997-98, an increase of almost 50 percent from 1996. About two-thirds of all public elementary and secondary schools students are white, while African Americans make up one-sixth and Hispanic students account for one-seventh. Only a tiny fraction of the student population was Asian American or Native American.

Six million students attended private elementary or secondary schools in 1997-98, representing 11 percent all students, down from 12 percent a decade earlier. The total number of such schools fell slightly during the mid-1990s, from 26,093 in 1994-95 to 23,066 in 1997. Catholic schools accounted for 50 percent of these students (though only 31 percent of those schools) while other religious schools accounted for 34 percent and nonsectarian schools claimed a 16 percent share. The proportion of students in private schools has changed little over the last ten years. The average private-school tuition in the mid-1990s was $3,116, though this figure is much lower among religious schools. Catholic schools, for instance, command $2,178 in tuition, while tuition at schools of other religious orientations totaled $2,915. Nonsectarian schools were by far the most expensive, at $6,631. Private schools altogether spent an average of $4,235 per student in 1997-98, up 0.7 percent form the year before.

The expenditures of public and private schools in the elementary and secondary grades were estimated to total $321 billion for the 1997-98 school year, up from $318 billion in 1995-96. Of this total, $296 billion was spent by the public school system. Local authorities provided 44.9 percent of school revenues, state governments provided 48.2 percent, and the federal government supplied 6.9 percent. Average per pupil expenditures amounted to $6,317, up 0.6 percent from the previous year. After being adjusted for inflation, this represented an increase in spending of 34 percent over the decade. Expenditures at public elementary and secondary schools was expected to reach $337.2 billion in 2007.

All 50 states have compulsory education statutes requiring children to attend school. Although such regulations vary state by state, in general attendance is mandated to begin by a specified age (typically between 5 and 8 years old) and children are required to remain in school until a specified age (typically between 14 and 18 years old) or until high school graduation is achieved.

Enrollment trends observed during the early 1990s led to projections of increased enrollment through the mid-2000s. The increase in elementary school enrollment will continue to be the most pronounced for several years but will taper off relative to secondary schools as those students reach high-school age. By 2009, an estimated 54.5 million students are expected to be enrolled in elementary and secondary schools in the United States, a figure analysts claim will necessitate about 6,000 new schools. Between fall 1996 and fall 2006, public enrollment was projected to grow by 2 percent, while public secondary school enrollment was expected to rise by 15 percent.

ORGANIZATION AND STRUCTURE

In the United States, schools are arranged into districts. Regular school districts are defined as those providing free public elementary and secondary education for the children living within them. Each school district functions under the auspices of a state-level regulatory agency and is responsible for the oversight and operation of the schools within its geographic boundaries. According to figures compiled by the National Center for Education Statistics, there were 14,990 regular school districts within the United States during the 1997-98 school year, down from 15,358 in 1990-91, which is consistent with the steady decrease in the number of districts operating in the United States. This trend reflects school district consolidation and reorganization in order to achieve greater efficiency in delivery of public school services. Over the long term, this trend is dramatically more pronounced; in 1930 there were more than 262,000 public elementary and secondary schools. The nation's five largest districts were New York City; Los Angeles Unified; City of Chicago Schools; Dade County, Florida; and Philadelphia City. Large metropolitan cities were home to about 1 out of every 8 elementary schools, but 1 out of 6 students. Districts with student populations of more than 25,000 accounted for only 1.1 percent of the nation's school districts but served 30 percent of the nation's public school students. California and Texas led the nation with respect to the number of school districts, each reporting more than 1,000 districts for 1997-98. Between 1970 and 1998, the percentage distribution of public elementary and secondary school enrollment increased in the South and the West but declined in both the Midwest and Northeast.

Comparison by region for fall 1997 demonstrated the variation in school district organization and distribution of enrollment. For example, the New England region had 8.3 percent of the nation's operating districts yet educated 4.4 percent of the nation's students. In contrast, the South operated 11 percent of the nation's districts but educated 24.2 percent of the total enrollment.

Different types of schools were established to serve students with different needs. According to U.S. Department of Education statistics for the school year ending June 1998, 98.2 percent of the nation's public schools were regular schools. The remaining schools offered special services such as vocational, alternative, or special education. Alternative schools were often operated in conjunction with regular schools and provided options for students whose needs were unmet in regular classroom settings; about 2,874 such schools, or 0.9 percent of the total, were in operation in 1997-98. Special education schools provided adapted curriculum to meet the needs of students with specific disabilities such as physical, emotional, or mental impairments; the 1,686 special education schools accounted for 0.5 percent of all schools. The nation's 335 vocational schools focused on providing education and training in semi-skilled or technical occupations. Regular schools, moreover, often provide programs such as those offered at these different types of institutions in addition to their standard course load.

BACKGROUND AND DEVELOPMENT

Education involves the process of transferring information from one generation to the next. Its origins are inseparable from the origins of civilization. Throughout history humankind has been concerned with the process of maintaining culture, preserving mores, and stimulating minds. The ancients passed on religious information; early science instruction took the form of indoctrination in the magical arts; and oral literary traditions developed before words were ever written down.

The roots of Western education can be traced to the ancient Greeks. Historians credited the Greeks with developing the study of science, art, literature, philosophy, ethics, and politics. Greek schools were designed to prepare the sons of Greek citizens for citizenship. This purpose represented a departure from older forms of education that focused on specialized instruction, such as the training of skilled craftsmen, priests, or government officials.

The expansion of the ensuing Roman Empire paved the way for the development of education throughout Europe. Roman schools consisted of three levels: elementary, secondary, and higher. Elementary schools taught reading, writing, morality, conduct, counting, and calculating. Secondary schools taught literature, language, astronomy, geometry, and ethics. Students in higher education learned rhetoric, mathematics, music, history, and law. The study of these subjects enabled students to lead effective public lives.

Christian schools, dating back to the second century, were developed to teach new believers about the doctrines, discipline, and morals of the church. Other religious schools were developed to teach theology, philosophy, and science. As early as the fourth century, controversy arose concerning the conflict between the pagan influence in Roman schools and the teachings of the Christian church. Gradually, the pagan schools closed and the center of learning shifted to monasteries. Monastic schools were devoted to preparing students for careers with the church. Pupils were taught discipline, and they received instruction in subjects such as Latin, music, grammar, composition, record keeping, law, logic, arithmetic, geometry, and astronomy. Advanced students also studied higher mathematics and science. The emperor Charlemagne (742-814) was credited with revitalizing education. He opened schools for common children and ordered priests to offer free instruction to anyone who came to learn letters.

Following the Middle Ages, Europe saw a rise in universities where students could receive instruction in the arts, law, medicine, and theology. The Renaissance brought a revival of classical studies combined with Christian ideals. Formal education focused on cultivating the mind and the body. In the New World, colonists copied the European model but lacked established institutions and had to build a structure for education. Early opportunities were limited to apprenticeships, schools for practical instruction in mathematics and surveying, and instruction in reading and religion. College bound students could arrange for training in Latin grammar.

Private schools in America developed during the eighteenth century and, following the Revolutionary War, the nation turned its attention to the idea of public education. Legislation in 1785 required new townships to set aside land for public education. Massachusetts was the first state to pass a compulsory education statute. Enacted in 1852, the law required that children between the ages of 8 and 14 attend school 12 weeks per year and that 6 of the 12 weeks had to be consecutive. As the complexity of public education grew, states created positions for superintendents. By 1861, 30 of the existing states and organized territories had state-level school officials. During the Reconstruction era following the Civil War, education reform spread from the North into the South. During the 1869-70 school year, 6.9 million students were enrolled in the nation's public elementary and secondary schools. The average school year was 132.2 days long, and the average number of days attended per pupil was 78.4 days. The system employed 201,000 people as supervisors, principals, teachers, and other nonsupervisory instructional staff. The average annual salary was $189.

At the end of the nineteenth century, primary education focused on the fundamentals of reading and mathematics and on the development of specific character qualities such as honesty and patriotism. Industrial expansion and growing middle-class ambition brought with them increased interest in expanding participation in the educational process.

Fundamental changes in educational philosophy occurred with the dawning of the twentieth century. W. F. Connell, author of *A History of Education in the Twentieth Century,* described the new attitude as one that ''sought more actively to question and to break with established traditions.'' The early years of the 1900s saw educational expansion in the sciences, modern languages, and history. The process of scientific inquiry ushered in an era of questioning that included the close examination of ideas and customs. John Dewey made a significant impact on the development of educational philosophy in the United States. Dewey's many written works included *The School and Society* and *Democracy & Education.* Dewey espoused the notion that the purpose of education was not to prepare students for future life but that it was part of an ongoing experience leading to social progress and reform. A Deweyan teacher was not one who merely educated a child, but one who changed society. Dewey's principles were promoted by the Progressive Education Association (PEA), which was founded in 1919. The PEA dissolved in the mid-1950s because its aims had largely been adopted by mainstream educators.

During the time between World War I and World War II, American educational establishments focused on expanding and providing universal secondary education. As a result, high school attendance increased from 915,000 during the 1909-10 school year to more than 4.4 million in 1929-30, and to 6.6 million by 1939-40. The increasing numbers of students involved in secondary education during the 1930s led to an expansion in course offerings. High schools, which had traditionally offered classes intended to prepare students for higher education, added courses in general education, commercial and industrial arts, and home economics.

Following World War II and through the 1950s, the American educational system was characterized by many changes. Rapid increases in enrollment occurred as children born in the post World War II era began entering elementary schools. In 1954 the Supreme Court's *Brown v. Board of Education* decision opened the way for racial integration. Curriculum changes reflected the intensified competition between Communist and Western nations, placing a heavy emphasis on scientific investigation and innovation. As a result, in 1958 Congress passed the National Defense Education Act to encourage the study of science, mathematics, foreign languages, and technology.

During the 1960s, school enrollment continued to climb. As mainstream education centered on programmed instruction, alternate programs based on the Montessori method experienced a revival. This educational philosophy was based on the work of Maria Montessori (1870-1952), an Italian educator. Montessori believed that education should encourage spontaneity and activity and that children needed freedom to develop. Legislative initiatives also impacted education during the decade. In 1964 the National Defense Education Act was expanded to include English, social sciences, and reading. Congress also passed the Economic Opportunity Act in 1964, intended to expand the availability of educational opportunities in disadvantaged areas. In 1965, the Elementary and Secondary Education Act (ESEA) was enacted as part of President Lyndon Johnson's War on Poverty. The purpose of ESEA was to give federal support to schools located in low-income communities. ESEA made provisions for the funding of counseling, remedial education, and experimental classes. In subsequent years, ESEA was expanded to include help for migrant, neglected, delinquent, non-English speaking, and other children with special needs. The education establishment also saw a shift back to classes focused on preparing students for life experiences during the 1960s. Courses were provided in areas such as community involvement, job performance, citizenship, and family life.

Educators of the 1970s were challenged by rapid changes in society and technology. The prevailing educational philosophy was characterized by a ''back to basics'' attitude. Critics charged that such an emphasis forced educators to focus on low-level skills and test children in accordance with minimum standards rather than striving to achieve excellence. Another challenge of the decade was the expansion of special services for handicapped children. In 1975 Congress passed the Education for All Handicapped Children Act. The act required school districts to identify students with special needs and provide educational opportunities for them. The four most commonly identified dysfunctions were learning disabilities, speech and language impairments, mental handicaps, and emotional disturbances. In the 1976-77 school year, 8.3 percent of the nation's children were served by special programs. By 1993-94, the most recent tabulation, the number had increased to 12 percent. The most significant increases were among children identified as learning disabled.

Although the Education for All Handicapped Children Act was intended to help foster educational opportunities for all students, it drew criticism during the late 1980s and early 1990s as courts interpreted its provisions to mean that school districts were required to pay for educational and support services irrespective of a child's ability to benefit from any education provided. Critics of the courts' actions claimed, without success, that the decisions placed an undue burden on school districts and that the cost of providing services for the severely disabled should be transferred to health care agencies.

During the early 1980s, a federal report titled *A Nation at Risk* analyzed the education system and concluded that schools were not doing an adequate job. The report led to the development of school reform efforts that continued into the 1990s. As a result, between 1982 and the early 1990s, 47 states instituted more stringent student testing practices, 42 implemented higher graduation requirements, and 39 established programs to test teachers. Changes were also made in vocational education philosophy. The Carl D. Perkins Vocational and Applied Technology Education Act of 1990 (Perkins Act) was aimed at restructuring vocational education through the integration of broad-based academic requirements. Because only 27 percent of secondary students completing high school with a major in a technical area ever worked in a related field, and because American workers generally changed occupations four to six times during a lifetime, the narrow training given to students in vocational programs was judged inadequate. Critics claimed it provided only obsolete skills that were not transferable. Under the provisions of the Perkins Act, vocational programs were required to help students experience and understand all aspects of an industry with the aim that graduating students be prepared to take an active role in community development.

Problems with vocational education were also raised by critics who claimed that a shortage of skilled workers would render the United States unable to remain competitive in the global economy. Some educators advocated the development of a high-tech preparatory program that would include provisions for transition into the work world through apprenticeships or would prepare students for further study at two-year community or technical colleges.

In addition to the problems associated with low academic achievement, schools continued to face challenges related to drug abuse and violence. According to the U.S. Department of Health and Human Services, the proportion of public and private high school seniors who reported ever using an illicit drug rose from 55 percent in 1975 to 66 percent in 1981. After 1981, that proportion fell to 41 percent in 1992 but rose again to 48 percent in 1995. The proportion of high school seniors who had ever used cocaine fell from 17 percent in 1985 to 6 percent in 1995. Alcohol remained the most often used drug with the proportion of seniors who had used alcohol within the past 30 days declining from 72 percent in 1980 to 51 percent in 1995. Cigarette and smokeless tobacco use increased from ninth to twelfth grades for all categories. However, alcohol, marijuana, and illegal drug use on school property increased for males while it declined for females.

CURRENT CONDITIONS

As the education establishment entered the 1990s, efforts aimed at improving learning opportunities for all of America's children intensified. The number of high school graduates in 1997-98 totaled about 2.7 million. Americans 25 years old and older holding high school diplomas or GED credentials increased from 69 percent to 82 percent between 1990 and 1977. The drop-out rate at U.S. high schools fell from 14 percent in 1977 to 11 percent 20 years later.

The 1990s were plagued by negative public perceptions about schools and inconsistent measurements of student achievement. For example, school records indicated that an increasing number of students were taking college preparatory classes in math, English, science, and social studies—up from 37.9 percent in 1982 to almost 50 percent in 1996. Moreover, state governments placed a great deal of emphasis on increasing standards, indica-

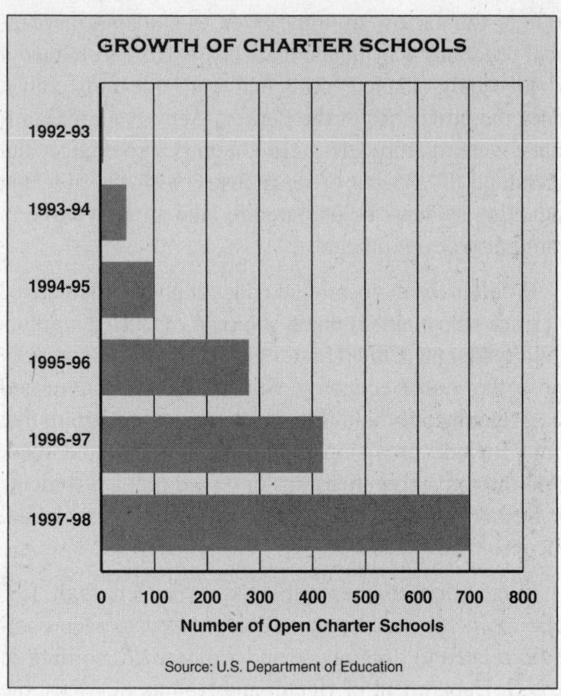

tive of the heightened primacy of scholastic assessment tests, both in evaluating school performance and for students entering colleges and advanced learning programs. But educators argued about the effect of these measures. SAT scores remained flat through the 1990s, still far below their mid-1960s peak, despite the fact that students taking advanced-placement courses in high school grew from 5 percent of seniors in 1984 to 13.1 percent in 1997. Geography and history performance among students at all levels remain dismal by international standards. In mathematics, 9- and 13-year-olds demonstrated improved skills in numeric operations between 1977 and 1997, while performance remained flat for the remainder of the 1990s. Meanwhile, more complex mathematical skills among 17-year-olds continued their 20-year disappointment though 1997, by which time complex procedures and reasoning were only proficiently tackled by 59 percent of high-school 17-year-olds, while adequacy in multi-step algebra was beyond the grasp of 93 percent of that age group.

Attempts aimed at increasing the quality of science education focused on curriculum changes. One program, sponsored by the National Science Foundation, provided obligatory units of science in each grade progressing from basic measurements in ninth grade to abstract and theoretical studies in the higher grades. This proposal was intended to replace traditional science studies in which students, on an elective basis, enrolled in biology in tenth grade, chemistry in eleventh grade, and physics in twelfth grade. Under traditional science programs, statistics for 1994 graduates revealed that although 94 percent had taken biology, only 56 percent had taken chemistry and only 24 percent had taken physics, though the average number of science courses completed in high school rose from 2.2 in 1980 to 3.0 in 1994.

Reading proficiency was another area of concern. The reading level among 9- and 13-year-olds improved markedly between 1970 and 1995, but little of the change occurred after 1980. By 1996, the reading level of high-school 17-year-olds was unchanged since 1971, while writing levels have declined gradually over that period. A Department of Education Study in the late 1990s reported that only 1 in 4 students sampled across fourth, eighth, and twelfth grades met the Department's standards of writing proficiency for those levels.

Despite improvements made by African-Americans and other minorities over the last 30 years, minority students continued to score below white students in many standardized tests and educational assessments. The most recent (1996) National Assessment of Educational Progress (NAEP) results in reading suggest that minority groups may be beginning to lose some of the earlier gains they had made relative to whites. The problem was heightened by the fact that minority students were statistically in the majority at 22 of the nation's largest 25 school districts. In such schools, classroom sizes tend to be larger and the level of economic prosperity markedly lower. Moreover, studies have revealed a positive correlation between students' levels of educational performance and the level of parents' educational attainment. According to statements made by the U.S. Department of Education, school reforms made under the Elementary and Secondary Education Act ''seldom triggered the kinds of transforming that our schools need—particularly in economically disadvantaged communities.''

Many school problems were associated with economically disadvantaged students. According to statistics, tenth grade students from districts with high rates of poverty were found to have drop out rates twice as high as those from schools in districts with little poverty. The U.S. Department of Education estimates that more than 50 percent of the students in schools containing the nation's highest concentrations of poverty were judged to be low achievers. In schools with the least poverty, only about 10 percent of the students were judged to be low achievers. Because of the ramifications of poverty on education, 30 states were involved in lawsuits over disparities in education spending created by differences in local property taxes during the mid-1990s. In two states, Alabama and Massachusetts, the courts ruled that disparities in school funding violated the states' constitutions.

In an effort to increase the quality of education for the economically disadvantaged, the Clinton Administration in 1994 reauthorized the Elementary and Secondary Education Act (ESEA) of 1965 and passed the Goals 2000: Educate America Act, aimed at setting exacting standards for poorer students that matched those for their more advantaged counterparts. Federal resources were thus directed toward helping states implement these performance standards. Texas, for instance, achieved among the highest gains in National Assessment of Educational Progress performance and further closed achievement levels between minority and white students.

Such measures were not without detractors, however. Critics of such educational spending proposals argued that states with the highest per-pupil spending had the lowest test scores. Instead of increasing financial assistance to schools, these analysts recommended core changes in school structure and curricula. Social scientists attribute much of the white-minority differences in achievement not only to poverty but to the lower average educational levels of their parents. While it is difficult for schools to compensate for such disadvantages, there is evidence that extraordinary schools and teachers make a difference in how all students perform. Research on early intervention and one-to-one tutoring suggests that at-risk students can achieve far higher levels and that taking more challenging courses is related to higher performance and achievement.

Other tools influencing student achievement are electronic computers and Internet access. By 1998, 89 percent of public schools were plugged into the Internet, an increase of 11 percent from a year earlier; only 35 percent of public schools were connected in 1994. Thus the elementary and secondary school systems were closing in on the Clinton Administration's goal of connecting all schools to the Internet by 2000. Nonetheless, schools in impoverished areas remained the least likely to maintain Internet access. In other technological developments, more than 90 percent of all elementary and secondary schools utilized computers in classrooms (as opposed to only in a separate computer room), while the number of students per computer dropped from 45.3 in the 1985-86 school year to 7.4 in 1996-97. A growing number of schools also maintained local area networks (LANs), CD-ROMs, and even satellite dishes. The Department of Education further maintains the Star Schools Program, which provides education-at-a-distance by utilizing telecommunications to transmit video and interactive instructionals, reaching about 1.6 million students.

School districts entered into periods of restructuring through the 1990s. Some individual schools were stepping up efforts to make the educational process more efficient and more profitable to students. For example, some schools experimented with having teachers move up with students so that students did not have to lose instruction time during the beginning of the school year as they adjusted to new teachers.

In addition to efforts to make the educational system more profitable to students, a growing movement was geared toward generating profits for the schools themselves. More than 200 for-profit schools were in operation in 1999, enrolling about 100,000 students. Edison Schools, based in New York, generated $217 million in revenues. Edison is also an expansion franchise; growing from four schools in 1995 to 79 schools across 16 states in 2000. By 2006 the company expected to operate 423 schools and enroll 260,000 students, for revenues of $1.8 billion in sales. Overall, a Merrill Lynch and Company analyst predicted that U.S. for-profit schools could maintain 10 percent of the elementary-school market by 2009.

Unsurprisingly, the trend toward profitability in the school system met with ethical concerns. While proponents of the trend argued that financial competitiveness would force schools to increase their efficiency and standards, essentially to offer a more superior product than their competitors, critics feared that the profit motive inherent in such moves would drastically alter the type of education students received, inviting companies to gear learning toward their economic interests and advertising.

The influence of commercialism in U.S. elementary and secondary schools is hardly limited to for-profit institutions, however. In order to garner increased funding to compensate for tight budgets and to gain a competitive edge, schools have sought investment from companies looking to peddle their products inside the schools. Zapme! Corp., for instance, donates computer equipment and software to schools in exchange for information about students that the company can use in marketing campaigns; meanwhile, the computers themselves display advertisements in the corner of the screen for companies such as PCGames.com, Amazon.com, and Lego. Channel One, the commercial-supported education channel introduced in 1991 and received in 12,000 U.S. schools, includes advertisements for acne medicine, breakfast cereals, candy, and other youth-oriented products in addition to shoe and apparel brands such as Nike and Gap.

The Cola wars, meanwhile, have shifted their battle ground to U.S. schools. Coca-Cola and Pepsi increasingly enjoy "official drink" status at schools, in which the companies install soda-dispenser machines in exchange for investing funds. This trend achieved a degree of notoriety in 1998 when an Atlanta high school student was suspended from school for wearing a Pepsi t-shirt on "Coca-Cola Day." Such reports raised the eyebrows of many educators, claiming that the influence of commercial enterprises had extended too far. The city of San Francisco prohibited its schools from contracting with beverage and snack companies.

Public schools also investigated the concept of charter schools. Charter schools are public schools set up to function independently of state regulation (except in regard to civil rights, health and safety, and financial accountability). Proponents of charter schools claim that the concept provides administrators with the freedom to offer the types of programs best suited to their students. The nation's first state-sanctioned charter school, City Academy, opened in St. Paul, Minnesota, in September 1992. Cleveland joined Milwaukee's six-year-old program of 1700 students. In this program, the private schools are not allowed to choose their students, however. By 1999 more than 30 states had passed charter-school legislation, and 160,000 students were educated in about 720 such schools. Nearly 35 percent of all charter-school students lived in California, followed by Arizona, with 15 percent, although Arizona had the highest proportion of its population enrolled in charter schools. According to studies, about 70 percent of charter schools were created to realize a vision of education that was alternative to that provided by the public-school system.

Home schooling, likewise, became increasingly attractive during the 1990s. The growth of home schooling follows years of negative perception of the public-school system. While home schooling traditionally was relegated to fringe religious groups, the practice has become increasingly common and mainstream. Strong performance results as measured by SAT scores and other standardized test have gained wide recognition. A precise figure is difficult to come by, but most observers agree that the total number of home-schooled students in 1999 lay somewhere between the Department of Education's estimate of 750,000 and home-schooling advocates' figure of 1.5 million.

School safety achieved a high priority in the late 1990s after a string of high-profile school shootings involving juvenile assailants. Public schools reported 6,093 expulsions for possession of firearms during 1996-97, while 57 percent of public elementary schools reported at least once incident of crime or violence that required reporting to officials (including police officers) outside the school. Moreover, 10 percent of public schools reported at least one serious crime, a classification that includes murder, rape, sexual battery, suicide, physical attack, fighting with a weapon, and robbery. Urban schools were twice as likely to experience incidences of violent crime. Particularly following the large-scale shooting at a high school in Littleton, Colorado, legislators debated fiercely over a range of issues relating to juvenile violence and schooling, ranging from gun control, enhanced punishment of juvenile offenders, and heightened disciplinary measures. Most broadly, the issue has triggered a wave of zero-tolerance rules, including sharp disciplinary action by school administrators for incidences, both inside and outside of the school, of dress and speech deemed inappropriate.

Educators came under criticism by some who claimed that by focusing on the needs of disadvantaged students they were failing to provide for the nation's brightest students. Proponents of special programming for gifted and talented students offered statistical evidence that the top performing students in the United States were behind their peers in other countries, particularly in mathematics and science. In response, legislatures in 45 states passed laws either mandating gifted and talented programs or making provisions for state support of programs serving gifted and talented students. Not all people, however, accepted the premise that special programs should be provided for bright children. Critics claimed the programs were elitist. As a result, although only two percent of the funds spent on K-12 education were spent on gifted and talented programs, funding in many states was in danger of being cut.

Debate over the implementation of school-choice programs has grown increasingly heated since the late 1980s. Many parents and politicians demanded public subsidies, such as school vouchers, to provide financial assistance to parents choosing private education. Proponents argued that such programs would afford parents greater freedom to provide their children with the highest-caliber education. Opponents, however, countered that vouchers and similar programs would not be able to cover the total costs of private education, and thus would afford greater leverage to the more economically advantaged while simultaneously gutting the public school system that the disadvantaged would have to rely on. There were three types of school-choice programs in the late 1990s: intradistrict, interdistrict, and magnet. Magnet schools, sometimes in conjunction with one of the other types, offer specialized programs aimed at drawing students with particular interests, abilities, or characteristics.

WORKFORCE

By 1998 a total of 3.1 million teachers worked at U.S. elementary and secondary schools, an increase of 17 percent from 1988, though flat from 1996 figures. The distribution, amounting to 1.9 million elementary school teachers and 1.2 million secondary school teachers, likewise held steady. The growth in public school teachers through the 1990s mirrored the escalating enrollment figures, maintaining a ratio of about 17 students per every teacher. At private schools, the ratio declined somewhat throughout the decade, from 15.2 students per teacher in 1990 to 14.9 in 1998.

Almost all teachers held at least a bachelor's degree by 1998, while 45 percent held a master's degree. Salaries escalated about 25 percent between 1990 and 1996, though overall teachers' salaries carried about the same purchasing power as they did in 1972. By 1998 inflation-adjusted salaries had declined slightly since 1990. The average salary for a public-school teacher in 1998 was

$39,385; private-school teachers, meanwhile, commanded an average of $26,000.

Most teachers work a 10-month schedule, with two months off during the summer. However, in addition to classroom duties, teachers' responsibilities include devising lesson plans, grading assignments and tests, and meeting with faculty, administrators, parents, and students. The combination of these tasks generally translates into significantly more than 40 hours of work per week.

Examples of nonteaching staff included principals and assistant principals, guidance counselors, librarians, teacher aides, and noninstructional staff. In private schools, the pupil/teacher ratio is 15:1.

AMERICA AND THE WORLD

The U.S. elementary and secondary school system has long met with sharp criticism from those who feel its success in transmitting basic knowledge to its students was falling behind other nations. Scholastic tests repeatedly reveal that U.S. students tend toward the bottom of the list of industrialized countries in mathematics and science, while history and geography scores remain, for many educators, embarrassingly low. While an ever-increasing number percentage of Americans are completing high school, literacy levels remain below many developed nations, including Sweden, Germany, and Japan.

According to the Third International Mathematics and Science Study conducted in 1997, U.S. students ranked twenty-first and sixteenth in these categories, respectively. The test is structured to accurately reflect the different educational emphases in various countries, and thus is widely accepted as an accurate comparative indicator of U.S. performance.

Only France and Germany spend a higher percentage of annual gross domestic product on education, while Sweden, Switzerland, and the United States spend the most per pupil. Schools in the United States, however, are structured differently from many schools overseas and offer wider educational opportunities to a more diverse student population. In the United States, elementary schools are structured to prepare students for secondary school, and secondary schools are structured to prepare students for higher education. In many other places, the progression of educational opportunity was less unified. Primary schools provide a basic education for the masses, and separate preparatory schools train children of the higher social classes for a secondary or higher education. Once committed to either a primary school or a preparatory school, very few students can move to the other system.

Despite these differences, critics of the American system claimed that even European and Japanese students in non-college bound courses of study receive better academic training and higher skills via apprenticeships and school-to-work transition programs than do their American counterparts. In Germany, beginning with the fifth grade, children are enrolled in vocational, technical, or college-prep schools. In the tenth grade, students in vocational and technical schools begin paid apprenticeship programs in which they work for approximately three years while completing their academic and skill-building schooling. Students in college-prep schools, called Gymnasien, prepare for stringent university entrance exams.

FURTHER READING

Cohen, Warren. "Zero-Tolerance Brawl." *U.S. News & World Report,* 22 November 1999.

"For-Profit Schools." *Business Week,* 7 February 2000.

Good, H. G. *A History of Western Education.* 2nd ed. New York: Macmillan, 1960.

Kaminer, Wendy. "The War on High Schools." *The American Prospect,* 20 December 1999.

"'Media Literacy' Sparks a New Debate Over Commercialism in Schools." *Wall Street Journal,* 17 December 1999.

The National Center for Education Statistics. *Digest of Education Statistics, 1998.* Available from http://nces.ed.gov/pubs99/digest98/.

Sale, Richard. "Lions Among Lambs? Schools Open Their Doors to Brand Promotion, But Also to a Controversy Over." *Promo,* February 1999.

"San Jose, Calif., School District Approves Deal with Pepsi." *San Jose Mercury News,* 22 October 1999.

"School Enrollment to Hit a Record of 53.2 Million." *Wall Street Journal,* 20 August 1999.

"Schools Taking Tougher Stance With Standards." *New York Times,* 6 September 1999.

Tice, Terrence N. "Research Report." *Education Digest,* November 1999.

SIC 8221

COLLEGES, UNIVERSITIES, AND PROFESSIONAL SCHOOLS

This classification covers colleges, universities, seminaries, and professional schools offering academic courses and granting academic degrees. The minimum requirement for admission is a high school diploma or equivalent general academic training.

NAICS CODE(S)

611310 (Colleges, Universities, and Professional Schools)

INDUSTRY SNAPSHOT

The U.S. higher educational system has long been the envy of the developed world. It plays a critical role in U.S. social and economic life and is a cornerstone of the nation's competitiveness on the world stage. By the end of the twentieth century, U.S. colleges and universities were increasingly coming to resemble traditional business entities by streamlining operations and aggressively competing for students and finances as a way of maintaining their vitality.

Colleges and universities are institutions of higher learning that admit post-secondary students for education and training in a vast number of disciplines. No central governing body oversees the administration of these institutions, although governments do contribute financial aid in the form of loans and grants to both students and schools. Private corporations donate substantial sums of money to colleges, universities, seminaries, and professional schools in the United States, supplementing public subsidies as a way of investing in research and development, and traditionally recruit employees from these institutions. Although primarily mandated to impart skills and knowledge to students, many colleges and universities are also major research institutions and have made significant contributions to medicine, technology, engineering, and a number of other fields.

About 11.9 million students were enrolled in public colleges and universities during the 1998-99 school year. An additional 3.4 million attended private schools. There were a total of about 3,500 post-secondary schools in the United States, of which community, junior, and technical colleges accounted for 1,600 and enrolled more than 5.4 million, or 34 percent of the entire postsecondary student population. About 1.64 million students were enrolled in graduate programs, a figure that escalated rapidly in the early and mid-1990s after holding steady around 1.3 million for over a decade. Students tended to gravitate toward very large or very small schools. Institutions with a student body of less than 1,000 enrolled about 41 percent of all postsecondary students; conversely, colleges and universities with more than 10,000 students enrolled about half the nation's total student population. The student-teacher ratio increased somewhat in the late 1990s to 15 students for every faculty member. Of the more than 500 universities in the United States, 488 offer doctoral degrees in at least one field.

U.S. colleges and universities enjoyed a combined endowment of $128.8 billion in 1996. The greatest beneficiaries included prestigious research universities such as Harvard University, with $9.06 billion; Yale University, with $4.86 billion; the University of Texas at Austin, with $4.34 billion; Stanford University, with $3.69 billion, and Princeton University, with $2.87 billion.

Federal studies show that U.S. colleges and universities recorded more than $221 billion in expenditures in 1997, up from $171 billion in 1992, including $138 billion by public schools and $83 billion by private schools. Average per-student expenditures rose 8 percent during the 1990s, reaching about $19,000 in 1997. This increase was especially pronounced for scholarships and fellowships, which increased 84 percent between 1986 and 1996. Less than one percent of all postsecondary institutions are under federal control, while state governments were responsible for about 28 percent, independent religious institutions for 25 percent and independent nonprofit organizations for 20 percent. The majority of college campuses are located in small towns, closely followed by urban settings and suburban areas, with the fewest located in rural areas.

Tuition rose steadily throughout the 1990s. Private four-year colleges and universities demand the highest annual tuition, followed by independent two-year institutes; public four-year institutions come next, and two-year public schools charge the lowest tuition. Average tuition ranged from $1,501 at public community colleges to $13,664 at private four-year universities. Moreover, private universities have experienced the fastest rise in tuition expenses, growing 28 percent between 1988 and 1998. Tuition at public universities increased 20 percent over the same period.

In 1996 about 26 percent of all college and university students were minorities, a substantial increase over the 16 percent in 1976. This trend is most notable among Hispanic and Asian students; Asian and Pacific students tripled their presence over this period, accounting for 6 percent of the student body in 1996, while Hispanic students doubled their proportion to 8 percent. African-American students accounted for about 11 percent of all students. Native Americans were the least represented minority group with enrollments averaging 1 percent on all campuses. Meanwhile, the number of women enrolled in higher education rose 20 percent between 1980 and 1996, while male enrollment increased 8 percent over that period. By 1998, female enrollment totaled 8 million while male enrollment reached 7.3 million. Students with either physical or mental disabilities totaled 428,300 in 1998. A final trend in higher education was the escalating numbers of adults entering or returning to colleges. Persons over 25 years of age accounted for 6 percent of the nation's college and university students in 1998.

ORGANIZATION AND STRUCTURE

Colleges and universities are either public or private. Public institutions are able to secure funding from government sources, while private institutions rely on tuition and private donations to operate. Universities are different from colleges in that they provide a greater number of areas of study, are larger in size, and are more involved in research activities. Universities also grant graduate, doctoral, and professional degrees in addition to undergraduate degrees, which colleges may or may not bestow.

The way a college or university is structured is in large part determined by the needs of the population it serves. Underscoring the objectives and operating strategies of every U.S. institution of higher learning is the fundamental belief that every interested and capable high school graduate should have the opportunity to attend post-secondary school. This philosophy has distinguished higher education in the United States and serves as a central tenet of its structure and organization.

Population growth, particularly the significant growth of the college-age population in the 1960s and 1970s, put increased pressure on institutions of higher learning. Private and public donations also increased the number and diversity of programs offered, as did the quality of teachers and technology available. In all, the landscape of the industry is remarkable for its sheer diversity and its ability to meet the needs of students, whether they seek a well-rounded liberal arts education or hands-on training in the most advanced computer sciences.

In terms of broad structure, coordinating boards are the primary feature in most colleges and universities. These boards, some elected, others appointed, may govern only senior institutions; others may govern all of the institutions in a state; still others are charged with compiling and analyzing data that is related to enrollment, curricula, staff appointments, institution investments and disbursements, and other issues related to the administration and management of the schools. Some states employ statewide governing boards charged with overseeing specific or all institutions of higher learning. An additional administrative arm of colleges and universities are voluntary consortia, both public and private. These advisory and governing bodies address such areas as faculty composition, teaching facilities, and library materials.

BACKGROUND AND DEVELOPMENT

The development of higher education in America had its genesis as far back as 1636, when the first colleges in the colonies began to take shape. These institutions were equipped with close ties to religious organizations, a condition that remained prevalent until early in the twentieth century when a number of these universities were secularized in administration and curriculum. (Many American colleges and universities, however, continue to cultivate a relationship with religious bodies.) During the latter stages of the eighteenth century, professional studies were first incorporated into these schools.

Harvard, the first institution of higher learning in America, was founded in 1636. The first colonial colleges attempted to foster the advancement of learning and the training of clergymen. These colleges offered curricula that featured classical studies such as rhetoric, mathematics, and logic. It was not until the emergence of the university that emphasis was placed on the total education of the individual, and the liberal arts education, with its emphasis on diversity of subject matter, took a prominent role in higher learning.

Professional schools, often referred to as technical or polytechnical schools, emerged alongside the growing popularity of liberal arts colleges. Professional schools were intended to provide students with "practical skills" that would prepare them for employment in a specialized field when they graduated. Prototypes of these applied science institutions include the Polytechnic Institute of Brooklyn and Cooper Union, and agricultural schools in Maryland, Pennsylvania, and Michigan. So successful were the experimental professional schools that traditional institutions that had ignored practical skills training began incorporating them into their programs. The federal government also recognized the utility of such training and indicated its approval by requiring institutions participating in the Morrill Land-Grant College Act of 1862 to include agriculture and the mechanic arts in their curricula.

A key piece of legislation in the history of American higher education was the passage of the Morrill Act in 1862, which permitted public lands to be appropriated by individual states in order to establish state agricultural and mechanical schools, forerunners of the modern state university.

The Land-Grant College Act of 1862 granted to each state 30,000 acres of land (or its equivalent) for each senator and representative in Congress. This allowed colleges and universities, particularly those that specialized in training students in agriculture and mechanical arts, enormous growth potential. The land-grant colleges and universities benefited the curriculum and overall structure of higher education in America in general; most notably, states realized the practical and long-term benefit of continued underwriting of institutions of higher learning. Equally as important, the breadth of subject matter available at these schools became increasingly diverse and wide-ranging as the institutions improved and expanded their faculties.

Normal schools, which traditionally trained teachers, also came into existence around 1840. As the training of elementary and secondary instructors became more specialized, teachers' colleges emerged and eventually became a vibrant part of the industry.

It was during the mid-1800s that the states began to exert more influence on colleges and universities and promote them as private, non-sectarian institutions of learning. State funding and development of colleges and universities heralded the end of the era of the public college and ushered in the industry of colleges and universities in its present form. The Universities of Georgia (1785), North Carolina (1789), and Vermont (1791) were the first state-chartered schools. This trend escalated dramatically around the time of the Civil War, until state colleges and universities became the standard route to higher education across the nation. It was not until late in the nineteenth century, however, that states began to assume financial responsibility on an ongoing basis for colleges and universities. It was also at this time that the municipal college or university came into being. These institutions were managed by city governments and partially funded by municipal taxes.

So specialized had the industry become that special colleges for women and for black Americans began operating in the nineteenth century. The overall trend in higher education, however, has been toward coeducation. Today, of course, admittance discrimination based on gender, race, or religion is outlawed. Still, there are about 130 single-sex colleges (men- or women-only) in the United States, and there are more than 100 historically black colleges.

Universities, as institutions of higher learning and scholarship, became fully entrenched after the founding of Johns Hopkins in 1876. Truly the renaissance in higher education in America, it was during this period as well that Yale, Columbia, Harvard, and the Universities of Michigan, Wisconsin, Minnesota, and California opened their doors. Endowments and grants from major corporations also established these institutions as the focus of corporate investment. With such fiscal leverage at their disposal, these universities quickly became forces to be reckoned with, both in the academic arena as well as in the overall economy. Research and the training of highly specialized professionals positioned the nation's universities as one of the primary resources big business and government relied on for a constant supply of technology and skilled labor. In addition, communities where colleges and universities were located became increasingly dependent on those institutions for the community's economic health and well-being.

Higher education became an even more dominant part of the American experience after World War II. Virtually anyone who qualified for the G.I. Bill of Rights and was armed with the necessary academic requirements could gain entrance to a college or university. Financial subsidies from the government increased attendance enormously and post-secondary institutions realized substantial growth in revenues. The surge in the popularity and fiscal growth of these institutions can be appreciated by comparing enrollment statistics of the past 40 years. The enrollment in the fall semester of 1950 for all students in institutions of higher education was 2.6 million; in 1990 that number had increased to 13.8 million. Industry analysts predict this trend will continue, and that the number of students enrolled in American colleges and universities at the turn of the century will far exceed previous levels of enrollment.

The exponential growth of two-year trade schools, or junior or community colleges, is indicative of the diversity that characterizes higher education in the twentieth century. Staggeringly popular since the middle of this century, these two-year programs, according to *American Universities and Colleges,* enrolled 217,572 students in 527 institutions in 1950-51; by the 1998-99 academic year, enrollment totaled approximately 5.4 million in more than 1,600 institutions.

As the twenty-first century approached, colleges and universities emphasized imparting practical skills and knowledge to as wide and diverse a population as possible. The technological and computer revolution has supplanted the traditional liberal arts education, stressing the importance of skills and knowledge that make students marketable in a computerized age. There has also been a strong emphasis placed on removing financial and racial barriers to a higher education. Government loan programs and equal opportunity initiatives have been very successful in these areas.

Current Conditions

The higher educational system faced the twenty-first century with a wide range of challenges and some significant transformations in the works. Many colleges and universities were financially troubled. Operating costs continue to soar in all areas—scholarships, administration, student services, faculty, research, and maintenance. As a result, tuition and room and board costs have grown, typically higher than the rate of overall inflation. Throughout the 1970s and 1980s, most universities attempted to mitigate these pressures by cutting expenses at the margins, such as maintenance and staff cuts, while raising tuition prices and boosting fund-raising efforts. An increasingly competitive industry, colleges and universities found that in order to maintain a competitive edge in this crowded field, they would need to begin thinking strategically in the manner of a typical corporation.

Appropriately, then, the presence of corporate America has grown highly visible on United States campuses. Marketing contracts, research funding, and other such deals between schools and powerful business skyrocketed in the mid- and late 1990s. Pennsylvania State University, for example, entered into a contract with Pepsi-Cola Co. whereby Pepsi agreed to donate $14 million to the university over a 10-year period in exchange for granting the soft drink company exclusive rights to market and sell its products on the school's campuses. Coca-Cola, Nike Inc., Rite Aid Corp., and a host of other firms have made similar deals with colleges and universities across the country. Other corporations have donated money to build academic facilities on campuses in exchange for the right to occupy parts of the buildings for their own operations.

Moreover, as businesses invest more heavily in colleges and universities, curricula have been increasingly tailored to gear students toward careers with the firms donating the money. The National Science Foundation in 1998 facilitated more than 20 partnerships between businesses and community colleges designed to ready students for jobs in the high-technology sector. As schools compete to retain top-notch programs in order to draw the highest caliber of students, they are expected to rely more on corporate investment to propel their research programs.

As postsecondary education comes to adopt the traditional business model, institutions have met with inflated pressures to streamline their operations and eliminate bureaucracies. By the end of the 1990s, one of the most notable examples of cost cutting was in the realm of faculty. Whereas traditionally colleges and universities prized the tenure status of professors, which guarantees permanent employment thereby allowing professor to concentrate on research, by the late 1990s tenure itself was under attack. Critics complained that tenure encouraged professors to diminish productivity and lose sight of their teaching responsibilities. However, cost pressures were the most widely recognized explanation for the decreased emphasis on tenured faculty. The temptation to register savings by filling vacancies with part-time faculty proved very powerful through the mid- and late 1990s.

The proliferation of qualified teachers has made the transition toward part-time, or adjunct, faculty especially attractive. The large potential employment pool from which departments and administrators can draw has resulted in a tremendous market for low-cost part-time teachers. The tendency toward fiscal austerity is most marked in the humanities and other liberal arts programs. These conditions do not bode well for the current record numbers of students enrolled in graduate programs in these areas. The number of adjunct faculty members leaped 30 percent between 1991 and 1995; over the longer term, the use of part-time teachers escalated 266 percent between 1970 and 1995, during which time the number of full-time faculty members declined 49 percent. A total of 10,732 new full-time faculty appointments were made in 1996, down 25 percent from 1989. By 1998 45 percent of all faculty at U.S. postsecondary schools were part-time; among community colleges, that figure jumps to 63 percent.

By the late 1990s, efforts to organize adjunct faculty members were intensifying in an effort to gain some leverage throughout the higher education system, including demand for health benefits. Adjuncts are typically

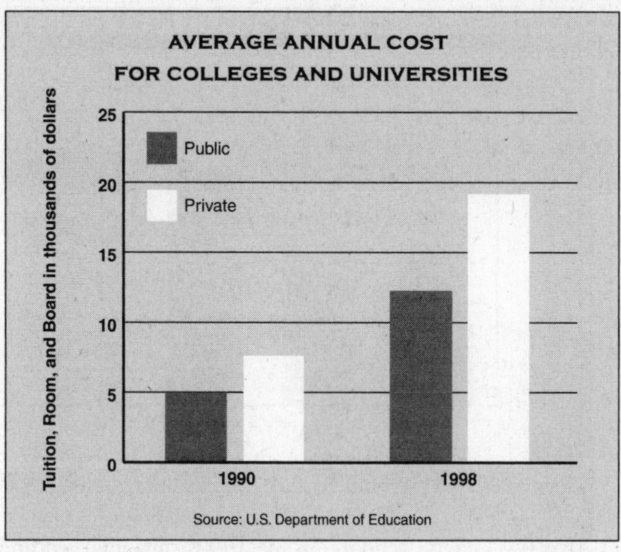

remunerated according to the number of credit hours they teach each semester, usually amounting to between $1,200 and $2,000 for a regular three-credit course. This usually translates into annual earnings of less than $12,000 per year. About 70 percent of part-time teachers, therefore, supplement their income with other employment, which must be balanced with recurrent job-application filings for their next teaching position. It was not uncommon for adjunct faculty to commute between positions at two or even three schools in a localized region.

Tuition. As a whole, tuition has risen twice the rate of inflation in the past two decades. In the late 1990s, tuition costs were rising about 4 percent annually. This trend has held true for all types of postsecondary institutions. For instance, the average annual at a four-year private institution was $13,664 during the 1997-98 academic year, compared to $10,994 in 1993-94 and $8,120 during 1984-85. Likewise, four-year public institutions cost $3,111 in 1997-98, up from $2,543 in 1993-94 and $1,748 in 1984-85. When combined with room and board prices, the total basic expenses at private schools reached $18,745 in 1997-98, compared with $6,788 at public institutions. These costs do not include books and supplies, health insurance, and personal expenses, which includes traveling between school and home. At public community colleges, tuition averaged $1,501 in 1997-98, up from $1,114 in 1993-94.

According to a March 1997 *Time* magazine special investigation by Erik Larson, tuition hikes can be attributed to high growth and expansion in the 1950s and 1960s, the slowing of federal funding in the mid-1970s, the rising energy costs of the late 1970s, high inflation in the 1970s and 1980s, and a phenomenon called the ''Chivas Regal effect'' in the 1980s, in which universities and parents began to equate higher tuition with higher educational quality, especially among the very competi-

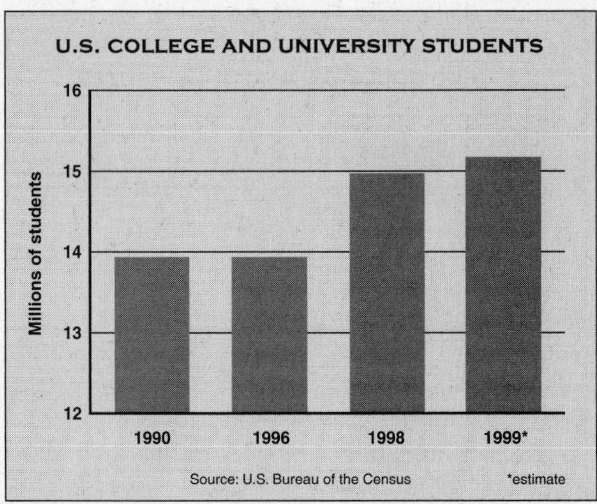

tive Ivy League schools. In the 1990s, financial aid and the expense of keeping up with technological advances were among the reasons for rising costs.

Pressure is causing tuition hikes to slow down. Indeed, some Ivy League schools may be losing many top-notch students who are unable to afford or unwilling to pay exorbitant tuition costs. In addition, the financial-aid process has grown increasingly convoluted. Still, since the 1980s a college education has been perceived to be a necessity, due to the significantly increased value an employee commands on the job market if in possession of a college degree. By the late 1990s, a college diploma translated into an average of 52 percent in additional wages when compared with an applicant with only a high school diploma. Moreover, real wages in some sectors, such as certain manufacturing fields, were actually lower than their 1960 level for those with only a high school education. Those with professional degrees, such as legal, medical, or business certificates, tend to garner the highest salaries, followed by doctoral and master degrees. As job security diminishes throughout the economy, moreover, a degree from a prestigious university is increasingly valued as an insurance policy against downsizing layoffs.

The federal government underwrites about 72 percent of the approximately $60 billion in financial aid benefits offered annually by federal, state, institutional, and private bodies. Lower-income students and families can receive assistance in paying for higher education through Pell Grants and Hope Scholarship tax credits. For adult students, moreover, the Lifelong Learning tax credit can supplement employment income while they retrain to upgrade their skills.

The Student Body. The composition of the student body has changed dramatically over the course of the last 30 years. In 1970 women made up 41 percent of the college and university student body. By 1998 this figure had increased to more than 53 percent. Minority enrollment has escalated as well. Moreover, an increasing number of minority high school students were pursuing college degrees by enrolling in college preparatory classes in secondary schools. Observers note that individuals with parents who attended colleges were far more likely to attend college themselves.

Racial and ethnic demographics underwent some interesting shifts in the 1990s. While African-Americans have come to enjoy nearly proportional enrollment in postsecondary education, the National Association for Equal Opportunity in Higher Education reported that enrollment at historically black colleges and universities (HBCUs) rose 11 percent between 1990 and 1998; notably, however, white enrollment at these institutions increased 16 percent during this period, while African American enrollment rose 6 percent. Most of this growth, analysts surmised, was due to the schools' lower average tuition cost ($6,600) when compared to other private schools, as well as the expanding number of degree offerings at HBCUs. Those schools, meanwhile, have greatly intensified their recruitment efforts in an effort to more readily meet their financial needs and, of course, to attract the best students.

Curriculum. Diversity is becoming key to the college curriculum. With the rising presence of minority students on college campuses has come the demand for more ethnic-studies and foreign-language courses, as well as minority instructors. According to the National Center for Education Statistics and the Asian-American Studies Program at Cornell University, in 1996 about 90 of 2,200 four-year colleges in the United States offered majors in African-American studies, 20 in Latino studies, 17 in Asian-American studies, and 12 in Native-American studies. Some conservatives challenge the academic legitimacy of these courses, fearing they will de-emphasize the core curriculum, while supporters question the assumptions that kept such studies out of the traditional curriculum and note that students can only benefit by diversifying their range of knowledge. At any rate, students of all races find ethnic studies popular and often these classes have long waiting lists. Moreover, many businesses emphasize the growing need for greater cultural awareness as the business community grows more international in character.

Most institutions of higher learning are attempting to tailor their programs according to the needs of students who will be job hunting into the twenty-first century. Land grant universities in particular are being urged to combine vocational training with general education. Throughout the country, in fact, institutions are finding that applications for admission increase proportionate to their ability to offer instruction in areas such as advanced business training, computer sciences, health sciences, engineering, and other professions that will be looking for qualified graduates in the near future.

Indicative of the situation facing college students, who will be seeking employment in an environment where many blue collar and white collar skills are becoming obsolete, vocational colleges and two-year trade schools have enjoyed increasing enrollments for a number of years. Since the 1960s and 1970s, these institutions have become a staple in most communities and show every indication of thriving well into the next century.

An important and increasingly popular component of the training these schools offer is upgrading and remedial education, which appeals to an American population that is discovering the value of re-education. Remedial skills training, taught in a wide variety of evening, weekend, summer and other adult education programs, are appealing to students who might have enrolled in a liberal arts college 15 or 20 years ago.

Government Financial Assistance. Retraining and educational upgrading have become priorities of both federal and local governments in the United States. Both the technical revolution, particularly related to the computer industry, and the obsolescence of many white collar, middle- and upper-management jobs have engendered a revolution in retraining in America. The public sector has been committing substantial amounts of money to the re-education of Americans who possess minimal training in the skills that are required in today's market. In 1998 federal funds for education and related activities amounted to contributions of more than $60 billion. Education analysts believe government will continue to support such efforts.

WORKFORCE

Approximately 2.7 million people are employed in U.S. colleges and universities. Faculty members, by far the largest and most visible component of the workforce, assume a number of diverse roles in higher education. Duties typically include teaching, appointment and promotion of colleagues, conferring tenure, curriculum planning, and student admission evaluations. Faculty usually operate within specific academic or administrative departments and are represented in faculties, senates, committees, and, in some cases, bargaining or arbitration units. Gender disparity continues to haunt the coveted tenure position; about 72 percent of male faculty had tenure in 1997, compared with 52 percent of women. Only 13 percent of faculty members belonged to an ethnic minority.

The average academic year salary for a full-ranking professor at a public university in 1998 was $65,400. An associate professor earned an average of $48,300; assistant professors brought in $40,100; and instructors earned

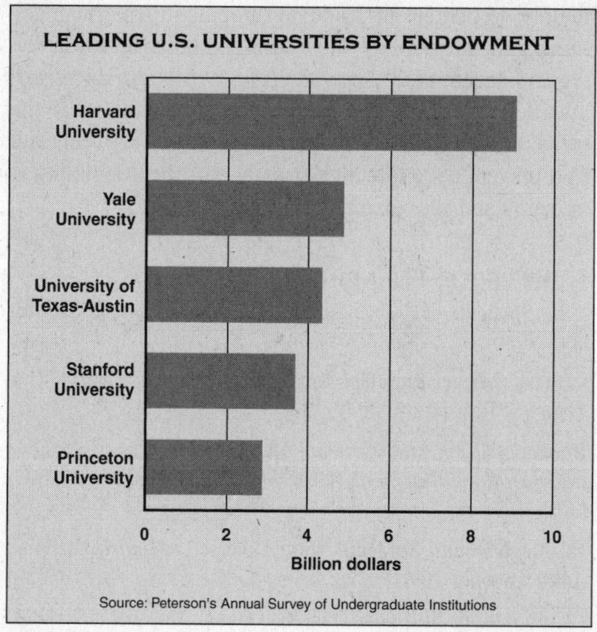

$30,800. These figures do not include fringe benefits, which can range between $10,000 and $12,000. Salaries are dependent upon expertise and standing. For all positions, faculty at private schools tend to earn higher salaries. The highest-paying fields include medicine, law, and engineering, while the lowest salaries are earned by those in the humanities and education.

AMERICA AND THE WORLD

Higher education in the United States continues to enjoy a great deal of prestige around the world. In 1995-96, the number of foreign students enrolled in U.S. colleges and universities reached an all-time high of 454,000, up from 407,530 in 1990-91.

Foreign students continue to value an American business education above all other forms of learning available in this country. Until recently, engineering was the most popular subject amongst foreigners. This discipline, though, has fallen behind programs such as the Masters of Business Administration. Twenty percent of foreign students were enrolled in business programs in 1997, while 15 percent studied engineering. Other popular areas of study for foreign students include mathematics, computer sciences, and physical life sciences.

The foreign student population in American universities and colleges is largely composed of students from China, Japan (the two leading senders of foreign students), Korea, and Taiwan. Overall, Asians constitute nearly two-thirds of all foreign students attending U.S. colleges and universities, while Europeans account for 15 percent. There has also been a relatively recent increase in the number of students coming from Latin America, Africa, and the Middle East. In the late 1990s, approximately 45 percent of graduate students in American colleges and universities were foreign students, while foreigners accounted for one-fourth of all doctorates awarded in the United States. Observers feel that this trend will continue and that foreign students will continue to represent a significant percentage of the population of colleges and universities.

Further Reading

''Big Spenders On US Campuses.'' *Business Week,* 27 December 1999.

''Black Colleges Enriched, Engulfed by White Students.'' *USA Today,* 3 February 2000.

Bureau of Labor Statistics. U.S. Department of Labor. *Occupational Outlook Handbook, 1998-99 Edition.* Washington, D.C.: GPO, 1998.

''College-Bound Students More Diverse.'' *Minority Markets Alert,* October 1998.

''Corporations Still Give, but Also Get.'' *New York Times,* 15 July 1998.

Feemster, Ron. ''Going the Distance.'' *American Demographics,* September 1998.

Garmon, John. ''The Full-Time Faculty Free Fall.'' *Community College Week,* 15 November 1999.

Heuberger, Barbara and Diane Gerber. ''Strength through Cultural Diversity.'' *College Teaching,* Summer 1999.

McKenna, Barbara. ''Vanishing professors.'' *Education Digest,* December 1999.

Rudolph, Frederick. *American College and University: A History.* Athens, GA: University of Georgia Press, 1991.

Stephens, Angela, and Scott W. Wright. ''The Part-time Faculty Paradox.'' *Community College Week,* 25 January 1999.

Thomas, Charlotte. *What's in the Future for Financial Aid?* Available from http://www.petersons.com/.

U.S. Department of Commerce. International Trade Administration. *U.S. Industry and Trade Outlook 1999.* New York: The McGraw Hill Companies, 1999.

''What the Numbers Say.'' *Curriculum Review,* January 2000.

SIC 8222

JUNIOR COLLEGES AND TECHNICAL INSTITUTES

This classification includes junior colleges and technical institutes offering academic or technical courses and granting Associate degrees, certificates, or diplomas. The minimum requirement for admission is a high school diploma or equivalent general academic training. Schools having junior college grades in conjunction with secondary grades are classified in **SIC 8211: Elementary and Secondary Schools.**

NAICS Code(s)

611210 (Junior Colleges)

Industry Snapshot

In 1998, more than 1,500 institutions in the United States offered courses at the junior, community, or technical college level to more than 6 million students. This type of institution is often referred to as a two-year college, though this designation only pertains to establishments that provide students with an Associate's degree. Students at these institutions pay relatively low tuition rates compared to amounts charged by colleges and universities. Federal, state, and local appropriations and grants support public community colleges, which account for the majority of these schools, while private community colleges receive funds from a variety of sources.

Community and technical colleges are considered more convenient for students because they offer options for full-time, part-time, day, evening, weekend, and co-op Associate degree programs, which are especially helpful to those with full-time employment and family obligations. In fact, the majority of students at these institutions are enrolled part-time. The open-door policy of these colleges (admission is open to individuals with a high school diploma or equivalent) provides higher education to people whose circumstances might otherwise prevent them from obtaining a degree. In addition to the comparably lower tuition fees, two-year college students' expenses are usually lower due to savings on room and board costs, since many students live at home rather than on campus.

Organization and Structure

Community colleges and technical institutes are either private or public. Among private schools, many are administered by religious groups. There are also independent nonprofit institutions and proprietary institutes that are owned by individuals or groups. Since the funding for these schools does not come from public funds, they are relatively free to set their own priorities and form their own curricula. If they wish to receive accreditation from the American Association of Community and Junior Colleges (AACJC), however, they must fulfill specific requirements.

Most community colleges are public. Federal funding for community colleges comes in the form of either appropriations or grants. The Vocational Education Act of 1963, Title III of the Higher Education Act of 1965, and the Comprehensive Employment and Training Act of 1973 established appropriations to be awarded to schools.

Federal grants are awarded to students for tuition and other needs. Forms and amounts of state and local funding vary widely. The amount of money the federal, state, or local community provides is a constant matter of controversy, along with the degree to which programming decisions are tied to funding. Members of a local school board may believe that they possess the greatest understanding of student needs and interests in their community, but when the state provides funding there is often a state board of education that exercises authority.

There are at least five functions performed by community colleges: academic transfer preparation, vocational education, continuing education, remedial education, and community service. Academic transfer preparation programs are designed for students whose academic performance in high school did not meet four-year college admission standards. These programs offer students an opportunity to prove their academic abilities and develop in a particular field of study, with the goal of gaining admission and transferring to a four-year college to earn a Baccalaureate degree. Some schools have established honors programs within academic transfer programs for those students who demonstrate high academic potential.

Vocational or technical education is designed for students who have a particular career goal in mind; subjects ranging from cosmetology to word processing are taught in these programs. Usually, the two-year degree offered by the community college will be the culmination of a vocational student's educational career.

Continuing education is designed for adults who are interested in taking courses for career or academic reasons. Continuing education students often maintain full-time jobs while attending community college. Remedial education is designed for students with developmental or learning disabilities, or students who received an inadequate secondary education. Community service programs consist of short courses, workshops, and non-credit courses.

BACKGROUND AND DEVELOPMENT

The community college is a strictly American phenomenon. It is the most substantial element of the nation's educational system that is not based on an European model. The first junior college was established in 1896 as a division of the University of Chicago by William Rainey Harper, the result of an idea that first emerged from the frustration of many university administrators who were concerned with devoting valuable class time to freshman and sophomores. Subsequent development of the junior college, however, occurred more at the grassroots level than within the university community. During the first decade of the twentieth century, some high schools began offering courses for graduates who remained in the area instead of attending college. As the idea spread from state to state, private junior colleges predominated over public ones and, depending on the region, certain colleges emphasized agricultural or industrial education. The two years after high school were regarded as the final stage in the transition into adulthood and, for that reason, many educators felt these years were best spent in the home and in the community.

The democratic ideal that education should be available to all who seek it fueled what became known as "The Junior College Movement." After World War II, many veterans took advantage of the GI Bill by pursuing a government-sponsored education without leaving their communities. As baby boomers reached the ages of 19 and 20 during the 1960s, they filled junior colleges beyond their capacity, which resulted in a simultaneous growth in the budgets and staffs at these institutions. With this growth, public junior colleges overtook private ones in number and size. California became the first state in the nation to establish a statewide junior college system. By the 1976-77 school year, there were 1,030 public junior colleges in the United States, compared to 203 private ones. By this time, the schools saturated almost every region of the country. Subsequent growth, however, became considerably slower. Many of the two-year colleges that opened were designated "community college" rather than "junior college," and administrators began to stress the change in focus that accompanied this change in name.

Two-year colleges tend to be much more diverse than their four-year counterparts because they comprise students of all ages, races, and economic backgrounds. Almost 50 percent of all undergraduates in the United States attend two-year institutions, and more than 50 percent of first-time freshman begin their higher education at a community college.

The issue of funding for community colleges was hotly debated during the economic recession of the early 1990s. Because this community concern has national ramifications, all three of the major presidential candidates visited community colleges during the campaign of 1992, pledging to uphold the institutions with tax dollars. Ross Perot, a former student in the community college system himself, was an especially vociferous supporter. Nevertheless, community colleges suffered along with all other recipients of federal dollars. In order to cope, many schools established fund-raising campaigns targeting former students, local businesses, and businesses with traditions of supporting educational growth.

Curriculum was another issue that divided community colleges, with student diversity presenting a key challenge. With such diversity came distinct and sometimes conflicting expectations of post-secondary education. Some students and faculty pushed for a new balance between vocational training and liberal education, which has always been an issue of debate for community college administrators.

As efforts to curtail government spending increased in the 1980s and early 1990s, funds for public community colleges began to fall short of their needs, and the schools began to turn to other sources for funding. Corporate donations became more common, especially at technical institutes. Some schools had success with fund-raising campaigns styled after those of colleges and universities. As financial woes continued, administrators began debating the possibility of increasing tuition or restricting admission. While both options would save money, they went against the principles of affordability and accessibility, upon which community colleges have rested since their creation early in the twentieth century. Other schools considered eliminating their special education divisions and facilities for students with learning disabilities, but again, it was feared that such decisions would undermine the intentions of the institutions.

With the proliferation of computer and video technology, some community colleges began experimenting with nontraditional teaching methods, including 24-hour learning laboratories; lectures delivered on closed-circuit, cable, or public television; and computer conferences. Such programs were aimed at meeting the needs of students whose work schedules conflicted with course schedules, as well as students who were unable to commute to school for a variety of other reasons. Such innovations were seen as a way of keeping pace with technological developments, especially in the field of computers.

Community colleges have reevaluated their curricula. In the early 1990s it was determined that fewer students were earning Associate degrees and less than a quarter were transferring to four-year colleges. The pattern that many students seemed to be following was horizontal rather than vertical. This behavior was attributed to student scheduling conflicts and career considerations, rather than a lack of ambition or inability to pursue a goal. Community colleges have tried to address these problems by providing alternative means of participating in class—often through the use of modern technology. For instance, community college libraries are being transformed into ''resource centers.''

While funding was readily available for computer and video equipment in the early 1980s, the recession of the late 1980s and early 1990s resulted in limited resources for community colleges. Consequently, community colleges have often been unable to maintain a constant investment in rapidly developing technology. Heavy investment in the area of computer software, for example, was seen as a risky endeavor since nobody could predict which systems would endure. In order to remain current, some colleges have initiated partnerships with local software companies or companies that target the offices and work places of their community. This allows community college students to develop computer literacy on the equipment of a particular company, often in a setting that resembles an office.

Mutual use of network communications technology, such as e-mail and the Internet, is another partnership with the corporate world that has been an effective way for community colleges to obtain expensive technology without relying on government funds.

Because community colleges have a large number of minority students, especially in urban areas, the question of changing curriculum—such as including an ethnic studies program—was raised starting in the late 1980s and early 1990s. The debate over curriculum was comparable to the question of revising the canon of literary classics at colleges and universities. Community colleges, however, did not prove to be a radical force for change in the academic curriculum. Students interested in vocational training were naturally not as insistent about bringing nontraditional works into the classroom, and students aiming at transferring to four-year institutions feared that the study of anything other than the established curriculum might jeopardize their chances. Students at many four-year universities, however, have demanded ethnic-studies programs and many institutions have implemented such programs.

In regard to growth in the community college industry, at least one expert, Arthur M. Cohen, long-time director of the Educational Resources Information Center (ERIC) Clearinghouse for Junior Colleges, believes that community colleges have reached a saturation point in the United States. Because these institutions are within easy access to virtually every community, no further dramatic growth is expected. According to Cohen, ''Few new institutions will open in the years ahead because a community college is now within commuting distance of most of the nation's population. There will be very little contraction in enrollment. . . . Funding for various programs will continue to be provided. . . . The colleges are here to stay in their current form.''

Current Conditions

Between 1971 and 1997, the percentage of high school graduates who had completed at least some college rose from 44 to 65 percent. The number of Associate degrees awarded during 1997-1998 was approximately 514,000. The 18- to 24-year-old population is expected to increase by 16 percent by the year 2007. However, the 25- to 29-year-old population is expected to decrease by 10 percent until 2002, when it will commensurately increase again. As junior college populations tend to carry large numbers of students in these age groups, total college enrollments are expected to increase at a more modest annual rate of between 1.1 and 1.3 percent. The number of associate degrees awarded annually is expected to increase to 587,000 by 2006-07. All in all, these statistical trends reflect America's growing emphasis on education as a means to better one's job opportunities, earnings, and community stature.

WORKFORCE

Community college faculty and administrators have long had to cope with the impression that their schools are somehow less legitimate or consequential than four-year institutions. According to Dale Parnell, a former chief executive officer of the AACJC, for too many educators, ''the highest calling in teaching is an Ivy League university. If you can't teach there, then in a state college or another four-year institution. If you can't do that, teach in a community college. If not there, then teach in high school.'' Frustration with this pecking order is often formidable. Along with being accorded less respect, teachers receive lower salaries than their counterparts at four-year colleges and universities. The level of aggravation, however, among two-year instructors is a great deal higher. The faculty at community colleges is often composed of younger teachers who, like their students, are looking to transfer to four-year institutions. Teachers complain that their students have not been adequately prepared during their secondary education to handle college material, that high student-to-teacher ratios make it extremely difficult to perform their classroom duties and still keep abreast of developments in their field, and that their reputation as second-rate professionals hampers their performance. To boost morale among teachers, some community colleges have established programs for recognizing and rewarding excellence.

FURTHER READING

Digest of Education Statistics, 1997. Available from http://nces.ed.gov/pubs/digest97t241.html.

''Earned Degrees Conferred.'' From *Projections of Education Statistics to 2007.* U.S. Department of Education, 1997. Available from http://nces.ed.gov/pubs/pj/p97c04.html.

El-Khawas, Elaine, Deborah J. Carter, and Cecilia A. Ottinger, eds. *Community College Fact Book.* New York: Macmillan Publishing Company, 1988.

Peterson's Guide to Two-Year Colleges, 1997. Princeton, NJ: Peterson's, 1996.

''Projections of Education Statistics to 2007,'' 1997. Available from http://nces.ed.gov/pubs/pj/p97c04.html.

SIC 8231

LIBRARIES

This category encompasses establishments primarily engaged in providing library services, including the circulation of books and other materials for reading, study, and reference. Establishments primarily engaged in operating motion picture film libraries are classified in **SIC 7829: Services Allied to Motion Picture Distribution.**

NAICS CODE(S)

514120 (Libraries and Archives)

INDUSTRY SNAPSHOT

More than 122,611 libraries provide services to the public and to specialized audiences. Libraries offer printed matter, electronic services, audio and video recordings, CD-ROM, lectures and similar adult programming, concerts, puppet shows as well as reading hours for children, bookmobiles and many other services. In 1998, total operating revenue for all American Library Association (ALA) members totaled $35.4 billion while total expenses were $34.1 billion. ALA membership reached 58,777.

In addition to public libraries (8,981), there are academic libraries at colleges and universities (3,303), school libraries (98,169), special libraries (9,898), armed forces libraries (363), government libraries (1,897), as well as corporate libraries, and collections tailored to specific needs like hospitals, religious organizations, and museums.

Probably the most visible libraries are the public facilities located in communities across the country. Americans borrow more than 1.6 billion items each year from such libraries, which total 15,994 including branch libraries. In addition to books, Americans borrow magazines, sound recordings (both tape and CD-ROM), videotapes, games, art work, computer software, and other materials.

The most recent figures available indicate that of all adults over the age of 17, 64 percent use public libraries. Similarly, almost 75 percent of children between the ages of three and nine visit a public library each year, and more than 40 million elementary and secondary school students use their school libraries—the fastest-growing segment of the industry—each week.

Public library circulation in 1996 reached 1.6 billion items, a per capita total of 6.5 per year. Total visits for 1996 numbered 1.0 billion. According to the most recent Gallup Poll, a majority of the population views the public library as a key educational institution and believes that it should be well-supported.

Respondents to the poll thought that public financing should more than double, and showed their support by approving 85 percent of referenda for public library capital campaigns in the 1990s. Public libraries are among the most efficient of tax-supported entities, serving more than half of the adult population while spending less than 1 percent of all tax dollars from the local, state, and federal levels,

Public, academic, and special libraries alike face great challenges. Libraries are usually the first to bear the brunt of budget cuts, whether in the public domain, at universities, or in corporations, despite their importance to users. Struggling to keep up with rapidly-evolving, costly, yet necessary technology, while striving to operate within budgets, libraries find themselves walking an increasingly fine line.

Although library budget cuts have received widespread press coverage, the institutions overall remain an attractive market to book publishers, according to *Publisher's Weekly.* Libraries continue to purchase more diversified materials in order to keep up with the demand for information. In an effort to economize and make the most of existing funds many institutions participate in cooperative arrangements known as interlibrary loan systems. Such programs enable school, public, and academic libraries to borrow materials from other libraries nationwide. As more libraries computerize their holdings, these arrangements will increase and sharing will become faster, economically workable and more practical, enhancing efforts to reduce costs and increase library offerings and services.

Organization and Structure

The American Library Association (ALA) divides the country's libraries into several main categories. These include government, public, academic, school, and special libraries.

The nation's largest library is the Library of Congress, which contains more than 83 million items, including approximately 22 million volumes, pamphlets, and other printed materials. Created in 1800, beginning with Thomas Jefferson's collection of some 6,000 volumes, the library's first priority is to serve the U.S. Congress; it also provides many services to the nation's other libraries as well as to the general public. The Library of Congress publishes the *National Union Catalog,* a guide to the location of books in more than 1,200 libraries across North America. In addition, the library compiles bibliographic data for published books that is made available to other libraries on magnetic tape or machine-readable cataloging (MARC) for use in their cataloging processes.

The National Archives houses documents and records of the nation's history to be used for research and study. In addition to textual documents, such items include photographs, audio and video recordings, and maps. Since about 1770, the archives has housed all aspects of the federal government, encompassing domestic and military activities as well as foreign relations. The National Archives is also responsible for organizing and preserving the items and making them available to the country's citizens.

The National Library of Medicine holds the distinction of being the world's largest research library devoted to a single scientific area, although material on such topics as physics, chemistry, botany, and zoology are also collected. The library developed an online network available to major libraries across the country that allows virtually instantaneous searches of more than five million bibliographic citations from current journals in the health sciences. The National Agricultural Library has been at the forefront of librarianship since it was founded in 1862 as part of the Department of Agriculture. The institution began printing a card catalog in 1899. A photocopier was developed in order to provide fast and inexpensive copies of materials, and it was the first library to test the feasibility of automated information storage and retrieval.

Establishing libraries in other countries is just one aspect of the United States Information Agency's objectives in promoting mutual understanding between Americans and citizens of foreign countries. The collections of such libraries introduce patrons to U.S. history, culture, and technology as well as American literary classics. Such libraries also serve as an example of the value of public libraries and free access to information.

School libraries represent perhaps the fastest-growing group of libraries. These libraries play an expanded role in education by offering enhanced methods of learning via audio and videotapes, printed materials, CD-ROM, the Internet, and reference volumes formerly unavailable in more remote areas. Automation of libraries continues to make these services more widely available.

Academic libraries provide more specialized information for the benefit of scholars. Typically, a group of libraries focusing on various disciplines is linked together within a college or university setting to provide materials to students seeking specific information. The Harvard University Library, the second largest library in the United States (founded in 1638), contains more than 11 million volumes. Harvard's library system includes branches specializing in topics ranging from music to divinity, as well as a renowned law library.

The United States began the practice of providing all of its citizens access to public libraries, and still strives to ensure that library services are made available to everyone. This goal was made more attainable by the Library Services and Construction Act, which made money available for the purpose of establishing libraries in smaller towns and rural areas. Similarly, branch libraries provide library service to neighborhoods in larger cities. Public libraries provide myriad services to their community of users. In addition to making books, periodicals, and audiovisual materials available, these libraries offer information and referral services. Voter registration, tax, employment, health and family services, and other assistance is also available, and librarians guide citizens to various agencies.

The New York Public Library was established in 1895 when the Astor and Lenox libraries and the Tilden Trust were consolidated, and is the largest public library in the United States. The library contains more than 30 million catalog items, including books, manuscripts, microfilm, CD-ROMs, video, audio recordings, and sheet music. The Library's 82 branches have more than 3.2 million circulating items classified as books, and 5 million nonbook items.

BACKGROUND AND DEVELOPMENT

Libraries have played an important role in preserving the history of civilization since the invention of writing. Alexandria, Egypt, was the site of the most comprehensive ancient library, where scholars could study manuscripts in Greek, Ethiopian, Persian, Hebrew, and Hindi. In Rome, educated citizens maintained personal libraries, and there were 28 public libraries in Rome by the beginning of the fourth century A.D..

During the Middle Ages, the libraries of monasteries preserved copies of Greek and Latin classics. During the Renaissance, collectors, kings, and noblemen preserved many works of literature and philosophy in their personal libraries. These collections became the foundations of some of Europe's great scholarly libraries.

Books received a larger circulation after Johannes Gutenberg invented the printing press in the mid-1440s. Prior to this invention, manuscripts were written by hand, an inefficient method. In addition, few members of the public were literate or had the leisure time to read books until the Industrial Revolution and other social changes in the eighteenth and nineteenth centuries. Because of these advances, libraries changed from institutions that preserved valuable works with a limited sphere of elite users to educational facilities for the common people.

In 1731, Benjamin Franklin and some of his friends organized the Library Company of Philadelphia, the earliest library of its kind in the American colonies. The first free public library supported by public funds opened in Peterborough, New Hampshire, in 1833. Additional libraries were soon opened in many other cities in the United States and Great Britain. By 1876, there were 342 public libraries in the United States, and by 1920, the number had grown to more than 6,500 institutions.

CURRENT CONDITIONS

The United States has the most extensive public library system in the world, with more than 15,994 outlets, including branches. Libraries were being used by record numbers of American citizens in the late-1990s, however, funding from government at the local, state, and federal levels was becoming increasingly difficult to secure, especially in certain geographic regions. In some places libraries have closed; in others, new libraries are being built, stocked with print materials and connected to the Internet.

Electronic information services play an increasing role in serving library users. Massive amounts of information are contained on these database systems, and people use the library as their primary source for health, employment, financial, educational, as well as entertainment needs.

In markets serving populations of 100,000 or more, the following computer-related services were available to the public in a majority of the centers: CD-ROM databases (71 percent); remote database searching (71 percent); microcomputers (62 percent), software (57 percent); and online public access catalogs (OPACs). Increasingly, libraries are offering access to the Internet, enabling libraries to serve those who do not otherwise have computer access—by providing information as well as instruction in the use of computers and other equipment.

The Internet. The biggest change in libraries during the 1990s was the rapidly increasing availability of access to computers generally, and to the Internet in particular. Nowhere has the change been more dramatic than in the nation's schools.

Through the efforts of local communities and upon the urging of the President, 'Net Days' have made possible wiring and connections to the Internet for many of the nation's schools and especially school libraries. In 1998, 89 percent of public schools were connected to the Internet.

As of 1997, the American Library Association reported that library staff have access to the Internet in virtually all academic libraries. Users have access to the Internet from terminals in the libraries of 93 percent of Doctorate granting institutions, 82 percent of Master's colleges, 76 percent of Baccalaureate colleges, and 61 percent of Associate of Arts colleges.

The World Wide Web is a significant vehicle for distributing information; web home pages have been developed by 87 percent Baccalaureate granting universities, 62 percent of Master's colleges, 51 percent Baccalaureate colleges, and 26 percent of Associate of Arts colleges.

According to the ALA, 74 percent of public libraries offer public access to the Internet. Of libraries serving populations greater than 100,000 people, 85 percent provide Internet access.

In 1998, the 461 public libraries that serve populations of 100,000 or more (the libraries that serve 57 percent of the U.S. population), 99.4 percent offer Internet access to library staff; 65 percent offer Internet access for their patrons with a staff member in attendance; 85.4 percent offer direct Internet access to their patrons; 31.1

percent offer modem access to the Internet from outside the library. As new technologies are integrated into the library system, public libraries will require additional financial support to make these options available to a wide range of users. *The New York Times* Internet edition, quotes Mary R. Somerville, President of the ALA saying, ''libraries may soon be the principal place where people . . . can gain access to the Internet.''

It is estimated that of the one-third of U.S. households that have computers, only half currently have access to the Internet. The issue is access to information; as more material is delivered online some information will no longer be available in print form. Those with no freely available Internet access will no longer be able to readily obtain public information.

In ''A Digital Metropolis,'' a *New York Times* Internet edition column by Jason Chervokas and Tom Watson, the NY Public Library is used as an example of the ''Quiet Revolution'' taking place in libraries. Eighty three branch libraries are equipped with 220 Internet equipped computers; the most (17) are located in the Mid-Manhattan branch. In the four research centers the library maintains there are 110 Internet equipped computers; the most (95) are in the Science, Industry, and Business library. The NY Public Library's extensive catalogue is available online through the Library Entrance Online (LEO) system. The system was made available in November of 1995, and by June of 1996, was recording nearly 30,000 visits a day.

Electronic media owners, seeking to protect their rights to the information in their databases, are trying to control access to data by selling the use of the material, unlike the one-time sale of a book or periodical. This has forced some libraries to charge users for access to this information—despite the basic tenets of the public library ensuring free and equal access to its patrons—based on relatively arbitrary fee structures. Karen Muller, spokesperson for the American Library Association, noted in *Technology Review,* ''proprietary information and copyright in the computer age run right up against American values of free access to information.'' Because libraries are protected by copyright law, works that have been purchased can be loaned and borrowed freely.

Public libraries' budgets rose by 4.4 percent in 1998, for the fifth straight year. Funding for these libraries was provided by local tax dollars (78 percent), state sources (12 percent), and donations (9 percent). Less than one percent of funding came from federal tax dollars.

WORKFORCE

There are approximately 125,522 librarians employed in the United States in 1998, the vast majority of whom are required to have a master's degree in library and/or information science. About 72,160 work in school libraries; 26,636, in public libraries; 26,726, in college and university libraries; and 18,600, in special libraries. More than 279,751 technical and clerical staff members support the librarians' labors. Librarians are overwhelmingly women. For academic libraries, 68 percent of librarians are women, 79 percent of public librarians are women, as well as 92 percent of school librarians.

The number of jobs is expected to increase more slowly through the first decade of the 2000s than the average of all occupations. The number of new positions decreased somewhat in the 1980s and are on the rise as information becomes a more valuable and vital commodity. Librarians who have special qualifications such as expertise in computerized systems, data searching, foreign languages, or children's services may expect an optimistic forecast for employment opportunities. Numerous career opportunities exist in libraries, including positions as library administrators; public service, reference, and acquisitions librarians; and catalogers, online data entry, information designers, and systems planners.

There are also many technical and clerical positions available that do not require library school training. For those who choose to pursue a career as a librarian, a background in liberal arts serves as a strong base for library science. So too, is an undergraduate degree in Computer Science as libraries become as aspect of the information available to users of the World Wide Web. After completing undergraduate studies, library science students study for at least a year in one of the approximately 56 schools in the United States that are accredited by the American Library Association.

RESEARCH AND TECHNOLOGY

Computers are increasingly important in the library as networks linking public, college and university, school, and special libraries are expanded. Librarians maintain records on computers, and card catalogs are now nearly all replaced by computer terminals that allow online access to the library's holdings, as well as data, abstracts, and texts contained in periodicals and journals. The electronic network enables libraries to economically facilitate interlibrary loans, thus expanding their collections, controlling cost, and improving service to users.

New software allows research to be completed and followed with a request for an interlibrary loan. David Churbuck predicted in *Forbes* that a system consisting of thousands of main libraries and branches will become obsolete with the advent of more sophisticated computer programs that allow users to obtain full-text versions of the volumes that they need. In addition, Churbuck believes that librarians will be replaced by programmers and database experts. The use of libraries as a prime source of access to the Internet for those who otherwise do not have access continues to grow.

University of Minnesota programmers have developed software called Gopher, which does not restrict its search to a specific server or component of the network. Gopher can conduct searches throughout a network and enables users to browse through myriad sources for specific information.

In order for such complex networks of the future to become reality, printed books must be digitized through the technique of scanning—an electronic procedure which translates material into a digitized format. Project Gutenberg, a program for digitizing books, is the creation of Michael Hart, professor of electronic text at Illinois Benedictine College in Lisle, Illinois.

The Library of Congress is also digitizing its collection and much is now currently available on the Internet. In addition, many periodicals have online editions.

Electronic resources will continue to enhance the information available to library users. On-line mediated searching, CD-ROM, and various databases provide references that were previously unavailable. Online searching is the most common electronic option and was the first electronic reference service to be offered by research librarians in the 1970s.

The use of online services continues to increase. CD-ROM is rapidly becoming more prevalent as an archival tool. Sometimes physical access to the discs is an issue; many libraries are making CD-ROMs available over a CD local area network.

FURTHER READING

America's Libraries: New Views in the '90s. Chicago: American Library Association, n.d.

American Library Association, 20 March 2000. Available from http://www.ala.org.

Churbuck, David C. "Good-bye, Dewey Decimals." *Forbes,* 15 February, 1993, 204-5.

Market Share Reporter. Detroit: Gale Research, 1997.

The New York Times, Online Edition, Cybertimes. Available from http://www.nytimes.com/library/.

U.S. Census Bureau. *1997 Economic Census—Information.* Washington, DC: GPO, 2000. Available from http://www.census.gov.

SIC 8243

DATA PROCESSING SCHOOLS

The data processing schools category encompasses establishments primarily engaged in offering data processing courses or training in computer programming and computer peripheral equipment operation, maintenance, and repair. Schools offering an academic degree in computer sciences are classified in **SIC 8221: Colleges, Universities, and Professional Schools.**

NAICS CODE(S)

611420 (Computer Training)

611519 (Other Technical and Trade Schools)

INDUSTRY SNAPSHOT

Data processing schools are profit-making institutions that teach specific skills required for computer-related jobs. The types of schools range from residential vocational training schools to correspondence school programs. The U.S. Census Bureau showed that there were 10 exclusive establishments in the data processing schools industry in 1992. By 1997, 2,785 establishments were listed as offering computer training, but not all were data processing schools exclusively. Most were headquartered in California, Connecticut, Illinois, New Jersey, New York, Pennsylvania, and Wisconsin. Several schools were subsidiaries of larger corporations.

Computer consulting and training is a multi-billion dollar industry. The growth of this industry, however, does not necessarily translate to the data processing schools industry, which is limited by competition from computer-related training in secondary and other post-secondary schools and the availability of self-tutorials. On the other hand, the market for data processing schools could increase as employers demand specialized skills from their workers and other post-secondary education becomes more expensive. Successful marketing of data processing schools as a less expensive and more job-specific alternative to college and university education is essential for growth.

INDUSTRY LEADERS

The National Education Training Group (NETG), a subsidiary of National Education Corporation, which was acquired by Sylvan Learning Systems in March 1997, is the global leader in information technology and interactive media-based learning. Its broad area of training ranges from programming to networking. NETG has been successful due to its diversified offerings, including multimedia products to train information technology professionals and end-user clients. NETG courses also include training to prepare professionals for vendor certification exams. NETG students may choose to combine media-based courses with classroom instruction. In February 1997, NETG was selected by Microsoft Corporation to provide computer-based training to its employees.

WORKFORCE

Most instructional staff members of data processing schools hold bachelor's degrees and have worked in the data processing field prior to becoming instructors. According to U.S. Census Bureau information released in 1999, employment in the industry in 1997 was listed as 28,848 people—from 8,200 in 1987. Industry payroll increased as well, from $165.3 million in 1987 to $970.2 million in 1997.

America and the World

The U.S. data processing network is among the world's largest, and much of the industry's growth potential exists in foreign markets. *U.S. Industrial Outlook* estimates that more than 28 percent of computer education and consulting revenues will come from foreign countries.

Data processing schools must continue to work closely with the computer industry to train workers adequately. Computer hardware and software change frequently, and the schools must strive to utilize state-of-the-art equipment to prepare students for employment in an increasingly computer-reliant business world.

Further Reading

Grubb, W. Norton. ''Local Systems of Vocational Education and Job Training: Diversity, Independence, and Effectiveness.'' Berkeley, CA: National Center for Research in Vocational Education Study, University of California, Berkeley, 1991.

National Education Training Group, 1999. Available from http://www.netg.com/.

U.S. Bureau of the Census. *Business and Industry Statistics,* 1999. Available from http://www.census.gov/ and http://www.factfinder.cen/.

SIC 8244

BUSINESS AND SECRETARIAL SCHOOLS

This category includes establishments offering courses in business machine operation, office procedures, and secretarial and stenographic skills. Schools offering academic degrees are classified in Industry Groups 821 and 822.

NAICS Code(s)

611410 (Business and Secretarial Schools)

Industry Snapshot

Independent business and secretarial schools, once widespread, have steadily decreased in number since the 1950s as business education has migrated to colleges and universities and secretarial training has undergone a transformation. Where secretaries were once responsible for typing, filing, and taking dictation, their tasks have grown to encompass computerized business systems. Secretarial training is typically part of vocational training offered at technical and community colleges, which have the financial resources to purchase business equipment for students. The term ''secretarial school'' itself has become antiquated in the United States; today most business and secretarial schools leave the word ''secretarial'' out of their name.

According to the latest data available from the U.S. Census Bureau, in 1997 there were 581 business and secretarial schools operating in the United States, employing 10,900 people and earning $554 million in revenues.

Background and Development

For centuries the profession of secretary was dominated by educated, economically lower-class males. Because there was no specialized equipment, a liberal arts education was considered adequate for a secretary's schooling. When the English gunsmith firm E. Remington and Sons began to produce typewriters in 1873, they employed young women to demonstrate the machines. As a result, the secretarial profession became associated with females. Remington and other companies established schools that offered typing instruction. These schools later evolved into secretarial schools. The Katharine Gibbs School—founded in 1911 in Providence, Rhode Island—became one of the most noteworthy names in the industry, branching into 11 separate locations by 1985. In the 1990s, Gibbs offered a one-year program, a two-year program, an Entre program for college graduates, and an Options program for those who were returning to work and wanted to improve particular skills.

Because some American executives believed that British secretaries were a status symbol, firms such as England's Brook Street Bureau of Mayfair, Ltd. trained secretaries and placed them in U.S. companies. Changes in immigration laws in the 1960s restricted such placement, and Brook Street established its own secretarial schools in the United States. The 1960s also saw the return of men into the American secretarial workforce. Men trained in secretarial schools were often hired by female executives who were eager to reverse conventional gender roles.

Secretarial training became a common facet of community college systems as these institutions grew in number and stature during the 1960s and 1970s. Government funding for community colleges provided all members of the community the opportunity to acquire valuable skills. As Charles Myers wrote in 1970 of a secretarial training program at the Southern Nevada Vocational Technical Center, ''The secretarial student who completes her course at the Las Vegas Vocational Center is entering the business world better equipped to handle today's modern business equipment than were any of her predecessors. . . . Thus, the community which has invested in her training gets its return at a higher interest rate than ever before.''

The 1980s brought sweeping changes to business and secretarial schools as new or refined technologies—photocopiers, fax machines, and personal computers—entered business offices. While technology eliminated or improved many secretarial tasks, they also required that secretaries receive new types of training. In 1981, Katharine Gibbs School Inc., then a subsidiary of Macmillan Inc., announced the formation of Gibbs Consulting Group, whose role included office-automation training. Recognizing that the role of secretaries had changed, Gibbs also focused on training managers to utilize their secretaries most effectively. In 1985, the publishing magnate Robert Maxwell acquired Macmillan and proceeded to rid the company of all non-publishing operations, including the Katharine Gibbs Schools.

CURRENT CONDITIONS

E-commerce was the buzz word at business schools during the latter 1990s, and those that offered courses in e-commerce and Internet business strategies had students lined up to register. Overall, technology courses such as MIS and computer science were most in demand, causing business schools to continue to move away from secretarial skills and move toward office automation and computer technology, accounting programs, court reporting programs, paralegal training, administrative training, legal (secretarial) programs, medical (secretarial) programs, and travel agent training in their curricula. Institutes offering these curricula include the Academy of Court Reporting, Michigan-based Dorsey Business Schools, and the renowned Wharton Business School.

According to a study completed by the Babson School of Executive Training in Massachusetts and the London School of Economics, in 1999, one in 12 persons in the United States was engaged in an entrepreneurial activity, compared to one in 30 in Britain. Consultants Ernst & Young believe that entrepreneurial activity in America will be the ''defining economic event'' of the millennium's first decade.

By catering to the needs of entrepreneurs in their curricular development, business schools may be able to create a niche for themselves in a market of educational services clamoring to gain the competitive edge over traditional institutions for the training of business and corporate skills.

INDUSTRY LEADERS

Dale Carnegie & Associates Inc., headquartered in Garden City, New York, is the provider of the well-known Dale Carnegie Courses. Founded in 1912 by Dale Carnegie, the company offers eight courses that have been translated in 20 different languages and made available in 70 countries. The firm has an annual average of more than 150,000 participants taught by approximately 2,700 instructors. Dale Carnegie Courses provide a unique type of business skills training that can be targeted to any employee at a business, management or non-management. Training is available at either a Dale Carnegie facility or on-site. The company offers courses that are designed to improve management and employee performance in areas such as sales presentation, public speaking, organizational planning, goal setting, working in teams, customer relations, and problem-solving.

DeVry Inc., headquartered in Oakbrook Terrace, Illinois, is another industry leader. It offers courses in electronics, data processing, accounting, telecommunications, and business. DeVry has 30 schools in seven states, an enrollment of 30,000 students, and 850 faculty members. It owns DeVry Institute, Keller Graduate School of Management, and Corporate Educational Services. In 1998, DeVry had sales of $308 million.

FURTHER READING

Brennan, Anne. ''Business Schools, Students Jump on the E-Commerce Bandwagon.'' *Chicago Tribune,* 9 November 1999.

Chambliss, Lauren. ''American Business Schools Supply Firms With Highly Skilled Workers.'' *Evening Standard, London.* 19 October 1999.

Dale Carnegie & Associates, Inc., 1999. Available from http://www.dale-carnegies.com.

Slater, Pamela. ''Business Schools Face Growing Demand for E-Commerce, Technology Courses.'' *The Sacramento Bee,* 13 November 1999.

SIC 8249

VOCATIONAL SCHOOLS, NOT ELSEWHERE CLASSIFIED

This classification covers establishments primarily engaged in offering specialized vocational courses, not elsewhere classified. Also included in this industry are establishments primarily engaged in offering educational courses by mail. Offices maintained by such schools for the sale of correspondence courses are included. Excluded from this classification are beauty schools, barber schools, schools offering flight instruction, and schools offering academic training.

NAICS CODE(S)

611513 (Apprenticeship Training)
611512 (Flight Training)

611519 (Other Technical and Trade Schools)

Industry Snapshot

Thousands of students have learned a new vocation, explored an avocation, or earned a certificate or degree from the establishments operating in this industry. Students can enroll in schools or correspondence courses that provide training in fields as varied as banking, commercial art, construction equipment operation, electronics, practical nursing, real estate, restaurant operation, and truck driving.

Vocational schools have existed for more than 200 years in the United States. Initially, a vocational education program was part of a high school education, but independent schools were established after the 1972 Education Amendments recognized technical education as part of post-secondary education.

Organization and Structure

Vocational schools train students in hundreds of occupations, ranging from automobile mechanic to practical nurse. Programs emphasize hands-on training and use modern equipment and professional teaching techniques. Some schools maintain a variety of industrial contacts in order to keep up with the latest technology and better match the curriculum to job demands. Programs usually take between six months to two years to complete, and students who successfully complete a program typically receive diplomas or certificates. Almost all privately owned post-secondary training schools are approved by an accreditation agency.

Post-secondary training schools usually qualify for federal and state financial aid programs, and a large percentage of the students who participate in specialized trade programs receive financial aid.

Many institutions offer home study or correspondence courses. Variously called ''distance learning,'' ''alternative,'' ''nontraditional,'' ''external,'' and ''off-campus'' education, the field began to grow rapidly beginning in the mid-1970s. Home study provides an alternative for people who want to pursue an educational goal but do not want to sit in a classroom. The programs are particularly popular with the disabled, parents of young children, and people living too far away from an educational institution's campus to attend regular classes.

Approximately 3 million students pursue their educational objectives each year through independent study. Students can usually enroll at any time of the year and sometimes have as long as a year to complete a course. While students may enroll simply to learn about a particular subject, most often they take courses in order to improve their employability or upgrade their skills. Courses vary greatly in subject matter, skill level, and duration. These courses offer students the advantages of studying at their own pace and with a reduction in expense—there are no room and board or transportation costs.

In the not-too-distant past, correspondence courses were solely delivered through postal mail. Technology has changed this practice. Improved and less expensive telecommunications technologies have contributed to increasing interest in distance learning education. Today, distance learning provides educational programs and course materials to off-site students via interactive telecommunications networks, such as a computer modem (Internet or Intranet) or computer and video conferencing. Some are provided by cable or satellite television, videotapes and audiotapes, fax machine, or other modes of electronic delivery. Courses are offered for credit, noncredit, or professional certification.

Privately owned and operated home study schools offer vocational correspondence programs, and U.S. colleges and universities offer numerous correspondence and distance learning classes. Private foundations, nonprofit organizations, and the U.S. military also operate correspondence schools. Students who complete correspondence or distance learning programs generally receive diplomas or certificates. Depending on the course, an institution may grant credits transferable to a formal degree program, an external degree, a certificate, or Continuing Education Units (CEUs). Continuing Education Units is a nationally recognized system that provides a standard measure for acknowledging, accumulating, and transferring credit in continuing education programs. One CEU is considered ten hours of participation in an organized continuing education course taught under qualified instruction.

The U.S. Department of Education recognizes several organizations that accredit institutions offering correspondence or distance learning programs. The National Home Study Council, six Regional Accrediting Commissions, and nationally recognized accrediting associations are among these organizations.

Current Conditions

One of the most interesting aspects of vocational education has been its ability to keep pace with demographic and socio-economic trends. As the booming economy in the latter 1990s gave Americans more leisure time and money to spend, vocational education in home improvement and culinary arts soared—so also did massage therapy, herbal medicine, landscaping, and gardening programs. One of the newest programs to enter the certification forum was in outdoor power equipment operation. As of late 1998, 18 schools were either certified or had certification pending by the Equipment & Engine Training Council (EETC) for the outdoor power equipment industry. ''Industry certification'' of programs have helped to bridge the gap between completing a vocational program and finding related employment.

The 1997 statistics released by the Bureau of the Census for business and industry indicate that there were 253 establishments in the United States that offered programs in apprenticeship training and more than 2,500 trade and technical schools. About as many establishments offered vocational rehabilitation services.

INDUSTRY LEADERS

The top vocational school company is National Education Corporation's subsidiary ICS Learning Systems, the world's largest provider of distance education in vocational, academic, and professional studies. In March 1997, National Education Corp. was acquired by educational services giant Sylvan Learning Systems, Inc. In the future, executives speculate that certain ICS courses could be migrated to technology platforms for learning center-based or Internet-based delivery.

Among technical institutes, DeVry Inc. headquartered in Oakbrook, Illinois, is an industry leader. In 1996 the institute earned $260 million in revenues. DeVry Inc. was founded in 1973 and owns and operates the DeVry Institutes of Technology, the Keller Graduate School of Management, Corporate Educational Services, and the Becker CPA Review. In 1996, 28,150 full- and part-time students were enrolled in the DeVry Institutes' Associate and Bachelor's degree day and evening programs in electronics, electronics engineering technology, computer information systems, technical management, telecommunications management, accounting, and business operations. DeVry's 1998 revenues were $308 million, with earnings of $24.2 million.

FURTHER READING

''Internet Connections.'' *Office Pro,* Aug/Sep 1998.

Kahmis, Jacob. ''Popularity of Vocational Schools Shifts According to Focus.'' *Pacific Business News,* 7 December 1998.

''Regional Education Training Group,'' 1999. Available from http://www.netg.com/.

''Schools Like Technician Certification Program.'' *Landscape Management,* 14 November 1998.

SIC 8299

SCHOOLS AND EDUCATIONAL SERVICES, NOT ELSEWHERE CLASSIFIED

This classification covers establishments primarily engaged in offering educational courses and services not elsewhere classified. Included in this industry are music schools, drama schools, language schools, short-term examination preparatory schools, student exchange programs, curriculum development, and vocational counseling, except rehabilitation counseling. Establishments primarily engaged in operating dance schools are classified in **SIC 7911: Dance Studios, Schools, and Halls;** and those providing rehabilitation counseling are classified in **SIC 8331: Job Training and Vocational Rehabilitation Services.**

NAICS CODE(S)

611512 (Flight Training)
611692 (Automobile Driving Schools)
611710 (Educational Support Services)
611691 (Exam Preparation and Tutoring)
611610 (Fine Arts Schools)
611630 (Language Schools)
611430 (Professional and Management Development Training Schools)
611699 (All other Miscellaneous Schools and Instruction)

INDUSTRY SNAPSHOT

Somewhere between traditional education at colleges or universities and adult enrichment classes at the local high school, there lies a vast array of schools, programs and educational services intended to educate students in areas where other schools may have left them out. Specialty schools and classes, often turning interests into careers, have enjoyed a steady following through the 1990s and into the millennium. In the periphery is a broad stratum of support services, all intended to assist the prospective student with informational, directional, or financial resources. This industry is segmented into three broad groupings: enrichment and avocational instruction, career development programs, and educational services.

ORGANIZATION AND STRUCTURE

The enrichment and avocational group is the largest in the industry. It encompasses art, ceramics, and cooking schools; baton, drama, and music schools; charm, diction, finishing, modeling, personal development, public speaking, and speed reading schools; as well as schools for those who want to learn to drive an automobile, fly an airplane, study the Bible, speak foreign languages, or survive in the wilderness. The depth of instruction varies and may range from appreciation of a subject all the way to mastery of that subject.

Career development programs include continuing education programs and civil service schools. Continuing education programs provide students with opportunities to learn or improve job and professional skills through participation in seminars and workshops. Civil service schools prepare students to successfully take the examinations required for employment in government positions. Other preparatory schools offer courses intended to enhance a prospective student's chances of being accepted into graduate or post-graduate schools.

Educational services organizations develop educational curricula, offer tutoring, or provide vocational counseling. Some also operate student exchange programs or provide other networking resources to facilitate a correct match between student and school.

Current Conditions

According to the most recent statistics available from the Business & Economics Department within the Bureau of the Census, there were 33,784 establishments listed in the educational services industry in 1997, employing more than 250,000 persons. The number of establishments did not include schools and educational institutions offering traditional diploma or degree programs, excepting those incidental to educational services.

Interest in private specialty schools has remained high. In 1997, *U.S. News & World Report* ranked leading music, drama, and fine arts (among other specialty) schools in the nation. Competing against their university counterparts, The Julliard School (New York), the Curtis Institute of Music (Pennsylvania), and the New England Conservatory of Music (Massachusetts) were three among the top six schools of music nationally. Independent drama schools also ranked successfully against competing universities offering comparable programs. In fact, during the spring of 1998, New York City drama schools had an unusually high number of applicants for the 1998-99 school year. The 1998 Tanglewood Festival in Lenox, Massachusetts, was also particularly crowded, and prospective students clamored to gain advice and lessons from celebrity performers and musicians.

Federal funds remained generally accessible for student loan financing through 1999. However, in 1998, a federal appeals court upheld the U.S. Department of Education's criteria for determining student loan default rates, which had been challenged by the American Association of Cosmetology Schools of Phoenix. The decision could adversely affect other small specialty schools because their smaller student bodies contribute to statistical anomalies when compared to larger student bodies from two- and four-year colleges. The challenged policy cuts federally guaranteed loans to any school which has a 25 percent default rate on loans for three straight years. In small specialty schools, a mere dozen students could represent a 25 percent default rate, for example, if that school has an enrollment of 50 per program.

Industry Leaders

Leading companies offering enrichment and avocational classes include the Braille Institute, Comair Aviation Academy, and Skip Barber Racing School. New York-based Barbizon International Inc., established in 1939, leads the modeling school industry. Barbizon schools serve more than 200 markets located around the world, and many of its graduates become professional models, actors, and actresses.

Of all the specialized instructional institutions, language schools are among the fastest growing. Berlitz International leads the field in teaching foreign languages to business executives and travelers around the world. The company's enrollment has increased significantly in the 1990s as corporations recognize the importance of foreign language skills when competing in global markets.

Some establishments in the industry offer job training. CareerTrack Inc. and Development Dimensions International are among the companies providing services in the area of career development programs.

Leading companies offering post-secondary educational services include Wilson Learning Corporation and Sylvan Learning Systems Inc., the world's leading educational services company. Sylvan, which acquired National Education Center in March 1997, holds chief market positions in supplemental education services for children, computer-based testing, adult professional education and training, and distance learning. In 1998, Sylvan bought out the stock of a German tutorial business and the Universidad Europea in Madrid, Spain. By the second quarter of 1999, Sylvan's earnings were up 49 percent, increasing it's quarterly earnings from $99 million to $148 million.

DeVry Inc., another fast-growing post-secondary education specialist, owns and operates Corporate Educational Services, a provider of on-site technical education and training services to businesses and government agencies, and Becker CPA Review prepares candidates to pass the Certified Public Accountant and Certified Management Accountant professional certification examinations. The company's revenues for fiscal year 1998 were $308 million, with earnings of $24.2 million. In 1999, DeVry planned to open three new DeVry Institutes—in San Francisco, New York, and Los Angeles. To mark its twenty-fifth anniversary, the successful company offered stock options to reward its employees.

Further Reading

Blumenthal, Ralph. ''You Want To Be a Star? Then Get In Line.'' *The New York Times,* 21 March 1998.

Holland, Bernard. ''As Teachers, The Modest Are Often The Best.'' *The New York Times,* 6 September 1998.

Hughlett, Roger. ''Sylvan Sets Record With 2Q Earnings.'' *Baltimore Business Journal,* 30 July 1999.

Koerner, Brendan. ''Top Graduate Art Schools in the U.S., 1997.'' *U.S. News & World Report,* 10 March 1997.

Mason, Edward. ''Beauty Schools Voice Concern Over Student Loan Cuts,'' 1998. Available from http://search.epnet.com.

Murphy, H. Lee. "Riding Learning Curve, DeVry Sets Up Growth." *Crain's Chicago Business,* 5 January 1998.

Wilson, Robin. "To Help Its Students Find Jobs, Eastman School Expands Its Musical Repertoire Beyond the Classical." *Chronicle of Higher Education,* 14 March 1997.

Wolff, Barry. "A Model Franchise." *Franchising World,* March/April 1998.

SIC 8322

INDIVIDUAL AND FAMILY SOCIAL SERVICES

This industry includes establishments primarily engaged in providing one or more of a wide variety of individual and family social, counseling, welfare, or referral services, including refugee, disaster, and temporary relief services. This industry includes offices of specialists providing counseling, referral, and other social services. Government offices directly concerned with the delivery of social services to individuals and families, such as issuing of welfare aid, rent supplements, food stamps, and eligibility casework, are included here, but central office administration of these programs is classified in **SIC 9441: Administration of Social, Human Resource and Income Maintenance Programs.**

NAICS CODE(S)

624110 (Child and Youth Services)
624210 (Community Food Services)
624229 (Other Community Housing Services)
624230 (Emergency and Other Relief Services)
624120 (Services for the Elderly and Persons with Disabilities)
624221 (Temporary Shelter)
922150 (Parole Offices and Probation Offices)
624190 (Other Individual and Family Services)

INDUSTRY SNAPSHOT

This industry covers the activities of both private and public nonprofit organizations and agencies, as well as federally funded welfare programs. These include individual and family service establishments that provide counseling and social services such as refugee, disaster, and temporary relief. It also includes state and local offices that distribute welfare benefits. Some private and public agencies offer adult day care, home-delivered meals, homemaking services, and in-home nursing. Other programs concentrate on children and youth, such as big brother/big sister organizations and protective and adoption services. The industry covers crisis centers, self-help organizations, parole offices, and probation services. In 1997, 45,970 establishments operated within this industry, employing 743,425 people and generating revenue of $32.5 billion.

The services within this industry can be classified as either public assistance programs or social service programs. In 1997, the largest public assistance program in the United States was Aid to Families with Dependent Children (AFDC), which, according to the Social Security Administration, provided federally funded cash aid to 10.9 million families ($27.7 billion). Interestingly, 1996 legislation was passed to transfer the public assistance offered by AFDC to the jurisdiction of state powers.

ORGANIZATION AND STRUCTURE

Public welfare programs fall under one of three general categories: social insurance, public assistance, or social services. Funded by mandatory contributions from employers and employees, social insurance programs are designed to protect people who experience a sudden loss of income due to the disability, temporary employment, retirement, or death of a wage-earner.

Public assistance programs are designed to help the financially needy with services commonly known as welfare, particularly through the Food Stamp program and the formerly federally-funded Aid to Families with Dependent Children (AFDC). Financed by federal, state, and local tax dollars, these programs provide benefits to people who show financial need and meet specific program qualifications.

Public social services were developed to meet needs through services such as counseling, day care, emergency youth shelters, alcohol and drug abuse services, and foster care. These programs are operated by state, county, and/or city governments, as well as public and private agencies.

The availability of these services, as well as the sources for their funding, vary greatly. Some programs are open to all people, while others are available for a fee. Some are accessible only to those already receiving assistance from other public assistance programs.

Federal Agencies. Until the passage of the Personal Responsibility and Work Opportunity Act of 1996, which transferred public assistance programs from federal agencies to state jurisdiction, many locally administered individual and family social services were under the jurisdiction of both state and federal agencies. Several public welfare programs were under the direction of the U.S. Department of Health and Human Services, including the largest social welfare program in the United States, Aid to Families with Dependent Children (AFDC). The AFDC has since been replaced by the Temporary Assistance for Needy Families (TANF) program.

TANF is a bipartisan creation that encourages welfare recipients to find jobs and become self-sufficient, while at the same time promoting strong family units. The program allocates a block grant of $16.8 billion to states and U.S. territories, which covers benefits, administrative expenses, and services. Individual states have a vast amount of power in determining their own programs, with the exception of a few federal mandates on eligibility. In general, recipients of aid must work after 2 years of assistance; families can only receive aid for 5 cumulative years; and food stamps can only be received for 3 consecutive months out of every 36.

Other Agencies. More than 100,000 social service organizations operate at the state, county, and local levels. For nearly 20 years, money from the private sector has made possible the activities and services of many of these groups. With the passage of the Personal Responsibility and Work Opportunity Act of 1996, most public assistance programs were operated at state, county, and local government levels.

Background and Development

Social welfare in the United States begins with the Social Security Act of 1935. The Great Depression, brought on by the 1929 stock market crash, led Americans to realize that unforeseen circumstances could lead anyone into poverty. The Social Security Act was established to circumvent this problem. The act provided protection against the loss of income due to old age, involuntary unemployment, and blindness; in 1956 it was amended to include disability. The act also established Aid to Dependent Children, a financial support program for children who had lost one or both parents.

The next major change in U.S. policy toward social welfare came during the 1960s and was known as the "War on Poverty." Precipitated by the civil rights movement that began in the 1950s, national social policy was changed during the 1960s to improve the standard of living for the poor. The federal government expanded existing programs such as AFDC and established new ones such as the Food Stamp Program.

During the 1970s, the federal government attempted to improve management and control over these public assistance programs. To eliminate variations of coverage among the states, uniform national standards were set for programs where the federal government and the states shared responsibility. Programs serving similar needs were consolidated into block grants to the states, where federal money was strictly limited in return for increased discretion in state spending.

Realizing that the current welfare system has been producing generations of recipients, both the state and federal governments began looking at welfare reform during the 1980s. President Reagan cut federally funded social spending by $20 billion in 1981. The Family Support Act of 1988 forced AFDC recipients into job training or education. But by the 1990s, state governments, whose federal funding was slashed during the 1980s, looked at more drastic measures, like cutting AFDC payments for mothers who have additional children while on welfare.

AFDC was a federally funded program that provided cash and noncash services to families with needy children. Available in all 50 states, the District of Columbia, the Virgin Islands, Guam, and Puerto Rico, AFDC aided children in families where need was brought by parental disability, death, continued absence, or unemployment. Financed by federal and state funds, payments usually were made directly to AFDC recipients. The federal government's share of AFDC payments was based on the need of each state. The government provided a higher percentage of federal matching funds to states with lower per capita incomes and a lower percentage to states with higher per capita incomes. The federal government also paid a certain percentage of costs related to program administration and training and the costs for acquiring and implementing management information systems. This public assistance program is now handled by individual state governments.

Current Conditions

In August 1996, President Clinton made good on his 1992 presidential campaign promise to "end welfare as we know it," by passing the Personal Responsibility and Work Opportunity Act of 1996. The legislation ended the 61-year federal guarantee of aid to the poor and children, giving states broad power to design their own welfare programs, imposing a five-year lifetime limit on receiving welfare, and requiring recipients to begin working within two years after receiving benefits. President Clinton stated that the reform "gives us a chance we haven't had before, to break the cycle of dependency" that affects millions of Americans.

TANF supplies an annual block grant to states to run their own programs. A five-year lifetime limit on receiving welfare requires recipients to work within two years, and half of all welfare recipients will eventually have to be working 30 hours a week. States that already have welfare programs in place under federal waivers will not have to comply with some federal work rules. The bill allows childless, able-bodied individuals ages 18 to 50 to receive Food Stamp benefits for only three months in any three-year period unless they are working part-time and undergoing job training. These people can receive food stamps for another three months in that time frame if they are laid off from a job.

Federal spending was expected to be reduced by about $60 billion into the beginning of the millenium, with the vast majority of savings coming from cutting

Food Stamp benefits. In January 1997, President Clinton asked business leaders to help move people from welfare to work, saying that a new welfare reform law ''cannot succeed by government action alone.'' Clinton also promised to submit incentives ''attractive to the private sector'' to encourage the hiring of welfare recipients. Referring to the provision of the new law that gives welfare recipients two years to find work or face a loss of benefits, Clinton stated, ''Unless we can create new jobs in the private sector within the two-year time frame, the welfare reform effort will not succeed.''

From 1993 to 1998, welfare recipients decreased by more than 41 percent—a total of 5.7 million people. The number of recipients is reduced by approximately 2 percent monthly. In fact, 1998 saw the lowest total number of welfare recipients (8.7 million) since 1970, the lowest number of families receiving aid (3.2 million) since 1972, and the lowest percentage of the population (3.2 percent) since 1968. In addition to the new legislation, these results were attributed to the nation's strong economy.

INDUSTRY LEADERS

Other than TANF, the largest programs in this industry are the Food Stamp program, disaster relief services, eldercare, adoption services, and self-help organizations.

Food Stamps. Established by the Food Stamp Act of 1964, the Food Stamp program is available in all 50 states, the District of Columbia, Guam, and the Virgin Islands. The Food Stamp Program assists more than 10 million households and 25 million individuals. Under this program, low-income individuals living in households meeting nationwide standards for income and assets may receive coupons redeemable at most grocery stores for food. As a result of the Personal Responsibility and Work Opportunity Act of 1996, the caseload for the food stamp program was reduced dramatically. From March 1994, a peak caseload year, the number of participants in the program fell to two-thirds by 1998. Moreover, the number of beneficiaries in the Food Stamp program dropped by 36 percent (5 million people). The U.S. Department of Agriculture administers the Food Stamp Program at the federal level through its Food and Consumer Service (FCS). State welfare agencies administer the program at the state and local levels.

Disaster Relief. Founded in 1881 by Clara Barton, The American Red Cross responds to thousands of tornadoes, hurricanes, floods, earthquakes, fires, hazardous materials spills, transportation accidents, and other calamities that occur in the United States each year by providing emergency and disaster assistance through their trained paid and volunteer staff. In 1997, a total of 1,500 American Red Cross chapters provided $215 million in financial and disaster assistance to individuals and families affected by disasters.

After a major disaster, the Red Cross supplies basic emergency shelter, food, medicine, and first aid to victims and distributes home clean-up items throughout affected areas. Red Cross disaster relief also includes feeding emergency workers; referring disaster victims to other available resources; handling inquiries from concerned family members outside the affected area; and supplying blood and blood products, as well as disaster-related counseling to victims.

The Red Cross enables disaster victims to resume independent living by assisting with the payment of groceries, clothing, basic household items, medicine, temporary housing, emergency home repairs, transportation, and tools. The American Red Cross provides all of its disaster assistance for free.

The Red Cross also offers assistance when other resources, such as insurance benefits and government assistance, are unavailable or inadequate in meeting disaster-related needs. All Red Cross assistance is provided on an individual basis, based on verified disaster-caused needs, and free of charge.

American Red Cross chapters also work within their communities to help the public prepare for, prevent, and cope with disasters and emergency situations. In 1999, total operating revenue amounted to $2.4 billion.

Eldercare. According to demographers, population trends predict that the needs of the rapidly growing elderly population will equal, if not exceed the needs for child care. U.S. workers have been left primarily to their own resources to find elderly care services. In fact, as the 1990s began, a Bureau of Labor Statistics' survey of medium and large firms indicated that only 3 percent of the 32.4 million employees contacted had an eldercare benefit program that included employer subsidies for day care or time off to handle eldercare needs. Although numerous private and public agencies exist that provide elder care, neither employers nor employees often know where to get assistance. Coordinated efforts have begun between employers and social service providers, however, to address the needs of those with eldercare responsibilities.

One option for eldercare has been senior citizen day care centers. A practical alternative to costly in-home care, day care centers provide social interaction and activities that improve the livelihood of the aged. According to the National Adult Day Services Association, more than 4,000 elderly day care centers existed in the United States by the end of the 1990s—almost three times the number of centers in 1991.

Adoption Services. Thousands of social service agencies work with adoption services, but only 250 handle most of the caseload, according to *Forbes*. Traditional agencies, such as Catholic Charities, manage about 70 percent of the business, while other intermediaries, usually attorneys, handle the remainder. According to the National Committee for Adoption, which represents over 100 non-profit agencies, nearly 1 million couples seek children to adopt. Based on the latest information available, the number of adoptions varied by decade—in 1951, unrelated adoptions rose from 33,800 in 1951 to an all-time high in 1970 of 89,200 children. From 1975, numbers dropped dramatically and averaged 49,000 yearly for the next ten years. Numbers rose to 61,600 in 1996. In general, the number of available babies affected the number of adoptions. Less than two-thirds of those were infants. The combined effects of legalized abortion and the declining social stigma of unwed mothers may have been possible reasons for the shortage of available babies.

Some couples wanting children have turned to private searches, claiming that traditional agencies have been too passive in their search for pregnant women considering adoption. This may be true as few traditional agencies have aggressively marketed their services. Many have not listed as adoption agencies in their local yellow pages and virtually none have used classified advertising.

Some people advocate turning over the entire adoption process to private practice, but current adoption statutes, which are complex and vary greatly from state to state, make this idea virtually impossible.

Self-help Organizations. The self-help movement, which began in 1935 with Alcoholics Anonymous (AA), has turned into a modern-day, low-cost alternative to expensive mental health services. Since self-help organizations have been inexpensive to operate, these publicly popular organizations have become appealing to lawmakers concerned with rising health care costs.

The AA formula of strict anonymity and its 12-step recovery program have proven to be quite successful. In 1999, AA chapters could be found in 133 countries with an estimated worldwide membership of 2 million people. Moreover, between 12 and 15 million Americans are estimated to have become involved in nonprofit self-help groups like AA.

Certain studies show that self-help membership has been increasing annually. Growth may be attributed to the anonymous nature of these groups, although anonymity has made accurate counting impossible. Most self-help participants have been white, middle-class baby boomers, but the movement itself has encompassed all kinds of Americans. The roster of groups includes Overeaters Anonymous, Gamblers Anonymous, and Debtors Anonymous.

Workforce

According to the Census Bureau, in 1998 taxable and tax-exempt individual and family social services establishments in the United States, employed 923,300 workers. (Almost half of all nongovernmental social service employees worked for individual and miscellaneous social service organizations.) According to the U.S. Department of Labor, projected employment levels over the next ten years was expected to reach 1.2 million.

Nearly two-thirds of all social service establishments have fewer than ten employees. However, half of all workers have been employed by larger establishments, those with 50 employees or more. The industry also has employed a high percentage of older workers, 36 percent being 45 years old or older.

One-third of nongovernmental jobs in social services have been in service occupations, such as homemaker/home health aides, food preparation workers, nurses aides, and child care or elderly care workers, according to the Department of Labor. These jobs usually have required little formal training in social services or an education beyond high school.

One-fourth of nongovernmental social service jobs have been professional specialty occupations, such as social workers, human services workers, adult education teachers, and counselors. These jobs usually have specific entrance requirements, similar to most professional specialty occupations. Some jobs required specific clinical knowledge, such as the duties of a licensed nurse.

Some of the fastest growing occupations in the United States can be found in the field of social services. By the year 2005, the number of homemaker/home health care aides in all industries has been projected to grow 88 percent, human service workers by 71 percent, and social workers by 34 percent, according to the Department of Labor. The anticipated growth in social service work has been based on the expanding needs of the elderly, disabled, mentally ill, mentally retarded, and families in crisis.

Research and Technology

The federal government has been actively involved in researching technological options available for use in an electronic system to deliver public assistance benefits. Targeted for implementation sometime within the next five to 15 years, the program would provide greater efficiency to the welfare system, especially in detecting fraud, waste, and abuse. The electronic delivery system would also reduce the costs associated with a paper-based, manual issuance and redemption public assistance program.

Further Reading

"Aid to Families with Dependant Children." Danbury, CT: Grolier, 1998. Available from http://ea.grolier.com.

"CARF and NADSA forge agreement to develop accreditation process for adult day services." Washington: National Council on the Aging, 1999. Available from http://www.ncoa.org.

"Facts on Adoption." Washington: National Council for Adoption, 2000. Available from http://familymedicine.about.com/health/familymedicine.

Red Cross Financial Statement, 5 May 2000. Available from http://www.redcross.org.

Temporary Assistance for Needy Families. "Fact Sheet," 5 May 2000. Available from http://www.acf.dhhs.gov.

"Trends in FSP Participation Rates: Focus on September 1997." Washington: U.S. Department of Agriculture, 2000. Available from http://www.fns.usda.gov.

True Stories: 1997 Annual Report. Washington: American Red Cross, 1997.

U.S. Bureau of Labor Statistics. *National Industry—Occupational Employment Matrix.* Washington: GPO, 2000. Available from http://stats.bls.gov.

U.S. Census Bureau. *1997 Economic Census—Health Care and Social Assistance.* Washington, DC: GPO, 2000.

U.S. Department of Health and Human Services. "The Administration for Children and Families Overview," 5 May 2000. Available from http://www.acf.dhhs.gov.

———. "Welfare Caseloads Decline/New Grants to Promote Job Retention," 5 May 2000. Available from http://www.acf.dhhs.gov.

Weinstein, Amy, ed. *1995/96 Public Welfare Directory.* Washington: American Public Welfare Association, 1995.

SIC 8331

JOB TRAINING AND VOCATIONAL REHABILITATION SERVICES

This category encompasses establishments primarily engaged in providing manpower training and vocational rehabilitation services for the unemployed, the underemployed, the disabled, and persons who have a job market disadvantage because of lack of education, job skills, or experience. Included in this industry are upgrading and job-development services, skill training, world-of-work orientation, and vocational rehabilitation counseling. This industry also includes offices of specialists providing rehabilitation and job counseling. Establishments primarily engaged in providing work experience for rehabilitates are also classified in this industry.

NAICS CODE(S)

624310 (Vocational Rehabilitation Services)

INDUSTRY SNAPSHOT

American industry spent tens of billions of dollars to train its employees each year. As industry becomes increasingly global and technology becomes more sophisticated, employers demand that workers sharpen their analytical, decision-making, and communication skills. In order to remain competitive, businesses need to provide their employees with continuous training. Likewise, to become employed and remain employable, individuals must be, at the minimum, literate and skilled. For many individuals—including those with vocational disadvantages such as illiteracy, a criminal record, former substance abuse, or physical and mental disabilities—education and training is received through job training and vocational rehabilitation centers.

According to the U.S. Census Bureau, there were an estimated 9,707 job training and vocational establishments operating in the United States in 1998, with combined operating revenues of almost $2.9 billion for taxable firms. These establishments employed 336,800 workers. The U.S. Department of Commerce, Bureau of Economic Analysis, estimated that there were about 4,000 non-tax-exempt private vocational schools in operation, which posted about $7.4 billion in revenues. Estimates of the cost of private-sector training vary widely, due to differences in the methods used and the difficulty of collecting cost data.

Job rehabilitation and training were expected to remain an important component of industry well into the 21st century as technological advances necessitated enhanced skills from new and current employees. Corporate downsizing and rapid technological change in the workplace promised to focus more attention on building and retaining a skilled workforce. Training was a key element in that process.

Workers once considered to have sufficient skills for lifetime employment found themselves learning new skills and processes to sustain their employment in an increasingly technological work environment. According to the U.S. Department of Education, in 1997, 76 percent of students in grades 1-12 used a computer at school (up from 62 percent in 1993), and 45 percent used one at home (up significantly from 25 percent in 1993). By the year 2000, a consequential number of both high school and college graduates used computers in their jobs. Technological growth raised the level of training required for the workforce in nearly all industries.

Based on the educational background of the unemployed and labor-market projections, the U.S. Office of Technology Assessment (OTA) found that a large segment of the U.S. labor force was fast becoming more prepared for employment in an increasingly high-tech workplace. Yet other groups, including the immigrants who made up 26 percent of the labor force growth in the 1980s and early 1990s, still had a need for more job training.

Additionally, employers and post-secondary institutions found that a number of high school graduates and college students needed remedial work in grammar, mathematics, and basic problem-solving skills before they could be ready for employment or college. As a result, efforts redoubled throughout the 1990s to ensure academic accountability through minimum proficiency requirements students had to pass to graduate. However, for those who had already been through the system and whose educational skills remained sub-par, job training and vocational rehabilitation services were designed to address needs for education and skill development and provide rehabilitative help and training for students and workers with insufficient knowledge and skills.

Organization and Structure

Nationally, the industry was composed of many small companies, a majority being non-profits and state-supported organizations. In the mid-1990s, the top 46 companies, which made up less than one percent of the total number of establishments in this industry, had sales of $1.03 billion. This figure represented approximately 25 percent of the entire industry's sales.

During the 1990s, however, there was a decrease in the number of state-run vocational rehabilitation service centers. In 1997, the U.S. Census Bureau reported 2,549 centers, compared to 2,643 in 1992—an elimination of 94 state centers. Speculation on the reasons for this was varied. Cutbacks in individual state spending and federal subsidies accounted for some of the decline. High technology in the workplace created a much more efficient system with which workers could be trained and/or retrained. That was a model employed by state-run program as well; many rehabilitation services were offered over the Internet and accessible from any computer.

Background and Development

Traditionally, training programs had been implemented in response to specific problems or situations, and little regard was given to previous programs or to the implications for the future. In general, most of the money spent on training programs went to programs for professional and managerial staff, ignoring other workers whose skill development would mandate more expenditure.

The number of individuals who lacked marketable skills fueled the growth of the rehabilitative and vocational training industry. Firms in this industry were formed as a result of the lack of training available to individuals without a college degree. Many of these companies operated on the premise that people would derive greater benefits from training programs if they were able to help themselves. This idea was the genesis of Goodwill Industries of America.

Goodwill Industries was started in the early 1900s by Edgar J. Helms, a Methodist minister working in Boston. Helms began collecting unwanted household items and hiring poor men and women to repair them for resale, and he paid workers through the sale of the goods. Goodwill Industries served not only low income people but also those with other ''barriers to employment including physical and mental disabilities, illiteracy, homelessness, inadequate education, and welfare dependency.'' Goodwill Industries offered training in many fields, which ranged from computer programming to janitorial positions.

The passage of the Americans with Disabilities Act (ADA), which removed many employment barriers faced by physically disabled individuals, was expected to increase the number of clients served by training centers. Implementation of the ADA met with some resistance from employers who feared that they would be required to meet hiring quotas, and by employees who believed that physically disabled workers would receive preferential treatment in the workplace. The training and development industry worked to resolve these issues by helping to create and sustain supportive work environments for all workers. Training was well received when the trainers were sensitive to employee attitudes and encouraged open discussion.

Passage of the ADA represented significant growth potential for the training industry. In addition to providing training to employees, professionals in this industry found a market in corporations making changes to meet the federal regulations and needing insights about hiring and training physically challenged employees.

Current Conditions

In August 1996, President Clinton signed and Congress passed the Personal Responsibility and Work Opportunity Act of 1996. The legislation ended a 61-year federal guarantee of aid to the poor, giving states the power to design their own welfare programs, imposing a five-year lifetime limit on receiving welfare, and requiring recipients to begin working within two years after receiving benefits. Childless, able-bodied people, aged 18 to 50, were limited to three months of welfare every three months. They were eligible to continue receiving food stamps on the condition that they secure a 20-hour per week job and participate in job training or volunteer programs. President Clinton promised to encourage companies to help welfare recipients find employment. In light of this welfare reform, businesses were increasingly focusing on the their roles in the education and training of adults, youth, and disadvantaged workers.

Continued corporate downsizing was another influence on the growth of the industry. As corporations continued to downsize their operations, they often demanded that remaining workers increase their performance and skill levels. More corporations required that job applicants possess high-level skills and that they cultivate these skills through on-going training. In manufacturing, for example, the tradition of using workers to perform routine, repetitive duties was being replaced by teaching employees a broader scope of skills and adding to their responsibilities. Companies were emphasizing teamwork and were cross-training their workers to make production more efficient.

The American Society for Training and Development estimated that nearly 50 million workers needed additional training just to perform their current jobs adequately.

INDUSTRY LEADERS

Goodwill Industries of America was one of the world's largest leaders in the industry. Goodwill Industries is a nonprofit corporation that serves more than 126,000 clients annually through its vocational rehabilitation programs. Goodwill receives clients through referrals, of which the state vocational rehabilitation system and the public welfare system provide more than 50 percent. Nearly 25,000 of these clients were placed in competitive employment by Goodwill Industries in 1995. Salaries and wages earned by clients in that year totaled $261 million. These people had previously depended upon some form of public assistance, but with their newly achieved employment, they became contributors to their local economies and returned about $32 million in tax revenues to government at federal, state, and local levels. In 1996, Goodwill Industries encompassed more than 185 independent member organizations in the United States, Canada, and the Pacific Basin. In addition, the company worked with more than 50 affiliated International Goodwill organizations.

Goodwill's largest client group included people with such vocational disadvantages as illiteracy, past substance abuse, a record of criminal behavior, physical and mental disabilities, and a lack of work experience. People with mental retardation made up the second-largest group of Goodwill's clients. Goodwill Industries divided its vocational services into four categories: vocational evaluation, vocational adjustment, job-seeking skills and placement, and sheltered employment for those who could not realistically expect to succeed in a competitive environment. Goodwill also assisted clients with social adjustment training, and many of its facilities provided rehabilitation for persons with industrial injuries. In late 1999, The U.S. Department of Labor awarded Goodwill Industries International Inc. a $20 million grant to provide training and support to place men and women on welfare in career-building Census 2000 jobs. The grant was the result of Goodwill's partnership with the Census Bureau; their goal was to recruit and hire 850,000 employees to conduct the census, and to place Goodwill graduates in jobs.

Goodwill Industries funded its job training programs through store, salvage, and contract sales; rehabilitation fees and grants; and public support funds. This revenue went directly to job-training services, vocational rehabilitation, and equipment required by people with disabilities and other special needs. An average of 84 percent of all revenue raised by Goodwill Industries from the sale of donated goods supported job-training and rehabilitation programs. The other 16 percent went toward overhead costs.

Another industry giant was Lions World Services for the Blind (LWSB), sponsored by various Lions Clubs. LWSB was formed to teach people who are blind or visually impaired independent living skills or job training skills. In the United States, 1.3 million Americans age 25 and older have severe visual impairments, causing them to make adjustments in areas of careers and everyday living situations. Since its founding in Little Rock, Arkansas, in 1947, LWSB has served more than 10,000 individuals in the United States and 54 other countries. LWSB offers a variety of vocational training programs to prepare individuals who are blind or visually impaired for careers in both white and blue-collar jobs. By the year 2000, LWSB offered 13 vocational programs, which included several courses that train students to work for the Internal Revenue Service. LWSB also provided a variety of other services, including a college preparatory program to prepare people for college work, job-seeking skills training, employer education workshops, job placement assistance on a selected basis, and in-service training for rehabilitation professionals.

WORKFORCE

According to the U.S. Census Bureau, the salary difference in taxed and tax-exempt establishments in this industry was significant in the 1990s. Workers in taxed organizations typically earned more than their counterparts employed by tax-exempt organizations. Based on limited information, starting salaries for these human services workers ranged from $13,000 to $20,000 a year in 1994. Experienced workers generally earned between $18,000 and $27,000 annually.

The industry relied on various instructors and workers to provide job training assistance to its diverse client base. Teachers and instructors in vocational education programs comprised a significant percentage of this industry's workforce, but other workers included counselors, social workers, and secretaries.

According to the U.S. Department of Labor, employment in this industry was expected to increase significantly by 2008. In 1998, job training and related services industry accounted for almost 370,000 workers; a 31 percent increase to over 483,000 workers was expected by 2008. When the 20th century ended, job training programs began to require more workers as the U.S. economy continued to grow at an unprecedented rate. Companies changed their mode of production more frequently, thus more workers needed to be retrained.

AMERICA AND THE WORLD

In addition to simply making corporations more efficient, job training is key to keeping the United States competitive in world markets. Skills training will enable American companies to exploit the benefits of available technology. Enhanced skills will be necessary to run advanced computers, including interactive software. Training will help close the gap between non-skilled workers and sophisticated technology.

With the exception of Goodwill Industries and Lions World Services for the Blind, most companies in this industry do not operate internationally. In general, training needs for vocational jobs vary widely from country to country. Many other countries have advanced systems of job training and apprenticeship. The United States relies heavily on on-the-job training, while European countries, particularly Germany, have more focused post-secondary education programs. Industry analysts expect that the United States will begin to follow Europe's example by establishing job-training programs in high schools and instituting a nationwide program of youth apprenticeship. Despite the attractiveness of a U.S. higher education to foreign students, the competitiveness of U.S. workers has declined compared with workers in some Asian and European countries because of weaker support for training and vocational education. These countries have used better-trained workers to shorten the production cycle and make incremental improvements in existing products, giving them a competitive edge over the United States.

Research and Technology

The industry did not rely on technology to function, but rather trained its clients to make use of existing technology. Advances in computer software and systems were fast becoming a primary focus of the job training industry, as corporations demanded that their employees improve their computer literacy.

Further Reading

Bureau of Labor Statistics. ''Table 1. Table A-1. National employment and wage data from the Occupational Employment Statistics survey by occupation, 1998.'' *Occupational Outlook Handbook.* Available from http://stats.bls.gov/news.release/ocwage.t01.htm.

U.S. Census Bureau. ''Service Annual Survey; Selected Social Services, Tables 8.1—8.6.,'' 1999. Available from http://www.census.gov.

SIC 8351

CHILD DAY CARE SERVICES

This industry includes establishments primarily engaged in the care of infants or children, or in providing pre-kindergarten education, where medical care or delinquency correction is not a major element. These establishments may or may not have substantial educational programs. These establishments generally care for pre-kindergarten or preschool children, but may also care for older children when they are not in school. Establishments providing baby-sitting services are classified in **SIC 7299: Miscellaneous Personal Services, Not Elsewhere Classified.** Head Start centers operating in conjunction with elementary schools are classified in **SIC 8211: Elementary and Secondary Schools.**

NAICS Code(s)

624310 (Child Day Care Services)

Industry Snapshot

In 1996, two thirds of women with pre-school aged children worked outside the home, up from 39 percent in 1975. As the twentieth century came to a close, the day care business had become by some estimates a $30 billion dollar industry and was poised to grow even further over the next several years.

Trends influencing the development of the industry in the late 1990s include the welfare-to-work program initiated under the Clinton administration. As several thousand mothers left their young children to take jobs, the already limited availability of affordable, quality child care worsened, calling national attention to the problem of decent child care.

Parents called upon employers and state and local government to provide assistance with child care, in the form of subsidies, training, better monitoring and regulations, and greater flexibility. As the labor shortage worsened, more and more employers found that child care was an important benefit for both employee retention and increased productivity. But because of the labor shortage, qualified child care workers became even more difficult to find.

Several studies released in the late 1990s caused frazzled parents even more worries. Although studies were mixed on the long-term effects of high quality child care versus staying home with a parent, surveys examining the standards of U.S. child care were unanimous: the majority of children in day care received mediocre to poor care.

As in most other sectors of the economy, major growth in the industry was achieved by mergers and acquisitions. Although large chains made up a very small portion of child care services in the 1990s, many were rapidly purchasing local chains and independent centers to expand operations, while others consolidated to increase their clout in the marketplace.

Organization and Structure

Day care services can be broadly divided into two groups: family day care homes and day care centers.

Family day care occurs in a private residence and typically serves four to six children. Most such providers operate unofficially, however, either because (1) they take care of four or fewer non-related children, and thus in many states are not required to register, or (2) they are subject to state regulation, but are wittingly or unwittingly operating underground. Estimates of these facilities naturally vary widely: a report of the National Association for the Education of Young Children places their number at anywhere from 500,000 to a million.

Day care centers, in contrast, operate outside homes and typically enroll more children, perhaps 50 to 100. The centers can be divided into for-profit and nonprofit facilities. For-profit centers comprise the large national or regional chains with hundreds of centers, such as KinderCare and Children's World Learning Centers, as well as thousands of smaller businesses. Nonprofit centers may be operated by churches, parent cooperatives, public schools, community centers, Head Start, YMCAs, and so forth; some may be operated by businesses for the benefit of their employees, or by the employees themselves.

In 1998, there were an estimated 60,117 establishments providing child day care services. Most of those were independent establishments, rather than chains, and most were nonprofits. In 1997, the Child Care Information Exchange estimated that 35 percent of centers were independent nonprofits, 29 percent were independent for-profit centers, 22 percent were nonprofits run by Head Start or a religious or community organization, 8 percent were run by public schools, and only 6 percent were chains. Industry watchers and investors both predicted that increasing need for child care and stiff competition for qualified child care workers would tend to favor large businesses in the future.

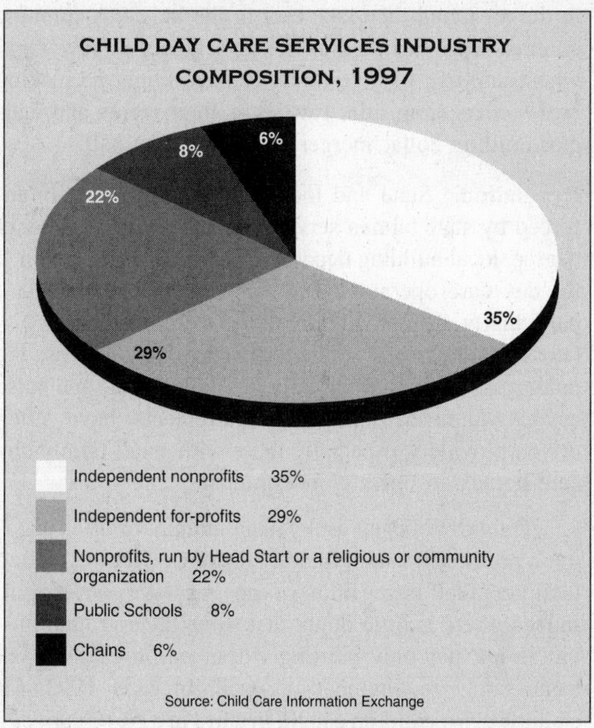

BACKGROUND AND DEVELOPMENT

During the seventeenth and eighteenth centuries, parents in America rarely had to face the problems of child-rearing alone because they could usually expect support from their extended families, many of whom lived and worked close by. Urbanization and changing social conditions in the nineteenth century created a need for child care for poor mothers who had to work. To this end, in 1828 a group of evangelical women established the Boston Infant School, often considered the first day care center in the United States. Similar schools were soon set up in New York and Philadelphia. As these centers were usually established under religious auspices, part of their care entailed instructing their charges in moral and religious belief.

Throughout the nineteenth century and the early 1900s, such centers generally provided care only for poor children. More affluent mothers rarely worked, and, if they did, they hired nannies to look after their kids. Thus, day care was generally seen as an issue confined to a relatively small segment of the population—until the Great Depression. The enormous rise in unemployment and the subsequent creation of the New Deal afforded a vast expansion of day care facilities through the Works Progress Administration. One of the primary objectives of these centers was to give jobs to the unemployed, especially laid-off schoolteachers.

Despite the dramatic social changes brought on by the Depression and World War II, most communities did not have full-day child care programs until the late 1960s. In the 1970s and 1980s the number of day care centers grew dramatically. The rise in the number of women working outside the home explains much of the story: in 1987, 67 percent of women in the United States were in the out-of-home work force, compared with 39 percent in 1970. According to government estimates, in 1991 employed mothers had almost 10 million children under the age of five. Nearly one quarter of these children received care in an organized facility such as a nursery school or a day care center. Forecasts indicate that women will account for 62 percent of the growth in the labor force through the year 2005, thus indicating a continued need for child day care services.

Demand also depends on local social conditions, including the strength of family ties. For example, a unit of KinderCare, the largest of the day care chains, surveyed 4,000 employees of an Ohio company and found that only 42 said they would use a corporate day care center. A KinderCare manager quoted in the *Wall Street Journal* remarked that "everybody's aunt and grandmother live in the area, and they take care of the kids.'' A stunning contrast is provided within the skyscrapers of New York, where children of investment bankers might be making bird feeders from milk cartons as their moms and dads close billion-dollar merger deals down the hall.

Regulation. State and local regulations, primarily enforced by state human services agencies and, to a lesser degree, local building departments, are a major challenge for day care operators. Day care regulation presents a particularly difficult dilemma for governments and legislators—and parents. While tough rules may increase the quality of care, they can also curtail supply and raise costs. Moreover, stringent requirements have often driven providers, especially those with small family day care homes, to operate underground.

Thus what began as a valiant attempt to offer maximum protection to children has had the effect of creating facilities that have little or no regulatory oversight. Indeed, there is little doubt that some underground providers are not only skirting extraneous regulation but basic safety requirements as well. In early 1993, for example, two children caught in a fire in a New York day care home were found dead in the cellar, next to a pile of mattresses and a nonworking smoke detector.

Some observers noted that often the rules may be sufficient, but the staff that enforces them can be small and inadequate, with a single inspector responsible for as many as 150 facilities. Providers complained that there were so many requirements that they were unable to discern which are essential and which are merely recommendations. Directors are often frustrated at having to compete with programs that are exempt from licensing, which often includes centers run by churches, local governments, or public schools.

The biggest regulatory hurdle for many day care centers is meeting child-to-staff ratio requirements, since wages usually account for well over half of all operating costs. To ensure that children receive proper supervision, state regulations require certain ratios of workers to children. The ratio varies with the age of the children. Child development experts generally recommend that a single caregiver be responsible for no more than three or four infants (less than one year old), five or six toddlers (one to two years old), or 10 preschool-age children (between two and five years old).

Health and Safety. During the mid-1980s, the insurance market for child care centers was in a crisis. Legal costs were climbing; insurers feared huge tort settlements; reports of child sex abuse, most notably at the McMartin Preschool, were on the rise; and a major insurer of child care services, Mission Insurance Co., became insolvent. By 1992, however, the Child Care Action Campaign was able to list 25 insurers that offered coverage, up from just a few providers available several years earlier.

Some day care centers are criticized for unsafe conditions identified on playgrounds, where climbing equipment is often too high or equipment is poorly maintained. While children do occasionally sustain injuries at centers, most of them are minor and result in only small claims. Indeed, it appears only 5 percent of accidents at centers lead to liability claims, versus 10 to 15 percent for accidents in general. On the downside, however, policies have become more expensive and insurers exclude some important risks. Most refuse to cover legal costs to defend against physical or sexual abuse charges.

Without attempting to minimize the horror of any instance of child abuse in a day care setting, some observers note that these incidents represent but a very small fraction of all child abuse cases. Indeed, statistically speaking, children are less likely to suffer abuse in a day care facility than they are in their own homes. Other commentators note that a child in day care is, again on a statistical basis, safer than at home because someone is always supervising the children, poisons are locked up, and there are no guns.

Whether small children are more likely to catch infectious diseases in a day care facility than in their own homes is a source of controversy. Some note the literature in medical journals that suggests several serious diseases, as well as less dangerous maladies, are more common among children in day care than those at home with a parent. A 1995 study found that an unsettling number of child care centers, both for-profit and nonprofit, are unhealthy for children. The study showed that one in eight centers is unhealthy, primarily because of unsanitary conditions that promote the spread of infectious diseases. According to researchers, the underlying cause of many child day care problems can be attributed to the low training of personnel and the high worker-to-child ratios.

Current Conditions

Welfare to Work. The welfare reforms of the Clinton administration during the 1990s raised new concerns about the quality and quantity of day care, as many women previously staying home to care for their children were compelled to work outside of the home. One company addressed the problem by hiring women recently off welfare to provide childcare. In 1997, Philadelphia-based Childspace Management Group employed such women at an hourly wage of $7 an hour—25 percent higher than the industry average. Employees paid a reduced rate to enroll their own children, and after one year were offered stock options in the company. The turnover rate for the company was more than 50 percent lower than the industry average. Another program, based in Chicago, that came about due to welfare reform efforts helped women getting off welfare to obtain licenses for running day care centers out of their homes.

For many of the working poor, mainly single mothers, help was not so forthcoming. Although some states offered child care assistance to working women, for some women their wages were too high to get public assistance, but too low to pay for child care bills as high as $600 per month for one child in the Seattle area—or up to $1,000 monthly for two. Some women requested lower wages or part-time work; others took lower paying jobs. Actually finding child care also presented challenges. Although women leaving welfare received priority, they still faced waiting lists nearing 400 families.

An additional hurdle facing workers starting in entry-level jobs was the difficulty of finding child care that matched their working hours. According to a survey by the National Association for the Education of Young Children, in the early 1990s only 10 percent of child care centers had weekend hours, and just 3 percent offered their services at night. According to the U.S. Census Bureau, less than one third of workers hold 9 to 5 jobs, and that proportion is much higher in entry-level positions. Cities working to move parents off welfare initiated programs and lessened restrictions to increase the number of hours child care was offered. In 1998, for example, the Chicago City Council rescinded a regulation requiring child care centers to close before 9:00 p.m. Rolling Meadows, a Chicago suburb, announced plans to open a center operating 24 hours a day, seven days a week.

Employer Support. Employer support may take several forms, which includes providing referral and information services; reimbursing employees, in varying degrees, through a benefits package; using a vendor system (the company buys places at day care centers, and then the employee pays all or part of the costs); contributing to local day care facilities; or opening a corporate child care center, as is the case with some corporations in the United States who have on-site facilities. Opening a day care center often yields much goodwill both within the firm, as well as favorable press. A 1997 study by Coopers & Lybrand L.L.P. reported that 43 percent of employers offered child care benefits, up from 30 percent the year before.

The study also reported that as many as 73 percent of companies with $1 billion or more in revenue provided some kind of child care benefits, while only 18 percent of companies with revenues under $10 million did the same. But as small business grew throughout the 1990s, so did their child care concerns. Tightening labor markets made retention of employees at all levels a crucial issue, more so in smaller firms, where losing one employee—either for a day or permanently—meant losing a substantial portion of the work force. Smaller firms lacking the resources for on-site child care often offered employees a payroll deduction permitting them to use pretax earnings for day care, through the federal Dependent Care Assistance Program. Union-based movements were also pushing state governments and individual employers to improve child care benefits.

A growing trend for employers was the provision of backup child care, allowing parents to work when their regular babysitter was not available: on weekends and evenings, or in case of an emergency. ChildrenFirst Inc. operated 14 backup care centers in major metropolitan areas in 1998. ''Sick day care,'' child care for children too ill to attend regular day care, was also subsidized by some major employers. Often, employers ''subscribe'' to the program by paying a flat annual fee; employees who use the service make a low co-payment for the days they use. Both types of providers rely primarily on corporate clients for support, rather than individual parents. According to benefits consultants, this sector of the industry was growing faster than on-site care.

Quality vs. Quantity. As more mothers entered the workforce throughout the 1990s, concerns about the effects of day care on children also increased. Several studies released in the late 1990s offered mixed reports. Widely publicized studies in 1997 reported that the most brain development happens prior to age three, and that it is highly dependent upon environmental factors including attachment to caregivers and mental stimulation. In 1999, the National Institute of Child Health and Human Development released another installment of a study of 1,300 children from birth to age three. The results suggested that using child care during the first year of life, particularly the first four months, disrupts ''the process of attachment, when mother and child learn to read one another's signals and expressions.'' Early reports from the National Institute's study provided parents better news. Findings released in 1998 indicated that ''toddlers in day care have fewer behavioral problems, like tantrums and hitting, than do those cared for alone with a nanny or in small groups.'' A 1997 report from that study claimed that children in high-quality day care begin school with enhanced language and social skills. A 27-year study at the University of North Carolina supported these findings by concluding that children in ''quality child care programs'' could maintain that advantage into adulthood.

With extreme shortages in affordable child care getting worse, however, quality was hard to come by. In 1999, the Consumer Products Safety Commission (CPSC) released the results of a study revealing unsafe practices and products in a majority of day care centers. Of the 200 licensed centers the CPSC examined, over two thirds had a least one major safety hazard. The findings, reported in *U.S. News and World Report,* listed several common safety hazards: ''At 38 percent of the centers, children were wearing clothing with neck drawstrings, which can become caught in playground equipment and can lead to strangulation. Twenty-four percent of the centers had unsafe playground surfacing, and 19 percent had cribs that contained soft bedding, which can smother children. Other dangers included poorly maintained playground surfaces, loops on the cords of window blinds, and failure to use child safety gates where necessary.'' The study offered no count of how many injuries were caused by these hazards, but the CPSC reported 56 deaths since 1990. A broader nationwide study, however, counted at least 76 deaths in the year 1996 alone.

Apart from safety concerns, many centers did not offer high quality care. A report published in 1996 by Suzanne Helburn and Carollee Howes found that 86 percent of child care centers were below average to bad. Home-based day care was not substantially better: the study found 35 percent to be inadequate and 56 percent to be no more than adequate. A 1999 article in *Time* cited a federal study with similar findings: ''85 percent of preschoolers who are cared for outside the home get poor or mediocre care, delivered by a hodgepodge of mostly unregulated providers.''

Other Programs. As private nursery schools began to proliferate in the postwar years, educators began to note that children were entering kindergarten with widely differing abilities. Project Head Start was conceived to give poorer children a ''head start'' on their education. The program was distinguished by its commitment to the total child: it included nutrition and health care assistance, and supported parents in their job searches. Unlike many of the programs initially funded during by the Johnson administration's War on Poverty campaign of the 1960s, Head Start continued to receive strong support from the government and the public.

In 1999, there were approximately 1,500 Head Start programs nationwide—some of which covered multiple sites—at an annual cost of $4.6 billion to the federal government. In the mid-1990s, the government became concerned with the quality of Head Start programs in many communities. According to the *National Journal,* ''Over time, many Head Start organizations became stale, entrenched bureaucracies, protected by local politics and politicians, with little accountability to anyone or close examination of their record in helping kids.'' Another challenge to the program was its strong affiliation with African-American communities, as the population of children being served by Head Start became more diverse, and more heavily Hispanic. In a Clinton administration initiative, hundreds of the poorest performing Head Start programs were closed down, and many others were reformed.

Child care for older children also became a bigger issue, as more parents sought structured after-school programs. Proposals included keeping schools open as late as 6 p.m., although conservatives have argued that such programs give government too much power. As a compromise, some suggest using public school facilities for community-based programs. As of 1999, 30 percent of public elementary schools offered after-school programs; 3.4 percent of eligible children made use of them. One publicly held child care provider sought to corner this market: Nobel Education Dynamics offered programs for children through the eight grade. The company announced in early 2000 that its net earnings for the six months ended December 31 1999, increased by over 153 percent from the same period last year.

Industry Leaders

Ranked according to capacity, the five largest child care organizations in 1998 were KinderCare Learning Centers (143,420), La Petite Academy (100,000), Children's World Learning Centers (74, 750), Tutor Time Learning Centers (37,305), and Childtime Learning Centers (27,740). Rankings by sales were nearly the same: KinderCare ($563 million), La Petite Holdings Corp. ($300 million), Children's World ($230 million), Children's Discovery Centers ($88 million), and Childtime Childcare Inc. ($74 million).

Bright Horizons is another large child care center chain, specializing in on-site child care. It operates centers in 24 states. Some of its clients include Allstate Insurance, Apple Computer, AT&T, Dunkin' Donuts, DuPont Company, Ernst & Young, Fidelity Investments, Hewlett Packard, IBM, Mattel Toys, MCA/Universal City Studios Inc., Merck & Co., Motorola Inc., Paramount Pictures, Procter & Gamble, Prudential Insurance Co., Sony Pictures Entertainment, Time Warner, United Nations, Women & Infants Hospital, and Xerox. Bright Horizons publicly announced that it was considering merging with Corporate Family Solutions, which would make it the nation's fifth-largest child care chain. Stock analysts suggested that the growing trend for employers to offer on-site child care made Bright Horizons an attractive investment opportunity.

As the industry has grown, these large firms have become targets for acquisition by other companies. In March of 1998, Knowledge Universe—an education investment concern organized by Michael Milken—purchased Children's Discovery Center for $82 million. In 1997, Chase Manhattan purchased La Petite Academy. The large chains have also begun going public as investor interest has grown. In 1998, New Horizons Kid Quest, Childtime Learning Centers, Bright Horizons, and Corporate Family Solutions were publicly traded; Childcare Network—the nations 14th largest firm—announced in 1998 its intent to hold an initial public offering.

As in other sectors of the economy, mergers and acquisitions were a popular growth strategy. KinderCare has continued to acquire additional centers to add to the chain, including 12 of Ohio-based Learning Enrichment Centers in early 2000. KinderCare's second quarter earnings for fiscal year 2000 were $2.6 million, compared to $2.2 million during the second quarter of fiscal 1999. That increase resulted not from higher occupancy rates—which went up by only 0.2 percent—but from the acquisition of centers that charged higher rates.

WORKFORCE

In 1996, child care workers, including preschool teachers, accounted for 1.2 million jobs, up from 1 million in 1994, and 500,000 in 1988. The majority of the workers in the industry are female, and about one-third of the workforce is composed of women of color. Job opportunities in the day care industry are expanding rapidly. The U.S. Department of Labor ranks child care worker as one of the fastest growing occupations and among those with the largest numerical growth. The Department of Labor expected the number of job openings for these workers to increase 358,000, or 33 percent, by the year 2005. Many child care workers work part time and about four out of 10 preschool teachers and child care workers are self-employed, most of whom are family day care providers. More than 60 percent of all salaried preschool teachers and child care personnel are found in child day care centers and preschools, and about 15 percent work for a religious institution. Others work in service organizations and in government.

Despite the increase in employment, child care wages remained among the lowest of all industries. In 1996, median weekly earnings of full-time, salaried child care workers were $250. The middle 50 percent of child care workers earned between $190 and $310. The top 10 percent earned at least $390; the bottom 10 percent earned less than $140. In 1997, the average yearly salary for a full-time child care provider was just over $12,000. Preschool teachers in privately funded child care centers generally earn much lower salaries than other comparably educated workers. Earnings of self-employed child care workers vary depending on the hours worked, number and ages of the children, and the location. The benefits for preschool teachers and child care workers also vary. Many employers offer free or discounted child care to employees. Some employers offer a full benefits package, including health insurance and paid vacations, but other employers offer no benefits at all. Some employers offer seminars and workshops to help workers improve upon or learn new skills.

In 1996, the low wages in the industry prompted a nationwide Worthy Wage Day, in an attempt to highlight the extremely low wages most child care providers earn. Many employees make a salary that is below the poverty level—causing over 40 percent to leave their jobs every year. According to the National Center for the Early Childhood Work Force, which supported Worthy Wage Day, one reason for the low wages was the United States' dismally low—compared to other industrialized nations—government or corporate subsidies for working parents to pay for child care. According to a 1996 *Wall Street Journal* study, ''People making less than $30,000 a year typically spend 25 percent to 30 percent of household income on child care,'' which limits how much child care providers can charge.

The training and qualifications required of preschool teachers and child care workers vary widely. Each state has licensing requirements that regulate caregiver training—ranging from a high school diploma, to community college courses, to a college degree in child development or early childhood education. Some states require continuing education for workers in this field. The state of Virginia, for example, requires that all day care center personnel receive eight hours of child care related courses each year. Formal education requirements in some private preschools and day care centers are often lower than in public programs since they are not bound by state requirements. Some states prefer preschool teachers and child care workers to have a Child Development Associate (CDA) credential, which is offered by the Council for Early Childhood Professional Recognition. The CDA credential is recognized as a qualification for teachers and directors in 46 states and the District of Columbia. The credential requires 120 hours of training, a high school diploma, and 480 hours of experience.

In 1999, the U.S. Department of Labor announced an apprenticeship program aimed at improved training of child care workers. The program awarded grants to the District of Columbia and 10 states: Kansas, $350,000; Washington, $350,000; New York, $350,000; New Hampshire, $257,570; Iowa, $191,316; Nevada, $349,316; Wisconsin, $212,000; Indiana, $349,970; Vermont, $303,750; Colorado, $375,000, and the District of Columbia, $340,000. In a press release about the program Secretary of Labor Alexis M. Herman said, ''One of the reasons so many parents have trouble finding quality child care is the shortage of workers with the right knowledge and experience. Apprenticeship is a great way to address this need.'' The program was funded through the Job Training Partnership Act.

AMERICA AND THE WORLD

Provisions for child care services are often part of the state insurance schemes of many European nations. As of 1990 the Swedish government provided day care for most children over 18 months. In Denmark about 50 percent of children under the age of three and nearly 90 percent of children between the ages of three and six were in publicly financed day care. Initially prompted by fears that the population would not produce enough soldiers, France has had state child care policies since the eighteenth century. Roughly 25 percent of French children under three years of age are in programs wholly or partly subsidized by the government, while 95 percent of three- to five-year-olds are in preschools. Belgium offers about the same level of state-sponsored care.

Britain, on the other hand, has few child care centers. Upper-income families employ nannies, while less affluent families rely on family members and so-called ''child minders.'' As the cost of domestic help rises, however, there has been increasing pressure on companies and the government to offer better care. Nevertheless, in 1990 there were only 120 day care centers operating in British workplaces.

FURTHER READING

Adelson, Andrea. ''Child Care Industry Set to Come of Age.'' *International Herald Tribune,* 27 July 1998.

Brownlee, Shannon. ''Day-care Kids May Act Up Less.'' *U.S. News & World Report,* 13 April 1998.

Casper, Lynne M. ''What Does It Cost To Mind Our Preschoolers?'' *Current Population Reports: Household Economic Studies.* Washington, DC: U.S. Census Bureau, 1995. Available from http://www.census.gov:80/population/www/socdemo/childcare.html.

Chetwynd, Josh. ''Day Care Gets a Muted Cheer.'' *U.S. News & World Report,* 14 April 1997.

Dickinson, Amy. ''The Mother Load: A New Study of Day Care Will Make Many Moms Feel Guilty for Using It. But They Shouldn't.'' *Time,* 15 November 1999.

Dionne, E. J. ''Freeing Childcare of Ideology.'' *Nation's Cities Weekly,*20 October 1997.

''Eleven Grants Awarded to Develop Apprenticeships for Child Care Workers.'' 27 October 1999. Available from http://www.dol.gov/dol/opa/public/media/press/eta/eta99310.

Erb, George. ''Child Care Dilemma: Cost Poses Hurdle for the Working Poor.'' *Puget Sound Business Journal,* 21 August 1998.

Fine, Andrea. ''Jobs in Day Care Help Moms Off Welfare.'' *Nation's Cities Weekly,* 21 April 1997.

Goldberg, Carol. ''Child Care: Does Business Recognize the Need?'' *LI Business News,* 6 October 1997.

Gordon, Julie. ''Children's World Cares for 70,000 Kids a Day.'' *Denver Business Journal,* 19 November 1999.

Hazlewood, Sara. ''Sick-Child Service Relieves Parents.'' *The Business Journal,* 16 March 1998.

Jacobson, Louis. ''Head Start on a Fresh Track.'' *National Journal,* 20 March 1999.

''KinderCare Announces Second Quarter of Fiscal Year 2000 Results.'' *PR Newswire,* 11 January 2000.

''KinderCare Learning Centers Announces Acquisition of 13 Ohio-Based Centers.'' *PR Newswire,* 1 February 2000.

Kyle, John E. ''National Campaign Highlights Wages for Child Care Providers.'' *Nation's Cities Weekly,* 13 May 1996.

Lacayo, Richard. ''The Kids Are All Right.'' *Time,* 14 April 1997.

Levy, Daniel S. ''In Brief.'' *Time,* 1 November 1999.

Maggs, John. ''Provide Day Care, and They Will Come.'' *National Journal,* 16 January 1999.

Market Share Reporter 2000 Detroit: Gale Group, 2000.

Milligan, Amanda. ''Backup Child Care Centers Help Parents Focus on Work.'' *Business Insurance,* 4 May 1998.

''Nobel Learning Communities, Inc. Announces a 153 Percent Increase in Its First Half Earnings.'' *PR Newswire,* 25 January 2000.

''Outside the Court, Chaos Too: Child Care.'' *The Economist,* 8 November 1997.

''Patterns of Behavior.'' *Florida Trend,* October 1997.

Prince, Michael. ''New York Unions Pushing for More Child Care Help.'' *Business Insurance,* 9 March 1998.

Rosellini, Lynn. ''The Risks of Day Care.'' *U.S. News & World Report,* 26 April 1999.

Rosenblum, Susan B. ''Cities Move to Make 'Day Care' a Night-Time Option.'' *Nation's Cities Weekly,* 17 August 1998.

Service Industries USA 4th ed. Detroit: Gale Group, 1998.

U.S. Department of Labor, Bureau of Labor Statistics. *Occupational Outlook Quarterly,* 15 January 1998. Available from http://www.bls.gov/ocohome.htm.

Whitman, David. ''Waiting for Mary Poppins.'' *U.S. News & World Report,* 24 November 1997.

SIC 8361

RESIDENTIAL CARE

This industry classification consists of establishments that provide residential social and personal care for children, senior citizens, and special categories of individuals with some limits on ability for self-care, but where medical care is not a major element. Included are group foster homes; halfway group homes; homes for the physically and mentally disabled; homes for the elderly; juvenile correctional homes; rehabilitation or residential centers; and children's boarding homes. Boarding schools providing elementary and secondary education are classified in **SIC 8211: Elementary and Secondary Schools.** Nursing homes and other providers of health-related personal care are classified in **SIC 8051: Skilled Nursing Care Facilities, SIC 8052: Intermediate Care Facilities,** and **SIC 8059: Nursing and Personal Care Facilities, Not Elsewhere Classified.**

NAICS CODE(S)

623312 (Homes for the Elderly)
623220 (Residential Mental Health and Substance Abuse Facilities)
623990 (Other Residential Care Facilities)

INDUSTRY SNAPSHOT

Facilities of many different types fall into the general category called residential care. The types of establishments in this classification include children's homes, rehabilitation facilities, group homes for people with a variety of limitations, halfway houses, and rest homes for the aged. For some segments of this industry, business has been booming in recent years. The market for space in retirement homes, for example, has expanded greatly due to the aging of the American population. Residential drug and alcohol treatment centers are overflowing. Orphanages have also been experiencing increased residency over the last several years. According to the U.S. Census Bureau, 10,869 establishments generated $9.4 billion in revenue in 1997.

Collectively, long-term care (LTC) facilities make up a multi-billion dollar industry in the United States. Long-term care industry forecasts are difficult to make because of continuing changes in federal and state legislation. In recent years, more than a dozen major long-term care companies and nursing facilities (containing more than 2,000 beds each) have been purchased by larger operators.

There are millions of people living in the various types of nursing homes and retirement communities that provide residential care for the elderly in the United States. The number of facilities continue to grow as America's population ages.

ORGANIZATION AND STRUCTURE

A broad range of residential care options exists for the elderly, making it possible for a client to choose a facility that is well-suited to his or her needs, both physical and financial. Traditional nursing homes provide continual shelter and 24-hour medical care for their elderly residents, who are unable to independently care for themselves. Nursing homes provide their residents with on-site meals and constant physical care, including assistance with bathing, grooming, and dressing. Nursing homes also often provide their residents with on-site social activities.

Retirement centers, increasingly referred to as assisted living communities, are designed for persons who are unable to function in an independent living setting, but do not need daily nursing care. In the late 1990s there were approximately 10,000 assisted living communities housing more than a million residents. Assisted living communities generally assist with bathing, dressing, housekeeping, and meals. The amount of help provided depends on individual need. Retirement homes offering assisted living can be considerably more affordable than nursing homes, primarily because 24-hour medical care is not required. The cost can range from $1,000 to more than $4,000 a month, about 30 percent less than the range for licensed nursing home care. Unlike nursing homes, however, most assisted living is not covered by private or government insurance. Independent operators and corporations in related industries such as hotel management are prevalent in assisted living.

Continuing-care retirement communities (CCRCs) are apartment complexes designed to meet the specific needs of the elderly, providing meals, social services, health care access, and sometimes housekeeping. CCRCs provide a somewhat higher degree of care than retirement centers, though health care is still secondary in these facilities. In the United States, there are about 700 CCRCs, housing more than 200,000 residents. Continuing care retirement communities offer seniors long-term contracts that ensure lifelong shelter and access to certain health care services. CCRC residents are able to enjoy an independent lifestyle with the knowledge that if they become sick or disabled, their needs will continue to be met. Residents usually pay an entrance fee and regular monthly payments for this service. Depending on the contract, the entrance fee may or may not be refundable. Most CCRCs enact requirements for incoming residents based on age, income level, financial assets, and physical health and mobility. Generally, residents are expected to move into the community while they are still fully able to care for themselves. Not-for-profit organizations, such as hospitals and religious groups, sponsor about 95 percent of the CCRCs in the United States.

Nearly two-thirds of drug and alcohol rehabilitation facilities, including outpatient and hospital programs not primarily engaged in the residential care industry, are privately owned, nonprofit operations. These institutions treat about 60 percent of the industry's substance abuse clients. The next largest segment consists of facilities run by state or local governments. These account for about 16 percent of rehabilitation operations, but treat nearly 25 percent of the industry's clients. The remainder of facilities are either privately-owned for profit (16.5 percent) or run by the federal government. The largest share of financial support for treatment services came from private third-party payers, such as HMOs and Blue Cross/Blue Shield. State governments contribute about one fourth of the industry's total funding. Only about 12 percent of funding comes from fees paid by clients.

Juvenile facilities make up another large block of institutions providing residential care. A steady rise in youth crime has led to an increasing demand for juvenile treatment services and providers who are qualified and experienced in serving troubled youth. The juvenile facilities segment of the industry, however, includes not only detention centers for delinquents, but also shelters, training schools, camps, ranches, and group homes.

Residential care for the mentally retarded and developmentally disabled has undergone a qualitative change since the 1970s. The shift has been away from large state institutions toward smaller, more flexible community-based group home settings. The number of residents in large state-operated institutions has shrunk by more than half since the late 1960s. Meanwhile, the number of people in facilities with less than 15 residents tripled during the 1980s and continues to rise. Numerous mental health professionals now consider group homes to be the most favorable residential environment for the mentally retarded. Throughout the 1990s, group homes had more than 100,000 residents nationwide, plus waiting lists with tens of thousands of additional names.

Background and Development

Orphanages. Each type of facility that is a part of the residential care industry has a distinct history. Orphanages, for example, have a history that is centuries old, as well as a brutal reputation based on Dickensian tales of squalor and abuse. By the 1970s, a large percentage of the bigger group homes had closed amid a flood of lawsuits and allegations of abuse and neglect. By the 1990s, however, orphanages began to reappear, as the need began to outdistance the availability of home-based foster care. The Hollywood-generated reputation of facilities such as Boys Town is somewhat more positive than that of the ordinary orphanage. Boys Town, which went co-ed in 1979, was founded by the legendary Father Flanagan in 1917. Located outside of Omaha, Nebraska, Boys Town covers 1,300 acres and has its own school, fire department, and zip code.

Residential Care for the Mentally Retarded. A history of poor conditions has also lead to great changes in the residential care of the mentally retarded. Historically, these individuals were not distinguished from insane or violent people, and therefore residential care resembled incarceration more than housing. The shift toward group homes began in the early 1970s as a reaction to growing dissatisfaction with the care that was being received in large institutions for the mentally retarded and developmentally disabled. Around 1972, lawsuits were brought in more than a dozen states, including New York, Illinois, Pennsylvania, and Texas, to protest the lack of adequate care in these facilities. As a result, scores of large institutions have since closed. The strongest resistance to the group home concept has come from the residents of neighborhoods that have been proposed sites for group homes. Some labor unions have also expressed concern, since many group home programs include vocational training that puts residents into competition with the unions for jobs.

Residential Care for the Elderly. The emergence of different levels of residential care for the elderly is a relatively recent phenomenon. Until the last few decades, nursing homes were the only option for those who could no longer care for themselves completely independently. CCRCs began to appear around 1960; however, they did not become common until the mid-1980s. In fact, about 80 percent of the CCRCs currently in existence opened between 1985 and 1989. Not surprisingly, this rapid expansion did meet with some resistance from nursing home organizations. Among the states, Oregon has been at the forefront of the movement for alternative housing for the elderly. In Oregon, several group homes, whose funding is aided by the state, house more than a thousand residents who might otherwise be in nursing homes. Most of these group homes are privately owned and licensed by the state.

Current Conditions

The current conditions of the residential care industry reflect the differing funding sources of its various segments. Although the demand for residential care seems to be increasing across the board, only those facilities funded through private investment seem able to meet the demand. Those relying on government funding are struggling with ways to meet the needs of their clients with the limited resources available to them.

Rehabilitation Facilities. Since the early 1990s, rehabilitation centers have been experiencing particularly strong growth. A number of large, multi-unit, investor-owned facilities have emerged. Several of the most successful rehabilitation chains have expanded through joint ventures with hospitals and nursing homes. At the same time, drug rehabilitation facilities run by public agencies are in crisis. Funding for public agencies has been frozen, and in some cases is being decreased, while the number of people seeking treatment in these facilities continues to increase.

Facilities for Children. Orphanages and other residential care for children is another area in which demand is skyrocketing, although very few of these facilities are run for profit. The main reason for the increase in this type of facility is the lack of space in foster homes. In 2000, an estimated 520,000 children were in foster care, 117,000 of whom were eligible for adoption. That year, there were about 1,000 group homes for children in operation. The AIDS epidemic has created a special need for abandoned children who have AIDS or HIV, or are born with a drug addiction. Residential care for parentless children can take a variety of forms, from the sprawling Boys Town, to home-like settings that house an average of eight children.

Facilities for the Elderly. Residential care for the elderly is an area that is expanding through the diversification of services offered. Advocacy groups estimate that as many as half of the residents in nursing homes could function adequately in facilities that placed less emphasis on medical attention. This fact, combined with the more rigid restrictions created by the National Nursing Home Reform Act of 1987 (passed to address the alarming increase in abuse cases), has led the emergence of a broad range of facilities that offer less intensive care. Residential care for the elderly is one segment of the industry in which both nonprofit and for-profit operations are well represented. As the elderly population is the fastest-growing segment of the American population, the need for residential care facilities is expected to grow. In 1997, 2,669 of these establishments generated $2 billion in revenue.

INDUSTRY LEADERS

Res-Care, Inc. is the leader among facilities that provide residential care and vocational training for mentally retarded and developmentally disabled people, as well as at-risk youths. Res-Care was founded in 1974 and is located in Louisville, Kentucky. In 1999, the organization served more than 12,000 people with developmental disabilities and 8,400 youths in 10 states and Puerto Rico. Res-Care has more than 29,000 employees.

Five Acres, The Boys' and Girls' Aid Society of Los Angeles County is a nationally recognized non-profit center for the prevention and therapeutic treatment of child abuse. It also serves as an educational facility for severely emotionally disturbed children. Founded in 1888 as one of Los Angeles' earliest orphanages, the Altadena, California-based agency served 1,037 children and 713 adults in 1999. Its services include residential treatment, a therapeutic school, emergency shelter, family group homes, a foster care program, in-home treatment and support for families in crisis, and deaf services programs for abused children. Their residential treatment program provides care and treatment for children ages 5 to 13 who have been removed from their homes by the courts because of severe behavior and emotional problems associated with abuse and neglect.

Sunrise Assisted Living, Inc., with 1999 sales of $255.2 million, was also a leading provider of assisted living for the elderly. Sunrise, founded in 1981, is a privately owned company that operates more than 120 projects in 22 states. Most of the residents in these facilities live in independent apartments where fewer services are available.

WORKFORCE

According to the U.S. Census Bureau there were more than 240,732 employees working for this industry in 1997. Approximately one-fourth of all residential care workers are employed by state and local governments, mostly in public welfare agencies and facilities for mentally disabled and developmentally delayed individuals. Another fourth work in private social or human services agencies offering a variety of services, including adult day-care, crisis intervention, counseling, and group meals. Many of these workers supervise residents of group homes and halfway houses. Others are employed in day treatment programs, detoxification units, community mental health centers, psychiatric hospitals, and sheltered workshops.

In the mid-1990s, starting salaries for residential care workers ranged from about $13,000 to $20,000 a year. Experienced workers generally earned between $18,000 and $27,000 annually.

Jobs in this industry are expected to increase significantly through the year 2005. More community-based programs, supported independent living sites, and group residences are expected to be established to shelter and assist the homeless and the chronically mentally ill, as well as provide housing and services for the elderly, disabled, and families and children in crisis.

FURTHER READING

Caywood, Hershel. ''Welcome to Nursing Home & Long Term Care Topics.'' Available from http://www.geocites.com.

Five Acres, The Boys' and Girls' Aid Society of Los Angeles County Homepage, 20 March 2000. Available from http://www.5acres.org/.

Guide to Retirement Living Online Homepage. Available from http://www.retirementliving.com/main.html.

National Adoption Information Clearinghouse. ''Adoption from Foster Care,'' 5 May 2000. Available from http://www.calib.com/naic/.

U.S. Census Bureau. *1997 Economic Census—Health Care and Social Assistance.* Washington, DC: GPO, 2000.

U.S. Department of Labor, Bureau of Labor Statistics. *Occupational Outlook Quarterly,* Spring 1996.

U.S. Department of Labor. Available from http://stats.bls.gov/ocooco2003.htm.

SIC 8399

SOCIAL SERVICES, NOT ELSEWHERE CLASSIFIED

This industry consists of establishments primarily engaged in providing social services, not elsewhere classified. This classification includes advocacy groups, anti-poverty boards, community action and development groups, councils for social agencies, fund-raising organizations (except on a fee basis), health and welfare councils, regional planning organizations, social change associations, and social service information exchanges (such as information on alcoholism or drug addiction). This industry does not include foundations and philanthropic trusts classified in **SIC 6732: Educational, Religious, and Charitable Trusts**; civic, social, and fraternal organizations classified in **SIC 8641: Civic, Social, and Fraternal Organizations**; political organizations classified in **SIC 8651: Political Organizations**; or companies that raise money on a fee or contract basis for organizations classified in **SIC 7389: Business Services, Not Elsewhere Classified.**

NAICS Code(s)

813212 (Voluntary Health Organizations)
813219 (Other Grantmaking and Giving Services)
813311 (Human Rights Organizations)
813312 (Environment Conservation and Wildlife Organizations)
813319 (Other Social Advocacy Organizations)

Industry Snapshot

There were an estimated 19,600 establishments in the social services industry in 1996—an increase of more than 47 percent from 1987. The majority of establishments were in New York and California. Industry employment increased by about 38 percent since 1987, reaching approximately 39,000 individuals by 1996. By January 2000, the entire social services industry employed 2,872,000. Tremendous growth was expected in the industry, with personal and home care aides and human services workers expected to increase 155 percent and 104 percent, respectively, by the year 2005.

Organization and Structure

The social service organizations within this industry consist of national organizations, state and regional associations, federal government agencies, state government agencies, and clearinghouses and information centers. National organizations include voluntary associations, advocacy groups, professional organizations, and other nonprofit groups providing services at the national level. State and regional associations are generally affiliates of national groups. State and federal government agencies are government owned and operated but often influence nongovernment organizations. Clearinghouses and information centers are a grouping of governmental and non-governmental services that collect, organize, and distribute information.

Organizations within this industry operate in many ways. For example, some establishments rely on fund-raising efforts, while others use membership dues as their primary means of support. Certain organizations conduct political lobbying on behalf of the social cause they represent.

A distinguishing factor of establishments in this industry is their use of money. Donations to establishments that primarily engage in charitable, educational, or research activities are tax-deductible to the donor. Establishments that conduct substantial lobbying activities, however, cannot receive tax-deductible donations. In addition, money collected for political election campaigns must be strictly accounted for and are heavily regulated by government bodies, such as the Federal Elections Commission.

Establishments in this industry are structured according to the types of activities they engage in, which are usually related to the services they provide. They are often referred to as social movements, improvement associations, pressure groups, citizen participation groups, or citizen action groups.

Social movements are groups that advocate changes in beliefs or practices of people within a relatively large geographical area. These establishments focus on increasing their membership and are usually managed by a paid professional staff. In addition, some social movement organizations lobby legislators, hold rallies, and promote their views through media-related activities.

Improvement associations advocate a belief or practice and foster it among their members to promote a better state of affairs within society as a whole or to improve conditions within their professions, religions, or patriotic societies. The larger organizations have paid staff, with a central office and branches throughout the country.

Pressure groups are organizations whose main feature is their advocacy of specific-issue legislative actions. On average, they are smaller than other groups working for social change. These establishments may be sponsored by companies whose products or political ideologies are under attack. These groups are often designed to conduct political lobbying activities and fund-raising for political candidates.

Citizen participation groups basically serve as advisory committees to community councils, charitable boards, and government agencies. Their staffs are made of a small group of professionals hired to run the administrative functions, as well as uncompensated members who act as advisors.

Citizen action associations (CAAs) are organized to protect and represent the rights of the community, particularly those with low-income and welfare recipients, protecting them in matters such as housing costs and conditions and unfair business practices. These non-profit groups were created in 1964 by the Economic Opportunity Act of 1964, and are managed by a small group of professional organizers who manage volunteers. As of 2000, there were almost 1,000 CAAs nationwide.

The primary source of money for CAAs comes from the Community Services Block Grant (CSBG), according to the National Association of Community Action Agencies. This block grant totals less than 10 percent of CAA funding.

BACKGROUND AND DEVELOPMENT

Social action organizations began in Victorian England when societies formed in the upper classes to give charity to people working in work houses and serving sentences in prisons. The idea soon caught on in the United States, and by the turn of the century philanthropy had developed into an industry. Social action organizations in America emerged with labor groups organizing to represent workers. At the same time, immigrant communities and new urban neighborhoods were developing groups and committees. These early groups were concerned with workers' rights and retaining a village life in newly developing cities. During the 1920s, local and community organizing expanded into social planning and fund-raising to support social agencies.

During the Great Depression, social agencies and community organizing took on new characteristics. Labor organizations became distinct political entities that elected their officers and organizers. Volunteer reform organizations worked toward getting citizen participation on issues such as women's rights. Rather than acting as organizers, social workers were working more within and through various government agencies, providing services for the public.

INDUSTRY LEADERS

Anti-poverty organizations seek to reduce poverty and hunger in the United States and other countries. They include organizations such as the Food and Agriculture Organization (FAO), created by the United Nations to help alleviate poverty and hunger by promoting agricultural development, improved nutrition, and food security; the Institute for Research on Poverty (IRP), established in 1966 at the University of Wisconsin-Madison by the U.S. Office of Economic Opportunity as a national center created to seek ways to reduce poverty in America; and the Food Industry Crusade Against Hunger (FICAH), a voluntary initiative of the American Food Industry to relieve hunger and malnutrition in the United States and around the world. There are hundreds of other anti-poverty organizations to help the poor and hungry.

Advocacy groups represent and defend the rights of others, particularly, but not limited to, those who do not have a voice to protect themselves, such as children, the sick, the disabled, the elderly, and animals. Organizations that fall into this enormous group include Children's Protection and Advocacy Coalition, the Center for Patient Advocacy, the National Alliance for Research on Schizophrenia and Depression, the 60 Plus Association, and the United States Humane Society. Several advocacy groups support issues such as education, the arts, homosexuality, abortion (both pro-life and pro-choice), and political matters.

High-profile associations that can be considered social change organizations include Mothers Against Drunk Driving (MADD), the National Organization for Women (NOW), and the National Gay and Lesbian Task Force.

Social service information exchanges provide the public with information on a specific topic of interest. These exchanges include the Community Information Exchange, a national nonprofit information service that provides community organizations with the information needed to successfully revitalize communities; and The Adoption Information Exchange, a Washington state nonprofit volunteer organization dedicated to making adoption information available to the public.

Welfare councils are designed to support and improve human rights. Health councils promote health issues. Many local and regional communities have their own health councils to improve the way health care services are delivered, paid for, and used; to address health issues; to promote disease prevention; and support health care industry workers. The National Safety Council is a major, nonprofit public service organization whose mission is to educate and persuade society concerning safety, health and environmental policies, and practices and procedures that prevent human suffering and economic loss.

An example of a community action group is Classical Action, an organization that uses the talents and resources of the performing arts community to raise money for AIDS-related services across the United States. A large community action group is the National Association of Community Action Agencies, a national forum for policy on poverty. Community action groups can consist of people of any age. The Youth Action Groups are comprised of young people who are supported by police, teachers, and youth workers to find solutions to community crime.

Citizen action groups are organized to protect and represent the rights of the community. The Association of Community Organizations for Reform Now (ACORN) is the nation's largest grassroots organization, acting to empower people earning low to moderate incomes. Its major concerns include housing, jobs, living wages, and banking. Citizen Action is a national federation of state citizen organizations with a combined membership of more than 2.5 million members. Citizen Action is a leading advocate for health care reform, environmental clean up, and campaign finance reform. Its state organizations consist of a coalition of community members organized in grassroots efforts to fight unfair business practices, such as high utility rates.

RESEARCH AND TECHNOLOGY

Generally, this industry has not been greatly affected by technological advances. However, computers have aided many of the office functions common to organizations in this industry, such as compiling membership databases, desktop publishing of newsletters and solicitation materials, and distributing clearinghouse mailings. In addition, technological developments in telemarketing have increased the effectiveness of calling campaigns used by lobbying groups and fund-raisers. The effect of the Internet has been felt by the industry as well. The Internet makes it far easier for organizations to disseminate information to donors, members, and the general public quickly and inexpensively. For the price of web development software or a web designer, an Internet connection, and someone to keep the site current, organizations can keep the public informed for sometimes less than the usual outreach expenses.

Further Reading

Adoption Information Exchange Homepage. Available from http://www.halcyon.com/adoption/exchange.html.

Association of Community Organizations for Reform Now Homepage, 10 March 2000. Available from http://www.igc.apc.org/community.

Classical Action Homepage, 10 March 2000. Available from http://www.classicalaction.org.

Community Information Exchange Homepage, 10 March 2000. Available from http://neighborlink.cc.duq.edu/cie/index.htm.

Food and Agriculture Organization Homepage, 10 March 2000. Available from http://www.fao.org.

Food Industry Crusade Against Hunger Homepage. Available from http://www.sugarplums.com/organizations/ficah/info.html.

Institute for Research on Poverty Homepage. Available from http://www.ssc.wisc.edu/irp.

National Association of Community Action Agencies Homepage, 10 March 2000. Available from http://www.nacaa.org.

National Safety Council Homepage, 10 March 2000. Available from http://www.nsc.org/nsc.

Social Services, SIC = 83: Total Employment, SA. Available from http://www.economagic.com/em-cgi/data.exe/blsee/ees80830001.

SIC 8412

MUSEUMS AND ART GALLERIES

This industry classification includes establishments primarily engaged in the operation of museums and art galleries. Art galleries and dealers primarily engaged in selling to the general public are classified in **SIC 5932: Used Merchandise Stores** and **SIC 5999: Miscellaneous Retail Stores, Not Elsewhere Classified.**

NAICS Code(s)

712110 (Museums)

712120 (Historical Sites)

Industry Snapshot

The numerous U.S. museums seem as permanent and stable a part of the cultural landscape as schools and libraries, but it was not until the late nineteenth century that they attained social respectability and civic solidity. Museums had existed since the founding of the country, but they were often small collections of odd paraphernalia, housed in someone's home or carted around by circus masters such as P.T. Barnum. But American museums grew as the country grew and, according to *Public Interest* contributor Michael Lind, ''The acquisition of an art museum by a city . . . has traditionally been a source of civic pride in communities across the country.''

Supported by government funding and private donations, twentieth-century museums became elaborate storehouses of America's and the world's artistic, scientific, historical, and technological past. In the process they became very big business, attracting more than 500 million visitors a year and employing more than 125,000 staff persons in the late 1990s. Contemporary museums are supported by billions of dollars of annual support from government sponsorship, corporate donations, and public membership, and they employ and educate a wide range of professionals.

In 1997, the U.S. Census Bureau reported that 3,434 museums were in the United States, as well as 814 historical sites. The establishments employed 60,122 and 6,757 people, respectively.

Organization and Structure

The museum world is fragmented and hard to summarize. The most recent comprehensive study is the 1989 National Museum Survey conducted by the American Association of Museums (AAM), the findings of which were presented in the 1994 report *Museums Count.* This survey, using information from fiscal 1988, counted 8,179 museums in the United States. About three-quarters of them have been founded since 1950 and less than 5 percent have origins in the nineteenth century. The AAM survey categorized American museums as follows—history museums (2,401); historic sites (2,083); art museums (1,214); general museums, or those in which two or more disciplines are equally represented (704); specialized museums, or those with a single distinct subject or for which no other category is appropriate (470); arboretum/botanical gardens (318); nature centers (297); natural history/anthropology museums (252); science museums (184); zoos (133); children's museums (64); planetariums (39); and aquariums (20). These institutions are distributed throughout the United States in roughly the same proportion as the population.

Fifty-nine percent of museums are privately run and 41 percent are run by the government, usually state or municipal authorities. Only 7 percent of the nation's museums are operated by the federal government. Government-run museums are most commonly found in southern and western states (slightly more than half of museums in these regions are public) and are least commonly found in the northeastern states (only about 27 percent of museums in the New England and Mid-Atlantic regions are public).

Museum budgets total some $4 billion, but this money is not evenly dispersed. Just eight 8 percent of museums have annual budgets of $1 million or more. Fifty-seven percent operate with $100,000 or less, and 38 percent have $50,000 or less to spend. Using budget size as an indicator, museums in the United States are generally small institutions. When budget size is adjusted to the differing operation costs of museum types (for example, a science museum needs a $5-million budget to be considered large, but a nature center requires only $800,000), 80 percent of museums can be described as small. About one-half of museums have endowment funds, with total museum endowments being valued at $14 billion. However, 93 percent of this endowment money is held by large museums, especially art museums which hold $10.6 billion, or 76 percent, of all endowment money. Personnel expenses account for the largest share of museum operating expenses, taking up a median of 54 percent of museum budgets. Despite this large investment in personnel, museums are still heavily dependent on volunteer staff to accomplish both day to day tasks and special functions. About 377,000 people were museum volunteers in 1988, with 10 percent of them working full-time schedules of 35 hours or more per week.

In addition to serving as conservators of the nation's cultural and scientific heritage, American museums have a strong commitment to education. Sherman Lee, former director of the Cleveland Museum of Art in Ohio, claimed in *Past, Present, East and West* that "in the world of visual images . . . the museum is the primary source for education. Merely by existing—preserving and exhibiting works of art—it is educational in the broadest and best sense, though it never utters a sound or prints a word."

Most museums provide educational programs for children as well as for adults, including guided tours, study groups, special lectures, and demonstrations. Forty-nine million children attended a museum as part of a school group in 1988. Historic sites, history museums, and zoos were the most likely choice for school groups. Many museums have joint programs with universities or colleges to provide work experience and research opportunities for college students. The American Association of Museums (AAM), a national membership organization representing all types of museums and museum professionals, provides an ongoing series of educational programs and seminars to ensure that museum professionals are as well educated as their visitors. Their 1991 publication, *Excellence and Equity: Education and the Public Dimension of Museums,* addressed the need for museums to continue their efforts at educating the museum-going public.

According to the AAM survey, 60 percent of museums are open to the public 52 weeks per year. Weekly operating schedules vary, with arboretums and botanical gardens tending to have the longest hours, and art museums and children's museums having the shortest. As is the case with funding dollars, attendance at museums is not evenly shared by institutions. Large museums, although they make up only 7 percent of museums, attract nearly 50 percent of all people who visit museums. Historic sites, zoos, and art museums are the types of museums most popular with the general public.

Museum attendance has increased in recent years. A 1979 survey by the AAM counted about 350 million museum visits. By the time of the 1989 Survey, that figure was up to 566 million visits. A study by the National Endowment for the Arts (NEA), which tracked participation in the arts between 1982 and 1992, concurs with the findings of the AAM survey. The NEA study, published in 1996, showed that younger Americans (those born in 1946 or after) attend art museums significantly more often than older people did when they were the same age. People born between 1951-55 and 1966-70 were the most likely to attend an art museum.

Increased attendance at art museums counters a general decline in arts participation among younger people, which was revealed in the NEA survey. Credit is given to art museums for doing a better job than other arts organizations in attracting new patrons. Some analysts, however, suspect that rising attendance at art museums is reflective of the decreasing interest in the arts rather than a refutation of it. "Unlike the performing arts, museum visits are an impulse buy. You don't need reservations, tickets, allocated time. You can look at what you like, or not look at anything at all. Increased museum attendance doesn't really tell us much about commitment to the fine arts," said Richard A. Peterson, one of the authors of the NEA report, to the *New York Times.*

In recent decades, many museums have greatly expanded their restaurants, gift shops, and parking facilities. Museums have also done much to shed their staid and elitist image, especially art museums, some of which are among the nation's oldest and most prestigious cultural institutions. In the late 1960s, it was considered a daring innovation for New York City's Metropolitan Museum of Art to hang a banner outside its door advertising its "Great Age of Frescoes" exhibit. The 1970s saw the advent of the ''blockbuster'' art museum show. The blockbuster exhibition, wrote Michael Conforti in *Art in America,* was created by Metropolitan Museum of Art director Thomas Hoving in 1971. ''Museums all over the country quickly adopted the formula established at the Met for self-supported exhibitions of popular and usually artistically credible subjects like impressionism, certain archeological objects, or treasures from foreign collections. Museums expected to fund these shows through revenues from admissions, merchandise, food, and also through grants from corporations and foundations seeking more positive public images.''

BACKGROUND AND DEVELOPMENT

Museums of one sort or another have played a part in the United States from the country's inception, and they have reflected the cultural variety and democratic tendencies of the country's diverse population. European collectors had always cultivated collections of artistic and historical importance, but their collections were reserved for their own personal enjoyment. In the United States, similar collections were made available to the public as early as 1773, when the Charleston Library Association in South Carolina announced the establishment of a museum to house specimens that would allow citizens to study the natural history of their colony. In 1785 a similar desire to make educational materials available to the public prompted artist and American Revolution officer Charles Willson Peale to display his collection of art and natural history specimens from his Philadelphia home. Within a decade his collection had grown so large and his visitors so numerous that the collection was moved to the larger quarters in Philadelphia's Philosophical Hall. Peale's example was soon followed in cities throughout the growing nation with the establishment of the Tammany Society Museum of Indian Relics in New York City, the Columbian Institute for the Promotion of Arts and Sciences in Washington, D.C., and the Columbian Museum in Boston, Massachusetts.

In the eighteenth and nineteenth centuries, many Americans eager to construct for themselves a sense of national identity found scientific, historical, and artistic value in nearly all aspects of their lives. Museums sprang up across America, housing collections of everything from Indian artifacts, stuffed animals, wax figures, and later, automobiles, airplanes, and art. Karl E. Meyer, author of *The Art Museum: Power, Money, Ethics,* noted that by the mid-nineteenth century there were two kinds of museums: ''One was the 'dime' museum, an emporium of curiosities operated for profit and dedicated to entertainment. The other was the impecunious but high-minded public gallery, usually an appendage of an art academy, library, historical society, college, or private club.'' Out of a combination of these two early progenitors, the modern museum was born.

In 1835 the U.S. government learned that it was the beneficiary of the will of British scientist James Smithson, who left slightly more than $508,000 to found ''the Smithsonian Institution, an Establishment for the increase and diffusion of knowledge among men.'' According to Paul H. Oehser's history, *The Smithsonian Institution,* the U.S. government hardly knew where to begin. By 1846, however, Senator John Quincy Adams had introduced legislation calling for the construction of a national museum in Washington, D.C., which would house all the objects of art and natural history belonging to the government, maintain a library, and encourage the study of science. By the mid-twentieth century, the Smithsonian Institution, with its numerous buildings spread across Washington's mall, and with additional sites at other locations, had become the largest museum in the world. By 1996 it boasted more than 25 million visitors annually.

In 1870 corporate lawyer Joseph H. Choate convinced the city of New York to finance the construction and operation of the Metropolitan Museum of Art, which was to be governed by a board of 21 private members and civic office-holding trustees, including the mayor. The museum charter, with its unique pairing of public funding and private control, became the model for most large U.S. museums that followed. Such an organization provided unique advantages to both the city and to the wealthy Americans who sat on the museum board. The greatest benefit for the city was the status that a world-class art museum conferred: New York City's cosmopolitan reputation rested in part on its museums, and even smaller cities could brag of the sophistication of their own local arts showcases. Museums bring money and people into the cities and often serve as a focal point for other cultural activities. According to former Smithsonian Secretary Dillon Ripley in *The Sacred Grove,* ''The art museum managed . . . to become a symbol of the community's rise to prominence and sophistication.''

Wealthy arts patrons and businessmen were equally enthusiastic about the new American institutions, which served as a culturally sanctioned storehouse for the surplus wealth of the country's industrial leaders. ''Of all the uses to which wealth can be put,'' wrote Lind, ''surely there are few that are less antisocial than endowing a public museum.'' America's first art museums were filled with the art collected by America's first multi-millionaires: J. Pierpont Morgan left his $60 million art collection to the Metropolitan Museum of Art in New York City; the Rockefeller family made cultural philanthropy a family tradition, and museums across the nation became the beneficiaries of private collectors. Changes in the U.S. tax structure in 1909 and 1913 made donations of art an appealing way for the wealthy to avoid paying taxes on their assets and to mollify critics who accused corporate giants of benefiting at the expense of society at large.

CURRENT CONDITIONS

Heavily advertised and often so expensive to mount that relatively small profits are common, blockbuster shows (such as those exhibiting Picasso, Van Gogh, Hopper, and Monet) draw in segments of the public who might rarely enter a museum otherwise. They can also raise a museum's status within the art world. Such shows are, in addition to being crowd pleasers, are considered valid, scholarly endeavors. One attraction expected to attract an enormous crowd, opening at Chicago's Field Museum in the summer of 2000, is the exhibit of ''Sue,'' the largest complete Tyrannosaurus Rex skeleton.

Although officially classified as privately or publicly funded, in reality most museums rely on a patchwork of funding sources, including government and corporate grants, private donations, interest from endowments, and earned income, such as admission fees, memberships, and revenues from food service and gift shops. The number of museums charging admission, either a fixed fee or a suggested donation at the door, went up from 32 percent in 1979 to 55 percent in 1988. Zoos are the most likely type of museum to charge admission (84.8 percent), and art museums the least likely (35.8 percent). Many museums in the late 1990s had moved to a ''suggested donation'' instead of admission.

Even well-endowed institutions are always in need of financial assistance. Museums have been hard hit by cut backs in government spending. The budget of the NEA, the largest source of government funds, was slashed by 40 percent in fiscal 1996. Private philanthropy is also down. To make up for this loss, museums have sought new ways of raising money. ''With less government money around, we all have to be more entrepreneurial and figure out ways to stretch our advertising dollars. We are slowly learning lessons others have known for years,'' David A. Ross, director of New York City's Whitney Museum of American Art, told the *New York Times.*

Museums have entered into alliances with hotels, airlines, phone card companies, and credit card operations. Corporations, which once considered underwriting museum activities as primarily a gesture of goodwill, are increasingly finding their connections with museums an effective form of advertising. Also, branches of museum gift shops have opened up in many malls across the United States, with a portion of the proceeds going to the museums. On a larger scale, the cable television shopping channel QVC began a series of museum programs in 1996. In addition to being able to purchase items from the featured museum's gift shop, QVC viewers were taken on a tour of the museum's exhibits. Among the museums showcased on QVC were the Smithsonian Institution, the Philadelphia Museum of Art, Colonial Williamsburg, and the Winterthur Museum of American Decorative Arts.

FURTHER READING

American Association of Museums. *Museums Count.* Washington, D.C.: American Association of Museums, 1994.

Levere, Jane L. ''Museums and QVC Find They Can Do Business Together By Going Beyond Typical Art Crowd.'' *New York Times,* 15 August 1996.

Miller, Judith. ''As Patrons Age, Future of Arts Is Uncertain.'' *New York Times,* 12 February 1996.

Vogel, Carol. ''Hustling High Culture with Fliers and Freebies.'' *New York Times,* 20 June 1996.

U.S. Department of Commerce. Economics and Statistics Administration. *1997 Economic Census-Arts, Entertainment, and Recreation.* Washington, D.C.: U.S. Census Bureau, November 1999.

SIC 8422

ARBORETA AND BOTANICAL OR ZOOLOGICAL GARDENS

This industry covers establishments primarily engaged in operating arboreta, botanical gardens, zoological gardens, and/or zoological exhibits.

NAICS CODE(S)

712130 (Zoos and Botanical Gardens)
712190 (Nature Parks and Other Similar Institutions)

INDUSTRY SNAPSHOT

In 1997, there were roughly 300 zoos and botanical gardens and aquariums and 276 nature parks in the United States. According to the American Zoo and Aquarium Association, such wildlife facilities in North America were visited by more than 130 million people in 1998. The growth and stability of this industry depends largely on the government's surplus funds and on the ability of U.S. families to afford attendance; this industry is closely linked to family entertainment and tourism. Helped in part by both the increase in the population and in leisure time since the start of the twentieth century, the number of establishments in this industry has increased by ten percent every five years.

ORGANIZATION AND STRUCTURE

This industry is organized according to the ownership and management of its establishments. There are five types of establishments: those owned and managed by the government (usually city and community); those owned by the government but managed by a nonprofit society; those owned by the government but jointly managed with a nonprofit society; those owned and managed by a nonprofit society; and those that are privately owned by corporations and individuals. In 1995, roughly 50 percent of the establishments in this industry were owned and managed by the government; nearly 25 percent were owned privately by nonprofit societies; and 25 percent were owned privately by individuals or corporations.

Internal management at these establishments was once loosely structured, often combining volunteers with city and privately hired employees. But during the early 1990s, the various types of owners developed new, more business-like, management styles to meet the competitive market. The San Diego Zoo, for example, went from managing 50 departments—such as animal keeping and maintenance—to managing diversified teams that claimed responsibility for one particular section of the zoo. Zoos have also modified their focus from merely allowing visitors to view animals to providing educational and hands-on opportunities.

Zoos constantly work to have more exciting, more natural habitat-like exhibits as well. Additionally, many zoos are heavily involved with the Species Survival Plan (SSP) program sponsored by the American Zoo and Aquarium Association (AZA).

The industry is served by many associations, including the AZA; the American Association of Zoo Keepers; the Consortium of Aquariums, Universities, and Zoos; and the California Association of Zoos and Aquariums (CAZA). These organizations reflect well on the industry. AZA reports that in the mid-1990s, its members supported more than 1,200 conservation efforts in approximately 60 countries. CAZA reports that its member zoos and aquariums receive more than 20 million visitors each year and contribute more than $1.8 billion (combined) to the state's economy each year.

Background and Development

The concept of the public zoo began in the mid-1800s. Prior to that time, zoos were the private property—and signal of power—of kings and queens. But with the growth of cities and the subsequent increase in the population's leisure time, zoos provided urban dwellers the opportunity to be closer to nature and wildlife and also served as a form of entertainment. Nearly the same can be said for botanical gardens and arboreta, but their origins as public facilities date back to Renaissance Europe. At this time, sculptured gardens were adopted as public art for the middle classes in Italy and later in England.

The first zoo in the United States was opened in 1876 by the Philadelphia Zoological Society as part of America's centennial exposition. Other major U.S. zoos also had their origins in international expositions, which often included animal exhibits from overseas. Zoos in the United States experienced considerable growth and restoration during the 1930s. Public works projects allowed new exhibits and landscaping grounds for zoos to be built. It was also during the 1930s that American zoos developed children's zoos, where children could learn about small animals through direct contact, such as petting, holding, and feeding the animals. These so-called petting zoos are now a standard feature at wildlife facilities around the world.

During the 1980s, the increase in attendance at U.S. zoos and botanical gardens was dramatic. The major wildlife facilities in the United States and Canada reported a 20 percent rise in attendance between 1980 and 1987. This increase beyond expected growth has been explained by three factors: baby-boom parents brought their children to facilities for educational reasons; establishments spent millions of dollars during the late 1970s and early 1980s upgrading their facilities (often as part of urban renewal projects); and the growth in city and suburban populations meant more attendance at local facilities.

Marketing. With increased competition within the arboreta and botanical or zoological gardens, establishments have become more involved in advertising their facilities. Each kind of facility has a different type of market. Zoos and botanical gardens are generally visited by local residents, while aquariums (which are more rare) are visited most often by tourists. Traditionally, marketing in this industry was low key. Zoological societies appealed to a small number of potential donors, and government zoos relied on a predictable portion of the government budget. However, the growth of U.S. cities limited city budgets, and an increase in competition from theme parks and other forms of family entertainment made these establishments invest considerably more in marketing starting in the late 1970s. Zoos saw their attendance increase with the birth of a new animal or the acquisition of certain endangered species. Promoting these events became an essential part of the marketing package for zoos and aquariums. In 1995, for example, the San Diego Zoo spent roughly $1.5 million on advertising annually.

Aquariums in the United States have advertised with the help of retail stores. Aquariums played an important part in the redevelopment of many of America's urban waterfronts where they have been placed near shopping districts and malls. In addition, these aquariums, even if privately owned, often received funding from the local governments. One of the largest aquariums in the United States, Monterey Bay National Marine Sanctuary, was built from a renovation of a sardine cannery. Zoos and aquariums have also attempted to increase their market share by expanding their facilities to include theme parks with rides and activities, such as video programs and birthday parties for the animals.

Current Conditions

Establishments in this industry experienced strong growth in the 1980s. Aquariums and zoo-aquariums did particularly well in attendance; according to *American Demographics,* these establishments represented more than 50 percent of all growth in this industry during the 1980s, and between 1980 and 1987 aquarium attendance increased by 50 percent and zoo-aquarium attendance by 80 percent. However, in the 1990s attendance seems to have leveled off, while still maintaining the growth of the 1980s.

Additionally, upon entering the late 1990s, the U.S. zoos, aquariums, and botanical gardens faced new financial problems as a result of less government funding and an increase in competition from theme parks and newly built aquariums. These concerns have been addressed with an increased emphasis on fund-raising campaigns and continued marketing for sales revenues. In 1997 expenses for zoos were $1.1 billion, while revenues were only $127.9 million. Nature parks had revenues of $129.4 million and expenses of only $107.5 million.

WORKFORCE

In 1997 there were approximately 15,727 workers in this industry. Of the total number of workers in this industry, slightly more than 3 percent were animal caretakers and nearly 4 percent were gardeners. Some of the larger portions of this workforce included guards (nearly 9 percent of the total workers), cashiers (more than 8 percent), curators and restorers (more than 7 percent), marketing and sales personnel (roughly 5 percent), instructors (more than 5 percent) and administrators and office workers (10 percent). The remaining employees were maintenance and food service workers.

Animal caretakers include the occupations of zoo caretaker and zoo veterinarian. Zoo caretakers feed, water, and clean the quarters of animals and birds; they also work closely with zoo veterinarians on the diets and medications for animals. Zoo veterinarians direct and carry out the health service program at a zoo. Their responsibilities include testing all incoming animals for the prevention of diseases, providing the needed medical attention for animals, and conducting reproduction programs for endangered species.

Gardeners include horticulturists, herbarium workers, and garden workers. Horticulturists determine methods for breeding, storing, and transporting plants (including flowers and vegetables) and trees. These specialists are also responsible for the techniques used in spraying, planting, and cultivating plants and trees. Herbarium workers maintain the records of botanical gardens and arboreta by pressing and mounting plant specimens, which are then kept on card files for loans and exchanges with other establishments. Garden workers cultivate and care for floral and ornamental plant arrangements; their duties include fertilizing, watering, and transplanting flowers and plants in greenhouses and outdoor growing areas.

Job prospects predicted to grow in this industry were mainly in the area of marketing research and development and in fund raising. In related industries, engineers and architects will be needed for the building of new establishments.

AMERICA AND THE WORLD

Worldwide, there are roughly 1,500 botanical gardens and arboreta and more than 3,000 zoos and aquariums. In general, the United States has fewer gardens and arboreta and more zoos and aquariums per capita than countries overseas. The royal places of Europe and the less extreme weather have kept botanical gardens an important part of the European tourism industry. As for zoos and aquariums, the general discrepancies between the United States and other countries can be explained to a large extent by the availability of open spaces in U.S. cities and the availability of larger funds through the family entertainment industry (often working with zoo and aquarium operators to create theme parks).

In 1993, the famous London Zoo closed; its attendance had dropped from three million to slightly more than one million between 1950 and 1990. During the 1980s, the zoo experienced a financial crisis due to a lack of government funded projects and the public's decreasing interest in zoos. (The British public, including its many animal rights groups, have come to prefer safari parks, where the animals roam around freely.) The London Zoo, unlike many U.S. zoos, had not adapted to animal conservationists' concerns for animals to be kept in more natural habitats.

RESEARCH AND TECHNOLOGY

Research in this industry includes the development of environmentally safe sprays and chemicals used in the soil at botanical gardens and arboreta. Aquariums are witnessing technological advances in the construction of their tanks, addressing such problems as materials resistant to salt water damage. Zoos have been investigating ways of making zoo environments more like natural habitats without posing dangers to the public. In addition, zoos are continually improving their care of animals with advances in veterinary medicine.

FURTHER READING

The American Zoo and Aquarium Association, 1999. Available from http://www.aza.org.

Callaghan, Will. "Sea Change." *RIBA,* July 1996.

Crispell, Diane. "Lleapin' Llamas." *American Demographics,* December 1996.

Dickinson, Rachel, and Brad Edmondson. "Golden Wings." *American Demographics,* December 1996.

"Private Caretakers Help Aging Zoo Turn Around." *American City & Country,* April 1996.

U.S. Department of Commerce. Economics and Statistics Administration. *1997 Economic Census-Arts, Entertainment, and Recreation.* Washington, D.C.: U.S. Census Bureau, November 1999.

SIC 8611

BUSINESS ASSOCIATIONS

This industry classification includes membership organizations engaged in promoting the business interests of their members. Associations owned by their members but organized to perform a specific business function, such as common marketing of crops or joint advertising, are classified according to the function performed.

NAICS Code(s)

813910 (Business Associations)

Industry Snapshot

In the mid-1990s, approximately 100,000 business associations operated at local, state, regional, and national levels in the United States, posting over a 40 percent increase since the 1980s. Associations annually contribute over $48 billion to the U.S. economy, provide nearly 500,000 jobs, and annually spend $30 billion to host meetings and conventions. According to an American Association of Retired Persons' (AARP) study in 1998, 9 out of 10 adult Americans in the United States belonged to at least one association, and one out of four belonged to four or more associations. As many as 1,000 new groups were being formed each year.

The term ''trade association'' has been broadly used to described most business associations. Trade associations are non-profit organizations representing a group of businesses within a particular segment of industry. The membership of these associations is composed primarily of individual company representatives. The oldest trade association in the United States is the New York Chamber of Commerce, which was founded in 1768. The U.S. Chamber of Commerce, headquartered in Washington, D.C. (the city with more associations than any other city), is the country's largest trade association. According to the American Society of Association Executives (ASAE), the largest national association convention in 1997 was that of the National Marine Manufacturers Association when over 170,000 members and guests attended. The Association for Manufacturing Technology was the second largest with over 100,000 attendees.

Trade association staff members perform activities that are too costly or time-consuming for an individual company to perform on its own. These activities include monitoring government regulations, conducting industry research, collecting statistical information, and producing educational programs and materials. Businesses and government depend heavily on associations for their statistical information, which is often not available elsewhere. This type of in-depth research has been spurred on by advances in computer technology, which have allowed trade associations to collect and disseminate industry information on a more timely basis and to a more targeted audience. In fact, by the late 1990s, the implementation of database programs and integrated systems became a necessity for all trade associations. Associations also publish newsletters, periodicals, and directories.

Associations rank as a major segment of the health insurance market and are the source of health insurance for more than 8 million people. They are also the originating source for codes of ethics and professional and safety standards, which govern such professions as law, medicine, banking, and manufacturing.

Organization and Structure

The following organizations are included under the classification of business associations: boards of trade, other than security and commodity exchanges; business associations, other than civic and social; chambers of commerce; contractors associations; growers associations, not engaged in contract buying or selling; growers marketing advisory services; industrial standards committees; junior chambers of commerce; manufacturers institutes; merchants associations, not engaged in credit investigations; public utility associations; real estate boards; shipping and steamboat company associations; and trade associations.

Business or trade associations can be organized at the local, state, regional, national, or international level. Groups with similar interests also can belong to a federation or a collection of associations under centralized leadership, such as the National Retail Federation. Most business associations, depending upon the nature of their membership, fall under one of the following tax-exempt categories defined by the Internal Revenue Service (IRS): Section 501(c)(3) includes religious, charitable, scientific, public safety testing, literacy, and educational organizations; Section 501(c)(4) covers civic or social welfare organizations and local associations of employees; Section 501(c)(5) includes labor, agricultural, and horticultural groups; Section 501(c)(6) includes business leagues, chambers of commerce, real estate boards, and boards of trade.

The structure of an association depends upon the size of its membership and its budget. A large national organization may include hundreds of people on its staff. Usually a board of directors sets the policies of an association, and the executives and staff members are responsible for the implementation of these policies. Divisions within an association include the legislative staff, meeting planners, publications executives, public relations personnel, information and research executives, membership services personnel, and fundraisers.

The primary goal of all trade associations has been to improve the business of its members. In pursuit of this goal, trade associations have conducted research, set industry standards, and represented their members' interests before legislative and regulatory bodies. Trade associations also have provided information to many audiences, including the general public, association members, and government officials.

BACKGROUND AND DEVELOPMENT

The origins of modern trade associations can be traced to the Middle Ages, when laborers and merchants formed guilds to ensure proper wages and maintain work standards. Associations in the United States began to grow during the Industrial Revolution. Due to the social and economic hardships caused by the Revolutionary War, local organizations developed more quickly than national groups. The rapid industrial growth America experienced after the Civil War created numerous new trade associations and local chambers of commerce. The following prominent organizations were formed during this time period: the American Bankers Association (1878), the National Association of Life Underwriters (1890), and the National Association of Manufacturers (1890).

By 1900, 100 national associations existed in the United States, and by the end of World War I that number had reached 1,000. World War II provided an opportunity for government and trade associations to work together to help meet wartime demands. Since 1945, many associations have changed, reflecting the country's evolving work environment. Those representing declining industries or technologies often merged with other organizations, became inactive, or formally dissolved.

CURRENT CONDITIONS

Two-thirds of all associations conducted research or engaged in statistical gathering in nearly all areas of public interest, including the environment, employment, and product safety. This work enabled businesses to improve their performance by comparing output to costs.

Membership education was also a primary trade association activity. Nearly 90 percent of surveyed associations offered educational programs and services to their members. More than 71 percent also disseminated industry information to the general public. By improving members' knowledge of their particular industry, associations contributed to the elevation of product and service quality and ultimately served the public interest.

Trade associations contributed greatly to setting, certifying, and meeting product safety and quality standards. Both the American Society for Testing and Materials (ASTM), and the American National Standards Institute (ANSI) have been devoted exclusively to standards testing.

One of the most visible activities of business associations in the 1990s was their legislative or lobbying efforts. Approximately 38 percent of national associations had at least one lobbyist, and 35 percent had political action committees. Business or trade associations allocated roughly 10 percent of their total annual expenditures to political education and providing industry information to Congress regarding legislative or regulatory proposals that could affect their membership. These political activities also served to provide association members with skills necessary for further political participation at the local and national level.

Other issues relevant to trade associations included the environment, energy conservation, health care costs, shifting values and attitudes in the workplace, technological innovations, declines in quality education, and a growing global economy.

INDUSTRY LEADERS

The largest trade association in the country, the United States Chamber of Commerce, is a national federation of business organizations and companies. Founded in 1912, the U.S. Chamber of Commerce maintained its headquarters in Washington, D.C., and had a staff of 1,200 and a $70 million budget. Its membership included local chambers of commerce, trade and professional associations, and private and public companies. More than 96 percent of its members, according to the Chamber, were small businesses with 100 or fewer employees, but almost all of the largest U.S. companies were members as well.

The Chamber of Commerce represents the political interests of the U.S. business community on national issues regarding the economy. For example, in 1996, the Chamber of Commerce successfully lobbied in the House of Representatives for passage of the Working Families Flexibility Act (H.R.1), which dealt with compensatory time for workers. The Chamber also informed and trained its members to participate in policymaking at the state and local levels and in legislative and political action at the national level.

The Chamber produced *Nation's Business Today,* a daily business-oriented newscast; *Ask Washington,* a daily national television program; and *It's Your Business,* a weekly televised debate program. This business association also published an annual analysis of workers' compensation laws; the *Congressional Handbook; Nation's Business,* a magazine covering national issues that especially affect small business; and numerous newsletters.

The National Retail Federation (NRF) was formed in 1990 with the merger of the American Retail Federation and the National Retail Merchants Association. The largest retail trade association, the NRF had 55,000 corporate members, including department, chain, mass merchandise, and specialty stores that sell men's, women's, and children's apparel, and home furnishings. Also included were the 32 national and 50 state affiliated associations. The NRF conducted conferences and workshops and provided an extensive collection of manuals, bulletins, and promotional materials. This business association offered advisory services regarding all aspects of retailing, such as financial planning, shortage control, electronic data processing, telecommunications, merchandise management, traffic, security, store planning and construction, personnel administration, recruitment and training, and advertising.

The NRF published *Retail Control,* a journal providing retail management and financial information. It also produced *Stores Magazine,* a publication covering current trends, concepts, and promotional activities of the retail industry, as well as association news. The NRF maintained a 1,000-volume library on retail management and fashion merchandising. Headquartered in New York, the National Retail Federation had a staff of about 100 and held its annual meeting every January in New York City.

The National Restaurant Association (NRA) is a trade association for restaurants, cafeterias, clubs, contract foodservice management, drive-ins, caterers, institutional food services, and other members of the foodservice industry. The group's annual convention has become the largest association gathering in the United States. The NRA supported foodservice education and research in several educational institutions and conducted traveling management courses and seminars for restaurant personnel. This trade association also sponsored the Educational Foundation of the NRA, which provides training and education for food and equipment operators, manufacturers, and distributors.

The NRA published the bi-weekly *Foodservice Information Abstracts; National Restaurant Association-Washington Weekly,* a report of legislative and regulatory issues; and *Restaurants USA,* a monthly magazine covering the trends and developments in the foodservice industry. Founded in 1919, the NRA had a staff of 115, membership of 30,000, and a $16 million budget. The association's headquarters were located in Washington, D.C., with 175,000 food service group affiliations worldwide.

The National Association of Manufacturers (NAM), also headquartered in Washington, D.C., represents manufacturers and non-manufacturers and voices the industry's political views on national and international problems. Founded in 1895, this trade also maintained the NAM National Division in Maryland, a field headquarters in Chicago, and eight regional offices throughout the United States. The NAM reviews current and proposed legislation, administrative rulings and interpretations, judicial decisions, and legal matters affecting the manufacturing industry. The organization maintained numerous policy groups including Government Regulation and Competition; Industrial Relations; International Economic Affairs; Resources and Technology; and Taxation and Fiscal Policy. The NAM was affiliated with 150 local and state trade associations of manufacturers through the National Industrial Council and 110 manufacturing associations.

The Council of Better Business Bureaus (CBBB), located in Arlington, Virginia, consisted of 250,000 businesses and professional firms from all industries and 130 local Better Business Bureaus operating autonomously in the United States, Canada, and Israel. The CBBB acted as a mouthpiece for business to consumers, assisted in expanding and upgrading local bureau capabilities, helped establish voluntary self-regulation of national advertising, provided pre-purchase information to consumers, strengthened consumer education programs, and settled consumer complaints through arbitration. Although its inception dates back to the Better Business Bureau system (founded in 1912), the CBBB was created in 1970 with the merger of the National Better Business Bureau and the Association of Better Business Bureaus. In 1997 the CBBB reported net assets and total liabilities of almost $6 million.

Workforce

More than 500,000 people were employed in different associations throughout the United States. Staff size and responsibilities largely reflect the membership size and budget of each association. Employment positions within associations generally have been divided evenly between executive and staff positions. As associations continued to grow in size and strength, so did the possibilities for employment within these organizations. Because staff members are exposed to a wide variety of functions and responsibilities, association employment can offer tremendous advancement potential.

Entry-level employment at associations generally can be found in the positions of conference planning, public relations, or membership services. Most jobs required that employees have a liberal arts degree and strong interpersonal and communication skills. Additional education, such as an MBA, legal training, or fund-raising experience, was sometimes necessary for financial services or legislative positions. An association executive could be designated a Certified Association Executive (CAE) upon the successful completion of a daylong written test.

Although associations were located across the United States, many were found in metropolitan areas. Boasting 2,500 organizations, Washington, D.C., served as headquarters for more associations than any other city, with Chicago in second place, and New York in third. Many trade associations also were located in or near state capitals.

AMERICA AND THE WORLD

The exchange of technology and the ability to generate business in new markets led many trade associations to venture into the international arena by developing new kinds of relationships. For example, some associations engaged in international networking by creating an umbrella organization incorporating trade associations of various countries. Other international formats include foreign partnerships and working with U.S. embassies overseas.

Some business organizations have been developed for the sole purpose of fostering international trade relations. For example, the U.S. Chamber of Commerce was probably one of the world's largest business federations. At the close of the century its represented membership included not only domestic (U.S.) chapters, but 850 business associations and 87 American Chambers of Commerce (AmChams) abroad. In addition to promoting business interests within the United States (through the auspices of AmChams), the chamber helped its members learn about the business environment and the general culture of a particular country. Membership services included supplying tax and credit information; arranging informal gatherings for foreign executives and their American counterparts; briefing U.S. employees new to the region; and counseling relocated families about schooling, housing, and health care.

In a message prepared for the general membership of AmCham Egypt, President Mohamed Hosni Mubarak opined that the beneficial function of ''Private sector organizations like AmCham . . . (had) consistently shown that economic growth is a result of a partnership between business and government.'' Such organizations facilitated international correspondence through a range of services, such as providing access to staff members who handle international relations issues. Such individuals usually possessed specialized expertise in overcoming language barriers, finding alternative delivery systems, and forming allied private sector organizations outside the United States.

The international aspect of trade associations was expected to grow along with the continued globalization of industry, trade, and technology. Associations view internationalism as a way of thinking and doing business. Carol Kinsey Goman noted in her book *Managing in a Global Organization,* ''Markets no longer stop at national boundaries, neither do corporations. . . . For organizations to flourish, let alone survive, their perspective must be global.''

RESEARCH AND TECHNOLOGY

Effective information management has become a vital function for the successful business association and was the driving force for the computerization of their office operations. On an annual basis, associations spent millions of dollars on computer technology. The average association dedicated as much as $28,500 annually to computer hardware and/or software purchases.

Most large business associations purchased mainframe systems in the 1970s to automate their record keeping. They added personal computers during the 1980s, and by the 1990s, they had amassed a collection of computers unable to communicate or interact with one another. Therefore, many associations started using local area networks (LANs) in order to share information among their departments. According to *Association Management,* ''By distributing programs and processing power among microcomputers, or PCs, no one unit needs the kind of power provided by a mainframe. Executives on networked PCs can communicate electronically using work group software applications, such as group editing, computer conferencing, project management, document design, electronic mail, and scheduling.'' With the use of LANs, many associations have begun to operate database management systems and experiment with a variety of software packages and hardware products. Some of these items include legislative affairs and grassroots software; relational database software and text-based information retrieval programs; and bar coding and document scanners.

Many business organizations also ventured into the CD-ROM arena. For example, the American Hotel and Motel Association (AHMA) has stored volumes of information in its Hospitality Index database on CD-ROM. Time required to perform research was reduced to one-fifth the amount of time that was needed previously.

Associations also used new technologies in educational programs that aided in expanding their audience and delivered information in a timely and cost-efficient way. Communication throughout the world was made easier through the Internet using the World Wide Web and e-mail. Some technologies being used in the year 2000 included online database services for up-to-date information; satellite down-links for conferencing; video recordings for standardized training; and portable computers, or laptops, for convenience when working at home or traveling. Many associations have a Web page so that members and others can receive important information. As Renata Webb, ASAE executive, remarked, ''Ultimately, technology adds options and alternatives.''

FURTHER READING

American Chamber of Commerce in Egypt. ''AmCham Highlights,'' 2000. Available from http://www.amcham.org.eg/.

"American Society of Association Executives." Available from http://www.asaenet.org/

Arnold, Pam. "Getting Members to Go Online." *Association Management,* August 1996.

The Better Business Bureau. "About the BBB," 2000. Available from http://www.bbb.org/.

Boyers, Carla. "Reach Out and Teach Someone." *Association Management,* June 1996.

Cook, Elizabeth Graham. "Associations Can Be Catalysts for Change." *Boston Business Journal,* 18 August 1995.

NAM—National Association of Manufacturers. "About the NAM," 2000. Available from http://www.uschamber.org/.

Svevo-Cianci, Kimberly A. *Associations and the Global Marketplace.* Washington: American Society of Association Executives, 1995.

U.S. Chamber of Commerce. "About Us,". 2000. Available from http://www.uschamber.org/.

SIC 8621

PROFESSIONAL MEMBERSHIP ORGANIZATIONS

This industry covers membership organizations of professional persons for the advancement of the interests of their profession.

NAICS Code(s)

813920 (Professional Organizations)

Industry Snapshot

Professional membership organizations spent the mid- and late 1990s stepping up efforts to attract members and remain the premier catalysts for their fields. These associations remain a vital source of information for individuals practicing in those fields, as well as for related businesses that take advantage of associations for client outreach and valuable marketing information. Among the chief concerns of associations was to establish a strong presence on the Internet, which has quickly become one of the primary sources of the type of rapidly evolving information in which major associations specialize. Moreover, an Internet presence afforded associations the opportunity to greatly streamline their operation by cutting down printing and meeting costs.

In 1999 there were approximately 135,000 associations operating in the United States, up from 100,000 in 1995. Of these, 110,000 were local, state, or regional associations; 23,000 were national; and 1,300 were international. Associations annually contribute more than $48 billion to the U.S. economy, provide some 295,000 jobs, and annually spend $56 billion to host meetings and conventions. According to the American Society of Association Executives (ASAE), the national organization for association managers, 9 out of 10 adults in the United States belonged to at least one association in the mid-1990s, and one in 4 belonged to four or more associations. As many as 1,000 new associations crop up each year.

Professional membership organizations are non-profit voluntary membership associations that represent individuals with a common background in a subject or profession such as law, medicine, or accounting. Three types of professional societies exist. The first includes any group with a common personal interest such as, the International Society of Stamp Collectors. The second type is dedicated to religious, charitable, public service, or fraternal causes such, as the National Council on Aging or the American Heart Association. The third classification covers organizations dealt with in this industry classification. This category includes scientific, engineering, and learned societies whose purpose is to advance knowledge related to their respective fields. Examples include the American Chemical Society, the Society of Automotive Engineers, and the National Association of Accountants.

The main responsibilities of professional membership organizations are to provide and enforce standards of professional practice and to conduct research. These organizations generally also provide educational programs to their members, and most supply current information and research materials to their members, governmental agencies, and the public. Since dissemination of timely information has been of the utmost importance, implementation of communications technology has become critical for effective association management.

Organization and Structure

Professional membership organizations include bar associations, dental associations, engineering associations, medical associations, professional standard review boards, and scientific membership associations. The memberships of professional societies are made up of individual doctors, dentists, or scientists. Membership services generally have been designed to benefit the individual members and include continued education, accreditation programs, government relations, publishing, and research.

Professional membership organizations can be organized at the local, state, regional, national, and international levels. Sometimes an individual may be a member of an organization at several different levels. For example, a doctor may belong to the local, state, and national levels of the American Medical Association. Groups with similar interests also can belong to a federation or collection of professional membership organizations, such as the American Association for the Advancement of Science.

Most professional societies, depending upon the nature of their membership, fall under one of the following tax-exempt categories defined by the Internal Revenue Service (IRS). Classification 501(c)(3) includes religious, charitable, scientific, public safety testing, literacy, and educational organizations. Section 501(c)(4) covers civic or social welfare organizations and local associations of employees. Section 501(c)(5) includes labor, agricultural, and horticultural groups.

The structure of a professional membership organization depends upon the size of its membership and its budget. A large national organization may have hundreds of people on its staff. Usually, a board of directors sets the policies of an organization, and the executives and staff members are responsible for the implementation of these policies. Divisions within a professional society include the legislative staff, meeting planners, publications executives, public relations personnel, information and research executives, membership services personnel, and fund-raisers.

BACKGROUND AND DEVELOPMENT

The formation of professional associations in the United States began during the Industrial Revolution. However, most of these groups were trade-related, not professional societies. As the United States began to develop urban areas in the mid-1800s, many professional and educational groups were established. Some organizations, such as those representing medicine, law, and accounting, were created specifically to develop and enforce standards of practice. The following organizations are among those formed during this period: the American Medical Association, founded in 1854; the American Dental Association, established in 1859; and the American Bar Association, created in 1878.

By 1900, 100 national associations existed in the United States, and by the end of World War I, that number had reached 1,000. After World War II, many trade associations changed their focus or evolved into new organizations due to technological advances in the modern business community. However, unlike trade groups, professional membership organizations maintain many of the same responsibilities as they did when they were first founded.

CURRENT CONDITIONS

By the late 1990s, associations were increasingly mirroring the behavior of the industries they represent. As merger activity sweeps across all industries, associations from different but related industries have likewise merged in order to maintain viable and effective membership. Seeking out new strategies to provide high-quality services to their members and the public, professional membership organizations have increasingly relied on non-dues income, such as fees derived from online information provision. At the same time, however, new associations have arisen quickly to serve the interests of emerging industries, particularly those related to technology. For example, twenty-five technology companies joined forces in 1999 to establish the ASP Industry Consortium to develop and implement guidelines for software service companies. Companies involved included as AT&T Corp., International Business Machines Corp., and Compaq Computer Corp.

Professional societies conduct research, set professional standards, collect statistical information, produce educational programs, and represent their members' interest before legislative and regulatory bodies. They also provide information about their respective fields of study to many audiences, including the general public, association members, and government officials.

Perhaps the most important responsibility of professional societies has been the development and enforcement of standards of practice and safety as well as ethical codes. These organizations provide education and testing for certification, accreditation, and licensing of their membership. They also encourage the peer review process, offer courses that meet legal requirements, and issue standards that form the basis for disciplinary action. Approximately 30 percent of all professional societies set professional standards and 15 percent certify that these standards are met.

Membership education has also played a critical role in professional societies, since the public interest is served by the quality of members' service and standardized accreditation. About 95 percent of professional membership organizations offer such educational programs, leading to annual expenditures of more than $3 billion on educational programs and services, while 46 percent offer scholarships. Seventy-one percent of all associations gather statistics and conduct research. For professional societies, the duty of research has been part of their very definition and purpose of existence. Research findings set important new directions and define the scope, standards, and trends within a particular field, and are often a primary source of government research and statistical compilations. This information usually is shared through some form of print or electronic journal published by the professional society. According to survey conducted by the ASAE, 62 percent of associations publish both periodicals and non-periodical literature; among these, 33 percent publish only periodicals, 82 percent publish newsletters, and 75 percent publish magazines and scholarly or research journals.

One of the most visible activities of professional membership organizations has been legislative or lobbying efforts. Approximately 40 percent of all national associations have at least one lobbyist and one-third maintain political action committees (PACs). PACs are particularly popular among smaller organizations; 52 percent of state and regional associations have political action committees. Professional societies allocate approximately 5 percent of their total annual expenditures to providing information to Congress regarding legislative or regulatory proposals that could affect the activities of their membership.

Other issues relevant to professional societies, as shown by advertising expenditures, include environmentalism, energy conservation, and health care costs. For example, in 1999 a coalition of scientific organizations pooled their resources to launch an $8 million campaign for television, radio, and print advertisements to raise public awareness of and spark political action against global warning. Future trends likely to affect these groups include, shifting values and attitudes in the workplace, technological innovations, decline in quality education, increased regulations, and a growing global economy.

Industry Leaders

American Medical Association. Founded in 1854, the American Medical Association's (AMA) membership totaled 295,000 in 1998. Headquartered in Chicago, the organization maintained 54 state groups representing physicians and county medical societies. In 1962, the AMA boasted 82.1 percent of the country's physicians as members. By 1998 that figure had dropped to slightly more than 40 percent; the number of total physicians, however, nearly tripled over that period.

With an annual budget of $190 million, the AMA disseminates a tremendous amount of information to both the public and members of the medical profession. The AMA informs members about medical and health legislation at the state and national levels, and represents its membership to legislative and regulatory bodies. It also assesses physicians' adherence to its uniform standards through the American Medical Accreditation Program and seeks to enforce ethical codes of conduct for use throughout the medical profession. In 1999 the AMA established a national labor organization, the Physicians for Responsible Negotiations, which represents practicing physicians to increase their leverage in patient-care management decisions.

With a $60-million publishing operation, the AMA is the world's largest publisher of medical and scientific information. Two of its most well-known publications are *American Medical News,* a weekly publication covering political, social, and economic issues as they pertain to medical care, and the *Journal of the American Medical Association,* (JAMA) a weekly publication devoted to topics in general medicine. The AMA also assists in setting standards for medical schools, hospitals, residency programs, and continuing medical education courses. In addition, the organization offers physician placement services and counseling regarding practice management issues.

American Bar Association. The American Bar Association (ABA) is the world's largest voluntary professional association, with a budget of $100 million in 1999. Founded in 1878, it is a national organization that represents all attorneys in good standing of the bar throughout the United States. The ABA is headquartered in Chicago, has 380,000 individual members, including 40,000 dues-paying associates and law students, and is affiliated with 20 other professional organizations.

The ABA addresses broad social concerns, which in the 1990s encompassed the high costs of litigation, legal services, domestic violence, and free press and fair trial issues. This organization conducts research, provides educational programs and public services, and seeks to improve the administration of civil and criminal justice. The ABA has 800 employees who operate 25 sections, including Criminal Justice, Economics of Law Practice, and Family Law. The organization's major publication is the monthly *ABA Journal,* which covers developments in law and association news.

American Dental Association. Founded in 1859, the American Dental Association (ADA) is a national professional society for dentists with 54 state or territorial and 529 local dental societies. Its membership of 141,000 gives the ADA a market share of 70 percent of all dentists in the United States. This organization promotes dental health issues to the public and dentistry issues regarding legislation, standards, and regulation. The ADA inspects and accredits dental schools and schools for dental hygienists, assistants, and laboratory technicians through its Commission on Dental Accreditation, which derives its authority from the U.S. Department of Education.

The ADA, which maintains a 50,000-volume library, conducts a vast amount of research and produces most of the dental health educational materials used in the United States. The organization also compiles statistics regarding personnel, practices, dental care needs, and attitudes of patients, as well as maintaining a biographical history of dentists in the United States. The ADA is headquartered in Chicago, operates with a staff of over 400, and has a $57.7 million budget. Its official publication is *The Journal of the American Dental Association,* as well as the *ADA News* and the *Index to Dental Literature.*

American Association for the Advancement of Science. The American Association for the Advancement of Science (AAAS) is the largest general organization representing all areas in the field of science. Its membership includes 143,000 individuals from 130 countries, including 120,000 members in the United States, and 296 societies, professional organizations, and state and city academies. Founded in 1848, the AAAS, headquartered in Washington, D.C., has a staff of 300 people, and a $44 million budget. It retains close links to 275 affiliated societies with more than 7 million additional members.

The goal of the AAAS is to promote the work of scientists and "improve the effectiveness of science in the promotion of human welfare." This professional membership organization conducts seminars and colloquia regarding scientific issues. The AAAS plays a role in settling crucial scientific questions and addresses issues such as population growth, environmental destruction, and viral infections. It also produces an annual report and a monograph series that provide information about proposed federal research and the development budget for the upcoming year, and maintains *Science Online* on the World Wide Web. Its highly respected weekly journal *Science* boasts a readership of more than 500,000 people.

American Institute of Certified Public Accountants. The American Institute of Certified Public Accountants (AICPA) is a professional society of accountants certified by the states and territories. The organization was founded in 1887, and in 1999 had 330,000 individual members, with 42.0 percent composed of accountants working in industry, 41.0 percent in public practice, 2.4 percent in education, and 4.4 percent in government. Headquartered in New York, the AICPA employs 700 people. This organization has become known for its preparation and grading of the national Uniform CPA Examination for state licensing bodies. Other responsibilities of the AICPA include, establishing, auditing, and reporting standards and determining the financial accounting standards included in the financial statements of U.S. companies. The AICPA also conducts research and continuing education programs and operates more than 135 boards, committees, and subcommittees that deal with issues ranging from accounting standards and professional ethics to computer services.

The AICPA publishes a number of newsletters and journals. The most prominent of these publications include: *CPA Client Bulletin,* a monthly publication for clients of AICPA members; *CPA Examinations,* a semiannual study package of past CPA examinations and unofficial answers; and the *Journal of Accountancy,* a monthly publication covering all aspects of accounting for practitioners and financial executives. It also produced the *CPA Client Tax Letter,* the *CPA Healthcare Client Letter,* and *Practicing CPA.*

National Society of Professional Engineers. Founded in 1934, the National Society of Professional Engineers (NSPE) is an organization representing professional engineers and engineers-in-training in all fields registered in the United States and Canada. The NSPE, headquartered in Alexandria, Virginia, has a staff of 49 and a $6 million budget. Qualified graduate engineers, student members, and registered land surveyors are among the organization's 60,000 members, who are organized in 500 chapters.

The NSPE is concerned with the social, professional, ethical, and economic considerations of engineering as a profession. It focuses on these issues through a number of public relations programs and provides continuing education programs. The organization also monitors legislative and regulatory actions of interest to the engineering profession. The NSPE publishes the monthly *Engineering Times.*

WORKFORCE

More than 295,000 people are employed in associations throughout the United States. This figure has declined gradually since the early 1990s, reflecting the consolidation forced by downsized and concentrated industries. Staff size and responsibilities largely reflect the membership size and budget of each association. Employment positions within associations generally have been divided evenly between executive and staff positions.

As associations continue to grow in size and strength, so have the possibilities for employment within these organizations. According to Ronald Krannich, author of *Jobs and Careers with Nonprofit Organizations,* all organizations need people with fund-raising skills. Professional organizations need communication specialists, researchers, writers, meeting planners, publicists, and lobbyists as well. Because staff members are exposed to a wide variety of functions and responsibilities, association employment can offer tremendous advancement potential. Executives can earn salaries nearing the $1 million mark.

Entry-level employment at associations generally can be found in the areas of conference planning, public relations, or membership services. Most jobs require that employees have a liberal arts degree with strong interpersonal and communication skills, and some computer knowledge. Additional education, such as an M.B.A. or legal training, may be necessary for financial services or legislative positions. Association executives may earn Certified Association Executive (CAE) designation upon the successful completion of a one-day, written test.

Although associations are located across the United States, many can be found in metropolitan areas. Perhaps reflecting the growing prominence of political action committees, Washington, D.C., is home to more professional membership organizations that any other city, boasting 2,500 association headquarters. New York City followed with 1,900, and Chicago placed third with 1,500. Moreover, many professional membership organizations have chapters located in or near state capitals.

AMERICA AND THE WORLD

The emerging global community has increased the interest and the need for U.S. professional membership organizations to share their talents overseas, especially with growing business communities in emerging democracies. Many organizations have begun to develop subcommittees or international task forces to deal with these expanding needs as they pertain to their respective profession. For example, the International Relations Task Force of the Government Financial Officers Association (GFOA) has begun to work with several international professional and financial organizations. This group has been providing education and networking opportunities with foreign officials, and has been assisting U.S. and Canadian finance officers in becoming competitive in the international economy. The GFOA has been especially active in Eastern Europe.

Staff members of professional societies who handle international relations issues usually have expertise in overcoming language barriers, finding alternative delivery systems, and forming chapters outside the United States. Most often, these people most often are contacted by members regarding international economic, social, and political issues.

Research and Technology

Effective information management has become a vital function for the successful professional society, and the driving force for the computerization of their office operations. Eighty-one percent of all professional organizations incorporated networked personal computers. More and more associations were bringing their information and operations online, often to generate additional revenues. For example, the AMA has made especially aggressive moves to tap into this resource, recognizing that health information represents one of the most commonly sought topics on the World Wide Web. In conjunction with six other medical associations, the AMA invested heavily to establish Medem.com to compete with the growing number of other major online heath-information services that do not promote physician-empowerment. The American Society of Association Executives, moreover, concluded an agreement with Microsoft Corp. in 1998 whereby the software giant agreed to build technological proficiency, resource access, and a model upon which associations can develop more effective networks with members. "Members only" sections on Web sites increasingly connect organization members beyond firewalls and generate additional revenue for the association from the online purchase of information materials and from advertisers. About two-thirds of the associations maintain Web sites, while more than three-fourths have e-mail.

Most large professional societies purchased mainframe systems in the 1970s to automate their record keeping. They added personal computers during the 1980s, and by the 1990s they had amassed a collection of computers unable to communicate or interact with one another. Therefore, many of these organizations have begun to use local area networks (LANs) in order to share information among their departments. For instance, the AMA has been converting its legal information system from a Wang VS 300 minicomputer to microcomputer LANs with the intention of simplifying the coordination of work groups and reducing downtime. The AMA also has moved from a proprietary system to an open client/server setup, hoping to unite a divided user community and consolidate several small data centers.

With the use of LANs, many professional membership organizations have begun to operate database management systems and experiment with a variety of software packages and hardware products. Some of these items include legislative affairs and grassroots software, relational database software, text-based information retrieval programs, and bar coding and document scanners.

Many associations are now involved in some kind of Internet interaction, whether it is a World Wide Web home page or other online research capabilities. Marketing their programs and products, recruiting new members, and providing educational information and services to members and the public can be easily accomplished on the Internet or other electronic databases, making technology of the 1990s an important tool for success.

Further Reading

"AMA Hopes Strategy Will Click." *Pharmaceutical Executive,* December 1999.

"Consortium Is Formed To Develop New Class Of Software Services." *Wall Street Journal,* 12 May 1999.

Dea, Don, and Hugh K. Lee. *Online Strategies: Association Models for Success.* Washington, D.C.: American Society of Association Executives, 1999.

"It's Lucrative At the Top." *Modern Healthcare,* 8 March 1999.

"Top Medical Bodies Join Net Gold Rush." *Online Reporter,* 1 November 1999.

SIC 8631

LABOR UNIONS AND SIMILAR LABOR ORGANIZATIONS

This industry includes membership organizations of workers that operate for the improvement of wages and working conditions.

NAICS Code(s)

813930 (Labor Unions and Similar Labor Organizations)

INDUSTRY SNAPSHOT

Labor unions enjoyed a slight but long-awaited resurgence in the late 1990s. After 20 years of sagging membership ranks and diminishing influence, labor unions managed to achieve small but significant gains in both size and power, fueled by a renewed militancy marked by a series of high-profile strikes. Membership numbers grew for the second straight year in 1999 for the first time since the late 1970s. Battered and bruised from years of intense anti-labor activity, including a proliferation of illegal firings during union election campaigns, U.S. labor unions were dusting themselves off and preparing the way for renewed activity in the twenty-first century.

Labor unions are organized on local and national levels, usually by industry or trade. The primary function of a labor union is to partake in collective bargaining, the negotiation process over the terms of employment between a union and management. Union officials use this procedure to determine the wages for workers of a particular industry and to settle other worker-related issues, such as health benefits, overtime compensation, and company policy and direction. Employee associations that use collective bargaining procedures have become a popular type of labor union among white-collar professionals and other workers who have shunned traditional unions. Additionally, new kinds of union membership have been offered to workers who would like to be affiliated with a union, but do not work in a union shop. These workers can become associate union members or join workplace organizations.

Though unions showed signs of reviving long-depressed spirits in the late 1990s, union vitality as a whole remained far below levels achieved in the past. In terms of membership, only 13.9 percent of the U.S. workforce was unionized in 1999, totaling 16.48 million members. Government workers were far more likely to be unionized, especially at the local level. After government, the most heavily unionized industries included transportation and public utilities, in which 26 percent of the workforce was organized, and construction, manufacturing, and mining. Men belong to unions slightly more than women, with respective unionization rates of 16.1 percent and 11.4 percent. Among all employed wage and salary workers, those not represented by unions earned an average of $499 per week, while union members earned $659.

Unions faced a number of challenges at the close of the twentieth century. Chief among these concerns was the nature of the labor union itself. The sharply diminishing ranks of unions during the past 30 years combined with the increasingly global and mobile nature of business sparked debate as to whether the organizational structures and practices of unions were applicable to the modern economy. At the other end of the spectrum, labor activists countered that while definite improvements and re-strategizing were indeed in order, unions were never more necessary than when faced with the constant threat of strongly leveraged management afforded by the increasing mobility of trade and investment. The challenge was thus to re-think labor practices to strengthen labor's position in the changed economic environment.

ORGANIZATION AND STRUCTURE

The American labor movement can be divided into two types of unions: craft and industrial. Craft unions were the first unions established in the United States and are comprised of workers who share a common occupation, skill, or trade. An industrial union includes all workers related to the production of a particular product, including skilled, semiskilled, and unskilled labor.

This distinction has been an important issue in the history of organized labor. The American Federation of Labor (AFL), founded by Samuel Gompers in 1886, favored craft unions. Over time and under the direction of various leaders, the Congress of Industrial Organizations (CIO) was created specifically for industrial unions. The differences between these two kinds of unions are not as apparent today because rapid changes in technology have blurred many remaining distinctions.

Probably the most recognizable name related to the American labor movement has been the AFL-CIO. This group is a ''union of unions,'' a federation of free and autonomous labor organizations. A voluntary membership group, the AFL-CIO includes 68 unions which represent a total of 13.8 million workers. Membership has been limited to national unions, although a few local unions also belong to the federation directly. National unions have been the backbone of the American labor movement. Membership has been concentrated in the largest national unions, such as the Teamsters, the Auto Workers, the Steelworkers, the Carpenters, and the United Mine Workers. Regardless of AFL-CIO affiliation, these groups have been responsible for collective bargaining.

In addition to setting the price of labor in a particular market, collective bargaining allows unions to share in decision-making processes with management. Collective bargaining establishes a system of checks and balances against the authority of management. With this negotiation strategy comes a new way of making and interpreting rules, known as the ''grievance procedure.'' This is essentially a judicial process which ensures that the collective bargaining agreement is being properly applied and interpreted.

The 63,000 local unions in the United States have been primarily responsible for grievance procedures. Nearly 98 percent of local unions are subdivisions or chapters of national unions, although a few are affiliated directly with the AFL-CIO or are completely independent.

Approximately 22,000 local unions are affiliated with six national unions that have 2,000 or more locals each.

Unlike the distant relationship between national unions and the AFL-CIO, locals typically are strictly controlled by their national leadership. The status of these locals lies entirely under the administration of the national leadership, who often disband locals deemed expendable or uneconomical to maintain. Generally, locals require permission from the national administration to call a strike, though unsanctioned ''wildcard'' strikes are not uncommon. National representatives are usually charged with engaging in collective bargaining on behalf of local chapters. Despite this ''top-down'' leadership, the local union has been a significant part of organized labor because it has been the point of contact between the member and the union. Nonetheless, recent years have witnessed heightened demand for greater direct or more representative democracy emanating from the local chapters up to the national administration.

Employee associations, like labor unions, participate in collective bargaining but they are less hierarchical than the unions. These groups may be the best way to organize professional and white-collar employees who are interested in collective bargaining, but have reservations about being identified with a union. Approximately 2.56 million people, or 10 percent of the total U.S. union membership, belong to employee associations. The largest employee association is the National Education Association (NEA). Boasting over 2.5 million members, the NEA has surpassed the Teamsters (1.6 million members as of 1999) as the largest union in the United States. Other employee associations with over 100,000 members include the American Nurses Association, Classified School Employees, the Fraternal Order of Police, and the California State Employees.

Background and Development

The beginnings of organized labor in the United States can be traced to the establishment of craft unions in the eighteenth century: shoemakers organized in Philadelphia in 1792; carpenters in Boston in 1793; and printers in New York in 1794. In the early nineteenth century, these groups tried to expand into other cities, with many crafts even boasting national organizations in the 1830s before being decimated by depression later that decade. Shortly before the Civil War, many national craft unions were re-established, and more importantly, survived.

By the end of the 1860s, approximately 30 national craft unions had been founded. In 1866, the National Labor Union, a national federation embracing both craft unionists and reform groups, was organized. The group lasted only six years before converting into a political party, which subsequently collapsed in 1872. The next national labor group was the Noble Order of the Knights of Labor. Founded in 1871 as a secret society, the Knights became a national organization in 1878. Their goal was to bring together in one organization all ''real'' producers, such as farmers, lower middle-class workers, and wage earners. The Knights were a centralized organization, which tried to prohibit national trade associations. The crafts membership of the Knights soon became disgruntled with this policy because the combination of skilled and unskilled workers weakened the craftsmen's ability to bargain effectively. Five years into its existence, the Knights had 50,000 members. At its peak year in 1886, the group had nearly 700,000 members—an all-time high. Four years later, the group had dwindled to 100,000, as the majority of the craftsmen became aligned with a new federation.

The AFL was the first union to achieve a lasting existence. Through various economic conditions, the AFL maintained a continuous presence from its inception until its merger with the CIO in 1955. Samuel Gompers, founder of the AFL, enforced two basic policies. National unions that belonged to the AFL were guaranteed ''trade autonomy'' and they were to be afforded ''exclusive jurisdiction'' over their particular craft or other occupation.

Trade autonomy allowed decision-making to be decentralized, with national unions retaining power. This was particularly important to the union's main function of collective bargaining. With exclusive jurisdiction, the AFL recognized the sole authority of its craft union members, and protected them against possible competition from other unions. The AFL assured its member groups that no other unions would be given overlapping jurisdiction, and no competitors would be recognized by the federation. These two policies proved to be extremely successful in attracting unions to the AFL. Between 1897 and 1904, the AFL issued 92 charters, doubling the number of affiliated unions to 120. By 1904, 85 percent of all national unions in the United States were affiliated with the AFL. By 1914, AFL membership exceeded 2 million. It rose briefly to 4 million before gradually declining throughout the 1920s. During the 1930s membership fell below 2.5 million.

The first two decades of the twentieth century were the period of labor radicalism, and unions' influence registered in American political life as they have not since. Labor leader and socialist Eugene Debs made strong third-party showings in successive U.S. presidential elections, while militant unions such as the Industrial Workers of the World (IWW) sought to organize all workers, including those unskilled and minority workers shunned by the AFL, into ''one big union'' with the aim of ending the capitalist system in favor of a socialist federation of syndicated labor organizations. After World War I and the Bolshevik overthrow of the Czar in Russia, the ''Red Scare'' in the United States produced a swift and harsh crackdown on labor militancy, and such radical unions were quickly dismantled.

In 1935, the dominance of craft unions was challenged by the establishment of a new organization that advocated a different kind of union. On 9 November 1935, John Lewis, president of the United Mine Workers, along with the presidents of seven other unions in the industrial block of the AFL, met and established the Congress of Industrial Organizations (CIO). This group promoted the collection of unorganized workers in mass-production industries on a per-industry basis. When the group was instructed by the AFL to disband the CIO or be suspended, the leaders ignored the order, broke away from the AFL, and became an independent federation.

The central legislation of U.S. labor-management relations is the National Labor Relations Act of 1935, usually referred to as the Wagner Act, which guaranteed the right of employees to join unions and engage in collective bargaining. Immediately a thorn in the side of businesses, the act prohibited employers from firing workers for joining or trying to organize a union and from refusing to negotiate with a union that represented a majority of workers. The act further established the National Labor Relations Board (NLRB) to enforce the law's provisions and mediate, at the federal level, broad legal disputes between labor and management. While business organizations quickly began working to amend the Wagner Act, union membership soared from 4 million in 1935 to 12 million in 1947.

Within a three-week period in early 1937, the CIO had penetrated the largest corporations in both the auto and steel industries—the core of mass production. Its first success came when General Motors, the largest auto maker at that time, recognized the United Auto Workers (UAW) as the bargaining agent for its members. The CIO also made its mark on other major industries in 1937, including electrical and radio manufacturing, rubber, men's and women's clothing, textiles, meat packing, petroleum and the maritime industry. By the end of that year, 33 national unions had become affiliated with the CIO. Moreover, its total membership reached nearly 2 million and it claimed five of the ten largest unions.

Wartime activities stimulated the growth of both the CIO and the AFL. During the Korean War in 1953, CIO membership reached its all-time high of nearly five million workers from the auto and steel, clothing, textiles, communications and electrical industries. The AFL also increased its membership from three million in 1937 to 6.8 million in 1944. Although CIO expansion leveled off in 1947, the AFL continued to grow from 8.5 million in 1947 to 10.5 million in 1955.

As strike activity skyrocketed following World War II, the U.S. business community, now recovered from the Depression, stepped up efforts to undo the Wagner Act, which was amended after President Truman intervened to settle disputes in the coal mining, railroad, and steel industries. The National Labor Relations Act of 1947, also called the Taft-Hartley Act, followed shortly thereafter, amending the controversial Section 8 by clarifying what were considered unfair labor practices by unions and employees; the Wagner Act had covered only unfair practices by employers, and allowed management greater opportunity to interfere with unions' choice of representatives for collective bargaining than had been allowed by the Wagner Act.

After a 20-year separation, the AFL and the CIO merged into a single organization, the American Federation of Labor and Congress of Industrial Organizations, on 5 December 1955. The new federation consisted of 138 unions, 108 from the AFL and 30 from the CIO, and a combined membership of 16.1 million. Two major union movements have occurred since the 1955 merger. The first was the expulsion of the Teamsters. Embarrassed by the alleged connection of Teamsters president Jimmy Hoffa with organized crime, the AFL told Teamsters leaders to remove Hoffa from office. The Teamsters refused, and in December 1957, they were suspended from the federation, and the AFL-CIO lost 1.5 million members and $900,000 in annual dues. Ten years later, the United Auto Workers left the federation due to disagreements between then-UAW president Walter Reuther and the leadership of the AFL-CIO under George Meany. However, both groups were reinstated into the AFL-CIO, the UAW in 1981 and the Teamsters in 1987.

Union membership expanded steadily in the post-World War II years until the recession of the late 1950s, when it declined from just over 17.5 million to 16.5 million members by the early 1960s. The period from the mid 1960s to the late 1970s saw a steady and substantial growth in the number of union members, peaking at about 24 million workers in 1977. From 1978 through the mid-1990s, however, union membership plummeted, reaching lower levels than in the worst years of the early 1960s. Looking at union membership as a percentage of the private sector labor force yields less of a roller coaster, since this ratio declined in almost all years after 1955, though at an accelerated rate after the mid-1970s. In 1997, only 14.1 percent of full-time wage and salaried employees were unionized.

The decline in union membership was associated with a number of other factors that led to a substantial transformation of labor-management relations in the United States. Among these factors were intensified global competition, substantially slower average growth rates for the economy as a whole, declining real wages, the deregulation of key industries, the shift in employment from the industrial to the service sector and from the union strongholds of the Midwest and Northeast to the Sunbelt states, greatly increased anti-union efforts on the part of employers, and reduced resources devoted to organizing on the part of unions.

CURRENT CONDITIONS

Membership Trends. In 1999, labor unions claimed 13.9 percent of the U.S. workforce, or 16.48 million members, an increase of 265,000 over 1998, and the largest annual membership growth in more than 20 years. Moreover, of the new members, 112,000 in 1999 were in the private sector, also a 20-year high. These numbers reflected the success of an aggressive campaign waged by organized labor, particularly the AFL-CIO, to boost union membership. After John Sweeney assumed the presidency of the AFL-CIO in 1996, the union refocused its efforts and financial resources away from lobbying and electing politicians through political action committees and toward the active recruitment of new members and building grass roots-commitments to labor.

These efforts were reflected in membership and union elections. Union representative elections totaled 3,229 in 1998, up 2.2 percent from 1997; of those, unions won 51.2 percent, compared with 50.3 percent in 1997. More notably, however, the number of workers participating in such elections escalated 8 percent in 1998, while in elections won by unions, that figure was 26.2 percent, demonstrating the heightened viability of participatory democracy in organizing activities. Unionization rates are highest among African Americans, at 17.2 percent; in comparison, 13.5 percent of whites and 11.9 percent of Hispanics are unionized.

Unions also created programs to focus recruitment efforts on industries with traditionally low union representation. In addition to agricultural workers, the occupations with the lowest unionization rates were in financial, insurance, and real estate sectors, where only 2.1 percent of the workforce was unionized. Another challenge was to make unionization more attractive to the booming high-tech sector.

While increasing union membership numbers constituted good news for labor leaders, the growing membership ranks in the late 1990s were commensurate with the expanding job market in the United States. The inability of new union membership to outpace job growth was generally attributed to mergers and acquisitions, which result in layoffs and increased leverage on the part of management, and to the closing of factories as companies shift production facilities overseas. The impact of NAFTA in the mid- and late 1990s had a tremendous influence on the number of union members, with many workers losing their jobs from foreign competition and downsizing as well as plants closing. Consequently, unions no longer dominate entire industries—like automobiles, steel and rubber—as they once did. The United Steelworkers even filed suit to have NAFTA declared unconstitutional, noting that the treaty failed to receive the two-thirds majority vote in the Senate necessary to ratify a treaty. While NAFTA is indeed a treaty, Congress had previously stipulated that trade pacts could be passed by a mere majority in both houses. While their petition was rejected, a federal judge ruled that the union did have the standing to bring such a suit to court. While only a marginal victory, the action was indicative labor's emboldened stance in rejecting the particular form of corporate globalization that has characterized the national and international economy in recent years.

Public vs. Private Sector. While union membership has declined in the private sector, it has grown in the public sector. In 1958 only 12 percent of the public sector was unionized; by 1999, approximately 37.3 percent of the public sector work force was unionized. By contrast, 35 percent of the private sector work force belonged to a union in 1958, while only 9.4 percent belonged in 1999. By 1999, approximately 42 percent of all union members worked in the public sector.

Merging Unions. Technological advances have made certain trades obsolete and have led many unions to merge with others in order to boost membership and power. For example, the Retail, Wholesale and Department Store Union was combined with the United Food and Commercial Workers. The Allied Industrial Workers joined the United Paper Workers. Additionally, Communication Workers of America (CWA) merged with the National Association of Broadcast Employees and Technicians, which absorbed the International Typographical Union earlier in 1993. The CWA spent the rest of the decade on a merger and organizational tear, incorporating small machine shops, newspaper guilds, and a host of other organizations into its ranks. The United Auto Workers, meanwhile, have scooped up occupations as diverse as writers, clerical employees, and farm-equipment manufacturers. As technological developments continue to squeeze out occupations and force workers to retrain, unions were likely to find it more economical to broaden their membership criteria and pool resources to cast a net over a wider area and keep pace with rapidly altering workplace conditions.

Emerging Unions. By the late 1990s, professions that traditionally found little use for unionization were beginning to see advantages in organizing. Health care workers, for example, greatly expanded their unionized ranks in 1999. The nation's largest union representing these occupations, the Service Employees International Union, doubled its rate of representation for this sector in the late 1990s, reaching 105,000 nurses, 20,000 physicians, and about 545,000 workers in healthcare-related positions.

Moreover, the American Medical Association, along with various associations representing nurses, doctors, and other health care workers, made moves toward unionizing in order to gain leverage against health care managers and insurance companies which, they felt, were exerting excessive influence over the health care system and thus compromising patient care. Meanwhile, unionization was being explored in the high-technology industry at such firms as AT&T and Microsoft.

Clinton Administration. Organized labor played an important role in electing Bill Clinton as president in both 1992 and in his re-election in 1996. After 12 years of strained relations with Republican administrations, initiated by President Reagan's firing of the striking air traffic controllers in 1981 and encompassing relaxed enforcement of laws against firing of organizing workers, labor unions hoped that the Democratic Clinton administration would be more sympathetic to their interests. Shortly thereafter, the administration convened the Dunlop Commission to study labor-management issues in the United States. The Commission's findings revealed extraordinary anti-union bias in the U.S. economy. Among its findings, the Commission reported that illegal firings occurred in one out of four union election campaigns, compared to one in every twenty elections in the 1950s; only two-thirds of union-certified elections were recognized by employers agreeing to negotiate contracts, while employers incur no monetary penalty for refusing to engage in good faith bargaining; and, in general, recourse to legal relief through the courts was not an option for a majority of employees, whose low income levels precluded them from paying the high costs and contingency fees required by private lawyers. In response to such reports, President Clinton issued an Executive Order in 1995 banning the hiring of permanent strike replacements by certain federal contractors, later called the Workplace Fairness Act.

While unions were generally pleased with such federal action, trade remained a sticking point between organized labor and the administration throughout the latter's terms. Clinton's strong endorsement of the North American Free Trade Agreement (NAFTA) in 1994 infuriated many union leaders, who worried about the dramatic shifting of U.S. production facilities to neighboring Mexico. Likewise, the administration's strong support of furthering the U.S. commitment to and reach of the World Trade Organization (WTO) alarmed unions, who saw in the WTO a vehicle through which businesses could force wages downward and jeopardize job security by seeking out the cheapest market worldwide in which to conduct their operations. Nonetheless, the AFL-CIO exhibited its desire for a continuation of Clinton-style policies with regard to labor, registering an early endorsement of Vice President Gore in his presidential-election campaign.

Associate Membership. In an attempt to expand its member base, the AFL-CIO created a new category of worker, called an "associate member." This type of membership was created for people who do not work in a union shop but want to be affiliated with a union and participate in its benefits program. Moreover, the AFL-CIO has become more like a social service organization offering credit cards, legal advice, life insurance, travel services, health benefits and high interest-yielding saving accounts. This associate status program was particularly designed to help attract white-collar workers who have been wary of unions because of their blue-collar, industrial image. The unions also hoped to attract former members who have taken nonunion jobs, as well as other union loyalists.

Labor leaders have also created worker associations as a strategy for attracting new union members. These are union-backed organizations that have refrained from collective bargaining and confrontation. Instead, they offer assistance with a variety of workplace issues, such as pay equity, health care, job training and family leave. These groups also provide legal advice, language tutoring, and skills training. Unions hoped that such associations will reach unorganized segments of the work force and give them a foot in the door at workplaces that have shut them out. By the late 1990s, these grassroots organizations had nearly 1 million members. Analysts believe that unions will have to continue with these alternative forms of membership and services if they want to keep pace with the expanding workforce.

Workers' Centers. Another form of labor organization that achieved growing popularity through the 1980s and 1990s were workers' centers. These organizations are centered on communities, rather than specific industries, and effectively bypass unions altogether and to incorporate workers in trades without much established union presence. Further, these centers were especially vibrant among immigrant and ethnic-minority laborers who face particular forms of discrimination in the workplace and often turned away of vilified by the larger unions. In the early 1980s, Korean, Chinese, Vietnamese, and Filipino women in San Francisco established the Asian Immigrant Women Advocates to conduct educational workshops on labor laws and rights for Asian women working in a variety of occupations, particularly in hotels. In New York, the Latino Workers Center conducted similar operations for workers in garment factories, groceries, health care institutions, and other occupations from the Latino community. The center also helped organize a series of protests against abusive labor practices, filed suit against employers to the Department of Labor, and even established radio and television networks to educate their community on labor and immigration issues.

The growing tendency among U.S. businesses to replace regular employees with lower-paid temporary workers has created a growing demand for organization of contingent employees. In Massachusetts, unions and community groups combined to form a Campaign on Contingent Work, establishing a workers center known as the Temporary Employees Meeting Place (TEMP) in 1996 to promote education for and solidarity among contingent workers, who have found it exceedingly difficult to organize in the past due to the unstable nature of their employment patterns.

Strikes. Strike activity generally paralleled the decline in union membership during the 1980s and 1990s. In 1997, for example, there were 29 strikes involving 1,000 or more workers, drawing a total of 339,000 workers. By way of comparison, 255 strikes of similar scale took place in 1979, involving a total of 1,021,000 workers.

The late 1990s, however, witnessed a resurgence of union militancy along with heightened emphasis on recruitment. In 1998 5.1 million working days were lost for workers involved in all strikes, representing the first time that figure had increased since 1994. Moreover, the 34 major strikes involved an expanded 387,000 workers. While these numbers remain low by historical standards, a series of high-profile work stoppages through the mid- and late 1990s helped garner labor unions renewed public acknowledgement as an influential force in the U.S. economy.

In the mid-1990s, amidst continued deflation of union membership and a general sense of decline in the significance of unions in general, situations emerged signaling that rumors of organized labor's demise had been premature. From 1995 to 1996, Bridgestone/Firestone Company squared off against the United Rubber Workers union in a strike that assumed symbolic import for the state of labor in the United States. The URW struck to maintain "pattern bargaining," whereby Bridgestone workers were to receive compensation and conditions on a par with workers at Goodyear, Bridgestone's more profitable competitor. Bridgestone rejected any such agreement, and the dispute evolved into a 27-month quagmire that saw the URW, by turns, nearly epitomize the death of organized labor and then symbolize its resurgence.

When Bridgestone mobilized several thousand strike breakers in 1995, some union locals voted to return to work without any concessions, though few workers were actually rehired initially. When Bridgestone registered a significant recovery through 1995 and more strikers were called back to work, the URW regrouped and merged allied with the sympathetic United Steel Workers. Subsequent pressure on the company threatened contagion, and proved embarrassing to the thriving Bridgestone. Soon all workers were re-hired by the company with massive concessions.

Following this display of union vitality, the Teamsters called a strike against United Parcel Service (UPS) in 1997. After accepting a two-tier wage system at the company in the early 1980s, whereby part-time workers received significantly lower wages than full-timers, UPS drastically reorganized its workforce, boosting its reliance on part-time employees from 42 percent of all workers in 1986 to more than 60 percent in 1997. More than 10,000 workers classified as part-time, furthermore, actually worked at least a full workweek. When UPS failed to sign a new contract creating more full-time jobs and subsequently proposed to assume control of the union's pension plan, the Teamsters initiated the largest U.S. strike in 20 years. The move proved extraordinarily successful for the union; while only 5 percent of all Teamsters crossed picket lines, UPS lost about $30 million daily, while public support for the strikers was markedly high, at 55 percent, compared with only 27 percent in favor of UPS, according to a *USA Today*-CNN-Gallup poll. After two weeks, UPS bowed to almost all the union's demands, and the strike initiated dramatically heightened public concern over the trend toward contingent labor.

After the UPS victory, strikes proliferated throughout the nation. Only a small handful achieved the kind of spotlight generated at UPS, such as the 54-day strike at General Motors in the summer of 1998. But clearly strikes returned as a popular and, in the eyes of labor unions, effective strategy for winning concessions and demands from management.

Labor-Management Relations. One factor encouraging the abundance of strikes was the tight labor market of the late 1990s. With unemployment at the lowest point since the early 1960s, businesses have found it difficult to hire replacement workers as the pool of available employees remains fairly shallow. Companies have thus reacted with greater reliance on networked production, whereby in-house operations are streamlined and downsized in favor of contracting work out to other companies both in the U.S. and abroad. General Motors, for example, spun off its Delphi Parts unit shortly after the 1998 strike, establishing it as a separate firm and replacing the factories with new models designed to make greater use of subcontractors, thus sidestepping its unions. Overall, companies trying to remain competitive in an ever-opening market, in which few restrictions are placed on investment and relocation of operations, are seeking the greatest cost-benefit efficiency and thus relying more heavily on cheaper foreign labor or contingent domestic labor.

Indeed, competitive pressures weighing on businesses have nearly guaranteed more drastic measures taken by unions. Constantly looking for the cheapest labor markets around the world, firms who fail to exploit available cost-savings opportunities risk losing market share to shrewder competitors. Recognizing the potential confrontations this situation could force with labor, corporate lockouts have been almost as numerous as employee strikes, as companies wield the power afforded by the ability to transport work elsewhere in order to stave off pressure from unions. This tactic carries the further advantage of denying unions the ability to strategize a strike in accordance with their resources.

INDUSTRY LEADERS

Since it was founded by Samuel Gompers in 1886, the American Federation of Labor (AFL), has been the leading voice of American organized labor. The organization's influence was expanded when it merged with the Congress of Industrial Organizations (CIO) in 1955. Headquartered in Washington, D.C., the AFL-CIO has a staff of over 400 employees. In 1999, the AFL-CIO was affiliated with 68 unions throughout the United States. Membership increased slightly from 13.6 million in 1996 to 13.8 million in 1999, but remained below the 1991 total of 13.9 million. The federation was expected to spend about $46 million on grass-roots lobbying during the 1999-2000 election cycle. Furthermore, the AFL-CIO embarked on a campaign, expected to cost $40 million by 2001, to raise awareness among its members of developments and legislation relating to social security, the minimum wage, and Medicare.

The AFL-CIO reorganized extensively in the mid- and late 1990s following Sweeney's ascendancy to the presidency. Abandoning its Cold-War-era anti-communism efforts, the union began to actively promote international solidarity. Domestic union solidarity also assumed heightened priority, as the federation aimed to reduce competition between unions by offering matching grants for joint-organization campaigns. In an attempt to help develop a strong work force for the future, the AFL-CIO has created programs through its Committee on the Evolution of Work, including training for a new generation of organizers. The federation also has developed Union Privilege, a benefits package that includes low-interest credit cards and home mortgage programs. In partnerships with the government and private groups, the AFL-CIO Housing and Building Investment Trust has begun to create jobs by building low-cost housing in urban areas.

The International Brotherhood of Teamsters, more commonly known as ''the Teamsters,'' was founded in 1903 and is headquartered in Washington, D.C. In 1991 the federal government forced the Teamsters' first democratic Election, in which Ronald Carey emerged as president of the organization. The Teamsters organization has been notorious for its corruption. Four of the six predecessors to Carey were indicted for embezzling union funds, and three leaders, including Jimmy Hoffa, were jailed. Jackie Presser was the fourth Teamsters leader to be indicted in 1986, but he died before his trial. In 1989 the union settled a racketeering suit, and in order to avoid government-imposed trusteeship the Teamsters agreed to open elections.

In the late 1990s, a series of presidential election disputes refocused attention on Teamsters controversy. Eventually, James P. Hoffa, son of the notorious Teamsters leader, emerged as president, and, after several years, was able to regalvanize the union somewhat. The union had 1.6 million members by the end of 1999, an increase of 200,000 workers from 1996, though still 300,000 fewer than its peak in the mid-1970s. Still, the Teamsters remain one of the largest unions in North America, with 596 locals and an annual budget of $1.4 million. The Teamsters continued to generate its share of controversy in the late 1990s; the union was sued for damages caused by its strike of the Overnite Transportation Company, which the Teamsters waged for alleged illegal harassment and termination of workers. Northwest Airlines likewise sued the Teamsters for its ''sick-out'' strike over the 1999 holiday season, though Teamsters officials countered that the lack of passengers, not the sick-out, was the primary cause of flight cancellations.

The National Education Association (NEA) has become the largest professional organization and labor union in the United States, more than doubling its membership since 1968 to 2.5 million in over 13,000 communities nationwide in 1999. By the late 1990s approximately 80 percent of NEA members were elementary or secondary school teachers. Another 88,000 were faculty members in institutions of higher education, and more than 160,000 were employed in such support positions as teacher assistants, bus drivers, cafeteria workers, and school custodians.

Founded as a professional association in 1857, the NEA became a labor union during the 1960s. The organization divides authority between rotating elected teachers, school employees, and permanent professional staff. The NEA also has 1,500 ''UniServ'' professionals to assist locals with collective bargaining. NEA dues were set at a fixed proportion of the average teacher's salary. The NEA political action committee donated $1.9 million to candidates during the 1997-98 feral election cycle. The union has been the largest single bloc at every Democratic convention since 1976. The organization is headquartered in Washington, D.C., and operates with a staff of 600.

AMERICA AND THE WORLD

While for years the sagging membership of unions seemed to be a distinctly American phenomenon, in recent decades unions in all countries have been under increased pressure due to slowing productivity and economic growth, rapid technical change, and a shift to a free-market ideology. The United Kingdom, for example, shed its long-standing strike-prone image as its unions became among the least militant in the industrialized world.

United States labor unions have generally been more successful than their foreign counterparts in winning wage increases for their members. This has provided enormous incentive for U.S. employers to oppose trade unions and set up nonunion shops. Foreign groups have been less focused on wage increases, and more concerned with worker council and plant-level decision-making, a direction that some U.S. unions already have begun to take.

Foreign labor organizations have, however, begun to take aim at U.S. corporations themselves. As U.S. business investment spreads over more of the world's markets, many unions have aligned to object to what they see as unfair labor practices and failure to comply with U.S. labor laws. In 1999 Asian garment workers filed class-action suits in U.S. federal courts against U.S. clothing retailers and manufacturers such as Wal-Mart Stores, Inc.; Sears Roebuck & Co.; Gap, Inc.; and a host of others for their reliance on sweatshop labor, low wages, and excessively long workweeks in their Asian manufacturing facilities.

This growing international labor solidarity was equally evident in opposition to the World Trade Organization. While many foreign government and business officials claim that the WTO will help foster greater investment in less developed countries, thereby raising wages and spurring development, labor groups in these countries have countered that the WTO's provision would force less developed countries to compete with each other for foreign investment based on lower labor costs and relaxed labor standards. For the same reason, many U.S. unions object to the WTO's policies, which they view as facilitating the outflow of U.S. jobs to foreign countries and diminishing job security and wages at home.

Research and Technology

Fearful of worker displacement caused by automation, many unions had been painfully slow to embrace the use of technology. Generally, unions have assumed that developing technology was not itself an antagonizing factor, but the unequal benefits of that technology between labor and management. Unions have looked at technology in one of two ways: proactive or reactive. The reactive position has been used during contract negotiations. For example, when the UAW was making concessions in 1982, one of the trade-offs was computer training. The union began efforts in 1983 and by 1990 had three main training centers, one each at Ford, Chrysler, and General Motors.

With the notable exceptions of the Airline Pilots Association and the International Association of Machinists and Aerospace Workers, most unions offer technology training in conjunction with employers. For example, after AT&T laid off thousands of union workers during 1988 and 1989, the company established a training center with the International Brotherhood of Electrical Workers and the Communication Workers of America. The Alliance for Employee Growth and Development Inc. has provided a variety of computer and other job skills to unemployed union workers.

Instead of trying to compensate for outdated skills, unions in a proactive position have welcomed technology to further the goals of their members. The United Steelworkers of America, for instance, developed the Institute for Career Development, which provides members with up to $2,500 in yearly tuition assistance for purposes of seeking additional technological training. The AFL-CIO, meanwhile, established an ambitious goal to provide low-cost computers with Internet access to all of its members, and was working with hardware and software firms to finance such a move. Relatedly, the union launched a World Wide Web site called Workingfamilies.com in 1999 to help build public awareness of the union and its activities and to promote union-made consumer items and keep members informed of important economic and legislative issues.

Further Reading

''AFL-CIO Launches Web Portal Service to Link Union's 13.3 Million Members.'' *Boston Globe,* 11 September 2000.

Bernstein, Aaron, and Paul Magnusson. ''Free Trade Needs a Nod From Labor.'' *Business Week,* 22 November 1998.

Brecher, Jeremy. *Strike!* 2d ed. Boston: South End Press, 1997.

Brecher, Jeremy, and Tim Costello. ''Labor's Day: The Challenge Ahead.'' *The Nation,* 21 November 1998.

''Campaign Fund-Raising Is at Record Pace.'' *New York Times,* 3 October 1999.

Dunne, Nancy. ''Steel Union Says Nafta 'Unconstitutional'.'' *Financial Times,* 14 July 1998.

Ettore, John. ''Unions Labor to Draw More: New Programs Seek to Battle Thinning Ranks.'' *Crain's Cleveland Business,* 30 August 1999.

Greenhouse, Steven. ''The Trade Deal: The American Worker; Union Leaders, Sensing Betrayal, Will Try to Block Agreement in Congress.'' *New York Times,* 17 November 1999.

Jaklevic, Mary Chris. '' Associations Join Pro-Union Ranks.'' *Modern Healthcare,* 5 July 1999.

Kovach, Kenneth A. *Strategic Labor Relations.* Lanham, MD: University Press of America, 1997.

Meyer, Bruce, and Brad Dawson. ''Strike Over: Workers at CGT Plant Approve Deal.'' *Tire Business,* 27 September 1999.

''News At Deadline: Employee Benefit Research Institute.'' *Modern Healthcare,* 24 May 1999.

''Supreme Court Rules Union Contracts Mean Membership.'' *Washington Times,* 4 November 1998.

''Unions Add Members in 1999, White-Collar, Service Workers Key to Growth.'' *Boston Globe,* 20 January 2000.

"Unions Won More Elections to Represent Employees in 1998." *Kansas City Star,* 10 August 1999.

"USWA Loses NAFTA Suit." *Rubber & Plastics News,* 2 August 1999.

Verespej, Michael A. "What's Behind The Strife?" *Industry Week,* 1 February 1999.

SIC 8641

CIVIC, SOCIAL, AND FRATERNAL ASSOCIATIONS

This category covers membership organizations engaged in civic, social, or fraternal activities, excluding homeowner groups primarily associated with property management and membership sports and recreation clubs, which are classified elsewhere.

NAICS CODE(S)

813410 (Civic and Social Organizations)
813990 (Other Similar Organizations)
921150 (American Indian and Alaska Native Tribal Governments)
624110 (Child and Youth Services)

Some of the most prominent civic, social, and fraternal organizations in the United States met with controversy in the late 1990s. Nonetheless, membership in such organizations increased nearly 20 percent between 1994 and 1999. This industrial classification encompasses nearly 50,000 local, national, and international nonprofit organizations, most of which are centered around a conception of altruism. It includes civic and fraternal associations, parent-teacher associations, singing societies, taxpayer's associations, veteran's organizations, youth groups, alumni associations, and booster clubs. The Internet has been instrumental in the establishment of new types of social organizations, including scores of activist groups, many devoted to social, environmental, and political causes. Their online networks facilitate organizing, letter-writing and fund-raising campaigns, and information sharing.

About 50 percent of all adults belong to civic clubs, with the percentage of women (50.5 percent) slightly outnumbering that of men (49.5 percent). However, males belong to fraternal organizations at a rate of nearly twice that of women (65.1 percent to 34.9 percent).

Civic and social associations are classified as tax-exempt corporations and are spared from federal, state, and local tax laws. They are usually not required to publish their income, expenses, or membership information. Most organizations rely primarily on volunteers to run their programs, and larger associations employ full-time administrative and management workers. About 460,000 workers were employed in the industry by the mid-1990s. The average association employee received an annual salary of approximately $11,500, less than half the service industry average.

Nonprofit associations generate income through dues, fund-raisers, and interest from investment funds, or by managing endowments. In addition, some associations employ nonprofit fund-raising firms. These companies usually work on a flat-fee basis and utilize direct marketing techniques to raise money, such as telephone and mail solicitation.

Although the industry is comprised primarily of community groups, some of the largest organizations stand out as major American institutions. These include the Freemasons, Boy Scouts, American Legion, the YMCA, and the United Way.

Freemasonry. Freemasons were increasing efforts to boost their membership ranks in the late 1990s. There were about 2 million Freemasons in the United States; although this is a significant number, membership numbers declined dramatically between 1987 to 1997, falling by 750,000 to 2 million members. One of the largest fraternal organizations in the world, freemasonry promotes public service and belief in the brotherhood of all men under a single God. Its basis and membership, however, remain predominantly Christian.

The physical foundation of Freemasonry is the lodge, which exists under a charter issued by the Grand Lodge. Lodges are informally linked and offer different service and achievement programs. All lodges offer three basic degrees which are achieved through service and learning: Entered Apprentice, Fellow Craft, and Master Mason. Groups of advanced Masons confer as many as 30 additional degrees.

Freemasonry is believed to have evolved from medieval guilds of stonemasons. The first formal lodge was formed in London in 1717, and the first American lodge was created in Philadelphia in 1730. Freemasons have endured religious and political criticism from various churches. The Roman Catholic Church, for example, originally claimed that Freemasonry was a religion and secret organization and banned membership, but this was overturned in 1983. Recently the Freemasons have relaxed the aura secrecy that has historically surrounded the organization in efforts to replenish membership ranks and to counter what they perceived as the widespread misconceptions about their organization among the general public.

In an effort to expand their social and charitable role, Freemasons have formed several other groups that are recognized among the largest U.S. civic organizations. The biggest of these is the Ancient Arabic Order of the Nobles of the Mystic Shrine—Shriners. Likewise, children's groups include De Molay for boys, and the Order of Job's Daughters and the Order of Rainbow for girls. Famous historical figures that were Freemasons include Benjamin Franklin, Wolfgang Amadeus Mozart, Henry Ford, Irving Berlin, Louis Armstrong, and Douglas MacArthur, along with George Washington and several other U.S. presidents.

Boy Scouts. One of the largest civic organizations in the world, the Boy Scouts is also the largest youth group; more than 99 million young males have been involved with the organization since its inception. Membership peaked at 4.8 million in 1972; the current membership contains 4.5 million youth and 1.2 million adult workers. The organization possesses a staff of about 1.1 million volunteers and a professional team of 4,000 scouters who provide training.

Founded in 1910, the Boy Scouts works to develop character, citizenship, and physical and mental fitness. It stresses duty to God, country, others, and self. The official Boy Scout slogan is ''Do a good turn daily,'' and the motto is ''Be prepared.'' Although the organization is nonsectarian, scouts must acknowledge a duty to God in the scout oath.

A boy is admitted to scouting under the supervision of adult volunteer leaders. Scout troops consist of patrols, which are made up of five to eight boys. Patrol leaders and troop leaders are elected. As a scout progresses in age and rank, his role becomes increasingly self-governing, and he develops leadership skills through interaction with other scouts. Character and achievement are nurtured through community service, outdoor activities, and the attainment of merit badges, which are earned by studying and passing tests on certain subjects.

Many Boy Scouts are introduced to scouting through the Tiger Scouts, for boys aged 7, and the Cub Scouts, for boys between the ages of 8 and 10. In addition, the Girl Scouts acts as a sister organization and offers activities and goals similar to the Boy Scouts. The Girl Scouts of America has recently embarked on a campaign to promote itself as responsive to contemporary changes in U.S. society that affect girls, with programs focused on sports, science, and the eradication of violence toward youth. Both boys and girls can continue scouting activities through the Explorers, an organization for members aged 14 to 20.

The Boy Scouts was started in 1907 by Robert Baden-Powell, a British officer. After writing a book for adults about scouting, Powell received such a demand for his book that he decided to write *Scouting for Boys.* This manual became the primer for his Boy Scouts organization. The Boy Scouts of America was formed in 1910.

The Boy Scouts came under attack in the early 1990s for its refusal to admit atheists and homosexuals as scouts and scoutmasters. Levi Strauss, BankAmerica, and Wells Fargo halted their donations in defiance of the group's homosexual ban. President Clinton became the first U.S. president in recent history to not address the national Jamboree or send his vice president. In addition, the city of Chicago canceled its sponsorship of the group. Nevertheless, the organization prevailed in several lawsuits filed by nonmembers for refusing to admit atheists, claiming that as a private organization, it is free to establish its own membership criteria. Critics often noted, however, that the group is sponsored by public schools and municipal organizations and should be subject to anti-discrimination provisions. In other countries, the theological portion of the oath has been either eliminated or made optional. Lawsuits and controversy have continued into the late 1990s. In 1999 New Jersey struck down the ban on homosexuals after four other states had upheld it. The Supreme Court expected to rule in 2000 on whether the Boy Scouts' denial of admission to a class of people amounts to a constitutional violation.

The highest rank attainable in the Boy Scouts is Eagle Scout. Many of the nation's most successful leaders hold this distinction, including astronauts, former presidents, business leaders, and creators. Gerald Ford, Sam Walton (founder of Wal-Mart), Steven Spielberg, and H. Ross Perot were examples of Eagle Scouts still living in the early 1990s. The 104th Congress of the United States has boasted 23 Eagle Scouts, with 302 members total having participated in scouting.

American Legion. The American Legion is the largest private U.S. organization for veterans. It is comprised of veterans from both world wars and the wars in Korea, Vietnam, and the Persian Gulf. The Legion is concerned primarily with the social and political interests of veterans, but it also sponsors numerous community and charitable programs, such as the Family Support Network. This program was launched in 1990 for the Persian Gulf War troops and remains active for other troops stationed around the world. Its four stated major areas of focus are: rehabilitation of veterans through medical and educational benefits; national security; child welfare; and Americanism. The organization strongly promotes respect for the U.S. flag, having drafted the U.S. Flag Code in 1923 establishing guidelines for the proper uses and treatment of the flag. The American Legion also works to fund and promote other civic associations included in this industry group, such as the Boy Scouts.

The American Legion represents 2.9 million male and female members in nearly 15,000 posts worldwide, with a full-time staff of 300. Membership is contingent upon performance of honorable service in the U.S. armed forces. The Legion's sister organization, the American Legion Auxiliary, founded in 1920, had approximately 1 million members. Its participants are women who are close relatives of Legionnaires or of deceased veterans and women who have served in the armed forces during peacetime. The Sons of the American Legion (about 180,500 members in 1995) is comprised of male descendants of Legionnaires and deceased veterans.

Because of its membership size and the percentage of its members that are registered to vote, the American Legion has constituted a powerful political block. It has served as a loud voice for veterans' rights and military preparedness. It has been a leading proponent of legislation against desecration of the American Flag since the 1960s, continuing into the 1990s. It has helped veterans receive proper medical care for illnesses that may be related to wartime environments, such as nerve gas during the Persian Gulf War in 1991. Recently the Legion has campaigned to increase hospital coverage funded by the Department of Veterans' Affairs to include veterans' dependents.

YMCA. The Young Men's Christian Association (YMCA) is one of the largest associations in the world. With 2,283 YMCAs, it is also the largest non-profit community-service organization in the United States. The YMCA is a network of nonsectarian organizations that offer athletic, recreational, cultural, educational, and health-related services to their members and local communities. YMCAs provide vocational instruction, organize sports programs, offer civic training, give night classes, and host social events. YMCAs also make their facilities available to community groups and rent cafeterias and rooms to transients and local residents.

The YMCA was founded in England in 1844, while the first YMCA in the United States was started in Boston in 1851. The World Alliance of YMCAs is head-quartered in Switzerland, serving more than 30 million international members in 120 countries. There were approximately 16.9 million members in the United States in 1999, up from 14.5 million just four years earlier. They rely on more 515,720 volunteers and 20,000 full-time staff, and are funded by a combined operating budget of $3.1 billion, drawn from fees for Y programs, membership dues, charitable contributions, and resident fees. Its sister organization, the Young Women's Christian Association (YWCA), was formed in 1855 to meet young women's physical, intellectual, and spiritual needs. But after World War II, women and girls were admitted to the YMCA, as well. By 1996, almost one-half of YMCA members and staff in the United States were women; also, one-half of all members were 18 years or under. The 326 YWCAs provide shelter for women and their families, and spearhead campaigns for domestic-violence prevention. They offer programs and services to about 700,000 women and children annually.

United Way. Another of the biggest organizations in this industry is the United Way, which is largely a fund-raising organization that gives money to national and community service groups. Raising $3.1 billion annually by their over 300,000 volunteers, it provided money to more than 50,000 agencies of health and human services needs in 1997. Fifty-two million people contribute annually to about 2,200 local United Way agencies.

Other Groups. The Knights of Columbus is a U.S. fraternal order of Roman Catholic men promoting itself as "the strong right arm of the Church." It was founded in 1882 by Michael J. McGivney, a Connecticut priest. Best known for their charity work within communities, it provides social activities, insurance, and other benefits for its members. It also sponsors athletic events, contributes to various charitable and educational projects, and works to promote Catholic interests. The group had approximately 1.6 million members in more than 12,000 local councils throughout the Americas in the late 1990s.

The Humane Society of the United States includes about 7 million supporters and established, with Salomon Brothers Asset Management, the Humane Equity Fund in the late 1990s, which refuses to invest in firms whose practices the Humane Society considers to be detrimental to the welfare of animals. The Humane Society has contributed $8 million to the fund.

Other organizations include university fraternities and sororities, the Elks Club, Lions Club, and the Parent-Teacher Association.

FURTHER READING

"Activists Without Borders." *Business Week,* 4 October 1999.

Gardner, Jonathan. "Legion Airs Proposal." *Modern Healthcare,* 29 June 1998.

"Girl Scouts Seek New Image." *Marketing News,* 25 May 1998.

Livingston, P. Hann. "Scout's Honor." *The American Lawyer,* September 1998.

"Women Belong to Religious Clubs, Men to Veterans' Groups." *About Women & Marketing,* April 1997.

Wrolstad, Mark. "To Rebuild, Freemasonry Crumbles Wall of Secrecy—Lodge Runs Spots on Radio to Recruit." *The Seattle Times,* 18 October 1998.

SIC 8651

POLITICAL ORGANIZATIONS

This classification includes membership organizations established to promote the interests of a national, state, or local political party or candidate, Also included are political groups organized to raise funds for a political party or individual candidates. Fund-raising organizations operating on a contract or fee basis are classified in **SIC 7389: Business Services, Not Elsewhere Classified.**

NAICS Code(s)

813940 (Political Organizations)

Industry Snapshot

The most prominent type of political organization is the political action committee, or PAC, which gradually came to replace the smaller localized political parties so prevalent in the nineteenth and early twentieth centuries. PACs are organized to pool the financial resources of a group of individuals or institutions with a common interest in order to disperse those funds toward political activities or candidates deemed by the PACs' organizers as conducive to the ends sought. PACs are usually, but not always, organized by corporations or people within an industry, such as oil companies, dairy farmers, banking institutions, or labor organizations. PACs contribute funds to politicians in hopes of gaining their support for legislation to advance the PACs' interests; some of the larger PACs focus on gun control, equal rights, or abortion rights. Corporate PACs have long been the leading contributors to political campaigns. Election-campaign funding has become a hot political topic in the late 1990s, as many question the political influence that PACs and other interests wield in the political process. The total cost of federal election campaigning in 2000 was expected to exceed $3 billion.

A 1974 law passed by Congress fueled a dramatic increase in the formation of PACs. In 1986, there were 608 PACs, but by the end of 1998, the number of PACs grew to more than 5,000. PACs delivered $219.9 million in contributions to federal candidates for the 1998 elections, up from $126.7 million in 1996. Nearly all of it went to candidates for the U.S. Congress. Republican candidates enjoyed $108.0 million in contributions, while Democrats trailed with $98.3 million. PACs raised a total of $502.6 million during the 1997-98 election cycle, a 15 percent increase from 1995-96.

In recent years ideological or issue-oriented PACs have become popular. In contrast to groups that contribute directly to candidates, these PACs donate funds to organizations aligned with their interests in an effort to sway public opinion. Such organizations typically produce radio and television commercials and direct mail campaigns on controversial issues, including the right to abortion, prayer in schools, and gun control. Unlike corporate and labor union PACs, which may use money from the treasuries of their members, ideological PACs foot their own administrative costs. Because these groups are not contributing directly to candidates, they are not bound by many of the usual limitations on PACs.

Organization and Structure

PACs fall into five general categories: those formed by unions; trade associations and industry groups; corporations; cooperatives; and ideological PACs, which pursue specific political causes. For the most part, PACs may only solicit their own members for contributions. PACs are heavily regulated by the Federal Election Commission (FEC) and must keep accurate and detailed records of receipts and expenditures. One of the most efficient ways of collecting donations for PACs is through automatic deductions from members' paychecks—the checkoff method. PACs may donate up to $35,000 to a particular candidate in an election season and $15,000 to a national party committee, as well as a maximum of $5,000 to another PAC.

While some commentators applaud the fact that PACs involve citizens in the political process, others argue that PACs rarely offer opportunities for people to do more than donate money. Most PACs have small boards or committees deciding how the contributions will be spent or which candidates will receive contributions. This structure has caused some to argue that control of PAC contributions is relinquished to just a few people within the organization, which may present opportunities for abuse or misrepresentation. Another common complaint about PACs, especially in recent years, concerns the perception that they often have enjoyed too much influence in America's legislative bodies.

In an attempt to maximize their influence, most PACs channel their energy to the most powerful members of the congressional committees affecting their industry. For example, in 1986, PACs advancing the interests of banks and other financial institutions made contributions totaling more than $3.4 million to members of the House and Senate banking committees. In 1998, the total contribution to the elections of congressional members sympathetic to financial causes was $35.2 million. PACs are also much more likely to donate monies to incumbents, who are historically difficult to unseat. Until 1994, incumbents seeking re-election in the U.S. House of Representatives had a 98 percent victory rate; since then, election results have continued to tilt overwhelmingly in favor of incumbents.

Background and Development

The development of modern campaign financing laws can be traced back to 1896, when scandals began to affect presidential elections. In the 1896 presidential campaign, assessments against corporations imposed by Republican National Chairman Mark Hanna filled William McKinley's campaign coffers. This was followed by the disclosure that McKinley's successor, Theodore Roosevelt, had received a secret $50,000 contribution from a New York insurance company in 1904. This election ignited national headlines and prompted Roosevelt to call for campaign reform, urging public financing of congressional and presidential elections. Congress responded by passing the Tillman Act of 1907, which prohibited business groups from making contributions to candidates for federal office. Campaign reform was broadened with passage of the Federal Corrupt Practices Act of 1925, which placed limits on contributions and required disclosure of receipts and expenditures by federal candidates.

The modern PAC is somewhat of a newcomer to the U.S. political scene. In the 1930s, newly formed labor unions began to see the advantages of becoming involved in politics. In 1936 organized labor contributed $750,000 to Democratic candidates, with most of the funds coming from union dues. But in 1943, Congress passed the Smith-Connally Act, which barred unions from making direct contributions in federal elections from their treasury funds. However, these laws were difficult to enforce. Both labor unions and corporations began to establish separate accounts with which to make political contributions—such activity foreshadowed the rise of the modern PAC.

The first PAC was formed by organized labor in 1943 when the AFL and CIO merged, forming the Committee on Political Education. These labor organizations were able to operate these PACs because they used political funds rather than union dues. This laid the groundwork for other labor PACs, which began to proliferate shortly thereafter. By 1956, 17 labor PACs contributed $2.1 million to political candidates. In 1982, the number had risen to 288 labor PACs, which contributed $20 million to federal candidates. In 1995, there were 332 labor PACs contributing $26 million to federal campaigns.

In the 1960s, corporations began to organize their own PACs. The first major PAC to be organized was the American Medical Political Action Committee (AMPAC), formed in 1961 by the American Medical Association, followed by the Business Industry Political Action Committee (BIPAC), organized in 1963 by the National Association of Manufacturers. Prior to this, most political contributions were made by wealthy individuals. For example, in 1956, 199 executives from 225 corporations contributed more than $1.9 million to federal candidates.

In 1972, Congress enacted the Federal Election Campaign Act, which superseded previous federal campaign regulations and was the catalyst for the tremendous growth of PACs in subsequent decades. The Federal Election Campaign Act (FECA) included the following key features: it limited the total amount a federal candidate could spend on media advertising to $50,000; it required disclosure of all contributions in excess of $100; it required committees and candidates to file reports of contributions and expenditures; and it required television stations to sell candidates time at the lowest unit cost provided to commercial advertising customers.

The most important part of the law for the PACs was the Hansen Amendment, which enabled union and corporate treasury money to be used for overhead in operating PACs. It also provided business and labor organizations with the right to solicit voluntary funds from members, employees, and stockholders. This gave PACs the power to be involved in federal elections and had the effect of institutionalizing the role of PACs within the political process. The Hansen Amendment became the springboard for the proliferation of PACs because it enabled corporate coffers to finance PACs' often considerable administrative expenses. It was estimated that in the 1984 election, some PACs spent $75 million, roughly one-fourth of their expenditures, on administrative expenses. And as television advertisements became the primary medium for articulating their viewpoints, campaign costs rose meteorically.

Concern about large monetary gifts to candidates peaked in the aftermath of the 1972 presidential election, when it was revealed that 124 donors gave $17 million to help re-elect Richard Nixon, and several individuals contributed a combined amount of $200,000 to George McGovern's campaign. This resulted in amendments to FECA in 1974 that established new contribution and spending limits. But in 1976, Senator James Buckley, together with Eugene McCarthy and philanthropist Stewart Mott, challenged the law, claiming that limits on campaign contributions were an infringement on the right to free speech. The U.S. Supreme Court agreed and struck down much of the law. Thereafter, groups and individuals could spend as much as they wanted to support or oppose a candidate. Later amendments to the law increased spending limits by candidates who accept public financing and required PACs and candidates to keep accurate records of receipts and expenditures.

A primary reason for the explosion of PACs is skyrocketing campaign costs. In 1974, all of the U.S. House and Senate candidates spent a combined total of $77.0 million on their campaigns. By 1982, that figure had jumped to $343.0 million—an increase of nearly 500 percent. And, according to the FEC, Congressional campaign spending climbed to $626.4 million during the 1996 elections.

CURRENT CONDITIONS

PACs increasingly dominate Congressional elections and provide security for incumbents. In 1996, PACs gave $98.3 million to Congressional incumbents but only $12.5 million to challengers. However, many legislators, including those who accept PAC contributions, regard PACs as a necessary evil because of the cost of campaigning. PACs, by their very nature, most often represent the interests of the wealthy and staunchly ideological.

For many years, Democrats enjoyed the majority of PAC contributions, but that trend reversed during the

1995-96 election cycle, when Republicans received $118.6 million compared with the Democrats' $98.85 million. Republicans continued to outpace their Democratic rivals in contributions receipts in 1997-98. This shift is primarily attributable to the enormous Republican gains in the congressional elections of 1994, which gave them a substantial majority in both houses. Since PAC contributions flow disproportionately to incumbents, Republicans were poised to enjoy healthy contributions through the 2000 elections.

Corporate PACs contributed a total of $78 million to candidates during the 1997-98 election cycle, of which 85 percent went to incumbents. Republicans received 68 percent of these donations, while Democrats received 32 percent.

Among industry groupings, contributions in 1997-98 were as follows: agribusiness contributed $15.6 million; communications and electronics gave $11.94 million; Construction interests donated $8.3 million; PACs representing the defense industry gave $5.8 million; energy and natural resources concerns contributed $14.85 million; finance and real estate bestowed $35.2 million; health PACs supplied candidates with $18.3 million; lawyers and lobbyists allotted $7.7 million; transportation interests contributed $14.4 million; and other business interests gave $17.3 million. With the exception of lawyers and lobbyists, all groups' contributions tilted heavily in favor of Republicans.

Labor PACs maintained a strong presence during 1997-98, contributing a total of $44.6 million. The vast majority of these donations (91 percent) went to Democrats, while most of the rest went to Republicans, with only a fraction left over for other candidates.

Trade and membership association PACs contributed $62.3 million, of which 81.0 percent was given to incumbents, 62.3 percent to Republicans, and 37.6 percent to Democrats.

Cooperative PACs donated 91 percent of their $2.4 million in total contributions to incumbents. Republicans took in 51 percent of the total, while Democrats received 48 percent.

Issue-oriented PACs fortified their growing influence in 1997-98, contributing a total of $28.15 million; 60.4 percent to Republicans and 39 percent to Democrats, and 61 percent to incumbents.

With the explosive growth of PACs came the cries for campaign finance reform in order to prevent special interest money from controlling the electoral process. Critics called for anti-PAC legislation aimed at curtailing campaign expenditures, worried that the influence of wealth would determine what candidates came to office and what policies they would support once elected. Moreover, critics contend, PAC sponsors enjoy disproportionate access to candidates, further marginalizing the general public from the political process. Opponents of such legislation have raised possible First Amendment concerns, asserting that contributing money to political campaigns amounts to free speech. Therefore, they claim, laws limiting such contributions would effectively infringe on contributors' constitutional rights

So long as members of Congress benefit from the contributions of PACs, reform will be difficult to achieve. Many bills designed to curb the influence of political action committees have been introduced in Congress, but none have been passed. PACs continue to influence legislation and elections, and polls show that Americans view PAC lobbying as a significant problem in the current legislative process. Studies by the U.S. Public Interest Research Group show that time and again, those who receive PAC donations from a particular industry are more likely to vote in alliance with that industry. Although the issue of campaign finance reform was discussed during the 1992 Presidential and 1994 Congressional elections, only after the 1996 campaign was it seriously brought before Congress and the public by both President Clinton and Congressional leaders. By 2000, however, the issue was far from solved and even more contentious. A poll conducted by Louis Harris and Associates found that about 83 percent of Americans felt that PACs wielded too much influence in national politics. The Alliance for Better Campaigns aimed their efforts at broadcasters, calling for increased television and radio coverage as well as free broadcast time for politicians, thus alleviating the necessity for enormous advertising expenditures. Political groups during the 1997-98 election cycle spent an estimated $260 million on radio and television advertising.

Political organizations have flourished on the World Wide Web, where a series of sites cropped up in the late 1990s devoted to mobilizing political support for issues and candidates. Furthermore, many sites, including Voter .com, Gay.com, Politicallyblack.com, and LatinoVota.com were designed specifically to raising political awareness and voter turnout among specific demographic groups.

Industry Leaders

The largest PACs by the late 1990s included those representing the Association Trial Lawyers of America, with contributions of $2.42 million during the 1997-98 election cycle; the American Federation of State and County Municipal Employees, with $2.37 million; the American Medical Association, with $2.34; as well as the National Association of Realtors, the American Institute of Certified Public Accountants, the National Rifle Association, United Parcel Service, AT&T, the National Automobile Dealers Association, and the United Auto

Workers. The fastest-growing political interest in Washington D.C. during 1997-98 was the credit-union lobby, who doubled their contributions to $1.6 million, fueled by consumer activism. Overall, business PACs donate more than three times as much money as labor PACs.

One of the most well-known and fastest growing individual PACs during the 1990s, the National Rifle Association, grew by 132 percent by 1992, giving more than $1.7 million to candidates. Although membership declined in the mid-1990s, increases in their PAC spending continued to grow, while public relations efforts intensified under the appointment of actor Charlton Heston as president of the association. The NRA Political Victory Fund raised $7.7 million during 1997-98, and contributed $2.05 million to congressional candidates, of which 86 percent went to Republicans.

FURTHER READING

Albiniak, Paige. ''Alliance Pushes for Airtime.'' *Broadcasting & Cable,* 13 December 1999.

Clymer, Adam. ''Court's Ruling Heartens Soft Money's Opponents.'' *New York Times,* 25 January 2000.

Federal Election Commission. ''FEC Releases Information on PAC Activity for 1997-98,'' 8 June 1999. Available from http://fec.gov/press/pacye98.htm.

''For-Profit Web Sites Give New Meaning to Campaign Financing.'' *New York Times,* 10 January 2000.

''Groups Spending $260 Million on Ads to Promote Agendas.'' *New York Times,* 15 October 1998.

Hicks, Daryl. ''Industry PACs Donate $10.8 Million.'' *New York Times,* 15 February 1999.

Knight, Danielle. ''Environment: Massive Ad Campaign Begins on Global Warming.'' *Interpress Service,* 6 October 1999.

''PAC Contributions to Federal Candidates 1997-1998.'' *Regulatory Compliance Watch,* 3 August 1998.

Stern, Philip M. *The Best Congress Money Can Buy.* New York: Random House, 1988.

Zuckerman, Edward, ed. *The Almanac of Federal PACs: 1998-99.* Arlington, VA: Amward Publications, Inc., 1998.

SIC 8661

RELIGIOUS ORGANIZATIONS

This category covers organizations operated for worship, for religious training or study, for government or administration of an organized religion, or for promotion of religious activities, including religious groups reaching the public through radio or television media. Other establishments maintained by religious organizations, such as educational institutions, hospitals, publishing houses, reading rooms, social services, and secondhand stores, are classified according to their primary activity. Establishments of such religious groups that produce taped religious programming for television are covered in **SIC 7812: Motion Picture and Video Tape Production;** and those that produce live religious programs are classified in **SIC 7922: Theatrical Producers (Except Motion Picture) and Miscellaneous Theatrical Services.** Radio or television stations operated by religious organizations are classified under **SIC 4832: Radio Broadcasting Stations** or **SIC 4833: Television Broadcasting Stations.**

NAICS CODE(S)

813110 (Religious Organizations)

INDUSTRY SNAPSHOT

Religious organizations in the United States have been involved in an innumerable range of activities. In recent years, these activities have included everything from organizing food drives to aid the poor, to solidarity campaigns to aid the victims of U.S. military operations in Central America, to grassroots measures to remove the teaching of biological evolution in U.S. science classes. On a comparative level, the greatest number of religious organizations, and those boasting the largest membership figures, remain overwhelmingly Christian. Between the mid-1960s and the end of the twentieth century, Catholicism and Evangelical Protestantism increased their membership as mainstream Protestant groups suffered significant losses in membership. This shift in numbers in America's religious groups has been especially painful for the largest, most well-established denominations. With membership a paramount concern for congregations across the country, many churches have adopted active philosophies designed to attract and keep worshippers.

In 1998, 70 percent of U.S. citizens aged 18 or older were members of a church or synagogue, up 3 percent from the year before, though that figure has not experienced much net change since the early 1980s. While 62 percent of Americans are of the opinion that religion is taking on a diminished influence in national life, up from 49 percent in 1989, the proportion who place a great priority on religion in their own lives held steady at 59 percent.

BACKGROUND AND DEVELOPMENT

The United States has long prided itself on its diversity of religious expression. Numerous faiths are practiced in America, ranging from the Abrahamic religions of Judaism, Catholicism, Protestantism, and Islam to the other major world religions like Hinduism and Buddhism, as well as myriad others. The church has traditionally functioned as a major institution for vast numbers of the American populace.

While churches do not have to pay government taxes, they still must secure income for a variety of purposes. Most churches sustain themselves financially through "tithes"—contributions made to the church by those who worship there. Tithing permits churches to meet their financial obligations in the realm of operating costs and payroll, as well as to contribute to charitable or social causes. In recent years, this primary source of income has risen in value but fallen as a proportion of the giver's income. By 1998 the average annual family income of Catholic homes was $43,000, but the contributions to the Church was a mere 0.6 percent of their income, a fact that observers attribute to factors such as a growing tendency for worshippers to disagree with the leadership's allocation of church resources.

The pilgrim fathers of the early seventeenth century created a powerful white Anglo-Saxon Protestant establishment. From about the mid-nineteenth century on, the nation's majority of Protestant denominations increasingly consolidated in churches that operated the financial aspect of their existence in a manner not unlike a corporate business.

In the 1970s and 1980s, however, Evangelical Protestant congregations increased in popularity. Long part of America but previously found among the poorest and least powerful sections of society, the numbers of Evangelical Protestants increased during this time, as did their socio-economic status. This provided an influx of wealth that brought further conversions, together with additional power and prestige in both the religious and political halls of the United States.

During this same period, six of the seven sister denominations of mainstream Protestantism collectively suffered significant membership losses. From 1965 to 1995, the membership in the United Methodist Church dropped from 11.0 to 8.5 million. Losses were posted by other Protestant groups as well: Evangelical Lutheran Church in America, from 5.7 to 5.2 million; Presbyterian Church (U.S.), from 4.2 to 3.7 million; Episcopal Church, from 3.5 to 2.5 million; and the Christian Church (Disciples of Christ) from 1.9 to 1.0 million. The American Baptist Church, however, grew from 1.3 to 1.5 million members. The general loss of membership should have created a corresponding drop in revenue, which would force many congregations to tighten budgets and curtail community programs, but according to the 1996 *Yearbook of American & Canadian Churches,* most religious denominations showed an increase in revenue despite attendance figures. For example, the Presbyterian Church (U.S.) having one of the biggest membership losses, still had an increase of 4.8 percent in contributions/revenue, totaling $2.1 billion.

Current Conditions

The top five religious groups by membership size account for 61 percent of all memberships in religious organizations in the United States. The Catholic Church is the largest religious body in the United States with 61.2 million members and 33,000 churches; the Southern Baptist Convention has 16 million members and 41,000 churches; United Methodist Churches have 8.5 million members and 33,000 churches; the National Baptist Convention, USA, has 8.5 million members and 36,170 churches; the Church of God in Christ has 5.5 million members and 15,300 churches; and the Evangelical Lutheran Church in America has 5.2 million members and 10,900 churches.

Among those Americans older than 18, 59 percent identified themselves as Protestant; 27 percent as Catholic; and 2 percent as Jewish. In addition, there were about 530,000 Muslims, 400,000 Buddhists, and 227,000 Hindus. Only 7 percent identified themselves as atheists or agnostics. Affiliation with a religious organization was directly correlated with age; among those 65 and older, 75 percent belong to a church, while the percentages drop among younger populations—to 63 percent for those between the ages of 18 and 29.

Protestantism, the most widely practiced religion in the United States, covered more than 70 denominations. Most Protestants identified with one of the five major bodies of Protestantism: Baptist, Lutheran, Methodist, Episcopalian, and Presbyterian. The leading Protestant denomination, the Southern Baptist Convention, was expected to split sometime in 2000 along ideological grounds between the conservatives and the moderates, the latter of whom sought greater tolerance of diversity in doctrinal, ethical, and social issues. Between 400 and 3,500 churches were likely to leave the organization.

While the Baptists were separating, other Protestant organizations were striking alliances. The nation's largest Lutheran congregation, the Evangelical Lutheran Church in America, and the Episcopal Church agreed in 1999 to fully accept each other's members and sacraments. While the two denominations would maintain their respective structures and practices, the alliance allowed for an exchange of clergy and collaboration of projects and services.

Religious organizations received about 60 percent of all household charitable contributions in 1998. Among the 70 percent of U.S. households that donated money to a church or religious organization, the average contribution was $1,022.

Workforce

Protestant ministers and diocesan priests have a wide array of duties. They read and study to prepare texts for preaching or publication, perform, offer religious instruction, and often are called upon to address various other community needs—conducting marriage and funeral services; visiting the elderly, sick, and handicapped; and responding to emergencies. Additional administrative, educational, and community service activities represent an unpredictable but typically heavy burden. Particular activities of course vary widely according to the religious group and the specific institution's mission and resources.

In 1997, there were more than 300,000 Protestant ministers leading individual congregations, as well as thousands of others with no fixed congregation. Other ministers worked in correctional institutions, universities, the military, hospitals, and other establishments. Other faiths had a considerable number of religious leaders in America as well. According to the *Occupational Outlook Handbook, 1999* there were approximately 4,300 rabbis in America (1,000 Orthodox, 1,250 Conservative, 1,800 Reform, and 250 Reconstructionist). By 1996, there were about 50,000 priests and 93,000 lay women and/or nuns associated with the Catholic Church in America.

Employment prospects were considered much more favorable for Evangelical ministers than for those in the mainstream, where the number of qualified candidates seemed likely to exceed the available positions, with the possible exception of congregations in rural areas. The Catholic Church requires that its priests remain celibate and does not allow women to serve the church in that capacity. These restrictions have been widely viewed as the primary reasons for the shortage of Catholic priests in America. And by the mid-1990s, with approximately 10 percent of the Catholic Churches without a resident priest, many of them began to rely on women to act as administrative pastors, changing the participatory numbers of women greatly.

According to the *Occupational Outlook Handbook, 1999,* the average salary (including such fringe benefits as housing and insurance) for Protestant ministers was $30,000, down from $40,000 a few years earlier. This figure, however, varied considerably, depending on age, experience, denomination, the size and wealth of the congregation served, and geographic location. Diocesan priests' salaries were typically as low as $11,000, but were usually supplemented with a comprehensive package of benefits including a retirement plan, free room and board, a transport allowance or car, and health benefits. Diocesan priests also often supplemented their income with teaching activities within the church parish; required to take a vow of poverty, priests were reliant on the support of their religious order. Annual earning of rabbis in America, generally, were between $45,000 and $75,000, including benefits such as above. Their income usually depended upon the size and financial capabilities of their congregation.

FURTHER READING

Condren, Dave. ''Empty Pulpits: Protestant Churches are Facing Dwindling Ranks of Clergy.'' *The Buffalo News,* 27 November 1999.

''The Heart of the Matter.'' *The Humanist,* May/June 1997.

Niebuhr, Gustav. '' A Religious Union May Beget Others.'' *The New York Times,* 29 August 1999.

'' Religion Is Important To A Large Majority of Americans.'' *Research Alert,* 3 December 1999.

Sheler, Jeffrey L.'' Christians, Unite!'' *U.S. News & World Report,* 15 November 1999.

''Southern Baptist Leader Predicts Split.'' *Los Angeles Times,* 11 December 1999.

SIC 8699

MEMBERSHIP ORGANIZATIONS, NOT ELSEWHERE CLASSIFIED

This category covers membership organizations, not elsewhere classified (NEC), such as art councils, automobile owner's associations and clubs, humane societies, and reading rooms.

NAICS CODE(S)

813410 (Civic and Social Organizations)
813910 (Business Associations)
813312 (Environment, Conservation, and Wildlife Organizations)
561599 (All Other Travel Arrangement and Reservation Services)
813990 (Other Similar Organizations)

The membership organizations (NEC) group was comprised of about 11,432 establishments with 108,600 paid employees in 1998. Many organizations, however, were staffed primarily with volunteer members. Most of the groups were small, local bodies, uniting people with common interests. In fact, many associations in this classification had no full-time staff members and only few hundred, or fewer, members. In the late 1980s, the average organization had eight workers and paid about $123,000 in payroll expenses, an average of only $15,000 per employee.

Almost all membership organizations in this classification are tax-exempt corporations. They generate revenues through dues, sales of insurance and other products and services, fund raising events and drives, endowment funds, and investments. Larger organizations often hire professional fund-raising firms. These companies usually charge a flat-fee or a percentage of proceeds and conduct direct marketing campaigns and events. The average establishment in this group generated tax-free income of $550,000 annually during the 1990s.

While most miscellaneous membership organizations are relatively small, there are a few large entities that warrant description. In 1998 the Boy Scouts of America (BSA) had 4.8 million members, 500 employees, and sales of $251 million. That same year, the Girl Scouts of the USA had 3.5 million members. YWCA of the USA reported 2 million members in 1998, $15 million in sales, and 90 employees. Rotary International reported 1.2 million members, 400 employees, and $72 million in sales.

American Automobile Association. With more than 40 million members, 90 clubs, and 1,000 offices, the American Automobile Association (AAA) is one of the largest and most successful enterprises in the United States. The only other organizations that compare in size to this behemoth are the U.S. Catholic Church and the American Association of Retired Persons. Unlike most organizations in this group, the AAA pays some taxes, but it still operates as a not-for-profit entity.

The AAA is a federation of 145 affiliated auto clubs. Members receive access to emergency road services, vacation and travel planning assistance, group insurance plans, and financial services. They also get periodic newsletters and magazines that keep them informed about automotive, travel, energy, environmental, and legislative topics. The AAA is the largest publisher of travel-related publications in the world. It produces more than 350 million copies of its publications each year, and consumes 22,000 tons of paper annually to produce its library of maps and books. The AAA also supports highway and road safety initiatives, and lobbies for membership interests.

The AAA was formed in 1902 when nine automobile clubs joined forces. As the automobile became a staple of American life during the twentieth century, AAA membership swelled to 20 million by 1980. During the 1980s, moreover, the AAA boosted its ranks at a rate of more than one million each year. It markets its services on a local basis, with each affiliate handling its own recruiting through direct mail and telephone sales. In-house local staffs provide individualized service. As a result, the AAA enjoys a membership renewal rate of 88 percent—much higher than the industry norm.

American Farm Bureau Federation. Another one of the largest membership organizations (NEC) is the American Farm Bureau Federation (AFBF). It represents the political interests of its members, and is recognized as a relatively powerful lobbying group in Washington. In the past, AFBF leadership has shown support for flexible price supports and minimal government interference in farming. The group has also promoted soil and water conservation, rural education programs, and rural electrification and infrastructure.

Farm bureaus emerged with the development of the county agricultural agent plan in the United States during the early 1900s. The AFBF was founded in 1919 to combine these bureaus into a single entity—to ''promote, protect, and represent the business, economic, social, and educational interests of the farmers of the nation.'' The AFBF had about 4 million members in 1996.

Further Reading

Darnay, Arsen J., ed. *Service Industries USA.* Detroit: Gale Group, 1999.

Elsbach, Kimberly D. ''Member's Responses to Organizational Identity Encountering and Countering the Business Week Rankings.'' *Administrative Science Quarterly,* September 1996.

Hoover's Company Capsules.*Hoover's Online.* 2000. Available from http://www.hoovers.com.

Kuttner, Robert. ''After Solidarity.'' *American Prospect,* May/June 1996.

Pisik, Betsy. ''The NRA's New Top Gun.'' *Working Woman,* April 1996.

Rubenstein, Edwin. ''Right Data.'' *National Review,* 9 December 1996.

''The Top 100.'' *Association Management,* May 1996.

SIC 8711

ENGINEERING SERVICES

This category covers establishments engaged primarily in providing professional engineering services. Civil, mechanical, electrical and electronic, chemical, sanitary, industrial, petroleum, mining, aeronautical, and marine engineering are among the disciplines included. Establishments primarily providing and supervising their own engineering staff on temporary contract to other firms are included in this industry. Establishments providing engineering personnel, but not general supervision, are classified in **SIC 7363: Help Supply Services.** Establishments primarily providing architectural services are classified in **SIC 8712: Architectural Services,** and those providing photogrammetric engineering are classified in Industry **SIC 8713: Surveying Services.**

NAICS Code(s)

541330 (Engineering Services)

Industry Snapshot

Engineering covers a vast array of specialties touching virtually all aspects of life. The profession is categorized into disciplines representing designated areas of interest, though not all commentators define the disciplines in the same way. Some choose many narrow descriptions while others rely on fewer, more broadly drawn, classifications. By far, the most significant modern trend in the industry was computerization. Computers equipped with CAD/CAM and 3-D software largely replaced calculators and drafting boards by the end of the 20th century.

In 1999, CorpTech estimated there were 44,623 U.S. establishments involved in the engineering services industry—an increase of 3.7 percent over 1996 figures. The industry employed approximately 1.64 million engineers, and 1.01 million technical personnel in 1997 including technicians, technologists drafters and estimators combined, according to U.S. Bureau of Labor Statistics (BLS).

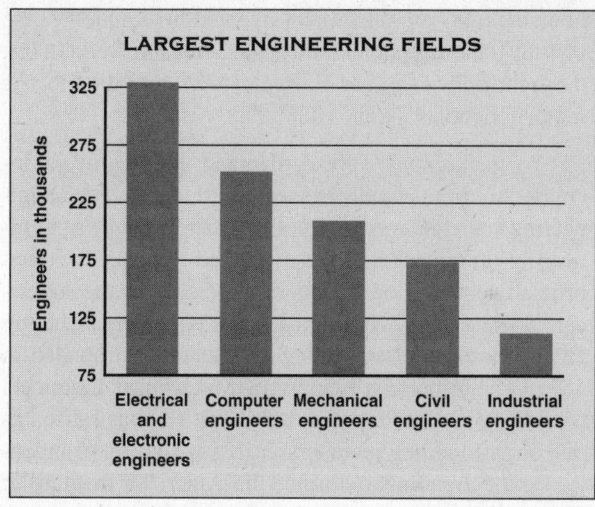

Organization and Structure

According to BLS approximately 329,070 electrical and electronic engineers comprise this field, which is the largest engineering discipline. The Institute of Electrical and Electronics Engineers, Inc., with 224,658 members in the United States in 1998, described itself as "the world's largest technical professional society."

The most populous classification of engineers after electrical and electronic engineers are computer engineers, which number 252,230, followed by mechanical engineers (209,490), civil engineers (173,690), and industrial engineers (112,400). The smallest groups of engineers are the 3,300 marine engineers and 3,440 mining engineers.

Engineering establishments serve two major classes of clients: government (representing 41.6 percent of fees charged) and industrial, commercial, and other firms (representing 35.4 percent). The remainder of engineering firm clients included architectural firms, construction companies, individuals, other engineering firms, and private institutions.

Projects undertaken by engineering establishments include industrial and processing plants and systems (19 percent); power generating and transmission facilities (18.9 percent); navel and aeronautical equipment (13.5 percent); water supply and sanitation facilities (8.1 percent); highways, roads, bridges, and streets (6.9 percent); commercial buildings (5.3 percent); and public and institutional facilities such as hospitals and educational facilities (3.3 percent).

Background and Development

The American Society for Engineering Education defined engineering as "the profession in which a knowledge of the mathematical and natural sciences gained by study, experience and practice is applied with judgement to develop ways to utilize the materials and forces of nature economically for the benefit of mankind." This interest in manipulating matter and power for society's welfare has its roots in antiquity. In many ways the progress of civilization provides a record of mankind's engineering achievements.

Throughout history, scientists have studied the world, its composition, its properties, its inhabitants, and its universe. As they discovered principles and truths, engineers applied these discoveries to construct a changed world. For example, chemists provided the information used by chemical engineers to create new building materials and pharmaceuticals. Biologists made discoveries that were put to use by engineers to increase crop production and offer improved medical services. Physical scientists contributed the knowledge needed to build pyramids and skyscrapers. Scientists identified electricity but engineers enabled the phenomenon.

Transitions from the Stone Age to the Bronze Age and then to the Iron Age were made possible by changes in mining and metallurgical engineering. When public works projects became too large for a single craftsman to accomplish, even with the help of family and apprentices, civil engineers coordinated and focused the efforts of thousands of workers. Their projects included roads, bridges, irrigation systems, government buildings, and religious structures.

Windmills and waterwheels were the work of archetypal mechanical engineers. Their progeny ushered in the Industrial Revolution during the late eighteenth and early nineteenth centuries. James Watt's invention of the steam engine in 1802 led to the development of steam locomotives, steam propelled boats, and the mechanization of agriculture.

The roots of electrical engineering extend back to the 1600s when William Gilbert, an English scientist, first described magnetism and static electricity. In 1800, Alexander Volta discovered that electric current could be made to flow. Throughout the nineteenth century, many scientists and inventors contributed to a growing body of knowledge about electricity. Some of its early applications included the telegraph (invented by Samuel Morse in 1838), the telephone (Alexander Graham Bell, 1876), the light bulb (Thomas Edison, 1878), and the electric motor (Nicholas Tesla, 1888).

As technology spread, demand for engineers increased. In time engineers specialized and founded engineering societies were to facilitate the exchange of engineering knowledge. In the United States, the first officially established engineering society was the American Society of Civil Engineers (ASCE), organized in 1852. The Society of Mining Engineers was founded in 1871. The American Society of Mechanical Engineers (ASME) was established in 1880 with Thomas Edison as one of its founding members. In 1884, a group of inventors and entrepreneurs formed the American Institute of Electrical Engineers.

The era also provided rapid advances in all disciplines of engineering. Civil engineers, for example, transformed bridge building technology. John Roebling, a pioneer in suspension bridge construction, designed and built an aqueduct over the Allegheny River to facilitate cargo transportation and a railway bridge over Niagara Falls Gorge. Roebling's most famous project, the Brooklyn Bridge, was completed in 1883—Roebling himself did not live to see the project finished. In addition to great landmark bridges, civil engineers erected hundreds of mass-produced metal truss bridges in many parts of the country.

Mechanical engineering, at the forefront of mass production, emerged from the domain of forges, iron smelters, and textile mills. Participants at the American Society of Mechanical Engineers' (ASME) first meeting discussed standardized sizes for screw threads, laying a necessary foundation for assembly-line technologies.

Material and metallurgical engineers also made rapid advances during the late 1800s. Innovations enabled the commercial production of aluminum, copper, zinc, and lead. Improved glass and stronger rubber products also became available. In addition, chemical engineers used scientific discoveries in the field of chemistry to produce an assortment of new materials. Some of the earliest commercial chemical products were manufactured for the nineteenth century textile dyeing industry.

In 1908, the American Institute of Chemical Engineers was founded. Throughout most of human history, people made items only with naturally occurring raw materials. Chemical engineers created new materials. They produced industrial chemicals, fertilizers, drugs, and paints. They improved stone, clay, glass, and ceramic building materials. They discovered processes to refine petroleum, preserve food, and make paper. Interest in U.S. chemical production intensified during the years preceding World War I because many industrial chemicals were imported from Germany.

During the war, an embargo of German materials led to a rapid expansion of the nation's domestic chemical industry. After the war, Arthur D. Little devised the concept of unit operations. Unit operations focused on the materials and energy undergoing changes inside a specific piece of equipment. By focusing on improving the efficiency of chemical reactions and preventing unwanted reactions, the concept enabled the development of techniques to produce chemicals in large continuous processes.

The World War I era also saw the birth of the electronic engineering field. As electrical knowledge developed, electricity was put to work in two distinct arenas. ''Heavy current'' was used for power and was manipulated by electrical engineers.''Light current,'' in contrast, was used for communication.

Electronics was born in 1907 when Lee De Forest invented the vacuum tube. Electronics engineers established the Institute of Radio Engineers in 1912 and the nation's first commercial radio stations began broadcasting during the 1920s. (The Institute of Radio Engineers and the American Institute of Electrical Engineers joined together to form the Institute of Electrical and Electronics Engineers, Inc. in 1963.)

As the machine age progressed, the need for codes and standards became apparent. To address the problem of boiler explosions, the ASME completed and published its first boiler code in 1915 and inaugurated a system for accrediting manufacturers of boiler equipment. The accrediting process involved reviewing manufacturing techniques, quality assurances, and materials. Manufacturers judged to be in compliance with the code were granted authorization to apply an ASME stamp to their products.

Three years later in 1918, the American National Standards Institute (ANSI) was founded. ANSI, the U.S. member of the International Standards Organization, served to coordinate development of voluntary standards by the various engineering disciplines.

Engineering disciplines became increasingly interrelated. Developments by electrical engineers impacted mechanical engineers. Demands for electricity by industrial engineers necessitated the development of improved means to generate and convey electric power. The growing automotive and aeronautical industries placed heavy demands on civil engineers to build the nation's infrastructure. They also relied on petroleum and chemical engineers to produce gasoline and aviation fuel.

During World War II, chemical engineers developed materials to help replace items, such as natural rubber, which were in short supply. DuPont researchers developed Nylon, a forerunner to the development of polymer plastics. Electronics engineers, spurred by military interests, developed advanced communication technologies including radar and sonar.

Following the war, electronics engineers created the transistor. Developed during the late 1940s and introduced commercially by Bell Labs in 1951, transistors replaced more fragile vacuum tubes. In the 1960s, engineers developed ways to build transistors on small chips of silicon. These innovations helped push the electronics industry into the computer era.

The 1960s also saw an event that was described by the National Academy of Engineering as the world's greatest engineering accomplishment—landing a man on the moon. NASA's Apollo project, begun in 1961, reached its primary objective in July 1969 when Neil Armstrong set foot on the lunar surface. His step was made possible by a variety of engineers who built the launch site; designed the spacecraft and lunar lander; generated the propulsion, guidance and life support systems; and fabricated space-durable textiles and other materials.

Another milestone in engineering history occurred in 1969 when the U.S. National Parks Service and the American Society of Civil Engineers established the Historic American Engineering Record (HAER) to chronicle America's engineering achievements. HAER's mission was to find structures of historic significance and document them, paying special attention to structures slated for demolition. HAER records were to be kept as part of the permanent collection of the Library of Congress.

David Brittan, writing for *Technology Review,* listed some of the artifacts included: blacksmith shops, bridges, canals, cider presses, coal mines, culverts, dams, electric power plants, foundries, granaries, ironworks, kilns, lighthouses, privies, sewage treatment plants, schooners, subways, tanneries, tunnels, viaducts, and waterworks.

In September 1971, ASME formed its own committee to begin a program to identify and recognize mechanical engineering artifacts. ASME noted that "machines are more likely than architecture or art to be moved, scrapped, or replaced by progressively efficient counterparts." They began a program of identifying three categories of designation: historic landmarks, heritage sites, and heritage collections. The 149 designations recognized in 34 states by 1992 included the Detroit Edison District Heating System (built in 1903), the Sikorsky VS-300 Helicopter (1939), the Experimental Breeder Reactor-1 (1951), the Shippingport Atomic Power Station (1958), the Disney Monorail System (1959), and the JFK Center's Crawler Transporters of Launch Complex 39 (1965).

Despite increased interest in preserving engineering history, engineers continued to forge the future. Advances in space technology led to improved communications. The first commercial satellite provided circuits for 240 telephone calls between the United States and Europe. By 1990, satellites provided communication systems between the United States and 40 other countries. Likewise, engineering advances made on behalf of medical providers led to the development of the computerized axial tomography (CAT) scan, based on X-ray technology that had been first used in Germany in 1895. The first CAT scanners were installed in Great Britain in 1971 and in the United States two years later. Subsequent advances led to ultrasound imaging and magnetic resonance imaging (MRI).

The increasing miniaturization of computer chips during the 1970s brought about a proliferation of electronic devices such as pocket calculators, personal computers, microwave ovens, and electronic toys. These miniature computer chips, no larger than a fingernail, also led to a growing sophistication of computer-controlled equipment including traffic lights, automobiles, and aircraft. More powerful computers resulted in the adoption of computer-aided design (CAD) and computer-aided manufacturing (CAM) techniques by many of the nation's major manufacturers.

Despite these accomplishments, the engineering industry faced some serious challenges during the 1980s. Some critics of modern technology blamed engineers for creating tools that wrought havoc on the environment. Others claimed that only engineering offered the potential for providing solutions to pollution. Within the arena of environmental engineering, researchers looked into ways to preserve, protect, and restore the environment. In addition, some industry watchers predicted a coming shortage of engineers. The number of male freshmen entering college with plans to earn an undergraduate degree in engineering fell from 22 percent to 17 percent between 1982 and 1987. Among women, the number dropped from 4 to 3 percent.

The Early 1990s. As the engineering industry entered the 1990s, the interdisciplinary nature of engineering increased. Many different types of engineering work were being done in many fields, and frequently the work done by an engineer in one discipline depended on or supplemented the work of an engineer in a different field. For example, mechanical engineering and electronic engineering combined to produce integrated machines with electronic components, and the field of robotics involved the integration of mechanical and electronic engineering.

Laser technology provided another example of an interdisciplinary expression of engineering skills. The creation of laser beams (beams of high-intensity light of one frequency, called "coherent" light) required input from electronics engineers, electrical engineers, chemical engineers, and mechanical engineers. Electronics engineers manipulated laser beams for use in office equipment. Other engineers used lasers to develop fiber optic technology. Mechanical engineers designed laser light shows. Engineers supplying the medical industry used lasers to create new types of surgical instruments.

Biochemical and biomedical chemical engineering during the 1990s also included work in genetic engineering, pharmaceutical research, and the development of agricultural chemicals. Other types of chemical engineering provided products to create advanced materials and polymer-based chemicals. In total, the chemical industry boasted sales of $268 billion in 1990.

The development of plastics and other materials by the chemical industry resulted in decreased demand for traditional mining and metallurgical products. For example, the automotive industry turned increasingly to plastics and new polymer materials to help speed production and improve fuel economy. Plastics, preferred by some manufacturers, could be injection-molded into a wider range of complex shapes with more precision than could be accomplished with metals. Ceramics were also being used with increasing frequency.

Political changes within the United States also impacted the engineering industry. As the nation shifted away from a policy of providing heavy funding for the development of defense technologies, engineers began to focus more on civilian undertakings. Research conducted in the private sector, however, typically carried more stringent economic restraints. As a result, some industry watchers predicted a slowing in the pace of technological development. Others disagreed, stating that the engineering industry would benefit from an emphasis on profitability.

In addition to the economic challenges brought about by a transforming political climate, the engineering industry faced economic difficulties as a result of global changes. The U.S. engineering establishment found itself as one of many competitors on a crowded global stage at a time when worldwide economies were in transition. According to some analysts, economies were shifting from being based on natural resources to being based on knowledge. The realization that industries involved in fast-moving technologies would be necessary to sustain a nation's future economic growth illustrated the need for continued U.S. strength in the field of engineering.

Within the United States, there were 36,086 establishments classified by the U.S. Department of Commerce as offering engineering services. In the *1987 Census of Service Industries,* their combined receipts totaled $41.6 billion. Of this amount, $35.3 billion represented receipts for consulting and design engineering services. Other sources of receipts included architectural and surveying services and construction management.

In the mid-1990s, engineering and design firms foresaw an end to the recession conditions that began in the early 1990s. A combination of factors such as the need for downsizing and limited resources in many industries increased the demand for engineering companies. Engineering companies were not only being sought after as consultants but as partners in day-to-day operations. The top 500 design firms garnered a collective total of $29.4 billion in billings during 1995, up 5.2 percent over the $27.95 billion seen in 1994. According to *ENR,* analysts and industry executives attributed the improvement to the international market, where some $5.21 billion in billings were seen in 1995.

Current Conditions

Numerous opportunities arose for U.S. environmental engineering firms, both in the United States and abroad as the 1990s came to a close. Worldwide demand for design and construction of petrochemical plants and refineries resulted in a boom for engineering and construction firms, although subsequent unexpected decreases in the price of oil resulted in cancellation of some petrochemical expansion projects and subsequent declines in stock prices. A survey conducted by *The Oil and Gas Journal* revealed that 59 percent of 291 sites were scheduled for the Asia/Pacific region, including 60 sites in China. Local construction firms also brought world class resources to clients by entering partnerships or by merging with global firms.

Domestically the deregulation of the utility industry created a competitive pressure among engineering firms; many were forced to take new risks to keep revenues flowing and to survive. An unanticipated slump in construction engineering caused stock prices to plummet in the late 1990s and aggravated already slow growth. Analysts attributed the slump to premature forecasts prompted by the passage in 1998 of the Transportation Equity Act, but when sizable injections of the appropriated $217 billion federal highway funding associated with the 1998 Act entered the economy near the end of 1999, the industry regrouped. Waning stock prices recovered and the construction industry stabilized. Two additional factors driving sales were economic recovery within the United States and the implementation of the North American Free Trade Agreement (NAFTA). NAFTA suspended residency requirements for obtaining Canadian and Mexican licenses—a move intended to create a new market for American engineers in Canada and Mexico. By the year 2000 the specific benefits of NAFTA remained inconclusive.

Industry Leaders

Fluor Corporation. Fluor Corporation of Irvine, California, with sales revenue at $12.4 billion in 1999, ranked as the largest company in the industry according to statistics compiled by CorpTech. The company employee count totaled 56,886 in 1998. The following year the company reported sales growth of 8.1 percent. Fluor Corporation operated from offices and locations on six continents and ranked in the top 15 of *Fortune* magazine's service companies. For more than eight consecutive years earnings from continuing operations grew an average of 15 percent.

Fluor Daniel, Incorporated, with $8.4 billion in operating revenue for fiscal year 1999, was Fluor's principal operating business. Fluor Daniel ranked third in the industry according to employee count and fourth according to annual sales. The company provides a broad range of engine construction and diversified services to clients in many industries and geographic locations. In February of 1996, Fluor Daniel, as part of an international consortium, won the contract to design and build a $4.8 billion high-speed rail system in Florida. This project was one of the largest single contracts for Fluor, and the project was the most ambitious public-private rail system in the United States, according to the *Los Angeles Times*. In December of that same year Fluor Daniel announced that Fluor Daniel India Pvt. Ltd., a wholly owned subsidiary in India, signed a memorandum of understanding to jointly undertake engineering, procurement, and construction work in core industrial sectors. The agreement, with Tata Technodyne Ltd., a company recently formed by the Indian steel giant Tata Steel, encompassed steel, power, hydrocarbons, ports and cement works.

Fluor participated in several nuclear cleanup efforts, most visibly at the Hanford Nuclear Reservation where the company outbid two imposing competitors to secure the contract for the cleanup project. The sprawling Hanford complex, at one-half the size of Rhode Island, provided storage for the largest collection of nuclear waste in the United States, including 65 million gallons of radioactive sludge stored in underground tanks. Additionally, until 1988, the Hanford Nuclear facility produced plutonium for nuclear weapons and housed 11 tons of potentially unstable plutonium. Fluor signed a five-year, $4.8 million contract to lead a team of contractors in the project, one of the two largest environmental awards in history. For the project, anticipated to utilize a work force of more than 9,000 employees, Fluor won a citation for its effort toward developing the local economy.

Bechtel Group, Incorporated. Bechtel Group, Incorporated was another large firm in the industry. The company, founded in 1898 by Warren Bechtel, remained a private, family-held firm 100 years later. With headquarters in San Francisco, California, Bechtel engineers had contributed to approximately 19,000 projects in 140 countries on seven continents. In 1998 Bechtel had overall sales revenue of $12.64 billion with a growth rate of 11.6 percent; the company employed a workforce of 30,000. Bechtel ranked ninth among the *Forbes* private 500.

Bechtel, during its early years, contracted largely with the railroad industry and later expanded into other arenas. In 1992 Bechtel reported a $2.5 billion contractual agreement with the U.S. Department of Energy to clean up low-level radioactive and chemical waste at 42 sites in 14 states.

Among Bechtel's overseas projects, in the early 1990s the contractor participated in the reconstruction of Kuwait's oil fields following the Persian Gulf War, a job that involved 10,000 workers from 35 nations. The project proceeded successfully and Kuwaiti oil production and exports returned to pre-war levels by September 1992. In the People's Republic of China, Bechtel was a key participant in the construction of the Daya Bay Nuclear Power Plant. According to projections the $4 billion Daya Bay project, located 30 miles northeast of Hong Kong, was expected to generate 1.5 billion kilowatt-hours of electricity annually. In Europe, Bechtel participated in the construction of the Eurotunnel between England and France, running 50 meters beneath the English Channel. In 1995, Bechtel's R&D's International Technology and Resources teamed with Southern Electric International and Arthur Andersen and Company in a consortium to assist 11 eastern European countries with energy programs under the auspices of the U.S. Agency for International Development's Regional Energy Efficiency Project.

Specialty Disciplines. Halliburton Company was recognized as the largest oil field services provider worldwide. The firm's sales revenues of $17.35 billion in 1998 constituted a 96.8 percent growth in the wake of a merger with Dresser Industries Incorporated that was finalized on September 29, 1998.

Additionally, USX Corporation's USX-U.S. Steel Group reported sales revenues of $6.2 billion in 1998 and was the largest steel maker in the United States according to Hoover's, with services ranging from engineering consulting, resource management and value-added product production. In November of 1999 U.S. Steel Gary Works, Indiana, received the Association of Iron and Steel Engineers' (AISE) Project Excellence Award. The award was in recognition of a *turnkey* (prefabricated) energy co-generation plant that was designed, constructed, and managed by Duke/Fluor Daniel through an ongoing alliance with Primary Energy Incorporated. The plant, for converting coke oven and blast furnace emissions into energy, commenced commercial operation in 1997.

WORKFORCE

BLS statistics released for 1997 reported an estimated 2.66 million workers in engineering and related

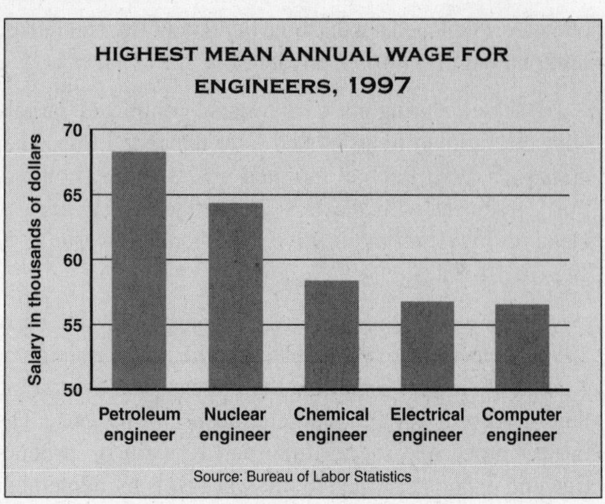

occupations including technicians, technologists, estimators and drafters. According to earlier projections by BLS most engineering disciplines expected to grow by the end of the century fell in reality. The number of electrical engineers, expected to rise from 439,000 in 1988 to 615,000 by the year 2000, fell to 329,070 according to 1997 figures. The number of mechanical engineers, expected to increase from 225,000 to 247,000, declined to 209,490. Likewise petroleum engineers, forecast to remain level at approximately 20,000 dropped significantly to 8,770 due to declining oil prices. Salaries for engineers varied according to discipline and education. Highest paid among the engineering disciplines were petroleum engineers with a mean salary of $68,300 per year, according BLS. Marine engineers ranked lowest in compensation, with a mean salary of $47,770 per year. Civil engineers, projected for significant growth during the mid- and late 1990s by the ASCE, earned $52,750 in 1997. Their numbers dropped significantly from 186,000 to 173,690 over the ten-year interim beginning in 1988, although analysts predicted an upsurge in conditions at the turn of the century as a result of a major infusion of federal highway funds late in 1999.

Despite national industrial decreases overall, employment fluctuations within the top performing engineering companies reflected a pattern of growth. Industry leader Fluor Corporation increased its employee count by 6.3 percent in 1998, and U.S. Steel gained 5.0 percent. Although Bechtel reported no growth in that area, neither did the company experience a loss of employees. Halliburton Corporation meanwhile reported employee growth of 52.4 percent in 1998 as the result of a merger with Dresser Industries.

Electronic News reported late in 1999 that the Department of Labor projected a need for nearly one-half million skilled scientists and technicians, including engineers, by 2006. The American Electronic Association at that same time reported a low 1.6 unemployment rate for engineers coupled with a significant drop in engineering graduates during the course of the 1990s. A report in *Crain's Cleveland Business* re-iterated the need for greater numbers of engineering professionals. The article indicated further that a dearth of skilled technicians and machinists also loomed heavily against the industry, in the absence of programs geared to elementary and secondary students to publicize the advantages of such careers. In an effort to meet future demand for engineers, the Cleveland Engineering Society developed the Internet-based "TOP RATE" program at www.toprate.org to encourage elementary and secondary students to enter the field of engineering. The Internet site was designed to provide links to database listings of scholarships, educational programs, and other career development resources.

America and the World

Demand for U.S. engineer services is closely tied to conditions in other countries. Increased competition from foreign nations pressured U.S. companies to expand productivity and reduce the cost of high-tech engineering services during the 1980s and 1990s. In 1970, the United States held a 51 percent share of the global high technology engineering services market. By 1986, U.S. market share had fallen to 42 percent. During the same time, the Japanese presence increased from 16 percent to 32 percent. In 1990, the National Science Board estimated that U.S. global competitors had science and engineering labor forces comparable to that of the United States and that the number of scientists and engineers in competing nations was rising faster than in the United States. In 1999 IEEE reported 67.1 percent of its total membership came from non-U.S. citizens.

Additionally U.S. construction engineers faced increased competition in the global marketplace. Asian factories suffered severely from a massive layoff of 8,000 employees by Seagate Technology in 1999. The cutbacks, attributed to automation, reflected a need for fewer assembly line workers in deference to greater numbers of skilled laborers at Seagate factories in Singapore, Thailand, Malaysia, and China. Elsewhere in Asia, electronics and electrical production constituted the biggest U.S. industry in Hong Kong, with $1.13 billion invested in that arena, totaling more than 5 percent of U.S. direct investment. Recent relaxation of restrictions prohibiting the employment of women in more dangerous trades, according to the U.S. Department of State, facilitated the escalation of heavier industries on the part of U.S. enterprises. The largest segment of the worldwide construction market—estimated at $3 trillion by the U.S. Department of Commerce in the 1990s—was in Japan. Yet the lucrative market, hindered by cartel-style pricing structures in the construction industry, remained largely closed to non-Japanese firms. Lee Chang-bok, president of Korea's Dong Ah Construction, cited his own company's ranking at the top of a Japanese governmental listing of the best foreign contractors, but noted that exclusionary government standards and restrictive business practices impeded what he termed an ''impregnable'' construction market. U.S.-based Bechtel Corporation ranked at number two on the listing.

Developing Nations. Overseas markets with the most growth potential for construction engineers were located in the Middle East where developing nations were expected to turn to foreign firms for help in developing their infrastructure and industrial base. Chang-bok focused on the Arabian markets as his company restructured in a rebound from the Asian monetary crisis of 1997. Among Dong Ah's largest projects, the firm held a 25 percent interest on the $1.2 billion Phase III of Libya's ''Great Man-Made River Authority.'' In order to compete, Dong Ah initiated a joint venture with local contractor, Al Hahr Company. Chang-bok noted that restrictive conditions in the Middle East precluded contractors from working in the absence of a joint venture agreement with another contractor local to the area. The government of Bahrain additionally required private contractors to register with the Ministry of Works and Agriculture. According to the *Herald,* Libyan leader Momar Khadafy announced an intent to assemble the nations of Northern Africa into a union modeled after the European Union, to be headquartered at Sirt, in the vicinity of Tripoli. Such a project would open major new markets in that part of the world.

In 1998 construction accounted for 10 percent of the $47.6 billion gross domestic product of Algeria; U.S. aid accounted for $209 million of that country's income. Thus an untapped potential market for contractors existed in that country, where a housing shortage persisted according to the U.S. Department of State Report on Economic Policy and Trade Practices. According to consulting engineer, Rodney Nohr, business opportunities abounded in developing nations. Nohr, cited by Jackie Elowsky in *Resource: Engineering & Technology for a Sustainable World,* faulted American engineering firms who ''. . . often fail to see profit in projects with non-U.S. companies. This leaves the global market open to smaller agencies . . .'' Nohr noted that improved communications technology had improved working conditions for American contractors working in developing nations. The ability to collaborate on a joint venture with local firms, often critical to such ventures, eliminated the restriction on foreign service industries. Such restrictions, common to Asian nations and others where significant barriers to trade were continually relaxed, were further augmented in Indonesia. There, according to law, foreign contractors must purchase local products as much as is feasible, except for goods purchased through financial aid resources.

South America. Substantial barriers preclude significant export of engineering services to Brazil. Among these, government contracting restraints prohibited contracting in technical service arenas unless domestic Brazilian contractors were unable to provide adequate facilities and services. Conspicuously complex registration procedures for foreign contractors applied in particular to the architectural and engineering industries.

RESEARCH AND TECHNOLOGY

The U.S. economy was built on technology and its continued health rests on technological advancement. The National Manufacturing Week trade show, held at McCormick Place in Chicago, offered engineers a chance to display new technology. Among the items featured in a booth sponsored by *Design News,* for example, were an ornithopter (a prototype airplane able to fly with sustained and controlled flapping wings), virtual reality technology, light weight insulators known as ''aerogels,'' and an improved lunar work vehicle.

Other projects under development during the 1990s by U.S. engineering teams involved superconductors, robotics, fuel cells, particle beams, magnetic levitation trains, radioactive waste storage, and advanced computer-integrated manufacturing. Chemical engineers continued investigating new materials for advanced information and communications, studying environmental issues, and contributing to public health technologies.

FURTHER READING

''Bechtel Group, Inc.'' Hoover's Online. Available from http://www.hoovers.com/co/capsule/9/0,2163,40059,00.html.

Berg, David R. *Meeting the Challenge: U.S. Industry Faces the 21st Century.* U.S. Department of Commerce, Office of Technology Policy. Washington, DC: 1998.

Berlow, Lawrence H. *The Reference Guide to Famous Engineering Landmarks of the World.* Phoenix: Oryx Press, 1998.

Bruner, Richard. ''Layoffs Persist Despite Labor Crunch,'' *Electronic News,* 29 November 1999.

''Design: Country Borders Are No Limit.'' *ENR,* 24 July 1995.

Elowsky, Jackie. ''Destination: The World: Consider Working in the Global Marketplace.'' *Vol. 5, Resource: Engineering & Technology for a Sustainable World,* American Society of Agricultural Engineers, 1 February 1998.

''Fluor Corporation.'' Hoover's Online. Available from http://www.hoovers.com/co/capsule/4/0,2163,10594,00.html.

''Fluor Reports FY 1999 Earnings,'' *Business Wire,* 11 November 1999.

''Global Work Requires Rethinking, Says U.S. Cleanup Firm Chief.'' *ENR,* 29 May 1995.

''Halliburton and Dresser Complete Merger,'' *Business Wire,* 28 September 1998.

''Halliburton Company.'' Hoovers' Online. Available from http://www.hoovers.com/co/capsule/7/0,2163, 10697,00.html.

Hunt, Charlie Deuel. *Information Sources in Science and Technology,* 3rd ed. Englewood, CO: Libraries Unlimited, Inc., 1998.

''IEEE State of the Membership Report-1998.'' 2 December 1999.

Ierley, Merritt. *The Comforts of Home: the American House and the Evolution of Modern Convenience.* New York: Clarkson Potter, 1999.

Jannazo, Mary Ann, ''New Site Will Look To Lure Future Tech Workers,'' *Crain's Cleveland Business,* 1 November 1999.

''After Rebound, Dong Ah at the Fore in Cracking Japan's Construction.'' *Korea Herald,* 10 November 1999.

Leder, Michelle. ''Investing.'' *New York Times,* 14 November 1999.

Mack, Pamela E., ed. ''From Engineering Science to Big Science: the NACA and NASA Collier Trophy Research Project Winners.'' National Aeronautics and Space Administration, 1998.

Man-Made Wonders. New York: Reader's Digest Association, 1998.

''Snapshot Report for Fluor Corporation (FLR).'' Market Guide, 1996-1999. Available from http://www.marketguide.com/mgi/snap/A0066.html.

Masters, Roger D. *Fortune Is a River: Leonardo da Vinci and Nicolo Machiavelli's Magnificent Dream to Change the Course of Florentine History.* New York: Plume, 1999.

Mowery, David C. *Paths of Innovation: Technological Change in 20th Century America.* New York: Cambridge University Press, 1998.

''Occupational Employment Statistics: 1997 National Occupational Employment and Wage Estimates.'' Available from http://stats.bls.gov/oes/national.

O'Dell, John. ''Fluor Wins Bid for High-Speed Rail in Florida.'' *Los Angeles Times,* 28 February 1996.

''Primary Energy-Duke/Fluor Daniel Cogeneration Plant at Gary Works Wins National Recognition.'' *PR Newswire,* 17 November 1999.

Shroyer, Jo Ann. *Secret Mesa: Inside Los Alamos National Laboratory.* New York: John Wiley & Sons, 1998.

''The Top 500 Design Firms.'' *ENR,* 1 April 1996.

Tulacz, Gary J. ''Asia Continues to Power International Design Quest.'' *ENR,* 3 April 1995.

Tuttle, Greg. ''Fluor Nabs Hanford Job.'' *Yakima Herald-Republic,* 7 August 1996.

''USAID Energy Program Aimed at East Europe, Baltics Via Bechtel Led Group.'' *Platt's Oilgram News,* 6 June 1995.

''USX-U.S. Steel Group.'' Hoover's Online. Available from http://www.hoovers.com/co/capsule/9/0,2163,12969,00.html.

Vartabedian, Ralph. ''Fluor Shares in Major Nuclear Cleanup Pacts.'' *Los Angeles Times.* 7 August 1996.

''What Does the Future Hold: Industry Leaders Say Labor Crunch Will Prove To Be Challenge of New Millennium.'' *Crain's Cleveland Business,*30 August 1999.

''1998 Country Reports on Economic Policy and Trade Practices.,'' Submitted to the Congress by the U.S. Department of State, 31 January 1999, Available from http://www.state.gov/www/issues/economic/trade_reports/98_toc.html (13 December 1999).

SIC 8712

ARCHITECTURAL SERVICES

This classification covers establishments primarily engaged in providing professional architectural services. Establishments primarily engaged in providing landscape architecture services are classified in **SIC 078: Landscape Counseling and Planning.** primarily engaged in providing graphic arts and related design services are classified in **SIC 7336: Commercial Art and Graphic Design**, and those providing drafting services are classified in **SIC 7389: Business Services, Not Elsewhere Classified.**

NAICS Code(s)

541310 (Architectural Services)

Industry Snapshot

Design firms primarily engaged in providing professional construction-related design services constitute the architectural services industry. This industry includes companies that offer engineering design services related to architectural work, but does not include civil engineering or ship and boat design companies. Landscape architecture, graphic arts, and drafting disciplines are covered in separate classifications.

Aside from actually designing structures, architects typically are employed throughout all phases of the building process—from conceptual planning through client construction. In 1998 an estimated 18,994 establishments employing 138,800 people existed in this industry. Seven percent of industry employment (9,716 employees) was attributed to licensed architects in 1996, with the percentage of architects projected to increase by 27.9 percent (to 12,426 architects by 2006. Licensure is the highest form of industry regulation, and all 50 states require architects to be licensed.

After suffering from a deep recession in the late 1980s and the early 1990s, the architectural services industry began a steady rise into the 1990s. Consumer confidence mounted throughout 1996, and the economy recovered. Home and office construction rose by an average of 4.8 percent for the year. That trend continued to the end of the decade, and the number of architectural establishments increased steadily at a rate of one percent per year.

ORGANIZATION AND STRUCTURE

Architecture firms design a multitude of different structures for all sectors of the market. Office and apartment buildings, schools, military installations, churches, factories, hospitals, houses, and airport terminals are but a few of the facilities that they design for commercial, government, and private nonprofit organizations. While some firms specialize in serving one niche or a few related segments of the market, others are highly diversified and offer a variety of design services to all types of clients.

The Design Process. Building design can be a complex, detailed, and painstaking endeavor. In addition to the important consideration of appearance, architects must also stress functionality, safety, and economy in the design process. Even one minuscule flaw in a volume of construction drawings can result in costly litigation and the erosion, or destruction, of a firm's reputation. More important than pleasing the potential users of any structure or satisfying personal design aspirations, architects must accommodate the client that commissions and funds a project.

Design programming is the first stage of the building process. Architects are often called upon at this point to determine what type of structure to erect. Marketing research, demographic analyses, regulatory constraints, and other factors all help to determine economically viable development options. Site selection and acquisition follow the design programming stage. The architect analyzes factors such as soils, drainage, utility availability, tax rates, and traffic patterns to determine where to build a project. If the client already has a parcel of land, the firm can help determine the financial and physical feasibility of developing the site.

After the client decides to build, the architect begins the conceptual design process. Schematic drawings and relational diagrams, prepared by the architect, allow the client to study possible options for developing the site. Crude models are often used to represent ideas in three dimensions. The conceptual design process eventually results in a hypothetical plan that is used to generate cost estimates and guide the development of more detailed elevations, cross-sections, models, and perspectives.

After developing a detailed design, the architect begins the bulk of the design work—detailed construction drawings. These highly-detailed drawings determine accurate construction cost estimates and bids by contractors. They also dictate the quality of craftsmanship and materials to be used by contractors. Architects cooperate with engineers and other professionals to insure that the design is technically appropriate and complies with legal guidelines. When the working drawings are complete, the architect usually takes bids on the project from contractors, awards a contract, and supervises construction to ensure that the contractor properly executes design details.

Although rates vary, most architects bill clients on a per-hour basis. The total bill for architecture and engineering design services is often in the range of 2 percent to 4 percent of the total construction cost of a project, but can be much more or less depending on the type of project or the level of involvement by the architect.

Types of Firms and Projects. Three types of companies are primarily engaged in providing architectural services: engineer/architecture (E/A) firms; architecture/engineer (A/E) companies; and architecture firms. Typically it is only an estimated 15 percent of the total billings by architectural firms that are rendered by firms in the architectural services industry. Engineering and construction firms and other companies that offer services related to architectural work such as surveying services consume the bulk of the revenues.

Purely architectural firms bill strictly for architectural design work. They do not have engineers on staff and often offer limited construction management expertise. *Building Design & Construction* reported in July of 1997 that the top ten firms of this type accounted for $327 million of industry billings in the prior year. Furthermore, this segment supplied only a small percentage of all architectural services rendered by U.S. companies.

A/E firms, while still emphasizing architectural skills, have engineers on staff with expertise related to architectural building design. Firms in this category typically account for 5 percent of all industry billings, as they service only a small percentage of the entire U.S. market for architectural services.

E/A firms maintain architects on staff but emphasize engineering design services that are related to construction work. These firms capture slightly more than half (approximately 54 percent) of all industry billings and furnish the highest percentage of all architectural services rendered by U.S. firms.

The market demand for architecture and engineering design services in the mid-1990s was concentrated in institutional facilities, which accounted for 40 percent of all billings. Within that percentage, educational facilities accounted for the single largest market sector with 18 percent, while health care facility design comprised about 15 percent. Commercial building design projects accounted for 30 percent of the total market, with 16 percent going to commercial space and 11 percent to the design of office buildings. Residential work accounted for 15 percent, with 8 percent of service billings from the design of single-family residences.

Background and Development

Architects have been designing structures in return for compensation for more than 3,000 years. Although several famous architects designed well-known projects during America's early history, such as Thomas Jefferson's Monticello in the early nineteenth century, an organized architectural profession did not exist in the United States until the 1850s. In fact, formal educational programs for architects were unavailable until the 1860s, with the establishment of the Massachusetts Institute of Technology, Cornell University, and the University of Illinois.

Prominent works that sprang from the fledgling architectural services industry in the middle and late nineteenth century included the Marshall Field & Company building in Chicago, the Wainright Building in St. Louis, St. Patrick's Cathedral in New York, and the Harvard Museum of Comparative Zoology in Cambridge. Prominent architects of the period who owned firms included James Renwick, Louis Agassiz, H. H. Richardson, and Louis H. Sullivan. Between 1900 and 1940, Frank Lloyd Wright, Mies van der Rohe, and Le Corbusier, among others, designed significant projects and had enormous influence on the profession. Famous works of this time included many office buildings, such as the Empire State Building and Rockefeller Center in New York.

It was not until after World War II that the U.S. architectural industry began to experience rapid growth and to become closely affiliated with building and construction industries. During that time, large corporations developed massive structures that projected wealth and distinction, and government expenditures for infrastructure and public works grew at an unprecedented rate. This development boom gave birth to many large architecture firms, like Hellmuth, Obata & Kassabaum and Perkins & Will, that employed hundreds of architects. Skidmore, Owings & Merrill, one of the larger firms in the post-war period, designed such projects as the Connecticut General Life and Inland Steel Buildings. The General Motors Technical Center and Frank Lloyd Wright's Guggenheim Museum were other prominent landmarks that characterized the progression of the industry from the 1950s through the 1970s.

By 1983, however, new development activity was leading the architectural services industry into an era of unprecedented profit and growth. Deregulation of lending institutions, an influx of foreign investment dollars, and new tax laws all combined to generate a massive injection of capital into the commercial development industry. Between 1982 and 1985 the total amount of commercial space designed by architects ballooned from less than 700 million square feet per year to over 1.3 billion. At the same time, residential markets were also booming and the demand for new public construction increased. As a result, the total number of establishments in the architectural services industry jumped over 20 percent, from 14,089 in 1985 to a peak of 17,777 by 1987. During the same period revenues leapt from $5.9 billion to over $9.8 billion and industry employment shot up to nearly 140,000 from only 105,000.

In the late 1980s the flow of capital for new design projects waned. The Tax Reform Act of 1986, which discouraged new construction, and a shortage of savings and loan capital were two of the various factors contributing to a slowdown in 1987. Architecture firms saw a significant decline in the number of design jobs available in many commercial and residential markets. In fact, by 1989 it was clear that their industry had fallen into a severe, and potentially sustainable, recession. Total new commercial development plunged to about 1 billion square feet in 1988, and fell to under 800 million square feet in 1989.

By the end of 1989, the market for architectural services appeared to many analysts to have bottomed out. But, while most firms were on the ropes and struggling to survive the industry shake-out, the development market continued to plummet in 1990 and 1991. In fact, many office buildings that architects had designed in the late 1980s opened in the early 1990s without a single tenant; these became known as "see-through buildings." The total demand for new construction continued to fall from only $410 billion in 1989 to about $358 billion in 1991. The market for residential design services was also hit hard, as new construction in that sector fell 14 percent in the same three-year period. Although many firms were able to stay afloat by emphasizing public works projects, which experienced expenditure increases of 9 percent between 1989 and 1991, most firms lost revenue.

In response to dour market conditions, the architectural services industry became increasingly competitive in the early 1990s. As hundreds of firms closed their doors, most remaining companies took sharp measures to increase their market share and to maintain profits. In some cities, about 50 percent of all architects were laid-off. Those hit hardest were young, inexperienced workers and older, highly paid employees. Firms were also reducing fees in an effort to undercut competitors. Most importantly, however, architecture firms were looking to new growth markets and technology to give them an edge in the 1990s.

Market conditions improved slightly from 1991 to 1992, indicating that the development drought was easing. The total value of new construction increased about 4 percent to about $423 billion. Although work in commercial markets, especially office building design, continued to decline, housing and public works design projects increased. Furthermore, spending in some commercial niche markets, such as health care, improved by as much as 5 percent. Importantly, remodeling, retrofit, and repair construction for all sectors reached record levels in 1992, allowing many firms to boost billings on small maintenance jobs.

A survey of 100 design firms by *Architectural Record* in 1992 revealed that nearly half the respondents had realized a reduction in the construction-dollar value of their commissions since 1990. The average decrease was 10 percent to 25 percent, although some firms lost as much as 90 percent. Of the survey respondents, 34 percent reported that their workload was down, 24 percent said it was up, and 42 percent felt that it had stabilized. A similar survey by *Engineering News-Record* showed a 20 percent decrease in design work backlogs from early 1991 levels, indicating that work was becoming more difficult to secure.

Firms were taking a variety of steps to improve internal operations and increase competitiveness. Most firms were increasing their workload-to-staff ratio to save money, and decreasing fees to attract more business. This was often accomplished by relying on part-time help from trained architects that were called on only when they were absolutely necessary. A popular trend was "hoteling," whereby employees would check into offices for short stints on special projects until their services were no longer needed, or several employees would use the same office but at different times of the day.

One of the most important internal changes for many companies was the increased use of technology to lower labor costs. In fact, 12 percent of respondents in the *Architectural Record* survey indicated that despite an increase in billings they had elected to diminish the size of their staff. Computer automated design (CAD) systems were a major factor in this increased productivity for some firms. "I've eliminated my whole office staff with a computer," said Philadelphia Architect David Steele in "Architectural Record," March 1993. Many companies were also eliminating clerical help with the aid of new office technology. For instance computers, answering machines, and cellular phones were replacing receptionists in some offices.

In addition to increasing the productivity of their internal operations, many firms in 1993 were expanding their service offerings. Some companies were going into project management, using their design expertise to streamline the construction process and save money for contractors and owners. Other architecture firms were expanding into interior design, facilities management, and environmental planning and engineering to increase revenues. Conversely, some firms were reducing their offerings, choosing instead to specialize in tiny niche markets where they held a competitive edge. Niche growth areas in the commercial market for architectural services included designs for privatized prisons, arenas, hospitals and other health care facilities, long-term care facilities, warehouses, and recreational structures around river boat gambling casinos.

Entering new markets was another way that architecture firms were trying to maintain profitability. As design work for commercial construction continued to decline through 1993, public works projects were allowing many firms to increase revenues. For instance, while the amount of new hotel space plummeted 40 percent in just one year between 1991 and 1992, the value of new public works projects steadily increased from $90.9 billion in 1989 to over $102 billion by 1992. Water supply facilities and miscellaneous public buildings, which grew in 1991 and 1992 at a rate of 5 percent and 7 percent respectively, offered the greatest potential for architecture firms competing for public works commissions. Design projects related to utility construction and conservation also offered increased opportunities.

After the recession of the early 1990s, the industry began to grow again, bringing in over $14.6 billion in 1994. Revenue was up 8.7 percent from 1993, and up by almost 20 percent from 1991, and industry strategists predicted the growth would continue well into the twenty-first century. According to the American Institute of Architects (AIA), building activity would increase by an average of 1 percent each year from the levels of the first half of the 1990s.

Social and Political Factors. Until the late 1990s, one of the most stable areas of growth for the industry had been retail construction sales, which increased a steady rate of 2.5 percent every year from 1980 to 1996. But several factors were pushing that figure down. Home shopping through network clubs and the Internet was taking away the need for retail centers. Also, as the baby-boomers aged, services became more of a concern than goods, lessening the need for retail centers even more. Some projected decline was offset by the effects of the Americans with Disabilities Act of 1990. Compliance with the Act required that many newer buildings be made handicap-accessible; this was expected to provide millions of dollars in architectural design contracts, along with rehabilitation and maintenance design work, especially for aging infrastructure.

Computerized Design. Two important advances in the architectural services field in the early 1990s were computer-aided design (CAD) software programs and 3-D modeling. As late as 1993, architects in many offices were still designing with ink or pencil on vellum or Mylar surfaces. Designers sat at a drafting board and used triangles and compasses to produce precise technical drawings. With the introduction of CAD, however, an increasing number of professionals moved away from the drawing board and onto the computer to develop their designs. Although both methods were extremely labor intensive, CAD offered the advantages of allowing architects to save their work, to duplicate and move parts of a design, and to make changes more easily. Additionally many tasks that were cumbersome on the drawing board were easily accomplished via CAD-involved calculations of surface areas and volumes for earthwork projects were among the functions made easy by the CAD software.

Critics of CAD argued that it was too costly for smaller firms to implement, that it stifled the design process and limited flexibility, and that it displaced architects. Others maintained, in contrast, that the implementation of CAD systems increased productivity for designers and reduced staffing requirements. For instance J. F. Borelli, a New York architect, increased billings at his firm by 125 percent in two years by 1992 when he expanded his CAD implementation. He maintained his staffing level at 65 employees and discovered that clients increasingly requested that projects be developed with the CAD software.

Even more sophisticated than CAD software were new 3-D modeling systems that allowed architects to design projects in three dimensions on computer. Three-dimensional modeling enabled architects to create ''virtual walk-through'' presentations of their projects, in order for clients and builders to ascertain a better sense of the reality of a structure. Through the implementation of three-dimensional animation, clients and builders might conveniently view the successive stages of a project, or they might view structures from different angles. By 1993, several larger firms used 3-D modeling regularly. The technology remained expensive, but the subsequent savings in construction time and improved communications between designer and client often justified the implementation of 3-D software and accelerated the recovery of equipment costs.

Current Conditions

Commercial development of suburban office space contributed to the life of the industry in the early 1990s, as commuters fled the cities and downtown office vacancy rates soared. Even when urban office vacancy rates stabilized by 1996, suburban office occupancy increased and vacancy rates in the suburbs dropped by 9 percent annually, as growing numbers of businesses abandoned their outmoded urban operations in favor of modern new quarters in the suburbs. At the turn of the century, however, conditions reversed and worsened for the commercial building industry, and construction lenders withdrew. Large projects, including office towers, suffered most severely as a result of conservative lending policies that brought an end to what some observers called speculative lending. Projections through 2006 indicate the likelihood of suppressed demand for office space.

In order to encourage a continued source of work contracts, engineering and construction companies devised ''one-stop shop'' (design-and-build) services. Often, these firms offered architectural services at very low or negligible costs, so as to help the company secure large construction and project management contracts. Of the top firms in the mid-1990s, only a handful offered the diversified design-and-build option, yet forecasters projected these services might grow to comprise 50 percent of all general construction in the United States by 2000, according to *Engineer News Record,* an East Coast based trade publication. Despite fears by some observers that the integration of design and construction services might eliminate important checks and balances, clients came to appreciate the economy of scale it offered. As a result, the market share of diversified competitors grew rapidly at the expense of A/E and purely architectural firms whose market shares plummeted respectively. Diversified companies thrived in comparison to traditional, specialized establishments. Less diversified operations—approximately two-thirds of the total number of firms—retained only 14 percent of all industry billings, leaving some doubt as to the future viability of traditional design practices.

Despite the slump in commercial construction in the late 1990s, projections of strong growth in the residential housing market—approximately 15 percent of total billings—held accurate. As the baby-boom generation moved into middle age they were the group most likely to own second homes or time-share condominiums. Additionally, new residential work increased along with population increases, and the market for home remodeling increased likewise. In 1999, 1.6 million houses were built, up from 1.35 in 1995. Some analysts predicted continued strength in the market during the first half of 2000, although a total decline of 6 to 8 percent was projected for the calendar year, bringing new starts to 1.5 million at best.

Turn-of-the Century Design Trends. As architects of the late twentieth century turned increasingly to new digital technologies for purposes of productivity, they experimented with 3-D technology to develop ''e-topia'' structures in modern communities, according to William J. Mitchell, in *Architectural Record.* In pursuit of e-topia, an expansion of the kiosk concept, designers undertook the design of virtual malls for on-line commerce, as well as virtual amusement parks and other conceptual structures that were previously limited to the physical realm. Through virtual reality technology, architects became further empowered in the arena of restorative construction. Modern designers ushered the art of structure restoration to a new level of evolution at the threshold of the 21st century by tapping the potential of 3-D systems and virtual reality to redefine the parameters of architectural restoration. Through the process of virtual reconstruction, historical structures became available for simulated viewing in their original state. Even ancient structures that ceased to exist altogether at some time in the past might be recreated in simulation form, through intensive application of the technique.

Increasingly, as the twentieth century drew to a close, what was once old became new again, including the architectural theories of feng shui, which experienced a revival in the United States during the 1990s. Progressive architectural firms, encouraged in part by academics at the University of Buffalo, subscribed to the ethereal concepts of the ancient Chinese art, the substance of which involves strategic placement of space and energy. Proper implementation of feng shui begins prior to construction of a building, with the selection of a site. During the design phase, the orientation of the structure must allow for consideration of the forces of wind and water, as implied in the words ''feng shui.'' Despite the ancient mystic and religious connotations of feng shui, adherence to the practice resulted in building designs not unlike those of mid twentieth century architects.

In stark contrast to feng shui, designer Gideon S. Golany in a 1997 publication discussed the use of geo-space (building underground) to squeeze more space for structures from cluttered landscapes in highly populated areas. Building groundward presents a number of advantages, according to Golany, for better protection from the elements and lower energy consumption. The practice is most advantageous as a means of conservation, and despite the speculative nature of underground construction for human occupation, geo-space designers implemented designs in Montreal, Paris, and Japan by the end of the 1990s. Geo-space designs were particularly well-disposed to the growing trend among architectural designers to become involved in community development from the initial inception, in order to create a customized and cohesive functionality of design, in coordination with existing regional demographics.

INDUSTRY LEADERS

Of the E/A firms that were not primarily engaged in the architectural services industry, companies such as Day & Zimmerman, ABB Lummus Crest, Incorporated, and Raytheon Engineers, each held a significant share of the market in 1998. Largest among them was Day & Zimmerman of Philadelphia, Pennsylvania, the largest firm in the industry, with total revenues estimated at $976 million. Second largest of the E/A firms was Sverdrup Corporation, with $920 million in billings for 1998. Other E/A leaders included Fluor Daniel, Incorporated of Sugar Land, Texas, with $800 million in billings; and Austin Company of Cleveland, Ohio, with $700 million in billings.

Extremely large among the architecture/engineer firms in 1998, Hellmuth, Obata & Kassabaum, Incorporated of St. Louis, Missouri, had estimated billings of $220 million in 1998. The company originated as a purely architectural firm in 1955, and by 1998 it had developed into an international firm with 2,000 employees. In contrast, the largest of the purely architectural design firms that year, according to *Service Industries USA,* was California-based Gensler & Associates/Architects, with $88 million in billings. Almost all companies offering purely architectural services had four or less employees, as the more lucrative contracts habitually went to the engineering/architecture firms.

Among the most notable architectural projects of the 1990s was the largest building in Europe, designed by American architect Cesar Pelli. The 800-foot building was part of London's massive Canary Wharf development, an office and retail project comprising over 6.45 million square feet of space. Illustrative of many commercial projects completed at that time, however, the project was a financial flop and contributed to the financial collapse of its developer.

WORKFORCE

Most architects complete a five-year accredited college program. They must then work for at least three years before becoming eligible for certification after a series of exams. The National Council of Architectural Registration Boards, which administers the licensing exams, recognized over 30,000 registered architects in 1999. Of all licensed architects in the mid-1990s, 82 percent worked in an architecture firm. That percentage was made up of about one-third solo practitioners, another third in firms with fewer than four people, and the last third in firms with more than four employees. Those that did not work in an architecture firm were employed in the commercial/industrial sector (5 percent), design firms (3 percent), government jobs (3 percent), universities or schools (2 percent), contractor firms (2 percent), and engineering firms (1 percent). Jobs for licensed architects were expected to grow about as fast as those in most other U.S. industries, with most job openings expected to result from professionals transferring to other occupations or leaving the work force.

With modern technologies affecting the industry, new jobs openings emerged for technical staff. In 1999 AIA reported 57,000 members nationwide, including students, interns, and other non-licensed professionals. As architecture firms hired drafters with CAD skills and other technical specialties, only 7 percent of industry workers in the mid-1990s were architects, although that number was projected to increase by 27.9 percent by the year 2006. The largest segment of the workforce in this industry was drafters, who comprised 12 percent of the total. Additionally, 9 percent of the workers were civil engineers, and an additional 8.2 percent were electrical engineers and electronics experts. By 2006 the number of electronics and computer specialists was anticipated to increase by a factor of 94.4 percent according to projections based on the U.S. Bureau of Labor Statistics. The clerical workforce combined, among the smallest segments of the industry except for computer programmers, comprised 5.5 percent of the total employment, with typists (including word processing personnel) projected to decline by 15.8 percent by 2006. Other occupations within the architectural services industry included surveyors, drafters, CAD operators, and specification writers.

Salaries. The total payroll increase for the industry between 1992 and 1998 was projected at 37 percent, with industry revenues projected to increase by 52 percent. Salaries in the industry rose throughout the duration of the 1990s at a rate slightly above inflation, averaging increases of only about 2 percent between 1990 and 1993 and 5 percent for the next three years, with smaller firms reporting salary increases at twice the rate of larger firms. Between 1990 and 1996 technical staff saw a 30 percent salary gain, the highest gain in the industry.

Salaries for architects are low compared to professions with similar training requirements. In the late 1990s the median annual salary for architects with only 3 to 5 years experience rose to $33,200, up from $33,000 in 1996. For an architect with eight to ten years experience, the median salary was $45,400, up from $45,000. Starting salaries ranged from $15,000 to $27,000 depending to a large degree on region. Salaries were highest in the Pacific Southwest where the average salary was 4 percent above the national average. In the West South Central region, salaries lagged behind the national average by 7 percent. Architects typically progress to senior draftsman, senior designer, job captain, and then to project manager, with salary ranges between $28,000 and $56,000 annually. A project manager might eventually progress to chief designer, which at a large company can pays up to $100,000 per year. Principals of firms can make between $75,000 and $250,000 depending on the size of the company.

America and the World

While American design markets sputtered in the early 1990s, international markets grew at a rapid pace and became a focal point for much of the architectural services industry. In fact, many U.S. companies were able to increase revenues and nurture their companies during the recession by means of international expansion. In the mid-1990s foreign companies sought the expertise of U.S. design firms for projects ranging from military installations and dams to golf courses and office buildings. Architecture, engineering, and construction services are all interrelated, and often grouped together in industry statistics. Architecture and engineering, however, accounted for most of the trade in architecture, engineering, and construction (AEC) services. Trade in AEC services is mostly undertaken by majority-owned affiliates in foreign markets. AEC firms that engage in international work often open an affiliate office in major foreign countries, as contracts regularly go to firms that have a local presence. Cross-border trade, trade with a U.S. firm instead of foreign affiliate, is generally limited to transporting blueprints and design over the phone or by mail.

Overall, surpluses on both cross-border and affiliate trade reflected the United States' strength in major market development and extensive experience in multiple foreign markets. Particularly the United States' widely acknowledged expertise in oil and gas construction and engineering would make countries like Venezuela, who was expanding its petroleum sector, and Saudi Arabia, already a powerful oil producer, even more in need of U.S. design expertise. U.S. exports to those two countries were expected to increase by up to 2 percent per year until 1998 because of anticipated privatization of major industrial sectors. Demand for services notwithstanding, cross-border trade remains subject to certain service barriers in many foreign countries. American architects and engineers who work in some countries are subject to the country's internal licensing requirements for those professions. In Venezuela and other countries, foreign engineers and architects must successfully complete the national professional examination process, including completion of a validation process through a Venezuelan university.

GATS. On January 1, 1995, the General Agreement on Trade in Services (GATS) went into effect. GATS was to be the first multilateral, legally enforceable agreement covering trade in the services industry. If passed, international trade rules would, for the first time, cover a sector that is 60 percent of the U.S. economy and 70 percent of U.S. jobs. GATS would also provide specific legal conditions for future negotiations aimed at breaking down market barriers that discriminate against services from other countries. The agreement would require little change in U.S. law, as the United States has regularly been one of the most open countries with regard to foreign trade. GATS negotiations had often been an effort by the United States to encourage other countries to open up trade markets. GATS would be most profitable to the United States as it has the largest services economy, and is the largest exporter of services.

The GATS Framework of Agreement, Article XXIV, created the Council for Trade in Services and charged the council with the duty to create guidelines to expedite international trade between the service industries. The council met in Uruguay in 1993 and scheduled a follow up session for 2000. Among the unfinished business on its agenda for 2000, the council planned to discuss a means to eliminate service trade barriers through mutual licensing agreements in certain professions, including architecture and engineering. While GATS had improved some foreign markets within architectural, engineering, and construction services, there was little or no change in foreign policies. A target date of 2005 was set for the negotiation of a ''Free Trade Area of the Americas'' that would substantially eliminate trade barriers within the Western Hemisphere. Although other countries, including those of Asia and the Pacific region, continued to restrict any foreign commercial presence, they remained involved in similar negotiations under the Party on Professional Services of the World Trade Organization. India, Malaysia, and Pakistan still had not made any steps toward opening their market to foreign ACE firms. Other countries opened up and were beginning to show an interest in U.S. firms. China, Japan, and Argentina all opened up as potentially significant markets, and China quickly became a top importer of U.S. ACE services.

Europe accounted for about half of the affiliate trade for the U.S. owned foreign firms. The United Kingdom, the Netherlands, Germany, and Canada accounted for about 67 percent of all exports. Europe was an even bigger source for imports from U.S. based foreign firms. France, Germany, and the United Kingdom accounted for half of U.S. imports, and Europe as a whole accounted for more than 85 percent of imports.

RESEARCH AND TECHNOLOGY

Climate Control. Peter Segalla, in *Buildings,* cited the issue of climate control as a critical concerns for designers at the turn of the century. In apartment buildings, office space, and private residence, the notion of individual preferences for what is ''too cold'' and ''too hot'' contribute to the basic comfort, livability, and usability of a design. Segalla further encouraged the refinement and use of underfloor air distribution technology based in modular, insulated floor space that affords individualized climate control within the flooring. Segalla operates Peter Segalla Design in New York City; he implemented the technology in his design of a 93,000-square-foot building in Salt Lake City.

In 1999 the National Renewable Engergy Lab (NREL) announced a promising new software tool called Energy-10. Energy-10 very quickly determines the most efficient energy and air flows within structures, to simplify the implementation of energy-saving designs for both climate control and lighting. NREL estimated that 40-70 percent energy savings might be realized with the use of Energy-10. The product can be applied toward the design of any type of structure, from a small residence to a large urban complex. Based on input regarding the size of a structure, in terms of floor space and number of stories, type of climate control system, and geographic location, Energy-10 assesses the potential rewards of designing solar heating, insulation, daylight and shading, and other features into a planned structure.

FURTHER READING

American Institute of Architects. ''AIA National Membership,'' 21 January 2000. Available from http://aiail.org/natmem.htm.

Dalal, Pradeep. *The Practice of Architecture: Industry Statistics.* Washington: American Institute of Architects, 1996.

Darnay, Arsen J., ed. *Service Industries USA.* Detroit: Gale Research Inc., 1999.

Dean, Daniela. ''Looking Ahead: Experts See Another Good Year, but Not Without Interest Rate Jitters,'' *Washington Post,* 8 January 2000.

English, Dale. ''Ancient Chinese concept finds modern Western discipline.'' *Business First of Buffalo,* 26 April 1999.

Emerson, Dan. ''Architects Enter Design-Build Arena.'' *Minneapolis/St.Paul City Business,* 24 February 1997.

Krasner, Jeffrey. *Wall Street Journal,* 19 January 2000.

Mitchell, William J.. ''The era of the E-topia: the right reactions to the digital revolution can produce lean and green cities.'' *Architectural Record,* March 1999.

''New Building Design Tool Saves Energy.'' *R & D,* August 1999.

Segalla, Peter. ''Raising the standard.'' *Buildings,* June 1999.

Siegmund, John E. ''Services in the WTO: recent developments and overview.'' *Business America,* April 1998.

Smith, Gina. ''Virtual to Reality.'' *Popular Science,* December 1996.

Turville-Heitz, Meg. ''Creating a Neighborhood from Scratch . . .'' *Wisconsin State Journal,* 6 June 1999.

U.S. Bureau of the Census *Service Annual Survey: 1994.* Washington: August 1995.

U.S. Bureau of Labor Statistics. *1998-99 Occupational Outlook Handbook.* 26 February 1999.

U.S. Department of State. *1998 Report on Economic Policy and Trade Practices.* January 31, 1999.

U.S. International Trade Commission *U.S. Trade Shifts in Selected Industries: Services.* Washington: June 1996.

Urban Studies, 1 June 1997.

Williams, Daniel. ''Architects need to expand the scale of the profession to include the design of regions.'' *Architectural Record,* August 1999.

SIC 8713

SURVEYING SERVICES

This industry is comprised of establishments primarily engaged in providing professional surveying services and photogrammetric engineering. Types of surveys produced include land, water, and aerial surveys.

NAICS CODE(S)

541360 (Geophysical Surveying and Mapping Services)
541370 (Surveying and Mapping (Except Geophysical) Services)

INDUSTRY SNAPSHOT

All physical characteristics and points on the earth's surface exist in positional relationship to other characteristics and points. Surveying is the process whereby these land relationships are measured and described. It uses the mathematical principles of geometry and trigonometry to identify horizontal and vertical placement and elevation. Surveys are primarily used in establishing property boundaries and in map making.

There are two major types of surveying: plane surveying and geodetic surveying. Plane surveying does not account for the curvature of the earth's surface. It is used primarily for smaller areas where this curvature produces insignificant deviations between the survey results and reality. According to information provided by *Public Works,* surveys of areas measuring "no more than 12 miles or so in any one direction" can be handled as if they were taken on a flat surface or plane. Geodetic surveying is used for larger areas in which it is necessary to make mathematical computations to account for the earth's curvature.

According to the U.S. Department of Commerce's *1992 Census of Service Industries,* there were 8,418 establishments in the United States offering surveying services, down from the 8,436 establishments in 1987. Their combined receipts were just under $3 billion in 1994, up 5.2 percent from the 1993 figure of $2.7 billion.

BACKGROUND AND DEVELOPMENT

Surveying techniques developed in the ancient world, when people began to describe the dimensions and shape of the earth. Homer (in approximately the ninth century B.C.) envisioned the earth as a flat disk surrounded by oceans. Pythagoras, a Greek philosopher of the sixth century B.C., imagined a spherical world. Gauging the circumference of the earth was first accomplished in 240 B.C. by the Greek astronomer Eratosthenes, who measured the angle of the sun from two points on earth separated by 500 miles. His calculations gave him an answer of 25,000 miles, remarkably close to the earth's actual circumference (24,901.55 miles around the equator and 24,859.82 miles through the poles).

Before men knew the earth's overall dimensions, however, they developed techniques for measuring and locating parts. As early as 3800 B.C., the Babylonians conducted land surveys for taxation purposes. In approximately 2900 B.C., the Egyptians used surveying techniques to site, level, and erect the pyramids. By 1400 B.C., they were able to survey the land along the Nile River and reestablish field boundaries when floods erased previously established markers. Ancient Greeks were also acquainted with surveying methods. Their knowledge was passed on to the Romans, who refined and further developed surveying techniques used in building roads, bridges, buildings, and monuments.

Early surveying instruments were designed to help technicians accurately measure the angles necessary to calculate precise distances. One instrument, developed by the Romans, was called a groma. The groma was a cross-shaped instrument used to make a right angle. It had plumb lines suspended from each of its four ends to aid in leveling.

Another early surveying tool, the astrolabe, was used to measure angular heights. Through the centuries innovators improved upon the astrolabe's basic design. Glass lenses were added to make sighting sharper and more accurate. Larger astrolabes were developed for astronomical use, and smaller ones were fashioned for mariners. Plumb bobs were added to help determine a true vertical line.

Some instruments that were originally developed to aid navigators were also used by surveyors and map makers. An instrument called a cross-staff, or sighting stick, was developed to identify latitude. It had a sliding crosspiece and three sight holes that could be lined up on the horizon and sun to measure the angle. Users of early cross-staffs had to mark this angle and perform complex mathematical calculations to determine their latitude. Later cross-staffs were marked for direct readings.

Both the astrolabe and cross-staff required their users to make direct sightings on the sun. Because of the visual problems associated with this task, results were not entirely accurate. In 1607, a device called a back staff was first described. The back staff was designed so that the sun, when placed directly behind the instrument, cast a thin shadow on its staff.

The first precise theodolite was built for the British Royal Society by Jesse Ramsden during the late 1700s. A theodolite was an instrument consisting of a transit (a device used to measure angles) and a level. Surveyors used the theodolite to measure land areas by determining horizontal and vertical angles and applying trigonometric principles in a process known as triangulation.

Surveying played an important role in the development of the United States. During the colonial period, land was often received by private citizens as a result of a grant from a governmental unit for specified purposes or as payment for services. Recipients would have the tract surveyed and defined for the purpose of establishing the boundaries of their legal ownership. This type of survey was called a ''metes and bounds'' survey. The word ''metes'' referred to the boundary lines or limits of the property. The word ''bounds'' also referred to the demarcation of property limits. Metes and bounds surveys were conducted by beginning at a specified point and describing the perimeter of the land by referencing natural or artificial markers, called monuments, then describing the geometric lines connecting these physical objects. Metes and bounds surveys sometimes resulted in disputes when subsequent and adjacent property owners defined overlapping tracts.

To help make the definition of property lines more uniform, a national grid survey pattern was established during the late eighteenth century, and was subsequently used to describe and define property limits in more than 70 percent of the continental United States. Under the Land Ordinance of 1785, townships were defined as square areas, six miles on each side, oriented to the compass points. Each township was subdivided into 36 sections, each containing 640 acres (one square mile). Sections were further subdivided to yield tracts of land that were sold to individuals.

During the 1930s, the United States began implementing state grid systems under which states would maintain State Plane Coordinate (SPC) systems. These would provide permanent point identification and would ultimately fall under the control of a national network. Two types of SPC systems were adopted. One, called the Lambert projection, was used by states with a greater East-West shape. The second, the Mercator projection, was used by states with a greater North-South shape.

Surveying distances in the United States were measured using foot and decimal parts. Angles were measured in degrees, minutes, and seconds. Positions were specified by identifying latitude and longitude or by referencing coordinates from an identified reference point. Elevation was measured from an established ''bench mark,'' which was a permanent marker (either artificial or natural) with a known elevation above or below a specified surface (such as sea level).

Surveyors were required to take meticulous notes concurrently with the process of conducting the survey. These notes were recorded in field notebooks, which were then permanently kept under carefully controlled conditions. In the United States, field notebooks were considered legal documents.

The precision of a survey and its cost were related. ''First Order'' surveys were the most precise and the most costly. Other orders of surveys, termed second, third, and fourth, descended in precision and expense. Specific types of surveys were used for different purposes. Topographic surveys described the shape of the ground; hydrographic surveys mapped the bottoms of water bodies; construction surveys marked areas for specific projects such as buildings, bridges, and highways; underground surveys were conducted for pipelines, tunnels, and mining operations.

INDUSTRY LEADERS

Most architectural and engineering firms offer surveying services, and do a majority of surveying work themselves. The pure surveying firms characteristically are small and have only a fraction of industry billings. The top pure surveying company in 1996 was BSC Group, Inc. with $10 million. Other leaders include Flood Data Services, Inc. ($9 million); Tobin Surveys, Inc. ($6 million); Towill, Inc. ($5 million); McIntosh and McIntosh PC ($5 million); and Toplis and Harding, Inc. ($5 million).

One of the largest surveying establishments in the United States was MSE Corporation. MSE, a privately held organization owned by Sol C. Miller, was first organized as a partnership in Indianapolis, Indiana, in 1960 and incorporated in 1962. In 1996, MSE expanded to 350 employees and completed its 300th project assignment.

WORKFORCE

Surveyors and mapping scientists held about 101,000 jobs in 1996. Engineering and architectural services firms employed about three-fifths of these workers. Federal, State, and local governmental agencies employed an additional quarter. Major Federal Governmental employers are the U.S. Geological Survey, the Bureau of Land Management, the Army Corps of Engineers, the Forest Service, the National Oceanic and Atmospheric Administration, and the National Imagery and Mapping Agency (NIMA), formerly the Defense Mapping Agency. Most surveyors in State and local government work for highway departments and urban planning and redevelopment agencies. Construction firms, mining and oil and gas extraction companies, and public utilities also employ surveyors and mapping scientists. About 8,000 were self-employed in 1996.

This is one of the few professional occupations in which employment is expected to decline. Employment of surveyors and mapping scientists is expected to decline slightly through the year 2006, as the widespread availability and use of advanced technologies, such as the Global Positioning System, Geographic Information Systems, and remote sensing, are increasing both the accuracy and productivity of survey and mapping work. Job openings, however, will continue to result from the need to replace workers who transfer to other occupations or leave the labor force altogether.

As technologies become more complex, opportunities will be best for surveyors and mapping scientists who have at least a bachelor's degree and strong technical skills. Increasing demand for geographic data, as opposed to traditional surveying services, will mean better opportunities for mapping scientists involved in the development and use of geographic and land information systems; however, upgraded licensing requirements will continue to limit opportunities for those with less education.

Even as demand is increasing in nontraditional areas such as urban planning and natural resource exploration and mapping, opportunities for surveyors and mapping scientists should remain concentrated in engineering, architectural, and surveying services firms. According to the *Occupational Outlook Handbook* published by the Bureau of Labor Statistics, growth in construction through the year 2006 should require surveyors to lay out streets, shopping centers, housing developments, factories, office buildings, and recreation areas. However, employment may fluctuate from year to year along with construction activity. In addition, employment of mapping scientists and surveyors by private firms and the federal government will continue to be affected by budget cutbacks and technological efficiency.

The median weekly earnings for surveyors and mapping scientists were about $694 a week in 1996. The middle 50 percent earned between $547 and $849 a week; 10 percent earned less than $446 a week; 10 percent earned more than $1,000 a week.

The median weekly earnings for survey technicians were about $461 a week in 1996. The middle 50 percent earned between $378 and $725 a week; 10 percent earned less than $294 a week; 10 percent earned more than $942 a week.

In 1997, the federal government hired high school graduates with little or no training or experience at salaries of about $14,240 annually for entry level jobs on survey crews. Those with one year of related post-secondary training earned about $15,540 a year. Those with an associate degree that included coursework in surveying generally started as instrument assistants with an annual salary of about $17,450. In 1997, entry level land surveyors or cartographers with the federal government earned about $19,520, $24,180 or $29,580 a year, depending on their qualifications. The average annual salary for federal land surveyors in early 1997 was about $47,850; for cartographers, about $52,500; and for geodesists, about $62,760. The average annual salary for federal surveying technicians was about $28,600; for cartographic technicians, about $34,840; and for geodetic technicians, about $45,050.

Research and Technology

In recent years, new technology has been changing the nature of the work of surveyors and survey technicians. For larger projects, surveyors are increasingly using the Global Positioning System (GPS), a satellite system that precisely locates points on the earth using radio signals transmitted by satellites. To use this system, a surveyor places a satellite signal receiver (a small instrument mounted on a tripod) on a desired point. The receiver simultaneously collects information from several satellites to locate a precise position. The receiver can also be placed in a vehicle for uses such as tracing out road systems. Since receivers now come in different sizes and shapes and the cost of the receivers has fallen, much more surveying work is being done by GPS.

Some surveyors perform specialized functions, which are closer to those of a mapping scientist than a traditional surveyor. For example, geodetic surveyors use high-accuracy techniques, including satellite observations, to measure large areas of the earth's surface. Geophysical prospecting surveyors mark sites for subsurface exploration, usually petroleum related. Marine surveyors survey harbors, rivers, and other bodies of water to determine shorelines, topography of the bottom, water depth, and other features. The work of surveyors and mapping scientists is changing due to advancements in technology. These advancements include not only the GPS, but also new earth resources data satellites, improved aerial photography, and geographic information systems (GIS), which are computerized data banks of spatial data. From the older specialties of photogrammetrist and cartographer, a new type of mapping scientist is emerging. The *geographic information specialist* combines the functions of mapping science and surveying into a broader field concerned with the collection and analysis of geographic information.

According to an estimate reported in *ENR* magazine, about 80 percent of future surveying would be accomplished using GPS. The remaining 20 percent of surveying tasks would be done by conventional methods only in areas in which GPS was not able to be used. These included underground locations, such as tunnels, and heavily congested urban regions.

Further Reading

Brown, Lloyd A. *Map Making: The Art That Became a Science.* Boston: Little Brown, 1960.

DeCamp, Lyon Sprague. *The Ancient Engineers.* Garden City, NY: Doubleday, 1963.

U.S. Department of Labor. *Occupational Outlook Handbook, 1999 Online Edition.* Available from http://www.bls.gov/.

U.S. Department of Commerce. *1992 Census of Service Industries.* Washington: GPO, February 1995.

U.S. Bureau of the Census. *Service Annual Survey: 1994.* Washington: GPO, 1995.

SIC 8721

ACCOUNTING, AUDITING, AND BOOKKEEPING SERVICES

This category covers establishments primarily engaged in furnishing accounting, bookkeeping, and related auditing services. It includes those businesses that use data processing and tabulating in connection with these services, but those whose primary aim is to provide such data processing and tabulating are classified in **SIC 7374: Computer Processing and Data Preparation and Processing Services.** Establishments providing tax preparation services without also providing accounting, auditing, or bookkeeping services are covered in **SIC 7291: Tax Return Preparation Services.**

NAICS CODE(S)

541211 (Offices of Certified Public Accountants)
541214 (Payroll Services)
541219 (Other Accounting Services)

INDUSTRY SNAPSHOT

Accounting, auditing, and bookkeeping services serve key functions in America's (and the world's) economic engine. In such publications as *The Bottom Line,* the global significance of the accounting profession has long been confirmed: "The world's capital markets rely on financial statements certified by independent auditors. If the integrity of those statements could not be trusted, investment would come to a halt and economic growth would be paralyzed." The extreme importance of this type of integrity had two opposing consequences for the practice of accounting in the United States toward the end of the twentieth century: accountants filled a wide range of positions in all sectors of business and government; at the same time, there was a strong pressure to define accounting activities as narrowly and as precisely as possible to ensure that accounting standards remained objective and trustworthy. It is expected that in the next century, CPAs will need to prepare for the effects of new technology and globalization on the accounting marketplace.

ORGANIZATION AND STRUCTURE

Different fields in the accounting profession represent different degrees of affiliation with the world of commerce. Public accountants run their own businesses or are employed by accounting firms to meet the particular accounting needs of their clients. Accountants employed by companies to record and summarize financial data are known variously as management, industrial, corporate, or private accountants. Internal auditors are employed by companies to check records for signs of inefficiency, mismanagement, or fraud. Accountants and auditors employed in government not only produce and check the financial records pertaining to the institution for which they work, they also audit persons or businesses regulated and taxed by government. Each of these broadly defined fields is further subdivided by choices of specialization, yielding a wide variety of niches for accountants to fill.

Associations. Numerous organizations within the accounting profession cater to the specialized needs of different groups of accountants, ranging from the Association of Black CPA Firms to the American Women's Society of Certified Public Accountants to the National Association of Accountants. By far the largest and most important of the organizations within the profession, however, has been the American Institute of Certified Public Accountants (AICPA), which not only represented more than 330,000 CPAs at the beginning of 2000, but also served as the voice of the profession as a whole through its activities, recognized by the Securities and Exchange Commission (SEC) as a self-regulating body and setter of standards. The AICPA's three special member divisions neither monitored competency nor provided accreditation, but served as outlets for volunteer members with particular interests; they were the Federal Tax Division (dating from 1983), and two divisions created in 1986—Personal Financial Planning, and Management Advisory Services.

In addition to the standards established by the AICPA's Auditing Standards Board (ASB) and by other standards boards, the standards that have governed the accounting profession are those known by the acronym GAAP—Generally Accepted Accounting Principles. According to *Principles of Accounting,* "The general acceptance of accounting principles is not determined by a formal vote or survey of practicing accountants. An accounting principle must have substantial authoritative support to qualify as generally accepted. References to a particular accounting principle in authoritative accounting literature constitute substantive evidence of its general acceptance."

BACKGROUND AND DEVELOPMENT

Through the earliest financial record—keeping dates back to the very origins of international trade—modern accounting methods developed with the introduction of the double entry technique, whereby debits are assigned to the left side of a ledger and credits to the right. The value of this fundamental method seems to have been grasped first in the commercial republics of Italy at some point before the fourteenth century.

More sophisticated accounting techniques were not needed until Great Britain's industrial revolution and ascent to global pre-eminence created business conditions of hitherto unprecedented scope and complexity. As noted in *Modern Accounting Theory,* "from about the beginning of the nineteenth century the rise of manufacturing, trading, shipping, and all the various subsidiary services (such as the provision of the many kinds of insurance), the vast ramifications of the London money market, and the opening of world markets (such as the Liverpool Cotton Exchange) made accurate financial accounting and reporting a prime necessity for the maintenance of Great Britain's commercial empire. " With the exception of the field of consolidated accounting, where, "practice in the United States developed before it did in Great Britain and was to provide the leadership for the latter," the early history of American accounting was therefore defined by the adaptation of British innovations and precedents to the novel conditions of business development in the United States.

In due course, as the United States increasingly assumed Great Britain's mantle as the world leader in economic affairs, still further developments took place in accounting methods. Many of the most important accounting principles were not introduced until the early decades of the twentieth century. These changes took place in response to the emergence of huge industrial firms, large stockholders' groups, government regulation, and continued economic growth. According to *Principles of Accounting,* all of these factors combined to help "create the large groups of interested parties who require a constant stream of reliable financial information concerning the economic entities they own, manage, or regulate," a type of information "meaningful only when prepared according to some agreed-on standards and procedures."

A further stimulus to the American accounting industry took place early in the twentieth century with the introduction of the national income tax in 1913. The American Bar Association took the position that income tax law fell entirely within the province of lawyers, and the resultant turf war between that association and the AICPA was not resolved until the mid-1950s, after a number of lawsuits, at which point the preparation of tax returns became solidly established as a key business area for American accountants.

The stock market crash of 1929 prompted the Federal Securities Act of 1933 and the Federal Securities Act of 1934. These pieces of legislation required that audits of the financial statements of public companies be made by independent certified public accountants, further bolstering the accounting profession. In addition to generating business for such accountants, these acts had the effect of raising the prestige of the accountancy profession, because the government neither insisted on providing auditors of its own nor set auditing standards, but rather accepted the integrity of the profession and the standards that it developed by means of self-regulation.

However, such self-regulation did not satisfy some critics, who took the view that government should play a more active part in such a highly critical area of the economy. Nor did it spell an end to controversy within the profession. At the end of the 1960s, especially, there was "a period of unprecedented stress for the individual members and institutions of the accounting profession," in the words of the March 1972 *Report of the Study on Establishment of Accounting Principles,* which cited the dramatic growth of accounting firms, new accounting issues and business practices, and corporate mergers as particular factors. According to *The Bottom Line,* that 1972 report proposed the establishment of an independent standard-setting body, the Financial Accounting Standards Board (FASB), whose scope was defined as follows by one of its former chairpersons: "FASB standards are binding on most companies and independent auditors, with stiff penalties for departures. The ethics rules of the American Institute of CPAs, the CPA licensing requirements of the 50 states, and the regulations of the Securities and Exchange Commission all mandate conformity with the Board's pronouncements."

But the establishment of the FASB in 1973 did not put an end to controversy, as it was a body perceived as having a bias in favor of business and the private sector. Therefore, the Governmental Accounting Standards Board (GASB) was instituted in 1984 for standard-setting in relation to state and local government, confining the FASB's jurisdiction to solely nongovernmental entities. Some analysts saw defects in this new arrangement, however, pointing out that institutions within the private sector and within the public sector were not always so different from each other as to justify the maintenance of different sets of standards for each, and that the entire idea of having different standards for the two sectors was by no means automatically a good thing—especially as still other sets of standards governed auditing procedures in federal government.

In recent years a number of the industry's largest companies have endured harsh criticism from some quarters. The savings and loan crisis of the 1980s, in which many of those institutions were felled by bankruptcy, tarnished the reputation of the industry-leading "Big Six" accounting firms, which were responsible for auditing most of the failed thrifts.

In the early 1990s, the accounting, auditing, and bookkeeping industry supported firms of vastly different economic status, from the giant accounting firms that comprised the Big Six to one-person operations. The difference in scale between the larger and smaller accounting businesses was so pronounced and led to such a difference in the type of services offered by each size of business that accountancy in the United States sometimes was viewed as ''two separate and distinct professions,'' according to *The Bottom Line,* which noted that ''major national firms were known for their audits of major publicly held companies and for the breadth of their management advisory services. The smallest firms, for the most part, emphasized personal attention to small businesses and individual taxpayers. The mid-size firms typically carved out a market niche in which they performed a variety of services.''

In theory, such a division of labor should have guaranteed the peaceful coexistence of accountancy firms of varying sizes. However, tension between firms had long been a characteristic of the modern accountancy profession in the United States, and reflected a variety of factors. For instance, there was a suspicion among the smaller firms that the larger ones were exploiting to their own advantage their ability to offer financial services at a loss-leading discount, thereby attracting potentially lucrative new clients in a way impossible for businesses with fewer resources to match. Moreover, the intermediate position occupied by mid-sized firms was an inherently unstable one: with smaller firms becoming more specialized, and larger ones having a matchless range and depth, mid-sized firms risked being left with no niche at all, and often ended up merging with larger outfits.

In addition, mergers among clients had a profound impact on the relative fortunes of larger and smaller accounting firms, especially as such mergers, already a cause for concern in some quarters during the 1970s, became a far more prominent feature of the business scene during the next decade. According to a study undertaken by the Senate Subcommittee on Reports, Accounting and Management of the Committee on Government Operations (1976), ''As a by-product of the corporate merger movement that has concentrated control over the Nation's economic resources among fewer and fewer institutions and individuals, small and medium-sized CPA firms have been displaced as independent auditors by large accounting firms.''

Moreover, as this same study reported, such displacement also tended to occur when companies decided to sell shares to the public: ''Underwriters and bankers often inform companies that a nationally known firm must be retained as independent auditor in order to sell securities to the public at the highest possible price, or obtain a necessary loan.''

Industry receipts grew by roughly 30 percent from 1992 to 1996, when they surpassed the $50 billion milestone. Annual growth in the 1990s was slower, however, than the double-digit percentage increases of the late 1980s. In the mid-1990s accounting firms moved toward confronting the ethical and legal problems of their clients, including such issues as corporate governance and accountability, according to *Oregon Business.*

Large international firms branched out into management consulting services. However, according to *The CPA Journal,* the attractive consulting fees may have led many firms to ignore potential conflicts of interest in serving as an auditor and as a management consultant to the same client. The profession's standards also were said to be jeopardized by the entrance of non-CPA partners and owners into influential accounting firms. Many companies facing these problems, like Arthur Andersen, split their accounting and management consulting operations into separate divisions or companies to avoid accusations of impropriety.

During the mid- to late 1990s, accounting firms evolved by restructuring their services and offering new services such as attestation and other assurance services, according to *The CPA Journal.* The growing internationalization of business was another important factor in changing the way the industry functioned. According to *Oregon Business,* international bookkeeping operations grew at a faster pace than domestic operations. The restructuring proved to be favorable for the continuation of mergers among accounting firms. By 1998, the Big Six had been reduced to the Big Five, with the merger of Price Waterhouse and Coopers & Lybrand.

CURRENT CONDITIONS

According to a news brief found on *AccountingNet,* a recent poll by RHI Management Resources found that ''51 percent of chief financial officers said they believe the consolidation trend among public accounting firms will continue over the next decade,'' with 34 percent saying there will be fewer than the current Big Five in the next 5 years.

Aside from the trend toward mergers among large national accounting firms, there was a movement during the late 1990's for other businesses, such as financial institutions, to aquire CPA firms, according to an article in the July 1999 issue of the *CPA Journal.* This may allow services traditionally offered exclusively by CPAs to be offered by non-CPAs. There still are many unresolved issues concerning regulation, licensing, state laws and peer reviews. The AICPA of the late 1990s was working to clarify and develop guidelines for some of these issues.

An area of expected growth into the next century involved consulting services, which were becoming increasingly important as businesses have sought to expand internationally. The trend toward one-stop shopping, as discussed by Barry Melancon, president and CEO of the AICPA, in an article in *Accounting Horizons,* puts an emphasis on firms able to provide multiple services to meet client expectations. This has put a strain on smaller firms that may not have the resources to provide a diversity of services. Smaller and mid-sized firms need to take note of the changes in the market in order to remain economically viable into the first part of the twenty-first century.

Industry Leaders

The Big Six accounting firms—KPMG Peat Marwick, Ernst & Young, Coopers & Lybrand, Arthur Andersen, Deloitte & Touche, and Price Waterhouse—continued to dominate the industry entering the late 1990s. While these firms were the most well-known in the profession, the American economy also supported regional and local firms as well as thousands of accountants that maintained their own small businesses. By 1998, the Big Six was reduced to the Big Five with the merger of Price Waterhouse and Coopers & Lybrand to form PricewaterhouseCoopers. Other industry leaders of the late 1990s included Century Business Services, American Express, H & R Block, Merrill Lynch and Oppenheimer.

Workforce

Because every state established its own licensing requirements, there were some differences in the type of education and experience required of a person seeking to become a CPA. Essentially, the requirements consisted of a four-year college degree, one or two years of on-the-job experience, and a passing grade on the CPA examination.

The shortage of teachers with doctoral degrees in accounting—largely attributable to the higher pay available to talented accountants in public and industrial accounting—presented a major hurdle to those who advocated the desirability of requiring a fifth year of education for CPAs, and prompted the AICPA to institute a financial aid program for doctoral candidates, in hopes of boosting the number of faculty in accounting.

Any student capable of meeting the existing educational requirements faced good prospects because of the anticipated healthy state of the American accounting profession in the twenty-first century. Through the year 2005, job growth in accounting was predicted to be higher than the average for all occupations tracked by the U.S. Department of Labor—and this in a context where the numbers of students graduating with degrees in accounting had remained essentially stable.

Though CPAs were expected to have a better choice among a greater range of employment activities, other accountants and accountants without college degrees could be expected to find niches in a growing market. Moreover, accountants of all levels of training and experience could take confidence from the fact that downturns in the national economy seldom had an adverse impact on their chosen profession, because even a poorly performing economy still generated data that had to be analyzed and interpreted.

Of the roughly 2 million clerks engaged in various forms of bookkeeping, about a third worked in wholesale and retail; about a quarter worked in social, educational, health, or business services; and about a quarter worked part-time. Their employment prospects were seen as vulnerable to increasing computerization of office functions.

At the beginning of the 1990s, the average starting salary for junior accountants in the federal government was $17,000 annually. By the close of the century, a college graduate who began working in public accounting could expect to earn $26,000 to $36,750; salaries offered in corporate accounting began at $27,000 and capped at $33,750. College graduates with a masters degree could expect to add 10 percent to their starting salary.

Unsurprisingly, members of the accounting profession who had greater experience earned significantly more during this same period. Managers and directors in accounting firms commanded an annual average salary of $56,250 in small accounting firms and could earn up to $92,000 in large firms (usually after a period of 5 to 8 years). In 8 to 12 years, once an individual reached partner status in an accounting firm, average first-year salaries were reported to be $175,000 (*1999 Robert Half and Accountemps Salary Guide*).

Demand for qualified accounting professionals continued to grow during the late 1990s. The target accounting firms for most fresh graduates were the Big Five. Accounting firms were in constant search of qualified personnel. Consequently, they were offering flexible working hours and a more democratic promotion system, according to *The Practical Accountant.*

According to a December 1998 article in *Accounting Horizons,* a publication of the American Accounting Association, there were approximately 45,000 accounting related firms in the United States, and about 150,000 CPAs in practice.

In her article on the changing roles of CPAs, Tami Kegley discussed the need for CPAs of the future to have knowledge of "the international market, technological applications and strategic knowledge management." Another area expected to grow is the consulting assurance area, according to Leigh Knopf of the AICPA. Other factors affecting the future of CPAs are increased competition with non-CPAs and the globalization of the accounting industry.

America and the World

The largest of the accountancy firms in the United States possessed the resources to conduct extensive business overseas. Some of the smaller firms worked in conjunction with similar outfits overseas by associating with them in cooperative networks. With the increasing trend toward a global economy that was apparent at the end of the twentieth century, the importance of such international transactions was sure to increase, stressing the desirability of essentially uniform worldwide accounting standards in making cross-border financial data as accurate and useful as possible.

Because the American way of doing business exerted a powerful influence on the rest of the world throughout the twentieth century, and because American accounting standards, building on British precedent and developed over the course of that century, had established a level of sophistication and authority recognized around the world, international accounting standards greatly conform to an American model.

FURTHER READING

"Accounting; Audit; Bookkeeping." *Britannica.com and Encyclopaedia, Inc.,* 1999. Available from http://www.britannica.com/bcom/eb/article/printable/1/0,5722,3491,00.

———. *Britannica.com and Encyclopaedia, Inc.,* 1999. Available from http://www.britannica.com/bcom/eb/article/printable/1/0,5722,11221,00.html

———. *Britannica.com and Encyclopaedia, Inc.,* 1999. Available from http://www.britannica.com/bcom/eb/article/printable/9/0,5722,80659,00.html.

"Accounting Salaries." AICPA Online (Search AICPA Online), 2000. Available from http://www.aicpa.org/.

Briloff, Abraham. "Our Profession's Jurassic Park." *The CPA Journal,* August 1994.

Demery, Paul. "The Changing Demographics of Accounting Firms." *The Practical Accountant,* March 1996.

Kegley, Tami. "Solutions: From Auditors to Consultants—the Changing Roles of CPAs." *AccountingNet,* 7 September, 1998. Available from http://accounting.pro2net.com/.

Kelly, Jim. "The People Who Really Count." *The Financial Times,* 22 February 1995.

Mastracchio, Nichols J., Jr. "A New Era For the Local CPA Firm." *The CPA Journal,* July 1999. Available from http://www.nysscpa.org/cpajournal/1999/0799/features/F20799.HTM.

Melancon, Barry C. "The Changing Strategy for the Profession, the CPA and the AICPA: What This Means for the Education Community." *Accounting Horizons.* American Accounting Association, Vol. 12, No. 4, December 1998. Available from http://www.rutgers.edu/Accounting/raw/aaa/pubs/12—98ah/securearea/5art 01.htm.

"News Briefs: Survey Predicts Continued Firm Consolidation." *AccountingNet,* 1 March, 1999. Available from wysiwyg://Forum.88/http://www.accountingne...m/news/press/industry/prin 990301survey.asp.

Oliverio, Mary Ellen, and Bernard H. Newman. *Auditing in Public Accounting Firms: A Preliminary Look to 1999.* February 1996.

Peloubet, Maurice E. "The Historical Development of Accounting." *Modern Accounting Theory.* Englewood Cliffs, NJ: Prentice-Hall, 1966.

"Professional Services: Global State of The Industry." *Oregon Business,* May 1996.

Walgenbach, Paul H., Ernest I. Hanson, and Norman E. Dittrich. *Principles of Accounting.* 4th ed. New York: Harcourt Brace Jovanovich, 1987.

Weinstein, Grace W. *The Bottom Line.* New York: NAL Penguin, 1987.

SIC 8731

COMMERCIAL PHYSICAL AND BIOLOGICAL RESEARCH

This industry classification covers establishments primarily engaged in commercial physical and biological research and development on a contract or fee basis. Noncommercial research establishments funded by endowments, grants, or contributions are classified in **SIC 8733: Noncommercial Research Organizations.** Separate establishments of aircraft, guided missile, or spacecraft manufacturers primarily engaged in research and development on these products are classified in several SICs concerned with transportation equipment manufacturing.

NAICS CODE(S)

541710 (Research and Development in the Physical Sciences and Engineering Sciences)

541720 (Research and Development in the Life Sciences)

Commercial physical and biological research organizations are supported by commercial firms and organizations that invest a portion of their annual budget in research and development (R&D). These industries apply the knowledge acquired through R&D toward developing products for domestic and international markets. Commercial physical and biological research is routinely undertaken in a vast array of subject categories, including agricultural, biological, chemical, engineering, physical, and industrial research. Studies in these arenas serve to improve already existing products as well as to develop new ones. Nearly every firm in every major industry has a division or subsidiary devoted to commercial physical research. Many products that arise out of these research efforts appear solely in the retail consumer market; others contribute to improving industrial processes.

Commercial, physical, and biological research surfaced among the fastest growing segments of the U.S.

economy beginning in the early 1990s and continuing into the turn of the 21st century. Research and development companies experienced explosive growth with associated high volatility. According to *R & D,* the total annual U.S. expenditures for research and development would grow by 7.75 percent in the year 2000, and in doing so would surpass $266 billion. Forecasters attributed an estimated $187 billion of that sum to the efforts of industrial organizations exclusive of supplier (in-house) research and development spending, with the industrial sector anticipated to grow by 10.6 percent in 2000. While other industries cut back during recession periods, commercial research and development divisions often enjoyed increased budgets. For instance, a fiercely competitive business environment in the early 1990s led companies to place a substantial premium on first-to-market technology, thus accentuating the importance of research and development for maintaining and expanding market share. Drug companies increased their R&D expenditures by 13 percent to about $11 billion or 16 percent of sales, in response to public concerns over physical and biological phenomena such as the spread of AIDS. In the latter years of the decade innovative new concepts—such as controversial experimentation with cloning—further fueled the R&D economy. The most anticipated spending increases for research and development existed in the industrial arenas: electronics; drugs and medicine; and computing and communications sciences for business purposes, with the lowest research and development investments expected among mature industries—including paper and pulp, industrial chemicals, petroleum refining and extraction.

At the end of the twentieth century the roster of R&D industry firms fluctuated drastically, although in 1997 *Ward's Business Directory of U.S. Private and Public Companies* named Science Applications International Corporation (SAIC) as the leader in this industry, and the company flourished. SAIC, a private company headquartered in San Diego, California, reported annual sales of $4.74 billion in 1999, for a 53.4 percent annual sales growth and more than double growth over a two-year period. SAIC employed 35,200 workers in 1999 and ranked at number 347 among the *Fortune* 500, and ranked 23rd among *Forbes* private 500. SAIC contracts an estimated 50 percent of its workload with government entities.

Also prominent was Quintiles Transnational Corporation, the largest research provider to pharmaceuticals manufacturers, which maintained operations in 30 countries worldwide. An S&P 500 company, Quintiles is headquartered in Durham, North Carolina. The company employed over 15,000 workers in 1998 and ranked among *Fortune* Magazine's Fastest Growing Companies in America, with $1.188 billion in sales in 1998, and 45.9 percent growth. Additionally, Chiron Corporation, devoted to pharmaceutical research, reported $762.6 billion in sales for 1999. Chiron, a public company headquartered in Emeryville, California, is largely owned (45 percent) by Novartis.

FURTHER READING

"Chiron Corp." *Hoover's Online,* 14 February 2000. Available from wysiwyg://29/http://www.hoovers.com/co/capsule/2/0,2163,12972,00.html.

"Quintiles Transnational Corp." *Hoover's Online,* 14 February 2000. Available from wysiwyg://74/http://www.hoovers.com/co/capsule/7/0,2163,17267,00.html.

Schwartz, Harry. "AIDS Research: Who Drives the Train?" *Pharmaceutical Executive*July 1995,7:3, 22-24.

"Science Applications International Corp." *Hoover's Online,* 14 February 2000. Available from wysiwyg://25/http://www.hoovers.com/co/capsule/7/0,2163,40417,00.html.

Studt, Tim, and Jules J. Duga. "Industry Spends Big on Development While Feds Focus on Research." *R & D,* January 2000.

SIC 8732

COMMERCIAL ECONOMIC, SOCIOLOGICAL, AND EDUCATIONAL RESEARCH

This classification includes establishments primarily engaged in performing commercial business, marketing, and other economic, sociological, and educational research on a contract or fee basis. Noncommercial economic, sociological, and educational research establishments funded from endowments, grants, or contributions are classified in **SIC 8733 Noncommercial Research Organizations.**

NAICS CODE(S)

541730 (Research and Development in the Social Sciences and Humanities)

541910 (Marketing Research and Public Opinion Polling)

Members of this classification gather and interpret data in the areas of business and economic research, educational research, market research, public opinion, and sociological research. Utilized to track such varied phenomena as product launches, television viewing habits, and political popularity, this industry has become an increasingly integral part of the sociological landscape of the United States. Demographic surveys and poll results are used to determine everything from a publication's advertising focus to the popularity of legislative initiatives under consideration. Indeed, the plethora of polls and surveys in the 1990s came under increased criticism from observers who charged that such polls, particularly with regard to politics, were in themselves forces that influenced public opinion.

Market research, routinely utilized by companies involved in myriad industries nationwide, grew and changed rapidly between the 1930s and the 1990s. The philosophical underpinnings of this growth were based on a consumer, market-driven orientation. Thus the emphasis was on discovering the needs and wants of the consumer and creating a product that fulfilled those needs and wants, as opposed to a product-driven philosophy centered on creating a product and trying to sell it without first consulting the marketplace to determine the appetite for the product.

In order to systematically gather such information and analyze it, larger corporations support marketing departments. Through a variety of means—mostly surveys—these departments evaluate a product's acceptance in the marketplace and track its sales. Many other corporations, large and small, contract with commercial research companies that specialize in such demographic studies.

Though some critics claim that the "scientific method" cannot be applied to inexact sciences such as anthropology, economics, geography, political science, psychology, and sociology, sociologists continue to use advanced mathematical statistics and other quantitative methods, as well as computer technology, to evaluate and interpret data. Much of their information is derived from a variety of sources such as census reports, government studies, and questionnaires from large samples of people. Commercial nonphysical research firms also employ qualitative methods such as direct observation and historical research.

As surveys and polls have become widely used tools for gathering demographic and other pertinent information, some of the best known firms in this industry—AC Nielsen, Gallup, and Harris—have become familiar names to the average consumer. By 1999, in fact, Nielsen had become the unquestioned leader. According to *Ward's Business Directory of U.S. Private and Public Companies,* other industry leaders included IMS International Inc., Gartner Group Inc., and Moody's Investors Service.

In 1998, there were an estimated 5,595 establishments in this industry, billing $9 billion, a 2 percent increase from the previous year. In 1999, 149,500 workers were employed, working just over 30 hours per week for average wages of $14.78 per hour.

FURTHER READING

Bradway, Bruce M., Mary Anne Frenzel, and Robert E. Pritchard. *Strategic Marketing: A Handbook for Entrepreneurs and Managers.* Reading, MA: Addison Wesley.

Darnay, Arsen J. *Service Industries, USA.* Detroit: Gale Group, 1999.

*Ward's Business Directory of U.S. Private and Public Companies.*Detroit: Gale Group, 1999.

U.S. Bureau of the Census. *Economic Census 1997,* 2000. Available from http://www.census.gov.

U.S. Bureau of Labor Statistics. *Employment Statistics,* 2000. Available from http://www.bls.gov.

SIC 8733

NONCOMMERCIAL RESEARCH ORGANIZATIONS

This category includes establishments primarily engaged in performing noncommercial research into and dissemination of information for public health, education, or general welfare. Establishments included here operate primarily on funds from endowments, contributions, and grants. The research is frequently contracted out and funded by these establishments. Establishments primarily engaged in commercial physical and biological research are classified in **SIC 8731: Commercial Physical and Biological Research,** and those engaged in commercial economic, sociological, and educational research are classified in **SIC 8732: Commercial Economic, Sociological, and Educational Research.**

NAICS CODE(S)

541710 (Research and Development in the Physical Sciences and Engineering Sciences)

541720 (Research and Development in the Life Sciences)

541730 (Research and Development in the Social Sciences and Humanities)

Colleges and universities are leaders in noncommercial research, with Stanford University, the University of Texas at Austin, Harvard University, the University of Arizona, Ohio State University, and the University of Chicago topping the list. These universities provide research on a variety of subjects, and the knowledge they gain benefits the whole of society. They specialize in technical research, such as engineering, physics, biochemistry, and biology. Academic aspects of universities are discussed in greater detail under **SIC 8221: Colleges, Universities, and Professional Schools.** Academic research in the United States is funded largely through taxpayer dollars in the form of government grants and occurs at the individual level rather than at the organizational level. Although federal funds are dispensed largely to individual researchers, educational institutions classified under the "Research I" category receive tens of millions of dollars annually in federal support. Additionally, ''Research II'' institutions receive between $15 million and $40 million every year.

Government Funding Sources. The National Institutes of Health (NIH) dispenses billions of research dollars each year in the form of grants. Twenty-two organizations, including the National Library of Medicine and the John F. Fogarty International Center, fall under the budgetary control of the National Institutes of Health. Most prominent among the research institutes are the National Cancer Institute, the National Heart, Lung, and Blood Institute, and the National Institute of Diabetes and Digestive and Kidney Research. According to U.S. budget estimates for the year 2001, NIH funds for research purposes total $18.172 billion, from a projected NIH budget of $20.068 billion. Of the total research funds, the top three research institutes will receive $3.25 billion, $2.07 billion, and $1.21 billion, respectively.

The U.S. National Science Foundation (NSF) controls an additional $3.641 billion in research funds. NSF research dollars go largely to the National Research Center. Research projects funded by NSF extend to biological sciences ($511 million), computer sciences ($529 million), polar programs ($223 million), geoscience ($583 million), and engineering, math, and physical sciences ($1.338 billion). In addition to NIH and NSF, the U.S. government provides funding to research efforts under the auspices of other departments including the Department of Energy, the Department of Agriculture, and the National Aeronautics and Space Administration.

One of the leading non-profit research organizations in the United States, the Smithsonian Institution receives approximately $200 million in U.S. taxpayer dollars annually for research and collections management purposes. Overall, the research budget of the Smithsonian comprises approximately one-third of the total budget of the Institute.

Private Sector Non-commercial Research. Silicon Valley in California is well known for its economic development in the high-tech industry. The community began as a collaborative effort between educational institutions and small businesses, in response to mutual concerns for technological innovation. State-of-the art technologies developed in the Valley afford nonprofit research researchers with online access to news and developments through the Internet. The American Association for the Advancement of Science's EurekAlert! is a World Wide Web site that provides research news from all over the world. This site was created with the intention of providing a bulletin for universities, nonprofit organizations, and corporations to post new discoveries and advancements in science. Researchers, journalists, and the public at large access information disseminated through this and other Internet-based sites.

The Better Business Bureau (BBB) is a nonprofit organization that provides reports and information that safeguard consumers against unscrupulous businesses. Another consumer information provider is the Consumers Union, established in 1936 ''to provide consumers with information and advice on goods, services, health and personal finance.''

FURTHER READING

''AAAS Launches On-line Service for Research News.'' *Science,* 31 May 1996.

Atkinson, Richard C. ''Universities: at the center of U.S. Research.'' *Science,* 6 June 1997.

Hoover's Handbook 1996. Austin, TX: Hoover's, Inc., 1996.

Kaiser, Jocelyn. ''New Law Could Open up Lab Books.'' *Science,* 6 November 1998.

Kornburg, Arthur. ''The NIH did it.'' *Science,* 12 December 1997.

Mervis, Jeffrey. ''NFS spells out an electronic future: grants management.'' *Science,* 9 October 1998.

Moy, Ernest; Anthony J. Mazzaschi, Rebecca J. Levin, David A. Blake, Paul F. Griner, ''Relationship between National Institutes of Health research awards to US medical schools and managed care market penetration.'' *JAMA,* 16 July 1997.

U.S. Department of Education. National Center for Educational Statistics. *Integrated Postsecondary Education Data System.* Washington, 1997.

Appendix, Budget of the United States Government, Fiscal Year 1002. Government Printing Office, 2000.

SIC 8734

TESTING LABORATORIES

This classification covers establishments primarily engaged in providing testing services. Establishments primarily engaged in performing clinical laboratory testing for the medical profession are classified in **SIC 8071: Medical Laboratories.**

NAICS CODE(S)

541940 (Veterinary Services)
541380 (Testing Laboratories)

Testing laboratories exist in both corporate in-house and independent settings and include varied services such as assaying; automobile proving and testing grounds; calibration and certification testing; dosimetry (measurement of radiation); film badge service (radiation detection); food testing; forensic services; hydrostatic testing services; product testing; metallurgical testing; pollution testing; radiographing welded joints on pipes and fittings; seed testing; veterinary testing; and industrial X-ray inspection.

As people in the twentieth century became increasingly aware of environmental and other physical hazards, they wanted to know about the quality of two very broad categories: substances that entered their bodies, and objects they came into contact with on a daily basis. In some cases, the constitution and/or reliability of substances and objects can be perceived easily, but the effects of radiation or toxic chemicals often are less immediately apparent or noticeable. For this reason, a broad range of testing laboratories developed in the twentieth century, especially where legislation mandated certain safety standards. The Food and Drug Administration (FDA), the Environmental Protection Agency (EPA), and the Food Safety and Inspection Service of the U.S. Department of Agriculture are the three best-known government agencies with which the testing laboratory industry is involved.

Because of the myriad federal regulations regarding food, drugs, equipment, and general products, testing for all kinds of substances and hazards has spawned its own industry. Food testing laboratories are among the most common testing laboratories. A number of laws directly relate to food: the Food, Drug, and Cosmetic Act; the Fair Packaging Act; Pure Food and Drug Laws; Consumer Product Safety Act; the Occupational Safety and Health Act; the Water Pollution Control Act; the Rodenticide Act; and the Clean Water Act. Companies that produce, package, and market food must be sure their products comply with all of the federal laws governing their products.

Devices that are used in hospitals and doctors' offices for diagnostic purposes, such as X-rays or mammography machines, must also be subjected to a wide range of tests on a regular basis to be sure they are functioning according to specifications and are calibrated properly. Some instruments used for detecting radiation intensity are the well-known Geiger-Muller counter, the Cutie Pie survey meter, and the scintillation counter. Some functions and calibrations must be tested on an annual basis, while others are tested on daily, weekly, or monthly schedules. Hospitals and other medical facilities contract with independent laboratories that provide trained professionals and physicists to perform such on-site inspections and to make repairs when necessary. They also train operators to complete the necessary daily tests that are mandated for peak performance and the optimum safety of both the operator and the patient.

Other laboratories work with the government, medical community, and other industries to provide a wide range of services in nearly every field from automobile testing to forensics and metallurgy. Many facilities feature mobile laboratories out of necessity and offer technicians cross-certified in accordance with the latest American Society for Nondestructive Testing (ASNT), American National Standards Institute (ANSI), and military requirements, enabling them to serve in technician, auditor, and inspector capacities.

The history of testing laboratories is a relatively short one. By the beginning of the twentieth century, members of the food manufacturing industry had begun adding untested chemicals to their products. Growing concern about such untested products prompted Congress to pass the Pure Food and Drug Act in 1906. This act established the Food and Drug Administration with jurisdiction over the safety of food additives and drugs that were already proven harmful. In 1938, the Cosmetic Act expanded that authority to drugs, which must undergo vigorous testing before reaching the marketplace. Subsequent legislation in 1957, 1958, and 1962 required additional testing and compliance with regulations regarding food, drugs, and cosmetics.

After 1945 and the dawning of the Atomic Age, people realized the dangers of radiation. They also realized that the use of radiation was not confined to warfare; the medical community was establishing a whole new use for the technology. X-rays, although no longer new, were in widespread use, as were the new radioisotopes (for diagnostic purposes), and radiation treatment for cancer therapy. Euphoria over the new treatments was soon tempered by concern, and public demand led to new legislation to set acceptable standards for exposure. Because of all the regulations regarding food, drugs, cosmetics, radiation, and related products, commercial testing laboratories materialized all over the country.

The development of varieties of lab tests seems to change historically along with society's concerns: first it was food, then radiation, and in the 1990s, the environment that raised concern. Thus, previously established labs have expanded their services to include environmental testing, and new, specialized labs have come into being specifically for environmental testing.

American Society for Testing and Material. In 1993 the American Society for Testing and Materials (ASTM) inaugurated a proficiency testing program. The program offers services to testing laboratories within all industries in an endeavor to coordinate testing standards worldwide. ASTM is a section of the International Association for Testing Materials and was founded in 1898 to encourage the development of materials standards for the railroad construction industry. Throughout the twentieth century ASTM expanded the scope of its programs and committees from steel and construction materials in 1898, to war-essential materials in the 1940s. ASTM branched into environmental and consumer product standards in the 1970s and established the Institute for Standards Research (ISR) in 1988. In the year 2000 ASTM published its *International Directory of Testing Laboratories,* listing more than 4,000 testing facilities. These included firms involved in acoustic and vibration testing, biological testing, chemical testing, chromatography, electrical and electronic testing, geotechnical testing, mechanical testing, metrology, nondestructive evaluation, optics and photometry, radiation and ionizing, surface analysis and microscopy, sensory evaluation, spectroscopy, thermal analysis, and thermal and fire testing. Facilities engaged in chemical testing were most populous, while radiation and ionizing testing labs were least prevalent. An overwhelming majority of laboratories were located in the United States and Canada.

Industry Leaders

LabOne Inc. of Lenexa, Kansas, earned $102 million in 1998, nearly doubling its 1997 revenues for the previous year. Also in 1998, the company experienced an overall sales growth of 29.5 percent, and increased its employee count by 34.6 percent. Other industry leaders in the late 1990s were Applied Bioscience International Inc., a public company based in Arlington, Virginia, which reported $183 million in sales for 1997; and Farmingdale, New York's Tyree Organization Inc., with $118 million. Market share was widespread, and some 36 companies claimed annual sales of $10 million or more.

Further Reading

''ASTM International Directory of Testing Laboratories, 1999,'' *American Society for Testing and Materials,* 12 February 2000. Available from http://www.astm.org/labs/index.html.

Darnay, Arsen J., ed. *Service Industries USA.* 3rd ed. Detroit: Gale Research, 1999.

''LabOne, Inc.'' *Hoover's Online,* 12 February 2000. Available from http://www.hoovers.com/.

U.S. Department of Commerce. *1995 Census of Service Industries.* Washington: GPO, 1997.

Ward's Business Directory of U.S. Private and Public Companies. Detroit: Gale Research, 1997.

SIC 8741

MANAGEMENT SERVICES

This category covers establishments primarily engaged in furnishing general or specialized management services on a day-to-day basis and on a contract or fee basis. Establishments in this industry do not provide operating staff. Management and operation of a business, where operating staff as well as management is provided, is classified according to the activity of the establishment managed.

NAICS Code(s)

561110 (Office Administrative Services)

Industry Snapshot

The management services industry is highly fragmented and unstructured. It consists of a conglomeration of different services for almost every sector of the economy. As a result, this entry presents examples of companies that are representative of different segments of the industry, and describes how the proliferation of management services is affecting the American economy and work force. Construction management services, which make up the largest single division of the industry, are highlighted.

The U.S. Bureau of the Census estimated that the management services industry generated revenues of about $13 billion and employed about 300,000 workers in the late 1980s. In the early 1990s, however, the industry continued to expand at a rapid pace, with some major segments growing by more than 30 percent per year. Plodding growth in the 1980s and early 1990s was a general shift in the dynamics of the American economy. Going into the mid-1990s, companies in all economic sectors were increasingly seeking the expertise and flexibility offered by professional management firms. By 1997 the U.S. Bureau of Census estimated that total receipt had reached $30.3 billion.

Organization and Structure

Management service firms benefit their customers by providing expertise in certain areas of the company's operations. In addition to expertise, companies may also benefit from increased flexibility. By contracting a service firm to manage a short-term project or administrative task, for instance, a company avoids the expensive and time-consuming chore of hiring, managing, and later eliminating workers.

Many service companies specialize in managing, or outsourcing, one niche of an organization's operations. Some companies, for instance, manage an establishment's mail room, or handle all electronic communications in an organization, such as voice and electronic mail. Other companies oversee various marketing and selling activities, or manage high-tech product development projects.

A construction supply manufacturer, for example, might consider its core competency to be the development and production of paving tiles and concrete forms. However, the company must also engage in several activities at which it may not be particularly adept, such as managing internal data and information systems, motivating its sales force, and handling administrative paperwork. By hiring service companies that specialize in managing each of these subordinate functions, the manufacturer is able to focus its resources on its competitive strengths, thereby increasing its overall productivity.

Within the service division, most of the projected job growth is in just two industry groups: business services, with a job gain of 3.6 million, and health services, with an increase of 3.2 million. Together, these industry groups account for 59 percent of the job growth in the services division and 38 percent of the increase in total non-farm wage and salary employment. The industry groups with the third and fourth largest projected job gains within the services division are social services, with a 1.1 million increase, and engineering, management, and related services, with an increase of 1 million jobs. Together, these four industry groups account for 78 percent of job growth in the services division and 50 percent of the total increase in non-farm wage and salary employment.

During 1988 approximately 508,000 jobs were reported in the management services industry. By 1998, a scant 10 years later, the number of jobs in this service sector doubled to over 1,034,000 jobs. Management services firms were primarily engaged in offering management services to almost every industrial, commercial, and nonprofit sector of the U.S. economy. In addition, many companies classified in other industries offered management services to their clients. Typical services included management of health care facilities, hotels and motels, all types of business offices, factories, research and charity organizations, theaters, restaurants, commercial and residential properties, and other operations.

Construction Management.

The largest single division of the management services industry was construction management. Firms practicing this discipline were hired to organize, staff, direct, plan, and control a development project. They also offered in-house design or construction services. By hiring a professional manager, developers usually hoped to speed up construction, lower development costs, and increase overall project quality. To achieve these goals, many management companies specialized in one type of development, such as power generation facilities, transportation infrastructure, office buildings, health care facilities, land reclamation, or renovations.

In the late 1980s construction managers were generating about $4 billion in revenue per year—roughly equivalent to 25 percent of total annual U.S. management service contracts. Engineering and construction firms accounted for 75 percent of all construction management services. Design firms captured about 10 percent of the market, general contractors held a 5 percent share, and pure construction management companies accounted for 10 percent of this segment's billings.

Industry Associations and Accreditation. There is no central licensing agency for management consultants. In fact, no guidelines or regulations exist in the industry at all as standards for operating practices. The only available form of acknowledgement of consulting expertise is the Certified Management Consultant designation which is granted by the trade association, the Institute of Management Consultants.

Another primary industry association is ACME (formerly Association of Consulting Management Engineers). Both ACME and the Institute of Management Consultants operate as divisions of the Council of Consulting Organizations (CCO). Other industry associations include the Society of Professional Management Consultants, the Association of Management Consulting Firms, the Association of Management Consultants, and the Association of Internal Management Consultants.

BACKGROUND AND DEVELOPMENT

Companies have offered management services in various forms for decades, such as construction firms that developed company facilities early in the Industrial Revolution. It was not until the 1970s and 1980s, however, that an identifiable management services industry gained stature in the United States.

Several developments led to the proliferation of management services. Significantly, as the rapid economic growth characteristic of the post-World War II boom years began to fade in the 1970s, large corporations began to seek ways to increase the efficiency of their operations and gain a competitive edge. While corporations had traditionally handled almost all of their administrative and office management activities with in-house staff, some firms began seeking the expertise and efficiency that management contractors offered. Particularly during the 1980s, as corporations restructured their organizations, reduced layers of management, and cut administrative overhead, the demand for specialized management services burgeoned. Likewise, as the economic representation of small businesses mushroomed during the 1980s, management services became important partners for many small companies that outsourced administrative tasks.

Also influencing industry growth was the proliferation of government regulations. New employment rules, safety and environmental regulations, financial reporting laws, and other constraints forced many firms to seek the assistance of outside professionals to handle administrative paperwork and to avoid litigation. Concurrent advances in computer, information, and communications technologies provided the tools many management services needed to serve their markets.

By 1992 U.S. management service firms were garnering nearly $23 billion per year and paying $9.7 billion in wages to just over 215,000 employees. Remarkably, annual receipts almost doubled (from $13 billion in 1988). More, the industry's reported 1988 payroll was nearly $7 billion and employment was over 280,000.

Fewer employees generated greater profits, perhaps due to the double-edged sword of an economic downturn in the late 1980s and early 1990s while, concurrently, increased global competition in all industries induced continued expansion of the management services industry.

According to the *U.S. Industrial Outlook 1994,* ''Demand for professional services will continue to increase through the 1990s, but at a slower rate than during the latter half of the past decade. A major force behind this growth will be the increased use of computers, integrated systems and other high technology.''

Industry Leaders

Indicative of a growing trend in the management services industry, ARAMARK Corp. provided management services in three divergent lines of business: food and support services, uniforms, and childcare. 1999 sales topped $6.7 million and their employee payroll included 152,000 workers. Two-thirds of company revenues derived from food, building maintenance, and housekeeping services provided to businesses, prisons, and colleges. ARAMARK also managed concessions at sports and other recreational facilities, operated before- and after-school programs, and provided employee on-site childcare via Children's World Learning Centers.

ServiceMaster L.P. of Downers Grove, Illinois, was characteristic of many management service firms in that it offered a broad range of related services. ServiceMaster was comprised of seven major divisions that were established to respond to the entire facility development process: strategic facility planning, architecture/engineering, interior design, equipment planning, construction services, project management and development, and computer-aided facility management. Formerly Maricia Capps & Associates, ServiceMaster's 51,740 employees earned their firm net income of $4.7 million during 1998.

Evidence of general industry growth in the late 1980s and early 1990s was Amerihost Properties, Inc., of Illinois—one of the fastest growing hotel and motel management firms in the United States. After beginning operations in 1987, Amerihost grew to manage 90 hotels. Although its operations were national, a majority of their hotels were in the Midwest and the South. Focusing on small communities, Amerihost sought out a market niche in midpriced hotel rooms. While operated under the AmeriHost Inn name, it also managed hotels under franchise agreements with Days Inn, Holiday Inn, Ramada Inn, and Hampton Inn. Franchised management services proved successful for AmeriHost: with a scant 1,820 employees, total revenues were $68.6 million in 1998. Capitalizing on this trend, the company planned to expand into the twenty-first century through a new franchising program under its signature operations.

Workforce

About 25 percent of the workforce was employed in secretarial, bookkeeping, and clerical jobs. Management and executive jobs represented about 15 percent of total employment, and management support, financial management, and administrative services jobs accounted for an additional 10 percent. Other occupations relate to computer programming and information systems management, engineering, marketing, and public relations.

Because the industry will likely realize strong growth, the U.S. Bureau of Labor Statistics estimated that most occupations in the industry will thrive between 1998 and 2008. In fact, almost every position in the industry will increase employment by more than 45 percent. Jobs for managers and administrators, for instance, should grow in addition to a marked increase in management support jobs. Positions for marketing and public relations professionals were also expected to take a dramatic increase by 2008. Total employment in this industry section was estimated at just over 1 billion jobs in 1998. By 2008, almost another half million jobs were expected to be created.

Research and Technology

New management techniques and advanced communications technologies will continue to propel the expansion of management services into the 2000s. The trend toward corporate reductions in middle management, renewed emphasis on core competencies, and expanded government regulations will encourage companies to increasingly employ and form partnerships with specialized services.

Wireless communication devices, electronic and voice mail, portable computers and digital devices, and advanced information management systems will allow companies to make greater use of outside consulting and management services. Construction management firms will especially benefit from portable electronic devices that can be used on-site. Scheduling, estimating, and field engineering activities will become more precise with the development of new software and communications technology.

Eventually, the division between management consulting services and the companies that hire them will become less distinct for several reasons. For instance, firms will retain a greater number of their employees as independent contractors and home-based workers. In addition, companies will form more partnerships with their competitors, or with firms in noncompeting industries, that resemble management service arrangements. Eventually, a large portion of U.S. companies will begin to view themselves as providers of specialized management services.

With the proliferation of Internet access throughout the 1990s, management services began to embrace a new paradigm, virtual service and outsource firms. No longer limited by geography, such enterprises could advertise, interact, communicate, and service clients from any place in the world. Coupled with an increased reliance by an ever-growing interglobal business culture, "virtual firms" could also engage in robust service support to international clients with subject-matter experts of international reputation. By expanding customer base and tapping into a worldwide labor force, the service management industry promised to revolutionize through the use of advanced wireless and communications technologies.

FURTHER READING

"AmeriHost Properties, Inc." *Hoover's Online,* 2000. Available from http://www.hoovers.com/co/capsule/1/0,2163,16211,00.html/.

"ARAMARK Corporation." *Hoover's Online,* 2000. Available from http://www.hoovers.com/co/capsule/8/0,2163,40038,00.html/.

"Employment and Output, by Detailed Industry." U.S. Bureau of Labor Statistics, 1999. Available from http://stats.bls.gov/emphome.htm/.

Office of Employment Projections (OEP). Economic and Employment Projections, 1998-2008. "Table 3a. The 10 Industries with the Fastest Wage and Salary Employment Growth, 1998-2008". Bureau of Labor Statistics, 1999. Available from http://stats.bls.gov/news.release/ecopro.t03.htm/.

"The Service Master Company." *Hoover's Online,* 2000. Available from http://www.hoovers.com/co/capsule/4/0,2163,11344,00.html/.

U.S. Bureau of the Census. "Current Business Reports BS/97." *Service Annual Survey: 1997.* Washington, D.C.: GPO, 1995.

U.S. Bureau of the Census. "1992 Economic Census, Summary of National Statistics." *1992 Economic Census, Definitions of Sectors, 1997.* Available from http://www.census.gov/epcd/www/ecensus.html/.

SIC 8742

MANAGEMENT CONSULTING SERVICES

This industry consists of establishments primarily engaged in furnishing operating counsel and assistance to management of private, nonprofit, and public organizations. These establishments generally perform a variety of activities, such as strategic and organizational planning; financial planning and budgeting; marketing objectives and policies; information systems planning, evaluation, and selection; human resource policies and practices planning; and production scheduling and control planning.

NAICS CODE(S)

541611 (Administrative Management and General Management Consulting Services)
541612 (Human Resources and Executive Search Consulting Services)
541613 (Marketing Consulting Services)
541614 (Process, Physical, Distribution, and Logistics Counseling)

INDUSTRY SNAPSHOT

In the late 1990s, management consulting was an $80-billion enterprise within the United States and a $100-billion industry worldwide. Nothing has funneled more money into the business than information technology consulting, which boomed in the 1990s as companies groped for ways to harness the benefits of office automation, network computing, and e-commerce. Other important consulting specialties include general strategy, marketing and branding, leadership, logistics, human resources, and industry-specific practices. All told, one standard reference on the industry lists 118 distinct types of consulting services offered and 98 industries served.

In many ways the industry has been propelled by what could be described as business fads—philosophies, events, and practices that ignite intense interest for a few years but gradually fade. An example is the sea of reengineering programs of the early and mid-1990s; reengineering was a form of organizational change dictated by management strategy. The idea was simple: change the way a company is structured and how it carries out its business so that both structure and process best serve strategic interests. Those interests usually centered around profitability and competitiveness with an eye toward customer needs. Corporate interest in reengineering channeled millions of dollars into the consulting business, notably at large firms like Ernst & Young that were vigorous advocates. By the late 1990s, though, executives' fascination with reengineering had waned, while other issues came to the fore.

More recently, corporate leaders have set their gaze on challenges like e-commerce and employee satisfaction. E-commerce entails consulting on many different levels, ranging from technology and logistics to marketing strategy. Human resources is a perennial concern, but attracting and retaining good workers has been especially worrisome in the United States while labor is in short supply.

ORGANIZATION AND STRUCTURE

Individual Firms. The most common organizational structure for a management consulting firm is that of a corporation. A typical consulting firm might employ research associates at the lower level, with consultants and senior consultants at the next level. Managing consultants are next in the hierarchy. At this level, individuals typically have greater degrees of client interaction, as well as responsibility for the success of consulting projects. Finally, at the top of a typical firm's hierarchy are partners. In addition to running the operations of the organization, partners are generally responsible for bringing new business into the firm.

Management consulting firms usually operate in project teams. Depending upon the firm and assignment, consultants on project teams often spend more time at the site of the client's offices than they do at their own. There, they gather data and interact extensively with personnel from the client organization, make recommendations, and often work on implementing solutions. Often, client personnel will work as part of the consulting team for the duration of the project to ensure that the organization has input into the process. Client participation increases the likelihood that the solutions will be implemented effectively.

Management consulting firms generally operate on a project fee or hourly fee basis. Fees in the consulting industry tend to run very high, due to the significance of the problems that consultants help their clients to overcome.

Industry Structure. Management consulting firms range in size from sole practitioners to large businesses. As far as areas of expertise, some firms are devoted to specific practice areas while others offer a broad range of services to varied clientele. For example, a consulting firm might specialize in providing clients with compensation and benefits packages, to the exclusion of all other services. Yet other firms might provide a broad range of advisory services—combining such varied forms of advice as consulting the chief executive officer on general business strategy and consulting a management information systems (MIS) executive on a new computer network. A major segment of the consulting market is occupied by consulting organizations that are part of Certified Public Accountant (CPA) firms. Such firms attempt to serve their tax and audit clients with management consulting services as well. Another type of consulting function is one that exists within a non-consulting organization. Such internal consultants provide specialized services for their corporations. An example is an internal human resources consulting department within a Fortune 500 corporation that serves the varied divisions of the organization as if they were external clients.

In addition to providing expertise or advice, many management consultants perform in the role of process consultant. This approach recognizes that the client firm already possesses knowledge of its own industry and internal corporate environment that exceeds the knowledge available to the consultant. Therefore, the role of the management consultant is one of facilitating the process of pulling solutions out from within the client organization and providing insight with an objective point of view.

Because the management consulting industry is unregulated, any individual or company that offers advice in exchange for compensation may be classified as a consultant. For this reason, the definition of a management consulting firm often varies, depending upon the source of information. Nonetheless, an understanding of the industry can be ascertained by separating consulting firms into distinct categories and contrasting the categories.

The following breakdown describes the most common and most widely recognized types of consulting organizations, first by organizational structure, and then by consulting specialty (also known as "practice area" within the industry).

Large Consulting Firms. This classification represents the largest players in the management consulting industry whose primary service is providing expertise and consultation to management. The broad heading of large consulting firms encompasses the larger of the generalist consulting firms and strategy consulting firms.

Big Five Accounting/Consulting Firms. A handful of large public accounting and consulting firms lead the industry on an international scale. These include the so-called Big Five: Andersen Worldwide, PricewaterhouseCoopers, Ernst & Young, Deloitte & Touche, and KPMG Peat Marwick. Consulting divisions of the Big Five are especially strong in information technology (IT) and management information systems (MIS) consulting. These firms typically offer strategic or generalist management consulting services as well. As of the late 1990s, though, the marriage of public accounting, particularly auditing services, and consulting was a troubled one; most of the top firms attempted to wall off their accounting and consulting practices to avoid appearing to have conflicts of interest.

Small Firms/Boutiques. Small firms or boutiques often provide specialized services or offer expertise that focuses on one industry or a single business practice area. These firms tend to be small, lesser-known niche players that do not regularly compete directly with the larger consulting organizations. Many of these firms operate in a single, geographic region. Some small or boutique firms service only one client.

Sole Practitioners. Perhaps the most difficult segment to define in the management consulting industry is that of the sole practitioner. This group encompasses many outplaced or retired executives and part-time consultants who offer expertise in areas where they have a great deal of experience. Sole practitioners are often engaged by smaller firms and even their previous employers. This classification of the consulting industry also includes university professors who provide consulting in their areas of teaching expertise.

Internal Consulting Organizations. Large corporations may have recurring project work for which the expertise of external management consultants would be required on an ongoing basis. Many such firms have developed internal consulting staffs in order to deal with this demand in a more cost-effective manner. Such internal organizations may be generalists or may specialize in corporate strategy, human resources issues, information technology, or other areas that are critical to the company's operation.

IT/MIS. The information technology segment is the largest segment of the consulting industry. The Big Five all provide expertise in this area and draw substantial revenue from it as well. Firms that specialize in information technology tackle business problems by applying technology to provide solutions. For example, a firm specializing in information technology might help a corporation to become more efficient in their order fulfillment operation by installing computers and equipment that automates the process. One of the firms that is best known in IT/MIS consulting is Andersen Consulting.

Compensation/Benefits Consulting. Compensation/benefits consulting firms represent the second largest independent segment of the industry in the United States. Firms that specialize in compensation/benefits consulting offer services related to human resource management with specific expertise in practices such as developing corporate grading and compensation schemes, titling plans, and benefits packages. Examples of firms that practice primarily in the compensation/benefits consulting practice area include the Hay Group and Hewitt Associates.

Generalist Consulting. Generalist management consulting firms typically provide advice on strategy to their clients but may also have internal expertise in specific industries, such as banking or health care, or in particular practice areas, such as new product development or operations. Generalist consulting firms often provide consulting in IT/MIS and compensation/benefits as well. Examples of generalist firms include McKinsey & Company, Inc.; Booz, Allen & Hamilton, Inc.; and Arthur D. Little, Inc.

Strategy Consulting. Strategy consulting firms specialize in providing advice on corporate strategy to senior executives—answering such questions as, "How can our firm improve profitability." Strategy firms compete with generalist firms for strategic engagements but do not provide the nonstrategy services of the broader, generalist firms. However, the larger strategy firms, as they have expanded their lines of business, have become more difficult to distinguish from the generalist firms. Examples of firms that have traditionally been regarded as strategy firms include the Boston Consulting Group and Bain & Company.

Specialty Consulting Practice Areas. This segment is by far the most difficult to define, for it encompasses so many different possible practice areas. Specialty consulting firms are often boutiques or small to medium size organizations that service a niche in the consulting market.

Marketing Consulting Firms. These firms provide marketing research, product test markets, target market selection and other services directly related to the marketing of client products or services. Perhaps the best known marketing consulting firm is Yankelovich, Skelly and White/Clancy Shulman Inc.

Business Reengineering/Organizational Effectiveness. This specialty in management consulting refers to the radical redesigning and rebuilding of the processes and functions of a business to recreate the company as a highly effective, cohesive whole that performs optimally. The concept of "Business Re-engineering" was originated by the Index Group (Now CSC/Index, Inc.). Increasingly, other consulting firms are also developing this line of business—most notably, Andersen Consulting.

Environmental Consulting Firms. With increased public attention on the environment, and increased governmental concern over hazardous waste, environmental consulting firms have seen increased demand for their services in recent years.

Health Care Consulting. There are two primary specialties that fall under the heading of health care consulting. The first practice area is providing general advisory services such as strategy consultation or cost-containment studies for health service agencies (e.g., Health Maintenance Organizations) and hospitals. The second practice area is in helping corporations to select employee health benefit plans that minimize costs and provide the best health care coverage for the organization.

As health care costs continue to rise in the United States and concern for health coverage increases, this consulting specialty has been experiencing growth as well. In addition to specialty firms that provide health care consulting, many of the larger consulting organizations also service this industry.

Changes in the economy can affect firms in different ways. For instance, if the economy slows and businesses become more concerned with the bottom line, they may put off decisions such as automating. This negatively impacts the information technology segment of management consulting. At the same time, however, executives of corporations in hard times might be more prone to call upon a consulting firm that can help them to find ways to increase their revenues, contain their costs, or reduce their head count.

For consulting firms, approximately 20 percent of their costs are consumed in new business development. Costs for marketing activities include the production and distribution of promotional materials, salaries of partners who are responsible for client development and new business, and association memberships. The area in which firms may expend the greatest amount of resources, however, is in the competitive bidding process, also known in the industry as the ''bake-off.''

A bake-off occurs when a client with a problem approaches several consulting firms. These firms each spend time and money becoming acquainted with the client's organization, attempting to develop internal champions for their firm. The bake-off often involves several personnel from each consulting firm, all dedicating their time, without pay, at the site of the potential client in order to gather a better understanding of the problem. At the end of the competitive bidding process, the client chooses one of the firms, or none, and the remainder have invested resources without remuneration.

Because of the expense involved in acquiring new clients, consulting firms try to become the ''house consultants'' for their existing clients. In doing so, the firm may become so trusted by the client that it can bypass the competitive bake-off and be engaged directly by client management. This is an enviable position for a consulting firm to be in, as it can minimize business development costs and ensure a more steady flow of income.

Industry Associations and Accreditation. There is no central licensing agency for management consultants. Nor are there any industry guidelines or regulations as standards for operating practices. The only form of acknowledgement for consulting expertise is the Certified Management Consultant designation which is granted by the trade association, the Institute of Management Consultants.

Another primary industry association is ACME (formerly Association of Consulting Management Engineers). Both ACME and the Institute of Management Consultants operate as divisions of the Council of Consulting Organizations (CCO). Other industry associations include the Society of Professional Management Consultants, the Association of Management Consulting Firms, the Association of Management Consultants, and the Association of Internal Management Consultants.

Background and Development

The practice of consulting began in the late 1880s. At that time, Frank Gilbreth was conducting time-and-motion studies to improve bricklaying techniques. At about the same time, Frank W. Taylor was applying time studies to improve the steel industry. In 1886, Arthur D. Little founded the consultancy that bears his name and is now one of the largest consulting firms in the world. Little began working in 1881 to bring scientific ideas to management practices. The next industry event was the introduction of a quality aspect to time and motion. In the 1920s, Charles Bedaux enabled his clients to make tremendous leaps in productivity by improving quality.

In the 1950s and 1960s, small firms began to proliferate as former sole practitioners expanded their business. Then, in 1963, the Boston Consulting Group was founded on the notion of giving strategic advice to clients. Management consultancy recognized this event as critical in changing the role that management consultants played. During the 1960s, CPA firms entered the fold and made the formal transition from offering advice related to their accounting activities to charging clients for business advice in a traditional consulting manner.

Current Conditions

Consulting revenues in the United States grew rapidly in the 1990s, rising from $28.9 billion in 1990 to $70.7 billion in 1998, according to estimates by the Census Bureau. Separate calculations by the Kennedy Information Research Group, which publishes newsletters, periodicals, and research reports on the industry, placed the global value of consulting services at $100 billion as of 1999. Information technology services, reported Kennedy Information, represented fully 60 percent of the industry's revenue. Based on estimates of 1998 consulting revenues, the top ten firms alone had more than $33 billion in consulting receipts.

E-commerce consulting was perhaps the most important trend of the late 1990s and early 2000s. A natural fit with the industry's well-developed IT consulting practices, e-commerce advice and implementation typically involves steering conventional businesses toward a successful Internet strategy. There is of course also a market for consultants within pure-play Internet firms that are trying to break into the business. Leading consulting firms like Andersen and Deloitte have found e-commerce such a potent consulting formula that they've raced to set up separate e-commerce units to cater to this market. By one estimate, as much as $20 billion would be spent on e-commerce consulting and deployment services in 2000.

Consolidation has had a major impact on management consulting, particularly among top-tier firms. Whereas observers used to speak of the Big Six or even the Big Eight, by the late 1990s consolidation had brought the top echelon down to five members. One of the most prominent mergers was between two members of the then-Big Six: Price Waterhouse and Coopers & Lybrand, which merged in 1998 to form PricewaterhouseCoopers. And in 2000, one of the remaining five, Ernst & Young, sold its consulting business to France-based Cap Gemini Group, effectively removing the Ernst & Young accounting practice from the consulting business.

Just as ethical worries have plagued the integrated accounting/consulting firms, a variety of other consulting practices have been attacked on ethical grounds. For one, as consultancies pursue growth aggressively, some have entertained the idea of going public to raise capital. However, if under such a scenario another company is both a client and a shareholder, the consulting firm may have a conflict of interest—doubly so if it's also doing audits. Another ethical quagmire is a proposal to allow consulting firms to dispense legal advice, or even merge with law firms. Although such combinations weren't permitted as of 2000 by the American Bar Association (ABA) and some states, some firms have lobbied strenuously for it and the ABA was considering the matter.

In contemporary business, management level employees are increasingly educated. Advanced degrees have become more common in business, especially in the large organizations that have traditionally called upon management consultants for an intellectual edge. Since many clients now have management personnel who attended graduate business school, management consulting organizations no longer have a monopoly on this type of experience. This has made the industry more competitive and has made clients more demanding of their consultants.

At the same time, clients increasingly insist that their high-priced advisors actually create change instead of simply producing thick reports filled with valuable insights that collect dust on a shelf. This led to an implementation orientation that pervades the industry. Practically every firm claims to be "the implementation firm." Client engagements now often include an implementation phase in which the consulting firm works with the client to bring the recommendations to reality.

INDUSTRY LEADERS

Andersen Consulting is the world's largest management consulting firm, with more than $7.1 billion in worldwide consulting revenue as of 1998. Under its parent company Andersen Worldwide, Andersen consulting is an offshoot of one of the Big Five accounting firms and has been offering some form of consulting services since at least the 1920s. The two Andersen segments have epitomized the struggle between the older accounting side of the business and the new consulting side; the consulting unit has been attempting for years to break away from the rest of Andersen. The original Arthur Andersen & Co. accounting firm dates to 1918. The consulting wing has grown to match the accounting business in terms of revenues, with big banks and communications companies as some of its largest clients. Thoroughly internationalized, Andersen brought in 44 percent of its 1998 sales from Europe and Asia. The same year it employed more than 53,400 consultants worldwide. In the early 2000s, Andersen was backing a major push into the e-commerce business, including a venture capital fund for start-ups.

A. T. Kearney, Inc. was founded in 1926 as a production and engineering consulting firm that served manufacturing clients. Over the years, A. T. Kearney has grown into a full service, generalist consulting firm employing more than 3500 professionals in 60 offices in 30 countries. In 1995 the firm was bought by Electronic Data Systems Corp., a large systems integration and technology service provider. In 1998 Kearney's worldwide consulting receipts were estimated at $1.2 billion, and it employed 2,880 consultants around the world.

Arthur D. Little is a generalist consulting firm that employs more than 2,100 advisers around the world. Although Little has been engaged in many consulting related activities, its main emphasis has been in research studies, including product and process design and development, and feasibility studies. The firm's clients have included such companies as Nabisco, Quaker Oats, Kodak, and Owens Illinois, which they have assisted by developing new products and product features. The company has also been contracted to assist in evaluating environmental control procedures. Its 1998 consulting revenues reached an estimated $608 million.

Booz, Allen & Hamilton, Inc. is another generalist consulting firm that was founded in 1914. Booz-Allen employs 6,540 consultants in more than 100 offices worldwide. The firm is organized around industry groups such as advanced technology, applied sciences, energy and chemicals, financial services, information and strategic systems, and marketing-intensive industries. It is split into two operating segments, the Worldwide Commercial Business unit and the Worldwide Technology Business unit. Global revenue in 1998 was $1.2 billion.

The Cap Gemini Group, Paris, France, is a global management consulting firm with fully integrated capabilities in strategy, operations, people, and information management. In 2000 the firm was catapulted to the consulting industry's top five with its purchase of Ernst & Young's consulting business. Based on 1998 results, Ernst had been the third-largest consultancy and Cap Gemini was eighth-largest. The combined company had an estimated 60,000 employees and a major presence throughout Western Europe and the United States.

McKinsey and Company, Inc., a generalist consulting firm, is perhaps the best known of the generalist management consulting organizations. Founded in 1926, McKinsey experienced tremendous growth in the 1980s and 1990s, expanding to more than 5,100 professionals and a total of 73 offices by 1998. Most of this growth for McKinsey came from international expansion. In the

United States, McKinsey has reported approximate sales at $2.5 billion in 1998. McKinsey provides consulting services that address top management issues for large organizations. The majority of their work is in the area of strategy and organization. The remainder is conducted in specialized practice areas such as marketing, manufacturing, and technology.

The second-largest consultancy as of 1998, PricewaterhouseCoopers was created by the high-profile 1998 merger of Big Six rivals Price Waterhouse and Coopers & Lybrand. Founded in London in the late 19th century, Price Waterhouse was one of the world's oldest and most prestigious accounting firms, and by the 1990s was a massive international management services purveyor. Coopers & Lybrand was a prominent accounting firm in its own right, dating to a 1957 merger of two multinational accounting concerns. Like Andersen and others, PricewaterhouseCoopers has suffered from internal tension between its accounting and consulting arms; the company was considering splitting into two separate entities. In 1998 worldwide consulting brought in an estimated $6 billion at the combined firm, and the firm had more than 40,000 consultants around the world.

Workforce

For the most part, large management consulting firms hire people with MBAs from top business schools as entry level consultants. For higher level positions, specialists may be recruited directly from the competition or from the industry. The latter is particularly true if an individual can offer industry expertise that would assist the consulting firm in expanding or servings its existing client base. Depending upon the industry and the needs of the particular firm, individuals with more advanced degrees or degrees in technical specialties (such as economics or computer science) may be selected as well. Some consulting firms will take academically strong candidates from top undergraduate schools as lower entry level consultants or analysts/researchers.

Overall, consultants in medium-to-large generalist or strategy firms are analytically oriented, well-educated individuals. In the past, management consultants in the United States were typically white males. Like other industries, consulting firms have been diversifying, especially as these firms increase their exposure in foreign markets.

The industry also comprises small firms, boutiques, and sole proprietorships that are composed of technical specialists such as information technologists or marketing consultants. These individuals may be displaced corporate professionals or individuals who have left larger consulting firms to start their own practices. It is also common for sole practitioners to perform consulting work on the side, in addition to their full-time positions with other companies.

Another segment of the consulting industry is that of university professors who consult to complement their full-time positions in teaching. These professors typically hold advanced degrees and are specialists in a particular field of research. This segment of the consulting population is self-regulating via the Academy of Management, Division of Managerial Consultation, which provides a code of ethics for its 800 members. The fastest growing segment of this market is systems analysis and administrative services managers; the areas seeing the least amount of growth by the year 2005 will be typists, word processors, secretaries, and bookkeeping/accounting clerks.

Research and Technology

The application of technology is a significant tool of the consulting industry. Many of the largest firms in the industry generate their revenue by applying technology solutions to business problems. An example of this is redesigning a distribution operation and inventory tracking system to automate the entire process with robotics, computers, scanners, and advanced software to control the system. Still other firms specialize in training corporate personnel to use technology.

Because of the high level of specialized knowledge that many management consulting firms possess, technical expertise may be the very reason for which a firm is engaged by a client. An example of such a rigorous application of technology and research is the type evidenced by Arthur D. Little, Inc. This historic consulting firm maintains research laboratories in the United States and in Europe. Arthur D. Little laboratories have produced advanced detection equipment for the U.S. Air Force and protective clothing for use by individuals who will be exposed to hazardous materials. Firms with technical expertise may be called in to assist in complex engineering or production problems that require the expertise of skilled scientists.

Further Reading

Delaney, Kevin J., and Elizabeth MacDonald. ''Cap Gemini Group Offers $10.7 Billion for Ernst & Young's Consulting Division.'' *Wall Street Journal,* 29 February 2000.

''Ethics Be Damned, Let's Merge.'' *Business Week,* 30 August 1999.

''HR Consulting Rides High.'' *HR Focus,* June 1999.

''Management Consultancy the New Witch Doctors.'' *Economist,* 13 February 1988.

Preston, Holly Hubbard. ''E-Commerce Explosion.'' *Computerworld,* 6 March 2000.

Seminerio, Maria. ''Large Consultancies Launch Venture Capital Units.'' *PC Week,* 3 January 2000.

''Top Consulting Firms.'' *Industry Week,* 24 January 2000.

U.S. Census Bureau. ''Business Services.'' *Service Annual Survey 1998.* Washington, D.C.: 2000. Available from www.census.gov.

SIC 8743

PUBLIC RELATIONS SERVICES

This category covers establishments primarily engaged in the preparation of materials, written or spoken, that are designed to influence the general public or other groups in promoting the interests of their clients.

NAICS CODE(S)

541820 (Public Relations Services)

INDUSTRY SNAPSHOT

The primary focus of the public relations industry is to project a favorable impression of a person, product, company, or organization and to win public confidence and approval. As a result, public relations involves communication with a variety of individuals and organizations, as well as the general public. Independent professionals, specialized companies, or in-house public relations departments carry out public relations services.

In 1991, the U.S. public relations industry consisted of approximately 4,400 firms and 345,000 employees. The majority of employees fell in the general managers and top executives category (7.3 percent); however, the largest anticipated change by 2005 was in the category of systems analysts (195.8 percent growth), and administrative services managers (118.2 percent growth). The primary form of organization within the public relations industry was the corporation, which in 1987 encompassed 60.6 percent of all establishments, with sole proprietorships accounting for 32 percent and partnerships for 7.3 percent.

The recession of the early 1990s greatly impacted the public relations firms and corporate communication professionals. The industry, which experienced 26 percent growth between 1980 and 1990, encountered significant downsizing in ensuing years. In spite of the downsizing, the industry saw a marked increase in billings from 1989 through 1994, when estimated earnings were $77 billion, up from $72 billion in 1993 and $68 billion in 1992.

In the mid-1990s, mergers and acquisitions continued to prevail, often prompted by a desire to gain leverage in the area of information technology. The area of management, consulting, and public relations services was expected to continue to grow at a significant pace as more corporations looked to outsourcing as a way to maximize efficiency and reduce operating costs.

ORGANIZATION AND STRUCTURE

About 98 percent of public relations firms were set up as taxed-based entities, with the remainder organized under the not-for-profit distinction. Giant advertising agencies, which have incorporated public relations functions into their consumer services, owned many of the larger public relations (PR) firms. In order to achieve an international presence, these multiple firms formed a network of independent companies, creating a trend within the public relations industry.

The majority of public relations firms made their headquarters in or around major metropolitan areas. International operations expanded more rapidly than domestic, with new markets in Eastern Europe and the Commonwealth of Independent States (former Soviet Union) proving to be very promising.

Certain basic activities common to all public relations efforts included the development of sound policies in the public interest, the implementation of a public relations campaign recognizing the importance of public goodwill, and the establishment and maintenance of the organization's integrity.

The annual Thomas L. Harris & Co. Public Relations Agency Survey of 1996 showed that media relations remained the most important capability of PR firms (97 percent). The second most frequent use of PR firms was to provide services for special events (93 percent), followed by international communications (92 percent), graphic design (89 percent) and community relations (88 percent).

With the current trends towards global marketing and frequent changes in communication technology, the accreditation of public relations experts took on greater importance. Universities offering post-graduate degrees in public relations provided courses on topics including the nature of human communication and the role of the media in public relations. Programs like those offered through Boston University and the University of Miami also provided areas of specialization in the fields of corporate, government, and non-profit sectors.

BACKGROUND AND DEVELOPMENT

The public relations industry was once synonymous with publicity, and for many years that was its chief mission. Many analysts claimed that the profession grew directly out of the boom-and-bust periods of the 1920s and 1930s. Indeed, during the Great Depression the public began to regard private industry as a failure and turned to big government for salvation. Due to these pressures, major business interests turned to public communication. The first public relations people were top newspaper journalists, practiced in the art of reporting and writing.

Due to the increased government regulation of business during the New Deal, the public relations industry grew following World War II. Additional factors affecting its growth included the growth of organized labor, the generally higher level of public education, and the recognition by all institutions of their dependence upon public approval. Until the 1950s, public relations was a business of generalists. The range of problems handled generally related to publicity, crisis management, financial public relations, speech writing, and community relations.

The Washington-based Public Affairs Council, established in 1954, focused its original mission to stimulate and train business executives to become active and effective in politics. At roughly the same time, companies such as Ford, General Electric, and Johnson and Johnson established political education and good citizen programs to get their own executives involved. The Public Affairs Council eventually became the professional association for corporate public officers.

By the end of the 1950s, a handful of companies had established public affairs departments. Their major priorities were to formalize the firms' federal government relations and to encourage executives to participate in political activities. The 1960s were experimental years of growth for public affairs. The Public Affairs Council estimated that during that decade, upwards of 500,000 business managers and executives attended formalized political education courses.

Toward the end of the 1960s, an outbreak of riots in some large cities triggered the development of urban affairs and social responsibility units in many firms. A concerned business community undertook new philanthropic and community initiatives organized under the directive of the corporate public affairs department. By the 1970s, these programs expanded to include job training for the disadvantaged, housing, transportation, law and order, health, education, and economic development initiatives. The Public Affairs Council doubled its membership during this time, and it was estimated that between 800 and 1,000 national companies had organized public relations departments.

Some critics regarded business responses to these social ills as cosmetic. For example, a large number of programs were undertaken to educate the public about how the economic system worked and its contribution to social wellbeing. Some companies undertook expensive advocacy-advertising programs to carry the business story to the public. Still others hoped that sponsorship of high-quality television programs, increased charitable contributions, and similar good works could replenish goodwill. Many of these efforts continue to the present day, but they are not regarded as a quick fix for perceptions of the citizens or the elected officials.

The growth of public affairs departments reflected business' recognition that managing business-society relations was a permanent task. Companies recognized that public relations strategy had to go beyond image building, political action, or social responsibility to be effective. A new term, "issues management," grew out of these needs and began to describe the public relations efforts of corporate entities in the late 1970s.

The election of Ronald Reagan in 1980 molded public relations programs for the next decade. Aspects of the political environment under Reagan included a reduced role of government in public life, substantial cutbacks in federal funding of social programs at the local level, and reform and relaxation of business regulation. Cutbacks in spending and reduced regulatory activity at the federal level required companies to pay more attention to state government relations activities. Even more challenging to companies was the growing pressure for business to assume the financial burden for the cost of social programs once paid for by the federal government.

By the early 1990s, workers in public relations specialized in many different areas, such as labor relations, financial relations, health care, and product publicity. Although the scope of its function broadened, the field of public relations became more specialized to accommodate the complex issues involved in an effective public relations campaign. The profession evolved from a "fire fighting" to a "fire prevention" role in the conduct of everyday corporate business.

The Internet. The public relations industry sustained a dramatic impact with the introduction of the Internet. In 1993, ProfNet, a collaboration of public information officers providing journalists with access to expert sources, was launched. Its members included colleges, corporations, nonprofit organizations, and law firms. ProfNet also included an online catalog of 2,000 leading experts across all disciplines.

As the use of the Internet continued to grow, the transition to interactive communications required a change in thinking and created new opportunities for building relationships between organizations and their public. The Internet could deliver messages combining various methods of communication: text, audio, graphics, still pictures, animation, and full-motion video. The challenge for the public relations professional was to use this tool to the organization's advantage, allowing for more one-to-one communication while maintaining the credibility and trust essential for the organization's wellbeing

The Internet also drove the increasing globalization of the marketplace. In 1999, the United States held an overwhelming lead in Internet users, with more than 110 million, which was nearly 43 percent of the total 259 million worldwide Internet users. By 2002, the United States was projected to have one-third of worldwide Internet users, declining to 27 percent by the end of 2005. The most notable impact on the public relations industry by the growth of the Internet was in the re-evaluating of the traditional marketplace. Conventional boundaries defining not only economic but geographic roles were being redefined with the increasingly expanding global market.

Public relations programs could constantly monitor the Internet in order to identify ways to communicate with targeted audiences through this new medium. Companies using the Internet could take advantage of the one-to-one marketing opportunities presented by the Internet to reach opinion leaders in industry. Extending the organizations' presence to the World Wide Web and commercial online services transcended traditional public relations. These communications efforts could combine the best of traditional PR—strategic consulting, marketing support, media relations, public affairs, crisis management, investor relations, even special events—with the vast reach of the Internet.

CURRENT CONDITIONS

The recession of the early 1990s had a negative effect on public relations firms and corporate communication professionals. The industry experienced a 26 percent jump in employment between 1980 and 1990, but this subsequently declined. For example, Hill and Knowlton Inc., one of the larger public relations firms, cut its work force by 25 percent in 1991, based on an 11.8 percent decline in billings.

In the 1980s, public relations agencies averaged 20 employees per $1 million in business, but that figure fell to 12 employees per million in the 1990s. The downsizing that occurred in the public relations industry required firms to outsource many tasks to independent public relations professionals. Firms realized savings on overhead, payroll taxes, and benefits under this arrangement.

A survey conducted by the Public Relations Society of America showed no growth in jobs in 1991 for the public relations industry as a whole, but many professionals in the field expected future industry growth. Specifically, 39 percent of public relations professionals surveyed expected their firms to expand in the next several years, while 45 percent predicted no change in employment, and only 5 percent anticipated additional downsizing. These numbers looked even better for the nonprofit sector, where expectations for staff expansion were 17 percent, compared to expectations of downsizing of 12 percent. Corporate public relations departments expected to experience downsizing as the reengineering process continued for American corporations. Sectors such as legal, health care, and environmental public relations were expected to achieve strong growth during the late 1990s.

By 1998, with the recession a distant memory and the economy booming, public relations services thrived. All of the top 10 agencies experienced growth.

INDUSTRY LEADERS

Burson-Marsteller, Hill and Knowlton, and Porter/Novelli were the big three in the public relations industry as of 1998. Burson-Marsteller, a company founded over 40 years ago, employed 2,200 professionals in over 30 countries. The firm had sustained billings of more than $200 million for three consecutive years and continued to enjoy a strong overseas market. Sales for 1998 were $258 million. Clients included multinational corporations, business organizations and professional associations, as well as governmental bodies and not-for-profit agencies. These have included Sun, Apple, TRW, Scott Paper and Sunbeam, BellSouth, Ford Motor Co., Westinghouse, and the U.S. Olympic Committee.

Hill and Knowlton was a member of the WPP Group integrated communications services family and operated globally with 59 offices in 34 countries. Having gained a reputation for exceptional service, Hill and Knowlton continued to enjoy continued growth increasing 9 percent to $206 million in 1998. The company employed 1,600 professionals around the world. The company had a strong European presence with a London office overseeing all administrative aspects for the firm. European income contributed 40 percent of worldwide business.

Porter/Novelli, which operated 83 offices in 45 countries around the world, saw tremendous growth in the mid-1990s, partly due to acquisitions of such firms as Brodeur & Partners and Copithorne & Bellows. The firm specialized in two growing marketplaces: health care and technology. Clients have included BASF Corporation, National Broiler Council and the Kids ThinkLink. Total sales for the company in 1998 were $813 million.

Steady growth continued to be common within the top 10 agencies. In fact, Burson-Marsteller, Hill and Knowlton, and Shandwick International were the only companies within the top 10 agencies to grow by less than 10 percent in 1998. Growth for 1998 continued to be the trend, with most companies enjoying 20-30 percent increases. The company with the largest percentage increase in sales was BSMG Worldwide, whose sales rose by 84.8 percent in 1998 to $130 million.

Other industry leaders included Shandwick International and Edelman Public Relations Worldwide. Peter Gummer founded Shandwick International in London, England, in 1974. In 1985 the company was listed on the London Stock Exchange and began expanding worldwide, mostly by acquiring other geographically dispersed public relations firms that complemented Shandwick in terms of culture, services offered and location. In 1998, Shandwick International boasted over 100 offices worldwide while employing over 1,700 public relations professionals. Shandwick International was itself acquired by The Interpublic Group of Companies Inc. (IPG) in October 1998.

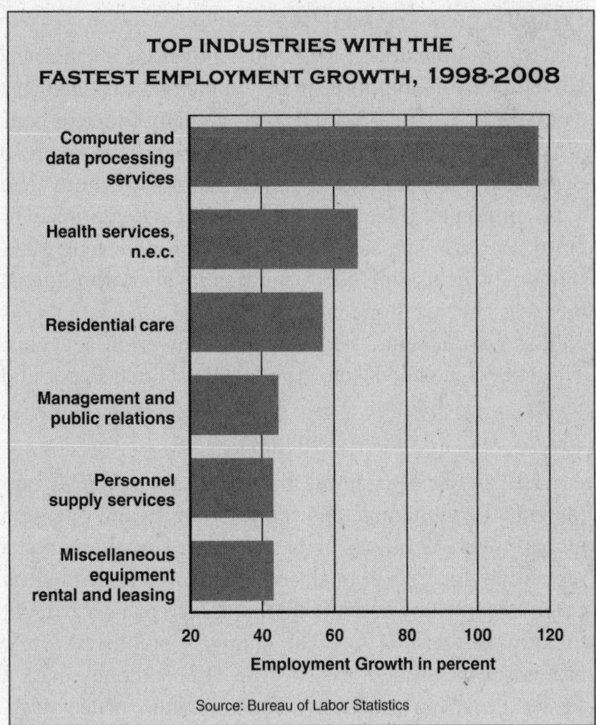

Founded in 1952, Edelman Public Relations Worldwide was a New York-based, privately held corporation with 32 offices in 20 countries. In 1998, the company was ranked fifth worldwide and was one of the largest independent public relations firms, with $161 million in annual fees and more than 1,600 staff members. About 65 percent of the firm's worldwide billings came from its U.S. operations, with 25 percent coming from Europe and 10 percent from elsewhere. Of the firms' 38 offices, 9 were located in the United States. Recognized as a technology leader, Edelman was the first of the major agencies to have its own home page.

Workforce

Public relations has been identified as one of the fastest growing industries. According to the Bureau of Labor Statistics, the number of people in public relations has been estimated to be as high as 716,000, and more than half of that number were women. Employment of marketing, advertising, and public relations managers was expected to increase faster than the average for all occupations through the year 2006, with a projected employment level of 1,049,000 in 2006. Increasingly intense domestic and global competition in products and services offered to consumers should require greater marketing, promotional, and public relations efforts by managers. Management and public relations firms may experience particularly rapid growth as businesses increasingly hire contractors for these services rather than support additional full-time staff.

The majority of occupations in the public relations field fell into the support category. General managers and top executives accounted for less than 10 percent, followed by secretaries at 6.8 percent, related workers not elsewhere classified (nec) at 4.5 percent, and general office clerks at 3.1 percent. The average entry-level salary in public relations for a person with a baccalaureate degree was approximately $18,000 - $22,000, while those with additional education or experience, as well as graduating members of the Public Relations Student Society of America, could qualify for higher salaries.

An account executive of a consulting firm could earn upwards of $35,000, as could a person with a comparable responsibility in a company's public relations department. A public relations director for a small- to medium-sized organization might earn $35,000 to $40,000, while the range for the large corporation was approximately $40,000 to $60,000. A salary survey performed by the Public Relations Society of America placed the median annual figure for public relations professionals at $46,204.

The largest categories of forecasted growth for public relations positions included systems analysts; administrative service managers; professional workers (nec); and marketing, advertising, and public relations staff. These professions were expected to grow by more than 100 percent by the year 2005. This trend was primarily due to the changing nature of the public relations industry and its adoption of technology into everyday business functions. Although all job categories within the public relations industry were forecast to grow into the next century, many positions stood to be eliminated due to the increase in technology in the operations of public relations firms. The occupational category most severely affected by this change was predicted to be typists/word processors.

America and the World

Public relations services took on a global perspective in the 1990s, and many corporations included public relations as part of their international marketing communications mix. This resulted in many larger firms establishing branch offices and affiliates in foreign countries. Independent firms formed exchanges with other firms in locations around the world, and countries took a fresh look at public relations in positioning themselves for future economic growth. Care was also taken to provide news distribution service and media relations in a format that was readily usable by using the native languages of the region.

In Europe, public relations firms helped to facilitate the unification of individual countries into the European Economic Community (EC). The impact of the EC on national life and corporate operations dramatically increased the need to lobby EC leadership, bureaucrats, and parliamentarians on an endless agenda of matters affecting virtually every business.

FURTHER READING

BSMG Worldwide. ''Clients and services, 1999.'' Available from http://www.bsmg.com/clients/c_frame.htm.

———. ''Company Profile, 1999.'' Available from http://www.bsmg.com/company/cp_frame.htm.

———. ''Our World, 1999.'' Available from http://www.bsmg.com/world/w_frame.htm.

Burson-Martstellar. ''Perception Management,'' 1999. Available from http://www.bm.com/files/perception/COR_FRAME.html.

Council of Public Relations Firms. ''Top Firms by Worldwide Income,'' 1998. Available from http://www.prfirms.org/infocenter/june99rankings-worldwide.html.

———. ''Top Firms by U.S. Income,'' 1998. Available from http://www.prfirms.org/infocenter/june99rankings-usincome.html.

Edelman Public Relations Worldwide. ''Global Strength,'' 1999. Available from http://www.edelman.com/global_strength/index.asp#top.

———. ''North America,'' 1999 Available from http://www.edelman.com/global_strength/north_america/index.asp#top.

Fleishman-Hillard. ''About FH,'' 1999. Available from http://www.fleishman.com/about/index.html.

Hill and Knowlton. ''Corporate Overview—Our Company,'' 1999. Available from http://www.hillandknowlton.com/our_company.asp.

———. ''Solutions-Technology,'' 1999. Available from http://www.hillandknowlton.com/tech.asp.

SIC 8744

FACILITIES SUPPORT MANAGEMENT SERVICES

This group covers establishments primarily engaged in furnishing personnel to perform a range of services in support of the operations of other establishments or in providing a number of different continuing services, on a contract or fee basis, within another establishment. Included in the industry are establishments primarily engaged in the private operation of jails and adult correctional facilities, whether or not providing both management and supporting staff.

NAICS CODE(S)

561210 (Facilities Support Services)

INDUSTRY SNAPSHOT

The facilities support services industry encompasses firms that provide facilities management services on a contract or fee basis. New government regulations enacted throughout the 1980s combined with efficiency efforts bolstered industry revenues past $5.3 billion annually in 1990 and $6.4 billion in 1995. Growth continued throughout the 1990s. By 1997, there were 2,490 establishments in this industry employing 112,137 employees. Annual receipts were nearly $7.6 billion.

ORGANIZATION AND STRUCTURE

Facilities support management service companies are involved in operating and managing sports complexes, jails, office buildings, stadiums, museums, hospitals, hotels, retail establishments, and almost any other type of facility. Contract facility managers are expected to reduce costs or improve the profitability and efficiency of the establishments or operations they oversee. Indeed, it is because of their expertise that they are expected to operate a facility more efficiently and safely than could a staff employed and managed by the facility owner. Many believe that the impartial opinion of the contract facility manager makes them more efficient.

The role of facility management firms has traditionally been associated with janitorial services, mailrooms, and security. Industry participants, however, in the 1990s, may also be responsible for facility design and construction, management of computer and communications systems, property acquisition, environmental oversight, and other factors related to the quality and functionality of a facility. A company hired to manage a firm's data processing systems, for example, may bring technical know-how that its employer would have great difficulty cultivating in-house. The ever-changing world of high technology and computers make it difficult for a company to keep staff continually educated. Soaring educational costs are often a detriment. Additionally, a company hired to operate a sports complex may bring a mix of knowledge related to grounds keeping, accounting and reporting, and sports marketing, among other functions.

Besides expertise and efficiency, establishments that employ facility managers receive other important benefits. A chief advantage of outsourcing facility management duties is that an entity is able to reduce liabilities related to personnel. A corporation that contracts a firm to manage one of its factories, for instance, is able to substantially reduce headaches related to staffing, training, workers compensation expenses and litigation, employee benefits, worker grievances, and general management and payroll responsibilities. Rather than tracking hours and writing checks for an entire staff, it simply pays the management company. In addition, an establishment can quickly reduce or increase its staff on an as-needed basis without worrying about hiring or severance legalities. In other words, a large portion of the benefit provided by contract managers is not directly related to facilities management.

Background and Development

Owners have employed managers to operate their facilities for centuries, and contract management services have been used throughout most of the twentieth century to handle grounds maintenance, janitorial responsibilities, food preparation, and other individual tasks. Only during the latter half of the 1900s, and particularly during the 1980s, has the use of large-scale management services that oversee entire facilities and complexes become widespread. Two dominant factors that have driven this trend are the proliferation of government regulation and the quest for corporate and institutional efficiency.

As government oversight at the federal, state, and local level mushroomed during the period from the 1960s to the early 1990s, many establishments became overwhelmed with complex rules and restrictions. Almost every industry was barraged with a separate set of regulations aimed at their niche. Hospitals, for example, were forced to comply with thousands of complex mandates related to waste disposal, malpractice liability and protection, and safety. But even general regulations that apply to all facilities have ballooned. Churches, schools, and factories alike must comply with stringent laws regarding staffing, employee and civil rights, patron and employee safety and comfort, recycling and energy conservation, and pension and health benefits. Adding to those are a profusion of environmental laws related to factors such as indoor air quality, grounds maintenance, and hazardous emissions.

The emphasis on efficiency, the second influence driving the use of contract facilities managers, emerged during the 1980s. An increasingly competitive global business environment, combined with slower domestic market growth and greater competition at home, forced U.S. companies in all industries to cut costs. Likewise, public pressure to reduce spending convinced many government entities, particularly at the local level, to farm out facilities management duties to more efficient firms in the private sector. Many entities found they could reduce personnel expenses through workforce cutbacks and at the same time boost efficiency by outsourcing tasks to specialized managers. "Outsourcing is a result of downsizing," said William L. Gregory, vice president of the International Facilities Management Association (IFMA).

Current Conditions

Facilities support service industry revenue shot up from about $2.25 billion per year in 1982 to $6.4 billion by 1995. The trend toward outsourcing continued during the 1990s as corporate cost-cutting and downsizing persisted and government regulatory activity accelerated. Between 1995 and 1997, the industry had grown and increase revenue by almost 16 percent. Indeed, a growing number of companies were viewing the act of employing and managing workers as a hefty liability. The shift in focus toward more employee benefits put a hold on aggressive hiring practices and put a greater demand on contract workers. Rather than risk exposure to lawsuits and workers compensation claims, many establishments were letting more adept facilities managers bear the risk of employing workers so they could concentrate on their core specialties.

Besides employee regulations, sweeping new mandates during the early 1990s that intensified the emphasis on facilities managers included the Americans with Disabilities Act (ADA) and Clean Air Act (CAA). The ADA decreed a long list of requirements related to disabled employee and patron access with which most facilities must comply. The CAA created new standards for indoor air quality and hazardous emissions. In addition to legislation, court rulings were forcing employers to respond to health risks, such as carpal tunnel syndrome and eye strain provoked by working with computers.

In addition to efficiency and regulatory factors, security issues were increasing the need for contract facilities managers in the mid-1990s. One of the fastest growing industry segments was corporate security services. Contractors were being called in to manage advanced electronic security and surveillance systems that controlled employee access to electronic information, reduced the possibility of work place violence, and discouraged theft and vandalism by employees and patrons. An abundance of outside security firms were enlisted by the retail industry to control theft problems such as shrinkage, an industry term used to describe shop lifting by both patrons and employees.

Industry Leaders

An example of a fast growing facilities support services firm in the mid-1990s was Wackenhut Corrections Corp., of Florida, a subsidiary of Wackenhut Corp. Established in 1984, Wackenhut Corrections Corp. emerged as a dominant international provider of prison design, construction, and management services. The company designs buildings; staffs prisons with guards, social workers, doctors, and cooks; and manages inmate education programs, among other tasks. By mid-1997, Wackenhut managed 28 prisons in the United States, 3 in Australia, 2 in England, 1 in Canada and 1 in Puerto Rico. Company revenue topped $312.8 million in 1998 and employees numbered approximately 8,000. "It is raining prison deals," said President George C. Zoley, in the February 18, 1994 issue of *South Florida Business Journal.* ". . . the business is growing exponentially."

Another successful facilities support company in the mid-1990s was Axiom Real Estate Management Inc., of Connecticut. Formed in 1992, Axiom was a joint venture between International Business Machines and Grub & Ellis Co., a national real estate company. Later, in September of 1997, Axiom became a wholly-owned subsidiary of Grub & Ellis; the venture was renamed to Grubb & Ellis Management Services, Inc. Although property management firms are excluded from this industry classification, Axiom provided a range of support services ranging from computer systems management to complete facilities oversight. The joint venture was established to take advantage of the corporate downsizing trend. Among other services, Axiom performs a full array of engineering, administrative, and financial duties.

About 800 companies competed in the facilities support services industry throughout the 1990s. Most of these companies were relatively large—the average industry participant had 80 workers, compared to an average of 13 for all U.S. service firms. The largest competitor by far was Ogden Corporation, a global provider of support services to energy and environmental agencies, airports and airlines, sports and entertainment facilities, industrial plants, office buildings, and government agencies. Ogden increased its net income 15 percent in 1993 to $17.5 million, but by 1998 its 21,970 employees helped bring in revenue of almost $1.7 billion.

During the 1990s, other large companies in the industry were Serv-Air Inc. of Texas; Canisco Resources, Inc. of Delaware; Nuclear Support Services of Pennsylvania; Bionetics Corp., of Virginia; and Antarctic Support Associates of Colorado. The median annual revenue of the top ten competitors during the 1990s typically ranged from $50 to $100 million.

Employment prospects for the industry are positive, since facilities management outsourcing is expected to proliferate. Jobs for secretaries and other clerical workers, which account for a large share of this industry's workforce, should increase more than 50 percent between 1990 and 2005, according to the U.S. Bureau of Labor Statistics. Most labor and management opportunities should increase similarly. Employment of computer programmers and systems analysts will leap by more than 100 percent by 2005, as will openings for management and financial analysts and marketing professionals. Furthermore, workers in this industry are well compensated. The average payroll per employee in the mid-1990s was about $33,000—35 percent higher than the average for all other U.S. service industries.

FURTHER READING

About Axiom. Available from http://www.axiom.com.

Darnay, Arsen J., ed. *Finance, Insurance, and Real Estate, USA.* Detroit: Gale Research, 1995.

Eyerdam, Rick. ''Wackenhut Goes Abroad for Prison Work.'' *South Florida Business Journal,* 18 February 1994.

Hoover's Company Capsules. Austin, TX: Hoover's Inc., 2000. Available from http://www.hoovers.com/.

U.S. Department of Commerce, Bureau of the Census. *1997 Economic Census: Administrative and Support and Waste Management and Remediation Services.* Washington: GPO, 2000.

Wackenhut Corporation Organizational History, 20 March 2000. Available from http://www.wackenhut.com.

SIC 8748

BUSINESS CONSULTING SERVICES, NOT ELSEWHERE CLASSIFIED

This category covers establishments primarily engaged in furnishing business consulting services, not elsewhere classified, on a contract or fee basis, including such specialties as agriculture, city planning, radio consulting, test development, and traffic consulting.

An important part of this classification's title and definition, ''not elsewhere classified,'' needs some clarification so that the classification may be properly understood. This classification is one of a group of five industries called Management and Public Relations Services. The largest service industry in this group is **SIC 8742: Management Consulting Services,** which is somewhat similar in function to this industry, but is several times larger in terms of its revenues and workforce.

NAICS CODE(S)

611710 (Educational Support Services)
541618 (Other Management Consulting Services)
541690 (Other Scientific and Technical Consulting Services)

ORGANIZATION AND STRUCTURE

Business consulting services, not elsewhere classified, includes businesses involved in supplying counsel and assistance to companies in the following areas: agricultural consulting; city planners, except professional engineering; economic consulting; educational consulting, except management; industrial development planning service; radio consultants; systems engineering consulting, except professional engineering or computer related; testing and test development and evaluation service, educational or personnel; and traffic consultants.

Hundreds of companies have reported activities in this industrial classification, including those involved in the testing of aptitude and skill for suitability in academic and vocational endeavors, and environmental consulting with or without testing. Other companies have offered

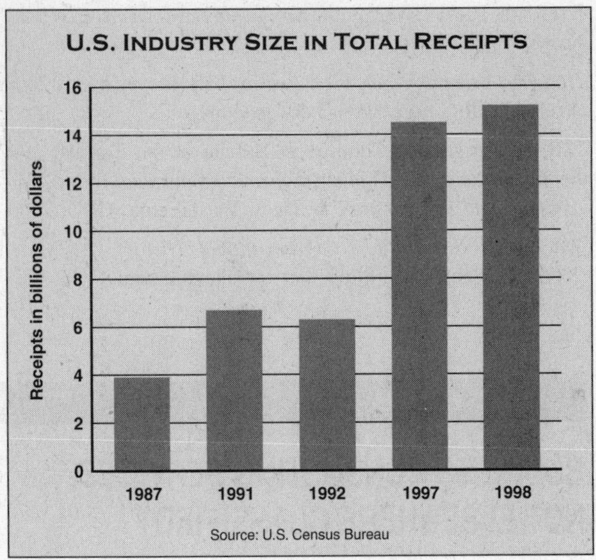

business consulting as adjuncts to their main functions, as in the fields of insurance or guard services.

Business consulting services, not elsewhere classified, provide a wide range of specialized technical assistance to businesses, nonprofit organizations, and government establishments. Some of these service firms are small, some are quite large, and others are small parts of large organizations whose major activities are in other fields.

Reasons for Using Consultants. As with all consulting, the specialties that have been successful are those where the client organizations require temporary expertise in areas where they have not found it feasible to employ a professional staff, or where a knowledgeable advisor may be wanted to give an authoritative independent opinion on an important matter. Profitable consultants usually have areas in which they are considered especially authoritative or skilled.

Industry Size. According to the most recent data available from the U.S. Census Bureau, total receipts for firms in the industry were approximately $15.2 billion in 1998, a 5 percent increase over the previous year. The number of employees in this service industry was estimated at 94,100 in 1998.

Industry Associations and Accreditation. There is no central licensing agency for management consultants. In fact, no guidelines or regulations exist in the industry at all as standards for operating practices. The only available form of acknowledgment of consulting expertise is the Certified Management Consultant designation, which is granted by the trade association, the Institute of Management Consultants.

Another primary industry association is ACME (formerly Association of Consulting Management Engineers). Both ACME and the Institute of Management Consultants operate as divisions of the Council of Consulting Organizations (CCO). Other industry associations include the Society of Professional Management Consultants, the Association of Management Consulting Firms, the Association of Management Consultants, and the Association of Internal Management Consultants.

Background and Development

Consulting grew slowly in the years before 1950, when there were less than 100 firms in the industry. The number of firms expanded rapidly after 1950, however, and by 1990 well over 1,000 firms were established. According to Service Industries USA, in 1998 there were an estimated 22,000 firms, representing an enormous increase during the 1990s.

Pre-World War II. The consulting field had its beginnings in the late 1880s. The Arthur D. Little Company, founded in Cambridge, Massachusetts in 1886 was among the first prominent consulting firms and was still an industry leader in the early 1990s. The company provides both business and management consulting and specializes in engineering-related research for its clients.

A new impetus in consulting came around World War I with the concepts of scientific management pioneered by Frederick W. Taylor and Frank and Lillian Gilbreth. Their studies of worker productivity in factories led to the widespread use of time studies. In 1929, a small group of firms joined together to form a trade association known as the Association of Consulting Management Engineers (ACME). In the 1930s and 1940s, such new consulting firms as McKinsey & Co. and Booz-Allen & Hamilton established themselves by broadening their scope of services to cover finance, organization, and policy issues. These firms, which have become among the most successful in the industry, also helped bolster troubled companies during and after the Depression.

Post-World War II. The consulting field grew rapidly in size, scope, and diversity from World War II to the mid-1990s. Many small firms were established and larger companies grew and branched out to meet ever-changing business needs. Many firms, for example, were hired to provide training and assistance for computer technology and methods. Public accounting firms initially offered consulting assistance as a sideline, but it has since come to represent a significant portion of revenues and profits.

In 1968, groups of consultants and consulting firms organized the Institute of Management Consultants (IMC), an individual membership organization that acts to further its members' interests as well as to certify and assure the ethics and capabilities of its members. In 1989, ACME and IMC established an overseeing umbrella organization, the Council of Consulting Organizations (CCO).

Growth and Change. This industry grew rapidly in the late 1980s and through the 1990s. Overall, the industry grew at an annual rate of nearly 20 percent between 1987 and 1991. In 1993, the industrygrew 11 percent from the previous year, then 22 percent in 1994, 16 percent in 1995, 3 percent in 1996, and 5 percent in 1997.

Several conditions have led to this growth. For example, an increasing number of firms were solicited to provide testing and analysis assistance on environmental issues. Additionally, psychological testing was in greater demand in the early 1990s as more academic and vocational organizations came to rely on such test results. In these areas, many companies found it more expedient and cost effective to use an outside service for a fee, rather than to hire a staff with the requisite skills. Companies also benefited from the further advantage of receiving an objective judgment from an independent outside service.

According to the *U.S. Industry and Trade Outlook,* "demand for professional services will continue to increase into 2000 but at a slower rate than during the latter half of the past decade." A major force behind this growth will be the increased use of computers, the Internet, integrated systems, and other high-technology equipment. The challenge for this industry will be to train and retain qualified consultants.

The leading firms mentioned below reflect the diversity in the specialties of professionals in the business consulting services field. Many of the smallest firms in the industry, not covered here, have very narrow specialties in which they have special expertise, or serve small geographical areas in which they have become well known.

INDUSTRY LEADERS

According to *Ward's Business Directory of U. S. Private and Public Companies*, the industry leader in 1998 was Prudential Resources Management of Valhalla, New York; second was National Shopping Service of Los Angeles, California; third was Post Buckley Schuss and Jeering Inc. of Miami, Florida; and fourth was Den Corp/ Information and Engineering Technology of Fairfax, Virginia.

WORKFORCE

Diversity of Skills. Because this industry is a field with many different types of functions, the work force is made up of individuals of many different specialties. For instance, environmental consulting requires engineers, psychological testing requires psychologists, economics consulting requires economists or MBAs, and city planning consulting requires architects, civil engineers, and landscape architects. The city planning consulting segment of the industry has 100 firms ranging in size from solo practitioners to businesses with over 5,000 employees.

FURTHER READING

Darnay, Arsen J.*Service Industries USA*. Detroit: Gale Research, 1999.

U.S. Bureau of the Census. *Economic Census 1997,* 2000. Available from http://www.census.gov.

U. S. Industry and Trade Outlook. The McGraw-Hill Companies, 1999.

Ward's Business Directory of U. S. Private and Public Companies. Detroit: Gale Research, 1999.

SIC 8811

PRIVATE HOUSEHOLDS

This industry consists of private households that employ workers on or about the premises who serve in occupations usually considered as domestic service. This classification includes baby-sitting; domestic service; private estates; noncommercial farmhouses; private households employing cooks, maids, chauffeurs, and gardeners; personal affairs management; and noncommercial residential farms.

NAICS CODE(S)

814110 (Private Households)

INDUSTRY SNAPSHOT

This industry, unlike most others, is comprised of individuals, not companies. More than half a million households paid employers' taxes on private household workers and more than 802,000 household workers were employed in the United States in 1996. General houseworkers accounted for about 63 percent of available jobs; 34 percent of this workforce were engaged in child care. Historically, demand for help in this industry has been greater than the supply of workers. The need for household workers increased during the latter part of the twentieth century as more women with children entered the workforce and as an aging population often required private attendants or companions. As the baby boomer generation ages, employment opportunities for personal attendants will continue to rise. In 1995, 40 percent of all persons employed in private households were involved in childcare and 4 percent were housekeepers, or butlers.

ORGANIZATION AND STRUCTURE

Generally, the organization of this industry can be defined by a simple employer and employee relationship, with one or more employers per household worker. In large households with sizable staff, a butler or head housekeeper manages the other workers. Some private household employees contract with placement agencies that act as a partial employer, often by offering benefits to the workers and acting as an intermediary between employer and employee.

Traditionally most U.S. domestics have been "general houseworkers" responsible for duties such as dusting; sweeping and vacuuming; and cleaning fixtures, ovens, and bathrooms. Some general houseworkers also take on such duties as cooking and childcare, although these are usually considered specialty areas. Another category of household workers includes those specifically involved in childcare. Workers employed on an hourly and casual basis are usually referred to as baby-sitters; those employed on a regular, ongoing basis who are in charge of infants are usually considered nannies; and workers in charge of older children are tutors or governesses. Household workers who assist the elderly or disabled are referred to as companions or personal attendants. Such employees generally prepare meals and do light housework, but, depending on the person's needs, may also help in bathing and dressing. Most household employees are also involved in the personal aspects of the employer's life. This is mainly true with nannies and personal attendants. Oftentimes, it is the household employee who is the stable figure in the lives of those being taken care of.

Large households employing workers may include a housekeeper, butler, cook, caretaker, and/or a launderer. Housekeepers and butlers are responsible for hiring and supervising household staff, and they normally do light housework. Butlers also answer phones, deliver messages, serve food and drinks, and act as personal attendants. Cooks are responsible for preparing and serving meals, ordering food supplies, and keeping the kitchen clean. Caretakers carry out heavy housework and maintenance, including light carpentry and plumbing.

Background and Development

Domestic workers have existed for centuries; early on, however, service often took the form of slavery or indentured servitude. In 1870 there were approximately 960,000 private household workers in the United States. Between 1870 and 1910, demand for such work increased rapidly because industrialization sparked a proliferation of middle- and upper-class families in urban areas. At this time, demand was easily met by the vast number of immigrants in the country. Yet, with this advance in industrialization, the status of household work declined. The gap between factory and domestic workers was widened by the emergence of benefits and legislation to protect factory workers.

For a short period, roughly between 1910 and 1920, the number of domestic workers in the United States declined. This drop was mainly due to the advent of compulsory education of children and the introduction of child labor laws. Between 1920 and 1940, the number of domestics working in the United States jumped from 1.36 million to a peak of 2.28 million. Domestic help was changing from a mostly live-in, full-time profession to one in which servants lived on their own and even worked on a part-time basis. This was spurred on, in part, because families living in small homes or apartments still hired household help. After World War I, this occupation drew immigrants with minimal language skills and African-Americans moving north, for whom domestic service was one of the few occupations available. Since 1940 the number of private household workers in the United States has decreased. Despite having long dominated the industry, women began to leave these jobs when outside opportunities increased and they were able to work in better occupations.

In the early 1990s, the treatment of household help, particularly nannies, was publicized as a result of lawsuits against employers involving sexual harassment and physical violence. An article in the *Wall Street Journal* claimed that "nannies are among the most exploited workers in the country." Stories of unfair wage practices, long hours, and physical abuse emerged in the media. However, nannies and other household workers have had few legal rights in fighting harsh working conditions. In 1993 most states did not place a limit on the number of consecutive hours or days a household worker could work. Moreover, sexual harassment of household workers has not been illegal in most states. In New York, human rights laws have prohibited sexual harassment and discrimination of employees, but has specifically excluded domestic workers.

In 1993, employers' tax obligations were highlighted when it was discovered that one of President Clinton's nominations for attorney general had hired an illegal alien and had not fully complied in paying social security taxes for an employee. As a result, President Clinton proposed simplifying the tax laws for employers to make it clearer if they are required to pay social security tax on wages. Unless a private household worker is an independent contractor—which is rarely the case—employers are required to pay social security tax on any employee earning more than $50 per quarter to the federal government and any additional taxes required by their states.

Current Conditions

Upon entering the 1990s, this industry continued to have a short supply of workers due primarily to the working conditions, low status, and lack of health and fringe benefits (although some placement agencies offered benefits). Also in the early 1990s, changes in immigration laws made work permits more difficult to obtain. The trend in the 1990s has been away from private household help for childcare and toward the use of nurseries, which are often sponsored by employers. Other trends for childcare have included more use of day care facilities, which are operated by private companies and individuals working out of their homes.

While the actual number of workers declined by 6,000 workers from 1992 to 1998, opportunities for employment in this industry sector was expected to remain robust through 2006. In essence, more lucrative employment was available due to a robust economy in which employers competed for a scarce labor pool. With an increasing number of women joining the workforce, demand for household help, child care, and (with an increasing population of senior citizens), elder care. In lieu of private household employers, the trend at the end of the 1990s was towards increasing dependence on domestic cleaning firms, child care establishments, and temporary help firms.

WORKFORCE

In the latter half of the 1990s, there were roughly 802,000 private household workers employed in the United States. More than half were general houseworkers, about 40 percent were child care workers, and about 4 percent were housekeepers, butlers, cooks, and launderers. Nearly two-thirds of household employees worked part-time (35 hours or less per week).

Experienced and highly recommended workers employed by wealthy families in major metropolitan areas may earn $800 to $1,200 a week. Private household workers who live with their employers may be given room and board, medical benefits, a car, vacation days, and education benefits. However, most private household workers receive very limited or no benefits.

Earnings of private household workers varied depending on household, staff size, geographic location, and experience. Generally, full-time live-in housekeepers, cooks, butlers, nannies, and governesses earned the highest remuneration. Experienced, well-referenced domestic workers serving wealthy families in large metropolitan areas were the highest paid household workers. For the most part, however, private household workers were employed part time and did not receive any benefits. Some workers lived with their employers and received room, board, and a package of benefits competitive with U.S. industry, but, in some states employers could deduct a minimal amount for room and board, making the salaries of some household workers lower than the minimum wage. The Bureau of Labor reported that, in 1996, median annual earnings for full-time private household workers were $11,600 for cleaners and servants, $11,100 for cooks, child care workers received $10,500, and $7,500 was the average wage for housekeepers and butlers.

AMERICA AND THE WORLD

In 1999, the Bureau of Labor Statistics indicated that a majority of household workers were women (62 percent). African-Americans composed 13 percent of all industry workers, while 9 percent were Latino.

According to the Center for Migration Studies, at least 10 percent of the United States' 3 million illegal immigrants worked in childcare in 1993, with roughly another 10 percent working in other private household occupations. Legally, over 10,000 Western Europeans work in the United States through cultural exchange programs.

Great Britain, like the United States, has reported shortages of child care help. In a 1990 study, 48 percent of British women who were unemployed said they had to stay at home to raise their children because they were unable to find help. Because of this shortage, salaries for nannies in Great Britain have increased significantly. In other European countries, childcare help is largely covered by the state, reducing the need for such workers. A study by the European Economic Commission showed that Denmark, France, Belgium, and Italy offered the most generous state assistance for childcare. In the Scandinavian countries, childcare is typically provided by employers.

FURTHER READING

Atkins, Andrea. "The Affordable Nanny." *Better Homes and Gardens,* January 1997.

"Clinton Wants to Amend the 'Nanny' Tax Law." *Wall Street Journal,* 26 April 1993.

Lipman, Joanne. "The Nanny Trap: Dark Side of Child Care Is How Poorly Workers Are Sometimes Treated." *Wall Street Journal,* 14 April 1993.

U.S. Bureau of Labor Statistics. "Private Household Workers." *Occupational Outlook Handbook.* Washington: GPO, 1998. Available from http://www.bls.gov/oco/ocos175.htm/.

SIC 8999

SERVICES, NOT ELSEWHERE CLASSIFIED

This group covers businesses that primarily provide services, not elsewhere classified (NEC), such as authors, lecturers, radio commentators, song writers, weather forecasters, writers, and artists working on their own account.

NAICS CODE(S)

711510 (Independent Artists, Writers, and Performers)
512210 (Record Production)
541690 (Other Scientific and Technical Consulting Services)
512230 (Music Publishers)

541612 (Human Resources and Executive Search Consulting Services)
514199 (All Other Information Services)
541620 (Environmental Consulting Services)

The services, NEC, group included many specialties ranging from inventors and lecturers to stained glass artists and cloud seeders. According to government statistics, 14,587 firms employed 81,136 people in this category in 1992. A majority of firms in this category had annual sales under $100,000, with 6,848 having sales below $49,000, and 8,607 with sales between $50,000 and $99,000. The size of such firms also favored the smaller firm, with 19,826 having less than 5 employees.

The largest industry sector was actuarial firms, with ten percent of the industry workforce in the 1990s. Actuaries use mathematical models and statistical techniques to analyze risk. They develop and price insurance products and financial instruments, analyze financial institutions, and help manage pension and employee benefit plans. Actuaries also perform other jobs requiring advanced statistical analysis and mathematical modeling, such as investment management.

Although their profession is considered rewarding and lucrative, actuaries typically must pass exams that may require several years of study during their employment. But experienced actuaries typically earn over $50,000 annually, and often make as much as $100,000 or more. Demand for actuaries was expected to rise more than 50 percent between 1990 and 2005, according to the Bureau of Labor Statistics.

Except for clerical workers, geology and geophysical services were the second largest industry category, accounting for about 6 percent of the workforce. Geologists study the earth's composition and structure. Geophysicists study matter and energy and how they interact. Members of both professions may consult on construction projects, such as dams and roadways; locating raw materials for extraction by mining and drilling companies; and predicting natural disasters. Salaries for experienced professionals in these fields were about $40,000 per year in 1992. Jobs for geologists and geophysicists could rise 70 percent by 2005, fed by more environmental research and the hunt for new mineral reserves.

Writers, editors, and technical writers made up 5 percent of the miscellaneous services workers in the mid 1990s. Often working as contractors or freelancers, writers and editors were hired by publishers, television and radio stations, and other media groups. They also worked for companies and individuals, writing speeches, marketing materials, manuals, and other compositions. Editors usually managed and reviewed the work of writers, and were often involved with the publishing process. While yearly salaries varied, experienced writers commonly earned $25,000 to $35,000 and editors generally drew $30,000 to $45,000.

While salary and employment prospects vary by occupation, the overall job outlook was positive for miscellaneous services workers through the 1990s. Demand for most occupations should rise more than 50 percent between 1990 and 2005. Computer programming services, which accounted for roughly two percent of the workforce, should rise nearly 100 percent. Job growth may also be strong for commercial artists, meteorologists, interior designers, and science and math technicians and managers.

FURTHER READING

U.S. Department of Commerce. *1992 Census of Service Industries & Geographic Area Series.* Washington, DC: Bureau of the Census, 1995.

Dun's Census of American Business 1997. Parsippany, NJ: Dun & Bradstreet, 1997.

Ward's Business Directory of U.S. Private and Public Companies, 1999. Detroit: Gale Research, 1999.

Public Administration

SIC 9111

EXECUTIVE OFFICES

This category covers offices of chief executives and their advisory and interdepartmental committees and commissions.

Executive offices are those held and directly controlled by mayors, governors, city managers, county supervisors, and the president of the United States. They encompass heads of local, state, and national governments. They formulate and project policy, prepare budgets, handle major emergencies, appoint and nominate leaders and judges, and work to improve the lot of constituents, among other activities.

NAICS Code(s)

921110 (Executive Offices)

Organization and Structure

According to a 1999 report released by Standard & Poor, local metropolitan areas drive the nation's economy. They accounted for 84 percent of the gross domestic product, and 89 percent of the nation's economic growth from 1992 to 1998. In 1997, there were 87,504 identified units of government operating in the United States, comprising 87,453 local governments, 50 state governments, and the federal government. Local governments were further subclassified as 3,043 county governments; 19,372 municipal governments; 16,629 town/township governments; 13,726 school districts; and 34,683 special districts. State and local governments took in more than $1.5 trillion dollars in revenues in 1997, and employed 954,600 persons (full-time equivalents) for government administration alone.

Local. The three basic types of municipal government structures in the United States are mayor-council, commission, and council-manager. While they typically oversee relatively small geographical units, local governments may exercise great control over the daily lives of their constituents. They are charged, for example, with providing fire and police protection, waste disposal, and other services.

In the mayor-council government, the mayor is elected as the executive and usually controls the council, which also is elected. The council formulates ordinances that the mayor enforces. Some systems use a weak-mayor system, in which the mayor is subordinate to the council. Examples of large cities with mayor-council organizations are Boston, New York, Chicago, and Seattle. In contrast, a commission government consists of several commissioners elected to serve as heads of city departments. The presiding commissioner usually acts as the mayor. Cities with commissioners include Tulsa and Salt Lake City.

A council-manager government has an elected council. The council hires a city manager to run various city departments. The city manager is the chief executive of the city and is ultimately responsible for running the government and advising the council. The council also elects a mayor to chair the council and officiate at major functions and events. Des Moines and Cincinnati have council-manager governments.

The United States Conference of Mayors was organized to improve municipal government through cooperation with the federal government. It is comprised of about 1,050 mayors from cities with a population of more than 30,000. As of 1999, the largest municipality (in area) was Jacksonville, Florida, covering 758.7 square miles. The largest *incorporated city* was Sitka, Alaska (2,881

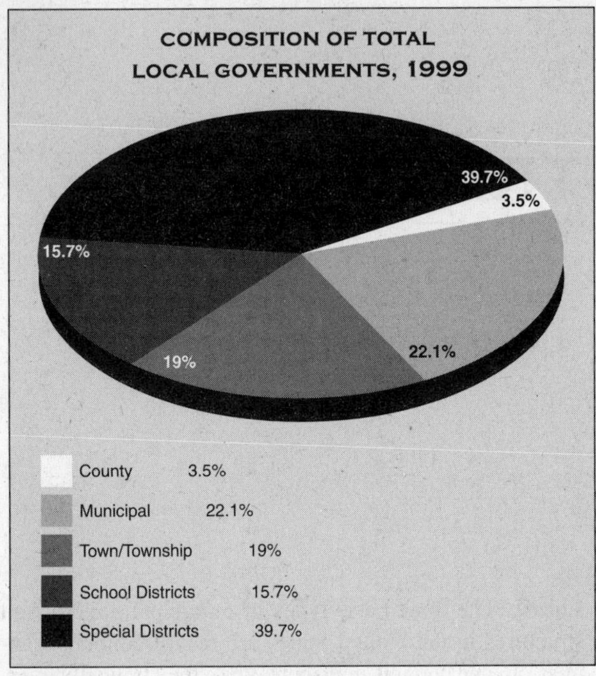

square miles). The nation's youngest mayor in 1999 was 18-year-old Jason Nastke, of Valatie, New York, a finance student at a local community college.

State. The 50 state governments are structured similarly to the government of the United States. Each state has an executive, legislative, and judicial branch, as well as its own constitution. The executive branch is headed by a governor whom the voters elect. Below the governor is the lieutenant governor. Among the primary duties of the governor's office are the preparation of a state budget and the guidance of new legislation. In addition, a governor acts as the commander-in-chief of the state militia (national guard) during times of peace.

In accomplishing his or her responsibilities, the governor enjoys the power to summon special sessions of the legislature, to veto legislation, and to issue pardons and commute sentences for most crimes. While the executive powers afforded most governors may seem extensive, their authority is often diminished by the existence of independent agencies over which they have little control.

Most governors are elected to four-year terms, but several states have a limit of two years. Other states set no limit on the number of terms a governor may serve. They may be forcibly removed from office, however, through impeachment or recall.

National. The United States has a presidential government, which is distinguished by the fact that it is practically independent of the federal legislative branch. This contrasts with cabinet governments, utilized in many European nations, in which the executive body is drawn from and responsible to the legislative arm. As a result, the president is solely responsible to the voters and theoretically is free from congressional control.

The president has expansive powers granted by the Constitution. Paramount are his duties as commander-in-chief of the armed forces, the authority to declare war and to make treaties, the ability to veto legislation, and his role as ceremonial head of state. In addition to the formal powers provided by the constitution, the office of the president has evolved into a much more powerful government entity than was conceived by the founding fathers. The president is responsible for conducting foreign affairs, appointing judges and other officials, and initiating and developing legislation. Furthermore, he has effectively become a guardian of the economy and is held largely responsible for factors such as the employment rate and standard of living.

The president is chosen through an electoral college. Voters choose electors on the state level who have been nominated by political parties and have pledged to vote for that party's candidate. Each state is allowed a number of electors equal to the combined total of its representatives and senators. The candidate who receives the majority of electoral votes receives the presidency. In the elections of 1800 and 1824, no candidate won a majority, so the House of Representatives selected the president.

The president serves a term of four years, and is limited to two elected terms and a total of 10 years in office. To be eligible for the office, he or she must be a natural-born citizen of at least 35 years of age, have resided in the United States for 14 or more years, and not have a felony conviction.

The office of the president has 12 offices. Among them are the office of the vice president; the White House office, which encompasses counselors, staff, and assistants; the National Security Council, which advises on military policy; the Council of Economic Advisers; and the Office of Management and Budget (OMB). The OMB is one of the most consequential executive offices. It evaluates, formulates, and coordinates management procedures and program objectives within federal departments and agencies. It also advises the president on relative legislation and proposals.

Although not clearly defined in the Constitution, the cabinet is described in the Twenty-Fifth Amendment as "the principal officers of the executive departments." An institution of tradition and custom dating back to George Washington, the cabinet is composed primarily of the heads of the 14 executive departments. It also may include the vice president and heads of other federal departments and agencies, as well as other individuals selected by the president. Cabinet appointments are subject to confirmation by the Senate. The Cabinet's sole function is to advise the president.

WORKFORCE

Although very few executive positions are available at the state or federal level, numerous opportunities to serve in executive positions exist within local governments. Many officials on the local level, such as mayors, do not hold full-time, year-round positions. They often have jobs, are retired, or have household responsibilities. Executives on the local, state, and federal level reach their positions in a number of ways. Many are attorneys, though public figures from all walks of life may be able to secure enough votes to capture an office.

City and county managers who are appointed by councils or commissions typically have a more definite career path than elected officials. While they come from a variety of backgrounds, many have a masters degree in public administration or business. Managers of larger jurisdictions are expected to exhibit expertise in financial, administrative, and personnel matters associated with public management. Because they often are appointed by revolving administrations, city and county managers also need keen political and interpersonal skills that will help to keep them employed. Job growth opportunities are very limited. Many existing local and municipal offices are expected to try to reduce expenses and personnel. Opportunities will be greatest in regions with growing populations, particularly in the Southwest. In addition, some communities have been hiring city managers for the first time in an effort to boost the efficiency of their government.

According to U.S. government Bureau of Labor statistics, there were 93,000 chief executives and legislators in 1996. The average annual salary for chief elected county officials was $25,600, while for city officials, it was $12,200. The average salary for city managers was $70,600, and county managers were paid an average $86,700. According to the Bureau's *Book of the States,* gubernatorial salaries ranged from $60,000 to $130,000 (plus a vehicle and an official residence).

FURTHER READING

Famighetti, Robert, ed. ''State and Local Government.'' *The World Almanac and Book of Facts.* Mahwah, New Hersey: World Almanac Books, 1996.

Occupational Outlook Handbook, 1998-1999 Edition, Washington: U.S. Department of Labor, 1999. Available from http://stats.bls.gov/oco/ocos013.htm.

''Timeline.'' *American City & County,* November 1999, 34.

U.S. Census Bureau. *Statistical Abstract of the United States: 1999.* Available from http://www.census/gov/prod/www/statistical-abstract-us.html.

Ward, Janet. ''Report Shows Metro Areas Drive Nation's Economy.'' *American City & County,* December 1999, 4.

SIC 9121

LEGISLATIVE BODIES

This category covers legislative bodies and their advisory and interdepartmental committees and commissions at the local, state, and national level.

NAICS CODE(S)

921120 (Legislative Bodies)

INDUSTRY SNAPSHOT

Legislative bodies (from the Latin *lex,* ''law,'' and *latio,* ''a bringing'') include the U.S. Congress, state legislative assemblies, and local commissions and boards. These entities are responsible for proposing, selecting, and amending the laws that govern all Americans. They have the authority to levy taxes, regulate commerce, borrow money, and exercise a number of additional powers.

Although it has been amended to alter the function of the legislature, the U.S. Constitution that became effective in 1789 defines the federal legislative branch. The Tenth Amendment to the Constitution expressly reserves to the states all powers not specifically granted to the federal government in the Constitution. *legislative* bodies have been likewise organized under state constitutions. The conceptual structure of most U.S. legislative bodies largely reflects European initiatives, such as the Magna Carta (1215) and the English Bill of Rights (1689).

The authoritative purview of U.S. legislative bodies is often challenged in legal efforts to clarify the scope, limits, and respective balancing of federal versus state power. This helps to maintain the vitality and viability of the Constitution when applied to contemporary issues and crises. Accordingly, the U.S. legislative system has remained a healthy model for democracies around the globe.

ORGANIZATION AND STRUCTURE

All U.S. governing bodies at the national and state levels—and most local governments—are distinguished by the fact that their executive, legislative, and judicial branches are practically independent of one another. This portentous difference contrasts with cabinet governments, utilized in many European nations, in which the executive body is drawn from and responsible to the legislative arm. As a result, the President is solely responsible to the voters and is theoretically free from direct legislative control. Likewise, legislative bodies are relatively unfettered by the executive branch. This separation of powers, combined with a system of checks and balances, serves to reduce the potential power of the government to domineer U.S. citizens. For example, chief executives can veto legislative initiatives, but legislators can override their vetoes.

State legislators initiate, draft, and vote on proposed state laws. Each state has two legislative bodies, an upper house (Senate) and a lower house. Nebraska, which has only one house, is the exception. The lower house is usually called the House of Representatives, or in some states the Assembly or the House of Delegates. The size of legislatures varies. For example, Georgia had 236 legislators in 1999 and Nevada had only 63. But within each state, all representatives are elected from districts with an almost equal number of citizens. About half of the legislators meet annually to vote on laws, and the other half meet twice each year. Upper house members are customarily elected for a term of four years and lower house members for a term of two-years.

Most community legislative bodies exist under one of three types of government. Under mayor and council systems—the most common type of local governing body in the United States—an elected council acts as the legislative body. Its ordinances are typically subject to confirmation by the mayor, who is the head of the executive branch. Conversely, in the commission form of government the elected commission essentially serves as both the legislative and executive body. The third type of system, council-manager government, operates similarly to the commission arrangement, the primary difference being that the council appoints a manager to oversee governmental departments rather than running the departments itself. Also at the local level are a variety of county legislators, who also receive their lawmaking authority from the state.

Congress. Congress constitutes the legislative branch of the federal government. It is the responsibility of Congress to develop, draft, amend, and vote on laws and proposed legislation that applies to the entire nation. In addition to their legislative duties, members of Congress also spend much of their time representing constituents in grievances against the federal bureaucracy. Congress convenes once each year, beginning on January 3, for a few months. It also holds special hearings on important public issues. In addition, the President may call special sessions of Congress.

Under the original U.S. Constitution, Congress is vested with the ''Power to lay and collect Taxes, Duties, Imposts and Excises, to pay the Debts and provide for the Common Defense and general Welfare of the United States.'' Some of the powers specifically outlined in Section 8, Powers of Congress, include the authority to: borrow money, regulate cross-border and interstate commerce, coin money, establish post offices and roads, grant creative (patent) rights, declare war, and ''make all Laws which shall be necessary and proper for carrying into Execution the foregoing Powers. . . .''

Congress is comprised of the Senate (upper house) and the House of Representatives (lower house). Both houses can introduce and amend bills. However, many of the laws on which Congress votes are written or proposed by the Executive Branch. To become law, bills must receive a majority vote from both houses and be signed by the President. If the President refuses to sign a bill, Congress can override the veto with a two-thirds majority vote from both houses.

The Senate was originally formed to represent the states and the upper class of society. Although its role has changed, it still retains some privileges, such as the power to approve or reject some presidential appointments, to try officials impeached by the House of Representatives, and to ratify or reject treaties. The Constitution allows each state two Senators. Senators are directly elected by the people of the state they represent, and serve a term of six years. Senate elections are staggered so that no more than one-third of all Senate seats are up for election during any year. Although the vice-president serves as the Senate president, the strongest Senate leaders are the majority floor leader and the minority floor leader, who are elected by caucuses of their respective political parties.

The House of Representatives was originally designed to represent the people. The proxies in this legislative body are elected from districts of approximately equal size in states throughout the United States. Each state gets at least one representative, and the total number of U.S. districts is limited to 435. ''Apportionment'' of House seats among the states is predicated upon U.S. Census results. Alaska, Montana, North Dakota, South Dakota, Vermont, Wyoming, and Delaware each had only one representative in 1999, while California, for example, had 52 House members. The House is led by the speaker, who is selected by the majority party. Among other duties, the speaker presides over debates and appoints some committee members.

Bills introduced by either Senate or House members are sent to standing—or permanent—committees. Committees meet in private to amend, hasten, delay, or kill the bills. There were 20 standing committees in the House and 16 in the Senate in 1999, each of which was concerned with a special subject, such as public works and transportation, foreign affairs, or agriculture. Committee chairpersons, who often possess significant power, are usually members of the majority party that have served the longest on their committee. In addition to standing committees, there are several special and select committees. In 1999, the Senate had three select committees: aging, ethics, and intelligence. The House, however, only had one: intelligence. Finally, joint committees unite members from both houses to draft compromises of conflicting bills that each house has passed. In 1999, there were four joint committees: economic, library, printing, and taxation.

After a bill is passed by a committee, the house votes on it. In the House of Representatives, the bill must also pass through the Rules Committee before it is put to a vote. If the bill passes, it is sent to the other house where it is again subjected to a committee. If changes are made, a joint committee develops a compromise bill that each house must accept. The final bill is sent to the President. If he does not sign or veto the bill within ten days, it becomes a law. On the other hand, if Congress adjourns before the ten day period expires the bill is effectively vetoed, or ''pocket vetoed.''

BACKGROUND AND DEVELOPMENT

The first Continental Congress was convened in Philadelphia in 1774. Representatives of all states except Georgia attended. The group passed intercolonial resolutions calling for a boycott of British trade. The Constitution of the United States of America was created between May and September of 1787, in Philadelphia, by a group of delegates from 12 of the original 13 states. That document, which became effective in 1789, outlined the structure of the legislative, as well as the executive and judicial, branches of the federal government.

The Constitution reflected a blend of British law, a general distrust of government, Pilgrim political heritage, and European political philosophy from authors like John Locke and Montesquieu. Manifest in the Constitution was the concept of legislative supremacy by a representative body, particularly in matters of economics. Legislative dominance related to taxes and other laws was tempered by the separation of powers and an innovative system of checks and balances. In addition, the framers of the Constitution were careful to retain independence of state and local legislative bodies.

The Constitution was also unique in that it established a system whereby lawmakers could amend the document. Amendments could be passed by a consensus of two-thirds of both houses, or by a state-supported national convention. By 1999, the Constitution had 27 additional amendments (the last in 1992). In addition, as the role of the United States in world politics expanded, particularly following World War II, the function of Congress changed. While the powers of the Federal Executive Branch increased, legislative dominance diminished in some areas, including fiscal control. However, the Congress remains the primary force in the U.S. government.

As the federal legislative branch changed during the twentieth century, so did the role of state and local legislative bodies. Early in the nation's history federal and state powers were succinctly delineated. The Constitution assigned exclusive powers to both state and federal legislatures, and provided for concurrent powers to be exercised by both levels of government. Federal courts, independent of the Congress, mediated disputes and helped to determine spheres of state and federal influence. States, meanwhile, delegated legislative authority to local governments.

But the autonomy of state legislatures declined during the mid-1900s as the federal government ballooned in massive proportions, particularly after World War II. After giving itself the power to tax the income of U.S. citizens in 1913 (16th amendment to the Constitution), Congress swelled its income tax revenues from $5.4 billion in 1920 to $360 billion by 1980, and then close to an estimated $trillion (individual and corporate income taxes) by 1995. As a result states became increasingly dependent on federal government resources, state and federal legislative bodies formed closer relationships.

Although they have evolved to meet the demands of a changing world, U.S. legislative bodies have remained relatively intact, from a Constitutional perspective. Besides a greater concentration of power at the federal level, several trends characterized the legislative process. One of the most dominant was an emphasis on legislative oversight. This entails the responsibility of state and national legislators to continually review, investigate, and evaluate how well the policies and programs of the government are being executed. The purpose of legislative oversight is to reduce excessive and inefficient laws and bureaucracy.

A primary oversight tool developed during the latter decades of the century was ''sunset legislation,'' which establishes a means of automatically terminating agencies, boards, and committees that are not specifically re-authorized by the legislature. Sunset laws had been adopted in 36 states by the mid-1980s. By the 1990s, however, several states had ceased using the sunset laws because of various logistical and political hindrances. The focus shifted to term limits and balanced-budget laws.

WORKFORCE

In 1999, there were 535 congresspersons, about 7,500 state legislators, and thousands of local legislative bodies. The numbers are not expected to increase before 2006, although some local governments may expand as a result of increased regulation and growth forecasting. Of the 535 U.S. Congressional members, 470 were male and

65 female. Caucasian members totalled 474, with 61 minorities. Ten members were over the age of 75, and nine members were under the age of 35. By far, the majority of members fell within the 40 to 60 year age group.

On a daily basis, legislators work with their voters, meet with lobbyists and special interest groups, read reports, write legislation, and meet with fellow legislators and other government workers. They may also appoint department heads and commission members, approve budgets, do research, and perform various ceremonial duties. National legislators, particularly, also spend time working to secure re-election. Local legislators often work part time—they hold another full time job, are retired, or run a household. State legislators usually work full time for a few months each year and then only part time. Congresspersons work long hours most of the year.

Eligibility requirements for local and state legislators vary, though residency is a common prerequisite. Likewise, Senators and House members in Congress must be residents of the state from which they are chosen. House members are typically residents of their districts, though that is not required by the Constitution. Senators must be 30 years old and have been U.S. residents for nine years or more, while House members must be 25 years of age and at least seven-year residents. Although there are many routes to becoming a legislator, it is common for state and national representatives to have law degrees, a history of public service, and/or a military background. But public figures from all walks of life, including astronauts, entertainers, and businessmen are commonly elected to serve.

According to the National Conference of State Legislatures, the average salary for state legislators in the 1990s ranged from $10,000 to $47,000 for those states that paid an annual salary. Only 10 states paid legislators for the days they were in session, and 2 of those states pay no expenses and only a nominal daily salary. In 1999, U.S. Congress voted to increase members' salaries to $141,300 annually for the year 2000. Minority and majority leaders, along with the speaker of the house earned considerably more. But congresspersons also enjoy a windfall of perks, and many representatives, after leaving their posts, are able to secure lucrative work as lobbyists, attorneys, and consultants. Gubernatorial salaries ranged from approximately $60,000 to $130,000.

America and the World

Most industrialized nations have a legislative federal arm that resembles the one in the United States. They are typically bicameral, allow for some system of checks and balances with executive and judicial branches, and represent the general population to varying degrees. However, checks and balances upon legislative powers varies greatly from country to country.

As of the close of the century, no global legislative body or entity yet existed. The United Nations continued to have its member nations adopt ''resolutions,'' and envisioned enforcement power under its newly-formed International Court of Justice, but its jurisdiction was limited to member nations only.

Of significance to the development of a global economy was the proliferation of multi-national corporations, organized under the laws of one country, but doing business world-wide. In the latter 1990s, Internet business continued to usurp conventional marketing strategies, raising new issues about the scope of intellectual property law (rights to Web sites, trademarks and service marks, computer software, etc.) and the ability to enforce such laws in other countries. The need for a global legislative body, in conjunction with a global enforcement entity, became a topic of discussion.

On the homefront, Congress entered the millennium with a balanced budget for the first time in decades. Several major pieces of legislation of global import were on the verge of final vote. The issues reflected the times: Year 2000 (''Y2K'') computer glitches, gun control, and interest rates. One of the most sensitive and politically charged issues for legislators was allocating funds for military efforts overseas, such as in peacekeeping missions, or in assisting new democracies rising from volatile beginnings.

Further Reading

''Congress by Sex, Race, Age.'' *The Political Reference Almanac.* Available from http://www.polisci.com/legis/compl.htm. March 1999.

Famighetti, Robert, ed. ''United States—105 Congress.'' *The World Almanac and Book of Facts.* Mahwah, New Jersey: World Almanac Books, 1996.

Famighetti, Robert, ed. ''State and Local Government.'' *The World Almanac and Book of Facts.* Mahwah, New Jersey: World Almanac Books, 1996.

''Federal Government Budget by Agency.'' From the Office of Management and Budget. 1999. Available from http://www.polisci.com/economy/agency.htm.

''Government Chief Executives and Legislators.'' *1998-1999 Occupational Outlook Handbook.* Bureau of Labor Statistics. Available from http://stats.bls.gov/oco/ocos013.htm.

''Hill Leaders Offer to Cut Their Pay as Part of Budget Cut.'' *Congressional News.* Available from http://207.153.197.247/oct99/ 102799.htm.

Standing Committees, 1999. Available from http://dir.yahoo.com/Government/ U_S_Government/Legislative_Branch/Senate/Committees.

"Table of Articles and Amendments [to the U.S. Constitution], November 1999." Available from http://www.law.cornell.edu/constitution/constitution.table.html.

"Y2K Issues." *Congressional Digest*, June-July 1999.

SIC 9131

EXECUTIVE AND LEGISLATIVE OFFICES COMBINED

This category covers councils and boards of commissioners or supervisors and such bodies where the chief executive is a member of the legislative body itself.

NAICS CODE(S)

921140 (Executive and Legislative Offices, Combined)

The U.S. government is distinguished by a strict separation of powers between federal and executive offices, as outlined in the U.S. Constitution. Likewise, most state constitutions embody this unique and important American division of legislative labor. It serves to reduce the power that government has over its citizens. However, many local governments are largely devoid of this separation of powers. For the sake of simplicity and efficiency, city and county governmental units often combine administrative and lawmaking functions.

The three primary types of city governments are: mayor-council, commission, and council-manager. Under the mayor-council arrangement, the mayor is technically charged with overseeing executive functions, such as formulating policy, presiding over functions, and preparing the budget. The council acts as the legislative body and establishes ordinances. In reality, however, the mayor often controls the actions of the council and ensures that laws are properly enforced. Most large cities still use a mayor-council government.

Under a commission form of city government, several commissioners are elected to serve as heads of city departments. A presiding commissioner usually acts as the mayor, but the commission oversees both administrative and lawmaking functions. Council-manager governments work similarly, but a council selects a city manager to run the government. City manager responsibilities vary, but many managers act in both legislative and executive roles to some extent.

Most county governments in the United States use the commission, or board, arrangement. In 1997, there were 3,043 county governments; 19,372 municipal governments, and 16,629 town/township governments in operation throughout the United States. At the county level, for example, more than one-fifth were structured with combined legislative and executive responsibilities. By 1999, slightly less than 60 percent of counties operated under the commission form.

County boards are typically comprised of 3 to 5 members elected from county districts, though boards range in size from 1 to more than 100 members. Consolidation of the three branches of government is most common in the South, but the majority of counties combine at least the executive and legislative offices—a legacy of the English governing system. In addition to traditional boards, an increasing number of states have moved to a county-manager system, in which the commission selects a manager to serve in a capacity similar to that of a city manager.

Also at the county level, voters typically elect several officials, or row officers, to handle specific executive functions. Elected county officer positions may include sheriff, prosecuting attorney, treasurer, county clerk, clerk of court, and many others. The degree of control that the county board or manager exercises over the row officers varies by county. But the responsibilities of the officers commonly include legislative and executive duties.

There were about 11,000 city and county managers in the United States in the late 1990s. City managers earned an average of $70,600; county managers earned an average $86,700. They commonly had a mix of education and experience related to public administration, business, and politics. Employment of city and county managers will likely increase as more entities adopt that form of government.

FURTHER READING

National Association of Counties (NACo), 1999. Available from http://www.naco.org.

U.S. Bureau of the Census. *Statistical Abstract of the United States: 1999.* Washington: GPO.

U.S. Department of Labor. *Occupational Outlook Handbook, 1996-1997 Edition.* Washington. Available from http://stats.bls.gov/ocohome.htm.

U.S. Department of Labor. *Occupational Outlook Handbook, 1998-1999 Edition.* Washington, 1999. Available from http://stats.bls.gov/oco/ocos013.htm.

SIC 9199

GENERAL GOVERNMENT, NOT ELSEWHERE CLASSIFIED

This group covers government establishments primarily engaged in providing general support for government, which include personnel, auditing, procurement services, and building management services, and other general government establishments, which cannot be classified in other industries. Public finance is classified in **SIC 9311: Public Finance, Taxation, and Monetary Policy.**

NAICS Code(s)

921190 (All Other General Government)

The general government not elsewhere classified (NEC) division includes several offices and agencies associated with civil rights, civil service, accounting, personnel, purchasing, and supply. Three of the largest of these offices, all on the federal level, are the General Accounting Office (GAO), the Office of Personnel Management (OPM), and the General Services Administration (GSA).

The GSA establishes policy for and provides economical and efficient management of government property and records. It oversees the construction and operation of buildings; purchasing and distribution of services and supplies; disposal and use of property; management of general transportation, traffic, and communications; and management of automatic data processing resources. Established in 1949, this massive federal bureaucracy ballooned into about 20 separate Washington, D.C., units and programs, and 11 regional offices with thousands of workers by the mid-1990s. The administrator of the GSA is supported by his deputy and chief of staff. Offices under GSA control range from the Office of Child Care and Development Programs to the Office of Business, Industry, and Governmental Affairs and the Office of Emerging Technology. The 1999 estimated budget for the GSA was $328 million dollars.

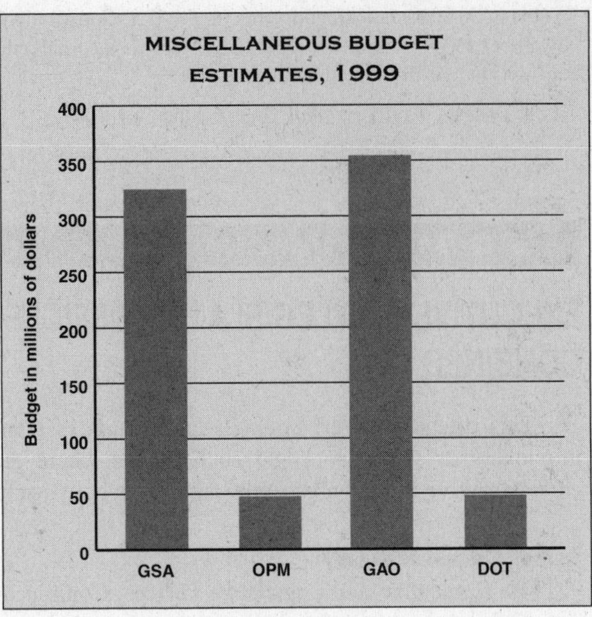

The OPM administers recruiting, examining, training, and promotion programs for federal workers. Its duty is to ensure that the federal government provides applicants and employees personnel services designed to develop and encourage the effectiveness of employees. The OPM also provides benefits to retired employees and their survivors. Established by the Civil Service Reform Act of 1978, the OPM inherited many of the responsibilities of the old Civil Service Commission. It is comprised of a director who oversees several offices, an Advisory committee, six functional groups (e.g. retirement and career entry), and five regional offices. OPM's estimated 1999 budget was $48 million.

The GAO is the investigate arm of Congress. Established in 1921 by the Budget and Accounting Act of 1921, it examines matters relating to the receipt and disbursement of public money. It supports Congress primarily by auditing and evaluating government programs and activities, usually at the request of house committees and members. The GAO is charged with finding inefficiency, waste, fraud, and illegality in government programs and bringing them to the attention of Congress. It also develops and prescribes accounting and fiscal policies, and provides legal counsel and services to Congress related to money and expenditures. The 1999 budget for the GAO was $354 million.

The Commission on Civil Rights, a smaller federal entity, collects and studies information on discrimination or denials of equal protection of the laws because of immutable physical characteristics, religion, or national origin. It was created in 1957 under the Civil Rights Act, and consists of 16 different offices, divisions, and units.

In addition to the GSA, OPM, GAO, and a few other separate entities, are numerous branches and divisions of large federal offices that conduct activities similar to the major offices. Likewise, numerous and varied counterpart offices and agencies operate in state and local governments. Although general government NEC offices account for a significant portion of overall government employment, prospects for job growth are slim given public pressure to eliminate new government spending.

At the state and local level, cumulative government expenditures on construction, equipment, land, and maintenance of existing structures came to $158.9 billion in 1996. State and local governments employed about 940,000 people in NEC administrative and otherwise unallocable positions during that year.

Further Reading

"Federal Government Budget by Agency." *The Political Reference Almanac,* March 1999. Published online at PoliSci.com, http://www.polisci.com/economy/agency.htm.

Office of the Federal Register. *The United States Government Manual 1996-1997.* Washington, D.C.: GPO, 1996.

U.S. Bureau of the Census. *Statistical Abstract of the United States: 1999.* Washington, D.C.: GPO, 1999.

U.S. Department of Labor. *Occupational Outlook Handbook.* Washington, D.C.: GPO, 1996.

SIC 9211

COURTS

This classification covers civilian courts of law. Military courts are classified in **SIC 9711: National Security.**

NAICS CODE(S)

922110 (Courts)

ORGANIZATION AND STRUCTURE

The law affects every aspect of modern society. It regulates the entire range of relationships among individuals, groups, businesses, and governments, defining rights and restrictions on conduct, communications, and transactions. Everything from paying taxes and entering into contracts to constructing buildings and punishing criminals is touched by the law. Even some aspects of personal relationships, such as divorce or child custody, are governed by law.

Because social needs and attitudes are continually changing, the law is also constantly changing. In many cases, the court system is the impetus for change. Judges play an important part in the development of the law by interpreting how particular laws apply to specific circumstances. When social mores have changed, judges—the interpreters of the law—can in effect rewrite the laws.

The court system is a vast network of federal, state, county, and local courts that provides a forum in which to interpret laws when disputes arise. Criminal matters are usually separated from civil matters, but a court of "general jurisdiction" may hear either. Issues that involve federal laws or the U.S. Constitution may be brought in federal district courts; matters between private parties are generally heard in a state's "circuit court" or court of common pleas. Courts may gain jurisdiction over foreign defendants who have committed a criminal or civil wrong while in this country. Likewise, through the Alien Tort Claims Act, illegal aliens may sue American companies for wrongs committed in other countries.

The court system encompasses a wide array of external support entities such as sentencing boards, Friends of the Court, probation and parole boards, local police and sheriff departments, state prosecutors and public defenders, lawyers, public service and community organizations, law schools, correctional institutions, and often, social services. Conversely, within a courtroom, there are bailiffs, court officers, court reporters, administrative staff and, importantly, the judge's clerk (a misnomer, as the clerk is usually a graduate law student or a full attorney, depending upon the level of court).

Judges. Judges oversee the legal process and resolve civil disputes or determine guilt in criminal cases for which there is no jury. They also determine the procedural process to be followed in the courts and provide instructions to juries in cases for which a jury is seated. Judges are responsible for assuring that trials are conducted fairly and that individual legal rights are safeguarded—particularly in criminal cases. Judges typically listen to the attorneys for each party while they argue their cases, examine witnesses, and present other evidence. Judges make rulings on the admissibility of evidence, methods of questioning witnesses, and legal validity of disputes between opposing attorneys.

Judges are also responsible for conducting pretrial hearings and other types of formal hearings. They may determine whether there is sufficient evidence to merit a criminal trial, establish whether bail will be allowed for criminal defendants, and set conditions for the release of an accused until trial. They may also rule whether certain evidence can be used at trial and whether television cameras will be allowed in the courtroom. Judges also decide whether a right to a trial by jury exists, and they make sentencing decisions.

Most judges have experience as lawyers prior to joining the bench. They are employed by local and county governments, state governments, and the federal government. Local judges are usually elected in local elections. State supreme court justices are appointed by the governor. Federal judges are appointed for life by the president, with the consent of the Senate. The prestige associated with being a judge fuels keen competition for these coveted positions.

Kinds of Courts. The Constitution of the United States divides the federal government into three branches of government: executive, legislative, and judicial. The executive branch includes the president, his cabinet, and certain federal agencies. The legislative branch is comprised of the U.S. Congress and certain federal agencies. The court system falls under the judicial branch, which is responsible for interpreting the laws passed by the legislative branch. While the judicial branch is the smallest of the three branches, its power is significant.

The court system in the United States includes federal courts, state courts, and county or municipal courts. Each of these courts serves a particular purpose. In some cases, a litigant must go to a particular court; in others, he

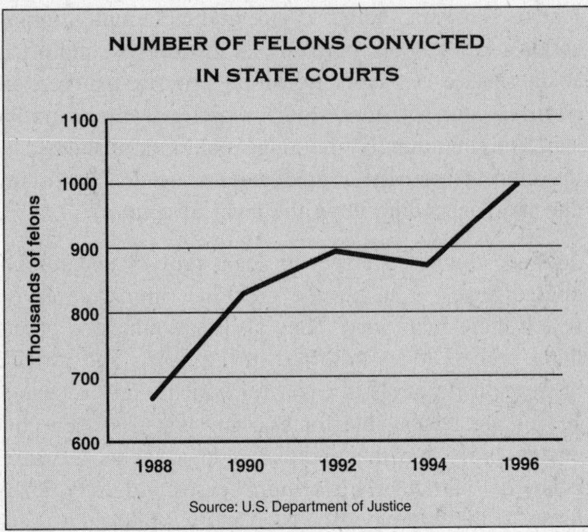

may, to some degree, choose his ''forum.'' Court systems are generally three-tiered, whether federal or state. First, there are the trial courts, then the courts of appeals and, finally, the supreme courts (the ultimate appellate courts).

The federal court system begins with the District Court, where trials are held for cases involving federal issues or where the parties to the case are from different states. If someone loses a case in District Court, he or she can appeal to the Court of Appeals in the appropriate district. The highest rung of the judicial branch is the U.S. Supreme Court—a body composed of nine justices, each appointed for life by the president. One justice serves as the chief justice.

The U.S. Supreme Court has discretionary authority to decide which cases it will hear. Cases come from more than 100 federal courts and scores of state courts. The court accepts only those cases that it believes are of significant public concern—issues like abortion, racial integration, and school prayer have all been decided by the Supreme Court. Nearly all cases reach the court by a petition for certiorari (a legal document to call up another court's records), and the vast majority are denied. In fact, no petition is even considered unless at least one justice believes it important enough, at which point at least four justices must vote in favor of granting the petition for the case to be heard.

Once a case has been accepted for review, the attorneys for the parties submit to the court written arguments known as briefs. They can then make their arguments in a public courtroom. The justices reflect upon the matter and hold weekly conferences to debate and discuss their ultimate decision. Only the justices are present during the conference in order to maintain complete secrecy until the decision is announced. After the conference, the chief justice makes assignments about who will write each opinion. However, if the chief justice votes with the minority, the most senior justice who votes with the majority will make the assignment.

The state court system operates both a civil court system, for civil disputes, and a criminal court system. The most minor civil suits begin at the local level with small claims court. This is a local court, usually serving a particular county, in which those with claims up to a certain amount of money (typically $3,000-$5,000), can go to court and have a judge decide their case without the cost or assistance of an attorney. In fact, attorneys are usually not allowed to represent the parties in a small claims action. The next level of state court is the municipal or justice court. Typically, this court covers a county-wide area in which the county is divided into judicial districts. Municipal courts usually hold preliminary hearings for criminal matters to determine whether there is enough evidence for a trial to proceed, conduct trials for misdemeanor violations, and hear civil actions up to the jurisdictional limit, which varies widely. The monetary limit for these courts is higher than small claims court, but usually lower than superior court, which is the next rung on the ladder.

Superior courts or circuit courts—generally one in each county—are where the majority of cases are heard, including felony trials, juvenile hearings, probate proceedings, divorce actions, and most other civil lawsuits, including business disputes, personal injury actions, and employment litigation. If a citizen loses a case in one of these trial courts, he or she typically can appeal to the court of appeals. If one still isn't satisfied with the decision, the highest state court is usually the state supreme court. State Supreme Court justices, appointed by the governor, review decisions of the court of appeal at their discretion, and are not obligated to accept all cases for review. However, all capital offense convictions are automatically appealed to the Supreme Court. After that, the court of last resort is the U.S. Supreme Court, which hears only those cases the court feels are of great public concern.

Litigants who do not wish to wait for their day in court may consider ''alternative dispute resolution,'' such as binding arbitration or court-directed mediation. In most state courts, less than ten percent of cases actually go to trial, by far the majority of them having been settled or adjudicated by alternative means. In 1998 the American Arbitration Association adopted measures to assist consumers who wished to arbitrate their claims by establishing a protocol which helps to equalize the respective parties: member companies who are being sued must pay $350.00 of the $500.00 arbitration fee.

BACKGROUND AND DEVELOPMENT

One of the first laws enacted by the first U.S. Congress was the Judiciary Act of 1789, which established a federal court system. It was somewhat of a duplication of the state court system, but the reasoning for the introduction of a federal system was sound. At that time, there was great fear of prejudice by the citizens of one state against another. It was believed that federal courts would assure out-of-state litigants a forum that would be free from local bias.

A landmark legal decision studied by law students across America is *Marbury v. Madison,* decided in 1803. One cannot study the court system of today without understanding the historical underpinnings of the entire system, for it was this legal decision upon which the system was founded. *Marbury* involved a struggle between different branches of government and found the judicial branch to wield the greatest power. The Supreme Court ruled that the judiciary had the power to review the constitutionality of a congressional law. This meant that while the legislative branch could pass a law, the judicial branch could review it and decide whether it was constitutional and how it should be applied to particular circumstances. This made the judicial branch the ''final arbiter'' of what the law is.

Another landmark decision affecting the court system was handed down in 1819, when the *McCulloch v. Maryland* decision established the supremacy of federal law over state law. It also enunciated a doctrine of implied powers for the federal government that has become the cornerstone of federal power and one of the most basic parts of American constitutional law.

The American court system of the late twentieth century operates, at least in theory, much the same way it always has. Little has changed in the way of formal structure and organization. However, across the nation, particularly in major metropolitan areas, the courts have become clogged with a morass of litigation, making it difficult for the system to keep up with demand. In many large cities, civil lawsuits can take as long as five years to go to trial. In the criminal arena, some accused must wait for periods of a year—or more—for their day in court. As a result, many prosecutors have increased the use of plea bargaining, wherein the accused pleads guilty, perhaps to a lesser charge, in order to try to alleviate the backlog of cases in the courts. In civil matters, divorce and child custody proceedings have caused significant backups on the courts' dockets, causing many state courts to establish separate divisions for ''domestic matters.'' Even the country's highest court, the U.S. Supreme Court, was dragged into controversy in 1999, when the National Association for the Advancement of Colored People (NAACP) and other African-American groups publicly denounced the high court's low representation of minority law clerks working for the judges.

CURRENT CONDITIONS

Between 1995 and 1999 the American public witnessed two major court events that changed perceptions of the legal system forever. First was the trial and ultimate acquittal of football celebrity O.J. Simpson for the murders of his wife, Nicole Simpson, and Ronald Goldman, who was with her at the time. Second was the televised impeachment trial of President Bill Clinton, also acquitted, for alleged perjury involving his illicit affair with White House intern Monica Lewinsky. In 1999, concerned that the general public believed trial outcome was more dependent upon money and ''who-you-knew'' than on truth and merit, the National Center for State Courts (NCSC) conducted a national survey, funded by the Hearst Corporation, to gauge public trust in court systems. The results were not altogether surprising:

- Americans are generally split on whether they believe the media's portrayal of courts is accurate.
- A full 81 percent of Americans believe that politics influences court decisions.
- Americans resoundingly (by 87 percent) believe that having a lawyer significantly adds to the cost of going to court, and a surprising six of ten Americans believe they could represent themselves in court if necessary.
- Most Americans (79 percent) believe that judges are honest and fair in deciding cases.
- Americans overwhelmingly believe that cases are not being resolved in a timely manner, and most give an ''average'' grade to court performance in their communities.

A major court trend in the 1990s was the proliferation of ''mass tort litigation,'' a term applied to multistate class actions by large groups of similarly situated litigants who have suffered common injuries: breast implant, tobacco, and asbestos cases are a few. In 1998 and 1999, after nearly a decade in court, the largest of the breast implant manufacturers and tobacco companies respectively entered into settlement agreements coordinated by several courts that had originally ''joined'' the cases.

An issue among state legislators in the 1990s was the enactment of laws establishing monetary ceilings or ''caps'' on the amount litigants could be awarded in personal injury court cases. This trend was abruptly halted in 1998 and 1999, when several states' high courts overturned the laws, finding them unconstitutional and violative of a person's fundamental right to have ''his day in court'' and be compensated for his actual loss, without limit.

By the end of the twentieth century, the highest courts of the land were still the arbiters of social, legal, and political disagreement, hearing and deciding issues unthinkable in earlier times: whether a woman may still be impregnated with frozen sperm if she is now divorced from the sperm donor; whether school districts may be sued by the parents of children harassed by other students; whether death by lethal injection constitutes "cruel and unusual punishment," or whether gun manufacturers may be sued for their roles in promoting violent crimes.

AMERICA AND THE WORLD

In 1998 the International Criminal Court, which was the world's first permanent war crimes tribunal, was established in the Hague (Netherlands). Created by international treaty and adopted by 60 nations, it was empowered to try cases of human rights violations and aggression. The court parallels the International Court of Justice (ICJ), under charter of the United Nations (UN) at the Peace Palace in The Hague. The ICJ hears matters involving international law and also renders advisory opinions. While these judicial efforts portended a significant international desire for a global "Big Brother," their enforcement powers are more specious than substantive: how do nations punish other nations for war crimes? Historically, trade bans and economic punishment have not worked and have often resulted in black market proliferation. Notwithstanding, the growing sentiment at the turn of the twenty-first century was for commonality and universal application of humanitarian law among civilized nations.

FURTHER READING

Berkman, Harvey. "10 Months after 'Koon,' Sentence Guidelines Intact." *The National Law Journal,* 14 April 1997.

"The Birth of a New World Court." *Maclean's,* 27 July 1998.

"How the Public Views the State Courts." Report from the National Center for State Courts, 1999. Available from http://www.ncsc.dni.us/PTC/results/nms4.htm.

Leo, John. "See Jane Sue Dick." *U.S. News & World Report,* 7 June 1999.

McMenamin, Brigid. "Bring Me Your Tired, Your Poor, Your Litigious." *Forbes,* 15 November 1999.

"No Suits for You." *U.S. News & World Report,* 7 June 1999.

"Note on the International Court of Justice," October 1999. Available from http://www.icj-cji.org.

SIC 9221

POLICE PROTECTION

This industry classification includes government establishments primarily engaged in law enforcement, traffic safety, police, and other activities related to the enforcement of the law and preservation of order. The National Guard and military police are classified in **SIC 9711: National Security.** Private establishments primarily engaged in law enforcement, traffic safety, police, and other activities related to law enforcement are classified in **SIC 7381: Detective, Guard, and Armored Car Services.** Government establishments primarily engaged in prosecution are classified in **SIC 9222: Legal Counsel and Prosecution.** Government establishments primarily engaged in the collection of law enforcement statistics are classified in **SIC 9229: Public Order and Safety, Not Elsewhere Classified.**

NAICS CODE(S)

922120 (Police Protection)

ORGANIZATION AND STRUCTURE

Police protection encompasses a wide range of protective services, involving many different municipal, state, and federal government agencies. These agencies often have overlapping authority, creating a vast network of law enforcement functions. The broadest authority possible is given to certain federal agencies.

Local police officers have many responsibilities and work in major metropolitan areas, small towns, and rural areas. They may investigate crimes, arbitrate domestic disputes, administer first aid, direct traffic, or investigate fires. Some areas use police on foot, bicycle, or motor patrol, while many other officers have desk assignments wherein the voluminous paperwork required for law enforcement is completed. Others may be assigned to special units such as mounted police who patrol on horseback, rescue teams, canine corps, helicopter patrol, or youth gang detail. Some officers become experts of another sort, working in a laboratory doing chemical or microscopic analysis, firearms identification, or handwriting or fingerprint identification. Nearly all police officers must write reports and maintain police records.

Most police organizations have a chain of command similar to that commonly utilized by American military organizations. In large cities, sergeants, lieutenants, and captains direct the work of squads or companies of officers. Ranking officers report to a chief of police or a police commissioner. In small towns, however, the chief of police naturally commands a small force; in some instances, he or she may be the only officer in town.

Generally, local police departments are covered by civil service regulations that require applicants to pass a test for the job. Because of the physical and character demands of the job, applicants must pass a rigorous physical and psychological examination, as well as a background investigation. Each promotion to a higher rank may also require passage of an additional civil service examination.

County sheriffs generally cover rural areas or the outskirts of an incorporated city. In many cases, they are the only local police force and, in others, they supplement the city police force. They often work as bailiffs, keeping order in courtrooms, and may work as guards in county jails. Many sheriffs' departments have fewer than 10 uniformed officers.

State police officers patrol highways to enforce traffic laws. They also provide aid to stranded motorists, call for emergency roadside services, and provide traffic control when road repairs are being made and during special events. State police have authority to enforce criminal laws and give traffic citations in local communities away from the highways, in most cases. They may also assist local police in crime investigations or provide crowd control during civil disturbances.

Federal law enforcement efforts include a vast network of special agents that work for various federal agencies and investigate particular types of criminal activity. Federal agents wield much authority because of their nationwide jurisdiction—they can cross state lines and negotiate with law representatives of foreign countries. Border Patrol agents are a good example of federal law enforcement efforts.

The Federal Bureau of Investigation (FBI) employs special agents who investigate serious crimes such as bank robberies, kidnapping, terrorism, organized crime, theft of government property, and espionage, among other transgressions. The FBI is one of the most technologically advanced law enforcement agencies in the country, and it concentrates its efforts on the most serious offenses. It also is called in to investigate crimes committed across state lines, where local police are unable to extend their authority. Agents for the FBI are graduates of accredited law schools or have accounting degrees or foreign-language skills.

Like the FBI, the Drug Enforcement Agency (DEA), the U.S. Marshals Service, and the Immigration and Naturalization Service (INS) are part of the U.S. Justice Department. DEA agents conduct investigations of illegal drug activity, often working undercover. They also may be involved in preparing documents to justify the seizure of financial and other assets gained by illegal activity. U.S. Marshals serve criminal warrants issued by federal judges and are often responsible for the safety and transport of jurors and prisoners. INS agents enforce laws regulating the entry of aliens into the country.

Several other law enforcement agencies are within the U.S. Department of the Treasury. For example, U.S. Customs agents enforce laws concerning smuggling of goods into the country, searching for banned items in tourists' belongings and among the cargo of ships and planes. Agents of the Bureau of Alcohol, Tobacco, and Firearms (ATF) investigate a range of illegal activity, from suspected illegal sales of guns, to underpayment of taxes by liquor importers, to illegal transport of cigarettes. Internal Revenue Service (IRS) agents investigate evasion of payment of federal taxes by U.S. taxpayers. The U.S. Secret Service not only protects the President, the Vice-President, their families, and visiting foreign dignitaries, but also investigates counterfeiting and the forgery of government checks or bonds.

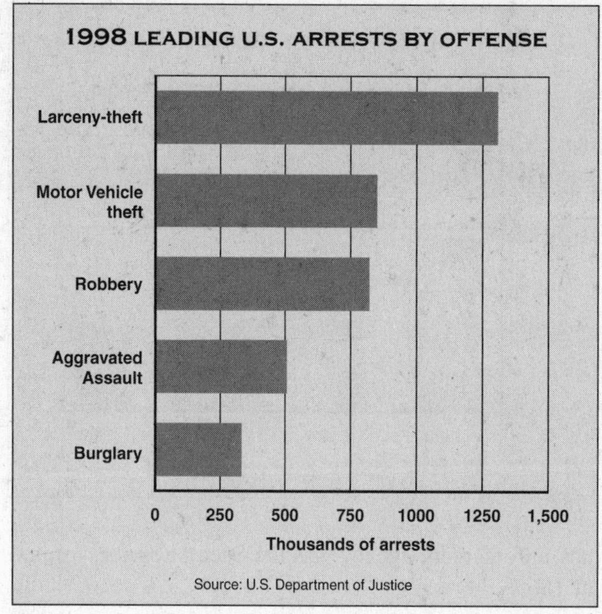

BACKGROUND AND DEVELOPMENT

The U.S. police system has its roots in England. The city of New York was so impressed with the efficiency of the London Metropolitan Police that it sent a delegation to London to study the department in 1833. The result was the formation of the New York City Police Department in 1844, the first of its kind in the United States. It was followed by the establishment of the Boston Police Department in 1850. Americans didn't adopt the English system entirely, however. The English and European systems favored strong, central government control. In contrast, Americans favored local control—the early settlers were suspicious of any type of centralized government control. Local autonomy was fiercely defended, which is probably why we still maintain local police forces.

The New England states became centers of commerce and industry, with a municipal-type government and a locally elected constable to enforce the laws. In the southern part of the country, which was more agricultural and rural, the county form of government was more suitable, and the county sheriff became the preferred law enforcement officer. The first state police agency was the Texas Rangers, created in 1835, and the first federal

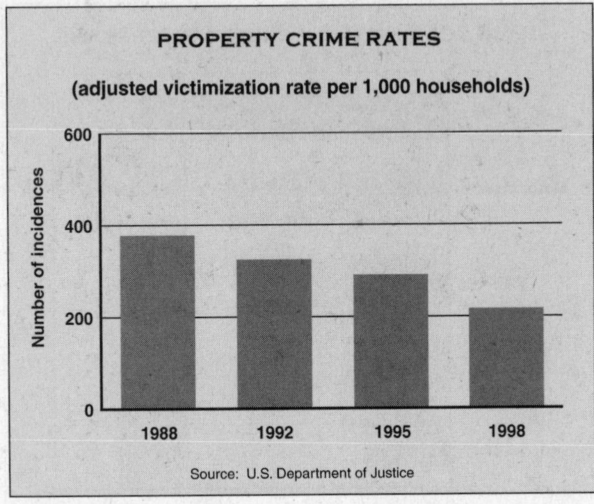

law enforcement agency was the Secret Service, formed in 1865.

CURRENT CONDITIONS

On July 24, 1998, Americans were shocked to learn that two policemen were gunned down in the line of duty while guarding our nation's Capitol in Washington, D.C. Thus, concern for protecting the protectors was justifiably heightened. In 1999, ten-year old Stephanie Taylor of Oceanside, California, made national news when she raised $3,000 to help purchase bulletproof vests for the city's local police dogs. In addition, the Police Executive Research Forum (PERF) remained very active in legislative lobbying on all matters involving gun control, a politically-charged issue for all American following a deadly rash of school shootings from 1996-1999 that killed dozens of students in various cities around the country.

Notwithstanding, stories of alleged police brutality continued to make headline news as the century came to a close. One of the most controversial stories involved New York police officer Justin Volpe who, in 1999, confessed to beating and sodomizing Haitian immigrant Abner Louima. Another politically charged matter was the string of appeals filed on behalf of death-row inmate Mumia Abu-Jamal, indicted for murdering a policeman back in the 1980s.

On a national level, with the booming stock market of 1998 and 1999, there was an epidemic rise in securities and investment fraud. In 1998, the FBI reported 865 securities fraud indictments and informations, with seizures of nearly $40 million and total restitution of over $1.2 billion. By 1999, Internet-related stock fraud was costing investors $10 billion per year. With an estimated 200 million Internet users in the year 2000, the number of online investors is expected to triple by 2003.

Another big crime market in the latter 1990s was a major increase in ''product counterfeiting,'' the unauthorized duplication and mass production of ''bootlegged'' videotapes, sound recordings, and computer software. In such matters, local police agencies often coordinate with the FBI in scam operations directed at containing the spread of this black market. The 1998 bombing of the United States Embassy in Nairobi, Kenya, the October 1999 crash of Egyptair Flight 990, and a rash of bombings at abortion clinics also resulted in the cohesive networking of local, state, and federal police authorities to combine resources for investigation and information processing.

Police agencies continually undergo intense changes on several fronts. Many local agencies are adopting a ''community policing'' approach in which officers build close, ongoing relationships with residents and neighborhood organizations. The intention is to establish trust, solve problems before they lead to crime, and draw on citizens as a resource for crime prevention. Also, many police agencies and departments have secured Internet Web sites that provide information to the general public about police work.

WORKFORCE

Police, detectives, and special agents held nearly 700,000 jobs in the late 1990s. Most were employed by local government agencies, as there are about 17,000 state and local police agencies in the country.

Job stress is common for police officers, whose work brings them in contact with some of society's worst members and conditions, sometimes in life-threatening circumstances. In 1995, 162 officers died in the line of duty, the highest number since 1989. By 1998, that number had come down to 137 police officers and detectives, but 38 of the 137 were homicide victims.

The Clinton Administration's efforts to put 100,000 more police officers on the street by the end of the century was readily accepted as good politics by a weary America.

RESEARCH AND TECHNOLOGY

Anyone who had not heard of ''DNA testing'' prior to the O.J. Simpson trial and President Clinton's impeachment trial probably learned more than he or she ever wanted to know about it during those few months of trial. Taxpayer dollars continue to help bring police agencies up to state-of-the-art technology in crime prevention and detection. New ways of identifying persons based on biological characteristics, such as ''biologic fingerprinting,'' have evolved, as have electronic devices for pinpointing an officer's location. Additionally, in 1999, many police agencies around the country started implementing test devices for remote gauging of blood alcohol levels. Using this technology, persons on probation for substance abuse offenses could breathe into their specially equipped telephones from their homes, and their blood-alcohol levels would be electronically measured and transmitted to local police authorities.

FURTHER READING

Anderson, David C. ''Crime Stoppers.'' *The New York Times Magazine,* 9 February 1997.

Bureau of Labor Statistics. ''Fatal Occupational Injuries by Occupation and Major Event or Exposure,'' 1998. Available from http://stats.bls. gov.news.release/cfoi.t02.htm.

''Case History: Mumia Abu-Jamal,'' 1998. Available from http:// www.danielfaulkner.com/Pages/casehistory.html.

Community Policing Consortium. ''About Community Policing,'' 1999. Available from http://www.communitypolicing.org/abtcp.html.

''Fulfilling Promise to Put New Police on Streets.'' *Crime Control Digest,* 10 January 1997.

Law Enforcement Links Directory, 1999. Available from http://www.leolinks.com/search/Law_ Enforcement/Sheriffs_ Departments/ index.shtml.

''Legislative Issues.'' The Police Executive Research Forum, 1999. Available from http://www.policeforum.org/home/legislative.html.

''NCIC 2000: Linking It All Together,'' 15 February 1996. Available from http://www.fbi.gov/2000/2ku1n1.htm.

''Operation Counter Copy,'' 1999. Available from http://www.fbi.gov/majcases/copy/copy.htm.

''Operation Investnet,'' 1999. Available from http://www.fbi.gov/majcases/investnet/investnet.htm.

Pilant, Lois. ''High-Technology Solutions.'' *The Police Chief,* May 1996.

''Police Must Be Held Accountable.'' *Newsweek,* 21 June 1999.

''Vested Interest.'' *People,* 26 July 1999.

SIC 9222

LEGAL COUNSEL AND PROSECUTION

This classification includes government establishments primarily engaged in providing legal counsel to or prosecution for their governments, and operation or administration of crime prevention programs. Government establishments primarily engaged in the collection of criminal justice statistics are classified in **SIC 9229: Public Order and Safety, Not Elsewhere Classified.**

NAICS CODE(S)

922130 (Legal Counsel and Prosecution)

Criminal practice and procedure is an area of law which encompasses both private and public employment. As further discussed, those accused of a crime may hire private legal counsel for their defense, or if they qualify as indigent, may request the trial court to appoint counsel for them (''public defenders''). Conversely, all prosecuting and ''district'' attorneys are public employees at the local, state, or federal level. This is because all crimes, even if committed against individuals, actually are violations of local, state, or federal laws. According to U.S. Census Bureau statistics, there were at least 419,000 judicial and legal employees working at all levels of government in 1997, including more than 400 federal magistrate judges. Magistrates render findings of probable cause, order warrants, and often conduct criminal misdemeanor trials.

Defense attorneys may represent clients accused of nearly any crime, including ''white-collar'' offenses such as fraud, stock manipulation, or tax evasion. Many defense attorneys work for a local office of the public defender—a state or county government agency established to provide legal representation for the accused who cannot afford to hire a private lawyer. Since the U.S. Constitution guarantees the right to adequate legal counsel, many people use this service. In fact, some offices are overwhelmed by the number of people in need of legal representation, in which case the court appoints an attorney from a private law firm—compensated at a given rate at government expense—to represent the accused. Defense attorneys also come from private law firms or from legal aid clinics established to provide legal services to the poor. Finally, public interest organizations, such as the American Civil Liberties Union (ACLU) and the National Association for the Advancement of Colored People (NAACP), to name a few, sometimes employ lawyers to represent clients in criminal court proceedings.

Prosecuting attorneys may work for federal government offices such as the Justice Department or the U.S. Attorney's Office, for state offices of the attorney general, or for a city or county in the office of the district attorney. The majority of prosecuting attorneys work at the county level as deputy district attorneys, representing the government against those accused of violating state and local laws, including the initiation of proceedings against inebriates, the mentally ill, narcotics addicts, and nonsupport of minor children cases.

The district attorney also is the legal advisor to the county grand jury, which is utilized to hear testimony and examine evidence for the purpose of determining whether an indictment will be pursued against the accused. District attorneys often maintain their own staff of investigators to pursue crimes of greater severity in efforts to assure a more successful prosecution. District attorneys may operate their own intelligence units to combat organized crime.

The Justice Department and U.S. attorney conduct investigations and prosecutions of serious federal crimes, such as political assassination, organized crime and racketeering, and crimes that take place on federal lands such as national parks, museums, and federal government buildings. Drug trafficking also falls within their jurisdiction. In 1999, there were 93 U.S. attorneys (appointed by the president of the United States) serving throughout the United States and its territories/possessions.

For lawyers interested in government service, job prospects may become brighter. Public concerns about crime and the administration of justice may lead to increased funding to payroll additional government-employed lawyers and judges. Government lawyers generally enjoy greater job security than lawyers in private practice, but may earn significantly less, at least in the early stages of a career.

By contrast, government lawyers frequently are given greater responsibility at an earlier stage of their career than their counterparts in private practice. They sometimes handle trials for significant criminal prosecutions early in their career, often battling skilled and prominent private lawyers in the courtroom. In addition, many government prosecutors and defense attorneys utilize the valuable experience gained through government service to successfully pursue careers in private law firms, elective office, or judgeships.

Prosecutors and defense attorneys primarily are employed by city and county government entities, as well as state and federal agencies. Some legal positions also are available in the armed forces. The majority of the lawyers who work for the government do so at the local level where judicial and legal employees outnumber their federal counterparts more than four to one. Most of the lawyers working for the federal government are employed by the departments of Justice, Treasury, and Defense, and advance through the civil service system.

Further Reading

American Bar Association. Chicago: American Bar Association. Available fromfrom http://www.aba.org. 1999.

U.S. Bureau of Labor Statistics. Available from http://stats.bls.gov/oco/ocos053.htm.

U.S. Census Bureau. *Statistical Abstract of the United States: 1999.* Washington: GPO, 1999.

U.S. Department of Justice, Bureau of Justice Statistics. *Comparing Case Processing Statistics.* Washington: U.S. Department of Justice, 1998. Available from http://www.usdoj.gov/usao.org.

SIC 9223

CORRECTIONAL INSTITUTIONS

This classification covers government establishments primarily engaged in the confinement and correction of offenders sentenced by a legal court. Private establishments primarily engaged in the confinement and correction of offenders sentences by a court are classified in **SIC 8744: Facilities Support Management Services.** Half-way houses for ex-convicts and homes for delinquents are classified in **SIC 8361: Residential Care.**

NAICS Code(s)

922140 (Correctional Institutions)

Industry Snapshot

According to a 1998 report released by the U.S. Justice Department, the incarceration rate in federal and state prisons and local jails has nearly doubled in the last decade, increasing by five to seven percent, or 60,000 new inmates per year. The report was updated in early 1999, at which time statistics indicated that as of December 1998, the overall prison population ratio constituted 627 inmates per 100,000 Americans. The prison rate was growing at a rate 13 times faster than that of the general population. Despite a slowing growth rate (down to 4.8 percent in 1998), America's prisons were filled to 97 percent capacity, notwithstanding the addition of 26,000 new beds the year before. By early 1999, federal and state prisons were operating at from 13 to 27 percent ''above'' capacity.

Americans are willing to pay for more correctional institutions, at a cost between $25,000 and $30,000 per prisoner per year in 1998 (not counting the burgeoning cost to the public for conviction appeals). Crime rates have steadily declined since peaking in 1991, although multiple reasons for the decline must be factored in. One has been the control of recidivism, or crimes repeatedly committed by the same criminal. A 1996 report revealed that as many as 80 percent of those released from prison return within one year. One in every three violent crimes is committed by someone on parole, probation, or pretrial release. In 1998, parole violators returned to prison increased by 39 percent.

Organization and Structure

The correctional system in America, just like the government, is operated on four different levels: federal, state, county, and city. Each has jurisdiction over certain areas, but they also have some overlapping zones of responsibility. In 1999, there were approximately 3,300 jails in the country, by far the majority of them under the auspices of county governments.

Federal Prisons. The federal prison system, administered by the Bureau of Prisons, includes approximately 40 institutions designed to house men and women who have, for the most part, violated federal laws. Federal prisons are among the most heavily guarded in the nation and provide maximum security. Begun in 1891, the federal prison system was formed when Congress passed legislation to establish three federal penitentiaries at Leavenworth, Kansas; McNeil's Island, off the coast of Washington state; and Atlanta, Georgia. Each remain a part of the federal prison system today. These institutions were intended to house those convicted of serious felonies—murder, rape, kidnapping, treason, and the like. These were generally considered to be the most serious of crimes and the criminals were considered to be the most violent and dangerous. The prisons built to house them were to provide the maximum amount of security against escapes, riots, or other disturbances. They were generally built away from cities and communities, often in rural areas, for few citizens want prisons located in their neighborhood.

But not all of the correctional institutions operated by the federal prison system are maximum security facilities. Medium security prisons exist in which prisoners may be afforded greater freedom of movement. Prisoners who have demonstrated good behavior may, in some cases, be transferred from a maximum security prison to a medium security facility or even a minimum security facility. At these facilities, often referred to as "country clubs," inmates are not subject to constant surveillance and are often housed in open, campus-like structures. They may have lounges, libraries, outdoor recreational facilities, and sleeping rooms rather than traditional cells. Golf courses, tennis courts, and swimming pools are not unheard of at these institutions, which house non-violent offenders. Those found guilty of such white-collar crimes as forgery, embezzlement, and tax evasion are often sent to minimum security correctional institutions.

Least restrictive of all federal institutions are the pre-release centers in metropolitan areas across the country. These centers were established to function as halfway houses to hold prisoners nearly due to be released. Prisoners housed at pre-release centers may hold jobs in the community, visit family, and receive counseling to prepare them for life on the outside.

The Bureau of Prisons was responsible for more than 45 prison facilities nationwide. Federal detention centers in New York and Arizona house those individuals awaiting trial on federal charges. Additionally, separate detention centers have been established to detain those suspected of entering the country illegally.

State Prisons. As for prison systems run by the states, each state has its own uniquely run prison system adapted to meet its own needs and the demands of its citizens. For example, states with expanding urban populations have experienced different crime problems than those in rural states.

City and County Jails. The city and county correctional facilities are known as jails, rather than prisons. There are literally thousands of local jails in cities and counties around the nation. These local jails include police precinct lockups where a person accused of a crime may spend a few hours, a few days, or several months. There is a technical distinction between prisons and jails. Prisons are for those people who have been convicted of a crime, typically a felony. Jails are generally reserved for those who have been accused of a crime and are awaiting trial or for those who are convicted of minor offenses, such as misdemeanors, where the period of incarceration is less than one year.

Background and Development

Punitive imprisonment has its roots as far back as ancient Rome, Egypt, China, and Babylon, and was firmly established in Europe during the Renaissance. But in many early societies, offenders were dealt with otherwise—exile, banishment, and barbaric physical punishments. The jail, the workhouse, the reformatory, and the convict ship all antedate the prison as we know it.

Throughout the eighteenth and nineteenth century, it was the Northern states that led the way in prison development in the United States. In the 1820s, Northern cities such as New York attracted large numbers of homeless boys and girls. Many of the older ones turned to crime to support themselves, so in 1825 New York became the first American city to open a House of Refuge for delinquent juveniles. Boston and Philadelphia quickly followed suit. Although the original House of Refuge was a city institution, it became the precursor to statewide juvenile institution systems.

After the Civil War, regional differences between the North and South became even more pronounced. In the South, the land was devastated and the economy was poor. Southern states had little time, money, energy or inclination to devote resources to their prison system, so the earlier custom of prisoners paying for their own upkeep was revived. Prisoners in the South were expected to earn their way by being thrust into labor-intensive work farms.

Clapped into leg irons and linked together with heavy chains—hence the term "chain gang"—prisoners throughout the South repaid the states for their room and board by building public roads and chopping brush near highways. Twelve-hour workdays were common and discipline was often enforced with a whip and a gun. Some prisoners were hired out to private companies as contract

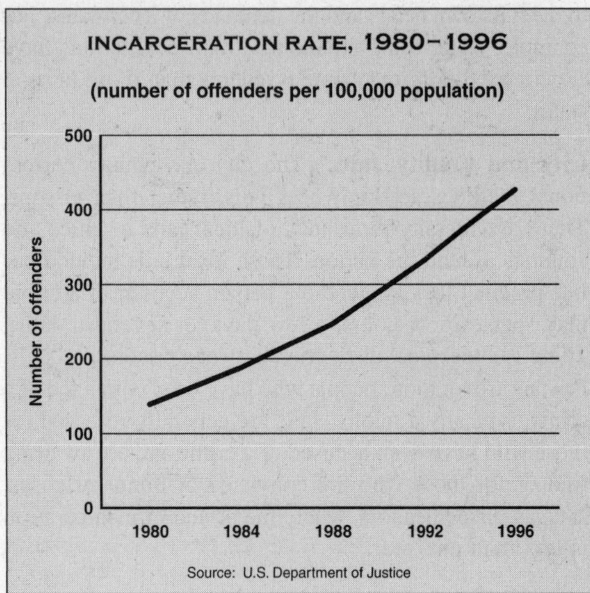

labor. The business owner assumed responsibility for clothing, housing, and feeding the prisoners, in exchange for the hard labor of the inmates. Some contractors saved money by nearly starving the prisoners and drove the men to work extremely hard. Contract labor and chain gangs were eventually outlawed.

As the number of female felons began to grow, Congress appropriated funds to construct the first federal prison for women in 1925—the Federal Reformatory for Women in West Virginia. These early federal prisons would prove to be only the beginning for the federal prison system and the 1920s saw a rapid increase in the male prison population, due in some measure to the introduction of the automobile and Prohibition. Auto theft became an increasingly common occurrence, and Congress made it a federal crime to transport a stolen car across state lines. Prohibition, which halted the legal manufacture, sale and transportation of alcoholic beverages, inspired bootleggers to commit many federal law violations. It was the crime wave during the Prohibition era in the 1920s that led to reorganization of the Federal Bureau of Investigation and creation of the Bureau of Prisons, which Congress established in 1930, to oversee the entire federal prison system.

Throughout the latter half of the twentieth century, the ideological emphasis has shifted away from the punishment methodology towards rehabilitation of offenders. The assumptions of rehabilitation point to forces such as poverty, unstable family life, and limited mental capacity as producing maladjusted individuals who have difficulty conforming to society's rules. Rehabilitation proponents argue that given proper treatment and social services—educational, vocational, and psychiatric—the criminal can be remolded into a well-adjusted and productive member of society.

Since World War II, the pace at which treatment and rehabilitative services have been offered to prisoners has quickened. In the 1990s vocational and educational training, individual psychological counseling, group therapy, halfway houses, work release programs, and other behavior modification programs have all been assimilated into the modern penal system. But the rehabilitative model has come under increased scrutiny. Some wonder whether its working, with the ever-increasing numbers of violent offenders in our society. Others wonder whether the causes of crime can ever really be diagnosed and treated. Critics point out that California, a state where the rehabilitative model has been firmly entrenched, has one of the highest recidivism rates in the country.

CURRENT CONDITIONS

While people in their twenties comprise only about 20 percent or less of the U.S. population, they represent more than 40 percent of convicted state felons. Of all convicted felons, roughly 51 percent are white, 48 percent are black, and 1 percent are of other races. In 1998, there were more than 84,000 incarcerated females, substantially outnumbered by approximately 1.2 million males. Notwithstanding, the ''growth'' rate for female inmates was higher (6.5 percent, compared to 4.7 percent for males). Drug offenders made up almost one-third of all felony convictions in state courts.

According to 1998 reports, the nation's jails processed more than 22 million people, who represented more of a transient inmate population than that found in prisons. Jail populations are typically comprised of many short-term offenders such as drunk drivers, domestic violence offenders, drug addicts, and weapons violators. At any given time, there may be half a million or less persons incarcerated in jails, compared to estimates ranging from 1.3 to 2.0 million federal prisoners serving lengthier sentences.

A controversial issue on the rise by the close of the century was the trend to ''privatize'' prisons, i.e., to house excess prisoners in privately-owned, for-profit facilities. Several states were even negotiating with neighboring states to take their excess prisoners. By the end of 1998, more than 132,300 beds in 186 facilities were under contract or construction in the United States, the United Kingdom, and Australia. Nationally, Texas and California had the greatest number of ''private secure adult facilities'' under contract. It should be mentioned that in 1998, California had the worst prison overcrowding problem in the nation.

Another sensitive, and disturbing, issue was the increasingly violent nature of juvenile crimes. From 1997 to 1999, America reeled from news that young pre-teens were gunning down schoolmates, murdering their parents, and engaging in violent acts of animal abuse. Of particular controversy was the varied treatment of juvenile offenders within the criminal justice system, as different laws applied in each state. Whether to try violent juveniles as adults and place them in prison, or to consider their ages as mitigating factors, carried heated arguments on both sides and across all strata of the academic and professional communities. Because society has not been successful in ''rehabilitating'' violent offenders (recidivism remains frighteningly high), the way in which society addresses juvenile crime in the coming years will remain a high priority in Congress, in the courts, and in our homes.

WORKFORCE

According to the 1998-1999 Occupational Outlook Handbook published by the Bureau of Labor and Statistics, job opportunities for correctional officers are expected to be favorable through the year 2006, increasing faster than the average for all occupations. The average annual salary for federal correctional officers was $33,500 in 1997. Because of the growth of privatized facilities, employee count in the correctional field was difficult to assess; however, it was estimated to be near 500,000.

Expansion and new construction of correctional facilities is expected to create even more new jobs. In addition, employment of correction officers is usually not affected by economic conditions or the overall level of government spending because security is vital at penal institutions. In approximately 36 out of 50 states, correction officers are represented by labor unions. It is the correctional officers who enforce the rules and regulations of the nation's prisons, negotiating a highly stressful work environment on a day-to-day basis. Other staffers at federal prisons include social workers, psychologists, vocational instructors, teachers, doctors, and nurses.

FURTHER READING

''1998-99 Occupational Outlook Handbook.'' U.S. Bureau of Labor Statistics, 1999. Available from http://stats.bls.gov/oco/ocos156.htm.

Gerrick, Aaron. ''Report Shows Record U.S. Prison Population,'' 1999. Available from http://www.policy.com/news/dbrief/dbriefarc307.asp.

Langan, Patrick A., and Jodi M. Brown. *Felony Sentences in State Courts, 1994.* Washington, D.C.: Bureau of Justice Statistics, 1997.

''Prisoners in 1998.'' U.S. Bureau of Justice Statistics reports, 1999. Available from http://www.ojp.usdoj.gov/bjs/abstract/p98.htm.

U.S. Bureau of Justice Statistics. *Lifetime Likelihood of Going to State or Federal Prisons.* Washington, D.C.: Bureau of Justice Statistics, 1997.

SIC 9224

FIRE PROTECTION

This classification covers government establishments primarily engaged in fire fighting and other related fire protection activities. Government and private establishments primarily engaged in forest fire fighting and fire protection services are classified in **SIC 0851: Forestry Services.** Private establishments primarily engaged in other fire fighting services are classified in **SIC 7389: Business Services, Not Elsewhere Classified.**

NAICS CODE(S)

922160 (Fire Protection)

INDUSTRY SNAPSHOT

Public fire departments responded to 1.75 million fires in 1998, according to the National Fire Protection Association (NFPA). Civilian deaths in 1998 dropped by 2.7 percent from the previous year (to 4,035), but property damage directly caused by fire was up 1.2 percent (to $8.6 billion). Overall trends, however, have been downward for more than a decade, due in part to improved fire code enforcement, mandatory sprinkler and smoke alarm laws, an increase in the utilization of other fire prevention methodologies, and innovations in fire fighting technology. On average, the number of fires decreased by nearly 17 percent from 1987-1996. Fire incidence in major cities was at its peak during the civil unrest of the 1960s and 1970s.

Even today, though, the United States has the highest fire death rate of any industrialized country. Researchers have linked this fact to a difference in attitudes, pointing out that families who experience fire loss are ostracized in countries such as Japan and Holland. Fire departments in other countries also tend to devote a much larger portion of resources on prevention rather than suppression.

ORGANIZATION AND STRUCTURE

Fire departments have two basic fire-related functions: prevention and suppression. Fire prevention activities aim to keep fires from starting. Fire suppression activities seek to put out fires once they have started, to rescue individuals, and to protect property from the paths of fires. More and more, fire departments also operate emergency medical services and air crash services that relate only tangentially to the problems of fires in structures.

In most urban areas of the United States, the fire fighting service is primarily the responsibility of the local government. In suburban and rural areas, either independent voluntary organizations or profit-making firms may provide the service instead. Most professional fire departments today have a past that includes volunteer elements, with traditions dating back, in some cases, to the nineteenth century or even colonial times.

The local nature of fire protection reinforces individual fire department identities. Variations in procedures also reflect regional differences in building construction and environmental conditions. The major influences at the national level are the National Fire Protection Association (NFPA), a consensus standard-making organization; the U.S. Fire Administration (USFA), a directorate within the Federal Emergency Management Administration; the USFA's National Fire Academy (NFA); the International Association of Fire Fighters (IAFF), the largest union; and the International Association of Fire Chiefs (IAFC).

Cities across the nation have made significant cuts in their budgets to adapt to a changing economic environment. Additional budget pressure has come from mandates for safer equipment and specialized training in such areas as hazardous materials and medical response. These demands have increased at the same time that the declining fire rate provides less actual fire fighting experience to younger members, thus creating the need for more training in fire fighting basics.

Current Conditions

Frequently the first emergency response teams to arrive on scene, fire departments are taking on larger roles in emergency medical treatment, natural disasters, and terrorist incidents. This also pus the fire department personnel at more risk. One bombing in the late 1990s involved a ''secondary bomb'' timed specifically to target responders arriving to provide aid in the wake of the initial attack. Additionally, responders at Columbine High School in Littleton, Colorado, came under attack while rescuing injured students. Many fire departments now are working closer with law enforcement to manage these mass casualty incidents.

Fire departments continue to struggle to meet tightened safety standards from two sometimes conflicting sources: voluntary standards promulgated in recent years by the NFPA, and mandatory standards of the U.S. Occupational Safety and Health Administration (OSHA). Newer equipment—such as insulated pants-and-jacket combinations—also has had physical and psychological effects on individual fire fighters. Meanwhile, changes in the built environment, such as synthetic materials and thermal-insulating windows, create fires of greater intensity and toxicity.

The U.S. Bureau of Labor Statistics forecasts that these pressures will move smaller departments from volunteer toward paid membership, creating new jobs. Larger, urban departments, however, are likely to have little job growth.

Workforce

Since fire fighting is such a specialized occupation, many people who begin their careers as fire fighters with a particular department will remain with that department for the duration of their career. Fire fighting is a uniformed, quasimilitary service. Fire fighters typically work swing shifts or long shifts and work in groups of 5 to 12 people. Most fire fighters rotate on a 24 hour work shift, with many fire fighters moonlighting in different trades during their off hours.

Important legislation passed in late 1999 amended the Fair Labor Standards Act (FLSA) to add a definition of a fire fighter. FLSA has a special overtime exemption to accommodate the unusual schedules of local government fire and emergency services agencies, in part used due to the unpredictable nature of emergencies. This exemption allows an average of 53 hours per week before overtime is due. However, prior to 1999, the FLSA did not explicitly define fire fighter, leading to inconsistent court interpretations on whether incidents involving emergency medical services were covered under the fire fighter exemption. The new legislation, supported by both labor and management, defined a fire fighter as an employee trained in fire suppression who has the authority and responsibility to engage in fire suppression and is employed by a fire department of a municipality, county fire district, or state. Under the legislation, the fire fighter is covered under the exemption whenever he or she is engaged in the prevention, control, and extinguishment of fires or response to emergency situations where life, property, or the environment is at risk. This definition of a fire fighter was also adopted under the Standard Occupational Classification (SOC) guidelines issued by the Department of Labor, Bureau of Labor Statistics.

In 1998, there were approximately 278,300 fire fighters on payroll in the United States, and 804,200 people were volunteer fire fighters. The fire service is overwhelmingly male and traditionally blue-collar. Entry to most career fire departments is based on competitive testing, with rigorous tests for physical strength and agility. Promotion is often based on a combination of competitive testing and seniority. Paid departments experience little turnover. Many departments are beginning to require some college education for promotion.

When full-time fire fighters are used exclusively, labor costs—including benefits—may exceed 90 percent of the total costs of fire service delivery. Nearly 80 percent of active fire fighters are union members. Fire departments have a low rate of turnover; most job openings result when fire fighters retire or change careers.

A major and legitimate concern of fire fighters is safety. The rate of deaths in the line of duty is much higher for fire fighters than for police officers or other city employees. The USFA reports that approximately 100 fire fighters die each year in duty-related incidents. Exposure to heat, smoke, and building collapse pose intense danger. Moreover, smoke inhalation may cause respiratory problems, heart failure, and cancer. One response to the danger has been more generous death, disability, and retirement benefits for fire fighters.

FURTHER READING

Downey, Ray. "Terrorism and the Fire Service: Analyzing the Problems." *Fire Engineering,* June 1996.

Gruenert, Jeffrey C. "Firefighting Occupations." *Occupational Outlook Handbook.* U.S. Bureau of Labor Statistics, 1999. Available from http://stats.bls.gov/oco/ocos158.htm.

Karter, Michael J., Jr. "U.S. Fire Department Profile Through 1998," 1999.

Petruzzello, Steven J., Denise L. Smith, David Clark, and Bradley G. Bone. "Psychological Responses to Working in Bunker Gear." *Fire Engineering,* February 1996.

Seaton, Michelle. "How Different Countries Teach Fire Safety." *NFPA Journal,* May/June 1996.

U.S. Fire Administration National Data Center. "Fire in the United States 1987-1996," 1999.

SIC 9229

PUBLIC ORDER AND SAFETY, NOT ELSEWHERE CLASSIFIED

This category covers miscellaneous government establishments primarily engaged in public order and safety, not elsewhere classified, including general administration of public order and safety programs. Collection of statistics on overall public safety also is included.

NAICS CODE(S)

922190 (All Other Justice, Public Order, and Safety)

This government group includes several miscellaneous safety, emergency preparedness, and statistical offices, most of which operate as components of other major government offices, centers, and bureaus. In addition to federal units, each state maintains its own safety, order, and statistical programs, often in cooperation with federal initiatives. Eight of 10 government inspection and compliance positions in the United States are for the purpose of preserving the general welfare and safety of its citizens. These include mine safety and health inspectors, consumer safety inspectors, and highway safety investigators. According to the U.S. Census Bureau, there were approximately 163,000 inspectors and compliance officers employed in 1996 (the latest available statistic). Of these, state governments employed about 34 percent, the federal government employed about 31 percent, and local governments about 18 percent. The remaining 17 percent were employed in various private sector positions.

Safety offices exist in a number of major U.S. federal government departments. The Food Safety and Inspection office, for example, is part of the Department of Agriculture and is directed by the Assistant Secretary of Marketing and Inspection Services. It was established in 1981 to regulate and enforce food safety in the meat and poultry industries. The responsibility to monitor the safety of egg products was added in 1994. Likewise, the Center for Food Safety and Applied Nutrition conducts research and develops standards for foods, including additives and colors. It is part of the federal Department of Health and Human Services.

In addition to food surety, several safety offices are operated within the U.S. Department of Transportation (DOT). The Port Safety and Security Program, for instance, is administered by the Coast Guard to enforce marine safety in ports and anchorages. The Federal Highway Administration, also a DOT office, operates a highway safety program that researches and constructs safer roadways. Similarly, the DOT's National Vehicle Safety Program conducts numerous driver and vehicle safety services and educational programs. Besides the DOT, other offices with major safety programs in this category include the Consumer Product Safety Commission, the Defense Nuclear Facilities Safety Board, the National Transportation Safety Board, and the Occupational Safety and Health Administration.

Federal public order offices and agencies also exist under several major departments. One of the largest of these departments is the Federal Emergency Management Agency (FEMA), which responds to national disasters. Established in 1979, it is the focal point within the federal government for emergency planning, preparedness, mitigation, and response. From its 10 regional offices, FEMA works closely with state and local governments to provide training and to administer relief programs. It also oversees a taxpayer-supported insurance program that provides inexpensive coverage for homeowners in flood plains destined for destruction. FEMA provided important emergency relief in the 1990s for victims of Hurricane Andrew, midwest floods, the Oklahoma bombing of a federal building, and a Los Angeles earthquake. The U.S. International Development Cooperation Agency's International Disaster Assistance Program provides relief for foreign catastrophe victims.

Like safety and public order offices falling under this classification, several federal departments maintain programs that collect and evaluate safety statistics. Among the largest of these offices is the Department of Commerce's Bureau of the Census, which keeps tabs on U.S. households and related demographic data. The Bureau of Justice Statistics collects crime data for the Department of Justice. The DOT has several safety data programs as well, such as the Office of Airline Statistics.

One of the greatest challenges of the century for public safety offices was "Y2K readiness," with intense focus on potential computer failures and "cyberterrorism." By 1999, computers across the nation controlled everything from hospital emergency power to wastewater treatment. A single failure could have affected large numbers of people. For this reason, an estimated 5 million Americans worked through the New Year's weekend in a state of preparedness for any disaster or catastrophe that might manifest. Two million of these were federal, state and local government employees. FEMA established 10 regional centers to monitor potential catastrophes, and in such an event, would have had backup support from 26 federal agencies and the Red Cross. The federal government also established 15 emergency command posts continuously feeding reports back to Washington throughout the holiday weekend.

FURTHER READING

Greenberg, Brigette. "Feds Stand Ready for Disaster." Associated Press Online, 30 December 1999.

Jackson, David and Jim Landers. "The Biggest Civil Defense Exercise in America Went Off Without a Hitch." *The Dallas Morning News,* 31 December 1999.

Office of the Federal Register. *The United States Government Manual.* Washington: GPO, 1996.

U.S. Department of Labor, Bureau of Labor Statistics. *Occupational Outlook Handbook: 1998-99.* Washington: GPO, 1999.

U.S. Bureau of the Census. *Statistical Abstract of the United States.* Washington: GPO, 1996.

U.S. Department of Labor. *Occupational Outlook Handbook.* Washington: GPO, 1996.

SIC 9311

PUBLIC FINANCE, TAXATION, AND MONETARY POLICY

This industry classification includes government establishments primarily engaged in financial administration and taxation including monetary policy; tax administration; collection, custody and disbursement of funds; debt and investment administration; government employee retirement and other trust funds; and the like. Income maintenance program administrations are classified in **SIC 9441: Administration of Educational Programs.** Government establishments primarily engaged in regulation of insurance and banking institutions are classified in **SIC 9651: Regulation, Licensing, and Inspection of Miscellaneous Commercial Sectors.**

NAICS CODE(S)

921130 (Public Finance)

INDUSTRY SNAPSHOT

The economic policy in the United States is determined by a complex web of organizations representing both the legislative and executive branches of government. The economic policies covered in this classification can be broadly divided into fiscal policies and monetary policies.

In general, fiscal policy is the policy of a government with respect to taxation, the public debt, public expenditures, and fiscal management. These policies serve to stabilize the national income of a country. In the United States, a policy of stability and growth has traditionally been pursued. The Employment Act of 1946 explicitly required the government to create and maintain "useful employment opportunities, including self-employment" and to promote production and a high standard of living in a manner that is consistent with free enterprise. The fiscal policy of the United States is determined and implemented by the Congress and the president by changing deficit expenditures and/or changing federal tax rates. Fiscal policies can be expansionary or contractionary. Expansionary policies can take the form of either a decrease in tax rates that increases private sector expenditures or an increase in government spending. Contractionary policies are decreases in deficit spending caused by either an increase in tax rates that decreases private expenditures or a decrease in public expenditures.

In general, monetary policies are government policies that relate to the supply or the use of money. This policy is implemented through the control of credit exercised through the central banking authority. Typically the objective of a monetary policy is to achieve price stability in the economy. In the United States, monetary policy is controlled by the board of governors of the Federal Reserve. The instruments used in the implementation of monetary policy include open market operations and variations in rates for rediscounts, loans, and advances in the legal reserve requirements. All of these have an impact on both the availability and cost of bank credit.

In setting its policies, the Federal Reserve Board looks at three measures of money. The first is called M1 and refers to the currency in the hands of the public, demand deposits, and interest-bearing checking accounts. Second, is M2, which includes assets in M1 plus all deposit liabilities of depository institutions, money market funds, overnight repurchase agreements, and overnight Eurodollars. Third, is M3, which includes M2 plus large denomination time deposits, term Eurodollars, and all other repurchase agreements. There is also broad measure of liquid assets, L, which is also regularly reported by the Federal Reserve.

ORGANIZATION AND STRUCTURE

The organizations responsible for public finance, taxation, and monetary policy can be divided into two categories: government agencies and legislative committees. The various agencies and departments are primarily responsible for implementing policy measures. The most important agencies are the Commerce Department, the Congressional Budget Office, the Council of Economic Advisors, the Federal Reserve System, the Internal Revenue Service, the Office of Management and Budget, Small Business Administration, the Treasury Department, and the U.S. Trade Representative. The most important legislative committees are the House Banking and Finance Committee; the House Budget Committee; the House Ways and Means Committee; the Joint Economic Committee; the Joint Taxation Committee; the Senate Banking, Housing, and Urban Affairs Committee; the Senate Budget Committee; and the Senate Finance Committee.

The Commerce Department. The U.S. Commerce Department provides business and government with relevant economic statistics research and analysis. The Commerce Department acts as the principal advisor to the president on federal policy affecting industry and commerce. The department develops and maintains macroeconomic models and other analytical tools necessary to analyze economic policy issues such as the effect of federal legislation, regulations, and programs. The department also promotes national economic growth and development, competitiveness, international trade, and technological development. As one of the government's main sources of economic data, the Commerce Department maintains the Economic Bulletin Board; the National Trade Data Bank; and the National Economic, Social, and Environmental Data Bank.

Created on March 4, 1913, the Commerce Department is headed by the secretary of commerce and is divided into five sections—each headed by an undersecretary. These sections are the National Oceanic and Atmospheric Administration (NOAA), the International Trade Administration (ITA), the Bureau of Export Administration, Economic Affairs, and the U.S. Travel and Tourism Administration.

The Congressional Budget Office. The Congressional Budget Office (CBO) is a nonpartisan office that provides the House and Senate with budget-related information and analyses of fiscal policies. The CBO does not make policy recommendations, but limits its activities to presenting options for consideration. The Balanced Budget and Emergency Deficit Control Act of 1985, also known as the Gram-Rudman-Holings Law, assigned the CBO the additional tasks of reporting whether the projected federal deficit exceeds the legal limits, calculating the amount of excess that must be removed to eliminate any deficit excess, and alerting the Congress to a recession in the economy that might require the suspension of deficit targets.

The CBO is divided into six divisions, each administered by a director and a deputy director. The directors are appointed to four-year renewable terms by the Speaker of the House and the president pro tempore of the Senate based on the recommendation of both budget committees.

The Council of Economic Advisors. The Council of Economic Advisors (CEA) is comprised of three members and a supporting staff of economists. The CEA advises the president on economic developments, trends, and policies, as well as preparing the Economic Report of the president for Congress. The CEA was established by the Employment Act of 1946 and is an agency within the Executive Office of the president. The members are appointed by the president with the advice and consent of the Senate.

The Federal Reserve System. The Federal Reserve System is responsible for setting U.S. monetary policy. The system is the central banking structure of the United States and was created by the Federal Reserve Act in 1913. It influences credit conditions through buying and selling treasury securities in the open market, fixing the amount of reserves depository institutions must maintain, and by determining interest rates. The Federal Reserve Board chairman and vice-chairman are appointed by the president for 4-year terms. The remaining seven members of the board are appointed for 14-year terms.

The Internal Revenue Service. The primary responsibility of the Internal Revenue Service (IRS) is the administration and enforcement of internal revenue laws except those related to firearms, alcohol, and tobacco. The IRS is a division of the Department of the Treasury and was established in 1962. The IRS develops national policies and programs for the administration of Internal Revenue laws.

The Office of Management and Budget. The Office of Management and Budget (OMB) prepares the president's annual budget and works with the CEA and Treasury Department to develop the government's fiscal program and oversee the administration of the budget. The OMB also reviews government regulations and coordinates administration procurement and management policy.

The Small Business Administration. The Small Business Administration (SBA) promotes small-business interests through financial aid, counseling, and ensuring that small businesses receive a fair portion of government contracts. The SBA is also involved in loan programs for small businesses. The agency acts in two manners: it can lend money directly to the small business or can cosign a loan through a lender.

The Treasury Department. The U.S. Treasury Department formulates and recommends domestic and international financial, economic, tax, and broad fiscal policies and manages the public debt. The Treasury Department is the chief financial department of the government and advisor to the president on economic policy. The Treasury Department also serves as the government's primary financial manager, taking responsibility for cash management and investment of government trust funds, credit administration, and debt collection. The Treasury Department was created on September 2, 1879, and is overseen by the secretary of the Treasury, a cabinet officer appointed by the president.

The U.S. Trade Representative. This office is a cabinet-level agency within the Office of the President. The U.S. Trade Representative acts as the president's chief advisor on international trade policy, has the primary responsibility for developing international trade policy and for coordinating its implementation, and is chief negotiator for international trade agreements. The office of the U.S. Trade Representative was created by the Trade Expansion Act of 1962 to negotiate all trade agreements on behalf of the United States.

The various legislative committees are responsible for setting economic policy through legislation. A brief discussion of each of the committees follows:

The House Banking, Finance, and Urban Affairs Committee. This committee has jurisdiction over legislation dealing with domestic monetary policy, including the Federal Reserve System. This committee also oversees financial aid to commerce and industry, the measurement of economic activity, federal loan guarantees, economic development and economic stabilization measures.

The House Budget Committee. The House Budget Committee exercises jurisdiction over congressional budget resolutions that fix levels for federal spending, revenues, deficit, and debt. The committee also has jurisdiction over reconciliation bills, which modify existing programs to meet budget goals.

The House Ways and Means Committee. The House Ways and Means Committee exercises jurisdiction over legislation dealing with the debt ceiling, investment policy, and taxes. The committee oversees the Internal Revenue Service and sets excise tax rates for the Bureau of Alcohol, Tobacco, and Firearms.

The Joint Economic Committee. The Joint Economic Committee studies and makes recommendations on economic policy, including fiscal policy. The committee also maintains data on aggregate economic activity.

The Joint Taxation Committee. The Joint Taxation Committee performs staff work for the House Ways and Means and Senate Finance Committees on domestic and international tax matters in the Internal Revenue Code, the public debt limit, and savings bonds. It also provides those committees with general economic and budgetary analysis, and provides revenue analysis for all tax legislation.

The Senate Banking, Housing, and Urban Affairs Committee. The Senate Banking, Housing, and Urban Affairs Committee exercises jurisdiction over legislation dealing with bank regulation, domestic monetary policy, financial aid to commerce and industry, the measurement of economic activity, federal loan guarantees, and economic stabilization measures. The Committee also oversees the Federal Reserve System.

The Senate Budget Committee. The Senate Budget Committee exercises jurisdiction over congressional budget resolutions, which set levels for federal spending, revenues, deficit, and debt. It also exercises jurisdiction over reconciliation bills, which modify existing programs to meet budget targets, and oversees the Congressional Budget Office.

The Senate Finance Committee. The Senate Finance Committee exercises jurisdiction over tax legislation. It oversees the Internal Revenue Service and sets excise tax rates for the Bureau of Alcohol, Tobacco, and Firearms.

Background and Development

On March 4, 1951, the board of governors of the Federal Reserve System and the Treasury Department reached an accord that established the coordination of monetary and fiscal policy in the United States. This was to be done in a manner consistent with the independence of monetary policy. The accord stated that the two offices had reached agreement with respect to debt management and monetary policies to be pursued in furthering their common purpose—to assure the successful financing of the government's requirements and, at the same time, to minimize monetization of the public debt.

The beginning of the Korean War in June of 1950 increased the government's requirements for debt financing. This increased the importance of a treasury policy that would ensure the availability of low-cost borrowing, stable money rates, adequate bank reserves, and stable markets for government securities.

The Federal Reserve System has tried to gain greater control over monetary policy. On October 6, 1979, the board of governors announced a new series of programs that would ''assure better control over the expansion of money and bank credit,'' curb speculation, and thus dampen inflationary forces. These policy objectives were met by placing greater emphasis on the supply of bank reserves and less emphasis on limiting fluctuations in the federal fund rates.

The early 1990s were marked by widespread public discontent with the economic policies of the U.S. government. Years of slow growth and recession were seen to be indicators that new policies should be developed and implemented. This sentiment was reinforced by the end of the Cold War and the resulting belief that American economic resources could be better deployed. The election of 1992 brought a Democrat to office for the first time in 12 years, largely on a platform that stressed new economic priorities and policies. That year also saw the political appearance of Ross Perot, who gained popularity by stressing the need to change U.S. economic policy for good reason: the federal deficit hit an all-time high of over $290 billion dollars in 1992. It has declined every year since.

CURRENT CONDITIONS

The nation prepared to enter the millennium with a balanced budget, an accomplishment first achieved in 1998, following years of overspending. The March 1999 Federal Budget Summary indicated that there was nearly $70 billion in surplus funds at the end of 1998. The projected figures for 1999 were: revenues of $1.8 trillion, expenditures of $1.72 trillion, and an estimated surplus of almost $80 billion. The same study also projected a Year 2000 surplus of $117 billion.

Where did all that money come from? The federal government expects to gain almost $869 billion dollars from personal income taxes and over $182 billion from corporate income taxes in 1999. When added to miscellaneous federal taxes such as excise, estate and gift, custom duties and fees, etc., the 1999 expected federal revenues exceed $1.8 trillion dollars.

Where does the money all go? In 1999 the budget for the Department of Defense was over $263 billion dollars; Department of Health and Human Services, over $375 billion; the Department of the Treasury (which includes the U.S. Secret Service, the Bureau of Alcohol, Tobacco and Firearms, and the U.S. Customs Office, among several others) was to receive just under $386 billion. On the other hand, the Department of Agriculture was budgeted for $63 billion, the Department of Labor, $36 billion, and the Department of Justice, just $16 billion. The list goes on.

All in all, 1999 was a very good year, according to the Federal Reserve Board's Humphrey-Hawkins Report. Economic expansion had moved into its ninth straight year, and unemployment was the lowest since 1970, at approximately four percent. Real gross domestic product was annualized at better than four percent growth, and stock indexes set world records in 1999—the Dow Jones Industrial Average breaking 10,000 points for the first time in history. Federal Reserve Board Chairman Alan Greenspan became a household name, as he carefully kept inflation in check by adjustments to the interest rate, and an aging America overwhelmingly supported extra protection for funds intended to keep the Social Security trust fund solvent.

FURTHER READING

"Congress: Stop Us Before We Spend Again." *U.S. News & World Report,* 7 June 1999.

"Federal Budget Summary." March 1999. Available from http://www.polisci.com/economy/budget.htm.

"Federal Government Budget by Agency." Office of Management and Budget. March 1999. Available from http://www.polisci.com/economy/agency/htm.

"Monetary Policy Report to the Congress." The Federal Reserve Board: Humphrey-Hawkins Report. 22 July 1999. Available from http://www.federalreserve. gov/boarddocs/hh/.

"U.S. Financial Indicators." Joint Economic Committee, March 1999. Available from http://www.polisci.com/economy/finance.htm.

SIC 9411

ADMINISTRATION OF EDUCATIONAL PROGRAMS

This category covers government establishments primarily engaged in central coordination, planning, supervision, and administration of funds, policies, intergovernmental activities, statistical reports and data collection, and centralized programs for educational administration. Government scholarship programs are classified here. Included are federal and state education departments, commissions, and similar educational organizations. Schools and local and state school boards operating schools are classified in educational services industries. Human resource training is classified in **SIC 8331: Job Training and Vocational Rehabilitation Services,** and administration of such programs is classified in **SIC 9440: Administration of Social, Human Resource and Income Maintenance Programs.**

NAICS CODE(S)

923110 (Administration of Educational Programs)

INDUSTRY SNAPSHOT

Virtually all of the functions conducted by the educational programs administration industry were connected in one way or another with the U.S. Department of Education, which administered more than 150 educational programs and guidelines for the nation's 110,000 schools. Despite carrying a legacy of controversy as old as the U.S. Constitution, the Department of Education grew from a meagerly funded agency charged with a single task—the gathering and dissemination of educational data—into a $34.4 billion federal program with widely varied responsibilities that changed with each presidency and each new session of Congress. The 1999 budget represented an increase of nearly $3 billion from 1998. Much of the debate in the 1990s about the Department's authority and goals centered around the question of state versus federal rights. So widespread was past resistance to a powerful, centralized department of education, not until 1979 was the century-old office granted cabinet-level status. Even then its survival was far from secure, for in Ronald Reagan's 1980 presidential campaign, he threatened to abolish the Department, saddled as it was with charges of mismanagement and ineffectiveness.

From the early 1980s forward, the education debate was shaped by a national call for fundamental reform, particularly at the elementary and secondary levels, where approximately half of the Department's spending went. The Department of Education only contributed around six percent of revenues to schools across the country, while the remaining 94 percent was divided between local and state sources. The Department of Education served as both mediator and scapegoat for a debate that showed no signs of ending.

When, where, and how meaningful and widespread reform would take place—and what role the Department would assume—were questions that would take years to answer. Private schools, small companies specializing in educational administration, and select public schools were paving the way and, in so doing, heightened public discussion of school choice, school vouchers, and a return to core curricula. President Bill Clinton's Goals 2000: the Educate America Act, criticized for its occasionally vague language, nevertheless gave clarity to the debate in 1994 and authorized the initial release of $647 million for experiments in reform.

During the latter half of the 1990s, statistics from the National Center for Education (part of the National Assessment of Educational Progress) indicated that academic achievement in the nation's schools had steadily turned upward. But it was readily apparent that no single solution would or will continue to turn achievement levels around for all students.

Organization and Structure

The Department of Education includes: the Secretary (OS), the Deputy Secretary (ODS), the Under Secretary (OUS), Intergovernmental and Interagency Affairs (OIIA), Inspector General (OIG), General Counsel (OGC), Bilingual Education and Minority Languages Affairs (OBEMLA), Human Resources and Administration (OHRA), Legislation and Congressional Affairs (OLCA), Civil Rights (OCR), Elementary and Secondary Education (OBESE), Educational Research and Improvement (OERI), Vocational and Adult Education (OVAE), Special Education and Rehabilitative Services (OSERS), Postsecondary Education (OPE), Chief Financial Officer (CFO), and Regional offices.

Although no overall plan or consistent philosophy for the federal government's education programs existed, they were divided into four general categories. The first was promoting equal educational opportunities for students. The Chapter 1 program under Title I of the Elementary and Secondary Education Act of 1965 (ESEA) was the largest federal program promoting equal educational opportunity. The 1999 Department of Education budget for Title I was $10.45 billion for disadvantaged students under the program. These included low-income children, migrant children with special needs, and children needing help with school readiness. Also included under the category of equal educational opportunity was funding for Immigrant Education, Bilingual Education, and Native American education grants.

Programs stimulating education reform were included in the second category of federal education programs. The Chapter 2 program of Title I of ESEA, blocking grants to state and local private and public educational authorities for improving schools, were included in this category. Also included were Safe and Drug-Free Schools and Communities grants, Eisenhower Mathematics and Science Education programs, and the Magnet Schools Assistance Program for desegregating schools.

The third category, general support, covered funding for school districts affected by federal activity, which limited the property tax revenues that would have gone to schools in that area. About 2,500 of the nation's 15,400 school districts, or about 16 percent, receive the federally legislated Impact Aid, with funds targeted to districts enrolling children living on Indian lands and children of members of the uniformed services who live on government property.

The final category was promoting educational preparation for employment. The focal point in this area was the Carl D. Perkins Vocational and Applied Technology Education Act for programs of instruction in areas such as business math, instructional arts, electronics, and office management. The Adult Education Act supported programs for adults wanting to complete high school education, to become literate, or to enroll in an employment-related training.

BACKGROUND AND DEVELOPMENT

Colonial education was controlled by churches and the economically privileged. Consequently, education was viewed as a personal, rather than a public, concern. Children of factory workers, farmers, and other laborers received very limited education, just enough to allow them to fulfill their roles in society. After the colonies won their freedom from England, the primary goal of the Constitution's framers was to protect the personal and religious freedoms of the people from central authorities. Therefore, education, discerned as a personal choice, was left to the discretion of local and state agencies. However, several early American leaders still wished to promote education, including George Washington, who sought support for a national university following the Revolutionary War. In 1785, the Continental Congress passed the Survey Ordinance, which provided for sections of land to be set aside for schools in newly created townships. The intention of this law was further bolstered by the passage two years later of the Northwest Ordinance, which offered educational land grants and stated that "schools and the means of education shall forever be encouraged."

During the nineteenth century, the Industrial Revolution and huge advances in science began to change public attitudes towards education. The quality of schools, then under the jurisdiction of individual schoolmasters, was now being questioned, and the radical idea of taxing citizens to support the education of everyone, regardless of class or income, was being debated openly.

Henry Barnard, who would become the first United States Commissioner of Education, was an early supporter of "common schools," the development of a school system, and its funding through taxation. He also was a fervent supporter of the need for the government to gather and distribute data on education. Barnard had been influenced by his contemporary Horace Mann, who crusaded for public education in Massachusetts. As a Connecticut legislator, Barnard created a commission to obtain facts about the state's common schools. The commission found less than one-half of the state's school-aged children were in school, three-fourths of its schools were unfit for use, and there were no standards for teachers. To make matters worse, Connecticut was considered to be one of the best states in terms of education. By 1840, Barnard convinced the U.S. Bureau of Census to include questions regarding the numbers of schools and colleges in the country and questions regarding the rate of illiteracy. He continued to promote the establishment of a federal agency to collect comprehensive education data.

The Civil War stymied the growing movement for a national education office except for one major piece of legislation. In July 1862, President Abraham Lincoln signed into law the Morrill Act. The legislation designated that money from the sale of federally owned lands should go to some of the nation's colleges and universities. This marked the true beginning of land-grant schools and was the first major step in legitimizing a role for the federal government in education.

After the Civil War, interest was high among educators to establish a federal office. Representative James A. Garfield, later President Garfield, introduced a bill into Congress to create such an office. After a year of contentious debate, the Department of Education was created through the Organic Act in March 1867. The Department's principal task was to gather and publish data on education with the intent to foster the growth and improvement of the nation's public schools. The Department also was to conduct related studies, two of which were mandated. The first was a federal land grant study and was included in the original bill. The second followed the appropriation of funds and mandated a study of education in the District of Columbia.

From its earliest days, the Garfield-sponsored law was controversial. In fact, to pacify supporters of state rights, the Department was downgraded to an office within the Department of Interior the year after it was formed and then renamed the Bureau of Education in 1870. In 1929, still within the Interior Department, the agency was renamed the Office of Education. In 1939, it became part of the Federal Security Agency, then, in 1953, it was assigned to the Department of Health, Education, and Welfare. All this movement was indicative of the ongoing debate about the role of the Federal Government in education. Overall, the first 75 years of the Department of Education were marked by lack of authority, lack of funding, and unpredictable support in Congress.

In addition, the early collection of information was extremely difficult because of the size of the nation and the suspicion of state and local officials and the educators themselves. Still, by 1875, the agency had collected information on nearly all grades of school and later added statistics on private schools, school expenditures, the value of physical plants of schools, and other types of data. In 1923, the agency added a team of field statisticians who visited schools and collected detailed and accurate information. The statistical component of the Department of Education, The National Center for Education Statistics, made these comprehensive visits until 1963. After World War II, the office began an annual survey of college and university enrollment. In the mid-1960s, these education statistics were used for legislative purposes for the first time. Then, at the end of the decade, data on educational outcomes or achievement was collected for the first time. Statistics comparing the United

States with international educational achievements were not added until the 1990s.

Federal involvement in education peaked at different times in U.S. history. The Department's first significant responsibilities came following passage of the Smith-Hughes Act in 1917 and the Smith-Bankhead Act in 1920, both of which provided grants to states for vocational education. This function became even more prominent during the years of the Great Depression. But it was not until the 1950s that significant changes began to take place in the Department. The advent of the space race and the Cold War during this decade accelerated federal spending on education through the National Defense Education Act of 1958. In addition, the 1954 *Brown v. Board of Education* Supreme Court desegregation case focused attention on both the equality of opportunity and the disparity among the nation's schools, followed by President Lyndon Johnson's Great Society programs of social reform and educational advancement during the 1960s. The Economic Opportunity Act of 1964, which created the Head Start program for preschool children, and the 1964 Civil Rights Act, which prohibited discrimination in the use of federal funds, included education funds. The Elementary and Secondary Education Act of 1965 (ESEA) was also passed to promote equality of education. All had an effect on the Department of Education, whose administrative budget grew from around $2 million in 1950 to more than $15 million by 1965 and total money disbursements then exceeded $760 million.

In 1972, the Emergency School Aid Act was passed to assist desegregating schools. The Education for All Handicapped Children Act of 1975 mandated free and appropriate education for disabled children. The elementary and secondary education legislation passed in the 1960s and 1970s mainly dealt with specific needs of small groups of students. Critics said the needs of the majority of students were being ignored by federal education programs, and the broad variety of programs lacked coordination.

When the Carter Administration came to power, a study group was formed to develop proposals for upgrading the Office of Education, which was then a part of the Office of Health, Education, and Welfare. After failure to get action on an education bill in 1978, a new bill was offered to Congress the following year. The Department of Education Organization Act created a cabinet-level department and authorized a budget of $14.2 billion for the 152 programs and 17,000 employees.

Opponents of the bill cited the loss of state and local control of education, the diminishment of civil rights protection, the increased influence of special interest groups, and a higher tax burden as major concerns. In order to address these issues, the legislation included the protection of state and local rights regarding education policy, programs, and administration; an Office of Civil Rights within the Department; and an Intergovernmental Advisory Council on Education, including state and local officials, public and private school representatives, and parents and students.

Combined public and private spending on education in the United States represented not only a mammoth industry, but a huge national investment amounting to 7.3 percent of the nation's gross domestic product. Only Canada spent more of its national gross domestic product (GDP) on education than the United States. The 1990 Census found that 6.3 million school children (ages 5-17) speak a language other than English at home. The same year, the Department of Education stated that 5 percent of the 41 million elementary and secondary students in the United States have ''limited English proficiency.'' Of those students speaking English as a second language, 37.8 percent speak English less than very well. But as William Dunn reported in April 1993, there was a steadily growing group of poor and uneducated immigrants in the United States, and students coming from these families were experiencing difficulty in the American educational system, despite English as a Second Language (ESL) programs.

Guaranteed Student Loans. An October 1992 *Financial World* article claimed that the Department of Education's biggest financial problem was the student loan program. In 1992, loans totaling $11 billion were made; that same year, $3.6 billion in previously made loans fell into default. To address the problem, the Department started to make some changes, including eliminating financing for schools with the largest student loan default rates. They also started monitoring for loans to students already in default and collaborating with the Internal Revenue Service (IRS) to collect payments from defaulters' tax refunds. Finally, the Department sought to upgrade its financial controls both for the student loan program and the Department in general.

In 1983, the National Commission on Education, a board appointed by Secretary of Education Terrel H. Bell, concluded that the American education system was in trouble and for younger Americans to compete internationally, reforms would need to take place. In response to the commission's influential *A Nation at Risk* report, a wave of school restructuring occurred. In 1989, the Bush Administration's Education Summit, which included the nation's governors, developed six national education goals to be met by the year 2000. President Bush's proposed education reform legislation, called America 2000: Excellence in Education, failed to pass in Congress, however. Instead, Congress created the National Council on Education Standards and Testing (NCEST), which recommended voluntary participation by the states in an education program that would compare students by means of "world class standards."

The Goals 2000 passed in Congress in March 1994. It authorized $647 million for school reforms nationwide, including $400 million in grants targeted for state and local school agencies. The Act also established the first national education goals and standards for education.

The eight national education goals for all students and schools included in Goals 2000 were: all children will start school ready to learn; at least 90 percent of students will finish high school; students will leave grades four, eight, and twelve with demonstrated competence in English, math, science, foreign languages, civics and government, economics, arts, history, and geography; teachers will have access to programs for the continued improvement of their skills; the United States will be first in the world in math and science achievement; every adult will be literate and possess the skills to compete in a global economy; every school will be free of drugs and violence; and every school will promote involvement of parents in their children's education.

The act also established a 19-member National Education Standards and Improvement Council (NESIC) to develop voluntary national curriculum content, student performance tests, and opportunity-to-learn programs. Funding for combating violent crime in schools and for new research institutes within the Office of Education Research and Improvement was authorized as well. Detractors of the act said that it was too general to bring any significant change to American education and that making the measures voluntary was a concession to the powerful national teachers' associations. Moreover, such goals had been put forth by previous administrations to no noticeable effect.

Current Conditions

By the end of the 1990s, states were aggressively forging ahead to make good on their promises. New York declared that by 2003, all students graduating from high school must pass a Regents Examination in mathematics, science, American history, and global history. For the 1998-1999 school year, California's controversial "Proposition 227," which replaced bilingual education programs with those emphasizing English as the primary language, was too new to gauge its efficacy, but appeared to be gaining ground.

In the last few months of 1999, Congress was completing work on fiscal-2000 legislation for the Department of Education, amid heavy lobbying by student loan providers and college lobbyists. President Clinton indicated that he would veto any budget that did not include funding for several of his proposed programs, including Americorps and the hiring of 100,000 new school teachers. Also contentious were efforts to remove certain fees attached to federal student direct-loan programs and raising the maximum Pell grant by $125, to $3,250.

The total 1999 budget for the Department of Education was $34.3 billion. This included $7.3 billion for the Office of Special Education and Rehabilitative Services, $1.3 billion for the Office of Vocational and Adult Education, and $386.0 million for the Office of Bilingual Education and Minority Language Affairs. (Its largest expenditure was for the Office of Postsecondary Education, at $14.1 billion.)

During its 1998-1999 term, the U.S. Supreme Court delivered an important decision affecting public education. In November 1998, the Court declined to review, and thus let stand, the decision of the Wisconsin Supreme Court that upheld the constitutionality of the Milwaukee school voucher program (*Jackson v. Benson*). In such programs, individual credit vouchers are given to parents by local, state, or federal government entities to be used for sending their children to a school of the parents' choosing. Often, this has meant private, parochial (including religious) schools. Two basic challenges against these vouchers have thus been defeated: the first, having to do with separation of church and state; and the second, involving the reality that such vouchering draws students away from the public school system, thus affecting federal funds to public schools.

America and the World

On another but related front, the majority of 1998 and 1999 winners of the prestigious international Nobel Prizes in Science were professors at American universities. In 1998, eight professors from various American universities won all the awards in chemistry, medicine, and physics. In October 1999, four of the five Nobel Prize winners (in chemistry, economics, medicine, and physics) were current or former professors at U.S. academic institutions. The sole sobering fact was that all the winning professors were foreign-born.

Further Reading

Digest of Education Statistics, 1992. Washington, D.C.: U.S. Department of Education, National Center for Education Statistics, 1996.

"Federal Government Budget by Agency," March 1999. Available from http://www.polisci.com/economy/agency.htm.

"House and Senate Negotiators Shape A Bill to Increase NIH Funds." *The Chronicle of Higher Education,* 29 October 1999.

"Looking Back, Looking Ahead." *The Phi Delta Kappan,* April 1999.

"Public Opinion and Public Education." *The Chronicle of Higher Education.* April 1999.

U.S. Bureau of the Census. *Statistical Abstract of the United States: 1996.* 116th ed. Washington, D.C.: U.S. Bureau of the Census, 1996.

"U.S. Dominates Nobel Prizes in Science, but All Winners are Foreign Born." *The Chronicle of Higher Education,* 22 October 1999.

SIC 9431

ADMINISTRATION OF PUBLIC HEALTH PROGRAMS

This category includes government establishments primarily engaged in planning, administration, and coordination of public health programs and services, including environmental health activities, mental health, categorical health programs (e.g., cancer control, communicable disease control, maternity, child health), health statistics, and immunization services.

NAICS CODE(S)

923120 (Administration of Public Health Programs)

The U.S. public health system consists of programs administered by federal, state, and local government agencies; voluntary health care and research associations, such as the American Red Cross and the American Cancer Society; and professional associations, such as the American Medical Association and American Dental Association. Although several agencies of the federal government had responsibility for aspects of public health, the U.S. Department of Health and Human Services (DDHS) is the principal federal health agency.

ORGANIZATION AND STRUCTURE

The Department of Health and Human Services oversees most of the U.S. government's health programs. It is headed by the Secretary of Health and Human Services, a Cabinet-level position appointed by the president and confirmed by the Senate. The surgeon general, the chief medical officer, and various agency heads report to the secretary. In 1999 the department employed a total of 59,800 persons and had a budget of $387 billion. Its operations are divided between Public Health Operating Divisions, which include much of what was formerly the Public Health Service, and Human Services Operating Divisions, which include Medicare, Medicaid, and the Administration for Children and Families. The human services divisions are discussed in greater detail under **SIC 9441: Administration of Social, Human Resource, and Income Maintenance Programs.**

Major divisions of the DHHS include the National Institutes of Health, the Food and Drug Administration, the Centers for Disease Control, the Substance Abuse and Mental Health Services Administration, the Health Resources and Services Administration, the Agency for Toxic Substances and Disease Registry, the Indian Health Service, and the Agency for Health Care Policy and Research.

The National Institutes of Health (NIH). This top-level agency includes the National Heart, Lung, and Blood Institute; the National Institute of Dental Research; the National Institute of Arthritis and Musculoskeletal and Skin Diseases; the National Institute of Diabetes and Digestive and Kidney Diseases; the National Institute of Neurological Disorders and Stroke; the National Institute of Allergy and Infectious Diseases; the National Institute of General Medical Sciences; the National Institute of Child Health and Human Development; the National Eye Institute; the National Institute of Environmental Health Sciences; the National Institute on Aging; the National Institute on Deafness and Other Communication Disorders; the National Institute on Alcohol Abuse and Alcoholism; the National Institute on Drug Abuse; the National Institute of Mental Health; the National Center for Nursing Research; and the National Center for Research Resources. All NIH institutes and research centers were located in Bethesda, Maryland, except for Environmental Health Sciences, which was located in Research Triangle Park, North Carolina. In 1999, the NIH had 16,010 employees, including more than 4,500 scientists and medical personnel, and a budget of $15.7 billion.

Food and Drug Administration (FDA). The FDA is responsible for enforcing the Food, Drug, and Cosmetic Act of 1938 and the Drug Amendments Act of 1962, which were designed to ensure the purity of food products and the safety and effectiveness of drugs, cosmetics, and therapeutic devices. The FDA inspects all food and drug manufacturing facilities, enforces sanitary standards at restaurants and other public eating places, establishes labeling requirements for food and drugs, and reviews test results on all drugs before they are approved for use in the United States. The FDA had more than 9,500 employees in 1999, including 2,000 scientists and 1,000 inspectors and investigators. The FDA's 1999 budget totaled $1.1 billion.

Centers for Disease Control (CDC). The CDC, located in Atlanta, Georgia, maintains records on the incidence of disease and provides information to health agencies worldwide. The agency also investigates the causes and works with state health care agencies to control the outbreak of diseases, and administers the U.S. quarantine program at ports of entry. The CDC includes the Center for Chronic Disease Prevention and Health Promotion; the Center for Environmental Health and Injury Control; the Center for Infectious Diseases; the Center for Prevention Services; the National Center for Health Statistics; and the National Institute for Occupational Safety and

Health. In 1999 the CDC employed a workforce of 7,100 people and had a budget of $2.7 billion.

Substance Abuse and Mental Health Services Administration. Created in 1992, the Substance Abuse and Mental Health Services Administration is responsible for developing substance abuse treatment and prevention programs in conjunction with state and local agencies, as well as programs to promote mental health. The division also supports efforts to develop local mental health facilities by providing leadership and federal grants. Approximately 690 persons staffed the agency in 1999 with a budget of $2.5 billion.

Health Resources and Services Administration (HRSA). The HRSA is charged with improving health care services in areas without adequate resources. The agency is responsible for the National Health Service Corps, which recruited and assigned physicians, dentists, and nurses to areas with a shortage of health care professionals. The agency also provides grants for health care education and administers well-child programs through the Bureau of Maternal and Child Health and Resources Development. In 1999 this agency's $4.3 billion budget was implemented by a workforce of 2,100 people.

Agency for Toxic Substances and Disease Registry. The Agency for Toxic Substances and Disease Registry was established in 1980 by the Comprehensive Environmental Response, Compensation, and Liability Act to clean up hazardous waste sites. The Public Health Service was responsible for identifying the health risks involved with toxic wastes and developing ways to lessen the danger of working with hazardous substances. Headquartered in Atlanta, the agency employed 413 workers in 1999 and had a budget of $74 million.

Indian Health Service (IHS). The IHS, with approximately 14,900 employees, including 1,000 physicians and dentists and 2,000 nurses in 1999, is responsible for providing health care to more than 1.5 million Native Americans. The IHS has more than 70 federally managed health care facilities and more than 350 health care facilities under the direction of Indian tribes or Alaska Native corporations, including seven hospitals and 173 Alaskan village clinics. The Bureau of Indian Affairs transferred responsibility for Native American health care to the Public Health Service in 1955. The Indian Health Service was elevated to agency status in 1988. Its 1999 expenditures were budgeted for $2.6 billion.

Agency for Health Care Policy and Research. Established in 1989, the Agency for Health Care Policy and Research focuses on improving patient care. It also assesses new health care technologies, promotes health care services in rural areas, and investigates questions of medical malpractice and liability. This agency employed 275 persons and had a $171 million budget in 1999.

Office of the Assistant Secretary for Health. Several public health programs are conducted by the Office of the Assistant Secretary for Health. These include population research and family planning by the Office of Population Affairs, the promotion of healthy lifestyles by the Office of Disease Prevention and Health Promotion, the President's Council on Physical Fitness and Sports, special health initiatives for minorities, and the National AIDS Program.

BACKGROUND AND DEVELOPMENT

Early efforts to provide for the public health in the United States were concerned with quarantine and sanitation. As early as 1795, the governor of New York appealed to the state medical society for help in controlling epidemics. The medical society recommended improving drainage in low-lying areas, collecting refuse from along river banks, controlling the air pollution from slaughter houses and soap factories, and generally cleaning up "the accumulation of filth in the street."

The U.S. Public Health Service traced its beginnings to 1798, when Congress authorized the Marine Hospital Fund for the "care and relief of sick and disabled seamen." The fund was financed by a 20-cents-per-month tax on merchant seamen and administered by the Treasury Department. The first Marine Hospital was established on Castle Island in Boston Harbor in 1799. Other hospitals, often small facilities located in boarding houses, were eventually established in port cities from Newport, Rhode Island, to Charleston, South Carolina. As the nation expanded west, Marine Hospitals also were established in Chicago, Cleveland, New Orleans, and several other cities along the Mississippi and Ohio rivers.

For much of the nineteenth century, the Marine Hospital Fund concerned itself primarily with caring for merchant seamen. It also was poorly managed. By 1869, when the first permanent public health department was created by Massachusetts, only nine of 31 Marine Hospitals built since 1798 were still in operation. In 1871, Dr. John Maynard Woodworth was appointed to the new position of Supervising Surgeon of the Marine Hospital Service. Woodworth, who envisioned a much broader role than caring for ill seamen, eliminated the patronage system and instituted examinations for all job applicants. Woodworth also had been General William T. Sherman's chief medical officer during the Civil War, and reorganized the Marine Hospital Service along military lines. He gave his "officers" military titles, put them in uniform, and assigned them where they were needed most. In 1873, Woodworth's title was changed to Surgeon General.

Meanwhile, the concept of public health developed slowly in the United States. New York, which was struck by an outbreak of yellow fever in 1798, received permission from the state legislature to pass its own health laws and appointed a city health inspector in 1804. But by 1830, only five major cities had established boards of health. In the mid-1840s, New York also became one of the first cities to pass legislation requiring the registration of births and deaths. In 1845, New York city health inspector John C. Grissom published a report entitled ''A Brief View of the Sanitary Conditions of the City,'' in which he found ''an immense amount of sickness, physical disability, and premature mortality among the poorer classes.'' Grissom also concluded ''that these are, to a large extent, unnecessary, being in a great degree the results of causes which are removable.''

Shattuck Report. When the American Medical Association was founded in 1847, one of its first endeavors was to collect information on sanitary conditions from around the country, which focused attention on the growth of slums in American cities. In 1850, the Massachusetts Sanitary Commission published what became known as the Shattuck Report, written by Lemuel Shattuck, a former teacher and bookseller.

Shattuck revealed the extent of communicable disease, especially among the poor, and recommended establishment of a state board of health and local boards in every community. The Shattuck Report also discussed the need for environmental sanitation, the inspection of food and drugs, well-child programs, vaccination against smallpox, air pollution, treatment of alcoholism, and city planning. Although Massachusetts did not implement the Shattuck Report for almost 20 years, it became a blueprint for later public health activities.

Metropolitan Board of Health. In 1857, Philadelphia organized a National Quarantine and Sanitary Convention, attended by 73 delegates from nine states. City health officers also met in Baltimore, New York, and Boston over the next three years, but the Civil War interrupted plans for a fifth conference scheduled for Cincinnati in 1861. After the war, the Council of Hygiene and Public Health, formed by a citizens group in New York, published a report on sanitary conditions that shocked the community into action. In 1866, the state legislature created a Metropolitan Board of Health with broad powers to improve sanitary conditions in a four-county area. Members of the board included four physicians who served as sanitary commissioners, the health officer for the port of New York, and four police commissioners.

In *A History of Public Health,* George Rosen called the Metropolitan Board of Health ''a turning point in the history of public health not only in New York City, but in the United States as a whole.'' Rosen noted that a ''change from a haphazard to an efficient administration was as essential to the development of a complicated urban industrial society as the provision of new scientific knowledge. In fact it was the provision of a stable administrative foundation which made it easier to incorporate new scientific knowledge into public health practice.''

Although Louisiana established the first state health department in 1855, it was largely ineffective. However, several states soon established boards of health patterned after the New York Metropolitan Board of Health. Massachusetts adopted the many of the ideas contained in the earlier Shattuck Report and established a state board of health in 1869. California followed in 1870, the District of Columbia in 1871, Minnesota and Virginia in 1872, Michigan in 1873, Maryland in 1874, Alabama in 1875, Wisconsin in 1876, and Illinois in 1877.

National Board of Health. In 1878, following an outbreak of yellow fever that killed an estimated 14,000 Americans, Congress passed the first Federal Quarantine Act. It assigned responsibility for enforcing port quarantines to the Marine Hospital Service. However, Congress failed to appropriate any money for enforcement and instructed Surgeon General Woodworth not to interfere with state laws.

Meanwhile, the American Public Health Association, founded in 1872, lobbied Congress to create a national health department. In 1879, Congress created a National Board of Health, comprised of nine members appointed by the president, including one each from the Army, Navy, and Marine Hospital Service. Quarantine responsibility was shifted to the National Board of Health, which also began monitoring outbreaks of disease and providing grants for states to create sanitary facilities.

Woodworth died 11 days after passage of the act creating the National Board of Health, which he had bitterly opposed. However, he was succeeded as surgeon general by Dr. John B. Hamilton, who continued the fight. Hamilton repeatedly accused board members of corruption or ineptitude. There also were growing complaints from the states, which felt the board was encroaching on their rights. In 1883, Congress refused to continue funding for the National Board of Health. Responsibility for port quarantines was returned to the Marine Hospital Service, which also was directed to investigate the origin and causes of epidemic diseases. Dr. Joseph J. Kinyuon established the first ''laboratory of hygiene,'' forerunner to the National Institutes of Health, at the Marine Hospital on Staten Island in 1887.

In 1889, following another deadly outbreak of yellow fever in the South, Congress officially created the Commissioned Corps of the Marine Hospital Service, a mobile force of physicians organized along military lines. The surgeon general was to be appointed by the president and confirmed by the Senate. The following year, Congress gave the Marine Hospital Service interstate quarantine authority. In 1891, when Dr. Walter Wyman became surgeon general, the Marine Medical Service had a budget of $600,000 and the Commissioned Corps consisted of 54 medical officers.

U.S. Public Health Service. This service has the responsibility for providing medical examinations to all immigrants. The Quarantine Act of 1893 charged the Marine Hospital Service with refusing admission to the United States to ''idiots, insane persons . . . persons likely to become a public charge, and persons suffering from a loathsome or a dangerous contagious disease.''

In 1902, the Marine Hospital Service officially became the Public Health and Marine Hospital Service, reflecting the widening scope of its activities. Forty of the 45 states then had some form of state health department, and the surgeon general also was directed by Congress to convene national conferences on public health annually or ''whenever in his opinion the interest of the public health would be promoted by such a conference.'' Five state health authorities also could require the surgeon general to convene a conference to discuss a public health emergency.

Also in 1902, Congress passed the Biologics Control Act, which made the Public Health and Marine Hospital Service responsible for regulating the transportation and sale of vaccines, serums, or other medical products designed for human use. The Hygienic Laboratory, which had begun the manufacturing of diphtheria antitoxin in 1894, was moved to Washington, D.C., where divisions of chemistry, zoology, and pharmacology were added to its facilities. When Surgeon General Wyman died in 1911, the Public Health and Marine Hospital Service budget was $1.75 million and the Commissioned Corps also had grown to 135 officers.

The Public Health and Marine Hospital Service officially became the Public Health Service in 1912, when Congress extended its authority to ''investigate the diseases of man and conditions influencing the propagation and spread thereof, including sanitation and sewage and the pollution either directly or indirectly of the navigable streams and lakes of the United States.'' Dr. Rupert Blue, who directed the agency's efforts to eradicate plague in San Francisco following the earthquake of 1906, became surgeon general. That same year saw the founding of the National Organization of Public Health Nursing.

World War I. On April 2, 1917, President Woodrow Wilson asked Congress to declare war on Germany. The following day, he issued an executive order making the Public Health Service part of the U.S. military. By that fall, more than half a million men were drafted and sent to makeshift training camps. The Public Health Service was set to work ensuring sanitary conditions, including drinking water and waste disposal.

The Public Health Service was also charged with controlling the spread of venereal disease among servicemen, which included treating infected prostitutes. In 1918, the Army Appropriation Act established a division of venereal disease within the Public Health Service with a budget of $2 million.

In 1918, following an outbreak of ''Spanish influenza'' that eventually spread to 46 states and killed half a million Americans, Congress created a Reserve Corps that allowed the Public Health Service to recruit health professionals other than physicians for emergency duty. More than 2,000 doctors, nurses, and clerks were recruited to the Public Health Service during the epidemic.

Federal Security Agency. The Federal Security Agency became responsible for the care of returning soldiers, and by 1921 the agency operated 62 hospitals. But in 1922, Congress established the Veteran's Bureau, later to become the Department of Veteran Affairs, which took over all but 24 Marine Service hospitals. The 1920s also saw new attempts to consolidate government services into a national department of health. However, Surgeon General Hugh S. Cumming opposed the move, which he believed would diminish the role of the Public Health Service, and the efforts failed.

In 1930, Congress passed two acts that would significantly affect public health administration in the United States. The first was the Parker Act, named for New York Congressman James S. Parker, which authorized the Public Health Service to recruit sanitary engineers, pharmacists, and dentists for the Commissioned Corps. The second was the Ransdell Act, named for Louisiana Senator Joseph Ransdell, which created an expanded National Institute of Health within the Public Health Service in place of the Hygienic Laboratory.

The Public Health Service continued to expand under President Franklin D. Roosevelt, whose New Deal programs included the Social Security Act, passed in 1935, which provided federal grants for states to develop public health programs in addition to benefits for retired workers. In 1936, the Public Health Service received applications for funds from every state, which ultimately led to creation of the Division of State Relations.

In 1937, Congress passed the National Cancer Act, which created the National Cancer Institute. In addition to setting up laboratories within the Public Health Service, the National Cancer Institute awarded research grants to individuals and nongovernmental institutions, establishing a pattern for federal support of biomedical research. In 1938, Congress passed the Venereal Disease

Control Act, which for the first time charged the Public Health Service with eradicating specific diseases.

In 1939, Roosevelt issued an executive order that brought the Public Health Service under the administration of the newly created Federal Security Agency, along with the Civilian Conservation Corps, National Youth Administration, Office of Education, U.S. Employment Service, and Social Security Board. The Food and Drug Administration was added in 1940.

World War II. At the start of World War II, Public Health Service officers were assigned to each of the Army Service Commands to oversee sanitary conditions. The Public Health Service also coordinated state emergency medical services, including a nationwide network of 300 hospitals to treat casualties, and commissioned officers served in war zones with the U.S. Coast Guard from 1941 to 1945. In 1942, the Public Health Service created the Office of Malaria Control in War Areas, based in Atlanta, which attempted to control the spread of disease in Southern states and the Caribbean by eradicating mosquito larvae and draining swamps. By 1943, the Office of Malaria Control, which extended its scope to include typhus, employed 4,300 people, including 300 commissioned officers. Between 1940 and 1945, the Public Health Service doubled in size, to 16,000 employees, while the Commissioned Corps quadrupled to 2,600 officers, two-thirds of whom were in the Reserve Corps.

As the war wound down, Congress began to enact legislation that would shape the future of the Public Health Service, beginning with the Public Health Service Act of 1944, which consolidated and revised most of the legislation then relating to the Public Health Service. The act also realigned the Public Health Service into four divisions: the Office of the Surgeon General, the Bureau of Medical Services, the Bureau of State Services, and the National Institute of Health. In 1946, the Office of Malaria Control became the Communicable Disease Center under the Bureau of State Services. The Public Health Service also assumed responsibility for national vital statistics, which had been a function of the Census Bureau.

A critical shortage of health care facilities after the war also led to creation of the National Hospital Survey and Construction Program in 1946, which provided grants for construction of state-run hospitals and positioned the Public Health Service as the lead agency in the planning, design, and operation of medical facilities. Between 1947 and 1971, the Public Health Service disbursed $3.7 billion in state grants, accounting for about 10 percent of all hospital construction in the United States. Under the National Mental Health Act, also passed in 1946, the Public Health Service established a broad program of grants for research, training, and creation of mental health services.

Health, Education, and Welfare. The research facility founded as the Hygiene Laboratory in 1887 became the National Institutes of Health in 1948 with creation of the National Heart Institute, National Institute of Dental Research, National Microbiological Institute (which would become the National Institute of Allergy and Infectious Diseases in 1955), and Experimental Biology and Medical Institute (which would be absorbed into the National Institute of Arthritis and Metabolic Disease in 1950). Other institutes of health would be created later, beginning with the National Institute of Mental Health in 1949 and concluding with the National Institute on Aging in 1974.

In the late 1940s, the Hoover Commission on Executive Reorganization also recommended creation of a Cabinet-level department for education and welfare. But it was not until 1953 that newly elected President Dwight D. Eisenhower created the Department of Health, Education, and Welfare (HEW) by executive order. The new department, which would become the Department of Health and Human Services in 1979 with the creation of the Department of Education, assumed all functions of the Federal Security Agency. Oveta Culp Hobby was appointed secretary of HEW, but administration of the Public Health Service remained with the surgeon general.

The Public Health Service faced a major crisis soon after the reorganization. In 1955, Surgeon General Leonard Scheele endorsed a new vaccine for polio developed by Dr. Jonas Salk, and HEW issued licenses to six pharmaceutical companies to begin distribution. Within two weeks, there were reports from across the country that vaccinated children were developing full-blown polio. Scheele issued a statement calling for a halt to all vaccinations while the vaccine was reexamined. The problem was quickly traced to one pharmaceutical company, but more than 70 children contracted polio from the vaccine and 11 died. Secretary Hobby and her special assistant for medical affairs resigned two months later.

Despite the polio scare, the Public Health Service continued to expand beginning in 1955, when the Bureau of Indian Affairs (BIA) in the U.S. Department of Interior transferred responsibility for Indian health care programs. Federal health care for Native Americans had begun in the early nineteenth century with Army doctors attempting to contain smallpox and other contagious diseases among tribes living near military posts. Originally part of the War Department, the BIA was transferred to the Department of the Interior in 1849, with the first federal hospital for Indians built in Oklahoma in the 1880s. By the mid-1950s, the BIA operated 48 hospitals and was responsible for the health of more than half a million Indians and Alaska natives.

The Armed Forces Medical Library, later known as the National Library of Medicine, became part of the

Public Health Service in 1956. Further expansions came with the Community Health Services and Facilities Act of 1961, the Vaccination Assistance Act and the Health Professionals Education Act of 1963, and the Nurse Training Act of 1964—each of which directed the Public Health Service to provide financial or research support for state health care programs.

Smoking. In the mid-1950s, the Public Health Service, the American Cancer Society, and the American Heart Association formed a panel to study the effect of smoking on health. In 1956, Surgeon General Leroy Burney wrote an obscure article for the *Journal of the American Medical Association* that concluded, ''The weight of evidence at present implicates smoking as the principal etiological factor in the increased incidence of lung cancer.''

In 1964 HEW published the results of a two-year study, entitled ''Smoking and Health: Report of the Advisory Committee to the Surgeon General of the Public Health Service,'' that reaffirmed the earlier conclusion. Dr. Terry Luther, who succeeded Burney, declared, ''Cigarette smoking is causally related to lung cancer in men. The magnitude of the effect of cigarette smoking far outweighs all other factors. The data for women, though less extensive, point in the same direction.''

Based on the Public Health Service report, Congress passed legislation in 1966 that required a warning label on all cigarette packaging. Cigarette ads were banned from radio and television in 1971, and cigarette companies were required to include a health warning in advertising in 1972.

Reorganization. After Lyndon Johnson became president in 1963, he presented Congress with a far-reaching program of social reform that included major health-related legislation. In 1965, Congress passed laws that expanded the role of the Public Health Service in the fight against heart disease, the care of migrant workers, the vaccination of children, and local health care planning. However, the most significant health care legislation, Medicare and Medicaid, did not involve the Public Health Service, which viewed the programs as medical insurance rather than the provision of health care.

In 1965 John Gardner became secretary of HEW and transferred the surgeon general's statutory authority to himself, although Dr. William Stewart, who had succeeded Terry as surgeon general, continued as head of the agency. Then in 1968, Wilbur Cohen replaced Gardner and initiated another reorganization. He created three agencies within the Public Health Service: the National Institutes of Health, the Food and Drug Administration, and the Health Services and Mental Health Administration. Cohen also assigned administrative responsibility to Dr. Philip Lee, then the assistant secretary for health and scientific affairs. The surgeon general was relegated to deputy administrator.

The changes continued after Richard Nixon was elected president in 1968. In 1969, Secretary of HEW Robert Finch appointed Dr. Jesse Steinfeld to be surgeon general, over the protests of many in the administration who thought the job should be left vacant. When Elliot Richardson replaced Finch in 1971, he appointed a committee chaired by former Undersecretary of HEW John Perkins to study the future of the Commissioned Corps. The committee concluded that the Commissioned Corps should be replaced by a civil service career system for health care professionals and that the position of surgeon general should be eliminated. The recommendation was never carried out, but the position of surgeon general was left unfilled for four years after Steinfeld resigned in 1973. The deputy surgeon general, Dr. S. Paul Ehrlich, Jr., fulfilled the ceremonial duties of the surgeon general until 1977.

Despite the controversy surrounding the role of the surgeon general, the Public Health Service expanded under the Nixon Administration. In 1970, Congress passed the Occupational Safety and Health Act, which created the Occupational Safety and Health Administration (OSHA) within the Department of Labor to establish and enforce workplace health and safety standards. The law also created a National Institute for Occupational Safety and Health under the Public Health Service to study the causes of employee illnesses and accidents. In 1970, the Public Health Service also established the Institute on Alcohol Abuse and Alcoholism and the National Health Service Corps, which recruited health care professionals for rural areas of the country with a critical shortage of health care services.

Tuskegee Project. The Public Health Service faced another controversy in 1972, when a former venereal disease program worker raised questions of ethics and racial prejudice in the Tuskegee syphilis project. In the early 1930s, the Public Health Service, the Macon County, Alabama, Health Department, and the Tuskegee Institute began studying syphilis in a group of black patients. They continued the study without medical intervention for almost 40 years, despite the fact that penicillin had proved effective against syphilis in the 1940s. The Center for Disease Control attempted to defend the study by claiming that penicillin sometimes led to adverse reactions in patients with advanced cases of syphilis. However, a medical review panel dismissed the claim and called for an immediate end to the project. The government later paid $10 million in out-of-court settlements to survivors of the program and families of those who had died.

Following revelations about the Tuskegee Project, the Public Health Service underwent another reorganization in 1973, when five operational level agencies were created under the Office of the Assistant Secretary for Health. The Centers for Disease Control was established as a separate agency, along with the Health Resources Administration, the Health Services Administration, the Food and Drug Administration, and the National Institutes of Health. A sixth agency, the Alcohol, Drug Abuse, and Mental Health Administration, was created in 1974. The name was later changed to the Substance Abuse and Mental Health Services Administration.

Swine Flu. Late in 1975, four Army recruits fell ill with a new strain of influenza, dubbed ''swine flu,'' that was believed related to the pandemic Spanish influenza of 1918 that killed more than half a million Americans. The swine flu virus was isolated in 1976, and the Public Health Service began preparing for a nationwide immunization program that fall. When more than 200 people came down with a respiratory illness after attending an American Legion convention in Philadelphia, the immunization program was put into effect. Almost 50 million Americans were inoculated between October and the middle of December.

However, by November there were also hundreds of reports of a rare condition known as Guillain-Barre Syndrome, which left its victims paralyzed. Horribly, the cause was traced to the swine flu vaccine. Moreover, researchers had proved that the ''Legionnaires disease'' was not swine flu, and there had not been any reports of swine flu in the United States since the four recruits had become ill a year earlier. The Public Health Service announced suspension of the immunization program on December 16, 1976. More than 1,000 people eventually developed Guillain-Barre Syndrome and the government paid more than $84 million in liability claims.

Healthy People. In 1977, President Jimmy Carter appointed Joseph Califano as secretary of HEW. Califano then recruited Dr. Julius Richmond, the first director of Project Head Start, as Assistant Secretary for Health. However, Richmond agreed to serve only if he also was appointed surgeon general, thus filling the vacancy that had existed since 1973 and avoiding the ambiguity of who ran the Public Health Service.

Richmond established an Office of Disease Prevention and Health Promotion to launch what he called a ''second health revolution'' that would address the issues of smoking, drinking, nutrition, sedentary living, and poor safety practices. In 1979, the Office of Disease Prevention and Health Promotion published ''The Surgeon General's Report on Health Promotion and Disease Prevention.''

The report, which became known as ''Healthy People,'' established goals for 1990 that included a 35 percent reduction in infant mortality, a 20 percent reduction in mortality among all age groups, and a 20 percent reduction in the number of days of illness among the elderly. In the forward, Califano said, ''You, the individual, can do more for your own health and well-being than any doctor, any hospital, any drug, any exotic medical device.'' A companion report, ''Objectives for the Nation,'' was published in 1980 and established specific targets by age group for several health categories.

During the 1980s, the Public Health Service continued to report that people were not adopting healthier lifestyles, and in 1990, the Office of Disease Prevention and Health Promotion extended its target date another decade with the publication of ''Healthy People 2000: National Health Promotion and Disease Prevention Objectives.'' The American Public Health Association published a guide, ''Eleven Steps to a Healthy Community,'' to assist states in achieving the ''Healthy People 2000'' objectives, and in 1993 reported that 41 states had adopted its model program.

AIDS. In 1981, doctors in the United States began reporting a strange new disease that left healthy young men susceptible to a variety of rare infections and cancers. In 1982, the Centers for Disease Control gave the disease a name, acquired immune deficiency syndrome (AIDS), after discovering that it weakened the body's disease-fighting immune system. In 1983, the Public Health Service issued its first set of guidelines on AIDS prevention, which urged high-risk individuals to change their sexual practices and refrain from donating blood. In 1986, Koop released a more controversial report, much of which he wrote himself, urging sex education beginning in grade school and the use of condoms. He also denounced the notion of quarantines and called for tolerance.

Meanwhile, other agencies within the Public Health Service also became involved in the campaign against AIDS. In 1985, the Centers for Disease Control announced that it was safe for children with the disease to attend school, however, it recommended precautions for younger children who might be more likely to bite or scratch each other. The Food and Drug Administration also approved a test to screen for AIDS among blood donors, and announced that the nation's blood supply was again safe.

Then in 1988, Koop took the dramatic step of writing and mailing an eight-page brochure on AIDS, ''Understanding AIDS,'' to all 107 million households in the United States—the largest public health educational campaign ever. In 1988, the Public Health Service also established the National AIDS Program to provide support and coordination for federal, local, and private-sector efforts. During Koop's tenure as surgeon general, he also issued the first surgeon general's report on the health hazards of smokeless tobacco and assumed formal command of the Commissioned Corps, then with 5,500 uniformed officers. The Public Health Service also closed the last of the Marine Hospitals and assumed responsibility for health aspects of the toxic waste clean-up program known as Superfund.

CURRENT CONDITIONS.

Further controversies with subsequent Clinton Administration nominees left the surgeon general's post vacant for more than two years. Shalala and Lee retained their posts in Clinton's second term.

As the century came to a close, it was easy, by funding and media coverage alone, to identify the most pressing public health issues: AIDS, tobacco-related disease and morbidity, food safety, and (more diffusely) the ability of the United States to respond to disease brought into the country from foreign sources. The World Health Organization had reported increases in infectious diseases, including a resurgence of tuberculosis, and U.S. pharmaceutical companies tried to keep pace with antimicrobials intended to defeat new strains of ''superbugs,'' a term applied to mutated viruses and bacterium that are resistant to conventional treatments.

A 1998 report from the CDC indicated that there were approximately 400,000 tobacco-use related deaths per year in the U.S. alone. The 1999 class action settlements with tobacco companies were allocated among federal and state agencies to assist in treatment and education programs to address this problem. The 1998 ''Fen Phen'' scare, as well as illnesses and deaths reportedly connected to contaminated herbal sprouts and pet chews (pig ears and animal hooves), were addressed by the FDA. The FDA also released statements in 1999 proposing new rules regarding nutrition labeling on food products and the safe handling of eggs and egg products. In September 1999 the FDA also issued a statement identifying a potential link between incidence of Down Syndrome and low maternal levels of folic acid.

Congress continued to negotiate a fiscal year 2000 budget that would increase NIH funding substantially (more than $2 billion) despite Clinton's budget request for only $320 million.

FURTHER READING

''1999 Food & Nutrition FDA Press Releases & Fact Sheets,'' 12 November 1999. Available from http://vm.cfsan.fda.gov/-lrd/press.html.

''House and Senate Negotiators Shape a Bill to Increase NIH Funds.'' *Chronicle of Higher Education,* 29 October 1999.

Mullan, Fitzhugh. *Plagues and Politics; The Story of the United States Public Health Service.* New York: Basic Books, 1989.

''State-Specific Prevalence Among Adults of Current Smoking and Smokeless Tobacco Use.'' *JAMA,* 6 January 1999.

''Stopping Microbial Killers.'' *The Futurist,* June-July 1998.

U.S. Department of Health and Human Services. ''HHS: What We Do.'' Washington, D.C.: 1999. Available from http://www.hhs.gov/about/profile.html.

SIC 9441

ADMINISTRATION OF SOCIAL, HUMAN RESOURCE, AND INCOME MAINTENANCE PROGRAMS

This category covers government agencies engaged in assistance to the elderly, child welfare, aid to families with dependent children, aid to the blind and disabled, medical assistance, human resource development, and related activities. The actual operations of the programs are classified in various social services industries. But both the administration and operation of Social Security, disability benefits under OASDI, Disability Insurance, Medicare, unemployment insurance, workman's compensation, and other social insurance programs for the aged, survivors, or disabled persons are classified under this industry. The offices that administer veterans' programs are classified in **SIC 9451: Administration of Veterans' Affairs, Except Health Insurance.** Local employment service offices are classified in Services under **SIC 7361: Employment Agencies.**

NAICS CODE(S)

923130 (Administration of Social, Human Resources and Income Maintenance Programs)

INDUSTRY SNAPSHOT

Federal activities directed toward the social welfare of Americans are overseen by divisions within the U.S. Department of Health and Human Services (HHS). It was created in 1953 as the Department of Health, Education, and Welfare (HEW). Following the Department of Education Organization Act, the Administration for Children and Families (ACF) is considered the largest (in terms of government-originated spending) and most expensive under HHS's umbrella. In 1999 this agency was expected to spend approximately $35 billion on programs and agency overhead. Fewer than 2 million families received aid to families with dependent children (AFDC) payments in 1970, but two decades later that number had grown to 4.6 million families. In 1997 the new welfare reform legislation was implemented, replacing the AFDC with Temporary Assistance to Needy Families, a state-federal program serving approximately 12 million people, including 8.4 million children. In August 1997 The Children's Health Insurance Program (CHIP) was enacted as Title XXI to the Social Security Act, to expand health insurance coverage for low-income children.

ORGANIZATION AND STRUCTURE

Social Security Administration. The National Old-Age, Survivors, and Disability Insurance (OASDI) program, commonly called Social Security, is the largest federal income maintenance program. The benefits, administered by the Social Security Administration (SSA), are for retired workers (Social Security Act of 1935), disabled workers (1956 amendment), and their dependents and survivors (1939 amendment). Compulsory tax withholdings from employees, employers, and the self-employed are put in the OASI and DI trust funds to be used for retirement, death or disability benefits, benefits for survivors, vocational rehabilitation, and administrative expenses.

Also administered by the SSA is the Supplemental Security Income program (SSI). Established in 1972, SSI replaced Old-Age Assistance (OAA), Aid to the Blind (AB), and Aid to the Permanently and Totally Disabled (APTD). The program was intended for people without any other source of income.

Health Care Financing Administration. Some 72 million Americans in 1997 were beneficiaries of Medicare and Medicaid programs administered by the Health Care Financing Administration (HCFA). Medicare recipients are the aged and disabled. Medicare consists of two programs: Hospital Insurance (HI) and Supplementary Medical Insurance (SMI). Medicare was the segment of the federal social security system in the most trouble in the early 1990s. Medicaid is for persons of limited means and is administered by the states.

Other Departments and Programs. The Office for Civil Rights within the Department of Health and Human Services is also responsible for the administration and enforcement of laws (e.g., the Americans with Disabilities Act of 1990 or the provisions of the Equal Employment Opportunity Acts) prohibiting discrimination in federally assisted health and human services programs.

Unemployment Insurance, a federal and state program, provides benefits for the involuntarily unemployed. Workers Compensation, mainly administered by the states, is for insured injured workers. Other work-related programs, such as Black Lung, are administered by the U.S. Department of Labor.

BACKGROUND AND DEVELOPMENT

The concept of social welfare has existed in some form or another throughout much of history. Some 4,000 years ago, Babylonian ruler Hammurabi was among the first in government to voice concern for protecting the needy. Ancient Greek and Roman philosophers, too, supported the concept of society helping those in need. And grounds for assistance of the poor are found in a number of religious traditions, including Judaism and Christianity.

America's Social Welfare Roots. In the European Middle Ages (476-1453) Christian monasteries served the needy. Their hospitals provided a broad range of services for the ill, homeless, aged, orphans, and even travelers. They were, of course, far removed from the acute care institutions of modern America. Under the laws of the day, the medieval church was responsible for public welfare and could collect taxes to support its activities.

Medieval life was characterized by feudalism and under this system most people were assured of at least minimal assistance for life. In the cities, those in need received some assistance from social, craft, and merchant guilds. Social stability, limited mobility, and a sense of obligation to the poor and needy of the community were essential to the social welfare activities of the Middle Ages. But eventually a series of upheavals resulted in a breakdown of this basic social welfare system. These included the bubonic plague (1348-49), which killed nearly one-third of the English population, and several other natural disasters. With the decline of the Church of England, which had been largely responsible for social welfare, a new system was needed.

In response the English government in the mid-fourteenth century began placing restrictions on the poor and unemployed, as well as taking some responsibility for organizing voluntary assistance. These early English laws regarding the needy included: restrictions on begging and later laws against it (with death as one possible consequence to repeat offenders), involuntary apprenticeships for the children of the poor, and taxes and assessments to help provide for the needy and the poor. Such laws were drawn together under the Elizabethan Poor Law of 1601. It was this law that became the basis for early social welfare laws in America.

Problems of the Old World arrived in the New World in spite of an abundance of land and opportunity. The needs of the poor, the aged, the sick, and others were at first taken care of by the individual colonies, but as towns grew so did needs, and the colonists turned to the English Poor Law for guidance. Another strong influence was the Puritan value and belief system regarding poverty—the poor were considered inferior but part of God's order and were to be assisted by the people higher up on God's natural hierarchy. Some colonies made decisions regarding the poor in town meetings. One application of aid was to place a needy person in a private home for a fee. Other colonies gave tax relief directly to the poor or to physicians aiding the poor.

In general, communities took care of their own but showed resistance to assisting a growing number of strangers or newcomers. Some colonies, such as early seventeenth-century Boston, passed laws allowing for forced removal of unemployed strangers, and the Plymouth Colony passed a residency statute regarding public assistance. Registering, bonding, fines, and whippings were other methods New England colonies used to deal with nonresidents they feared would become dependent on or destructive to the community.

Yet by the late 1700s, just prior to the American Revolution, certain colonies were spending as much as 35 percent of municipal funds on urban poverty. Urban problems had been exacerbated by war refugees and disabled soldiers from the French and Indian War in Canada, illegitimate children (up to one-half of all births during the Revolutionary period), widows of seafaring workers, and people affected by economic depressions, fires, and epidemics.

Religious, ethnic, and fraternal groups, as well as wealthy philanthropists, played major roles in assisting the poor: it was a period of cooperation between the public and private sectors, influenced by the humanitarian tenets of the Great Awakening (an evangelistic religious movement that occurred around 1740) and the Enlightenment (a philosophical movement that generally took place in Europe and elsewhere from 1700 to about 1789, or the beginning of the French Revolution). But the tradition of local assistance was widely disrupted following the American Revolution. Immigrants came in huge numbers; and industrialization, the spread of wage labor, and the growth of urban areas resulted in increased burdens on local governments.

In addition, broader social and economic changes in the Western world were transforming the traditional view of poverty. Classical economists of the eighteenth century supported the concept of an unregulated economy and saw social welfare programs as interfering with a natural economic process. In England the Poor Law of 1601 was revised to reflect these new views. The law that had upheld the belief that the needy should be assisted came to an end after nearly 250 years. The new view was that poverty was a moral, not a social, problem. Such factors of the work environment as low wages, depressed industries, limited opportunity, and seasonal and technological unemployment were dismissed as barriers to individual achievement. Communities became reluctant to assist the needy and larger county- and state-run institutions were formed to take care of the problem. In 1824 the New York legislature passed the County Poor House Act and thus marked a shift from the towns to the counties as social-service providers. During the same period mental hospitals, prisons, and orphanages also were being established.

Another shift in American attitudes toward social welfare came during the Civil War. The needy benefited from the general understanding that in war, circumstances were beyond the control of the individual. Significantly, the first national public-health group was formed and mainly operated by women. The United States Sanitary Commission organized local voluntary organizations to provide health education programs for soldiers. For the first time, the federal government was seen as the coordinator of social welfare needs that were universal in nature.

Problems that the United States faced prior to the war, such as those created by industrialization and urbanization, had to be contended with following the war; in addition, the nation was faced with the urgent needs of ex-slaves. The Congress created the first federal welfare agency, the Bureau of Refugees, Freedmen, and Abandoned Lands in the U.S. Department of War, to help during the transition from slavery to freedom. In existence from 1865 to 1872, the Bureau distributed food and assisted with employment, educational costs, and medical care. The federal government would not get as deeply involved in social welfare again until almost 100 years later. The nation continued to depend on voluntary organizations and local, county, and state governments for social welfare services.

Mothers' Pensions. Mothers' (or widows') pensions were early twentieth-century programs to assist single or widowed women with children. These programs marked yet another turning point in the debate between the deserving and the undeserving poor. The programs set some precedents for America's social welfare policy-to-come by keeping children with their mothers and keeping mothers at home rather than in the workplace.

The Birth of Social Security. In March 1933 Franklin Delano Roosevelt assumed the presidency and, with it, the daunting task of bringing the nation out of the Great Depression. Within his first hundred days in office he oversaw the passage of much of his New Deal program. But it was not until 1935 that the Social Security Act was passed. In its original form, this law established unemployment relief and old-age assistance, or social insurance, for American workers and designated that monthly benefits begin in 1940. The system was designed to return at least as much in benefits as an individual worker had paid in to the government. However, a 1939 amendment to the act weakened this commitment by instituting a formula in which benefits received would be based on average earnings during a confined period. The act also extended benefits to survivors and dependents, as well as the retired. In essence, social security was made to benefit a large cross-section of the population at the expense of its original intent.

In 1972 Congress added an automatic cost-of-living index to social security, so that benefits would rise accordingly. However, due to an error in the indexing plan, benefits began to rise faster than earnings. Despite 1977 legislation designed to correct the error, the social security fund continued to experience problems, largely due to high inflation and unemployment. Further legislation was introduced in 1983 to ensure OASDI's long-term health by, among other things, requiring a rise in the retirement age from 65 to 67, to take place between the years 2003 and 2027.

With the majority of American workers still under 45 years of age and years away from retirement, public sentiment during the early 1990s was toward changing social-security policy to deal with the staggering financial burden. Changes suggested included: increasing retirement age to 72 years of age to delay payments; elimination of income limits on retirees in order to increase tax revenue; and the termination of surplus social-security funds held in Treasury bills that are costly to redeem. Other changes suggested included separating out low-income old age benefits from benefits related to contributions to the social security system. The federal social security retirement fund solvency was guaranteed until 2010 by 1983 congressional amendments, but the program's future beyond that date was considered uncertain.

Current Conditions.

With unemployment rates dropping in 1999 to the lowest levels since the 1970s (approximately 4 percent), America's attention shifted from welfare programs to retirement benefits. The Social Security Solvency Act of 1998, a contentious piece of legislation, never made it through in its proposed form. Notwithstanding, by 1999 the use of an estimated $2.5 trillion Social Security surplus was hotly debated in Congress, resolved by a joint measure (referred to as the "lockbox" bill) to secure the trust fund from congressional meandering. Beginning in October 1999, the SSA intends to provide annual updates to the nation's employed, aged 25 and older, timed to arrive three months before an annual birthday. The statements, at a cost of $75 million annually, will show current personal balances in each individual's account and project estimated retirement benefits. For those born after 1970, there will be a gradual increase in age requirement before full retirement benefits may be withdrawn: from 65 to 67. This measure is expected to affect 96 percent of the employed population in 2000.

Because of the extreme 1998-1999 bull market in stocks, the "privatization" of social security accounts gained much attention—and political exposure. Two schools of thought emerged: one giving the federal government the authority to invest social security funds into speculative growth funds, and another allowing individuals to direct the destiny of their own funds, equal to an amount currently deducted from their paychecks. Negative consequences attach to both alternatives, so the twentieth century ended without any major changes to policy.

By 1999 all 50 states and the District of Columbia had complied with CHIP's requirement to develop plans for children's health insurance. Some 18 states chose to implement this under Medicaid, while 17 states developed programs independent of Medicaid. By the year 2007, nearly $40 billion will be earmarked for this program.

Another critical issue in 1999 was Medicaid reimbursements to nursing homes, affecting 70 percent of nursing-home residents in the country. Average reimbursement rates in 1998 varied from $329 per day in Alaska, down to just $62 per day in Nebraska. The disparity was the result of the Balanced Budget Act of 1997, giving block grants to states to control their own Medicaid costs. On the agenda are plans for legislators to tie reimbursement funds to quality of care received.

America and the World

The social security systems of many countries around the world were experiencing a period of crisis during the 1990s. What had once been used as a financial reserve for some industrial governments had now become a costly problem. George Kopits wrote in *Finance and Development,* "Until the 1970s, social insurance schemes prospered financially and gained considerable popularity, as the first generations of enrolled retirees and employed were able to benefit in amounts that often far exceeded their contributions during relatively short service periods." Inflation, rising oil prices, and economic slowdowns stressed even the most affluent nations.

Further Reading

"Congress: Stop Us Before We Spend Again." *U.S. News & World Report,* 7 June 1999.

Franklin, Mary Beth. "Still Think You Can Retire at 65?" *Kipplinger's Personal Finance Magazine,* September 1999.

Kilborn, Peter T., and Sam Howe Verhovek. "Welfare Shift Reflects New Democrat." *New York Times,* 2 August 1996.

"The National Debt." *Business Week,* 9 August 1999.

"Social Security Privatization:CBO's Crippen Slams Clinton Plan." Washington, D.C.: The Cato Institute, November 13-14, 1999. Available from http://www.socialsecurity.org/.

Ullman, Frank, Ian Hill, and Ruth Almeida. "CHIP: A Look at Emerging State Progams." Washington, D.C.: The Urban Institute, 1999. Available from http://newfederalism.urban.org/html/anf_135.html.

Wiener, Joshua M., and David G. Stevenson. ''Repeal of the *Boren Amendment:* Implications for Quality of Care in Nursing Homes.'' Washington, D.C.: The Urban Institute, 1999. Available from http://newfederalism.urban.org/html/anf30.html.

SIC 9451

ADMINISTRATION OF VETERANS AFFAIRS, EXCEPT HEALTH AND INSURANCE

This category includes government establishments primarily engaged in administration of programs of assistance, training, counseling, and other services to veterans and their dependents, heirs, or survivors. Also included are offices that maintain liaison and coordinate activities with other service organizations and governmental agencies. Veterans hospitals are classified in Hospitals categories, and veterans' insurance in the Insurance Carriers industries.

NAICS CODE(S)

923140 (Administration of Veteran's Affairs)

INDUSTRY SNAPSHOT

In 1999, there were an estimated 25.6 million veterans in the United States, most of whom served during periods of armed conflict. More than 70 million Americans, including veterans and their dependents, were potentially eligible for veterans benefits provided by the U.S. government, representing approximately one-third of the nation's population.

Veterans' benefits were administered by the Department of Veterans Affairs, second in size only to the Department of Defense among government departments. In 1999, the Department of Veterans Affairs had a budget of $43.7 billion. Department-wide employment totaled 235,300, down from 266,000 in 1993. About $23.5 billion of the department's budget went to veterans or their dependents in the form of disability payments, pensions, and educational benefits. Another $18.3 billion went for medical care. The remaining $1.6 billion was divided among housing credit assistance programs, life insurance benefits, cemetery maintenance, and administration.

ORGANIZATION AND STRUCTURE

The U.S. Department of Veterans Affairs is organized into three functional agencies: the Veterans Health Administration, the Veterans Benefits Administration, and the National Cemetery System. The Veterans Health Administration operates the largest health care system in the nation, including 173 medical centers, 133 nursing homes, 40 domiciliary care units, and 398 outpatient clinics. An estimated 3.6 million veterans received medical treatment in 1999. Combat veterans also received counseling at more than 200 Vietnam Veteran Outreach Centers for a variety of problems, including post-traumatic stress disorder. The budget for medical programs in 1999 totaled more than 40 percent of the total budget.

The Veterans Benefits Administration is responsible for most nonmedical benefit programs, including disability compensation, pensions, burial benefits, rehabilitation assistance, home loan guarantees, and insurance. These entitlement programs amounted to $20.1 billion in 1999, when the agency processed approximately 3.5 million claims by veterans seeking disability compensation or pensions. Another 631,640 widows, children, or parents of deceased veterans were receiving survivor benefits. In addition, more than 370,000 veterans or their dependents were receiving educational benefits, and about 343,954 veterans had received home loan guarantees for new mortgages as well as refinancing. Since the GI Bill of Rights was passed in 1944, the government has guaranteed home loans for more than 15 million veterans and their dependents. About 20.7 million veterans and dependents have attended college or received job training. The Veterans Benefits Administration also administers the fourth largest insurance program in the United States, with 2.2 million policyholders.

The National Cemetery System consists of 114 cemeteries and 34 memorials and monuments to veterans of the nation's wars. More than 2 million veterans and family members are buried in these national cemeteries, which occupy more than 5,000 developed acres. The U.S. Department of Veterans Affairs also provides headstones and markers for veterans' graves in private cemeteries. In 1999, the National Cemetery System's 1,300 employees provided more than 61,370 interments. The agency projects that its interments will increase nearly 50 percent by 2008.

BACKGROUND AND DEVELOPMENT

The United States has provided veterans' benefits since 1818, when Congress finally agreed to pay veterans of the Revolutionary War pensions they had been promised for more than 40 years. During the War, the Continental Congress had encouraged enlistments by promising pensions for soldiers who were disabled in the fighting. It also approved a lifetime pension amounting to half pay for all officers. However, since the Continental Congress did not have the power to raise money through taxes, there was no practical way to fulfill either promise.

In 1780, the Continental Congress voted to give officers who served until the end of the war half-pay for life, but according to Richard Severo and Lewis Milford, authors of *The Wages of War,* few officers ever expected to receive pensions since the Continental Congress lacked the resources to pay soldiers even their regular wages. In December 1817, after several other failed efforts, President James Monroe asked Congress to approve pensions for all veterans of the Revolutionary War and the War of 1812. Monroe told Congress, "In contemplating the happy situation of the United States our attention is drawn, with peculiar interest, to the surviving officers and soldiers of our Revolutionary Army, who so eminently contributed, by their services, to lay its foundation." Congress passed a bill the following year to give enlisted men $8 per month and officers $20.

Nearly 19,000 veterans applied for pensions in 1818. However, following the Panic of 1819, Congress amended the law to require that veterans be indigent before they qualified for a pension. More than 6,000 veterans were dropped from the pension rolls when they failed to prove poverty. These first pensions were administered by the office of the Secretary of War from 1818 until 1833, when Congress created the Bureau of Pensions, also within the Department of War. Prior to the Civil War, the administration of veterans' benefits was criticized for encouraging ex-soldiers to live at the government's expense and for encouraging graft and corruption.

Civil War. In many ways, the treatment of veterans after the Civil War was similar to what followed the Revolutionary War. By 1866, nearly 1 million Union soldiers had been demobilized and returned to their homes only to find there were no jobs available. The average Union soldier received about $250 when he was discharged, but very little else. By 1868, New York Governor Reuben E. Fenton lamented that homeless veterans in his state "are numbered by the thousands, and are altogether beyond the power of Executive and Legislative relief." He added that "their needs cannot be postponed," and called upon charitable organizations to help. The *North American Review* also estimated that in 1866 more than 5,000 former Union or Confederate soldiers were in state prisons, and one prison physician reported, "They have come to us with constitutions shattered by wounds, disease or intemperance." An estimated 45,000 veterans were addicted to morphine or heroin, which they had been given during the war for their injuries, and drug addiction came to be known as "the soldier's disease."

The United States did provide an annual pension for those who lost a limb: $75 for a leg or $50 for an arm. And in 1866, Congress funded the National Home for Disabled Voluntary Soldiers, which housed soldiers in 13 homes. However, the Commission of Inquiry and Advice in Respect to the Sanitary Interests of the United States Armed Forces advised that the government could not afford to pay for medical treatment of Civil War veterans.

When the Civil War ended, the United States had imposed a 5-year cutoff on disability claims. The Arrears Act of 1879 allowed Civil War veterans to file new claims and collect pensions retroactively. John Sherman, then Secretary of the Treasury, estimated the pensions would cost as much as $150 million, and the *New York Tribune* predicted "a grand scramble by a horde of hungry claims agents to get their hands on vast unearned portions of the national treasury." President Rutherford B. Hayes signed the bill into law despite the pressure to veto it. More than 47,000 new claims were filed in 1879 and nearly 140,000 in 1880, thus creating the first large veterans' administration bureaucracy. The Pension Building in Washington, D.C., was built in 1882 for the 1,500 clerks then needed to administer military pensions.

Grand Army of the Republic. Civil War veterans soon banded together to help influence governmental decisions concerning veterans' affairs. One such association was the secretive Grand Army of the Republic, founded in 1866, which was open to all honorably discharged members of the Union armed forces who served between April 12, 1861, and April 9, 1865. The Grand Army of the Republic began as a fellowship, but soon took a more active role in petitioning the government to provide pensions and homes for veterans. By 1885, the Grand Army of the Republic had nearly 250,000 members and was a powerful force in national politics.

Following the Civil War, veterans' benefits were the largest single item in the federal budget, accounting for almost 18 percent of the total. Nevertheless, when President Grover Cleveland vetoed a bill in 1887 that would have provided all disabled veterans with pensions, regardless of whether their disabilities were caused by military service, the Grand Army of the Republic launched a campaign to defeat him in the next election. When Benjamin Harrison was elected in 1888, the*National Tribune,* newspaper of the Grand Army of the Republic, bragged that veterans had "vetoed the great vetoer." Harrison, a brigadier general in the Civil War, was mindful of the support he received from the Grand Army of the Republic and appointed James Tanner, commander of the G.A.R.'s New York Department, to head the Pension Bureau. Tanner, who had lost both legs in the Civil War, immediately promised to review all pensions of less than $3.75 a month.

In May 1889, the *Nation* noted that veterans' pensions already cost more than $88 million a year and estimated they would rise to $95 million in 1890. The magazine, which called Tanner a "loud-mouthed Grand Army stump speaker," added, "This is a greater amount than the cost of the entire military establishment of Germany, under which the people of that nation groan so loudly.'' Many of the nation's leading newspapers also expressed concern. The *Philadelphia Press* complained that Tanner ''would apparently like to pension everybody and everything.'' Tanner also irritated powerful people in Washington—he once told Representative Thomas Flood of New York that if the congressman's brain ''was blown into the eye of a mosquito, it would not make the mosquito blink''—and ignored the Secretary of the Interior, to whom he nominally reported. That proved to be his undoing. Six months after taking office, Tanner submitted his resignation.

Tanner was succeeded by another Civil War veteran, Green B. Raum. Although less vociferous than Tanner, Raum was more effective. Congress passed the Dependent Pension Act of 1890, which provided a pension for any veteran of the Union army who had served at least 90 days and was unable to earn a living, for any reason, by his own labor. The law also applied to widows, and by 1893 more than a million Union veterans or their widows were receiving more than $150 million in benefits. The United States also operated seven National Soldiers' Homes with more than 14,000 residents. In contrast, about 26,000 Confederate veterans were sharing about $1 million from various state pensions. The Grand Army of the Republic eventually grew to more than 500,000 members. Although its influence began to fade around the turn of the century, the Grand Army of the Republic continued to exist until 1956, a year after the last Civil War veteran died.

Veterans Bureau. During World War I, Congress established the Bureau of War Risk Insurance, under the jurisdiction of the Treasury Department, to insure U.S. ships and their cargoes against the risk of mines, warships, and submarines. When the United States entered the war in 1917, the law was amended to provide death and disability benefits for members of the Armed Forces and their families. Congress also created a Federal Board for Vocational Education to provide job training for disabled veterans. In 1921, Congress combined the Bureau of War Risk Insurance and the Federal Board for Vocational Education to create the Veterans' Bureau. Charles R. Forbes, who had been appointed by President Warren G. Harding to head the Bureau of War Risk Insurance, became the first director of the new Veterans Bureau.

Forbes, however, proved to be a corrupt administrator who ignored the needs of veterans, padded the agency's payroll, and cheated the government out of millions of dollars. In the span of a few months, he embezzled millions of dollars and sold nearly $7 million worth of medical supplies to private interests for $600,000. Forbes later fled to Europe, leaving more than 200,000 unopened pieces of mail from veterans, and officially resigned in 1923. When he returned to the United States in 1924, he was convicted of conspiracy to defraud the U.S. government.

A Senate investigation of Forbes later revealed that the Veterans Bureau had disallowed thousands of legitimate claims. While more than 300,000 U.S. soldiers had been wounded in combat, the Veterans Bureau had approved only 47,000 claims for disability insurance and even fewer veterans received any vocational training. The Senate concluded, ''Neither Congress nor the people of the country intended that bureau employees should split hairs when the claimants affected are men who were wounded in battle.'' In 1925, a columnist for the *American Mercury* wrote that ''Congress little realizes that its creature, the Veterans Bureau, has probably made wrecks of more men since the war than the war itself took in dead and maimed.''

In 1930, Congress authorized President Herbert Hoover to ''consolidate and coordinate government activities affecting war veterans.'' The Veterans Administration, created by executive order, consolidated the Veterans Bureau, the Bureau of Pensions, and the National Home for Disabled Volunteer Soldiers. Brigadier General Frank T. Hines, who had been director of the Veterans Bureau under Hoover, became the first administrator, a position he would hold until 1945.

Bonus Army. In 1924, Congress overrode a veto by President Calvin Coolidge to pass a ''bonus bill'' that provided 3.5 million World War I veterans with Adjusted Compensation Certificates. These certificates, which amounted to about $1,000 each, were to mature in 1945. However, in May 1932, during the Great Depression, more than 15,000 veterans calling themselves the Bonus Expeditionary Force marched on Washington, D.C., demanding immediate payment. President Herbert Hoover refused to meet with leaders of the Bonus Army and promised to veto any bill that authorized early payment. Finally, when the Bonus Army camped out on the Potomac River and staged public protests, Hoover ordered the Army to disperse the men whom he labeled ''Communists and persons with criminal records.''

General Douglas MacArthur, then Army Chief of Staff, assembled 600 troops, including 200 cavalry under the command of Major George S. Patton. MacArthur ordered the troops to advance on the protesters with tear gas and bayonets. At one point, when the protesters resisted with bricks and curses, Patton led the last mounted charge of the U.S. Cavalry against homeless Americans. One of the veterans roused by the cavalry was Joseph T. Agelino, who won the Distinguished Service Cross in 1918 for saving Patton's life. After dispersing the protesters at the armory, MacArthur turned his attention to Anacostia Flats and marched on the camp.

More than 300 veterans and family members were injured in the confrontation.

Afterwards, President Hoover accepted responsibility for MacArthur's actions, but he claimed the protesters were rabble-rousers bent on insurrection, not veterans. However, an investigation by the Veterans' Administration revealed that 94 percent of the marchers had been veterans, almost 70 percent had served overseas, and 20 percent were disabled. In New York, an outraged Governor Franklin D. Roosevelt said of Hoover, ''There is nothing inside the man but jelly.'' Roosevelt was swept to victory in the presidential election that fall.

Ironically, Roosevelt persuaded Congress to pass the Economy Act of 1933, which among other measures cut service-related disabilities by 25 percent, thus triggering another bonus march. This time, however, Roosevelt had the Veterans' Administration establish a camp for protesters 15 miles outside Washington, thus avoiding confrontations with police or the Army. Congress eventually passed a bonus bill over Roosevelt's veto.

GI Bill of Rights. In July 1943, two years before World War II would come to an end, President Roosevelt told the American people during one of his radio ''fireside chats,'' ''While concentrating on military victory, we are not neglecting the planning of things to come. . . . Among other things, we are . . . laying plans for the return to civilian life of our gallant men and women of the armed services. They must not be demobilized into an environment of inflation and unemployment.'' In October, he proposed legislation that would finance one year of education for veterans who were honorably discharged, with the possibility that those with ''exceptional ability and skill'' might be able to attend college for three years at government expense.

Despite the fear expressed by Robert M. Hutchins, then president of the University of Chicago, that ''colleges and universities will find themselves converted into educational hobo jungles,'' Roosevelt's proposal became the Serviceman's Readjustment Act, largely written by the American Legion and passed unanimously by Congress in 1944. Roosevelt signed the law, better known as the GI Bill of Rights, on June 22, 1944.

As passed, the GI Bill provided veterans with up to 52 weeks of unemployment compensation following their discharge from the service. The law, considered one of the most significant pieces of social legislation ever enacted, also provided veterans with job training and counseling, educational grants, loans to establish small businesses and farms, and mortgage assistance to buy homes. Eventually, more than 2 million World War II veterans would go to college on the GI Bill, which paid full tuition plus $50 a month for those with more than 2 years of military service. By 1948, the government was paying tuition for nearly half of all male college students. In addition, by 1950, 20 percent of new homes were purchased with low-interest Veterans Administration loans. Between 1943 and 1956, more than 600,000 disabled veterans also took advantage of job training under the Vocational Rehabilitation Act. According to Severo and Milford, ''Whatever its shortcomings, the GI Bill . . . produced a generation of well-educated professionals, businessmen, and homeowners who became the basis for a greatly strengthened American middle class.''

The post-war administration of veterans' benefits was not without controversy, however. Early in 1945, Frank T. Hines, who had run the Veterans Administration since 1923, came under increasing criticism for his failure to adjust to the changing needs of American veterans. When President Harry S. Truman announced plans to ''modernize'' the Veterans Administration late in 1945, Hines resigned. In his place, Truman appointed General Omar N. Bradley, who had been in command of all U.S. ground troops in Europe since the D-day invasion of Normandy in 1944. Bradley took over the Veterans Administration in August 1945. He told his staff, which then numbered 65,000, ''Our job is to give the veterans service, and we must not forget that the service we give them they have earned by sweat and blood. It is a service they have paid for. We must realize that it is not a charity service.''

In *Wounded Men, Broken Promises,* Robert Klein wrote that ''Complaints about the treatment afforded veterans virtually disappeared'' under Bradley. However, his tenure as head of the Veterans Administration would be short lived, as key leaders within the American Legion criticized Bradley's failure to respond to their demands as Hines had. Bradley resigned as head of the Veterans Administration in 1947 and returned to the Army, where he became Army Chief of Staff in 1948 and the first chairman of the Joint Chiefs of Staff a year later. Bradley was replaced at the Veterans Administration by Carl R. Gray Jr., a former officer and vice president of the Chicago and Northwestern Railroad who was considered one of the most ineffectual administrators ever to run the agency.

Korean War. When President Truman ordered U.S. troops into Korea early in 1950, the government's initial position was that veterans of the ''police action'' would be entitled only to the peacetime benefits. Eventually, Congress extended the rehabilitation and vocational training offered to World War II veterans to those fighting in Korea under the Veterans' Readjustment Assistance Act, a GI Bill of Rights for Korean War veterans that provided fewer benefits than World War II veterans had received. When the Korean War ended in 1953 with a truce rather than victory, there was a general feeling in the United States that perhaps Korean War soldiers had not fought as hard as their World War II counterparts. The Army even refused to pay many former prisoners of war the $2.50 per day they were entitled to in back pay.

Korean War veterans were not immune from the fear of communism that gripped the nation in the mid-1950s. Charges that hundreds of American prisoners of war had collaborated with the Communist enemy prompted the Veterans Administration, invoking a 1943 law that denied benefits to anyone found guilty of treason, mutiny, or sabotage, to establish a committee in 1955 to examine the political activities of veterans. The first and last veteran the committee moved against was James Kutcher, a former Veterans Administration clerk who had been fired in 1948 for espousing the beliefs of Leon Trotsky, a leader of the 1917 Bolshevik revolution in Russia. In December 1955, the Veterans Administration notified Kutcher that it also was cutting off his disability checks. However, Kutcher hired an attorney, Joseph Rauh, who pressured the Veterans Administration into holding a hearing. Public sentiment was overwhelmingly with Kutcher and the Veterans Administration was forced restore his benefits. In 1956, a federal appeals court ordered the Veterans Administration to rehire Kutcher and pay him back pay.

Vietnam War. Veterans returning from Vietnam also received a less than enthusiastic welcome by the government and the American people. In particular, educational benefits were substantially less than those offered to veterans of World War II or the Korean War. In addition, the country was suffering through a period of high inflation and recession. In the early 1970s, President Richard Nixon vetoed a bill that would have increased the number of doctors at Veterans Administration hospitals, urged Congress to cut funds for vocational education, and impounded money that Congress had intended to help veterans attend college. After Nixon resigned in 1974, Congress overrode a veto by President Gerald Ford to increase educational benefits.

Poor administrators also contributed to the sorry reception offered to returning Vietnam War veterans. Nixon had appointed Donald Johnson, former national commander of the American Legion, to head the Vietnam-era Veterans Administration. However, Johnson later resigned amid charges that he pressured employees into contributing to Nixon's reelection campaign. Johnson's replacement, Richard Roudebush, was so disliked by veterans that a few weeks after he took office three of them sneaked into his office in Washington, D.C., nailed the door shut, and forced him to discuss plans to cut educational benefits in the hallway. When Jimmy Carter became president in 1977, he named Max Cleland, a Vietnam veteran and multiple amputee, to head the Veterans' Administration. But organizations like the Vietnam Veterans of America remained critical of government efforts to help soldiers who had fought in Southeast Asia.

U.S. Department of Veterans Affairs. In 1988, Congress approved legislation to elevate the Veterans Administration to Cabinet level, which proponents argued would give veterans a stronger voice in government. The Department of Veterans Affairs came into existence in March 1989, with former Illinois Congressman Edward J. Derwinski sworn in as the first secretary. Derwinski was succeeded in 1993 by Jesse Brown, former executive director of the Disabled American Veterans and an ex-Marine who was seriously wounded in Vietnam.

The Veterans Education, Employment, and Training Amendments of 1991 provided educational and vocational counseling for veterans who were not eligible for other educational benefits, extended the deadline for Vietnam veterans to take advantage of employment assistance until 1994, and gave preference to veterans for federal jobs. After years of debate, in 1994, the Department of Veterans' Affairs agreed to provide benefits to veterans who had been exposed to Agent Orange, a defoliant that had been used extensively in Vietnam.

Persian Gulf War. In 1991, Congress approved legislation extending GI Bill benefits, including educational benefits and home-loan guarantees, to servicemen and women who fought in the Persian Gulf War. It also passed legislation making Gulf War veterans eligible for non-service-connected pension benefits and authorized the U.S. Department of Veterans Affairs to provide readjustment counseling to veterans who served in armed conflicts since May 1975. The government continued to deny the existence of a distinct Gulf War syndrome, a variety of ailments that veterans' organizations claimed were the result of bacterial warfare in the Persian Gulf. But it agreed to provide benefits to suffering veterans, providing that they had become ill within two years of their return from the conflict. This deadline, which eliminated 95 percent of applicants from eligibility, was extended to 2001 in 1997. Public debate over the causes and treatment of these illnesses continued.

Cutting costs while improving service to its core constituency were the paramount concerns of the Department of Veterans Affairs (VA) in the early and mid-1990s. The Veterans Health Administration was a particular focus of criticism and reform. Some observers called for the wholesale dismantling of the health care system. Bob Helms of the American Enterprise Institute told *Insight on the News* magazine's Gayle M.B. Hanson that "If you took all of the money the VA spends on health care, and provided it directly to veterans in the form of vouchers, they would be getting much, much better service." And while veterans justifiably complained about long waits, poor service, and the deteriorating physical condition of many facilities, lobbying groups staunchly opposed privatization.

Under the leadership of Secretary for Health Care Dr. Kenneth Kizer, the Veterans Health Administration embarked on a vast reorganization dubbed the ''Prescription for Change.'' In 1996, the organization was decentralized from a 4-region system into 22 Veterans Integrated Service Networks (VISNs), in an effort to slim the bureaucracy. The VHA, as well as the VA as a whole, adopted a more businesslike approach to management, complete with ''organizational goals,'' ''performance measures,'' and ''core values.'' Since 1986, in fact, the VA has published an ''accountability report'' laid out much like a corporate annual report. Whether these efforts result in real improvements in service and resource allocation remains to be seen.

Current Conditions

On November 11, 1998, President Clinton signed into law the Veterans Programs Enhancement Act of 1998, representing the 105th Congress' joint efforts to improve benefits and services to veterans. Among its key provisions are an extension of the VA's authority to provide medical care to Persian Gulf veterans through December 31, 2001, and provisions for additional evaluation of evidence linking illnesses of veterans with service in the Persian Gulf War.

The VA-HUD Appropriations Act of 1999 increased the President's requested budget by $439 million, to be applied to various programs. Another important piece of legislation was the Veterans Benefits Act of 1998, which increases the full-time GI Bill monthly rate from $440 to $528; increases education benefits for spouses and children of veterans killed on active duty; and allows surviving spouses of deceased disabled veterans to again be eligible for benefits if their subsequent remarriage ends. Still to be signed into law during the 106th Congress was the Arlington National Cemetery Burial Eligibility Act, overwhelmingly passed by the House.

An increase of $1.7 billion dollars was recommended by the Conference Report on the Congressional Budget for U.S. Government for fiscal year 2000.

Further Reading

''Acts on Behalf of America's Veterans By The 105th Congress.'' Available from http://veterans.house.gov/Legislat/105/update105-2/vetaction11-18-98.htm.

''Annual Report of the Secretary of Veterans' Affairs.'' Department of Veterans' Affairs, Washington, 1998.

Gravely, Bob. ''Compensation for Gulf Syndrome Elusive as Hearings Continue.'' *Congressional Quarterly Weekly Report,* 15 February 1997, 430-32.

Hanson, Gayle M.B. ''Is It Time To Overhaul VA Hospitals?'' *Insight on the News,* 3 July 1995, 8-11.

Kizer, Kenneth W. and Garth L. Nicolson. ''Q: Is the Government Taking the Right Approach Toward Gulf War Illness?'' *Insight on the News,* 27 January 1997, 24-7.

U.S. Department of Veterans Affairs. ''Facts About the Department of Veterans Affairs.'' 1999. Available from http://www.va.gov/pressrel/99fsva.htm. Also available from http:www.va.gov/sumedpr/fy98/stotls.98.html.

SIC 9511

AIR AND WATER RESOURCE AND SOLID WASTE MANAGEMENT

This category includes government agencies primarily engaged in regulation, planning, protection, and conservation of air and water resources; solid waste management; water and air pollution control and prevention; flood control; drainage development and consumption of water resources; coordination of these activities at intergovernmental levels; research necessary for air pollution abatement, and control and conservation of water resources. Water systems are classified in **SIC 4941: Water Supply.** Sewage and refuse systems and other sanitary services are classified in **SIC 4950: Sanitary Services.** Irrigation systems are classified in **SIC 4971: Irrigation Systems.**

NAICS Code(s)

924110 (Air and Water Resource and Solid Waste Management)

Industry Snapshot

Management of air and water resources and regulation of solid waste disposal was a broadly distributed function at all levels of municipal, state, and federal government. This category included agencies within most Cabinet-level departments of the federal government, most notably the Departments of Agriculture, Interior, and Defense. However, the Environmental Protection Agency (EPA) became the lead federal agency involved in air and water resource and solid waste management when it was created in 1970. The environment industry is expected to grow to $300 billion per year by 2000. The total budget for the EPA was set at $6.7 billion for 1999.

The EPA was an independent agency of the executive branch of the federal government that was charged with implementing environmental legislation passed by Congress, including the Clean Air Act, the Clean Water Act, and the Comprehensive Environmental Response, Compensation, and Liability Act, better known as ''Superfund.'' Beginning in the early 1990s, the EPA focused on researching and establishing standards for acceptable levels of pollution, while delegating implementation to state environmental protection agencies. The EPA also administered low-interest loan and grant programs to encourage state compliance with federal anti-pollution legislation.

ORGANIZATION AND STRUCTURE

The EPA was organized principally along media lines. It included an Office of Water, which administered wastewater, ground water, and drinking water programs; an Office of Solid Waste and Emergency Response, which administered solid waste and toxic waste programs, including Superfund hazardous waste cleanup; an Office of Air and Radiation, which administered air quality programs, including clean air and automobile exhaust reduction efforts; and an Office of Prevention, Pesticides, and Toxic Substances, which administered the agency's chemical pollution control programs.

In addition, the EPA also was organized functionally and geographically. It included an Office of Enforcement and Compliance Assurance, Office of Research and Development, Office of the General Counsel, and several administrative divisions that supported the media program offices. The EPA also operated ten regional divisions that mirrored the national organizational structure. The EPA was headed by an administrator nominated by the president and confirmed by Congress. Carol Browner, former director of the Florida Department of Environmental Regulation, became the seventh person to head the EPA in January 1993.

BACKGROUND AND DEVELOPMENT

In 1899, Congress passed the Refuse Act, the first significant federal legislation directed at controlling the pollution of natural resources. The Refuse Act made it illegal to discharge ''any refuse matter . . . other than that flowing from streets and sewers and passing therefrom in a liquid state'' into any navigable waters of the United States, unless authorized by the secretary of the Army. However, the Refuse Act was seldom enforced, and the federal government would do little to control pollution for another 60 years. For the first half of the twentieth century, pollution was considered primarily an urban problem to be dealt with by local officials. Federal efforts dealt primarily with conservation of wilderness spaces.

National outrage over environmental pollution often was traced to *Silent Spring,* the classic 1962 book by Rachel Carson that detailed the poisoning of man and nature with pesticides. Congress actually began to take more interest in the environment soon after World War II. In 1948, Congress passed the Water Pollution Control Act, which allowed the federal government to investigate sources of pollution. However, the Justice Department was required to obtain approval from state authorities before bringing suit against polluters. Since major employers were often the worst polluters, states often blocked legal action that could result in a loss of jobs, and the law was generally ineffectual.

In 1955, Congress passed the Air Pollution Control Act which, for the first time, authorized federal funds to assist states in air-pollution research and technical training. The Act also acknowledged that automobile exhaust was a major source of air pollution. In 1956, Congress revised the earlier Water Pollution Control Act and for the first time gave the Public Health Service the authority to order the clean-up of polluted waters. The Act also authorized $500 million over ten years to help cities build sewage treatment plants and provided $15 million over five years for states to expand their pollution control agencies.

In 1961, the U.S. Surgeon General appointed a Committee on Environmental Health Problems, which recommended establishing an Office of Environmental Health Sciences. The committee also called for extensive study of air and water pollution, urban crowding, food safety, and occupational health hazards from chemical pollutants. That same year, Stewart L. Udall, then secretary of the Interior, wrote *The Quiet Crisis,* which traced land management from colonial times to 1960. The book opened with a warning: ''America today stands poised on a pinnacle of wealth and power, yet we live in a land of vanishing beauty, of increasing ugliness, of shrinking open space, of an over-all environment that is diminished daily by pollution and noise and blight. This, in brief, is the quiet conservation crisis of the 1960s.''

Air Pollution Legislation. In 1963, Congress passed the first federal Clean Air Act, which gave the Public Health Service responsibility for establishing national air quality standards but, again, enforcement was limited. The Public Health Service could regulate only interstate air pollution. As *Newsweek* noted, ''If the smell of boiling chicken offal had not wafted across the nearby Delaware line from Maryland, the first prosecution under the Federal Clean Air Act of 1963 never would have gone to trial.''

In 1965, Congress moved cautiously to address the problem of automobile emissions by passing the Motor Vehicle Air Pollution Control Act, which allowed, but did not mandate, the Department of Health, Education, and Welfare (HEW) to establish emission standards for new motor vehicles. Later that year, Congress approved an amendment to the Clean Air Act that directed HEW to establish emission standards. Nevertheless, as late as 1966, meteorologists addressing the annual meeting of the Air Pollution Control Association characterized the atmosphere as ''a free system, available for use as a dispersive mechanism,'' and concluded that using the atmosphere for waste disposal ''has been the traditional method since the caveman's bonfire, and has been generally successful.''

In 1967, Congress passed the Air Quality Act, which required states to establish air quality control regions that were to deal with common air pollution problems much as regional watersheds would deal with water pollution. The Act also directed HEW to publish research data on the adverse effects of air pollution on health so states could set their own air quality standards, and it directed the National Center for Air Pollution Control, an agency of HEW, to develop pollution-control techniques.

Water Pollution Legislation. There also was growing concern in the mid-1960s over water pollution, especially the dumping of municipal sewage. In 1965, Congress passed the Water Quality Act, which provided funds for wastewater treatment demonstration projects at the municipal level. The law also required states to establish minimum water quality standards for portions of interstate waters lying within their borders. The following year, Congress passed the Clean Waters Restoration Act, which provided $3.4 billion in federal aid for cities to construct sewage treatment plants. Meanwhile, the Department of the Interior established a Water Pollution Control Administration to provide federal coordination of pollution control efforts.

In 1967, Interior Secretary Udall called upon detergent makers to eliminate the use of phosphates, which were polluting rivers and lakes. In addition to a film residue, studies showed that phosphates contributed to eutrophication, the process by which freshwater lakes eventually became clogged with organic material, causing fish and other marine life to die. Although Udall had no authority to force compliance, several communities and states responded by banning phosphates.

Ironically, many of the first substitutes developed by detergent makers were more harmful to humans and the environment than phosphates. Eventually, environmentalists also came to agree that sewage was probably more to blame for eutrophication than phosphates, but the controversy over phosphates illustrated that people were concerned about water pollution and were willing to suffer some inconvenience to combat the problem.

National Environmental Policy Act. In 1967, a HEW task force urged Americans ''to think of their planetary home as a kind of huge spacecraft.'' ''For thousands of years,'' the task force said, ''man has treated this planet as a dumping ground, boundless in its ability to absorb insults.'' The task force also urged the government to establish a Council of Ecological Advisors to create a national policy on environmental management.

Two years later, President Richard Nixon created a Cabinet Committee on Environmental Quality, headed by Dr. Lee A. DuBridge, then director of the Office of Science and Technology. Nixon also asked Roy Ash, the founder of Litton Industries who was then heading a task force on executive organization, to consider whether all federal environmental activities should be consolidated in one agency.

As 1969 came to a close, Congress passed the National Environmental Policy Act (NEPA), which was to have a far-reaching effect. Barely five pages long, the act directed the president to establish a permanent three-person Council on Environmental Quality and declared ''a national policy that will encourage productive and enjoyable harmony between man and his environment and enrich the understanding of the ecological systems and natural resources important to the Nation.''

The National Environmental Policy Act clearly positioned the federal government as the protector of the environment. It also required federal agencies to prepare an environmental impact statement before taking any major action that could conceivably harm the environment. Although NEPA did not prevent federal agencies from going ahead with those actions, it ensured that they knew and acknowledged the consequences. Environmental impact statements would become a major weapon in public and private efforts to protect the environment.

Environmental Protection Agency. Nixon signed the National Environmental Policy Act on January 1, 1970, and pledged his administration to a ''now or never'' fight against pollution. Nixon declared, ''The 1970s absolutely must be the years when America pays its debt to the past by reclaiming the purity of its air, its waters, and our living environment.'' On February 10, 1970, Nixon presented Congress with a 37-point proposal for cleaning up the environment, including a request for $4 billion to construct municipal wastewater treatment facilities, the establishment of national air-quality standards, stringent guidelines on motor-vehicle emissions, and an end to the dumping of wastes in the Great Lakes.

However, Nixon stopped short of endorsing the creation of an independent agency within the executive branch to deal with environmental problems, as many congressional leaders were then urging. As the *New York Times* reported, ''A formidable obstacle to an integrated attack on environmental problems is the absence of centralized responsibility. More than a dozen departments and agencies are involved in various environmental programs.'' The newspaper noted that Senator Edmund Muskie ''would rectify this situation by setting up an independent agency . . . that would be a 'watchdog agency to exercise the regulatory functions associated with environmental protection.'''

By mid-summer, the Ash committee on executive organization had also joined the call for an independent agency, and on July 10, 1970, Nixon announced that he would create two new organizations within the executive branch. One, the National Oceanic and Atmospheric Administration, would be a part of the Department of Commerce and be responsible for scientific research involving the atmosphere and oceans. The other, the Environmental Protection Agency (EPA), would be an independent agency and consolidate all federal pollution control activities.

Both the Senate and House held hearings on the proposed EPA during the summer of 1970. The only serious objection was raised by Representative John Dingell, who wanted to create a Cabinet-level Department of Environmental Quality.

The EPA officially came into existence on December 2, 1970, with 6,673 employees and a budget of $1.28 billion. It assumed the environmental responsibilities of 63 existing agencies, including the National Air Pollution Control Administration, Bureau of Solid Waste Management, Bureau of Water Hygiene, the Air Quality Advisory Board, portions of the Bureau of Radiological Health, and the pesticide control functions of the Food and Drug Administration—all previously part of the Department of Health, Education, and Welfare.

From the Department of the Interior, the EPA also gained responsibility for the Federal Water Quality Administration, Water Pollution Control Advisory Board, Gulf Breeze (Florida) Biological Laboratory managed by the Bureau of Commercial Fisheries, and pesticide research functions of the Fish and Wildlife Service. The EPA also assumed responsibility for setting environmental radiation standards from the Atomic Energy Commission, the pesticides registration program from the Department of Agriculture, all functions of the Federal Radiation Council, and the study of ecological systems from the Council on Environmental Quality, which continued in existence as a statutory agency.

Nixon nominated William D. Ruckelshaus, then an assistant attorney general, to head the EPA. He was confirmed by Congress on December 2, 1970 and sworn in as EPA administrator on December 4, 1970. Ruckelshaus, who guided the EPA from 1970 to 1973 and again from 1983 to 1985, later recalled that Nixon created the EPA "because of public outrage about what was happening to the environment. Not because Nixon shared that concern, but because he didn't have any choice. People have often said, isn't that a terrible motive. But that's the way democracy is supposed to work."

Enforcement. Seven days after becoming EPA administrator, Ruckelshaus delivered a speech to the annual Congress of Cities at which he announced that Atlanta, Detroit, and Cleveland were being given 180 days to stop violating federally sponsored state water quality standards. Although Ruckelshaus preferred negotiated settlements, the three cities were woefully behind on previous commitments to stop using waterways as waste dumps, and he made it clear that the EPA would be willing to call in the Department of Justice if the cities did not comply. In Ruckelshaus' words, the EPA would be the "gorilla in the closet" to support state regulators who were attempting to enforce pollution-control laws. Although the cities were outraged by the EPA's move, they were forced to comply.

The EPA referred 152 cases to the Department of Justice in 1971, but perhaps the most critical was that against Armco Steel. In September, several months after receiving the case, a federal district court judge found Armco guilty of dumping half a ton of toxic chemicals into the Houston Ship Canal on a daily basis. The judge ordered Armco to desist, which would have forced the company to shut down its blast furnaces. Armco responded by complaining to the White House, which tried to pressure the EPA into agreeing to a compromise. However, the *Washington Star* published a story about Armco's contributions to President Nixon's election campaign, which embarrassed the White House into backing down, and Armco agreed to install pollution control equipment.

Another highly publicized battle of wills took place between the EPA and U.S. Steel in Gary, Indiana. In 1971, U.S. Steel agreed to replace its open-hearth furnaces with more modern equipment to reduce air pollution. But when the company failed to meet an EPA deadline, the agency ordered U.S. Steel to close down its last open-hearth furnace or pay a $2,300-a-day fine. Vowing never to "pay tribute to the government," U.S. Steel shut down the furnace, which put 500 people out of work. The EPA refused to rescind its order, and John Quarles, then EPA deputy administrator, told *Newsweek,* "In this job, you either stare down companies like U.S. Steel or lose the entire program." In 1976, *Newsweek* reported the air over Gary, "once the classic example of massive industrial pollution . . . just about meets national standards designed to protect public health."

Air Quality. With the Clean Air Act of 1970, the EPA became responsible for establishing and enforcing national air-quality standards. Those standards were issued in 1972, and cities were given until 1975 to reduce pollutants, including ozone and carbon monoxide, to acceptable levels. The EPA also set auto-emission standards and ordered manufacturers to reduce industrial pollution or shut down their factories. *Newsweek* reported, "it has become increasingly clear that the nation is committed to the environmental battle in a massive way. And nowhere is the battle being waged more fiercely than in EPA.''

However, as the enormity of the clean air challenge became clear, the EPA extended many of its deadlines. Strict enforcement of the air-quality standards could have banished automobiles from many major cities and forced a halt to economic development. In 1977, the agency formalized an ''offset'' policy that allowed development in areas that did not meet air quality standards if other industrial sources of air pollution had reduced their emissions and the net effect was an overall improvement. In 1980, Administrator Douglas M. Costle told *Business Week* that the EPA's history ''has been one of trying to catch up with an overly ambitious legislative agenda.'' EPA action also was often delayed by legal challenges, either from industrial polluters who believed the EPA standards were too strict or from environmentalists who believed the EPA was being too lax.

In 1987, the EPA reported that more than 70 municipalities still failed to meet minimum air quality standards. In 1990, more than 100 urban areas failed to meet national standards for at least one of six pollutants, including sulfur dioxide, nitrogen oxide, carbon monoxide, lead, volatile organic compounds, and total suspended particulates. The major cause of urban air pollution continued to be motor vehicle exhaust. Per-vehicle emissions were cut by 90 percent between 1970 and 1990, but the number of vehicles doubled during the same period and Americans were driving more.

In 1990, Congress passed a revised Clean Air Act, which added 189 chemicals to the original list of air pollutants regulated by the EPA. The Act also ordered the agency to reduce air pollution that was being blamed for acid rain, smog, and damage to the ozone. It directed the EPA to propose a strategy to reduce urban cancer risk from air pollutants by 75 percent and required the EPA to ban production of the five worst ozone-depleting chlorofluorocarbons (CFCs) by 2000.

When fully implemented, the Clean Air Act of 1990 was expected to reduce air pollution emissions by 56 billion pounds annually, about 224 pounds of pollutants for every person in the United States. Most of the regulations were to take effect in the mid-1990s, with all regions of the country expected to attain national air quality standards by 2010.

Water Quality. In 1972, Congress passed major revisions to the 1965 Water Pollution Control Act that made the EPA responsible for eliminating all discharge of pollutants into navigable streams and waterways by 1985. The Water Pollution Control Act also established a National Commission on Water Quality to study the technical, economic, social, and environmental ramifications of meeting the mandate. The commission issued its report in 1976, which led to the passage of the Clean Water Act of 1977. The Clean Water Act of 1977 strengthened controls on some toxic pollutants, but it also extended the deadlines for achieving water-quality standards.

In 1987, Congress again amended the Clean Water Act, extending federal aid for the construction of municipal sewage treatment facilities. However, the grant program was phased out in 1991 and replaced with state-managed revolving loan funds.

Meanwhile, in 1974 Congress also made the EPA responsible for setting and enforcing drinking water standards for municipal water systems. The Safe Drinking Water Act, amended in 1986 to encompass 105 contaminants commonly found in drinking water, also made the EPA responsible for protecting aquifers from underground contamination. In 1987, the EPA issued standards for drinking water taken from lakes and rivers and released acceptable levels on the first eight contaminants contained in the Safe Drinking Water Act. However, in general, the EPA delegated responsibility for ensuring safe drinking water to state authorities. As of 1997, 71 percent of all rivers in the United States were deemed unsafe recreational areas.

Superfund. The federal government first became involved with the disposal of solid waste in 1965, when Congress passed the Solid Waste Disposal Act, which channeled money to the states for operating municipal dumps. During the early 1970s, attention turned to the disposal of toxic wastes, which resulted in the passage of the Resource Conservation and Recovery Act (RCRA) in 1976, an attempt to create a ''cradle-to-grave management system'' for hazardous wastes. The law also established criteria for disposal of solid wastes.

However, in 1978 the nation learned just how ill-prepared it was to deal with hazardous wastes when foul smelling chemicals began seeping into the basements of houses in the Love Canal neighborhood of Niagara Falls, New York. An investigation showed that the residential complex and a nearby school had been built over an abandoned industrial dump that contained more than 21,000 tons of toxic wastes. The federal government declared a ''health emergency'' and relocated 237 families.

Another result of Love Canal was the passage of the Comprehensive Environmental Response, Compensation, and Liability Act, better known as Superfund, which put the EPA in the position of policing past acts of pollution as well as preventing future pollution. Under the 1980 law, the EPA was charged with determining who was responsible for dumping toxic wastes and forcing them to clean up the country's worst hazardous waste sites, or for conducting its own clean-up actions and then suing the responsible parties. In 1984, Congress amended the law to bring more than 130,000 small sources of toxic wastes, previously exempted, under EPA jurisdiction. The revised law also covered more than one million underground storage tanks, many of which were leaking gasoline or other toxic fluids into the soil.

In 1985, in the largest settlement in EPA history, Westinghouse Electric Co. agreed to spend $100 million to clean up six toxic waste sites near Bloomington, Indiana, that were contaminated with polychlorinated biphenyls (PCBs). The EPA also began requiring hazardous waste landfills to monitor the quality of water resources beneath the dumps. However, by the end of 1986, only 13 hazardous waste sites, out of more than 800 identified by the EPA, had been cleaned up under the Superfund program at a cost of $780 million. In 1986, President Ronald Reagan signed the Superfund Amendments and Reauthorization Act, which directed the EPA to clean up at least 375 hazardous waste sites over the next five years, and authorized $9 billion for the effort. The law also affirmed the public's right to know by requiring chemical companies to report emission levels to local authorities.

Through 1992, the EPA had identified more than 37,000 potentially hazardous waste sites, with 1,252 placed on the Superfund National Priorities List. However, only about 150 sites had been cleaned up under the Superfund program, with work underway at another 500. More than $3.7 billion had been spent in the effort. As of 1996 one in four Americans lived within 4 miles of a Superfund Site. The program did have the effect of forcing would-be polluters to more carefully select waste treatment and disposal methods to limit their future liability, however. More than 209 million tons of municipal solid waste are produced in the United States each year. Part of the $195.7 million assigned to the Hazardous Waste Program will be used in efforts to reduce that amount.

Anne Gorsuch. In 1981, President Reagan appointed Anne M. Gorsuch to head the EPA, which by then had grown to more than 12,000 employees and had a budget exceeding $5 billion. Nicknamed the ''Ice Queen'' within the agency for her cold managerial style, Gorsuch also angered environmentalists by reaching lenient, out-of-court settlements with industrial polluters. Only 10 cases were referred to the Department of Justice in 1981, leading *Newsweek* to conclude, ''EPA's enforcement of Federal air- and water-pollution laws has slowed to a crawl . . . .After a decade of vigorous enforcement in most areas, [the] EPA seems to be taking a sharp right turn.''

The EPA's budget was cut by $30 million between 1981 and 1983, and the hazardous waste enforcement staff was reduced from more than 300 people to about 75. Under Gorsuch, the EPA also was hit with accusations of malfeasance against several high ranking administrators, including Rita Lavelle, then chief of the toxic waste division, who was seen as being too cozy with the industries she was supposed to be regulating. There were also charges that the EPA had misused more than $50 million earmarked for toxic waste clean-up. James Scheuer, then a congressman from New York, told *Newsweek,* ''At best, EPA officials have been sloppy and incompetent. At worst, they may have knowingly looted Superfund.''

When a House committee subpoenaed Superfund documents, Gorsuch, at Reagan's direction, claimed executive privilege and refused to provide the information. However, as irregularities within the agency continued to surface, Reagan ordered Gorsuch to cooperate with Congress. He also fired Lavelle and ordered an investigation by the Department of Justice. By February 1983, the EPA was being investigated by six congressional committees, the Department of Justice, and the FBI. *Business Week* reported, ''For all intents and purposes, the Environmental Protection Agency is no longer a functioning federal agency. Like a leaky drum of toxic waste, the infighting and backbiting that have torn the agency since Anne M. Gorsuch took command two years ago are now poisoning the whole operation.''

Gorsuch (then known as Anne Burford, after marrying Robert Burford, then head of the Bureau of Land Management) resigned in March. *Newsweek* reported, ''Burford can . . . be faulted for presiding over a wide range of administrative actions that have hamstrung the EPA's effectiveness: a budget cut of more than 30 percent in real dollars since 1980, a 50 percent reduction in research grants and the resignation or firing of so many career officials that critics say EPA has been stripped of considerable expertise. But these policies have been Reagan's, not simply Burford's.'' In all, a dozen top EPA officials resigned or were fired during the scandal. The EPA also lost about 3,500 employees.

Looking for someone of integrity to restore confidence in the EPA, Reagan tapped William D. Ruckelshaus, who had served as EPA's first administrator from 1970 to 1973. Ruckelshaus left the EPA initially to become acting director of the FBI, but he soon became assistant attorney general. He was fired in 1973 by then-President Nixon for refusing to fire special prosecutor Archibald Cox during the Watergate investigation. Since leaving government service, Ruckelshaus had become senior vice president of corporate and legal affairs at Weyerhaeuser Co., a timber and paper-products company. He returned to the EPA on May 5, 1983. Ruckelshaus later said, ''What the Burford political appointees had done was terrible. I mean, it was really awful. If anything the press underplayed its seriousness.''

Ruckelshaus once said, ''There probably isn't enough money in the whole federal budget to do everything Congress assigns to the EPA.'' However, there was no doubt that the EPA played a significant role in improving the quality of air and water resources in the United States after it was formed in 1970. The EPA was also the lead agency in efforts to address the growing problem of solid waste disposal in the United States, setting standards for municipal dumps as well as toxic waste sites. As EPA Administrator Carol Browner said in 1994, ''Perhaps no agency . . . has a greater impact on the lives and the livelihoods of Americans. Citizens across our nation are counting on the EPA to make their lives safer and healthier, and to ensure that economic development and environmental protection go hand in hand.''

Current Conditions

As the century came to a close, the EPA was making some headway in waste management—more waste was being recycled than disposed of, by a 60:40 ratio. In 1998, the EPA published a report that incorporated data from the National Sewage Sludge Survey (NSSS), data from the Needs Surveys, and data from the 1997 Water Environment Federation (WEF). The report estimated that 6.9 million U.S. dry tons of biosolids were generated in 1998. Of this, 60 percent was recycled in the form of fertilizer, compost, or pellets for soil enrichment. The remaining 40 percent was disposed of—50 percent by incineration and about 17 percent by landfill. The most important part of the study was the projection of waste use for the next ten years. By 2005, the EPA projects that 66 percent will be put to beneficial use and, by 2010, it will be up to 70 percent. In the same ten-year period, the EPA projects that landfill disposal will diminish from 17 percent to 10 percent.

In November 1999, the EPA announced new action under the Clean Water Action Plan directed at storm water runoff—one of the greatest sources of water pollution. The runoff is comprised of rain or snow that runs off from city streets, buildings and construction sites into nearby storm drains. These, in turn, discharge into local streams and waterways. The new rules will mandate the issuing of ''discharge permits'' limiting the storm water runoff permitted by land improvement. In its expanded stage, the program is expected to control the sediment discharges from 97.5 of new acreage under development across the country.

With respect to the Clean Air Act, in November 1999, the Justice Department, in an unprecedented action, filed several joint lawsuits against several utilities companies in midwestern and southern states. The suits charge that the power plants released massive quantities of pollutants into the air—nearly three million tons per year, creating smog, acid rain, and soot that will take years to rectify. Such air emissions affect not only human health, but have been linked to forest degradation, reservoir contamination, and deterioration of stone and copper as well. In addition to money damages in the form of fines, which will assist clean-up measures, the Department seeks to force the utilities to install appropriate air pollution control technology.

Further Reading

Environmental Protection Agency. *Environmental Protection Agency FY 1999 Budget.* Washington, DC: Environmental Protection Agency, 1997. Available from http://www.polisci.com/economy/agency/htm.

Environmental Quality: The Twenty-Second Annual Report of the Council on Environmental Quality. Washington, D.C.: Council on Environmental Quality, 1992.

''EPA Expands Controls on Polluted Runoff to Further Protect Nation's Drinking Water and Waterways.'' EPA Press Release, 1 November 1999.

''Generation, Use, and Disposal of Biosolids in 1998,'' 1998. Available from http://www.epa.gov/epaoswer/non-hw/compost/biosolids.pdf.

''U.S. Sues Electric Utilities in Unprecedented Action to Enforce the Clean Air Act.'' EPA Press Release, 3 November 1999.

SIC 9512

LAND, MINERAL, WILDLIFE, AND FOREST CONSERVATION

This industry includes government establishments primarily engaged in the regulation, supervision, and control of land use, including recreational areas; conservation and preservation of natural resources; control of wind and water erosion; pest control on public lands; and the administration and protection of publicly and privately owned forest lands. The planning, management, regulation, and conservation of game, fish, and wildlife populations, as well as refuges and other areas relating to their protection, are also classified here. Parks are classified in **SIC 7999: Amusement and Recreation Services, Not Elsewhere Classified.** Operators of forest property are classified in **SIC 0811: Timber Tracts.** Game preserves are classified **SIC 0971: Hunting and Trapping, and Game Propagation.** Fish preserves are classified in **SIC 0921: Fish Hatcheries and Preserves.**

NAICS Code(s)

924120 (Land, Mineral, Wildlife and Forest Conservation)

Industry Snapshot

An elaborate web of public and private establishments work together to manage and protect natural resources in the United States. Private membership groups, professional societies, industry representatives, and community groups voice a variety of concerns in their efforts to influence federal, state, and local policy on natural resource management. The principal governmental agency charged with the management of land, mineral, wildlife and forest conservation is the U.S. Department of the Interior (DOI). As such, the DOI manages more than 500 million acres of federal land—approximately 30 percent of the nation's total land area—and is responsible for the collection and disbursement of all revenues generated from the use of public lands and the leasing of mineral deposits and offshore oil drilling sites.

An intensifying debate over the nation's economic and environmental interests has shaped the increasingly complex and often incongruent governmental policies on environmental stewardship in the last half of the twentieth century. One result of this debate has been a proliferation of bureaucracies designed to address the concerns of both industry leaders and environmentalists. By 1999 the U.S. government's federal budget allotted $8.7 billion to the expansion and protection of America's national parks, wildlife refuges, forests, and other public lands under the auspices of the Department of the Interior. That figure represented a 15 percent increase from 1998's $7.2 billion budget. Key efforts being undertaken by the DOI in the 1990s included restoration projects in the Florida Everglades, California Bay Delta, and Appalachian Mountains; forestry management, especially in the Pacific Northwest; ongoing revisions of the Endangered Species Act of 1973; infrastructure improvement at national parks; and national biological research.

ORGANIZATION AND STRUCTURE

As the primary guardian of the nation's natural resources, the Department of the Interior's jurisdiction is enormous. The secretary of the Department of the Interior is appointed by the president and supervises all activities of the department. Responsibilities are divided among five assistant secretaries who manage nine bureaus within the DOI.

Fish and Wildlife. The assistant secretary for Fish and Wildlife and Parks is responsible for the conservation and use of fish, wildlife, recreational and historical sites, and the national parks. Under the assistant secretary's supervision, these duties are carried out by the U.S. Fish and Wildlife Service and the National Park Service.

Responsibilities of the Bureau of Fisheries, established as an independent agency in 1871, and the Bureau of Biological Survey, established in 1885 as part of the U.S. Department of Agriculture (USDA), were combined and transferred to the DOI in 1939 by Reorganization Plan 3. The two bureaus were consolidated into the Fish and Wildlife Service in 1940, and in 1956 the Service was divided into the Bureau of Commercial Fisheries and the Bureau of Sport Fisheries and Wildlife. The Bureau of Commercial Fisheries was transferred to the U.S. Department of Commerce in 1970, while the DOI maintained the responsibilities of the Bureau of Sport Fisheries and Wildlife. In 1974 the Bureau was renamed the U.S. Fish and Wildlife Service.

The U.S. Fish and Wildlife Service is the principal bureau for the management of fish and wildlife and performs its responsibilities through an extensive infrastructure. It operates regional offices in the lower 48 states and Alaska and manages over 500 National Wildlife Refuges on more than 92 million acres of land. The bureau operates 25 fish and wildlife laboratories, 36 university research units, 76 National Fish Hatcheries, and employs a nationwide network of wildlife enforcement agents.

According to the *U.S. Government Manual,* the U.S. Fish and Wildlife Service "assists in the development of an environmental stewardship ethic for our society based on ecological principles, scientific knowledge of wildlife, and a sense of moral responsibility. . . ." The Service performs a variety of environmental assessment projects on fish and wildlife populations and their habitat areas in its efforts to protect species and ensure that the public enjoys continued benefits from these resources. The Service also compiles the Endangered and Threatened Species List and coordinates national and international efforts on species protection and propagation. In 1999 the Fish and Wildlife Service's $1.4 billion budget was approximately $100 million more than in 1998.

Also under the direction of the assistant secretary for Fish and Wildlife and Parks is the National Park Service. Established in the U.S. Department of the Interior in 1916, the primary objective of the National Park Service is the preservation of natural scenic parks and historic and natural monuments for the enjoyment of future generations. The National Park Service maintains more than 370 parks, many of which contain campgrounds and visitor facilities. The Service seeks to enhance the public enjoyment of wildlife and natural scenery through educational tours, films, and exhibits.

The Park Service is also responsible for the determination and preservation of historic sites and landmarks and maintenance of the National Register of Historic Places. The State portion of the Land and Water Conservation Fund is also under the Park Service's jurisdiction. The Park Service received $1.9 billion of the DOI's budget in 1999.

Indian Affairs. The assistant secretary for Indian Affairs heads the Bureau of Indian Affairs, which is intended to address the needs and concerns of Indian and Alaskan Native people. The bureau works directly with tribal governments in efforts to manage the use of resources on Indian lands and develop economic and social programs for their people. At $1.77 billion, this office's budget constituted the largest item in the DOI's 1999 allocation.

Land and Minerals Management. The assistant secretary for Land and Minerals Management oversees the maintenance and planning of public land, and monitors the collection and disbursement of revenues from government leases of mineral sites and rent and royalty payments from lessees of Outer Continental Shelf drilling sites. The Bureau of Land Management, the Minerals Management Service, and the Office of Surface Mining Reclamation and Enforcement carry out these tasks under the direction of the assistant secretary.

The Bureau of Land Management (BLM) was established within the DOI in 1946. It performs the combined functions of two predecessor agencies—the General Land Office (created in 1812) and the U.S. Grazing Service (created in 1934). Most of the 270 million acres of federal land over which the BLM has total jurisdiction are located in the western states and Alaska, and are original public domain land that was acquired in the territory expansion purchases of the nineteenth century. The Bureau is also responsible for the management of subsurface mineral resources found on an additional 300 million acres of public and private land, where the federal government maintains mineral rights. BLM policy is driven by the multiple use and sustained yield philosophies of resource management, which are designed to promote ''utilitarian conservation'' principles. These policies are implemented with the intent that the public will use resources to sustain production of crops or livestock indefinitely without environmental deterioration. The Bureau also manages the issuance of energy and mineral leases and is responsible for monitoring compliance with the terms of these leases. The BLM's budget for 1999 totaled $1.1 billion.

The Minerals Management Service (MMS) was created in 1982 to manage the development of both onshore and offshore mineral resources, and was also given all leasing responsibilities of Outer Continental Shelf drilling sites. In 1983 management responsibilities of all onshore minerals were transferred to the Bureau of Land Management, while all royalty and mineral revenue management duties were given to the MMS. Through its Offshore Minerals Management Program, the MMS performs resource evaluation of existing reserves, completes environmental impact assessments, and publishes estimates of undiscovered offshore oil and gas deposits. According to the *U.S. Government Manual,* the MMS ''works in consultation with the Congress, the 23 coastal States, local government, environmental groups, and the public'' to develop five-year leasing programs of sites on the Outer Continental Shelf. Through the Royalty Management Program, the MMS collects and disburses all revenues generated from the development and extraction of onshore, offshore, and Outer Continental Shelf mineral resources. This is the federal government's largest source of income other than the Treasury Department's tax revenues. ''From 1953 through 1990, MMS collected offshore oil royalties totaling $18.5 billion and gas royalties of $21.3 billion. The biggest source of offshore revenue has been lease sale bonuses, which were $55.8 billion during the period, giving the government a total of $96.3 billion from offshore operations through 1990,'' according to Patrick Crow in *Oil and Gas Journal.* The $691 million budget administered by the MMS in 1999 was distributed to states and Indian tribes from whose land the minerals are extracted, and to the Land and Water Conservation Fund, the Historic Preservation Fund, and the general Treasury.

The Office of Surface Mining Reclamation and Enforcement (OSM), created in 1977, is also under the supervision of the assistant secretary for Land and Minerals Management. Through its 13 field offices and 8 area offices, the OSM coordinates efforts of state and federal government agencies to protect the public and the environment from the adverse effects of coal mining. As many states have assumed these primary responsibilities, much of OSM's activities involve the reclamation of mines abandoned prior to 1977. The OSM's 1999 budget totaled $341 million.

Territorial and International Affairs. The assistant secretary for Territorial and International Affairs is responsible for the formulation of public policy pertaining to the U.S. territories of Guam, American Samoa, the Virgin Islands, the Northern Mariana Islands, the Republic of the Marshall Islands, and Federated States of Micronesia.

Water and Science. The assistant secretary for Water and Science monitors the performance of the U.S. Geological Survey and the Bureau of Reclamation. The U.S. Geological Survey (USGS) was created in 1879 to classify public lands and examine the geological structure and mineral resources of the nation. Under the assistant secretary's direction, the USGS performs quality assessments of the nation's water supply, analyzes potential for such natural hazards as volcanoes, earthquakes, and landslides, studies energy and mineral resources, and is responsible for the National Mapping Program. The USGS has water resource offices in all 50 states, Puerto Rico, and Guam; it also performs research at 13 earth science information centers. In 1962 the USGS was given authorization to perform geological research beyond the boundaries of U.S. jurisdiction. The USGS administered a budget of $806 million in 1999.

The Bureau of Reclamation was initially established as the Reclamation Service within the U.S. Geological Survey in 1902. Its original objective was to ensure a year-round water supply and irrigation system for the 17 contiguous western states. In 1907 the service was established as an independent department and renamed the Bureau of Reclamation. The Bureau's responsibilities have expanded to meet the growing demands of the West's increasing population. Its main functions include the generation of hydroelectric power, flood control, and planning for the design and construction of dam systems. The Bureau also provides technical assistance to foreign countries that are working to improve their water management systems. According to the *U.S. Government Manual,* the Bureau of Reclamation was responsible for the operation of 355 storage reservoirs; 69,400 miles of canals, pipeline, tunnels, and project drains; and 52 hydroelectric power plants in the mid-1990s. Its 1999 budget totaled $1.2 billion.

Established in 1910, the Bureau of Mines was for more than 80 years a research-oriented agency concerned with the extraction, use, and recycling of nonfuel mineral deposits. The Bureau also provided statistical data and economic information on resource availability. The federal government's downsizing efforts virtually eliminated this office in 1995, cutting about 1,200 employees from the DOI roster. Some of its operations and personnel were transferred to the Department of Energy's Fossil Energy Office, while other functions moved to the U.S. Geological Survey's newly created Office of Minerals Information. In 1999 the Bureau operated small skeleton operations only and was the smallest recipient of DOI's funds, just $4 million.

Background and Development

Along with the nation's enormous territory acquisitions of the nineteenth century came the daunting task of establishing a system of resource and land management. Federal bureaus were created to manage such concerns as mineral extraction, timber production, water resources, Indian affairs, and railroad land grants. As America's settlers reached the Pacific Ocean, and California was petitioning for statehood, land distribution issues and the realization that the nation's resources were finite prompted a coalition of Whigs and public-land state Democrats to create the Department of the Interior as an umbrella agency charged with the supervision of the nation's natural resources. Upon its creation in 1849, the Department of the Interior was given jurisdiction over the General Land Office, the Office of Indian Affairs, the Pension Office, and the Patent Office. The DOI was then divided into three units, each headed by a unit chief, that focused on Lands and Railroads, Indians, and Patents and Miscellaneous programs. The Patents and Miscellaneous division quickly expanded, and the DOI was given responsibility for supervision of the commissioner of Public Buildings, the warden of the Penitentiary of the District of Columbia, the Census Bureau, and the Labor and Education Departments. By the end of the nineteenth century, the DOI had become a sprawling repository for miscellaneous governmental bureaus.

The Department of the Interior was in a state of extreme disarray in the early twentieth century. Over the next fifty years, the DOI underwent dramatic organizational and administrative changes that shaped its current role as steward of the nation's natural resources. Major administrative reforms were implemented by James R. Garfield in 1907, Hubert Work during the 1920s, and Julius Krug and Oscar Chapman during the Truman administration. ''The principal value of Krug's reforms,'' according to Thomas G. Alexander in *The Greenwood Encyclopedia of American Institutions: Government Agencies,* ''seems to have been the closer contact promoted between the department and representatives of interest groups.'' Alexander also notes that departmental restructuring since the Truman administration has built on the reforms initiated by Interior Secretary Krug and his successor, Oscar Chapman.

Although the Department of the Interior was an extremely amorphous agency in its early years, the management of public lands has been one of the DOI's principal functions throughout its existence. Increasingly in the nineteenth and twentieth centuries, the Department has faced two significant policy problems in resource management. The first predicament stemmed from its responsibilities for managing resources that were covered by conflicting legislation. The Department was unable to dispense land to settlers for livestock grazing and agriculture because such large land tracts had to be purchased from railroads and other grantees. Meanwhile, the Department's hesitancy to allocate more land to industry indirectly slowed the subletting of that same land to settlers. The passage of the Taylor Grazing Act of 1935 gave the DOI authority to establish and manage, rather than simply sell off, land leases and grazing districts to industry and private citizens. The Federal Land Policy and Management Act of 1976 increased the Department's responsibilities in managing the nation's natural resources.

The second policy dilemma concerned differing opinions on the necessity and methods of resource preservation. A conservation movement driven by two differing rationales began in the nineteenth century and has continued to shape DOI policy through the twentieth century. ''Utilitarian conservation'' was promoted by John Wesley Powell and William E. Smyth in the nineteenth century, and Gifford Pinchot and Theodore Roosevelt in the twentieth century. Preservation of resources for the aesthetic enrichment of the nation was espoused by conservationists such as George Perkins Marsh, John Muir, and Aldo Leopold. The General Revision Act of 1891 has been described as the most important first step in steering the Department toward the promotion of conservation. The Act repealed the Timber Culture and Preemption Acts and allowed the Interior Department to establish forest reserves.

Since the passage of the Wilderness Act in 1964 and the National Environmental Policy Act in 1970, the Department of the Interior's responsibilities in the area of resource conservation have continued to expand. The DOI, because of its status as an arbiter of what constitutes a fair balance between environmental and economic concerns, is often a subject of controversy. Conservationists harshly criticized the DOI during the 1980s, a period that they felt was marked by the sacrifice of environmental needs to satisfy various industrial desires. Conversely, many members of manufacturing and other industries decried what they perceived as the inordinate and growing influence of the agency, whose budget increased by more than 36 percent in the late 1980s, from $6.2 billion in 1986 to nearly $8.5 billion in 1990.

The expanding influence of government institutions involved in the conservation of America's natural resources has rippling effects on the profits and growth of many industries. The logging, oil, fishing, and real estate industries have become increasingly embroiled in conflicts over resource use. Government establishments such as the U.S. Department of Agriculture and the U.S. Department of Energy, involved in resource use, rather than conservation, have also been pressured to incorporate conservation strategies into their policies. According to the Energy Information Administration, increased conservation measures, coupled with the passage of the Energy Policy Act of 1992, are expected to slow the growth rate of energy demand to less than 1.5 percent per year until 2021.

Disputes between conservationists and the logging industry drew national attention in the late 1980s and early 1990s. According to *Industry Surveys'* 1992 analysis of the wood products industry, "the most important factor affecting prices and the future balance between supply and demand is the conflict between the logging companies and the environmentalists." Conservationists waged a campaign against the lumber industry in an effort to ensure the protection of the endangered spotted owl and old growth forests in the Pacific Northwest. The dispute between industry leaders, government representatives, and conservation groups erupted in an intense national controversy over the use of timberlands in 1988. Lumber industry representatives tried to sway public opinion and government policy in their favor by emphasizing that increased regulation will result in increased worker lay-offs. In fact, the National Forest Products Association (NFPA) reported that more than 100 sawmills in the Pacific Northwest closed in the early 1990s. In the short term, this has resulted in substantially higher profits for surviving logging companies, as lumber prices rose dramatically due to environmentalists' success in limiting logging on millions of acres of government timberlands. Permanently higher wood prices are the likely result of continued logging bans and pressures from environmental groups. The NFPA projects that an estimated 60 percent of logging on government lands will ultimately be suspended.

Likewise, the oil industry has been seriously affected by disputes over resource conservation. The leasing of oil drilling sites located in the Arctic National Wildlife Refuge and off the Florida and California coastlines has prompted intense debate. Conservationists tried to prohibit all oil drilling in the Arctic National Wildlife Refuge, but the federal government has approved limited leasing in the area. Threats of targeted product boycotts from private conservation groups in Florida and California have resulted in fewer lease bids from oil companies. According to Patrick Crow in *Oil and Gas Journal,* "from 1979 through 1984, the Minerals Management Service averaged nearly six offshore sales a year, gleaning average bonuses of $4.9 billion per year." However, increasing attacks on offshore leasing resulted in an average of only three lease sales per year between 1985 and 1990, and a reduction in revenue to $778 million per year for the five-year period.

Extensive environmental damage to Prince William Sound and the Gulf of Alaska resulting from the March 1989 oil spill of the Exxon *Valdez* has added to the controversy over the expansion of oil drilling sites. Conservationists argue that potential costs in environmental damage outweigh the benefits of continued expansion of oil drilling sites. The $900 million Exxon *Valdez* settlement was the largest resource damage settlement in history. The monies were applied to several projects, including the restoration of Prince William Sound and its environs; the North American Wetlands Conservation Fund; and for land acquisition to augment Alaska's Kodiak Island wildlife habitat.

Under the direction of former Arizona Governor Bruce Babbitt during the Clinton administration, the Department of the Interior continued to tread a fine line between environmentalists and economic interests. Babbitt envisioned himself not only as the nation's chief conservator, but also as a modern-day King Solomon who would use science to find solutions to the nation's resource dilemmas. During the first four years of his tenure, Babbitt faced ongoing disputes over grazing fees in the West, oil and gas leases on public property, and—after the Republican Party gained control of Congress in 1994—threats to reform environmental regulations.

CURRENT CONDITIONS

In late 1999 the Clinton administration announced that some 40 million acres currently protected in our national forests will gain additional protections by the prohibition of any roads going through them. It was also announced that the nonprofit Wildlands Conservancy had donated to the nation an additional 14,000 acres within Southern California's Joshua Tree National Park, where multimillion acres of land in the Mojave and Colorado Deserts are likewise protected. It is hoped that this will secure protection from further development in the area. Also purchased was the 95,000-acre Baca Ranch in New Mexico's Jemez Mountains, west of Sante Fe. Located on the ranch's acreage is the world-renowned Valles Caldera, a collapsed crater from an ancient volcano. The ranch is also home to one of the nation's largest herds of wild elk.

Unfortunately, there were casualties as well: some of the controversies surrounding Babbitt's tenure at the end of 1999 included: allowing major oil companies to pay below-market royalties for oil taken from federal lands; the environmental impact of oil drilling off the coast of California (a Babbitt legacy); and diminished funds for the Florida Everglades National Park and some earmarked Civil War Battlefields. Another 425 oil-rich tracts on 3.9 million acres of Alaskan wilderness were offered in a lease sale by the Bureau of Land Management on May 5, 1999. Six major oil companies purchased the bulk of them.

Following a study conducted by the Office of the Inspector General, which found that Indian schools were in worse shape than inner-city schools, the fiscal year (FY) 2000 budget request for the Bureau of Indian Affairs was increased by $155 million from 1999. Indian school children represent the seventh generation of Native Americans to occupy reserved land since the system began, and in 1999 there were 53,000 students in 185 Indian schools within the reservation system. Also included in the FY 2000 budget is a $100 million appropriation for a ''Bring Back the Bison'' campaign.

In October 1999 the U.S. Fish and Wildlife Service published its Candidate Notice of Review, naming 258 plant and animal species considered likely to warrant protection under the Endangered Species Act. This was the first update since 1997.

September 25, 1999, was National Public Lands Day. Over 30,000 volunteers across America dedicated their time and energy for one day to make needed improvements in some 200 parks, wildlife refuges, forests, lakes and recreation areas around the country. Of inspiration was the dramatic growth of this popular program—from just 1700 volunteers in 1996. The 1999 event was sponsored by Toyota, but is actually a partnership event shared by NEETF and several of DOI's departments. The program listed a toll-free number for volunteering, 800-VOL-TEER (1-800-865-8337) or a Web site address of www.npld.com.

AMERICA AND THE WORLD

America has developed an extensive network of conservation establishments since the mid-nineteenth century. However, it has done so only after incurring significant resource depletion and wildlife extinctions. Consequently, the United States' pleas that Third World countries begin to focus more on conservation have been largely ignored, as the people of undeveloped nations try to improve their economic conditions. At the same time, the United States has been harshly criticized by the international community for its refusal to sign a biodiversity treaty that every other attending nation signed at 1991's international Earth Summit in Rio de Janeiro. The treaty was intended to encourage developing nations via financial incentives to protect their natural resources.

Despite an increasing international acknowledgment of the necessity for conservation, global land, mineral, wildlife, and forest resources are continually imperiled by reckless exploitation. According to Edward O. Wilson in his *The Diversity of Life* ''only 4.3 percent of the earth's land surface is currently under legal protection, divided among national parks, scientific stations, and other classes of reserves.''

The cultivation of rain forest plants with medicinal properties is one strategy that could prove enormously lucrative for several nations. For example, two alkaloids produced by the rosy periwinkle of Madagascar have been proven to cure Hodgkin's disease and lymphocytic leukemia. According to Wilson, ''the income from the manufacture and sale of these two substances exceeds $180 million a year.'' By destroying unknown species of plants in the rain forest, South American people may be depriving themselves of future wealth. The creation of an ecotourism industry that promotes the enjoyment of interesting fauna and flora endemic to rain forests may provide other economic incentives for rain forest conservation.

Contributions from government organizations are essential for the initiation of conservation-oriented strategies. One of the most significant organizations involved in the promotion of conservation in undeveloped nations is the Global Environment Facility (GEF). GEF was established in 1990 by the United Nations Development Program, the World Bank, and the United Nations Environmental Program, and by 1992 the organization had committed more than $450 million to set up national parks, promote sustainable forestry, and establish conservation trust funds in developing countries. Among the countries being considered for the allocation of these funds are Bhutan, Indonesia, Papua, New Guinea, the Philippines, Vietnam, and the Central African Republic.

Prospects for the Future. Increasingly sophisticated technology has yielded more detailed information on the state of natural resources and environmental conditions around the world. Environmentalists charge that this information has overwhelmingly revealed that the world's resources and wildlife have been critically depleted. An increased sense of urgency has thus characterized the conservation debate. The number of conflicts between developers and conservationists is likely to increase as researchers classify more and more species as endangered. Continued advances made by scientists may help enlarge the framework of economic and environmental debate. A growing number of environmental economists and scientists are working together to explore prospects that would allow industries to thrive through conservation-oriented use of land, minerals, and wildlife. Innovative arbitration techniques will have to be implemented by governments to promote a compatible relationship between economic growth and resource conservation.

Further Reading

Freedman, Allan. ''After Interior's Smooth Ride, Some Issues Left Behind.'' *Congressional Quarterly Weekly Report,* October 5, 1996, 2858-2859.

''FY 2000 Budget Press Release.'' *News,* February 1, 1999. U.S. Dept. of Interior. Bureau of Indian Affairs. Available from http://www.doi.gov/bia/news/2000budg.html.

''National Public Lands Day.'' 1999. Available from http://www/nps.gov/pub_aff/press/npld.html.

Nelson, Robert H. ''Environmental Creationism.'' *Forbes,* 8 April 1996, 76.

''News Releases of the BLM.'' October 1999. Available from http://www.blm.gov/nhp/news/press/.

''President Clinton and Vice President Al Gore: Protecting Our Environment, Not Special Interests.'' EPA News Release, November 2, 1999. Available from http://epainotes1.rtpnc.epa.gov:7777/.../ceecdd1ce605eb158525681d006ee23f?OpenDocumen.

''U.S. Fish and Wildlife Service Publishes List of Candidates for Endangered Species Act Protection.'' News Release, October 25, 1999. Available from http://news.fws.gov/newsreleases/Display.cfm?ID = 178&Time Period = 30.

Williams, Ted. ''On the Fire Line for Conservation.'' *Outdoor Life,* October 1996, 12-15.

SIC 9531

ADMINISTRATION OF HOUSING PROGRAMS

This category covers government establishments engaged in the administration, planning, and development of housing programs. The category also includes government building standards agencies and nonoperating government housing agencies and housing authorities. Insurance and finance areas are classified in Finance, Division H. The operation and rental of apartments and houses is classified in Finance, Insurance, and Real Estate **SIC 6510: Real Estate Operators (Except Developers) and Lessors. SIC 9532: Administration of Urban Planning and Community and Rural Development** covers government agencies and commissions, with the private establishments engaged in this work classified in services in the major group for engineering, accounting, research, management, and related services.

NAICS Code(s)

925110 (Administration of Housing Programs)

Industry Snapshot

Administration of housing programs is the central task of the Department of Housing and Urban Development (HUD), which was created by an act of Congress in 1965. Other governmental housing programs include the Veterans Administration housing program and the Farmers Home Administration, which are overseen by the Department of Veterans Affairs and the Department of Agriculture, respectively. The original legislation broadly mandated HUD to administer federal housing programs, promote the solution of urban problems, and provide funding for housing via private institutions. Consistent with that mandate, HUD's major focus continues to be on increasing home ownership across the country, providing assistance for the homeless, improving public housing and administering block grants for economic and urban development of targeted areas. Major issues for the organization have been lack of funding, inconsistent presidential support, and conflicting congressional directives.

Organization and Structure

The secretary of housing and urban development is assisted by a deputy secretary. Together they oversee a chief of staff, as well as assistant secretaries for administration, community planning and development, congressional and intergovernmental relations, fair housing and equal opportunity, housing and federal housing, policy development and research, public and Native American housing, and public affairs, in addition to an overall support staff of several thousand employees. HUD deals with approximately 3,100 public housing agencies that disperse around 80 percent of all HUD funds and manage 1.3 million housing units. The FHA and the Government National Mortgage Association, or Ginnie Mae, operate within HUD, but do so with considerable autonomy. The private Federal National Mortgage Association, or Fannie Mae, is the corporate "sister" of Ginnie Mae and is subject to regulation by HUD.

BACKGROUND AND DEVELOPMENT

Since the birth of the nation, government has been concerned with the growth and distribution of its population. During the mid-nineteenth century the Department of Agriculture was created to address the many needs of farming families and agricultural laborers, who then constituted two-thirds of American society. A century later, the United States had largely completed its transition from a predominantly agrarian to a predominantly urban economy and population. With this transition came a growing demand for an agency, or agencies, to address the many problems associated with urban expansion.

New Deal Era. The economic disaster caused by the Great Depression forced urban and housing problems to a federal level for the first time in American history. In 1932, under Herbert Hoover, the Federal Home Loan Bank system was created in an attempt to shore up the housing industry and keep savings and loan associations above water. With Franklin Delanoe Roosevelt's inauguration came the New Deal, a massive series of programs that, among other things, restructured the country's housing finance and regulatory system. In 1934 the FHA was created to provide mortgage insurance to banks and other financial institutions. In 1935 the Resettlement Administration was created in order to begin a number of housing and resettlement projects, including those related to eliminating unproductive farms. Two years later the U.S. Housing Authority was created to support and oversee public housing.

In the 1940s the federal government's foray into urban policy was also driven by pressing national problems. The National Housing Agency (NHA) was created to provide housing for World War II workers. Once the war ended the agency began housing planning, but soon became a casualty in a new political war, for in 1946 a Republican-led congress denied permanent status to the NHA. So instead of becoming an independent department, housing was placed under the Housing and Home Finance Agency (HHFA). The HHFA was not strongly positioned in the structure of the federal government and continued to shift with the political winds of the day. Nonetheless, FHA by itself played a fundamental postwar role in managing suburban housing growth and freeing up money for new, lower-income homeowners.

The federal housing policy finally was clearly stated under the Housing Act of 1949, which said there should be "a decent home in a suitable living environment for every American family." This law was closely tied to the Employment Act of 1946, but neither were ever made part of a larger, cohesive national policy for both promoting and controlling urban growth.

Legislation for a cabinet-level department to deal with urban renewal problems was first introduced in 1954, but it lacked necessary support of the public and the Eisenhower administration to become law. Yet momentum continued to gather within the National Housing Conference (NHC), a liberal organization devoted to the expansion of federal redevelopment and housing policies. William L. C. Wheaton, once with the NHA, was an avid supporter of the NHC proposals and understood the need to tie them to a strong constituency. He knew that it had to be a segment that already had some clout in Washington, like the private sector groups that were already involved in housing: thrift institutions, realtors, home builders, and mortgage bankers. Wheaton also was aware that there was a tide of support in Congress for new suburban housing and development that also would assist the cause.

John F. Kennedy's election in 1960 further increased the momentum toward the creation of the department. Kennedy planned to work with Robert Weaver, his new administrator of the HHFA, toward that end. However, according to Rachel G. Bratt and W. Dennis Keating in *Urban Affairs Quarterly,* "conservative southern opposition to the likely appointment of Weaver as the first black cabinet officer resulted in rejection of the administration's legislation in January 1962 by the House Rules Committee." Other efforts under Kennedy also failed.

Original Legislation. By 1965, with Lyndon Johnson in office, political and public support finally was in place. The real estate industry was the last group that strongly opposed the creation of a department of housing. Congress passed the legislation in August of 1965 just as a period of widespread urban unrest (1965 to 1968) was ignited, first in the Watts neighborhood of Los Angeles. Weaver was appointed to be the first HUD Secretary the following January, after the passage of ground-breaking civil rights legislation. In 1968, some concrete goals were established for HUD. These included the creation over the next 10 years of 26 million new and rehabilitated housing units, 6 million of which were to be for low- and moderate-income Americans.

HUD made its mark on the urban environment in the 1960s and early 1970s through the development of multifamily housing in inner city areas where whole blocks were razed under the auspices of urban renewal and slum clearance. The federal government encouraged local nonprofit agencies and residents to join in the process. The FHA, the government's mortgage insurance underwriter and a part of HUD, opposed the role the inexperienced nonprofits were playing. The FHA had a history of conservative underwriting that clashed with the social mission of getting housing into low-income, high-risk areas. In addition, as William Harris wrote in the *Journal of Housing,* "The issue of who controlled the delivery of the Department's program at the regional and local levels became a critical element in determining how these programs would be administered—HUD vs. FHA, liberal voice vs. conservative." This was a conflict that paralleled the organization's history.

Richard Nixon, elected in 1968, set the tone for how HUD money would be used to build housing by supporting a "supply-side" housing strategy. The construction of low-rent housing was spurred on by such subsidized interest programs as Section 235 (home ownership) and Section 236 (rental). Interest rates as low as one percent were available for builders of low-income housing projects. Subsidies would be handled through the newly formed Ginnie Mae, and private investment would be stimulated through the National Corporation for Housing Partnerships and the Federal Home Loan Mortgage Association, or Freddie Mac. Yet, according to Bratt and Keating, "the infusion of funds, without sufficient federal safeguards and oversight, created a situation prone to disaster. In numerous congressional hearings, a string of scandals, and abuses on the part of private real estate brokers, home builders, mortgage lenders, and FHA appraisers was disclosed, constituting the first major scandal to rock the young agency."

HUD's subsidized housing programs were put on hold in 1973, and the Department was realigned by the Housing and Community Development Act of 1974. Section 236 was replaced by Section 8 rent subsidies for multi-unit housing. Also under this act the Community Development Block Grant program was developed to consolidate urban development grants for water and sewer, streets, and other public service improvement projects. The result was a separation of the housing and community development units.

The support that successfully brought HUD into existence was not there to sustain the agency in reaching its 10-year goal, which ended in 1978. Although 80 percent of the units outlined in the goal were created (when including mobile homes in that count), only 45 percent of the 6 million low- and moderate-income units were actually built or rehabilitated. Some speculated that part of the reason low income public housing programs failed to be fully implemented was due to the contemporary social views regarding public housing and the costs involved with the Vietnam War. In addition, the initial urgency of the mission fueled by the urban unrest of the time died down with the cessation of violence and the election of conservative presidents. As it turned out, HUD housing production peaked in 1972.

Section 8 Housing. Developed under the administrations of Richard Nixon and Gerald Ford, Section 8 housing was intended to reduce government housing assistance costs by shifting money away from long-term to short-term rent subsidies. Instead, the funding for additional public housing fell on Section 221 money that was loaned at 3 percent interest. Not only did Section 8 ultimately cost much more than section 236, but the philosophical differences—sound fiscal policy voice and social responsibility—still raged on within the department.

Section 8 was unpopular due to its cost and also due to its "spatial concentration" provision. Johnson's Great Society programs were implemented in a manner that perpetuated racial and economic segregation by razing and then rebuilding whole neighborhoods. Section 8 provided economic incentives for builders and local governments to bring low income housing to a broader diversity of neighborhoods and not just to concentrate them in poor non-white areas. Section 8 was terminated in 1983 following the election of Ronald Reagan.

HUD under Reagan. Support for many social change programs was dramatically reduced during the Reagan years. Eric Addison in the *Journal of Housing* wrote, "Perhaps no federal agency was more affected by the Reagan administration's attempt to reduce federal spending than the Department of Housing and Urban Development (HUD). Between 1981 and 1988, the department's spending authority dropped from $33.4 billion to just over $15 billion per year." Rather than focusing on subsidizing new rental unit construction, as had been done previously, the Reagan administration directed HUD to rehabilitate existing housing and assist tenants through a housing voucher system and rent subsidies. The administration also sponsored Enterprise Zones, a program that encouraged businesses to locate within economically depressed areas in exchange for tax and regulatory breaks.

Unfortunately, in 1989 another HUD scandal came to light. Just as in the early 1970s, the scandal revolved around realtors, mortgage lenders, and the co-insured. A general lack of supervision of federal contracting, according to some critics, allowed for discretionary funds to be funneled to favored developers. Samuel R. Pierce, Jr., head of HUD under Ronald Reagan, took the Fifth Amendment, refusing to testify at the hearings regarding the misuse of funds. However, in 1992 two of Pierce's assistants were indicted in what appeared to be an influence peddling conspiracy.

Indications that something was amiss in HUD were ignored in spite of early warning signs. ''A GAO report in 1984—five years before the scandals—should have alerted Congress and HUD to the severity of its problems,'' reported *Financial World.* The article went on to quote Judy England-Joseph, director of housing and community development issues at the General Accounting Office (GAO): ''Until you have a smoking gun, people don't understand what's at stake when you don't have the right information systems in place or the right financial management systems. People aren't willing to spend a lot of money to bring a department like HUD on track.''

The HUD Reform Act of 1989 followed the disclosure of the HUD abuses of the 1980s. Among the changes was the addition of a chief financial operator and a comptroller for each major operating division. In addition, the secretary's discretionary fund was eliminated and waivers of HUD rules became subject to disclosure. Improvements implemented by HUD Secretary Jack Kemp, under the George Bush administration, included a system to track the sale of single family homes and a plan to improve the information and financial management systems. All improvements were related to preventing a repeat of past abuses. The primary focus of HUD during the Bush years was damage repair. And there were a lot of problems with image control as well. For many, HUD had become virtually synonymous with mismanaged and misdirected big government programs.

Long-term problems still remained in spite of Kemp's actions; Kemp himself was hampered from fully implementing such promising ideas as revamping HUD operations through tenant ownership of public housing. In general, poor financial and data management systems and an organizational structure that allowed for too much freedom in the local and regional offices were cited as reasons for HUD's poor performance. Examples of the severity of the problems were illustrated by the fact that contracts of rent records had not been reconciled for 15 years. HUD's 1991 financial statement was so inaccurate and lacking in current financial information that the auditor, Price Waterhouse, could not file an opinion.

Nonetheless, wrote Addison, ''in the public mind, HUD is public housing. Media descriptions of HUD as the federal agency responsible for public housing have led many to believe that the reports of scandal referred to the activities of local housing and development officials. In that respect, the real victims of the HUD abuses have been the local officials, managers, and administrators—those far removed from the machinations at HUD Central.'' Addison claimed the real HUD scandal was the emphasis put on the unethical practices of the few, and neglect of the success of the department. ''Indeed, when it comes to providing housing for low- and moderate-income people, no other group, not even the private sector, has been shown to perform as effectively and efficiently as the public housing industry.''

Reinventing HUD. In July of 1993 a *National Journal* article described the task facing the new HUD secretary, Henry G. Cisneros, and his staff as follows: ''The mission: Bring order out of management chaos. Turn a frustrated, cynical, and defensive bureaucracy into an active partner in urban innovation. Recast controversial old programs such as public housing into models of new Democratic effectiveness, while creating and implementing forward-looking programs such as empowerment zones. And, by the way, don't spend any more money.''

During Cisneros's first few months as HUD secretary, much was written about his commitment to social change via federal housing and urban development policy. When Los Angeles was devastated by riots in 1992 following the acquittal of L.A. police officers on trial for beating motorist Rodney King, Cisneros, though out of public office at the time, was on the scene calling for changes in urban policy. Laurie McGinley, in an April 1993 *Wall Street Journal* article, described the hopes Cisneros brought with him to HUD. ''In his first months in office, Mr. Cisneros has developed 'principles' for retooling urban programs, including reducing the concentration of the poor in the inner city; using housing policy to provide 'an economic ladder'; and trying to change 'self destructive behaviors on both sides of the racial divide.''' In September of 1993 William Fulton wrote in *Planning* that Cisneros ''recommended that public housing regulations be reformed to support four values he believes HUD should promote: community, family, economic 'lift,' and individual rights and responsibilities.'' And at the end of 1993, Cisneros issued a memo to President Bill Clinton calling for ''a multifaceted urban policy,'' with tax and housing credits for the working poor, expanded home ownership programs, and economic empowerment zones to encourage business investment.

Actions taken by Cisneros in 1993, as part of his ''Reinventing HUD'' initiative, included: fostering cooperation, through the National Community Development Training Institute, among local governments and community organizations for better delivery of services; launching a $100 million public-private initiative to create a leadership fund; and generating half a billion dollars in pension money for Section 8 housing, through a joint program with the AFL-CIO.

Wavering support in Washington, not to mention around the country, has been tied directly to HUD's generally poor performance record. As Bruce Reed, deputy assistant to the president for domestic policy, said in an April 1993 *Wall Street Journal* article, ''This country has spent billions and billions over the last 30 years with relatively little impact. Our goal is to empower communities to develop their own recovery plans and become economically viable.'' Empowerment Zones, the Clinton administration's $5 billion, 4-year plan for inner-city areas such as South Central L.A., was preceded by Truman's Urban Renewal, Kennedy's War on Poverty, Johnson and Nixon's Model Cities, Ford's Community Development Block Grants, Jimmy Carter's Urban Development Action Grants, and Reagan and Bush's Enterprise Zones. Nicholas Lemann has posited that all such programs have promised the illusion of wholesale economic development when, in fact, such basic social services as housing and day-care for ghetto dwellers have been the most urgently needed and the most easily provided. As he wrote for *New York Times Magazine* in January 1994, ''Economic revitalization efforts pass every test but one, the reality test. They are popular among all the key players in antipoverty policy; they sound good; they have bipartisan appeal; they are based on tax breaks rather than on spending so are easier to pass. The only problem is that so far they haven't worked—which creates a larger problem.''

HUD problems are perhaps rooted essentially in the broadness of the departmental goals as set forth in the 1965 legislation, but perhaps also in the very structure of the agency, which lacks interdepartmental control over such related federal agencies as the Farmers Home Administration, the Veterans Administration housing program, and the Federal Home Loan Bank Board. HUD, the department that in Cisneros's words ''has the explicit responsibility for America's cities and urban places,'' has virtually no control over farm and veterans housing or thrift financing and has always had limited control over its public-private partnerships and relationships with state and local agencies.

It is this very type of government inefficiency and inadequacy that was the subject of *The Gore Report on Reinventing Government,* which offered broad restructuring recommendations for a number of departments, including HUD. In particular, the report placed a new emphasis on competition among public housing managers and creating market-rate housing that would serve both publicly subsidized and market-rate tenants. Vice President Al Gore, as chairman of the newly created Community Enterprise Board, promised to play a key role in implementing the Clinton administration's housing policy, which in 1994 was focused on targeting a number of impoverished inner-city areas for economic revitalization through tax breaks and other incentives. In addition, HOME, a matching grant program for state and local governments that was created by the 1990 housing act, was being allowed greater latitude and authority to make its own contributions toward reinventing the housing administration industry.

A government financial analysis of HUD completed in 1996 showed that FHA (Federal Housing Administration) cumulative losses with both GI (General Insurance) and SRI (Special Risk Insurance) mortgage insurance funds was greater than the appropriated capital in both 1994 and 1995. During 1995, the FHA and Ginnie Mae loss reserves amounted to $11.51 billion. This was a decrease of approximately $1.1 billion from 1994. Still, premiums generated by GI and SRI funds will not be enough to offset these losses. MMI (Mutual Mortgage Insurance) showed a loss of approximately $318 billion; CHMO (Cooperative Management Housing Insurance) $298 million; GI almost $75 billion; and SRI more than $10 billion.

CURRENT CONDITIONS

During Clinton's second term as president, Andrew Cuomo took over as the secretary of HUD. With Cuomo at the helm, the president pledged a goal of 67.5 percent homeownership by 2000. The 1997 national homeownership rate was a record 66 percent. By the end of 1998, HUD was ''back in business'' with the best budget (for fiscal year 1999) it had seen in a decade: $24.5 billion. Key provisions of the budget legislation were the creation of 50,000 new housing vouchers under Section 8, the raising of loan limits on home mortgages insured by FHA, an increase in funding for Community Development Block Grants (CDBGs), and expanding HUD's award-winning ''Continuum of Care Program'' for the homeless. The budget was increased by 33 percent over the previous year for Fair Housing activities as well.

Again in the fall of 1999, Congress appropriated major increases for HUD programs in its fiscal year 2000 budget. A total of 60,000 new Section 8 vouchers were to be funded (10,000 more than had been appropriated by the fiscal year 1999 budget), and public housing funds were increased from $2.8 billion to $3.1 billion. Another increase of $45 million for the homeless ensured the uninterrupted success of The Continuum of Care Program. There also was a $7 million increase in funds for the Housing for Persons With AIDS Program (HOPWA).

FURTHER READING

Addison, Eric. ''HUD: The Real Scandal.'' *The Journal of Housing,* November/December 1989.

''A New HUD: Opportunity For All.'' HUD 1997 Consolidated Report, Available from http://www.hud.gov/conrept.html.

''Back in Business.'' HUD Press Release, 15 November 1999. Available from http://www.hud.gov/pressrel/backnbiz.html.

Famighetti, Ed. *The World Almanac and Book of Facts 1997.* Mahwah, NJ: World Almanac Books, 1996.

HUD. ''What Are Hud's Major Programs?'' 1997. Available from http://hud.gov.

———. ''CFO Financial Notes.'' 1997. Available from http://entp.hud.gov/cfo/cfofin2c.html.

''President Clinton Signs Best HUD Budget In A Decade.'' HUD Press Release, 21 October 1998. Available from http://www.hud.gov/pressrel/pr98-509.html.

U.S. Department of Housing and Urban Development. Office of Community Planning and Development. *Perspectives on National Growth and Development, a Compact History, 1776-1976.* 1976, 1-11.

SIC 9532

ADMINISTRATION OF URBAN PLANNING AND COMMUNITY AND RURAL DEVELOPMENT

This category covers government establishments primarily engaged in planning, administration, and research for the development of urban and rural areas, including programs for slum clearance, community redevelopment, urban renewal and land clearance. Also included are zoning boards and commissions. Private establishments primarily engaged in urban planning, rural planning, and community development planning are covered by several SICs in the Engineering, Accounting, Research, Management, and Related Services category.

NAICS Code(s)

92512 (Adminstration of Urban Planning and Community and Rural Development)

Industry Snapshot

In *U.S. Metropolitan Economies: The Engines of America's Growth,* (prepared by Standard and Poor's in 1999 on behalf of the U.S. Conference of Mayors and the National Association of Counties), the role that U.S. cities have played in generating national and global economic growth could not have been emphasized more. It is generally understood that the United States is first-named on any list of the world's largest economies. What is less known is that, if an urban equivalent to ''gross domestic product'' (referred to in the study as *gross metropolitan product*) were used as the primary ranking criterion, 46 of the world's top 100 economies would be U.S. metropolitan areas. Thus, the health of America's cities and metropolitan communities remains vital to the health of this country.

Accordingly, each year, Congress allocates billions of dollars to ensure the continued well-being and development of urban and rural communities, through economic incentive programs such as block grants, matching funds, and the creation of ''empowerment zones,'' selected areas deemed worthy of special attention, either for renewal or stimulated growth. Another area of focus is the ''enterprise zone.'' An enterprise zone program targets economically distressed areas and cuts the taxes of businesses within those areas to attract investment, raise employment, and foster economic development.

Organization and Structure

The phrases ''community development'' and ''planning'' refer to the processes by which cities, towns, and rural communities consciously shape the course of their physical and economic growth to improve their economic health and the quality of their residents' lives. Community development is used to describe a wide range of strategies for improving conditions within a community, while planning usually describes the process of managing the details of a community's physical environment so that they conform to a comprehensive scheme for the community's future development. The planning and development process involves many different governmental activities, from constructing streets to regulating banks; therefore, it is conducted by a variety of separate, loosely coordinated governing bodies and agencies.

Government administration of planning and development takes place on both the federal level and the state and local level. At every level, government agencies must work closely with organizations outside of the government—from private companies and trade organizations to neighborhood associations. In the 1990s there were approximately 3,500 special governmental districts devoted to housing and community development in the United States, the vast majority on the local level.

At the federal level, agencies and cabinet departments in the executive branch put into practice policies mandated by acts of Congress or by the president. While the Department of Housing and Urban Development (HUD) enacts most national community development programs, a wide variety of development activities are conducted by administrative entities outside of HUD. The U.S. Department of Agriculture, for example, runs the Rural Electrification Administration, which provides loans for the creation of power supply systems, telephone services, and job development projects in rural areas. The Appalachian Regional Commission and the Tennessee Valley Authority conduct development programs targeted at specific geographic regions.

Federal agencies can implement planning and development initiatives primarily through either loans and grants, or legislation and regulation. Loans and grants may be given to private individuals (home buyers or real estate developers, for example) or to state or local governments and involve varying degrees of restrictions on the uses of funds. HUD's Rental Rehabilitation program, for example, grants funds to residential property owners specifically for improving the stock of low-income housing. HUD therefore specifies that program funds must be used to rehabilitate housing in neighborhoods whose residents have a median income no higher than 80 percent of the median income for the region surrounding the neighborhood. Community Development Block Grants, in contrast, are provided to state and local governments with few restrictions on use. Some loan programs involve collaboration between government and private financial institutions. Through its coinsurance program, for example, HUD aimed to encourage private lending for development purposes by offering to help private lenders absorb the cost of defaulted loans.

In addition to distributing financial aid, the federal government can shape community development through direct regulation. The Community Reinvestment Act of 1977 (CRA) was designed to penalize banks that drain capital away from economically distressed or minority neighborhoods by refusing to extend credit to the residents of these neighborhoods (a practice known as redlining). Under CRA, banks are required to serve "the convenience and needs" of their communities by providing credit services tailored to suit the needs of low-income community residents. The Board of Governors of the Federal Reserve System, the Office of the Comptroller of the Currency, the Federal Deposit Insurance Corporation, and the Office of Thrift Supervision enforce the act through regular examinations of financial institutions. These agencies can, if necessary, deny a financial institution permission to open, relocate, merge, or acquire a deposit facility on the basis of that institution's CRA record.

Through the allocation of aid and the creation of regulations, the federal government can try to guide communities toward very general goals, such as universal access to housing and equitable distribution of credit. But the U.S. national government has little power to decide where to locate public housing projects, which slums to demolish and rebuild, whether to devote a given area to industrial uses or to residences, what the direction of a city's growth will be, or any of the more detailed questions involved in a community's development. With the exception of a few experiments in national and regional planning, responsibility for resolving questions such as these falls on local governments' planning process.

In a typical community, the state or local government grants a local planning commission the power to create a master plan that makes proposals concerning the city's growth, the purposes for which its various sections of land will be used, how utilities such as water and electricity will be provided, where to build schools and libraries, how to lay out new streets, and other similar issues. The planning commission then recommends the master plan to the local governing body, which decides whether or not to adopt the plan. Once a plan has been adopted, it becomes a guideline for policy and a blueprint for possible municipal legislation. Parks, roads, and other facilities constructed by the city often must be approved by the planning commission to insure that all municipal construction follows the master plan.

In order to harmonize private development with the master plan, subdividers are frequently required to gain the approval of the planning commission before dividing their property into streets, lots, and blocks. The master plan also provides guidelines for municipal zoning ordinances, which designate whether or not particular areas of land can be used for residential construction, industrial development, or other specific uses.

Municipal governments are not limited to guiding the course of future development. They may also compel property owners to sell developed land to the local governing body so that existing construction can be demolished and redeveloped—a procedure known as urban redevelopment or urban renewal. It is frequently used to replace substandard or unsightly slum housing, in which case it is called slum clearance.

Municipalities frequently delegate responsibility for redevelopment to limited-dividend corporations—corporations that agree both to limit their investment returns and to abide by the regulations of the agency in charge of the renewal project in exchange for tax breaks and mortgage credits. Once a property has been redeveloped, the limited-dividend corporation can usually then sell it or lease it. Limited-dividend housing corporations have been created and operated by cooperatives, unions, reform groups, and private entrepreneurs.

Background and Development

The first city planners in America were the Puritans, who anticipated zoning restrictions by requiring that all residences be within a mile and a half of the town church. Contemporary methods of urban planning and community development originated in the nineteenth century, however. Planning experiments in private industry preceded any extensive effort on the part of federal or local government to solve the problems posed by urban development. Industrialists such as Francis Cabot Lowell (1775-1817) planned and built factory towns designed to provide a morally uplifting, rural environment for factory workers. Ultimately, however, the fate of the factory town of Lowell, Massachusetts, simply illustrated the difficulty of yoking the public welfare to private interests. As Lowell grew, and as the economic pressures of the 1837-1840 depression diverted resources away from the project of moral reform, it became more and more difficult to distinguish the planned factory town from the urban industrial environment it was intended to replace.

Ultimately, urban social problems prompted government intervention in urban development. In 1858 Frederick Law Olmstead and Calvert Vaux pioneered public urban planning by offering their own solution to the problems of urban industrialization: New York City's Central Park. Olmstead believed that the growth of cities should be carefully planned to protect the public interest rather than guided solely by market forces. In the case of Central Park, he hoped that a public park accessible to all of a city's residents would exert a moral influence on the city by providing urbanites with a pastoral escape from the hectic city street. For the first twelve years of its existence, an independent board of commissioners devoted to preserving Olmstead's moral purpose oversaw the park's maintenance. In 1870, however, the political machine of ''Boss'' William M. Tweed replaced the board with the Department of Public Parks, bringing Central Park under the city's system of management through political patronage. This sort of management proved much more characteristic of early municipal urban development efforts than Olmstead's ideal of careful planning for the public good. Informal systems of political influence, bribery, and covert cooperation between businesses and city officials managed to organize a makeshift response to the increasing need for transportation, utilities, and other public services in a time of ballooning urban growth.

Toward the end of the nineteenth century, municipal governments began to develop more systematic approaches to the management of community growth. Reform organizations such as the Tenement House Commission managed to move some cities toward more formal development policies, using fact-finding missions and statistical studies of tenement life to lobby for the municipal regulation of housing standards. These reformers achieved their most significant contributions to planning methods when they joined forces with the business sector. The increasing importance of scientific management techniques in industry gave rise to a distaste among industrialists for the informal planning procedures of political machines and attracted business leaders to the statistical methods of early social workers and sociologists. Some industrialists joined organizations like the League for Social Service to promote social reform through planning in the hope that improved planning and community development would improve the economic health of cities.

While reform-minded business leaders and business-minded reformers rarely advocated direct government intervention in community development, they did create model residential communities that set important patterns for future government planning by pioneering zoning and championing suburbanization. Corporations building company towns could give planners a centralized power unavailable to most city governments, and planners often used that power to experiment with zoning. Many reform groups advocated moderate cost suburban housing as an escape from the city's ills. The New York City and Suburban Homes Company, a limited-dividend corporation formed for reform purposes, built the prototype suburban development of Homewood, believing that the privacy of a single-family dwelling removed from the urban environment would foster the individualistic values required for a successful capitalist economy. To insure this morally elevating privacy, the company created rudimentary zoning regulations which excluded saloons, factories, and multiple-family residences from the area.

Municipal governments soon began implementing similar plans for separating residential neighborhoods from other types of land use. In 1909 Los Angeles enacted the first zoning legislation, an ordinance which divided land into heavy industrial, light industrial, and residential areas. In the landmark 1926 Supreme Court case *Village of Euclid v. Ambler Realty Company,* an Ohio town successfully defended its right to use zoning ordinances to reserve neighborhoods exclusively for single-family residential housing. By the end of the decade, 981 American communities were using zoning ordinances.

In addition to excluding industrial development from residential neighborhoods, early attempts to shape patterns of residential development frequently involved efforts to exclude racial minorities from designated areas. In 1917 the Supreme Court ruled that municipal governments could not enforce segregation. After this decision, segregationists were forced to rely on contracts between private individuals (such as a home buyer and a seller) which placed racial restrictions on future real estate transactions within particular neighborhoods. These ''restrictive covenants'' were struck down by the Supreme Court in 1948.

During the 1920s the Hoover administration helped promote the suburban ideal, and the use of zoning to enforce it, by creating a system of government agencies designed to help local communities guide and control their own development. The Bureau of Home Economics, the Advisory Committee on Building Codes, the Division of Building and Housing, and other agencies contributed to an increasing federal involvement in community development issues while avoiding direct federal intervention. Rather than regulating or funding development, these agencies served as information sources for municipal governments and private organizations. The Division of Building and Housing, for example, developed hypothetical zoning legislation for state and municipal governments, which these governments could then use as blueprints for their own legislation. By chairing the advisory council of Better Homes in America, Inc., a private organization devoted to improving moderate income housing standards, President Hoover hoped to realize his ideal of a collaboration between government and the private sector for development purposes. Like many advocates of suburban development, Better Homes in America saw ethnic and racial homogeneity as an important element of the suburban neighborhood and approved of the use of restrictive covenants to shape the demographic profiles of suburban communities.

The New Deal programs of the 1930s gave the U.S. government a much more direct role in community planning and development, setting the stage for future federal aid programs. President Franklin D. Roosevelt created extensive public works programs in an effort to relieve the massive unemployment of the Depression, and many of these programs involved urban redevelopment and the construction of planned communities. New Deal community development policy tended to encourage migration out of urban areas while trying to shore up decaying central cities. Forty out of 99 communities developed under the New Deal were in rural or suburban areas. The Subsistence Homestead Division funded experimental farm communities while moving industrial workers to rural communities planned, constructed, and managed by the U.S. government. The Resettlement Administration, run by Rex Tugwell, constructed planned communities named ''greenbelt'' towns after the band of deliberately undeveloped land which surrounded them. The planners of greenbelt towns like Greenbelt, Greendale, and Greenhills (located in Maryland, Wisconsin, and Ohio, respectively) were influenced by the ideas of pioneering British planner Ebenezer Howard, who saw the ideal community as a combination of urban and rural environments. In 1937 the newly created Farm Security Administration (FSA) absorbed the Resettlement Administration and undertook rural development programs designed to help tenant farmers become land owners. After the 1937 Dust Bowl, the FSA provided housing, health care, cooperative stores, and a variety of community services to migrant farm workers.

Meanwhile, the Public Works Administration (PWA) was conducting urban redevelopment projects. For a time the PWA itself bought and demolished slums in order to replace them with public housing, but a 1935 court ruling eventually prohibited the federal government from condemning private lands. After 1935 the PWA handed over to local housing authorities the task of purchasing slum property for urban redevelopment. The Wagner-Steagall Housing Act of 1937 further continued this trend toward local control of urban redevelopment by replacing federal government ownership of public housing projects with ownership by local government. Under Wagner-Steagall, the federal government restricted its involvement in public housing and urban redevelopment to regulatory guidance and financial assistance administered through the U.S. Housing Authority.

Federally assisted urban redevelopment, renamed ''urban renewal'' by the Housing Act of 1954, remained a widespread development strategy long after the New Deal. While members of the private sector had objected to the public housing projects of the PWA as a step toward socialism, some businessmen saw investment potential in the urban redevelopment initiatives of the Housing Act of 1949 and the Urban Renewal Act of 1954. Developers could take advantage of federal funds to turn ''blighted'' urban neighborhoods into upscale housing, office buildings, or other profitable projects. City governments benefited from this approach to redevelopment, for it turned decayed neighborhoods into sources of tax revenue.

The stock of low-income housing often suffered from this sort of urban renewal, however, and dislocated slum residents faced the difficult task of finding new housing that was as cheap as their previous dwellings. The 425,000 units of low-income housing destroyed for redevelopment from 1949 to 1968 far outweighed the 125,000 new units constructed during the same period. Faced with a shortage of low-income housing and a federal public housing budget depleted by the Korean War, many urban communities in the 1950s opted for large high-rise public housing projects which offered economies of scale.

Relocation of displaced slum-dwellers remained a problem, however. In the late 1960s, the Johnson administration emphasized the need to make low-income housing an integral part of all urban renewal projects, and the Housing Acts of 1968 and 1969 required that one low- or moderate-income housing unit be constructed for every unit that was demolished. In an effort to give a voice to residents of areas affected by urban renewal, HUD made local renewal agencies create and consult Project Area Committees composed of neighborhood representatives.

In the process of trying to create the comprehensive network of social services that he called the ''Great Society,'' President Johnson also increased funding to community development programs and attempted to restructure them. Through umbrella organizations such as the Office of Economic Opportunity and the Model Cities Administration, the Johnson administration tried to coordinate a wide variety of federal development programs. In theory, such a coordinated development strategy would be able to address urban decay as part of a web of interrelated social problems rather than as an isolated crisis, and so would be able to deal with it more effectively. In practice, however, the complexity and politicized nature of the relationships between different agencies and levels of government precluded a coordinated effort. The Vietnam War further weakened Great Society programs by draining away funds.

The simplification of the bureaucratic structure of federal social programs became an important element of the Nixon administration's domestic policy. Nixon's primary solution to bureaucratic complexity was to give state and local governments greater control over the allocation of federal funds, a proposal known as revenue sharing. The Community Development Block Grant (CDBG) proved to be the primary vehicle for revenue sharing in community development programs. The CDBG remained an important source of federal community development aid into the 1990s.

The Reagan administration cut back sharply on community development outlays in the early 1980s. The Reagan administration also saw a wave of scandals undermine the credibility of HUD. Ineffective management and accounting procedures allowed HUD employee Marilyn Louise Harrell—dubbed ''Robbin HUD'' by the press—to embezzle $5 million from the agency.

Abuses of HUD loan programs by private financial institutions were perhaps more significant than the highly publicized Robbin HUD scandal. The coinsurance program, for example, allowed irresponsible financial institutions to profit from large high-risk loans while leaving the federal government responsible for the bulk of the losses from defaulted loans. The program was designed to encourage private lending for development purposes by helping lenders absorb the risk while shifting the bureaucratic burden for processing loans off of HUD and onto the private lender. But because the private lenders handled the processing of coinsured loans, HUD had no way of assessing the risk of the loans it was guaranteeing. As a result, lenders like DRG Funding could make huge, obviously dangerous loans, profit from the fees involved, and lose relatively little when the borrower failed to repay the loan. President Bush's Secretary of Housing and Urban Development sought to reform the management methods of the department to prevent such abuses. Supported by the president, he also lobbied for an approach to federal community development assistance, which became the premise for the later development of empowerment zone and enterprise zone legislation.

President Clinton proposed a community development plan that adapted the enterprise zone proposals of the Bush administration. Initially, Clinton advocated both enterprise zones and a network of community development banks designed to foster economic development in distressed neighborhoods. The comprehensive development proposal presented by the Clinton administration on May 4, 1993, however, abandoned the community development bank idea. Instead, it outlined a system of grants and tax incentives to be offered to 10 ''empowerment zones'' and 100 ''enterprise neighborhoods.'' The empowerment zones would receive the most heavily concentrated aid, primarily in the form of wage-tax credits. According to the May 4 proposal, a company within a zone could receive a $5,000 tax credit for the first $20,000 of wages paid to a zone resident employed by the company. Businesses outside of the zone could receive a $2,400 credit for every employee living in the zone. This emphasis on wage credits represented a departure from the Bush administration's enterprise zone proposals, which focused instead on cuts in capital gains taxes for companies in the zones. President Clinton's plan would also try to attract small- and medium-sized businesses to the empowerment zones by allowing companies within the zones to deduct as much as $75,000 worth of equipment purchases from their taxes in the first year. Six of the empowerment zones would be in urban areas, three would be in rural areas, and one would be on a Native American reservation.

The winning cities were announced in late 1994 and by early 1997, the Clinton administration was calling its program an unqualified success. In Detroit, for example, more than $2 billion had been pledged by private investors toward redevelopment of that city's 18-square-mile zone. Critics questioned how successful such programs really were; they pointed out that other public and private redevelopment efforts over the years, from urban renewal in the 1950s to downtown pedestrian malls in the 1970s, had failed to eradicate poverty, which indeed was worse by some measures in the 1990s than twenty years earlier. But there was no denying the enthusiasm in designated cities for the empowerment zone policy.

CURRENT CONDITIONS

Notwithstanding congressional appropriation of substantial funds for three fiscal years in a row (1998, 1999, 2000), pockets of problem areas remained. In April 1999 HUD released a report, *Now Is the Time: Places Left Behind in the New Economy,* which identified several communities still struggling with poverty, unemployment, and population depletion. The Year 2000 Census will have tremendous impact on future funding of all programs dealing with urban and rural community development, as such funds are tied to census results and other demographic data. (The 1999 budget for the Bureau of the Census was approximately $1.24 billion.) One of the anticipated findings of the Census Report is expected to be the growth of large communities of immigrant populations clustered near major metropolitan areas. For example, in 1999 the city of Lowell, Massachusetts, not far from Boston, was home to the country's second largest population of Cambodian immigrants. Demands on social services and educational needs in cities like these are far different than those needed in communities such as those found in the Plains states. Thus, the interrelationship and interdependency of social and educational programs with urban planning and development initiatives are all too apparent.

In President Clinton's 1999 State of the Union Address, he drew attention to the urban challenges that still remain in many of our historically prosperous regions, such as Boston and New York. While Sun Belt states experienced great increases in population (with commensurate growing pains related to water, sewage, and transportation needs), the Northeast region of the United States was losing its urban populations by an average of more than five percent. As population declines, so also does funding, thereby creating a circular problem facing many large metropolises across the country.

Between 1992 and 1998, unemployment in central cities dropped overall from 8.5 to 5.1 percent. During the same time frame, 14.3 million new jobs (comprising 84 percent) were created in major metropolitan areas. Again, the importance of maintaining the health and vitality of urban communities is readily apparent. The Department of Commerce spent approximately $438 million in 1999 on its Economic Development Administration, and another 32 million on its Minority Business Development Agency. HUD's *State of the Cities 1999* report incorporated the Clinton Administration's ''21st Century Agenda for Cities and Suburbs,'' which outlined a formula for expanded home ownership, employment stimulus, affordable rental housing, and regional problem solving to ensure an investment return on America's cities.

The National Rural Development Partnership (NDRP) represents a collaborative effort between government and private sector interests working toward improving the quality of life for rural communities. In 1999 NRDP had 36 State Rural Development Councils, a National Council representing over 40 federal agencies in addition to private sector organizations, and The National Partnership Office as its administrative center. Examples of NRDP activities include those of the FORVM for Rural Maryland, which in 1999 worked with state legislators to ensure that rural communities would share in the benefits of the $4.9 billion settlement fund from the tobacco industry's national class action settlement. In Michigan the Rural Development Council sponsored a five-day tour of 163,000 acres of farmland in Maryland, Pennsylvania, and New Jersey, highlighting successful farming preservation projects and other leading land-use efforts in order to bring back new ideas for their own communities.

Further Reading

''Federal Government Budget by Agency.'' Office of Management and Budget, 1999. Available from http://www.polisci.com/economy/agency.htm

''HUD: Back in Business.'' U.S. Department of Housing and Urban Development,1999. Available from http://www.hud.gov/bkfact1.html.

The NRDP Update. October 1999. Available from http://www.rurdev.usda.gov/nrdp/update.html.

''Recent Evidence on the State of the Nation's Cities and Regions.'' *Now Is The Time: Places Left Behind in the New Economy.* U.S. Department of Housing and Urban Development, 1999. Available from http://www.hud.gov/pressrel/nowtime.html.

SIC 9611

ADMINISTRATION OF GENERAL ECONOMIC PROGRAMS

This group covers government establishments primarily engaged in promoting and developing economic resources of all kinds, including tourism, business, and industry. Included are establishments responsible for the development of general statistical data and analyses and promotion of general economic well-being.

NAICS Code(s)

926110 (Administration of General Economic Programs)

In 1999, the five largest economies in the world were the United States, China, Japan, Germany, and India. The primary U.S. federal agency supporting general economic programs is the Department of Commerce (DOC). Established in 1931, the DOC encourages and serves the nation's international trade, economic growth, and technological advancement. In 1999, the DOC had a budget of $5.5 billion dollars and 47,200 (full-time equivalent) employees.

Within the context of fostering competitive free enterprise, the DOC administers a wide variety of social and economic programs. For instance, it conducts research for technological advancements, grants patents, encourages growth of minority-owned businesses, works to improve the utilization of natural resources, and promotes travel to the United States by foreigners. The Secretary of Commerce oversees more than 30 offices and bureaus.

In 1997, the DOC published its ''Strategic Plan for 1997-2002,'' addressing its five-year priorities. In that Plan, it identified three basic areas of focus, which it referred to as ''themes.'' Theme 1 of the Plan addressed the nation's economic infrastructure, and DOC's role in developing jobs to support our economy. Theme 2 focused on the promotion of science and technology, and their roles in contributing to a competitive global economy. Finally, Theme 3 outlined the DOC's responsibilities for the management of national resources and assets, such as intellectual property rights, the radio frequency spectrum, and ocean and coastal resources.

To better manage these objectives and responsibilities, the Department of Commerce is charged with the periodic conducting of the national census. In preparation for the 2000 census, an additional 80,000 (mostly temporary) employees were hired for the Bureau of the Census, bringing its total employment to 104,900 for the year. Its budget also jumped from $1.3 million in 1999 to $4.7 million in 2000.

The DOC's Economic Development Administration (EDA) was created to generate new jobs, to protect existing jobs, and to stimulate commercial and industrial growth in economically distressed areas of the United States. It provides loan guarantees, public works grants, land and resource planning grants, and specialized technical assistance and consultation programs. It particularly concentrates on rural and urban areas of high unemployment, low income, and severe economic distress. EDA's 2000 budget was $387 million, with approximately 270 employees.

Conversely, the DOC's International Trade Administration (ITA) promotes world trade and investments in the interests of the United States. It advises the president on international economic policy, enforces fair import trade practices, works to foster U.S. export competitiveness, and gathers data and conducts research. In 1999, ITA maintained several U.S. Export Assistance Centers, 99 domestic Commercial Service Offices, and 138 worldwide posts and commercial centers in 70 countries. Its biggest challenge, possibly to date, was the U.S.-China WTO (World Trade Organization) Accession Deal. The ITA's 2000 budget was $307.0 million, with 2,400 employees.

Other commerce responsibilities are administered under numerous offices, such as the National Oceanic & Atmospheric Administration, and the National Telecommunications and Information Administration, which advises the president on telecommunications policy and promotes U.S. communications interests globally, among other activities.

The Patent and Trademark Office (PTO), also a responsibility of the Commerce Department, was created by the U.S. Constitution. It protects inventors' rights to the results of their creative efforts. In 1999, the PTO granted 169,154 patents, including 153,493 for inventions and 14,732 for design. Of these, 55.6 percent went to U.S. inventors, with California and New York claiming the highest numbers. The 2000 budget for the PTO was $115.0 million, with 7,200 employees.

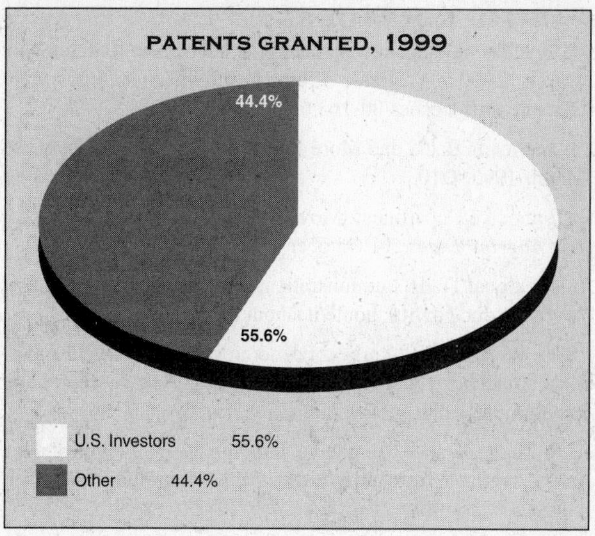

The National Institute of Standards and Technology assists industry in developing technology to improve products and manufacturing processes. Several other DOC offices collect data, provide technical assistance to various industries, and work to increase minority commerce.

Like the DOC, the Federal Trade Commission (FTC) strives to sustain the economic health of the nation. But its duties center around protecting the free enterprise system from monopolies, unnecessary trade restraints, and unfair or deceptive trade practices. Specifically, it regulates price-fixing, boycotting, and other competitive market influences; pricing discrimination; truth in advertising and labeling; and consumer credit policies. It also conducts research, enforces laws, and issues various trade regulations.

Besides the DOC and FTC, several smaller federal and state offices work to promote economic activity, protect consumers and businesses from fraud and negligence, and promote fair world trade. Within the Department of Energy, for instance, are several offices that work to develop energy programs, and to conserve resources for future economic goals.

Likewise, the U.S. International Development Cooperation Agency devises and coordinates international economic policy to ensure that development goals are considered in executive branch trade policies affecting less-developed nations, and provides strong direction for U.S. economic policies toward the developing world.

Similarly, the U.S. International Trade Commission furnishes studies, reports, and recommendations to the president, Congress, and other government entities regarding international trade and tariffs. It also conducts related investigations and public hearings.

FURTHER READING

''1999 Patent Statistics Announced.'' PTO Press Release, 2 March 2000. Available from http://www.uspto.gov/web/offices/com/speeches/00-16.htm.

''America Is Back, and More Inventive.'' *New York Times,* 25 March 1996, D10.

''Commerce Department, Moving Closer to Chopping Block.'' *Los Angeles Times,* 14 October 1995, D1.

International Trade Administration, 2000. Available from http://www.ita.doc.gov/ita_home/itaabout.htm.

''The World's Fifty Largest Economies.'' *The Political Reference Almanac,* 1999. Available from http://www.polisci.com/economy/fifty.htm.

U.S. Department of Commerce. Funding and employment data, 2000. Available from http://www.doc.gov/bmi/budget/PB2001/pdf.

SIC 9621

REGULATION AND ADMINISTRATION OF TRANSPORTATION PROGRAMS

This group covers government establishments primarily engaged in regulation, licensing, planning, inspection, and investigation of transportation services and facilities. Motor vehicle and operator licensing is classified here. Establishments of the Coast Guard that perform functions related to the regulation, administration, and operation of transportation are likewise included. Also included in this industry are civilian government air traffic control and aircraft inspection establishments. Parking authorities are classified here, but the operators of lots and garages are classified in **SIC 7521: Automobile Parking.** Operators of railroads, subways, depots, ports, toll roads and bridges, and other transportation facilities are classified in the Transportation, Communications, Electric, Gas, and Sanitary Services division. Highway construction and maintenance are classified in **SIC 1611: Highway and Street Construction, Except Elevated Highways.** Military establishments primarily engaged in air traffic control operations are classified in **SIC 9711: National Security** and private establishments engaged in air traffic control operations are classified in **SIC 4581: Airports, Flying Fields, and Airport Terminal Services.**

NAICS CODE(S)

488110 (Air Traffic Control)

926120 (Regulation and Administration of Transportation Programs)

The regulation and administration of transportation programs includes numerous offices and agencies at the federal, state, and local levels. These offices build roadways, railways, canals, and other transportation routes; manage vehicle licensing and safety programs; collect data; inspect vehicles and equipment; regulate traffic; and enforce and propose laws. In 1999, the federal government budgeted $48.4 billion for transportation. The Department of Transportation has more than 100,000 employees throughout the world.

DOT. The Department of Transportation (DOT) was the main transportation arm of the U.S. government. Formed in April of 1967, this massive bureaucracy encompassed several major government functions and wielded significant influence over state governments that relied on its transportation funds. The DOT was comprised of seven administrations, the U.S. Coast Guard, the Saint Lawrence Seaway Development Corp., the Office of the Inspector General, and the Office of the Secretary. The DOT was charged with establishing the nation's overall transportation policy, and was organized into major task groups that oversaw railroads; aviation; safety of waterways, ports, highways, and oil and gas pipelines; highway planning, development, and construction; and urban mass transit.

The largest entity within the DOT was the U.S. Coast Guard, which becomes part of the Department of the Navy during wartime. The Coast Guard enforces maritime laws; sets standards for and inspects commercial vessels; investigates marine accidents and misconduct, including pollution; and enforces port safety. According to the DOT, the Coast Guard's mission is to ''protect the public, U.S. economic interests and the environment—at sea, along the nation's coasts, in U.S. ports and waterways, and internationally.'' The Coast Guard also ran boating safety programs, operated icebreaking vessels, and trained military reserves. One of its chief responsibilities was maintaining a navigation system, which included long-range satellite radio-navigation aids positioned around the globe. Similar to but separate from the Coast Guard was the Maritime Administration, established in 1950, which helped to develop and promote the U.S. merchant marine.

The Federal Aviation Administration (FAA), also under the auspices of the DOT, was established in 1958 to regulate air commerce, control the use of navigable U.S. airspace, promote and encourage civil aeronautics, maintain navigation facilities, develop and operate an air traffic control system, conduct research, and regulate the environmental effects of aviation, such as noise. The FAA has offices throughout the world. The budget for the FAA was $9.8 billion in 1999.

In 1967, the giant Federal Highway Administration (FHA) administered a number of transportation programs related to the total operation and environment of highway systems and motor carriers. For example, the FHA tried to create uniform state trucking standards and implement trucking safety programs. The 1999 budget for the FHA was $28.7 billion.

The FHA's notable Federal-Aid Highway Program (FAHP), established in 1968 as the Urban Mass Transportation Administration, promoted mass transportation initiatives. The Federal Transit Administration (FTA) helped to develop technology and plans for new systems and carriers, encouraged the planning and creation of urban transit systems, provided financial assistance and consultation to state and local governments, and strove to implement national goals related to people who were elderly, handicapped, or economically disadvantaged. It operated largely through grant programs that disbursed federal dollars. The goal of the FTA is to provide public transit to all Americans. More than 10 million people utilize some form of public transit each working day. The budget for the FTA was set at $5.7 billion for 1999.

The Federal Railroad Administration, formed in 1966, enforced rail safety, administered railway financial assistance programs, and generally supported rail transportation activities. Its 8 regional offices conducted a variety of safety, freight, research, and policy programs related to railroads. In the 1999 budget, the Federal Railroad Administration received $740 million.

The National Highway Traffic Safety Administration (NHTSA) supports numerous federal and state governmental entities served to fulfill American transportation-related needs. The 1999 budget for the NHTSA was set at $361.0 million; $745,000 of the allocated funds are to be spent on a campaign to promote child safety seats, and $152.0 million for Campaign Safe and Sober, which educates the community about the perils of drinking and driving. The Federal Maritime Commission, for example, regulated waterborne foreign and domestic offshore commerce to assure that international trade was open to all nations. It also discouraged unauthorized activities and enforced equitable carrier rates.

The Interstate Commerce Commission (ICC) was established in 1979, and operated, maintained, and improved the Panama Canal in an effort to ensure safe, efficient, and economical transit service for the benefit of global commerce. It ceded its duties to the Republic in 2000.

Outlook. Expenditures for transportation were forecast to increase as the nation sought to revitalize and maintain its aging highways and roads. Federal spending on all transportation-related programs increased from $31 billion in 1991 to $48.4 billion in 1999.

In June of 1998, the Transportation Equity Act for the 21st Century became Public Law 105-178. It authorizes the federal surface transportation programs for highways, highway safety, and transit for the 6-year period from 1998-2003. Some of the department's stated goals are to increase seat belt use to 86 percent (from 70 percent in 1998); to reduce the percent of alcohol-related highway fatalities from 38 percent in 1998 to 34 percent; to increase Amtrak ridership from 21 million to 25 million; to decrease mobile source emissions from on-road vehicles; and to decrease the number of U.S. residents exposed to significant aircraft noise levels.

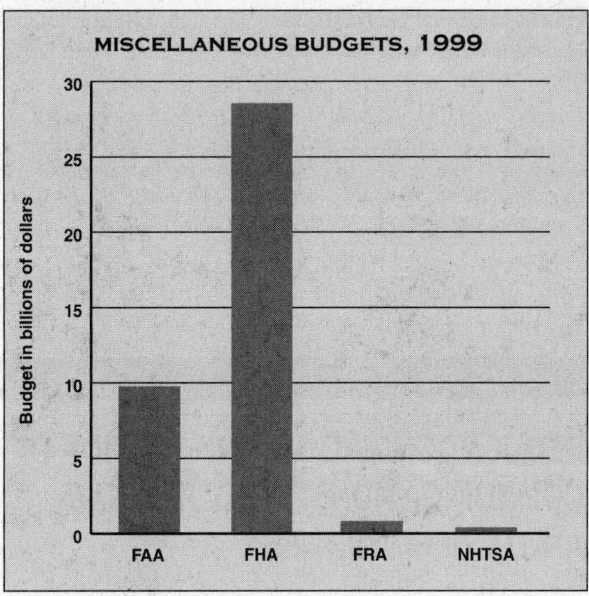

The DOC's NHTSA also worked to get anti-lock braking systems (ABS) installed on U.S. trucks, and to mandate new mirror systems on school buses that would increase a driver's field of vision.

The NHTSA published its 1998 statistics in 1999, showing a slight decrease (1 percent) in traffic fatalities (41,471) from the previous year. The sad statistic was that an average of 114 persons died each day in motor vehicle crashes—one every 13 minutes. Traffic fatalities increased significantly in Wyoming, South Dakota, and South Carolina in 1998. They decreased in Montana, North Dakota, New Mexico, New York, Delaware, Massachusetts, Oklahoma, and Michigan.

Although 49 states and the District of Columbia had seat belt laws in effect in 1998, the NHTSA found that 42 percent of those killed in crashes were not wearing seat belts. Motor vehicle accidents remained the leading cause of death for children in the United States (2,549 in 1998), as well as for adults under the age of 29. Intoxicated drivers accounted for the highest single group of fatalities, an alarming 56 percent. Speeding was the second highest contributing factor in fatalities, at 30 percent.

FURTHER READING

Federal Highway Administration, 1999. Available from http://www.fhwa.dot.gov/.

"Traffic Safety Facts 1998." National Center for Statistics & Analysis. Available from http://www.nhtsa.dot.gov.

U.S. Department of Transportation. *Highlights of the FY 1999 Transportation Budget.* Washington: GPO, 1999.

SIC 9631

REGULATION AND ADMINISTRATION OF COMMUNICATIONS, ELECTRIC, GAS AND OTHER UTILITIES

The primary participants in this industry grouping are government establishments which regulate, license and inspect utilities. The utility operations include the generation and delivery of electricity regardless of fuel, and the delivery of gas, water and sewer services.

NAICS CODE(S)

926130 (Regulation and Administration of Communications, Electric, Gas, and Other Utilities)

INDUSTRY SNAPSHOT

Utility operations directly affect almost everyone in the United States. The way they do business and how much they charge for their services is determined by federal, state and municipal commissions through a complex series of often overlapping regulations. Utility services include potable water, sewer facilities, electricity, natural gas, telephone, and cable television. The industry participants also monitor and regulate air and water quality and nuclear reactors. The U.S. Department of Energy budgeted nearly $5.7 billion on energy programs in 1999, including, but not limited to, regulation, monitoring, and research for alternative energy.

Of increasing interest and concern over the years is whether commodities which, at one time, were optional indulgences to make life easier or more enjoyable, but which now have become absolute necessities in today's world, should be regulated by any government entity, or should be left alone to operate within the free enterprise system upon which capitalism is built. The answer lies somewhere in between. Governmental "deregulation" of utilities during the 1990s was both contentious and problematic in many areas, yet ostensibly served to control price gouging and unfair market practices by utilities owners and suppliers.

ORGANIZATION AND STRUCTURE

The following organizations are the main national regulatory commissions:

The Federal Energy Regulatory Commission (FERC), which was established in 1977, replaced the Federal Power Commission (FPC) which was formed in 1935. FERC controls all electric generation, distribution and transmission involving wholesale transactions.

The Nuclear Regulatory Commission (NRC), which replaced the Atomic Energy Commission, was established in 1975. The NRC regulates all nuclear generation power plants and the transport and disposal of nuclear waste.

The Federal Communications Commission (FCC) consolidated the telecommunications authority of the Federal Radio Commission (1927) and the Interstate Commerce Commission in 1934. The FCC regulates telephone and telegraph services, satellites, broadcast and cable television, and newspapers.

The Environmental Protection Agency came into being in 1970 as an independent agency of the federal executive. It consolidated all federal environmental laws into a single administrative body.

The National Association of Regulatory Utility Commissioners (NARUC) provides a forum for state and municipal regulators.

BACKGROUND AND DEVELOPMENT

The evolution of the current regulatory system began with a concept referred to by Paul Gioia in an April 1989 issue of *Public Utilities Fortnightly* as "the regulatory compact." By the beginning of the twentieth century, utility services were seen as essential to the welfare of the public and the growth of the economy. Since their intricate distribution systems required large investments of capital and public lands for right-of-ways, control of such early utilities became concentrated in a few hands. This tendency toward a "natural monopoly" prompted experiments in utility regulation that continue today.

The extensive land requirements of transmission systems gave control of most gas, water and electric utilities to municipal governments before the turn of the century. This was primarily because, by 1880, most states turned over control of public streets to their cities. However, U.S. law required special permits or franchises for the use of such public property. Consequently, the municipalities controlled the privately owned utilities by granting franchises and sought to maintain control through competition by issuing overlapping franchises. This system predominated between 1879 and 1907, but complaints of excessively high prices, poor service, discriminatory marketing practices, and unsafe systems sparked public investigations that resulted in regulatory changes.

Matters came to a head in New York State when Charles Evans Hughes was elected governor. Despite the findings of his own investigation a year earlier, which confirmed all the charges against private utilities, Hughes favored continuing the system and adding a strong regulatory oversight commission manned with a professional staff. He had been opposed by William Randolph Hearst who proposed public ownership of all utilities. By 1907, however, Hughes established the first public utility commission. Wisconsin did the same and was followed by 27 other states between 1907 and 1914.

These policies shifted power away from the municipalities into the hands of state regulatory commissions and insulated legislators from the influence of utility operators. Consequently, legislators were able to enforce more uniform regulation and stem corruption and competitive waste. State regulations granted monopoly powers to utilities in specific regions in exchange for the ability to protect the public by setting price schedules which yielded a ''fair rate of return'' to the companies, while pushing costs down by taking advantage of the natural monopoly. Here, the important characteristic of the natural monopoly was that one company could operate more efficiently than two, thus minimizing costs for both the utility and the public.

However, current moves to deregulate utilities have prompted reexaminations of such concepts. Gregg A. Jarrell examined prices and profits for electric utilities around 1917. His study showed utilities in states which adopted regulation before 1917 were already the most efficient in the industry. The move to state regulation brought them, on average, a 25 percent increase in price and 40 percent increase in profits. In a 1992 article in *Regulation,* R. Richard Geddes quoted Jarrell and argued that the municipal system of overlapping franchises did foster competition and proved more effective than state regulation in controlling utilities. In fact, the move to state regulation actually insulated utilities from competition and allowed them to operate more freely as monopolies.

By 1925, the move to state regulation essentially was complete, but the abuses continued. In 1928, Congress reacted by ordering the Federal Trade Commission to investigate the gas and electric utilities and their holding companies. It found that such companies typically had a pyramid structure: the operating utility was at the bottom and was owned by intermediate holding companies, which were in turn held by another parent company. Apparently, the arrangement provided operating capital for the utility, but in reality the parent companies were siphoning off profits with imaginative bookkeeping techniques. Parent companies were able to make far more profits than the utilities alone, because regulations essentially stipulated a limit on utility profits.

The Public Utility Holding Company Act of 1935 (PUHCA) attacked the pyramid structure for the electric and gas utilities, but left the telephone holding companies alone. The act requires all such companies to register with the Securities and Exchange Commission (SEC) and file reports on their organization, financial structure, and operations. The SEC then broke up the large companies with interests in several states, requiring all surviving companies to operate as coordinated, integrated systems within a confined geographic area. This reorganization, however, was not completed until 1960.

The effect of PUHCA was to overlay federal authority onto state regulation of electric and gas utilities. It also established control of wholesale power distribution with the creation of the FPC in 1935. The FPC became the FERC in 1977. Wholesale electricity sales are transactions between the producer and the utility, and often involve interstate transmission of power. The federal government also began producing its own power with the Tennessee Valley Authority (TVA) and promoted the spread of electric services outside of cities with the Rural Electrification Administration (REA). That program provided farm cooperatives with subsidized loans and access to federal power.

Between 1925 and 1970, the cost of generating electricity dropped steadily as technology and economies of scale improved. In response, the utilities regularly requested and received rate decreases from regulators, but decreases took time to implement because of the regulatory process itself. The ''regulatory lag'' allowed utilities to realize returns on investment which exceeded their cost of capital.

In the early 1970s, the system suffered its first major challenge and failed. During the 1960s, growing public concerns about the environment prompted increased environmental regulation, which escalated the cost of power plant and transmission line construction and the average construction time. Technological innovation had slowed and nuclear power was proving far more expensive and unreliable than first thought. Subsequently, the OPEC oil embargo of 1974 doubled the cost of oil and affected the plants directly by dramatically increasing the price of all fossil fuels and the cost of generating electricity. It also affected the economy as a whole, slowing economic activity and reducing demand for electricity. Still operating on optimistic demand forecasts of the 1950s and 1960s, however, the utilities continued to replace inefficient oil and gas turbine plants with modern coal and nuclear facilities. The industry moved from a position of no-excess generation capacity in 1973 to 12-percent excess in 1975. Moreover, during this period electric rates increased 49 percent. This resulted in increasing rate-payer hostility and a growing tendency on the part of regulators to resist further price jumps. New construction began to tail off by the end of the decade when the second OPEC oil shock hit. Between 1972 and 1982, utilities canceled 100 nuclear plants.

The traditional rate-setting practice that allowed utilities to earn a fair rate of return on their operations began to unravel as consumers demanded an accounting of management practices. In 1985, regulatory commissions began to impose "prudence reviews" on new plant construction. Under these reviews, any questionable decisions that resulted in waste in the form of construction delays or cost overruns could come back to haunt the utility. The cost of these mistakes had to be absorbed by the utility company and were not allowed to be passed on to consumers through rate increases. This became particularly important to companies involved in nuclear plant construction. Changes in safety regulations mandated by the NRC forced utilities to make expensive alterations or sometimes complete reconstruction of plant facilities. Regulators also adopted the "used-and-useful rule" to bar the inclusion of abandoned plants in the rate base. This policy penalized utilities for stopping construction on plants and in many cases disallowed some or all of the output from new plants because a surplus of generating capacity existed. By 1991, utilities had been forced to write off about $14.7 billion worth of new generating capacity. That figure represents about 13 percent of all shareholder investment in utilities. As Gioia points out, this policy satisfied rate-payers by keeping current costs down, but it also convinced utilities to not engage in long-term capital investments like new generating equipment. Gioia believes that this situation foreshadows the possibility of shortages and reductions in service levels early in the twenty-first century.

This policy also created an opening for the increasingly important non-utility generators (NUGS). NUGS are small producers of electricity, usually industrial users, who supply their own power and sell the excess to utilities. Utilities always have viewed the NUGS' contributions as unreliable and too expensive compared to their own large scale operations. The Carter administration's Public Utility Regulatory Policies Act of 1978 (PURPA) has led many in the industry to consider NUGS as the wave of the future. The original intent of the act was to encourage the development of alternate fuels like solar, wind, hydroelectric, and garbage, as well as promoting cogeneration and other conservation initiatives. Utilities were required to buy power from these small generators at a rate equal to their avoided costs, which are costs associated with producing or buying power normally available to the utility.

Initially, the utilities objected to the NUGS incursion into the generating domain. Subsequently, however, they discovered they could use the act to build small plants in other franchise areas. The strategy allowed them to make higher profits because these new plants were not subject to regulatory rate approval. It also answered the capacity problem. By 1990, the amount of new generating capacity brought into service by the utilities through the traditional rate base construction programs dipped to less than that built by independent producers. By 1992, non-utility generating capacity amounted to 45,000 Mw, or 5 percent of all U.S. generating capacity, and displaced the equivalent output of 40 nuclear plants.

Until the mid-1980s, gas pipeline companies bought gas on long-term contracts, and sold it to local distribution customers under "take-or-pay" contracts. In the early 1980s, the supply of natural gas turned into a glut and resulted in the creation of a low-priced spot market. In response, the FERC abolished the take-or-pay arrangements and mandated open transmission access for the pipelines. Local distributors were no longer financially prohibited from abandoning long term contracts in favor of spot market purchases, and pipelines were required to transport the gas for them at a reasonable rate.

Similar developments occurred in the communications sector of the industry. Regulation in this segment began with the Manns-Elkins Act, which placed control of telephones and telegraphs into the hands of the Interstate Commerce Commission in 1910. The move, supported by AT&T, reduced competition from local telephone companies and reestablished AT&T's predominance, especially in the long-distance market, after its major Bell telephone patents expired. In 1934, the Commissions Act transferred regulatory authority to the FCC. As the FCC allowed private users to obtain transmission licenses in the late 1950s, AT&T's monopoly position began to erode. In the 1960s and 1970s, the courts forced the FCC to end the AT&T equipment monopoly by allowing clients to attach their own equipment to phone lines. Finally, in 1984, an antitrust decree forced AT&T to divest from all its local operating companies.

For the cable companies, the FCC control began to slip in 1984 with the Cable Communications Policy Act. The act deregulated pricing in competitive markets which were deemed to comprise all but the very smallest. It also prohibited phone companies from offering cable television services on their lines. When the average cost of cable service rose more than 40 percent, Congress, in 1992, allowed states and municipalities to reestablish rate regulation.

In the early 1990s, the movement toward deregulation was picking up steam as more utility operations faced competitive challenges. However, critics warned that deregulation policies would jeopardize supplies, quality, and safety. They have pointed out that base-load electric generating facilities like nuclear plants and large coal-fired plants are not being built. Instead, gas turbines are becoming popular because natural gas is relatively inexpensive. Such systems are less efficient than the base-load plants and consequently, the price of gas could rise. More importantly, unlike utilities which are able to switch fuels, gas turbines cannot operate if the supply of gas is curtailed.

Electric companies also found themselves embroiled in deregulation controversies. A bill was introduced to Congress in 1996 that would mandate federal retail wheeling of electric power by December 15, 2000. According to Eastern Maine Electric, ''generation utilities will no longer have ownership or control of transmission and/or distribution facilities.'' The new legislation is intended to break up ''vertical monopolies,'' which control generation, transmission, and distribution of electricity. Basically, the new proposal will lead to competition between retail electric companies. Consumers will have the right to choose which company they will purchase electricity from. Critics worried utility companies will no longer be able to initiate new development because of the uncertainty of the number of base clients.

Also in 1996, Congress passed the Telecommunications Reform Act. This act substantially deregulated the cable TV industry, along with other services. One of its key components was the introduction of the V-chip for TV sets, which allows parents to block programs they feel are inappropriate for their children.

CURRENT CONDITIONS

Electric power generation has become an industry twice the size of the global auto industry, bringing in an estimated $800 billion in revenues annually. As such, it is no wonder that the century ended without the complicated and contentious deregulation that many had hoped for. Notwithstanding, Congress appeared poised to act soon thereafter on a bill which would, in fact, deregulate the industry. In 1999, Congress accelerated activity on issues attendant to deregulation: viability of competition to drive prices down; antitrust concerns; and the reality of electricity restructuring in a deregulated industry. As of late November, 1999, H.R. 2944, the Electricity Competition and Reliability Act of 1999, had gone through its second draft and was headed for a full legislative hearing. Studies by consumer advocate groups and academia assert that utility companies have held back on power output to control prices, and that the industry could realize between 13 to 25 percent more output annually without adding any more equipment. They believe that deregulation of the industry would equate to a real-world savings of about $30 per month on the average household electric bill.

In the communications arena, antitrust concerns over the pending mergers between AT&T and Tele-Communications Inc., Bell Atlantic and GTE, and Ameritech with SBC Communications Inc. dominated the 1999 calendar. To be avoided were the ''vertical monopolies'' so characteristic of the electricity industry. There were an estimated 65 million mobile phone users by early 1999, and 70 million Internet users. As fast as fiber-optic technology hit the global market, its biggest competitor, satellite communications technology, also entered the arena of soon-to-be-deregulated industries.

Natural gas consumption is expected to continue growing at about 2 percent per year, and according to EOG Resources, will nearly double by 2020. The Gas Research Institute predicts that the natural gas share of the total energy market will jump from 24 percent in 1997 to 28 percent in 2015. The largest demand growth is in the electric power generation sector.

AMERICA AND THE WORLD

The deregulation of the gas pipeline industry is straining relations with gas producers in Canada. Shifting from long-term contracts to purchases on the spot-market, many Canadian contract holders were left in the lurch. They appealed to the provincial government, which issued an order forbidding sales of spot-market gas to California until the original contracts were satisfied. The California Public Utilities Commission responded by charging the move was in violation of the 1988 Canada-U.S. Free Trade Agreement.

Domestic natural gas production has plateaued, despite rising demand. Industry reports from the second quarter of 1999 show a 3.3 percent fall in production for the 14 major companies, as compared to the same period in 1998. Canada was experiencing the same trend. Low-cost imported gas will help to maintain supply levels until new technology can rise to a level capable of addressing demand.

On September 30, 1999, the worst nuclear accident in years occurred at a power generation plant near Tokyo, Japan, exposing some 70 persons to direct radiation, and causing the quarantine sheltering of 320,000 local residents. Three workers who were gravely injured were said to have received more than 17,000 times the average yearly dose of radiation allowed per worker. While the accident was said to have been caused by the workers, it raised new concerns about the safety of nuclear power-generating plants, when considering the modest cost savings they, in fact, produce.

In the area of cable and telephone companies, American regulatory policy has created one of the most restrictive systems in the world. France and Germany have no regulatory barriers for cable-telephone interaction, while Britain, Canada, and Japan enforce some regulatory controls on joint agreements between the two industries.

RESEARCH AND TECHNOLOGY

Much of the impetus for deregulation is coming from advances in technology. Traditionally, utilities and communications have been seen as natural monopolies because of the size and unwieldy nature of their transmission systems. If FCC regulations are relaxed, fiber-optics technology would allow the telephone company to deliver hundreds of television channels, voice and two-way video, information services, and home banking and shopping services over phone lines. Similarly, the use of computers in electric transmissions allows greater control and reliability in accepting power from alternative and changing sources.

FURTHER READING

Abel, Amy and Parker, Larry. ''IB10006: Electricity: The Road Toward Restructuring.'' 12 August 1999. Available from http://www.cnie.org/nle/eng-7.html.

''Barton Introduces H.R. 2944, The Electricity Competition and Reliability Act.'' News Release, 15 October 1999. Available from http://www.house/gov/barton/hr2944release.html.

Burke, Robert G. ''Deregulation changing structure of satellite communications.'' *Offshore,* July 1998, 100.

Chambers, Ann. ''Natural Gas Use Rising, Prices May Follow.'' *Power Engineering,* 1 October 1999.

Famighetti, Robert, ed. *The World Almanac and Book of Facts 1997.* Mahway, New Jersey: World Almanac Books, 1996.

''Federal Government Budget by Agency, 1999.'' Available from http://www.polisci.cpm/economy/agency.htm.

Geddes, R. Richard. ''A Historical Perspective on Electrical Utility Regulation.'' *Regulation,* Winter 1992.

''Japanese Nuclear Accident Victim Turns Sharply Worse.'' *Power Engineering News,* 19 November 1999. Available from http://pe.pennwellnet.com/content/news/readnews.cfm?ID=63285.

Maloney, Michael T., Robert E. McCormick and Raymond D. Sauer. ''Customer Choice, Consumer Value.'' Prepared for Citizens for a Sound Economy Foundation. Available from http://hubcap.clemson edu/customer choice. 1998.

Silva, Jeffrey. ''Kennard Hints at More Deregulation.'' *Radio Communications Report,* 11 January 1999, 4.

''Top Cable Industry News Stories of the Day.'' *CableNET Extra Archive,* 31 March 1997. Available from http://www.cablenet.org/Cablenet/extra.html.

''Utility Deregulation for Beginners.'' Eastern Maine Electric, 1997. Available from http://www.emec.com/deregulation/dereg1.htm.

SIC 9641

REGULATION OF AGRICULTURAL MARKETING AND COMMODITIES

This category covers government establishments primarily engaged in the planning, administration, and coordination of agricultural programs for production, marketing, and utilization, including related research, education, and promotion activities. Establishments responsible for regulation and control of the grading, inspection, and warehousing of agricultural products; the grading and inspection of foods; and the handling of plants and animals are classified here. This government group also includes such entities as agricultural extension services, fair boards, marketing, and consumer services.

NAICS CODE(S)

926140 (Regulation of Agricultural Marketing and Commodities)

Government establishments primarily engaged in the administration of programs for developing economic data about agriculture and trade in agricultural products are classified in **SIC 9611: Administration of General Economic Programs.** Government establishments primarily engaged in programs for conservation of agricultural resources are classified in **SIC 9512: Land, Mineral, Wildlife, and Forest Conservation.** Government establishments primarily engaged in programs to provide food to people are classified in **SIC 9441: Administration of Social, Human Resource, and Income Maintenance Programs.**

INDUSTRY SNAPSHOT

The major federal agency in this category is the U.S. Department of Agriculture (USDA). This cabinet-level agency, established in 1862, works to improve and maintain farms, to cultivate markets for U.S. agricultural exports, and to regulate the integrity of farm commodities. These goals are accomplished through its various programs (e.g., loans and subsidy payments), marketing and outreach efforts, research, and regulations. The USDA works in conjunction with agriculture departments in states and territories.

BACKGROUND AND DEVELOPMENT

While many of the early U.S. presidents considered themselves farmers, a cabinet department to address the needs of the country's largely agrarian society did not come into existence until the mid-nineteenth century. In 1839, Congress appropriated $1,000 for the collection of agriculture-related statistics and the distribution of seeds; this function was assigned to the U.S. Patent Office because Commissioner of Patents Henry L. Ellsworth supported aid to agriculture and the number of agricultural patents being handled by that office was larger than any other category of inventions.

Farming in America gradually shifted from subsistence cultivation to more commercial operations by the mid-1800s, and at the urging of the U.S. Agricultural Society (organized in 1852), a formal agriculture agency (not a cabinet department) was established on May 15, 1862. The first commissioner of the new agency was Isaac Newton, a personal friend of President Lincoln and a farmer. It was during this time the department began to regularly publish statistical and research reports, send scientists to Europe and Asia to observe agriculture abroad, and take some initial steps toward regulation of commodities. In 1887, passage of the Hatch Act authorized experimental stations in the states, and in 1989, raised the agriculture bureau to cabinet status.

Much of the Department of Agriculture's proactive work began during the Great Depression, when farmers faced tremendous challenges and hard times. In 1933, the Agricultural Adjustment Act was passed, its purpose being to adjust production to meet demand, and ultimately establish marketing conditions that would raise farm prices to parity. While this legislation was declared unconstitutional by the U.S. Supreme Court in 1936, many of the functions assigned to the Agricultural Adjustment Administration were incorporated into USDA operations. In the post-World War II period, farmers and the USDA began addressing the problems of crop surpluses, subsidies, and development of new opportunities to maintain farmer income.

Divisions within the USDA that are involved with the marketing and regulation of commodities are the following:

- The Agricultural Marketing Service. Established on April 2, 1972, the service concerns itself with grading, inspection, certification, market news, marketing orders, and the research and promotion of regulatory programs. Grading standards are in place for nearly 240 agricultural commodities. These standards are developed to certify quality of the commodities being purchased.
- Animal and Plant Health Inspection Service. Established in 1977, this service conducts regulatory and control programs designed to protect and improve animal and plant health. Working with state agencies, the inspection service is concerned with humane treatment of animals, the control and elimination of pests and diseases, and animal and plant quarantines. This agency also is involved in border inspection of agricultural products coming in to the United States.
- Grain Inspection, Packers, and Stockyards Administration. The former Federal Grain Inspection Service and the former Packers and Stockyards Administration were merged to form this USDA office. The agency is responsible for establishing standards for grains and other assigned commodities and for administering a nationwide inspection and weighing system.
- Cooperative State Research, Education, and Extension Service. This agency works closely with research colleges and universities, agricultural stations, and state agencies, focusing on research, extension, and higher education in the food and agricultural sciences and in related environmental and human sciences. Among this agency's concerns are improvement of agricultural productivity, creation of new products, and addressing of agriculture-related problems as they surface. It has been involved in plant and animal genome, food safety, and sustainable agriculture research projects throughout the country.

One of the most important developments in commodities and price regulation has no direct connection to the USDA—the closing of the National Cheese Exchange. Located in Green Bay, Wisconsin, the cheese exchange was a nonprofit organization that helped to determine the price of cheese throughout the nation. In response to complaints from Wisconsin farmers about declining prices, and following a research study conducted by the University of Wisconsin that suggested the exchange was being inappropriately dominated by large traders such as Kraft Foods, Wisconsin's two U.S. senators (Russ Feingold and Herb Kohl) called for an investigation into the exchange's operations. Kraft Foods denied charges of cheese "dumping" in order to lower milk prices, and the Federal Trade Commission's 1996 investigation found no evidence of antitrust violations. But rather than fight what it labeled "assaults from farmers' organizations, politicians, and the media," the cheese exchange's functions have been shifted to the Chicago Mercantile Exchange. Although cheese futures trading was adopted by a New York commodity exchange several years ago, it has had little impact on pricing.

CURRENT CONDITIONS

In 1999, the USDA had a budget of more than $65 billion and employed 110,000 persons. It continued to serve the nation's 2 million farmers and 69 million rural residents. The agency also was responsible for providing 25 million lunches to the nation's school children each day. The USDA estimated that in 1999, the number of U.S. commercial farms was between 300,000 and 500,000. Commercial grain storage was estimated at approximately 8 billion bushels, with another 11 billion bushels stored on the farms.

Although there was a one-year increase in 1999 (for emergency funding to address the farm economic crisis and the President's Food Aid Initiative), the USDA's budget outlays have declined steadily from $63.1 billion in 1993 to an estimated $55.2 billion for 2000. The department's stated strategic goals for the FY2000 budget were to expand economic and trade opportunities for agricultural producers; to ensure food for the hungry and an accessible supply of safe, nutritious, and affordable food; and to promote sensible management of our natural resources. In furthering these goals, early in 2000 the USDA announced new criteria for the labeling of ''organic foods,'' eliminating from that category all genetically-engineered products and those which have been irradiated.

Highlights of specific program budgets for 2000 included $25.0 billion for the Farm Service Agency, $6.4 billion for the Foreign Agricultural Service, $1.7 billion for the Risk Management Agency, $10.9 billion for rural development programs, $21.7 billion for the Food Stamp Program, $742.0 million for the Food Safety and Inspection Service, $4.9 billion for natural resources and environment, $825.0 million for marketing and regulatory programs, and $2.1 billion for research and education.

FURTHER READING

Kendell, Keith, President of the National Grain and Feed Association. ''Competitiveness in Agriculture and Food Marketing.'' FDCH Congressional Testimony, 20 October 1999.

National Archives and Records Administration. *The United States Government Manual 1996/1997,* Washington: GPO, 1996, 119-123.

''National Cheese Exchange Folds.'' *Wisconsin State Journal,* 26 April 1997, 8B.

Onken, John. ''Will New Cheese System Really Change Things?'' *The Capital Times,* 24 April 1997, 1B.

Rinard, Amy. ''Cheese Exchange Closes Its Doors; Trading to Resume Next Week after Shift from Green Bay to Chicago.'' *The Milwaukee Journal Sentinel,* 26 April 1997, 1D.

U.S. Department of Agriculture (USDA). Available from http://www.usda.gov/ 1999.

SIC 9651

REGULATION, LICENSING, AND INSPECTION OF MISCELLANEOUS COMMERCIAL SECTORS

This category covers government establishments primarily engaged in regulation, licensing, and inspection of other commercial sectors, such as retail trade, professional occupations, manufacturing, mining, construction, and services. Also covered are physical standards, regulating hazardous conditions not elsewhere classified, and alcoholic beverage control.

NAICS CODE(S)

926150 (Regulation and Inspection of Miscellaneous Commercial Sectors)

ORGANIZATION AND STRUCTURE

The primary purpose of regulation is to prevent harm—either physical, pecuniary, or restrictive—to persons or entities. It follows that statistical data on harm, damage, or injury is necessary to amend, delete, or provide regulatory structure to an industry. Analysis and application of data provide justification for agencies and regulatory boards to exercise jurisdiction over private and public sectors in order to reduce such injuries. Examples include vehicular safety belt and speeding laws, minimum age requirements for tobacco and alcohol products, maximum weight loads in elevators, airplanes, and freight trucks, nutritional analysis on food packages, and control of pharmaceuticals by prescription only.

From the federal regulations commercial truck drivers must meet, to the deposit requirements banks must follow, government agencies—at both the state and national level—present a mosaic of requirements that promote safety and stability for the general public and for the employees in regulated industries. Regulatory responsibilities are assigned to a wide range of federal agencies. Following are some of the most active and high-profile agencies.

The U.S. Occupational Safety and Health Administration (OSHA). This agency, part of the U.S. Department of Labor, came into being in 1970. Its stated mission is ''to assure so far as possible every working man and woman in the nation safe and healthful working conditions.''

OSHA, working in conjunction with state agencies, utilizes 2,100 inspectors and additional complaint-discrimination investigators, engineers, physicians, educators, standards writers, and other technical and support personnel throughout the country. The agency's regulations generally do not apply to miners, transportation workers, the self-employed, and some public employees.

Through its investigations and its enforcement of regulations and standards, and through its public outreach and training efforts, OSHA works to reduce workplace injuries and deaths. An estimated 6,000 Americans die each year from injuries sustained at their places of work. An additional 50,000 people die from illnesses brought on by chemical exposures in the workplace, and an estimated 6 million people suffer nonfatal workplace injuries—injuries that carry a $110 billion price tag annually.

OSHA strictly monitors: asbestos in the workplace, bloodborne pathogens, and carbon monoxide poisoning, as well as control of hazardous energy sources, cotton dust, employee rights and responsibilities, lead exposure, exposure to formaldehyde, safety of video display terminals, and workplace fire safety.

A recent study of the impact of OSHA inspections showed the positive impact such regulation efforts have had. According to the study, in the three years following an OSHA inspection, penalties, injuries, and illnesses fell an average of 22 percent. In addition, overall injury and illness rates dropped in industries where OSHA has concentrated its attention but remained unchanged or actually increased in industries where OSHA had less presence. OSHA's 1999 budget was estimated at $349 million.

The Federal Deposit Insurance Corporation (FDIC). This agency is an independent organization created by Congress as part of the 1933 Banking Act. Along with its related regulatory agency, the Federal Savings and Loan Insurance Corporation (and, to a lesser degree, the Federal Reserve), the FDIC's mission is "to maintain stability and public confidence" in the nation's banking system.

Issues connected to banking have played integral roles in American history: the stock market collapse of 1929 and its effect on banks prompted the establishment of the FDIC. During Franklin D. Roosevelt's first 100 days in office, legislation establishing the FDIC was passed by Congress, as a way to stave off the collapse of banks and the loss of depositor savings.

The big news in 1999, following a record-breaking stock market boom lasting for several months, was the historic restructuring of banking law by Congress and the White House in October-November 1999. Intended to dissolve restrictions placed upon banks, insurance companies, and stockbrokerages by the Glass-Steagall Act of 1933, the new legislation was promoted as an offensive rather than defensive measure to meet the rising global economy. It essentially allows integration of commerce and banking—mutually exclusive industries following the market collapse of the Great Depression. Banks and financial firms may engage in commercial activities such as the marketing of insurance and investment portfolios, and commercial firms will be allowed to purchase banks and financial entities.

The FDIC requires banks and other financial institutions included in its regulatory purview to protect their money supplies through the provision of insurance coverage for bank deposits. Accounts are protected up to $100,000. The FDIC also conducts periodic examinations of banks that do not belong to the Federal Reserve System. In 1998 and 1999 the Department of the Treasury's Bureau of Engraving and Printing issued new paper currency for all but the dollar bill, intended to ensure the continued containment of high-tech counterfeiting, which costs billions of dollars each year.

The Bureau of Alcohol, Tobacco, and Firearms (ATF). This agency is part of the U.S. Treasury Department. While the portion of its mission dealing with the reduction of crime and provision of law enforcement assistance to local entities receives the greatest public attention, ATF also enforces regulations dealing with the sale of alcohol, tobacco, and firearms; in particular, ATF is concerned with the fair and proper collection of revenues and taxes on those items.

The history of ATF goes back to the beginnings of U.S. history. The taxing of alcohol has generally been seen as a way to generate needed revenue. But not surprisingly, those required to pay the tax weren't always supportive of those efforts. The Whiskey Rebellion of 1794 (when farmers vigorously protested the imposition of a federal excise tax on whiskey) was only one in a continuing series of episodes in which the federal government met the resistance of general citizens. With the end of Prohibition, alcohol was once again seen as a possible revenue source. In 1934 the Alcohol Tax Unit within the Bureau of Internal Revenue was created. In 1935, the Federal Alcohol Administration Act was passed, creating licensing and permit requirements and establishing regulations to ensure an open and fair marketplace for the legal manufacturers of distilled spirits and their customers. In 1940 the Federal Alcohol Administration merged with ATF; that merger combined law enforcement and regulatory authority into one agency. Firearms became a part of the organization's responsibilities, and oversight of tobacco taxes was added in 1951. From the mid-1960s into the 1980s, ATF's mission came to include law enforcement duties.

While it may appear that its regulatory functions have taken a back seat to its law enforcement activities, ATF, which regulates some of the most important and controversial industries in this country, collected more than $18.2 billion in revenues in 1998. The agency also conducts seminars to ensure the market and product integrity of alcoholic beverages. And, consistent with its history, ATF is expected to expand into the area of electronic commerce. A 1995 test project that allowed industries to electronically submit and monitor applications for non-beverage alcohol formula was deemed successful and will likely be expanded to include other areas under ATF jurisdiction. The 1999 budget for the ATF was approximately $743 million.

The issue of industry regulation in general has prompted considerable political debate. A key theme of the Clinton administration has been the need to get rid of regulations and requirements that are ''burdensome'' to U.S. industry, particularly to small businesses. The movement from regulation to deregulation or self-regulation came to a head during the Reagan administration. And while federal agencies continued to enunciate their desire to move away from ''over-regulation,'' or at least make the regulations more user-friendly, a trend appears to be emerging that would increase the federal government's regulatory role.

For example, the U.S. Environmental Protection Agency ranks as a priority the reduction of tiny air particles believed to pose risks to children. Nelson Litterst, a lobbyist for the National Federation of Independent Business suggests such rules could cost $16 billion annually, double the EPA's estimate. Also, OSHA recognized its need to respond to public perceptions that it has been an agency enmeshed in red tape and a ''one-size-fits-all'' approach to regulation. At the same time, OSHA continued its efforts to require workplace ergonomic standards, in order to reduce back injuries and problems resulting from repetitive stress syndrome. However, a GOP-controlled Congress blocked OSHA's move in 1995, but that ban was not renewed in 1996. Thomas J. Donahue, president of the American Trucking Association, has said the kinds of regulations being considered would cost truckers $6.4 billion a year. OSHA's estimate of costs in this area was $257 million. Furthermore, it was expected that OSHA would be turning its attention toward convenience stores and fast-food restaurants in an attempt to reduce nighttime crime. With the National Highway Traffic Safety Administration developing new standards for automobile airbags and the Food and Drug Administration offering new regulations to prevent a U.S. outbreak of mad-cow disease, the pendulum may be swinging back toward regulation.

CURRENT CONDITIONS

The National Safety Council released its annual report in November 1999, *Report on Injuries in America,* containing highlights from its 1999 edition of *Injury Facts.* According to the report, in 1998 alone, there were 19.4 *million* injuries from unintentional causes which resulted in disability. During the same year, 92,200 people died of fatal injuries.

The leading causes for injury-related fatalities in 1998 were motor vehicle accidents, falls, poisonings, drownings, and burns by fire. The leading causes of noninjury related fatalities were heart disease, cancer, stroke, and pulmonary disease. At the workplace, a fatality occurs every 103 minutes and a disabling injury every 8 seconds. A total of 3.8 million workers suffered disabling injuries in 1998 alone, costing Americans $125.1 billion. At home, the leading cause of death was by falling, resulting in 10,700 fatalities for 1998 alone. Deaths and injuries in public places (including sports, recreation, and building access) totaled 20,100 in 1998.

The total cost to the American public of medical expenses, property loss, and employer expense was an estimated $480.5 billion, or the equivalent of 59 cents for every one dollar spent on food in 1998. It is from statistical data such as this that regulatory entities decide whether to further regulate, deregulate, or leave intact the controlling laws and rules that govern major industries across the nation.

FURTHER READING

''Bentsen Amendments Strengthen Banking Overhaul Legislation.'' Press Release, June 20, 1997. Available from http://www.house.gov/bentsen/pr62097.htm.

''Fatal Occupational Injuries and Employment by Industry, 1998.'' Bureau of Labor and Statistics: Safety & Health Statistics, Table 3. Available from http://stats.bls.gov/news.release/cfoi.t03.htm.

''Federal Government Budget by Agency.'' Office of Management and Budget, 1999. Available from http://www.polisci.com/economy/agency.htm.

''Greenspan Backs Bank Reform.'' *CNN Financial Network,* 11 February 1999. Available from http://www.cnnfn.com/hotstories/economy/9902/11/greenspan/.

Hopkins, Thomas. ''Cost-Benefit Paralysis.'' *National Review,* 2 September 1996, 69.

''Unintentional Injuries Are Among Leading Causes of Death in the U.S.'' National Safety Council News Release, November 5, 1999. Available from http://www.nsc.org/news/nrrptinj.htm.

''U.S. Congress, White House Reach Agreement on Banking Reform.'' Yahoo News, 23 October 1999. Available from http://ink.yahoo.com/bin/query?p = %22glass-steagall + act.

Yang, Catherine, and John Carey. ''The Regulators Are Back at Business.'' *Business Week,* 20 January 1997, 41.

SIC 9661

SPACE RESEARCH AND TECHNOLOGY

This category includes government establishments primarily engaged in programs for manned and unmanned space flights and space exploration. Research and development laboratories operated by the National Aeronautics and Space Administration (NASA) are classified as auxiliaries to this industry. Private establishments primarily engaged in operation of space flights on their own account are classified in **SIC 4789: Transportation Services, Not Elsewhere Classified.**

NAICS CODE(S)

927110 (Space Research and Technology)

INDUSTRY SNAPSHOT

The National Aeronautics and Space Administration (NASA) is the primary U.S. government agency involved in space research and technology. The Department of Defense also operates extensive space research programs, many of them classified, including the Strategic Defense Initiative, better known as Star Wars.

Other government agencies involved in space research include the Department of Commerce, which operates the National Institute of Standards and Technology and the Office of Space Commerce; the National Science Foundation, which operates several Earth-based observatories; and the Smithsonian Institute, which operates the Smithsonian Astrophysical Observatory, the Center for Earth and Planetary Sciences, and the Laboratory for Astrophysics.

The federal space program came to prominence during the 1960s as a result of the "space race," which pitted the United States against the Soviet Union in a contest to be first to land a man on the moon. Over the years, the space program has enjoyed spectacular successes, but also suffered several disappointments, including the tragic explosion of the Challenger shuttle.

ORGANIZATION AND STRUCTURE

NASA, the government's largest space research organization, is divided into several "offices," each responsible for a different aspect of the U.S. space program. These include the Office of Aeronautics, the Office of Space Science, the Office of Mission to Planet Earth, the Office of Life and Microgravity Sciences and Applications, the Office of Space Flight, the Office of Space System Development, the Office of Advanced Concepts and Technology, and the Office of Space Communications.

Office of Aeronautics. The Office of Aeronautics is primarily involved in aeronautical research, including development of high-speed aircraft and air-traffic control aids for civil transport, rather than space flight. However, it also is responsible for NASA's participation in the National Aero-Space Plane program, whose goal was to develop vehicles that would take off horizontally, fly into orbit, and then return for a runway landing. The Office of Aeronautics also managed the Ames Research Center, Dryden Flight Research Facility, and Lewis Research Center.

In 1997, NASA's Office of Aeronautics announced new goals for the agency's aeronautics program. These goals included improved aeronautics safety and traffic handling and reductions in aircraft emissions and noise-levels.

The Ames Research Center in Mountain View, California, was established in 1939 by the National Advisory Committee for Aeronautics (NACA) to conduct aircraft research. It was named for Dr. Joseph S. Ames, NACA chairman from 1927 to 1939. The center became part of NASA in 1958. The center has continued to conduct a broad range of research, including computer space-flight simulations.

The Hugh L. Dryden Flight Research Facility at the Edwards Air Force Base in Edwards, California, was established in 1946. Dryden is involved in testing high-speed aircraft and wingless lifting bodies. Dryden developed the Lunar Landing Research Vehicle during the Apollo program and was involved in developing and testing the space shuttle Enterprise. Space shuttles that land at Edwards Air Force Base were supported by the Dryden Research Facility.

The Lewis Research Center in Cleveland, Ohio, was established in 1941. It was named for George W. Lewis, NACA director of research from 1924 to 1947. The research center is best known for its work in jet propulsion, although it also was instrumental in developing liquid hydrogen as a fuel for space flight in the 1960s. Lewis was responsible for developing an electrical power system for the space station program. The center also includes the Microgravity Materials Science Laboratory, which reviews potential space projects and operates a Zero-Gravity Drop Tower.

Office of Space Sciences. The Office of Space Sciences is primarily responsible for programs involving the unmanned scientific investigation of the solar system and deep space. NASA's Space Science Program seeks to understand the nature of the Universe, to explore the solar system, to better understand the relationship between the Earth and sun, and to study the origin and possible distribution of life in the Universe.

The Office of Space Sciences conducts many of its projects at the Jet Propulsion Laboratory (JPL) in Pasadena, California. NASA operates the JPL under contract with the California Institute of Technology. Founded in 1944, JPL built the first U.S. satellite, Explorer I, in 1958. JPL also was responsible for the Ranger probes that provided the first close-up pictures of the moon between 1964 and 1965. Since then, probes launched by JPL have explored every planet in the solar systems except Pluto. Projects under its direction have included Voyager, Galileo, Magellan, Mars Observer, and Ulysses. JPL also developed a wide-field planetary camera for the Hubble Space Telescope that was launched in 1990.

The Office of Space Sciences is responsible for upgrading the Hubble telescope to include a Near Infrared Camera and Multi-Object Spectrometer (NICMOS) and the Space Telescope Imaging Spectrograph (STIS). These enhancements extend HST's wavelength range into the near infrared and greatly enhance its ability for ultraviolet spectroscopy.

Office of Mission to Planet Earth. Mission to Planet Earth is responsible for NASA's earth science and environmental programs, which included space-based research. The division also has responsibility for the Goddard Space Flight Center. The Center, located in Greenbelt, Maryland, boasted the largest scientific staff of all NASA centers. It was named for Robert H. Goddard, considered the father of modern rocketry. In the early 1990s, the Goddard center was responsible for monitoring more than 20 major space projects, including the Cosmic Background Explorer, which was launched in 1989 to investigate the origins of the universe, and the Hubble Space Telescope. Other projects managed by Goddard included the Compton Gamma Ray Observatory, the International Ultraviolet Explorer, and the Upper Atmosphere Research Satellite, launched in 1991 as part of the U.S. Global Change Research Program. The center also operated the Goddard Institute for Space Studies in New York.

The Office of Mission Earth has funded research projects including: Synthesis and Modeling Project of the U.S. Joint Global Ocean Flux Study; Satellite Remote Sensing Measurement, Accuracy, Variability, and Validation Studies; The Effects of Tropical Forest Conversion: Ecological Research in the Large-Scale Biosphere-Atmosphere Experiment in Amazonia (LBA); and Remote Sensing Research—Biological Oceanography.

Office of Life and Microgravity Sciences and Applications. Life and Microgravity Sciences and Applications is responsible for researching the effect of zero gravity and space flight on humans and other biological organisms.

Office of Space Flight. The Office of Space Flight is responsible for the operation of the space shuttle. It also is responsible for Spacelab, a research laboratory that was carried inside the space shuttle cargo bay, and for operational planning for the proposed U.S. space station. It has managerial oversight for the Kennedy Space Center, Marshall Space Flight Center, Johnson Space Center, and the Stennis Space Center.

The Kennedy Space Center on Florida's Cape Canaveral is NASA's primary launch facility. The Air Force established a missile test center on Cape Canaveral in 1949, and the first U.S. manned space flights were launched from there. The Kennedy Space Center, named for President John F. Kennedy, was built in the early 1960s for the Apollo program. The main complex was on Merritt Island, separated from Cape Canaveral by the Banana River, but the actual launch sites were on the cape. The first space shuttle was launched from the Kennedy Space Center in 1981.

The Marshall Space Flight Center at the Army's Redstone Arsenal in Huntsville, Alabama, was NASA's primary rocket research center and played a key role in the development of the space shuttle. The center continued to be responsible for the space shuttle's main engines and operated the Spacelab Mission Operations Control Center. Marshall also managed the Michoud Assembly Facility, the Slidell Computer Complex, and the Advanced Rocket Motor program. Originally part of the Army Ballistic Missile Agency, Marshall became part of NASA in 1960. It was named for George C. Marshall, who served as Army chief of staff during World War II and later as secretary of both Defense and State.

The Johnson Space Center in Houston, Texas, is NASA's primary center for the design and testing of space craft for manned flight. Mission Control for all manned space flights is also located at the Johnson Space Center, as are most astronaut training facilities. The center also is responsible for operation of the White Sands Test Facility at Las Cruces, New Mexico. The center was established in 1961, and later named for President Lyndon B. Johnson.

Stennis Space Center in Hancock County, Mississippi, is responsible for testing the space shuttle's main engines, the same role it filled for the Saturn V rocket during the Apollo space program. The center was named for Congressman John C. Stennis.

Office of Space System Development. Space System Development is responsible for defining and planning future space systems and capabilities, which includes the proposed manned space station and the Advanced Solid Rocket Motor. The space station was expected to be sent aloft aboard the space shuttle and assembled in orbit beginning in 1996.

Office of Advanced Concepts and Technology. The Office of Advanced Concepts and Technology works with the academic and business communities to promote commercial use of space technologies. It administers several technology transfer programs, including Small Business Innovative Research and the Defense Conversion Act.

Office of Space Communications. The Office of Space Communications is responsible for communications, navigation and control, data acquisition, telemetry, and data processing systems for all NASA activities, including space flights and interplanetary probes.

The Commercial Development and Technology Transfer Division. The Commercial Development and Technology Transfer Division at NASA Headquarters oversees NASA's development of commercial partnerships. This includes the commercial development of technology for NASA missions and the transfer and NASA-funded research and technology to private industry.

BACKGROUND AND DEVELOPMENT

Robert H. Goddard. The U.S. government took its first tentative step into space research in 1916, when the federally chartered Smithsonian Institute began to subsidize the work of physicist Robert Hutchings Goddard. During World War I, Goddard engaged in weapons research for the U.S. military, working primarily with solid-fuel rockets. After the war, he returned to experimenting with liquid-fuel rockets, which seemed to hold greater promise. He continued to receive $100 a month from the Navy Bureau of Ordnance.

In 1920, the Smithsonian published a treatise by Goddard entitled ''A Method of Reaching Extreme Altitudes.'' The Smithsonian also issued a press release mentioning the possibility that rockets developed for atmospheric research might one day land a magnesium flare on the moon that would be visible from Earth.

Later that same year, the Smithsonian published another treatise by Goddard entitled ''Report on Further Developments of the Rocket Method of Investigating Space.'' In the treatise, Goddard discussed such visionary topics as the control of unmanned space vehicles, ion propulsion, and a ''solar sail''—a giant mirror up to 600 feet square—that could be unfurled in space to collect solar energy. He also suggested that spacecraft carrying metal plates engraved with diagrams of the solar system could be sent into deep space in search of extraterrestrial life—a plan that was carried out in 1972 with Pioneer 10. At the time, however, many influential newspapers openly ridiculed Goddard's ideas.

Goddard severed his relationship with the U.S. military in 1923 and returned to Clark University, in Massachusetts, where he was professor of physics. In 1926, Goddard launched the world's first liquid-fuel rocket on a farm near Auburn, Massachusetts. The awkward-looking mechanism of tanks and tubes reached a height of 41 feet and traveled 184 feet down range. The flight lasted just 2.5 seconds.

In 1929, Goddard was introduced to Charles Lindbergh, the celebrated American pilot who had made the first solo nonstop flight across the Atlantic two years earlier. Lindbergh later persuaded both the Guggenheim Foundation and the Carnegie Institute to back Goddard, which enabled him to leave his teaching position and devote full-time to rocket research at a ranch near Roswell, New Mexico. In 1935, Goddard launched a rocket that reached an altitude of 7,500 feet and flew faster than the speed of sound.

When the United States entered World War II, Goddard again turned his attention to developing rockets for the military. He died in 1945. Although little known outside the research community, Goddard was the first to develop the mathematics of rocket action and prove that rockets would work in a vacuum. He also was the first to develop a gyroscope-based control mechanism. In 1960, NASA and the U.S. military awarded $1 million to Goddard's estate and the Guggenheim Foundation for use of his patents. NASA also named its primary research and engineering facility the Goddard Space Flight Center.

Wernher von Braun. About 1930, a group of rocket enthusiasts who had formed the German space society, known as the Verein fur Raumschiffsfahrt or VFR, approached the German government with a proposal to develop the rockets as an alternative to traditional artillery. One of those enthusiasts was Wernher von Braun, who later would be responsible for developing the Saturn V rocket that would take U.S. astronauts to the moon.

Under the Treaty of Versailles, which ended World War I, the German military was reduced to little more than a police force. Among the restrictions, Germany was prohibited from developing heavy artillery, building tanks, or possessing an air force. Rockets, however, were not mentioned in the treaty, and in 1932 von Braun became an advisor to the fledgling German rocket program.

During World War II, a team of scientists led by von Braun developed the V-2 rocket that was used to bomb England. They also began developing a larger rocket that would have been able to reach the United States. However, by early 1945, it was clear that Germany was losing the war, and von Braun began to prepare for the future.

At the time, von Braun's research facility was on an isolated peninsula near the Baltic Sea, and it appeared likely that he would be captured by the Russian army. However, von Braun and most of his team preferred to be captured by American forces. Von Braun convinced the beleaguered German military that he needed to move the research center to Mittelwerk in the central German highlands, where the scientists buried tons of documents and waited to be captured. In what became known as Operation Paperclip, von Braun, more than 100 of his staff members, most of the documents, and about 100 V-2 rockets were eventually taken to the United States.

Space Race. Von Braun and most of the other German scientists became part of various U.S. military research programs. However, following World War II, the United States placed more emphasis on developing long-range bombers than intercontinental ballistic missiles (ICBM), which many military leaders felt would never be able to deliver warheads the size of an atomic bomb. Even when the Soviet Union launched the first Sputnik satellite in

1957, most U.S. military leaders were unconcerned. President Dwight D. Eisenhower told the news media, "One small ball in the air . . . does not raise my apprehensions, not one iota."

However, the public outcry at being bested by the Soviet Union did cause the military to step up rocket research. In 1955, the Navy had initiated Project Vanguard, basically a civilian research program, to develop a rocket for launching unmanned satellites for the International Geophysical Year. Late in 1957, a month after Sputnik 2 was launched with the dog Laika aboard, the Navy attempted to quiet public concerns about Soviet superiority by sending its own satellite into orbit. However, the Vanguard rocket rose only a few feet before exploding.

Attention then turned to the Redstone rocket, which the Army was developing at Huntsville, Alabama, under the direction of von Braun. Initially, the Redstone was to be a long-range ICBM, and the Army was under orders from the Pentagon not to interfere with Project Vanguard by attempting to launch a satellite. However, following the launch of Sputnik 1, von Braun was given the go-ahead to develop a rocket capable of reaching outer space.

In January 1958, a modified Redstone rocket, known as the Jupiter-C, lifted off with Explorer 1, the first U.S. satellite to successfully reach orbit. Almost immediately, Explorer 1 made a startling discovery when it sent back evidence of two regions of electrically charged particles high above the Earth, which became known as the Van Allen Belts. Although still trailing the Soviet Union, the Army and von Braun had taken the clear lead in the U.S. space program.

NASA. By 1958 two things had become clear: the Soviet Union was planning to put a man into orbit, and most Americans favored the United States joining the space race. Although the Navy's Vanguard succeeded in carrying a satellite into orbit in March 1958, the rocket was clearly too small and too unreliable for a manned space program. Only 3 of the 11 Vanguard rockets were ever launched successfully. The Air Force proposed a "Man in Space Soonest" program using supersonic aircraft that could reach outer space, but would not be able to go into orbit. Meanwhile, von Braun and the Army began developing a rocket known as the Saturn that would be more powerful than either the Vanguard or the Redstone.

However, President Eisenhower and his scientific advisor, James Killian, then president of the Massachusetts Institute of Technology, believed the space program should be a civilian effort focused on scientific exploration rather than military purposes. To achieve that goal, they turned to the National Advisory Committee for Aeronautics (NACA), a panel of scientists created by Congress in 1915 to promote development of civilian aircraft. In the mid-1950s, NACA was operated two aeronautical laboratories and the Jet Propulsion Laboratory in Pasadena, California. Then chaired by General Jimmy Doolittle, NACA also moved into space research and was in the process of building the first hydrogen-fueled rocket engine. In 1957, one fifth of NACA's budget was devoted to space research.

In April 1958 NACA was renamed the National Aeronautics and Space Agency. Six months later, the organization was absorbed by the National Aeronautics and Space Administration (NASA), created when Congress passed the National Aeronautics and Space Act. NASA was charged with the peaceful exploration of space "for the benefit of all mankind," which included the efforts to put a man into space that had been started by the military. NASA also was given control of the Jet Propulsion Laboratory. NASA's budget in 1959, its first full year of operation, was $331 million.

Manned Space Program. During its first three years, the U.S. space agency achieved little success. Of 28 satellites sent aloft, only 8 achieved orbit, including the first communications satellite, Project Score, launched in December 1958. The manned space program, Project Mercury, was equally unsuccessful. The first unmanned test of a Mercury-Redstone rocket lasted just 58 seconds before the rocket failed. The second Mercury-Redstone rocket never left the launching pad. Meanwhile, in 1959, the Soviet Union launched Luna 2, the first probe to reach the moon, and Luna 3, which took the first pictures of the far side of the moon. In 1960, the Soviet Union launched several dogs into space aboard Sputnik 5 and returned them safely to the Earth.

Although Eisenhower had opposed manned space flight as too expensive, the pressure mounted for NASA to match the Soviet Union. In January 1961, Ham, a chimpanzee who had been taught to perform simple tasks, was launched into space on a sub-orbital flight. NASA then scheduled the first manned flight for the middle of March. However, von Braun cautiously decided the Mercury-Redstone rocket needed further testing and postponed the flight until May. On April 12, Soviet cosmonaut Yuri Gagarin became the first man in space, less than a month before astronaut Alan B. Shepard, Jr., rocketed into space on May 5.

Three weeks later, on May 25, President John F. Kennedy addressed Congress and declared, "I believe that this nation should commit itself to achieving the goal, before the decade is out, of landing a man on the moon and returning him safely to Earth." NASA's budget was nearly doubled from $964 million in 1961 to $1.8 billion in 1962. The Department of Defense budget for space activities also increased by more than 50 percent, from $814 million to $1.3 billion.

Nine years later, on July 20, 1969, astronauts Neil A. Armstrong and Edwin E. ''Buzz'' Aldrin, Jr., eased a spidery-looking craft known as the Lunar Module 3 onto the surface of the moon, while astronaut Michael Collins continued to orbit above them in Apollo 11. Armstrong and Aldrin spent nearly 24 hours on the moon, including more than two hours outside their space craft. The three astronauts returned to Earth on July 24. A total of 14 men have set foot on the moon.

Between Shepard's 15-minute suborbital flight in 1961 and the historic, 8-day Apollo 11 mission to the moon in 1969 there were many spectacular moments. For example, during the flight of Apollo 8 in 1968, astronaut Frank Borman read from the Book of Genesis while orbiting the moon on Christmas Eve. The space program also experienced tragedy in 1976 when astronauts Virgil I. Grissom, Edward H. White II, and Roger Chaffee were killed in a fire during a pre-flight test of the Apollo capsule. NASA's budget averaged $5 billion a year from 1964 through 1968.

As Apollo 11 was on its way to the moon in 1969, then-Vice President Spiro T. Agnew announced that NASA's next goal would be to land men on Mars, and the Space Task Group was created to formulate a plan. However, less than a year later, in the midst of the Vietnam War, President Richard Nixon issued a statement that shocked NASA officials. After a decade of spectacular achievements in space, Nixon declared, ''Space must take its place with other national priorities.''

By the time the Apollo program ended in 1972, NASA's budget had dropped to $3.3 billion. There were only six more missions to the moon, beginning with Apollo 12 in November 1969 and ending with Apollo 17 in December 1972. The Apollo 13 mission was aborted when an oxygen tank aboard the service module exploded, disabling the spacecraft en route to the moon. The astronauts averted disaster by using the moon's gravity to slingshot the spacecraft back to Earth. The last men to walk on the moon were astronauts Eugene A. Cernan and Harrison H. Schmitt. Although often talked about, there still were no manned missions to Mars planned in the mid-1990s.

Skylab. When Apollo ended, NASA turned its attention to Skylab. Conceived in 1969, the 85-ton Skylab, the first U.S. space station, actually consisted of the third stage of a Saturn V rocket modified to provide work space and living quarters for three astronauts who would stay in orbit for extended periods of times. Skylab, considered the first serious opportunity to conduct industrial research in space, was launched in May 1973.

However, a heat shield and one of two solar panels that would produce electricity for Skylab were lost during launch, and a second solar panel only partially opened once Skylab was in orbit. The first astronauts to use the space station, Charles Conrad, Joseph P. Kerwin, and Paul J. Weitz, who followed Skylab into space a few days later, had to erect a large aluminum ''parasol'' to protect the area of Skylab where the heat shield had been torn away from the heat of the sun. They also repaired the remaining solar panel.

Eventually, Skylab demonstrated that humans could live and work in space for extended periods of time without harmful effects. Three teams of astronauts ultimately spent a total of 171 days aboard Skylab, with the last crew staying 84 days. The astronauts also conducted significant astrological research, including observations of the stars and planets without the visually distorting effect of the Earth's atmosphere. The industrial research was less successful. For example, in the gravity-free environment of Skylab, the astronauts were able to create perfectly round ball bearings. However, they were unable to remove the bearings from the crucible without producing a tail.

In 1978, NASA discovered Skylab, abandoned since 1974, was in a deteriorating orbit and eventually would fall back to Earth. Several unsuccessful attempts were made to trigger Skylab's thrusters from Earth and boost the space station into a more stable orbit. NASA also considered a manned rescue mission using the shuttle spacecraft then under development. However, the shuttle was not completed in time, and on July 11, Skylab plunged into the Earth's atmosphere and broke up over the South Pacific and Indian Oceans.

Unmanned Space Research. While the manned space program captured most of the public's attention, NASA also launched numerous unmanned planetary probes. The first of these probes to successfully complete its mission was Mariner II, launched in 1962, which passed within 22,000 miles of Venus. It revealed that the planet's surface was about 800 degrees Fahrenheit—too hot for any earthly plants or animals to survive.

Mariner IV, launched in 1964, discovered that Mars had a thin atmosphere, and sent back pictures as it passed within 6,120 miles of the planet. Mariner V, launched in 1967, was another mission to Venus, while Mariners VI and VII, launched in 1969, and Mariner IX, launched in 1971, provided more information about Mars.

In 1972, two more unmanned probes, Viking I and II, landed softly on the surface of Mars, where they sent back photographs and analyzed the plant's soil and atmosphere. In 1972, NASA also launched Pioneer X, a nuclear-powered probe that reached Jupiter 21 months later. After flying past Jupiter, Pioneer X continued on toward

Uranus. Pioneer XI, launched in 1973, also flew by Jupiter, but used the planet's gravity in a slingshot effect to send it on toward Saturn. Mariner X, also launched in 1973, flew by Venus and then used the planet's gravity to send it on to Mercury.

Perhaps the most ambitious probes were Voyagers I and II, both launched in 1977. They reached Jupiter in 1979 and transmitted spectacular pictures revealing, among other things, a ring similar to the one around Saturn and giant active volcanos on Io, one of Jupiter's moons. They also took time-lapse motion pictures of the swirling gases surrounding the planet. As they left Jupiter, both probes headed for Saturn, where they revealed more information about the planet's rings and took pictures of previously unknown moons. Voyager I then headed out into the universe, while Voyager II headed for Uranus, which it reached in 1986; and Neptune, which it reached in 1989. Voyager II came within 3,000 miles of Neptune, 2.8 billion miles from Earth, and revealed for the first time six new moons and four rings circling the planet.

Space Shuttle. In 1972, Congress approved NASA's plan to build a reusable spacecraft that came to be known as the shuttle. The shuttle was a four-piece launch vehicle that consisted of a delta-winged orbiter, a strap-on fuel tank, and two solid-fuel boosters. The 122-foot long orbiter would be launched into space as a rocket, but would return to the Earth as an airplane.

It took almost as long to develop the shuttle as it did to put a man on the moon, but on April 12, 1981, the twentieth anniversary of Soviet cosmonaut Yuri Gagarin's first flight into space, the shuttle Columbia lifted off from Cape Kennedy with astronauts John Young and Robert Crippen aboard. After one orbit, the shuttle landed at Edwards Air Force Base in the Mojave Desert.

In July 1982, after two more test flights and a classified mission for the military, the shuttle Columbia was declared operational. In November 1982, Columbia carried two privately owned communications satellites aloft in its cargo bay and placed them into orbit. A year later, Columbia lifted off with Spacelab, a research laboratory built by the European Space Agency, tucked neatly into its cargo bay. Spacelab could be removed between flights and prepared for the next research mission.

By 1985, NASA had added three more shuttles to the Space Transportation System—Challenger (1983), Discovery (1984), and Atlantis (1985). The cost of the program since its inception in the early 1970s was more than $13 billion. NASA's budget had climbed steadily from a post-Apollo low of $3 billion in 1974 to $7.5 billion in 1985. NASA also completed nine shuttle missions in 1985 and announced the sale of the first products made in space—perfectly round, microscopic bits of plastic. James M. Beggs, then NASA administrator, announced, ''This material is the first of what we expect will be a long line of products to carry the made-in-space label.''

However, NASA, which once predicted nearly 60 shuttle flights per year by 1990, was forced to cut back to less than a dozen flights because of higher costs and greater preparation time. In addition, NASA, which had hoped to support the shuttle program by carrying commercial satellites into orbit, began to face competition from the European Space Agency and other space programs. The United States also began to emphasize its military space program, and by 1986 the $14.1 billion budgeted for military space activities was almost twice the $7.2 billion allocated to NASA.

Challenger. Less than two minutes after liftoff from the Kennedy Space Center on January 28, 1986, the space shuttle Challenger exploded, killing all seven crew members. NASA had scheduled 13 more shuttle flights for 1986, but it immediately shut down the program until the cause of the explosion was determined. An official investigation later found that a rubber seal on one of the shuttle's two booster rockets had failed because of unusually cool temperatures at the launch site. But the investigation also placed blame for the tragedy on mismanagement at NASA and Morton Thiokol, Inc., which built the booster.

According to the Rogers Commission report, NASA and Morton Thiokol had been aware of the effect cool temperatures could have on the rubber seals for some time, but had done nothing to correct the problem. The investigation also found that more than a dozen engineers at Morton Thiokol attempted to warn NASA about the dangers immediately preceding the launch, but had been blocked by poor internal communications at NASA. The report criticized the political and economic pressure on NASA to schedule frequent shuttle flights, and more than a dozen senior executives at NASA and Morton Thiokol ultimately resigned because of the Challenger disaster.

To reduce the number of shuttle flights, President Ronald Reagan directed NASA to stop carrying commercial payloads and to concentrate on scientific missions. The Air Force was given responsibility for unmanned military launches, while commercial payloads were to be carried aloft by private corporations.

The shuttle program remained grounded until late 1988, when both Discovery and Atlantis flew successful missions. There were only four shuttle missions in 1989, but two were especially significant for space research. In May, astronauts aboard the Atlantis achieved the first launch of a planetary probe, the Venus-bound Magellan, from the shuttle's cargo bay. In October, the Atlantis launched the Galileo on a six-year mission to Jupiter. In

1990, radar signals from Magellan began penetrating the thick clouds surrounding Venus and transmitting clear images of the surface back to Earth.

Fuel leaks discovered aboard Columbia and Atlantis grounded the space shuttles for much of 1990. As a result, the National Space Council reversed the policy instituted in 1986 that NASA concentrate on manned space flight. The Council recommended that NASA develop new unmanned launch vehicles and reduce its dependence on the space shuttles.

Hubble Telescope. In January 1990, astronauts aboard the shuttle Columbia successfully retrieved a satellite, known as the Long Duration Exposure Facility, which had been launched in 1984 to test the long-term effect of space on various materials. In April, the shuttle Discovery lifted-off with the long-delayed Hubble Space Telescope. The $1.5 billion telescope, named for American astronomer Edwin P. Hubble, was to provide the clearest views ever of stars, galaxies, and other space phenomenon. However, the images sent back to Earth were blurred, and scientists discovered that the main 95-inch mirror had been ground to the wrong optical specifications.

NASA was able to restore some clarity, producing images beyond the capability of Earth-based telescopes, by using a computer technique known deconvolution, but the Hubble Space Telescope remained an embarrassing disappointment. An official investigation criticized both the manufacturer and management at NASA. In 1993, astronauts aboard the shuttle Endeavor were able to correct many of the problems with the Hubble telescope by installing new optics.

Mars Observer. After the Hubble telescope embarrassment, NASA appeared back on track in 1992, which was celebrated worldwide as ''International Space Year.'' There were several successful shuttle flights involving military and scientific missions, including experiments aboard the International Microgravity Laboratory carried aloft in Discovery's cargo bay in January. On the Endeavor's maiden voyage in May, astronauts retrieved a communications satellite that had been stranded in a useless orbit since 1990 and boosted it into the proper orbit.

NASA also used an unmanned Titan 3 rocket to launch the Mars Observer, a probe designed to spend a full Martian year, or 687 earth days, orbiting the planet and mapping its surface. However, after making the 450-million mile trip in 11 months, the Mars Observer stopped transmitting, and NASA speculated it may have exploded when the braking rockets fired.

In 1993, the White House also instructed NASA to redesign the proposed space station to reduce the cost over the next three years from an estimated $17 billion to $9 billion or less. More than $8 billion already had been spent on the program since 1984, when the project was endorsed by then-President Ronald Reagan.

In 1994, President Bill Clinton reduced NASA's budget by about $250 million for 1995, from $15.55 billion to $14.3 billion—the first reduction in the agency's budget since 1972. Most of the reduction came in space shuttle operations, which were pegged at $3.3 billion. Under the proposal, there was a slight increase in science programs, which would account for about 24 percent of the total NASA budget.

In 1996, NASA stunned the world by announcing that they had discovered evidence of life on Mars. Earlier, in 1984, scientists discovered the remnants of an asteroid that struck the Earth approximately 13,000 years ago. Analysis of gas trapped in the rock indicated a Martian origin; and unusual mineral compounds surrounding carbonate globules indicate biological activity. Various dating methods placed the rock's age at 4.5 billion years, and the carbonate globules at 3.6 billion years. Critics remained skeptical, saying that these minerals could also be formed by inorganic processes. They wanted to see evidence of cell division and life cycles. NASA is continuing its investigation.

Shuttle missions have continued, but with more focus on scientific and defense missions. Throughout the 1990s, NASA has faced increasing competition from foreign competitors for commercial payloads.

In 1996, NASA awarded a contract to Lockheed Martin to develop a new reusable launch vehicle, the X-33. NASA expected that this vehicle would eventually replace the space shuttle as their primary manned spacecraft.

NASA has been developing new ways to remote planetary surfaces. By combining a Full Immersion Telepresence Testbed (FITT) and a Dexterous Anthropomorphic Robotic Testbed (DART) technologies, NASA hopes to accomplish more ambitious surveys of Mars. A DART robot could travel the surface of Mars carrying its own laboratory, while a person sits in a safe, remote location controlling the robot with the FITT gear.

CURRENT CONDITIONS

NASA's successes for 1998 included the in-orbit assembly of two units for the International Space Station (ISS), two launches to Mars, and a Space Shuttle science research mission that put Senator John Glenn back in orbit. At the same time, NASA was reorganizing and reducing the number of its full-time employees, dropping 440 FTEs (full-time equivalents) in fiscal year 1998 and an estimated 350 more for fiscal year 1999. At the end of 1998, the NASA workforce totaled 18,924 FTEs.

In 1999, NASA continued its efforts to develop and refine a next-generation Reusable Launch Vehicle. It also focused on support for logistics launches and the launch of the Russian Service Module. MEIT activities for Z1 truss, the photovoltaic arrays on P6, MEIT for the Lab, and the Space Station Remote Manipulator System (SSRMS) were also priorities. Seven additional U.S. assembly and logistics flights were planned for FY 2000.

A growing use of NASA's space force has been in the area of medical research. Scientists have been growing antibody crystals aboard the Space Shuttle, which effectively treat many viral illnesses of humans such as the common cold and flu. Because of the weightless environment, known as microgravity, protein crystals grow larger and are of better quality than those grown on earth. In late 1999, NASA announced that it was working on another protein crystal to combat human diabetes, not associated with viral infection.

Another important use of space technology has been in the tracking of weather. The U.S.-France collaboration known as the TOPEX/Poseidon Satellite was used to track the 1997-1998 El Nino event, from a distance of 800 miles above earth.

Disppointing news came in September 1999, when NASA's Mars Climate Orbiter, launched in December 1998, smashed into Mars after a final rocket firing intended to put the spacecraft in orbit around Mars. The Orbiter was supposed to relay signals from the Mars Polar Lander, scheduled to land on Mars in December 1999. In early November, NASA issued a press release, identifying human error as the cause of the loss: failure to convert English measures into metric values.

AMERICA AND THE WORLD

Representing a massive collaboration between the United States, Russia, and 14 other nations, the International Space Station (ISS) has been going through assembly stages since 1998 and is scheduled for completion by 2004. The ISS is a permanent space research laboratory, the size of a football field, which will orbit the earth at 17,500 miles per hour with a minimum life expectancy of ten years. Boeing North America is the sole contractor for the project, managed by NASA's Johnson Space Center. When completed, the $40-billion spacecraft will house up to seven astronauts at a time, for as long as six months. It has been dubbed ''the window to the universe.'' It represents the world's largest peace-time engineering effort.

FURTHER READING

Asker, James. ''For Myriad Woes, NASA Calls X-38 to the Rescue.'' *Aviation Week & Space Technology,* 11 November 1996.

Chang, Maria. ''Space City.'' *Science World,* 9 September 1998.

Key, Sandra W., Daniel J. DeNoon, and Salynn Boyles. ''Space Research May Accelerate Flu-Fighting Drug Development.'' *World Disease Weekly Plus,* 29 March 1999.

Miller, Ryder W. ''Reflections on the 'Year of the Ocean'.'' *Mercury,* July 1999.

''My Favorite Martian.'' *Ad Astra,* September/October 1996.

''NASA: Human Error Caused Loss of Mars Orbiter.'' *CNN News,* 10 November 1999. Available from http://www.cnn.com/TECH/space/9911/10/orbiter.02.

Oberg, James. ''NASA's Russian Payload.'' *American Spectator,* August 1998.

''Space Research Aids Study of Deadly Virus.'' *USA Today Magazine,* October 1998.

SIC 9711

NATIONAL SECURITY

This classification covers establishments of the armed forces, including the National Guard, primarily engaged in national security and related activities. Establishments primarily engaged in manufacturing ordnance, ships, and other military goods are classified in the manufacturing division. Service academies are classified in **SIC 8221: College, Universities, and Professional Schools,** but military training schools are classified here. Military hospitals are classified in **SIC 8060: Hospitals.** Establishments of the Coast Guard primarily engaged in administration, operation, or regulation of transportation are classified in **SIC 9621: Regulation and Administration of Transportation Programs.**

NAICS CODE(S)

928110 (National Security)

INDUSTRY SNAPSHOT

National security depends not only on the latest defense technology, but more importantly, upon the human workforce that creates and develops the technology and carries it into action to defend our country. The United States has one of the only major armed forces in world history that has never been used against its own citizens or to permanently annex other nations.

ORGANIZATION AND STRUCTURE

The U.S. Department of Defense is charged with providing the military force needed to deter war and protect the security and interests of the United States and its citizens. Besides its defensive role, the military is the country's largest employer. It provides important training that its employees often utilize in the private sector. The Department of Defense is also a primary source of research and development funding for private sector technology efforts.

The major components of its force are the Army, Air Force, Navy, and Marine Corps. The President of the United States is the Commander in Chief of the armed forces. The Secretary of Defense serves under the President and controls the Department of Defense. Under the Secretary and his Deputy are the Joint Chiefs of Staff, who provide military advice to the President and Secretary. Subordinate to the Chairman of the Joint Chiefs of Staff are the Chiefs of Staff for the Army, Air Force, and Navy, as well as the Commandant of the Marine Corps. Also under the immediate direction of the Secretary of Defense and Deputy are the Department of the Army, U.S. Department of the Air Force, and Department of the Navy. Each department is headed by a Secretary. The Marine Corps is under the jurisdiction of the Secretary of the Navy.

When a person enters one of the armed forces, he or she forfeits many rights granted by the U.S. Constitution. Military personnel are governed under a legal system that is completely different from that in the private sector. Personnel are subject to the Uniform Code of Military Justice, though the Department of Justice and other federal and state agencies may become involved with some legal matters.

Divisions of the Armed Forces. The Army is recognized as the major land fighting division of the U.S. armed forces and is the largest segment of the military. Besides combat-related functions, it conducts intelligence gathering and counterintelligence, formulation of strategy, and numerous other responsibilities. In peacetime, the Army's sole duty is to train its reserves and plan for mobilization in the event of a war. The Army has 18 active and 10 reserve divisions. The Army also administers environmental management and construction programs and provides disaster relief assistance. The Army employed 483,880 of all active duty military personnel in 1998.

The Navy is the dominant sea-based fighting division, though it also represents a major share of U.S. air power. The second largest armed forces division, it had about 382,338 members in 1998. The Air Force, which specializes in air and space defense functions, had about 367,470 members. The Marine Corps, which had 173,000 members in 1998, fights on land, sea, and in the air. This elite combat division is usually the ''first to fight'' on land in a military conflict.

The two types of employees in the military are enlisted personnel and officers. Each service has nine enlisted grades and ten officer ranks. Officers account for approximately 15 percent of the armed forces. Only a fraction of the enlisted personnel are designated combat troops.

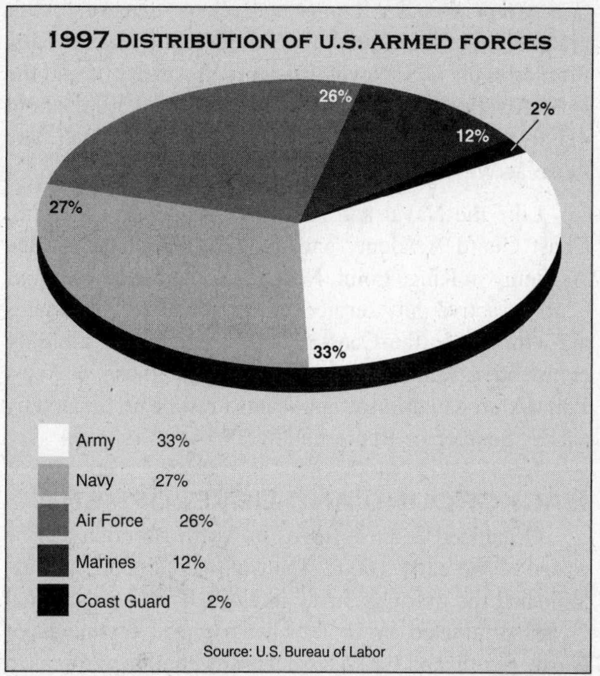

In addition to a large fighting force, the Department of Defense oversees the largest arsenal of weaponry and equipment in the world. Tens of thousands of tanks, jets, bombers, missiles, guns, armored personnel carriers, and other equipment complement its troops. Furthermore, its nuclear arsenal is the largest in the world.

Reserve Forces. In addition to active duty personnel and Department of Defense employees, the U.S. military is backed by 1.8 million reserve and guard forces in the National Guard and Coast Guard. During times of peace, the Coast Guard operates under the Department of Transportation. It promotes marine safety and enforces federal maritime laws. In the event of war, the President can place the Coast Guard under the jurisdiction of the Navy.

The National Guard consists of the Army Guard and the Air Force Guard. Although the Guard utilizes many part-time personnel with military training, it is a major component of the U.S. defense force. The Army Guard, for example, represented about 45 percent of the Army's fighting capability in 1998. The Guard is commanded by state or territory governors during peacetime and is commonly used in state emergencies or civil disturbances. During a war, the President or Congress can call the Guard into active duty.

Military Academies. There are five major U.S. military academies. The U.S. Military Academy (West Point) enrolls about 1,200 candidates each year in its elite institution. Candidates must be unmarried U.S. citizens between the ages of 17 and 22 and must present a nomination from a U.S. Representative or Senator. After graduation, officers must serve in the Army for six years. Similarly, the U.S. Naval Academy in Annapolis and the U.S. Air Force Academy in Denver each have about 4,500 students. Entrance requirements are much like those at West Point, though slightly less selective.

Like the Naval and Air Force academies, the U.S. Coast Guard Academy and the U.S. Merchant Marine Academy in Kings Point, New York, require at least four years of active duty service after graduation. Candidates are admitted to the Coast Guard Academy via a highly competitive national competition. Like those at West Point, Merchant Marine applicants must be nominated by a U.S. Senator or Representative.

Background and Development

Organized defense forces in North America can be traced to the early 1600s. The Continental Congress established the first U.S. army in 1775. The U.S. National Guard originated in 1636, when isolated regiments of North, South, and East Massachusetts combined forces to defend their new-found territory. The National Guard is commonly recognized as the oldest U.S. fighting force and has served the nation in every major conflict since colonial times.

The first national military defense force founded by the United States was the New England Armies—later called the Continental Army. The Continental Congress established this army on June 14, 1775 to fight Britain. The U.S. Navy and Marine Corps were concurrently started in late 1775 to complement the Continental Army's efforts. General George Washington commanded the group of colonial volunteers, which essentially consisted of a band of slightly trained rebels. The Navy started with two vessels.

During the Revolutionary War, which lasted from 1775 to 1783, 4,435 U.S. soldiers died, and more than 6,000 were seriously wounded. A band of only 700 soldiers was left after the war to form a standing army. This force was increased in the early 1790s to meet threats from Native Americans and to defend against French aggression. Congress authorized the construction of six navy frigates in 1794, and launched its first ship, the United States, on May 10, 1797. The Revenue Marine was also established in the 1790s with ten boats; it was renamed the Coast Guard in 1915. In 1802, Congress established the U.S. Military Academy at West Point.

The first major U.S. military conflict after the Revolution was the War of 1812, when the United States resisted British interference with sea trade. The U.S.S. Constitution sank a British frigate, and the United States gained more independence as a result of that conflict. Besides the Mexican American War (1846-1848), in which 1,700 U.S. service people died, the next war of consequence was the Civil War (1861-1865). By the time General Lee surrendered to General Grant at Appamatox, the Civil War had taken 365,000 lives, or about 17 percent of the total number of soldiers who fought in that war.

Although World War I (1917-1918) involved nearly 5 million U.S. service people and resulted in 116,516 American deaths, World War II (1941-1946) soon overshadowed that war's statistics. It was during World War II that the Marines, Navy, and Air Force grew in importance in relation to the Army. As the Army tripled in size over World War I levels, the Navy and Marine Corps swelled about 700 percent and 850 percent, respectively. The Air Force, which was part of the Army, grew so much that it became its own division in 1947. World War II engaged 16 million U.S. service people, 405,399 of whom were killed.

The Cold War. World War II put an end to global military conflicts in the twentieth century, and the United States reduced its active military forces to only 1.5 million people. But the Cold War between the Soviet Union and the United States, with its war-ravaged allies, soon necessitated American military leadership. By 1950, U.S. services were again engaged in battle. This time they were countering Communist expansion in Korea. In the Korean War, 5.7 million Americans served in the armed forces, and 54,246 were killed. To discourage future Communist aggression, the United States maintained a force of about 3 million troops throughout the 1950s.

After World War II, the United States began to reduce its emphasis on military manpower and started to stress high-tech armaments. As the U.S. military budget escalated during the next three decades, the number of Americans employed in the armed forces dwindled. Even the war in Vietnam during the late 1960s through 1975 had only a modest effect on troop numbers in comparison to previous conflicts. More importantly, American forces utilized new aircraft, including jet-powered fighters and bombers, which had been developed and tested since the Korean War. As a result, U.S. casualties as a percentage of soldiers engaged in battle declined dramatically. Nevertheless, 58,135 of the 8.7 million soldiers sent to Vietnam were killed.

After the Vietnam War, no major military conflicts confronted U.S. forces through the 1980s. The number of U.S. troops remained steady during the late 1970s and 1980s, at about 2 million. By this time, U.S. forces had been deployed across the globe. Most of them were strategically positioned to thwart Soviet aggression. Indeed, more than 25 percent of U.S. military personnel lived outside U.S. borders by the 1980s.

Despite stable troop strength during the 1980s, the U.S. military budget continued to balloon. Spending on high-tech armaments and nuclear weaponry pushed annual defense expenditures to a staggering $300 billion annually by the late 1980s. In an effort to foil the Soviet nuclear threat, the United States proposed massive expenditures for its Strategic Defense Initiative (SDI). In the early 1990s, U.N. allies hammered Iraqi ground forces with air strikes. Four days after the commencement of a ground war on February 24, 1991, Iraqi troops fled Kuwait. High-tech weaponry and advanced military training contributed to the lowest casualty rate in U.S. war history. Of 532,000 U.S. forces deployed in the Gulf, only 374 were killed.

The Department of Defense planned to retain military dominance through the development of high-tech weapons. While personnel and nuclear warheads had been reduced, spending on advanced armaments continued at relatively high levels in 1996. The Department of Defense continued the development and testing of new jet fighters, for example, and was also engaged in the creation of new satellite and missile systems.

U.S. service men and women now are well educated and trained. Despite the Department of Defense's increased emphasis on technology, its people remained the centerpiece of the U.S. military machine. And they were becoming even more qualified, as 1996 proved. In contrast to the soldiers in Vietnam, who often suffered from low pay, weak morale, and poor leadership, military personnel in the 1990s more closely reflected the private sector work force. In addition, the armed forces were comprised solely of volunteers, resulting in a highly motivated force.

The move to higher standards began in the early 1980s, when about 65 percent of all incoming military personnel were high school dropouts. Congress boosted military pay and benefits and upped the entry requirements. By the early 1990s, 96 percent of new enlistees had a high school diploma, compared to just 82 percent of entrants into the civilian workforce. The number of recruits scoring in the highest categories on the government's aptitude test doubled between 1980 and 1987.

In addition to payroll cutbacks, the Department of Defense was also conducting a significant reduction in its nuclear arsenal. For the first time, the Army and Marines will not control nuclear weapons. The Navy and Air Force will split the arsenal. U.S. nuclear warheads were already being dismantled at a rapid pace in the early 1990s. Although 11,500 warheads remained in stock in 1992, 7,000 nuclear devices had been retired since 1990. Furthermore, the total stockpile is scheduled to be reduced to 6,300 by the late 1990s. As of 1997, no new nuclear warheads had been produced in the United States since 1990.

CURRENT CONDITIONS

After peaking at nearly 12 million during World War II, total employment in all areas of the armed forces stood at less than 4 million in 1999. Of that amount, 1.37 million were working for the Department of Defense, and 1.35 million belonged to reserve and guard forces. The defense budget for fiscal year 1999 was $270 billion. Moreover, the Department of Defense maintained 519 fixed facilities in 1998, covering 18 million acres in more than 140 countries.

Notwithstanding such a powerful presence in the world, in October 1999, the U.S. Commission on National Security/21st Century advised the House Armed Services Committee that in the twenty-first century, superiority in size will not insulate U.S. citizens from attack. The Committee warned that increased resentment toward the United States and its overseas involvement may hasten attacks on civilians, at home and abroad. Overseas deployments will become more difficult as alliances with other countries shifts. It also warned that the number of troops will not serve to deter cyber attacks and the use of biotechnology by adversaries.

WORKFORCE

As the largest American employer, the U.S. military employs 1.7 percent of the nation's workforce in active duty positions. It is an important source of training for individuals who eventually enter the nation's civilian workforce, and it helps millions of recruits and veterans pay to attend college. More than 2,000 occupational specialties are available for enlisted personnel, along with 1,600 for officers. In addition, more than 75 percent of these occupations have civilian counterparts offering opportunities for trained veterans.

Infantrymen, gun crews, and seamanship specialists are the heart of the armed forces. Combat officers plan and direct military actions and lead troops. Among other jobs, enlisted personnel engage in hand-to-hand combat, drive tanks and other combat equipment, demolish enemy equipment and infrastructure, and serve as aircraft crew members. Combat jobs accounted for about 18 percent of all enlisted personnel and 40 percent of officers in the 1990s.

Electronic equipment repair personnel maintain avionics, missile, radio, navigation, data processing, telephone, and other equipment. Mechanical equipment repair people work with tanks, personnel carriers, planes, and other machines. Together, electrical and mechanical repair people make up about 25 percent of the armed forces. Communications and intelligence specialists account for 8 percent of military workers. These enlisted personnel often work as air traffic controllers, computer programmers, radar and sonar operators, interpreters and translators, intelligence gatherers, and cryptoligists.

About 25 percent of all military jobs are classified as administrative and functional support. This group includes many traditional private sector occupations, such as lawyers, accountants, hospital administrators, chaplains, typists, and storekeepers. Health care specialists and medical officers are another large part of the military, representing about 7 percent of active duty forces. This group includes doctors, dentists, veterinarians, optometrists, and other medical professionals and assistants. Other occupational groups include craftsmen, supply handlers, scientists, and numerous technical specialists.

Getting Hired. To qualify as an enlistee, you must be between the ages of 17 and 35 (the Marine Corps only accepts enlistees aged 17 to 24). In addition, you must pass a physical exam and have no felony convictions. Most divisions of the armed forces accept applications only from U.S. citizens with high school diplomas or equivalencies. Enlisted personnel typically sign up for an eight year stint. At least two years must be served on active duty, the remainder in the reserves.

Most commissioned officer positions require a college degree. There are several routes to obtaining a commission. The best way to become an officer is to graduate from one of the military service academies. Those institutions provide recruits with free education and a monthly stipend, and graduates are practically guaranteed a commission. In return, students typically sign a contract to serve five years or more after graduation.

The most common route to a commission, however, is through the Reserve Officer Training Corps (ROTC) at one of 400 colleges in the United States. For example, the ROTC program at Texas A&M, College Station, has produced more military officers than West Point. ROTC programs also offer free tuition and monthly stipends for qualified students. Enlistees who qualify can leave the military, get a free college education, and return as officers. College graduates who do not participate in ROTC can go through Officer Candidate School (OCS) in any of the 6 military branches to obtain a commission. Finally, some health professionals may qualify for a direct appointment as an officer.

Minority Opportunities. The policy of the U.S. military is to offer equal opportunity to its members. About 28 percent of all new enlistees in the 1990s were racial minorities—33.2 percent of all armed forces personnel were African-American or another minority. Of military women, 52 percent are minorities. Although African American representation in the officer ranks is relatively small, it has continued to rise since 1995.

Women have also availed themselves of military opportunities. Although there were only 41,500 active duty women in the armed forces in 1970, their numbers ballooned to above 200,000 by the 1990s. Women are eligible to enter about 90 percent of all military specialties. They serve as mechanics, heavy equipment operators, technicians, and intelligence personnel, for example. Although federal law has traditionally barred women from direct combat, the military was skirting that restriction in 1994 by allowing women to fly combat aircraft and serve at sea on Navy ships. Women have challenged the combat restriction, pointing out that combat experience is often a factor in promotions.

The armed forces will likely recruit 15,000 officers and more than 200,000 enlisted personnel per year through the 1990s to replace those leaving the service or retiring. Educational requirements will continue to rise as the military seeks enlisted personnel with some college training.

America and the World

The United States spends more money on defense and is better equipped than any other armed force in the world, although some nations, such as China and the former Soviet Union, have larger forces. The United States also has the most geographically diverse military machine.

The Department of Defense began implementing overseas force reductions in the early 1990s. It planned significant withdrawals of European NATO forces, for example, and shifted its focus to the development of a U.S. regional defense system. A principal Department of Defense objective in the 1990s was the development of significant force that could be quickly deployed anywhere in the world.

Research and Technology

Several separate agencies within the Department of Defense serve to develop and promote new military technologies. Through the Defense Advanced Research Projects Agency's (DARPA) efforts and expenditures, the United States maintains a significant technological lead in weapons and defense systems. This advantage allowed them to vanquish most of their adversaries since World War II, and to literally dominate, with few casualties, every military conflict since the Vietnam War. When the arms race escalated during the 1980s, America's technological superiority increased as Soviet military investments lagged. Indeed, in the 1990s, the United States maintained a lethal arsenal of high-tech weaponry.

Some of the most impressive weapons were utilized in the Persian Gulf War. General Norman Schwarzkopf even called it ''the technology war,'' and some observers hailed it as the transition from the traditional bloody ground war to a new era of combat strategy. For the first time, a warring nation was able to directly attack its adversary's political and military infrastructure from long range with pinpoint accuracy. This tactic essentially guaranteed U.N. air superiority in the Gulf and reduced the probability of a protracted ground war.

High-Tech Weapons. The M-1 Abrams Main Battle Tank is the Army's most powerful land-based vehicle. It was developed at a cost of $20.4 billion, and each tank costs $4.4 million to produce. The tank is designed to absorb direct hits from certain armor-piercing shells and is powered by a turbine engine that allows the massive vehicle to cruise at 60 miles per hour. A damper allows the 120 mm cannon to ''float'' as the tank plows across the terrain so that the operator can fire laser-aimed projectiles with accuracy. Tank operators can wear infrared headgear for night vision, an option also available to some ground forces and pilots.

Another important weapon of the Gulf War was the HARM Air-To-Ground Antiradar Missile. At a program cost of $7.1 billion and about $260,000 per unit, these missiles are designed to lock in on an enemy radar signal and follow the beam to the target. U.S. planes can then enter enemy territory undetected. The Tomahawk Sea-Launched Cruise Missile ($9.8 billion to develop, and $1.35 million to produce) also proved effective. Originally designed to deliver nuclear warheads to the Soviet Union, the missiles can be retrofitted to carry large conventional payloads to small targets. Designed just in time for the Persian Gulf War, the Patriot Missile utilized state-of-the-art homing and propulsion technology to chase and destroy enemy missiles in the air.

The Gulf War also gave U.S. forces an opportunity to test the AW-64 Apache Attack Helicopter. This jet-powered contraption is capable of cruising through battlefields at high speeds and simultaneously launching a barrage of cannon fire, rockets, and laser-guided missiles in multiple directions. The Apache's fatal Hellfire missile system allows a pilot to unleash an armor piercing missile that is aimed and guided by a soldier on the ground, thus allowing the Apache pilot to seek other targets. Similarly, the F-117A Stealth Fighter, at a cost of $118 million each, allows pilots to enter enemy territory and deliver its bombs before being detected on radar.

In addition to its high-tech weaponry, some of the most advanced U.S. defense devices include high-flying planes and satellite systems that gather intelligence and help ground forces communicate. Advanced military imaging satellites, for example, are capable of reading a car's license plate from space. The armed forces' early warning satellite systems detect launched missiles and relay their flight patterns to observers on the ground. Importantly, the Airborne Warning & Control System (AWACS) is used to monitor and control air battles from a plane in the air.

The Future. The U.S. military establishment will retain its technological lead into the twenty-first century. Despite its uncontested supremacy, U.S. research and development of new weapons continued in the late 1990s. For example, the Air Force was funding the development of a new bomb called the Sensor-Fuzed Weapon. The device consists of a canister with 40 separate warheads. When dropped from a plane, the warheads separate and use infrared sensors to locate and destroy multiple battlefield targets, such as tanks.

Likewise, the Army was contributing to the creation of the Silent Soldier. This robotic weapon lies on the ground and uses microcomputers to locate and destroy oncoming tanks. Meanwhile, DARPA was developing Thirsty Saber, an undetectable air-launched cruise missile that incorporates stealth technology. Tacit Rainbow, another advanced missile under development in the mid-1990s, is a jet-powered weapon that can circle for up to an hour waiting for the enemy to activate its radar. In the late 1990s, the Army continued to build up its fleet of Crusaders, self-propelled computer-aimed howitzer cannons built for rapid fire while maintaining 60 mph speed. The most advanced military technology continued to be developed in secrecy.

FURTHER READING

Barry, John, and Evan Thomas. ''Not Your Father's Army.'' *Newsweek,* 22 November 1999.

''DOD at a Glance,'' 1999. Available from http://www.defenselink.mil/pubs/almanac.

''Federal Government Budget by Agency,'' 1999. Available from http://www.polisci.com/economy/agency/htm.

Occupational Outlook Handbook, 1998-1999 Edition. Washington, D.C.: U.S. Department of Labor, 1999.

''Panel Warns Military Could Be Inadequate.'' *Army Times,* 25 October 1999.

Wright, John W., ed. *The Universal Almanac 1997.* Andrews and McNeel, 1997.

SIC 9721

INTERNATIONAL AFFAIRS

This industry consists of establishments of U.S. and foreign governments primarily engaged in international affairs and programs related to other nations and peoples.

NAICS CODE(S)

928120 (International Affairs)

INDUSTRY SNAPSHOT

The sovereign states of the world, with their mutual inter-dependence in the midst of economic and political forces, have put new emphasis on the need for friendly relations among nations. The creation of the United Nations at the end of World War II has facilitated consultations and negotiations between the community of states; nevertheless, bilateral contacts through U.S. consular and diplomatic missions remain a key force in official relations between governments. The Department of State works concurrently with U.S. consular and diplomatic missions to represent U.S. interests abroad.

ORGANIZATION AND STRUCTURE

Three main organizations comprise and assist United States foreign relations: the United Nations, the Diplomatic Mission, and Consular Officers and Consular Posts. The United Nations (UN) formally came into existence on October 24, 1945. It was created as a union of nations working to maintain international peace and security and cooperating in establishing political, economic, and social security. The adoption of the 1961 Vienna Convention on Diplomatic Relations established diplomatic relations, by mutual consent, for one person to act as the envoy of two or more states. An envoy, or diplomatic agent, represents the home state, acts as a government agent, and is an official channel of communication between the governments of the sending and receiving state. The Consular Officer is a representative of the sending state and is primarily concerned with the improvement of commercial and economic relations between the sending and receiving state.

The United Nations. Membership in the UN is open to all peace-loving states that accept the obligations of the United Nations Charter. The purposes of the United Nations, as set forth in the Charter, are to develop friendly relations among nations; to maintain international peace and security; to cooperate internationally to promote respect for human rights; and to solve international economic, social, and humanitarian problems.

The UN functions in accordance with the following principles: members are sovereign and equal; members are to act according to their charter obligations; members are to refrain in the use of force against any other state; members are to settle international disputes without endangering international peace; members shall not work against the UN in its efforts to act in accordance with the charter; the UN shall ensure that states, which are not members, act accordingly to ensure international peace; and the UN may not interfere within the domestic jurisdiction of any state.

The UN is composed of six principal organs—the General Assembly, the Security Council, the Economic and Social Council, the Trusteeship Council, the International Court of Justice, and the Secretariat.

The General Assembly consists of all the representatives of the member states. Each member has one vote, and decisions on important matters require a two-thirds majority vote. The General Assembly considers principles of cooperation in the maintenance of international peace and security; works with the UN budget; elects the non-permanent members of the Security Council and the members of the Economic and Social Council; jointly elects with the Security Council the judges of the International Court of Justice; and appoints the Secretary-General. In addition, the General Assembly makes recommendations for the peaceful settlement of situations that might impede friendly relations among nations. The Assembly also discusses and makes recommendations on questions relating to international peace and security and international political cooperation.

The Security Council consists of five permanent members and ten members elected by the General Assembly for two terms. The five permanent members are China, France, Russia, the United Kingdom, and the United States. Each state has one vote. The functions and powers of the Security Council are to take military action against an aggressor; to maintain international peace and security; to formulate plans to regulate armaments; and to recommend action when there is a threat to peace. The Security Council also investigates disputes which might threaten international peace; recommends terms of settlement to such disputes; proposes economic sanctions in order to prevent aggression; recommends the admission of new members; utilizes the trusteeship functions in strategic areas; recommends to the General Assembly the appointment of the Secretary-General; and elects the judges of the International Court.

The Economic and Social Council is responsible for carrying out the functions of the UN with regard to international economic, social, cultural, educational, and health matters. The functions and powers of the Economic and Social Council are making reports and recommendations on international economic, social, cultural, educational, and health matters; serving as the primary forum for the discussion of international economic and social issues; promoting human rights; and consulting with nongovernmental groups concerned with the matters of the council.

The Trusteeship Council consists of one member administering trust territories—the United States. This council provides for an international trusteeship system to protect the interests of the inhabitants of territories that are not yet self-governing. The primary function of the Trusteeship Council is to promote the advancement of the inhabitants of the Trust Territories and their development towards self-government.

The International Court of Justice consists of 15 judges elected by the General Assembly and the Security Council. No two judges can be nationals of the same state. In deciding disputes, the International Court of

Justice applies international conventions—establishing rules recognized by the contesting states, the general principles of law recognized by nations, international custom as evidence of general practice accepted as law, and judicial decisions and teachings of qualified publicists—as means for determining the rules of law.

The Secretariat is composed of the secretary-general and an international staff appointed under regulations of the General Assembly. The Secretariat carries out the daily work of the UN both at its headquarters in New York and in its offices abroad. The Secretariat administers peace-keeping operations; monitors international economic and social trends; organizes conferences on international problems and concerns; prepares studies on human rights, disarmament, and development; and translates information about the UN and supplies that information to the world media.

Special Agencies. The United Nations system has created 15 specialized agencies to assist in providing international economic, social, and technical services. These organizations have separate budgets, statutes, and memberships, but they are all tied to the UN with a varying degree of affiliation. The UN family of organizations includes the International Bank for Reconstruction and Development (IBRD); International Civil Aviation Organization (ICAO); International Development Association (IDA); Inter-Governmental Maritime Consultative Organization (IMCO); International Monetary Fund (IMF); International Telecommunications Union (ITU); World Meteorological Organization (WMO); World Intellectual Property Organization (WIPO); World Health Organization (WHO); Universal Postal Union (UPU); UN Educational, Scientific, and Cultural Organization (UNESCO); Food and Agriculture Organization of the United Nations (FAO); International Labor Organization (ILO); International Finance Corporation (IFC); and the International Fund for Agricultural Development (IFAD).

Embassies. A U.S. diplomatic mission is classified as an embassy if the chief of the mission holds the rank of ambassador. Members of the Foreign Service and the Department of State staff U.S. embassies. The ambassador, as head of the diplomatic mission, represents the diplomat's native country by acting as a representative of his or her government and as an official channel of communication between the government and the state to which he has been assigned. The diplomatic agent must report on conditions and developments in the appointed state; protect the interests of his or her home state and its nationals in that state; promote friendly relations between the represented state and the host state; and help develop economic, cultural, and scientific relations.

The heads of a U.S. diplomatic mission are the chief of the mission—ambassador, minister, or charge d'affaires—and the deputy of the mission. Many diplomats are successful business people who offer specialized expertise and understanding of their countries, cultures, and societies.

Consular Officers. In the 1990s, separate consular services were abolished in favor of combined foreign service for both diplomatic and consular officers. Although many traditional functions of the consular have been taken by diplomatic agents, the consular plays an important role in connection with trading and commercial interests of the sending state. According to the 1963 Vienna Convention on Consular Relations, consular functions are concerned with promoting the development of commercial, economic, cultural, and scientific relations; protecting the interests of the state he or she represents and its nationals; issuing passports and travel documents to persons wishing to travel to the consular's native state; assisting nationals, both individuals and corporations, in their interactions with the host state; acting as notary and civil registrar; arranging appropriate representation for nationals before the authorities of the host state in order to preserve the rights and interests of the nationals; and exercising rights of supervision and inspection in respect to vessels and aircraft having the nationality of the state the consular represents.

Consular officers are appointed with the host government's permission and may be withdrawn at any time. They hold the rank of consul-general, consul, or vice-consul and are divided into two categories—career consular officers and honorary consular officers. Career consular officers are full time employees of their government and are appointed by their head of state. Conversely, honorary consular officers are non-career officials for whom consular functions are usually a part-time occupation.

BACKGROUND AND DEVELOPMENT

The organizations that comprise U.S. foreign relations derive their power and authority from the executive branch of the government. The Constitution of the United States grants the president the authority to negotiate treaties and appoint diplomatic and consular officials. Foreign policy is conducted primarily through the U.S. Department of State. The Secretary of State, as head of the department, is the primary advisor to the president on foreign affairs issues.

Consular and diplomatic missions had a small role in world affairs for the first 100 years of the existence of the United States. In 1893, the United States and several European countries began ambassador reciprocation. President Woodrow Wilson had attempted to reduce U.S. involvement abroad during the isolationist period after

World War I, but that policy gradually disappeared during the terms of successive presidents. In 1924, the Rogers Act combined consular and diplomatic service into the Foreign Service.

With the start of World War II, international conditions demanded that the United States take a leading role in world affairs. Under the direction of President Franklin D. Roosevelt, the United States proceeded with a program of foreign aid designed to promote world trade and cooperation. The Foreign Service Act of 1946 reorganized the Foreign Service, raised pay, and launched a promotion system based on merit.

As international responsibilities grew and world affairs became more complex, the responsibilities of the foreign relations departments increased. The Department of Defense—along with the Departments of Agriculture, Commerce, and Treasury—took on new responsibilities in world affairs. Under the direction of the Secretary of State, the Agency for International Development and the International Development Cooperation Agencies were created to assist in controlling and directing foreign aid.

During the mid-1990s, Madeleine K. Albright succeeded Warren Christopher as Secretary of State, and the presidency of William (Bill) Clinton continued into its second term. Secretary Albright reiterated the Clinton Administration's aim of making commercial affairs and the promotion of American business interests abroad one of the highest priorities of foreign relations policies and officers. During this time, significant changes occurred in several important areas that affected U.S. foreign policy and international relations. Key among them were changes to the U.S. Immigration and Naturalization Service's provisions regarding illegal immigrants; U.S.-proposed changes to the United Nations system; changes and expansions of international trade agreements that affected U.S. global trade policies; and a focused and structured effort to include policies and programs to advance opportunities for women throughout the world.

The Immigration and Naturalization Service (INS). In September 1996, President Clinton signed into law the Illegal Immigration Reform and Immigrant Responsibility Act. The 1996 Act was targeted at reducing the flood of illegal immigrants along the U.S.-Mexico border. The Act contained provisions to increase the number of border agents and to strengthen enforcement efforts; increase penalties for alien smuggling and document fraud; enhance inspection, capture, retention, status review, and deportation of aliens; decrease the numbers of illegal aliens; restrict alien benefits; and implement new parole and safehaven procedures. Many of the Act's provisions—particularly those pertaining to retention, deportation, and to persons seeking safehaven—became effective April 1, 1997.

The United States and the United Nations. The United States played a pivotal role in the formation of the UN after World War II and was the UN's single largest contributor; total U.S. contributions to the UN in 1995 was $1.84 billion. The Clinton Administration took the lead during the mid-1990s to propose changes to the UN system to increase overall efficiency and effectiveness. U.S. proposed changes targeted more effective use of UN funds, greater accountability to UN members, and tighter focus on key UN objectives. In addition, the U.S. revised its decades-long history of participation in multilateral peace operations. These changes resulted in President Clinton's Presidential Decision Directive (PDD 25), which emphasizes that the President will never give up command of U.S. troops. Changes focused on peacekeeping activities as one means of serving U.S. interests abroad by promoting international security, democracy, and economic growth. Within this framework, several changes were to be made. These changes would affect decisions concerning which peacekeeping missions to support; the increased goal of reducing the U.S. cost burden from 31.7 percent down to 25 percent; re-examination of the circumstances under which U.S. troops would be under operational command of a foreign commander; provisions to improve the UN's ability to manage peacekeeping missions; and improving communications between Congress, the Executive Office, and the American public concerning U.S. participation in such missions.

U.S. Trade Policy. Building on the goal of promoting American commercial and business interests abroad as a cornerstone of American foreign policy, the United States became an active participant in the World Trade Organization (WTO), which succeeded the General Agreement on Tariffs and Trade (GATT) as the legal basis of the multilateral trading system. Formed in January 1995, WTO made provisions to open national markets, administer and monitor trade relations among countries, and served as a forum for settlement of trade-related disputes covered under its jurisdiction. WTO incorporated the structure of GATT and also consolidated governmental trade policies with regard to trade in goods, services, and intellectual property rights. Associated multilateral agreements focused on environmental, health, and safety issues. By mid-1996, 120 countries were WTO members, and an additional 30 countries were in the process of joining.

Big Emerging Markets (BEMs). Having historically focused its foreign commercial policies on Europe and Japan during the mid-1990s, the United States started shifting focus to 12 countries dubbed the "Big Emerging Markets" (BEMs). These countries consisted of Argentina; Brazil; the Chinese Economic Area, which included China, Hong Kong, and Taiwan; India; Indonesia; Mexico; Poland; South Africa; South Korea; and Turkey. The U.S. Department of Commerce, International Trade Administration anticipated that the BEMs' average gross domestic product (GDP) growth rate would increase by 6.5 percent from 1995 to 2000, in comparison to an average of 2.9 percent among the developed countries. In addition, BEMs' imports of goods and services were expected to increase by 75 percent over the same timeframe, compared to a 38 percent expected rise among the developed countries.

The U.S. Commercial Service. Today U.S. diplomatic officers work in accord with private organizations to develop strong and aggressive trade policies. New laws and greater cooperation between government agencies and private interests help promote U.S. business by increasing exports and appealing unfair trade practices. Diplomatic officers work with commercial officers at the U.S. Commercial Service—part of the United States International Trade Administration—to ensure that U.S. business interests are a central part of their embassy and consulate operations. The Commercial Service maintains more than 70 U.S. offices and operates in nearly 70 countries. The result of a collaboration among the Commercial Service, the Small Business Administration, and the Export-Import Bank, U.S. Export Assistance Centers are located throughout the United States and provide consulting services, market research, and trade information. A recent addition to the Commercial Service family of programs and initiatives is the creation of commercial centers—usually located outside U.S. embassies and within key business districts. They offer full business services, such as office space and equipment, when conducting business abroad. In addition, commercial officers serve the financial assistance needs of American businesses through a network of five multilateral development banks: the European Bank for Reconstruction and Development, Asian Development Bank, the World Bank, African Development Bank, and the Inter-American Development Bank. The National Trade Data Bank (NTDB) supports the efforts of U.S. diplomatic and commercial officers and American businesses and serves as the U.S. Government's premier source of global trade information contained in more than 130 separate databases from more than 20 federal sources.

Ambassadors assist the U.S. business community by lending their time at trade events, interceding on behalf of U.S. bidders for major contracts, providing current foreign market information, and informing business leaders of new opportunities in foreign markets. During the 1990s, ambassadors focused their negotiating efforts on three areas in which the United States was a major international competitor: services, agriculture, and intellectual property rights. Two multilateral agreements: the Information Technology Agreement (ITA) and the Agreement on Basic Telecommunications were expected to reduce global trade barriers in these high-technology industries, significantly reduce international taxes, increase U.S. jobs, and save American consumers billions of dollars. By 1999, U.S. ambassadors expected to be entrenched in negotiations to further open the $526-billion global agricultural market, considered to be a key component on the U.S. trade agenda. Negotiations to further open the $1.2-trillion global financial services market were expected to begin in January 2000.

Intellectual Property Rights. Increasingly aware of the international tensions created and exacerbated by differing global standards, protection, and enforcement of intellectual property rights, the World Trade Organization's (WTO) agreement on Trade-Related Aspects of Intellectual Property Rights (TRIPS) was implemented to address these issues. Among its numerous provisions were the recognition of computer programs as literary works and the rights of authors of computer programs and audio recordings to authorize or prohibit commercial rental of their work to the public. In addition, the agreement protected industrial designs for ten years and patents for 20 years in nearly all fields of technology, whether for a product or a process. TRIPS was to apply to existing as well as new intellectual property, and a council monitored countries' timely implementation of the new agreement and their compliance with it. Further negotiations to protect the interests of U.S. copyright industries, which exported over $400 billion annually, were to be continued into the year 2000.

Women. Reflecting the rapidly increasing integration, contributions, and growing acceptance of women into all aspects of the global community, Secretary of State Albright included the advancement of women throughout the world as another integral part of America's foreign relations policies. During the mid-1990s, the President's Interagency Council on Women was formed to coordinate and implement the Platform for Action adopted at the UN's Fourth World Conference on Women held in Beijing in early fall 1995. Following up on the Beijing conference, the Clinton Administration outlined additional specific commitments in areas pertaining to working women, violence against women, discrimination, women entrepreneurs, health, women's political participation, and education. In 1997, the UN launched an Internet site called "Womenwatch" as an entry into its vast array of information pertaining to women throughout the globe. The three UN organizations that created Womenwatch—the Division for the Advancement of Women in the Department for Policy Coordination and Sustainable Development (DPCSD), the United Nations Development Fund for Women (UNIFEM), and the International Research and Training Institute for the Advancement of Women (INSTRAW)—also launched Internet sites accessible via the Womenwatch gateway.

CURRENT CONDITIONS

The decision on whether or not to pay its long outstanding dues to the UN was a politically-polarized controversy for the United States in the late 1990s. Congress had been fighting to continue withholding the payments in arrears—conditioning payment on contentious anti-abortion restrictions (''riders'') attached to the bill authorizing payment. President Clinton, eager to have his Administration remembered for cleaning up debts, fought to have the dues paid. Consequences of continued nonpayment included the loss of voting rights in the General Assembly.

Another polarizing issue in 1999 was the admission of China into the World Trade Organization. China ranked second of the world's largest economies, based on gross domestic product. The ostensibly-accidental bombing of the Chinese embassy in May 1999, coupled with the Report of the House Select Committee on U.S. National Security (''The Cox Report''), which cited recent and repeated incidence of Chinese espionage at U.S. nuclear laboratories, kept scholars and politicians uncertain of the propriety of continuing fortification of Chinese capability. China remained the only nation to have its nuclear warheads aimed at the United States.

Finally, the U.S. refused to join other nations in ratifying the Comprehensive Test Ban Treaty, a decision the consequences of which were too early to gauge.

FURTHER READING

''America's New I-Word.'' *Economist,* 6 November 1999.

A Diplomat's Handbook of International Law and Practice. Boston: Martin Nihoff Publications, 1989.

Freymann. ''Is U.S. Feeding Mouths That Will Bite Us?'' *San Antonio Business Journal,* 19 Sept 1999.

Richelson, Jeffrey T. ''Uncertain Damage.'' *Bulletin of the Atomic Scientists,* September/October 1999.

Segal, Gerald.''Does China Matter?'' *Foreign Affairs,* September/October 1999.

''World Economy and Trade: International Trade Agreements.'' *Peace Research Abstracts Journal,* August 1999.

Contributor Notes

Adams, Mary Alice: Coordinator of Telecommunicated Instruction at Troy State University, Montgomery, Alabama; freelance writer, researcher, and editor for various publications including *Business Leaders for Students, Notable Black American Men,* and *Encyclopedia of World Biographies.*

Alberts, Daniel J: Technical writer based in Sterling Heights, Michigan; author of computer software and hardware operations manuals; a recognized member of the Society for Technical Communication.

Alexanian, Christine: Freelance copyeditor based in Spokane, Washington; B.A. in English and a Publishing Certificate from the University of Denver's Publishing Institute; does work for the State University of New York Press and the University of Pennsylvania Press, as well as the Gale Group.

Amato, Sara: Electronic Services and Web Development Librarian at Bowdoin College; degrees in library sciences and change management; has written for publications in the area of Internet organization, use, and research.

Amerman, Don: Freelance writer, editor, and owner of A&M Editorial Services based in Saylorsburg, Pennsylvania; has written extensively for *The Journal of Commerce;* work for the Gale Group includes *Encyclopedia of Emerging Industries, Women in World History, Notable Hispanic-American Women,* and *The African-American Almanac.*

Armstrong, Robin: Freelance writer; contributor to *Contemporary Musicians, Contemporary Black Biography,* and *International Dictionary of Opera.*

Azzata, Gerry: Freelance writer and researcher based in Medford, Massachusetts; former academic reference librarian with graduate degrees in law and Library Science; has written numerous materials in the areas of law, business, health, and online research.

Baker, Sandy: Freelance writer, researcher, and editor from Normal, Illinois; work experience in employee communications, university public relations, textbook publishing, and newspaper reporting.

Baker, Suzanne: Freelance writer; MBA, University of Michigan, Ann Arbor.

Balch, Trudy: Freelance writer.

Ballard, Andrew: Freelance writer.

Banks, Leslie: Freelance writer and publicist based in Chicago, Illinois; experienced in public relations, Web site content development, and business writing.

Barduson, Thomas: MBA and freelance writer and researcher.

Barnett, Kris: Freelance writer based in Portland, Connecticut; adjunct English instructor at the University of New Haven.

Baue, William D: Freelance writer who has published articles on William Faulkner and Toni Morrison, as well as on business topics, such as work apprenticeships; has taught writing and literature to both college and high school students.

Beard, James L: Freelance writer and essay author; CPA and MBA candidate, Oral Roberts University, Tulsa, Oklahoma.

Bellenir, Karen: Freelance writer and editor.

Bennett, Bill: Business writer and researcher; MBA, University of Oregon.

Berger, Percy Lee: J.D. and MBA candidate, University of Michigan, Ann Arbor; associate editor, *Michigan Journal of International Law;* freelance writer.

Berry, Pamela: Freelance writer and editor.

Bianco, David P: Freelance writer, editor, and publishing consultant; editor of several reference books; graduate degrees in business and English.

Bilas, Wendy Johnson: Freelance writer; MBA in marketing, Wake Forest University; director of marketing for the Charlotte Symphony Orchestra.

Black, Virginia Mayo: Freelance reporter and editor based in Madison, Wisconsin; writer for newspapers and magazines covering business and general news topics.

Blumenfield, Steven: MBA candidate, University of Chicago; managing editor, *Chicago Business.*

Bodine, Paul S: Freelance writer and editor based in Milwaukee, Wisconsin; has edited for McGraw-Hill Professional Publishing, New York University Press, and the University of Michigan Press; his work has appeared in the *Milwaukee Journal* and the *Baltimore Sun.*

Boyer, Dean: Former newspaper reporter; freelance writer in Seattle area.

Brennan, Carol: Freelance writer and regular contributor to numerous Gale Group titles, as well as *Hour Detroit.*

Briggs, Karen: Freelance writer and editor based in Toronto, Ontario; has written for more than 20 general-interest magazines in Canada, the United States, Great Britain, and Bermuda.

Brinker, Kaye: Freelance writer based in Brooklyn Heights, New York; former advertising copywriter; contributor to *Discount Merchandiser, Advertising Career Directory,* and *Bank Security Report.*

Brooke, Bob: Freelance writer and author of six books; writes weekly for the *Philadelphia Business Journal* and has also been published in *Business Traveler (US/UK), Mexico Business, The Rotarian, Delta Sky,* and the Rand McNally *Guide to World Business.*

Brooks, Jeanette: Technical writer and editor specializing in technical training and manufacturing.

Brown, Susan: Freelance writer.

Broyles, Michael J: Ph.D. ABD working on his thesis at the University of Western Ontario; has also written for the *Encyclopedia of Latin American History.*

Brussel, Marika: Freelance writer and editor, specializing in food and dance articles, based in Santa Fe, New Mexico.

Burke, Andrew: Freelance writer.

Burnett-Balga, Beth: Freelance writer and full-time communications manager based in Atlanta, Georgia; has published articles in *Resource, American City and County,* and *World Wastes* magazines.

Burton-Faulkner, Kimberly: Freelance writer and editor based in Ann Arbor, Michigan; has written for the *Detroit Free Press Magazine;* masters candidate, University of Michigan, Ann Arbor.

Calhoun, Lisa: Freelance writer based in San Antonio, Texas; has written for a range of magazines on subjects from new media to Russian mafia; degree in professional writing from Baylor University, Waco, Texas.

Casey, Jim: Freelance technical writer based in Galveston, Texas; systems operator of CompuServe forums; former computer programmer and electrical engineer.

Chittick, Paul: Freelance writer; M.D. candidate at Wayne State University, Detroit, Michigan.

Clark, Margaret: Freelance writer.

Cohen, Kerstan B: Freelance writer and French translator; editor for *Letter-Ex* poetry review.

Cohen, Paula Hartman: Freelance writer.

Cohn, Lynne M: Writer, poet, and editor; has written for *New York Newsday, Michigan Living,* and *Woman's Own,* as well as publishing her own poetry.

Collins, Cheryl: Freelance writer and researcher.

Cook, Allan R: Freelance writer and journalist; graduate student in English, Oakland University, Rochester, Michigan.

Cooksey, Gloria: Freelance writer; earned a certificate in programming and operations from Data Control Institute and is certified as a network engineer; holds associate degrees in electronic communications and computer electronics and is licensed by the FCC to repair aircraft and marine communications equipment.

Costilow, Donald R: Graphic artist/illustrator, Monongahela Power Company; instructor of business, Fairmont State College, Fairmont, West Virginia.

Covell, Jeffrey L: Freelance writer and corporate history contractor.

Creighton, Kevin: Freelance writer; MBA, University of Michigan, Ann Arbor.

Cuene, Jim: Freelance writer; graduate student in American Studies, Purdue University, West Lafayette, Indiana.

Daily, Kristine: Freelance writer; MBA candidate, Boston College.

Daniels, Garth K: Business consultant in corporate strategy and new venture development; adjunct faculty member, Westminster College, Salt Lake City, Utah.

Day, Holly L: Freelance writer and editor living in Minneapolis, Minnesota; her fiction and nonfiction writing has appeared in more than 800 publications internationally.

Dee, James P: Freelance writer based in Pittsburgh, Pennsylvania; specialist in business and legal writing, editing, and project management.

DeShantz-Cook, Lisa: Freelance writer and editor.

Distelzweig, Howard: Freelance writer and researcher based in Ann Arbor, Michigan; former educator currently working in Quality Assurance Documentation; has written numerous materials in the areas of business, industry, and technology.

Dorman, Evelyn: Freelance journalist, as well as French teacher, tutor, and graduate student; Contributor to *Brides Today, Lerner-Pulitzer* newspapers, the *Chicago Sun Times,* and the *International Directory of Company Histories.*

Dougal, April S: Archivist and freelance writer specializing in business and social history in Cleveland, Ohio.

Eigo, Tim: Freelance business and law writer based in Phoenix, Arizona; M.A. from the University of Notre Dame and J.D. from the University of California, Hastings College of Law.

Estioco, Rose M: Freelance writer and editor based in Detroit, Michigan, with writing experience on a variety of subjects including health care, science, aging, and business.

Evans, Ken: Doctoral candidate in Economics, University of Michigan, Ann Arbor.

Fagan, Dave: Business and technical writer and freelance journalist in Seattle, Washington; writes regularly for *Downtown Source,* a weekly newspaper owned by *The Seattle Times;* his professional honors include writing awards from the Society of Professional Journalists in 1995 and 1996.

Fee, Joe: Freelance writer.

Fishel, Larry: Freelance writer and chemist based in East Lansing, MI.

Fisher, Rogene M: Freelance writer and editor.

Frick, Lisa: Freelance writer based in Columbia, Missouri; former newspaper reporter, copyeditor, and research assistant for the *Missouri Historical Review;* contributor to *Marketing Missouri History;* specializes in writing business features for the *Columbia Daily Tribune.*

Fujinaka, Marika: Freelance writer and editor living in the central coast region of California.

Gallagher, Elizabeth A: Freelance writer.

Gallagher, John: Freelance writer.

Gallman, Jason: Freelance writer; graduate student in literature, Purdue University, West Lafayette, Indiana.

Gasbarre, April Dougal: Freelance writer specializing in business and social history in Cleveland, Ohio.

Genaway, David C: Library Director Emeritus, Youngstown State University, Ohio; president of Genaway & Associates, Inc. based in Canfield, Ohio; founded the national Conference on Integrated Online Library Systems, editor/compiler/publisher of the proceedings of seven national conferences; author of several books and articles; Ph.D., University of Minnesota.

Giglierano, Joan: Independent information professional and former business librarian based in Columbus, Ohio.

Glover, Beaird: Freelance writer.

Gluskin, Lisa: Writer and editor based in San Francisco; editor of *And . . .* arts and culture magazine.

Goldfarb, Kathie: Freelance writer; librarian and Webmaster at Florida State University Libraries.

Grant, Tina: Freelance writer and editor.

Grensing-Pophal, Lin: Business author and consultant in Chippewa Falls, Wisconsin; B.A. in psychology and M.A. in organizational management; author of four books on employee management and marketing issues; frequent contributor to business and trade publications.

Griffin, Attrices Dean: Freelance researcher and writer; former owner of research and technical writing firm.

Gundersen, Linda: Freelance editor and writer based in Doylestown, Pennsylvania; contributor to *The Strategic Healthcare Atlas,* freelancer for Aetna/U.S. Healthcare and Springhouse Corp., a publisher of nursing textbooks.

Gustafson, Randy: Freelance writer; MBA, University of Michigan, Ann Arbor.

Haas, Leslie M: Head of General Reference Department at the Marriott Library at the University of Utah; has written several articles on the subject of business research and products.

Hammond, Nancy: Freelance writer and researcher working in the Detroit, Michigan area.

Harding, Lauri: Freelance writer and editor.

Harris, Lisa: Graduate student in business, Chattanooga, Tennessee.

Harrison, Susan R: Writer and educator.

Harvey, Dan: Freelance writer and editor based in Wilmington, Delaware; former newspaper and magazine editor specializing in news and features on business, medicine, and health.

Hedden, Heather: Senior staff writer, *Middle East Times,* Cairo Bureau, 1991-92.

Heil, Karl: Freelance writer; M.A. in linguistics, Eastern Michigan University, Ypsilanti, Michigan.

Hemingway, Lloyd: Freelance writer.

Henderson, Tona: Freelance consultant, Internet trainer, and business researcher; business librarian at Pennsylvania State University, University Park, Pennsylvania.

Hernandez, Rolando: Computer systems analyst, project leader, and knowledge engineer.

Hillstrom, Laurie Collier: Freelance writer and editor; MBA, University of Michigan, Ann Arbor; former editor of *Authors and Artists for Young Adults,* and *Major Authors and Illustrators for Young Children and Young Adults.*

Hillyer, Richard: Freelance writer and editor, poet, and part-time English teacher; Ph.D. in English, University of Michigan, Ann Arbor.

Hogan, Beatrice: Freelance writer based in New York City.

Holm, Catherine Dybiec: Freelance writer, researcher, and editor based in Cook, Minnesota; former planner with degrees in natural resource management; areas of writing and publication include: business, career development, trade and industry, trends, sociology, fiction, and fantasy.

Holmes, Gillian S: Freelance writer and engineer in Hayward, California.

Hornbeck, Diane M: Co-owner of Home Based Data Services, Inc., offering services to the publishing industry; graduate of Wayne State University, Detroit, Michigan, with a degree in mass communications.

Hoyt, Douglas: Freelance writer.

Huerster, Paricia G: Freelance writer and editor.

Hunt, Christopher: Freelance writer and editor; former advertising copyeditor in Japan; contributor to *Mainichi Daily News, The Japan Times, Canadian Biker, Exile,* and *Intertext.*

Ingram, Frederick: Freelance writer based in Sumter, South Carolina; contributor to *Encyclopedia of Business, Encyclopedia of Consumer Brands,* and *The Disaster Planning Handbook.*

Isaacs, McAllister III: Freelance writer and editor of *Textile World.*

Jaffe, Roger: Received a bachelor's degree in mathematics from UCLA and a master's in statistics from San Diego State University; has been involved in the real estate development industry; currently teaches middle- and high-school mathematics in San Diego, California.

Jacobson, Robert R: Freelance writer and musician.

Jeffrey, Tim: Playwright, short story writer, and freelance writer based in Detroit, Michigan.

Jochnowitz, Marinell: Writer and editor based in San Francisco, California.

Jones, Allison: Freelance writer.

Jones, J. Jacob: Graduate student in American history, Purdue University, West Lafayette, Indiana.

Joseph, Leslie: Freelance writer and editor based in Birmingham, Michigan; worked on *Lifetime Book of Money Management, Chronology of 20th Century Eastern European History,* and *Contemporary Heroes and Heroines, Book II* as an editor for Gale Research.

Kalfatovic, Mary C: Freelance writer and librarian in the Washington, DC area; has written on film, theater, and entertainment for a variety of publications and is the author of *Montgomery Clift: A Bio-bibliography.*

Karl, Lisa: Editor at LifeServ.com, a life-events software and Internet company in Chicago, Illinois; freelance writer and editor in business, parenting, and sports; has written for numerous regional newspapers and magazines, sports teams, reference publishers, and national magazines.

Kaufman, Scott: Freelance writer.

Kelley, Christine: Freelance writer.

King, Brett Allan: Freelance writer.

King, Daniel: Freelance writer; doctoral candidate in economics, New School for Social Research, New York, New York.

King, Susan Wood: Freelance writer and communications specialist based in Research Triangle Park, North Carolina.

Kirchner, Joseph: Freelance writer based in Alexandria, Virginia.

Kirn, Kathy: Freelance writer and owner of KMK Communications based in Baltimore, Maryland; experienced in corporate communications, public relations, and technical writing.

Kiser, Helene: Graduate of Purdue University's and Warren Wilson College's writing programs; freelance writer and former teacher of learning disabled children and college students.

Kitsuse, Alicia: Freelance writer and editor based in Boulder, Colorado.

Kleiman, Robert T., Ph.D: Professor of finance at Oakland University, Rochester, Michigan, and a nationally known consultant; frequently used as a source in such publications as *Money* magazine and the *Wall Street Journal.*

Kline, Trish: Freelance writer experienced in business script writing, public relations and advertising/marketing; author of children's books, teacher's guides, and educational software.

Knes, Michael E: Freelance writer.

Knight, Judson: Freelance writer and editor; partner in the Knight Agency, specializing in literary representation.

Kody, John: Freelance writer.

Kolberg, Sharyn: Freelance writer and editor based in New York, New York; has written and ghostwritten dozens of non-fiction books, articles, and audio tapes.

Koserowski, Laurette: Freelance writer and assistant editor of *Traditional Quilter* magazine.

Kucera, David: Ph.D. candidate in economics, New School for Social Research, New York, New York.

Kuhn, Karyn Bober: Freelance writer and editor.

Lawrie, Laura: Freelance writer, editor, and publishing consultant based in Arizona; has worked on *The Association of MBAs Guide to Business Schools, The New Grove Dictionary of Opera,* and *The Macmillian Dictionary of Art.* Currently the managing editor of *American Behavioral Scientist.*

Leahy, Norman W: Writer and researcher living in Richmond, Virginia; his work has appeared in such publications as the *Christian Science Monitor, USA Today, The San Diego Union-Tribune,* and the *Washington Times;* M.A. in writing from Johns Hopkins University, Baltimore, Maryland.

Leotta, Joan: Freelance business and travel writer and storyteller in Burke, Virginia; published a book on writing techniques for hotel managers; writes poetry, fiction, and nonfiction for children.

Levine, David: Freelance writer based in New York City specializing in gay, lesbian, and medical topics.

Levine, Kathie: Attorney and freelance writer; contributing editor for *California Employer Advisor;* contributor to *San Francisco Business Times* and *Marin Independent Journal.*

Lewis, Scott M: Freelance writer and editor; contributing editor, *Option;* staff editor, *Security, Distributing and Marketing,* 1989-90.

MacFarlane, K. Thomas: Freelance writer.

Malkin, Shula: Freelance writer.

Mandeville, Gertrude: Freelance writer.

Marshall, Mary: Publications editor for a trade association in Fairfax, Virginia; has worked in publishing, researching, writing, and editing for more than 10 years; former project editor at *Congressional Quarterly* in Washington, DC.

Maschinot, Michael: Freelance writer.

Mason, Todd: Manager of Information Systems at Michigan Credit Union League and freelance writer/computer consultant.

Maxfield, Doris: Freelance editor, writer, and owner of Max's Word Services, an editorial services business based in Linden, Michigan; has contributed to numerous reference publications in diverse fields and has extensive experience editing grant proposals.

McDonald, Avril: Freelance writer.

McInerney, Merry: Freelance writer.

McKelvey, Paul S: Principal, McKelvey & Associates, Slidell, Louisiana; extensive writing on international commerce, inland waterways and ports, and shipbuilding; member of New Orleans Press Club, International Association of Business Communicators, Public Relations Society of America, and Society for Technical Communication.

McNulty, Mary: Freelance writer and editor based in Chicago, Illinois; regular Gale contributor since 1988 whose work has also appeared in the *Chicago Tribune.*

Meyer, Bruce: Senior Editor for *Rubber & Plastics News,* Akron, Ohio.

Milite, George A: Philadelphia-based independent writer and editor specializing in business management issues; longtime contributing editor with the American Management Association; past president of the Editorial Freelancers Association.

Mogelonsky, Marcia: Freelance writer.

Mogul, Jonathan: Freelance writer based in Washington DC; Ph.D. in history from the University of Michigan, Ann Arbor.

Moncada, Patricia: Freelance editor based in Burke, Virginia; M.A. in English and American Literature from Southern Illinois University at Edwardsville.

Mote, Dave: Freelance writer and editor based in Indianapolis, Indiana; president of information retrieval company Performance Database.

Mote, Michelle: Freelance writer and professional educator.

Motta, Paolo: Freelance writer.

Mumma, Lisa: Freelance writer based in Raleigh, North Carolina; experienced in corporate communications and public relations.

Nash, Margo: Freelance writer.

Neilson, Susan: Business reference librarian at the Charleston County Library, Charleston, South Carolina.

Nelson, Roxanne: Freelance writer based in San Francisco, California; regular contributor to *Living Healthy;* currently writing a book on sleep disorders.

Neubauer, Joan R: Owner, Word Wright International, Houston, Texas; public speaker, teacher, author of *Tell Them Like it Really Was: The Five Step Method to Writing Your Story,* and publisher of *The Last Word.*

Norman, Bill: Former newspaper reporter and editor based in northern Illinois.

O'Donnell, Sondra E: University of Michigan graduate; translates from the Spanish language and freelance writes from her home in Ann Arbor, Michigan.

Oleck, Joan: Freelance writer in Brooklyn, New York; contributor to *New York Times, New Woman, Washington Journalism Review,* and business publications.

Opdycke, Betty: Freelance writer.

Ossip, Kathleen: Freelance writer.

Paulson, Linda: Graduate of Columbia University Graduate School of Journalism, New York, New York; currently a contributor for numerous regional and national publications on a variety of topics.

Peck, Matthew C: M.A., Wayne State University, Detroit, Michigan; faculty member at the University of North Alabama, Florence.

Pederson, Jay P: Freelance writer and editor.

Pendergast, Sara: Freelance writer and copyeditor.

Pendergast, Tom: Freelance writer and editor; graduate student in American studies, Purdue University, West Lafayette, Indiana.

Pennie, Ariel: Freelance writer.

Pennington-Boyce, Amy: Consultant, researcher, and freelance business writer based in Ypsilanti, Michigan; provides services to profit and nonprofit organizations and to individuals regarding commercial and philanthropic development in the former Soviet Union, international business, healthcare, and public relations.

Pitts, Lee: Executive editor, *Livestock Market Digest;* author of several books and a syndicated humor column.

Plamondon, Scott: Freelance writer.

Poss, Andrew: Freelance writer based in Buffalo, New York; Ph.D. in chemistry from the University of Rochester, New York.

Powell, Tami L: Freelance writer based in La Crescent, Minnesota; specializing in technical writing and editing, including computer software manuals.

Przybylo, Christine: Freelance writer and researcher based in Dearborn, Michigan.

Quagliana, Catherine A: Freelance writer and editor based in Austin, Texas.

Ratcliffe, Mary: Freelance writer and editor; author of brochures, newsletters, press releases, and advertising copy.

Rhodes, Scott: Freelance writer and funeral director based in Burlington, North Carolina.

Risland, Susan: Writer whose work experience has appeared in *Ferguson's Guide to Apprenticeship Programs, Exploring Tech Careers,* and other publications; is an associate editor for the *Missouri River Basin,* and was once co-owner and editor of an equine magazine.

Rooks, Alan: Freelance writer.

Ross-Flanigan, Nancy: Freelance writer based in Belleville, Michigan; has written for *Technology Review, The Dallas Morning News, The Harley-Davidson Enthusiast,* and other national publications; former science writer for the *Detroit Free Press.*

Rothman, Howard: Book author, magazine writer, and Web content provider based in Colorado; books include *RX Inc.: The Small Business Handbook for Building a Healthier Workforce, Companies with a Conscience: Intimate Portraits of Twelve Firms That Make a Difference,* and *All That Once Was Good: Inside America's National Pastime.*

Roy, Soumya: Freelance writer; MBA candidate, Temple University, Philadelphia, Pennsylvania.

Salamie, Dave: Co-owner of InfoWorks Development Group, a reference publication development and editorial services company; contributor to such reference works as *International Directory of Company Histories* and *International Dictionary of Films and Filmmakers.*

Saporito, Kathy: Freelance writer based in Warren, Michigan, specializing in technical writing and corporate communications; has more than 12 years of experience in the communications field and has written for various forms of media including reference materials, user manuals, newsletters, newspapers, videos, and online help.

Sarich, John A: Freelance writer and editor; graduate student in economics, New School for Social Research, New York, New York.

Schneider, Bob: Freelance writer and Japanese translator; CPA, MBA, and New York Stock Exchange supervisory analyst.

Scott, Paula Pyzik: Freelance writer and video producer based in Ada, Ohio; contributed to numerous reference publications including *Contemporary Authors, Native American Tribes,* and *Newsmakers.*

Seablom, Kathy: Freelance writer.

Sharp, Arthur G: Business faculty member of Naugatuck Valley Community/Technical College, Waterbury, Connecticut.

Sharp, Kim: Freelance writer and information developer based in Houston, Texas; academic medical librarian with a graduate degree in library and information science; has published book reviews, articles, and presented papers in the area of medical library science.

Sheil, Richard: Freelance writer, MBA candidate, University of Wisconsin—Madison.

Sheldon, AnnaMarie: Freelance writer.

Shelton, Sonya: Freelance writer and editor based in Seattle, Washington; former editor of *RadioActive, Screamer,* and *Image* magazines; has written for various consumer and business magazines, corporate marketing, and reference books for more than 12 years.

Shepherd, Kenneth R: Freelance writer based in Detroit, Michigan; history teacher at Henry Ford Community College, Dearborn.

Sheppard, Laurel: Freelance writer and owner of Lash Publications International, based in Hilliard, Ohio; has an engineering background and writes for a variety of trade and association publications including *SWE Magazine* (Society of Women Engineers), *Software Strategies, Refractories Applications, Photonics Spectra,* and *Ceramic Industry;* also contributes to Gale's *How Products Are Made* and *Notable Women Scientists.*

Sherman, Fran Shonfeld: Freelance writer and editor; former contributor to *Compton's Encyclopedia* and *Britannica Book of the Year;* has worked on the online version of *Compton's Interactive Encyclopedia.*

Shostak, Elizabeth: Freelance writer.

Shugg, Elizabeth P: Freelance writer and editor specializing in corporate communications literature and feature writing for magazines and newspapers; she writes for regional newspapers in North Carolina as well as national magazines such as *Coastal Living* and *Web-Guide.*

Slick, Scott: Freelance writer and attorney from Lakeville, Minnesota; practiced for four years as public defender in Minnesota's Third Judicial District; writes a monthly column for "Beyond the Bar;" frequent contributor to Gale Group publications.

Spencer, Dorothy: Freelance writer and editor.

Sprinkle, David: Freelance writer and editor.

Stanfel, Rebecca: Freelance writer living in Helena, Montana; her work has appeared in several other business-oriented texts, including the *Encyclopedia of Major Marketing Campaigns.*

Stanley, Jill: Freelance writer.

Stansell, Christina: Freelance writer and editor based in Farmington Hills, Michigan; experienced in business writing and online research.

Steward, Celeste: Reference librarian for Contra Costa County Library, Pinole, California; former news reporter and contributor to *What Do I Read Next* CD-ROM.

Stong, Jennifer: Freelance writer.

Straub, Deborah: Freelance writer and editor based near Grand Rapids, Michigan; has compiled several reference works published by Gale, including *Voices of Multicultural America* and *Contemporary Heroes and Heroines.*

Strohmer, Shaun: Freelance writer and editor based in Minneapolis, Minnesota; former instructor at the University of Michigan with a doctoral degree in English; author of numerous essays and articles on literature, theatre, music, education, biography, business, and science.

Sturzenacker, Gloria: Freelance writer and editor based in New York, New York; former editor of the New York City Fire Department training magazine and local government reporter in public radio; editor of a variety of consumer and trade magazines.

Summers, Shannon: Freelance writer.

Sunder, Aaron: Freelance writer; MBA, University of Michigan, Ann Arbor.

Swartz, Mark: Manuscript editor for the journals division of the University of Chicago Press.

Theodoroff, Mike: Freelance writer.

Thor, Angela: Information specialist based in Syracuse, New York; indexed *Higher & Higher* magazine and several historical books.

Thuermer, Karen: Editor and writer on international topics for 16 years; former editor of *Global Trade Magazine;* currently contributes to *International Business, Journal of Commerce,* and *World Trade* among others; masters degree in journalism form Pennsylvania State University, Hershey, Pennsylvania.

Tilak, Visi: Freelance writer based in Detroit, Michigan.

Trimarco, Paola: Freelance business and health writer based in Washington, DC; Ph.D., University of Edinburgh, Scotland.

Untener, Deborah J: Freelance writer and editor based in Broomfield, Colorado; eight years of experience with reference products, including directories, encyclopedias, and essay collections.

Urbiel, Martha: Librarian based in Hillsdale, New Jersey; regular contributor to Gale Group publications including *Children's Book Review Index.*

Vecchiolla, Richard R: Freelance writer and researcher focusing on shareholders rights and total quality management issues; J.D. candidate, Georgetown University, Washington, DC.

Viswanathan, Shoba: Freelance writer and editor currently working as a senior editor in an electronic publishing company based in the San Francisco Bay area, California.

Von Heitman, Khatanga: Freelance writer.

Vyn, Kathleen: Freelance writer based in Chicago, Illinois; M.A. in creative writing from San Francisco State University, California; has written two nonfiction books and had articles published in the *Chicago Tribune,* the *San Francisco Examiner, American Health, Omni,* and other publications.

Waters, John K: Freelance writer and editor based in California; author of *Silicon Valley: Inventing the Future* and *The Bay Area: California Gateway to the Future;* contributor to *San Jose Magazine, South Bay Accent,* and *The Silicon Valley Insider.*

Wagner, Katherine: Freelance writer and editor based in Chicago, Illinois; correspondent for a variety of general-interest and business publications and has edited catalogs, brochures, and travel guides.

Weaver, Danialle: Professional business and technology writer in Port Orange, Florida; has covered the energy and electricity industries since 1986 for publications such as *The Electric Daily, The Energy Daily,* and *Warfield's Business & Technology.*

Weber, Nathan: Freelance writer.

Weisman, Charlotte: Freelance writer and editor located in Wayne, Pennsylvania; has worked on various publications in Miami and Philadelphia.

Wellner, Margot: Freelance writer.

Westbrook, M. David: Freelance writer.

Wilson, Valerie: Freelance writer.

Wingett, Jeffery T: Freelance writer; MBA from California Polytechnic State University, San Luis Obispo.

Winters, Elaine: Award winning writer whose work has appeared in print and online; currently based in Berkeley, California; has also worked in Asia and the South Pacific.

Withem, Karen: Freelance writer.

Wolf, Gillian: Freelance writer based in Evanston, Illinois; ten years of experience in history, corporate history, and biography.

Wolfe, Joanne: Freelance writer, editor, and desktop publishing service provider based in Springfield, Oregon.

Woodward, Angela: Freelance writer.

Woodward, Nancy Hatch: Freelance writer based in Chattanooga, Tennessee; contributes regularly to several business- and health-oriented publications.

Yocca, Beth: Freelance writer.

York, Leslee: Freelance writer.

Yu, Simone: Assistant Bibliographer and Research Librarian at the Graduate School of Business, Stanford University.

Zrinsky, Christine M: Freelance writer and editor; director of individual gifts, Chicago Symphony Orchestra.

NAICS to SIC Conversion Guide

The following guide cross-references six-digit 1997 North American Industry Classification System (NAICS) codes with four-digit 1987 Standard Industrial Classification (SIC) codes. Because the systems differ in specificity, some NAICS categories correspond to more than one SIC category. Please refer to the **Introduction** *under "About Industry Classification" for more information.*

Agriculture, Forestry, Fishing, & Hunting

111110 Soybean Farming *see* SIC 0116: Soybeans

111120 Oilseed (except Soybean) Farming *see* SIC 0119: Cash Grains, NEC

111130 Dry Pea and Bean Farming *see* SIC 0119: Cash Grains, NEC

111140 Wheat Farming *see* SIC 0111: Wheat

111150 Corn Farming *see* SIC 0115: Corn

111150 Corn Farming *see* SIC 0119: Cash Grains, NEC

111160 Rice Farming *see* SIC 0112: Rice

111191 Oilseed and Grain Combination Farming *see* SIC 0119: Cash Grains, NEC

111199 All Other Grain Farming *see* SIC 0119: Cash Grains, NEC

111211 Potato Farming *see* SIC 0134: Irish Potatoes

111219 Other Vegetable (except Potato) and Melon Farming *see* SIC 0139: Field Crops, Except Cash Grains, NEC; SIC 0161: Vegetables and Melons

111310 Orange Groves *see* SIC 0174: Citrus Fruits

111320 Citrus (except Orange) Groves *see* SIC 0174: Citrus Fruits

111331 Apple Orchards *see* SIC 0175: Deciduous Tree Fruits

111332 Grape Vineyards *see* SIC 0172: Grapes

111333 Strawberry Farming *see* SIC 0171: Berry Crops

111334 Berry (except Strawberry) Farming *see* SIC 0171: Berry Crops

111335 Tree Nut Farming *see* SIC 0173: Tree Nuts

111336 Fruit and Tree Nut Combination Farming *see* SIC 0179: Fruits and Tree Nuts, NEC

111339 Other Noncitrus Fruit Farming *see* SIC 0175: Deciduous Tree Fruits; SIC 0179: Fruits and Tree Nuts, NEC

111411 Mushroom Production *see* SIC 0182: Food Crops Grown Under Cover

111419 Other Food Crops Grown Under Cover *see* SIC 0182: Food Crops Grown Under Cover

111421 Nursery and Tree Production *see* SIC 0181: Ornamental Floriculture and Nursery Products; SIC 0811: Timber Tracts

111422 Floriculture Production *see* SIC 0181: Ornamental Floriculture and Nursery Products

111910 Tobacco Farming *see* SIC 0132: Tobacco

111920 Cotton farming *see* SIC 0131: Cotton

111930 Sugarcane Farming *see* SIC 0133: Sugarcane and Sugar Beets

111940 Hay Farming *see* SIC 0139: Field Crops, Except Cash Grains, NEC

111991 Sugar Beet Farming *see* SIC 0133: Sugarcane and Sugar Beets

111992 Peanut Farming *see* SIC 0139: Field Crops, Except Cash Grains, NEC

111998 All Other Miscellaneous Crop Farming *see* SIC 0139: Field Crops, Except Cash Grains, NEC; SIC 0191: General Farms, Primarily Crop; SIC 0831: Forest Nurseries and Gathering of Forest Products; SIC 0919: Miscellaneous Marine Products; SIC 2099: Food Preparations, NEC

112111 Beef Cattle Ranching and Farming *see* SIC 0212: Beef Cattle, Except Feedlots; SIC 0241: Dairy Farms

112112 Cattle Feedlots *see* SIC 0211: Beef Cattle Feedlots

112120 Dairy Cattle and Milk Production *see* SIC 0241: Dairy Farms

112210 Hog and Pig Farming *see* SIC 0213: Hogs

112310 Chicken Egg Production *see* SIC 0252: Chicken Eggs

112320 Broilers and Other Meat-Type Chicken Production *see* SIC 0251: Broiler, Fryers, and Roaster Chickens

112330 Turkey Production *see* SIC 0253: Turkey and Turkey Eggs

112340 Poultry Hatcheries *see* SIC 0254: Poultry Hatcheries

112390 Other Poultry Production *see* SIC 0259: Poultry and Eggs, NEC

112410 Sheep Farming *see* SIC 0214: Sheep and Goats

112420 Goat Farming *see* SIC 0214: Sheep and Goats

112511 Finfish Farming and Fish Hatcheries *see* SIC 0273: Animal Aquaculture; SIC 0921: Fish Hatcheries and Preserves

112512 Shellfish Farming *see* SIC 0273: Animal Aquaculture; SIC 0921: Fish Hatcheries and Preserves

112519 Other Animal Aquaculture *see* SIC 0273: Animal Aquaculture

112910 Apiculture *see* SIC 0279: Animal Specialties, NEC

112920 Horse and Other Equine Production *see* SIC 0272: Horses and Other Equines

112930 Fur-bearing Animal and Rabbit Production *see* SIC 0271: Fur-Bearing Animals and Rabbits

112990 All Other Animal Production *see* SIC 0219: General Livestock, Except Dairy and Poultry; SIC 0279: Animal Specialties, NEC; SIC 0291: General Farms, Primarily Livestock and Animal Specialties

113110 Timber Tract Operations *see* SIC 0811: Timber Tracts

113210 Forest Nurseries and Gathering of Forest Products *see* SIC 0831: Forest Nurseries and Gathering of Forest Products

113310 Logging *see* SIC 2411: Logging

114111 Finfish Fishing *see* SIC 0912: Finfish

114112 Shellfish Fishing *see* SIC 0913: Shellfish

114119 Other Marine Fishing *see* SIC 0919: Miscellaneous Marine Products

114210 Hunting and Trapping *see* SIC 0971: Hunting, Trapping, and Game Propagation

115111 Cotton Ginning *see* SIC 0724: Cotton Ginning

115112 Soil Preparation, Planting and Cultivating *see* SIC 0711: Soil Preparation Services; SIC 0721: Crop Planting, Cultivating and Protecting

115113 Crop Harvesting, Primarily By Machine *see* SIC 0722: Crop Harvesting, Primarily by Machine

115114 Postharvest Crop Activities (except Cotton Ginning) *see* SIC 0723: Crop Preparation Services For Market, except Cotton Ginning

115115 Farm Labor Contractors and Crew Leaders *see* SIC 0761: Farm Labor Contractors and Crew Leaders

115116 Farm Management Services *see* SIC 0762: Farm Management Services

115210 Support Activities for Animal Production *see* SIC 0751: Livestock Services, Except Veterinary; SIC 0752: Animal Specialty Services, Except Veterinary; SIC 7699: Repair Shops and Related Services, NEC

115310 Support Activities for Forestry *see* SIC 0851: Forestry Services

MINING

211111 Crude Petroleum and Natural Gas Extraction *see* SIC 1311: Crude Petroleum and Natural Gas

211112 Natural Gas Liquid Extraction *see* SIC 1321: Natural Gas Liquids

212111 Bituminous Coal and Lignite Surface Mining *see* SIC 1221: Bituminous Coal and Lignite Surface Mining

212112 Bituminous Coal Underground Mining *see* SIC 1222: Bituminous Coal Underground Mining

212113 Anthracite Mining *see* SIC 1231: Anthracite Mining

212210 Iron Ore Mining *see* SIC 1011: Iron Ores

212221 Gold Ore Mining *see* SIC 1041: Gold Ores

212222 Silver Ore Mining *see* SIC 1044: Silver Ores

212231 Lead Ore and Zinc Ore Mining *see* SIC 1031: Lead and Zinc Ores

212234 Copper Ore and Nickel Ore Mining *see* SIC 1021: Copper Ores; SIC 1061: Ferroalloy Ores, Except Vanadium

212291 Uranium-Radium-Vanadium Ore Mining *see* SIC 1094: Uranium-Radium-Vanadium Ores

212299 Other Metal Ore Mining *see* SIC 1061: Ferroalloy Ores, Except Vanadium; SIC 1099: Miscellaneous Metal Ores, NEC

212311 Dimension Stone Mining and Quarry *see* SIC 1411: Dimension Stone

212312 Crushed and Broken Limestone Mining and Quarrying *see* SIC 1422: Crushed and Broken Limestone

212313 Crushed and Broken Granite Mining and Quarrying *see* SIC 1423: Crushed and Broken Granite

212319 Other Crushed and Broken Stone Mining and Quarrying *see* SIC 1429: Crushed and Broken Stone, NEC; SIC 1499: Miscellaneous Nonmetallic Minerals, Except Fuels

212321 Construction Sand and Gravel Mining *see* SIC 1442: Construction Sand and Gravel

212322 Industrial Sand Mining *see* SIC 1446: Industrial Sand

212324 Kaolin and Ball Clay Mining *see* SIC 1455: Kaolin and Ball Clay

212325 Clay and Ceramic and Refractory Minerals Mining *see* SIC 1459: Clay, Ceramic, and Refractory Minerals, NEC

212391 Potash, Soda, and Borate Mineral Mining *see* SIC 1474: Potash, Soda, and Borate Minerals

212392 Phosphate Rock Mining *see* SIC 1475: Phosphate Rock

212393 Other Chemical and Fertilizer Mineral Mining *see* SIC 1479: Chemical and Fertilizer Mineral Mining, NEC

212399 All Other Non-Metallic Mineral Mining *see* SIC 1499: Miscellaneous Nonmetallic Minerals, Except Fuels

213111 Drilling Oil and Gas Wells *see* SIC 1381: Drilling Oil and Gas Wells

213112 Support Activities for Oil and Gas Field Exploration *see* SIC 1382: Oil and Gas Field Exploration Services; SIC 1389: Oil and Gas Field Services, NEC

213113 Support Activities for Coal Mining *see* SIC 1241: Coal Mining Services

213114 Support Activities for Metal Mining *see* SIC 1081: Metal Mining Services

213115 Support Activities for Non-metallic Minerals, (except Fuels) *see* SIC 1481: Nonmetallic Minerals Services Except Fuels

UTILITIES

221111 Hydroelectric Power Generation *see* SIC 4911: Electric Services; SIC 4931: Electric and Other Services Combined; SIC 4939: Combination Utilities, NEC

221112 Fossil Fuel Electric Power Generation *see* SIC 4911: Electric Services; SIC 4931: Electric and Other Services Combined; SIC 4939: Combination Utilities, NEC

221113 Nuclear Electric Power Generation *see* SIC 4911: Electric Services; SIC 4931: Electric and Other Services Combined; SIC 4939: Combination Utilities, NEC

221119 Other Electric Power Generation *see* SIC 4911: Electric Services; SIC 4931: Electric and Other Services Combined; SIC 4939: Combination Utilities, NEC

221121 Electric Bulk Power Transmission and Control *see* SIC 4911: Electric Services; SIC 4931: Electric and Other Services Combined; SIC 4939: Combination Utilities, NEC

221122 Electric Power Distribution *see* SIC 4911: Electric Services; SIC 4931: Electric and Other Services Combined; SIC 4939: Combination Utilities, NEC

221210 Natural Gas Distribution *see* SIC 4923: Natural Gas Transmission and Distribution; SIC 4924: Natural Gas Distribution; SIC 4925: Mixed, Manufactured, or Liquefied Petroleum Gas Production and/or Distribution; SIC 4931: Electric and Other Services Combined; SIC 4932: Gas and Other Services Combined; SIC 4939: Combination Utilities, NEC

221310 Water Supply and Irrigation Systems *see* SIC 4941: Water Supply; SIC 4971: Irrigation Systems

221320 Sewage Treatment Facilities *see* SIC 4952: Sewerage Systems

221330 Steam and Air-Conditioning Supply *see* SIC 4961: Steam and Air-Conditioning Supply

CONSTRUCTION

233110 Land Subdivision and Land Development *see* SIC 6552: Land Subdividers and Developers, Except Cemeteries; SIC 1521: General Contractors-Single-Family Houses; SIC 1531: Operative Builders

233220 Multi-Family Housing Construction *see* SIC 1522: General Contractors-Residential Buildings, Other Than Single-Family; SIC 1531: Operative Builders

233310 Manufacturing and Light Industrial Building Construction *see* SIC 1531: Operative Builders; SIC 1541: General Contractors-Industrial Buildings and Warehouses

233320 Commercial and Institutional Building Construction *see* SIC 1522: General Contractors-Residential Buildings, Other Than Single-Family; SIC 1531: Operative Builders; SIC 1541: General Contractors-Industrial Buildings and Warehouses; SIC 1542: General Contractors-Nonresidential Buildings, Other than Industrial Buildings and Warehouses

234110 Highway and Street Construction *see* SIC 1611: Highway and Street Construction, Except Elevated Highways

234120 Bridge and Tunnel Construction *see* SIC 1622: Bridge, Tunnel, and Elevated Highway Construction

234910 Water, Sewer and Pipeline Construction *see* SIC 1623: Water, Sewer, Pipeline, and Communications and Power Line Construction

234920 Power and Communication Transmission Line Construction *see* SIC 1623: Water, Sewer, Pipeline, and Communications and Power Line Construction

234930 Industrial Nonbuilding Structure Construction *see* SIC 1629: Heavy Construction, NEC

234990 All Other Heavy Construction *see* SIC 1629: Heavy Construction, NEC; SIC 7353: Heavy Construction Equipment Rental and Leasing

235110 Plumbing, Heating and Air-Conditioning Contractors *see* SIC 1711: Plumbing, Heating, and Air-Conditioning

235210 Painting and Wall Covering Contractors *see* SIC 1721: Painting and Paper Hanging; SIC 1799: Special Trade Contractors, NEC

235310 Electrical Contractors *see* SIC 1731: Electrical Work

235410 Masonry and Stone Contractors *see* SIC 1741: Masonry, Stone Setting and Other Stone Work

235420 Drywall, Plastering, Acoustical, and Insulation Contractors *see* SIC 1742: Plastering, Drywall, Acoustical and Insulation Work; SIC 1743: Terrazzo, Tile, Marble, and Mosaic Work; SIC 1771: Concrete Work

235430 Tile, Marble, Terrazzo and Mosaic Contractors *see* SIC 1743: Terrazzo, Tile, Marble, and Mosaic Work

235510 Carpentry Contractors *see* SIC 1751: Carpentry Work

235520 Floor Laying and Other Floor Contractors *see* SIC 1752: Floor Laying and Other Floor Work, NEC

235610 Roofing, Siding, and Sheet Metal Contractors *see* SIC 1761: Roofing, Siding, and Sheet Metal Work

235710 Concrete Contractors *see* SIC 1771: Concrete Work

235810 Water Well Drilling Contractors *see* SIC 1781: Water Well Drilling

235910 Structural Steel Erection Contractors *see* SIC 1791: Structural Steel Erection

235920 Glass and Glazing Contractors *see* SIC 1793: Glass and Glazing Work; SIC 1799: Special Trade Contractors, NEC

235930 Excavation Contractors *see* SIC 1794: Excavation Work

235940 Wrecking and Demolition Contractors *see* SIC 1795: Wrecking and Demolition Work

235950 Building Equipment and Other Machinery Installation Contractors *see* SIC 1796: Installation or Erection of Building Equipment, NEC

235990 All Other Special Trade Contractors *see* SIC 1799: Special Trade Contractors, NEC

FOOD MANUFACTURING

311111 Dog and Cat Food Manufacturing *see* SIC 2047: Dog and Cat Food

311119 Other Animal Food Manufacturing *see* SIC 2048: Prepared Feed and Feed Ingredients for Animals and Fowls, Except Dogs and Cats

311211 Flour Milling *see* SIC 2034: Dried and Dehydrated Fruits, Vegetables, and Soup Mixes; SIC 2041: Flour and Other Grain Mill Products

311212 Rice Milling *see* SIC 2044: Rice Milling

311213 Malt Manufacturing *see* SIC 2083: Malt

311221 Wet Corn Milling *see* SIC 2046: Wet Corn Milling

311222 Soybean Processing *see* SIC 2075: Soybean Oil Mills; SIC 2079: Shortening, Table Oils, Margarine, and Other Edible Fats and Oils, NEC

311223 Other Oilseed Processing *see* SIC 2074: Cottonseed Oil Mills; SIC 2076: Vegetable Oil Mills, Except Corn, Cottonseed, and Soybeans; SIC 2079: Shortening, Table Oils, Margarine, and Other Edible Fats and Oils, NEC

311225 Fats and Oils Refining and Blending *see* SIC 2074: Cottonseed Oil Mills; SIC 2075: Soybean Oil Mills; SIC 2076: Vegetable Oil Mills, Except Corn, Cottonseed, and Soybeans; SIC 2077: Animal and Marine Fats and Oils; SIC 2079: Shortening, Table Oils, Margarine, and Other Edible Fats and Oils, NEC

311230 Breakfast Cereal Manufacturing *see* SIC 2043: Cereal Breakfast Foods

311311 Sugarcane Mills *see* SIC 2061: Cane Sugar, Except Refining

311312 Cane Sugar Refining *see* SIC 2062: Cane Sugar Refining

311313 Beet Sugar Manufacturing *see* SIC 2063: Beet Sugar

311320 Chocolate and Confectionery Manufacturing from Cacao Beans *see* SIC 2066: Chocolate and Cocoa Products

311330 Confectionery Manufacturing from Purchased Chocolate *see* SIC 2064: Candy and Other Confectionery Products

311340 Non-Chocolate Confectionery Manufacturing *see* SIC 2064: Candy and Other Confectionery Products; SIC 2067: Chewing Gum; SIC 2099: Food Preparations, NEC

311411 Frozen Fruit, Juice, and Vegetable Processing *see* SIC 2037: Frozen Fruits, Fruit Juices, and Vegetables

311412 Frozen Specialty Food Manufacturing *see* SIC 2038: Frozen Specialties, NEC

311421 Fruit and Vegetable Canning *see* SIC 2033: Canned Fruits, Vegetables, Preserves, Jams, and Jellies; SIC 2035: Pickled Fruits and Vegetables, Vegetables Sauces and Seasonings, and Salad Dressings

311422 Specialty Canning *see* SIC 2032: Canned Specialties

311423 Dried and Dehydrated Food Manufacturing *see* SIC 2034: Dried and Dehydrated Fruits, Vegetables, and Soup Mixes; SIC 2099: Food Preparations, NEC

311511 Fluid Milk Manufacturing *see* SIC 2026: Fluid Milk

311512 Creamery Butter Manufacturing *see* SIC 2021: Creamery Butter

311513 Cheese Manufacturing *see* SIC 2022: Natural, Processed, and Imitation Cheese

311514 Dry, Condensed, and Evaporated Dairy Product Manufacturing *see* SIC 2023: Dry, Condensed, and Evaporated Dairy Products

311520 Ice Cream and Frozen Dessert Manufacturing *see* SIC 2024: Ice Cream and Frozen Desserts

311611 Animal (except Poultry) Slaughtering *see* SIC 0751: Livestock Services, Except Veterinary; SIC 2011: Meat Packing Plants; SIC 2048: Prepared Feed and Feed Ingredients for Animals and Fowls, Except Dogs and Cats

311612 Meat Processed From Carcasses *see* SIC 2013: Sausages and Other Prepared Meats; SIC 5147: Meats and Meat Products

311613 Rendering and Meat By-product Processing *see* SIC 2077: Animal and Marine Fats and Oils

311615 Poultry Processing *see* SIC 2015: Poultry Slaughtering and Processing

311711 Seafood Canning *see* SIC 2077: Animal and Marine Fats and Oils; SIC 2091: Canned and Cured Fish and Seafood

311712 Fresh and Frozen Seafood Processing *see* SIC 2077: Animal and Marine Fats and Oils; SIC 2092: Prepared Fresh or Frozen Fish and Seafoods

311811 Retail Bakeries *see* SIC 5461: Retail Bakeries

311812 Commercial Bakeries *see* SIC 2051: Bread and Other Bakery Products, Except Cookies and Crackers; SIC 2052: Cookies and Crackers

311813 Frozen Bakery Product Manufacturing *see* SIC 2053: Frozen Bakery Products, Except Bread

311821 Cookie and Cracker Manufacturing *see* SIC 2052: Cookies and Crackers

311822 Flour Mixes and Dough Manufacturing from Purchased Flour *see* SIC 2045: Prepared Flour Mixes and Doughs

311823 Pasta Manufacturing *see* SIC 2098: Macaroni, Spaghetti, Vermicelli, and Noodles

311830 Tortilla Manufacturing *see* SIC 2099: Food Preparations, NEC

311911 Roasted Nuts and Peanut Butter Manufacturing *see* SIC 2068: Salted and Roasted Nuts and Seeds; SIC 2099: Food Preparations, NEC

311919 Other Snack Food Manufacturing *see* SIC 2052: Cookies and Crackers; SIC 2096: Potato Chips, Corn Chips, and Similar Snacks

311920 Coffee and Tea Manufacturing *see* SIC 2043: Cereal Breakfast Foods; SIC 2095: Roasted Coffee; SIC 2099: Food Preparations, NEC

311930 Flavoring Syrup and Concentrate Manufacturing *see* SIC 2087: Flavoring Extracts and Flavoring Syrups NEC

311941 Mayonnaise, Dressing, and Other Prepared Sauce Manufacturing *see* SIC 2035: Pickled Fruits and Vegetables, Vegetables Sauces and Seasonings, and Salad Dressings; SIC 2099: Food Preparations, NEC

311942 Spice and Extract Manufacturing *see* SIC 2087: Flavoring Extracts and Flavoring Syrups NEC; SIC 2095: Roasted Coffee; SIC 2099: Food Preparations, NEC; SIC 2899: Chemicals and Chemical Preparations, NEC

311991 Perishable Prepared Food Manufacturing *see* SIC 2099: Food Preparations, NEC

311999 All Other Miscellaneous Food Manufacturing *see* SIC 2015: Poultry Slaughtering and Processing; SIC 2032: Canned Specialties; SIC 2087: Flavoring Extracts and Flavoring Syrups NEC; SIC 2099: Food Preparations, NEC

Beverage & Tobacco Product Manufacturing

312111 Soft Drink Manufacturing *see* SIC 2086: Bottled and Canned Soft Drinks and Carbonated Waters

312112 Bottled Water Manufacturing *see* SIC 2086: Bottled and Canned Soft Drinks and Carbonated Waters

312113 Ice Manufacturing *see* SIC 2097: Manufactured Ice

312120 Breweries *see* SIC 2082: Malt Beverages

312130 Wineries *see* SIC 2084: Wines, Brandy, and Brandy Spirits

312140 Distilleries *see* SIC 2085: Distilled and Blended Liquors

312210 Tobacco Stemming and Redrying *see* SIC 2141: Tobacco Stemming and Redrying

312221 Cigarette Manufacturing *see* SIC 2111: Cigarettes

312229 Other Tobacco Product Manufacturing *see* SIC 2121: Cigars; SIC 2131: Chewing and Smoking Tobacco and Snuff; SIC 2141: Tobacco Stemming and Redrying

Textile Mills

313111 Yarn Spinning Mills *see* SIC 2281: Yarn Spinning Mills; SIC 2299: Textile Goods, NEC

313112 Yarn Texturing, Throwing and Twisting Mills *see* SIC 2282: Yarn Texturizing, Throwing, Twisting, and Winding Mills

313113 Thread Mills *see* SIC 2284: Thread Mills; SIC 2299: Textile Goods, NEC

313210 Broadwoven Fabric Mills *see* SIC 2211: Broadwoven Fabric Mills, Cotton; SIC 2221: Broadwoven Fabric

Mills, Manmade Fiber and Silk; SIC 2231: Broadwoven Fabric Mills, Wool (Including Dyeing and Finishing); SIC 2299: Textile Goods, NEC

313221 Narrow Fabric Mills *see* SIC 2241: Narrow Fabric and Other Smallware Mills: Cotton, Wool, Silk, and Manmade Fiber; SIC 2299: Textile Goods, NEC

313222 Schiffli Machine Embroidery *see* SIC 2397: Schiffli Machine Embroideries

313230 Nonwoven Fabric Mills *see* SIC 2297: Nonwoven Fabrics; SIC 2299: Textile Goods, NEC

313241 Weft Knit Fabric Mills *see* SIC 2257: Weft Knit Fabric Mills; SIC 2259: Knitting Mills, NEC

313249 Other Knit Fabric and Lace Mills *see* SIC 2258: Lace and Warp Knit Fabric Mills; SIC 2259: Knitting Mills, NEC

313311 Broadwoven Fabric Finishing Mills *see* SIC 2231: Broadwoven Fabric Mills, Wool (Including Dyeing and Finishing); SIC 2261: Finishers of Broadwoven Fabrics of Cotton; SIC 2262: Finishers of Broadwoven Fabrics of Manmade Fiber and Silk; SIC 2269: Finishers of Textiles, NEC; SIC 5131: Piece Goods, Notions, and Other Dry Goods

313312 Textile and Fabric Finishing (except Broadwoven Fabric) Mills *see* SIC 2231: Broadwoven Fabric Mills, Wool (Including Dyeing and Finishing); SIC 2257: Weft Knit Fabric Mills; SIC 2258: Lace and Warp Knit Fabric Mills; SIC 2269: Finishers of Textiles, NEC; SIC 2282: Yarn Texturizing, Throwing, Twisting, and Winding Mills; SIC 2284: Thread Mills; SIC 2299: Textile Goods, NEC; SIC 5131: Piece Goods, Notions, and Other Dry Goods

313320 Fabric Coating Mills *see* SIC 2295: Coated Fabrics, Not Rubberized; SIC 3069: Fabricated Rubber Products, NEC

Textile Product Mills

314110 Carpet and Rug Mills *see* SIC 2273: Carpets and Rugs

314121 Curtain and Drapery Mills *see* SIC 2391: Curtains and Draperies; SIC 5714: Drapery, Curtain, and Upholstery Stores

314129 Other Household Textile Product Mills *see* SIC 2392: Housefurnishings, Except Curtains and Draperies

314911 Textile Bag Mills *see* SIC 2392: Housefurnishings, Except Curtains and Draperies; SIC 2393: Textile Bags

314912 Canvas and Related Product Mills *see* SIC 2394: Canvas and Related Products

314991 Rope, Cordage and Twine Mills *see* SIC 2298: Cordage and Twine

314992 Tire Cord and Tire Fabric Mills *see* SIC 2296: Tire Cord and Fabrics

314999 All Other Miscellaneous Textile Product Mills *see* SIC 2299: Textile Goods, NEC; SIC 2395: Pleating, Decorative and Novelty Stitching, and Tucking for the Trade; SIC 2396: Automotive Trimmings, Apparel Findings, and Related Products; SIC 2399: Fabricated Textile Products, NEC

Apparel Manufacturing

315111 Sheer Hosiery Mills *see* SIC 2251: Women's Full-Length and Knee-Length Hosiery, Except Socks; SIC 2252: Hosiery, NEC

315119 Other Hosiery and Sock Mills *see* SIC 2252: ,Hosiery, NEC

315191 Outerwear Knitting Mills *see* SIC 2253: Knit Outerwear Mills; SIC 2259: Knitting Mills, NEC

315192 Underwear and Nightwear Knitting Mills *see* SIC 2254: Knit Underwear and Nightwear Mills; SIC 2259: Knitting Mills, NEC

315211 Men's and Boys' Cut and Sew Apparel Contractors *see* SIC 2311: Men's and Boys' Suits, Coats and Overcoats; SIC 2321: Men's and Boys' Shirts, Except Work Shirts; SIC 2322: Men's and Boys' Underwear and Nightwear; SIC 2325: Men's and Boys' Trousers and Slacks; SIC 2326: Men's and Boys' Work Clothing; SIC 2329: Men's and Boys' Clothing, NEC; SIC 2341: Women's, Misses, Children's, and Infants' Underwear and Nightwear; SIC 2361: Girls', Children's and Infants' Dresses, Blouses and Shirts; SIC 2369: Girls', Children's and Infants' Outerwear, NEC; SIC 2384: Robes and Dressing Gowns; SIC 2385: Waterproof Outerwear; SIC 2389: Apparel and Accessories, NEC; SIC 2395: Pleating, Decorative and Novelty Stitching, and Tucking for the Trade

315212 Women's and Girls' Cut and Sew Apparel Contractors *see* SIC 2331: Women's, Misses', and Juniors' Blouses and Shirts; SIC 2335: Women's, Misses', and Junior's Dresses; SIC 2337: Women's, Misses', and Juniors' Suits, Skirts and Coats; SIC 2339: Women's, Misses', and Juniors' Outerwear, NEC; SIC 2341: Women's, Misses, Children's, and Infants' Underwear and Nightwear; SIC 2342: Brassieres, Girdles, and Allied Garments; SIC 2361: Girls', Children's, and Infants' Dresses, Blouses, and Shirts; SIC 2369: Girls', Children's, and Infants' Outerwear, NEC; SIC 2384: Robes and Dressing Gowns; SIC 2385: Waterproof Outerwear; SIC 2389: Apparel and Accessories, NEC; SIC 2395: Pleating, Decorative and Novelty Stitching, and Tucking for the Trade

315221 Men's and Boys' Cut and Sew Underwear and Nightwear Manufacturing *see* SIC 2322: Men's and Boys' Underwear and Nightwear; SIC 2341: Women's, Misses, Children's, and Infants' Underwear and Nightwear; SIC 2369: Girls', Children's and Infants' Outerwear, NEC; SIC 2384: Robes and Dressing Gowns

315222 Men's and Boys' Cut and Sew Suit, Coat, and Overcoat Manufacturing *see* SIC 2311: Men's and Boys' Suits, Coats and Overcoats; SIC 2369: Girls', Children's and Infants' Outerwear, NEC; SIC 2385: Waterproof Outerwear

315223 Men's and Boys' Cut and Sew Shirt, (except Work Shirt) Manufacturing *see* SIC 2321: Men's and Boys' Shirts, Except Work Shirts; SIC 2361: Girls', Children's and Infants' Dresses, Blouses and Shirts

315224 Men's and Boys' Cut And Sew Trouser, Slack, And Jean Manufacturing *see* SIC 2325: Men's and Boys' Trousers and Slacks; SIC 2369: Girls', Children's and Infants' Outerwear, NEC

315225 Men's and Boys' Cut and Sew Work Clothing Manufacturing *see* SIC 2326: Men's and Boys' Work Clothing

315228 Men's and Boys' Cut and Sew Other Outerwear Manufacturing *see* SIC 2329: Men's and Boys' Clothing, NEC; SIC 2369: Girls', Children's and Infants' Outerwear, NEC; SIC 2385: Waterproof Outerwear

315231 Women's and Girls' Cut and Sew Lingerie, Loungewear, and Nightwear Manufacturing *see* SIC

2341: Women's, Misses, Children's, and Infants' Underwear and Nightwear; SIC 2342: Brassieres, Girdles, and Allied Garments; SIC 2369: Girls', Children's and Infants' Outerwear, NEC; SIC 2384: Robes and Dressing Gowns; SIC 2389: Apparel and Accessories, NEC

315232 Women's and Girls' Cut and Sew Blouse and Shirt Manufacturing *see* SIC 2331: Women's, Misses', and Juniors' Blouses and Shirts; SIC 2361: Girls', Children's and Infants' Dresses, Blouses and Shirts

315233 Women's and Girls' Cut and Sew Dress Manufacturing *see* SIC 2335: Women's, Misses' and Junior's Dresses; SIC 2361: Girls', Children's and Infants' Dresses, Blouses and Shirts

315234 Women's and Girls' Cut and Sew Suit, Coat, Tailored Jacket, and Skirt Manufacturing *see* SIC 2337: Women's, Misses' and Juniors' Suits, Skirts and Coats; SIC 2369: Girls', Children's and Infants' Outerwear, NEC; SIC 2385: Waterproof Outerwear

315238 Women's and Girls' Cut and Sew Other Outerwear Manufacturing *see* SIC 2339: Women's, Misses' and Juniors' Outerwear, NEC; SIC 2369: Girls', Children's and Infants' Outerwear, NEC; SIC 2385: Waterproof Outerwear

315291 Infants' Cut and Sew Apparel Manufacturing *see* SIC 2341: Women's, Misses, Children's, and Infants' Underwear and Nightwear; SIC 2361: Girls', Children's and Infants' Dresses, Blouses and Shirts; SIC 2369: Girls', Children's and Infants' Outerwear, NEC; SIC 2385: Waterproof Outerwear

315292 Fur and Leather Apparel Manufacturing *see* SIC 2371: Fur Goods; SIC 2386: Leather and Sheep-Lined Clothing

315299 All Other Cut and Sew Apparel Manufacturing *see* SIC 2329: Men's and Boys' Clothing, NEC; SIC 2339: Women's, Misses' and Juniors' Outerwear, NEC; SIC 2389: Apparel and Accessories, NEC

315991 Hat, Cap, and Millinery Manufacturing *see* SIC 2353: Hats, Caps, and Millinery

315992 Glove and Mitten Manufacturing *see* SIC 2381: Dress and Work Gloves, Except Knit and All-Leather; SIC 3151: Leather Gloves and Mittens

315993 Men's and Boys' Neckwear Manufacturing *see* SIC 2323: Men's and Boys' Neckwear

315999 Other Apparel Accessories and Other Apparel Manufacturing *see* SIC 2339: Women's, Misses' and Juniors' Outerwear, NEC; SIC 2385: Waterproof Outerwear; SIC 2387: Apparel Belts; SIC 2389: Apparel and Accessories, NEC; SIC 2396: Automotive Trimmings, Apparel Findings, and Related Products; SIC 2399: Fabricated Textile Products, NEC

Leather & Allied Product Manufacturing

316110 Leather and Hide Tanning and Finishing *see* SIC 3111: Leather Tanning and Finishing; SIC 3999: Manufacturing Industries, NEC

316211 Rubber and Plastics Footwear Manufacturing *see* SIC 3021: Rubber and Plastics Footwear

316212 House Slipper Manufacturing *see* SIC 3142: House Slippers

316213 Men's Footwear (except Athletic) Manufacturing *see* SIC 3143: Men's Footwear, Except Athletic

316214 Women's Footwear (except Athletic) Manufacturing *see* SIC 3144: Women's Footwear, Except Athletic

316219 Other Footwear Manufacturing *see* SIC 3149: Footwear, Except Rubber, NEC

316991 Luggage Manufacturing *see* SIC 3161: Luggage

316992 Women's Handbag and Purse Manufacturing *see* SIC 3171: Women's Handbags and Purses

316993 Personal Leather Good (except Women's Handbag and Purse) Manufacturing *see* SIC 3172: Personal Leather Goods, Except Women's Handbags and Purses

316999 All Other Leather Good Manufacturing *see* SIC 3131: Boot and Shoe Cut Stock and Findings; SIC 3199: Leather Goods, NEC

Wood Product Manufacturing

321113 Sawmills *see* SIC 2421: Sawmills and Planing Mills, General; SIC 2429: Special Product Sawmills, NEC

321114 Wood Preservation *see* SIC 2491: Wood Preserving

321211 Hardwood Veneer and Plywood Manufacturing *see* SIC 2435: Hardwood Veneer and Plywood

321212 Softwood Veneer and Plywood Manufacturing *see* SIC 2436: Softwood Veneer and Plywood

321213 Engineered Wood Member (except Truss) Manufacturing *see* SIC 2439: Structural Wood Members, NEC

321214 Truss Manufacturing *see* SIC 2439: Structural Wood Members, NEC

321219 Reconstituted Wood Product Manufacturing *see* SIC 2493: Reconstituted Wood Products

321911 Wood Window and Door Manufacturing *see* SIC 2431: Millwork

321912 Cut Stock, Resawing Lumber, and Planing *see* SIC 2421: Sawmills and Planing Mills, General; SIC 2426: Hardwood Dimension and Flooring Mills; SIC 2429: Special Product Sawmills, NEC; SIC 2439: Structural Wood Members, NEC

321918 Other Millwork (including Flooring) *see* SIC 2421: Sawmills and Planing Mills, General; SIC 2426: Hardwood Dimension and Flooring Mills; SIC 2431: Millwork

321920 Wood Container and Pallet Manufacturing *see* SIC 2441: Nailed and Lock Corner Wood Boxes and Shook; SIC 2448: Wood Pallets and Skids; SIC 2449: Wood Containers, NEC; SIC 2499: Wood Products, NEC

321991 Manufactured Home (Mobile Home) Manufacturing *see* SIC 2451: Mobile Homes

321992 Prefabricated Wood Building Manufacturing *see* SIC 2452: Prefabricated Wood Buildings and Components

321999 All Other Miscellaneous Wood Product Manufacturing *see* SIC 2421: Sawmills and Planing Mills, General; SIC 2426: Hardwood Dimension and Flooring Mills; SIC 2429: Special Product Sawmills, NEC; SIC 2499: Wood Products, NEC; SIC 3131: Boot and Shoe Cut Stock and Findings; SIC 3999: Manufacturing Industries, NEC

Paper Manufacturing

322110 Pulp Mills *see* SIC 2611: Pulp Mills

322121 Paper (except Newsprint) Mills *see* SIC 2611: Pulp Mills

322121 Paper (except Newsprint) Mills *see* SIC 2621: Paper Mills

322122 Newsprint Mills *see* SIC 2621: Paper Mills

322130 Paperboard Mills *see* SIC 2611: Pulp Mills

322130 Paperboard Mills *see* SIC 2631: Paperboard Mills

322211 Corrugated and Solid Fiber Box Manufacturing *see* SIC 2653: Corrugated and Solid Fiber Boxes

322212 Folding Paperboard Box Manufacturing *see* SIC 2657: Folding Paperboard Boxes, Including Sanitary

322213 Setup Paperboard Box Manufacturing *see* SIC 2652: Setup Paperboard Boxes

322214 Fiber Can, Tube, Drum, and Similar Products Manufacturing *see* SIC 2655: Fiber Cans, Tubes, Drums, and Similar Products

322215 Non-Folding Sanitary Food Container Manufacturing *see* SIC 2656: Sanitary Food Containers, Except Folding; SIC 2679: Converted Paper and Paperboard Products, NEC

322221 Coated and Laminated Packaging Paper and Plastics Film Manufacturing *see* SIC 2671: Packaging Paper and Plastics Film, Coated and Laminated

322222 Coated and Laminated Paper Manufacturing *see* SIC 2672: Coated and Laminated Paper, NEC; SIC 2679: Converted Paper and Paperboard Products, NEC

322223 Plastics, Foil, and Coated Paper Bag Manufacturing *see* SIC 2673: Plastics, Foil, and Coated Paper Bags

322224 Uncoated Paper and Multiwall Bag Manufacturing *see* SIC 2674: Uncoated Paper and Multiwall Bags

322225 Laminated Aluminum Foil Manufacturing for Flexible Packaging Uses *see* SIC 3497: Metal Foil and Leaf

322231 Die-Cut Paper and Paperboard Office Supplies Manufacturing *see* SIC 2675: Die-Cut Paper and Paperboard and Cardboard; SIC 2679: Converted Paper and Paperboard Products, NEC

322232 Envelope Manufacturing *see* SIC 2677: Envelopes

322233 Stationery, Tablet, and Related Product Manufacturing *see* SIC 2678: Stationery, Tablets, and Related Products

322291 Sanitary Paper Product Manufacturing *see* SIC 2676: Sanitary Paper Products

322292 Surface-Coated Paperboard Manufacturing *see* SIC 2675: Die-Cut Paper and Paperboard and Cardboard

322298 All Other Converted Paper Product Manufacturing *see* SIC 2675: Die-Cut Paper and Paperboard and Cardboard; SIC 2679: Converted Paper and Paperboard Products, NEC

PRINTING & RELATED SUPPORT ACTIVITIES

323110 Commercial Lithographic Printing *see* SIC 2752: Commercial Printing, Lithographic; SIC 2771: Greeting Cards; SIC 2782: Blankbooks, Loose-leaf Binders and Devices; SIC 3999: Manufacturing Industries, NEC

323111 Commercial Gravure Printing *see* SIC 2754: Commercial Printing, Gravure; SIC 2771: Greeting Cards; SIC 2782: Blankbooks, Loose-leaf Binders and Devices; SIC 3999: Manufacturing Industries, NEC

323112 Commercial Flexographic Printing *see* SIC 2759: Commercial Printing, NEC; SIC 2771: Greeting Cards; SIC 2782: Blankbooks, Loose-leaf Binders and Devices

323112 Commercial Flexographic Printing *see* SIC 3999: Manufacturing Industries, NEC

323113 Commercial Screen Printing *see* SIC 2396: Automotive Trimmings, Apparel Findings, and Related Products; SIC 2759: Commercial Printing, NEC; SIC 2771: Greeting Cards; SIC 2782: Blankbooks, Loose-leaf Binders and Devices; SIC 3999: Manufacturing Industries, NEC

323114 Quick Printing *see* SIC 2752: Commercial Printing, Lithographic; SIC 2759: Commercial Printing, NEC

323115 Digital Printing *see* SIC 2759: Commercial Printing, NEC

323116 Manifold Business Form Printing *see* SIC 2761: Manifold Business Forms

323117 Book Printing *see* SIC 2732: Book Printing

323118 Blankbook, Loose-leaf Binder and Device Manufacturing *see* SIC 2782: Blankbooks, Loose-leaf Binders and Devices

323119 Other Commercial Printing *see* SIC 2759: Commercial Printing, NEC; SIC 2771: Greeting Cards; SIC 2782: Blankbooks, Loose-leaf Binders and Devices; SIC 3999: Manufacturing Industries, NEC

323121 Tradebinding and Related Work *see* SIC 2789: Bookbinding and Related Work

323122 Prepress Services *see* SIC 2791: Typesetting; SIC 2796: Platemaking and Related Services

PETROLEUM & COAL PRODUCTS MANUFACTURING

324110 Petroleum Refineries *see* SIC 2911: Petroleum Refining

324121 Asphalt Paving Mixture and Block Manufacturing *see* SIC 2951: Asphalt Paving Mixtures and Blocks

324122 Asphalt Shingle and Coating Materials Manufacturing *see* SIC 2952: Asphalt Felts and Coatings

324191 Petroleum Lubricating Oil and Grease Manufacturing *see* SIC 2992: Lubricating Oils and Greases

324199 All Other Petroleum and Coal Products Manufacturing *see* SIC 2999: Products of Petroleum and Coal, NEC; SIC 3312: Steel Works, Blast Furnaces (Including Coke Ovens), and Rolling Mills

CHEMICAL MANUFACTURING

325110 Petrochemical Manufacturing *see* SIC 2865: Cyclic Organic Crudes and Intermediates, and Organic Dyes and Pigments; SIC 2869: Industrial Organic Chemicals, NEC

325120 Industrial Gas Manufacturing *see* SIC 2813: Industrial Gases; SIC 2869: Industrial Organic Chemicals, NEC

325131 Inorganic Dye and Pigment Manufacturing *see* SIC 2816: Inorganic Pigments; SIC 2819: Industrial Inorganic Chemicals, NEC

325132 Organic Dye and Pigment Manufacturing *see* SIC 2865: Cyclic Organic Crudes and Intermediates, and Organic Dyes and Pigments

325181 Alkalies and Chlorine Manufacturing *see* SIC 2812: Alkalies and Chlorine

325182 Carbon Black Manufacturing *see* SIC 2816: Inorganic Pigments; SIC 2895: Carbon Black

325188 All Other Inorganic Chemical Manufacturing *see* SIC 2819: Industrial Inorganic Chemicals, NEC; SIC 2869: Industrial Organic Chemicals, NEC

325191 Gum and Wood Chemical Manufacturing *see* SIC 2861: Gum and Wood Chemicals

325192 Cyclic Crude and Intermediate Manufacturing *see* SIC 2865: Cyclic Organic Crudes and Intermediates, and Organic Dyes and Pigments

325193 Ethyl Alcohol Manufacturing *see* SIC 2869: Industrial Organic Chemicals, NEC

325199 All Other Basic Organic Chemical Manufacturing *see* SIC 2869: Industrial Organic Chemicals, NEC; SIC 2899: Chemicals and Chemical Preparations, NEC

325211 Plastics Material and Resin Manufacturing *see* SIC 2821: Plastics Material Synthetic Resins, and Nonvulcanizable Elastomers

325212 Synthetic Rubber Manufacturing *see* SIC 2822: Synthetic Rubber

325221 Cellulosic Manmade Fiber Manufacturing *see* SIC 2823: Cellulosic Manmade Fibers

325222 Noncellulosic Organic Fiber Manufacturing *see* SIC 2824: Manmade Organic Fibers, Except Cellulosic

325311 Nitrogenous Fertilizer Manufacturing *see* SIC 2873: Nitrogenous Fertilizers

325312 Phosphatic Fertilizer Manufacturing *see* SIC 2874: Phosphatic Fertilizers

325314 Fertilizer (Mixing Only) Manufacturing *see* SIC 2875: Fertilizers, Mixing Only

325320 Pesticide and Other Agricultural Chemical Manufacturing *see* SIC 2879: Pesticides and Agricultural Chemicals, NEC

325411 Medicinal and Botanical Manufacturing *see* SIC 2833: Medicinal Chemicals and Botanical Products

325412 Pharmaceutical Preparation Manufacturing *see* SIC 2834: Pharmaceutical Preparations; SIC 2835: In Vitro and In Vivo Diagnostic Substances

325413 In-Vitro Diagnostic Substance Manufacturing *see* SIC 2835: In Vitro and In Vivo Diagnostic Substances

325414 Biological Product (except Diagnostic) Manufacturing *see* SIC 2836: Biological Products, Except Diagnostic Substances

325510 Paint and Coating Manufacturing *see* SIC 2851: Paints, Varnishes, Lacquers, Enamels, and Allied Products; SIC 2899: Chemicals and Chemical Preparations, NEC

325520 Adhesive and Sealant Manufacturing *see* SIC 2891: Adhesives and Sealants

325611 Soap and Other Detergent Manufacturing *see* SIC 2841: Soaps and Other Detergents, Except Specialty Cleaners; SIC 2844: Perfumes, Cosmetics, and Other Toilet Preparations

325612 Polish and Other Sanitation Good Manufacturing *see* SIC 2842: Specialty Cleaning, Polishing, and Sanitary Preparations

325613 Surface Active Agent Manufacturing *see* SIC 2843: Surface Active Agents, Finishing Agents, Sulfonated Oils, and Assistants

325620 Toilet Preparation Manufacturing *see* SIC 2844: Perfumes, Cosmetics, and Other Toilet Preparations

325910 Printing Ink Manufacturing *see* SIC 2893: Printing Ink

325920 Explosives Manufacturing *see* SIC 2892: Explosives

325991 Custom Compounding of Purchased Resin *see* SIC 3087: Custom Compounding of Purchased Plastics Resins

325992 Photographic Film, Paper, Plate and Chemical Manufacturing *see* SIC 3861: Photographic Equipment and Supplies

325998 All Other Miscellaneous Chemical Product Manufacturing *see* SIC 2819: Industrial Inorganic Chemicals, NEC; SIC 2899: Chemicals and Chemical Preparations, NEC; SIC 3952: Lead Pencils, Crayons, and Artist's Materials; SIC 3999: Manufacturing Industries, NEC

Plastics & Rubber Products Manufacturing

326111 Unsupported Plastics Bag Manufacturing *see* SIC 2673: Plastics, Foil, and Coated Paper Bags

326112 Unsupported Plastics Packaging Film and Sheet Manufacturing *see* SIC 2671: Packaging Paper and Plastics Film, Coated and Laminated

326113 Unsupported Plastics Film and Sheet (except Packaging) Manufacturing *see* SIC 3081: Unsupported Plastics Film and Sheet

326121 Unsupported Plastics Profile Shape Manufacturing *see* SIC 3082: Unsupported Plastics Profile Shapes; SIC 3089: Plastics Products, NEC

326122 Plastics Pipe and Pipe Fitting Manufacturing *see* SIC 3084: Plastic Pipe; SIC 3089: Plastics Products, NEC

326130 Laminated Plastics Plate, Sheet, and Shape Manufacturing *see* SIC 3083: Laminated Plastics Plate, Sheet, and Profile Shapes

326140 Polystyrene Foam Product Manufacturing *see* SIC 3086: Plastics Foam Products

326150 Urethane and Other Foam Product (except Polystyrene) Manufacturing *see* SIC 3086: Plastics Foam Products

326160 Plastics Bottle Manufacturing *see* SIC 3085: Plastics Bottles

326191 Plastics Plumbing Fixtures Manufacturing *see* SIC 3088: Plastics Plumbing Fixtures

326192 Resilient Floor Covering Manufacturing *see* SIC 3069: Fabricated Rubber Products, NEC; SIC 3996: Linoleum, Asphalted-Felt-Base, and Other Hard Surface Floor Coverings, NEC

326199 All Other Plastics Product Manufacturing *see* SIC 3089: Plastics Products, NEC; SIC 3999: Manufacturing Industries, NEC

326211 Tire Manufacturing (except Retreading) *see* SIC 3011: Tires and Inner Tubes

326212 Tire Retreading *see* SIC 7534: Tire Retreading and Repair Shops

326220 Rubber and Plastics Hoses and Belting Manufacturing *see* SIC 3052: Rubber and Plastics Hose and Belting

326291 Rubber Product Manufacturing for Mechanical Use *see* SIC 3061: Molded, Extruded, and Lathe-Cut Mechanical Rubber Products

326299 All Other Rubber Product Manufacturing *see* SIC 3069: Fabricated Rubber Products, NEC

Nonmetallic Mineral Product Manufacturing

327111 Vitreous China Plumbing Fixture and China and Earthenware Fitting and Bathroom Accessories Manufacturing *see* SIC 3261: Vitreous China Plumbing Fixtures and China and Earthenware Fittings and Bathroom Accessories

327112 Vitreous China, Fine Earthenware and Other Pottery Product Manufacturing *see* SIC 3262: Vitreous China Table and Kitchen Articles; SIC 3263: Fine Earthenware (Whiteware) Table and Kitchen Articles; SIC 3269: Pottery Products, NEC

327113 Porcelain Electrical Supply Manufacturing *see* SIC 3264: Porcelain Electrical Supplies

327121 Brick and Structural Clay Tile Manufacturing *see* SIC 3251: Brick and Structural Clay Tile

327122 Ceramic Wall and Floor Tile Manufacturing *see* SIC 3253: Ceramic Wall and Floor Tile

327123 Other Structural Clay Product Manufacturing *see* SIC 3259: Structural Clay Products, NEC

327124 Clay Refractory Manufacturing *see* SIC 3255: Clay Refractories

327125 Nonclay Refractory Manufacturing *see* SIC 3297: Nonclay Refractories

327211 Flat Glass Manufacturing *see* SIC 3211: Flat Glass

327212 Other Pressed and Blown Glass and Glassware Manufacturing *see* SIC 3229: Pressed and Blown Glass and Glassware, NEC

327213 Glass Container Manufacturing *see* SIC 3221: Glass Containers

327215 Glass Product Manufacturing Made of Purchased Glass *see* SIC 3231: Glass Products, Made of Purchased Glass

327310 Cement Manufacturing *see* SIC 3241: Cement, Hydraulic

327320 Ready-Mix Concrete Manufacturing *see* SIC 3273: Ready-Mixed Concrete

327331 Concrete Block and Brick Manufacturing *see* SIC 3271: Concrete Block and Brick

327332 Concrete Pipe Manufacturing *see* SIC 3272: Concrete Products, Except Block and Brick

327390 Other Concrete Product Manufacturing *see* SIC 3272: Concrete Products, Except Block and Brick

327410 Lime Manufacturing *see* SIC 3274: Lime

327420 Gypsum and Gypsum Product Manufacturing *see* SIC 3275: Gypsum Products; SIC 3299: Nonmetallic Mineral Products, NEC

327910 Abrasive Product Manufacturing *see* SIC 3291: Abrasive Products

327991 Cut Stone and Stone Product Manufacturing *see* SIC 3281: Cut Stone and Stone Products

327992 Ground or Treated Mineral and Earth Manufacturing *see* SIC 3295: Minerals and Earths, Ground or Otherwise Treated

327993 Mineral Wool Manufacturing *see* SIC 3296: Mineral Wool

327999 All Other Miscellaneous Nonmetallic Mineral Product Manufacturing *see* SIC 3272: Concrete Products, Except Block and Brick; SIC 3292: Asbestos Products; SIC 3299: Nonmetallic Mineral Products, NEC

PRIMARY METAL MANUFACTURING

331111 Iron and Steel Mills *see* SIC 3312: Steel Works, Blast Furnaces (Including Coke Ovens), and Rolling Mills; SIC 3399: Primary Metal Products, NEC

331112 Electrometallurgical Ferroalloy Product Manufacturing *see* SIC 3313: Electrometallurgical Products, Except Steel

331210 Iron and Steel Pipes and Tubes Manufacturing from Purchased Steel *see* SIC 3317: Steel Pipe and Tubes

331221 Cold-Rolled Steel Shape Manufacturing *see* SIC 3316: Cold-Rolled Steel Sheet, Strip, and Bars

331222 Steel Wire Drawing *see* SIC 3315: Steel Wiredrawing and Steel Nails and Spikes

331311 Aluminum Refining *see* SIC 2819: Industrial Inorganic Chemicals, NEC

331312 Primary Aluminum Production *see* SIC 3334: Primary Production of Aluminum

331314 Secondary Smelting and Alloying of Aluminum *see* SIC 3341: Secondary Smelting and Refining of Nonferrous Metals; SIC 3399: Primary Metal Products, NEC

331315 Aluminum Sheet, Plate, and Foil Manufacturing *see* SIC 3353: Aluminum Sheet, Plate, and Foil

331316 Aluminum Extruded Product Manufacturing *see* SIC 3354: Aluminum Extruded Products

331319 Other Aluminum Rolling and Drawing, *see* SIC 3355: Aluminum Rolling and Drawing, NEC; SIC 3357: Drawing and Insulating of Nonferrous Wire

331411 Primary Smelting and Refining of Copper *see* SIC 3331: Primary Smelting and Refining of Copper

331419 Primary Smelting and Refining of Nonferrous Metals (except Copper and Aluminum) *see* SIC 3339: Primary Smelting and Refining of Nonferrous Metals, Except Copper and Aluminum

331421 Copper (except Wire) Rolling, Drawing, and Extruding *see* SIC 3351: Rolling, Drawing, and Extruding of Copper

331422 Copper Wire Drawing *see* SIC 3357: Drawing and Insulating of Nonferrous Wire

331423 Secondary Smelting, Refining, and Alloying of Copper *see* SIC 3341: Secondary Smelting and Refining of Nonferrous Metals; SIC 3399: Primary Metal Products, NEC

331491 Nonferrous Metal (except Copper and Aluminum) Rolling. Drawing, and Extruding *see* SIC 3356: Rolling, Drawing, and Extruding of Nonferrous Metals, Except Copper and Aluminum; SIC 3357: Drawing and Insulating of Nonferrous Wire

331492 Secondary Smelting, Refining, and Alloying of Nonferrous Metals (except Copper and Aluminum) *see* SIC 3313: Electrometallurgical Products, Except Steel; SIC 3341: Secondary Smelting and Refining of Nonferrous Metals; SIC 3399: Primary Metal Products, NEC

331511 Iron Foundries *see* SIC 3321: Gray and Ductile Iron Foundries; SIC 3322: Malleable Iron Foundries

331512 Steel Investment Foundries *see* SIC 3324: Steel Investment Foundries

331513 Steel Foundries (except Investment) *see* SIC 3325: Steel Foundries, NEC

331521 Aluminum Die-Castings *see* SIC 3363: Aluminum Die-Castings

331522 Nonferrous (except Aluminum) Die-Castings *see* SIC 3364: Nonferrous Die-Castings, Except Aluminum

331524 Aluminum Foundries *see* SIC 3365: Aluminum Foundries

331525 Copper Foundries *see* SIC 3366: Copper Foundries

331528 Other Nonferrous Foundries *see* SIC 3369: Nonferrous Foundries, Except Aluminum and Copper

FABRICATED METAL PRODUCT MANUFACTURING

332111 Iron and Steel Forging *see* SIC 3462: Iron and Steel Forgings

332112 Nonferrous Forging *see* SIC 3463: Nonferrous Forgings

332114 Custom Roll Forming *see* SIC 3449: Miscellaneous Structural Metal Work

332115 Crown and Closure Manufacturing *see* SIC 3466: Crowns and Closures

332116 Metal Stamping *see* SIC 3469: Metal Stamping, NEC

332117 Powder Metallurgy Part Manufacturing *see* SIC 3499: Fabricated Metal Products, NEC

332211 Cutlery and Flatware (except Precious) Manufacturing *see* SIC 3421: Cutlery; SIC 3914: Silverware, Plated Ware, and Stainless Steel Ware

332212 Hand and Edge Tool Manufacturing *see* SIC 3423: Hand and Edge Tools, Except Machine Tools and Handsaws; SIC 3523: Farm Machinery and Equipment; SIC 3524: Lawn and Garden Tractors and Home Lawn and Garden Equipment; SIC 3545: Cutting Tools, Machine Tool Accessories, and Machinists' Precision Measuring Devices; SIC 3799: Transportation Equipment, NEC; SIC 3999: Manufacturing Industries, NEC

332213 Saw Blade and Handsaw Manufacturing *see* SIC 3425: Saw Blades and Handsaws

332214 Kitchen Utensil, Pot and Pan Manufacturing *see* SIC 3469: Metal Stamping, NEC

332311 Prefabricated Metal Building and Component Manufacturing *see* SIC 3448: Prefabricated Metal Buildings and Components

332312 Fabricated Structural Metal Manufacturing *see* SIC 3441: Fabricated Structural Metal; SIC 3449: Miscellaneous Structural Metal Work

332313 Plate Work Manufacturing *see* SIC 3443: Fabricated Plate Work (Boiler Shops)

332321 Metal Window and Door Manufacturing *see* SIC 3442: Metal Doors, Sash, Frames, Molding, and Trim Manufacturing; SIC 3449: Miscellaneous Structural Metal Work

332322 Sheet Metal Work Manufacturing *see* SIC 3444: Sheet Metal Work

332323 Ornamental and Architectural Metal Work Manufacturing *see* SIC 3446: Architectural and Ornamental Metal Work; SIC 3449: Miscellaneous Structural Metal Work; SIC 3523: Farm Machinery and Equipment

332410 Power Boiler and Heat Exchanger Manufacturing *see* SIC 3443: Fabricated Plate Work (Boiler Shops)

332420 Metal Tank (Heavy Gauge) Manufacturing *see* SIC 3443: Fabricated Plate Work (Boiler Shops)

332431 Metal Can Manufacturing *see* SIC 3411: Metal Cans

332439 Other Metal Container Manufacturing *see* SIC 3412: Metal Shipping Barrels, Drums, Kegs and Pails; SIC 3429: Hardware, NEC; SIC 3444: Sheet Metal Work; SIC 3499: Fabricated Metal Products, NEC; SIC 3537: Industrial Trucks, Tractors, Trailers, and Stackers

332510 Hardware Manufacturing *see* SIC 3429: Hardware, NEC; SIC 3499: Fabricated Metal Products, NEC

332611 Steel Spring (except Wire) Manufacturing *see* SIC 3493: Steel Springs, Except Wire

332612 Wire Spring Manufacturing *see* SIC 3495: Wire Springs

332618 Other Fabricated Wire Product Manufacturing *see* SIC 3315: Steel Wiredrawing and Steel Nails and Spikes; SIC 3399: Primary Metal Products, NEC; SIC 3496: Miscellaneous Fabricated Wire Products

332710 Machine Shops *see* SIC 3599: Industrial and Commercial Machinery and Equipment, NEC

332721 Precision Turned Product Manufacturing *see* SIC 3451: Screw Machine Products

332722 Bolt, Nut, Screw, Rivet, and Washer Manufacturing *see* SIC 3452: Bolts, Nuts, Screws, Rivets, and Washers

332811 Metal Heat Treating *see* SIC 3398: Metal Heat Treating

332812 Metal Coating, Engraving, and Allied Services (except Jewelry and Silverware) to Manufacturing *see* SIC 3479: Coating, Engraving, and Allied Services, NEC

332813 Electroplating, Plating, Polishing, Anodizing, and Coloring *see* SIC 3399: Primary Metal Products, NEC; SIC 3471: Electroplating, Plating, Polishing, Anodizing, and Coloring

332911 Industrial Valve Manufacturing *see* SIC 3491: Industrial Valves

332912 Fluid Power Valve and Hose Fitting Manufacturing *see* SIC 3492: Fluid Power Valves and Hose Fittings; SIC 3728: Aircraft Parts and Auxiliary Equipment, NEC

332913 Plumbing Fixture Fitting and Trim Manufacturing *see* SIC 3432: Plumbing Fixture Fittings and Trim

332919 Other Metal Valve and Pipe Fitting Manufacturing *see* SIC 3429: Hardware, NEC; SIC 3494: Valves and Pipe Fittings, NEC; SIC 3499: Fabricated Metal Products, NEC

332991 Ball and Roller Bearing Manufacturing *see* SIC 3562: Ball and Roller Bearings

332992 Small Arms Ammunition Manufacturing *see* SIC 3482: Small Arms Ammunition

332993 Ammunition (except Small Arms) Manufacturing *see* SIC 3483: Ammunition, Except for Small Arms

332994 Small Arms Manufacturing *see* SIC 3484: Small Arms

332995 Other Ordnance and Accessories Manufacturing *see* SIC 3489: Ordnance and Accessories, NEC

332996 Fabricated Pipe and Pipe Fitting Manufacturing *see* SIC 3498: Fabricated Pipe and Pipe Fittings

332997 Industrial Pattern Manufacturing *see* SIC 3543: Industrial Patterns

332998 Enameled Iron and Metal Sanitary Ware Manufacturing *see* SIC 3431: Enameled Iron and Metal Sanitary Ware

332999 All Other Miscellaneous Fabricated Metal Product Manufacturing *see* SIC 3291: Abrasive Products; SIC 3432: Plumbing Fixture Fittings and Trim; SIC 3494: Valves and Pipe Fittings, NEC; SIC 3497: Metal Foil and Leaf; SIC 3499: Fabricated Metal Products, NEC; SIC 3537: Industrial Trucks, Tractors, Trailers, and Stackers; SIC 3599: Industrial and Commercial Machinery and Equipment, NEC; SIC 3999: Manufacturing Industries, NEC

MACHINERY MANUFACTURING

333111 Farm Machinery and Equipment Manufacturing *see* SIC 3523: Farm Machinery and Equipment

333112 Lawn and Garden Tractor and Home Lawn and Garden Equipment Manufacturing *see* SIC 3524: Lawn and Garden Tractors and Home Lawn and Garden Equipment

333120 Construction Machinery Manufacturing *see* SIC 3531: Construction Machinery and Equipment

333131 Mining Machinery and Equipment Manufacturing *see* SIC 3532: Mining Machinery and Equipment, Except Oil and Gas Field Machinery and Equipment

333132 Oil and Gas Field Machinery and Equipment Manufacturing *see* SIC 3533: Oil and Gas Field Machinery and Equipment

333210 Sawmill and Woodworking Machinery Manufacturing *see* SIC 3553: Woodworking Machinery

333220 Rubber and Plastics Industry Machinery Manufacturing *see* SIC 3559: Special Industry Machinery, NEC

333291 Paper Industry Machinery Manufacturing *see* SIC 3554: Paper Industries Machinery

333292 Textile Machinery Manufacturing *see* SIC 3552: Textile Machinery

333293 Printing Machinery and Equipment Manufacturing *see* SIC 3555: Printing Trades Machinery and Equipment

333294 Food Product Machinery Manufacturing *see* SIC 3556: Food Products Machinery

333295 Semiconductor Manufacturing Machinery *see* SIC 3559: Special Industry Machinery, NEC

333298 All Other Industrial Machinery Manufacturing *see* SIC 3559: Special Industry Machinery, NEC; SIC 3639: Household Appliances, NEC

333311 Automatic Vending Machine Manufacturing *see* SIC 3581: Automatic Vending Machines

333312 Commercial Laundry, Drycleaning, and Pressing Machine Manufacturing *see* SIC 3582: Commercial Laundry, Drycleaning, and Pressing Machines

333313 Office Machinery Manufacturing *see* SIC 3578: Calculating and Accounting Machines, Except Electronic Computers; SIC 3579: Office Machines, NEC

333314 Optical Instrument and Lens Manufacturing *see* SIC 3827: Optical Instruments and Lenses

333315 Photographic and Photocopying Equipment Manufacturing *see* SIC 3861: Photographic Equipment and Supplies

333319 Other Commercial and Service Industry Machinery Manufacturing *see* SIC 3559: Special Industry Machinery, NEC; SIC 3589: Service Industry Machinery, NEC; SIC 3599: Industrial and Commercial Machinery and Equipment, NEC; SIC 3699: Electrical Machinery, Equipment, and Supplies, NEC

333411 Air Purification Equipment Manufacturing *see* SIC 3564: Industrial and Commercial Fans and Blowers and Air Purification Equipment

333412 Industrial and Commercial Fan and Blower Manufacturing *see* SIC 3564: Industrial and Commercial Fans and Blowers and Air Purification Equipment

333414 Heating Equipment (except Electric and Warm Air Furnaces) Manufacturing *see* SIC 3433: Heating Equipment, Except Electric and Warm Air Furnaces; SIC 3634: Electric Housewares and Fans

333415 Air-Conditioning and Warm Air Heating Equipment and Commercial and Industrial Refrigeration Equipment Manufacturing *see* SIC 3443: Fabricated Plate Work (Boiler Shops); SIC 3585: Air-Conditioning and Warm Air Heating Equipment and Commercial and Industrial Refrigeration Equipment

333511 Industrial Mold Manufacturing *see* SIC 3544: Special Dies and Tools, Die Sets, Jigs and Fixtures, and Industrial Molds

333512 Machine Tool (Metal Cutting Types) Manufacturing *see* SIC 3541: Machine Tools, Metal Cutting Type

333513 Machine Tool (Metal Forming Types) Manufacturing *see* SIC 3542: Machine Tools, Metal Forming Type

333514 Special Die and Tool, Die Set, Jig, and Fixture Manufacturing *see* SIC 3544: Special Dies and Tools, Die Sets, Jigs and Fixtures, and Industrial Molds

333515 Cutting Tool and Machine Tool Accessory Manufacturing *see* SIC 3545: Cutting Tools, Machine Tool Accessories, and Machinists' Precision Measuring Devices

333516 Rolling Mill Machinery and Equipment Manufacturing *see* SIC 3547: Rolling Mill Machinery and Equipment

333518 Other Metalworking Machinery Manufacturing *see* SIC 3549: Metalworking Machinery, NEC

333611 Turbine and Turbine Generator Set Unit Manufacturing *see* SIC 3511: Steam, Gas, and Hydraulic Turbines, and Turbine Generator Set Units

333612 Speed Changer, Industrial High-Speed Drive, and Gear Manufacturing *see* SIC 3566: Speed Changers, Industrial High-Speed Drives, and Gears

333613 Mechanical Power Transmission Equipment Manufacturing *see* SIC 3568: Mechanical Power Transmission Equipment, NEC

333618 Other Engine Equipment Manufacturing *see* SIC 3519: Internal Combustion Engines, NEC; SIC 3699: Electrical Machinery, Equipment, and Supplies, NEC

333911 Pump and Pumping Equipment Manufacturing *see* SIC 3561: Pumps and Pumping Equipment; SIC 3743: Railroad Equipment

333912 Air and Gas Compressor Manufacturing *see* SIC 3563: Air and Gas Compressors

333913 Measuring and Dispensing Pump Manufacturing *see* SIC 3586: Measuring and Dispensing Pumps

333921 Elevator and Moving Stairway Manufacturing *see* SIC 3534: Elevators and Moving Stairways

333922 Conveyor and Conveying Equipment Manufacturing *see* SIC 3523: Farm Machinery and Equipment; SIC 3535: Conveyors and Conveying Equipment

333923 Overhead Traveling Crane, Hoist, and Monorail System Manufacturing *see* SIC 3531: Construction Machinery and Equipment; SIC 3536: Overhead Traveling Cranes, Hoists and Monorail Systems

333924 Industrial Truck, Tractor, Trailer, and Stacker Machinery Manufacturing *see* SIC 3537: Industrial Trucks, Tractors, Trailers, and Stackers

333991 Power-Driven Hand Tool Manufacturing *see* SIC 3546: Power-Driven Handtools

333992 Welding and Soldering Equipment Manufacturing *see* SIC 3548: Electric and Gas Welding and Soldering Equipment

333993 Packaging Machinery Manufacturing *see* SIC 3565: Packaging Machinery

333994 Industrial Process Furnace and Oven Manufacturing *see* SIC 3567: Industrial Process Furnaces and Ovens

333995 Fluid Power Cylinder and Actuator Manufacturing *see* SIC 3593: Fluid Power Cylinders and Actuators

333996 Fluid Power Pump and Motor Manufacturing *see* SIC 3594: Fluid Power Pumps and Motors

333997 Scale and Balance (except Laboratory) Manufacturing *see* SIC 3596: Scales and Balances, Except Laboratory

333999 All Other General Purpose Machinery Manufacturing *see* SIC 3569: General Industrial Machinery and Equipment, NEC; SIC 3599: Industrial and Commercial Machinery and Equipment, NEC

COMPUTER & ELECTRONIC PRODUCT MANUFACTURING

334111 Electronic Computer Manufacturing *see* SIC 3571: Electronic Computers

334112 Computer Storage Device Manufacturing *see* SIC 3572: Computer Storage Devices

334113 Computer Terminal Manufacturing *see* SIC 3575: Computer Terminals

334119 Other Computer Peripheral Equipment Manufacturing *see* SIC 3577: Computer Peripheral Equipment, NEC; SIC 3578: Calculating and Accounting Machines, Except Electronic Computers; SIC 3699: Electrical Machinery, Equipment, and Supplies, NEC

334210 Telephone Apparatus Manufacturing *see* SIC 3661: Telephone and Telegraph Apparatus

334220 Radio and Television Broadcasting and Wireless Communications Equipment Manufacturing *see* SIC 3663: Radio and Television Broadcasting and Communication Equipment; SIC 3679: Electronic Components, NEC

334290 Other Communication Equipment Manufacturing *see* SIC 3669: Communications Equipment, NEC

334310 Audio and Video Equipment Manufacturing *see* SIC 3651: Household Audio and Video Equipment

334411 Electron Tube Manufacturing *see* SIC 3671: Electron Tubes

334412 Printed Circuit Board Manufacturing *see* SIC 3672: Printed Circuit Boards

334413 Semiconductor and Related Device Manufacturing *see* SIC 3674: Semiconductors and Related Devices

334414 Electronic Capacitor Manufacturing *see* SIC 3675: Electronic Capacitors

334415 Electronic Resistor Manufacturing *see* SIC 3676: Electronic Resistors

334416 Electronic Coil, Transformer, and Other Inductor Manufacturing *see* SIC 3661: Telephone and Telegraph Apparatus; SIC 3677: Electronic Coils, Transformers, and Other Inductors; SIC 3825: Instruments for Measuring and Testing of Electricity and Electrical Signals

334417 Electronic Connector Manufacturing *see* SIC 3678: Electronic Connectors

334418 Printed Circuit/Electronics Assembly Manufacturing *see* SIC 3661: Telephone and Telegraph Apparatus; SIC 3679: Electronic Components, NEC

334419 Other Electronic Component Manufacturing *see* SIC 3679: Electronic Components, NEC

334510 Electromedical and Electrotherapeutic Apparatus Manufacturing *see* SIC 3842: Orthopedic, Prosthetic, and Surgical Appliances and Supplies; SIC 3845: Electromedical and Electrotherapeutic Apparatus

334511 Search, Detection, Navigation, Guidance, Aeronautical, and Nautical System and Instrument Manufacturing *see* SIC 3812: Search, Detection, Navigation, Guidance, Aeronautical, and Nautical Systems and Instruments

334512 Automatic Environmental Control Manufacturing for Regulating Residential, Commercial, and Appliance Use *see* SIC 3822: Automatic Controls for Regulating Residential and Commercial Environments and Appliances

334513 Instruments and Related Product Manufacturing for Measuring Displaying, and Controlling Industrial Process Variables *see* SIC 3823: Industrial Instruments for Measurement, Display, and Control of Process Variables; and Related Products

334514 Totalizing Fluid Meter and Counting Device Manufacturing *see* SIC 3824: Totalizing Fluid Meters and Counting Devices

334515 Instrument Manufacturing for Measuring and Testing Electricity and Electrical Signals *see* SIC 3825: Instruments for Measuring and Testing of Electricity and Electrical Signals

334516 Analytical Laboratory Instrument Manufacturing *see* SIC 3826: Laboratory Analytical Instruments

334517 Irradiation Apparatus Manufacturing *see* SIC 3844: X-Ray Apparatus and Tubes and Related Irradiation Apparatus; SIC 3845: Electromedical and Electrotherapeutic Apparatus

334518 Watch, Clock, and Part Manufacturing *see* SIC 3495: Wire Springs; SIC 3579: Office Machines, NEC; SIC 3873: Watches, Clocks, Clockwork Operated Devices and Parts

334519 Other Measuring and Controlling Device Manufacturing *see* SIC 3829: Measuring and Controlling Devices, NEC

334611 Software Reproducing *see* SIC 7372: Prepackaged Software

334612 Prerecorded Compact Disc (Except Software), Tape and Record Reproducing *see* SIC 3652: Phonograph Records and Prerecorded Audio Tapes and Disks; SIC 7819: Services Allied to Motion Picture Production

334613 Magnetic and Optical Recording Media Manufacturing *see* SIC 3695: Magnetic and Optical Recording Media

Electrical Equipment, Appliance, & Component Manufacturing

335110 Electric Lamp Bulb and Part Manufacturing *see* SIC 3641: Electric Lamp Bulbs and Tubes

335121 Residential Electric Lighting Fixture Manufacturing *see* SIC 3645: Residential Electric Lighting Fixtures; SIC 3999: Manufacturing Industries, NEC

335122 Commercial, Industrial, and Institutional Electric Lighting Fixture Manufacturing *see* SIC 3646: Commercial, Industrial, and Institutional Electric Lighting Fixtures

335129 Other Lighting Equipment Manufacturing *see* SIC 3648: Lighting Equipment, NEC; SIC 3699: Electrical Machinery, Equipment, and Supplies, NEC

335211 Electric Houseware and Fan Manufacturing *see* SIC 3634: Electric Housewares and Fans

335212 Household Vacuum Cleaner Manufacturing *see* SIC 3635: Household Vacuum Cleaners; SIC 3639: Household Appliances, NEC

335221 Household Cooking Appliance Manufacturing *see* SIC 3631: Household Cooking Equipment

335222 Household Refrigerator and Home and Farm Freezer Manufacturing *see* SIC 3632: Household Refrigerators and Home and Farm Freezers

335224 Household Laundry Equipment Manufacturing *see* SIC 3633: Household Laundry Equipment

335228 Other Household Appliance Manufacturing *see* SIC 3639: Household Appliances, NEC

335311 Power, Distribution, and Specialty Transformer Manufacturing *see* SIC 3548: Electric and Gas Welding and Soldering Equipment; SIC 3612: Power, Distribution, and Specialty Transformers

335312 Motor and Generator Manufacturing *see* SIC 3621: Motors and Generators; SIC 7694: Armature Rewinding Shops

335313 Switchgear and Switchboard Apparatus Manufacturing *see* SIC 3613: Switchgear and Switchboard Apparatus

335314 Relay and Industrial Control Manufacturing *see* SIC 3625: Relays and Industrial Controls

335911 Storage Battery Manufacturing *see* SIC 3691: Storage Batteries

335912 Dry and Wet Primary Battery Manufacturing *see* SIC 3692: Primary Batteries, Dry and Wet

335921 Fiber Optic Cable Manufacturing *see* SIC 3357: Drawing and Insulating of Nonferrous Wire

335929 Other Communication and Energy Wire Manufacturing *see* SIC 3357: Drawing and Insulating of Nonferrous Wire

335931 Current-Carrying Wiring Device Manufacturing *see* SIC 3643: Current-Carrying Wiring Devices

335932 Noncurrent-Carrying Wiring Device Manufacturing *see* SIC 3644: Noncurrent-Carrying Wiring Devices

335991 Carbon and Graphite Product Manufacturing *see* SIC 3624: Carbon and Graphite Products

335999 All Other Miscellaneous Electrical Equipment and Component Manufacturing *see* SIC 3629: Electrical Industrial Apparatus, NEC; SIC 3699: Electrical Machinery, Equipment, and Supplies, NEC

Transportation Equipment Manufacturing

336111 Automobile Manufacturing *see* SIC 3711: Motor Vehicles and Passenger Car Bodies

336112 Light Truck and Utility Vehicle Manufacturing *see* SIC 3711: Motor Vehicles and Passenger Car Bodies

336120 Heavy Duty Truck Manufacturing *see* SIC 3711: Motor Vehicles and Passenger Car Bodies

336211 Motor Vehicle Body Manufacturing *see* SIC 3711: Motor Vehicles and Passenger Car Bodies; SIC 3713: Truck and Bus Bodies; SIC 3714: Motor Vehicle Parts and Accessories

336212 Truck Trailer Manufacturing *see* SIC 3715: Truck Trailers

336213 Motor Home Manufacturing *see* SIC 3716: Motor Homes

336214 Travel Trailer and Camper Manufacturing *see* SIC 3792: Travel Trailers and Campers; SIC 3799: Transportation Equipment, NEC

336311 Carburetor, Piston, Piston Ring and Valve Manufacturing *see* SIC 3592: Carburetors, Pistons, Piston Rings and Valves

336312 Gasoline Engine and Engine Parts Manufacturing *see* SIC 3714: Motor Vehicle Parts and Accessories

336321 Vehicular Lighting Equipment Manufacturing *see* SIC 3647: Vehicular Lighting Equipment

336322 Other Motor Vehicle Electrical and Electronic Equipment Manufacturing *see* SIC 3679: Electronic Components, NEC; SIC 3694: Electrical Equipment for Internal Combustion Engines; SIC 3714: Motor Vehicle Parts and Accessories

336330 Motor Vehicle Steering and Suspension Components (except Spring) Manufacturing *see* SIC 3714: Motor Vehicle Parts and Accessories

336340 Motor Vehicle Brake System Manufacturing *see* SIC 3292: Asbestos Products; SIC 3714: Motor Vehicle Parts and Accessories

336350 Motor Vehicle Transmission and Power Train Part Manufacturing *see* SIC 3714: Motor Vehicle Parts and Accessories

336360 Motor Vehicle Fabric Accessories and Seat Manufacturing *see* SIC 2396: Automotive Trimmings, Apparel Findings, and Related Products; SIC 2399: Fabricated Textile Products, NEC; SIC 2531: Public Building and Related Furniture

336370 Motor Vehicle Metal Stamping *see* SIC 3465: Automotive Stamping

336391 Motor Vehicle Air Conditioning Manufacturing *see* SIC 3585: Air-Conditioning and Warm Air Heating Equipment and Commercial and Industrial Refrigeration Equipment

336399 All Other Motor Vehicle Parts Manufacturing *see* SIC 3519: Internal Combustion Engines, NEC; SIC 3599: Industrial and Commercial Machinery and Equipment, NEC; SIC 3714: Motor Vehicle Parts and Accessories

336411 Aircraft Manufacturing *see* SIC 3721: Aircraft

336412 Aircraft Engine and Engine Parts Manufacturing *see* SIC 3724: Aircraft Engines and Engine Parts

336413 Other Aircraft Part and Auxiliary Equipment Manufacturing *see* SIC 3728: Aircraft Parts and Auxiliary Equipment, NEC

336414 Guided Missile and Space Vehicle Manufacturing *see* SIC 3761: Guided Missiles and Space Vehicles

336415 Guided Missile and Space Vehicle Propulsion Unit and Propulsion Unit Parts Manufacturing *see* SIC 3764: Guided Missile and Space Vehicle Propulsion Units and Propulsion Unit Parts

336419 Other Guided Missile and Space Vehicle Parts and Auxiliary Equipment Manufacturing *see* SIC 3769: Guided Missile Space Vehicle Parts and Auxiliary Equipment, NEC

336510 Railroad Rolling Stock Manufacturing *see* SIC 3531: Construction Machinery and Equipment; SIC 3743: Railroad Equipment

336611 Ship Building and Repairing *see* SIC 3731: Ship Building and Repairing

336612 Boat Building *see* SIC 3732: Boat Building and Repairing

336991 Motorcycle, Bicycle, and Parts Manufacturing *see* SIC 3751: Motorcycles, Bicycles, and Parts; SIC 3944: Games, Toys, and Children's Vehicles, Except Dolls and Bicycles

336992 Military Armored Vehicle, Tank, and Tank Component Manufacturing *see* SIC 3711: Motor Vehicles and Passenger Car Bodies; SIC 3795: Tanks and Tank Components

336999 All Other Transportation Equipment Manufacturing *see* SIC 3799: Transportation Equipment, NEC

Furniture & Related Product Manufacturing

337110 Wood Kitchen Cabinet and Counter Top Manufacturing *see* SIC 2434: Wood Kitchen Cabinets; SIC 2541: Wood Office and Store Fixtures, Partitions, Shelving, and Lockers; SIC 5712: Furniture Stores

337121 Upholstered Wood Household Furniture Manufacturing *see* SIC 2512: Wood Household Furniture, Upholstered; SIC 2515: Mattresses, Foundations, and Convertible Beds; SIC 5712: Furniture Stores

337122 Nonupholstered Wood Household Furniture Manufacturing *see* SIC 2511: Wood Household Furniture, Except Upholstered; SIC 5712: Furniture Stores

337124 Metal Household Furniture Manufacturing *see* SIC 2514: Metal Household Furniture

337125 Household Furniture (except Wood and Metal) Manufacturing *see* SIC 2519: Household Furniture, NEC

337127 Institutional Furniture Manufacturing *see* SIC 2531: Public Building and Related Furniture; SIC 2599: Furniture and Fixtures, NEC; SIC 3952: Lead Pencils, Crayons, and Artist's Materials; SIC 3999: Manufacturing Industries, NEC

337129 Wood Television, Radio, and Sewing Machine Cabinet Manufacturing *see* SIC 2517: Wood Television, Radio, Phonograph and Sewing Machine Cabinets

337211 Wood Office Furniture Manufacturing *see* SIC 2521: Wood Office Furniture

337212 Custom Architectural Woodwork, Millwork, and Fixtures *see* SIC 2541: Wood Office and Store Fixtures, Partitions, Shelving, and Lockers

337214 Nonwood Office Furniture Manufacturing *see* SIC 2522: Office Furniture, Except Wood

337215 Showcase, Partition, Shelving, and Locker Manufacturing *see* SIC 2426: Hardwood Dimension and Flooring Mills; SIC 2541: Wood Office and Store Fixtures, Partitions, Shelving, and Lockers; SIC 2542: Office and Store Fixtures, Partitions Shelving, and Lockers, Except Wood; SIC 3499: Fabricated Metal Products, NEC

337910 Mattress Manufacturing *see* SIC 2515: Mattresses, Foundations, and Convertible Beds

337920 Blind and Shade Manufacturing *see* SIC 2591: Drapery Hardware and Window Blinds and Shades

Miscellaneous Manufacturing

339111 Laboratory Apparatus and Furniture Manufacturing *see* SIC 3821: Laboratory Apparatus and Furniture

339112 Surgical and Medical Instrument Manufacturing *see* SIC 3829: Measuring and Controlling Devices, NEC; SIC 3841: Surgical and Medical Instruments and Apparatus

339113 Surgical Appliance and Supplies Manufacturing *see* SIC 2599: Furniture and Fixtures, NEC; SIC 3842: Orthopedic, Prosthetic, and Surgical Appliances and Supplies

339114 Dental Equipment and Supplies Manufacturing *see* SIC 3843: Dental Equipment and Supplies

339115 Ophthalmic Goods Manufacturing *see* SIC 3851: Ophthalmic Goods; SIC 5995: Optical Goods Stores

339116 Dental Laboratories *see* SIC 8072: Dental Laboratories

339911 Jewelry (including Precious Metal) Manufacturing, *see* SIC 3469: Metal Stamping, NEC; SIC 3479: Coating, Engraving, and Allied Services, NEC; SIC 3911: Jewelry, Precious Metal

339912 Silverware and Plated Ware Manufacturing *see* SIC 3479: Coating, Engraving, and Allied Services, NEC; SIC 3914: Silverware, Plated Ware, and Stainless Steel Ware

339913 Jewelers' Material and Lapidary Work Manufacturing *see* SIC 3915: Jewelers' Findings and Materials, and Lapidary Work

339914 Costume Jewelry and Novelty Manufacturing *see* SIC 3479: Coating, Engraving, and Allied Services, NEC; SIC 3499: Fabricated Metal Products, NEC; SIC 3961: Costume Jewelry and Costume Novelties, Except Precious Metals

339920 Sporting and Athletic Good Manufacturing *see* SIC 3949: Sporting and Athletic Goods, NEC

339931 Doll and Stuffed Toy Manufacturing *see* SIC 3942: Dolls and Stuffed Toys

339932 Game, Toy, and Children's Vehicle Manufacturing *see* SIC 3944: Games, Toys, and Children's Vehicles, Except Dolls and Bicycles

339941 Pen and Mechanical Pencil Manufacturing *see* SIC 3951: Pens, Mechanical Pencils and Parts

339942 Lead Pencil and Art Good Manufacturing *see* SIC 2531: Public Building and Related Furniture; SIC 3579: Office Machines, NEC; SIC 3952: Lead Pencils, Crayons, and Artist's Materials

339943 Marking Device Manufacturing *see* SIC 3953: Marking Devices

339944 Carbon Paper and Inked Ribbon Manufacturing *see* SIC 3955: Carbon Paper and Inked Ribbons

339950 Sign Manufacturing *see* SIC 3993: Signs and Advertising Specialties

339991 Gasket, Packing, and Sealing Device Manufacturing *see* SIC 3053: Gaskets, Packing, and Sealing Devices

339992 Musical Instrument Manufacturing *see* SIC 3931: Musical Instruments

339993 Fastener, Button, Needle, and Pin Manufacturing *see* SIC 3131: Boot and Shoe Cut Stock and Findings; SIC 3965: Fasteners, Buttons, Needles, and Pins

339994 Broom, Brush and Mop Manufacturing *see* SIC 2392: Housefurnishings, Except Curtains and Draperies; SIC 3991: Brooms and Brushes

339995 Burial Casket Manufacturing *see* SIC 3995: Burial Caskets

339999 All Other Miscellaneous Manufacturing *see* SIC 2499: Wood Products, NEC; SIC 3999: Manufacturing Industries, NEC

Wholesale Trade

421110 Automobile and Other Motor Vehicle Wholesalers *see* SIC 5012: Automobiles and Other Motor Vehicles; SIC 5013: Motor Vehicle Supplies and New Parts

421130 Tire and Tube Wholesalers *see* SIC 5014: Tires and Tubes

421140 Motor Vehicle Part (Used) Wholesalers *see* SIC 5015: Motor Vehicle Parts, Used

421210 Furniture Wholesalers *see* SIC 5021: Furniture

421220 Home Furnishing Wholesalers *see* SIC 5023: Home Furnishings

421310 Lumber, Plywood, Millwork, and Wood Panel Wholesalers *see* SIC 5031: Lumber, Plywood, Millwork, and Wood Panels; SIC 5211: Lumber and Other Building Materials Dealers

421320 Brick, Stone and Related Construction Material Wholesalers *see* SIC 5032: Brick, Stone and Related Construction Materials

421330 Roofing, Siding, and Insulation Material Wholesalers *see* SIC 5033: Roofing, Siding, and Insulation Materials

421390 Other Construction Material Wholesalers *see* SIC 5039: Construction Materials, NEC

421410 Photographic Equipment and Supplies Wholesalers *see* SIC 5043: Photographic Equipment and Supplies

421420 Office Equipment Wholesalers *see* SIC 5044: Office Equipment

421430 Computer and Computer Peripheral Equipment and Software Wholesalers *see* SIC 5045: Computers and Computer Peripheral Equipment and Software

421440 Other Commercial Equipment Wholesalers *see* SIC 5046: Commercial Equipment, NEC

421450 Medical, Dental and Hospital Equipment and Supplies Wholesalers *see* SIC 5047: Medical, Dental, and Hospital Equipment and Supplies

421460 Ophthalmic Goods Wholesalers *see* SIC 5048: Ophthalmic Goods

421490 Other Professional Equipment and Supplies Wholesalers *see* SIC 5049: Professional Equipment and Supplies, NEC

421510 Metals Service Centers and Offices *see* SIC 5051: Metals Service Centers and Offices

421520 Coal and Other Mineral and Ore Wholesalers *see* SIC 5052: Coal and Other Minerals and Ores

421610 Electrical Apparatus and Equipment, Wiring Supplies and Construction Material Wholesalers *see* SIC 5063: Electrical Apparatus and Equipment Wiring Supplies, and Construction Materials

421620 Electrical Appliance, Television and Radio Set Wholesalers *see* SIC 5064: Electrical Appliances, Television and Radio Sets

421690 Other Electronic Parts and Equipment Wholesalers *see* SIC 5065: Electronic Parts and Equipment, Not Elsewhere Classified

421710 Hardware Wholesalers *see* SIC 5072: Hardware

421720 Plumbing and Heating Equipment and Supplies (Hydronics) Wholesalers *see* SIC 5074: Plumbing and Heating Equipment and Supplies (Hydronics)

421730 Warm Air Heating and Air-Conditioning Equipment and Supplies Wholesalers *see* SIC 5075: Warm Air Heating and Air-Conditioning Equipment and Supplies

421740 Refrigeration Equipment and Supplies Wholesalers *see* SIC 5078: Refrigeration Equipment and Supplies

421810 Construction and Mining (except Petroleum) Machinery and Equipment Wholesalers *see* SIC 5082: Construction and Mining (Except Petroleum) Machinery and Equipment

421820 Farm and Garden Machinery and Equipment Wholesalers *see* SIC 5083: Farm and Garden Machinery and Equipment

421830 Industrial Machinery and Equipment Wholesalers *see* SIC 5084: Industrial Machinery and Equipment; SIC 5085: Industrial Supplies

421840 Industrial Supplies Wholesalers *see* SIC 5085: Industrial Supplies

421850 Service Establishment Equipment and Supplies Wholesalers *see* SIC 5087: Service Establishment Equipment and Supplies

421860 Transportation Equipment and Supplies (except Motor Vehicles) Wholesalers *see* SIC 5088: Transportation Equipment and Supplies, Except Motor Vehicles

421910 Sporting and Recreational Goods and Supplies Wholesalers *see* SIC 5091: Sporting and Recreational Goods and Supplies

421920 Toy and Hobby Goods and Supplies Wholesalers *see* SIC 5092: Toys and Hobby Goods and Supplies

421930 Recyclable Material Wholesalers *see* SIC 5093: Scrap and Waste Materials

421940 Jewelry, Watch , Precious Stone, and Precious Metal Wholesalers *see* SIC 5094: Jewelry, Watches, Precious Stones, and Precious Metals

421990 Other Miscellaneous Durable Goods Wholesalers *see* SIC 5099: Durable Goods, NEC; SIC 7822: Motion Picture and Video Tape Distribution

422110 Printing and Writing Paper Wholesalers *see* SIC 5111: Printing and Writing Paper

422120 Stationery and Office Supplies Wholesalers *see* SIC 5112: Stationery and Office Supplies

422130 Industrial and Personal Service Paper Wholesalers *see* SIC 5113: Industrial and Personal Service Paper

422210 Drugs, Drug Proprietaries, and Druggists' Sundries Wholesalers *see* SIC 5122: Drugs, Drug Proprietaries, and Druggists' Sundries

422310 Piece Goods, Notions, and Other Dry Goods Wholesalers *see* SIC 5131: Piece Goods, Notions, and Other Dry Goods

422320 Men's and Boys' Clothing and Furnishings Wholesalers *see* SIC 5136: Men's and Boys' Clothing and Furnishings

422330 Women's, Children's, and Infants' Clothing and Accessories Wholesalers *see* SIC 5137: Women's Children's and Infants' Clothing and Accessories

422340 Footwear Wholesalers *see* SIC 5139: Footwear

422410 General Line Grocery Wholesalers *see* SIC 5141: Groceries, General Line

422420 Packaged Frozen Food Wholesalers *see* SIC 5142: Packaged Frozen Foods

422430 Dairy Products (except Dried or Canned) Wholesalers *see* SIC 5143: Dairy Products, Except Dried or Canned

422440 Poultry and Poultry Product Wholesalers *see* SIC 5144: Poultry and Poultry Products

422450 Confectionery Wholesalers *see* SIC 5145: Confectionery

422460 Fish and Seafood Wholesalers *see* SIC 5146: Fish and Seafoods

422470 Meat and Meat Product Wholesalers *see* SIC 5147: Meats and Meat Products

422480 Fresh Fruit and Vegetable Wholesalers *see* SIC 5148: Fresh Fruits and Vegetables

422490 Other Grocery and Related Product Wholesalers *see* SIC 5149: Groceries and Related Products, NEC

422510 Grain and Field Bean Wholesalers *see* SIC 5153: Grain and Field Beans

422520 Livestock Wholesalers *see* SIC 5154: Livestock

422590 Other Farm Product Raw Material Wholesalers *see* SIC 5159: Farm-Product Raw Materials, NEC

422610 Plastics Materials and Basic Forms and Shapes Wholesalers *see* SIC 5162: Plastics Materials and Basic Forms and Shapes

422690 Other Chemical and Allied Products Wholesalers *see* SIC 5169: Chemicals and Allied Products, NEC

422710 Petroleum Bulk Stations and Terminals *see* SIC 5171: Petroleum Bulk Stations and Terminals

422720 Petroleum and Petroleum Products Wholesalers (except Bulk Stations and Terminals) *see* SIC 5172: Petroleum and Petroleum Products Wholesalers, Except Bulk Stations and Terminals

422810 Beer and Ale Wholesalers *see* SIC 5181: Beer and Ale

422820 Wine and Distilled Alcoholic Beverage Wholesalers *see* SIC 5182: Wine and Distilled Alcoholic Beverages

422910 Farm Supplies Wholesalers *see* SIC 5191: Farm Supplies

422920 Book, Periodical and Newspaper Wholesalers *see* SIC 5192: Books, Periodicals, and Newspapers

422930 Flower, Nursery Stock and Florists' Supplies Wholesalers *see* SIC 5193: Flowers, Nursery Stock, and Florists' Supplies

422940 Tobacco and Tobacco Product Wholesalers *see* SIC 5194: Tobacco and Tobacco Products

422950 Paint, Varnish and Supplies Wholesalers *see* SIC 5198: Paint, Varnishes, and Supplies; SIC 5231: Paint, Glass, and Wallpaper Stores

422990 Other Miscellaneous Nondurable Goods Wholesalers *see* SIC 5199: Nondurable Goods, NEC

Retail Trade

441110 New Car Dealers *see* SIC 5511: Motor Vehicle Dealers (New and Used)

441120 Used Car Dealers *see* SIC 5521: Motor Vehicle Dealers (Used Only)

441210 Recreational Vehicle Dealers *see* SIC 5561: Recreational Vehicle Dealers

441221 Motorcycle Dealers *see* SIC 5571: Motorcycle Dealers

441222 Boat Dealers *see* SIC 5551: Boat Dealers

441229 All Other Motor Vehicle Dealers *see* SIC 5599: Automotive Dealers, NEC

441310 Automotive Parts and Accessories Stores *see* SIC 5013: Motor Vehicle Supplies and New Parts; SIC 5531: Auto and Home Supply Stores

441310 Automotive Parts and Accessories Stores *see* SIC 5731: Radio, Television, and Consumer Electronics Stores

441320 Tire Dealers *see* SIC 5014: Tires and Tubes; SIC 5531: Auto and Home Supply Stores

442110 Furniture Stores *see* SIC 5021: Furniture; SIC 5712: Furniture Stores

442210 Floor Covering Stores *see* SIC 5023: Home Furnishings; SIC 5713: Floor Covering Stores

442291 Window Treatment Stores *see* SIC 5714: Drapery, Curtain, and Upholstery Stores; SIC 5719: Miscellaneous Homefurnishings Stores

442299 All Other Home Furnishings Stores *see* SIC 5719: Miscellaneous Homefurnishings Stores; SIC 5722: Household Appliance Stores

443111 Household Appliance Stores *see* SIC 5999: Miscellaneous Retail Stores, NEC; SIC 7623: Refrigeration and Air-Conditioning Services and Repair Shops; SIC 7629: Electrical and Electronic Repair Shops, NEC

443112 Radio, Television, and Other Electronics Stores *see* SIC 5731: Radio, Television, and Consumer Electronics Stores; SIC 5999: Miscellaneous Retail Stores, NEC; SIC 7622: Radio and Television Repair Shops

443120 Computer and Software Stores *see* SIC 5045: Computers and Computer Peripheral Equipment and Software; SIC 5734: Computer and Computer Software Stores; SIC 7378: Computer Maintenance and Repair

443130 Camera and Photographic Supplies Stores *see* SIC 5946: Camera and Photographic Supply Stores

444110 Home Centers *see* SIC 5211: Lumber and Other Building Materials Dealers

444120 Paint and Wallpaper Stores *see* SIC 5198: Paint, Varnishes, and Supplies; SIC 5231: Paint, Glass, and Wallpaper Stores

444130 Hardware Stores *see* SIC 5251: Hardware Stores

444190 Other Building Material Dealers *see* SIC 5031: Lumber, Plywood, Millwork, and Wood Panels; SIC 5032: Brick, Stone and Related Construction Materials; SIC 5039: Construction Materials, NEC; SIC 5063: Electrical Apparatus and Equipment Wiring Supplies, and Construction Materials; SIC 5074: Plumbing and Heating Equipment and Supplies (Hydronics); SIC 5211: Lumber and Other Building Materials Dealers; SIC 5231: Paint, Glass, and Wallpaper Stores

444210 Outdoor Power Equipment Stores *see* SIC 5083: Farm and Garden Machinery and Equipment; SIC 5261: Retail Nurseries, Lawn and Garden Supply Stores

444220 Nursery and Garden Centers *see* SIC 5191: Farm Supplies; SIC 5193: Flowers, Nursery Stock, and Florists' Supplies; SIC 5261: Retail Nurseries, Lawn and Garden Supply Stores

445110 Supermarkets and Other Grocery (except Convenience) Stores *see* SIC 5411: Grocery Stores

445120 Convenience Stores *see* SIC 5411: Grocery Stores

445210 Meat Markets *see* SIC 5421: Meat and Fish (Seafood) Markets, Including Freezer Provisioners; SIC 5499: Miscellaneous Food Stores

445220 Fish and Seafood Markets *see* SIC 5421: Meat and Fish (Seafood) Markets, Including Freezer Provisioners

445230 Fruit and Vegetable Markets *see* SIC 5431: Fruit and Vegetable Markets

445291 Baked Goods Stores *see* SIC 5461: Retail Bakeries

445292 Confectionery and Nut Stores *see* SIC 5441: Candy, Nut, and Confectionery Stores

445299 All Other Specialty Food Stores *see* SIC 5451: Dairy Products Stores; SIC 5499: Miscellaneous Food Stores

445310 Beer, Wine and Liquor Stores *see* SIC 5921: Liquor Stores

446110 Pharmacies and Drug Stores *see* SIC 5912: Drug Stores and Proprietary Stores

446120 Cosmetics, Beauty Supplies, and Perfume Stores *see* SIC 5087: Service Establishment Equipment and Supplies

446120 Cosmetics, Beauty Supplies, and Perfume Stores *see* SIC 5999: Miscellaneous Retail Stores, NEC

446130 Optical Goods Stores *see* SIC 5995: Optical Goods Stores

446191 Food (Health) Supplement Stores *see* SIC 5499: Miscellaneous Food Stores

446199 All Other Health and Personal Care Stores *see* SIC 5047: Medical, Dental, and Hospital Equipment and Supplies; SIC 5999: Miscellaneous Retail Stores, NEC

447110 Gasoline Stations with Convenience Stores *see* SIC 5411: Grocery Stores; SIC 5541: Gasoline Service Stations

447190 Other Gasoline Stations *see* SIC 5541: Gasoline Service Stations

448110 Men's Clothing Stores *see* SIC 5611: Men's and Boys' Clothing and Accessory Stores

448120 Women's Clothing Stores *see* SIC 5621: Women's Clothing Stores

448130 Children's and Infants' Clothing Stores *see* SIC 5641: Children's and Infants' Wear Stores

448140 Family Clothing Stores *see* SIC 5651: Family Clothing Stores

448150 Clothing Accessories Stores *see* SIC 5611: Men's and Boys' Clothing and Accessory Stores; SIC 5632: Women's Accessory and Specialty Stores; SIC 5699: Miscellaneous Apparel and Accessory Stores

448190 Other Clothing Stores *see* SIC 5632: Women's Accessory and Specialty Stores; SIC 5699: Miscellaneous Apparel and Accessory Stores

448210 Shoe Stores *see* SIC 5661: Shoe Stores

448310 Jewelry Stores *see* SIC 5944: Jewelry Stores; SIC 5999: Miscellaneous Retail Stores, NEC

448320 Luggage and Leather Goods Stores *see* SIC 5948: Luggage and Leather Goods Stores

451110 Sporting Goods Stores *see* SIC 5941: Sporting Goods Stores and Bicycle Shops; SIC 7699: Repair Shops and Related Services, NEC

451120 Hobby, Toy and Game Stores *see* SIC 5945: Hobby, Toy, and Game Shops

451130 Sewing, Needlework and Piece Goods Stores *see* SIC 5714: Drapery, Curtain, and Upholstery Stores; SIC 5949: Sewing, Needlework, and Piece Goods Stores

451140 Musical Instrument and Supplies Stores *see* SIC 5736: Musical Instrument Stores

451211 Book Stores *see* SIC 5942: Book Stores

451212 News Dealers and Newsstands *see* SIC 5994: News Dealers and Newsstands

451220 Prerecorded Tape, Compact Disc and Record Stores *see* SIC 5735: Record and Prerecorded Tape Stores

452110 Department Stores *see* SIC 5311: Department Stores

452910 Warehouse Clubs and Superstores *see* SIC 5399: Miscellaneous General Merchandise Stores; SIC 5411: Grocery Stores

452990 All Other General Merchandise Stores *see* SIC 5331: Variety Stores; SIC 5399: Miscellaneous General Merchandise Stores

453110 Florists *see* SIC 5992: Florists

453210 Office Supplies and Stationery Stores *see* SIC 5049: Professional Equipment and Supplies, NEC; SIC 5112: Stationery and Office Supplies; SIC 5943: Stationery Stores

453220 Gift, Novelty and Souvenir Stores *see* SIC 5947: Gift, Novelty, and Souvenir Shops

453310 Used Merchandise Stores *see* SIC 5932: Used Merchandise Stores

453910 Pet and Pet Supplies Stores *see* SIC 5999: Miscellaneous Retail Stores, NEC

453920 Art Dealers *see* SIC 5999: Miscellaneous Retail Stores, NEC

453930 Manufactured (Mobile) Home Dealers *see* SIC 5271: Mobile Home Dealers

453991 Tobacco Stores *see* SIC 5993: Tobacco Stores and Stands

453998 All Other Miscellaneous Store Retailers (except Tobacco Stores) *see* SIC 5261: Retail Nurseries, Lawn and Garden Supply Stores; SIC 5999: Miscellaneous Retail Stores, NEC

454110 Electronic Shopping and Mail-Order Houses *see* SIC 5961: Catalog and Mail-Order Houses

454210 Vending Machine Operators *see* SIC 5962: Automatic Merchandising Machine Operator

454311 Heating Oil Dealers *see* SIC 5171: Petroleum Bulk Stations and Terminals; SIC 5983: Fuel Oil Dealers

454312 Liquefied Petroleum Gas (Bottled Gas) Dealers *see* SIC 5171: Petroleum Bulk Stations and Terminals; SIC 5984: Liquefied Petroleum Gas (Bottled Gas) Dealers

454319 Other Fuel Dealers *see* SIC 5989: Fuel Dealers, NEC

454390 Other Direct Selling Establishments *see* SIC 5421: Meat and Fish (Seafood) Markets, Including Freezer Provisioners; SIC 5963: Direct Selling Establishments

TRANSPORTATION & WAREHOUSING

481111 Scheduled Passenger Air Transportation *see* SIC 4512: Air Transportation, Scheduled

481112 Scheduled Freight Air Transportation *see* SIC 4512: Air Transportation, Scheduled

481211 Nonscheduled Chartered Passenger Air Transportation *see* SIC 4522: Air Transportation, Nonscheduled

481212 Nonscheduled Chartered Freight Air Transportation *see* SIC 4522: Air Transportation, Nonscheduled

481219 Other Nonscheduled Air Transportation *see* SIC 0721: Crop Planting, Cultivating and Protecting; SIC 7319: Advertising, NEC; SIC 7335: Commercial Photography

482111 Line-Haul Railroads *see* SIC 4011: Railroads, Line-haul Operating

482112 Short Line Railroads *see* SIC 4013: Railroad Switching and Terminal Establishments

483111 Deep Sea Freight Transportation *see* SIC 4412: Deep Sea Foreign Transportation of Freight

483112 Deep Sea Passenger Transportation *see* SIC 4481: Deep Sea Transportation of Passengers, Except by Ferry

483113 Coastal and Great Lakes Freight Transportation *see* SIC 4424: Deep Sea Domestic Transportation of Freight; SIC 4432: Freight Transportation on the Great Lakes-St. Lawrence Seaway; SIC 4492: Towing and Tugboat Services

483114 Coastal and Great Lakes Passenger Transportation *see* SIC 4481: Deep Sea Transportation of Passengers, Except by Ferry; SIC 4482: Ferries

483211 Inland Water Freight Transportation *see* SIC 4449: Water Transportation of Freight, NEC; SIC 4492: Towing and Tugboat Services

483212 Inland Water Passenger Transportation *see* SIC 4482: Ferries; SIC 4489: Water Transportation of Passengers, NEC

484110 General Freight Trucking, Local *see* SIC 4212: Local Trucking Without Storage; SIC 4214: Local Trucking with Storage

484121 General Freight Trucking, Long-Distance, Truckload *see* SIC 4213: Trucking, Except Local

484122 General Freight Trucking, Long-Distance, Less Than Truckload *see* SIC 4213: Trucking, Except Local

484210 Used Household and Office Goods Moving *see* SIC 4212: Local Trucking Without Storage; SIC 4213: Trucking, Except Local; SIC 4214: Local Trucking with Storage

484220 Specialized Freight (except Used Goods) Trucking, Local *see* SIC 4212: Local Trucking Without Storage; SIC 4214: Local Trucking with Storage

484230 Specialized Freight (except Used Goods) Trucking, Long-Distance *see* SIC 4213: Trucking, Except Local

485111 Mixed Mode Transit Systems *see* SIC 4111: Local and Suburban Transit

485112 Commuter Rail Systems *see* SIC 4111: Local and Suburban Transit

485113 Bus and Motor Vehicle Transit Systems *see* SIC 4111: Local and Suburban Transit

485119 Other Urban Transit Systems *see* SIC 4111: Local and Suburban Transit

485210 Interurban and Rural Bus Lines *see* SIC 4131: Intercity and Rural Bus Transportation

485310 Taxi Service *see* SIC 4121: Taxicabs

485320 Limousine Service *see* SIC 4119: Local Passenger Transportation, NEC

485410 School and Employee Bus Industry *see* SIC 4119: Local Passenger Transportation, NEC; SIC 4151: School Buses

485510 Charter Bus Industry *see* SIC 4141: Local Bus Charter Service; SIC 4142: Bus Charter Service, Except Local

485991 Special Needs Transportation *see* SIC 4119: Local Passenger Transportation, NEC

485999 All Other Transit and Ground Passenger Transportation *see* SIC 4111: Local and Suburban Transit; SIC 4119: Local Passenger Transportation, NEC

486110 Pipeline Transportation of Crude Oil *see* SIC 4612: Crude Petroleum Pipelines

486210 Pipeline Transportation of Natural Gas *see* SIC 4922: Natural Gas Transmission; SIC 4923: Natural Gas Transmission and Distribution

486910 Pipeline Transportation of Refined Petroleum Products *see* SIC 4613: Refined Petroleum Pipelines

486990 All Other Pipeline Transportation *see* SIC 4619: Pipelines, NEC

487110 Scenic and Sightseeing Transportation, Land *see* SIC 4119: Local Passenger Transportation, NEC; SIC 4789: Transportation Services, NEC; SIC 7999: Amusement and Recreation Services, NEC

487210 Scenic and Sightseeing Transportation, Water *see* SIC 4489: Water Transportation of Passengers, NEC; SIC 7999: Amusement and Recreation Services, NEC

487990 Scenic and Sightseeing Transportation, Other *see* SIC 4522: Air Transportation, Nonscheduled; SIC 7999: Amusement and Recreation Services, NEC

488111 Air Traffic Control *see* SIC 4581: Airports, Flying Fields, and Airport Terminal Services; SIC 9621: Regulations and Administration of Transportation Programs

488119 Other Airport Operations *see* SIC 4581: Airports, Flying Fields, and Airport Terminal Services; SIC 4959: Sanitary Services, NEC

488190 Other Support Activities for Air Transportation *see* SIC 4581: Airports, Flying Fields, and Airport Terminal Services

488210 Support Activities for Rail Transportation *see* SIC 4013: Railroad Switching and Terminal Establishments; SIC 4741: Rental of Railroad Cars; SIC 4789: Transportation Services, NEC

488310 Port and Harbor Operations *see* SIC 4491: Marine Cargo Handling; SIC 4499: Water Transportation Services, NEC

488320 Marine Cargo Handling *see* SIC 4491: Marine Cargo Handling

488330 Navigational Services to Shipping *see* SIC 4492: Towing and Tugboat Services; SIC 4499: Water Transportation Services, NEC

488390 Other Support Activities for Water Transportation *see* SIC 4499: Water Transportation Services, NEC; SIC 4785: Fixed Facilities and Inspection and Weighing Services for Motor Vehicle Transportation; SIC 7699: Repair Shops and Related Services, NEC

488410 Motor Vehicle Towing *see* SIC 7549: Automotive Services, Except Repair and Carwashes

488490 Other Support Activities for Road Transportation *see* SIC 4173: Terminal and Service Facilities for Motor Vehicle Passenger Transportation; SIC 4231: Terminal and Joint Terminal Maintenance Facilities for Motor Freight Transportation; SIC 4785: Fixed Facilities and Inspection and Weighing Services for Motor Vehicle Transportation

488510 Freight Transportation Arrangement *see* SIC 4731: Arrangement of Transportation of Freight and Cargo

488991 Packing and Crating *see* SIC 4783: Packing and Crating

488999 All Other Support Activities for Transportation *see* SIC 4729: Arrangement of Passenger Transportation, NEC; SIC 4789: Transportation Services, NEC

491110 Postal Service *see* SIC 4311: United States Postal Service

492110 Couriers *see* SIC 4215: Couriers Services Except by Air; SIC 4513: Air Courier Services

492210 Local Messengers and Local Delivery *see* SIC 4215: Couriers Services Except by Air

493110 General Warehousing and Storage Facilities *see* SIC 4225: General Warehousing and Storage; SIC 4226: Special Warehousing and Storage, NEC

493120 Refrigerated Storage Facilities *see* SIC 4222: Refrigerated Warehousing and Storage; SIC 4226: Special Warehousing and Storage, NEC

493130 Farm Product Storage Facilities *see* SIC 4221: Farm Product Warehousing and Storage

493190 All Other Warehousing and Storage Facilities *see* SIC 4226: Special Warehousing and Storage, NEC

Information

511110 Newspaper Publishers *see* SIC 2711: Newspapers: Publishing, or Publishing and Printing

511120 Periodical Publishers *see* SIC 2721: Periodicals: Publishing, or Publishing and Printing

511130 Book Publishers *see* SIC 2731: Books: Publishing, or Publishing and Printing

511140 Database and Directory Publishers *see* SIC 2741: Miscellaneous Publishing

511191 Greeting Card Publishers *see* SIC 2771: Greeting Cards

511199 All Other Publishers *see* SIC 2741: Miscellaneous Publishing

511210 Software Publishers *see* SIC 7372: Prepackaged Software

512110 Motion Picture and Video Production *see* SIC 7812: Motion Picture and Video Tape Production

512120 Motion Picture and Video Distribution *see* SIC 7822: Motion Picture and Video Tape Distribution; SIC 7829: Services Allied to Motion Picture Distribution

512131 Motion Picture Theaters, Except Drive-In *see* SIC 7832: Motion Picture Theaters, Except Drive-In

512132 Drive-In Motion Picture Theaters *see* SIC 7833: Drive-In Motion Picture Theaters

512191 Teleproduction and Other Post-Production Services *see* SIC 7819: Services Allied to Motion Picture Production

512199 Other Motion Picture and Video Industries *see* SIC 7819: Services Allied to Motion Picture Production; SIC 7829: Services Allied to Motion Picture Distribution

512210 Record Production *see* SIC 8999: Services, NEC

512220 Integrated Record Production/Distribution *see* SIC 3652: Phonograph Records and Prerecorded Audio Tapes and Disks

512230 Music Publishers *see* SIC 2731: Books: Publishing, or Publishing and Printing; SIC 2741: Miscellaneous Publishing; SIC 8999: Services, NEC

512240 Sound Recording Studios *see* SIC 7389: Business Services, NEC

512290 Other Sound Recording Industries *see* SIC 7389: Business Services, NEC; SIC 7922: Theatrical Producers (Except Motion Picture) and Miscellaneous Theatrical Services

513111 Radio Networks *see* SIC 4832: Radio Broadcasting Stations

513112 Radio Stations *see* SIC 4832: Radio Broadcasting Stations

513120 Television Broadcasting *see* SIC 4833: Television Broadcasting Stations

513210 Cable Networks *see* SIC 4841: Cable and Other Pay Television Services

513220 Cable and Other Program Distribution *see* SIC 4841: Cable and Other Pay Television Services

513310 Wired Telecommunications Carriers *see* SIC 4813: Telephone Communications, Except Radiotelephone; SIC 4822: Telegraph and Other Message Communications

513321 Paging *see* SIC 4812: Radiotelephone Communications

513322 Cellular and Other Wireless Telecommunications *see* SIC 4812: Radiotelephone Communications; SIC 4899: Communications Services, NEC

513330 Telecommunications Resellers *see* SIC 4812: Radiotelephone Communications; SIC 4813: Telephone Communications, Except Radiotelephone

513340 Satellite Telecommunications *see* SIC 4899: Communications Services, NEC

513390 Other Telecommunications *see* SIC 4899: Communications Services, NEC

514110 New Syndicates *see* SIC 7383: News Syndicates

514120 Libraries and Archives *see* SIC 8231: Libraries

514191 On-Line Information Services *see* SIC 7375: Information Retrieval Services

514199 All Other Information Services *see* SIC 8999: Services, NEC

514210 Data Processing Services *see* SIC 7374: Computer Processing and Data Preparation and Processing Services

FINANCE & INSURANCE

521110 Monetary Authorities-Central Banks *see* SIC 6011: Federal Reserve Banks

522110 Commercial Banking *see* SIC 6021: National Commercial Banks; SIC 6022: State Commercial Banks; SIC 6029: Commercial Banks, NEC; SIC 6081: Branches and Agencies of Foreign Banks

522120 Savings Institutions *see* SIC 6035: Savings Institutions, Federally Chartered; SIC 6036: Savings institutions, Not Federally Chartered

522130 Credit Unions *see* SIC 6061: Credit Unions, Federally Chartered; SIC 6062: Credit Unions, Not Federally Chartered

522190 Other Depository Intermediation *see* SIC 6022: State Commercial Banks

522210 Credit Card Issuing *see* SIC 6021: National Commercial Banks; SIC 6022: State Commercial Banks; SIC 6141: Personal Credit Institutions

522220 Sales Financing *see* SIC 6141: Personal Credit Institutions; SIC 6153: Short-Term Business Credit Institutions, Except Agricultural; SIC 6159: Miscellaneous Business Credit Institutions

522291 Consumer Lending *see* SIC 6141: Personal Credit Institutions

522292 Real Estate Credit *see* SIC 6162: Mortgage Bankers and Loan Correspondents

522293 International Trade Financing *see* SIC 6081: Branches and Agencies of Foreign Banks; SIC 6082: Foreign Trade and International Banking Institutions; SIC 6111: Federal and Federally Sponsored Credit Agencies; SIC 6159: Miscellaneous Business Credit Institutions

522294 Secondary Market Financing *see* SIC 6111: Federal and Federally Sponsored Credit Agencies

522298 All Other Non-Depository Credit Intermediation *see* SIC 5932: Used Merchandise Stores; SIC 6081: Branches and Agencies of Foreign Banks; SIC 6111: Federal and Federally Sponsored Credit Agencies; SIC 6153: Short-Term Business Credit Institutions, Except Agricultural; SIC 6159: Miscellaneous Business Credit Institutions

522310 Mortgage and Other Loan Brokers *see* SIC 6163: Loan Brokers

522320 Financial Transactions Processing, Reserve, and Clearing House Activities *see* SIC 6019: Central Reserve Depository Institutions, NEC; SIC 6099: Functions Related to Deposit Banking, NEC; SIC 6153: Short-Term Business Credit Institutions, Except Agricultural; SIC 7389: Business Services, NEC

522390 Other Activities Related to Credit Intermediation *see* SIC 6099: Functions Related to Deposit Banking, NEC; SIC 6162: Mortgage Bankers and Loan Correspondents

523110 Investment Banking and Securities Dealing *see* SIC 6211: Security Brokers, Dealers, and Flotation Companies

523120 Securities Brokerage *see* SIC 6211: Security Brokers, Dealers, and Flotation Companies

523130 Commodity Contracts Dealing *see* SIC 6099: Functions Related to Deposit Banking, NEC; SIC 6221: Commodity Contracts Brokers and Dealers; SIC 6799: Investors, NEC

523140 Commodity Brokerage *see* SIC 6221: Commodity Contracts Brokers and Dealers

523210 Securities and Commodity Exchanges *see* SIC 6231: Security and Commodity Exchanges

523910 Miscellaneous Intermediation *see* SIC 6211: Security Brokers, Dealers, and Flotation Companies; SIC 6799: Investors, NEC

523920 Portfolio Management *see* SIC 6282: Investment Advice; SIC 6371: Pension, Health, and Welfare Funds; SIC 6733: Trusts, Except Educational, Religious, and Charitable; SIC 6799: Investors, NEC

523930 Investment Advice *see* SIC 6282: Investment Advice

523991 Trust, Fiduciary and Custody Activities *see* SIC 6021: National Commercial Banks; SIC 6022: State Commercial Banks; SIC 6091: Nondeposit Trust Facilities; SIC 6099: Functions Related to Deposit Banking, NEC; SIC 6289: Services Allied With the Exchange of Securities or Commodities, NEC; SIC 6733: Trusts, Except Educational, Religious, and Charitable

523999 Miscellaneous Financial Investment Activities *see* SIC 6099: Functions Related to Deposit Banking, NEC; SIC 6211: Security Brokers, Dealers, and Flotation Companies; SIC 6289: Services Allied With the Exchange of Securities or Commodities, NEC; SIC 6792: Oil Royalty Traders; SIC 6799: Investors, NEC

524113 Direct Life Insurance Carriers *see* SIC 6311: Life Insurance

524114 Direct Health and Medical Insurance Carriers *see* SIC 6321: Accident and Health Insurance; SIC 6324: Hospital and Medical Service Plans

524126 Direct Property and Casualty Insurance Carriers *see* SIC 6331: Fire, Marine, and Casualty Insurance; SIC 6351: Surety Insurance

524127 Direct Title Insurance Carriers *see* SIC 6361: Title Insurance

524128 Other Direct Insurance Carriers (except Life, Health, and Medical) *see* SIC 6399: Insurance Carriers, NEC

524130 Reinsurance Carriers *see* SIC 6311: Life Insurance; SIC 6321: Accident and Health Insurance; SIC 6324: Hospital and Medical Service Plans; SIC 6331: Fire, Marine, and Casualty Insurance; SIC 6351: Surety Insurance; SIC 6361: Title Insurance

524210 Insurance Agencies and Brokerages *see* SIC 6411: Insurance Agents, Brokers, and Service

524291 Claims Adjusters *see* SIC 6411: Insurance Agents, Brokers, and Service

524292 Third Party Administration for Insurance and Pension Funds *see* SIC 6371: Pension, Health, and Welfare Funds; SIC 6411: Insurance Agents, Brokers, and Service

524298 All Other Insurance Related Activities *see* SIC 6411: Insurance Agents, Brokers, and Service

525110 Pension Funds *see* SIC 6371: Pension, Health, and Welfare Funds

525120 Health and Welfare Funds *see* SIC 6371: Pension, Health, and Welfare Funds

525190 Other Insurance and Employee Benefit Funds *see* SIC 6321: Accident and Health Insurance; SIC 6324: Hospital and Medical Service Plans; SIC 6331: Fire, Marine, and Casualty Insurance; SIC 6733: Trusts, Except Educational, Religious, and Charitable

525910 Open-End Investment Funds *see* SIC 6722: Management Investment Offices, Open-End

525920 Trusts, Estates, and Agency Accounts *see* SIC 6733: Trusts, Except Educational, Religious, and Charitable

525930 Real Estate Investment Trusts *see* SIC 6798: Real Estate Investment Trusts

525990 Other Financial Vehicles *see* SIC 6726: Unit Investment Trusts, Face-Amount Certificate Offices, and Closed-End Management Investment Offices

Real Estate & Rental & Leasing

531110 Lessors of Residential Buildings and Dwellings *see* SIC 6513: Operators of Apartment Buildings; SIC 6514: Operators of Dwellings Other Than Apartment Buildings

531120 Lessors of Nonresidential Buildings (except Mini-warehouses) *see* SIC 6512: Operators of Nonresidential Buildings

531130 Lessors of Mini-warehouses and Self Storage Units *see* SIC 4225: General Warehousing and Storage

531190 Lessors of Other Real Estate Property *see* SIC 6515: Operators of Residential Mobile Home Sites; SIC 6517: Lessors of Railroad Property; SIC 6519: Lessors of Real Property, NEC

531210 Offices of Real Estate Agents and Brokers *see* SIC 6531: Real Estate Agents and Managers

531311 Residential Property Managers *see* SIC 6531: Real Estate Agents and Managers

531312 Nonresidential Property Managers *see* SIC 6531: Real Estate Agents and Managers

531320 Offices of Real Estate Appraisers *see* SIC 6531: Real Estate Agents and Managers

531390 Other Activities Related to Real Estate *see* SIC 6531: Real Estate Agents and Managers

532111 Passenger Cars Rental *see* SIC 7514: Passenger Car Rental

532112 Passenger Cars Leasing *see* SIC 7515: Passenger Car Leasing

532120 Truck, Utility Trailer and RV (Recreational Vehicle) Rental and Leasing *see* SIC 7513: Truck Rental and Leasing, Without Drivers; SIC 7519: Utility Trailer and Recreational Vehicle Rental

532210 Consumer Electronics and Appliances Rental *see* SIC 7359: Equipment Rental and Leasing, NEC

532220 Formal Wear and Costumes Rental *see* SIC 7299: Miscellaneous Personal Services, NEC; SIC 7819: Services Allied to Motion Picture Production

532230 Video Tapes and Disc Rental *see* SIC 7841: Video Tape Rental

532291 Home Health Equipment Rental *see* SIC 7352: Medical Equipment Rental and Leasing

532292 Recreational Goods Rental *see* SIC 7999: Amusement and Recreation Services, NEC

532299 All Other Consumer Goods Rental *see* SIC 7359: Equipment Rental and Leasing, NEC

532310 General Rental Centers *see* SIC 7359: Equipment Rental and Leasing, NEC

532411 Commercial Air, Rail, and Water Transportation Equipment Rental and Leasing *see* SIC 4499: Water Transportation Services, NEC; SIC 4741: Rental of Railroad Cars; SIC 7359: Equipment Rental and Leasing, NEC

532412 Construction, Mining and Forestry Machinery and Equipment Rental and Leasing *see* SIC 7353: Heavy Construction Equipment Rental and Leasing; SIC 7359: Equipment Rental and Leasing, NEC

532420 Office Machinery and Equipment Rental and Leasing *see* SIC 7359: Equipment Rental and Leasing, NEC; SIC 7377: Computer Rental and Leasing

532490 Other Commercial and Industrial Machinery and Equipment Rental and Leasing *see* SIC 7352: Medical Equipment Rental and Leasing; SIC 7359: Equipment Rental and Leasing, NEC; SIC 7819: Services Allied to Motion Picture Production; SIC 7922: Theatrical Producers (Except Motion Picture) and Miscellaneous Theatrical Services

533110 Owners and Lessors of Other Non-Financial Assets *see* SIC 6792: Oil Royalty Traders; SIC 6794: Patent Owners and Lessors

Professional, Scientific, & Technical Services

541110 Offices of Lawyers *see* SIC 8111: Legal Services

541191 Title Abstract and Settlement Offices *see* SIC 6541: Title Abstract Offices

541199 Other Legal Services *see* SIC 7389: Business Services, NEC

541211 Offices of Certified Public Accountants *see* SIC 8721: Accounting, Auditing, and Bookkeeping Services

541213 Tax Preparation Services *see* SIC 7291: Tax Return Preparation Services

541214 Payroll Services *see* SIC 7819: Services Allied to Motion Picture Production; SIC 8721: Accounting, Auditing, and Bookkeeping Services

541219 Other Accounting Services *see* SIC 8721: Accounting, Auditing, and Bookkeeping Services

541310 Architectural Services *see* SIC 8712: Architectural Services

541320 Landscape Architectural Services *see* SIC 0781: Landscape Counseling and Planning

541330 Engineering Services *see* SIC 8711: Engineering Services

541340 Drafting Services *see* SIC 7389: Business Services, NEC

541350 Building Inspection Services *see* SIC 7389: Business Services, NEC

541360 Geophysical Surveying and Mapping Services *see* SIC 1081: Metal Mining Services; SIC 1382: Oil and Gas Field Exploration Services; SIC 1481: Nonmetallic Minerals Services Except Fuels; SIC 8713: Surveying Services

541370 Surveying and Mapping (except Geophysical) Services *see* SIC 7389: Business Services, NEC; SIC 8713: Surveying Services

541380 Testing Laboratories *see* SIC 8734: Testing Laboratories

541410 Interior Design Services *see* SIC 7389: Business Services, NEC

541420 Industrial Design Services *see* SIC 7389: Business Services, NEC

541430 Graphic Design Services *see* SIC 7336: Commercial Art and Graphic Design; SIC 8099: Health and Allied Services, NEC

541490 Other Specialized Design Services *see* SIC 7389: Business Services, NEC

541511 Custom Computer Programming Services *see* SIC 7371: Computer Programming Services

541512 Computer Systems Design Services *see* SIC 7373: Computer Integrated Systems Design; SIC 7379: Computer Related Services, NEC

541513 Computer Facilities Management Services *see* SIC 7376: Computer Facilities Management Services

541519 Other Computer Related Services *see* SIC 7379: Computer Related Services, NEC

541611 Administrative Management and General Management Consulting Services *see* SIC 8742: Management Consulting Services

541612 Human Resources and Executive Search Consulting Services *see* SIC 7361: Employment Agencies; SIC 8742: Management Consulting Services; SIC 8999: Services, NEC

541613 Marketing Consulting Services *see* SIC 8742: Management Consulting Services

541614 Process, Physical, Distribution and Logistics Consulting *see* SIC 8742: Management Consulting Services

541618 Other Management Consulting Services *see* SIC 4731: Arrangement of Transportation of Freight and Cargo; SIC 8748: Business Consulting Services, NEC

541620 Environmental Consulting Services *see* SIC 8999: Services, NEC

541690 Other Scientific and Technical Consulting Services *see* SIC 0781: Landscape Counseling and Planning; SIC 8748: Business Consulting Services, NEC; SIC 8999: Services, NEC

541710 Research and Development in the Physical Sciences and Engineering Sciences *see* SIC 8731: Commercial Physical and Biological Research; SIC 8733: Noncommercial Research Organizations

541720 Research and Development in the Life Sciences *see* SIC 8731: Commercial Physical and Biological Research; SIC 8733: Noncommercial Research Organizations

541730 Research and Development in the Social Sciences and Humanities *see* SIC 8732: Commercial Economic, Sociological, and Educational Research; SIC 8733: Noncommercial Research Organizations

541810 Advertising Agencies *see* SIC 7311: Advertising Agencies

541820 Public Relations Services *see* SIC 8743: Public Relations Services

541830 Media Buying Agencies *see* SIC 7319: Advertising, NEC

541840 Media Representatives *see* SIC 7313: Radio, Television, and Publishers' Advertising Representatives

541850 Display Advertising *see* SIC 7312: Outdoor Advertising Services; SIC 7319: Advertising, NEC

541860 Direct Mail Advertising *see* SIC 7331: Direct Mail Advertising Services

541870 Advertising Material Distribution Services *see* SIC 7319: Advertising, NEC

541890 Other Services Related to Advertising *see* SIC 5199: Nondurable Goods, NEC; SIC 7319: Advertising, NEC; SIC 7389: Business Services, NEC

541910 Marketing Research and Public Opinion Polling *see* SIC 8732: Commercial Economic, Sociological, and Educational Research

541921 Photographic Studios, Portrait *see* SIC 7221: Photographic Studios, Portrait

541922 Commercial Photography *see* SIC 7335: Commercial Photography; SIC 8099: Health and Allied Services, NEC

541930 Translation and Interpretation Services *see* SIC 7389: Business Services, NEC

541940 Veterinary Services *see* SIC 0741: Veterinary Service For Livestock; SIC 0742: Veterinary Services for Animal Specialties; SIC 8734: Testing Laboratories

541990 All Other Professional, Scientific and Technical Services *see* SIC 7389: Business Services, NEC

Management of Companies & Enterprises

551111 Offices of Bank Holding Companies *see* SIC 6712: Offices of Bank Holding Companies

551112 Offices of Other Holding Companies *see* SIC 6719: Offices of Holding Companies, NEC

Administrative & Support, Waste Management & Remediation Services

561110 Office Administrative Services *see* SIC 8741: Management Services (Except Construction Management Services)

561210 Facilities Support Services *see* SIC 8744: Facilities Support Management Services

561310 Employment Placement Agencies *see* SIC 7361: Employment Agencies; SIC 7819: Services Allied to Motion Picture Production; SIC 7922: Theatrical Producers (Except Motion Picture) and Miscellaneous Theatrical Services

561320 Temporary Help Services *see* SIC 7363: Help Supply Services

561330 Employee Leasing Services *see* SIC 7363: Help Supply Services

561410 Document Preparation Services *see* SIC 7338: Secretarial and Court Reporting Services

561421 Telephone Answering Services *see* SIC 7389: Business Services, NEC

561422 Telemarketing Bureaus *see* SIC 7389: Business Services, NEC

561431 Other Business Service Centers (including Copy Shops) *see* SIC 7389: Business Services, NEC; SIC 7334: Photocopying and Duplicating Services

561439 Private Mail Centers *see* SIC 7389: Business Services, NEC

561440 Collection Agencies *see* SIC 7322: Adjustment and Collection Services

561450 Credit Bureaus *see* SIC 7323: Credit Reporting Services

561491 Repossession Services *see* SIC 7322: Adjustment and Collection Services; SIC 7389: Business Services, NEC

561492 Court Reporting and Stenotype Services *see* SIC 7338: Secretarial and Court Reporting Services

561499 All Other Business Support Services *see* SIC 7389: Business Services, NEC

561510 Travel Agencies *see* SIC 4724: Travel Agencies

561520 Tour Operators *see* SIC 4725: Tour Operators

561591 Convention and Visitors Bureaus *see* SIC 7389: Business Services, NEC

561599 All Other Travel Arrangement and Reservation Services *see* SIC 4729: Arrangement of Passenger Transportation, NEC; SIC 7389: Business Services, NEC; SIC 7999: Amusement and Recreation Services, NEC; SIC 8699: Membership Organizations, NEC

561611 Investigation Services *see* SIC 7381: Detective, Guard, and Armored Car Services

561612 Security Guards and Patrol Services *see* SIC 7381: Detective, Guard, and Armored Car Services

561613 Armored Car Services *see* SIC 7381: Detective, Guard, and Armored Car Services

561621 Security Systems Services (except Locksmiths) *see* SIC 1731: Electrical Work; SIC 7382: Security Systems Services

561622 Locksmiths *see* SIC 7699: Repair Shops and Related Services, NEC

561710 Exterminating and Pest Control Services *see* SIC 4959: Sanitary Services, NEC; SIC 7342: Disinfecting and Pest Control Services

561720 Janitorial Services *see* SIC 4581: Airports, Flying Fields, and Airport Terminal Services; SIC 7342: Disinfecting and Pest Control Services; SIC 7349: Building Cleaning and Maintenance Services, NEC

561730 Landscaping Services *see* SIC 0782: Lawn and Garden Services; SIC 0783: Ornamental Shrub and Tree Services

561740 Carpet and Upholstery Cleaning Services *see* SIC 7217: Carpet and Upholstery Cleaning

561790 Other Services to Buildings and Dwellings *see* SIC 7389: Business Services, NEC; SIC 7699: Repair Shops and Related Services, NEC

561910 Packaging and Labeling Services *see* SIC 7389: Business Services, NEC

561920 Convention and Trade Show Organizers *see* SIC 7389: Business Services, NEC

561990 All Other Support Services *see* SIC 7389: Business Services, NEC

562111 Solid Waste Collection *see* SIC 4212: Local Trucking Without Storage; SIC 4953: Refuse Systems

562112 Hazardous Waste Collection *see* SIC 4212: Local Trucking Without Storage; SIC 4953: Refuse Systems

562119 Other Waste Collection *see* SIC 4212: Local Trucking Without Storage; SIC 4953: Refuse Systems

562211 Hazardous Waste Treatment and Disposal *see* SIC 4953: Refuse Systems

562212 Solid Waste Landfills *see* SIC 4953: Refuse Systems

562213 Solid Waste Combustors and Incinerators *see* SIC 4953: Refuse Systems

562219 Other Nonhazardous Waste Treatment and Disposal *see* SIC 4953: Refuse Systems

562910 Remediation Services *see* SIC 1799: Special Trade Contractors, NEC; SIC 4959: Sanitary Services, NEC

562920 Materials Recovery Facilities *see* SIC 4953: Refuse Systems

562991 Septic Tank and Related Services *see* SIC 7359: Equipment Rental and Leasing, NEC; SIC 7699: Repair Shops and Related Services, NEC

562998 All Other Miscellaneous Waste Management *see* SIC 4959: Sanitary Services, NEC

Educational Services

611110 Elementary and Secondary Schools *see* SIC 8211: Elementary and Secondary Schools

611210 Junior Colleges *see* SIC 8222: Junior Colleges and Technical Institutes

611310 Colleges, Universities and Professional Schools *see* SIC 8221: Colleges, Universities, and Professional Schools

611410 Business and Secretarial Schools *see* SIC 8244: Business and Secretarial Schools

611420 Computer Training *see* SIC 8243: Data Processing Schools

611430 Professional and Management Development Training Schools *see* SIC 8299: Schools and Educational Services, NEC

611511 Cosmetology and Barber Schools *see* SIC 7231: Beauty Shops; SIC 7241: Barber Shops

611512 Flight Training *see* SIC 8249: Vocational Schools, NEC; SIC 8299: Schools and Educational Services, NEC

611513 Apprenticeship Training *see* SIC 8249: Vocational Schools, NEC

611519 Other Technical and Trade Schools *see* SIC 8243: Data Processing Schools; SIC 8249: Vocational Schools, NEC

611610 Fine Arts Schools *see* SIC 7911: Dance Studios, Schools, and Halls; SIC 8299: Schools and Educational Services, NEC

611620 Sports and Recreation Instruction *see* SIC 7999: Amusement and Recreation Services, NEC

611630 Language Schools *see* SIC 8299: Schools and Educational Services, NEC

611691 Exam Preparation and Tutoring *see* SIC 8299: Schools and Educational Services, NEC

611692 Automobile Driving Schools *see* SIC 8299: Schools and Educational Services, NEC

611699 All Other Miscellaneous Schools and Instruction *see* SIC 8299: Schools and Educational Services, NEC

611710 Educational Support Services *see* SIC 8299: Schools and Educational Services, NEC; SIC 8748: Business Consulting Services, NEC

Health Care & Social Assistance

621111 Offices of Physicians (except Mental Health Specialists) *see* SIC 8011: Offices and Clinics of Doctors of Medicine; SIC 8031: Offices and Clinics of Doctors of Osteopathy

621112 Offices of Physicians, Mental Health Specialists *see* SIC 8011: Offices and Clinics of Doctors of Medicine; SIC 8031: Offices and Clinics of Doctors of Osteopathy

621210 Offices of Dentists *see* SIC 8021: Offices and Clinics of Dentists

621310 Offices of Chiropractors *see* SIC 8041: Offices and Clinics of Chiropractors

621320 Offices of Optometrists *see* SIC 8042: Offices and Clinics of Optometrists

621330 Offices of Mental Health Practitioners (except Physicians) *see* SIC 8049: Offices and Clinics of Health Practitioners, NEC

621340 Offices of Physical, Occupational, and Speech Therapists and Audiologists *see* SIC 8049: Offices and Clinics of Health Practitioners, NEC

621391 Offices of Podiatrists *see* SIC 8043: Offices and Clinics of Podiatrists

621399 Offices of All Other Miscellaneous Health Practitioners *see* SIC 8049: Offices and Clinics of Health Practitioners, NEC

621410 Family Planning Centers *see* SIC 8093: Specialty Outpatient Facilities, NEC; SIC 8099: Health and Allied Services, NEC

621420 Outpatient Mental Health and Substance Abuse Centers *see* SIC 8093: Specialty Outpatient Facilities, NEC

621491 HMO Medical Centers *see* SIC 8011: Offices and Clinics of Doctors of Medicine

621492 Kidney Dialysis Centers *see* SIC 8092: Kidney Dialysis Centers

621493 Freestanding Ambulatory Surgical and Emergency Centers *see* SIC 8011: Offices and Clinics of Doctors of Medicine

621498 All Other Outpatient Care Facilities *see* SIC 8093: Specialty Outpatient Facilities, NEC

621511 Medical Laboratories *see* SIC 8071: Medical Laboratories

621512 Diagnostic Imaging Centers *see* SIC 8071: Medical Laboratories

621610 Home Health Care Services *see* SIC 8082: Home Health Care Services

621910 Ambulance Service *see* SIC 4119: Local Passenger Transportation, NEC; SIC 4522: Air Transportation, Nonscheduled

621991 Blood and Organ Banks *see* SIC 8099: Health and Allied Services, NEC

621999 All Other Miscellaneous Ambulatory Health Care Services *see* SIC 8099: Health and Allied Services, NEC

622110 General Medical and Surgical Hospitals *see* SIC 8062: General Medical and Surgical Hospitals; SIC 8069: Specialty Hospitals, Except Psychiatric

622210 Psychiatric and Substance Abuse Hospitals *see* SIC 8063: Psychiatric Hospitals; SIC 8069: Specialty Hospitals, Except Psychiatric

622310 Specialty (except Psychiatric and Substance Abuse) Hospitals *see* SIC 8069: Specialty Hospitals, Except Psychiatric

623110 Nursing Care Facilities *see* SIC 8051: Skilled Nursing Care Facilities; SIC 8052: Intermediate Care Facilities; SIC 8059: Nursing and Personal Care Facilities, NEC

623210 Residential Mental Retardation Facilities *see* SIC 8052: Intermediate Care Facilities

623220 Residential Mental Health and Substance Abuse Facilities *see* SIC 8361: Residential Care

623311 Continuing Care Retirement Communities *see* SIC 8051: Skilled Nursing Care Facilities; SIC 8052: Intermediate Care Facilities; SIC 8059: Nursing and Personal Care Facilities, NEC

623312 Homes for the Elderly *see* SIC 8361: Residential Care

623990 Other Residential Care Facilities *see* SIC 8361: Residential Care

624110 Child and Youth Services *see* SIC 8322: Individual and Family Social Services; SIC 8641: Civic, Social, and Fraternal Associations

624120 Services for the Elderly and Persons with Disabilities *see* SIC 8322: Individual and Family Social Services

624190 Other Individual and Family Services *see* SIC 8322: Individual and Family Social Services

624210 Community Food Services *see* SIC 8322: Individual and Family Social Services

624221 Temporary Shelter *see* SIC 8322: Individual and Family Social Services

624229 Other Community Housing Services *see* SIC 8322: Individual and Family Social Services

624230 Emergency and Other Relief Services *see* SIC 8322: Individual and Family Social Services

624310 Vocational Rehabilitation Services *see* SIC 8331: Job Training and Vocational Rehabilitation Services

624410 Child Day Care Services *see* SIC 7299: Miscellaneous Personal Services, NEC; SIC 8351: Child Day Care Services

Arts, Entertainment, & Recreation

711110 Theater Companies and Dinner Theaters *see* SIC 5812: Eating and Drinking Places; SIC 7922: Theatrical Producers (Except Motion Picture) and Miscellaneous Theatrical Services

711120 Dance Companies *see* SIC 7922: Theatrical Producers (Except Motion Picture) and Miscellaneous Theatrical Services

711130 Musical Groups and Artists *see* SIC 7929: Bands, Orchestras, Actors, and Other Entertainers and Entertainment Groups

711190 Other Performing Arts Companies *see* SIC 7929: Bands, Orchestras, Actors, and Other Entertainers and Entertainment Groups; SIC 7999: Amusement and Recreation Services, NEC

711211 Sports Teams and Clubs *see* SIC 7941: Professional Sports Clubs and Promoters

711212 Race Tracks *see* SIC 7948: Racing, Including Track Operations

711219 Other Spectator Sports *see* SIC 7941: Professional Sports Clubs and Promoters; SIC 7948: Racing, Including Track Operations; SIC 7999: Amusement and Recreation Services, NEC

711310 Promoters of Performing Arts, Sports, and Similar Events with Facilities *see* SIC 6512: Operators of Nonresidential Buildings; SIC 7922: Theatrical Producers (Except Motion Picture) and Miscellaneous Theatrical Services; SIC 7941: Professional Sports Clubs and Promoters

711320 Promoters of Performing Arts, Sports, and Similar Events without Facilities *see* SIC 7922: Theatrical Producers (Except Motion Picture) and Miscellaneous Theatrical Services; SIC 7941: Professional Sports Clubs and Promoters

711410 Agents and Managers for Artists, Athletes, Entertainers and Other Public Figures *see* SIC 7389: Business Services, NEC; SIC 7922: Theatrical Producers (Except Motion Picture) and Miscellaneous Theatrical Services; SIC 7941: Professional Sports Clubs and Promoters

711510 Independent Artists, Writers, and Performers *see* SIC 7819: Services Allied to Motion Picture Production; SIC 7929: Bands, Orchestras, Actors, and Other Entertainers and Entertainment Groups; SIC 8999: Services, NEC

712110 Museums *see* SIC 8412: Museums and Art Galleries

712120 Historical Sites *see* SIC 8412: Museums and Art Galleries

712130 Zoos and Botanical Gardens *see* SIC 8422: Arboreta and Botanical or Zoological Gardens

712190 Nature Parks and Other Similar Institutions *see* SIC 7999: Amusement and Recreation Services, NEC; SIC 8422: Arboreta and Botanical or Zoological Gardens

713110 Amusement and Theme Parks *see* SIC 7996: Amusement Parks

713120 Amusement Arcades *see* SIC 7993: Coin Operated Amusement Devices

713210 Casinos (except Casino Hotels) *see* SIC 7999: Amusement and Recreation Services, NEC

713290 Other Gambling Industries *see* SIC 7993: Coin Operated Amusement Devices; SIC 7999: Amusement and Recreation Services, NEC

713910 Golf Courses and Country Clubs *see* SIC 7992: Public Golf Courses; SIC 7997: Membership Sports and Recreation Clubs

713920 Skiing Facilities *see* SIC 7999: Amusement and Recreation Services, NEC

713930 Marinas *see* SIC 4493: Marinas

713940 Fitness and Recreational Sports Centers *see* SIC 7991: Physical Fitness Facilities; SIC 7997: Membership Sports and Recreation Clubs; SIC 7999: Amusement and Recreation Services, NEC

713950 Bowling Centers *see* SIC 7933: Bowling Centers

713990 All Other Amusement and Recreation Industries *see* SIC 7911: Dance Studios, Schools, and Halls; SIC 7993: Coin Operated Amusement Devices; SIC 7997: Membership Sports and Recreation Clubs; SIC 7999: Amusement and Recreation Services, NEC

Accomodation & Foodservices

721110 Hotels (except Casino Hotels) and Motels *see* SIC 7011: Hotels and Motels; SIC 7041: Organization Hotels and Lodging Houses, on Membership Basis

721120 Casino Hotels *see* SIC 7011: Hotels and Motels

721191 Bed and Breakfast Inns *see* SIC 7011: Hotels and Motels

721199 All Other Traveler Accommodations *see* SIC 7011: Hotels and Motels

721211 RV (Recreational Vehicle) Parks and Campgrounds *see* SIC 7033: Recreational Vehicle Parks and Campsites

721214 Recreational and Vacation Camps *see* SIC 7032: Sporting and Recreational Camps

721310 Rooming and Boarding Houses *see* SIC 7021: Rooming and Boarding Houses; SIC 7041: Organization Hotels and Lodging Houses, on Membership Basis

722110 Full-Service Restaurants *see* SIC 5812: Eating and Drinking Places

722211 Limited-Service Restaurants *see* SIC 5499: Miscellaneous Food Stores; SIC 5812: Eating and Drinking Places

722212 Cafeterias *see* SIC 5812: Eating and Drinking Places

722213 Snack and Nonalcoholic Beverage Bars *see* SIC 5461: Retail Bakeries; SIC 5812: Eating and Drinking Places

722310 Foodservice Contractors *see* SIC 5812: Eating and Drinking Places

722320 Caterers *see* SIC 5812: Eating and Drinking Places

722330 Mobile Caterers *see* SIC 5963: Direct Selling Establishments

722410 Drinking Places (Alcoholic Beverages) *see* SIC 5813: Drinking Places (Alcoholic Beverages)

Other Services

811111 General Automotive Repair *see* SIC 7538: General Automotive Repair Shops

811112 Automotive Exhaust System Repair *see* SIC 7533: Automotive Exhaust System Repair Shops

811113 Automotive Transmission Repair *see* SIC 7537: Automotive Transmission Repair Shops

811118 Other Automotive Mechanical and Electrical Repair and Maintenance *see* SIC 7539: Automotive Repair Shops, NEC

811121 Automotive Body, Paint, and Upholstery Repair and Maintenance *see* SIC 7532: Top, Body, and Upholstery Repair Shops and Paint Shops

811122 Automotive Glass Replacement Shops *see* SIC 7536: Automotive Glass Replacement Shops

811191 Automotive Oil Change and Lubrication Shops *see* SIC 7549: Automotive Services, Except Repair and Carwashes

811192 Car Washes *see* SIC 7542: Carwashes

811198 All Other Automotive Repair and Maintenance *see* SIC 7534: Tire Retreading and Repair Shops; SIC 7549: Automotive Services, Except Repair and Carwashes

811211 Consumer Electronics Repair and Maintenance *see* SIC 7622: Radio and Television Repair Shops; SIC 7629: Electrical and Electronic Repair Shops, NEC

811212 Computer and Office Machine Repair and Maintenance *see* SIC 7378: Computer Maintenance and Repair; SIC 7629: Electrical and Electronic Repair Shops, NEC; SIC 7699: Repair Shops and Related Services, NEC

811213 Communication Equipment Repair and Maintenance *see* SIC 7622: Radio and Television Repair Shops; SIC 7629: Electrical and Electronic Repair Shops, NEC

811219 Other Electronic and Precision Equipment Repair and Maintenance *see* SIC 7629: Electrical and Electronic Repair Shops, NEC; SIC 7699: Repair Shops and Related Services, NEC

811310 Commercial and Industrial Machinery and Equipment (except Automotive and Electronic) Repair and Maintenance *see* SIC 7623: Refrigeration and Air-Conditioning Services and Repair Shops; SIC 7694: Armature Rewinding Shops; SIC 7699: Repair Shops and Related Services, NEC

811411 Home and Garden Equipment Repair and Maintenance *see* SIC 7699: Repair Shops and Related Services, NEC

811412 Appliance Repair and Maintenance *see* SIC 7623: Refrigeration and Air-Conditioning Services and Repair Shops; SIC 7629: Electrical and Electronic Repair Shops, NEC; SIC 7699: Repair Shops and Related Services, NEC

811420 Reupholstery and Furniture Repair *see* SIC 7641: Reupholster and Furniture Repair

811430 Footwear and Leather Goods Repair *see* SIC 7251: Shoe Repair Shops and Shoeshine Parlors; SIC 7699: Repair Shops and Related Services, NEC

811490 Other Personal and Household Goods Repair and Maintenance *see* SIC 3732: Boat Building and Repairing; SIC 7219: Laundry and Garment Services, NEC; SIC 7631: Watch, Clock, and Jewelry Repair; SIC 7692: Welding Repair; SIC 7699: Repair Shops and Related Services, NEC

812111 Barber Shops *see* SIC 7241: Barber Shops

812112 Beauty Salons *see* SIC 7231: Beauty Shops

812113 Nail Salons *see* SIC 7231: Beauty Shops

812191 Diet and Weight Reducing Centers *see* SIC 7299: Miscellaneous Personal Services, NEC

812199 Other Personal Care Services *see* SIC 7299: Miscellaneous Personal Services, NEC

812210 Funeral Homes *see* SIC 7261: Funeral Services and Crematories

812220 Cemeteries and Crematories *see* SIC 6531: Real Estate Agents and Managers; SIC 6553: Cemetery Subdividers and Developers

812220 Cemeteries and Crematories *see* SIC 7261: Funeral Services and Crematories

812310 Coin-Operated Laundries and Drycleaners *see* SIC 7215: Coin-Operated Laundry and Drycleaning

812321 Laundries, Family and Commercial *see* SIC 7211: Power Laundries, Family and Commercial

812322 Drycleaning Plants *see* SIC 7216: Drycleaning Plants, Except Rug Cleaning

812331 Linen Supply *see* SIC 7213: Linen Supply; SIC 7219: Laundry and Garment Services, NEC

812332 Industrial Launderers *see* SIC 7218: Industrial Launderers

812391 Garment Pressing and Agents for Laundries *see* SIC 7212: Garment Pressing, and Agents for Laundries

812399 All Other Laundry Services *see* SIC 7219: Laundry and Garment Services, NEC

812910 Pet Care (except Veterinary) Services *see* SIC 0752: Animal Specialty Services, Except Veterinary

812921 Photo Finishing Laboratories (except One-Hour) *see* SIC 7384: Photofinishing Laboratories

812922 One-Hour Photo Finishing *see* SIC 7384: Photofinishing Laboratories

812930 Parking Lots and Garages *see* SIC 7521: Automobile Parking

812990 All Other Personal Services *see* SIC 7299: Miscellaneous Personal Services, NEC; SIC 7389: Business Services, NEC

813110 Religious Organizations *see* SIC 8661: Religious Organizations

813211 Grantmaking Foundations *see* SIC 6732: Education, Religious, and Charitable Trusts

813212 Voluntary Health Organizations *see* SIC 8399: Social Services, NEC

813219 Other Grantmaking and Giving Services *see* SIC 8399: Social Services, NEC

813311 Human Rights Organizations *see* SIC 8399: Social Services, NEC

813312 Environment, Conservation and Wildlife Organizations *see* SIC 8399: Social Services, NEC; SIC 8699: Membership Organizations, NEC

813319 Other Social Advocacy Organizations *see* SIC 8399: Social Services, NEC

813410 Civic and Social Organizations *see* SIC 8641: Civic, Social, and Fraternal Associations; SIC 8699: Membership Organizations, NEC

813910 Business Associations *see* SIC 8611: Business Associations; SIC 8699: Membership Organizations, NEC

813920 Professional Organizations *see* SIC 8621: Professional Membership Organizations

813930 Labor Unions and Similar Labor Organizations *see* SIC 8631: Labor Unions and Similar Labor Organizations

813940 Political Organizations *see* SIC 8651: Political Organizations

813990 Other Similar Organizations *see* SIC 6531: Real Estate Agents and Managers; SIC 8641: Civic, Social, and Fraternal Associations; SIC 8699: Membership Organizations, NEC

814110 Private Households *see* SIC 8811: Private Households

PUBLIC ADMINISTRATION

921110 Executive Offices *see* SIC 9111: Executive Offices

921120 Legislative Bodies *see* SIC 9121: Legislative Bodies

921130 Public Finance *see* SIC 9311: Public Finance, Taxation, and Monetary Policy

921140 Executive and Legislative Offices, Combined *see* SIC 9131: Executive and Legislative Offices, Combined

921150 American Indian and Alaska Native Tribal Governments *see* SIC 8641: Civic, Social, and Fraternal Associations

921190 All Other General Government *see* SIC 9199: General Government, NEC

922110 Courts *see* SIC 9211: Courts

922120 Police Protection *see* SIC 9221: Police Protection

922130 Legal Counsel and Prosecution *see* SIC 9222: Legal Counsel and Prosecution

922140 Correctional Institutions *see* SIC 9223: Correctional Institutions

922150 Parole Offices and Probation Offices *see* SIC 8322: Individual and Family Social Services

922160 Fire Protection *see* SIC 9224: Fire Protection

922190 All Other Justice, Public Order, and Safety *see* SIC 9229: Public Order and Safety, NEC

923110 Administration of Education Programs *see* SIC 9411: Administration of Educational Programs

923120 Administration of Public Health Programs *see* SIC 9431: Administration of Public Health Programs

923130 Administration of Social, Human Resource and Income Maintenance Programs *see* SIC 9441: Administration of Social, Human Resource and Income Maintenance Programs

923140 Administration of Veteran's Affairs *see* SIC 9451: Administration of Veteran's Affairs, Except Health Insurance

924110 Air and Water Resource and Solid Waste Management *see* SIC 9511: Air and Water Resource and Solid Waste Management

924120 Land, Mineral, Wildlife, and Forest Conservation *see* SIC 9512: Land, Mineral, Wildlife, and Forest Conservation

925110 Administration of Housing Programs *see* SIC 9531: Administration of Housing Programs

925120 Administration of Urban Planning and Community and Rural Development *see* SIC 9532: Administration of Urban Planning and Community and Rural Development

926110 Administration of General Economic Programs *see* SIC 9611: Administration of General Economic Programs

926120 Regulation and Administration of Transportation Programs *see* SIC 9621: Regulations and Administration of Transportation Programs

926130 Regulation and Administration of Communications, Electric, Gas, and Other Utilities *see* SIC 9631: Regulation and Administration of Communications, Electric, Gas, and Other Utilities

926140 Regulation of Agricultural Marketing and Commodities *see* SIC 9641: Regulation of Agricultural Marketing and Commodities

926150 Regulation, Licensing, and Inspection of Miscellaneous Commercial Sectors *see* SIC 9651: Regulation, Licensing, and Inspection of Miscellaneous Commercial Sectors

927110 Space Research and Technology *see* SIC 9661: Space Research and Technology

928110 National Security *see* SIC 9711: National Security

928120 International Affairs *see* SIC 9721: International Affairs

999990 Unclassified Establishments *see* SIC 9999: Nonclassified Establishments

SIC TO NAICS CONVERSION GUIDE

The following guide cross-references four-digit 1987 Standard Industrial Classification (SIC) codes with six-digit 1997 North American Industry Classification System (NAICS) codes. Because the systems differ in specificity, some SIC categories correspond to more than one NAICS category. Please refer to the **Introduction** *under "About Industry Classification" for more information.*

AGRICULTURE, FORESTRY & FISHING

0111 Wheat *see* NAICS 111140: Wheat Farming

0112 Rice *see* NAICS 111160: Rice Farming

0115 Corn *see* NAICS 111150: Corn Farming

0116 Soybeans *see* NAICS 111110: Soybean Farming

0119 Cash Grains, NEC *see* NAICS 111130: Dry Pea and Bean Farming; NAICS 111120: Oilseed (except Soybean) Farming; NAICS 111150: Corn Farming; NAICS 111191: Oilseed and Grain Combination Farming; NAICS 111199: All Other Grain Farming

0131 Cotton *see* NAICS 111920: Cotton Farming

0132 Tobacco *see* NAICS 111910: Tobacco Farming

0133 Sugarcane and Sugar Beets *see* NAICS 111991: Sugar Beet Farming; NAICS 111930: Sugarcane Farming

0134 Irish Potatoes *see* NAICS 111211: Potato Farming

0139 Field Crops, Except Cash Grains, NEC *see* NAICS 111940: Hay Farming; NAICS 111992: Peanut Farming; NAICS 111219: Other Vegetable (except Potato) and Melon Farming; NAICS 111998: All Other Miscellaneous Crop Farming

0161 Vegetables and Melons *see* NAICS 111219: Other Vegetable (except Potato) and Melon Farming

0171 Berry Crops *see* NAICS 111333: Strawberry Farming; NAICS 111334: Berry (except Strawberry) Farming

0172 Grapes *see* NAICS 111332: Grape Vineyards

0173 Tree Nuts *see* NAICS 111335: Tree Nut Farming

0174 Citrus Fruits *see* NAICS 111310: Orange Groves; NAICS 111320: Citrus (except Orange) Groves

0175 Deciduous Tree Fruits *see* NAICS 111331: Apple Orchards; NAICS 111339: Other Noncitrus Fruit Farming

0179 Fruits and Tree Nuts, NEC *see* NAICS 111336: Fruit and Tree Nut Combination Farming; NAICS 111339: Other Noncitrus Fruit Farming

0181 Ornamental Floriculture and Nursery Products *see* NAICS 111422: Floriculture Production; NAICS 111421: Nursery and Tree Production

0182 Food Crops Grown Under Cover *see* NAICS 111411: Mushroom Production; NAICS 111419: Other Food Crops Grown Under Cover

0191 General Farms, Primarily Crop *see* NAICS 111998: All Other Miscellaneous Crop Farming

0211 Beef Cattle Feedlots *see* NAICS 112112: Cattle Feedlots

0212 Beef Cattle, Except Feedlots *see* NAICS 112111: Beef Cattle Ranching and Farming

0213 Hogs *see* NAICS 112210: Hog and Pig Farming

0214 Sheep and Goats *see* NAICS 112410: Sheep Farming; NAICS 112420: Goat Farming

0219 General Livestock, Except Dairy and Poultry *see* NAICS 112990: All Other Animal Production

0241 Dairy Farms *see* NAICS 112111: Beef Cattle Ranching and Farming; NAICS 112120: Dairy Cattle and Milk Production

0251 Broiler, Fryers, and Roaster Chickens *see* NAICS 112320: Broilers and Other Meat-Type Chicken Production

0252 Chicken Eggs *see* NAICS 112310: Chicken Egg Production

0253 Turkey and Turkey Eggs *see* NAICS 112330: Turkey Production

0254 Poultry Hatcheries *see* NAICS 112340: Poultry Hatcheries

0259 Poultry and Eggs, NEC *see* NAICS 112390: Other Poultry Production

0271 Fur-Bearing Animals and Rabbits *see* NAICS 112930: Fur-bearing Animal and Rabbit Production

0272 Horses and Other Equines *see* NAICS 112920: Horse and Other Equine Production

0273 Animal Aquaculture *see* NAICS 112511: Finfish Farming and Fish Hatcheries; NAICS 112512: Shellfish Farming; NAICS 112519: Other Animal Aquaculture

0279 Animal Specialties, NEC *see* NAICS 112910: Apiculture; NAICS 112990: All Other Animal Production

0291 General Farms, Primarily Livestock and Animal Specialties *see* NAICS 112990: All Other Animal Production

0711 Soil Preparation Services *see* NAICS 115112: Soil Preparation, Planting and Cultivating

0721 Crop Planting, Cultivating and Protecting; NAICS 481219: Other Nonscheduled Air Transportation; NAICS 115112: Soil Preparation, Planting, and Cultivating

0722 Crop Harvesting, Primarily by Machine *see* NAICS 115113: Crop Harvesting, Primarily By Machine

0723 Crop Preparation Services For Market, except Cotton Ginning *see* NAICS 115114: Postharvest Crop Activities (except Cotton Ginning)

0724 Cotton Ginning *see* NAICS 115111: Cotton Ginning

0741 Veterinary Service For Livestock *see* NAICS 541940: Veterinary Services

0742 Veterinary Services for Animal Specialties *see* NAICS 541940: Veterinary Services

0751 Livestock Services, Except Veterinary *see* NAICS 311611: Animal (except Poultry) Slaughtering NAICS 115210: Support Activities for Animal Production

0752 Animal Specialty Services, Except Veterinary; NAICS 115210: Support Activities for Animal Production; NAICS 812910: Pet Care (except Veterinary) Services

0761 Farm Labor Contractors and Crew Leaders *see* NAICS 115115: Farm Labor Contractors and Crew Leaders

0762 Farm Management Services *see* NAICS 115116: Farm Management Services

0781 Landscape Counseling and Planning *see* NAICS 541690: Other Scientific and Technical Consulting Services; NAICS 541320: Landscape Architectural Services

0782 Lawn and Garden Services *see* NAICS 561730: Landscaping Services

0783 Ornamental Shrub and Tree Services *see* NAICS 561730: Landscaping Services

0811 Timber Tracts *see* NAICS 111421: Nursery and Tree Production; NAICS 113110: Timber Tract Operations

0831 Forest Nurseries and Gathering of Forest Products; NAICS 111998: All Other Miscellaneous Crop Farming; NAICS 113210: Forest Nurseries and Gathering of Forest Products

0851 Forestry Services *see* NAICS 115310: Support Activities for Forestry

0912 Finfish *see* NAICS 114111: Finfish Fishing

0913 Shellfish *see* NAICS 114112: Shellfish Fishing

0919 Miscellaneous Marine Products *see* NAICS 114119: Other Marine Fishing; NAICS 111998: All Other Miscellaneous Crop Farming

0921 Fish Hatcheries and Preserves *see* NAICS 112511: Finfish Farming and Fish Hatcheries; NAICS 112512: Shellfish Farming

0971 Hunting, Trapping, and Game Propagation *see* NAICS 114210: Hunting and Trapping

MINING INDUSTRIES

1011 Iron Ores *see* NAICS 212210: Iron Ore Mining

1021 Copper Ores *see* NAICS 212234: Copper Ore and Nickel Ore Mining

1031 Lead and Zinc Ores *see* NAICS 212231: Lead Ore and Zinc Ore Mining

1041 Gold Ores *see* NAICS 212221: Gold Ore Mining

1044 Silver Ores *see* NAICS 212222: Silver Ore Mining

1061 Ferroalloy Ores, Except Vanadium *see* NAICS 212234: Copper Ore and Nickel Ore Mining; NAICS 212299: Other Metal Ore Mining

1081 Metal Mining Services *see* NAICS 213114: Support Activities for Metal Mining; NAICS 541360: Geophysical Surveying and Mapping Services

1094 Uranium-Radium-Vanadium Ores *see* NAICS 212291: Uranium-Radium-Vanadium Ore Mining

1099 Miscellaneous Metal Ores, NEC *see* NAICS 212299: Other Metal Ore Mining

1221 Bituminous Coal and Lignite Surface Mining *see* NAICS 212111: Bituminous Coal and Lignite Surface Mining

1222 Bituminous Coal Underground Mining *see* NAICS 212112: Bituminous Coal Underground Mining

1231 Anthracite Mining *see* NAICS 212113: Anthracite Mining

1241 Coal Mining Services *see* NAICS 213113: Support Activities for Coal Mining

1311 Crude Petroleum and Natural Gas *see* NAICS 211111: Crude Petroleum and Natural Gas Extraction

1321 Natural Gas Liquids *see* NAICS 211112: Natural Gas Liquid Extraction

1381 Drilling Oil and Gas Wells *see* NAICS 213111: Drilling Oil and Gas Wells

1382 Oil and Gas Field Exploration Services *see* NAICS 541360: Geophysical Surveying and Mapping Services; NAICS 213112: Support Activities for Oil and Gas Field Exploration

1389 Oil and Gas Field Services, NEC *see* NAICS 213112: Support Activities for Oil and Gas Field Exploration

1411 Dimension Stone *see* NAICS 212311: Dimension Stone Mining and Quarry

1422 Crushed and Broken Limestone *see* NAICS 212312: Crushed and Broken Limestone Mining and Quarrying

1423 Crushed and Broken Granite *see* NAICS 212313: Crushed and Broken Granite Mining and Quarrying

1429 Crushed and Broken Stone, NEC *see* NAICS 212319: Other Crushed and Broken Stone Mining and Quarrying

1442 Construction Sand and Gravel *see* NAICS 212321: Construction Sand and Gravel Mining

1446 Industrial Sand *see* NAICS 212322: Industrial Sand Mining

1455 Kaolin and Ball Clay *see* NAICS 212324: Kaolin and Ball Clay Mining

1459 Clay, Ceramic, and Refractory Minerals, NEC *see* NAICS 212325: Clay and Ceramic and Refractory Minerals Mining

1474 Potash, Soda, and Borate Minerals *see* NAICS 212391: Potash, Soda, and Borate Mineral Mining

1475 Phosphate Rock *see* NAICS 212392: Phosphate Rock Mining

1479 Chemical and Fertilizer Mineral Mining, NEC *see* NAICS 212393: Other Chemical and Fertilizer Mineral Mining

1481 Nonmetallic Minerals Services Except Fuels *see* NAICS 213115: Support Activities for Non-metallic Minerals, (except Fuels); NAICS 541360: Geophysical Surveying and Mapping Services

1499 Miscellaneous Nonmetallic Minerals, Except Fuels *see* NAICS 212319: Other Crushed and Broken Stone Mining and Quarrying; NAICS 212399: All Other Non-Metallic Mineral Mining

CONSTRUCTION INDUSTRIES

1521 General Contractors-Single-Family Houses *see* NAICS 233210: Single-Family Housing Construction

1522 General Contractors-Residential Buildings *see* NAICS 233320: Commercial and Institutional Building Construction; NAICS 233220: Multi-Family Housing Construction

1531 Operative Builders *see* NAICS 233210: Single-Family Housing Construction; NAICS 233220: Multi-Family Housing Construction; NAICS 233310: Manufacturing and Light Industrial Building Construction; NAICS 233320: Commercial and Institutional Building Construction

1541 General Contractors-Industrial Buildings and Warehouses *see* NAICS 233320: Commercial and Institutional Building Construction; NAICS 233310: Manufacturing and Light Industrial Building Construction

1542 General Contractors-Nonresidential Buildings, Other than Industrial Buildings and Warehouses *see* NAICS 233320: Commercial and Institutional Building Construction

1611 Highway and Street Construction, Except Elevated Highways *see* NAICS 234110: Highway and Street Construction

1622 Bridge, Tunnel, and Elevated Highway Construction *see* NAICS 234120: Bridge and Tunnel Construction

1623 Water, Sewer, Pipeline, and Communications and Power Line Construction *see* NAICS 234910: Water, Sewer and Pipeline Construction; NAICS 234920: Power and Communication Transmission Line Construction

1629 Heavy Construction, NEC *see* NAICS 234930: Industrial Nonbuilding Structure Construction; NAICS 234990: All Other Heavy Construction

1711 Plumbing, Heating, and Air-Conditioning *see* NAICS 235110: Plumbing, Heating and Air-Conditioning Contractors

1721 Painting and Paper Hanging *see* NAICS 235210: Painting and Wall Covering Contractors

1731 Electrical Work *see* NAICS 561621: Security Systems Services (except Locksmiths); NAICS 235310: Electrical Contractors

1741 Masonry, Stone Setting and Other Stone Work *see* NAICS 235410: Masonry and Stone Contractors

1742 Plastering, Drywall, Acoustical and Insulation Work *see* NAICS 235420: Drywall, Plastering, Acoustical and Insulation Contractors

1743 Terrazzo, Tile, Marble, and Mosaic Work *see* NAICS 235420: Drywall, Plastering, Acoustical and Insulation Contractors; NAICS 235430: Tile, Marble, Terrazzo and Mosaic Contractors

1751 Carpentry Work *see* NAICS 235510: Carpentry Contractors

1752 Floor Laying and Other Floor Work, NEC *see* NAICS 235520: Floor Laying and Other Floor Contractors

1761 Roofing, Siding, and Sheet Metal Work *see* NAICS 235610: Roofing, Siding, and Sheet Metal Contractors

1771 Concrete Work *see* NAICS 235420: Drywall, Plastering, Acoustical and Insulation Contractors; NAICS 235710: Concrete Contractors

1781 Water Well Drilling *see* NAICS 235810: Water Well Drilling Contractors

1791 Structural Steel Erection *see* NAICS 235910: Structural Steel Erection Contractors

1793 Glass and Glazing Work *see* NAICS 235920: Glass and Glazing Contractors

1794 Excavation Work *see* NAICS 235930: Excavation Contractors

1795 Wrecking and Demolition Work *see* NAICS 235940: Wrecking and Demolition Contractors

1796 Installation or Erection of Building Equipment, NEC *see* NAICS 235950: Building Equipment and Other Machinery Installation Contractors

1799 Special Trade Contractors, NEC *see* NAICS 235210: Painting and Wall Covering Contractors; NAICS 235920: Glass and Glazing Contractors; NAICS 562910: Remediation Services; NAICS 235990: All Other Special Trade Contractors

FOOD & KINDRED PRODUCTS

2011 Meat Packing Plants *see* NAICS 311611: Animal (except Poultry) Slaughtering

2013 Sausages and Other Prepared Meats *see* NAICS 311612: Meat Processed From Carcasses

2015 Poultry Slaughtering and Processing *see* NAICS 311615: Poultry Processing; NAICS 311999: All Other Miscellaneous Food Manufacturing

2021 Creamery Butter *see* NAICS 311512: Creamery Butter Manufacturing

2022 Natural, Processed, and Imitation Cheese *see* NAICS 311513: Cheese Manufacturing

2023 Dry, Condensed, and Evaporated Dairy Products *see* NAICS 311514: Dry, Condensed, and Evaporated Dairy Product Manufacturing

2024 Ice Cream and Frozen Desserts *see* NAICS 311520: Ice Cream and Frozen Dessert Manufacturing

2026 Fluid Milk *see* NAICS 311511: Fluid Milk Manufacturing

2032 Canned Specialties *see* NAICS 311422: Specialty Canning; NAICS 311999: All Other Miscellaneous Food Manufacturing

2033 Canned Fruits, Vegetables, Preserves, Jams, and Jellies *see* NAICS 311421: Fruit and Vegetable Canning

2034 Dried and Dehydrated Fruits, Vegetables, and Soup Mixes *see* NAICS 311423: Dried and Dehydrated Food Manufacturing; NAICS 311211: Flour Milling

2035 Pickled Fruits and Vegetables, Vegetables Sauces and Seasonings, and Salad Dressings *see* NAICS 311421: Fruit and Vegetable Canning; NAICS 311941: Mayonnaise, Dressing, and Other Prepared Sauce Manufacturing

2037 Frozen Fruits, Fruit Juices, and Vegetables *see* NAICS 311411: Frozen Fruit, Juice, and Vegetable Processing

2038 Frozen Specialties, NEC *see* NAICS 311412: Frozen Specialty Food Manufacturing

2041 Flour and Other Grain Mill Products *see* NAICS 311211: Flour Milling

2043 Cereal Breakfast Foods *see* NAICS 311920: Coffee and Tea Manufacturing; NAICS 311230: Breakfast Cereal Manufacturing

2044 Rice Milling *see* NAICS 311212: Rice Milling

2045 Prepared Flour Mixes and Doughs *see* NAICS 311822: Flour Mixes and Dough Manufacturing from Purchased Flour

2046 Wet Corn Milling *see* NAICS 311221: Wet Corn Milling

2047 Dog and Cat Food *see* NAICS 311111: Dog and Cat Food Manufacturing

2048 Prepared Feed and Feed Ingredients for Animals and Fowls, Except Dogs and Cats *see* NAICS 311611: Animal (except Poultry) Slaughtering; NAICS 311119: Other Animal Food Manufacturing

2051 Bread and Other Bakery Products, Except Cookies and Crackers *see* NAICS 311812: Commercial Bakeries

2052 Cookies and Crackers *see* NAICS 311821: Cookie and Cracker Manufacturing; NAICS 311919: Other Snack Food Manufacturing; NAICS 311812: Commercial Bakeries

2053 Frozen Bakery Products, Except Bread *see* NAICS 311813: Frozen Bakery Product Manufacturing

2061 Cane Sugar, Except Refining *see* NAICS 311311: Sugarcane Mills

2062 Cane Sugar Refining *see* NAICS 311312: Cane Sugar Refining

2063 Beet Sugar *see* NAICS 311313: Beet Sugar Manufacturing

2064 Candy and Other Confectionery Products *see* NAICS 311330: Confectionery Manufacturing from Purchased Chocolate; NAICS 311340: Non-Chocolate Confectionery Manufacturing

2066 Chocolate and Cocoa Products *see* NAICS 311320: Chocolate and Confectionery Manufacturing from Cacao Beans

2067 Chewing Gum *see* NAICS 311340: Non-Chocolate Confectionery Manufacturing

2068 Salted and Roasted Nuts and Seeds *see* NAICS 311911: Roasted Nuts and Peanut Butter Manufacturing

2074 Cottonseed Oil Mills *see* NAICS 311223: Other Oilseed Processing; NAICS 311225: Fats and Oils Refining and Blending

2075 Soybean Oil Mills *see* NAICS 311222: Soybean Processing; NAICS 311225: Fats and Oils Refining and Blending

2076 Vegetable Oil Mills, Except Corn, Cottonseed, and Soybeans *see* NAICS 311223: Other Oilseed Processing; NAICS 311225: Fats and Oils Refining and Blending

2077 Animal and Marine Fats and Oils *see* NAICS 311613: Rendering and Meat By-product Processing; NAICS 311711: Seafood Canning; NAICS 311712: Fresh and Frozen Seafood Processing; NAICS 311225: Fats and Oils Refining and Blending

2079 Shortening, Table Oils, Margarine, and Other Edible Fats and Oils, NEC *see* NAICS 311225: Fats and Oils Refining and Blending; NAICS 311222: Soybean Processing; NAICS 311223: Other Oilseed Processing

2082 Malt Beverages *see* NAICS 312120: Breweries

2083 Malt *see* NAICS 311213: Malt Manufacturing

2084 Wines, Brandy, and Brandy Spirits *see* NAICS 312130: Wineries

2085 Distilled and Blended Liquors *see* NAICS 312140: Distilleries

2086 Bottled and Canned Soft Drinks and Carbonated Waters *see* NAICS 312111: Soft Drink Manufacturing; NAICS 312112: Bottled Water Manufacturing

2087 Flavoring Extracts and Flavoring Syrups NEC *see* NAICS 311930: Flavoring Syrup and Concentrate Manufacturing; NAICS 311942: Spice and Extract Manufacturing; NAICS 311999: All Other Miscellaneous Food Manufacturing

2091 Canned and Cured Fish and Seafood *see* NAICS 311711: Seafood Canning

2092 Prepared Fresh or Frozen Fish and Seafoods *see* NAICS 311712: Fresh and Frozen Seafood Processing

2095 Roasted Coffee *see* NAICS 311920: Coffee and Tea Manufacturing; NAICS 311942: Spice and Extract Manufacturing

2096 Potato Chips, Corn Chips, and Similar Snacks *see* NAICS 311919: Other Snack Food Manufacturing

2097 Manufactured Ice *see* NAICS 312113: Ice Manufacturing

2098 Macaroni, Spaghetti, Vermicelli, and Noodles *see* NAICS 311823: Pasta Manufacturing

2099 Food Preparations, NEC *see* NAICS 311423: Dried and Dehydrated Food Manufacturing; NAICS 111998: All Other Miscellaneous Crop Farming; NAICS 311340: Non-Chocolate Confectionery Manufacturing; NAICS 311911: Roasted Nuts and Peanut Butter Manufacturing; NAICS 311991: Perishable Prepared Food Manufacturing; NAICS 311830: Tortilla Manufacturing; NAICS 311920: Coffee and Tea Manufacturing; NAICS 311941: Mayonnaise, Dressing, and Other Prepared Sauce Manufacturing; NAICS 311942: Spice and Extract Manufacturing; NAICS 311999: All Other Miscellaneous Food Manufacturing

Tobacco Products

2111 Cigarettes *see* NAICS 312221: Cigarette Manufacturing

2121 Cigars *see* NAICS 312229: Other Tobacco Product Manufacturing

2131 Chewing and Smoking Tobacco and Snuff *see* NAICS 312229: Other Tobacco Product Manufacturing

2141 Tobacco Stemming and Redrying *see* NAICS 312229: Other Tobacco Product Manufacturing; NAICS 312210: Tobacco Stemming and Redrying

Textile Mill Products

2211 Broadwoven Fabric Mills, Cotton *see* NAICS 313210: Broadwoven Fabric Mills

2221 Broadwoven Fabric Mills, Manmade Fiber and Silk *see* NAICS 313210: Broadwoven Fabric Mills

2231 Broadwoven Fabric Mills, Wool (Including Dyeing and Finishing) *see* NAICS 313210: Broadwoven Fabric Mills; NAICS 313311: Broadwoven Fabric Finishing Mills; NAICS 313312: Textile and Fabric Finishing (except Broadwoven Fabric) Mills

2241 Narrow Fabric and Other Smallware Mills: Cotton, Wool, Silk, and Manmade Fiber *see* NAICS 313221: Narrow Fabric Mills

2251 Women's Full-Length and Knee-Length Hosiery, Except Socks *see* NAICS 315111: Sheer Hosiery Mills

2252 Hosiery, NEC *see* NAICS 315111: Sheer Hosiery Mills; NAICS 315119: Other Hosiery and Sock Mills

2253 Knit Outerwear Mills *see* NAICS 315191: Outerwear Knitting Mills

2254 Knit Underwear and Nightwear Mills *see* NAICS 315192: Underwear and Nightwear Knitting Mills

2257 Weft Knit Fabric Mills *see* NAICS 313241: Weft Knit Fabric Mills; NAICS 313312: Textile and Fabric Finishing (except Broadwoven Fabric) Mills

2258 Lace and Warp Knit Fabric Mills *see* NAICS 313249: Other Knit Fabric and Lace Mills; NAICS 313312: Textile and Fabric Finishing (except Broadwoven Fabric) Mills

2259 Knitting Mills, NEC *see* NAICS 315191: Outerwear Knitting Mills; NAICS 315192: Underwear and Nightwear Knitting Mills; NAICS 313241: Weft Knit Fabric Mills; NAICS 313249: Other Knit Fabric and Lace Mills

2261 Finishers of Broadwoven Fabrics of Cotton *see* NAICS 313311: Broadwoven Fabric Finishing Mills

2262 Finishers of Broadwoven Fabrics of Manmade Fiber and Silk *see* NAICS 313311: Broadwoven Fabric Finishing Mills

2269 Finishers of Textiles, NEC *see* NAICS 313311: Broadwoven Fabric Finishing Mills; NAICS 313312: Textile and Fabric Finishing (except Broadwoven Fabric) Mills

2273 Carpets and Rugs *see* NAICS 314110: Carpet and Rug Mills

2281 Yarn Spinning Mills *see* NAICS 313111: Yarn Spinning Mills

2282 Yarn Texturizing, Throwing, Twisting, and Winding Mills *see* NAICS 313112: Yarn Texturing, Throwing and Twisting Mills; NAICS 313312: Textile and Fabric Finishing (except Broadwoven Fabric) Mills

2284 Thread Mills *see* NAICS 313113: Thread Mills; NAICS 313312: Textile and Fabric Finishing (except Broadwoven Fabric) Mills

2295 Coated Fabrics, Not Rubberized *see* NAICS 313320: Fabric Coating Mills

2296 Tire Cord and Fabrics *see* NAICS 314992: Tire Cord and Tire Fabric Mills

2297 Nonwoven Fabrics *see* NAICS 313230: Nonwoven Fabric Mills

2298 Cordage and Twine *see* NAICS 314991: Rope, Cordage and Twine Mills

2299 Textile Goods, NEC *see* NAICS 313210: Broadwoven Fabric Mills; NAICS 313230: Nonwoven Fabric Mills; NAICS 313312: Textile and Fabric Finishing (except Broadwoven Fabric) Mills; NAICS 313221: Narrow Fabric Mills; NAICS 313113: Thread Mills; NAICS 313111: Yarn Spinning Mills; NAICS 314999: All Other Miscellaneous Textile Product Mills

Apparel & Other Finished Products Made From Fabrics & Similar Materials

2311 Men's and Boys' Suits, Coats and Overcoats *see* NAICS 315211: Men's and Boys' Cut and Sew Apparel Contractors; NAICS 315222: Men's and Boys' Cut and Sew Suit, Coat, and Overcoat Manufacturing

2321 Men's and Boys' Shirts, Except Work Shirts *see* NAICS 315211: Men's and Boys' Cut and Sew Apparel Contractors; NAICS 315223: Men's and Boys' Cut and Sew Shirt, (except Work Shirt) Manufacturing

2322 Men's and Boys' Underwear and Nightwear *see* NAICS 315211: Men's and Boys' Cut and Sew Apparel Contractors; NAICS 315221: Men's and Boys' Cut and Sew Underwear and Nightwear Manufacturing

2323 Men's and Boys' Neckwear *see* NAICS 315993: Men's and Boys' Neckwear Manufacturing

2325 Men's and Boys' Trousers and Slacks *see* NAICS 315211: Men's and Boys' Cut and Sew Apparel Contractors; NAICS 315224: Men's and Boys' Cut And Sew Trouser, Slack, And Jean Manufacturing

2326 Men's and Boys' Work Clothing *see* NAICS 315211: Men's and Boys' Cut and Sew Apparel Contractors; NAICS 315225: Men's and Boys' Cut and Sew Work Clothing Manufacturing

2329 Men's and Boys' Clothing, NEC *see* NAICS 315211: Men's and Boys' Cut and Sew Apparel Contractors; NAICS 315228: Men's and Boys' Cut and Sew Other Outerwear Manufacturing; NAICS 315299: All Other Cut and Sew Apparel Manufacturing

2331 Women's, Misses', and Juniors' Blouses and Shirts *see* NAICS 315212: Women's and Girls' Cut and Sew Apparel Contractors; NAICS 315232: Women's and Girls' Cut and Sew Blouse and Shirt Manufacturing

2335 Women's, Misses' and Junior's Dresses *see* NAICS 315212: Women's and Girls' Cut and Sew Apparel Contractors; NAICS 315233: Women's and Girls' Cut and Sew Dress Manufacturing

2337 Women's, Misses' and Juniors' Suits, Skirts and Coats *see* NAICS 315212: Women's and Girls' Cut and Sew Apparel Contractors; NAICS 315234: Women's and Girls' Cut and Sew Suit, Coat, Tailored Jacket, and Skirt Manufacturing

2339 Women's, Misses' and Juniors' Outerwear, NEC *see* NAICS 315999: Other Apparel Accessories and Other Apparel Manufacturing; NAICS 315212: Women's and Girls' Cut and Sew Apparel Contractors; NAICS 315299: All Other Cut and Sew Apparel Manufacturing; NAICS 315238: Women's and Girls' Cut and Sew Other Outerwear Manufacturing

2341 Women's, Misses, Children's, and Infants' Underwear and Nightwear *see* NAICS 315212: Women's and Girls' Cut and Sew Apparel Contractors; NAICS 315211: Men's and Boys' Cut and Sew Apparel Contractors; NAICS 315231: Women's and Girls' Cut and Sew Lingerie, Loungewear, and Nightwear Manufacturing; NAICS 315221: Men's and Boys' Cut and Sew Underwear and Nightwear Manufacturing; NAICS 315291: Infants' Cut and Sew Apparel Manufacturing

2342 Brassieres, Girdles, and Allied Garments *see* NAICS 315212: Women's and Girls' Cut and Sew Apparel Contractors; NAICS 315231: Women's and Girls' Cut and Sew Lingerie, Loungewear, and Nightwear Manufacturing

2353 Hats, Caps, and Millinery *see* NAICS 315991: Hat, Cap, and Millinery Manufacturing

2361 Girls', Children's and Infants' Dresses, Blouses and Shirts *see* NAICS 315291: Infants' Cut and Sew Apparel Manufacturing; NAICS 315223: Men's and Boys' Cut and Sew Shirt (except Work Shirt) Manufacturing;

NAICS 315211: Men's and Boys' Cut and Sew Apparel Contractors; NAICS 315232: Women's and Girls' Cut and Sew Blouse and Shirt Manufacturing; NAICS 315233: Women's and Girls' Cut and Sew Dress Manufacturing; NAICS 315212: Women's and Girls' Cut and Sew Apparel Contractors

2369 Girls', Children's and Infants' Outerwear, NEC *see* NAICS 315291: Infants' Cut and Sew Apparel Manufacturing; NAICS 315222: Men's and Boys' Cut and Sew Suit, Coat, and Overcoat Manufacturing; NAICS 315224: Men's and Boys' Cut and Sew Trouser, Slack, and Jean Manufacturing; NAICS 315228: Men's and Boys' Cut and Sew Other Outerwear Manufacturing; NAICS 315221: Men's and Boys' Cut and Sew Underwear and Nightwear Manufacturing; NAICS 315211: Men's and Boys' Cut and Sew Apparel Contractors; NAICS 315234: Women's and Girls' Cut and Sew Suit, Coat, Tailored Jacket, and Skirt Manufacturing; NAICS 315238: Women's and Girls' Cut and Sew Other Outerwear Manufacturing; NAICS 315231: Women's and Girls' Cut and Sew Lingerie, Loungewear, and Nightwear Manufacturing; NAICS 315212: Women's and Girls' Cut and Sew Apparel Contractors

2371 Fur Goods *see* NAICS 315292: Fur and Leather Apparel Manufacturing

2381 Dress and Work Gloves, Except Knit and All-Leather *see* NAICS 315992: Glove and Mitten Manufacturing

2384 Robes and Dressing Gowns *see* NAICS 315231: Women's and Girls' Cut and Sew Lingerie, Loungewear, and Nightwear Manufacturing; NAICS 315221: Men's and Boys' Cut and Sew Underwear and Nightwear Manufacturing; NAICS 315211: Men's and Boys' Cut and Sew Apparel Contractors; NAICS 315212: Women's and Girls' Cut and Sew Apparel Contractors

2385 Waterproof Outerwear *see* NAICS 315222: Men's and Boys' Cut and Sew Suit, Coat, and Overcoat Manufacturing; NAICS 315234: Women's and Girls' Cut and Sew Suit, Coat, Tailored Jacket, and Skirt Manufacturing; NAICS 315228: Men's and Boys' Cut and Sew Other Outerwear Manufacturing; NAICS 315238: Women's and Girls' Cut and Sew Other Outerwear Manufacturing; NAICS 315291: Infants' Cut and Sew Apparel Manufacturing; NAICS 315999: Other Apparel Accessories and Other Apparel Manufacturing; NAICS 315211: Men's and Boys' Cut and Sew Apparel Contractors; NAICS 315212: Women's and Girls' Cut and Sew Apparel Contractors

2386 Leather and Sheep-Lined Clothing *see* NAICS 315292: Fur and Leather Apparel Manufacturing

2387 Apparel Belts *see* NAICS 315999: Other Apparel Accessories and Other Apparel Manufacturing

2389 Apparel and Accessories, NEC *see* NAICS 315999: Other Apparel Accessories and Other Apparel Manufacturing; NAICS 315299: All Other Cut and Sew Apparel Manufacturing; NAICS 315231: Women's and Girls' Cut and Sew Lingerie, Loungewear, and Nightwear Manufacturing; NAICS 315212: Women's and Girls' Cut and Sew Apparel Contractors; NAICS 315211: Men's and Boys' Cut and Sew Apparel Contractors

2391 Curtains and Draperies *see* NAICS 314121: Curtain and Drapery Mills

2392 Housefurnishings, Except Curtains and Draperies *see* NAICS 314911: Textile Bag Mills; NAICS 339994: Broom, Brush and Mop Manufacturing; NAICS 314129: Other Household Textile Product Mills

2393 Textile Bags *see* NAICS 314911: Textile Bag Mills

2394 Canvas and Related Products *see* NAICS 314912: Canvas and Related Product Mills

2395 Pleating, Decorative and Novelty Stitching, and Tucking for the Trade *see* NAICS 314999: All Other Miscellaneous Textile Product Mills; NAICS 315211: Men's and Boys' Cut and Sew Apparel Contractors; NAICS 315212: Women's and Girls' Cut and Sew Apparel Contractors

2396 Automotive Trimmings, Apparel Findings, and Related Products *see* NAICS 336360: Motor Vehicle Fabric Accessories and Seat Manufacturing; NAICS 315999: Other Apparel Accessories, and Other Apparel Manufacturing; NAICS 323113: Commercial Screen Printing; NAICS 314999: All Other Miscellaneous Textile Product Mills

2397 Schiffli Machine Embroideries *see* NAICS 313222: Schiffli Machine Embroidery

2399 Fabricated Textile Products, NEC *see* NAICS 336360: Motor Vehicle Fabric Accessories and Seat Manufacturing; NAICS 315999: Other Apparel Accessories and Other Apparel Manufacturing; NAICS 314999: All Other Miscellaneous Textile Product Mills

Lumber & Wood Products, Except Furniture

2411 Logging *see* NAICS 113310: Logging

2421 Sawmills and Planing Mills, General *see* NAICS 321912: Cut Stock, Resawing Lumber, and Planing; NAICS 321113: Sawmills; NAICS 321918: Other Millwork (including Flooring); NAICS 321999: All Other Miscellaneous Wood Product Manufacturing

2426 Hardwood Dimension and Flooring Mills *see* NAICS 321918: Other Millwork (including Flooring); NAICS 321999: All Other Miscellaneous Wood Product Manufacturing; NAICS 337215: Showcase, Partition, Shelving, and Locker Manufacturing; NAICS 321912: Cut Stock, Resawing Lumber, and Planing

2429 Special Product Sawmills, NEC *see* NAICS 321113: Sawmills; NAICS 321912: Cut Stock, Resawing Lumber, and Planing; NAICS 321999: All Other Miscellaneous Wood Product Manufacturing

2431 Millwork *see* NAICS 321911: Wood Window and Door Manufacturing; NAICS 321918: Other Millwork (including Flooring)

2434 Wood Kitchen Cabinets *see* NAICS 337110: Wood Kitchen Cabinet and Counter Top Manufacturing

2435 Hardwood Veneer and Plywood *see* NAICS 321211: Hardwood Veneer and Plywood Manufacturing

2436 Softwood Veneer and Plywood *see* NAICS 321212: Softwood Veneer and Plywood Manufacturing

2439 Structural Wood Members, NEC *see* NAICS 321912: Cut Stock, Resawing Lumber, and Planing; NAICS 321214: Truss Manufacturing; NAICS 321213: Engineered Wood Member (except Truss) Manufacturing

2441 Nailed and Lock Corner Wood Boxes and Shook *see* NAICS 321920: Wood Container and Pallet Manufacturing

2448 Wood Pallets and Skids *see* NAICS 321920: Wood Container and Pallet Manufacturing

2449 Wood Containers, NEC *see* NAICS 321920: Wood Container and Pallet Manufacturing

2451 Mobile Homes *see* NAICS 321991: Manufactured Home (Mobile Home) Manufacturing

2452 Prefabricated Wood Buildings and Components *see* NAICS 321992: Prefabricated Wood Building Manufacturing

2491 Wood Preserving *see* NAICS 321114: Wood Preservation

2493 Reconstituted Wood Products *see* NAICS 321219: Reconstituted Wood Product Manufacturing

2499 Wood Products, NEC *see* NAICS 339999: All Other Miscellaneous Manufacturing; NAICS 321920: Wood Container and Pallet Manufacturing; NAICS 321999: All Other Miscellaneous Wood Product Manufacturing

Furniture & Fixtures

2511 Wood Household Furniture, Except Upholstered *see* NAICS 337122: Nonupholstered Wood Household Furniture Manufacturing

2512 Wood Household Furniture, Upholstered *see* NAICS 337121: Upholstered Wood Household Furniture Manufacturing

2514 Metal Household Furniture *see* NAICS 337124: Metal Household Furniture Manufacturing

2515 Mattresses, Foundations, and Convertible Beds *see* NAICS 337910: Mattress Manufacturing; NAICS 337121: Upholstered Wood Household Furniture Manufacturing

2517 Wood Television, Radio, Phonograph and Sewing Machine Cabinets *see* NAICS 337129: Wood Television, Radio, and Sewing Machine Cabinet Manufacturing

2519 Household Furniture, NEC *see* NAICS 337125: Household Furniture (except Wood and Metal) Manufacturing

2521 Wood Office Furniture *see* NAICS 337211: Wood Office Furniture Manufacturing

2522 Office Furniture, Except Wood *see* NAICS 337214: Nonwood Office Furniture Manufacturing

2531 Public Building and Related Furniture *see* NAICS 336360: Motor Vehicle Fabric Accessories and Seat Manufacturing; NAICS 337127: Institutional Furniture Manufacturing; NAICS 339942: Lead Pencil and Art Good Manufacturing

2541 Wood Office and Store Fixtures, Partitions, Shelving, and Lockers *see* NAICS 337110: Wood Kitchen Cabinet and Counter Top Manufacturing; NAICS 337212: Custom Architectural Woodwork, Millwork, and Fixtures; NAICS 337215: Showcase, Partition, Shelving, and Locker Manufacturing

2542 Office and Store Fixtures, Partitions Shelving, and Lockers, Except Wood *see* NAICS 337215: Showcase, Partition, Shelving, and Locker Manufacturing

2591 Drapery Hardware and Window Blinds and Shades *see* NAICS 337920: Blind and Shade Manufacturing

2599 Furniture and Fixtures, NEC *see* NAICS 339113: Surgical Appliance and Supplies Manufacturing; NAICS 337127: Institutional Furniture Manufacturing

Paper & Allied Products

2611 Pulp Mills *see* NAICS 322110: Pulp Mills; NAICS 322121: Paper (except Newsprint) Mills; NAICS 322130: Paperboard Mills

2621 Paper Mills *see* NAICS 322121: Paper (except Newsprint) Mills; NAICS 322122: Newsprint Mills

2631 Paperboard Mills *see* NAICS 322130: Paperboard Mills

2652 Setup Paperboard Boxes *see* NAICS 322213: Setup Paperboard Box Manufacturing

2653 Corrugated and Solid Fiber Boxes *see* NAICS 322211: Corrugated and Solid Fiber Box Manufacturing

2655 Fiber Cans, Tubes, Drums, and Similar Products *see* NAICS 322214: Fiber Can, Tube, Drum, and Similar Products Manufacturing

2656 Sanitary Food Containers, Except Folding *see* NAICS 322215: Non-Folding Sanitary Food Container Manufacturing

2657 Folding Paperboard Boxes, Including Sanitary *see* NAICS 322212: Folding Paperboard Box Manufacturing

2671 Packaging Paper and Plastics Film *see* NAICS 322221: Coated and Laminated Packaging Paper and Plastics Film Manufacturing; NAICS 326112: Unsupported Plastics Packaging Film and Sheet Manufacturing

2672 Coated and Laminated Paper, NEC *see* NAICS 322222: Coated and Laminated Paper Manufacturing

2673 Plastics, Foil, and Coated Paper Bags *see* NAICS 322223: Plastics, Foil, and Coated Paper Bag Manufacturing; NAICS 326111: Unsupported Plastics Bag Manufacturing

2674 Uncoated Paper and Multiwall Bags *see* NAICS 322224: Uncoated Paper and Multiwall Bag Manufacturing

2675 Die-Cut Paper and Paperboard and Cardboard *see* NAICS 322231: Die-Cut Paper and Paperboard Office Supplies Manufacturing; NAICS 322292: Surface-Coated Paperboard Manufacturing; NAICS 322298: All Other Converted Paper Product Manufacturing

2676 Sanitary Paper Products *see* NAICS 322291: Sanitary Paper Product Manufacturing

2677 Envelopes *see* NAICS 322232: Envelope Manufacturing

2678 Stationery, Tablets, and Related Products *see* NAICS 322233: Stationery, Tablet, and Related Product Manufacturing

2679 Converted Paper and Paperboard Products, NEC *see* NAICS 322215: Non-Folding Sanitary Food Container Manufacturing; NAICS 322222: Coated and Laminated Paper Manufacturing; NAICS 322231: Die-Cut Paper and Paperboard Office Supplies Manufacturing; NAICS 322298: All Other Converted Paper Product Manufacturing

Printing, Publishing, & Allied Industries

2711 Newspapers: Publishing, or Publishing and Printing *see* NAICS 511110: Newspaper Publishers

2721 Periodicals: Publishing, or Publishing and Printing *see* NAICS 511120: Periodical Publishers

2731 Books: Publishing, or Publishing and Printing *see* NAICS 512230: Music Publishers; NAICS 511130: Book Publishers

2732 Book Printing *see* NAICS 323117: Book Printing

2741 Miscellaneous Publishing *see* NAICS 511140: Database and Directory Publishers; NAICS 512230: Music Publishers; NAICS 511199: All Other Publishers

2752 Commercial Printing, Lithographic *see* NAICS 323114: Quick Printing; NAICS 323110: Commercial Lithographic Printing

2754 Commercial Printing, Gravure *see* NAICS 323111: Commercial Gravure Printing

2759 Commercial Printing, NEC *see* NAICS 323113: Commercial Screen Printing; NAICS 323112: Commercial Flexographic Printing; NAICS 323114: Quick Printing; NAICS 323115: Digital Printing; NAICS 323119: Other Commercial Printing

2761 Manifold Business Forms *see* NAICS 323116: Manifold Business Form Printing

2771 Greeting Cards *see* NAICS 323110: Commercial Lithographic Printing; NAICS 323111: Commercial Gravure Printing; NAICS 323112: Commercial Flexographic Printing; NAICS 323113: Commercial Screen Printing; NAICS 323119: Other Commercial Printing; NAICS 511191: Greeting Card Publishers

2782 Blankbooks, Loose-leaf Binders and Devices *see* NAICS 323110: Commercial Lithographic Printing; NAICS 323111: Commercial Gravure Printing; NAICS 323112: Commercial Flexographic Printing; NAICS 323113: Commercial Screen Printing; NAICS 323119: Other Commercial Printing; NAICS 323118: Blankbook, Loose-leaf Binder and Device Manufacturing

2789 Bookbinding and Related Work *see* NAICS 323121: Tradebinding and Related Work

2791 Typesetting *see* NAICS 323122: Prepress Services

2796 Platemaking and Related Services *see* NAICS 323122: Prepress Services

CHEMICALS & ALLIED PRODUCTS

2812 Alkalies and Chlorine *see* NAICS 325181: Alkalies and Chlorine Manufacturing

2813 Industrial Gases *see* NAICS 325120: Industrial Gas Manufacturing

2816 Inorganic Pigments *see* NAICS 325131: Inorganic Dye and Pigment Manufacturing; NAICS 325182: Carbon Black Manufacturing

2819 Industrial Inorganic Chemicals, NEC *see* NAICS 325998: All Other Miscellaneous Chemical Product Manufacturing; NAICS 331311: Aluminum Refining; NAICS 325131: Inorganic Dye and Pigment Manufacturing; NAICS 325188: All Other Inorganic Chemical Manufacturing

2821 Plastics Material Synthetic Resins, and Nonvulcanizable Elastomers *see* NAICS 325211: Plastics Material and Resin Manufacturing

2822 Synthetic Rubber *see* NAICS 325212: Synthetic Rubber Manufacturing

2823 Cellulosic Manmade Fibers *see* NAICS 325221: Cellulosic Manmade Fiber Manufacturing

2824 Manmade Organic Fibers, Except Cellulosic *see* NAICS 325222: Noncellulosic Organic Fiber Manufacturing

2833 Medicinal Chemicals and Botanical Products *see* NAICS 325411: Medicinal and Botanical Manufacturing

2834 Pharmaceutical Preparations *see* NAICS 325412: Pharmaceutical Preparation Manufacturing

2835 In Vitro and In Vivo Diagnostic Substances *see* NAICS 325412: Pharmaceutical Preparation Manufacturing; NAICS 325413: In-Vitro Diagnostic Substance Manufacturing

2836 Biological Products, Except Diagnostic Substances *see* NAICS 325414: Biological Product (except Diagnostic) Manufacturing

2841 Soaps and Other Detergents, Except Specialty Cleaners *see* NAICS 325611: Soap and Other Detergent Manufacturing

2842 Specialty Cleaning, Polishing, and Sanitary Preparations *see* NAICS 325612: Polish and Other Sanitation Good Manufacturing

2843 Surface Active Agents, Finishing Agents, Sulfonated Oils, and Assistants *see* NAICS 325613: Surface Active Agent Manufacturing

2844 Perfumes, Cosmetics, and Other Toilet Preparations *see* NAICS 325620: Toilet Preparation Manufacturing; NAICS 325611: Soap and Other Detergent Manufacturing

2851 Paints, Varnishes, Lacquers, Enamels, and Allied Products *see* NAICS 325510: Paint and Coating Manufacturing

2861 Gum and Wood Chemicals *see* NAICS 325191: Gum and Wood Chemical Manufacturing

2865 Cyclic Organic Crudes and Intermediates, and Organic Dyes and Pigments *see* NAICS 325110: Petrochemical Manufacturing; NAICS 325132: Organic Dye and Pigment Manufacturing; NAICS 325192: Cyclic Crude and Intermediate Manufacturing

2869 Industrial Organic Chemicals, NEC *see* NAICS 325110: Petrochemical Manufacturing; NAICS 325188: All Other Inorganic Chemical Manufacturing; NAICS 325193: Ethyl Alcohol Manufacturing; NAICS 325120: Industrial Gas Manufacturing; NAICS 325199: All Other Basic Organic Chemical Manufacturing

2873 Nitrogenous Fertilizers *see* NAICS 325311: Nitrogenous Fertilizer Manufacturing

2874 Phosphatic Fertilizers *see* NAICS 325312: Phosphatic Fertilizer Manufacturing

2875 Fertilizers, Mixing Only *see* NAICS 325314: Fertilizer (Mixing Only) Manufacturing

2879 Pesticides and Agricultural Chemicals, NEC *see* NAICS 325320: Pesticide and Other Agricultural Chemical Manufacturing

2891 Adhesives and Sealants *see* NAICS 325520: Adhesive and Sealant Manufacturing

2892 Explosives *see* NAICS 325920: Explosives Manufacturing

2893 Printing Ink *see* NAICS 325910: Printing Ink Manufacturing

2895 Carbon Black *see* NAICS 325182: Carbon Black Manufacturing

2899 Chemicals and Chemical Preparations, NEC *see* NAICS 325510: Paint and Coating Manufacturing; NAICS 311942: Spice and Extract Manufacturing; NAICS 325199: All Other Basic Organic Chemical Manufacturing; NAICS 325998: All Other Miscellaneous Chemical Product Manufacturing

PETROLEUM REFINING & RELATED INDUSTRIES

2911 Petroleum Refining *see* NAICS 324110: Petroleum Refineries

2951 Asphalt Paving Mixtures and Blocks *see* NAICS 324121: Asphalt Paving Mixture and Block Manufacturing

2952 Asphalt Felts and Coatings *see* NAICS 324122: Asphalt Shingle and Coating Materials Manufacturing

2992 Lubricating Oils and Greases *see* NAICS 324191: Petroleum Lubricating Oil and Grease Manufacturing

2999 Products of Petroleum and Coal, NEC *see* NAICS 324199: All Other Petroleum and Coal Products Manufacturing

RUBBER & MISCELLANEOUS PLASTICS PRODUCTS

3011 Tires and Inner Tubes *see* NAICS 326211: Tire Manufacturing (except Retreading)

3021 Rubber and Plastics Footwear *see* NAICS 316211: Rubber and Plastics Footwear Manufacturing

3052 Rubber and Plastics Hose and Belting *see* NAICS 326220: Rubber and Plastics Hoses and Belting Manufacturing

3053 Gaskets, Packing, and Sealing Devices *see* NAICS 339991: Gasket, Packing, and Sealing Device Manufacturing

3061 Molded, Extruded, and Lathe-Cut Mechanical Rubber Products *see* NAICS 326291: Rubber Product Manufacturing for Mechanical Use

3069 Fabricated Rubber Products, NEC *see* NAICS 313320: Fabric Coating Mills; NAICS 326192: Resilient Floor Covering Manufacturing; NAICS 326299: All Other Rubber Product Manufacturing

3081 Unsupported Plastics Film and Sheet *see* NAICS 326113: Unsupported Plastics Film and Sheet (except Packaging) Manufacturing

3082 Unsupported Plastics Profile Shapes *see* NAICS 326121: Unsupported Plastics Profile Shape Manufacturing

3083 Laminated Plastics Plate, Sheet, and Profile Shapes *see* NAICS 326130: Laminated Plastics Plate, Sheet, and Shape Manufacturing

3084 Plastic Pipe *see* NAICS 326122: Plastics Pipe and Pipe Fitting Manufacturing

3085 Plastics Bottles *see* NAICS 326160: Plastics Bottle Manufacturing

3086 Plastics Foam Products *see* NAICS 326150: Urethane and Other Foam Product (except Polystyrene) Manufacturing; NAICS 326140: Polystyrene Foam Product Manufacturing

3087 Custom Compounding of Purchased Plastics Resins *see* NAICS 325991: Custom Compounding of Purchased Resin

3088 Plastics Plumbing Fixtures *see* NAICS 326191: Plastics Plumbing Fixtures Manufacturing

3089 Plastics Products, NEC *see* NAICS 326122: Plastics Pipe and Pipe Fitting Manufacturing; NAICS 326121: Unsupported Plastics Profile Shape Manufacturing; NAICS 326199: All Other Plastics Product Manufacturing

LEATHER & LEATHER PRODUCTS

3111 Leather Tanning and Finishing *see* NAICS 316110: Leather and Hide Tanning and Finishing

3131 Boot and Shoe Cut Stock and Findings *see* NAICS 321999: All Other Miscellaneous Wood Product Manufacturing; NAICS 339993: Fastener, Button, Needle, and Pin Manufacturing; NAICS 316999: All Other Leather Good Manufacturing

3142 House Slippers *see* NAICS 316212: House Slipper Manufacturing

3143 Men's Footwear, Except Athletic *see* NAICS 316213: Men's Footwear (except Athletic) Manufacturing

3144 Women's Footwear, Except Athletic *see* NAICS 316214: Women's Footwear (except Athletic) Manufacturing

3149 Footwear, Except Rubber, NEC *see* NAICS 316219: Other Footwear Manufacturing

3151 Leather Gloves and Mittens *see* NAICS 315992: Glove and Mitten Manufacturing

3161 Luggage *see* NAICS 316991: Luggage Manufacturing

3171 Women's Handbags and Purses *see* NAICS 316992: Women's Handbag and Purse Manufacturing

3172 Personal Leather Goods, Except Women's Handbags and Purses *see* NAICS 316993: Personal Leather Good (except Women's Handbag and Purse) Manufacturing

3199 Leather Goods, NEC *see* NAICS 316999: All Other Leather Good Manufacturing

STONE, CLAY, GLASS, & CONCRETE PRODUCTS

3211 Flat Glass *see* NAICS 327211: Flat Glass Manufacturing

3221 Glass Containers *see* NAICS 327213: Glass Container Manufacturing

3229 Pressed and Blown Glass and Glassware, NEC *see* NAICS 327212: Other Pressed and Blown Glass and Glassware Manufacturing

3231 Glass Products, Made of Purchased Glass *see* NAICS 327215: Glass Product Manufacturing Made of Purchased Glass

3241 Cement, Hydraulic *see* NAICS 327310: Cement Manufacturing

3251 Brick and Structural Clay Tile *see* NAICS 327121: Brick and Structural Clay Tile Manufacturing

3253 Ceramic Wall and Floor Tile *see* NAICS 327122: Ceramic Wall and Floor Tile Manufacturing

3255 Clay Refractories *see* NAICS 327124: Clay Refractory Manufacturing

3259 Structural Clay Products, NEC *see* NAICS 327123: Other Structural Clay Product Manufacturing

3261 Vitreous China Plumbing Fixtures and China and Earthenware Fittings and Bathroom Accessories *see* NAICS 327111: Vitreous China Plumbing Fixture and China and Earthenware Fitting and Bathroom Accessories Manufacturing

3262 Vitreous China Table and Kitchen Articles *see* NAICS 327112: Vitreous China, Fine Earthenware and Other Pottery Product Manufacturing

3263 Fine Earthenware (Whiteware) Table and Kitchen Articles *see* NAICS 327112: Vitreous China, Fine Earthenware and Other Pottery Product Manufacturing

3264 Porcelain Electrical Supplies *see* NAICS 327113: Porcelain Electrical Supply Manufacturing

3269 Pottery Products, NEC *see* NAICS 327112: Vitreous China, Fine Earthenware, and Other Pottery Product Manufacturing

3271 Concrete Block and Brick *see* NAICS 327331: Concrete Block and Brick Manufacturing

3272 Concrete Products, Except Block and Brick *see* NAICS 327999: All Other Miscellaneous Nonmetallic Mineral Product Manufacturing; NAICS 327332: Concrete Pipe Manufacturing; NAICS 327390: Other Concrete Product Manufacturing

3273 Ready-Mixed Concrete *see* NAICS 327320: Ready-Mix Concrete Manufacturing

3274 Lime *see* NAICS 327410: Lime Manufacturing

3275 Gypsum Products *see* NAICS 327420: Gypsum and Gypsum Product Manufacturing

3281 Cut Stone and Stone Products *see* NAICS 327991: Cut Stone and Stone Product Manufacturing

3291 Abrasive Products *see* NAICS 332999: All Other Miscellaneous Fabricated Metal Product Manufacturing; NAICS 327910: Abrasive Product Manufacturing

3292 Asbestos Products *see* NAICS 336340: Motor Vehicle Brake System Manufacturing; NAICS 327999: All Other Miscellaneous Nonmetallic Mineral Product Manufacturing

3295 Minerals and Earths, Ground or Otherwise Treated *see* NAICS 327992: Ground or Treated Mineral and Earth Manufacturing

3296 Mineral Wool *see* NAICS 327993: Mineral Wool Manufacturing

3297 Nonclay Refractories *see* NAICS 327125: Nonclay Refractory Manufacturing

3299 Nonmetallic Mineral Products, NEC *see* NAICS 327420: Gypsum and Gypsum Product Manufacturing; NAICS 327999: All Other Miscellaneous Nonmetallic Mineral Product Manufacturing

Primary Metals Industries

3312 Steel Works, Blast Furnaces (Including Coke Ovens), and Rolling Mills *see* NAICS 324199: All Other Petroleum and Coal Products Manufacturing; NAICS 331111: Iron and Steel Mills

3313 Electrometallurgical Products, Except Steel *see* NAICS 331112: Electrometallurgical Ferroalloy Product Manufacturing; NAICS 331492: Secondary Smelting, Refining, and Alloying of Nonferrous Metals (except Copper and Aluminum)

3315 Steel Wiredrawing and Steel Nails and Spikes *see* NAICS 331222: Steel Wire Drawing; NAICS 332618: Other Fabricated Wire Product Manufacturing

3316 Cold-Rolled Steel Sheet, Strip, and Bars *see* NAICS 331221: Cold-Rolled Steel Shape Manufacturing

3317 Steel Pipe and Tubes *see* NAICS 331210: Iron and Steel Pipes and Tubes Manufacturing from Purchased Steel

3321 Gray and Ductile Iron Foundries *see* NAICS 331511: Iron Foundries

3322 Malleable Iron Foundries *see* NAICS 331511: Iron Foundries

3324 Steel Investment Foundries *see* NAICS 331512: Steel Investment Foundries

3325 Steel Foundries, NEC *see* NAICS 331513: Steel Foundries (except Investment)

3331 Primary Smelting and Refining of Copper *see* NAICS 331411: Primary Smelting and Refining of Copper

3334 Primary Production of Aluminum *see* NAICS 331312: Primary Aluminum Production

3339 Primary Smelting and Refining of Nonferrous Metals, Except Copper and Aluminum *see* NAICS 331419: Primary Smelting and Refining of Nonferrous Metals (except Copper and Aluminum)

3341 Secondary Smelting and Refining of Nonferrous Metals *see* NAICS 331314: Secondary Smelting and Alloying of Aluminum; NAICS 331423: Secondary Smelting, Refining, and Alloying of Copper; NAICS 331492: Secondary Smelting, Refining, and Alloying of Nonferrous Metals (except Copper and Aluminum)

3351 Rolling, Drawing, and Extruding of Copper *see* NAICS 331421: Copper (except Wire) Rolling, Drawing, and Extruding

3353 Aluminum Sheet, Plate, and Foil *see* NAICS 331315: Aluminum Sheet, Plate, and Foil Manufacturing

3354 Aluminum Extruded Products *see* NAICS 331316: Aluminum Extruded Product Manufacturing

3355 Aluminum Rolling and Drawing, NEC *see* NAICS 331319: Other Aluminum Rolling and Drawing

3356 Rolling, Drawing, and Extruding of Nonferrous Metals, Except Copper and Aluminum *see* NAICS 331491: Nonferrous Metal (except Copper and Aluminum) Rolling, Drawing, and Extruding

3357 Drawing and Insulating of Nonferrous Wire *see* NAICS 331319: Other Aluminum Rolling and Drawing; NAICS 331422: Copper Wire Drawing; NAICS 331491: Nonferrous Metal (except Copper and Aluminum) Rolling, Drawing, and Extruding; NAICS 335921: Fiber Optic Cable Manufacturing; NAICS 335929: Other Communication and Energy Wire Manufacturing

3363 Aluminum Die-Castings *see* NAICS 331521: Aluminum Die-Castings

3364 Nonferrous Die-Castings, Except Aluminum *see* NAICS 331522: Nonferrous (except Aluminum) Die-Castings

3365 Aluminum Foundries *see* NAICS 331524: Aluminum Foundries

3366 Copper Foundries *see* NAICS 331525: Copper Foundries

3369 Nonferrous Foundries, Except Aluminum and Copper *see* NAICS 331528: Other Nonferrous Foundries

3398 Metal Heat Treating *see* NAICS 332811: Metal Heat Treating

3399 Primary Metal Products, NEC *see* NAICS 331111: Iron and Steel Mills; NAICS 331314: Secondary Smelting and Alloying of Aluminum; NAICS 331423: Secondary Smelting, Refining and Alloying of Copper; NAICS 331492: Secondary Smelting, Refining, and Alloying of Nonferrous Metals (except Copper and Aluminum); NAICS 332618: Other Fabricated Wire Product Manufacturing; NAICS 332813: Electroplating, Plating, Polishing, Anodizing, and Coloring

Fabricated Metal Products, Except Machinery & Transportation Equipment

3411 Metal Cans *see* NAICS 332431: Metal Can Manufacturing

3412 Metal Shipping Barrels, Drums, Kegs and Pails *see* NAICS 332439: Other Metal Container Manufacturing

3421 Cutlery *see* NAICS 332211: Cutlery and Flatware (except Precious) Manufacturing

3423 Hand and Edge Tools, Except Machine Tools and Handsaws *see* NAICS 332212: Hand and Edge Tool Manufacturing

3425 Saw Blades and Handsaws *see* NAICS 332213: Saw Blade and Handsaw Manufacturing

3429 Hardware, NEC *see* NAICS 332439: Other Metal Container Manufacturing; NAICS 332919: Other Metal Valve and Pipe Fitting Manufacturing; NAICS 332510: Hardware Manufacturing

3431 Enameled Iron and Metal Sanitary Ware *see* NAICS 332998: Enameled Iron and Metal Sanitary Ware Manufacturing

3432 Plumbing Fixture Fittings and Trim *see* NAICS 332913: Plumbing Fixture Fitting and Trim Manufacturing; NAICS 332999: All Other Miscellaneous Fabricated Metal Product Manufacturing

3433 Heating Equipment, Except Electric and Warm Air Furnaces *see* NAICS 333414: Heating Equipment (except Electric and Warm Air Furnaces) Manufacturing

3441 Fabricated Structural Metal *see* NAICS 332312: Fabricated Structural Metal Manufacturing

3442 Metal Doors, Sash, Frames, Molding, and Trim Manufacturing *see* NAICS 332321: Metal Window and Door Manufacturing

3443 Fabricated Plate Work (Boiler Shops) *see* NAICS 332313: Plate Work Manufacturing; NAICS 332410: Power Boiler and Heat Exchanger Manufacturing; NAICS 332420: Metal Tank (Heavy Gauge) Manufacturing; NAICS 333415: Air-Conditioning and Warm Air Heating Equipment and Commercial and Industrial Refrigeration Equipment Manufacturing

3444 Sheet Metal Work *see* NAICS 332322: Sheet Metal Work Manufacturing; NAICS 332439: Other Metal Container Manufacturing

3446 Architectural and Ornamental Metal Work *see* NAICS 332323: Ornamental and Architectural Metal Work Manufacturing

3448 Prefabricated Metal Buildings and Components *see* NAICS 332311: Prefabricated Metal Building and Component Manufacturing

3449 Miscellaneous Structural Metal Work *see* NAICS 332114: Custom Roll Forming; NAICS 332312: Fabricated Structural Metal Manufacturing; NAICS 332321: Metal Window and Door Manufacturing; NAICS 332323: Ornamental and Architectural Metal Work Manufacturing

3451 Screw Machine Products *see* NAICS 332721: Precision Turned Product Manufacturing

3452 Bolts, Nuts, Screws, Rivets, and Washers *see* NAICS 332722: Bolt, Nut, Screw, Rivet, and Washer Manufacturing

3462 Iron and Steel Forgings *see* NAICS 332111: Iron and Steel Forging

3463 Nonferrous Forgings *see* NAICS 332112: Nonferrous Forging

3465 Automotive Stamping *see* NAICS 336370: Motor Vehicle Metal Stamping

3466 Crowns and Closures *see* NAICS 332115: Crown and Closure Manufacturing

3469 Metal Stamping, NEC *see* NAICS 339911: Jewelry (including Precious Metal) Manufacturing; NAICS 332116: Metal Stamping; NAICS 332214: Kitchen Utensil, Pot, and Pan Manufacturing

3471 Electroplating, Plating, Polishing, Anodizing, and Coloring *see* NAICS 332813: Electroplating, Plating, Polishing, Anodizing, and Coloring

3479 Coating, Engraving, and Allied Services, NEC *see* NAICS 339914: Costume Jewelry and Novelty Manufacturing; NAICS 339911: Jewelry (including Precious Metal) Manufacturing; NAICS 339912: Silverware and Plated Ware Manufacturing; NAICS 332812: Metal Coating, Engraving, and Allied Services (except Jewelry and Silverware) to Manufacturing

3482 Small Arms Ammunition *see* NAICS 332992: Small Arms Ammunition Manufacturing

3483 Ammunition, Except for Small Arms *see* NAICS 332993: Ammunition (except Small Arms) Manufacturing

3484 Small Arms *see* NAICS 332994: Small Arms Manufacturing

3489 Ordnance and Accessories, NEC *see* NAICS 332995: Other Ordnance and Accessories Manufacturing

3491 Industrial Valves *see* NAICS 332911: Industrial Valve Manufacturing

3492 Fluid Power Valves and Hose Fittings *see* NAICS 332912: Fluid Power Valve and Hose Fitting Manufacturing

3493 Steel Springs, Except Wire *see* NAICS 332611: Steel Spring (except Wire) Manufacturing

3494 Valves and Pipe Fittings, NEC *see* NAICS 332919: Other Metal Valve and Pipe Fitting Manufacturing; NAICS 332999: All Other Miscellaneous Fabricated Metal Product Manufacturing

3495 Wire Springs *see* NAICS 332612: Wire Spring Manufacturing; NAICS 334518: Watch, Clock, and Part Manufacturing

3496 Miscellaneous Fabricated Wire Products *see* NAICS 332618: Other Fabricated Wire Product Manufacturing

3497 Metal Foil and Leaf *see* NAICS 322225: Laminated Aluminum Foil Manufacturing for Flexible Packaging Uses; NAICS 332999: All Other Miscellaneous Fabricated Metal Product Manufacturing

3498 Fabricated Pipe and Pipe Fittings *see* NAICS 332996: Fabricated Pipe and Pipe Fitting Manufacturing

3499 Fabricated Metal Products, NEC *see* NAICS 337215: Showcase, Partition, Shelving, and Locker Manufacturing; NAICS 332117: Powder Metallurgy Part Manufacturing; NAICS 332439: Other Metal Container Manufacturing; NAICS 332510: Hardware Manufacturing; NAICS 332919: Other Metal Valve and Pipe Fitting Manufacturing; NAICS 339914: Costume Jewelry and Novelty Manufacturing; NAICS 332999: All Other Miscellaneous Fabricated Metal Product Manufacturing

Industrial & Commercial Machinery & Computer Equipment

3511 Steam, Gas, and Hydraulic Turbines, and Turbine Generator Set Units *see* NAICS 333611: Turbine and Turbine Generator Set Unit Manufacturing

3519 Internal Combustion Engines, NEC *see* NAICS 336399: All Other Motor Vehicle Parts Manufacturing; NAICS 333618: Other Engine Equipment Manufacturing

3523 Farm Machinery and Equipment *see* NAICS 333111: Farm Machinery and Equipment Manufacturing; NAICS 332323: Ornamental and Architectural Metal Work Manufacturing; NAICS 332212: Hand and Edge Tool Manufacturing; NAICS 333922: Conveyor and Conveying Equipment Manufacturing

3524 Lawn and Garden Tractors and Home Lawn and Garden Equipment *see* NAICS 333112: Lawn and Garden Tractor and Home Lawn and Garden Equipment Manufacturing; NAICS 332212: Hand and Edge Tool Manufacturing

3531 Construction Machinery and Equipment *see* NAICS 336510: Railroad Rolling Stock Manufacturing; NAICS 333923: Overhead Traveling Crane, Hoist, and Monorail System Manufacturing; NAICS 333120: Construction Machinery Manufacturing

3532 Mining Machinery and Equipment, Except Oil and Gas Field Machinery and Equipment *see* NAICS 333131: Mining Machinery and Equipment Manufacturing

3533 Oil and Gas Field Machinery and Equipment *see* NAICS 333132: Oil and Gas Field Machinery and Equipment Manufacturing

3534 Elevators and Moving Stairways *see* NAICS 333921: Elevator and Moving Stairway Manufacturing

3535 Conveyors and Conveying Equipment *see* NAICS 333922: Conveyor and Conveying Equipment Manufacturing

3536 Overhead Traveling Cranes, Hoists, and Monorail Systems *see* NAICS 333923: Overhead Traveling Crane, Hoist, and Monorail System Manufacturing

3537 Industrial Trucks, Tractors, Trailers, and Stackers *see* NAICS 333924: Industrial Truck, Tractor, Trailer, and Stacker Machinery Manufacturing; NAICS 332999: All Other Miscellaneous Fabricated Metal Product Manufacturing; NAICS 332439: Other Metal Container Manufacturing

3541 Machine Tools, Metal Cutting Type *see* NAICS 333512: Machine Tool (Metal Cutting Types) Manufacturing

3542 Machine Tools, Metal Forming Type *see* NAICS 333513: Machine Tool (Metal Forming Types) Manufacturing

3543 Industrial Patterns *see* NAICS 332997: Industrial Pattern Manufacturing

3544 Special Dies and Tools, Die Sets, Jigs and Fixtures, and Industrial Molds *see* NAICS 333514: Special Die and Tool, Die Set, Jig, and Fixture Manufacturing; NAICS 333511: Industrial Mold Manufacturing

3545 Cutting Tools, Machine Tool Accessories, and Machinists' Precision Measuring Devices *see* NAICS 333515: Cutting Tool and Machine Tool Accessory Manufacturing; NAICS 332212: Hand and Edge Tool Manufacturing

3546 Power-Driven Handtools *see* NAICS 333991: Power-Driven Hand Tool Manufacturing

3547 Rolling Mill Machinery and Equipment *see* NAICS 333516: Rolling Mill Machinery and Equipment Manufacturing

3548 Electric and Gas Welding and Soldering Equipment *see* NAICS 333992: Welding and Soldering Equipment Manufacturing; NAICS 335311: Power, Distribution, and Specialty Transformer Manufacturing

3549 Metalworking Machinery, NEC *see* NAICS 333518: Other Metalworking Machinery Manufacturing

3552 Textile Machinery *see* NAICS 333292: Textile Machinery Manufacturing

3553 Woodworking Machinery *see* NAICS 333210: Sawmill and Woodworking Machinery Manufacturing

3554 Paper Industries Machinery *see* NAICS 333291: Paper Industry Machinery Manufacturing

3555 Printing Trades Machinery and Equipment *see* NAICS 333293: Printing Machinery and Equipment Manufacturing

3556 Food Products Machinery *see* NAICS 333294: Food Product Machinery Manufacturing

3559 Special Industry Machinery, NEC *see* NAICS 333220: Rubber and Plastics Industry Machinery Manufacturing; NAICS 333319: Other Commercial and Service Industry Machinery Manufacturing; NAICS 333295: Semiconductor Manufacturing Machinery; NAICS 333298: All Other Industrial Machinery Manufacturing

3561 Pumps and Pumping Equipment *see* NAICS 333911: Pump and Pumping Equipment Manufacturing

3562 Ball and Roller Bearings *see* NAICS 332991: Ball and Roller Bearing Manufacturing

3563 Air and Gas Compressors *see* NAICS 333912: Air and Gas Compressor Manufacturing

3564 Industrial and Commercial Fans and Blowers and Air Purification Equipment *see* NAICS 333411: Air Purification Equipment Manufacturing; NAICS 333412: Industrial and Commercial Fan and Blower Manufacturing

3565 Packaging Machinery *see* NAICS 333993: Packaging Machinery Manufacturing

3566 Speed Changers, Industrial High-Speed Drives, and Gears *see* NAICS 333612: Speed Changer, Industrial High-Speed Drive, and Gear Manufacturing

3567 Industrial Process Furnaces and Ovens *see* NAICS 333994: Industrial Process Furnace and Oven Manufacturing

3568 Mechanical Power Transmission Equipment, NEC *see* NAICS 333613: Mechanical Power Transmission Equipment Manufacturing

3569 General Industrial Machinery and Equipment, NEC *see* NAICS 333999: All Other General Purpose Machinery Manufacturing

3571 Electronic Computers *see* NAICS 334111: Electronic Computer Manufacturing

3572 Computer Storage Devices *see* NAICS 334112: Computer Storage Device Manufacturing

3575 Computer Terminals *see* NAICS 334113: Computer Terminal Manufacturing

3577 Computer Peripheral Equipment, NEC *see* NAICS 334119: Other Computer Peripheral Equipment Manufacturing

3578 Calculating and Accounting Machines, Except Electronic Computers *see* NAICS 334119: Other Computer Peripheral Equipment Manufacturing; NAICS 333313: Office Machinery Manufacturing

3579 Office Machines, NEC *see* NAICS 339942: Lead Pencil and Art Good Manufacturing; NAICS 334518: Watch, Clock, and Part Manufacturing; NAICS 333313: Office Machinery Manufacturing

3581 Automatic Vending Machines *see* NAICS 333311: Automatic Vending Machine Manufacturing

3582 Commercial Laundry, Drycleaning, and Pressing Machines *see* NAICS 333312: Commercial Laundry, Drycleaning, and Pressing Machine Manufacturing

3585 Air-Conditioning and Warm Air Heating Equipment and Commercial and Industrial Refrigeration Equipment *see* NAICS 336391: Motor Vehicle Air Conditioning Manufacturing; NAICS 333415: Air Conditioning and Warm Air Heating Equipment and Commercial and Industrial Refrigeration Equipment Manufacturing

3586 Measuring and Dispensing Pumps *see* NAICS 333913: Measuring and Dispensing Pump Manufacturing

3589 Service Industry Machinery, NEC *see* NAICS 333319: Other Commercial and Service Industry Machinery Manufacturing

3592 Carburetors, Pistons, Piston Rings and Valves *see* NAICS 336311: Carburetor, Piston, Piston Ring and Valve Manufacturing

3593 Fluid Power Cylinders and Actuators *see* NAICS 333995: Fluid Power Cylinder and Actuator Manufacturing

3594 Fluid Power Pumps and Motors *see* NAICS 333996: Fluid Power Pump and Motor Manufacturing

3596 Scales and Balances, Except Laboratory *see* NAICS 333997: Scale and Balance (except Laboratory) Manufacturing

3599 Industrial and Commercial Machinery and Equipment, NEC *see* NAICS 336399: All Other Motor Vehicle Part Manufacturing; NAICS 332999: All Other Miscellaneous Fabricated Metal Product Manufacturing; NAICS 333319: Other Commercial and Service Industry Machinery Manufacturing; NAICS 332710: Machine Shops; NAICS 333999: All Other General Purpose Machinery Manufacturing

Electronic & Other Electrical Equipment & Components, Except Computer Equipment

3612 Power, Distribution, and Specialty Transformers *see* NAICS 335311: Power, Distribution, and Specialty Transformer Manufacturing

3613 Switchgear and Switchboard Apparatus *see* NAICS 335313: Switchgear and Switchboard Apparatus Manufacturing

3621 Motors and Generators *see* NAICS 335312: Motor and Generator Manufacturing

3624 Carbon and Graphite Products *see* NAICS 335991: Carbon and Graphite Product Manufacturing

3625 Relays and Industrial Controls *see* NAICS 335314: Relay and Industrial Control Manufacturing

3629 Electrical Industrial Apparatus, NEC *see* NAICS 335999: All Other Miscellaneous Electrical Equipment and Component Manufacturing

3631 Household Cooking Equipment *see* NAICS 335221: Household Cooking Appliance Manufacturing

3632 Household Refrigerators and Home and Farm Freezers *see* NAICS 335222: Household Refrigerator and Home and Farm Freezer Manufacturing

3633 Household Laundry Equipment *see* NAICS 335224: Household Laundry Equipment Manufacturing

3634 Electric Housewares and Fans *see* NAICS 335211: Electric Houseware and Fan Manufacturing; NAICS 333414: Heating Equipment (except Electric and Warm Air Furnaces) Manufacturing

3635 Household Vacuum Cleaners *see* NAICS 335212: Household Vacuum Cleaner Manufacturing

3639 Household Appliances, NEC *see* NAICS 335212: Household Vacuum Cleaner Manufacturing; NAICS 333298: All Other Industrial Machinery Manufacturing; NAICS 335228: Other Household Appliance Manufacturing

3641 Electric Lamp Bulbs and Tubes *see* NAICS 335110: Electric Lamp Bulb and Part Manufacturing

3643 Current-Carrying Wiring Devices *see* NAICS 335931: Current-Carrying Wiring Device Manufacturing

3644 Noncurrent-Carrying Wiring Devices *see* NAICS 335932: Noncurrent-Carrying Wiring Device Manufacturing

3645 Residential Electric Lighting Fixtures *see* NAICS 335121: Residential Electric Lighting Fixture Manufacturing

3646 Commercial, Industrial, and Institutional Electric Lighting Fixtures *see* NAICS 335122: Commercial, Industrial, and Institutional Electric Lighting Fixture Manufacturing

3647 Vehicular Lighting Equipment *see* NAICS 336321: Vehicular Lighting Equipment Manufacturing

3648 Lighting Equipment, NEC *see* NAICS 335129: Other Lighting Equipment Manufacturing

3651 Household Audio and Video Equipment *see* NAICS 334310: Audio and Video Equipment Manufacturing

3652 Phonograph Records and Prerecorded Audio Tapes and Disks *see* NAICS 334612: Prerecorded Compact Disc (Except Software), Tape and Record Reproducing; NAICS 512220: Integrated Record Production/Distribution

3661 Telephone and Telegraph Apparatus *see* NAICS 334210: Telephone Apparatus Manufacturing; NAICS 334416: Electronic Coil, Transformer, and Other Inductor Manufacturing; NAICS 334418: Printed Circuit/Electronics Assembly Manufacturing

3663 Radio and Television Broadcasting and Communication Equipment *see* NAICS 334220: Radio and Television Broadcasting and Wireless Communications Equipment Manufacturing

3669 Communications Equipment, NEC *see* NAICS 334290: Other Communication Equipment Manufacturing

3671 Electron Tubes *see* NAICS 334411: Electron Tube Manufacturing

3672 Printed Circuit Boards *see* NAICS 334412: Printed Circuit Board Manufacturing

3674 Semiconductors and Related Devices *see* NAICS 334413: Semiconductor and Related Device Manufacturing

3675 Electronic Capacitors *see* NAICS 334414: Electronic Capacitor Manufacturing

3676 Electronic Resistors *see* NAICS 334415: Electronic Resistor Manufacturing

3677 Electronic Coils, Transformers, and Other Inductors *see* NAICS 334416: Electronic Coil, Transformer, and Other Inductor Manufacturing

3678 Electronic Connectors *see* NAICS 334417: Electronic Connector Manufacturing

3679 Electronic Components, NEC *see* NAICS 334220: Radio and Television Broadcasting and Wireless Communications Equipment Manufacturing; NAICS 334418: Printed Circuit/Electronics Assembly Manufacturing; NAICS 336322: Other Motor Vehicle Electrical and Electronic Equipment Manufacturing; NAICS 334419: Other Electronic Component Manufacturing

3691 Storage Batteries *see* NAICS 335911: Storage Battery Manufacturing

3692 Primary Batteries, Dry and Wet *see* NAICS 335912: Dry and Wet Primary Battery Manufacturing

3694 Electrical Equipment for Internal Combustion Engines *see* NAICS 336322: Other Motor Vehicle Electrical and Electronic Equipment Manufacturing

3695 Magnetic and Optical Recording Media *see* NAICS 334613: Magnetic and Optical Recording Media Manufacturing

3699 Electrical Machinery, Equipment, and Supplies, NEC *see* NAICS 333319: Other Commercial and Service Industry Machinery Manufacturing; NAICS 333618: Other Engine Equipment Manufacturing; NAICS 334119: Other Computer Peripheral Equipment Manufacturing; NAICS 335129: Other Lighting Equipment Manufacturing; NAICS 335999: All Other Miscellaneous Electrical Equipment and Component Manufacturing

TRANSPORTATION EQUIPMENT

3711 Motor Vehicles and Passenger Car Bodies *see* NAICS 336111: Automobile Manufacturing; NAICS 336112: Light Truck and Utility Vehicle Manufacturing; NAICS 336120: Heavy Duty Truck Manufacturing; NAICS 336211: Motor Vehicle Body Manufacturing; NAICS 336992: Military Armored Vehicle, Tank, and Tank Component Manufacturing

3713 Truck and Bus Bodies *see* NAICS 336211: Motor Vehicle Body Manufacturing

3714 Motor Vehicle Parts and Accessories *see* NAICS 336211: Motor Vehicle Body Manufacturing; NAICS 336312: Gasoline Engine and Engine Parts Manufacturing; NAICS 336322: Other Motor Vehicle Electrical and Electronic Equipment Manufacturing; NAICS 336330: Motor Vehicle Steering and Suspension Components (except Spring) Manufacturing; NAICS 336340: Motor Vehicle Brake System Manufacturing; NAICS 336350: Motor Vehicle Transmission and Power Train Part Manufacturing; NAICS 336399: All Other Motor Vehicle Parts Manufacturing

3715 Truck Trailers *see* NAICS 336212: Truck Trailer Manufacturing

3716 Motor Homes *see* NAICS 336213: Motor Home Manufacturing

3721 Aircraft *see* NAICS 336411: Aircraft Manufacturing

3724 Aircraft Engines and Engine Parts *see* NAICS 336412: Aircraft Engine and Engine Parts Manufacturing

3728 Aircraft Parts and Auxiliary Equipment, NEC *see* NAICS 332912: Fluid Power Valve and Hose Fitting Manufacturing; NAICS 336413: Other Aircraft Part and Auxiliary Equipment Manufacturing

3731 Ship Building and Repairing *see* NAICS 336611: Ship Building and Repairing

3732 Boat Building and Repairing *see* NAICS 811490: Other Personal and Household Goods Repair and Maintenance; NAICS 336612: Boat Building

3743 Railroad Equipment *see* NAICS 333911: Pump and Pumping Equipment Manufacturing; NAICS 336510: Railroad Rolling Stock Manufacturing

3751 Motorcycles, Bicycles, and Parts *see* NAICS 336991: Motorcycle, Bicycle, and Parts Manufacturing

3761 Guided Missiles and Space Vehicles *see* NAICS 336414: Guided Missile and Space Vehicle Manufacturing

3764 Guided Missile and Space Vehicle Propulsion Units and Propulsion Unit Parts *see* NAICS 336415: Guided Missile and Space Vehicle Propulsion Unit and Propulsion Unit Parts Manufacturing

3769 Guided Missile Space Vehicle Parts and Auxiliary Equipment, NEC *see* NAICS 336419: Other Guided Missile and Space Vehicle Parts and Auxiliary Equipment Manufacturing

3792 Travel Trailers and Campers *see* NAICS 336214: Travel Trailer and Camper Manufacturing

3795 Tanks and Tank Components *see* NAICS 336992: Military Armored Vehicle, Tank, and Tank Component Manufacturing

3799 Transportation Equipment, NEC *see* NAICS 336214: Travel Trailer and Camper Manufacturing; NAICS 332212: Hand and Edge Tool Manufacturing; NAICS 336999: All Other Transportation Equipment Manufacturing

MEASURING, ANALYZING, & CONTROLLING INSTRUMENTS

3812 Search, Detection, Navigation, Guidance, Aeronautical, and Nautical Systems and Instruments *see* NAICS 334511: Search, Detection, Navigation, Guidance, Aeronautical, and Nautical System and Instrument Manufacturing

3821 Laboratory Apparatus and Furniture *see* NAICS 339111: Laboratory Apparatus and Furniture Manufacturing

3822 Automatic Controls for Regulating Residential and Commercial Environments and Appliances *see* NAICS 334512: Automatic Environmental Control Manufacturing for Regulating Residential, Commercial, and Appliance Use

3823 Industrial Instruments for Measurement, Display, and Control of Process Variables; and Related Products *see* NAICS 334513: Instruments and Related Product Manufacturing for Measuring Displaying, and Controlling Industrial Process Variables

3824 Totalizing Fluid Meters and Counting Devices *see* NAICS 334514: Totalizing Fluid Meter and Counting Device Manufacturing

3825 Instruments for Measuring and Testing of Electricity and Electrical Signals *see* NAICS 334416: Electronic Coil, Transformer, and Other Inductor Manufacturing; NAICS 334515: Instrument Manufacturing for Measuring and Testing Electricity and Electrical Signals

3826 Laboratory Analytical Instruments *see* NAICS 334516: Analytical Laboratory Instrument Manufacturing

3827 Optical Instruments and Lenses *see* NAICS 333314: Optical Instrument and Lens Manufacturing

3829 Measuring and Controlling Devices, NEC *see* NAICS 339112: Surgical and Medical Instrument Manufacturing; NAICS 334519: Other Measuring and Controlling Device Manufacturing

3841 Surgical and Medical Instruments and Apparatus *see* NAICS 339112: Surgical and Medical Instrument Manufacturing

3842 Orthopedic, Prosthetic, and Surgical Appliances and Supplies *see* NAICS 339113: Surgical Appliance and Supplies Manufacturing; NAICS 334510: Electromedical and Electrotherapeutic Apparatus Manufacturing

3843 Dental Equipment and Supplies *see* NAICS 339114: Dental Equipment and Supplies Manufacturing

3844 X-Ray Apparatus and Tubes and Related Irradiation Apparatus *see* NAICS 334517: Irradiation Apparatus Manufacturing

3845 Electromedical and Electrotherapeutic Apparatus *see* NAICS 334517: Irradiation Apparatus Manufacturing;

NAICS 334510: Electromedical and Electrotherapeutic Apparatus Manufacturing

3851 Ophthalmic Goods *see* NAICS 339115: Ophthalmic Goods Manufacturing

3861 Photographic Equipment and Supplies *see* NAICS 333315: Photographic and Photocopying Equipment Manufacturing; NAICS 325992: Photographic Film, Paper, Plate and Chemical Manufacturing

3873 Watches, Clocks, Clockwork Operated Devices and Parts *see* NAICS 334518: Watch, Clock, and Part Manufacturing

MISCELLANEOUS MANUFACTURING INDUSTRIES

3911 Jewelry, Precious Metal *see* NAICS 339911: Jewelry (Including Precious Metal) Manufacturing

3914 Silverware, Plated Ware, and Stainless Steel Ware *see* NAICS 332211: Cutlery and Flatware (except Precious) Manufacturing; NAICS 339912: Silverware and Plated Ware Manufacturing

3915 Jewelers' Findings and Materials, and Lapidary Work *see* NAICS 339913: Jewelers' Material and Lapidary Work Manufacturing

3931 Musical Instruments *see* NAICS 339992: Musical Instrument Manufacturing

3942 Dolls and Stuffed Toys *see* NAICS 339931: Doll and Stuffed Toy Manufacturing

3944 Games, Toys, and Children's Vehicles, Except Dolls and Bicycles *see* NAICS 336991: Motorcycle, Bicycle, and Parts Manufacturing; NAICS 339932: Game, Toy, and Children's Vehicle Manufacturing

3949 Sporting and Athletic Goods, NEC *see* NAICS 339920: Sporting and Athletic Good Manufacturing

3951 Pens, Mechanical Pencils, and Parts *see* NAICS 339941: Pen and Mechanical Pencil Manufacturing

3952 Lead Pencils, Crayons, and Artist's Materials *see* NAICS 337127: Institutional Furniture Manufacturing; NAICS 325998: All Other Miscellaneous Chemical Product Manufacturing; NAICS 339942: Lead Pencil and Art Good Manufacturing

3953 Marking Devices *see* NAICS 339943: Marking Device Manufacturing

3955 Carbon Paper and Inked Ribbons *see* NAICS 339944: Carbon Paper and Inked Ribbon Manufacturing

3961 Costume Jewelry and Costume Novelties, Except Precious Metals *see* NAICS 339914: Costume Jewelry and Novelty Manufacturing

3965 Fasteners, Buttons, Needles, and Pins *see* NAICS 339993: Fastener, Button, Needle and Pin Manufacturing

3991 Brooms and Brushes *see* NAICS 339994: Broom, Brush and Mop Manufacturing

3993 Signs and Advertising Specialties *see* NAICS 339950: Sign Manufacturing

3995 Burial Caskets *see* NAICS 339995: Burial Casket Manufacturing

3996 Linoleum, Asphalted-Felt-Base, and Other Hard Surface Floor Coverings, NEC *see* NAICS 326192: Resilient Floor Covering Manufacturing

3999 Manufacturing Industries, NEC *see* NAICS 337127: Institutional Furniture Manufacturing; NAICS 321999: All Other Miscellaneous Wood Product Manufacturing; NAICS 316110: Leather and Hide Tanning and Finishing; NAICS 335121: Residential Electric Lighting Fixture Manufacturing; NAICS 325998: All Other Miscellaneous Chemical Product Manufacturing; NAICS 332999: All Other Miscellaneous Fabricated Metal Product Manufacturing; NAICS 326199: All Other Plastics Product Manufacturing; NAICS 323112: Commercial Flexographic Printing; NAICS 323111: Commercial Gravure Printing; NAICS 323110: Commercial Lithographic Printing; NAICS 323113: Commercial Screen Printing; NAICS 323119: Other Commercial Printing; NAICS 332212: Hand and Edge Tool Manufacturing; NAICS 339999: All Other Miscellaneous Manufacturing

TRANSPORTATION, COMMUNICATIONS, ELECTRIC, GAS, & SANITARY SERVICES

4011 Railroads, Line-haul Operating *see* NAICS 482111: Line-Haul Railroads

4013 Railroad Switching and Terminal Establishments *see* NAICS 482112: Short Line Railroads; NAICS 488210: Support Activities for Rail Transportation

4111 Local and Suburban Transit *see* NAICS 485111: Mixed Mode Transit Systems; NAICS 485112: Commuter Rail Systems; NAICS 485113: Bus and Motor Vehicle Transit Systems; NAICS 485119: Other Urban Transit Systems; NAICS 485999: All Other Transit and Ground Passenger Transportation

4119 Local Passenger Transportation, NEC *see* NAICS 621910: Ambulance Service; NAICS 485410: School and Employee Bus Industry; NAICS 487110: Scenic and Sightseeing Transportation; NAICS 485991: Special Needs Transportation; NAICS 485999: All Other Transit and Ground Passenger Transportation; NAICS 485320: Limousine Service

4121 Taxicabs *see* NAICS 485310: Taxi Service

4131 Intercity and Rural Bus Transportation *see* NAICS 485210: Interurban and Rural Bus Lines

4141 Local Bus Charter Service *see* NAICS 485510: Charter Bus Industry

4142 Bus Charter Service, Except Local *see* NAICS 485510: Charter Bus Industry

4151 School Buses *see* NAICS 485410: School and Employee Bus Industry

4173 Terminal and Service Facilities for Motor Vehicle Passenger Transportation *see* NAICS 488490: Other Support Activities for Road Transportation

4212 Local Trucking Without Storage *see* NAICS 562111: Solid Waste Collection; NAICS 562112: Hazardous Waste Collection; NAICS 562119: Other Waste Collection; NAICS 484110: General Freight Trucking, Local; NAICS 484210: Used Household and Office Goods Moving; NAICS 484220: Specialized Freight (except Used Goods) Trucking, Local

4213 Trucking, Except Local *see* NAICS 484121: General Freight Trucking, Long-Distance, Truckload; NAICS 484122: General Freight Trucking, Long-Distance, Less Than Truckload; NAICS 484210: Used Household and Office Goods Moving; NAICS 484230: Specialized Freight (except Used Goods) Trucking, Long-Distance

4214 Local Trucking with Storage *see* NAICS 484110: General Freight Trucking, Local; NAICS 484210: Used Household and Office Goods Moving; NAICS 484220: Specialized Freight (except Used Goods) Trucking, Local

4215 Couriers Services Except by Air *see* NAICS 492110: Couriers; NAICS 492210: Local Messengers and Local Delivery

4221 Farm Product Warehousing and Storage *see* NAICS 493130: Farm Product Storage Facilities

4222 Refrigerated Warehousing and Storage *see* NAICS 493120: Refrigerated Storage Facilities

4225 General Warehousing and Storage *see* NAICS 493110: General Warehousing and Storage Facilities; NAICS 531130: Lessors of Mini-warehouses and Self Storage Units

4226 Special Warehousing and Storage, NEC *see* NAICS 493120: Refrigerated Storage Facilities; NAICS 493110: General Warehousing and Storage Facilities; NAICS 493190: All Other Warehousing and Storage Facilities

4231 Terminal and Joint Terminal Maintenance Facilities for Motor Freight Transportation *see* NAICS 488490: Other Support Activities for Road Transportation

4311 United States Postal Service *see* NAICS 491110: Postal Service

4412 Deep Sea Foreign Transportation of Freight *see* NAICS 483111: Deep Sea Freight Transportation

4424 Deep Sea Domestic Transportation of Freight *see* NAICS 483113: Coastal and Great Lakes Freight Transportation

4432 Freight Transportation on the Great Lakes-St. Lawrence Seaway *see* NAICS 483113: Coastal and Great Lakes Freight Transportation

4449 Water Transportation of Freight, NEC *see* NAICS 483211: Inland Water Freight Transportation

4481 Deep Sea Transportation of Passengers, Except by Ferry *see* NAICS 483112: Deep Sea Passenger Transportation; NAICS 483114: Coastal and Great Lakes Passenger Transportation

4482 Ferries *see* NAICS 483114: Coastal and Great Lakes Passenger Transportation; NAICS 483212: Inland Water Passenger Transportation

4489 Water Transportation of Passengers, NEC *see* NAICS 483212: Inland Water Passenger Transportation; NAICS 487210: Scenic and Sightseeing Transportation, Water

4491 Marine Cargo Handling *see* NAICS 488310: Port and Harbor Operations; NAICS 488320: Marine Cargo Handling

4492 Towing and Tugboat Services *see* NAICS 483113: Coastal and Great Lakes Freight Transportation; NAICS 483211: Inland Water Freight Transportation; NAICS 488330: Navigational Services to Shipping

4493 Marinas *see* NAICS 713930: Marinas

4499 Water Transportation Services, NEC *see* NAICS 532411: Commercial Air, Rail, and Water Transportation Equipment Rental and Leasing; NAICS 488310: Port and Harbor Operations; NAICS 488330: Navigational Services to Shipping; NAICS 488390: Other Support Activities for Water Transportation

4512 Air Transportation, Scheduled *see* NAICS 481111: Scheduled Passenger Air Transportation; NAICS 481112: Scheduled Freight Air Transportation

4513 Air Courier Services *see* NAICS 492110: Couriers

4522 Air Transportation, Nonscheduled *see* NAICS 621910: Ambulance Services; NAICS 481212: Nonscheduled Chartered Freight Air Transportation; NAICS 481211: Nonscheduled Chartered Passenger Air Transportation; NAICS 487990: Scenic and Sightseeing Transportation

4581 Airports, Flying Fields, and Airport Terminal Services *see* NAICS 488111: Air Traffic Control; NAICS 488119: Other Airport Operations; NAICS 561720: Janitorial Services; NAICS 488190: Other Support Activities for Air Transportation

4612 Crude Petroleum Pipelines *see* NAICS 486110: Pipeline Transportation of Crude Oil

4613 Refined Petroleum Pipelines *see* NAICS 486910: Pipeline Transportation of Refined Petroleum Products

4619 Pipelines, NEC *see* NAICS 486990: All Other Pipeline Transportation

4724 Travel Agencies *see* NAICS 561510: Travel Agencies

4725 Tour Operators *see* NAICS 561520: Tour Operators

4729 Arrangement of Passenger Transportation, NEC *see* NAICS 488999: All Other Support Activities for Transportation; NAICS 561599: All Other Travel Arrangement and Reservation Services

4731 Arrangement of Transportation of Freight and Cargo *see* NAICS 541618: Other Management Consulting Services; NAICS 488510: Freight Transportation Arrangement

4741 Rental of Railroad Cars *see* NAICS 532411: Commercial Air, Rail, and Water Transportation Equipment Rental and Leasing; NAICS 488210: Support Activities for Rail Transportation

4783 Packing and Crating *see* NAICS 488991: Packing and Crating

4785 Fixed Facilities and Inspection and Weighing Services for Motor Vehicle Transportation *see* NAICS 488390: Other Support Activities for Water Transportation; NAICS 488490: Other Support Activities for Road Transportation

4789 Transportation Services, NEC *see* NAICS 488999: All Other Support Activities for Transportation *see* NAICS 487110: Scenic and Sightseeing Transportation, Land; NAICS 488210: Support Activities for Rail Transportation

4812 Radiotelephone Communications *see* NAICS 513321: Paging; NAICS 513322: Cellular and Other Wireless Telecommunications; NAICS 513330: Telecommunications Resellers

4813 Telephone Communications, Except Radiotelephone *see* NAICS 513310: Wired Telecommunications Carriers; NAICS 513330: Telecommunications Resellers

4822 Telegraph and Other Message Communications *see* NAICS 513310: Wired Telecommunications Carriers

4832 Radio Broadcasting Stations *see* NAICS 513111: Radio Networks; NAICS 513112: Radio Stations

4833 Television Broadcasting Stations *see* NAICS 513120: Television Broadcasting

4841 Cable and Other Pay Television Services *see* NAICS 513210: Cable Networks; NAICS 513220: Cable and Other Program Distribution

4899 Communications Services, NEC *see* NAICS 513322: Cellular and Other Wireless Telecommunications; NAICS 513340: Satellite Telecommunications; NAICS 513390: Other Telecommunications

4911 Electric Services *see* NAICS 221111: Hydroelectric Power Generation; NAICS 221112: Fossil Fuel Electric Power Generation; NAICS 221113: Nuclear Electric Power Generation; NAICS 221119: Other Electric Power Generation; NAICS 221121: Electric Bulk Power Transmission and Control; NAICS 221122: Electric Power Distribution

4922 Natural Gas Transmission *see* NAICS 486210: Pipeline Transportation of Natural Gas

4923 Natural Gas Transmission and Distribution *see* NAICS 221210: Natural Gas Distribution; NAICS 486210: Pipeline Transportation of Natural Gas

4924 Natural Gas Distribution *see* NAICS 221210: Natural Gas Distribution

4925 Mixed, Manufactured, or Liquefied Petroleum Gas Production and/or Distribution *see* NAICS 221210: Natural Gas Distribution

4931 Electric and Other Services Combined *see* NAICS 221111: Hydroelectric Power Generation; NAICS 221112: Fossil Fuel Electric Power Generation; NAICS 221113: Nuclear Electric Power Generation; NAICS 221119: Other Electric Power Generation; NAICS 221121: Electric Bulk Power Transmission and Control; NAICS 221122: Electric Power Distribution; NAICS 221210: Natural Gas Distribution

4932 Gas and Other Services Combined *see* NAICS 221210: Natural Gas Distribution

4939 Combination Utilities, NEC *see* NAICS 221111: Hydroelectric Power Generation; NAICS 221112: Fossil Fuel Electric Power Generation; NAICS 221113: Nuclear Electric Power Generation; NAICS 221119: Other Electric Power Generation; NAICS 221121: Electric Bulk Power Transmission and Control; NAICS 221122: Electric Power Distribution; NAICS 221210: Natural Gas Distribution

4941 Water Supply *see* NAICS 221310: Water Supply and Irrigation Systems

4952 Sewerage Systems *see* NAICS 221320: Sewage Treatment Facilities

4953 Refuse Systems *see* NAICS 562111: Solid Waste Collection; NAICS 562112: Hazardous Waste Collection; NAICS 562920: Materials Recovery Facilities; NAICS 562119: Other Waste Collection; NAICS 562211: Hazardous Waste Treatment and Disposal; NAICS 562212: Solid Waste Landfills; NAICS 562213: Solid Waste Combustors and Incinerators; NAICS 562219: Other Nonhazardous Waste Treatment and Disposal

4959 Sanitary Services, NEC *see* NAICS 488119: Other Airport Operations; NAICS 562910: Remediation Services; NAICS 561710: Exterminating and Pest Control Services; NAICS 562998: All Other Miscellaneous Waste Management

4961 Steam and Air-Conditioning Supply *see* NAICS 221330: Steam and Air-Conditioning Supply

4971 Irrigation Systems *see* NAICS 221310: Water Supply and Irrigation Systems

Wholesale Trade

5012 Automobiles and Other Motor Vehicles *see* NAICS 421110: Automobile and Other Motor Vehicle Wholesalers

5013 Motor Vehicle Supplies and New Parts *see* NAICS 441310: Automotive Parts and Accessories Stores; NAICS 421120: Motor Vehicle Supplies and New Part Wholesalers

5014 Tires and Tubes *see* NAICS 441320: Tire Dealers; NAICS 421130: Tire and Tube Wholesalers

5015 Motor Vehicle Parts, Used *see* NAICS 421140: Motor Vehicle Part (Used) Wholesalers

5021 Furniture *see* NAICS 442110: Furniture Stores; NAICS 421210: Furniture Wholesalers

5023 Home Furnishings *see* NAICS 442210: Floor Covering Stores; NAICS 421220: Home Furnishing Wholesalers

5031 Lumber, Plywood, Millwork, and Wood Panels *see* NAICS 444190: Other Building Material Dealers; NAICS 421310: Lumber, Plywood, Millwork, and Wood Panel Wholesalers

5032 Brick, Stone and Related Construction Materials *see* NAICS 444190: Other Building Material Dealers; NAICS 421320: Brick, Stone and Related Construction Material Wholesalers

5033 Roofing, Siding, and Insulation Materials *see* NAICS 421330: Roofing, Siding, and Insulation Material Wholesalers

5039 Construction Materials, NEC *see* NAICS 444190: Other Building Material Dealers; NAICS 421390: Other Construction Material Wholesalers

5043 Photographic Equipment and Supplies *see* NAICS 421410: Photographic Equipment and Supplies Wholesalers

5044 Office Equipment *see* NAICS 421420: Office Equipment Wholesalers

5045 Computers and Computer Peripheral Equipment and Software *see* NAICS 421430: Computer and Computer Peripheral Equipment and Software Wholesalers; NAICS 443120: Computer and Software Stores

5046 Commercial Equipment, NEC *see* NAICS 421440: Other Commercial Equipment Wholesalers

5047 Medical, Dental, and Hospital Equipment and Supplies *see* NAICS 421450: Medical, Dental and Hospital Equipment and Supplies Wholesalers; NAICS 446199: All Other Health and Personal Care Stores

5048 Ophthalmic Goods *see* NAICS 421460: Ophthalmic Goods Wholesalers

5049 Professional Equipment and Supplies, NEC *see* NAICS 421490: Other Professional Equipment and Supplies Wholesalers; NAICS 453210: Office Supplies and Stationery Stores

5051 Metals Service Centers and Offices *see* NAICS 421510: Metals Service Centers and Offices

5052 Coal and Other Minerals and Ores *see* NAICS 421520: Coal and Other Mineral and Ore Wholesalers

5063 Electrical Apparatus and Equipment Wiring Supplies, and Construction Materials *see* NAICS 444190: Other Building Material Dealers; NAICS 421610: Electrical Apparatus and Equipment, Wiring Supplies and Construction Material Wholesalers

5064 Electrical Appliances, Television and Radio Sets *see* NAICS 421620: Electrical Appliance, Television and Radio Set Wholesalers

5065 Electronic Parts and Equipment, Not Elsewhere Classified *see* NAICS 421690: Other Electronic Parts and Equipment Wholesalers

5072 Hardware *see* NAICS 421710: Hardware Wholesalers

5074 Plumbing and Heating Equipment and Supplies (Hydronics) *see* NAICS 444190: Other Building Material Dealers; NAICS 421720: Plumbing and Heating Equipment and Supplies (Hydronics) Wholesalers

5075 Warm Air Heating and Air-Conditioning Equipment and Supplies *see* NAICS 421730: Warm Air Heating and Air-Conditioning Equipment and Supplies Wholesalers

5078 Refrigeration Equipment and Supplies *see* NAICS 421740: Refrigeration Equipment and Supplies Wholesalers

5082 Construction and Mining (Except Petroleum) Machinery and Equipment *see* NAICS 421810: Construction and Mining (except Petroleum) Machinery and Equipment Wholesalers

5083 Farm and Garden Machinery and Equipment *see* NAICS 421820: Farm and Garden Machinery and Equipment Wholesalers; NAICS 444210: Outdoor Power Equipment Stores

5084 Industrial Machinery and Equipment *see* NAICS 421830: Industrial Machinery and Equipment Wholesalers

5085 Industrial Supplies *see* NAICS 421830: Industrial Machinery and Equipment Wholesalers; NAICS 421840: Industrial Supplies Wholesalers

5087 Service Establishment Equipment and Supplies *see* NAICS 421850: Service Establishment Equipment and Supplies Wholesalers; NAICS 446120: Cosmetics, Beauty Supplies, and Perfume Stores

5088 Transportation Equipment and Supplies, Except Motor Vehicles *see* NAICS 421860: Transportation Equipment and Supplies (except Motor Vehicles) Wholesalers

5091 Sporting and Recreational Goods and Supplies *see* NAICS 421910: Sporting and Recreational Goods and Supplies Wholesalers

5092 Toys and Hobby Goods and Supplies *see* NAICS 421920: Toy and Hobby Goods and Supplies Wholesalers

5093 Scrap and Waste Materials *see* NAICS 421930: Recyclable Material Wholesalers

5094 Jewelry, Watches, Precious Stones, and Precious Metals *see* NAICS 421940: Jewelry, Watch, Precious Stone, and Precious Metal Wholesalers

5099 Durable Goods, NEC *see* NAICS 421990: Other Miscellaneous Durable Goods Wholesalers

5111 Printing and Writing Paper *see* NAICS 422110: Printing and Writing Paper Wholesalers

5112 Stationery and Office Supplies *see* NAICS 453210: Office Supplies and Stationery Stores; NAICS 422120: Stationery and Office Supplies Wholesalers

5113 Industrial and Personal Service Paper *see* NAICS 422130: Industrial and Personal Service Paper Wholesalers

5122 Drugs, Drug Proprietaries, and Druggists' Sundries *see* NAICS 422210: Drugs, Drug Proprietaries, and Druggists' Sundries Wholesalers

5131 Piece Goods, Notions, and Other Dry Goods *see* NAICS 313311: Broadwoven Fabric Finishing Mills; NAICS 313312: Textile and Fabric Finishing (except Broadwoven Fabric) Mills; NAICS 422310: Piece Goods, Notions, and Other Dry Goods Wholesalers

5136 Men's and Boys' Clothing and Furnishings *see* NAICS 422320: Men's and Boys' Clothing and Furnishings Wholesalers

5137 Women's Children's and Infants' Clothing and Accessories *see* NAICS 422330: Women's, Children's, and Infants' Clothing and Accessories Wholesalers

5139 Footwear *see* NAICS 422340: Footwear Wholesalers

5141 Groceries, General Line *see* NAICS 422410: General Line Grocery Wholesalers

5142 Packaged Frozen Foods *see* NAICS 422420: Packaged Frozen Food Wholesalers

5143 Dairy Products, Except Dried or Canned *see* NAICS 422430: Dairy Products (except Dried or Canned) Wholesalers

5144 Poultry and Poultry Products *see* NAICS 422440: Poultry and Poultry Product Wholesalers

5145 Confectionery *see* NAICS 422450: Confectionery Wholesalers

5146 Fish and Seafoods *see* NAICS 422460: Fish and Seafood Wholesalers

5147 Meats and Meat Products *see* NAICS 311612: Meat Processed from Carcasses; NAICS 422470: Meat and Meat Product Wholesalers

5148 Fresh Fruits and Vegetables *see* NAICS 422480: Fresh Fruit and Vegetable Wholesalers

5149 Groceries and Related Products, NEC *see* NAICS 422490: Other Grocery and Related Product Wholesalers

5153 Grain and Field Beans *see* NAICS 422510: Grain and Field Bean Wholesalers

5154 Livestock *see* NAICS 422520: Livestock Wholesalers

5159 Farm-Product Raw Materials, NEC *see* NAICS 422590: Other Farm Product Raw Material Wholesalers

5162 Plastics Materials and Basic Forms and Shapes *see* NAICS 422610: Plastics Materials and Basic Forms and Shapes Wholesalers

5169 Chemicals and Allied Products, NEC *see* NAICS 422690: Other Chemical and Allied Products Wholesalers

5171 Petroleum Bulk Stations and Terminals *see* NAICS 454311: Heating Oil Dealers; NAICS 454312: Liquefied Petroleum Gas (Bottled Gas) Dealers; NAICS 422710: Petroleum Bulk Stations and Terminals

5172 Petroleum and Petroleum Products Wholesalers, Except Bulk Stations and Terminals *see* NAICS 422720: Petroleum and Petroleum Products Wholesalers (except Bulk Stations and Terminals)

5181 Beer and Ale *see* NAICS 422810: Beer and Ale Wholesalers

5182 Wine and Distilled Alcoholic Beverages *see* NAICS 422820: Wine and Distilled Alcoholic Beverage Wholesalers

5191 Farm Supplies *see* NAICS 444220: Nursery and Garden Centers; NAICS 422910: Farm Supplies Wholesalers

5192 Books, Periodicals, and Newspapers *see* NAICS 422920: Book, Periodical and Newspaper Wholesalers

5193 Flowers, Nursery Stock, and Florists' Supplies *see* NAICS 422930: Flower, Nursery Stock and Florists' Supplies Wholesalers; NAICS 444220: Nursery and Garden Centers

5194 Tobacco and Tobacco Products *see* NAICS 422940: Tobacco and Tobacco Product Wholesalers

5198 Paint, Varnishes, and Supplies *see* NAICS 422950: Paint, Varnish and Supplies Wholesalers; NAICS 444120: Paint and Wallpaper Stores

5199 Nondurable Goods, NEC *see* NAICS 541890: Other Services Related to Advertising; NAICS 422990: Other Miscellaneous Nondurable Goods Wholesalers

RETAIL TRADE

5211 Lumber and Other Building Materials Dealers *see* NAICS 444110: Home Centers; NAICS 421310: Lumber, Plywood, Millwork, and Wood Panel Wholesalers; NAICS 444190: Other Building Material Dealers

5231 Paint, Glass, and Wallpaper Stores *see* NAICS 422950: Paint, Varnish, and Supplies Wholesalers; NAICS 444190: Other Building Material Dealers; NAICS 444120: Paint and Wallpaper Stores

5251 Hardware Stores *see* NAICS 444130: Hardware Stores

5261 Retail Nurseries *see* NAICS 444220: Nursery and Garden Centers; NAICS 453998: All Other Miscellaneous Store Retailers (except Tobacco Stores); NAICS 444210: Outdoor Power Equipment Stores

5271 Mobile Home Dealers *see* NAICS 453930: Manufactured (Mobile) Home Dealers

5311 Department Stores *see* NAICS 452110: Department Stores

5331 Variety Stores *see* NAICS 452990: All Other General Merchandise Stores

5399 Miscellaneous General Merchandise Stores *see* NAICS 452910: Warehouse Clubs and Superstores; NAICS 452990: All Other General Merchandise Stores

5411 Grocery Stores *see* NAICS 447110: Gasoline Stations with Convenience Stores; NAICS 445110: Supermarkets and Other Grocery (except Convenience) Stores; NAICS 452910: Warehouse Clubs and Superstores; NAICS 445120: Convenience Stores

5421 Meat and Fish (Seafood) Markets, Including Freezer Provisioners *see* NAICS 454390: Other Direct Selling Establishments; NAICS 445210: Meat Markets; NAICS 445220: Fish and Seafood Markets

5431 Fruit and Vegetable Markets *see* NAICS 445230: Fruit and Vegetable Markets

5441 Candy, Nut, and Confectionery Stores *see* NAICS 445292: Confectionery and Nut Stores

5451 Dairy Products Stores *see* NAICS 445299: All Other Specialty Food Stores

5461 Retail Bakeries *see* NAICS 722213: Snack and Nonalcoholic Beverage Bars; NAICS 311811: Retail Bakeries; NAICS 445291: Baked Goods Stores

5499 Miscellaneous Food Stores *see* NAICS 445210: Meat Markets; NAICS 722211: Limited-Service Restaurants; NAICS 446191: Food (Health) Supplement Stores; NAICS 445299: All Other Specialty Food Stores

5511 Motor Vehicle Dealers (New and Used) *see* NAICS 441110: New Car Dealers

5521 Motor Vehicle Dealers (Used Only) *see* NAICS 441120: Used Car Dealers

5531 Auto and Home Supply Stores *see* NAICS 441320: Tire Dealers; NAICS 441310: Automotive Parts and Accessories Stores

5541 Gasoline Service Stations *see* NAICS 447110: Gasoline Stations with Convenience Stores; NAICS 447190: Other Gasoline Stations

5551 Boat Dealers *see* NAICS 441222: Boat Dealers

5561 Recreational Vehicle Dealers *see* NAICS 441210: Recreational Vehicle Dealers

5571 Motorcycle Dealers *see* NAICS 441221: Motorcycle Dealers

5599 Automotive Dealers, NEC *see* NAICS 441229: All Other Motor Vehicle Dealers

5611 Men's and Boys' Clothing and Accessory Stores *see* NAICS 448110: Men's Clothing Stores; NAICS 448150: Clothing Accessories Stores

5621 Women's Clothing Stores *see* NAICS 448120: Women's Clothing Stores

5632 Women's Accessory and Specialty Stores *see* NAICS 448190: Other Clothing Stores; NAICS 448150: Clothing Accessories Stores

5641 Children's and Infants' Wear Stores *see* NAICS 448130: Children's and Infants' Clothing Stores

5651 Family Clothing Stores *see* NAICS 448140: Family Clothing Stores

5661 Shoe Stores *see* NAICS 448210: Shoe Stores

5699 Miscellaneous Apparel and Accessory Stores *see* NAICS 448190: Other Clothing Stores; NAICS 448150: Clothing Accessories Stores

5712 Furniture Stores *see* NAICS 337122: Nonupholstered Wood Household Furniture Manufacturing; NAICS 337110: Wood Kitchen Cabinet and Counter Top Manufacturing; NAICS 337121: Upholstered Wood Household Furniture Manufacturing; NAICS 442110: Furniture Stores

5713 Floor Covering Stores *see* NAICS 442210: Floor Covering Stores

5714 Drapery, Curtain, and Upholstery Stores *see* NAICS 442291: Window Treatment Stores; NAICS 451130: Sewing, Needlework, and Piece Goods Stores; NAICS 314121: Curtain and Drapery Mills

5719 Miscellaneous Homefurnishings Stores *see* NAICS 442291: Window Treatment Stores; NAICS 442299: All Other Home Furnishings Stores

5722 Household Appliance Stores *see* NAICS 443111: Household Appliance Stores

5731 Radio, Television, and Consumer Electronics Stores *see* NAICS 443112: Radio, Television, and Other Electronics Stores; NAICS 441310: Automotive Parts and Accessories Stores

5734 Computer and Computer Software Stores *see* NAICS 443120: Computer and Software Stores

5735 Record and Prerecorded Tape Stores *see* NAICS 451220: Prerecorded Tape, Compact Disc, and Record Stores

5736 Musical Instrument Stores *see* NAICS 451140: Musical Instrument and Supplies Stores

5812 Eating and Drinking Places *see* NAICS 722110: Full-Service Restaurants; NAICS 722211: Limited-Service Restaurants; NAICS 722212: Cafeterias; NAICS 722213: Snack and Nonalcoholic Beverage Bars; NAICS 722310: Foodservice Contractors; NAICS 722320: Caterers; NAICS 711110: Theater Companies and Dinner Theaters

5813 Drinking Places (Alcoholic Beverages) *see* NAICS 722410: Drinking Places (Alcoholic Beverages)

5912 Drug Stores and Proprietary Stores *see* NAICS 446110: Pharmacies and Drug Stores

5921 Liquor Stores *see* NAICS 445310: Beer, Wine and Liquor Stores

5932 Used Merchandise Stores *see* NAICS 522298: All Other Non-Depository Credit Intermediation; NAICS 453310: Used Merchandise Stores

5941 Sporting Goods Stores and Bicycle Shops *see* NAICS 451110: Sporting Goods Stores

5942 Book Stores *see* NAICS 451211: Book Stores

5943 Stationery Stores *see* NAICS 453210: Office Supplies and Stationery Stores

5944 Jewelry Stores *see* NAICS 448310: Jewelry Stores

5945 Hobby, Toy, and Game Shops *see* NAICS 451120: Hobby, Toy and Game Stores

5946 Camera and Photographic Supply Stores *see* NAICS 443130: Camera and Photographic Supplies Stores

5947 Gift, Novelty, and Souvenir Shops *see* NAICS 453220: Gift, Novelty, and Souvenir Stores

5948 Luggage and Leather Goods Stores *see* NAICS 448320: Luggage and Leather Goods Stores

5949 Sewing, Needlework, and Piece Goods Stores *see* NAICS 451130: Sewing, Needlework, and Piece Goods Stores

5961 Catalog and Mail-Order Houses *see* NAICS 454110: Electronic Shopping and Mail-Order Houses

5962 Automatic Merchandising Machine Operator *see* NAICS 454210: Vending Machine Operators

5963 Direct Selling Establishments *see* NAICS 722330: Mobile Caterers; NAICS 454390: Other Direct Selling Establishments

5983 Fuel Oil Dealers *see* NAICS 454311: Heating Oil Dealers

5984 Liquefied Petroleum Gas (Bottled Gas) Dealers *see* NAICS 454312: Liquefied Petroleum Gas (Bottled Gas) Dealers

5989 Fuel Dealers, NEC *see* NAICS 454319: Other Fuel Dealers

5992 Florists *see* NAICS 453110: Florists

5993 Tobacco Stores and Stands *see* NAICS 453991: Tobacco Stores

5994 News Dealers and Newsstands *see* NAICS 451212: News Dealers and Newsstands

5995 Optical Goods Stores *see* NAICS 339115: Ophthalmic Goods Manufacturing; NAICS 446130: Optical Goods Stores

5999 Miscellaneous Retail Stores, NEC *see* NAICS 446120: Cosmetics, Beauty Supplies, and Perfume Stores; NAICS 446199: All Other Health and Personal Care Stores; NAICS 453910: Pet and Pet Supplies Stores; NAICS 453920: Art Dealers; NAICS 443111: Household Appliance Stores; NAICS 443112: Radio, Television, and Other Electronics Stores; NAICS 448310: Jewelry Stores; NAICS 453998: All Other Miscellaneous Store Retailers (except Tobacco Stores)

FINANCE, INSURANCE, & REAL ESTATE

6011 Federal Reserve Banks *see* NAICS 521110: Monetary Authorities-Central Banks

6019 Central Reserve Depository Institutions, NEC *see* NAICS 522320: Financial Transactions Processing, Reserve, and Clearing House Activities

6021 National Commercial Banks *see* NAICS 522110: Commercial Banking; NAICS 522210: Credit Card Issuing; NAICS 523991: Trust, Fiduciary, and Custody Activities

6022 State Commercial Banks *see* NAICS 522110: Commercial Banking; NAICS 522210: Credit Card Issuing; NAICS 522190: Other Depository Intermediation; NAICS 523991: Trust, Fiduciary, and Custody Activities

6029 Commercial Banks, NEC *see* NAICS 522110: Commercial Banking

6035 Savings Institutions, Federally Chartered *see* NAICS 522120: Savings Institutions

6036 Savings institutions, Not Federally Chartered *see* NAICS 522120: Savings Institutions

6061 Credit Unions, Federally Chartered *see* NAICS 522130: Credit Unions

6062 Credit Unions, Not Federally Chartered *see* NAICS 522130: Credit Unions

6081 Branches and Agencies of Foreign Banks *see* NAICS 522293: International Trade Financing; NAICS 522110: Commercial Banking; NAICS 522298: All Other Non-Depository Credit Intermediation

6082 Foreign Trade and International Banking Institutions *see* NAICS 522293: International Trade Financing

6091 Nondeposit Trust Facilities *see* NAICS 523991: Trust, Fiduciary, and Custody Activities

6099 Functions Related to Deposit Banking, NEC *see* NAICS 522320: Financial Transactions Processing, Reserve, and Clearing House Activities; NAICS 523130: Commodity Contracts Dealing; NAICS 523991: Trust, Fiduciary, and Custody Activities; NAICS 523999: Miscellaneous Financial Investment Activities; NAICS 522390: Other Activities Related to Credit Intermediation

6111 Federal and Federally Sponsored Credit Agencies *see* NAICS 522293: International Trade Financing; NAICS 522294: Secondary Market Financing; NAICS 522298: All Other Non-Depository Credit Intermediation

6141 Personal Credit Institutions *see* NAICS 522210: Credit Card Issuing; NAICS 522220: Sales Financing; NAICS 522291: Consumer Lending

6153 Short-Term Business Credit Institutions, Except Agricultural *see* NAICS 522220: Sales Financing; NAICS 522320: Financial Transactions Processing, Reserve, and Clearing House Activities; NAICS 522298: All Other Non-Depository Credit Intermediation

6159 Miscellaneous Business Credit Institutions *see* NAICS 522220: Sales Financing; NAICS 522293: International Trade Financing; NAICS 522298: All Other Non-Depository Credit Intermediation

6162 Mortgage Bankers and Loan Correspondents *see* NAICS 522292: Real Estate Credit; NAICS 522390: Other Activities Related to Credit Intermediation

6163 Loan Brokers *see* NAICS 522310: Mortgage and Other Loan Brokers

6211 Security Brokers, Dealers, and Flotation Companies *see* NAICS 523110: Investment Banking and Securities Dealing; NAICS 523120: Securities Brokerage; NAICS 523910: Miscellaneous Intermediation; NAICS 523999: Miscellaneous Financial Investment Activities

6221 Commodity Contracts Brokers and Dealers *see* NAICS 523130: Commodity Contracts Dealing; NAICS 523140: Commodity Brokerage

6231 Security and Commodity Exchanges *see* NAICS 523210: Securities and Commodity Exchanges

6282 Investment Advice *see* NAICS 523920: Portfolio Management; NAICS 523930: Investment Advice

6289 Services Allied With the Exchange of Securities or Commodities, NEC *see* NAICS 523991: Trust, Fiduciary, and Custody Activities; NAICS 523999: Miscellaneous Financial Investment Activities

6311 Life Insurance *see* NAICS 524113: Direct Life Insurance Carriers; NAICS 524130: Reinsurance Carriers

6321 Accident and Health Insurance *see* NAICS 524114: Direct Health and Medical Insurance Carriers; NAICS 525190: Other Insurance and Employee Benefit Funds; NAICS 524130: Reinsurance Carriers

6324 Hospital and Medical Service Plans *see* NAICS 524114: Direct Health and Medical Insurance Carriers; NAICS 525190: Other Insurance and Employee Benefit Funds; NAICS 524130: Reinsurance Carriers

6331 Fire, Marine, and Casualty Insurance *see* NAICS 524126: Direct Property and Casualty Insurance Carriers; NAICS 525190: Other Insurance and Employee Benefit Funds; NAICS 524130: Reinsurance Carriers

6351 Surety Insurance *see* NAICS 524126: Direct Property and Casualty Insurance Carriers; NAICS 524130: Reinsurance Carriers

6361 Title Insurance *see* NAICS 524127: Direct Title Insurance Carriers; NAICS 524130: Reinsurance Carriers

6371 Pension, Health, and Welfare Funds *see* NAICS 523920: Portfolio Management; NAICS 524292: Third Party Administration for Insurance and Pension Funds; NAICS 525110: Pension Funds; NAICS 525120: Health and Welfare Funds

6399 Insurance Carriers, NEC *see* NAICS 524128: Other Direct Insurance Carriers (except Life, Health, and Medical)

6411 Insurance Agents, Brokers, and Service *see* NAICS 524210: Insurance Agencies and Brokerages; NAICS 524291: Claims Adjusters; NAICS 524292: Third Party Administrators for Insurance and Pension Funds; NAICS 524298: All Other Insurance Related Activities

6512 Operators of Nonresidential Buildings *see* NAICS 711310: Promoters of Performing Arts, Sports and Similar Events with Facilities; NAICS 531120: Lessors of Nonresidential Buildings (except Mini-warehouses)

6513 Operators of Apartment Buildings *see* NAICS 531110: Lessors of Residential Buildings and Dwellings

6514 Operators of Dwellings Other Than Apartment Buildings *see* NAICS 531110: Lessors of Residential Buildings and Dwellings

6515 Operators of Residential Mobile Home Sites *see* NAICS 531190: Lessors of Other Real Estate Property

6517 Lessors of Railroad Property *see* NAICS 531190: Lessors of Other Real Estate Property

6519 Lessors of Real Property, NEC *see* NAICS 531190: Lessors of Other Real Estate Property

6531 Real Estate Agents and Managers *see* NAICS 531210: Offices of Real Estate Agents and Brokers; NAICS 813990: Other Similar Organizations; NAICS 531311: Residential Property Managers; NAICS 531312: Nonresidential Property Managers; NAICS 531320: Offices of Real Estate Appraisers; NAICS 812220: Cemeteries and Crematories; NAICS 531390: Other Activities Related to Real Estate

6541 Title Abstract Offices *see* NAICS 541191: Title Abstract and Settlement Offices

6552 Land Subdividers and Developers, Except Cemeteries *see* NAICS 233110: Land Subdivision and Land Development

6553 Cemetery Subdividers and Developers *see* NAICS 812220: Cemeteries and Crematories

6712 Offices of Bank Holding Companies *see* NAICS 551111: Offices of Bank Holding Companies

6719 Offices of Holding Companies, NEC *see* NAICS 551112: Offices of Other Holding Companies

6722 Management Investment Offices, Open-End *see* NAICS 525910: Open-End Investment Funds

6726 Unit Investment Trusts, Face-Amount Certificate Offices, and Closed-End Management Investment Offices *see* NAICS 525990: Other Financial Vehicles

6732 Education, Religious, and Charitable Trusts *see* NAICS 813211: Grantmaking Foundations

6733 Trusts, Except Educational, Religious, and Charitable *see* NAICS 523920: Portfolio Management; NAICS 523991: Trust, Fiduciary, and Custody Services; NAICS 525190: Other Insurance and Employee Benefit Funds; NAICS 525920: Trusts, Estates, and Agency Accounts

6792 Oil Royalty Traders *see* NAICS 523999: Miscellaneous Financial Investment Activities; NAICS 533110: Owners and Lessors of Other Non-Financial Assets

6794 Patent Owners and Lessors *see* NAICS 533110: Owners and Lessors of Other Non-Financial Assets

6798 Real Estate Investment Trusts *see* NAICS 525930: Real Estate Investment Trusts

6799 Investors, NEC *see* NAICS 523910: Miscellaneous Intermediation; NAICS 523920: Portfolio Management; NAICS 523130: Commodity Contracts Dealing; NAICS 523999: Miscellaneous Financial Investment Activities

SERVICE INDUSTRIES

7011 Hotels and Motels *see* NAICS 721110: Hotels (except Casino Hotels) and Motels; NAICS 721120: Casino Hotels; NAICS 721191: Bed and Breakfast Inns; NAICS 721199: All Other Traveler Accommodations

7021 Rooming and Boarding Houses *see* NAICS 721310: Rooming and Boarding Houses

7032 Sporting and Recreational Camps *see* NAICS 721214: Recreational and Vacation Camps

7033 Recreational Vehicle Parks and Campsites *see* NAICS 721211: RV (Recreational Vehicle) Parks and Campgrounds

7041 Organization Hotels and Lodging Houses, on Membership Basis *see* NAICS 721110: Hotels (except Casino Hotels) and Motels; NAICS 721310: Rooming and Boarding Houses

7211 Power Laundries, Family and Commercial *see* NAICS 812321: Laundries, Family and Commercial

7212 Garment Pressing, and Agents for Laundries *see* NAICS 812391: Garment Pressing and Agents for Laundries

7213 Linen Supply *see* NAICS 812331: Linen Supply

7215 Coin-Operated Laundry and Drycleaning *see* NAICS 812310: Coin-Operated Laundries and Drycleaners

7216 Drycleaning Plants, Except Rug Cleaning *see* NAICS 812322: Drycleaning Plants

7217 Carpet and Upholstery Cleaning *see* NAICS 561740: Carpet and Upholstery Cleaning Services

7218 Industrial Launderers *see* NAICS 812332: Industrial Launderers

7219 Laundry and Garment Services, NEC *see* NAICS 812331: Linen Supply; NAICS 811490: Other Personal and Household Goods Repair and Maintenance; NAICS 812399: All Other Laundry Services

7221 Photographic Studios, Portrait *see* NAICS 541921: Photographic Studios, Portrait

7231 Beauty Shops *see* NAICS 812112: Beauty Salons; NAICS 812113: Nail Salons; NAICS 611511: Cosmetology and Barber Schools

7241 Barber Shops *see* NAICS 812111: Barber Shops; NAICS 611511: Cosmetology and Barber Schools

7251 Shoe Repair Shops and Shoeshine Parlors *see* NAICS 811430: Footwear and Leather Goods Repair

7261 Funeral Services and Crematories *see* NAICS 812210: Funeral Homes; NAICS 812220: Cemeteries and Crematories

7291 Tax Return Preparation Services *see* NAICS 541213: Tax Preparation Services

7299 Miscellaneous Personal Services, NEC *see* NAICS 624410: Child Day Care Services; NAICS 812191: Diet and Weight Reducing Centers; NAICS 532220: Formal Wear and Costumes Rental; NAICS 812199: Other Personal Care Services; NAICS 812990: All Other Personal Services

7311 Advertising Agencies *see* NAICS 541810: Advertising Agencies

7312 Outdoor Advertising Services *see* NAICS 541850: Display Advertising

7313 Radio, Television, and Publishers' Advertising Representatives *see* NAICS 541840: Media Representatives

7319 Advertising, NEC *see* NAICS 481219: Other Nonscheduled Air Transportation; NAICS 541830: Media Buying Agencies; NAICS 541850: Display Advertising; NAICS 541870: Advertising Material Distribution Services; NAICS 541890: Other Services Related to Advertising

7322 Adjustment and Collection Services *see* NAICS 561440: Collection Agencies; NAICS 561491: Repossession Services

7323 Credit Reporting Services *see* NAICS 561450: Credit Bureaus

7331 Direct Mail Advertising Services *see* NAICS 541860: Direct Mail Advertising

7334 Photocopying and Duplicating Services *see* NAICS 561431: Other Business Service Centers (including Copy Shops)

7335 Commercial Photography *see* NAICS 481219: Other Nonscheduled Air Transportation; NAICS 541922: Commercial Photography

7336 Commercial Art and Graphic Design *see* NAICS 541430: Graphic Design Services

7338 Secretarial and Court Reporting Services *see* NAICS 561410: Document Preparation Services; NAICS 561492: Court Reporting and Stenotype Services

7342 Disinfecting and Pest Control Services *see* NAICS 561720: Janitorial Services; NAICS 561710: Exterminating and Pest Control Services

7349 Building Cleaning and Maintenance Services, NEC *see* NAICS 561720: Janitorial Services

7352 Medical Equipment Rental and Leasing *see* NAICS 532291: Home Health Equipment Rental; NAICS 532490: Other Commercial and Industrial Machinery and Equipment Rental and Leasing

7353 Heavy Construction Equipment Rental and Leasing *see* NAICS 234990: All Other Heavy Construction; NAICS 532412: Construction, Mining and Forestry Machinery and Equipment Rental and Leasing

7359 Equipment Rental and Leasing, NEC *see* NAICS 532210: Consumer Electronics and Appliances Rental; NAICS 532310: General Rental Centers; NAICS 532299: All Other Consumer Goods Rental; NAICS 532412: Construction, Mining and Forestry Machinery and Equipment Rental and Leasing; NAICS 532411: Commercial Air, Rail, and Water Transportation Equipment Rental and Leasing; NAICS 562991: Septic Tank and Related Services; NAICS 532420: Office Machinery and Equipment Rental and Leasing; NAICS 532490: Other Commercial and Industrial Machinery and Equipment Rental and Leasing

7361 Employment Agencies *see* NAICS 541612: Human Resources and Executive Search Consulting Services; NAICS 561310: Employment Placement Agencies

7363 Help Supply Services *see* NAICS 561320: Temporary Help Services; NAICS 561330: Employee Leasing Services

7371 Computer Programming Services *see* NAICS 541511: Custom Computer Programming Services

7372 Prepackaged Software *see* NAICS 511210: Software Publishers; NAICS 334611: Software Reproducing

7373 Computer Integrated Systems Design *see* NAICS 541512: Computer Systems Design Services

7374 Computer Processing and Data Preparation and Processing Services *see* NAICS 514210: Data Processing Services

7375 Information Retrieval Services *see* NAICS 514191: On-Line Information Services

7376 Computer Facilities Management Services *see* NAICS 541513: Computer Facilities Management Services

7377 Computer Rental and Leasing *see* NAICS 532420: Office Machinery and Equipment Rental and Leasing

7378 Computer Maintenance and Repair *see* NAICS 443120: Computer and Software Stores; NAICS 811212: Computer and Office Machine Repair and Maintenance

7379 Computer Related Services, NEC *see* NAICS 541512: Computer Systems Design Services; NAICS 541519: Other Computer Related Services

7381 Detective, Guard, and Armored Car Services *see* NAICS 561611: Investigation Services; NAICS 561612: Security Guards and Patrol Services; NAICS 561613: Armored Car Services

7382 Security Systems Services *see* NAICS 561621: Security Systems Services (except Locksmiths)

7383 News Syndicates *see* NAICS 514110: New Syndicates

7384 Photofinishing Laboratories *see* NAICS 812921: Photo Finishing Laboratories (except One-Hour); NAICS 812922: One-Hour Photo Finishing

7389 Business Services, NEC *see* NAICS 512240: Sound Recording Studios; NAICS 512290: Other Sound Recording Industries; NAICS 541199: Other Legal Services; NAICS 812990: All Other Personal Services; NAICS 541370: Surveying and Mapping (except Geophysical) Services; NAICS 541410: Interior Design Services; NAICS 541420: Industrial Design Services; NAICS 541340: Drafting Services; NAICS 541490: Other Specialized Design Services; NAICS 541890: Other Services Related to Advertising; NAICS 541930: Translation and Interpretation Services; NAICS 541350: Building Inspection Services; NAICS 541990: All Other

Professional, Scientific and Technical Services; NAICS 711410: Agents and Managers for Artists, Athletes, Entertainers and Other Public Figures; NAICS 561421: Telephone Answering Services; NAICS 561422: Telemarketing Bureaus; NAICS 561439: Private Mail Centers; NAICS 561431: Other Business Service Centers (including Copy Shops); NAICS 561491: Repossession Services; NAICS 561910: Packaging and Labeling Services; NAICS 561790: Other Services to Buildings and Dwellings; NAICS 561599: All Other Travel Arrangement and Reservation Services; NAICS 561920: Convention and Trade Show Organizers; NAICS 561591: Convention and Visitors Bureaus; NAICS 522320: Financial Transactions, Processing, Reserve and Clearing House Activities; NAICS 561499: All Other Business Support Services; NAICS 561990: All Other Support Services

7513 Truck Rental and Leasing, Without Drivers *see* NAICS 532120: Truck, Utility Trailer and RV (Recreational Vehicle) Rental and Leasing

7514 Passenger Car Rental *see* NAICS 532111: Passenger Cars Rental

7515 Passenger Car Leasing *see* NAICS 532112: Passenger Cars Leasing

7519 Utility Trailer and Recreational Vehicle Rental *see* NAICS 532120: Truck, Utility Trailer and RV (Recreational Vehicles) Rental and Leasing

7521 Automobile Parking *see* NAICS 812930: Parking Lots and Garages

7532 Top, Body, and Upholstery Repair Shops and Paint Shops *see* NAICS 811121: Automotive Body, Paint, and Upholstery Repair and Maintenance

7533 Automotive Exhaust System Repair Shops *see* NAICS 811112: Automotive Exhaust System Repair

7534 Tire Retreading and Repair Shops *see* NAICS 326212: Tire Retreading; NAICS 811198: All Other Automotive Repair and Maintenance

7536 Automotive Glass Replacement Shops *see* NAICS 811122: Automotive Glass Replacement Shops

7537 Automotive Transmission Repair Shops *see* NAICS 811113: Automotive Transmission Repair

7538 General Automotive Repair Shops *see* NAICS 811111: General Automotive Repair

7539 Automotive Repair Shops, NEC *see* NAICS 811118: Other Automotive Mechanical and Electrical Repair and Maintenance

7542 Carwashes *see* NAICS 811192: Car Washes

7549 Automotive Services, Except Repair and Carwashes *see* NAICS 811191: Automotive Oil Change and Lubrication Shops; NAICS 488410: Motor Vehicle Towing; NAICS 811198: All Other Automotive Repair and Maintenance

7622 Radio and Television Repair Shops *see* NAICS 811211: Consumer Electronics Repair and Maintenance; NAICS 811213: Communication Equipment Repair and Maintenance; NAICS 443112: Radio, Television and Other Electronics Stores

7623 Refrigeration and Air-Conditioning Services and Repair Shops *see* NAICS 443111: Household Appliance Stores; NAICS 811310: Commercial and Industrial Machinery and Equipment (except Automotive and Electronic) Repair and Maintenance; NAICS 811412: Appliance Repair and Maintenance

7629 Electrical and Electronic Repair Shops, NEC *see* NAICS 443111: Household Appliance Stores; NAICS 811212: Computer and Office Machine Repair and Maintenance; *see* NAICS 811213: Communication Equipment Repair and Maintenance; NAICS 811219: Other Electronic and Precision Equipment Repair and Maintenance; NAICS 811412: Appliance Repair and Maintenance; NAICS 811211: Consumer Electronics Repair and Maintenance

7631 Watch, Clock, and Jewelry Repair *see* NAICS 811490: Other Personal and Household Goods Repair and Maintenance

7641 Reupholster and Furniture Repair *see* NAICS 811420: Reupholstery and Furniture Repair

7692 Welding Repair *see* NAICS 811490: Other Personal and Household Goods Repair and Maintenance

7694 Armature Rewinding Shops *see* NAICS 811310: Commercial and Industrial Machinery and Equipment (except Automotive and Electronic) Repair and Maintenance; NAICS 335312: Motor and Generator Manufacturing

7699 Repair Shops and Related Services, NEC *see* NAICS 561622: Locksmiths; NAICS 562991: Septic Tank and Related Services; NAICS 561790: Other Services to Buildings and Dwellings; NAICS 488390: Other Support Activities for Water Transportation; NAICS 451110: Sporting Goods Stores; NAICS 811310: Commercial and Industrial Machinery and Equipment (except Automotive and Electronic) Repair and Maintenance; NAICS 115210: Support Activities for Animal Production; NAICS 811212: Computer and Office Machine Repair and Maintenance; NAICS 811219: Other Electronic and Precision Equipment Repair and Maintenance; NAICS 811411: Home and Garden Equipment Repair and Maintenance; NAICS 811412: Appliance Repair and Maintenance; NAICS 811430: Footwear and Leather Goods Repair; NAICS 811490: Other Personal and Household Goods Repair and Maintenance

7812 Motion Picture and Video Tape Production *see* NAICS 512110: Motion Picture and Video Production

7819 Services Allied to Motion Picture Production *see* NAICS 512191: Teleproduction and Other Post-Production Services; NAICS 561310: Employment Placement Agencies; NAICS 532220: Formal Wear and Costumes Rental; NAICS 532490: Other Commercial and Industrial Machinery and Equipment Rental and Leasing; NAICS 541214: Payroll Services; NAICS 711510: Independent Artists, Writers, and Performers; NAICS 334612: Prerecorded Compact Disc (Except Software), Tape, and Record Manufacturing; NAICS 512199: Other Motion Picture and Video Industries

7822 Motion Picture and Video Tape Distribution *see* NAICS 421990: Other Miscellaneous Durable Goods Wholesalers; NAICS 512120: Motion Picture and Video Distribution

7829 Services Allied to Motion Picture Distribution *see* NAICS 512199: Other Motion Picture and Video Industries; NAICS 512120: Motion Picture and Video Distribution

7832 Motion Picture Theaters, Except Drive-In *see* NAICS 512131: Motion Picture Theaters, Except Drive-In

7833 Drive-In Motion Picture Theaters *see* NAICS 512132: Drive-In Motion Picture Theaters

7841 Video Tape Rental *see* NAICS 532230: Video Tapes and Disc Rental

7911 Dance Studios, Schools, and Halls *see* NAICS 713990: All Other Amusement and Recreation Industries; NAICS 611610: Fine Arts Schools

7922 Theatrical Producers (Except Motion Picture) and Miscellaneous Theatrical Services *see* NAICS 561310: Employment Placement Agencies; NAICS 711110: Theater Companies and Dinner Theaters; NAICS 711410: Agents and Managers for Artists, Athletes, Entertainers and Other Public Figures; NAICS 711120: Dance Companies; NAICS 711310: Promoters of Performing Arts, Sports, and Similar Events with Facilities; NAICS 711320: Promoters of Performing Arts, Sports, and Similar Events without Facilities; NAICS 512290: Other Sound Recording Industries; NAICS 532490: Other Commercial and Industrial Machinery and Equipment Rental and Leasing

7929 Bands, Orchestras, Actors, and Other Entertainers and Entertainment Groups *see* NAICS 711130: Musical Groups and Artists; NAICS 711510: Independent Artists, Writers, and Performers; NAICS 711190: Other Performing Arts Companies

7933 Bowling Centers *see* NAICS 713950: Bowling Centers

7941 Professional Sports Clubs and Promoters *see* NAICS 711211: Sports Teams and Clubs; NAICS 711410: Agents and Managers for Artists, Athletes, Entertainers, and Other Public Figures; NAICS 711320: Promoters of Performing Arts, Sports, and Similar Events without Facilities; NAICS 711310: Promoters of Performing Arts, Sports, and Similar Events with Facilities; NAICS 711219: Other Spectator Sports

7948 Racing, Including Track Operations *see* NAICS 711212: Race Tracks; NAICS 711219: Other Spectator Sports

7991 Physical Fitness Facilities *see* NAICS 713940: Fitness and Recreational Sports Centers

7992 Public Golf Courses *see* NAICS 713910: Golf Courses and Country Clubs

7993 Coin Operated Amusement Devices *see* NAICS 713120: Amusement Arcades; NAICS 713290: Other Gambling Industries; NAICS 713990: All Other Amusement and Recreation Industries

7996 Amusement Parks *see* NAICS 713110: Amusement and Theme Parks

7997 Membership Sports and Recreation Clubs *see* NAICS 713910: Golf Courses and Country Clubs; NAICS 713940: Fitness and Recreational Sports Centers; NAICS 713990: All Other Amusement and Recreation Industries

7999 Amusement and Recreation Services, NEC *see* NAICS 561599: All Other Travel Arrangement and Reservation Services; NAICS 487990: Scenic and Sightseeing Transportation, Other; NAICS 711190: Other Performing Arts Companies; NAICS 711219: Other Spectator Sports; NAICS 713920: Skiing Facilities; NAICS 713940: Fitness and Recreational Sports Centers; NAICS 713210: Casinos (except Casino Hotels); NAICS 713290: Other Gambling Industries; NAICS 712190: Nature Parks and Other Similar Institutions; NAICS 611620: Sports and Recreation Instruction; NAICS 532292: Recreational Goods Rental; NAICS 487110: Scenic and Sightseeing Transportation, Land; NAICS 487210: Scenic and Sightseeing Transportation, Water; NAICS 713990: All Other Amusement and Recreation Industries

8011 Offices and Clinics of Doctors of Medicine *see* NAICS 621493: Freestanding Ambulatory Surgical and Emergency Centers; NAICS 621491: HMO Medical Centers; NAICS 621112: Offices of Physicians; NAICS 621111: Offices of Physicians (except Mental Health Specialists)

8021 Offices and Clinics of Dentists *see* NAICS 621210: Offices of Dentists

8031 Offices and Clinics of Doctors of Osteopathy *see* NAICS 621111: Offices of Physicians (except Mental Health Specialists); NAICS 621112: Offices of Physicians, Mental Health Specialists

8041 Offices and Clinics of Chiropractors *see* NAICS 621310: Offices of Chiropractors

8042 Offices and Clinics of Optometrists *see* NAICS 621320: Offices of Optometrists

8043 Offices and Clinics of Podiatrists *see* NAICS 621391: Offices of Podiatrists

8049 Offices and Clinics of Health Practitioners, NEC *see* NAICS 621330: Offices of Mental Health Practitioners (except Physicians); NAICS 621340: Offices of Physical, Occupational, and Speech Therapists and Audiologists; NAICS 621399: Offices of All Other Miscellaneous Health Practitioners

8051 Skilled Nursing Care Facilities *see* NAICS 623311: Continuing Care Retirement Communities; NAICS 623110: Nursing Care Facilities

8052 Intermediate Care Facilities *see* NAICS 623311: Continuing Care Retirement Communities; NAICS 623210: Residential Mental Retardation Facilities; NAICS 623110: Nursing Care Facilities

8059 Nursing and Personal Care Facilities, NEC *see* NAICS 623311: Continuing Care Retirement Communities; NAICS 623110: Nursing Care Facilities

8062 General Medical and Surgical Hospitals *see* NAICS 622110: General Medical and Surgical Hospitals

8063 Psychiatric Hospitals *see* NAICS 622210: Psychiatric and Substance Abuse Hospitals

8069 Specialty Hospitals, Except Psychiatric *see* NAICS 622110: General Medical and Surgical Hospitals; NAICS 622210: Psychiatric and Substance Abuse Hospitals; NAICS 622310: Specialty (except Psychiatric and Substance Abuse) Hospitals

8071 Medical Laboratories *see* NAICS 621512: Diagnostic Imaging Centers; NAICS 621511: Medical Laboratories

8072 Dental Laboratories *see* NAICS 339116: Dental Laboratories

8082 Home Health Care Services *see* NAICS 621610: Home Health Care Services

8092 Kidney Dialysis Centers *see* NAICS 621492: Kidney Dialysis Centers

8093 Specialty Outpatient Facilities, NEC *see* NAICS 621410: Family Planning Centers; NAICS 621420: Outpatient Mental Health and Substance Abuse Centers; NAICS 621498: All Other Outpatient Care Facilities

8099 Health and Allied Services, NEC *see* NAICS 621991: Blood and Organ Banks; NAICS 541430: Graphic Design Services; NAICS 541922: Commercial Photography; NAICS 621410: Family Planning Centers; NAICS 621999: All Other Miscellaneous Ambulatory Health Care Services

8111 Legal Services *see* NAICS 541110: Offices of Lawyers

8211 Elementary and Secondary Schools *see* NAICS 611110: Elementary and Secondary Schools

8221 Colleges, Universities, and Professional Schools *see* NAICS 611310: Colleges, Universities, and Professional Schools

8222 Junior Colleges and Technical Institutes *see* NAICS 611210: Junior Colleges

8231 Libraries *see* NAICS 514120: Libraries and Archives

8243 Data Processing Schools *see* NAICS 611519: Other Technical and Trade Schools; NAICS 611420: Computer Training

8244 Business and Secretarial Schools *see* NAICS 611410: Business and Secretarial Schools

8249 Vocational Schools, NEC *see* NAICS 611513: Apprenticeship Training; NAICS 611512: Flight Training; NAICS 611519: Other Technical and Trade Schools

8299 Schools and Educational Services, NEC *see* NAICS 611512: Flight Training; NAICS 611692: Automobile Driving Schools; NAICS 611710: Educational Support Services; NAICS 611691: Exam Preparation and Tutoring; NAICS 611610: Fine Arts Schools; NAICS 611630: Language Schools; NAICS 611430: Professional and Management Development Training Schools; NAICS 611699: All Other Miscellaneous Schools and Instruction

8322 Individual and Family Social Services *see* NAICS 624110: Child and Youth Services; NAICS 624210: Community Food Services; NAICS 624229: Other Community Housing Services; NAICS 624230: Emergency and Other Relief Services; NAICS 624120: Services for the Elderly and Persons with Disabilities; NAICS 624221: Temporary Shelter; NAICS 922150: Parole Offices and Probation Offices; NAICS 624190: Other Individual and Family Services

8331 Job Training and Vocational Rehabilitation Services *see* NAICS 624310: Vocational Rehabilitation Services

8351 Child Day Care Services *see* NAICS 624410: Child Day Care Services

8361 Residential Care *see* NAICS 623312: Homes for the Elderly; NAICS 623220: Residential Mental Health and Substance Abuse Facilities; NAICS 623990: Other Residential Care Facilities

8399 Social Services, NEC *see* NAICS 813212: Voluntary Health Organizations; NAICS 813219: Other Grantmaking and Giving Services; NAICS 813311: Human Rights Organizations; NAICS 813312: Environment, Conservation and Wildlife Organizations; NAICS 813319: Other Social Advocacy Organizations

8412 Museums and Art Galleries *see* NAICS 712110: Museums; NAICS 712120: Historical Sites

8422 Arboreta and Botanical or Zoological Gardens *see* NAICS 712130: Zoos and Botanical Gardens; NAICS 712190: Nature Parks and Other Similar Institutions

8611 Business Associations *see* NAICS 813910: Business Associations

8621 Professional Membership Organizations *see* NAICS 813920: Professional Organizations

8631 Labor Unions and Similar Labor Organizations *see* NAICS 813930: Labor Unions and Similar Labor Organizations

8641 Civic, Social, and Fraternal Associations *see* NAICS 813410: Civic and Social Organizations; NAICS 813990: Other Similar Organizations; NAICS 921150: American Indian and Alaska Native Tribal Governments; NAICS 624110: Child and Youth Services

8651 Political Organizations *see* NAICS 813940: Political Organizations

8661 Religious Organizations *see* NAICS 813110: Religious Organizations

8699 Membership Organizations, NEC *see* NAICS 813410: Civic and Social Organizations; NAICS 813910: Business Associations; NAICS 813312: Environment, Conservation, and Wildlife Organizations; NAICS 561599: All Other Travel Arrangement and Reservation Services; NAICS 813990: Other Similar Organizations

8711 Engineering Services *see* NAICS 541330: Engineering Services

8712 Architectural Services *see* NAICS 541310: Architectural Services

8713 Surveying Services *see* NAICS 541360: Geophysical Surveying and Mapping Services; NAICS 541370: Surveying and Mapping (except Geophysical) Services

8721 Accounting, Auditing, and Bookkeeping Services *see* NAICS 541211: Offices of Certified Public Accountants; NAICS 541214: Payroll Services; NAICS 541219: Other Accounting Services

8731 Commercial Physical and Biological Research *see* NAICS 541710: Research and Development in the Physical Sciences and Engineering Sciences; NAICS 541720: Research and Development in the Life Sciences

8732 Commercial Economic, Sociological, and Educational Research *see* NAICS 541730: Research and Development in the Social Sciences and Humanities; NAICS 541910: Marketing Research and Public Opinion Polling

8733 Noncommercial Research Organizations *see* NAICS 541710: Research and Development in the Physical Sciences and Engineering Sciences; NAICS 541720: Research and Development in the Life Sciences; NAICS 541730: Research and Development in the Social Sciences and Humanities

8734 Testing Laboratories *see* NAICS 541940: Veterinary Services; NAICS 541380: Testing Laboratories

8741 Management Services *see* NAICS 561110: Office Administrative Services

8742 Management Consulting Services *see* NAICS 541611: Administrative Management and General Management Consulting Services; NAICS 541612: Human Resources and Executive Search Consulting Services; NAICS 541613: Marketing Consulting Services; NAICS 541614: Process, Physical, Distribution, and Logistics Consulting

8743 Public Relations Services *see* NAICS 541820: Public Relations Services

8744 Facilities Support Management Services *see* NAICS 561210: Facilities Support Services

8748 Business Consulting Services, NEC *see* NAICS 611710: Educational Support Services; NAICS 541618: Other Management Consulting Services; NAICS 541690: Other Scientific and Technical Consulting Services

8811 Private Households *see* NAICS 814110: Private Households

8999 Services, NEC *see* NAICS 711510: Independent Artists, Writers, and Performers; NAICS 512210: Record Production; NAICS 541690: Other Scientific and Technical Consulting Services; NAICS 512230: Music Publishers; NAICS 541612: Human Resources and Executive Search Consulting Services; NAICS 514199: All Other Information Services; NAICS 541620: Environmental Consulting Services

PUBLIC ADMINISTRATION

9111 Executive Offices *see* NAICS 921110: Executive Offices

9121 Legislative Bodies *see* NAICS 921120: Legislative Bodies

9131 Executive and Legislative Offices, Combined *see* NAICS 921140: Executive and Legislative Offices, Combined

9199 General Government, NEC *see* NAICS 921190: All Other General Government

9211 Courts *see* NAICS 922110: Courts

9221 Police Protection *see* NAICS 922120: Police Protection

9222 Legal Counsel and Prosecution *see* NAICS 922130: Legal Counsel and Prosecution

9223 Correctional Institutions *see* NAICS 922140: Correctional Institutions

9224 Fire Protection *see* NAICS 922160: Fire Protection

9229 Public Order and Safety, NEC *see* NAICS 922190: All Other Justice, Public Order, and Safety

9311 Public Finance, Taxation, and Monetary Policy *see* NAICS 921130: Public Finance

9411 Administration of Educational Programs *see* NAICS 923110: Administration of Education Programs

9431 Administration of Public Health Programs *see* NAICS 923120: Administration of Public Health Programs

9441 Administration of Social, Human Resource, and Income Maintenance Programs *see* NAICS 923130: Administration of Social, Human Resource, and Income Maintenance Programs

9451 Administration of Veteran's Affairs, Except Health Insurance *see* NAICS 923140: Administration of Veteran's Affairs

9511 Air and Water Resource and Solid Waste Management *see* NAICS 924110: Air and Water Resource and Solid Waste Management

9512 Land, Mineral, Wildlife, and Forest Conservation *see* NAICS 924120: Land, Mineral, Wildlife, and Forest Conservation

9531 Administration of Housing Programs *see* NAICS 925110: Administration of Housing Programs

9532 Administration of Urban Planning and Community and Rural Development *see* NAICS 925120: Administration of Urban Planning and Community and Rural Development

9611 Administration of General Economic Programs *see* NAICS 926110: Administration of General Economic Programs

9621 Regulations and Administration of Transportation Programs *see* NAICS 488111: Air Traffic Control; NAICS 926120: Regulation and Administration of Transportation Programs

9631 Regulation and Administration of Communications, Electric, Gas, and Other Utilities *see* NAICS 926130: Regulation and Administration of Communications, Electric, Gas, and Other Utilities

9641 Regulation of Agricultural Marketing and Commodities *see* NAICS 926140: Regulation of Agricultural Marketing and Commodities

9651 Regulation, Licensing, and Inspection of Miscellaneous Commercial Sectors *see* NAICS 926150: Regulation, Licensing, and Inspection of Miscellaneous Commercial Sectors

9661 Space Research and Technology *see* NAICS 927110: Space Research and Technology

9711 National Security *see* NAICS 928110: National Security

9721 International Affairs *see* NAICS 928120: International Affairs

9999 Nonclassified Establishments *see* NAICS 999990: Unclassified Establishments

INDEX

Citations in this index are followed by the volume number and page number(s) in which the indexed term is referenced.

INDEX

INDEX

B

INDEX

C

INDEX

INDEX

INDEX

INDEX

INDEX

E

INDEX

INDEX

INDEX

F

INDEX

INDEX

INDEX

INDEX

INDEX

H

INDEX

INDEX

INDEX

L

INDEX

INDEX

INDEX

INDEX

N

INDEX

INDEX

O

INDEX

P

INDEX

INDEX

INDEX

Q

R

INDEX

INDEX

INDEX

INDEX

INDEX

INDEX

U

INDEX

INDEX

X